Merriam-Webster's
Essential
LEARNER'S
English Dictionary

Merriam-Webster's
Essential
LEARNER'S
English Dictionary

Merriam-Webster, Incorporated
Springfield, Massachusetts, U.S.A.

A GENUINE MERRIAM-WEBSTER

The name *Webster* alone is no guarantee of excellence. It is used by a number of publishers and may serve mainly to mislead an unwary buyer.

Merriam-Webster™ is the name you should look for when you consider the purchase of dictionaries or other fine reference books. It carries the reputation of a company that has been publishing since 1831 and is your assurance of quality and authority.

Contents

Contents

Preface

Merriam-Webster's Essential Learner's English Dictionary is a new dictionary that is intended to serve as an affordable and compact reference for learners of English as a second or foreign language. It is based on *Merriam-Webster's Advanced Learner's English Dictionary* and includes many of the features found in that larger book. It provides coverage of both American and British English, with a particular emphasis on American English.

The more than 54,000 entries in this dictionary include the most essential words and phrases that people are likely to need and encounter in their daily lives. The choice of entries was based mainly on the evidence in our database of citation text, which now includes more than 100 million words. We also made frequent use of online resources, such as the databases of Lexis-Nexis, which provided editors with ready access to vast amounts of material from a very wide variety of sources.

The definitions in this dictionary are written in simple language. Notes of various kinds are also used to help clarify aspects of usage that cannot be easily captured or expressed in a definition. The inclusion of examples showing how words are used is an important feature in any dictionary, and it is particularly important in a learner's dictionary. Most of the entries and senses in this book therefore include at least one example, and many include more than one. The examples have been carefully chosen to show words being used in appropriate contexts which accurately reflect their uses in actual speech and writing. Many of the examples are enhanced by the inclusion of highlighted phrases, explanatory glosses, and synonyms.

Merriam-Webster's Essential Learner's English Dictionary was created by the editorial staff of a company that has been publishing dictionaries for more than 160 years. The dozens of people who worked on our *Advanced Learner's English Dictionary* can also be said to have contributed to this abridgment. The people who worked specifically on this project as definers were Penny L. Couillard-Dix, Benjamin T. Korzec, Emily A. Brewster, Rebecca Bryer-Charette, Karen L. Wilkinson, Susan L. Brady, and Kory L. Stamper. The task of checking cross-references was handled by Maria Sansalone, Donna L. Rickerby, and Adrienne M. Scholz. Pronunciations were provided by Joshua S. Guenter. Copyediting was done by Stephen J. Perrault and Penny L. Couillard-Dix. The final review of the manuscript was by Stephen J. Perrault.

Proofreading was done by most of the editors mentioned above. Donna L. Rickerby keyed revisions to the data file and provided technical assistance. Susan L. Brady directed the steps that turned the manuscript into pages ready to be printed. Project coordination and scheduling were handled by Madeline L. Novak. Page design and layout were chiefly handled by editors Brady and Novak. Company president John M. Morse assisted in the book's initial planning and was supportive throughout the project.

Learning a new language is a difficult challenge. We believe that *Merriam-Webster's Essential Learner's English Dictionary* contains a wealth of useful and practical information that will help students of English to better understand the words and expressions that they hear and read, and to choose the best way to express themselves in their own speech and writing.

Using the Dictionary

Entries

The entries in the dictionary are arranged in alphabetical order according to their **headwords**.

Headwords are the boldface words at the beginning of an entry.

> **boon** /'bu:n/ *n* [C] : something pleasant or helpful ▪ *The new tax cut is a boon for married couples.*

Dots within headwords show the places where you can break a word and add a hyphen if all of it will not fit at the end of a line of print or writing.

> **gar·gan·tuan** /gɑə'gænt∫əwən/ *adj* : very large in size or amount ▪ *a gargantuan appetite*

You will sometimes find two or more headwords that are spelled exactly alike and that have small numbers attached to them. These entries are called **homographs**.

Homographs often are related words that have different parts of speech. For example, the noun *gel* and the verb *gel* are entered in this dictionary as separate homographs.

> ¹**gel** /'dʒɛl/ *n* [C/U] : a thick substance that is like jelly and that is used in various products ▪ *hair gels* [=gels used for styling hair]
> ²**gel** *vb* **gelled; gel·ling** **1** [I] : to change into a thick substance that is like jelly ▪ *The mixture will gel as it cools.* **2** [I] : to become clear and definite ▪ *Our plans are finally starting to gel.* **3** [T] : to style (hair) with gel ▪ *She gelled her hair.*

Some homographs are words that are spelled the same way but are pronounced differently or have other important differences. For example, there are two different nouns in English that are spelled *primer*. Those two nouns are pronounced differently and are not related to each other, so they are treated as separate entries in this dictionary.

> ¹**prim·er** /'prɪmə, *Brit* 'praɪmə/ *n* [C] **1** *chiefly US* : something that gives basic information on a subject ▪ *The article is a good primer on economics.* **2** : a small book that helps teach children how to read — compare ²PRIMER
> ²**prim·er** /'praɪmə/ *n* [C/U] : a kind of paint that is used to prepare a surface for a final layer of a different paint — compare ¹PRIMER

Idioms and **phrasal verbs** are shown in alphabetical order at the end of the entry that they relate to.

> [1]**die** /ˈdaɪ/ *vb* **died; dy·ing** /ˈdajɪŋ/   1 a [*I*] : to stop living • *She claims she's not afraid to die.* • *More than a hundred people died* [=were killed] *in the crash. . . .* — **die down** [*phrasal vb*] : to gradually become less strong • *She waited for the noise/wind to die down.* — **die hard** : to take a long time to die or end : to continue for a long time • *That kind of determination dies hard.* — **die laughing** *informal* : to laugh very hard • *If the guys hear about this, they're going to die laughing.* — **die off** [*phrasal vb*] : to die one after another so that fewer and fewer are left • *The remaining members of her family gradually died off.*

Some words are shown without definitions at the very end of an entry. The meaning of these words can be understood when you know the meaning of the main entry word that they are related to. For example, when a word ends in a suffix like -*ly* or -*ness*, you can understand the word's meaning by combining the meaning of the base word (the main entry) and the meaning of the suffix.

> **con·cise** /kənˈsaɪs/ *adj* : using few words • *a concise account/summary/definition* — **con·cise·ly** *adv* — **con·cise·ness** *n* [*U*]

Pronunciations

The **pronunciations** in this dictionary are written using the International Phonetic Alphabet (IPA). The symbols used are listed in a chart on page 22a.

Pronunciations are shown between a pair of slashes // following the entry word. Only one pronunciation is given for most words. This is the most commonly used pronunciation.

> **band·wag·on** /ˈbænd₊wægən/ *n*

Additional pronunciations are shown when the word can be pronounced in different ways that are equally common.

> **apri·cot** /ˈæprə₊kɑːt, ˈeɪprə₊kɑːt/ *n*

Pronunciations are not shown at every entry. If homographs have the same pronunciation, the pronunciation is written only at the first homograph (as the entries above for *gel* show). If the homographs are pronounced differently, a pronunciation is written at each homograph.

> [1]**pres·ent** /ˈprɛznt/ *n* **1** [C] : something that you give to someone especially as a way of showing affection or thanks : GIFT ▪ *a birthday present*
> [2]**pre·sent** /prɪˈzɛnt/ *vb* **1** [T] : to give something to someone in a formal way ▪ *He presented the queen with a diamond necklace.*

Pronunciations are not usually shown for entries like *gag order* that are compounds of two or more words which have their own entries.

> **gag order** *n* [C] *chiefly US, law* : an order by a judge or court saying that the people involved in a legal case cannot talk about the case or anything related to it in public — called also (*Brit*) *gagging order*

Pronunciations are not shown for most undefined words that end in a common suffix, such as *-ly* or *-ness*.

> **meek** /ˈmiːk/ *adj* : having or showing a quiet and gentle nature ▪ *a meek child/reply* — **meek·ly** *adv* — **meek·ness** *n* [U]

When only the last part of a pronunciation is shown, the missing part can be found in a full pronunciation shown earlier in that same entry. In this example, only the last syllable is shown for the pronunciation of the plural *formulae*. The pronunciation of the first two syllables of *formulae* is the same as the pronunciation of the first two syllables of the singular *formula*.

> **for·mu·la** /ˈfoɚmjələ/ *n, pl* **-las** *also* **-lae** /-ˌliː/

Most of the pronunciations in this dictionary should be considered standard American pronunciations, showing how words are typically pronounced in many parts of the United States. For some words, a British pronunciation is also provided.

British pronunciations are shown when the most common British pronunciation is very different from the American pronunciation.

> **flask** /ˈflæsk, *Brit* ˈflɑːsk/ *n*

Spelling

Some words can be spelled in different ways. These additional spellings are called **variants** and are entered after the main entry words and after either *or* or *also*.

The word *or* is used when the variant is as common as the main entry word.

> **han·kie** *or* **han·ky** /ˈhæŋki/ *n, pl* **-kies** [C] *informal* : HANDKERCHIEF

The word *also* is used when the variant is less common than the main entry word.

> **Ha·nuk·kah** *also* **Cha·nu·kah** /ˈhɑːnəkə/ *n* [C/U] : an eight-day Jewish holiday that is celebrated in November or December

A label in parentheses ( ) after a headword tells you where that spelling is used. The example shown here indicates that the spelling *catalog* is used in U.S. English. Notice that the spelling *catalogue* does not have a *US* or *Brit* label. This means that it is common in both U.S. and British English.

> ²**catalog** (*US*) *or* **catalogue** *vb* **-loged** *or* **-logued; -log·ing** *or* **-logu·ing** [*T*] : to list or describe (something) in an organized way • *They use the computer to catalog books.* — **cat·a·log·er** (*US*) *or* **cat·a·logu·er** *n* [C]

The word *chiefly* is used to tell you that a word or variant is very common in a specified country or region but that it is also sometimes used in other countries or regions. The example shown here indicates that the British spellings *grey*, *greyish*, and *greyness* are also sometimes used in U.S. English.

> ¹**gray** (*US*) *or chiefly Brit* **grey** /ˈgreɪ/ *adj* **1** : having a color between black and white • *gray hair/socks* **2** : having gray hair • *He's gone gray.* **3** : not bright or cheerful • *a cold, gray day* • *the gray faces of the people in the crowd* — **gray** (*US*) *or chiefly Brit* **grey** *n* [C/U] • *shades of gray* — **gray·ish** (*US*) *or chiefly Brit* **grey·ish** /ˈgreɪʃ/ *adj* — **gray·ness** (*US*) *or chiefly Brit* **grey·ness** *n* [U]

Definitions

The definitions in this dictionary are written in simple and clear language. If you are unsure about the meaning of a word that is used in a definition, you can look that word up at its own entry in the dictionary and find its meaning explained there.

Most definitions begin with a boldface colon.

gait /ˈgeɪt/ *n* [C] **:** a particular way of walking • *an easy/unsteady/awkward gait*

Some definitions are written as notes that describe how a word or phrase is used. Those definitions are preceded by a dash.

hel·lo /həˈloʊ/ *n* **1** — used as a greeting • *Hello, my name is Linda.*

Some definitions are written as complete sentences and begin with the ◇ symbol.

²**beach** *vb* [T] **1** : to cause (a boat or ship) to go out of the water and onto a beach • *The pirates beached the ship on the island.* **2** ◇ When a large ocean animal, such as a whale, is *beached* or has *beached itself*, it has come out of the water onto land and is unable to return to the water. • *a beached whale*

Synonyms

Synonyms are words that have the same meaning. A word that is shown in small capital letters in a definition is a synonym of the word that is being defined. The example shown here indicates that the word *know-how* has the same meaning as *expertise*.

know–how /ˈnoʊˌhaʊ/ *n* [U] : knowledge of how to do something well : EXPERTISE • *technical know-how*

For some words, the only definition shown is a synonym. You can read a full definition by looking at the entry for its synonym.

DJ /ˈdiːˌdʒeɪ/ *n* [C] : DISC JOCKEY

The synonyms of an entry are often shown at the end of the entry or sense in a **called also** note.

disc jockey *n* [C] : a person who plays popular recorded music on the radio or at a party or nightclub — called also *DJ*

Synonyms are also sometimes shown in square brackets within examples.

¹**act** /ˈækt/ *n* **1** [C] : something that is done • *His first official act [=action] as President was to sign the bill.*

Examples

Examples of how a word is used are provided at most of the entries and are printed in italic type.

> **²junk** vb [T] informal : to get rid of (something) because it is worthless, damaged, etc. ▪ *We junked our old computer.*

Some examples have explanations that are given in square brackets.

> **ga·lore** /gəˈloɚ/ adj, always after a noun, informal : in large numbers or amounts ▪ *bargains galore* [=lots of bargains]

Some examples show different ways of saying the same thing.

> **mis·chief** /ˈmɪstʃəf/ n [U] **1** : behavior or activity that is annoying but that is not meant to cause serious harm or damage ▪ *He's always up to some mischief.* = *He's always getting into mischief.*

Many **common phrases** are highlighted in examples and are sometimes followed by explanations.

> **¹bolt** /ˈboʊlt/ n [C] **1** : a flash of lightning ▪ *a bolt of lightning* = *a lightning bolt* ▪ (figurative) *The news came as/like* ***a bolt from the blue.*** [=it was surprising and unexpected]

Examples that show collocations and other common word groups are often introduced by a brief note.

> **li·a·ble** /ˈlajəbəl/ adj **1** : legally responsible for something ▪ *They are liable for any damage.* **2** : likely to be affected or harmed by something — + to ▪ *liable to injury* **3** : likely to do something — + to ▪ *You're liable to fall if you're not more careful.*

Words that are shown in parentheses in an example are optional words, which means that they can be included or omitted without changing the basic meaning of the example.

> **jam–packed** /ˈdʒæmˈpækt/ adj : filled completely ▪ *The theater was jam-packed (with people).*

A slash / is used between words in an example or phrase when either of the words can be used in the same place in that example or phrase. Words separated by slashes in examples do not always have the same meaning.

> **flu·o·res·cent** /fluˈrɛsn̩t/ adj **1** : producing light when electricity flows through a tube that is filled with a type of gas ▪ *a fluorescent light/lamp* **2** : very bright ▪ *fluorescent colors/paint* — **flu·o·res·cence** /fluˈrɛsn̩s/ n [U]

Forms and Tenses

The **plural form** of most nouns in English is formed by adding *-s* or *-es* to the base word. For example, the plural of *book* is *books*, and the plural of *latch* is *latches*. Plural forms are only shown in this dictionary when they are unusual or when it is likely that the dictionary user will be uncertain about them. Often just the last part of the plural form is shown.

> **flur·ry** /ˈfləri/ *n, pl* **-ries** [C]   **1** : a brief, light snowfall   **2** : a brief period of excitement or activity ▪ *a flurry of trading/requests*

The **present third-person singular** form of most English verbs is formed by adding *-s* or *-es* to the base verb, so that *look* becomes *looks* and *touch* becomes *touches*. The **past tense** is usually formed by adding *-ed* (*looked, touched*) and the **present participle** is formed by adding *-ing* (*looking, touching*). In this dictionary, these forms are only shown when they are unusual or when it seems likely that the user will be uncertain about them. In many cases, only the last parts of the forms are shown.

> **clas·si·fy** /ˈklæsə,faɪ/ *vb* **-fies; -fied; -fy·ing** [T]   **1** : to arrange (people or things) into groups based on ways that they are alike ▪ *They classified the books into different categories.* ▪ *The parts were classified according to size.*   **2** : to consider (someone or something) as belonging to a particular group ▪ *I would classify her as a jazz singer.*
>
> ¹**dive** /ˈdaɪv/ *vb* **dived** /ˈdaɪvd/ *or chiefly US* **dove** /ˈdoʊv/; **div·ing** [I]   **1** : to jump into water with your arms and head going in first ▪ *She dove into the pool.*   **2** : to swim underwater usually while using special equipment to help you breathe ▪ *Many people enjoy diving on the island's coral reefs.*

When the **past participle** and the past tense of a verb are different, the past participle is also shown after the past tense.

> ¹**drive** /ˈdraɪv/ *vb* **drove** /ˈdroʊv/; **driv·en** /ˈdrɪvən/; **driv·ing**   **1 a** [T/I] : to direct the movement of (a car, truck, bus, etc.) ▪ *He drove the car down the road.* ▪ *She drives a taxi.* [=her job is driving a taxi] ▪ *He is learning to drive.*   **b** [I] *of a car, truck, etc.* : to move in a specified manner or direction ▪ *The car drove away/off.*   **c** [T/I] : to travel in a car ▪ *We drove all night.* ▪ *We drove (for) 160 miles.* ▪ *I drive (on/along) this route every day.*   **d** [T] : to take (someone or something) to a place in a car, truck, etc. ▪ *I drove her to the station.*

Some **adjectives** and **adverbs** have **comparative** and **superlative** forms which are normally formed by adding *-er* or *-est* to the base word; for example, the comparative and superlative forms of *cold* are *colder* and *coldest*. In this dictionary, such forms are only shown when they are unusual or when they require a change in spelling that is more than just the addition of *-er* and *-est*. The example shown here indicates that the comparative form of *fancy* is *fancier* and that the superlative form is *fanciest*.

¹fan·cy /ˈfænsi/ *adj* **fan·ci·er; -est**

Sometimes the comparative and superlative forms are very different from the main entry word.

¹good /ˈgʊd/ *adj* **bet·ter** /ˈbɛtɚ/; **best** /ˈbɛst/

Grammatical Labels

In addition to having a part of speech label, such as *n* (for *noun*), *vb* (for *verb*), and *adj* (for *adjective*), many entries include one or more **grammatical labels** which are shown in square brackets and which tell you the different forms or uses of a particular noun, verb, adjective, etc. When these labels appear in the beginning of the entry, they describe the entire entry. They can also appear at individual senses in an entry.

Most **nouns** are labeled [*C*], [*U*], [*C/U*], [*singular*], or [*plural*].

The label [*C*] stands for "count noun" and indicates that a noun entry or sense has both a singular and plural form and refers to something that can be counted.

heart·beat /ˈhɑɚtˌbiːt/ *n* [*C*] : the action or sound of the heart as it pumps blood • *irregular/rapid heartbeats*

The label [*U*] stands for "uncountable" and indicates a noun entry or sense that does not have a plural form and that refers to something that cannot be counted.

heart·burn /ˈhɑɚtˌbɚn/ *n* [*U*] : an unpleasant hot feeling in your chest caused by something that you ate

When a noun can be used as both a count and an uncountable (or "noncount") noun, it is given a [*C/U*] label.

heart·break /ˈhɑɚtˌbreɪk/ *n* [*C/U*] : a very strong feeling of sadness, disappointment, etc. ▪ *He recently suffered a string of romantic heartbreaks.*

An entry or sense for a noun that is always used in its plural form is labeled [*plural*].

long johns /ˈlɑːŋˌdʒɑːnz/ *n* [*plural*] : underwear that covers your legs — called also (*US*) long underwear

An entry or sense for a noun that refers to one thing and is never used in a plural form is labeled [*singular*].

²**glow** *n* [*singular*] **1** : a soft and steady light ▪ *the glow of the lamp* **2** : a pink color in your face from exercising, being excited, etc. ▪ *the rosy glow of health* **3** : a pleasant feeling ▪ *the glow of victory*

These labels are sometimes combined in different ways.

cav·al·ry /ˈkævəlri/ *n, pl* **cavalry** [*U, plural*] : the part of an army that in the past had soldiers who rode horses and that now has soldiers who ride in vehicles or helicopters ▪ *The cavalry was/were brought in to support the mission.* ▪ *cavalry forces/officers/troops*

Most **verbs** in this dictionary are labeled as either [*T*] or [*I*] or both. Other types of verbs have these labels: [*modal vb*], [*linking vb*], or [*auxiliary vb*]. Verbs labeled [*phrasal vb*] are entered as phrases at the end of a verb entry.

An entry or sense for a verb that has an object is labeled [*T*]. A verb of this kind is known as a **transitive verb**.

²**grease** *vb* **greased; greas·ing** [*T*] : to put grease or oil on (something) ▪ *Grease the pan then pour in the cake batter.*

An entry or sense for a verb that does not have an object is labeled [*I*]. A verb of this kind is known as an **intransitive verb**.

²**lapse** *vb* **lapsed; laps·ing** [*I*] **1** : to stop for usually a brief time ▪ *After a few polite words the conversation lapsed.*

When a verb entry or sense can be used both with and without an object, it is given a [*T/I*] label.

> **nav·i·gate** /ˈnævəˌgeɪt/ *vb* **-gat·ed; -gat·ing** **1** [*T/I*] : to find the way to get to a place when you are traveling in a ship, airplane, car, etc. ▪ *You can drive and I'll navigate.* ▪ *I'd need a map to navigate the city.* ▪ *(figurative) We navigated (our way) through all the rules and regulations.*

An entry or sense that is labeled [*linking vb*] does not express action but is used to say that something exists or is in a particular state. It connects an object with an adjective or noun that describes or identifies a subject.

> **be·come** /bɪˈkʌm/ *vb* **-came** /-ˈkeɪm/; **-come; -com·ing** **1** [*linking vb*] : to begin to be or come to be something specified ▪ *We didn't become close friends until recently.* ▪ *They both became teachers.* ▪ *The book has become quite popular.* ▪ *It eventually became clear that he had lied.*

An entry or sense that is labeled [*auxiliary vb*] is used with another verb in order to show the verb's tense, to form a question, etc.

> **be** /ˈbi/ *vb . . .*
> **10** [*auxiliary vb*] — used with the past participle of a verb to form passive constructions ▪ *The money was found by a child.* ▪ *They were [=got] married by a priest.* ▪ *Please be seated.* [=please sit down]

An entry or sense that is labeled [*modal vb*] is used with another verb to express an idea about what is possible, necessary, etc.

> **¹can** /kən, ˈkæn/ *vb, past tense* **could** /kəd, ˈkʊd/; *present tense for both singular and plural* **can**; *negative* **can·not** /ˈkænɑt, kəˈnɑːt, Brit* ˈkænət/ *or* **can't** /ˈkænt, Brit* ˈkɑːnt/ [*modal vb*] **1** : to be able to (do something) ▪ *I can do it myself.* ▪ *I can't decide what to do.* ▪ *The car can hold five people.* ▪ *I visit her whenever I can.* ▪ *She can play the piano.* ▪ *I can't lift the box.*

A verb that is labeled [*phrasal vb*] is a verb that is used with a preposition, an adverb, or both.

> **²pal** *vb* **palled; pal·ling** — **pal around with** [*phrasal vb*] *chiefly US, informal* : to spend time with (someone) as a friend ▪ *She's been palling around with a girl from her school.*

Other Labels

Many entries include labels such as *formal, informal, US, Brit,* etc. [See page 21a for a list of the labels that are commonly used in this dictionary.]

When a label appears at the beginning of an entry, it describes the entire entry, including any undefined words that may appear at the end of the entry. In the example shown here, the label *formal* means that both senses of *defile* are formal, and that the noun *defilement* is also a formal word.

> **de·file** /dɪˈfajəl/ *vb* **-filed; -fil·ing** [*T*] *formal* **1** : to make (something) dirty • *a lake defiled by pollution* **2** : to take away or ruin the purity, honor, or goodness of (something or someone important) • *Vandals defiled the church.* — **de·file·ment** /dɪˈfajəlmənt/ *n* [*U*]

When a label is used at a specific part of an entry (such as a particular sense or example), it relates only to that specific part.

> **¹grit** /ˈgrɪt/ *n* [*U*] **1** : very small pieces of sand or stone **2** *informal* : mental toughness and courage • *the resourcefulness and grit of pioneers*

Cross-references

Many entries include notes that direct you to another entry or sense for additional information.

Compare notes are placed at the entries of words that are similar or that may be confused with each other.

> **²effect** *vb* [*T*] *formal* **1** : to make (something) happen • *She could not effect a change in policy.* **2** : to cause (something) to produce the desired result • *The duty of the legislature is to effect the will of the people.* — compare AFFECT

When two or more homographs have the same part of speech, a *compare* note is included at the end of each entry.

> **¹re·count** /riˈkaʊnt/ *vb* [*T*] : to count (something) again • *They recounted the votes/money.* — compare ³RECOUNT
> **³re·count** /rɪˈkaʊnt/ *vb* [*T*] *formal* : to tell someone about (something that happened) • *He recounted the conversation he'd had earlier.* — compare ¹RECOUNT

See also notes often direct you to another entry that uses a form of the word you were looking up.

> **ef·face** /ɪˈfeɪs/ *vb* **-faced; -fac·ing** [*T*] *formal* : to cause (something) to fade or disappear • *a memory effaced by time* — see also SELF-EFFACING

See also notes can also direct you to a phrase that is defined at another entry.

> **¹do** /ˈduː/ *vb* **does** /ˈdʌz/; **did** /ˈdɪd/; **done** /ˈdʌn/; **do·ing** /ˈduːwɪŋ/ **1 a** [*T/I*] : to perform (an action or activity) • *This crime was done deliberately.* • *I have to do some chores.* . . . — **do by** [*phrasal vb*] : to deal with or treat (someone) well or badly • *She feels that they did poorly/badly by her.* [=that they treated her poorly/badly] — see also *hard done by* at ²HARD

A **see** cross-reference tells you that more information can be found at another entry.

> **goes** see GO
>
> **gold·en** /ˈgoʊldən/ *adj* ... — **silence is golden** see ¹SILENCE — **the golden goose** or **the goose that lays the golden egg** see ¹GOOSE

Other Features

Problems and questions that relate to the use of a particular word are discussed in *usage* paragraphs.

> **ain't** /ˈeɪnt/ *informal* ...
>
> *usage* *Ain't* is usually regarded as an error, but it is common in the very informal speech of some people and it is also used in informal and humorous phrases.

Many entries include notes that explain the **origins** of a word or provide other kinds of information.

> **cf** *abbr* compare — used to direct a reader to another idea, document, etc. ◆ *Cf* comes from the Latin *conferre*, which means "to compare."

Labels Used in This Dictionary

Parts of Speech

abbr — abbreviation
adj — adjective
adv — adverb
combining form
conj — conjunction
definite article
indefinite article

interj — interjection
n — noun
prefix
prep — preposition
pronoun
suffix
vb — verb

Grammatical Labels

(See pages 16a-19a for explanations and examples.)
for nouns: [*C*], [*U*], [*C/U*], [*singular*], [*plural*]
for verbs: [*T*], [*I*], [*T/I*] [*auxiliary vb*], [*linking vb*], [*modal vb*], [*phrasal vb*]

Usage labels

Regional Labels:

US — common only in American English
chiefly US — common in American English and sometimes used in British English
Brit — common only in British English
chiefly Brit — common in British English and sometimes used in American English

Status Labels:

slang — used in very informal, spoken English usually by a small group of people
offensive — likely to offend many people and usually avoided
impolite — not used in polite speech and writing

Register Labels:

informal — used in informal speech and writing
formal — used in formal speech and writing
literary — used in novels, poetry, etc., and rarely used in ordinary speech and writing
old-fashioned — not often used today but used by people in the recent past or by older people
humorous — having a funny or amusing quality
technical — used by people who have special knowledge about a particular subject
disapproving — used to show that you do not like or approve of someone or something
approving — used to show that you like or approve of someone or something

Subject Labels

Labels like *medical, law,* and *baseball* are used to show the specific subject that a definition relates to.

Pronunciation Symbols

VOWELS

Note: when two symbols are separated by / in the list below (eɪ/ej, oʊ/ow, etc.), the second symbol is used when the sound occurs immediately before another vowel and the first symbol is used elsewhere. The symbols /ɑ: i: u:/ are written as /ɑ i u/ when found in unstressed syllables.

æ	ask, bat, glad
ɑ:	cot, bomb, paw
ɛ	bet, fed
ə	about, banana, collide
i:/i:j	eat, bead, bee
ɪ	id, bid, pit
ʊ	foot, should, put
u:/u:w	boot, two, coo
ʌ	under, putt, bud
ɚ/ɚr	merge, bird, further
eɪ/ej	eight, wade, play
aɪ/aj	ice, bite, tile
aʊ/aw	out, gown, owl
ɔɪ/oj	oyster, coil, boy
oʊ/ow	oat, own, zone
ɑɚ/ɑr	car, heart, star
eɚ/er	bare, fair, wear
iɚ/ir	near, deer, mere
oɚ/or	boar, port, door
uɚ/ur	boor, tour

Note: The symbols below are for vowels that occur in British English. British pronunciations are shown in this dictionary when the most common British pronunciation is very different from the American pronunciation.

ɒ	*British*	cot, bomb
ɔ:	*British*	caught, paw, port
ə:	*British*	merge, bird
əʊ	*British*	oat, own, zone
ɪə	*British*	near, deer
ɛə	*British*	bare, fair
ʊə	*British*	boor, tour

CONSONANTS

b	baby, labor, cab
d	day, kid, riddle
dʒ	just, badger, fudge
ð	then, either, bathe
f	foe, tough, buff
g	go, dagger, bag
h	hot, ahead
j	yes, vineyard
k	cat, flock, skin
l	law, hollow
l̩	pedal, battle, final
m	mat, hemp, hammer
n	new, tent, tenor, run
n̩	button, satin, kitten
ŋ	rung, hang, swinger
p	top, speed, pay
r	rope, arrive
s	sad, mist, kiss
ʃ	shoe, mission, slush
t	stick, late, later
tʃ	batch, nature, choose
θ	thin, ether, bath
v	vat, never, cave
w	wet, software
z	zoo, easy, buzz
ʒ	vision, azure, beige

OTHER SYMBOLS

ˈ	high stress: **pen**manship
ˌ	low stress: pen**man**ship
Brit	indicates British pronunciation
/	slash used in pairs to mark the beginning and end of a pronunciation or set of pronunciations /ˈpɛn/

22a

A

¹**a** *or* **A** /ˈeɪ/ *n, pl* **a's** *or* **as** *or* **A's** *or* **As** 1 [C/U] : the first letter of the English alphabet • *a word that begins with (an) a* 2 [C/U] : a musical note or key referred to by the letter A : the sixth tone of a C-major scale • *play/sing an A* • *a song in the key of A* 3 [C] : a grade that is given to a student for doing excellent work • *She got an A on the exam.* • *He's an A student.* [=a student who gets A's] — **an A for effort** see EFFORT — **from (point) A to (point) B** : from one place to another • *traveling from A to B*

²**a** /ə, ˈeɪ/ *or* **an** /ən, ˈæn/ *indefinite article* ✧ *A* is used before a consonant sound, and *an* is used before a vowel sound. • *a door* • *a human* • *a union* • *an icicle* • *an honor* • *an FBI investigation*
1 — used before singular nouns when the person or thing is being mentioned for the first time • *He bought a house.* 2 a — used like *one* before some number words, units of measure, etc. • *a million dollars* • *This is a third the size of that.* • *a foot and a half of water* = *one and a half feet of water* b : one single — used with *no*, *not*, etc. • *"Did she say anything?" "Not a word."* 3 — used before a word or phrase that indicates a type or class of person or thing • *My uncle is a plumber.* • *a torrential rain* • *She has a warmth that puts people at ease.* 4 — used like *any* to refer in a general way to people or things • *A person who is sick can't work well.* [=people can't work well if they are sick] 5 — used before a proper noun to indicate limited knowledge about the person or thing being mentioned • *A Mr. Smith* [=a man named Mr. Smith] *called.* 6 a — used before a proper noun that is acting as an example or type • *His friends say he's an Einstein in regard to science.* b — used before the name of a day of the week to refer to one occurrence of it • *My birthday falls on a Tuesday this year.* 7 a — used before the name of a person when the name is being used to refer to something created by that person • *a Rembrandt* [=a painting by Rembrandt] b — used before a family name to show that someone is a member of that family • *She's a Kennedy.* 8 — used with words like *bit* and *little* to describe a quantity, amount, or degree • *It's getting a bit/little late.* 9 — used in phrases that describe speed, frequency, etc. • *They meet twice a* [=each] *week.* • *ten miles an* [=per] *hour*

a- *or* **an-** *prefix* : not : without • *asexual*

AA *abbr* 1 Alcoholics Anonymous 2 Brit Automobile Association

AAA *abbr, US* American Automobile Association

aah /ˈɑː/ *interj* — used to express pleasure, surprise, or happiness • *Aah, that feels good.* — **aah** *vb* [I] *informal* • *We all oohed and aahed at/over the fireworks.* — **aah** *n* [C]

aard·vark /ˈɑːdˌvɑːk/ *n* [C] : an African animal that has a long nose and that eats ants and other insects

AARP *abbr, US* American Association of Retired Persons

ab /ˈæb/ *n* [C] *informal* : an abdominal muscle — usually plural • *exercises that tone your abs*

ab. *abbr* about

aback /əˈbæk/ *adv* : by surprise • *She was taken aback* [=she was very surprised] *by his rude response.*

aba·cus /ˈæbəkəs/ *n, pl* **-cus·es** *also* **-ci** /-ˌsaɪ/ [C] : a device used for calculating by sliding small balls along rods or in grooves

¹**aban·don** /əˈbændən/ *vb* [T] 1 a : to leave and never return to (someone who needs protection or help) • *He abandoned his family.* • *an abandoned baby* b : to leave and never return to (something) • *an old, abandoned house* 2 : to leave (a place) because of danger • *People were forced to abandon their homes.* 3 : to stop doing or having (something) • *We abandoned hope of ever getting back.* — **aban·don·ment** /əˈbændənmənt/ *n* [U]

²**abandon** *n* [U] : a feeling of wild or complete freedom • *They danced with (wild) abandon.* • *With reckless abandon* [=in a very wild and reckless way], *she quit her job and moved to Tahiti.*

abashed /əˈbæʃt/ *adj* : embarrassed or ashamed • *She seemed a little abashed when they asked about her job.*

abate /əˈbeɪt/ *vb* **abat·ed; abat·ing** [I] : to become weaker • *The excitement has abated.* — **abate·ment** /əˈbeɪtmənt/ *n* [C/U] • *continuing without abatement* • *a tax abatement* [=an amount by which a tax is reduced]

ab·at·toir /ˈæbəˌtwɑːr/ *n* [C] *chiefly Brit* : SLAUGHTERHOUSE

ab·bey /ˈæbi/ *n, pl* **-beys** [C] : a church that is connected to other buildings where monks or nuns live or once lived • *Westminster Abbey*

ab·bot /ˈæbət/ *n* [C] : a man who is the head of a monastery

abbr *or* **abbr.** *abbr* abbreviation

ab·bre·vi·ate /əˈbriːviˌeɪt/ *vb* **-at·ed; -at·ing** [T] : to make (something, such as a word) shorter • *an abbreviated version of the story* • *"United Kingdom" is commonly abbreviated to/as "UK."*

ab·bre·vi·a·tion /əˌbriːviˈeɪʃən/ *n* [C] : a shortened form of a word or name • *"UK" is an abbreviation of/for "United Kingdom."*

¹**ABC** /ˌeɪˌbiːˈsiː/ *n, pl* **ABCs** *or* **ABC's** [U, plural] 1 : the letters of the English alphabet • *(US) We learned our ABC's.* = *(Brit) We learned our ABC.* 2 : the most basic or important information about a subject • *(US) learning the ABC's of wine*

²**ABC** *abbr* 1 American Broadcasting

Corporation 2 Australian Broadcasting Corporation

ab·di·cate /ˈæbdɪˌkeɪt/ vb -cat·ed; -cat·ing 1 [T/I] : to leave the position of being a king or queen • *The king was forced to abdicate (the throne).* 2 [T] formal : to fail to do what is required by (a duty or responsibility) • *He has abdicated his parental responsibilities.* — **ab·di·ca·tion** /ˌæbdɪˈkeɪʃən/ n [C/U]

ab·do·men /ˈæbdəmən/ n [C] 1 : the part of the body below the chest that contains the stomach and other organs 2 : the rear part of an insect's body — **ab·dom·i·nal** /æbˈdɑːmən̩/ adj • *abdominal muscles*

ab·duct /æbˈdʌkt/ vb [T] : to take (someone) away from a place by force • *He was abducted from his home.* — **ab·duct·ee** /ˌæbdʌkˈtiː/ n [C] • *alien abductees* [=people who say they were abducted by creatures from another world] — **ab·duc·tion** /æbˈdʌkʃən/ n [C/U] — **ab·duc·tor** /æbˈdʌktɚ/ n [C] • *She escaped from her abductors.*

ab·er·rant /əˈberənt/ adj, formal : AB-NORMAL • *aberrant behavior*

ab·er·ra·tion /ˌæbəˈreɪʃən/ n [C/U] : something (such as a problem or a type of behavior) that is unusual or unexpected • *For her, such a low grade on an exam was an aberration.*

abet /əˈbɛt/ vb abet·ted; abet·ting [T] formal : to help or encourage someone in a criminal act • *She is charged with aiding and abetting the bank robbers.*

abey·ance /əˈbeɪəns/ n — **in abeyance** formal : in a temporary state of being stopped • *The plans are (being held) in abeyance.*

ab·hor /əbˈhoɚ/ vb -horred; -hor·ring [T] formal : to dislike (someone or something) very much • *They abhor violence.* — **ab·hor·rence** /əbˈhorəns/ n [U]

ab·hor·rent /əbˈhorənt/ adj, formal : causing or deserving hatred • *an abhorrent crime*

abide /əˈbaɪd/ vb abid·ed; abid·ing [T] : to accept or bear (someone or something bad, unpleasant, etc.) • *I can't abide* [=stand] *his bad moods.* — **abide by** [phrasal vb] : OBEY • *We have to abide by their rules/decision.*

abid·ing /əˈbaɪdɪŋ/ adj, always before a noun, formal : continuing for a long time • *an abiding love/friendship*

abil·i·ty /əˈbɪləti/ n, pl -ties [C/U] : the power or skill to do something • *a teacher's ability to inspire his students* • *a woman of great artistic/athletic ability* • *He works to the best of his ability.* [=as well as he can]

ab·ject /ˈæbˌdʒɛkt/ adj 1 : extremely bad or severe • *abject poverty* • *an abject failure* 2 a : feeling or showing shame • *an abject apology* b : lacking courage or strength • *an abject coward* — **ab·ject·ly** /ˈæbˌdʒɛktli/ adv

ab·jure /æbˈdʒʊɚ/ vb -jured; -jur·ing [T] formal : to reject (something) formally • *He abjured allegiance to his native country.*

ablaze /əˈbleɪz/ adj, not before a noun : burning or on fire • *Lightning set the house ablaze.* • (figurative) *Her eyes were ablaze with anger.*

able /ˈeɪbəl/ adj 1 not before a noun : having the power, skill, money, etc., that is needed to do something • *Is he able to swim?* [=can he swim?] • *They weren't able to afford a vacation.* **b** : not prevented from doing something • *Will you be able to visit soon?* 2 abler; ablest : having skill or talent • *a very able editor/leader/soldier*

-able also **-ible** adj suffix 1 : fit for or worthy of being • *lovable* • *collectible* 2 : likely to • *breakable* 3 : having a certain quality • *knowledgeable*

able—bod·ied /ˌeɪbəlˈbɑːdid/ adj : having a healthy and strong body • *able-bodied men and women*

ably /ˈeɪbəli/ adv : skillfully and well • *She was ably assisted by two helpers.*

ab·nor·mal /æbˈnoɚməl/ adj : different from what is normal especially in a way that causes problems • *abnormal behavior* • *The results of the blood test were abnormal.* — **ab·nor·mal·i·ty** /ˌæbnɚˈmæləti/ n [C/U] • *genetic abnormalities* — **ab·nor·mal·ly** adv

¹**aboard** /əˈboɚd/ adv : on a train, ship, plane, etc. • *Climb aboard before the train leaves.* • *Everyone aboard was injured in the accident.*

²**aboard** prep : on or into (a train, ship, etc.) • *We went/got aboard (the) ship.*

abode /əˈboʊd/ n [C] formal + humorous : the place where someone lives • *Welcome to my humble abode.*

abol·ish /əˈbɑːlɪʃ/ vb [T] : to officially end or stop (something, such as a law) • *They abolished the death penalty.* — **ab·o·li·tion** /ˌæbəˈlɪʃən/ n [U] • *the abolition of slavery*

ab·o·li·tion·ist /ˌæbəˈlɪʃnɪst/ n [C] : a person who wants to abolish slavery

A–bomb /ˈeɪˌbɑːm/ n [C] : ATOMIC BOMB

abom·i·na·ble /əˈbɑːmənəbəl/ adj, formal : very bad or unpleasant • *abominable crimes/weather* — **abom·i·na·bly** /əˈbɑːmənəbli/ adv

abom·i·na·tion /əˌbɑːməˈneɪʃən/ n [C] : something that causes disgust or hatred • *She thinks the sculpture is an abomination.*

ab·orig·i·nal /ˌæbəˈrɪdʒən̩/ adj, always before a noun 1 : of or relating to the people and things that have been in a region from the earliest time • *aboriginal plants/tribes* 2 : of or relating to Australian aborigines • *the aboriginal peoples of Australia*

ab·orig·i·ne /ˌæbəˈrɪdʒəni/ n [C] 1 : a member of the original people to live in an area • *North American aborigines* 2 or **Aborigine** : a member of any of the native peoples of Australia

abort /əˈboɚt/ vb 1 [T] : to end a pregnancy deliberately by causing the death of the fetus • *They decided to abort the pregnancy/fetus.* 2 [T/I] : to stop something before it is completed because of problems or danger • *The project had to be aborted.* • *an aborted mission/attempt*

abor·tion /əˈboɚʃən/ n [C/U] : a medical procedure used to end a pregnancy and cause the death of the fetus ▪ *She had/got an abortion.* ▪ *abortion laws/rights*

abor·tion·ist /əˈboɚʃənɪst/ *n* [C] : a person who performs abortions

abor·tive /əˈboɚtɪv/ *adj* : failing to achieve the desired result ▪ *an abortive coup*

abound /əˈbaʊnd/ *vb* [I] : to be present in large numbers or amounts ▪ *business opportunities abound.* — **abound in/with** [*phrasal vb*] : to contain a very large amount of (something) ▪ *The region abounds in/with oil.*

¹**about** /əˈbaʊt/ *adv* **1 a** : almost or nearly ▪ *We're about ready to go.* ▪ *That's about all the time we have.* ▪ *We tried just about everything we could think of.* ▪ *"Is there anything else to do?" "No, that's about it/ all."* [=there is nothing else to do] **b** — used to indicate that a number, amount, time, etc., is not exact or certain ▪ *It should cost about $200.* **2** : very close to doing something ▪ *She is about to leave.* [=she will be leaving very soon] — often used with *not* to stress that someone will not do something ▪ *I'm not about to quit.* [=I will not quit] **3** *chiefly Brit* **a** : in many different directions or places : AROUND ▪ *They wandered about for several hours.* **b** : in or near a particular area or place : AROUND ▪ *There was no one about.* — **out and about** see ¹OUT

²**about** *prep* **1 a** — used to indicate the object of a thought, feeling, or action ▪ *We did something about the problems.* ▪ *I'm worried about her.* **b** — used to indicate the subject of something said or written ▪ *What's he talking about?* ▪ *books about birds* **2** : as part of (someone or something) ▪ *There's something weird about that guy.* [=that guy is weird] **3** — used to indicate the most important or basic part or purpose of something ▪ *A good marriage is (all) about trust.* **4** *chiefly Brit* **a** : in the area near (something or someone) ▪ *Fish are abundant about* [=around] *the reefs.* **b** : over or in different parts of (a place) ▪ *He traveled all about* [=around] *the country.* **c** : on every side of (something or someone) ▪ *She wrapped the blanket about* [=around] *herself.* **5 a** — used to say that something is done quickly or slowly ▪ *If you're going to do that, be quick about it.* [=do it quickly] **b** *chiefly Brit* : in the act or process of doing (something) ▪ *He seems to know what he's about.* [=to know what he's doing] — **how about** see ¹HOW — **what about** see ¹WHAT

about–face /əˈbaʊtˈfeɪs/ *n* [C] **1** : an act of turning to face in the opposite direction ▪ *The soldiers were ordered to do an about-face.* **2** : a complete change of attitude or opinion ▪ *After saying that he didn't want the job, he did an about-face and accepted the offer.*

about–turn /əˈbaʊtˈtɚn/ *n* [C] *Brit* : ABOUT-FACE

¹**above** /əˈbʌv/ *adv* **1** : in or to a higher place ▪ *The stars shone above.* ▪ *up above and down below* **2** : in or to a higher rank or number ▪ *Groups of six and above* [=of six or more] *need reservations.* **3** : above zero ▪ *Temperatures range from 5*

below to 5 above. **4** : higher, further up, or earlier on the same page or on a preceding page ▪ *the person named above = the above-named person* — **from above** **1** : from a higher place or position ▪ *It looks like a cross when viewed from above.* **2** : from someone with greater power or authority ▪ *waiting for orders from above*

²**above** *prep* **1** : in or to a higher place than (something) : OVER ▪ *Put your hands above your head.* ▪ *We rented an apartment above a restaurant.* **2** : greater in number, quantity, or size than (something) ▪ *Temperatures were above average all week.* **3** : in a higher or more important position than (something) ▪ *He puts his child's needs above his own.* ▪ *Above all, we must consider what is best for the children.* **4** : having more importance or power than (someone) ▪ *A captain is above a lieutenant.* **5** : too important to be affected by (something) ▪ *She thinks that she's above criticism.* [=that she cannot be criticized] — see also *above the law* at LAW **6** : too good for (some type of behavior, work, etc.) ▪ *He was not above cheating* [=he would cheat] *when it served his purposes.* **7** : more loudly and clearly than (another sound) ▪ *I heard the whistle above* [=over] *the roar of the crowd.* — **above and beyond** : further than what is required ▪ *He went above and beyond the call of duty.* [=he did more than his duty required him to do] — **over and above** see ²OVER

³**above** *adj* : written at an earlier point in the same document ▪ *You can contact me at the above address.* — **the above** : something that is mentioned at an earlier point in the same document ▪ *If any of the above is incorrect, please let me know.* ▪ *The correct answer is "none of the above."*

above·ground /əˈbʌvˌgraʊnd/ *adj, US* : located or occurring above the ground ▪ *an aboveground pool*

abra·sion /əˈbreɪʒən/ *n* [C] : a mark or an injury caused by something that rubs or scrapes against a surface (such as the skin) ▪ *She had abrasions on her knees.*

abra·sive /əˈbreɪsɪv/ *adj* **1** : having a rough texture ▪ *an abrasive surface* ▪ *abrasive cleaners* **2** : very unpleasant or irritating ▪ *an abrasive comment/personality* — **abra·sive·ly** *adv* — **abra·sive·ness** *n* [U]

abreast /əˈbrɛst/ *adv* — used to describe people or things that are next to each other in a line ▪ *rows of five men abreast* — **abreast of** **1** : next to (someone or something) ▪ *Another runner drew abreast of her.* **2** : informed about (new events, facts, etc.) ▪ *He likes to keep/stay abreast of the news.*

abridge /əˈbrɪdʒ/ *vb* **abridged; abridg·ing** [T] : to shorten (a book, a play, etc.) by removing some parts ▪ *an abridged dictionary* — **abridg·ment** *or* **abridge·ment** /əˈbrɪdʒmənt/ *n* [C/U]

abroad /əˈbrɑːd/ *adv* : in or to a foreign country ▪ *both at home and abroad* ▪ *He hopes to study abroad next year.* ▪ *They moved here from abroad.* [=from a foreign country]

abrupt /ə'brʌpt/ *adj* **1** : very sudden and not expected • *an abrupt change in the weather* • *The road came to an abrupt end.* **2 a** : talking to other people in a very brief and unfriendly way • *He tends to be abrupt with his employees.* **b** : rudely brief • *an abrupt reply* — **abrupt·ly** *adv* • *The party ended abruptly.* — **abrupt·ness** *n* [U, singular]

ab·scess /'æb,sɛs/ *n* [C] *medical* : a painful area of tissue that is filled with pus — **ab·scessed** /'æb,sɛst/ *adj* • *an abscessed tooth* [=an infected tooth that has caused an abscess in the gum]

ab·scond /əb'skɑːnd/ *vb* [I] *formal* **1** : to leave a place secretly • *The suspect absconded to Canada.* **2** : to leave and take something that does not belong to you — + *with* • *a banker who absconded with all the money*

ab·sence /'æbsəns/ *n* **1** [*singular*] : a state in which something is not present or does not exist • *an absence of enthusiasm* • *In the absence of any objections, the plan will proceed.* **2 a** [C] : a failure to be present at a usual or expected place • *I expected to see her and was surprised by her absence.* **b** [C/U] : a period of time when someone is not present at a place, job, etc. • *She returned to the company after a prolonged absence.* • *I won't see him for a week, but absence makes the heart grow fonder.* • *The study was completed in her absence.* [=while she was away] — see also LEAVE OF ABSENCE

¹**ab·sent** /'æbsənt/ *adj* **1** : not present at a usual or expected place • *an absent father who is not home most of the time* • *She was absent (from school) yesterday.* • *The soldier was absent without leave.* [=AWOL; absent without having permission to be absent] **2** : not present at all • *a landscape in which vegetation is entirely absent* **3** : showing a lack of attention to what is happening or being said • *There was an absent look on her face.* — **ab·sent·ly** *adv*

²**ab·sent** /æb'sɛnt/ *vb* — **absent yourself** *formal* : to go or stay away from something • *He absented himself from the meeting.*

³**ab·sent** /'æbsənt/ *prep, US, formal* : in the absence of (something) : WITHOUT • *Absent any objections, the plan will proceed.*

ab·sen·tee /,æbsən'tiː/ *n* [C] : a person who is not present in a usual or expected place • *There were 10 sick absentees that day.*

absentee ballot *n* [C] *US* : a vote that is submitted before an election by a voter who will not be present when the election occurs

ab·sen·tee·ism /,æbsən'tiː,ɪzəm/ *n* [U] : a tendency to be away from work or school • *Her office has a high rate of absenteeism.* [=people in her office are frequently absent from work]

ab·sent·mind·ed /,æbsənt'maɪndəd/ *adj* : tending to forget things or to not notice things • *Her absentminded husband forgot their anniversary.* — **ab·sent·mind·ed·ly** *adv* — **ab·sent·mind·ed·ness** *n* [U]

ab·so·lute /'æbsə,luːt/ *adj* **1** *always be-*fore a noun : complete and total • *I have absolute faith/confidence in her.* • *absolute freedom* • (*informal*) *That's absolute nonsense/rubbish!* • (*US*) *That was the absolute best movie ever!* **2 a** : not limited in any way • *absolute power/authority* **b** : having unlimited power • *an absolute dictator/monarchy* **3** : not depending on or compared with anything else • *The company has grown in absolute terms, but its share of the market has decreased.* — **ab·so·lute·ness** *n* [U]

ab·so·lute·ly /'æbsə,luːtli/ *adv* **1** : completely or totally • *Are you absolutely certain?* • *I absolutely love the car.* **2** : with unlimited power • *The king ruled absolutely.* **3** — used in speech as a forceful way of saying "yes" • *"Do you want to go?" "Absolutely!"* • *"We all need to work harder." "Absolutely!"* ◆ **Absolutely not** is used in speech as a forceful way of saying "no." • *"Do you think he's right?" "Absolutely not!"*

ab·solve /əb'zɑːlv/ *vb* **-solved; -solving** [T] *formal* **1** : to make (someone) free from guilt, responsibility, etc. • *His youth does not absolve him (of guilt) for these crimes.* **2** : to give forgiveness to (someone who has sinned) or for (a sin) • *He asked the priest to absolve (him of) his sins.* — **ab·so·lu·tion** /,æbsə'luːʃən/ *n* [U]

ab·sorb /əb'soəb/ *vb* [T] **1 a** : to take in (liquids, vitamins, etc.) in a gradual way • *a material that absorbs moisture like a sponge* • *Water is absorbed by plants through their roots.* **b** : to take in (heat, light, etc.) • *These special walls absorb sound.* • *The frame of the car absorbed much of the impact.* **2** : to learn (something) • *She is good at absorbing information.* **3** : to take all of the interest or attention of (someone) • *I was so absorbed by her story that I lost track of time.* • *She was (completely) absorbed in* [=fully involved in] *thought.* **4** : to accept or deal with (something that is difficult, harmful, etc.) • *The company has had to absorb many setbacks recently.* **5** : to use up or consume (something) • *His work absorbs most of his time.* — **ab·sorb·er** *n* [C] — see also SHOCK ABSORBER — **ab·sorb·ing** *adj* • *an absorbing story* [=a very interesting story] — **ab·sorp·tion** /əb'soəpʃən/ *n* [U]

ab·sor·bent /əb'soəbənt/ *adj* : able to absorb liquid • *very absorbent paper towels* — **ab·sor·ben·cy** /əb'soəbənsi/ *n* [U]

ab·stain /əb'steɪn/ *vb* [I] **1** : to choose not to do or have something • *He abstained from taking part in the discussion.* • *abstain from (drinking) alcohol* **2** : to choose not to vote • *Ten members voted for the proposal, six voted against it, and two abstained.* — **ab·stain·er** *n* [C] — **ab·sten·tion** /əb'stɛnʃən/ *n* [C/U] • *abstention from drugs and alcohol* • *There were 10 ayes, 6 nays, and 2 abstentions.*

ab·sti·nence /'æbstənəns/ *n* [U] : the practice of not doing or having something that is wanted or enjoyable • *sexual abstinence* — **ab·sti·nent** /'æbstənənt/ *adj*

¹**ab·stract** /æbˈstrækt, ˈæbˌstrækt/ *adj* **1** : relating to or involving general ideas or qualities rather than specific people, objects, or actions ▪ *abstract thinking* ▪ *abstract concepts such as love and hate* **2** *of art* : expressing ideas and emotions without attempting to create a realistic picture ▪ *abstract art* ▪ *an abstract painter* — **ab·stract·ly** /æbˈstræktli/ *adv* — **abstract·ness** /æbˈstræktnəs/ *n* [U]

²**ab·stract** /ˈæbˌstrækt/ *n* [C] : a brief written statement of the main points in a longer report, speech, etc. : SUMMARY — **in the abstract** : without referring to a specific person, object, or event : in a general way ▪ *thinking about freedom in the abstract*

³**ab·stract** /æbˈstrækt/ *vb* [T] **1** : to make a summary of the main parts of (a report, speech, etc.) ▪ *abstract an academic paper* **2** : to obtain or remove (something) *from a source* ▪ *Data for the study was abstracted from hospital records.*

ab·strac·tion /æbˈstrækʃən/ *n* **1** [U] : the act of obtaining or removing something from a source ▪ *the abstraction of data from hospital records* **2** [C/U] *formal* : a general idea or quality rather than an actual person, object, or event ▪ *"Beauty" and "truth" are abstractions.*

ab·struse /əbˈstruːs/ *adj, formal* : hard to understand ▪ *abstruse theories* — **ab·struse·ly** *adv* — **ab·struse·ness** *n* [U]

ab·surd /əbˈsəd/ *adj* : extremely silly, foolish, or unreasonable ▪ *an absurd situation/idea* ▪ *The charges against him are absurd.* — **the absurd** **1** : a condition of extreme silliness or foolishness ▪ *Her ideas verge on the absurd.* **2** : things that are absurd ▪ *a filmmaker who is fascinated with the absurd* — **ab·sur·di·ty** /əbˈsədəti/ *n, pl* **-ties** [C/U] — **ab·surd·ly** *adv*

abun·dance /əˈbʌndəns/ *n* [U, singular] : a large amount of something ▪ *a plant with an abundance of flowers* ▪ *a time of great abundance* [=a time when there is much food, money, etc.] — **in abundance** : in large amounts ▪ *The city has fine restaurants in abundance.*

abun·dant /əˈbʌndənt/ *adj* : existing or occurring in large amounts ▪ *an abundant supply of food* — **abun·dant·ly** *adv*

¹**abuse** /əˈbjuːz/ *vb* **abused; abus·ing** [T] **1** : to treat (a person or animal) in a harsh or harmful way ▪ *He abused his wife both mentally and physically.* ▪ *an abused child* **2** : to use or treat (something) in a way that causes damage ▪ *She abused her body with years of heavy drinking.* **3** : to use (something) wrongly ▪ *abuse a privilege* ▪ *She abused her friend's trust.* **4** : to use too much of (a drug, alcohol, etc.) ▪ *He abused alcohol.* **5** : to attack (someone) using words ▪ *The fans were verbally abusing the referee.* — **abus·er** *n* [C]

²**abuse** /əˈbjuːs/ *n* **1** : the act or practice of abusing someone or something: such as **a** [U, plural] : harmful treatment of a person or animal ▪ *child abuse* ▪ *a government accused of human rights abuses* [=of violating the basic rights of people]

b [U] : the use or treatment of something in a way that causes damage ▪ *These toys can handle a lot of abuse.* **c** [C/U] : the act or practice of using something wrongly ▪ *the governor's abuse of power* **d** [U] : the act or practice of using too much of a drug, alcohol, etc. ▪ *drug/substance abuse* **2** [U] : harsh and insulting language ▪ *verbal abuse*

abu·sive /əˈbjuːsɪv/ *adj* **1** : using harsh and insulting language ▪ *a verbally abusive fan* **2** : using or involving physical violence or emotional cruelty ▪ *an abusive parent* ▪ *people in abusive relationships* — **abu·sive·ly** *adv* — **abu·sive·ness** *n* [U]

abut /əˈbʌt/ *vb* **abut·ted; abut·ting** [T/I] *formal* : to touch along an edge ▪ *Their property abuts (on) our property.* [=an edge of their property touches an edge of our property] — **abut·ter** /əˈbʌtɚ/ *n* [C]

abut·ment /əˈbʌtmənt/ *n* [C] *technical* : a heavy structure that supports something (such as a bridge)

a·buzz /əˈbʌz/ *adj, informal* : filled with excited talk about something ▪ *Washington is abuzz with rumors of a scandal.*

abys·mal /əˈbɪzməl/ *adj* : extremely poor or bad ▪ *abysmal living conditions* ▪ *Her grades were abysmal.* — **abys·mal·ly** *adv*

abyss /əˈbɪs/ *n* [C] : a hole so deep or a space so great that it cannot be measured ▪ *the ocean's abysses* ▪ *(figurative) an abyss of despair*

AC *abbr* **1** *US* air-conditioning **2** alternating current

ac·a·de·mia /ˌækəˈdiːmijə/ *n* [U] : the world of teachers, schools, and education ▪ *The business world is very different from academia.*

¹**ac·a·dem·ic** /ˌækəˈdɛmɪk/ *adj* **1** : of or relating to schools and education ▪ *academic achievements* ▪ *I spent my academic career at one school.* **2** : having no practical importance ▪ *a purely academic question* — **ac·a·dem·i·cal·ly** /ˌækəˈdɛmɪkli/ *adv*

²**academic** *n* **1** [C] : a teacher in a college or university ▪ *The book only appeals to academics.* **2** [plural] *chiefly US* : courses of study taken at a school or college ▪ *She excelled at academics but not at sports.*

acad·e·my /əˈkædəmi/ *n, pl* **-mies** [C] **1 a** : a school that provides training in special subjects or skills ▪ *a military/tennis academy* **b** *US* : a private high school ▪ *a student at Smith Academy* **2** : an organization that supports art, science, or literature ▪ *the National Academy of Sciences*

Academy Award *trademark* — used for an award given by part of the U.S. film industry to the best actors, directors, etc., of the year

a cap·pel·la /ˌɑːkəˈpɛlə, Brit ˌækæˈpɛlə/ *adv* : without instrumental music ▪ *singing a cappella* — **a cappella** *adj*

ac·cede /ækˈsiːd/ *vb* **-ced·ed; -ced·ing** [I] *formal* **1** : to agree to a request or a demand ▪ *We were forced to* **accede** *to their demands.* **2** : to enter a high office or position — usually + *to* ▪ *He acceded* *to the throne* [=he became king] *in 1838.*

ac·cel·er·ate /ɪkˈsɛləˌreɪt/ *vb* **-at·ed; -at·ing** [*T/I*] **1** : to move faster • *The plane accelerated down the runway.* • *She accelerated the car.* **2** : to cause (something) to happen sooner or more quickly • *He says that cutting taxes accelerated economic growth.* • *Changes occurred at an accelerated rate.* — **ac·cel·er·a·tion** /ɪkˌsɛləˈreɪʃən/ *n* [*U, singular*]

ac·cel·er·a·tor /ɪkˈsɛləˌreɪtə/ *n* [*C*] : a pedal in a vehicle that is pressed down to make the vehicle go faster • *step on the accelerator* — called also (*US*) **gas pedal**

¹ac·cent /ˈækˌsɛnt, *Brit* ˈæksənt/ *n* [*C*] **1** : a way of pronouncing words that occurs among the people in a particular region or country • *She spoke with a heavy/ thick Southern accent.* **2** : greater stress given to a syllable of a word in speech • *The word "before" has the accent on the last syllable.* **3 a** : a mark (such as ' or) used to show the part of a word that should be given greater stress when it is spoken — called also **accent mark b** : a mark placed above a letter to show how it should be pronounced • *the accents in the French word "émigré"* — called also **accent mark 4** : special concern or attention : EMPHASIS • *The TV shows put/ place the/an accent on youth.* **5** : a small decorative object or detail that is different from the things that are around it • *accent colors/lighting/plants*

²ac·cent /ˈækˌsɛnt, *Brit* əkˈsɛnt/ *vb* [*T*] **1** : to give special attention to (something) • *His speech accented positive parts of the plan.* **2** : to say part of a word with greater stress • *Accent the word "before" on the second syllable.* • *an accented syllable*

ac·cen·tu·ate /ækˈsɛntʃəˌweɪt/ *vb* **-at·ed; -at·ing** [*T*] : to make (something) more noticeable • *His clothes accentuate his muscular build.* • *accentuate the positive* — **ac·cen·tu·a·tion** /ɪkˌsɛntʃuˈweɪʃən/ *n* [*U*]

ac·cept /ɪkˈsɛpt/ *vb* **1 a** [*T/I*] : to receive or take (something offered) • *accept a gift/proposal/offer* • *They offered him the job, and he accepted.* **b** [*T*] : to take (something) as payment • *The store doesn't accept credit cards.* **2** [*T*] : to agree to receive or allow (something) • *accept a telephone call* • *I accept your apology.* **3** [*T*] **a** : to think of (something) as true, proper, or normal • *This treatment is now accepted by many doctors.* • *an accepted practice* **b** : to stop denying or resisting (something true or necessary) • *learning to accept change* • *The truth can be hard to accept.* • *He has to accept (the fact) that his baseball career is over.* **c** : to admit that you have or deserve (something, such as blame) • *I accept responsibility for the accident.* **d** : to be willing to have or experience (something) • *Investors have to accept some risk.* • *She accepted the challenge.* **4** [*T*] **a** : to allow (someone) to join a club, to attend a school, etc. • *She was accepted at/by Yale University.* **b** : to regard (someone) as belonging to a group • *They were accepted into the community.*

— **ac·cep·tance** /ɪkˈsɛptəns/ *n* [*U*] • *The college sent me a letter of acceptance.* • *Her theories have won widespread acceptance.* • *He delivered an acceptance speech at the party's convention.*

ac·cept·able /ɪkˈsɛptəbəl/ *adj* **1** : capable or worthy of being accepted • *socially acceptable behavior* **2** : fairly good : SATISFACTORY • *an acceptable performance* — **ac·cept·abil·i·ty** /ɪkˌsɛptəˈbɪləti/ *n* [*U*] — **ac·cept·ably** /ɪkˈsɛptəbli/ *adv*

¹ac·cess /ˈækˌsɛs/ *n* [*U*] **1** : a way of getting near, at, or to something or someone • *a building with wheelchair access* [=a way for people in wheelchairs to enter] **2** : a way of being able to use or get something • *Internet access* • *I don't have access to a car.* [=I don't have a car that I can use] **3** : permission or the right to enter, get near, or make use of something or to have contact with someone • *Investigators are trying to gain/get access to her financial records.* [=trying to get the right to see her financial records] • *He was granted/denied access to his children.*

²access *vb* [*T*] : to gain access to (something): such as **a** : to be able to use, enter, or get near (something) • *accessing the money in your bank account* **b** : to open or load (a computer file, an Internet site, etc.) • *You'll need a password to access the database.*

ac·ces·si·ble /ɪkˈsɛsəbəl/ *adj* **1** : able to be reached or approached • *The inn is accessible by car.* **2** : able to be used or obtained • *The information is accessible to all.* **3** : easy to appreciate or understand • *accessible art* **4** *of a person* : easy to speak to or deal with • *The teachers here are quite accessible.* — **ac·ces·si·bil·i·ty** /ɪkˌsɛsəˈbɪləti/ *n* [*U*] — **ac·ces·si·bly** /ɪkˈsɛsəbli/ *adv*

ac·ces·sion /ɪkˈsɛʃən/ *n* [*U*] *formal* : the act or process by which someone rises to a powerful and important position • *the accession of Queen Elizabeth II* • *her accession to the crown/throne*

ac·ces·so·rize (*US*) *or Brit* **ac·ces·so·rise** /ɪkˈsɛsəˌraɪz/ *vb* **-rized; -riz·ing** [*T/I*] : to add accessories to (something, such as clothing) • *an outfit accessorized with a red purse*

ac·ces·so·ry /ɪkˈsɛsəri/ *n, pl* **-ries** [*C*] **1** : something added to something else to make it more useful or attractive • *fashion accessories such as jewelry and scarves* • *automotive/computer accessories* **2** *law* : someone who helps another person commit a crime • *an accessory to murder*

ac·ci·dent /ˈæksədənt/ *n* **1** [*C*] : a sudden event (such as a crash) that is not intended and that causes damage or injury • *a car/traffic/fatal accident* • *He got in an accident at work.* • *My clumsy brother is an accident waiting to happen.* [=he is very likely to have a bad accident] **2** [*C/U*] : an event that is not planned or intended • *Their meeting was an accident. They met by accident* [=in a way that was not planned or intended] • *It is no accident that the woman he married is wealthy.* [=he deliberately chose a wealthy woman to marry] — **ac·ci·den·tal** /ˌæksəˈdɛntl̩/ adj ▪ *The discovery was purely accidental.* ▪ *an accidental shooting* — **ac·ci·den·tal·ly** /ˌæksəˈdɛntl̩i/ adv ▪ *He accidentally deleted the file.*

accident–prone adj : tending to have many accidents ▪ *He is clumsy and accident-prone.*

¹**ac·claim** /əˈkleɪm/ n [U] : strong approval or praise ▪ *Her performance earned her critical acclaim.*

²**acclaim** vb [T] : to praise (someone or something) in a very strong and enthusiastic way ▪ *He was acclaimed as one of the best players in the league.* ▪ *a highly/widely acclaimed play* — **ac·cla·ma·tion** /ˌækləˈmeɪʃən/ n [U] ▪ *shouts of acclamation from the audience*

ac·cli·mate /ˈækləˌmeɪt, Brit əˈklaɪmət/ vb -mat·ed; -mat·ing [T/I] US : to adjust or adapt to a new climate, place, or situation ▪ *He couldn't acclimate to the hot weather.* ▪ *getting acclimated to the high altitude* ▪ *We needed a few days to get acclimated to our new teacher.* — **ac·cli·ma·tion** /ˌækləˈmeɪʃən/ n [U]

ac·cli·ma·tize also Brit **ac·cli·ma·tise** /əˈklaɪməˌtaɪz/ vb -tized; -tiz·ing [T/I] : ACCLIMATE — **ac·cli·ma·ti·za·tion** also Brit **ac·cli·ma·ti·sa·tion** /əˌklaɪmətəˈzeɪʃən, Brit əˌklaɪməˌtaɪˈzeɪʃən/ n [U]

ac·co·lade /ˈækəˌleɪd/ n [C] : an award or an expression of praise ▪ *She has been winning accolades for her performances.*

ac·com·mo·date /əˈkɑːməˌdeɪt/ vb -dat·ed; -dat·ing [T] **1 a** : to provide a place to sleep and sleep for (someone) ▪ *The hotel can only accommodate about 100 people.* **b** : to have room for (someone or something) ▪ *The table accommodates [=seats] 12 comfortably.* **2** : to provide what is needed or wanted for (someone or something) ▪ *He changed his schedule to accommodate his clients.* ▪ *accommodating the special needs of the elderly*

accommodating adj : willing to do what someone else wants or requests ▪ *The chef can be very accommodating.*

ac·com·mo·da·tion /əˌkɑːməˈdeɪʃən/ n **1 a** [plural] US : a place (such as a room in a hotel) where travelers can sleep and find other services ▪ *overnight accommodations for four people* ▪ *The ship's accommodations are a bit cramped.* **b** [U] chiefly Brit : a place where people can live, stay, or work ▪ *overnight accommodation for four people* **2** [U, singular] formal **a** : an agreement that allows people, groups, etc., to work together ▪ *He hoped to reach an accommodation with the new owners.* **b** : something done to provide what is needed or wanted for someone or something ▪ *Changes were made for the accommodation of differing viewpoints.*

ac·com·pa·ni·ment /əˈkʌmpənimənt/ n **1** [C/U] : music played to support a person who is singing or playing a musical instrument **2** [C] : something that is added to or used with another thing to make it better ▪ *This wine is a good accompaniment for/of spicy foods.*

ac·com·pa·nist /əˈkʌmpənɪst/ n [C] : someone who plays a musical accompaniment ▪ *her accompanist on the piano*

ac·com·pa·ny /əˈkʌmpəni/ vb -nies; -nied; -ny·ing [T] **1** : to go somewhere with (someone) ▪ *Children under 17 must be accompanied by an adult to see this movie.* **2 a** : to be included with (something) ▪ *A delicious sauce accompanied the fish.* **b** : to happen at the same time as (something) ▪ *The thunderstorm was accompanied by high winds.* **3** : to play music with (someone who is singing or playing the main tune) ▪ *He accompanied her on the piano.*

accompli SEE FAIT ACCOMPLI

ac·com·plice /əˈkɑːmpləs/ n [C] : a person who helps someone do something wrong or illegal ▪ *a murderer's accomplice*

ac·com·plish /əˈkɑːmplɪʃ/ vb [T] : to succeed in doing (something) ▪ *They accomplished a lot in a short period of time.*

ac·com·plished /əˈkɑːmplɪʃt/ adj **1** : very skillful ▪ *an accomplished athlete/writer* **2** : having done or achieved many good or important things ▪ *an accomplished scientist*

ac·com·plish·ment /əˈkɑːmplɪʃmənt/ n **1** [C] : something done, achieved, or accomplished successfully ▪ *her academic accomplishments* **2** [U] : the successful completion of something ▪ *the accomplishment of all our goals*

¹**ac·cord** /əˈkoəd/ n **1** [C] : a formal or official agreement ▪ *a peace accord* **2** [U] : a situation or state in which people or things agree ▪ *His ideas and mine were in accord.* = *His ideas were in accord with mine.* — **of your own accord** ◇ If you do something *of your own accord,* you do it because you want to, not because someone has asked you or forced you to do it. ▪ *They left of their own accord.*

²**accord** vb [T] formal : to give (something, such as special treatment) to someone or something ▪ *He was accorded certain favors because of his age.* — **accord with** [phrasal vb] : to be in agreement with (something) ▪ *His plans for the company did not accord with my own.*

ac·cor·dance /əˈkoədn̩s/ n — **in accordance with** : in a way that follows (something, such as a rule or request) ▪ *His funeral will be private, in accordance with his wishes.*

ac·cord·ing·ly /əˈkoədɪŋli/ adv **1** : in a proper or appropriate way ▪ *She is a manager and is paid accordingly.* **2** : as a result : THEREFORE ▪ *They wanted to find out how people felt. Accordingly, they took a poll.*

according to prep **1** : as stated or reported by (someone or something) ▪ *According to rumors, he was fired for stealing from the company.* **2** : as directed by (rules, directions, etc.) ▪ *Cook the rice according to the directions on the box.* ▪ *Everything went according to plan.* [=the way it had been planned] **3** : in a way that is based on (something) ▪ *books arranged according to their size*

ac·cor·di·on /əˈkoədijən/ n [C] : a musical instrument that is played by pulling its sides apart and then pushing them to- gether while pressing buttons and keys — **ac·cor·di·on·ist** /ə'kɔərdijənɪst/ n [C]

ac·cost /ə'kɑːst/ vb [T] : to approach and speak to (someone) often in an angry, aggressive, or unwanted way • *He was ac- costed by three gang members on the sub- way.*

¹**ac·count** /ə'kaʊnt/ n **1 a** [C] : a record of money that has been paid and money that has been received : BILL • *the debit and credit sides of an account* **b** [plural] : records of income and expenses • *The company's accounts show a profit this year.* **2** [C] : an arrangement in which a bank keeps a record of the money that a person puts in and takes out of the bank • *We opened new bank accounts.* • *My wife and I have a joint account.* [=an ac- count that both of us can use] • *your ac- count balance/number* **3** [C] : a compa- ny's record of the products or services used by a customer and of the money that the customer owes or has paid to the company • *I don't have the money right now. Put it on my account.* • *Charge it to my account.* **4** [C] : a business arrange- ment in which a person or company reg- ularly buys products or services from a particular company • *That company is one of our biggest/best accounts.* • *She is our account manager.* [=the person who manages our account] **5** [C] : an ar- rangement in which a person uses the In- ternet or e-mail services of a particular company • *I use two separate e-mail ac- counts.* **6** [C] : a description of an event or situation • *eyewitness accounts from the war* • *a written account of his trip* **7** [C/U] : a reason or explanation for an ac- tion • *You will be asked to give an account of your actions.* [=to explain the reasons for your actions] • *He was called/brought to account* [=required to explain what he did and accept punishment] *for his mis- take.* — **by/from all accounts** : accord- ing to all of the different descriptions of something • *She was, by all accounts, good at her job.* — **by your own ac- count** : according to what you have said about your own life or experiences • *They had, by their own account, a won- derful time.* — **on account of** : because of • *The game was canceled on account of the rain.* — **on no account** or **not on any account** chiefly Brit : for no reason • *On no account should the children be left at home alone.* — **on someone's ac- count** : because of someone • *Don't leave on our account.* — **on your own ac- count** : by yourself or for your own sake • *He left the company on his own account.* • *I'm doing it on my own account, not for anyone else.* — **take (something) into account** or **take account of (some- thing)** : to think about (something) be- fore doing something (such as making a decision) : CONSIDER • *Try to take our feelings into account.* • *The plan fails to take account of the fact that we have very little money.*

²**account** vb — **account for** [phrasal vb] **1 a** : to give a reason or explanation for

(something) • *How do you account for your success?* **b** : to be the cause of (something) • *The disease accounted for over 10,000 deaths last year.* **c** : to make up or form (a part of something) • *Wom- en account for 45 percent of our employ- ees.* **d** US : to think about (something) before doing something • *The researchers failed to account for the hot weather.* **2 a** : to show what happened to (someone or something) • *I'll have to account for the money I spent.* **b** : to know the location of (someone or something) • *Is everyone accounted for?* [=do we know where ev- eryone is?]

ac·count·able /ə'kaʊntəbəl/ adj, not be- fore a noun **1** : required to explain ac- tions or decisions to someone • *Politi- cians are accountable to the people they represent.* **2** : responsible for something • *If anything goes wrong, I will hold you accountable!* — **ac·count·abil·i·ty** /ə- ˌkaʊntə'bɪləti/ n [U]

ac·coun·tant /ə'kaʊntn̩t/ n [C] : some- one who keeps the financial records of a business or person

ac·count·ing /ə'kaʊntɪŋ/ n [U] : the sys- tem or job of keeping the financial records of a business or person • *an ac- counting firm*

ac·cou·tre·ment or US **ac·cou·ter- ment** /ə'kuːtrəmənt, ə'kuːtəmənt/ n [C] : a piece of clothing or equipment that is used in a particular place or for a partic- ular activity • *all the accoutrements of a first-class hotel*

ac·cred·it /ə'krɛdət/ vb [T] **1** : to say that something is good enough to be giv- en official approval • *an accredited col- lege* **2** : to give (someone) credit for something : CREDIT • *The invention of scuba gear is accredited to Jacques Cousteau.* — **ac·cred·i·ta·tion** /ə- ˌkrɛdə'teɪʃən/ n [U]

ac·cre·tion /ə'kriːʃən/ n **1** [U] : a grad- ual process in which things are added in small amounts over time • *The accretion of detail creates a complex story.* **2** [C] : something that has grown or accumu- lated slowly • *strangely shaped limestone accretions*

ac·crue /ə'kruː/ vb **-crued; -cru·ing** [T/I] : to increase in value or amount gradually as time passes • *investments that have accrued interest and dividends* — **ac·cru·al** /ə'kruːwəl/ n [C/U]

ac·cu·mu·late /ə'kjuːmjəˌleɪt/ vb **-lat- ed; -lat·ing 1** [T] : to gather or acquire (something) gradually • *slowly accumu- lating a fortune* **2** [I] : to increase gradu- ally in amount as time passes • *Debris has accumulated in the corner.* — **ac·cu- mu·la·tion** /əˌkjuːmjə'leɪʃən/ n [C/U]

ac·cu·mu·la·tive /ə'kjuːmjələtɪv/ adj : growing or increasing over time • *the accumulative effect of his injuries*

ac·cu·rate /'ækjərət/ adj **1** : free from mistakes or errors • *an accurate descrip- tion/throw* • *historically accurate* **2** : not making mistakes • *an accurate reporter/ thermometer* — **ac·cu·ra·cy** /'ækjərəsi/ n [U, singular] — **ac·cu·rate·ly** adv

ac·cu·sa·tion /ˌækju'zeɪʃən/ n [C/U] : a claim that someone has done something wrong or illegal ▪ *The police are investigating serious accusations of wrongdoing against him.* ▪ *a false accusation*

ac·cu·sa·tive /əˈkʰjuːzətɪv/ *n* [U] *grammar* : the form of a noun or pronoun when it is the direct object of a verb or the object of a preposition ▪ *a noun in the accusative (case)* — called also *objective*

ac·cu·sa·to·ry /əˈkjuːzəˌtori, *Brit* əˈkjuːzətri/ *adj* : accusing or blaming someone ▪ *He pointed an accusatory finger at the suspect.*

ac·cuse /əˈkjuːz/ *vb* **-cused; -cus·ing** [T] : to blame (someone) for something wrong or illegal ▪ *She is/stands accused of murder.* ▪ *(humorous)* No one could accuse him of being modest. [=he is not modest] — **ac·cus·er** *n* [C] — **accusing** *adj* ▪ *She gave him a very accusing look.* — **ac·cus·ing·ly** /əˈkʰjuːzɪŋli/ *adv*

accused *n* — **the accused** : a person who is charged with a crime ▪ *The accused was found not guilty.* : a group of people who are charged with a crime ▪ *The accused were found not guilty.*

ac·cus·tom /əˈkʌstəm/ *vb* [T] : to cause (someone) to become adjusted to or familiar with something — + *to* ▪ *trying to accustom the students to their new surroundings*

ac·cus·tomed /əˈkʌstəmd/ *adj* : familiar with something so that it seems normal or usual ▪ *She is accustomed to life/living on the farm.*

¹**ace** /ˈeɪs/ *n* [C] **1** : a playing card that has one figure in its center and that can have either the highest or lowest value ▪ *the ace of clubs* ▪ *(figurative)* The company holds all the aces [=has a strong advantage] *in its negotiations with the strikers.* ▪ *(US, figurative)* His popularity among elderly voters gives him an ace in the hole [=a powerful and often secret weapon, advantage, etc.] *for the coming election.* **2** : a person who is very skilled at something ▪ *a computer ace* ▪ *an ace reporter* **3** : a point scored on a serve that an opponent fails to hit in tennis **4** *US, golf* : HOLE IN ONE ▪ *He got/shot/scored an ace on the eighth hole.*

²**ace** *vb* **aced; ac·ing** [T] **1** *US, informal* : to earn a grade of A on (an exam) ▪ *He aced the test.* **2** *tennis* : to score an ace against (an opponent) ▪ *He aced his opponent on the last point of the match.* **3** *US, golf* : to score an ace on (a hole) ▪ *She aced the 14th hole.*

acer·bic /əˈsɝbɪk/ *adj* : expressing harsh or sharp criticism in a clever way ▪ *his acerbic wit* — **acer·bi·cal·ly** /əˈsɝbɪkli/ *adv*

¹**ache** /ˈeɪk/ *vb* **ached; ach·ing** [I] **1** : to hurt in a way that is constant but not severe ▪ *Her muscles ached from shoveling snow.* ▪ *(figurative)* His heart ached. [=he felt sad and sorry] **2** : to want or desire something or someone very much ▪ *Her heart ached for him.* ▪ *I've been aching to see you.*

²**ache** *n* [C] : a pain that is not sharp but continues for a long time ▪ *He had a dull ache in his back.* ▪ *the many aches and pains of old age* — **achy** /ˈeɪki/ *adj* **ach·i·er; -est**

achieve /əˈtʃiːv/ *vb* **achieved; achiev·ing 1** [T] : to get or reach (something) by working hard ▪ *achieve goals/success* **2** [I] : to become successful ▪ *the skills students need in order to achieve in college* — **achiev·able** /əˈtʃiːvəbəl/ *adj* — **achieve·ment** /əˈtʃiːvmənt/ *n* [C/U] : *major scientific achievements* ▪ *a high level of artistic/academic achievement* — **achiev·er** /əˈtʃiːvə/ *n* [C]

Achil·les' heel /əˈkɪliːz-/ *n* [C] : a fault or weakness that causes or could cause someone or something to fail ▪ *The team's Achilles' heel is its poor pitching.*

Achilles tendon *n* [C] : the body part that joins the muscles of the lower leg to the bone of the heel

achoo /əˈtʃuː/ *interj* — used to represent the sound of a sneeze

¹**ac·id** /ˈæsəd/ *n* **1** [C/U] *chemistry* : a chemical with a sour taste and a pH of less than 7 ▪ *the acids in your stomach* **2** [U] *slang* : LSD ▪ *dropping acid* [=taking LSD]

²**acid** *adj* **1** *always before a noun* : of, relating to, or having the qualities of an acid ▪ *an acid solution of vinegar and water* ▪ *Pizza gives me acid indigestion.* [=a burning feeling in the stomach] **2** : sharp, strong, and critical in tone ▪ *acid comments/remarks* — **acid·i·ty** /əˈsɪdəti/ *n* [U]

acid·ic /əˈsɪdɪk/ *adj* **1** : having a sour or sharp taste ▪ *an acidic sauce* **2** : containing acid ▪ *acidic soil*

acid rain *n* [U] : rain that contains dangerous chemicals

acid test *n* [*singular*] : a difficult situation or task that shows if someone or something is good enough to succeed ▪ *The new team passed its first acid test when it played the national champions.*

ac·knowl·edge /ɪkˈnɑːlɪdʒ/ *vb* **-edged; -edg·ing** [T] **1** : to say that you accept the truth or existence of (something) : ADMIT ▪ *They acknowledged their mistake.* ▪ *He refuses to acknowledge the authority of the court.* **2** : to regard or describe (someone or something) as having or deserving a particular status ▪ *She is acknowledged to be one of the world's best chefs.* **3** : to tell someone that a letter, message, etc., has been received ▪ *She acknowledged the gift with a card.* **4** : to look at or talk to (someone) ▪ *She walked by me without even acknowledging me.* **5** : to express thanks or appreciation for (something or someone) ▪ *They acknowledge the important work done by past scholars.*

ac·knowl·edg·ment *also* **ac·knowl·edge·ment** /ɪkˈnɑːlɪdʒmənt/ *n* **1** [C/U] : the act of showing that you know, admit, or accept that something exists or is true ▪ *(an) acknowledgment of his guilt* **2** [C/U] : the act of praising or thanking someone for an action or achievement ▪ *He hasn't received the acknowledgment he deserves.* ▪ *an award in acknowledgment of his charitable work* **3** [*plural*] : a section of a book, article, etc., in which people are thanked for their help ▪ *She was mentioned in the book's acknowledgments.* **4** [C] : a usually written statement saying that a letter or message was received ▪ *He never received an acknowledgment of his payment.*

ac·me /'ækmi/ *n* [*singular*] : the highest point of something ▪ *His career was at its acme.*

ac·ne /'ækni/ *n* [*U*] : a condition in which the skin has many pimples ▪ *a teenager with bad acne*

ac·o·lyte /'ækə,laɪt/ *n* [*C*] *formal* : someone who follows and admires a leader ▪ *a popular professor dining with a few of her acolytes*

acorn /'eɪ,koərn/ *n* [*C*] : the nut of the oak tree

acorn squash *n* [*C/U*] *US* : a round vegetable with dark skin and yellow flesh

acous·tic /ə'ku:stɪk/ *also US* **acous·ti·cal** /ə'ku:stɪkəl/ *adj* **1** : of or relating to sound ▪ *acoustic vibrations* **2 a** *of a musical instrument* : not having its sound changed by electrical devices ▪ *an acoustic guitar* **b** : made with or using acoustic instruments ▪ *acoustic folk music* — **acous·ti·cal·ly** /ə'ku:stɪkli/ *adv*

acous·tics /ə'ku:stɪks/ *n* [*plural*] : the qualities of a room that make it easy or difficult for people inside to hear sounds clearly ▪ *a room with great acoustics*

ac·quaint /ə'kweɪnt/ *vb* [*T*] *formal* : to cause (someone) to know and become familiar *with* something ▪ *The lawyer took a few days to acquaint herself with* [=to learn about] *the facts of a case.*

ac·quain·tance /ə'kweɪntəns/ *n* **1** [*C*] : someone who is known but who is not a close friend ▪ *Is he an acquaintance of yours?* [=have you met him?] **2** [*U*] *formal* : the state of knowing someone in a personal or social way ▪ *It's a pleasure to make your acquaintance.* [=(*less formally*) *it's nice to meet you*] ▪ *She made the acquaintance of* [=she met] *the city's mayor.* **3** [*U, singular*] : knowledge about something — + *with* ▪ *While he has some acquaintance with the subject, he is not an expert.*

acquaint·ed *adj, not before a noun* **1** *formal* : having knowledge about something ▪ *I am* (*well*) *acquainted with his books.* [=I have read his books] **2** : knowing each other in a personal or social way ▪ *Are you two acquainted* (*with each other*)? [=have you met before?] ▪ *intimately/casually acquainted* ▪ *I'll let you two get better acquainted.* [=get to know each other better]

ac·qui·esce /,ækwi'ɛs/ *vb* **-esced; -escing** [*I*] *formal* : to accept, agree, or allow something to happen by staying silent or by not arguing ▪ *She acquiesced to her husband's plans.* — **ac·qui·es·cence** /,ækwi'ɛsn̩s/ *n* [*U*] — **ac·qui·es·cent** /,ækwi'ɛsn̩t/ *adj* ▪ *an acquiescent wife*

ac·quire /ə'kwajɚ/ *vb* **-quired; -quir·ing** [*T*] **1** *formal* : to get (something) ▪ *acquire a new home* ▪ *She acquired control of the company.* ▪ *The old word has acquired a new meaning.* **2** : to gain (a new skill, ability, etc.) ▪ *acquire knowledge* ▪ *He has acquired a reputation as a good worker.* [=people regard him as a good worker] ▪ *Her art is an acquired taste.* [=it is something that is not easily

or immediately liked]

acquired immune deficiency syndrome *n* [*U*] : AIDS

ac·qui·si·tion /,ækwə'zɪʃən/ *n* **1** [*U*] : the act of acquiring something ▪ *the acquisition of wealth* **2** [*C*] : something valuable that is acquired ▪ *the museum's latest acquisitions*

ac·quis·i·tive /ə'kwɪzətɪv/ *adj, formal* : GREEDY ▪ *our increasingly acquisitive society*

ac·quit /ə'kwɪt/ *vb* **-quit·ted; -quit·ting** [*T*] : to decide that someone is not guilty of a crime ▪ *The jury acquitted him* (*of the crime*) *because there wasn't enough evidence to convict him.* — **acquit yourself** : to perform or behave in a specified way ▪ *The soldiers acquitted themselves well/honorably in battle.* — **ac·quit·tal** /ə'kwɪt̬l̩/ *n* [*C/U*] ▪ *The case resulted in* (*an*) *acquittal of the defendant.*

acre /'eɪkɚ/ *n* [*C*] : a measure of land area in the U.S. and Britain that equals 4,840 square yards (about 4,047 square meters)

acre·age /'eɪkərɪdʒ/ *n* [*U*] : land measured in acres ▪ *Most of the park's acreage is forest.*

ac·rid /'ækrəd/ *adj* : bitter and unpleasant in taste or smell ▪ *acrid smoke*

ac·ri·mo·ny /'ækrə,mouni, *Brit* 'ækrəməni/ *n* [*U*] *formal* : angry and bitter feelings ▪ *They separated without acrimony.* — **ac·ri·mo·ni·ous** /,ækrə'mounijəs/ *adj* ▪ *an acrimonious divorce/dispute* — **ac·ri·mo·ni·ous·ly** *adv*

ac·ro·bat /'ækrə,bæt/ *n* [*C*] : someone who entertains people by performing difficult and often dangerous acts ▪ *circus acrobats* — **ac·ro·bat·ic** /,ækrə'bætɪk/ *adj* — **ac·ro·bat·i·cal·ly** /,ækrə'bætɪkli/ *adv*

ac·ro·bat·ics /,ækrə'bætɪks/ *n* [*plural*] : difficult and dangerous acts done by an acrobat or other kind of performer ▪ *a singer's vocal acrobatics*

ac·ro·nym /'ækrə,nɪm/ *n* [*C*] : a word formed from the first letters of each one of the words in a phrase ▪ *The North Atlantic Treaty Organization is known by the acronym "NATO."*

¹across /ə'krɑːs/ *prep* **1 a** : from one side to the other side of (something) ▪ *We were walking across the street.* ▪ *She reached across the table to shake his hand.* **b** : on the other side of (something) ▪ *They live across the street (from us).* **2** : so as to reach or spread over or throughout (something) ▪ *looking out across the ocean* **3** : in every part of (a country, region, etc.) ▪ *Newspapers* (*all*) *across the world reported the story.*

²across *adv* **1** : from one side to the other ▪ *The streams are small enough to jump across.* **2** : in a measurement from one side to the other side ▪ *The hole was 10 feet across.* [=10 feet wide] **3** : on the opposite side ▪ *I saw them crossing the street and I waited until they were safely across.* ▪ *She sat* (*directly*) *across from* [=on the opposite side from] *me at the table.*

across–the–board *adj, always before a noun* : affecting everyone or everything in a group ▪ *an across-the-board tax cut*

acryl·ic /ə'krɪlɪk/ *n* **1** [*U*] : a material

that is made from a chemical process and that is used for making many different products ▪ *acrylic fabrics/paint* **2** [*plural*] : paints that contain acrylic ▪ *a painting done in acrylics*

¹**act** /ˈækt/ *n* **1** [*C*] : something that is done ▪ *His first official act* [=*action*] *as President was to sign the bill.* ▪ *an act of kindness/bravery* ▪ *He was* **caught in the act** *of robbing a bank.* [=he was caught while he was robbing a bank] **2** [*C*] : a law made by a group of legislators ▪ *an act of Congress/Parliament* ▪ *the Civil Rights Act of 1964* **3** [*C*] : one of the main divisions of a play or opera ▪ *the play's first/opening act* **4** [*C*] **a** : one of the performances in a show ▪ *a circus/magic act* **b** : a show that a person or group performs often ▪ *a stand-up/comedy act* **c** : a person or group that performs in shows ▪ *The band was one of this summer's best live acts.* **5** [*singular*] : a way of behaving that is not honest or sincere ▪ *He said he was sorry, but it was all just an act.* ▪ *He was* **putting on an act.** — **clean up your act** see *clean up* at ²CLEAN — **get into the act** or **get in on the act** : to start to participate in an activity ▪ *We started selling last year, and now other stores are getting into the act.* [=now other stores are also selling them] — **get your act together** see *get together* at GET

²**act** *vb* **1** [*I*] : to do something ▪ *We have to act quickly/fast.* ▪ *The firefighters acted courageously.* ▪ *The killer acted alone.* **2** [*T/I*] : to behave in a particular way ▪ *He was acting funny/strangely this morning.* ▪ *Now that he's rich he certainly* **acts the part.** [=behaves like a rich person] ▪ *John, act your age.* [=don't act like a younger person] ▪ *I acted like a fool.* [=I behaved foolishly] **3 a** [*I*] : to behave in a way that is not sincere or honest ▪ *Stop acting. We know you're guilty.* **b** [*linking vb*] : to pretend to be something ▪ *He did his best to act excited.* **c** [*I*] : to pretend that something is true — usually used in the phrases **act as if, act as though,** and (*chiefly US*) **act like** ▪ *She acted as if nothing had happened.* **4** [*T/I*] : to perform the words and actions of a character in a play, movie, etc. ▪ *She can sing, dance, and act.* ▪ *He'll be acting the part of Romeo in tonight's play.* **5** [*I*] : to do the work of a particular kind of person or thing — *as* ▪ *She'll be acting as her own attorney during the trial.* ▪ *The trees act as a source of shade.* **6** [*I*] : to have a particular effect ▪ *The chemical acts by destroying the cells in the brain.* ▪ *These medicines act on the heart.* — **act on/upon** [*phrasal vb*] : to use (something, such as a feeling or suggestion) as a reason or basis for doing something ▪ *They never acted on the information they had.* — **act out** [*phrasal vb*] **1** : to behave badly especially because you are feeling painful emotions ▪ *What can parents do when their kids start acting out?* **2 act out (something)** or **act (something) out a** : to show that you are feeling (a painful emotion) by behaving badly ▪ *He tries not to act out his anger/frustrations.* **b** : to

perform (a play, a character in a movie, etc.) ▪ *She skillfully acted out the role of a young queen.* **c** : to do and say the things that happen in (a movie, past event, etc.) ▪ *They acted out scenes from old movies.* ▪ *adults acting out their childhood dreams* [=doing what they wanted to do when they were children] — **act up** [*phrasal vb*] **1** : to behave in a way that is not polite or acceptable ▪ *The kids are acting up again.* **2** *of a machine* : to not work properly ▪ *The camera started acting up after I dropped it.* **3** *of a disease* : to become worse ▪ *Whenever it rains, my arthritis starts acting up.*

¹**act·ing** /ˈæktɪŋ/ *adj, always before a noun* : holding a temporary job or position ▪ *The college's acting president was replaced with a permanent one.*

²**acting** *n* [*U*] : the art or profession of performing the role of a character in a play, movie, etc. ▪ *Her acting is superb in this film.* ▪ *an acting career*

ac·tion /ˈækʃən/ *n* **1** [*C*] : something that a person or group does ▪ *He criticized/defended the government's actions.* ▪ *The school has* **taken actions** *to fix the problem.* ▪ *They say they want peace, but* **actions speak louder than words.** [=the things that you do are more important than the things that you say] **2** [*U*] : things done to achieve a particular purpose ▪ *The situation demanded immediate action.* ▪ *No further action was necessary.* ▪ *Let's agree on a* **plan/course of action.** [=let's agree on what we will be doing] ▪ *The company failed to* **take appropriate action.** ▪ *He was a* **man of action.** [=a man who works in an active way to do things] **3** [*U*] : fighting that happens in a war ▪ *killed/wounded in action* [=while fighting in a battle] ▪ *soldiers who are* **missing in action** [=cannot be found after a battle] **4 the action** : the most exciting activities happening in a place ▪ *I moved to New York City to be (a) part of the action.* **5** [*U*] *informal* : an opportunity to make money ▪ *Do you want to* **get in on the action?** [=participate in a plan to make money] ▪ *She wanted to get a* **piece/cut/slice of the action.** [=a portion of the money that can be earned by something] **6** [*U*] : the events that happen in a story, movie, etc. ▪ *The play's action takes place in a bar.* **7** [*U*] : events that happen quickly and that cause feelings of danger and excitement ▪ *The movie is two hours of nonstop action.* ▪ *action movies* **8** — used as a command to start filming part of a movie or TV show ▪ *Lights, camera, action!* **9** [*C/U*] *law* : the process of having a court of law make a decision about an argument ▪ *She filed an action against the company.* **10** [*U*] : the way that something works or moves ▪ *the mechanical action of a pulley* — **in action** : performing a usual job or function ▪ *fans who came to see their favorite players in action* — **into action** : to an active state ▪ *Put the plan into action.* [=start using the plan] ▪ *As a doctor, she can be* **called into action** [=asked to start working] *at any time of the day.*

action–packed *adj* : filled with action,

danger, and excitement ▪ *an action-packed movie*

action replay *n* [C] *Brit* : INSTANT REPLAY

ac·ti·vate /ˈæktəˌveɪt/ *vb* **-vat·ed; -vat·ing** [T] **1** : to cause (a device) to start working ▪ *The bomb was activated by remote control.* **2** *chemistry* : to cause (a natural process) to begin ▪ *Sunlight activates a chemical reaction in the plant's leaves.* **3** *chiefly US* : to order (soldiers) to serve in a war ▪ *The President has activated the reserves.* — **ac·ti·va·tion** /ˌæktəˈveɪʃən/ *n* [U]

ac·tive /ˈæktɪv/ *adj* **1** : doing things that require physical movement and energy ▪ *We stay/keep active during winter by skiing and ice skating.* **2 a** : involved in the activities of a group ▪ *We are active members of our church.* : participating in an activity ▪ *politically active people* ▪ *active in the civil rights movement* **b** : involving action or participation ▪ *They take an active interest/role in their children's education.* **3** : marked by regular action or use ▪ *an active bank account* ▪ *sexually active teenagers* [=teenagers who have sex] **4** *of a volcano* : capable of erupting ▪ *active and inactive volcanoes* **5** *of a disease* : becoming worse or continuing to have bad effects ▪ *active tuberculosis* **6** : having a chemical effect on the body ▪ *The medicine has two active ingredients.* **7** *US* : involving service in the military as a main job ▪ *After two years of active duty* [=of being a full-time member of the military] *she entered the reserves.* **8** *grammar* **a** *of a verb or voice* : showing that the subject of a sentence is the one doing the action expressed by the verb ▪ *"She hits the ball" is in the active voice, while "The ball was hit" is in the passive.* **b** *of a verb* : expressing action rather than describing the state of something ▪ *Words like "walk," "sing," and "eat" are active verbs.* — **ac·tive·ly** *adv*

ac·tiv·ist /ˈæktɪvɪst/ *n* [C] : a person who uses strong actions (such as public protests) to help make changes in politics or society ▪ *political activists* — **ac·tiv·ism** /ˈæktɪˌvɪzəm/ *n* [U]

ac·tiv·i·ty /ækˈtɪvəti/ *n, pl* **-ties 1** [U] : behavior or actions usually of a particular kind ▪ *the sexual activity of married couples* ▪ *Police monitored criminal/gang/drug activity in the area.* ▪ *physical activity* **2** [C] : something that is done as work or for a particular purpose ▪ *business/political/illegal activities* **3** [C] : something that is done for pleasure usually with a group of people ▪ *We planned an activity for the children.* ▪ *social/recreational activities*

ac·tor /ˈæktɚ/ *n* [C] : a person who acts in a play, movie, etc.

ac·tress /ˈæktrəs/ *n* [C] : a woman or girl who acts in a play, movie, etc.

ac·tu·al /ˈæktʃəwəl/ *adj* **1** : real and not merely possible or imagined ▪ *The movie is based on actual events.* **2** : known to be correct or precise ▪ *The actual cost of the repair was higher than the estimate.* **3** — used for emphasis ▪ *This is the actual room where he was born.* — **ac·tu·al·i·ty** /ˌæktʃəˈwæləti/ *n, pl* **-ties** [C/U] ▪ *the actualities of war* ▪ *I thought they just arrived, but in actuality* [=actually] *they'd been here for an hour.*

ac·tu·al·ly /ˈæktʃəwəli/ *adv* **1** — used to refer to what is true or real ▪ *What actually happened?* ▪ *It's hard to believe that we're actually finished.* **2** — used to say that the truth differs from what was thought or expected ▪ *I didn't think I'd like the movie, but it was actually pretty good.*

ac·tu·ary /ˈæktʃəˌweri, Brit ˈæktʃuəri/ *n, pl* **-ar·ies** [C] : a person who tells insurance companies how much they should charge people for insurance — **ac·tu·ar·i·al** /ˌæktʃəˈwerijəl/ *adj*

acu·ity /əˈkjuːwəti/ *n* [U] *formal* : the ability to see, hear, or understand something easily ▪ *mental/visual/political acuity*

acu·men /əˈkjuːmən/ *n* [U] : the ability to think clearly and make good decisions ▪ *political acumen*

acu·punc·ture /ˈækjəˌpʌŋktʃɚ/ *n* [U] : a method of relieving pain or curing illness by placing needles into a person's skin at particular points on the body

acute /əˈkjuːt/ *adj* **acut·er; -est 1** : requiring serious attention or action ▪ *an acute fuel shortage* ▪ *an acute crisis* **2** : having or showing an ability to think clearly and to understand what is not obvious or simple about something ▪ *an acute observer/observation/understanding* **3** : very strong and sensitive ▪ *acute hearing/vision/awareness* **4** : strongly felt or experienced ▪ *acute distress/embarrassment* **5** *medical* **a** : very sharp and severe ▪ *acute pain/infection/symptoms* **b** : becoming very severe very quickly ▪ *an acute disease* **6** *mathematics* : measuring less than 90 degrees ▪ *an acute angle* **7** *of an accent mark* : having the form ´ ▪ *"Café" has an acute accent over the "e."* — **acute·ly** *adv* — **acute·ness** *n* [U]

ad /ˈæd/ *n* [C] : ADVERTISEMENT ▪ *I saw your ad in the newspaper.*

AD *or chiefly US* **A.D.** *abbr* — used to refer to the years since the birth of Jesus ▪ *550 A.D. = A.D. 550* ▪ *the first century A.D.*

ad·age /ˈædɪdʒ/ *n* [C] : an old and well-known saying that expresses a general truth ▪ *the (old) adage, "Two heads are better than one"*

ad·a·mant /ˈædəmənt/ *adj* : not willing to change an opinion or decision ▪ *He's adamant about staying here.* ▪ *an adamant refusal* — **ad·a·mant·ly** *adv*

Adam's apple *n* [C] : the lump that sticks out in the front of a person's neck and that is larger in men than in women

adapt /əˈdæpt/ *vb* [T/I] **1** : to change your behavior so that it is easier to live in a particular place or situation ▪ *She has adapted (well) to college life.* **2** [T] : to change (something) so that it functions better or is better suited for a purpose ▪ *The teachers adapted the lessons to the needs of their students.* **3** [T] : to change (a movie, book, play, etc.) so that it can be presented in another form ▪ *adapting the movie for television* — **adapt·abil·i-**

ty /ə,dæptə'bıləti/ n [U] — **adapt·able** /ə'dæptəbəl/ adj

ad·ap·ta·tion /ˌæ,dæp'teɪʃən/ n **1** [C] : something that is adapted; especially : a movie, book, play, etc., that is changed so that it can be presented in another form **2** [U] : the process of changing to fit some purpose or situation • a tool designed for easy adaptation

adapt·er also **adap·tor** /ə'dæptə/ n [C] : a device that is used to connect two pieces of equipment that were not designed to be connected

add /'æd/ vb **1** [T] **a** : to put (something) with another thing or group of things • She's planning to add some new flowers to the garden. **b** : to mix or combine (an ingredient) with other ingredients • Add one cup of sugar to the mixture. **2** [T] : to cause something to have (a usually good quality or characteristic) • In this dish, fresh herbs add lots of color and flavor. **3** [T/I] : to put (two or more numbers or amounts) together to find a total or sum • Add these numbers together. • schoolchildren learning how to add and subtract **4** [T] : to say or write (something more or extra) • That's all I have to say. Do you have anything (else/more) to add? • It was a long project and, I might add, an expensive one. — **add on** [phrasal vb] **add (something) on or add on (something)** : to put (something) with another thing or group of things • We're going to add on a new garage. — **add to** [phrasal vb] : to make (something) larger, better, or greater • Her research has greatly added to our knowledge of the subject. • The funny characters really add to the story. [=they make the story better] — **add up** [phrasal vb] **1 a** : to equal the expected or correct total • The numbers just don't add up. **b** : to seem to be logical or true • Their story doesn't add up. **c** : to slowly increase and become a large number or amount • A soda may only cost a dollar, but those dollars add up quickly. **2 add (something) up or add up (something)** : to count (the number or amount of something) to find the total • Let's add up all of the money we saved. **3 add up to a** : to have (a number) as a total • The amount she spends on coffee adds up to $2.75 a day. **b** : to produce (a specified result) • All of the team's hard work didn't add up to a win. — **add·ed** adj • added value • an added advantage

ADD abbr attention deficit disorder

ad·den·dum /ə'dɛndəm/ n, pl **-den·da** /-'dɛndə/ or **-den·dums** [C] : a section of a book that is added to the main or original text

ad·dict /'ædɪkt/ n [C] **1** : a person who is not able to stop taking drugs • a heroin addict **2** informal : a person who enjoys something very much and spends a large amount of time doing it, watching it, etc. • television/basketball addicts

ad·dict·ed /ə'dɪktəd/ adj : having an addiction: such as **a** : unable to stop using a harmful substance • He's addicted to heroin/nicotine. **b** : unable to stop doing something that is harmful • He's addicted to smoking. **c** : having an unusually

great interest in something • He's addicted to (playing/watching) basketball.

ad·dic·tion /ə'dɪkʃən/ n **1** [C/U] : a strong and harmful need to regularly have something or do something • He has a gambling addiction. — often + to • addiction to heroin **2** [C] : an unusually great interest in something • his surfing addiction

ad·dic·tive /ə'dɪktɪv/ adj : causing addiction • highly addictive drugs

ad·di·tion /ə'dɪʃən/ n **1** [U] : the act or process of adding something • The school welcomed the addition of three new teachers. **2** [U] : the act or process of adding numbers • learning addition and subtraction **3** [C] : something or someone that is added • an addition to the family [=a new member of the family] **4** [C] US : a part of a building that is built after the original part has been completed — **in addition** — used for adding information to a statement • The city has the largest population in the country and in addition is a major shipping port. • There were six people at the meeting in addition to me.

ad·di·tion·al /ə'dɪʃənəl/ adj : more than is usual or expected • an additional charge/fee — **ad·di·tion·al·ly** /ə'dɪʃənli/ adv

ad·di·tive /'ædətɪv/ n [C] : something that is added in small amounts to a substance to improve it • preservatives and other food additives

ad·dle /'ædl/ vb **ad·dled; ad·dling** [T] : to make (someone's mind) unable to think clearly • Their brains were addled with/by fear/drugs.

add–on /'æd,ɑːn/ n [C] : an extra part or device that can be added to something else to improve it • add-on components/ equipment

¹**ad·dress** /ə'drɛs/ vb [T] **1** : to write on an envelope, package, etc., the name and address of the person or business it is being sent to • The letter was addressed incorrectly. **2 a** : to speak to (a person or group) • She addressed me directly. **b** : to use a specified name or title when speaking or writing to (someone) — + as • Address the queen as "Your Majesty." **c** : to direct (spoken or written words) to someone • She addressed her comments to him. [=she spoke to him] **3** : to give a formal speech to (a group of people) • Before the awards were given, the mayor addressed the crowd. **4** formal : to deal with (an issue, problem, etc.) • How do you plan to address the issue?

²**ad·dress** /ə'drɛs, 'æ,drɛs/ n [C] **1 a** : the words and numbers that are used to describe the location of a building and that are written on letters, envelopes, and packages so that they can be mailed to that location • My address is 82 Third Street. • Put the return address [=the address of the person sending the letter] on the envelope. **b** : the letters, numbers, and symbols that are used to direct an e-mail message or to show the location of a site on the Internet • an e-mail address **2** : a formal speech • the President's inaugural address — **form/term of address** : a word, name, or title that is used when speaking or writing to some-

one • *"Honey" is an affectionate term of address in U.S. English.*

ad·dress·ee /ˌæˌdrɛˈsiː/ n [C] : the person to whom mail is addressed

adept /əˈdɛpt/ adj : very good at doing something that is not easy • *He's adept at/in several languages.* — **adept·ly** adv — **adept·ness** n [U]

ad·e·quate /ˈædɪkwət/ adj **1** : enough for some need or requirement • *The plants need adequate water.* **2** : good enough : of a quality that is good or acceptable • *Millions of people lack adequate health care.* : of a quality that is acceptable but not better than acceptable • *His work was barely adequate.* — **ad·e·qua·cy** /ˈædɪkwəsi/ n [U] — **ad·e·quate·ly** adv

ad·here /ædˈhɪr/ vb **-hered; -her·ing** [I] : to stick or attach firmly to something • *The stamp failed to adhere (to the envelope).* — **adhere to** [phrasal vb] : to act in the way that is required by (a rule, belief, etc.) • *She adheres to a strict vegetarian diet.* — **ad·her·ence** /ædˈhɪrəns/ n [U] • *adherence to religious laws*

ad·her·ent /ædˈhɪrənt/ n [C] : a person who is loyal to a leader, group, or religion • *adherents of Islam* : a person who supports a system or set of principles • *an adherent of free trade*

ad·he·sion /ædˈhiːʒən/ n [U] : the act of adhering; *especially* : the act of sticking or attaching to something • *the adhesion of the mud to my shoes*

¹**ad·he·sive** /ædˈhiːsɪv/ adj : designed to stick to something • *adhesive bandages/tape*

²**adhesive** n [C] : a substance (such as glue or cement) that is used to make things stick together

ad hoc /ˈædˈhɑːk/ adj : formed, used, or done for a special purpose • *The mayor appointed an ad hoc committee to study the project.* • *We made some ad hoc changes to the plans.*

adieu /əˈduː, əˈdjuː/ interj, formal + literary : goodbye or farewell • *Adieu, my friends.* — **adieu** n, pl **adieus** or **adieux** /əˈduːz, əˈdjuːz/ [C] • *She bid/wished me adieu.* [=farewell]

adj abbr adjective

ad·ja·cent /əˈdʒeɪsn̩t/ adj : close or near : sharing a border, wall, or point • *They are in the adjacent room.* [=the room that is next to this room] • *adjacent houses*

ad·jec·tive /ˈædʒɪktɪv/ n [C] : a word that describes a noun or a pronoun • *The words "blue" in "the blue car" and "deep" in "the water is deep" are adjectives.* — abbr. *adj* — **ad·jec·ti·val** /ˌædʒɪkˈtaɪvəl/ adj — **ad·jec·ti·val·ly** adv

ad·join /əˈdʒɔɪn/ vb [T/I] of a building, room, area of land, etc. : to be next to or joined with something • *The two rooms adjoin (each other).* • *adjoining rooms*

ad·journ /əˈdʒɚn/ vb [T/I] : to end something (such as a meeting or session) for a period of time • *Court is adjourned until 10:00 tomorrow.* — **adjourn to** [phrasal vb] : to leave one place and go to (another place) after the end of a meeting, discussion, etc. • *After the ceremony, we adjourned to the garden.* — **ad·journ-**

ment /əˈdʒɚnmənt/ n [C/U]

ad·ju·di·cate /əˈdʒuːdɪˌkeɪt/ vb **-cat·ed; -cat·ing** [T/I] formal : to make an official decision about who is right in a dispute • *The case was adjudicated in the state courts.* — **ad·ju·di·ca·tion** /əˌdʒuːdɪˈkeɪʃən/ n [U] — **ad·ju·di·ca·tor** /əˈdʒuːdɪˌkeɪtɚ/ n [C]

¹**ad·junct** /ˈædˌdʒʌŋkt/ n [C] : something that is joined or added to another thing but is not an essential part of it • *The Web site is designed as an adjunct to the book.*

²**adjunct** adj, always before a noun **1** : added or joined in order to be used with something • *an adjunct treatment* **2** : added to a teaching staff for only a short time or in a lower position than other staff • *adjunct faculty/professors*

ad·just /əˈdʒʌst/ vb **1** [T] **a** : to change (something) in a minor way so that it works better • *I adjusted the volume on the radio.* **b** : to change the position of (something) • *He adjusted his glasses/tie.* **2** [T/I] : to change in order to work or do better in a new situation • *The kids will eventually adjust (to the new school).* **3** [T/I] : to make an amount or number more exact by considering other information — usually + for • *He makes less money now when you adjust (his salary) for inflation.* — **ad·just·able** /əˈdʒʌstəbəl/ adj — **ad·just·er** n [C] — **ad·just·ment** /əˈdʒʌstmənt/ n [C/U] • *She made some adjustments to the recipe.* • *We went through a period of adjustment at the new school.*

ad–lib /ˈædˈlɪb/ vb **-libbed; -lib·bing** [T/I] : to make up words or music in a performance instead of saying or playing something that has been planned • *The actor often ad-libs (his lines).* — **ad–lib** n [C] • *a clever ad-lib*

ad·min·is·ter /ədˈmɪnɪstɚ/ vb [T] **1** : to manage the operation or use of (something) • *She's been hired to administer the fund.* **2** : to put (something) into effect • *administer justice/punishment* **3** : to give or present (something) officially • *The assistant will administer the test.* **4** : to give (a drug or treatment) to someone • *The drug is administered by injection.*

ad·min·is·tra·tion /ədˌmɪnəˈstreɪʃən/ n **1 a** [U] : the activities that relate to running an organization • *a degree in business administration* **b** [C] : a group of people who manage the way an organization functions • *The editorial criticizes the college's administration.* **2** or **Administration** [C] **a** : a government or part of a government that is identified with its leader • *during the Reagan Administration* [=during the time when Reagan was President] • *Administration officials refused to comment.* **b** : a U.S. government department • *the U.S. Food and Drug Administration* **3** [U] : the act or process of administering something • *the administration of justice*

ad·min·is·tra·tive /ədˈmɪnəˌstreɪtɪv/ adj : of or relating to the management of an organization • *administrative duties/assistants* — **ad·min·is·tra·tive·ly** adv

ad·min·is·tra·tor /ədˈmɪnəˌstreɪtɚ/ n [C]

1 : a person whose job is to manage an organization • *a hospital administrator* 2 : a person who controls the use of something • *the administrator of the estate*

ad·mi·ra·ble /ˈædmrəbəl/ *adj* : deserving to be admired : very good • *admirable qualities/motives* — **ad·mi·ra·bly** /ˈædmrəbli/ *adv*

ad·mi·ral /ˈædmrəl/ *n* [C] : a high-ranking officer in the navy

ad·mi·ra·tion /ˌædməˈreɪʃən/ *n* [U, *singular*] : a feeling of great respect and approval • *She earned/won the admiration of her coworkers.*

ad·mire /ədˈmajɚ/ *vb* -mired; -mir·ing [T] 1 : to feel respect or approval for (someone or something) • *We all admire (her for) her courage.* 2 : to look at (something or someone) with enjoyment • *We admired the scenery.* — **ad·mir·er** *n* [C] • *She has many admirers.* — **admir·ing** *adj* • *an admiring glance* — **ad·mir·ing·ly** /ədˈmaɪrɪŋli/ *adv*

ad·mis·si·ble /ədˈmɪsəbəl/ *adj* : able to be allowed or considered in a legal case • *admissible evidence*

ad·mis·sion /ədˈmɪʃən/ *n* 1 [U] : the act of allowing something • *the admission of evidence* 2 [C] : a statement or action by which someone admits a weakness, fault, etc. • *an admission of guilt* • *By his own admission, he is a bad cook.* [=he admits that he is a bad cook] 3 a [U] : the right or permission to enter a place or to join a club, group, etc. • *He was refused admission.* b [C/U] : the act or process of accepting a patient in a hospital for treatment • *a large number of hospital admissions* c [C/U] : the act or process of accepting someone as a student at a school • *college/university admissions* • *an* **admissions** *officer* [=an official at a school who is in charge of admitting students] 4 [C/U] : the cost of entering a theater, museum, etc. • *Admission (to the museum) is free on Tuesdays.*

ad·mit /ədˈmɪt/ *vb* -mit·ted; -mit·ting [T] 1 : to say usually in an unwilling way that you accept or do not deny the truth or existence of (something) • *He admitted (to me) that he didn't know the answer.* • *He admitted his guilt.* = *He admitted that he was guilty.* • *I have to admit that the movie was good.* = *It was good, I must admit.* • *She refused to admit defeat.* 2 a : to allow (someone) to enter a place • *This ticket admits one person.* b : to allow (someone) to join a club, group, etc. • *They refused to admit her to/into the club.* c : to accept (someone) as a patient in a hospital • *He was admitted (to the hospital) last night.* d *law* : to allow (something) to be considered as evidence in a legal case • *The judge decided to admit the evidence.* — **admit to** [*phrasal vb*] : to acknowledge the truth or existence of (something) • *He admitted to his guilt.* = *He admitted to being guilty.* — **admitted** *adj* • *He is an admitted liar.* [=he has admitted that he lied] — **ad·mit·ted·ly** /ədˈmɪtədli/ *adv* • *Admittedly, it was worse than expected.*

ad·mit·tance /ədˈmɪtns/ *n* [U] *formal*

: permission to enter a place or to become a member of a club, group, etc. • *gain admittance*

ad·mon·ish /ædˈmɑːnɪʃ/ *vb* [T] *formal* 1 : to speak to (someone) in a way that expresses disapproval or criticism • *We were admonished for arriving late.* 2 : to tell or urge (someone) to do something • *She admonished them to keep trying.* — **ad·mon·ish·ment** /ædˈmɑːnɪʃmənt/ *n* [C/U] — **ad·mo·ni·tion** /ˌædməˈnɪʃən/ *n* [C/U] • *a stern admonition*

ad nau·se·am /ædˈnɑːzijəm/ *adv* — used to say that something happens or is done so many times or for such a long time that it makes people annoyed, disgusted, etc. • *We debated the issue ad nauseam.*

ado /əˈduː/ *n* [U] : foolish or unnecessary talk, trouble, or activity • *The controversy turned out to be much ado about nothing.* • *Without further ado* [=without waiting any longer], *I'd like to introduce our speaker.*

ado·be /əˈdoʊbi/ *n* [U] : a type of brick made of a mixture of mud and straw that is dried by the sun • *adobe bricks/houses*

ad·o·les·cence /ˌædəˈlɛsns/ *n* [U] : the period of life when a child develops into an adult • *in early/late adolescence*

ad·o·les·cent /ˌædəˈlɛsnt/ *n* [C] : a young person who is developing into an adult • *a troubled adolescent* • *an adolescent boy/girl*

adopt /əˈdɑːpt/ *vb* 1 [T/I] : to take a child of other parents legally as your own child • *They decided to adopt (a child).* • *an adopted child* 2 [T] a : to begin to use or have a (different manner, name, etc.) • *We adopted some of the local customs.* • *The author Samuel Clemens adopted the name "Mark Twain."* b : to live in (a country that is not your original country) and regard it as your home • *Canada is his adopted country.* 3 [T] : to accept or approve (something) in a formal or official way • *The assembly adopted a new constitution.*

adop·tion /əˈdɑːpʃən/ *n* 1 [C/U] : the act or process of adopting a child • *an adoption agency* • *She decided to put/give the baby up for adoption.* [=to allow other people to adopt the baby] 2 [U] : the act or process of beginning to use something new or different • *the company's adoption of new technology* 3 [U] : the act or process of giving official acceptance or approval to something • *the adoption of the resolution by the Senate*

adop·tive /əˈdɑːptɪv/ *adj, always before a noun* — used to describe a parent who has adopted a child • *They are her adoptive parents.* [=they adopted her]

ador·able /əˈdorəbəl/ *adj* : very appealing or attractive : very lovable • *an adorable child/cottage* — **ador·ably** /əˈdorəbli/ *adv*

adore /əˈdoɚ/ *vb* adored; ador·ing [T] 1 : to love or admire (someone) very much • *She adores her son.* 2 : to like or desire (something) very much • *She adores chocolate.* — **ad·o·ra·tion** /ˌædəˈreɪʃən/ *n* [U] • *He has earned the adoration of his fans.* — **adoring** *adj* •

his adoring fans [=his fans who adore him]

adorn /ə'doən/ *vb* [T] *somewhat formal* : to make (someone or something) more attractive by adding something beautiful • *Her paintings adorn the walls.* • *a dress adorned with lace* — **adorn·ment** /ə-'doənmənt/ *n* [C/U] • *Her room has little adornment.*

adren·a·line *or chiefly Brit* **adren·a·lin** /ə'drɛnələn/ *n* [U] : a substance that is released in the body of a person who is feeling a strong emotion and that gives the person more energy • *The game got our adrenaline going.* [=got us very excited] • *I felt a* **rush of adrenaline.** [=I felt very excited and full of energy]

adrift /ə'drɪft/ *adj* **1** *of a boat* : floating on the water without being tied to anything or controlled by anyone • *a ship adrift in the storm* **2** : without guidance, purpose, or support • *Many workers were* **cast adrift** *by the layoffs.*

adroit /ə'drɔɪt/ *adj* : very clever or skillful • *an adroit negotiator* — **adroit·ly** *adv* — **adroit·ness** *n* [U]

ad·u·la·tion /ˌædʒə'leɪʃən/ *n* [U] : extreme admiration or praise • *He enjoyed the adulation of his fans.*

¹adult /ə'dʌlt, 'æˌdʌlt/ *n* [C] : a fully grown person or animal • *Her books appeal both to children and to adults.*

²adult *adj* **1** : fully grown and developed • *an adult student/learner* • *adult birds* • *my* **adult** *life* [=my life since I became an adult] **2** : mature and sensible • *We need to approach this in an adult way.* **3** : of or intended for adults • *adult literacy/education* **4** : dealing with sexual material • *adult movies* — **adult·hood** /ə'dʌlt-ˌhʊd/ *n* [C/U]

adul·ter·ate /ə'dʌltəˌreɪt/ *vb* -at·ed; -at·ing [T] : to add something of poor quality to (something, such as a food or drink) • *The company adulterates its products with additives.* • *adulterated food* — **adul·ter·a·tion** /əˌdʌltə'reɪʃən/ *n* [U]

adul·ter·er /ə'dʌltərɚ/ *n* [C] : a person who commits adultery

adul·tery /ə'dʌltəri/ *n* [U] : sex between a married person and someone who is not that person's wife or husband • *She accused her husband of (committing) adultery.* — **adul·ter·ous** /ə'dʌltərəs/ *adj*

adv *abbr* **adverb**

¹ad·vance /əd'væns, *Brit* əd'vɑːns/ *vb* -vanced; -vanc·ing **1 a** [I] : to move forward • *The car advanced slowly down the street.* • *Enemy soldiers are* **advancing on** *the city.* [=are approaching the city in order to attack it] **b** [T] : to move (someone or something) forward • *The team advanced the ball steadily down the field.* **2** [I] : to go forward : to make progress • *The team did not advance beyond the first round of the play-offs.* • *advancing technology* : to continue in a process of development, aging, etc. • *As he advanced in age, he advanced in knowledge.* **3** [T/I] : to increase in amount or rate • *Wages have continued to advance.* • *a sign of advancing age* **4** [T] **a** : to help the progress of (something) • *They used propaganda to advance their*

cause. **b** : to make (something) higher or better • *trying to advance your career* **5** [T/I] : to rise to a higher rank or position • *He advanced quickly through the ranks.* **6** [T] : to give money to someone as a loan or before the usual time • *advance an employee a week's pay* **7** [T] : to suggest (something) for consideration or acceptance • *advance a new plan/theory* **8** [T] : to cause (something) to occur earlier or more quickly • *advance the date of a meeting* — **ad·vance·ment** /əd'vænsmənt, *Brit* əd-'vɑːnsmənt/ *n* [C/U] • *the advancement of enemy troops* • *economic advancement* • *advancements in technology*

²advance *n* **1** [C/U] : forward movement • *trying to halt the enemy's advance* **2** [C/U] : progress in the development or improvement of something • *recent advances in medicine* • *economic advance* **3** [C] : a rise in price, value, or amount • *wage advances* **4** [C] : the act of speaking to someone in an effort to start a sexual relationship — usually plural • *She rebuffed/rejected his advances.* **5** [C] : money given to someone as a loan or before the usual time of payment • *a cash advance on your salary* — **in advance** : before something happens • *There was no way to know in advance what would occur.* : before a future event or time • *Call in advance to make an appointment.* • *They were ready several days* **in advance of** [=before] *her arrival.*

³advance *adj, always before a noun* **1** : made, sent, or provided at an early time • *an advance payment/warning* **2** : going or placed before others • *an advance guard/scout*

ad·vanced /əd'vænst, *Brit* əd'vɑːnst/ *adj* **1** : beyond the basic level • *advanced mathematics* • *an advanced course in English* • *an advanced degree* [=a degree (such as a master's degree or a PhD) that is higher than a bachelor's degree] **2 a** : having developed more than others • *a highly advanced civilization* **b** : having or using new and modern methods • *advanced technology/weapons* **c** : having reached a bad state or condition • *The disease is in an advanced stage.* **d** : far along in a process of aging • *She began painting* **at an advanced age.** [=when she was old] • *He is rather* **advanced in age/ years.** [=rather old]

ad·van·tage /əd'væntɪʤ, *Brit* əd-'vɑːntɪʤ/ *n* **1** [C] **a** : something (such as a good position or condition) that helps to make someone or something better or more likely to succeed than others • *His wealth gives him an unfair advantage over us.* • *He is at an advantage because of his wealth.* • *This plan has the advantage of being less expensive than others.* **b** : a good or desirable quality or feature • *the advantages of owning a business* **2** [U] : benefit or gain • *There isn't any advantage in/to leaving early.* • *The error was* **to our advantage.** [=we were helped by the error] — **take advantage of 1** : to use (something) in a way that helps you • *We took advantage of the warm weather and did some yard work.*

2 a : to ask for or expect more than is fair or reasonable from (someone) ▪ *She was trying to take advantage of me.* **b** : to use (something) unfairly for personal gain ▪ *She took advantage of our generosity.* — **ad·van·ta·geous** /ˌæd·vænˈteɪdʒəs/ *adj* : advantageous changes — **ad·van·ta·geous·ly** *adv*

ad·vent /ˈædˌvɛnt/ *n* **1** [*singular*] : the first appearance of something ▪ *the advent of spring* **2 Advent** [*U*] *Christianity* : the period of time beginning four Sundays before Christmas ▪ *services during Advent*

ad·ven·ture /ədˈvɛntʃɚ/ *n* **1** [*C*] : an exciting or dangerous experience ▪ *He told us about his camping adventures.* ▪ *an adventure story/novel* **2** [*U*] : danger or excitement ▪ *They were looking for adventure.*

ad·ven·tur·er /ədˈvɛntʃɚrɚ/ *n* [*C*] : someone who likes dangerous or exciting experiences

ad·ven·ture·some /ədˈvɛntʃɚsəm/ *adj, chiefly US* : liking to do dangerous and exciting things ▪ *an adventuresome explorer*

ad·ven·tur·ous /ədˈvɛntʃɚəs/ *adj* **1 a** : not afraid to do new and dangerous or exciting things ▪ *adventurous travelers* **b** : exciting or unusual ▪ *an adventurous menu* **2** : full of danger and excitement ▪ *an adventurous lifestyle/vacation*

ad·verb /ˈædˌvɚb/ *n* [*C*] : a word that describes a verb, an adjective, another adverb, or a sentence and that often shows time, manner, place, or degree ▪ *In "stayed home" and "works hard," the words "home" and "hard" are adverbs.* — **ad·ver·bi·al** /ædˈvɚbijəl/ *adj* — **ad·ver·bi·al·ly** *adv*

ad·ver·sary /ˈædvɚˌseri, *Brit* ˈædvəsri/ *n, pl* **-sar·ies** [*C*] *formal* : an enemy or opponent ▪ *political adversaries* — **ad·ver·sar·i·al** /ˌædvɚˈserijəl/ *adj* ▪ *an adversarial relationship*

ad·verse /ædˈvɚs, ˈædˌvɚs/ *adj* : bad or unfavorable ▪ *adverse criticism/remarks* ▪ *Budget cuts may have an adverse effect on education.* — **ad·verse·ly** *adv*

ad·ver·si·ty /ædˈvɚsəti/ *n, pl* **-ties** [*C/U*] : a difficult situation or condition ▪ *courage in the face of adversity*

ad·vert /ˈædˌvɚt/ *n* [*C*] *Brit, informal* : ADVERTISEMENT

ad·ver·tise /ˈædvɚˌtaɪz/ *vb* **-tised; -tis·ing 1** [*T/I*] : to make the public aware of something that is being sold ▪ *advertise a new product* ▪ *businesses that advertise on the radio* **2** [*T/I*] : to make a public announcement about something that is wanted or available ▪ *We advertised the job in the paper.* **3** [*T*] : to cause people to notice (something) ▪ *Don't advertise the fact that we arrived late.* — **ad·ver·tis·er** *n* [*C*]

ad·ver·tise·ment /ˌædvɚˈtaɪzmənt, *Brit* ədˈvɚːtəsmənt/ *n* **1** [*C*] : something that is shown or presented to the public to help sell a product or to make an announcement ▪ *He learned about the job from an advertisement in the newspaper.* ▪ *a magazine/television/radio advertisement for a new car* **2** [*U*] : the act or process

of advertising ▪ *They spent a lot on advertisement.*

ad·ver·tis·ing /ˈædvɚˌtaɪzɪŋ/ *n* [*U*] **1** : published or broadcast advertisements ▪ *There is a lot of advertising in that magazine.* **2** : the business of creating advertisements ▪ *a job in advertising*

ad·vice /ədˈvaɪs/ *n* [*U*] : an opinion or suggestion about what someone should do ▪ *Take my advice and sell your old car.* ▪ *Let me offer you a bit/piece/word of advice.* ▪ *I lost some weight **on the advice of** my doctor.*

ad·vis·able /ədˈvaɪzəbəl/ *adj* : wise, sensible, or reasonable ▪ *My doctor said it was advisable for me to lose weight.* — **ad·vis·abil·i·ty** /ədˌvaɪzəˈbɪləti/ *n* [*U*]

ad·vise /ədˈvaɪz/ *vb* **-vised; -vis·ing 1 a** [*T/I*] : to give advice to (someone) ▪ *We advised them to save their money.* ▪ *We were thinking of buying that house, but our lawyer **advised (us) against** it.* **b** [*T*] : to recommend or suggest (something) ▪ *He advises patience when dealing with children.* **2** [*T*] *formal* : to give information to (someone) ▪ *The police advised them of their rights.* [=told them what their legal rights were] ▪ *Keep me advised about/on how the project is going.* — **ad·vise** *also* **ad·vi·sor** /ədˈvaɪzɚ/ *n* [*C*] ▪ *a financial/legal/medical adviser*

ad·vise·ment /ədˈvaɪzmənt/ *n* — **take (something) under advisement** *US, formal* : to consider (something) carefully ▪ *We'll take your suggestion under advisement.*

¹ad·vi·so·ry /ədˈvaɪzɚi/ *adj* : having the power or right to give advice ▪ *an advisory committee/board/panel*

²advisory *n, pl* **-ries** [*C*] *US* : a report that gives information or a warning about something ▪ *a traffic/weather advisory*

¹ad·vo·cate /ˈædvəkət/ *n* [*C*] **1 a** : a person who argues for or supports a cause or policy ▪ *a civil rights advocate* **b** *US* : a person who works for a cause or group ▪ *She works as a consumer advocate.* **2** : LAWYER

²ad·vo·cate /ˈædvəˌkeɪt/ *vb* **-cat·ed; -cat·ing** [*T*] : to support or argue for (a cause, policy, etc.) ▪ *The plan is advocated by the president.* — **ad·vo·ca·cy** /ˈædvəkəsi/ *n* [*U*]

ae·gis /ˈiːdʒəs/ *n* [*singular*] *formal* : the power to protect, control, or support something or someone ▪ *Their rights are protected **under the aegis** [=authority] of the law.*

ae·on *chiefly Brit spelling of* EON

aer·ate /ˈeəˌreɪt/ *vb* **-at·ed; -at·ing** [*T*] : to put air or a gas into (something) ▪ *Aerate the soil before planting.* → **aer·a·tion** /ˌeəˈreɪʃən/ *n* [*U*]

¹ae·ri·al /ˈerijəl/ *adj* **1** : performed in the air ▪ *aerial acrobatics* **2** : performed using an airplane ▪ *aerial combat/photography* : taken or seen from an airplane ▪ *aerial photographs/views*

²aerial *n* [*C*] **1** *chiefly Brit* : ANTENNA 2 **2** : a movement performed by an athlete (such as a skier) in the air

aer·o·bic /ˌeəˈroʊbɪk/ *adj* **1** *of exercise* : strengthening the heart and lungs by making them work hard for several minutes or more ▪ *aerobic exercises* **2** *technical* : using oxygen ▪ *aerobic organisms such as bacteria*

aer·o·bics /ˌeə'oʊbɪks/ *n* [*U*] : a system of exercises often done by a group of people while music is playing ▪ *She does aerobics twice a week.* ▪ *an aerobics class*

aero·dy·nam·ics /ˌeroʊdaɪ'næmɪks/ *n* **1** [*U*] : a science that studies the movement of air and the way that airplanes, cars, etc., move through air **2** [*plural*] : the qualities of an object that affect how easily it is able to move through the air ▪ *a car with improved aerodynamics* — **aero·dy·nam·ic** /ˌeroʊdaɪ'næmɪk/ *adj* — **aero·dy·nam·i·cal·ly** /ˌeroʊdaɪ'næmɪkli/ *adv*

aero·nau·tics /ˌerə'nɑːtɪks/ *n* [*U*] : a science that deals with airplanes and flying — **aero·nau·ti·cal** /ˌerə'nɑːtɪkəl/ *adj*

aero·plane /'erə,pleɪn/ *n* [*C*] *Brit* : AIRPLANE

aero·sol /'erə,sɑːl/ *n* [*C/U*] : a substance (such as hair spray) that is kept in a container under pressure and that is released as a fine spray when a button is pressed

aero·space /'eroʊ,speɪs/ *n* [*U*] : an industry that deals with travel in and above the Earth's atmosphere ▪ *aerospace technology*

aes·thet·ic *also US* **es·thet·ic** /es'θetɪk, *Brit* iːs'θetɪk/ *adj* : of or relating to art or beauty ▪ *making aesthetic improvements to the building* ▪ *aesthetic values* — **aes·thet·i·cal·ly** *also US* **es·thet·i·cal·ly** /es'θetɪkli, *Brit* iːs'θetɪkli/ *adv* ▪ *an aesthetically pleasing design*

afar /ə'fɑ/ *adv* — **from afar** : from a great distance ▪ *the Earth as it is seen from afar* ▪ *He admired her from afar.* [=without telling her]

AFC *abbr, US* American Football Conference ◇ The *AFC* and the NFC make up the NFL.

af·fa·ble /'æfəbəl/ *adj, formal* : friendly and easy to talk to ▪ *an affable host* — **af·fa·bil·i·ty** /ˌæfə'bɪləti/ *n* [*U*] — **af·fa·bly** /'æfəbli/ *adv*

af·fair /ə'feə/ *n* **1** [*plural*] : work or activities done for a purpose ▪ *The group conducts its affairs* [=*business*] *in private.* ▪ *the current/present* **state of affairs** [=*situation*] ▪ *the company's director of* **public affairs** [=the person who manages a company's relationship with the public] ▪ *an expert in* **foreign/world/international/domestic affairs 2** [*C*] : a secret sexual relationship between two people ▪ *She discovered that her husband was* **having an affair** *with her coworker.* **3** [*C*] **a** : a social event or activity ▪ *Their wedding day was an affair to remember.* [=a very special event] **b** : an event or series of events that usually involves well-known people ▪ *the Iran-Contra affair* **4** [*C*] : an object or thing ▪ *The bridge was a flimsy affair of ropes and rotten wood.*

af·fect /ə'fekt/ *vb* [*T*] **1** : to produce an effect on (someone or something): such as **a** : to act on (someone or something) and cause a change ▪ *His decisions could affect the lives of millions of people.* ▪ *This medication may affect your ability to drive a car.* ▪ *The scandal adversely affected*

[=*hurt*] *her political career.* **b** : to cause strong emotions in (someone) ▪ *We were all greatly affected* [=we were all very upset] *by the terrible news.* **c** : to cause a change in (a part of the body) ▪ *drugs that affect the nervous/immune system* **d** : to cause illness in (someone) ▪ *a disease primarily affecting older women* — compare EFFECT **2** *formal* : to pretend that a false behavior or feeling is natural or genuine ▪ *He affected (a look of) surprise.* [=he pretended to be surprised]

af·fec·ta·tion /ˌæˌfek'teɪʃən/ *n* [*C/U*] : an unnatural form of behavior that is meant to impress others ▪ *His French accent is just an affectation.*

af·fect·ed /ə'fektəd/ *adj* : not natural or genuine ▪ *an affected French accent*

af·fect·ing /ə'fektɪŋ/ *adj* : causing a feeling of sadness or sympathy ▪ *a powerful, affecting performance* — **af·fect·ing·ly** *adv*

af·fec·tion /ə'fekʃən/ *n* **1** [*U, singular*] : a feeling of liking and caring for someone or something ▪ *feelings of love and affection* ▪ *She developed a deep affection for that country.* **2** [*plural*] : a person's romantic feelings ▪ *They competed for the affections of the same man.* ▪ *She's been the object of his affections* [=he has loved her] *since they were children.*

af·fec·tion·ate /ə'fekʃənət/ *adj* : feeling or showing love and affection ▪ *an affectionate nickname* — **af·fec·tion·ate·ly** *adv*

af·fi·da·vit /ˌæfə'deɪvət/ *n* [*C*] *law* : a written report which is signed by a person who promises that the information is true ▪ *a signed affidavit from an eyewitness*

¹**af·fil·i·ate** /ə'fɪliˌeɪt/ *vb* **-at·ed; -at·ing** [*T*] : to closely connect (something or yourself) with or to a program, organization, etc., as a member or partner ▪ *Their group is not affiliated with/to any political party.* ▪ *the TV network's affiliated stations* — **af·fil·i·a·tion** /əˌfɪli'eɪʃən/ *n* [*C/U*] ▪ *political affiliations*

²**af·fil·i·ate** /ə'fɪlijət/ *n* [*C*] : an organization (such as a TV station) that is a member of a larger organization (such as a national network) ▪ *the network's local affiliates*

af·fin·i·ty /ə'fɪnəti/ *n, pl* **-ties** *formal* **1** [*U, singular*] : a feeling of closeness and understanding that someone has for another person because of their similar qualities, ideas, or interests ▪ *They felt a close affinity (for/to/with each other).* **2** [*singular*] **a** : a liking for something ▪ *We share an affinity for* [=we both like] *foreign films.* **b** : a quality that makes people or things suited to each other ▪ *Fish and white wine have a natural affinity for/to each other.*

af·firm /ə'fɝm/ *vb* [*T*] **1** *formal* : to say that something is true in a confident way ▪ *They neither affirmed nor denied their guilt.* **2** *formal* : to show a strong belief in or dedication to (something, such as an important idea) ▪ *laws affirming the equality of all peoples* **3** *law* : to decide that the judgment of another court is correct ▪ *The decision was affirmed by a* higher court. — **af·fir·ma·tion** /ˌæfə-ˈmeɪʃən/ n [C/U]

¹**af·fir·ma·tive** /əˈfɚmətɪv/ adj, formal : saying or showing that the answer is "yes" rather than "no" ▪ an affirmative answer — **af·fir·ma·tive·ly** adv

²**affirmative** n — **in the affirmative** formal : with a reply that means "yes" ▪ He answered (the question) in the affirmative. [=he said "yes"]

affirmative action n [U] chiefly US : the practice of improving the educational and job opportunities of members of groups that have not been treated fairly in the past because of their race, sex, etc.

¹**af·fix** /əˈfɪks/ vb [T] formal : to attach (something) to something else ▪ affix a stamp to [=put a stamp on] an envelope

²**af·fix** /ˈæˌfɪks/ n [C] grammar : a prefix or suffix

af·flict /əˈflɪkt/ vb [T] formal : to cause pain or suffering to (someone or something) ▪ Much of the region is afflicted by poverty. ▪ people afflicted with cancer — **af·flic·tion** /əˈflɪkʃən/ n [C/U] ▪ He died from a mysterious affliction. ▪ her affliction with polio

af·flu·ent /ˈæfluwənt/ adj : RICH, WEALTHY ▪ an affluent country/neighborhood/family — **af·flu·ence** /ˈæfluwəns/ n [U]

af·ford /əˈfoɚd/ vb [T] 1 : to be able to pay for (something) ▪ Don't spend more than you can afford. ▪ They couldn't afford (to buy) new coats. 2 : to be able to do (something) without having problems or being seriously harmed ▪ We can't afford to wait any longer. ▪ She càn ill afford to lose any more weight. 3 formal : to supply or provide (something needed or wanted) to someone ▪ He was afforded [=given] the opportunity to work for a judge. — **af·ford·abil·i·ty** /əˌfoɚdə-ˈbɪləti/ n [U] — **af·ford·able** /əˈfoɚdəbəl/ adj

¹**af·front** /əˈfrʌnt/ n [C] formal : an action or statement that insults or offends someone ▪ He regarded her rude behavior as a personal affront.

²**affront** vb [T] formal : to do or say something that shows a lack of respect for (someone or someone's feelings) ▪ He was affronted [=offended] by her rude behavior.

af·ghan /ˈæfˌgæn/ n [C] chiefly US : a blanket made of wool or cotton knitted in patterns

afi·cio·na·do /əˌfɪʃijəˈnɑːdoʊ/ n, pl -dos [C] : a person who likes and knows a lot about something ▪ sports/poetry aficionados

afield /əˈfiːld/ adv : away from home : away from here or there — used with far, farther, or further ▪ People came from as far afield as New York to see the show.

afire /əˈfajɚ/ adj, not before a noun : burning : on fire ▪ The house was afire. — **afire** adv

aflame /əˈfleɪm/ adj, not before a noun : burning : on fire ▪ The entire town was aflame. ▪ (figurative) The fields are aflame with flowers of every color. — **aflame** adv

afloat /əˈfloʊt/ adj, not before a noun 1 : floating on water ▪ Our boat was still

afloat. 2 : having enough money to continue ▪ trying to keep the business afloat

aflut·ter /əˈflʌtɚ/ adj, not before a noun : nervously excited ▪ Her heart was aflutter at the thought of his return.

afoot /əˈfʊt/ adj, not before a noun : developing or happening now ▪ There's trouble afoot.

afore·men·tioned /əˈfoɚˈmɛnʃənd/ adj, always before a noun, formal : mentioned before ▪ The aforementioned book is the author's most famous work.

afoul of /əˈfaʊləv/ adv — **fall/run afoul of** chiefly US : to get into trouble because of (the law, a rule, etc.) ▪ He fell afoul of the law. [=he was arrested for breaking the law]

afraid /əˈfreɪd/ adj, not before a noun 1 : feeling fear ▪ Don't be afraid (of the dog)—he won't hurt you. ▪ She's afraid of failing/failure. ▪ He wasn't afraid to say what he thought. ▪ We were all afraid (that) she wouldn't live. = We were all afraid for her life. 2 — used in the phrase **I'm afraid** as a polite way of showing that you are sorry about a disappointing, negative, or critical statement ▪ She tries hard, but I'm afraid (to say) that her work just isn't very good. ▪ "Is it raining?" "I'm afraid so." [=yes, it is] ▪ "Can you come to our party?" "I'm afraid not." [=no, I can't come] 3 — used with not to say that someone is willing to do something ▪ She's not afraid of hard work. = She's not afraid to work hard. [=she's willing to work hard]

afresh /əˈfrɛʃ/ adv : from a new beginning ▪ Let's stop now and start afresh in the morning.

Af·ri·can /ˈæfrɪkən/ n [C] 1 : a person born, raised, or living in Africa 2 : a descendant of Africans — **African** adj

Af·ri·can–Amer·i·can /ˌæfrɪkənəˈmerɪkən/ n [C] : an American who has African ancestors — **African–American** adj

African violet n [C] : a tropical plant that has fuzzy leaves and purple, pink, or white flowers

Af·ro /ˈæfroʊ/ n, pl -ros [C] : a hairstyle in which very curly hair is shaped into a smooth round ball

Af·ro–Amer·i·can /ˌæfrowəˈmerəkən/ n [C] : AFRICAN-AMERICAN — **Afro–American** adj

aft /ˈæft, Brit ˈɑːft/ adv : towards or at the back part of a boat, ship, or plane ▪ The plane's exits are located fore and aft.

¹**af·ter** /ˈæftɚ, Brit ˈɑːftə/ adv : at a later time ▪ He ate lunch and left immediately after.

²**after** prep 1 a : at a time following (something or someone) ▪ We arrived shortly after six o'clock. ▪ He left after lunch. ▪ He finished the exam after me. ▪ I'm expecting her to arrive the day after tomorrow. ▪ They earned $30,000 after (paying) taxes. ▪ He left after an hour. ▪ The job got easier **after a while.** [=after some time had passed] b US — used to describe a time following a specified hour ▪ It's 20 (minutes) after 12. [=it's 12:20] 2 a : following (something or

someone) in order or in a series ▪ *It's the highest mountain after Mount Everest.* ▪ *You go first and I'll go/follow after you.* ▪ *The children marched out one after the other.* ◇ The phrase *after you* is used as a polite way of saying that someone should go ahead of you or do something before you do it. ▪ *After you, Madam!* **b** — used in phrases to describe something that happens many times or for a long period of time ▪ *They have suffered misfortune after misfortune.* ▪ *She does her job day after day without complaining.* ▪ *He's done the same thing time after time.* **3** : trying to catch or get (something or someone) ▪ *The dog ran after the ball.* ▪ *The police are after him.* [=are trying to catch him] ▪ *What is she after?* [=what does she want?] ▪ *Mom was after me* [=Mom repeatedly told me] *to clean my room.* **4** : following the actions or departure of (someone) ▪ *She shouted after him* [=she shouted at/toward him] *as he walked away.* ▪ *They made a mess and didn't clean up after themselves.* [=didn't clean up the mess they made] **5 a** : with the name of (someone or something) ▪ *She was named after her grandmother.* **b** : in the manner of (someone or something) ▪ *a building patterned after a cathedral* **6** : about (someone or something) ▪ *One of your old friends was asking/inquiring after you.* [=she was asking how you are] — **after all 1** : even though the opposite was expected ▪ *It didn't rain after all.* **2** — used to emphasize something that needs to be considered ▪ *You should apologize. After all, she is your best friend.*

³after *conj* : later than the time that ▪ *Call me after you arrive.* ▪ *He finished the exam after I did.*

af·ter·care /ˈæftəˌkeɚ, *Brit* ˈɑːftəˌkɛə/ *n* [U] : the care, treatment, etc., given to people after they leave a place (such as a hospital or prison) ▪ *aftercare services*

af·ter·ef·fect /ˈæftəɹɪˌfɛkt, *Brit* ˈɑːftəɹɪˌfɛkt/ *n* [C] : an effect that occurs after time has passed ▪ *the aftereffects of his injury*

af·ter·glow /ˈæftəˌgloʊ, *Brit* ˈɑːftəˌgləʊ/ *n* [*singular*] **1** : a glowing light remaining in the sky after the sun has set **2** : a happy feeling that remains after a successful or emotional event ▪ *We basked in the afterglow* [=enjoyed the satisfaction] *of the victory.*

af·ter·life /ˈæftəˌlaɪf, *Brit* ˈɑːftəˌlaɪf/ *n* [*singular*] : a life that some people believe exists after death ▪ *Does he believe in an/the afterlife?*

af·ter·math /ˈæftəˌmæθ, *Brit* ˈɑːftəˌmæθ/ *n* [C] : the period of time after a bad and usually destructive event ▪ *in the aftermath of the war* ▪ *divorce and its aftermath*

af·ter·noon /ˌæftəˈnuːn, *Brit* ˌɑːftəˈnuːn/ *n* [C] : the part of the day between noon and evening ▪ *It was early/late afternoon when I left.* ▪ *She spent the/her afternoon at the library.* ▪ *We went for a walk this afternoon.* [=during the afternoon today] ▪ *an afternoon drive* ▪ *afternoon tea*

af·ters /ˈæftəz, *Brit* ˈɑːftəz/ *n* [U] *Brit, informal* : DESSERT ▪ *What's for afters?*

af·ter·shave /ˈæftəˌʃeɪv, *Brit* ˈɑːftəˌʃeɪv/

n [C/U] : a liquid that some men put on their faces after they have shaved

af·ter·shock /ˈæftəˌʃɑːk, *Brit* ˈɑːftəˌʃɒk/ *n* [C] : a smaller earthquake that occurs after a larger one ▪ *(figurative) the aftershocks of being laid off*

af·ter·taste /ˈæftəˌteɪst, *Brit* ˈɑːftəˌteɪst/ *n* [*singular*] : a taste that remains after something is eaten or drunk ▪ *The wine has a sweet aftertaste.*

af·ter·thought /ˈæftəˌθɑːt, *Brit* ˈɑːftəˌθɔːt/ *n* [C] : something done or said after other things because it was not thought of earlier ▪ *The lounge was added to the office as an afterthought.*

af·ter·ward /ˈæftəwəd, *Brit* ˈɑːftəwəd/ *or* **af·ter·wards** /ˈæftəwədz, *Brit* ˈɑːftəwədz/ *adv* : after something has happened ▪ *I felt better afterward.*

af·ter·word /ˈæftəˌwəd, *Brit* ˈɑːftəˌwəːd/ *n* [C] : a final section that comes after the main part of a book ▪ *The novel has an afterword by the author.*

again /əˈgɛn/ *adv* **1** : one more time ▪ *It was nice to see you again.* ▪ *Never again will I be so foolish.* ▪ *Oh no! Not again!* ▪ *She won yet again.* ▪ *It'll just be the same thing all over again.* ▪ *I told him over and over again to be careful.* = *I told him again and again to be careful.* **2** : to a previous position or place ▪ *We flew from Boston to Chicago and back again.* [=back to Boston] **3** — used to introduce a thought or possibility that differs from a preceding one ▪ *He might go, and (then) again, he might not.* **4** — used when repeating and stressing something previously said ▪ *Again, this is a serious problem.* **5** — used to ask someone to repeat something ▪ *What was your name again?* — **once again** see ¹ONCE — **time and again** see ¹TIME

against /əˈgɛnst/ *prep* **1 a** : in opposition to (someone or something) ▪ *Everyone was against them.* ▪ *She voted against the proposal.* ▪ *They fought against each other in World Wars I and II.* ▪ *He borrowed the car against their wishes.* [=even though they did not want him to] ▪ *Against my advice* [=even though I advised her not to], *she quit her job.* ▪ *He was taken against his will.* [=he was taken by force even though he didn't want to go] **b** : in competition with (someone or something) ▪ *two runners racing against each other* **2** — used to indicate the person or thing that is affected or harmed by something ▪ *The evidence against him is convincing.* **3** : not agreeing with or allowed by (something, such as a law) ▪ *Touching the ball with your hands is against the rules.* **4** : as a reason for disliking (someone or something) ▪ *I have nothing against her.* [=I have no reason for disliking her] ▪ *We disagree, but I don't hold it/that against him.* [=I don't dislike you because of it/that] **5** — used to say that one thing is being compared with another ▪ *Weigh the risk against the possible benefit.* **6** : as a defense or protection from (something) ▪ *injections against flu* **7** — used to describe hitting or touching something or someone ▪ *I hit my head against the shelf.*

• *leaning against the wall* **8** : in a direction opposite to the movement of (something) • *sailing against the wind* **9** : with the background of (something) • *The tree's red leaves stood out against the gray sky.* — **up against** see ²UP

agape /ə'geɪp/ *adj, not before a noun* : having the mouth open because of wonder, surprise, or shock • *He stood there with his mouth agape.*

¹**age** /'eɪdʒ/ *n* **1** [*C/U*] **a** : the amount of time during which a person or animal has lived • *What is your age?* [=how old are you?] • *She died at a young age.* • *a man (of) your age* • *He is twice her age.* • **Act your age.** [=act in a way that is appropriate for a person of your age] • *She showed remarkable musical talent at/from an early age.* [=when she was young] • *The movie appeals to people of all ages.* • *She is starting to feel her age.* [=starting to feel old] • *He left home at the tender age of 18.* [=when he was only 18 years old] • *She died at the ripe old age of 90.* • *He learned to paint in his old age.* [=when he was old] • *Our son is small for his age.* [=he's smaller than most children are at his age] • *She was 20 years of age.* [=was 20 years old] • *He joined the company at age 35.* • *He was over the age limit.* [=he was too old] **b** : the amount of time during which a thing has existed • *What is the age of your car?* **2** [*C/U*] : the time of life when a person does something or becomes legally able to do something • *The voting age is 18.* [=people may vote when they are 18] • *They are approaching retirement age.* • *college-age students* • *He received his full inheritance when he came of age.* [=became an adult] • *(figurative) a political movement that has come of age* [=has become fully formed and effective] **3** [*U*] **a** : the process of becoming old or older • *a wine that has improved with age* **b** : the condition of being old • *She died of old age.* **4** [*C*] : a period of history • *a symbol of the modern age* • *a bygone/past age* • *How can such behavior still be tolerated in this day and age?* : a period of time that is associated with a particular thing or person • *the age of the Internet* — **5** [*C*] *informal* : a long period of time — usually plural • *It's been ages since we last saw them.*

²**age** *vb* **aged; ag·ing** *or chiefly Brit* **age·ing 1** [*I*] : to become old or older • *As he aged he grew more bitter.* • *an aging population* **2** [*T*] : to cause (someone or something) to become old or to appear to be old • *The sun has aged her skin.* **3** [*T/I*] *of food or drink* : to be stored for a period of time in order to gain desired qualities • *The wine is aged in oak barrels.*

aged *adj* **1** /'eɪdʒəd/ : very old • *an aged oak* **2** /'eɪdʒd/ *not before a noun* : having reached a specified age • *a child aged 10* — **the aged** : old people • *the aged and the sick*

age·ism /'eɪˌdʒɪzəm/ *n* [*U*] : unfair treatment of old people • *He accused his former employer of ageism.* — **age·ist** /'eɪdʒɪst/ *adj*

age·less /'eɪdʒləs/ *adj* **1** : not growing old or showing the effects of age • *a* seemingly ageless athlete **2** : lasting forever • *ageless truths* — **age·less·ness** *n* [*U*]

agen·cy /'eɪdʒənsi/ *n, pl* **-cies** [*C*] **1** : a business that provides a particular service • *an insurance/travel/employment agency* **2** : a government department that is responsible for a particular activity, area, etc. • *federal law enforcement agencies* — **through the agency of** *formal* : by using the help of (something or someone) • *a treaty ratified through the agency of a neutral country*

agen·da /ə'dʒɛndə/ *n* [*C*] **1** : a list of things to be considered or done • *They set the agenda for the meeting.* • *What's next on the agenda?* **2** : a plan or goal that guides someone's behavior and that is often kept secret • *She had no hidden agenda.*

agent /'eɪdʒənt/ *n* [*C*] **1** : a person who does business for another person • *A travel agent helped plan their vacation.* • *The actor got the role through his agent.* **2** : a person who tries to get secret information about another country, government, etc. : SPY • *a government agent* **3** : a person or thing that causes something to happen • *agents of social change* **4** : something that is used to produce a particular effect or result • *Flour is used as a thickening agent in sauces.*

age-old /'eɪdʒˌoʊld/ *adj, always before a noun* : having existed for a very long time • *an age-old problem*

ag·glom·er·a·tion /əˌglɑːməˈreɪʃən/ *n* [*C*] *formal* : a large group or pile of different things • *an agglomeration of homes and businesses*

ag·gran·dize·ment *also Brit* **ag·gran·dise·ment** /ə'grændəzmənt/ *n* [*U*] *disapproving* : advancement or increase in power or importance • *self-aggrandizement*

ag·gra·vate /'ægrəˌveɪt/ *vb* **-vat·ed; -vat·ing** [*T*] **1** : to make (an injury, problem, etc.) more serious or severe • *She aggravated an old knee injury.* • *aggravating an already bad situation* **2** *informal* : to make (someone) angry or annoyed • *These delays really aggravate me.* — **aggravating** *adj* • *a slow and aggravating process* — **ag·gra·vat·ing·ly** *adv* — **ag·gra·va·tion** /ˌægrə'veɪʃən/ *n* [*C/U*] • *I don't need all this aggravation.*

aggravated *adj* **1** : annoyed or angry • *I get very aggravated with her.* **2** *always before a noun, law* : made more serious by the use of violence or the threat of violence • *convicted of aggravated assault*

¹**ag·gre·gate** /'ægrɪgət/ *n* [*C/U*] *formal* : a total amount • *They won the two games by an aggregate of 40 points.* • *Spending amounted to 25 million dollars* **in the aggregate** [=all together] *to 25 million dollars.*

²**ag·gre·gate** /'ægrɪgət/ *adj* : formed by adding together two or more amounts • *The team with the highest aggregate score wins.*

³**ag·gre·gate** /'ægrɪˌgeɪt/ *vb* **-gat·ed; -gat·ing** [*T/I*] *formal* : to join or combine into one group • *The Web site aggregates content from many other sources.* • *insects that aggregate in dark, moist places*

— **ag·gre·ga·tion** /ˌægrɪˈgeɪʃən/ n [C/U]

ag·gres·sion /əˈgrɛʃən/ n [U] **1** : angry or violent behavior or feelings ▪ *a display of aggression* **2** : hostile action against another country, government, etc. ▪ *military aggression* ▪ *an act of aggression*

ag·gres·sive /əˈgrɛsɪv/ adj **1** : ready and willing to fight, argue, etc. ▪ *an aggressive dog* ▪ *aggressive behavior* **2** : using forceful methods to succeed or to do something ▪ *an overly aggressive salesman* ▪ *They took aggressive steps to discourage trespassing.* **3** medical **a** : very severe ▪ *an aggressive form of cancer* **b** : very strong or intense ▪ *aggressive chemotherapy* — **ag·gres·sive·ly** adv — **ag·gres·sive·ness** n [U]

ag·gres·sor /əˈgrɛsɚ/ n [C] : a person or country that attacks another ▪ *Which country was the aggressor?*

ag·grieved /əˈgriːvd/ adj : feeling anger because of unfair treatment ▪ *an aggrieved victim*

ag·gro /ˈægroʊ/ n [U] Brit, informal **1** : something that annoys or bothers someone ▪ *It wasn't worth the aggro.* [=*aggravation*] **2** : angry and violent behavior : AGGRESSION

aghast /əˈgæst, Brit əˈgɑːst/ adj, not before a noun : shocked and upset ▪ *They were aghast at how awful the play was.*

ag·ile /ˈædʒəl/ adj **1** : able to move quickly and easily ▪ *an agile athlete* **2** : quick, smart, and clever ▪ *an agile mind/thinker* — **ag·ile·ly** adv — **agil·i·ty** /əˈdʒɪləti/ n [U]

ag·i·tate /ˈædʒəˌteɪt/ vb -tat·ed; -tat·ing **1** [T] : to disturb, excite, or anger (someone) ▪ *Talking about the problem just agitates him even more.* **2** [I] : to try to get people to support or oppose something ▪ *agitate for equal rights* **3** [T] technical : to move or stir up (a liquid) ▪ *water agitated by wind* — **agitated** adj ▪ *She became very agitated.* — **ag·i·ta·tion** /ˌædʒəˈteɪʃən/ n [U]

ag·i·ta·tor /ˈædʒəˌteɪtɚ/ n [C] **1** : a person who tries to get people angry or upset so that they will support an effort to change something ▪ *antigovernment agitators* **2** : a device for stirring or shaking something in a machine (such as a washing machine)

aglit·ter /əˈglɪtɚ/ adj, not before a noun : sparkling brightly ▪ *The tree was aglitter with decorations.*

aglow /əˈgloʊ/ adj, not before a noun **1** : glowing with light or color ▪ *The room was aglow with candlelight.* **2** : very excited or happy ▪ *The children were aglow with excitement.*

ag·nos·tic /æɡˈnɑːstɪk/ n [C] : a person who does not have a definite belief about whether God exists or not ▪ (*figurative*) *a political agnostic* [=a person who lacks strong political beliefs] — **agnostic** adj — **ag·nos·ti·cism** /æɡˈnɑːstəˌsɪzəm/ n [U]

ago /əˈgoʊ/ adv : before now ▪ *She arrived a few hours ago.* ▪ *He long ago learned to be patient.* ▪ *It happened a while ago.* = *It happened (quite) some time ago.*

agog /əˈgɑːɡ/ adj, not before a noun : full of interest or excitement because of something ▪ *Her supporters were agog at/over the idea.*

ag·o·nize also Brit **ag·o·nise** /ˈægəˌnaɪz/ vb -nized; -niz·ing [I] : to think or worry very much about something ▪ *She agonized about/over what she was going to do.*

agonizing also Brit **agonising** adj : very mentally or physically painful ▪ *an agonizing decision* ▪ *He was in agonizing pain.* — **ag·o·niz·ing·ly** also Brit **ag·o·nis·ing·ly** adv ▪ *agonizingly slow*

ag·o·ny /ˈægəni/ n, pl -nies [C/U] : extreme mental or physical pain ▪ *He died in agony.* ▪ *the agony of defeat* ▪ *He suffered no agonies of guilt/remorse/regret over his decision.* [=he did not feel guilty about his decision]

ag·o·ra·pho·bia /ˌægərəˈfoʊbijə/ n [U] : a fear of being in open or public places — **ag·o·ra·pho·bic** /ˌægərəˈfoʊbɪk/ adj — **agoraphobic** n [C]

agrar·i·an /əˈɡrerijən/ adj : of or relating to farms and farming ▪ *an agrarian economy/society*

agree /əˈɡriː/ vb agreed; agree·ing **1** [T/I] : to have the same opinion ▪ *Do you agree or disagree (with me/that)?* ▪ *I agree completely.* = *I couldn't agree more.* ▪ *We all agree that the law needs to be changed.* ▪ *We* **are** *all* **agreed** *that the law needs to be changed.* ▪ *Do you agree with* [=do you approve of] *the death penalty?* ▪ *I'm not going to change my mind, so we're going to have to* **agree** *to* **disagree/differ.** [=to agree not to argue anymore about a difference of opinion] **2** [T/I] : to say that you will do, accept, or allow something that is suggested or requested by another person ▪ *He agreed to their proposal/plan.* ▪ *She agreed to be interviewed.* **3** [T/I] of two or more people or groups : to decide to accept something after discussing what should or might be done ▪ *We* **agreed** *on/upon a plan.* ▪ *They met at the* **agreed-upon** *time.* ▪ (*Brit*) *The jurors were unable to* **agree** *a verdict.* **4** [I] : to be alike ▪ *These results agree with earlier studies.* **5** [I] grammar : to be alike in gender, number, case, or person ▪ *A verb should agree with its subject.* **6** [I] : to be suitable for or pleasing to someone ▪ *Spicy food doesn't* **agree with** *me.* [=it makes me feel unwell]

agree·able /əˈɡriːjəbəl/ adj **1** : pleasing to the mind or senses ▪ *a very agreeable young man* ▪ *They spent an agreeable evening together.* **2** : ready or willing to agree ▪ *She seemed agreeable to (the idea of) leaving early.* **3** : able to be accepted ▪ *Is the schedule agreeable to you?* [=do you agree to it?] — **agree·able·ness** n [U] — **agree·ably** /əˈɡriːjəbli/ adv

agree·ment /əˈɡriːmənt/ n **1** [U] **a** : the act of agreeing ▪ *She nodded her head in* **agreement.** [=to show that she agreed] **b** : a situation in which people share the same opinion ▪ *There is widespread agreement on this issue.* **2** [C] : an arrangement, contract, etc., by which people agree about what is to be done ▪ *I thought we had an agreement.* ▪ *a formal/contractual agreement* ▪ *a peace/*

trade agreement • *They have come to an agreement.* = *They have reached an agreement.* **3** [U] *grammar* : the fact or state of being alike in gender, number, case, or person • *The subject and the verb need to be in agreement (with each other).*

ag·ri·busi·ness /ˈægrəˌbɪznəs/ *n* [U] : farming thought of as a large business • *a giant agribusiness corporation*

ag·ri·cul·ture /ˈægrɪˌkʌltʃɚ/ *n* [U] : the science or occupation of farming • *land used for agriculture* — **ag·ri·cul·tur·al** /ˌægrɪˈkʌltʃərəl/ *adj* • *agricultural machinery/products* • *an agricultural society* — **ag·ri·cul·tur·al·ly** *adv* — **ag·ri·cul·tur·ist** /ˌægrɪˈkʌltʃərɪst/ *or* **ag·ri·cul·tur·al·ist** /ˌægrɪˈkʌltʃərəlɪst/ *n* [C]

agron·o·my /əˈgrɑːnəmi/ *n* [U] : a science that deals with farming — **agron·o·mist** /əˈgrɑnəmɪst/ *n* [C]

aground /əˈgraʊnd/ *adv* : on or onto the ground • *The boat ran aground on a reef.*

ah /ˈɑː/ *interj* — used to express pleasure, relief, etc. • *Ah, that feels good.* • *Ah, yes, now I remember.*

aha /ɑˈhɑː/ *interj* — used when something is suddenly seen, found, or understood • *Aha! So that's how it's supposed to work.*

ahead /əˈhɛd/ *adv* **1 a** : in or toward the front • *There's a gas station (up) ahead.* • *He was looking straight ahead.* [=directly forward] **b** : to or toward the place where someone is going • *You go on ahead. I'll catch up later.* **2** : in, into, or for the future • *We need to think/plan ahead.* • *in the weeks ahead* • *We don't know what lies ahead.* **3** : in the lead in a race or competition • *They're ahead by 7 points.* • *a politician who is ahead in the polls* **4** : in or toward a better position • *He'll do anything to get ahead.* [=to become successful] **5** : at an earlier time • *She prepared most of the food ahead.*

ahead of *prep* **1** : in, at, or to a place before (someone or something) • *They are several miles ahead of us.* **2** : in the future for (someone or something) • *We have some hard work ahead of us.* **3** : having a lead or advantage over (a competitor) • *The company stays one step ahead of the competition.* • *They're ahead of us by 7 points.* **4 a** : better than (something) • *The company's earnings are (way/far) ahead of forecasts.* **b** : in a more advanced position than (someone or something) • *He was a year ahead of me in school.* [=he finished school a year before I did] • *As a poet, she was ahead of her time.* [=she was too advanced or modern to be understood or appreciated during the time when she lived or worked] **5** : at an earlier time than (someone or something) • *They arrived ahead of us.* • *She prepared the food ahead of time.* • *We finished the project ahead of schedule.* [=earlier than planned]

ahem /əˈhɛm/ *interj* — used in writing to represent a sound that people make to attract attention, to express disapproval, etc.

ahoy /əˈhɔɪ/ *interj* — used by a sailor who is calling out to a passing boat • *Ahoy there, mate!*

¹aid /ˈeɪd/ *vb* [T/I] : to provide what is useful or necessary : HELP • *She aided them in their efforts.* • *aiding the poor* • *His research aided in the discovery of a new treatment for cancer.* • *She is charged with aiding and abetting* [=helping and encouraging] *the thief in his getaway.*

²aid *n* **1** [U] : help or assistance given to someone • *The work was done with the aid of a computer.* • *A rescue party was sent to their aid.* [=was sent to help/rescue them] **2** [U] : something (such as money, food, or equipment) that is given by a government or an organization to help a country or area where many people are suffering because of poverty, disease, etc. • *millions of dollars in economic/foreign/humanitarian aid* • *international aid organizations* **b** : money that is given to a student to help pay for the cost of attending a school • *financial/student aid* **3** [C] : a device, object, etc., that makes something easier to do • *instructional/learning aids* • *a pill used as a sleeping aid* **4** [C] *chiefly US* : a person whose job is to assist someone : AIDE • *a teacher's aid*

aide /ˈeɪd/ *n* [C] : a person whose job is to assist someone • *a nurse's/teacher's aide* • *congressional aides*

AIDS /ˈeɪdz/ *n* [U] : a serious disease of the immune system that is caused by a virus ✧ *AIDS* is an abbreviation of "acquired immune deficiency syndrome."

ail /ˈeɪl/ *vb* **1** [T] : to cause pain or trouble for (someone) • *This medicine is good for what/whatever ails you.* • *What ails public education these days?* **2** [I] : to suffer bad health • *her ailing husband* • (*figurative*) *The company is ailing financially.*

ail·ment /ˈeɪlmənt/ *n* [C] : a sickness or illness • *a chronic ailment*

¹aim /ˈeɪm/ *vb* **1** [T/I] **a** : to point (a weapon) at a target • *He aimed the gun carefully.* • *Ready, aim, fire!* **b** : to point (a device) at something • *aim a camera/telescope* • *She aimed at me with her camera.* **c** : to direct (something, such as a ball or a kick) at a target • *a badly aimed punch* **2** [T/I] : to have a specified goal or purpose • *a political movement that aims at promoting world peace* • *We aim to please.* • *You need a goal to aim for.* • *If you want to be successful, you have to aim high.* [=you have to be ambitious] **3** [T] : to direct (something) at a particular goal, group of people, etc. • *His criticism was aimed primarily at parents.* • *changes aimed at reducing costs*

²aim *n* **1** [C] : a goal or purpose • *Their aim is to promote peace.* • *I started this business with the aim of making a profit.* **2** [U] : the ability to hit a target • *His aim was off/bad and he missed.* — **take aim 1** : to point a weapon at a target • *He took aim at the target.* **2** *US* : to have a specified goal or intention • *The runners took aim at setting a record.* [=their goal was to set a record] **3** : to have something as the object of an action or effort • *Investigators are taking aim at* [=are intending to punish/stop] *health-care fraud.*

aim·less /ˈeɪmləs/ *adj* : not having a goal or purpose ▪ *an aimless conversation* — **aim·less·ly** *adv* ▪ *wander aimlessly* — **aim·less·ness** *n [U, singular]*

ain't /ˈeɪnt/ *informal* **1** : am not ▪ *I ain't worried.* : are not ▪ *They ain't interested.* : is not ▪ *Say it ain't so!* **2** : have not ▪ *They ain't got a clue.* ▪ *You ain't seen nothing yet!* : has not ▪ *She ain't never been the same.*

> *usage Ain't* is usually regarded as an error, but it is common in the very informal speech of some people and it is also used in informal and humorous phrases.

¹**air** /ˈeɚ/ *n* **1** [U] **a** : the invisible gases that surround the Earth and that people and animals breathe ▪ *outdoors in the open air* ▪ *fresh/stale air* ▪ *High in the mountains the air is thin.* ▪ *My keys vanished/disappeared into thin air.* [=vanished in a very sudden and mysterious way] **b** : the space or sky that is filled with air ▪ *land, water, and air* ▪ *The balloon rose up into the air.* **2** [U] : methods of travel that involve flying ▪ *travel by air* [=by flying in airplanes] **3** [*singular*] : a quality that a person or thing has ▪ *a dignified air* ▪ *He has an air of mystery about him.* [=he has a mysterious quality] **4** [U] *US* : AIR-CONDITIONING ▪ *a house with central air* — **clear the air** : to talk about problems, feelings, etc., in order to reach agreement or understanding — **floating/walking on air** : feeling very happy ▪ *After he won, he was walking on air.* — **in the air 1** : felt or sensed by many people ▪ *There was anticipation in the air.* **2** : expected to happen soon ▪ *Change is in the air.* — **off the air** of a radio or TV station, program, etc. : not being broadcast ▪ *My favorite show went off the air* [=stopped being broadcast] *last year.* — **on the air** also *on air* of a radio or TV station, program, etc. : being broadcast ▪ *The interview will be on the air tomorrow.* — **put on airs** : to act in a way that shows you think you are better than other people ▪ *She has been putting on airs since she became wealthy.* — **up in the air** : not yet settled or decided ▪ *Our vacation plans are still up in the air.* — **air·less** /ˈeɚləs/ *adj*

²**air** *vb* **1** [T/I] **a** : to place something in an open area where there is a lot of moving air to make it cool, dry, or clean ▪ *air a blanket* ▪ *The blankets were left outside to air.* **b** : to allow air from the outside to enter something ▪ *She opened the windows to air out the room.* **2** [T] : to make (something) known in public ▪ *publicly airing their differences* **3** [T/I] : to broadcast something on radio or TV ▪ *The interview will be aired tomorrow.* = *It will air tomorrow.*

air bag *n [C]* : a bag that fills with air to protect a driver or passenger when a vehicle crashes

air·borne /ˈeɚˌboɚn/ *adj* **1** : moving or being carried through the air ▪ *airborne dust particles* **2** of soldiers : specially trained to jump from airplanes into enemy territory for battle ▪ *airborne forces*

air·brush /ˈeɚˌbrʌʃ/ *n [C]* : a device that is used to spray a liquid (such as paint) onto a surface — **airbrush** *vb [T]* ▪ *His blemishes were airbrushed out in the photograph.* [=an airbrush was used to change the photograph so that his blemishes could not be seen]

air conditioner *n [C]* : a machine that is used to cool and dry the air in a building, room, etc.

air–con·di·tion·ing /ˌeɚkənˈdɪʃənɪŋ/ *n [U]* : a system used for cooling and drying the air in a building, room, etc. ▪ *a car with air-conditioning* — abbr. *AC* — **air–con·di·tioned** /ˌeɚkənˈdɪʃənd/ *adj*

air·craft /ˈeɚˌkræft, Brit ˈeɚˌkrɑːft/ *n, pl* **aircraft** [C] : a machine (such as an airplane or a helicopter) that flies through the air ▪ *military aircraft*

aircraft carrier *n [C]* : a military ship that has a large deck where aircraft take off and land

air·drop /ˈeɚˌdrɑːp/ *n [C]* : the act or action of delivering supplies by parachute from an airplane during an emergency ▪ *an airdrop of food for refugees* — **air·drop** /ˈeɚˌdrɑːp/ *vb* **-dropped; -dropping** [T] ▪ *air-dropping supplies*

air·fare /ˈeɚˌfeɚ/ *n [C]* : the money paid to travel on an airplane ▪ *round-trip airfare*

air·field /ˈeɚˌfiːld/ *n [C]* : a field or airport where airplanes take off and land

air force *n [C]* : the part of a country's military forces that fights with airplanes ▪ *the U.S./British Air Force*

air·head /ˈeɚˌhɛd/ *n [C] informal* : a silly and stupid person

air·lift /ˈeɚˌlɪft/ *n [C]* : an occurrence in which people or things are carried to or from a place by airplanes during an emergency ▪ *an airlift to deliver supplies to the refugees* — **airlift** *vb [T]* ▪ *airlifting supplies to refugees*

air·line /ˈeɚˌlaɪn/ *n [C]* : a company that owns and operates many airplanes used for carrying passengers and goods ▪ *a major airline* ▪ *airline passengers*

air·lin·er /ˈeɚˌlaɪnɚ/ *n [C]* : a large airplane used for carrying passengers

air·mail /ˈeɚˌmeɪl/ *n [U]* : the system used for sending mail by aircraft ▪ *The package was sent by/via airmail.* — **airmail** *vb [T]* ▪ *He airmailed the letter/package.*

air mattress *n [C]* : a soft plastic case that can be filled with air and used as a bed

air·plane /ˈeɚˌpleɪn/ *n [C] US* : a machine that has wings and an engine and that flies through the air ▪ *traveling on/in an airplane* — called also *plane*, (Brit) *aeroplane*

air·play /ˈeɚˌpleɪ/ *n [U]* : time when a musical recording is played by a radio station ▪ *Her latest song is getting a lot of airplay.*

air·port /ˈeɚˌpoɚt/ *n [C]* : a place where aircraft land and take off and where there are buildings for passengers to wait in and for aircraft to be sheltered

air raid *n [C]* : an attack in which a place is bombed by military airplanes

air rifle *n* [C] : a rifle that uses air pressure to shoot small pellets

air·sick /'eɚ,sɪk/ *adj* : feeling sick in the stomach while riding in an airplane — **air·sick·ness** *n* [U]

air·space /'eɚ,speɪs/ *n* [U] : the space that is above a country and that is legally controlled by that country • *flying through U.S. airspace*

air·speed /'eɚ,spi:d/ *n* [U] : the speed at which an aircraft moves through the air

air strike *n* [C] : an attack in which military airplanes drop bombs • *air strikes on key targets*

air·strip /'eɚ,strɪp/ *n* [C] : an area of land used as a runway for airplanes to take off and land

air·tight /'eɚ,taɪt/ *adj* **1** : tightly sealed so that no air can get in or out • *an airtight container* **2** : too strong or effective to fail or to be defeated • *an airtight argument*

air·time /'eɚ,taɪm/ *n* [U] : time during a radio or TV broadcast • *buy radio/TV airtime for campaign ads*

air traffic control *n* [U] : a system in which people on the ground give instructions by radio to aircraft pilots — **air traffic controller** *n* [C] • *She's an air traffic controller.*

air·waves /'eɚ,weɪvz/ *n* [plural] : the signals used to broadcast radio and television programs • *The band's new recording hit the airwaves* [=was broadcast for the first time] *yesterday.*

air·way /'eɚ,weɪ/ *n* [C] **1** *medical* : the area in the throat through which air passes to and from the lungs • *a blocked airway* **2** — used in the names of some airlines • *British Airways*

air·wor·thy /'eɚ,wɚði/ *adj* : fit or safe for flying • *an airworthy helicopter* — **air·wor·thi·ness** *n* [U]

airy /'eri/ *adj* **air·i·er; -est** **1** : having a lot of open space through which air can move freely • *an airy room* **2** : showing a lack of concern • *He refused with an airy wave of his hand.* **3** : very light or delicate • *an airy fabric* — **air·i·ly** /'erəli/ *adv* — **air·i·ness** /'erinəs/ *n* [U]

aisle /'ajəl/ *n* [C] : a passage where people walk: such as **a** : a passage between sections of seats in a church, theater, airplane, etc. • *The bride walked down the aisle.* • *(figurative) She says she'll never walk down the aisle.* [=get married] • *The likes to sit **on the aisle.** = He likes to sit in the aisle seat.* [=in the seat next to the aisle] • *People were dancing in the aisles.* • *a new comedy that has audiences **rolling in the aisles*** [=laughing a lot] **b** : a passage where people walk through a store, market, etc. • *supermarket aisles*

ajar /ə'dʒɑɚ/ *adj, not before a noun* : slightly open • *He left the door ajar.*

AK *abbr* Alaska

aka /,eɪ,keɪ'eɪ/ *abbr* also known as • *Elvis Presley, aka "The King"*

akim·bo /ə'kɪmboʊ/ *adj, not before a noun* : with the hands on the hips and the elbows turned outward • *She stood with arms akimbo.*

akin /ə'kɪn/ *adj, not before a noun* : similar or related • *a feeling akin to loneliness* [=a feeling that resembles loneliness]

AL *abbr* Alabama

à la /,ɑ:,lɑ:/ *prep* : in the manner or style of (someone or something) • *walking with a swagger à la John Wayne*

al·a·bas·ter /'ælə,bæstɚ, *Brit* 'ælə,bɑ:stə/ *n* [U] : a white stone that is used to make vases and decorations • *(figurative) her alabaster skin* [=her smooth and white skin]

à la carte /,ɑ:lə'kɑɚt/ *adv* : with a separate price for each item on the menu • *order à la carte* — **à la carte** *adj* • *an à la carte menu*

alac·ri·ty /ə'lækrəti/ *n* [U, *singular*] : a quick and cheerful readiness to do something • *She accepted the invitation with alacrity.*

à la mode /,ɑ:lə'moʊd/ *adj, not before a noun, US* : topped with ice cream • *apple pie à la mode*

¹**alarm** /ə'lɑɚm/ *n* **1** [C] **a** : a device that makes a loud sound as a warning or signal • *The alarm went off when he opened the door.* • *a car alarm* **b** : ALARM CLOCK • *She set the alarm for six o'clock.* **2** [U] : a feeling of fear caused by a sudden sense of danger • *The new developments are being viewed with alarm.* • *There's no cause for alarm.* [=no reason to be worried or afraid] **3** [C] : a warning of danger • *Economists have raised/sounded the alarm* [=have warned people] *about a possible recession.*

²**alarm** *vb* [T] : to worry or frighten (someone) • *I didn't mean to alarm you.* • *I was alarmed to see how sick he is.* • *an alarming number of problems* — **alarm·ing·ly** /ə'lɑɚmɪŋli/ *adv*

alarm clock *n* [C] : a clock that can be set to sound an alarm at any desired time • *She set the alarm clock for six o'clock.*

alarm·ist /ə'lɑɚmɪst/ *n* [C] : a person who spreads unnecessary fear about something that is not truly dangerous • *He didn't want to sound like an alarmist.* — **alarm·ism** /ə'lɑɚ,mɪzəm/ *n* [U] — **alarm·ist** /ə'lɑɚmɪst/ *adj*

alas /ə'læs/ *interj, old-fashioned + literary* — used to express sadness, sorrow, disappointment, etc. • *Life, alas, is all too short.*

al·ba·tross /'ælbə,trɑ:s/ *n* [C] **1** : a large white ocean bird **2** : a continuing problem that makes it difficult or impossible to do or achieve something • *Fame has become an albatross that prevents her from leading a normal and happy life.*

al·be·it /ɑl'bi:jət/ *conj, formal* : even though • *She appeared on the show, albeit briefly.*

al·bi·no /æl'baɪnoʊ, *Brit* æl'bi:noʊ/ *n, pl* **-nos** [C] : a person or animal born with a medical condition that results in very pale skin, white hair, and pink eyes — **albino** *adj* • *an albino mouse*

al·bum /'ælbəm/ *n* [C] **1** : a book with blank pages in which you put a collection of photographs, stamps, etc. • *a photo/stamp album* • *our wedding/family album* [=our book of wedding/family photographs] **2** : a long musical recording on a record, CD, etc., that usually includes a set of songs ▪ *a song on the group's latest album*

al·che·my /ˈælkəmi/ *n* [*U*] : a science that was used in the Middle Ages with the goal of changing ordinary metals into gold — **al·che·mist** /ˈælkəmɪst/ *n* [*C*]

al·co·hol /ˈælkəˌhɑːl/ *n* 1 [*C/U*] : a clear liquid that has a strong smell and that is the substance in beer, wine, etc., that can make a person drunk ▪ *cough medicine that contains alcohol* ▪ *drug and alcohol abuse* 2 [*U*] : drinks containing alcohol ▪ *She doesn't drink alcohol.*

¹**al·co·hol·ic** /ˌælkəˈhɑːlɪk/ *adj* 1 : of, containing, or caused by alcohol ▪ *alcoholic drinks/beverages* 2 : affected with alcoholism ▪ *She has an alcoholic uncle.*

²**alcoholic** *n* [*C*] : a person who is affected with alcoholism ▪ *a recovering alcoholic*

al·co·hol·ism /ˈælkəˌhɑːˌlɪzəm/ *n* [*U*] : a medical condition in which someone frequently drinks too much alcohol and becomes unable to live a normal and healthy life

al·cove /ˈælˌkoʊv/ *n* [*C*] : a small section of a room that is set back from the rest of it

al den·te /ɑlˈdɛnteɪ/ *adj* : cooked but still firm ▪ *al dente carrots/pasta* — **al dente** *adv* ▪ *The pasta was cooked al dente.*

al·der·man /ˈɑːldərmən/ *n, pl* **-men** /-mən/ [*C*] : a member of a city government in the U.S., Canada, and Australia ▪ *the board of aldermen*

ale /ˈeɪl/ *n* [*C/U*] : an alcoholic drink that is similar to beer ▪ *a glass of ale*

aleck see SMART-ALECK

¹**alert** /əˈlɚt/ *adj* : able to think clearly and to notice things ▪ *An alert guard stopped the robbers.* ▪ *He was tired and had trouble staying alert.* — **alert·ly** *adv* — **alert·ness** *n* [*U*]

²**alert** *n* 1 [*C*] : something (such as a message or loud sound) that tells people there is some danger or problem ▪ *The government has issued a terrorism/security alert.* 2 [*U*] : the state of being ready for something you have been warned about (such as an attack) ▪ *We need to be* **on (full/high) alert** *for any sudden changes.* ▪ *I'm always* **on the alert for** [=looking for] *a good bargain.*

³**alert** *vb* [*T*] 1 : to give (someone) important information about a possible problem, danger, etc. ▪ *Several neighbors alerted the authorities/police when they noticed strangers acting suspiciously.* 2 : to make (someone) aware of something ▪ *She alerted me to the existence of a new museum.*

A level *n* [*C*] *Brit* : an advanced test in a particular subject that students in England, Wales, and Northern Ireland take usually at the age of 18 ▪ *The university requires at least three A levels.*

al·fal·fa /ælˈfælfə/ *n* [*U*] : a type of plant that is grown mostly as food for farm animals

al·fres·co /ælˈfrɛskoʊ/ *adv* : in the open air ▪ *We dined alfresco.* — **alfresco** *adj*

al·gae /ˈældʒi/ *n* [*plural*] : simple plants that have no leaves or stems and that grow in or near water

al·ge·bra /ˈældʒəbrə/ *n* [*U*] : a branch of mathematics that uses numbers and letters that represent numbers — **al·ge·bra·ic** /ˌældʒəˈbrejɪk/ *adj*

al·go·rithm /ˈælgəˌrɪðəm/ *n* [*C*] *technical* : a set of steps that are followed in order to solve a mathematical problem or to complete a computer process

¹**ali·as** /ˈeɪlijəs/ *adv* : otherwise known as ▪ *The thief was identified as John Smith, alias Richard Jones.* [=John Smith, who is also known as Richard Jones]

²**alias** *n* [*C*] : an additional name that a person (such as a criminal) sometimes uses ▪ *He was traveling* **under an alias**. [=using a name that was not his real name]

al·i·bi /ˈæləˌbaɪ/ *n* [*C*] 1 : a claim that you cannot be guilty of a crime because you were somewhere else when the crime was committed ▪ *His alibi was that he was at the movies.* 2 : an excuse for not being somewhere or doing something ▪ *She made up an alibi for why she missed the meeting.*

¹**alien** /ˈeɪlijən/ *adj* 1 : different from the things you have known ▪ *an alien environment* ▪ *The whole idea of having a job was alien to him.* 2 : from another country ▪ *alien residents* 3 : too different from something to be acceptable or suitable ▪ *ideas alien to democracy* 4 : from somewhere other than the planet Earth ▪ *an alien spaceship*

²**alien** *n* [*C*] 1 : a person who was born in a different country and is not a citizen of the country in which he or she now lives ▪ *illegal aliens* [=foreign people who live in a country without having official permission to live there] 2 : a creature that comes from somewhere other than the planet Earth ▪ *space aliens*

alien·ate /ˈeɪlijəˌneɪt/ *vb* **-at·ed; -at·ing** [*T*] 1 : to cause (someone) to stop being friendly, helpful, etc., towards you ▪ *Her position on this issue has alienated many former supporters.* 2 : to cause (someone) to feel that she or he no longer belongs in a particular group, society, etc. ▪ *His drug problems have alienated him from his partners.* ▪ *alienated young people* [=young people who do not feel that they have a part in society] — **alien·ation** /ˌeɪlijəˈneɪʃən/ *n* [*U*]

¹**alight** /əˈlaɪt/ *vb* [*I*] 1 : to stop on a surface after flying ▪ *A butterfly alighted on her hat.* 2 : to step down from a boat, vehicle, etc. ▪ *Tourists alighted from the train.* — **alight on/upon** [*phrasal vb*] : to see, notice, or think of (something) ▪ *Her eye/eyes alighted on his face.*

²**alight** *adj, not before a noun* : full of light : lighted up ▪ *(figurative) a face alight with excitement*

align /əˈlaɪn/ *vb* 1 [*T/I*] : to arrange things so that they form a line or are in proper position ▪ *He aligned the two holes so he could put the screw through them.* ▪ *The two parts of the machine don't align properly.* 2 [*T*] : to change (something) so that it agrees with or matches something else ▪ *Schools aligned their programs with state requirements.* 3 [*T/I*] : to join a group that is supporting or opposing something • *He has aligned himself with the protesters.* — **align·ment** /ə'laɪnmənt/ *n* [C/U] • *The parts were not in alignment.* = *They were out of alignment.* • *The school brought its programs into alignment with state requirements.* • *his alignment with the protesters*

¹alike /ə'laɪk/ *adj, not before a noun* : similar in appearance, nature, or form • *The two cars are much alike.*

²alike *adv* : in the same way • *We think alike.* • *a film intended for parents and kids alike* [=intended for both parents and kids]

al·i·men·ta·ry canal /ˌæləˈmɛntri-/ *n* [C] : the long tube in the body through which food passes after it is eaten

al·i·mo·ny /ˈæləˌmoʊni, *Brit* ˈæləməni/ *n* [U] : money that a court orders someone to pay regularly to a former wife or husband after a divorce

alive /ə'laɪv/ *adj, not before a noun* **1** : living : not dead • *The patient was barely alive.* • *She must be the happiest woman alive.* [=the happiest woman in the world] • *He managed to stay alive for a week without any food.* **2 a** : continuing to exist • *keeping hope alive* **b** : not yet defeated • *The legislation is still alive in the Senate.* **3 a** : filled with life and energy • *Her face was alive with joy/happiness.* **b** : filled with activity • *The city comes alive at night.* — usually + *with* • *The city streets are alive with shoppers.* — **alive and well 1** : living and healthy • *She found out that her aunt is alive and well and living in Arizona.* **2** : still popular : continuing to be used • *Many of the old traditions are still alive and well.* — **bring (something) alive** : to make (something) seem more real or interesting • *The play brings the old fairy tale alive.* — **eat (someone or something) alive** see EAT

al·ka·li /ˈælkəˌlaɪ/ *n, pl* **-lies** *or* **-lis** [C/U] *chemistry* : a substance that has a bitter taste and a pH of more than 7

al·ka·line /ˈælkəˌlaɪn/ *adj* : containing an alkali • *alkaline soil* — **al·ka·lin·i·ty** /ˌælkəˈlɪnəti/ *n* [U]

¹all /ˈɑːl/ *adj* **1** : the whole, entire, total amount, quantity, or extent of • *She worked hard all day.* [=throughout the entire day] • *He had to walk all the way home.* • *Don't take all the candy.* • *I think about her all the time.* [=constantly] **2 a** : every member or part of • *All my friends were there.* • *Not all teenagers are alike.* = *Teenagers are not all alike.* • *They were up till/until all hours.* [=they were up very late] • *She has to deal with all kinds/sorts/types of people.* **b** : the whole number or sum of • *It was great to see him again after all these years.* **3** : any whatever • *She denied all responsibility for the accident.* **4 a** : as much as possible of (something) • *He spoke in all seriousness.* [=in a completely serious way] **b** : having or showing only (some quality, feature, etc.) • *He was all smiles with the boss.* [=he was smiling constantly when he was with the boss] **5** *US, chiefly Southern, informal* — used in speech to refer to a group of people or things •

Who all is coming? [=who is coming?] — **for all** : in spite of (something) • *For all his faults, she still loves him.* — **of all (the)** *informal* — used to express surprise, disapproval, anger, etc. • *Why did my car break down now of all times?!* • *"He called you a fool!" "Of all the nerve!"* [=I am shocked and offended that he called me a fool]

²all *adv* **1** : entirely or completely • *She sat all alone.* • *I forgot all about it.* • *These problems have been occurring all too often.* [=much too often] **2** : for each side or player • *We're tied at 3–all after seven innings.* **3** *informal* : very • *The kids got all excited when they saw Santa Claus.* — **all along** see ²ALONG — **all around** (*US*) *or chiefly Brit* **all round** : for everyone • *It was a good deal all around.* • *Let's have drinks all around, bartender.* — **all of 1** : not more than — used to stress that an amount is surprisingly small • *She learned to fly a plane when she was all of 16 years old.* **2** : as much as — used to stress that an amount is somewhat large • *The prize is now worth all of 10 million dollars.* — **all over 1 a** : over an entire area • *We looked all over for you.* • *People came from all over.* [=from many places] **b** : in every part of (something) • *He's lived all over Texas.* • *There are books piled all over the place.* [=everywhere] **2** *informal* : very critical of (someone) • *She was all over me for being late.* **3** *informal* : crowding around or touching (someone) in a very eager or aggressive way • *His fans were all over him.* **4** *chiefly Brit, informal* : in every way • *She's her mother all over.* [=she's just like her mother] — **all that** : to a high degree • *It wasn't all that bad.* [=wasn't that/very bad] — **all the** — used to give added force to a word like "more" or "better" • *If we arrive early, all the better.* [=it will be even better if we arrive early] — **all told** : with everything considered or included • *All told, it took us three days to get there.* — **go all out** see ¹GO — **not all there** *informal* — used to describe a person who is somewhat strange or stupid • *She's sweet but not all there (mentally).*

³all *pron* **1** : the entire number or amount • *All* [=everything] *that I have is yours.* • *She told us all about what happened.* • *Her latest book is the best of all.* [=the best one of all her books] • *All are welcome!* [=everyone is welcome] • *"Is there anything else to be done?" "No, that's all."* **2** : the only thing • *That's all I can do to help.* — **after all** see ²AFTER — **all in all** *informal* : in a general way : when everything is thought of or considered • *All in all, I like the way things have gone.* — **all told** : including everything or everyone • *The cost of the repairs came to about $300 all told.* — **and all** : and everything else • *He endured everything, insults and all, without getting angry.* — **at all** — used to make a statement or question more forceful • *He will go anywhere at all to get a job.* • *"Did she say anything?" "No, nothing at all."* • *I wasn't tired at all.* = *I wasn't at all tired.* [=I wasn't even slightly tired] •

"Thank you for all your trouble." "Not at all." [=it wasn't any trouble at all] — **for all I know** see ¹KNOW — **for all (someone) cares** see ²CARE — **give (it) your all** : to do or give as much as you can to achieve something, to support a cause, etc. ▪ *You'll never succeed in this business unless you give it your all.* — **in all** : including everything or everyone ▪ *There were about a thousand people there in all.* — **once and for all** see ¹ONCE — **when all is said and done** : after considering or doing everything ▪ *It won't be easy, but when all is said and done, we'll be glad we did it.*

all- *combining form* **1** : entirely ▪ *an all-wool suit* ▪ *an all-woman band* **2** : including everything ▪ *Her all-consuming passion was music.*

Al·lah /ˈɑːlə, ˈæləˈ/ *n* [*singular*] — used as the name of God in Islam

all-Amer·i·can /ˌɑːləˈmerəkən/ *adj* **1** : having qualities that are thought to be typical of people in the U.S. or that are widely admired in the U.S. ▪ *her all-American optimism* **2** *sports* : selected as one of the best in the U.S. in a particular sport ▪ *an all-American football player* ▪ *He was all-American in football.* **3** : consisting entirely of Americans or of American elements ▪ *an all-American tennis final* [=a final in which both players are American] — **all-American** *n* [*C*] ▪ *He was an all-American in football.*

all-around /ˌɑːləˈraund/ *adj, always before a noun, US* **1** : relating to or involving many different things ▪ *an all-around improvement in her work* ▪ *He is an all-around good guy.* **2** : skillful or useful in many ways ▪ *She's the best all-around player on the team.*

al·lay /æˈleɪ/ *vb* [*T*] *formal* : to make (something) less severe or strong ▪ *allay fears/suspicions*

all but *adv* : very nearly : ALMOST ▪ *We had all but given up hope.*

all clear *n* — **the all clear** : a signal telling you that a situation is no longer dangerous ▪ *Doctors have given her the all clear.* [=have told her that she is healthy]

all-day /ˈɑːlˈdeɪ/ *adj, always before a noun* : lasting throughout the day ▪ *an all-day event*

al·le·ga·tion /ˌæləˈgeɪʃən/ *n* [*C*] : a statement saying that someone has done something wrong or illegal ▪ *They are investigating allegations that the mayor accepted bribes.* ▪ *He denies the allegations (made) against him.*

al·lege /əˈlɛdʒ/ *vb* **-leged; -leg·ing** [*T*] : to state without definite proof that someone has done something wrong or illegal ▪ *He alleged that the mayor accepted bribes.* ▪ *an alleged thief* ▪ *alleged abuse* — **al·leg·ed·ly** /əˈlɛdʒədli/ *adv*

al·le·giance /əˈliːdʒəns/ *n* [*C/U*] *formal* : loyalty to a person, country, group, etc. ▪ *I pledge allegiance to my country.* ▪ *switch allegiances* — **the Pledge of Allegiance** see ¹PLEDGE

al·le·go·ry /ˈæləˌgori, *Brit* ˈæləgri/ *n, pl* **-ries** [*C/U*] : a story in which the characters and events are symbols that stand for ideas about human life or for a political or historical situation ▪ *an allegory of/about love and jealousy* — **al·le·gor·i·cal** /ˌæləˈgorɪkəl/ *adj* — **al·le·gor·i·cal·ly** /ˌæləˈgorɪkli/ *adv*

all-encompassing *adj* : including everything or everyone ▪ *an all-encompassing solution*

Al·len wrench /ˈælən-/ *n* [*C*] *US* : a small tool that is used to turn a special type of screw

al·ler·gen /ˈælədʒən/ *n* [*C*] : a substance that causes an allergy ▪ *common allergens, such as pollen* — **al·ler·gen·ic** /ˌæləˈdʒenɪk/ *adj* ▪ *a highly allergenic substance*

al·ler·gic /əˈlədʒɪk/ *adj* **1** : of or relating to an allergy ▪ *an allergic reaction* **2** : having an allergy ▪ *I'm allergic to cats/nuts.* ▪ *(figurative)* He's allergic to hard work.* [=he does not like hard work]

al·ler·gist /ˈælədʒɪst/ *n* [*C*] : a doctor who is an expert in the treatment of allergies

al·ler·gy /ˈælədʒi/ *n, pl* **-gies** [*C/U*] : a medical condition that causes someone to become sick after eating, touching, or breathing something that is harmless to most people ▪ *food allergies*

al·le·vi·ate /əˈliːviˌeɪt/ *vb* **-at·ed; -at·ing** [*T*] : to make (something) less painful, difficult, or severe ▪ *ways to alleviate stress* ▪ *alleviating poverty* — **al·le·vi·a·tion** /əˌliːviˈeɪʃən/ *n* [*U*]

al·ley /ˈæli/ *n, pl* **-leys** [*C*] : a narrow street or passage between buildings ▪ *a dark alley* — **up someone's alley** *chiefly US, informal* : suited to someone's tastes or abilities ▪ *A job like that would be right up my alley!* [=would suit me very well]

al·ley·way /ˈæliˌweɪ/ *n* [*C*] : ALLEY

al·li·ance /əˈlajəns/ *n* **1** [*C*] : a relationship in which people, countries, etc., agree to work together ▪ *We need to form a closer alliance between government and industry.* **2** [*U*] : the state of being joined in some activity or effort ▪ *one nation working in alliance with another* **3** [*C*] : a group of people, countries, etc., that are joined together in some activity or effort ▪ *a disagreement within the alliance*

al·lied /əˈlaɪd, ˈæˌlaɪd/ *adj* **1 a** : joined in a relationship in which people, groups, countries, etc., agree to work together ▪ *allied nations* = nations that are allied to/with each other **b** *Allied always before a noun* : of or relating to the nations that fought together against Germany in World War I and World War II ▪ *Allied soldiers/troops/forces* **2** : related or connected ▪ *two families allied by marriage*

al·li·ga·tor /ˈæləˌgeɪtə/ *n* **1** [*C*] : a large reptile that is similar to crocodiles and that lives in the tropical parts of the U.S. and China **2** [*U*] : the skin of an alligator used for making shoes and other products ▪ *an alligator purse*

all-im·por·tant /ˌɑːlɪmˈpoətnt/ *adj* : very important ▪ *an all-important question*

all-in·clu·sive /ˌɑːlɪnˈkluːsɪv/ *adj* : sold for one price that includes charges and fees that are often added separately ▪ *The* *resort is all-inclusive so you don't worry about money while you're there.*

al·lit·er·a·tion /ə‚lɪtəˈreɪʃən/ n [U] : the use of words that begin with the same sound near one another (as in *a babbling brook*) — **al·lit·er·a·tive** /əˈlɪtərətɪv/ adj

all–night·er /ˈɑːlˈnaɪtə/ n [C] *informal* : a night during which someone works on something instead of sleeping ▪ *He pulled an all-nighter* [=he stayed up all night] *to study for the exam.*

al·lo·cate /ˈæləˌkeɪt/ vb **-cat·ed; -cat·ing** [T] : to divide and give out (something) for a special reason or to particular people, companies, etc. ▪ *the best way to allocate our funds/resources* — **al·lo·ca·tion** /‚æləˈkeɪʃən/ n [C/U]

al·lot /əˈlɑːt/ vb **-lot·ted; -lot·ting** [T] : to give someone (an amount of something) to use or have ▪ *Each speaker will be allotted 15 minutes.* ▪ *We finished in the allotted time.* — **al·lot·ment** /əˈlɑːtmənt/ n [C/U] ▪ *an allotment of time*

all–out /ˈɑːlˈaʊt/ adj, *always before a noun* **1** : made or done with as much effort as possible ▪ *an all-out attack/assault/ effort* **2** : fully developed ▪ *an all-out war*

al·low /əˈlaʊ/ vb [T] **1 a** : to treat (something) as acceptable ▪ *They don't allow smoking here.* **b** : to permit (someone) to have or do something ▪ *He allowed her to leave.* [=he let her leave] — used in the phrase **allow me** to make a polite offer to help someone ▪ *Allow me to get/open the door for you.* **c** : to permit (someone) to go or come in, out, etc. ▪ *Women were not allowed in/into the club.* ▪ *The hospital doesn't allow visitors after 8 p.m.* **2 a** : to make it possible for someone or something to have or do something ▪ *The system allows you to transfer data between computers.* **b** : to make it possible for something to happen ▪ *a password that allows access to the system* **c** : to fail to prevent something or someone from being, becoming, or doing something ▪ *They allowed the plants to die.* ▪ *She allowed herself to get fat.* **3** : to include (a quantity of time, money, etc.) as an appropriate amount ▪ *We need to allow (ourselves) enough time to finish the job.* **4 a** : to accept (something) ▪ *The judge decided to allow the evidence.* **b** : to admit (something) ▪ *She allowed that the work was hard.* **5** *sports* : to let an opposing team or player have or score (a goal, a hit, etc.) ▪ *The pitcher allowed three runs in the first inning.* — **allow for** [*phrasal vb*] **1 a** : to think about or plan for (something that will or might happen in the future) ▪ *We'll leave early to allow for the rush hour traffic.* **b** : to consider (something) when you make a calculation ▪ *The total traveling time, allowing for traffic, is about 10 hours.* **2** : to make (something) possible ▪ *The design of the system allows for easy upgrades.* — **al·low·able** /əˈlaʊəbəl/ adj

al·low·ance /əˈlaʊəns/ n **1** [C] **a** : an amount of money that is given to someone regularly or for a specific purpose ▪ *a monthly allowance for household expenses* **b** *chiefly US* : a small amount of

money that is regularly given to children by their parents ▪ *Each of their kids gets a weekly allowance of five dollars.* **2** [C] **a** : an amount of something (such as time) that is allowed or available ▪ *a generous allowance of time for sightseeing* **b** : an amount that is regarded as acceptable or desirable ▪ *the recommended daily allowance of vitamin C* **c** : an amount that is subtracted from the price of something ▪ *We got a trade-in allowance of $2,000 on our old car.* [=the price of our new car was reduced by $2,000 because we traded in our old car] **d** *Brit* : an amount of your earnings that you do not have to pay taxes on ▪ *the tax allowance for married couples* **3 a** [U] : the act of thinking about or including something when you make a plan, calculation, etc. ▪ *His theory makes no allowance for* [=does not allow for] *the possibility that the disease may be genetic.* **b** [C/U] : the act of regarding bad behavior or a mistake as less serious or bad because of some special situation or condition ▪ *She performed poorly, but we should make some allowance for her inexperience.* [=because she is inexperienced, we should not blame her too much for performing poorly] ▪ *Allowances should be made for her inexperience.*

al·loy /ˈæˌlɔɪ/ n [C/U] : a metal made by melting and mixing two or more metals or a metal and another material together ▪ *(an) aluminum alloy* — **al·loy** /əˈlɔɪ/ vb [T] ▪ *alloying steel with chromium*

all–pow·er·ful /ˈɑːlˈpaʊəfəl/ adj : able to do anything — often used in an exaggerated way to describe people or organizations that are very powerful ▪ *an all-powerful leader*

all–pur·pose /ˈɑːlˈpɚpəs/ adj, *always before a noun* : suitable for many uses ▪ *an all-purpose tool* ▪ (*US*) *all-purpose flour*

¹all right adv **1** : fairly well : well enough ▪ *She does all right in school.* ▪ *He was pretty sick, but he's doing all right now.* **2** — used to stress that a preceding statement is true or accurate ▪ *"Is this the one you wanted?" "Yes, that's it all right."* **3 a** — used to ask for or express agreement, acceptance, or understanding ▪ *I'll meet you at noon, all right?* ▪ *All right, I'll meet you at noon.* — often used in a way that shows annoyance or reluctance ▪ *"Hurry up!" "All right, all right, I'm coming!" = "All right already, I'm coming!"* **b** *chiefly US* — used to express pleasure or excitement ▪ *"They won!" "All right! That's great!"* **c** — used for emphasis at the beginning of a statement ▪ *All right everyone, let's get started.*

²all right adj, *not before a noun* **1** : fairly good : SATISFACTORY ▪ *The movie wasn't great, but it was all right.* **2 a** : acceptable or agreeable ▪ *Whatever you decide to do is all right (with/by me).* **b** : suitable or appropriate ▪ *Is this movie all right for children?* **3 a** : not ill, hurt, unhappy, etc. ▪ *"Are you hurt?" "No, I'm all right."* **b** : not marked by problems, danger, etc. — used to tell someone not to be worried or concerned ▪ *Everything will be all right.* ▪ *"I'm so sorry that I'm* late." "It's/That's all right." **4** *informal* : likable, good, or honest • *You'll like him. He's all right.*

all-round /'ɑːl'raund/ *adj, chiefly Brit* : ALL-AROUND

all·spice /'ɔːl,spaɪs/ *n* [U] : a spice that is made from the berries of a tree and that is often used in baking

all-star /'ɑːl,stɑɚ/ *adj, always before a noun* : including only performers who are famous or very skillful • *the movie's all-star cast* — **all-star** *n* [C] • *He was selected as an all-star.* [=a member of an all-star team]

all-terrain vehicle *n* [C] : a small open vehicle with three or four large wheels that is used to drive over very rough ground — called also *ATV*

all-time /'ɑːl,taɪm/ *adj, always before a noun* : more than all others have ever been • *It's my all-time favorite movie.* • *The price of gasoline has hit an all-time high.* [=it is higher than it has ever been]

al·lude /ə'luːd/ *vb* **-lud·ed; -lud·ing** — **allude to** [*phrasal vb*] : to speak of or mention (something or someone) in an indirect way • *She alluded to her first marriage.*

al·lure /ə'luɚ/ *n* [U] : a quality that attracts people • *the allure of fame*

al·lur·ing /ə'luɚ/ *adj* : very attractive • *an alluring offer/smile/aroma*

al·lu·sion /ə'luːʒən/ *n* [C/U] : a statement that refers to something without mentioning it directly • *She made an allusion to her first marriage, but said nothing more about it.* — **al·lu·sive** /ə'luːsɪv/ *adj*

al·lu·vi·al /ə'luːvijəl/ *adj, geology* : made up of or found in the materials that are left by the water of rivers, floods, etc. • *an alluvial plain/deposit*

¹**al·ly** /'æ,laɪ/ *n, pl* **-lies** **1 a** [C] : a country that supports and helps another country in a war • *the nation's closest ally* **b the Allies** [*plural*] : the nations that fought together against Germany in World War I or World War II **2** [C] : a person or group that gives help to another person or group • *her allies in the state legislature*

²**al·ly** /ə'laɪ/ *vb* **-lies; -lied; -ly·ing** [T/I] : to join (yourself) with another person, group, etc., in order to get or give support — often + *with* • *She's allied herself with the moderates on this issue.*

al·ma ma·ter /,ælmə'mɑːtɚ/ *n* [C] : the school, college, or university that someone attended • *I visited my old alma mater.*

al·ma·nac /'ɑːlmə,næk/ *n* [C] **1** : a book published every year that contains facts about the movements of the sun and moon, changes in the tides, the weather, etc. **2** : a book published every year that contains detailed information on a special subject • *a hunter's almanac*

al·mighty /ɑl'maɪti/ *adj* **1 or Al·mighty** : having complete power • *Almighty God* = *God Almighty* **2** *always before a noun* : having a lot and often too much power or importance • *the almighty dollar*

Almighty *n* — **the Almighty** : GOD 1 • *worshipping the Almighty*

al·mond /'ɑːmənd/ *n* [C] : a nut with a sweet flavor; *also* : the tree that produces almonds

al·most /'ɑːl,moʊst/ *adv* : a little less than : NEARLY • *"Are you finished?" "Almost."* • *Prices rose by almost 40 percent.* • *She's almost always late.* • *I have* **almost no** *money.*

alms /'ɑːmz/ *n* [*plural*] *old-fashioned* : money, food, etc., given to poor people

al·oe /'æloʊ/ *n* [C] : a tropical plant with long, heavy leaves which produce a thick liquid used in medicines, cosmetics, etc.

aloe vera /'æloʊ'verə/ *n* [U] : a thick liquid that is made by an aloe plant and used in medicines, cosmetics, etc.

aloft /ə'lɑːft/ *adv* : in the air • *The balloon stayed aloft for days.*

alo·ha /ə'loʊ,hɑː/ *interj* — used in Hawaii to say hello or goodbye

¹**alone** /ə'loʊn/ *adj, not before a noun* **1 a** : without anyone or anything else : separate from other people or things • *This wine goes well with food, but it is also very good alone.* • *She lived alone for many years.* **b** : without people that you know or that usually are with you • *He traveled alone* [=*by himself*] *to visit his grandparents when he was only seven.* • *She's worried about losing her job, and she's* **not alone.** [=other people are also worried about losing their jobs] **2** : feeling unhappy because of being separated from other people • *He felt very alone when he went away to school.*

²**alone** *adv* **1** : without help from anyone or anything else • *She raised six children alone.* • *The criminal acted alone.* • *Medication alone won't relieve all the symptoms.* • *If no one's willing to help me, I'll just have to* **go it alone.** [=do it by myself] **2** : without another — used for emphasis • *You alone are responsible.* • *The blame is mine and mine alone.* [=I am the only one who should be blamed] **3** : without including or needing anything more • *The special effects alone make the movie worth seeing.*

¹**along** /ə'lɑːŋ/ *prep* **1** : in a line matching the length or direction of (something) • *We walked along (the side of) the road.* • *Chairs were lined up along the wall.* **2** : at a point on (something) • *a house along the river* • *We stopped along the way for lunch.*

²**along** *adv* **1** : in a forward direction • *I was just walking along, minding my own business.* • *Let's hurry this process along.* [=make this process go faster] **2** — used to say that someone or something is brought or taken with you when you go somewhere • *He brought his son along with him to the bank.* **3** : at or to an advanced point • *Plans for a new stadium are already far along.* • *She is* **well/far along in years.** [=she is old] **4** : at a particular place • *I'll be along* [=I'll be there] *in a few minutes.* • *Another bus should be along* [=should be here] *soon.* **5** : from one person to another • *Word was passed along that the attack was coming.* — **all along** : during the entire time since something began • *I knew the truth all along.* • *They knew all along who was*

guilty. — **along with** : together with (something or someone) ▪ *All my cousins were there along with my aunts and uncles.*

¹**along·side** /ə'lɑːŋ'saɪd/ *adv* 1 : along or close at the side ▪ *Another boat came alongside.* ▪ *(chiefly US, informal) The police car pulled up* **alongside** *of our car.*

²**alongside** *prep* 1 : next to (someone or something) ▪ *The children work alongside their parents.* 2 : along the side of (something) ▪ *Bring the boat alongside the dock.* 3 : at the same time as (something) ▪ *one theory taught alongside the other*

aloof /ə'luːf/ *adj* 1 : not involved with or friendly toward other people ▪ *She remained aloof despite their efforts to make friends.* 2 : not involved in or influenced by something ▪ *They keep/remain/stand aloof from politics.* — **aloof·ness** *n* [U]

aloud /ə'laʊd/ *adv* : in a voice that can be heard ▪ *read aloud* ▪ *She wondered aloud [=out loud] where they'd gone.*

al·paca /æl'pækə/ *n* 1 [C] : an animal that is related to the llama and has long woolly hair 2 [U] : wool of the alpaca

al·pha *adj, always before a noun* 1 : having the most power in a group of animals or people ▪ *a wolf pack's* **alpha male** [=the most powerful male] 2 — used to describe the first version of a product that is being developed and tested ▪ *the alpha version of the software*

al·pha·bet /'ælfə,bɛt/ *n* [C] : the letters of a language arranged in their usual order ▪ *The Roman alphabet begins with "A" and ends with "Z."* — **al·pha·bet·i·cal** /,ælfə'bɛtɪkəl/ *also* **al·pha·bet·ic** /,ælfə-'bɛtɪk/ *adj* ▪ *The words in the dictionary are listed/shown in* **alphabetical order.** — **al·pha·bet·i·cal·ly** /,ælfə'bɛtɪkli/ *adv*

al·pha·bet·ize *also Brit* **al·pha·bet·ise** /'ælfəbə,taɪz/ *vb* **-ized; -iz·ing** [T] : to arrange (items) in alphabetical order ▪ *She alphabetized the books according to their authors.* — **al·pha·bet·i·za·tion** *also Brit* **al·pha·bet·i·sa·tion** /,ælfə-,bɛtə'zeɪʃən, Brit* ,ælfə,bɛ,taɪ'zeɪʃən/ *n* [U]

al·pha·nu·mer·ic /,ælfənʊ'mɛrɪk, Brit* ,ælfənjʊ'mɛrɪk/ *adj* : having or using letters and numbers ▪ *an alphanumeric system* — **al·pha·nu·mer·i·cal·ly** /,ælfə-nʊ'mɛrɪkli, Brit* ,ælfə,njʊ'mɛrɪkli/ *adv*

al·pine /'æl,paɪn/ *adj* 1 : of or existing in high mountains and especially the Alps ▪ *an alpine lake* 2 : done in high mountains ▪ *alpine sports*

al·ready /ɑ:l'rɛdi/ *adv* 1 : before now ▪ *I have already told him the news.* ▪ *before that time* ▪ *I'd already left by the time you called.* 2 : so soon ▪ so early ▪ *Do you have to go already?* ▪ *Is it already midnight?* 3 — used to describe a situation that exists now and that will continue to exist ▪ *The exhibit has already caused quite a stir.* 4 *US, informal* — used to express impatience or annoyance ▪ *Enough, already!* ▪ *All right already!*

al·right /,ɑ:l'raɪt/ *adv or adj, informal* : ALL RIGHT

al·so /'ɑːl,soʊ/ *adv* 1 : in addition — used for adding information to a statement ▪ *She's a singer and also a fine actress.* ▪ *Not only is it dark outside, but it's also snowing.* 2 : in a similar way ▪ *"I grew up in Iowa." "Really? I'm also from Iowa."* [=I'm from Iowa too]

al·so–ran /'ɑːl,soʊ,ræn/ *n* [C] : a person who has participated in a contest and did not win ▪ *He was an also-ran in last year's election.*

al·tar /'ɑːltɚ/ *n* [C] 1 : a raised place on which sacrifices and gifts are offered in some religions ▪ *(figurative) She sacrificed honesty* **on the altar of success.** [=she chose to be dishonest in order to achieve success] 2 : a platform or table used as a center of worship in Christian ceremonies and services ▪ *Her fiancé* **left her at the altar.** [=her fiancé decided at the last moment not to marry her]

altar boy *n* [C] : a boy who helps the priest during a Catholic service

al·ter /'ɑːltɚ/ *vb* [T] 1 : to change (something) ▪ *He altered his will to leave everything to his sister.* ▪ *an event that altered the course of history* ▪ *an altered state of consciousness* 2 : to make a change to (a piece of clothing) so that it will fit better ▪ *She had/got the dress altered.* 3 *US* : to remove the sex organs of (an animal) so that the animal is unable to reproduce ▪ *The puppies had been altered.* — **al·ter·a·tion** /,ɑːltɚ'reɪʃən/ *n* [C/U] ▪ *He made alterations in/to his will.*

al·ter·ca·tion /,ɑːltɚ'keɪʃən/ *n* [C] *formal* : a noisy or angry argument ▪ *She got into an altercation with the coach.*

alter ego *n* [C] 1 : a different version of yourself ▪ *the actor's alter ego of Agent 007* 2 : a close friend who thinks or feels the same way you think or feel ▪ *a trusted adviser who is the President's alter ego*

¹**al·ter·nate** /'ɑːltɚ,neɪt/ *vb* **-nat·ed; -nat·ing** [T/I] : to place or do (different things) so that one follows the other in a repeated series ▪ *The appetizer alternates layers of tomatoes and cheese.* ▪ *The shirt has alternating blue and red stripes.* ▪ *Light woods alternate with dark woods to form an elegant pattern on the floor.* ▪ *He alternates between riding his bike and taking the bus to work.* — **al·ter·na·tion** /,ɑːltɚ'neɪʃən/ *n* [C/U]

²**al·ter·nate** /'ɑːltɚnət, Brit* ɔːl'təːnət/ *adj* 1 : occurring in or forming a repeated series ▪ *alternate red and blue stripes* 2 — used to describe something that happens one time, does not happen the next time, happens again, etc. ▪ *The fair is held on alternate years.* [=it is held every other/second year] 3 *chiefly US* : other than the usual ▪ ALTERNATIVE ▪ *We took an alternate route because of the traffic.* — **al·ter·nate·ly** *adv*

³**al·ter·nate** /'ɑːltɚnət/ *n* [C] *US* : someone who takes another person's place if that person is not able to be present or to do a required job ▪ *The relay team has two alternates.* ▪ *an alternate juror*

alternating current *n* [U] : an electric current that changes its direction very frequently at regular intervals — *abbr.* AC

¹al·ter·na·tive /ɑlˈtɝnətɪv/ adj 1 always before a noun : offering or expressing a choice • alternative plans • We took an alternative route [=a different route] to avoid the traffic. 2 : not usual or traditional • alternative rock music • alternative energy/fuel • alternative medicine [=methods of healing or treating disease that are different from the usual methods taught in Western medical schools] 3 : existing or functioning outside of the established society • alternative newspapers/lifestyles — al·ter·na·tive·ly adv

²alternative n [C] : something that can be chosen instead of something else • They left me no alternative but to call the police. [=I had to call the police] • alternatives to the usual treatment

al·ter·na·tor /ˈɑltɚˌneɪtɚ/ n [C] : a device that produces electricity (as in the engine of a vehicle)

al·though /ɑlˈðoʊ/ conj 1 : despite the fact that : THOUGH — used to introduce a fact that makes another fact unusual or surprising • Although we rarely see each other, we're still very good friends. • He's their best player although he's the shortest one on the team. 2 — used when making a statement that differs from or contrasts with a statement you have just made • I don't believe we've met before, although you do look familiar.

al·tim·e·ter /ælˈtɪmətɚ/ n [C] : an instrument used for measuring the altitude of an airplane, a mountain, etc.

al·ti·tude /ˈæltəˌtuːd, Brit ˈæltəˌtjuːd/ n [C/U] : the height of something above the level of the sea • We're now flying at an altitude of 20,000 feet. • the city's high altitude • The plane lost/gained altitude rapidly.

¹al·to /ˈæltoʊ/ n, pl -tos [C] music : a singer with a singing voice that is lower than the voice of a soprano and higher than the voice of a tenor

²alto adj, always before a noun : having a range that is lower than a soprano and higher than a tenor • an alto voice • the alto saxophone

al·to·geth·er /ˌɑltəˈgɛðɚ/ adv 1 : completely and fully : TOTALLY, ENTIRELY • an altogether new idea • It stopped raining altogether. • That's a different question altogether. • It is not altogether clear why she left. 2 : when everything is added up • They spent a thousand dollars altogether. 3 : when everything is considered • Altogether, I'd say this was our best vacation ever.

al·tru·ism /ˈæltruˌɪzəm/ n [U] : feelings and behavior that show a desire to help other people and a lack of selfishness • charitable acts motivated purely by altruism — al·tru·is·tic /ˌæltruˈɪstɪk/ adj — al·tru·is·tic·al·ly /ˌæltruˈɪstɪkli/ adv

alum /əˈlʌm/ n [C] US, informal : ALUMNUS, ALUMNA • a Harvard alum

alu·mi·num (US) /əˈluːmənəm/ or Brit al·u·min·i·um /ˌæljəˈmɪnijəm/ n [U] : a silver metal that is strong and light • aluminum cans • aluminum foil [=a very thin sheet of aluminum used for wrapping food]

alum·na /əˈlʌmnə/ n, pl -nae /-niː/ [C]

chiefly US : a woman who was a student at a particular school, college, or university • a group of Harvard alumnae

alum·nus /əˈlʌmnəs/ n, pl -ni /-naɪ/ [C] chiefly US : someone who was a student at a particular school, college, or university • the college's alumni [=all of the men and women who attended the college] • the alumni association

al·ways /ˈɑlˌweɪz/ adv 1 a : at all times : in a way that does not change • She's almost always smiling. • This area is always filled with tourists. • You should always wear your seat belt. • You're always welcome to stay with us. b : at all times in the past • He has always been a good friend to me. • They didn't always like each other. [=they like each other now, but they didn't in the past] 2 : for a very long time • You'll always be my best friend. • I've always wanted to own a restaurant. 3 : often, frequently, or repeatedly • My parents always told me not to speak to strangers. — often used to describe repeated behavior that is annoying • Must you always be so rude?! 4 — used to suggest another possibility • If we don't win today, there's always tomorrow. [=we might win tomorrow] • If you don't have enough money now, you can/could always use your credit card. — as always — used to say that something was expected because it always happens • As always, dinner was delicious. [=dinner was delicious, as it always is]

Alz·hei·mer's disease /ˈɑlts,haɪmɚz-/ n [U] : a disease of the brain that causes people to slowly lose their memory and mental abilities as they grow old — called also Alzheimer's

am see BE

AM /ˈeɪ,ɛm/ n [U] : a system for sending radio signals • a show broadcast on AM • AM radios/stations ◇ AM is an abbreviation of "amplitude modulation."

a.m. or AM or Brit am abbr in the morning — used with numbers to show the time of day • She woke up at 6 a.m. ◇ The abbreviation a.m. stands for the Latin phrase ante meridiem, which means "before noon." — compare P.M.

amal·gam /əˈmælgəm/ n [C] formal : a combination or mixture of different things • an amalgam [=amalgamation] of different styles of music

amal·gam·ate /əˈmælgəˌmeɪt/ vb -at·ed; -at·ing [T] formal : to unite (two or more things, such as two businesses) into one thing • The hospital was amalgamated with the university. — amal·gam·ation /əˌmælgəˈmeɪʃən/ n [U, singular] • an amalgamation of different styles of music

amass /əˈmæs/ vb [T] : to gather or collect (a usually large amount of something) especially for yourself • By the time he was 21, he had already amassed a great fortune.

am·a·teur /ˈæmə,tɚ/ n [C] 1 : a person who does something (such as a sport or hobby) for pleasure and not as a job • photos taken by both amateurs and professionals • amateur athletes 2 : a person who does something poorly • Only ama-

teurs make this kind of mistake. — **am·a·teur·ism** /ˈæməˌtəˌɪzəm/ n [U]

am·a·teur·ish /ˌæməˈtərɪʃ/ adj : lacking experience or skill ▪ *His acting is hopelessly amateurish.* — **am·a·teur·ish·ly** adv

amaze /əˈmeɪz/ vb **amazed; amaz·ing** [T/I] : to surprise and sometimes confuse (someone) very much ▪ *He has amazed audiences with his magic tricks.* ▪ *It amazes me that no one noticed the error.* = *I'm amazed that no one noticed the error.* ▪ *They were amazed at/by the size of the place.* — **amaze·ment** /əˈmeɪzmənt/ n [U] ▪ *The crowd watched the magic tricks in amazement.*

amazing adj : causing great surprise or wonder ▪ *She gave an amazing performance.* ▪ *It's amazing* [=difficult to believe] *how/that many adults in this country don't know how to read.* — **amaz·ing·ly** adv

am·a·zon /ˈæməˌzɑːn/ n [C] : a tall and strong woman

am·bas·sa·dor /æmˈbæsədə/ n [C] : the highest-ranking person who represents his or her own government while living in another country ▪ *the American ambassador to Italy* ▪ *(figurative) a baseball player who is an effective ambassador for his sport* ▪ *a goodwill ambassador* [=a person who travels to different places to promote friendship and goodwill] — **am·bas·sa·do·ri·al** /æmˌbæsəˈdorijəl/ adj

am·ber /ˈæmbə/ n [U] **1** : a hard orange-yellow substance that can be used for decorations **2** : a dark orange-yellow color

am·bi·dex·trous /ˌæmbɪˈdɛkstrəs/ adj : able to use both hands equally well ▪ *an ambidextrous baseball player*

am·bi·ence or **am·bi·ance** /ˈæmbijəns/ n [singular] formal : the mood or feeling of a particular place ▪ *Candlelight gives the restaurant a romantic ambience.*

am·bi·ent /ˈæmbijənt/ adj : surrounding on all sides ▪ *ambient light*

am·big·u·ous /æmˈbɪgjəwəs/ adj **1** : having more than one possible meaning ▪ *We were confused by the ambiguous wording of the message.* **2** : not expressed or understood clearly ▪ *His role in the company was becoming more ambiguous.* — **am·bi·gu·i·ty** /ˌæmbəˈgjuːwəti/ n, pl -ties [C/U] ▪ *moral ambiguity* [=lack of certainty about whether something is right or wrong] ▪ *the ambiguities in his answers* — **am·big·u·ous·ly** adv

am·bi·tion /æmˈbɪʃən/ n **1** [C] : something that a person hopes to do or achieve ▪ *She had literary ambitions.* [=she wanted to be a writer] ▪ *She fulfilled her life's ambition* [=the thing she most wanted to do in her life] *by starting her own business.* **2** [U] : a desire to be successful, powerful, or famous ▪ *He lacked ambition.* **3** [U] US : a desire to do things and be active ▪ *I had no ambition and just spent the weekend watching TV.*

am·bi·tious /æmˈbɪʃəs/ adj **1** : having a desire to be successful, powerful, or famous ▪ *ambitious politicians/lawyers* **2** : not easily done or achieved ▪ *ambitious goals/plans* — **am·bi·tious·ly** adv — **am·bi·tious·ness** n [U]

am·biv·a·lent /æmˈbɪvələnt/ adj : having or showing very different feelings (such as love and hate) about someone or something at the same time ▪ *He felt ambivalent about his job.* [=he both liked and disliked his job] — **am·biv·a·lence** /æmˈbɪvələns/ n [U]

am·ble /ˈæmbəl/ vb **am·bled; am·bling** [I] : to walk slowly in a free and relaxed way ▪ *They ambled down/up/along the road.*

am·bu·lance /ˈæmbjələns/ n [C/U] : a vehicle used for taking hurt or sick people to the hospital especially in emergencies ▪ *They called (for) an ambulance.* ▪ *She was taken to the hospital by ambulance.* [=in an ambulance]

¹**am·bush** /ˈæmˌbʊʃ/ n **1** [C] : a surprise attack ▪ *Many soldiers were killed in the ambush.* **2** [U] : a hidden place from which a surprise attack can be made ▪ *a snake lying/waiting in ambush*

²**ambush** vb [T] : to attack (someone or something) by surprise from a hidden place ▪ *The soldiers were ambushed.* ▪ *(figurative) She was ambushed by a group of reporters.*

ameba variant spelling of AMOEBA

ame·lio·rate /əˈmiːljəˌreɪt/ vb **-rat·ed; -rat·ing** [T] formal : to make (something, such as a problem) better, less painful, etc. ▪ *trying to ameliorate the suffering of poor people* — **ame·lio·ra·tion** /əˌmiːljəˈreɪʃən/ n [U]

amen /ɑˈmɛn, eɪˈmɛn/ interj **1** — used at the end of a prayer **2** — used to express agreement or approval ▪ *"We need change!" "Amen!"* ▪ *"Amen to that!"* [=I agree very much with that]

ame·na·ble /əˈmiːnəbəl/ adj **1** : willing to agree or to accept something that is wanted or asked for ▪ *a government that is not amenable to change* **2** formal : able to be controlled, organized, or affected by something ▪ *The disease is not amenable to surgery.* [=it cannot be fixed by surgery]

amend /əˈmɛnd/ vb [T] **1** : to change some of the words and often the meaning of (a law, document, etc.) ▪ *amend the constitution* **2** : to change and improve (something) ▪ *He tried to amend the situation by apologizing to me.*

amend·ment /əˈmɛndmənt/ n **1** [C] : a change in the words or meaning of a law or document ▪ *constitutional amendments* ▪ *They proposed an amendment to the law.* **2** [U] : the act or process of amending something ▪ *rights granted by amendment of the Constitution*

amends /əˈmɛndz/ n — **make amends** : to do something to correct a mistake or a bad situation that you have caused ▪ *She tried to make amends by apologizing.*

ame·ni·ty /əˈmɛnəti/ n, pl **-ties** [C] : something that makes life easier or more pleasant ▪ *The hotel has other amenities such as a restaurant and a swimming pool.* ▪ *The town lacks basic amenities.* [=basic things such as roads, running water, and electricity]

¹Amer·i·can /ə'merəkən/ *n* [C] **1** : a person born, raised, or living in the U.S. ▪ *Americans in all 50 states* **2** : a person born, raised, or living in North America or South America

²American *adj* **1** : of or relating to the U.S. or its citizens ▪ *American history* ▪ *their American friends* **2** : of or relating to North America, South America, or the people who live there ▪ *the American continents*

Amer·i·ca·na /ə,merə'kɑːnə/ *n* [U] : things produced in the U.S. and thought to be typical of the U.S. or its culture ▪ *collectors of Americana*

American football *n* [U] : FOOTBALL 1a

American Indian *n* [C] : NATIVE AMERICAN

Amer·i·can·ism /ə'merəkə,nɪzəm/ *n* [C] : a word or meaning that is common only in U.S. English

Amer·i·can·ize *also Brit* **Amer·i·can·ise** /ə'merəkə,naɪz/ *vb* -**ized**; -**iz·ing** [T] : to cause (something or someone) to have Americanized characteristics ▪ *an Americanized city* — **Amer·i·can·i·za·tion** *also Brit* **Amer·i·can·i·sa·tion** /ə,merəkənə'zeɪʃən, *Brit* ə,merəkə,naɪ'zeɪʃən/ *n* [U]

American Revolution *n* — **the American Revolution** : the war of 1775–83 in which 13 British colonies became the United States of America

am·e·thyst /'æməθəst/ *n* [C] : a clear purple stone used as a gem

ami·a·ble /'eɪmijəbəl/ *adj* : friendly and pleasant ▪ *an amiable person/conversation* — **ami·a·bil·i·ty** /,eɪmijə'bɪləti/ *n* [U, singular] — **ami·a·bly** /'eɪmijəbli/ *adv*

am·i·ca·ble /'æmɪkəbəl/ *adj* : showing a friendly desire to avoid disagreement and argument ▪ *an amicable discussion/agreement* — **am·i·ca·bly** /'æmɪkəbli/ *adv*

amid /ə'mɪd/ *or* **amidst** /ə'mɪdst/ *prep* : in or into the middle of (something) ▪ *The investigation comes amid growing concerns.* ▪ *a single dark bird amid a flock of white pigeons*

ami·no acid /ə'miːnoʊ-/ *n* [C] *biology* : any one of many acids that occur naturally in living things and that include some which form proteins

Amish /'ɑːmɪʃ/ *adj* : of or relating to a Christian religious group in America whose members live in a traditional way on farms ▪ *an Amish community* — **Amish** *n* [plural] ▪ *a tradition among the Amish*

¹amiss /ə'mɪs/ *adj, not before a noun* : not proper or correct : WRONG ▪ *Something is amiss here.*

²amiss *adv* : in the wrong way ▪ *Now, don't take this remark amiss.* [=don't misunderstand this remark]

am·i·ty /'æməti/ *n* [U] *formal* : friendly relations between nations or groups ▪ *international amity*

am·mo /'æmoʊ/ *n* [U] *informal* : AMMUNITION

am·mo·nia /ə'moʊnjə/ *n* [U] : a gas or liquid that has a strong smell and that is used especially in cleaning products

am·mu·ni·tion /,æmjə'nɪʃən/ *n* [U] : the objects (such as bullets) that are shot from weapons ▪ *(figurative) His error gave his opponents more ammunition to use against him in the campaign.*

am·ne·sia /æm'niːʒə/ *n* [U] : a condition in which a person is unable to remember things because of brain injury, shock, or illness — **am·ne·si·ac** /æm'niːʒi,æk/ *adj* — **amnesiac** *n* [C] ▪ *a friendless amnesiac* [=a person who has amnesia]

am·nes·ty /'æmnəsti/ *n, pl* -**ties** [C/U] : a decision that a group of people will not be punished or will be allowed to go free ▪ *The government gave/granted amnesty to/for all political prisoners.* ▪ *an amnesty from fines* — **amnesty** *vb* -**tied**; -**ty·ing** [T] ▪ *They amnestied all political prisoners.*

am·nio·cen·te·sis /,æmnijoʊ,sɛn'tiːsəs/ *n, pl* -**te·ses** /-'tiː,siːz/ [C] *medical* : a test that is done to check for possible health problems in a baby that is not yet born

amoe·ba *also US* **ame·ba** /ə'miːbə/ *n, pl* -**bas** *or* -**bae** /-,biː/ [C] : a tiny living thing that consists of a single cell — **amoe·bic** *also US* **ame·bic** /ə'miːbɪk/ *adj*

amok *also* **amuck** /ə'mʌk/ *adv* : in a wild or uncontrolled manner ▪ *After the attack, looters were running amok.*

among /ə'mʌŋ/ *also* **amongst** /ə'mʌŋst/ *prep* **1** : in or through (a group of people or things) ▪ *There were ducks among the geese.* **2** : in the presence of (a group of people) ▪ *The people of the town learned that a killer had been living among them.* ▪ *We were joking among ourselves.* [=as a group without involving others] **3** — used to talk about the opinions, feelings, etc., of a group of people ▪ *a TV show that is popular among women* ▪ *He is known among his colleagues as a good worker.* **4** — used to indicate the group of people or things involved in or affected by something ▪ *a high rate of illness among the town's children* **5** — used to say that a person or thing is part of a larger group ▪ *He is among her greatest admirers.* [=is one of her greatest admirers] ▪ *Among other things* she was president of her college class. **6** — used to indicate the group of people or things being considered, compared, etc. ▪ *We chose (from) among several options.* **7** : in shares to each of (a group of people) ▪ *The food was distributed among the people.* **8** — used to describe someone who is unusual or excellent in some way ▪ *He was a giant among men.* [=he was very powerful, successful, etc.]

amor·al /eɪ'morəl/ *adj* : having or showing no concern about whether behavior is morally right or wrong ▪ *amoral politicians* — **amo·ral·i·ty** /,eɪmə'ræləti/ *n* [U] — **amor·al·ly** /,eɪ'morəli/ *adv*

am·o·rous /'æmərəs/ *adj* : having or showing strong feelings of sexual attraction or love ▪ *an amorous glance/woman* — **am·o·rous·ly** *adv* — **am·o·rous·ness** *n* [U]

amor·phous /ə'moəfəs/ *adj* : having no definite or clear shape or form ▪ *amorphous clouds*

am·or·tize *also Brit* **am·or·tise** /'æmə-,taɪz, *Brit* ə'mɔː,taɪz/ *vb* **-tized; -tiz·ing** [*T*] *business* : to pay money that is owed for something (such as a mortgage) by making regular payments over a long period of time ▪ *amortize a debt/loan* — **am·or·ti·za·tion** *also Brit* **am·or·ti·sa·tion** /,æmətə'zeɪʃən, *Brit* æ,mɔː,taɪ-'zeɪʃən/ *n* [*U*]

¹**amount** /ə'maʊnt/ *n* [*C*] **1** : a quantity of something ▪ *The drug is not being produced in adequate amounts.* — usually + *of* ▪ *Be sure to add the right amount of salt.* ▪ *large amounts of time/money/research* ▪ *No amount of money can make up for their loss.* [=money cannot make up for their loss] **2** : a quantity of money ▪ *An amount was finally agreed upon.* ▪ *The new law limits the amount a candidate can spend.*

²**amount** *vb* — **amount to** [*phrasal vb*] **1** : to produce (a total) when added together ▪ *They have debts amounting to thousands of dollars.* **2** : to turn out to be (something or someone important, impressive, etc.) ▪ *The problems didn't amount to much.* [=they were not very bad] ▪ *He'll never amount to anything.* [=achieve success] **3** : to be the same in meaning or effect as (something) ▪ *acts that amount to treason*

amp /'æmp/ *n* [*C*] **1** : AMPERE ▪ *a 15-amp current* **2** *informal* : AMPLIFIER ▪ *a guitar amp*

am·per·age /'æmprɪdʒ/ *n* [*U*] *technical* : the strength of a current of electricity expressed in amperes

am·pere /'æm,pɪə, *Brit* 'æm,peə/ *n* [*C*] *technical* : a unit for measuring the rate at which electric current flows ▪ *a current of 15 amperes* — called also *amp*

am·per·sand /'æmpə,sænd/ *n* [*C*] : a character & that is used for the word *and* ▪ *Mr. & Mrs. Joe Smith*

am·phet·amine /æm'fɛtə,miːn/ *n* [*C*] : a drug that causes a person to feel more energy and mental excitement

am·phib·i·an /æm'fɪbijən/ *n* [*C*] : an animal (such as a frog or toad) that can live both on land and in water

am·phib·i·ous /æm'fɪbijəs/ *adj* **1** : able to live both on land and in water ▪ *amphibious plants/animals* **2** : able to be used both on land and water ▪ *amphibious airplanes/vehicles* **3** : done by soldiers who are brought to land in special boats ▪ *an amphibious assault*

am·phi·the·a·ter (*US*) *or chiefly Brit* **am·phi·the·a·tre** /'æmfə,θiːjətə/ *n* [*C*] : a large building with seats rising in curved rows around an open space on which games, concerts, and plays take place

am·ple /'æmpəl/ *adj* **am·pler** /'æmplə/; **am·plest** /'æmpləst/ **1 a** : having or providing enough or more than enough of what is needed ▪ *They had ample money for the trip.* ▪ *You will have ample time to finish the test.* **b** : quite large ▪ *There was room for an ample garden.* **2** — used to describe a person's body as being large in usually an attractive way ▪ *a*

woman with an ample bosom — **am·ply** /'æmpli/ *adv* ▪ *You will be amply rewarded* [=you will be given a large reward] *for your efforts.*

am·pli·fi·er /'æmplə,fajə/ *n* [*C*] : a device that causes sounds played through an electronic system to be louder

am·pli·fy /'æmplə,faɪ/ *vb* **-fies; -fied; -fy·ing** [*T*] **1 a** : to increase the strength of (an electric signal) ▪ *amplify a weak radio signal* **b** : to make (something) louder by increasing the strength of electric signals ▪ *amplify an electric guitar* **2** *formal* : to speak or write about (something) in a more complete way ▪ *I'd like to amplify my earlier remarks.* **3** : to make (something) stronger ▪ *Salt amplifies the food's flavors.* — **am·pli·fi·ca·tion** /,æmpləfə-'keɪʃən/ *n* [*C/U*]

am·pli·tude /'æmplə,tuːd, *Brit* 'æmplə-,tjuːd/ *n* [*C/U*] *technical* : a measurement that indicates the movement or vibration of a sound wave or a radio wave

am·pu·tate /'æmpjə,teɪt/ *vb* **-tat·ed; -tat·ing** [*T*] *medical* : to cut off (part of a person's body) ▪ *His arm had to be amputated.* — **am·pu·ta·tion** /,æmpjə'teɪʃən/ *n* [*C/U*]

am·pu·tee /,æmpjə'tiː/ *n* [*C*] : a person who has had an arm or leg amputated

amuck *variant spelling of* AMOK

am·u·let /'æmjələt/ *n* [*C*] : a small object worn to protect the person wearing it against illness, bad luck, etc.

amuse /ə'mjuːz/ *vb* **amused; amus·ing** **1** [*T/I*] : to entertain (someone) in a light and pleasant way ▪ *His silly jokes amused the audience.* ▪ *She was amused by his appearance.* **2** [*T*] : to get the attention of (someone) in a pleasant way as time passes ▪ *We need to find something to amuse the children.* ▪ *He amused himself with a game of solitaire.* — **amuse·ment** /ə'mjuːzmənt/ *n* [*C/U*] ▪ *a source of great amusement* ▪ *plays, movies, and other amusements* — **amus·ing** /ə'mjuːzɪŋ/ *adj* ▪ *an amusing story/joke* — **amus·ing·ly** *adv*

amusement park *n* [*C*] : a place that has many games and rides (such as roller coasters and merry-go-rounds) for entertainment

an /'æn, ən/ *indefinite article* : ²A — used before words beginning with a vowel sound ▪ *an oak* ▪ *an hour*

an- see ²A-

¹**-an** *or* **-ian** *also* **-ean** *n suffix* : someone or something that belongs to ▪ *Bostonian* [=a person who lives in or is from Boston]

²**-an** *or* **-ian** *also* **-ean** *adj suffix* **1** : of or belonging to ▪ *American* **2** : characteristic of : resembling ▪ *Herculean* [=resembling Hercules]

an·a·bol·ic steroid /,ænə'baːlɪk-/ *n* [*C*] : a drug that is sometimes used illegally by athletes to help them become stronger

anach·ro·nism /ə'nækrə,nɪzəm/ *n* [*C*] **1** : something (such as a word, an object, or an event) that is mistakenly placed in a time where it does not belong in a story, movie, etc. ▪ *The novel is full of anachronisms.* **2** : a person or a thing that seems to belong to the past and not to fit in the present • *He's an old-fashioned politician who is seen as an anachronism.* — **anach·ro·nis·tic** /ə,nækrə'nıstık/ *adj*

anaemia, anaemic *chiefly Brit spellings of* ANEMIA, ANEMIC

an·aer·o·bic /,ænə'roubık/ *adj* : not aerobic: such as **a** *of exercise* : strengthening muscles by forcing them to work very hard for a brief time • *anaerobic sports/training* **b** *technical* : not using oxygen • *anaerobic bacteria*

anaesthesia, anaesthetic *Brit spellings of* ANESTHESIA, ANESTHETIC

an·a·gram /'ænə,græm/ *n [C]* : a word or phrase made by changing the order of the letters in another word or phrase • *"Secure" is an anagram of "rescue."*

anal /'eınl/ *adj* **1** *biology* : of or relating to the anus **2** *informal* : ANAL-RETENTIVE — **anal·ly** *adv*

an·al·ge·sic /,ænl'dʒi:zık/ *n [C] medical* : a drug that relieves pain • *a powerful analgesic* — **analgesic** *adj* • *an analgesic drug*

an·a·log (*chiefly US*) *or chiefly Brit* **an·a·logue** /'ænə,lɑ:g/ *adj* **1** *technical* : of or relating to a device or process in which data is represented by physical quantities that change continuously • *analog video signals* • *an analog computer* **2** *of a clock or watch* : having hour and minute hands • *an analog watch*

anal·o·gous /ə'næləgəs/ *adj, formal* : similar in some way • *I could not think of an analogous situation.* • *It's analogous to riding a bike.* — **anal·o·gous·ly** *adv*

an·a·logue *or US* **an·a·log** /'ænə,lɑ:g/ *n [C] formal* : something that is similar to something else in design, origin, use, etc. • *the synthetic analog of a chemical found in nature*

anal·o·gy /ə'nælədʒi/ *n, pl* **-gies** **1** *[C]* : a comparison of two things that are alike in some way • *He drew/made an analogy between flying a kite and fishing.* [=he compared flying a kite to fishing] **2** *[U]* : the act of comparing two things that are alike • *reasoning by analogy*

anal–re·ten·tive /'eınlrı'tentıv/ *adj* : overly neat, careful, or precise • *He's anal-retentive about keeping his office neat.*

anal·y·sis /ə'næləsıs/ *n, pl* **-y·ses** /-ə,si:z/ *[C/U]* **1** : a careful study of something to learn about its parts • *the scientific analysis of data* • *perform a chemical analysis of the soil* **2** : an explanation of the nature and meaning of something • *a detailed analysis of each candidate's positions* • *a problem that requires careful analysis* • *It was a difficult decision but, in the final/last analysis* [=after considering everything]*, it was the right choice.*

an·a·lyst /'ænələst/ *n [C]* **1** : a person who studies or analyzes something • *a financial/legal/political analyst* **2** : PSYCHOANALYST • *My analyst felt that I was making good progress.*

an·a·lyt·i·cal /,ænə'lıtıkəl/ *or* **an·a·lyt·ic** /,ænə'lıtık/ *adj* **1** : of or relating to the careful examination of something • *an analytical examination of the text* **2** : having or showing skill in thinking or reasoning •

developing social and analytical skills in children • *an analytical mind* — **an·a·lyt·i·cal·ly** /,ænə'lıtıkli/ *adv*

an·a·lyze (*US*) *or Brit* **an·a·lyse** /'ænə,laız/ *vb* **-lyzed; -lyz·ing** *[T]* **1** : to study (something) closely and carefully • *analyze a problem* • *The sample was chemically analyzed by a lab.* **2** : to study the emotions and thoughts of (someone) by using psychoanalysis

an·ar·chist /'ænə,kıst/ *n [C]* : a person who believes that government and laws are not necessary — **an·ar·chism** /'ænə,kızəm/ *n [U]* — **an·ar·chis·tic** /,ænə'kıstık/ *adj*

an·ar·chy /'ænəki/ *n [U]* : a situation of confusion and wild behavior in which the people in a country, group, etc., are not controlled by rules or laws • *There was complete anarchy in the classroom.* — **an·ar·chic** /æ'nɑəkık/ *adj*

anath·e·ma /ə'næθəmə/ *n [U, singular] formal* : someone or something that is very strongly disliked • *ideas that are (an) anathema to me* [=ideas that I strongly dislike]

anat·o·my /ə'nætəmi/ *n, pl* **-mies** **1** *biology* **a** *[U]* : the study of the structure of living things • *We took a class on/in anatomy.* **b** *[C/U]* : the parts that form a living thing (such as an animal or plant) • *human anatomy and physiology* **2** *[C] informal* : a person's body • *parts of her anatomy* **3** *[U]* : the parts or causes that form or create something • *the anatomy of a storm* — **an·a·tom·i·cal** /,ænə'tɑ:mıkəl/ *also US* **an·a·tom·ic** /,ænə'tɑ:mık/ *adj* — **an·a·tom·i·cal·ly** /,ænə'tɑ:mıkli/ *adv* • *anatomically correct dolls* [=dolls that have body parts like those of actual people]

an·ces·tor /'æn,sestəʳ/ *n [C]* **1** : a person who was in someone's family in past times • *My ancestors came to America during the 1800s.* **2** : an animal in the past from which a modern animal developed • *the ancestor of the modern horse* **3** : something in the past from which something else has developed • *Latin is the ancestor of French.* — **an·ces·tral** /æn'sestrəl/ *adj* • *our ancestral home* [=the home of our ancestors]

an·ces·try /'æn,sestri/ *n, pl* **-tries** *[C/U]* : a person's ancestors • *an Englishman of German/noble/unknown ancestry*

¹**an·chor** /'æŋkəʳ/ *n [C]* **1** : a heavy device that is attached to a boat or ship by a rope or chain and that is thrown into the water to hold the boat or ship in place • *The ship dropped anchor in a harbor.* • **2** : a person or thing that provides strength and support • *She was the emotional anchor of his life.* **3** *chiefly US* : someone who reads the news on a television broadcast • *a TV/network news anchor*

²**anchor** *vb* **1** *[T/I]* : to keep a ship or boat from moving by using an anchor • *They anchored (the ship) in the bay.* **2** *[T]* : to connect (something) to a solid base • *The bridge's cables are anchored to the hillside.* • (*figurative*) *Her authority is anchored in more than 20 years of experience.* **3** *[T]* : to be the strongest and

most important part of (something) ▪ *The quarterback has anchored the team for many years.* **4** [T] *US* : to be the anchorman or anchorwoman on (a news program) ▪ *She anchors the nightly news broadcast.*

an·chor·age /ˈæŋkərɪʤ/ *n* [C/U] **1** : a place where boats and ships are anchored ▪ *(a) safe anchorage* **2** : something that provides a strong hold or connection ▪ *A heavy metal ring provides (an) anchorage for the cable.*

an·chor·man /ˈæŋkəˌmæn/ *n, pl* -men /-ˌmɛn/ [C] *chiefly US* : a man who reads the news on a television news program

an·chor·wom·an /ˈæŋkəˌwʊmən/ *n, pl* -wom·en /-ˌwɪmən/ [C] *chiefly US* : a woman who reads the news on a television news program

an·cho·vy /ˈænˌʧoʊvi/ *n, pl* an·cho·vies *also* anchovy [C] : a small fish that has a salty flavor ▪ *pizza with anchovies*

an·cient /ˈeɪnʃənt/ *adj* **1** : very old ▪ *ancient customs/traditions* — often used in an exaggerated way ▪ *She finally replaced her ancient computer.* **2** : of, coming from, or belonging to a time that was long ago in the past ▪ *in ancient times* ▪ *life in ancient Egypt/Rome* ▪ *ancient and modern history* ▪ *(informal) Our relationship is ancient history.* [=it happened a long time ago and is no longer important]

an·cients /ˈeɪnʃənts/ *n* — **the ancients** : the people who lived in ancient times ▪ *the gods of the ancients*

an·cil·lary /ˈænsəˌleri, *Brit* ænˈsɪləri/ *adj, formal* : providing something additional to a main part or function ▪ *ancillary services/expenses*

and /ˈænd, ənd, ən/ *conj* **1** — used to join words or groups of words ▪ *cake and ice cream* ▪ *He walked into the room and sat down.* **2** : added to : plus ▪ *2 and 2 equals 4.* **3 a** — used to describe an action that is repeated or that occurs for a long time ▪ *She cried and cried.* **b** — used to repeat a word for emphasis ▪ *You and you alone are responsible for this mess.* ▪ *more and more expensive* **4 a** — used to describe actions that occur at the same time ▪ *We sat and waited for hours.* **b** — used to describe an action that occurs after another action ▪ *He promised to come and didn't.* **c** — used to describe an action that occurs after and is caused by another action ▪ *I told him to go and he went.* **5** — used after *go, come,* etc., to indicate the purpose of an action ▪ *Why don't you go/come and see her?* [=go/come to see her] **6** — used to indicate a choice ▪ *You have to choose between him and me.* **7** — used to start a new sentence or clause that continues or adds to a previous sentence or clause ▪ *"Well, I've spoken to him . . . " "And?" "And he said yes!"* **8 a** — used after *hundred, thousand,* etc., when saying a number aloud ▪ *a hundred and twenty-four* [=124] **b** — used when saying aloud a number that is followed by a fraction ▪ *one and a half years = a year and a half* **9** — used to indicate the point where two streets

meet or cross ▪ *located at (the corner of) Main Street and First Avenue*

an·drog·y·nous /ænˈdrɑːʤənəs/ *adj* **1** : having both male and female characteristics or qualities ▪ *androgynous rock stars* **2** : suitable for both men and women ▪ *androgynous clothes* — **an·drog·y·ny** /ænˈdrɑːʤəni/ *n* [U]

an·droid /ˈænˌdrɔɪd/ *n* [C] *in stories* : a robot that looks like a person

an·ec·dote /ˈænɪkˌdoʊt/ *n, pl* -dotes [C] : a short story about an interesting or funny event ▪ *humorous anecdotes about his childhood* — **an·ec·dot·al** /ˌænɪkˈdoʊtl/ *adj* ▪ *anecdotal evidence* [=evidence in the form of stories that people tell about what has happened to them] — **an·ec·dot·al·ly** *adv*

ane·mia (*US*) *or Brit* **anae·mia** /əˈniːmijə/ *n* [U] : a condition in which a person has fewer red blood cells than normal and feels very weak and tired

ane·mic (*US*) *or Brit* **anae·mic** /əˈniːmɪk/ *adj* **1** : relating to or suffering from anemia ▪ *a slightly anemic patient* **2** : not strong, forceful, or impressive ▪ *They are worried about the stock's anemic performance.* — **ane·mi·cal·ly** (*US*) *or Brit* **anae·mi·cal·ly** /əˈniːmɪkli/ *adv*

an·es·the·sia (*US*) *or Brit* **an·aes·the·sia** /ˌænəsˈθiːʒə/ *n* [U] *medical* : loss of feeling in a person's body through the use of drugs ▪ *an injection to induce general anesthesia* [=to make someone unconscious and unable to feel pain] ▪ *The patient was under local anesthesia.* [=the patient had been given drugs that took away feeling in only a particular part of the body]

an·es·the·si·ol·o·gist /ˌænəsˌθiːziˈɑːləʤɪst/ *n* [C] *US, medical* : a doctor who specializes in anesthesia and anesthetics

an·es·thet·ic (*US*) *or Brit* **an·aes·thet·ic** /ˌænəsˈθɛtɪk/ *n* [C] *medical* : a drug that causes a person to lose feeling and to feel no pain in part or all of the body

anes·the·tist (*US*) *or Brit* **anaes·the·tist** /əˈnɛsθətɪst/ *n* [C] *medical* : a doctor or nurse who gives an anesthetic to a patient

anes·the·tize (*US*) *or Brit* **anaes·the·tize** *or* **anaes·the·tise** /əˈnɛsθəˌtaɪz/ *vb* **-tized; -tiz·ing** [T] *medical* : to give drugs to (a patient) so that no pain can be felt ▪ *She was anesthetized before the operation.*

anew /əˈnuː, *Brit* əˈnjuː/ *adv, somewhat formal* **1** : over again : once more ▪ *The process begins anew each spring.* **2** : in a new or different form ▪ *The poem has been translated anew for this new book.*

an·gel /ˈeɪnʤəl/ *n* [C] **1** : a spiritual being that serves especially as a messenger from God or as a guardian of human beings ▪ *an angel from heaven* ▪ *the angel of death* [=an angel that comes when someone dies] **2** *informal* : a person who is very good, kind, beautiful, etc. ▪ *Their young son is such an angel!* — **an·gel·ic** /ænˈʤɛlɪk/ *adj* ▪ *an angelic face/voice* ▪ *angelic behavior* [=very good behavior] — **an·gel·i·cal·ly** /ænˈʤɛlɪkli/ *adv*

angel food cake *n [C/U] US* : a soft and light white cake

¹an·ger /ˈæŋgɚ/ *n [U]* : a strong feeling of being upset or annoyed : the feeling of being angry ▪ *You could hear the anger in his voice.* ▪ *She was shaking/trembling in/with anger.*

²anger *vb [T]* : to make (someone) angry ▪ *He's not easily angered.*

an·gi·na /ænˈʤaɪnə/ *n [U]* : a heart disease that causes brief periods of intense chest pain ▪ *an attack of angina*

¹an·gle /ˈæŋgəl/ *n [C]* **1 a** : the space or shape formed when two lines or surfaces meet each other ▪ *The two lines meet at a 30-degree angle.* = *There is a 30-degree angle between the two lines.* ▪ *The lines are at sharp angles to each other.* **b** — used to describe a surface that is not level ▪ *The hill slopes down/up at a 30-degree angle.* **c** — used to describe something that leans or goes to the side rather than straight up or directly forward ▪ *The pole stood at an angle.* **2** : the position from which something is approached, looked at, etc. ▪ *She took several pictures from different angles.* **3** : a way of thinking about, describing, or discussing something ▪ *They considered the question from a different angle.* **4** *chiefly US, informal* : a clever and often improper way of doing or getting something ▪ *a salesman who's always looking for an angle* [=looking for a way to convince people to buy the things he is selling]

²angle *vb* **an·gled; an·gling 1 a** *[T/I]* : to turn, move, or point something so that it is not straight or flat ▪ *One spotlight was angled down toward the floor.* **b** *[T]* : to present (something, such as a news story) in a particular way ▪ *The story was angled to appeal to younger readers.* **2** *[I] informal* : to try to get what you want in a clever or indirect way ▪ *She's angling for a promotion.* **3** *[I]* : to fish with a hook and line ▪ *go angling for trout*

an·gler /ˈæŋglɚ/ *n [C]* : a person who catches fish for pleasure

An·gli·can /ˈæŋglɪkən/ *n [C]* : a member of the Church of England — **Anglican** *adj*

An·gli·can·ism /ˈæŋglɪkəˌnɪzəm/ *n [U]* : the beliefs and practices of the Church of England

an·gli·cize *also Brit* **an·gli·cise** /ˈæŋglɪˌsaɪz/ *vb* **-cized; -ciz·ing** *[T]* : to make (something or someone) English or more English ▪ *anglicize a French word/name*

an·gling /ˈæŋglɪŋ/ *n [U]* : the activity or sport of fishing for pleasure ▪ *an angling trip*

An·glo /ˈæŋgloʊ/ *n, pl* **-glos** *[C] chiefly US* : a white person who lives in the U.S. and is not Hispanic ▪ *blacks, Anglos, and Hispanics*

An·glo- *combining form* : English or British ▪ *Anglo-American* ▪ *Anglophile*

An·glo–Amer·i·can /ˌæŋgloʊˈmerəkən/ *n [C]* : an American whose family comes originally from England — **Anglo–American** *adj*

An·glo·phile /ˈæŋgləˌfaɪl/ *n [C]* : a non-English person who greatly likes and admires England and English things

An·glo–Sax·on /ˌæŋgloʊˈsæksən/ *n* **1 a** *[C]* : a member of the Germanic people who conquered Britain in the fifth century A.D. **b** *[U]* : the language of the Anglo-Saxons **2** *[C]* : a person whose ancestors were English — **Anglo–Saxon** *adj* ▪ *a white Anglo-Saxon Protestant*

an·go·ra /ænˈgorə/ *n* **1** *[U]* : a kind of soft yarn or wool that is made from the hair of the Angora goat or the Angora rabbit ▪ *an angora sweater* **2** *[C]* : a type of cat, goat, or rabbit that has long, soft hair

an·gry /ˈæŋgri/ *adj* **an·gri·er; -est 1 a** : filled with anger ▪ *I've never seen her look so angry.* ▪ *an angry crowd* ▪ *He was angry at/with her for staying out so late.* ▪ *She's still angry about/over the way she's been treated.* **b** : showing anger ▪ *She gave me an angry look.* **2** *literary* : seeming to show anger ▪ *angry clouds* **3** : very red and painful ▪ *an angry rash/sore/scratch* — **an·gri·ly** /ˈæŋgrəli/ *adv*

angst /ˈɑːŋst, ˈæŋst/ *n [U]* : a feeling of being worried or nervous about your life or situation ▪ *teenage angst*

an·guish /ˈæŋgwɪʃ/ *n [U]* : extreme grief or pain ▪ *mental anguish* ▪ *They watched in anguish as fire spread through the house.* — **an·guished** /ˈæŋgwɪʃt/ *adj*

an·gu·lar /ˈæŋgjələ/ *adj* **1** : thin and bony ▪ *He has an angular face.* **2** : having one or more angles ▪ *an angular mountain* — **an·gu·lar·i·ty** /ˌæŋgjəˈlerəti/ *n [U]*

¹an·i·mal /ˈænəməl/ *n [C]* **1** : a living thing that is not a human being or plant ▪ *the animals in the zoo* ▪ *She loves all kinds of animals.* **2** : any living thing that is not a plant ▪ *Fish, birds, insects, reptiles, mammals, and human beings are all animals.* **3** : a person who behaves in a wild, aggressive, or unpleasant way ▪ *You're all acting like animals.* **4** *somewhat informal* : a person or thing of a particular kind ▪ *The sport has changed. It's a very different animal today.* [=it's very different today] ▪ *She is a political animal.* [=she is very interested in politics]

²animal *adj* **1** *always before a noun* : of or relating to animals ▪ *studying animal behavior* ▪ *milk, meat, and other animal products* ▪ *the animal kingdom* [=a basic group of living things that includes all animals] ▪ *She's a supporter of animal rights.* [=she believes that all animals should be treated in a fair and kind way] **2** : of or relating to the body and not to the mind ▪ *animal instincts/passion/desires* ▪ *Women were drawn to his animal magnetism.* [=his strong physical or sexual attractiveness]

¹an·i·mate /ˈænəmət/ *adj, formal* : alive or living ▪ *animate and inanimate objects*

²an·i·mate /ˈænəˌmeɪt/ *vb* **-mat·ed; -mat·ing** *[T]* **1** : to make (someone or something) lively or excited ▪ *A smile animated his face.* **2** : to make (something, such as a drawing) appear to move by using the process of animation ▪ *The film's dinosaurs were animated on computers.*

an·i·mat·ed /ˈænəˌmeɪtəd/ *adj* **1** : full of life and energy ▪ *After dinner, the discussion got more animated.* **2** : produced through the process of animation ▪ *animated films/cartoons/characters* — **an·i·mat·ed·ly** *adv*

an·i·ma·tion /ˌænəˈmeɪʃən/ *n* [U] **1** : a lively or excited quality ▪ *He talked with animation* [=in an excited way] *about his vacation.* **2** : a way of making a movie by creating a series of drawings, photographs, etc., that are slightly different from one another and showing them quickly one after another to create the appearance of movement ▪ *The animation for the film took two years to complete.* ▪ *computer animation*

an·i·ma·tor /ˈænəˌmeɪtɚ/ *n* [C] : a person who creates animated movies and cartoons

an·i·me /ˈænəˌmeɪ/ *n* [U] : a style of animation that was created in Japan

an·i·mos·i·ty /ˌænəˈmɑːsəti/ *n, pl* **-ties** [C/U] : a strong feeling of dislike or hatred ▪ *There has always been animosity between them.* [=they have always disliked each other] ▪ *our personal animosities*

an·ise /ˈænəs/ *n* [U] : a plant with seeds that are used in cooking

an·kle /ˈæŋkəl/ *n* [C] : the joint where the foot joins the leg ▪ *I twisted/sprained my ankle.*

an·klet /ˈæŋklət/ *n* [C] : a band, ring, or chain that is worn around the ankle — called also *ankle bracelet*

an·nals /ˈænəlz/ *n* [plural] **1** : historical records ▪ *This event will go down in the annals of sports/war/medicine.* [=it will be remembered as part of the history of sports/war/medicine] **2** : records of the activities of an organization — often used in the titles of publications ▪ *the Annals of Family Medicine*

¹**an·nex** /əˈnɛks/ *vb* [T] : to add (an area or region) to a country, state, etc. ▪ *The United States annexed Texas in 1845.* — **an·nex·a·tion** /ˌæˌnɛkˈseɪʃən/ *n* [C/U]

²**an·nex** (*chiefly US*) *or Brit* **an·nexe** /ˈæˌnɛks/ *n* [C] **1** : a building that is attached to or near a larger building and usually used as part of it ▪ *We store our old files in the annex.* **2** *chiefly Brit* : a section or statement added at the end of a document : APPENDIX

an·ni·hi·late /əˈnajəˌleɪt/ *vb* **-lat·ed; -lat·ing** [T] **1** : to destroy (something or someone) completely ▪ *Bombs annihilated the city.* **2** : to defeat (someone) completely ▪ *He annihilated his opponent in the last election.* — **an·ni·hi·la·tion** /əˌnajəˈleɪʃən/ *n* [U]

an·ni·ver·sa·ry /ˌænəˈvɚsəri/ *n, pl* **-ries** [C] : a date that is remembered or celebrated because a special or notable event occurred on that date in a previous year ▪ *the anniversary of the invasion* ▪ *We are celebrating our fifth (wedding) anniversary this year.*

an·no·tate /ˈænəˌteɪt/ *vb* **-tat·ed; -tat·ing** [T] : to add notes or comments to a (book, drawing, etc.) ▪ *She annotated the text at several places.* ▪ *a fully annotated diagram*

an·no·ta·tion /ˌænəˈteɪʃən/ *n* **1** [C] : a note added to a book, drawing, etc., as a comment or explanation ▪ *the text's annotations* **2** [U] : the act of adding notes or comments to something ▪ *her annotation of the diagram*

an·nounce /əˈnaʊns/ *vb* **-nounced; -nounc·ing** **1** [T] : to make (something) known in a public or formal way ▪ *They announced plans to shut down the factory.* ▪ *She announced that the store would be closing in 10 minutes.* ▪ *Their engagement was announced in the newspaper.* **2** [T] : to say (something) in a loud and definite way ▪ *He stood up and announced that he was leaving.* **3** [T] : to say in a formal or official way that something or someone has arrived or is present or ready ▪ *Our flight was just announced over the loudspeaker.* **4** [I] *US* : to say that you are a candidate for a political office ▪ *He announced for president* [=he said that he is going to run for president] *yesterday.* **5** [T] *US* : to describe (a sports event) on radio or television ▪ *Who's going to announce tonight's game?* — **an·nounce·ment** /əˈnaʊnsmənt/ *n* [C/U] ▪ *She made an announcement that the store would be closing in 10 minutes.* ▪ *the announcement of the contest's winners* — **an·nounc·er** /əˈnaʊnsɚ/ *n* [C] ▪ *a radio/sports announcer*

an·noy /əˈnoɪ/ *vb* [T] : to cause (someone) to feel slightly angry ▪ *Her constant questions annoyed us.* — **an·noyed** /əˈnoɪd/ *adj* ▪ *She's very annoyed at/with me.* ▪ *He had an annoyed expression on his face.* — **an·noy·ing** /əˈnojɪŋ/ *adj* ▪ *an annoying habit.* — **an·noy·ing·ly** *adv*

an·noy·ance /əˈnojəns/ *n* **1** [U] : slight anger : the feeling of being annoyed ▪ *She expressed annoyance at the slow service.* **2** [C] : something that causes feelings of slight anger or irritation ▪ *The long wait was a minor annoyance.*

¹**an·nu·al** /ˈænjəwəl/ *adj* **1** : happening once a year ▪ *The annual meeting is in July.* ▪ *the company's annual report* **2** : covering the period of a year ▪ *the area's average annual rainfall* ▪ *an annual fee of $45* — **an·nu·al·ly** *adv* ▪ *We meet annually in July.*

²**annual** *n* [C] **1** : a plant that lives for only one year or season ▪ *annuals and perennials* **2** : a book or magazine that is published once a year

an·nu·ity /əˈnuːəti, *Brit* əˈnjuːəti/ *n, pl* **-ities** [C] **1** : a fixed amount of money that is paid to someone each year **2** : an insurance policy or an investment that pays someone a fixed amount of money each year

an·nul /əˈnʌl/ *vb* **-nulled; -nul·ling** [T] : to say officially that something is no longer valid ▪ *Their marriage was annulled.* — **an·nul·ment** /əˈnʌlmənt/ *n* [C/U]

an·ode /ˈæˌnoʊd/ *n* [C] *technical* : the part of an electrical device (such as a battery) from which electrons leave

anoint /əˈnoɪnt/ *vb* [T] **1** : to put oil on

(someone) as part of a ceremony • *The priest anointed them (with oil).* **2** : to officially choose (someone) to do or to be something • *He anointed her his successor.* — **anoint·ment** /ə'nɔɪntmənt/ *n* [U]

anom·a·ly /ə'nɑːməli/ *n, pl* **-lies** [C] *somewhat formal* : something that is unusual or unexpected • *The blizzard was an anomaly for this area.* — **anom·a·lous** /ə'nɑːmələs/ *adj* • *anomalous test results* — **anom·a·lous·ly** *adj*

anon /ə'nɑːn/ *adv, literary* : in a short time : SOON

anon. *abbr* anonymous; anonymously

anon·y·mous /ə'nɑːnəməs/ *adj* **1** : not named or identified • *The donor wishes to remain anonymous.* **2** : made or done by someone unknown • *He made an anonymous phone call to the police.* **3** : not distinct or noticeable • *His was just another anonymous face in the crowd.* — **an·o·nym·i·ty** /ˌænə'nɪmətɪ/ *n* [U] • *She agreed to speak to the reporter only on condition of anonymity.* [=only if her name would not be revealed by the reporter] — **anon·y·mous·ly** *adv*

an·orex·ia /ˌænə'rɛksijə/ *n* [U] : a serious physical and emotional illness especially among young women in which an abnormal fear of being fat leads to very poor eating habits and dangerous weight loss — **an·orex·ic** /ˌænə'rɛksɪk/ *adj* • *an anorexic teenager* — **anorexic** *n* [C] • *She's an anorexic.* [=a person suffering from anorexia]

¹an·oth·er /ə'nʌðɚ/ *adj* **1** : one more in addition • *They opened another bottle of wine.* • *It will take another two years* [=two more years] *to finish the building.* • *We had dinner at another one of the city's fine restaurants.* • *This is yet another example of government waste.* • *He's just another overpaid athlete.* [=he's one of many overpaid athletes] **2** : different from the first or other one • *We'll have to meet again (at) another time.* • *I need another cup. This one is chipped.* • *Complaining is one thing, but finding solutions is another thing altogether/entirely.* [=it is more difficult to find solutions than to complain] **3** : similar or equal to a particular person or thing • *He thought of himself as another Napoleon.* [=as a person who was like Napoleon]

²another *pron* **1** : one more of the same kind • *I've had only one drink, but I think I'll have another.* • *One thief carried a gun, another (carried) a knife.* • *The buses kept arriving, one after another.* [=in a continuing series] **2** : one that is different • *moving from one city to another* — used in phrases with *one* to refer to something that is not specified • *We all do foolish things at one time or another.* • *We will succeed (in) one way or another.* [=we will find a way to succeed] • *a lock of one kind/sort/type or another* [=some kind/sort/type of lock]

¹an·swer /'ænsɚ, Brit 'ɑːnsə/ *n* **1** [C] **a** : something you say or write when someone asks you a question • *I asked him a simple question and he gave me a long and confusing answer.* **b** : a response to

a question that is meant to show whether or not you know something • *What's the right/correct answer to question number 5?* **c** : the correct response to a question • *The answers are listed in the back of the book.* **2** [C/U] : something you say or write as a reaction to something someone else has said or done • *I sent a letter and got an answer two weeks later.* • *In answer to your request, we are sending a catalog.* **3** [C] : something you do in response to something that has happened • *I called but there was no answer.* [=no one answered the phone when I called] • *The company had no answer when its competitors lowered their prices.* **4** [C] : something that makes a bad situation better • *More money is not the answer (to our problems).* • *She thinks she has/knows all the answers.* [=she thinks that she knows the solution to every problem] **5** [C] : something or someone that resembles a successful thing or person — + *to* • *The show is TV's answer to news magazines.* [=the show is similar to a news magazine]

²answer *vb* **1 a** [T/I] : to say or write something when someone asks you a question • *She answered only three of the test questions correctly.* • *When the police asked him his name, he refused to answer.* **b** [T] : to say or write (something) as a reply • *When asked if she would run for office, she answered that she would.* • *When asked if she would run, she answered "Yes."* **c** [T] : to reply to (someone) • *When I ask you a question, I expect you to answer me!* **2** [T/I] **a** : to write a response to a letter, e-mail message, etc. • *I sent her a letter, but she never answered (me).* • *She never answered my letter.* **b** : to pick up (a ringing telephone) • *The phone rang repeatedly, but no one answered (it).* **c** : to open a door when someone knocks on it • *No one answered (the door).* **3** [T/I] : to act in response to (something) • *I got the job by answering a "help wanted" ad in the newspaper.* **4** [T] : to defend yourself against (something) • *The mayor will appear in court today to answer charges of corruption.* — **answer back** [*phrasal vb*] **1** *somewhat informal* : to reply to someone especially in a rude way • *impolite children who answer back when their teacher corrects them* **2 answer (someone) back** : to reply rudely to (someone) • *He became angry when she answered him back.* — **answer for** [*phrasal vb*] **1 a** : to take responsibility for (something) • *I can't answer for their safety.* [=I can't promise that they will be safe] **b** : to be punished for (something) • *He must answer for his crimes.* **2** : to give the opinion of (someone else) • *I like the idea myself, but I can't answer for my boss.* — **answer someone's prayers** : to provide what someone hopes or prays for • *Their prayers were answered when their son's health was restored.* — **answer to** [*phrasal vb*] **1** : to be required to explain your actions to (someone) • *He has to answer to a tough boss.* **2** : to respond when called by a particular name • *This dog answers to the name (of) "Rover."* — **an·swer·er** /ˈænsərə/ *n [C]*

an·swer·able /ˈænsərəbəl, Brit ˈɑːnsərəbəl/ *adj* **1** *not before a noun* **a** : required to explain actions or decisions *to* someone • *a powerful businesswoman who thinks she's answerable to no one* **b** : responsible *for* something • *The company is answerable for any damage caused by its employees.* **2** : capable of being answered • *an easily answerable question*

answering machine *n [C]* : a machine that answers the telephone and records messages left by the people who call

answering service *n [C]* : a business that answers telephone calls and takes messages for the people and businesses that hire it

an·swer·phone /ˈænsəˌfoʊn, Brit ˈɑːnsəˌfəʊn/ *n [C] Brit* : ANSWERING MACHINE

ant /ˈænt/ *n [C]* : a kind of small insect that lives in an organized social group • *an ant colony*

ant·ac·id /æntˈæsəd/ *n [C/U]* : medicine that prevents or lessens the pain caused by having too much acid in your stomach

an·tag·o·nism /ænˈtægəˌnɪzəm/ *n [U, plural]* : a desire to oppose something you dislike or disagree with • *There is a long history of antagonism between the two nations.* • *I never felt any antagonism toward her.* • *ethnic antagonisms* — **an·tag·o·nist** /ænˈtægənɪst/ *n [C]* • *He faced his antagonist in a series of debates.* — **an·tag·o·nis·tic** /ænˌtægəˈnɪstɪk/ *adj* • *Many people are antagonistic to the idea of renovating the building.* • *The two groups were antagonistic toward each other.*

an·tag·o·nize *also Brit* **an·tag·o·nise** /ænˈtægəˌnaɪz/ *vb* **-nized; -niz·ing** *[T]* : to cause (someone) to feel hostile or angry • *Her comments antagonized many people.*

ant·arc·tic *or* **Ant·arc·tic** /æntˈɑəktɪk/ *adj, always before a noun* : of or relating to the South Pole or the region around it • *Antarctic exploration*

Antarctic Circle *n* — **the Antarctic Circle** : an imaginary line that goes around the Earth near the South Pole

¹**an·te** /ˈænti/ *n [C]* : the amount of money that a player must bet at the beginning of play in a poker game • *The dealer called for a dollar ante.* — **up/raise the ante** : to increase an amount or level: such as **a** : to raise the cost or price • *She said she would accept $5,000 for the car but then kept upping the ante.* **b** : to increase the possible harm that could result from something • *The new law ups the ante on people who cheat on their taxes.* **c** : to set a higher standard or goal • *The film ups the ante on special effects.*

²**ante** *vb* **an·ted; an·te·ing** *[T/I]* : to pay the amount of money required to start play in a poker game • *The dealer waited until everyone had anted up before he dealt the cards.* • *(figurative)* They had to ante up [=*pay*] $5,000 to attend the senator's banquet.

ant·eat·er /ˈæntˌiːtə/ *n [C]* : an animal that has a very long nose and tongue and eats ants

an·te·bel·lum /ˌænti·ˈbɛləm/ *adj, formal* : occurring in the southern U.S. before the American Civil War • *the antebellum South*

an·te·ced·ent /ˌæntəˈsiːdənt/ *n* **1** *[C] grammar* : a word or phrase that is represented by another word (such as a pronoun) • *"John" is the antecedent of the pronoun "him" in "Mary saw John and thanked him."* **2** *[C] formal* : something that came before something else and may have influenced or caused it • *The events were antecedents of/to the war.* [=the events helped to cause the war] **3** *[plural] formal* : the people in a family who lived in past times • *his Scottish antecedents*

an·te·cham·ber /ˈæntiˌtʃeɪmbə/ *n [C] formal* : ANTEROOM

an·te·date /ˌæntiˈdeɪt/ *vb* **-dat·ed; -dat·ing** *[T] formal* **1** : to give an earlier date rather than the actual date to (something) • *antedate a check* **2** : to be earlier or older than (something) • *The church antedates the village itself.*

an·te·di·lu·vi·an /ˌæntidəˈluːvijən/ *adj, formal* : very old or old-fashioned • *antediluvian ideas*

an·te·lope /ˈæntiˌloʊp/ *n, pl* **an·te·lopes** *or* **antelope** *[C]* : an animal in Africa and Asia that looks like a deer, has horns pointing up and back, and runs very fast

an·te·na·tal /ˌæntiˈneɪtl/ *adj, Brit* : PRENATAL

an·ten·na /ænˈtɛnə/ *n, pl* **-nae** /-ni/ *or* **-nas** *[C]* **1** : a thin sensitive organ on the head of an insect, crab, etc., that is used mainly to feel and touch things **2** *chiefly US* : a device (such as a wire or a metal rod) for sending or receiving radio or television signals • *TV antennas*

an·te·ri·or /ænˈtirijə/ *adj, technical* : near or toward the front of something (such as the body) • *the anterior part of the brain*

an·te·room /ˈæntiˌruːm/ *n [C]* : a small room in which people wait before going into a larger room

an·them /ˈænθəm/ *n [C]* **1** : a formal song of loyalty, praise, or happiness • *patriotic anthems* — see also NATIONAL ANTHEM **2** : a song that is important to a particular group of people • *teen anthems* — **an·the·mic** /ˌænˈθiːmɪk/ *adj* • *anthemic songs*

ant·hill /ˈæntˌhɪl/ *n [C]* : a mound of dirt made by ants

an·thol·o·gy /ænˈθɑːlədʒi/ *n, pl* **-gies** *[C]* **1** : a published collection of poems, short stories, etc., by different authors • *an anthology of American poetry* **2** : a collection of works of art or music • *an anthology of the band's earlier albums*

an·thra·cite /ˈænθrəˌsaɪt/ *n [U]* : a hard type of coal

an·thrax /ˈænˌθræks/ *n [U]* : a serious disease that affects animals (such as cattle and sheep) and sometimes people

an·thro·pol·o·gy /ˌænθrəˈpɑːlədʒi/ *n [U]* : the study of human origins, societies, and cultures — **an·thro·po·log·i·cal**

/ˌænθrəpəˈlɑːdʒɪkəl/ *adj* — **an·thro·po·log·i·cal·ly** /ˌænθrəpəˈlɑːdʒɪkli/ *adv* — **an·thro·pol·o·gist** /ˌænθrəˈpɑːlədʒɪst/ *n [C]*

an·thro·po·mor·phic /ˌænθrəpəˈmoɾfɪk/ *adj* **1** : described or thought of as being like human beings in appearance, behavior, etc. ▪ *The story's characters are anthropomorphic animals.* **2** : considering animals, objects, etc., as having human qualities ▪ *anthropomorphic beliefs about nature*

an·ti /ˈænti, ˈænˌtaɪ/ *prep, informal* : opposed to (something or someone) ▪ *She's anti big corporations.*

an·ti- /ˌæn·taɪ, ˌænti; sometimes ˌænti before consonants/ *prefix* **1** : opposite to something ▪ *antisocial* **2** : against someone or something ▪ *antiwar* ▪ *antismoking* — often used with a hyphen ▪ *anti-American* **3** : acting to prevent something ▪ *antitheft*

an·ti·air·craft /ˌæntiˈeəˌkræft, Brit ˌæntiˈeəˌkrɑːft/ *adj, always before a noun* : used for defense against military aircraft ▪ *antiaircraft missiles*

an·ti·bac·te·ri·al /ˌænˌtaɪbækˈtiɾijəl/ *adj* : able to kill bacteria ▪ *antibacterial soap*

an·ti·bi·ot·ic /ˌænˌtaɪbaɪˈɑːtɪk/ *n [C] medical* : a drug that is used to kill harmful bacteria and to cure infections — **antibiotic** *adj*

an·ti·body /ˈæntiˌbɑːdi/ *n, pl* **-bod·ies** *[C]* : a substance produced by the body to fight disease

an·tic·i·pate /ænˈtɪsəˌpeɪt/ *vb* **-pat·ed; -pat·ing** *[T]* **1** : to think of (something that will or might happen in the future) ▪ *They do not anticipate any major problems.* **2** : to expect (something) with pleasure ▪ *He eagerly anticipated her arrival.*

an·tic·i·pa·tion /ænˌtɪsəˈpeɪʃən/ *n [U]* **1** : a feeling of excitement about something that is going to happen ▪ *He looked forward to the party with anticipation.* **2** : the act of preparing for something ▪ *They hired extra police officers in anticipation of* [=because they expected] *a big crowd.* — **an·tic·i·pa·to·ry** /ænˈtɪsəpəˌtori, Brit ænˌtɪsəˈpeɪtri, ænˈtɪsəpətri/ *adj, formal* ▪ *anticipatory measures*

an·ti·cli·max /ˌænˌtaɪˈklaɪˌmæks/ *n [C/U]* : an ending or result that is much less exciting or dramatic than it was expected to be ▪ *The movie ended in (an) anticlimax.* — **an·ti·cli·mac·tic** /ˌænˌtaɪˌklaɪˈmæktɪk/ *adj*

an·ti·clock·wise /ˌænˌtaɪˈklɑːk,waɪz/ *adj or adv, Brit* : COUNTERCLOCKWISE

an·tics /ˈæntɪks/ *n [plural]* : playful actions or behavior ▪ *I'm tired of his childish antics.*

an·ti·de·pres·sant /ˌænˌtaɪdɪˈprɛsnt/ *n [C]* : a drug that relieves or prevents depression in a person — **antidepressant** *adj*

an·ti·dote /ˈæntiˌdoʊt/ *n [C]* **1** : a substance that stops the harmful effects of a poison **2** : something that corrects or improves the bad effects of something ▪ *an antidote to/for boredom*

an·ti·freeze /ˈæntiˌfriːz/ *n [U]* : a sub-

stance that is added to the water in a vehicle's engine to prevent it from freezing

an·ti·gen /ˈæntɪdʒən/ *n [C]* : a harmful substance that causes the body to produce antibodies

an·ti·he·ro /ˈænˌtaɪˌhiroʊ/ *n, pl* **-roes** *[C]* : a main character in a book, movie, etc., who lacks the usual good qualities of a hero

an·ti·his·ta·mine /ˌæntiˈhɪstəˌmiːn/ *n [C/U]* : a drug used to treat allergic reactions and colds

an·ti·lock /ˈænˌtaɪˌlɑːk/ *adj, always before a noun* : made to keep the wheels of a vehicle from causing a skid when the vehicle stops suddenly ▪ *antilock brakes*

an·tip·a·thy /ænˈtɪpəθi/ *n, pl* **-thies** *[C/U] formal* : a strong feeling of dislike ▪ *The author has (an) antipathy to/toward other cultures.*

an·ti·per·spi·rant /ˌæntiˈpəspɾənt/ *n [C/U]* : a substance that is used to prevent sweating

an·ti·quar·i·an /ˌæntəˈkwerijən/ *adj* : relating to the collection and study of valuable old things (such as old books) ▪ *antiquarian bookstores*

an·ti·quat·ed /ˈæntəˌkweɪtəd/ *adj* : very old and no longer useful, popular, or accepted ▪ *antiquated technologies/opinions*

¹**an·tique** /ænˈtiːk/ *adj* : old and often valuable ▪ *antique furniture/cars*

²**antique** *n [C]* : art, furniture, etc., that was made at an earlier time and is often valuable ▪ *an antique collector/dealer/shop*

an·tiq·ui·ty /ænˈtɪkwəti/ *n, pl* **-ties** **1** *[U]* : ancient times ▪ *Greek/Roman antiquity* **2** *[plural]* : objects from ancient times ▪ *a museum of Roman antiquities*

an·ti–Sem·i·tism /ˌænˌtaɪˈsɛməˌtɪzəm/ *n [U]* : hatred of Jewish people — **an·ti–Sem·ite** /ˌænˌtaɪˈsɛˌmaɪt/ *n [C]* — **an·ti–Se·mit·ic** /ˌænˌtaɪsəˈmɪtɪk/ *adj*

an·ti·sep·tic /ˌæntəˈsɛptɪk/ *n [C/U]* : a substance that prevents infection in a wound by killing bacteria — **antiseptic** *adj* ▪ *antiseptic cream/lotion/soap*

an·ti·so·cial /ˌænˌtaɪˈsoʊʃəl/ *adj* **1** : violent or harmful to people ▪ *antisocial behavior* **2** : not friendly to other people ▪ *My neighbor is antisocial.*

an·tith·e·sis /ænˈtɪθəsəs/ *n, pl* **-e·ses** /-əˌsiːz/ *[C] formal* **1** : the exact opposite of something or someone ▪ *His lifestyle is the antithesis of healthy living.* **2** : the state of two things that are directly opposite to each other ▪ *the antithesis of/between good and evil*

an·ti·trust /ˌæntaɪˈtrʌst/ *adj, always before a noun, law* : protecting against unfair business practices that limit competition or control prices ▪ *antitrust laws*

an·ti·vi·rus /ˌænti·vaɪrəs/ *adj* : used to protect a computer from viruses ▪ *antivirus software*

ant·ler /ˈæntlɚ/ *n [C]* : the horn of a deer or similar animal

an·to·nym /ˈæntəˌnɪm/ *n [C]* : a word with a meaning that is opposite to the meaning of another word ▪ *"Hot" and "cold" are antonyms.*

ant·sy /ˈæntsi/ *adj* **ant·si·er; -est** *chiefly US, informal* **1** : impatient and unable to stay still ▪ *The children were getting antsy.* **2** : nervous about what might happen ▪ *They are antsy about the stock market.*

anus /ˈeɪnəs/ *n* [C] : the opening through which solid waste leaves the body

an·vil /ˈænvəl/ *n* [C] : an iron block on which hot metal is shaped by hitting it with a hammer

anx·i·ety /æŋˈzajəti/ *n, pl* **-et·ies** [C/U] : fear or nervousness about what might happen ▪ *feelings of anger and anxiety* ▪ *anxieties about/over terrorism*

anx·ious /ˈæŋkʃəs/ *adj* **1 a** : afraid or nervous especially about what may happen : feeling anxiety ▪ *They were anxious about/for* [=they were worried about what might happen to] *their daughter.* **b** : causing or showing fear or nervousness ▪ *anxious moments* ▪ *an anxious expression/look on his face* **2** : wanting to do or have something very much especially because of fear or nervousness ▪ *It was snowing hard and we were anxious to get home.* — **anx·ious·ly** *adv* — **anx·ious·ness** *n* [U]

¹**any** /ˈɛni/ *adj, always before a noun* **1** — used to indicate a person or thing that is not particular or specific ▪ *Ask any woman you meet, and she will tell you the same thing.* ▪ *We can meet any day but Monday.* ▪ *They won't let* ***just any*** *person into their club.* **2** — used to indicate an amount greater than zero or none; usually used in negative statements, in questions, and in statements with *if* or *whether* ▪ *I can't find any stamps.* ▪ *The company has denied any responsibility for the accident.* ▪ *Do you have any money?* ▪ *He asked if/whether we had any money.* ▪ *If there are any errors, report them to me. = Report any errors to me.*

²**any** *pron* **1** : any one of the people or things in a group ▪ *Any of them could answer the question.* **2** : any amount ▪ *"I'd like some more coffee." "I'm sorry, but there isn't any left."* ▪ *You haven't eaten any of your salad.*

³**any** *adv* : to the least amount or degree ▪ *I could not walk any farther.* ▪ *Do you want any* [=some] *more pizza?* ▪ *(US, informal) You aren't helping me any.* [=you aren't helping me at all] ▪ *We can't ignore these problems* ***any*** *longer.* [=we must stop ignoring these problems]

any·body /ˈɛniˌbɑːdi, ˈɛniˌbʌdi/ *pron* **1** : any person : ANYONE ▪ *Did anybody call?* ▪ *If anybody calls, take a message.* ▪ *There wasn't anybody there.* [=no one was there] ▪ *It could happen to anybody.* ▪ *She arrived before* ***anybody else.*** [=before any other person] **2** — used when asking a question that could be answered by any of the people in a group ▪ *Would anybody like more coffee?*

any·how /ˈɛniˌhaʊ/ *adv, informal* : ANYWAY ▪ *I wasn't that interested in seeing the movie anyhow.*

any·more /ˌɛniˈmoɚ/ *adv* : in the recent or present period of time — usually used in negative statements and in questions ▪ *I never see them anymore.* ▪ *Does she live there anymore?*

any·one /ˈɛniˌwʌn/ *pron* **1** : any person

▪ *Did anyone call?* ▪ *It could happen to anyone.* ▪ *There wasn't anyone there.* ▪ *She arrived before* ***anyone else.*** **2** — used when asking a question that could be answered by any one of the people in a group ▪ *Would anyone like more coffee?*

any·place /ˈɛniˌpleɪs/ *adv, US* : ¹ANYWHERE **1** ▪ *We wouldn't want to live anyplace else.*

any·thing /ˈɛniˌθɪŋ/ *pron* **1** : a thing of any kind ▪ *That dog will eat almost/practically/virtually anything.* ▪ *She didn't say anything at all.* [=she said nothing] ▪ *I've never seen anything like it.* ▪ *I'll do anything I can to help.* ▪ *We're ready for anything (that might happen).* ▪ *I'd do/give anything to see her again.* ▪ *She dresses conservatively at work, but on the weekends,* ***anything goes.*** [=there are no rules that have to be followed] **2** : ¹SOMETHING — used in questions ▪ *Would you like anything else?* ▪ *Is there anything (good/interesting) on TV tonight?* ▪ *(informal) Do you want some pretzels or anything?* [=or a similar thing] — ***anything but*** : not at all ▪ *She looked anything but happy.* [=she looked very unhappy] — ***anything like*** **1** : at all like — used in negative statements ▪ *He doesn't look anything like his brother.* **2** or ***anything near*** : at all — used in negative statements ▪ *We don't have anything like/near enough time.* [=we don't have nearly enough time] — ***as anything*** *informal* : as any person or thing — used to make a statement more forceful ▪ *He was as calm as anything.* [=he was very calm] — ***for anything*** : for any reason — used in negative statements ▪ *I wouldn't change my life for anything.* — ***if anything*** see ¹IF — ***like anything*** *informal* : very much ▪ *She was hoping like anything that the weather would be good.* — ***more than anything*** : very much ▪ *I wanted to believe her more than anything (in the world)* [=I very much wanted to believe her], *but I couldn't.*

any·time /ˈɛniˌtaɪm/ *adv* : at any time ▪ *You can call me anytime. I'm always home.* ▪ *We should arrive anytime between 5 and 6 p.m.*

any·way /ˈɛniˌweɪ/ *adv* **1** : despite something that has been stated before ▪ *He's not perfect, but she loves him anyway.* **2** — used to give added force to a question ▪ *How do they do it anyway?* **3** — used to add something to a previous statement ▪ *It's too expensive,* ***and anyway*** [=and besides], *we don't have enough time to do it.* **4** — used to correct or slightly change a previous statement ▪ *For a brief time, anyway, they seemed to be happy. The weather will improve next week. Anyway, that's what I've heard.* **5** — used to say that something stated is not important ▪ *It doesn't matter anyway.* **6** — used to introduce a statement that begins a new subject or that goes on to the next part of a story ▪ *Anyway, what do you want to do next?*

¹**any·where** /ˈɛniˌweɚ/ *adv* **1** : in, at, or to any place ▪ *You can sit anywhere you like.* ▪ *He's at home anywhere in the world.* ▪ *I'd know/recognize her anywhere.* ▪ *I*

wouldn't want to live anywhere else. ▪ *(figurative) Their idea never went anywhere.* [=never produced any useful results] ▪ *(figurative) We're working hard but don't seem to be getting anywhere.* [=making progress] **2** : ¹SOMEWHERE — used in questions ▪ *Have you been anywhere (else) in Europe?* **3** — used to give added emphasis to *near* and *close* ▪ *The dog barks if you come anywhere near him.* ▪ *The movie was not anywhere near as good* [=was not nearly as good] *as I expected it to be.* **4** — used to indicate a range of amounts, values, etc. ▪ *The procedure can take anywhere from/between two to four hours to complete.*

²**anywhere** *n* [U] **1** : any place ▪ *It's a short drive from anywhere in the region.* **2** : ²SOMEWHERE — used in questions ▪ *Do you know anywhere I can buy cheap furniture?*

A–OK /ˌeɪoʊˈkeɪ/ *adj, US, informal* : entirely good or satisfactory ▪ *Everything is A-OK.* — **A–OK** *adv* ▪ *Everything went A-OK.*

A1 /ˈeɪˈwʌn/ *adj, informal + old-fashioned* : very good or excellent ▪ *The car's in A1 condition.*

aor·ta /eɪˈoɚtə/ *n* [C] : the large artery that brings blood from the heart to the rest of the body — **aor·tic** /eɪˈoɚtɪk/ *adj*

apace /əˈpeɪs/ *adv* : at a fast speed or pace ▪ *Development on the project continued/proceeded apace.*

¹**apart** /əˈpɑɚt/ *adv* **1** : separated by an amount of space ▪ *They live five miles apart (from each other).* ▪ *The referee had to pull the boxers apart (from each other).* [=to separate them] ▪ *(figurative) Her technique sets her apart from* [=makes her different from] *other singers.* ▪ *(figurative) They were close friends once, but they have drifted/grown apart* [=they are no longer close friends] ▪ *(figurative) The city is a world apart from* [=is completely different from] *the small town where she grew up.* **2** : separated by an amount of time ▪ *Their children were born two years apart.* **3** : not together ▪ *We are unhappy when we're apart.* **4** : into parts or pieces ▪ *He took the clock apart.* ▪ *cut/pry/pull it apart* — **apart from 1** : not including (something) ▪ *The potatoes were salty, but apart from that, the food was very good.* **2** : other than (something) ▪ *Apart from his work, his only real interest is baseball.* **3** : separately from (something) ▪ *This problem needs to be considered apart from the other issues.*

²**apart** *adj, not before a noun* : separate or different from others ▪ *in a place apart* ▪ *They are a breed apart.* [=they are not like other people] — **apart·ness** *n* [U]

apart·heid /əˈpɑɚˌteɪt/ *n* [U] : a former social system in South Africa in which people from other racial groups did not have the same political and economic rights as white people

apart·ment /əˈpɑɚtmənt/ *n* [C] **1** *chiefly US* : a usually rented room or set of rooms that is part of a building and is used as a place to live **2** *Brit* : a large

and impressive set of rooms — usually plural ▪ *the Royal apartments*

ap·a·thy /ˈæpəθi/ *n* [U, singular] : the feeling of not having much emotion or interest ▪ *People have shown (a) surprising apathy toward/about these important social problems.* — **ap·a·thet·ic** /ˌæpə-ˈθɛtɪk/ *adj* ▪ *the apathetic attitude of the public* ▪ *He was apathetic about his future.* [=he didn't care about his future] — **ap·a·thet·ic·al·ly** /ˌæpəˈθɛtɪkli/ *adv*

¹**ape** /ˈeɪp/ *n* [C] **1** : a type of animal (such as a gorilla) that is related to monkeys and humans and that is covered in hair and has no tail or a very short tail **2** *informal* : a large and stupid or rude person ▪ *Her boyfriend's a big ape.* — **go ape** *informal* **1** : to become very excited ▪ *The kids go ape when they hear that song.* **2** : to become very angry ▪ *Mom went ape when I got home late.* — **ape·like** /ˈeɪpˌlaɪk/ *adj*

²**ape** *vb* **aped; ap·ing** [T] *often disapproving* : to copy or imitate (something or someone) ▪ *She apes the speech and manners of the rich.*

aper·i·tif /əˌperəˈtiːf/ *n* [C] : an alcoholic drink that people drink before eating a meal ▪ *They drank champagne as an aperitif.*

ap·er·ture /ˈæpɚtʃɚ/ *n* [C] *formal* : a hole or small opening ▪ *We entered the cave through a narrow aperture.* ▪ *adjusting the aperture of a camera lens*

apex /ˈeɪˌpeks/ *n* [C] : the top or highest point of something ▪ *the mountain's apex* ▪ *(figurative) She died at the apex of her career.*

aphid /ˈeɪfəd/ *n* [C] : a very small insect that harms plants

aph·o·rism /ˈæfəˌrɪzəm/ *n* [C] : a short phrase that expresses a true or wise idea ▪ *When decorating, remember the aphorism, "less is more."*

aph·ro·di·si·ac /ˌæfrəˈdiːziˌæk/ *n* [C] : something (such as a food or drug) that increases sexual desire — **aphrodisiac** *adj*

apiece /əˈpiːs/ *adv, always after a noun* : for or to each person or thing ▪ *She gave the kids a dollar apiece.* [=she gave a dollar to each kid]

aplenty /əˈplɛnti/ *adj, always after a noun* : in a large number or amount ▪ *We found mistakes aplenty in their story.*

aplomb /əˈplɑːm/ *n* [U] : confidence and skill shown especially in a difficult situation ▪ *He showed great aplomb in handling the reporters.* = *He handled the reporters with (great) aplomb.*

apoc·a·lypse /əˈpɑːkəˌlɪps/ *n* [singular] : a great disaster ▪ *an environmental apocalypse* ▪ *waiting for the apocalypse* [=the end or destruction of the world] — **apoc·a·lyp·tic** /əˌpɑːkəˈlɪptɪk/ *adj* ▪ *apocalyptic predictions/warnings*

apoc·ry·phal /əˈpɑːkrəfəl/ *adj* : well-known but probably not true ▪ *an apocryphal story/tale*

apo·lit·i·cal /ˌeɪpəˈlɪtɪkəl/ *adj* : not interested or involved in politics ▪ *Although her parents are politicians, she's completely apolitical.*

apol·o·get·ic /əˌpɑːləˈdʒɛtɪk/ *adj* : feeling or showing regret ▪ *an apologetic letter* ▪ *They were apologetic about the mistake.* — **apol·o·get·i·cal·ly** /ˌǝˌpɑːlǝˈdʒetɪkli/ *adv*

apol·o·gist /ǝˈpɑːlǝdʒɪst/ *n* [C] : a person who defends or supports something (such as a cause or organization) that is being criticized or attacked by other people ▪ *an apologist for the film industry*

apol·o·gize *also Brit* **apol·o·gise** /ǝˈpɑːlǝˌdʒaɪz/ *vb* **-gized; -giz·ing** [I] : to express regret for doing or saying something wrong ▪ *He apologized (to us) for the mistake and promised that it won't happen again.*

apol·o·gy /ǝˈpɑːlǝdʒi/ *n, pl* **-gies** **1** [C/U] : a statement saying that you are sorry about something ▪ *Please accept our sincerest/humblest apologies.* ▪ *I owe you an apology.* ▪ *a letter of apology* ▪ *She* **makes no apologies** *for her lifestyle.* [=she does not believe that her lifestyle is wrong] **2** [C] *formal* : something that is said or written to defend something that other people criticize ▪ *The book is an apology for capitalism.*

ap·o·plexy /ˈæpǝˌpleksi/ *n* [U] **1** *medical, old-fashioned* : STROKE **2** *informal* : great anger and excitement ▪ *Her speech caused apoplexy among the audience members.* — **ap·o·plec·tic** /ˌæpǝˈplektɪk/ *adj* ▪ *She was apoplectic with anger/rage.* ▪ *(old-fashioned)* He suffered an apoplectic fit. [=he suffered a stroke]

apos·tle /ǝˈpɑːsǝl/ *n* [C] **1** : any one of the 12 men chosen by Jesus Christ to spread the Christian religion **2** : some·one who believes in or supports an idea, cause, etc. ▪ *an apostle of democracy* — **ap·os·tol·ic** /ˌæpǝˈstɑːlɪk/ *adj*

apos·tro·phe /ǝˈpɑːstrǝfi/ *n* [C] : the punctuation mark ' used to show that letters or numbers are missing (as when "did" and "not" are combined into "didn't" or when the date 1776 is written as '76), the possessive form of a noun (as in "Lee's book"), and the plural forms of letters or numbers (as in "the 1960's")

app /ˈæp/ *n* [C] *chiefly US, computers, informal* : APPLICATION 4 ▪ *a popular app*

ap·pall *(US) or Brit* **ap·pal** /ǝˈpɑːl/ *vb* [T] : to cause (someone) to feel fear, shock, or disgust ▪ *She was appalled by/at their behavior.*

ap·pall·ing /ǝˈpɑːlɪŋ/ *adj* : very bad in a way that causes fear, shock, or disgust ▪ *an appalling accident* ▪ *Your behavior has been appalling.* — **ap·pall·ing·ly** *adv*

ap·pa·ra·tus /ˌæpǝˈrætǝs/ *n, pl* **ap·pa·ra·tus·es** *or* **apparatus** **1** [C/U] : a tool or piece of equipment used for specific activities ▪ *an expensive (piece of) construction apparatus* **2** [C] : the organization or system used for doing or operating something ▪ *The party apparatus* [=machinery] *supported his ideas.*

ap·par·el /ǝˈperǝl/ *n* [U] *formal* : clothing of a particular kind ▪ *fine apparel* ▪ *All children's apparel is now on sale.* ▪ *athletic apparel* [=clothing for exercising or playing sports]

ap·par·ent /ǝˈperǝnt/ *adj* **1** : easy to see or understand ▪ *They were in no apparent danger.* [=they did not appear to be in

any danger] ▪ *It soon/quickly became apparent (to us) that something was wrong.* ▪ *He started yelling for* **no apparent reason.** **2** *always before a noun* : seeming to be true but possibly not true ▪ *He died of an apparent heart attack.* [=it appears that a heart attack caused his death]

ap·par·ent·ly /ǝˈperǝntli/ *adv* — used to describe something that appears to be true ▪ *Their apparently happy marriage ended after only two years.* ▪ *Apparently, he died of a heart attack.* ▪ *He apparently died of a heart attack.* ▪ *"Did the bus leave without us?" "Apparently (so)."* [=yes, that seems/appears to be the case]

ap·pa·ri·tion /ˌæpǝˈrɪʃǝn/ *n* [C] *formal* : a ghost or spirit of a dead person ▪ *ghostly apparitions*

¹**ap·peal** /ǝˈpiːl/ *n* **1** [U] : a quality that causes people to like someone or something ▪ *Her jokes are quickly losing their appeal.* ▪ *The movie has/holds great appeal to/for children.* [=children like the movie] **2** [C] **a** : a serious request for help, support, etc. ▪ *They made a desperate appeal to the government for help.* **b** : an attempt to make someone do or accept something as right or proper by saying things that are directed at a person's feelings, attitudes, etc. — **+ to** ▪ *The author makes an appeal to the reader's emotions/intellect.* **c** : an organized effort to raise money ▪ *We made a donation during the school's annual appeal.* **3** [C/U] : a process in which a decision is studied and accepted or rejected by a higher court or by someone in authority ▪ *My lawyer said that we should file for an appeal.* ▪ *Her conviction was thrown out* **on appeal.** [=a higher court decided that she should not have been convicted] ▪ *The case is currently* **under appeal.** [=it is being reviewed by a higher court]

²**appeal** *vb* **1** [I] : to be pleasing or attractive to someone ▪ *music that appeals to a wide variety of people* ▪ *The idea appealed to him greatly.* [=he liked the idea very much] **2** [I] **a** : to ask for help, support, etc., in a serious way ▪ *They appealed for calm.* = *They appealed to everyone to stay calm.* **b** : to try to make someone do or accept something as right or proper by saying things that are directed at a person's feelings, attitudes, etc. — **+ to** ▪ *We got them to help by appealing to their sense of duty.* **3** [T/I] : to make a formal request for a higher court or for someone in authority to review and change a decision ▪ *She lost the case and decided to appeal.* ▪ *(US) We plan to appeal the court's decision.* = *(Brit) We plan to* **appeal against** *the court's decision.*

ap·peal·ing /ǝˈpiːlɪŋ/ *adj* : pleasing or attractive ▪ *appealing colors* ▪ *an idea that most people will* **find appealing** [=that most people will like] — **ap·peal·ing·ly** *adv*

ap·pear /ǝˈpiǝ/ *vb* **1** [*linking vb*] *somewhat formal* : to make someone think that a person or thing has a particular characteristic : LOOK, SEEM ▪ *She appears (to be) angry.* ▪ *"Is she angry?" "It appears so."* ▪ *Winning the election appears* *unlikely at this point.* **2** [I] : to become able to be seen • *The sun began to appear from behind the clouds.* • *He often appears to her in her dreams.* [=she often sees him in her dreams] **3** [I] : to arrive at a place • *One of the guests appeared an hour late.* **4** [I] : to begin to exist • *The disease first appeared in the late 1970s.* **5** [I] **a** : to go where people can see you give a speech, answer questions, etc. • *a politician appearing before a group of reporters* **b** : to work as an actor or performer in a movie, on the radio, etc. • *The two actors appeared together in the film.* • *Guest musicians appeared on his latest album.* **c** : to be published or made available to the public • *The story appeared in today's newspaper.* **6** [I] : to go in front of a person or group that has authority especially in order to answer questions • *I appeared in front of the committee during its last meeting.* • *She appeared in court as a witness.*

ap·pear·ance /ə'pirəns/ *n* **1** [C/U] *somewhat formal* : the way that someone or something looks • *The general appearance of the house is quite good.* • *Have you noticed any changes in her physical appearance?* • *They are very similar in appearance.* [=they look the same] **2** [C] : a way of looking that is not true or real • *She appears to be happy, but appearances can be deceiving.* • *He was, to/by all (outward) appearances, a happily married man.* [=he seemed to be a happily married man, but he wasn't] • *His white beard gave him the appearance of an old man.* [=made him look like an old man] • *Although they were getting a divorce, my parents thought it was important to keep up appearances.* [=to hide something bad by pretending that nothing is wrong] **3** [C] : the fact that something or someone arrives or begins to be seen • *The appearance of buds on the trees tells us that spring has arrived.* • *I was surprised by his sudden appearance.* [=I was surprised when he suddenly appeared] **4** [C] : the time when something begins to exist or is seen for the first time • *The technology made its first appearance* [=appeared for the first time] *in the early 1980s.* **5** [C] : an act of being seen or heard by the public as an actor, politician, athlete, etc. — often used with *make* • *She is making her first appearance at/in the championships.* • *This is his first public appearance since winning the award.* **6** [C] : the formal act of going in front of a person or group to speak, answer questions, etc. • *She made an appearance before Congress last year.* • *They are awaiting court appearances.* [=waiting to go to court] — **make an appearance** or **put in an appearance** : to go to an event, gathering, etc., usually for a short period of time • *The candidate made an appearance at the rally.*

ap·pease /ə'pi:z/ *vb* **-peased; -peas·ing** [T] *formal* **1** *often disapproving* : to make (someone) pleased or less angry by giving or saying something desired • *His critics were not appeased by this last speech.* **2** : to make (a pain, a problem,

etc.) less painful or troubling • *She appeased her guilty conscience by telling him the truth.* — **ap·pease·ment** /ə'pi:zmənt/ *n* [U]

ap·pel·lant /ə'pɛlənt/ *n* [C] *law* : someone who requests that a higher court review and change the decision of a lower court

ap·pel·late /ə'pɛlət/ *adj, always before a noun, law* : able to review and change the decisions of a lower court • *an appellate court/judge*

ap·pel·la·tion /ˌæpə'leɪʃən/ *n* [C] *formal* : a name or title • *an honorary appellation*

ap·pend /ə'pɛnd/ *vb* [T] *formal* : to add (something) to a piece of writing • *Read the notes **appended** to each chapter.*

ap·pend·age /ə'pɛndɪdʒ/ *n* [C] **1** : a body part (such as an arm or a leg) connected to the main part of the body **2** : something connected to a larger or more important thing • *an appendage of a larger political party*

ap·pen·dec·to·my /ˌæpən'dɛktəmi/ *n, pl* **-mies** [C] *medical* : an operation to remove a person's appendix

ap·pen·di·ci·tis /əˌpɛndə'saɪtəs/ *n* [U] : a condition in which a person's appendix is infected

ap·pen·dix /ə'pɛndɪks/ *n* [C] **1** *pl* **-dix·es** or **-di·ces** /-dɪˌsiːz/ : a section of extra information added at the end of a book • *Turn to Appendix 3: Glossary of Terms.* **2** *pl* **-dixes** : a small tube at the beginning of the large intestine

ap·per·tain /ˌæpə'teɪn/ *vb* [I] *formal* : to belong to or be related to something • *the rights that appertain to marriage*

ap·pe·tite /'æpəˌtaɪt/ *n* **1** [C/U] : a physical desire for food • *He has a healthy/good/hearty appetite.* • *The aroma **whetted our appetites**.* [=made us hungry] • *I just **lost my appetite**.* [=I no longer want to eat] • *loss of appetite* **2** [C] : a desire or liking for something • *She has an appetite for adventure.* [=she likes adventure]

ap·pe·tiz·er *also Brit* **ap·pe·tis·er** /'æpəˌtaɪzə/ *n* [C] : a small dish of food served before the main part of a meal

ap·pe·tiz·ing *also Brit* **ap·pe·tis·ing** /'æpəˌtaɪzɪŋ/ *adj* : having a good smell or appearance that makes people want to eat • *an appetizing meal/aroma* — **ap·pe·tiz·ing·ly** *also Brit* **ap·pe·tis·ing·ly** *adv*

ap·plaud /ə'plɑːd/ *vb* **1** [T/I] : to strike the hands together over and over to show approval or praise • *The audience stood and applauded (her performance).* **2** [T] : to express approval of or support for (something or someone) • *We applaud their decision/efforts to lower taxes.*

ap·plause /ə'plɑːz/ *n* [U] : a show of approval or appreciation at a play, sporting event, etc., in which people strike their hands together over and over • *The announcement was greeted with applause.* • *a big round of applause*

ap·ple /'æpəl/ *n* [C/U] : a round fruit with red, yellow, or green skin and firm white flesh • *crisp, juicy apples* • *apple pie/juice/trees* • *(figurative) The day was ru-*

ined for us by one bad/rotten apple. [=one bad member of a group who causes problems for the rest of the group] • *Baseball is as American as apple pie.* [=it is very American] — *the apple of someone's eye* : a person or thing that someone loves very much • *His daughter is the apple of his eye.* — *upset the apple cart* see ²UPSET

ap·ple–cheeked /ˈæpəlˌtʃiːkt/ *adj* : having red or pink cheeks • *apple-cheeked youngsters*

ap·ple·sauce /ˈæpəlˌsɑːs/ *n* [U] : a sweet sauce made from cooked apples

ap·pli·ance /əˈplajəns/ *n* [C] : a machine that is powered by electricity and that is used in people's houses to perform a particular job • *stoves, microwaves, and other appliances*

ap·pli·ca·ble /ˈæplɪkəbəl/ *adj* : able to be applied or used in a particular situation • *This method is applicable to a variety of problems.* • *all applicable laws* — **ap·pli·ca·bil·i·ty** /ˌæplɪkəˈbɪləti/ *n* [U]

ap·pli·cant /ˈæplɪkənt/ *n* [C] : someone who formally asks for something (such as a job or admission to a college) • *We need qualified applicants for the job.*

ap·pli·ca·tion /ˌæpləˈkeɪʃən/ *n* **1 a** [C/U] : a formal and usually written request for something (such as a job, a loan, etc.) • *Our loan application has been approved/denied.* **b** [C] : a document that is used to make a formal request for something • *Please fill out this application.* **2 a** [C/U] : the act of putting something on a surface, a part of the body, etc. • *the application of heat/lotion/ointment* • *repeated applications of fertilizer* **b** [C/U] : the use of an idea, method, law, etc., in a particular situation or for a particular purpose • *the creative application of new technology* **c** [U] : the use of a word, name, etc., to describe someone or something • *the application of "baby boomer" to people born right after World War II* **3** [C/U] : the ability to be used for practical purposes • *The technique has limited application.* [=it cannot be used for many purposes] • *a tool with a wide range of applications* **4** [C] *computers* : a computer program that performs a particular task (such as word processing) • *How many applications is your computer currently running?* **5** [U] *formal* : effort made to work hard in order to complete something successfully • *I admire her application and intelligence.*

ap·pli·ca·tor /ˈæpləˌkeɪtɚ/ *n* [C] : a tool that is used to put something (such as paint or makeup) on a surface • *a paint applicator*

ap·plied /əˈplaɪd/ *adj* : having or relating to practical use • *applied linguistics/physics/psychology*

ap·pli·qué /ˌæpləˈkeɪ, *Brit* əˈpliːkeɪ/ *n* [C/U] : a decoration that is sewn onto a larger piece of cloth — **appliqué** *vb* **-quéd; -qué·ing** [T] • *I appliquéd the sweater.*

ap·ply /əˈplaɪ/ *vb* **-plies; -plied; -ply·ing 1** [I] : to ask formally for something (such as a job, a loan, etc.) usually in writing • *Anyone can apply for membership.* = *Anyone can apply to become a member.* • *She started applying for college.* • *High school dropouts need not apply (for this job).* **2** [T] : to put or spread (something) on a surface, a part of the body, etc. • *Apply at least two coats of paint.* • *applying ointment to a cut* **3** [T] : to cause (force, pressure, etc.) to have an effect or to be felt • *Stop the bleeding by applying pressure to the wound.* [=by pressing on/against the wound] • *The police dealt with the situation without applying force.* **4** [T] : to use (an idea, method, law, etc.) in a particular situation • *They apply what they learned in school to their everyday lives.* **5** [T] : to cause (the brakes of a vehicle) to work • *Take your foot off the gas pedal and apply the brakes.* **6** [I] : to have an effect on someone or something • *The rule no longer applies.* • *These rules apply to everyone.* [=everyone must obey these rules] **7** [T/I] : to use a word, name, etc., to describe someone or something • *The term "baby boomer" is usually applied to people born right after World War II.* — *apply yourself* : to make yourself work hard in order to do something successfully • *She applied herself to learning the language.*

ap·point /əˈpɔɪnt/ *vb* [T] **1** : to choose (someone) to have a particular job • *The President appointed him (to serve as) Secretary of Education.* • *appointing women to positions of power* • *a committee appointed by Congress* **2** *formal* **a** : to decide or establish (something) in an official way • *accomplishing your appointed tasks* [=the things that you are supposed to do] **b** : to decide (the time or place at which something will happen or be done) • *We were there at the appointed time/hour.* **3** : to decorate and put furniture in (a room or space) • *the hotel's beautifully appointed rooms* — **ap·point·ee** /əˌpɔɪnˈtiː/ *n* [C] • *presidential appointees* [=people chosen by the President to fill a position]

ap·point·ment /əˈpɔɪntmənt/ *n* **1** [C/U] : an agreement to meet with someone at a particular time • *I'm late for an appointment.* • *I have a dentist's appointment tomorrow.* • *She made an appointment (to meet) with her professor.* • *The museum is open to visitors by appointment only.* [=you have to make an appointment to visit the museum] **2** [U] : the act of giving a particular job or position to someone • *the appointment of the new Secretary of State* **3** [C] : a position to which someone is appointed • *He now holds an appointment from the President.* • *academic appointments*

ap·por·tion /əˈpɔɚʃən/ *vb* [T] *formal* : to give (a part or portion of something) to a number of people • *The proceeds from the auction will be apportioned between/among the couple's children.* • *There is no point in trying to apportion blame.* [=to say who should be blamed] — **ap·por·tion·ment** /əˈpɔɚʃənmənt/ *n* [C/U]

ap·po·site /ˈæpəzət/ *adj, formal* : very appropriate • *an apposite quotation* — **ap·po·site·ly** *adv*

ap·praise /ə'preɪz/ vb -praised; -prais·ing [T] 1 : to say how much something is worth after you have carefully examined it ▪ She appraised the painting at [=she said that the painting is worth] $1.2 million. 2 : to give your opinion about the condition, quality, or importance of (something or someone that you have studied or examined) ▪ In the book, he appraises the current economic situation. — **ap·prais·al** /ə'preɪzəl/ n [C/U] ▪ real estate appraisal ▪ The book is an excellent appraisal of the situation. — **ap·prais·er** n [C] ▪ The appraiser gave us a report on the value of the property.

ap·pre·cia·ble /ə'priːʃəbəl/ adj : large enough to be noticed or measured ▪ The chemical made no appreciable difference in the results. — **ap·pre·cia·bly** /ə-'priːʃəbli/ adv

ap·pre·ci·ate /ə'priːʃiˌeɪt/ vb -at·ed; -at·ing 1 [T] : to admire and value (something or someone) ▪ They make their employees feel appreciated. ▪ She appreciates fine wine. 2 [T] a : to be grateful for (something) ▪ Your help was greatly appreciated. ▪ I don't appreciate being ignored. [=I do not like to be ignored] b — used to make a polite request ▪ I would appreciate it if you would wait. [=please wait] 3 [T] : to recognize or understand (something) ▪ I don't think you appreciate the seriousness of the situation. ▪ I appreciate what you are trying to do, but I don't think it will work. 4 [I] : to increase in value ▪ Your investment will appreciate (in value) over time. — **ap·pre·cia·tive** /ə-'priːʃətɪv/ adj ▪ I'm very appreciative of [=very grateful for] your efforts. — **ap·pre·cia·tive·ly** adv

ap·pre·ci·a·tion /əˌpriːʃiˈeɪʃən/ n 1 [U] : a feeling of being grateful for something ▪ He showed his appreciation by cooking a meal for her. ▪ We'd like to present you with this gift in appreciation of your hard work. [=to show that we are grateful for your hard work] 2 [singular] : an ability to understand the worth, quality, or importance of something ▪ developing an appreciation for/of exotic foods ▪ a music appreciation class 3 [U, singular] : full awareness or understanding of something ▪ (an) appreciation for/of the seriousness of the situation 4 [U, singular] : an increase in the value of something ▪ There's been no appreciation in the stock's value.

ap·pre·hend /ˌæprɪˈhɛnd/ vb [T] formal 1 of police : to arrest (someone) for a crime ▪ Police have apprehended the thief. 2 : to notice and understand (something) ▪ subtle differences that are difficult to apprehend

ap·pre·hen·sion /ˌæprɪˈhɛnʃən/ n 1 [C/U] : fear that something bad or unpleasant is going to happen ▪ The thought fills me with apprehension. 2 formal : the act of apprehending someone or something; such as a [C/U] : the act of arresting someone for a crime ▪ the sheriff's apprehension of the criminal b [U] : the act of noticing and understanding something ▪ the apprehension of danger

ap·pre·hen·sive /ˌæprɪˈhɛnsɪv/ adj

: afraid that something bad or unpleasant is going to happen ▪ He was apprehensive about the surgery. — **ap·pre·hen·sive·ly** adv — **ap·pre·hen·sive·ness** n [U]

¹**ap·pren·tice** /ə'prɛntəs/ n [C] : a person who learns a job or skill by working for someone who is very good at that job or skill ▪ a carpenter's apprentice = an apprentice carpenter — **ap·pren·tice·ship** /ə'prɛntəsˌʃɪp/ n [C] ▪ He obtained an apprenticeship with a carpenter.

²**apprentice** vb -ticed; -tic·ing 1 [T] : to make (someone) an apprentice ▪ He was apprenticed to a carpenter [=he became a carpenter's apprentice] at the age of 15. 2 [I] : to work as an apprentice ▪ He is apprenticing with a carpenter.

ap·prise /ə'praɪz/ vb -prised; -pris·ing [T] formal : to give information to (someone) — usually + of ▪ Please apprise me of any changes. = Please keep me apprised of any changes. [=please let me know if any changes happen]

¹**ap·proach** /ə'proʊtʃ/ vb 1 [T/I] a : to move or become near or nearer to something or someone ▪ We approached (the dog) cautiously. ▪ a train approaching a tunnel b : to become near or nearer in time to something ▪ She is approaching retirement. [=she will soon be retiring from her job] ▪ Your birthday is fast approaching. [=your birthday is soon] 2 [T] a : to get close to (an amount or level) ▪ We're expecting temperatures approaching 100 degrees. b : to be almost the same as (something or someone) ▪ a reproduction that approaches the quality of the original painting 3 [T] : to start talking to (someone) for some purpose (such as to ask a question or make a request) ▪ She is easy to approach. ▪ Don't be too aggressive when approaching a potential client. ▪ He was approached about the job, but he didn't take it. 4 [T] : to begin to deal with or think about (something) ▪ She approached the problem from a different angle.

²**approach** n 1 [C] : a way of doing or thinking about something ▪ I admire your direct approach (to the problem). 2 [singular] : the act of becoming near or nearer to someone or something ▪ the noisy approach of a motorboat ▪ the approach of summer 3 [C] : the act of speaking to someone to ask a question, make a request, etc. ▪ They made approaches to the car's owner with an offer (to buy). 4 [C] : a road or path that leads to a place ▪ This road is the only approach to the cabin. 5 [C] : the final part of a flight just before landing ▪ a plane making its final approach

ap·proach·able /ə'proʊtʃəbəl/ adj 1 : easy to talk to or deal with ▪ She is quite approachable, so don't hesitate to ask her your questions. ▪ The book makes this complex topic very approachable. 2 not before a noun : able to be reached or approached ▪ The cabin is approachable by one road. — **ap·proach·abil·i·ty** /əˌproʊtʃəˈbɪləti/ n [U]

ap·pro·ba·tion /ˌæprəˈbeɪʃən/ n [U] *formal* : praise or approval ▪ *winning the approbation of voters*

¹**ap·pro·pri·ate** /əˈprouprijət/ *adj* : right or suited for some purpose or situation ▪ *It's a formal occasion and appropriate attire is expected.* [=you are expected to wear formal clothing] ▪ *Is the movie appropriate for children (to see)? = Is it appropriate for children to see the movie?* — **ap·pro·pri·ate·ly** *adv* — **ap·pro·pri·ate·ness** *n* [U]

²**ap·pro·pri·ate** /əˈproupriˌeɪt/ *vb* **-at·ed; -at·ing** [T] **1** : to get or save (money) for a specific use or purpose ▪ *The town has appropriated funds to repair the bridge.* **2** : to take or use (something) especially in a way that is illegal, unfair, etc. ▪ *Corrupt officials have appropriated the country's resources for their own use.*

ap·pro·pri·a·tion /əˌproupriˈeɪʃən/ *n, formal* **1** [U] : the act of appropriating something ▪ *the appropriation of funds/resources* **2** [C] : an amount of money that is used or provided by a government for a specific purpose ▪ *the Senate Appropriations Committee*

ap·prov·al /əˈpruːvəl/ *n* **1** [U] : the belief that something or someone is good or acceptable ▪ *children looking for their parents' approval* ▪ *I hope that these arrangements* **meet with your approval.** [=I hope that they are acceptable to you] **2** [C/U] : permission to do something ▪ *Do I have your approval to make the changes?* ▪ *The company is seeking approval of the drug.* [=is seeking official permission to sell the drug]

ap·prove /əˈpruːv/ *vb* **-proved; -prov·ing** **1** [I] : to believe that something or someone is good or acceptable ▪ *I don't* **approve of** *the way he treats his wife.* **2** [T] : to officially accept (an idea, action, plan, etc.) ▪ *The state approved the building plans.* ▪ *Your application has been approved.*

approving *adj* : showing that you believe that something or someone is good or acceptable ▪ *an approving smile* — **ap·prov·ing·ly** /əˈpruːvɪŋli/ *adv*

approx. *abbr* approximate; approximately

¹**ap·prox·i·mate** /əˈprɑːksəmət/ *adj* : almost correct or exact ▪ *her approximate age* ▪ *Can you give me the approximate cost of the repair?* — **ap·prox·i·mate·ly** *adv*

²**ap·prox·i·mate** /əˈprɑːksəˌmeɪt/ *vb* **-mat·ed; -mat·ing** **1** [T/I] : to be very similar to but not exactly like (something) ▪ *The colors in the pictures can only approximate the real thing.* = *(chiefly Brit) The colors in the pictures can only approximate to the real thing.* **2** [T] : to calculate the almost exact value or position of (something) ▪ *approximating the distance between the Earth and the planets*

ap·prox·i·ma·tion /əˌprɑːksəˈmeɪʃən/ *n* [C] **1** : an amount, figure, etc., that is almost correct and is not intended to be exact ▪ *a rough approximation of the land's value* **2** : something that is similar to something else ▪ *The paint is a close approximation off/to the actual color of the flowers.*

appt. *abbr* appoint; appointed; appointment

ap·pur·te·nance /əˈpətənəns/ *n* [C] *formal* : an object that is used with or for something — usually plural ▪ *all the appurtenances of a well-equipped office*

Apr. *abbr* April

APR /ˌeɪˌpiːˈɑɚ/ *n* [singular] *business* : annual percentage rate : the rate at which interest on a loan is calculated over the period of a year

apri·cot /ˈæprəˌkɑːt, ˈeɪprəˌkɑːt/ *n* [C] : a small orange-colored fruit that is related to the peach and plum

April /ˈeɪprəl/ *n* [C/U] : the fourth month of the year ▪ *in (early/mid-/late) April* ▪ *We arrived on April the fourth.* = *(US) We arrived on April fourth.* = *We arrived on the fourth of April.* — abbr. **Apr.**

April Fools' Day *or* **April Fool's Day** *n* [singular] : April 1 celebrated as a day on which people play tricks on each other ▪ *an April Fool's (Day) joke/trick*

apron /ˈeɪprən/ *n* [C] : a piece of clothing that is worn on the front of the body over clothes to keep them from getting dirty ▪ *a cook's apron*

apron string *n* [C] : either one of a pair of strings that are attached to an apron and are used to keep it close to your body ▪ *(figurative) The company has relied on government support, but the government is now threatening to* **cut the apron strings.** [=to stop providing support to the company]

¹**ap·ro·pos** /ˌæprəˈpou/ *adj* : suitable or appropriate ▪ *an apropos comment*

²**apropos** *or* **apropos of** *prep* : with regard to (something) ▪ *Apropos (of) the proposed changes, I think more information is needed.*

apt /ˈæpt/ *adj* **1** : likely or tending *to do* something ▪ *He's apt to become angry if you wake him up.* **2** : appropriate or suitable ▪ *an apt remark* **3** : quick to learn ▪ *a very apt student* — **apt·ly** *adv* — **apt·ness** *n* [U]

apt. *abbr* **1** apartment **2** aptitude

ap·ti·tude /ˈæptəˌtuːd, Brit ˈæptəˌtjuːd/ *n* [C/U] : a natural ability to do something or to learn something ▪ *She has (an) aptitude for (learning) languages.* ▪ *an* **aptitude test** [=a test that shows how easily someone will be able to learn certain skills]

aqua·ma·rine /ˌɑːkwəməˈriːn/ *n* [C/U] : a light greenish-blue color — **aquamarine** *adj*

aquar·i·um /əˈkwerijəm/ *n, pl* **-i·ums** *or* **-ia** /-ijə/ [C] **1** : a glass or plastic container in which fish and other water animals and plants can live **2** : a building people can visit to see water animals and plants

Aquar·i·us /əˈkwerijəs/ *n* **1** [U] : the 11th sign of the zodiac that comes between Capricorn and Pisces and is symbolized by a person carrying a jug of water **2** [C] : a person born between January 20th and February 18th

aquat·ic /əˈkwɑːtɪk/ *adj* **1** : living or

found in or near water • *aquatic animals/ plants* **2** : of or relating to animals and plants that live in or near water • *aquatic biology* **3** : done in or on water • *aquatic sports*

aq·ue·duct /'ækwə,dʌkt/ *n* [C] : a structure that looks like a bridge and that is used to carry water over a valley; *also* : a pipe or channel that is used to bring water to an area

aqui·fer /'ækwəfər/ *n* [C] *technical* : a layer of rock or sand that can absorb and hold water

aq·ui·line /'ækwə,laɪn/ *adj* : like an eagle • *He has an aquiline nose.* [=a nose that has an angular shape like the beak of an eagle]

AR *abbr* Arkansas

Ar·ab /'erəb/ *n* [C] : a member of the people who are originally from the Arabian Peninsula — **Arab** *adj* • *Arab history*

Ara·bi·an /ə'reɪbijən/ *adj* : from or in Arabia • *the Arabian Desert* : connected with the Arab people • *Arabian culture*

Arabian horse *n* [C] : a type of horse originally from Arabia

Ar·a·bic /'erəbɪk/ *n* [U] : the language of the Arab people — **Arabic** *adj* • *the Arabic alphabet*

Arabic numeral *n* [C] : any one of the number symbols 1, 2, 3, 4, 5, 6, 7, 8, 9, and 0

ar·a·ble /'erəbəl/ *adj* : suitable for farming • *arable land*

arach·nid /ə'ræknəd/ *n* [C] *technical* : a kind of animal that has eight legs and a body formed of two parts • *Spiders, scorpions, and ticks are arachnids.*

ar·bi·ter /'ɑɚbətɚ/ *n* [C] **1** : a person who is considered to be an authority on what is right, good, or proper • *an arbiter of taste and style* **2** : a person who has the power to settle an argument between people • *She will act as the* **final arbiter** *in the matter.*

ar·bi·trary /'ɑɚbə,treri, Brit* 'ɑːbətrəri/ *adj* **1** : not made, planned, or chosen for a particular reason • *a completely arbitrary decision* **2** : done without concern for what is fair or right • *arbitrary arrests* — **ar·bi·trari·ly** /,ɑɚbə'treɪrəli, Brit* 'ɑːbətrərəli/ *adv* — **ar·bi·trari·ness** /'ɑɚbə,treɪrɪnəs, Brit* 'ɑːbətrərɪnəs/ *n* [U]

ar·bi·trate /'ɑɚbə,treɪt/ *vb* **-trat·ed; -trat·ing** [T/I] : to settle an argument between two people or groups after hearing the opinions and ideas of both • *arbitrate (a dispute) between managers and staff* — **ar·bi·tra·tion** /,ɑɚbə'treɪʃən/ *n* [U] • *a dispute settled by arbitration* — **ar·bi·tra·tor** /'ɑɚbə,treɪtɚ/ *n* [C]

ar·bor (*US*) *or Brit* **ar·bour** /'ɑɚbɚ/ *n* [C] : a shelter in a garden that plants grow over

ar·bo·re·al /ɑɚ'borijəl/ *adj* **1** *formal* : of or relating to trees • *arboreal images* **2** *technical* : living in trees • *an arboreal monkey*

ar·bo·re·tum /,ɑɚbə'ri:təm/ *n, pl* **-re·tums** *or* **-re·ta** /-'ri:tə/ [C] : a place where trees and plants are grown in order to be studied or seen by the public

¹**arc** /'ɑɚk/ *n* [C] : a line or shape that is curved like part of a circle • *He bent the twig into an arc.*

²**arc** *vb* **arced** /'ɑɚkt/; **arc·ing** /'ɑɚkɪŋ/ [I] : to move or lie in a curving path • *The arrow arced through the air.*

ar·cade /ɑɚ'keɪd/ *n* [C] **1** : a row of arches that are supported by columns **2** : a passageway or building with many shops **3** : a place with many games that can be played by putting coins in them • *an arcade game*

ar·cane /ɑɚ'keɪn/ *adj* : known or understood by only a few people • *an arcane ritual*

¹**arch** /'ɑɚtʃ/ *n* [C] **1** : a usually curved part of a structure that is over an opening **2** : the raised area on the bottom of the foot **3** : something that has a curved shape • *the slight arch of her eyebrows*

²**arch** *vb* [T/I] : to bend into the shape of an arch • *She arched her back.* • *The cat's back arched in fear.* • *arched ceilings*

³**arch** *adj* : having or showing an amused feeling of being superior to other people • *The book is never mocking or arch in its tone.* — **arch·ly** *adv* — **arch·ness** *n* [U]

arch- /,ɑɚtʃ/ *prefix* **1** : main or chief • *archbishop* • *archrival* **2** : extreme • *archconservative*

ar·chae·ol·o·gy *or chiefly US* **ar·che·ol·o·gy** /,ɑɚki'ɑːlədʒi/ *n* [U] : a science that studies the bones, tools, etc., of ancient people — **ar·chae·o·log·i·cal** *or* **ar·che·o·log·i·cal** /,ɑɚkiə'lɑːdʒɪkəl/ *adj* — **ar·chae·ol·o·gist** *or* **ar·che·ol·o·gist** /,ɑɚki'ɑːlədʒɪst/ *n* [C]

ar·cha·ic /ɑɚ'keɪɪk/ *adj* **1** : old and no longer used • *archaic words/customs* **2** : old and no longer useful • *an archaic computer system*

arch·an·gel /'ɑɚtʃ,eɪndʒəl/ *n* [C] : an angel of the highest rank

arch·bish·op /ɑɚtʃ'bɪʃəp/ *n* [C] : the bishop of highest rank in a particular area

arch·con·ser·va·tive /ɑɚtʃkən'sɚvətɪv/ *n* [C] : a person who is very conservative in politics — **archconservative** *adj*

arch·di·o·cese /ɑɚtʃ'dajəsəs/ *n* [C] : the area an archbishop is in charge of

arch·duch·ess /ɑɚtʃ'dʌtʃəs/ *n* [C] **1** : a princess of the royal family of Austria **2** : the wife of an archduke

arch·duke /ɑɚtʃ'du:k, Brit* ɑtʃ'dju:k/ *n* [C] : a prince of the royal family of Austria

arch·en·e·my /ɑɚtʃ'ɛnəmi/ *n, pl* **-mies** [C] : someone's main enemy • *The two men were archenemies.*

archeology *chiefly US spelling of* ARCHAEOLOGY

ar·chery /'ɑɚtʃəri/ *n* [U] : the sport or skill of shooting with a bow and arrow • *an archery contest* — **ar·cher** /'ɑɚtʃɚ/ *n* [C] • *a skilled archer*

ar·che·type /'ɑɚkɪ,taɪp/ *n* [C] : a perfect example of something • *an archetype of the modern family* — **ar·che·typ·al** /,ɑɚkɪ'taɪpəl/ *adj*

ar·chi·pel·a·go /,ɑɚkə'pɛlə,goʊ/ *n, pl* **-goes** *or* **-gos** [C] : a group of islands

ar·chi·tect /'ɑɚkə,tɛkt/ *n* [C] **1** : a person who designs buildings **2** : a person who designs and guides a plan, project, etc. ▪ *He is the chief architect of the country's foreign policy.*

ar·chi·tec·ture /ˈɑɚkəˌtɛktʃɚ/ *n* [U] **1** : the art or science of designing and creating buildings **2** : a method or style of building ▪ *The architecture of the building is modern.* — **ar·chi·tec·tur·al** /ˌɑɚkəˈtɛktʃərəl/ *adj* — **ar·chi·tec·tur·al·ly** *adv*

¹ar·chive /ˈɑɚˌkaɪv/ *n* [C] : a place in which public records or historical materials are kept ▪ *The original movie was stored in a film archive.; also* : the material that is stored in an archive ▪ *reading through the town's historical archives* — **ar·chi·val** /ɑɚˈkaɪvəl/ *adj*

²archive *vb* **-chived; -chiv·ing** [T] : to collect and store materials (such as recordings, documents, or computer files) so that they can be found and used when they are needed ▪ *cataloging and archiving printed materials*

ar·chi·vist /ˈɑɚkəvɪst/ *n* [C] : a person who has the job of collecting and storing the materials in an archive

arch·ri·val /ɑɚtʃˈraɪvəl/ *n* [C] : someone's main rival or opponent ▪ *The two teams are archrivals.*

arch·way /ˈɑɚtʃˌweɪ/ *n* [C] : a passage that goes under an arch

arc·tic /ˈɑɚktɪk/ *adj* **1** *or* **Arctic** *always before a noun* : of or relating to the region around the North Pole ▪ *Arctic exploration* **2** : very cold ▪ *arctic temperatures*

Arctic Circle *n* — **the Arctic Circle** : an imaginary line that goes around the Earth near the North Pole

ar·dent /ˈɑɚdnt/ *adj* : having or showing very strong feelings ▪ *ardent fans/supporters* — **ar·dent·ly** *adv*

ar·dor *(US) or chiefly Brit* **ar·dour** /ˈɑɚdɚ/ *n* **1** [C/U] : a strong feeling of energy or eagerness ▪ *She preached with the ardor of a true believer.* **2** [U] : a strong feeling of love ▪ *young love, with all its ardor and intensity*

ar·du·ous /ˈɑɚdʒəwəs/ *adj* : very difficult ▪ *arduous tasks* ▪ *an arduous journey across the desert* — **ar·du·ous·ly** *adv* — **ar·du·ous·ness** *n* [U]

are *see* BE

ar·ea /ˈerijə/ *n* **1** [C] **a** : a part or section of a larger place ▪ *the area surrounding the lake* ▪ *in many areas of the world* ▪ *a residential area* **b** : a section of space within a building, room, etc. ▪ *a work area in the kitchen* ▪ *The park had several picnic areas.* **2** [C] : a part of the surface of something (such as a person's body or a piece of cloth) ▪ *Choose a small area of the fabric to test first.* ▪ *pain in the shoulder/abdominal area* **3** [C] : a field of activity or study ▪ *Your question falls outside my area of expertise.* ▪ *areas of disagreement between the two sides* **4** [C/U] : the amount of space inside a shape, surface, region, room, etc. ▪ *calculating the area of a triangle* ▪ *The park is 2 square miles in area.* — **in the area of** : close to (an amount) ▪ *The project will cost (somewhere) in the area of $50,000.*

area code *n* [C] : a number that represents each telephone service area in a country

are·na /əˈriːnə/ *n* [C] **1** : a building for sports, concerts, etc., that has a large central area surrounded by seats ▪ *a basketball arena* **2** : an area of activity, interest, or competition ▪ *a tough political arena*

aren't /ˈɑɚnt, ˈɑɚənt/ **1** — used as a contraction of *are not* ▪ *We aren't ready to leave.* **2** — used in questions as a contraction of *am not* ▪ *Aren't I included too?* = *I'm included too, aren't I?* [=am I not also included?]

ar·gu·able /ˈɑɚgjuwəbəl/ *adj* **1** : able to be questioned ▪ *That is an arguable point of view.* **2** — used to say that there are good reasons for believing that a statement is true ▪ *It's arguable that he's the best writer of his generation.*

ar·gu·ably /ˈɑɚgjuwəbli/ *adv* — used to say that a statement is very possibly true even if it is not certainly true ▪ *He is arguably the best writer of his generation.*

ar·gue /ˈɑɚgju/ *vb* **-gued; -gu·ing 1** [T/I] : to give reasons for or against something : to say or write things in order to change someone's opinion about what is true, what should be done, etc. ▪ *She argued for/against the law.* ▪ *She argued that the war should end.* ▪ *You argue your case well.* ▪ *He argued in favor of lowering taxes.* **2** [I] : to disagree or fight by using angry words ▪ *Their neighbors often argue (with each other).* ▪ *They were arguing about/over politics.* **3** [I] : to express doubt or disagreement about something ▪ *You can't argue with her success.* [=you can't deny that she is successful] **4** [I] : to show that something is or is not necessary, appropriate, etc. ▪ *The result argues for/against a new approach.* [=shows that we do/don't need a new approach] — **ar·gu·er** *n* [C]

ar·gu·ment /ˈɑɚgjəmənt/ *n* **1 a** [C] : a statement or series of statements for or against something ▪ *They made a compelling argument for/against building a new school.* ▪ *the lawyer's closing argument at the trial* **b** [U] : a discussion in which people express different opinions about something ▪ *Let us accept, for the sake of argument, that she is right.* ▪ *I want to hear both sides of the argument.* **2** [C/U] : an angry disagreement ▪ *getting into arguments about/over politics* ▪ *They settled an argument that started in class.* ▪ *You'll get no argument from me.* [=I won't disagree] **3** [singular] : something which shows that something is or is not necessary, appropriate, etc. ▪ *The result is an argument for/against a new approach.* [=the result shows that we do/don't need to try a new approach]

ar·gu·men·ta·tion /ˌɑɚgjəmənˈteɪʃən/ *n* [U] *formal* : the act or process of making and presenting arguments ▪ *legal argumentation*

ar·gu·men·ta·tive /ˌɑɚgjəˈmɛntətɪv/ *adj* : having or showing a tendency to disagree with other people in an angry way ▪ *an argumentative person/essay*

ar·gy-bar·gy /ˌɑɚdʒiˈbɑɚdʒi/ *n* [U, singu-

lar] Brit, informal : an argument or disagreement • *They got into a bit of an argybargy.*

aria /ˈɑriə/ *n [C]* : a song sung by one person in an opera

ar·id /ˈerəd/ *adj* **1** : having very little rain or water • *an arid desert* **2** : lacking in interest and life • *an arid textbook —* **arid·i·ty** /əˈrɪdəti/ *n [U]*

Ar·i·es /ˈeriz/ *n, pl* **Aries** **1** *[U]* : the sign of the zodiac that comes between Pisces and Taurus and has a ram as its symbol **2** *[C]* : a person born between March 21 and April 19

arise /əˈraɪz/ *vb* **arose** /əˈrouz/; **aris·en** /əˈrɪzn/; **aris·ing** *[I]* **1 a** : to begin to occur or to exist • *A new opportunity arose.* • *The problems/conflict arose because of a misunderstanding.* • *Jobs will be created as/when the need arises.* [=jobs will be created when they are needed] **b** : to begin at a source • *The disease probably arose from a virus.* **2 a** : to get up from sleep or after lying down • *He arose refreshed after his nap.* **b** : to stand up • *She arose from her chair.* **3** : to move upward • *Mist arose from the valley.*

ar·is·toc·ra·cy /ˌerəˈstɑːkrəsi/ *n, pl* **-cies** *[C]* : the highest social class in some countries • *The duke was a member of the country's wealthy and powerful aristocracy.*

aris·to·crat /əˈrɪstəˌkræt/ *n [C]* : a member of an aristocracy • *an aristocrat by birth —* **aris·to·crat·ic** /əˌrɪstəˈkrætɪk/ *adj* • *aristocratic titles like "duke" and "duchess"*

arith·me·tic /əˈrɪθməˌtɪk/ *n [U]* **1** : mathematics that deals with addition, subtraction, multiplication, and division **2** : the act or process of calculating a number • *doing simple arithmetic —* **arith·met·ic** /ˌerɪθˈmetɪk/ *or* **ar·ith·met·i·cal** /ˌerɪθˈmetɪkəl/ *adj —* **ar·ith·met·i·cal·ly** /ˌerɪθˈmetɪkli/ *adv*

Ark /ˈɑɚk/ *n [singular] in the Bible* : the ship in which Noah and his family were saved from a great flood in ancient times • *Noah's Ark*

¹arm /ˈɑɚm/ *n [C]* **1 a** : either one of the two long body parts that join the top of your body at the shoulder and that end at the hand or wrist • *He has strong, muscular arms.* • *She stood with her arms crossed/folded.* • *She sat cradling the baby in her arms.* • *He took her in/into his arms* [=he embraced her] *and kissed her.* • *She found him in the arms of* [=being embraced by] *another woman.* • *He showed up at the party with a young woman on his arm.* [=holding his arm] • *walking down the street arm in arm* [=next to each other with the arm of one person linked at the elbow to the arm of another person] • *We were welcomed back with open arms.* [=in a very kind and friendly way] **b** : a part of a machine, structure, etc., that looks or moves like a human arm • *the robot's mechanical arm* **2 a** : the part of a shirt, coat, etc., that covers the arm • *The jacket's arms are too tight.* **b** : a part of a chair, couch, etc., that gives support for a person's arm • *the arm of the sofa* **3** : a gun or other weapon that is used especially in a war — usually plural • *The government was selling arms to other countries.* • *the right of individuals to carry/bear arms* [=firearms] • *an arms agreement/deal* • *an arms race* [=a situation in which countries that are enemies each try to build or collect weapons faster than the other can] • *The soldiers refused to lay down their arms.* [=to put down their weapons and stop fighting] • *They took up arms* [=they picked up weapons and became ready to fight] *to defend their city.* **4** : the part of a group or organization that performs a specific job or function — usually singular • *the organization's political arm* • *the military arm of the government —* **an arm and a leg** *informal* : a very large amount of money • *The car doesn't cost an arm and a leg.* [=it isn't too expensive] *— a shot in the arm* see **¹SHOT** *— at arm's length* : from a distance that is the length of a person's arm • *holding a candle at arm's length* • *(figurative) She kept him at arm's length.* [=she avoided being very close or friendly with him] *— call to arms* : a request or command to become ready to fight — often used for something that tries to make people fight for a cause • *Her book is a political call to arms.* *— in arms* ✧ If someone is your **brother/sister/comrade in arms**, that person has helped you fight an enemy especially in a war. • *He and I were brothers in arms.* [=we fought in a war together] *— the long arm of the law* : the ability of the police to find and catch people who commit crimes • *The long arm of the law finally caught up with him* [=the police caught him] *30 years later.* *— twist someone's arm* see **¹TWIST** *— up in arms* : angry and ready to fight or argue • *Voters were up in arms over the new taxes.*

²arm *vb* **1** *[T/I]* : to provide (yourself, a country, etc.) with weapons especially in order to fight a war or battle • *The fighters were armed by a foreign government.* • *She armed herself with a kitchen knife.* • *arming for battle* **2** *[T]* : to provide (someone) *with* a way of fighting, competing, or succeeding • *arming women with the right to vote* **3** *[T]* : to make (a bomb, weapon, etc.) ready for use • *Once the bomb has been armed, we have five minutes to escape.*

ar·ma·da /ɑɚˈmɑːdə/ *n [C]* : a large group of ships, boats, etc. • *an armada of fishing boats*

ar·ma·dil·lo /ˌɑɚməˈdɪloʊ/ *n, pl* **-los** *[C]* : a small American animal whose head and body are protected by a hard shell

Ar·ma·ged·don /ˌɑɚməˈgedn/ *n [U, singular]* : a final destructive battle or conflict • *the threat of (a) nuclear Armageddon* [=a nuclear war that would destroy the world]

ar·ma·ment /ˈɑɚməmənt/ *n* **1** *[U]* : the process of preparing for war by producing and obtaining weapons • *The country's armament will take years.* **2** *[plural]* : military weapons that are used to fight a war • *a nation with adequate armaments*

¹**arm·chair** /ˈɑəmˌtʃeɚ/ n [C] : a chair with supports for your arms

²**armchair** adj, always before a noun **1** — used to describe people who like to read about or watch the dangerous or exciting activities of other people ▪ an armchair adventurer/traveler **2** — used to describe people who like to give opinions about matters they do not have to deal with themselves ▪ armchair strategists

¹**armed** /ˈɑəmd/ adj **1** : involving the use of weapons ▪ an armed conflict/uprising ▪ He's in jail for armed robbery. [=robbery while carrying a gun or other weapon] **2** : carrying weapons ▪ The building is surrounded by armed guards/soldiers. ▪ She wasn't armed. [=she wasn't carrying a weapon] ▪ The car was armed with explosives. ▪ The police said that the suspects are armed and dangerous. ▪ heavily armed men = men who are armed to the teeth [=men who are carrying many dangerous weapons] **3** : having something that provides security or strength ▪ journalists armed with cameras and notebooks

²**armed** adj : having arms of a specific kind or number — used in combination ▪ a long-armed boxer

armed forces n [plural] : the military organizations (such as the army, navy, and air force) of a country ▪ a long career in the armed forces — called also armed services

arm·ful /ˈɑəmˌfʊl/ n, pl **arm·fuls** also **arms·ful** /ˈɑəmzˌfʊl/ [C] : an amount that can be carried in a person's arm or arms ▪ carrying an armful of books

arm·hole /ˈɑəmˌhoʊl/ n [C] : an opening for the arm in a piece of clothing

arm·mi·stice /ˈɑəmstəs/ n [C] : an agreement to stop fighting a war

ar·moire /ɑəmˈwɑɚ/ n [C] : a tall piece of furniture that usually has two doors and that is used to store things (such as clothes)

ar·mor (US) or Brit **ar·mour** /ˈɑəmə/ n [U] **1** : special clothing that people wear to protect their bodies from weapons ▪ The officers wear bulletproof body armor. ▪ the heavy metal suits of armor worn by medieval knights ▪ (figurative) We've found some **chinks in its/their armor**. [=weaknesses that might cause it/them to fail or to be defeated] **2** : a hard covering that protects something (such as a vehicle or an animal) ▪ The shots penetrated/pierced the tank's armor. ▪ an armor-plated vehicle [=a vehicle that is covered in flat pieces of metal]

ar·mored (US) or Brit **ar·moured** /ˈɑəmə·d/ adj **1** : covered in flat pieces of metal for protection ▪ armored cars/ trucks **2** a : having soldiers and vehicles that are protected with armor ▪ Additional armored divisions were deployed. **b** : using soldiers and vehicles that are protected with armor ▪ an armored assault/ attack

ar·mory (US) or Brit **ar·moury** /ˈɑəməri/ n, pl **-mor·ies** [C] **1** : a supply of weapons ▪ the nation's nuclear armory **2** : a place where weapons are made or kept; especially, US : a place where weapons

are kept and where soldiers are trained ▪ a National Guard armory

arm·pit /ˈɑəmˌpɪt/ n [C] **1** : the hollow area on a person's body beneath the place where the arm and the shoulder meet — called also underarm **2** US, informal : the worst area in a place ▪ The area is the armpit of the city.

arm·rest /ˈɑəmˌrɛst/ n [C] : the part of a seat in a car, an airplane, etc., that supports your arm

arm–twist·ing /ˈɑəmˌtwɪstɪŋ/ n [U] informal : the act of using pressure to make people do things that they do not want to do ▪ There was a lot of political arm-twisting before the Senate vote.

arm wrestling n [U] : a contest in which two people sit facing each other and join usually their right hands together and then try to force each other's arm down — **arm wrestler** n [C]

ar·my /ˈɑəmi/ n, pl **-mies** [C] **1 a** : a large group of soldiers organized to fight battles on land ▪ the armies of Alexander the Great **b** : the part of a country's military forces that includes soldiers who are trained to fight on land ▪ He joined the army. ▪ the U.S. Army, Navy, Air Force, and Marines **2** : a large number of people or things that are involved in some activity together ▪ a dedicated army of volunteers

aro·ma /əˈroʊmə/ n [C] : a usually pleasant smell ▪ the aroma of fresh-baked bread

aro·ma·ther·a·py /əˌroʊməˈθerəpi/ n [U] : the use of oils that have a pleasant smell to make a person feel better

ar·o·mat·ic /ˌerəˈmætɪk/ adj : having a pleasant smell ▪ aromatic herbs/oils

arose past tense of ARISE

¹**around** /əˈraʊnd/ adv **1 a** : in a circle ▪ The wheel went/turned around (and around). **b** : in, along, or through a curving path ▪ Don't take the long way around: I know a shortcut. **c** chiefly US — used to indicate a measurement that is made along the outer surface of something circular ▪ "How big around is the tree?" "It's five feet around." **2** — used to indicate that a number, amount, time, etc., is not exact or certain ▪ The repair should cost around $200. ▪ We got home at around 8 o'clock. **3 a** : in close from all sides so as to surround someone or something ▪ People crowded around to hear her. **b** : in many different directions ▪ They wandered around for hours. ▪ He entered the room and looked around. **c** : in or to many different places ▪ His tools were scattered around carelessly. ▪ Welcome to our home: let me show you around. **d** : in or near a particular area or place ▪ We went inside, but no one was around. [=no one was there] ▪ Let's wait/ stick around awhile. ▪ So long, then! (I'll) **See you around!** [=I'll see you later] **e** : to a particular place ▪ Why don't you come around (to my house) for dinner? **4** : in the opposite direction ▪ She turned (completely) around. **5** — used with some verbs to indicate repeated or continued action or behavior that does not have a clear or definite purpose ▪ He's al-

ways joking around when he should be serious. • *Don't play/fool around with your food!* • *I was just standing around, waiting for the bus.* **6** — used to describe something that returns in a regular or repeated way • *Winter has come around again.* **7** — used to describe how two things are arranged or ordered • *You put the fork on the right and the knife on the left. They should be the other way around.* [=the fork should be on the left and the knife on the right]

²**around** *prep* **1 a :** on all sides of (something or someone) • *a house with trees (all) around it* • *They stood around the table.* **b :** so as to circle or surround (something or someone) • *He tied the rope around his waist.* : moving so as to circle (something or someone) • *sailing around the world* **c :** over or in different parts of (a place) • *She traveled (all) around the country.* • *You can find lots of good restaurants around here.* • *I often help her around the house.* **d :** on or to another side of (something) • *There's another door around near to the back of the house.* **2 a :** in the area near to (something or someone) • *Fish are abundant around* [=about, near] *the reefs.* • *I feel happier when I'm around her.* • *He's not from around here.* **b :** near or not far from (something) in time • *The company was founded (at) around the turn of the century.* **3 :** so as to avoid or get past (something) • *She went around the puddle.* • *We found a way around their objections.* **4** — used to indicate the central part or idea used for building or organizing something • *a society built around kinship ties*

³**around** *adj, not before a noun* **:** existing or active • *She is among the best artists around today.* • *This building has been around* [=has existed] *for hundreds of years.* • *I can tell you've been around.* [=that you have had many different experiences and know a lot about the world] — *up and around* see ²UP

around–the–clock *adj, always before a noun, chiefly US* **:** happening or continuing all day and all night • *The patient requires around-the-clock care.*

arouse /ə'raʊz/ *vb* **aroused; arous·ing** [T] **1 :** to cause (an arousal or mental state) • *He tried to sneak about without arousing suspicion.* [=without making people suspicious] • *Their comments aroused our curiosity.* [=made us curious] **2 :** to excite (someone) sexually • *The sound of her voice always aroused him.* **3 a :** to wake (someone) from sleep • *I was aroused by a loud noise.* **b :** to cause (someone) to become active, ready, or upset • *Their proposal is certain to arouse the opposition.* — **arous·al** /ə'raʊzəl/ *n* [U] • *sexual arousal* — **arousing** *adj*

ar·raign /ə'reɪn/ *vb* [T] *law* **:** to state the charges against someone who is accused of a crime in a formal procedure before a judge • *He was arraigned on charges of manslaughter.* — **ar·raign·ment** /ə'reɪnmənt/ *n* [C/U]

ar·range /ə'reɪndʒ/ *vb* **-ranged; -ranging** **1** [T] **a :** to move and organize

(things) into a particular order or position • *arranging flowers in a vase* • *The books are arranged according to their subject.* = *The books are arranged by subject.* **b :** to give a particular order or position to the parts of (something) • *They arranged the room around a fireplace.* **2** [T/I] **:** to organize the details of something before it happens • *All of the details were arranged in advance.* • *I think we can arrange a deal.* • *She arranged for a car to pick us up at our house.* • *They arranged to meet each other at the restaurant.* **3** [T] *music* **:** to change (a song, a musical, etc.) so that it can be performed by particular voices or instruments • *He arranged her last two albums.* — **ar·rang·er** /ə'reɪndʒɚ/ *n* [C] • *a funeral arranger* • *a talented arranger of musicals*

arranged marriage *n* [C] **:** a marriage in which the husband and wife are chosen for each other by their parents

ar·range·ment /ə'reɪndʒmənt/ *n* **1** [C/U] **:** the way that things or people are organized for a particular purpose or activity • *the arrangement of furniture in the room* • *a chronological arrangement of historical events* • *The family had very unusual living arrangements.* • *the seating arrangements for the dinner party* **2** [C/U] **:** something that is done to prepare or plan for something in the future • *She has her secretary handle/make all of her travel arrangements.* **3** [C] **:** a usually informal agreement • *business/financial arrangements* • *Our band has an arrangement with the club's manager.* **4** [C] **:** something made by putting things together and organizing them • *a flower/floral arrangement* = *an arrangement of flowers* **5** [C] *music* **:** a piece of music that has been changed so that it can be performed by particular types of voices or instruments • *orchestral/vocal arrangements*

ar·rant /'erənt/ *adj, always before a noun, somewhat old-fashioned + literary* **:** of the worst kind — used to make a statement more forceful • *This is arrant nonsense!*

¹**ar·ray** /ə'reɪ/ *n* [C] **1 :** a large group or number of things — usually singular • *They offer a wide array of products.* **2** *technical* **:** a group of devices that together form a unit • *an array of batteries*

²**array** *vb* [T] *formal* **1 :** to place a group of things in a particular position so that they are in order or so that they look attractive • *The table was arrayed with fruits and cheeses.* [=fruits and cheeses were placed attractively on the table] **2** *literary* **:** to dress (someone, especially yourself) in fine clothing • *She arrayed herself in rich velvets and satins.* **3 :** to put (soldiers) in a place or position so that they are ready to attack • *The troops were arrayed along the hilltop.*

ar·rears /ə'riɚz/ *n* [*plural*] **1 :** money that is owed and that has not been paid when it should be • *He's been trying to pay off the arrears on his mortgage.* **2** — used to describe a situation in which someone has failed to make a regular payment at the required time • *He is two months in arrears with his mortgage pay-*

ments. ▪ *He has fallen* **into arrears** *on his mortgage payments.* **3** — used to describe a situation in which someone is paid money that was earned at an earlier time ▪ *construction workers paid in* **arrears** *for their work*

¹**ar·rest** /ə'rɛst/ *vb* [T] **1 :** to use the power of the law to take and keep (someone, such as a criminal) usually in a jail ▪ *The police arrested him on drug charges.* ▪ *He got/was arrested.* **2** *formal* **:** to stop the progress or movement of (something) ▪ *The drugs can't arrest the disease's progress.* **3** *formal* **:** to attract and hold the attention of (someone or something) ▪ *My attention was arrested by a sudden movement.* — **ar·rest·ing** /ə'rɛstɪŋ/ *adj* ▪ *an arresting* [=eye-catching] *painting/image*

²**arrest** *n* [C/U] **1 :** the act of legally taking and keeping someone (such as a criminal) ▪ *The police are investigating the case but they have not yet made any arrests.* ▪ *She was charged with resisting arrest.* ▪ *The police placed/put her* **under arrest.** [=the police arrested her] **2** *medical* **:** an occurrence in which a part of the body suddenly stops working ▪ *The patient went into* **cardiac arrest.** [=the patient's heart stopped beating]

ar·riv·al /ə'raɪvəl/ *n* **1** [C/U] **:** the act of coming to or reaching a place : the act of arriving ▪ *awaiting the arrival of guests* ▪ *We checked into the hotel upon (our) arrival.* ▪ *The flight's estimated time of arrival is 11:30.* ▪ *airport arrivals and departures* **2** [C] **:** someone or something that has arrived at a place ▪ *They were late arrivals at the party.* ▪ *We went to the hospital to see the family's* **new arrival.** [=the family's new baby] **3** [U] **:** the time when something begins or happens ▪ *They are eagerly awaiting the arrival of their wedding day.*

ar·rive /ə'raɪv/ *vb* **-rived; -riv·ing** [I] **1 :** to come to or reach a place after traveling, being sent, etc. ▪ *Their flight is due to arrive in Boston at 11:30.* ▪ *The train from New York is now arriving.* ▪ *The mail hasn't arrived yet.* **2 a** *of a day, season, time, etc.* **:** to happen or begin ▪ *The day of their wedding has almost arrived.* **b** *of a baby* **:** to be born ▪ *When is their baby expected to arrive?* **3 :** to become successful — used with a form of *have* ▪ *After years of climbing the corporate ladder, he felt he had finally arrived.* — **arrive at** [*phrasal vb*] **:** to make or reach (a decision, conclusion, etc.) after a lot of thought or effort ▪ *I hope we can arrive at some sort of understanding.*

ar·ro·gance /'ɛrəgəns/ *n* [U, *singular*] **:** an insulting way of thinking or behaving that comes from believing that you are better, smarter, or more important than other people ▪ *Her arrogance has earned her a lot of enemies.* — **ar·ro·gant** /'ɛrəgənt/ *adj* ▪ *an arrogant person/remark/attitude* — **ar·ro·gant·ly** *adv*

ar·row /'ɛroʊ/ *n* [C] **1 :** a weapon that is made to be shot from a bow and that is usually a stick with a point at one end and feathers at the other end ▪ *shoot an*

arrow **2 :** a mark (such as →) that is shaped like an arrow and that is used to show direction ▪ *The arrow on the map points north.* — see also STRAIGHT ARROW

ar·row·head /'ɛroʊˌhɛd/ *n* [C] **:** a piece of stone or metal that forms the point of an arrow

ar·row·root /'ɛroʊˌruːt/ *n* [U] **:** a powdery substance that is used in cooking to make liquids thicker

arse /'ɑɚs/ *n* [C] *Brit, informal + offensive* **:** ASS 3

ar·se·nal /'ɑɚsənəl/ *n* [C] **1 a :** a collection of weapons ▪ *the nation's nuclear arsenal* **b :** a place where weapons are made or stored ▪ *a federal arsenal* **2 :** a group of things or people that are available to be used ▪ *the team's arsenal of talented players*

ar·se·nic /'ɑɚsənɪk/ *n* [U] **:** a poisonous chemical

ar·son /'ɑɚsn/ *n* [C/U] **:** the crime of burning a building or other property ▪ *committing arson* — **ar·son·ist** /'ɑɚsnɪst/ *n* [C] ▪ *The fire was set by an arsonist.*

art /'ɑɚt/ *n* **1** [U] **:** something that is created with imagination and skill and that is beautiful or that expresses important ideas or feelings ▪ *a piece of modern/contemporary art* **2** [U] **:** works created by artists ▪ *the art of Picasso* ▪ *African art* ▪ *an art museum/collector* **3** [U] **:** the methods and skills used for painting, sculpting, drawing, etc. ▪ *He studied art in college.* ▪ *an art teacher* **4 a** [C] **:** an activity that is done to create something beautiful or to express important ideas or feelings ▪ *the art of painting/dance* ▪ *the performing/visual arts* **b the arts :** painting, music, theater, etc., considered as a group of activities done by people with skill and imagination ▪ *funding for the arts* **5** [C] **:** a skill that someone learns through experience or study — usually singular ▪ *the art of conversation* ▪ *Writing letters has become a* **lost art.** [=not many people write letters anymore] **6** [C] **:** an activity that requires special knowledge or skill ▪ *Cooking is both an art and a science.* **7** [*plural*] **:** areas of study (such as history, language, and literature) that are intended to develop the mind in a general way ▪ *the College of Arts and Sciences*

Art de·co *or* **Art Deco** /ˌɑɚt'dɛkoʊ/ *n* [U] **:** a style of art, design, and architecture that was popular in the U.S. and Europe in the 1920s and 1930s ▪ *an Art Deco vase/building*

artefact *chiefly Brit spelling of* ARTIFACT

ar·te·rio·scle·ro·sis /ɑɚˌtɪrioʊskləˈroʊsəs/ *n* [U] **:** a disease in which the walls of arteries become thick and hard

ar·tery /'ɑɚtəri/ *n, pl* **-ter·ies** [C] **1 :** any one of the tubes that carry blood from the heart to all parts of the body ▪ *clogged/coronary arteries* **2 :** a large road, railroad line, etc. ▪ *local roads and major arteries* — **ar·te·ri·al** /ɑɚ't ̄irijəl/ *adj* ▪ *arterial walls/pressure*

art·ful /'ɑɚtfəl/ *adj* **1 :** done with or showing artistic skill ▪ *an artful performance* **2** *sometimes disapproving* **:** getting or achieving things in ways that are clever and not noticeable • *artful questioning/deception* • *an artful politician* — **art·ful·ly** /ˈɑətfəli/ *adv* — **art·ful·ness** *n* [U]

ar·thri·tis /ɑəˈθraɪtəs/ *n* [U] : a disease that causes the joints of the body to become swollen and painful — **ar·thrit·ic** /ɑəˈθrɪtɪk/ *adj* — **arthritis** *n* [C] • *medicines for arthritics* [=for people who have arthritis]

ar·ti·choke /ˈɑətəˌtʃoʊk/ *n* [C] : a vegetable with a soft middle part that is surrounded by thick, pointed leaves

ar·ti·cle /ˈɑətɪkəl/ *n* [C] **1** : a piece of writing about a particular subject that is included in a magazine, newspaper, etc. • *a magazine/newspaper article on/about the city's history* **2** : a particular kind of object • *an article of clothing* • (*figurative*) *an article of faith* [=something that is believed without being questioned or doubted] • (*figurative*) *Some people pretend to be cowboys, but he's* **the genuine article.** [=he's a real cowboy] **3** : a separate part of a legal document that deals with a single subject • *Article 3 of the U.S. Constitution* **4** *grammar* : a word (such as *a, an,* or *the*) that is used with a noun to show whether or not the noun refers to a specific person or thing

¹**ar·tic·u·late** /ɑəˈtɪkjələt/ *adj* : able to express ideas clearly and effectively in speech or writing • *She's an intelligent and articulate speaker.* **2** : clearly expressed and easily understood • *an articulate argument/essay/speech* • *The baby is now forming articulate words.* — **ar·tic·u·late·ly** *adv*

²**ar·tic·u·late** /ɑəˈtɪkjəˌleɪt/ *vb* **-lat·ed; -lat·ing** **1** [T] : to express (something, such as an idea) in words • *He had some trouble articulating his thoughts.* **2** [T/I] : to say or pronounce (something, such as a word) in a way that can be clearly heard and understood • *She spoke slowly, articulating each syllable.* **3** [I] *technical* : to connect with a joint • *the bones that articulate with the knee*

ar·tic·u·lat·ed /ɑəˈtɪkjəˌleɪtəd/ *adj* **1** : connected by a joint • *dolls with articulated limbs* [=arms and legs that can be moved because they are connected by joints] **2** *of a vehicle* : having front and back sections that are connected by means of a joint that allows sharp turns • (*Brit*) *articulated lorries*

ar·tic·u·la·tion /ɑəˌtɪkjəˈleɪʃən/ *n* **1** *formal* : the act of expressing an idea, thought, etc., in words • *The book is the articulation of his vision.* **b** : the act of saying or pronouncing something in a way that can be clearly heard and understood • *the articulation of consonants* **2** [C] : a joint that allows connected parts (such as bones) to move • *the articulations between vertebrae*

ar·ti·fact (*chiefly US*) *or Brit* **ar·te·fact** /ˈɑətɪˌfækt/ *n* [C] **1** : a simple object that was made by people in the past • *The caves contained prehistoric tools and other artifacts.* **2** : an accidental effect that causes incorrect results • *The drop in scores was just an artifact of the way the test was given.*

ar·ti·fice /ˈɑətəfəs/ *n* [C/U] : dishonest behavior or speech that is meant to deceive someone • *He spoke without artifice or pretense.* • *political/legal artifices*

ar·ti·fi·cial /ˌɑətəˈfɪʃl/ *adj* **1** : not natural or real • *artificial lighting/plants* **2** : created or caused by people • *The country's borders are artificial.* **3** : not sincere • *an artificial smile* — **ar·ti·fi·ci·al·i·ty** /ˌɑətəˌfɪʃiˈæləti/ *n* [U] — **ar·ti·fi·cial·ly** *adv* • *artificially flavored/colored foods*

artificial insemination *n* [U] : a medical process in which semen is used to make a woman or female animal pregnant without having sex

artificial intelligence *n* [U] *computers* : the power of a machine to copy intelligent human behavior • *a robot with artificial intelligence* — abbr. *AI*

artificial respiration *n* [U] *medical* : a process in which air is forced into and out of the lungs of a person who has stopped breathing

ar·til·lery /ɑəˈtɪləri/ *n* [U] **1** : large guns that are used to shoot over a great distance • *The troops were being bombarded by artillery.* • *heavy artillery fire* • (*figurative*) *His first argument didn't work, so he brought out the* **heavy artillery.** [=he started using a more powerful argument] **2** : the part of an army that uses artillery • *artillery units*

ar·ti·san /ˈɑətəzən, *Brit* ˌɑːtɪˈzæn/ *n* [C] : a person who is skilled at making things by hand • *rugs made by local artisans*

art·ist /ˈɑətɪst/ *n* [C] **1** : a person who creates art especially by painting, drawing, etc. • *famous artists and musicians* **2** : a skilled performer • *a trapeze artist* • *recording artists* [=singers and musicians who record their music] **3** : a person who is very good at something • *a scam artist*

ar·tiste /ɑəˈtiːst/ *n* [C] *chiefly Brit* : a skilled performer

ar·tis·tic /ɑəˈtɪstɪk/ *adj* **1** : relating to art or artists • *He has real artistic talent.* **2** : having or showing the skill of an artist • *She's an artistic person.* [=a creative person] — **ar·tis·ti·cal·ly** /ɑəˈtɪstɪkli/ *adv*

art·ist·ry /ˈɑətəstri/ *n* [U] **1** : artistic ability or skill • *the singer's artistry* **2** : a quality that results from artistic ability or skill • *the artistry of her novel*

art·less /ˈɑətləs/ *adj* : not false or artificial • *her simple artless charm* — **art·less·ly** *adv* — **art·less·ness** *n* [U]

art nou·veau *or* **Art Nouveau** /ˌɑətnuˈvoʊ/ *n* [U] : a style of art, design, and architecture that was popular in the U.S. and Europe in the late 1800s • *an Art Nouveau lamp*

arts and crafts *n* [*plural*] : objects that are meant to be both useful and beautiful • *They sell local arts and crafts, such as pottery and baskets.*

art·sy /ˈɑətsi/ *adj* **art·si·er; -est** *chiefly US, informal* + *usually disapproving* : ARTY • *The movie is too artsy for me.*

art·work /ˈɑətˌwək/ *n* **1** [C/U] : a piece of art • *an original artwork* • *A local painter was selling her artwork on the street.* **2**

[U] : drawings, photographs, etc., included in books, magazines, and newspapers

art·y /'ɑɚti/ *adj* **art·i·er; -est** *informal + usually disapproving* : artistic in a way that seems insincere or too extreme ▪ *an arty intellectual*

aru·gu·la /ə'ru:gələ, *Brit* ə'ru:gjələ/ *n* [U] *US* : a plant with strongly flavored leaves that are eaten in salads

¹**as** /'æz, əz/ *adv* : to the same degree or amount ▪ *He has a lot of time but I don't have as much.* [=I have less time than he has] ▪ *He was angry, but she was just as angry.* [=she was angry to the same degree that he was angry]

²**as** *conj* **1 a** — used to make comparisons ▪ *The fabric was soft as silk.* [=the softness of the fabric was like the softness of silk] — usually used in the phrase **as . . . as** ▪ *The fabric was as soft as silk.* ▪ *Her second book is twice as long as her first one.* ▪ *There are as many books here as (there are) there.* **b** — used in the phrase **as . . . as** to say when something should be done, how often something should happen, etc. ▪ *Come back as often as you like.* ▪ *Please call me as soon/early/quickly as possible.* **2 a** : in the way that ▪ *The letter "k" is sometimes silent, as (it is) in "knee."* ▪ *I'll do it as I planned (to).* ▪ *We planned a picnic but, as it happened, it rained that day.* [=it happened to rain that day] ▪ *As it turned out, all the tickets were already sold.* [=we learned that all the tickets were already sold] **b** — used to introduce a statement which indicates that something being mentioned was known, expected, etc. ▪ *Just as I suspected/thought! You've been drinking!* **c** — used in phrases with *same* ▪ *He works in the same building as my sister.* [=he and my sister work in the same building] ▪ *She was fooled the same as I was.* [=she and I were both fooled] **3** : while or when ▪ *I met him as I was leaving.* **4** : regardless of the degree to which ▪ *Improbable as it seems, it's still true.* ▪ (*chiefly US*) *As much as I respect him, I still disagree with him.* ▪ *Try as she might* [=no matter how hard she tried], *she couldn't do it.* **5** *formal* : for the reason that : BECAUSE ▪ *She stayed home as she had no car.* **6** — used to indicate that one relationship is like another relationship ▪ *A puppy is to a dog as a kitten is to a cat.* **7** — used with *so* or *such* to indicate the result or effect of something ▪ *The evidence is such as to leave* [=the evidence leaves] *no doubt of his guilt.* ▪ *He is so clearly guilty as to leave no doubt.* — **as for** : with regard to ▪ *She's here. As for the others, they'll arrive later.* [=the others will arrive later] — **as from** *chiefly Brit* — used to indicate the time or date when something begins ▪ *The new law takes effect as from* [=as of] *July 1.* — **as if or as though 1** : the way it would be if ▪ *The plane looked as if it was going to crash.* ▪ *It seemed as though the day would never end.* **2** : as someone would do if ▪ *He ran as if ghosts were chasing him.* **3** — used in spoken phrases to say that something is not true, will not happen, etc. ▪ *"She's afraid you might quit." "As if I ever would!"* [=I never would] ▪ *"He'll never come back, you know!" "As if I cared!"* [=I don't care] **4** ◆ The phrase *as if* is sometimes used informally as an interjection to say that something suggested or claimed is impossible or very unlikely. ▪ *"He thinks you like him." "As if!"* [=I don't like him at all] — **as is** *chiefly US* : in the present condition without any changes ▪ *The car is being sold as is.* — **as it is 1** : in the present condition ▪ *Leave everything exactly/just as it is.* **2** : with the situation that exists now ▪ *We have enough to do as it is without your latest orders!* — **as it were** — used to say that a statement is true in a certain way even if it is not completely true ▪ *His retirement was, as it were, the beginning of his real career.* — **as of** — used to indicate the time or date when something begins ▪ *The new law takes effect as of July 1.* — **as to 1** : ²ABOUT ▪ *I'm at a loss as to how to explain the error.* [=I don't know how to explain the error] **2** : ACCORDING TO, BY ▪ *The eggs are graded as to size and color.* — **so as** — used to indicate the purpose of something ▪ *He defended himself so as to prove his innocence.*

³**as** *prep* **1** — used to indicate how a person or thing appears, is thought of, etc. ▪ *They regarded/described the situation as (being) a disaster.* ▪ *Many people now think of him as a traitor.* **2** — used to indicate the condition, role, job, etc., of someone or something ▪ *She has a job as an editor.* ▪ *The policeman disguised himself as a beggar.* ▪ *his performance as Othello* ▪ *Everyone rose as one.* [=everyone rose together]

ASAP /ˌeɪˌɛsˌeɪ'pi:, 'eɪˌsæp/ *abbr* as soon as possible — used in informal contexts ▪ *Write ASAP.*

as·bes·tos /æs'bɛstəs/ *n* [U] : a soft gray mineral that was used as a building material in the past and that can cause serious diseases of the lungs when people breathe its dust

as·cend /ə'sɛnd/ *vb* **1** [T/I] *formal* : to go up toward the sky ▪ *balloons slowly ascending into the sky* ▪ *The climbers ascended the mountain in less than four hours.* **2** [I] : to slope or lead upward ▪ *stairs ascending to the attic* **3** [T/I] : to rise *to* a higher or more powerful position in a government, company, etc. ▪ *A new national government ascended to power.* [=it gained control of the country] ▪ *John Adams ascended to the presidency in 1797.* ▪ *He ascended (to) the throne* [=he became the king] *after the death of his father.* — **in ascending order** : arranged in a series that begins with the least or smallest and ends with the greatest or largest ▪ *The children were lined up in ascending order of height.* — **as·cen·dance** /ə'sɛndəns/ *n* [U] *chiefly US* ▪ *his ascendance to the throne*

as·cen·dan·cy *also* **as·cen·den·cy** /ə'sɛndənsi/ *n* [U] *formal* : a position of power in which someone can control or influence other people ▪ *She gained (the) ascendancy in the debate.*

as·cen·dant /ə'sɛndənt/ *n* — **in the as-**

cendant formal : becoming more powerful ▪ *Their party is no longer in the ascendant.*

as·cen·sion /əˈsɛnʃən/ n [singular] : the act of rising or ascending; *especially* : the act of moving to a higher or more powerful position ▪ *the ascension of women in society*

as·cent /əˈsɛnt/ n [C] **1** : the act or process of ascending: such as **a** : the act or process of rising, moving, or climbing up ▪ *The elevator began its ascent to the top floor.* **b** : the act or process of moving to a higher or more powerful position ▪ *the ascent and decline of the world's great civilizations* **2** : an upward slope, path, etc. ▪ *They followed a steep ascent to the top of the hill.*

as·cer·tain /ˌæsərˈteɪn/ vb [T] formal : to learn or find out (something, such as information or the truth) ▪ *The police are attempting to ascertain his whereabouts.* [=to find out where he is]

as·cet·ic /əˈsɛtɪk/ adj, formal : relating to or having a strict and simple way of living that avoids physical pleasure ▪ *the ascetic life of monks* — **ascetic** n [C] ▪ *the life of an ascetic* — **as·cet·i·cism** /əˈsɛtəˌsɪzəm/ n [U]

as·cribe /əˈskraɪb/ vb **-cribed; -crib·ing** — **ascribe to** [phrasal vb] **ascribe (something) to** formal : to say or think that (something) is caused by, comes from, or is associated with (something or someone) ▪ *The author ascribes the economy's success to the government.* [=the author says that the government is responsible for the economy's success] ▪ *qualities that are usually ascribed to men*

asex·u·al /eɪˈsɛkʃəwəl/ adj **1** : not having or including sex ▪ *an asexual relationship* **2** technical : of or relating to a kind of reproduction that does not involve the combining of male and female cells ▪ *asexual plants/reproduction* — **asex·u·al·ly** /eɪˈsɛkʃəwəli/ adv

ash /ˈæʃ/ n **1 a** [C/U] : the soft gray powder that remains after something has been completely destroyed by fire ▪ *hot volcanic ash* ▪ *cigarette ashes* **b** [plural] : the burned parts that remain when something is destroyed ▪ *The city was reduced/burned to ashes by the fire.* ▪ (figurative) *The nation rose from the ashes of war and began to rebuild itself.* **c** [plural] : the remains of a dead human body after it has been burned or cremated ▪ *He asked to have his ashes scattered along the river.* **2 a** [C] : a type of tree that grows in northern parts of the world **b** [U] : the hard wood of an ash tree ▪ *baseball bats made of ash*

ashamed /əˈʃeɪmd/ adj, not before a noun **1** : feeling shame or guilt ▪ *He was deeply ashamed of/about his behavior.* ▪ *You ought to be ashamed (of yourself)!* **2** : not wanting to do something because of shame or embarrassment ▪ *We were too ashamed to go back to school.* ▪ *I'm ashamed to admit it, but I still don't know how to ride a bicycle.*

ash·en /ˈæʃən/ adj : having a pale light gray color because of sickness, fear, etc. ▪ *She was ashen with fear.*

ashore /əˈʃoɚ/ adv : on or to the shore of an ocean, sea, lake, or river ▪ *We docked our boat and went ashore.*

ash·tray /ˈæʃˌtreɪ/ n [C] : a small dish or other container that is used as a place to put cigarettes and cigars and their ashes

Ash Wednesday n [U] : the first day of the Christian holy period of Lent

Asian /ˈeɪʒən/ n [C] : a person born, raised, or living in Asia : a person whose family is from Asia ▪ *There are many Asians living in South America.* — **Asian** adj ▪ *Asian cities/culture/food*

Asian–Amer·i·can /ˈeɪʒənəˈmɛrəkən/ n [C] : an American who was born in Asia or whose family is from Asia — **Asian–American** adj

Asi·at·ic /ˌeɪʒiˈætɪk/ adj, always before a noun : of or relating to Asia ▪ *Asiatic plants/countries* ◇ *Asiatic* should not be used to describe people.

¹**aside** /əˈsaɪd/ adv **1** : to or toward the side ▪ *He stepped aside and let her pass.* ▪ *She laid/set the book aside.* ▪ (figurative) *Their objections were swept/brushed/cast/thrown aside.* [=were quickly dismissed or disregarded] **2** — used with put or set to describe something that is being kept or saved for a future use ▪ *She's been setting/putting money aside* [=has been saving money] *for school.* **3** — used to say that something is not included in a statement that follows ▪ *A few minor problems aside* [=except for a few minor problems], *the party went well.* — **aside from** chiefly US **1** : not including (something) ▪ *Aside from a few pieces of bread, the food is gone.* **2** : in addition to (something) ▪ *Aside from being well written, the book is also beautifully illustrated.*

²**aside** n [C] **1** : a comment spoken by a character in a play that is heard by the audience but is supposedly not heard by other characters on stage **2** : a comment that is spoken quietly to someone so that it cannot be heard by other people who are present ▪ *She whispered an aside to her husband.*

as·i·nine /ˈæsəˌnaɪn/ adj, formal : very stupid and silly ▪ *a completely asinine question*

ask /ˈæsk, Brit ˈɑːsk/ vb **1** [T/I] : to request an answer to a question ▪ *I need to ask (you) a question.* ▪ *Did you ask her about it?* ▪ *"Have you seen the movie yet?" he asked.* ▪ *He asked (them) if they had seen the movie.* ▪ *The police were here asking about you.* **2** [T/I] : to tell someone in the form of a question that you want to be given something or that you want something to happen : to request something ▪ *I would have given it to him, but he never asked.* ▪ *We had to stop and ask (someone) for directions.* ▪ *I asked permission.* = *I asked her (for) permission.* = *I asked for (her) permission.* ▪ *She asked me not to say anything about it.* **3** [T] : to invite (someone) to go somewhere or do something ▪ *She's asking just a few friends to the party.* ▪ *I asked him to lunch.* ▪ *I asked her out (on a date), but she turned me down.* **4** [T] **a** : to believe that you should receive (something) from someone ▪ *She asks very little in return for her* *hard work.* ▪ *The school asks much of its students.* [=the school expects its students to do a lot] **b :** to set (a specific amount of money) as a price ▪ *They're asking $100 or more per concert ticket.* — **ask after** [*phrasal vb*] **:** to ask about (someone or something) ▪ *He asked after my wife's health.* — **ask around** [*phrasal vb*] **:** to ask many people to tell you information about someone or something ▪ *We usually ask around before trying a new restaurant.* — **ask for** [*phrasal vb*] **1 :** to request to see or talk to (someone) ▪ *There's someone on the phone asking for you.* **2 ask for it** *informal* **:** to behave in a way that makes someone want to hurt or punish you ▪ *All right. You asked for it!* **3 ask for trouble** *informal* **:** to behave in a way that is likely to result in trouble ▪ *If you invest your money without doing careful research, you're just asking for trouble.* — **ask yourself** ✧ To *ask yourself* something is to think about the true answer to a question. ▪ *Ask yourself what you would do in that situation.* — **don't ask** *informal* — used to say that something is too strange, embarrassing, or complicated to explain ▪ *"How did you manage to lose both sets of keys?" "Don't ask."* — **don't ask me** *informal* — used to say that you do not know the answer to a question ▪ *Don't ask me why they're changing the system. I think it's fine the way it is.* — **for the asking** ✧ If something is yours *for the asking,* you can have it if you want it or ask for it. ▪ *This job is hers for the asking.* — **I ask you** — used before or after a question when you want someone to agree or sympathize with you ▪ *(Now) I ask you, is that fair? [=I don't think it's fair; do you?] — if you ask me* **:** in my opinion ▪ *She looks ridiculous in that hat, if you ask me.* — **who asked you?** *informal + impolite* — used as a response when someone gives an opinion that is not wanted ▪ *"I think you should break up with that guy." "Who asked you?"*

askance /ə'skæns/ *adv* **:** in a way that shows a lack of trust or approval ▪ *Most scientists looked askance at the new discovery.* [=most scientists were doubtful about the new discovery]

askew /ə'skju:/ *adv* **:** not straight **:** at an angle ▪ *The picture hung askew on the wall.* — **askew** *adj, not before a noun* ▪ *His tie is slightly askew.*

asking price *n* [*singular*] **:** the price that is asked for by a person who is selling something ▪ *The original asking price for/ of the car was $20,000, but I bought it for $18,000.*

asleep /ə'sli:p/ *adj, not before a noun* **:** in a state of sleep ▪ *"Are you asleep?" "No, I'm awake."* ▪ *Everyone was fast/ sound asleep.* [=sleeping very deeply] ▪ *I was still half asleep* [=very tired and not completely awake] *when I went to work this morning.* **2 :** lacking any feeling ✧ If a part of your body is *asleep,* it is not able to feel anything for a brief time, usually because you have kept it in an awkward position for too long. ▪ *My*

foot's asleep. — **fall asleep :** to begin sleeping ▪ *I woke up and I couldn't fall back asleep.*

asp /'æsp/ *n* [*C*] **:** a small poisonous snake from Egypt

as·par·a·gus /ə'sperəgəs/ *n* [*U*] **:** a green vegetable with long stems and tiny leaves at one end

as·pect /'æ,spɛkt/ *n* **1** [*C*] **:** a part of something ▪ *Our proposal differs from theirs in one important aspect.* ▪ *Computers now influence all aspects of American life.* **2** [*U, singular*] *formal* **:** the way a person, place, or thing appears ▪ *The old house took on a dark and lonely aspect at night.* **3** [*singular*] *formal* **:** the direction that something (such as a room or building) faces or points towards ▪ *The house has a southern aspect.* [=the front of the house faces the south] ▪ *(figurative) We studied the situation from every aspect.*

as·pen /'æspən/ *n* [*C*] **:** a kind of tree whose leaves move easily when the wind blows

as·per·i·ty /ə'sperəti/ *n* [*U*] *formal* **:** harshness of behavior or speech that expresses bitterness or anger ▪ *She spoke about him with asperity.*

as·per·sions /ə'spɜˑʒənz/ *n* — **cast aspersions** *formal* **:** to criticize someone harshly or unfairly ▪ *He avoided casting aspersions on (the motives/integrity of) his political opponents.*

as·phalt /'æs,fɑ:lt/ *n* [*U*] **:** a black substance used for making roads

as·phyx·i·ate /æs'fɪksi,eɪt/ *vb* **-at·ed; -at·ing** [*T*] **:** to cause (someone) to stop breathing ▪ *The murder victim was asphyxiated.* — **as·phyx·i·a·tion** /æs-,fɪksi'eɪʃən/ *n* [*U*]

as·pi·rant /'æspərənt/ *n* [*C*] *formal* **:** a person who wants or aspires to do or to be something ▪ *a presidential aspirant* [=someone who wants to become president]

as·pi·ra·tion /,æspə'reɪʃən/ *n* [*C*] **:** something that a person wants very much to achieve ▪ *What are your aspirations for the future?* [=what do you want to accomplish in the future?] ▪ *political/social/literary/romantic aspirations* — **as·pi·ra·tion·al** /,æspə'reɪʃənəl/ *adj, Brit* ▪ *aspirational people*

as·pire /ə'spajɚ/ *vb* **-pired; -pir·ing** [*I*] **:** to want to have or achieve something (such as a particular career or level of success) ▪ *She aspires to a career in medicine.* ▪ *He never aspired to become famous.* ▪ *an aspiring actor* [=a person who wants to be an actor]

as·pi·rin /'æspərən/ *n, pl* **aspirin** or **as·pi·rins** [*C/U*] **:** a medicine that reduces pain and fever ▪ *I had a headache so I took an/some aspirin.* [=one or more aspirin pills]

ass /'æs/ *n* [*C*] **1** *old-fashioned* **:** a donkey **2** *informal + impolite* **:** a foolish, stupid, or stubborn person ▪ *I made an ass of myself at the party.* ▪ *I behaved very foolishly at the party* **3** *chiefly US, informal + impolite* **:** BUTTOCKS ▪ *She slipped and fell on her ass.* [=(Brit) arse]

as·sail /ə'seɪl/ *vb* [*T*] **:** to attack or criticize (someone or something) in a violent or angry way • *The movie was assailed by critics.* • *(figurative) We were assailed by fears/doubt.*

as·sail·ant /ə'seɪlənt/ *n* [C] *formal* : a person who attacks someone violently • *Her assailant* [=the person who attacked her] *was wearing a mask.*

as·sas·sin /ə'sæsn/ *n* [C] : a person who assassinates someone • *the President's assassin* [=the person who killed the President]

as·sas·si·nate /ə'sæsə,neɪt/ *vb* **-nat·ed; -nat·ing** [T] : to kill (someone, such as a famous person) usually for political reasons • *a secret plot/plan to assassinate the governor* — **as·sas·si·na·tion** /ə,sæsə-'neɪʃən/ *n* [C/U]

¹**as·sault** /ə'sɑːlt/ *n* **1 a** [U] *law* : the crime of trying or threatening to hurt someone physically • *She was charged with assault with a deadly weapon.* • *He was found guilty of sexual assault.* [=the crime of touching someone in an unwanted sexual way] **b** [C] : a violent physical attack • *He was injured in a brutal assault.* **2** [C/U] : a military attack • *They launched an air assault* [=an attack using airplanes] *against the enemy.* • *(figurative) They saw the change as an assault on the values of their society.* • *The city is under assault from enemy troops.*

²**assault** *vb* [T] : to violently attack (someone or something) • *He was arrested for assaulting a police officer.* • *She was sexually assaulted.* [=touched or hurt in a sexual way]

assault and battery *n* [U] *law* : the crime of threatening and physically attacking someone

assault rifle *n* [C] : a gun that can shoot many bullets quickly — called also *assault weapon*

as·sem·blage /ə'sɛmblɪdʒ/ *n* [C] *formal* : a group of people or things • *an assemblage of tools/students*

as·sem·ble /ə'sɛmbəl/ *vb* **-sem·bled; -sem·bling** **1** [T] : to collect (things) or gather (people) into one place or group • *She assembled all of her old photos into an album.* • *assemble a team of scientists* **2** [I] : to meet together in one place • *A crowd assembled in front of the courthouse.* **3** [T] : to connect or put together the parts of (something, such as a toy or machine) • *She helped them assemble their new bicycles.*

as·sem·bly /ə'sɛmbli/ *n, pl* **-blies** **1** [U] : the act of connecting together the parts of a toy, machine, etc. • *No assembly (is) required.* [=this product is already put together] **2** [C] : a group of people who make and change laws for a government or organization • *a legislative assembly* **3** [C] **a** : a group of people who have gathered together • *an assembly of armed men* **b** : a meeting of all the teachers and students of a school • *School assemblies were usually held in the cafeteria.* **4** [U] : the act of gathering together to talk about issues • *Freedom of assembly is protected by the U.S. Constitution.*

assembly line *n* [C] : PRODUCTION LINE

as·sem·bly·man /ə'sɛmblimən/ *n, pl* **-men** /-mən/ [C] : a person (especially a man) who is a member of a legislative assembly

as·sem·bly·wom·an /ə'sɛmbli,wʊmən/ *n, pl* **-wom·en** /-,wɪmən/ [C] : a woman who is a member of a legislative assembly

as·sent /ə'sɛnt/ *vb* [I] *formal* : to agree to or approve of something (such as an idea or suggestion) • *She refused to assent to the new rules.* — **assent** *n* [U] • *A contract requires the assent of both parties.*

as·sert /ə'sət/ *vb* [T] **1** : to state (something) in a strong and definite way • *The authors assert that poverty is the city's most serious problem.* **2** : to demand that other people accept or respect (something) • *She asserted her independence by getting her own apartment.* — **assert yourself 1** *of a person* : to speak or act in a strong and definite way • *You need to learn how to assert yourself.* **2** *of a thing* : to start to be clearly seen or known • *Doubts about the plan began to assert themselves.* — **as·ser·tion** /ə-'səʃən/ *n* [C/U] • *an assertion of innocence*

as·ser·tive /ə'sətɪv/ *adj* : confident in behavior or style • *an assertive attitude/woman* • *an assertive foreign policy* — **as·ser·tive·ly** *adv* — **as·ser·tive·ness** *n* [U]

as·sess /ə'sɛs/ *vb* [T] **1** : to make a judgment about (something) • *The school assesses the students' progress each year.* **2** : to officially say what the amount, value, or rate of (something) is • *Damage to the boat was assessed at $5,000.* **3 a** : to require (a person, business, etc.) to pay an amount of money • *The company was assessed $12 million in fines.* **b** : to require a person, business, etc., to pay (a tax, fee, fine, etc.) • *The bank assesses a fee for some services.* — **as·ses·sor** /ə-'sɛsə/ *n* [C] • *a tax assessor* — **as·sess·ment** /ə'sɛsmənt/ *n* [C/U] • *I don't agree with his assessment of the problem.* • *the tax assessment on their house* [=the amount of tax they are required to pay on their house]

as·set /'æ,sɛt/ *n* [C] **1** : a valuable person or thing • *She is a great asset to the team.* [=a valuable member of the team] • *His sense of humor is one of his best assets.* **2** : something that is owned by a person, company, etc. — usually plural • *a bank with billions of dollars in assets* • *business assets and liabilities*

as·sid·u·ous /ə'sɪdʒəwəs/ *adj, formal* : showing great care, attention, and effort • *The project required assiduous planning.* • *assiduous students* — **as·si·du·ity** /,æsə'duːwəti, Brit ,æsə'djuːwəti/ *n* [U] — **as·sid·u·ous·ly** *adv* — **as·sid·u·ous·ness** *n* [U]

as·sign /ə'saɪn/ *vb* [T] **1** : to give someone a particular job or duty • *I was assigned the job of cleaning the equipment.* • *Our teacher assigned us 50 math problems for homework!* **2** : to send (someone) to a particular group or place as part of a job • *She was assigned to the embassy in India.* **3** : to choose someone to be the person who will use or have something •

Parts in the play were assigned to each student. • *our assigned positions/seats* **4** : to say that someone has (something, such as responsibility) • *They have assigned blame to the wrong people.* **5** : to give a particular value, identity, etc., to something • *The computer program assigns a number to each image.*

as·sig·na·tion /ˌæsɪgˈneɪʃən/ *n* [C] *formal* : a meeting between lovers • *a secret assignation*

as·sign·ment /əˈsaɪnmənt/ *n* **1** [C/U] : a job or duty that is given to someone • *homework assignments* • *The reporter is here on (an) assignment.* **2** [U] : the act of assigning something or someone • *her assignment to the embassy in India* • *the assignment of blame/responsibility* **3** [C] : something (such as a particular role or seat) that is chosen for you to use or have • *May I change my seating assignment?*

as·sim·i·late /əˈsɪməˌleɪt/ *vb* **-lat·ed; -lat·ing 1** [T] : to learn and fully understand (something) • *assimilating new ideas/concepts* **2** [T/I] : to cause (a person or group) to become part of a different society, country, etc. • *Schools were used to assimilate the children of immigrants.* • *They found it hard to assimilate to/into American society.* — **as·sim·i·la·tion** /əˌsɪməˈleɪʃən/ *n* [U]

¹**as·sist** /əˈsɪst/ *vb* [T/I] : to give support or help • *The device assists those who can't climb stairs.* • *Another doctor assisted (him) with the operation.* — **as·sis·tance** /əˈsɪstəns/ *n* [U] • *She offered her assistance.* *She asked, "Can I be of (any) assistance?"* [=can I help you?]

²**assist** *n* [C] *sports* : an action (such as passing a ball or puck) that helps a teammate to score • *He had 3 goals and 2 assists in the hockey game.*

¹**as·sis·tant** /əˈsɪstənt/ *n* [C] **1** : a person who helps someone; *especially* : a person whose job is to help another person to do work • *a dental assistant* [=a person whose job is to help a dentist] • *a wealthy executive who has a personal assistant* **2** : a person whose job is to help the customers in a store • *She's a **sales assistant** at Macy's.*

²**assistant** *adj, always before a noun* : having a lower rank or position than others in a group, organization, etc. • *an assistant manager*

assisted living *n* [U] : a system that provides a place to live and medical care for people (such as elderly or disabled people) who need help with daily activities • *an assisted-living facility/residence*

assn. *abbr* association

assoc. *abbr* associate; ¹associated; association

¹**as·so·ci·ate** /əˈsoʊʃiˌeɪt/ *vb* **-at·ed; -at·ing 1** [T] : to think of one person or thing when you think of another person or thing — usually + *with* • *She associates that place with her childhood.* ◇ When one thing is **associated with** another, they happen together or are related or connected in some way. • *There are several dangers/risks associated with that approach.* **2** [T/I] : to be together with an-

other person or group as friends, partners, etc. • *She associates with some pretty strange people.* • *He was associated with a terrorist group.* • *He is reluctant to **associate himself with** [=to show or say that he supports and agrees with] the government's position.*

²**as·so·ci·ate** /əˈsoʊʃiət/ *n* [C] **1** : a person who you work with or spend time with • *business associates* **2** : a member of a group or organization who is at a level that is below the highest level • *She started as an associate at the law firm.*

³**as·so·ci·ate** /əˈsoʊʃiət/ *adj, always before a noun* : having a rank or position that is below the highest level in a group, organization, etc. • *an associate editor/professor*

associate's degree *n* [C] : a degree that is given to a student who has completed two years of study at a college or university in the U.S.

as·so·ci·a·tion /əˌsoʊsiˈeɪʃən/ *n* **1** [C] : an organized group of people who have the same interest, job, etc. • *an association of local business leaders* **2** [C/U] : a connection or relationship between things or people • *They denied having any association with terrorists.* • *The book was produced by the publisher **in association with** the museum.* [=the publisher and the museum were both involved in making the book] **3** [C] : a feeling, memory, or thought that is connected to a person, place, or thing — usually plural • *His former school has only bad/negative associations for him.* [=he has only unhappy memories of his former school]

as·sort·ed /əˈsoɑtəd/ *adj* : including several kinds • *assorted colors/flavors/sizes/styles*

as·sort·ment /əˈsoɑtmənt/ *n* [C] : a group or collection of different things or people • *a wide assortment of options*

asst. *abbr* assistant • *asst. coach*

as·suage /əˈsweɪdʒ/ *vb* **-suaged; -suag·ing** [T] *formal* : to make (something, such as an unpleasant feeling) less painful, severe, etc. • *The company tried to assuage investors' fears/concerns.*

as·sume /əˈsuːm/ *vb* **-sumed; -sum·ing** [T] **1** : to think that something is true or probably true without knowing that it is true • *"Is he coming?" "I assume so."* • *I think we can safely assume that he's coming.* • *Assuming (that) she says no, what will you do?* [=what will you do if she says no?] **2 a** : to begin (a role, duty, etc.) as a job or responsibility • *He assumed the throne* [=he became the king] *when he was very young.* **b** : to take or begin to have (power, control, etc.) in a job or situation • *She assumed control of the organization.* **3** : to begin to have (a particular appearance or quality) • *The sky assumed an otherworldly glow.* **4 a** : to make yourself have (an appearance that does not show your true feelings) in order to deceive someone • *She assumed a look of innocence.* [=she made herself look innocent] **b** : to place yourself in (a particular position or posture) • *She assumed a sitting position* [=she sat down] *on the floor.* **5** : to accept (a responsibility, debt, etc.) • *When they purchased the company, they had to assume its debts.*

as·sumed /əˈsuːmd/ *adj* : not true or real • *He traveled under an assumed name.* [=he used a false name when he traveled]

as·sump·tion /əˈsʌmpʃən/ *n* **1** [C] : something that is believed to be true or probably true but that is not known to be true • *He's coming. At least, that's my assumption.* • *We are operating* **on/under/with the assumption** [=we are behaving as though we know] *that the loan will be approved.* **2** [U] : the act of assuming something • *her assumption of the presidency* • *the assumption of control/authority*

as·sur·ance /əˈʃʊrəns/ *n* **1** [U] : the state of being sure or certain about something • *He has the assurance of full support from his boss.* **2** [U] : a strong feeling of confidence about yourself or about being right • *She spoke with quiet assurance about her future plans.* **3** [C] : a strong and definite statement that something will happen or that something is true • *She gave him every assurance that she would be there.*

as·sure /əˈʃʊr/ *vb* **-sured; -sur·ing** [T] **1** : to make (something) certain : ENSURE • *We must assure that every child gets a proper education.* • *Success is by no means assured.* [=is definitely not certain] • *A victory in this game will* **assure them of finishing** [=it will make it certain that they will finish] *the season with a winning record.* **2** : to tell someone in a very strong and definite way that something will happen or that something is true • *She assured me (that) she was OK.* • *It won't happen again, I (can) assure you.* • *He tried opening the door to* **assure himself** [=to make himself sure] *that it was locked.*

as·sured /əˈʃʊrd/ *adj* **1** : very confident : SELF-ASSURED • *an assured voice/ manner* **2** : sure that something is certain or true • *You can* **rest assured** [=you can be sure] *that these mistakes won't happen again.* — **assured of** : certain to have or get (something) • *They are not assured of being paid.* [=it is not certain that they will be paid] — **as·sur·ed·ly** /əˈʃʊrədli/ *adv* • *The merger will (most) assuredly* [=certainly] *lead to job layoffs.* • *She moved/walked assuredly across the stage.*

as·ter /ˈæstər/ *n* [C] : a type of plant that is grown in gardens for its colorful flowers

as·ter·isk /ˈæstəˌrɪsk/ *n* [C] : a symbol * that is used in printed text especially to tell someone to read a note that can be found at the bottom of a page

as·ter·oid /ˈæstəˌrɔɪd/ *n* [C] : any one of thousands of small planets that circle around the sun

asth·ma /ˈæzmə, *Brit* ˈæsmə/ *n* [U] *medical* : a condition that makes it difficult for someone to breathe — **asth·mat·ic** /æzˈmætɪk, *Brit* æsˈmætɪk/ *adj* • *an asthmatic cough/patient* — **asthmatic** *n* [C] • *My son is an asthmatic.*

astig·ma·tism /əˈstɪɡməˌtɪzəm/ *n* [U]

medical : a problem with the eye that prevents a person from seeing clearly

as·ton·ish /əˈstɑːnɪʃ/ *vb* **-ished; -ish·ing** [T/I] : to cause a feeling of great wonder or surprise in (someone) • *His great intelligence never fails to astonish (me).* • *We were astonished by/at all the changes in the town's appearance.* • *an astonishing performance* [=a performance that was surprisingly good] — **as·ton·ish·ing·ly** /əˈstɑːnɪʃɪŋli/ *adv* • *an astonishingly beautiful scene* — **as·ton·ish·ment** /əˈstɑːnɪʃmənt/ *n* [U]

as·tound /əˈstaʊnd/ *vb* [T] : to cause a feeling of great surprise or wonder in (someone) • *What astounds me is that they never apologized.* • *We were astounded* [=very surprised] *to discover a valuable painting in the attic.* • *He ate an astounding amount* [=an amazingly large amount] *of food.* — **as·tound·ing·ly** /əˈstaʊndɪŋli/ *adv*

astray /əˈstreɪ/ *adv* **1** : off the right path or route • *They marked the trail so hikers wouldn't* **go astray.** [=become lost] **2** : away from what is right, good, or desirable — usually used with *go* or *lead* • *His friends led him astray.* [=made him behave badly] • *Their plans have gone astray.* [=have failed]

astride /əˈstraɪd/ *prep* : with one leg or part on each side of (something) • *sitting astride a horse* • *The town lies astride the river.*

as·trin·gent /əˈstrɪndʒənt/ *adj* **1** *medical* : causing body tissues (such as skin) to tighten • *astringent cleansers* **2** : having a sharp or bitter quality • *an astringent taste* **3** : very critical in a sharp and often clever way • *an astringent critic/ comment* — **as·trin·gen·cy** /əˈstrɪndʒənsi/ *n* [U] — **astringent** *n* [C] • *She used an astringent on her face.*

as·trol·o·gy /əˈstrɑːlədʒi/ *n* [U] : the study of how the positions of the stars and movements of the planets have a supposed influence on events and on the lives and behavior of people — **as·trol·o·ger** /əˈstrɑːlədʒər/ *n* [C] • *She consulted an astrologer to see if she would ever get married.* — **as·tro·log·i·cal** /ˌæstrəˈlɑːdʒɪkəl/ *adj* • *astrological signs*

as·tro·naut /ˈæstrəˌnɑːt/ *n* [C] : a person who travels in a spacecraft into outer space

as·tro·nom·i·cal /ˌæstrəˈnɑːmɪkəl/ *also* **as·tro·nom·ic** /ˌæstrəˈnɑːmɪk/ *adj* **1** : of or relating to astronomy • *astronomical research* **2** : extremely large • *The cost of the building was astronomical.* • *an astronomical phone bill* — **as·tro·nom·i·cal·ly** /ˌæstrəˈnɑːmɪkli/ *adv* • *The cost of health care rose astronomically.*

as·tron·o·my /əˈstrɑːnəmi/ *n* [U] : the scientific study of stars, planets, and other objects in outer space — **as·tron·o·mer** /əˈstrɑːnəmər/ *n* [C]

As·tro·turf /ˈæstrəˌtərf/ *trademark* — used for an artificial surface that resembles grass

as·tute /əˈstuːt, *Brit* əˈstjuːt/ *adj* : having or showing an ability to notice and understand things clearly • *an astute politi-*

cal observer/observation — **as·tute·ly**
adv — **as·tute·ness** *n* [U]

asun·der /ə'sʌndə/ *adv, literary* : into
parts • *The government was torn asunder*
[=deeply divided] *by scandal.*

asy·lum /ə'saɪləm/ *n* **1** [U] : protection
given by a government to someone who
has left another country in order to escape being harmed • *She asked for political asylum.* **2** [C] *old-fashioned* : a mental hospital

asym·met·ri·cal /ˌeɪsə'mɛtrɪkəl/ *or*
asym·met·ric /ˌeɪsə'mɛtrɪk/ *adj* : having two sides or halves that are not the
same • *an asymmetrical design* — **asym-
met·ri·cal·ly** /ˌeɪsə'mɛtrɪkli/ *adv* —
asym·me·try /eɪ'sɪmətri/ *n, pl* **-tries**
[C/U]

at /'æt, ət/ *prep* **1** — used to indicate the
place where someone or something is •
The kitchen is at the back of the house. •
He was sitting at the table. • *Is your father
at home or at work?*

> The word *at* is used in speech in e-mail
> addresses. • *"Our address is 'comments
> at Merriam-Webster dot com.'"* When
> an e-mail address is written rather than
> spoken, the symbol @ is used instead. •
> *comments@Merriam-Webster.com*

2 — used to indicate the person or thing
toward which an action, motion, or feeling is directed • *She looked/laughed/
shouted at me.* • *He's angry at his brother.*
3 — used to indicate something that is
being tried or attempted • *I took a shot at
doing it myself.* [=I tried to do it myself]
4 : because of or in reaction to (something) • *They laughed at my joke.* • *I was
surprised at the result.* [=the result surprised me] • *They came here at our invitation.* **5** — used to indicate an activity •
children who are at play [=children who
are playing] • *She's good at (playing)
chess.* [=she plays chess well] **6** — used
to indicate a situation or condition • *two
nations that are at war* • *people who are at
risk* • *He is now at peace.* **7 a** — used to
indicate position on a scale or in a series
• *driving at 80 miles an hour* **b** — used
to indicate a rate • *They sell at a dollar
each.* [=each costs one dollar] **8** — used
to indicate an age or time • *He retired at
(age) 65.* • *She called us at 9 o'clock on
Thursday.* **9 a** — used in phrases like *at
best, at worst*, etc., to indicate a possible
result or condition that is considered
best, worst, etc. • *The company will make
a small profit at best.* [=the company will
earn no more than a small profit] • *We'll
arrive by noon at the latest.* [=we will not
arrive later than noon] **b** — used in
phrases like *at its best, at its worst*, etc.,
to indicate that something or someone is
as good, bad, etc., as possible • *This is
baseball at its best.* — **at it** : doing some
activity • *My neighbors are always arguing, and they were at it again last night.*
[=they were arguing again last night] •
*We'll clean the kitchen and maybe wash
the floor while we're at it.* [=we may wash
the floor when we clean the kitchen]

ate *past tense of* EAT

athe·ist /'eɪθijɪst/ *n* [C] : a person who

believes that God does not exist — **athe-
ism** /'eɪθiˌɪzəm/ *n* [U] — **athe·is·tic**
/ˌeɪθi'ɪstɪk/ *adj*

ath·lete /'æθˌliːt/ *n* [C] : a person who is
trained in or good at sports, games, or
exercises that require physical skill and
strength • *amateur/professional athletes*

athlete's foot *n* [U] *medical* : a condition that affects the skin around the toes

ath·let·ic /æθ'lɛtɪk/ *adj* **1** *always before
a noun* **a** : of or relating to athletes • *an
athletic association* **b** : of or relating to
sports, games, or exercises • *athletic
events* • *She has great athletic ability.* **2**
always before a noun : used by athletes •
athletic shoes • *an athletic field* **3 a**
: strong and muscular • *She has an athletic build.* **b** : active in sports, games, or
exercises • *He's very athletic.* — **ath·let·i-
cal·ly** /æθ'lɛtɪkli/ *adv* — **ath·let·i·cism**
/æθ'lɛtəˌsɪzəm/ *n* [U] • *He has speed and
athleticism.*

ath·let·ics /æθ'lɛtɪks/ *n* **1** [*plural*] *US*
: athletic activities ◇ *Athletics* is used
with both plural and singular verbs. •
*College athletics attract/attracts students
from many backgrounds.* **2** [U] *Brit*
: TRACK AND FIELD

Atl. *abbr* Atlantic

at·las /'ætləs/ *n* [C] : a book of maps • *a
world/road atlas*

ATM /ˌeɪˌtiː'ɛm/ *n* [C] : a machine that
people use to get money from their bank
accounts by using a special card • *ATM
cards/machines* ◇ *ATM* is an abbreviation of "automatic teller machine."

at·mo·sphere /'ætməˌsfiːə/ *n* **1 a** [*singular*] : the mass of air that surrounds
the Earth • *meteors that pass through
Earth's atmosphere* **b** [C] : a mass of
gases that surround a planet or star • *the
planets' different atmospheres* **2 a** [C]
: the particular way a place or situation
makes you feel — usually singular • *a
restaurant with a romantic/relaxed atmosphere* • *The news created an atmosphere
of fear/excitement/confusion.* **b** [U] : an
interesting or pleasing quality or effect •
a country inn with lots of atmosphere —
at·mo·spher·ic /ˌætmə'sfiːrɪk, *Brit*
ˌætmə'sfɛrɪk/ *adj* • *atmospheric gases/
conditions/pressure*

atoll /'æˌtɑːl/ *n* [C] : an island that is
shaped like a ring

at·om /'ætəm/ *n* [C] **1** : the smallest particle of a substance that can exist by itself • *carbon/hydrogen atoms* **2** : a very
small amount of something • *There is not
an atom of truth to what he said.*

atom·ic /ə'tɑːmɪk/ *adj* **1** : of or relating
to atoms • *atomic particles* **2** : of, relating to, or using the energy that is produced when atoms are split apart • *an
atomic weapon/reactor*

atomic bomb *n* [C] : a bomb that produces an extremely powerful explosion
when atoms are split apart — called also
atom bomb

atomic energy *n* [U] *physics* : NUCLEAR
ENERGY

atone /ə'toʊn/ *vb* **atoned; aton·ing** [I]
formal : to do something good as a way
to show that you are sorry about doing
something bad — usually + *for* • *He*

wants to atone for the sins of his youth. — **atone·ment** /ə'toʊnmənt/ *n* [U]

atop /ə'tɑːp/ *prep, chiefly US* : on top of ▪ *The house sits atop a hill.*

atri·um /'eɪtrijəm/ *n, pl* **atria** /'eɪtrijə/ *also* **atriums** [C] **1** : an open area inside a tall building that has windows to let light in from above **2** *technical* : one of two sections of the heart that take in blood from the veins

atro·cious /ə'troʊʃəs/ *adj* **1** : very evil or cruel ▪ *atrocious crimes* **2** : very bad ▪ *atrocious weather* ▪ *His performance was atrocious.* — **atro·cious·ly** *adv*

atroc·i·ty /ə'trɑːsəti/ *n, pl* **-ties** [C/U] : a very cruel or terrible act or action ▪ *the atrocities of war*

at·ro·phy /'ætrəfi/ *n* [U] *medical* : gradual loss of muscle or flesh usually because of disease or lack of use ▪ *atrophy of the leg muscles* — **atrophy** *vb* **-phied; -phy·ing** [I] ▪ *Her muscles atrophied during her illness.*

att. *abbr* **1** attached **2** attention **3** attorney

at·tach /ə'tætʃ/ *vb* **1 a** [T] : to fasten or join one thing *to* another ▪ *She attached a note to the package.* ▪ *The file is attached to this e-mail.* ▪ *(figurative)* *They attached the blame to the boys.* [=said the boys should be blamed] **b** [I] : to be or become joined or connected ▪ *The handle attaches here on the top.* **2** [T] **a** : to associate or connect one thing with another — + *to* ▪ *He attaches great importance to appearance.* [=he thinks appearance is very important] **b** : to associate or connect (yourself) with someone or something — + *to* ▪ *He attached himself to an older, wealthy woman.*

at·ta·ché /ˌætə'ʃeɪ, *Brit* ə'tæˌʃeɪ/ *n* [C] : a person who works at an embassy as an expert on a particular subject ▪ *a cultural/military attaché*

attaché case *n* [C] : a small, thin suitcase that is used especially for carrying papers

at·tached /ə'tætʃt/ *adj* **1** : connected or joined to something ▪ *The house has an attached garage.* **2** : having strong feelings of affection ▪ *She's very attached to her cousin.* [=she likes her cousin very much]

at·tach·ment /ə'tætʃmənt/ *n* **1** [C] : an extra part that can be used with a machine to make it do a particular job ▪ *vacuum cleaner attachments* **2** [C/U] : strong feelings of affection or loyalty for someone or something ▪ *They have a deep attachment to the old house.* ▪ *emotional attachment* **3** [C] : a document or file that is sent with e-mail ▪ *I'll send the document as an attachment to my next e-mail.* **4 a** [C] : a part that is used to attach something ▪ *the attachments that connect the rack to the car* **b** [U] : the act of attaching something ▪ *There are two brackets for attachment of the shelf.* — **on attachment** *Brit* : working for a limited time in a particular place ▪ *She's on attachment to Rome for a month.*

¹**at·tack** /ə'tæk/ *vb* **1** [T/I] : to try to hurt, injure, or destroy (something or someone) ▪ *Troops attacked (the fortress) at*

dawn. ▪ *She was attacked by a dog.* **2** [T] : to criticize (someone or something) in a very harsh and severe way ▪ *He was attacked for his position on the issue.* **3** [T] **a** : to begin to work on or deal with (something, such as a problem) in a determined and eager way ▪ *We eagerly attacked the problem.* **b** : to begin to eat (food) eagerly ▪ *The kids attacked the pizza.* **4** [T] : to begin to harm, injure, or destroy (something) ▪ *The virus attacks the body's immune system.* **5** [T/I] *sports* : to try to score points or goals by moving forward in a very forceful way ▪ *The team began to attack.* — **at·tack·er** *n* [C] ▪ *He identified his attacker.* [=the person who attacked him]

²**attack** *n* **1 a** [C] : a violent, harmful, or destructive act against someone or something ▪ *dog/shark attacks* ▪ *the victim of a knife attack* [=an attack made using a knife] ▪ *attacks on women* **b** [C/U] : harmful or destructive action against something by a disease, insect, chemical, etc. ▪ *attacks by common pests* **2** [C/U] : an attempt by a military force to defeat an enemy ▪ *a surprise air/ground attack* ▪ *the threat of nuclear attack* **3** [C] : strong or severe criticism ▪ *a verbal attack* ▪ *The editorial is an attack on policymakers.* **4** [C] : a sudden short period of suffering from an illness or of being affected by a strong emotion ▪ *a panic/anxiety attack* ▪ *an attack of the flu* **5** [C] : an attempt to destroy or end something ▪ *They called for an attack on poverty.* **6** [C/U] : a method of dealing with something (such as a problem) ▪ *We need a new plan of attack.* [=a new idea of how to do what we are trying to do] **7** *sports* **a** [C] : an attempt by a player or group of players to score points, goals, or runs ▪ *They had a sustained attack but could not score.* **b** [U, singular] *Brit* : the players on a team who try to score : OFFENSE ▪ *He will play in attack.* [=(US) on offense] — **on the attack** : making an attack ▪ *The soldiers were on the attack.* ▪ *Both candidates went on the attack.* [=began to attack each other] — **under attack** : being affected or hurt by an attack ▪ *The troops were under attack.* ▪ *The new policy has come under attack.* [=has been strongly criticized]

at·tain /ə'teɪn/ *vb* [T] *somewhat formal* **1** : to accomplish or achieve (something) ▪ *The injury kept her from attaining her goal of being in the Olympics.* **2** : to grow or increase to (a particular amount, size, etc.) ▪ *a tree that attains a height of 20 feet within three years* — **at·tain·able** /ə-'teɪnəbəl/ *adj* — **at·tain·ment** /ə-'teɪnmənt/ *n* [C/U] ▪ *the attainment of her goals* ▪ *scientific attainments*

¹**at·tempt** /ə'tɛmpt/ *vb* [T] : to try to do (something) ▪ *The book attempts to prove their innocence.* ▪ *She attempted suicide.* ▪ *an attempted robbery/murder/suicide*

²**attempt** *n* [C] **1** : an act of trying to do something ▪ *In an attempt to save money, they started using coupons.* ▪ *She failed her driving test on the first attempt.* ▪ *We both made an attempt* [=tried] *to be friendly.* ✧ *Attempt often suggests that the effort*

made was unsuccessful. • *a suicide/assassination attempt* • *Someone made an attempt on her life.* [=someone tried to kill her] **2** : something that results from trying to do something • *Her attempt at a home-cooked meal consisted of a can of soup.*

at·tend /ə'tɛnd/ *vb* **1 a** [*T/I*] : to go to and be present at (an event, meeting, etc.) • *He won't be attending the wedding.* • *One hundred people attended.* **b** [*T*] : to regularly go to (classes, church services, etc.) • *We attend the same church.* **2** [*T*] : to help or care for (someone, such as a patient) • *Each nurse attends 15 patients.* **3** [*T*] *formal* : to go with or be with (someone) as a helper or adviser • *ministers who attend the king* — **attend to** [*phrasal vb*] **1** : to deal with (something) • *I've got some business I must attend to.* **2** : to give needed help or attention to (someone or something) • *The hotel staff attended to my every need.*

at·ten·dance /ə'tɛndəns/ *n* **1** [*C/U*] : the number of people present at an event, meeting, etc. • *Museum attendance is down so far this season.* **2** [*U*] : the act of being present at a place • *Attendance (at all classes) is mandatory.* • *A number of celebrities were in attendance at the party.* [=attended the party] **b** : a record of how often a person goes to classes, meetings, etc. • *a student who has perfect attendance* [=who has been present at every class] • *The teacher takes attendance* [=makes a record of who is present] *every day.*

¹at·ten·dant /ə'tɛndənt/ *n* [*C*] **1** : an assistant or servant • *the royal family's attendants* **2** : an employee who serves or helps customers • *She let the parking attendant park her car.*

²attendant *adj, formal* : coming with or following as a result • *high population growth and the attendant increase in traffic* • *the problems attendant on/upon the introduction of new technology*

at·tend·ee /ˌətɛn'diː/ *n* [*C*] : a person who is present at an event, meeting, etc., or at a particular place • *There were 300 attendees at the conference.*

at·tend·er /ə'tɛndə/ *n* [*C*] *Brit* : ATTENDEE

at·ten·tion /ə'tɛnʃən/ *n* **1** [*C/U*] : the act or power of carefully thinking about, listening to, or watching someone or something • *Attention, please!* [=please give me your attention] • *Please give me your full/undivided attention.* [=please listen carefully and concentrate on what I am saying and doing] • *The movie keeps/holds your attention to the very end.* • *It's time to turn/give our attention to the next project.* • *Pay (close/careful) attention to what he says.* • *Don't pay any attention to them.* [=ignore them] • *(US) She's been focusing her attentions on making sales.* **2** [*U*] : notice, interest, or awareness • *He avoids drawing attention to himself.* • *The book has received/attracted national attention.* • *Your hard work has not escaped my attention.* [=I have noticed your hard work] • *The book's title grabbed/caught my attention.* [=the title caused me to look at the book] • *We tried to get your attention* [=we tried to get you to see us], *but you didn't hear us calling you.* • *I would like to call/bring your attention to a problem we are having.* • *Thank you for bringing the matter to my attention.* [=making me aware of the matter] • *New information has come to my attention.* [=I have been made aware of new information] • *He loves being the center of attention.* [=being noticed and watched by many people] **3** [*U*] : special care or treatment • *Be sure the dog gets plenty of attention.* • *The victim needed medical attention.* **4** [*plural*] : acts of kindness, care, or courtesy • *She found his attentions flattering.* **5** [*U*] : the way a soldier stands with the body stiff and straight, the feet together, and both arms at the sides — often used as a command • *Attention!* • *(US) The troops stood at attention.* = *(Brit) The troops stood to attention.*

attention deficit disorder *n* [*U*] *medical* : a condition in which someone (such as a child) has problems with learning and behavior because of being unable to pay attention to things for very long — abbr. *ADD*

attention span *n* [*C*] : the length of time during which someone is able to think about or remain interested in something • *people with short attention spans*

at·ten·tive /ə'tɛntɪv/ *adj* **1** : thinking about or watching something carefully : paying careful attention to something • *an attentive audience* • *He's very attentive to details.* **2** : very concerned about the needs of others • *Our waiter was very attentive.* — **at·ten·tive·ly** *adv* — **at·ten·tive·ness** *n* [*U*]

at·ten·u·ate /ə'tɛnjəˌweɪt/ *vb* -**at·ed**; -**at·ing** [*T*] *formal* : to make (something) weaker or less in amount, effect, or force • *an attenuated virus* — **at·ten·u·a·tion** /əˌtɛnjə'weɪʃən/ *n* [*U*]

at·test /ə'tɛst/ *vb* [*T/I*] *formal* : to show, prove, or state that something is true or real • *The plant's presence during that time is attested by fossil evidence.* • *I can attest to the truth of his statement.* — **at·tes·ta·tion** /ˌæˌtɛs'teɪʃən/ *n* [*C/U*]

at·tic /'ætɪk/ *n* [*C*] : a room or space that is just below the roof of a building

at·tire /ə'tajə/ *n* [*U*] *formal* : clothing • *beach/business/golf attire* • *Proper attire is required.*

at·tired /ə'tajəd/ *adj, formal* : dressed in a particular way • *He was attired in his uniform.*

at·ti·tude /'ætəˌtuːd, Brit 'ætəˌtjuːd/ *n* **1** [*C*] : the way you think and feel about someone or something • *He has a positive/negative attitude about the changes.* • *her attitude to/toward/towards money* **2** [*C*] : a feeling or way of thinking that affects a person's behavior • *You need to change your (bad) attitude.* • *She has an attitude problem.* [=she is not friendly or cooperative] **3** *informal* **a** [*C/U*] : a way of thinking and behaving that people regard as unfriendly, rude, etc. • *She has a real attitude.* **b** [*U*] : a strong, confident, or impressive quality • *a movie with attitude*

attn. *abbr* attention

at·tor·ney /əˈtɚni/ *n, pl* **-neys** [C] *chiefly US* : LAWYER

attorney general *n, pl* **attorneys general** *or* **attorney generals** [C] : the chief lawyer of a country or state who represents the government in legal matters

at·tract /əˈtrækt/ *vb* [T] **1** : to cause (someone) to be interested in or involved in something • *The company has difficulty attracting good employees.* • *What attracted you to a career as a flight attendant?* **2** : to cause (someone or something) to go to or move to or toward a place • *The museum attracts visitors from all over the world.* **3** : to cause sexual or romantic feeling in (someone or something) • *Her bright blue eyes attracted me.* • *The bird's colorful feathers are used to attract a mate.* • *She is attracted to short men.* **4** : to get or create (notice, interest, etc.) • *Her comment attracted criticism.* **5** *physics* : to pull (something) to or toward something else • *A magnet attracts iron.*

at·trac·tion /əˈtrækʃən/ *n* **1** [C] **a** : something interesting or enjoyable that people want to visit, see, or do • *The waterfall is the main attraction at the park.* • *the city's tourist attractions* [=things tourists usually like to see or do] • *Before the movie began, we saw previews of coming attractions.* [=movies that are going to be available soon] **b** : a performer who people want to see • *She is the star attraction of the show.* **2** [*singular*] : a feeling that makes someone romantically or sexually interested in another person • *There's a strong sexual attraction between them.* **3** [C/U] : a feature or quality that makes someone or something interesting or enjoyable • *I don't understand the attraction of skydiving.* **4** [C/U] *physics* : a force that pulls something to or toward something else • *magnetic attraction*

at·trac·tive /əˈtræktɪv/ *adj* **1** : having a pleasing appearance • *an attractive flower arrangement* • *an attractive person/smile* **2** : having a feature or quality that people like • *a very attractive offer/proposition/price* • *His ideas are attractive to many people.* — **at·trac·tive·ly** *adv* — **at·trac·tive·ness** *noun* [U]

¹at·trib·ute /əˈtrɪˌbjuːt/ *vb* **-ut·ed; -ut·ing** — **attribute to** [*phrasal vb*] **attribute (something) to** **1** : to say that (something) is because of (someone or something) • *His doctor attributes his health problems to a poor diet.* **2** : to think of (something) as being a quality of (someone or something) • *She attributes some importance to the research.* [=she thinks that the research is important] **3** : to think of (something) as being made or created by (someone) • *The poem is usually attributed to Shakespeare.* — **at·trib·ut·able** /əˈtrɪbjutəbəl/ *adj, not before a noun* • *His health problems are attributable to a poor diet.* — **at·tri·bu·tion** /ˌætrəˈbjuːʃən/ *n* [C/U]

²at·tri·bute /ˈætrəˌbjuːt/ *n* [C] : a usually good quality or feature that someone or something has • *She possesses the attributes we want in a leader.*

at·trib·u·tive /əˈtrɪbjətɪv/ *adj, grammar* : joined directly to a noun in order to describe it • *In "airplane pilot" the noun "airplane" is attributive.* — **at·trib·u·tive·ly** *adv*

at·tri·tion /əˈtrɪʃən/ *n* [U] *formal* **1** *chiefly US* : a reduction in the number of employees or participants that occurs when people leave because they resign, retire, etc., and are not replaced • *The staff has been thinned through attrition.* **2** : the act or process of weakening and defeating an enemy through attacks and pressure over a long period of time • *They fought a long war of attrition.*

at·tune /əˈtuːn, *Brit* əˈtjuːn/ *vb* **-tuned; -tun·ing** [T] : to cause (a person, company, etc.) to have a better understanding of what is needed or wanted by a particular group or person • *The company is attuned to the needs of its customers.*

atty. *abbr* attorney

ATV /ˌeɪˌtiːˈviː/ *n* [C] : ALL-TERRAIN VEHICLE

atyp·i·cal /eɪˈtɪpɪkəl/ *adj* : not usual or normal • *This book is atypical of her previous work.* [=is not like her previous work] — **atyp·i·cal·ly** /eɪˈtɪpɪkli/ *adv*

au·ber·gine /ˈoubɚˌʒiːn/ *n* [C/U] *Brit* : EGGPLANT

au·burn /ˈɑːbɚn/ *adj* : reddish brown • *auburn hair*

¹auc·tion /ˈɑːkʃən/ *n* [C/U] : a public sale at which things are sold to the people who offer to pay the most • *She bought the desk at an auction.* • *The house is being sold at auction.* — **on the (auction) block** *see* **¹BLOCK**

²auction *vb* [T] : to sell (something) at an auction • *The house was auctioned (off) last week.*

auc·tion·eer /ˌɑːkʃəˈniɚ/ *n* [C] : a person who runs an auction

au·da·cious /ɑːˈdeɪʃəs/ *adj* : very confident and daring : very bold and surprising or shocking • *audacious plans/decisions/behavior* — **au·da·cious·ly** *adv* — **au·da·cious·ness** *n* [U] — **au·dac·i·ty** /ɑːˈdæsəti/ *n* [U] • *He had the audacity to suggest that it was all my fault.* [=he rudely suggested that it was all my fault]

au·di·ble /ˈɑːdəbəl/ *adj* : heard or able to be heard • *Her voice was barely audible.* — **au·di·bil·i·ty** /ˌɑːdəˈbɪləti/ *n* [U] — **au·di·bly** /ˈɑːdəbli/ *adv*

au·di·ence /ˈɑːdijəns/ *n* [C] **1** : the people who attend a performance • *The concert attracted a large audience.* • *an audience member = a member of the audience* **2** : the people who watch, read, or listen to something • *The film is intended for a young audience.* [=for young viewers] **3** : a formal meeting with an important person • *They were granted an audience with the Pope.*

au·dio /ˈɑːdiˌou/ *adj, always before a noun* : of or relating to the sound that is heard on a recording or broadcast • *audio equipment* [=equipment used for recording sound or listening to recorded sound] • *They listened to an audio record-*

ing of the speech. — **audio** *n* [U] • *The picture was clear but the audio was very poor.*

au·dio·tape /'ɑːdijou,teip/ *n* [C/U] : tape on which sound is recorded • *The program was recorded on (an) audiotape.*

au·dio·vi·su·al /,ɑːdijou'vɪʒəwəl/ *adj* : of, relating to, or using both sound and sight • *audiovisual equipment* — abbr. *AV*

¹**au·dit** /'ɑːdət/ *n* 1 [C/U] : a complete and careful examination of the financial records of a business or person • *The Internal Revenue Service selected us for (an) audit.* 2 [C] : a careful check or review of something • *Investigators called for an audit of flight safety standards.*

²**audit** *vb* [T] 1 : to check the financial records of (a business or person) • *They audit the company books every year.* 2 *US* : to attend a course at a college or university without receiving credit • *I audited a Biology class last year.* — **au·di·tor** /'ɑːdətər/ *n* [C] • *The auditor checked our books.*

¹**au·di·tion** /ɑː'dɪʃən/ *n* [C] : a short performance to show the talents of someone (such as an actor or a musician) who is being considered for a role in a play, a position in a band, etc. • *Auditions will be held next week.*

²**audition** *vb* 1 [I] *of a performer* : to perform in an audition • *She auditioned for the lead role.* 2 [T] : to test (someone) in an audition • *They auditioned several girls for the role.*

au·di·to·ri·um /,ɑːdə'torijəm/ *n, pl* -to·ri·ums *also* -to·ria /-'torijə/ [C] 1 *US* : a large room or building where people gather to watch a performance, hear a speech, etc. 2 : the part of a building (such as a theater) where an audience sits

au·di·to·ry /'ɑːdə,tori, Brit 'ɔːdətri/ *adj, technical* : relating to hearing or the ears • *the auditory nerve*

Aug. *abbr* August

au·ger /'ɑːgər/ *n* [C] : a tool for making holes

aug·ment /ɑːg'mɛnt/ *vb* [T] *formal* 1 : to increase the size or amount of (something) • *Heavy rains augmented the water supply.* 2 *US* : to add something to (something) in order to improve or complete it • *Job training will augment the class work.* — **aug·men·ta·tion** /,ɑːgmən'teɪʃən/ *n* [U]

au·gur /'ɑːgər/ *vb* [T/I] *formal* : to show or suggest something that might happen in the future • *The decision doesn't augur well.*

au·gust /ɑː'gʌst/ *adj, formal* : having a formal and impressive quality • *an august mansion*

Au·gust /'ɑːgəst/ *n* [C/U] : the eighth month of the year • *in (early/mid/late) August* • *We arrived on August (the) fourth.* = *We arrived on the fourth of August.* — abbr. *Aug.*

aunt /'ænt, 'ɑːnt/ *n* [C] : the sister of your father or mother or the wife of your uncle • *my Aunt Mary*

aunt·ie /'ænti, 'ɑːnti/ *n* [C] *informal* : AUNT

au·ra /'orə/ *n* [C] : a special quality that

seems to come from a person, place, or thing • *His presence brought an aura of dignity to the proceedings.*

au·ral /'orəl/ *adj* : relating to the ear or sense of hearing • *aural sensations* — **au·ral·ly** *adv*

Aus. *abbr* Austria, Austrian

aus·pic·es /'ɑːspəsəz/ *n* — *under the auspices of* *formal* : with the help and support of (someone or something) • *research done under the auspices of the federal government*

aus·pi·cious /ɑː'spɪʃəs/ *adj, formal* : showing or suggesting that future success is likely • *It was an auspicious time to open a new business.* • *an auspicious debut* — **aus·pi·cious·ly** *adv*

Aus·sie /'ɑːsi, Brit 'ɒzi/ *n* [C] *informal* : a person who lives in or is from Australia — **Aussie** *adj*

aus·tere /ɑː'stiər/ *adj* 1 : simple or plain • *austere furnishings* • *her austere style of writing* 2 *of a person* : having a serious and unfriendly quality • *an austere man* 3 : having few pleasures • *They lived an austere life in the country.* — **aus·tere·ly** *adv*

aus·ter·i·ty /ɑː'sterəti/ *n* [U] 1 : a simple and plain quality • *the austerity of the furnishings* 2 : a situation in which there is not much money and it is spent only on things that are necessary • *They lived through years of austerity after the war.* • *a series of austerity measures* [=things done to save money during difficult economic times]

Aus·tra·lian /ɑː'streɪljən/ *n* [C] : a person from Australia — **Australian** *adj*

Aus·tri·an /'ɑːstrijən/ *n* [C] : a person from Austria — **Austrian** *adj*

au·then·tic /ə'θɛntɪk/ *adj* 1 : real or genuine • *The document is authentic.* 2 : true and accurate • *an authentic account of what happened* 3 : made to be or look just like an original • *authentic medieval costumes* • *an authentic Mexican meal* — **au·then·ti·cal·ly** /ə-'θɛntɪkli/ *adv* — **au·then·tic·i·ty** /,ɑː-,θɛn'tɪsəti/ *n* [U]

au·then·ti·cate /ə'θɛntɪ,keɪt/ *vb* -cat·ed; -cat·ing [T] : to prove that something is real, true, or genuine • *Experts authenticated the painting.* — **au·then·ti·ca·tion** /ə,θɛntɪ'keɪʃən/ *n* [U]

¹**au·thor** /'ɑːθər/ *n* [C] 1 : a person who has written something • *The author of the article didn't check his facts.*; *especially* : a person who has written a book or who writes many books • *a best-selling author* 2 : a person who starts or creates something (such as a plan or idea) • *She is the author of the plan.*

²**author** *vb* [T] : to be the author of (something, such as a book) • *She authored several magazine articles.*

au·thor·i·tar·i·an /ə,θorə'terijən/ *adj* : not allowing personal freedom • *an authoritarian government/regime* — **au·thoritarian** *n* [C] • *His father was an authoritarian.* — **au·thor·i·tar·i·an·ism** /ə,θorə'terijə,nɪzəm/ *n* [U]

au·thor·i·ta·tive /ə'θorə,teɪtɪv/ *adj* 1 : having or showing impressive knowledge about a subject • *an authoritative* *source of information* **2** : having the confident quality of someone who is respected or obeyed by other people ▪ *His manner is polite but authoritative.* — **au·thor·i·ta·tive·ly** *adv*

au·thor·i·ty /əˈθɔrəti/ *n, pl* **-ties** **1** [U] : the power to give orders or make decisions ▪ *Does she have (the) authority to do this?* ▪ *You don't have authority over me.* [=you don't have the power to give me orders] ▪ *He was acting under the authority of the company president.* [=the company president gave him the power to do it] ▪ *No one in (a position of) authority objected to the plan.* ▪ *an authority figure* [=a person who has authority over other people] **2** [U] **a** : the confident quality of someone who knows a lot about something or who is respected or obeyed by other people ▪ *She has an air of authority.* ▪ *He spoke with authority about the situation.* **b** : a quality that makes something seem true or real ▪ *Her accent lent authority to her performance.* **3** [plural] : people who have power to make decisions and enforce rules and laws ▪ *Local authorities are investigating the accident.* ▪ *He complained to the authorities* [=the police] *about the noise.* **4** [C] : a person who is an expert on a subject ▪ *He is an authority on local history.* **5** [C] : a government organization that has control of a specified activity or area ▪ *the city's housing authority* — **have it on good authority** ◊ If you *have it on good authority* that something is true, you have been told that it is true by someone you trust and believe. ▪ *I have it on good authority that she is writing a novel.*

au·tho·rize *also Brit* **au·tho·rise** /ˈɑːθəˌraɪz/ *vb* **-rized; -riz·ing** [T] **1** : to give power or permission to (someone or something) ▪ *She was authorized to act for her husband.* ▪ *Only authorized personnel* [=people who have been given special permission] *can enter this area.* **2** : to give legal or official approval to or for (something) ▪ *The city council authorized the sale of the land.* — **au·tho·ri·za·tion** *also Brit* **au·tho·ri·sa·tion** /ˌɑːθərəˈzeɪʃən/ *n* [C/U]

au·thor·ship /ˈɑːθərˌʃɪp/ *n* [U] **1** : the identity of the person who has written something ▪ *The authorship of the novel is unknown.* **2** : the job or profession of writing ▪ *his first attempt at authorship*

au·tism /ˈɑːˌtɪzəm/ *n* [U] *medical* : a condition or disorder that begins in childhood and that causes problems in forming relationships and in communicating with other people — **au·tis·tic** /ɑːˈtɪstɪk/ *adj*

au·to /ˈɑːtoʊ/ *n, pl* **-tos** [C] *chiefly US* : AUTOMOBILE — usually before another noun ▪ *an auto accident/mechanic/ show* ▪ *auto parts*

au·to·bi·og·ra·phy /ˌɑːtəˌbaɪˈɑːgrəfi/ *n, pl* **-phies** [C] : a biography written by the person it is about ▪ *I read her autobiography last year.* — **au·to·bi·og·ra·pher** /ˌɑːtəˌbaɪˈɑːgrəfər/ *n* [C] — **au·to·bio·graph·i·cal** /ˌɑːtəˌbaɪəˈgræfɪkəl/ *adj*

au·toc·ra·cy /ɑːˈtɑːkrəsi/ *n, pl* **-cies** **1**

[U] : a form of government in which a country is ruled by a person or group with total power **2** [C] : a country that is ruled by a person or group with total power — **au·to·crat** /ˈɑːtəˌkræt/ *n* [C] ▪ *The country is ruled by an autocrat.* — **au·to·crat·ic** /ˌɑːtəˈkrætɪk/ *adj*

¹au·to·graph /ˈɑːtəˌgræf, *Brit* ˈɔːtəˌgrɑːf/ *n* [C] : the signature of a famous person ▪ *We asked her for her autograph.*

²autograph *vb* [T] *of a famous person* : to write your signature in or on (something) ▪ *We asked her to autograph her book.* ▪ *an autographed photo*

au·to·mak·er /ˈɑːtoʊˌmeɪkər/ *n* [C] *US* : a company that makes and sells cars ▪ *American automakers*

automata *plural of* AUTOMATON

au·to·mate /ˈɑːtəˌmeɪt/ *vb* **-mat·ed; -mat·ing** [T/I] : to run or operate (something, such as a factory or system) by using machines, computers, etc., instead of people to do the work ▪ *The company recently automated its filing process.* ▪ *a factory that has not yet automated* ▪ *a fully automated factory* ▪ *automated machinery* — **au·to·ma·tion** /ˌɑːtəˈmeɪʃən/ *n* [U]

automated teller machine *n* [C] *US* : ATM

¹au·to·mat·ic /ˌɑːtəˈmætɪk/ *adj* **1** *of a machine or device* : having controls that allow something to work or happen without being directly controlled by a person ▪ *an automatic door* [=a door that opens without being pushed] ▪ *The car has an automatic transmission.* [=a system that changes gears at different speeds without direct control by the driver] **2** *of a gun* : shooting many bullets very quickly when the trigger is pulled ▪ *an automatic rifle/weapon* **3** : happening or done without deliberate thought or effort ▪ *He gave an automatic reply.* **4** : always happening because of a rule, law, previous agreement, etc. ▪ *He had to pay an automatic fine.* — **au·to·mat·i·cal·ly** /ˌɑːtəˈmætɪkli/ *adv*

²automatic *n* [C] **1** : an automatic weapon **2** : a car with automatic transmission ▪ *Is the car a manual or an automatic?*

automatic pilot *n* [C/U] : AUTOPILOT

automatic teller machine *n* [C] *US* : ATM

au·tom·a·ton /ɑːˈtɑːmətən/ *n, pl* **-a·tons** *or* **-a·ta** /-ətə/ [C] **1** : ROBOT **2** : a person who acts in a machinelike way ▪ *an unfeeling automaton*

au·to·mo·bile /ˌɑːtəmoʊˈbiːl/ *n* [C] : a vehicle used for carrying passengers on streets and roads : CAR

au·to·mo·tive /ˌɑːtəˈmoʊtɪv/ *adj, always before a noun* : of, relating to, or concerned with cars and other vehicles ▪ *the automotive industry*

au·ton·o·my /ɑːˈtɑːnəmi/ *n* [U] **1** : the state of existing or acting separately from others ▪ *a teacher who encourages individual autonomy* **2** : the power or right of a country, group, etc., to govern itself ▪ *The territory has been granted autonomy.* — **au·ton·o·mous** /ɑːˈtɑːnəməs/ *adj*

au·to·pi·lot /'ɑːtoʊˌpaɪlət/ *n* [C/U] : a device that steers a ship, aircraft, or spacecraft in place of a person • *The plane was flying on autopilot.* • *(figurative) She performed her chores on autopilot.* [=in a mechanical way without thinking about what she was doing]

au·top·sy /'ɑːˌtɑːpsi/ *n, pl* **-sies** [C] : an examination of a dead body to find out the cause of death • *The coroner performed an autopsy on the victim's body.* — **autopsy** *vb* **-sied; -sy·ing** [T] *US* • *The body has not yet been autopsied.*

au·tumn /'ɑːtəm/ *n* 1 [C/U] : the season between summer and winter • *I saw her last autumn.* • *in early/late autumn* • *the autumn harvest* — called also *(US)* **fall** 2 [C] : the later part of someone's life or of something's existence • *in the autumn of his life* — **au·tum·nal** /ɑˈtʌmnəl/ *adj* • *autumnal colors*

¹**aux·il·ia·ry** /ɑɡˈzɪljəri/ *adj* : available to provide extra help, power, etc., when it is needed • *auxiliary fuel tanks*

²**auxiliary** *n, pl* **-ries** [C] 1 : a group that provides help or assistance • *She joined the women's auxiliary.* [=a group of women who do work to support a church, hospital, etc.] 2 : AUXILIARY VERB • *a verbal auxiliary*

auxiliary verb *n* [C] *grammar* : a verb (such as *have, be, may, do, shall, will, can,* or *must*) that is used with another verb to show the verb's tense, to form a question, etc. — called also *helping verb*

AV *abbr* audiovisual

¹**avail** /əˈveɪl/ *vb* [T/I] *literary* : to be useful or helpful to (someone or something) • *This knowledge availed (her) little.* [=it was not very helpful or useful (to her)] — **avail yourself of** *formal* : to make use of (something) • *They availed themselves of his services.*

²**avail** *n* [U] : help toward reaching a goal • *What I learned then is of no/little avail* [=is not very helpful] *to me now.* • *They tried to discuss the issue calmly, but to no avail.* [=they were unable to discuss the issue calmly]

avail·able /əˈveɪləbəl/ *adj* 1 : easy or possible to get or use • *The medication is available at any drugstore.* • *Is the dress available in larger sizes?* • *The report will soon be made available to the public.* 2 a : present or ready for use • *All available resources were used.* • *Tickets are now available.* b : present and able or willing to talk to someone • *She was not available for comment.* 3 a : not being used or occupied by someone or something else • *the last available seat* b : free to do something • *Are you available for lunch next Tuesday?* c : not involved in a romantic relationship • *a great way to meet available men/women/singles* — **avail·abil·i·ty** /əˌveɪləˈbɪləti/ *n* [U]

av·a·lanche /ˈævəˌlæntʃ/ *n* 1 [C] : a large amount of snow and ice or of dirt and rocks that slides suddenly down the side of a mountain • *He was buried by an avalanche.* 2 [*singular*] : a sudden great amount of something • *an avalanche of praise/publicity*

avant–garde /ˌɑːˌvɑːntˈgɑːd, *Brit* ˌævɒn-**'gɑːd/ *n* [C] : a group of people who develop new and often very surprising ideas in art, literature, etc. • *the literary avant-garde* — **avant–garde** *adj* • *avant-garde art*

av·a·rice /ˈævərəs/ *n* [U] *formal* : GREED • *He was driven by avarice.* — **av·a·ri·cious** /ˌævəˈrɪʃəs/ *adj*

av·a·tar /ˈævəˌtɑːr/ *n* [C] 1 *Hinduism* : the human or animal form of a Hindu god on earth • *an avatar of Vishnu* 2 *computers* : a small picture that represents a computer user in a game, on the Internet, etc. • *A penguin is her personal avatar in the chat room.*

ave. *abbr* avenue

avenge /əˈvɛndʒ/ *vb* **avenged; aveng·ing** [T] : to harm or punish someone who has harmed you or someone or something that you care about • *The brothers vowed to avenge (the death of) their father.* — **aveng·er** *n* [C]

av·e·nue /ˈævəˌnuː, *Brit* ˈævəˌnjuː/ *n* [C] 1 a : a wide street • *Sixth Avenue in Manhattan* b *chiefly Brit* : a path or driveway that leads to a house located off a main road • *a tree-lined avenue* 2 : a way of achieving something or of reaching a goal • *a new avenue of research*

aver /əˈvɚ/ *vb* **averred; aver·ring** [T] *formal* : to say (something) in a very strong and definite way • *He averred that he was innocent.*

¹**av·er·age** /ˈævrɪdʒ/ *n* 1 [C/U] : a number that is calculated by adding quantities together and then dividing the total by the number of quantities • *To find the average of 16, 8, and 6, add them together and divide the total by 3.* • *An average of 2,000 people attend the show each night.* • *On average, women live longer than men.* — see also *the law of averages* at LAW 2 [C/U] : a level that is typical of a group, class, or series • *His work has been better/ worse than average.* • *It has been above/ below average.* 3 [C] *baseball* : BATTING AVERAGE

²**average** *adj* 1 : calculated by adding quantities together and then dividing by the number of quantities • *The average age of the company's employees is 36.* 2 : ordinary or usual • *the average American family* • *(informal) It wasn't your average snowstorm.* [=it was worse than an ordinary snowstorm] 3 a : not unusually large or small • *Sales were about average for the industry.* b : not unusually good or bad • *She was an average student.*

³**average** *vb* **-aged; -ag·ing** [T] 1 : to have (a specified number) as an average • *We average six calls a day.* [=we usually get about six calls a day] 2 : to calculate the average of (something) • *The teacher averaged the students' grades.* — **average out** [*phrasal vb*] 1 : to produce a result that is even and balanced when looked at over a period of time • *Sometimes you win, and sometimes you lose. It all averages out in the end.* 2 **average out to** : to be equal to (a specified average amount) over a period of time • *The gain averaged out to 20 percent.*

averse /əˈvɚs/ *adj* — **averse to** : having a feeling of not liking (something) • *She* *is not averse to taking chances.* [=she is willing to take chances] — **aver·sion** /əˈvɚʒən/ n [C/U] • *(an) aversion to exercise*

avert /əˈvɚt/ vb [T] **1** : to turn (your eyes, gaze, etc.) away or aside • *She had to avert her eyes* [=to look away] *from the TV.* **2** : to prevent (something bad) from happening • *He sped up and averted an accident.*

avi·ary /ˈeɪviˌeri, Brit ˈeɪviəri/ n, pl **-ar·ies** [C] : a place (such as a large cage or a building) where many birds are kept • *The zoo has an outdoor aviary.*

avi·a·tion /ˌeɪviˈeɪʃən/ n [U] : the business or practice of flying airplanes, helicopters, etc. • *commercial/military aviation*

avi·a·tor /ˈeɪviˌeɪtɚ/ n [C] : a person who flies airplanes, helicopters, etc. • *a naval aviator*

av·id /ˈævəd/ adj **1** : very eager or enthusiastic • *an avid fan/golfer/reader* **2** : wanting something very much • *He was avid for power.* — **avid·i·ty** /əˈvɪdəti/ n [U, singular] — **av·id·ly** adv

av·o·ca·do /ˌɑːvəˈkɑːdoʊ, Brit ˌævəˈkɑːdəʊ/ n, pl **-dos** also **-does** [C/U] : a fruit with rough dark green or purple skin, smooth light green flesh, and a large seed in the middle

av·o·ca·tion /ˌævəˈkeɪʃən/ n [C] : HOBBY • *My favorite avocation is reading.* — **av·o·ca·tion·al** /ˌævəˈkeɪʃənəl/ adj

avoid /əˈvɔɪd/ vb [T] **1** : to stay away from (someone or something) • *She took a detour to avoid the traffic jam.* • *They avoided each other for days.* **2** : to prevent the occurrence of (something bad, unpleasant, etc.) • *We need to avoid further delays.* **3** : to keep yourself from doing (something) or participating in (something) • *I'm not going to be late if I can avoid it.* — **avoid·able** /əˈvɔɪdəbəl/ adj — **avoid·ance** /əˈvɔɪdns/ n [C/U] • *(an) avoidance of sentimentality*

avow /əˈvaʊ/ vb [T] formal : to declare or state (something) in an open and public way • *She avowed her innocence.* • *Their avowed aim/goal is to win the trophy.* • *an avowed* [=openly declared] *liberal/conservative* — **avow·al** /əˈvaʊəl/ n [C] • *her avowal of innocence* — **avow·ed·ly** /əˈvaʊədli/ adv

aw /ˈɑː/ interj, US + Scotland, informal — used to express mild disappointment or sympathy • *Aw, that's too bad.*

await /əˈweɪt/ vb [T] **1** : to wait for (someone or something) • *We're eagerly awaiting her arrival.* • *He is in prison awaiting trial.* **2** : to be ready or waiting for (someone or something) • *The same fate awaits us all.*

¹awake /əˈweɪk/ vb awoke /əˈwoʊk/; awo·ken /əˈwoʊkən/; awak·ing [T/I] somewhat formal : to stop sleeping : to wake up • *He awoke suddenly.* • *They were awoken by a loud bang.*

²awake adj, not before a noun : not asleep • *I am so tired I can barely stay awake.* • *She was wide awake.*

awak·en /əˈweɪkən/ vb [T/I] somewhat formal : to stop sleeping : to wake up • *I was awakened by a loud noise.* •

(figurative) Her arrival awakened old memories. — **awaken to** [phrasal vb] **awaken to** or **awaken (someone or something) to** : to become aware of (something) or to make (someone or something) aware of (something) • *They finally awakened to the possibility of war.* — **awak·en·ing** /əˈweɪkənɪŋ/ n [C] • *He thinks he's going to win, but he is in for a rude awakening.* [=he will learn that he is mistaken]

¹award /əˈwoɚd/ vb [T] **1** : to give (a reward or prize) to someone or something • *The judges awarded a prize to the best speaker.* **2** : to officially decide that someone should get (something) • *The company awarded the contract to the lowest bidder.*

²award n [C] : something (such as a prize) that is given to someone or something for being excellent or for doing something that is admired • *She has won numerous awards for her books.* • *an awards ceremony* • *an award-winning film/writer* = *an award-winner*

aware /əˈweɚ/ adj **1 a** not before a noun : knowing that something (such as a situation, condition, or problem) exists • *He was made aware of the situation.* • *Is she aware that you are upset?* • *acutely/keenly/completely aware* **b** : feeling, experiencing, or noticing something (such as a sound, sensation, or emotion) • *I was aware* [=I had noticed] *that he was following me.* **2** : knowing and understanding a lot about what is happening in the world or around you • *They are very aware about the environment.* = *They are very environmentally aware.* — **aware·ness** n [U, singular] • *He is trying to raise public awareness of/about the problem.*

awash /əˈwɑːʃ/ adj, not before a noun **1** : flooded with or covered by water or another liquid — usually + with or (US) in • *a floor awash with/in water* **2** US : floating in a large amount of water or another liquid — + in • *chicken awash in a tasteless broth* • *(figurative) They were awash in debt.*

¹away /əˈweɪ/ adv **1** : in or to another place or direction • *The family next door moved away.* • *We rowed away from the shore.* • *Stay away from that dog.* **2** : toward another direction • *She turned her face away.* **3** : in a safe or secure place • *The will was locked away in the safe.* **4** : into a state of being completely gone • *The memory is fading away.* **5** : from someone's possession • *She gave away a fortune to charity.* **6** : without stopping or slowing down • *The clocks are ticking away.* **7** sports : on the field or court of an opponent • *The team plays away tonight.*

²away adj **1** not before a noun : not at home or in a usual or expected place • *They are away for the weekend.* • *away from home* **2** not before a noun — used to describe how distant something is in space or time • *The lake is 10 miles away.* • *The holidays are two months away.* **3** always before a noun : played on the field or court of an opponent ▪ *The team played both home games and away games.*

¹**awe** /ˈɑː/ *n* [*singular*] : a strong feeling of fear or respect and also wonder ▪ *The experience filled me with awe.* ▪ *an awe-inspiring sight* ▪ *We watched in awe as the building collapsed.* ▪ *I stand in awe of their courage.*

²**awe** *vb* **awed; aw·ing** [*T*] : to fill (someone) with awe ▪ *He was awed by the beauty of the canyon.*

awe·some /ˈɑːsəm/ *adj* **1** : causing feelings of fear and wonder ▪ *Raising a child is an awesome responsibility.* **2** *informal* : extremely good ▪ *She's a totally awesome singer.* ▪ *You did an awesome job.* — **awe·some·ly** *adv* — **awe·some·ness** *n* [*U*]

awe·struck /ˈɑːˌstrʌk/ *adj* : filled with feelings of fear and wonder ▪ *They were awestruck by the size of the project.*

¹**aw·ful** /ˈɑːfəl/ *adj* : extremely bad or unpleasant ▪ *The weather was awful.* ▪ *an awful disease* ▪ *That's an awful thing to say.* ▪ *I felt awful* [=very sick] *and didn't go to school.* ▪ *I feel awful* [=very sorry] *about what happened.* — **an awful lot** *informal* **1** : a large amount ▪ *an awful lot of money* **2** : very much ▪ *I like him an awful lot.* — **aw·ful·ness** *n* [*U*]

²**awful** *adv, chiefly US, informal* : very or extremely ▪ *I'm awful tired.* ▪ *an awful long time*

aw·ful·ly /ˈɑːfəli, ˈɑːfli/ *adv* **1** : very or extremely ▪ *That's awfully nice of you.* ▪ *It's awfully cold out.* **2** : in a very bad or unpleasant way ▪ *He sings awfully.*

awhile /əˈwajəl/ *adv* : for a short while ▪ *Sit and rest awhile.*

awk·ward /ˈɑːkwəd/ *adj* **1 a** : not graceful : CLUMSY ▪ *awkward dancing/movements/writing* ▪ *She is an awkward writer.* **2** : difficult to use or handle ▪ *an awkward tool* **3 a** : not easy to deal with ▪ *It was an awkward moment for everyone.* ▪ *an awkward pause in the conversation* **b** : not socially confident or comfortable ▪ *I feel awkward (about) asking you to help.* ▪ *awkward with/around strangers* — **awk·ward·ly** *adv* — **awk·ward·ness** *n* [*C/U*]

awl /ˈɑːl/ *n* [*C*] : a pointed tool used for making holes in leather, wood, etc.

aw·ning /ˈɑːnɪŋ/ *n* [*C*] : a piece of cloth on a frame that sticks out over a door or window and gives shelter from sun, rain, etc.

awoke *past tense of* ¹AWAKE

awoken *past participle of* ¹AWAKE

AWOL /ˈeɪˌwɑːl/ *adj* : leaving the armed forces without permission ▪ *The soldiers went AWOL.*; *broadly* : absent or missing ▪ *The Senator has been AWOL for the last three votes.* ❖ *AWOL* comes from a military phrase: *absent without leave.*

awry /əˈraɪ/ *adj, not before a noun* **1** : not working correctly or happening in the expected way ▪ *Something was awry with the machine.* **2** : not straight or neat ▪ *Her hair was all awry.* — **awry** *adv* ▪ *Something went dreadfully/terribly awry.*

¹**ax** (*US*) *or* **axe** /ˈæks/ *n* **1** [*C*] : a tool that has a heavy metal blade and a long handle and that is used for chopping wood **2** [*singular*] *informal* **a** : the act of removing someone from a job ▪ *His boss gave him the ax.* [=fired him] ▪ *She got the ax.* [=was fired from her job] **b** : the act of cutting or removing something ▪ *The school program escaped the ax this year.* [=the school program was not cut/eliminated this year] ▪ *Congress took an ax to the program.* [=Congress made severe cuts in the program] — **ax to grind** : a hidden and often selfish purpose for doing something ▪ *He had a political ax to grind with his opponent.*

²**ax** *or* **axe** *vb* **axed; ax·ing** [*T*] *informal* **1** : to cut or remove (something) ▪ *The TV show was axed from the new schedule.* **2** : to fire (someone) ▪ *The boss told him that he had been axed.*

ax·i·om /ˈæksijəm/ *n* [*C*] *formal* : a rule or principle that many people accept as true ▪ *one of the key axioms of the theory of evolution*

ax·i·om·at·ic /ˌæksijəˈmætɪk/ *adj, formal* : obviously true ▪ *an axiomatic truth/assumption*

ax·is /ˈæksəs/ *n, pl* **ax·es** /ˈækˌsiːz/ [*C*] **1** : the imaginary straight line that something (such as the Earth) turns around ▪ *The Earth spins on its axis.* **2** : a straight line that divides a shape evenly into two parts — called also *axis of symmetry*

ax·le /ˈæksəl/ *n* [*C*] : a bar on which a wheel or a pair of wheels turns

¹**aye** *also* **ay** /ˈaɪ/ *adv* **1** — used especially in the language of sailors ▪ *"Take the helm." "Aye, aye, Captain!"* **2** — used to indicate a spoken yes vote ▪ *All in favor, say "aye."*

²**aye** *also* **ay** *n, pl* **ayes** [*C*] : a yes vote ▪ *We have six nays and 12 ayes, so the ayes have it.* [=the "yes" votes win]

AZ *abbr* Arizona

aza·lea /əˈzeɪljə/ *n* [*C*] : a type of bush that has colorful flowers that bloom in the spring

azure /ˈæʒɚ/ *n* [*C/U*] : the blue color of the sky — **azure** *adj*

B

b or **B** /ˈbiː/ n, pl **b's** or **bs** or **B's** or **Bs**
1 [C/U] : the second letter of the English
alphabet • *words that begin with (a) b* **2**
[C/U] : a musical note or key referred to
by the letter B • *play/sing a B* • *a song in
the key of B* **3** [C] : a grade that is given
to a student for doing good work • *got a
B in math* • *He's a B student.* [=a student
who gets B's for his schoolwork] **4** [U]
— used to refer to the second of two or
more things being considered • *We chose
option B over option A.*

B.A. (US) or **BA** abbr bachelor of arts •
*He received a B.A. (degree) in philosophy
from Harvard.*

baa /ˈbæ, ˈbɑː/ n [singular] : the sound
made by a sheep

bab·ble /ˈbæbəl/ vb **bab·bled; bab·
bling** [I] **1 a** : to talk foolishly or too
much • *babbling (on) about sports* • *a babbling idiot* **b** : to make speech sounds
that do not make sense to the hearer •
The baby babbled happily. **2** : to make
the quiet sound of water flowing over
rocks • *a babbling brook* — **babble** n
[U] • *the babble of a brook* — **bab·bler**
/ˈbæbələ/ n [C]

babe /ˈbeɪb/ n [C] **1** : BABY • *I've known
her since she was a babe in arms.* [=an in-
fant] • (*figurative*) *I was a mere babe in
the woods.* [=a person who lacks experi-
ence] **2** slang **a** : a sexually attractive
person • *hot babes in bikinis* **b** — used
as an informal way of addressing a lover,
close friend, etc. • *Hey babe, how've you
been?*

ba·boon /bæˈbuːn/ n [C] : a large African or Asian monkey

¹ba·by /ˈbeɪbi/ n, pl **-bies** [C] **1 a** : a very
young child • *She had the baby yesterday.*
= *She gave birth to the baby yesterday.* •
Are you expecting a baby? [=are you pregnant?] • *a baby girl/boy* • *baby clothes/pic-
tures* • *She has a baby face.* [=a face that
looks young and innocent] **b** : a very
young animal • *a baby bird/deer* **2 a**
: the youngest member of a group • *My
sister is the baby of the family.* • *my baby
sister* **b** : someone who is young in comparison with others • *"Only 32? Oh, you're
just a baby!"* **c** : someone who is afraid
or who complains a lot • *When it comes
to getting shots, I'm a real baby.* **3** slang
a : a lover or sweetheart • *My baby left
me.* **b** — used as an informal way of addressing a lover, close friend, etc. • *I
missed you, baby.* **4** : something that
someone has created and developed •
This project is my baby. — **ba·by·hood**
/ˈbeɪbiˌhʊd/ n [U] • *from babyhood to
adulthood*

²baby adj, always before a noun : much
smaller than usual • *a baby grand piano* •
Take baby steps.

³baby vb **-bies; -bied; -by·ing** [T] **1** : to
be kind or too kind to (someone) • *She
babies her children.* • *I babied myself with*
a trip to the spa. **2** : to treat (something)
in a very careful way • *baby a car*

baby blue n **1** [U] : a very light blue
color **2** [plural] informal : blue eyes •
She gazed into his baby blues. — **baby
blue** adj

baby boom n [C] : a time when there is a
great increase in the number of babies
born • *the U.S. baby boom after World
War II* — **baby boomer** n [C] • *American baby boomers* [=Americans who
were born in the period after World War
II]

baby buggy n [C] **1** US : BABY CAR-
RIAGE **2** Brit : STROLLER 1

baby carriage n [C] US : a vehicle in
which a baby lies while someone pushes
it from place to place — called also (Brit)
pram

baby fat n [U] US : the extra fat that a
healthy baby or young child has • *He still
has his baby fat.*

ba·by·sit /ˈbeɪbiˌsɪt/ vb **-sat** /-ˌsæt/; **-sit·
ting** [T/I] : to take care of a child while
the child's parents are away • *She
babysits (their kids) on Saturday nights.*
— **ba·by·sit·ter** n [C]

baby talk n [U] : the speech used by very
young children

baby tooth n, pl **~ teeth** [C] : a tooth
from the first set of teeth that a child develops

bach·e·lor /ˈbætʃələ/ n [C] : a man who
is not married • *an eligible bachelor* [=an
unmarried man who is regarded as a desirable husband] • *a confirmed bachelor*
[=a man who shows no interest in marry-
ing] • *His friends threw him a bachelor
party the night before his wedding.* —
bach·e·lor·hood /ˈbætʃələˌhʊd/ n [U]

bach·e·lor·ette /ˌbætʃələˈrɛt/ n [C] US
: a woman who is not married • *Her
friends threw the bride a bachelorette party at a night club.*

bachelor's degree n [C] : a degree giv-
en to a student by a college or university
usually after four years of study

¹back /ˈbæk/ n [C] **1 a** : the rear part of
the body that goes from the neck to the
top of the legs • *She was carrying her little
son on her back.* • *She suffered a back injury.* • *I patted him on his/the back to congratulate him.* • *His hands were tied behind his back.* **b** : the part of an animal
that is like a person's back • *riding on the
back of a horse* **2** : the rear side, surface,
or area of something — usually singular
• *the back of the head/hand/mirror/couch*
• *He signed his name on the back of the
check.* **3** : the part of a chair or seat that
supports a person's back • *a chair with a
padded seat and back* **4** : the section of
a book, magazine, etc., that includes the
last pages — usually singular • *There is
an index in/at the back of the book.* **5**
sports : a player in some games (such as
soccer and American football) who is

positioned behind the front line of players • *a defensive back* — **a pat on the back** see ¹PAT — **a stab in the back** see ¹STAB — **at/in the back of your mind** : in the part of your mind where thoughts and memories are kept • *Somewhere in the back of my mind I knew I'd met him before.* — **back is to/against the wall** ✧ When *your back is to/against the wall* or *you have your back to/against the wall*, you are in a bad position in which you are forced to do something in order to avoid failure. • *With our backs to the wall we made a last desperate effort to finish the project on time.* — **back to back 1** : with backs opposite or against each other • *The soldiers stood back to back.* **2** : happening one after the other • *I scheduled two appointments back to back.* — see also BACK-TO-BACK — **behind someone's back** : without someone's knowledge • *You shouldn't gossip about people behind their back(s).* • *She went behind his back and spoke directly to his supervisor.* — **break the back of** : to greatly weaken (something you are trying to stop or defeat) • *new policies that will break the back of inflation* — **get your back up** : to become angry or annoyed and want to fight or argue • *He gets his back up whenever someone questions his work.* — **in back** : in an area at the back of something • *There were two available seats in back.* — **in back of** *chiefly US* : directly behind (something or someone) • *There's a small yard in back of the house.* — **on the back of 1** : because of (something) • *Profits have increased on the back of improved sales.* **2** *disapproving* : by using the efforts of (other people) • *They achieved record profits on the back of cheap labor.* — **on/off your back** ✧ Someone who is frequently criticizing you or telling you what to do is *on your back* and won't **get off your back**. • *My boss is always on my back about getting more work done.* • *Get off my back! I'm working as hard as I can!* — **on your back** ✧ If you are *(flat)* on *your back*, you are lying down on your back. • *The accident left him (lying) flat on his back (in bed) for two weeks.* • *(figurative) The stock market has been flat on its back [=has been doing very poorly] in recent weeks.* — **out back** : in the area behind a house, building, etc. • *The house has a shed out back.* — **put someone's back up** : to make someone angry or ready to argue • *Questioning his decision will just put his back up.* — **put your back into** : to work very hard at (something) • *He put his back into scrubbing the floor.* — **see the back of** ✧ In British English, to be *glad/happy (etc.) to see the back of* someone is to be glad to see someone finally going away. • *He's a troublemaker and I'll be glad to see the back of him!* — **stab (someone) in the back** see ²STAB — **the shirt off your back** see SHIRT — **turn your back** : to turn so that you are facing away from someone • *She turned her back (on me) and walked away.* • *(figurative) His fans have turned their backs on him.* [=have

abandoned him] — **watch/have someone's back** : to protect someone who is doing something that is dangerous or risky • *Don't worry, I've got your back.* — **watch your back** : to be careful • *The boss is in a bad mood this morning, so watch your back.* — **back·less** /ˈbækləs/ *adj* • *a backless evening gown*

²back *adv* **1 a** : in, toward, or at the back or rear • *The police asked the crowd to move/step back.* • *He left his friends two miles back.* • *She looked back toward him.* **b** : to, toward, or in the place where someone or something was previously • *He left and never went back (home).* • *She forgot to put the book back.* • *She should be back* [=return] *soon.* **2** : in or into the past • *an event back in the last century* • *It happened several years back.* **3 a** : to or toward a former state or condition • *I wish things could go back to how they used to be.* **b** : in return or reply • *He gave the money back (to me).* • *He hit me and I hit him right back.* **c** — used to describe someone or something that is being stopped from moving forward or happening • *He tried to jump, but his friends held him back.* • *He didn't allow poverty to hold/keep him back.* [=to keep him from succeeding] • *The project was set back* [=it was delayed] *many days.* **d** — used to describe something that is being kept instead of being given or revealed • *They held/kept back part of the money.* **4** : to or at an angle • *lie back on the couch* [=lie down on the couch] • *After work, I like to just sit/lean back and relax.*

³back *adj, always before a noun* **1** : located at the back • *the back door/entrance* [=the door/entrance at the back of a building] • *his back pocket* • *She likes to sit in the back row.* **2** : far from a central or main area • *We used the back roads instead of the highway.* • *a back alley* **3** : owed from an earlier time • *The company owes him several months in back pay.* • *back rent* **4** : published at an earlier time • *a back issue of a magazine* **5** *golf* — used to refer to the final 9 holes of an 18-hole golf course • *She was three over par on the back nine.*

⁴back *vb* **1** [*T*] **a** : to give help or support to (someone) • *I'm backing him for President.* **b** : to bet on (someone or something) • *She backed the winner of the race and won a lot of money.* **c** : to provide evidence that supports (something) • *She backed her argument with written evidence.* **d** : to provide the money that is needed for (something) • *back a new company* **e** : to sing or play music that supports (a main singer or musical instrument) • *A guitarist backed (up) the singer.* **2** [*T/I*] : to move backward • *She backed (her car) into a parking space.* • *(figurative) The reporter backed her into a corner* [=put her into a difficult position that was hard to get out of] *with his questions.* **3** [*I*] : to have the back toward something • *The house backs onto/on* [=the back of the house faces] *the golf course.* — **back away** [*phrasal vb*] : to move away from something or someone by walking backward • *She told him to

back away (from the growling dog). •
*(figurative) The governor is now backing
away from her earlier position.* — **back
down** [phrasal vb] : to stop arguing or
fighting for something • *The strike will
continue until one side backs down.* • *He'll
never back down from a fight.* — **back off**
[phrasal vb] **1** : to stop arguing or fighting for something • *He refused to back off.*
2 : to stop bothering someone • *She was
getting irritated, so I backed off.* — **back
out** [phrasal vb] : to decide not to do
something that you had agreed to do •
*The agreement fell through when investors
backed out (of the deal).* — **back up**
[phrasal vb] **1 a** : to move backward •
*Could you back up a little to give me some
room?* • *(figurative) Wait, let's back up for
a second.* [=let's go back to what we were
discussing earlier] **b** *back (a vehicle) up
or back up (a vehicle)* : to move (a vehicle) backward • *He backed his car up into
the garage.* **2** *back up or back (something) up or back up (something)* : to become blocked or to cause (something) to
become blocked • *The accident backed
up traffic for miles.* = *Traffic was backed
up for miles because of the accident.* •
Traffic backed up for miles. • *The drain
was backed up.* **3** *back (someone or
something) up or back up (someone or
something)* **a** : to give help or support
to (someone or something) • *I'll back you
up if I think you're right.* • *She backed up
her argument with written evidence.* **b**
computers : to make a copy of (a computer file or data) to protect it from being lost • *Remember to back up your work
before you log off.*

back·ache /'bæk,eɪk/ *n* [C/U] : pain in
the back • *a patient suffering from (a)
backache*

back and forth *adv* **1** : backward and
forward • *The chair rocked back and
forth.* **2** : between two places or people •
They threw the ball back and forth.

back-and-forth *n* [U] : talk or discussion about something • *An agreement was
finally reached after a lot of back-and-
forth between the two sides.*

back·bit·ing /'bæk,baɪtɪŋ/ *n* [U] : unkind talk about someone who is not
present • *petty backbiting among employees*

back·board /'bæk,bɔəd/ *n* [C] *basketball* : the board behind the basket

back·bone /'bæk,boʊn/ *n* **1** [C] : the
row of bones that go down the middle of
the back and protect the spinal cord —
called also *spinal column, spine* **2** [C]
: the most important or strongest part of
something • *She is the backbone of the
family.* **3** [U] : strength and courage •
*He showed some backbone by refusing to
compromise his values.*

back·break·ing /'bæk,breɪkɪŋ/ *adj* : involving very difficult physical work or
effort • *backbreaking work*

back burner *n* — **on the back burner**
chiefly US : in the position of not receiving immediate attention and action • *She
put her singing career on the back burner
to pursue acting.*

back·chat /'bæk,tʃæt/ *n* [U] *Brit, informal* : BACK TALK

back·drop /'bæk,drɑːp/ *n* [C] **1** : a
painted cloth that is hung across the
back of a stage **2** : the scenery that is in
the background • *The mountains were a
perfect backdrop for the wedding photos.*
3 : the setting or conditions within which
something happens • *The novel unfolds
against a backdrop of war.*

-backed *combining form* **1** : having a
particular kind of back • *a high-backed
chair* **2** : supported by a particular
group, organization, etc. • *government-
backed programs*

back·er /'bækɚ/ *n* [C] : a person or
group that gives support to someone or
something • *the candidate's backers* •
backers of the plan

back·fire /'bæk,fajɚ/ *vb* **-fired; -fir·ing**
[I] **1** *of an engine or vehicle* : to make a
loud sound when fuel is not burned
properly • *The car backfired.* **2** : to have
the opposite result of what was desired
or expected • *Our plans backfired (on us).*

back·gam·mon /'bæk,gæmən/ *n* [U] : a
board game in which two players throw
dice and try to move all of their pieces
around the board

back·ground /'bæk,graʊnd/ *n* **1** [C]
: the scenery behind a main figure or object in a picture • *a photograph of a house
with mountains in the background* • *background scenery* **b** : a surface or color
that is behind or around something • *red
letters printed on a white background* **2**
[singular] **a** : a position that attracts little attention • *He tried to keep/stay in the
background.* [=tried to avoid attracting
attention] **b** — used to describe something that happens without requiring attention • *The software was automatically
updated in the background while we continued to work on the data.* **c** — used to
describe something that is heard while
something else is being listened to • *I
could hear a dog barking in the background.* • *There was a lot of background
noise.* [=unwanted sound heard in a radio broadcast, a tape recording, etc.] •
background music [=music played in a
movie, television show, etc., to add to the
story or mood] **3 a** [C] : the events and
conditions that help to explain why
something happens — usually singular •
*the social and economic background of
the American Civil War.* **b** [U] : information needed to understand a problem or
situation • *background information* **4**
[C] : the experiences, knowledge, education, etc., in a person's past • *people with
different educational/social/ethnic backgrounds* • *They ran a background check to
make sure she had no criminal record.*

back·hand /'bæk,hænd/ *n* [C] *sports* **1**
: a way of hitting a ball or puck in which
the back of the hand is turned in the direction of the ball or puck • *She has a
good backhand.* • *He hit a backhand shot
into the net.* **2** : a catch in baseball and
similar games that is made on the side of
the body that is opposite the hand being
used • *The shortstop made a backhand*

catch. — **back·hand** *vb* [T] • *She backhanded the ball over the net.*

back·hand·ed /ˈbækˈhændəd/ *adj* **1** : not direct or sincere • *a backhanded apology* • *She paid me a backhanded **compliment** [=a compliment that was not really a compliment] when she said my work was "surprisingly good."* **2** *sports* : using or done with a backhand • *a backhanded shot*

back·hoe /ˈbækˌhoʊ/ *n* [C] *US* : a large machine that digs into the ground with a metal scoop

back·ing /ˈbækɪŋ/ *n* **1** [U] : support or aid • *The project got financial backing from several investors.* **2** [C] : something that forms a back • *The tape has an adhesive backing.*

back·lash /ˈbækˌlæʃ/ *n* [C] : a strong public reaction against something • *a backlash against feminism*

back·log /ˈbækˌlɑːg/ *n* [C] : a large number of jobs that are waiting to be finished • *We have a huge backlog of orders to be filled.*

back order *n* [C/U] *chiefly US, business* : a product that has been ordered but not sent to the customer because it is not yet available • *The book is on back order and won't be shipped for three weeks.* — **back–or·der** *vb* [T] • *The book has been back-ordered.*

¹**back·pack** /ˈbækˌpæk/ *n* [C] *chiefly US* : a bag for carrying things that has two shoulder straps and is carried on the back

²**backpack** *vb* [I] : to hike or travel with a backpack • *backpacking through Europe* — **back·pack·er** *n* [C]

back·ped·al /ˈbækˌpɛdl̩/ *vb, US* **-ped-aled** *or chiefly Brit* **-ped-alled;** *US* **-ped-al·ing** *or chiefly Brit* **-ped-al·ling** [I] : to move backward with quick steps • *She backpedaled a few steps to catch the ball.* *(figurative) The governor backpedaled from his previous position.*

back·seat /ˈbækˈsiːt/ *n* [C] : a seat in the back of a car, bus, etc. — **take a backseat** : to be or become less important, active, or powerful • *He refuses to take a backseat to anyone.* [=to let anyone have more power or control than he has]

backseat driver *n* [C] : a passenger in a car who gives driving advice to the driver

back·side /ˈbækˌsaɪd/ *n* [C] *informal* : BUTTOCKS

back·slash /ˈbækˌslæʃ/ *n* [C] : a mark \ used for separating written items

back·slide /ˈbækˌslaɪd/ *vb* **-slid** /-ˌslɪd/; **-slid·ing** [I] : to start doing something bad again after you have stopped it • *backsliding into old bad habits* — **back·slid·er** /ˈbækˌslaɪdɚ/ *n* [C]

back·space /ˈbækˌspeɪs/ *n* [C] : a key pressed on a computer keyboard to move backward on a line of text — **backspace** *vb* **-spaced; -spac·ing** [I]

back·spin /ˈbækˌspɪn/ *n* [U] : a backward spinning motion of a ball • *put backspin on the ball*

back·stab·bing /ˈbækˌstæbɪŋ/ *n* [U] *US* : harmful and unfair things that are said or done to hurt someone • *the backstab-*

bing of her former friend — **back·stab·ber** /ˈbækˌstæbɚ/ *n* [C] — **backstab·bing** *adj* • *a backstabbing liar*

back·stage /ˈbækˌsteɪdʒ/ *adv* : behind the stage of a theater • *We went backstage to meet the band.* — **backstage** *adj* • *a backstage pass* [=a card that gives permission to go backstage and usually to meet the performers]

back·stop /ˈbækˌstɑːp/ *n* **1** [C] *baseball* : a fence or screen behind the catcher **2** [singular] : something that is kept so that it can be used if it is needed • *a backstop line of credit*

back·stretch /ˈbækˌstrɛtʃ/ *n* [C] : the far side of a racetrack • *The horses are in the backstretch.* — called also (*Brit*) **backstraight** /ˈbækˌstreɪt/

back·stroke /ˈbækˌstroʊk/ *n* [singular] : a way of swimming by floating on your back; *also* : a race in which the swimmers do the backstroke • *the 50-meter backstroke*

back·swing /ˈbækˌswɪŋ/ *n* [C] : a movement of the arm backwards before swinging a club, bat, etc. • *a golfer with a short backswing*

back talk *n* [U] *US, informal* : rude speech in reply to someone who should be spoken to with respect • *Don't give me any back talk!* — called also (*Brit*) **backchat**

back–to–back *adj* **1** : facing in opposite directions and often touching • *back-to-back seats* **2** : happening one after another in time • *back-to-back victories/appointments* — **back to back** *adv* • *standing back to back*

back·track /ˈbækˌtræk/ *vb* [I] **1** : to go back over a course or path • *We made a wrong turn and had to backtrack.* **2** : to return to something that was mentioned before • *Let me backtrack and return to your first question.* **3** : to completely change what you think or say about something • *He backtracked* [=he reversed his position] *on the issues.*

back·up /ˈbækˌʌp/ *n* **1 a** [C] : a person or thing that can be used to replace or support another person or thing • *We have an extra radio as a backup in case this one doesn't work.* • *a backup quarterback* • *a backup plan* **b** [U] : help or support provided by additional people or things • *The policeman called for backup.* [=called for other police to come and help him] **2** [C] *US* : a situation in which the flow of something becomes blocked • *a traffic backup* [=(*Brit*) *tailback*] **3** [U] : a musical part that is sung to support the main singer • *She sang backup on his CD.* • *a backup singer* **4** [C] : a copy of information stored on a computer • *Be sure to make a backup of your work.* • *a backup file/copy*

¹**back·ward** (*chiefly US*) /ˈbækwɚd/ *or* **back·wards** /ˈbækwɚdz/ *adv* **1** : toward the back • *I glanced backward over my shoulder.* • *She took a step backward.* • *driving backward* **2** : opposite to the usual way • *Count backward from 10.* **3** : toward the past • *a journey backward in time* **4** : toward a worse condition • *His new job, which paid less, felt like a step*

backward. — **bend/fall/lean over back-ward** : to make a great effort to help someone or to reach agreement with someone • *The salesman said he would bend over backward to make the deal.*

²**backward** *adj* **1 a** : directed or turned toward the back • *a backward glance/movement* **b** : done backward • *a backward somersault* **2** : behind others : not as advanced as others in learning or development • *a backward village with no running water* — **back·ward·ly** *adv* — **back·ward·ness** *n* [U]

back·wa·ter /ˈbækˌwɑːtə/ *n* [C] : a quiet place where there is little activity, excitement, progress, etc. • *The once sleepy backwater is now a thriving city.*

back·woods /ˈbækˈwʊdz/ *n* [plural] : an area that is far from cities • *the back-woods of Canada*

back·yard /ˈbækˈjɑəd/ *n* **1** [C] : an area behind someone's house • *The kids were playing in the backyard.* • *a backyard bar-becue/garden* **2** [U] : the general area near and around someone's home • *They want to build a new prison in our own backyard.* [=near our homes]

ba·con /ˈbeɪkən/ *n* [U] : thin strips of salted and smoked meat from a pig • *a slice of bacon* — **bring home the bacon** *informal* : to earn the money that is needed to live • *He brings home the bacon for his family.* — **save someone's ba-con** see ¹SAVE

bacteria *plural of* BACTERIUM

bac·te·ri·um /bækˈtirijəm/ *n, pl* **-te·ria** /-ˈtirijə/ [C] : any one of a group of very small living things that often cause disease — usually plural • *Keep the wound clean and free of bacteria.* — **bac·te·ri-al** /bækˈtirijəl/ *adj*

¹**bad** /ˈbæd/ *adj* **worse** /ˈwəs/; **worst** /ˈwəst/ **1 a** : low or poor in quality • *bad work* • *The house is in bad condition/shape.* **b** : not correct or proper • *bad manners/grammar* • *a bad check* [=a check that cannot be cashed] • *She scolded the children for using* **bad language.** [=language that is offensive or dirty] **2 a** : not pleasant, pleasing, or enjoyable • *bad weather* • *He had a bad day/dream.* • *The food tastes/smells bad.* • *bad breath* [=breath that smells bad] • *I look bad in this hat.* = *This hat looks bad on me:* **b** : having, marked by, or relating to problems, troubles, etc. • *bad news* • *in good times and bad (times)* • *bad luck/fortune* • *I have a bad feeling about this.* • *Stay away from him—he's* **bad news.** [=a bad, unpleasant, or dangerous person or thing] • *There's been a lot of* **bad blood** [=feelings of dislike] *between them since their fight.* **c** : not adequate or suitable • *a bad day for a picnic* • *Is this a bad time to talk with you?* **d** : not producing or likely to produce a good result • *a bad idea/plan* • *a bad loan* [=a loan that will not be repaid] **e** : expressing criticism or disapproval • *The movie got bad reviews.* **3 a** : marked or affected by injury or disease • *His health is bad.* = *He's in bad health.* • *She has a bad back/leg.* [=a back/leg that is often painful] • *bad eye-sight/hearing* **b** : causing harm or trou-

ble • *a bad diet/influence* — often + *for* • *Smoking is bad for you.* • *Eating too much candy is bad for your teeth.* • **4 a** : morally evil or wrong • *bad people/behavior/deeds* • *It's hard to tell the good guys from the* **bad guys** *in this movie.* **b** : not behaving properly • *Your son has been a very* **bad boy.** **5 a** : not skillful : not doing or able to do something well • *a bad musician/doctor* — often + *at* • *He's bad at express-ing his feelings.* **b** : having a tendency not to do something — + *about* • *I'm bad about remembering* [=I often forget] *peo-ple's birthdays.* **6 a** : feeling regret or guilt about something • *I feel bad about what happened.* • *She felt bad that she for-got to call.* **b** : not cheerful or calm • *She's in a bad mood.* • *He has a bad tem-per.* [=he becomes angry easily] **7** : seri-ous or severe • *a bad cough/cold* • *How bad is the pain?* **8** : no longer fresh enough to eat or drink • *Is the milk still good or has it* **gone bad?** **9 bad·der; bad·dest** *chiefly US, informal* **a** : very good • *He's the baddest guitar player ever!* **b** : very tough or dangerous • *Don't mess with him. He's a bad dude.* — **from bad to worse** : from a bad state or condition to an even worse state or condition • *Things have gone from bad to worse for the struggling company.* — **in a bad way** : in a bad condition • *Without enough funding, public services are in a bad way right now.* — **not bad** : fairly good or quite good • *She's really not a bad singer.* [=she's a pretty good singer] • *"How are you?" "Not (too/so) bad, thanks. And you?"* — **too bad 1** — used to show that you are sorry or feel bad about something • *It's too bad that John and Mary are getting divorced.* • *"I can't come to the party." "(That's) Too bad. I was hoping you'd come."* **2** — used in an ironic way to show that you do not feel bad about something • *"But I need your help!" "Too bad."* — **bad·ness** *n* [U]

²**bad** *adv* **worse; worst** *US, informal* : BADLY • *She hasn't succeeded because she doesn't want it bad enough.* • *He cut himself real bad.* [=very badly] • *He's* **got it bad** *for her.* [=he's extremely in love with her] — **bad off** *US* **1** : having little money • *They're* **bad off** *(for money) now that he's lost his job.* **2** : in a bad or diffi-cult situation or condition • *This state isn't too* **bad off** *compared to other places.*

³**bad** *n* **1** [U] : EVIL • *the difference be-tween good and bad* **2 the bad a** [sin-gular] : the unpleasant things that hap-pen to people • *You have to* **take the good with the bad.** [=accept the bad things that happen to you as well as the good things] **b** [plural] : morally bad people • *He be-lieves that the bad go to hell when they die.*

bad·ass /ˈbædˌæs/ *adj, always before a noun, chiefly US, informal + sometimes offensive* **1** : likely to cause trouble • *a badass criminal* **2** : very skillful or im-pressive • *a badass musician* — **badass** *n* [C] • *He thought of himself as a real badass.*

bade *past tense of* ¹BID

bad faith *n* [U] : lack of honesty in deal-ing with other people • *She accused her* landlord of bad faith. — **in bad faith** : in a dishonest and improper way ▪ She signed the contract in bad faith. [=with no intention of following the contract]

badge /ˈbædʒ/ n [C] **1** : a small tag, pin, or metal shield that is worn or held up by a person in order to show who the person is ▪ The policeman flashed his badge. ▪ She had on an employee/visitor's badge. **2** : a cloth patch that can be sewn onto clothing and that is awarded to a person for doing something ▪ She earned 10 Girl Scout merit badges. **3** Brit : ¹BUTTON 2 ▪ She wore a badge that read "Vote." **4** : something that represents or is a sign of something else ▪ He wore his ethnicity as a **badge** of honor/pride. [=he was proud of his ethnicity]

¹**bad·ger** /ˈbædʒɚ/ n [C] : a type of animal that lives in the ground and has long claws on its front feet

²**badger** vb [T] **1** : to bother or annoy (someone) with many comments or questions ▪ She was being badgered by reporters. **2** : to ask or tell someone many times to do something ▪ Stop badgering me. I'll do it.

bad·lands /ˈbædˌlændz/ n [plural] : a region where there are large rocks with strange shapes and very few plants ▪ the badlands of South Dakota

bad·ly /ˈbædli/ adv **worse** /ˈwɚs/; **worst** /ˈwɚst/ **1** : in a bad manner ▪ We played badly. ▪ The failure reflects badly on us. ▪ children behaving badly ▪ a badly planned project ▪ "How are you doing?" "Not (too/so) badly. [=fairly or quite well] And you?" ▪ Will you think badly of [=have a bad or low opinion of] me if I take the last cookie? **2 a** : very much ▪ She wanted the job badly. ▪ I'm badly in need of a vacation. **b** : severely or seriously ▪ Was she hurt badly? — **badly off 1** : having little money ▪ I'm not badly off. [=I'm pretty well off] **2** : in bad condition ▪ Other patients were more badly off than me. ▪ (Brit) The team is badly off for young players. [=the team has a strong need for young players]

bad·min·ton /ˈbædˌmɪntn/ n [U] : a game in which a shuttlecock is hit over a net by players using light rackets

bad–mouth /ˈbædˌmaʊθ/ vb [T] informal : to say bad things about (someone or something) ▪ She won't bad-mouth her colleagues.

bad–tempered adj : easily annoyed or angered ▪ a bad-tempered old man

baf·fle /ˈbæfəl/ vb **baf·fled; baf·fling** [T] : to confuse (someone) completely ▪ Her behavior baffles me. ▪ a baffled look [=a look that shows confusion] — **baf·fle·ment** /ˈbæfəlmənt/ n [U] — **baffling** adj ▪ a baffling array of choices — **baf·fling·ly** /ˈbæflɪŋli/ adv

¹**bag** /ˈbæg/ n **1** [C] **a** : a container made of paper, plastic, cloth, etc., that opens at the top and is used for holding or carrying things ▪ She packed her lunch in a paper bag. ▪ **shopping bags** = (Brit) **carrier bags** [=bags used for holding items bought at a store] ▪ (US) **grocery bags b** : HANDBAG ▪ She put the pencil in her bag. **c** : a container used for car-

rying personal things (such as clothes) when you are going somewhere ▪ an overnight/gym bag ▪ We carried our bags to the hotel room. **2** [C] : the amount of something that is inside a bag ▪ We ate two bags of chips. **3** [plural] : an area of swollen skin under a person's eyes ▪ a tired old man with bags under his eyes **4** [singular] : a collection of different things (such as ideas) ▪ They tried using their usual **bag of tricks**. **5** [C] informal — used as an insulting word for an old woman ▪ Shut up, you old bag! — **hold the bag** informal : sure to happen ▪ Their success was in the bag. : certain to be successful ▪ She has the election in the bag. [=she is sure to win the election] — **let the cat out of the bag** see CAT — **bag·ful** /ˈbægˌfʊl/ n [C] ▪ a bagful of apples

²**bag** vb **bagged; bag·ging** [T] **1** : to put (something) into a bag ▪ He got a job bagging groceries. **2** : to kill or catch (an animal) while hunting, fishing, etc. ▪ We bagged 10 fish today. **3** informal : to get (something desired) ▪ She's expected to bag the award. **4** US, informal : to give up or leave (something) ▪ He bagged his acting career and went back to school.

ba·gel /ˈbeɪgəl/ n [C] : a bread roll shaped like a ring

bag·gage /ˈbægɪdʒ/ n [U] **1** chiefly US : LUGGAGE ▪ Please collect your baggage. **2** : the feelings, problems, or past events that can make life difficult for a person or group ▪ He has a lot of personal/emotional baggage from his childhood.

bag·gy /ˈbægi/ adj **bag·gi·er; -est** of clothing : very loose ▪ baggy jeans/sweaters

bag lady n, pl ~ **ladies** [C] : a homeless woman who carries her possessions in a bag

bag lunch n [C] US : a lunch that is made at home, packed inside a bag or box, and eaten at a job, at school, etc. — called also box lunch

bag of bones n [singular] informal : a very thin person or animal ▪ He's just a bag of bones.

bag·pipe /ˈbægˌpaɪp/ n [C] : a musical instrument that is played especially in Scotland and that has a bag, a tube for blowing air into the bag, and pipes where the air leaves and makes sounds — usually plural ▪ He plays the bagpipes.

¹**bail** /ˈbeɪl/ n [U] : an amount of money given to a court so that a prisoner is allowed to leave jail and return later for a trial ▪ The judge/court **set bail** at $1 million. [=decided that the person must pay $1 million in order to get out of jail until a trial] ▪ He is now **free/out on bail**. [=he has paid the court money and is out of jail and waiting for his trial] ▪ He didn't have enough money to **make/post bail**. [=to give enough money to the court in order to leave jail until his trial] ▪ He **jumped/skipped bail**. [=he paid money to get out of jail and then failed to return for his trial]

²**bail** vb **1** [T] : to remove or throw water from a boat ▪ bailing water out of a canoe = bailing out (water from) a canoe **2** [I]

US, informal : to leave a difficult situation ▪ She bailed when things got tough. — **bail out** [phrasal verb] chiefly US **1 a** : to jump out of an airplane with a parachute ▪ The pilot bailed out [=(Brit) baled out] before the plane crashed. **b** : to leave or escape a harmful or difficult situation ▪ They bailed out [=(Brit) baled out] of the deal. **2 bail (someone or something) out** or **bail out (someone or something) a** : to make it possible for (someone) to leave jail by paying bail ▪ She bailed him out (of jail). **b** : to help (someone) solve a problem or leave a difficult situation ▪ They bailed their son out of trouble. ▪ to help (a business, an organization, etc.) by giving or lending money ▪ The government bailed out [=gave money to] their company.

bai·liff /ˈbeɪləf/ n [C] **1** US : an officer in a court of law who helps the judge control the people in the courtroom **2** Brit : someone hired by a sheriff to bring legal documents to people and to take away possessions when people cannot pay for them **3** Brit : someone who manages the land and property of another person

bail·out /ˈbeɪlˌaʊt/ n [C] : the act of saving or rescuing something (such as a business) from money problems ▪ government bailouts of large corporations

¹**bait** /ˈbeɪt/ n [C/U] : something that is used to attract fish or animals so they can be caught ▪ fishing with live bait [=worms that are alive] ▪ cheese used for/as bait in mousetraps ▪ (figurative) The police waited for the bank robbers to **take the bait**. [=to be tricked into doing the thing that would cause them to be trapped or caught]

²**bait** vb [T] **1** : to put a piece of food on (a hook) or in (a trap) in order to attract and catch fish or animals ▪ She used cheese to bait the traps. **2** : to try to make (someone) angry by using criticism or insults ▪ The interviewer baited him by asking him if he was lying.

bake /ˈbeɪk/ vb **baked**; **bak·ing 1 a** [T/I] : to make bread, cake, etc., by preparing a dough or batter and cooking it in an oven using dry heat ▪ I baked you a cake. ▪ freshly baked bread ▪ He likes to bake. = He enjoys baking. [=he likes making pies, cookies, etc.] **b** [T/I] : to cook (food) in an oven using dry heat ▪ Put the chicken in the oven and bake (it) for 30 minutes. ▪ baked potatoes **c** [I] : to be cooked in an oven ▪ How long has the cake been baking? **2** [T] : to make clay, mud, etc., dry and hard by using heat ▪ They baked the bricks in the sun. **3** [I] : to be or become very hot ▪ We stood baking in/under the hot desert sun. ▪ The streets were baking hot. [=very hot]

baked beans n [plural] : beans that have been boiled and then baked usually in a sweet brown sauce

bak·er /ˈbeɪkə/ n [C] : someone who bakes bread, cakes, etc. ▪ I'm a good baker. ▪ I got this bread fresh from the baker's. [=from the bakery]

baker's dozen n [singular] : thirteen of something

bak·ery /ˈbeɪkəri/ n, pl **-er·ies** [C] : a place where bread, cakes, cookies, and other baked foods are made or sold

bake sale n [C] US : an event in which people try to earn money by selling cookies, pies, etc.

baking powder n [U] : a white powder that is used to make cakes, breads, etc., light and fluffy ▪ a teaspoon of baking powder

baking sheet n [C] : a flat piece of metal used for baking cookies, biscuits, etc., in an oven — called also (chiefly US) cookie sheet

baking soda n [U] : a kind of salt that is used to make cookies, breads, etc., light and fluffy — called also sodium bicarbonate

¹**bal·ance** /ˈbæləns/ n **1** [U] **a** : the state of having your weight spread equally so that you do not fall ▪ She held on to the rail for balance. = She held on to the rail to **keep/maintain her balance**. ▪ The skater suddenly **lost his balance** and fell. ▪ Another skater bumped into him and **knocked/threw him off balance**. ▪ (figurative) The sudden change in the schedule knocked/threw me off balance. **b** : the ability to move or to remain in a position without losing control or falling ▪ She has a good **sense of balance**. **2** [U, singular] : a state in which different things occur in equal or proper amounts or have an equal or proper amount of importance ▪ To provide balance in her news story, she interviewed members of both political parties. ▪ Temperature changes could upset the delicate balance of life in the forest. ▪ He needs to achieve/create/strike a better balance between his work life and his family life. [=to spend less time at work and more time with his family] ▪ He's trying to keep his work life **in balance** with his family life. ▪ His life is **out of balance**. **3 a** [C] : the amount of money in a bank account ▪ You must maintain a minimum balance of $1,000 [=you must keep at least $1,000] in your bank account. **b** [C] : the amount of money that still needs to be paid ▪ the unpaid balances on your credit cards **c the balance** : something that remains after other things have been done or used ▪ We stayed there for the balance [=the rest] of the summer. **4** [C] : a device that shows how heavy things are : SCALE — see also CHECKS AND BALANCES — **in the balance** ◇ If something (such as your future) **hangs in the balance** or is **in the balance**, it will soon be known or decided. ▪ Our future hangs in the balance as we await their decision. [=their decision will control our future] ▪ With her job in the balance, she went to ask her boss for a raise. — **on balance** : in general ▪ The meeting went well on balance. — **tip the balance** see ¹TIP

²**balance** vb **-anced**; **-anc·ing 1** [T/I] : to make something steady by keeping weight equal on all sides — usually + on ▪ The waiters balanced the food on large trays. ▪ balancing on one foot **2 a** [T] : to adjust (an account or budget) so that the amount of money available is more than

or equal to the amount of money that has been spent • *The legislature is still trying to balance the state's budget.* **b** [*T/I*] : to check and make adjustments to financial records so that they are accurate • *He balances his checkbook every month.* **3** [*T/I*] : to make (different or opposite things) equal in strength or importance • *She's able to balance her career with her family life.* • *The article gave a balanced* [=*fair, unbiased*] *account of the event.* • *a balanced diet* [=a diet having all the kinds of food needed to be healthy] • *The good times and the bad times balanced out* [=happened in equal amounts] *in the end.* **4** [*T*] : to make (a different or opposite thing) less powerful, noticeable, etc. • *The movie's serious subject matter is balanced (out) with humor.* **5** [*T*] : to think about (different things) and decide which is better or more important — usually + *against* or *with* • *They'll have to balance the risks against/with the rewards.* [=to decide if the possible good results are worth the possible bad results]

balance beam *n* [*C*] : a thick bar of wood used in gymnastics for displays of balance

balance of power *n* [*singular*] : a situation in which two countries, political parties, etc., have equal amounts of power • *Their party's loss of two members shifted/tipped/tilted* **the balance of power** *in the legislature.*

balance sheet *n* [*C*] : a statement that shows the money and property that a company has and the money it owes

bal·co·ny /ˈbælkəni/ *n, pl* **-nies** [*C*] **1** : a raised platform that is connected to the side of a building and surrounded by a low wall or railing • *a hotel room with a balcony* **2** : a floor above the main floor of a theater • *Our seats are on/in the balcony.*

bald /ˈbɑːld/ *adj* **1 a** *of a person* : having no hair or very little hair on the head • *a completely bald man* • *He's starting to go bald.* [=to become bald] **b** *of a part of the body* : not covered with hair • *There are bald spots/patches in the cat's fur.* • *a bald head* **2** : not covered with trees and plants • *a bald mountaintop* **3** *of a tire* : having a smooth surface because of use • *a car with bald tires* **4** : said or given in a very direct way without extra details or explanations • *She repeated her bald assertion that her son was innocent.* — **bald·ly** *adv* • *To put it baldly* [=to say it in a harsh and honest way], *I don't like you.* — **bald·ness** *n* [*U*]

bald eagle *n* [*C*] : a large bird of North America that has a white head and white tail feathers ✧ The bald eagle is a symbol of the U.S.

bald–faced /ˈbɑːldˈfeɪst/ *adj, chiefly US* **1** : easy to see and understand as being bad • *a bald-faced lie* **2** : showing no guilt or shame • *a bald-faced liar*

bald·ing /ˈbɑːldɪŋ/ *adj* : becoming bald • *a balding head/man*

¹**bale** /ˈbeɪl/ *n* [*C*] : a large amount of a material (such as hay or wool) that is pressed together tightly and then tied or

wrapped • *a bale of cotton/paper*

²**bale** *vb* **baled; bal·ing** [*T*] **1** : to press together and tightly tie or wrap (something) into a bale • *baling hay* **2** *Brit* : ²BAIL 1 • *baling water out of a canoe* — **bale out** [*phrasal vb*] *Brit* **1** : to jump out of an airplane with a parachute • *The pilot baled out.* [=bailed out] **2** : to leave a harmful or difficult situation • *They baled out* [=bailed out] *of the deal.*

bale·ful /ˈbeɪlfəl/ *adj, formal* **1** : threatening harm or evil • *He gave us a baleful glare/look.* **2** : harmful or deadly • *the baleful effects of water pollution* — **bale·ful·ly** *adv*

¹**balk** *also Brit* **baulk** /ˈbɑːk/ *vb* [*I*] **1** : to refuse to do what someone else wants you to do • *The union balked at accepting the new contract.* **2 a** : to stop quickly and refuse to continue going • *The horse balked and would not jump the fence.* **b** : to fail to work in the usual or expected way • *The car's engine balked.* [=refused to start] **3** *baseball* : to stop suddenly after starting to throw a pitch • *The pitcher balked.* [=committed a balk]

²**balk** *n* [*C*] *baseball* : an occurrence in which a pitcher stops suddenly or makes an illegal movement after starting to throw a pitch • *He committed a balk.*

balky /ˈbɑːki/ *adj* **balk·i·er; -est** *chiefly US* : not doing what is wanted or expected • *a balky horse/engine*

¹**ball** /ˈbɑːl/ *n* **1** [*C*] : a usually round object that is used in a game or sport or as a toy • *a tennis/soccer ball* • *golf/billiard/bowling balls* **2** [*C*] : something that has a round shape • *a ball of string* • *cotton balls* **3** [*C*] : the rounded part of the human foot that is at the bottom of the foot and behind the toes • *He stood on the balls of his feet.* **4** *informal* + *often offensive* **a** [*C*] : TESTICLE **b** [*plural*] : the courage that is needed to do something • *You don't have the/enough balls to fight me.* **5** [*C*] *a sports* : a ball that is thrown or hit • *She hit a high arching ball over the net.* **b** *baseball* : a pitch that does not go through the proper area and that the batter does not swing at • *The pitcher threw a ball followed by two strikes.* — **carry the ball** *US, informal* : to have the responsibility for doing something • *It's up to you to carry the ball.* — **drop the ball** *US, informal* : to make a mistake especially by not doing something important • *The mayor dropped the ball by not hiring more police officers.* — **get/set/start/keep the ball rolling** *informal* : to cause an activity or process to begin or continue • *She got the ball rolling by asking him a few questions.* — **keep your eye on the ball** *informal* : to continue thinking about or giving attention to something important that you want to do or achieve • *Keep your eye on the ball* [=stay focused] *if you want to finish on time.* — **on the ball** *informal* : mentally prepared • *With such smart students, the teacher really has to be on the ball.* — **play ball!** **1** : to begin or continue to play baseball, basketball, etc. • *Let's play some ball.* **2** : to cooperate with other people • *He refused to play ball with the*

police. — **the ball is in your court** ✧ If *the ball is in your court*, you are the person who is expected or required to do something. ▪ *What should we do now? The ball is in your court.* — compare ³BALL

²ball *vb* [T] : to form (something) into a ball ▪ *balling your hands into fists* ▪ *He balled up the letter and threw it in the trash.*

³ball *n* [C] : a large formal party for dancing ▪ *She went to the ball and danced with the prince.* ▪ *the governor's ball* — **have a ball** *informal* : to have fun ▪ *We had a ball at the party.* — compare ¹BALL

bal·lad /ˈbæləd/ *n* [C] **1** : a slow popular song that is typically about love **2** : a kind of poem or song that tells a story ▪ *a ballad about King Arthur*

bal·last /ˈbæləst/ *n* [U] : heavy material (such as rocks or water) that is put on a ship to make it steady or on a balloon to control its height in the air ▪ *(figurative) His wife provided the ballast* [=the steadiness or stability] *he needed in times of stress.*

ball bearing *n* [C] **1** : a part of a machine in which another part (such as a metal pole) turns easily ✧ A ball bearing is made up of several small metal balls that fit between two metal rings. **2** : one of the balls in a ball bearing

bal·le·ri·na /ˌbæləˈriːnə/ *n* [C] : a woman who is a ballet dancer

bal·let /bæˈleɪ, ˈbæˌleɪ/ *n* **1** [U] : a kind of dancing that is performed on a stage and that uses light flowing movements to tell a story ▪ *She teaches tap dancing and ballet.* ▪ *ballet dancers/shoes/lessons* **2** [C/U] : a show in which ballet is performed ▪ *one of my favorite ballets* ▪ *We enjoy going to the ballet.* [=going to ballet performances] **3** [C] : a group of dancers who perform ballets together ▪ *the New York City Ballet* — **bal·let·ic** /bæˈlɛtɪk/ *adj* ▪ *balletic movements/grace*

ball game *n* [C] **1** *US* : a baseball game ▪ *Dad took us to a ball game.* **2** *informal* — used in phrases like **a whole new ball game** and **a different ball game** to describe a situation or activity that has changed ▪ *Raising children is a different ball game now.*

bal·lis·tic /bəˈlɪstɪk/ *adj* — **go ballistic** *informal* **1** : to become very angry ▪ *Dad went ballistic when he saw the dent in his car.* **2** *US* : to become very excited ▪ *The crowd was going ballistic.*

ballistic missile *n* [C] : a weapon that is shot through the sky over a great distance and then falls to the ground and explodes

bal·lis·tics /bəˈlɪstɪks/ *n* [plural] : the science that studies the movement of bullets, rockets, etc.

ball of wax *n* [singular] *US, informal* **1** : a situation or set of conditions ▪ *Playing basketball at the professional level is a different ball of wax.* **2** : a collection of items or objects ▪ *He won the car, the furniture, and the vacation—the whole ball of wax!* [=everything]

¹bal·loon /bəˈluːn/ *n* [C] : a thin usually rubber bag that becomes larger when it is filled with air or gas ▪ *balloons and oth-*

er party decorations — see also HOT-AIR BALLOON — **go over like a lead balloon** (*US*) or *Brit* **go down like a lead balloon** *informal, of a joke, suggestion, etc.* : to fail completely ▪ *His joke went over like a lead balloon.* [=no one laughed at his joke]

²balloon *vb* [I] : to become bigger quickly ▪ *His weight ballooned to 300 pounds.* = *He ballooned to 300 pounds.* ▪ *ballooning credit card debt*

bal·loon·ing /bəˈluːnɪŋ/ *n* [U] : the activity of traveling in a hot air balloon ▪ *We went ballooning.* — **bal·loon·ist** /bəˈluːnɪst/ *n* [C]

bal·lot /ˈbælət/ *n* **1** [C] : a ticket or piece of paper used to vote in an election ▪ *The issue was on the ballot.* [=people voted on the issue] ▪ *I cast my ballot for her.* [=I voted for her] **2** [C/U] : a process that allows people to vote in secret so that other people cannot see their votes ▪ *She was elected by (a) secret ballot.* **3** [U] **a** : the total number of votes in an election ▪ *He won 65 percent of the ballot.* **b** : an election ▪ *He claims that his opponent won by rigging the ballot.* [=by dishonestly controlling the results of the election]

ballot box *n* **1** [C] : a box that holds the ballots used for voting in an election ▪ *(US) Fans stuffed the ballot box* [=voted more than once] *for their favorite players.* **2** [singular] : an act of voting using secret ballots ▪ *winning at the ballot box* [=in an election]

bal·lot·ing *n* [U] : an act or process of voting ▪ *the balloting for class president*

¹ball·park /ˈbɑːlˌpɑːrk/ *n* [C] : a park in which baseball games are played ▪ *hit a home run out of the ballpark* — **in the ballpark** *informal* : close to the correct or exact number, price, etc. ▪ *My first guess wasn't even in the ballpark.* [=it was not close to being correct]

²ballpark *adj, always before a noun* : approximately correct ▪ *She gave us a ballpark price of $5,000.* [=she said it could cost about $5,000]

ball·play·er /ˈbɑːlˌpleɪjɚ/ *n* [C] *US* : a baseball player

ball·point pen /ˈbɑːlˌpɔɪnt-/ *n* [C] : a pen whose tip is a small metal ball

ball·room /ˈbɑːlˌruːm/ *n* [C] : a large room used for dances

ballroom dancing *n* [U] : a style of dancing in which couples perform formal dances (such as the tango or the waltz) — **ballroom dance** *n* [C]

ball·sy /ˈbɑːlzi/ *adj* **ball·si·er; -est** *informal, sometimes offensive* : very tough or brave ▪ *That was a ballsy thing to say!* ▪ *a ballsy lawyer*

bal·ly·hoo /ˈbæliˌhuː/ *n* [U] *informal* : talk or writing that is designed to get people excited or interested in something ▪ *Despite all the ballyhoo* [=hype]*, their new album is terrible.* — **ballyhoo** *vb* [T] ▪ *a ballyhooed new album*

balm /ˈbɑːm/ *n* **1** [C/U] : an oily substance that is used for healing or protecting the skin **2** [singular] : something that gives comfort or support ▪ *Music is a balm to the soul.*

balmy /ˈbɑːmi/ *adj* **balm·i·er; -est** *of air,*

weather, etc. : warm, calm, and pleasant • *a balmy evening*

ba·lo·ney /bə'louni/ *n* [U] **1** *informal* : NONSENSE • *Don't believe all of that baloney.* • *That's a bunch/load of baloney.* **2** *US* : BOLOGNA • *a baloney sandwich*

bal·sa /'baːlsə/ *n* [U] : the very light wood of a tropical American tree

bal·sam fir /'baːlsəm-/ *n* [C] : a small American evergreen tree

bal·sam·ic vinegar /bɑl'sæmɪk-/ *n* [U] : a type of vinegar that has a dark color and a sweet taste

bal·us·trade /'bæləˌstreɪd/ *n* [C] : a low wall at the sides of staircases, bridges, etc., that is made of a row of posts topped by a long rail

bam /'bæm/ *n* [C] *informal* : a sudden loud noise — often used as an interjection • *I was driving along when, bam, I hit a pothole.*

bam·boo /bæm'buː/ *n* [C/U] : a tall plant with hard hollow stems — **bamboo** *adj* • *bamboo furniture* • *eating bamboo shoots* [=young bamboo plants]

bam·boo·zle /bæm'buːzəl/ *vb* **-boo·zled**; **-boo·zling** [T] *informal* : to trick or confuse (someone) • *The salesperson bamboozled us into getting a more expensive item.*

¹**ban** /'bæn/ *vb* **banned**; **ban·ning** [T] **1** : to say that something cannot be used or done • *The city banned smoking in all public buildings.* • *a list of banned books* **2** : to forbid (someone) from doing or being part of something • *She was banned from the team.*

²**ban** *n* [C] : an official rule saying that people are not allowed to use or do something • *a smoking ban = a ban on smoking*

ba·nal /bə'næl, bə'nɑːl, 'beɪnəl/ *adj* : boring or ordinary : not interesting • *banal remarks about the weather* — **ba·nal·i·ty** /bə'næləti/ *n, pl* **-ties** [C/U] • *banalities about the weather* • *the banality of daily life*

ba·nana /bə'nænə, Brit bə'nɑːnə/ *n* [C/U] : a long curved fruit with a thick peel that is yellow when it is ripe • *a bunch of bananas* • *a banana peel*

ba·nan·as /bə'nænəz, Brit bə'nɑːnəz/ *adj, not before a noun, informal* : CRAZY • *You're driving me bananas.* • *The crowd went bananas.* [=became very excited] *when the concert began.*

¹**band** /'bænd/ *n* [C] **1 a** : a usually small group of musicians who play popular music together • *The band's drummer is also the lead singer.* • *a jazz/rock-and-roll band* **b** : a group of people or animals • *a band of hunters* **2 a** : a flat, straight piece of plastic, metal, etc., that forms a circle around something • *A band of plastic holds the lid on the container.* • *They placed a metal band on the bird's leg.* • *a wedding band* [=wedding ring] **b** : a thick line • *The dress has a band (of white) at the hem.*

²**band** *vb* — **band together** [phrasal vb] : to form a group in order to do or achieve something • *They banded together for protection.*

¹**ban·dage** /'bændɪʤ/ *n* [C] : a strip of cloth, plastic, etc., that covers part of the body that has been hurt • *He wrapped a bandage around his knee.* • *She put a bandage on/over the cut.*

²**bandage** *vb* **-daged**; **-dag·ing** [T] : to cover or wrap (something) with a bandage • *She bandaged (up) their wounds.*

¹**Band–Aid** /'bændˌeɪd/ *trademark* — used for a small bandage

²**Band–Aid** *adj, disapproving* : able to help something only for a short time • *a Band-Aid solution to the problem*

ban·dan·na *also* **ban·dana** /bæn'dænə/ *n* [C] : a square piece of cloth that is worn on the head or around the neck

B and B *n* [C] : BED-AND-BREAKFAST

band·ed /'bændəd/ *adj* : having narrow strips of different color • *a banded tail*

ban·dit /'bændət/ *n* [C] : a criminal who attacks and steals from travelers • *a famous bandit of the 19th century* — **ban·dit·ry** /'bændətri/ *n* [U]

band·lead·er /'bændˌliːdə/ *n* [C] : the leader of a band that plays jazz or dance music

ban·do·lier *or* **ban·do·leer** /ˌbændə'liə/ *n* [C] : a belt that is worn over the shoulder and that holds bullets

band·stand /'bændˌstænd/ *n* [C] : a covered or raised platform on which a band or orchestra plays

band·wag·on /'bændˌwægən/ *n* [C] : a popular activity, effort, cause, etc., that attracts growing support — usually singular • *Many companies are getting/jumping/climbing on the bandwagon and offering flexible work schedules.*

band·width /'bændˌwɪdθ/ *n* [C/U] *technical* : a measurement of the ability of a computer, computer network, etc., to send and receive information • *Graphics use more bandwidth than text does.*

ban·dy /'bændi/ *vb* **-dies**; **-died**; **-dy·ing** — **bandy about/around** [phrasal vb] **bandy (something) about/around** *or* **bandy (something) about/around** : to discuss or mention (something) in a casual or informal way • *The idea is being bandied about.* — **bandy words** *old-fashioned* : to say angry words in an argument : ARGUE • *I don't want to bandy words with you.*

bane /'beɪn/ *n* [singular] : a cause of trouble, annoyance, or unhappiness • *She was the bane of my existence.* [=she made my life very unhappy, difficult, etc.]

bane·ful /'beɪnfəl/ *adj, formal* : causing destruction or serious harm • *the baneful effects/consequences of inflation*

¹**bang** /'bæŋ/ *vb* **1 a** [T] : to cause or allow (something) to hit something in a way that makes a loud noise • *She accidentally banged her elbow.* • *He banged his empty glass on the counter.* **b** [T/I] : to hit (something or someone) in a way that makes a loud noise • *The chair fell over and banged (into/against) the wall.* • *Someone banged into her.* **2** [T/I] : to use your hand or a tool to beat or hit (something) in a way that makes a loud noise • *He banged (on) the drum.* • *She banged (on) the table with her fist.* — see also *bang the drum for* at ¹DRUM **3** [I] : to make a sudden loud noise • *The door*

banged shut. **4** [T] *informal + offensive* : to have sex with (someone) — **bang away** [*phrasal vb*] *US, informal* : to work hard at something • *We have to keep banging away (at this) if we want to finish on time.* — **bang on about** [*phrasal vb*] *Brit, informal* : to talk about (something) repeatedly or for a long time • *She's always banging on about the need for change.* — **bang out** [*phrasal vb*] **bang out (something)** or **bang (something) out** *informal* **1** : to produce (something) quickly • *banging out an agreement* **2** : to play (a song, melody, etc.) loudly on a piano • *She banged out a song on the piano.* — **bang up** [*phrasal vb*] **bang up (something or someone)** or **bang (something or someone) up 1** *US, informal* : to injure or damage (something or someone) • *She banged up her knee.* • *The car was pretty banged up.* **2** *Brit slang* : to put (someone) in prison • *He got banged up for robbery.*

²**bang** *n* **1 a** [C] : a sudden loud noise • *The door shut with a bang.* **b** — used as an interjection to imitate a loud noise (such as the sound of a gun being fired) • *"Bang, bang! You're dead."* **2** [C] : a hard hit or blow • *She got a nasty bang on her head.* — **bang for the/your buck** *US, informal* — used to describe how much value is received when money is spent • *This restaurant offers people the most bang for the buck.* [=offers more than other restaurants for the same price] — **get a bang out of** *US, informal* : to enjoy (something) very much • *You'll get a bang out of this story.* — **with a bang** : in a sudden and exciting way • *The movie starts with a bang.*

³**bang** *adv, Brit, informal* : exactly or directly • *It was bang in front of us!* — see also *bang to rights* at ³RIGHT — **bang on** *Brit, informal* : exactly right • *His answer was bang on.*

bang·er /ˈbæŋɚ/ *n* [C] *Brit, informal* **1** : SAUSAGE • *bangers and mash* [=sausages and mashed potatoes] **2** : FIRECRACKER **3** : JALOPY

ban·gle /ˈbæŋgəl/ *n* [C] : a stiff bracelet worn around your arm, wrist, or ankle

bangs /ˈbæŋz/ *n* [*plural*] *US* : the front section of a person's hair when it is cut short and worn over the forehead — called also (*Brit*) *fringe*

bang–up /ˈbæŋˌʌp/ *adj, always before a noun, US, informal* : very good or excellent • *She did a bang-up job.*

ban·ish /ˈbænɪʃ/ *vb* [T] **1** : to force (someone) to leave a country as punishment • *He was banished (from the country) for life.* **2** : to send (someone or something) away • *They want to banish her from the sport.* • *The reporters were banished to another room.* **3** : to cause (something) to leave • *She banished him from her mind.* [=she did not think about him] — **ban·ish·ment** /ˈbænɪʃmənt/ *n* [U]

ban·is·ter *also* **ban·nis·ter** /ˈbænəstɚ/ *n* [C] : a structure like a fence with a bar on top that is built next to a set of stairs

ban·jo /ˈbændʒoʊ/ *n, pl* **-jos** [C] : an instrument like a guitar with a round body and long neck • *playing (the) banjo*

¹**bank** /ˈbæŋk/ *n* [C] **1** : a business where people keep their money, borrow money, etc. • *Our paychecks are deposited into the bank automatically.* • *How much money is in your bank account?* **2** : a small closed container in which money is saved — see also PIGGY BANK **3** : a place where a particular thing is stored until it is needed • *information stored in a computer's memory banks* — see also BLOOD BANK, SPERM BANK **4** : the higher ground that is along the edge of a river, stream, etc. • *The stream overflowed its banks.* **5 a** : the side of a hill • *climbing up a steep bank* **b** : a small hill that is built next to a road along a curve **6** : a thick mass of clouds or fog • *a fog bank* **7** : a group of objects that are arranged close together in a row • *a bank of file cabinets* — **break the bank** : to be very expensive or too expensive • *a dependable car that won't break the bank*

²**bank** *vb* **1 a** [I] : to have money in a bank • *We bank locally.* **b** [T] : to put (something) in a bank • *bank a check* **2** [T/I] : to cause an airplane, motorcycle, etc., to tilt or lean to one side when turning • *The pilot banked (the plane) to the right.* **3** [T] *US* : to cause (something) to bounce off a surface • *She banked the basketball off the backboard.* **4** [T] : to form (something) into a pile • *banking sand (up) along the river to prevent flooding* — **bank on** [*phrasal vb*] : to feel confident or sure about (something) • *We're banking on fair weather for the trip.*

bank·able /ˈbæŋkəbəl/ *adj* : certain to make a profit • *a bankable director/star* [=a director/star who makes movies that earn a profit]

bank card /ˈbæŋkˌkɑɚd/ *n* [C] **1** *US* : a card from your bank that you use to pay for things or to get money from an ATM **2** *Brit* : a card that you show when you pay for something with a check to prove that the bank will pay the amount of the check

bank·er /ˈbæŋkɚ/ *n* [C] : a person who owns or has an important job in a bank

bank holiday *n* [C] *Brit* : LEGAL HOLIDAY

bank·ing *n* [U] : the business of operating a bank • *a career in banking*

bank·note /ˈbæŋkˌnoʊt/ *n* [C] : a piece of paper money • *a $10 banknote*

¹**bank·roll** /ˈbæŋkˌroʊl/ *vb* [T] *chiefly US, informal* : to supply money for (a business, project, person, etc.) • *The company is bankrolling the film.*

²**bankroll** *n* [*singular*] *chiefly US* : a supply of money • *They started the business with a small bankroll.*

bank·rupt /ˈbæŋkˌrʌpt/ *adj* **1** : unable to pay debts • *The company went bankrupt.* [=became unable to pay its debts] **2** : completely lacking a good or desired quality • *emotionally/morally bankrupt* [=having no emotions/morals] — **bankrupt** [T] • *Several risky deals bankrupted the company.* — **bank·rupt·cy** /ˈbæŋkˌrʌptsi/ *n, pl* **-cies** [C/U] • *moral/ethical bankruptcy* • *The number of bankruptcies was high last year.* • *The company* *filed for bankruptcy.* [=officially asked to be legally recognized as bankrupt] ▪ *He declared bankruptcy.* [=formally said that he was bankrupt in a legal document]

¹**ban·ner** /ˈbænə/ *n* [C]   **1 a** : a large strip of cloth usually with writing on it ▪ *He helped carry a banner in the parade.* ▪ *(figurative) changes made **under the banner of** "restoring order"* [=for the officially stated purpose of restoring order]   **b** : FLAG ▪ *The Star-Spangled Banner*   **2** : an advertisement that is across the top of a page on a Web site

²**banner** *adj, always before a noun, US* : unusually good ▪ *It was a banner year for the sales department.*

bannister *variant spelling of* BANISTER

ban·quet /ˈbæŋkwət/ *n* [C] : a formal dinner for many people usually to celebrate a special event ▪ *They held a banquet in his honor.* ▪ *a banquet hall/table*

ban·shee /ˈbænˌʃiː/ *n* [C] : a female spirit in stories who cries loudly ▪ *wailing/screaming like a banshee*

ban·tam·weight /ˈbæntəmˌweɪt/ *n* [C] : a boxer who weighs from 112 to 119 pounds (51 to 54 kilograms) ▪ *a bantamweight fighter*

ban·ter /ˈbæntɚ/ *n* [U] : talk in which people make jokes about each other in a friendly way ▪ *good-natured banter* — **banter** *vb* [I] ▪ *We bantered with each other.*

bap /ˈbæp/ *n* [C] *Brit* : ²ROLL 2a

bap·tism /ˈbæpˌtɪzəm/ *n* [C/U] : a Christian ceremony in which water is placed on a person's head or in which a person's body is briefly placed under water ✧ *A baptism officially makes someone a member of the Christian religion.* ▪ *the sacrament of baptism* ▪ *(figurative) The interview was a baptism into journalism for the young writer.* [=was the young writer's first experience as a journalist] ▪ *(figurative) a baptism of/by fire* [=a first experience that is very difficult or painful] — **bap·tis·mal** /bæpˈtɪzməl/ *adj*

Bap·tist /ˈbæpˌtɪst/ *n* [C] : a member of a Christian church in which members are baptized only as adults — **Baptist** *adj* ▪ *a Baptist preacher*

bap·tize *also Brit* **bap·tise** /ˈbæpˌtaɪz, bæpˈtaɪz/ *vb* **-tized; -tiz·ing** [T] : to perform a baptism for (someone) ▪ *The priest baptized the baby.* ▪ *He was baptized* [=*christened*] *"John" when he was two months old.*

¹**bar** /ˈbɑɚ/ *n*   **1** [C]   **a** : a building or room where alcoholic drinks and sometimes food are served ▪ *We went to a bar for a drink.*   **b** : a counter where alcoholic drinks are served ▪ *We sat at the restaurant's bar.* ▪ *He tends bar.* [=works as a bartender]   **2** [C] : a long, narrow piece of metal, wood, etc. ▪ *There were bars across all the windows.* ▪ *The pole-vaulter cleared the bar.* [=jumped over the long bar set at a specific height] ▪ *(US, figurative) The company's new software* **raises the bar** *for its competitors.* = *It* **sets the bar** *higher for its competitors.* [=the company's new software is very good and competitors will have to produce better

software to compete with it] ▪ *He has been **behind bars** [=in jail] for 10 years.*   **3** [C] : a solid piece of something that is shaped like a rectangle ▪ *a chocolate/candy bar* ▪ *a bar of soap*   **4** [C] : a straight line, stripe, or section that is longer than it is wide ▪ *a menu bar* [=a section across the screen in a computer program that shows available menus] — *see also* TASK BAR, TOOLBAR   **5** [C] *formal* : something that makes it difficult or impossible to do or achieve something ▪ *His poor attitude was a bar to his success.* [=his poor attitude prevented him from succeeding]   **6** *the bar* a *US* : the profession of a lawyer ▪ *She is a member of the bar.* [=she is a lawyer] ▪ *the American Bar Association*   **b** *or the Bar Brit* : the profession of a barrister   **c** *US* : the test that a person must pass in order to be a lawyer ▪ *the bar exam*   **7** [C] *music*   **a** : a line in written music that shows where a measure begins   **b** : the beats between two bars in a piece of music : MEASURE

²**bar** *vb* **barred; bar·ring** [T]   **1** : to put a bar or a set of bars in front of a door, window, etc. ▪ *He shut and barred the door.*   **2** : to put something in a road, path, etc., so that people cannot get by ▪ *A cow was barring the road.*   **3 a** : to prevent or forbid (someone) *from* doing something ▪ *Reporters were barred from (attending) the meeting.*   **b** : to prevent or forbid (something) ▪ *forms of punishment barred by the Constitution* — *no holds barred see* ²HOLD

³**bar** *prep* — used in the phrase *bar none* to emphasize that a statement is completely true ▪ *She is the brightest student I've ever known, bar none.*

barb /ˈbɑɚb/ *n* [C]   **1** : a sharp point that sticks out and backward from the point of an arrow, a fishhook, etc.   **2** : a clever insult or criticism ▪ *The candidates exchanged barbs during the debate.* — **barbed** *adj* ▪ *a barbed fishhook* ▪ *barbed comments*

bar·bar·i·an /bɑɚˈberijən/ *n* [C]   **1** : a member of a violent or uncivilized group of people especially in past times ▪ *The city was invaded by barbarians.*   **2** : a rude or uneducated person ▪ *They behaved like barbarians.*

bar·bar·ic /bɑɚˈberɪk/ *adj*   **1 a** : very rude or offensive ▪ *barbaric manners*   **b** : very cruel ▪ *The treatment of the prisoners was barbaric.*   **2** : of or relating to barbarians ▪ *Barbaric tribes invaded the area.* — **bar·bar·i·cal·ly** /bɑɚˈberɪkli/ *adv*

bar·ba·rism /ˈbɑɚbəˌrɪzəm/ *n*   **1** [C/U] : cruel and violent behavior ▪ *a dictator accused of barbarisms*   **2** [U] : very rude behavior ▪ *acts of social barbarism*

bar·ba·rous /ˈbɑɚbərəs/ *adj*   **1** : very rude or offensive ▪ *barbarous behavior/language*   **2** : very cruel and violent ▪ *a barbarous crime* — **bar·bar·i·ty** /bɑɚˈberəti/ *n, pl* **-ties** [C/U] ▪ *the barbarity of the attack* ▪ *unimaginable barbarities* — **bar·ba·rous·ly** *adv*

¹**bar·be·cue** /ˈbɑɚbɪˌkjuː/ *n*   **1** [C] : a flat metal frame that is used to cook food over hot coals or a fire ▪ *grill a steak on*

the barbecue **2** [C] : an outdoor meal or party at which food is cooked on a barbecue ▪ *We had a barbecue last weekend.* — abbr. *BBQ* **3** [U] *chiefly US, informal* : food that has been cooked on a barbecue ▪ *We ate some barbecue.* ▪ **barbecue sauce** [=a spicy sauce usually eaten with barbecued food]

²**barbecue** *vb* **-cued; -cu·ing** [T/I] : to cook (food) on a barbecue ▪ *We barbecued (chicken) last night.* ▪ *We ate barbecued chicken.*

barbed wire *n* [U] : wire that has sharp points ▪ *a barbed-wire fence* — called also (*US*) **barbwire**

bar·bell /ˈbɑɚˌbɛl/ *n* [C] : a metal bar with weights at each end that is used for exercise

bar·ber /ˈbɑɚbɚ/ *n* [C] : a person whose job is to cut men's hair

bar·ber·shop /ˈbɑɚbɚˌʃɑːp/ *n* [C] *chiefly US* : a place where a barber works

barbershop quartet *n* [C] : a group of four male singers who sing in an old-fashioned style without instruments

bar·bie /ˈbɑɚbi/ *n* [C] *chiefly Brit + Australia, informal* : ¹BARBECUE

bar·bit·u·rate /bɑɚˈbɪtʃərət/ *n* [C] *medical* : a type of drug that is used to calm people or make them sleep

barb·wire /ˈbɑɚbˈwajɚ/ *n* [U] *US* : BARBED WIRE

bar chart *n* [C] : BAR GRAPH

bar code *n* [C] : a group of thick and thin lines that is placed on a product so that a computer can get information about the product

¹**bare** /ˈbeɚ/ *adj* **bar·er; bar·est 1 a** : not having a covering ▪ *The walls were bare.* ▪ (*figurative*) *The book lays bare* [=reveals] *the secrets of this political family.* **b** : not covered by clothing, shoes, a hat, etc. ▪ *Her feet were bare.* = *She had bare feet.* [=she wasn't wearing shoes or socks on her feet] ▪ *He bent the pipe with his bare hands.* [=using only his hands and no tools] **c** : not covered by leaves, grass, trees, or plants ▪ *bare branches* ▪ *The ground was bare where the statue had stood.* **2 a** : not containing anything ▪ *a bare cupboard/shelf* **b** : having little or no furniture ▪ *Her office was pretty bare.* **3** *always before a noun* : including only what is most basic or needed ▪ *He only told me the bare facts about what happened.* ▪ *the bare essentials/necessities* ▪ *the bare minimum* [=the least amount possible] — **bare·ness** *n* [U]

²**bare** *vb* **bared; bar·ing** [T] : to remove the covering from (something) ▪ *The dog growled and bared its teeth.* ▪ *She was asked to bare (it) all* [=to pose nude] *for the magazine.* ▪ (*figurative*) *He bared his soul to me.* [=he told me his most private thoughts and feelings]

bare·back /ˈbeɚˌbæk/ *adv* : without a saddle ▪ *We rode (the horses) bareback.* — **bareback** *adj* ▪ *bareback riding*

bare bones *n* — **the bare bones** : the most basic or important facts or parts of something ▪ *What are the bare bones of the story?*

bare–bones *adj* : including only what is most basic or needed ▪ *a bare-bones Web*

site ▪ *The hotel rooms are bare-bones.*

bare·faced /ˈbeɚˌfeɪst/ *adj, always before a noun, disapproving* : completely obvious ▪ *a barefaced lie/liar*

bare·foot /ˈbeɚˌfʊt/ *or* **bare·foot·ed** /ˈbeɚˌfʊtəd/ *adv* : without shoes ▪ *We walked barefoot in the stream.* — **barefoot** *or* **barefooted** *adj* ▪ *barefoot children*

bare–hand·ed /ˈbeɚˌhændəd/ *adv* : without using a tool, weapon, glove, etc. ▪ *She caught the ball bare-handed.* — **bare–handed** *adj* ▪ *a bare-handed catch*

bare·head·ed /ˈbeɚˌhɛdəd/ *adv* : without a hat ▪ *He left the house bareheaded.* — **bareheaded** *adj* ▪ *a bareheaded man*

bare–knuck·le /ˈbeɚˌnʌkəl/ *also* **bare–knuck·led** /ˈbeɚˌnʌkəld/ *or* **bare–knuck·les** /ˈbeɚˌnʌkəlz/ *adj, always before a noun* : without boxing gloves ▪ *a bare-knuckle fight/fighter/punch* ▪ (*figurative*) *bare-knuckle politics* [=very tough and aggressive politics]

bare·ly /ˈbeɚli/ *adv* **1 a** — used to say that something was almost not possible or almost did not happen ▪ *She could barely walk/read/see.* [=she was almost unable to walk/read/see] ▪ *I barely recognized her.* ▪ *He barely made it on time.* [=he almost was too late] **b** : having only a specified small size, age, length, etc. ▪ *He's (just) barely a teenager.* ▪ *barely four feet tall* **c** : having reached a specified condition or happened only a short time before ▪ *They had barely set up the tents when it started to rain.* **2 a** : almost not at all ▪ *I barely knew him.* **b** : almost not ▪ *There is barely any difference between them.*

barf /ˈbɑɚf/ *vb* [I] *US, informal* : VOMIT ▪ *The smell made me want to barf.*

bar·fly /ˈbɑɚˌflaɪ/ *n, pl* **-flies** [C] *US, informal* : a person who spends a lot of time drinking in bars

¹**bar·gain** /ˈbɑɚgən/ *n* [C] **1** : an agreement in which people or groups say they will do or give something in exchange for something else ▪ *Everyone involved seemed satisfied with the bargain we made.* ▪ *You can go to the party, but you have to keep your side of the bargain* [=do what you agreed to do] *and clean your room.* ▪ *You drive a hard bargain* [=you do not agree easily to what other people want and are very determined to get what you want], *but I'll accept your terms.* — see also PLEA BARGAIN **2** : something bought or sold for a low price ▪ *I got a (real) bargain on the tickets.* = *The tickets were a bargain.* ▪ *bargain prices* — **in/into the bargain** : in addition to what has been said ▪ *Locally grown food is fresher, and cheaper in the bargain.* [=it is also cheaper]

²**bargain** *vb* [I] : to discuss an agreement or price in order to make it more appealing ▪ *The price is high, but the seller might be willing to bargain.* ▪ *Teachers are bargaining for higher salaries.* — **bargain away** [*phrasal vb*] **bargain (something) away** *or* **bargain away (something)** : to lose or give up (something) as part of an agreement ▪ *The union may bargain away wage increases for other benefits.* — **bar-**

gain for/on [*phrasal vb*] : to expect or plan on (something) ▪ *No one bargained for/on the change in weather.* ▪ *The job ended up being more than I had bargained for.* [=more difficult than I had expected] — **bar·gain·er** *n* [C] ▪ *He's a hard bargainer.* — **bargaining** *n* [U] ▪ *After some hard bargaining, they came to an agreement.* ▪ *bargaining power*

bar·gain–base·ment /ˈbɑɚɡənˈbeɪsmənt/ *adj* **1** *of a price* : very low ▪ *bargain-basement prices* **2** : having a low cost and often having poor quality ▪ *worthless bargain-basement products*

bargaining chip *n* [C] : something that can be used to gain an advantage when you are trying to make a deal or an agreement ▪ *The workers used the threat of a strike as a bargaining chip in their negotiations.*

¹**barge** /ˈbɑɚdʒ/ *n* [C] : a large boat that is used to carry goods on rivers, canals, etc.

²**barge** *vb* **barged; barg·ing** [*I*] : to move or push in a fast, awkward, and often rude way ▪ *She barged through the door without even knocking.* ▪ *You can't just barge in here.* [=enter suddenly and rudely] — **barge in on** [*phrasal vb*] : to suddenly and rudely interrupt or disturb (something or someone) ▪ *She kept barging in on our conversation.*

bar graph *n* [C] : a graph or chart that uses narrow columns of different heights to show and compare different amounts

¹**bar·i·tone** /ˈberəˌtoʊn/ *n* [C] *music* : a man's singing voice that is higher than a bass and lower than a tenor; *also* : a singer who has such a voice

²**baritone** *adj* : having a range that is higher than a bass and lower than a tenor ▪ *a baritone voice/saxophone*

¹**bark** /ˈbɑɚk/ *vb* **1** [*I*] *of a dog* : to make a short, loud sound ▪ *A dog started barking.* **2** [*T/I*] : to shout or say (something) in a loud and angry way ▪ *The captain barked (out) orders/commands to the crew.* — **barking up the wrong tree** *informal* : trying to do something in a way that will not be successful ▪ *She claims that researchers are barking up the wrong tree.*

²**bark** *n* [C] **1** : the short, loud sound made by a dog ▪ *a loud bark* ▪ (*figurative*) *Don't get upset if the boss yells at you. His bark is worse than his bite.* [=he appears to be more angry or dangerous than he really is] **2** : the outer covering of a tree

bar·keep /ˈbɑɚˌkiːp/ *also* **bar·keep·er** /ˈbɑɚˌkiːpɚ/ *n* [C] *US* : BARTENDER

barking mad *adj, Brit, informal* : completely crazy ▪ *He's barking mad.*

bar·ley /ˈbɑɚli/ *n* [U] : a kind of grain used for food and to make beer and whiskey

bar·maid /ˈbɑɚˌmeɪd/ *n* [C] : a woman who serves drinks at a bar

bar·man /ˈbɑɚmən/ *n, pl* **-men** /-mən/ [C] *chiefly Brit* : BARTENDER

bar mitz·vah /bɑɚˈmɪtsvə/ *n* [C] : a ceremony and celebration for a Jewish boy on his 13th birthday when he takes on the religious duties and responsibilities of an adult; *also* : a boy for whom a bar mitzvah is held — compare BAT MITZVAH

barmy /ˈbɑɚmi/ *adj* **barm·i·er; -est** *chiefly Brit, informal* : crazy or foolish ▪ *a barmy idea*

barn /ˈbɑɚn/ *n* [C] : a building on a farm that is used for storing grain and hay and for housing farm animals or equipment

bar·na·cle /ˈbɑɚnɪkəl/ *n* [C] : a kind of small shellfish that attaches itself to rocks and the bottoms of boats underwater — **bar·na·cled** /ˈbɑɚnɪkəld/ *adj* ▪ *barnacled rocks*

barn·storm /ˈbɑɚnˌstoɚm/ *vb* [T/I] *chiefly US* : to travel to different places to give speeches, perform, etc. ▪ *barnstorming politicians* ▪ *The national soccer team barnstormed (around/across/through) the country.*

barn·storm·ing /ˈbɑɚnˌstoɚmɪŋ/ *adj, always before a noun, Brit* : very exciting and thrilling ▪ *a barnstorming performance*

¹**barn·yard** /ˈbɑɚnˌjɑɚd/ *n* [C] : an area of ground near a barn that usually has a fence around it

²**barnyard** *adj, always before a noun* **1** : of or relating to a farm ▪ *barnyard animals* **2** *US, informal* : not polite : somewhat crude or rude ▪ *barnyard jokes/humor*

ba·rom·e·ter /bəˈrɑːmətɚ/ *n* [C] **1** : an instrument that is used to measure air pressure and predict changes in the weather **2** : something that is used to indicate or predict something ▪ *The test is used as a barometer to measure a student's reading level.* ▪ *Wealth is not a barometer of happiness.* — **baro·met·ric** /ˌberəˈmetrɪk/ *adj* ▪ *barometric pressure*

bar·on /ˈberən/ *n* [C] **1 a** : a man who is a member of a low rank of British nobility **b** : a man who is a member of various ranks of nobility in other countries **2** : a man who has a lot of power or influence ▪ *a cattle/oil baron* — **ba·ro·ni·al** /bəˈroʊnijəl/ *adj* ▪ *baronial privileges* ▪ *a baronial estate* [=a very large and impressive estate]

bar·on·ess /ˈberənəs/ *n* [C] **1 a** : a woman who is a member of a low rank of British nobility **b** : a woman who is a member of various ranks of nobility in other countries **2** : the wife or widow of a baron

ba·roque /bəˈroʊk/ *adj* **1** : of or relating to a dramatic style of art and music that was common in the 17th and early 18th centuries ▪ *baroque paintings/music/cathedrals* **2** : having many details or too many details ▪ *a book filled with baroque descriptions* — **baroque** *n* [U] ▪ *paintings from the baroque* [=the baroque period]

bar·rack /ˈberək/ *vb* **1** [T/I] *Brit* : to bother or interrupt (someone, such as a performer or speaker) by shouting comments or criticism ▪ *The crowd barracked* [=heckled] *the visiting team.* **2** [I] *chiefly Australia* : to shout in support of a person or group ▪ *barracking for the home team*

bar·racks /ˈberəks/ *n* [C] : a building or group of buildings in which soldiers live ▪ *The soldier was moved to a different barracks.*

bar·ra·cu·da /ˌberəˈkuːdə/ n, pl **barracuda** or **bar·ra·cu·das** [C] **1** : a kind of fierce tropical fish that has strong jaws and sharp teeth **2** US, informal + disapproving : someone who uses aggressive, harsh, and sometimes improper ways to achieve something ▪ *The company's lawyers are a bunch of barracudas.*

¹bar·rage /bəˈrɑːʒ, Brit ˈbæˌrɑːʒ/ n **1** [C] : a heavy and continuous firing of weapons during a battle ▪ *a barrage of machine-gun fire* **2** [singular] : a great amount of something that comes quickly and continuously ▪ *a barrage of questions*

²barrage vb **-raged; -rag·ing** [T] chiefly US : to cause (someone) to receive a great amount of something — usually + with ▪ *The office has been barraged with phone calls.*

barred /ˈbɑɚd/ adj **1** : covered by a bar or a set of bars ▪ *barred windows* **2** : having bands or stripes of different colors ▪ *a bird with a barred tail*

¹bar·rel /ˈberəl/ n [C] **1 a** : a round usually wooden container with curved sides and flat ends **b** : the amount of something in a barrel ▪ *a barrel of oil/rum* **2** : the part of a gun that the bullets go through when it is fired — see also *lock, stock, and barrel* at ¹LOCK — **a barrel of laughs** informal : someone or something that is very funny — often used in negative statements or in an ironic way ▪ *The office isn't exactly a barrel of laughs these days.* — **over a barrel** : in a situation where you are forced to do something you do not want to do ▪ *My landlord has me over a barrel.* — **the bottom of the barrel** see ¹BOTTOM

²barrel vb **-reled** also **-relled; -rel·ing** also **-rel·ling** [I] US, informal : to move very fast and often in an uncontrolled or dangerous way ▪ *The truck went barreling down Main Street.*

bar·rel–chest·ed /ˈberəlˌtʃɛstəd/ adj, of a man : having a large, round chest that usually suggests great strength ▪ *a big, barrel-chested football player*

bar·ren /ˈberən/ adj **1 a** : having very few plants ▪ *a barren landscape/desert* **b** : not producing fruit or not able to produce fruit ▪ *a barren tree/orchard* **2** old-fashioned, of a woman or female animal : not able to produce children or offspring : INFERTILE **3** : not exciting or interesting ▪ *She lived a barren life.* **4** : not producing good or useful things, ideas, etc. ▪ *an artist who is going through a barren period* — **barren of** formal : not having (something) : WITHOUT ▪ *an area barren of trees* — **bar·ren·ness** n [U]

bar·rette /bəˈrɛt/ n [C] US : a decorative clip or bar that is used to hold a girl's or woman's hair in place — called also (Brit) *hair slide*

¹bar·ri·cade /ˈberəˌkeɪd/ n [C] : a temporary wall, fence, etc., that is built to prevent people from entering a place or area ▪ *Police erected barricades to keep the crowds away.*

²barricade vb **-cad·ed; -cad·ing** [T] : to block (something) so that people or things cannot enter or leave ▪ *The police*

barricaded the area. — **barricade yourself** ◇ If you barricade yourself in/inside something, you prevent other people from entering the place where you are by locking the door or by putting up a barricade. ▪ *The students barricaded themselves in the cafeteria.*

bar·ri·er /ˈberijɚ/ n [C] **1** : something (such as a fence or natural obstacle) that prevents or blocks movement from one place to another ▪ *Concrete barriers surround the racetrack.* **2 a** : a law, rule, problem, etc., that makes something difficult or impossible ▪ *trade barriers* ▪ *a barrier to progress* **b** : something that makes it difficult for people to understand each other ▪ *Age can be a big barrier between parents and children.* ▪ *a language barrier* [=a problem caused when people do not understand each other because they speak different languages] **3** : a level, amount, or number that is difficult to get past ▪ *a price barrier* — see also SOUND BARRIER

bar·ring /ˈbɑrɪŋ/ prep — used to say that something will happen unless something else happens ▪ *She's going to lose the election barring a miracle.* [=unless a miracle occurs]

bar·rio /ˈbɑrijoʊ/ n, pl **-rios** [C] : a neighborhood in a city or town in the U.S. in which many people who speak Spanish live

bar·ris·ter /ˈberəstɚ/ n [C] : a lawyer in Britain who has the right to argue in higher courts of law — compare SOLICITOR

bar·room /ˈbɑɚˌruːm/ n [C] : a place where alcoholic drinks are served : BAR

bar·tend·er /ˈbɑɚˌtɛndɚ/ n [C] US : a person who serves drinks at a bar or restaurant — **bar·tend** /ˈbɑɚˌtɛnd/ vb [I] ▪ *He bartends on weekends.*

bar·ter /ˈbɑɚtɚ/ vb [T/I] : to exchange things (such as products or services) for other things instead of for money ▪ *The farmers bartered for supplies with their crops.* ▪ *They barter eggs for cheese with the neighboring farm.* — **barter** n [U] ▪ *The tribes use a system of barter.*

ba·salt /bəˈsɑːlt/ n [U] : a type of dark gray to black rock — **ba·sal·tic** /bəˈsɑːltɪk/ adj

¹base /ˈbeɪs/ n **1** [C] : the bottom or lowest part of something : the part on which something rests or is supported ▪ *The lamp has a heavy base.* ▪ *He planted flowers around the stone's base.* ▪ (figurative) *The tour was informative, thanks to the guide's broad base of knowledge.* **2** [C] : something (such as a group of people or things) that provides support for a place, business, etc. ▪ *The economic base of the village is tourism.* ▪ *The company has a solid customer base.* [=a set of customers it can depend on] ▪ *a sport with a large fan base* [=group of fans] **3** [C] : a main ingredient to which other things are added to make something ▪ *She uses chicken broth as the base of the soup.* **4 a** [C] : the main place in which a person works or lives or a business operates ▪ *The company's base (of operations) is in London.* ▪ *The band's home base is Chi-*

cago. **b** [C/U] : a place where a military force keeps supplies and where people in the military live and work • *a naval/army base* **5** [C/U] *baseball* : any one of the four places a runner must touch in order to score • *There's a runner on base.* **6** [C] *chemistry* : a chemical that reacts with an acid to form a salt — **cover all the bases** *also* **cover every base** *or chiefly US* **touch all the bases** *or* **touch every base** : to do or include everything that needs to be done or included • *They reviewed the contract to make sure that it covered all the bases.* • *She touched all the bases in her report.* — **off base** *US, informal* **1** : not correct • *The estimate was (way) off base.* **2** : in an unprepared state • *He was caught off base by the accusations.* — **touch base** *informal* : to meet and talk as a way of learning about recent news • *Have you touched base with him?*

²**base** *vb* **based; bas·ing** [T] : to have a particular place as the main place where a person works or lives or where a business operates • *They based their new company in Seattle.* • *The company is based in London.* [=the company's main offices are in London] — **base on/upon** [phrasal vb] **base (something) on/upon** : to form, make, or develop (an opinion, decision, etc.) by using (something) as a basis or starting point • *You've based your opinion on faulty information.* [=the information that you used to form your opinion is wrong] • *The story is based on real-life events.* • *The island's economy is based on tourism.*

³**base** *adj* **bas·er; -est** *formal + literary* : not honest or good • *base motives/criminals* **2** *technical* : having low quality and value • *Iron is a base metal.* — **base·ly** *adv* — **base·ness** *n* [U]

base·ball /ˈbeɪsˌbɑːl/ *n* **1** [U] : a game played on a large field by two teams of nine players who try to score runs by hitting a small ball with a bat and then running to each of the four bases without being put out • *a baseball player/team/game/bat* **2** [C] : the ball used in baseball

baseball cap *n* [C] : a rounded cap that fits close to the head and that has a long visor

base·board /ˈbeɪsˌbɔəd/ *n* [C] *US* : a narrow board along the bottom of a wall

based *adj* — used to describe the base or basis of something • *a soundly based argument* [=an argument that has a sound basis]

base hit *n* [C] *baseball* : a hit that allows a batter to reach a base safely

base·less /ˈbeɪsləs/ *adj* : not based on facts • *a baseless accusation/fear*

base·line /ˈbeɪsˌlaɪn/ *n* [C] **1** *technical* : information that is used as a starting point by which to compare other information • *The experiment provided a baseline for other studies.* **2** : a line at either end of the playing area in games like basketball and tennis **3** *baseball* : either one of the lines that lead from home plate to first base and third base

base·ment /ˈbeɪsmənt/ *n* [C] : the part of

a building that is entirely or partly below the ground

base on balls *n* [C] *baseball* : a movement to first base that is awarded to a batter who does not swing at four pitches that are balls — called also *walk*

base pay *n* [C/U] : the amount of money paid to someone for work at a job that does not include any added payments for bonuses, overtime, etc.

base runner *n* [C] *baseball* : a player who is on base or is trying to reach a base — **base·run·ning** *n* [U]

bases *plural of* ¹BASE *or of* BASIS

¹**bash** /ˈbæʃ/ *vb* **1 a** [T] : to cause or allow (something) to hit something very hard or forcefully • *She fell down and bashed her knee against a rock.* **b** [T/I] : to hit someone or something very hard • *Someone bashed him over/on the head with a chair.* **c** [T] : to hurt or damage (something) by hitting or beating • *They tried to bash the door open/down/in.* **2** [T] : to criticize or attack (a person or group) • *an editorial bashing the president* • *celebrity bashing* — **bash away** [phrasal vb] *Brit, informal* : to work hard at something • *The children are bashing away at their homework.* — **bash out** [phrasal vb] **bash out (something)** *or* **bash (something) out** *Brit, informal* : to produce (something) quickly • *He bashed out an angry letter to the editor.* — **bash·er** *n* [C]

²**bash** *n* [C] **1** : a big or exciting party • *a birthday bash* **2** : a hard and powerful hit or blow • *a bash on the head* — **have a bash at** *Brit, informal* : to try or attempt (something) • *I've never done it before, but I'll have a bash at it.*

bash·ful /ˈbæʃfəl/ *adj* : afraid to talk to people because of a lack of confidence • *a very bashful* [=shy] *child* — **bash·ful·ly** *adv* • *He smiled bashfully.* — **bash·ful·ness** *n* [U]

¹**ba·sic** /ˈbeɪsɪk/ *adj* **1** : forming or relating to the most important part of something • *the basic principles of chemistry* • *The basic difference between the two companies is their size.* • *These ingredients are basic to Indian cooking.* **2** : forming or relating to the first or easiest part of something • *basic English/mathematics* • *basic skills* **3** : not including anything extra • *a very basic computer*

²**basic** *n* **1** [plural] : the simplest and most important parts of something • *the basics of Japanese cooking* • *computer basics* • *We need to get back to basics.* [=return to a simpler way of doing or thinking about something] **2** [U] *chiefly US* : BASIC TRAINING

BA·SIC /ˈbeɪsɪk/ *n* [U] *computers* : a simple language used for programming computers

ba·si·cal·ly /ˈbeɪsɪkli/ *adv* **1** : in a general or basic way — used to say that something is true or correct as a general statement even if it is not entirely true or correct • *It's basically a very good book.* • *a basically healthy person* • *Basically, all people are the same.* **2** — used to show that a statement is expressing the most important reason for something • *"Why* *don't you like him?" "Basically, I think he's crazy."* **3** : in a simple way ▪ *people who are trying to live more basically*

basic training *n* [*U*] : the first few weeks of training for someone who has recently joined the military

ba·sil /ˈbæzəl, ˈbeɪzəl/ *n* [*U*] : an herb that has a sweet smell

ba·sin /ˈbeɪsn/ *n* [*C*] **1 a** *chiefly Brit* : a kitchen sink **b** *Brit* : a large bowl that is used for mixing, cooking, or serving food **c** : the amount contained in a basin ▪ *a basin of cold water* **2** : the area of land around a large river and the small rivers that flow into it ▪ *the Amazon Basin* **3** : a large area of the Earth's surface that is lower than the area around it ▪ *the Great Basin of the western U.S.*

ba·sis /ˈbeɪsəs/ *n, pl* **ba·ses** /ˈbeɪˌsiːz/ **1** [*C/U*] : something from which another thing develops or can develop ▪ *This principle forms the basis of the country's economic policies.* ▪ *These stories have no basis in fact/reality.* [=are not supported by facts/reality] **2** [*U*] : a reason for doing something ▪ *The news provides some basis for hope.* ▪ *On what basis were the students selected?* [=how were the students selected?] ▪ *Students were selected on the basis of their test scores.* **3** [*singular*] **a** : a pattern or system for doing something — used with *on* ▪ *He visits his grandmother on a regular basis.* [=regularly] ▪ *The company updates its Web site on a daily/weekly/hourly basis.* [=every day/week/hour] **b** — used to describe the way people act with each other ▪ *They compete on a friendly basis.* [=in a friendly way]

bask /ˈbæsk, Brit ˈbɑːsk/ *vb* [*I*] **1** : to lie or relax in a bright and warm place ▪ *We sat basking in the sun.* **2** : to enjoy the attention and good feelings expressed by others ▪ *He stood before the audience, basking in their applause.*

bas·ket /ˈbæskɪt, Brit ˈbɑːskɪt/ *n* [*C*] **1 a** : a container usually made by weaving together long thin pieces of material ▪ *wicker/straw/wire baskets* ▪ *a laundry/picnic basket* **b** : the amount contained in a basket ▪ *a basket of eggs* **2** *basketball* **a** : a net hanging from a thin metal ring that the ball must go through in order to score points **b** : a successful shot ▪ *She made/scored a basket.* — **put all your eggs in one basket** see ¹EGG — **bas·ket·ful** *n* [*C*]

bas·ket·ball /ˈbæskɪtˌbɑːl, Brit ˈbɑːskɪtˌbɔːl/ *n* **1** [*U*] : a game in which two teams of five players bounce a ball and try to score points by throwing the ball through one of the raised nets at each end of a rectangular court ▪ *a basketball game/team/player/coach* **2** [*C*] : a large ball that is used in the game of basketball

basket case *n* [*C*] *informal* **1** : a person who is very nervous, tired, etc., and is not able to think or act normally ▪ *I was so worried that I was a complete basket case.* **2** : a company, government, etc., that is in very bad condition and close to failure ▪ *a financial basket case*

bas mitz·vah /bɑsˈmɪtsvə/ *n* [*C*] : BAT MITZVAH

¹**bass** /ˈbeɪs/ *n, music* **1** [*U, singular*] : the lowest range of sounds used in music ▪ *The song has a loud/heavy/booming bass.* **2** [*C*] : the lowest male singing voice; *also* : a singer who has such a voice **3** [*C/U*] : a kind of guitar that usually has four strings and that makes low sounds ▪ *an electric/acoustic bass* — called also *bass guitar* — compare ³BASS

²**bass** /ˈbeɪs/ *adj, always before a noun* : having or indicating a low sound or range ▪ *his deep bass voice* ▪ *a bass drum/clarinet*

³**bass** /ˈbæs/ *n, pl* **bass** [*C/U*] : a kind of fish that people catch for food — compare ¹BASS

bas·set hound /ˈbæsət-/ *n* [*C*] : a kind of dog that has short legs and long ears and that is used for hunting — called also *basset*

bas·si·net /ˌbæsəˈnɛt/ *n* [*C*] : a bed for a baby that looks like a basket and that usually has a hood over one end

bas·soon /bəˈsuːn/ *n* [*C*] : a large musical instrument that is shaped like a tube and makes low sounds — **bas·soon·ist** /bəˈsuːnɪst/ *n* [*C*]

bas·tard /ˈbæstəd, Brit ˈbɑːstəd/ *n* [*C*] **1** *informal* **a** *offensive* : a very bad or unpleasant man ▪ *You dirty bastard!* **b** *sometimes offensive* : a man who you think is lucky, unlucky, etc. ▪ *His wife left him, the poor bastard.* **2** *usually offensive* : an illegitimate child

baste /ˈbeɪst/ *vb* **bast·ed**; **bast·ing** [*T*] **1** : to pour hot juices, melted fat, etc., over (meat) while it is cooking ▪ *Baste the turkey every half hour.* **2** : to sew together (pieces of cloth) with long, loose stitches ▪ *She basted the hem of the dress.*

bas·tion /ˈbæstʃən, Brit ˈbæstiən/ *n* [*C*] : a place or system in which something continues to survive ▪ *a bastion of racial inequality* ▪ *bastions of democracy*

¹**bat** /ˈbæt/ *n* [*C*] **1 a** : a long rounded stick that is used to hit the ball in baseball **b** : a long flattened stick that is used to hit the ball in cricket **c** *Brit* : ¹PADDLE 2 **2** : an animal that has wings and a furry body like a mouse **3** *informal* : an unpleasant old woman ▪ *an old bat* — **(as) blind as a bat** see ¹BLIND — **at bat** *baseball* **1** — used to describe the player or team that is batting ▪ *He got a home run on his first time at bat.* ▪ *The home team is at bat.* **2** : the act of batting ▪ *She has two hits in three at bats.* — **go to bat** *baseball* : to be the player or team that is batting ▪ *The visiting team goes to bat first.* — **go to bat for US, informal** : to try to help, support, or defend (someone or something) in an active way ▪ *Many of his friends went to bat for him when he was accused of fraud.* — **like a bat out of hell** *informal* : very quickly ▪ *He ran out of the house like a bat out of hell.* — **off the bat** *chiefly US, informal* : without any delay : IMMEDIATELY ▪ *I could tell it was right off the bat.* — **off your own bat** *Brit, informal* : through your own efforts ▪ *He made good off his own bat.*

²**bat** *vb* **bat·ted**; **bat·ting** **1 a** [*T/I*] : to hit or try to hit something (such as a ball)

with a bat, club, etc., or with your hand ▪ *The ball was batted down.* ▪ *It's your turn to bat.* **b** [*I*] *baseball* : to have a specified batting average ▪ *He's batting* [=*hitting*] *.300.* [=his batting average is .300] ▪ *She's batting a thousand.* [=her batting average is 1.000] ▪ *(figurative) So far in her career, she's batting a thousand.* [=she has succeeded in everything she has done in her career] **2** [*T*] : to close and open (your eyes or eyelashes) very quickly several times ▪ *She batted her eyelashes at him.* ▪ *(figurative) He thought the news would upset her, but she never batted an eye.* [=she did not appear to be upset at all] — **bat around** [*phrasal vb*] **bat (something) around** or **bat around (something)** *informal* : to think about or talk about (something) for a period of time ▪ *The plan was batted around for a while, but it was finally rejected.* — **bat in** [*phrasal vb*] **bat in (a run)** also **bat (a run) in** *in baseball* : to hit the ball in a way that makes it possible for a run to score ▪ *He batted in 70 runs last year.* — **batting** *adj,* always before a noun ▪ *batting practice/gloves*

batch /ˈbætʃ/ *n* [*C*] **1** : an amount of something that is made at one time ▪ *a batch of cookies* ▪ *Mix the cement in batches.* [=mix one amount and then another amount and so on] **2** : a group of people or things ▪ *a new batch of television shows*

bat·ed /ˈbeɪtəd/ *adj* — **with bated breath** : in a nervous and excited state ▪ *They waited for the answer with bated breath.*

¹**bath** /ˈbæθ, *Brit* ˈbɑːθ/ *n* **1** [*C*] **a** : the act of washing the body usually by sitting or lying in a container filled with water ▪ *I was taking a bath when the phone rang.* ▪ *bath towels* [=large towels used after a bath or shower] **b** : the water used for a bath ▪ *Would you like me to draw/run a bath* [=to fill the bathtub with water] *for you?* **c** *chiefly Brit* : BATHTUB ▪ *He slipped in the bath.* **2** [*C*] *chiefly US* : BATHROOM ▪ *a room with a private bath* **3** [*plural*] : a public building where people in the past went to wash or soak their bodies ▪ *ancient Roman baths* **4** [*C*] *technical* : a container filled with a liquid in which an object is placed to be cleaned, treated, etc. ▪ *She dipped the metal in a bath of acid.* — **take a bath** *US, informal* : to lose a large amount of money in a business deal ▪ *The movie studio took a bath on his last picture.*

²**bath** *vb* **bathed; bath·ing** *Brit* **1** [*T*] : to give a bath to (someone) ▪ *She baths* [=(*US*) *bathes*] *the baby in the kitchen sink.* **2** [*I*] *formal* : to wash yourself in a bath ▪ *I usually bath before going to bed.*

¹**bathe** /ˈbeɪð/ *vb* **bathed; bath·ing 1** [*I*] *chiefly US* : to wash yourself in a bath ▪ *I always bathe in the morning.* **2** [*T*] *chiefly US* : to give a bath to (someone) ▪ *We'll bathe the baby later.* **3** [*I*] *somewhat old-fashioned* : to swim for pleasure ▪ *We bathed in the ocean.* **4** [*T*] : to cover (an area or surface) with light ▪ *The town was bathed in moonlight.* — **bathed in sweat** : covered with sweat ▪ *He was*

bathed in sweat when he finished exercising. — **bath·er** /ˈbeɪðɚ/ *n* [*C*] ▪ *a beach crowded with bathers* [=*swimmers*] — **bathing** *n* [*U*] ▪ *a beach where bathing* [=*swimming*] *is not allowed*

²**bathe** *n* [*C*] *Brit* : the act of swimming for pleasure : SWIM ▪ *We went for a bathe in the sea.*

bath·house /ˈbæθˌhaʊs, *Brit* ˈbɑːθˌhaʊs/ *n* [*C*] **1** : a public building where people go to take baths, showers, etc. **2** *US* : a public building at a beach where people go to put on the clothes they use for swimming

bathing costume *n* [*C*] *Brit* : SWIMSUIT

bathing suit *n* [*C*] *chiefly US* : SWIMSUIT

bath·robe /ˈbæθˌroʊb, *Brit* ˈbɑːθˌrəʊb/ *n* [*C*] : a loose piece of clothing that wraps around your body and is worn especially before or after a bath

bath·room /ˈbæθˌruːm, *Brit* ˈbɑːθˌruːm/ *n* [*C*] : a room with a sink and toilet and usually a bathtub or shower ✧ In U.S. English, a bathroom is mainly thought of as a room with a toilet. In British English, a bathroom is mainly thought of as a room with a bathtub or shower. — **go to the bathroom** or **use the bathroom** *US* : to use the toilet ▪ *The little boy told his mother that he had to go to the bathroom.*

bath·tub /ˈbæθˌtʌb, *Brit* ˈbɑːθˌtʌb/ *n* [*C*] *chiefly US* : a large, long container in which people take baths or showers

bath·wa·ter /ˈbæθˌwɑːtɚ, *Brit* ˈbɑːθˌwɔːtə/ *n* [*U*] : water used for a bath

bat mitz·vah /ˌbɑtˈmɪtsvə/ *n* [*C*] : a ceremony and celebration for a Jewish girl usually on her 13th birthday when she takes on the religious duties and responsibilities of an adult; *also* : a girl for whom a bat mitzvah is held — called also *bas mitzvah;* compare BAR MITZVAH

ba·ton /bəˈtɑːn, *Brit* ˈbæˌtɒn/ *n* [*C*] **1** : a thin stick that is used to lead a band or orchestra **2** : a long thin stick that is carried by someone who performs with or leads a marching band **3** : NIGHTSTICK **4** : a stick that is passed from one runner to the next runner in a relay race ▪ *The runner dropped the baton.* ▪ *(figurative) The chef recently passed the baton* [=gave the job and responsibility that had been hers] *to her young assistant.*

bats·man /ˈbætsmən/ *n, pl* -**men** [*C*] : a player who is batting especially in the game of cricket

bat·tal·ion /bəˈtæljən/ *n* [*C*] : a large organized group of soldiers

bat·ten /ˈbætn/ *vb* — **batten down** [*phrasal vb*] **1** : to prepare for possible trouble or difficulty ▪ *People are battening down in preparation for a hard winter.* **2 batten down (something)** or **batten (something) down** : to tie, close, or cover (something) in order to prevent it from moving or becoming damaged ▪ *Everything on the ship's deck was battened down.* **3 batten down the hatches** : to prepare a boat or ship for stormy weather by closing and covering the openings in the deck ▪ *(figurative) As the economy grows worse, investors need to batten down the hatches.*

¹bat·ter /ˈbætɚ/ vb [T] **1** : to hit (something or someone) forcefully many times in a way that causes much damage or injury • *Storms battered the shore.* • *children who are abused and battered by their parents* • (figurative) *a country battered by years of war and poverty* • *He tried to batter down the door* [=to force the door to open] *by kicking it.* **2** : to cover (food) in a batter and then fry it • *lightly/thickly battered pieces of fish* — **bat·tered** /ˈbætɚd/ adj • *a battered old hat* • *a shelter for battered wives* — **bat·ter·er** /ˈbætɚɚ/ n [C] — **bat·ter·ing** /ˈbætɚɪŋ/ n [singular] • *He suffered/took a vicious battering in the ring.* • (figurative) *The stock market took a battering.*

²batter n **1** [C/U] : a mixture of flour and other ingredients (such as sugar, eggs, and oil) that is cooked and eaten • *(a) thin pancake batter* • *coat the fish with batter* **2** [C] baseball : a player who is trying to hit the ball : a player who is batting • *a left-handed batter*

battering ram n [C] : a large, heavy piece of wood or other material that is used to hit and break through walls and doors

bat·tery /ˈbætɚi/ n, pl -ter·ies **1** [C] : a device that is placed inside a clock, toy, car, etc., to supply it with electricity • *The car's battery is dead.* **2** [C] : a usually large group of similar people, things, or ideas • *a battery of tests* **3** [C] : a group of two or more big guns used by the military • *an artillery battery* **4** [U] law : the crime of hitting or touching someone in a way that is meant to cause harm or injury — see also ASSAULT AND BATTERY **5** [C] baseball : the pitcher and catcher on a particular team — **recharge your batteries** see RECHARGE

batting average n [C] baseball : a number that shows how often a batter gets a base hit • *an excellent hitter with a batting average above .300*

¹bat·tle /ˈbætl/ n **1 a** [C/U] : a military fight between groups of soldiers, ships, airplanes, etc. • *the battle of Gettysburg* • *the field of battle* [=the battlefield] • *brave soldiers who died/fell in battle* [=while fighting in a war] **b** [C] : a violent fight in which people use weapons • *a gun battle* **2** [C] : a long, hard struggle or contest • *a legal battle* • *a battle for the presidency* • *Last year, he lost his 10-year battle with/against AIDS.* [=he died of AIDS after being sick with the disease for 10 years] • *In this movie, it's a battle of wits as the bank robbers try to outsmart the city's detectives.* • *She tried to stay awake, but it was a losing battle.* [=she wasn't able to stay awake] — **do battle** : to fight or struggle • *doing battle* [=battling] *with the enemy* — **half the battle** : an important and necessary part of doing or achieving something • *When you're opening a new restaurant, good advertising is half the battle.* — **in the heat of (the) battle** : while fighting in a battle • (figurative) *He apologized for the angry things he had said in the heat of battle.* [=while arguing]

²battle vb bat·tled; bat·tling **1** [I] : to fight with weapons • *The army battled for control of the bridge.* **2** [I] : to try, fight, or struggle very hard • *They battled to keep their son out of jail.* • *The two families battled for control of the land.* • *They constantly battled (with each other) over how to spend their money.* **3** [T] **a** : to fight, compete, or argue with (someone or something) • *The two teams will battle each other for the championship.* **b** : to try to stop or defeat (something) • *Firefighters battled the forest fire.* • *She's been battling cancer for 10 years.* — **battle it out** : to argue or fight • *The two sides are battling it out in the courtroom.*

battle fatigue n [U] : a mental illness that is caused by the experiences of fighting in a war

bat·tle·field /ˈbætlˌfiːld/ n [C] **1** : a place where a military battle is fought **2** : an area of conflict or disagreement • *a political battlefield*

bat·tle·ground /ˈbætlˌɡraʊnd/ n [C] : BATTLEFIELD

bat·tle·ship /ˈbætlˌʃɪp/ n [C] : a large ship that has many big guns and is used in fighting wars

bat·ty /ˈbæti/ adj bat·ti·er; -est informal : CRAZY • *batty ideas* • *She's a little batty.*

bau·ble /ˈbɑːbəl/ n [C] **1** : an inexpensive piece of jewelry **2** Brit : a shiny ball that is hung on a Christmas tree

baulk Brit spelling of ¹BALK

bawdy /ˈbɑːdi/ adj bawd·i·er; -est : dealing with sex in a way that is meant to be funny • *bawdy jokes*

bawl /ˈbɑːl/ vb **1** [I] : to cry very loudly • *a bawling baby* **2** [T/I] informal : to say or shout (something) very loudly • *"Get in the car!" he bawled.* — **bawl out** [phrasal vb] bawl out (someone) or bawl (someone) out chiefly US, informal : to yell at (someone) for doing something bad or wrong • *His boss bawled him out for forgetting about the meeting.* — **bawl your eyes out** : to cry loudly especially for a long time

¹bay /ˈbeɪ/ n [C] **1** : a large area of water that is part of an ocean or lake and partly surrounded by land • *San Francisco Bay* **2** : a section of a ship, airplane, etc., that is used for a special purpose (such as storing things) • *a cargo bay on a ship* **3** : a kind of European tree that has leaves which are used in cooking **4** : a horse that is a reddish-brown color — **at bay** : in the position of being unable to move closer • *The soldiers kept/held the attackers at bay.* [=prevented the attackers from coming closer] • (figurative) *The doctors kept her illness at bay* [=prevented her illness from becoming worse] *for a few months, but then the disease began to spread again.*

²bay vb [I] **1** : to bark with long sounds • *The dog was baying at the moon.* **2** : to shout or cry out in a loud and often angry way • *an angry mob baying for blood* [=angrily demanding or threatening violence]

bay leaf n [C] : a dried leaf from the bay tree that is used in cooking

bay·o·net /ˈbeɪənət/ n [C] : a long knife that is attached to the end of a rifle —

bayonet vb [T] • *The soldier was bayoneted in the chest.*

bay·ou /ˈbaɪuː/ n [C] : an area of water in the southern U.S. in which the water moves very slowly and is filled with many plants • *Louisiana bayous*

bay window n [C] : a large window or set of windows that sticks out from the outside wall of a building

ba·zaar /bəˈzɑɚ/ n [C] **1** : a type of market found especially in Middle Eastern countries that has rows of small shops which sell many different kinds of things **2** : an event at which things are sold to raise money for people or an organization • *a charity/church bazaar*

ba·zoo·ka /bəˈzuːkə/ n [C] : a military weapon that fires small rockets

BB /ˈbiːˌbiː/ n [C] : a small metal ball that is fired from a BB gun

BBC abbr British Broadcasting Corporation

BB gun n [C] chiefly US : a gun that uses air pressure to fire small metal balls (called BBs)

BBQ abbr barbecue

BC or chiefly US **B.C.** abbr before Christ — used to refer to the years that came before the birth of Jesus Christ • *550 B.C.* • *in the fifth century B.C.*

BCE or chiefly US **B.C.E.** abbr before the Christian Era; before the Common Era — used to refer to the years that came before the birth of Jesus Christ ✧ *B.C.E.* is now often used instead of *B.C.* especially in scientific writing. • *550 B.C.E.* • *in the fifth century B.C.E.*

be /ˈbiː/ vb, present first singular **am** /ˈæm, əm/ second singular **are** /ˈɑɚ, ɚ/ third singular **is** /ˈɪz, əz/ pl **are**; past tense first and third singular **was** /ˈwɑz/ second singular **were** /ˈwɚ/ pl **were**; past participle **been** /ˈbɪn, Brit ˈbiːn/ present participle **be·ing** /ˈbiːjɪŋ/ **1** [linking vb] **a** — used to indicate the identity of a person or thing • *Today is Wednesday.* • *John is my brother.* • *"There's someone at the door." "Who is it?" "It's David."* **b** — used to describe the qualities of a person or thing • *My hands are cold.* • *He is 35 years old.* • *The leaves are green.* • *Don't be such a fool!* • *To be perfectly honest (with you), I didn't like the movie.* [=I am speaking honestly when I say that I didn't like the movie] • *I'd do it if I were you.* [=I think you should do it] **c** — used to indicate the condition of a person or thing • *"Hi. How are you?" "Fine, thanks. How are you?"* **2** [linking vb] — used to indicate the group, class, category, etc., that a person or thing belongs to • *I'm a doctor and my sister is a lawyer.* • *Apes are mammals.* **3** [linking vb] — used to indicate the place, situation, or position of a person or thing • *The book is on the table.* • *"Where's John?" "He's in the living room."* **4** [linking vb] **a** — used in phrases with there to describe a situation, occurrence, etc. • *There is a book on the table.* [=a book is on the table] • *There's someone at the door.* **b** — used in phrases with it to indicate a time or place or to describe a current, past, or future condition • *It's 12 o'clock.* [=the time is 12 o'clock] • *It's Wednesday today.* [=today is Wednesday] • *It's raining.* **5** [linking vb] — used to say how much something costs • *"I like this painting. How much is it?" "It's 600 dollars."* [=it costs 600 dollars] **6** [linking vb] — used to say that one amount or number is the same as another • *Three plus two is [=equals] five.* **7** [I] : to happen or take place • *The concert is tomorrow night.* [=the concert will take place tomorrow night] • *"When is Christmas?" "It's on a Wednesday this year."* **8** [I] : to come or go — used in perfect tenses • *Have you ever been [=gone] to Rome?* • *Where have you been?* [=where were you?; why weren't you here?] **9** [I] somewhat formal : to exist or live • *I think, therefore I am.* • *There once was a man who dwelt alone in a small village.* **10** [auxiliary vb] — used with the past participle of a verb to form passive constructions • *The money was found by a child.* • *They were [=got] married by a priest.* • *Please be seated.* [=please sit down] **11** [auxiliary vb] **a** — used with the present participle of a verb to express continuous action • *He was reading.* **b** — used with the present participle of a verb to express future or later action • *We are leaving soon.* [=we will leave soon] **12** [auxiliary vb] **a** — used with to + verb to say what will happen or was going to happen in the future • *The best is yet/still to come.* • *She was never/never to see him again.* [=she would never see him again] **b** — used with to + verb to say what should happen or be done • *People like that are to be pitied, not hated.* • *What am I to do?* **c** — used in negative statements with to + verb to say what is or was possible • *The truth of their argument was not to be denied.* **d** — used with to + verb to say that one thing must happen or be true so that another thing can happen or be true • *He must study if he is to pass his exams.* **13** [auxiliary vb] — used like have with the past participle of some verbs to form perfect tenses • *He isn't here; he is [=has] gone.* — **be yourself** : to behave in a normal or natural way • *You're not yourself today. What's the matter?* — **leave (someone or something) be** see ¹LEAVE — **let (someone or something) be** see LET — **the best is yet to be** see ³BEST — **to be sure** see ¹SURE

¹beach /ˈbiːtʃ/ n [C] : an area covered with sand or small rocks that is next to an ocean or lake • *We spent the day at the beach.*

²beach vb [T] **1** : to cause (a boat or ship) to go out of the water and onto a beach • *The pirates beached the ship on the island.* **2** ✧ When a large ocean animal, such as a whale, is *beached* or has *beached itself*, it has come out of the water onto land and is unable to return to the water. • *a beached whale*

beach ball n [C] : a large ball that is filled with air

beach buggy n [C] : DUNE BUGGY

beach·comb·er /ˈbiːtʃˌkoʊmɚ/ n [C] : a person who walks along beaches looking for things (such as seashells or items that can be sold)

beach towel *n* [*C*] : a large towel made for use at the beach

bea·con /ˈbiːkən/ *n* [*C*] **1** : a strong light that can be seen from far away and that is used to help guide ships, airplanes, etc. **2** : a radio signal that is broadcast to help guide ships, airplanes, etc. ▪ *a radio beacon* **3** : someone or something (such as a country) that guides or gives hope to others ▪ *This new medicine is a beacon of hope for/to thousands of people.*

bead /ˈbiːd/ *n* [*C*] **1** : a small, usually round piece of glass, wood, stone, etc., that has a hole through its center by which it can be put on a string or sewn onto clothing ▪ *a string of beads* ▪ *She was wearing beads.* [=a necklace of beads] **2** : a small, round drop of liquid ▪ *beads of sweat* — **draw a bead on** also US **get/take a bead on** : to aim at (someone or something) ▪ *He lifted the rifle and drew a bead on the target.*

bead·ed /ˈbiːdəd/ *adj* **1** : decorated with beads ▪ *fancy beaded dresses* **2** : covered with small drops of sweat ▪ *Her forehead was beaded with sweat/perspiration.*

beady /ˈbiːdi/ *adj* **bead·i·er; -est** *disapproving* — used to describe eyes that are small, round, and shiny and that usually suggest greed, dishonesty, etc. ▪ *the boss's beady little eyes*

bea·gle /ˈbiːgəl/ *n* [*C*] : a type of small dog used for hunting that has smooth black, brown, and white fur

beak /ˈbiːk/ *n* [*C*] **1** : the hard usually pointed parts that cover a bird's mouth ▪ *the beak of a hawk* **2** *informal + humorous* : a person's nose ▪ *an actor with a big beak* — **beaked** /ˈbiːkt/ *adj* ▪ *a long-beaked bird*

bea·ker /ˈbiːkɚ/ *n* [*C*] **1** : a wide glass with a lip for pouring that is used for holding and measuring liquids **2** *chiefly Brit* : a large drinking cup with a wide opening

be–all and end–all /ˈbiːˌɑːlənd̩ˈɛnd̩ˌɑːl/ *n* — **the be-all and end-all** : the most important part of something or the reason for something ▪ *He acts as if making money is the be-all and end-all of human existence.*

¹**beam** /ˈbiːm/ *n* [*C*] **1 a** : a line of light coming from the sun, a headlight, etc. ▪ *a bright beam of light* ▪ *a laser beam* — see also HIGH BEAM, LOW BEAM **b** : a line of energy, particles, etc., that cannot be seen ▪ *a beam of electrons* **2** : a long, heavy piece of wood or metal that is used as a support in a building or ship ▪ *the building's steel support beams* — **off beam** *Brit, informal* : incorrect or mistaken ▪ *My guess was way off beam.* — **on the beam** *informal* : exactly correct ▪ *His description of the problem was right on the beam.* — **beamed** *adj* ▪ *a beamed ceiling* [=a ceiling that is supported with beams]

²**beam** *vb* **1 a** [*I*] : to smile happily ▪ *They stood beaming with satisfaction.* **b** [*T*] : to say (something) while smiling happily ▪ *"We're getting married!" he beamed.* **2** [*T/I*] : to send out beams of light or energy ▪ *Sunlight was beaming* [=*shining*] *through the window.* **3** [*T*] : to send out (information, television signals, etc.) through wires or the air ▪ *Pictures of the distant planet were beamed back to the Earth.* **4** [*T*] *in stories* : to send (someone) to another place instantly by using a special machine ▪ *The explorers were beamed onto the surface of the planet.*

¹**bean** /ˈbiːn/ *n* [*C*] **1 a** : a seed that is eaten as a vegetable and that comes from any one of many different kinds of climbing plants **b** : a part of a plant that contains very young seeds and that is eaten as a vegetable **c** : a plant that produces beans **2** : a seed that looks like a bean but that does not come from a climbing plant ▪ *coffee/cocoa beans* — see also JELLY BEAN — **a hill of beans** see HILL — **full of beans** *informal* **1** : full of energy and life ▪ *We were young and full of beans.* **2** *US* : full of nonsense ▪ *If that's what he's been saying, then he's full of beans.* — **not know beans about** *US, informal* : to not know anything about (something) ▪ *I don't know beans about computers.* — **spill the beans** *informal* : to reveal secret information ▪ *He refused to spill the beans.*

²**bean** *vb* [*T*] *informal* : to hit (someone) on the head with something ▪ *He beaned me with an eraser.* [=threw an eraser that hit my head]

bean·bag /ˈbiːnˌbæg/ *n* [*C*] **1** : a small bag that is filled with dried beans or pieces of another material and used as a toy **2** : a large bag that is filled with small round pieces of material and used as a soft chair

bean counter *n* [*C*] *informal + disapproving* : a person who helps to run a business and who only cares about money ▪ *corporate bean counters*

bean curd *n* [*U*] : TOFU

bean·ie /ˈbiːni/ *n* [*C*] : a small, round, tight-fitting hat or cap

bean sprouts *n* [*plural*] : very young plants that come from bean seeds and that are eaten as a vegetable

¹**bear** /ˈbeɚ/ *n, pl* **bear** *or* **bears** [*C*] **1** : any one of a group of large, heavy animals that have thick hair and sharp claws and that can stand on two legs like a person ▪ *a mother bear and her cubs* ▪ *(figurative) a tall, friendly bear of a man* **2** *finance* : a person who expects the price of stocks to go down and who sells them to avoid losing money — compare BULL **3** *US, informal* : something that is difficult to do or deal with ▪ *The oven is a bear to clean.*

²**bear** *vb* **bore** /ˈboɚ/; **borne** /ˈboɚn/; **bear·ing 1** [*T/I*] : to accept or endure (something) ▪ *He bore their insults patiently.* ▪ *I can't bear the suspense.* ▪ *His behavior was more than I could bear.* ▪ *(US) I couldn't bear for you to get the wrong idea.* **2** [*T*] : to be worthy of (something) ▪ *a joke too silly to bear repeating* ▪ *suspicious behavior that bears watching* [=that should be watched] **3** [*T*] : to assume or accept (something) ▪ *The company agreed to bear the costs/expenses.* ▪ *They must bear full responsibility for their*

actions. **4** [T] *somewhat formal + literary* : to carry (something) ▪ *They arrived bearing gifts.* ▪ *disease-bearing germs* [=germs that carry and spread diseases] ▪ *the right to bear arms* [=to carry weapons] **5** [T] **a** : to have (something) as a feature or characteristic ▪ *His face bears marks/signs of suffering.* ▪ *The cornerstone bears a Latin inscription.* ▪ *a letter bearing the date of 1900* ▪ *She bore a resemblance to her aunt.* [=she looked like her aunt] **b** : to have or hold (a feeling) in the mind ▪ *She still bears a grudge against him.* = *She still bears him a grudge.* **6** [T] *a formal* : to give birth to (a child) ▪ *She has borne three children.* **b** : to produce (something) ▪ *a bank account that bears interest* = *an interest-bearing bank account* ▪ *trees that bear fruit* ▪ *All his plans have finally borne fruit.* [=all his plans have finally been realized] **7** [T] : to support the weight of (something) ▪ *How much weight can that wall bear?* **8** [I] : to go, move, or turn in a specified direction ▪ *The road bears (to the) right.* ▪ *When you get to the fork in the road, you should bear left.* — **bear down** [*phrasal vb*] *US* : to try very hard to do something ▪ *The pitcher bore down and struck out the last batter.* — **bear down on** [*phrasal vb*] **1** : to push or lean down on (something) ▪ *She bore down hard on her pencil.* **2** : to approach or move toward (something or someone) quickly ▪ *The enemy battleship bore down on us.* — **bear in mind** see [1]MIND — **bear on** [*phrasal vb*] *formal* **1** : to have an effect on (something) ▪ *Personal feelings did not bear on our decision.* **2** : to apply or relate to (something) ▪ *What are the facts bearing directly on this matter?* — **bear out** [*phrasal vb*] **bear out (something or someone) or bear (something or someone) out** : to show the correctness of (something or someone) ▪ *The facts bore out* [=confirmed] *her story.* ▪ *Research has fully borne him out.* [=has shown that he was completely correct] — **bear up** [*phrasal vb*] : to not be overwhelmed during a time of trouble, pain, etc. ▪ *She's been going through a tough time, but she's bearing up pretty well.* — **bear with** [*phrasal vb*] : to be patient with (someone) ▪ *Please bear with me for another minute.* — **bear witness** see [1]WITNESS — **bear yourself** *formal* : to move, stand, or behave in a specified way ▪ *He always bore himself* [=behaved] *like a gentleman.* — **bring (something) to bear** : to cause (something) to have an effect or influence ▪ *The demonstrators will continue to bring pressure to bear on the government.* — **cross to bear** see [1]CROSS

bear·able /ˈberəbəl/ *adj* : able to be accepted or endured ▪ *The pain was bad but bearable.*

beard /ˈbiəd/ *n* [C] **1** : the hair that grows on a man's cheeks and chin ▪ *He grew a beard and mustache.* **2** : the long hair that grows on the chin of some animals ▪ *the beard of a goat* — **beard·ed** /ˈbiədəd/ *adj* ▪ *a bearded man*

bear·er /ˈberə/ *n* [C] : a person who has or carries something ▪ *the bearer of a U.S.*

passport ▪ *the bearer of glad/bad tidings* [=the person who brings good/bad news]

bear hug *n* [C] : a strong and rough but friendly hug ▪ *He gave his brother a bear hug.*

bearing *n* **1** [U, *singular*] *formal* : the way in which a person moves, stands, or behaves ▪ *a man of military/dignified/regal bearing* **2** [U, *singular*] *formal* : a relation or connection — + *on* ▪ *These facts have a direct bearing on the question.* ▪ *Personal feelings had no bearing on our decision.* **3** [C] *technical* : a machine part in which another part turns or slides — see also BALL BEARING **4** [C] *technical* : a measurement taken with a compass that indicates the direction or position of something ▪ *take/get a compass bearing* — **get/find your bearings** : to find out your position ▪ *Let's stop here and find our bearings.* ▪ (*figurative*) *Our course for new employees will help you get/find your bearings at work.* — **lose your bearings** : to become lost ▪ *The ship lost its bearings in the fog.* ▪ (*figurative*) *I feel I've lost my bearings in life.*

bear·ish /ˈberɪʃ/ *adj* **1** : having qualities like a bear ▪ *a grumpy, bearish old man* **2** : expecting the price of stocks to go down ▪ *bearish investors* : characterized by falling stock prices ▪ *a bearish market* — compare BULLISH — **bear·ish·ly** *adv* — **bear·ish·ness** *n* [U]

bear market *n* [C] : a market (such as a stock market) in which prices are going down — compare BULL MARKET

beast /ˈbiːst/ *n* [C] **1** *old-fashioned* : an animal ▪ *the birds and beasts of the forest* ▪ *a conflict between man and beast* [=between human beings and animals] ▪ *They were attacked by a savage beast.* **2** *old-fashioned* : an unkind or cruel person ▪ *He's a cruel, hateful beast!* **3** *informal* : a person or thing of a particular kind ▪ *a powerful political beast* [=a powerful politician]

beast·ly /ˈbiːstli/ *adj* **beast·li·er; -est** *chiefly Brit* : very unpleasant ▪ *beastly* [=terrible] *weather/behavior* — **beast·li·ness** *n* [U]

beast of burden *n* [C] : an animal that people use to carry heavy things

[1]**beat** /ˈbiːt/ *vb* **beat; beat·en** /ˈbiːtn̩/ *or chiefly US* **beat; beat·ing** **1** [T/I] : to hit (something) repeatedly ▪ *He beat the dusty rug with a stick.* ▪ *The dented metal was beaten flat.* ▪ *He beat (at/against/on) the door with his fists.* **2** [T] : to hit (someone) repeatedly in order to cause pain or injury ▪ *They beat him with clubs.* ▪ *a man accused of beating his wife* ▪ *He was beaten to death.* **3** [T/I] : to hit (a drum) repeatedly in order to produce music or a signal ▪ *The drummer kept beating his drum.* ▪ *the sound of a beating drum* — see also beat the drum for at [1]DRUM **4** [T/I] *cooking* : to stir or mix (something) in a forceful way ▪ *She used a whisk to beat the eggs.* **5** [T/I] : to move (wings) with an up and down motion ▪ *The bird was beating* [=flapping] *its wings.* **6** [I] *of the heart* : to make the regular movements needed to pump blood ▪ *My heart was beating wildly with*

excitement! **7** [T] **a** : to defeat (someone) in a game, contest, etc. • *We beat them 14 to 3.* • *She was beaten in the election.* ✧ People say **if you can't beat them, join them** or **if you can't beat 'em, join 'em** when they decide to do what other people are doing and to stop opposing them. **b** : to do better than (something) • *She managed to beat the old record by several seconds.* • *His performance will be* **hard/tough to beat.** • *They managed to* **beat the odds.** [=to succeed even though they did not have a good chance of succeeding] ✧ People say **can you beat that?** when they are surprised or angry about something. • *Can you beat that?! A person like him being elected mayor!* **c** : to be better than (something) • *For sheer luxury* **you can't beat** *a nice hot bath.* **d** : to control or overcome (something) • *By working together we can beat crime!* • (*US*) *His favorite way of* **beating the heat** [=remaining cool in hot weather] *is to have a couple of cold beers.* **e** : to be too difficult for (someone) • *This problem has beaten everyone.* • (*informal*) *"How did she manage to fix the problem so quickly?" "It beats me."* [=I don't know] **8** [T] **a** : to come, arrive, or act before (someone or something) • *I beat him to the finish line.* [=I reached the finish line before he did] • *I wondered which of us would finish our work first, but she* **beat me to it** *by two days.* [=she finished two days before I did] **b** : to avoid having problems with (something) by acting earlier • *We left early so that we could* **beat the traffic/rush.** — **beat a dead horse** see ¹HORSE — **beat a path** : to make (a path) by walking over the ground many times • (*figurative*) *If you work hard, success will* **beat a path to your door.** [=you will be very successful] — **beat a retreat** : to leave quickly • *They* **beat a hasty retreat** *when the cops arrived.* — **beat around/about the bush** see BUSH — **beat back** [*phrasal vb*] **beat back (someone)** or **beat (someone) back** : to force (someone) to go back or to retreat by fighting • *Our troops were beaten back by enemy forces.* — **beat down** [*phrasal vb*] **1** *of the sun* : to shine down with great heat and strength • *The blazing sun was beating down on us.* **2 beat (something or someone) down** or **beat down (something or someone) a** : to hit (something) repeatedly so that it falls down • *The police beat down the door.* • (*figurative*) *Years of failure had beaten him down.* [=caused him to lose hope or spirit] **b** *chiefly Brit* : to cause someone to lower a price • *I beat her down from £30 to £15.* — **beat off** *informal* : to go away quickly • *The teenagers beat it when the cops arrived.* — **beat off** [*phrasal vb*] **1 beat off (someone or something)** or **beat (someone or something) off** : to force (someone or something) to go away by fighting • *She managed to beat off her attacker.* • (*figurative*) *The company has managed to beat off* [=fight off] *its competitors.* **2** *US, informal* + *impolite, of a man* : MASTURBATE — **beat out** [*phrasal vb*] **beat out (something or**

someone) or **beat (something or someone) out 1** : to put out (a fire) by beating • *She used a towel to beat out the fire.* **2** *baseball* : to turn (a ground ball) into a base hit by running fast to first base • *He beat out a bunt.* **3** *US* : to defeat or overcome (a person, team, etc.) • *She thought she'd get the job, but someone else beat her out.* [=someone else got the job] — **beat the clock** see ¹CLOCK — **beat the rap** see ¹RAP — **beat up** [*phrasal vb*] **beat up (someone)** or **beat (someone) up** : to hurt or injure (someone) by hitting repeatedly • *A gang of bullies threatened to beat him up.* • (*figurative*) *a politician who is getting beat/beaten up by liberal/conservative critics* • (*figurative*) *He's been* **beating himself up** [=harshly blaming or criticizing himself] *because of the failure of his marriage.* — **beat up on** [*phrasal vb*] *US, informal* : to hit (someone) repeatedly in order to cause pain or injury • *A gang of bullies was beating up on him.* —

beat·able /ˈbiːtəbəl/ *adj* • *an easily beatable opponent* [=an opponent that can be easily defeated]

²beat *n* **1 a** [C] : the act of beating • *a single beat on a drum* • *with every beat of his heart* **b** [*singular*] : a sound produced by beating • *They danced to the beat of the drums.* **2 a** [C] : a loud or strong sound that occurs regularly in music or poetry • *music that has four beats to a bar* **b** [*singular*] : the regular pattern of sounds in music or poetry : RHYTHM • *music with a Latin/steady beat* **3** [C] : a place or area that someone regularly goes to, walks through, or covers as part of a job • *a policeman patrolling/on his/ the beat* • *a reporter's beat* — **miss a beat** *chiefly US* : to stop or hesitate briefly • *He answered their questions* **without missing a beat.** [=he answered all their questions very easily]

³beat *adj, not before a noun, informal* : very tired • *I'm absolutely beat!*

beat·en /ˈbiːtn̩/ *adj, always before a noun* **1** : formed into a desired shape by being hit with a hammer • *beaten gold* **2** : walked on by many people • *a beaten path* **3** : having lost all hope or spirit • *a beaten* [=defeated] *man* — **off the beaten track** or *US* **off the beaten path** : in or to a place that is not close to the places where people usually go • *The restaurant is a little off the beaten track.*

beat·er /ˈbiːtɚ/ *n* [C] **1** : a device or tool that is used for beating something • *a carpet beater* **2** : someone who repeatedly hits another person • *a wife beater* [=a man who beats his wife]

be·atif·ic /ˌbiːjəˈtɪfɪk/ *adj, formal* : showing complete happiness • *a beatific smile*

be·at·i·fy /biˈætəˌfaɪ/ *vb* **-fies; -fied; -fy·ing** [T] *in the Roman Catholic Church* : to give a dead person a title of honor for being very good and holy • *She was beatified by the Pope.* — **be·at·i·fi·ca·tion** /biˌætəfəˈkeɪʃən/ *n* [U]

beat·ing /ˈbiːtɪŋ/ *n* [C] : the act of repeatedly hitting someone to cause pain or injury • *He threatened to give the boys a (good) beating for stealing the apples.* • (*figurative*) *Many investors took quite a* *(bad) beating* [=lost a lot of money] *when the stock market crashed.*

beat·nik /ˈbiːtˌnɪk/ *n* [C] : a young person in the 1950s and early 1960s who rejected the traditional rules of society

beat–up /ˈbiːtˌʌp/ *adj, informal* : old and badly worn or damaged ▪ *a beat-up old car*

beau /ˈboʊ/ *n, pl* **beaux** /ˈboʊz/ *or* **beaus** [C] *old-fashioned* : a woman's male lover or friend ▪ *her latest beau*

beaut /ˈbjuːt/ *n* [C] *US + Australia + New Zealand, informal* : a very good or attractive thing or person ▪ *His new car is a real beaut.* [=beauty]

beau·te·ous /ˈbjuːtijəs/ *adj, literary* : BEAUTIFUL ▪ *a beauteous evening*

beau·ti·cian /bjuˈtɪʃən/ *n* [C] : a person whose job is to give beauty treatments by washing and cutting hair, applying makeup, etc.

beau·ti·ful /ˈbjuːtɪfəl/ *adj* **1** : having beauty: such as **a** : very attractive in a physical way ▪ *a beautiful woman/smile* **b** : giving pleasure to the mind or the senses ▪ *a beautiful song/dress/house/view* **2** : very good or pleasing ▪ *They did a beautiful job.* ▪ *a beautiful friendship* — **beau·ti·ful·ly** /ˈbjuːtɪfli/ *adv* ▪ *You sang beautifully.*

beau·ti·fy /ˈbjuːtəˌfaɪ/ *vb* **-fies**; **-fied**; **-fy·ing** [T] : to make (something) beautiful or more beautiful ▪ *Fresh flowers beautify every room.* — **beau·ti·fi·ca·tion** /ˌbjuːtəfəˈkeɪʃən/ *n* [U]

beau·ty /ˈbjuːti/ *n, pl* **-ties** **1** [U] : the quality of being physically attractive ▪ *Her beauty is beyond compare.* [=no one is as beautiful as she is] ▪ *beauty products* [=soaps, makeup, and other things that help make people more physically attractive] **2** [U, plural] : the qualities that give pleasure to the senses or the mind ▪ *the beauty of the stars* ▪ *the beauty of poetry* ▪ *We explored the natural beauties of the island.* **3** [C] : a beautiful woman ▪ *She was one of the great beauties of her time.* **4** [C] *informal* : a very good example of something ▪ *That was a beauty of a catch.* [=that was an excellent catch] ▪ *(ironic) That mistake was a beauty.* [=a very bad mistake] **5** [C/U] : a good or appealing part of something ▪ *The beauty of the game is that everyone can play.*

beauty contest *n* [C] : a contest in which people judge a group of women or girls and decide which one is the most beautiful — called also *beauty pageant*

beauty queen *n* [C] : a woman or girl who is a winner of a beauty contest

beauty salon *n* [C] : a shop where women get beauty treatments (such as haircuts) — called also *beauty parlor, beauty shop*

beauty spot *n* [C] **1** : a small dark mark (such as a mole) on a woman's face — called also *(US)* **beauty mark** **2** *Brit* : a beautiful place

¹**bea·ver** /ˈbiːvɚ/ *n, pl* **beaver** *or* **bea·vers** **1** [C] : a small animal that has thick, brown fur and that cuts down trees with its teeth and builds dams and underwater houses with mud and branches ▪ *a beaver dam* [=a dam built by

beavers] — see also EAGER BEAVER **2** [U] : the fur of a beaver ▪ *a coat made of beaver = a beaver coat*

²**beaver** *vb* — **beaver away** [*phrasal vb*] *informal* : to work in a very active and energetic way ▪ *They're still beavering away at the problem.*

be·bop /ˈbiːˌbɑːp/ *n* [U] : a fast and complex type of jazz music

became *past tense of* BECOME

be·cause /bɪˈkɑːz, bɪˈkʌz/ *conj* : for the reason that ▪ *I ran because I was afraid.* ▪ *We can't assume it will rain today just because it rained yesterday.* — **because of** : for the reason of ▪ *The picnic has been canceled because of bad weather.* ▪ *Because of you, we missed the bus* [=you caused us to miss the bus]

beck /ˈbɛk/ *n* — **at someone's beck and call** : always ready to do whatever someone asks ▪ *He expects his employees to be at his beck and call day and night.*

beck·on /ˈbɛkən/ *vb* [T/I] **1** : to signal (someone) with your arm or hand ▪ *She beckoned (to) the waiter to come over.* **2** : to attract (someone or something) ▪ *(figurative) The wilderness beckoned (to) him.* ▪ *a beckoning smile*

be·come /bɪˈkʌm/ *vb* ◆**-came** /-ˈkeɪm/; **-come**; **-com·ing** **1** [*linking vb*] : to begin to be or come to be something specified ▪ *We didn't become close friends until recently.* ▪ *They both became teachers.* ▪ *The book has become quite popular.* ▪ *It eventually became clear that he had lied.* **2** [T] *formal* **a** : to look attractive on (someone) ▪ *That dress becomes you.* **b** : to be suitable or proper for (someone) ▪ *This kind of behavior hardly becomes a person of your age.* — **become of** : to happen to ▪ *Whatever became of our old friend?*

be·com·ing /bɪˈkʌmɪŋ/ *adj, formal* **1** : causing someone to look attractive ▪ *That jacket is very becoming on you.* ▪ *a becoming new hairstyle* **2** : suitable or appropriate ▪ *She accepted the award with a becoming humility.* — **be·com·ing·ly** *adv*

¹**bed** /ˈbɛd/ *n* **1 a** [C/U] : a piece of furniture that people sleep on ▪ *There are two beds in the hotel room.* ▪ *a hospital bed* ▪ *Don't forget to* **make the bed.** [=to neatly arrange the sheets, blankets, etc., on the bed] ▪ *She usually* **goes to bed** [=lies down in her bed to sleep] *around 11:00.* ▪ *It's time to* **get out of bed.** [=get up] ▪ *She lay/stayed* **in bed** *all morning.* ▪ *The kids like to hear a story* **before bed.** [=before they go to sleep] ▪ *Have you put the children to bed?* [=have you prepared the children to go to sleep and put them in their beds?] ▪ *It's time for bed.* [=bedtime; time to sleep] **b** [C] : something that is used to sleep on ▪ *The blanket by the fireplace is the dog's bed.* **2** — used in phrases that describe having sexual relations ◇ Someone who is **good in bed** is a skillful lover. To **go to bed** with someone is to have sex with someone. When two people are **in bed,** they are in the act of having sex. ▪ *She caught her husband in bed with his secretary.* Phrases like these are also used figuratively. ▪ *a politician*

who is **in bed with** the oil industry [=who has an improperly close relationship with the oil industry] **3** [C] : a small area of ground specially prepared for plants • *a bed of flowers* = *a flower bed* — see also BED OF ROSES **4** [C] : a flat pile or layer of something • *a bed of coals* **5** [C] : an area of ground at the bottom of a sea, lake, etc. • *the ocean bed* [=*floor*] **6** [C] *technical* : a layer of rock or some other material from inside the earth • *fossil beds* **7** [C] : the platform or box in the back of some kinds of trucks — **get up on the wrong side of the bed** (*US*) or *chiefly Brit* **get out of bed on the wrong side** : to be in a bad mood throughout the day — **make your bed and lie in it** ✧ Expressions like *you've made your bed, and now you must lie in it* mean that you have done something that causes problems and now you must accept and deal with those problems.

²**bed** *vb* **bed·ded; bed·ding** — **bed down** [*phrasal vb*] **bed down** or **bed down (someone or something) down** or **bed down (someone or something)** : to lie down for sleep or to provide (a person or animal) with a place to sleep • *I bedded down on the couch.* • *We fed and bedded down the animals.*

bed and board *n* [U] *chiefly Brit* : food and a place to sleep

bed–and–breakfast *n* **1** [C] : a house or small hotel in which someone can rent a room to sleep in for a price that includes breakfast the next morning — called also *B and B* **2** [U] *chiefly Brit* : a service in which the price of a room also includes breakfast the next morning • *a small hotel that offers bed-and-breakfast*

be·daz·zle /bɪˈdæzəl/ *vb* **-daz·zled; -daz·zling** [T] : to thrill or excite (someone) very much • *fans bedazzled by movie stars* — **be·daz·zle·ment** /bɪˈdæzəlmənt/ *n* [U]

bed·clothes /ˈbɛdˌkloʊz/ *n* [*plural*] : BEDDING 1

bed·ding /ˈbɛdɪŋ/ *n* [U] **1** : the sheets and blankets that are used on a bed **2** : something used for an animal's bed • *straw bedding*

be·deck /bɪˈdɛk/ *vb* [T] : to decorate (someone or something) • *She was bedecked in jewels.* • *The hall was bedecked with flowers.*

be·dev·il /bɪˈdɛvəl/ *vb*, *US* **-iled** or *Brit* **-illed**; *US* **-il·ing** or *Brit* **-il·ling** [T] : to cause trouble or repeated problems for (someone or something) • *The project has been bedeviled by problems.*

bed·fel·low /ˈbɛdˌfɛloʊ/ *n* [C] : a person or thing that is associated or connected with another • *Politics makes strange bedfellows.* [=people who are very different sometimes work together for political reasons]

bed·head /ˈbɛdˌhɛd/ *n* [C] *Brit* : HEADBOARD

bed·lam /ˈbɛdləm/ *n* [U] : a very noisy and confused state or scene • *The classroom was total/complete bedlam.*

bed of roses *n* [*singular*] : a place or situation that is pleasant or easy • *Her life is no bed of roses.*

bed·pan /ˈbɛdˌpæn/ *n* [C] : a shallow pan used as a toilet by a person who is too ill to get out of bed

bed·post /ˈbɛdˌpoʊst/ *n* [C] : any one of the four main supporting posts at each corner of an old-fashioned bed

be·drag·gled /bɪˈdrægəld/ *adj* : wet or dirty from being in rain or mud • *a bedraggled hitchhiker*

bed·rid·den /ˈbɛdˌrɪdn̩/ *adj* : forced to stay in bed because of illness or weakness • *bedridden patients*

bed·rock /ˈbɛdˌrɑːk/ *n* [U] **1** : the solid rock that lies under the surface of the ground **2** : a strong idea, principle, or fact that supports something • *His religious beliefs are/form the bedrock on which his life is based.* • *bedrock beliefs/ values*

¹**bed·room** /ˈbɛdˌruːm/ *n* [C] : a room used for sleeping • *a house with three bedrooms* = *a 3-bedroom house* — **bedroomed** /ˈbɛdˌruːmd/ *adj*, *Brit* — used in combination • *a three-bedroomed house*

²**bedroom** *adj*, *always before a noun* **1** *US* : lived in by people who go to another town or city to work • *a bedroom community* **2** : dealing with sexual relationships • *bedroom humor*

bed·side /ˈbɛdˌsaɪd/ *n* [*singular*] : the place next to a person's bed • *She sat at his bedside.* • *a bedside table/lamp* • *a doctor with a warm bedside manner* [=a doctor who treats patients in a warm and friendly way]

bed·sit /ˌbɛdˈsɪt/ *n* [C] *Brit* : an apartment with only one room that is used for both sleeping and living in — called also *bedsitter, bedsitting room*

bed·spread /ˈbɛdˌsprɛd/ *n* [C] : a decorative cover for a bed

bed·time /ˈbɛdˌtaɪm/ *n* [C/U] : the usual time when someone goes to bed • *It's almost bedtime.* • *a bedtime story* [=a story that is read or told to children when they go to bed]

bee /ˈbiː/ *n* [C] **1** : a black and yellow flying insect that can sting and that is often kept in hives for the honey that it produces • *flowers pollinated by bees* • *(figurative) My mom is a real busy bee.* = *My mom is (as) busy as a bee.* [=she is very busy and active] **2** *US* : a gathering of people for the purpose of spending time together while working on similar projects • *a quilting bee* — see also SPELLING BEE — **have a bee in your bonnet** *informal* : to talk and think a lot about something • *He always has a bee in his bonnet about safety.* — **the birds and the bees** see BIRD

beech /ˈbiːtʃ/ *n*, *pl* **beech·es** or **beech** [C] : a kind of tree that has smooth gray bark and small nuts

¹**beef** /ˈbiːf/ *n* **1** [U] : meat from a cow • *ground beef* • *the beef industry* • *beef stew* [=a stew made with beef] **2** [C] *informal* : COMPLAINT • *What's your beef?*

²**beef** *vb* [I] *informal* : COMPLAINT • *She's always beefing about something.* — **beef up** [*phrasal vb*] **beef (something) up** or **beef up (something)** *informal* : to add weight, strength, or power to (some-

thing) ▪ *Security will be beefed up during the event.*

beef·bur·ger /'bi:f₊bɚgɚ/ *n* [C] *chiefly Brit* : HAMBURGER

beef·cake /'bi:f₊keɪk/ *n* [U] *informal* : men who are muscular and attractive ▪ *The movie has a lot of beefcake.* ▪ *beefcake photos/posters*

Beef·eat·er /'bi:f₊iːtɚ/ *n* [C] : a guard at the Tower of London

beef·steak /'bi:f₊steɪk/ *n* [C/U] : a thick slice of beef : STEAK

beefy /'bi:fi/ *adj* **beef·i·er; -est 1** : large, strong, and often fat ▪ *a beefy football player* **2** *US* : strongly built ▪ *a beefy truck* **3** *chiefly US* : of or relating to beef ▪ *a beefy flavor*

bee·hive /'bi:₊haɪv/ *n* [C] **1** : a nest for bees : HIVE **2** : a place filled with busy activity ▪ *The office was a beehive of activity.* **3** : a woman's hairdo in which long hair is piled high on top of the head

bee·keep·er /'bi:₊kiːpɚ/ *n* [C] : a person who raises bees — **bee·keep·ing** *n* [U]

bee·line /'bi:₊laɪn/ *n* — **make a beeline for** *informal* : to go quickly and directly at or to (something or someone) ▪ *He made a beeline for the kitchen.* — **beeline** *vb* **-lined; -lin·ing** [I] *US, informal* ▪ *He beelined out the door.*

been *past participle of* BE

¹**beep** /'bi:p/ *n* [C] : a short, high sound made by a horn, an electronic device, etc.

²**beep** *vb* [T/I] : to cause (a horn, an electronic device, etc.) to make a beep ▪ *She beeped (her horn) at me.* ▪ *a beeping noise*

beep·er /'bi:pɚ/ *n* [C] *chiefly US* : PAGER

beer /'biɚ/ *n* **1** [C/U] : an alcoholic drink made from malt and flavored with hops ▪ *a glass of beer* ▪ *a beer mug* **2** [U] : a drink made from roots or other parts of plants ▪ *a glass of birch/ginger beer* — see also ROOT BEER — **beery** /'biri/ *adj* **beer·i·er; -est** ▪ *a beery flavor/smell*

beer belly *n* [C] *informal* : a fat belly caused by drinking a lot of beer — called also *beer gut*

bees·wax /'bi:z₊wæks/ *n* [U] : wax made by bees — **none of your beeswax** *US, informal* — used as a way of telling someone that you will not provide information because it is private ▪ *"How old are you?" "That's none of your beeswax."* [=none of your business]

beet /'bi:t/ *n* [C] **1** *US* **a** : a garden plant with thick leaves and a rounded red root — called also (*Brit*) *beetroot* **b** : the root of the beet plant that is eaten as a vegetable ▪ *sliced beets* — called also (*Brit*) *beetroot* **2** *Brit* : SUGAR BEET — **beet red** or **red as a beet** : red in the face especially from embarrassment ▪ *When she realized her mistake, she turned beet red.*

¹**bee·tle** /'bi:tl/ *n* [C] : a type of insect with wings that form a hard cover on its back when it is not flying

²**beetle** *vb* **bee·tled; bee·tling** [I] *chiefly Brit, informal* : to move quickly ▪ *Everybody beetled off home.*

beet·root /'bi:t₊ru:t/ *n* [C/U] *Brit* : BEET

be·fall /bɪ'fɑːl/ *vb* **-fell** /-'fɛl/; **-fall·en** /-'fɑːlən/; **-fall·ing** [T] *formal* : to happen to (someone or something) ▪ *the unhappy fate that befell him*

be·fit /bɪ'fɪt/ *vb* **-fit·ted; -fit·ting** [T] *formal* : to be suitable to or proper for (someone or something) ▪ *She has a mind for serious inquiry, as befits a scientist.* ▪ *clothes befitting the occasion* — **be·fit·ting·ly** /bɪ'fɪtɪŋli/ *adv*

¹**be·fore** /bɪ'foɚ/ *adv* **1** : at an earlier time ▪ *Haven't we met before?* ▪ *the day before* **2** *formal* + *old-fashioned* : to or toward the place where someone is going ▪ *marching on before* [=ahead]

²**before** *prep* **1 a** : at a time earlier than (something or someone) ▪ *We arrived shortly before six o'clock.* ▪ *before dinner* ▪ *Call me before your arrival.* ▪ *You can go before me.* ▪ *They earned 50,000 dollars before taxes.* **b** *US* — used to describe a time earlier than a specified hour ▪ *It's 20 (minutes) before 12.* [=it's 11:40] **2** : at a place earlier than (something or someone) in order or in a series ▪ *Your name is listed before mine.* ▪ *The number 2 comes before 3 and after 1.* **3 a** : in front of (someone or something) ▪ *The Great Plains stretched endlessly before them.* ▪ *The game took place before a crowd of thousands.* ▪ *The defendant stood before the judge.* **b** : being considered by (someone or something) ▪ *The case before the court involves a robbery.*

³**before** *conj* **1** : earlier than the time that : earlier than when ▪ *He left long before morning came.* ▪ *Call me before you arrive.* ▪ *I finished the exam before he did.* ▪ *He left before I could thank him.* [=I wasn't able to thank him because he left too soon] ▪ *I'll resign before I give in!* [=I would rather resign than give in] ▪ *Before I forget, will you give me your telephone number?* [=I'm asking for your telephone number now because I might forget to do it later] ▪ *You have to complete an introductory class before you can take the advanced class.* **2** : until the time that ▪ *It did not take long before he had earned their trust.* [=he earned their trust quickly]

be·fore·hand /bɪ'foɚ₊hænd/ *adv* : at an earlier time ▪ *We paid for our tickets beforehand.*

be·foul /bɪ'fawəl/ *vb* [T] *formal* : to make (something) dirty ▪ *pollutants that befoul* [=foul] *the air*

be·friend /bɪ'frɛnd/ *vb* [T] : to become a friend to (someone) ▪ *He befriended the new student.*

be·fud·dled /bɪ'fʌdld/ *adj* : unable to think clearly : very confused ▪ *The paperwork left me completely befuddled.*

beg /'bɛg/ *vb* **begged; beg·ging 1** [T/I] : to ask people for money or food ▪ *children begging (strangers) for food* = *children begging food from strangers* **2** [T/I] : to ask someone in a very serious and emotional way for something ▪ *He begged the doctor for medicine.* ▪ *He begged (for) forgiveness.* = *He begged to be forgiven.* ▪ *I beg (of) you to help them!* = *Help them, I beg you!* ▪ *He's too proud to beg.* **3** [T] : to seem perfect for some purpose : to be very well suited for something ▪ *a scene begging to be photo-*

graphed — **beg leave** formal + old-fashioned : to ask for permission to do something • I beg leave to differ with you, sir. — **beg off** [phrasal vb] informal : to say that you cannot or can no longer do something • He originally said he'd go to the party, but he later begged off (going), claiming he had to work that night. — **beg the question 1** : to cause someone to ask a specified question as a reaction or response • The quarterback's injury begs the question of who will start in his place. **2** formal : to ignore a question or issue by assuming it has been answered or settled • Their proposed solution begs the question of whether the changes are actually a problem. — **beg to differ** : to politely disagree with someone • You say that the candidates are the same, but I beg to differ. [=I do not agree] — **beg your pardon** ✧ The phrase I beg your pardon is used to apologize when you have done something impolite or when you have made a mistake. • I beg your pardon. [=sorry, excuse me] I didn't mean to bump into you. It can be used to show that you are annoyed or offended by something • "That boy isn't very bright." "I beg your pardon! That's my son!" It can also be used when you have not heard or understood something clearly. • I beg your pardon? What did you say? — **go begging** chiefly Brit : to be something that few or no people want • With the poor economy, many expensive restaurants now have tables that go begging.

began past tense of BEGIN

be-get /bɪˈgɛt/ vb **-got** /-ˈgɑːt/ also **-gat** /-ˈgæt/; **-got-ten** /-ˈgɑːtn̩/ or **-got**; **-get-ting** [T] **1** formal : to cause (something) to happen or exist • Violence begets more violence. **2** old-fashioned + literary : to become the father of (someone) • He died without begetting an heir.

¹beg-gar /ˈbɛgɚ/ n [C] **1** : a person who lives by begging for money, food, etc. **2** Brit, informal : a person who is regarded as lucky, unlucky, lazy, etc. • He's a lazy beggar. — **beggars can't be choosers** ✧ The saying beggars can't be choosers means that people who need something must be satisfied with whatever they get even if it is not exactly what they wanted.

²beggar vb **-gared; -gar-ing** [T] chiefly Brit — used in the phrases **beggar belief** and **beggar description** to talk about something that is very difficult to believe or describe • It almost beggars belief that anyone can be so cruel.

be-gin /bɪˈgɪn/ vb **-gan** /-ˈgæn/; **-gun** /-ˈgʌn/; **-gin-ning** **1 a** [T/I] : to start doing something • They will begin construction on the new school soon. • She'll begin the lecture at 10. • He began his career at the local newspaper. • I had just begun eating when the phone rang. • She interrupted as soon as I began to speak. • I began (working on) the quilt last month. • You'll have to begin again. [=start over] **b** [T] : to start to have a feeling, thought, etc. • She began to feel dizzy. = She began feeling dizzy. • I'm beginning to think the oversight was intentional. **2** [T/I] : to

start to happen, to exist, to be done, etc. • The meeting began in the morning and finished/ended at noon. • Our problems were just beginning. • His passion for music began at the age of six. • "Where does the river begin?" "It begins in the mountains to the north." • The English alphabet begins with A and ends with Z. • Prices for the hotel rooms begin at 85 dollars. [=85 dollars is the lowest price for a hotel room] • It's beginning to rain. • He began as a clerk. [=he was a clerk when he started working] **3** [T] : to start speaking by saying (something) • "Allow me to introduce myself," he began. **4** — used in an exaggerated way to say that something is not possible • I can't even begin to describe how good the food was. [=the food was very good] • I can hardly begin to thank you for all you've done. — **to begin with 1** : as the first thing to be thought about or considered • "I don't think we should buy the car." "Why not?" "To begin with, I'm not sure we can afford it." **2** : at the start • She has lost a lot of weight, and she wasn't very heavy to begin with.

be-gin-ner /bɪˈgɪnɚ/ n [C] : a person who is beginning something or doing something for the first time • a swimming class for beginners = a beginner class • His success was beginner's luck. [=he succeeded because he was lucky, as beginners sometimes are]

¹be-gin-ning /bɪˈgɪnɪŋ/ n **1** [C] : the point or time at which something begins • He has been working there since the beginning of the year. • It was clear from the (very) beginning that she would eventually win. • The company was very small in the beginning [=when it began], but it eventually became a giant corporation. • The argument marked the beginning of the end of their marriage. [=the argument was the start of a series of events that led to the end of their marriage] **2** [C] : the first part of something • the beginning of a song/movie **3** [plural] **a** : an early stage or period • I have the beginnings of a sore throat. [=my throat is starting to feel sore] **b** : the origins or background of a person or thing • He came from humble beginnings. • The organization had its beginnings in a small Midwestern town.

²beginning adj : involving or learning about the simple or basic parts of a subject • beginning mathematics • courses for beginning [=elementary], intermediate, and advanced students

begot past tense and past participle of BEGET

begotten past participle of BEGET

be-grudge /bɪˈgrʌdʒ/ vb **-grudged; -grudg-ing** [T] : to think that someone does not deserve something • You shouldn't begrudge (her) her success.

begrudging adj : said, done, or given in a reluctant way • begrudging acceptance/admiration/respect — **be-grudg-ing-ly** /bɪˈgrʌdʒɪŋli/ adv • She agreed begrudgingly.

be-guile /bɪˈgajəl/ vb **-guiled; -guil-ing** formal **1** [T] : to trick or deceive (someone) • She beguiled her classmates into *doing the work for her.* **2** [T/I] : to attract or interest someone • *The audience was beguiled by his smooth, seductive voice.* — **beguiling** *adj* • *a beguiling melody/temptress* — **be·guil·ing·ly** /bɪˈgaɪlɪŋli/ *adv*

begun *past participle of* BEGIN

be·half /bɪˈhæf, *Brit* bɪˈhɑːf/ *n* — **on behalf of someone** *or* **on someone's behalf 1** : as a representative of someone • *The teacher accepted the award on behalf of the whole class.* **2** *or US* **in behalf of someone** *or* **in someone's behalf** : in support of someone • *They're willing to do anything on their child's behalf.* **3** : because of someone • *Don't get up on my behalf.*

be·have /bɪˈheɪv/ *vb* **-haved; -hav·ing 1** [T/I] : to act in an acceptable or proper way • *If you can't behave in the store, we'll have to leave.* • *I wish those children would* **behave themselves. 2** [I] : to act in a particular way • *He behaves like a child!* • *The experiment tested how various metals behave under heat and pressure.* — **behaved** *adj* • *a well-behaved child* [=a child who behaves well; a polite child]

be·hav·ior (*US*) *or Brit* **be·hav·iour** /bɪˈheɪvjɚ/ *n* [C/U] : the way a person, animal, or thing acts or behaves • *Students are rewarded for good behavior.* • *studying the behavior of elephants* • *(a) normal adolescent behavior* • *an interesting pattern of behavior = an interesting behavioral pattern* • *The children were all on their best behavior.* [=behaving very well and politely] • *behaviors that can put people at increased risk for skin cancer* — **be·hav·ior·al** (*US*) *or Brit* **be·hav·iour·al** /bɪˈheɪvjərəl/ *adj* • *behavioral problems/patterns*

be·head /bɪˈhɛd/ *vb* [T] : to cut off the head of (someone) especially as a punishment • *Louis XVI was beheaded in 1793.*

beheld *past tense and past participle of* BEHOLD

be·he·moth /bɪˈhiːməθ/ *n* [C] : something very big and powerful • *a corporate behemoth* [=a giant corporation]

be·hest /bɪˈhɛst/ *n* — **at the behest of someone** *or* **at someone's behest** *formal* : because of being asked or ordered by someone • *A meeting was held at the senator's behest.*

[1]**be·hind** /bɪˈhaɪnd/ *adv* **1 a** : in or toward the back • *look behind* **b** : in the place that someone is going away from • *She* **stayed behind** *after the other guests left.* • *They* **left behind** *everything they owned.* • *(figurative) She wanted to* **leave the past behind.** [=forget about the past] **2** : in a losing position in a race or competition • *We were ahead in the first half, but now we're behind.* • *A politician who is behind in the polls* • *She was losing the race, but she* **came from behind** *and is now in front.* **3 a** — used to describe something that is not happening or proceeding as quickly as it should • *We're running about five minutes behind with tonight's schedule.* **b** — used to describe someone who is not doing something (such as paying a debt) as quickly as required or expected • *He got a bit behind in/with his payments.*

[2]**behind** *prep* **1** : in or to a place at the back of or to the rear of (someone or something) • *Look behind you.* • *The house is behind some trees.* **2** : losing to (someone or something) in a race or competition • *They were ahead of us by 5 points, but now they're behind us by 7.* • *The company is now behind the competition.* **3** : in a less advanced position than (someone or something) • *He was a year behind me in school.* [=he finished school a year after I did] : not happening or proceeding as quickly as (someone or something) • *He was behind the other students in his studies.* • *We're running about five minutes* **behind schedule.** [=*late*] **4** : in the past for (someone or something) • *Those problems are behind us now.* • *Let's put our troubles behind us.* [=let's stop thinking/worrying about our troubles] **5 a** : providing the reason or explanation for (something) • *What was really behind his murder?* [=what was the real reason for his murder?] **b** : responsible for (something) • *We'll find out who's behind this conspiracy!* **6 a** : in support of (someone or something) • *We're behind you all the way!* • *I encourage everyone to* **get behind** *these proposals.* [=to support these proposals] **b** : with the support of (something) • *They won the game behind brilliant pitching.* [=brilliant pitching made it possible for them to win the game]

[3]**behind** *n* [C] *informal* : BUTTOCKS • *kicked him in the behind*

behind-the-scenes *adj, always before a noun* **1** : working or happening without being known or seen by the public • *behind-the-scenes lobbying/influence* • *an effective behind-the-scenes operator* **2** : revealing or reporting on things that usually happen without being known or seen by the public • *a behind-the-scenes account*

be·hold /bɪˈhoʊld/ *vb* **-held** /-ˈhɛld/; **-hold·ing** [T] *formal + literary* : to look at or see (something) • *Have you ever beheld such beauty?* • *The canyon was a* **sight/wonder to behold.** [=an impressive thing to see] — see also *lo and behold* at LO — **be·hold·er** *n* [C] • *Beauty is in the eye of the beholder.* [=different people have different ideas about what is beautiful]

be·hold·en /bɪˈhoʊldən/ *adj* — **beholden to** *formal* : owing a favor or gift to (someone) • *politicians who are beholden to special interest groups*

be·hoove (*US*) /bɪˈhuːv/ *or Brit* **be·hove** /bɪˈhoʊv/ *vb* **-hooved; -hoov·ing** [T] *formal* : to be necessary or proper for (someone) • *It behooves a good citizen to obey the law.* [=a good citizen should obey the law]

beige /ˈbeɪʒ/ *n* [C/U] : a light yellowish-brown color — **beige** *adj*

[1]**be·ing** /ˈbiːjɪŋ/ *n* **1** [C] : a living thing • *sentient beings* — see also *HUMAN BEING* **2** [U] : EXISTENCE • *theories about how the universe* **came into being** [=began to exist] **3** [U] *formal* : the most im-

portant or basic part of a person's mind or self • *He loved her with his whole being.* [=he deeply loved her]

²be·ing *present participle of* BE

be·jew·eled (*US*) *or Brit* **be·jew·elled** /bɪˈʤuːld/ *adj* : decorated with jewels • *a bejeweled princess/sword*

be·la·bor (*US*) *or Brit* **be·la·bour** /bɪˈleɪbɚ/ *vb* [T] : to talk about (something) for too long • *Please don't belabor the point.*

be·lat·ed /bɪˈleɪtəd/ *adj* : happening or coming very late or too late • *a belated birthday card* — **be·lat·ed·ly** *adv* • *I belatedly realized my mistake.* — **be·lat·ed·ness** *n* [U]

belch /ˈbɛltʃ/ *vb* **1** [I] : to let out air from the stomach through the mouth very loudly • *He finished his beer and belched (loudly).* **2** [T/I] : to push or throw (something) out with force • *trucks belching (out) exhaust* • *Smoke belched (out) from the factories.* — **belch** *n* [C]

be·lea·guer /bɪˈliːgɚ/ *vb* [T] *formal* : to cause constant or repeated trouble for (a person, business, etc.) • *The company is beleaguered by debt.*

bel·fry /ˈbɛlfri/ *n, pl* **-fries** [C] : a tower or part of a tower where a bell hangs • (*chiefly US, figurative*) *an old woman with bats in her belfry* [=a crazy/batty old woman]

Bel·gian /ˈbɛldʒən/ *n* [C] : a person from Belgium — **Belgian** *adj*

be·lie /bɪˈlaɪ/ *vb* **-lied; -ly·ing** [T] *formal* **1** : to give a false idea of (something) • *Her appearance belies her age.* [=she looks much younger than she is] **2** : to show (something) to be false or wrong • *Their actions belie their words.*

be·lief /bəˈliːf/ *n* **1 a** [U, singular] : a feeling of being sure that someone or something is real or true • *his belief in God* • *It's my belief* [=I believe] *that this policy will fail.* • *She bought the stock in the (mistaken) belief that it would make her rich.* • *Contrary to popular belief* [=although many people do not think so]*, the economy has improved.* **b** [singular] : a feeling that something is good, right, or valuable • *a (firm/strong) belief in democracy* **c** [singular] : a feeling of trust in someone's worth or ability • *He has a strong belief in himself.* [=he strongly believes that he will succeed] **2** [C] : a strongly held opinion about something • *religious/political beliefs* **3** [U] : the state of being accepted as true • *a story that is worthy of belief* [=a believable story] • *a story that defies belief = a story that is beyond belief*

be·lieve /bəˈliːv/ *vb* **-lieved; -liev·ing 1 a** [T/I] : to accept (something) as true or real • *We believed her story.* • *Her story is hard/difficult to believe.* • *I didn't think it could happen, but seeing is believing.* [=I saw it happen, so now I believe it's possible] **b** [T] : to accept the truth of what is said by (someone) • *He says he'll help, but I don't believe him.* **2** [T] : to have a (specified) opinion : THINK • *She (clearly/firmly/honestly) believes (that) it is possible.* • *We were led to believe* [=someone

or something made us think] *that it was true.* **3** [I] : to regard the existence of God as a fact • *She went to church, but she didn't really believe.* **4** *informal* **a** — used to express certainty • *"Do you think they can win?" "You('d) better believe it!"* [=yes, definitely!] • *Believe (you) me, that kid has talent.* **b** — used to express annoyance • *You broke the window? I can't believe you guys!* [=I am very annoyed at you] • *I don't believe it! The floor is already dirty again!* **c** — used to express surprise • *I can't believe it* [=I am very surprised] *that he quit his job.* • *You won't/wouldn't believe* [=you will be very surprised by] *what I just heard!* • *Can/Would you believe it? He quit his job! = He quit his job, if you can believe it/that.* • *Believe it or not* [=although it is surprising]*, it's true.* • *He's going to quit? I'll believe it/that when I see it.* [=I do not believe he will quit] • *I could hardly believe my eyes/ears!* [=I was shocked by what I was seeing/hearing] — **believe in** [phrasal vb] **1 a** : to have faith or confidence in the existence of (something) • *Do you believe in ghosts?* **b** : to have trust in the goodness or value of (something) • *She believes in regular exercise. = She believes in exercising regularly.* • *I don't believe in* [=I disapprove of] *using pesticides.* **2** : to have trust in the goodness or ability of (someone) • *His parents have always believed in him.* — **make believe** : PRETEND • *The children like to make believe (that) they're soldiers.* — *see also* MAKE-BELIEVE — **be·liev·able** /bəˈliːvəbəl/ *adj* — **be·liev·ably** /bəˈliːvəbli/ *adv* — **be·liev·er** *n* [C] • *devout (religious) believers* • *She's a firm/great/strong believer in education.* [=she thinks education is very useful and important]

be·lit·tle /bɪˈlɪtl̩/ *vb* **-lit·tled; -lit·tling** [T] : to describe (someone or something) as little or unimportant • *The critic belittled the author's work.* — **belittling** *adj* • *a very belittling description*

bell /ˈbɛl/ *n* [C] **1** : a hollow usually cup-shaped metal object that makes a ringing sound when it is hit • *ring/sound/toll a bell* • *church bells* **2** : an electronic device that makes a ringing sound • *We rang the bell* [=doorbell] *twice, but no one was home.* • (*figurative*) *Warning/alarm bells went off (in my head) as I read her letter.* [=there was something in her letter that alarmed me] **3** : something that is shaped like a bell — **ring a bell** *see* ³RING

bell-bot·toms /ˈbɛlˌbɑːtəmz/ *n* [plural] : pants with legs that become much wider at the bottom — **bell-bottom** *adj* • *bell-bottom jeans*

bell·boy /ˈbɛlˌbɔɪ/ *n* [C] : BELLHOP

belle /ˈbɛl/ *n* [C] *old-fashioned* : a very attractive and popular girl or woman • *a Southern belle*

bell·hop /ˈbɛlˌhɑːp/ *n* [C] *chiefly US* : a boy or man who takes hotel guests to their rooms, carries luggage, etc. — called also *bellboy*

bel·li·cose /ˈbɛlɪˌkoʊs/ *adj, formal* : having or showing a tendency to argue or fight • *a bellicose general* • *bellicose be-*

havior/language — **bel·li·cos·i·ty** /ˌbɛlɪˈkɑːsəti/ n [U]

¹bel·lig·er·ent /bəˈlɪdʒərənt/ adj **1** : feeling or showing readiness to fight ▪ He was drunk and belligerent. **2** always before a noun, formal : fighting a war ▪ belligerent nations/states — **bel·lig·er·ence** /bəˈlɪdʒərəns/ n [U] — **bel·lig·er·ent·ly** adv

²belligerent n [C] formal : a group or country that is fighting a war ▪ negotiating a cease-fire between the belligerents

bel·low /ˈbɛloʊ/ vb [T/I] : to shout in a deep voice ▪ He bellowed at/to/for her to come at once. ▪ bellowing orders — **bellow** n [C] ▪ a bellow of anger/rage

bel·lows /ˈbɛloʊz/ n [plural] : a device that produces a current of air when its sides are pressed together

bell pepper n [C] chiefly US : a large pepper with a mild flavor

bells and whistles n [plural] informal : parts and features that are appealing but not necessary ▪ The car comes with all the bells and whistles.

bell·weth·er /ˈbɛlˌwɛðɚ/ n [C] : someone or something that leads others or shows what will happen in the future ▪ She is a bellwether of fashion.

¹bel·ly /ˈbɛli/ n, pl **-lies** [C] **1 a** : a person's stomach or abdomen ▪ My belly was full. ▪ He crawled on his belly. **b** : the part of an animal's body that is like a person's belly ▪ a gray squirrel with a white belly **2** : a curved or rounded surface or part ▪ the belly of an airplane/ship — **bel·lied** adj — used in combination ▪ a red-bellied woodpecker

²belly vb **-lies; -lied; -ly·ing** [T/I] : to cause (something) to curve or bulge outward ▪ The wind bellied (out) the sails. = The sails bellied out in the wind. — **belly up to** [phrasal vb] US, informal : to walk to or toward (someone or something) ▪ The men bellied up to the bar.

¹bel·ly·ache /ˈbɛliˌeɪk/ n [C/U] : STOMACHACHE

²bellyache vb **-ached; -ach·ing** [I] informal : to complain in an annoying way ▪ He's always bellyaching about something. — **bellyaching** n [U] ▪ I'm tired of his bellyaching.

belly button n [C] informal : NAVEL

belly dance n [C] : a type of Middle Eastern dance done by a woman who makes rhythmic movements with her hips and belly — **belly dance** vb [I] — **belly dancer** n [C]

bel·ly·ful /ˈbɛliˌfʊl/ n [singular] informal : a large amount of something ▪ a bellyful of laughs

belly laugh n [C] : a deep and loud laugh

bel·ly-up /ˈbɛliˈʌp/ n — **go belly-up** informal : to fail completely ▪ The business went belly-up. [=went bankrupt]

be·long /bɪˈlɑːŋ/ vb [I] **1** — used to say that someone or something should be in a particular place or situation ▪ This book belongs on the top shelf. ▪ Those kids belong in school. ▪ She and her husband truly belong together. **2** : to be accepted and liked by the other people in a group ▪ She was here for 15 years, but she never

really belonged. — **belong to** [phrasal vb] **1** : to be owned by (someone) ▪ The money/watch belongs to him. **2 a** : to be a member of (a club, organization, etc.) ▪ They belong to a country club. **b** : to be included in (a category, group, etc.) ▪ What family does that bird belong to? **c** : to be a part of (something) ▪ all of the pieces belonging to the puzzle — **belonging** n [U] ▪ Her neighbors' kindness gave her a sense/feeling of belonging.

be·long·ings /bɪˈlɑːŋɪŋz/ n [plural] : POSSESSIONS ▪ They gathered their (personal) belongings and left.

be·loved /bɪˈlʌvəd, bɪˈlʌvd/ adj : dearly loved ▪ my own beloved grandmother ▪ an actor beloved by/of millions — **beloved** n [C] literary ▪ She saw her beloved [=the person she loved] approaching.

¹be·low /bɪˈloʊ/ adv **1** : in or to a lower place ▪ The pilot looked down at the sea far below. **2** : on or to a lower deck on a ship or boat ▪ The captain ordered the men (to go) below. **3** : in or to a lower rank or number ▪ children at age 10 and below **4** : lower than zero ▪ The temperature ranged from 5 below to 10 above. [=from −5 degrees to 10 degrees Fahrenheit] **5** : at a later point in the same document ▪ See the graph below. — **from below** : from a lower place ▪ I felt a draft (coming) from below.

²below prep **1** : in or to a lower place than (something) : BENEATH ▪ Our apartment is (directly) below theirs. ▪ The sun disappeared below the horizon. **2** : less than (something) ▪ Temperatures were below average/normal. ▪ children below [=younger than, under] the age of 10 **3** : having a lower rank than (someone) ▪ A lieutenant is/ranks below a captain.

¹belt /ˈbɛlt/ n [C] **1** : a band of leather, cloth, etc., that is worn around a person's waist ▪ fasten/buckle your belt **2** : a band that runs around wheels or other parts in a machine **3** : a region that has a lot of a particular thing ▪ the corn/cotton belt [=a region with many farms growing corn/cotton] — see also BIBLE BELT, SUNBELT **4** informal : a hard hit ▪ Some drunk threatened to give me a belt. **5** US, informal : a drink of alcohol ▪ He had a few belts (of whiskey). — **below the belt** informal : too harsh and unfair ▪ That remark was below the belt. = That remark really hit (him) below the belt. — **tighten your belt** : to make changes in order to save money ▪ Many companies are tightening their belts during the recession. — **under your belt** : as an achievement or as part of your experience ▪ an actor who has several films under his belt [=who has appeared in several films] — **belt·ed** /ˈbɛltəd/ adj ▪ a belted coat/robe

²belt vb **1** [T] : to fasten (something) with a belt ▪ His bathrobe was loosely belted. **2** [T] informal : to hit (someone or something) hard ▪ Some drunk threatened to belt me. **3** [T] informal : to sing (a song) in a loud and forceful way ▪ a singer belting out tunes **4** [T] US, informal : to drink (something) quickly ▪ He belted down/back a shot of whiskey. **5** [I] chiefly Brit, informal : to go at a high speed ▪ a car belting down/along the road — **belt up** [phrasal vb] Brit **1** : to fasten a seat belt • When you're riding in a car, you should always belt up. [=(US) buckle up] **2** informal : to stop talking • Will you just belt up? [=shut up]

belt-tight·en·ing /ˈbɛltˌtaɪtnɪŋ/ n [U] : changes that are made in order to save money • Many companies are doing some belt-tightening. • a belt-tightening measure/policy

belt·way /ˈbɛltˌweɪ/ n **1** [C] US : a highway that goes around a city **2 the Beltway** : the political and social world of Washington, D.C. • politics inside the Beltway — **Beltway** adj, always before a noun • Beltway politicians/politics

be·moan /bɪˈmoʊn/ vb [T] : to say that you are unhappy about (something) • critics bemoaning the state of the language

be·muse /bɪˈmjuːz/ vb -mused; -mus·ing [T] : to cause (someone) to be confused and often also somewhat amused • He was bemused by all the attention that he was receiving. — **bemused** adj • She had a bemused expression/smile on her face. — **be·mus·ed·ly** /bɪˈmjuːzədli/ adv — **be·muse·ment** /bɪˈmjuːzmənt/ n [U]

¹**bench** /ˈbɛntʃ/ n **1** [C] : a long seat for two or more people • a park bench **2 the bench** law **a** : the place where a judge sits in a court of law • The lawyers approached the bench. **b** : the position or rank of a judge • her appointment to the bench **3** [C] : a long table for holding tools and work • a carpenter's bench **4** sports **a the bench** : a long seat where the members of a sports team wait for a chance to play • He spent most of his season on the bench. [=he did not play in many games] **b** [C] chiefly US : the players on a team who do not usually play at the start of a game • The team has a deep bench. [=the team has many good players in addition to its main players]

²**bench** vb [T] US, sports : to not allow (a player) to play in a game • He was benched for several games by a leg injury.

bench·mark /ˈbɛntʃˌmɑɚk/ n [C] : something that can be used as a way to judge the quality or level of other, similar things • a stock whose performance is a benchmark

bench press n [C] : a lift or exercise in which a weight is raised by pushing your arms upward while you lie on a bench — **bench-press** vb [T] • He can bench-press 350 pounds.

bench·warm·er /ˈbɛntʃˌwɑɚmɚ/ n [C] US, sports : a player who is not among the best players on a team and does not often play

¹**bend** /ˈbɛnd/ vb bent /ˈbɛnt/; bend·ing [T/I] **1** : to curve out of a straight line or position • The road bends to the left. • I bent the wire into a circle. • His glasses got bent. • (figurative) I think we can bend the rule(s) [=be less strict/exact about the rule(s)] in this case. • (figurative) She was bending the truth a little. [=she was being somewhat but not completely truthful] **2** : to move your body or a part of your body so that it is not straight • She bent

down/over/forward. • **bend a knee/leg/arm** • (figurative) They pressured her, but she refused to bend (to their will). • (figurative, formal) He bent himself to/toward the task. = He bent his strength/energy/efforts to/toward the task. [=he worked very hard to do the task] — **bend over backward** see ¹BACKWARD] — **bend someone's ear** informal : to talk to someone for a long time • He just wanted to bend my ear about his own problems. — **on bended knee** also **on bended knees** : in the position of someone who is kneeling on one knee • He proposed to her on bended knee.

²**bend** n **1** [C] : a curved part of something • a bend in a road/stream **2** [C] : the act or process of bending something • doing knee bends **3 the bends** medical : a painful and dangerous condition caused by rising to the surface too quickly after being deep underwater — **around the bend** (chiefly US) or chiefly Brit **round the bend** informal **1** : CRAZY • The stress nearly drove him around the bend. **2** US : occurring soon • The end of summer is just/right around the bend. — **bendy** /ˈbɛndi/ adj, chiefly Brit, informal • a bendy toy/road

bend·er /ˈbɛndɚ/ n [C] informal : a period when someone gets very drunk • He went on a bender last weekend. — see also FENDER BENDER

¹**be·neath** /bɪˈniːθ/ adv : BELOW • the sky above and the earth beneath

²**beneath** prep **1 a** : BELOW • the sky above us and the earth beneath us **b** : directly under (something or someone) • The paper was hidden beneath some books. **2** : not worthy of (someone) • He thinks the work is beneath him. **3** : under the pressure or influence of (something) • The chair sagged beneath his weight. [=his weight made the chair sag] **4** : hidden under (something) • He has a warm heart beneath his gruff manner. — **from beneath** : from a place below or under (something) • She gazed at us from beneath the brim of her hat.

ben·e·fac·tor /ˈbɛnəˌfæktɚ/ n [C] : someone who helps a person, group, etc., by giving money • a rich/anonymous benefactor

be·nef·i·cent /bəˈnɛfəsənt/ adj, formal : doing or producing good • a beneficent leader — **be·nef·i·cence** /bəˈnɛfəsəns/ n [U]

ben·e·fi·cial /ˌbɛnəˈfɪʃəl/ adj : producing good or helpful results or effects • The new drug is beneficial to/for many people. • the beneficial effects of exercise — **ben·e·fi·cial·ly** adv

ben·e·fi·ci·ary /ˌbɛnəˈfɪʃiˌeri, Brit ˌbɛnəˈfɪʃəri/ n, pl -ar·ies [C] **1** : a person, organization, etc., that is helped by something • The college was a beneficiary of the private grant. **2** : a person, organization, etc., that receives money or property when someone dies • Her daughter is her sole beneficiary.

¹**ben·e·fit** /ˈbɛnəˌfɪt/ n **1** [C/U] : a good or helpful result or effect • The benefits outweigh the risks. • Soon she'll reap the benefits of all her hard work. • changes

that are of benefit to you = *changes that are to your benefit* [=changes that will help/benefit you] ▪ *I'm doing this for your benefit.* [=to help you] ▪ *I'm going to give him the benefit of the doubt.* [=I am going to treat him as if he is worthy of trust] **2 a** [C/U] : money that is paid by insurance, the government, etc., when someone dies, becomes sick, etc. ▪ *retirement/disability benefits* ▪ (*Brit*) *to be on benefits* [=(US) *on welfare*] **b** [C] : FRINGE BENEFIT ▪ *The job doesn't pay much, but the benefits are good.* ▪ *a benefit plan/package/program* **3** [C] : a social event to raise money for a person or cause ▪ *have/hold a benefit* ▪ *a benefit concert/dinner/performance* — **have the benefit** : to be helped by (something) ▪ *She has the benefit of years of experience.* — **without the benefit of** or US **without benefit of** : without the help of (something or someone) ▪ *He succeeded without (the) benefit of formal schooling.* — **with the benefit of** : with the help of (something) ▪ *She'll do better with the benefit of experience.*

²**benefit** *vb* **-fit·ed** *also* **-fit·ted**; **-fit·ing** *also* **-fit·ting 1** [T] : to be useful or helpful to (someone or something) ▪ *medicines that benefit thousands of people* ▪ *All of you will be benefited by these changes.* **2** [I] : to be helped ▪ *Many people will benefit from the new drug.*

be·nev·o·lent /bə'nɛvələnt/ *adj* **1** : kind and generous ▪ *a benevolent company/donor* **2** : organized to do good things for other people ▪ *a benevolent* [=*philanthropic*] *society* — **be·nev·o·lence** /bə'nɛvələns/ *n* [U] — **be·nev·o·lent·ly** *adv*

be·nign /bɪ'naɪn/ *adj* **1** *medical* **a** : not causing death or serious injury ▪ *a benign infection/disease* **b** : not cancerous ▪ *The tumor is benign.* — opposite MALIGNANT **2** : HARMLESS ▪ *a benign habit* **3** : mild and pleasant ▪ *a benign climate* — **be·nign·ly** *adv*

¹**bent** /'bɛnt/ *adj* **1** : not straight ▪ *a bent metal wire* ▪ *bent arms/elbows* ▪ *He was bent double* [=bent forward from the waist] *with pain.* ▪ (*US, figurative, informal*) *Don't get all bent out of shape!* [=angry or upset] **2** *chiefly Brit, informal* : not honest ▪ *a bent* [=*corrupt*] *cop* — **bent on/upon** : having a strong desire to do (something) ▪ *She seems bent on winning.*

²**bent** *n* [C] : an attraction to or an interest in something ▪ *an organization with a strong religious bent* ▪ *students with a creative/scientific bent*

³**bent** *past tense and past participle of* ¹BEND

be·numbed /bɪ'nʌmd/ *adj, formal* : feeling numb : unable to have strong emotions ▪ *After years of war, they were benumbed* [=*numb*] *to violence.*

be·queath /bɪ'kwiːθ, bɪ'kwiːð/ *vb* [T] *formal* **1** : to say in a will that (your property) will be given to (a person or organization) after you die ▪ *He bequeathed his paintings to the museum.* **2** : to give (ideas, knowledge, etc.) to (younger people) as part of their history ▪ *These stories*

were bequeathed to us by our ancestors.

be·quest /bɪ'kwɛst/ *n* [C] : the property or money that you promise in your will to give to another person or organization after you die ▪ *He made a bequest of his paintings to the museum.*

be·rate /bɪ'reɪt/ *vb* **-rat·ed**; **-rat·ing** [T] *formal* : SCOLD ▪ *She berated him for coming home late.*

be·reaved /bɪ'riːvd/ *adj, formal* : sad because a family member or friend has died ▪ *the bereaved parents/families of the victims* ▪ *The minister tried to comfort the bereaved.* [=the bereaved person/people]

be·reave·ment /bɪ'riːvmənt/ *n, formal* **1** [U] : the state of being sad because a family member or friend has died ▪ *a period of bereavement* **2** [C/U] : the death of a family member or friend ▪ *people who have recently suffered bereavements*

be·reft /bɪ'rɛft/ *adj* — **bereft of** : not having (something that is needed, wanted, or expected) ▪ *They are completely bereft of new ideas.* ▪ *bereft of hope/reason*

be·ret /bə'reɪ/ *n* [C] : a round hat with a tight band around the head and a top that is flat and loose

berk /'bək/ *n* [C] *Brit slang* : a stupid or foolish person ▪ *He's acting like a berk.*

ber·ry /'bɛri/ *n, pl* **-ries** [C] : a small fruit (such as a strawberry or raspberry) that has many small seeds

ber·serk /bɚ'sɚk, bə'zɚk/ *adj* : crazy and violent especially because of anger ▪ *berserk behavior* — **go berserk 1** : to become very angry, crazy, and violent ▪ *A worker went berserk and killed his boss.* **2** : to become very excited ▪ *The crowd was going berserk.*

¹**berth** /'bəθ/ *n* [C] **1** : a place to sleep on a ship, train, etc. ▪ *an upper/lower berth* **2** : a place near the shore where a ship stops and stays **3** *chiefly US* : a place on a team ▪ *She won/earned an Olympic berth.* — **give (someone or something) a wide berth** : to stay away from (someone or something) ▪ *She was in a bad mood, so I gave her a wide berth.*

²**berth** *vb* [T/I] : to bring (a ship) into a place where it can stop and stay ▪ *The ship (was) berthed at this pier.*

be·seech /bɪ'siːtʃ/ *vb* **-sought** /-sɑːt/ *or* **-seeched**; **-seech·ing** [T] *formal + literary* : to beg (someone) for something ▪ *I beseech you, let me live!* [=please, don't kill me]

be·set /bɪ'sɛt/ *vb* **-set**; **-set·ting** [T] : to cause many difficulties for (someone or something) ▪ *He was beset by/with injuries this season.*

be·side /bɪ'saɪd/ *prep* **1** : by the side of (someone or something) ▪ *The man (sitting) beside her was reading.* ▪ *Their house is beside a lake.* **2** : in comparison with (something) ▪ *These problems seem minor beside the potential benefits.* — **beside the point** see ¹POINT — **beside yourself** : not thinking clearly because you are feeling very strong emotions ▪ *We were beside ourselves (with anger/worry/joy).*

¹**be·sides** /bɪ'saɪdz/ *prep* **1** : other than (someone or something) ▪ *There's no one here besides* [=except, but] *me.* ▪ *The traf-*

fic was heavy but, besides that, the trip went well. **2** : in addition to (something) ▪ *She wants to learn other languages besides English.*

²**besides** *adv* **1** : as well ▪ ALSO ▪ *They serve pasta and other foods besides.* **2** : in addition to what has been said ▪ *The play is excellent, and besides, the tickets don't cost much.*

be·siege /bɪˈsiːʤ/ *vb* -**sieged**; -**sieg·ing** [T] **1** : to surround a city, building, etc., with soldiers and try to take control of it ▪ *The army besieged the castle.* **2** : to gather around (someone) in a way that is aggressive, annoying, etc. ▪ *They were besieged by reporters.* **3** : to overwhelm (someone) with too many questions or requests ▪ *Our office was besieged with letters/questions/complaints.*

be·smirch /bɪˈsmɚʧ/ *vb* [T] : to cause harm to (the reputation of someone or something) ▪ *His lies have besmirched her reputation/name/honor.*

be·sot·ted /bɪˈsɑːtəd/ *adj* : loving someone or something so much that you cannot think clearly ▪ *He was completely besotted with/by her.*

be·speak /bɪˈspiːk/ *vb* -**spoke** /-ˈspoʊk/; -**spo·ken** /-ˈspoʊkən/; -**speak·ing** [T] *formal* : to be evidence of (something) ▪ *Her newest album bespeaks a great talent.*

be·spec·ta·cled /bɪˈspɛktəkəld/ *adj* : wearing glasses ▪ *a bespectacled student*

¹**best** /ˈbɛst/ *adj, superlative form of* ¹GOOD *or of* ²WELL **1 a** : better than all others in quality or value ▪ *the (very) best foods/wines* ▪ *our best customers* ▪ *Which of these tastes best?* ▪ *He's my best friend.* [=my closest/dearest friend] **b** : most skillful, talented, or successful ▪ *the team's best player* ▪ *She's the best player, and he's the next/second best player.* **2** : most appropriate, useful, or helpful ▪ *the best thing to do* ▪ *He's the best man for the job.* ▪ *We want to do what's best for you.* ▪ *You should do whatever you think is best.* = *You should do whatever you think best.* ▪ *It's fast, it's easy, and best of all, it's free!* ▪ *Talking on the telephone is the next best thing to visiting in person.*

²**best** *adv, superlative form of* ¹WELL **1** : in a way that is better than all others ▪ *The sauce is best served cold.* ▪ *with the most success or benefit* ▪ *I work best under pressure.* **2** : to the greatest degree or extent : MOST ▪ *That's the one we liked (the) best.* — **as best you can or the best (that) you can** : as well, skillfully, or accurately as you can ▪ *She answered their questions as best she could.* — **had best** ◆ If you *had best* do something, you should do it. ▪ *You'd best get ready for school.*

³**best** *n* [*singular*] **1 the best** : the best person or thing ▪ *Our company is the best in the business.* ▪ *Thanks, Dad. You're the best!* ▪ *the best group of those or things* ▪ *We sell only the best.* [=the best products] ▪ *They want the best for their children.* ▪ *Even in the best of times, we had trouble paying our bills.* ▪ *the best of all possible worlds* ▪ *We were the best of friends.* [=we were very good friends] ▪ *Problems can occur in/under the*

best of circumstances. **2** : someone's or something's most effective, capable, or successful condition — used in phrases like **at your best** and **at its best** ▪ *She's at her best in the morning.* ▪ *This is democracy at its best.* **3** : the highest level that you can do or achieve ▪ *Was that your best?* = *Was that the best you could do?* ▪ *Just do your best.* = *Just do the best you can.* ▪ *Her time in the race was a personal best.* [=it was her fastest time ever] — **(all) for the best** : having or producing a better result ▪ *I won't be able to go, but maybe it's all for the best.* [=just as well] *I have a lot of work to do anyway.* — **(all) the best** — used to wish someone happiness, success, etc. ▪ *We wish you all the best in your new job.* — **at best** — used to refer to a result, condition, etc., that is the best one possible even though it is not very good ▪ *We won't make a profit this year. At best, we'll break even.* — **bring out the best in** ◆ A person or thing that *brings out the best in you* helps you to use or show your best qualities. — **feel your best** : to feel very healthy ▪ *Exercise helps you look and feel your best.* — **get the best of** ◆ If an emotion *gets the best of you*, it causes you to do something that you should not do. — **know (what's) best** see ¹KNOW — **look your best** : to look as attractive and pleasant as possible ▪ *Try to look your best when interviewing for a job.* — **make the best of 1** : to use (something) in an effective way ▪ *We need to make the best of this opportunity.* **2** : to deal with (a bad situation) as well as possible ▪ *We're trying to make the best of it/things.* — **the best is yet to come/be** — used to say that good things have happened but that even better things will happen in the future — **to the best of my knowledge** see KNOWLEDGE — **to the best of your ability** : as well as you are able to ▪ *Our team always plays to the best of our ability.*

⁴**best** *vb* [T] : to defeat or outdo (someone or something) ▪ *He was bested* [=*beaten*] *by his opponent.*

bes·tial /ˈbɛstʃəl/ *adj, formal* : very cruel, violent, etc. ▪ *bestial behavior/violence* — **bes·ti·al·i·ty** /ˌbɛstʃiˈæləti/ *n* [U]

best man *n* [*singular*] : the most important male friend or relative who helps a groom at his wedding

be·stow /bɪˈstoʊ/ *vb* [T] *formal* : to give (something) as a gift or honor ▪ *The university bestowed on/upon her an honorary degree.*

best seller *n* [C] : a popular product (such as a book) that many people have bought ▪ *She has written several best sellers.* ▪ *the best-seller list* — **best-sell·ing** /ˈbɛstˈsɛlɪŋ/ *adj* ▪ *his best-selling novel*

¹**bet** /ˈbɛt/ *n* **1** [C] : an agreement in which people try to guess what will happen and the person who guesses wrong has to give something to the person who guesses right ▪ *lose/win a bet* ▪ *settle/pay a bet* ▪ *He made/has a bet with his brother.* = *He and his brother made/have a bet.* **2** [C] : the money or other valuable thing that you could win or lose in a bet ▪ *She placed/laid a $10 bet.* [=*wager*] **3** [*singu-*

lar] : a choice made by thinking about what will probably happen ▪ *Your best/surest/safest bet* [=the best/surest/safest thing for you to do] *is to avoid the high-way.* ▪ *It's a good/safe/sure bet* [=it is very likely] *that they'll win.* ▪ *All bets are off on the election.* [=it is impossible to guess who will win the election] ▪ *My bet is* [=my guess is] *that they'll say yes.* — *hedge your bets* see ²HEDGE

²**bet** *vb* **bet** *also* **bet·ted; bet·ting 1** [*T/I*] : to make a bet ▪ *He bet $5 on the game.* ▪ *I'll bet (you) a dollar that he makes the next shot.* ▪ *betting on football games* ▪ *He always bets on the favorite (to win).* ▪ *I bet against the favorite and I lost.* **2** [*T*] : to risk losing (something) when you try to do or achieve something ▪ *She's willing to bet* [=risk] *everything on winning this election.* **3** [*T*] : to make decisions based on the belief that something will happen or is true ▪ *We're betting (that) the price of houses will drop.* **4** [*T*] *informal* : to think that something will probably or certainly happen ▪ *I bet (that) it'll rain to-morrow.* ▪ *I bet (you) she doesn't do it.* [=I don't believe that she'll do it] : to think that something is probably or certainly true ▪ *I bet you that no one knows we're here.* ▪ *I'll bet you're tired.* [=you must be tired] ▪ *I'd bet my life on it.* [=I am entire-ly sure] **5** *informal* — used in phrases as an enthusiastic way of saying "yes" ▪ *"Are you going to be there?" "You bet (I'll be there)!"* = *"You can bet on it!"* = *"You bet your life (I will)!"* [=I'll certainly be there] **6** *informal* — used in phrases that ex-press doubt about what will happen ▪ *"She'll be here soon." "I wouldn't bet on it (if I were you)."* = *"Don't bet on it!"* [=I don't think she'll be here soon] — **bet-ting** *adj* ▪ *I'm not a betting man.* [=I'm not a man who likes to bet] — **betting** *n* [*U*] ▪ *No betting* [=gambling] *is allowed.*

be·ta /ˈbeɪtə, *Brit* ˈbiːtə/ *n* **1** [*singular*] : the second letter of the Greek alphabet — B or β **2** [*U*] : a version of a product that is almost finished and that is used for testing ▪ *the beta version of a computer program* ▪ *beta testing*

be·to·ken /bɪˈtoʊkən/ *vb* [*T*] *formal* : to be a sign of (something) ▪ *His strong handshake betokens his self-confidence.*

be·tray /bɪˈtreɪ/ *vb* [*T*] **1** : to give infor-mation about (a person, group, country, etc.) to an enemy ▪ *They betrayed their own country/people.* **2** : to hurt (some-one who trusts you) by not giving help or by doing something morally wrong ▪ *She would never betray a friend.* ▪ *He betrayed his wife with another woman.* [=he was unfaithful to his wife] **3 a** : to show (a feeling, desire, etc.) without wanting or trying to ▪ *His eyes betrayed his happi-ness.* ▪ *The expression on his face betrayed nothing.* [=did not show what he was feeling or thinking] **b** : to reveal (some-thing that should not be revealed) ▪ *be-tray a secret* **4** : to do something that does not agree with (your beliefs, princi-ples, etc.) ▪ *He would be betraying his principles if he accepted the money.* — **be·tray·al** /bɪˈtreɪəl/ *n* [*C/U*] ▪ *acts of be-trayal* — **be·tray·er** /bɪˈtreɪə/ *n* [*C*]

be·troth·al /bɪˈtroʊðəl/ *n* [*C*] *formal + old-fashioned* : the act of promising to marry someone : ENGAGEMENT ▪ *They kept their betrothal a secret.*

be·trothed /bɪˈtroʊðd/ *adj, formal + old-fashioned* : engaged to be married ▪ *a be-trothed couple* — **betrothed** *n* [*singular*] ▪ *a man and his betrothed* [=*fiancée*]

¹**bet·ter** /ˈbetə/ *adj, comparative form of* ¹GOOD *or of* ²WELL **1** : higher in quality ▪ *Her second book is better than her first one.* ▪ *This one is no better than that one.* **2** : more skillful ▪ *She's a better golfer than I am.* **3** : more attractive, appeal-ing, effective, useful, etc. ▪ *a better solu-tion* ▪ *a better* [=more accurate and com-plete] *understanding of the problem* ▪ *Her work is getting better.* ▪ *There's nothing better than a cold drink on a hot day.* ▪ *It's not much, but it's better than nothing.* ◇ People say *the sooner the better, the big-ger the better,* etc., when they want something to happen as soon as possible, to be as big as possible, etc. ▪ *"They say the cold weather will end soon." "Well, the sooner the better."* **4** : more morally right or good ▪ *You're a better man than I am.* ▪ *He's hardly/little/no better than a common criminal.* **5 a** : improved in health ▪ *I was sick but now I'm (all) better.* [=now I'm well] ▪ *I hope you feel/get bet-ter soon.* **b** : happier or more pleased ▪ *"You did the right thing." "Thanks. That makes me feel better."* **6** — used to sug-gest that something should or should not be done ▪ *It would be better (not) to wait.* — *the better part of* see ¹PART

²**better** *adv, comparative form of* ¹WELL **1** : in a better way ▪ *She sings better than I do.* ▪ *You could write to her, or, even/still better, visit her in person.* **2** — used to suggest that something should or should not be done ▪ *Some things are better left unsaid.* [=it is better not to say some things] **3** : to a higher or greater degree ▪ *Her paintings have recently become bet-ter known.* **4** : greater in distance or amount : MORE ▪ *It is better than nine miles to the next town.* — **(had) better** ◇ If you *(had) better* do something, you should do it. ▪ *You'd better leave early.* ▪ *(formal) Hadn't you better leave early?* [=shouldn't you leave early?] ▪ *You'd bet-ter not do that.* ▪ *"I'm sorry." "You'd better be!"* = *(informal)* *"You better be!"*

³**better** *n* [*U*] : something that is better : better behavior ▪ *I expected better from them.* ▪ *He deserves better.* — *all the bet-ter* or *so much the better* — used to say that something makes a good situa-tion even better ▪ *I love painting. If I can earn money by doing it, so much the bet-ter!* — *for better or (for) worse* : whether good or bad things happen ▪ *We have to stick to our decision for better or worse.* — *for the better* : so as to pro-duce improvement ▪ *The new policy is a change for the better.* [=an improve-ment] ▪ *His health has taken a turn for the better.* [=has improved] — *get the bet-ter of* : to defeat or trick (someone) by being clever ▪ *It would be hard to get the better of someone as smart as she is.* ▪ *(figurative) His temper/curiosity got the*

better of him. [=caused him to do something that he should not have done] — **know better** see ¹KNOW — **think better of** see THINK — **your betters** somewhat old-fashioned : people who are more important than you or who have a higher social position than you ▪ *His parents always told him to respect his betters.*

⁴**better** vb [T] **1** : to make (something) better : IMPROVE ▪ *They are trying to better the lives of working people.* **2** : to be or do better than (something or someone) ▪ *I can better their offer.* [=I can make you a better offer] ▪ *a record that has never been bettered* — **better yourself** : to do things that will make you a better or more successful person ▪ *She has worked hard to better herself.*

⁵**better** variant spelling of BETTOR

better half n [C] old-fashioned + humorous : someone's wife or husband ▪ *Please come to our party—and bring your better half, too!*

bet·ter·ment /ˈbɛtɚmənt/ n [U] : the act or result of making something better : IMPROVEMENT ▪ *working for the betterment of the lives of working people*

better off adj, comparative form of WELL-OFF **1** : having more money and possessions ▪ *The better off he became, the less he thought about other people.* **2** : in a better position ▪ *He'd be better off with a new job.*

bet·tor also **bet·ter** /ˈbɛtɚ/ n [C] : a person who makes a bet ▪ *Thousands of bettors were at the racetrack last weekend.*

¹**be·tween** /bɪˈtwiːn/ prep **1** : in the space that separates (two things or people) ▪ *The ball rolled between the desk and the wall.* ▪ *There's a fence between their house and their neighbor's house.* ▪ *There are fences in between all the houses.* ▪ *(figurative) the line/boundary between fact and fiction* **2** : in the time that separates (two actions, events, etc.) ▪ *We arrived between 9 and 10 o'clock.* ▪ *Between bites of food, they talked to their teacher.* **3** — used to indicate the beginning and ending points of a range ▪ *a number between 1 and 20* **4** : in shares to each of (two or more people) ▪ *His estate was divided equally between his son and daughter.* **5** — used to indicate two or more people or things considered together ▪ *Between her work and family life, she has no time for hobbies.* **6** — used to indicate two people or teams that are involved in a game, activity, etc. ▪ *There's a game tonight between the Red Sox and the Yankees.* **7** — used to indicate two or more people or things that are related or connected in some way ▪ *There are many connections between linguistics and psychology.* ▪ *the passageway between the two rooms* **8** — used to indicate two or more people or things that are being considered, compared, etc. ▪ *There are few differences between the two cars.* ▪ *choosing between two/several options* — used to indicate movement from one place to another place ▪ *The airline provides service between New York and Paris.* **10** : known only by (two people) ▪ *They shared a secret between them.* — **often**

used to ask someone to keep something you have said a secret ▪ *(Just) between you and me, I think he's wrong.* ▪ *What I've told you should be kept between us/ ourselves.*

²**between** adv : in the space separating two things or people ▪ *The office has two desks with a table (in) between.* — **few and far between** see ¹FEW

bev·el /ˈbɛvəl/ n [C] : a slanted surface or edge on a piece of wood, glass, etc. ▪ *the bevel of the mirror* — **bev·eled** (US) or Brit **bev·elled** /ˈbɛvəld/ adj ▪ *a mirror with a beveled edge*

bev·er·age /ˈbɛvrɪdʒ/ n [C] somewhat formal : a liquid for drinking ▪ *alcoholic beverages* [=drinks]

bevy /ˈbɛvi/ n, pl **bev·ies** [C] : a large group of people or things ▪ *A bevy of girls waited outside.*

be·wail /bɪˈweɪl/ vb [T] literary + humorous : to express great sadness about (something) ▪ *Many people bewailed the changes.*

be·ware /bɪˈweɚ/ vb [T/I] : to be careful about possible danger, trouble, etc. — used only as beware or to beware ▪ *Let the buyer beware.* ▪ *He told them to beware.* ▪ *The sign said "Beware of the dog."* ▪ *Beware the chili! It's very spicy.*

be·wil·der /bɪˈwɪldɚ/ vb [T] : to confuse (someone) very much ▪ *His decision bewildered her.* = *She was bewildered by his decision.* — **bewildered** adj ▪ *He had a bewildered expression on his face.* — **bewildering** adj ▪ *a bewildering number of choices* — **be·wil·der·ing·ly** adv — **be·wil·der·ment** /bɪˈwɪldɚmənt/ n [U] ▪ *She stared at them in bewilderment.*

be·witch /bɪˈwɪtʃ/ vb [T] **1** : to use a magic spell to make someone do, think, or say something ▪ *People believed she had been bewitched.* **2** : to attract or delight (someone) in a way that seems magical ▪ *They were bewitched by her beauty.* — **be·witch·ing** adj ▪ *a bewitching smile* [=captivating]

¹**be·yond** /biˈɑːnd/ adv **1** : on or to the farther part or side ▪ *We could see the valley and the hills beyond.* **2** : to or until a later time ▪ *through their school years and beyond*

²**beyond** prep **1** : on or to the farther part or side of (something) ▪ *The parking area is just beyond those trees.* **2** : outside the limits or range of (something) ▪ *The job is beyond his ability.* [=the job is too hard for him] ▪ *She became rich beyond her wildest dreams.* [=became very rich] ▪ *We need to stop living beyond our means.* [=spending more money than we earn] **3** — used to say that something cannot be changed, understood, etc. ▪ *The circumstances are beyond our control.* [=we cannot control the circumstances] ▪ *The stories she tells are beyond belief.* [=are not believable] ▪ *His actions are beyond comprehension/understanding.* [=cannot be understood] ▪ *Why anyone would do that is beyond me.* [=I do not understand why anyone would do that] **4** : for a period of time that continues after (a particular date, age, etc.) ▪ *She continued working beyond the usual*

retirement age. **5** : in addition to (something) ▪ *I knew nothing about him beyond* [=except] *what he told me.* — **above and beyond** see [2]ABOVE

bi- /baɪ/ *prefix* **1** : two ▪ *bilingual* **2 a** : coming or happening every two ▪ *bimonthly* **b** : coming or happening two times ▪ *biannual*

bi·an·nu·al /baɪˈænjəwəl/ *adj, always before a noun* **1** : happening twice a year : SEMIANNUAL ▪ *biannual meetings in December and July* **2** : happening every two years : BIENNIAL ▪ *A biannual event that won't happen again for two more years* — **bi·an·nu·al·ly** *adv*

[1]**bi·as** /ˈbajəs/ *n* **1** [C/U] : a tendency to believe that some people, ideas, etc., are better than others that usually results in treating some people unfairly ▪ *a strong liberal/conservative bias* ▪ *a bias towards/against someone* ▪ *She showed no bias toward older clients.* **2** [*singular*] : a strong interest in something or ability to do something ▪ *a student with a natural bias towards the arts* — **on the bias** [=in a slanted direction] ▪ *The material for the dress was cut on the bias.*

[2]**bias** *vb* **-ased; -as·ing** [T] : to have a strong and often unfair influence on (someone or something) ▪ *I don't want to bias you against the movie, but I liked the book better.* — **biased** *adj* ▪ *She is too biased to be objective.*

bib /ˈbɪb/ *n* [C] **1** : a piece of cloth or plastic that is worn under a baby's chin while the baby is eating **2** : the part of a piece of clothing (such as an apron) that covers the area above a person's waist

bi·ble /ˈbaɪbəl/ *n* **1 the Bible a** : the book of sacred writings used in the Christian religion **b** : the book of sacred writings used in the Jewish religion **2** *Bible* [C] : a copy or edition of the Bible **3** [C] : a book, magazine, etc., that contains the most important information about a particular thing ▪ *Her cookbook has become the gourmet's bible.*

Bible Belt *n* — **the Bible Belt** : an area chiefly in the southern U.S. where there are many people who have very strong and strict Christian beliefs

bib·li·cal /ˈbɪblɪkəl/ *adj* : relating to, taken from, or found in the Bible ▪ *a biblical passage/reference* ▪ *events in biblical times*

bib·li·og·ra·phy /ˌbɪbliˈɑːgrəfi/ *n, pl* **-phies** [C] **1** : a list of books, magazines, articles, etc., about a particular subject ▪ *Our instructor gave us a bibliography on local history.* **2** : a list of the books, magazines, articles, etc., that are mentioned in a text ▪ *the book's bibliography* — **bib·lio·graph·ic** /ˌbɪblijəˈgræfɪk/ *also* **bib·lio·graph·i·cal** /ˌbɪblijəˈgræfɪkəl/ *adj*

bi·carb /baɪˈkɑːb/ *n* [U] : BAKING SODA

bi·car·bon·ate of soda /baɪˈkɑːbəˌneɪt-/ *n* [U] : BAKING SODA

bi·cep /ˈbaɪˌsɛp/ *n* [C] : BICEPS ▪ *She flexed her left bicep.*

bi·ceps /ˈbaɪˌsɛps/ *n, pl* **biceps** [C] : a large muscle at the front of the upper arm — usually plural ▪ *His biceps were huge.*

bick·er /ˈbɪkɚ/ *vb* [I] : to argue in a way that is annoying about things that are not important ▪ *They bickered about/over how to decorate the room.* — **bick·er·ing** /ˈbɪkərɪŋ/ *n* [U] ▪ *their constant bickering*

[1]**bi·cy·cle** /ˈbaɪsɪkəl/ *n* [C] : a 2-wheeled vehicle that a person rides by pushing on foot pedals ▪ *She rode her bicycle* [=bike] *to school.* ▪ *touring Europe by bicycle*

[2]**bicycle** *vb* **-cy·cled; -cy·cling** [I] : to ride a bicycle ▪ *She bicycles* [=bikes] *to work.* — **bi·cy·cler** /ˈbaɪsɪklɚ/ *n* [C] *US* ▪ *a group of bicyclers* — **bicycling** *n* [U] ▪ *Bicycling is his favorite sport.* — **bi·cy·clist** /ˈbaɪsɪklɪst/ *n* [C] ▪ *a group of bicyclists*

[1]**bid** /ˈbɪd/ *vb* **bade** /ˈbæd, ˈbeɪd/ *or* **bid; bid·den** /ˈbɪdn̩/ *or* **bid; bid·ding 1** *past tense and past participle* **bid a** [T/I] : to offer to pay (a particular amount) for something that is being sold at an auction ▪ *She bid ($100) for/on the lamp.* **b** [I] *US* : to offer to do work for a particular price ▪ *Several companies are bidding for/on the job/contract.* **2** *past tense and past participle* **bid** [T/I] : to say how many points you are trying to win in a card game ▪ *He bid (two) and I passed.* **3** [T] *formal* : to order or command (someone) to do something ▪ *She bid/bade them enter.* [=told them to come in] **4** [T] *formal* : to express (greetings or good wishes) to (someone) ▪ *They bid/bade me farewell.* [=they said goodbye to me] — **bid fair** : to seem likely ▪ *a movie that bids fair to become a big hit* — **bid up** [*phrasal vb*] **bid up (something)** *or* **bid (something) up** : to raise the price of (something that is being sold) by repeatedly offering more money than other people ▪ *bidding stock prices up* — **bid·der** *n* [C] ▪ *the highest bidder* [=the person who offers to pay the most]

[2]**bid** *n* [C] **1 a** : an offer to pay a particular amount of money for something ▪ *the highest bid* ▪ *He made a bid of $100.* **b** : an offer to do a job for a particular price ▪ *The company is accepting bids for the project.* **2** : an attempt to win, get, or do something ▪ *make a bid for power/re-election* ▪ *their bid to take over the company* — *their takeover bid* [=their attempt to gain control of the company by buying most of its stock] **3** : a statement of how many points a player is trying to win in a card game

bidding *n* [U] **1** : the act of making bids at an auction ▪ *Bidding started at $1,000.* **2** : the act of offering to do a job for a particular price ▪ *Bidding for the project begins soon.* **3** : the act of telling or ordering someone to do something ▪ *She attended law school at her father's bidding.* [=because her father told her to do it] ▪ *He was always willing to do her bidding.* [=to do what she told him to do]

bid·dy /ˈbɪdi/ *n, pl* **-dies** [C] *informal + disapproving* : a silly or annoying old woman ▪ *a couple of old biddies*

bide /ˈbaɪd/ *vb* **bid·ed; bid·ing** — **bide your time** : to wait for the right time before you do something ▪ *He is biding his time before asking his parents for a loan.*

bi·en·ni·al /baɪˈɛnijəl/ *adj, always before*

a noun **1** : happening every two years • *a biennial show* **2** *of a plant* : living for only two years or seasons • *biennial plants/herbs/flowers* — **bi·en·ni·al·ly** *adv*

bi·fo·cal /ˈbaɪˌfoʊkəl, Brit baɪˈfəʊkəl/ *adj, of eyeglasses* : divided into two parts that help you see things that are nearby and things that are far away • *bifocal lenses/glasses* — **bi·fo·cals** /ˈbaɪˌfoʊkəlz, Brit baɪˈfəʊkəlz/ *n [plural]* • *She wears bifocals.*

¹**big** /ˈbɪg/ *adj* **big·ger; -gest** **1** : large in size • *a big house/room/field* • *a big man* • *the biggest city in the state* • *a great big* [=*very large, huge*] *truck* • *She uses too many big words.* [=*long and difficult words*] **2** : large in number or amount • *a big group* • *earning big money* [=a lot of money] — see also BIG BUCKS **3** : involving or including many people, things, etc. • *a big company* **4** *always before a noun* **a** : tending to do something more often or to a larger degree than most people • *He's a big eater.* **b** : feeling or showing a lot of excitement or enthusiasm • *I'm a big fan of their music.* • *a big smile/hug* **5** : important or significant • *He's big in local politics.* • *a big (movie) star* • *our biggest concern* • *a big* [=*serious*] *mistake/problem* • *They have big plans.* • *I hear you're getting married! When is the big day?* **6** *always before a noun, informal* — used to express strong disapproval • *You're nothing but a big sissy/bully!* **7** *informal* : older or more grown up • *my big sister/brother* • *He's a big boy now.* [=he is less like a baby now] — see also BIG BOYS, BIG BROTHER **8** : very popular • *That toy is a big seller.* • *Her books are big with teenagers.* • *the next big thing* [=a future trend] *in home decorating* **9** : generous or kind • *It was big of him to forgive them.* • *She was big about it and invited him.* • *He has a big heart.* [=he is kind] **10** : very strong, forceful, etc. • *There was a big storm last night.* — **(as) big as life** see LIFE — **big fish in a small/little pond** see ¹FISH — **big on** *informal* : very enthusiastic about (something) • *She's not (very) big on dancing.* — **too big for your britches** (*US*) or chiefly Brit **too big for your boots** *informal* : too confident or proud • *He's gotten too big for his britches.* — **big·ness** /ˈbɪgnəs/ *n [U]*

²**big** *adv* **1** : in a big way • *They won/lost big.* [=they won/lost a large amount] **2** : in a way that is meant to impress people • *He talks big, but he hasn't done much yet.* — **go over big** *informal* : to be successful or well-liked • *a recipe that goes over big with kids* [=that children like a lot] — **make it big** or **hit (it) big** *informal* : to become very successful • *musicians who dream of making it big* — **think big** : to think about doing things that involve a lot of people, money, effort, etc. • *If we're going to start our own business, we should think big.*

big·a·my /ˈbɪgəmi/ *n [U]* : the crime of marrying one person while you are still legally married to another — **big·a·mist** /ˈbɪgəmɪst/ *n [C]* — **big·a·mous** /ˈbɪgəməs/ *adj* • *a bigamous marriage*

Big Apple *n* — **the Big Apple** *informal* — used as a name for New York City • *She moved to the Big Apple.*

big band *n [C]* : a large musical group that usually plays jazz music that people dance to

big bang *n* — **the big bang** : a huge explosion that might have happened when the universe began • *scientists who support the big bang theory*

big boys *n* — **the big boys** *informal* : the most powerful people or companies • *He'll have to work hard if he wants to compete with the big boys.*

Big Brother *n [singular]* : a powerful government or organization that watches and controls what people say and do • *"Be careful what you say," she warned, "Big Brother is listening!"*

big bucks *n [plural] US, informal* : a large amount of money • *A car like that costs big bucks.*

big business *n [U]* **1** : large companies considered together as a powerful group • *The tax proposal benefits big business.* **2** : an activity or product that makes a large amount of money • *Tourism is big business here.*

big cheese *n* — **the big cheese** *informal* : the most powerful or important person • *Who's the big cheese around here?*

big–city *adj, always before a noun* : of or relating to a large city • *big-city problems* • *a big-city school/hospital/mayor*

big deal *n [singular]* : something that is very important • *The party was a big deal.* • *The cost is a big deal for many people.* • *"She's going to be angry." "Big deal."* [=I don't care] • *Don't worry, it's no big deal.* [=it's not a problem] • *So I'm late. What's the big deal?* [=why is that important?] • *Whenever I'm late, she always makes a big deal out of it.* = *She always makes it into a big deal.* [=she treats it as more important than it really is]

big dipper *n* **1** *the Big Dipper US* : a group of seven stars in the northern sky that form a shape like a large dipper or ladle **2** [C] *Brit, old-fashioned* : ROLLER COASTER 1

Big·foot or **big·foot** /ˈbɪgˌfʊt/ *n [singular]* : SASQUATCH

big game *n [U]* : large animals that are hunted for sport • *They traveled to Africa to hunt big game.* • *a big-game hunter*

big·gie /ˈbɪgi/ *n [C] informal* : someone or something that is very big or important • *This problem's a real biggie.* • (*chiefly US*) *"Sorry I'm late." "No biggie."* [=it's not a problem]

big gun *n* — **the big guns** *informal* : the most powerful people, companies, etc. • *They called in the big guns to deal with the problem.*

big–headed *adj* **1** : having a large head • *a big-headed dinosaur* **2** *disapproving* : sure that you are better or more important than other people • *big-headed celebrities*

big–hearted *adj* : generous and kind • *a big-hearted person*

big house n — **the big house** US slang : PRISON

big leagues n — **the big leagues** US : MAJOR LEAGUES • *playing in the big leagues* • (*figurative*) *She's in the big leagues now, working for a major law firm.* — **big-league** adj, always before a noun • *big-league [=major-league] baseball* — **big leagu·er** n [C]

big mouth n [C] informal — used to describe a person who cannot keep a secret or who talks too much • *Be careful what you tell her. She's a big mouth. = She has a big mouth.* • *Why did you have to open your big mouth and tell everyone?* — **big-mouthed** adj

big name n [C] informal : a very famous person • *There were many big names [=celebrities] at the party.* — **big-name** adj, always before a noun • *a big-name movie star*

big noise n [C] Brit, informal : BIG SHOT • *She's a big noise in local politics.*

big·ot /ˈbɪgət/ n [C] disapproving : a person who hates or refuses to accept the members of a particular race, religion, etc. • *He was labeled a bigot after making some offensive comments.* — **big·ot·ed** /ˈbɪgətəd/ adj • *a bigoted person/comment* — **big·ot·ry** /ˈbɪgətri/ n [U] • *religious/racial bigotry*

big picture n — **the big picture** : everything that relates to or is involved in a situation or issue • *We need to stop focusing on details and look at the big picture.*

big screen n — **the big screen** : movies and the movie industry especially when they are being compared to television • *The novel was adapted for the big screen.* [=was made into a movie]

big shot n [C] informal : a powerful or important person • *corporate big shots*

big-tick·et /ˈbɪgˌtɪkət/ adj, chiefly US, informal : having a high price • *big-ticket items like cars and appliances*

big time n — **the big time** : the highest or most successful level of an activity • *a basketball player who never made (it to) the big time* • *They finally hit the big time.* [=became very successful] — **big-time** /ˈbɪgˌtaɪm/ adj, always before a noun • *big-time [=major] college sports* — **big-time** adv, chiefly US, informal • *The show bombed big-time.* [=it was very unsuccessful] • *You owe me big-time.* [=in a big way; very much or very badly]

big toe n [C] : the largest toe on a person's foot

big top n [singular] : a large circus tent • *performing under the big top* [=in/with the circus]

big wheel n [C] **1** chiefly US, informal : BIG SHOT **2** Brit : FERRIS WHEEL

big·wig /ˈbɪgˌwɪg/ n [C] informal : BIG SHOT • *corporate bigwigs*

¹**bike** /ˈbaɪk/ n [C] **1** : BICYCLE • *She rode her bike to school.* • *a bike path* **2** : MOTORCYCLE

²**bike** vb biked; bik·ing [I] : to ride a bicycle • *We biked to the park.* — **biking** n [U] • *Biking is a great form of exercise.*

bik·er /ˈbaɪkə/ n [C] **1** : MOTORCYCLIST **2** chiefly US : BICYCLIST

bi·ki·ni /bəˈkiːni/ n [C] : a swimsuit that

has two parts and that does not cover much of the body

bi·lat·er·al /baɪˈlætərəl/ adj : involving two groups or countries • *a bilateral treaty*

bile /ˈbajəl/ n [U] **1** : a yellow or greenish liquid that is made by the liver and that helps to digest fats **2** : anger or hatred • *He spewed bile at/on his political enemies.*

bilge /ˈbɪldʒ/ n **1** [C] : the bottom part of the inside of a ship or boat • *water in the bilge* **2** [U] informal : NONSENSE • *That magazine prints a lot of bilge.*

bi·lin·gual /baɪˈlɪŋgwəl/ adj **1** : able to speak and understand two languages • *bilingual students* **2** : using or expressed in two languages • *a bilingual dictionary* • *bilingual education* — **bi·lin·gual·ism** /baɪˈlɪŋgwəˌlɪzəm/ n [U]

bilk /ˈbɪlk/ vb [T] chiefly US, informal : to cheat or trick (a person or organization) especially by taking money • *They bilked the company (out) of a lot of money.*

¹**bill** /ˈbɪl/ n [C] **1** : a document that says how much money you owe for something you have bought or used • *the telephone/water/electric bill* • *We barely had enough (money) to pay the bills.* **2** : a written description of a new law that is being suggested and that lawmakers must vote to accept before it becomes law • *The Senate passed/rejected the bill.*; also : such a bill after it has become a law • *the GI bill* — see also BILL OF RIGHTS **3** chiefly US : a piece of paper money • *a 5-dollar bill* **4** : a poster or piece of paper that advertises a play, movie, or concert • *a double bill* [=a performance that has two parts] **5** : a bird's beak • *a duck's bill* **6** US : the part of a cap that sticks out in front — **fill the bill** or **fit the bill** : to be exactly what is needed • *Our hotel room isn't fancy, but it fits the bill.* — **foot the bill** see ²FOOT — **give (someone) a clean bill of health** : to officially say that someone is healthy • *The doctor gave him a clean bill of health.* • (*figurative*) *The technician gave the system a clean bill of health.*

²**bill** vb [T] **1** : to send a bill to (someone or something) for money owed • *They billed me for the repairs.* **2** : to describe or advertise (someone or something) as something very good, important, etc. • *She was billed as the next big movie star.* **3** : to officially say that someone is going to do something • *Both writers are billed to appear at the conference.*

bill·board /ˈbɪlˌboəd/ n [C] : a large sign for advertisements that is next to a road, on the side of a building, etc.

bil·let /ˈbɪlət/ n [C] : a private home where a soldier lives temporarily with the people who live there — **billet** vb [T] • *The soldiers were billeted [=quartered, housed] throughout the town.*

bill·fold /ˈbɪlˌfould/ n [C] US : a small folding case that holds paper money and credit cards : WALLET

bil·liards /ˈbɪljədz/ n [U] : any one of several games that are played on a large table by hitting balls into one another with the end of a long stick — **bil·liard**

/'bɪljəd/ *adj, always before a noun* • **billiard balls** • **a billiard table**

bill·ing /'bɪlɪŋ/ *n* [U] : the things that are said or written to advertise a show, performer, etc. • *The film didn't live up to its advance billing.* [=it was not as good as people said it would be]

bil·lion /'bɪljən/ *n, pl* **billion** *or* **bil·lions** [C] **1** : the number 1,000,000,000 • *a/one/two billion (of them)* • *a hundred billion = 100 billion* • *hundreds of billions (of them)* • *The company is worth billions.* [=worth billions of dollars, pounds, euros, etc.] **2** : a very large amount or number • *billions (and billions) of stars* — **bil·lionth** /'bɪljənθ/ *adj* • *our (one) billionth customer* — **billionth** *n* [C] • *one billionth of a second*

bil·lion·aire /ˌbɪljə'neɚ/ *n* [C] : a rich person who has at least a billion dollars, pounds, etc.

bill of fare *n* [C] *somewhat formal + old-fashioned* : a restaurant's menu

bill of rights *or* **Bill of Rights** *n* [*singular*] : a written statement that lists the basic rights of the citizens of a country ◆ The first 10 amendments to the U.S. Constitution are called **the Bill of Rights**.

bill of sale *n* [C] : a document saying that something has been sold to a new owner • *Do you have the bill of sale for the car?*

¹**bil·low** /'bɪloʊ/ *n* [C] : a moving cloud or mass • *billows of smoke/fog/steam*

²**billow** *vb* [I] **1** : to move as a large cloud or mass • *Clouds of smoke billowed (up) from the chimney.* **2** : to be pushed outward by air • *sails billowing (out) in the breeze*

billy goat *n* [C] : a male goat

bim·bo /'bɪmboʊ/ *n, pl* **-bos** [C] *informal* : an attractive but stupid woman • *Her husband ran off with some bimbo.*

bi·month·ly /baɪ'mʌnθli/ *adj* **1** : occurring every two months • *We hold bimonthly meetings in January, March, May, and so on.* **2** : occurring twice a month : SEMIMONTHLY • *We hold bimonthly meetings on the first and third Tuesday of each month.* — **bimonthly** *adv*

¹**bin** /'bɪn/ *n* [C] **1** : a box that is used for storing things • *a storage/laundry/recycling bin* **2** *chiefly Brit* : a can for trash or garbage : DUSTBIN

²**bin** *vb* **binned; bin·ning** [T] *Brit, informal* : to put (something) in the trash • *binning old newspapers*

bi·na·ry /'baɪnəri/ *adj, technical* **1** : relating to or consisting of two things or parts • *binary stars* **2** : relating to or involving a method of calculating and of representing information by using the numbers 0 and 1 • *binary digits/numbers*

¹**bind** /'baɪnd/ *vb* **bound** /'baʊnd/; **bind·ing** **1** [T] : to tie or wrap (something) with rope, string, etc. • *She bound her hair in a ponytail.* **2** [T] : to tie the hands or feet of a person • *He bound the prisoner's wrists (together) with rope.* • *The captives were bound and gagged.* **3** [I] *of clothing* : to prevent free movement by fitting too tightly • *clothes that bind* **4** [T] : to wrap or cover (something) with a

bandage • *The doctor bound (up) the injured ankle.* **5** [T] : to make (someone) have to do something because of a promise, agreement, etc. • *By signing here, you agree to be bound by the terms of the contract.* — see also ²BINDING, ²BOUND 5 **6** [T] : to make (something, such as an agreement) certain • *A handshake binds the deal.* **7** [T] : to cause (people) to be joined together • *the emotional ties that bind us* **8** [T/I] : to cause (something) to form a mass that stays together • *The mayonnaise binds the salad together.* • *Without the eggs, the dough won't bind.* **9** [T/I] *technical* : to combine with (something) by chemical forces • *particles that bind to/with one another* **10** [T] : to put a cover on or binding on (a book) • *This book was bound by hand.* — see also ²BOUND 6

²**bind** *n* [*singular*] **1** : a difficult situation • *I've gotten myself into a (bit of a) bind.* **2** *Brit* : an annoying problem : NUISANCE • *It's a real bind having to meet all these deadlines.*

bind·er /'baɪndɚ/ *n* [C] **1** : a cover for holding together sheets of paper • *a loose-leaf binder* **2** : a material that is used to hold things together • *The egg in the recipe acts as a binder.* **3** : a person or machine that puts books together **4** *US* : a temporary insurance contract that provides coverage until a policy is issued **5** *US* : a payment given to make an agreement official and legal

¹**bind·ing** /'baɪndɪŋ/ *n* **1** [C] : the cover of a book • *a leather binding* **2** [C/U] : a narrow strip of cloth attached along the edge of something • *a carpet edged with (a) canvas binding* **3** [C] : a device that attaches a boot to a ski

²**binding** *adj* : forcing or requiring someone to do something because of a promise, agreement, etc. • *The contract is legally binding.*

¹**binge** /'bɪndʒ/ *n* [C] : a short period of time when you do too much of something • *a drinking/shopping binge* • *binge drinking* — often used in the phrase **go on a binge** • *He went on an eating binge.*

²**binge** *vb* **binged; binge·ing** *or* **bing·ing** [I] : to eat, drink, etc., too much in a short period of time • *He binges on beer now and then.* — **binge and purge** : to eat a lot of food and then force yourself to vomit so that you do not gain weight — **bing·er** *n* [C]

bin·go /'bɪŋɡoʊ/ *n* [U] : a game in which players match numbered squares on a card with numbers that are called out until someone wins by matching five squares in a row • *play bingo* • *bingo halls/parlors/games*

²**bingo** *interj* **1** — used to announce that you have won the game in bingo **2** — used to announce a successful result that is quick or unexpected • *Then, bingo! The idea hit me.* **3** — used to indicate that another person's statement is correct • *"You mean he lied to us?" "Bingo!"*

bin·oc·u·lar /baɪ'nɑːkjələ/ *adj* : involving or designed for both eyes • *binocular vision*

bin·oc·u·lars /bə'nɑːkjələz/ *n* [*plural*]

: a device that you hold up to your eyes to see things that are far away • *looking through (a pair of) binoculars*

bio- *combining form* : relating to or living things • *biochemistry*

bio·chem·is·try /ˌbajoʊˈkɛməstri/ *n* [U] : the chemistry of living things • *advances in the field of biochemistry* — **bio·chem·i·cal** /ˌbajoʊˈkɛmɪkəl/ *adj* — **bio·chem·ist** /ˌbajoʊˈkɛmɪst/ *n* [C]

bio·de·grad·able /ˌbajoʊdɪˈgreɪdəbəl/ *adj* : capable of being slowly broken down into very small parts by natural processes • *biodegradable trash bags*

bio·di·ver·si·ty /ˌbajoʊdəˈvəsəti/ *n* [U] : the existence of many different kinds of plants and animals in an environment • *efforts to preserve biodiversity*

bio·feed·back /ˌbajoʊˈfiːdˌbæk/ *n* [U] : the technique of controlling things in your body (such as heartbeats or brain waves) with your conscious mind

bio·graph·i·cal /ˌbajəˈgræfɪkəl/ *adj* : relating to or telling the story of a real person's life • *biographical information* • *a biographical essay*

bi·og·ra·phy /baɪˈɑːgrəfi/ *n, pl* **-phies** [C] : the story of a real person's life written by someone other than that person • *a new biography of Abraham Lincoln* — **bi·og·ra·pher** /baɪˈɑːgrəfə/ *n* [C] • *Lincoln's biographers*

bi·o·log·i·cal /ˌbajəˈlɑːdʒɪkəl/ *adj* **1** : of or relating to biology or to life and living things • *biological processes/research* **2** : related through birth • *an adopted child who finally found her biological mother* — **bi·o·log·i·cal·ly** /ˌbajəˈlɑːdʒɪkli/ *adv* • *a biologically diverse region*

biological clock *n* [C] : a system in the body that controls how and when the body does certain things (such as sleeping and aging) — often used to describe a woman's desire to have children before she is too old • *She felt her biological clock ticking away.*

biological warfare *n* [U] : the use of harmful living things (such as germs that cause disease) as weapons in a war

biological weapon *n* [C] : a harmful living thing (such as a germ that causes disease) used as a weapon in a war

bi·ol·o·gy /baɪˈɑːlədʒi/ *n* [U] **1** : a science that deals with things that are alive (such as plants and animals) • *advances in the field of biology* • *a professor of biology* **2** : the plant and animal life of a particular place • *the biology of the rain forest* **3** : the processes that occur in a living thing • *human biology* — **bi·ol·o·gist** /baɪˈɑːlədʒɪst/ *n* [C]

bi·op·sy /ˈbaɪˌɑːpsi/ *n, pl* **-sies** [C] *medical* : the removal of tissue, cells, or fluids from someone's body in order to check for illness • *a skin biopsy*

bio·rhythm /ˈbajoʊˌrɪðəm/ *n* [C] : a natural, repeated pattern of changes that occur in the body

bio·sphere /ˈbajəˌsfiə/ *n* [*singular*] : the part of the Earth in which life can exist • *the effects of pollution on the biosphere*

bio·tech /ˈbajoʊˌtɛk/ *n* [U] : BIOTECHNOLOGY

bio·tech·nol·o·gy /ˌbajoʊtɛkˈnɑːlədʒi/ *n* [U] : the use of living cells, bacteria, etc., to make useful products (such as stronger crops or new kinds of medicine) — **bio·tech·no·log·i·cal** /ˌbajoʊˌtɛknəˈlɑːdʒɪkəl/ *adj*

bi·par·ti·san /baɪˈpɑːtəzən, *Brit* ˌbaɪˌpɑːtəˈzæn/ *adj* : relating to or involving members of two political parties • *a bipartisan effort/commission* — **bi·par·ti·san·ship** /baɪˈpɑːtəzənˌʃɪp, *Brit* ˌbaɪˌpɑːtəˈzænˌʃɪp/ *n* [U]

bi·plane /ˈbaɪˌpleɪn/ *n* [C] : an old type of airplane that has two sets of wings with one placed above the other

bi·ra·cial /baɪˈreɪʃəl/ *adj* : of, relating to, or involving people from two races • *a biracial coalition/couple*

birch /ˈbətʃ/ *n* **1** [C] : a type of tree that has outer bark which can be pulled off easily — called also *birch tree* **2** [U] : the hard, pale wood of the birch

bird /ˈbəd/ *n* [C] **1** : an animal that has wings and is covered with feathers • *The birds were singing.* • *a flock of birds* **2** *informal* : PERSON • *He's a tough old bird.* **3** *Brit, informal + sometimes offensive* : a young woman — *a bird in the hand is worth two in the bush* — used to say that it is better to keep something you have than to risk losing it by trying to get something better — *birds of a feather* see [1]FEATHER — *for the birds informal* : worthless or ridiculous • *This town is for the birds.* — *give (someone) the bird informal* **1** or *flip (someone) the bird US* : to make an offensive gesture at someone by pointing the middle finger upward while keeping the other fingers folded down • *He flipped them the bird.* [*=gave them the finger*] **2** *Brit* : to loudly shout at, laugh at, or boo someone (such as a performer) in order to show disapproval — *the birds and the bees informal + humorous* : the facts about sex that are told to children — *the early bird catches/gets the worm* see [2]EARLY

bird·bath /ˈbədˌbæθ, *Brit* ˈbɜːdˌbɑːθ/ *n* [C] : a bowl that is filled with water in a yard or garden so birds can bathe in it

bird·brain /ˈbədˌbreɪn/ *n* [C] *US, informal* : a stupid person • *He's a real birdbrain.* — **bird-brained** /ˈbədˌbreɪnd/ *adj* • *her birdbrained brother*

bird·cage /ˈbədˌkeɪdʒ/ *n* [C] : a cage for birds

bird dog *n* [C] *US* : a dog that has been trained to help people hunt birds

bird·er /ˈbədə/ *n* [C] : BIRD-WATCHER — **bird·ing** /ˈbədɪŋ/ *n* [U] • *She goes birding [=bird-watching] with her friends.*

bird·house /ˈbədˌhaʊs/ *n* [C] : a small covered box that is made as a place for wild birds to nest

[1]**bird·ie** /ˈbədi/ *n* **1** [C] : a small bird — used especially by children or when speaking to children • *Look at the little birdies.* **2** [C/U] *golf* : a score of one stroke less than par on a hole • *I made/scored a birdie.* **3** [C] *US* : SHUTTLECOCK

[2]**birdie** *vb* **bird·ied; bird·ie·ing** [T] : to score a birdie on (a hole in golf) • *She birdied the second hole.*

bird of paradise *n* [C] : any one of

many brightly colored birds that live in New Guinea and on nearby islands

bird of prey n [C] : a bird (such as an eagle or a hawk) that hunts and eats other animals

bird·seed /'bəd,si:d/ n [U] : seeds that are used for feeding birds

bird's–eye /'bədz,aɪ/ adj, always before a noun : seen from high above • a bird's-eye view of the city

bird–watch·er /'bəd,wɑːtʃə/ n [C] : a person who watches and identifies wild birds — called also **birder** — **bird–watch·ing** /'bəd,wɑːtʃɪŋ/ n [U] • She goes bird-watching [=birding] with her friends.

birth /'bəθ/ n 1 [C/U] : the time when a baby comes out from the body of its mother • the birth of his daughter • Please indicate your date of birth. • a disease that is present at birth • She's Canadian by birth. [=she was born in Canada] 2 [U] : the beginning or origin of something • We are witnessing the birth of a new era. 3 [U] — used to describe the kind of family a person comes from • a person of noble/low/humble birth — **give birth** 1 of a mother : to produce a baby from the body • His wife just gave birth (to their daughter). 2 : to cause the beginning of something — + to • a revolution that gave birth to a new nation

birth canal n [C] : the part of a mother's body that a baby passes through when it is born

birth certificate n [C] : an official document that says where and when a person was born and who the parents are

birth control n [U] : things that are done to keep a woman from becoming pregnant • modern methods of birth control [=contraception] • a birth control pill

birth·day /'bəθ,deɪ/ n [C] 1 : the day when someone was born or the anniversary of that day • Her birthday is September 30th. • Today is his 21st birthday. • Happy Birthday! • a birthday party/gift 2 : the day when something began • The company just celebrated its 50th birthday. — **birthday suit** informal + humorous ◊ If you are wearing your birthday suit, you are naked.

birth father n [C] : the natural father of a child who has been adopted

birth·ing /'bəθɪŋ/ n [U] : the act of giving birth • pregnancy and birthing • a birthing room/center • the birthing process

birth·mark /'bəθ,mɑək/ n [C] : a mark that is present on the skin from the time when someone is born

birth mother n [C] : a woman who gave birth to a child who has been adopted

birth·place /'bəθ,pleɪs/ n [C] : the place where someone was born or where something began • his grandmother's birthplace • the birthplace of jazz

birth·rate /'bəθ,reɪt/ n [C] : a number that shows how many babies are born in a particular place or during a particular time • nations with high birthrates

birth·right /'bəθ,raɪt/ n [C] : a right that you have because you were born into a particular position, family, place, etc., or because it is a right of all people • the freedom that is our birthright

bis·cuit /'bɪskət/ n [C] 1 US : a small, light roll that is eaten as part of a meal 2 Brit : COOKIE

bi·sect /'baɪ,sɛkt/ vb [T] : to divide (something) into two equal parts • The city is bisected by the highway.

bi·sex·u·al /baɪ'sɛkʃəwəl/ adj 1 : sexually attracted to both men and women • She's bisexual. 2 : relating to or involving two sexes • bisexual reproduction — **bisexual** n [C] — **bi·sex·u·al·i·ty** /baɪ,sɛkʃə'wæləti/ n [U]

bish·op /'bɪʃəp/ n [C] 1 : an official in some Christian religions who ranks higher than a priest • the Bishop of New York 2 : a piece in the game of chess that moves across the board at an angle

bi·son /'baɪsn/ n, pl bison also **bi·sons** [C] : a large, hairy wild animal that has a big head and short horns — called also (US) buffalo

bisque /'bɪsk/ n [C/U] : a thick, creamy soup • lobster bisque

bis·tro /'bi:stroʊ/ n, pl -tros [C] : a small restaurant or bar

¹**bit** /'bɪt/ n 1 [C] : a small piece of something • Put all the broken bits back together. • He ate every last/single bit of his food. 2 [C] a chiefly Brit : a part of something (such as a book, play, etc.) • There are some good bits near the end of the story. b chiefly US : a brief comic performance or joke • The comedian did a funny bit about going to the dentist. c : a very short performance in a movie, play, etc. • a bit part/role/player 3 [singular] informal : all the things that are connected to an activity, a process, etc. • He's tired of his job, his boss, his coworkers, **the whole bit**. [=everything] 4 [C] : the part of a tool (such as a drill) that is used for cutting, drilling, etc. 5 [C] : a piece of metal that is put in the mouth of a horse and that is part of the device (called a bridle) that is used to control the horse • (figurative) He's been **champing/chomping at the bit** [=waiting in an impatient way] to start the project. • (figurative) He can be lazy, but when he **gets the bit between his teeth** [=when he starts doing something in a very enthusiastic and determined way] there's no stopping him. 6 [C] computers : a single unit of computer information that is represented as either 1 or 0 — compare BYTE — **a bit** 1 : a little • His house is down the street a bit further. • I'm feeling a bit better today. 2 : a small amount or quantity • They saved money a bit at a time. • Only a (very little) bit of milk is left. — often + of • The car caused me a bit of trouble. 3 a : a short period of time • Let's wait a (little/wee) bit longer. b : for a short period of time • Please stay here with me a bit. — **a bit much** informal — used to describe a person or thing that is regarded as annoying, excessive, or unfair • I find him a bit much. — **a bit of a/an** chiefly Brit — used to make a statement or description less forceful or definite • I had a bit of a shock when I saw him. — **a little bit** see ³LITTLE — **bit by bit** : GRADUALLY • The situation im-

proved bit by bit. — **bits and pieces** 1 : small pieces ▪ *There were bits and pieces of broken glass on the floor.* 2 *or Brit* **bits and bobs** : things or objects of different kinds ▪ *a few bits and pieces* [=*odds and ends*] *of furniture* — **do your bit** *chiefly Brit* : to do your share of a job or task ▪ *We all did our bit* [=*did our part*] *to help.* — **every bit** : in every way ▪ *Her second book was every bit* [=*just*] *as good as her first.* — **not a/one bit** *or* **not (in) the least/smallest/slightest/tiniest bit** : not at all ▪ *That was not a/one bit funny.* [=*was not funny at all*] — **not a bit of it** *Brit, informal* — used to say that something expected or possible did not happen or is not true ▪ *I thought she'd be angry, but not a bit of it.* [=*she wasn't angry at all*] — **quite a bit** *or chiefly Brit* **a good/fair bit** : a lot ▪ *He knows quite a bit about it.* ▪ *There's still a fair bit (of food) left.* — **to bits** 1 : to pieces ▪ *The bridge was blown/smashed to bits by the explosion.* 2 *informal* : to a very great degree ▪ *She was thrilled to bits.* [=*she was very thrilled*]

²**bit** *past tense of* ¹BITE

¹**bitch** /ˈbɪtʃ/ *n* 1 [C] : a female dog 2 [C] *informal + offensive* : a very bad or unpleasant woman 3 [*singular*] *informal* : something that is very difficult or unpleasant ▪ *Divorce is a bitch.* — **bitchy** /ˈbɪtʃi/ *adj* **bitch·i·er; -est** *informal* ▪ *a bitchy salesclerk/attitude/comment* — **bitch·i·ness** *n* [U]

²**bitch** *vb* [I] *informal + disapproving* : to complain about something in a repeated and annoying way ▪ *He bitched constantly about his old car.*

¹**bite** /ˈbaɪt/ *vb* **bit** /ˈbɪt/; **bit·ten** /ˈbɪtn̩/; **bit·ing** /ˈbaɪtɪŋ/ 1 [T/I] *of a person or animal* **a** : to press down on or cut into (someone or something) with the teeth ▪ *He bit (into) the apple.* ▪ *The child bit off a corner of the cracker.* ▪ *A wild animal may bite if it is frightened.* ▪ *Go talk to him. He won't bite.* [=you should not be afraid to go talk to him] **b** *of an insect or snake* : to wound (someone) by pushing a stinger, fang, etc., into the skin ▪ *He was bitten by a snake.* ▪ (*figurative*) *He was bitten by the travel bug* [=he became very interested in traveling] 2 [I] : to grab and hold something without slipping — usually + *into* ▪ *The anchor bit into the ocean floor.* 3 [I] **a** *of a fish* : to take a fishhook and bait into the mouth and usually to get caught ▪ *Are the fish biting today?* **b** *somewhat informal* : to respond to or accept something that is being offered ▪ *We offered them a great deal, but they wouldn't bite.* [=they wouldn't accept the deal] ◆ *Someone gets you to bite by offering something you want so that you will do something desired.* 4 [I] *US slang, impolite* : to be extremely bad ▪ *This movie really bites.* — **bite off more than you can chew** *informal* : to try to do too much ▪ *I bit off more than I could chew with this project.* — **bite someone's head off** *informal* : to yell at someone or to be very critical of someone especially very suddenly and without a good reason ▪ *I asked him one* simple question and he bit my head off.* — **bite the bullet** *informal* : to do something unpleasant or painful because it is necessary ▪ *We need to bite the bullet and make some budget cuts.* — **bite the dust** *informal* : to die or stop functioning ▪ *My old car finally bit the dust.* — **bite the hand that feeds you** *informal* : to harm someone who has helped or supported you — **bite your tongue** *also* **bite your lip** *informal* : to not say something that you want to say ▪ *I thought she was acting foolishly, but I bit my tongue and didn't say anything.* — **come back to bite you** : to cause problems at a later time ▪ *That decision may come back to bite them someday.* — **once bitten, twice shy** ◆ The expression *once bitten, twice shy* means that a person who has failed or been hurt when trying to do something is careful or fearful about doing it again. — **bit·er** *n* [C]

²**bite** *n* 1 [C] **a** : an act of biting ▪ *He ate the candy bar in three quick bites.* **b** : the way the upper and lower teeth come together ▪ *I wore a special device at night to correct my bite.* 2 **a** [C] : the amount of food eaten with a bite ▪ *He took a bite (out) of the apple.* **b** [*singular*] *informal* : a snack or a small informal meal ▪ *We grabbed a quick bite (to eat) before the show.* 3 [C] : a wound made by biting ▪ *a mosquito bite* 4 [U] : a bad effect ▪ *feeling the bite of budget cuts* 5 [U] **a** : a sharp feeling or taste ▪ *the bite of the cold wind* **b** : a sharp quality in something written, spoken, or performed ▪ *the bite of his humor* — see also SOUND BITE

bite-size /ˈbaɪtˌsaɪz/ *also* **bite-sized** /ˈbaɪtˌsaɪzd/ *adj* : small enough to be eaten in one bite ▪ *bite-size pieces*

bit·ing /ˈbaɪtɪŋ/ *adj* 1 : unpleasantly cold ▪ *a biting wind* ▪ *biting cold* 2 : having a sharply critical and often clever quality ▪ *biting accusations/wit*

bitten *past participle of* ¹BITE

¹**bit·ter** /ˈbɪtɚ/ *adj* 1 : having a strong and often unpleasant flavor that is the opposite of sweet ▪ *a bitter flavor/aftertaste* 2 : causing painful emotions ▪ *a bitter disappointment/defeat* ▪ *The defeat was a bitter pill to swallow.* [=was difficult and painful to accept] 3 : angry and unhappy because of unfair treatment ▪ *She's very bitter toward her ex-husband.* ▪ *He's the bitterest man I know.* 4 : feeling or showing a lot of hatred or anger ▪ *bitter enemies* 5 : very cold ▪ *a bitter wind* ▪ *bitter cold* — **to/until the bitter end** : until the end of something that may be very bad, unpleasant, etc. ▪ *He vowed that he would fight until the bitter end.* — **bit·ter·ly** *adv* ▪ *bitterly disappointed* — **bit·ter·ness** *n* [U]

²**bitter** *n* 1 [*plural*] : a bitter alcoholic liquid that is used especially in mixed drinks ▪ *a dash of bitters* 2 [C/U] *Brit* : a type of beer that has a slightly bitter flavor ▪ *a pint of bitter*

bit·ter·sweet /ˌbɪtɚˈswiːt/ *adj* 1 : having both bitter and sweet flavors ▪ *bittersweet chocolate* 2 : combining sadness and happiness ▪ *a bittersweet memory/story*

bi·week·ly /ˌbaɪˈwiːkli/ *adj* 1 : happening every two weeks **2** : happening twice a week : SEMIWEEKLY — **bi·weekly** adv

biz /ˈbɪz/ n [singular] informal : BUSINESS • the music biz • a career in show biz [=show business]

bi·zarre /bəˈzɑɚ/ adj : very unusual or strange • His behavior was bizarre. • a bizarre story/outfit — **bi·zarre·ly** adv — **bi·zarre·ness** n [U]

blab /ˈblæb/ vb **blabbed; blab·bing** informal **1** [T/I] : to say something that was supposed to be kept secret • Don't tell Mary. She'll blab it all over town. **2** [I] : to talk too much • He kept blabbing about politics.

blab·ber·mouth /ˈblæbəˌmaʊθ/ n [C] informal : someone who reveals secrets or talks too much

¹**black** /ˈblæk/ adj **1 a** : having the very dark color of coal or the night sky • black ink **b** : very dark because there is no light • a black night **2** or **Black** : of or relating to a race of people who have dark skin and who come originally from Africa • black people/culture ✧ In the U.S., the term African-American is often preferred over black when referring to Americans of African descent. **3** : very dirty • His hands were black with grime. **4** : served without cream or milk • black coffee **5** literary : evil or wicked • a black deed **6** : very tragic or unhappy • a black day in our country's history **7** : marked by anger or hatred • a black mood **8** — used to describe humor that deals with subjects which are usually regarded as very serious or unpleasant • a black comedy • black humor — **black·ly** adv — **black·ness** n [U]

²**black** n **1** [C/U] : the dark color of coal or the night sky • the black of night **2** [U] : black clothing • She was dressed in black. **3** [C] : a person belonging to a race of people who have dark skin : a black person ✧ The singular form black in this sense is rarely used and is often considered offensive. The plural form blacks is commonly used to refer to black people as a group or community. • His policies are supported by both blacks and whites. — **in the black** : making a profit • The company is finally in the black. — compare with ²RED

³**black** vb [T] **1** old-fashioned + literary : to make (something) black • He blacked his boots with polish. **2** Brit : to refuse to work for or with (a business, employer, etc.) or to buy (goods, services, etc.) • Labor union members have blacked the company. — **black out** [phrasal vb] **1** : to suddenly become unconscious • Someone hit me and I blacked out. **2 black (something) out** or **black out (something) a** : to cover (something written) with a black or dark mark so that it cannot be read • They blacked out some sections of the report. **b** : to cause (a place) to become dark • They blacked out the stage by turning off all the lights. **c** : to prevent the broadcast of (a televised sports event) • The game was blacked out in this area, so I couldn't watch it.

black–and–blue /ˌblækənˈbluː/ adj

: having dark marks (called bruises) on your skin because of being hit or injured • She had black-and-blue marks [=dark bruises] all over her legs.

black–and–white /ˌblækənˈwaɪt/ adj **1** : partly black and partly white in color • a black-and-white dog **2** : having, showing, or producing pictures that do not have colors except for black, white, and shades of gray • black-and-white movies/photos **3** : involving a simple choice between things that are clearly opposite and especially between good and bad or right and wrong • The truth is not always black-and-white.

black and white n — **in black and white 1** : in written or printed form • I want to see it in black and white. **2** : in a way that involves a simple choice between two opposite things • She sees everything in black and white. **3** : using equipment that produces only black-and-white pictures • a movie filmed in black and white

black·ball /ˈblækˌbɑːl/ vb [T] : to prevent (someone) from joining a group, club, etc., by voting against him or her • He was blackballed by the fraternity.

black belt n [C] : an expert in karate, judo, etc. • She is a karate black belt. ; also : the rank of such an expert • He has a black belt in judo.

black·ber·ry /ˈblækˌberi/ n, pl -ries [C] : a black or dark purple berry that is sweet and juicy; also : the plant that blackberries grow on

black·bird /ˈblækˌbɚd/ n [C] **1** : any one of several American birds with males that are mostly black **2** : a common European bird with males that have black feathers and an orange bill

black·board /ˈblækˌbɔɚd/ n [C] : a smooth, dark surface that is used for writing on with chalk in a classroom

black box n [C] : a device used in an airplane to record flight information (such as altitude or airspeed) or the voices of the pilots and crew

black death n — **the black death** or **the Black Death** : a deadly disease (called bubonic plague) that spread through Asia and Europe in the 14th century

black·en /ˈblækən/ vb **1** [T/I] : to make something dark or black or to become dark or black • The sky blackened as the storm approached. **2** [T] : to hurt the reputation of (someone or something) • His presidency/reputation/character was blackened by scandal.

black eye n [C] : a dark area of skin around the eye caused by being hit hard • He gave me a black eye. • (figurative) The scandal gave the team a black eye. [=caused people to think badly of the team]

black–eyed pea /ˈblækˌaɪd-/ n [C] chiefly US : a type of small, light bean that has a dark spot on it — called also (chiefly Brit) black-eyed bean

black·guard /ˈblægəd/ n [C] old-fashioned + literary : a rude or dishonest man • a cowardly blackguard

black·head /ˈblækˌhed/ n [C] : a small,

inflamed area on the skin with a dark spot in the middle

black hole n [C] : an invisible area in outer space with gravity so strong that light cannot get out of it • (*figurative*) The project turned out to be a financial black hole. [=something that uses up a large amount of money without producing a good result]

black·jack /ˈblækˌdʒæk/ n **1** [U] : a card game in which the players try to get a score that is higher than that of the dealer but less than or equal to 21 **2** [C] : a small leather-covered metal club used as a hand weapon

¹**black·list** /ˈblækˌlɪst/ n [C] : a list of people, organizations, etc., that are disapproved of or that are to be punished or avoided • He's on the FBI's blacklist.

²**blacklist** vb [T] : to say that a person, company, etc., should be avoided or not allowed to do something • In the 1950s, many Hollywood actors were blacklisted for suspected involvement with the Communist Party.

black magic n [U] : magic that is associated with the devil or with evil spirits

black·mail /ˈblækˌmeɪl/ n [U] : the crime of threatening to tell secret information about someone unless the person being threatened gives you money or does what you want • She was a victim of blackmail. • (*figurative*) He used emotional blackmail to get what he wanted from her. [=he unfairly made her feel guilty or upset] — **blackmail** vb [T] • He was being blackmailed by his nephew. — **black·mail·er** n [C]

black mark n [C] : something that makes something else less perfect or less appealing • The suspension was a black mark on her record.

black market n [C] : a system through which things are bought and sold illegally • a thriving black market for prescription drugs — **black marketeer** n [C]

black·out /ˈblækˌaʊt/ n [C] **1** : a period when lights are kept off or are hidden from view to guard against enemy airplane attack in a war **2** : a period when lights are off because of an electrical power failure **3** : a sudden and temporary loss of consciousness, vision, or memory • He told his doctor he had been experiencing blackouts. **4** : a situation in which some kinds of information are deliberately kept from the public • The government imposed a news blackout during the war.

black pepper n [U] : PEPPER 1

black sheep n [C] : someone who does not fit in with the rest of a group and is often considered to be a troublemaker or an embarrassment • She was the black sheep of the family.

black·smith /ˈblækˌsmɪθ/ n [C] : a person who makes or repairs things made of iron (such as horseshoes)

black spot n [C] Brit : a dangerous place or a place where a particular problem or difficulty is very common • The intersection is a notorious (accident) black spot.

black–tie adj — used to describe a formal social event at which men wear black ties and tuxedos and women wear formal dresses • a black-tie dinner

black·top /ˈblækˌtɑːp/ n [U] chiefly US **1** : black material that is used for making roads **2** : a surface that is covered with blacktop • cars lining the blacktop

black widow n [C] : a poisonous American spider — called also black widow spider

blad·der /ˈblædɚ/ n [C] **1** : the organ in the body that holds urine after it passes through the kidneys and before it leaves the body **2** : a soft bag (such as the rubber bag inside a football) that is filled with water or air

blade /ˈbleɪd/ n [C] **1** : the flat, sharp part of a weapon or tool that is used for cutting • a knife blade **2** : one of the flat spinning parts that are used on some machines to push air or water • a propeller blade **3** : the wide, flat part of an oar or paddle **4** : the sharp metal piece on the bottom of an ice skate **5** : a single piece of grass or a similar plant • a blade of grass — see also SHOULDER BLADE

¹**blah** /ˈblɑː/ adj, chiefly US, informal **1** : dull or boring • a blah winter day **2** : without energy or enthusiasm • She felt blah all day.

²**blah** n, informal **1** the blahs [plural] chiefly US : a feeling of being bored, tired, etc. • She had a bad case of the blahs. **2** [U] — used to suggest that what someone is saying is unimportant or boring • He got tired of hearing his mother tell him to brush his teeth, clean his room, blah, blah, blah.

¹**blame** /ˈbleɪm/ vb blamed; blam·ing [T] : to say or think that a person or thing is responsible for something bad that has happened • Don't blame me for your problems. = Don't blame your problems on me. • The company blames the poor economy for its losses. • She has only herself to blame for her problems. [=her problems are her own fault] — not blame ✧ If you say that you wouldn't/don't/can't blame someone or can hardly blame someone, you think that person has a good reason for doing something. • After the way he treated you, I wouldn't blame you if you never spoke to him again. • You can hardly blame her for being angry. — to blame : responsible for something bad • Who's to blame for these problems?

²**blame** n [U] : responsibility for something that fails or is wrong • The blame lies with me. [=I am at fault; I am to blame] • He tried to put/lay/pin the blame on me. • The coach took the blame for the defeat. [=the coach said he was responsible for the defeat] — **blame·less** /ˈbleɪmləs/ adj • The police were blameless in the man's death. [=were not responsible for his death] — **blame·wor·thy** /ˈbleɪmˌwɚði/ adj, formal • His conduct was judged (to be) blameworthy. [=deserving of blame]

blanch /ˈblænʧ/ Brit ˈblɑːnʧ/ vb **1** [T] : to put (food items) in boiling water or steam for a short time • Blanch the potatoes. **2** [I] : to suddenly have less color in your face because you are afraid, embarrassed, etc. • She blanched when the *store owner accused her of stealing.*

blanche see CARTE BLANCHE

bland /ˈblænd/ *adj* **1** : not interesting or exciting • *a bland film* **2** : lacking strong flavor • *The soup was rather bland.* **3** : showing no emotion, concern, etc. • *a bland expression/face* — **bland·ly** *adv* — **bland·ness** *n* [U]

¹**blank** /ˈblæŋk/ *adj* **1 a** : without any writing, marks, or pictures • *a blank sheet of paper* • *Leave that line blank.* [=don't write on that line] **b** : having empty spaces to be filled in with information • *a blank application/form* **2** : without any recorded sound or information • *a blank tape/disk/CD* **3** : not showing any emotion • *a blank expression/stare* — **go blank** **1** : to suddenly stop showing letters, images, etc. • *The computer screen went blank.* **2** ✧ If your *mind goes blank*, you are unable to remember or think of something. • *My mind went blank when I heard the question.* — **blank·ly** *adv* — **blank·ness** *n* [U]

²**blank** *n* **1** [C] : an empty space on a document where you put information • *Please fill in the blanks.* [=put information in the blank spaces] **2** [*singular*] : a period of time that you cannot remember anything about • *He says that the first hour after the accident is a complete blank.* ✧ If your *mind draws a blank* or if you *draw a blank*, you are unable to remember or think of something. • *I should know the answer, but my mind's a blank.* **3** [C] : a gun cartridge that is filled with powder but that does not contain a bullet • *The actors are shooting/firing blanks.*

³**blank** *vb* — **blank out** [*phrasal vb*] **blank out (something)** or **blank (something) out** **1** : to completely hide or cover (something) • *They blanked out parts of the document before making it public.* **2 a** : to cause (something) to be forgotten • *The injury blanked out parts of his memory.* **b** : to completely forget (something) • *She blanked out what happened that night.*

blank check (*US*) or *Brit* **blank cheque** *n* [C] : a signed check that does not have the amount of money written on it yet

¹**blan·ket** /ˈblæŋkət/ *n* [C] **1** : a covering made of cloth that is used especially on a bed to keep you warm • *a wool blanket* **2 a** : a mass of something that covers an area • *a blanket of snow/fog/ice/flowers/grass* **b** : a general mood — usually singular • *A blanket of gloom spread over the crowd.*

²**blanket** *vb* [T] : to cover (something) • *The field was blanketed with flowers/snow.*

³**blanket** *adj, always before a noun* : affecting or applying to everyone or everything • *a blanket ban on use of the chemical*

blank slate *n* [C] **1** : someone or something that is still in an original state and that has not yet been changed by people, experiences, etc. • *She saw her students as blank slates, ready to be filled with knowledge.* **2** : something that does not show or express anything • *Her face was a blank slate.*

blank verse *n* [U] : poetry that is not rhymed but that has a regular rhythm

¹**blare** /ˈbleɚ/ *vb* **blared**; **blar·ing** [T/I] : to make a loud and usually unpleasant sound • *Rock music blared (out) from the loudspeakers.*

²**blare** *n* [*singular*] : a loud and usually unpleasant noise • *the blare of the radio*

bla·sé /blɑˈzeɪ, *Brit* ˈblɑːˌzeɪ/ *adj* : having or showing a lack of excitement or interest in something especially because it is very familiar • *a blasé reaction/traveler*

blas·pheme /blæsˈfiːm/ *vb* **-phemed**; **-phem·ing** [T/I] *formal* : to talk about God or religion in a way that does not show respect • *He did not curse or blaspheme.* — **blas·phem·er** *n* [C]

blas·phe·my /ˈblæsfəmi/ *n, pl* **-mies** **1** [U] : great disrespect shown to God or to something holy • *acts of blasphemy* **2** [C] : something said or done that is disrespectful to God or to something holy • *The church condemned her for uttering blasphemies.* — **blas·phe·mous** /ˈblæsfəməs/ *adj* • *blasphemous language*

¹**blast** /ˈblæst, *Brit* ˈblɑːst/ *n* [C] **1** : a powerful explosion • *a bomb/shotgun blast* **2** : a mass of air, heat, etc., that moves very quickly and forcefully • *a blast of wind/heat* **3** : the loud sound made by a horn or a whistle • *a blast of the car horn* **4** *informal* : a very enjoyable and exciting experience • *I had a blast at the party.* — **blast from the past** *informal* : something that reminds you of an earlier time • *Hearing that song again was a real blast from the past.* — **full blast** *informal* : with as much loudness or power as possible • *The stereo was going full blast.*

²**blast** *vb* **1 a** [T/I] : to destroy, break apart, or remove (something) with an explosive • *The rock has been blasted away.* **b** [T] : to create (a space or opening) with explosives • *The explosion blasted a hole in the side of the ship.* **2** [T] : to strongly criticize (someone or something) especially in public • *The mayor was blasted by the local press.* **3** [T/I] : to shoot (something or someone) with a weapon • *They blasted the enemy plane out of the sky.* **4** [T] : to hit or kick (something) with great force • *He blasted the puck past the goalie.* **5** [T/I] : to make a loud and usually unpleasant sound • *A radio was blasting music in the next room.* — **blast off** [*phrasal vb*] *of a missile, rocket, or spacecraft* : to leave the ground and begin flight • *The rocket will blast off tomorrow.* — **blast·er** *n* [C]

blast-off /ˈblæstˌɑːf, *Brit* ˈblɑːstˌɒf/ *n* [C] : the time when a rocket, missile, etc., begins to rise into the air

bla·tant /ˈbleɪtn̩t/ *adj* : very obvious and offensive • *a blatant lie* — **bla·tant·ly** *adv*

blath·er /ˈblæðɚ/ *n* [U] : foolish or dull talk or writing that continues for a long time • *listening to a lot of blather from politicians* — **blather** *vb* [I] • *blathering politicians*

¹**blaze** /ˈbleɪz/ *n* **1** [C] *somewhat formal* : an intense and dangerous fire • *The family escaped the blaze.* **2** [*singular*] : a

very bright area of light or color ▪ *a blaze of light* **3** [*singular*] **:** a sudden appearance or expression of something ▪ *a blaze of fury/publicity/controversy* ▪ *The soldier went down in a blaze of glory.* [=the soldier died doing something important and worthy of great respect] **4** [*plural*] *informal + somewhat old-fashioned* — used to make a statement or question more forceful ▪ *It's hot as blazes.* [=it's very hot] ▪ *What in blazes are you doing?* **5** [*C*] **a :** a stripe of white fur on the center of an animal's face **b :** a mark made on a tree to show where there is a trail

²**blaze** *vb* **blazed; blaz·ing** [*I*] **1 :** to burn very brightly and intensely ▪ *A fire blazed in the stove.* **2 a :** to shine very brightly ▪ *The sun blazed down on us.* **b :** to be extremely bright or colorful like fire ▪ *The field was blazing with flowers.* **c** *of the eyes* **:** to show anger ▪ *His eyes blazed with anger/fury.* **3 :** to shoot very quickly and constantly ▪ *They rushed outside with their guns blazing.* **4 :** to move very quickly ▪ *A comet blazed across the sky.* ▪ *a blazing fastball* — **blaze a trail 1 :** to show where a trail is with marks on trees ▪ *They blazed a trail through the woods.* **2 :** to be the first one to do something and to show others how to do it ▪ *She blazed a trail for other women in politics.*

blaz·er /ˈbleɪzɚ/ *n* [*C*] **:** a jacket that is worn over a shirt and that looks like a suit jacket but is not part of a suit

¹**bleach** /ˈbliːtʃ/ *vb* [*T*] **:** to make (something) whiter or lighter in color ▪ *She bleached her hair blonde.*

²**bleach** *n* [*U*] **:** a strong chemical that is used to make something clean or white

bleach·ers /ˈbliːtʃɚz/ *n* [*plural*] *US* **:** a set of benches arranged like steps for people to sit on while they watch a sporting event or performance ▪ *stadium bleachers* ▪ *The ball bounced into the bleachers.* — **bleach·er** /ˈbliːtʃɚ/ *adj, always before a noun* ▪ *bleacher seats*

bleak /ˈbliːk/ *adj* **1 :** not warm, friendly, cheerful, etc. ▪ *a bleak day/landscape* **2 :** not hopeful or encouraging ▪ *The future looks bleak.* — **bleak·ly** *adv* — **bleak·ness** *n* [*U*]

bleary /ˈbliri/ *adj* **blear·i·er; -est :** very tired and unable to see clearly ▪ *bleary eyes* ▪ *bleary-eyed travelers* — **blear·i·ly** /ˈblirəli/ *adv*

bleat /ˈbliːt/ *vb* **1** [*I*] **:** to make the sound that a sheep or goat makes ▪ *The lamb bleated.* **2** [*T/I*] *disapproving* **:** WHINE ▪ *He's always bleating about his boss.* — **bleat** *n* [*C*]

bleed /ˈbliːd/ *vb* **bled** /ˈblɛd/; **bleed·ing 1** [*I*] **:** to lose or release blood because of a cut, injury, etc. ▪ *Her lip is bleeding.* ▪ *He almost bled to death.* [=almost died because he lost too much blood] **2** [*T*] **:** to remove air or liquid from something ▪ *We bled air from the tank.* **3** [*I*] **a** *of dye, ink, paint, etc.* **:** to spread from one area into another ▪ *The shirt's colors bled when I washed it.* **b :** to gradually spread into or become something else ▪ *Her professional life began to bleed into her personal life.* **4** [*T*] *informal* **:** to take

a lot of money from (someone) over a period of time ▪ *His ex-wife is bleeding him of all his money.* ▪ *Many people complain that the new taxes are bleeding them dry.* [=are taking all their money] — *your heart bleeds for* see HEART

¹**bleed·ing** /ˈbliːdɪŋ/ *n* [*U*] **:** the process of losing blood ▪ *She tried to stop the bleeding.*

²**bleeding** *adj, always before a noun, Brit, informal + offensive* — used to make an angry or critical statement more forceful ▪ *a bleeding idiot*

bleeding–heart *adj, always before a noun, disapproving* **:** feeling too much sympathy for people who you think do not deserve sympathy or help ▪ *Some conservatives call him a bleeding-heart liberal.*

bleep /ˈbliːp/ *vb* **1** [*T*] *US* **:** to replace (offensive words on radio or television) with an electronic sound ▪ *The radio station bleeped (out) the swearwords.* **2** [*I*] **:** to make a short, high sound **:** BEEP ▪ *The monitor bleeped.*

bleep·er /ˈbliːpɚ/ *n* [*C*] *Brit* **:** PAGER

blem·ish /ˈblɛmɪʃ/ *n* [*C*] **1 :** an unwanted mark on the surface of something ▪ *a skin blemish* ▪ *The table had a few scratches and minor blemishes.* **2 :** a fact or event that causes people to respect someone or something less ▪ *The incident left a blemish on his reputation.* — **blemish** *vb* [*T*] ▪ *The incident blemished his reputation.*

¹**blend** /ˈblɛnd/ *vb* **1** [*T*] **:** to mix (things) thoroughly and usually with good results ▪ *Blend the fruit, yogurt, and milk (together).* ▪ *The music blends traditional and modern melodies.* **2** [*I*] **:** to exist together as a combination ▪ *The flavor of the sauce blends well with the fruit.* [=the sauce and fruit taste good together] — **blend in** [*phrasal vb*] **1 :** to look like what is around you ▪ *The bird blends in perfectly with the leaves.* **2 :** to look like you belong with a particular group ▪ *She tried to blend in by dressing like the other girls.* **3 blend (something) in** or **blend in (something) :** to add (something) to a mixture or substance and mix it thoroughly ▪ *Combine the dry ingredients, then blend in the cream.* — **blend into** [*phrasal vb*] **1 :** to gradually become the same as or part of (something) ▪ *where the city blends into the suburbs* **2 :** to look like (what is around you) ▪ *The animal's dark fur lets it blend into its surroundings.* **3 :** to look like you belong in (something) ▪ *He tried to blend into the crowd.* — **blended** *adj* ▪ *blended tobacco/coffee* — **blending** *n* [*singular*]

²**blend** *n* [*C*] **:** something produced by mixing or combining different things ▪ *a blend of traditional and modern styles*

blend·er /ˈblɛndɚ/ *n* [*C*] **:** an electric kitchen machine that is used to cut food and ice into very small pieces and to make soft foods (such as fruits) into a liquid — called also (*Brit*) liquidizer

bless /ˈblɛs/ *vb* [*T*] **1 a :** to make (something or someone) holy by saying a special prayer ▪ *The priest blessed their marriage at the wedding.* **b :** to ask God to care for and protect (someone or something) • *The priest blessed the baby/house/ food.* **2 a** — used in the phrase *God bless* to express good wishes or appreciation for someone or something • *(May) God bless this country.* — see also GOD BLESS YOU (below) **b** — used in phrases like *bless his/her heart* and *bless him/ her* to express affection, appreciation, or understanding • *She tries so hard, bless her heart.* **3** : to provide (a person, place, etc.) *with* something good or desirable • *I have been blessed with good health.* **4** : to give approval to (something) • *The committee has not yet blessed the plan.* — **bless you** or **God bless you 1** — used in speech to express thanks or good wishes • *"I'll be happy to help." "Oh, bless you!"* **2** — said to someone who has just sneezed

bless·ed /ˈblɛsəd/ *adj* **1** : connected with God : HOLY • *the blessed Trinity* **2** *always before a noun* : very welcome, pleasant, or appreciated • *The rain brought blessed relief from the heat.* **3** *informal + somewhat old-fashioned* — used to make a statement more forceful • *You don't know a blessed thing.* — **bless·ed·ly** *adv* — **bless·ed·ness** *n* [U]

bless·ing /ˈblɛsɪŋ/ *n* **1** [U] **a** : approval that allows or helps you to do something • *He gave his blessing to the plan.* • *She was acting with the government's blessing.* **b** : help and approval from God • *We asked the Lord's blessing.* **2** [C] : something that helps you or brings happiness — usually singular • *My daughter is a blessing to me in my old age.* ◇ Something that is **a blessing in disguise** seems to be a bad thing at first but actually is a good thing. • *Losing my job turned out to be a blessing in disguise, since I got a much better job soon afterward.* ◇ If something is **a blessing and a curse** or **a mixed blessing** there are both good and bad things about it. • *Being famous can be a blessing and a curse.* **3** [C] : a short prayer **4** [U] : the act of asking God to care for and protect someone or something • *The priest performed the blessing of the fishing boats.* — **count your blessings** : to make a special effort to appreciate the good things in your life

blew *past tense of* ¹BLOW

¹**blight** /ˈblaɪt/ *n* **1** [C] : a disease that makes plants dry up and die • *potato blight* **2 a** [C] : something that causes harm or damage like a disease — usually singular • *The abandoned factory is a blight on the neighborhood.* **b** [U] : a damaged condition • *the city's spreading urban blight*

²**blight** *vb* [T] **1** : to damage (plants) with a disease • *The trees were blighted by fungus.* **2** : to damage (a thing or place) • *Builders blighted the land with malls and parking lots.* • *a blighted neighborhood*

blight·er /ˈblaɪtə/ *n* [C] *Brit, informal* **1** : a person (especially a man) who is unpleasant **2** : a man who you think is lucky, unlucky, etc. • *that lucky little blighter*

bli·mey /ˈblaɪmi/ *interj, Brit, informal* —

used to express surprise or amazement

blimp /ˈblɪmp/ *n* [C] : a large aircraft without wings that floats because it is filled with gas

¹**blind** /ˈblaɪnd/ *adj* **1** : unable to see • *a blind person* • *She went blind* [=she became unable to see] *at age 67.* • *providing assistance to the blind* [=blind people] **2** : unable to notice or judge something • *She is blind to his faults.* **3 a** *usually disapproving* : accepting the actions or decisions of someone or something without any questions or criticism • *blind faith/ loyalty/allegiance/obedience* **b** — used to describe strong emotions that make someone unable to think clearly or to act reasonably • *a blind fury/rage* **4** : done in a way that prevents people from seeing or knowing certain things that might influence them • *a blind taste test* [=a test in which people taste something without knowing what it is, who made it, etc.] **5** : difficult for a driver to see • *a blind driveway/drive* — **(as) blind as a bat** *informal* : unable to see well • *Without glasses I'm blind as a bat.* — **love is blind** see ¹LOVE — **turn a blind eye** : to ignore a problem instead of dealing with it • *Colleges can't afford to turn a blind eye to alcohol abuse.* — **blind·ness** *n* [U]

²**blind** *vb* [T] **1** : to cause (someone) to be unable to see • *The accident blinded me in one eye.* **2** : to cause (someone) to be unable to see for a short time • *I was blinded by the sun.* **3** : to cause (someone) to be unable to think clearly or to act reasonably • *He was blinded by love.*

³**blind** *n* [C] **1** : something that is used to cover a window from the inside of a room; *especially* : a roll of cloth or plastic that is hung at the top of a window and pulled down over the window • *Raise/lower/open/close the blinds.* **2** *US* : a place where hunters hide from animals while they are hunting • *a duck blind* — called also (*chiefly Brit*) *hide*

⁴**blind** *adv* **1** : using only a plane's instruments • *They had to fly blind through heavy rain.* **2** *informal* : to the degree that you are unable to think clearly or to act reasonably • *He was blind drunk.* — **rob (someone) blind** see ROB

blind alley *n* [C] : a narrow path between two buildings that can only be entered at one end • *(figurative) Police had been down several blind alleys* [=had tried several methods that did not produce useful results] *in the investigation before they solved the case.*

blind date *n* [C] : an occasion for two people who do not know each other to meet and decide if they may want to have a romantic relationship • *She went on a blind date with her friend's cousin.*

blind·er /ˈblaɪndə/ *n* **1** [*plural*] *chiefly US* : leather pieces that are placed on either side of a horse's head next to its eyes in order to keep the horse from seeing what is beside it • *(figurative) Many parents put on blinders* [=choose not to think about what might be happening] *when their teenagers start staying out late.* — called also (*chiefly Brit*) *blinkers* **2** [*singular*] *Brit, informal* : a very exciting or impressive performance or action in a game such as cricket or soccer ▪ *They played a blinder.*

blind·fold /ˈblaɪndˌfoʊld/ *n* [C] : a piece of cloth that covers the eyes — **blind·fold** *vb* [T] ▪ *They tied him up and blindfolded him.* ▪ *a blindfolded prisoner* — **blind·fold·ed** /ˈblaɪndˌfoʊldəd/ *also* **blindfold** *adv* ▪ *He was led blindfolded* [=with his eyes covered by a blindfold] *into the woods.* ▪ *I could find that house blindfolded.* [=I could find it very easily because I know exactly where it is]

blind·ing /ˈblaɪndɪŋ/ *adj* **1** : very bright or strong ▪ *a blinding color* ▪ *a blinding headache* [=a very painful headache]; *especially* : so bright or strong that you cannot see ▪ *a blinding light* **2** : very fast ▪ *blinding speed* — **blind·ing·ly** /ˈblaɪndɪŋli/ *adv*

blind·ly /ˈblaɪndli/ *adv* **1** : without seeing ▪ *She stumbled blindly in the dark.* **2** : without noticing or seeming to see anything ▪ *He stared blindly at the wall.* **3** : without thinking or questioning ▪ *They blindly obeyed orders.*

blind·side /ˈblaɪndˌsaɪd/ *vb* -**sid·ed**; -**sid·ing** [T] *US* **1** : to hit (someone who is facing in another direction) suddenly and very hard ▪ *The quarterback was blindsided.* **2** : to surprise or shock (someone) in a very unpleasant way ▪ *We were blindsided by the decision.*

blind side *n* [C] : the side that is not the side you are facing ▪ *He was hit on his blind side.*

blind spot *n* [C] **1** : an area around a car, truck, etc., that the driver cannot see **2** : a tendency to ignore something especially because it is difficult or unpleasant ▪ *She has a blind spot concerning her son's behavior.*

¹**blink** /ˈblɪŋk/ *vb* [T/I] : to close and then open your eyes very quickly ▪ *She blinked (her eyes) when the light flashed.* **2** [I] : to shine with a light that goes on and off ▪ *The light was blinking.* **3** [I] : to show that you are surprised or upset ▪ *She didn't (even) blink at the news.* **4** [I] : to show that you are willing to agree to or accept what someone else wants or says ▪ *When threatened, the government blinked* [=gave in] *and agreed to move the missiles.* — **blink away/back tears** : to prevent yourself from crying or to make your tears go away by blinking ▪ *He blinked back (his) tears as he told us the bad news.*

²**blink** *n* [C] : the act of closing and then opening your eyes very quickly — **in the blink of an eye** : very quickly ▪ *She finished her work in the blink of an eye.* — **on the blink** *informal* : not working properly ▪ *The TV is on the blink.*

blink·er /ˈblɪŋkɚ/ *n* **1** [C] *US, informal* : a light on a car, truck, etc., that goes off and on and that is used as a warning or as a signal that the vehicle will be turning **2** [*plural*] *chiefly Brit* : BLINDERS

blip /ˈblɪp/ *n* [C] **1** : a bright dot on the screen of an electronic device (such as a radar) ▪ *The approaching ship appeared as a blip on the screen.* ▪ (*figurative*) *The organization was only a blip on the politi-*

cal radar screen two years ago.* **2** : a very short high sound made by an electronic device **3** : something that is small or unimportant or that does not last a long time ▪ *The company's problems were just a temporary blip.*

bliss /ˈblɪs/ *n* [U] : complete happiness ▪ *marital/wedded/domestic bliss* [=complete happiness in marriage] — **ignorance is bliss** see IGNORANCE

bliss·ful /ˈblɪsfəl/ *adj* : extremely or completely happy ▪ *Their time together was blissful.* ▪ *existing in blissful ignorance* [=a state of not knowing and not wanting to know about unhappy things or possible problems] — **bliss·ful·ly** *adv*

blis·ter /ˈblɪstɚ/ *n* [C] **1** : a raised area on the skin that contains clear liquid and that is caused by injury to the skin **2** : a raised area on a surface (such as a painted wall) that is filled with air — **blister** *vb* [T/I] ▪ *Her skin was blistered by the sun.*

blis·ter·ing /ˈblɪstɚɪŋ/ *adj* : very harsh or powerful ▪ *blistering heat/sun* ▪ *blistering criticism* — **blistering** *adv* ▪ *a blistering hot day* — **blis·ter·ing·ly** *adv*

blithe /ˈblaɪθ, ˈblaɪð/ *adj* **blith·er**; -**est 1** : showing a lack of proper thought or care ▪ *a blithe disregard for safety* **2** *literary* : CAREFREE ▪ *a blithe spirit* — **blithe·ly** *adv*

blith·er·ing /ˈblɪðɚɪŋ/ *adj, informal* : very foolish or stupid ▪ *a blithering idiot*

blitz /ˈblɪts/ *n* [C] **1** : a military attack in which many bombs are dropped from airplanes **2** : a fast and powerful effort ▪ *an advertising/marketing/media blitz* **3** *American football* : a play in which many defensive players rush toward the quarterback — **blitz** *vb* [T/I] ▪ (*American football*) *The linebackers blitzed the quarterback.*

bliz·zard /ˈblɪzɚd/ *n* [C] **1** : a severe snowstorm that goes on for a long time ▪ *a raging/fierce blizzard* **2** : a large amount of something that comes suddenly ▪ *a blizzard of mail/questions*

bloat *n* [U] *chiefly US* : too much growth ▪ *budget/corporate bloat*

bloat·ed /ˈbloʊtəd/ *adj* : very swollen : too full of liquid, gas, food, etc. ▪ *a bloated body* ▪ *I felt bloated from eating too much.* ▪ (*figurative*) *a bloated budget/ego* — **bloat·ed·ness** *n* [U]

blob /ˈblɑːb/ *n* [C] *somewhat informal* : a usually small amount of something thick and wet ▪ *a blob of paint*

bloc /ˈblɑːk/ *n* [C] : a group of people or countries that are connected by a treaty or agreement or by common goals ▪ *the communist bloc* ▪ *a Senate voting bloc*

¹**block** /ˈblɑːk/ *n* **1** [C] : a solid piece of material (such as rock or wood) that has flat sides and is usually square or rectangular in shape ▪ *a block of ice/cheese* ▪ *concrete blocks* **2** [C] **a** : an area of land surrounded by four streets in a city ▪ *She lived on our block.* **b** *US* : the length of one city block ▪ *The store is three blocks down on the right.* **3** [C] : a large building divided into separate apartments, shops, etc. ▪ *an apartment block* **4** [*singular*] : something that stops the progress or achievement of

something • *They put a block on future development of the area.* **5** [C] *sports* : an action or movement that stops or slows down an opponent • *a shoulder block* • (*American football*) *The lineman threw a block.* [=the lineman hit an opposing player to prevent him from making a tackle] **6** [*singular*] : something that stops a person from thinking about certain things • *a mental/emotional block* — see also STUMBLING BLOCK **7** [C] **a** : a number of similar things that form a group • *a block of seats* **b** : an amount or section of something • *a big block of time* — **chip off the old block** see ¹CHIP — **knock someone's block off** see ¹KNOCK — **on the (auction) block** : for sale especially at an auction • *Some valuable paintings went on the block today.*

²**block** *vb* **1** [T] **a** : to be placed in front of a road, path, etc., so that people or things cannot pass through • *A truck was blocking the road.* **b** : to place something in front of (something, such as a road) so that people or things cannot go into the area • *Police blocked (off) the road.* **2** [T] **a** : to stop (someone or something) from moving through or going by • *An accident was blocking traffic.* **b** : to stop (something) from getting through to someone or something • *You're blocking my light.* **c** : to be in front of (something) so that it cannot be seen • *Their house blocks our view.* **3** [T] **a** : to not allow (something, such as progress or an action) to occur • *His vote blocked the treaty.* **b** : to stop the way of (something) • *blocking access to information* **4** [T/I] *sports* : to stop the movement of (an opponent, a shot, etc.) • *She blocked the shot!* — **block in** [*phrasal vb*] **block in** (*someone or something*) *or* **block** (*someone or something*) **in** : to put something in front of (someone or something) so that person or thing cannot leave • *My car is blocked in.* [=someone has parked in a way that makes it impossible for me to move my car] — **block out** [*phrasal vb*] **block out** (*something*) *or* **block** (*something*) **out 1** : to hide or cover (something) so that it cannot be seen, felt, or heard • *Clouds blocked out the sun.* **2** : to force yourself not to think about (something) • *blocking out distractions* — **block-er** *n* [C]

block-ade /blɑˈkeɪd/ *n* [C] : an act of war in which one country uses ships to stop people or supplies from entering or leaving another country • *a naval blockade* — **blockade** *vb* -ad-ed; -ad-ing [T] • *They blockaded the country's ports.*

block-age /ˈblɑːkɪdʒ/ *n* **1** [C] : something that stops something (such as blood) from moving through something (such as a blood vessel) • *a blockage in the arteries* **2** [U] : the state of being blocked • *trying to prevent blockage of the artery*

block and tackle *n* [*singular*] : a simple machine that is used to help lift heavy objects

block-bust-er /ˈblɑːkˌbʌstɚ/ *n* [C] : something that is very large, expensive,

or successful • *a blockbuster product/movie*

block-head /ˈblɑːkˌhɛd/ *n* [C] *informal* : a stupid person • *Don't be such a blockhead!*

block party *n* [C] *US* : a party that is held outdoors for all the people who live in a neighborhood or city block

blog /ˈblɑːg/ *n* [C] : a Web site on which someone writes about personal opinions, activities, and experiences — **blog-ger** *n* [C] — **blog-ging** *n* [U]

bloke /ˈbloʊk/ *n* [C] *chiefly Brit, informal* : a man • *an ordinary bloke*

¹**blond** *or* **blonde** /ˈblɑːnd/ *adj* **blond-er; -est** : of a yellow or very light brown color • *blond hair; also* : having blond hair • *a blond actor* ✧ When used to describe a boy or man, the word is spelled *blond*. When used for a girl or woman, the word is often spelled *blonde*.

²**blond** *or* **blonde** *n* [C] : a person who has yellow or very light brown hair ✧ The word is spelled *blond* when used for a boy or man, and it is usually spelled *blonde* when used for a girl or woman. • *She's a natural blonde.* [=her hair has not been dyed blonde]

blood /ˈblʌd/ *n* [U] **1** : the red liquid that flows through the bodies of people and animals • *the blood in your veins* • *She donates/gives blood twice a year.* [=twice a year she has blood taken out of her body so that it can be put into the body of a person who needs it] **2** — used to say that a person's ancestors were of a particular kind • *There's some Italian blood in her family.* [=one or more of her family's ancestors was Italian] **3** : members of a team, company, or organization • *Our company needs some new blood.* [=new employees] — **blood and guts** see ¹GUT — **blood is thicker than water** — used to say that a person's family is more important than a person's other relationships or needs — **blood is up** — used in British English to say that someone is angry and wants to fight or argue • *It's best to avoid her when her blood is up.* — **blood on your hands** ✧ If someone's *blood is on your hands*, you are responsible for that person's death. — **by blood** : by a relationship that connects two people through their natural parents, grandparents, etc. • *My aunt and I are related by blood.* [=my aunt is the sister of one of my parents] — **draw blood 1** : to take blood from a person's body for medical reasons • *We need to draw some blood to test you for the virus.* **2** : to cause blood to flow from a person's body • *The punch to his nose drew blood.* [=caused his nose to bleed] — **flesh and blood** see ¹FLESH — **in cold blood** : in a deliberate, planned way • *They were killed in cold blood.* — **in your blood** ✧ If an ability, activity, etc., is *in your blood*, it is part of your nature and is often shared by your family members. • *With two parents who are painters, art is in her blood.* — **make someone's blood boil** : to make someone very angry — **make someone's blood curdle** *or* **make someone's blood run cold** : to cause someone to be very afraid or disgusted • *The news made our blood run cold.* — **out for blood** ◇ If you are *out for (someone's) blood*, you are very angry and you want to kill someone or to cause someone pain or discomfort. • *Those soldiers were out for blood.* — **spill/shed blood** : to kill people violently — **sweat blood** *informal* : to care a lot about something and work very hard for it • *basketball players who sweat blood for their teams*

blood bank *n* [C] : a place where blood is stored so that it later can be given to people who are ill

blood·bath /ˈblʌdˌbæθ, *Brit* ˈblʌdˌbɑːθ/ *n* [C] : a violent and cruel killing of many people • *The battle became a bloodbath.* • *(figurative) a political bloodbath*

blood clot *n* [C] : a thick and sticky clump of dried blood that stops blood from flowing through a blood vessel in a person or an animal — called also *clot*

blood·cur·dling /ˈblʌdˌkɚdlɪŋ/ *adj* : causing great horror or fear • *a blood-curdling scream*

blood feud *n* [C] : a very long fight between two families or groups in which each group kills members of the other group in order to punish the group for earlier murders

blood group *n* [C] : BLOOD TYPE

blood·hound /ˈblʌdˌhaʊnd/ *n* [C] : a large dog that has very long ears and a very good sense of smell and that is often used for finding people and for hunting

blood·less /ˈblʌdləs/ *adj* **1** : done without killing people • *a bloodless coup* **2** : pale in color • *His face was bloodless with fear.* — **blood·less·ly** *adv*

blood·line /ˈblʌdˌlaɪn/ *n* [C] : the ancestors of a person or animal • *her family's German bloodlines*

blood money *n* [U] : money wrongly obtained by killing someone or because someone has died • *the blood money earned by people who profited from the tragedy*

blood pressure *n* [C/U] : the force with which blood moves through a person's body • *high/low blood pressure*

blood relative *n* [C] *US* : someone who has the same parents or ancestors as you — called also *(Brit) blood relation*

blood·shed /ˈblʌdˌʃɛd/ *n* [U] : the killing of people especially in a war • *years of violence and bloodshed*

blood·shot /ˈblʌdˌʃɑːt/ *adj, of eyes* : having many red lines from lack of sleep, drunkenness, etc.

blood sport *n* [C] : a sport (such as hunting) in which birds or animals are killed

blood·stain /ˈblʌdˌsteɪn/ *n* [C] : a spot of blood on something (such as a piece of clothing) — **blood·stained** /ˈblʌdˌsteɪnd/ *adj*

blood·stream /ˈblʌdˌstriːm/ *n* [singular] : the flow of blood that moves through the heart and body

blood sugar *n* [U] : the amount of sugar in your blood

blood·thirsty /ˈblʌdˌθɚsti/ *adj* : eager to hurt or kill • *bloodthirsty soldiers* —

blood·thirst·i·ness /ˈblʌdˌθɚstinəs/ *n* [U]

blood type *n* [C] *chiefly US* : one of the eight different blood categories into which humans are separated ◇ These categories of blood are labeled A, B, AB, or O and each of these is either Rh-positive or Rh-negative. • *Her blood type is B negative.* — called also *blood group*

blood vessel *n* [C] : a small tube that carries blood to different parts of a person or animal's body ◇ Arteries, veins, and capillaries are kinds of *blood vessels.*

¹**bloody** /ˈblʌdi/ *adj* **blood·i·er; -est** **1** : bleeding or covered with blood • *a bloody nose* • *a bloody knife/towel* **2** : violent and causing the death or injury of many people • *a bloody battle/war* **3** *always before a noun, Brit, informal + sometimes offensive* — used to make an angry or critical statement more forceful • *He's a bloody fool!* — **blood·i·ly** /ˈblʌdəli/ *adv*

²**bloody** *adv, Brit, informal + sometimes offensive* : VERY, EXTREMELY — used to make a statement more forceful • *We all had a bloody good time.*

³**bloody** *vb* **blood·ies; blood·ied; bloody·ing** [T] : to make (something) bloody • *He hit me and bloodied my nose.* • *His face was bloodied and bruised.*

Bloody Mary /-ˈmɛri/ *n* [C] : an alcoholic drink made with vodka, tomato juice, and usually spices

bloody–mind·ed /ˌblʌdiˈmaɪndəd/ *adj, chiefly Brit, informal* : not willing to be helpful • *Stop being so bloody-minded and give me a hand here!* — **bloody-mind·ed·ness** *n* [U]

¹**bloom** /ˈbluːm/ *n* **1** [C] : ¹FLOWER 1 • *a plant with purple blooms* **2** [U] : a state or time of beauty, health, and strength • *the bloom of youth* — **in (full) bloom** : having flowers • *The bushes should be in bloom soon.*

²**bloom** *vb* [I] **1** : to produce flowers • *trees that bloom in the spring* **2** : to change, grow, or develop fully • *Their love was just beginning to bloom.*

bloom·er /ˈbluːmɚ/ *n* [C] : a plant that blooms at a specified time • *These plants are spring bloomers.* — **late bloomer** *US* : someone who becomes successful, attractive, etc., at a later time in life than other people • *She was a late bloomer as a writer.*

bloo·mers /ˈbluːmɚz/ *n* [plural] : long and loose underpants worn by women and girls especially in the past

bloom·ing /ˈbluːmən/ *adj, always before a noun, Brit, informal* — used to make an angry or critical statement more forceful • *Don't be a blooming idiot!* — **blooming** *adv*

bloop·er /ˈbluːpɚ/ *n* [C] *US* : an embarrassing mistake usually made in public • *The mayor's blooper was shown on every TV channel.*

¹**blos·som** /ˈblɑːsəm/ *n* [C] : a flower especially of a fruit tree • *apple/cherry/orange blossoms*

²**blossom** *vb* [I] **1** : to produce flowers • *blossoming trees* **2** : to change, grow, and develop fully • *Their friendship blos-*

somed [=bloomed] *during the summer.* ▪ *a blossoming romance/talent*

¹**blot** /'blɑːt/ *vb* **blot·ted; blot·ting** [*T*] : to dry (something, such as wet ink) by pressing a piece of cloth or paper over it ▪ *Blot the spill with a paper towel.* — **blot out** [*phrasal vb*] **blot out (something)** or **blot (something) out** : to hide or block (something): such as **a** : to make (something) difficult to see ▪ *Clouds blotted out the sun.* **b** : to try to forget (an event or memory) ▪ *blotting out bad memories*

²**blot** *n* [*C*] **1 a** : a spot or stain ▪ *a blot of ink* [=an ink blot] **b** : something that makes something else dirty or unattractive ▪ *The tower is a blot on the landscape.* **2** : a mark of shame or dishonor ▪ *Slavery is a blot on the nation's history.*

blotch /'blɑːtʃ/ *n* [*C*] : a usually dark-colored spot especially on the skin ▪ *She has brown blotches on her hands.* — **blotched** /'blɑːtʃt/ *adj, Brit* — **blotchy** /'blɑːtʃi/ *adj* **blotch·i·er; -est**

blot·ter /'blɑːtɚ/ *n* [*C*] **1** : a large piece of soft, thick paper that is used to dry wet ink **2** : a book used in a police station for writing down information about people or events ▪ *a police blotter*

blot·to /'blɑːtoʊ/ *adj, slang* : very drunk ▪ *He came home blotto after the party.*

blouse /'blaʊs/ *n* [*C*] : an often somewhat formal shirt for women and girls

¹**blow** /'bloʊ/ *vb* **blew** /'bluː/; **blown** /'bloʊn/; **blow·ing** **1 a** [*I*] *of air, wind, etc.* : to move with speed or force ▪ *The wind is blowing hard.* **b** [*T*] : to cause (air or something carried by air) to move ▪ *The fan blew the smoke out the window.* **c** [*T/I*] : to be moved or affected in a specified way by the wind ▪ *The leaves were blowing around in the wind.* ▪ *The wind blew his hat off.* **2 a** [*T/I*] : to create a current of moving air by breathing ▪ *She blew air into the balloon.* ▪ *He blew on his soup to cool it off.* **b** [*T*] : to produce or shape (something) by blowing air ▪ *blowing bubbles* **3 a** [*I*] *of a musical instrument, whistle, etc.* : to produce a loud sound ▪ *The whistle blew loudly.* **b** [*T*] : to play or produce a sound with (a musical instrument, whistle, etc.) ▪ *blow a trumpet/whistle* **4** [*T/I*] : to damage or destroy (something) with an explosion ▪ *The bomb blew the bridge to bits/smithereens.* [=completely destroyed the bridge] ▪ *The window blew out in the explosion.* ▪ (*figurative*) *The prosecution's case was blown apart by new evidence.* **5** [*T/I*] : to cause (a tire) to suddenly lose air and become flat ▪ *He drove over a nail and blew (out) a tire.* **6** [*T/I*] *of an electric fuse* : to melt and stop the flow of electricity when an electric current is too strong ▪ *What blew the fuse?* ▪ *The light went off because a fuse had blown.* ▪ (*figurative, informal*) *She blew a fuse* [=became very angry] *when I came home late.* **7** [*T*] : to clear (your nose) by forcing air through it quickly ▪ *He blew his nose into his handkerchief.* **8** [*T*] *informal* : to spend or waste (a large amount of money) in a foolish way ▪ *He blew his whole paycheck at the racetrack.* **9** [*T*] *informal* **a** : to make a mistake in doing

or handling (something) ▪ *The actress blew her lines.* [=she said her lines incorrectly] **b** : to lose or miss (an opportunity) by acting in a stupid or clumsy way ▪ *I blew my chance.* ▪ *They should have won the game but they blew it.* **10** [*T*] *US, informal* : to leave (a place) very quickly ▪ *Let's blow this joint.* ▪ *He packed his bags and blew town.* [=left town] **11** [*T*] *US, informal* : to throw (a ball) with great force and speed ▪ *The pitcher blew a fastball by/past the batter.* **12** *Brit, informal* — used to express surprise, annoyance, etc. ▪ *He washed the dishes? Well blow me down!* ▪ *Blow it!* I forgot to buy milk. — **blow a gasket** see GASKET — **blow away** [*phrasal vb*] **blow (someone) away** or **blow away (someone)** *informal* **1** : to kill (someone) by shooting ▪ *a gangster who got blown away by a hit man* **2** : to impress (someone) in a very strong and favorable way ▪ *I was really blown away by her latest movie.* **3** *US* : to defeat (someone) very badly ▪ *They blew their rivals away in the first game 34–7.* — **blow in** [*phrasal vb*] *informal* : to arrive in a sudden or unexpected way ▪ *He just blew in, asking for a place to stay.* — **blow into** [*phrasal vb*] **blow into (a place)** *informal* : to arrive at (a place) in a sudden or unexpected way ▪ *He just blew into town.* — **blow off** [*phrasal vb*] *US, informal* **blow (someone or something) off** or **blow off (someone or something)** **1 a** : to refuse to notice or deal with (someone) ▪ *I tried to say hello to him, but he just blew me off.* **b** : to fail to meet (someone) at an expected time ▪ *She was supposed to meet me for lunch but she blew me off.* **2** : to fail to attend or show up for (something) ▪ *He blew off math class again.* — **blow off (some) steam** see ¹STEAM — **blow out** [*phrasal vb*] **1 blow out** or **blow (something) out** or **blow out (something)** : to go out or to cause (something, such as a candle) to go out by blowing ▪ *She blew out the candles on her birthday cake.* **2** *of a storm* : to come to an end ▪ *The storm eventually blew (itself) out.* [=the storm eventually ended] — **blow over** [*phrasal vb*] *of a storm* : to come to an end ▪ *The storm eventually blew over.* ▪ (*figurative*) *The scandal blew over and was quickly forgotten.* — **blow smoke** see ¹SMOKE — **blow someone's brains out** see ¹BRAIN — **blow someone's cover** see ²COVER — **blow someone's mind** see ¹MIND — **blow the whistle** see ¹WHISTLE — **blow up** [*phrasal vb*] **blow up** or **blow (something) up** or **blow up (something)** **1** : to fill (something) with air or gas ▪ *blow up a balloon/tire* **2 a** : to explode or to cause (something, such as a bomb) to explode ▪ *The bomb blew up.* **b** : to be destroyed or to destroy (something) by an explosion ▪ *The bridge blew up (in the explosion).* ▪ *The soldiers blew up the bridge with a bomb.* ▪ (*figurative*) *The whole situation has blown up in his face.* [=has gone terribly wrong] **3** : to become very angry ▪ *The boss blew up when the shipment arrived late.* **4** : to make (a photograph) larger ▪ *We had the* *picture blown up for framing.* : to make (something) seem larger or more important than it really is ▪ *It was just a minor mistake that got blown up into something much worse.* **5** *of the wind, a storm, etc.* : to begin blowing ▪ *A storm blew up suddenly.* — **blow your cool** see ³COOL — **blow your own horn** see ¹HORN — **blow your own trumpet** see ¹TRUMPET — **blow your top** or US **blow your stack** *informal* : to become very angry

²**blow** *n* [C] : the act of blowing something (such as your nose) ▪ *He gave his nose a blow.* [=he blew his nose]

³**blow** *n* [C] **1** : a hard hit using a part of the body or an object ▪ *a blow with a hammer* = *a hammer blow* ▪ *The boxers exchanged blows.* [=hit each other] — see also LOW BLOW **2 a** : something that is done to fight for or against something ▪ *They struck a blow for freedom and against tyranny.* [=they did something that helped freedom and opposed tyranny] **b** : a sudden event that causes trouble, damage, sorrow, etc. ▪ *Her injury was a serious blow to the team's chances.* ▪ *She was disappointed, but the promise of another job cushioned/softened the blow.* — **come to blows** : to begin hitting each other ▪ *They almost came to blows during the argument.*

blow-by-blow /ˈbloʊbaɪˈbloʊ/ *adj, always before a noun* : describing each thing that happens in a series ▪ *a blow-by-blow account/description of the meeting*

blow-dry-er /ˈbloʊˌdraɪər/ *n* [C] : a device that blows air and is used for drying hair — **blow-dry** /ˈbloʊˌdraɪ/ *vb* **-dries; -dried; -dry-ing** [T/I] ▪ *She washed and blow-dried her hair.* — **blow-dry** *n, pl* **-dries** [C] ▪ *She gave her hair a quick blow-dry.*

blow-er /ˈbloʊər/ *n* [C] : a device that blows air ▪ *a leaf blower* [=a device that is used for clearing away leaves from the ground by producing a strong current of air] — **on the blower** *Brit, informal* : on the telephone ▪ *I finally got him on the blower.*

blow-hard /ˈbloʊˌhɑərd/ *n* [C] *US, informal + disapproving* : a person who talks too much and who has strong opinions that other people dislike ▪ *an arrogant blowhard*

blow-lamp /ˈbloʊˌlæmp/ *n* [C] *Brit* : BLOWTORCH

blown *past participle of* ¹BLOW

blow-out /ˈbloʊˌaʊt/ *n* [C] **1** : a sudden loss of air caused by a hole or cut in a tire ▪ *The left front tire had a blowout.* **2** *informal* : a big party ▪ *We had a big blowout to celebrate his promotion.* **3** *US, informal* : a game or contest in which the winner defeats the loser by a large amount

blow-torch /ˈbloʊˌtoərtʃ/ *n* [C] *US* : a device that produces a very hot, narrow flame for doing work (such as melting metal to join parts together) — called also (*Brit*) **blowlamp**

blow-up /ˈbloʊˌʌp/ *n* [C] **1** : a photograph that has been made larger **2 a** : an angry argument ▪ *They had a big blowup.* **b** : an occurrence in which

someone becomes very angry ▪ *The coach's latest blowup occurred when one of his players arrived late.*

BLT /ˌbiːˌɛlˈtiː/ *n* [C] *US* : a bacon, lettuce, and tomato sandwich

¹**blub-ber** /ˈblʌbər/ *n* [U] : the fat on whales and some other animals that live in the water

²**blubber** *vb* [I] : to cry in a noisy and annoying way ▪ *Oh, stop blubbering, you big baby!*

¹**blud-geon** /ˈblʌdʒən/ *vb* [T] : to hit (someone or something) very hard ▪ *The victim was bludgeoned to death with a hammer.*

²**bludgeon** *n* [C] : a heavy stick that usually has one thick end and is used as a weapon

¹**blue** /ˈbluː/ *adj* **blu-er; blu-est 1** : having the color of the clear sky ▪ *a blue house/car/shirt/pen* **2** : sad or unhappy ▪ *Are you feeling blue?* — see also BLUES — **blue in the face** ✧ If you do something until you are *blue in the face*, you do it for a very long time without having any success or making any difference. ▪ *I talked to him until I was blue in the face, but he wouldn't listen to me.* — **talk a blue streak** *US* : to talk rapidly and without stopping — **blue-ness** [U]

²**blue** *n* **1** [C/U] : the color of the clear sky ▪ *Her favorite color is blue.* ▪ *A mixture of blues and greens* **2** *the blue literary* : the sky or the sea ▪ *They sailed off into the blue.* — **out of the blue** : in a surprising or unexpected way ▪ *Then, out of the blue, he sold his house and left the country.*

blue-ber-ry /ˈbluːˌberi/ *n, pl* **-ries** [C] : a small round fruit with blue, purple, or blackish skin ▪ *a blueberry muffin/pie/bush*

blue-bird /ˈbluːˌbəd/ *n* [C] : a small North American bird that is mostly blue

blue blood *n* **1** [U] : membership in a royal or socially important family ▪ *a woman of blue blood* **2** [C] : a member of a royal or socially important family ▪ *a gathering place for the city's blue bloods* — **blue–blood-ed** /ˈbluːˈblʌdəd/ *adj*

blue book *n* **1** [*singular*] : a report that is published by the government **2** [C] *US* : a thin booklet with a blue cover and empty pages that is used for writing the answers to test questions in college **3** [*singular*] *US* : a book that lists the current value of certain products (such as used cars)

blue cheese *n* [C/U] : a kind of cheese that is white with lines of blue mold and that has a strong flavor

blue–chip *adj, always before a noun* **1** : valuable and likely to make a good profit ▪ *blue-chip companies/stocks* **2** *chiefly US* : very good ▪ *a blue-chip artist/athlete*

blue–col-lar /ˈbluːˈkɑːlər/ *adj* : requiring physical work ▪ *blue-collar jobs* [=jobs making things in a factory, fixing machines, building things, etc.] : relating to or having jobs that require physical work ▪ *blue-collar workers/families* — compare WHITE-COLLAR

blue-grass /ˈbluːˌgræs, *Brit* ˈbluːˌgrɑːs/ *n*

[U] : a type of traditional American music that is played on stringed instruments (such as banjos and fiddles)

blue jay n [C] : a common American bird that is mostly blue

blue jeans n [plural] : pants made of a strong blue cloth (called denim) ▪ He was wearing (a pair of) blue jeans.

blue law n [C] US : an old law that forbids people from doing certain things (such as working or selling alcohol) on Sundays

blue moon n — **once in a blue moon** : very rarely ▪ It happens once in a blue moon.

blue·print /'blu:ˌprɪnt/ n [C] 1 : a photographic print that shows how something (such as a building) will be made ✧ Blueprints are often sheets of blue paper with white lines on them. ▪ architectural blueprints ▪ (figurative) Each cell contains the organism's genetic blueprint. 2 : a detailed plan of how to do something ▪ a blueprint for success

blue ribbon n [C] chiefly US : a decorative piece of blue cloth that is given to the winner in a contest or competition — called also (Brit) blue rib·and /'rɪbənd/

blue–ribbon adj, always before a noun, US : made up of people who have special knowledge, abilities, etc. ▪ a blue-ribbon committee/panel

blues /'blu:z/ n 1 **the blues** [plural] : a feeling of sadness or depression ▪ I've got (a case of) the blues. 2 [U] : a style of music that was created by African-Americans in the southern U.S. and that often expresses feelings of sadness ▪ a band that plays blues and jazz ▪ a blues singer ▪ (figurative) He's been singing the blues [=feeling sad and discouraged] since he lost his job. — see also RHYTHM AND BLUES — **blue·sy** /'blu:zi/ adj blues·i·er; -est ▪ bluesy music

¹bluff /'blʌf/ vb 1 [T/I] : to pretend that you will do something or that you know or have something in order to trick or persuade someone into doing what you want ▪ Don't listen to his threats—he's just bluffing (you). [=he will not really do what he threatens to do] 2 [T] US : to pretend to do or make (something) ▪ The catcher bluffed a throw to first base.

²bluff n [C] 1 : a false threat or claim that is meant to get someone to do something ▪ Her threat to quit was just a bluff. ▪ When she threatened to quit her job, I called her bluff. [=told her to do it because I did not believe that she really would] 2 : CLIFF

³bluff adj : having a very open, honest, and direct way of talking that is friendly but not always polite ▪ a bluff, easygoing fellow

blu·ish /'blu:wɪʃ/ adj : somewhat blue ▪ a bluish green

¹blun·der /'blʌndɚ/ vb [I] 1 : to move in an awkward or confused way ▪ Another runner blundered in his path. 2 : to make a stupid or careless mistake ▪ The government blundered by not acting sooner. ▪ a blundering fool

²blunder n [C] : a bad mistake made because of stupidity or carelessness ▪ a po-

litical/tactical blunder

¹blunt /'blʌnt/ adj 1 : not sharp or pointed ▪ scissors with blunt ends ▪ He was hit over the head with a blunt instrument. 2 : saying or expressing something in a very direct way that may upset some people ▪ To be perfectly blunt, I find her annoying. — **blunt·ly** adv — **blunt·ness** n [U]

²blunt vb [T] : to make (something) less sharp ▪ a weapon blunted by use ▪ (figurative) He tried to blunt [=soften] his criticism.

¹blur /'blɚ/ n 1 [C] : something that you cannot see clearly — usually singular ▪ The letters are just a blur without my glasses. 2 [singular] : something that is difficult to remember ▪ The whole weekend is just a blur to me. — **blur·ry** /'blɚi/ adj blur·ri·er; -est

²blur vb blurred; blur·ring 1 [T] : to make (something) unclear or difficult to see or remember ▪ The tears in my eyes blurred my vision. ▪ The novel blurs the line/distinction between fact and fiction. 2 [I] : to become unclear or difficult to see or remember ▪ The two events have blurred together in my mind. — **blurred** adj : a blurred memory ▪ The symptoms include blurred vision.

blurb /'blɚb/ n [C] : a short description that praises something (such as a book) so that people will want to buy it

blurt /'blɚt/ vb [T] : to say (something) suddenly and without thinking about how people will react ▪ He accidentally blurted (out) an obscenity.

¹blush /'blʌʃ/ vb [I] : to become red in your face because you are ashamed, embarrassed, confused, etc. ▪ He blushed at the compliment.

²blush n 1 [C] : the red color that spreads over your face when you are ashamed, embarrassed, confused, etc. ▪ The comment brought a blush to her cheeks. 2 [U] US : a cream or powder that some people put on their cheeks to make their cheeks pink or reddish ▪ She put on a little lipstick and blush. — called also (chiefly Brit) blush·er /'blʌʃɚ/ — **at first blush** see ¹FIRST

¹blus·ter /'blʌstɚ/ vb 1 [T/I] : to speak in a loud and aggressive or threatening way ▪ a blustering bully 2 [I] of wind : to blow loudly and violently ▪ a strong storm with blustering winds

²bluster n [U] : words that are loud and aggressive ▪ We were all tired of his macho bluster.

blus·tery /'blʌstəri/ adj : blowing loudly and violently ▪ blustery winds

blvd. abbr boulevard

B movie n [C] : a movie that costs little money to make and that is usually not considered to be very good

BO abbr body odor ▪ She had horrible BO.

boa /'bowə/ n [C] 1 : BOA CONSTRICTOR 2 : a long scarf that is made of fur, feathers, or cloth ▪ a feather boa

boa constrictor n [C] : a large brown snake of Central and South America that crushes the animals it eats by squeezing them with its body

boar /'boɚ/ n [C] 1 : a male pig 2 : a

wild pig — called also **wild boar**

¹board /ˈboəd/ n 1 [C] : a long, thin, flat piece of wood ▪ *They nailed some boards over the broken window.* 2 [C] a : a flat piece of material (such as wood or cardboard) that is used for a special purpose ▪ *They covered the board in fabric and pinned photographs to it.* b : BULLETIN BOARD 1 — see also MESSAGE BOARD c : a large, smooth surface for writing on ▪ *The teacher wrote her name on the board.* 3 [C] a : a group of people who manage or direct a company or organization ▪ *She sits on the bank's board of directors.* ▪ *a board member* b : a group of people who have been chosen to learn information about something, to give advice, etc. ▪ *an advisory/planning/zoning board* 4 [U] : daily meals that you pay for when you are paying to stay at a hotel, school, etc. ▪ *a place that provides board and lodging* — see also ROOM AND BOARD 5 [C] : CIRCUIT BOARD — **across the board** : in a way that includes or affects everyone or everything ▪ *We will cut spending across the board.* — see also ACROSS-THE-BOARD — **go by the board** *or US* **go by the boards** : to no longer be used or considered ▪ *Many of his original theories have gone by the board in recent years.* — **on board** 1 : in or on a train, boat, etc. ▪ *The passengers are all on board.* 2 : included among the group of people who support a particular goal, project, etc. ▪ *They needed to get more senators on board for the bill to pass.* — **sweep the board** see ¹SWEEP — **take (something) on board** *Brit* : to decide to accept or deal with (something, such as a suggestion or idea) ▪ *We have taken your suggestions on board in formulating the policy.*

²board vb 1 [T/I] a : to get into or onto (an airplane, a bus, a train, etc.) ▪ *We boarded (the train) at 8:00.* b : to put or allow (someone) into or onto an airplane, a bus, a train, etc. ▪ *The flight is about to begin boarding (passengers).* 2 [T] : to cover or close (something) with pieces of wood ▪ *The workers boarded (up) the windows.* 3 a [T] : to provide (someone) with daily meals and a place to live in exchange for money ▪ *They board guests during the summer.* b [I] : to pay for daily meals and a place to live ▪ *Many students board at the college.*

board-er /ˈboədə/ n [C] 1 : a person who pays to live and have daily meals at another person's house or at a school 2 : a person who uses a snowboard ▪ *an amateur boarder*

board game n [C] : a game (such as chess) that is played by moving pieces on a special board

board-ing-house /ˈboədɪŋˌhaʊs/ n [C] : a house where people pay to live and have daily meals

boarding pass n [C] *US* : a special piece of paper that you must have in order to be allowed to get onto an airplane — called also (*Brit*) **boarding card**

boarding school n [C/U] : a school where students can live during the school term ▪ *She was sent to (a) boarding school when she was nine.*

board-room /ˈboədˌruːm/ n [C] : a room where the group of people who manage or direct a company or organization have meetings

board-walk /ˈboədˌwɑːk/ n [C] *chiefly US* : a wooden path along a beach

¹boast /ˈboʊst/ vb 1 [T/I] : to express too much pride in yourself or in something you have, have done, or are connected to in some way ▪ *He liked to boast that he was the richest man in town.* ▪ *That score is nothing to boast about.* [=you shouldn't be proud of that score] 2 [T] : to have (something that is impressive) ▪ *The museum boasts some of the rarest gems in the world.*

²boast n [C] 1 : a statement in which you express too much pride in yourself or in something you have, have done, or are connected to in some way ▪ *an idle/empty boast* 2 : something impressive that someone or something has or has done ▪ *The museum's proudest boast is its collection of rare gems.* — **boast-ful** /ˈboʊstfəl/ adj — **boast-ful-ly** /ˈboʊstfəli/ adv — **boast-ful-ness** n [U]

boat /ˈboʊt/ n [C] 1 a : a small vehicle that is used for traveling on water ▪ *a fishing boat* b : a vehicle of any size that is used for traveling on water ▪ *traveling by boat across the ocean* — compare SHIP 2 : a long and narrow container that is used for serving a sauce with a meal ▪ *a gravy/sauce boat* — **in the same boat** *informal* : in the same unpleasant or difficult situation ▪ *We're all in the same boat.* — **miss the boat** *informal* : to fail to use an opportunity ▪ *We missed the boat on the investment.* — **push the boat out** *Brit, informal* : to spend a lot of money ▪ *We're going to push the boat out and throw a big party to celebrate his recovery.* — **rock the boat** *informal* : to cause trouble by changing or trying to change a situation that other people do not want to change ▪ *Don't rock the boat.* — **boat-ful** /ˈboʊtfəl/ n [C]

boat-er /ˈboʊtə/ n [C] 1 : a person who travels in a boat 2 : a stiff straw hat that has a brim and a flat top

boat-ing /ˈboʊtɪŋ/ n [U] : the activity of going or traveling in a boat for pleasure ▪ *She enjoys hiking, boating, and fishing.* ▪ *We went boating on the lake.*

boat-load /ˈboʊtˌloʊd/ n [C] : an amount or number that will fill a boat ▪ *a boatload of passengers* ▪ *(figurative) boatloads of money* [=a lot of money]

boat people n [plural] : people who leave their country in boats in order to get away from a dangerous situation

¹bob /ˈbɑːb/ vb **bobbed**; **bob-bing** 1 [T/I] : to move up and down quickly or repeatedly ▪ *The bird bobbed (its head) up and down.* ▪ *We bobbed for apples* [=tried to catch floating or hanging apples with our teeth] *at the party.* 2 [T] a : to cut (something) shorter ▪ *They bobbed the horse's tail.* b : to cut (a person's hair) so that it is all one length and usually as long as the person's chin • *She bobbed her hair.*

²**bob** *n* [*C*] **1** : a quick up-and-down motion • *a bob of his head* **2** : a woman's or child's haircut in which the hair is all one length and usually as long as the person's chin **3** *pl* **bob** *Brit, informal* • SHILLING • *It costs five bob.* **4** : ²FLOAT 1a — **bits and bobs** see ¹BIT

bob·bin /ˈbɑːbən/ *n* [*C*] : a tube that has wide flat ends around which thread or yarn is wound

¹**bob·ble** /ˈbɑːbəl/ *vb* **bob·bled; bob·bling** [*T*] *US* : to handle (something, such as a ball) in a clumsy or awkward way • *The shortstop bobbled the ball.*

²**bobble** *n* [*C*] **1** *US* : an instance of failing to catch or handle the ball properly in baseball, football, etc. • *a bobble that cost them the game* **2** *chiefly Brit* : a small ball of fabric that is used for decoration • *a hat with a bobble* [=(*US*) *pompom*] *on top*

bob·by /ˈbɑːbi/ *n, pl* **-bies** [*C*] *Brit, old-fashioned + informal* : POLICE OFFICER

bobby pin *n* [*C*] *US* : a thin piece of bent metal that is used for holding hair in place — called also (*Brit*) *hairgrip*

bob·cat /ˈbɑːbˌkæt/ *n* [*C*] : a kind of large wild cat that has a short tail and that lives in North America

bob·sled /ˈbɑːbˌsled/ *n* [*C*] *US* : a small vehicle for two or four people that slides over snow and ice and is used for racing • *an Olympic bobsled team* — called also (*Brit*) **bob·sleigh** /ˈbɑːbˌsleɪ/ — **bob·sled·ding** /ˈbɑːbˌsledɪŋ/ *n* [*U*] • *He competed in bobsledding at the Olympics.*

bod /ˈbɑːd/ *n* [*C*] *informal* **1** *chiefly US* : BODY • *guys with hot bods* **2** *Brit* : FELLOW • *He's a bit of an odd bod.*

bode /ˈboʊd/ *vb* **bod·ed; bod·ing** [*T/I*] : to be a sign of (a future event or situation) • *a change that could bode disaster* • *This bodes well/ill.* [=this is a sign that something good/bad will happen]

bod·ice /ˈbɑːdəs/ *n* [*C*] : the upper part of a dress

¹**bodi·ly** /ˈbɑːdəli/ *adj* : relating to the body • *bodily functions/fluids* • *bodily injury/harm*

²**bodily** *adv* : by moving someone's body • *The police removed them bodily.*

body /ˈbɑːdi/ *n, pl* **bod·ies** **1** [*C*] **a** : a person's or animal's whole physical self • *the human body* • *body weight/fat* **b** : a dead person or animal • *The body* [=*corpse*] *was shipped home for burial.* **c** : the main physical part of a person or animal • *She held her arms against her body.* **2** [*C*] : the main or most important part of something • *the (main) body of the text/letter* • *There was damage to the car's body.* **3** [*C*] : an object that is separate from other objects • *heavenly/celestial bodies* [=the moon, planets, etc.] • *The X-ray showed a foreign body* [=something in a place it should not be] *in his stomach.* **4** [*C*] : a large area of water • *This lake is the largest body of water in the state.* **5** [*C*] : a group of people or things that are connected together in some way • *a body of troops* • *the student body* • *a large body of evidence/work* **6**

[*U*] *of hair* : a thick and appealing quality • *hair that lacks body* — **body and soul** : with all of your energy and enthusiasm • *He devoted himself body and soul to the cause.* — **over my dead body** — used to say that you are very determined to not let something happen • *"We're getting married." "Over my dead body!"*

body·build·ing /ˈbɑːdiˌbɪldɪŋ/ *n* [*U*] : the activity of doing exercises to make the muscles of your body larger and stronger • *competitive bodybuilding* • *a bodybuilding competition* — **body·build·er** /ˈbɑːdiˌbɪldər/ *n* [*C*]

body·guard /ˈbɑːdiˌgɑːrd/ *n* [*C/U*] : a person or group of people whose job is to protect someone • *They were surrounded by bodyguards.*

body language *n* [*U*] : movements or positions of the body that express thoughts or feelings • *I saw from his body language that he was nervous.*

body odor *n* [*U*] : an unpleasant smell from the body of a person who has been sweating or is not clean — abbr. *BO*

body shop *n* [*C*] : a place where the bodies of vehicles are repaired • *My car is at the body shop.*

¹**bog** /ˈbɑːg/ *n* [*C/U*] : an area of soft, wet land : MARSH • *(a) peat bog* — **bog·gy** /ˈbɑːgi/ *adj* **bog·gi·er; -est** • *boggy soil*

²**bog** *vb* **bogged; bog·ging** — **bog down** [*phrasal vb*] **1** *bog (something) down or bog down (something)* : to cause (something) to sink in wet ground • *The car got bogged down in the mud.* • (*figurative*) *Don't get bogged down* [=slowed down] *by the details.* **2** : to become stuck in wet ground • *The car bogged down in the mud.* • (*figurative*) *The story bogs down* [=slows down] *in the middle.*

¹**bo·gey** *also* **bo·gie** *or* **bo·gy** /ˈboʊgi/ *n, pl* **-geys** *also* **-gies** **1** [*C*] *golf* : a score of one stroke over par on a hole • *He made/scored (a) bogey on the second hole.* **2** [*C*] : something that causes fear or worry • *the economic bogey of recession* **3** [*C*] *Brit, informal* : BOOGER

²**bogey** *vb* **-geyed; -gey·ing** [*T*] *golf* : to score a bogey on (a hole) • *She bogeyed the second hole.*

bo·gey·man /ˈbʊgiˌmæn/ *n, pl* **-men** /-ˌmɛn/ [*C*] **1** : an imaginary monster that is used to frighten children • *The bogeyman will get you!* **2** : a person who is hated or feared by a group of people • *a politician who is the bogeyman of conservatives*

bog·gle /ˈbɑːgəl/ *vb* **bog·gled; bog·gling** [*T/I*] *informal* : to cause the mind to be amazed or overwhelmed • *It boggles the/my mind to think of it.* • *The/my mind boggles at the thought of it.* — see also MIND-BOGGLING

bog-standard *adj, Brit, informal* : having no special or interesting qualities • *a bog-standard speech/school*

bo·gus /ˈboʊgəs/ *adj, informal* : fake or false • *bogus claims/experiments*

bo·he·mi·an /boʊˈhiːmijən/ *n* [*C*] : a person (such as an artist or writer) who does not follow society's accepted rules of behavior — **bohemian** *adj* ▪ *a bohemian way of life*

¹**boil** /ˈbojəl/ *vb* **1 a** [*I*] : to become so hot that bubbles form in a liquid and rise to the top ▪ *a pot of boiling water* **b** [*T*] : to heat (a liquid or a container with liquid in it) so that bubbles form and rise to the top ▪ *Boil (up) some water.* **2** [*T/I*] : to cook (something) in water that is boiling ▪ *Boil the eggs/vegetables.* ▪ *The pasta is boiling.* **3** [*I*] : to feel a strong emotion (such as anger) ▪ *The crowd boiled [=seethed] with anger.* — **boil down** [*phrasal vb*] **1 a** : to become reduced in amount by boiling ▪ *Let the sauce boil down.* **b boil (something) down or boil down (something)** : to reduce the amount of (a liquid) by boiling it ▪ *Boil down the sauce.* **2 boil (something) down or boil down (something)** : to make (something) shorter or simpler by removing some parts ▪ *He boiled down the report to a brief summary.* **3 boil down to** : to have (something) as the main or basic part ▪ *His speech boiled down to a plea for more money.* — **boil over** [*phrasal vb*] **1** : to flow over the side of a container while boiling ▪ *The pot (of water) is boiling over.* **2 a** : to lose control because of anger ▪ *He's so mad that he's ready to boil over.* **b** : to change into something more violent ▪ *Their disagreement finally boiled over into a fight.* — **boil up** [*phrasal vb*] : to grow toward a dangerous level ▪ *He could feel the anger boiling up inside him.* — **make someone's blood boil** see BLOOD

²**boil** *n* **1** [*singular*] *of a liquid* : the act or state of boiling ▪ *(US) Bring the water to a boil.* = *(chiefly Brit) Bring the water to the boil.* [=boil the water] **2** [*C*] : a painful, swollen area under the skin that is caused by infection

boil·er /ˈbojlɚ/ *n* [*C*] **1** : a large container in which water is heated to produce steam in an engine, a furnace, etc. **2** *chiefly Brit* : FURNACE b

boil·er·plate /ˈbojlɚˌpleɪt/ *n* [*U*] *US* : phrases or sentences that are a standard way of saying something and are often used ▪ *a boilerplate speech that she has given many times*

boil·ing /ˈbojlɪŋ/ *adj* : very hot ▪ *a boiling summer day* — **boiling** *adv* ▪ *a boiling hot sun* ▪ *He was boiling mad.* [=very angry]

boiling point *n* [*C/U*] : the temperature at which a liquid begins to boil ▪ *the boiling point of water* ▪ *(US, figurative) Tensions were at a/the boiling point.* [=the situation was very tense and people were angry] ▪ *(Brit, figurative) Tempers are reaching boiling point.*

bois·ter·ous /ˈbojstrəs/ *adj* : very noisy and active in a lively way ▪ *a boisterous party/crowd* — **bois·ter·ous·ly** *adv*

¹**bold** /ˈbould/ *adj* **1 a** : not afraid of danger or difficult situations ▪ *a bold adventurer* **b** : showing or needing confidence or lack of fear ▪ *a bold plan/strategy* **2** : very confident in a way that may seem rude or foolish ▪ *I'd like to offer a few criticisms, if I may be so bold.* ▪ *He was (as) bold as brass.* [=very bold] **3** : very no-

ticeable or easily seen ▪ *a dress with bold stripes/colors* **4** : having thick, dark lines ▪ *bold [=bold-faced] type/lettering* — **bold·ly** *adv* — **bold·ness** *n* [*U*]

²**bold** *n* [*U*] : BOLDFACE

bold·face /ˈbouldˌfeɪs/ *n* [*U*] : letters that are printed in thick, dark lines ▪ *The headline was printed in boldface.* — **boldfaced** /ˈbouldˌfeɪst/ *adj, chiefly US* ▪ *a boldfaced headline*

bol·lard /ˈbɑːlɚd/ *n* [*C*] *Brit* : a post that prevents vehicles from going into an area where people can wait in the middle of a road

bol·locks /ˈbɑːləks/ *n, Brit, informal + impolite* **1** [*U*] : NONSENSE ▪ *It's all bollocks.* **2** [*plural*] : TESTICLES ▪ *She kicked him in the bollocks.*

bo·lo·gna /bəˈlouni/ *n* [*U*] : a wide cooked sausage that is cut into thin pieces and eaten in sandwiches ▪ *a bologna sandwich*

Bol·she·vik /ˈboulʃəˌvɪk, ˈbɑːlʃəˌvɪk/ *n* [*C*] : a member of the political party that started to rule Russia in 1917 or a member of a similar political party — **Bolshevik** *adj* ▪ *the Bolshevik revolution/state/leader*

¹**bol·ster** /ˈboulstɚ/ *vb* [*T*] : to make (something) stronger or better ▪ *trying to bolster his image/career/confidence*

²**bolster** *n* [*C*] : a long pillow or cushion

¹**bolt** /ˈboult/ *n* [*C*] **1** : a flash of lightning ▪ *a bolt of lightning = a lightning bolt* ▪ *(figurative) The news came as/like a bolt from the blue.* [=it was surprising and unexpected] **2** : a sliding bar that is used to lock a door or window and that is sometimes moved by a key — see also DEAD BOLT **3** : a long, round piece of metal that has a wider part at one end and is like a screw at the other end ▪ *(figurative) still learning the nuts and bolts* [=the basic parts or details] *of the business* **4** : a large roll of cloth

²**bolt** *vb* **1** [*I*] **a** : to move or go very suddenly and quickly from or to a particular place, position, or condition ▪ *He bolted up from the chair.* ▪ *She bolted awake.* ▪ *Reporters bolted for the door.* **b** : to run away suddenly and quickly ▪ *The horse bolted.* **2** [*T/I*] *US* : to suddenly leave a political party, team, etc. ▪ *Some members threatened to bolt (from) the party.* **3 a** [*T/I*] : to lock (something) with a bolt ▪ *She closed and bolted the door.* ▪ *The door bolts on the inside.* **b** [*T*] : to attach (something) with a bolt ▪ *The bench was bolted to the floor.* **4** [*T*] : to eat (food) quickly ▪ *Don't bolt your food.*

³**bolt** *adv* : with the back in a very straight position ▪ *She sat bolt upright.*

¹**bomb** /ˈbɑːm/ *n* **1 a** [*C*] : a device that is designed to explode in order to injure or kill people or to damage or destroy property ▪ *A bomb went off.* ▪ *a suicide bomb* [=a bomb carried by someone who plans to be killed by it when it explodes] ▪ *a bomb threat* [=a message saying that a bomb is located in a particular place] ▪ *a bomb squad* [=a group of people who try to keep bombs from exploding] **b the bomb** : nuclear weapons ▪ *countries that have the bomb* **2** [*C*] *US, informal*

: something that is a complete failure ▪ *The movie was a bomb.* **3 the bomb** *US slang* : something or someone that is very good ▪ *Their new album is the bomb.* **4** [*C*] *sports* : a long pass, shot, home run, etc. ▪ *The quarterback threw a bomb to the wide receiver.* ▪ *shooting three-point bombs from center court* **5** [*singular*] *Brit, informal* : a large amount of money ▪ *She paid a bomb for the car.* — **drop a/the bomb** *informal* : to do or say something that is very shocking and unexpected ▪ *She dropped a bomb with her resignation.*

²**bomb** *vb* **1** [*T*] : to attack (a place or people) with a bomb or many bombs ▪ *The city was heavily bombed.* **2 a** [*I*] *informal* : to fail completely ▪ *The movie bombed.* **b** [*T*] *US slang* : to fail (a test) ▪ *I bombed my exam.* **3** [*I*] *informal* : to move or go very quickly ▪ *A car was bombing down the highway.* — **bombing** /ˈbɑːmɪŋ/ *n* [*C/U*] ▪ *The city was destroyed by bombing(s) during the war.*

bom·bard /bɑmˈbɑɚd/ *vb* [*T*] **1** : to attack (a place) with bombs, large guns, etc. ▪ *The navy bombarded the shore.* **2** : to hit or attack (something or someone) constantly or repeatedly ▪ *Scientists bombarded the sample with X-rays.* ▪ *(figurative) He is being bombarded by offers.* — **bom·bard·ment** /bɑmˈbɑɚdmənt/ *n* [*C/U*]

bom·bar·dier /ˌbɑːmbɚˈdiɚ/ *n* [*C*] *chiefly US* : the person in a military aircraft who controls when the bombs are dropped

bom·bast /ˈbɑːmˌbæst/ *n* [*U*] *formal* : speech or writing that is meant to sound impressive but is not sincere or meaningful ▪ *political bombast* — **bom·bas·tic** /bɑmˈbæstɪk/ *adj* ▪ *a bombastic speech/speaker* — **bom·bas·ti·cal·ly** /bɑmˈbæstɪkli/ *adv*

bombed /ˈbɑːmd/ *adj, not before a noun, US, informal* : very drunk or intoxicated ▪ *I got bombed last night.*

bomb·er /ˈbɑːmɚ/ *n* [*C*] **1** : a military aircraft designed for dropping bombs **2** : a person who bombs a place ▪ *a suicide bomber* [=someone who takes a bomb to a place and expects to be killed by it when it explodes]

bomb·shell /ˈbɑːmˌʃɛl/ *n* [*C*] **1** : something that is very surprising or shocking ▪ *The book/news was a political bombshell.* ▪ *She dropped a bombshell* [=she surprised everyone] *when she said she was quitting.* **2** *informal* : a very attractive woman ▪ *a blonde bombshell who looks like a movie star*

bo·na fide /ˈboʊnəˌfaɪd, ˌboʊnəˈfaɪdi/ *adj* **1** : real or genuine ▪ *a bona fide celebrity/hit* **2** *law* : made or done in an honest and sincere way ▪ *a bona fide claim/claim*

bo·nan·za /bəˈnænzə/ *n* [*C*] **1** : something that produces very good results ▪ *The movie turned out to be a box-office bonanza.* [=the movie made a great deal of money] **2** : a large amount of something valuable ▪ *Her research resulted in a bonanza of information.*

¹**bond** /ˈbɑːnd/ *n* **1** [*C*] : an idea, interest, experience, feeling, etc., that is shared between people or groups and forms a connection between them ▪ *the bonds of friendship* ▪ *Recent events strengthened the bonds between our countries.* ▪ *We share a common bond because we both grew up in the Midwest.* **2** [*C*] *finance* : an official document in which a government or company promises to pay back money that it has borrowed and to pay interest for the borrowed money ▪ *stocks and bonds* **3** [*C*] *formal* : a chain or rope that is used to prevent someone from moving or acting freely ▪ *The prisoner broke free from his bonds.* ▪ *(figurative) the bonds of oppression* **4** [*C*] : the condition of being held together or joined ▪ *The glue provides a good/strong bond.* **5** [*C*] *chemistry* : a force that holds together the atoms in a molecule ▪ *chemical bonds* **6** [*U*] *chiefly US, law* : the amount of money that someone promises to pay if a prisoner who is allowed to leave jail does not return later for a trial or to prison ▪ *He was released on $10,000 bond.* [=he was released from jail because someone promised to pay $10,000 if he does not appear for the trial]

²**bond** *vb* **1** [*T/I*] : to join (things) together ▪ *bond sheets of plastic (together)* **2** [*I*] : to form a close relationship with someone ▪ *We were strangers at first, but we bonded quickly.* — **bond·ing** /ˈbɑːndɪŋ/ *n* [*U*] ▪ *mother-child bonding* ▪ *He and his brother did some male bonding last weekend.*

bond·age /ˈbɑːndɪdʒ/ *n* [*U*] **1** *formal + literary* : SLAVERY ▪ *He delivered them from bondage.* [=he freed them] ▪ *a population held/kept in bondage* **2** : sexual activity that involves tying a person up for pleasure

¹**bone** /ˈboʊn/ *n* **1** [*C*] : any one of the hard pieces that form the frame (called a skeleton) inside a person's or animal's body ▪ *He broke a bone in his left arm.* ▪ *(figurative) He doesn't have a selfish/jealous bone in his body.* [=he is not selfish/ jealous at all] ▪ *(figurative) My aching bones!* [=my body is tired and sore] ▪ *(figurative) I'll be glad to have a chance to rest my weary bones.* ▪ *(figurative) He knew/felt in his bones* [=had a strong feeling] *that he was wrong.* **2** [*U*] : the hard material that bones are made of ▪ *flesh and bone* — **bone to pick** *informal* : something to argue or complain about with someone ▪ *I have a bone to pick with you!* — **bred in the bone** see ¹**BREED** — **make no bones about** : to be very sure about (something) ▪ *Make no bones about it—we will win.* — **skin and bones** see ¹**SKIN** — **throw (someone) a bone** *informal* : to offer (someone) something that is not very important or valuable especially to stop complaints ▪ *He made us work overtime but threw us a bone by buying lunch.* — **to the bone 1** : very much ▪ *We were frozen to the bone.* [=we were very cold] ▪ *It chilled me to the bone.* [=made me feel very fearful] **2** : as much as possible ▪ *The company has cut costs to the bone.* — **work your fingers to the bone** see ¹**FINGER** — **bone·less** /ˈboʊnləs/ *adj*

²**bone** *vb* **boned; bon·ing** [*T*] : to remove

the bones from (a fish or meat) ▪ *bone a fish* — **bone up** [*phrasal vb*] *informal* **1** : to try to learn a lot of information quickly for a test, exam, etc. ▪ *She boned up for the exam.* **2** : to study something again ▪ *I have to bone up on my French.*

³**bone** *adv, always before an adjective* : extremely or very ▪ *bone tired/lazy/idle* ▪ *a bone-dry desert climate*

boned /'boʊnd/ *adj* **1** : having bones of a specified type ▪ *She is small-boned.* **2** : with the bones removed ▪ *boned chicken/fish*

bone·head /'boʊnˌhɛd/ *n* [*C*] *informal* : a stupid or foolish person ▪ *Don't be a bonehead.* — **bone·head·ed** /'boʊnˌhɛdəd/ *adj*

bone marrow *n* [*U*] : a soft substance that fills the bones of people and animals — called also **marrow**

bon·er /'boʊnə/ *n* [*C*] *US, informal* **1** : a foolish or careless mistake ▪ *They pulled a boner.* [=made a stupid mistake] **2** *impolite* : an erection of the penis

bon·fire /'bɑːnˌfajə/ *n* [*C*] : a large outdoor fire

bong /'bɑːŋ/ *n* [*C*] : a deep loud sound that is made by a large bell

bon·go /'bɑːŋgoʊ/ *n, pl* **-gos** [*C*] : one of a pair of small drums that are joined together and played with the hands

bonk /'bɑːŋk/ *vb* [*T*] *informal* **1** : to hit (someone or something) ▪ *He bonked him on the head.* **2** *Brit* : to have sexual intercourse with (someone)

bonk·ers /'bɑːŋkəz/ *adj, not before a noun, informal* : CRAZY ▪ *You are driving me bonkers!* ▪ *They went bonkers when their team won.*

bon·net /'bɑːnət/ *n* [*C*] **1** : a hat that ties under the chin ▪ *a baby bonnet* **2** *Brit* : HOOD 2b ▪ *He lifted the car's bonnet.* — **have a bee in your bonnet** See BEE

bon·ny *also* **bon·nie** /'bɑːni/ *adj* **bon·ni·er; -est** *chiefly Scotland* : very pretty or attractive ▪ *a bonny lass/baby*

bo·nus /'boʊnəs/ *n* [*C*] **1** : something good that is more than what was expected or required ▪ *The product has the added bonus of providing extra vitamins.* **2** : an extra amount of money that is given to an employee ▪ *We were given a bonus for finishing on schedule.*

bon voy·age /ˌbɑːnvɔɪˈɑːʒ/ *n* [*U*] : ²GOODBYE 1 — usually used to wish someone a good journey ▪ *Bon voyage! Have a safe trip.*

bony /'boʊni/ *adj* **bon·i·er; -est** **1** : resembling bone ▪ *a bony substance* **2** : full of bones ▪ *a bony piece of fish* **3** : having large or noticeable bones ▪ *bony fingers/knees* **4** : very thin ▪ *She's bony.*

¹**boo** /'buː/ *n, pl* **boos** [*C*] : a sound that people make to show they do not like or approve of someone or something ▪ *The announcement was greeted by/with boos.* — **boo** *vb* **booed; boo·ing** [*T/I*] ▪ *People booed when the announcement was made.* ▪ *They booed her off the stage.*

²**boo** *interj* **1** — used to show dislike or disapproval of someone or something ▪ *Boo! Get off the stage!* ❖ When people say "Boo!" with this meaning, they say it very slowly. **2** — used when a person

frightens someone ▪ *She jumped out from behind the door and shouted "Boo!"* ❖ When people say "Boo!" with this meaning, they say it very quickly.

¹**boob** /'buːb/ *n* [*C*] *informal* **1** *US* : a stupid or foolish person ▪ *an incompetent boob* **2** *sometimes offensive* : a woman's breast ▪ *a boob job* [=a surgical operation to increase the size of a woman's breasts]

²**boob** *vb* [*I*] *Brit, informal* : to make a foolish or careless mistake : GOOF

boo-boo /'buːˌbuː/ *n* [*C*] *informal* **1** : a small injury (such as a bruise or scratch) — used especially by children or when speaking to children ▪ *Did you get a boo-boo?* **2** : a foolish or careless mistake ▪ *a major diplomatic boo-boo*

boob tube *n* — **the boob tube** *US, informal + often disapproving* : TELEVISION ▪ *watching the boob tube*

booby prize [*C*] *informal* : a prize that is given as a joke to the person who finishes last in a competition ▪ *(figurative) The company gets the booby prize for worst customer service.*

booby trap *n* [*C*] : a hidden bomb that explodes when the object connected to it is touched, moved, etc. — **boo·by–trap** *vb* **-trapped; -trap·ping** [*T*] ▪ *Someone booby-trapped the car.* ▪ *The house is booby-trapped.*

boog·er /'bu·gə/ *n* [*C*] *US, informal* : a piece of mucus from the nose — used especially by children

boo·gey·man /'bugiˌmæn/ *n, pl* **-men** /-ˌmɛn/ [*C*] *US* : BOGEYMAN 1, 2

boo·gie /'bugi, *Brit* 'buːgi/ *vb* **-gied; -gie·ing** [*I*] *informal* : to dance especially to rock music ▪ *Everyone was boogying (down).*

¹**book** /'buk/ *n* **1** [*C*] : a set of printed sheets of paper that are held together inside a cover : a long written work ▪ *a book about plumbing* ▪ *a hardcover/paperback book* **2** [*C*] : a set of sheets of paper that are inside a cover and that you can write information on ▪ *an appointment/address book* **3** [*C*] : a major section of a long written work (such as the Bible) ▪ *the Book of Job* **4** [*C*] : a set of things held together inside a cover like the pages of a book ▪ *a book of stamps/matches* **5** [*plural*] : the financial records of a business ▪ *The company's books show a profit.* **6** **the book** *informal* : PHONE BOOK ▪ *I'm in the book.* [=my telephone number is listed in the telephone book] — **a closed book** : a person or thing that is difficult to understand — **an open book** : a person or thing that is easy to learn about and understand ▪ *My life is an open book.* [=I do not hide anything about my life] — **bring (someone) to book** *chiefly Brit, formal* : to require (someone) to explain and accept punishment or criticism for bad or wrong behavior ▪ *The criminals must be brought to book.* — **by the book** : by following the rules very strictly ▪ *She does everything by the book.* — **every trick in the book** see ¹TRICK — **hit the books** *informal* : to study or begin studying very intensely ▪ *I've got to hit the books this weekend.* — **in my book** *infor-*

mal : in my opinion • *He isn't that smart, at least not in my book.* — **in someone's good/bad books** *chiefly Brit, informal* : in a state in which you are liked/disliked by someone • *He remains in her bad/good books.* [=she is still displeased/pleased with him] — **one for the books** : a very unusual, important, or surprising situation, statement, event, etc. • *His trial was one for the books.* — **on the books** : part of the set of official laws • *a law on the books* — **read someone like a book** see ¹READ — **throw the book at** *informal* : to punish (someone) as severely as possible • *The judge threw the book at him.* — **write the book on** see WRITE

²**book** *vb* **1** [T/I] : to make arrangements so that you will be able to use or have a (a room, table, seat, etc.) at a later time • *We booked* [=reserved] *a hotel room.* ✧ When a hotel, restaurant, etc., is *booked (up), booked solid,* or *fully booked,* there are no more rooms, tables, etc., available. • *The flight was fully booked.* **2** [T] : to make arrangements for (someone) to do, use, or have something at a later time • *She booked me on a flight from Oslo to Paris.* **3** [T] : to schedule a performance or appearance by (someone, such as a musician) • *book a singer/band* **4** [T] *law* : to write down in an official police record the name of (a person who is being charged with a crime) • *She was booked on suspicion of murder.* **5** [T] *Brit, of a soccer referee* : to write down in an official book the name of (a player who has broken the rules in a game) • *He was booked for a late tackle.* — **book in/into** [*phrasal vb*] *Brit* : to arrive at and be given a room in a hotel, an inn, etc. • *We booked in* [=checked in] *shortly after noon.* — **book·able** /ˈbʊkəbət/ *adj, chiefly Brit* • *a bookable offense* — **booking** /ˈbʊkɪŋ/ *n* [C/U] • *vacation/hotel bookings*

book·case /ˈbʊkˌkeɪs/ *n* [C] : a piece of furniture with shelves to hold books

book·end /ˈbʊkˌɛnd/ *n* [C] : something placed at the end of a row of books to hold them up • *a pair of bookends*

book·ie /ˈbʊki/ *n* [C] *informal* : BOOK-MAKER

booking office *n* [C] *Brit* : a place in a train station, bus station, etc., where people can buy tickets

book·ish /ˈbʊkɪʃ/ *adj, sometimes disapproving* : more interested in reading books and studying than doing more physical activities (such as sports) • *a bookish fellow*

book·keep·er /ˈbʊkˌkiːpɚ/ *n* [C] : a person whose job is to keep the financial records for a business — **book·keep·ing** /ˈbʊkˌkiːpɪŋ/ *n* [U]

book·let /ˈbʊklət/ *n* [C] : a book with only a few pages that contains information on one subject

book·mak·er /ˈbʊkˌmeɪkɚ/ *n* [C] : a person who decides how likely it is that an event will occur and receives and pays off bets about it — called also (*informal*) *bookie* — **book·mak·ing** /ˈbʊkˌmeɪkɪŋ/ *n* [U]

¹**book·mark** /ˈbʊkˌmɑɚk/ *n* [C] **1** : something (such as a piece of paper) that is put in a book to show the place where you stopped reading **2** *computers* : something (such as a menu entry or icon) that allows you to go quickly and directly to something (such as an Internet site) that you have seen before

²**bookmark** *vb* [T] *computers* : to create a computer bookmark for (something, such as an Internet site) • *I bookmarked the site.*

book·mo·bile /ˈbʊkmoʊˌbiːl/ *n* [C] *US* : a large vehicle that contains many library books and that goes to different places so that people can borrow the books — called also (*Brit*) *mobile library*

book·shelf /ˈbʊkˌʃɛlf/ *n, pl* **-shelves** [C] : a shelf that is used for books

book·shop /ˈbʊkˌʃɑːp/ *n* [C] : BOOK-STORE

book·store /ˈbʊkˌstoɚ/ *n* [C] *chiefly US* : a store that sells books

book·worm /ˈbʊkˌwɚm/ *n* [C] : a person who likes to read books and who spends a lot of time reading and studying • *She was a bookworm as a kid.*

¹**boom** /ˈbuːm/ *vb* **1 a** [I] : to make a deep and loud sound • *His voice boomed across the field.* • *his booming voice* **b** [T] : to say (something) in a deep and loud voice • *"What's going on here?" he boomed.* **2** [I] *of a business or industry* : to grow or expand suddenly • *New home construction has boomed in the past year.* • *Business is booming.*

²**boom** *n* [C] **1** : a deep and loud sound or cry • *the boom of a gun* — often used as an interjection to indicate that something has happened suddenly • *She was there and then—boom!—she was gone.* **2** : a rapid increase in growth or economic success • *the population boom* • *a boom in tourism = a tourism boom* — see also BABY BOOM

boom box *n* [C] : a large portable radio and often tape deck or CD player with two attached speakers

boom·er /ˈbuːmɚ/ *n* [C] : a person born during a baby boom • *a show popular among boomers* [=baby boomers]

¹**boo·mer·ang** /ˈbuːməˌræŋ/ *n* [C] : a curved, flat, wooden tool that can be thrown in such a way that it returns to the thrower

²**boomerang** *vb* [I] : to have an effect that is the opposite of the desired or expected effect • BACKFIRE • *His attempt to discredit his opponent boomeranged.*

boom·town /ˈbuːmˌtaʊn/ *n* [C] : a town that experiences a sudden growth in business and population • *a former boomtown*

boon /ˈbuːn/ *n* [C] : something pleasant or helpful • *The new tax cut is a boon for/ to married couples.*

boon·docks /ˈbuːnˌdɑːks/ *n* — **the boondocks** *US, informal* : an area that is not close to any towns or cities • *She grew up in the boondocks.*

boon·dog·gle /ˈbuːnˌdɑːgəl/ *n* [C] *US* : an expensive and wasteful project usually paid for with public money

boon·ies /ˈbuːniz/ *n* — **the boonies** *US,*

informal : BOONDOCKS ▪ *We live (out) in the boonies.*

boor /ˈbuɚ/ n [C] : a rude and rough person ▪ *He's such a boor.* — **boor·ish** /ˈburɪʃ/ adj ▪ *boorish behavior* — **boor·ish·ly** adv

¹**boost** /ˈbuːst/ vb [T] **1** : to increase the force, power, or amount of (something) ▪ *They have boosted [=increased] production.* ▪ *ways to boost [=strengthen] your immune system* **2** : to push or shove (something or someone) up from below ▪ *I boosted the boy onto my shoulders.*

²**boost** n [C] **1** : an increase in amount ▪ *a boost in production/sales* **2** : something that provides help or encouragement ▪ *The product has been a boost to the entire industry.* **3** : a push upward ▪ *He gave her a boost up onto the horse.*

boost·er /ˈbuːstɚ/ n [C] **1 a** : an action or substance that makes something stronger or more effective ▪ *a metabolism booster* **b** : something that helps or encourages someone or something ▪ *a mood/confidence booster* **c** : BOOSTER SHOT **2** US : someone who supports an idea or organization ▪ *the football team's boosters* **3** : part of a rocket that provides force for the launch and the first part of the flight ▪ *rocket boosters*

booster seat n [C] : a high seat that raises a child to a higher position at a table, in a car, etc. — called also *booster chair*, (Brit) *booster cushion*

booster shot n [C] chiefly US : an extra amount of a vaccine that is injected into a person or animal to help protect against a particular disease ▪ *a tetanus booster shot*

¹**boot** /ˈbuːt/ n **1** [C] : a covering usually of leather or rubber for the entire foot and the lower part of the leg ▪ *a pair of hiking boots* **2** [C] : a forceful kick with the foot ▪ *She gave the ball a boot.* **3** *the boot informal* : a sudden dismissal from a job ▪ *He got the boot.* [=got fired] ▪ *They gave her the boot.* [=they fired her] **4** [C] Brit : the trunk of a car — *to boot* : BESIDES, ALSO ▪ *He's smart, funny, and handsome to boot.* — *too big for your boots* see ¹BIG — *to put the boot in* Brit, informal **1** : to treat someone in a cruel or critical way **2** : to kick someone again and again

²**boot** vb **1** [T] : to kick (something) forcefully ▪ *She booted the ball.* **2** [T] informal **a** : to force (someone) to leave a place or situation ▪ *Voters booted him from office.* [=he was not reelected] ▪ *She was booted from the game.* ▪ *He got booted out.* **b** : to dismiss (someone) suddenly from a job ▪ *She got booted [=fired] (from her job).* **3** [T/I] : to start a computer ▪ *Did you boot (your computer) yet?* ▪ *She booted (up).*

boot camp n [C/U] US **1** : a camp where people who have recently joined the U.S. Army, Navy, or Marine Corps receive their basic training **2** : a short but very difficult training program ▪ *business boot camp*

bootee chiefly Brit spelling of BOOTIE

booth /ˈbuːθ, Brit ˈbuːð/ n, pl **booths** /ˈbuːðz/ [C] **1** : a partially enclosed area or a small and usually temporary building where things are sold or displayed or services are provided ▪ *a booth at the county fair* ▪ *visit the information booth* [=a booth where general information about a place or event is provided] ▪ *Traffic slowed as we approached the toll booth.* [=a booth at which drivers pay a fee for using a particular road or bridge] ▪ *the broadcast booth* [=a booth from which a radio broadcast is made] **2** : a small area that is enclosed in order to provide privacy for one person ▪ *a voting booth* **3** chiefly US : a table in a restaurant between benches with high backs

boo·tie or chiefly Brit **boo·tee** /ˈbuːti/ n [C] **1** : a short and thick sock for a baby **2** : a sock, slipper, or boot that covers the foot and ankle

¹**boot·leg** /ˈbuːtˌlɛg/ vb **-legged; -leg·ging** [T] **1** : to illegally record or copy (a video, CD, concert, etc.) ▪ *bootleg a DVD* **2** : to make or sell (alcoholic liquor) illegally ▪ *bootlegging booze* — **boot·leg·ger** n [C]

²**bootleg** n **1** [C] : an illegal copy or recording of a video, CD, concert, etc. ▪ *a bootleg album/DVD/copy* **2** [U] : alcohol that is made or sold illegally ▪ *bootleg whiskey/bourbon*

boot·straps /ˈbuːtˌstræps/ n — *by your own bootstraps* : without help from other people ▪ *She has pulled herself up by her own bootstraps.*

boo·ty /ˈbuːti/ n [U] **1** : money or goods stolen or taken in war **2** : a valuable gain or prize ▪ *His booty from the sale included several antiques.*

¹**booze** /ˈbuːz/ n [U] informal : alcoholic drinks ▪ *We bought some booze for the party.*

²**booze** vb **boozed; booz·ing** [T/I] informal : to drink a lot of alcohol ▪ *He was out boozing with his friends.* ▪ *They boozed it up.* [=got drunk]

booz·er /ˈbuːzɚ/ n [C] informal **1** : a person who drinks a lot of alcohol ▪ *He's a real boozer.* **2** Brit : PUB ▪ *go to the boozer for a beer*

bop /ˈbɑːp/ vb **bopped; bop·ping** **1** [T] : to hit (someone or something) especially in a playful way ▪ *She bopped him on the head.* **2** [I] informal a US : to walk or move like a person who is dancing to lively music ▪ *He was bopping down the street.* **b** Brit : to dance to popular music ▪ *We're going bopping tonight.* — **bop** n [C] ▪ *She gave him a bop on the head.*

bor·del·lo /boɚˈdɛloʊ/ n, pl **-los** [C] somewhat literary : BROTHEL

¹**bor·der** /ˈboɚdɚ/ n [C] **1 a** : a line separating one country or state from another ▪ *the border between Poland and Slovenia* ▪ *a border dispute* ▪ *border guards* ▪ (US) *I've never been south of the border.* [=the U.S. border with Mexico] **b** : a boundary between places ▪ *the border of the Sahara/park* **2** : a decorative design along the edge of something ▪ *The quilt is plain except for a colorful border.* ▪ *the photograph's white border*

²**border** vb [T] **1** : to be next to or share a border with (a country, state, or area) ▪

Slovenia borders Poland. ▪ *Their house borders the park.* **2** : to form a border at the edge of (something) ▪ *streets (that are) bordered by oak trees* — **border on** [*phrasal vb*] **1** : to lie on the border of (something) ▪ *The area she comes from borders on the Atacama Desert.* **2** : to come very close to being (something) ▪ *The play's dialogue borders on the ridiculous.*

bor·der·land /'boɚdɚˌlænd/ *n* [C] : the land on either side of a border between countries ▪ *the Slovenian-Polish borderlands*

¹bor·der·line /'boɚdɚˌlaɪn/ *adj* **1** : having some but not all characteristics of something ▪ *In borderline cases, the best course of action is difficult to determine.* **2** : not quite as severe as what is usual or expected ▪ *a borderline diabetic* ▪ *borderline alcoholics*

²borderline *n* [C] : the point at which one thing changes to another thing : the point *between* two different things ▪ *the borderline between fact and fiction*

¹bore /'boɚ/ *vb* **bored; bor·ing** [*T*] : to make (someone) tired and annoyed by being uninteresting or too much the same ▪ *He was bored by the lecture. = The lecture bored him.* ▪ *She got bored and left.* ▪ *I was bored stiff. = I was bored to death/tears.* [=I was very bored] — compare ³BORE — **bored** *adj* ▪ *bored teenagers* ▪ *I'm bored.* — **boring** *adj* ▪ *This lecture is boring.* ▪ *a boring teacher/subject/lesson*

²bore *n* [C] : a person or thing that makes people feel tired and annoyed ▪ *They're a bunch of bores!* — compare ⁴BORE

³bore *vb* **bored; bor·ing** [*T/I*] : to make (a hole, tunnel, etc.) in something with a tool or by digging ▪ *bore a hole through rock* ▪ *Insects have bored into the tree.* ▪ *(figurative) The teacher's eyes bored into me.* [=the teacher stared at me] ▪ *(figurative) We bored through the crowd.* [=we moved forward through the crowd] — compare ¹BORE

⁴bore *n* [C] **1** : a hole made by boring — called also **borehole** **2** : the space inside a gun barrel that is shaped like a tube — compare ²BORE

⁵bore *past tense of* ²BEAR

bore·dom /'boɚdəm/ *n* [U] : the state of being bored ▪ *overwhelmed by boredom*

bore·hole /'boɚˌhoʊl/ *n* [C] : ⁴BORE 1; *especially* : a hole dug into the earth in order to find water or oil

bor·er /'boɚɚ/ *n* [C] : an insect that digs holes in the woody parts of plants

born /'boɚn/ *adj* **1** *not before a noun* : brought into life by the process of birth ▪ *She was born in a hospital.* ▪ *The baby was born on July 31st.* **2** : having certain qualities or characteristics from the time of birth ▪ *born blind/deaf* ▪ *The author Mark Twain was born Samuel Clemens.* [=was named Samuel Clemens at birth] ▪ *She's a born teacher. = She was born to teach. = She was born to be a teacher.* [=she has natural talents or qualities that make her a good teacher] **3** *not before a noun* — used to describe the place where someone was born ▪ *He's American born.* [=he was born in America] ▪ *He was born*

and bred in Mexico. [=his birth and childhood took place in Mexico] **4** *not before a noun* — used to describe the social conditions or situations that exist when people are born ▪ *They were born in/into slavery.* **5** *not before a noun* : brought into existence ▪ *a mentality born in the age of computers* ▪ *Their relationship was born of necessity.* [=established because it was necessary in some way] ▪ *The recent unrest in the city is born out of* [=has occurred because of] *poverty.* — **born too late** ◇ Someone who was *born too late* seems to be better suited for life in an earlier time period. — **born with a silver spoon in your mouth** ◇ If you were *born with a silver spoon in your mouth,* you were born into a very wealthy family. — **in all your born days** *informal + somewhat old-fashioned* : in your entire life ▪ *I never saw anything like it in all my born days.* — **there's one born every minute** *or* **there's a sucker born every minute** *informal* — used to say that there are many people who are foolish and can be easily deceived — **wasn't born yesterday** — used to say that someone is unlikely to believe something that is not true or to trust someone who is not trustworthy ▪ *He asked me for money, but I refused. I wasn't born yesterday.*

born–again /ˌboɚnə'gɛn/ *adj* **1** : having a new or stronger belief in the Christian religion ▪ *She's born-again now.* ▪ *a born-again Christian* **2** : newly interested in and enthusiastic about something ▪ *a born-again fitness buff*

borne *past participle of* ²BEAR

bor·ough /'bɚoʊ/ *n* [C] **1** : a village, town, or part of a large city that has its own government **2** : one of the five main sections of New York City ▪ *the borough of Brooklyn*

bor·row /'bɑːˌroʊ/ *vb* **1** [*T*] **a** : to take and use (something that belongs to someone else) for a period of time before returning it ▪ *Can I borrow your camera?* [=will you lend me your camera?] **b** : to take and use up (something) with the promise to give back something of equal value ▪ *borrow a cup of sugar from the neighbors* ▪ *borrow money from the bank* **2** [*T/I*] : to use (an idea, saying, etc.) that was thought up by someone else ▪ *She borrowed the technique from local artisans.* ▪ *The company is borrowing a page from* [=using a technique or idea first used by] *its largest competitor.* **3** [*T*] — used to use (a word or phrase from another language) in a language ▪ *The English word "entrepreneur" was borrowed from (the) French.* — **be living on borrowed time** : to continue to be alive after you were expected to die ▪ *After his heart attack, he was living on borrowed time.* — **bor·row·er** /'bɑːrəwɚ/ *n* [C]

bor·row·ing /'bɑːrəwɪŋ/ *n* **1** [C] : something that is borrowed; *especially* : a word or phrase from one language that is used in another language ▪ *a list of Japanese borrowings in English* **2** [U] : the act of borrowing something (such as money) • *increases in government borrowing*

Bor·stal /ˈboəstl/ *n [C/U] Brit* : a special prison formerly used for people too young to go to a regular prison

¹**bos·om** /ˈbuzəm/ *n* **1** [C] : a person's chest • *He clutched the flowers to his bosom.* **2** [C] *somewhat old-fashioned* **a** : a woman's breasts • *her large bosom* **b** : one of a woman's breasts • *a woman's bosoms* **3** [*singular*] : a safe and comfortable place or situation • *the bosom of your family*

²**bosom** *adj, always before a noun* : very close • *very dear* • *bosom friends/buddies*

¹**boss** /ˈbɑːs/ *n [C]* **1** : the person whose job is to tell other workers what to do • *I asked my boss for a raise.* • *She wanted to* ***be her own boss.*** [=have no boss except for herself] **2** : a person who has a lot of power in an organization • *a union/studio/warehouse boss* **3** : the person who has more power or control in a relationship • *He wants to show them who's (the) boss.* [=who's in charge]

²**boss** *vb [T]* : to give orders to (someone) • ***Don't boss*** *me around!* — ***bossy*** /ˈbɑːsi/ *adj* **boss·i·er; -est** *informal* • *Quit being so bossy!*

bo·tan·i·cal /bəˈtænɪkəl/ *adj* : of or relating to plants or the study of plants • *botanical specimens* • *botanical extracts* — **bo·tan·i·cal·ly** /bəˈtænɪkli/ *adv*

bot·a·ny /ˈbɑːtəni/ *n [U]* : a branch of science that deals with plant life — **bot·a·nist** /ˈbɑːtənɪst/ *n [C]*

botch /ˈbɑːtʃ/ *vb [T]* : to do (something) badly : to ruin (something) because of carelessness or a lack of skill • *The store botched (up) the order.* • *a botched robbery/experiment*

¹**both** /ˈboʊθ/ *adj* — used to indicate that two things or people are being referred to rather than just one • *She put both feet in the stream.* • *Both countries have agreed to the treaty.*

²**both** *pron* : each one of two things or people • *There were two for sale, and he bought (them) both.* • *We were both tired.* = *Both of us were tired.* • *He read both of the books.* [=he read both books]

³**both** *conj* — used before two words or phrases connected with *and* to stress that each is included • *The show will be in both New York and London.* • *Both he and his wife play golf.*

¹**both·er** /ˈbɑːðɚ/ *vb* **1** [T] : to cause (someone) to feel troubled, worried, or concerned • *Nothing seems to bother him.* • *It didn't bother him in the least.* • ***Don't bother your head with that.*** [=don't worry about that] • *He decided he **wasn't** going to* ***bother himself** about the problem.* [=he wasn't going to worry about the problem] **2** [T] : to annoy (someone) • *It bothers her when people throw trash on the ground.* **3** [I] **a** : to make an effort to do something • *She doesn't bother to cook big meals anymore.* • *Why bother talking if no one is listening?* • *"Should I call later?" "No, don't bother."* • *He **can't be bothered** [=he is too busy or uninterested] to send us a picture.* **b** : to be concerned with or about something •

I'm not going to bother with that. • *We were told not to bother about the data.* [=not to consider or use the data] **4** [T] : to interrupt or talk to (someone who is working or who wants to be alone) • *I hate to bother you, but I need some assistance.* **5** [T] **a** : to make (someone) feel sick or uncomfortable • *His stomach/arthritis was bothering him.* **b** : to cause a painful or unpleasant feeling in (part of someone's body) • *The light bothered her eyes.*

²**bother** *n* **1** [*singular*] : someone or something that is annoying or that causes trouble • *I'm sorry to be a bother* [=*nuisance*], *but I need some help.* **2** [U] : trouble or difficulty : INCONVENIENCE • *He doesn't want the bother of filling out those forms again.* — **both·er·some** /ˈbɑːðɚsəm/ *adj* • *the bothersome task of applying for a passport*

¹**bot·tle** /ˈbɑːtl/ *n* **1** [C] **a** : a glass or plastic container that has a narrow neck and usually has no handle ⬦ Bottles are usually used to store liquid or tablets. • *a bottle of wine* • *an aspirin bottle* **b** : the amount contained in a bottle • *We drank a whole bottle of wine.* **2** ***the bottle*** : alcoholic drink • *Her struggles with the bottle affected her entire family.* • *He took* ***to the bottle.*** = *He hit the bottle.* [=he began to drink a lot of alcohol] **3** [C] : a special bottle for feeding babies that contains milk or a drink which contains milk • *(US) a baby bottle* = *(Brit) a baby's bottle* **4** [U] *Brit slang* : courage or strength of spirit • *I don't think he's got bottle* [=*guts*] *enough to do it.* — ***bring your own bottle*** *(US)* or *Brit* ***bring a bottle*** — used to tell the people who are invited to a party that they should bring their own alcoholic drinks — ***catch/capture lightning in a bottle*** see ¹LIGHTNING — **bot·tle·ful** /ˈbɑːtlˌfʊl/ *n* [*singular*] • *a bottleful of water*

²**bottle** *vb* **bot·tled; bot·tling** [T] : to put (something) into a bottle so that it can be sold or so that it is easier to use • *The restaurant bottles its own ginger ale.* • *bottled oxygen/water/beer* — ***bottle out*** [*phrasal vb*] *Brit slang* : to become too afraid to do something • *I was going to ask him but then I bottled out.* — ***bottle up*** [*phrasal vb*] ***bottle (something) up*** or ***bottle up (something)*** : to keep (a feeling or emotion) inside of you instead of expressing it • *I know he's angry, but he bottles it up inside.* — **bot·tler** *n* [C] • *soft drink bottlers*

bottle bank *n* [C] *Brit* : a large container that people put empty bottles in so that the glass or plastic the bottles are made from can be used again

bot·tle-feed /ˈbɑːtlˌfiːd/ *vb* **-fed; -feed·ing** [T] : to feed (a baby or young animal) with a bottle instead of from its mother's breast • *All her children were bottle-fed.*

bot·tle·neck /ˈbɑːtlˌnɛk/ *n* [C] **1** : a section of road or highway where the traffic moves very slowly • *Construction has created a bottleneck on Main Street.* **2** : something that slows down a process • *All decisions must be approved by the* committee, and that's where the bottleneck is.

¹bot·tom /'bɑ:təm/ n **1 a** [C] : the lowest part, point, or level of something • the bottom of the stairs/hill • Please sign your name at the bottom of the form. **b** [C] : the part of something that is below or under the other parts • the bottom of his foot • a ship's bottom **c** [C] : the lowest point or surface inside something • the bottom of the box/container/jar/pool **d** [singular] chiefly Brit : the part of something that is furthest away • the bottom of the garden **2** [C] : BUTTOCKS • The baby has a rash on his bottom. **3 a** [singular] : a position of little power in a company or organization • He started at the bottom of the company and worked his way up. **b** [singular] : a low rank or position • the team at the bottom of the league • She graduated at the bottom of her/the class. [=her grades were among the lowest in her class] **c** [U] : the worst position, level, or condition • at the bottom of the pay scale • The company's stocks have hit bottom. [=reached the bottom; lost all value] **4** [singular] : the surface that is under a body of water • the bottom of the ocean/lake/river **5** [C] : a piece of clothing that is worn on the lower part of the body • a bikini bottom • pajama bottoms **6** [singular] : the second half of an inning in baseball • the bottom of the ninth inning **7** [U] chiefly Brit : the lowest gear of a car • Stay in bottom (gear). — **at bottom** chiefly Brit : in truth : REALLY • The song is, at bottom, a lullaby. — **be/lie at the bottom of** chiefly Brit : to be the source or originator of (something) • I know who's at the bottom of these pranks. — **bottoms up** informal — used as a toast or to tell people to finish their drinks • Bottoms up! — **from the bottom of your heart** see HEART — **from top to bottom** see ¹TOP — **get to the bottom of** : to find out the true reason for or cause of (something) • I'm determined to get to the bottom of this problem. — **the bottom drop/fall out** ◇ If the bottom drops/falls out of something, it suddenly fails or becomes unable to continue in a normal and effective way. • The bottom dropped out of the oil market. [=the oil market collapsed] — **the bottom of the barrel** : the lowest possible condition, level, etc. • Salaries are scraping/hitting the bottom of the barrel. [=salaries are very low] — **bottom** adj, always before a noun • the bottom rung of the ladder • the bottom drawer/shelf — **bot·tomed** /'bɑ:təmd/ adj • flat bottomed boats

²bottom vb — **bottom out** [phrasal vb] : to reach a lowest or worst point usually before beginning to rise or improve • Real estate prices seem to have bottomed out.

bottom feeder n [C] **1** : a fish that feeds at the bottom of a lake, pond, etc. **2** US, disapproving : someone who uses other people's troubles, weakness, etc., as an opportunity to make money • media bottom feeders whose secrets would sell magazines **3** US, informal : someone or something that has a very

low status or rank • Our team lost to one of the league's bottom feeders.

bot·tom·land /'bɑ:təm,lænd/ n [C] : flat low land along a river or stream • the bottomlands

bot·tom·less /'bɑ:təmləs/ adj **1** : seeming to have no limit • a bottomless supply of money **2** : very deep • a bottomless pit

bottom line n **1 the bottom line** : the most important thing to consider • We can't miss the flight. That's the bottom line. **2** [singular] : a company's profits or losses • changes that affect our bottom line **3** [singular] : the least amount of money you are willing to accept for something • My bottom line is $120,000.

bot·u·lism /'bɑ:tʃə,lɪzəm/ n [U] : a serious illness that is caused by eating food that has not been preserved correctly and that is filled with bacteria

bou·doir /'bu:ˌdwɑːr/ n [C] old-fashioned : a woman's bedroom or private room for dressing or resting

bough /'baʊ/ n [C] : a main branch of a tree

bought past tense and past participle of ¹BUY

bouil·la·baisse /ˌbu:jəˈbeɪs/ n [C/U] : a stew made with strong spices and two or more kinds of fish

bouil·lon /'bu:ˌljɑːn, Brit 'bu:ˌjɒn/ n [C/U] : a clear liquid in which meat, chicken, fish, or vegetables have been cooked and which is eaten as soup or used to make sauces • beef bouillon

bouillon cube n [C] : a small cube of dried meat or vegetables that is used to add flavor to soup

boul·der /'boʊldər/ n [C] : a very large stone or rounded piece of rock

bou·le·vard /'bʊləˌvɑːrd/ n [C] : a wide and usually important street that often has trees, grass, or flowers planted down its center or along its sides — abbr. blvd.

¹bounce /'baʊns/ vb **bounced**; **bouncing 1 a** [T] : to cause (a ball, rock, etc.) to hit against a surface and quickly move in a different and usually opposite direction • He was bouncing a ball against/off the garage door. **b** [I] : to move in one direction, hit a surface (such as a wall or the floor), and then quickly move in a different and usually opposite direction • The ball bounced (off the wall). **2 a** [I] : to move with a lot of energy and excitement • He bounced [=bounded] into the room to welcome his guests. • a bouncing [=very active and healthy] baby boy **b** [T/I] : to move or jump up and down • bounce on a bed/trampoline • He bounced the baby on his knee. **3 a** [I] of a check : to be returned by a bank because there is not enough money in the bank account to pay the amount that is on the check • Her check bounced and I never got the money. **b** [T] : to write (a check) that is returned without payment by the bank • He bounced a check at the grocery store. **4** [I] : to go quickly and repeatedly from one job, place, etc., to another • bouncing from one job to another **5** [T/I] : to return (an e-mail) to the sender instead of delivering it • I tried to send you an e-mail, but it (was) bounced back to *me.* [=the e-mail or computer system was not able to deliver it] — **bounce around** [*phrasal vb*] **bounce (something) around** *or* **bounce around (something)** *informal* : to talk about (something, such as an idea) in an informal way in order to get different opinions about it • *We were bouncing some ideas around.* — **bounce back** [*phrasal vb*] : to return quickly to a normal condition after a difficult situation or event • *She bounced back* [=recovered] *easily from her surgery.* • *After losing, they bounced back to win their next eight games.* — **bounce off** [*phrasal vb*] **bounce (something) off** *informal* : to talk about (something, such as an idea) with (someone) in an informal way in order to get an opinion • *I wanted to bounce some ideas off you.*

²**bounce** *n* **1** [C] : the act or action of bouncing off the ground or another surface • *He caught the ball on the first bounce.* **2** [U] **a** : the ability to move quickly in a different direction after hitting a surface • *a basketball that has lost all its bounce* **b** : a quality that makes a person's hair look healthy, full, and attractive • *The shampoo will give your hair lots of bounce.* **3** [*singular*] : a sudden increase • *a bounce in earnings* **4** [U, *singular*] : energy and liveliness • *He has plenty of bounce* [=spring] *in his step.*

bounce pass *n* [C] *basketball* : a pass to a teammate that is made by bouncing the ball once

bounc·er /ˈbaʊnsɚ/ *n* [C] **1** : a person whose job is to force anyone who causes a problem in a bar, nightclub, etc., to leave that place **2** : a ball that bounces on the ground • *The batter hit a bouncer to the shortstop.*

bouncy /ˈbaʊnsi/ *adj* **bounc·i·er; -est** **1** : able to bounce well • *a bouncy rubber ball* **2** : lively, cheerful, and full of energy • *a bouncy host* • *bouncy music* **3** : quickly returning to a full, rounded shape after being made flat • *a bouncy seat cushion* • *bouncy hair*

¹**bound** *past tense and past participle of* ¹BIND

²**bound** /ˈbaʊnd/ *adj* **1** *not before a noun* : very likely or certain *to do or to be* something • *It's bound to rain soon.* • *It was bound to happen.* **2** : unlikely or unable to change, develop, move, etc., because of being held or controlled by something • *an organization that is bound by tradition* = *a tradition-bound organization* **3** : tied together with something (such as a string or rope) • *a neatly/tightly/loosely bound stack of papers* **4** *not before a noun* : closely joined or connected to other people • *She and I are bound (together) by our shared past.* [=we are connected to each other because we have the same past] **5** *not before a noun* : required by law or duty to do something • *The state is legally bound* [=obligated] *to provide each child with an education.* • *He was duty/honor bound* [=it was his duty or moral obligation] *to help.* • (*chiefly Brit*) *The experiment, I am bound to say* [=I must say/admit], *seems to have succeeded.* **6** : held together or covered

with a particular type of material • *books bound in leather/velvet* **7** : going or planning to go to a specified place • *We were homeward bound.* [=we were going towards our home] • *college-bound teenagers* [=teenagers who are planning to go to college] • *a ship bound for Africa* — **bound and determined** : very determined • *We were bound and determined to finish the project.* — **bound up** : closely involved or associated • *Their lives are closely bound up with their religion.*

³**bound** *n* **1** [C] : a leap or long jump • *He leapt over the puddle in/with a single bound.* **2** [*plural*] : the limit of what is correct or proper • *The play goes beyond the bounds of decency.* = *The play exceeds the bounds of decency.* • *within the bounds of reason* • *The police officers exceeded/overstepped their bounds and broke the law.* **3** [C] : something that shows where one area ends and another area begins • *the bounds* [=boundaries] *of the nature reserve* — *by/in leaps and bounds* see ²LEAP — **in bounds** : inside the area where players or the ball must stay in sports like basketball and American football • *The receiver was in bounds when he caught the pass.* — **know no bounds** : to have no limit • *His generosity knows no bounds.* [=he is very generous] — **out of bounds 1** : outside the area where players or the ball must stay in sports like basketball and American football • *The ball was kicked out of bounds.* **2** : not good or acceptable • *The teacher's comment was completely out of bounds.* [=unacceptable, inappropriate] **3** — used to describe a place where people are not allowed to go • *The auditorium is out of bounds during the renovations.* **4** — used to describe something that people are not allowed to discuss or mention • *The subject of politics is out of bounds* [=off limits] *when our family gets together.*

⁴**bound** *vb* **1** [I] : to walk or run with long, energetic steps • *She came bounding down the stairs.* • *The deer bounded over the fence.* **2** [T] : to form a border around (an area) • *a quiet village bounded* [=surrounded, enclosed] *by mountains*

bound·ary /ˈbaʊndri/ *n, pl* **-ar·ies 1** [C] : something that shows where an area ends and another area begins • *Those two trees mark the boundary of our property.* • (*figurative*) *a story at/on the boundary between fact and fiction* **2** [*plural*] : limits that define acceptable behavior • *You need to set boundaries with your children.* • *They're pushing the boundaries of* [=doing things that are unusual in] *traditional French cooking.* — **know no boundaries** : to have no limits • *My admiration for him knows no boundaries.*

bound·less /ˈbaʊndləs/ *adj* : not limited in any way • *the boundless* [=limitless, endless] *sky* • *Her love for her family was boundless.*

boun·te·ous /ˈbaʊntijəs/ *adj, formal* : BOUNTIFUL • *a bounteous harvest*

boun·ti·ful /ˈbaʊntɪfəl/ *adj, formal* **1** : giving or providing many desired things • *bountiful harvests* **2** : given or existing in large amounts • *a bountiful supply of water* — **boun·ti·ful·ly** *adv*

boun·ty /ˈbaʊnti/ *n, pl* **-ties** **1** [*U, singular*] *literary* : good things that are given or provided freely and in large amounts • *the bounty of nature = nature's bounty* • *a bounty of flowers* **2** [*C*] : an amount of money given to someone as a reward for catching a criminal • *A bounty of 500 dollars was put on his head.* [=anyone who captured him would receive a 500-dollar bounty]

bounty hunter *n* [*C*] : someone who catches criminals who have not been caught by the police in exchange for a reward

bou·quet /boʊˈkeɪ, buːˈkeɪ/ *n* [*C*] **1** : a group of flowers that are picked and often tied together • *a bouquet of roses* **2** : a particular and usually pleasant smell of flowers or wine • *The wine has a lovely bouquet.*

bour·bon /ˈbɚbən/ *n* [*C/U*] : a type of American whiskey made from corn, malt, and rye

bour·geois /ˈbʊɚˌʒwɑː/ *adj* **1** : relating to or belonging to the middle class of society • *the bourgeois class* • *bourgeois families/businessmen* **2** *disapproving* : too concerned about wealth, possessions, and respectable behavior • *bourgeois attitudes/values* — **bourgeois** *n, pl* **bourgeois** /ˈbʊɚˌʒwɑːz/ [*C*] • *a philosopher who had no sympathy for the bourgeois*

bour·geoi·sie /ˌbʊɚˌʒwɑːˈziː/ *n* — **the bourgeoisie** : the middle class of society : the social class of skilled workers, business and professional people, and government officials • *members of the bourgeoisie*

bout /ˈbaʊt/ *n* [*C*] **1** : a period of time during which someone suffers from something (such as an illness or disease) • *a bout of fever/depression* • (*US*) *She survived a 5-year bout with cancer.* **2** : a short period of time during which something is done or happening • *a drinking bout* • *a bout of unemployment* **3** : a wrestling or boxing contest

bou·tique /buːˈtiːk/ *n* [*C*] : a small store that sells stylish clothing or other usually expensive things

bo·vine /ˈboʊˌvaɪn/ *adj* **1** *technical* : relating to cows • *bovine growth hormones* **2** *disapproving* : looking or acting like a cow • *She stared at us with a stupid, bovine expression.*

¹bow /ˈbaʊ/ *vb* **1** [*I*] : to bend forward at the neck or waist as a formal way of greeting someone or showing respect • *He bowed (to us) politely and introduced himself.* • *You must bow (down) before the king.* **2** [*T*] : to turn (your head) down so that you are looking toward the ground • *people bowing their heads in prayer* **3** [*I*] : to stop trying to fight or resist something • *The President bowed* [=gave in, yielded] *to political pressure.* • *She finally bowed to the inevitable and accepted their decision.* — **bow and scrape** : to treat someone who is powerful or wealthy in an extremely respectful way especially in order to get approval, friendship, etc. • *politicians who bow and*

scrape before wealthy contributors — **bow down to** [*phrasal vb*] : to show weakness by agreeing to the demands or following the orders of (someone or something) • *I will bow down to no one.* — **bow out** [*phrasal vb*] : to stop doing something • *He decided to bow out of the presidential race.* — compare ⁴BOW

²bow *n* [*C*] **1** : the act of bending forward at the neck or waist in order to greet someone or show respect : the act of bowing • *He smiled and made/gave a bow.* **2** : the front part of a boat or ship • *The deck was cleaned from bow to stern.* [=from the front end to the back end] — **take a bow** : to bow towards an audience that is applauding for you • *The actors lined up to take a bow.* • (*figurative*) *The people who organized the festival should take a bow* [=should be praised] *for its remarkable success.* — compare ³BOW

³bow /ˈboʊ/ *n* [*C*] **1** : a knot that is made by tying a ribbon or string into two or more loops and that is used for tying shoelaces or for decoration • *She tied/wore a bow in her hair.* **2** : a weapon used for shooting arrows that is made of a long, thin piece of wood which is bent with its ends connected by a tight, strong string • *They hunted with bows and arrows.* **3** : a tool that is used for playing a violin or similar musical instrument — compare ²BOW

⁴bow *vb* **1** [*T*] : to use a bow to play (a violin or similar musical instrument) • *bowing the violin strings* **2** [*T/I*] : to bend or curve • *The wall bows out at the bottom.* • *People with this disorder often have bowed legs.* — compare ¹BOW

bow·el /ˈbawəl/ *n* **1** [*C*] : the long tube in the body that helps digest food and carries solid waste out of the body • *a disease that affects the bowels* ✧ To have a **bowel movement** or to **move your bowels** or (*Brit*) **open your bowels** is to pass solid waste from your body. **2** **the bowels** *literary* : the deep inner parts of something • *the bowels of the earth/ship*

bow·er /ˈbawɚ/ *n* [*C*] *literary* : a pleasant shady place in a garden or forest • *resting in the shade of the bower*

¹bowl /ˈboʊl/ *n* **1** [*C*] **a** : a round container that has tall, curving sides and that is used for preparing or serving foods and liquids • *a soup/salad/pasta bowl* • *the dog's water bowl* **b** : the amount of food or liquid served in a bowl • *I ate two bowls of soup for dinner.* **2** [*C*] : a part of something that is shaped like a bowl • *toilet bowl* [=the round bottom part of a toilet] • *the bowl of a spoon/pipe* **3** [*singular*] *US* : a large stadium or theater that is shaped like a bowl • *a concert at the Hollywood Bowl* **4** [*C*] *American football* : a game that is played after the regular season between college teams that have been specially invited • *college bowl games* • *the Orange Bowl* **5** [*plural*] *Brit* : LAWN BOWLING

²bowl *vb* **1** [*T*] : to roll (a ball) towards something especially in the game of bowling or lawn bowling • *I don't think I can bowl a 12-pound ball.* **2 a** [*I*] : to play the game of bowling ▪ *Do you like to bowl?* **b** [*T*] : to get (a score) in a game of bowling ▪ *She usually bowls around 150.* **3** [*T*] *cricket* **a** : to throw (a ball) to the batsman **b** : to force (a batsman) to leave the field by throwing a ball that hits the wicket behind the batsman ▪ *He was bowled (out) for 47.* **4** [*I*] *chiefly Brit* : to move or go very quickly ▪ *We were bowling along the motorway.* — **bowl over** [*phrasal vb*] **bowl (someone or something) over** or **bowl over (someone or something) 1** : to hit and push down (someone or something) while quickly moving past ▪ *We were almost bowled over by the wind.* **2** : to surprise or impress (someone) very much ▪ *He was completely bowled over by the news.*

bow·leg·ged /ˈboʊˌlɛgəd/ *adj* : having legs that curve outward at the knee ▪ *He's short and bowlegged.*

bowl·er /ˈboʊlə/ *n* [*C*] **1** : someone who plays the game of bowling ▪ *She's a great bowler.* [=she bowls very well] **2** *cricket* : the player who throws the ball to the batsman **3** *chiefly Brit* : DERBY **4**

bowl·ful /ˈboʊlˌfʊl/ *n* [*C*] : the amount of food or liquid that fits in a bowl ▪ *a bowlful of peanuts*

bowl·ing /ˈboʊlɪŋ/ *n* [*U*] : a game played by rolling a large, heavy ball down a smooth floor (called a lane) towards a set of pins in order to knock down as many pins as possible ▪ *We're going bowling.* ▪ *a bowling ball/lane*

bowling alley *n* [*C*] : a room or building in which people play the game of bowling

bow·string /ˈboʊˌstrɪŋ/ *n* [*C*] : the strong, tight string that is used on a bow for shooting arrows

bow tie *n* [*C*] : a narrow length of cloth that is worn by men around the neck and tied into a bow at the throat

¹box /ˈbɑːks/ *n* **1** [*C*] **a** : a container that is made of a hard material and that usually has four straight sides ▪ *a cardboard box* ▪ *a box of tools* ▪ *a box of chocolates.* **2** [*C*] : a container used for holding mail or papers especially in an office ▪ *I put the memo in your box.* ▪ *a post office box* **3 a** [*C*] : a piece of electronic equipment that is contained inside a box ▪ *a control/cable box* **b** **the box** *Brit, informal* : a television **4** [*C*] : a small area or section of seats that is separated from other seats inside a theater, stadium, or courtroom ▪ *the jury box* **5** [*C*] : a closed shape with four sides on a piece of paper, a Web page, etc. ▪ *If you are over 18 years old, check this box.* **6** [*C*] *chiefly Brit* : an area where two streets cross that is marked by painted lines to show where cars are not allowed to stop but can only pass through — **think outside the box** ✧ If you *think outside the box*, your thoughts are not limited or controlled by rules or tradition, and you have ideas that are creative and unusual.

²box *vb* **1** [*T*] : to put (something) in a box ▪ *Ask the clerk to box it (up) for you.* ▪ *a boxed set* [=a set of things that are sold

together in a box] **2** [*I*] : to participate in the sport of boxing ▪ *His father taught him how to box.* — **box in** [*phrasal vb*] **box (someone or something) in** : to surround (someone or something) and make movement difficult ▪ *Our car got boxed in and we couldn't get out of our parking space.* ▪ (*figurative*) *I feel boxed in by all these rules.* — **box someone's ears** *old-fashioned* : to hit someone on the sides of the head or on the ears

box·car /ˈbɑːksˌkɑɚ/ *n* [*C*] *US* : a section of a train that has a roof and large, sliding doors and that carries goods and supplies rather than people

box·er /ˈbɑːksɚ/ *n* **1** [*C*] : someone who participates in the sport of boxing **2** [*C*] : a type of dog that has a short, square face and a tail that is usually cut short when the dog is young **3** [*plural*] : BOXER SHORTS

boxer shorts *n* [*plural*] : loose shorts that are worn as underwear by men and boys ▪ *a pair of boxer shorts*

box·ing /ˈbɑːksɪŋ/ *n* [*U*] : the sport of fighting someone with your hands while wearing very thick gloves ▪ *a boxing glove/match*

Boxing Day *n* [*C/U*] *chiefly Brit* : a holiday that is celebrated especially in England and Canada on the first day after Christmas that is not a Sunday

box lunch *n* [*C*] *US* : BAG LUNCH

box office *n* **1** [*C*] : an area in a theater where tickets are sold for a movie, play, etc. **2** [*singular*] — used to describe how many tickets have been sold for a movie, play, etc. ▪ *The movie did well at the box office.* [=many people bought tickets to see the movie] ▪ *a box office hit/success*

box score *n* [*C*] *US* : a small chart that shows the players, score, and other details of a baseball game

box seat *n* [*C*] : a seat in a small area or section of seats that is separated from the other seats in a theater or stadium

box spring *n* [*C*] *US* : a wide, flat box that is filled with metal springs and covered with cloth and that is put under a mattress for support

box·wood /ˈbɑːksˌwʊd/ *n* [*C/U*] *US* : an evergreen bush or small tree that has small dark leaves

¹boy /ˈboɪ/ *n* **1** [*C*] **a** : a male child ▪ *a baby/little boy* ▪ *Calm down, boys and girls.* **b** : SON ▪ *our oldest/youngest boy* **2** [*C*] **a** : a young man ▪ *teenage boys* ▪ *boy wonder* [=a young man who has achieved many great things] **b** : a usually young man from a specified kind of place ▪ *city/country boys* ▪ *a local/farm boy* **3 a the boys** [*plural*] *informal* : the male friends or work partners of a man viewed as a group ▪ *He's out with the boys.* **b** [*singular*] *chiefly Brit, old-fashioned* : a man of any age ✧ The phrases **my dear boy** and **old boy** are used as friendly ways for one man to address another man. ▪ *Cheer up, old boy.* **4** [*C*] : a man or boy who does a particular job ▪ *a messenger boy* ✧ *Boy* is often offensive in this sense when the person being described is an adult. — **boys will be**

boys — used to say that it is not surprising or unusual when men or boys behave in energetic, rough, or improper ways — **boy·hood** /ˈbɔɪˌhʊd/ *n* [U] • *the president's early boyhood* • *my boyhood home* [=where I lived when I was a boy] — **boy·ish** /ˈbɔɪɪʃ/ *adj* • *his boyish good looks* — **boy·ish·ly** *adv* • *boyishly handsome* — **boy·ish·ness** *n* [U]

²**boy** *interj* — used to express surprise or enthusiasm • *Boy, I sure am hungry!*

boy·cott /ˈbɔɪˌkɑːt/ *vb* [T] : to refuse to buy, use, or participate in (something) as a way of protesting • *plans to boycott American products* • *They boycotted* [=did not attend] *the event.* : to stop using the goods or services of (a company, country, etc.) until changes are made • *boycotting companies that pollute the environment* — **boycott** *n* [C] • *the country's boycott of the Olympics*

boy·friend /ˈbɔɪˌfrɛnd/ *n* [C] : a man that someone has a romantic or sexual relationship with • *She has a new boyfriend.*

Boy Scout *n* [C] : a member of an organization for boys ages 11 to 17 ✧ Boy Scouts participate in group activities, learn skills, and are encouraged to have good morals and be good citizens. — called also *Scout*

bo·zo /ˈboʊzoʊ/ *n, pl* **bo·zos** [C] *informal* : a stupid or foolish person • *Some bozo forgot to shut the door.*

Br *abbr* 1 Britain 2 British

bra /ˈbrɑː/ *n* [C] : a piece of clothing that is worn by women under other clothes to cover and support the breasts — called also *brassiere*

¹**brace** /ˈbreɪs/ *vb* **braced**; **brac·ing** [T/I] : to get ready for something difficult or unpleasant • *We braced ourselves for the storm.* • *(chiefly US) The town is bracing for a busy tourist season.* 2 [T] : to give added physical support or strength to (something) • *Steel columns brace the structure.* 3 [T] **a** : to support (yourself) by leaning against something or holding something • *She braced herself with one hand and reached up with the other.* **b** : to place (your feet, hands, etc.) against something for support • *He braced his foot against the wall.*

²**brace** *n* 1 [C] : a part that adds physical strength or support • *a brace to hold the shelf in place* 2 [C] **a** : a device that supports a part of the body • *a back/neck brace* **b** : a device that is attached to teeth to make them straight • *(Brit) She has a brace on her teeth.* — plural in U.S. English • *She has braces on her teeth.* 3 [C] : either one of the marks { or } that are used as a pair around words or items that are to be considered together 4 [*plural*] *Brit* : SUSPENDERS

brace·let /ˈbreɪslət/ *n* [C] : a piece of jewelry worn on the wrist

brac·ing /ˈbreɪsɪŋ/ *adj* : pleasantly cool or refreshing • *clean, bracing air* • *(figurative) the bracing honesty of her remarks* — **brac·ing·ly** *adv*

brack·en /ˈbrækən/ *n* [U] : a large kind of fern

¹**brack·et** /ˈbrækət/ *n* [C] 1 : an object that is attached to a wall and used to support or hold up something (such as a shelf) 2 : a category that includes a certain range of incomes, ages, etc. • *an age bracket* • *a higher tax bracket* 3 **a** : either one of a pair of marks [ ] or ⟨ ⟩ used to enclose words or mathematical symbols **b** *Brit* : PARENTHESIS

²**bracket** *vb* [T] 1 : to place (words, symbols, etc.) within brackets • *She bracketed (off) portions of the text.* • *bracketed information* 2 : to be located at each side of (something) • *The door is bracketed by tall bushes.* 3 : to put (two or more people or things) into the same category, group, etc. • *two composers whose names are often bracketed together*

brack·ish /ˈbrækɪʃ/ *adj* : somewhat salty • *brackish water/ponds*

brag /ˈbræg/ *vb* **bragged**; **brag·ging** [T/I] : to talk about yourself, your achievements, your family, etc., in a way that shows too much pride • *She kept bragging about how she'd won the race.*

brag·ga·do·cio /ˌbrægəˈdoʊsiˌoʊ/ *n* [U] *literary* : the annoying or exaggerated talk of someone who is trying to sound very proud or brave

brag·gart /ˈbrægət/ *n* [C] : a person who brags a lot

bragging rights *n* [*plural*] *US* : a good reason to talk with pride about something you have done • *She earned bragging rights for completing the work on time.*

Brah·man *or* **Brah·min** /ˈbrɑːmən/ *n* [C] : a member of the highest priestly class of Hindu society

braid /ˈbreɪd/ *n* 1 [C] *chiefly US* : an arrangement of hair made by weaving three sections together • *She wore her hair in a long braid.* [=(chiefly Brit) plait] 2 [U] : a piece of cord or ribbon made of three or more strands woven together — **braid** *vb* [T] • *braiding hair/ribbons* • *a braided rug*

braille *or* **Braille** /ˈbreɪl/ *n* [U] : a system of writing for blind people in which letters are represented by raised dots

¹**brain** /ˈbreɪn/ *n* [C] 1 : the body organ in the head that controls functions, movements, sensations, and thoughts • *the human brain* • *brain surgery* • *brain cells/tissue* 2 *informal* : the ability to think : INTELLIGENCE • *He'd do it if he had half a brain.* [=if he was at all smart] • *She has both brains and beauty.* 3 *informal* : a very intelligent person • *the brains in the class* ✧ If you use **the brains** *of/behind* something, you are the person who thinks of plans or makes important decisions for a group. • *She's the brains of the organization.* — **beat/bash someone's brains out** *or US* **beat/bash someone's brains in** *informal* : to hit someone on the head in a way that causes serious injury or death — **blow someone's brains out** *informal* : to kill someone with a shot to the head — **on the brain** *informal* : always in your thoughts • *I've had pizza on the brain all day.* — **pick someone's brain/brains** *informal* : to talk to someone in order to get helpful information or advice • *I need to pick your brain about something.* —

rack your brain/brains see ²RACK

²**brain** *vb* [T] *informal* : to hit (someone) on the head very hard • *The tree limb fell and nearly brained me.*

brain·child /ˈbreɪnˌtʃaɪəld/ *n* [*singular*] : an idea, plan, or creation of one person • *The museum is the brainchild of a wealthy art collector.*

brain–dead /ˈbreɪnˌdɛd/ *adj* **1** *medical* : having no brain function • *Doctors determined that she was brain-dead.* **2** *informal* : very stupid or unable to think • *brain-dead politicians* • *I was so tired I was/felt brain-dead.*

brain·i·ac /ˈbreɪniˌæk/ *n* [C] *informal* : a very intelligent person • *the class brainiac*

brain·less /ˈbreɪnləs/ *adj, informal* : very stupid or silly • *my brainless coworkers*

brain·pow·er /ˈbreɪnˌpawɚ/ *n* [U] : the ability to think intelligently • *The herb is supposed to boost brainpower.*

¹**brain·storm** /ˈbreɪnˌstoɚm/ *n* [C] **1** *US* : an idea that someone thinks of suddenly • *Her latest brainstorm is to convert the garage into an apartment.* **2** *Brit* : a temporary state of confusion

²**brainstorm** *vb* [T/I] : to discuss a problem and suggest solutions • *a meeting to brainstorm (about) ideas/strategies* — **brain·storm·ing** *n* [U] • *a brainstorming session*

brain·teas·er /ˈbreɪnˌtiːzɚ/ *n* [C] : a puzzle that is difficult to figure out or solve

brain trust *n* [C] *US* : a group of people who give advice to a leader about what should be done • *the president's brain trust* — called also (*Brit*) *brains trust*

brain·wash /ˈbreɪnˌwɑːʃ/ *vb* [T] : to cause (someone) to think or believe something by using methods that make a person unable to think normally • *Does advertising brainwash children?* • *people brainwashed into donating all their money to cults*

brain wave *n* [C] **1** : a pattern or cycle of electrical activity in the brain • *monitoring the patient's brain waves* **2** *chiefly Brit* : ¹BRAINSTORM 1

brainy /ˈbreɪni/ *adj* **brain·i·er; -est** *informal* : very intelligent • *a brainy kid* — **brain·i·ness** *n* [U]

braise /ˈbreɪz/ *vb* [T] : to cook (food) slowly in fat and a small amount of liquid in a covered pot • *beef braised in red wine*

¹**brake** /ˈbreɪk/ *n* [C] **1** : a device for slowing or stopping something (such as a wheel or vehicle) • *Release the brake slowly.* • *Take your foot off the brake (pedal).* • *The car needs new brakes.* • *I slammed/jammed on the brakes very quickly.* **2** : something used to slow or stop movement or activity • *economic policies that will act as a brake on inflation* [=that will slow the rate of inflation] • *trying to put the brakes on inflation/crime*

²**brake** *vb* **braked; brak·ing** [I] : to use the brake on a vehicle • *I had to brake suddenly/quickly when a cat ran in front of the car.*

bram·ble /ˈbræmbəl/ *n* [C] **1** *US* : a rough bush or vine that usually has sharp thorns on its branches **2** *Brit* : BLACKBERRY

bran /ˈbræn/ *n* [U] : the outer coat of the seed of a grain • *bran cereal/muffins* [=cereal/muffins containing bran]

¹**branch** /ˈbræntʃ, *Brit* ˈbrɑːntʃ/ *n* [C] **1** : a part of a tree that grows out from the trunk • *the branches of a tree = tree branches* **2 a** : a local office or shop of a company or organization • *The bank has a branch in our area.* • *one of the bank's branch offices* **b** : a major part of a government • *the executive/legislative/judicial branch of the United States government* **3** : a part of an area of knowledge or study • *Pathology is a branch of medicine.* **4** : a part of a family that is descended from a particular family member in the past **5** : something that goes outward from a main line or source • *the west branch of the river* — **branched** /ˈbræntʃt, *Brit* ˈbrɑːntʃt/ *adj*

²**branch** *vb* [I] : to separate into branches • *The river branches near their house.* — **branch off** [*phrasal vb*] : to separate from something and move in a different direction • *Roads branch off from both sides of the highway there.* — **branch out** [*phrasal vb*] : to begin to do more different kinds of activities or work • *The company is branching out into formal wear.*

¹**brand** /ˈbrænd/ *n* [C] **1** : a category of products that are all made by a particular company and all have a particular name • *a brand of jeans* **2** : a particular kind or type of something • *I don't like his brand of humor.* **3** : a mark that is burned into the skin of an animal (such as a cow) to show who owns the animal

²**brand** *vb* [T] **1** : to put a mark on the skin of (an animal) by burning to show who owns it • *They branded their cattle.* **2** : to describe or identify (someone or something) with a word that expresses strong criticism • *They branded him a coward.* [=they said he was a coward] • *The newspaper was branded (as) racist for publishing the article.*

brand·ed /ˈbrændəd/ *adj, always before a noun* : having a well-known brand name • *branded* [=*brand-name*] *products*

bran·dish /ˈbrændɪʃ/ *vb* [T] : to wave or swing (something, such as a weapon) in a threatening or excited manner • *an intruder brandishing a knife*

brand name *n* [C] : a name that is given to a product by the company that produces or sells it

brand–name /ˈbrændˈneɪm/ *adj* : having a well-known brand name • *brand-name products*

brand–new /ˈbrændˈnuː, *Brit* ˈbrændˈnjuː/ *adj* : completely new • *a brand-new car/baby*

bran·dy /ˈbrændi/ *n, pl* **-dies** [C/U] : an alcoholic drink made from wine

brash /ˈbræʃ/ *adj* **1** : confident and aggressive in usually a rude or unpleasant way • *a brash young executive* **2** : very strong or harsh • *brash colors/lighting* — **brash·ly** *adv* — **brash·ness** *n* [U]

brass /ˈbræs, *Brit* ˈbrɑːs/ *n* **1** [U] : a yellow metal that is made by combining copper and zinc • *a candlestick made of* *brass = a brass candlestick*　**2** [*U, plural*] : musical instruments (such as trumpets and tubas) that are made of brass ▪ *a brass instrument* ▪ *The brasses began to play.* — see also BRASS BAND　**3** [*U*] : bright metal objects made of brass ▪ *polishing the brass and the silver*　**4** [*U*] *chiefly US, informal* : the people in the highest positions in the military, a business, etc. ▪ *Navy brass [=top brass] met earlier today.* — used with both plural and singular verbs ▪ *The company brass have/has decided that no action is necessary.* — **get down to brass tacks** *informal* : to start to discuss or consider the most important details or facts about something

brass band *n* [*C*] : a band (such as a marching band or a military band) in which most of the musicians play brass instruments

brassed off *adj, Brit, informal* : annoyed and unhappy ▪ *feeling a bit brassed off*

bras·siere /brəˈzɪɚ, *Brit* ˈbræziə/ *n* [*C*] *formal* : BRA

brass ring *n* — **the brass ring** *US, informal* : a very desirable prize, goal, or opportunity ▪ *This job offer is her chance to grab the brass ring.*

brassy /ˈbræsi, *Brit* ˈbrɑːsi/ *adj* **brass·i·er; -est**　**1** : very confident and aggressive in a loud and sometimes annoying way ▪ *a brassy reporter*　**2** : having a loud and often harsh sound ▪ *a big, brassy voice*　**3** : resembling or suggesting brass ▪ *a brassy color/shine*

brat /ˈbræt/ *n* [*C*] *informal*　**1** *disapproving* : a child who behaves very badly ▪ *a bunch of little brats* ▪ *a spoiled brat*　**2** *US* : the child of a person whose career is in the army, navy, etc. ▪ *I was an army/navy/military brat.* — **brat·ty** /ˈbræti/ *adj* **brat·ti·er; -est** ▪ *a bratty child* — **brat·ti·ness** *n* [*U*]

bra·va·do /brəˈvɑːdoʊ/ *n* [*U*] : confident or brave talk or behavior that is intended to impress other people ▪ *youthful/macho bravado*

¹**brave** /ˈbreɪv/ *adj* : feeling or showing no fear : not afraid ▪ *a brave soldier/smile/fight* ▪ *She put on/up a brave face/front* [=she appeared brave or calm] *despite the pain.* — **the brave** : brave people ▪ *the home of the brave* — **brave·ly** *adv*

²**brave** *vb* **braved; brav·ing** [*T*] : to face or deal with (something dangerous or unpleasant) ▪ *Thousands of fans braved rush-hour traffic to see the concert.*

³**brave** *n* [*C*] *old-fashioned* : a Native American warrior

brave new world *n* [*singular*] : a situation or area of activity that is created by the development of something completely new and different ▪ *the brave new world of computer technology*

brav·ery /ˈbreɪvəri/ *n* [*U*] : the quality that allows someone to do things that are dangerous or frightening ▪ *an act of bravery* [=a brave act]

bra·vo /ˈbrɑːvoʊ/ *interj* — used to express approval of a performance ▪ *Shouts of "Bravo!" continued after the curtain fell.*

bra·vu·ra /brəˈvjʊrə/ *n* [*U*] : great skill and energy in doing something (such as

performing on a stage) ▪ *a bravura performance*

brawl /ˈbrɑːl/ *vb* [*I*] : to fight noisily in usually a public place ▪ *Fans were brawling in the streets.* — **brawl** *n* [*C*] ▪ *A brawl broke out among the fans.* ▪ *a barroom brawl* [=a fight in a bar] — **brawl·er** *n* [*C*]

brawn /ˈbrɑːn/ *n* [*U*] : muscular strength — usually used to compare physical strength to intelligence ▪ *women who prefer brains over brawn* [=like smart men better than muscular ones] — **brawny** /ˈbrɑːni/ *adj* **brawn·i·er; -est** ▪ *his brawny* [=*muscular*] *arms*

bray /ˈbreɪ/ *vb*　**1** [*I*] : to make the loud sound that a donkey makes ▪ *The donkey brayed loudly (at us).*　**2** [*T/I*] : to speak or laugh in a very loud and unpleasant way ▪ *a braying voice/laugh* ▪ *"I'm the best!" she brayed.* — **bray** *n* [*C*] ▪ *the bray of a donkey*

bra·zen /ˈbreɪzn̩/ *adj* : acting or done in a very open and shocking way without shame or embarrassment ▪ *a brazen liar/lie* — **bra·zen·ly** *adv* — **bra·zen·ness** *n* [*U*]

¹**breach** /ˈbriːtʃ/ *n*　**1** [*C/U*] : a failure to do what is required by a law, an agreement, or a duty — usually + *of* ▪ *He was fined for committing a breach of the peace.* [=for making a lot of noise or behaving violently in public] ▪ *They sued her for breach of contract.* [=for failing to do what the contract required]　**2** ◆ A **breach of security** or a **security breach** is an occurrence in which someone is able to get into a place that is guarded or is able to get secret information.　**3** [*C*] : a break in friendly relations between people or groups ▪ *The breach between them developed years ago.*　**4** [*C*] : a hole or opening in something (such as a wall) made by breaking through it ▪ (*figurative*) *When the company needed new leadership, she stepped/leaped/jumped into the breach.* [=she provided help that was badly needed; she became a leader]

²**breach** *vb* [*T*]　**1** : to fail to do what is required by (a law, agreement, contract, etc.) ▪ *The city breached an agreement by selling the property.*　**2** : to make a hole or opening in (something) ▪ *The army breached the castle wall.*

¹**bread** /ˈbrɛd/ *n*　**1** [*C/U*] : a baked food made from a mixture of flour and water ▪ *a loaf/slice/piece/hunk of bread* ▪ *bread crumbs*　**2** [*U*] *old-fashioned, slang* : MONEY ▪ *I took the job because I need the bread.* — **break bread** : to have a meal together ▪ *Will you break bread with me?* — **know which side your bread is buttered on** *informal* : to know how to act or how to treat others in order to get what you want

²**bread** *vb* [*T*] : to cover (food) with bread crumbs before cooking it ▪ *Bread the pork chops before frying them.* ▪ *breaded chicken*

bread and butter *n* [*singular*] : a dependable source of income or success ▪ *Casual clothing has always been the company's bread and butter.*

bread–and–butter *adj, always before a*

noun **1** : basic and important ▪ *bread-and-butter economic issues* **2** : dependable as a source of income or success ▪ *the company's bread-and-butter products*

bread·bas·ket /'brɛd,bæskət, Brit 'brɛd,bɑːskət/ *n* [C] : a region that provides large amounts of food ▪ *The area is the nation's breadbasket.*

bread·box /'brɛd,bɑːks/ *n* [C] chiefly US : a container in someone's kitchen where bread and other baked goods are stored to keep them fresh — often used informally to describe the size of something ▪ *It's not much bigger than a breadbox.*

bread·line /'brɛd,laɪn/ *n* **1** [C] chiefly US : a line of people who are waiting to receive free food **2** **the breadline** Brit : the level of income at which someone is considered poor ▪ *people living below/near/on the breadline* [=the poverty line]

breadth /'brɛtθ/ *n* [U] **1** : the distance from one side to the other side of something : WIDTH ▪ *Measure the height, breadth, and depth of each cabinet.* — see also HAIR'S BREADTH **2** : the wide scope or range of something ▪ *your breadth of knowledge/experience/achievement* — **the length and breadth of** see LENGTH

bread·win·ner /'brɛd,wɪnɚ/ *n* [C] : a person who earns money to support a family ▪ *the family/family's breadwinner*

¹**break** /'breɪk/ *vb* **broke** /'broʊk/; **broken** /'broʊkən/; **break·ing** **1** [T/I] : to separate (something) into parts or pieces often in a sudden and forceful or violent way ▪ *She broke the cup when she dropped it.* = *The cup broke when she dropped it.* **2** [T/I] : to cause (a bone) to separate into two or more pieces ▪ *He broke his arm in the accident.* [=one of the bones in his arm was broken in the accident] **3** [I] : to open suddenly especially because of pressure from inside ▪ *The blister broke.* **4** **a** [T] : to cause (something, such as a machine) to stop working or being damaged ▪ *I somehow broke the phone.* **b** [I] : to stop working because of being damaged ▪ *The pump broke.* **5** [T/I] : to split or divide (something) into smaller units or parts ▪ *The word "singing" can be broken (up) into the two syllables "sing-" and "-ing."* ▪ *The corporation broke (up) into several smaller companies.* **6** [T] **a** : to go through or make a hole in (a surface, someone's skin, etc.) ▪ *A large fish broke the surface of the water.* **b** : to go through (something) by using force ▪ *Use a knife to break the seal.* ▪ *(figurative) people who broke racial barriers in the music industry* **c** : to cut into and turn over the surface of (the ground, soil, etc.) ▪ *The farmer uses a plow to break the soil.* **7** [T] : to fail to do what is required by (a law, a promise, etc.) ▪ *They broke the law.* ▪ *break a promise/rule/contract* **8** **a** [T] : to destroy or defeat (something) by using force or pressure ▪ *They couldn't break his spirit/determination/resistance.* ▪ *His spirit/determination will never break.* **b** [T] : to cause (someone) to fail or to stop trying or fighting ▪ *They put pressure on him, but they couldn't break him.* ▪ *This film could make or break her career.*

[=the success or failure of her career could depend on the success or failure of this film] **c** [I] : to lose your health, mental or physical strength, or control ▪ *The witness broke under questioning.* **d** [T] : to train (a wild animal) to behave in a way that is useful to people ▪ *special equipment used to break horses* **9** [T] **a** : to cause the end of (something that is strong or that has continued for a long time) ▪ *trying to break the deadlock in Congress* ▪ *break a bad habit* **b** : to cause (someone) to give up a habit — + *of* ▪ *His friends are trying to break him of his smoking habit.* **10** [T] : to interrupt (something) ▪ *The silence was broken by a sudden shout.* ▪ *The noise broke my concentration.* [=made it impossible for me to concentrate] **11** [I] : to stop an activity for a brief time ▪ *Let's break for lunch.* **12** **a** [T] : to tell (bad news) to someone in a kind or gentle way ▪ *I'll try to break the news to her gently.* **b** [T] : to make (something, such as news) publicly known for the first time ▪ *The local TV station broke the news about the President's visit.* **c** [I] of news : to become publicly known ▪ *The story broke yesterday.* **13** [T] : to reduce the speed or force of (something) ▪ *The bushes helped to break his fall.* [=helped make his fall less forceful] ▪ *She never broke (her) stride.* [=never paused or slowed down] **14** [T] **a** : to be higher or more than (a specified number, measurement, etc.) ▪ *The temperature broke 90 (degrees Fahrenheit) today.* **b** : to do better than (a record, a particular total, etc.) ▪ *She almost broke the world record.* ▪ *golfers trying to break 90* [=to have a score below 90] **15** [T] **a** : to find or provide an explanation or solution for (something, such as a criminal case) ▪ *The detective finally broke* [=solved] *the case.* **b** : to find the meaning of (a secret code) ▪ *They couldn't break the code.* **16** [I] **a** of the weather : to change by becoming rainy, clear, cool, etc., after a long time ▪ *The heat wave finally broke.* [=ended] **b** of clouds : to separate so that the sky or sun can be seen ▪ *The clouds broke, revealing blue sky above.* **c** of a storm : to start suddenly ▪ *Everyone ran inside when the storm broke.* **17** [I] literary : to begin when the sun rises ▪ *They left just as day/dawn was breaking* [=just as the sun was rising] **18** [I] : to begin running quickly ▪ *Everyone broke* [=dashed, ran] *for cover.* **19** [T] **a** : to give smaller bills or coins for (a large bill) ▪ *Can you break a $20 bill for me?* **b** : to use (a large bill) to pay for something that costs much less than the value of the bill ▪ *I didn't want to break a $20 bill just to buy something for a dollar.* **20** [I] of a wave : to curl over and fall onto or near land ▪ *waves breaking against/over/on the rocks* **21** [I] **a** of someone's voice : to change sharply in tone or pitch because of strong emotion ▪ *Her voice was breaking (with emotion) as she said goodbye.* **b** of a boy's voice : to change from the high voice of a boy to the lower voice of a man **22** [I] sports, of a thrown or struck ball : to turn or

curve ▪ *The putt broke to the left.* **23**
[*T/I*] *tennis* : to win against (an opponent
who is serving) ▪ *The challenger broke
(the champion) in the final set.* **24** [*I*] : to
happen or develop ▪ *For the team to succeed, everything has to break* [=go] *right
for them.* [=they have to be lucky] —
break a leg see ¹LEG — **break a sweat**
see ²SWEAT — **break away** [*phrasal vb*]
1 : to get away from someone or something especially by using force or effort ▪
Pieces of the rock ledge have broken away.
▪ *She broke away from the other runners to
win the race.* ▪ *(figurative) young people
breaking away from traditional values* **2**
: to separate or become separate from a
larger group, country, etc. ▪ *a faction that
has broken away from the main political
party* — **break bread** see ¹BREAD —
break down [*phrasal vb*] **1 a** *of a machine* : to stop working properly ▪ *Our
car broke down on the highway.* **b** : to
fail or stop usually in a complete and
sudden way ▪ *Negotiations have broken
down.* **2 a** : to become overwhelmed by
strong emotions ▪ *She broke down and
started to cry.* = *She broke down in tears.*
b break down or **break (someone) down**
or **break down (someone)** : to lose or
cause (someone) to lose strength or the
ability to resist or fight ▪ *The prisoner finally broke down under intensive questioning.* ▪ *She finally broke down and got a
cell phone.* [=she bought a cell phone after resisting the desire to buy one for a
long time] **3 break down** or **break
(something) down** or **break down (something) a** : to become separated or to
separate (something) into simpler substances ▪ *Water can be broken down into
hydrogen and oxygen.* **b** : to be able to
be divided or to divide (something) *into*
parts or groups ▪ *The report breaks down
into three sections.* = *The report is broken
down into three sections.* [=the report has
three sections] **c** : to use force to push
(something) to the ground ▪ *break down
a door* ▪ *(figurative) trying to break down
legal barriers to integration* — **break
even** : to take in as much money as you
spend ▪ *The company is finally breaking
even and hopes to make a profit soon.* —
break faith with see FAITH — **break
free** : to become able to move or escape
by using force or effort ▪ *The prisoner
struggled to break free.* — **break from**
[*phrasal vb*] : to end a relationship, connection, or agreement with (someone or
something) ▪ *breaking from tradition/ste-
reotypes* — **break ground** see ¹GROUND
— **break in** [*phrasal vb*] **1** : to enter a
house, building, etc., illegally ▪ *Someone
tried to break in while we were away.* **2**
: to interrupt or disturb someone or
something ▪ *We were having a chat when
he rudely broke in (on it).* **3 break in** or
break (someone or something) in or
break in (someone or something) a : to
start or help (someone) to start a new activity, job, etc. ▪ *We try to break new employees in gradually.* **b** : to use (something) for a period of time so that it
becomes comfortable ▪ *I'm breaking in a
new pair of shoes.* **c** : to operate (a new

machine) carefully for a period of time
until it is ready for regular use ▪ *Don't
drive too fast while you're breaking the car
in.* — **break into** [*phrasal vb*] **1** : to enter (a house, building, etc.) illegally and
especially by using force ▪ *Someone tried
to break into our house.* **2** : to begin to
do or have (something) suddenly ▪ *She
broke into tears.* [=began to cry] ▪ *The audience broke into applause.* [=began ap-
plauding] **3** : to enter or get started in
(something, such as a profession) ▪ *trying
to break into show business* **4** : to interrupt (something) ▪ *The network broke
into the program with a special news report.* — **break loose 1** : to suddenly
stop being attached to something ▪ *One
of the shutters broke loose during the
storm.* **2** : to get away from someone or
something by using force or effort ▪ *The
prisoner broke loose and ran away.* — see
also *all hell breaks loose* at HELL —
break new ground see ¹GROUND —
break off [*phrasal vb*] **1 break off** or
break off (something) or **break (something) off** or **break (something) off
(something)** : to become separated or
cause (something) to become separated
because of force or violence ▪ *The handle
broke off when I dropped the cup.* ▪ *I broke
[=tore] a piece of bread off (the loaf) and
ate it.* **2** : to stop or end suddenly or
cause (something) to stop or end suddenly ▪ *The speaker broke off (speaking) in the
middle of a sentence.* ▪ *The two countries
have broken off diplomatic relations.* ▪
They broke off their engagement. —
break open [*phrasal vb*] **break open** or
break open (something) or **break (something) open** : to open or to cause (something) to open suddenly ▪ *The pods broke
open and the seeds scattered on the wind.* ▪
The burglars broke open the locked safe.
— **break out** [*phrasal vb*] **1** : to begin
happening suddenly ▪ *A fire/riot had broken out.* ▪ *War could break out soon.* **2 a**
: to suddenly begin to have sweat, a rash,
etc., on your skin ▪ *He broke out in a
sweat.* [=he began to sweat] ▪ *Eating
strawberries makes her break out (in
hives).* **b** : to appear on the skin suddenly ▪ *Sweat broke out on his forehead.* **3**
: to escape from a prison, jail, etc. ▪ *Six
prisoners were caught attempting to break
out (of the jail).* ▪ *(figurative) We need to
break out of the financial rut we're in.* **4
break (something) out** or **break out
(something)** : to take (something) from
the place where it is stored so that it can
be used ▪ *We broke out the champagne to
celebrate our victory.* — **break rank** see
¹RANK — **break someone's heart** see
HEART — **break the back of** see ¹BACK
— **break the bank** see ¹BANK — **break
the ice** see ¹ICE — **break the mold** see
¹MOLD — **break through** [*phrasal vb*]
1 : to use force to get through (something, such as a barrier) ▪ *The enemy finally broke through (our defenses) and defeated us.* ▪ *(figurative) trying to help
people break through the barriers of poverty* **2** *of the sun* : to shine through
(clouds) ▪ *The sun finally began to break
through (the clouds).* — **break up** [*phras-*

al vb] **1 break up** or **break (something) up** or **break up (something) a** : to separate into parts or pieces ▪ *The asteroid broke up when it hit the Earth's atmosphere.* ▪ *break up a large estate* **b** : to end or cause (something) to end ▪ *The demonstration broke up when the police arrived.* ▪ *break up a fight* **2** : to end a romantic relationship, marriage, etc. ▪ *He and his wife have broken up.* ▪ *She broke up with him yesterday.* **3 break up** or **break (someone) up** *US, informal* : to begin laughing or cause (someone) to begin laughing suddenly and in a way that is difficult to control ▪ *Everyone broke up when they saw what he was wearing.* ▪ *That joke always breaks me up.* **4 break (something) up** or **break ŭp (something) a** : to change the regular quality or appearance of (something) ▪ *break up a dull routine* **b** : to separate the parts of (something) so that it is not complete ▪ *She was unwilling to break up the dining room set by selling one of the chairs.* **5** *Brit, of a school* : to come to the end of a period of instruction (such as a term) ▪ *School broke up for the summer last Friday.* — **break wind** see ¹WIND — **break with** [*phrasal vb*] : to end a relationship, connection, or agreement with (someone or something) ▪ *a desire to break with tradition* — **break·able** /ˈbreɪkəbəl/ *adj* ▪ *an easily breakable object*

²**break** *n* **1** [*C*] **a** : a crack, hole, etc., that is caused by damage, injury, or pressure ▪ *The tank is reinforced to prevent breaks and leaks.* **b** : an opening or space *in* something ▪ *There was a break in the clouds/hedge/fence.* ▪ *a break in traffic* **2** [*C*] : something that causes a change or interruption ▪ *a break in routine* [=something that changes/interrupts a routine] **3** [*C*] **a** : a time when something stops ▪ *It rained for five days without a break.* ▪ *a break in the game* **b** : a brief period of time during which someone stops an activity ▪ *Let's take a break.* [=let's stop doing what we are doing for a short period of time]; *especially* : a brief period of time during which a worker is allowed to rest, eat, etc., instead of working ▪ *We've been working all day without a break.* — see also COFFEE BREAK **c** : a longer period of time when someone is not working or doing some other activity ▪ *The weekend provided her with a much-needed break (from her job).* **d** : a time when many people are not working or going to school because of a holiday, vacation, etc. ▪ *What are your plans for the Thanksgiving break?* **4** [*C*] : a planned interruption in a radio or television program ▪ *a break for a commercial* = *a commercial break* **5** [*singular*] : a sudden fast run ▪ *The runner made a break for second base.* [=suddenly ran toward second base]; *especially* : a fast run by someone who is trying to escape ▪ *She made a (sudden) break for the door.* **6** [*C*] : a situation or event that is lucky or unlucky ▪ *a series of unlucky/bad breaks*; *especially* : a lucky situation or event that makes success possible ▪ *She gets all the breaks.* [=she is very lucky] ▪ *(US) I just can't*

seem to catch a break. [=I am unlucky] **7** [*C*] : something that helps a particular person or group ▪ *Can you give me a break on the price?* [=can you lower the price for me?] ▪ *a tax break* [=permission to pay less in taxes than other people] **8** [*singular*] **a** : a sudden ending of a relationship ▪ *The crisis has caused a break (in diplomatic relations) between the two countries.* **b** : a change from what was done before ▪ *a sharp break with tradition* ▪ *We need to make a clean break with the past.* [=to start doing things in a completely new way] **9** [*U*] *literary* — used in the phrase **break of day** to refer to the time of morning when the sun can first be seen ▪ *We left at (the) break of day.* **10** [*U*] *sports* : a curve in the path of a thrown or hit ball ▪ *The putt had a lot of break.* [=the putt curved a lot] **11** [*C*] *tennis* : the act defeating an opponent who is serving ▪ *a service break* — **give me a break** *informal* **1** — used to tell someone to stop bothering you or treating you unfairly **2** — used to say that you do not believe or are disgusted about what someone has said or done ▪ *"She says she went to Harvard." "Give me a break! I doubt she even finished high school!"* — **give (someone) a break** : to stop treating (someone) in a strict or harsh way ▪ *Why don't you give him a break and stop criticizing him?*

break·age /ˈbreɪkɪʤ/ *n* [*C/U*] : the act of breaking or being broken ▪ *The cups are prone to breakage.* [=they break easily]

break·away /ˈbreɪkəˌweɪ/ *adj, always before a noun* : having become separate from a larger group, country, etc. ▪ *a breakaway republic/province*

break·down /ˈbreɪkˌdaʊn/ *n* **1** [*C/U*] : an occurrence in which a machine (such as a car) stops working ▪ *We had a breakdown on the highway.* **2 a** [*C*] : the failure of a relationship or of an effort to discuss something ▪ *a breakdown of/in in negotiations* **b** [*C/U*] : a failure that prevents a system from working properly ▪ *(a) breakdown of the health-care system* **3** [*C*] : a sudden failure of mental or physical health ▪ *He suffered/had a breakdown after his wife died.* — see also NERVOUS BREAKDOWN **4** [*C/U*] : the process or result of showing the different parts of something in order to understand it more clearly ▪ *She did/provided a breakdown of the statistics into categories.* **5** [*U*] : the process or result of separating a substance into simpler parts ▪ *the breakdown of water into hydrogen and oxygen*

breakdown lane *n* [*C*] *US* : an area along the side of a highway where vehicles are able to stop for an emergency

break·er /ˈbreɪkɚ/ *n* [*C*] **1** : someone or something that breaks something ▪ *a breaker of records* = *a record-breaker* **2** : a wave that is curling over and falling onto the shore, rocks, etc. ▪ *breakers crashing on the shore*

¹**break·fast** /ˈbrɛkfəst/ *n* [*C/U*] : the first meal of the day ▪ *a big/good/hearty breakfast* ▪ *breakfast cereals* — **a dog's breakfast** see ¹DOG

²**breakfast** vb [I] : to eat breakfast ▪ We breakfasted on cereal and toast.

break-in /'breɪkˌɪn/ n [C] : the act or crime of illegally entering a house, building, etc., especially by using force ▪ an attempted break-in

breaking and entering n [U] law : the crime of illegally entering a house, building, etc., especially by using force

breaking point — **the breaking point** (US) or Brit **breaking point** 1 : the time when a person can no longer accept or deal with a situation because of too much pressure or stress ▪ I had just about reached the breaking point. 2 : the time when a situation has become so difficult, dangerous, etc., that it cannot continue ▪ Tensions between them had reached the breaking point.

break-neck /'breɪkˌnɛk/ adj, always before a noun : very fast : dangerously fast ▪ driving at breakneck speed

¹**break-out** /'breɪkˌaʊt/ n [C] : an escape from a prison, jail, etc., especially by a group of prisoners ▪ Three people were killed during an attempted breakout (from the prison).

²**breakout** adj, always before a noun, US : having, causing, or marked by sudden and great success that comes usually after a time without much success ▪ The company had a breakout year last year.

break-through /'breɪkˌθru:/ n [C] 1 : an important discovery that happens after trying for a long time to understand or explain something ▪ Researchers have made/achieved a major breakthrough in cancer treatment. ▪ breakthrough ideas/products 2 : a person's first important success ▪ This job is the breakthrough she's been waiting for. ▪ a breakthrough performance/role/album

break-up /'breɪkˌʌp/ n 1 [C/U] : the end of a relationship, marriage, etc. ▪ She went through a bad/painful breakup with her boyfriend. ▪ the breakup of his marriage 2 [U] : the separation of something into smaller parts or pieces ▪ the breakup of the Roman Empire

break-wa-ter /'breɪkˌwɑːtɚ/ n [C] : a wall that is built out into the sea to protect a harbor or beach from the force of waves

breast /'brɛst/ n 1 [C] : either one of the two soft parts on a woman's chest that produce milk when she has a baby ▪ breast cancer ▪ breast tissue/milk 2 [C] a old-fashioned + literary : the front part of a person's body between the neck and the stomach : CHEST ▪ She clasped the child to her breast. b literary : the chest thought of as the place where emotions are felt ▪ Dark thoughts lurked within his breast. 3 a [C] : the front part of a bird's body below the neck ▪ a bird with an orange breast b [C/U] : meat from the front part of a bird's or animal's body ▪ a few slices of turkey breast 4 [C] : the part of a piece of clothing that covers a person's chest ▪ the breast of a jacket ▪ the coat's breast pocket — **make a clean breast of** : to speak openly and honestly about (something that you have previously lied about or kept secret) ▪ I made

a clean breast of it/things and admitted that I was to blame. — **breast·ed** /'brɛstəd/ adj ▪ a red-breasted bird [=a bird with a red breast] ▪ bare-breasted women

breast·bone /'brɛstˌboʊn/ n [C] : a flat, narrow bone in the middle of the chest to which the ribs are connected — called also sternum

breast–feed /'brɛstˌfi:d/ vb -fed /-ˌfɛd/; -feed·ing [T/I] : to feed a baby from a mother's breast ▪ mothers who breast-feed (their children)

breast–stroke /'brɛstˌstroʊk/ n [singular] : a way of swimming in which the swimmer's face is in the water and the arms move in a large motion from front to back as the feet kick outward

breath /'brɛθ/ n 1 [U] : the air that you take into your lungs and send out from your lungs when you breathe ▪ It's so cold outside that I can see my breath. ▪ I smelled alcohol on his breath. [=his breath smelled of alcohol] ▪ bad breath [=breath that smells unpleasant] 2 a [U] : the ability to breathe freely ▪ He was fighting/struggling/gasping for breath. [=he was having a lot of difficulty breathing] ▪ I'm out of breath [=I'm breathing hard] from walking up all those stairs. ◇ To **catch your breath** or (Brit) **get your breath back** is to rest until you are able to breathe normally. ▪ Give me a moment to catch my breath. ◇ Someone who is **short of breath** or who has **shortness of breath** has difficulty breathing in enough air especially because of a physical or medical condition. b [C] : an amount of air that you take into your lungs ▪ The patient was taking shallow breaths. [=breathing in small amounts of air] ▪ Take a deep breath. [=breathe deeply] ▪ her last/dying breath [=the breath that she took just before she died] ◇ If someone say two different things in the same breath, or if you say one thing and then something else in the next breath, it means that you say these things very close together. ▪ It's unusual to hear "promotions" mentioned in the same breath as "layoffs." ◇ If someone says that you are wasting your breath or tells you to save your breath, it means that the things you say will not make someone behave or think differently and that you should not bother to try. 3 [C] : a slight breeze ▪ a hot day with scarcely a breath of wind 4 [singular] : a very small amount of something ▪ There was never even the slightest breath of suspicion. — **a breath of fresh air** 1 : clean or cool outside air after you have been in a building for a period of time ▪ We went outside to get a breath of fresh air. 2 : someone or something that is different in a way that is interesting, exciting, enjoyable, etc. ▪ Our new supervisor is a breath of fresh air. — **hold your breath** 1 : to keep the air that you have breathed in your lungs for a short time instead of breathing out ▪ How long can you hold your breath? 2 informal — used to say that you do not believe that something will happen soon or at all ▪ "She says she'll do it." "Well, don't hold *your breath."* — **take your breath away** ✧ Something that *takes your breath away* is extremely exciting, beautiful, or surprising. — **under your breath** ✧ If you say something *under your breath*, you say it quietly so that it is difficult to hear. ▪ *She muttered something under her breath.* — **with bated breath** see BATED

breathe /ˈbriːð/ *vb* **breathed; breathing 1** [*T/I*] : to move air into and out of your lungs ▪ *Relax and breathe deeply.* ▪ *I want to live where I can breathe clean/ fresh air.* **2** [*T/I*] **a** : to send (something) out from your lungs through your mouth or nose ▪ *a dragon that breathes fire* ▪ *Breathe out through your nose.* **b** : to take (something) into your lungs through your mouth or nose ▪ *People usually contract the virus by breathing contaminated air.* ▪ **breathing in** [=*inhaling*] *fumes* **3** [*I*] : to be alive ▪ *a living, breathing human being* **4** [*I*] : to pause and rest before continuing ▪ *Let's stop to breathe for a moment.* **5** [*T*] : to bring (something) *into* a thing ▪ *Their leadership breathed new life into* [=gave new energy to] *the movement.* **6** [*I*] : to feel able to think or act freely ▪ *I need room to breathe.* = *I need breathing room/space.* **7** [*I*] : to allow air to pass through ▪ *a fabric that breathes* **8** [*T*] : to say (something) very quietly ▪ *Don't breathe a word of/about this to anyone!* [=do not say anything about this to anyone] — **breathe a sigh of relief** : to relax because something you have been worrying about is not a problem or danger anymore — **breathe down someone's neck 1** : to chase after someone closely ▪ *The cops were breathing down our necks.* **2** : to watch someone carefully and constantly ▪ *My parents are always breathing down my neck.* — **breathe easy/easier/ easily/freely** : to feel relief from pressure, danger, etc. ▪ *I'll breathe easier once this whole ordeal is over.* — **live and breathe** ✧ If you *live and breathe* something, you spend a great deal of time, thought, or effort on that thing. ▪ *She lives and breathes music.* — **breath·able** /ˈbriːðəbəl/ *adj* ▪ *a breathable fabric* [=a fabric that allows air to pass through] — **breathing** *n* [*U*] ▪ *Her breathing is heavy/ shallow/labored.* ▪ *breathing exercises/ problems*

breath·er /ˈbriːðɚ/ *n* [*C*] : a pause for rest : BREAK ▪ *Let's take a breather.*

breath·less /ˈbrɛθləs/ *adj* **1** : breathing very hard because you are trying to get more air ▪ *The hike left me breathless.* [=*out of breath*] **2 a** : full of emotion ▪ *They were breathless with anticipation.* **b** : very fast ▪ *driving at a breathless pace* — **breath·less·ly** *adv* — **breath·less·ness** *n* [*U*]

breath·tak·ing /ˈbrɛθˌteɪkɪŋ/ *adj* **1** : very exciting : THRILLING ▪ *a breathtaking performance/ view* **2** : very great or surprising ▪ *breathtaking arrogance* — **breath·tak·ing·ly** *adv*

breathy /ˈbrɛθi/ *adj* **breath·i·er; -est** : spoken or sung with the sound of a person's breath ▪ *a breathy whisper/voice*

bred *past tense and past participle of* ¹BREED

breech·es /ˈbrɪtʃəz/ *n* [*plural*] : short pants that are fastened at or just below the knee ▪ *riding breeches*

¹**breed** /ˈbriːd/ *vb* **bred** /ˈbrɛd/; **breed·ing 1** [*T*] : to keep and take care of animals or plants in order to produce more animals or plants of a particular kind ▪ *breeding cattle* ▪ *The plants are bred to resist disease.* **2** [*I*] : to produce young animals, birds, etc. ▪ *areas where mosquitoes breed* [=*reproduce*] **3** [*T*] : to take care of and teach (a child who is growing up) ▪ *children who are bred* [=*raised, brought up*] *in poverty* **4** [*T*] : to cause or lead to (something) ▪ *Despair often breeds violence.* — **bred in the bone** — used to describe a personal quality that is a deep or basic part of someone's nature ▪ *His love of sports is bred in the bone.* ▪ *a bred-in-the-bone conservative* — **breed·er** *n* [*C*] ▪ *cattle/dog breeders*

²**breed** *n* [*C*] **1** : a particular kind of dog, cat, horse, etc. ▪ *different breeds of cattle* **2** : a kind of person ▪ *a new/different breed of athlete* ▪ *People like them are a dying breed.* [=there are not many people like them anymore]

breeding *n* [*U*] **1** : the process by which young animals, birds, etc., are produced by their parents ▪ *the breeding season* **2** : the activity of keeping and caring for animals or plants in order to produce more animals or plants of a particular kind ▪ *horse/dog/plant breeding* ▪ *a breeding program* **3** *somewhat old-fashioned* : the way a person was taught in childhood to behave ▪ *Politeness shows good breeding.* : good manners that come from being raised correctly ▪ *a person who lacks breeding*

breeding ground *n* [*C*] **1** : a place where animals go to breed ▪ *a breeding ground for seals* **2** : a place or situation that helps or allows something to grow, develop, etc. ▪ *The company is a breeding ground for innovation.*

¹**breeze** /ˈbriːz/ *n* **1** [*C*] : a gentle wind ▪ *a cool breeze* **2** [*singular*] *informal* : something that is easy to do ▪ *The test was a breeze.* — **shoot the breeze** see ¹SHOOT

²**breeze** *vb* **breezed; breez·ing** [*I*] **1** : to move quickly and confidently ▪ *He breezed past/by us.* **2** : to easily succeed at something ▪ *She breezed through the test.*

breeze–block *n* [*C*] *Brit* : CINDER BLOCK

breeze·way /ˈbriːzˌweɪ/ *n* [*C*] *US* : a narrow structure with a roof and no walls that connects two buildings (such as a house and garage)

breezy /ˈbriːzi/ *adj* **breez·i·er; -est 1** : having strong winds : WINDY ▪ *a breezy day/beach* **2** : informal and lively ▪ *the author's breezy style* **3** : relaxed in a way that shows you are not concerned about or interested in something ▪ *breezy indifference* — **breez·i·ly** /ˈbriːzəli/ *adv*

breth·ren /ˈbrɛðrən/ *plural of* BROTHER — used especially to begin to talk in a formal way to a group of people or to refer to the members of a particular group • *our church brethren*

brev·i·ty /ˈbrɛvəti/ *n* [U] : the quality of being brief • *I've omitted some passages for the sake of brevity.* [=because I want to be brief] • *the brevity of youth*

¹**brew** /ˈbruː/ *vb* **1** [T/I] : to make (beer, ale, etc.) • *They brew their own beer.* • *the brewing process* **2** [T/I] : to make (coffee, tea, etc.) • *I'll brew (up) another pot of tea.* • *The coffee is brewing.* [=the coffee is being brewed] **3** [I] : to start to form • *There's a storm brewing.* • *Trouble is brewing.* — **brew·er** /ˈbruːwɚ/ *n* [C]

²**brew** *n* **1** [C/U] *chiefly US* : a drink (such as beer or ale) that is made by brewing • *a bottle of brew* • *one of my home brews* [=a beer/ale that I made at home] • *a* [U] *US* : COFFEE • *a perfect cup of brew* **b** [C] *Brit* : a cup of tea **3** [C] : a mixture of different things • *a strange brew of jazz, classical, and bluegrass music* • *a dangerous brew*

brew·ery /ˈbruːwəri/ *n, pl* **-er·ies** [C] : a place where beer is made or a company that makes beer

bri·ar *also* **bri·er** /ˈbrajɚ/ *n* [C] : a wild plant that has many sharp points (called thorns) on its branches • *a thicket of briars*

¹**bribe** /ˈbraɪb/ *n* [C] : something valuable (such as money) that is given in order to get someone to do something usually illegal or dishonest • *a police officer accused of taking/accepting bribes* — **brib·ery** /ˈbraɪbəri/ *n* [U] • *arrested on charges of bribery*

²**bribe** *vb* **bribed; brib·ing** [T] : to try to get someone to do something by giving or promising something valuable (such as money) • *She attempted to bribe a judge.*

bric–a–brac /ˈbrɪkəˌbræk/ *n* [U] : small objects that are used for decoration and are not usually valuable • *shelves full of bric-a-brac*

¹**brick** /ˈbrɪk/ *n* **1** [C/U] : a small, hard block of baked clay that is used to build structures (such as houses) and sometimes to make streets, paths, etc. • *a pile of bricks* • *a house/wall made of brick/bricks = a brick house/wall* **2** [C] **a** : a block of something • *a brick of ice cream* **b** *Brit* : a child's toy block — **bricks and mortar** *Brit* : houses and other buildings especially when people consider buying them because of their possible future value • *people rushing to invest in bricks and mortar* — see also BRICK-AND-MORTAR — **like a ton of bricks** *informal* : very hard or severely • *The loss of his job hit him like a ton of bricks.* [=made him very upset, unhappy, etc.]

²**brick** *vb* — **brick up** [*phrasal vb*] **brick (something) up** *or* **brick up (something)** : to cover or block (something) with bricks • *They bricked up the windows.*

brick–and–mortar *or* **bricks–and–mortar** *adj* — used to describe a traditional store or business that is in a building instead of on the Internet • *They have a Web site as well as several brick-and-mortar stores.*

brick·bat /ˈbrɪkˌbæt/ *n* [C] : a criticism

or rude comment • *politicians hurling brickbats at one another*

brick·lay·er /ˈbrɪkˌlejɚ/ *n* [C] : a person whose job is to build things with bricks — **brick·lay·ing** /ˈbrɪkˌlejɪŋ/ *n* [U]

brick red *n* [U] : a brownish-red color — **brick–red** *adj* • *a brick-red scarf*

brick·work /ˈbrɪkˌwɚk/ *n* [U] : the part of something that is made with bricks • *the building's decorative brickwork*

brid·al /ˈbraɪdl̩/ *adj* : of or relating to a bride or a wedding • *a bridal shop/gown* • *the bridal party* [=the bride and groom and the people who stand with them during the wedding ceremony] • *the hotel's bridal suite* [=a special set of rooms for a couple who have just been married]

bride /ˈbraɪd/ *n* [C] : a woman who has just married or is about to be married • *a new bride*

bride·groom /ˈbraɪdˌgruːm, ˈbraɪdˌgrʊm/ *n* [C] : ¹GROOM 1 • *the bride and bridegroom*

brides·maid /ˈbraɪdzˌmeɪd/ *n* [C] : a female friend or relative who helps a bride at her wedding

bride–to–be *n, pl* **brides–to–be** [C] : a woman who is going to be married soon

¹**bridge** /ˈbrɪdʒ/ *n* **1** [C] : a structure built over something (such as a river) so that people or vehicles can get across • *the Brooklyn Bridge* • *a railroad bridge* [=a bridge for trains] **2** [C] : something that joins or connects different people or things • *Her work serves as a bridge between the past and the present.* • *trying to build a bridge between two cultures* **3** [C] : the place on a ship where the ship is steered **4** [C] **a** : the upper part of the nose • *He broke the bridge of his nose.* **b** : the part of a pair of eyeglasses that rests on a person's nose **5** [C] : the part of a guitar, violin, or similar musical instrument that raises the strings away from the surface **6** [C] : part of a song that connects one section to the next section **7** [C] : a false tooth or row of false teeth that fits between two real teeth **8** [U] : a card game for four players in two teams — **burn your bridges** see ¹BURN — **cross that bridge when you come to it** ◇ If you say you will *cross that bridge when you come to it*, you mean that you will not worry about a possible problem until it actually happens. — **water under the bridge** see ¹WATER

²**bridge** *vb* **bridged; bridg·ing** [T] : to make a bridge over or across (something) • *(figurative) styles that bridge the gap between fashion and practicality*

¹**bri·dle** /ˈbraɪdl̩/ *n* [C] : a device that fits on a horse's head and that is used for guiding and controlling the horse

²**bridle** *vb* **bri·dled; bri·dling** **1** [T] : to put a bridle on (a horse) • *(figurative) She was forced to bridle her anger.* **2** [I] : to react in an angry way • *He bridled at their criticism.*

¹**brief** /ˈbriːf/ *adj* **1** : lasting only a short time • *The meeting will be brief.* • *a brief period (of time)* **2** : using only a few words • *I promise to be brief.* [=to say what I need to say quickly] • *a brief description/summary* • *I'd like to say a brief*

word [=a few words] *about the issue.* **3** *of clothing* : covering less of the body than is usual ▪ *a brief bikini*

²brief *n* **1** [*C*] : a brief statement or report ▪ *a news brief* **2** [*C*] *US, law* : a document that states the facts a lawyer plans to use in a court case ▪ *a legal brief* **3** [*C*] *chiefly Brit* : instructions that explain what a person is supposed to do ▪ *Her brief is to manage the sales department.* **4** [*plural*] : short underpants for men, women, or children that fit close to the body ▪ *a pair of briefs* — **in brief** : in a few words ▪ *the news in brief* [=a brief report of the news]

³brief *vb* [*T*] : to give information or instructions to (someone) ▪ *The captain briefed the crew on the new procedures.* — **brief·ing** *n* [*C*] ▪ *a military briefing*

brief·case /ˈbriːfˌkeɪs/ *n* [*C*] : a flat case that is used for carrying papers or books

brief·ly /ˈbriːfli/ *adv* **1** : in only a few words ▪ *The issue was only briefly mentioned.* ▪ *The party, to put it briefly, was a disaster.* **2** : for a short period of time ▪ *We briefly considered canceling the trip.*

brier *variant spelling of* BRIAR

¹brig /ˈbrɪg/ *n* [*C*] : a ship with square sails and two masts

²brig *n* [*C*] : a jail or prison of the U.S. Navy

bri·gade /brɪˈgeɪd/ *n* [*C*] **1** : a large group of soldiers that is part of an army **2** : a group of people organized to act together ▪ *a fire brigade*

brig·a·dier /ˌbrɪɡəˈdiɚ/ *n* [*C*] : a British army officer who is in charge of a brigade

brigadier general *n* [*C*] : an officer in the U.S. Army, Air Force, or Marine Corps who is ranked above a colonel

bright /ˈbraɪt/ *adj* **1** : producing or having a lot of light ▪ *a bright light* ▪ *It's too bright in here.* ▪ *a bright, sunny day* **2** : having a very light and strong color ▪ *a bright red* **3 a** : able to learn things quickly : INTELLIGENT ▪ *a bright child* **b** : showing intelligence : CLEVER ▪ *a bright idea* **4** : happy and lively ▪ *a bright smile* **5** : providing a reason for hope ▪ *a bright future* ▪ *Brighter days are ahead.* [=things will improve in the future] — **bright and early** : very early ▪ *We'll be leaving bright and early.* — **bright spot** *informal* : a good thing that occurs during a bad or difficult time ▪ *Exports are one of the few bright spots in the economy now.* — **on the bright side** — used to refer to the good part of something that is mostly bad ▪ *Replacing the roof is expensive, but look on the bright side. You won't have any more leaks.* — **bright·ly** *adv* ▪ *candles glowing brightly* ▪ *a brightly lit room* ▪ *brightly colored toys* — **bright·ness** *n* [*U*]

bright·en /ˈbraɪtn̩/ *vb* **1** [*T*] : to add more light to (something) ▪ *Brighten the picture on the television.* **2 a** [*T*] : to make (something) more colorful or cheerful ▪ *Flowers brighten any room.* ▪ *You really brightened (up) my day.* **b** [*I*] : to become brighter or more cheerful ▪ *The sky brightened.* ▪ *Her mood/eyes brightened.*

brill /ˈbrɪl/ *adj, Brit, informal* : BRILLIANT **4** ▪ *We had a brill time.*

bril·liant /ˈbrɪljənt/ *adj* **1** : very bright ▪ *a brilliant star* **2** : very impressive or successful ▪ *a brilliant career/performance* **3 a** : extremely intelligent ▪ *a brilliant scientist/mind* **b** : showing extreme intelligence ▪ *a brilliant idea* **4** *Brit, informal* : very good : wonderful or excellent ▪ *a brilliant film/dinner* — **brilliance** /ˈbrɪljəns/ *n* [*U*] ▪ *intellectual brilliance* — **bril·liant·ly** *adv*

¹brim /ˈbrɪm/ *n* [*C*] **1** : the top edge of a glass or a similar container ▪ *Fill the glass to the brim.* [=to the top] ▪ *(figurative) Her heart was filled to the brim with joy.* **2** : the part of a hat that sticks out around the lower edge — **brim·ful** /ˈbrɪmˌfʊl/ *adj* ▪ *The book is brimful of funny jokes.* [=is filled with funny jokes] — **brimmed** /ˈbrɪmd/ *adj* ▪ *a wide-brimmed hat*

²brim *vb* **brimmed; brim·ming** [*I*] : to be completely filled *with* something ▪ *a boy brimming (over) with energy* ▪ *Her eyes brimmed with tears.* [=tears filled her eyes]

brim·stone /ˈbrɪmˌstoʊn/ *n* [*U*] *old-fashioned* : SULFUR — now usually used in the phrase *fire and brimstone* to refer to descriptions of hell ▪ *sermons full of fire and brimstone* [=sermons warning of the punishment of hell]

brine /ˈbraɪn/ *n* [*U*] **1** : a mixture of salty water used especially to preserve or add flavor to food **2** : the salty water of the ocean ▪ *ocean brine*

bring /ˈbrɪŋ/ *vb* **brought** /ˈbrɑːt/; **bring·ing** [*T*] **1** : to come with (something or someone) to a place ▪ *I'll bring some wine (with me).* ▪ *She brought her boyfriend home to meet her parents.* ▪ *I'll bring you another drink.* = *I'll bring another drink to you.* **2** : to cause (something or someone) to come ▪ *Her screams brought the neighbors running.* [=the neighbors ran to help her when they heard her screams] **3** : to cause (something) to exist, happen, or start ▪ *Can anything bring peace to this troubled region?* ▪ *The sad story brought tears to our eyes.* [=made us cry] **4** : to cause (something or someone) to reach a specified state, place, condition, etc. ▪ *The dancer brought his hands up to his face.* ▪ *The snow brought traffic to a stop.* **5** : to have (a particular talent, quality, etc.) when you start to do something (such as a job) — + *to* ▪ *She brings years of experience to the position.* [=she comes to the position with years of experience] **6** *law* : to start a case against someone in a court of law ▪ *They are going to bring charges against him.* [=they are going to charge him with a crime] **7** : to cause (something) to reach a total — + *to* ▪ *Last week's sales brought our profits for the year to just over $35,000.* **8** : to be sold for (a price) ▪ *The painting brought* [=fetched] *a high price.* — **bring about** *(something)* [*phrasal vb*] **bring about** *(something)* also **bring** *(something)* **about** : to cause (something) ▪ *the various factors that brought about the current crisis* — **bring around** *(chiefly US)* or *chiefly Brit* **bring**

round [*phrasal vb*] **1 bring (someone) around** : to cause (someone) to come around ▪ *We'll bring her around (to our way of thinking) eventually.* [=we'll convince/persuade her to support us eventually] ▪ *It took the doctor several minutes to bring him around.* [=to make him conscious again] **2 bring (something) around** : to cause (something, such as a conversation) to go *to* a desired subject or area ▪ *We gradually brought the conversation around to politics.* — **bring back** [*phrasal vb*] **bring (something or someone) back or bring back (something or someone) 1** : to come back with (something or someone) ▪ *What did you bring back (with you) from your vacation?* **2** : to cause (something or someone) to return ▪ *a former policy that is being brought back* ▪ *a story about a man who is brought back (to life) from the dead* **3** : to cause (something or someone) to return *to* a condition, subject, etc. ▪ *That question brings us back (again) to the issue of poverty.* **4** : to cause (something) to return to someone's memory ▪ *Seeing her again brought back a lot of happy memories.* — **bring down** [*phrasal vb*] **1 bring down (someone or something) or bring (someone or something) down a** : to cause (someone or something) to fall down onto the ground ▪ *a plane brought down by enemy fire* ▪ (*figurative*) *a politician who was brought down by scandal* **b** : to cause (something) to become lower ▪ *An increase in supply should bring prices down.* **2 bring (someone) down** *informal* : to cause (someone) to become sad or depressed ▪ *This rainy weather is really bringing me down.* — **bring forth** [*phrasal vb*] *somewhat formal* : to produce (something) ▪ *The tree brought forth an abundance of flowers.* — **bring forward** [*phrasal vb*] **bring (something) forward or bring forward (something) 1** : to talk about or show (something) so that it can be seen or discussed by others ▪ *The police have brought new evidence forward.* **2** : to make the time of (something) earlier or sooner ▪ *We're bringing the meeting forward from 3 p.m. to noon.* — **bring in** [*phrasal vb*] **bring in (someone or something) or bring (someone or something) in 1** : to cause (someone) to become involved in a process, activity, etc. ▪ *The company is bringing in outside experts to help on the project.* **2** : to produce or earn (an amount of money) ▪ *Each sale brought in $5.* ▪ *He brings in a good salary.* **3** *chiefly Brit* : to introduce (a new law, rule, etc.) ▪ *The government may bring in legislation to make such practices illegal.* **4** : to cause (someone or something) to come to a place ▪ *The sale should bring in* [=attract] *new customers/business.* — **bring off** [*phrasal vb*] **bring (something) off also bring off (something)** : to achieve or accomplish (something) ▪ *It's a tough job, but she has enough talent to bring it off.* — **bring on** [*phrasal vb*] **1 bring on (something) or bring (something) on** : to cause (something) to appear or occur ▪ *The crisis was brought on by many factors.* **2 bring (something) on (someone)** : to

cause (something bad) to happen to (someone) ▪ *You've brought this trouble on yourself.* — **bring out** [*phrasal vb*] **bring out (something) or bring (something) out 1** : to cause (something) to appear or to be more easily seen ▪ *The debate brought out* [=highlighted] *the differences between the two candidates.* ▪ *That blue sweater brings out the color in your eyes.* ▪ *A crisis brings out the best in some people and brings out the worst in others.* [=causes some people to behave very well and other people to behave very badly] **2** : to produce (something, such as a book) ▪ *a writer who brought out a new novel last year* — **bring to** [*phrasal vb*] **bring (someone) to** : to cause (someone) to become awake again after being unconscious ▪ *It took the doctor several minutes to bring him to.* — **bring together** [*phrasal vb*] **bring (people) together or bring together (people)** : to cause (people) to come together ▪ *They were brought together by a shared love of nature.* — **bring up** [*phrasal vb*] **1 bring (someone) up or bring up (someone)** : to take care of and teach (a child who is growing up) ▪ *I was born and brought up* [=raised, reared] *here.* ▪ *My grandparents brought me up.* **2 bring (something) up or bring up (something) a** : to mention (something) when talking ▪ *Did you bring up* [=introduce, raise] *the subject of his unpaid bills?* **b** *computers* : to cause (something, such as a file or picture) to appear on a computer screen ▪ *The system makes it easy to bring up (on the screen) information about any customer.* **3 bring (someone) up** : to cause (someone) to stop suddenly — used in phrases like **bring up short** and **bring up suddenly** ▪ *He was just starting to argue when her scream brought him up short.* — **bring yourself** : to force yourself *to do* something that you do not want to do ▪ *He wanted to apologize, but he couldn't bring himself to do it.* — **bring·er** *n* [C]

brink /ˈbrɪŋk/ *n* — **the brink** : the edge at the top of a steep cliff — usually used figuratively to refer to a point that is very close to the occurrence of something ▪ *The two nations are on the brink of war.* [=are very close to war] ▪ *The other team brought them to the brink of defeat.* [=came very close to defeating them]

briny /ˈbraɪni/ *adj* **brin·i·er; -est** : SALTY ▪ *a briny flavor*

brisk /ˈbrɪsk/ *adj* **1** : quick and efficient ▪ *a brisk manner/voice* **2** : pleasantly cool or cold ▪ *brisk autumn weather* **3 a** : done with quickness and energy ▪ *They went for a brisk walk.* **b** : very active and steady ▪ *Business is brisk at the store.* — **brisk·ly** *adv* — **brisk·ness** *n* [U]

bris·ket /ˈbrɪskət/ *n* [C/U] : beef from the chest of a cow

¹bris·tle /ˈbrɪsəl/ *n* [C] : a short, stiff hair, fiber, etc. ▪ *the bristles of a brush* — **bris·tly** /ˈbrɪsli/ *adj* **bris·tli·er; -est** ▪ *a bristly mustache*

²bristle *vb* **bris·tled; bris·tling** [I] **1** *of hair* : to rise up and become stiff ▪ *Electricity makes your hair bristle.* **2** : to become angry ▪ *She bristled at the insult.* —

bristle with [*phrasal vb*] **1** : to be covered with (something) ▪ *a bush bristling with thorns* **2** : to be full of (something) ▪ *a performance bristling with energy*

Brit /ˈbrɪt/ *n* [*C*] *informal* : a British person

britch·es /ˈbrɪtʃəz/ *n* [*plural*] *chiefly US, informal + old-fashioned* : PANTS ▪ *an old pair of britches* — *too big for your britches* see ¹BIG

Brit·ish /ˈbrɪtɪʃ/ *adj* : of or relating to Great Britain and especially England ▪ *British newspapers* — **the British** : the people of Great Britain and especially England

Brit·on /ˈbrɪtn̩/ *n* [*C*] *somewhat formal* : a British person

brit·tle /ˈbrɪtl̩/ *adj* **brit·tler; brit·tlest 1** : easily broken or cracked ▪ *brittle glass/bones* **2** : easily damaged ▪ *a brittle* [=*fragile*] *alliance* **3** : sharp in sound ▪ *a high, brittle voice* — **brit·tle·ness** /ˈbrɪtlnəs/ *n* [*U*]

bro /ˈbroʊ/ *n* [*C*] **1** *informal* : BROTHER ▪ *my big bro* **2** *US slang* — used as a friendly way of addressing a man or boy ▪ *Catch you later, bro.*

¹**broach** /ˈbroʊtʃ/ *vb* [*T*] : to introduce (a subject, issue, etc.) for discussion ▪ *She broached the idea of getting another cat.*

²**broach** *n* [*C*] : BROOCH

¹**broad** /ˈbrɑːd/ *adj* **1 a** : large from one side to the other side : WIDE ▪ *broad shoulders* ▪ *a broad stripe/avenue* **b** *chiefly Brit* : having a specified width ▪ *three metres broad* [=*wide*] **2** : including or involving many things or people ▪ *a broad selection/variety* ▪ *broad appeal* **3** : relating to the main parts of something : GENERAL ▪ *the broad outlines of a problem* **4** : easily seen or noticed ▪ *a broad Midwestern accent* — **in broad daylight** : during the day when people and things can be easily seen rather than at night ▪ *The crime was committed in broad daylight.* — **broad·ly** *adv* ▪ *He smiled broadly.* [=*with a big smile*]

²**broad** *n* [*C*] *US slang, old-fashioned + often offensive* : WOMAN

broad·band /ˈbrɑːdˌbænd/ *n* [*U*] : a fast electronic network that carries more than one type of communication (such as Internet and cable television signals) — **broadband** *adj* ▪ *broadband Internet access*

broad bean *n* [*C*] *chiefly Brit* : FAVA BEAN

¹**broad·cast** /ˈbrɑːdˌkæst, *Brit* ˈbrɔːdˌkɑːst/ *vb* -**cast; -cast·ing** [*T*] **1** : to send out (signals, programs, etc.) by radio or television ▪ *The interview was broadcast from London.* **2** : to tell (something that is private or secret) to many people ▪ *I'll tell you, but don't broadcast it to everyone in the office.* — **broad·cast·er** *n* [*C*] ▪ *radio/television broadcasters* — **broadcasting** *n* [*U*] ▪ *a career in broadcasting*

²**broadcast** *n* **1** [*C*] : a radio or television program ▪ *a live/recorded broadcast* **2** [*U*] : the act of broadcasting something ▪ *The judge will allow broadcast of the trial.* ▪ *a career in broadcast journalism* [=a career in broadcasting]

broad·en /ˈbrɑːdn̩/ *vb* **1** [*T*] : to make (something) wider or more general ▪ *The police have broadened the scope of the investigation.* ▪ *Travel can broaden your horizons/mind.* [=increase the range of your knowledge, understanding, or experience] **2** [*I*] : to become wider or more general ▪ *Her smile broadened.* ▪ *The investigation has broadened.*

broad jump *n* — **the broad jump** *US* see LONG JUMP — **broad jumper** *n* [*C*]

broad–mind·ed /ˈbrɑːdˈmaɪndəd/ *adj* : willing to accept opinions, beliefs, or behaviors that are unusual or different from your own ▪ *a broad-minded view of racial issues* — **broad–mind·ed·ness** *n* [*U*]

broad·sheet /ˈbrɑːdˌʃiːt/ *n* [*C*] *chiefly Brit* : a newspaper that has large pages and that usually deals with serious subjects — compare TABLOID

¹**broad·side** /ˈbrɑːdˌsaɪd/ *n* [*C*] : a very strong and harsh spoken or written attack ▪ *The senator delivered a broadside against the President.*

²**broadside** *adv* **1** : with the side facing forward ▪ *Turn the ship broadside.* **2** *chiefly US* : directly from the side ▪ *The car was hit broadside.*

³**broadside** *vb* -**sid·ed; -sid·ing** [*T*] *US* : to hit (a vehicle) very hard from the side ▪ *My car was broadsided by a truck.*

Broad·way /ˈbrɑːdˌweɪ/ *n* [*U*] : a street in New York City where there are many theaters — used to refer to the world of the theater in New York City ▪ *a play/star on Broadway* ▪ *a Broadway play/star*

bro·cade /broʊˈkeɪd/ *n* [*U*] : a cloth with a raised design in gold or silver thread — **bro·cad·ed** /broʊˈkeɪdəd/ *adj*

broc·co·li /ˈbrɑːkəli/ *n* [*U*] : a common vegetable that has green branches and many small green or purple flowers

bro·chure /broʊˈʃʊr, *Brit* ˈbrəʊʃə/ *n* [*C*] : a small, thin book or magazine that usually has many pictures and information about a product, a place, etc. ▪ *a travel brochure*

brogue /ˈbroʊg/ *n* [*C*] : the way that English is pronounced in Ireland or Scotland : an Irish or Scottish accent

broil /ˈbrojəl/ *vb, US* **1** [*T*] : to cook (food) directly over or under extremely high heat ▪ *a broiled steak* **2** [*I*] *informal* : to be extremely hot ▪ *workers broiling in the hot sun*

broil·er /ˈbrojlə/ *n* [*C*] **1** *US* : a part of an oven that becomes very hot and that food is placed under to be broiled **2** *chiefly US* : a young chicken that is suitable for broiling

¹**broke** *past tense of* ¹BREAK

²**broke** /ˈbroʊk/ *adj, not before a noun, informal* : not having any money ▪ *Can I borrow 10 dollars? I'm broke until payday.* ▪ (*informal*) *The company could go broke* [=lose all its money] *if the economy doesn't improve soon.* ▪ *I'm flat broke.* = (*Brit*) *I'm stony broke.* [=I have no money at all] — **go for broke** *informal* : to do something that is dangerous or that could result in complete failure in order to try to achieve success ▪ *She decided to go for broke and start her own restaurant.*

— *if it ain't broke, don't fix it* *informal*
— used to say that you should not try to
change something that is working

¹**broken** *past participle of* ¹BREAK

²**bro·ken** /ˈbroʊkən/ *adj* 1 : separated
into parts or pieces by being hit, damaged, etc. • *broken glass/bones* • *a broken
leg/arm* [=a leg/arm that has a broken
bone] 2 : not working properly • *a broken camera* 3 : not kept or honored • *a
broken promise* 4 : without hope or
strength because of having suffered very
much • *a broken spirit/heart* • *a broken
man* 5 : spoken with many mistakes
: not fluent • *speaking in broken English*
6 — used to describe a relationship
(such as a marriage) that has ended • *a
broken marriage/engagement* • *children
from broken homes* [=children whose
parents are divorced]

broken–down *adj* : in a bad or weak
condition because of being old, not well
cared for, etc. • *a broken-down car*

bro·ken·heart·ed /ˌbroʊkənˈhɑɚtəd/ *adj*
: filled with great sadness especially because someone you love has left you, has
died, etc. • HEARTBROKEN • *I was bro-
kenhearted when he died.*

¹**bro·ker** /ˈbroʊkɚ/ *n* [C] : a person who
helps other people to reach agreements,
to make deals, or to buy and sell property (such as stocks or houses) • *an insurance broker* • *a marriage broker* [=a person who helps to arrange the marriages
of other people]

²**broker** *vb* [T] : to help people, countries,
etc., to make a deal or to reach an agreement • *broker a deal/compromise*

bro·ker·age /ˈbroʊkərɪdʒ/ *n* [C] : the
business of a broker • *a brokerage firm*

bro·mide /ˈbroʊˌmaɪd/ *n* 1 [C/U] : a
drug that makes a person calm 2 [C] : a
statement that is intended to make people feel happier or calmer but that is not
original or effective • *a speech offering
nothing more than the usual bromides*

bron·chi·al /ˈbrɑːnkijəl/ *adj* : relating to
or involving the tubes that carry air into
the lungs • *a bronchial infection*

bron·chi·tis /brɑnˈkaɪtəs/ *n* [U] *medical*
: an illness in which your bronchial tubes
become sore or damaged and you cough
a lot

bron·co /ˈbrɑːŋkoʊ/ *n, pl* **-cos** [C] : a
wild horse of western North America • *a
rodeo featuring bucking broncos*

bron·to·sau·rus /ˌbrɑːntəˈsorəs/ *n* [C]
: a very large dinosaur that had a long
neck and tail

bronze /ˈbrɑːnz/ *n* 1 [U] : a metal that is
made by combining copper and tin 2
[C] **a** : something (such as a statue) that
is made of bronze • *a bronze of the president* **b** : BRONZE MEDAL • *She won a
bronze in skiing.* 3 [U] : a yellowish-
brown color — **bronze** *adj* • *a bronze
statue*

Bronze Age *n* — **the Bronze Age** : a
period of time that began between 4000
and 3000 B.C. in which people used
bronze to make weapons and tools

bronzed /ˈbrɑːnzd/ *adj* 1 : having skin
that has been made brown by the sun •
bronzed [=tanned] *bodies* 2 : covered

with a material that makes something
appear to be made of bronze • *bronzed
baby shoes*

bronze medal *n* [C] : a medal made of
bronze that is awarded as the prize for
third place in a sports competition

brooch /ˈbroʊtʃ/ *n* [C] : a piece of jewelry
that is held on clothing by a pin and
worn by a woman at or near her neck —
called also *broach*

¹**brood** /ˈbruːd/ *n* [C] 1 : a group of
young birds (such as chickens) that were
all born at the same time • *a hen and her
brood of chicks* 2 *informal* : the children
in someone's family • *Mrs. Smith took her
brood to church every Sunday.*

²**brood** *vb* [I] : to think a lot about something in an unhappy way • *hours spent
brooding about/on/over her misfortune* —
brood·er *n* [C]

brood·ing /ˈbruːdɪŋ/ *adj* : very serious
and sad • *a brooding artist/essay* —
brood·ing·ly *adv*

broody *adj* **brood·i·er; -est** 1 : serious
and sad : BROODING 2 **a** *of a hen*
: ready to lay and sit on eggs **b** *Brit, informal, of a woman* : wanting to have a
baby • *feeling broody*

¹**brook** /ˈbrʊk/ *vb* [T] : to allow (something) to exist or happen • *a government
that brooks no criticism*

²**brook** *n* [C] : a small stream

broom /ˈbruːm/ *n* [C] : a brush that has a
long handle and that is used for sweeping
floors

broom·stick /ˈbruːmˌstɪk/ *n* [C] : the
handle of a broom

Bros. *abbr* brothers — used in company
names • *Smith Bros.*

broth /ˈbrɑːθ/ *n* [C/U] : liquid in which
food (such as meat) has been cooked •
chicken broth

broth·el /ˈbrɑːθəl/ *n* [C] : a building in
which prostitutes are available

broth·er /ˈbrʌðɚ/ *n* [C] 1 : a boy or man
who has one or both of the same parents
as you • *her big/older brother* 2 : a man
who is from the same group or country
as you • *We must support our brothers and
sisters fighting overseas.* 3 *pl* **broth·ers**
or **breth·ren** /ˈbrɛðrən/ : a male member
of a religious group — used especially as
a title • *Brother John* 4 *US, informal* : a
black man — used especially by African-
Americans 5 *US, informal* — used
when talking to a man • *Brother, you have
got to relax.* 6 *chiefly US, informal* —
used as an interjection to express surprise or annoyance • *Oh, brother! What a
ridiculous thing to say.*

broth·er·hood /ˈbrʌðɚˌhʊd/ *n* 1 [U]
: feelings of friendship, support, and understanding between people • *the brotherhood of humankind* 2 [C] : a group or
organization of people who have the
same interests, jobs, etc. — often used in
the names of labor unions • *the International Brotherhood of Electrical Workers*

broth·er–in–law /ˈbrʌðərənˌlɑː/ *n, pl*
broth·ers–in–law /ˈbrʌðəzənˌlɑː/ [C]
1 : the brother of your husband or wife
2 : the husband of your sister

broth·er·ly /ˈbrʌðɚli/ *adj* : showing or
suggesting the love and closeness of a

brother • *a brotherly hug* • *brotherly support* — **broth·er·li·ness** *n* [*U*]

brought *past tense and past participle of* BRING

brou·ha·ha /ˈbruːˌhɑːˌhɑː/ *n* [*U, singular*] *informal + usually disapproving* : great excitement or concern about something • *the/a brouhaha over where to put the new statue*

brow /ˈbraʊ/ *n* [*C*] **1** : EYEBROW **2** : FOREHEAD • *She wiped the sweat from her brow.* **3** : the upper edge of a steep slope — **knit your brow** *see* ¹KNIT

brow·beat /ˈbraʊˌbiːt/ *vb* **-beat**; **-beat·en** /-ˌbiːtn̩/; **-beat·ing** [*T*] : to use threats or angry speech to make (someone) do or accept something • *I refuse to be browbeaten into making unnecessary changes.*

¹**brown** /ˈbraʊn/ *adj* : having a color like coffee or chocolate • *a brown cow/door/sweater* — **brown** *n* [*C/U*] • *a shade of brown* — **brown·ish** /ˈbraʊnɪʃ/ *adj* • *brownish-red*

²**brown** *vb* [*T/I*] : to make (something) brown or to become brown especially by cooking or heating • *Brown the chicken in a pan with butter.* • *skin browned by the sun*

brown·ie /ˈbraʊni/ *n* [*C*] **1** *Brownie* : a member of an organization of Girl Scouts or Girl Guides for girls ages 7 through 10 — *compare* CUB SCOUT **2** : a short, square piece of rich, chocolate cake that often contains nuts

brownie points *n* [*plural*] *informal* : praise, credit, or approval that a person gets from someone (such as a boss or a teacher) for doing something good or helpful • *trying to earn/win/get brownie points (from the boss) by working overtime*

brown-nose /ˈbraʊnˌnoʊz/ *vb* **-nosed**; **-nos·ing** [*T*] *informal + disapproving* : to try to get the approval of (an important or powerful person) by praise, flattery, etc. • *trying to get a promotion by brownnosing the boss* — **brown·nos·er** *n* [*C*]

brown·stone /ˈbraʊnˌstoʊn/ *n* **1** [*U*] : a reddish-brown type of stone that is used for building **2** [*C*] *US* : a house that is covered with a layer of brownstone • *a neighborhood of brownstones*

browse /ˈbraʊz/ *vb* **browsed**; **brows·ing** **1** [*T/I*] : to look at many things in a store, in a newspaper, etc., to see if there is something interesting or worth buying • *customers browsing in a bookstore* • *browsing (through) shops* **2** [*T*] : to use a special program (called a browser) to find and look at information on the Internet • *browse* [=surf] *the Web/Internet* **3** [*I*] *of an animal* : to eat grass, plants, etc. : GRAZE • *cows browsing in the pasture*

brows·er /ˈbraʊzɚ/ *n* [*C*] **1** : a person who looks at the things being sold in a store to see if there is something worth buying • *There were a few browsers in the bookstore.* **2** : a computer program that is used to find and look at information on the Internet • *a Web browser*

¹**bruise** /ˈbruːz/ *n* [*C*] **1** : a dark and painful area on your skin that is caused by an injury **2** : a dark area on a plant or piece of fruit that has been damaged • *a bruise on an apple*

²**bruise** *vb* **bruised**; **bruis·ing** **1 a** [*T*] : to cause a bruise on (part of a person's body, a piece of fruit, etc.) • *I bruised my knee.* • *His arm was bruised in the accident.* **b** [*I*] : to get a bruise • *She bruises easily.* **2** [*T*] : to hurt (someone's confidence, feelings, etc.) through speech or actions • *I don't want to bruise anyone's feelings.* — **bruising** *n* [*U, singular*] • *My ego took a bruising when I lost.*

bruis·er /ˈbruːzɚ/ *n* [*C*] *informal* : a large, strong man • *a 250-pound bruiser*

bruising *adj* : extremely rough or painful • *a bruising battle*

brunch /ˈbrʌntʃ/ *n* [*C*] : a meal that combines breakfast and lunch and that is usually eaten in late morning

bru·nette *also* **bru·net** /bruˈnɛt/ *n* [*C*] : a person who has brown or black hair • *a beautiful brunette* ✧ This word usually refers to a woman or a girl and is spelled *brunette.* When it refers to a man or a boy, it is usually spelled *brunet.* — **brunette** *also* **brunet** *adj* • *brunette hair*

brunt /ˈbrʌnt/ *n* — **the brunt of** : the main force or effect of (something harmful or dangerous) • *Cities on the coast felt/bore the brunt of the storm.* • *The brunt of his criticism was directed at me.*

¹**brush** /ˈbrʌʃ/ *n* **1** [*C*] : a tool with many stiff hairs, fibers, etc., that is used for cleaning, smoothing, or painting something **2** [*C*] **a** : an act of cleaning or smoothing something with a brush • *I gave her hair a quick brush.* **b** : a quick, light movement • *She wiped the crumbs off the table with a brush of her hand.* **3** [*C*] : a situation in which you briefly experience or almost experience something bad, dangerous, exciting, etc. • *She had a brush with fame/greatness/death.* **4** [*U*] **a** : wood from small branches on a tree • *a pile of brush* **b** : small bushes or trees • *dense brush*

²**brush** *vb* [*T*] **1 a** : to clean or smooth (something) with a brush • *brush your teeth/hair* **b** : to put (something) on or onto something with a brush • *He brushed the butter onto the fish.* **2** : to remove (something) with a brush or with a quick movement of your hand, fingers, etc. • *Brush the dirt off your pants.* **3** : to touch gently against (something) when going past it • *Leaves brushed my cheek.* • *The two men brushed shoulders* [=touched at the shoulders] *as they walked past each other.* **4** : to move quickly past someone without stopping or paying attention • *The governor brushed by/past the reporters.* — **brush aside** [*phrasal vb*] **brush (something) aside** *or* **brush aside (something)** : to treat (something) as not important • *brushing aside questions about the arrest* — **brush off** [*phrasal vb*] **brush (something or someone) off** *or* **brush off (something or someone)** **1** : to refuse to deal with or talk about (something) in a serious way • *The company brushed off reports that it couldn't pay its bills.* **2** : to respond to (someone) in a rude way that

shows you are not interested in what is being asked for or suggested • *I asked him for help, but he just brushed me off.* — **brush up** [*phrasal vb*] : to improve your skill at (something) or increase your knowledge of (something) • *I need to brush up (on) my Spanish.*

brush-off /ˈbrʌʃˌɑːf/ *n* — **the brush-off** *informal* : rude treatment or behavior by someone who is not interested at all in what another person wants or asks for • *The mayor's assistant gave me the brush-off.*

brush-stroke /ˈbrʌʃˌstrouk/ *n* [C] : the paint left on a painting by a movement of the artist's brush

brusque /ˈbrʌsk/ *adj* : talking or behaving in a very direct, brief, and unfriendly way • *a brusque reply* — **brusque-ly** *adv* — **brusque-ness** *n* [U]

brus-sels sprout *or* **Brus-sels sprout** /ˈbrʌsəl-/ *n* [C] : a small, green vegetable that looks like a very small cabbage

bru-tal /ˈbruːtl/ *adj* **1** : extremely cruel or harsh • *a brutal dictatorship* • *a brutal attack/murder/assault* **2** : very direct and accurate in a way that is harsh or unpleasant • *brutal honesty* **3** *informal* : very bad or unpleasant • *Traffic was brutal last night.* • *a brutal headache* — **bru-tal-ly** *adv*

bru-tal-i-ty /bruˈtæləti/ *n, pl* **-ties** [C/U] : cruel, harsh, and usually violent treatment of another person • *police brutality* • *the brutalities of slavery*

bru-tal-ize *also Brit* **bru-tal-ise** /ˈbruːtlˌaɪz/ *vb* **-ized; -iz-ing** [T] **1** : to cause (someone) to lose ordinary human kindness or feelings • *people brutalized by the experience of war* **2** : to treat (someone) in a very harsh and usually violent way • *prisoners brutalized by their handlers*

¹**brute** /ˈbruːt/ *n* [C] : a cruel, rough, or violent man • *Let go of me, you brute!*

²**brute** *adj, always before a noun* **1** : very strong or forceful • *brute force/strength* **2** : very harsh • *the brute fact of getting old*

brut-ish /ˈbruːtɪʃ/ *adj* : cruel, violent, and stupid • *brutish behavior* — **brut-ish-ness** *n* [U]

BS *abbr, US* **1** *or* **B.S.** bachelor of science • *a B.S. (degree) in chemistry* **2** *informal + impolite* bullshit

BSc *abbr, Brit* bachelor of science

¹**bub-ble** /ˈbʌbəl/ *n* [C] **1 a** : a tiny, round ball of air or gas inside a liquid • *champagne bubbles* **b** : a very light ball of air inside a thin layer of soap • *soap bubbles* • *children blowing bubbles* [=making soap bubbles by blowing air through a thin layer of soap] **2** : a period when many people invest money in something and cause its value to rise to a level that is much higher than its real value until finally its value drops very suddenly • *a stock market bubble* — **burst someone's bubble** *informal* : to cause someone to suddenly realize that something is not really good, true, etc. • *I'm sorry to burst your bubble, but the job is not really that exciting.*

²**bubble** *vb* **bub-bled; bub-bling** [I] **1** : to form or produce bubbles • *Oil bubbled (up) through the ground.* **2** : to flow

with the quiet sound of water moving over rocks • *a bubbling brook* **3** : to be very happy and excited • *bubbling over with enthusiasm/excitement*

bubble bath *n* [C] : a bath in which bubbles are made by a special type of soap

bubble gum *n* [U] : a type of gum that you chew and that can be blown into large bubbles

bubble–gum *adj, always before a noun* : intended to appeal to young teenagers • *bubble-gum music*

¹**bub-bly** /ˈbʌbli/ *adj* **bub-bli-er; -est** **1** : full of bubbles • *a bubbly liquid* **2** : very happy, cheerful, and lively • *bubbly music*

²**bubbly** *n* [U] *informal* : CHAMPAGNE • *a glass of bubbly*

bu-bon-ic plague /bjuˈbɑːnɪk-/ *n* [U] : a very serious disease that is spread especially by rats and that killed many people in the Middle Ages

buc-ca-neer /ˌbʌkəˈniɚ/ *n* [C] : ¹PIRATE 1

¹**buck** /ˈbʌk/ *n* [C] **1** *informal* **a** : DOLLAR • *I owe you a buck.* **b** : MONEY • *That car costs big bucks.* [=a lot of money] • *working hard, trying to make a buck* [=to earn money] • *a fast/quick buck* [=money earned or gotten quickly] **2** : a male animal (such as a male deer) — **bang for the/your buck** see ²BANG — **look/feel like a million bucks** see MILLION — **pass the buck** : to avoid a responsibility by giving it to someone else • *The federal government passed the buck to the state governments.* — **the buck stops here** ◇ Expressions like *the buck stops here* are used to say that you accept a responsibility and will not try to give it to someone else.

²**buck** *vb* **1** [I] *of a horse* : to jump violently into the air with the back bent upward • *a bucking horse/bronco* **2** [T] : to oppose or resist (something or someone) • *The local decline in crime bucked a nationwide trend.* [=crime declined locally but is increasing nationally] • *trying to buck the system* [=opposing the rules of the system; doing things that are not allowed] — **buck for** [*phrasal vb*] *US, informal* : to try very hard or work very hard to get (something) • *bucking for a promotion* — **buck up** [*phrasal vb*] *informal* **1** : to become happier or more confident • *Buck up, buddy. You'll feel better soon.* **2** **buck (someone) up** *or* **buck up (someone)** : to cause (someone) to be happier or more confident • *trying to buck up the (morale of the) troops*

¹**buck-et** /ˈbʌkət/ *n* **1** [C] **a** : an open container with a handle that is used especially to hold and carry water and other liquids • *a bucket and mop* **b** : the amount contained in a bucket • *a bucket of water* **2** [C] : a large container that is part of a machine (such as a tractor) and that is used for digging or carrying dirt, rocks, and other material **3** [*plural*] *informal* : a large amount especially of a liquid • *It's raining buckets.* [=it's raining very hard] **4** [C] *basketball* : a successful shot : BASKET • *She scored/sank five*

buckets. — *a drop in the bucket* see ¹DROP — *kick the bucket* see ¹KICK

²**bucket** *vb* — **bucket down** [*phrasal vb*] *Brit, informal* : to rain very heavily ▪ *The rain is bucketing down.*

bucket seat *n* [*C*] : a low, separate seat for one person in a car or other vehicle

¹**buck·le** /ˈbʌkəl/ *n* [*C*] : a metal or plastic device that is attached to one end of a belt or strap and that is used to connect it to the other end ▪ *a belt buckle*

²**buckle** *vb* **buck·led; buck·ling** **1** [*T*] : to fasten or attach (something) with a buckle ▪ *Buckle your seat belt.* ▪ *She buckled the horses into their harness.* **2** [*T/I*] : to bend or collapse from pressure, heat, etc. ▪ *The pavement buckled in the heat.* = *Heat buckled the pavement.* ▪ *My knees/legs buckled.* [=my knees bent and I began to fall down] ▪ *(figurative) He finally buckled under the pressure/strain of his job.* — **buckle down** [*phrasal vb*] *informal* : to start to work hard ▪ *You had better buckle down if you want to get good grades.* — **buckle up** [*phrasal vb*] *US* : to fasten your seat belt in a car or other vehicle ▪ *Buckle up* [=(Brit) *belt up*] *before you start driving.*

buck·shot /ˈbʌkˌʃɑːt/ *n* [*U*] : small lead balls that are fired by a shotgun — called also *shot*

buck·skin /ˈbʌkˌskɪn/ *n* [*U*] : a soft type of leather that is made especially from the skin of a deer or similar animal ▪ *a buckskin jacket*

buck teeth *n* [*plural*] : upper teeth that stick out in the front of the mouth ▪ *She has buck teeth.* — **buck–toothed** /ˈbʌkˌtuːθt/ *adj*

buck·wheat /ˈbʌkˌwiːt/ *n* [*U*] : a plant with dark seeds that are used to make grain and flour; *also* : grain or flour made from the seeds of the buckwheat plant

bu·col·ic /bjuˈkɑːlɪk/ *adj, literary + formal* : of or relating to the country or country life ▪ *a bucolic farmhouse/landscape*

¹**bud** /ˈbʌd/ *n* [*C*] **1** : a small part that grows on a plant and develops into a flower, leaf, or branch ✧ *If a plant is in bud it is beginning to grow buds.* **2** *US, informal* — **nip (something) in the bud** see ¹NIP

²**bud** *vb* **bud·ded; bud·ding** [*I*] : to produce buds ▪ *The trees budded early this spring.*

Bud·dhism /ˈbuːˌdɪzəm, ˈbuˌdɪzəm/ *n* [*U*] : a religion that is based on the teachings of Gautama Buddha — **Bud·dhist** /ˈbuːdɪst, ˈbudɪst/ *n* [*C*] — **Buddhist** *adj* ▪ *Buddhist monks/temples*

bud·ding /ˈbʌdɪŋ/ *adj* : beginning to develop ▪ *a budding romance/career*

¹**bud·dy** /ˈbʌdi/ *n, pl* **-dies** **1** [*C*] *informal* : a close friend — used especially of men or boys ▪ *We've been buddies since childhood.* **2** [*singular*] *US, informal + sometimes impolite* — used to address a man or boy ▪ *Hey, buddy, slow down!* **3** [*C*] : a person who does an activity with you ▪ *his fishing buddy*

²**buddy** *vb* **-dies; -died; -dy·ing** — **buddy up** [*phrasal vb*] *US, informal* : to become friendly especially in order to get help or some advantage ▪ *businessmen buddying up with/to politicians*

bud·dy–bud·dy /ˌbʌdiˈbʌdi/ *adj, US, informal* : very friendly or too friendly ▪ *He's a little too buddy-buddy with his professors.*

budge /ˈbʌdʒ/ *vb* **budged; budg·ing** [*T/I*] **1** : to move slightly ▪ *The horse refused to budge.* ▪ *The door wouldn't budge.* ▪ *I can't budge the door.* **2** : to change your opinion or decision ▪ *They wouldn't budge on the issue.*

¹**bud·get** /ˈbʌdʒət/ *n* **1** [*C/U*] : an amount of money available for spending ▪ *living on a budget of $1,500 a month* ▪ *a movie with a big budget* = a **big-budget** *movie* [=a movie that costs a lot of money to make] ▪ *a low-budget movie* ▪ *The project was completed under budget.* [=for less money than had been planned] ▪ *We're within budget.* [=we're not spending more money than we had planned] ▪ *They went over budget.* [=spent more money than was planned] ▪ *a budget deficit/surplus/crisis* ▪ *budget cuts* **2** [*C*] : a plan used to decide the amount of money that can be spent and how it will be spent ▪ *We worked out a budget.* ▪ *The government needs to balance the budget.* [=to plan to collect as much money as it spends] ✧ *If you are on a budget, you have planned how you will spend your money usually because you do not have a lot to spend and need to save money.* ▪ *She started her business on a small/tight/shoestring budget.* [=she did not have much money when she started her business] — **bud·get·ary** /ˈbʌdʒəˌteri, Brit ˈbʌdʒətri/ *adj, formal* ▪ *budgetary constraints*

²**budget** *vb* **1** [*T*] : to plan to spend (an amount of money) for a particular purpose ▪ *He budgets $50 for entertainment each month.* **2** [*I*] : to make and follow a plan for spending your money ▪ *If we budget carefully, we'll be able to go on the trip.* **3** [*T*] : to plan how to use (something, such as your time) ▪ *I need to budget my time more wisely.*

³**budget** *adj, always before a noun* : low in price ▪ *budget hotels*

¹**buff** /ˈbʌf/ *n* **1** [*C*] : a person who is very interested in something and who knows a lot about it ▪ *history/movie/music buffs* **2** [*U*] : a light, somewhat yellow or orange color — **in the buff** *informal* : NAKED ▪ *They sunbathe in the buff.*

²**buff** *adj, US, informal* : having a strong, muscular body or form ▪ *a buff bodybuilder*

³**buff** *vb* [*T*] : to make (a surface) smooth and shiny by rubbing it ▪ *We waxed and buffed the floors.* — **buff up** [*phrasal vb*] **buff up** *or* **buff** (*someone or something*) **up** *or* **buff up** (*someone or something*) *informal* : to become stronger and more muscular or to make (someone or something) stronger and more muscular ▪ *She is buffing up for summer.* — **buffed-up** *bodies*

buf·fa·lo /ˈbʌfəˌlou/ *n, pl* **buffalo** *or* **buf·fa·loes** [*C*] **1** *US* : BISON **2** : WATER BUFFALO

¹buff·er /ˈbʌfɚ/ *n* [C] **1** : something that gives protection by separating things ▪ *Thick walls serve as a buffer from/against sound.* ▪ *(figurative) She acted as a buffer between the two brothers when they argued.* **2** *computers* : a place in the memory of a computer where information is stored for a short time

²buffer *vb* [T] **1** : to protect (something) from something ▪ *The trees buffer the house from the hot summer sun.* **2** *computers* : to put (something, such as data) in a buffer

buffer zone *n* [C] : an area that keeps two things separated ▪ *a 500-foot buffer zone between the river and the buildings*

¹buf·fet /bəˈfeɪ, *Brit* ˈbʊˌfeɪ/ *n* [C] **1** : a meal for which different foods are placed on a table so that people can serve themselves ▪ *a breakfast buffet* ▪ *a buffet table/meal/lunch/dinner* **2** *chiefly Brit* : a place in a train, a bus station, etc., where people can buy food and drinks **3** *chiefly US* : SIDEBOARD 1

²buf·fet /ˈbʌfət/ *vb* [T] : to hit (something) with great force many times ▪ *Waves buffeted the shore.* ▪ *(figurative) The schools have been buffeted by budget cuts.*

buf·foon /bəˈfuːn/ *n* [C] : a stupid or foolish person who tries to be funny — **buf·foon·ery** /bəˈfuːnəri/ *n* [U] ▪ *silly buffoonery*

¹bug /ˈbʌg/ *n* **1** [C] *chiefly US, informal* : a usually small insect ▪ *bug bites* ▪ *2* : a usually mild illness (such as a cold) that can be passed from one person to another ▪ *an intestinal/stomach/flu bug* **3** [C] : a problem that prevents a computer program or system from working properly ▪ *trying to work/get the bugs out of the system* [=trying to fix the system's problems] **4** [C] : a small hidden microphone that is used to secretly listen to and record people ▪ *The government put a bug in her telephone.* **5 the bug** *informal* : a sudden, strong interest in a particular activity ▪ *He's been bitten by the acting bug.* [=he's become very interested in acting]

²bug *vb* **bugged; bug·ging** **1** [T] *informal* : to bother or annoy (someone) ▪ *Quit bugging me!* **2** [T] : to put a hidden microphone in (a room, telephone, etc.) in order to secretly hear what people are saying ▪ *The cops bugged his apartment.* **3** [I] *of the eyes* : to stick out more than is normal especially because of surprise or fear ▪ *Their eyes were bugging out as if they saw a ghost.* — **bug off** [*phrasal vb*] *US, informal* — used in speech as a rude or angry way to tell someone to leave you alone and to stop bothering you ▪ *She told him to bug off.*

bug·a·boo /ˈbʌgəˌbuː/ *n, pl* **-boos** [C] *US* : something that makes people very worried or upset ▪ *that old bugaboo, high oil prices*

bug·bear /ˈbʌgˌbeɚ/ *n* [C] : something that causes problems or annoys people ▪ *Clutter is her biggest bugbear.*

bug–eyed /ˈbʌgˌaɪd/ *adj* : having eyes that stick far out of the head ▪ *She was bug-eyed with amazement.*

bug·ger /ˈbʌgɚ/ *n* [C] *informal* **1** : an annoying or difficult but usually small thing ▪ *I put down my keys, and now I can't find the buggers.* **2** *chiefly Brit* **a** *offensive* : a person (especially a man) who is strongly disliked **b** : an annoying or playful person or animal ▪ *You cheeky bugger!*

¹bug·gy /ˈbʌgi/ *n, pl* **-gies** [C] : a light carriage that is usually pulled by one horse ▪ *a horse and buggy* — see also BABY BUGGY, DUNE BUGGY

²buggy *adj* **bug·gi·er; -est** **1** *US* : having many insects ▪ *a buggy swamp* **2** *chiefly US, of a computer program, system, etc.* : having many problems or errors that prevent proper operation ▪ *buggy software*

bu·gle /ˈbjuːgəl/ *n* [C] : a musical instrument like a trumpet that is used especially for giving military signals — **bu·gler** /ˈbjuːglɚ/ *n* [C]

¹build /ˈbɪld/ *vb* **built** /ˈbɪlt/; **build·ing** **1** [T/I] : to make (something) by putting together parts or materials ▪ *build a house/bridge/plane* ▪ *build a fire* ▪ *He built a dollhouse for the children.* = *He built the children a dollhouse.* ▪ *You'll need permission to build here.* **2** [T] : to develop or form (something) gradually ▪ *They are building a legal case against him.* ▪ *build friendships* ▪ *building a career/reputation* ▪ *She has built up a large collection of awards.* **3** [T] : to increase the amount of (something) ▪ *Lifting weights helps build muscle.* ▪ *a program that helps build confidence/character* ▪ *She is trying to build up (her) endurance.* **4** [I] : to grow or increase to a high point, level, number, etc. ▪ *The excitement is beginning to build.* ▪ *The story slowly builds to a climax.* [=slowly reaches a climax] ▪ *Her anger has been building up for years.* — **build around** [*phrasal vb*] **build (something) around** : to develop (something) by using (something else) as its main or central part ▪ *Their lives are built around their children.* [=their children are the most important things in their lives] — **build in/into** [*phrasal vb*] **build in (something)** or **build (something) in** or **build (something) in/into** : to make (something) a part of (something else) ▪ *We've built bookshelves into the wall.* ▪ *There are special provisions for bonuses built into the contract.* — **build on/upon** [*phrasal vb*] **1** : to use (something that has been done in the past) as a basis for further work, development, etc. ▪ *The class helps students build on what they already know.* **2 build (something) on/upon** : to develop or create (something) by using (something else) as its basis ▪ *She has built her artistic reputation on the strength of her earlier paintings.* — **build up** [*phrasal vb*] **1** : to increase gradually in amount as time passes ▪ *Dangerous chemicals are building up in our lakes and ponds.* **2 build (something or someone) up** or **build up (something or someone)** : to say many good things about (something or someone) ▪ *political candidates trying to build themselves up* [=promote themselves]

²build *n* [C/U] : the shape and size of a person's body • *a thin/slender/slight/strong/ muscular build [=physique]* • *a man of average build*

build·er /ˈbɪldɚ/ *n [C]* **1** : a person or company that builds or repairs houses, ships, bridges, etc. **2** : something that helps to develop or increase something • *a character/confidence builder*

build·ing /ˈbɪldɪŋ/ *n* **1** [C] : a structure with a roof and walls that is used as a place for people to live, work, do activities, store things, etc. • *a small brick building* • *office/apartment buildings* [=buildings with offices/apartments inside] **2** [U] : the act or process of making structures by putting together materials • *The building of the bridge took 10 years.* • *building materials/supplies*

building block *n [C]* : an important part that is grouped together with similar things to form something larger • *Families are the building blocks of our society.*

building society *n [C]* : a British business that is like a bank, that holds and invests the money saved by its members, and that provides loans and mortgages

build·up /ˈbɪldˌʌp/ *n* **1** [C/U] : an increase in something that occurs as time passes • *the country's military buildup* [=an increase in the size of its military] • *a buildup of tension/pressure/stress* **2** [C/U] : things that are said so that people will feel excited about something or someone • *After all the buildup, I expected the movie to be better than it was.* **3** [U, singular] : a series of things that lead to an important event or occurrence • *The story has a great buildup to a terrific ending.*

¹built *past tense and past participle of* ¹BUILD

²built /ˈbɪlt/ *adj* **1** *not before a noun* — used to say that someone or something has the right qualities *for* or *to* do something • *This horse is built for speed.* • *These tools are built to last.* [=these tools will last a long time] **2** : made, formed, or shaped in a specified way • *a powerfully built wrestler* • *a Japanese-built car* [=a car made in Japan]

built-in /ˈbɪltˈɪn/ *adj, always before a noun* **1** : included as a part of something • *a camera with a built-in flash* **2** : forming a natural part of someone or something • *All humans have a built-in ability to learn their native language.*

built-up /ˈbɪltˈʌp/ *adj* : having many buildings in a small area • *a built-up area of the city*

bulb /ˈbʌlb/ *n [C]* **1** : LIGHT BULB **2** : a rounded part of some plants that is under the ground and that grows into a new plant • *tulip bulbs* **3** : a part that has a rounded shape • *the bulb of the thermometer/eyedropper*

bul·bous /ˈbʌlbəs/ *adj* : big and round often in an unattractive way • *a big, bulbous nose*

¹bulge /ˈbʌldʒ/ *n [C]* : a rounded lump on the surface of something • *I'm exercising to get rid of this bulge around my middle.*

²bulge *vb* **bulged; bulg·ing** [I] **1** : to stick out in a rounded lump • *His eyes bulged (out).* • *bulging eyes/muscles* **2**

: to be completely filled *with* something • *Their bags were bulging with books and papers.*

bu·lim·ia /buˈliːmijə, *Brit* bjuˈlɪmiə/ *n [U]* : a serious physical and emotional illness in which people and especially young women eat large amounts of food and then vomit in order to not gain weight — **bu·lim·ic** /buˈliːmɪk, *Brit* bjuˈlɪmɪk/ *adj* — **bulimic** *n [C]*

¹bulk /ˈbʌlk/ *n* **1** **the bulk** : most of something • *We spent the bulk of the summer at the beach.* **2** [U] : the large size of someone or something • *Despite his bulk, he's a very fast runner.* — **in bulk** : in large containers or in large amounts • *The restaurant buys rice and flour in bulk.*

²bulk *adj, always before a noun* : of or relating to things that are sent or sold in large amounts • *bulk purchases/shipments/rates/mailings*

³bulk *vb* — **bulk up** [*phrasal vb*] **1** : to gain weight often by becoming more muscular • *He's bulked up to 200 pounds.* **2 a** *bulk (someone) up* : to cause (someone) to gain weight • *He's trying to bulk himself up.* **b** *bulk up (something)* or *bulk (something) up* : to make (something) bigger or thicker by adding more material • *He bulked up the report with a lot of graphs.*

bulk·head /ˈbʌlkˌhɛd/ *n [C]* : a wall that separates the different parts of a ship or aircraft

bulky /ˈbʌlki/ *adj* **bulk·i·er; -est** **1** : large and difficult to carry or store • *a bulky sweater/package* **2** *of a person* : large and fat or muscular • *a bulky football player* — **bulk·i·ness** *n [U]*

bull /ˈbʊl/ *n* **1** [C] **a** : an adult male animal of the ox and cow family **b** : an adult male of some other large animals • *a bull elephant/moose/whale* **2** [C] *finance* : a person who tries to make money by buying stocks and selling them after their price has gone up — compare ¹BEAR **3** [U] *informal* : NONSENSE **1** • *That's a lot/load/bunch of bull!* — **take the bull by the horns** : to deal with a difficult situation in a very direct or confident way

bull·dog /ˈbʊlˌdɑːg/ *n [C]* : a type of short, strong, muscular dog

bull·doze /ˈbʊlˌdoʊz/ *vb* **-dozed; -doz·ing** [T] **1 a** : to use a bulldozer to move, destroy, or knock down (something) • *The houses were bulldozed (flat).* **b** : to create (something) by using a bulldozer • *They bulldozed a road through the hills.* **2 a** : to force (something) to be done or accepted in an aggressive or harsh way • *The governor bulldozed the law through the legislature.* **b** : to force (someone) to do something • *She bulldozed her partners into accepting the agreement.* — **bulldoze your way** : to move forward while forcing other people to move out of your way • *They bulldozed their way through the crowd.*

bull·doz·er /ˈbʊlˌdoʊzɚ/ *n [C]* : a powerful and heavy vehicle that has a large curved piece of metal at its front and that is used for moving dirt and rocks and pushing over trees and other structures

bul·let /ˈbʊlət/ n [C] 1 : a small piece of metal or another material that is shot out of a gun • *a stray bullet* [=a bullet that misses its target] • *He took a bullet to the head.* [=he was shot in the head] • *a bullet hole/wound* 2 : a large dot in a document, book, etc., that brings attention to separate pieces of information in a list 3 US, *sports* : a hit or thrown ball or puck that is moving very fast • *The quarterback threw a bullet to the receiver.* — **bite the bullet** see ¹BITE — **dodge a/the bullet** see ¹DODGE — **sweat bullets** see ¹SWEAT — **bul·let·ed** /ˈbʊlətəd/ adj • *a bulleted list*

bul·le·tin /ˈbʊlətən/ n [C] 1 : a quick announcement from an official source about an important piece of news • *a news bulletin* 2 : NEWSLETTER • *a church bulletin*

bulletin board n [C] 1 US : a board on the wall of a classroom, office, etc., where things (such as written notices) are put so that they can be seen by many people — called also (Brit) *noticeboard* 2 : MESSAGE BOARD

bullet point n [C] : an item in a list that has a large dot (called a bullet) in front of it to show that it is important

bul·let·proof /ˈbʊlətˌpruːf/ adj : made to stop bullets from going through • *a bulletproof window/vest*

bull·fight /ˈbʊlˌfaɪt/ n [C] : an event that is popular especially in Spain in which a person fights with and usually kills a bull for public entertainment — **bull·fight·er** /ˈbʊlˌfaɪtɚ/ n [C] — **bull·fight·ing** /ˈbʊlˌfaɪtɪŋ/ n [U]

bull·frog /ˈbʊlˌfrɑːg/ n [C] : a large frog that makes a loud, deep sound

bull·head·ed /ˈbʊlˈhɛdəd/ adj, chiefly US : very stubborn in a foolish or annoying way • *a bullheaded old man*

bull·horn /ˈbʊlˌhoɚn/ n [C] US : an electrical device that is used for making your voice much louder so that you can be heard over a large distance — called also (Brit) *loudhailer*

bul·lion /ˈbʊljən/ n [U] : bars of gold or silver

bull·ish /ˈbʊlɪʃ/ adj 1 : hopeful or confident that something or someone will be successful • *Many people are bullish on/about the company's future.* 2 : expecting the price of stocks to go up • *bullish investors* : characterized by rising stock prices • *a bullish market* — compare BEARISH

bull market n [C] : a market (such as a stock market) in which prices are going up — compare BEAR MARKET

bull·pen /ˈbʊlˌpɛn/ n [C] 1 : a place on a baseball field where pitchers practice throwing the ball before they start pitching in a game 2 : the pitchers on a baseball team who can replace another pitcher during a game • *The team has a strong bullpen.*

bull session n [C] US, informal : an informal conversation in which a group of people talk about something

bull's-eye /ˈbʊlzˌaɪ/ n, pl **bull's-eyes** [C] 1 : the small circle at the center of a target toward which people throw darts or shoot arrows or bullets • *(figurative) Her comments hit the bull's-eye.* [=her comments were exactly correct] 2 : a shot that hits the center of a target • *I got/threw/shot/scored a bull's-eye!*

¹**bull·shit** /ˈbʊlˌʃɪt/ n [U] informal + offensive : NONSENSE 1

²**bullshit** vb -shit; -shit·ting [T/I] informal + offensive : to say foolish or untrue things to (someone) — **bull·shit·ter** n [C]

¹**bul·ly** /ˈbʊli/ n, pl -lies [C] : someone who frightens, hurts, or threatens smaller or weaker people • *classroom bullies*

²**bully** vb -lies; -lied; -ly·ing [T] 1 : to frighten, hurt, or threaten (a smaller or weaker person) • *A group of girls were bullying her at the playground.* 2 : to cause (someone) to do something by making threats or insults or by using force — usually + *into* • *His boss bullied him into working overtime.* — **bullying** n [U]

bul·ly·boy /ˈbʊliˌbɔɪ/ n [C] chiefly Brit : an aggressive or violent man • *political bullyboys* • *bullyboy tactics*

¹**bum** /ˈbʌm/ n [C] 1 chiefly US, informal + disapproving : a person who has no place to live and no job and who asks people for money 2 informal : a person who is lazy or who does something badly • *Get to work, you lazy bum!* 3 : a person who spends a lot of time relaxing and doing something fun rather than working • *a beach bum* [=a person who spends a lot of time at the beach] 4 informal : BUTTOCKS • *He fell on his bum.*

²**bum** vb bummed; bum·ming [T] informal 1 : to get (something) for free by asking • *She bummed a cigarette off him.* 2 US : to cause (someone) to feel sad or disappointed — usually + *out* • *The news really bummed me out.* — **bum around** or Brit **bum about** [phrasal vb] informal 1 : to spend time relaxing in (a place) instead of working • *bumming around the house* 2 : to spend time living and traveling in (a place) without a job or much money • *After graduation, she bummed around Mexico.* — **bummed** adj, US • *He's bummed (out) about losing the game.*

³**bum** adj, always before a noun, informal 1 : of bad quality • *a bum deal* • *bum* [=bad] *advice/luck* 2 : not legally acceptable : not valid • *writing/passing bum checks* 3 US : injured or damaged • *a bum knee/ankle/leg*

bum·ble /ˈbʌmbəl/ vb bum·bled; bum·bling [T/I] 1 : to act, move, or speak in an awkward or confusing way • *He bumbled (his way) through the speech.* 2 US : to do, make, or handle (something) badly • *I had one chance and I bumbled* [=bungled] *it.* • *a bumbling fool* — **bum·bler** /ˈbʌmblɚ/ n [C]

bum·ble·bee /ˈbʌmbəlˌbiː/ n [C] : a large, hairy bee

bumf also **bumph** /ˈbʌmf/ n [U] Brit, informal : material that is not important or interesting • *public relations bumf*

bum·mer /ˈbʌmɚ/ n [singular] informal : something that is unpleasant or disappointing • *You can't go? What a bummer!*

¹**bump** /ˈbʌmp/ *vb* **1** [T] **a** : to hit (something, such as part of your body) against an object in a sudden and forceful way ▪ *He bumped his head against the shelf.* **b** : to hit and move (someone or something) ▪ *Don't bump the vase.* ▪ *He accidentally bumped me.* **2** [I] : to move into or against (someone or something) in a sudden and forceful way ▪ *The boat bumped (up) against the pier.* **3** [T] **a** : to move (someone or something) to a different level, position, rank, etc. ▪ *The TV show will be bumped to a new time.* **b** : to remove (someone or something) from a group or position ▪ *The loss bumped us out of first place.* ▪ *The flight was overbooked, and I was bumped.* [=I was not given a seat on the flight] **4** [I] : to move in an up and down motion over a rough surface ▪ *The truck bumped along the dirt road.* — **bump into** [*phrasal vb*] *informal* : to meet (someone) by chance ▪ *I bumped into a friend at the store.* — **bump off** [*phrasal vb*] **bump (someone) off** or **bump (someone) off** *informal* : to murder (someone) ▪ *He knew too much, so they bumped him off.* — **bump up** [*phrasal vb*] **bump up (something or someone)** or **bump (something or someone) up** *informal* : to move (something or someone) to a higher level, position, rank, etc. ▪ *They're bumping her up* [=promoting her] *to district manager.*

²**bump** *n* [C] **1** : an area of skin that is raised because it was hit, injured, etc. ▪ *a few minor bumps and bruises* **2** : a small raised area on a surface ▪ *The car hit a bump (in the road).* ▪ *(US, figurative) His career has hit a few bumps (in the road).* [=things have happened that have slowed the progress of his career] **3** : an act of something hitting against something else ▪ *The airplane landed with a bump.* [=it went up again and then down when it hit the ground]

¹**bum·per** /ˈbʌmpɚ/ *n* [C] : a bar across the front or back of a car, truck, etc., that reduces the damage if the vehicle hits something

²**bumper** *adj, always before a noun* **1** : unusually large ▪ *a bumper crop of tomatoes* **2** : very good or successful ▪ *a bumper harvest/season*

bumper sticker *n* [C] : a strip of paper or plastic that has a printed message and that is made to be stuck on the bumper of a car, truck, etc.

bumper–to–bumper *adj* : made up of long lines of cars that are very close to each other ▪ *bumper-to-bumper traffic*

bumph *variant spelling of* BUMF

bump·kin /ˈbʌmpkən/ *n* [C] *informal* : a person who lives in the country far away from cities and who is regarded as stupid ▪ *country bumpkins*

bump·tious /ˈbʌmpʃəs/ *adj* : proud or confident in a loud and rude way that annoys other people ▪ *bumptious people/behavior*

bumpy /ˈbʌmpi/ *adj* **bump·i·er**, **-est** **1** : having or covered with bumps ▪ *a bumpy road* **2** : having sudden up and down movements ▪ *a bumpy flight/ride/*

journey **3** : having a lot of problems ▪ *a bumpy relationship* ▪ *The project got off to a bumpy start.* — **bump·i·ness** *n* [U]

bun /ˈbʌn/ *n* **1** [C] : ²ROLL 2a ▪ *a hamburger/hotdog bun* **2** [C] : a small, usually round sweet cake ▪ *cinnamon buns* **3** [C] : a way of arranging long hair by twisting it into a round shape against the head ▪ *She wears her hair in a bun.* **4** [*plural*] *US, informal* : BUTTOCKS ▪ *This exercise will firm up your buns.* — **have a bun in the oven** *informal* : to be pregnant

¹**bunch** /ˈbʌntʃ/ *n* **1** [C] : a group of things of the same kind that are held or tied together or that grow together ▪ *a bunch of flowers/grapes/keys* **2** [C] *somewhat informal* : a group of people or things that are together or are associated with each other in some way ▪ *a nice/wild bunch of people* **3** [C] *chiefly US, somewhat informal* : a large amount : LOT ▪ *Thanks a bunch.* ▪ *a bunch of money/problems/nonsense* ▪ *They make bunches of money.* **4** [*plural*] *Brit* : a way of arranging hair by separating it into two sections and tying these at each side of the head ▪ *She wore her hair in bunches.* [=(US) ponytails]

²**bunch** *vb* **1 a** [T] : to put (things or people) together in a group or bunch ▪ *The words were all bunched together at the bottom of the page.* ▪ *We bunched the youngest kids together in one group.* **b** [I] : to form a group ▪ *The baby birds bunched together for warmth.* **2** [T/I] *of clothing* : to form a group of tight folds on or around part of your body ▪ *The tights (were) bunched (together) at the ankles.* ▪ *The sweater's sleeves kept bunching up around her wrists.*

¹**bun·dle** /ˈbʌndəl/ *n* [C] **1** : a group of things that are fastened, tied, or wrapped together ▪ *a bundle of straw/newspapers/clothes* **2** *informal* : a person who has a lot of some quality or who is known for a particular kind of behavior — + *of* ▪ *He's a bundle of contradictions.* ▪ *She's a bundle of energy.* [=she's very energetic] ▪ *I was a bundle of nerves.* [=I was very nervous] ◆ The phrase *(little) bundle of joy* is used as a humorous or affectionate way of referring to a baby. ▪ *He's our little bundle of joy.* **3** *informal* : a large amount of money ▪ *He made/lost a bundle (of money) on the stock market.* **4** : a group of products or services that are sold together at a single price ▪ *software bundles*

²**bundle** *vb* **bun·dled**; **bun·dling** **1** [T] : to fasten, tie, or wrap a group of things together ▪ *I bundled the papers together.* ▪ *Bundle up the newspapers.* **2** [T/I] : to move or push (someone) *into* a place quickly ▪ *She bundled the children into the car.* **3** [T] : to include (a product or service) with another product or service so that they are sold together ▪ *The software is bundled with the computer.* — **bundle off** [*phrasal vb*] **bundle (someone) off** or **bundle off (someone)** : to send (someone) to a place quickly or suddenly ▪ *She was bundled off to summer camp.* — **bundle up** [*phrasal vb*] **bundle**

up or bundle (someone) up or bundle up (someone) : to dress (yourself or someone else) warmly ▪ *Be sure to bundle up.* ▪ *He was (all) bundled up in a hat and scarf.*

bung *vb* [T] *Brit, informal* : to put (something) *in* or *into* a place in a quick and careless way ▪ *Just bung it in the oven for 20 minutes.* — **bung up** [*phrasal vb*] **bung up (something)** or **bung (something) up** *Brit, informal* : to block (something) so that liquid, air, etc., cannot move through it ▪ *Leaves had bunged up the drain.*

bun·ga·low /ˈbʌŋgəˌloʊ/ *n* [C] **1** : a house that is all on one level **2** *US* : a house that has one main level and a second smaller level above

bun·gee cord /ˈbʌndʒi-/ *n* [C] : a very strong rope that can be stretched and that has hooks on either end — called also *bungee*

bungee jump *vb* [I] : to jump from a very high place while you are attached to a strong, long rope that stretches and that keeps you from hitting the ground ▪ *People were bungee jumping off the bridge.* — **bungee jump** *n* [C] — **bungee jumper** *n* [C] — **bungee jumping** *n* [U] ▪ *He likes daring sports like bungee jumping.*

bun·gle /ˈbʌŋgəl/ *vb* **bun·gled; bun·gling** [T/I] : to make mistakes in doing (something) ▪ *The police bungled the investigation.* ▪ *a bungled robbery* ▪ *They bungled badly.* — **bun·gler** *n* [C] — **bungling** *adj* ▪ *a bungling attempt at humor* — **bungling** *n* [U] ▪ *The investigation was ruined by their bungling.*

bun·ion /ˈbʌnjən/ *n* [C] : a painful swelling on the side of the big toe

¹**bunk** /ˈbʌŋk/ *n* [C] **a** : either one of the beds in a bunk bed **b** : a narrow bed attached to a wall on a train, train, etc. **2** [U] *informal* : NONSENSE 1 ▪ *His story is pure bunk.*

²**bunk** *vb* [I] *chiefly US* : to stay overnight at a place ▪ *We'll bunk here for the night.* — **bunk off** [*phrasal vb*] *Brit, informal* : to not go to (school, work, etc.) ▪ *We used to bunk off school as kids.* : to leave early from school, work, etc. ▪ *He bunked off early last Friday.*

bunk bed *n* [C] : a type of bed for two people that has two single beds placed so that one is above the other

bun·ker /ˈbʌŋkɚ/ *n* [C] **1** : a strong building that is mostly below ground and that is used to keep soldiers, weapons, etc., safe from attacks **2** *golf* : SAND TRAP **3** : a container for holding coal, oil, etc., on a ship or outside a house

bunk·house /ˈbʌŋkˌhaʊs/ *n* [C] : a building in which workers sleep

bun·ny /ˈbʌni/ *n, pl* **-nies** [C] *informal* : a rabbit — used especially by children or when talking to children ▪ *Look at the cute little bunny!* — called also *bunny rabbit*

Bun·sen burner /ˈbʌnsən-/ *n* [C] : a piece of equipment that produces a hot flame and that is used in scientific experiments

bunt /ˈbʌnt/ *vb* [T/I] *baseball* : to hit a baseball lightly with the bat so that the

ball rolls only for a short distance ▪ *The batter bunted (the ball).* — **bunt** *n* [C] — **bunt·er** *n* [C]

bun·ting /ˈbʌntɪŋ/ *n* [U] : flags or decorations that are made of thin cloth or paper

¹**buoy** /ˈbuːwi, ˈbɔɪ/ *n* [C] : an object that floats on water in a lake, bay, etc., to show areas that are safe or dangerous for boats

²**buoy** *vb* [T] **1** : to cause (someone) to feel happy or confident ▪ *Buoyed (up) by the success of her first novel, she began work on a second.* **2** : to lift or improve (something) ▪ *buoy the economy* ▪ *His spirits were buoyed (up) by the good news.*

buoy·ant /ˈbɔɪjənt/ *adj* **1 a** : able to float ▪ *a buoyant material* **b** : able to cause things to float ▪ *Warm air is more buoyant than cool air.* **2** : happy and confident ▪ *a buoyant mood* **3** : able to stay at a regular or high level ▪ *a buoyant economy/market* — **buoy·an·cy** /ˈbɔɪjənsi/ *n* [U] ▪ *the natural buoyancy of cork* — **buoy·ant·ly** *adv*

bur *variant spelling of* BURR 1

burbs /ˈbɚbz/ *n* — **the burbs** *US, informal* : the suburbs ▪ *a house in the burbs*

¹**bur·den** /ˈbɚdn/ *n* [C] **1** : something heavy that is carried : LOAD ▪ *a heavy burden* **2** : someone or something that is very difficult to accept, do, or deal with ▪ *She had to bear/shoulder the burden of caring for her aging parents.* ▪ *His illness has placed a huge financial burden on the family.* ▪ *The burden of proof is on the plaintiff.* [=the plaintiff must prove that the defendant is guilty]

²**burden** *vb* [T] **1** : to make (someone) hold or carry something heavy or accept or deal with something difficult ▪ *I don't wish to burden you with my problems.* ▪ *She was burdened by guilt.* ▪ *burdened with supplies and equipment*

bur·den·some /ˈbɚdnsəm/ *adj* : causing difficulty or worry ▪ *a burdensome task/load/responsibility*

bu·reau /ˈbjɚoʊ/ *n, pl* **-reaus** *also Brit* **-reaux** /-ˌroʊz/ *n* [C] **1 a** : a government department or part of a government in the U.S. ▪ *the Federal Bureau of Investigation* **b** : an office of a newspaper, magazine, etc., that is not the main office but is in an important city ▪ *the newspaper's Washington/Moscow bureau* **c** : an office or organization that provides services or information to the public ▪ *a credit/travel bureau* **2 a** *US* : CHEST OF DRAWERS **b** *Brit* : WRITING DESK

bu·reau·cra·cy /bjʊˈrɑːkrəsi/ *n, pl* **-cies** **1** [C] : a large group of people who are involved in running a government but who are not elected ▪ *state/city bureaucracies* **2** [U] *often disapproving* : a system of government or business that has many complicated rules and ways of doing things ▪ *She was fed up with all the red tape and bureaucracy.*

bu·reau·crat /ˈbjɚrəˌkræt/ *n* [C] *often disapproving* : a person who is one of the people who run a government or big company and who does everything according to the rules of that government or company ▪ *government bureaucrats*

bu·reau·crat·ic /ˌbjɚrəˈkrætɪk/ adj : using or connected with many complicated rules and ways of doing things • *bureaucratic hassles/power/procedures* — **bu·reau·crat·i·cal·ly** /ˌbjɚrəˈkrætɪkli/ adv

bur·geon /ˈbɚdʒən/ vb [I] formal : to grow or develop quickly • *a burgeoning industry*

bur·ger /ˈbɚgɚ/ n [C] **1** : HAMBURGER **2** : a food that is like a hamburger but that is not made from beef • *a turkey/tofu burger*

bur·glar /ˈbɚglɚ/ n [C] : a person who illegally enters a building in order to steal things

burglar alarm n [C] : a device that makes a loud noise (such as a ringing sound) if someone tries to enter a building by using force

bur·glar·ize /ˈbɚgləˌraɪz/ vb -ized; -iz·ing [T] US : to illegally enter (a building) and steal things • *Their house was burglarized.*

bur·glary /ˈbɚgləri/ n, pl -glar·ies [C/U] : the act of illegally entering a building in order to steal things

bur·gle /ˈbɚgəl/ vb bur·gled; bur·gling [T] : BURGLARIZE

bur·gun·dy /ˈbɚgəndi/ n, pl -dies [C/U] **1** *Burgundy* : a red or white wine made in Burgundy, France **2** : a reddish-purple color

buri·al /ˈberijəl/ n **1** [C/U] : the act or ceremony of burying a dead person in a grave • *preparing a body for burial* • *She wanted to give him a proper burial.* • *burial rites/customs* **2** [U] : the act of burying something in the ground • *The law prohibits the burial of toxic substances.*

bur·lap /ˈbɚˌlæp/ n [U] US : a strong, rough fabric • *a burlap bag* — called also (Brit) hessian

bur·lesque /bɚˈlɛsk/ n **1** [C/U] : a play, novel, etc., that makes a serious subject seem funny or ridiculous • *The book is a burlesque of Victorian society.* **2** [U] : a kind of entertainment that was popular in the U.S. in the late 19th and early 20th centuries and that included funny performances, singing, dancing, etc. • *a performer who got her start in burlesque* • *a burlesque dancer/show*

bur·ly /ˈbɚli/ adj bur·li·er; -est of a man : strong and heavy • *a big, burly man*

¹burn /ˈbɚn/ vb burned /ˈbɚnd/ or burnt /ˈbɚnt/; burn·ing ✧ *Burned* is more common in U.S. English; *burnt* is more common in British English. **1** [I] of a fire or flame : to give off heat, light, and gases • *A small fire burned in the fireplace.* **2** [I] : to be on fire : to have or produce a flame • *I smell smoke. Is something burning?* **3** [T/I] **a** : to destroy or damage (something) by fire or heat • *The wildfire burned acres of forest.* • *burnt pieces of wood* • *a material that burns slowly/easily* **b** : to injure or damage (someone or a part of the body) by fire, heat, acid, etc. • *She burned her hand on the stove.* = *She burned herself on the hot stove.* = *The hot stove burned her hand.* • *She has to stay out of the sun because her skin burns easily.* [=she gets sunburned easily] • *Several people were trapped in the building*

and (were) *burned to death.* [=were killed by fire] **4** [T/I] : to ruin (food) by cooking it too long or with too much heat • *She burned the toast.* **5 a** [T/I] of an acid, chemical, etc. : to damage (something) by causing a strong chemical reaction • *The acid burned his hand.* • *The acid burned into/through the metal.* • (figurative) *Her words were burned into his memory.* [=he always remembered her words] **b** [T] : to produce (something, such as a hole) by fire, heat, acid, etc. • *The acid burned a hole in the cloth.* ✧ If you have money and you want to spend it, the money is **burning a hole in your pocket.** **6** [I] : to be very hot • *The pavement was burning.* **7 a** [T/I] : to have or produce an unpleasantly hot and painful feeling • *The hot peppers burned my mouth.* = *My mouth is burning from the hot peppers.* **b** [I] : to feel a pain that is like being injured by heat or fire • *My ears were burning from the cold.* **c** [I] : to have a high fever • *She was burning (up) with fever.* **8** [I] **a** : to feel a strong emotion • *She was burning for a chance to prove herself.* — often + with • *burning with anger/ambition* **b** : to become hot and red because of a strong emotion • *Her cheeks were burning (with anger/shame).* **9** [T] US, informal **a** : to cheat or deceive (someone) • *I've been/gotten burned by him in the past.* **b** : to make (someone) angry • *It really burns me (up) to see people being treated so badly.* **10** [T] **a** : to use (something) as fuel • *This furnace burns oil/gas.* **b** : to use (food, calories, etc.) as a source of energy • *exercising to burn (up/off) fat* [=exercising to lose fat by using it to produce energy] **11** [I] : to give off light • *There was a light burning in the window.* **12** [T] computers : to record information or music on a disk • *burn a CD/DVD* • *burn songs onto a CD* — **burn down** [phrasal vb] **burn down** or **burn (something) down** or **burn down (something)** of a building or other structure : to be destroyed or to destroy (something) by fire • *The hotel burned down in 1922.* — **burn off** [phrasal vb] **burn off** or **burn (something) off** or **burn off (something)** **1** US, of fog, smoke, etc. : to go away because of the sun's heat • *The fog burned off.* = *The sun burned off the fog.* **2** : to be removed or to remove (something) by fire or heat • *The hot sun had burned the paint off the sign years before.* — **burn out** [phrasal vb] **1** **burn out** or **burn (itself) out** of a fire : to stop burning • *The campfire eventually burned out.* • (figurative) *His anger finally burned itself out.* [=he finally stopped being angry] **2** **burn (a building) out** or **burn out (a building)** : to destroy the inside of (a building) by fire • *The factory was completely burned out by the fire.* **3** **burn out** or **burn (something or someone) out** or **burn out (something or someone)** **a** : to stop working or cause (something) to stop working because of too much use or careless use • *The engine burned out.* **b** : to become or cause (someone) to become very physically and emotionally tired after doing a difficult job for a long time ▪ *Many teachers eventually burn out.* = *Many teachers eventually burn themselves out.* — **burn rubber** see ¹RUBBER — **burn the candle at both ends** : to do too much by being active late at night and during the day — **burn the midnight oil** : to work or study until very late at night — **burn through** [*phrasal vb*] *informal* : to use all of (something) quickly ▪ *They've burned through all the money already.* — **burn up** [*phrasal vb*] **burn up** or **burn (something) up** or **burn up (something)** : to be destroyed or cause (something) to be destroyed by fire ▪ *Most asteroids burn up upon entering the Earth's atmosphere.* — **burn your bridges** also Brit **burn your boats** : to do something that makes you unable to go back to a previous situation ▪ *He tried to stay friendly with his former boss because he didn't want to burn his bridges.*

²**burn** *n* **1** [*C*] **a** : an injury caused by fire, heat, acid, etc. ▪ *He suffered severe/serious burns in the accident.* **b** : a burned area ▪ *There's a small burn (mark) on the tabletop.* **2** [*C*] : a painful red mark on the skin caused by rubbing against something ▪ *rope/friction burns* **3** [*singular*] : a sharp, hot pain ▪ *the burn of iodine on a cut* ▪ *Continue doing the exercise until you feel the burn in your muscles.* — **do a slow burn** *US, informal* : to slowly become very angry

burned out or **burnt out** *adj* **1** of a building : having the inside destroyed by fire — usually hyphenated ▪ *an empty, burned-out building* **2** : feeling very physically and emotionally tired after doing a difficult job for a long time ▪ *I was burned out after 25 years as a corporate lawyer.* ▪ *a burned-out novelist*

burn·er /ˈbɚnɚ/ *n* [*C*] **1 a** : the part of a furnace, stove, etc., where the flame or heat is produced ▪ **b** : a device that burns something ▪ *a propane/gas/oil burner* : a device in which something is burned ▪ *an incense burner* — see also BACK BURNER, BUNSEN BURNER, FRONT BURNER **2** *computers* : a device that is used to record information or music on a CD or DVD ▪ *a CD burner*

burn·ing /ˈbɚnɪŋ/ *adj, always before a noun* **1** : producing or having a flame ▪ *a burning fire/candle/city* **2** : very strong ▪ *a burning hatred/desire* **3 a** : very hot ▪ *burning sand/pavement* ▪ *The pavement was burning hot.* [=extremely hot] **b** : similar to the feeling caused by something hot ▪ *itchy, burning eyes* ▪ *a burning sensation* **4** : very important ▪ *a burning issue/question*

bur·nish /ˈbɚnɪʃ/ *vb* [*T*] *formal* : ¹POLISH **1** ▪ *Burnish the metal with a soft cloth.* ▪ *burnished gold/leather* ▪ (*figurative*) *trying to burnish her image/reputation*

burn·out /ˈbɚnˌaʊt/ *n* **1** [*U*] : the condition of someone who has become very physically and emotionally tired after doing a difficult job for a long time ▪ *Many teachers eventually suffer/experience burnout.* **2** [*C*] : a person who suffers burnout ▪ *academic burnouts*

burnt *past tense and past participle of* ¹BURN

burnt out *variant spelling of* BURNED OUT

burp /ˈbɚp/ *vb* **1** [*I*] : to let out air from the stomach through the mouth with a sound **2** [*T*] : to help (a baby) let out air from the stomach especially by patting or rubbing the baby's back — **burp** *n* [*C*] ▪ *He let out a burp.*

burr /ˈbɚ/ *n* [*C*] **1** *also* **bur** : a rough covering of a nut or seed **2** : a rough area on a piece of metal that is left after the metal is cut **3** : a strong way of pronouncing *r* that is used by some speakers of English especially in northern England and in Scotland ▪ *He speaks with a Scottish burr.*

bur·ri·to /bəˈriːˌtoʊ/ *n, pl* **-tos** [*C*] : a Mexican food that consists of a flour tortilla that is rolled or folded around a filling of meat, beans, cheese, etc.

bur·ro /ˈbɚoʊ/ *n, pl* **-ros** [*C*] *chiefly US* : a small donkey

¹**bur·row** /ˈbɚoʊ/ *n* [*C*] : a hole or tunnel in the ground that an animal (such as a rabbit or fox) makes to live in or for safety

²**burrow** *vb* [*T/I*] **1** : to make a hole or tunnel in the ground by digging ▪ *The rabbit burrowed (its way) into the side of the hill.* ▪ *burrowing animals/rodents* **2** : to move or press under, through, or into something ▪ *She burrowed deep under the blankets.* ▪ *The baby burrowed* [=nestled] *her head into/against her mother's chest.*

¹**burst** /ˈbɚst/ *vb* **burst** *also* **burst·ed; burst·ing 1** [*T/I*] : to break open or into pieces in a sudden and violent way ▪ *The balloon burst.* ▪ *bombs bursting* [=exploding] ▪ *Be careful not to burst the balloon.* **2** [*I*] : to come or go very quickly and suddenly ▪ *The sun burst through the clouds.* ▪ *They burst in on us.* [=they suddenly entered the room we were in] ◆ To **burst onto/on/upon the scene** is to suddenly become very well known. ▪ *a rock band that (first) burst onto the music scene in 1995* **3** [*T*] of a river, stream, etc. : to flow over the surrounding land because of a flood ▪ *The stream burst its banks.* — **be bursting 1** : to be filled with something ▪ *The crate was bursting with fruit.* ▪ *She was bursting with energy/excitement/pride.* **2** : to want very much to do (something you are not yet able to do) ▪ *I'm bursting to tell you the news.* — **be bursting at the seams** : to be very full or crowded ▪ *The nightclub was bursting at the seams.* — **burst into** [*phrasal vb*] : to begin to produce or do (something) suddenly ▪ *She burst into laughter/tears/song.* ▪ *The house burst into flame(s).* — **burst open** : to open suddenly ▪ *The doors burst open.* ▪ *The cops burst the door open.* — **burst out** [*phrasal vb*] **burst out (doing something)** : to begin (doing something) suddenly ▪ *They both burst out* [=busted out] *laughing.* — **burst someone's bubble** see ¹BUBBLE

²**burst** *n* [*C*] **1** : a short period of producing or doing something that begins suddenly ▪ *a (sudden) burst of speed/laughter/*

energy **2** : an act of breaking open or into pieces • *the burst of a bubble*

bury /'beri/ *vb* **bur·ies; bur·ied; bury·ing** [T] **1** : to put (a dead person or animal) in a grave • *She was buried in the local cemetery.* **2 a** : to hide (something) in the ground • *The dog buried her bone.* • *buried treasure* **b** : to hide (something) so that it cannot be seen or is difficult to see • *He buried his feelings.* • *She buried her face in her hands.* **3** : to cover (someone or something) with something • *Snow had buried the car.* • *The car was buried under the snow.* • *Three skiers were buried alive in the avalanche.* **4** : to push (something) *in* or *into* something • *He buried his face/head in the pillow.* • (*figurative*) *He buried himself in his studies.* [=he gave his studies all of his attention] **5** : to stop being angry or upset about (something) • *bury the past —*
bury the hatchet see HATCHET

1bus /'bʌs/ *n, pl* **bus·es** *also US* **bus·ses** [C/U] : a large vehicle that is used for carrying passengers especially along a particular route at particular times • *We boarded the bus.* • *a bus driver/station* • *a bus stop* [=a place where a bus stops for passengers to get on or off]

2bus *vb* **buses** *also US* **busses; bused** *also US* **bussed; bus·ing** *also US* **bussing** [T] **1** : to transport (someone) in a bus • *The children are bused to school.* **2** *US* **a** : to remove dirty dishes from (a table at a restaurant) • *He buses tables at the diner.* **b** : to remove (something, such as dirty dishes) • *Be sure to bus your own trays.*

bus·boy /'bʌs,bɔɪ/ *n* [C] : a man or boy whose job is to remove dirty dishes, clean tables, etc., at a restaurant

bush /'bʊʃ/ *n* **1** [C] : a plant that has stems of wood and is smaller than a tree • *a rose bush* **2 the bush** : a large area (such as in Australia or Africa) that has not been cleared and that is not used for farming — *a bird in the hand is worth two in the ·bush* see BIRD — *beat around the bush* or *Brit* **beat about the bush** : to avoid saying something by talking about other things • *Stop beating around the bush and tell me why you're here.*

bushed /'bʊʃt/ *adj, not before a noun, informal* : very tired • *I'm bushed.* [=beat, exhausted]

bush·el /'bʊʃəl/ *n* **1** [C] : a unit for measuring an amount of fruit and grain that is equal to about 35.2 liters in the U.S. and to about 36.4 liters in the U.K. • *a bushel of wheat/apples* **2** [*plural*] *US, informal* : a large amount of something • *bushels of money* — *hide your light under a bushel* : to not tell others about your talents, successes, ideas, etc.

bush league *n* [C] *informal* : MINOR LEAGUE — **bush leagu·er** *n* [C]

bush·whack /'bʊʃ,wæk/ *vb* **1** [I] : to clear a path through thick woods by cutting down bushes and low tree branches • *bushwhacking through the jungle* **2** [T] : to attack (someone) suddenly • *He was bushwhacked by enemy soldiers.*

bushy /'bʊʃi/ *adj* **bush·i·er; -est** **1**

: very thick and full • *a bushy beard/tail* **2** *of a plant* : having a lot of branches and leaves • *a bushy tree* — **bush·i·ness** *n* [U]

busi·ness /'bɪznəs/ *n* **1** [U] **a** : the activity of making, buying, or selling goods or providing services in exchange for money • *The store will be open for business soon.* [=will be ready for customers soon] • *These changes are bad (for) business.* • *She works in the fashion/music/publishing/restaurant business.* • *business opportunities/contacts/interests* • *We do business with* [=sell to or buy from] *companies overseas.* • *He decided to go into business with his brother.* • *a place of business* [=a place, such as a store, bank, etc., where business is done] • *regular business hours* [=the hours when an office is open to do business] • *a business meeting* [=a meeting at which matters of business are discussed] **b** : work that is part of a job • *I went to New York City on/for business.* • *a business trip* **c** : the amount of activity that is done by a store, company, factory, etc. • *Business has been slow/bad lately.* [=there have been few customers, sales, etc., lately] **2** [C] : an organization (such as a store, company, or factory) that makes, buys, or sells goods or provides services in exchange for money • *He wants to start a business.* • *local businesses* • *the business district* [=the part of a city or town where there are many businesses] • *the business community* [=people involved in the upper levels of businesses] **3** [*singular*] : something that concerns a particular person, group, etc. • *Is there any other business to discuss?* • *What's this business I hear about you moving away?* • *Who I choose to vote for is my business.* • *He's decided to make it his business* [=make it his goal] *to improve local schools.* • *"Who did you vote for?" "That's none of your business."* [=that's private information that you should not be asking about] • *It's no business of yours who I voted for.* • *It's nobody's business who I voted for.* • *You have no business telling me* [=you have no right to tell me] *what I can do!* • *I was minding my own business* [=not bothering or talking to anyone] *when she suddenly started yelling at me.* ◇ The phrase *mind your own business* is used as an informal and often somewhat impolite way to tell someone to stop watching or asking about something that is private. **4** [U] : something that must be done • *I have some business in town.* [=I have to do something in town] • *He has to attend to some unfinished business.* • *Let's get down to business.* [=start working] • *I was just going about my business* [=doing what I usually do] *when I heard a big crash.* • *Sarah is good at taking care of business.* [=doing what needs to be done] • *A public library is in the business of providing information.* [=the job/purpose of a public library is to provide information] **5** [*singular*] : a matter, event, or situation • *Divorce is a messy business.* • *a risky/tricky business* — **business as usual** — used to say that something is working or continuing in the normal or usual way ▪ *Some people lost electricity in the storm, but for us it was business as usual.* — **business is business** — used to say that in order for a business to be successful it is necessary to do things that may hurt or upset people ▪ *I'm sorry I have to let you go, but business is business.* — **in business** 1 : operating as a business ▪ *The hotel has been in business for over 150 years.* 2 *informal* : ready to begin doing or using something ▪ *Just plug in the computer and you're in business!* [=you will be able to use the computer] ▪ *He quickly changed the tire, and was back in business.* [=ready to drive again] — **like nobody's business** *informal* : very well or quickly or in very large amounts ▪ *She can design computer programs like nobody's business.* — **mean business** : to be serious about doing something ▪ *We thought he was joking, but then we saw that he meant business.* — **out of business** : closed down ▪ *My favorite shop is out of business.* ▪ *The store has gone out of business.*

business card *n* [C] : a small card printed with a person's name and information about that person's company and job

business end *n* — **the business end** *informal* : the part of a tool, weapon, or instrument that is used most directly for the object's purpose ▪ *the business end of a rifle* [=the end where the bullets come out]

busi·ness·like /ˈbɪznəsˌlaɪk/ *adj* : having or showing qualities that are considered good in business : serious, polite, and practical ▪ *a businesslike approach/manner*

busi·ness·man /ˈbɪznəsˌmæn/ *n, pl* **-men** /-ˌmɛn/ [C] : a man who works in business especially in a high position

busi·ness·per·son /ˈbɪznəsˌpɚsn̩/ *n, pl* **-peo·ple** /-ˌpiːpəl/ [C] : a man or woman who works in business

busi·ness·wom·an /ˈbɪznəsˌwʊmən/ *n, pl* **-wom·en** /-ˌwɪmən/ [C] : a woman who works in business especially in a high position

bus·ing /ˈbʌsɪŋ/ *n* [U] *US* : the act or practice of bringing children by buses to a school that is far from the area where they live so that the school will have many children of different races

busk /ˈbʌsk/ *vb* [I] *chiefly Brit, informal* : to play music in a public place in order to earn money from people who are passing by — **busk·er** /ˈbʌskɚ/ *n* [C]

¹**bust** /ˈbʌst/ *n* [C] 1 : a sculpture of a person's head and neck and usually a part of the shoulders and chest ▪ *a marble/bronze bust* 2 **a** : a woman's breasts **b** : a measurement taken around a woman's chest and back ▪ *bust size* 3 *US, informal* : a complete failure : FLOP ▪ *The product/play was a bust.* 4 *informal* : an occurrence in which the police catch and arrest people committing a crime ▪ *a drug bust*

²**bust** *vb* **bust·ed** *also Brit* **bust**; **bust·ing** [T] *informal* 1 : to break (something) ▪ *He busted his watch.* ▪ *The camera is busted.* 2 **a** : to arrest (someone) ▪ *Police*

busted 12 men on weapons charges. **b** : to catch (someone) doing something wrong ▪ *Two students got busted for smoking in the bathroom.* 3 *US, impolite* — used in phrases like *bust your butt/ass* to describe working very hard ▪ *She's been busting her butt at her job.* 4 *US* : to hit or punch (someone) ▪ *I felt like busting him in the nose.* — **bust out** [*phrasal vb*] *informal* 1 **bust out (doing something)** : to begin (doing something) suddenly ▪ *She busted out laughing.* 2 **bust out (something) or bust (something) out** : to take (something) from the place where it is stored so that it can be used ▪ *He busted out the champagne.* 3 : to escape from a prison, jail, etc. ▪ *They busted out of jail.* — **bust up** [*phrasal vb*] *informal* 1 : to end a relationship ▪ *Their marriage busted up after three years.* 2 **bust up (something) or bust (something) up** : to cause (something) to end ▪ *The police busted the party up.* — **or bust** *informal* — used to say that you will do everything possible to get somewhere ▪ *The sign on the car said "New Orleans or bust!"*

³**bust** *adj* — **go bust** *informal* : to spend or lose all of your money ▪ *The company has gone bust.*

bust·er /ˈbʌstɚ/ *n* 1 [C] **a** : a person or thing that stops or prevents something ▪ *crime-busters* **b** : a person or thing that breaks something apart ▪ *The new drug acts as a clot-buster.* [=it causes blood clots to break apart] 2 *US, informal + somewhat old-fashioned* — used to address a man who is behaving in a way you do not like ▪ *Wait a minute, buster.*

bus·tier /ˌbuːstiˈeɪ, *Brit* ˈbʌstiˌeɪ/ *n* [C] : a tight piece of clothing that covers the upper part of a woman's body

¹**bus·tle** /ˈbʌsl̩/ *vb* **bus·tled**; **bus·tling** [I] 1 : to move or go in a busy or hurried way ▪ *She bustled around the kitchen.* 2 : to have a lot of busy activity ▪ *a bustling town* ▪ *The pier was bustling with people.*

²**bustle** *n* [U] : noisy or busy activity ▪ *The countryside seems very quiet after the hustle and bustle of the city.*

bust-up /ˈbʌstˌʌp/ *n* [C] *informal* 1 : the end of a relationship, marriage, etc. ▪ *the bust-up of their marriage* 2 *Brit* : a very bad argument or disagreement ▪ *They had a bust-up over money.*

busty /ˈbʌsti/ *adj* **bust·i·er; -est** *informal, of a woman* : having large breasts ▪ *a busty blonde*

¹**busy** /ˈbɪzi/ *adj* **bus·i·er; -est** 1 : actively doing something ▪ *Are you busy?* ▪ *He's been busy in the kitchen all afternoon.* ▪ *She's as busy as a bee.* [=very busy] 2 **a** : full of activity or work ▪ *My week has been busy!* ▪ *They live/lead busy lives.* ▪ *a busy schedule* **b** : full of people or things ▪ *a busy street/store* 3 *chiefly US, of a telephone or telephone line* : being used ▪ *The line/phone is busy.* [=(*chiefly Brit*) *engaged*] ◆ When you dial a telephone line that is already in use, you hear a sound that is called a *busy signal*. 4 : full of many details ▪ *busy wallpaper* — **get busy** : to start doing work ▪ *We'd better get busy.* — **busi·ly** /ˈbɪzəli/ *adv*

— **busy·ness** /'bɪzinəs/ n [U]

²**busy** vb **bus·ies; bus·ied; busy·ing** — **busy yourself** : to make or keep (yourself) busy with work or an activity ▪ *The children busied themselves with puzzles all day.*

busy·body /'bɪzi,bɑːdi/ n, pl **-bod·ies** [C] *disapproving* : a person who is too interested in the private lives of other people

busy·work /'bɪzi,wək/ n [U] US : work that is given to you only to keep you busy ▪ *Students were given busywork for the last few minutes of class.*

¹**but** /'bʌt, bət/ conj **1** — used to introduce a statement that adds something to a previous statement and usually contrasts with it in some way ▪ *He wants to go to the movies, but I want to go to the museum.* ▪ *She plans to visit Boston but not New York.* ▪ *I'd love to come to the party, but* [=however] *I'll be away that weekend.* **2** : other than : EXCEPT ▪ *They've done nothing but argue all day.* **3** — used in speech at the beginning of a sentence that expresses surprise, shock, etc. ▪ *They've arrived? But I thought they were coming Tuesday.* **4** — used with a repeated word for emphasis ▪ *Nobody but nobody could solve the riddle.* — **but then 1** — used to introduce a statement that adds another and different thought to a preceding statement ▪ *I'm surprised to hear that Tom has left the army. But then he never was the type to obey orders.* **2** — used to introduce a statement that tells about something different or surprising that happened next ▪ *They won the first two games, but then lost the next five.*

²**but** prep : other than (something or someone) : EXCEPT ▪ *We had nothing but rain all week.* [=it rained for the entire week] ▪ *I didn't tell anyone but my sister.* — **but for** : if not for (something or someone) ▪ *The score would have been higher but for some excellent goaltending.*

³**but** adv, formal **1** : ²ONLY ▪ *They have but two weeks to get ready.* ▪ *She is but a child.* **2** — used in negative statements to say that something must happen ▪ *I cannot but* [=it is impossible that I would not] *feel sympathy for him.* ▪ *I could not (help) but wonder* [=I could not help wondering] *why she had lied.* — see also ALL BUT

⁴**but** /'bʌt/ n [C] : a reason someone gives for not doing or agreeing with something — usually plural ▪ (*US*) *She's the most qualified candidate, and there are no* **ifs, ands, or buts** *about it!* = (*Brit*) *There are no ifs and buts about it!* [=it is certain that she is the most qualified candidate]

bu·tane /'bju:,teɪn/ n [U] : a type of gas that is used in a liquid form as a fuel

butch /'bʊtʃ/ adj, informal **1** sometimes offensive : having a very masculine appearance and way of behaving — used especially to describe homosexuals **2** of hair : cut very short ▪ *a butch haircut*

¹**butch·er** /'bʊtʃə/ n [C] **1 a** : someone who cuts and sells meat in a shop **b** : someone who kills animals and prepares their meat to be eaten **2** : a shop that sells meat **3** : someone who kills a lot of people or animals in a brutal or cruel way ▪ *a bunch of butchers who gained power by slaughtering their enemies* **4** informal : someone who does something very roughly and badly ▪ *That surgeon is a butcher!*

²**butcher** vb [T] **1** : to kill (an animal) and prepare its meat for sale ▪ *butcher the hogs* **2** : to kill (people or animals) in a brutal and cruel way ▪ *Many innocent people were butchered under his regime.* **3** informal : to do (something) very badly ▪ *The band butchered the song.*

but·ler /'bʌtlə/ n [C] : the main male servant in the home of a wealthy person

¹**butt** /'bʌt/ n [C] **1** chiefly US, informal + sometimes impolite : BUTTOCKS ▪ *He slipped and landed on his butt.* ▪ *Why don't you* **get off your butt** [=stop being so lazy] *and do something?* **2** : the thicker end of a weapon or tool ▪ *the butt (end) of a rifle* **3 a** : the end part of a cigarette or cigar that is not smoked **b** informal : a cigarette ▪ *She went out to buy some butts.* **4** : a person who is treated badly or is made fun of ▪ *She was the butt of their jokes.* [=they made unkind jokes about her] **5** : a forceful hit or push with the head ▪ *a head butt in/to the ribs*

²**butt** vb [T/I] **1** : to hit or push (something) forcefully with the head ▪ *She got butted by an angry goat.* **2** US : to place something right next to something else or to be right next to something else ▪ *The floorboards (were) butted against each other.* ▪ *The apartment building butts up against an old church.* — **butt heads** chiefly US, informal : to disagree about how something should be done ▪ *They're butting heads over the issue.* — **butt in** [phrasal vb] informal : to get involved in something (such as a conversation or someone else's activities) especially in a rude way ▪ *Sorry to butt in (on you) like this, but I need to ask you a question.* — **butt out** [phrasal vb] chiefly US, informal : to stop being involved in something (such as a conversation or someone else's affairs) ▪ *This has nothing to do with you! I wish you would just butt out!*

¹**but·ter** /'bʌtə/ n **1** [U] : a solid yellow substance made from milk or cream that is spread on food or used in cooking — see also BREAD AND BUTTER **2** [C/U] : a food made from cooked fruit or roasted nuts that have been ground up ▪ *apple butter* — see also PEANUT BUTTER

²**butter** vb [T] : to spread or put butter on (something) ▪ *butter a piece of bread* — **butter up** [phrasal vb] **butter up (someone)** or **butter (someone) up** informal : to treat (someone) very well or kindly in order to get something ▪ *butter up potential clients* — **know which side your bread is buttered** on see ¹BREAD

but·ter·cup /'bʌtə,kʌp/ n, pl **-cups** [C] : a wild plant that has small yellow flowers that are shaped like cups

but·ter·fin·gers /'bʌtə,fɪŋgəz/ n [singular] informal : a person who often drops things — **but·ter·fin·gered** /'bʌtə,fɪŋgəd/ adj

but·ter·fly /'bʌtə,flaɪ/ n, pl **-flies 1** [C]

: a kind of insect that has a long thin body and brightly colored wings and that flies mostly during the day **2** [C] *often disapproving* : a person who goes to many parties and other social events ▪ *a **social butterfly** 3* [*singular*] : a way of swimming in which the swimmer's face is in the water and the arms move together in a circular motion while the legs kick up and down **4** [*plural*] *informal* : a nervous feeling in your stomach ▪ *She gets butterflies (in her stomach) before she goes on stage.*

butter knife *n* [C] : a small knife with a rounded blade that is used especially for spreading butter on bread during a meal

but·ter·milk /ˈbʌtɚˌmɪlk/ *n* [U] : the liquid that is left after butter has been made from milk or cream

but·ter·scotch /ˈbʌtɚˌskɑːtʃ/ *n* [U] : a candy made by boiling butter, sugar, and water ▪ *butterscotch pudding*

but·tery /ˈbʌtɚi/ *adj* **1** : resembling butter ▪ *a buttery flavor/texture* **2** : containing or covered with butter ▪ *buttery popcorn*

but·tock /ˈbʌtək/ *n* [C] : either of the two soft parts of the body that a person sits on — usually plural ▪ *He fell and landed on his buttocks.*

¹but·ton /ˈbʌtn̩/ *n* [C] **1** : a small, usually round piece of plastic, metal, etc., that is sewn to a piece of clothing and is pushed through a loop or hole to fasten one part of the clothing to another part **2** *US* : a small, usually round sign that has a picture or words on the front and a pin on the back ▪ *She wore a button that read "Support your local library." ▪ a **campaign button** [=a button that shows support for someone's political campaign] — called also* (*Brit*) **badge 3 a** : a small part of a machine that you push to make the machine work ▪ *the on/off button* **b** : a small area on a computer screen that you click on to make the computer software do something — **(as) cute as a button** *informal* : very cute — **on the button** *US, informal* **1** : exactly at the specified time ▪ *They arrived at noon on the button.* **2** : perfectly accurate ▪ *Your guess was (right) on the button.* — **push your buttons** *informal* : to do or say something just to make you angry or upset ▪ *Don't pay any attention to her. She's just trying to push your buttons.*

²button *vb* **1** [T] : to attach (a button) by passing it through a hole ▪ *button the top button on a shirt* **2** [T/I] : to close or fasten (something) with buttons ▪ *Button your shirt. ▪ Be sure to button up (your coat) before you go outside.* **3** [I] : to have buttons for fastening ▪ *The skirt buttons on the side.*

but·ton-down /ˈbʌtn̩ˌdaʊn/ *adj, always before a noun* **1 a** *of a collar* : having the ends fastened to the shirt with buttons ▪ *a button-down collar* **b** *of a shirt* : having a button-down collar ▪ *a button-down shirt* **2** *or* **but·toned-down** /ˈbʌtn̩dˌdaʊn/ *often disapproving* : having a very traditional and formal way of dressing, behaving, etc. ▪ *a buttoned-down* [=*conservative*] *businessman*

¹but·ton·hole /ˈbʌtn̩ˌhoʊl/ *n* [C] : a hole in clothing through which a button is passed in order to fasten something

²buttonhole *vb* [T] *informal* : to force (someone who is going somewhere) to stop and talk to you ▪ *When I tried to leave I was buttonholed by a coworker.*

¹but·tress /ˈbʌtrəs/ *n* [C] : a structure built against a wall in order to support or strengthen it

²buttress *vb* [T] : to support, strengthen, or defend (something) ▪ *The treaty will buttress the cause of peace.*

but·ty /ˈbʌti/ *n, pl* **-ties** [C] *Brit, informal* : a sandwich

bux·om /ˈbʌksəm/ *adj, of a woman* : healthy and attractive with large breasts ▪ *a buxom blonde*

¹buy /ˈbaɪ/ *vb* **bought** /ˈbɑːt/; **buy·ing 1** [T/I] : to get (something) by paying money for it ▪ *I bought a computer. ▪ He bought dinner for us. ▪ He bought us dinner. ▪ Stock prices are low, so now is a good time to buy.* **2** [T] *of money* : to be able to get something ▪ *Money can't buy love.* **3** [T] *informal* : to accept or believe (something) as true ▪ *I don't buy what he's saying.* **4** [T] *informal* : BRIBE ▪ *an honest man who can't be bought* — **buy into** [*phrasal vb*] **1** : to pay money in order to own part of (something) ▪ *buying into a company* **2** : to accept or believe (something) as true ▪ *I don't buy into the idea that money brings happiness.* — **buy it** *or US* **buy the farm** *informal* : to die ▪ *I nearly bought the farm when my car crashed.* — **buy off** [*phrasal vb*] **buy off (someone)** *or* **buy (someone) off** : to give money to (someone) for illegal or dishonest help ▪ *He bought off the police.* — **buy out** [*phrasal vb*] **buy out (someone)** *or* **buy (someone) out** : to pay money to (someone) for his or her part of a company or team ▪ *She bought out her partners.* — **buy time** : to get more time for someone or something ▪ *The medication may buy patients some time.* [=it may allow patients to live longer] — **buy up** [*phrasal vb*] **buy up (something)** *or* **buy (something) up** : to pay money for all or a large part of (something) ▪ *She is buying up all the artist's early work.* — **buy·er** /ˈbajɚ/ *n* [C] ▪ *The buyer and seller must agree on a price for the property.*

²buy *n* [C] — used to describe something that is being sold ▪ *The shoes were a great buy.* [=*deal*]

buy·out /ˈbaɪˌaʊt/ *n* [C] : the act of gaining control of a company by buying the parts of it you do not own ▪ *an employee buyout = a buyout by the employees of the company*

¹buzz /ˈbʌz/ *vb* **1** [I] **a** : to make the low, continuous sound of a flying insect ▪ *a buzzing bee* **b** : to make a low, continuous sound ▪ *The doorbell buzzed.* **c** : to be filled with a low, continuous sound ▪ *My ears are still buzzing* [=*ringing*] *from the concert.* **2** [I] : to be filled with activity, excitement, etc. ▪ *The room buzzed with excitement.* **3 a** [T/I] : to send for or signal (someone) by using an electric device (called a buzzer) that produces a loud, low sound ▪ *The nurse buzzed (for) the doctor.* **b** [*T*] : to let (someone) go into or out of a place by using an electric device that produces a loud, low sound as it unlocks a door, gate, etc. ▪ *Someone will buzz you into the building.* **4** [*T*] *US, informal* : to call (someone) on the telephone ▪ *Buzz me when you get there.* **5** [*T*] : to fly an airplane low over (something or someone) ▪ *The plane/pilot buzzed the people watching the show.* **6** [*I*] : to go or move quickly ▪ *She was buzzing around the office.* — **buzz off** *informal* — used as a rude or angry way to tell someone to go away — **buzz·ing** /ˈbʌzɪŋ/ *n* [*U*] ▪ *the buzzing of bees*

²**buzz** *n* **1** [*C*] **a** : the low, continuous sound made by a flying insect (such as a bee) ▪ *the buzz of the bees* **b** : a low, continuous sound ▪ *The machine makes a quiet buzz.* **2** [*singular*] : a low sound caused by many people talking at the same time ▪ *a buzz of voices* **3** *informal* **a** [*U*] : the things that are being said about something ▪ *the latest buzz about their marriage* **b** [*U, singular*] : excited talk about something ▪ *There's been a lot of buzz about the new movie.* **4** [*singular*] *informal* **a** : a feeling of excitement ▪ *I get a buzz out of this game.* **b** : a feeling of being somewhat drunk or intoxicated ▪ *He had a buzz after only two drinks.* **5** [*singular*] *informal* : a telephone call ▪ *Give me a buzz.* [=call me]

buz·zard /ˈbʌzɚd/ *n* [*C*] **1** *US* : a kind of large bird that eats animals that are already dead **2** *Brit* : a kind of large hawk

buzz cut *n* [*C*] *US* : CREW CUT

buzz·er /ˈbʌzɚ/ *n* [*C*] : an electric device that makes a loud sound ▪ *The buzzer signaled the end of the game.*

buzz saw *n* [*C*] *US* : CIRCULAR SAW

buzz·word /ˈbʌzˌwɚd/ *n* [*C*] : a word or phrase that becomes very popular for a period of time ▪ *At that time, the new buzzword in the computer industry was "multitasking."*

¹**by** /ˈbaɪ, bə/ *prep* **1** : close to or next to (something or someone) : NEAR ▪ *She was standing by the window.* **2 a** : up to and beyond (something or someone) : PAST ▪ *The bus went right by him without stopping.* **b** : at or to (someone's home) ▪ *Why don't you come by my place later?* **3 a** — used following a passive verb to indicate the person or thing that does something ▪ *The decision was made by me.* [=I made the decision] ▪ *I was surprised by the result.* [=the result surprised me] **b** — used to indicate the thing that is used to do something ▪ *He opened the door by (using) force.* [=he used force to open the door] **c** — used to indicate an action that is done for a particular purpose ▪ *Reset the machine by pressing this button.* ▪ *He began his speech by thanking the President.* **4** — used to indicate the person who wrote or created something ▪ *a play/painting by a famous writer/artist* **5 a** — used to indicate the method used to go somewhere, send something, etc. ▪ *We came by train/car.* ▪ *a message sent by e-mail* **b** — used to indicate the method used to enter or leave a place ▪ *We en-*

tered by the front door. **6 a** — used to indicate the name that is used for someone or something ▪ *Her full name is Elizabeth but she goes by (the nickname) "Lizzie."* **b** — used to indicate how someone is spoken to, identified, etc. ▪ *He called her by name.* [=he used her name when he spoke to her] **c** — used to introduce the name of someone or something important as proof that you are speaking the truth ▪ *I swear by all that's sacred that I'm not lying.* — often used in phrases like *by God* to add emphasis ▪ *He said he'd go, and by God, he did!* **d** : when using (a specified word or phrase) ▪ *What do you mean by "acceptable levels?"* **7** — used to indicate the part of something or of a person's body that is held, grasped, etc. ▪ *She grabbed him by the arm.* **8** : during the time of (day or night) ▪ *New York by night is very different from New York by day.* **9 a** : not later than (a specified time) ▪ *We need to leave by noon.* **b** : during the time until (a specified time) ▪ *By her 10th birthday she had lived in 15 countries.* **10 a** : in a way that agrees with or follows (something, such as a rule) ▪ *They didn't play by the rules.* **b** : in a way that is based on (something) ▪ *You shouldn't judge people by (their) appearances.* **11 a** — used to indicate units of measurement or quantity ▪ *sold by the dozen* ▪ *paid by the hour* **b** — used to indicate the number that multiplies or divides another number ▪ *multiply/divide 10 by 4* **c** — used to indicate the numbers of a measurement ▪ *The room is 15 feet by 20 feet.* **12** — used to indicate an amount, length, etc. ▪ *The price increased by five dollars.* **13** — used to indicate someone's job, origin, character, etc. ▪ *He's French by birth.* ▪ *I'm an optimist by nature.* [=it is my nature to be optimistic] **14 a** — used in phrases to describe the speed at which something happens or changes ▪ *The work is getting done bit by bit.* [=gradually in small amounts] ▪ *His health is growing worse day by day.* [=every day] ▪ *The situation is getting more dangerous by the hour.* **b** — used in phrases to describe how a series of people or things proceed or are dealt with ▪ *I solved the problems one by one.* [=I solved the first problem, then the second one, etc.] **15** *informal* : in the opinion of (someone) ▪ *Whatever you want to do is fine/okay by me.* [=I will agree to whatever you want to do] — **by the by** or **by the bye** *old-fashioned* — used to introduce a statement that provides added information or that mentions another subject ▪ *I met his wife who, by the by [=by the way], is a well-known author.* — **by yourself** : without others : ALONE ▪ *He sat (all) by himself, reading the newspaper.*

²**by** /ˈbaɪ/ *adv* **1** : ⁴PAST ▪ *The bus drove by without stopping.* ▪ *This year went by* [=passed] *quickly.* **2** — used with *put* to describe something that is being kept or saved for a future use ▪ *You should be putting some money by* [=saving some money] *for your old age.* **3** : at or to someone's home ▪ *Some friends stopped/*

came by for a chat. **4** : close or near ▪ *She lives close by.* [=*nearby*] — **by and by** *literary* + *old-fashioned* : EVENTUAL-LY ▪ *I feel sure that we'll succeed by and by.* — **by and large** **1** : in a general way ▪ *By and large, I like the way things have gone.* **2** : in most cases ▪ *By and large it takes a month for the shipment to arrive.*

bye /'baɪ/ *interj, informal* : [1]GOODBYE ▪ *Bye. I'll see you tomorrow.*

bye–bye /'baɪ,baɪ/ *interj, informal* : [1]GOODBYE ▪ *Bye-bye! See you later!* — often used by children or when speaking to children ▪ *Say/Wave bye-bye.* — **go bye-bye** *US, informal* : to go away — used in imitation of children's speech ▪ *Investors watched their money go bye-bye.*

by–elec·tion /'baɪə,lɛkʃən/ *n* [C] *Brit* : a special election that is held to replace someone who has died or resigned

by·gone /'baɪ,gɑːn/ *adj, always before a noun* : from a time in the past ▪ *a bygone age/era*

by·gones /'baɪ,gɑːnz/ *n* — **let bygones be bygones** : to forgive someone and forget about past disagreements ▪ *I think it's time we let bygones be bygones.*

by·law /'baɪ,lɑː/ *n* [C] **1** *US* : a rule that an organization (such as a club or company) makes and that its members must follow **2** : a law or regulation that is made by a local government and that applies only to the local area

by·line /'baɪ,laɪn/ *n* [C] : a line at the beginning of a newspaper or magazine article that gives the writer's name

[1]**by·pass** /'baɪ,pæs, *Brit* 'baɪ,pɑːs/ *n* [C] **1** : a road that goes around a blocked or very crowded area **2** *medical* : a procedure done to allow blood to flow past a blocked blood vessel to reach the heart ▪ *heart bypass surgery* ▪ *a double/triple/ quadruple bypass* [=a procedure done when two/three/four blood vessels are blocked]

[2]**bypass** *vb* [T] **1** : to go around or avoid (a place or area) ▪ *Is there a way to bypass the city/construction?* **2** : to avoid or ignore (someone or something) especially to get something done quicker ▪ *He bypassed the manager and talked directly to the owner.*

by–prod·uct /'baɪ,prɑːdəkt/ *n* [C] **1** : something that is produced during the production or destruction of something else ▪ *Carbon monoxide is a by-product of burning fuel.* **2** : something that happens as a result of something else ▪ *The loss of jobs was a by-product of other changes in the industry.*

by·stand·er /'baɪ,stændə/ *n* [C] : a person who is standing near but not taking part in what is happening ▪ *innocent bystanders*

byte /'baɪt/ *n* [C] : a unit of computer information that is equal to eight bits

by·way /'baɪ,weɪ/ *n* [C] : a road that is not used very much ▪ *He's traveled the highways and byways of this country.*

by·word /'baɪ,wəd/ *n* [C] : someone or something that is closely connected with a particular quality ▪ *The hotel's name has become a byword for hospitality.*

C

c *or* **C** /'siː/ *n, pl* **c's** *or* **cs** *or* **C's** *or* **Cs** **1** [C/U] : the third letter of the English alphabet ▪ *words that begin with (a) c* **2** [C] : the Roman numeral that means 100 **3** [C/U] : a musical note or key referred to by the letter C ▪ *play/sing a C* ▪ *a song in the key of C* **4** [C] : a grade that is given to a student for doing average work ▪ *She got a C on the exam.*

c. *abbr* **1** *also* **ca.** circa — used to indicate that a date is not exact ▪ *c. 1600 = ca. 1600* **2** *US* cup ▪ *2 c. flour*

C *abbr* **1** Celsius **2** centigrade **3** copyright **4** count noun

CA *abbr* California

cab /'kæb/ *n* [C] **1** : [1]TAXI **2** : the part of a truck, tractor, etc., in which the driver sits

cab·a·ret /,kæbə'reɪ/ *n* [C] : a restaurant where you can buy alcohol and see a musical show

cab·bage /'kæbɪdʒ/ *n* [C/U] : a leafy usually green vegetable that grows in a tight round shape

cab·bie *or* **cab·by** /'kæbi/ *n, pl* **-bies** [C] *informal* : CABDRIVER

cab·driv·er /'kæb,draɪvə/ *n* [C] : a person who drives a taxi

cab·in /'kæbən/ *n* [C] **1** : a small, simple house made of wood ▪ *a cabin in the woods* ▪ *a log cabin* **2 a** : a room that you can sleep in on a ship or boat **b** : the part of an airplane in which the passengers sit

cabin cruiser *n* [C] : CRUISER 3

cab·i·net /'kæbnɪt/ *n* [C] **1** : a piece of furniture that is used for storing things and usually has doors and shelves ▪ *a kitchen/medicine cabinet* **2** *or* **Cabinet** : a group of people who give advice to the leader of a government ▪ *a member of the President's Cabinet*

cabin fever *n* [U] : an unhappy and impatient feeling that comes from being indoors for too long

[1]**ca·ble** /'keɪbəl/ *n* **1 a** [C/U] : a thick, strong rope made of wires that are twisted together ▪ *a bridge held up by cables* **b** [C] : a wire that moves a part in a machine ▪ *a brake cable* **2** [C/U] : a group of wires, glass fibers, etc., covered in plastic or rubber and used to carry electricity or electrical signals ▪ *battery/computer cables* **3** [C] : a message sent by telegraph **4** [U] : CABLE TELEVISION ▪

The game was shown on cable. • *cable networks/companies*

²**cable** *vb* **ca·bled; ca·bling** [*T/I*] : to send a message by telegraph • *She cabled the news to the United States.*

cable car *n* [*C*] **1** : a vehicle that hangs in the air from a cable that pulls it up and down mountains **2** : a vehicle that is pulled along tracks by a cable

cable modem *n* [*C*] : a device that connects a computer to a network (such as the Internet) through the same kind of cable used for cable television

cable television *n* [*U*] : a system in which television signals are sent through cables rather than through the air — called also *cable, cable TV*

ca·boo·dle /kəˈbuːdl/ *n* — **the whole (kit and) caboodle** *US, informal* : EVERYTHING • *Her father owned 5 houses and 12 cars, and when he died he left her the whole kit and caboodle.*

ca·boose /kəˈbuːs/ *n* [*C*] *US* : a part of a train that is attached at the back end

ca·cao /kəˈkaʊ/ *n* [*U*] : the dried seeds of a tropical tree that are used to make cocoa and chocolate

cache /ˈkæʃ/ *n* [*C*] : a group of things that have been hidden in a secret place because they are illegal or have been stolen • *a weapons cache* • *a cache of stolen goods*

ca·chet /ˌkæˈʃeɪ/ *n* [*U, singular*] — used to say that someone or something is liked or respected by people • *a movie director with great artistic cachet*

cack·le /ˈkækəl/ *vb* **cack·led; cack·ling** [*I*] **1** : to make loud, unpleasant sounds • *cackling hens* **2** : to laugh noisily • *I could hear them cackling in the next room.* — **cackle** *n* [*C*]

ca·coph·o·ny /kæˈkɑːfəni/ *n* [*singular*] : unpleasant loud sounds • *a cacophony of voices*

cac·tus /ˈkæktəs/ *n, pl* **cac·ti** /ˈkæk,taɪ/ *or* **cac·tus·es** *also US* **cactus** [*C*] : a plant that lives in the desert and that has many sharp points (called spines)

cad /ˈkæd/ *n* [*C*] *old-fashioned* : a rude and selfish man — **cad·dish** /ˈkædɪʃ/ *adj* : *caddish men/behavior*

ca·dav·er /kəˈdævə/ *n* [*C*] *formal* : a dead body : CORPSE

cad·die *or* **cad·dy** /ˈkædi/ *n, pl* **-dies** [*C*] : a person who carries a golfer's clubs on the golf course — **caddie** *or* **caddy** *vb* **-dies; -died; -dy·ing** [*I*]

ca·dence /ˈkeɪdns/ *n* **1** [*C/U*] : a regular beat or rhythm • *the steady cadence of the drums* **2** [*C*] : the way a person's voice changes by gently rising and falling while he or she is speaking • *He speaks with a soft Southern cadence.*

ca·det /kəˈdɛt/ *n* [*C*] : a student at a military school who is preparing to be an officer • *a naval cadet*

caesarean, caesarean section *variant spellings of* CESAREAN, CESAREAN SECTION

ca·fé *also* **ca·fe** /kæˈfeɪ, *Brit* ˈkæˌfeɪ/ *n* [*C*] : a small restaurant where you can get simple meals and drinks (such as coffee)

caf·e·te·ria /ˌkæfəˈtiriə/ *n* [*C*] : a place where people get food at a counter and carry it to a table for eating • *a school cafeteria*

caf·fein·at·ed /ˈkæfəˌneɪtəd/ *adj* : containing caffeine • *caffeinated beverages*

caf·feine /kæˈfiːn, *Brit* ˈkæˌfiːn/ *n* [*U*] : a substance that is found especially in coffee and tea and that makes you feel more awake

cage /ˈkeɪdʒ/ *n* [*C*] : a box made of wire or metal bars in which people keep animals or birds — see also RIB CAGE — **rattle someone's cage** *informal* : to make someone feel worried or upset

caged /ˈkeɪdʒd/ *adj* : kept in a cage • *a caged lion*

ca·gey *also* **ca·gy** /ˈkeɪdʒi/ *adj* **ca·gi·er; -est** **1** : not willing to say everything that you know about something • *She's being cagey about her plans.* **2** : careful to avoid being trapped or tricked • *a cagey lawyer* **3** : very clever • *a cagey prisoner/move* — **cag·i·ness** *n* [*U*]

ca·hoots /kəˈhuːts/ *n* — **in cahoots** *informal* : working together or making plans together in secret • *He was robbed by a man who was in cahoots with the bartender.*

Cain *see* raise Cain at ¹RAISE

ca·jole /kəˈdʒoʊl/ *vb* **-joled; -jol·ing** [*T*] : to persuade someone to do something or to give you something by making promises or saying nice things • *She cajoled her husband into going with her.* • *My roommate cajoled money from me.*

Ca·jun /ˈkeɪdʒən/ *n* [*C*] : a person from Louisiana whose ancestors were French Canadian — **Cajun** *adj* • *Cajun music/culture/food*

¹**cake** /ˈkeɪk/ *n* **1** [*C/U*] : a sweet baked food made from a mixture of flour, sugar, and other ingredients (such as eggs and butter) • *I made/baked a cake.* • *a piece of chocolate cake* — see also PIECE OF CAKE **2** [*C*] : a mixture of food that has been shaped into a ball or a flat round shape and baked or fried • *crab/rice/potato cakes* **3** [*C*] : something that is shaped like a rectangular block • *a cake of soap* — **have your cake and eat it too** (*US*) *or Brit* **have your cake and eat it** : to have or enjoy the good parts of something without having or dealing with the bad parts — **icing on the cake** see ICING — **take the cake** *chiefly US* : to win the prize in a contest — used to describe something that is extremely surprising, foolish, annoying, etc. • *You've done some silly things, but this one really takes the cake!*

²**cake** *vb* **caked; cak·ing** **1** [*T*] : to cover something with an outer layer that becomes hard as it dries • *Mud was caked all over his truck.* = *His truck was caked in/with mud.* **2** [*I*] : to become dry and hard • *The mud had caked on his boots.*

cake·walk /ˈkeɪk,wɑːk/ *n* [*singular*] : something that is very easy to win or do

• *She expected the election to be a cakewalk.*

cal·a·mine /ˈkæləˌmaɪn/ *n* [U] : a pink liquid that is used to treat skin that is sore, itchy, sunburned, etc. — called also *calamine lotion*

ca·lam·i·ty /kəˈlæməti/ *n, pl* **-ties** [C/U] *formal* : an event that causes great harm and suffering : DISASTER • *floods, earthquakes, and other calamities* — **ca·lam·i·tous** /kəˈlæmətəs/ *adj* • *a calamitous oil spill*

cal·ci·um /ˈkælsijəm/ *n* [U] : a substance that is found in most plants and animals and that is especially important in people for strong healthy bones

cal·cu·late /ˈkælkjəˌleɪt/ *vb* **-lat·ed; -lat·ing** [T] **1** : to find (a number, answer, etc.) by using mathematical processes • *We calculated the cost of the repairs.* **2** : to get a general idea about the value, size, or cost of (something) : ESTIMATE • *We need to calculate our chances of success.*

cal·cu·lat·ed /ˈkælkjəˌleɪtəd/ *adj* : carefully planned for a particular and often improper purpose • *a calculated attempt to deceive voters* • *a calculated risk* [=a risk that is accepted after careful thought]

cal·cu·lat·ing /ˈkælkjəˌleɪtɪŋ/ *adj* : carefully thinking about and planning actions for selfish or improper reasons • *a cold, calculating criminal*

cal·cu·la·tion /ˌkælkjəˈleɪʃən/ *n* [C/U] **1** : a process or result of calculating something • *The computer can do millions of calculations each second.* • *Careful calculation was required.* **2** : careful thought and planning that is done usually for selfish reasons • *The book reveals the cold calculations behind the government's policies.*

cal·cu·la·tor /ˈkælkjəˌleɪtəʳ/ *n* [C] : a small electronic device that is used for adding, subtracting, etc.

cal·cu·lus /ˈkælkjələs/ *n* [U] : an advanced branch of mathematics that deals mostly with rates of change and with finding lengths, areas, and volumes

caldron *variant spelling of* CAULDRON

cal·en·dar /ˈkæləndəʳ/ *n* [C] **1** : a document, chart, etc., that shows the days, weeks, and months of a year **2** : a list or schedule of events or activities that occur at different times throughout the year • *The university's academic calendar runs from September to May.* **3** : a particular system for organizing the days of the year by month • *the Jewish calendar*

calendar year *n* [C] : the period of time from January 1 to December 31

calf /ˈkæf, *Brit* ˈkɑːf/ *n, pl* **calves** /ˈkævz, *Brit* ˈkɑːvz/ [C] **1 a** : a very young cow **b** : the young of various other large animals (such as the elephant or whale) **2** : the muscular back part of the leg below the knee

cal·i·ber (*US*) *or Brit* **cal·i·bre** /ˈkæləbəʳ/ *n* **1** [U] : level of excellence, skill, etc. • *teachers of the highest caliber* **2** [C] : a measurement of the width of a bullet or a gun barrel • *a .22-caliber bullet* [=a bul-

let that is 22 hundredths of an inch in diameter]

cal·i·brate /ˈkæləˌbreɪt/ *vb* **-brat·ed; -brat·ing** [T] : to adjust, mark, or measure (something) in an accurate and exact way • *calibrate a thermometer* — **cal·i·bra·tion** /ˌkæləˈbreɪʃən/ *n* [C/U]

cal·i·co /ˈkælɪˌkoʊ/ *n, pl* **-coes** *or* **-cos** **1** [U] *US* : a light, printed cotton cloth **2** [U] *Brit* : a heavy, plain white cotton cloth **3** [C] *US* : a cat that has white, brown, and black fur — called also *calico cat*

cal·i·per (*US*) *or Brit* **cal·li·per** /ˈkæləpəʳ/ *n* **1** [C] : a tool that has two narrow legs which can be adjusted to measure the thickness or width of something • *a pair of calipers* **2** [*plural*] *Brit* : metal devices that are worn to support legs that have been weakened by injury or disease

cal·is·then·ics (*chiefly US*) *or Brit* **cal·lis·then·ics** /ˌkæləsˈθɛnɪks/ *n* [*plural*] : physical exercises that are done without special equipment

¹**call** /ˈkɑːl/ *vb* **1 a** [T/I] : to speak in a loud voice • *He called (out) to them for help.* • *He called (out) her name in his sleep.* **b** [T] : to announce or read (something) in a loud voice • *They're calling our flight: it's boarding at gate 57.* [I] : to make the sound that is usual for a particular type of bird or animal • *The birds were calling as the sun rose.* **2** [T/I] : to make a telephone call • *I call once a week to talk to my parents.* = *I call my parents once a week.* • *In an emergency you should call* [=dial] *911.* **3** [T] **a** : to tell, order, or ask (someone or something) to come • *I called the waiter over (to my table).* • *He's not home because he was called away on business.* **b** : to make a telephone call to tell, order, or ask (someone or something) to come • *We had to call an ambulance.* **4** [T] **a** : to give a name to (someone or something) • *Her parents called* [=named] *her Katherine.* **b** : to talk to or refer to (someone or something) with a specified name • *Her friends all call her "Kitty."* • *a large group of animals called "mammals"* **c** : to regard or think of (someone or something) in a certain way • *He's not what you would call a generous man.* [=he's not a generous man] • *He calls them like he sees them!* [=he states his opinion in an open, honest, and direct way] **5** [T] : to give the order for (something) • *call a meeting* • *The union has threatened to call a strike.* **6** [I] : to make a brief visit • *He called to pay his respects.* **7** [T] : to say or guess what the result of something will be • *You called it!* [=you correctly said what would happen] • *The election is still too close to call.* **8** [T] *sports* **a** : to stop or cancel (a game) because of bad conditions • *The game was called on account of rain.* **b** : to make an official ruling or decision about (something, such as a pitched ball or a player's action) • *The pitch was called a strike.* [=the umpire said the pitch was a strike] • *call a serve in/out* **c** *American football* : to say or decide what kind of play will be used • *The quarterback

called a running play. **9** [T/I] *poker* : to require (a player) to show a hand by making an equal bet ▪ *I call (you).* — **call at** [*phrasal vb*] : to stop at (a place) briefly ▪ *The ship called at the port.* — **call for** [*phrasal vb*] **1 a** : to say or demand publicly that something is needed or should be done ▪ *The opposition has called for an investigation.* **b** : to indicate that something is needed or should be done ▪ *You've won! That calls for a celebration!* **c** : to require or demand (something) as necessary or proper ▪ *The job calls for typing skills.* ▪ *His rude behavior was not called for.* [=was not appropriate] **2** : to go to a place to get (someone or something) ▪ *I'll call for you (at your house) after dinner.* — **call forth** [*phrasal vb*] **call forth (something) or call (something) forth** : to bring (a memory, image, etc.) into the mind ▪ *These events call forth strong feelings.* — **call in** [*phrasal vb*] **1 a** : to make a telephone call to a place (such as the place where you work) ▪ *She called in sick yesterday.* [=she telephoned the place where she works to say that she was sick] **b** : to make a telephone call to a radio or television program ▪ *Thousands of people called in to make a donation.* **c** : **call (something) in or call in (something)** : to deliver (a message, order, etc.) by making a telephone call ▪ *He called in an order for pizza.* **2** : to make a brief visit ▪ *I called in on an old friend* [=I visited an old friend] *while I was in New York.* **3** : **call (something or someone) in or call in (something or someone) a** : to demand payment of (a loan) ▪ *The bank has called in the loan.* **b** : to ask for the help or services of (someone) ▪ *They may have to call in a mediator to settle the strike.* — **call into question** *also US* **call into doubt** : to make people doubt something ▪ *This news calls her loyalty into question.* — **call it a day/night** : to stop an activity (such as work) for the remainder of the day or night ▪ *It's getting late. I think we should call it a night.* — **call it quits** see QUITS — **call off** [*phrasal vb*] **call off (something or someone) or call (something or someone) off 1** : to stop doing or planning to do (something) ▪ *We had to call off* [=cancel] *our trip.* **2** : to cause or tell (a person or animal) to stop attacking, chasing, etc. ▪ *Its owner called the dog off.* — **call on/upon** [*phrasal vb*] **1 a** : to ask (someone or something) to do something ▪ *The opposition has called on/upon the governor to resign.* **b** : to ask (someone) for something ▪ *Is there anyone you can count on (for help) in an emergency?* ▪ *The teacher called on me for the answer, but I didn't know it.* **2** : to use (something, such as a talent or skill) ▪ *She had to call on/upon all her reserves of strength.* **3** : to make a brief visit to (someone) ▪ *call on an old friend* **4 call (someone) on (something)** *US, informal* : to directly criticize (someone) for (something) ▪ *He's incredibly rude, but no one ever calls him on it.* [=no one ever tells him that he should stop being so rude] — **call the shots** see ¹SHOT

— **call the tune** see ¹TUNE — **call time** see ¹TIME — **call up** [*phrasal vb*] **call (someone or something) up or call up (someone or something) 1** *chiefly US* : to make a telephone call to (someone) ▪ *I called her up last night.* **2 a** : to bring (something, such as a memory) into the mind ▪ *The sound of the ocean called up memories of my childhood.* **b** : to bring (strength, courage, etc.) from within yourself ▪ *He will have to call up all his reserves of strength to meet this challenge.* **c** : to get (something) from the memory of a computer and show it on the screen ▪ *call up an old document for revision* **3 a** : to order or tell (someone) to come or appear ▪ *The prisoner was called up before a magistrate.* ▪ *call up the army reserves* **b** : to bring (an athlete) to a higher league ▪ *a minor-league player called up to the major leagues* — **call·er** /ˈkɑːlɚ/ *n* [C] : telephone callers ▪ *She's had several callers* [=visitors] *at her house today.*

²**call** *n* **1** [C] : an act of speaking or trying to speak to someone using the telephone ▪ *a local/long-distance phone/telephone call* ▪ *I got a call from my brother.* ▪ *"There's someone on the phone for you, sir." "Tell them I can't take their call now* [=I can't speak to them on the phone now] *but I'll return their call* [=I'll call them back] *as soon as I can."* ▪ *Give me a call when you get back.* [=call me when you get back] **2** [C] **a** : a loud cry or shout ▪ *He shouted but no one heard his call.* **b** : the sound made by an animal or bird ▪ *The bird has an unusual call.* **c** : a loud sound or signal made with a musical instrument ▪ *a bugle call* **3 a** [C] : a public request or statement that asks or tells people to do something ▪ *a call for reform* ▪ *The political party has issued a call to action.* **b** [C/U] : a request for something ▪ *We get many calls for Christmas stories.* ▪ *There's not much call for ice cream at this time of year.* **c** [U] : a reason for doing something ▪ *There was no call for your rudeness.* [=you were wrong to behave so rudely] **4** [C] : a brief visit ▪ *I made/paid a brief social call on an old friend.* — see also HOUSE CALL, PORT OF CALL **5** [C] : something that is called or announced ▪ *This is the last call for Flight 139.* **6** [C] : a decision ▪ *The runner was called out by the umpire, and the manager came out to argue about the call.* ▪ *(chiefly US) It's a tough call (to make).* ▪ *(chiefly US)* **It's your call.** — see also CLOSE CALL, JUDGMENT CALL **7** [*singular*] : the appeal or attraction of something ▪ *sailors who cannot resist the call of the open ocean* **8** [C] : something that requires a person's attention or effort ▪ *There are many calls on the time of a busy housewife.* [=there are many things that a busy housewife must spend time doing] — **at someone's beck and call** see BECK — **on call** : ready to come when needed ▪ *a doctor on call*

call girl *n* [C] : a prostitute who arranges to meet with men who call her on the telephone

cal·lig·ra·phy /kəˈlɪɡrəfi/ *n* [U] : artistic or beautiful handwriting; *also* : the art of making such handwriting — **cal·lig·ra·pher** /kəˈlɪgrəfə/ n [C]

call–in /ˈkɑːlˌɪn/ n [C] US : a radio or television show in which telephone calls from listeners are included as part of the broadcast ▪ a call-in radio show

call·ing /ˈkɑːlɪŋ/ n [C] **1** : a strong desire to spend your life doing a certain kind of work (such as religious work) ▪ He had always felt a calling to help others. **2** : the work that a person does or should be doing ▪ He feels he **missed his calling** [=did not have the career he should have] by not becoming a doctor.

calling card n [C] US **1** : a plastic card that allows a person to charge telephone calls to an account — called also phone card **2** old-fashioned : a small card presented when making a formal visit to someone that has the name and sometimes the address of the visitor

cal·lous /ˈkæləs/ adj, disapproving : not feeling or showing any concern about the problems or suffering of other people ▪ a callous remark/person — **cal·lous·ly** adv — **cal·lous·ness** n [U]

cal·loused /ˈkæləst/ adj : having hard and thick skin : having calluses ▪ calloused hands/feet

cal·low /ˈkælou/ adj : not having much experience and not knowing how to behave the way adults behave ▪ a callow youth — **cal·low·ness** n [U]

cal·lus /ˈkæləs/ n [C] : a hard and thickened area on the skin and especially on the hands or feet

call waiting n [U] : a service that makes it possible for someone who is speaking on the telephone to receive another call without ending the first one

¹**calm** /ˈkɑːm/ adj **1** : not angry, upset, excited, etc. ▪ Please try to remain/stay calm. ▪ a calm discussion **2** — used to describe weather that is not windy, stormy, etc. ▪ a calm day — **calm·ly** adv — **calm·ness** n [U]

²**calm** n **1** [U, singular] : a quiet and peaceful state or condition ▪ A quiet calm settled over the city. ▪ Police tried to restore calm after the riot. **2** [C] : a peaceful mental or emotional state ▪ The coach kept his calm during the game.

³**calm** vb [T/I] **1** : to become or to cause (someone) to become less upset, emotional, excited, etc. ▪ The mayor tried to calm the protesters. ▪ calm someone's fears ▪ He needs to **calm down**. **2** : to become or to cause (something) to become less active, violent, forceful, etc. ▪ The winds calmed (down) overnight. ▪ The medicine helped calm her breathing.

cal·o·rie /ˈkæləri/ n [C] : a unit of heat used to indicate the amount of energy that foods will produce in the human body ▪ foods with high/low calories ▪ a low-calorie diet — **ca·lo·ric** /kəˈlorɪk/ adj ▪ caloric intake/restriction/values

calves plural of CALF

ca·lyp·so /kəˈlɪpsou/ n [U] : a lively musical style from the West Indies that usually has humorous lyrics concerning current topics (such as politics)

cam /ˈkæm/ n [C] technical : a part of a machine (such as an engine) that chang-

es circular motion into another type of motion (such as forward motion)

ca·ma·ra·de·rie /kɑmˈrɑːdəri, Brit ˌkæmərɑːdəri/ n [U, singular] : a feeling of good friendship among the people in a group

cam·cord·er /ˈkæmˌkoədə/ n [C] : a small video camera

came past tense of COME

cam·el /ˈkæməl/ n [C] : a large animal of Africa and Asia that has a long neck and one or two large humps on its back and that is often used for desert travel — **the straw that breaks the camel's back** see STRAW

cam·eo /ˈkæmiˌou/ n [C] **1** : a small role in a movie, play, etc., that is performed by a well-known actor **2** : a piece of jewelry that has a carved design shown against a background of a different color

cam·era /ˈkæmrə/ n [C] : a device that is used for taking photographs or for making movies, television programs, etc. — **off camera** : not on television or in a movie ▪ He is a different person (when he's) off camera. — **on camera** : on television or in a movie ▪ He looks very relaxed (when he's) on camera.

cam·era·man /ˈkæmrəˌmæn/ n, pl -men /-mən/ [C] : someone who uses a camera to film a movie or television show

cam·i·sole /ˈkæməˌsoul/ n [C] : a light piece of clothing for women that is worn on the top part of the body and that does not have sleeves

camomile variant spelling of CHAMOMILE

¹**cam·ou·flage** /ˈkæməˌflɑːʒ/ n **1** [U] **a** : a way of hiding something (such as military equipment) by painting it or covering it with leaves or branches to make it harder to see **b** : the green and brown clothing that soldiers and hunters wear to make them harder to see ▪ troops in full camouflage ▪ a camouflage jacket **2** [U, singular] : something (such as color or shape) that protects an animal from attack by making the animal difficult to see in the area around it ▪ The rabbit's white fur acts as (a) camouflage in the snow.

²**camouflage** vb -flaged; -flag·ing [T] : to hide (something) by covering it up or making it harder to see ▪ camouflaged soldiers/animals ▪ She camouflaged her feelings well.

¹**camp** /ˈkæmp/ n **1 a** [C/U] : a place that is usually far away from cities and that has tents, small houses, etc., that people can live in for a short period of time ▪ a fishing camp ▪ army/refugee camps ▪ We pitched/made camp by the lake. ▪ They set up camp for the night. ▪ The soldiers broke camp. [=took down the tents and other parts of the camp] **b** [C] : a town that has been set up so people can live there and work nearby ▪ a logging/mining camp **2** [C/U] **a** : a place usually in the mountains or by a lake where young people can do different activities during the summer ▪ The kids are away at (summer) camp. ▪ day camps [=camps where children spend the day and then return

home at the end of the day] **b** : a place where athletes train before the beginning of a season ▪ *He injured his arm in training camp.* **3** [C] : a group of people who support or believe in certain ideas ▪ *the Democratic/Republican camp* **4** [U] — used of art and entertainment when qualities that are normally considered bad (such as excessive emotion and bad acting) are exaggerated so much that they become interesting and funny ▪ *movie fans who appreciate camp* ▪ *a camp classic*

²**camp** *vb* [I] **1** : to sleep outdoors usually in a tent ▪ *We camped (out) by the lake.* ▪ *a camping trip* ▪ *She likes to **go camping**.* **2** *informal* : to live or stay in a place for a period of time — + *out* ▪ *I camped out at a friend's apartment for a few days.*

¹**cam·paign** /kæmˈpeɪn/ *n* [C] : a series of activities designed to produce a particular result ▪ *an election campaign* ▪ *the campaign against drugs* ▪ *campaign contributions/promises/slogans*

²**campaign** *vb* [I] : to lead or be involved in a campaign to support or oppose someone or something or to achieve something ▪ *She campaigned to save the town library.* ▪ *He campaigned for president.* [=he tried to be elected president] — **cam·paign·er** *n* [C]

camp bed *n* [C] *Brit* : COT 1

camp·er /ˈkæmpɚ/ *n* [C] **1** : a person who sleeps outdoors, in a tent, or in a simple shelter usually for enjoyment for a short period of time — see also HAPPY CAMPER **2** *US* : a type of vehicle or special trailer that people can live and sleep in when they are traveling or camping — called also (*Brit*) **camper van**, (*Brit*) **caravan** **3** : a young person who goes to a camp during the summer to do different activities

camp·fire /ˈkæmpˌfajɚ/ *n* [C] : a fire that is built outdoors at a camp or picnic area

camp·ground /ˈkæmpˌgraʊnd/ *n* [C] *chiefly US* : an area or place that is used for camping

camp·site /ˈkæmpˌsaɪt/ *n* [C] **1** *US* : a place where people can put up a tent **2** *Brit* : CAMPGROUND

cam·pus /ˈkæmpəs/ *n* [C/U] : the area and buildings around a university, college, school, etc. ▪ *We toured the campus.* ▪ *campus events/life/politics* ▪ *living **on/off campus***

campy /ˈkæmpi/ *adj* **camp·i·er; -est** *US* : having the qualities of camp (sense 4) ▪ *a campy comedy*

cam·shaft /ˈkæmˌʃæft, *Brit* ˈkæmˌʃɑːft/ *n* [C] *technical* : a metal shaft or bar to which a cam is attached

¹**can** /kən, ˈkæn/ *vb, past tense* **could** /kəd, ˈkʊd/; *present tense for both singular and plural* **can**; *negative* **can·not** /ˈkænɑt, kəˈnɑːt, *Brit* ˈkænɑt/ *or* **can't** /ˈkænt, *Brit* ˈkɑːnt/ [*modal vb*] **1** : to be able to (do something) ▪ *I can do it myself.* ▪ *I can't decide what to do.* ▪ *The car can hold five people.* ▪ *I visit her whenever I can.* ▪ *She can play the piano.* ▪ *I can't lift the box.* **2** — used to describe what someone sees, feels, thinks, etc. ▪ *"Can you see him yet?" "Yes, I can see him clearly."* **3 a** — used

to say that something is or is not possible ▪ *She can be very rude at times.* [=she is sometimes very rude] ▪ *The weather can change quickly.* [=the weather often changes quickly] ▪ (*informal + humorous*) *"Can you give me a ride to work tomorrow?" "Sorry—no can do."* [=I can't do it] ▪ *They seemed as happy **as can be**.* [=they seemed extremely happy] **b** — used in speech to express surprise or disbelief ▪ *You can't/cannot (possibly) be serious!* ▪ *That can't be right.* [=that must be wrong] **4 a** : to have permission to (do something) ▪ *You can do it tomorrow if you like.* ▪ *"Can I leave now?" "No, you can't."* **b** — used in speech to make a request or suggestion ▪ *Can [=could] I have another cookie?* ▪ *You can sit here if you like.* **5** — used to say what should or should not be done ▪ *You can't leave now! The party is just getting started!*

²**can** /ˈkæn/ *n* [C] **1 a** : a closed metal container that is usually shaped like a cylinder and that holds food or drink ▪ *a tin can* ▪ *a soda/beer can* **b** : the food or drink that is in a can ▪ *He ate the whole can of beans.* **2 a** : a metal or plastic container that has a removable top and that is used for holding liquid, trash, etc. ▪ *a garbage/trash can* : SPRAY CAN — **can of worms** : a complicated situation in which doing something to correct a problem leads to many more problems ▪ *I don't want to change the policy now because that might **open a can of worms**.* — **carry the can** *Brit, informal* : to accept blame or responsibility for something that you did not cause ▪ *He made the error, but she was left to carry the can.* — **in the can** : completed and ready to be released ▪ *a movie that is in the can* — **the can** *US, informal* **1** : BUTTOCKS ▪ *a kick in the can* **2 a** : BATHROOM ▪ *He locked himself in the can.* **b** : TOILET ▪ *sitting on the can* **3** : a prison or jail ▪ *The cops threw him in the can.*

³**can** /ˈkæn/ *vb* **canned; can·ning** [T] **1** *chiefly US* : to preserve food by putting it in a metal or glass container ▪ *canning tomatoes* **2** *US, informal* : to dismiss (someone) from a job ▪ *He got canned for being late to work.* **3** *US, informal* : to stop or end (something) ▪ *The boss angrily told him to can the jokes.*

Ca·na·di·an /kəˈneɪdijən/ *n* [C] : a person who is from Canada — **Canadian** *adj* ▪ *the Canadian government*

ca·nal /kəˈnæl/ *n* [C] **1** : a long, narrow area of water built for boats to pass through or to supply fields, crops, etc., with water ▪ *the Panama Canal* ▪ *irrigation canals* **2** *medical* : a tube or passageway in the body

ca·nary /kəˈneri/ *n, pl* **-nar·ies** [C] : a small usually yellow or green tropical bird that is often kept in a cage

can·cel /ˈkænsəl/ *vb, US* **-celed** *or Brit* **-celled**; *US* **-cel·ing** *or Brit* **-cel·ling** **1** [T/I] : to stop doing or planning to do (something) ▪ *The event/game/flight was canceled.* **2** [T/I] : to cause (something) to end or no longer produce a certain effect ▪ *Please cancel my order.* **3** [T] : to put a mark with a set of ink lines on

172

something (such as a stamp) so that it cannot be used again • *a canceled stamp* — **cancel out** *[phrasal vb]* **cancel out (something)** or **cancel (something) out** : to be equal to (something) in force or importance but have an opposite effect • *The costs cancel out the benefits.* — **can·cel·la·tion** *also US* **can·cel·a·tion** /ˌkænsəˈleɪʃən/ *n [C/U]* • *flight cancellations*

can·cer /ˈkænsɚ/ *n* **1** *[C/U]* : a serious disease caused by cells that are not normal and that can spread to one or many parts of the body • *breast/lung cancer* • *cancer patients/treatments* **2** *[C]* : something bad or dangerous that causes other bad things to happen • *Drugs and violence have become a cancer in the city.* **3 Cancer a** *[U]* : the fourth sign of the zodiac that comes between Gemini and Leo and has a crab as its symbol **b** *[C]* : a person born between June 22nd and July 22nd — **can·cer·ous** /ˈkænsərəs/ *adj* • *a cancerous tumor*

can·de·la·bra /ˌkændəˈlɑːbrə/ *n [C]* : an object with several branches for holding candles or lights

can·did /ˈkændəd/ *adj* **1** : expressing opinions and feelings in an honest and sincere way • *a candid person/confession/interview/opinion* **2** *photography* : showing people acting in a natural way because they do not know that they are being photographed • *a candid snapshot* — **can·did·ly** *adv* — **can·did·ness** *n [U]*

can·di·da·cy /ˈkændədəsi/ *n, pl* **-cies** *[C/U]* : the position of a person who is trying to be elected • *She is expected to announce her candidacy for president.*

can·di·date /ˈkændəˌdeɪt, ˈkændədət/ *n [C]* **1** : a person who is trying to be elected • *a presidential candidate = a candidate for president* **2** : a person who is being considered for a job, position, award, etc. • *He is a candidate for the job/award.* **3** : a student in the process of meeting final requirements for a degree • *a Ph.D. candidate in linguistics* • *doctoral candidates* **4** *Brit* : someone who is taking an exam

can·di·da·ture /ˈkændədəˌtʃɚ/ *n [C] Brit* : CANDIDACY

can·died /ˈkændid/ *adj, always before a noun* : cooked in or covered with sugar • *candied fruit/yams*

can·dle /ˈkændl̩/ *n [C]* : wax that has been formed into a stick or another shape and has a string in the middle that can be burned • **burn the candle at both ends** see ¹BURN — **hold a candle to** : to be on the same level as or as good as (something or someone) • *The new movie doesn't hold a candle to the original version.*

can·dle·light /ˈkændl̩ˌlaɪt/ *n [U]* : the light of a candle • *We dined by candlelight.* — **can·dle·lit** /ˈkændl̩ˌlɪt/ *adj* • *a romantic candlelit dinner*

can·dle·stick /ˈkændl̩ˌstɪk/ *n [C]* : an object with a small hole in the middle for holding a candle

can–do /ˈkænˈduː/ *adj, always before a noun, informal* : having or showing an

ability to do difficult things • *her can-do attitude/spirit*

can·dor *(US)* or *Brit* **can·dour** /ˈkændɚ/ *n [U]* : the quality of being open, sincere, and honest • *She spoke with candor about racism.*

can·dy /ˈkændi/ *n, pl* **-dies** *[C/U] US* : a sweet food made with sugar or chocolate • *a box/piece of candy* • *chewy candies* • *a candy bar*

candy cane *n [C] US* : a stick of hard red and white candy with a curve at the top

candy floss *n [U] Brit* : COTTON CANDY

¹**cane** /ˈkeɪn/ *n* **1** *[C]* : a stick that often has a curved handle and is used to help someone walk **2** *[U]* : the hard hollow stem of a plant (such as bamboo or reed) that is used to make furniture and baskets • *woven strips of cane*

²**cane** *vb* **caned; can·ing** *[T]* : to hit (someone) with a cane or stick as a form of punishment

¹**ca·nine** /ˈkeɪˌnaɪn/ *adj* : of or relating to dogs • *canine behavior/loyalty* • *a canine companion* [=a dog that is kept as a pet]

²**canine** *n [C]* **1** *formal* : a dog • *poodles and other canines* **2** : a pointed tooth — called also *canine tooth*

can·is·ter /ˈkænəstɚ/ *n [C]* **1** : a container with a lid that is used for keeping dry products • *a flour/sugar/tea canister* **2** : a plastic or metal container that is used for keeping a roll of film **3** : a metal case that contains gas or chemical substances and that bursts when it is fired from a gun • *tear gas canisters*

can·ker /ˈkæŋkɚ/ *n* **1** *[C] US* : a small, painful sore inside the mouth — called also *canker sore* **2** *[C]* : something that causes bad things to happen • *Poverty is the canker of this neighborhood.* **3** *[C/U]* : any one of various plant diseases

canned /ˈkænd/ *adj* **1** : preserved in a metal or glass container • *canned goods/tomatoes/tuna* **2 a** : prepared or recorded at an earlier time for use in television, radio, etc. • *canned laughter/music* **b** *US* : not original or special • *a canned speech*

can·nery /ˈkænəri/ *n, pl* **-ner·ies** *[C]* : a factory where food is put into cans

can·ni·bal /ˈkænəbəl/ *n [C]* : a person who eats the flesh of human beings or an animal that eats its own kind — **can·ni·bal·ism** /ˈkænəbəˌlɪzəm/ *n [U]* — **can·ni·bal·is·tic** /ˌkænəbəˈlɪstɪk/ *adj*

¹**can·non** /ˈkænən/ *n, pl* **cannons** or **cannon** *[C]* **1** : a large gun that shoots heavy metal or stone balls and that was once a common military weapon — see also LOOSE CANNON **2** : a large automatic gun that is shot from an aircraft

²**cannon** *vb [I] Brit* : to suddenly and forcefully hit or move into or against someone or something • *The ball cannoned off the goalpost.*

can·non·ade /ˌkænəˈneɪd/ *n [C]* : an attack with cannons that continues for a long time

can·non·ball /ˈkænənˌbɑːl/ *n [C]* : a heavy metal or stone ball that is shot from a cannon

cannon fodder *n [U]* : soldiers who are sent into battle even though it is likely that they will die

can·not /'kænɑt, kə'nɑːt, Brit 'kænət/ — used as the negative form of *can* ▪ *We cannot* [=*can't*] *allow that to happen.*

can·ny /'kæni/ *adj* **can·ni·er; -est** : very clever and showing an ability to make intelligent decisions ▪ *canny investors/investments* — **can·ni·ly** /'kænəli/ *adv* — **can·ni·ness** /'kæninəs/ *n* [U]

ca·noe /kə'nuː/ *n* [C] : a long narrow boat that is pointed at both ends and that is moved by a paddle with one blade — **canoe** *vb* **-noed; -noe·ing** [T/I] ▪ *We canoed (on) the river.* ▪ *We went canoeing.* — **ca·noe·ist** /kə'nuːwɪst/ *n* [C] — **ca·no·er** *n* [C] *US*

ca·no·la oil /kə'noʊlə-/ *n* [U] *chiefly US + Canada* : a type of oil that is obtained from the seeds of the rape plant and used for cooking

can·on /'kænən/ *n* [C] **1** *formal* : an accepted rule or guide about how people should behave or how something should be done ▪ *the canons of good taste* **2 a** : a group of books, poems, plays, etc., that are traditionally considered to be very important ▪ *the American literary canon* **b** : a list of books that are considered to be part of a religion's official text ▪ *the Jewish canon* — **ca·non·i·cal** /kə-'nɑːnɪkəl/ *adj* ▪ *canonical procedures/texts*

can·on·ize *also Brit* **can·on·ise** /'kænə-ˌnaɪz/ *vb* **-ized; -iz·ing** [T] *in the Roman Catholic Church* : to declare (someone) to be a saint — **can·on·i·za·tion** *also Brit* **can·on·i·sa·tion** /ˌkænənə'zeɪʃən, Brit ˌkænəˌnaɪ'zeɪʃən/ *n* [U]

canon law *n* [U] : the laws of a religion

can opener *n* [C] *chiefly US* : a device that is used to open cans of food

can·o·py /'kænəpi/ *n, pl* **-pies** [C] **1 a** : a piece of cloth that hangs over a bed, throne, etc., as a decoration or shelter ▪ *a canopy bed* [=a bed that has a piece of cloth above it like a roof] **2 a** : something that hangs or spreads out over an area ▪ *a theater canopy* [=the part of a theater building that extends over the sidewalk] ▪ *(figurative) the canopy of the sky* **b** : the highest layer of branches in a forest or on a tree ▪ *the jungle's thick canopy* — **can·o·pied** /'kænəpid/ *adj* ▪ *a canopied bed/forest*

cant /'kænt/ *n* [U] : words that are supposed to sound like serious statements about important issues (such as religion or morality) but that are not honest or sincere ▪ *political hypocrisy and cant*

can't /'kænt, Brit 'kɑːnt/ — used as a contraction of *cannot* ▪ *I can't do it.*

can·ta·loupe *also* **can·ta·loup** /'kæntə-ˌloup, Brit 'kæntəˌluːp/ *n* [C/U] : a type of large melon that has a hard, rough skin and orange flesh

can·tan·ker·ous /kæn'tæŋkərəs/ *adj* : often angry and annoyed ▪ *a cantankerous old man*

can·teen /kæn'tiːn/ *n* [C] **1** : a store in a camp, school, etc., in which food, drinks, and small supplies are sold **2 a** *chiefly US* : a place where drinks and entertainment are provided for soldiers at a military base or camp **b** *chiefly Brit* : a place where food is served in a factory,

school, etc. : CAFETERIA **3** : a small container for carrying water or other liquids **4** *Brit* : a box for storing knives, forks, spoons, etc.

can·ter /'kæntɚ/ *n* **1** [*singular*] : the way a horse moves when it is running fairly fast ▪ *He set off at a canter towards the stable.* **2** [C] : a ride or run at a canter ▪ *a canter through the fields* — **canter** *vb* [I] ▪ *The horses cantered across the grass.*

can·ti·le·ver /'kæntəˌliːvɚ/ *n* [C] : a long piece of wood, metal, etc., that sticks out from a wall or other structure to support something above it (such as a balcony or bridge) — **cantilever** *vb* [T/I] ▪ *cantilevered beams/floors*

can·tor /'kæntɚ/ *n* [C] **1** : a person who sings and leads people in prayer in a Jewish religious service **2** : a person who leads a group of singers in a church

Ca·nuck /kə'nʌk/ *n* [C] *informal* : a person who is from Canada

can·vas /'kænvəs/ *n* **1** [C/U] : a strong, rough cloth that is used to make bags, tents, sails, etc. ▪ *a canvas bag* ▪ *(chiefly Brit) sleeping under canvas* [=in a tent] **2 a** [C/U] : a specially prepared piece of cloth on which a picture can be painted by an artist ▪ *a fresh/blank canvas* **b** [C] : a painting made on canvas ▪ *canvases by Rubens*

can·vass /'kænvəs/ *vb* [T/I] : to ask or talk to the people in an area about a candidate, project, idea, etc. ▪ *Volunteers are canvassing the voters/city.* — **can·vass·er** *n* [C]

can·yon /'kænjən/ *n* [C] : a deep valley with steep rock sides and often a stream or river flowing through it ▪ *the Grand Canyon*

¹**cap** /'kæp/ *n* [C] **1 a** : a small, soft hat that often has a hard curved part (called a visor) that extends out over your eyes — see also BASEBALL CAP **b** : a covering for a person's head that is worn for a special purpose ▪ *a shower/bathing cap* **c** : a hat that people with particular jobs wear while working ▪ *a surgeon's cap, gown, and gloves* **2** : a part or object that covers the end or top of something ▪ *a bottle/lens cap* **3** : a part that forms the top of something ▪ *a mushroom cap* [=the top part of a mushroom] **4** : a limit on the amount of money that can be spent, given, charged, etc., for something ▪ *a spending cap* ▪ *a cap on political donations* **5** : a paper or metal container that holds an explosive substance ▪ *a blasting cap* **6** *informal* : a capital letter ▪ *e-mails written in all caps* **7** : a hard substance that is shaped to look like a healthy tooth and used to cover a damaged tooth **8** *Brit, sports* **a** : an opportunity to play for your school or country ▪ *He won his first cap against Columbia when he was 22.* **b** : a player chosen to play for a country's team **9** *Brit* : DIAPHRAGM 3

²**cap** *vb* **capped; cap·ping** [T] **1** : to cover the top or end of (something) ▪ *a mountain capped with snow = a snow-capped mountain* : to put a cap on (something) ▪ *cap a pen/marker* **2 a** : to end (something) in usually an exciting or

impressive way ▪ *The report caps a ten-year study of lung cancer.* ▪ *(US) The band* **capped off** *the show with their classic hit.* **b** : to follow (something) with something that is better, worse, etc. ▪ *a concert capped by a fireworks display* **3** : to put an upper limit on (something) ▪ *capping interest rates* **4** : to put a cap on (a tooth) ▪ *He had two of his teeth capped.* **5** *Brit, sports* : to choose (someone) to play for a national team ▪ *He was first capped for Ireland at age 12.*

ca·pa·ble /ˈkeɪpəbəl/ *adj* **1** : able to do something ▪ *The train is capable of (reaching) very high speeds.* ▪ *I don't believe that she's capable of murder.* **2** : able to do something well ▪ *a very capable* [=*skilled*] *student/pilot* ▪ *I'll leave the store in your* **capable hands** *while I'm gone.* — **ca·pa·bil·i·ty** /ˌkeɪpəˈbɪləti/ *n, pl* **-ties** [*C/U*] ▪ *The job is beyond my capabilities.* [=it is too difficult for me] ▪ *a cell phone with Internet capability* ▪ *countries with* **nuclear capability** [=with nuclear weapons] — **ca·pa·bly** /ˈkeɪpəbli/ *adv*

ca·pa·cious /kəˈpeɪʃəs/ *adj, formal* : able to hold or contain a lot : SPACIOUS ▪ *capacious rooms* — **ca·pa·cious·ness** *n* [*U*]

ca·pac·i·tor /kəˈpæsətɚ/ *n* [*C*] *technical* : a device that is used to store electrical energy

ca·pac·i·ty /kəˈpæsəti/ *n, pl* **-ties** **1 a** [*C*] : the ability to hold or contain people or things ▪ *The restaurant has a large seating capacity.* [=there are seats for many people] ▪ *a hard drive's storage capacity* **b** [*C/U*] : the largest amount or number that can be held or contained ▪ *a bottle with a capacity of two liters* ▪ *The auditorium was* **filled to capacity.** [=was completely full] **2** [*C/U*] : a mental, emotional, or physical ability ▪ *breathing capacity* ▪ *a character with a great capacity for love* [=a character who is able to love people very deeply] **3** [*C*] : a usually official position or job ▪ *He was acting in his capacity as judge.* ▪ *She's worked for the company in various capacities.* **4** [*U*] : the amount of something that can be produced or managed by a factory, company, etc. ▪ *a plan to double the factory's capacity* ▪ *The airport has not yet reached capacity.*

cape /ˈkeɪp/ *n* [*C*] **1** : a piece of clothing that does not have sleeves and that fits closely at the neck and hangs over the shoulders, arms, and back ▪ *a superhero's mask and cape* **2** : a large area of land that sticks out into a sea, bay, etc. ▪ *the Cape of Good Hope* ▪ *Cape Cod* **3** *US* : a small house that has one or one-and-a-half levels and a steep roof — called also *Cape Cod cottage*

¹**ca·per** /ˈkeɪpɚ/ *n* [*C*] **1** *informal* : an illegal or improper activity that is usually seen as amusing or not very serious ▪ *a jewelry caper* [=*theft, heist*] **2** : a small flower bud or young berry that is preserved in vinegar and used to flavor food

²**caper** *vb* **-pered; -per·ing** [*I*] : to jump around in a lively way

cap·il·lary /ˈkæpəˌleri, *Brit* kəˈpɪləri/ *n, pl* **-lar·ies** [*C*] : one of the many very small tubes that carry blood within the body

¹**cap·i·tal** /ˈkæpətl/ *adj* **1** *of a letter* : in the form A, B, C, etc., rather than a, b, c, etc. : UPPERCASE ▪ *capital letters* ▪ *a capital D* — sometimes used informally to give emphasis to a description ▪ *He is conservative* **with a capital C!** [=he is very conservative] **2** : having the main offices of a government ▪ *the state's capital city* **3** *of a crime* : having death as a possible punishment ▪ *a capital crime/offense* — see also CAPITAL PUNISHMENT **4** *chiefly Brit, old-fashioned* : EXCELLENT ▪ *a capital idea*

²**capital** *n* **1** [*U*] : money, property, etc., that is used to start or operate a business or that a person or business owns ▪ *the accumulation of capital* ▪ *Her house is her biggest capital asset.* ▪ *(figurative) the governor wasted his political capital on an unpopular cause.* **2** [*C*] : a letter in the form A, B, C, etc. **3** [*C*] **a** : a city in which the main offices of a government are located ▪ *Austin is the capital of Texas.* **b** : the most important city for an activity or product ▪ *New York City is the media capital of the United States.*

capital gains *n* [*plural*] : money that you get by selling property at a higher price than the price that you paid to buy it ▪ *the capital gains tax*

cap·i·tal·ism /ˈkæpətəˌlɪzəm/ *n* [*U*] : a way of organizing an economy so that the things that are used to make and transport products (such as land, oil, factories, ships, etc.) are owned by individual people and companies rather than by the government — **cap·i·tal·ist** /ˈkæpətəlɪst/ *also* **cap·i·tal·is·tic** /ˌkæpətəˈlɪstɪk/ *adj* ▪ *a capitalist society/nation* — **capitalist** *n* [*C*] ▪ *a wealthy capitalist*

cap·i·tal·ize *also Brit* **cap·i·tal·ise** /ˈkæpətəˌlaɪz/ *vb* **-ized; -iz·ing** [*T*] **1 a** : to use a capital letter to write, print, or type (a letter of the alphabet) ▪ *Remember to capitalize the "I" in "Internet."* **b** : to begin (a word or name) with a capital letter ▪ *Capitalize the first word of your sentence.* **2** : to provide the money that is needed to start or develop (a business) ▪ *They're seeking investors to capitalize the business.* — **capitalize on** [*phrasal vb*] : to use (something) in a way that helps you ▪ *They were able to capitalize on* [=*take advantage of*] *our mistakes.* — **cap·i·tal·i·za·tion** *also Brit* **cap·i·tal·i·sa·tion** /ˌkæpətələˈzeɪʃən, *Brit* ˌkæpətəˌlaɪˈzeɪʃən/ *n* [*U*]

capital punishment *n* [*U*] : punishment by death for committing serious crimes (such as murder)

cap·i·tol /ˈkæpətl/ *n* **1** [*C*] : the building in which the people who make the laws of a U.S. state meet ▪ *the dome of the state capitol (building)* **2** *the Capitol* : the building in which the U.S. Congress meets in Washington, D.C.

Capitol Hill *n* [*singular*] : the group of people who make the federal laws in the United States : the U.S. Congress ▪ *The organization is lobbying Capitol Hill for increased funding.*

ca·pit·u·late /kəˈpɪtʃəˌleɪt/ vb -lat·ed; -lat·ing [I] formal **1** : SURRENDER • *The army was forced to capitulate.* **2** : to agree to do or accept something that you have been resisting or opposing • *Officials eventually capitulated to the protesters' demands.* — **ca·pit·u·la·tion** /kəˌpɪtʃəˈleɪʃən/ n [C/U]

cap·puc·ci·no /ˌkæpəˈtʃiːnoʊ/ n, pl -nos [C/U] : a drink of strong coffee (called espresso) that has a bubbly layer of hot milk on top

ca·price /kəˈpriːs/ n [C/U] : a sudden change especially in someone's mood or behavior • *Employees are at the mercy of the manager's every whim and caprice.*

ca·pri·cious /kəˈprɪʃəs/ adj, formal : changing often and quickly • *capricious weather/winds; especially* : often changing suddenly in mood or behavior • *a capricious boss* — **ca·pri·cious·ly** adv — **ca·pri·cious·ness** n [U]

Cap·ri·corn /ˈkæprɪˌkoɚn/ n **1** [U] : the sign of the zodiac that comes between Sagittarius and Aquarius and that has a goat as its symbol **2** [C] : a person born between December 22 and January 19

cap·size /ˈkæpˌsaɪz/ vb -sized; -siz·ing [T/I] : to turn over (a boat) so that the bottom is on top • *They capsized the canoe.* • *The canoe suddenly capsized.*

cap·sule /ˈkæpsəl, Brit ˈkæpˌsjuːl/ n [C] **1 a** : a very small container that is filled with medicine and swallowed whole **b** : a small glass or plastic container that has something (such as a liquid) inside of it **2** : a small part of a spacecraft that is separate from the rest of the spacecraft and that is where people live and work

Capt. abbr captain

¹cap·tain /ˈkæptən/ n [C] **1** : a person who is in charge of a ship or an airplane **2** : an officer of high rank in some branches of the military **3** chiefly US : an officer of high rank in a police or fire department **4** : an athlete who is chosen to be the leader of a team • *the captain of a team = the team captain* — **cap·tain·cy** /ˈkæptənsi/ n, pl -cies [C/U]

²captain vb [T] : to be the captain of (something) • *The ship was captained by John Smith.* • *She captained last year's team.*

captain of industry n, pl **captains of industry** [C] : someone who owns or manages a large, successful business or company

cap·tion /ˈkæpʃən/ n [C] : a sentence or group of words that is written on or next to a picture to explain what is being shown • *The caption on the picture says "This year's contest winners."* — **caption** vb [T] • *The picture is captioned "This year's contest winners."*

cap·ti·vate /ˈkæptəˌveɪt/ vb -vat·ed; -vat·ing [T] : to attract and hold the attention of (someone) by being interesting, pretty, etc. • *He was captivated by her beauty.* • *a captivating story/smile*

cap·tive /ˈkæptɪv/ adj **1** : captured and kept in a prison, cage, etc. • *captive animals* • *Enemy forces took/held them captive.* **2** always before a noun : forced to

watch or listen to something because you cannot leave • *a captive audience* — **captive** n [C] • *They set their captives free.* — **cap·tiv·i·ty** /kæpˈtɪvəti/ n [U] • *The prisoners were released from captivity.* • *The lions were bred in captivity.* [=while living in a zoo]

cap·tor /ˈkæptɚ/ n [C] : someone who has captured a person and is keeping that person as a prisoner

¹cap·ture /ˈkæptʃɚ/ vb -tured; -tur·ing [T] **1 a** : to take and hold (someone) as a prisoner especially by using force • *captured by enemy soldiers* **b** : to catch (an animal) • *using traps to capture mice* **2 a** : to get control of (a place) especially by using force • *The city was captured by the Romans.* **b** : to win or get (something) through effort • *She captured 60 percent of the vote.* **3** : to get and hold (someone's attention, interest, etc.) • *The story captured our imaginations.* [=the story was very interesting and exciting] **4** : to describe or show (someone or something) in a very accurate way • *The story captures the essence of the holiday.* **5 a** : to record (something) • *The robbery was captured (on film) by the security cameras.* **b** : to get and put (information) into a form that can be read or used by a computer • *capture data*

²capture n [U] : the act of capturing someone or something • *The soldiers avoided/eluded/escaped capture.* • *the capture of the city by enemy forces* • *data/image capture*

car /ˈkɑɚ/ n **1** [C/U] : a vehicle that has an engine and moves on four wheels • *drive/park a car* • *a car dealer/accident* — called also (US) **automobile 2** [C] US : a separate section of a train • *a railroad car*

ca·rafe /kəˈræf/ n [C] : a glass container that has a wide mouth and is used to serve wine, water, etc., during a meal

car·a·mel /ˈkɑɚməl, ˈkerəməl/ n **1** [C/U] : a light brown candy made from butter, sugar, and milk or cream **2** [U] : sugar that is cooked until it is burnt and that is used to give color and flavor to food

car·a·mel·ize also Brit **car·a·mel·ise** /ˈkɑɚməˌlaɪz, ˈkerəməˌlaɪz/ vb -ized; -iz·ing [T/I] **1** : to cook (something, such as a fruit or vegetable) slowly until it becomes brown and sweet • *caramelized onions* **2** : to change (sugar) into caramel by cooking it • *Continue stirring until the sugar caramelizes.*

¹car·at /ˈkerət/ n [C] : a unit for measuring the weight of jewels (such as diamonds) that is equal to 200 milligrams

²carat chiefly Brit spelling of KARAT

car·a·van /ˈkerəˌvæn/ n [C] **1 a** : a group of people or animals traveling together especially through the desert **b** : a group of vehicles traveling together **2** Brit : CAMPER 2

car·a·van·ning /ˈkerəˌvænɪŋ/ n [U] Brit : the activity of taking a vacation in a trailer or camper

car·a·way /ˈkerəˌweɪ/ n [U] : the seeds of a plant related to the carrot that are used to flavor foods

carb /ˈkɑɚb/ n [C] US, informal : CARBO-

HYDRATE • *a diet low in carbs = a low-carb diet*

car·bine /ˈkɑɚˌbiːn, ˈkɑɚˌbaɪn/ *n* [*C*] : a short, light rifle

car·bo·hy·drate /ˌkɑɚbouˈhaɪˌdreɪt/ *n* [*C/U*] : any one of various substances found in certain foods (such as bread, rice, and potatoes) that provide your body with heat and energy and are made of carbon, hydrogen, and oxygen

car·bon /ˈkɑɚbən/ *n* **1** [*U*] : a chemical element that forms diamonds and coal and that is found in petroleum and in all living plants and animals **2** [*C*] : CARBON COPY 1 • *a carbon of the document*

car·bon·at·ed /ˈkɑɚbəˌneɪtəd/ *adj* : having many tiny bubbles that rise to the top : containing carbon dioxide • *soda and other carbonated beverages* — **car·bon·ation** /ˌkɑɚbəˈneɪʃən/ *n* [*U*]

carbon copy *n* [*C*] **1** : a copy of a document, letter, etc., that is made by using carbon paper **2** : a person or thing that is very similar to another person or thing • *She's a carbon copy of her mother.*

carbon di·ox·ide /-daɪˈɑːkˌsaɪd/ *n* [*U*] : a gas that is produced when people and animals breathe out or when certain fuels are burned and that is used by plants for energy

carbon mon·ox·ide /-məˈnɑːkˌsaɪd/ *n* [*U*] : a poisonous gas that is formed when carbon is not completely burned and especially when gasoline is burned in car engines

carbon paper *n* [*U*] : paper with a dark substance on one side that is placed between two other pieces of paper and used to make copies of documents

car·bun·cle /ˈkɑɚˌbʌŋkəl/ *n* [*C*] : a large painful swelling under the skin

car·bu·re·tor (*US*) *or Brit* **car·bu·ret·tor** /ˈkɑɚbəˌreɪtɚ, *Brit* ˌkɑəˈbjʊˈrɛtɚ/ *n* [*C*] : the part of an engine in which gasoline is mixed with air so it will burn and provide the engine with power

car·cass *also Brit* **car·case** /ˈkɑɚkəs/ *n* [*C*] **1** : the body of a dead animal **2** *informal + humorous* : a person's body • *He hauled his carcass out of bed.* [=he got out of bed] **3** : the remaining parts of an old vehicle, structure, etc. • *the rusting carcass of an old truck*

car·cin·o·gen /kɑɚˈsɪnədʒən/ *n* [*C*] : a substance that can cause cancer — **car·ci·no·gen·ic** /ˌkɑɚsənouˈdʒɛnɪk/ *adj* • *a carcinogenic compound/chemical*

car·ci·no·ma /ˌkɑɚsəˈnoumə/ *n* [*C/U*] : a type of cancer

¹card /ˈkɑɚd/ *n* **1 a** [*C*] : a small piece of stiff paper that is marked with symbols or pictures to show its value, comes in a set, and is used for playing games (such as poker) • *deal/shuffle the cards* • *card tricks/games* • *a deck/pack of cards* — called also *playing card* **b** [*plural*] : a game played with a deck of cards • *Do you want to play (a game of) cards?* **c** [*C*] — used figuratively to refer to something that gives you an advantage when you are trying to make a deal or reach an agreement • *His support from big firms was his strongest/best card during the negotiations.* **d** [*singular*] — used figura-

tively to refer to an emotional issue (such as race) that is mentioned in a particular situation in order to give you an advantage • *She used/played the gender card and said we didn't hire her because she's a woman.* **2** [*C*] **a** : a thick piece of paper that is usually folded in half and decorated on one side and that contains a greeting, an invitation, etc. • *a birthday card* • *a card shop/store* — see also GREETING CARD **b** : POSTCARD **3** [*C*] : a rectangular piece of plastic that is used to buy goods or services or to get money from a bank or a machine • *an ATM card* **4** [*C*] **a** : a rectangular piece of paper or plastic with information about a person written on it • *Let me give you my card.* [=business card] • *a membership/library card* **b** : a small piece of paper that is used for writing down information • *He wrote his notes on 3 x 5 cards.* [=cards that are 3 inches tall and 5 inches wide] **5** [*C*] : TRADING CARD • *a collection of baseball cards* **6** [*C*] : a thin, hard board that has small electronic devices on it and that can be added to the inside of a computer to make the computer perform different tasks • *a memory/sound/video card* **7** [*C*] : a list of the competitions that will happen at a sports event • *a racing card* [=a list of races] **8** [*C*] *informal + old-fashioned* : a funny or amusing person • *He's such a card!* **9** [*U*] *Brit* : CARDBOARD • *a piece of card* — **hold (all/all of) the cards** : to be in control of a situation and have the power to make decisions — **in the cards** (*US*) *or Brit* **on the cards** : certain or likely to happen in the future • *It's not in the cards for him to win the election.* [=he's not going to win the election] — **lay/put (all/all of) your cards on the table** : to be completely honest and open • *Before we can talk further, you need to put all your cards on the table.* [=to tell me what you are really thinking] — **play/hold/keep your cards close to the/your chest/vest** : to keep your plans, ideas, etc., hidden from other people — **play your cards right** : to do things in an intelligent and well-planned way • *If I play my cards right, I'll be able to graduate next year.*

²card *vb* [*T*] **1** *US, informal* : to ask (someone) to show a form of identification (such as a driver's license) in order to prove that the person is old enough to do something (such as to drink alcohol) • *He carded me when I bought cigarettes/beer.* **2** : to achieve (a score) in golf • *She carded a birdie on the second hole.*

car·da·mom /ˈkɑɚdəməm/ *n* [*U*] : the seeds of an Asian plant that are used as a spice

¹card·board /ˈkɑɚdˌboɚd/ *n* [*U*] : a stiff and thick kind of paper that is used especially for making boxes

²cardboard *adj* **1** : made out of cardboard • *cardboard boxes* **2** : not acting or seeming real • *The play had cardboard characters.*

card–car·ry·ing /ˈkɑɚdˌkerijɪŋ/ *adj*, always before a noun : known as an active member of a group or organization • *a* *card-carrying liberal/conservative*

card catalog *n [C] US* : a set of cards in a library that have information about books, journals, etc., written on them and are arranged in alphabetical order — called also (*Brit*) **card index**

card·hold·er /ˈkɑɚdˌhoʊldə/ *n [C]* : someone who has a credit card

car·di·ac /ˈkɑɚdiˌæk/ *adj, always before a noun* : of or relating to the heart • *cardiac problems/disease/surgery*

car·di·gan /ˈkɑɚdɪgən/ *n [C]* : a sweater that opens like a jacket and that is fastened in the front with buttons — called also (*US*) **cardigan sweater**

¹**car·di·nal** /ˈkɑɚdənəl/ *n [C]* **1** : a priest of the Roman Catholic Church who ranks immediately below the Pope **2** : a common North American bird ✧ The male cardinal is red and the female is mostly light brown.

²**cardinal** *adj, always before a noun, formal* : basic or most important • *My cardinal rule is to always be honest.* • *The cardinal points on a compass are North, South, East, and West.*

cardinal number *n [C]* : a number (such as 1, 2, or 3) that is used in simple counting and shows quantity — compare OR-DINAL NUMBER

cardinal sin *n [C]* : a very bad or serious sin in Christianity • (*figurative*) *Giving false information is a cardinal sin in news reporting.*

card index *n [C] chiefly Brit* : a set of cards that have information written on them and are arranged in alphabetical order; *especially* : CARD CATALOG

car·di·ol·o·gy /ˌkɑɚdiˈɑːlədʒi/ *n [U]* : the study of the heart and of diseases that affect the heart — **car·di·ol·o·gist** /ˌkɑɚdiˈɑːlədʒɪst/ *n [C]*

car·dio·pul·mo·nary resuscitation /ˌkɑɚdijoʊˈpʊlməˌneri-, *Brit* ˌkɑːdɪəʊˈpʊlmənri-/ *n [U]* : CPR

car·dio·vas·cu·lar /ˌkɑɚdijoʊˈvæskjələ/ *adj* : of or relating to the heart and blood vessels • *the cardiovascular system* • *cardiovascular disease*

card·sharp /ˈkɑɚdˌʃɑɚp/ *n [C]* : someone who makes money by cheating at card games — called also **card shark**

¹**care** /ˈkeɚ/ *n* **1** [*U*] : effort made to do something correctly, safely, or without causing damage • *She used care in selecting a doctor for her son.* • *a box marked "Handle With Care"* [=handle carefully] **2** [*U*] **a** : things that are done to keep someone healthy, safe, etc. • *inadequate medical/dental care* • *He is under a doctor's care.* [=is being treated by a doctor] • *The boys were in the care of* [=being looked after by] *their grandparents.* **b** : things that are done to keep something in good condition • *an article on car/skin care* • *the care and feeding of horses* • *The machine needs a lot of care and feeding.* [=maintenance] **3** [*U*] : something that causes you to feel worried or unhappy • *He doesn't have a care in the world.* [=he has no worries] — **care of** : at the address of • *You can write to him care of his fan club.* [=you can write to him by sending a letter to him at his fan club] — abbr. **c/o** —

take care : to be careful • *He took care not to upset anyone.* — often used informally to express good wishes when someone is leaving or at the end of a letter • *I'll see you next week. Take care!* — **take care of 1** : to do the things that are needed to help or protect (someone) or to keep (something) in good condition • *taking care of a sick child* • *taking care of a machine* • *I'm old enough to take care of myself.* **2** : to deal with or do (something that requires effort or attention) • *Don't worry about that mess. I'll take care of it.* [=I'll clean it up]

²**care** *vb* **cared; car·ing 1** [*T/I*] : to feel interest or concern about something • *He doesn't care if he gets fired.* • *I don't care about your problems.* • *I care what happens to her.* • *"She says she doesn't want to talk to you." "As if I cared!"* [=I don't care at all] **2** [*I*] : to feel affection for someone • *He sent her flowers to show that he cares.* **3** [*I*] *somewhat formal* : to want to do something or to be something • *I wouldn't care to be in your shoes right now.* • *I'm going for a walk. Would you care to join me?* — **care for** [*phrasal vb*] **1** : to do the things that are needed to help or protect (a person or animal) • *She cares for* [=takes care of] *elderly patients.* • *I cared for his cat while he was away.* **2** : to feel affection for (someone) • *He sent flowers to show that he cares for you.* **3** *somewhat formal* **a** : to like or enjoy (something) • *He doesn't care for sports.* **b** : to want (something) • *Would you care for some pie?* — **could/couldn't care less** *informal* ✧ If you *could care less* (*US*) or *couldn't care less*, you are not at all concerned about or interested in something. • *I could care less what happens.* [=I don't care what happens] — **for all (someone) cares** *informal* — used to say that someone does not care at all about something • *For all I care, he can leave today.* [=I don't care if he leaves today] — **see if I care** *informal* — used in angry speech to say that you do not care at all about something • *Go ahead and call her. See if I care!* — **what does (someone) care?** *informal* — used to say that you do not think someone should have any interest in something • *"She said we should go." "Well, what does she care?"* — **who cares?** *informal* — used to stress that something is not important • *Who cares what she says?* [=what she says is not important]

ca·reen /kəˈriːn/ *vb [I] US* : to go forward quickly without control • *The car careened down the hill.*

¹**ca·reer** /kəˈriɚ/ *n [C]* **1** : a job or profession that someone does for a long time • *I want to make teaching my career.* • *She hopes to have/pursue a medical career.* • *a career soldier* [=a soldier for all or most of his working life] **2** : a period of time spent in a job or profession • *My career as a waitress lasted only one day.*

²**career** *vb [I]* : CAREEN

ca·reer·ism /kəˈriɚˌɪzəm/ *n [U] disapproving* : an attitude or way of behaving that involves trying to do whatever you can to make more money or get promoted at your job — **ca·reer·ist** /kəˈrɪrɪst/ n [C]

care·free /ˈkeɚˌfri/ adj : having no worries or problems ▪ a carefree person/attitude

care·ful /ˈkeɚfəl/ adj 1 : using care ▪ a careful driver ▪ Be careful! The stove is hot! ▪ They are very careful with their money. [=they only spend what they can afford] ▪ The police were careful to leave the room exactly as they found it. 2 always before a noun : made, done, or said with care ▪ We kept careful records of the project. — **care·ful·ly** adv ▪ He opened the door carefully. — **care·ful·ness** n [U]

care·giv·er /ˈkeɚˌgɪvɚ/ n [C] : a person who gives help and protection to someone ▪ When she got sick, her husband became her primary caregiver. — called also (Brit) **carer**

care·less /ˈkeɚləs/ adj 1 : not using care : not careful ▪ a careless worker ▪ She was careless with my things. 2 : done, made, or said without enough thought or attention ▪ a careless mistake/remark — **care·less·ly** adv — **care·less·ness** n [U]

care package n [C] US : a package of useful or enjoyable items (such as candy or baked goods) that is sent or given as a gift to someone who is away from home

car·er /ˈkeɚ/ n [C] Brit : CAREGIVER

ca·ress /kəˈrɛs/ vb [T] : to touch (someone or something) in a gentle or loving way ▪ She caressed the baby's cheek. — **caress** n [C] ▪ a gentle caress

¹**care·tak·er** /ˈkeɚˌteɪkɚ/ n [C] 1 : a person who takes care of buildings or land while the owner is not there 2 chiefly US : a person who gives physical or emotional care to someone 3 Brit : JANITOR

²**caretaker** adj, always before a noun : doing a job for a short time before another is chosen to take the job officially ▪ a caretaker government

care worker n [C] Brit : a person whose job is to give care to people who are ill, disabled, etc.

care·worn /ˈkeɚˌwoɚn/ adj : looking sad, tired, or worried ▪ a careworn face

car·fare /ˈkaɚˌfeɚ/ n [C] : the money a person pays to travel by bus, taxi, etc.

car·go /ˈkaɚˌgoʊ/ n, pl **-goes** also **-gos** [C/U] : something that is carried from one place to another by boat, airplane, etc. ▪ The ship was carrying a cargo of crude oil. ▪ a cargo ship/plane

Ca·rib·be·an /ˌkeɚəˈbiːjən, kəˈrɪbijən/ adj : of or relating to the Caribbean Sea or its islands or to the people of the islands ▪ the Caribbean islands ▪ Caribbean food/customs

car·i·bou /ˈkeɚəˌbu:/ n, pl **caribou** or **car·i·bous** [C] : a large type of deer : a reindeer that lives in the northern parts of North America

¹**car·i·ca·ture** /ˈkerɪkəˌtʃɚ/ n [C] 1 : a drawing that makes someone look funny or foolish because some part of the person's appearance is exaggerated 2 : someone or something that is very exaggerated in a funny or foolish way ▪ His performance was a caricature of a hard-boiled detective. — **car·i·ca·tur·ist** /ˈkerɪkəˌtʃɚɪst/ n [C]

²**caricature** vb **-tured; -tur·ing** [T] : to draw or describe (someone or something) in a funny or exaggerated way ▪ The press caricatured him as clumsy and forgetful.

caring adj 1 : feeling or showing concern for other people ▪ a caring child/teacher/gesture 2 always before a noun, Brit : of or relating to work that involves helping people ▪ the caring professions

car·jack·ing /ˈkaɚˌdʒækɪŋ/ n [C] : the crime of using violence or threats to steal a car from its driver or to force the driver to take you someplace — **car·jack** /ˈkaɚˌdʒæk/ vb [T] — **car·jack·er** /ˈkaɚˌdʒækɚ/ n [C]

car·load /ˈkaɚˌloud/ n [C] : the amount of people or things that will fit in a car ▪ a carload of people

car·mak·er /ˈkaɚˌmeɪkɚ/ n [C] : a company that makes and sells cars

car·nage /ˈkaɚnɪdʒ/ n [U] : the killing of many people ▪ The highway accident was a scene of carnage.

car·nal /ˈkaɚnl/ adj, formal : of or relating to the body : sexual or sensual ▪ carnal desires/pleasures

car·na·tion /kaɚˈneɪʃən/ n [C] : a pink, white, yellow, or red flower that has a sweet smell

car·ni·val /ˈkaɚnəvəl/ n 1 or **Carnival** [C/U] : a festival held before Lent that includes music and dancing 2 [C] US a : a form of entertainment that travels to different places and includes rides and games you can play to win prizes b : FESTIVAL ▪ the school's annual winter carnival 3 [C] : a time or place that is exciting, lively, colorful, etc. ▪ The garden was a carnival of color.

car·ni·vore /ˈkaɚnəˌvoɚ/ n [C] : an animal that eats meat — **car·niv·o·rous** /kaɚˈnɪvɚəs/ adj

¹**car·ol** /ˈkerəl/ n [C] : a song sung during the Christmas season

²**carol** vb, US **-oled** or chiefly Brit **-olled**; US **-ol·ing** or chiefly Brit **-ol·ling** [I] : to go from place to place singing Christmas carols ▪ Last night, we went caroling with our friends. — **carol·er** (US) or chiefly Brit **carol·ler** /ˈkerələ/ n [C]

ca·rouse /kəˈrauz/ vb **-roused; -rous·ing** [I] : to drink alcohol, make noise, and have fun with other people ▪ My brother and his friends went out carousing last night.

car·ou·sel also **car·rou·sel** /ˌkerəˈsɛl/ n [C] 1 : MERRY-GO-ROUND 1 2 : a machine or device with a moving belt or part that carries things around in a circle ▪ the luggage carousel at the airport

¹**carp** /ˈkaɚp/ vb [I] : to complain in an annoying way ▪ He's always carping about his boss. ▪ She's always being carped at by her critics.

²**carp** n, pl **carp** or **carps** [C] : a type of large fish that lives in rivers and lakes and is often used for food

car park n [C] Brit 1 : PARKING LOT 2 : PARKING GARAGE

car·pen·ter /ˈkaɚpəntɚ/ n [C] : a person whose job is to make or fix wooden objects or wooden parts of buildings

car·pen·try /ˈkɑɚpəntri/ *n* [*U*] : the skill or work of making or fixing wooden objects or wooden parts of buildings

¹car·pet /ˈkɑɚpət/ *n* **1** [*C/U*] : a heavy fabric cover for a floor **2** [*C*] : a thick covering or layer ▪ *a carpet of leaves/snow* — **call (someone) on the carpet** *US, informal* : to criticize someone for doing something wrong ▪ *He was/got called on the carpet for missing the deadline.*

²carpet *vb* [*T*] **1** : to put a carpet on the floor of a room ▪ *carpet the bedroom/floor* ▪ *a carpeted room* **2** : to cover (something) with a thick layer ▪ *The lawn was carpeted with leaves.*

car·pet·bag·ger /ˈkɑɚpətˌbæɡɚ/ *n* [*C*] *disapproving* : a person from the northern United States who went to the South after the American Civil War to make money

carpet–bomb *vb* [*T*] : to drop many bombs in order to cause great destruction over (an area) ▪ *a city destroyed by carpet-bombing*

car·pet·ing /ˈkɑɚpətɪŋ/ *n* [*U*] : carpets or the material used for carpets ▪ *The house has wall-to-wall carpeting in the bedrooms.*

car pool *n* [*C*] : a group of people who regularly share a car when they are going to and from their jobs or who take turns driving each other other's children to school, activities, etc. — **car·pool** /ˈkɑɚˌpuːl/ *vb* [*I*] ▪ *She carpools to work with her neighbor.* — **car·pool·er** *n* [*C*]

car·port /ˈkɑɚˌpoɚt/ *n* [*C*] : a shelter for a car that has open sides and that is usually attached to the side of a building

car·riage /ˈkerɪdʒ/ *n* **1** [*C/U*] : a large vehicle with four wheels that is pulled by a horse **2** [*C*] : a wheeled structure that is used to carry and move something heavy (such as a large gun) **3** [*C*] *US* : BABY CARRIAGE **4** [*C*] *Brit* : a separate section of a train ▪ *a passenger carriage* **5** [*C*] : a moving part of a machine that supports or carries some other movable object or part ▪ *a typewriter carriage* **6** [*U*] *somewhat old-fashioned* : the way in which a person's body is positioned ▪ *a dancer noted for her elegant carriage* [=*posture*] **7** [*U*] *Brit* : the process or cost of carrying or transporting goods ▪ *payment of carriage charges*

car·ri·er /ˈkerijɚ/ *n* [*C*] **1** : someone or something that carries something: such as **a** : MAIL CARRIER **b** : a container used to move something from one place to another ▪ *a pet carrier* **c** : AIRCRAFT CARRIER **2** : a company that moves people or goods from one place to another ▪ *The airline is the nation's largest carrier.* **3** : a person or animal that can give a disease or a gene to others but is not affected by it ▪ *Mosquitoes can be carriers of malaria.* **4** *US* : a company that provides a specified service (such as insurance or long-distance telephone service) ▪ *We switched to a different long-distance carrier.*

carrier bag *n* [*C*] *Brit* : a bag that a store gives you to carry items you have bought there

carrier pigeon *n* [*C*] : a type of pigeon

that is trained to carry messages

car·ri·on /ˈkerijən/ *n* [*U*] : the flesh of dead animals

car·rot /ˈkerət/ *n* **1** [*C/U*] : the long orange root of a plant that is eaten as a vegetable ▪ *grated carrot(s)* **2** [*C*] *informal* : something that is offered as a reward or advantage to persuade a person to do something ▪ *The company offered a carrot in the form of additional vacation time to workers who met their deadlines.* ❖ This sense of *carrot* is often contrasted with *stick*, which suggests a punishment for not doing something. ▪ *He'll have to choose between the carrot and the stick.*

¹car·ry /ˈkeri/ *vb* **-ries; -ried; -ry·ing** **1** [*T*] : to move (something) while holding and supporting it ▪ *I'll carry your luggage to your room.* ▪ *The wind carried the smoke away.* ▪ *These planes can carry up to 300 passengers.* ▪ *(figurative) Your talent will carry you far.* [=it will make you very successful] **2** [*T*] : to contain and direct the flow of (water, electricity, etc.) ▪ *The gutters carry water away from the house.* ▪ *These cables carry electricity to hundreds of homes.* **3** [*T*] : to have (something) with you or on your body ▪ *police officers carrying guns* ▪ *I always carry $20 in case of an emergency.* **4** [*T*] : to be able to give (a disease or a gene) to others even though you may not be affected by it ▪ *One percent of the population carries the virus.* **5** [*T*] : to be pregnant with (a baby) ▪ *She's carrying her second child.* **6** [*T*] : to hold (your body or head) in a particular way ▪ *You should walk tall and carry your head high!* ▪ *She carries herself with dignity.* **7** [*T*] : to have (something) in a store and ready to be sold ▪ *The store carries a good selection of wines.* **8** [*T*] : to have (something) as a quality or characteristic ▪ *Our products carry a lifetime guarantee.* **9** [*T*] : to have (something) as a result or consequence ▪ *The surgery does carry certain risks.* ▪ *The job carries with it great responsibility.* **10** [*T*] : to have (something) as a duty or responsibility ▪ *I'm carrying a full course load this semester.* **11** [*T*] : to be responsible for the success of (something or someone) ▪ *He's capable of carrying a team on his own.* **12 a** [*T*] : to make (something) continue ▪ *He realized that he had carried the joke too far and hurt her feelings.* **b** [*I*] : to travel a long distance ▪ *His deep voice carries well.* **13** [*T*] : to sing (a tune) correctly ▪ *I've never been able to carry a tune.* **14** [*T*] : to present (something) to the public ▪ *Channel 9 will carry the game.* ▪ *The trial was carried live on television.* **15 a** [*T/I*] : to cause (a bill or an official proposal) to be passed or adopted ▪ *The bill was carried in the Senate by a vote of 75–25.* **b** [*T*] *chiefly US* : to win a majority of votes in (a state, legislature, etc.) ▪ *The bill carried the Senate by a vote of 75–25.* — **be/get carried away** : to be so excited that you are no longer in control of your behavior ▪ *I shouldn't have behaved like that. I just got carried away.* — **carry off** [*phrasal vb*] **carry off (something) or carry (something) off 1** : to do (some-

thing difficult) successfully ▪ *He tried to
look cool but couldn't carry it off.* [=*pull it
off*] **2** : to win (something) ▪ *We carried
off the prize.* — **carry on** [*phrasal vb*] **1
a** : to continue to do what you have been
doing ▪ *She carried on as if nothing had
happened.* ▪ *Please carry on with what
you were doing.* **b** : to continue (something) ▪ *The money allows us to carry on
our research.* ▪ *carry on a tradition* **c** : to
manage or be involved in (an activity) ▪
carry on an investigation ▪ *She carried on
an affair with her boss.* **2** : to behave or
speak in an excited or foolish way ▪ *We
were embarrassed by the way he was carrying on.* — **carry out** [*phrasal vb*] **carry
(something) out** *or* **carry out (something)**
: to do and complete (something) ▪ *We
carried out several experiments to test the
theory.* ▪ *She failed to carry out* [=*fulfill*]
her promise. ▪ *carry out your orders/duties*
— **carry over** [*phrasal vb*] **carry over** *or*
carry (something) over *or* **carry over
(something)** : to continue or cause
(something) to continue to exist or be
seen in another place or situation ▪ *His
unhappiness at home carried over into/to
his work.* = *He carried his unhappiness
over into/to his work.* — **carry the day**
see DAY — **carry through** [*phrasal vb*]
1 carry through to : to continue into or
to (something) ▪ *Our conversation carried
through to dessert.* ▪ *Though extremely
tired, she managed to carry through to the
finish.* **2 carry through with/on US** : to
do (something that you said you would
do) ▪ *The mayor carried through on her
promise to clean up the city.* ▪ *We're beginning to carry through with our plans.* **3
carry (something) through** : to successfully finish or complete (something that
you have begun or said you will do) ▪
They carried the project through to completion. **4 carry (someone) through** : to
help or allow (someone) to survive or
continue ▪ *We had enough supplies to carry us through (until spring).* ▪ *His faith carried him through a difficult time.*

²**carry** *n, pl* **-ries** [*C*] *American football*
: the act of running with the ball ▪ *He averaged four yards per carry this season.*

car·ry·all /ˈkeriˌɑːl/ *n* [*C*] *US* : a large bag
or carrying case

car·ry·on /ˈkeriˌɑːn/ *n* [*C*] *US* : a small
piece of luggage that a passenger can
carry onto an airplane ▪ *I packed the
book in my carry-on.* ▪ *carry-on baggage/
luggage*

car·ry·out /ˈkeriˌaʊt/ *n, chiefly US* **1** [*U*]
: TAKEOUT 1 ▪ *We ordered Chinese
carryout.* **2** [*C*] : TAKEOUT 2 ▪ *She works
in a Chinese carryout.* — **carryout** *adj* ▪
carryout food

car·ry·over /ˈkeriˌoʊvɚ/ *n* [*C*] : something that existed in one time or place
and continues in another ▪ *superstitions
that are carryovers from ancient times*

car·sick /ˈkɑɚˌsɪk/ *adj* : feeling sick
while riding in a car because of the
movement of the vehicle — **car·sick·ness** *n* [*U*]

¹**cart** /ˈkɑɚt/ *n* [*C*] **1** : a wagon with two
wheels that is pulled by an animal (such
as a horse or donkey) **2** : a small

wheeled vehicle that is pushed ▪ *a grocery/shopping cart* **3** : GOLF CART —
put the cart before the horse : to do
things in the wrong order ▪ *He is putting
the cart before the horse by planning on
how to spend the money before he even
has it.*

²**cart** *vb* [*T*] **1** : to carry or move (something) in a cart ▪ *We carted some dirt to
the garden.* **2** : to carry or move (something) ▪ *I carted the books home.* **3** : to
take (someone) away by force ▪ *They
carted him off to jail.*

carte blanche /ˌkɑɚtˈblɑːntʃ/ *n* [*U*] : permission to do something in any way you
choose to do it ▪ *We gave the decorator
carte blanche to furnish the house.*

car·tel /kɑɚˈtɛl/ *n* [*C*] : a group of businesses that agree to fix prices so they all
will make more money ▪ *an illegal drug
cartel*

car·ti·lage /ˈkɑɚtəlɪdʒ/ *n* [*U*] : a strong
but flexible material found in some parts
of the body (such as the nose, the outer
ear, and some joints) — **car·ti·lag·i·nous** /ˌkɑɚtəˈlædʒənəs/ *adj*

car·tog·ra·phy /kɑɚˈtɑːgrəfi/ *n* [*U*] : the
process or skill of making maps — **car·tog·ra·pher** /kɑɚˈtɑːgrəfɚ/ *n* [*C*] —
car·to·graph·ic /ˌkɑɚtəˈgræfɪk/ *adj*

car·ton /ˈkɑɚtn/ *n* [*C*] **1** : a light box or
container usually made of cardboard or
plastic ▪ *a carton of ice cream* **2** *US* : a
box containing things that have been
packed together so they can be sold or
moved ▪ *a carton of cigarettes/books*

car·toon /kɑɚˈtuːn/ *n* [*C*] **1 a** : a drawing in a newspaper or magazine intended
as a humorous comment on something ▪
a political cartoon **b** : COMIC STRIP **2**
: a film or television show made by photographing a series of drawings ▪ *The kids
are watching cartoons.* — **car·toon·ist**
/kɑɚˈtuːnɪst/ *n* [*C*]

car·tridge /ˈkɑɚtrɪdʒ/ *n* [*C*] **1** : a tube
which you put into a gun and which contains a bullet and explosive material **2**
: a case or container that you put into a
machine to make it work ▪ *The printer
needs a new ink cartridge.*

¹**cart·wheel** /ˈkɑɚtˌwiːl/ *n* [*C*] : an athletic
movement in which you move sideways
by placing one hand and then the other
on the ground, lifting your feet into the
air, and then landing on one foot and
then the other foot ▪ *do/turn cartwheels*

²**cartwheel** *vb* [*I*] **1** : to do a cartwheel ▪
She cartwheeled across the floor. **2** : to
spin or turn over in a violent and uncontrolled way ▪ *The car hit the pole and then
cartwheeled across the road.*

carve /ˈkɑɚv/ *vb* **carved**; **carv·ing** **1**
[*T*] : to make (a sculpture, design, etc.)
by cutting off pieces of the material it is
made of ▪ *We carved an ice sculpture.* **2**
[*T*] **a** : to cut (something, such as a pattern or design) into a surface ▪ *Their initials are carved into the tree.* **b** : to create
(something) by cutting into a surface ▪
*The Colorado River carved out the Grand
Canyon.* **3** [*T/I*] : to cut (cooked meat)
into pieces or slices ▪ *carve a turkey* **4**
[*T*] : to create (a job, a fortune, a way of
life, etc.) for yourself usually through

hard work • *She worked hard to* **carve out** *a career in education.* — **carve up** [*phrasal vb*] **carve up (something)** or **carve (something) up** *usually disapproving* : to divide something into small parts • *The old farm was carved up by developers.* — **carv·er** *n* [C]

carv·ing /ˈkɑɚvɪŋ/ *n* [C] : a carved object, design, or figure • *a small wooden carving*

car wash *n* [C] **1** : an area or building with equipment for washing cars **2** *US* : an event at which people pay to have their cars washed in order to raise money for some purpose

cas·cade /kæˈskeɪd/ *n* [C] **1** : a small, steep waterfall **2** : a large amount *of* something that flows or hangs down • *a cascade of water* **3** : a large number of things that happen quickly in a series • *a cascade of events* — **cascade** *vb* -**cad·ed**; -**cad·ing** [*I*] • *The water cascaded over the rocks.*

¹**case** /ˈkeɪs/ *n* **1** [C] : a particular situation or occurrence • *We usually ask for a deposit, but* **in this case** *we'll make an exception.* • *a classic case* [=a typical example] *of sibling rivalry* **2** [C] : a situation that is being investigated or managed by someone in an official way • *Police detectives are on the case.* • *a murder/rape/kidnapping case* **3** [C] *grammar* : a form of a noun, pronoun, or adjective showing its relationship to other words in a sentence • *the possessive case of a noun* **4** *the case* : what actually exists or happens • *Is it not the case* [=isn't it true] *that she took the car without permission?* **5** [C] *law* : a situation that will be talked about and decided in court • *a civil/criminal/court case* **6** [C] : a box or container to hold something • *a cigarette/pencil case* **7** [C] : a convincing argument • *He makes a good case for cutting expenses.* **8** [C] : an occurrence of a disease, an injury, etc. • *a bad/severe/slight case of the flu* • *a bad case of nerves* **9** [*singular*] : a particular person and his or her condition or character • *You are a sad case.* — **in any case** — used to indicate that something is true or certain regardless of what else has happened or been said • *I'm not sure if I'll be there tomorrow, but I'll see you Sunday in any case.* [=I'll definitely see you Sunday] — **in case** **1** : for the purpose of being ready for something that might happen • *Bring an umbrella (just) in case it rains.* **2** — used to talk about something that might have happened or that might be true • *Today is my birthday, in case you've forgotten.* — **in case of** : if (something) happens • *That door is for use in case of fire.* — **in that case** : because of that • *"The traffic could be heavy tomorrow." "In that case, we better leave early."* — **on/off your case** *informal* ✧ Someone who often criticizes you or tells you what to do is *on your case* and won't *get off your case.* • *He's always on her case about the clothes she wears.*

²**case** *vb* **cased; cas·ing** [*T*] : to study or watch (a house, store, etc.) with plans to rob it • *A couple of robbers were casing the joint.*

case history *n* [C] : a record that shows a person's past illnesses, treatments, and other information for use by doctors, social workers, etc.

case·load /ˈkeɪsˌloʊd/ *n* [C] : the number or amount of cases handled by a court, social worker, etc. • *a heavy/light caseload*

case study *n* [C] : a published report about a person, group, or situation that has been studied over time • *a case study of prisoners*

case·work /ˈkeɪsˌwɚk/ *n* [U] : the work done by a social worker to help fix the problems of a person or family — **case·work·er** /ˈkeɪsˌwɚkɚ/ *n* [C]

¹**cash** /ˈkæʃ/ *n* [U] **1** : money in the form of coins and bills • *He paid cash for the truck.* • *cash payments/prizes/sums* **2** : money along with other things (such as stocks) that can be quickly changed into money • *The company has $4 million in cash.*

²**cash** *vb* [T] : to give or get cash for (a check) • *He cashed his paycheck at the bank.* — **cash in** [*phrasal vb*] **1 cash in (something)** or **cash (something) in** : to obtain money for (something that you own) • *She cashed in her stocks.* **2 a cash in on** : to take advantage of (something) in order to make money • *Builders cashed in on the construction boom.* **b** : to make money from something • *He cashed in big* [=made a lot of money] *when he sold his house.*

cash card *n* [C] *Brit* : an ATM card

cash cow *n* [C] : someone or something that makes a lot of money for a business, organization, etc. • *The football team was a cash cow for the university.*

cash crop *n* [C] : a crop (such as tobacco or cotton) that is grown to be sold rather than for use by the farmer

cash·ew /ˈkæʃu, kəˈʃu/ *n* [C] : a type of roasted nut that has a curved shape

cash flow *n* [C/U] : the movement of money in and out of a business • *new ways to generate cash flow*

cash·ier /kæˈʃiɚ/ *n* [C] : a person whose job is to take in or give out money in a store, bank, etc.

cashier's check *n* [C] : a check that is written by a bank and signed by a cashier

cash·mere /ˈkæʒˌmiɚ, ˈkæʃˌmiɚ/ *n* [U] **1** : fine wool from a kind of goat from India **2** : a soft fabric made from cashmere wool • *a cashmere sweater*

cash·point /ˈkæʃˌpoɪnt/ *n* [C] *Brit* : ATM

cash register *n* [C] : a machine used in a store, restaurant, etc., that calculates the amount of cash due for a sale and has a drawer for holding money

cas·ing /ˈkeɪsɪŋ/ *n* [C] **1** : a layer on the outside of something that covers and protects it • *a sausage casing* **2** : a frame around a door or window

ca·si·no /kəˈsiːnoʊ/ *n, pl* -**nos** [C] : a building or room that has games (such as roulette or blackjack) for gambling

cask /ˈkæsk, Brit ˈkɑːsk/ *n* [C] : a container that is shaped like a barrel and is used for holding liquids • *a wine cask*

cas·ket /'kæskət, Brit 'kɑːskət/ *n* [C] **1** *chiefly US* : COFFIN **2** : a small chest or box for jewelry or other valuable things

cas·se·role /'kæsə,roʊl/ *n* **1** [C/U] : food (such as meat, noodles, and vegetables) baked together and served in a deep dish • *a seafood casserole* **2** [C] : a deep dish used for baking • *meat and noodles served in a casserole (dish)*

cas·sette /kə'sɛt/ *n* [C] : a thin case that holds audio tape or videotape and in which the tape passes from one reel to another when being played • *a cassette player/recorder*

¹**cast** /'kæst, Brit 'kɑːst/ *vb* **cast; cast·ing** [T] **1 a** : to throw or move (something) in a forceful way • *cast a stone* **b** : to throw (a fishing line, hook, etc.) into the water by using a fishing pole **2 a** : to send or direct (something) toward or at someone or something • *He cast a glance toward the door.* • *The witch cast a spell on him.* **b** : to send (something) out or forward • *The tree cast a long shadow on the lawn.* • *(figurative) The incident casts doubt on her honesty.* **3** : to make (a vote) formally • *cast a ballot/vote* **4** : to assign roles for a play, movie, etc., to actors • *cast a play* • *She was cast as the lead.* **5 a** : to shape (a substance) by pouring it into a mold and letting it harden • *molds used for casting steel* **b** : to form (something, such as a sculpture) by casting metal, plaster, etc. • *The statue was cast in bronze.* **6** : to arrange (something) into parts or into a proper form • *He cast the story in the form of a diary.* **7** : to talk about or think of (someone or something) in a particular way • *The war was cast as a battle against terrorism.* — **cast about/around for** [*phrasal vb*] : to look in many places for (something) • *They cast about for new ways to make money.* — **cast aside** [*phrasal vb*] **cast aside (something)** or **cast (something) aside** : to stop thinking about (something) • *She tried to cast aside her worries.* — **cast away** [*phrasal vb*] **cast away (someone)** or **cast (someone) away** : to leave (someone) alone somewhere (such as on an island) as a result of a storm, shipwreck, etc. • *They were cast away on a desert island.* — **cast off** [*phrasal vb*] **1** **cast off (something)** or **cast (something) off** : to get rid of (something) • *She cast off her fears.* **2** : to untie the rope that is holding a boat near the land • *We cast off and headed out to sea.* — **cast out** [*phrasal vb*] **cast out (someone or something)** or **cast (someone or something) out** : to force (someone or something) to go away • *He was cast out of the tribe.*

²**cast** *n* **1** [C] : the actors in a play, film, or television show • *a strong supporting cast* [=the actors other than the main stars] • *an interesting cast of characters* [=group of people who have important roles in a book, story, or event] **2** [C] : a hard covering that is put on an arm, leg, etc., so that a broken bone can heal **3** [C] : a container that is used to give its form or shape to something that is

poured or pressed into it **4** [*singular*] : a slight bit of color • *old photographs with a reddish cast* **5** [C] : the act of throwing a fishing line into water with a pole

cas·ta·nets /,kæstə'nɛts/ *n* [*plural*] : a musical instrument that consists of two small, round parts that are clicked together by the fingers

cast·away /'kæst,əweɪ, Brit 'kɑːstə,weɪ/ *n* [C] : a person who is left alone in a place (such as an island) as a result of a storm, shipwreck, etc.

caste /'kæst, Brit 'kɑːst/ *n* **1** [C] : one of the classes into which the Hindu people of India were traditionally divided **2** [C/U] : a division of society based upon differences of wealth, rank, or occupation

cast·er (*US*) or Brit **cas·tor** /'kæstə, Brit 'kɑːstə/ *n* [C] : a small wheel attached to the bottom of something (such as a piece of furniture) to make it easier to move

cas·ti·gate /'kæstə,geɪt/ *vb* **-gat·ed; -gat·ing** [T] *formal* : to criticize (someone) harshly • *The judge castigated the lawyers for their lack of preparation.* — **cas·ti·ga·tion** /,kæstə'geɪʃən/ *n* [U]

cast·ing /'kæstɪŋ, Brit 'kɑːstɪŋ/ *n* [C] : something made from material that hardens in a mold • *metal castings for machine parts*

cast iron *n* [U] : a very hard type of metal that is made into different shapes by being melted and poured into special containers (called casts or molds) • *a fence made of cast iron*

cast–iron *adj* **1** : made of cast iron • *a cast-iron stove* **2** : very strong or tough • *a cast-iron stomach/will* **3** *Brit* : not likely to fail or be broken • *a cast-iron promise*

cas·tle /'kæsəl, Brit 'kɑːsəl/ *n* [C] **1** : a large building usually with high, thick walls and towers that was built in the past to protect against attack **2** : a piece in the game of chess that looks like a castle tower

cast·off /'kæst,ɑːf, Brit 'kɑːst,ɒf/ *n* [C] : something or someone that is thrown out or replaced • *The books were mostly castoffs from other schools.* — **cast–off** *adj* • *cast-off clothes*

castor Brit spelling of CASTER

cas·tor oil /'kæstə-, Brit 'kɑːstər-/ *n* [U] : a thick oil made from a tropical plant and used in the past as a medicine

cas·trate /'kæ,streɪt, Brit kæ'streɪt/ *vb* **-trat·ed; -trat·ing** [T] : to remove the testes of (a person or animal) — **cas·tra·tion** /kæ'streɪʃən/ *n* [U]

ca·su·al /'kæʒəwəl/ *adj* **1** : not formal • *casual clothes/restaurants* **2** *always before a noun* : not planned or expected • *a casual encounter* **3 a** : done without much thought, effort, or concern • *a casual remark* **b** : not involving a close or serious relationship • *casual sex* • *They are only casual acquaintances.* **c** : having some interest but not a lot • *a casual sports fan* **4** : happening at certain times but not on a regular basis • *She found only casual work.* — **ca·su·al·ly** *adj* — **ca·su·al·ness** *n* [U]

ca·su·al·ty /'kæʒəwəlti/ *n, pl* **-ties**

[C] : a person who is hurt or killed during an accident, war, etc. ▪ *The battle resulted in heavy casualties.* **2** [C] : a person or thing that is harmed, lost, or destroyed ▪ *The tree was a casualty of the high winds.* **3** [U] *Brit* : EMERGENCY ROOM

cat /'kæt/ *n* [C] **1 a** : a small animal that is related to lions and tigers and that is often kept by people as a pet **b** : a lion, tiger, leopard, or similar wild animal **2** *old-fashioned slang* : a man ▪ *He's a cool cat.* — **Cat got your tongue?** *informal* — used to ask someone why he or she is not saying anything — **let the cat out of the bag** : to reveal a secret ▪ *We wanted the party to be a surprise, but he let the cat out of the bag.* — **rain cats and dogs** see ²RAIN — **cat-like** /'kæt,laɪk/ *adj*

cat·a·clysm /'kætə,klɪzəm/ *n* [C/U] : something that causes great destruction, violence, etc. ▪ *the cataclysm of war* — **cat·a·clys·mic** /,kætə'klɪzmɪk/ *adj*

cat·a·comb /'kætə,koʊm, *Brit* 'kætə-,kuːm/ *n* [C] : an underground place where people are buried

¹**cat·a·log** (*chiefly US*) *or* **cat·a·logue** /'kætə,lɑːg/ *n* [C] **1** : a book containing a list of things that you can buy, use, etc., and often pictures ▪ *I buy clothes through a (mail-order) catalog.* ▪ *a college/course catalog* **2** : a group of similar or related things ▪ *the band's catalog of hits*

²**catalog** (*US*) *or* **catalogue** *vb* **-loged** *or* **-logued; -log·ing** *or* **-logu·ing** [T] : to list or describe (something) in an organized way ▪ *They use the computer to catalog books.* — **cat·a·log·er** (*US*) *or* **cat·a·logu·er** *n* [C]

cat·a·lyst /'kætələst/ *n* [C] **1** *technical* : a substance that causes a chemical reaction to happen more quickly **2** : a person or event that quickly causes change or action ▪ *the catalyst for war*

cat·a·lyt·ic converter /,kætə'lɪtɪk-/ *n* [C] : a part of an automobile exhaust system that removes harmful chemicals

cat and mouse *n* [U] : behavior that is like the way a cat chases a mouse or plays with a mouse before killing it — used especially to describe a situation in which someone says or does different things to deceive or control other people, to avoid being caught, etc.; usually used with *play* ▪ *The governor has been playing (a game of) cat and mouse with the media, refusing to say definitely whether he will run for reelection.*

¹**cat·a·pult** /'kætə,pʌlt/ *n* [C] **1 a** : an ancient weapon used for throwing large rocks **b** *Brit* : SLINGSHOT **2** : a device for launching an airplane from the deck of an aircraft carrier

²**catapult** *vb* **1** [T] : to throw (something) with a catapult ▪ *They catapulted rocks toward the castle.* **2 a** [T] : to cause (someone or something) to quickly move up or ahead or to a better position ▪ *The publicity catapulted her CD to the top of the charts.* **b** [I] : to quickly move up or ahead ▪ *He catapulted to fame after his first book.*

cat·a·ract /'kætə,rækt/ *n* [C] : a condition in which a part of your eye (called the lens) becomes cloudy and you cannot see well

ca·tas·tro·phe /kə'tæstrəfi/ *n* [C/U] : a terrible disaster ▪ *an economic/environmental catastrophe* ▪ *an area on the brink of catastrophe* — **cat·a·stroph·ic** /,kætə'strɑːfɪk/ *adj* — **cat·a·stroph·i·cal·ly** /,kætə'strɑːfɪkli/ *adv*

cat burglar *n* [C] : a thief who enters buildings by climbing up a wall and going in through a window without being seen

cat·call /'kæt,kɑːl/ *n* [C] : a sound or noise that someone (such as an audience member) makes toward a speaker, performer, athlete, etc., that he or she does not like

¹**catch** /'kætʃ, 'kɛtʃ/ *vb* **caught** /'kɑːt/; **catch·ing** **1 a** [T/I] : to use your hands to stop and hold (an object that is moving through the air) ▪ *catch a ball* **b** [T] : to use your hands to grasp and hold onto (someone or something) ▪ *He caught [=grabbed] her by the wrist.* **2** [T] : to capture and not allow (a person, animal, or fish) to escape ▪ *The police worked hard to catch the criminals.* ▪ *I caught 10 fish today.* **3** [T] **a** : to manage to find, meet, or reach (someone) at a particular time or in a particular state or condition ▪ *I caught her just as she was leaving for work.* **b** : to find (someone who is doing something wrong) ▪ *My teacher caught me cheating on a test.* ▪ *They caught him in the act (of stealing the painting).* = *He was caught red-handed.* **4** [T] : to affect (someone) in a sudden and surprising way ▪ *They were caught unprepared by the crisis.* [=they were not prepared when the crisis occurred] ▪ *The news caught me by surprise.* [=I was surprised by the news] **5** [T] **a** : to suddenly stop (yourself) before you do something ▪ *Luckily, he caught himself before he said something foolish.* **b** : to suddenly become aware that you are doing something ▪ *He caught himself staring at her.* **6** [T] : to cause (someone) to be stopped, delayed, etc. ▪ *I got/was caught in traffic.* **7** [T/I] : to cause (something) to become stuck and unable to move ▪ *The kite got caught in a tree.* ▪ *My sleeve caught on a nail.* **8** [T] **a** : to hit or touch (someone or something) ▪ *His last punch caught me in the jaw.* **b** : to be hit or touched by (something) ▪ *The trees catch the light as the sun sets.* **9** [T] : to become affected with (a sickness or disease) ▪ *I caught a cold.* **10** [T] : to begin to feel excitement or interest about something ▪ *I haven't caught the holiday spirit yet this year.* **11** [T] : to attract and hold (someone's attention, interest, etc.) ▪ *trying to catch a waiter's attention* ▪ *Her books caught the imagination of children from around the world.* ▪ *a dress that caught my eye* [=a dress that I noticed] **12** [T] : to see, smell, or notice (something) ▪ *I caught a whiff of her perfume.* ▪ *You might catch a glimpse of some movie stars in Hollywood.* ▪ *I caught sight of a deer in the back yard.* **13** [T] *informal* : to hear or understand (something) ▪ *I didn't catch your name.* **14** [T] : to be-

come aware of (something, such as an illness) • *The disease is curable if caught [=detected] early.* **15** [*T*] : to have or do (something) • *You can catch a quick nap on the train.* **16** [*T*] : to get (something) through effort • *I'll try to catch a ride with some friends.* **17** [*T*] *informal* : to meet with (someone) • *I'll catch you later.* **18** [*T*] : to move fast enough to be next to or in front of (someone) • *She caught the leader in the final meters of the race.* **19** [*T*] : to get on a bus, train, etc., before it leaves • *I have a plane to catch.* **20** [*T*] : to see or hear (a show, game, etc.) • *I only caught the last few minutes of the game.* — **catch fire 1** or *US* **catch on fire** : to begin to burn • *Their house caught fire and burned to the ground.* **2** : to become very popular or effective • *a new technology that has caught fire with the public* — **catch hell** see HELL — **catch on** [*phrasal vb*] **1** : to become popular • *Soccer is finally starting to catch on in America.* **2** : to learn or understand something • *Once he started playing the game, he caught on quickly.* — **catch out** [*phrasal vb*] **catch (someone) out** *chiefly Brit* : to show that (someone) does not know something or is doing something bad • *They tried to catch him out in a lie.* — **catch up** [*phrasal vb*] **1** : to move fast enough to join someone or something that is in front of you • *They went so fast we couldn't catch up.* • *She couldn't catch up with me.* — (*US*) *She couldn't catch up to me.* • (*figurative*) *She missed several months of school and may never catch up with the other children in her class.* **2** : to learn about recent events • *He reads the newspaper on Sunday mornings to catch up on the news.* **3** **catch up on** : to do (something) that you could have done earlier • *She has to catch up on her homework.* **4** **catch (someone) up** *Brit* : to join someone who is ahead of you • *Go on ahead: I'll catch you up later.* **5** **catch up with a** : to begin to affect (someone) usually in a bad way • *All those late nights are really starting to catch up with me!* **b** : to find and arrest (someone) • *The police finally caught up with him in Texas.* **c** *informal* : to meet with (someone) • *I've got to go. I'll catch up with you later.* — **catch your breath** see BREATH — **caught up in 1** : involved in (a difficult or confusing situation) • *How did you get caught up in this mess?* **2** : excited about something and having trouble thinking about anything else • *Everyone was caught up in the excitement.* — **catch·a·ble** /ˈkætʃəbəl, ˈketʃəbəl/ *adj*

²**catch** *n* **1** [*C*] : a hidden problem that makes something more complicated or difficult to do • *He said he would let me borrow his car, but I knew there had to be a catch.* **2 a** [*C*] : the act of stopping a moving object (such as a ball) and holding it in your hands • *The shortstop made a tough catch.* **b** [*U*] : a game in which two or more people throw and catch a ball • *She likes to play catch with her dad.* **3** [*C*] : an amount of fish that has been caught • *a catch of about 20 fish* **4** [*C*] *old-fashioned* : a person who would be

very desirable as a husband or wife • *He was an excellent catch.* **5** [*C*] : something that holds an object or stops the parts of an object from moving • *She fastened the catch on her purse.*

catch-all /ˈkætʃˌɑːl, ˈketʃˌɑːl/ *n* [*singular*] : something that holds or includes many different things • *They used the drawer as a catchall for kitchen items.* • *a catchall phrase/term*

catch·er /ˈkætʃɚ, ˈketʃɚ/ *n* [*C*] **1** : someone or something that catches something • *a dog catcher* **2** *baseball* : the player who plays behind home plate and catches the pitches thrown by the pitcher

catching *adj, not before a noun* : able to be passed quickly from one person or animal to another • *"I have a cold." "Is it catching?"*

catch·phrase /ˈkætʃˌfreɪz, ˈketʃˌfreɪz/ *n* [*C*] : a word or phrase that is easy to remember and is commonly used to represent or describe a person, group, idea, etc.

catch-22 or **Catch-22** /ˈkætʃˌtwɛntiˈtuː, ˈketʃˌtwɛntiˈtuː/ *n, pl* **-22's** or **-22s** [*C*] : a difficult situation for which there is no easy or possible solution • *I'm in a catch-22: to get the job I need experience, but how do I get experience if I can't get the job?* • *a catch-22 dilemma/situation*

catch-up /ˈkætʃˌʌp, ˈketʃˌʌp/ *n* — **play catch-up** : to try to reach the same position, score, etc., as a competitor after you have fallen behind • *The team fell behind in the second inning and has had to play catch-up ever since.*

catch·word /ˈkætʃˌwəd, ˈketʃˌwəd/ *n* [*C*] : CATCHPHRASE

catchy /ˈkætʃi, ˈketʃi/ *adj* **catch·i·er; -est** : appealing and easy to remember • *a catchy song/tune/slogan/title*

cat·e·chism /ˈkætəˌkɪzəm/ *n* [*U*] : a collection of questions and answers that are used to teach people about the Christian religion

cat·e·gor·i·cal /ˌkætəˈgorɪkəl/ also **cat·e·gor·ic** /ˌkætəˈgorɪk/ *adj* : said in a very strong, clear, and definite way • *a categorical denial/statement* — **cat·e·gor·i·cal·ly** /ˌkætəˈgorɪkli/ *adv*

cat·e·go·rize also *Brit* **cat·e·go·rise** /ˈkætɪgəˌraɪz/ *vb* **-rized; -riz·ing** [*T*] : to put (people or things) into categories • *This software lets you categorize your photographs in many different ways.* — **cat·e·go·ri·za·tion** also *Brit* **cat·e·go·ri·sa·tion** /ˌkætɪgərəˈzeɪʃən, *Brit* ˌkætɪgərəˈraɪˈzeɪʃən/ *n* [*C/U*]

cat·e·go·ry /ˈkætəˌgori, *Brit* ˈkætəgri/ *n, pl* **-ries** [*C*] : a group of people or things that are similar in some way • *She competed for the award in her age category.*

ca·ter /ˈkeɪtɚ/ *vb* [*T/I*] : to provide food and drinks at a party, meeting, etc., especially as a job • *The restaurant caters (for) parties/banquets/receptions.* — **cater to** (*chiefly US*) or *chiefly Brit* **cater for** [*phrasal vb*] : to provide what is wanted or needed by (someone or something) • *The inn caters exclusively to foreign tourists.* • *His parents catered to his every need.* — **ca·ter·er** /ˈkeɪtərɚ/ *n* [*C*] — **cater·ing** *n* [*U*]

cat·er·pil·lar /'kætə,pɪlə/ n [C] : a small creature that is like a worm with many legs and that changes to become a butterfly or moth

cat·er·waul /'kætə,wɑːl/ vb [I] : to make a very loud and unpleasant sound ▪ *a caterwauling animal/singer* — **caterwaul** n [C]

cat·fight /'kæt,faɪt/ n [C] *informal* : an angry fight or argument between two women

cat·fish /'kæt,fɪʃ/ n, pl **cat·fish** [C/U] : a type of fish that has a large head and long thin parts that look like a cat's whiskers around its mouth

ca·thar·sis /kə'θɑːsɪs/ n [U, singular] *formal* : the act or process of releasing a strong emotion (such as pity or fear) especially by expressing it in an art form ▪ *Acting is a means of catharsis for her.* — **ca·thar·tic** /kə'θɑːtɪk/ adj ▪ *a cathartic experience*

ca·the·dral /kə'θiːdrəl/ n [C] : the main church of an area that is headed by a bishop

cathedral ceiling n [C] : a high ceiling that has two sides that slant downwards from a pointed top

cath·e·ter /'kæθətə/ n [C] *medical* : a thin tube that is put into the body to remove or inject a liquid or to keep a passage open — **cath·e·ter·i·za·tion** *also Brit* **cath·e·ter·i·sa·tion** /,kæθətərə-'zeɪʃən, Brit ,kæθətə,raɪ'zeɪʃən/ n [C/U] ▪ *The patient underwent cardiac catheterization.*

cath·ode /'kæ,θoʊd/ n [C] *technical* : the part of an electrical device (such as a battery) where electrons enter

cathode–ray tube n [C] : a large tube that shows a picture on a screen (such as a television or computer screen)

cath·o·lic /'kæθlɪk/ adj **1** Catholic : of or relating to the Roman Catholic Church ▪ *a Catholic bishop/nun/priest/school* **2** *formal* : including many different things ▪ *He has catholic tastes in art.* — **Catholic** n [C]

Ca·thol·i·cism /kə'θɑːlə,sɪzəm/ n [U] : the Roman Catholic religion

cat·nap /'kæt,næp/ n [C] : a short nap ▪ *He took/had a catnap.* — **cat·nap** vb **-napped**; **-nap·ping** [I] ▪ *I catnapped while she drove the car.*

cat·nip /'kæt,nɪp/ n [U] : a type of mint that has a strong smell which is attractive to cats

CAT scan /'kæt-/ n [C] *medical* : a picture of the inside of a part of your body that is made by a computerized machine — called also *CT scan* — **CAT scanner** n [C]

cat·sup /'kɛtʃəp/ n [U] *US* : KETCHUP

cat·tail /'kæt,teɪl/ n [C] *US* : a tall plant that has long flat leaves and that grows in wet areas

cat·tle /'kætl/ n [plural] : cows, bulls, or steers that are kept on a farm or ranch for meat or milk ▪ *a herd of cattle* ▪ *a cattle ranch*

cattle prod n [C] : a device that is used to make cattle move by giving them an electric shock

cat·ty /'kæti/ adj **cat·ti·er**; **-est** *disap-*proving : unkind or critical ▪ *a catty remark* — **cat·ti·ly** /'kætəli/ adv — **cat·ti·ness** /'kætinəs/ n [U]

cat·ty-cor·ner /'kæti,kɔənə/ or **cat·ty-cor·nered** /'kæti,kɔənəd/ adv, US : KITTY-CORNER

cat·walk /'kæt,wɑːk/ n [C] **1** : a narrow structure for people to walk on along a bridge or high up on the side of a building **2** : the raised structure that models walk along in a fashion show

Cau·ca·sian /kɑ'keɪʒən, Brit kɔ'keɪziən/ n [C] : a white person — **Caucasian** adj

¹**cau·cus** /'kɑːkəs/ n [C] **1** : a meeting of members of a political party for the purpose of choosing candidates for an election ▪ *a presidential caucus* **2** : a group of people (such as members of the U.S. Congress) who meet to discuss a particular issue or to work together for a shared, usually political goal

²**caucus** vb [I] *US* : to meet in a caucus ▪ *Democrats/Republicans caucused last week to choose their candidates.*

caught *past tense and past participle of* ¹CATCH

caul·dron *also US* **cal·dron** /'kɑːldrən/ n [C] : a large pot ▪ *a witch's cauldron* ▪ *(figurative) The area was a cauldron of violence.*

cau·li·flow·er /'kɑːlɪ,flawə/ n [C/U] : a plant that is grown for its head of white flowers which is eaten as a vegetable

caulk /'kɑːk/ vb [T] : to fill the cracks or holes in (something) with a substance that keeps out water ▪ *He caulked the area around the windows.* — **caulk** n [U] ▪ *He filled the cracks with caulk.*

caus·al /'kɑːzəl/ adj, *formal* : relating to or showing the cause of something ▪ *a causal link/connection/relationship* — **cau·sal·i·ty** /kɑ'zæləti/ n [U] — **caus·al·ly** adv

cau·sa·tion /kɑ'zeɪʃən/ n [U] *formal* : the act or process of causing something to happen or exist ▪ *the causation of cancer*

caus·ative /'kɑːzətɪv/ adj, *formal* : causing something ▪ *a causative agent/factor*

¹**cause** /'kɑːz/ n **1** [C] : something or someone that makes something happen or exist ▪ *What was the cause of the accident/fire?* ▪ *He died off/from natural causes.* [=he died because of old age or an illness] **2** [U, singular] : a reason for doing or feeling something ▪ *There is some/no cause for concern.* ▪ *a cause for celebration* **3** [C] : something (such as an organization, belief, idea, or goal) that a group of people support or fight for ▪ *donating money to a good/worthy cause* — **lost cause** : a person or thing that is certain to fail ▪ *She decided her acting career was a lost cause.*

²**cause** vb **caused**; **caus·ing** [T] **1** : to make (something) happen or exist ▪ *cause an accident* ▪ *The illness is caused by a virus.* **2** : to make (someone) feel, have, or do something ▪ *His nervous behavior caused me to question his innocence.*

cause cé·lè·bre *also* **cause ce·le·bre** /,kɑːz'lɛbrə/ n, pl **causes cé·lè·bres**

also **causes ce·le·bres** /ˌkɑz:sə'lebrə/ [C] *formal* : a legal case or an event that a lot of people become interested in • *The case became a cause célèbre for/ among environmentalists.*

cause·way /'kɑːzˌweɪ/ *n* [C] : a raised road or path that goes across wet ground or water

caus·tic /'kɑːstɪk/ *adj* **1** : able to destroy or burn something by chemical action • *a caustic chemical* **2** : very harsh and critical • *caustic humor/wit* — **caus·ti·cal·ly** /'kɑːstɪkli/ *adv*

¹**cau·tion** /'kɑːʃən/ *n* **1** [U] : care taken to avoid danger or risk • *You should use/ exercise caution when operating the electric saw.* **2** [C/U] : a warning telling someone to be careful • *Her comments were intended as a caution to us.* • *He offered a* **note/word of caution**. [=a warning to be careful] **3** [C] *Brit, law* : a spoken official warning given to someone who has done something illegal but has not committed a serious crime • *She was given a caution by the magistrate.* — **throw/ fling/cast caution to the wind** : to stop being careful and do something that is dangerous or that might result in failure • *He finally threw caution to the wind, quit his job, and started his own company.*

²**caution** *vb* **1** [T/I] : to warn or tell (someone) about a possible danger, problem, etc. • *She cautioned me not to decide too quickly.* • *I would* **caution against** *getting involved with him.* **2** [T] *Brit, law* : to give a caution to (someone) • *He was cautioned for speeding.*

cau·tion·ary /'kɑːʃəˌneri, *Brit* 'kɔːʃənri/ *adj* : giving a warning about a possible danger, problem, etc. • *a cautionary tale*

cau·tious /'kɑːʃəs/ *adj* : careful about avoiding danger or risk • *a cautious driver/reply* — **cau·tious·ly** *adv* — **cau·tious·ness** *n* [U]

cav·al·cade /ˌkævəl'keɪd/ *n* [C] **1** : a line of riders, vehicles, etc., moving along in the same direction • *a cavalcade of antique cars* **2** *literary* : a series of similar or related things • *a cavalcade of natural disasters*

cav·a·lier /ˌkævə'liə/ *adj, disapproving* : having or showing no concern for something that is important or serious : CARELESS • *a cavalier attitude* — **cav·a·lier·ly** *adv*

cav·al·ry /'kævəlri/ *n, pl* **cavalry** [U, *plural*] : the part of an army that in the past had soldiers who rode horses and that now has soldiers who ride in vehicles or helicopters • *The cavalry was/were brought in to support the mission.* • *cavalry forces/officers/troops*

cav·al·ry·man /'kævəlrimən/ *n, pl* **-men** /-mən/ [C] : a soldier who is in the cavalry

¹**cave** /'keɪv/ *n* [C] : a large hole that was formed by natural processes in the side of a cliff or hill or under the ground

²**cave** *vb* **caved; cav·ing** — **cave in** [*phrasal vb*] **1 a** : to fall down or inward • *The tunnel caved in on them.* **b cave (something) in** or **cave in (something)** : to cause (something) to fall down or inward • *The weight of the snow caved in the*

roof. **2** *informal* : to stop trying to resist or oppose something • *He caved in to the pressure to resign.* — sometimes used in informal U.S. English without *in* • *We kept asking her to come and she finally caved.*

ca·ve·at /'kæviˌɑːt, *Brit* 'kæviæt/ *n* [C] *formal* : an explanation or warning that should be remembered when you are doing or thinking about something

cave–in /'keɪvˌɪn/ *n* [C] : an occurrence in which something (such as the roof or walls of a building or cave) suddenly falls down or inward

cave·man /'keɪvˌmæn/ *n, pl* **-men** /-mən/ [C] : a person who lived in a cave in ancient times

cav·er /'keɪvə/ *n* [C] : a person who explores caves

cav·ern /'kævən/ *n* [C] : a large cave

cav·ern·ous /'kævənəs/ *adj, of a building or room* : very large • *a cavernous auditorium*

cav·i·ar /'kæviˌɑə/ *n* [U] : the eggs of a large fish (such as the sturgeon) that are salted and eaten as food

cav·i·ty /'kævəti/ *n, pl* **-ties** [C] **1** : a hole or space inside something • *the abdominal/chest/nasal cavity* **2** : a hole formed in a tooth by decay

ca·vort /kə'voət/ *vb* [I] **1** : to jump or move around in a lively manner • *Dogs cavorted in the grass.* **2** : to spend time in an enjoyable and often wild or improper way • *The governor was criticized for cavorting with celebrities.*

caw /'kɑː/ *n* [C] : the loud sound made by a crow or a similar bird — **caw** *vb* [I]

cay·enne pepper /ˌkaɪ'en-, ˌkeɪ'en-/ *n* [U] : a red powder that is made from hot peppers and that is used as a spice to give a hot taste to food

CB /ˌsiː'biː/ *n* [U] : a range of radio frequencies that people and especially truck drivers use to talk to each other over short distances often while driving • *a CB radio* ◇ *CB* is an abbreviation of "citizens band."

CBS *abbr* Columbia Broadcasting System ◇ CBS is one of the major television networks in the U.S.

¹**cc** *abbr* **1** cubic centimeter • *a 250cc engine* **2** carbon copy — used to show that a copy of a business letter or an e-mail is also being sent to someone else • *to Meg Thomas, cc Ben Phipps*

²**cc** /ˌsiː'siː/ *vb* **cc's; cc'd; cc'ing** [T] : to send a copy of a business letter or an e-mail to someone in addition to the person addressed • *Please cc the letter to me.* • *He cc'd the entire staff.*

CD /ˌsiː'diː/ *n* **1** [C/U] : a small plastic disk on which information (such as music or computer data) is recorded • *The singer released a new CD* [=a new set of songs recorded on CDs] *last month.* • *a CD player* • *The album is now available on CD.* — called also **compact disc 2** [C] : CERTIFICATE OF DEPOSIT

CD–ROM /ˌsiːˌdiː'rɑːm/ *n* [C/U] : a small plastic disk on which large amounts of information (such as books, pictures, or computer programs) are stored in a form that cannot be changed

CE or chiefly US **C.E.** abbr Christian Era; Common Era — used to refer to the years that come after the birth of Jesus Christ ◇ *C.E.* is now often used instead of *A.D.* especially in scientific writing. — *the first century C.E.* ▪ *883 C.E.*

cease /'si:s/ vb **ceased; ceas·ing** formal **1** [*I*] : to end ▪ *The fighting there has ceased.* [=stopped] ▪ *The court ordered the company to cease and desist from selling the photographs.* [=to immediately stop selling the photographs] **2** [*T*] : to stop doing (something) ▪ *The factory ceased operations last year.* ▪ *Her courage never ceases to amaze me.* [=I am always amazed by her courage] ▪ *The soldiers were ordered to cease fire.* [=to stop shooting their weapons]

cease–fire /'si:s'fajɚ/ n [*C*] : an agreement to stop fighting a war for a period of time

cease·less /'si:sləs/ adj, somewhat formal : seeming to never stop ▪ *ceaseless efforts* — **cease·less·ly** adv

ce·dar /'si:dɚ/ n **1** [*C*] : a very tall evergreen tree **2** [*U*] : the hard, reddish, and pleasant-smelling wood of a cedar ▪ *cedar shingles*

cede /'si:d/ vb **ced·ed; ced·ing** [*T*] formal : to give control of (something) to another person, group, government, etc. ▪ *They ceded their authority.*

ceil·ing /'si:lɪŋ/ n [*C*] **1** : the inside surface at the top of a room ▪ *high/low ceilings* ▪ (figurative) *a ceiling of stars/clouds* **2** : an upper limit ▪ *a price ceiling* — see also GLASS CEILING **3** technical : the greatest height at which an aircraft can fly ▪ *The airplane has a ceiling of 32,000 feet.*

ce·leb /sə'lɛb/ n [*C*] informal : CELEBRITY 1 ▪ *Hollywood celebs*

cel·e·brant /'sɛləbrənt/ n [*C*] formal : a person who performs, leads, or participates in a religious ceremony

cel·e·brate /'sɛlə,breɪt/ vb **-brat·ed; -brat·ing** **1** [*T/I*] : to do something special or enjoyable for an important event, occasion, holiday, etc. ▪ *We celebrated (my birthday) by going out to dinner.* **2** [*T*] formal : to say that (someone or something) is great or important ▪ *He is celebrated for his contributions to modern science.* **3** [*T*] formal : to perform (a religious ceremony) ▪ *A priest celebrates Mass there daily.* — **cel·e·bra·tor** /'sɛlə,breɪtɚ/ n [*C*] — **ce·leb·ra·to·ry** /'sɛlɛbrə,tori, Brit ,sɛlə'breɪtri/ adj ▪ *a celebratory drink/dinner*

celebrated adj : known and praised by many people ▪ *a celebrated artist/book/film/writer*

cel·e·bra·tion /,sɛlə'breɪʃən/ n **1** [*C*] : a party or other special event that you have for an important occasion, holiday, etc. ▪ *a victory/birthday/holiday celebration* **2** [*U*] : the activity of doing special, enjoyable things for an important occasion, achievement, etc. ▪ *It was a night of celebration.* ▪ *We're having a dinner in celebration of their anniversary.* **3** [*C*] : the performance of a religious ceremony ▪ *a celebration of Mass*

ce·leb·ri·ty /sə'lɛbrəti/ n, pl **-ties** **1** [*C*]

: a person who is famous ▪ *There were many celebrities at the party.* ▪ *a celebrity chef/interview* **2** [*U*] formal : FAME ▪ *The actress lived a life of celebrity.*

cel·ery /'sɛləri/ n [*U*] : a vegetable that is grown for its long light green stems ▪ *a stalk of celery*

ce·les·tial /sə'lɛstʃəl, Brit sə'lɛstiəl/ adj : of or relating to the sky or to heaven ▪ *stars, planets, and other celestial bodies* ▪ *celestial beings/music*

cel·i·bate /'sɛləbət/ adj — used to describe a person who is not married and does not have sex ▪ *celibate monks and nuns* ▪ *They lead celibate lives.* — **cel·i·ba·cy** /'sɛləbəsi/ n [*U*] — **celibate** n [*C*]

cell /'sɛl/ n [*C*] **1 a** : a room in a prison, jail, etc., where prisoners live or are kept ▪ *a prison/jail cell* **b** : a small room that one person (such as a monk or a nun) lives in **2** : any one of the very small parts that together form all living things ▪ *blood/brain/skin cells* ▪ *cancer cells* **3** : any one of many similar sections that together form a larger structure ▪ *a honeycomb cell* **4** technical **a** : a container for holding substances that are used for producing electricity by chemical action ▪ *a fuel cell* **b** : a device for changing light (such as sunlight) into electricity ▪ *a solar cell* **5** : a small group of people who work secretly as part of a larger organization or group ▪ *terrorist cells* **6** US, informal : CELL PHONE **7** computers : a space where information can be entered in an organized arrangement of rows and columns — **celled** /'sɛld/ adj ▪ *single-celled organisms*

cel·lar /'sɛlɚ/ n [*C*] : the part of a building that is entirely or partly below the ground

cel·list /'tʃɛlɪst/ n [*C*] : a person who plays the cello

cel·lo /'tʃɛloʊ/ n, pl **-los** [*C*] : a large musical instrument like a violin that is held between the player's knees while the player sits

cel·lo·phane /'sɛlə,feɪn/ n [*U*] : a thin transparent material that is used for wrapping things

cell phone n [*C*] chiefly US : a small telephone that people can take with them and use outside their homes

cel·lu·lar /'sɛljəlɚ/ adj **1** : of, relating to, or made of the cells of living things ▪ *He studied the disease at the cellular level.* **2** : relating to a system that uses radio waves instead of wires to send telephone signals ▪ *a cellular network*

cellular phone n [*C*] chiefly US : CELL PHONE

cel·lu·loid /'sɛljə,lɔɪd/ n [*U*] **1** : a tough kind of plastic that was used in the past to make photographic film and other products **2** : the film used to make movies ▪ *The event was captured on celluloid.* [=was filmed] ▪ *celluloid stars of old Hollywood*

cel·lu·lose /'sɛljə,loʊs/ n [*U*] : a substance that is the main part of the cell walls of plants and that is used in making various products (such as paper)

Cel·si·us /'sɛlsijəs/ adj : relating to or having a scale for measuring temperature on which the boiling point of water is at 100 degrees and the freezing point of water is at 0 degrees • *The Celsius scale* • *The temperature was 23 degrees Celsius.* — abbr. *C*; compare FAHRENHEIT

Celt /'kɛlt, 'sɛlt/ *n* [C] : a member of a group of people (such as the Irish or Welsh) who lived in ancient Britain and parts of western Europe — **Celt·ic** /'kɛltɪk, 'sɛltɪk/ *adj* • *Celtic music/history/languages*

¹**ce·ment** /sɪ'mɛnt/ *n* [U] **1 a** : a soft gray powder that is mixed with water and other substances to make concrete **b** : the hard substance that is made when cement is mixed with water and allowed to dry : CONCRETE • *cement blocks* • *a cement floor* **2** : a substance that is used to make things stick together : GLUE • *rubber cement*

²**cement** *vb* [T] **1** : to join (things) together with cement • *The parts are cemented together.* **2** : to make (something) stronger • *Working together helped to cement their relationship.*

cem·e·tery /'sɛmə,teri, *Brit* 'sɛmətri/ *n, pl* **-ter·ies** [C] : a place where dead people are buried

cen·sor /'sɛnsɚ/ *vb* [T] : to examine books, movies, letters, etc., in order to remove things that are considered to be offensive, immoral, harmful to society, etc. • *His report was heavily censored.* — **censor** *n* [C] • *a government censor* [=a person who censors books, movies, etc., for the government]

cen·sor·ship /'sɛnsɚ,ʃɪp/ *n* [U] : the system or practice of censoring books, movies, letters, etc. • *censorship of the press/media*

¹**cen·sure** /'sɛnʃɚ/ *n* [U] *formal* : official strong criticism • *The country faces international censure for its policies.*

²**censure** *vb* **-sured; -sur·ing** [T] *formal* : to officially criticize (someone or something) strongly and publicly • *He was censured by the committee.*

cen·sus /'sɛnsəs/ *n* [C] : the official process of counting the number of people in a country, city, or town and collecting information about them

cent /'sɛnt/ *n* [C] : a unit of money that is equal to ¹⁄₁₀₀ of the basic unit of money in many countries • *A dime is worth 10 cents.* — **two cents** *US, informal* : someone's opinion about something • *He'll offer his two cents on any topic.*

cen·taur /'sɛn,toɚ/ *n* [C] : a creature in Greek mythology that is part human and part horse

cen·ten·a·ry /sɛn'tɛnəri, *Brit* sɛn'ti:nri/ *n, pl* **-ries** [C] *Brit* : CENTENNIAL — **centenary** *adj*

cen·ten·ni·al /sɛn'tɛniəl/ *n* [C] *US* : the 100th anniversary of something (such as an important event) — **centennial** *adj, always before a noun* • *a centennial year/celebration*

¹**cen·ter** (*US*) *or Brit* **cen·tre** /'sɛntɚ/ *n* **1** [C] : the middle point or part of something • *the center of the room/circle* • *candies with a soft center* • *the center aisle/lane* **2** [*singular*] **a** : a person or thing that is causing a lot of interest, argu-

ment, etc. • *a center of controversy* • *He likes to be the* **center of attention.** [=he likes to be noticed and watched by many people] **b** : the position of a person or thing that is causing a lot of interest, argument, etc. • *They are at the center of the debate.* **3** [C] : a building or set of buildings used by the people of a city, town, area, etc., for a particular purpose • *a day-care center* **4** [C] : a place where a particular activity happens • *the city's financial/business/cultural center* **5** [C] : an area where many people live • *a population/urban center* **6** [C] : the main part of a town or city where there are many stores, restaurants, offices, etc. • *the town/city center* **7** [*singular*] : a moderate political position between the positions of people who are conservative and liberal • *political views that are right/left of center* **8** [C] *sports* : someone who plays a middle position on a team in sports like basketball, hockey, football, and soccer

²**center** (*US*) *or Brit* **centre** *vb* **1** [T] : to place (something) in the middle of something • *Center the picture on the wall.* • *The pain is centered around/in his lower back.* **2 a** [*I*] : to be mainly concerned about or involved with someone or something • *Her life centers on/around her children.* **b** [T] : to cause (something) to be mainly concerned about or involved with something • *She centers his life on/around her children.* **3** [T] : to have the main or most important part of (something, such as an organization or activity) *in* or *at* a specified place • *an organization that is centered in Cairo* — see also CENTERED

cen·tered (*US*) *or Brit* **cen·tred** /'sɛntɚd/ *adj* **1** : mainly concerned about or involved with something specified • *a family-centered hotel* **2** : having a specified kind of center • *a dark-centered flower* **3** : emotionally healthy and calm • *She's more centered now.*

center field *n* [U] : the part of the baseball outfield between right field and left field; *also* : the position of the player defending center field • *She plays center field.* — **center fielder** *n* [C]

cen·ter·fold (*US*) *or Brit* **cen·tre·fold** /'sɛntɚ,foʊld/ *n* [C] **1** : the pages that face each other in the middle of a magazine or newspaper **2** : a picture of a person (such as a woman who is not wearing clothes) that is in the centerfold of a magazine

center of gravity (*US*) *or Brit* **centre of gravity** *n* [*singular*] : the point at which the entire weight of something can be balanced • *Its low center of gravity makes the car very stable.*

cen·ter·piece (*US*) *or Brit* **cen·tre·piece** /'sɛntɚ,pi:s/ *n* **1** [C] : a decoration (such as a group of flowers) that is placed in the center of a table **2** [U] : the most important part of something • *the centerpiece of her campaign/speech*

center stage (*US*) *or Brit* **centre stage** *n* [*singular*] **1** : the middle section of a theater's stage **2** : a main or very important position • *The issue is expected to* *take center stage in the elections.*

cen·ti·grade /'sɛntəˌgreɪd/ *adj* : CELSIUS

cen·ti·gram /'sɛntəˌgræm/ *n* [C] : a weight equal to ¹⁄₁₀₀ gram

cen·ti·li·ter (*US*) *or Brit* **cen·ti·li·tre** /'sɛntəˌliːtə/ *n* [C] : a unit for measuring the volume of a liquid or gas that is equal to ¹⁄₁₀₀ liter or 10 cubic centimeters

cen·ti·me·ter (*US*) *or Brit* **cen·ti·me·tre** /'sɛntəˌmiːtə/ *n* [C] : a length equal to ¹⁄₁₀₀ meter

cen·ti·pede /'sɛntəˌpiːd/ *n* [C] : a small creature that is like an insect and that has a long, thin body and many legs

¹**cen·tral** /'sɛntrəl/ *adj* **1** *always before a noun* : in the middle of something ▪ *a country in central Africa* **2** : main or most important ▪ *the novel's central character* ▪ *a central belief/claim* **3** *always before a noun* : controlling all other parts ▪ *local and central governments* **4** : designed to reach all parts of a building — **central heat/air-conditioning** — **cen·tral·i·ty** /sɛn'træləti/ *n* [U] — **cen·tral·ly** /'sɛntrəli/ *adv* ▪ *centrally located*

²**central** *n* [*singular*] *US, informal* : a place where an activity takes place or a group meets ▪ *Their house is party central on weekends.*

cen·tral·ize *also Brit* **cen·tral·ise** /'sɛntrəˌlaɪz/ *vb* **-ized; -iz·ing** [T] **1** : to bring (things that are in different places) together at a single point or place ▪ *Shipping operations are centralized at the Miami office.* **2** : to bring (something) under the control of one authority ▪ *centralize control/power* ▪ *a centralized authority/government* — **cen·tral·i·za·tion** *also Brit* **cen·tral·i·sa·tion** /ˌsɛntrələ'zeɪʃən, *Brit* ˌsɛntrəˌlaɪ'zeɪʃən/ *n* [U]

central nervous system *n* [C] : the part of the nervous system that includes the brain and spinal cord

central processing unit *n* [C] : CPU

centre *Brit spelling of* CENTER

cen·trif·u·gal force /sɛn'trɪfjəgəl-, *Brit* ˌsɛntrɪ'fjuːgəl-/ *n* [C/U] *physics* : a force that causes an object moving in a circular path to move out and away from the center of its path

cen·tri·fuge /'sɛntrəˌfjuːdʒ/ *n* [C] : a machine that uses centrifugal force to separate substances or parts of substances

cen·trist /'sɛntrɪst/ *n* [C] : a person whose political opinions are not extreme — **centrist** *adj*

cen·tu·ry /'sɛntʃəri/ *n, pl* **-ries** [C] **1** : a period of 100 years **2** : a period of 100 years counted from the beginning of the Christian era ▪ *the third century A.D.* ▪ *the crime/wedding of the century*

CEO /ˌsiːˌiːˈoʊ/ *n* [C] : the person who has the most authority in an organization or business ◇ *CEO* is an abbreviation of "chief executive officer."

ce·ram·ic /sə'ræmɪk/ *adj* : made of clay that has been heated to a very high temperature so that it becomes hard ▪ *a ceramic bead/bowl/tile*

ce·ram·ics /sə'ræmɪks/ *n* **1** [U] : the art of making things out of clay ▪ *a ceramics class* **2** [*plural*] : ceramic objects ▪ *ancient Greek ceramics*

ce·re·al /'sɪrijəl/ *n* **1** [C] : a plant (such as a grass) that produces grain that can be eaten **2** [C/U] : a breakfast food made from grain ▪ *a bowl of cereal* ▪ *breakfast cereals*

cer·e·bel·lum /ˌsɛrə'bɛləm/ *n, pl* **-lums** *or* **-la** /-lə/ [C] : the back part of the brain that controls balance and the use of muscles

ce·re·bral /sə'riːbrəl, 'sɛrəbrəl/ *adj* **1** *always before a noun* : of or relating to the brain ▪ *a cerebral hemorrhage* **2** : intellectual and not emotional ▪ *a very cerebral comedian/novel*

cerebral pal·sy /-'pɑːlzi/ *n* [U] : a disease that causes a person to have problems moving and speaking

ce·re·brum /sə'riːbrəm, 'sɛrəbrəm/ *n, pl* **-brums** *or chiefly Brit* **-bra** /-brə/ [C] : the front part of the brain that is believed to be where thoughts occur

cer·e·mo·ni·al /ˌsɛrə'moʊnijəl/ *adj* **1 a** : used in or done as part of a ceremony ▪ *a ceremonial dance/mask* **b** : including a ceremony ▪ *a ceremonial occasion* **2** : without real power or influence ▪ *a ceremonial position* — **cer·e·mo·ni·al·ly** *adv*

cer·e·mo·ni·ous /ˌsɛrə'moʊnijəs/ *adj* : formal and serious ▪ *She read the announcement in a very ceremonious way.* — **cer·e·mo·ni·ous·ly** *adv*

cer·e·mo·ny /'sɛrəˌmoʊni/ *n, pl* **-nies** **1** [C] : a formal act or event that is a part of a social or religious occasion ▪ *graduation/wedding ceremonies* **2** [U] : very polite or formal behavior ▪ *She presented the gifts with great ceremony.* ▪ *He told them abruptly and without ceremony that they would have to leave.*

¹**cer·tain** /'sɚtn/ *adj* **1** *not before a noun* : not having any doubt about something : SURE ▪ *Are you certain you want to do this?* **2** — used to say that something will definitely happen or that someone will definitely do something ▪ *Her defeat/victory seems certain.* ▪ *It is certain that the company will lay off workers.* **3** *always before a noun* — used to refer to something or someone that is not named specifically ▪ *She's allergic to certain foods.* — **a certain 1** — used to refer to a quality that is noticed but that is difficult to explain or describe ▪ *The house has a certain charm.* **2** *formal* — used with the name of a person you do not know ▪ *In 1889, a certain Mr. Kelly made a large donation to the church.* — **for certain** : definitely or certainly ▪ *No one knows for certain what happened.* — **make certain** : to do something or find out something so that you have no doubt about whether something is true, correct, will happen, etc. ▪ *Make certain (that) you lock the door when you leave.*

²**certain** *pron, formal* : certain members of a group ▪ *Certain of his ideas are quite good.*

cer·tain·ly /'sɚtnli/ *adv* **1** : without doubt ▪ *It will certainly rain tomorrow.* ▪ *The new version is most certainly easier to use.* — sometimes used for emphasis ▪ *I certainly didn't mean to offend anyone.* **2** : of course — used to answer questions

cer·tain·ty /ˈsɝtnti/ n, pl **-ties** 1 [U] : the state of being or feeling certain about something ▪ *We cannot predict the outcome with absolute/any certainty.* ▪ *It is difficult to say with certainty when they met.* 2 [C] : a fact about which there is no doubt ▪ *We live in a world without certainties.*

cer·ti·fi·able /ˈsɝtəˌfajəbəl/ adj 1 *informal* : crazy or insane ▪ *certifiable behavior* 2 *always before a noun, chiefly US* : real or genuine ▪ *a certifiable expert/masterpiece*

cer·tif·i·cate /sɚˈtɪfɪkət/ n [C] 1 : a document that is official proof that something has happened 2 : a document that is official proof that you have finished school or a course of training ▪ *a teaching certificate* 3 : a document which shows that you own something ▪ *a stock certificate*

cer·tif·i·cat·ed /sɚˈtɪfɪˌkeɪtəd/ adj, Brit : CERTIFIED 1 ▪ *a certificated teacher*

certificate of deposit n [C] chiefly US : an official document in which a bank promises to pay a specified amount of interest when you deposit money in the bank for a specified period of time — called also CD

cer·ti·fied /ˈsɝtəˌfaɪd/ adj 1 : having met the official requirements that are needed to do a particular type of work ▪ *a certified instructor* 2 chiefly US **a** : officially approved as having met a standard ▪ *certified organic vegetables* **b** *informal* : real or genuine ▪ *a certified celebrity*

certified check (US) or Brit **certified cheque** n [C] : a check that is guaranteed by a bank

certified public accountant n [C] US : an accountant who has finished the schooling or tests required by law — abbr. CPA

cer·ti·fy /ˈsɝtəˌfaɪ/ vb **-fies; -fied; -fy·ing** [T] 1 : to say officially that something is true, correct, or genuine ▪ *A judge must certify the contract.* 2 : to say officially that something or someone has met certain standards or requirements ▪ *Has your doctor been certified?* — **cer·ti·fi·ca·tion** /ˌsɝtəfəˈkeɪʃən/ n [C/U]

cer·ti·tude /ˈsɝtəˌtuːd, Brit ˈsɝːtəˌtjuːd/ n [U] : the state of being or feeling certain ▪ *moral certitude*

cer·vi·cal /ˈsɝvɪkəl/ adj 1 : of or relating to a cervix of the uterus ▪ *cervical cancer* 2 : of or relating to the neck ▪ *cervical vertebrae*

cer·vix /ˈsɝvɪks/ n, pl **-vi·ces** /-vəˌsiːz/ or **-vix·es** [C] : the narrow end at the opening of a woman's uterus

ce·sar·e·an or **cae·sar·e·an** /sɪˈzerijən/ n [C] medical : CESAREAN SECTION — **cesarean** or **caesarean** adj ▪ *a cesarean birth*

cesarean section also **caesarean section** n [C] medical : a surgical operation for giving birth in which a cut is made in the mother's body so that the baby can be removed through the opening — called also C-section

ces·sa·tion /sɛˈseɪʃən/ n [C/U] formal : a stopping of some action ▪ *a cessation of hostilities*

cess·pit /ˈsɛsˌpɪt/ n [C] chiefly Brit : CESSPOOL

cess·pool /ˈsɛsˌpuːl/ n [C] 1 : an underground hole or container for holding liquid waste (such as sewage) from a building 2 : a place or situation that is very dirty, evil, or corrupt ▪ *a cesspool of corruption*

cf abbr compare — used to direct a reader to another idea, document, etc. ✧ *Cf* comes from the Latin *conferre*, which means "to compare."

CFC abbr chlorofluorocarbon

CFO abbr chief financial officer

chafe /ˈtʃeɪf/ vb **chafed; chaf·ing** 1 [I] : to feel irritated or annoyed ▪ *She chafed at being stuck in an office all day.* 2 [T/I] : to cause soreness or damage by rubbing against something (such as your skin) ▪ *If the strap is too tight, it can chafe (the baby's skin).* **b** [I] : to become sore or damaged from rubbing ▪ *The baby's skin will chafe if the strap is too tight.*

chaff /ˈtʃæf, Brit ˈtʃɑːf/ n [U] : the seed coverings and other plant parts that cannot be eaten and are removed from grain

cha·grin /ʃəˈɡrɪn, Brit ˈʃæɡrɪn/ n [U] : a feeling of being frustrated or annoyed because of failure or disappointment ▪ *She had gained five pounds, much to her chagrin.* — **cha·grined** also **cha·grinned** /ʃəˈɡrɪnd, Brit ˈʃæɡrɪnd/ adj ▪ *They were chagrined to find that they were wrong.*

¹**chain** /ˈtʃeɪn/ n 1 **a** [C/U] : a series of usually metal links or rings that are connected to each other in a line ▪ *Their dog is kept on a chain.* ▪ *She wore a beautiful gold chain around her neck.* ▪ *a bicycle chain* **b** [C] : a chain that is attached to the arms or legs of a prisoner — usually plural ▪ *The prisoners were kept in chains.* 2 [C] : a series or group of things or people that are connected to each other in some way ▪ *a chain of islands* ▪ *a mountain chain* ▪ *a chain of events* ▪ *The protesters formed a human chain.* [=they stood next to each other with their arms linked] — see also FOOD CHAIN 3 [C] : a group of businesses (such as stores, restaurants, or hotels) that have the same name and basic appearance and sell the same products or services ▪ *fast-food/clothing chains* ▪ *a hotel chain* — **pull/yank someone's chain** US, informal : to deceive someone in a friendly or playful way ▪ *I thought he was really angry but he was only pulling my chain.*

²**chain** vb [T] : to fasten, hold, or connect (someone or something) with a chain ▪ *She chained her bicycle to the post.* ▪ *The prisoners were chained together.* ▪ (figurative) *She spends the day chained to the computer.* [=she works with a computer all day]

chain gang n [C] : a group of prisoners who are chained together while they do work outside the prison

chain letter n [C] : a letter that is sent to

a certain number of people and that asks each of those people to send a copy of the letter to the same number of people

chain–link fence n [C] : a fence of heavy steel wire that is woven to form a pattern of large diamond-shaped spaces

chain mail n [U] : a kind of protective armor that was worn by knights and soldiers in the Middle Ages

chain of command n [C] : a series of positions of authority or rank within an organization that are ordered from lowest to highest • *the head of the military chain of command*

chain reaction n [C] **1** : a series of events in which each event causes the next one **2** *technical* : a chemical or nuclear change that causes other changes of the same kind to happen

chain saw n [C] : a tool that cuts wood with a circular chain that is driven by a motor and made up of many connected sharp metal teeth

chain–smoke /ˈtʃeɪnˌsmoʊk/ vb **-smoked; -smoking** [T/I] : to smoke cigarettes continuously one after another • *She chain-smokes (cigarettes).* — **chain–smok·er** n [C]

¹**chair** /ˈtʃeɚ/ n [C] **1** : a seat for one person that has a back and usually four legs • *sitting in a chair by the window* **2 a** : the person who is the head of a department at a college or university • *He is now (the) chair of the English department.* **b** : the person who is the leader of a meeting, organization, committee, or event • *She's (the) chair of the school board.*

²**chair** vb [T] : to be in charge of a meeting, organization, committee, or event • *He will chair the task force on school violence.*

chair·lift /ˈtʃeɚˌlɪft/ n [C] : a series of seats that hang from a moving cable and that carry people (such as skiers) up and down a mountain

chair·man /ˈtʃeɚmən/ n, pl **-men** /-mən/ [C] **1** : the person (especially a man) who is in charge of a meeting, committee, or event • *the chairman of the task force* **2** : the person who is in charge of a company or organization • *the chairman of the airline/company* — **chair·man·ship** /ˈtʃeɚmənˌʃɪp/ n [C] • *She took over the chairmanship of the company.*

chair·per·son /ˈtʃeɚˌpɚsn/ n [C] : the person who leads a meeting, organization, committee, or event

chair·wom·an /ˈtʃeɚˌwʊmən/ n, pl **-wom·en** /-ˌwɪmən/ [C] : a woman who leads a meeting, organization, committee, or event

chaise longue /ˈʃeɪzˈlɑːŋ/ n, pl **chaise longues** or **chaises longues** /ˈʃeɪzˈlɑːŋ/ [C] **1** : a long low chair with a back along half its length and one arm **2** *US* : a long chair with a back that can be moved so that you can sit up or lie down — called also (*US*) *chaise lounge*

cha·let /ʃæˈleɪ/ n [C] : a type of house that has a steep roof that extends past the walls • *a ski chalet*

chal·ice /ˈtʃæləs/ n [C] : a special cup for holding wine; *especially* : the cup used in the Christian ceremony of Communion

¹**chalk** /ˈtʃɑːk/ n **1** [U] : a type of soft, light-colored rock **2 a** [U] : a substance that is made into white or colored sticks and used for writing or drawing **b** [C] : a piece of chalk • *They drew on the sidewalk with colored chalks.* — **chalky** /ˈtʃɑːki/ adj **chalk·i·er; -est**

²**chalk** vb [T] : to write or draw with chalk • *She chalked a message on the side of the barn.* — **chalk up** [phrasal vb] **chalk (something) up** or **chalk up (something) 1** : to earn or achieve (something) • *The team chalked up another victory.* **2** *chalk (something) up to chiefly US* : to say that (something) was caused by (something) • *Her early mistakes can be chalked up to inexperience.*

chalk·board /ˈtʃɑːkˌboɚd/ n [C] *chiefly US* : BLACKBOARD

¹**chal·lenge** /ˈtʃæləndʒ/ vb **-lenged; -leng·ing** [T] **1** : DISPUTE • *Many doctors challenged the study's claims.* **2** : to question the action or authority of (someone) • *He challenged the referee on the call.* **3** : to test the ability, skill, or strength of (someone or something) • *The work doesn't challenge him anymore.* **4** : to invite (someone) to compete in a game, fight, etc. • *I challenge you to a rematch.* — **chal·leng·er** n [C] • *The champion defeated the/his challenger.*

²**challenge** n **1** [C/U] : a difficult task or problem • *Teaching adolescents can be quite a challenge.* • *seeking ways to* **meet the challenge** *of future growth* **2** [C] : a refusal to accept something as true, correct, or legal • *challenges to her authority* **3** [C] **a** : an invitation to compete in a game, fight, etc. • *I accepted his challenge to a rematch.* **b** : an attempt to defeat someone in a competition • *The senator faced a challenge from within her own party.*

challenged adj, *chiefly US* : having a physical or mental problem that makes it difficult to do things as easily as other people do — used as a polite way to say that a person has a disability • *an advocate for the mentally and physically challenged* [=*disabled*]

chal·leng·ing /ˈtʃæləndʒɪŋ/ adj : difficult in a way that is usually interesting or enjoyable • *Teaching is challenging but rewarding work.* — **chal·leng·ing·ly** adv

cham·ber /ˈtʃeɪmbɚ/ n [C] **1** : a small space inside something (such as a machine or your body) • *the chambers of the heart* **2** : a usually large room where members of a government group (such as a legislature) have meetings • *the Senate chamber* **3** : a group of people who form part of a government • *The U.S. legislature is separated into two chambers: the Senate and the House of Representatives.* **4** : a room where a judge goes to do official business or to discuss cases with lawyers outside of the courtroom — usually plural • *the judge's chambers* **5** *formal + old-fashioned* : a person's bedroom or other private room • *the queen's personal chambers* **6** : a room used for a special purpose • *a burial/torture chamber*

cham·ber·maid /ˈʧeɪmbɚˌmeɪd/ n [C] : a woman who cleans bedrooms in hotels

chamber music n [U] : classical music written for a small number of musicians

chamber of commerce n [C] : a group of businesspeople who work together to try to help businesses in their town or city

cha·me·leon /kəˈmiːljən/ n [C] **1 :** a type of lizard that can change the color of its skin to look like the colors that are around it **2** usually disapproving : a person who often changes his or her beliefs or behavior in order to please others or to succeed • a political chameleon

cham·o·mile or **cam·o·mile** /ˈkæməˌmaɪl/ n [U] : a plant that has a strong smell and small white and yellow flowers that are often used in making tea and medicine • chamomile tea

¹champ /ˈʧæmp/ n [C] informal : CHAMPION

²champ vb [T/I] : to bite and chew on (something) in a noisy way : CHOMP • He champed (on) his pipe angrily. — **champing at the bit** : waiting in an impatient way to do something • We've all been champing at the bit to get started on the project.

cham·pagne /ʃæmˈpeɪn/ n [C/U] : a French white wine that has many bubbles and that people often drink on special occasions

¹cham·pi·on /ˈʧæmpijən/ n [C] **1 :** someone or something (such as a team or an animal) that has won a contest or competition especially in sports • the heavyweight boxing champion of the world • the current/national/world/Olympic champions • a champion boxer/skier/swimmer **2 :** someone who fights or speaks publicly in support of a person, belief, cause, etc. • She is a champion of children's rights.

²champion vb [T] : to fight or speak publicly in support of (a person, belief, cause, etc.) • a lawyer who champions children's rights

cham·pi·on·ship /ˈʧæmpijənˌʃɪp/ n [C] **1 :** an important competition that decides which player or team is the best in a particular sport, game, etc. • the heavyweight boxing championship • this year's basketball championships • a championship game/race/match/competition **2 :** the title of champion in a sport or game • The team hasn't won a championship in 30 years.

¹chance /ˈʧæns, Brit ˈʧɑːns/ n **1** [C/U] : an opportunity to do something • I wanted to call you, but I never got/had the chance (to). • I go there every chance I get. [=whenever I can] • Give me a chance to explain. • We didn't have much chance to talk about it. • He still has a fighting chance to succeed. [=he may still be able to succeed by making a great effort] **2** [C/U] : the possibility that something will happen • a 50 percent chance of rain • They have no/little chance of winning. • Chances are [=it is very likely that] she has already heard the news. • I like their chances. [=I think they have a good

chance. of succeeding/winning] ◆ The phrase **by any chance** is used when asking questions in a polite way. • Are you free tonight, by any chance? ◆ The informal phrases **fat chance** and **not a chance** are used as a forceful way of saying that there is no possibility that something will happen. • "He says that he'll be on time." "Fat chance!" **3** [U] : LUCK • We planned for everything and left nothing to chance. [=we prepared for everything possible] ◆ If something happens **by chance**, people have not planned it or tried to make it happen. • We found the house entirely by chance. ◆ A **game of chance** is a game (such as a dice game) in which luck rather than skill decides who wins. — **on the off chance** — used to talk about something that might happen or be true but that is not likely • I called his office on the off chance that he would still be there. — **stand a chance** : to have a possibility of succeeding • I think she **stands a good chance** of winning the election. • She **stands no chance** of winning. — **take a chance** : to do something that could have either good or bad results • He said he couldn't afford to take any chances. • He's not afraid to take chances. [=to do things that are risky or dangerous]

²chance vb chanced; chanc·ing **1** [T] : to accept the danger of (doing something) • We knew it might rain, but we decided to chance it. **2** [I] formal — used to describe something that happens because of luck or chance • We chanced [=happened] to arrive at the same time. — **chance upon** also **chance on** [phrasal vb] formal : to find (something) or meet (someone) by chance • She chanced upon a copy of the book.

³chance adj, always before a noun : happening without being planned or controlled • a chance event/occurrence/discovery/encounter

chan·cel·lery or **chan·cel·lory** /ˈʧænsələri, Brit ˈʧɑːnsələri/ n, pl **-ler·ies** or **-lor·ies** [C] : the department of a chancellor or the building where a chancellor's office is located

chan·cel·lor /ˈʧænsələ, Brit ˈʧɑːnsələ/ n [C] **1 :** the highest government official in Germany and Austria **2 a :** the head of some U.S. universities **b :** the head of a British university who represents the school but who does not have many responsibilities **3** Brit : CHANCELLOR OF THE EXCHEQUER

Chancellor of the Exchequer n [C] : an official in the British government who is in charge of taxes and the money that the government spends

chan·cery /ˈʧænsəri, Brit ˈʧɑːnsəri/ n [singular] **1 :** a government office where public documents are kept **2 a :** a type of court in the U.S. **b** Chancery : a part of the High Court in England and Wales **3 :** the office of an embassy

chancy /ˈʧænsi, Brit ˈʧɑːnsi/ adj chanc·i·er; -est informal : RISKY • Opening a new restaurant can be chancy.

chan·de·lier /ˌʃændəˈliɚ/ n [C] : a large, decorated light that hangs from a ceiling and has branches for holding many light bulbs or candles

¹change /ˈʧeɪnʤ/ vb **changed; changing** 1 a [I] : to become different • *The leaves change (in color) from green to red in the fall.* • *The town has changed little in recent years.* • *the changing times* b [T] : to make (someone or something) different • *He's changed his appearance with a new haircut.* • *You can't change human nature.* • *(US, informal) She changed up her daily routine.* c [I] : to become something else • *Winter changed to/into spring.* 2 [T/I] a : to replace one thing or person with another • *She changed her name when she got married.* • *She's going to change jobs/dentists.* • *change the channel on the TV* • *Let's change the subject.* [=let's talk about a different subject] b : to move from one position, place, etc., to another • *I changed places/seats with him.* • *He opposed the parlace at first, but then he changed sides and voted in favor of it.* 3 [T] a : to exchange one kind of money for another kind • *change dollars into/for pounds* b : to exchange a larger bill for an equal amount in smaller bills or coins • *I need to change a $10 bill: can you give me a five and five ones?* 4 a [T/I] : to put on different clothes • *Let me change (out of this suit) into something more comfortable.* • *I need to change my clothes.* b [T] : to put clean clothes on (a baby) • *change a baby = change a baby's diaper* c [T] : to put a fresh covering on (a bed) • *change a bed = change the sheets on a bed* 5 [T/I] : to move from one plane, train, etc., to another in order to continue a journey • *We had to change (planes) in Chicago.* — **change around** or Brit **change round** [phrasal vb] **change (something) around/round** or **change around/round (something)** : to change the order or positions of the parts of (something) • *The schedule has been changed around a little.* — **change down** [phrasal vb] Brit : to change to a lower gear in a motor vehicle — **change hands** : to go from one owner to another • *The restaurant recently changed hands.* [=the restaurant was recently bought by a new owner] — **change over** [phrasal vb] **change over** or **change over** (something) **over** or **change over** (something) : to go from one system, method, etc., to another or to change (one system, method, etc.) to another • *We are changing over to a new computer network.* — **change someone's/your mind** see **¹MIND** — **change up** [phrasal vb] Brit : to change to a higher gear in a motor vehicle — **chang·er** n [C] • *a CD changer*

²change n 1 [C/U] : the act, process, or result of changing • *a change in her routine* • *making changes in/to the system* • *a change of address/name* • *There's been a change of plan.* [=we have changed our plans] • *a change for the better/worse* 2 [singular] : something that is different from what is usual or expected • *We've been so busy that a quiet day at home was a welcome change.* • *(chiefly Brit) So you've done the cooking for once in your life! Well, that makes a change!* • *I could really use a change of scene/scenery.* [=I would like to go somewhere else for a time] 3 [U] a : smaller bills or coins that are given for a larger bill • *Have you got change for a $10 bill?* b : the money returned when a payment is more than the amount needed • *It cost $9 and I gave you $10, so I should be getting $1 in change.* • *(US) Can you make change for a twenty?* [=can you give me change if I pay with a $20 bill?] c : money in the form of coins • *a pocketful of loose change* d US, informal : MONEY • *She inherited a large/hefty/nice chunk of change.* [=a large amount of money] 4 [C] : a clean set of clothes that someone can wear if they are needed • *a change of underwear* — **and change** US, informal : and a very small additional amount • *There's only six minutes and change* [=only a little more than six minutes] *left in the game.* — **for a change** : as something different from what is usual • *Let's eat out for a change.*

change·able /ˈʧeɪnʤəbəl/ adj 1 : able to change or to be changed • *The terms of this contract are easily changeable.* 2 : changing often or suddenly • *changeable people/weather*

change·less /ˈʧeɪnʤləs/ adj : never changing • *the changeless rhythms of nature* • *changeless values*

change of heart n [singular] : an important change in the way a person feels or thinks about something • *He had a change of heart about retiring and decided to continue working.*

change of pace n [C] 1 : a new activity or situation that comes after another activity or situation which has lasted for a long time • *Their vacation was a much-needed change of pace.* 2 baseball : CHANGEUP

change·over /ˈʧeɪnʤˌoʊvɚ/ n [C] : a change from one condition, system, method, etc., to another • *the changeover from the franc to the euro*

change purse n [C] US : a very small bag for carrying coins

change·up /ˈʧeɪnʤˌʌp/ n [C] baseball : a slow pitch that is thrown with the same motion as a fastball in order to fool the batter

changing room n [C] : a room where people can change their clothes in a public place (such as a store); especially, Brit : LOCKER ROOM

changing table n [C] : a table used for changing a baby's clothes or diapers

¹chan·nel /ˈʧænl/ n [C] 1 : a television or radio station • *The TV program airs at 8:00 p.m. on Channel 5.* • *a movie/news/ sports channel* 2 a : a system used for sending something (such as information or supplies) from one place or person to another • *a channel of communication* • *the army's distribution/supply channels* b : a way of expressing your ideas, feelings, etc., to other people • *Art provides a channel for creativity.* 3 : a path, tube, or long narrow place where water flows • *a system of irrigation channels* 4 : a deep part of a river, harbor, or other body of water where ships can go • *a narrow channel of the Mississippi River* **5** : a narrow area of the sea between two large areas of land that are close together • *crossing the English Channel*

²**channel** *vb, US* -neled *or Brit* -nelled; *US* -nel·ing *or Brit* -nel·ling [T] **1** : to express (your ideas, thoughts, feelings, energy, etc.) through a particular behavior or action • *She's started channeling her anger towards me.* • *His aggression was channeled into playing football.* **2** : to send (food, money, etc.) to someone or something • *Food, clothes, and money were channeled through churches to people in need.* **3** : to carry and move (something, such as water) in or through a tube, passage, etc. • *Pipes channel water to the fields.*

channel surfing *n* [U] : the activity of using a remote control to change television stations quickly as you look for something to watch — called also *channel-hopping*

¹**chant** /ˈtʃænt, *Brit* ˈtʃɑːnt/ *vb* [T/I] **1** : to say (a word or phrase) many times in a rhythmic way usually loudly and with other people • *The crowd was chanting her name.* **2** : to sing words and especially religious prayers by using a small number of musical notes that are repeated many times • *Priests chanted the Catholic Mass in Latin.*

²**chant** *n* **1** [C] : a word or phrase that is repeated in a rhythmic way usually loudly and by a group of people **2** [C/U] : a kind of singing that uses a small number of musical notes that are repeated- many times • *a religious chant*

Chanukah *variant spelling of* HANUKKAH

cha·os /ˈkeɪˌɑːs/ *n* [U] : complete confusion and disorder • *The loss of electricity caused chaos throughout the city.*

cha·ot·ic /keɪˈɑːtɪk/ *adj* : in a state of complete confusion or disorder • *a chaotic political race* • *His life became chaotic.* — **cha·ot·i·cal·ly** /keɪˈɑːtɪkli/ *adv*

chap /ˈtʃæp/ *n* [C] *chiefly Brit, informal + somewhat old-fashioned* : a man • *He's a friendly sort of chap.*

chap. *abbr* chapter

chap·el /ˈtʃæpəl/ *n* **1** [C] : a small church • *a wedding chapel* **2** [C] : a room or small building that is used for private church services or prayer by a family or group • *school/hospital/prison chapels* **3** [C] : a room or area in a church that is used for prayer or small religious services **4** [U] : Christian religious services held in a chapel • *We went to chapel every day.*

chap·er·one *also* **chap·er·on** /ˈʃæpəˌroʊn/ *n* [C] **1** *US* : someone (such as a teacher or parent) who goes with children on a trip or to a school dance to make sure that the children behave properly **2** : a person in the past who went with a young unmarried woman to social events in order to make sure that the woman behaved properly — **chaperone** *also* **chaperon** *vb* -oned; -on·ing [T] • *Two parents chaperoned the children.*

chap·lain /ˈtʃæplən/ *n* [C] : a priest or other Christian religious leader who performs religious services for a military group (such as the army) or for a prison, hospital, etc.

chapped /ˈtʃæpt/ *adj, of the skin or lips* : red, dry, and cracked usually because of cold air or wind • *chapped lips/skin*

chaps /ˈʃæps, ˈtʃæps/ *n* [*plural*] : leather coverings for the legs that cowboys and cowgirls wear over their pants when they ride horses • *a pair of chaps*

chap·ter /ˈtʃæptɚ/ *n* [C] **1** : one of the main sections of a book • *Chapter three deals with the country's economy.* **2** : a period of time that is very different from the period of time before it • *a difficult/new chapter in her life* **3** : the people in a certain area who make up one section of a large organization • *local/regional chapters of the American Red Cross* — **chapter and verse** : exact information or details about something • *He can give chapter and verse about/on the dangers of smoking.*

char /ˈtʃɑɚ/ *vb* **charred**; **char·ring** [T/I] : to burn or cook (something) until it is black • *Dad charred the hamburgers on the grill.*

char·ac·ter /ˈkerɪktɚ/ *n* **1** [C] : a person's personality and behavior • *the different aspects/facets of her character* • *character flaws/traits* **2** [C] : a set of qualities that are shared by many people in a group, country, etc. • *the character of a nation* **3** *a* [C/U] : a set of qualities that make a place or thing different from other places or things • *the unique character of the town/city/region* • *This room is not really in character with the rest of the house.* [=is not like the rest of the house] *b* [U] : the qualities or characteristics that make something interesting or special • *The room lacks character.* **4** [C] : a person who appears in a story, book, play, movie, or television show • *the film's lead/main/central character* **5** [C] *informal* *a* : a particular type of person • *He's a strange/interesting character.* *b* : a person who says or does funny or unusual things • *He's a real character!* **6** [U] *a* : the good qualities of a person that usually include moral or emotional strength, honesty, and fairness • *a person of good character* • *He is admired for his **strength of character**.* • *Playing sports is seen as a way to **build character** in young people.* *b* : the usually good beliefs or opinions that most people have about a particular person • *They defended his character.* [=reputation] **7** [C] : a symbol (such as a letter or number) that is used in writing or printing • *the Chinese character for "water"* — **in character, out of character** — used to say that some action or behavior is or is not like someone's usual way of behaving • *It was entirely in character for her to give him the money.* • *His rudeness was completely out of character.* — **char·ac·ter·less** /ˈkerɪktɚləs/ *adj* : *rows of characterless houses*

character actor *n* [C] : an actor who is known for playing many different and unusual characters

character assassination n [U] : the act of saying false things about a person usually in order to make the public stop liking or trusting that person

¹**char·ac·ter·is·tic** /ˌkerɪktəˈrɪstɪk/ adj : typical of a person, thing, or group • his characteristic good humor • Such behavior is not characteristic of her. — **char·ac·ter·is·ti·cal·ly** /ˌkerɪktəˈrɪstɪkli/ adv

²**characteristic** n [C] : a special quality or trait that makes a person, thing, or group different from others • physical/genetic characteristics

char·ac·ter·ize also Brit **char·ac·ter·ise** /ˈkerɪktəˌraɪz/ vb **-ized**; **-iz·ing** [T] somewhat formal **1** : to describe the character or special qualities of (someone or something) • How would you characterize the situation/problem? **2** : to be a typical feature or quality of (someone or something) • Humor and intelligence characterize his writing. • The disease is characterized by a rise in blood pressure. — **char·ac·ter·i·za·tion** also Brit **char·ac·ter·i·sa·tion** /ˌkerɪktərəˈzeɪʃən, Brit ˌkærɪktəˌraɪˈzeɪʃən/ n [C/U]

cha·rade /ʃəˈreɪd, Brit ʃəˈrɑːd/ n **1** [C] : something that is done in order to pretend something is true when it is not really true • Her concern was just a charade. [=she pretended to be concerned but she was not] **2** [plural] : a game in which players try to guess a word or phrase from the actions of another player who is not allowed to speak

char·broil /ˈtʃɑːˌbrojəl/ vb [T] US : to cook (something) on a rack above charcoal • charbroiled steak/chicken

char·coal /ˈtʃɑːˌkoʊl/ n [U] **1** : a hard black material that is made by burning wood with a small amount of air ◊ Charcoal is burned for cooking food and is also made into sticks that are used for drawing pictures. **2** : a dark gray color

Char·don·nay /ˌʃɑːrdnˈeɪ/ n [C/U] : a type of dry white wine

¹**charge** /ˈtʃɑːdʒ/ vb **charged**; **charg·ing** **1** [T] : to put electricity into a battery so that a machine or device will run • We tried to charge the car's battery. **2** [T] formal : to give a job or responsibility to (a person or group) • She works in the department charged with helping veterans. **3** [T] **a** : to formally accuse (someone) of a crime • She was charged with murder. **b** : to say that someone has done something wrong • It is not clear if he violated the rules, as his critics have charged. **c** : to say that a player has broken the rules in a game • The basketball player was charged with a foul. **4 a** [T] : to rush toward (a person, place, etc.) • The bull charged the matador. **b** [I] : to rush in a particular direction • People charged toward the stage. **5** [T] : to create a record of an amount of money that is owed • The clerk charged the purchase to my account. **6** [T/I] : to ask for money in return for providing or doing something • Do you charge (a fee) for fixing flat tires? • The shop charged (me) $100 for the repairs.

²**charge** n **1** [C] **a** : an amount of electricity • an electrical charge **b** : the amount of an explosive material (such as dynamite) that is used in a single blast • He set off a charge that destroyed the mountain. **2** [U] : the responsibility of managing or watching over something • He has charge of the building. • He wanted to **take charge** of the organization. **3** [C] : an amount of money that someone asks for in return for providing or doing something • There is no charge for fixing the tire. • a delivery charge • The concert is **free of charge**. [=costs nothing to attend] • A second member of your family can join **at no charge**. [=without paying] **4** [C] : a law : a formal accusation that someone committed a crime • They dropped the charges against him. • He decided not to **bring/press charges**. [=to formally accuse someone of a crime] **b** : an accusation or criticism • The senator rejects charges that he is too liberal. **5** [C] formal : a person (such as a child) that another person must guard or take care of • She loved to play with her young charges at the day-care center. **6** [C] : a judge's instructions to a jury before it begins deciding a verdict • The judge delivered his charge to the jury. **7** [C] : an act of running or rushing forward especially in order to make an attack • a cavalry charge **8** [singular] US, informal : a feeling of joy or excitement • The children got a **charge out of** [=were amused by] the juggler. — **in charge** : having control of or responsibility for something • She is in charge of hiring new employees.

charge·able /ˈtʃɑːdʒəbəl/ adj **1** : able to be charged • chargeable interest **2** : able to be treated as a crime • a chargeable offense

charge account n [C] US : an arrangement in which a bank, store, etc., allows a customer to buy things with a credit card and pay for them later

charge card n [C] : CREDIT CARD

charged /ˈtʃɑːdʒd/ adj **1** technical : having an amount of electricity • a charged particle **2** : showing or causing strong feelings • a politically charged subject • The crowd was all **charged up**. [=was very excited]

charg·er /ˈtʃɑːdʒɚ/ n [C] **1** : a device that is used to add electricity to batteries **2** literary : a horse that a knight or soldier rides in battle

charge sheet n [C] Brit : RAP SHEET

char·i·ot /ˈtʃerijət/ n [C] : a carriage with two wheels that was pulled by horses and was raced and used in battle in ancient times

char·i·o·teer /ˌtʃerijəˈtiɚ/ n [C] : a driver of a chariot

cha·ris·ma /kəˈrɪzmə/ n [U] : a special charm or appeal that causes people to feel attracted and excited by someone (such as a politician)

char·is·mat·ic /ˌkerəzˈmætɪk/ adj **1** : having great charm or appeal • a charismatic leader **2** — used to describe Christian religious groups whose members believe that they can communicate directly with God to receive help and guidance and the power to heal others • charismatic sects

char·i·ta·ble /ˈʧerət̬əbəl/ adj 1 : done or designed to help people who are poor, sick, etc. ▪ charitable donations/contributions/organizations/causes 2 : showing kindness in talking about or judging other people ▪ She has tried to be charitable about her sister's problems. — **char·i·ta·bly** /ˈʧerət̬əbli/ adv

char·i·ty /ˈʧerət̬i/ n, pl -ties 1 [U] : the act of giving money, food, or other kinds of help to people who are poor, sick, etc. ▪ The holidays are a time for charity and good will.; also : something (such as money or food) that is given to people who are poor, sick, etc. ▪ She refused to accept charity. ◇ The phrase charity begins at home means you should take care of yourself and your family before helping others. 2 a [C] : an organization that helps people who are poor, sick, etc. ▪ a local charity that gives books to children b [U] : the organizations that help people in need ▪ All the money will go to charity. ▪ a charity concert/dinner/event [=a concert/dinner/event held to raise money for a charity]

charity shop n [C] Brit : a store that sells used clothes, goods, etc., in order to raise money for people who are poor, sick, etc.

char·la·tan /ˈʃɑːlət̬ən/ n [C] : a person who pretends to know or be something in order to deceive people

¹**charm** /ˈʧɑːm/ n 1 [C] : something that is believed to have magic powers and especially to prevent bad luck ▪ a good luck charm 2 [C] : a small object that is worn on a chain or bracelet ▪ a gold charm ▪ a charm bracelet 3 [C/U] : a quality that causes someone or something to be very likeable ▪ He fell under the spell of her charms. ▪ The new curtains add charm to the room. — **work like a charm** : to produce a desired result very easily and effectively ▪ The cleaning fluid worked like a charm on the carpet stain. — **charm·less** adj

²**charm** vb [T] 1 : to put a spell on (someone or something) ▪ The snake was charmed by the music. 2 a : to cause (someone) to like you or to do what you want by being nice, friendly, etc. ▪ He charmed the committee into approving his proposal. b : to attract (someone) by being beautiful or welcoming ▪ I was charmed by the cozy country inn. — **charm·er** n [C] ▪ Your little girl is a real charmer. [=she is sweet, cute, etc.] ▪ a snake charmer

charmed /ˈʧɑːmd/ adj : very lucky ▪ She has always lived/led a charmed life.

charmed circle n [C] : a group of people who are special or powerful in some way

charm·ing /ˈʧɑːmɪŋ/ adj : very pleasing or appealing ▪ a charming café/man — **charm·ing·ly** adv

charred /ˈʧɑːd/ adj : made black from burning ▪ charred wood

¹**chart** /ˈʧɑːt/ n [C] 1 a : information in the form of a table, diagram, etc. ▪ a chart showing the area's annual rainfall b : a record of information about a medical patient ▪ The doctor consulted my chart. 2 : a map used by pilots, sailors,

etc. 3 : a list that shows which music recordings have sold the most during a recent period of time ▪ The record went to the top of the (pop/rock) charts.

²**chart** vb [T] 1 : to make a chart of (an area) ▪ They charted the bay.; also : to mark (something) on a chart ▪ charting the ship's course 2 : to make a plan for (something) ▪ He is charting a new course for the company. 3 : to note the changes, progress, etc., in (something) ▪ chart trends in the stock market

¹**char·ter** /ˈʧɑːt̬ə/ n [C] 1 : a document issued by a government that gives rights to a person or group 2 a : a document which declares that a city, town, school, or corporation has been established ▪ a corporate charter b : a document that describes the basic laws, principles, etc., of a group ▪ the United Nations Charter

²**charter** vb [T] 1 : to give a charter to (a government, corporation, etc.) ▪ The city was chartered in 1837. 2 : to hire (a ship, bus, etc.) for temporary use ▪ The team chartered a plane.

³**charter** adj, always before a noun : hired for temporary use ▪ a charter flight/plane

char·tered /ˈʧɑːt̬əd/ adj, always before a noun, Brit : certified to work in a certain job ▪ a chartered accountant/engineer

charter member n [C] US : FOUNDING MEMBER

chary /ˈʧeri/ adj **char·i·er**; **-est** : cautious about doing something ▪ She is chary about/of spending money.

¹**chase** /ˈʧeɪs/ n [C/U] : the act of following and trying to catch a person, animal, etc. ▪ a high-speed car/police chase ▪ The officer saw the thief and **gave chase** (to him). [=started to chase him] 2 [singular] : an eager attempt to get something ▪ He's trying to find a new girlfriend and seems to enjoy the thrill of the chase. — **cut to the chase** : to go directly to the important points of a story, argument, etc. ▪ Skip the details and cut to the chase.

²**chase** vb **chased**; **chas·ing** 1 [T/I] : to follow and try to catch (someone or something) ▪ The cops chased (after) the thief. 2 [T/I] a : to try very hard to get (someone or something) ▪ a journalist chasing (after) a big story b : to try to attract (someone) for a romantic or sexual relationship ▪ He chases (after) women half his age. 3 [T] : to cause (someone or something) to go away ▪ She chased a dog off the lawn. ▪ chasing away our fears — **chase down** [phrasal vb] **chase (someone or something) down** or **chase down (someone or something)** 1 : to follow and catch (someone or something) ▪ Police chased down the robber. 2 : to search for and find (someone or something) ▪ I finally chased down that recipe. — **chase up** [phrasal vb] Brit **chase (someone or something) up** or **chase up (someone or something)** : to search for and find (someone or something) ▪ His landlord had to chase him up for his rent.

chas·er /ˈʧeɪsə/ n [C] : an alcoholic drink that is drunk immediately after a different one ▪ *He ordered whiskey with a beer chaser.*

chasm /'kæzəm/ *n* [C] : a deep opening in the surface of the Earth

chas·sis /'ʃæsi, 'ʃæsiz/ *n, pl* **chas·sis** /'ʃæsiz, 'ʃæsiz/ [C] : a frame upon which the main parts of an automobile are built

chaste /'ʃeɪst/ *adj* **chast·er; -est** **1** *old-fashioned* : not having sex ▪ *a chaste young woman* **2** : morally pure or decent ▪ *a chaste kiss on the cheek* — **chaste·ly** *adj*

chas·ten /'ʃeɪsn/ *vb* [T] : to cause (someone) to feel sad or embarrassed about something that has happened ▪ *She was chastened by her defeat.* ▪ *a chastening [=humbling] experience*

chas·tise /'ʃæ'staɪz/ *vb* **-tised; -tis·ing** [T] *formal* : to criticize (someone) harshly for doing something wrong ▪ *The coach chastised the players.* — **chas·tise·ment** /'ʃæ'staɪzmənt/ *n* [U]

chas·ti·ty /'ʃæstəti/ *n* [U] : the state of not having sex with anyone ▪ *a vow of chastity* [=a promise never to have sex]

chat /'ʃæt/ *vb* **chat·ted; chat·ting** [I] **1** : to talk with someone in a casual way ▪ *We chatted about sports.* **2** : to send messages back and forth in a chat room ▪ *chatting online* — **chat up** [*phrasal vb*] **chat (someone) up** *or* **chat up (someone)** *informal* : to talk informally with (someone you are attracted to) ▪ *He tried to chat up a girl at the dance.* — **chat** *n* [C/U] ▪ *I need to have a chat with you.* ▪ *live chat sessions*

châ·teau /ʃæ'tou, Brit 'ʃætəʊ/ *n, pl* **châ·teaus** *or* **châ·teaux** /ʃæ'touz, Brit 'ʃætəʊz/ [C] : a castle or a large house especially in France

chat room *n* [C] : a Web site or computer program that allows people to send messages to each other instantly over the Internet

chat·ter /'ʃætɚ/ *vb* [I] **1** : to talk in a quick or casual way ▪ *chattering away on a cell phone* **2** : to make clicking sounds by knocking together rapidly ▪ *My teeth were chattering from the cold.* **3** : to make fast and usually high-pitched sounds ▪ *Birds chattered in the trees.* — **chatter** *n* [U] ▪ *listening to their chatter about celebrities* ▪ *the chatter of squirrels*

chat·ter·box /'ʃætɚˌbaːks/ *n* [C] *informal* : a person who talks a lot

chat·ty /'ʃæti/ *adj* **chat·ti·er; -est** **1** : tending to talk a lot ▪ *a chatty neighbor* **2** : having a style that is similar to friendly speech ▪ *a chatty book* — **chat·ti·ness** *n* [U]

¹chauf·feur /'ʃoufɚ, ʃou'fɚ/ *n* [C] : a person whose job is to drive people in a car — **chauf·feured** /'ʃoufɚd, ʃou'fɚd/ *adj* ▪ *a chauffeured limousine* [=a limousine driven by a chauffeur]

²chauffeur *vb* **1** [T/I] : to work as a chauffeur ▪ *He chauffeurs (for) a millionaire.* **2** [T] : to drive (someone) in a car to a certain place ▪ *She was chauffeured to the airport.*

chau·vin·ism /'ʃouvəˌnɪzəm/ *n* [U] *disapproving* : an attitude that the members of your sex, country, race, etc., are always better than members of other

groups ▪ *American chauvinism* ▪ **male chauvinism** [=a belief that men are superior to women] — **chau·vin·ist** /'ʃouvənɪst/ *or* **chau·vin·is·tic** /ˌʃouvə'nɪstɪk/ *adj* ▪ *chauvinistic attitudes* — **chauvinist** *n* [C] ▪ *a male chauvinist*

¹cheap /'ʃiːp/ *adj* **1 a** : low in price ▪ *a good, cheap meal* ▪ *cheap imported goods* **b** : of low quality ▪ *cheap clothes/perfume* **2** : charging low prices ▪ *a cheap store/restaurant* **3** : not willing to share or spend money ▪ *He was too cheap (with his money) to pay for dinner.* **4** : not hard to do or get ▪ *He likes to harass the dog as a cheap thrill.* [=a minor thing done for entertainment] **5** : having little or no self-respect ▪ *She felt cheap letting other people treat her like that.* — **on the cheap** *informal* : at the lowest possible cost ▪ *The movie was made on the cheap.* — **cheap·ly** *adv* ▪ *The radio was cheaply made.* — **cheap·ness** *n* [U]

²cheap *adv* : at a low cost ▪ *The film was made cheap.* : for a low price ▪ *The house sold cheap.* ▪ *His services* **don't** *come cheap.* [=they are expensive]

cheap·en /'ʃiːpən/ *vb* [T] : to cause (something) to have or to seem to have less value, meaning, or importance ▪ *The wedding ceremony was cheapened by the best man's tasteless jokes.*

cheap·ie /'ʃiːpi/ *n* [C] *informal* : something that is inexpensive and usually of low quality ▪ *Her first camera was a cheapie.*

cheapo /'ʃiːpou/ *adj, informal* : ¹CHEAP ▪ *a cheapo radio/movie*

cheap shot *n* [C] *disapproving* **1** *sports* : an unfair hit made against an opponent ▪ *He took a cheap shot at the quarterback.* **2** : a critical, unkind, and unfair comment ▪ *The remark about his weight was a cheap shot.*

cheap·skate /'ʃiːpˌskeɪt/ *n* [C] *informal* : a person who does not like to spend money

¹cheat /'ʃiːt/ *vb* **1** [I] : to break a rule or law usually to gain an advantage at something ▪ *She was caught cheating (on a test).* ▪ *He cheats (at cards).* **2** [T] **a** : to take something from (someone) by lying or breaking a rule — usually + *out of* ▪ *I was cheated out of 20 dollars.* **b** : to prevent (someone) from having something that he or she deserves or was expecting to get ▪ *Tourists felt cheated when they learned the cathedral was closed.* **3** [T] : to avoid (something bad, dangerous, etc.) by being clever or lucky ▪ *He has cheated death/fate many times.* — **cheat on** [*phrasal vb*] *informal* : to break a promise made to (your girlfriend, husband, etc.) by having sex with someone else ▪ *He cheated on his wife.* — **cheat·er** *n* [C]

²cheat *n* [C] : a person who cheats ▪ *He's a liar and a cheat.*

¹check /'ʃɛk/ *vb* **1** [T/I] : to look at (something) carefully to make sure there is nothing wrong with it ▪ *Check your spelling (for any mistakes).* ▪ *The guards checked my passport.* **2 a** [T/I] : to get information by looking at something, asking about something, etc. ▪ *I'll check*

the map to see where we are. • *She was fine last time I checked.* • *I think the door is locked, but I'll check (to be sure).* **b** [T/I] : to look at or in (a place) in order to find or get something or someone • *I checked (in) the closet, but my hat wasn't there.* **c** [T] : to find out if you have any (mail, messages, etc.) • *Did you check the mail today?* • *She checked her e-mail/messages.* **3** [T/I] : to talk *with* someone in order to get approval, information, etc., about something • *Check with your doctor to find out which drugs are safe.* **4** [T] **a** : to slow or stop (something or someone) from doing something • *She started to speak but then checked herself.* **b** *hockey* : to stop or hit (an opponent) • *He was checked by the defender.* **5** [T] *US* **a** : to leave (something you own) with a worker in a checkroom • *I checked my hat and coat.* **b** : to give (your bags, suitcases, etc.) to a worker so that they can be loaded onto a plane or train • *We checked our bags before boarding.* **c** : to take (someone's bags, suitcases, etc.) to load them onto a plane or train • *The airline checked our bags.* **6** [T] *US* : to mark (something) with a check (✔) to show that it has been done, approved, etc. • *Check (off) each item on the list after you've completed it.* — **check back** [*phrasal vb*] *informal* : to return to a place, person, etc., in order to try something again or to get more information • *We are not hiring today, but check back next month.* • *I'll* **check back with you** [=talk to your again] *in about a week.* — **check in** [*phrasal vb*] **1** : to report to someone when you arrive at a place (such as an airport or convention) to let them know you are there • *Passengers must check in one hour before the flight leaves.* • *Hotel guests cannot check in before 4:00 p.m.* **2** *US, informal* : to talk with someone in order to report or find out new information • *I'm just checking in (with you) to see how things are going.* **3** **check (something) in** or **check in (something)** : to leave or take bags, suitcases, etc., so that they can be loaded onto a plane or train • *We checked our bags in at the station.* — **check into** [*phrasal vb*] **1** : to arrive at and be given a room in (a hotel, motel, etc.) • *We checked into a hotel.* **2** : to look for information about (something) • *The police are checking into* [=investigating] *his activities.* — **check off on** [*phrasal vb*] *US, informal* : to give official approval for (something) • *My boss will have to check off on my decision.* — **check on** [*phrasal vb*] **1** : to look at or examine (someone or something) to see if there are any problems • *The nurse checked on the patients regularly.* **2** : to look for information about (someone or something) • *I asked the waiter to check on* [=find out what was happening with] *my order.* — **check out** [*phrasal vb*] **1** : to leave and pay for your room at a hotel, motel, etc. • *We checked out (of the hotel) early.* **2** *US, informal* **a** : to be proven to be accurate, true, etc. • *Her story/alibi checked out.* **b** **check out (something)** or **check**

(something) out : to find out if (something) is true • *The police are checking out his alibi.* **3** **check out (something or someone)** or **check (something or someone) out** : to look at (something or someone) in order to find problems, mistakes, etc. • *We checked the car out for defects.* • *He got checked out by a doctor.* **b** *informal* : to look at (someone or something that is attractive or interesting) • *When she walked into the room, all the guys were checking her out.* • *Check out that car!* **4** **check out (something)** or **check (something) out a** : to borrow (something) from a library • *He checked out a book on farming.* **b** *US* : to add up the cost of the goods that someone buys in a store and accept payment for them • *She checks out groceries at the supermarket.; also* : to pay for the goods that you buy in a store • *She checked out quickly using her debit card.* — **check over** [*phrasal vb*] **check (something or someone) over** or **check over (something or someone)** : to look at (something or someone) in a careful way to find problems, mistakes, etc. • *She checked herself over in the mirror.* — **check through** [*phrasal vb*] : to look at the parts of (a group of things) • *I checked through his letters but found nothing useful.* — **check up on** [*phrasal vb*] : to find or look for information about (someone or something) often in order to find out the truth • *My parents often check up on me.* — **check·able** *adj*

²**check** *n* **1** [C] : the act or process of looking at or examining something to find out information or see if there are mistakes • *I gave the list a quick check.* • *She ran/did a quick check of the computer to make sure it was working properly.* • *They did a* **sound check** [=tested the sound equipment] *before the concert.* • *All employees are subject to a* **security check.** [=they are investigated to see if they can be trusted] **2** [C] **a** : something that stops or limits another thing • *The store hired a guard to* **put a check on** [=reduce or stop] *shoplifting.* **b** *hockey* : an act of hitting or stopping a player • *He was penalized for an illegal check.* **3** *US* **check** or *Brit* **cheque** [C] : a piece of paper that is used to pay someone using the money in a bank account • *He made out the check to me and I cashed it.* — see also BLANK CHECK, TRAVELER'S CHECK **4** [C] *US* : a bill for the items served in a restaurant • *She asked the waiter for the check.* **5 a** [C] *US* : a mark ✔ that is used to show that something (such as an item on a list) has been noted, done, etc. — called also (*US*) **check mark,** (*chiefly Brit*) **tick b** *informal* — used in speech to say that something has been noted, done, etc. • *"Do you have the camera?" "Check." "The umbrella?" "Check."* **6** [C] *US* : a ticket that is given to you when you leave something that you will return for later • *a baggage check* **7** [C] : a pattern of squares in different colors • *a fabric with a blue and yellow check (pattern)* **8** [U] *chess* : a situation in which a play-

er's king can be captured on the opponent's next turn ▪ *He moved his bishop and said, "Check!"* — **in check** : under control — used with *keep* or *hold* ▪ *The government is trying to keep inflation in check.*

check·book (*US*) *or Brit* **cheque·book** /ˈtʃɛkˌbʊk/ *n* [C] : a book of checks for use with a checking account

checked *adj* : having a pattern made up of squares of different colors ▪ *a checked pattern/fabric/shirt*

check·er /ˈtʃɛkɚ/ *n* [C] **1** *US* : a person in a store whose job is to add up the cost of customers' purchases and take payment for them ▪ *a grocery/supermarket checker* **2** : someone or something that looks at things to find problems ▪ *a fact checker* [=a person whose job is to make sure that the facts in a book, magazine, etc., are correct] ▪ *The software includes a grammar checker.* [=a feature that finds grammatical errors] — see also SPELL-CHECKER **3** *US* : any one of the round pieces that are used in the game of checkers — called also (*Brit*) *draught*

check·er·board /ˈtʃɛkɚˌboɚd/ *n* [C] *US* **1** : a board used in checkers that has squares in two colors **2** : something that looks like a checkerboard ▪ *a checkerboard pattern*

check·ered (*chiefly US*) *or Brit* **che·quered** /ˈtʃɛkɚd/ *adj* **1** : having a pattern made up of squares of different colors ▪ *a checkered fabric/tablecloth* **2 a** : including good parts and bad parts ▪ *a checkered career* **b** : including many problems or failures ▪ *The senator has a checkered past.* [=he has done bad things in the past]

check·ers /ˈtʃɛkɚz/ *n* [U] *US* : a game played on a checkerboard by two players who each have 12 checkers — called also (*Brit*) *draughts*

check-in /ˈtʃɛkˌɪn/ *n* **1** [U] : the act or process of checking in at a hotel, airport, etc. ▪ *Check-in was delayed.*; *also* : the time when people are allowed to check in ▪ *When is check-in (time)?* **2** [C] : the place where people go when they arrive at a hotel, airport, etc. ▪ *a long line at the check-in (desk/counter)*

checking account *n* [C] *US* : a bank account from which you can take money by writing checks — called also (*Brit*) *current account*

check·list /ˈtʃɛkˌlɪst/ *n* [C] : a list of things to be checked or done

check mark *n* [C] *US* : ²CHECK 5a

check·mate /ˈtʃɛkˌmeɪt/ *n* [C/U] *chess* : a situation in which a player loses the game because that player's king cannot escape ▪ *a move that resulted in (a) checkmate*

check·out /ˈtʃɛkˌaʊt/ *n* **1 a** [C/U] : the act of leaving your room in a hotel, motel, etc., after you are finished staying there ▪ *She paid for the room at checkout.* ▪ *the checkout desk* **b** [U] : the time by which you must leave your room in a hotel, motel, etc. ▪ *Checkout (time) is at 11:00.* **2** [C] : the place or area where goods are paid for in a store ▪ *a long line at the checkout (counter)*

check·point /ˈtʃɛkˌpɔɪnt/ *n* [C] : a place where people or vehicles are searched by a guard, police officer, etc., before being allowed to continue ▪ *a police/military/security checkpoint*

check·room /ˈtʃɛkˌruːm/ *n* [C] *US* : a room in a restaurant, theater, etc., where you can leave something that you do not want to carry or wear while you are there — called also (*chiefly Brit*) *cloakroom*

checks and balances *n* [*plural*] : a system in which the different parts of a government have powers that affect and control the other parts so that no part can become too powerful

check·up /ˈtʃɛkˌʌp/ *n* [C] : an examination made by a doctor to make sure a person is healthy ▪ *a yearly checkup*

ched·dar /ˈtʃɛdɚ/ *n, often* **Cheddar** [U] : a type of hard yellow, white, or orange cheese

cheek /ˈtʃiːk/ *n* **1** [C] : the part of the face that is below the eye and to the side of the nose and mouth ▪ *He kissed her on the cheek.* ▪ *They danced* **cheek to cheek.** [=with their cheeks touching] **2** [U, *singular*] *Brit* : a way of behaving that is rude and does not show proper respect ▪ *He had the cheek to say that our gift was cheap.* **3** [C] *informal* : BUTTOCKS — **cheek by jowl** : very close together ▪ *cheap knickknacks displayed cheek by jowl with fine antiques* — **turn the other cheek** : to choose not to hurt or insult someone who has hurt or insulted you

cheek·bone /ˈtʃiːkˌboʊn/ *n* [C] : a bone of the face that is located below the eye

cheeky /ˈtʃiːki/ *adj* **cheek·i·er; -est** *chiefly Brit, informal* : rude and showing a lack of respect often in a way that seems playful or amusing ▪ *a cheeky grin* — **cheek·i·ness** /ˈtʃiːkinəs/ *n* [U]

cheep /ˈtʃiːp/ *vb* [I] *of a bird* : CHIRP ▪ *chicks cheeping for food* — **cheep** *n* [C]

¹cheer /ˈtʃiɚ/ *n* **1** [C] : a shout of praise or encouragement ▪ *The actress was greeted with cheers.* ▪ *Three cheers for our team!* [=hooray for our team] **2** [U] *somewhat formal* : a happy feeling or attitude ▪ *Let's spread a little holiday cheer.* **3** [C] : a special song or chant that is performed to encourage a team during a game of American football, basketball, etc. ▪ *The cheerleaders did/led a victory cheer.*

²cheer *vb* **1 a** [T/I] : to shout with joy, approval, or enthusiasm ▪ *We will be cheering for you!* **b** [T] : to express enthusiastic approval of (something) ▪ *Supporters cheered the court's decision.* **2** [T] : to cause (someone) to feel happier or more hopeful ▪ *Investors were cheered by good economic news.* — **cheer on** [*phrasal vb*] **cheer (someone) on** *or* **cheer on (someone)** : to encourage (someone) with shouts or cheers ▪ *Their fans cheered them on from the sidelines.* — **cheer up** [*phrasal vb*] **1 cheer up** *or* **cheer (someone) up** *or* **cheer up (someone)** : to become happier or to make (someone) happier ▪ *Cheer up—things will get better!* ▪ *We tried to cheer her up.* **2 cheer (something) up** *or* **cheer up**

(something) : to make (something) more cheerful or pleasant ▪ *Bright colors really cheer up a room.*

cheer·ful /ˈtʃirfəl/ *adj* **1 a** : feeling or showing happiness ▪ *a cheerful outlook on life* ▪ *He seems more cheerful today.* **b** : feeling or showing that you are willing to do something without complaining ▪ *cheerful obedience* **2 a** : causing good feelings or happiness ▪ *cheerful words/news* **b** : bright and pleasant to look at ▪ *cheerful colors* — **cheer·ful·ly** *adv* — **cheer·ful·ness** *n* [U]

cheer·io /ˌtʃiriˈoʊ/ *interj*, *Brit, old-fashioned* : ¹GOODBYE

cheer·lead·er /ˈtʃiəˌliːdɚ/ *n* [C] **1** : a member of a group who shout out songs or chants to encourage the team and entertain the crowd during a game of American football, basketball, etc. **2** : a person who encourages other people to do or support something ▪ *a cheerleader for the new economic plan* — **cheer·lead·ing** *n* [U] ▪ *She's on a cheerleading team/squad.*

cheer·less /ˈtʃiələs/ *adj* : not causing happiness or warm feelings ▪ *a cheerless office*

cheers /ˈtʃiəz/ *interj* **1** — used as a toast to wish everyone happiness **2** *Brit* — used as an informal way to say "thank you" or "goodbye"

cheery /ˈtʃiri/ *adj* **cheer·i·er; -est** : having or causing happy feelings ▪ *cheery words/colors* — **cheer·i·ly** /ˈtʃirəli/ *adv* — **cheer·i·ness** /ˈtʃirinəs/ *n* [U]

cheese /ˈtʃiːz/ *n* [C/U] : a yellow or white solid food that comes from milk ▪ *a piece of cheese* ▪ *grated/melted cheeses* ▪ *cheese sandwiches/sauces* — **say cheese** ✧ Someone who is taking your photograph and wants you to smile may tell you to *say cheese.* — see also BIG CHEESE

cheese·burg·er /ˈtʃiːzˌbɚgɚ/ *n* [C] : a hamburger with a piece of cheese on the meat

cheese·cake /ˈtʃiːzˌkeɪk/ *n* [C/U] : a cake with a sweet filling usually made of cheese, eggs, and sugar

cheese·cloth /ˈtʃiːzˌklɑːθ/ *n* [U] : a very thin cotton cloth used in preparing food

cheesed off /ˌtʃiːzdˈɑːf/ *adj, Brit, informal* : angry or annoyed ▪ *He's a bit cheesed off.*

cheese·steak /ˈtʃiːzˌsteɪk/ *n* [C] *US* : a sandwich made with thin slices of beef and melted cheese

cheesy /ˈtʃiːzi/ *adj* **chees·i·er; -est 1 a** : resembling cheese ▪ *a cheesy texture/odor* **b** : containing cheese ▪ *a cheesy sauce* **2** *informal* : lacking style or good taste ▪ *cheesy pop songs*

chee·tah /ˈtʃiːtə/ *n* [C] : a large, spotted wild cat that can run very fast

chef /ˈʃɛf/ *n* [C] **1** : a professional cook who is in charge of a kitchen ▪ *She's the head chef at a five-star restaurant.* **2** : ¹COOK ▪ *She's an excellent chef.*

¹chem·i·cal /ˈkɛmɪkəl/ *adj* **1** : of or relating to chemistry ▪ *chemical elements/reactions* ▪ *the compound's chemical structure/composition/properties* **2** : working by means of chemicals ▪ *chem-*

ical pesticides/weapons — **chem·i·cal·ly** /ˈkɛmɪkli/ *adv*

²chemical *n* [C] : a substance that is made by a chemical process ▪ *toxic/industrial chemicals*

chemical engineering *n* [U] : engineering that deals with the use of chemistry in industry — **chemical engineer** *n* [C]

chemical warfare *n* [U] : the use of chemical substances as weapons in a war

chem·ist /ˈkɛmɪst/ *n* [C] **1** : a person who studies or does research in chemistry **2** *Brit* : PHARMACIST

chem·is·try /ˈkɛməstri/ *n* [U] **1** : a science that deals with the structure and properties of substances and with the changes that they go through ▪ *a professor of chemistry* **2** : the structure and properties of a substance ▪ *the chemistry of gasoline/iron* **3 a** : a strong attraction between people ▪ *They tried dating, but they had no chemistry.* **b** : the way the people in a group work together and feel about each other ▪ *The team lacks chemistry.*

che·mo·ther·a·py /ˌkiːmoʊˈθɛrəpi/ *n* [U] *medical* : the use of chemicals to treat cancer ▪ *She underwent (a course of) chemotherapy.*

cheque *Brit spelling of* ²CHECK 3

cheque·book *Brit spelling of* CHECK-BOOK

che·quered *Brit spelling of* CHECKERED

cher·ish /ˈtʃɛrɪʃ/ *vb* [T] **1** : to feel or show great love for (someone or something) ▪ *She cherishes her friends/family.* **2** : to remember or hold (an idea, belief, etc.) in a deeply felt way ▪ *a cherished memory*

cher·ry /ˈtʃɛri/ *n, pl* **-ries 1 a** [C] : a small round fruit that is usually red or black ▪ *cherry pie* **b** [C] : a tree that grows cherries **c** [U] : the wood of a cherry tree ▪ *cherry cabinets* **2** [U] : a bright red color

cherry tomato *n* [C] : a very small tomato

cher·ub /ˈtʃɛrəb/ *n, pl* **cher·ubs** *or* **cher·u·bim** /ˈtʃɛrəˌbɪm/ *[C]* : a type of angel that is shown in art as a chubby child with small wings — **che·ru·bic** /tʃəˈruːbɪk/ *adj* ▪ *a child with a cherubic face*

chess /ˈtʃɛs/ *n* [U] : a game for two players in which each player moves 16 pieces across a board and tries to place the opponent's king in a position from which it cannot escape ▪ *a chess player/match*

chess·board /ˈtʃɛsˌboəd/ *n* [C] : a board used in chess that has 64 squares in two colors

chess·man /ˈtʃɛsˌmæn/ *n, pl* **-men** /-mən/ *[C]* : any one of the playing pieces used in chess

chest /ˈtʃɛst/ *n* [C] **1** : a box or case for holding or moving things ▪ *a linen/tool/treasure chest* **2** : the front part of the body between the neck and the stomach ▪ *He has a broad chest.* ▪ *She's been complaining of chest pains.* — **close to your chest** see ²CLOSE — **get (something) off your chest** : to tell someone about something that has been making you upset or unhappy ▪ *Is there something you'd*

like to get off your chest? — **chest·ed**
/'tʃɛstəd/ *adj* • *flat-chested* • *bare-chested*

¹chest·nut /'tʃɛs,nʌt/ *n* **1** [C] : a type of tree that produces large, sweet nuts that can be eaten **2** [C] : the nut of a chestnut tree • *roasted chestnuts* — see also WATER CHESTNUT **3** [U] : the wood of a chestnut tree

²chestnut *adj* : of a reddish-brown color • *chestnut hair* • *a chestnut horse*

chest of drawers *n* [C] : a piece of furniture that contains drawers for storing clothes

chew /'tʃuː/ *vb* **1** [T/I] **a** : to crush food with your teeth before you swallow it • *Don't chew (your food) with your mouth open.* **b** : to bite on (something) repeatedly with the teeth • *chew gum/tobacco* • *a dog chewing on a bone* **2** [T] : to make (a hole) by chewing • *Mice chewed holes in the boxes.* — **bite off more than you can chew** see ¹BITE — **chew off** [*phrasal vb*] **chew off (something) or chew (something) off** : to remove (something) by chewing • *The dog chewed the doll's arm off.* — **chew on** [*phrasal vb*] *informal* : to think about (something) • *Chew on it for a while before you decide.* — **chew out** [*phrasal vb*] **chew (someone) out or chew out (someone)** *US, informal* : to speak in an angry and critical way to (someone) • *The coach chewed him out.* — **chew over** [*phrasal vb*] **chew (something) over or chew over (something)** *informal* : to think about (something) • *He chewed the problem over in his mind.* — **chew the fat/rag** *informal* : to talk together in a friendly and casual way — **chew up** [*phrasal vb*] **chew (something) up or chew up (something)** **1** : to destroy (something) by chewing it • *The puppy chewed up my shoes.* **2** *informal* : to destroy or defeat (someone or something) • *The truck chewed up the grass.* • *They chewed up the competition.* — **chew·able** /'tʃuː·wəbəl/ *adj* — **chew·er** *n* [C] • *gum chewers*

chewing gum *n* [U] : a type of soft candy that you chew but do not swallow • *a piece/stick of chewing gum*

chewy /'tʃuːwi/ *adj* **chew·i·er; -est** : requiring a lot of chewing • *chewy meat/candy*

chic /'ʃiːk/ *adj* : following the current fashion or style • *chic new clothes*

Chi·ca·na /tʃɪˈkɑːnə/ *n* [C] : an American woman or girl whose family came from Mexico — **Chicana** *adj*

chi·ca·nery /ʃɪˈkeɪnəri/ *n* [U] *formal* : deception or trickery • *using chicanery to win votes*

Chi·ca·no /tʃɪˈkɑːnoʊ/ *n, pl* **-nos** [C] : an American whose family came from Mexico — **Chicano** *adj*

chick /'tʃɪk/ *n* [C] **1** : a baby bird; *especially* : a baby chicken **2** *informal, sometimes offensive* : a woman or girl

chick·a·dee /'tʃɪkəˌdiː/ *n* [C] : a common, small American bird

¹chick·en /'tʃɪkən/ *n* **1 a** [C] : a bird that is raised for its eggs and meat **b** [U] : the meat of the chicken used as food • *fried/roasted chicken* • *chicken soup/salad* **2** [C] *informal* : COWARD • *Don't be such*

a chicken. — **count your chickens (before they hatch)** : to believe that something you want to happen will definitely happen before you know for certain that it really will • *Don't count your chickens before they hatch—we don't know yet if she will accept our offer.*

²chicken *adj, not before a noun, informal* : too afraid to do something • *You're chicken, aren't you?*

³chicken *vb* — **chicken out** [*phrasal vb*] *informal* : to decide not to do something because you are afraid • *He was going to ask her on a date, but he chickened out.*

chicken feed *n* [U] *informal* : an amount of money that is too small to be considered important • *The project cost almost a million dollars, which isn't exactly chicken feed.*

chicken pox *n* [U] : a disease that causes a fever and red spots on the skin

chicken wire *n* [U] : a type of wire used especially to make fences

chick flick *n* [C] *informal* : a movie intended to appeal to women

chick·pea /'tʃɪkˌpiː/ *n* [C] : a pale round seed that is cooked and eaten as a vegetable

chic·o·ry /'tʃɪkəri/ *n, pl* **-ries** [C/U] : a plant with bitter leaves that are often used in salads

chide /'tʃaɪd/ *vb* **chid·ed** /'tʃaɪdəd/; **chid·ing** /'tʃaɪdɪŋ/ [T] : to express mild disapproval of (someone) • *She chided us for arriving late.*

¹chief /'tʃiːf/ *n* [C] : the person who is the leader of a group of people, of an organization, etc. • *the police chief = the chief of police* • *an Indian chief* [=the leader of a tribe of Native Americans]

²chief *adj* **1** : highest in rank or authority • *the company's chief executive* **2** : most important • *the country's chief export* — **chief·ly** *adv* • *We're chiefly concerned with helping the poor.* • *The disease occurs chiefly in children.*

chief executive officer *n* [C] : CEO

chief justice or **Chief Justice** *n* [C] : the most powerful judge especially of the U.S. Supreme Court

chief of staff *n* [C] **1** : a person of high rank in the U.S. Army, Navy, Air Force, or Marines who advises the person in charge of military operations — see also JOINT CHIEFS OF STAFF **2** : a person of high rank who advises a leader (such as the U.S. President) on important matters

chief·tain /'tʃiːftən/ *n* [C] : a leader of a tribe or clan

chif·fon /ʃɪˈfɑːn, 'ʃɪˌfɑːn/ *n* [U] : a very thin cloth • *a chiffon scarf*

Chi·hua·hua /tʃəˈwɑːwɑ/ *n* [C] : a type of very small dog with large ears

child /'tʃaɪld/ *n, pl* **chil·dren** /'tʃɪldrən/ [C] **1** : a young person • *the birth of a child* • *a movie for both children and adults* • *I went there as a child.* [=when I was a child] • *a child actor/psychologist* **2** : a son or daughter • *the couple's adult children* **3** : an adult who acts like a child • *Men are such children sometimes.* **4** : a person who has been strongly influenced by a certain place or time • *a child of WWII* — **with child** *old-fashioned*

: PREGNANT • *She was with child.* —
child·ish /ˈtʃaɪldɪʃ/ *adj, usually disapproving* • *I'm tired of their childish games/behavior.* — **child·ish·ly** *adv* — **child·ish·ness** *n* [U] — **child·like** /ˈtʃaɪld,laɪk/ *adj* • *a childlike voice/face* • *childlike innocence/wonder/enthusiasm*

child·bear·ing /ˈtʃaɪld,berɪŋ/ *n* [U] : CHILDBIRTH — **childbearing** *adj* • *women of childbearing age* [=women who are old enough to give birth to children]

child·birth /ˈtʃaɪld,bɚθ/ *n* [C/U] : the act or process of giving birth to children • *(a) difficult childbirth*

child·care /ˈtʃaɪld,keɚ/ *n* [U] : the care of children especially when their parents are at work • *childcare costs/centers/workers*

child·hood /ˈtʃaɪld,hʊd/ *n* [C/U] : the period of time when a person is a child • *I remember them from (my) childhood.* • *childhood friends/diseases*

child·less /ˈtʃaɪldləs/ *adj* : having no children • *childless couples*

child·proof /ˈtʃaɪld,pruːf/ *adj* 1 : made so that a child cannot open it • *a childproof bottle* 2 : made safe for children • *a childproof home* — **childproof** *vb* [T] • *tips on how to childproof a home* [=make a home safe for children]

children *plural of* CHILD

child's play *n* [U] : something that is very easy to do • *Writing songs is child's play for him.*

child support *n* [U] : money that a former husband or wife must pay regularly to help raise a child

chili (*US*) *or Brit* **chil·li** *also US* **chile** /ˈtʃɪli/ *n, pl* **chil·ies** *or Brit* **chil·lies** *also US* **chil·es** 1 [C/U] : a small pepper with a very hot flavor — called also *chili pepper* 2 [U] : a spicy dish made of ground beef, hot peppers or chili powder, and usually beans • *a bowl of chili*

chili dog *n* [C] *US* : a hot dog with chili on top of it

chili powder (*US*) *or Brit* **chilli powder** *n* [U] : a powder made of chilies and other spices

chili sauce *n* [U] *US* : a spicy sauce made with tomatoes and hot peppers

¹**chill** /ˈtʃɪl/ *n* 1 [*singular*] : a cold feeling • *There was a chill in the air.* 2 [C] : a feeling of being cold • *Her symptoms include chills and a fever.* 3 [C] : a sudden feeling of fear • *The photograph gave him the chills.* • *Her words sent chills down my spine.* 4 [*singular*] : a cold and unfriendly quality • *I felt the chill of my opponent's stare.*

²**chill** *vb* 1 a [T] : to make (someone or something) cold or cool • *Chill the dessert for one hour before serving it.* • *I was chilled to the bone/marrow.* [=very cold] b [I] : to become cold or cool • *Let the dessert chill for one hour.* 2 [T] : to cause (someone) to feel afraid • *Her screams chilled me to the bone.* 3 [I] *informal* a : to become less tense, anxious, or angry • *Chill (out), man.* b : to spend time in a relaxed manner • *Let's stay home and chill (out) tonight.*

³**chill** *adj, somewhat formal* : unpleasantly cold • *a chill wind*

chilli *chiefly Brit spelling of* CHILI

chill·ing /ˈtʃɪlɪŋ/ *adj* : very disturbing or frightening • *a chilling tale* — **chill·ing·ly** *adv*

chilly /ˈtʃɪli/ *adj* **chill·i·er; -est** 1 : noticeably cold • *a chilly morning/breeze* 2 : feeling cold • *I'm a bit chilly.* 3 : noticeably unfriendly • *They gave him a chilly reception.* — **chill·i·ness** *n* [U, *singular*]

¹**chime** /ˈtʃaɪm/ *n* [C] 1 : a device that makes a sound like bells • *door chimes* 2 : the sound made by a set of bells • *the chime of church bells*

²**chime** *vb* **chimed; chim·ing** 1 [I] : to make the sound of a ringing bell • *The door bell chimed.* 2 [T/I] *of a clock* : to make a sound that indicates the time • *The clock chimed (midnight).* — **chime in** [*phrasal vb*] : to add a comment to a conversation that you have been listening to • *He kept chiming in with his opinions.*

chi·me·ra /kaɪˈmɪrə/ *n* [C] *formal* : something that exists only in the imagination and is not possible in reality • *Economic stability in that country is a chimera.* — **chi·mer·i·cal** /kaɪˈmerəkəl/ *adj*

chim·ney /ˈtʃɪmni/ *n, pl* **-neys** [C] : a part of a building through which smoke rises into the outside air

chimney sweep *n* [C] : a person who cleans chimneys

chimp /ˈtʃɪmp/ *n* [C] : CHIMPANZEE

chim·pan·zee /ˌtʃɪmˌpænˈziː/ *n* [C] : an intelligent ape that lives mostly in trees in Africa

chin /ˈtʃɪn/ *n* [C] : the part of the face below the mouth and above the neck — **keep your chin up** : to stay cheerful and hopeful during difficult times • *He's still keeping his chin up despite all his health problems.* — **take it on the chin** *informal* 1 *US* : to be badly affected by something • *Many investors took it on the chin as stocks dropped sharply.* 2 *Brit* : to accept something unpleasant without complaining • *The criticism was harsh but he took it on the chin.*

chi·na /ˈtʃaɪnə/ *n* [U] 1 : a hard white material that is used to make plates, bowls, etc. • *This vase is (made of) china.* 2 : plates, bowls, cups, etc., that are made of china • *She uses her good china on special occasions.*

Chi·nese /tʃaɪˈniːz/ *n* 1 **the Chinese** : the people of China • *customs of the Chinese* 2 [U] : any one of the languages spoken in China • *He speaks Chinese.* — **Chinese** *adj* • *Chinese history/food* • *She is Chinese.*

Chinese checkers (*US*) *or Brit* **Chinese chequers** *n* [U] : a game in which players move marbles across a board shaped like a star

chink /ˈtʃɪŋk/ *n* [C] 1 : a small crack or opening • *a chink in the fence* • (*figurative*) *We've found some chinks in their armor.* [=weaknesses that might cause them to fail or be defeated] 2 : the short sharp sound made when objects made of metal or glass hit each other • *the chink of our wine glasses*

chintz /ˈtʃɪnts/ *n* [U] : a shiny cotton fabric with a flowery pattern printed on it • *chintz curtains*

chintzy /ˈʧɪntsi/ *adj* **chintz·i·er; -est** **1** *US, informal* **a** : not tasteful or stylish • *chintzy decorations* **b** : of low quality • *chintzy movies* **2** *US, informal* : not willing to give or spend money • *The boss is chintzy about raises.* **3** *chiefly Brit* : decorated in or covered with chintz • *chintzy furniture*

chin–up /ˈʧɪnˌʌp/ *n* [C] *US* : PULL-UP

¹**chip** /ˈʧɪp/ *n* [C] **1** : a small piece that has been broken off from something larger • *wood chips* **2** : a place where a small piece of something has broken off • *The cup has a chip in/on it.* **3** : a small piece of candy used in baking • *chocolate chips* **4** **a** : a thin, hard, and usually salty piece of food • *tortilla chips; especially, US* : POTATO CHIP • *a bag of chips* **b** *Brit* : FRENCH FRY **5** : a small, flat, round piece of plastic that is used to represent money in gambling games like poker • *a poker chip* **6** : a very small piece of hard material that contains many electronic circuits • *computer/silicon chips* — **chip off the old block** *informal* : someone who looks or behaves like his or her parent • *His son is a real chip off the old block.* — **have a chip on your shoulder** *informal* : to have an angry or unpleasant attitude or way of behaving caused by a belief that you have been treated unfairly in the past • *He has had a chip on his shoulder ever since he didn't get the promotion he was expecting.* — **let the chips fall where they may** *US, informal* : to allow events to happen without trying to change them • *I will do the best I can, then let the chips fall where they may.* — **when the chips are down** *informal* : in a difficult situation • *True friends will support you when the chips are down.*

²**chip** *vb* **chipped; chip·ping** **1 a** [T] : to break off a small piece from (something) • *I chipped my tooth on a piece of candy.* • *a chipped cup* **b** [I] : to break off in small pieces • *The paint had chipped off/away.* **2 a** [T] : to break off (something) especially with a tool • *The sculptor chipped away/off bits of stone.* **b** [I] : to hit something with a tool in order to break off small pieces • *The sculptor chipped away at the stone.* • (*figurative*) *His failures chipped away at his self-confidence.* **3** [T/I] : to hit or kick a chip shot • *The golfer chipped (the ball) onto the green.* • *She chipped the soccer ball over the goalie's head.* — **chip in** [*phrasal vb*] **1** : to give something (such as money) to help a person, group, or cause • *We all chipped in (10 dollars) to buy him a gift.* **2** *chiefly Brit* : to add your comment or opinion to a conversation or discussion

chip·munk /ˈʧɪpˌmʌŋk/ *n* [C] : a small North American animal that is related to the squirrel

¹**chip·per** /ˈʧɪpə/ *adj, informal* + *old-fashioned* : cheerful and lively • *My, you're looking chipper today.*

²**chip·per** *n* [C] : a piece of equipment that is used to cut wood into small pieces • *a wood chipper*

chip·py /ˈʧɪpi/ *n, pl* **-pies** [C] *Brit, informal* : CHIP SHOP

chip shop *n* [C] *Brit* : a restaurant that sells fish and chips and other fried foods for people to take away and eat somewhere else

chip shot *n* [C] **1** *golf* : a very short shot that is made from an area near the green **2** *soccer* + *rugby* : a short kick that lifts a ball high in the air **3** *American football* : a short and easy field goal

chi·ro·prac·tic /ˈkaɪrəˌpræktɪk/ *n* [U] : a method of treating people who are sick or in pain by pushing bones in the spine and joints — **chiropractic** *adj* — **chi·ro·prac·tor** /ˈkaɪrəˌpræktɚ/ *n* [C]

chirp /ˈʧɚp/ *vb* **1** [I] : to make a short high-pitched sound • *The birds/crickets were chirping.* **2** [T] : to say (something) in a cheerful and lively way • *"Good morning!" she chirped.* — **chirp** *n* [C]

chirpy /ˈʧɚpi/ *adj* **chirp·i·er; -est** *informal* : cheerful and lively • *a chirpy student* — **chirp·i·ness** /ˈʧɚpinəs/ *n* [U]

¹**chis·el** /ˈʧɪzl/ *n* [C] : a metal tool with a flat, sharp end that is used to shape stone, wood, etc.

²**chisel** *vb, US* **-eled** *or Brit* **-elled;** *US* **-el·ing** *or Brit* **-el·ling** [T] : to cut or shape (something) with a chisel • *She chiseled her name into the wood.*

chis·eled (*US*) *or Brit* **chis·elled** /ˈʧɪzld/ *adj* **1** : having an attractive well-formed shape • *a handsome actor's chiseled face/jaw/nose* **2** : having a strong, muscular body or form • *a chiseled body/athlete*

chit–chat /ˈʧɪtˌʧæt/ *n* [U, singular] *informal* : friendly conversation about things that are not very important • *a/some chitchat about the weather* — **chitchat** *vb* **-chat·ted; -chat·ting** [I] • *chitchatting with my neighbors*

chiv·al·ry /ˈʃɪvəlri/ *n* [U] **1** : the system of values (such as loyalty and honor) of knights • *medieval chivalry* **2** : an honorable and polite way of behaving especially toward women • *He paid her fare as an act of chivalry.* — **chiv·al·rous** /ˈʃɪvəlrəs/ *adj* • *chivalrous behavior/acts/men* — **chiv·al·rous·ly** *adv*

chive /ˈʧaɪv/ *n* **1** [C] : a plant that is related to the onion **2** [*plural*] : the long thin leaves of the chive plant that are cut into small pieces and used for flavoring food • *a baked potato with butter and chives*

chiv·vy /ˈʧɪvi/ *vb* **-vies; -vied; -vy·ing** [T] *Brit, informal* : to try to make (someone) do something more quickly • *They chivvied the children along.*

chlo·ri·nate /ˈklorəˌneɪt/ *vb* **-nat·ed; -nat·ing** [T] *technical* : to add chlorine to (something) • *chlorinated water* — **chlo·ri·na·tion** /ˌklorəˈneɪʃən/ *n* [U]

chlo·rine /ˈkloɹˌiːn/ *n* [U] : a chemical that has a strong smell and that is often used to keep water clean

chlo·ro·flu·o·ro·car·bon /ˌklorouˌflorouˈkɑɚbən/ *n* [C] *technical* : a chemical that was once commonly used in various products (such as aerosols) but that is believed to cause damage to the ozone layer in the Earth's atmosphere — abbr. **CFC**

chlo·ro·form /'klorə,foəm/ n [U] : a poisonous liquid that was used in the past to make patients unconscious during medical operations

chlo·ro·phyll /'klorə,fɪl/ n [U] : the green substance in the cells of plants

chock·a·block /'tʃɑːkə,blɑːk/ adj, not before a noun : very full — usually + with • shelves chockablock with books

chock–full or **chock·ful** /'tʃɑːkˈfʊl/ adj, not before a noun : completely full • This article is chock-full of good ideas.

choc·o·hol·ic also **choc·a·hol·ic** /,tʃɑːkəˈhɑːlɪk/ n [C] informal : a person who loves chocolate

choc·o·late /'tʃɑːklət/ n 1 [U] : a sweet food that is made from cacao beans • a bar of chocolate • chocolate milk/cake 2 [C] : a candy made or covered with chocolate • a box of chocolates 3 [U] : a dark brown color — called also chocolate brown — **choc·o·laty** also **choc·o·lat·ey** /'tʃɑːkləti/ adj

¹**choice** /'tʃois/ n 1 [C] : the act of choosing : the act of deciding between two or more possibilities • You can either go or not. It's your choice. • She was faced with a difficult choice. • You made a good/bad choice. 2 [U, singular] : the opportunity or power to make a decision • He had no choice. = He did not have a choice. • You leave me (with) no choice. • They gave/offered me a choice between red or blue. • I live here by choice. [=because I want/choose to] • The meal is served with a beverage of your choice. [=a beverage that you choose] 3 a [U, singular] : a range of things that can be chosen • You have the choice of coffee or tea. b [C] : one of the things that you can choose • a wide range of choices 4 [C] : the person or thing that someone chooses • That was the right choice. • She is my first choice for the job. • She is the one I most want for the job] — **of choice** : favorite or most often chosen • Wine was his beverage of choice.

²**choice** adj **choic·er; -est** 1 : very good • only the choicest [=best] fruits 2 of words or phrases : carefully chosen especially for the purpose of expressing anger or disapproval • I had a few choice words for him. [=I said a few angry words to him]

choir /'kwajə/ n [C] : a group of singers especially in a church — **preach to the choir** see PREACH

choir·boy /'kwajə,boi/ n [C] : a boy who is a member of a church choir

¹**choke** /'tʃouk/ vb **choked; chok·ing** 1 [I] : to become unable to breathe usually because something gets stuck in your throat • She choked to death. • We were choking on fumes. 2 [T] **a** : to squeeze the throat of (someone) • The murderer choked his victim (to death). **b** : to make (someone) unable to breathe normally • The thick smoke was choking me. • She was so **choked with emotion/anger** that she couldn't speak. 3 [T] : to stop (something) from growing or developing • The flowers were choked (out) by the weeds. 4

[T] : to fill (something) completely so that movement is stopped or slowed • The streets were choked (up) with traffic. 5 [I] informal : to fail to do something well because you are very nervous • athletes who choke at the Olympics — **choke back** [phrasal vb] ✧ If you are **choking back tears, rage, anger, etc.**, you are finding it very hard not to cry or express emotion. • He choked back tears as he talked about his late wife. — **choke down** [phrasal vb] **choke down (something)** or **choke (something) down** informal : to eat (something) with difficulty or without enjoyment • I managed to choke down a few bites. — **choke off** [phrasal vb] **choke off (something)** also **choke (something) off** 1 : to cause (something) to slow down or stop • Rising interest rates choked off consumer spending. 2 : to prevent (something) from flowing • choking off the enemy's supply lines — **choke out** [phrasal vb] **choke (something) out** or **choke out (something)** : to say (something) with difficulty because of strong emotion • She tearfully choked out an apology. — **choke up** [phrasal vb] ✧ If you **choke up** or **get/become (all) choked up**, you are almost crying and have trouble talking because of strong emotion. • He chokes up when he tries to talk about the accident.

²**choke** n [C] : a part in a vehicle that controls the flow of air into the engine

choke hold n [C] chiefly US 1 : a method of holding someone by putting your arm around the person's neck • He put the suspect in a choke hold. 2 : a force or influence that stops something from growing or developing : STRANGLEHOLD • The state has a choke hold on the city's finances.

chok·er /'tʃoukə/ n [C] 1 : a necklace that fits closely around the neck 2 informal : a person who fails to do something because of nervousness : a person who chokes

chol·era /'kɑːlərə/ n [U] : a disease that causes vomiting and diarrhea and that often results in death

chol·er·ic /'kɑːlərɪk/ adj, formal : made angry easily • a choleric temperament

cho·les·ter·ol /kə'lɛstə,rɑːl/ n [U] : a substance that is found in the bodies of people • She is on medication to lower her cholesterol (level). [=to lower the amount of cholesterol in her blood]

chomp /'tʃɑːmp/ vb [T/I] informal : to chew or bite on something • The dog was chomping (on) a bone. — **chomping at the bit** : waiting in an impatient way to do something • We're all chomping at the bit to get started.

choose /'tʃuːz/ vb **chose** /'tʃouz/; **cho·sen** /'tʃouzn/; **choos·ing** [T/I] 1 : to decide that a particular person or thing is the one that you want • They chose her as the team captain. • Choose your words carefully. • You'll have to choose between the two of them. • There are several books to choose from. 2 : DECIDE • We chose to go by train. • They have chosen not to believe it. • Do as you choose. [=do what you want to do] — **choose sides** : to divide a group into two teams that will play against each other ▪ *When we chose sides in gym class, I was always the last person to be picked to be on a team.* ▪ (figurative) *They are forcing us to choose sides in the dispute.* — **choos·er** n [C] — see also **beggars can't be choosers** at BEGGAR

choosy also **choos·ey** /'tʃuːzi/ adj **choos·i·er; -est** : liking only certain things ▪ *You can't be too choosy if you want a job right away.*

¹**chop** /'tʃɑːp/ vb **chopped; chop·ping** [T] : to cut (something) into pieces by hitting it with an ax, knife, etc. ▪ *chopping vegetables/firewood* ▪ *two cups of chopped onions* ▪ (figurative) *They chopped [=lowered] prices for the sale.* — **chop down** [phrasal vb] **chop (something) down** or **chop down (something)** : to cut (a tree, bush, etc.) at the bottom so that it falls to the ground ▪ *He chopped the tree down.* — **chop off** [phrasal vb] **chop (something) off** or **chop off (something)** : to remove (something) by cutting ▪ *She chopped off a hunk of bread.* — **chop up** [phrasal vb] **chop (something) up** or **chop up (something)** : to cut (something) into small pieces ▪ *She chopped up the walnuts.*

²**chop** n [C] **1 a** : a small piece of meat that usually includes a bone ▪ *lamb/pork chops* **2 a** : the act of hitting something with an ax, knife, etc. ▪ *He cut off the branch with a single chop.* **b** : the act of hitting someone or something with the side of your hand ▪ *He broke the boards with a karate chop.* — **the chop** Brit, informal : the act of removing someone from a job : AX ▪ *More than 100 jobs are for the chop.* [=are going/likely to be eliminated] ▪ *Eight employees got the chop.* [=were fired] ▪ *His boss gave him the chop.* [=fired him]

chopped liver n [U] US slang : someone or something that is not important or appealing ▪ *"Wow, she's gorgeous!" "And what am I . . . chopped liver?"*

chop·per /'tʃɑːpɚ/ n **1** [C] : someone or something that chops something ▪ *a food chopper* **2** [C] informal : HELICOPTER **3** [C] chiefly US, informal : a type of motorcycle **4** [plural] chiefly US slang : TEETH ▪ *The dentist checked my choppers.*

chopping block n [C] US : a wooden block on which pieces of meat, wood, etc., are chopped ▪ (figurative, informal) *There were several programs on the chopping block.* [=programs that were going to be eliminated]

chopping board n [C] chiefly Brit : CUTTING BOARD

chop·py /'tʃɑːpi/ adj **chop·pi·er; -est 1** : rough with small waves ▪ *choppy seas/waters* **2** : marked by sudden stops and starts ▪ *quick choppy strides* — **chop·pi·ness** n [U]

chops /'tʃɑːps/ n [plural] **1 a** : the part of an animal's face that covers the jaws ▪ *The dog was licking its chops.* **b** informal : a person's jaw ▪ *I'm going to break/bust your chops.* ▪ (figurative) *My brother likes to bust my chops.* [=to tease me] **2**

chiefly US, informal : skill in a particular field or activity ▪ *showing off his acting chops* [=showing his talents as an actor] — **lick your chops** see ¹LICK

chop·stick /'tʃɑːpˌstɪk/ n [C] : either one of a pair of thin sticks that are used to pick up and eat food

chop su·ey /ˌtʃɑːpˈsuːwi/ n [U] : a dish of vegetables and meat or fish that is served with rice in Chinese restaurants

cho·ral /'korəl/ adj : of or relating to a choir or chorus ▪ *choral groups/music*

chord /'koɚd/ n [C] : a group of three or more musical notes that are played or sung at the same time — **strike/touch a chord** ◇ If something strikes/touches a chord in/with you, you think that it is true and have strong feelings about it. ▪ *Her speech on reform clearly struck a chord with many voters.*

chore /'tʃoɚ/ n [C] **1** : a small job that is done regularly ▪ *children doing household chores* **2** : a dull, unpleasant, or difficult job or experience ▪ *Doing taxes can be a real chore.*

cho·re·og·ra·phy /ˌkori'ɑːgrəfi/ n [U] : the art or job of deciding how dancers will move in a performance; *also* : the movements that are done by dancers in a performance — *a show with excellent choreography* — **cho·re·o·graph** /'korijəˌgræf, Brit 'kɒrijəˌgrɑːf/ vb [T] ▪ *She was hired to choreograph the ballet.* ▪ (figurative) *a carefully choreographed meeting* — **cho·re·og·ra·pher** /ˌkori'ɑːgrəfɚ/ n — **cho·re·o·graph·ic** /ˌkorijəˈgræfɪk/ adj

chor·tle /'tʃoɚtl/ vb **chor·tled; chor·tling** [T/I] : to laugh because you are amused or pleased by something ▪ *She chortled with delight.* — **chortle** n [C]

cho·rus /'korəs/ n [C] **1 a** : a group of singers and dancers in a play, musical show, etc. **b** : CHOIR **2 a** : a part of a song that is repeated between verses **b** : a piece of music that is sung by a large group ▪ *Handel's "Hallelujah Chorus"* **3 a** : a sound made by many people or animals at the same time ▪ *a loud chorus of boos* [=the sound of many people booing] **b** : a group of people or animals that are all heard at the same time ▪ *a chorus of critics/frogs* — **in chorus** : all at the same time ▪ *The phones rang in chorus.*

chorus girl n [C] : a young woman who sings or dances in a musical show

chose past tense of CHOOSE

¹**chosen** past participle of CHOOSE

²**cho·sen** /'tʃoʊzn/ adj : selected to do or receive something special ▪ *Only the/a chosen few* [=only a few people] *will get to go on the trip.*

¹**chow** /'tʃaʊ/ n [U] informal : FOOD 1 ▪ *Let's grab some chow.*

²**chow** vb — **chow down** [phrasal vb] US, informal : EAT 1 ▪ *The kids chowed down (on pizza).*

chow·der /'tʃaʊdɚ/ n [C/U] : a kind of thick soup ▪ *clam/corn chowder*

chow mein /'tʃaʊˈmeɪn/ n [U] : a combination of meat and vegetables with fried noodles that is served in Chinese restaurants

Christ /'kraɪst/ n [singular] : JESUS

CHRIST — **Christ·like** /ˈkraɪstˌlaɪk/ adj
— **Christ·ly** adj

chris·ten /ˈkrɪsn/ vb [T] **1** : to baptize
(someone) • The baby will be christened
today. **2 a** : to name (someone) at baptism • They christened her Anna. **b** : to
officially give (something) a name in a
ceremony • She was chosen to christen the
new ship. **3** : to use (something new) for
the first time • They christened the new
ball park with a win.

Chris·ten·dom /ˈkrɪsndəm/ n [U] : the
part of the world where most people are
Christians

chris·ten·ing /ˈkrɪsənɪŋ/ n [C] **1** : the
ceremony of baptizing and naming a
child **2** : the official ceremony in which
something is named • a ship's christening

¹**Chris·tian** /ˈkrɪstʃən/ n [C] : a person
who believes in the teachings of Jesus
Christ

²**Christian** adj **1** : of or relating to Jesus
Christ or the religion based on his teachings • Christian scriptures/ethics/burials
2 : of, relating to, or being Christians • a
Christian country/family **3** : treating
other people in a kind and generous way
• That was not a very Christian thing to do.

Christian era n [U] : the time starting
from the birth of Jesus Christ — abbr.
CE

Chris·ti·an·i·ty /ˌkrɪstʃiˈænəti/ n [U] : the
religion that is based on the teachings of
Jesus Christ

Christian name n [C] : a person's first
name • Her Christian name is Anna.

Christ·mas /ˈkrɪsməs/ n [C/U] : a Christian holiday that is celebrated on December 25 in honor of the birth of Jesus
Christ • Merry Christmas! • Christmas
cards/carols/trees — **Christ·mas·sy**
/ˈkrɪsməsi/ adj • Christmassy decorations

Christmas tree n [C] : an evergreen tree
that is decorated in people's houses for
Christmas

chrome /ˈkroʊm/ n [U] : a type of shiny
metal

chro·mi·um /ˈkroʊmijəm/ n [U] : a bluewhite metallic element

chro·mo·some /ˈkroʊməˌsoʊm/ n [C]
: the part of a cell that contains the genes
of an animal or plant — **chro·mo·som·al** /ˌkroʊməˈsoʊməl/ adj

chron·ic /ˈkrɑːnɪk/ adj **1** medical : continuing or occurring again and again for
a long time • chronic diseases/pain **2 a**
: happening or existing frequently or
most of the time • a chronic need for attention • chronic warfare **b** : always or
often doing something specified • a
chronic gambler/complainer — **chron·i·cal·ly** /ˈkrɑːnɪkli/ adv

¹**chron·i·cle** /ˈkrɑːnɪkəl/ n [C] : a description of events in the order that they happened • a chronicle of the American Civil
War

²**chronicle** vb **-i·cled; -i·cling** [T] : to describe a series of events in the order that
they happened • a magazine that chronicles the lives of the rich and famous —
chron·i·cler n [C]

chro·nol·o·gy /krəˈnɑːlədʒi/ n, pl **-gies**
1 [U] : the order in which a series of
events happened • We tried to reconstruct

the chronology of the accident. **2** [C] : a
record of the order in which a series of
events happened • a chronology of the
American Civil War — **chro·no·log·i·cal** /ˌkrɑːnəˈlɑːdʒɪkəl/ adj • His art is displayed in chronological order. — **chro·no·log·i·cal·ly** /ˌkrɑːnəˈlɑːdʒɪkli/ adv

chrys·a·lis /ˈkrɪsələs/ n, pl **chrys·al·i·ses** also **chrys·a·lid·es** /krɪˈsæləˌdiːz/
[C] biology : a hard case that protects a
moth or butterfly while it is turning into
an adult

chry·san·the·mum /krɪˈsænθəməm/ n
[C] : a plant that has brightly colored
flowers and that is often grown in gardens — called also (US) **mum**

chub·by /ˈtʃʌbi/ adj **chub·bi·er; -est**
: somewhat fat • a baby with chubby
cheeks — **chub·bi·ness** /ˈtʃʌbinəs/ n
[U]

¹**chuck** /ˈtʃʌk/ vb [T] informal **1** : to
throw or toss (something) • She chucked
a snowball at me. **2** : to get rid of (something) • Use what you need and chuck the
rest. **3** : to give up (something) • He decided to chuck his career/job. — **chuck
out** [phrasal vb] **chuck (someone) out** or
chuck out (someone) : to force (someone) to leave • The landlord chucked
them out of the apartment.

²**chuck** n **1** [U] : a piece of beef from a
cow's neck and shoulders • a chuck roast
2 [C] : a part of a machine that holds
something so that it does not move • To
remove the drill bit, loosen the chuck.

chuck·le /ˈtʃʌkl/ vb **chuck·led; chuck·ling** [I] : to laugh in a quiet way • She
chuckled to herself. — **chuckle** n [C] • I
got a good chuckle out of the joke.

chuffed /ˈtʃʌft/ adj, Brit, informal : very
pleased • She's (feeling) quite chuffed.

chug /ˈtʃʌg/ vb **chugged; chug·ging 1**
[I] : to move or go while making a sound
like the engine on a train • The train
chugged up the hill. • (figurative) Business
is chugging along quite nicely. **2** [T] US,
informal : to drink all the beer, soda,
etc., in a can or bottle without stopping •
He chugged a few beers at the party.

¹**chum** /ˈtʃʌm/ n [C] informal + oldfashioned : a close friend • a couple of old
chums

²**chum** vb **chummed; chum·ming** [I]
chiefly US, informal : to spend time with
someone as a friend — usually + around
• She often chums around with celebrities.
— **chum up** [phrasal vb] Brit, informal
: to become friendly • businessmen
chumming up to politicians

chum·my /ˈtʃʌmi/ adj **chum·mi·er; -est**
informal : very friendly • getting chummy
with celebrities

chump /ˈtʃʌmp/ n [C] informal : a person
who is easy to trick • Don't be a chump.

chump change n [U] US, informal : a
small amount of money • Her share of the
profits was chump change.

chunk /ˈtʃʌŋk/ n [C] **1** : a thick piece of
something • She cut the fruit/meat/wood
into large chunks. **2** : a large amount or
part of something • She spends a good
chunk of her day on the phone.

chunky /ˈtʃʌŋki/ adj **chunk·i·er; -est**
: heavy, thick, and solid • chunky ear-

rings **2** : somewhat fat • *She was a bit chunky as a child.* **3** : containing chunks • *chunky peanut butter*

church /ˈtʃɚtʃ/ *n* **1 a** [*C*] : a building that is used for Christian religious services **b** [*U*] : religious services held in a church • *They go to church* [=attend church services] *every Sunday.* • *She's at/in church.* **2** *or* **Church** [*C*] : a particular Christian group • *a member of the Catholic/Anglican Church* **3** [*U*] : the Christian religion as an organization • *the separation of church and state*

church·go·er /ˈtʃɚtʃˌgowɚ/ *n* [*C*] : someone who regularly goes to church — **church·go·ing** *adj* • *churchgoing people*

church·yard /ˈtʃɚtʃˌjɑɚd/ *n* [*C*] : a piece of land that belongs to a church and that is often used as a cemetery

churl·ish /ˈtʃɚlɪʃ/ *adj, formal* : not polite : RUDE • *churlish behavior*

¹**churn** /ˈtʃɚn/ *vb* **1** [*T/I*] : to stir or mix something with force • *The tractors churned (up) the soil.* **2** [*I*] : to move in a circle • *The gears began to churn.* **3** [*T*] : to make (butter) by stirring cream • *They churn their own butter.* **4** [*I*] : to experience a lot of confused activity • *Her emotions were churning inside her.* • *The movie made my stomach churn.* = *It churned my stomach.* [=it made me feel sick from nervousness, disgust, etc.] — **churn out** *[phrasal vb]* **churn out (something)** *or* **churn (something) out** : to produce (something, especially something of low quality) quickly as part of a continuous process • *He churns out a new novel every year.*

²**churn** *n* [*C*] : a container in which cream is stirred to make butter

chute /ˈʃuːt/ *n* [*C*] **1** : a narrow passage that things or people go down or through • *a mail/laundry chute* **2** *informal* : PARACHUTE — **out of the chute** *US, informal* : since the very beginning • *He was successful (right) out of the chute.*

chut·ney /ˈtʃʌtni/ *n, pl* **-neys** [*C/U*] : a sauce made from fruits, vinegar, sugar, and spices

chutz·pah /ˈhʊtspə/ *n* [*U*] *approving* : personal confidence or courage • *It took a lot of chutzpah to do what she did.*

CIA *abbr* Central Intelligence Agency • *The group is being investigated by the CIA.* • *a CIA agent* ◊ The Central Intelligence Agency is a part of the U.S. federal government that collects information about other countries or foreign groups.

ci·ca·da /səˈkeɪdə, səˈkɑːdə/ *n* [*C*] : a large insect that makes a loud, high-pitched sound

ci·der /ˈsaɪdɚ/ *n* [*C/U*] : a drink made from apples • *a cup of apple cider*

ci·gar /sɪˈgɑɚ/ *n* [*C*] : a roll of tobacco leaves that is smoked

cig·a·rette /ˌsɪgəˈrɛt/ *n* [*C*] : a small roll of paper that is filled with cut tobacco and smoked • *a pack of cigarettes*

¹**cinch** /ˈsɪntʃ/ *n* [*singular*] **1** *informal* : something that is very easy to do • *This dish is a cinch to make.* **2** *chiefly US, informal* — used to say that something will certainly happen • *He's a cinch to win* [=he will easily win] *the election.*

²**cinch** *vb* [*T*] *US* **1** : to fasten (something, such as a belt or strap) tightly around someone or something • *The coat is cinched at the waist.* • *She cinched the horse's saddle.* **2** *informal* : to make (something) certain to happen • *He cinched the nomination by winning the major primary elections.*

cin·der /ˈsɪndɚ/ *n* [*C*] : a very small piece of burned wood, coal, etc. • *Cinders from the fire floated through the air.*

cinder block *n* [*C*] *US* : a block made of cement and coal cinders and used in building — called also (*Brit*) breeze-block

Cin·der·el·la /ˌsɪndəˈrɛlə/ *n* [*C*] : someone or something that is not expected to do well but that succeeds in a very exciting way • *The Cinderella of the tournament* • *Their win was a classic Cinderella story.*

cin·e·ma /ˈsɪnəmə/ *n* **1** [*U*] **a** : the film industry • *She had a long career in (the) cinema.* **b** : the art or technique of making movies • *a student of French cinema* **2** [*C*] *chiefly Brit* : a movie theater • *They are going to the cinema* [=(*US*) going to the movies] *tonight.* — **cin·e·mat·ic** /ˌsɪnəˈmætɪk/ *adj* — **cin·e·mat·i·cal·ly** /ˌsɪnəˈmætɪkli/ *adv*

cin·e·ma·tog·ra·phy /ˌsɪnəməˈtɑːgrəfi/ *n* [*U*] : the art, process, or job of filming movies • *The film's cinematography is breathtaking.* — **cin·e·ma·tog·ra·pher** /ˌsɪnəməˈtɑːgrəfɚ/ *n* [*C*]

cin·na·mon /ˈsɪnəmən/ *n* [*U*] : a sweet spice used in cooking and baking • *a cinnamon roll/stick*

ci·pher *also chiefly Brit* **cy·pher** /ˈsaɪfɚ/ *n* [*C/U*] *technical* : a way of changing a message to keep it secret : CODE • *The message was written in (a) cipher.* **2** [*C*] *formal* + *disapproving* : a person who has no power or is not important

cir·ca /ˈsɚkə/ *prep, formal* : about or around • *He was born circa 1600.* — abbr. *c., ca.*

¹**cir·cle** /ˈsɚkəl/ *n* [*C*] **1 a** : a perfectly round shape • *Draw a circle around the correct answer.* **b** : a path that goes around a central point • *She walked (around) in a circle.* • (*figurative*) *We've been trying to make a decision, but we just keep going/running around in circles.* [=we are not making any progress] • (*figurative*) *The new product will run circles around* [=will be much better than] *the competition.* **2 a** : an arrangement of people or things that forms a circle • *We formed a circle around the campfire.* **b** : something that is shaped like part of a circle • *He had dark circles under his eyes.* **3** : a group of people who do something together, are friends, belong to the same profession, etc. • *She has a large circle of friends.* • *She is well-known in literary/political circles.*

²**circle** *vb* **cir·cled; cir·cling** **1 a** [*T/I*] : to form a circle around (something) • *There are trees circling our little house.* **b** [*T*] : to draw a circle around (something) • *She circled the correct answer.* **2** [*T/I*] : to move or go around (someone or something) in a circle • *The pilot circled the airport before landing.* • *I circled back* [=returned] *to the house to get my book.*

cir·cuit /ˈsəkət/ n [C] 1 : a series of performances, sports events, lectures, etc., that are held or done at many different places ▪ *the tennis/racing circuit* 2 : a path or trip around something ▪ *the Earth completing one circuit around the sun* 3 : the complete path that an electric current travels along ▪ *electric/electronic circuits* 4 or Circuit US, law : a legal district ▪ *the chief judge for the circuit*

circuit board n [C] : a board with many electrical circuits that is used in a computer, TV, etc.

circuit breaker n [C] : a switch that automatically stops the flow of electricity to a place or device if a dangerous problem occurs

circuit court n [C] US, law : a court of law that meets at two or more places within a particular area

circuit judge n [C] US, law : a judge who works in a circuit court

cir·cu·i·tous /səˈkjuːwətəs/ adj, formal 1 : not straight, short, and direct ▪ *a circuitous route* 2 : not said or done simply or clearly ▪ *a circuitous explanation* — **cir·cu·i·tous·ly** adv

cir·cuit·ry /ˈsəkətri/ n [U] : a system of electric circuits ▪ *computer circuitry*

¹**cir·cu·lar** /ˈsəkjələ/ adj 1 : shaped like a circle or part of a circle ▪ *a circular table* 2 : moving or going around in a circle ▪ *a circular motion/staircase* 3 : incorrectly using a statement that may not be true to prove an idea that would be false if the original statement was not true ▪ *circular logic/reasoning* — **cir·cu·lar·i·ty** /ˌsəkjəˈlerəti/ n [U]

²**circular** n [C] : a printed advertisement that is sent to many people at the same time ▪ *the sales in this week's circular*

circular saw n [C] : an electric tool that has a sharp round blade and is used for cutting wood

cir·cu·late /ˈsəkjəˌleɪt/ vb -lat·ed; -lat·ing [T/I] 1 : to move without stopping through a system, place, etc. ▪ *Blood circulates through the body.* ▪ *Fans circulate the air.* 2 : to go or spread from one person or place to another ▪ *Rumors (were) circulated around the town.*

cir·cu·la·tion /ˌsəkjəˈleɪʃən/ n 1 [U] a : the movement of blood through the body that is caused by the pumping action of the heart ▪ *He has bad circulation in his legs.* b : movement of air, water, etc., through the different parts of something ▪ *The attic has poor air circulation.* 2 [U] : the act of passing money, information, etc., from person to person or place to place ▪ *This memo is not meant for circulation.* ▪ *That rumor has been in circulation* [=has been going around] *for a long time.* ▪ *The magazine has been taken out of circulation.* [=the magazine will no longer be made and sold] 3 [U] : the state of being actively involved in social activities (such as parties or dates) ▪ *She's finally getting back in/into circulation after her divorce.* 4 [C] : the average number of copies of a newspaper, magazine, etc., that are sold over a particular period ▪ *The newspaper has the largest circulation in the country.*

cir·cu·la·to·ry /ˈsəkjələˌtori, Brit ˌsəːkjəˈletri, ˈsəːkjəlɑtri/ adj, medical : of or relating to the circulation of blood through the body ▪ *the circulatory system*

cir·cum·cise /ˈsəkəmˌsaɪz/ vb -cised; -cis·ing [T] : to cut off the foreskin of (a man or boy) ▪ *The baby was circumcised at the hospital.* — **cir·cum·ci·sion** /ˌsəkəmˈsɪʒən/ n [C/U]

cir·cum·fer·ence /səˈkʌmfrəns/ n 1 [C/U] : the length of a line that goes around a circle or other round shape ▪ *The tree/circle is 38 inches in circumference.* 2 [C] : the outer edge of a shape or area ▪ *The fence goes around the circumference of the field.*

cir·cum·flex /ˈsəkəmˌflɛks/ n [C] : a mark ˆ used to show how to pronounce a vowel

cir·cum·lo·cu·tion /ˌsəkəmlouˈkjuːʃən/ n [C/U] formal : the use of many words to say something that could be said using fewer words ▪ *Try to avoid circumlocutions.*

cir·cum·nav·i·gate /ˌsəkəmˈnævəˌgeɪt/ vb -gat·ed; -gat·ing [T] formal : to travel all the way around (something) ▪ *The ship circumnavigated the world.* — **cir·cum·nav·i·ga·tion** /ˌsəkəmˌnævəˈgeɪʃən/ n [C/U]

cir·cum·scribe /ˈsəkəmˌskraɪb/ vb -scribed; -scrib·ing [T] 1 formal : to limit the size or amount of (something) ▪ *His role as president was circumscribed by the board.* 2 technical : to draw a shape around (another shape) ▪ *a circle circumscribed by a square*

cir·cum·spect /ˈsəkəmˌspɛkt/ adj, formal : thinking carefully about possible risks before doing or saying something ▪ *a circumspect businesswoman* — **cir·cum·spec·tion** /ˌsəkəmˈspɛkʃən/ n [U]

cir·cum·stance /ˈsəkəmˌstæns/ n 1 [C] : a condition or fact that affects a situation ▪ *adapting to changing circumstances* ▪ *It is impossible under these/the circumstances to meet our deadline.* 2 [plural] : the specific details of an event ▪ *The circumstances of his death are suspicious.* 3 [U, plural] : an event or situation that you cannot control ▪ *She says that her client is a victim of circumstance/circumstances.* 4 [plural] : the conditions in which someone lives ▪ *Their (financial) circumstances changed greatly after she lost her job.* — **pomp and circumstance** see POMP

cir·cum·stan·tial /ˌsəkəmˈstænʃəl/ adj, law : based on information which suggests that something is true but does not prove that it is true ▪ *The evidence is purely circumstantial.*

cir·cum·vent /ˌsəkəmˈvɛnt/ vb [T] formal : to avoid being stopped by a law, rule, etc. ▪ *We found a way to circumvent the problem.* — **cir·cum·ven·tion** /ˌsəkəmˈvɛnʃən/ n [U]

cir·cus /ˈsəkəs/ n [C] 1 : a traveling show that typically includes trained animals, clowns, acrobats, etc. ▪ *We're going to the circus.* ▪ *She wants to join the circus.* [=to become a performer in a circus] 2 informal : a situation that is busy, lively, and confusing and that attracts a lot of

attention • *The trial became a media circus.*

cir·rho·sis /səˈroʊsəs/ *n* [U] : a disease of the liver often caused by drinking too much alcohol

cissy *Brit spelling of* SISSY

cis·tern /ˈsɪstən/ *n* [C] : an often underground container that holds a supply of water

cit·a·del /ˈsɪtədl/ *n* [C] : a castle or fort • *(figurative) The magazine is a citadel* [=*stronghold*] *of conservatism.*

ci·ta·tion /saɪˈteɪʃən/ *n* [C] **1** *US* : an official order to appear before a court of law : SUMMONS • *She was issued a citation for reckless driving.* **2** : a formal public statement that praises a person for doing something good or brave • *a citation for bravery* **3** : a line or short section taken from a piece of writing or a speech • *She includes citations from the book in her report.*

cite /ˈsaɪt/ *vb* **cit·ed; cit·ing** [T] **1** : ¹QUOTE 1a • *The article cites several experts on the subject.* **2** : to mention (something) especially as an example or to support an idea or opinion • *He cited the data as evidence.* **3** *law* : to order (someone) to appear before a court of law • *She was cited for reckless driving.* **4** : to officially and publicly honor (someone) for doing something • *She was cited for bravery.*

cit·i·zen /ˈsɪtəzən/ *n* [C] **1** : a person who legally belongs to a country and has the rights and protection of that country • *Japanese citizens living in the U.S.* • *I've been treated like a second-class citizen.* [=*someone who is not given the same rights as other people*] **2** : a person who lives in a particular place • *the citizens of Boston* — **cit·i·zen·ship** /ˈsɪtəzənˌʃɪp/ *n* [U] • *He applied for Canadian citizenship.* • *good citizenship*

cit·i·zen·ry /ˈsɪtəzənri/ *n, pl* **-ries** [C] *formal* : all the citizens of a place • *an educated citizenry*

cit·ric acid /ˈsɪtrɪk-/ *n* [U] : an acid that occurs in citrus fruit

cit·rus /ˈsɪtrəs/ *n, pl* **citrus** *or* **cit·rus·es** [C] : a juicy fruit (such as an orange or lemon) that has a thick skin • *citrus trees* — **cit·rusy** /ˈsɪtrəsi/ *adj*

city /ˈsɪti/ *n, pl* **cit·ies** **1** [C] : a place where people live and work that is larger or more important than a town • *major cities like London and Tokyo* • *Mexico City* • *We spent the day in the city.* [=in the nearest big city] **2 a** [C] : the people in a city • *The whole city was celebrating.* **b** *the city* : the government of a city • *The city needs to make the streets safer.* **3** *the City* : the section of London that is Great Britain's financial and business center

city council *n* [C] : the group of people who determine the laws of a city

city hall *or* **City Hall** *n* [C] *US* : a city government's main building • *They were married at City Hall.*

city slicker *n* [C] *informal* : someone who lives in a city and does not understand life outside a city

city·wide /ˈsɪtiˌwaɪd/ *adj* : involving all parts of a city • *a citywide smoking ban*

civ·ic /ˈsɪvɪk/ *adj* **1** : of or relating to a city or town • *civic pride* • *civic leaders/groups* **2** : relating to citizenship • *Voting is your civic duty/responsibility.*

civ·ic-mind·ed /ˌsɪvɪkˈmaɪndəd/ *adj* : tending to do things that help your city or town • *civic-minded businesses/individuals* — **civ·ic-mind·ed·ness** *n* [U]

civ·ics /ˈsɪvɪks/ *n* [U] *chiefly US* : the study of how government works

civ·il /ˈsɪvəl/ *adj* **1** : of or relating to the people who live in a country • *civil liberties/duties* • *a period of civil unrest* [=a time when groups of people in a country fight one another] **2** : of or relating to the business of a city, state, etc., and not connected to the military or to a religion • *a civil wedding ceremony at city hall* **3** *not before a noun* : polite but not friendly • *Try to at least be civil to her.* **4** *law* : relating to laws that describe a person's rights rather than to laws about crime • *They filed a civil suit against the company.* • *civil cases/law* — **civ·il·ly** /ˈsɪvəli/ *adv* • *Let's discuss this civilly.* [=*politely*]

civil defense *(US)* or *Brit* **civil defence** *n* [U] : a group of people who are not part of the military but are trained to protect and help people if their country is attacked, suffers an earthquake, etc.

civil disobedience *n* [U] : refusal to obey laws as a way of protesting in a nonviolent way • *an act of civil disobedience*

civil engineering *n* [U] : a type of engineering that deals with roads, bridges, large buildings, etc. — **civil engineer** *n* [C]

ci·vil·ian /səˈvɪljən/ *n* [C] : a person who is not a member of the military or of a police or firefighting force — **civilian** *adj* • *civilian casualties*

ci·vil·i·ty /səˈvɪləti/ *n* [U] *formal* : polite, reasonable, and respectful behavior • *They were treated with civility.*

civ·i·li·za·tion *also Brit* **civ·i·li·sa·tion** /ˌsɪvələˈzeɪʃən, *Brit* ˌsɪvɪˌlaɪˈzeɪʃən/ *n* **1** [U] : the condition that exists when people have an advanced and well-organized society • *modern civilization* **2** [C/U] : a particular well-organized and developed society • *ancient/modern civilizations* • *Egyptian civilization* **3** [U] : all the societies of the world • *threats to civilization* **4** [U] *informal* : a place where there is electricity, hot water, etc. • *He was sick of camping and wanted to get back to civilization.*

civ·i·lize *also Brit* **civ·i·lise** /ˈsɪvəˌlaɪz/ *vb* **-lized; -liz·ing** [T] **1** : to teach (a person or group) to behave in a more polite and gentle way • *a teacher who tried to civilize her students* **2** : to make (something) more gentle, fair, reasonable, etc. • *efforts to civilize public education* **3** : to cause (a group of people) to have a more modern way of living • *They wanted to civilize the native people.*

civilized *also Brit* **civilised** *adj* **1** : marked by well-organized laws and rules about how people behave with each other • *a more civilized culture* **2** : polite, reasonable, and respectful • *civilized behavior/conversations* **3 a** : pleasant and comfortable • *Please call back at a more civilized hour.* [=at a time that is not so early in the morning] **b** : showing concern for what is correct according to social rules • *a more civilized era* [=a time when people were more concerned with what was proper]

civil liberty *n* [*C*] : the right of people to do or say things that are not illegal without being stopped or interrupted by the government • *freedom of speech and other civil liberties*

civil rights *n* [*plural*] : the rights that every person should have regardless of his or her sex, race, or religion • *Martin Luther King, Jr., fought for civil rights.*

civil servant *n* [*C*] : a person who works for the government

civil service *n* [*U*] : the administrative part of a government • *a civil service employee*

civil war *n* [*C/U*] : a war between groups of people in the same country • *The country is on the brink of (a) civil war.*

cl *abbr* centiliter

clack /'klæk/ *vb* [*T/I*] : to make a short sharp sound • *I heard her heels clacking down the hall.* — **clack** *n* [*C*] • *the clack of typewriter keys*

¹**clad** /'klæd/ *adj, literary* **1** : covered with something specified • *ivy-clad buildings* **2** — used to describe the way someone is dressed • *scantily clad dancers*

²**clad** *past tense and past participle of* CLOTHE

clad·ding /'klædɪŋ/ *n* [*U*] *chiefly Brit* : SIDING

¹**claim** /'kleɪm/ *vb* [*T*] **1** : to say that (something) is true when some people may say it is not true • *They claim (that) the drug prevents hair loss.* • *He claims to know nothing about the robbery.* **2 a** : to say that you have (something) • *The organization claims 10,000 members.* **b** : to say that (something) belongs to you or that you deserve (something) • *The terrorist group claimed responsibility for the attack.* • *Both of them claimed credit for the idea.* **3** : to say that you have a legal right to be given (something) • *You can claim these expenses as* [=you can say that these expenses should be] *tax deductions.* **4** : to take (something that belongs to you or that you deserve) • *She claimed her luggage and left the airport.* **5** — used to say that someone's attention, time, etc., is being given to something • *This issue has claimed too much of our time.* [=we have spent too much time on this issue] **6** : to cause the end of someone's life • *The illness claimed her life.* [=caused her death]

²**claim** *n* **1** [*C*] : a statement saying that something is true when some people may say it is not true • *He made false claims about his past.* • *She disputes/denies the claim* [=she says it isn't true] *that she cheated.* **2** [*C*] : an official request for money that is owed to you • *file an insurance claim = make a claim on an insurance policy* • *a claim form* [=a document with information about why you should be given money] **3** [*C/U*] : a right to have something • *The bank has a claim* on/to their property. • *The community lays claim to being* [=claims to be] *the oldest city in the country.* • *The restaurant's claim to fame* [=the thing that makes it important, famous, or interesting] *is its barbecue sauce.* — **baggage claim** : the area in an airport or bus station where you pick up your luggage after traveling

claim·ant /'kleɪmənt/ *n* [*C*] *formal* : a person who believes that he or she has a right to something (such as an amount of money) • *They are claimants to the dead man's estate.*

clair·voy·ance /ˌkleəˈvojəns/ *n* [*U*] : an ability to communicate with dead people or to know about things that you did not actually see happen or hear about — **clair·voy·ant** /ˌkleəˈvojənt/ *adj* • *clairvoyant powers/people* — **clairvoyant** *n* [*C*] • *psychics and clairvoyants*

¹**clam** /'klæm/ *n* [*C*] : a type of shellfish that has a shell with two parts • *steamed clams* • *clam chowder* — **(as) happy as a clam** *US, informal* : very happy

²**clam** *vb* **clammed; clam·ming** — **clam up** [*phrasal vb*] *informal* : to stop talking or refuse to talk • *They clammed up when the detectives started asking questions.*

clam·ber /'klæmbə/ *vb* [*I*] : to climb in an awkward way • *The children clambered over the rocks.*

clam·my /'klæmi/ *adj* **clam·mi·er; -est** : unpleasantly wet and cold • *clammy hands* — **clam·mi·ness** *n* [*U*]

clam·or (*US*) *or Brit* **clam·our** /'klæmə/ *vb* [*I*] **1** : to be loud and noisy • *The children clamored around us.* **2** : to ask for or demand something in a loud way • *Fans clamored for autographs.* — **clamor** (*US*) *or Brit* **clamour** *n* [*U, singular*] • *a clamor of voices/bells* • *There is growing clamor for reform.* — **clam·or·ous** /'klæmrəs/ *adj*

¹**clamp** /'klæmp/ *n* [*C*] : a device that holds or presses parts tightly together

²**clamp** *vb* [*T*] **1** : to fasten or tighten (something) with a clamp • *The surgeon clamped the vein.* • *Clamp the boards together.* **2** : to press or squeeze (something) • *He clamped his mouth shut.* **3** *Brit* : ²BOOT 4 — **clamp down on** [*phrasal vb*] : to try harder to stop (a crime) or punish (people) • *The state is clamping down on drug trafficking/traffickers.* — **clamp on** [*phrasal vb*] *chiefly US* **clamp (something) on** : to officially set (a limit, rule, etc.) for (someone or something) • *The mayor clamped a curfew on the area after the riots.*

clamp·down /'klæmpˌdaʊn/ *n* [*C*] : an increased effort to make sure that people obey laws and rules • *a clampdown on drug trafficking*

clan /'klæn/ *n* [*C*] : a large group of people who are related • *Scottish clans*

clan·des·tine /klænˈdɛstən/ *adj, formal* : done secretly • *a clandestine meeting/marriage* — **clan·des·tine·ly** *adv*

clang /'klæŋ/ *vb* [*T/I*] : to make or cause (something) to make the loud sound of metal hitting against something • *He clanged a spoon against his cup.* • *The pots clanged together.* — **clang** *n* [*C*] • *the clang of cymbals*

clang·er /ˈklæŋɚ/ n [C] Brit, informal : a bad and embarrassing mistake : BLUNDER ▪ a verbal clanger

clank /ˈklæŋk/ vb [T/I] : CLANG ▪ The empty can clanked along the sidewalk. — **clank** n [C]

¹clap /ˈklæp/ vb clapped; clap·ping **1** [T/I] : to hit the palms of your hands together usually more than once ▪ They cheered and clapped [=applauded] for the band. ▪ She clapped her hands twice. **2** [T] : to suddenly put the palm of your hand on someone or something ▪ He clapped his friend on the shoulder. **3** [T/I] : to hit (something) together in a way that makes a loud noise ▪ She clapped the two boards together. — **clap·ping** n [U] ▪ The clapping [=applause] died down.

²clap n **1** [C] **a** : a sound made by clapping your hands ▪ a series of hand claps **b** : a loud, sharp sound ▪ a clap of thunder **2** [C] : a friendly hit with the palm of your hand ▪ He gave me a clap on the back. **3 the clap** slang : GONORRHEA

clap·board /ˈklæbɚd, ˈklæpˌboɚd/ n [U] chiefly US : a set of narrow boards covering the outside of a building ▪ a clapboard house [=a house covered in clapboard]

clap·per /ˈklæpɚ/ n [C] : a piece of metal that hangs inside a bell to make it ring

clap·trap /ˈklæpˌtræp/ n [U] informal : NONSENSE ▪ Her speech was nothing but claptrap.

clar·i·fy /ˈklerəˌfaɪ/ vb -fies; -fied; -fy·ing [T] : to make (something) clear or clearer ▪ Her explanation did not clarify matters much. ▪ clarified butter [=butter that is made purer by a process that involves heating it] — **clar·i·fi·ca·tion** /ˌklerəfəˈkeɪʃən/ n [C/U] ▪ Your argument needs some clarification. — **clar·i·fi·er** /ˈklerəˌfajɚ/ n [C]

clar·i·net /ˌkleɚˈnɛt/ n [C] : a musical instrument that is shaped like a straight tube and played by blowing into the top — **clar·i·net·ist** or **clar·i·net·tist** /ˌkleɚˈnɛtɪst/ n [C]

clar·i·on call /ˈkleɚijən-/ n [C] : a strong request for something to happen ▪ the leader's clarion call to action

clar·i·ty /ˈkleɚəti/ n [U] : the quality of being clear ▪ Many legal documents lack clarity. [=they are difficult to understand] ▪ She remembered what happened with surprising clarity. ▪ the clarity of the photographs/water

¹clash /ˈklæʃ/ vb [I] **1** : to be in a situation in which you are fighting or disagreeing ▪ Police and protesters clashed. = Protesters clashed with the police. ▪ clashing over politics **2 a** : to look bad or ugly together ▪ Those colors clash. ▪ Does this shirt clash with these pants? **b** : to be very different in a way that makes being together difficult ▪ Their personalities/ideas clash. **3** : to make the loud sound of a metal object hitting another metal object ▪ Their swords clashed.

²clash n [C] **1 a** : a short fight between groups of people ▪ a clash with the police ▪ violent clashes between the factions **b** : an argument or disagreement ▪ a clash between the two leaders **2** : a difference that makes it difficult for people or things to be together or work together ▪ a clash of opinions/cultures/personalities **3** : a loud sound of two metal objects clashing ▪ the clash of swords/cymbals

¹clasp /ˈklæsp, Brit ˈklɑːsp/ n [C] : a device for holding together objects or parts of a purse, necklace, etc.

²clasp vb [T] **1** : to fasten (something) with a clasp ▪ She clasped her purse shut. **2** : to hold (someone or something) tightly with your hands or arms ▪ He clasped her hand gently/firmly.

class /ˈklæs, Brit ˈklɑːs/ n **1 a** [C] : a group of students who meet regularly to be taught a particular subject or activity ▪ The class is going on a field trip. **b** [C] : a series of meetings in which students are taught ▪ She is teaching a class on psychology. ▪ taking dance classes **c** [C/U] : one of the meetings in which students are taught ▪ I have an English class this morning. ▪ Class starts at 8:00 a.m. **d** [C] US : students who graduate together ▪ a member of the class of 2006 ▪ the freshman class [=the group of students who are freshmen this year] ▪ She's running for class president. **2 a** [C] : a group of people in a society who are at the same economic and social level ▪ the ruling class ▪ class struggles **b** [U] : the way people in a society are divided into different social and economic groups ▪ a discussion about class and race **3** [U] **a** : a quality that makes something or someone seem special and attractive ▪ The hotel has class. [=it is very elegant] **b** : a quality that makes someone seem very good, kind, etc. ▪ She showed a lot of class by donating her prize money to charity. **4** [C] **a** : a group of people or things that are similar in some way ▪ There are other good players, but she is **in a class by herself**. [=she is far better than the other good players] **b** : one of the sections of seats on an airplane, train, etc. ▪ I am traveling **business class**. [=in a section of an airplane that is more comfortable than the main section but less comfortable than first class]

class act n [C] informal : an admirable person ▪ She's a real class act.

class action n [C] US, law : a lawsuit in which many people join together to sue the same person or group for the same reason — **class–action** adj ▪ a class-action suit against a car company

¹clas·sic /ˈklæsɪk/ adj **1 a** — used to say that something is one of the best of its kind ▪ classic movies/cars **b** — used to say that something is an example of excellence ▪ His winning goal was classic. **c** — used to describe something that has been popular for a long time ▪ a new version of a classic dish **2** : having a graceful design with simple lines ▪ It's a classic suit that won't go out of style. **3** : very typical ▪ a classic error

²classic n [C] **1** : something that has been considered to be excellent for a long time ▪ I like to read the classics. **2** : a traditional event ▪ The football game is a Thanksgiving classic.

clas·si·cal /ˈklæsɪkəl/ adj 1 : of a kind that has been respected for a long time ▪ classical ballet 2 : of or relating to the ancient Greek and Roman world ▪ classical literature/art/scholars 3 : relating to music in a European tradition that includes opera and symphony ▪ classical music/composers 4 : teaching art, science, etc., rather than practical skills ▪ a classical education — **clas·si·cal·ly** /ˈklæsɪkli/ adv

clas·si·cism /ˈklæsəˌsɪzəm/ n [U] formal 1 : the ideas and styles that are common in ancient Greece and Rome ▪ Roman classicism 2 : a traditional style of art, literature, music, architecture, etc. ▪ the classicism of the building — **clas·si·cist** /ˈklæsəsɪst/ n [C] ▪ a well-trained classicist

¹**clas·si·fied** /ˈklæsəˌfaɪd/ adj 1 : arranged in groups with similar things ▪ a classified directory 2 : kept secret from all but a few people in the government ▪ classified information/documents

²**classified** n [C] : a small advertisement that is grouped with others like it — usually plural ▪ newspaper/online classifieds — called also **classified ad**, **classified advertisement**

clas·si·fy /ˈklæsəˌfaɪ/ vb **-fies; -fied; -fy·ing** [T] 1 : to arrange (people or things) into groups based on ways that they are alike ▪ They classified the books into different categories. ▪ The parts were classified according to size. 2 : to consider (someone or something) as belonging to a particular group ▪ I would classify her as a jazz singer. — **clas·si·fi·ca·tion** /ˌklæsəfəˈkeɪʃən/ n [C/U] ▪ a system of classification ▪ racial/ethnic classifications

class·less /ˈklæsləs, Brit ˈklɑːsləs/ adj 1 : without social or economic classes ▪ a classless society 2 : rude in an annoying way ▪ classless behavior

class·mate /ˈklæsˌmeɪt, Brit ˈklɑːsˌmeɪt/ n [C] : a member of the same class in a school, college, or university ▪ We were classmates in high school.

class·room /ˈklæsˌruːm, Brit ˈklɑːsˌruːm/ n [C] : a room where classes are taught

class·work /ˈklæsˌwɜːk, Brit ˈklɑːsˌwɔːk/ n [U] : the part of a student's work that is done in a class and not at home

classy /ˈklæsi, Brit ˈklɑːsi/ adj **class·i·er; -est** 1 : having qualities that make someone or something special and attractive ▪ classy hotels/spas/clients 2 : very good, kind, etc. ▪ a classy guy — **class·i·ness** /ˈklæsinəs/ n [U]

clat·ter /ˈklætər/ vb [I] : to make a quick series of short loud sounds ▪ The wagon clattered down the road. — **clatter** n [C] ▪ the clatter of dishes

clause /ˈklɑːz/ n [C] 1 grammar : a part of a sentence that has its own subject and verb 2 : a separate part of a legal document ▪ a clause in a will/contract

claus·tro·pho·bia /ˌklɑːstrəˈfoʊbijə/ n [U] 1 : a fear of being in closed or small spaces 2 : an unhappy or uncomfortable feeling caused by being in a situation that limits or restricts you ▪ the claustrophobia of life in a small town — **claus·tro·pho·bic** /ˌklɑːstrəˈfoʊbɪk/ adj ▪ a small, claustrophobic room ▪ She

hates elevators because she's claustrophobic.

¹**claw** /ˈklɑː/ n [C] 1 : a sharp curved part on the toe of some animals ▪ a bear's/eagle's claws 2 : a body part of an animal (such as a lobster or crab) that is used for gripping and holding things 3 : a part on a tool or machine that is used for gripping, digging, etc. ▪ the claw of a hammer — **clawed** /ˈklɑːd/ adj ▪ a clawed foot

²**claw** vb [T/I] : to scratch, grip, or dig with claws or fingers ▪ The cat was clawing (at) the door. — **claw back** [phrasal vb] **claw (something) back** or **claw back (something)** chiefly Brit : to get back (something, such as money or business) by acting in a forceful way or by doing something that requires a lot of effort ▪ The government is trying to claw back some of the money it promised to state agencies. — **claw your way** : to move ahead slowly by grabbing onto things ▪ The climbers clawed their way up the steep terrain. ▪ (figurative) The company is clawing its way out of bankruptcy.

clay /ˈkleɪ/ n [C/U] : a heavy, sticky material from the earth that is made into different shapes and that becomes hard when it is baked or dried ▪ a clay pot/pipe/tablet

clay pigeon n [C] : a circular object made of baked clay that people throw into the air and shoot at to practice their shooting skills

¹**clean** /ˈkliːn/ adj 1 : free from dirt, marks, etc. : not dirty ▪ a clean floor/table ▪ clean laundry/socks/towels ▪ wiping the baby's face clean 2 : tending to keep clean ▪ Cats are very clean animals. 3 a : free from pollution or other dangerous substances ▪ clean air/water ▪ b : not causing pollution ▪ clean fuels/energy 4 : not yet used ▪ a clean piece/sheet of paper 5 : pleasingly simple ▪ the clean simplicity of the chair's design ▪ a suit with clean lines 6 : having edges that are straight and smooth ▪ a clean cut/break 7 : completely and quickly done ▪ The thief made a clean getaway. ▪ He made a clean break with the past. 8 : not showing evidence of any broken rules or laws ▪ a clean driving record 9 a : not connected with or involving anything illegal or morally wrong ▪ clean living ▪ good, clean fun ▪ b : not referring to anything sexual or offensive ▪ clean jokes/language 10 not before a noun : no longer using drugs ▪ clean and sober — **clean slate** also Brit **clean sheet** 1 : a person's record from a school, job, etc., that shows no evidence of any problems or broken rules ▪ Everyone who comes to this school starts with a clean slate. 2 clean sheet Brit : a game in which the opposing team is prevented from scoring : SHUTOUT — **come clean** informal : to tell the truth about what happened ▪ Eventually she came clean and admitted what she'd done. — **clean·ness** /ˈkliːnnəs/ n [U]

²**clean** vb 1 a [T/I] : to make (something) clean ▪ The carpet needs to be cleaned. ▪ In our house, I clean and my husband

cooks. **b** [*I*] : to become clean • *a surface that cleans easily* [=that is easy to clean] **2** [*T*] : to make (something, such as a room) neat and orderly • *Clean your room.* **3** [*T*] : to remove the organs from the inside of (an animal) before cooking • *skin and clean a rabbit/deer* — **clean house** see ¹HOUSE — **clean out** [*phrasal vb*] **1 clean (something) out** or **clean out (something)** : to remove unwanted things from (a room, closet, etc.) • *cleaning out the garage* **2 clean (someone or something) out** or **clean out (someone or something)** *informal* : to steal or take everything from (someone or something) • *The thieves broke in and cleaned out the store.* **3 clean (someone) out** or **clean out (someone)** *informal* : to use up all or most of someone's money • *Buying the house really cleaned us out.* — **clean up** [*phrasal vb*] **1 clean (something) up** or **clean up (something)** **a** : to remove (dirt, spilled substances, etc.) • *I'll clean this mess up.* **b** or **clean up** : to make (a room or space) clean and orderly • *Would you help me clean up (the kitchen) after dinner?* ✧ To **clean up after** someone is to make a place clean after someone has made it dirty or messy. . **c** : to remove pollution from (something) • *trying to clean up the bay* **2 clean up** or **clean (yourself) up** : to wash your face and hands • *I need a few minutes to clean (myself) up before dinner.* **3 clean (something) up** or **clean up (something)** : to remove whatever is illegal or immoral from (something) • *a mayor who will clean up city hall* **4** *informal* : to make a large amount of money • *She really cleaned up in the stock market.* **5 clean up your act** *informal* : to behave in a way that is more acceptable • *It's time to clean up your act and get a real job.* — **clean your plate** : to eat all the food on your plate

³**clean** *adv, informal* : completely or entirely • *The nail went clean through the wall.*

⁴**clean** *n* [*singular*] *informal* : an act of removing dirt from something • *She gave the tub a good clean.* [=she cleaned it thoroughly]

clean–cut /ˈkliːnˈkʌt/ *adj* : having a neat appearance that suggests you are someone who does not break rules or cause trouble • *a clean-cut guy*

clean·er /ˈkliːnɚ/ *n* **1** [*C*] : a person whose job is to clean something • *street/window/house cleaners* **2** [*C*] : a substance, device, or machine used for cleaning things • *an air cleaner* **3 the cleaners** or **the cleaner's** : a shop where clothes are cleaned : DRY CLEANER • *My suit is at the cleaners.* — **take (someone) to the cleaners** *informal* : to get all or most of someone's money or possessions usually in a dishonest or unfair way • *His ex-wife really took him to the cleaners in the divorce.*

cleaning lady *n* [*C*] : a woman whose job is to clean offices or houses — called also *cleaning woman*

cleaning person *n* [*C*] : a woman or man whose job is to clean offices or houses

clean·li·ness /ˈklɛnlinəs/ *n* [*U*] **1** : the state of being clean • *restaurants being inspected for cleanliness* **2** : the practice of keeping yourself and your surroundings clean • *the virtues of cleanliness and honesty*

clean·ly /ˈkliːnli/ *adv* **1** : easily and completely • *a knife that cuts cleanly* **2** : without causing pollution • *a fuel that burns cleanly*

cleanse /ˈklɛnz/ *vb* to make (someone or something) clean • *The cut should be cleansed gently with mild soap and water.*

cleans·er /ˈklɛnzɚ/ *n* [*C/U*] : a substance (such as a powder or cream) that is used for cleaning something • *a skin cleanser*

clean–shaven *adj, of a man* : having no beard or mustache

clean·up /ˈkliːnˌʌp/ *n* [*C*] : the process of cleaning something • *The children helped with the cleanup.* • *cleanup costs*

¹**clear** /ˈkliɚ/ *adj* **1** : very obvious • *The show was a clear failure.* [=there is no doubt that the show was a failure] • *I see clear differences between them.* • *It's clear that changes are necessary.* • *The work needs to be finished by this afternoon.* **Is that clear?** **2** : easily understood • *a clear writer/definition/message* **3 a** : free from doubt or confusion • *a clear understanding of the problem* • *Are you clear on/about what you need to do?* [=do you understand what you need to do?] **b** : able to think in an accurate way without confusion • *a clear thinker* • *a clear head* [=an ability to think clearly] **4** : having small parts and details that can be easily seen and identified • *This picture is blurry, but that one is clear.* **5** : easily heard • *a very clear sound* : easily heard and understood • *a clear pronunciation/voice* **6** : easily seen through • *clear glass/plastic* • *clear soup/broth* **7** : not blocked or covered by anything • *a clear view/path* • *The aisles must be kept clear.* • *Wait until the street is clear of traffic.* [=until there is no traffic on the street] **8** *of weather or the sky* : not having any clouds, fog, etc. • *a clear blue sky* **9 a** : free of marks or spots • *clear, healthy skin* **b** : having a distinct and bright color • *clear blue eyes* **10** : free from feelings of guilt or blame — used with *conscience* • *My conscience is clear.* [=I do not feel guilty because I did not do anything wrong] **11** *finance* — used to describe the amount that remains after costs, taxes, etc., have been paid • *a clear profit of $500* **12** : not having any planned or scheduled activities • *My schedule is clear on Friday afternoon.* — **(as) clear as a bell** : very clear • *a sound as clear as a bell* — **clear of** : away from (something dangerous, harmful, etc.) • *Stand clear of the closing doors!* — **see your way clear to** see ¹WAY — **clear·ness** *n* [*U*] • *the clearness* [=clarity] *of the water/explanation*

²**clear** *vb* **1** [*I*] **a** *of weather or the sky* : to change so that there are no clouds, fog, etc. • *The sky cleared after the rain.* **b** *of clouds, fog, smoke, etc.* : to go away • *The*

smoke gradually cleared. **c** *of a liquid* : to become transparent or more transparent • *The water cleared after the mud had settled.* **d** *of the skin* : to become free of marks or spots • *My skin cleared when I started using the cream.* **e** ✧ When your **head clears** or when something **clears your head**, you become more awake or alert and are able to think in a normal way without confusion. **f** ✧ When your **vision/eyesight clears** you become able to see things correctly. **2 a** [*T*] : to remove something entirely from an area or place • *clearing the snow off/from the driveway* = *clearing the driveway of snow* • *She cleared the dishes from the table.* = *She cleared the table (of dishes).* **b** [*T/I*] : to cause the people in an area or place to leave • *The alarm cleared* [=emptied] *the room (of people).* • *The room cleared quickly when the alarm sounded.* **c** [*T*] : to leave (an area or place) so that it is empty • *ordered by police to clear the area* **3** [*T*] : to make (a path, road, open space, etc.) by removing things that block or cover an area or surface • *clearing a path through the jungle* • *Clear a space on the table for the books.* **4** [*T*] : to go over, under, or past (something) without touching • *The horse cleared* [=jumped over] *the fence easily.* **5** [*T*] : to prove that (someone) is not guilty of a crime • *The investigation cleared him of all the charges.* • *He wants an opportunity to clear his name.* [=to prove that he is innocent] **6** [*T*] **a** : to get approval for (something) • *You should clear the article with your boss before trying to get it published.* **b** : to give approval for (something) • *Her boss cleared the article for publication.* **c** : to say that (someone) has official permission to do something • *The flight/plane/pilot was cleared to land.* • *We were cleared (to go) through customs.* = *We cleared customs.* **d** : to be passed or officially approved by (a group) • *The bill has finally cleared the Senate.* **7** [*T*] *finance* **a** : to pay all the money that is owed for (a debt or loan) • *clear a debt* **b** : to gain (an amount of money) after paying all costs, taxes, etc. • *clear a profit* **c** ✧ When a **check clears** or **is cleared**, it goes through the process of being reviewed and accepted by a bank, and the money for the check is taken from the bank's account. — **clear away** [*phrasal vb*] **clear (something) away** or **clear away (something)** : to remove (something) from an area or surface • *Let me clear away these papers.* — **clear off** [*phrasal vb*] **1 clear off (something)** or **clear (something) off** : to remove things from (an area or surface) • *I'll clear off my desk so that you can use it.* **2** *chiefly Brit, informal* **a** : to leave quickly • *Clear off and leave me alone.* **b** **clear off (a place)** : to leave (a place) quickly • *I ordered the hikers to clear off my land.* — **clear out** [*phrasal vb*] **1** : to leave quickly • *We'll clear out first thing tomorrow.* **2 clear (something) out** or **clear out (something)** : to remove unwanted things from (an area or place) • *clear out a cluttered closet*

— **clear the air** see **¹AIR** — **clear up** [*phrasal vb*] **1** : to become clear: such as **a** *of weather or the sky* : to change so that there are no clouds, fog, etc. **b** *of the skin* : to become free of marks or spots **2 clear up** or **clear (something) up** or **clear up (something)** : to go away or cause (something) to go away • *My symptoms have cleared up.* **3 clear (something) up** or **clear up (something) a** : to make (something) clear by explaining it • *clear up a mystery* **b** : to cause the end of (something) by talking about it or dealing with it • *clearing up misunderstandings* **4** *Brit* : to make an area clean or tidy • *Let's clear up* [=clean up] *before we leave.* — **clear your throat** : to make a noise in your throat for attention or to be able to speak more clearly • *He cleared his throat and began to speak.*

³clear *adv* **1** : in a clear manner — used in the phrase **loud and clear** • *"Can you hear me?" "Loud and clear."* [=I can hear you clearly] **2** *chiefly US, informal* : completely or entirely • *We drove clear across the state.*

⁴clear *n* — **in the clear** : free from guilt or suspicion • *He's not in the clear yet. The police still consider him a suspect.*

clear·ance /ˈklirəns/ *n* **1** [*C/U*] **a** : an official decision saying that someone has permission to do something • *You'll have to get clearance from management.* • *people with* **security clearance** [=special permission to know about or see secret things] **b** : official permission for an aircraft, pilot, etc., to do something • *The pilot got clearance to land.* **2** [*C/U*] : the amount of space between two things • *There was only 10 inches of clearance between the car and the side of the tunnel.* **3** [*U*] : the act or process of removing things (such as trees or old buildings) from an area • *the clearance of forests for farming*

¹clear–cut /ˈkliərˌkʌt/ *adj* : very obvious or definite • *a clear-cut distinction/victory*

²clear–cut /ˈkliərˌkʌt/ *n* [*C*] *US* : an area of land in which all the trees have been cut down — **clear–cut** *vb* **-cut;** **-cut·ting** [*T/I*] • *an area of forest that has been clear-cut*

clear·head·ed /ˈkliərˌhedəd/ *adj* : having or showing an ability to think clearly • *a clearheaded person/analysis* — **clear·head·ed·ness** *n* [*U*]

clear·ing /ˈklirɪŋ/ *n* **1** [*U*] : the act or process of making something clear or of becoming clear • *the clearing of the table* **2** [*C*] : an open area of land in which there are no trees • *a clearing in the forest*

clear·ing·house /ˈklirɪŋˌhaʊs/ *n* [*C*] **1** : a business that banks use to exchange checks and money between them **2** : an organization that collects and gives out information about a specific thing • *an online clearinghouse for information on museums around the world*

clear·ly /ˈkliərli/ *adv* **1** : in a way that is easy to see, hear, or understand • *Speak/ Write more clearly.* • *The mountain was clearly visible.* **2** : in a way that is certain • *The project was clearly a failure.* • *Clearly, a new approach is needed.*

cleat /ˈkliːt/ n **1** [C] : a metal or wooden object that is attached to something (such as a boat or dock) and around which a rope can be tied **2 a** [C] : a piece of rubber, wood, or metal that is fastened to the bottom of a shoe or boot to prevent slipping **b** [plural] US : shoes that have cleats on them ▪ a football player wearing cleats

cleav·age /ˈkliːvɪdʒ/ n **1** [U] informal : the space between a woman's breasts especially when it can be easily seen ▪ The dress reveals some cleavage. **2** [C/U] : a division between two things or groups ▪ the cleavage between the rich and poor **3** [C] technical : the act of splitting apart ▪ the cleavages of an egg as an embryo develops

cleav·er /ˈkliːvə/ n [C] : a heavy knife with a wide blade used for cutting up large pieces of meat

cleft /ˈklɛft/ n [C] **1** : a narrow space in the surface of something ▪ water trickling from a cleft in a rock **2** : a narrow area that looks like a small dent in someone's chin — **cleft** adj ▪ a cleft chin

clem·en·cy /ˈklɛmənsi/ n [U] : kind or merciful treatment of someone who could be given harsh punishment ▪ a plea for clemency [=mercy]

clench /ˈklɛntʃ/ vb **1** [T/I] : to set (something) in a tightly closed position ▪ He clenched his fists in anger. ▪ clenched teeth **2** [T] : to hold (something) tightly ▪ dancing with a rose clenched in her teeth

cler·gy /ˈkləːdʒi/ n [plural] : people (such as priests) who are the leaders of a religion and who perform religious services ▪ a member of the clergy

cler·gy·man /ˈkləːdʒimən/ n, pl **-men** /-mən/ [C] : a man who is a member of the clergy

cler·ic /ˈklɛrɪk/ n [C] : a member of the clergy

cler·i·cal /ˈklɛrɪkəl/ adj **1** : of or relating to a clerk or office worker ▪ clerical work ▪ a clerical error **2** : of or relating to members of the clergy ▪ clerical leaders

¹clerk /ˈkləːk, Brit ˈklɑːk/ n [C] **1** : a person whose job is to keep track of records and documents for a business, office, etc. ▪ a bank/office/law clerk **2** US **a** : a person who works in a store ▪ a sales/grocery clerk **b** : a person who works at the main desk of a hotel assisting the people who are staying there ▪ a hotel clerk = a desk clerk

²clerk vb [I] US : to work as a clerk and especially as a law clerk ▪ She clerked for a judge for a year.

clev·er /ˈklɛvə/ adj **1** : intelligent and able to learn things quickly ▪ clever students **2** : showing intelligent thinking ▪ a clever design/invention/idea **3** : funny in a way that shows intelligence ▪ the play's clever dialogue — **clev·er·ly** adv — **clev·er·ness** n [U]

cli·ché /kliˈʃeɪ, ˈkliːˌʃeɪ/ n [C] **1** : a phrase or expression that has been used so often that it is no longer original or interesting **2** : something that is so commonly used in books, stories, etc., that is no longer effective ▪ The macho cop

has become a Hollywood cliché. — **cli·chéd** /kliˈʃeɪd/ adj ▪ clichéd phrases/characters

¹click /ˈklɪk/ vb **1** [T/I] : to make a short, sharp sound or to cause (something) to make a short, sharp sound ▪ He clicked his heels together. ▪ a clicking noise/sound **2** [T/I] computers : to press a button on a mouse or some other device in order to make something happen on a computer ▪ Click the left mouse button. ▪ Click (on) the icon. **3** [I] informal : to like and understand each other ▪ They met at a party and clicked [=hit it off] right away. **4** [I] informal : to get the attention or interest of people ▪ an issue that has really clicked with the voters this year **5** [I] informal — used to describe what happens when you suddenly understand or remember something ▪ I worked on it for days, and then finally something clicked and I knew what to do.

²click n [C] **1** : a short, sharp sound ▪ the click of her heels on marble **2** : the act of selecting something on a computer screen by clicking a mouse or some other device ▪ a mouse click

cli·ent /ˈklaɪənt/ n [C] **1** : a person who pays a professional person or organization for services ▪ a lawyer's clients **2** : a customer in a shop or hotel **3** computers : a computer in a network that uses the services provided by a server

cli·en·tele /ˌklaɪənˈtɛl/ n [singular] : the group of people who are regular customers at a particular business ▪ The restaurant attracts an older clientele.

cliff /ˈklɪf/ n [C] : a high, steep surface of rock, earth, or ice

cliff–hang·er /ˈklɪfˌhæŋə/ n [C] : a story, contest, or situation that is very exciting because what is going to happen next is not known ▪ The election was a real cliffhanger.

cli·mac·tic /klaɪˈmæktɪk/ adj : most exciting and important ▪ the movie's climactic moment

cli·mate /ˈklaɪmət/ n [C] **1 a** : a region with particular weather patterns or conditions ▪ living in a cold/dry/mild/hot climate **b** : the usual weather conditions in a particular place or region ▪ a climate ideal for growing grapes **2** : the usual or most widespread mood or conditions in a place ▪ the country's economic/political climate — **cli·mat·ic** /klaɪˈmætɪk/ adj : climatic conditions

¹cli·max /ˈklaɪˌmæks/ n [C] **1 a** : the most exciting and important part of a story, play, or movie that occurs usually at or near the end ▪ The movie's climax is a fantastic chase scene. **b** : the most interesting and exciting part of something ▪ the tournament's climax **2** : ORGASM

²climax vb **1 a** [I] : to reach the most exciting or important part in something ▪ The movie climaxes with a chase scene. **b** [T] : to occur at the end as the most exciting or important part of (something) ▪ The protest climaxed a series of demonstrations. **2** [I] : to have an orgasm

¹climb /ˈklaɪm/ vb **1** [T] : to move or go up (something) using your feet and often your hands ▪ climb a ladder/tree ▪ climb the stairs **2** [T/I] : to go up mountains, cliffs, etc., as a sport ▪ *She began climbing (mountains) several years ago.* **3** [I] : to move yourself in a way that usually involves going up or down ▪ *climb over a fence* ▪ *She climbed in through the window.* **4 a** [I] : to go higher : to go upward ▪ *smoke climbing [=rising] into the sky* ▪ *a steeply climbing trail* **b** [T/I] : to move to a higher position ▪ *The album is climbing the charts.* ▪ *The book tells how the senator climbed to power.* **5** [I] : to increase in amount, value, or level ▪ *The temperature is climbing.* **6** [T/I] *of plants* : to grow up or over something ▪ *ivy climbing the walls of the building* ▪ *a climbing plant* [=a plant that attaches itself to something, such as a wall, as it grows up it] — **climb down** [*phrasal vb*] *chiefly Brit* : to admit that you have made a mistake and change your position or opinion ▪ *His statement is an attempt to climb down from the denial he made yesterday.* — **climbing the walls** *informal* : feeling very anxious or frustrated because you have a lot of energy and are unable to do something you want to do ▪ *Being stuck at home had me climbing the walls.* — **climb·er** /ˈklaɪmɚ/ *n* [C] — **climb·ing** *n* [U] ▪ *She enjoys mountain climbing.*

²**climb** *n* [C] **1** : the act or process of climbing a mountain, hill, etc. ▪ *It's a 20-minute climb.* **2** : the act or process of moving upward ▪ *the plane's climb to 30,000 feet* **3** : the act or process of going to a higher level or position ▪ *her climb to power*

climb·down /ˈklaɪmˌdaʊn/ *n* [*singular*] *Brit* : an act of admitting that you have made a mistake and are changing your position or opinion ▪ *His statement is a climbdown from the denial he made yesterday.*

clinch /ˈklɪntʃ/ *vb* [T] **1** : to make (something) certain or final ▪ *His home run clinched the victory.* **2** : to make certain the winning of (something) ▪ *If they win this game they'll clinch the pennant.* — **clinch·er** /ˈklɪntʃɚ/ *n* [*singular*]

cling /ˈklɪŋ/ *vb* **clung** /ˈklʌŋ/; **cling·ing** [I] **1** : to hold onto something or someone very tightly ▪ *The children clung together under the little umbrella.* ▪ *The cat clung to/onto the narrow branch.* ▪ (*figurative*) *still clinging to the idea that the marriage can be saved* ▪ (*figurative*) *an aging leader clinging to power* **2** *often disapproving* : to stay very close to someone for emotional support, protection, etc. ▪ *parents who cling to their children* **3** : to stick to something or someone ▪ *The shirt clung to his wet shoulders.* — **clingy** /ˈklɪŋi/ *adj* **cling·i·er**; **-est** ▪ *a clingy dress/child*

clin·ic /ˈklɪnɪk/ *n* [C] **1** : a place where people get medical help ▪ *a drug rehab clinic* **2** : a place where professional services are offered to people for a lower cost than is usual ▪ *a legal clinic* — **put on a clinic** *US, informal* : to perform or play extremely well ▪ *watching the team put on a clinic*

clin·i·cal /ˈklɪnɪkəl/ *adj* **1** *always before*

a noun : of or relating to the medical treatment that is given to patients in hospitals, clinics, etc. ▪ *experimental and clinical evidence* ▪ *a clinical study* ▪ *a clinical psychologist* [=a psychologist who works with patients] **2** : requiring treatment as a medical problem ▪ *clinical depression* **3** *always before a noun* : of or relating to a place where medical treatment is given ▪ *clinical offices* **4** : not showing emotion or excitement ▪ *Her voice was almost clinical as she told us what happened.* **5** : very exact or skillful ▪ *clinical precision* — **clin·i·cal·ly** /ˈklɪnɪkli/ *adv*

cli·ni·cian /klɪˈnɪʃən/ *n* [C] : a person (such as a doctor or nurse) who works directly with patients

clink /ˈklɪŋk/ *n* [C] : a short, sharp sound made when glass or metal objects hit each other ▪ *the clink of glasses* — **clink** *vb* [T/I] ▪ *The bottles clinked together.*

¹**clip** /ˈklɪp/ *n* **1** : a usually small piece of metal or plastic that holds things together or keeps things in place ▪ *a hair/tie clip* **2** [C] : a short piece of a movie, TV show, etc. ▪ *video/audio clips* **3** [*singular*] : the speed at which something happens ◆ If something moves or happens **at a fast/rapid/steady/good clip**, it moves or happens quickly. ▪ *We were moving at a good clip.* **4** [C] : a container that is filled with bullets and that is placed inside a gun so that the bullets can be fired ▪ *an ammunition clip* **5** [*singular*] *US, informal* : one time or instance ▪ *She can bicycle 30 miles at a clip.*

²**clip** *vb* **clipped; clip·ping** **1** [T/I] : to hold or attach things with a clip ▪ *clip the papers together* ▪ *Clip this microphone to/onto your shirt.* ▪ *The radio clips to/onto your belt.* **2** [T] : to make (something) shorter or neater by cutting off small pieces ▪ *clipping* [=trimming] *the hedges/bushes* ▪ *The bird's wings have been clipped so that it can't fly away.* **3** [T] : to cut (an article, a picture, etc.) out of a newspaper or magazine ▪ *clipping (out) recipes from a magazine* ▪ *clipping coupons* **4** [T] : to hit the side of (something) while going past it ▪ *The car skidded off the road and clipped a tree.*

clip·board /ˈklɪpˌboɚd/ *n* [C] **1** : a small board that has a clip at the top for holding papers **2** : a feature of a computer program that holds a copy of some data (such as words or a picture) and allows the user to move the data to another document or program

clip-on /ˈklɪpˌɑːn/ *adj, always before a noun* : attached to something with a clip ▪ *clip-on earrings*

clipped *adj* — used to describe speech that is fast, that uses short sounds and few words, and that is often unfriendly or rude ▪ *a clipped voice/tone* ▪ *clipped speech*

clip·per /ˈklɪpɚ/ *n* [C] **1** : a device used for cutting something ▪ *fingernail/wire/hedge clippers* **2** : a person who clips something ▪ *a coupon clipper* **3** : a very fast type of sailing ship that was used especially in the 1800s

clip·ping /ˈklɪpɪŋ/ *n* [C] **1** *chiefly US*

: something (such as an article or a picture) that has been cut out of a newspaper or magazine • *a newspaper/magazine clipping* **2** : a small piece that has been cut off of something • *grass clippings*

clique /ˈklɪk, ˈkliːk/ *n* [C] *disapproving* : a small group of people who spend time together and who are not friendly to other people • *high school cliques* — **cliqu·ish** /ˈklɪkɪʃ, ˈkliːkɪʃ/ *also* **cliqu·ey** /ˈklɪki, ˈkliːki/ *adj*

cli·to·ris /ˈklɪtərəs/ *n* [C] : a female sexual organ that is small, sensitive, and located on the outside of the body in front of the opening of the vagina — **cli·to·ral** /ˈklɪtərəl/ *adj*

¹**cloak** /ˈkloʊk/ *n* **1** [C] : a piece of clothing that is used as a coat, that has no sleeves, and that is worn over the shoulders and attached at the neck **2** [*singular*] : a thing that hides or covers someone or something • *a cloak of secrecy/darkness*

²**cloak** *vb* [T] *literary* **1** : to cover (someone or something) • *a field cloaked in snow* **2** : to hide or disguise (something) • *plans cloaked in secrecy*

cloak–and–dagger *adj* : relating to or showing actions or behavior in which people or governments try to protect their important secrets or try to learn the secrets of others • *cloak-and-dagger operations*

cloak·room /ˈkloʊkˌruːm/ *n* [C] **1** *Brit* : a room in a public building that has toilets and sinks **2** *chiefly Brit* : CHECKROOM

¹**clob·ber** /ˈklɑːbɚ/ *vb* [T] *informal* **1** : to hit (someone or something) very hard • *If you say anything I'll clobber you.* **2** : to defeat (a person or team) very easily • *She was/got clobbered in the election.* **3** : to have a very bad effect on (someone or something) • *businesses being/getting clobbered by the bad economy*

²**clobber** *n* [U] *Brit, informal* : someone's clothes, supplies, or equipment • *Just dump your clobber anywhere.*

¹**clock** /ˈklɑːk/ *n* **1** [C] : a device that shows what time it is and that is usually placed in a room or attached to a wall **2** **the clock** : a clock that is used in sports and that shows how much time remains for a particular part of a game • *They were winning by 2 points with 10 seconds (left) on the clock.* ◆ In U.S. English, to **eat up the clock** or **run out the clock** or **kill the clock** is to keep control of the ball or puck near the end of a game so that your opponent will not have a chance to score. **3** **the clock** : TIME CLOCK • *I punched the clock at 8:45 and started working right away.* — **against the clock 1** : in order to do or finish something before a particular time • *working/racing against the clock* **2** ◆ If a race is *against the clock*, the time of each racer is measured and the racer with the fastest time wins. — **around the clock** *also* **round the clock** : throughout the entire day and night • *The store is open around the clock.* — **beat the clock** : to do or finish something quickly before a particular time — **put/turn back the**

clock *also* **put/turn the clock back** : to return to a condition that existed in the past • *I wish that we could turn back the clock and start over.*

²**clock** *vb* **1** [T] **a** : to measure the amount of time it takes for (a person) to do something or for (something) to be completed • *She clocked her first mile at 5 minutes and 20 seconds.* **b** : to finish a race in (an amount of time) • *He clocked 3 hours and 15 minutes in his last marathon.* **2 a** [T] : to measure or show (the speed of something) with a measuring device • *The cop clocked her going 95 miles per hour.* **b** [I] : to have a particular speed or to continue for a particular amount of time • *The movie clocked in at over two hours.* [=it was more than two hours long] — **clock in** [*phrasal vb*] : to record on a special card the time that you start working — **clock out** [*phrasal vb*] : to record on a special card the time that you stop working — **clock up** [*phrasal vb*] *chiefly Brit* : to gain or reach (a particular number or amount) • *Our company clocked up a record number of sales this year.*

clock·wise /ˈklɑːkˌwaɪz/ *adv* : in the direction that the hands of a clock move when you look at it from the front — **clockwise** *adj* • *in a clockwise direction*

clock·work /ˈklɑːkˌwɚk/ *n* [U] **1** : the system of moving wheels inside something (such as a clock or an old-fashioned toy) that makes its parts move **2** — used to describe something that happens or works in a very regular and exact way • *Every morning, like clockwork, customers line up outside the bakery.* • *clockwork precision/regularity*

clod /ˈklɑːd/ *n* [C] **1** : a lump of dirt or clay **2** *informal* : a stupid and dull person — **clod·dish** /ˈklɑːdɪʃ/ *adj* • *cloddish behavior*

clog /ˈklɑːg/ *vb* **clogged; clog·ging** [T/I] : to slowly form a block in (something) so that things cannot move through quickly or easily • *a sink clogged by/with dirt and grease* • *a clogged pipe* • *Traffic clogged (up) the streets.* • *arteries that have clogged (up)* • (*figurative*) *too many legal cases clogging (up) the court system*

²**clog** *n* [C] **1** : a shoe or sandal that has a thick usually wooden sole **2** : something that blocks or clogs a pipe

clois·ter /ˈklɔɪstɚ/ *n* [C] **1** : a place where monks or nuns live **2** : a covered path or hall with arches that is on the side of a monastery, church, etc.

clois·tered /ˈklɔɪstɚd/ *adj* : separated from the rest of the world • *a private, cloistered life in the country*

¹**clone** /ˈkloʊn/ *n* [C] **1** *biology* : a plant or animal that is grown from one cell of its parent and that has exactly the same genes as its parent **2** : a product (such as a computer) that is a copy of another product produced by a well-known company **3** : a person or thing that appears to be an exact copy of another person or thing • *He's almost a clone of his father.*

²**clone** *vb* **cloned; clon·ing** [T/I] : to make a clone of (something or someone)

• *cloning animals* • *a plant produced by cloning*

¹close /'klouz/ *vb* **closed; clos·ing 1** [T/I] : to move (a door, window, etc.) so that things cannot pass through an opening : SHUT • *Please close the door/window/gate.* • *The door opened and closed quietly.* **2** [T] : to cover the opening of (something) : SHUT • *Close the box when you're done.* **3** [T/I] **a** : to bring together the parts or edges of (something open) • *close a book* • *Close your mouth/eyes.* • *Her eyes closed, and she fell asleep.* **b** : to bring together the edges of (a wound) so that it can heal • *It took 10 stitches to close the wound.* **4** [T/I] : to not allow (a road, park, etc.) to be used for a period of time • *They closed the bridge to traffic.* • *The park closes at dusk.* **5** [T/I] **a** : to stop the services or activities of (a business, school, etc.) for a period of time • *They closed the school today because of the storm.* • *What time does the library close?* **b** : to stop the services or activities of (a business, school, etc.) permanently • *They closed [=closed down] the school last year.* **6** [T/I] : to end (something) • *I'd like to close (the meeting) by thanking you all for your help.* **7** [T] : to stop keeping money in (an account at a bank) • *I closed my savings account.* **8** [T] : to end the use of (a file, document, or program) on a computer • *Save the file before closing it.* **9** [T] : to formally accept (an agreement) • *close a deal* **10** [I] : to reach a specified price or level at the end of the day • *The stock opened at $19 a share and closed at $22.* **11** [T/I] : to reduce the amount of distance or difference between two things, people, or groups • *trying to close the gap between the richest and the poorest countries* • *She has closed to within two points of the champion.* — **close down** [*phrasal vb*] **1 a** : to permanently stop operating • *The factory closed down in the 1980s.* **b** *Brit* : to stop broadcasting from a radio or television station for the day **2 close down (something) or close (something) down** : to permanently stop the services or activities of (a business, school, etc.) • *They closed down the school.* — **close in** [*phrasal vb*] **1** : to come or move nearer or closer • *The storm is closing in fast.* • *The camera closed in on the actor's face.* • *Researchers are closing in on* [=are close to finding] *a cure.* — **close off** [*phrasal vb*] **close off (something) or close (something) off** : to not allow (something) to be used for a period of time • *The city closed off the beach to tourists.* — **close on** [*phrasal vb*] *US* : to formally and legally agree to and complete (an important financial arrangement, such as the purchase of a house) • *We're going to close on our house next Friday.* — **close out** [*phrasal vb*] **1** *US* : to quickly sell (all of a particular type of product in a store) at a lower price • *The store is closing out its entire stock of clothing.* **2** : to stop keeping money in (a bank account) • *She closed out her account.* **3** : to end (something) in a specified way • *The team*

closed out the series with a 2–1 win over New York. — **close ranks** see ¹RANK — **close up** [*phrasal vb*] **1 a** : to close and lock all the doors of a building usually for a short period of time • *Many businesses closed up early today.* **b close (something) up or close up (something)** : to close and lock all the doors of (a house, store, etc.) • *They closed up the house and left.* ◇ To **close up shop** is to go out of business forever or stop performing all services or activities for a period of time. **2** : to move closer together • *The troops closed up.* **3** *of a wound* : to become completely healed • *The cut eventually closed up on its own.* **4** : to stop talking about your thoughts or emotions with other people • *She closes up when people ask her about it.* **5 close (something) up or close up (something)** : to bring (people or things) closer together • *Close up the space between these numbers.*

²close /'klous/ *adj* **clos·er; -est 1** : near in space • *We're not there yet, but we're getting close.* • *standing close together* • *Stay close to me.* • *a gun shot* **at close range** [=from a short distance] **2** : near in time • *Summer is getting closer.* • *It's close to midnight.* **3** *not before a noun* : very similar : almost the same • *Their daughters are close in age.* • *He bears a* **close resemblance** *to his father.* [=he looks very much like his father] **4** *not before a noun* : almost correct • *"I'd guess that you're 29 years old." "You're close. I'm 30."* **5 a** — used to say that someone or something has almost reached a particular condition; + *to* • *He was close to death.* • *I was close to tears.* [=I was almost crying] **b** : almost *doing* something — + *to* • *She was/came close to crying.* **6** — used to say that something bad almost happened • *That was close! We almost missed our plane.* • *That was a* **close one.** **7** — used to describe the people you are most directly related to • *a close relative* **8** — used to describe people who know each other very well and care about each other very much • *close friends* • *We're very close.* • *He's close to his mom.* **9** : connected in a direct way • *sources close to the president* • *She stays in close touch/contact with her friends back home.* **10** : very careful, complete, or precise • *close attention/supervision* • *a closer look* • *Keep (a)* **close watch/eye** *on the baby.* [=watch the baby closely] **11** — used to describe a race, contest, game, etc., in which one person, group, or team defeats the other or is leading the other by only a small amount • *a very close election/race* • *The election is* **too close to call.** [=it is not clear who will win] **12** : very short or near to the skin • *a close shave* **13** : having no extra space • *a close* [=*tight*] *fit* **14** : not having enough fresh air • *It's close in here: let's open a window.* — **close to your chest** *or US* **close to the vest** ◇ If you hold, keep, or play something *close to your chest* or *close to the vest*, you do not tell other people about it. — **close·ly** *adv* • *houses crowded closely together* • *She closely re-*

sembles her mother. ▪ *suspects watched closely by police* — **close·ness** *n* [U]

³**close** /ˈkloʊs/ *adv* **clos·er; -est** : at or to a short distance or time away ▪ *Stay/keep close to me.* ▪ *Look close* [=*closely*] *and tell me what you see.* ▪ *Election day is drawing closer.* ▪ *They sat **close** together.* — **close at hand** : near in time or place ▪ *I keep a pen close at hand.* [=near me] — **close by** : at a short distance away ▪ *They're building a school close by.* — **close on** Brit : almost or nearly ▪ *walking for close on five miles* — **close to** 1 : almost or nearly ▪ *It cost close to a million dollars.* ▪ *waiting for close to an hour* 2 Brit : from a short distance ▪ *She's even more beautiful when seen close to.* — **close up** or **up close** : from a short distance ▪ *looking at the painting close up* ▪ *It looks different up close.* — **come close** 1 : to almost do something ▪ *We didn't win, but we came close (to winning).* 2 : to be similar to something or as good as expected ▪ *This sugar-free candy doesn't come close to the real thing.* — **cut it close** see ¹CUT

⁴**close** /ˈkloʊz/ *n* [*singular*] *formal* : the end of an activity or a period of time ▪ *the close of the school year* ▪ *as the year drew/came to a close* [=as the end of the year got closer] ▪ *She brought the show to a close with a final song.*

close call /ˈkloʊs-/ *n* [C] : an escape that was almost not successful ▪ *We were almost too late. It was a pretty close call.*

closed /ˈkloʊzd/ *adj* 1 : covering an opening ▪ *The windows are closed.* [=shut] : having an opening that is covered ▪ *Keep your eyes closed.* ▪ *a closed container/umbrella* 2 : not operating or open to the public ▪ *a closed road/bridge* 3 a : not being worked on anymore ▪ *The case is closed.* b : no longer able to be discussed ▪ *The question/discussion is closed.* 4 : including only people from a particular group ▪ *a closed circle of advisers* 5 : not allowing the public to participate or know what is being said or done ▪ *a meeting closed to the public* ▪ *a closed session of Congress* 6 : not willing to listen to or accept different ideas or opinions ▪ *a closed mind* — **behind closed doors** : in a private room or place ▪ *decisions made behind closed doors*

closed–cir·cuit /ˈkloʊzdˈsɚkət/ *adj*, *always before a noun* — used to describe a television system that sends its signal through wires to a limited number of televisions ▪ *The store's closed-circuit television monitors shoppers.*

closed–mind·ed /ˈkloʊzdˈmaɪndəd/ *adj*, *chiefly US, disapproving* : not willing to consider different ideas or opinions ▪ *He's too closed-minded.*

close–knit /ˈkloʊsˈnɪt/ *adj* — used to describe a group of people who care about each other and who are very friendly with each other ▪ *a close-knit family*

close–mind·ed /ˈkloʊzˈmaɪndəd/ *adj*, *US* : CLOSED-MINDED ▪ *close-minded people*

close·out /ˈkloʊzˌaʊt/ *n* [C] *US* : a sale in which a store tries to sell all of its prod-

ucts because the store is going out of business

close shave *n* [C] : CLOSE CALL

¹**clos·et** /ˈklɑːzət/ *n* 1 [C] *chiefly US* : a usually small room that is used for storing clothing, towels, dishes, etc. ▪ *broom/coat closets* ▪ *a walk-in closet* [=a large closet usually for clothes] 2 [U] : a state in which someone will not talk about something or admit something; *especially* : a state in which someone will not admit being a homosexual ▪ *He's still in the closet.* [=he has not told people that he is gay] ▪ *She came out of the closet in college.*

²**closet** *adj*, *always before a noun* : hiding the fact that you are a particular type of person ▪ *a closet homosexual/racist*

³**closet** *vb* [T] 1 : to put (yourself) in a room in order to be alone ▪ *He closeted himself in his apartment for several days.* 2 : to bring (someone) into a room in order to talk privately ▪ *The manager was closeted with two employees for an hour.*

close–up /ˈkloʊsˌʌp/ *n* [C/U] : a photograph or movie picture taken very close to an object or person ▪ *a close-up of her face* ▪ *a close-up shot* ▪ *a scene shot in close-up*

¹**clos·ing** /ˈkloʊzɪŋ/ *n* [C] 1 : a situation or occurrence in which a business or organization shuts down and stops its operations ▪ *factory/plant/store closings* 2 : the last part of a letter or speech 3 : a meeting in which the owners of a house formally give ownership of the house to other people ▪ *closing costs* [=the extra amounts of money that people need to pay when they buy a house] — **in closing** *formal* : at the end of a speech, letter, etc. ▪ *"Thank you all for your help," she said in closing.*

²**closing** *adj*, *always before a noun* : forming the last part or end of something ▪ *the book's closing chapters/pages/lines*

clo·sure /ˈkloʊʒɚ/ *n* 1 [C] : a situation or occurrence in which a business, factory, etc., closes forever ▪ *a school/factory closure* 2 [U] a : a feeling that something has been completed or that a problem has been solved ▪ *I need to get some closure on this issue.* b : a feeling that a bad experience has ended and that you can start to live again in a calm and normal way ▪ *The memorial service for Grandma helped us achieve (a sense of) closure.* 3 [C] : the way that something (such as a jacket) is closed together ▪ *a coat with a zipper closure* [=a coat that closes with a zipper]

¹**clot** /ˈklɑːt/ *n* [C] : BLOOD CLOT

²**clot** *vb* **clot·ted; clot·ting** [T/I] : to become thick and partly solid : to develop clots ▪ *medications that prevent blood from clotting* — **clotted** *adj* ▪ *clotted arteries* [=arteries that are blocked by blood clots]

cloth /ˈklɑːθ/ *n* 1 [C/U] : material that is made by weaving together threads of cotton, wool, nylon, etc., and that is used to make clothes, sheets, etc. ▪ *a piece of cloth* [=*fabric*] ▪ *cloth napkins/diapers* 2 [C] : a piece of cloth that is used for a particular purpose (such as cleaning things) • *Wipe the surface with a clean cloth.* **3 the cloth** : Christian priests and ministers : CLERGY • *a man of the cloth* [=a priest or minister]

clothe /'klouð/ *vb* **clothed** *also* **clad** /'kʰlæd/; **cloth·ing** [*T*] : to provide (someone) with clothes • *the cost of feeding and clothing my children*

clothed *adj* **1** : wearing clothes • *He fell into the lake fully clothed.* • *dancers clothed entirely in red* **2** : covered in something • *land clothed in dense green forests*

clothes /'klouz/ *n* [*plural*] : the things that people wear to cover their bodies and that are usually made from cloth • *winter/new clothes* [=clothing] • *Change your clothes.* • *a clothes dryer/washer*

clothes·horse /'klouz,hoɚs/ *n* [*C*] *informal + sometimes disapproving* : a person who likes to wear stylish clothing

clothes·line /'klouz,laɪn/ *n* [*C*] : a piece of rope or a wire that people hang wet clothes on to dry

clothes·pin /'klouz,pɪn/ *n* [*C*] *US* : a small object used for holding clothes on a clothesline — called also (*Brit*) **clothes peg**

cloth·ing /'klouðɪŋ/ *n* [*U*] : the things that people wear to cover their bodies • *a new article/item/piece of clothing* • *women's/men's/children's clothing* [=clothes] • *clothing stores*

¹**cloud** /'klaud/ *n* [*C*] **1** : a white or gray mass in the sky that is made of many very small drops of water • *rain clouds* • *flying above the clouds* **2** : a large amount of smoke, dust, etc., that hangs in the air • *a cloud of cigarette smoke* • *dust clouds* **3** : a feeling or belief that a person or organization has done something wrong • *She remains under a cloud (of suspicion).* [=people believe she did something wrong] • *a cloud of controversy/uncertainty/doubt* • *The scandal cast a (dark) cloud over his presidency.* — **cloud on the horizon** : a problem that could appear in the future • *The only cloud on the horizon for the team is the age of its key players.* — **in the clouds** ✧ If you are *in the clouds* or you **have your head in the clouds**, you spend too much time thinking about love or about ideas that are not practical. • *walking around with your head in the clouds* — **on cloud nine** *informal* : very happy • *He's been on cloud nine since he won.* — **cloud·less** /'klaudləs/ *adj* • *a cloudless sky*

²**cloud** *vb* **1** [*T*] : to confuse (a person's mind or judgment) • *The alcohol clouded my judgment/mind.* [=made me unable to think clearly] **2** [*T*] : to make (something, such as an issue or situation) difficult to understand • *These points only cloud the issue further.* **3** [*T*] : to affect (something) in a bad way • *a scandal that continues to cloud his reputation* **4** [*I*] *of the sky* : to become covered with clouds • *The sky clouded over, and it began to rain.* **5** [*T*] : to cover or fill (a room, the sky, etc.) with large amounts of smoke, dust, etc. • *a room clouded with cigarette smoke* **6** [*T*] : to cover (glass, a window, etc.) with many very small drops of water •

Steam clouded the bathroom mirror. **7** [*I*] *of a person's face or eyes* : to show that someone is worried or unhappy • *a face clouded with concern*

cloud·burst /'klaud,bɚst/ *n* [*C*] : a sudden rainstorm

cloudy /'klaudi/ *adj* **cloud·i·er; -est 1** : having many clouds in the sky • *a cloudy day* • *cloudy weather/skies* **2** : not clean or clear • *cloudy water* • *cloudy eyes* — **cloud·i·ness** *n* [*U*]

¹**clout** /'klaut/ *n* **1** [*U*] : the power to influence or control situations • *political/financial clout* **2** [*C*] *chiefly Brit, informal* : a hit especially with the hand

²**clout** *vb* [*T*] **1** *baseball* : to hit (the ball) very hard • *He clouted 19 home runs last year.* **2** *chiefly Brit* : to hit (someone or something) hard especially with your hand

clove /'klouv/ *n* [*C*] **1** : any one of the small sections that are part of a large head of garlic **2** : a small, dried flower bud that is used in cooking as a spice

cloven hoof *n* [*C*] : a foot of some animals (such as sheep, goats, or cows) that is divided into two parts

clo·ver /'klouvɚ/ *n* [*C/U*] : a small plant that has usually three leaves on each stem • *a four-leaf clover* [=a clover with four leaves instead of three]

¹**clown** /'klaun/ *n* [*C*] **1** : someone who performs in a circus, who wears funny clothes and makeup, and who tries to make people laugh **2** : someone who often does funny things to make people laugh • *She was the class clown.* [=a student who tried to make other students laugh] **3** *informal* : a rude or stupid person • *those clowns at the state capital* — **clown·ish** /'klaunɪʃ/ *adj* • *clownish behavior*

²**clown** *vb* [*I*] : to act like a clown : to say funny things or act in a silly way • *Stop clowning (around). We've got work to do.*

cloy·ing /'klojɪŋ/ *adj, disapproving* : too sweet, pleasant, or emotional • *a cloying romantic comedy* — **cloy·ing·ly** *adv* • *cloyingly cute/sweet*

¹**club** /'klʌb/ *n* **1** [*C*] **a** : a group of people who meet to participate in an activity (such as a sport or hobby) • *a social/men's club* **b** : the place where the members of a club meet • *I'll see you at the club.* **2** [*C*] : a sports team or organization • *a boxing/football/hockey club* **3** [*C*] : an organization in which people agree to buy things (such as books, DVDs, or CDs) regularly in order to receive a benefit (such as lower prices) • *a book club* **4** [*C*] : NIGHTCLUB • *a dance/jazz club* **5** [*C*] : GOLF CLUB **6** [*C*] : a heavy usually wooden stick that is used as a weapon • *swords and wooden clubs* **7 a** [*C*] : a playing card that is marked with a black shape that looks like three round leaves • *one heart and two clubs* **b** [*plural*] : the suit in a deck of playing cards that consists of cards marked by a black shape that looks like three round leaves • *the nine of clubs* **8** [*C*] *informal* : CLUB SANDWICH • *a turkey club* — **join the club** *also* **welcome to the club** *informal* — used to say that the problems

or feelings someone is having are problems or feelings that you have had yourself ▪ *If you don't understand the rules, join the club: no one else does either!*

²**club** *vb* **clubbed; club·bing** [*T*] **:** to hit (a person or animal) with a heavy stick or object ▪ *He was clubbed to death.* [=killed by being hit with a heavy object] — **club together** [*phrasal vb*] *Brit* : to combine your money with the money of other people ◇ If a group of people *club together* to do something, each member of the group gives some money to pay for something.

club·bing /ˈklʌbɪŋ/ *n* [*U*] : the activity of going to nightclubs in order to dance, drink alcohol, etc. ▪ *We went (out) clubbing last night.*

club·by /ˈklʌbi/ *adj* **club·bi·er; -est** *US* : friendly only to people who belong to a high social class ▪ *the restaurant's clubby atmosphere*

club·foot /ˈklʌbˌfʊt/ *n, pl* **-feet** [*C/U*] : a badly twisted or deformed foot that someone is born with — **club—foot·ed** /ˈklʌbˌfʊtəd/ *adj*

club·house /ˈklʌbˌhaʊs/ *n* [*C*] **1 :** a building used by a club for its activities **2 :** a building or set of rooms with lockers and showers that are used by a sports team

club sandwich *n* [*C*] : a sandwich that has three slices of bread with two layers of meat (such as turkey) and other cold foods (such as lettuce, tomato, and mayonnaise) between them

club soda *n* [*U*] *US* : SODA WATER

¹**cluck** /ˈklʌk/ *n* [*C*] **1 a :** a short, low sound that is made by a chicken **b :** a short, low sound that is used to show disapproval or sympathy ▪ *clucks of disapproval* **2** *US, informal* : a stupid or foolish person ▪ *a dumb cluck*

²**cluck** *vb* **1** [*I*] *of a chicken* : to make a low sound ▪ *The hen clucked at her chicks.* **2** [*T/I*] : to make a low sound with the tongue ▪ *She clucked (her tongue) in disapproval.* **3** [*I*] *informal* : to talk about something in an excited and often disapproving way ▪ *commentators clucking over/about the controversy*

¹**clue** /ˈkluː/ *n* **1** [*C*] : something that helps a person find something, understand something, or solve a mystery or puzzle ▪ *The book gives the reader plenty of clues to solve the mystery.* ▪ *a crossword puzzle clue* **2** [*singular*] *informal* : an understanding of something ▪ *Get a clue!* [=don't be so stupid or clueless] ▪ *When it comes to computers, I don't have a clue.* [=I don't understand computers at all]

²**clue** *vb* **clued; clue·ing** *or* **clu·ing** — **clue in** [*phrasal vb*] **clue (someone) in** *also* **clue in (someone)** *informal* : to give information to (someone) ▪ *The public should be clued in to what's happening.* [=should be told about what's happening] ▪ *She'll clue you in on the latest news.*

clued up *adj, Brit, informal* : having a lot of information about something ▪ *He's totally clued up (on/about the latest computer developments).*

clue·less /ˈkluːləs/ *adj, informal* : not having knowledge about something ▪

When it comes to computers, I'm clueless.

¹**clump** /ˈklʌmp/ *n* [*C*] **1 a :** a small ball or mass of something ▪ *a clump of roots/grass/mud* **b :** a group of things or people that are close together ▪ *a clump of bushes/trees* **2 :** a loud, heavy sound made by footsteps ▪ *the clump of footsteps*

²**clump** *vb* **1** [*T/I*] : to form a mass or clump ▪ *The virus causes the cells to clump (together).* **2** [*I*] : to walk with loud, heavy steps ▪ *someone clumping down/up the stairs*

clum·sy /ˈklʌmzi/ *adj* **clum·si·er; -est** **1 :** moving or doing things in a very awkward way and tending to drop or break things ▪ *He's very clumsy.* = *He's a very clumsy person.* **2 :** badly or awkwardly made or done ▪ *a clumsy attempt at a joke* **3 :** awkward to handle ▪ *a clumsy tool* — **clum·si·ly** /ˈklʌmzəli/ *adv* — **clum·si·ness** /ˈklʌmzinəs/ *n* [*U*]

clung *past tense and past participle of* CLING

clunk /ˈklʌŋk/ *n* [*C*] : a loud, dull sound that is made when a heavy object hits another object or a surface — **clunk** *vb* [*T/I*] ▪ *The lid clunked shut.*

clunk·er /ˈklʌŋkɚ/ *n* [*C*] *chiefly US, informal* : an old car or machine that does not work well

clunky /ˈklʌŋki/ *adj* **clunk·i·er; -est** *informal* **1 :** large and awkward in form or appearance ▪ *clunky shoes* **2 :** old and not working well ▪ *a clunky old station wagon* **3 :** badly or awkwardly made or done ▪ *clunky dialogue*

¹**clus·ter** /ˈklʌstɚ/ *n* [*C*] : a group of things or people that are close together ▪ *a cluster of cottages/grapes*

²**cluster** *vb* [*I*] : to come together to form a group ▪ *The children clustered around her.*

¹**clutch** /ˈklʌtʃ/ *vb* **1** [*T*] : to hold onto (someone or something) tightly with your hand ▪ *I clutched her hand firmly.* **2** [*I*] : to try to hold onto someone or something by reaching with your hand ▪ *She clutched at his shoulder.* — **clutch at straws** see STRAW

²**clutch** *n* [*C*] **1 :** the act of holding or gripping something or someone tightly ▪ *The hawk had the mouse in its clutches.* [=in its claws] **2 a :** a pedal that is pressed to change gears in a vehicle **b :** the part of a vehicle that is controlled by a clutch **3 a :** a group of eggs that is laid by a bird at one time ▪ *a clutch of eggs* **b :** a small group of things or people ▪ *a clutch of buildings/onlookers* — **in the clutch** *US* : in a very important situation especially during a sports competition ▪ *She scored a basket in the clutch.*

³**clutch** *adj, US* **1** *always before a noun* : happening during a very important time especially in a sports competition ▪ *a clutch hit/play/goal/basket* **2 :** able to perform well in a very important situation ▪ *a clutch hitter/player*

¹**clut·ter** /ˈklʌtɚ/ *vb* [*T*] : to fill or cover (something) with a crowded or disordered collection of things ▪ *Tools cluttered the garage.* ▪ *Avoid cluttering (up) your desk with books and papers.* — **clut-**

tered adj • a very cluttered attic/desk/office/room

²**clutter** n [U] : a crowded or disordered collection of things • There's a lot of unnecessary clutter in the house.

cm abbr centimeter

Cmdr. abbr commander

co. abbr 1 company 2 county

CO abbr 1 Colorado 2 commanding officer

c/o abbr care of ✧ This abbreviation is used in addresses when you are sending a letter or package to a person by using someone else's address or the address of a company. • Address the letter to "John Smith c/o Merriam-Webster, Inc."

co- prefix 1 : with : together • coexist 2 : associated with another • coworker

¹**coach** /'koutʃ/ n 1 [C] **a** : a person who teaches and trains an athlete or performer • a vocal/voice/drama coach **b** : a person who teaches and trains the members of a sports team • a football/basketball/soccer coach 2 [C] Brit : a private teacher who gives someone lessons in a particular subject 3 [C/U] : a large four-wheeled vehicle that is pulled by horses : CARRIAGE 4 [C/U] chiefly Brit : a large bus with comfortable seating that is used for long trips 5 [U] US : the section of least expensive seats on an airplane or train • seats in coach = coach seats • I usually fly coach. 6 [C] Brit : a separate section of a train

²**coach** vb 1 [T/I] **a** : to teach and train (an athlete or performer) • She coaches singers. **b** : to teach, train, and direct (a sports team) • He coaches football. = He coaches a football team. 2 [T] chiefly Brit : to teach (a student) privately rather than in a class 3 [T] : to give (someone) instructions on what to do or say in a particular situation • The witness had been coached on how to answer the questions.

co·ag·u·late /kou'ægjəˌleɪt/ vb -lat·ed; -lat·ing [T/I] : to become thick and partly solid • The blood coagulated. — **co·ag·u·la·tion** /kouˌægjə'leɪʃən/ n [U]

coal /'koul/ n 1 [U] : a black or brownish-black hard substance within the earth that is used as a fuel 2 [C] **a** : a piece of coal or charcoal especially when burning • hot coals 2 US : a glowing piece of wood from a fire : EMBER • the glowing coals of the campfire — haul/rake (someone) over the coals informal : to criticize (someone) very severely

co·a·lesce /ˌkowə'lɛs/ vb -lesced; -lesc·ing [I] formal : to come together to form one group or mass • reformers who gradually coalesced into a political movement — **co·a·les·cence** /ˌkowə'lɛsns/ n [U, singular]

co·a·li·tion /ˌkowə'lɪʃən/ n 1 [C] : a group of people, groups, or countries who have joined together • a coalition of businesses • a coalition government/party 2 [U] : the action or process of joining together with another or others for a common purpose • We're working in coalition with other environmental groups.

coarse /'koɚs/ adj **coars·er; -est** 1 : made up of large pieces : not fine •

coarse sand/salt 2 : having a rough quality • coarse wild grass 3 : rude or offensive • coarse language/humor — **coarse·ly** adv • coarsely ground pepper — **coarse·ness** n [U]

coars·en /'koɚsn/ vb [T/I] 1 : to become rough or rougher or to make (something) rough or rougher • hands coarsened by years of hard work 2 : to become rude or offensive or to cause (someone or something) to become rude or offensive • offensive words that coarsen the English language

¹**coast** /'koust/ n 1 [C/U] : the land along or near a sea or ocean • sea/rocky coasts [=shores] • a long stretch of coast 2 **the Coast** US, informal : the area along or near the Pacific Ocean — from coast to coast : from one coast to the other coast of a country or continent • They traveled from coast to coast across the U.S. — the coast is clear ✧ When the coast is clear you can go somewhere or do something without being caught or seen because no one is in the area. — **coast·al** /'koustl/ adj • coastal areas/regions/waters

²**coast** vb [I] 1 **a** : to move forward using no power or very little power • The car coasted to a stop. **b** : to move downhill by the force of gravity • The children coasted on sleds down the snowy hill. 2 : to progress or have success without special effort • After taking a big lead, the team coasted to victory.

coast·er /'koustɚ/ n [C] 1 : a small, flat object on which a glass, cup, or dish is placed to protect the surface of a table 2 chiefly US : ROLLER COASTER 1

coast guard (US) or Brit **coast·guard** n 1 US **the Coast Guard** or Brit **the Coastguard** : an organization that has the job of guarding the area along a country's coast and helping people, boats, and ships that are in danger on the sea ✧ The U.S. Coast Guard is a military organization. 2 [C] Brit : a member of the Coastguard

coast·line /'koustˌlaɪn/ n [C/U] : the land along the edge of a coast • a rocky/sandy coastline

coast–to–coast /'koustə'koust/ adj 1 : going across an entire nation or continent from one coast to another • a coast-to-coast flight/broadcast 2 US, informal : going from one end of a playing surface (such as a basketball court) to the other • a coast-to-coast play — **coast–to–coast** adv

¹**coat** /'kout/ n [C] 1 **a** : an outer piece of clothing that can be long or short and that is worn to keep warm or dry • a winter/fur/wool coat **b** chiefly US : a piece of clothing that is worn over a shirt as part of a suit : JACKET • wearing a coat and tie • a sport coat 2 : the outer covering of fur, hair, or wool on an animal • the dog's thick/smooth/shaggy coat 3 : a thin layer of paint covering a surface • a coat of paint

²**coat** vb [T] : to cover (something or someone) with a thin layer of something • shoes coated with mud • Coat the chicken with flour.

coat hanger n [C] : a device that is used

for hanging clothes in a closet : HANGER

coat·ing /'koʊtɪŋ/ n [C] : a thin layer or covering of something • *The fabric has a coating that prevents liquids from soaking through.*

coat of arms n [C] : a special group of pictures that belong to a person, family, or group of people and that are shown on a shield

coat·tail /'koʊt₊teɪl/ n **1** [C] : a long piece of cloth that hangs down at the back of a man's formal coat — usually plural **2** [*plural*] : the help or influence of another person's work, ideas, or popularity • *They were elected to Congress by riding (on) the coattails of the President.* [=they were elected because they belong to the same political party as the President, who is very popular]

coax /'koʊks/ vb [T] **1** : to influence or persuade (a person or animal) to do something by talking in a gentle and friendly way • *coaxing a cat down from a tree* • *Can we coax her into singing?* **2** : to get (something) by talking in a gentle and friendly way • *trying to coax an answer out of her*

cob /'kɑːb/ n [C] : CORNCOB • *Cut the corn from the cob.* • *We had corn on the cob.*

co·balt /'koʊ₊bɑːlt/ n [U] : a hard, shiny, silver-white metal that is often mixed with other metals

cob·ble /'kɑːbəl/ vb **cob·bled**; **cob·bling** [T] **1** : to make (something) by putting together different parts in a quick way • *a speech cobbled together from papers and lectures* • *working quickly to cobble up a temporary solution* **2** *old-fashioned* : to make or repair (shoes) • *shoes cobbled in Italy*

cobbled adj : covered with cobblestones • *a cobbled street*

cob·bler /'kɑːblə/ n **1** [C] *old-fashioned* : a person who makes or repairs shoes **2** [C/U] *US* : a dessert made of cooked fruit covered with a thick crust • *peach cobbler*

cob·ble·stone /'kɑːbəl₊stoʊn/ n [C] : a round stone that is used in paving streets — **cob·ble·stoned** /'kɑːbəl₊stoʊnd/ adj • *cobblestoned streets*

co·bra /'koʊbrə/ n [C] : a very poisonous snake found in Asia and Africa

cob·web /'kɑːb₊wɛb/ n [C] : the threads of old spider webs that are found in areas that have not been cleaned for a long time • *a barn filled with cobwebs* • (*figurative*) *trying to clear the cobwebs from her mind* [=to clear her mind] — **cob·webbed** /'kɑːb₊wɛbd/ adj • *a cobwebbed attic*

co·caine /koʊ'keɪn/ n [U] : a powerful drug that is used in medicine to stop pain or is taken illegally for pleasure

¹**cock** /'kɑːk/ n [C] **1** : an adult male chicken : ROOSTER **2** *informal + impolite* : PENIS

²**cock** vb [T] **1** : to pull back the hammer of (a gun) to get ready to shoot • *He cocked the pistol.* **2** : to pull or bend back (something) to get ready to throw or hit a ball • *The hitter stood with the bat cocked, waiting for a pitch.* **3** : to turn,

tip, or raise (part of your body or face) upward or to one side • *She cocked an eyebrow in disbelief.* • *The dog sat with one ear cocked.* **4** : to move (a hat) so that it is tilted on your head • *a hat cocked to one side* — **cock up** [*phrasal vb*] *Brit, informal* **cock up** or **cock up (something)** or **cock (something) up** : to make a mistake or mistakes in doing or making (something) • *Someone had cocked up the arrangements.*

cock·a·ma·my or **cock·a·ma·mie** /₊kɑːkə'meɪmi/ adj, *US, informal* : ridiculous or silly • *a cockamamie idea/scheme*

cock-and-bull story /'kɑːkən'bʊl-/ n [C] *informal* : a ridiculous story that is used as an explanation or excuse

cock·a·too /'kɑːkə₊tuː/ n [C] : a type of large parrot from Australia

cocker spaniel n [C] : a type of small dog that has long ears and long fur

cock-eyed /'kɑːk₊aɪd/ adj, *informal* **1** : turned or tilted to one side • *a cockeyed grin* **2** : crazy or foolish • *a cockeyed idea*

cock·le /'kɑːkəl/ n [C] : a type of shellfish with a shell that has two parts and is shaped like a heart — **warm the cockles of your heart** ✧ If something *warms the cockles of your heart*, it makes you have warm and happy feelings.

cock·ney or **Cock·ney** /'kɑːkni/ n, pl **-neys 1** [C] : a person from the East End of London **2** [U] : the way of speaking that is typical of cockneys — **cockney** adj • *a cockney accent*

cock·pit /'kɑːk₊pɪt/ n [C] : the area in a boat, airplane, etc., where the pilot or driver sits

cock·roach /'kɑːk₊roʊtʃ/ n [C] : a black or brown insect that is sometimes found in people's homes — called also (*US*) **roach**

cock·sure /'kɑːk'ʃʊɚ/ adj : having or showing confidence in a way that is annoying to other people • *cocksure arrogance*

cock·tail /'kɑːk₊teɪl/ n **1** [C] : an alcoholic drink that is a mixture of one or more liquors and other ingredients (such as fruit juice) **2** [C] : a mixture of different things • *treatment involving a cocktail of powerful drugs* — see also MOLOTOV COCKTAIL **3** [C/U] : a small dish of a particular food that is served usually at the beginning or end of a meal • *fruit/shrimp cocktail*

cocktail party n [C] : a usually formal party at which alcoholic drinks are served

cock-up /'kɑːk₊ʌp/ n [C] *Brit, informal* : a situation that is complicated, unpleasant, or difficult to deal with because of someone's mistake • *an administrative cock-up*

cocky /'kɑːki/ adj **cock·i·er**; **-est** *informal* : having or showing confidence in a way that is annoying to other people • *a cocky young athlete* — **cock·i·ness** /'kɑːkinəs/ n [U]

co·coa /'koʊkoʊ/ n **1** [U] : a brown powder made from roasted cocoa beans that is used to give a chocolate flavor to foods — called also *cocoa powder* **2**

[C/U] : a hot drink of milk or water mixed with cocoa • *a cup of cocoa*

cocoa bean *n* [C] : the seed of a tropical tree (called the cacao) that is used in making cocoa, chocolate, and cocoa butter

cocoa butter *n* [U] : a pale fat made from cocoa beans that is used in making chocolate and in various products (such as soaps and skin lotions)

co·co·nut /ˈkoʊkəˌnʌt/ *n* 1 [C] : a large fruit that has a thick shell with white flesh and liquid inside it and that grows on a palm tree 2 [U] : the white flesh of a coconut • *shredded coconut*

coconut milk *n* [U] : the liquid that is inside a coconut

co·coon /kəˈkuːn/ *n* [C] 1 : a covering usually made of silk which some insects (such as caterpillars) make around themselves to protect them while they grow 2 : something that covers or protects a person or thing • *The child was wrapped in a cocoon of blankets.* — **cocoon** *vb* [T] • *We were comfortably cocooned in our sleeping bags.*

cod /ˈkɑːd/ *n* [C/U] : a large fish that lives in the northern Atlantic Ocean and is often eaten as food

COD *or* **C.O.D.** *abbr* cash on delivery; collect on delivery — used to indicate that payment must be made when something is delivered • *merchandise shipped C.O.D*

cod·dle /ˈkɑːdl/ *vb* **cod·dled; cod·dling** [T] *disapproving* : to treat (someone) with too much care or kindness • *judges accused of coddling criminals*

¹**code** /ˈkoʊd/ *n* 1 [C] **a** : a set of laws or regulations • *the state's criminal/tax code* • *a dress code* [=rules about what a person can wear] **b** : a set of ideas or rules about how to behave • *a moral code* • *a strict code of ethics/conduct/behavior* 2 **a** [C/U] : a set of letters, numbers, symbols, etc., that is used to secretly send messages to someone • *trying to break/crack a secret code* • *a message sent in code* **b** [C] : a set of letters, numbers, symbols, etc., that identifies or gives information about something or someone • *a product code* • *a code number* 3 [U] : a set of instructions for a computer • *lines of code*

²**code** *vb* **cod·ed; cod·ing** [T] 1 : to put (a message) into the form of a code so that it can be kept secret • *a coded message* 2 : to mark (something) with a code so that it can be identified • *Each product has been coded.* 3 : to change (information) into a set of letters, numbers, or symbols that can be read by a computer • *Programmers coded the data.*

code name *n* [C] : a name that is used to keep someone's or something's real name a secret — **code-name** /ˈkoʊdˌneɪm/ *vb* **-named; -nam·ing** [T] • *The military operation is code-named "Clean Sweep."*

code word *n* [C] : a word or phrase that has a secret meaning or that is used instead of another word or phrase to avoid speaking directly • *The code word "con-*

flict" has been used for what some people are calling a war.

cod·ger /ˈkɑːdʒɚ/ *n* [C] *informal* : an old man • *a feisty old codger*

cod·i·fy /ˈkɑːdəˌfaɪ/ *vb* **-fies; -fied; -fy·ing** [T] : to put (laws or rules) together as a code or system • *The convention codified the rules of war.* — **cod·i·fi·ca·tion** /ˌkɑːdəfəˈkeɪʃən/ *n* [C/U]

cod–liver oil *n* [U] : an oil from the liver of cod that is used in medicine as a source of vitamin A and D

¹**co·ed** /ˈkoʊˌɛd/ *n* [C] *US, somewhat old-fashioned* : a female student at a college that has both male and female students

²**coed** *adj* 1 : COEDUCATIONAL • *a coed dormitory* 2 *US* : having or including both men and women • *The softball team is coed.*

co·ed·u·ca·tion·al /ˌkoʊˌɛdʒəˈkeɪʃənl/ *adj, formal* : having both male and female students • *a coeducational institution*

co·erce /koʊˈɚs/ *vb* **-erced; -erc·ing** [T] 1 : to make (someone) do something by using force or threats • *I was coerced into signing the confession.* 2 : to get (something) by using force or threats • *A confession was coerced from the suspect.* — **co·er·cion** /koʊˈɚʒən, koʊˈɚʃən/ *n* [U]

co·er·cive /koʊˈɚsɪv/ *adj, formal* : using force or threats to make someone do something : using coercion • *coercive measures/techniques/policies*

co·ex·ist /ˌkoʊɪɡˈzɪst/ *vb* [I] 1 : to exist together or at the same time • *proof that dinosaurs and turtles coexisted (with each other)* 2 : to live in peace with each other • *Can the two countries peacefully coexist?* — **co·ex·is·tence** /ˌkoʊɪɡˈzɪstəns/ *n* [U]

cof·fee /ˈkɑːfi/ *n* 1 [C/U] : a dark brown drink made from ground coffee beans and boiled water • *a cup of coffee* • *Would you like another coffee?* [=another cup of coffee] • *a coffee cup/mug* 2 [U] : coffee beans • *a pound of coffee*

coffee bean *n* [C] : the bean of a tropical tree or bush from which coffee is made

coffee break *n* [C] : a short period of time in which you stop working to rest and have coffee, tea, simple foods, etc.

coffee cake *n* [C] *US* : a sweet, rich bread usually made with fruit, nuts, and spices and often eaten with coffee

cof·fee·house /ˈkɑːfiˌhaʊs/ *n* [C] : a business that sells coffee and usually other drinks and simple foods

cof·fee·mak·er /ˈkɑːfiˌmeɪkɚ/ *n* [C] : a small electrical machine that makes coffee

cof·fee·pot /ˈkɑːfiˌpɑːt/ *n* [C] : a pot that is used for making and pouring coffee

coffee shop *n* [C] : a small restaurant that serves coffee and other drinks as well as simple foods

coffee table *n* [C] : a long, low table that is usually placed in front of a sofa in someone's home

cof·fer /ˈkɑːfɚ/ *n* 1 [C] : a box for holding money or other valuable things 2 [plural] : money that is available for spending • *the city's coffers*

cof·fin /ˈkɑːfən/ *n* [C] : a box in which a

dead person is buried

cog /'kɑːg/ *n* [C] **1** : any one of the small parts that stick out on the outer edge of a wheel or gear and that allow it to turn along with another wheel or gear **2** : someone or something that is thought of as being like a small part of a machine ▪ *She's an electrician for a film studio: a minor cog in the Hollywood machine.*

co·gent /'kouʤənt/ *adj, formal* : very clear and easy for the mind to accept and believe ▪ *a cogent argument* — **co·gen·cy** /'kouʤənsi/ *n* [U] — **co·gent·ly** *adv*

cog·i·tate /'kɑːʤəˌteɪt/ *vb* **-tat·ed; -tat·ing** [I] *formal* : to think carefully and seriously about something ▪ *I was cogitating about/on my chances of failing.* — **cog·i·ta·tion** /ˌkɑːʤəˈteɪʃən/ *n* [C/U] ▪ *a problem requiring further cogitation* [=thought]

co·gnac /'koʊnˌjæk, 'kɑːnˌjæk/ *n* [C/U] : a kind of brandy that is made in France

cog·nate /'kɑːgˌneɪt/ *adj, linguistics* : having the same origin ▪ *Spanish and French are cognate languages.* — **cog·nate** *n* [C]

cog·ni·tion /kɑːgˈnɪʃən/ *n* [U] *technical* : the activities of thinking, understanding, learning, and remembering

cog·ni·tive /'kɑːgnətɪv/ *adj, technical* : of, relating to, or involving conscious mental activities (such as thinking, understanding, learning, and remembering) ▪ *cognitive development/psychology/impairment* — **cog·ni·tive·ly** *adv*

cog·ni·zance *also Brit* **cog·ni·sance** /'kɑːgnəzəns/ *n* [U] *formal* : knowledge or awareness of something ▪ *She has no cognizance of the crime.* — **take cognizance of** : to notice or give attention to (something) ▪ *He should take cognizance of those who disagree with his theory.*

cog·ni·zant *also Brit* **cog·ni·sant** /'kɑːgnəzənt/ *adj, not before a noun, formal* : aware of something ▪ *cognizant of the potential dangers*

cog·no·scen·ti /ˌkɑːnjəˈʃɛnti/ *n* — **the cognoscenti** : the people who know a lot about something ▪ *the jazz cognoscenti*

co·hab·it /koʊˈhæbət/ *vb* [I] *formal* : to live together and have a sexual relationship — **co·hab·i·ta·tion** /koʊˌhæbəˈteɪʃən/ *n* [U]

co·her·ent /koʊˈhɪrənt/ *adj* **1** : logical and well-organized : easy to understand ▪ *a coherent plan/argument/essay* **2** : able to talk or express yourself in a clear way that can be easily understood ▪ *too drunk to be coherent* **3** : working closely and well together ▪ *a coherent group/team* — **co·her·ence** /koʊˈhɪrəns/ *n* [U] — **co·her·ent·ly** *adv*

co·he·sion /koʊˈhiːʒən/ *n* [U] : a condition in which people or things are closely united : UNITY ▪ *the team's lack of cohesion*

co·he·sive /koʊˈhiːsɪv/ *adj* **1** : closely united ▪ *a small but cohesive group* **2** : causing people to be closely united ▪ *Religion can be a cohesive social force.* — **co·he·sive·ly** *adv* — **co·he·sive·ness** *n* [U]

co·hort /'koʊˌhoɜt/ *n* [C] *often disapproving* : a friend or companion ▪ *the gang's*

leader and his cohorts

coif /'kwɑːf/ *vb* **coiffed** *also* **coifed; coiffing** *also* **coif·ing** [T] : to cut and arrange someone's hair ▪ *her perfectly coiffed hair*

coif·fure /kwɑːˈfjuɚ/ *n* [C] *formal* : HAIR-DO

¹**coil** /'kojəl/ *vb* [T/I] : to wind (something) into circles ▪ *The snake coiled (itself) around its prey.* ▪ *coiled wire*

²**coil** *n* [C] **1** : a long, thin piece of material (such as a wire, string, or piece of hair) that is wound into circles ▪ *a coil of wire* **2** *technical* : a wire wound into circles that carries electricity

¹**coin** /'kojn/ *n* [C] : a small, flat, and usually round piece of metal issued by a government as money ▪ *gold/silver/copper coins* — **the other/opposite/flip side of the coin** : a different way of looking at or thinking about a situation ▪ *The economy is improving, but the other side of the coin is that inflation is becoming a bigger problem.* — **toss/flip a coin** : to decide something by throwing a coin up in the air and seeing which side is shown after it lands — **two sides of the same coin** : two things that are regarded as two parts of the same thing ▪ *These problems are two sides of the same coin.*

²**coin** *vb* [T] **1** : to create (a new word or phrase) that other people begin to use ▪ *an author who coined many words* ✧ The phrase **to coin a phrase** is sometimes used in a joking way to say that you know you are using a very common expression. ▪ *They lived happily ever after, to coin a phrase.* **2** : to make (money in the form of coins) ▪ *The nation plans to coin more money.* — **coin it** *or* **coin money** *Brit, informal* : to earn a lot of money quickly or easily

coin·age /'kojnɪʤ/ *n* **1 a** [U] : the act of creating a new word or phrase that other people begin to use ▪ *"Blog" is a word of recent coinage.* [=a word that was recently created] **b** [C] : a word that someone has created ▪ *The word "blog" is a recent coinage.* **2** [U] **a** : money in the form of coins ▪ *Coinage was scarce in the colonies.* **b** : the act or process of creating coins ▪ *the coinage of money*

co·in·cide /ˌkowənˈsaɪd/ *vb* **-cid·ed; -cid·ing** [I] **1** : to happen at the same time as something else ▪ *The population increase coincided with rapid industrial growth.* **2** : to agree with something exactly ▪ *Her job coincided well with her career goals.*

co·in·ci·dence /koʊˈɪnsədəns/ *n* [C/U] : a situation in which events happen at the same time in a way that is not planned or expected ▪ *It was (a) mere/pure/sheer coincidence that brought them together.* ▪ *By coincidence, every man in the room was named Fred.* **2** [*singular*] *formal* : the occurrence of two or more things at the same time ▪ *Scientists have no explanation for the coincidence of these phenomena.*

co·in·ci·dent /koʊˈɪnsədənt/ *adj, formal* : happening at the same time ▪ *Animal hibernation is coincident with the approach of winter.*

co·in·ci·den·tal /ˌkoʊˌɪnsəˈdɛntl̩/ adj : happening because of a coincidence : not planned • *a purely coincidental meeting* — **co·in·ci·den·tal·ly** adv • *Coincidentally, they were both graduates of the same college.*

co·i·tus /ˈkoʊətəs/ n [U] technical : SEXUAL INTERCOURSE — **co·i·tal** /ˈkoʊətl̩/ adj

coke /ˈkoʊk/ n [U] **1** : a black material made from coal that is used as fuel for heating **2** informal : COCAINE

Coke /ˈkoʊk/ trademark — used for a cola drink

col. abbr column

Col. abbr colonel

co·la /ˈkoʊlə/ n [C/U] : a sweet brown drink that contains many bubbles

col·an·der /ˈkɑːləndər/ n [C] : a bowl that has many small holes and that is used for washing or draining food

¹cold /ˈkoʊld/ adj **1** : having a very low temperature • *cold water/weather* • *a cold climate/winter* • *It's cold outside.* **2** : having a feeling of low body heat • *Are you cold?* **3** *of food* : not heated • *cold cereal/sandwiches/meats* **4** : causing a cold or unhappy feeling • *the cold gray sky* **5** : not friendly or emotional • *Why is he so cold toward me?* • *a cold stare* **6** : not changed or affected by personal feelings or emotions • *the cold facts* **7** : unconscious or sleeping very deeply • *He passed out cold.* • *She was out cold by eight o'clock.* **8** : no longer easy to follow • *The police had been hot on their trail, but then the trail went cold.* **9** : not close to finding something or solving a puzzle — used especially in children's games • *You're getting warmer! Oh, now you're getting colder!* **10** : not having success or good luck • *The team was hot in the first half, but their shooting turned cold in the second half.* [=they missed a lot of shots in the second half] — **in the cold light of day** : in the day when things can be seen clearly rather than at night • *The house that had looked so sinister at night seemed much less frightening in the cold light of day.* — **leave you cold** ⬦ Something that *leaves you cold* does not interest or excite you. • *His movies leave me cold.* — **cold·ly** adv • *She looked at me coldly.* — **cold·ness** n [U]

²cold n **1** [U] : a cold condition • *I mind cold more than heat.* **2** *the cold* : cold weather • *Come in out of the cold.* **3** [C] : a common illness that affects the nose, throat, and eyes and that usually causes coughing, sneezing, etc. • *He got/caught a cold.* • *cold symptoms/remedies* — **the common cold** — **come in from the cold** : to become part of a group or of normal society again after you have been outside it • *a former spy who has come in from the cold* — **leave (someone) out in the cold** : to not give (someone) the rights or advantages that are given to others • *The changes benefit management but leave the workers out in the cold.*

³cold adv **1** chiefly US **a** : in a very clear, complete, and definite way • *She turned the offer down cold.* **b** : in a sudden way

• *He stopped cold.* **2** : without practicing or preparing before doing something • *She was asked to perform the song cold.*

cold–blood·ed /ˈkoʊldˈblʌdəd/ adj **1** : showing no sympathy or mercy • *cold-blooded murderers* : done in a planned way without emotion • *a cold-blooded killing* **2** : not affected by emotions • *a cold-blooded assessment of the situation* **3** biology : having a body temperature that is similar to the temperature of the environment • *Reptiles are cold-blooded.* — **cold–blood·ed·ly** adv — **cold–blood·ed·ness** n [U]

cold comfort n [U] : something that is good for a situation but does not make someone happy because the whole situation is still bad • *The good news about the economy is cold comfort to people who have lost their jobs.*

cold cream n [U] : a cream that people use to clean the face or soften the skin

cold cuts n [plural] chiefly US : cold cooked meats (such as turkey, roast beef, or ham) that have been cut into thin slices

cold–eyed /ˈkoʊldˈaɪd/ adj **1** : not affected by emotions • *a cold-eyed analysis of the data* **2** : having a cold or unfriendly appearance • *a cold-eyed businessman*

cold feet n [plural] : a feeling of worry or doubt that is strong enough to stop you from doing something that you planned to do • *I got cold feet and couldn't go through with it.*

cold fish n, pl ~ **fish** [C] : an unfriendly person • *Her husband's a bit of a cold fish.*

cold–heart·ed /ˈkoʊldˈhɑtəd/ adj : lacking kindness, sympathy, or sensitivity • *a coldhearted criminal* — **cold–heart·ed·ly** adv — **cold–heart·ed·ness** n [U]

cold shoulder n — **the cold shoulder** : cold and unfriendly treatment from someone who knows you • *Most of the other professors gave him the cold shoulder.* — **cold–shoul·der** vb [T] • *He was cold-shouldered by the other professors.*

cold sore n [C] : a small sore area around or inside the mouth that is caused by a virus

cold storage n [U] : the state of being kept in a cold place for later use • *food that has been taken out of cold storage* • (figurative) *a project being kept/put in cold storage until funds become available*

cold sweat n [singular] : a condition in which someone is sweating and feeling cold at the same time because of fear, illness, etc. • *I break out in a cold sweat when I think about it.*

cold turkey n [U] informal : the act of stopping a bad habit (such as taking drugs) in a sudden and complete way — **cold turkey** adv • *quitting cold turkey* • *Some people have to go cold turkey to stop.*

cold war n **1** *the Cold War* : the nonviolent conflict between the U.S. and the former U.S.S.R. after 1945 **2** [C] : a conflict or dispute between two groups that does not involve actual fighting • *the cold war between the party's more liberal* *and conservative members* — **cold-war** or **Cold-War** *adj, always before a noun* • *cold-war diplomacy*

cold warrior *n* [C] : a person who supported or participated in the Cold War between the U.S. and the U.S.S.R.

cole·slaw /'koʊlˌslɑː/ *n* [U] : a salad made with chopped raw cabbage

col·ic /'kɑːlɪk/ *n* [U] : a physical condition in which a baby is very uncomfortable and cries for long periods of time — **col·icky** /'kɑːlɪki/ *adj* • *a colicky baby*

col·i·se·um /ˌkɑːlə'siːjəm/ *n* [C] *chiefly US* : a large stadium or building for sports or entertainment

co·li·tis /koʊ'laɪtəs/ *n* [U] : an illness that causes pain and swelling in the colon

col·lab·o·rate /kə'læbəˌreɪt/ *vb* **-rat·ed; -rat·ing** [*I*] **1** : to work with another person or group in order to achieve or do something • *They collaborated (with each other) on a book about dogs.* **2** *disapproving* : to give help to an enemy who has invaded your country during a war • *He was suspected of collaborating with the enemy.* — **col·lab·o·ra·tion** /kəˌlæbə'reɪʃən/ *n* [C/U] • *a collaboration between two writers* • *an artistic collaboration* • *They worked in close collaboration (with each other).* — **col·lab·o·ra·tor** /kə'læbəˌreɪtɚ/ *n* [C]

col·lab·o·ra·tive /kə'læbərətɪv/ *adj* : involving or done by two or more people or groups working together to achieve or do something • *a collaborative project/study/effort* — **col·lab·o·ra·tive·ly** *adv*

col·lage /kə'lɑːʒ/ *n* **1** [C/U] : a work of art that is made by attaching pieces of different materials (such as paper, cloth, or wood) to a flat surface **2** [C] : a collection of different things • *The album is a collage of several musical styles.*

¹**col·lapse** /kə'læps/ *vb* **-lapsed; -laps·ing** **1** [*I*] : to break apart and fall down suddenly • *The chair he was sitting in collapsed.* **2** [*I*] **a** : to fall down or become unconscious because you are sick or exhausted • *He collapsed on stage and had to be rushed to the hospital.* **b** : to completely relax the muscles of your body because you are very tired, upset, etc. • *She came home from work and collapsed on the sofa.* **3** [*I*] **a** : to fail or stop working suddenly • *Negotiations have completely collapsed.* **b** : to lose almost all worth • *Oil prices have collapsed.* **4** [*I*] *medical* : to become flat and empty • *a collapsed lung* **5** [T/I] : to fold together • *The stroller collapses easily.* = *You can collapse the stroller easily.* — **col·laps·ible** /kə'læpsəbəl/ *adj* • *a collapsible chair/table/stroller*

²**collapse** *n* [C/U] : a situation or occurrence in which something or someone collapses, fails, etc. • *a fatal bridge collapse* • *She was on the verge of collapse.* • *the collapse of negotiations* • *a collapse in the value of their currency*

¹**col·lar** /'kɑːlɚ/ *n* [C] **1** : a part of a piece of clothing that fits around a person's neck and is usually folded down • *a shirt with a tight collar* **2** : a band worn around an animal's neck • *a dog's collar* **3** *technical* : a ring or band used to hold

something (such as a pipe or a part of a machine) in place — **hot under the collar** see HOT

²**collar** *vb* [T] *informal* : to catch or arrest (someone) • *The police collared him outside his home.*

col·lar·bone /'kɑːlɚˌboʊn/ *n* [C] : a bone that connects the shoulder to the base of the neck

col·late /kə'leɪt, 'koʊˌleɪt/ *vb* **-lat·ed; -lat·ing** [T] **1** : to gather information from different sources in order to study it carefully • *collating data* **2** : to arrange (sheets of paper) in the correct order • *The photocopier will collate the pages of the report.* — **col·la·tion** /kə'leɪʃən/ *n* [C/U]

col·lat·er·al /kə'lætərəl/ *n* [U] : something that you promise to give someone if you cannot pay back a loan • *She put up her house as collateral for the loan.*

collateral damage *n* [U] : forms of damage including deaths and injuries that happen to people who are not in the military as a result of the fighting in a war

col·league /'kɑːˌliːg/ *n* [C] *somewhat formal* : a person who works with you • *a colleague of mine*

¹**col·lect** /kə'lɛkt/ *vb* **1 a** [T/I] : to get (things) from different places and bring them together • *They collected information about the community.* • (*Brit*) *I collected up* [=*picked up*] *the dishes and brought them to the kitchen.* **b** [T] : to get (someone or something) from a place • *We collected our baggage from/at the baggage claim at the airport.* • *She collected the children after school.* **2** [T/I] : to get (similar things) and bring them together as a hobby • *He collects postage stamps.* **3** [T] : to get control of (your thoughts, emotions, etc.) • *I took a minute to collect my thoughts.* • *She stopped briefly to collect herself.* **4** [T/I] **a** : to ask for and get (money or other things) • *collect rent/taxes/contributions* • *I am collecting for the local women's shelter.* **b** : to be given or paid (money) • *She collects social security benefits.* • *He is collecting* on *his disability insurance.* **5** [T/I] : to come together in a large amount as time passes • *Dust had collected on the dashboard.*

²**collect** *adj, US* : paid for by the person who is receiving the call • *a collect phone call* — **collect** *adv* • *You can call me collect.*

col·lect·ed /kə'lɛktəd/ *adj* **1** *always before a noun* : brought together in a group • *the collected works of Shakespeare* **2** *not before a noun* : calm and in control of your emotions • *She was cool, calm, and collected.*

col·lect·ible *or chiefly Brit* **col·lect·able** /kə'lɛktəbəl/ *adj* : considered valuable by collectors • *The shop sells antiques and various collectible items.* — **collectible** *or chiefly Brit* **collectable** [C]

col·lec·tion /kə'lɛkʃən/ *n* **1** [C/U] : the act or process of getting things from different places and bringing them together • *tax/data collection* • *weekly trash collections* **2** [C] : a group of interesting or beautiful objects brought together in order to show or study them or as a hobby • *a stamp collection* • *(figurative) She has quite a collection of friends/stories.* **3** [*C*] : a request for money in order to help people or to pay for something important • *We took up a collection for the school renovations.; also* : the money collected in this way • *Ten percent of the collection goes to the city's homeless shelters.* • *a collection plate/box* **4** [*C*] : a group of clothes that a fashion designer has created • *the designer's spring collection* **5** [*C*] : a group of different writings that are brought together in one book • *a collection of her short stories*

¹**col·lec·tive** /kə'lɛktɪv/ *adj, always before a noun* : shared or done by a group of people • *a collective decision/effort* • *the collective wisdom of generations* — **col·lec·tive·ly** *adv*

²**collective** *n* [*C*] : a business or organization that is owned by the people who work there

collective bargaining *n* [*U*] : talks between an employer and the leaders of a union about how much a group of workers will be paid, how many hours they will work, etc.

collective noun *n* [*C*] : a word (such as *family* or *herd*) that names a group of people or things

col·lec·tor /kə'lɛktə/ *n* [*C*] **1** : a person who collects certain things as a hobby • *a stamp collector* **2** : a person whose job is to collect something • *tax/bill/debt/trash collectors*

collector's item *n* [*C*] : an object that people want because it is rare or valuable

col·lege /'kɑːlɪdʒ/ *n* **1** [*C/U*] : a school in the U.S. that you go to after high school • *She attended a business college.* • *college students/courses/graduates* **2** [*C*] : a part of an American university that offers courses in a specified subject • *the university's college of dentistry/engineering/medicine* **3 a** [*C/U*] : a school in Britain that offers advanced training in a specified subject • *an arts college* **b** [*C*] : a separate part of a large British university where students live and take courses **4** [*C*] *formal* : an organized group of people who have similar jobs or interests • *the American College of Cardiology* — see also ELECTORAL COLLEGE

col·le·giate /kə'liːdʒət/ *adj* : of or relating to a college or its students • *collegiate athletics*

col·lide /kə'laɪd/ *vb* **-lid·ed; -lid·ing** [*I*] **1** : to hit something or each other with strong force • *Two players collided (with each other) on the field.* **2** — used of situations in which people or groups disagree or are very different from each other • *Their ideas for the company often collide.* [=clash]

col·lie /'kɑːli/ *n* [*C*] : a large type of dog with long hair and a long pointed nose

col·liery /'kɑːljəri/ *n, pl* **-lier·ies** [*C*] *chiefly Brit* : a coal mine and the buildings that are near it

col·li·sion /kə'lɪʒən/ *n* [*C*] **1** : a crash in which two or more things or people hit each other • *a head-on collision* [=a

crash of two vehicles that are moving directly toward each other] **2** : a situation in which people or groups disagree • *the latest collision between the two leaders*

collision course *n* — **on a collision course** ✧ Two people or things that are *on a collision course* are moving and will crash into each other if one of them does not change direction. • *The two airplanes were on a collision course (with each other).* • *(figurative) The decision put us on a collision course with economic disaster.*

col·lo·cate /'kɑːlə,keɪt/ *vb* **-cat·ed; -cat·ing** [*I*] *technical* : to appear often with another word • *The word "college" collocates with "student."* — **col·lo·ca·tion** /ˌkɑːlə'keɪʃən/ *n* [*C/U*] • *a common collocation*

col·lo·qui·al /kə'loʊkwijəl/ *adj* : used when people are speaking in an informal way • *a colloquial word/expression* — **col·lo·qui·al·ly** *adv*

col·lo·qui·al·ism /kə'loʊkwijə,lɪzəm/ *n* [*C*] : a colloquial word or phrase

col·lude /kə'luːd/ *vb* **-lud·ed; -lud·ing** [*I*] *disapproving* : to work with others secretly • *The companies colluded to fix prices.* • *colluding with criminals* — **col·lu·sion** /kə'luːʒən/ *n* [*U*] • *collusion between city officials and local businesses* • *The company acted in collusion with manufacturers to inflate prices.*

co·logne /kə'loʊn/ *n* [*C/U*] : a liquid that has a light, pleasant smell and that people put on their skin

co·lon /'koʊlən/ *n* [*C*] **1** : the punctuation mark : used to direct attention to what follows it (such as a list, explanation, or quotation) **2** : the main part of the large intestine

col·o·nel /'kɚnl/ *n* [*C*] : a military officer who ranks above a major

¹**co·lo·ni·al** /kə'loʊnijəl/ *adj* **1 a** : of or relating to a colony • *colonial possessions/administration* **b** : owning or made up of colonies • *a colonial empire* **2** *or* **Colonial** : of or relating to the original 13 colonies forming the United States • *Colonial America* • *colonial architecture/furniture* **3** : in a style that was popular during the American colonial period (before 1776) • *They live in a colonial (style) house.*

²**colonial** *n* [*C*] **1** *or* **Colonial** : a two-story house built in a style that was first popular during the American colonial period (before 1776) **2** : a person who is part of a colony : COLONIST

co·lo·ni·al·ism /kə'loʊnijə,lɪzəm/ *n* [*U*] : control by one country over another area and its people — **co·lo·ni·al·ist** /kə'loʊnijəlɪst/ *n* [*C*] — **colonialist** *adj* • *the colonialist past*

col·o·nist /'kɑːlənɪst/ *n* [*C*] : a person who lives in or helps to create a colony • *an area settled by British colonists*

col·o·nize *also Brit* **col·o·nise** /'kɑːlə,naɪz/ *vb* **-nized; -niz·ing** [*T*] : to create a colony in or on (a place) • *The area was colonized in the 18th century.* — **col·o·ni·za·tion** *also Brit* **col·o·ni·sa·tion** /ˌkɑːlənə'zeɪʃən, *Brit* ˌkɒlə,naɪ'zeɪʃən/ *n* [*U*] — **col·o·niz·er** *also Brit* **col·o·nis·er** *n* [*C*]

col·on·nade /ˌkɑːləˈneɪd/ n [C] : a row of columns usually holding up a roof

co·lo·nos·co·py /ˌkoʊləˈnɑːskəpi/ n, pl **-pies** [C] : a medical procedure in which a special tube-shaped instrument is used to take pictures of the inside of someone's colon

col·o·ny /ˈkɑːləni/ n, pl **-nies** [C] : 1 : an area that is controlled by or belongs to a country ▪ a former French colony in Africa 2 : a group of plants or animals living or growing in one place ▪ an ant colony 3 : a group of people who are similar in some way and who live in a certain area ▪ an artist colony

¹**col·or** (US) or Brit **col·our** /ˈkʌlə/ n 1 [C/U] : a quality such as red, blue, green, yellow, etc., that you see when you look at something ▪ The color of blood is red. ▪ The pillows are all different colors. ▪ The room needs more color. 2 [C/U] : something used to give color to something ▪ She's using a new lip/nail color. 3 [U] a : the use or combination of colors ▪ a painter who is a master of color b — used to describe a photograph, televison picture, etc., that includes colors and that is not black and white ▪ The book includes over 100 photographs in (full) color. ▪ a color photograph ▪ color printing/television 4 [U] : the color of a person's skin as a mark of race ▪ discrimination on the basis of sex or color ✧ A person of color is a person who is not white. 5 [U] : a pink or red tone in a person's face especially because of good health, excitement, or embarrassment ▪ The color drained from her face. [=she became very pale] 6 [plural] : something (such as a flag) that shows that someone or something belongs to a specific group ▪ The ship sails under Swedish colors. 7 [U] : interest or excitement ▪ Her comments added color to the broadcast. — see also LOCAL COLOR — **show your true colors** : to show what you are really like ▪ He seemed nice at first, but he showed his true colors during the crisis. — **with flying colors** see ¹FLYING — **col·or·less** (US) or Brit **col·our·less** /ˈkʌlələs/ adj

²**color** (US) or Brit **colour** vb 1 [T] : to give color to (something) ▪ We colored the water with red ink. ▪ She colors [=dyes] her hair. 2 [T/I] : to fill in a shape or picture using crayons, markers, etc. ▪ The children were coloring in their coloring books. ▪ The child colored the sky blue. 3 [T] : to change (someone's ideas, opinion, etc.) in some way ▪ His feelings about divorce are colored [=influenced] by his own experiences.

col·or·a·tion (chiefly US) or Brit **col·our·a·tion** /ˌkʌləˈreɪʃən/ n [C/U] : the color of or patterns of color on something ▪ the coloration of a bird/flower

col·or-blind (US) or Brit **col·our-blind** /ˈkʌlərˌblaɪnd/ adj 1 : unable to see the difference between certain colors 2 : treating people of different skin colors equally ▪ color-blind companies/policies — **color blindness** (US) or Brit **colour blindness** [U]

col·ored (US) or Brit **col·oured** /ˈkʌləd/ adj 1 : having color : not black or white ▪ colored glass/pencils/lights 2 old-fashioned + sometimes offensive : of or relating to a race other than white; especially : ¹BLACK 2

col·or·fast (US) or Brit **col·our·fast** /ˈkʌlərˌfæst, Brit ˈkʌləˌfɑːst/ adj : able to keep the same color even if washed, placed in light, etc. ▪ a colorfast carpet

col·or·ful (US) or Brit **col·our·ful** /ˈkʌlərfəl/ adj 1 : having a bright color or a lot of different colors ▪ a colorful outfit 2 : interesting or exciting ▪ a colorful story/person/personality ✧ If you use colorful language, you use words that are usually considered rude or offensive. — **col·or·ful·ly** (US) or Brit **col·our·ful·ly** /ˈkʌləfli/ adv

col·or·ing (US) or Brit **col·our·ing** /ˈkʌlərɪŋ/ n 1 [C/U] : something that produces color ▪ hair colorings ▪ blue food coloring 2 [U] a : the color of a person's skin and hair ▪ He has very light coloring. b : the color of an animal or plant ▪ a bird's bright coloring

coloring book (US) or Brit **colouring book** n [C] : a book of pictures that you color in with crayons, markers, etc.

color line n [singular] US : a set of customs or laws that does not allow black people to do the same things or be in the same places as white people ▪ Jackie Robinson broke American baseball's color line. [=he was the first black man to play professional baseball with white players] — called also (Brit) colour bar

co·los·sal /kəˈlɑːsəl/ adj : very large or great ▪ a colossal statue/failure

co·los·sus /kəˈlɑːsəs/ n, pl **-los·si** /-ˈlɑːˌsaɪ/ [C] 1 : a huge statue 2 : a very large or important person or thing ▪ a corporate colossus

colour Brit spelling of COLOR

colt /ˈkoʊlt/ n [C] : a young male horse

Co·lum·bus Day /kəˈlʌmbəs-/ n [singular] : the second Monday in October observed as a legal holiday in many states of the U.S. in honor of the arrival of Christopher Columbus in the Bahamas in 1492

col·umn /ˈkɑːləm/ n [C] 1 : a long post made of steel, stone, etc., that is used as a support in a building 2 a : a group of printed or written items (such as numbers or words) shown one under the other on a page b : any one of two or more sections of print that appear next to each other on a page 3 : an article in a newspaper or magazine that appears regularly and that is written by a particular writer or deals with a particular subject ▪ a weekly sports/gossip column 4 : something that is tall and thin in shape ▪ columns of smoke 5 : a long row of people or things ▪ a column of troops/cars

col·um·nist /ˈkɑːləmnɪst/ n [C] : a person who writes a newspaper or magazine column

com /ˈkɑːm/ abbr commercial organization — used in an Internet address to show that it belongs to a company or business ▪ www.Merriam-Webster.com

co·ma /ˈkoʊmə/ n [C/U] : a state in which a sick or injured person is unconscious for a long time • *She was in a coma for a year.*

co·ma·tose /ˈkoumə₁tous/ *adj* : in a coma • *comatose patients*

¹comb /ˈkoum/ *n* [C] **1** : a flat piece of plastic or metal with a row of thin teeth that is used for making hair neat **2** : a soft part on top of the head of some birds (such as chickens)

²comb *vb* **1** [T] : to smooth, arrange, or separate (hair) with a comb • *He combed his hair.* **2** [T/I] : to search very thoroughly for something • *We combed the beach for shells.* • *They got the information by* **combing** *through old records.* — **comb out** [*phrasal vb*] **comb out** (*hair*) *or* **comb** (*hair*) **out** : to make (hair) neat and smooth with a comb • *She combed out (the tangles in) her hair.*

¹com·bat /ˈkɑːm₁bæt/ *n* [U] : active fighting especially in a war • *troops ready for combat* • *combat boots/missions*

²com·bat /kəmˈbæt/ *vb* -bat·ed *also* -bat·ted; -bat·ing *also* -bat·ting [T] **1** : to try to stop (something) from happening or getting worse • *combating poverty/ crime* **2** *formal* : to fight against (someone) • *combating the rebels*

com·bat·ant /kəmˈbætənt, Brit ˈkɒmbə₁tənt/ *n* [C] : a person, group, or country that fights in a war or battle

combat fatigue *n* [U] : BATTLE FATIGUE

com·bat·ive /kəmˈbætɪv, Brit ˈkɒmbətɪv/ *adj* : having or showing a willingness to fight or argue • *a combative person/attitude* — **com·bat·ive·ness** *n* [U]

com·bi·na·tion /₁kɑːmbəˈneɪʃən/ *n* **1** [C] : a result or product of combining two or more things or people • *Water is a combination of hydrogen and oxygen.* • *color combinations* • *A combination of factors led to her decision.* **2** [C/U] : an act of combining two or more things • *The combination of these chemicals can cause an explosion.* • *The drugs should not be taken in* **combination** (*with each other*). [=should not be taken together] **3** [C] : a particular series of numbers or letters that is used to open a lock • *the safe's combination* • *a combination lock* [=a lock opened by using its combination] **4** — used to describe something that can be used in more than one way • *The tool is a combination jackknife and bottle opener.*

¹com·bine /kəmˈbaɪn/ *vb* -bined; -bin·ing **1** *a* [T] : to cause (two or more things) to be together or to work together • *The groups have combined forces.* • *Combine* [=mix] *the ingredients (together) in a large bowl.* • *combining oxygen and/ with hydrogen* *b* [I] : to come together or act together • *Atoms combine to form molecules.* • *Many factors combined to cause the recession.* **2** [T] : to have (two or more different things) at the same time • *She found it difficult to combine a career and family.*

²com·bine /ˈkɑːm₁baɪn/ *n* [C] **1** : a group of people or organizations that work together **2** : a machine that cuts crops and separates the seeds of the plant from the rest of the plant

com·bined /kəmˈbaɪnd/ *adj, always be-*

fore a noun **1** : formed or produced by adding two or more things or amounts together • *They've raised a combined total of one thousand dollars.* **2** : acting together • *the combined effects of stress and fatigue*

combining form *n* [C] : a form of a word (such as *mal-* in *malodorous*) that only occurs as a part of other words

com·bo /ˈkɑːm₁bou/ *n, pl* -bos [C] **1** : a small musical group that plays jazz or dance music **2** *informal* : a combination of different things • *color combos* • *a washer-dryer combo*

com·bus·ti·ble /kəmˈbʌstəbəl/ *adj* : able to be burned easily • *highly combustible gases* • (*figurative*) *a combustible situation* [=a situation in which people are angry and could become violent] — **combustible** *n* [C]

com·bus·tion /kəmˈbʌstʃən/ *n* [U] *technical* : the act of burning

come /ˈkʌm/ *vb* **came** /ˈkeɪm/; **come; com·ing** **1** [I] : to move toward someone or something • *Please come here.* • *Here he comes.* [=he is approaching us] • *The dogs kept coming at me.* • (*figurative*) *We need to come at the problem from a different angle.* **2** [I] : to go or travel to a place • *People come from all over the country to see him.* • (*figurative*) *We've come so far* [=we've made so much progress]; *we can't stop now.* • (*figurative*) *Medicine has* **come** *a long way* [=has made great progress] *in recent years.* **3** [I] : to be delivered to a place • *A letter came for you.* **4** [I] *a* : to have or form an opinion, attitude, etc., after time passes • *I eventually came to regard him as a friend.* • *The food wasn't as good as I've come to expect.* *b* : to do something specified • *How did she come to be there?* [=why was she there?] **5** [I] : to reach a specified level, part, etc. • *The water came almost up to the window.* **6** [*linking vb*] : to reach a specified state or condition • *My shoe came untied.* • *The party suddenly* **came** *alive.* [=suddenly became lively] • *an old house that is* **coming** *apart at the seams* [=that is in very bad condition] **7** [I] *a* : to happen or occur • *These changes couldn't have come at a better time.* • *No harm will come to you.* • *the people and things that came before us* • *Success didn't* **come** *easy for her.* *b* : to arrive or happen after time has passed • *She'll be back in school come September.* = *She'll be back in school when September comes.* • *in the days to come* [=in the future] **8** [I] *a* : to be available • *The product comes in a variety of colors.* • : to have something as a feature, quality, ability, etc. • *The car comes (equipped/ complete) with air-conditioning.* **9** [I] *a* : to have a specified position or place in a series • *The letter D comes after C and before E.* *b Brit* : to end a race or competition in a specified position • *Joan won the race and her sister came second.* **10** [I] *informal* + *impolite* : to experience an orgasm — **as . . . as they come** — used to describe someone or something as very good, bad, etc. • *She's as clever as they come.* [=she's very clever] — **come**

about [*phrasal vb*] **1** : to happen ▪ *Their meeting came about by accident/chance.* **2** *of a boat or ship* : to turn to a different direction ▪ *The captain gave the order to come about.* — **come across** [*phrasal vb*] **1** : to seem to have a particular quality or character ▪ *He came across as a nice guy.* **2** : to be expressed to someone ▪ *Her enthusiasm really came across when she talked about her job.* **3** : to meet or find (something or someone) by chance ▪ *Researchers have come across important new evidence.* — **come after** [*phrasal vb*] : to try to find or capture (someone you want to hurt or punish) ▪ *They're worried that the government might be coming after them.* — **come again** *informal* — used to ask someone to repeat something that was not heard or understood clearly ▪ *"Her name is Hermione." "Come again?"* — **come along** [*phrasal vb*] **1** : to go somewhere with someone ▪ *They asked me to come along (with them) on the trip.* **2** : to make progress in a desired or specified way ▪ *The project is coming along (slowly).* **3** : to happen or appear ▪ *An opportunity like this doesn't come along too often.* — **come around** *or chiefly Brit* **come round** [*phrasal vb*] **1** : to start to accept and support something (such as an idea) after opposing it ▪ *People are starting to come around (to the idea).* **2** : to become conscious ▪ *He was knocked out. When he came around, he didn't remember what had happened.* **3** : to make a visit to someone ▪ *Why don't you come around (to my house) after work today?* **4** : to occur in the usual way as time passes ▪ *I always feel a little sad when the end of the school year comes around.* **5** *of a boat or ship* : to turn to a different direction — **come at** [*phrasal vb*] **1** : to move toward (someone) in a threatening or aggressive way ▪ *They kept coming at me.* **2** : to begin to deal with or think about (something) ▪ *We need to come at these problems from a different angle.* — **come back** [*phrasal vb*] **1** : to return to a place ▪ *I hope you'll come back soon.* **2** *(figurative)* : to return to someone ▪ *come back to haunt us* [=*that may cause problems for us in the future*] **2 a** : to return to a former good position or condition ▪ *an athlete trying to come back* [=*recover*] *from an injury* **b** : to become popular or fashionable again ▪ *Short skirts are coming back.* **c** : to be successful in a game, sport, etc., after being behind ▪ *The team came back and won in the second half.* **3** : to return to someone's memory ▪ *I had forgotten what she said, but it's all coming back to me now.* — **come between** [*phrasal vb*] : to cause disagreement between (people or groups) ▪ *We shouldn't let these problems come between us.* — **come by** [*phrasal vb*] **1** : to make a visit to someone ▪ *Why don't you come by after dinner?* **2** : to get or acquire (something) ▪ *I asked him how he came by the money.* ▪ *A good job is* **hard to come by.** — **come down** [*phrasal vb*] **1** : to move, fall, or go downward ▪ *The curtain/branch came down.* ▪ *She watched the rain come down.* ▪ *Stock prices have*

come down. **2** : to decide or say in an official or public way that you support or oppose someone or something ▪ *The committee* **came down in favor of** *the proposal.* [=*the committee approved the proposal*] **3 ✧** An announcement or decision that **comes down** is an announcement or decision from someone who has power or authority. ▪ *The decision came down in his favor.* **4 ✧** Something that **comes down from** the past is something that has existed for a very long time. ▪ *The story comes down from ancient times.* — **come down on** [*phrasal vb*] : to criticize, punish, or oppose (someone or something) ▪ *The governor has promised to* **come down hard on** *corrupt officials.* [=*to severely punish corrupt officials*] — **come down to** [*phrasal vb*] : to have (something) as the most important part ▪ *The company's failure comes down to one thing: a lack of leadership.* ▪ *It's nice to be rich, but* **when you come (right) down to it,** *it's more important to be healthy and happy.* — **come down with** [*phrasal vb*] : to begin to have or suffer from (an illness) ▪ *She came down with measles.* — **come forward** [*phrasal vb*] : to say openly or publicly that you should get something or can do something ▪ *No one has yet come forward to claim the reward.* — **come from** [*phrasal vb*] **1** : to have (something or someone) as an origin or source ▪ *Wine comes from grapes.* ▪ *English words come from a wide variety of sources.* ▪ *She comes from a wealthy family.* ▪ *This information comes from a person I trust.* ▪ *(figurative) I understand where you're coming from.* [=*I understand your point of view*] **2 a** : to have been born or raised in (a place) ▪ *She comes (originally) from a small southern town.* : to live in (a place) ▪ *The people who attend the convention come from countries all around the world.* **b** : to be produced in (a place) ▪ *Where did this wine come from?* ▪ *a bad smell coming from the basement* — **come in** [*phrasal vb*] **1** : to enter or arrive at a particular place ▪ *Please come in.* ▪ *Some new products are coming in next week.* **2** : to be received ▪ *The election results should start coming in soon.* ▪ *The broadcast was coming in loud and clear.* **3** : to end a race or competition in a specified position ▪ *He came in* [=*finished*] *first/last.* **4** : to have a particular role or function ▪ *We need someone to help with the cooking, and* **that's where you come in.** [=*your job will be to help with the cooking*] — **come in handy** [=*be very useful*] — **come in for** [*phrasal vb*] : to get or be given (something unpleasant) ▪ *The government's policies are coming in for increasing criticism.* — **come in on** [*phrasal vb*] *informal* : to become involved in (something) ▪ *He'd like to come in (with us) on the deal.* — **come into** [*phrasal vb*] **1** : to enter (a place or position) ▪ *Everyone watched her as she came into the room.* ▪ *A ship* **came into view.** **2** : to get (something) as a possession ▪ *He came into a fortune when he inherited his father's estate.* **3** : to be involved in (something) • *You shouldn't allow personal feelings to come into your decision.* — **come into your own** : to begin to have the kind of success that you are capable of having — **come of** [*phrasal vb*] : to be the result of (something) • *the excitement that comes of meeting new people* • *They had discussions about possible new products, but nothing came of it.* — **come off** [*phrasal vb*] **1** : to stop being attached to something • *The handle came off (the suitcase).* **2** : to produce a desired result • *His plans to start his own business never came off.* **3** : to happen • *The meeting came off as scheduled.* **4** : to do or perform well or badly • *He came off well/badly in the debate.* **5** : to seem to have a specified quality or character • *He came off as a stuffy old man.* **6 a** *US* : to have recently completed or recovered from (something) • *a company coming off a very successful year* **b** : to have recently stopped using (an illegal drug) • *an addict coming off heroin* **7** *US, informal* — used in phrases like **where do you come off?** to express anger or annoyance at what someone has said or done • *Where do you come off talking to me like that?* • *I don't know where he comes off making those kinds of accusations.* — **come off it** *informal* : to stop talking or acting in a foolish way • *"I could be a pro golfer if I really tried." "Oh, come off it!"* — **come on** [*phrasal vb*] **1 a** : to happen or progress as time passes • *Darkness came on rapidly.* **b** : to begin to happen • *I feel a headache coming on.* **2 a** : to begin to work or function • *The lights came on briefly and then went out again.* **b** *of a TV or radio program* : to start • *That program you like is coming on in a few minutes.* **3** *informal* **a** — used in speech to ask or urge someone to do something • *"I don't feel like going out." "Oh, come on! It'll do you good."* **b** — used in speech to tell someone to hurry or to go faster • *Come on, let's go.* **c** — used in speech to express surprise, disbelief, etc. • *"I think she could win the election." "Come on! She doesn't have a chance!"* — **come on strong 1** : to be very forceful in talking to or dealing with someone • *She didn't like him because she felt that he came on too strong.* **2** : to become stronger or more successful in a continuing contest, race, etc. • *The team has been coming on strong lately.* — **come on to** [*phrasal vb*] **1** *informal* : to try to start a sexual relationship with (someone) • *She complained that her boss has been coming on to her.* **2** *Brit* : to start to talk about or deal with (something) • *We'll come on to that question later.* — **come out** [*phrasal vb*] **1** : to become available, obvious, or known • *The book/movie comes out next month.* • *His pride came out in his refusal to accept help.* • *The truth finally came out.* **2 a** : to say something openly or publicly • *Why don't you just come out and say what you really think?* • *She came out in favor of the proposal.* **b** : to say openly that you are a homosexual • *Last year she came out (as a lesbian) to her parents.* **3** : to appear after being hid-

den • *The rain stopped and the sun came out.* **4 a** : to end or finish in a specified way • *How did the game come out?* [=who won the game?] • *Everything came out all right.* • *He's confident that he'll come out a winner.* **b** *of a photograph* : to produce a good picture • *Those pictures I took yesterday didn't come out.* **c** — used to describe the quality that something has when it is finished • *The brownies came out a little too dry.* **5** : to be said, expressed, or understood in a particular way • *He was trying to make a joke, but it came out wrong.* — **come out of** [*phrasal vb*] **1** : to result from (something) • *It's hard to see how anything good can come out of this.* **2** : to go through the experience of (something) • *I was lucky to come out of the accident alive.* — **come out with** [*phrasal vb*] **1** : to say or express (something) • *Why don't you just come out with it and say what you really think?* **2** : to publish or produce (something) • *coming out with a new series of children's books* — **come over** [*phrasal vb*] **1** : to make a visit to someone • *Why don't you come over (to my place) after work?* **2** : to change from one side to the other in a disagreement, competition, etc. • *She agreed to come over to our side.* **3** *Brit, informal* : BECOME • *He suddenly came over all bashful.* **4** : to affect (someone) in a sudden and strong way • *A feeling of dread came over me.* • *I don't know what's come over him lately.* — **come through** [*phrasal vb*] **1** : to succeed in doing something : to do what is needed or expected • *an athlete who is known for coming through in the clutch* **2 a** : to be received and understood • *The message/signal came through loud and clear.* **b** : to be expressed to someone • *Her enthusiasm really came through when she talked about her job.* **3** : to be given or made official in a formal and final way • *waiting for approval of our loan application to come through* **4** : to have the experience of living through (something) • *It was a very difficult illness, but he came through it.* — **come to** [*phrasal vb*] **1** : to become conscious • *He was knocked out. When he came to, he didn't remember what had happened.* **2 a** : to reach or approach (something) • *We came to a fork in the road.* • *That was easy. Now we come to the hard part.* • *The water came slowly to a boil.* • *The two sides came to an agreement/understanding.* • *I've **come to the conclusion** [=I've decided] that we need to try a different method.* • *The project suddenly **came to a stop/halt**.* **b** : to result in (something) • *His plans never came to much.* • *She talked about learning to fly, but it all **came to nothing** in the end.* [=she never did learn to fly] **3** ◇ People say that they **don't know what the world is coming to** or they ask **What is the world coming to?** when they are shocked or disgusted by something that has happened in the world. **4** ◇ The phrase **when it comes to** is used to identify the specific topic that is being talked about. • *When it comes to playing chess, he's the best I know.* **5** : to produce (an amount) when added together ▪ *The bill came to 10 dollars.* **6** : to be thought of by (someone) ▪ *The answer suddenly came to me.* **7** ◇ Something that is *coming to* you is something that is owed to you. ▪ *I have another dollar coming to you.* ◇ If you *get what's coming to you,* you get the punishment that you deserve. ◇ If you *have it coming (to you),* you deserve to get something bad, such as punishment. ▪ *I'm not sorry to hear that he lost his job. He had it coming.* — **come together** [*phrasal vb*] **1** : to join or meet *the place where two rivers come together* ▪ *people coming together to try to find a solution* **2** : to begin to work or proceed in the desired way ▪ *The project is starting to come together.* — **come to pass** *formal + literary* : to happen ▪ *Many of the things he predicted never came to pass.* — **come to think of it** — used in speech to say that you have just remembered or thought of something ▪ *The meeting is next Tuesday, which, come to think of it, is also the date of my doctor's appointment.* — **come under** [*phrasal vb*] **1** : to be subjected to (something) ▪ *The troops suddenly came under attack.* [=were suddenly attacked] ▪ *His policies have been coming under criticism/fire.* **2** : to be affected, controlled, or influenced by (something) ▪ *an area that has come under the control of rebel forces* **3** — used to identify the group or category that something belongs to ▪ *These matters come under the heading of classified information.* — **come up** [*phrasal vb*] **1** : to move near to someone or something ▪ *He came (right) up (to me) and introduced himself.* **2 a** : to be mentioned or thought of ▪ *That issue/question never came up.* **b** : to occur in usually a sudden or unexpected way ▪ *Something has come up and I won't be able to attend the meeting.* **3** of the sun or moon : to become visible in the sky : to rise ▪ *She was already awake when the sun came up.* **4** : to first appear above the ground ▪ *The daffodils and tulips are coming up.* **5** : to finish in a specified condition or state ▪ *I flipped the coin and it came up heads/tails.* ▪ *The shot came up short.* [=the shot did not go far enough] **6** ◇ Something that is *coming up* will happen soon or will appear soon. ▪ *With the election coming up, both candidates are spending all their time on the campaign trail.* ▪ *Our interview with the mayor is coming (right) up after this commercial.* — **come up against** [*phrasal vb*] : to be stopped or slowed by (something) ▪ *The proposal has come up against some opposition.* — **come up empty** : to fail to get or find something or someone ▪ *The police searched the area for clues but came up empty.* — **come upon** [*phrasal vb*] *somewhat formal* **1** : to meet or find (someone or something) by chance ▪ *As they turned the corner, they came upon an unexpected scene.* **2** : to affect (someone) suddenly ▪ *An urge to travel suddenly came upon him.* — **come up to** [*phrasal vb*] : to be as good as (something) ▪ *The movie didn't come up to our expectations.*

[=was not as good as we expected it to be] — **come up with** [*phrasal vb*] : to get or think of (something) ▪ *We finally came up with a solution (to our problem).* — **come what may** : regardless of what happens ▪ *He promised to support her, come what may.* — **easy come, easy go** see ²EASY — **first come, first served** see ²FIRST — **how come** see ¹HOW

come·back /ˈkʌmˌbæk/ *n* [C] **1 a** : a return to being popular, fashionable, successful, etc. ▪ *Short skirts are making/staging a comeback.* **b** : a new effort to win or succeed after being close to defeat or failure ▪ *The team made/staged/mounted a comeback in the second half of the season.* **2** : a quick reply or response ▪ *a clever comeback*

co·me·di·an /kəˈmiːdijən/ *n* [C] **1** : a performer who makes people laugh by telling jokes or funny stories or by acting in a funny way **2** : a person who is funny or makes people laugh

co·me·di·enne /kəˌmiːdiˈɛn/ *n* [C] : a woman who is a comedian

come·down /ˈkʌmˌdaʊn/ *n* [C] : a situation in which a person falls to a lower level of importance, popularity, etc. ▪ *For a man who was once a star, working in a nightclub is quite a comedown.*

com·e·dy /ˈkɑːmədi/ *n, pl* **-dies 1** [C] : a play, movie, television program, novel, etc., that is meant to make people laugh **2** [U] : things that are done and said to make an audience laugh ▪ *The movie includes a lot of physical comedy.* ▪ *a comedy show/club* **3** [U] : the funny or amusing part of something : HUMOR ▪ *We could see the comedy of the situation.* — **co·me·dic** /kəˈmiːdɪk/ *adj* ▪ *comedic talent*

come·ly /ˈkʌmli/ *adj, old-fashioned + literary* : pretty or attractive ▪ *a comely young lady*

come–on /ˈkʌmˌɑːn/ *n* [C] **1** *informal* : something that a person says or does to try to start a sexual relationship with someone **2** : something that is done to get customers for a business ▪ *This special sale is a come-on to bring in new customers.*

com·er /ˈkʌmɚ/ *n* [C] : a person who goes to a place to take part in an activity ▪ *The class is open to all comers.* [=to anyone who comes to the class]

com·et /ˈkɑːmət/ *n* [C] : an object in outer space that develops a long, bright tail when it passes near the sun

come·up·pance /kəmˈʌpəns/ *n* [*singular*] : punishment that someone deserves to receive ▪ *One of these days, he'll get his comeuppance for treating people so badly.*

¹**com·fort** /ˈkʌmfɚt/ *n* **1** [U] : a state or situation in which you are relaxed and do not have any physically unpleasant feelings caused by pain, heat, cold, etc. ▪ *The car's seats are designed for comfort.* ▪ *I found a cozy chair where I could read in comfort.* **2** [U] : a state or feeling of being less worried, upset, frightened, etc., about something ▪ *He turned to her for comfort and support when he lost his job.* ▪

We found little/no comfort in their words. [=their words did not make us feel better] • *I take comfort in the knowledge that I'm not alone.* — see also COLD COMFORT **3** [C] : a person or thing that makes someone feel less worried, upset, frightened, etc. • *Her grandchildren were a great comfort to her.* • *It's a comfort to know that you're here.* **4** [*plural*] : the things that make you more comfortable and your life easier and more pleasant • *a country inn with all the comforts of home* — see also CREATURE COMFORT **5** [U] : a state or situation in which you have all the money and possessions that you need • *They lived a life of comfort and ease.* — *too close for comfort* also *too near for comfort* ◇ Something or someone that is *too close/near for comfort* is close enough to make you feel nervous, worried, or upset. • *That bus came a little too close for comfort!*

²**comfort** *vb* [T] : to cause (someone) to feel less worried, upset, frightened, etc. • *She comforted the crying child.* — **comfort·ing** *adj* • *a comforting thought* • **com·fort·ing·ly** *adv*

com·fort·able /ˈkʌmfɚtəbəl/ *adj* **1** : not causing or having any physically unpleasant feelings • *a comfortable bed/temperature/position* • *comfortable clothes* • *Are you comfortable in that chair?* **2 a** : causing no worries, difficulty, or uncertainty • *a comfortable routine/pace* • *The team has a comfortable lead.* **b** : feeling relaxed and happy • *I'm not very comfortable with the idea of flying.* • *I felt comfortable with her as soon as I met her.* **3** : having or providing enough money for everything you need to live well • *a comfortable job/income* — **com·fort·ably** /ˈkʌmfɚtəbli/ *adv*

com·fort·er /ˈkʌmfɚtɚ/ *n* [C] **1** : someone who helps you to feel less worried, upset, frightened, etc. **2** *US* : a soft, thick bed covering

com·fy /ˈkʌmfi/ *adj* **-fi·er; -est** *informal* : physically comfortable • *a comfy bed*

¹**com·ic** /ˈkɑːmɪk/ *adj* **1** : of or relating to a comedy • *a comic actor/writer* **2** : causing laughter or amusement • *a comic monologue*

²**comic** *n* **1** [C] : COMEDIAN **2** *US* **a** [C] : COMIC STRIP **b** *the comics* : the comic strips in a newspaper • *Did you read the comics today?* **3** [C] *chiefly Brit* : COMIC BOOK

com·i·cal /ˈkɑːmɪkəl/ *adj* : causing laughter • *a comical performance* • *You looked comical* [=*funny*] *in that big hat.* — **com·i·cal·ly** *adv*

comic book *n* [C] : a magazine that is made up of a series of comic strips

comic strip *n* [C] : a series of drawings that tell a story or part of a story

¹**com·ing** /ˈkʌmɪŋ/ *adj, always before a noun* : happening soon or next • *the coming days/year*

²**coming** *n* [C] : the time when something begins • *the coming* [=*arrival*] *of spring* — see also SECOND COMING — *comings and goings* : the activity of people arriving at and leaving a place • *the comings and goings of customers*

coming–of–age *n* [U] : the time when a person becomes an adult • *The film is about a young man's coming-of-age.* • (*figurative*) *The album marked her coming-of-age as a singer.* [=the album showed that she had developed her talents fully as a singer]

com·ma /ˈkɑːmə/ *n* [C] : a punctuation mark , that is used to separate words or groups of words in a sentence

¹**com·mand** /kəˈmænd/ *vb* **1** [T/I] : to give (someone) an order • *She commanded us to leave.* • *She commanded that work begin immediately.* **2** [T] : to have authority and control over (a group) • *He commands a platoon of 60.* **3** [T] **a** : to deserve or be able to get or receive (something) • *a reputation that commands attention/respect* • *He can command a high salary.* **b** : to have and be able to use or control (something) • *They command many resources.* **4** [T] *formal* : to be in a place in which you can clearly see (something) • *a hill that commands an excellent view of the valley*

²**command** *n* **1** [C/U] : an order to do something • *He shouted out commands to the crew.* • *The dog will only attack on command.* [=when it is told/commanded to] **2** [C] : an instruction in the form of a code or signal that tells a computer to do something • *keyboard/voice commands* **3** [U] **a** : the power to give orders and control a group • *He was relieved of his command.* • *He has 100 troops under his command.* • *Who is the officer in command of the unit?* — see also CHAIN OF COMMAND **b** : control of something • *I assumed command of the business after my father's death.* • *She seems to be in (full) command of the situation.* **4** [*singular*] : knowledge and skill that allows you to do or use something well • *She has a good command of French.* [=she speaks French well] **5** [C] : a group of military officers of high rank who give orders • *The order came down from Naval Command.* — *at your command* : available for your use • *They used every resource at their command.*

com·man·dant /ˈkɑːmənˌdɑːnt, Brit ˌkɒmənˈdænt/ *n* [C] : an officer who is in charge of a group of soldiers

com·man·deer /ˌkɑːmənˈdiɚ/ *vb* [T] *formal* : to take (something) by force • *The soldiers commandeered civilian vehicles to help transport the injured.*

com·mand·er /kəˈmændɚ/ *n* [C] **1** : a person who is in charge of a group • *the platoon/battalion commander* **2** : an officer of high rank in the U.S. Navy, the U.S. Coast Guard, or the British Royal Navy

commander in chief *n* [C] : a person who is in charge of all the armed forces of an entire country • *the President's power as commander in chief*

com·mand·ing /kəˈmændɪŋ/ *adj* **1** : having a powerful or important quality • *a commanding figure in American literature* • *a commanding voice/manner/presence* **2** *always before a noun* : very likely to result in victory • *She holds a commanding lead in the polls.* **3** *always be-*

fore a noun : allowing you to see an area very well • *The castle is in a **commanding** position at the top of the hill.* • *a **commanding** view*

commanding officer n [C] : an officer who is in charge of a group

com·mand·ment /kəˈmændmənt/ n [C] : an important rule given by God that tells people how to behave

com·man·do /kəˈmændoʊ/ n, pl **-dos** or **-does** [C] : a soldier who is trained to make surprise attacks

command performance n [C] : a special performance of a concert, play, etc., that is done at the request of an important person (such as a king)

com·mem·o·rate /kəˈmɛməˌreɪt/ vb **-rat·ed; -rat·ing** [T] **1** : to exist or be done in order to remind people of (an important event or person from the past) • *The festival commemorates the town's founding.* **2** : to do something special in order to remember and honor (an important event or person from the past) • *Each year we commemorate our ancestors with a special ceremony.* — **com·mem·o·ra·tion** /kəˌmɛməˈreɪʃən/ n [C/U] • *A service was held in commemoration of the battle.* — **com·mem·o·ra·tive** /kəˈmɛmrətɪv/ adj • *a commemorative postage stamp*

com·mence /kəˈmɛns/ vb **-menced; -menc·ing** [T/I] formal : to begin • *Their contract commences in January.* • *The court commenced criminal proceedings.*

com·mence·ment /kəˈmɛnsmənt/ n, formal **1** [U] : the time when something begins : BEGINNING • *the commencement of the trial* **2** [C/U] US : a ceremony during which degrees or diplomas are given to students who have graduated from a school or college

com·mend /kəˈmɛnd/ vb [T] formal **1** : to praise (someone or something) in a serious and often public way • *He commended her for her bravery.* **2** : RECOMMEND • *Their theory **has much to commend it**.* [=there are many good things about it] • *His ideas are not likely to **commend themselves** to most voters.* [=most voters will not approve of his ideas] — **com·mend·able** /kəˈmɛndəbəl/ adj • *a commendable effort* — **com·mend·ably** /kəˈmɛndəbli/ adv — **com·men·da·tion** /ˌkɑːmənˈdeɪʃən/ n [C/U]

com·men·su·rate /kəˈmɛnsərət/ adj, formal : equal or similar in size, amount, or degree • *The punishment should be commensurate with the offense.*

¹**com·ment** /ˈkɑːˌmɛnt/ n **1** [C/U] : a spoken or written statement that expresses an opinion about someone or something • *The most frequent comment was that the service was slow.* • *We haven't gotten any comments on/about the new design.* • *She couldn't be reached for comment.* ◇ The phrase **no comment** is used to tell someone (such as a reporter) that you do not wish to answer a question. **2** [U] : spoken or written discussion about something • *The trial drew widespread comment.* **3** [C] : something that shows or makes a statement about the true state or condition of something • *She sees*

the film as a comment on modern values.

²**comment** vb [T/I] : to make a statement about someone or something • *Several people commented on her new dress.* • *"The service seems slow today," she commented.*

com·men·tary /ˈkɑːmənˌteri, Brit ˈkɒməntri/ n, pl **-tar·ies** [C/U] : spoken or written discussion in which people express opinions about someone or something • *The magazine includes humor and social commentary.* • *The book is a commentary on her experiences abroad.* **2** [C/U] : a spoken description of an event (such as a sports contest) as it is happening • *He provided commentary during the game.* • *a running commentary* **3** [C] : something that shows or makes a statement about the true state or condition of something • *The students' poor performance on the tests is a sad commentary on the current state of education.*

com·men·tate /ˈkɑːmənˌteɪt/ vb **-tat·ed; -tat·ing** [T/I] : to provide a description on a radio or television program of an event (such as a sports contest) as it is happening • *He will be commentating on tomorrow night's game.*

com·men·ta·tor /ˈkɑːmənˌteɪtɚ/ n [C] **1** : a person who discusses important people and events on television, in newspapers, etc. • *a political commentator* **2** : a person who provides a description on a radio or television program of an event (such as a sports contest) as it is happening • *a sports commentator*

com·merce /ˈkɑːmɚs/ n [U] : activities that relate to the buying and selling of goods and services • *interstate commerce* [=trade] — see also CHAMBER OF COMMERCE

¹**com·mer·cial** /kəˈmɚʃəl/ adj **1** : related to or used in the buying and selling of goods and services • *commercial property/regulations/vehicles* • *a commercial airliner* **2 a** : concerned with earning money • *Their music is too commercial.* **b** always before a noun : relating to or based on the amount of profit that something earns • *The play was a commercial success.* **3** always before a noun : paid for by advertisers • *commercial television/broadcasting* — **com·mer·cial·ly** adv

²**commercial** n [C] : an advertisement on radio or television • *a commercial for a new kind of soap*

com·mer·cial·ism /kəˈmɚʃəˌlɪzəm/ n [U] disapproving : the attitude or actions of people who are influenced too strongly by the desire to earn money or buy goods • *the commercialism of modern society*

com·mer·cial·ize also Brit **com·mer·cial·ise** /kəˈmɚʃəˌlaɪz/ vb **-ized; -iz·ing** [T] disapproving : to use (something) as an opportunity to earn money • *She hates to see Christmas commercialized.* — **com·mer·cial·i·za·tion** also Brit **com·mer·cial·i·sa·tion** /kəˌmɚʃələˈzeɪʃən, Brit kəˌmɔːʃəˌlaɪˈzeɪʃən/ n [U]

com·mie or **Com·mie** /ˈkɑːmi/ n [C] chiefly US, informal + disapproving : COMMUNIST

com·mis·er·ate /kəˈmɪzəˌreɪt/ vb **-at·ed;**

-at·ing [I] formal : to express sadness or sympathy for someone ▪ *The players commiserated (with each other) over/about their loss.* — **com·mis·er·a·tion** /kəˌmɪzəˈreɪʃən/ *n* [U, plural]

com·mis·sary /ˈkɑːməˌseri, *Brit* ˈkɒməsri/ *n, pl* **-sar·ies** [C] *US* : a store that sells food and basic household supplies on a military base or in a prison

¹**com·mis·sion** /kəˈmɪʃən/ *n* **1** [C] : a group of people who have been given the official job of finding information about something or controlling something ▪ *the city's water commission* **2** [C/U] : an amount of money paid to an employee for selling something ▪ *She gets a commission for each car she sells.* = *She sells cars* **on commission. 3** [U] *formal* : the act of committing a crime ▪ *the commission of a felony* **4** [C/U] : a request or order for someone to do something for money ▪ *a commission to paint a portrait* ▪ *an artist working* **on commission 5** [C] : a position of high rank in the military — **in commission** or **into commission** : able to function properly ▪ *Our Internet connection is back in commission.* — **out of commission** : not able to function properly ▪ *The elevator was out of commission.* ▪ (*figurative*) *He was out of commission for three days with the flu.*

²**commission** *vb* [T] **1** : to order or request something to be made or done ▪ *The report on poverty was commissioned by the governor.* ▪ *The king commissioned the artist to paint his portrait.* **2** : to make (someone) an officer in the military ▪ *She was commissioned as a captain.* **3** : to make (a ship) officially active and ready for use ▪ *The ship was commissioned in 2004.*

com·mis·sion·er /kəˈmɪʃənɚ/ *n* [C] **1** : a member of a commission ▪ *a library commissioner* **2** : an official who is in charge of a government department or part of a government department ▪ *the police commissioner* **3** *US* : an official who is in charge of a major professional sport ▪ *the baseball commissioner*

com·mit /kəˈmɪt/ *vb* **-mit·ted; -mit·ting 1** [T] : to do (something that is illegal or harmful) ▪ *commit a crime* ▪ *commit suicide/murder* **2** [T] : to decide to use (a person, money, etc.) for something ▪ *The city committed millions of dollars to/for the housing project.* **3** [T/I] : to say that (someone or something) will definitely do something ▪ *I'm committed to a meeting on Thursday.* [=I have said that I will definitely go to a meeting on Thursday] ▪ *The contract commits the company to finishing by next fall.* ▪ *They have not yet committed to a particular course of action.* ▪ *He doesn't want to* **commit himself. 4** [T/I] : to decide to give your love, support, or effort to someone or something in a serious or permanent way ▪ *My girlfriend just can't seem to commit!* ▪ *They are committing themselves to the cause.* ▪ *We're very committed to the cause.* ▪ *a committed environmentalist* **5** [T] : to cause (someone) to be put in a prison or mental hospital ▪ *She was committed to a state mental hospital.* **6** [T] *Brit, law* : to

order (someone) to be tried in a court of law ▪ *He was committed for trial.* — **commit (something) to memory** : to memorize (something) ▪ *I committed the poem to memory.* — **commit (something) to paper/writing** : to write (something) down ▪ *She committed her thoughts to writing.*

com·mit·ment /kəˈmɪtmənt/ *n* **1** [C] : a promise to do or give something ▪ *the government's commitment of troops to the region* ▪ *a financial commitment* ▪ *Getting a dog is a* **big commitment.** [=something that requires you to do a lot] **2** [C/U] : a promise to be loyal to someone or something ▪ *She isn't ready to make a lifelong commitment to another person.* ▪ *the company's commitment to safety* ▪ *He's afraid of commitment.* **3** [U] : the attitude of someone who works very hard to do or support something ▪ *No one doubts your commitment to the cause/team.*

com·mit·tee /kəˈmɪti/ *n* [C/U] : a group of people who are chosen to do a particular job or to make decisions about something ▪ *the Olympic Committee* ▪ *the advisory/ethics committee*

com·mode /kəˈmoud/ *n* [C] **1** : a low piece of furniture with drawers or sometimes a door and shelves **2 a** : a chair with a hole in the seat and a pot underneath that is used as a toilet **b** *US* : TOILET 1

com·mo·di·ous /kəˈmoudijəs/ *adj, formal* : having a lot of space ▪ *a commodious apartment*

com·mod·i·ty /kəˈmɑːdəti/ *n, pl* **-ties** [C] **1** : something that is bought and sold ▪ *agricultural commodities like grain and corn* **2** : something or someone that is useful or valued ▪ *Patience is a rare commodity.*

com·mo·dore /ˈkɑːməˌdoɚ/ *n* [C] : a high-ranking officer in the navy

¹**com·mon** /ˈkɑːmən/ *adj* **1** : belonging to or shared by two or more people or groups ▪ *a common ancestor/goal/interest* ▪ *the* **common good** [=the public good; the advantage of everyone] **2 a** : done by many people ▪ *a common practice/mistake* **b** : occurring or appearing frequently ▪ *a common disease/cold/bird* ▪ *"Smith" is a common name.* **3** : not having special or high rank or status ▪ *a common soldier/thief* ▪ **common** [=*ordinary, regular*] *people* **4** : expected from polite and decent people ▪ *It is common courtesy to say "thank you."* **5** *Brit, old-fashioned + disapproving* : of or belonging to a low social class ▪ *She thought him common and uneducated.* — **common-or-garden** *chiefly Brit, informal* : not unusual ▪ *a common-or-garden nightclub* — **com·mon·ly** *adv* ▪ *a medicine commonly used to treat the flu* — **com·mon·ness** /ˈkɑːmənnəs/ *n* [U]

²**common** *n* **1** [C] : a public area or park ▪ *the town common* ▪ *Boston Common* **2** [plural] *US* : a place where meals are served at a school, college, etc. ▪ *a/several* **dining commons 3 the Commons** : HOUSE OF COMMONS — **in common** : shared together ▪ *We have a lot in common (with each other).* ▪ *We have* **nothing**

in common. [=we share no interests, opinions, etc.]

com·mon·al·i·ty /ˌkɑːməˈnæləti/ *n, pl* **-ties** **1** [*U*] : the fact of sharing features or qualities • *commonality of origin* **2** [*C*] : a shared feature or quality • *commonalities among the various religions*

common denominator *n* [*C*] **1** *mathematics* : a number that can be divided by each of the denominators of a group of fractions • *36 is a common denominator of ¼ and ⅓.* **2** : something that is shared by all the members of a group • *Drugs seem to be the common denominator in these crimes.* — see also LOWEST COMMON DENOMINATOR

com·mon·er /ˈkɑːmənə/ *n* [*C*] : a person who is not a member of the nobility

Common Era *n* [*C*] : CHRISTIAN ERA

com·mon-law /ˈkɑːmənˌlɑː/ *adj, always before a noun* — used to describe a relationship between a man and a woman that is considered to be a marriage because the man and woman have lived together for a long period of time • *a common-law marriage* • *his common-law wife*

common law *n* [*U*] : the laws that developed from English court decisions and customs and that form the basis of laws in the U.S.

common market *n* [*C*] : a group of countries that allows free trade among its members

common noun *n* [*C*] : a word (such as "singer" or "car") that refers to a person, place, or thing but that is not the name of a particular person, place, or thing — compare PROPER NOUN

¹**com·mon·place** /ˈkɑːmənˌpleɪs/ *adj* : very common or ordinary • *Drug use has become commonplace at rock concerts.* • *commonplace objects like lamps*

²**commonplace** *n* [*C*] *formal* : something that is often said, seen, etc. • *It is a commonplace that we only use a small part of our brain's capacity.* • *We accept cell phones as commonplaces of everyday life.*

common room *n* [*C*] : a room that may be used by all members of a school, residential community, etc.

common sense *n* [*U*] : the ability to think and behave in a reasonable way and to make good decisions • *She's very smart but she doesn't have a lot of common sense.* — **com·mon·sense** *adj, always before a noun* • *commonsense solutions/wisdom*

com·mon·wealth /ˈkɑːmənˌwɛlθ/ *n* [*C*] : a group of countries or states that have political or economic connections with one another • *a commonwealth of states* **2 a** *the Commonwealth* : a U.S. state — used officially of Kentucky, Massachusetts, Pennsylvania, and Virginia • *the Commonwealth of Kentucky* **b** [*C*] : a political unit that is like a U.S. state but that pays no federal taxes and has only a representative in Congress who does not vote — used officially of Puerto Rico and of the Northern Mariana Islands **3** *the Commonwealth* : the

countries that were once part of the British Empire

com·mo·tion /kəˈmoʊʃən/ *n* [*U, singular*] : noisy excitement and confusion • *There was a sudden commotion when the actress entered the restaurant.*

com·mu·nal /kəˈmjuːnl̩, ˈkɑːmjənl̩/ *adj* **1 a** : shared or used by members of a group • *a communal meal/bathroom* • *communal property* **b** : relating to or involving members of a commune • *a communal living arrangement* **2** *formal* : involving people from different racial or cultural groups • *communal violence* — **com·mu·nal·ly** *adv* • *Nuns live communally.*

¹**com·mune** /kəˈmjuːn/ *vb* **-muned; -mun·ing** [*I*] *formal* : to communicate *with* someone or something in a very personal or spiritual way • *commune with God/nature*

²**com·mune** /ˈkɑːmˌjuːn/ *n* [*C*] : a group of people who live together and share responsibilities, possessions, etc. • *a religious/hippie commune*

com·mu·ni·ca·ble /kəˈmjuːnɪkəbəl/ *adj* : able to be passed to another person • *communicable diseases*

com·mu·ni·cant /kəˈmjuːnɪkənt/ *n* [*C*] : a person who is a member of a Christian church

com·mu·ni·cate /kəˈmjuːnəˌkeɪt/ *vb* **-cat·ed; -cat·ing** **1** [*T/I*] : to give information about (something) by speaking, writing, moving your hands, etc. • *He communicated the news to the rest of the people.* • *She communicates with her sister by e-mail.* **2** [*T/I*] : to get someone to understand your thoughts or feelings • *The couple has trouble communicating.* • *He communicated his dissatisfaction to the staff.* **3** [*T*] : to pass (a disease) from one person or animal to another • *The disease is communicated through saliva.* — **com·mu·ni·ca·tor** /kəˈmjuːnəˌkeɪtə/ *n* [*C*]

com·mu·ni·ca·tion /kəˌmjuːnəˈkeɪʃən/ *n* **1** [*U*] : the act or process of using words, sounds, signs, or behaviors to express or exchange information or to express your ideas, thoughts, feelings, etc. • *human/insect/nonverbal communication* • *communication problems/skills* • (*formal*) *We are in communication by e-mail.* • *television and other means of mass communication* **2** [*C*] *formal* : a message that is given to someone • *We received an important communication.* **3** *communications* [*U*] : the ways of sending information to people by using technology • *radio/wireless/electronic communications* • *Communications is a growing industry.*

com·mu·ni·ca·tive /kəˈmjuːnəˌkeɪtɪv, kəˈmjuːnəkətɪv/ *adj, formal* **1** : willing to talk to people • *He wasn't very communicative.* **2** : relating to communication • *communicative disorders*

com·mu·nion /kəˈmjuːnjən/ *n* [*U*] **1** *Communion* : a Christian ceremony in which bread is eaten and wine is drunk as a way of showing devotion to Jesus Christ • *take/receive/celebrate Communion* — called also *the Eucharist* **2** *formal* : a close relationship with someone or something • *He sat alone on the mountain, in communion with the wilderness.*

com·mu·ni·qué /kə'mju:nə,keɪ/ *n* [C] *formal* : an official announcement about a usually very important piece of news

com·mu·nism *or* **Communism** /'ka:-mjə,nɪzəm/ *n* [U] : a way of organizing a society in which the government owns the things that are used to make and transport products (such as land, oil, factories, ships, etc.) and there is no privately owned property

com·mu·nist *or* **Communist** /'ka:mjə-nɪst/ *n* [C] : a person who believes in communism or is a member of a political party that supports communism — **communist** *or* **Communist** *adj* • *communist ideology/leaders/countries*

com·mu·ni·ty /kə'mju:nəti/ *n, pl* **-ties** **1** [C] : a group of people who live in the same area • *members of the local community* • *Many communities are facing budget problems.* • *community leaders* **2** [C] : a group of people who have the same interests, religion, race, etc. • *'artistic/business/medical communities* **3** [C] : a group of nations • *the international community* **4** [U] : a feeling of wanting to be with other people or of caring about the other people in a group • *The school encourages a sense/feeling of community in its students.*

community college *n* [C] *US* : a college that offers courses leading to an associate's degree

community service *n* [U] : work that is done without pay to help people in a community ◇ People do community service because they want to or because a court of law has ordered them to do it as a form of punishment for a crime.

¹com·mute /kə'mju:t/ *vb* **-mut·ed; -mut·ing** **1** [I] : to travel regularly to and from a place and especially between where you live and where you work • *He commutes to work every day by train.* **2** [T] *law* : to change (a punishment) to a less severe one • *The judge commuted his death sentence to life imprisonment.* — **com·mut·er** /kə'mju:tə/ *n* [C] • *busy commuters on their way to work* • *a commuter train*

²commute *n* [C] : the journey that you make when you travel to or from a place that you go to regularly • *a long commute to work/school*

¹com·pact /kəm'pækt/ *adj* **1** : smaller than other things of the same kind • *a compact camera/design* • *a compact car* **2** : closely or firmly packed or joined together • *compact dirt* **3** : short but solid and strong • *a compact body* — **compact·ly** *adv* • *a compactly built hockey player* — **com·pact·ness** /kəm-'pæktnəs/ *n* [U]

²com·pact /kəm'pækt/ *vb* [T/I] : to press (something) so that it is harder and fills less space • *The snow had compacted into a hard icy layer.* • *compacted soil* — **com·pac·tor** *also* **com·pact·er** /kəm-'pæktə/ *n* [C]

³com·pact /'ka:m,pækt/ *n* [C] **1** : a small flat case containing powder or makeup for a woman's face **2** *US* : a small car

3 *formal* : an agreement between two or more people or groups

compact disc *n* [C] : CD

com·pan·ion /kəm'pænjən/ *n* [C] **1 a** : a person or animal you spend time with or enjoy being with • *close companions* • *The dog has been her constant companion for over 12 years.* **b** : someone you are with • *traveling companions* **2 a** : something that is meant to be used with something else • *The workbook is a companion to the textbook.* **b** — used in the titles of books that give information about a particular subject • *The Gardener's Companion*

com·pan·ion·able /kəm'pænjənəbəl/ *adj, formal + literary* : FRIENDLY • *a companionable young man* — **com·pan·ion·ably** /kəm'pænjənəbli/ *adv*

com·pan·ion·ship /kəm'pænjən,ʃɪp/ *n* [U] : the good feeling that comes from being with someone else • *She missed her husband's companionship after he died.*

com·pa·ny /'kʌmpəni/ *n, pl* **-nies** **1** [C] : a business organization that makes, buys, or sells goods or provides services in exchange for money • *record/insurance/computer companies* • *company policy/profits* **2** [U] : the state or condition of being with another person • *I enjoy her company.* • [=I enjoy being with her] • *I felt nervous being in the company of such important people.* • *I'll keep you company* [=I'll stay with you] *while you wait.* • *He has been keeping company with* [=associating with] *criminals.* • *It's not something you should talk about in polite company.* [=in formal settings; with people you do not know well] **3** [U] **a** : someone or something you spend time with or enjoy being with • *He's good company.* • [=he's enjoyable to be around] **b** : the people you spend time with • *You can tell a lot about people by the company they keep.* ◇ If you are *in good company* or have *plenty of company*, you are in the same situation or have the same problem or opinion as many other people. **4** [U] : guests or visitors especially at your home • *We're having/expecting company for dinner.* **5** [C] : a group of people who act or perform together • *the soldiers of Company C* • *a theater/ballet company* **6** [U] : people who are not named but are part of a group • *the law firm of Smith and Company* — **part company** see ²PART — **two's company, three's a crowd** — used to say that a third person is not welcome when two people want to be alone with each other

com·pa·ra·ble /'ka:mpərəbəl/ *adj* : very similar or about the same • *The two houses are comparable in size.* • *Her scores were comparable to/with mine.* — **com·pa·ra·bil·i·ty** /,ka:mpərə'bɪləti/ *n* [U] — **com·pa·ra·bly** /'ka:mpərəbli/ *adv* • *The cars are comparably equipped.*

¹com·par·a·tive /,kəm'perətɪv/ *adj, always before a noun* **1** : seeming to be something when compared with others • *She is a comparative newcomer.* • [=she is not really a newcomer but is more of a newcomer than many others] **2** : involving the act of looking at the ways that things are alike or different ▪ *a comparative study of classical and modern art* **3** : of or relating to the form of an adjective or adverb that is used to indicate more of a particular quality ▪ *The comparative form of "happy" is "happier."* — **com·par·a·tive·ly** *adv* ▪ *a comparatively small amount*

²comparative *n* [C] : the comparative form of an adjective or adverb ▪ *"Taller" is the comparative of "tall."*

¹com·pare /kəm'peə/ *vb* **-pared; -paring** **1** [T] : to say that (something) is similar to something else ▪ *The poet compared his sweetheart to a beautiful rose.* **2** [T] : to look at (two or more things) to see what is similar or different about them or to decide which one is better ▪ *I compared several bicycles before buying one.* **3** [I] : to be as good or as bad as something else ▪ *Skiing is fun but it can't compare with snowboarding.* [=snowboarding is better] ▪ *Spraining an ankle hurts but doesn't compare to breaking a leg.* [=breaking a leg is worse] **4** [I] : to seem better or worse in comparison to something else ▪ *How does your new job compare to the last one?* ▪ *Her scores compare well with mine.* — **compared to** or **compared with** : measured or judged against (someone or something else) ▪ *I'm a slob compared to my roommate.* ▪ *Today's quiz was easy compared with the last one.* — **compare notes** : to talk to someone about something that you and that person have each done, experienced, etc. ▪ *I phoned a coworker after the meeting to compare notes.*

²compare *n* — **beyond compare** also **without compare** : better or greater than any other ▪ *beauty beyond compare*

com·par·i·son /kəm'perəsən/ *n* [C/U] **1** : the act of looking at things to see how they are similar or different ▪ *a comparison of the data from the two studies* ▪ *The Web site allows consumers to make direct comparisons between competing products.* ▪ *The wine stands/bears comparison with* [=is as good as] *more expensive wines.* **2** : the act of suggesting that two or more things are similar ▪ *I don't think comparisons of her situation and/with/to mine are appropriate.* ▪ *There's really no comparison between the two models.* [=they are very different] ▪ *His poetry evokes/invites comparison with* [=is similar to] *the work of Robert Frost.* — **by/in comparison** : when compared with another ▪ *Yesterday's weather was very cold. Today's weather is mild by comparison.*

com·part·ment /kəm'paətmənt/ *n* [C] : an enclosed space or area that is usually part of something larger ▪ *The refrigerator has a separate compartment for meats.* ▪ *the baggage/engine compartment of the airplane*

com·part·men·tal·ize *also Brit* **compart·men·tal·ise** /kəm,paət'mentə,laız/ *vb* **-ized; -iz·ing** [T] *somewhat formal* : to separate things into sections or categories ▪ *He compartmentalizes his life by keeping his job and his personal life separate.* ▪ *The company has compartmentalized its services.* — **com·part-**

men·tal·i·za·tion *also Brit* **com·part-men·tal·i·sa·tion** /kəm,paət,mentələ-'zeıʃən, *Brit* kəm,pɑ:t,mentə,laı'zeıʃən/ *n* [U]

com·pass /'kʌmpəs/ *n* **1** [C] : a device that is used to find direction by means of a needle that always points north **2** [C] : something that helps a person make choices about what is right, effective, etc. ▪ *He had no moral compass to tell him that stealing was wrong.* **3** [C] : a tool that consists of two pointed sticks joined at the top and that is used for measuring distances ▪ *a pair of compasses; also* : a similar tool that is used for drawing circles **4** [U] : a specialized area of knowledge, skill, experience, etc. ▪ *That topic falls beyond/within the compass of their research.*

com·pas·sion /kəm'pæʃən/ *n* [U] : a feeling of wanting to help someone ▪ *He felt compassion for the lost child.* ▪ *She shows compassion to the sick.*

com·pas·sion·ate /kəm'pæʃənət/ *adj* : feeling or showing concern for someone who is sick, hurt, poor, etc. ▪ *a very compassionate person/act* — **com·pas·sion·ate·ly** *adv*

com·pat·i·ble /kəm'pætəbəl/ *adj* **1** : able to exist together without trouble or conflict ▪ *compatible colors/people/personalities* ▪ *a policy that is compatible with my beliefs* **2** : able to be used together ▪ *compatible computers* ▪ *This printer is compatible with most PCs.* — **com·pat-i·bil·i·ty** /kəm,pætə'bıləti/ *n* [U]

com·pa·tri·ot /kəm'peıtrijət, *Brit* kəm-'pætriət/ *n* [C] : a person from the same country, group, etc., as someone else

com·pel /kəm'pel/ *vb* **-pelled; -pel·ling** [T] : to force someone to do something ▪ *Illness compelled him to stay in bed.* ▪ *We took steps to compel their cooperation.* ▪ *I feel compelled to respond.*

com·pel·ling /kəm'pelıŋ/ *adj* **1** : very interesting ▪ *a compelling novel* **2** : capable of causing someone to believe, agree to, or do something ▪ *a compelling argument/desire/reason* — **com·pel·ling·ly** *adv*

com·pen·sate /'kɑ:mpən,seıt/ *vb* **-sat·ed; -sat·ing** *somewhat formal* **1** [I] : to provide something good as a balance against something bad or undesirable ▪ *His enthusiasm compensates for his lack of skill.* **2** [T] : to give money or something else of value to (someone) in return for something or as payment for something lost, damaged, etc. ▪ *compensate workers for their labor* ▪ *She was not compensated for the damage done to her car.* — **com·pen·sa·tion** /,kɑmpən'seıʃən/ *n* [C/U] ▪ *The court awarded the victims millions of dollars in compensation.* ▪ *Moving has some drawbacks, but there are also compensations.* — **com·pen·sa·to·ry** /kəm'pensə,tori, *Brit* kəm'pensətri, kɔmpən'seıtri/ *adj*

com·pete /kəm'pi:t/ *vb* **-pet·ed; -pet·ing** [I] : to try to get or win something that someone else is trying to get or win ▪ *They competed against each other for the same job.* ▪ *We are competing with companies that are twice our size.* ▪ *competing* *teams/products* ▪ *Store-bought cookies* **can't** *compete with homemade ones.* [=homemade cookies are much better than store-bought ones]

com·pe·tence /ˈkɑːmpətəns/ *n* [U] : the ability to do something well ▪ *He trusts in the competence of his doctor.*

com·pe·ten·cy /ˈkɑːmpətənsi/ *n* [U] : COMPETENCE

com·pe·tent /ˈkɑːmpətənt/ *adj* : having the necessary ability or skills ▪ *a competent teacher/worker* — **com·pe·tent·ly** *adv*

com·pe·ti·tion /ˌkɑːmpəˈtɪʃən/ *n* 1 [U] : the act or process of competing ▪ *There was intense/fierce competition for the job.* ▪ *competition among/between different stores* ▪ *These products are in* **competition** *with each other.* 2 **the competition** : a person or group that you are competing with ▪ *Don't let the competition know our secrets.* 3 [C] : a contest in which people compete ▪ *a gymnastics/dance/talent competition*

com·pet·i·tive /kəmˈpɛtətɪv/ *adj* 1 : of or relating to a situation in which people or groups are trying to win or succeed ▪ *competitive sports* ▪ *a competitive job market* ▪ *a competitive advantage/edge* 2 : having a strong desire to win or succeed ▪ *She is a very competitive player.* 3 : as good as or better than others of the same kind ▪ *We offer great service at competitive rates.* ▪ *a competitive team* [=a team with a good chance to win] — **com·pet·i·tive·ly** *adv* — **com·pet·i·tive·ness** *n* [U]

com·pet·i·tor /kəmˈpɛtətə/ *n* [C] : someone who is trying to win or do better than all others especially in business or sports ▪ *We offer better rates than our competitors.*

com·pile /kəmˈpajəl/ *vb* **-piled; -pil·ing** [T] : to create a CD, book, list, etc., by gathering things (such as songs or pieces of writing or information) ▪ *She compiled a list of names.* ▪ *We compiled our findings in the report.* — **com·pi·la·tion** /ˌkɑːmpəˈleɪʃən/ *n* [C/U] ▪ *The CD is a compilation of hits.* ▪ *the compilation of data* — **com·pil·er** /kəmˈpajlə/ *n* [C]

com·pla·cent /kəmˈpleɪsnt/ *adj, disapproving* : satisfied with how things are and not wanting to change them ▪ *The strong economy has made people complacent.* — **com·pla·cen·cy** /kəmˈpleɪsnsi/ *n* [U] — **com·pla·cent·ly** *adv*

com·plain /kəmˈpleɪn/ *vb* 1 [I] : to say or write that you are unhappy, sick, uncomfortable, etc., or that you do not like something ▪ *He works hard but never complains.* ▪ *He complained about the poor service.* ▪ *She complained of a sore throat.* [=she said she had a sore throat] ▪ *"How are you feeling?" "I can't complain."* [=I am fine] 2 [T] : to say (something that expresses annoyance or unhappiness) ▪ *The students complained that the test was too hard.* — **com·plain·er** *n* [C]

com·plain·ant /kəmˈpleɪnənt/ *n* [C] : a person who makes a formal charge in court saying that someone has done something wrong

com·plaint /kəmˈpleɪnt/ *n* 1 **a** [C] : a statement that you are unhappy or not satisfied with something ▪ *We've received many complaints about the new policy.* **b** [U] : the act of saying or writing that you are unhappy or dissatisfied ▪ *She did her chores without complaint.* ▪ *a letter of complaint* 2 [C] : something that people complain about ▪ *I have no complaints with/about the service.* 3 [C] : a pain or sickness in the body ▪ *a stomach complaint* 4 [C] : a formal charge saying that someone has done something wrong ▪ *He filed a complaint against his employer.*

¹**com·ple·ment** /ˈkɑːmpləmənt/ *n* [C] 1 : something that completes something else or makes it better ▪ *The scarf is a perfect complement to her outfit.* 2 : the usual number or quantity of something that is needed or used ▪ *a ship's complement of officers* 3 *grammar* : a word or group of words added to a sentence to make it complete ▪ *"President" in "they elected her president" is a complement.* — **com·ple·men·ta·ry** /ˌkɑːmpləˈmɛntəri/ *adj* ▪ *complementary flavors* [=flavors that go together well]

²**com·ple·ment** /ˈkɑːmpləˌmɛnt/ *vb* [T] : to complete something else or make it better ▪ *The shirt complements the suit nicely.*

¹**com·plete** /kəmˈpliːt/ *adj* **-plet·er; -est** 1 : having all necessary parts : not lacking anything ▪ *a complete set of encyclopedias* ▪ *a complete sentence/list* 2 : not limited in any way ▪ *She has complete control of the business.* ▪ *The movie was a complete failure.* 3 *not before a noun* : not requiring more work : entirely done or completed ▪ *The construction is complete.* [=finished] 4 *American football* : caught by the player the ball was thrown to ▪ *The pass was complete.* — **complete with** : having or including (something good or desirable) ▪ *a birthday cake complete with candles* — **com·plete·ly** *adv* ▪ *I completely agree.* ▪ *We are completely different.* — **com·plete·ness** *n* [U]

²**complete** *vb* **-plet·ed; -plet·ing** [T] 1 : to finish making or doing (something) ▪ *I have completed my research.* = *My research is now completed.* 2 : to make (something) whole or perfect ▪ *The new baby completed their family.* 3 *American football* : to throw (a pass) to a teammate who catches it ▪ *The quarterback completed 12 out of 15 passes.*

com·ple·tion /kəmˈpliːʃən/ *n* 1 [U] : the act or process of completing something : the state of being complete ▪ *He will receive his degree upon completion of his studies.* ▪ *The project is near completion.* [=almost finished] 2 [C] *American football* : a pass made to a teammate who catches it

¹**com·plex** /kəmˈplɛks, Brit ˈkɒmˌplɛks/ *adj* 1 : having parts that connect or go together in complicated ways ▪ *a complex system* 2 : not easy to understand or explain ▪ *a complex problem/situation* — **com·plex·i·ty** /kəmˈplɛksəti/ *n, pl* **-ties** [C/U] ▪ *the complexities of the English language* — **com·plex·ly** *adv*

²com·plex /ˈkɑːmˌplɛks/ *n* [*C*] **1** : a group of buildings that are located near each other and used for a particular purpose ▪ *an industrial/apartment complex* **2** : an emotional problem that causes someone to think or worry too much about something ▪ *She has a complex about her appearance.* — see also INFERIORITY COMPLEX **3** : a group of things that are connected in complicated ways ▪ *a complex of protein molecules*

com·plex·ion /kəmˈplɛkʃən/ *n* [*C*] **1** : the color or appearance of the skin especially on the face ▪ *She has a dark/fair/light complexion.* **2** : the general appearance or character of something ▪ *The complexion of the neighborhood has changed.* ▪ *That information puts a (whole) new/different complexion on the case.* [=changes the way the case is thought about]

com·pli·ance /kəmˈplajəns/ *n* [*U*] *formal* : the act or process of doing what you have been asked or ordered to do ▪ *a high rate of compliance* ▪ *They were not in compliance with the rules.* [=were not following the rules]

com·pli·ant /kəmˈplajənt/ *adj* : willing to do whatever you are asked or ordered to do ▪ *a compliant servant*

com·pli·cate /ˈkɑːmpləˌkeɪt/ *vb* **-cat·ed; -cat·ing** [*T*] : to make (something) more difficult or less simple ▪ *Changing jobs now would complicate life.* ▪ *a disease complicated by infection*

com·pli·cat·ed /ˈkɑːmpləˌkeɪtəd/ *adj* : hard to understand, explain, or deal with ▪ *The rules of the game are too complicated.* ▪ *a very complicated situation/issue/design/plan*

com·pli·ca·tion /ˌkɑːmpləˈkeɪʃən/ *n* [*C*] **1** : something that makes something harder to understand, explain, or deal with ▪ *The negotiations stalled when complications arose.* **2** : a problem that makes a disease or condition more dangerous or harder to treat ▪ *The patient died of complications from surgery.*

com·plic·i·ty /kəmˈplɪsəti/ *n* [*U*] *formal* : the act of helping to commit a crime or do wrong ▪ *There's no proof of her complicity in the murder.*

¹com·pli·ment /ˈkɑːmpləmənt/ *n* **1** [*C*] : a remark or action that expresses admiration or approval ▪ *She gave/paid me a compliment.* [=she said something nice about me] ▪ *She returned/repaid the compliment by saying I looked good too.* **2** [*plural*] — used politely to express praise, welcome, or good wishes ▪ *Our compliments to the chef!* ▪ *Please accept this gift with our compliments.* ✦ The phrase *compliments of* is often used to identify the giver of something that has been provided for free. ▪ *free drinks compliments of the casino*

²com·pli·ment /ˈkɑːmpləˌmɛnt/ *vb* [*T*] : to say nice things about (someone or something) ▪ *She complimented (me on) my outfit.*

com·pli·men·ta·ry /ˌkɑːmpləˈmɛntəri/ *adj* **1** : expressing praise or admiration for someone or something ▪ *a complimentary remark* **2** : given for free ▪ *complimentary tickets*

com·ply /kəmˈplaɪ/ *vb* **-plies; -plied; -ply·ing** [*I*] : to do what you have been asked or ordered to do ▪ *We complied with the request/law.*

¹com·po·nent /kəmˈpoʊnənt/ *n* [*C*] : a piece or part of something ▪ *computer/electrical components* ▪ *Hard work has been a major component of his success.*

²component *adj, always before a noun* : forming or being a part of something ▪ *the component parts of a machine*

com·port /kəmˈpoʊɹt/ *vb* — **comport yourself** *formal* : to behave in a certain way ▪ *He comported himself with dignity.*

com·port·ment /kəmˈpoʊɹtmənt/ *n* [*U*] *formal* : the way in which someone behaves ▪ *the comportment of a gentleman*

com·pose /kəmˈpoʊz/ *vb* **-posed; -pos·ing** **1** [*T*] : to come together to form or make (something) ▪ *Minorities composed about a third of the group.* ▪ *a group composed of 5 women* **2 a** [*T*] : to create and write (a piece of music or writing) ▪ *compose a song/letter* **b** [*I*] : to practice the art of writing music ▪ *He is in his studio composing.* **3** [*T*] : to arrange the appearance of (a picture, image, etc.) in an orderly or careful way ▪ *an elegantly composed photograph* **4** [*T*] : to make (yourself) calm ▪ *Take a moment to compose yourself before you speak.* ▪ *She struggled to* ***compose her feelings***.

com·posed /kəmˈpoʊzd/ *adj* : not feeling or showing anger, fear, nervousness, etc. ▪ *He seemed perfectly composed* [=calm] *when he walked onto the stage.*

com·pos·er /kəmˈpoʊzɚ/ *n* [*C*] : a person who writes music ▪ *Mozart is my favorite composer.*

¹com·pos·ite /kəmˈpɑːzət, *Brit* ˈkɒmpəzɪt/ *adj* : made of different parts or elements ▪ *a composite photograph/material*

²composite *n* [*C*] **1** : something that is made up of different parts ▪ *a composite of minerals/styles* **2** *US* : a drawing of someone who is wanted by the police that is made using descriptions given by witnesses

com·po·si·tion /ˌkɑːmpəˈzɪʃən/ *n* **1** [*U*] : the way in which something is put together, formed, or arranged ▪ *the painting's composition* ▪ *the composition of a chemical compound* **2** [*C*] : a piece of writing ▪ *Is this an original composition?* [=did you write this yourself?]; *especially* : a brief essay written as a school assignment **3** [*C*] : a written piece of music and especially one that is very long or complex ▪ *a classical composition* **4** [*U*] : the art or process of writing words or music ▪ *She studies musical theory and composition.*

com·post /ˈkɑːmˌpoʊst, *Brit* ˈkɒmˌpɒst/ *n* [*U*] : a decayed mixture of plant materials that is used to improve the soil in a garden ▪ *a compost heap/pile* [=a pile of plant materials that are kept in a garden and allowed to decay to create compost] — **compost** *vb* [*T/I*] ▪ *We compost leaves in our backyard.*

com·po·sure /kəmˈpoʊʒɚ/ *n* [*U*] : calmness especially of mind, manner, or appearance ▪ *She never loses her composure.* [=she always appears calm]

¹**com·pound** /ˈkɑːmˌpaʊnd/ *n* [C] **1 a** : something that is formed by combining two or more parts; *especially* : a substance created when the atoms of two or more chemical elements join together ▪ *chemical/organic compounds* ▪ *a compound of sodium and chlorine* **b** : a word (such as *rowboat* or *high school*) formed by combining two or more words **2** : an enclosed area that contains a group of buildings ▪ *a prison compound*

²**com·pound** /kəmˈpaʊnd/ *vb* **1** [T] : to make (an error, problem, etc.) worse ▪ *He compounded his mistake by telling her about it.* **2** [T/I] *finance* : to pay interest on both an amount of money and the interest it has already earned ▪ *The interest (was) compounded quarterly.* **3** [T] : to form (something) by combining separate things ▪ *compound a medicine* ▪ *an attitude compounded of greed and arrogance*

³**com·pound** /ˈkɑːmˌpaʊnd/ *adj* **1** : made up of two or more parts ▪ *a compound leaf/microscope* **2** : made by combining two or more words ▪ *"Steamboat" is a compound noun.*

compound interest *n* [U] *finance* : interest paid both on the original amount of money and on the interest it has already earned

com·pre·hend /ˌkɑːmprɪˈhɛnd/ *vb* [T] *somewhat formal* : to understand (something) ▪ *She is unable to fully comprehend what happened.*

com·pre·hen·si·ble /ˌkɑːmprɪˈhɛnsəbəl/ *adj, somewhat formal* : able to be understood ▪ *a comprehensible explanation* — **com·pre·hen·si·bil·i·ty** /ˌkɑːmprɪˌhɛnsəˈbɪləti/ *n* [U] — **com·pre·hen·si·bly** /ˌkɑːmprɪˈhɛnsəbli/ *adv*

com·pre·hen·sion /ˌkɑːmprɪˈhɛnʃən/ *n* [U, singular] : ability to understand ▪ *reading/language comprehension* ▪ *I don't have a clear comprehension* [=*understanding*] *of how it works.* ▪ *The war caused suffering beyond comprehension.* [=suffering that is impossible to imagine] ▪ *mysteries that are beyond our comprehension*

com·pre·hen·sive /ˌkɑːmprɪˈhɛnsɪv/ *adj* : including many, most, or all things ▪ *a comprehensive list/guide/course* — **com·pre·hen·sive·ly** /ˌkɑːmprɪˈhɛnsɪvli/ *adv* — **com·pre·hen·sive·ness** *n* [U]

comprehensive school *n* [C] *Brit* : a school in Britain for children of all different levels of ability who are over the age of 11

¹**com·press** /kəmˈprɛs/ *vb* [T/I] **1** : to press or squeeze (something) so that it is smaller or fills less space ▪ *compress the air in a closed chamber* ▪ *a material that compresses easily* **2** [T] : to make (something) shorter or smaller ▪ *The author compressed 80 years of history into 15 pages.* **3** [T/I] : to reduce the size of (a computer file) by using special software ▪ *compress a digital photograph* — **com·press·ible** /kəmˈprɛsəbəl/ *adj* —

com·pres·sion /kəmˈprɛʃən/ *n* [U]

²**com·press** /ˈkɑːmˌprɛs/ *n* [C] : a folded cloth that is pressed against a part of the body to reduce pain or stop bleeding from an injury ▪ *a cold compress*

com·pres·sor /kəmˈprɛsɚ/ *n* [C] : a machine that compresses air or gas

com·prise /kəmˈpraɪz/ *vb* **-prised**; **-pris·ing** [T] **1** : to be made up of (something) ▪ *The play comprises three acts.* **2** : to make up or form (something) ▪ *The play is comprised of* [=*composed of*] *three acts.*

¹**com·pro·mise** /ˈkɑːmprəˌmaɪz/ *n* **1** [C/U] : a way of reaching agreement in which each person or group gives up something that was wanted in order to end an argument or dispute ▪ *seeking compromise* ▪ *a compromise agreement* ▪ *Both boys will have to make compromises.* [=they will each have to give up something] ▪ *The two sides were unable to reach a compromise.* [=unable to come to an agreement] **2** [C] : something that combines two different qualities ▪ *The style is a compromise between formal and informal.* **3** [C/U] : a change that makes something worse and that is not done for a good reason ▪ *artistic compromise* ▪ *Accepting their proposal would be a compromise of my principles.*

²**compromise** *vb* **-mised**; **-mis·ing** **1** [I] : to give up something that you want in order to reach an agreement ▪ *The two sides are unwilling to compromise (on this issue).* **2** [T] : to expose (something) to risk or danger ▪ *actions that could compromise national security* **3** [T] : to damage or weaken (something) ▪ *The disease compromised her immune system.* **4** [T] : to damage (your reputation, integrity, etc.) by doing something that causes people to lose respect for you ▪ *He refused to do anything that might compromise his reputation/principles.* ▪ *She compromised herself by refusing to answer their questions.* — **com·pro·mis·er** *n* [C]

compromising *adj* : revealing something that is improper or embarrassing ▪ *a compromising letter/situation/position*

comp·trol·ler /kənˈtroʊlɚ/ *n* [C] : a person who is in charge of the financial accounts of a company or organization

com·pul·sion /kəmˈpʌlʃən/ *n* **1** [C] : a very strong desire to do something ▪ *I felt a compulsion to say something.* **2** [U] : the act of using force or pressure to make someone do something ▪ *They used compulsion to get us to cooperate.* ▪ *He was acting under compulsion.* [=he was being forced to act]

com·pul·sive /kəmˈpʌlsɪv/ *adj* **1 a** : caused by a desire that is too strong to resist ▪ *compulsive behavior* **b** : not able to stop or control doing something ▪ *a compulsive gambler/liar* **2** *chiefly Brit* : very interesting ▪ *The book made compulsive* [=*compelling*] *reading.* — **com·pul·sive·ly** *adv* — **com·pul·sive·ness** *n* [U]

com·pul·so·ry /kəmˈpʌlsəri/ *adj* **1** : required by a law or rule ▪ *compulsory education* **2** : having the power of forcing someone to do something ▪ *a compulsory*

243   compunction • concentration camp

law — **com·pul·so·ri·ly** /kəm-ˈpʌlsərəli/ *adv*

com·punc·tion /kəmˈpʌŋkʃən/ *n* [C/U] : a feeling of guilt or regret ▪ *He feels/has no compunction about his crimes.* ▪ (*chiefly US*) *He has no compunctions about his crimes.*

com·pu·ta·tion /ˌkɑːmpjʊˈteɪʃən/ *n* [C/U] : the act or process of computing or calculating something ▪ *the computation of taxes* ▪ *mental computations*

com·pute /kəmˈpjuːt/ *vb* **-put·ed; -put·ing** [T] : CALCULATE 1 ▪ *compute your income tax* ◇ In informal U.S. English, something that *does not compute* does not make sense.

com·put·er /kəmˈpjuːtə/ *n* [C] : an electronic machine that can store and work with large amounts of information ▪ *a personal/desktop/laptop computer* ▪ *computer software*

com·put·er·ize *also Brit* **com·put·er·ise** /kəmˈpjuːtəˌraɪz/ *vb* **-ized; -iz·ing** [T] 1 : to use a computer to make, do, or control (something) ▪ *We computerized our billing system.* 2 : to provide (something) with computers ▪ *The office is being computerized.* 3 : to put (something) into a form that a computer can use ▪ *We are computerizing our records.* — **com·put·er·i·za·tion** *also Brit* **com·put·er·i·sa·tion** /kəmˌpjuːtərəˈzeɪʃən, Brit kəmˌpjuːtəˌraɪˈzeɪʃən/ *n* [U]

com·rade /ˈkɑːmˌræd, Brit ˈkɒmˌreɪd/ *n* [C] 1 : a close friend you have worked with, been in the military with, etc. ▪ *his old army comrades* ▪ *his old comrades in arms* [=the people he fought alongside or worked together with to achieve something] 2 **Comrade** — used as a title for a member of a communist party — **com·rade·ly** *adj* ▪ *a warm and comradely feeling* — **com·rade·ship** /ˈkɑːmˌrædˌʃɪp, Brit ˈkɒmˌreɪdˌʃɪp/ *n* [U]

¹con /ˈkɑːn/ *n* [C] 1 *informal* : a dishonest trick that is done to get someone's money ▪ *victims of a con* [=*scam*] 2 : an argument against something ▪ *Each plan has its pros and cons.* [=its good parts and its bad parts] 3 *informal* : CONVICT, PRISONER ▪ *an ex-con* [=a former prisoner]

²con *vb* **conned; con·ning** [T] *informal* : to deceive or to trick (someone) ▪ *She conned them out of their savings.* ▪ [=deceived them in order to take their savings]

con artist *n* [C] : a person who tricks other people in order to get their money

con·cave /ˌkɑːnˈkeɪv/ *adj* : having a shape like the inside of a bowl ▪ *a concave lens* — **con·cav·i·ty** /kɑːnˈkævəti/ *n, pl* **-ties** [C/U]

con·ceal /kənˈsiːl/ *vb* [T] 1 : to hide (something or someone) from sight ▪ *The sunglasses conceal her eyes.* ▪ *a concealed* [=*hidden*] *weapon.* 2 : to keep (something) secret ▪ *concealing the truth* ▪ *She tried to conceal her anger.* — **con·ceal·ment** /kənˈsiːlmənt/ *n* [U]

con·cede /kənˈsiːd/ *vb* **-ced·ed; -ced·ing** [T] : to say that you accept or do not deny the truth or existence of (something) ▪ *I concede that the work has been*

slow. 2 [T/I] : to admit that you have been defeated and stop trying to win ▪ *He refuses to concede (the election).* ▪ *They were forced to concede defeat.* 3 [T] : to give away (something) usually in an unwilling way ▪ *The former ruler was forced to concede power to a new government.*

con·ceit /kənˈsiːt/ *n* 1 [U] : too much pride in your own worth or goodness ▪ *She disdains his conceit.* 2 [C] *literary* : an idea that shows imagination ▪ *an artistic conceit*

con·ceit·ed /kənˈsiːtəd/ *adj* : having or showing too much pride in your own worth or goodness ▪ *a conceited musician* — **con·ceit·ed·ly** *adv* — **con·ceit·ed·ness** *n* [U]

con·ceiv·able /kənˈsiːvəbəl/ *adj* : able to be imagined ▪ *We discussed the issue from every conceivable angle.* — **con·ceiv·ably** /kənˈsiːvəbli/ *adv*

con·ceive /kənˈsiːv/ *vb* **-ceived; -ceiv·ing** [T/I] 1 : to think of or create (something) in the mind ▪ *The system was conceived* [=*invented*] *by a Swedish engineer.* ▪ *I can't conceive of a reason to support this policy.* 2 : to become pregnant ▪ *a woman who has been unable to conceive (a child)*

¹con·cen·trate /ˈkɑːnsənˌtreɪt/ *vb* **-trat·ed; -trat·ing** 1 [I] : to give your attention to something ▪ *The noise makes it hard to concentrate (on my work).* 2 [T] : to cause (attention, efforts, strength, etc.) to be used or directed for a single purpose ▪ *She's concentrating her attention on her studies.* 3 [T] : to make (something, such as a liquid) stronger by removing water ▪ *The sauce should be simmered to concentrate its flavors.*

²concentrate *n* [C/U] : a substance that is made stronger or more pure by removing water ▪ (*a*) *frozen orange juice concentrate*

concentrated *adj* 1 : made stronger or more pure by removing water ▪ *concentrated orange juice* 2 : existing or happening together in one place ▪ *a highly concentrated beam of light* ▪ *Power was concentrated in the hands of a few men.* [=a few men had most of the power] 3 *always before a noun* : done in a way that involves a lot of effort and attention ▪ *a concentrated effort*

con·cen·tra·tion /ˌkɑːnsənˈtreɪʃən/ *n* 1 [U] : the ability to give your attention or thought to a single object or activity ▪ *The noise disturbed my concentration.* ▪ *The job required her full concentration.* 2 [U, *singular*] : the act of giving your attention to a single object or activity ▪ *a student who chose law as his field/area of concentration* [=his main area of study] 3 a [C/U] : a large amount of something in one place ▪ *There is a concentration of wealth in the cities.* b [C] : a large number of people in one place ▪ *a heavy/high concentration of tourists* 4 [C] : the amount of an ingredient in a mixture ▪ *They detected high concentrations of pollutants in the water.*

concentration camp *n* [C] : a type of prison where large numbers of people who are not soldiers are kept during a war and are usually forced to live in very bad conditions

con·cen·tric /kən'sɛntrɪk/ *adj* : having the same center • *concentric circles*

con·cept /'kɑːnˌsɛpt/ *n* [C] : an idea of what something is or how it works • *the basic concepts of psychology*

con·cep·tion /kən'sɛpʃən/ *n* 1 [U] : the process of forming an idea • *He directed the project from conception to production.* 2 [U] : the process that occurs within a woman's body when she becomes pregnant • *the moment of conception* 3 [C/U] : an idea of what something is or should be : CONCEPT • *I have a clear conception of the process.* • *He has no conception* [=he does not understand] *the problems we face.*

con·cep·tu·al /kən'sɛptʃəwəl/ *adj* : based on or relating to ideas or concepts • *a conceptual framework/model* • *conceptual art* [=art that expresses an idea] — **con·cep·tu·al·ly** *adv*

¹**con·cern** /kən'sən/ *n* 1 a [C/U] : a feeling of worry • *They raised concerns about the project.* • *There is some concern among voters that the economy might worsen.* • *There is no cause for concern.* [=no reason to worry] b [C] : something that causes people to worry • *Her health is a constant concern.* 2 [C/U] : a feeling of being interested in and caring about a person or thing • *(a) genuine/deep concern for the poor* 3 [C] : something that is regarded as important • *Our main concern is to finish on time.* 4 [C] : something that a person is responsible for or involved in • *That bill is your concern* [=responsibility], *not mine.* 5 [C] *formal* : a business or company • *a going concern* [=a successful business]

²**concern** *vb* [T] 1 : to be about (something or someone) • *The novel concerns three soldiers.* 2 : to affect or involve (someone) • *This conversation doesn't concern you.* ◇ The phrase **To whom it may concern** is used at the beginning of a formal letter when the name of the person who will read it is not known. 3 : to make (someone) worried • *Our mother's illness concerns us.* — **concern yourself** : to become involved or interested in something • *There's no need for you to concern yourself with/in her problem.*

con·cerned /kən'sənd/ *adj* 1 : feeling worry or concern • *Her family was very concerned for/about her safety.* 2 a : having an interest or involvement in something • *a discussion that will be of interest to everyone concerned* • *She was more concerned with* [=interested in] *winning than with playing fair.* b : having a relation to something • *The memo is concerned with hiring policies.* [=is about hiring policies] — **as far as (someone) is concerned** : in the opinion of (someone) • *As far as I'm concerned, everything he says is a lie.* — **as far as (something) is concerned** : with regard to (something) • *He has no worries as far as money is concerned.* [=he has no worries about money]

con·cern·ing /kən'sənɪŋ/ *prep* : relating to (something or someone) : ABOUT •

There is some confusion concerning his current location.

con·cert /'kɑːnsət/ *n* [C] : a public performance of music • *a rock/classical concert* • *a concert hall/pianist* — **in concert** 1 *formal* : TOGETHER • *The FBI and the local police acted in concert (with each other) to solve the case.* 2 : performing at a concert • *I heard that band in concert.*

con·cert·ed /kən'sətəd/ *adj, always before a noun* : done in a planned and deliberate way usually by several or many people • *a concerted effort/action/campaign*

con·cer·to /kən'tʃeɹˌtou/ *n, pl* **-cer·ti** /-ˌtiː/ *or* **-cer·tos** [C] : a piece of music for one or more main instruments with an orchestra • *a violin concerto*

con·ces·sion /kən'sɛʃən/ *n* 1 [C] a : the act of giving up something or doing something in order to reach agreement • *The company had to make concessions (to the strikers) during negotiations.* • *The strikers won/gained some major concessions from the company.* b : the act of admitting that you have been defeated in a contest • *The candidate made an emotional concession speech.* 2 [C] : something that is done because a particular situation makes it necessary or desirable • *He takes afternoon naps now in/as a concession to his old age.* 3 *US* a [C] : the right to sell something or do business on a property • *a mining concession* b [C] : a small business or shop where things are sold in a public place (such as a sports stadium) • *He runs a concession that sells hot dogs at the ballpark.* • *We got hot dogs at the concession stand.* c [plural] : things sold at a concession stand • *a license to sell concessions* 4 [C] *Brit* : a special lower price or rate • *tax concessions*

conch /'kɑːŋk, 'kɑːntʃ/ *n, pl* **conchs** /'kɑːŋks/ *or* **conch·es** /'kɑːntʃəz/ [C] : a type of shellfish that lives in a large shell which has the form of a spiral; *also* : the shell of a conch

con·cierge /ˌkɑːnsiˈeɹ3/ *n* [C] 1 : a person in an apartment building who takes care of the building and checks the people who enter and leave 2 *chiefly US* : a person whose job is to provide help and information to the people staying at a hotel

con·cil·i·ate /kən'sɪliˌeɪt/ *vb* **-at·ed; -at·ing** [T] *formal* : to make (someone) more friendly or less angry • *The company's attempts to conciliate the strikers have failed.* — **con·cil·i·a·tion** /kənˌsɪliˈeɪʃən/ *n* [U] — **con·cil·i·a·tor** /kən'sɪliˌeɪtə/ *n* [C]

con·cil·i·a·to·ry /kən'sɪliˌjəˌtori, *Brit* kən'sɪliətri/ *adj* : intended to make someone less angry • *a conciliatory note/message/ statement*

con·cise /kən'saɪs/ *adj* : using few words • *a concise account/summary/definition* — **con·cise·ly** *adv* — **con·cise·ness** *n* [U]

con·clave /'kɑːnˌkleɪv/ *n* [C] *formal* : a private or secret meeting or group • *conclave of bishops*

con·clude /kən'kluːd/ vb **-clud·ed; -clud·ing 1 a** [I] : to stop or finish ▪ *The meeting concluded at noon.* **b** [T] : to cause (something) to stop or finish ▪ *conclude a speech/meeting* **2** [T] : to decide (something) after a period of thought or research ▪ *Many studies have concluded that smoking is dangerous.* **3** [T] : to complete (something, such as a business deal) ▪ *conclude a sale*

concluding adj, always before a noun : ¹FINAL 1 ▪ *a concluding remark*

con·clu·sion /kən'kluːʒən/ n **1** [C] : an opinion or decision that is formed after a period of thought or research ▪ *The evidence does not support the report's conclusions.* ▪ *We came to the conclusion* [=we decided] *that we shouldn't go.* ▪ *They haven't yet reached a conclusion.* ▪ *Is it possible to draw conclusions from this evidence?* ▪ *We should hear his explanation before we jump/leap to the conclusion* [=decide too quickly] *that he's to blame.* ▪ *Let's not jump to conclusions.* [=make a quick and possibly incorrect judgment] **2** [C] : the last part of something : END — usually singular ▪ *the conclusion of the meeting* ▪ *The strike has finally reached its conclusion.* [=ended] ▪ *His victory is a foregone conclusion.* [=he will certainly win] **3** [U, singular] : the act of concluding or finishing something or the state of being finished ▪ *We hoped for a quick conclusion of/to the war.* ▪ *the conclusion of a business deal* ▪ *The case was finally brought to (a) conclusion last week.* — **in conclusion** — used to introduce final comments ▪ *In conclusion, I would like to thank you for inviting me to speak tonight.*

con·clu·sive /kən'kluːsɪv/ adj : showing that something is certainly true ▪ *conclusive evidence/proof* — **con·clu·sive·ly** adv — **con·clu·sive·ness** n [U]

con·coct /kən'kɑːkt/ vb [T] **1** : to make (a food or drink) by mixing different things together ▪ *concoct a stew* **2** : to invent or develop (a plan, story, etc.) especially in order to trick or deceive someone ▪ *They concocted a scheme to steal money from the company.*

con·coc·tion /kən'kɑːkʃən/ n [C] : something (such as a food or drink) that is made by mixing together different things

con·com·i·tant /kən'kɑːmətənt/ adj, formal : happening at the same time as something else ▪ *changes that are concomitant with population growth*

con·cord /'kɑːnˌkoɚd/ n [U] formal : a state in which people or things agree with each other and exist together in a peaceful way ▪ *They lived in peace and concord.*

con·cord·ance /kən'koɚdəns/ n **1** [U] formal : a state in which things agree and do not conflict with each other ▪ *The witness's testimony was not in concordance with* [=did not agree with] *the rest of the evidence.* **2** [C] : an alphabetical list of all of the words in a book or in a set of works written by an author ▪ *a concordance of Shakespeare's plays*

con·course /'kɑːnˌkoɚs/ n [C] : a large open space or hall in a public building ▪ *an airport concourse*

¹**con·crete** /'kɑːnˌkriːt/ n [U] : a hard, strong material that is used for building and made by mixing cement, sand, and broken rocks with water

²**con·crete** /kən'kriːt/ adj **1** : made of concrete ▪ *concrete blocks/floors/walls* **2** : relating to or involving specific people, things, or actions rather than general ideas or qualities ▪ *concrete examples/suggestions/results* ▪ *The police had no concrete evidence against him.* — **con·crete·ly** adv — **con·crete·ness** n [U]

³**con·crete** /'kɑːnˌkriːt/ vb **-cret·ed; -cret·ing** [T] Brit : to cover or form (something) with concrete ▪ *They concreted (over) their drive.*

con·cur /kən'kɚ/ vb **-curred; -cur·ring** [I] formal : to agree with someone or something ▪ *She concurred with the judge's ruling.* = *She concurred with the judge.*

con·cur·rence /kən'kɚəns/ n, formal **1** [U] : the state of agreeing with someone or something ▪ *The bill passed with the full concurrence of the Senate.* **2** [C] : a situation in which two or more things happen at the same time ▪ *a concurrence of events*

con·cur·rent /kən'kɚənt/ adj, formal : happening at the same time ▪ *concurrent events* — **con·cur·rent·ly** adv

con·cus·sion /kən'kʌʃən/ n [C/U] : an injury to the brain that is caused by something hitting the head very hard ▪ (US) *She suffered a severe concussion.* ▪ (Brit) *He went to hospital with concussion.*

con·demn /kən'dɛm/ vb [T] **1** : to say in a strong and definite way that someone or something is bad or wrong ▪ *The government condemns all acts of terrorism.* ▪ *They were condemned as criminals.* **2 a** : to give (someone) a severe punishment ▪ *The jury condemned* [=sentenced] *her to death.* **b** : to cause (someone) to suffer or live in difficult or unpleasant conditions — + *to* ▪ *His lack of education condemned him to a life of poverty.* **3** : to close (a building, house, etc.) for not being safe or clean enough for people to use ▪ *City officials condemned the building.*

con·dem·na·tion /ˌkɑːndəm'neɪʃən/ n [C/U] : a statement or expression of very strong and definite criticism or disapproval ▪ *a condemnation of all acts of terrorism*

con·den·sa·tion /ˌkɑːndən'seɪʃən/ n **1** [U] : small drops of water that form on a cold surface ▪ *Condensation formed on the windows.* **2** [U] technical : the process by which a gas cools and becomes a liquid **3** [C/U] : the act, process, or result of making something (such as a piece of writing) shorter ▪ (a) *condensation of a play/novel*

con·dense /kən'dɛns/ vb **-densed; -dens·ing 1** [T] : to make (something) shorter or smaller by removing parts that are less important ▪ *I've condensed the story down to a few pages.* ▪ *The book condenses 50 years of history into 200 pages.* **2** [I] : to change from a gas into a liquid ▪

The cooler temperatures cause the gas to condense into a liquid. **3** [*T*] : to remove water from (something) to make it thicker ▪ *a can of condensed soup* [=soup that has had much of the water removed and that is served by heating it with milk or water]

condensed milk *n* [*U*] : canned milk with sugar added and much of the water removed

con·dens·er /kən'dɛnsɚ/ *n* [*C*] *technical* **1** : a device used for changing a gas into a liquid **2** : a device used for storing electrical energy

con·de·scend /ˌkɑːndɪ'sɛnd/ *vb* [*I*] *formal* + *disapproving* **1** : to show that you believe you are more intelligent or better than other people ▪ *The author never condescends (to her readers).* **2** : to do something that you usually do not do because you believe you are too important to do it ▪ *She condescends to speak to me only when she needs something.* — **con·de·scen·sion** /ˌkɑːndɪ'sɛnʃən/ *n* [*U*] ▪ *She writes without condescension.*

con·de·scend·ing /ˌkɑːndɪ'sɛndɪŋ/ *adj, disapproving* : showing that you believe you are more intelligent or better than other people ▪ *a condescending tone/attitude/comment* — **con·de·scend·ing·ly** *adv*

con·di·ment /'kɑːndəmənt/ *n* [*C*] : something (such as salt, mustard, or ketchup) that is added to food to give it more flavor

¹**con·di·tion** /kən'dɪʃən/ *n* **1** [*U*] : a way of living or existing ▪ *Happiness is the state or condition of being happy.* **2** [*C/U*] : the physical state of something ▪ *They restored the painting to its original condition.* ▪ *The car is in excellent condition.* **3** [*U, singular*] : the physical or mental state of a person or animal ▪ *The accident victim was reported to be in (a) good/stable/critical condition.* ▪ *The players are all in good/excellent (physical) condition.* [=shape] ▪ *She runs every day to stay in condition.* [=healthy and strong] ▪ *He's overweight and out of condition.* [=unhealthy and weak] ▪ *He is in no condition to drive.* [=he is too drunk, ill, upset, etc., to drive] **4** [*C*] : a sickness or disease that a person has for a long time ▪ *a serious heart condition* **5** [*plural*] **a** : the situation in which someone or something lives, works, etc. ▪ *The organization is working to improve (living) conditions for the poor.* ▪ *dangerous driving conditions* **b** : the things that affect the way something is or happens ▪ *favorable economic conditions* **c** : the type of weather that occurs at a particular time ▪ *weather/atmospheric conditions* **6** [*C*] : something that you must do or accept in order for something to happen ▪ *Joining the union was a condition of employment.* [=I had to join the union in order to get the job] ▪ *You can go on one condition: you have to finish your homework.* [=you can go only if you finish your homework] **7** [*C*] : something that must happen or exist in order for something else to happen ▪ *Hard work is a necessary condition for/of success.* — **under no**

condition — used to say that something is definitely not allowed ▪ *Under no condition are you to answer the phone.*

²**condition** *vb* [*T*] **1** : to train or influence (a person or an animal) to do something or to think or behave in a certain way because of a repeated experience ▪ *We have been conditioned to expect immediate results.* ▪ *conditioned behavior/responses* **2** : to make (hair, leather, etc.) softer and less dry by applying a liquid ▪ *She conditions her hair daily.*

con·di·tion·al /kən'dɪʃənl/ *adj* — used to describe something that will happen only if something else also happens ▪ *a conditional agreement/sale* ▪ *Our agreement is conditional on/upon your raising the needed money.* — **con·di·tion·al·ly** *adv*

con·di·tion·er /kən'dɪʃənɚ/ *n* [*C/U*] : a thick liquid that you put on your hair after washing it to make it softer and less dry

con·di·tion·ing /kən'dɪʃənɪŋ/ *n* [*U*] **1** *chiefly US* : the process of becoming stronger and healthier by following a regular exercise program and diet ▪ *aerobic conditioning* [=training] ▪ *a conditioning workout* **2** : the act or process of training a person or animal to do something or to behave in a certain way in a particular situation ▪ *With the proper conditioning, the horse will learn to trust and obey its handler.*

con·do /'kɑːndoʊ/ *n, pl* **-dos** [*C*] *US* : CONDOMINIUM

con·do·lence /kən'doʊləns/ *n* [*C/U*] : a feeling or expression of sympathy and sadness especially when someone is suffering because of the death of a family member, a friend, etc. ▪ *Please accept my condolences.* ▪ *a letter/statement of condolence*

con·dom /'kɑːndəm/ *n* [*C*] : a thin rubber covering that a man wears on his penis during sex in order to prevent a woman from becoming pregnant or to prevent the spread of diseases

con·do·min·i·um /ˌkɑːndə'mɪnijəm/ *n* [*C*] *chiefly US* **1** : a room or set of rooms that is owned by the people who live there and that is part of a larger building containing other similar sets of rooms **2** : a building that contains condominiums

con·done /kən'doʊn/ *vb* **-doned; -don·ing** : to forgive, approve, or allow (something that is considered wrong) ▪ *a government accused of condoning racism* ▪ *We cannot condone that kind of behavior.*

con·dor /'kɑːnˌdoɚ/ *n* [*C*] : a very large black bird from South America or a related bird from North America

con·du·cive /kən'duːsɪv, *Brit* kən'djuːsɪv/ *adj, not before a noun, formal* : making it easy, possible, or likely for something to happen or exist ▪ *an atmosphere (that is) conducive to learning* [=an atmosphere that makes learning easier]

¹**con·duct** /kən'dʌkt/ *vb* **1** [*T*] : to plan and do (something, such as an activity) ▪ *conduct an investigation* ▪ *conduct a survey/meeting* ▪ *conduct research/business*

2 [T/I] : to direct the performance of (musicians or singers) ▪ *conduct a choir* **3** [T] *formal* : to guide or lead (someone) through or around a place ▪ *Our guide conducted us through the museum.* **4** [T] *technical* : to allow (heat or electricity) to move from one place to another ▪ *Metals conduct electricity well.* — **conduct yourself** : to behave especially in a public or formal situation ▪ *I don't like the way he conducts himself.*

²**con·duct** /ˈkɑːnˌdʌkt/ *n* [U] *somewhat formal* **1** : the way that a person behaves in a particular place or situation ▪ *A panel investigated her conduct and she was subsequently fired.* **2** : the way that something is managed or directed ▪ *laws that control the conduct of business and trade*

con·duc·tiv·i·ty /ˌkɑːnˌdʌkˈtɪvəti/ *n* [U] *technical* : the ability to move heat or electricity from one place to another ▪ *measuring the conductivity of different metals* — **con·duc·tive** /kənˈdʌktɪv/ *adj*

con·duc·tor /kənˈdʌktɚ/ *n* [C] **1** : a person who stands in front of people while they sing or play musical instruments and directs their performance **2** : a person who collects money or tickets from passengers on a train or bus **3** : a material or object that allows electricity or heat to move through it ▪ *Metal is a good conductor of electricity.*

con·duit /ˈkɑːnˌduːwət, Brit ˈkʌndɪt/ *n* [C] **1** *technical* : a pipe or tube through which something (such as water or wire) passes **2** *formal* : someone or something that is used as a way of sending information, money, etc., from one place or person to another ▪ *a conduit of information* ▪ *a conduit for trade*

cone /ˈkoʊn/ *n* [C] **1** : a shape that has a pointed top and sides that form a circle at the bottom **2** : a hard and dry part that is the fruit of a pine tree or other evergreen plant **3 a** : something that looks like a cone ▪ *a paper cone* **b** : the top of a volcano **4** : a thin crisp cookie that is usually shaped like a cone and that is used to hold ice cream ▪ *an ice-cream cone*

con·fec·tion /kənˈfɛkʃən/ *n* [C] : a very sweet food ▪ *cakes and other confections* ▪ *a confection of cream, chocolate, and nuts*

con·fec·tion·er /kənˈfɛkʃənɚ/ *n* [C] : a person or business that makes or sells confections

confectioners' sugar *n* [U] *US* : POWDERED SUGAR

con·fed·er·a·cy /kənˈfɛdərəsi/ *n, pl* **-cies** **1** [C] : a group of countries, organizations, etc., that are joined together in some activity or effort ▪ *a confederacy of tribes* **2 the Confederacy** : the group of 11 southern states that separated themselves from the U.S. during the American Civil War

con·fed·er·ate /kənˈfɛdərət/ *n* [C] **1** *formal* : a person who helps someone do something ▪ *He turned to his confederates for help.* **2 Confederate** : a soldier, citizen, or supporter of the Confederacy during the American Civil War — **Con-**

federate *adj* ▪ *Confederate states/soldiers* ▪ *the Confederate flag/army*

con·fed·er·a·tion /kənˌfɛdəˈreɪʃən/ *n* [C] : a group of countries, organizations, etc., that are joined together in some activity or effort ▪ *a loose confederation of businesses*

con·fer /kənˈfɚ/ *vb* **-ferred; -fer·ring** *formal* **1** [I] : to discuss something important in order to make a decision ▪ *The lawyer and judge conferred (with each other).* **2** [T] : to give (something, such as a degree, award, title, right, etc.) to someone or something ▪ *The university conferred an honorary degree on the governor.* — **con·fer·ment** /kənˈfɚmənt/ *n* [U] ▪ *the conferment of degrees/privileges*

con·fer·ence /ˈkɑːnfərəns/ *n* **1** [C] : a formal meeting in which many people gather in order to talk about ideas or problems related to a particular topic usually for several days ▪ *national conferences on women's health* ▪ *an international peace conference* ▪ *a conference center* [=a large building where conferences are held] **2** [C/U] : a formal meeting in which a small number of people talk about something ▪ *Our boss called a conference.* ▪ *a conference room/table* ▪ *He spent an hour in conference with the president.* — see also NEWS CONFERENCE, PRESS CONFERENCE **3** [C] *US* : a group of sports teams that play against each other and that are part of a larger league of teams ▪ *a football conference*

conference call *n* [C] : a telephone call in which someone talks to several people at the same time

con·fess /kənˈfɛs/ *vb* [T/I] **1** : to admit that you did something wrong or illegal ▪ *He confessed (to the crime) after being questioned for many hours.* ▪ *He confessed his crime/guilt.* ▪ *She confessed that she did it.* **2** : to talk about or admit something that makes you embarrassed, ashamed, etc. ▪ *He confessed (that) he had forgotten to call.* ▪ *He confessed his love for her.* [=he admitted that he loved her] ▪ *I confess to being unsure about what to do.* **3** : to tell (your sins) to God or to a priest ▪ *I confessed my sins to the priest.* — **confessed** /kənˈfɛst/ *adj* ▪ *a confessed murderer*

con·fes·sion /kənˈfɛʃən/ *n* **1** [C] : a written or spoken statement in which you say that you have done something wrong or committed a crime ▪ *She made/gave a full confession.* **2** [C] : the act of telling people something that makes you embarrassed, ashamed, etc. ▪ *I have a confession to make: I've never done this before.* **3** [C/U] : the act of telling your sins to God or to a priest ▪ *The priest will hear confessions after mass.* ▪ *I haven't gone/been to confession in three years.*

¹**con·fes·sion·al** /kənˈfɛʃənl/ *n* [C] : a private place inside a church where a priest hears confessions

²**confessional** *adj* : telling private information about a person's life ▪ *confessional poetry/writing*

con·fes·sor /kənˈfɛsɚ/ *n* [C] : a priest who listens to a person's confession

con·fet·ti /kənˈfɛti/ *n* [U] : small pieces

of brightly colored paper that people sometimes throw at parties, weddings, etc.

con·fi·dant /ˈkɑːnfəˌdɑːnt/ *n* [C] : a trusted friend you can talk to about personal and private things • *a trusted confidant of the president*

con·fi·dante /ˈkɑːnfəˌdɑːnt/ *n* [C] : a woman who is a trusted friend • *my closest friend and confidante*

con·fide /kənˈfaɪd/ *vb* **-fid·ed; -fid·ing** [T] : to tell (something that is secret or private) to someone you trust • *She confided (to me) that she couldn't read.* — **confide in** [*phrasal vb*] : to tell personal and private things to (someone) • *She often confides in me.*

con·fi·dence /ˈkɑːnfədəns/ *n* **1** [U] : a feeling or belief that you can do something well or succeed at something • *The experience gave her the confidence to start her own business.* • *He has a lot of confidence (in himself).* **2** [U] : a feeling or belief that someone or something is good or has the ability to succeed at something • *She has earned/gained/won/lost my confidence.* • *I have complete/full confidence in you.* **3** [U] : the feeling of being certain that something will happen or that something is true • *I have confidence that the problem will be resolved.* • *We have every confidence* [=we are sure] *that you'll succeed.* **4** [U] : a relationship in which you tell personal and private information to someone • *Doctors cannot betray the confidence of their patients.* [=cannot reveal their patients' personal information to other people] • *He told me about it in confidence.* • *She took me into her confidence.* [=shared private information with me] **5** [C] : a secret that you tell someone you trust • *She accused him of betraying a confidence.* [=of telling her secret to other people]

confidence game *n* [C] *US* : ¹CON 1
confidence man *n* [C] *US* : CON ARTIST
confidence trick *n* [C] *Brit* : ¹CON 1

con·fi·dent /ˈkɑːnfədənt/ *adj* **1 a** : having a feeling or belief that you can do something well or succeed at something • *a confident young businesswoman* • *I am confident about/in my ability.* **b** : showing that you have confidence • *a confident smile* **2** *not before a noun* : certain that something will happen or that something is true • *We are confident that we will succeed.* — **con·fi·dent·ly** *adv*

con·fi·den·tial /ˌkɑːnfəˈdɛnʃəl/ *adj* **1** : secret or private • *confidential documents/records/information* **2** : showing that you are saying something that is secret or private • *He spoke in a confidential tone/voice.* **3** *always before a noun* : trusted with secret or private information • *a confidential secretary/clerk* — **con·fi·den·ti·al·i·ty** /ˌkɑːnfəˌdɛnʃiˈæləti/ *n* [U] • *All medical records are treated with complete confidentiality.* [=are kept completely private] — **con·fi·den·tial·ly** *adv* • *Confidentially, I don't think she's very good at her job.*

con·fig·u·ra·tion /kənˌfɪɡjəˈreɪʃən, *Brit* kənˌfɪɡəˈreɪʃən/ *n* [C] : the way the parts of something are arranged • *airplane seating configurations* • *the configuration of the room*

con·fig·ure /kənˈfɪɡjɚ, *Brit* kənˈfɪɡə/ *vb* **-ured; -ur·ing** [T] *technical* : to arrange or prepare (something) so that it can be used • *configure a computer* • *The plane is configured for military use.*

con·fine /kənˈfaɪn/ *vb* **-fined; -fin·ing** [T] **1** : to keep (someone or something) within a particular limit, area, etc. — usually + *to* • *Students need not confine themselves to a single area of study.* • *The city's poverty is not confined to just one neighborhood.* **2** : to keep (a person or animal) in a place (such as a prison) • *She was confined to a psychiatric hospital.* • *a camp where prisoners were confined during the war* **3** : to force or cause (someone) to stay in something (such as a bed or wheelchair) • *a sick friend who is confined at home* [=who cannot leave home because of being sick] • *confined to a wheelchair* — **con·fine·ment** /kənˈfaɪnmənt/ *n* [U] • *the confinement of violent criminals* • *The dog was kept in confinement.* — see also SOLITARY CONFINEMENT — **confining** *adj* • *She thinks the job is too confining.* [=restrictive]

confined *adj*, of a space or area : very small • *confined spaces*

con·fines /ˈkɑːnˌfaɪnz/ *n* [*plural*] *formal* : the limits or edges of something • *Stay within the confines of the city.*

con·firm /kənˈfɚm/ *vb* **1** [T] : to state or show that (something) is true or correct • *The tests confirmed our suspicions/fears.* • *I cannot confirm the story.* **2** [T/I] : to tell someone that something has definitely happened or is going to happen • *confirm an appointment* • *confirm a reservation* **3** [T] *formal* : to make (a feeling, desire, etc.) stronger or more certain • *His attitude only confirmed her resolve to leave.* • *She was confirmed in her determination to leave.* **4** [T/I] : to give official approval to (something or someone) • *confirm a treaty* • *confirm a political appointee* **5** [T] : to make (someone) a full member of a church or synagogue • *Our son will be confirmed in the spring.*

con·fir·ma·tion /ˌkɑːnfɚˈmeɪʃən/ *n* **1** [U] : proof which shows that something is true or correct • *confirmation of a theory* • *confirmation of a person's identity* **2** [C/U] : a response which shows that information is received and understood • *You will receive an e-mail confirmation of your order.* **3** [U] : the act of giving official approval to something or someone • *his confirmation as a federal judge* • *Senate confirmation hearings* **4** [C/U] : a ceremony in which someone becomes a full, adult member of a religion

con·firmed /kənˈfɚmd/ *adj, always before a noun* : not likely to change • *a confirmed optimist* • *a confirmed bachelor* [=a man who seems happy to remain unmarried]

con·fis·cate /ˈkɑːnfəˌskeɪt/ *vb* **-cat·ed; -cat·ing** [T] : to take (something) away from someone especially as punishment or to enforce the law or rules • *Police confiscated the weapons.* — **con·fis·ca-**

tion /ˌkɑːnfəˈskeɪʃən/ n [U]

con·fla·gra·tion /ˌkɑːnfləˈgreɪʃən/ n [C] *formal* : a large destructive fire

¹con·flict /ˈkɑːnˌflɪkt/ n **1** [C/U] : a struggle for power, property, etc. ▪ *an armed conflict* ▪ *years of conflict* **2** [C/U] : strong disagreement between people, groups, etc., that results in often angry argument ▪ *He tries to avoid conflict.* ▪ *There was (a) conflict over the budget.* **3** [C/U] : a difference that prevents agreement ▪ *We need to resolve the conflict between your plans and mine.* ▪ *inner conflicts* [=ideas, feelings, etc., that disagree with one another] **4** [C] *chiefly US* : a situation in which you are unable to do something because there is something else you have already agreed to do at that same time ▪ *a scheduling conflict* — **come into conflict** **1** : to be different in a way that prevents agreement ▪ *The rules sometimes come into conflict with each other.* [=contradict each other] **2** : to enter a situation in which there is a struggle for power, property, etc. ▪ *come into conflict with neighboring tribes* — **in conflict** **1** : different in a way that prevents agreement ▪ *Her ideas were in direct conflict with mine.* **2** : in a struggle for power, property, etc. ▪ *The two clans were in constant conflict (with one another).*

²con·flict /kənˈflɪkt/ vb [I] **1** : to be different in a way that prevents agreement : DISAGREE ▪ *Their stories conflict.* ▪ *His statement conflicts with the facts.* ▪ *conflicting reports/views* **2** : to happen at the same time as something else ▪ *The appointment conflicts with an important meeting.*

con·flict·ed /kənˈflɪktəd/ *adj, chiefly US* : having or showing feelings that disagree with one another ▪ *She was still conflicted about her ex-husband's remarriage.*

conflict of interest n [C] *formal* : a problem caused by having official responsibilities that involve things that might be helpful or harmful to you ▪ *The involvement of her husband's company creates a conflict of interest for the senator.*

con·flu·ence /ˈkɑːnˌfluːwəns/ n [*singular*] **1** : a place where two rivers or streams join to become one **2** : a situation in which two things come together or happen at the same time ▪ *a confluence of styles/events*

con·form /kənˈfoɚm/ vb [I] **1** : to be similar to or the same as something ▪ *Her behavior conforms to a pattern.* ▪ *The results conform with the estimates.* **2** : to obey or agree with something ▪ *The building conforms to regulations.* ▪ *We have to conform with the rules.* **3** : to behave in a way that is accepted by most people ▪ *Many teenagers feel pressure to conform.*

con·form·ist /kənˈfoɚmɪst/ n [C] *often disapproving* : a person who behaves in a way that is considered acceptable by most people and who avoids doing things that could be considered different or unusual — **conformist** *adj* ▪ *a conformist attitude/society*

con·for·mi·ty /kənˈfoɚməti/ n [U] **1** : behavior that is the same as the behavior of most other people in a society, group, etc. ▪ *mindless conformity* **2** : the fact or state of agreeing with or obeying something ▪ *the building's conformity to regulations* ▪ *in conformity with tradition*

con·found /kənˈfaʊnd/ vb [T] **1** : to surprise and confuse (someone or something) ▪ *The strategy confounded our opponents.* **2** : to prove (someone or something) wrong ▪ *The team confounded all predictions.*

con·front /kənˈfrʌnt/ vb [T] **1 a** : to oppose or challenge (someone) especially in a direct and forceful way ▪ *The mayor was confronted by angry protesters.* **b** : to directly question the action or authority of (someone) ▪ *She confronted him about his smoking.* **2 a** : to deal with (a problem, danger, etc.) ▪ *Firemen regularly confront danger.*; *especially* : to deal with (something) in an honest and direct way ▪ *confront a problem* **b** : to force (someone) to see or deal with (something, such as a problem) in a direct way ▪ *I confronted her with the evidence.* **c** : to be a problem for (someone or something) ▪ *the financial problems confronting local schools*

con·fron·ta·tion /ˌkɑːnfrənˈteɪʃən/ n [C/U] : a situation in which people, groups, etc., fight, oppose, or challenge each other in an angry way ▪ *confrontations between rival gangs* ▪ *a confrontation with the authorities*

con·fron·ta·tion·al /ˌkɑːnfrənˈteɪʃənl/ *adj* : challenging or opposing someone especially in an angry way ▪ *She's become confrontational with her parents.* ▪ *a confrontational approach*

con·fuse /kənˈfjuːz/ vb [T] **1** : to make (someone) uncertain or unable to understand something ▪ *He's trying to confuse us.* ▪ *I was confused by her words.* **2** : to make (something) difficult to understand ▪ *Stop confusing the issue.* **3** : to mistakenly think that one person or thing is another person or thing ▪ *You must be confusing me with someone else.*

con·fused /kənˈfjuːzd/ *adj* **1** : unable to understand or think clearly ▪ *I'm confused about what to do.* **2** : difficult to understand ▪ *a confused explanation*

confusing *adj* : difficult to understand ▪ *The instructions were confusing.* — **con·fus·ing·ly** *adv*

con·fu·sion /kənˈfjuːʒən/ n **1** [C/U] : a situation in which people are uncertain about what to do or are unable to understand something clearly ▪ *There is a great deal of confusion about what happened.* **2** [U] : the feeling that you have when you do not understand what is happening, what is expected, etc. ▪ *She was overwhelmed by confusion.* **3** [U] : a state or situation in which many things are happening in a way that is not controlled or orderly ▪ *There was total/mass confusion in the streets.* **4** [U] : the act of mistakenly thinking that one person or thing is another ▪ *Write clearly on the labels to avoid confusion.*

con game n [C] *US* : ¹CON 1

con·geal /kən'dʒiːl/ vb [I] of a liquid : to become thick or solid • The gravy began to congeal in the pan.

con·ge·nial /kən'dʒiːnijəl/ adj, somewhat formal **1 a** : suitable or appropriate • a congenial place for raising children **b** : pleasant and enjoyable • He found the work to be congenial. **2** : very friendly • a congenial host/companion — **con·ge·ni·al·i·ty** /kən͵dʒiːni'æləti/ n [U]

con·gen·i·tal /kən'dʒɛnətəl/ adj **1** : existing since birth • a congenital defect/disease **2** always before a noun, informal : naturally having a specified character • a congenital liar [=someone who lies a lot and has always lied] — **con·gen·i·tal·ly** adv

con·gest·ed /kən'dʒɛstəd/ adj **1** : too full or crowded with vehicles, people, etc. • congested highways/stores **2** of a part of the body : blocked with fluid (such as blood or mucus) • a congested nose — **con·ges·tion** /kən'dʒɛstʃən/ n [U]

con·glom·er·ate /kən'glɑːmərət/ n [C] : a large business that is made of different kinds of companies

con·glom·er·a·tion /kən͵glɑːmə'reɪʃən/ n [C] : a group or mixture of different things • a conglomeration of shops and restaurants

con·grat·u·late /kən'grætʃə͵leɪt, kən'grædʒə͵leɪt/ vb -lat·ed; -lat·ing [T] **1** : to tell (someone) that you are happy because of his or her success or good luck • I'd like to congratulate you on/for your success. **2** : to feel pleased with (yourself) • She congratulated herself for finishing the race.

con·grat·u·la·tion /kən͵grætʃə'leɪʃən, kən͵grædʒə'leɪʃən/ n **1** [plural] **a** : a message telling someone that you are happy because of his or her success or good luck • Let me offer you my congratulations. **b** — used to tell someone that you are happy because of his or her success or good luck • "I won!" "Congratulations!" • Congratulations on your win! **2** [U, plural] formal : the act of telling someone that you are happy because of his or her success or good luck • a letter/message of congratulation(s)

con·grat·u·la·to·ry /kən'grætʃələ͵tori, kən'grædʒələ͵tori, Brit kən͵grætʃə'leɪtri/ adj, formal : showing someone that you are happy because of his or her success or good luck • a congratulatory phone call

con·gre·gate /'kɑːngrɪ͵geɪt/ vb -gat·ed; -gat·ing [I] : to come together in a group or crowd • Students began to congregate in the hall.

con·gre·ga·tion /͵kɑːngrɪ'geɪʃən/ n [C] : the people who attend religious services • The priest addressed the congregation. • a member of a small congregation

con·gre·ga·tion·al /͵kɑːngrɪ'geɪʃənl/ adj **1** : involving or done by the people who attend religious services • congregational singing **2** Congregational : relating to a group of Christian churches that believe that the people who attend each church should make their own decisions,

rules, etc. • a Congregational church

con·gress /'kɑːngrəs, Brit 'kɑːŋgrɛs/ n **1** [C] : a formal meeting of representatives or experts • a Communist Party congress **2 a** [C/U] : the group of people who are responsible for making the laws of a country in some governments • the congresses of Mexico and Chile **b** Congress [singular] : the congress of the United States that includes the Senate and the House of Representatives • The bill passed both houses of Congress. — **con·gres·sion·al** /kən'grɛʃənl/ adj • a congressional committee

con·gress·man /'kɑːngrəsmən/ n, pl -men /-mən/ [C] : someone (especially a man) who is a member of a congress and especially of the U.S. House of Representatives • Congressman Smith

con·gress·wom·an /'kɑːngrəs͵wumən/ n, pl -wom·en /-͵wimən/ [C] : a woman who is a member of a congress and especially of the U.S. House of Representatives • Congresswoman Jones

con·i·cal /'kɑːnɪkəl/ adj : shaped like a cone • a conical cap/shape

con·i·fer /'kɑːnəfɚ/ n [C] : a bush or tree (such as a pine) that produces cones and that usually has leaves that are green all year — **co·nif·er·ous** /kou'nɪfərəs/ adj • coniferous trees/forests

conj abbr conjunction

¹con·jec·ture /kən'dʒɛktʃɚ/ n [C/U] formal : an opinion or idea formed without proof or sufficient evidence • The book includes a lot of conjecture(s) about her private life. — **con·jec·tur·al** /kən'dʒɛktʃərəl/ adj

²conjecture vb -tured; -tur·ing [T/I] formal : to form an opinion or idea without proof or sufficient evidence • Some have conjectured that the distant planet could sustain life.

con·ju·gal /'kɑːndʒɪgəl/ adj, formal : relating to marriage or to a married couple • conjugal bliss/happiness

con·ju·gate /'kɑːndʒə͵geɪt/ vb -gat·ed; -gat·ing [T] grammar : to list the different forms of a verb • Conjugate the verb "go."

con·ju·ga·tion /͵kɑːndʒə'geɪʃən/ n **1** [U] : the way a verb changes form to show number, person, tense, etc. • a lesson on verb conjugation **2** [C] : a group of verbs that change in the same way to show number, person, tense, etc. • Latin conjugations

con·junc·tion /kən'dʒʌŋkʃən/ n [C] **1** grammar : a word (such as and, but, or although) that joins together sentences, clauses, phrases, or words **2** formal : a situation in which two or more things happen at the same time or in the same place • a conjunction of events — **in conjunction with** formal : in combination with • The medicine is typically used in conjunction with other treatments.

con·junc·ti·vi·tis /kən͵dʒʌŋktə'vaɪtəs/ n [U] : a disease that causes the eye to become pink and sore

con·jure /'kɑːndʒɚ, Brit 'kʌndʒɚ/ vb -jured; -jur·ing [T] **1** : to make (something) appear or seem to appear by using magic — usually + up • In the movie she has the power to *conjure up* storms, fires, and earthquakes. **2 a** : to make you think of (something) — usually + *up* • *The photos conjure up memories of a simpler time.* **b** : to create or imagine (something) — usually + *up* • *They conjured up a clever scheme.*

con·jur·er *or* **con·ju·ror** /ˈkɑːndʒərɚ, Brit ˈkʌndʒərə/ *n* [C] : a person who performs magic tricks

conk /ˈkɑːŋk/ *vb* [T] *informal* : to strike or hit (someone or something) hard • *He conked his brother on the head.* — **conk out** [*phrasal vb*] *informal* **1** *of a machine* : to stop working properly • *The engine conked out.* **2** : to fall asleep • *I conked out early last night.*

con man *n, pl* **— men** [C] : CON ARTIST

con·nect /kəˈnɛkt/ *vb* **1 a** [T] : to join (two or more things) together • *Connect the hose to the sprinkler.* • *A hallway connects the two rooms.* = *The two rooms are connected by a hallway.* • *The stories are connected by a common theme.* **b** [I] : to join with or become joined to something else • *The bedroom connects to the kitchen.* **2** [T] **a** : to think of (something or someone) as being related to or involved with another person, thing, event, or idea • *In my mind, the two places are connected.* **b** : to show or prove that a person or thing is related to or involved with something • *There's no evidence connecting her to the crime.* **3** [T/I] : to join or become joined to a system, network, etc., through a telephone, computer, or other device • *connect to the Internet* • *The operator connected me to the front desk.* [=linked my telephone with the telephone at the front desk] **4** [I] — used to say that an airplane, train, etc., stops at a particular place where passengers get onto another airplane, train, etc., in order to continue their journey • *Our flight connects in Chicago.* • *a connecting flight* **5** [I] *chiefly US, informal* : to have or share a feeling of affection and understanding • *We really connected on our first date.* **6** [I] *chiefly US, sports* : to make a successful shot, hit, or throw • *He connected for a home run.* — **connect the dots** *chiefly US, informal* : to learn or understand how different things are related • *The information was all there but no one had ever connected the dots.* — **connect up** [*phrasal vb*] **connect up (something)** *or* **connect (something) up** : to join or link (a device, piece of equipment, etc.) to something • *I'm having trouble connecting the speakers up to the TV.*

con·nect·ed /kəˈnɛktəd/ *adj* **1** : joined or linked together • *connected rooms* **2** : having useful social, professional, or commercial relationships • *a politically connected businessman* [=a businessman who has relationships with people who have political power] — **con·nect·ed·ness** /kəˈnɛktədnəs/ *n* [U]

con·nec·tion /kəˈnɛkʃən/ *n* **1** [C] : something that joins or connects two or more things • *pipe/hose connections* **2** [U] : the act of connecting two or more things or the state of being connected •

All classrooms are wired for connection to the Internet. **3** [C] **a** : a situation in which two or more things have the same cause, origin, goal, etc. • *Investigators found no connection between the two fires.* • *The school has no connection with the museum.* **b** : a situation in which one thing causes another • *the connection between smoking and lung cancer* **4** [C] **a** : something that allows you to become connected to a system, network, etc., through a telephone, computer, or other device • *a high-speed Internet connection* • *We have a bad connection.* [=a problem with the way our phones are connected] **b** : a place where two parts or wires meet and touch • *an electrical connection* **5** [C] : a train, bus, or airplane that you get onto after getting off another train, bus, or airplane as part of the same journey • *We have to make a connection in Chicago.* **6** [C] **a** : a relationship between people who are part of the same family, who do business together, etc. • *He has no connection with that law firm.* • *a connection to the royal family* **b** : a shared feeling of affection and understanding • *an emotional connection* **7** [C] : a powerful person who you know and who can help you • *She has some connections in the banking industry.* — **in connection with** : for reasons that relate to (something) • *Police arrested four men in connection with the robbery.* — **make a/the connection** : to understand that there is a relationship between two or more things • *It didn't take long for us to make the connection between the missing money and our partner's new car.*

connective tissue *n* [C/U] *medical* : the parts of the body (such as ligaments, tendons, and cartilage) that support and hold together muscles, bones, etc.

con·nec·tor /kəˈnɛktɚ/ *n* [C] **1** : a device or a part of a device that connects two computers, pieces of equipment, etc. • *an electrical connector* **2** : a road that connects two places, roads, etc.

con·nive /kəˈnaɪv/ *vb* **-nived; -niv·ing** [I] *disapproving* : to secretly help someone do something dishonest or illegal • *She connived with him to fix the election.* • *a conniving swindler* — **con·niv·ance** /kəˈnaɪvəns/ *n* [U]

con·nois·seur /ˌkɑːnəˈsɚ/ *n* [C] : an expert in a specified subject • *wine connoisseurs = connoisseurs of wine*

con·no·ta·tion /ˌkɑːnəˈteɪʃən/ *n* [C] : an idea or quality that a word makes you think about in addition to its meaning • *The word "fat" has negative connotations.*

con·note /kəˈnoʊt/ *vb* **-not·ed; -not·ing** [T] *formal, of a word* : to make you think about (something) in addition to the word's meaning • *For her, the word "family" connotes love and comfort.*

con·quer /ˈkɑːŋkɚ/ *vb* [T] **1** : to take control of (a country, city, etc.) through the use of force • *conquer a city* **2** : to defeat (someone or something) through the use of force • *They conquered their enemies.* **3** : to gain control of (a problem or difficulty) through great effort • *She conquered* [=overcame] *her fear.* **4**

: to become successful in (a place, situation, etc.) ▪ *an actress who has conquered Hollywood* **5** : to succeed in climbing (a mountain) ▪ *the first climbers to conquer Mount Everest* — **con·quer·or** /ˈkɑːŋkərɚ/ *n* [C]

con·quest /ˈkɑːnˌkwɛst/ *n* **1** [C/U] : the act of taking control of a country, city, etc., through the use of force ▪ *tales of military conquest(s)* **2** [C] : a country, city, etc., that an army has taken control of through the use of force ▪ *Napoleon's conquests* **3** [C] : a person someone has succeeded in having a romantic and especially a sexual relationship with ▪ *She was one of his many conquests.* **4** [U] : success in defeating or dealing with something difficult or dangerous ▪ *the conquest of space*

con·science /ˈkɑːnʃəns/ *n* **1** [C/U] : the part of the mind that makes you aware of your actions as being either morally right or wrong ▪ *Her conscience was bothering her, so she told the truth.* ▪ *I can't do anything that is/goes against my conscience.* [=that I believe is morally wrong] ▪ *a guilty/troubled conscience* [=a feeling of guilt] ▪ *a clear conscience* [=an absence of guilt] ▪ *a company that has no social conscience* [=that does not care about important social issues] **2** [U] : a feeling that something you have done is morally wrong ▪ *She felt a pang/prick of conscience.* — **in (all/good) conscience** *formal* ✧ If you cannot do something *in (all/good) conscience,* you cannot do it because you think that it is morally wrong. ▪ *She could not in good conscience remain silent.* — **on your conscience** ✧ If something is *on your conscience,* it makes you feel guilty.

con·sci·en·tious /ˌkɑːnʃiˈɛnʃəs/ *adj* : very careful about doing what you are supposed to do ▪ *a conscientious worker* — **con·sci·en·tious·ly** *adv* — **con·sci·en·tious·ness** *n* [U]

conscientious objector *n* [C] : a person who refuses to serve in the military because of moral or religious beliefs

con·scious /ˈkɑːnʃəs/ *adj* **1** : awake and able to understand what is happening around you ▪ *Is the patient conscious yet?* **2** *not before a noun* : aware of something (such as a fact or feeling) ▪ *She was very conscious of the time.* ▪ *He was conscious that they were watching him.* **3** : known or felt by yourself ▪ *conscious guilt/thought* **4** : caring about something specified ▪ *environmentally conscious* [=caring about the health of the environment] ▪ *cost-conscious* [=concerned about the price of things] **5** : done after thinking about facts and reasons carefully ▪ *a conscious decision/effort/attempt* — **con·scious·ly** *adv* ▪ *I wasn't consciously aware of having laughed.*

con·scious·ness /ˈkɑːnʃəsnəs/ *n* **1** [U] : the normal state of being awake and able to understand what is happening around you ▪ *She briefly lost consciousness.* [=became unconscious] ▪ *He slowly regained consciousness.* **2 a** [C/U] : a person's mind and thoughts ▪ *an altered*

state of consciousness **b** [U] : knowledge that is shared by a group of people ▪ *The events have become part of the national/public consciousness.* **3** [C/U] : awareness or knowledge of something specified ▪ *trying to increase public consciousness of the disease* ▪ *She has a strong social consciousness.* [=she is aware of important social issues]

con·script /kənˈskrɪpt/ *vb* [T] : to force (someone) to serve in the armed forces ▪ *He was conscripted into the army.* — **con·script** /ˈkɑːnˌskrɪpt/ *n* [C] ▪ *army conscripts* — **con·scrip·tion** /kənˈskrɪpʃən/ *n* [U]

con·se·crate /ˈkɑːnsəˌkreɪt/ *vb* **-crat·ed; -crat·ing** [T] **1** : to officially make (a place, building, etc.) holy through a special religious ceremony ▪ *The church was consecrated in 1856.* **2** : to officially make (someone) a priest, bishop, etc., through a special religious ceremony ▪ *He was recently consecrated (as) a priest.* — **con·se·cra·tion** /ˌkɑːnsəˈkreɪʃən/ *n* [C/U]

con·sec·u·tive /kənˈsɛkjətɪv/ *adj* : following one after the other in a series ▪ *We had rain for five consecutive days.* — **con·sec·u·tive·ly** *adv*

con·sen·su·al /kənˈsɛnʃəwəl/ *adj* : agreed to by the people involved ▪ *consensual sex* — **con·sen·su·al·ly** *adv*

con·sen·sus /kənˈsɛnsəs/ *n* [C/U] : an idea or opinion that is shared by all the people in a group ▪ *The consensus of the group was to leave today.* ▪ *a lack of consensus* [=agreement] ▪ *They have reached a consensus.* [=come to an agreement] ▪ *What is the consensus of opinion?* [=what do all or most people say?] ▪ *a decision made by consensus* [=by a group of people who have come to an agreement]

¹**con·sent** /kənˈsɛnt/ *vb* [I] *formal* : to agree to do or allow something ▪ *He consented to the plan/marriage/meeting.*

²**consent** *n* [U] *somewhat formal* **1** : permission for something to happen or be done ▪ *Students must have the consent of their parents to go on the trip.* ▪ *written consent* [=a document giving permission] **2** : agreement about an opinion or about something that will happen or be done ▪ *This restaurant is, by common consent, the best in the city.* [=people agree that this restaurant is the best in the city] ▪ *The contract was canceled by mutual consent.* [=the people involved agreed to cancel the contract]

consenting adult *n* [C] *law* : a person who is legally considered old enough to decide to have sex

con·se·quence /ˈkɑːnsəˌkwɛns/ *n* **1** [C] : something that happens as a result of a particular action or set of conditions ▪ *The error had serious consequences.* ▪ *the economic consequences of war* ✧ If you **face/suffer the consequences** of something, you deal with the results of something that you have done. **2** [U] *formal* : importance or value ▪ *a man of consequence* [=an important man] — **in consequence** *or* **as a consequence** *formal* : as a result of something ▪ *Many people* *became sick as a consequence of the poor sanitary conditions.*

con·se·quent /ˈkɑːnsəkwənt/ *adj, always before a noun, somewhat formal* : happening as a result of a particular action or set of conditions ▪ *heavy rains and consequent flooding* — **con·se·quent·ly** /ˈkɑːnsəˌkwentli/ *adv* ▪ *The state's economy was poor. Consequently, many college graduates moved away.*

con·ser·va·tion /ˌkɑːnsɚˈveɪʃən/ *n* [U] **1** : the protection of animals, plants, and natural resources ▪ *wildlife conservation* ▪ *the conservation of the environment* ▪ *conservation efforts/groups* **2** : the careful use of natural resources (such as trees, oil, etc.) to prevent them from being lost or wasted ▪ *water/forest/energy conservation* **3** : the things that are done to keep works of art or things of historical importance in good condition ▪ *the conservation of religious shrines*

con·ser·va·tion·ist /ˌkɑːnsɚˈveɪʃənɪst/ *n* [C] : someone who works to protect animals, plants, and natural resources or to prevent the loss or waste of natural resources

con·ser·va·tism /kənˈsɚvəˌtɪzəm/ *n* [U] **1** : belief in the value of established and traditional practices in politics and society ▪ *political conservatism* **2** : dislike of change or new ideas in a particular area ▪ *cultural/religious conservatism*

¹con·ser·va·tive /kənˈsɚvətɪv/ *adj* **1** : believing in the value of established and traditional practices in politics and society ▪ *conservative politicians/policies* **2** *Conservative* : of or relating to the conservative party in countries like the United Kingdom and Canada ▪ *the Conservative candidate* **3** : not liking or accepting changes or new ideas ▪ *She's more conservative now than she was in college.* ▪ *conservative ideas* **4** — used to describe a guess, estimate, etc., that is probably lower than the actual amount will be ▪ *a conservative estimate of how much repairs will cost* **5** : traditional in taste, style, or manners ▪ *Her taste in art/clothes is fairly conservative.* **6** : not willing to take risks ▪ *a conservative investor* **7** *or Conservative* : accepting and following many of the traditional beliefs and customs of a religion ▪ *Conservative Judaism* — **con·ser·va·tive·ly** *adv*

²conservative *n* [C] **1** : a person who believes in the value of established and traditional practices in politics and society ▪ *His message was well received by conservatives.* **2** *Conservative* : a member or supporter of a conservative political party in countries like the United Kingdom and Canada

con·ser·va·toire /kənˈsɚvəˌtwɑɚ/ *n* [C] *Brit* : CONSERVATORY 1

con·ser·va·to·ry /kənˈsɚvəˌtori, *Brit* kənˈsɚːvətri/ *n, pl* **-ries** [C] **1** *US* : a school in which students are taught music, theater, or dance **2** : GREENHOUSE

con·serve /kənˈsɚv/ *vb* **-served; -serving** [T] **1** : to keep (something) safe or from being damaged or destroyed ▪ *The organization works to conserve our national forests/wildlife.* **2** : to use (something)

carefully in order to prevent loss or waste ▪ *conserving fuel/energy/water* ▪ *You need to conserve your strength.*

con·sid·er /kənˈsɪdɚ/ *vb* **1 a** [T/I] : to think about (something or someone) carefully especially in order to make a choice or decision ▪ *We are considering you for the job.* ▪ *She refused to consider my request.* **b** [T] : to think about (something that is important in understanding something or in making a decision or judgment) ▪ *When you consider her background, her decision is not surprising.* **2** [T] : to think about (a person or a person's feelings) before you do something in order to avoid making someone upset, angry, etc. ▪ *You never consider my feelings.* **3** [T] : to think of or regard (someone or something) in a specified way ▪ *We consider it an honor to have you here with us tonight.* ▪ *an actor who is considered talented* ▪ *Consider yourself lucky/fortunate that your survived.* [=you are lucky to have survived] **4** [T] *formal* : to look at (someone or something) carefully and thoughtfully ▪ *He stepped back to consider the whole painting.* — **all things considered** — used for saying that a statement is true when you think about all the good and bad parts or results of something ▪ *It was a pretty good vacation, all things considered.*

con·sid·er·able /kənˈsɪdɚəbəl/ *adj* : large in size, amount, or quantity ▪ *She was in considerable pain.* ▪ *a considerable amount of time/money/attention* — **con·sid·er·ably** /kənˈsɪdɚəbli/ *adv* ▪ *considerably* [=*much*] *more expensive*

con·sid·er·ate /kənˈsɪdɚət/ *adj* : thinking about the rights and feelings of other people ▪ *a very considerate person* ▪ *She is always considerate of other people's feelings.* — **con·sid·er·ate·ly** *adv*

con·sid·er·a·tion /kənˌsɪdəˈreɪʃən/ *n* **1** [U] : the act of thinking carefully about something you will make a decision about ▪ *I will give the matter some serious/careful consideration.* ▪ *Her suggestion is still under consideration.* [=is still being thought about and discussed] **2** [U] : a desire to avoid doing something that will make another person sad, upset, angry, etc. ▪ *Out of consideration for the victim's family, no photos will be shown.* ▪ *He has no consideration for her feelings.* **3** [C] : something that you think about when you make a choice or decision ▪ *an important consideration* — **take (something) into consideration** : to think about (something) before you make a decision or form an opinion

con·sid·ered /kənˈsɪdɚd/ *adj, always before a noun, formal* : resulting from careful thought ▪ *a considered opinion/response*

con·sid·er·ing /kənˈsɪdɚɪŋ/ *prep* : when you think about or consider (something) — used to indicate a fact or situation that is being thought of when a statement is made ▪ *He did very well, considering his lack of preparation.* — sometimes used informally in speech without a following object ▪ *He didn't win, but he did* *very well, considering.* — **considering** *conj* ▪ *He did well, considering (that) he had no experience.*

con·sign /kən'saɪn/ *vb* [T] *formal* **1** : to put (someone) in a usually unpleasant place or situation — + *to* ▪ *The prisoners were consigned to labor camps.* **2** : to put (something that is not wanted or used) in a place where old things are stored or thrown away — + *to* ▪ *She consigned his letter to the wastebasket.* [=she threw away his letter]

con·sign·ment /kən'saɪnmənt/ *n* **1** [C] : a quantity of goods that are sent to a person or place to be sold ▪ *a consignment of books/goods/cars* **2** [U] : the act or process of sending goods to a person or place to be sold ▪ *the consignment of goods* — **on consignment** — used to describe a situation in which goods are sent to a person who pays only for what is sold and who may return what is not sold ▪ *goods sold on consignment*

con·sist /kən'sɪst/ *vb* — **consist in** [*phrasal vb*] *formal* : to have (something) as an essential or main part ▪ *Happiness consists in being satisfied with what you have.* — **consist of** [*phrasal vb*] : to be formed or made up of (specified things or people) ▪ *Breakfast consisted of cereal, fruit, and orange juice.*

con·sis·ten·cy /kən'sɪstənsi/ *n, pl* -**cies** **1** [U] **a** : the quality or fact of staying the same at different times ▪ *consistency of behavior; especially* : the quality or fact of being good each time ▪ *Customers expect consistency in the quality of service they receive.* **b** : the quality or fact of having parts that agree with each other ▪ *Her argument lacks consistency.* **2** [C/U] : the quality of being thick, firm, smooth, etc. ▪ *The batter should have/be the consistency of pudding.*

con·sis·tent /kən'sɪstənt/ *adj* **1 a** : always acting or behaving in the same way ▪ *We need to be more consistent in handling this problem.* ▪ *consistent results* **b** : of the same quality; *especially* : good each time ▪ *His pitching is very consistent.* **2** : continuing to happen or develop in the same way ▪ *Your grades have shown consistent improvement.* **3** : having parts that agree with each other ▪ *She is not being consistent in her argument.* ▪ *His statements were not consistent with the truth.* [=were not true] — **con·sis·tent·ly** *adv*

con·so·la·tion /ˌkɑːnsə'leɪʃən/ *n* **1** [C/U] : something that makes a person feel less sadness, disappointment, etc. ▪ *She found/took great consolation in his words.* = *His words were a consolation to/ for her.* **2** [C] : a contest in which people or teams that have previously lost compete against each other ▪ *a consolation game/match/race*

consolation prize *n* [C] : a prize that is given to someone who has not won a contest

¹con·sole /kən'soʊl/ *vb* -**soled**; -**sol·ing** [T] : to try to make (someone) feel less sadness or disappointment ▪ *She consoled him after his wife died.* ▪ *I consoled myself with the thought that things could be much worse.*

²con·sole /'kɑːnˌsoʊl/ *n* [C] **1** : a flat surface that contains the controls for a machine, for a piece of electrical equipment, etc. **2** : a cabinet for a stereo or television that stands on the floor

con·sol·i·date /kən'sɑːlə‚deɪt/ *vb* -**dat·ed**; -**dat·ing 1** [T/I] : to join or combine together into one thing ▪ *The two companies consolidated.* [=merged] ▪ *I consolidated my loans.* **2** [T] : to make (something, such as a position of power or control) stronger or more secure ▪ *The team consolidated their lead.* — **con·sol·i·da·tion** /kən‚sɑːlə'deɪʃən/ *n* [C/U]

con·som·mé /ˌkɑːnsə'meɪ, *Brit* kən'sɒmeɪ/ *n* [U] : a clear soup that is usually made with seasoned meat

con·so·nant /'kɑːnsənənt/ *n* [C] **1** : a speech sound (such as /p/, /d/, or /s/) that is made by partly or completely stopping the flow of air breathed out from the mouth **2** : a letter that represents a consonant

¹con·sort /kən'soɚt/ *vb* — **consort with** [*phrasal vb*] *formal* + *disapproving* : to spend time with (someone) ▪ *consorting with criminals*

²con·sort /'kɑːnˌsoɚt/ *n* [C] *formal* : a wife or husband of a king, queen, emperor, etc.

con·sor·tium /kən'soɚʃəm, kən'soɚtijəm/ *n, pl* **con·sor·tia** /-ʃə, -tijə/ *also* **con·sor·tiums** [C] : a group of people, companies, etc., that agree to work together ▪ *a consortium of universities/ banks*

con·spic·u·ous /kən'spɪkjəwəs/ *adj* **1** : very easy to see or notice ▪ *She felt very conspicuous in her pink coat.* ▪ *conspicuous changes* ▪ *a conspicuous spot/position* **2** : attracting attention by being great or impressive ▪ *a conspicuous success* ▪ *conspicuous bravery* — **con·spic·u·ous·ly** *adv* — **con·spic·u·ous·ness** /kən'spɪkjəwəsnəs/ *n* [U]

con·spir·a·cy /kən'spɪrəsi/ *n, pl* -**cies 1** [C] : a secret plan made by two or more people to do something that is harmful or illegal ▪ *a conspiracy against the government* **2** [U] : the act of secretly planning to do something that is harmful or illegal ▪ *They were accused of conspiracy to commit murder.*

conspiracy theory *n* [C] : a theory that explains an event or situation as the result of a secret plan by usually powerful people or groups ▪ *Conspiracy theories sprung up soon after the leader's assassination.*

con·spir·a·tor /kən'spɪrətɚ/ *n* [C] : a person who is involved in a secret plan to do something harmful or illegal

con·spir·a·to·ri·al /kən‚spɪrə'torijəl/ *adj* **1** : involving a secret plan by two or more people to do something that is harmful or illegal ▪ *conspiratorial plots/ plans* **2** : suggesting that something secret is being shared ▪ *a conspiratorial smile/wink* — **con·spir·a·to·ri·al·ly** *adv*

con·spire /kən'spajɚ/ *vb* -**spired**; -**spir·ing** [I] **1** : to secretly plan with someone to do something that is harmful or illegal ▪ *They conspired to overthrow the*

government. • *They conspired against him.*
2 : to happen in a way that produces bad or unpleasant results • *The weather conspired against us.*

con·sta·ble /ˈkɑːnstəbəl, ˈkʌnstəbəl/ *n* [C] **1** *US* : a public official whose job is similar to that of a police officer but who is elected or appointed rather than hired **2** *chiefly Brit* : POLICE CONSTABLE

¹**con·stant** /ˈkɑːnstənt/ *adj* **1** : happening all the time or very often over a period of time • *He suffers from constant headaches.* • *constant attention/care* **2** : staying the same : not changing • *a constant temperature/weight/speed* **3** *formal + literary* : always loyal • *They remained constant friends throughout their lives.* — **con·stan·cy** /ˈkɑːnstənsi/ *n* [U] — **con·stant·ly** *adv* • *He talked/complained constantly.*

²**constant** *n* [C] **1** : something that stays the same • *Her job was the one constant in her life.* **2** *technical* : a quantity or number whose value does not change

con·stel·la·tion /ˌkɑːnstəˈleɪʃən/ *n* [C] : a group of stars that forms a particular shape in the sky and has been given a name

con·ster·na·tion /ˌkɑːnstəˈneɪʃən/ *n* [U] *formal* : a strong feeling of surprise or sudden disappointment that causes confusion • *Much to her parents' consternation, she decided to not go to college.*

con·sti·pa·tion /ˌkɑːnstəˈpeɪʃən/ *n* [U] : the condition of being unable to easily release solid waste from your body — **con·sti·pat·ed** /ˈkɑːnstəˌpeɪtəd/ *adj*

con·stit·u·en·cy /kənˈstɪtʃəwənsi/ *n, pl* **-cies** [C] **1** : a group of people who support or who are likely to support a politician or political party • *the governor's conservative/liberal constituency* **2 a** : the people who live and vote in an area • *The senator's constituency includes a large minority population.* **b** *Brit* : a district with an elected representative • *He was elected to represent a Liverpool constituency.*

con·stit·u·ent /kənˈstɪtʃəwənt/ *n* [C] **1** : any one of the people who live and vote in an area • *Many of the senator's constituents want her to vote in favor of the law.* **2** : one of the parts that form something • *the chemical constituents of the liquid* — **constituent** *adj* • *constituent parts/elements* [=parts/elements that form something]

con·sti·tute /ˈkɑːnstəˌtuːt, *Brit* ˈkɒnstəˌtjuːt/ *vb* **-tut·ed**; **-tut·ing** *formal* **1** [*linking vb*] : to make up or form something • *Women constitute 70 percent of the group.* • *Twelve months constitute a year.* **2** [*linking vb*] : to be the same as something : to be equivalent to something • *The search of their house constituted a violation of their rights.* **3** [T] : to establish or create (an organization, a government, etc.) • *The recently constituted government will hold elections in May.*

con·sti·tu·tion /ˌkɑːnstəˈtuːʃən, *Brit* ˌkɒnstəˈtjuːʃən/ *n* [C] **a** : the system of beliefs and laws by which a country, state, or organization is governed **b** : a document that describes this system •

The state's original constitution is on display at the museum. **2** [C] : the physical health and condition of a person or animal • *a robust/weak/tough/strong constitution* **3** [U] *formal* : the form or structure of something • *the constitution of the chemical*

con·sti·tu·tion·al /ˌkɑːnstəˈtuːʃənl, *Brit* ˌkɒnstəˈtjuːʃənl/ *adj* **1** *always before a noun* : of or relating to the system of beliefs and laws that govern a country • *a constitutional amendment* • *constitutional law* **2** : allowed by a country's constitution • *a constitutional right* **3 a** : of or relating to the health and strength of a person's body • *constitutional symptoms* **b** : of or relating to a person's basic nature or character • *a constitutional dislike of controversy* — **con·sti·tu·tion·al·i·ty** /ˌkɑːnstəˌtuːʃəˈnæləti, *Brit* ˌkɒnstəˌtjuːʃəˈnæləti/ *n* [U] • *He questions the constitutionality of the proposed law.* — **con·sti·tu·tion·al·ly** *adv*

con·strain /kənˈstreɪn/ *vb* [T] **1** : to limit or restrict (something or someone) • *We were constrained by rules.* **2** *formal* : to use pressure to force (someone) to do something • *She felt constrained to apologize.*

con·straint /kənˈstreɪnt/ *n* **1** : something that limits or restricts someone or something • *Budget/time constraints forced me to revise my plans.* **2** [U] : control that limits or restricts someone's actions or behavior • *working under constraint*

con·strict /kənˈstrɪkt/ *vb* **1** [T/I] : to make or become narrower, smaller, or tighter • *The drug constricts blood vessels.* = *The drug causes the blood vessels to constrict.* **2** [T] : to prevent or keep (something or someone) from developing freely • *a life constricted by poverty* • *He felt constricted by the rules.* — **con·stric·tion** /kənˈstrɪkʃən/ *n* [C/U]

constrictor see BOA CONSTRICTOR

¹**con·struct** /kənˈstrʌkt/ *vb* [T] **1** : to build or make (a road, building, etc.) • *construct a bridge* • *a newly constructed building* **2** : to make or create (something, such as a story or theory) by organizing ideas, words, etc. • *a well-constructed story/argument* — **con·struc·tor** /kənˈstrʌktɚ/ *n* [C]

²**con·struct** /ˈkɑːnˌstrʌkt/ *n* [C] *formal* : something (such as an idea or a theory) that is formed in people's minds • *Class distinctions are social constructs.* [=ideas that have been created and accepted by the people in a society]

con·struc·tion /kənˈstrʌkʃən/ *n* **1** [U] **a** : the act or process of building something (such as a house or road) • *Construction of the new bridge will begin soon.* • *construction costs/equipment/materials* • *The new school is now under construction.* [=being built] **b** : the business of building houses, roads, etc. • *the construction industry* **2** [U] : the way something is built or made • *the sturdy construction of the furniture* **3** [C] : the way words in a sentence or phrase are arranged • *passive/positive/negative constructions*

construction paper *n* [*U*] *US* : a kind of thick paper that comes in many colors and is used especially by children in school to create art

con·struc·tive /kən'strʌktɪv/ *adj* : helping to develop or improve something ▪ *constructive criticism/suggestions/comments/feedback* ▪ *a former prisoner who now plays a constructive role in society* — **con·struc·tive·ly** *adv*

con·strue /kən'stru:/ *vb* -**strued**; -**struing** [*T*] *somewhat formal* 1 : to understand (an action, event, remark, etc.) in a particular way — usually + *as* ▪ *He construed my actions as hostile.* 2 : to understand the meaning of (a word, phrase, or sentence) ▪ *The way the court construes various words has changed over time.*

con·sul /'ka:nsəl/ *n* [*C*] 1 : a government official whose job is to live in a foreign country and protect and help the citizens of his or her own country who are traveling, living, or doing business there 2 : a chief official of the ancient Roman republic — **con·sul·ar** /'ka:nsələ, *Brit* 'kɒnsjələ/ *adj*

con·sul·ate /'ka:nsələt, *Brit* 'kɒnsjələt/ *n* [*C*] : the building where a consul lives and works

con·sult /kən'sʌlt/ *vb* 1 [*T/I*] : to ask (someone) for advice or his or her opinion ▪ *consult a lawyer/accountant/doctor about the matter* ▪ *I expect to be consulted on important decisions.* ▪ *I'll need to consult with* [=talk with] *my husband before I sign the papers.* 2 [*T*] : to look for information in (something) ▪ *consult a dictionary/map* 3 [*I*] *chiefly US* : to give professional advice for a fee ▪ *She consults for a living.* ▪ *a consulting firm* — **con·sul·ta·tion** /,ka:nsəl'teɪʃən/ *n* [*C/U*] ▪ *After their consultation with the judge, the lawyers decided to drop the case.* ▪ *a consultation of the city records* ▪ *The book was chosen in consultation with* [=after consulting] *a panel of experts.*

con·sul·tan·cy /kən'sʌltnsi/ *n, pl* -**cies** [*C*] : a company that gives professional advice for a fee

con·sult·ant /kən'sʌltnt/ *n* [*C*] 1 : a person who gives professional advice or services for a fee ▪ *an advertising/management consultant* 2 *Brit* : a hospital doctor who is an expert in a particular area of medicine ▪ *a cardiology consultant* [=*specialist*]

con·sum·able /kən'su:məbəl, *Brit* kən'sju:məbəl/ *adj* : needing to be replaced after being used for a period of time ▪ *paper, pencils, and other consumable goods* — **consumable** *n* [*C*]

con·sume /kən'su:m, *Brit* kən'sju:m/ *vb* -**sumed**; -**sum·ing** [*T*] 1 : to eat or drink (something) ▪ *consume a lot of food* 2 : to use (fuel, time, etc.) ▪ *The new lights consume less electricity.* ▪ *The car repair consumed* [=*used up*] *his entire paycheck.* 3 : to destroy (something) with fire ▪ *Fire consumed the building.* 4 : to take all of a person's attention, energy, time, etc. ▪ *Work on the project has consumed his attention for months.* ▪ *He was consumed with/by jealousy.* ▪ *a consuming interest in* politics ▪ *Her all-consuming passion was music.*

con·sum·er /kən'su:mɚ, *Brit* kən'sju:mə/ *n* [*C*] : a person who buys goods and services ▪ *products that appeal to young consumers* ▪ *consumer spending/goods*

consumer price index *n* — **the consumer price index** *US* : a list of prices of goods and services that shows how much prices have changed in a given period of time — *abbr.* CPI

¹**con·sum·mate** /'ka:nsəmət, kən'sʌmət/ *adj, always before a noun* 1 : very good or skillful ▪ *a consummate actor* 2 : very bad ▪ *consummate cruelty/evil* — **con·sum·mate·ly** *adv*

²**con·sum·mate** /'ka:nsə,meɪt/ *vb* -**mated**; -**mat·ing** [*T*] *formal* 1 : to make (a marriage or romantic relationship) complete by having sex 2 : to make (something) perfect or complete ▪ *consummate an alliance* — **con·sum·ma·tion** /,ka:nsə'meɪʃən/ *n* [*U*]

con·sump·tion /kən'sʌmpʃən/ *n* [*U*] 1 : the act of eating or drinking something ▪ *alcohol/chocolate consumption = the consumption of alcohol/chocolate* ▪ *This food is not fit for human consumption.* [=*not fit to be eaten by people*] 2 : the use of something (such as fuel) ▪ *electricity/gas consumption* 3 : the act of buying things ▪ *increasing rates of consumption*

con·sump·tive /kən'sʌmptɪv/ *n* [*C*] *old-fashioned* : a person who has tuberculosis — **consumptive** *adj*

cont. *also* **cont'd** *abbr* continued

¹**con·tact** /'ka:n,tækt/ *n* 1 [*U*] : the state or condition that exists when two people or things physically touch each other ▪ *physical contact between a mother and child* ▪ *diseases spread by sexual contact* ▪ *The players made contact (with each other).* ▪ *Don't let your skin come in/into contact with* [=*touch*] *the acid.* 2 [*C/U*] : the state or condition that exists when people see and communicate with each other ▪ *There has been no contact between them recently.* ▪ *Contacts between the two leaders have been frequent.* ▪ *native people coming into/in contact with the settlers* ▪ *human contact* [=interaction with other people] ▪ *"Are you in contact with them?" "No, I haven't talked to them in years."* ▪ *I lost contact with her years ago.* ▪ *We made/established contact by radio.* ✧ Your *contact information* is the information (such as your telephone number, address, or e-mail address) that tells someone how to communicate with you. — *see also* EYE CONTACT 3 [*C*] : a person who you know and who can be helpful to you especially in business ▪ *business contacts* 4 [*C*] : CONTACT LENS 5 [*C*] : the connection of two objects that allows an electrical current to pass through them

²**contact** *vb* [*T*] : to call or write to (someone or something) ▪ *For more information, contact the city's tourism office.* ▪ *We contacted them by radio.*

³**contact** *adj, always before a noun* : allowing players to touch or hit each other ▪

Ice hockey is a contact sport.

contact lens *n* [C] : a thin piece of round plastic that is worn on the eye to improve vision

con·ta·gion /kənˈteɪʤən/ *n* 1 [U] : the process by which a disease is passed from one person or animal to another by touching • *a disease that spreads by contagion* 2 [C] : a contagious disease • *a deadly contagion*

con·ta·gious /kənˈteɪʤəs/ *adj* 1 : able to be passed from one person or animal to another by touching • *a contagious disease/virus* 2 : having a sickness that can be passed to someone else by touching • *I'm sick, but the doctor says I'm not contagious.* 3 : causing other people to feel or act a similar way • *She has a contagious smile.* • *contagious enthusiasm* — **con·ta·gious·ly** *adv* — **con·ta·gious·ness** *n* [U]

con·tain /kənˈteɪn/ *vb* [T] 1 : to have (something) inside • *The box contains old papers.* 2 : to have or include (something) • *The book contains over 200 recipes.* • *foods that contain a high level of fat* 3 : to keep (something) from spreading • *Firefighters contained the wildfires.* 4 : to keep (a feeling or yourself) under control • *They could barely contain their excitement.* • *She could not contain herself and broke into tears of relief.* — **con·tain·able** /kənˈteɪnəbəl/ *adj* — **con·tain·ment** /kənˈteɪnmənt/ *n* [U] • *the containment of hazardous waste*

con·tain·er /kənˈteɪnɚ/ *n* [C] : an object (such as a box or can) that can hold something • *bowls, boxes, jars, and other containers*

con·tam·i·nant /kənˈtæmənənt/ *n* [C] : something that contaminates a place or substance • *a water contaminant*

con·tam·i·nate /kənˈtæməˌneɪt/ *vb* **-nat·ed; -nat·ing** [T] : to make (something) dangerous, dirty, or impure by adding something harmful or undesirable to it • *The water was contaminated with chemicals.* • *contaminated food* • *(figurative) Racist ideas have contaminated their minds.* — **con·tam·i·na·tion** /kənˌtæməˈneɪʃən/ *n* [U]

cont'd see CONT.

con·tem·plate /ˈkɑːntəmˌpleɪt/ *vb* **-plat·ed; -plat·ing** 1 [T/I] : to think deeply or carefully about (something) • *contemplated the meaning of a poem* 2 [T] : to think about doing (something) : CONSIDER • *They're contemplating marriage.* 3 [T] : to look carefully at (something) • *She stood and quietly contemplated the scene.* — **con·tem·pla·tion** /ˌkɑːntəmˈpleɪʃən/ *n* [U] — **con·tem·pla·tive** /kənˈtɛmplətɪv, ˈkɑːntəmˌpleɪtɪv/ *adj* • *a contemplative mood*

con·tem·po·ra·ne·ous /kənˌtɛmpəˈreɪnijəs/ *adj, formal* : existing or happening during the same time period • *contemporaneous events* — **con·tem·po·ra·ne·ous·ly** *adv*

con·tem·po·rary /kənˈtɛmpəˌreri, Brit kənˈtɛmpərəri/ *adj* 1 : happening or beginning now or in recent times • *contemporary poetry/art/furniture* 2 : existing or happening in the same time period •

contemporary events — **contemporary** *n, pl* **-rar·ies** [C] • *He was a contemporary of George Washington.* [=he lived during the same time as George Washington]

con·tempt /kənˈtɛmpt/ *n* [U, singular] 1 : a feeling that someone or something is not worthy of any respect or approval • *She has contempt for them.* = *She holds them in contempt.* • *a liar who is beneath contempt* 2 : a lack of respect for or fear of something • *He has (a) contempt for danger.* [=he is not afraid of doing dangerous things] • *She was arrested for (being in) contempt of court.* [=for acting disrespectfully toward a court or judge]

con·tempt·ible /kənˈtɛmptəbəl/ *adj* : not worthy of respect or approval • *a contemptible liar* — **con·tempt·ibly** /kənˈtɛmptəbli/ *adv*

con·temp·tu·ous /kənˈtɛmptʃəwəs/ *adj, somewhat formal* : feeling or showing deep hatred or disapproval • *a contemptuous attitude/smile/remark* — **con·temp·tu·ous·ly** *adv*

con·tend /kənˈtɛnd/ *vb* 1 [T] : to argue or state (something) in a strong and definite way • *She contends (that) the new law will only benefit the wealthy.* 2 [I] : to compete with someone or for something • *A number of groups are contending (with each other) for power.* • *The team is contending for the championship this year.* — **contend with** [*phrasal vb*] : to deal with (something difficult or unpleasant) • *Customers should not have to contend with delays.*

con·tend·er /kənˈtɛndɚ/ *n* [C] : a person who has a good chance of winning • *the top/leading presidential contenders*

[1]**con·tent** /ˈkɑːnˌtɛnt/ *n* 1 [*plural*] : the things that are in something • *He emptied the contents of the package/box/drawer onto the floor.* ✧ A **table of contents** is a list at the beginning of some books that shows how the book is divided into sections and at which page each section begins. 2 [U] : the ideas, facts, or images that are in a book, movie, etc. • *a summary of the book's content* • *movies with violent content* 3 [U] : the amount of something that is in something else • *the fat/fiber content of food* — compare [4]CONTENT

[2]**con·tent** /kənˈtɛnt/ *adj, not before a noun* : pleased and satisfied • *I don't need more. I'm content with what I have.* • *She's content to stay out of the spotlight.* — **con·tent·ment** /kənˈtɛntmənt/ *n* [U] • *finding peace and contentment in living simply*

[3]**con·tent** /kənˈtɛnt/ *vb* [T] *formal* : to make (someone) pleased and satisfied • *The weather was rainy, so we had to content ourselves with* [=had to be satisfied with] *a relaxing day at home.*

[4]**con·tent** /kənˈtɛnt/ *n* [U] : a feeling of being pleased and satisfied • *There was a look of perfect content* [=contentment] *on his face.* — compare [1]CONTENT

con·tent·ed /kənˈtɛntəd/ *adj* : happy and satisfied • *a contented smile/child* — **con·tent·ed·ly** *adv*

con·ten·tion /kənˈtɛnʃən/ *n* 1 [C] : something that is argued or stated • *It is* *her contention that the new law will only benefit the wealthy.* **2** [*U*] : anger and disagreement • *a point/source of contention = a bone of contention • an issue that is still in contention* [=still being argued about] **3** [*U*] : a situation in which you have a chance to win something that you are trying to win • *The loss means that she's now out of contention for the world title.* • *He is in contention for the Olympic medal.*

con·ten·tious /kənˈtɛnʃəs/ *adj* **1 a** : likely to cause people to argue or disagree • *a contentious topic/issue* **b** : involving a lot of arguing • *a contentious debate* **2** : likely or willing to argue • *a contentious student* — **con·ten·tious·ly** *adv* — **con·ten·tious·ness** *n* [*U*]

¹**con·test** /ˈkɑːnˌtɛst/ *n* [*C*] **1** : an event in which people try to win by doing something better than others • *a fishing/singing contest • a contest to see who can jump highest* **2** : a struggle or effort to win or get something • *She hopes to win the contest for mayor.* — **no contest 1** *informal* — used to say that someone or something is much better than another or can easily defeat another • *It's no contest. The book is much better than the movie.* **2** *US* : a statement in a court of law in which someone who has been charged with a crime does not admit guilt but also does not dispute the charge • *He pleaded no contest to (the charge of) driving while intoxicated.*

²**con·test** /kənˈtɛst/ *vb* **1** [*T*] : to make (something) the subject of an argument or a legal case • *contest a will • contest the results of an election* **2** [*T*] : to try to win (something) • *a hotly/bitterly contested election* **3** [*I*] : to struggle or fight for or against something • *contesting for power*

con·test·ant /kənˈtɛstənt/ *n* [*C*] : a person who takes part in a contest • *a game-show contestant*

con·text /ˈkɑːnˌtɛkst/ *n* [*C/U*] **1** : the words that are used with a certain word or phrase and that help to explain its meaning • *Use the word in context.* [=in a sentence with other words] ◇ If the words that someone has said are taken or quoted *out of context,* they are repeated without explaining the situation in which they were said so that their meaning is changed. **2** : the group of conditions that exist where and when something happens • *The book puts the events in their proper historical and social contexts.* — **con·tex·tu·al** /kənˈtɛkstʃəwəl/ *adj* • *contextual information* — **con·tex·tu·al·ly** *adv*

con·tig·u·ous /kənˈtɪgjəwəs/ *adj, formal* : touching or immediately next to each other • *the 48 contiguous states in the U.S.*

con·ti·nent /ˈkɑːntənənt/ *n* **1** [*C*] : one of the great divisions of land (such as North America, South America, Europe, Asia, Australia, or Antarctica) of the Earth **2 the Continent** *chiefly Brit* : the countries of Europe except for Great Britain and Ireland

¹**con·ti·nen·tal** /ˌkɑːntəˈnɛntl̩/ *adj* **1** : of, relating to, or located on a continent • *the continental U.S.* [=the part of the U.S.

that is on the North American continent] **2** *Continental* : of or relating to the countries of Europe except for Great Britain and Ireland • *Continental Europe* **3** : characteristic of Europe • *The hotel combines American comfort with continental elegance.*

²**continental** *n* [*C*] *Brit, somewhat old-fashioned* : a person from Continental Europe

continental breakfast *n* [*C*] : a light breakfast in a hotel, restaurant, etc., that usually includes baked goods, jam, fruit, and coffee

con·tin·gen·cy /kənˈtɪndʒənsi/ *n, pl* **-cies** [*C*] : something (such as an emergency) that might happen • *trying to plan for any contingency • a contingency plan* [=a plan that can be followed if an original plan is not possible for some reason]

¹**con·tin·gent** /kənˈtɪndʒənt/ *adj, formal* : depending on something else that might or might not happen • *Our plans are contingent on/upon the weather.*

²**contingent** *n* [*C*] : a group of people who go to a place together, do something together, or share some quality, interest, etc. • *The largest contingent of voters in the area is the elderly.* • *A British contingent was sent to assist the security forces.*

con·tin·u·al /kənˈtɪnjuwəl/ *adj* **1** : happening without stopping • *continual sunshine • a continual state of war* **2** : happening again and again within short periods of time • *continual interruptions* — **con·tin·u·al·ly** *adv*

con·tin·u·ance /kənˈtɪnjuwəns/ *n, formal* **1** [*U*] : the act of continuing for a long period of time • *the continuance* [=continuation] *of good relations between the two countries* **2** [*U*] : the period of time when something continues • *No changes are allowed during the continuance of the lease.* **3** [*C*] *US* : a legal decision that a court case will continue at a later date

con·tin·u·a·tion /kənˌtɪnjəˈweɪʃən/ *n* **1** [*C*] : something that starts where something else ends and adds to or continues the first part • *The book is a continuation of her first novel.* **2** [*C/U*] : the act of continuing or of causing something to continue • *the continuation of therapy*

con·tin·ue /kənˈtɪnju/ *vb* **-ued; -u·ing** **1** [*T/I*] : to do or keep doing something without stopping or changing • *She should continue with her studies.* • *Do you plan to continue working?* = *Do you plan to continue to work?* • *I continue to believe* [=I still believe] *that we can win.* • *She will continue as director* [=stay in her job as the director] *for another year.* • *We are thankful for your continuing support.* **2** [*I*] : to keep happening or existing • *The good weather continued for several days.* • *I'm surprised by the film's continuing popularity.* • *Please accept our best wishes for your continued success.* **3** [*I*] **a** : to go or move ahead in the same direction • *continue along a path/road* **b** : to go onward • *The plot gets more intricate as the story continues.* **4** [*T/I*] : to start again after an interruption or pause • *The article continues on the next page.* • *We will* *continue (on) our journey in the morning.* • *The teacher continued (talking) only when all the students were quiet.*

con·tin·u·ing education n [U] : classes taken by adult students usually in the evenings — called also *continuing ed, adult education*

con·ti·nu·i·ty /ˌkɑntə'nuːwəti, Brit ˌkɒntə'njuːəti/ n [U] **1** : the quality or state of being continuous • *maintaining continuity of effort* **2** : the arrangement of the parts in a story, movie, etc., in a way that is logical • *a problem with the movie's continuity*

con·tin·u·ous /kən'tɪnjuwəs/ adj **1** : happening or existing without stopping or changing • *a continuous stream of air* • *a continuous line of traffic* • *continuous use/effort* **2** grammar : PROGRESSIVE **4** • *The phrases "am seeing" and "had been seeing" are in continuous tenses.* — **con·tin·u·ous·ly** adv

con·tin·u·um /kən'tɪnjuwəm/ n, pl **-tin·ua** /-juwə/ also **-tin·u·ums** [C] formal : a range or series of things that are slightly different from each other and that exist between two different possibilities • *a continuum of temperatures ranging from very cold to very hot*

con·tort /kən'toət/ vb [T/I] : to twist into an unusual appearance or shape • *His body contorted with/in pain.* • *Her face was contorted with/in rage.* — **con·tor·tion** /kən'toəʃən/ n [C/U] • *body contortions*

con·tor·tion·ist /kən'toəʃənɪst/ n [C] : a performer who twists his or her body into unusual positions

con·tour /'kɑːnˌtuə/ n [C] : the outline or outer edge of something • *the sleek/smooth contours of the car*

con·toured /'kɑːnˌtuəd/ adj **1** : shaped to fit the outline of something • *the contoured seats of the car* • *a dress with a contoured waist* **2** : having a smooth shape or outer edge • *a nicely contoured vase*

con·tra·band /'kɑːntrəˌbænd/ n [U] : things that are brought into or out of a country illegally

con·tra·cep·tion /ˌkɑːntrə'sɛpʃən/ n [U] : BIRTH CONTROL

con·tra·cep·tive /ˌkɑːntrə'sɛptɪv/ n [C] : a drug or device that is used to prevent a woman from becoming pregnant — **contraceptive** adj • *a contraceptive device/pill*

¹**con·tract** /'kɑːnˌtrækt/ n **1 a** [C/U] : a legal agreement between people, companies, etc. • *If he breaks the contract, he will get sued.* • *contract negotiations* • *She's under contract with the company for three more years.* **b** [C] : a document on which the words of a contract are written • *sign a contract* **2** [C] informal : an agreement to kill a person for money • *His enemies put/took out a contract on him.* [=paid someone to kill him]

²**con·tract** /kən'trækt/ vb **1** [T/I] : to become smaller or make (something) smaller or shorter • *The metal contracts as it cools.* • *contract a muscle* **2** [T] : to become ill with (a disease) • *He contracted a cold.* **3** [T/I] : to agree to work or to pay someone to work according to the

terms stated in a contract • *The carpenter contracted (with them) to do the work on their house.* • *We contracted a lawyer.* **4** /'kɑːnˌtrækt/ [T] formal : to agree to (a marriage, an alliance, etc.) formally • *a legally contracted marriage* — **contract out** /'kɑːnˌtrækt/ [phrasal vb] **contract out (something) out** or **contract out (something)** : to agree to pay someone to perform a job according to the terms stated in a contract • *The company contracted out its manufacturing jobs.*

con·trac·tion /kən'trækʃən/ n **1** [U] : the act or process of making something smaller or of becoming smaller • *The metal undergoes contraction as it cools.* **2** [C] : a movement of a muscle that causes it to become tight and that is sometimes painful; *especially* : a movement of muscles in the womb when a woman is giving birth to a child **3** [C] : a short form of a word or word group that is made by leaving out a sound or letter • *The word "don't" is a contraction of "do not."*

con·trac·tor /'kɑːnˌtræktə/ n [C] : a person who is hired to perform work or to provide goods at a certain price or within a certain time

con·trac·tu·al /kən'træktʃəwəl/ adj : of or relating to the things that are required by a contract • *contractual requirements* — **con·trac·tu·al·ly** adv

con·tra·dict /ˌkɑːntrə'dɪkt/ vb [T] **1** : to say the opposite of (something) : to deny the truth of (something) • *contradict a rumor* **2** : to deny or disagree with what is being said by (someone) • *She doesn't like being contradicted.* • *He contradicted himself.* [=made a statement that disagreed with what he said earlier] **3** : to not agree with (something) in a way that shows or suggests that it is false, wrong, etc. • *The evidence contradicts his testimony.* — **con·tra·dic·tion** /ˌkɑːntrə'dɪkʃən/ n [C/U] • *a contradiction between statements* • *What he said yesterday is in direct contradiction to what he said today.* • *I think "working vacation" is a contradiction in terms.* [=a phrase having words with opposite or different meanings] — **con·tra·dic·to·ry** /ˌkɑːntrə'dɪktəri/ adj • *contradictory statements*

con·tral·to /kən'træltou/ n, pl **-tos** [C] : the lowest female singing voice; *also* : a female singer with such a voice

con·trap·tion /kən'træpʃən/ n [C] : a piece of equipment or machinery that is unusual or strange

con·trar·i·an /kən'treɪriən/ n [C] : a person who takes an opposite or different position or attitude

¹**con·trary** /'kɑːnˌtreri, Brit 'kɑːntrəri/ n — **on the contrary** also **quite the contrary** — used to state that the opposite of what was said before is true • *The test will not be easy; on the contrary, it will be very difficult.* — **the contrary** : an opposite or different fact, event, or situation • *He was sure he was right, but the contrary was true: she was right and he was wrong.* — **to the contrary** : stating or proving the opposite of something • *He was no fool, despite talk to the contrary.*

²**con·trary** /ˈkɑːnˌtreri, Brit ˈkɑːntrəri/ adj
1 : opposite to or different from something else • contrary answers/opinions •
*Contrary to popular belief, these animals
are not dangerous to humans.* **2** : against
or opposed to something • *Going over the
speed limit is contrary to traffic laws.* **3**
: not favorable or helpful • *The boat
sailed against a contrary wind.* **4** /kən-
ˈtreri/ : unwilling to obey or behave well
• *a contrary child* — **con·trar·i·ly** /kən-
ˈtrerəli/ adv — **con·trar·i·ness** /kən-
ˈtrerinəs/ n [U]

¹**con·trast** /kənˈtræst, Brit kənˈtrɑːst/ vb
1 [I] : to be very different • *contrasting
opinions/colors* • *Her black dress contrasts
with the white background.* **2** [T] : to
compare (people or things) to show how
they are different • *His essay contrasted
his life in America with/to his life in India.* —
con·trast·ing·ly adv

²**con·trast** /ˈkɑːnˌtræst, Brit ˈkɒnˌtrɑːst/ n
1 [C] : something that is different from
another thing • *Today's weather is quite a
contrast to yesterday's.* **2** [C/U] : a difference
between people or things that
are being compared • *a contrast in teaching
styles* • *the contrasts between the books*
• **His comments were in stark/marked/
sharp contrast with/to** [=very different
from] *his earlier statements.* **3** [U] : the
act of comparing people or things to
show the differences between them • *In
contrast to/with last year's profits, the
company is not doing very well.* • *The
queen's wit and humor made the prince
seem dull by contrast.* **4** [U] : the difference
between the dark and light parts of
a painting or photograph • *a picture with
a lot of contrast*

con·tra·vene /ˌkɑːntrəˈviːn/ vb **-vened;
-ven·ing** [T] formal : to fail to do what is
required by (a law or rule) • *The crowded
club contravened safety regulations.* —
con·tra·ven·tion /ˌkɑːntrəˈvɛnʃən/ n
[C/U] • *(a) contravention of school policy*

con·trib·ute /kənˈtrɪbjuːt/ vb **-ut·ed; -ut·
ing** [T/I] **1** : to give (money, goods,
time, etc.) to help a person, group, cause,
or organization • *He contributed (100 dollars)
to the charity.* • *The volunteers contributed
their time towards cleaning up the
city.* **2** [I] : to help to cause something
to happen • *Many players have contributed
to the team's success.* • *Heavy drinking
contributed to her death.* = *Heavy drinking
was a contributing factor in her death.* **3**
[T/I] : to write (something) for a magazine
• *He contributed (many poems) to the
magazine.* • *a contributing writer/editor*
— **con·tri·bu·tion** /ˌkɑːntrəˈbjuːʃən/ n
[C/U] • *a 100-dollar contribution to breast
cancer research* • *voluntary contribution*
— **con·trib·u·tor** /kənˈtrɪbjətə/ n [C]
— **con·trib·u·to·ry** /kənˈtrɪbjəˌtori,
Brit kənˈtrɪbjətri/ adj, always before a
noun • *Car exhaust is a major contributory
factor in air pollution.*

con·trite /ˈkɑːnˌtraɪt, kənˈtraɪt/ adj, formal
: feeling or showing regret for bad
behavior • *a contrite criminal/apology* —
con·trite·ly adv — **con·tri·tion** /kən-
ˈtrɪʃən/ n [U] • *Her tears were a sign of
contrition.*

con·triv·ance /kənˈtraɪvəns/ n **1** [C/U]
usually disapproving : something that
causes things to happen in a story in a
way that does not seem natural or believable
• *a plot contrivance* **2** [C] : a machine
or piece of equipment • *a clever
contrivance* **3** [C/U] : a clever plan or
trick • *a contrivance to get out of doing the
work*

con·trive /kənˈtraɪv/ vb **-trived; -triv·
ing** [T] **1** : to form or think of (something)
• *Natives invented weapons out of
stone, wood, and bone.* • *The prisoners
contrived a way to escape.* **2** : to make
(something) happen in a clever way or
with difficulty • *He contrived (to arrange)
a meeting with the president.*

contrived adj : having an unnatural or
false appearance or quality • *The movie's
contrived ending was a big disappointment.*

¹**con·trol** /kənˈtroʊl/ vb **-trolled; -trol·
ling** [T] **1** : to cause (a person or animal)
to do what you want • *The parents
could not control their child.* **2** : to have
power over (something) • *Her family controls
the business.* **3 a** : to cause (something)
to act or function in a certain way
• *The lights are controlled by a computer.*
b : to set or adjust the amount, degree,
or rate of (something) • *He controlled the
volume by turning the radio's knob.* **4**
: to limit the amount or growth of
(something) • *using insecticides to control
pests* • *controlling pollution* **5 a** : to keep
(emotions, desires, etc.) from becoming
too strong or from being shown • *Please
control your temper.* [=keep yourself
calm] • *He tried hard to control his laughter.*
b : to keep or make (yourself) calm
• *He couldn't control himself any longer.*
— **con·trol·la·ble** /kənˈtroʊləbəl/ adj

²**control** n **1** [U] : the power to make decisions
• *I have no control over what happens.*
• *He took control of the family farm.*
• *The market is in/under the control of
three companies.* [=is controlled by three
companies] • *He always wants to be in
control.* [=to be the one who makes decisions]
• *She is in control of the sales department.*
• *The weather is not in/under
our control. = The weather is beyond our
control.* **2** [U] : the ability to direct the
actions of someone or something • *muscle
control* • *a teacher with good control of
her students* • *He felt calm and in control
(of himself).* • *The driver lost control (of
the car) and hit a tree.* • *He lost control (of
himself) and yelled at his students.* ✧ If
people or things are **out of control**, they
cannot be handled or managed with success.
✧ If people or things are **under control**,
they can be handled or managed
with success. • *She remained calm and
kept the situation under control.* **3** [C/U]
: an action, method, or law that limits
the amount or growth of something •
pest/price controls • *They want stricter
control on immigration.* **4** [C] : a device
or piece of equipment used to operate a
machine, vehicle, or system • *the volume
control on a television* • *a control panel* •
The copilot was at the controls. [=controlling
the plane] — see also REMOTE

CONTROL **5** [*singular*] : the group of people who direct or control something (such as the flight of an aircraft) ▪ *pilots communicating with air traffic control* ▪ *a control tower/room*

control freak *n* [C] *informal* : a person who has a strong need to control people or things

con·trolled /kənˈtroʊld/ *adj* **1** : not overly angry or emotional ▪ *They talked in a calm, controlled manner.* **2** : done or organized according to certain rules, instructions, or procedures ▪ *living in a controlled environment* **3** — used to describe a drug that is illegal to have or use without permission from a doctor ▪ *a controlled drug/substance*

con·trol·ler /kənˈtroʊlɚ/ *n* [C] **1** : a person who is in charge of the money received and paid out by a business or college **2** : a person who directs the action of something ▪ *an air traffic controller* **3** : a device or piece of equipment used to operate a machine, vehicle, or system ▪ *a volume controller*

con·tro·ver·sial /ˌkɑːntrəˈvɚʃəl/ *adj* : relating to or causing much discussion, disagreement, or argument ▪ *a highly controversial subject/author* — **con·tro·ver·sial·ly** *adv*

con·tro·ver·sy /ˈkɑːntrəˌvɚsi, *Brit* ˈkɒntrəˌvɜːsi, kənˈtrɒvəsi/ *n, pl* **-sies** [C/U] : strong disagreement about something among a large group of people ▪ *There is (a) controversy over the new law.*

con·tu·sion /kənˈtuːʒən, *Brit* kənˈtjuːʒən/ *n* [C] : ¹BRUISE 1 ▪ *leg contusions*

co·nun·drum /kəˈnʌndrəm/ *n* [C] : a confusing or difficult problem ▪ *an ethical conundrum*

con·ur·ba·tion /ˌkɑːnɚˈbeɪʃən/ *n* [C] *chiefly Brit* : a large area of cities or towns with very little room between them

con·va·lesce /ˌkɑːnvəˈlɛs/ *vb* **-lesced; -lesc·ing** [I] : to become healthy and strong again after illness, weakness, or injury ▪ *He is convalescing from his leg injuries.* — **con·va·les·cence** /ˌkɑːnvəˈlɛsns/ *n* [U, singular] ▪ *a period of convalescence*

con·va·les·cent /ˌkɑːnvəˈlɛsnt/ *adj* : going through or used for the process of becoming well again after an illness or injury ▪ *convalescent patients* ▪ *a convalescent hospital ward* — **convalescent** *n* [C] ▪ *a hospital ward for convalescents*

con·vec·tion /kənˈvɛkʃən/ *n* [U] *technical* : movement in a gas or liquid in which the warmer parts move up and the colder parts move down ▪ *foods cooked by convection*

convection oven *n* [C] : an oven with a fan that moves hot air around so that food cooks evenly

con·vene /kənˈviːn/ *vb* **-vened; -ven·ing** [T/I] : to come together in a group for a meeting ▪ *The students convened in the gym.* ▪ *convene a meeting*

con·ve·nience /kənˈviːnjəns/ *n* **1** [U] : a quality or situation that makes something easy or useful for someone ▪ *I enjoy the convenience of living on campus.* ▪ *For*

your convenience, you can pay your bills over the Internet. **2** [U] : a time that is appropriate for doing something or that is suitable for someone ▪ *I'll be happy to meet with you at your convenience.* **3** [C] : something that makes you more comfortable or allows you to do things more easily ▪ *modern conveniences* ▪ *Frozen pizza is a popular convenience food.*

convenience store *n* [C] *chiefly US* : a small store that is open for many hours of the day

con·ve·nient /kənˈviːnjənt/ *adj* **1** : allowing you to do something easily or without trouble ▪ *a convenient time/location* ▪ *It is more convenient to use a calculator.* **2** : located in a place that is nearby and easy to get to ▪ *a convenient drugstore* **3** : giving you a reason to do something that you want to do ▪ *The power failure was a convenient excuse to leave work early.* — **con·ve·nient·ly** *adv*

con·vent /ˈkɑːnvənt/ *n* [C] : a group of nuns who live together or the house or buildings that they live in

con·ven·tion /kənˈvɛnʃən/ *n* **1** [C] : a large meeting of people who come to a place to do work, make decisions, discuss their interests, etc. ▪ *the weeklong annual teachers' convention* **2** [C/U] : a custom or a way of acting or doing things that is widely accepted and followed ▪ *the conventions of punctuation* ▪ *artistic/social conventions* ▪ *a director who has always defied convention* [=done unexpected or unusual things] *in his movies* **3** [C] *formal* : a formal agreement between two groups ▪ *an international convention banning the spread of nuclear weapons*

con·ven·tion·al /kənˈvɛnʃənəl/ *adj* **1** : used, accepted, or done by most people : usual, common, or traditional ▪ *conventional methods/views* ▪ *conventional detective stories* **2** *always before a noun* : not nuclear ▪ *conventional weapons/warfare* — **con·ven·tion·al·i·ty** /kənˌvɛnʃəˈnæləti/ *n* [C] — **con·ven·tion·al·ly** *adv*

con·verge /kənˈvɚdʒ/ *vb* **-verged; -verg·ing** [I] : to come together and meet ▪ *The two roads converge in the center of town.* ▪ *Six police cars converged on the accident scene.* — **con·ver·gence** /kənˈvɚdʒəns/ *n* [U] — **con·ver·gent** /kənˈvɚdʒənt/ *adj* ▪ *convergent lines*

con·ver·sant /kənˈvɚsənt/ *adj, not before a noun* **1** *formal* : having knowledge about or experience with something ▪ *He is conversant with* [=familiar with] *the facts of the case.* **2** *US* : able to talk in a foreign language ▪ *conversant in several languages*

con·ver·sa·tion /ˌkɑːnvɚˈseɪʃən/ *n* [C/U] : an informal talk involving two people or a small group of people ▪ *a casual/telephone/private conversation* ▪ *The topic came up in conversation.* ▪ *They were deep in conversation.* ▪ *a perfect spot to have/hold a quiet conversation* [=talk quietly] ▪ *She was trying to make conversation.* [=start a conversation] — **con·ver·sa·tion·al** /ˌkɑːnvɚˈseɪʃənl/ *adj* ▪ *conversa-*

tional skills — **con·ver·sa·tion·al·ly** adv

con·ver·sa·tion·al·ist /ˌkɑːnvəˈseɪʃənlɪst/ n [C] : a person who likes or is good at conversation • *a good/lively/witty conversationalist*

¹**con·verse** /kənˈvɚs/ vb -versed; -versing [I] formal : to talk usually informally with someone • *They conversed (with each other) in Spanish.*

²**con·verse** /ˈkɑːnˌvɚs/ n — **the converse** formal : something that is the opposite of something else • *They need our help, but the converse is also true: we need their help as well.*

³**con·verse** /kənˈvɚs, ˈkɑːnˌvɚs/ adj, formal : opposite or reverse • *a converse effect* — **con·verse·ly** adv

con·ver·sion /kənˈvɚʒən, Brit kənˈvɚːʃən/ n 1 [C/U] **a** : the act or process of changing from one form, state, etc., to another • *(a) conversion of the old school into apartments* **b** : the act or process of changing from one religion, belief, political party, etc., to another • *(a) conversion from Catholicism to Judaism* 2 [C] : a successful attempt at scoring extra points in rugby or American football • *a 2-point conversion*

¹**con·vert** /kənˈvɚt/ vb [T/I] 1 : to change into or to something different • *convert light to energy* • *convert pounds to grams* • *We converted the attic into a bedroom.* • *The sofa converts into a bed.* 2 : to change or persuade (someone) to change from one religion, belief, etc., to another • *He converted to Islam.* • *They tried to convert us to their way of thinking.* 3 sports : to use (an opportunity, such as an opportunity to score points) successfully • *They failed to convert (the field goal).*

²**con·vert** /ˈkɑːnˌvɚt/ n [C] : a person who has changed to a different religion, belief, etc. • *a religious convert*

con·vert·er also **con·vert·or** /kənˈvɚtɚ/ n [C] : a piece of equipment that changes radio signals, radio frequencies, data, etc., from one form to another — see also CATALYTIC CONVERTER

¹**con·vert·ible** /kənˈvɚtəbəl/ adj : able to be changed into another form • *The bonds are convertible into stock.* — **con·vert·ibil·i·ty** /kənˌvɚtəˈbɪləti/ n [U]

²**convertible** n [C] : a car with a roof that can be lowered or removed

con·vex /kɑnˈvɛks, ˈkɑːnˌvɛks/ adj : having a shape like the outside of a bowl : curving outward • *a convex lens* — **con·vex·i·ty** /kənˈvɛksəti/ n, pl -ties [C/U]

con·vey /kənˈveɪ/ vb [T] 1 formal : to take or carry (someone or something) from one place to another • *She was conveyed from her hotel to the airport by limousine.* • *The pipes convey water to the fields.* 2 : to make (something) known to someone • *Words convey meaning.* • *Her appearance conveys self-confidence.*

con·vey·ance /kənˈveɪəns/ n, formal 1 [U] : the act of conveying someone or something • *the conveyance of goods/passengers/meaning* 2 [C] : something that carries people or things from one place

to another • *public conveyances*

con·vey·or also **con·vey·er** /kənˈveɪɚ/ n [C] : someone or something that conveys something • *the conveyor of good news*; especially : a long strip of material that moves continuously and carries packages, luggage, etc., from one place to another — called also *conveyor belt*

¹**con·vict** /kənˈvɪkt/ vb [T/I] : to prove that someone is guilty of a crime in a court of law • *There is sufficient evidence to convict (her).* • *a convicted criminal*

²**con·vict** /ˈkɑːnˌvɪkt/ n [C] : a person who has been found guilty of a crime and sent to prison

con·vic·tion /kənˈvɪkʃən/ n 1 [C/U] : the act of proving that a person is guilty of a crime in a court of law • *In light of the evidence, (a) conviction seems certain.* • *drunk-driving convictions* 2 **a** [C/U] : a strong belief or opinion • *religious convictions* **b** [U] : the feeling of being sure that what you believe or say is true • *She spoke with conviction.*

con·vince /kənˈvɪns/ vb -vinced; -vincing [T] 1 : to cause (someone) to believe that something is true • *They convinced us of their innocence.* 2 : to cause (someone) to agree to do something • *We convinced her to stay.*

convinced adj, not before a noun : completely certain or sure about something • *I was never fully convinced of his innocence.* • *She's convinced that we're wrong.*

convincing adj 1 : causing someone to believe that something is true or certain • *a convincing argument/story* 2 : easily achieved : clearly showing that one person or team is better than the other • *a convincing victory/win* — **con·vinc·ing·ly** adv

con·viv·i·al /kənˈvɪvijəl/ adj, formal : of or relating to social events where people can eat, drink, and talk in a friendly way • *a convivial atmosphere/gathering/host* — **con·viv·i·al·i·ty** /kənˌvɪviˈæləti/ n [U]

con·vo·ca·tion /ˌkɑːnvoˈkeɪʃən/ n, formal 1 [C] : a large formal meeting of people 2 [U] : the act of calling a group of people to a formal meeting

con·voke /kənˈvoʊk/ vb -voked; -voking [T] formal : to call a group of people to a formal meeting • *The assembly was convoked for a special session.*

con·vo·lut·ed /ˈkɑːnvəˌluːtəd/ adj : very complicated and difficult to understand • *convoluted logic* • *a convoluted plot*

¹**con·voy** /ˈkɑːnˌvɔɪ/ n [C/U] : a group of vehicles or ships that are traveling together usually for protection • *a military convoy*

²**convoy** vb [T] formal : to travel with and protect (someone or something) • *The tankers were convoyed by warships.*

con·vulse /kənˈvʌls/ vb -vulsed; -vulsing [T/I] : to shake in a sudden violent way that you are not able to control • *The patient began convulsing.* • *(figurative) The audience (was) convulsed with laughter.*

con·vul·sion /kənˈvʌlʃən/ n [C] 1 medical : a sudden violent shaking of your muscles that you are unable to control • *He suddenly went into convulsions.* •

(figurative) The joke sent the audience into **convulsions** *of laughter.* **2** : a sudden change or disturbance ▪ *an era of political convulsions*

con·vul·sive /kən'vʌlsɪv/ *adj* **1** : involving or causing a sudden violent shaking of your muscles that you are unable to control ▪ *a convulsive seizure/disorder* **2** : causing the entire body to shake ▪ *convulsive laughter* — **con·vul·sive·ly** *adv*

coo /'ku:/ *vb* **1** [*I*] : to make the soft sound of a dove or pigeon; *also* : to make a similar sound ▪ *The baby cooed quietly.* **2** [*T/I*] : to talk in a soft, quiet, and loving way ▪ *They all cooed over the baby pictures.* — **coo** *n* [*C*]

¹**cook** /'kʊk/ *n* [*C*] : someone who prepares and cooks food for eating at home, in a restaurant, etc. ▪ *He's a good cook.*

²**cook** *vb* **1** [*T/I*] : to prepare (food) for eating especially by using heat ▪ *Cook the onions over low heat.* ▪ *She cooked a great meal.* ▪ *I'll cook tonight.* **2** [*I*] : to go through the process of being cooked ▪ *The rice is still cooking.* — **be cooking** *informal* **1** : to be happening ▪ *What's cooking?* ▪ *There's something cooking, but he won't say what.* **2** : to be performing or doing something well ▪ *That's it! Now you're cooking!* — **cook someone's goose** *informal* : to make it certain that someone will fail, lose, etc. ▪ *That last goal really cooked their goose.* — **cook the books** *informal* : to dishonestly change official records of how much money was spent and received — **cook up** [*phrasal vb*] **cook up (something)** *or* **cook (something) up** **1** : to prepare (food) for eating especially quickly ▪ *I cooked up some hamburgers.* **2** : to invent (an idea, excuse, etc.) to deal with a particular situation ▪ *They cooked up a scheme to fool their neighbor.*

cook·book /'kʊkˌbʊk/ *n* [*C*] *chiefly US* : a book of cooking recipes and directions — called also (*Brit*) *cookery book*

cook·er /'kʊkɚ/ *n* [*C*] **1** *US* : a piece of equipment that is used to cook food ▪ *a* **slow cooker** [=an electric pot that slowly cooks food] — see also PRESSURE COOKER **2** *Brit* : ¹RANGE 10 ▪ *a gas cooker*

cook·ery /'kʊkəri/ *n* [*U*] : the art or activity of cooking food

cook·ie /'kʊki/ *n* [*C*] *chiefly US* : a small, sweet, flat baked food that is made from flour and sugar — see also FORTUNE COOKIE **2** *informal* : PERSON ▪ *She's a tough/smart cookie.* **3** : a file that may be added to your computer when you visit a Web site and that contains information about you (such as an identification code or a record of the Web pages you have visited) — **that's the way the cookie crumbles** *informal* — used when something bad has happened to say that you must accept things the way they are ▪ *I'm disappointed that I didn't get the job, but that's the way the cookie crumbles.*

cookie cutter *n* [*C*] *chiefly US* : a metal or plastic object that is used to make cookies that have a certain shape

cookie–cutter *adj*, *US*, *disapproving*

: very similar to other things of the same kind : not original or different ▪ *cookie-cutter houses*

cookie sheet *n* [*C*] *chiefly US* : BAKING SHEET

¹**cooking** *n* [*U*] **1** : the act of preparing and cooking food ▪ *I do most of the cooking in our house.* **2** : food that is cooked ▪ *Don't you like my cooking?* ▪ **home cooking** [=food cooked at home]

²**cooking** *adj*, *always before a noun* : suitable for or used in cooking : involving or having to do with cooking ▪ *Cooking time is about 20 minutes.* ▪ *cooking methods* ▪ *cooking oil*

cook·out /'kʊkˌaʊt/ *n* [*C*] *US* : a meal or party at which food is cooked and served outdoors

cook·top /'kʊkˌtɑːp/ *n* [*C*] *US* : a flat piece of equipment for cooking that is built into a kitchen countertop and that usually has four devices (called burners) that become hot when turned on

cook·ware /'kʊkˌweɚ/ *n* [*U*] : the pots, pans, etc., that are used in cooking

¹**cool** /'ku:l/ *adj* **1** : somewhat cold : not warm or hot ▪ *a cool breeze/drink* ▪ *The weather is cool today.* **2** : made of a light, thin material that helps you stay cool ▪ *cool clothes* **3** : able to think and act in a calm way ▪ *It's important to keep a cool head* [=remain calm] *in a crisis.* = *It's important to keep/stay cool in a crisis.* ❖ *If you are (as) cool as a cucumber, you are very calm and able to think clearly often in a difficult situation.* **4** : not friendly ▪ *a cool reply/reception* ▪ *She is cool toward strangers.* **5** *informal* **a** : very fashionable, stylish, or appealing in a way that is generally approved of especially by young people ▪ *cool sunglasses* ▪ *You look cool in those jeans.* ▪ *"I got a job as a lifeguard this summer." "Cool."* **b** — used to suggest acceptance, agreement, or understanding ▪ *"Is getting together Friday cool with you?" "Yeah, I'm cool with that."* **6** : suggesting cool things ▪ *Blue is a cool color.* **7** *informal* — used for emphasis in referring to a large amount of money ▪ *He's worth a cool million.* — **cool·ly** *adv* ▪ *"Is that so?" she asked coolly.* ▪ *My idea was received coolly.* — **cool·ness** *n* [*U*]

²**cool** *vb* [*T/I*] **1** : to make (someone or something) cool or to become cool ▪ *The fan cools the engine.* ▪ *Allow the cake to cool before slicing.* ▪ *The weather has cooled off/down a little.* ▪ *the car's cooling system* ▪ *the cooling of the ocean waters* **2** : to become less strong or intense or to make (an emotion) less strong or intense ▪ *His interest in her has cooled somewhat.* ▪ *His friends tried to cool him off/down.* [=calm him down] — **cool it** *informal* : to stop being excited, angry, noisy, etc. ▪ *They were being too noisy, so he told them to cool it.* — **cool your heels** see ¹HEEL

³**cool** *n* — **keep your cool** *also chiefly US* **maintain your cool** *informal* : to remain calm — **lose your cool** *also US* **blow your cool** *informal* : to suddenly become very angry ▪ *He lost his cool and yelled at me.* — **the cool** : a cool time or

cool • copious

place • *the cool of the evening/night*

⁴cool *adv, informal* : in a calm manner • *Here comes Mom. Act cool and she won't suspect a thing.* • *She didn't want to seem too eager, so she tried to* **play it cool***.*

cool·ant /ˈkuːlənt/ *n* [C/U] : a liquid that is used to cool an engine or machine

cool·er /ˈkuːlɚ/ *n* **1** [C] : a container for keeping food or drinks cool **2** [C] *US* : a cold drink that usually contains alcohol • *a wine cooler* **3** *the cooler informal + somewhat old-fashioned* : a prison or jail

cool·head·ed /ˈkuːlˌhɛdəd/ *adj* : able to think and act in a calm way • *a coolheaded leader*

coon /ˈkuːn/ *n* [C] *US, informal* : RACCOON

coon·skin /ˈkuːnˌskɪn/ *n* [C/U] : the skin and fur of a raccoon • *a coonskin cap*

¹coop /ˈkuːp/ *n* [C] : a cage or small building in which chickens or other small animals are kept — **fly the coop** see ¹FLY

²coop *vb* — **coop up** [phrasal vb] **coop up** (someone or something) or **coop** (someone or something) **up** : to keep (a person or animal) inside a building or in a small space especially for a long period of time • *We were cooped up in the house all day.*

co–op /ˈkouˌɑːp/ *n* [C] : COOPERATIVE • *a farmers' co-op*

coo·per /ˈkuːpɚ/ *n* [C] : a person who makes or repairs wooden casks or barrels

co·op·er·ate /kouˈɑːpəˌreɪt/ *vb* **-at·ed; -at·ing** [I] **1** : to work together in order to do something • *It will be much easier if everyone cooperates (with each other).* **2** : to be helpful by doing what someone asks or tells you to do • *He refused to co-operate with the police.* • *(figurative)* We can barbecue on Sunday if the weather cooperates. [=if the weather is good enough] — **co·op·er·a·tion** /kouˌɑːpəˈreɪʃən/ *n* [U] • *Thank you for your cooperation.*

¹co·op·er·a·tive /kouˈɑːprətɪv/ *adj* **1** : willing to be helpful by doing what someone wants or asks for • *a cooperative witness* **2** : involving two or more people or groups working together to do something • *a cooperative effort* — **co·op·er·a·tive·ly** *adv* — **co·op·er·a·tive·ness** *n* [U]

²cooperative *n* [C] : a business or organization that is owned and operated by the people who work there or who use its services • *the farmers' cooperative*

co–opt /kouˈɑːpt/ *vb* [T] *formal* **1** : to cause or force (someone or something) to become part of your group, movement, etc. • *The national organization has co-opted many local groups.* **2** : to use or take control of (something) for your own purposes • *Advertisers co-opted the team's slogan.*

¹co·or·di·nate /kouˈoɚdəˌneɪt/ *vb* **-nat·ed; -nat·ing** **1** [T/I] **a** : to make arrangements so that two or more people or groups can work together • *She'll be coordinating the relief effort.* • *You'll have to coordinate with the sales department.* • *a coordinated effort/attack* **b** : to work or move together properly and well •

Since his illness, he has had trouble coordinating his arms and legs. • *I would take dance lessons, but I'm not very coordinated.* **2** [T] : to cause (two or more things) to be the same or to go together well • *We need to coordinate our schedules.* **3** [I] : to look good with another color, pattern, style, etc. • *This color coordinates with your outfit.* • *coordinating styles/colors/patterns* — **co·or·di·na·tion** /kouˌoɚdəˈneɪʃən/ *n* [U] : coordination between departments • *Playing sports improves strength and coordination.* • *The FBI worked in coordination with local police.*

²co·or·di·nate /kouˈoɚdənət/ *n* [C] *technical* : one of a set of numbers that is used to locate a point on a map, graph, etc. • *latitude and longitude coordinates*

coordinating conjunction *n* [C] *grammar* : a conjunction (such as *and*, *or*, or *but*) that joins together words, phrases, or clauses of equal importance

co·or·di·na·tor /kouˈoɚdəˌneɪtɚ/ *n* [C] : a person who organizes people or groups so that they work together properly and well • *She is the program/project coordinator.*

coot /ˈkuːt/ *n* [C] **1** : a type of black and gray bird that lives on or near the water **2** *US, informal* : a strange and usually old man • *a crazy old coot*

¹cop /ˈkɑːp/ *n* [C] *informal* : POLICE OFFICER • *He threatened to call the cops.*

²cop *vb* **copped; cop·ping** [T] *informal* **1** : to get or receive (something) • *I managed to cop an invitation.* **2** *US* : to steal or take (something) • *Somebody copped my watch.* — **cop an attitude** *US, informal* : to show that you believe you are more important or better than other people by behaving in a rude or unpleasant way • *The students tried to cop an attitude with the new teacher.* — **cop a plea** *US, informal* : to admit to doing a less serious crime than the one you are accused of : to agree to a plea bargain • *Her lawyers convinced her to cop a plea.* — **cop it** *Brit, informal* : to be punished for doing something wrong — **cop out** [phrasal vb] *informal* : to not do something that you are expected to do • *She said she'd come, but then she copped out (on us) at the last minute.* — **cop to** [phrasal vb] *US slang* : to admit to doing (something) • *He agreed to cop to a misdemeanor.*

co–pay·ment /ˈkouˌpeɪmənt/ *n* [C] : an amount of money that a person with health insurance is required to pay at the time of each visit to a doctor or when purchasing medicine

cope /ˈkoup/ *vb* **coped; cop·ing** [I] : to deal with problems and difficult situations • *coping with stress*

cop·i·er /ˈkɑːpijɚ/ *n* [C] : a machine that makes paper copies of printed pages, pictures, etc.

co–pi·lot /ˈkouˌpaɪlət/ *n* [C] : a pilot who helps the main pilot operate an airplane, helicopter, etc.

co·pi·ous /ˈkoupijəs/ *adj, always before a noun* : very large in amount or number • *She took copious notes during the lecture.* — **co·pi·ous·ly** *adv*

cop–out /'kɑːˌpaʊt/ n [C] informal + disapproving : an excuse for not doing something ▪ He played poorly and used his recent illness as a cop-out.

cop·per /'kɑːpɚ/ n **1** [U] : a reddish-brown metal that allows heat and electricity to pass through it easily ▪ copper wire **2** [U] : a reddish-brown color ▪ copper hair/skin **3** [C] chiefly Brit, informal : a copper or bronze coin that has little value **4** [C] chiefly Brit, informal : POLICE OFFICER — **cop·pery** /'kɑːpəri/ adj ▪ a coppery red

cop·ter /'kɑːptɚ/ n [C] chiefly US, informal : HELICOPTER

cop·u·late /'kɑːpjəˌleɪt/ vb **-lat·ed; -lat·ing** [I] formal : to have sexual intercourse — **cop·u·la·tion** /ˌkɑːpjəˈleɪʃən/ n [U]

¹copy /'kɑːpi/ n, pl **cop·ies** **1** [C] : something that is or looks exactly or almost exactly like something else ▪ The paintings at the museum are originals, not copies. ▪ a copy of the receipt/file — see also CARBON COPY, HARD COPY **2** [C] : one of the many books, magazines, albums, DVDs, etc., that are exactly the same and are sold or given to the public ▪ The novel has sold more than a million copies. ▪ a free copy of our catalog **3** [U] : written information that is to be published in a newspaper, magazine, etc. ▪ She got a job writing advertising copy. ▪ Political scandals make **good copy**. [=interesting news stories]

²copy vb **copies; cop·ied; copy·ing** **1** [T/I] : to make a copy of (something) ▪ copy a document ▪ The page did not copy well. **2 a** [T/I] : to write (something) down exactly as it is seen or heard ▪ We caught him copying (the answers) out of the book. ▪ Are you copying this down? ▪ I copied out the equations from the book on a piece of paper. **b** [T] : to use (someone else's words or ideas) as your own ▪ The speech was copied word for word. **3** [T] **a** : to do the same thing as (someone) ▪ She's always copying her older sister. **b** : to make or do something the same way as (something else) ▪ Their competitors soon copied the idea.

copy·cat /'kɑːpiˌkæt/ n [C] **1** informal : a person who does the same thing as someone else ▪ She called me a copycat for wearing the same dress. **2** : something that is very similar to another thing ▪ a copycat crime

copy editor n [C] US : a person whose job is to prepare a book, newspaper, etc., for printing by making sure the words are correct — called also (Brit) subeditor — **copy·ed·it** /'kɑːpiˌɛdət/ vb [T] ▪ copyedit a manuscript

copy machine or **copying machine** n [C] : COPIER

¹copy·right /'kɑːpiˌraɪt/ n [C/U] : the legal right to be the only one to reproduce, publish, and sell a book, musical recording, etc., for a certain period of time ▪ His family holds the copyright to his songs. ▪ The book is under copyright.

²copyright vb [T] : to get a copyright for (something) ▪ He has copyrighted all of his plays. ▪ copyrighted materials

copy·writ·er /'kɑːpiˌraɪtɚ/ n [C] : someone whose job is to write the words for advertisements

cor·al /'korəl/ n [U] : a hard material formed on the bottom of the sea by the skeletons of small creatures

coral reef n [C] : a long line of coral that lies in warm, shallow water

cord /'koɚd/ n **1** [C/U] : material that is like a thin rope ▪ She wore the key on a cord around her neck. — see also BUNGEE CORD, RIP CORD **2** [C] : an electrical wire that is wrapped in a protective covering ▪ a telephone/lamp cord — see also EXTENSION CORD **3** [C] : a part of the body that is like a string or rope ▪ a nerve cord — see also SPINAL CORD, UMBILICAL CORD, VOCAL CORDS **4** [C] US : an amount of wood that has been cut for burning in a fireplace, stove, etc. ▪ a cord of firewood **5** [plural] : pants made of corduroy ▪ a pair of black cords

¹cor·dial /'koɚdʒəl, Brit 'kɔːdiəl/ adj : politely pleasant and friendly ▪ a cordial greeting/relationship — **cor·di·al·i·ty** /ˌkoɚdʒiˈæləti, Brit ˌkɔːdiˈæləti/ n [U] — **cor·dial·ly** adv ▪ You are cordially invited to attend the wedding of our daughter.

²cordial n [C/U] **1** US : a sweet alcoholic drink **2** Brit : a drink of heavy fruit juice that is mixed with water

cord·less /'koɚdləs/ adj : powered by a battery rather than by electricity through a cord ▪ a cordless phone/drill

¹cor·don /'koɚdn̩/ n [C] : a line of people or objects that are placed around or in front of a person or place to keep people away ▪ a cordon of police

²cordon vb — **cordon off** [phrasal vb] **cordon off (something)** or **cordon (something) off** : to form a line around or in front of (a place) to keep people away ▪ Police cordoned off the street.

cor·du·roy /'koɚdəˌroɪ/ n **1** [U] : strong cotton cloth with straight raised lines ▪ a corduroy skirt **2** [plural] : pants made of corduroy

¹core /'koɚ/ n [C] **1** : the central part of a fruit (such as an apple) that contains the seeds **2** : the central part of something ▪ the core of a golf ball ▪ the Earth's core ▪ the reactor core **3** : the most important or basic part of something ▪ Lack of money is (at) the core of the problem. ▪ The company's core business is lending money. ▪ the core vocabulary of a language — **to the core** : in a very complete or extreme way ▪ patriotic to the core ▪ He's rotten to the core. [=he's a very bad person]

²core vb **cored; cor·ing** [T] : to remove a core from (a fruit) ▪ core an apple — **cor·er** n [C]

co·ri·an·der /'koriˌændɚ/ n [U] **1** : a plant whose leaves and seeds are used in cooking **2** : the dried seed of the coriander plant used as a flavoring

¹cork /'koɚk/ n **1** [U] : a material that is made from the soft bark of a kind of oak tree **2** [C] : a piece of cork or similar material that is put in the opening of a bottle to close it ▪ the cork of a wine bottle ▪ She popped the cork on the champagne.

[=she opened the bottle of champagne by removing the cork] — **put a cork in it** *chiefly US, informal* — used as a rude way to tell someone to stop talking and especially to stop complaining

²**cork** *vb* [T] **1** : to close (something, such as a bottle) with a cork • *Please cork the wine.* **2** : to put cork inside (something, such as a baseball bat) • *a corked bat*

cork·er /ˈkoɚkɚ/ *n* [C] *informal + old-fashioned* : a very good or amusing person or thing

cork·screw /ˈkoɚkˌskruː/ *n* [C] : a tool that is used to pull corks from bottles

cor·mo·rant /ˈkoɚmərənt/ *n* [C] : a type of dark-colored bird that has a long neck and that eats fish that it catches in the ocean

corn /ˈkoɚn/ *n* **1** [U] *US* **a** : a tall plant that produces yellow seeds (called kernels) that are eaten as a vegetable, used to produce many food products, and used as food for animals — called also *maize* **b** : the seeds of the corn plant eaten as a vegetable • *a dish of buttered corn* — called also (*Brit*) *sweetcorn* **2** [U] *Brit, somewhat old-fashioned* : a plant (such as wheat or barley) that produces seeds which are used for food; *also* : the seeds of such a plant : GRAIN **3** [C] : a painful hard spot on the skin of the foot **4** [U] *US, informal* : something (such as writing, music, or acting) that is old-fashioned and silly or sentimental : something that is corny • *The movie's humor is pure corn.* [=is very corny]

corn·ball /ˈkoɚnˌbaːl/ *adj, US, informal* : old-fashioned and silly or sentimental • *a cornball sense of humor*

corn bread *n* [C/U] : bread made with cornmeal

corn·cob /ˈkoɚnˌkaːb/ *n* [C] : the long, hard, center part of corn that the kernels grow on

cor·nea /ˈkoɚnijə/ *n* [C] : the clear outer covering of the eyeball — **cor·ne·al** /ˈkoɚnijəl/ *adj*

corned beef *n* [U] : beef that has been preserved in salt water

¹**cor·ner** /ˈkoɚnɚ/ *n* [C] **1** : the point or area where two lines, edges, or sides of something meet • *the corner of a box/table/page* • *a table in a corner of the room* **2 a** : the place where two streets or roads meet • *a street corner* • *The hotel is at the corner of Fifth Avenue and 59th Street.* • *the grocery store around the corner from the bank* **b** : a curve in a road • *There is a gas station just around the corner.* [=after the curve] **3** : the side of your mouth or eye • *He said something out of the corner of his mouth.* • *I saw something out of the corner of my eye.* [=I saw something to the side of where I was looking] **4** : one of four parts of a boxing ring where the sides meet • *The boxers returned to their corners when the round ended.* • (*figurative*) *In one corner you have the music industry, and in the other, those who want music but don't want to pay for it.* • (*figurative*) *I am going to need you in my corner* [=need your help and support] *when I go to court.* **5 a** : a quiet place that few people visit • *a*

quiet corner of the town* • (*figurative*) *the dark corners of his mind* **b** : a place that is far away • *She is famous in every corner of the world.* [=throughout the world] • *People came from the four corners of the earth.* [=from places throughout the world] **6** : a position that you cannot easily get out of : a difficult situation • *The city is in a tight corner financially.* • *He backed/painted himself into a corner.* [=put himself in a bad position] **7** : CORNER KICK — **cut corners** *often disapproving* : to save time or money by doing less than you usually do or than you should do — **have/get a corner on** : to have or get enough of (something) to be able to control its price • *He has a corner on the silver market.* — **(just) around the corner** : coming or happening very soon • *Summer vacation is around the corner.* — **turn the corner** : to get past the most difficult area or period and begin to improve • *The company claims it has turned the corner and will be profitable soon.*

²**corner** *adj, always before a noun* : located at a corner • *a corner office/store*

³**corner** *vb* **1** [T] : to force (a person or animal) into a place or position from which escape is very difficult or impossible • *Police cornered the suspect in a backyard.* **2** [T] : to get control of a particular type of product that is being bought and sold • *They have cornered the market in wheat.* **3** [I] : to turn a corner • *The car corners well.*

corner kick *n* [C] *soccer* : a free kick from the corner of the field near the opponent's goal

cor·ner·stone /ˈkoɚnɚˌstoʊn/ *n* [C] **1** : a stone that forms part of a corner in a wall of a building and that often shows the date when the building was built **2** : something of basic importance • *Trust is the cornerstone of their relationship.*

cor·net /koɚˈnɛt, Brit ˈkɔːnɪt/ *n* [C] : a brass musical instrument that is similar to a trumpet but smaller

corn·flakes /ˈkoɚnˌfleɪks/ *n* [plural] : toasted flakes made from kernels of corn (sense 1) and used as a breakfast cereal

corn flour *n* [U] *Brit* : CORNSTARCH

corn·flow·er /ˈkoɚnˌflawɚ/ *n* [C] : a wild plant that usually has blue flowers

cor·nice /ˈkoɚnəs/ *n* [C] : the decorative top edge of a building, column, or wall

corn·meal /ˈkoɚnˌmiːl/ *n* [U] : a coarse flour made from crushed corn (sense 1)

corn·rows /ˈkoɚnˌroʊz/ *n* [plural] : a hairstyle in which hair is twisted together in tight rows that lie close to the skin

corn·starch /ˈkoɚnˌstaɚtʃ/ *n* [U] *US* : a fine powder made from corn (sense 1) that is used in cooking especially to make liquids thicker

corn syrup *n* [U] : a sweet, thick liquid made from corn (sense 1)

cor·nu·co·pia /ˌkoɚnəˈkoʊpijə, ˌkoɚnjəˈkoʊpijə/ *n* [singular] : a great amount or source of something • *The book includes a cornucopia of wonderful stories.*

corny /ˈkoɚni/ *adj* **corn·i·er; -est** *informal + usually disapproving* : old-fashioned and silly or sentimental • *a corny joke*

cor·ol·lary /ˈkorəˌleri, *Brit* kəˈrɒləri/ *n, pl* **-lar·ies** [C] *formal* : something that naturally follows or results from another thing • *A corollary of increased poverty is more crime.*

co·ro·na /kəˈrounə/ *n* [C] *technical* : a bright circle seen around the sun or the moon

[1]**cor·o·nary** /ˈkorəˌneri, *Brit* ˈkɒrənri/ *adj* : of or relating to the heart or the vessels that supply blood to the heart • *a coronary artery* • *coronary surgery*

[2]**coronary** *n, pl* **-nar·ies** [C] *informal* : HEART ATTACK • *I almost had a coronary when I heard the news.*

cor·o·na·tion /ˌkorəˈneiʃən/ *n* [C] : a ceremony in which a crown is placed on the head of a new king or queen

cor·o·ner /ˈkorənər/ *n* [C] : a public official whose job is to find out the cause of death when people die in ways that are violent, sudden, etc.

cor·o·net /ˌkorəˈnɛt, *Brit* ˈkɒrənit/ *n* [C] : a small crown

Corp. *abbr* corporation

corpora *plural of* CORPUS

cor·po·ral /ˈkoəpərəl/ *n* [C] : an officer in the army or marines with a rank below sergeant

corporal punishment *n* [U] : punishment that involves hitting someone • *physical punishment*

cor·po·rate /ˈkoəpərət/ *adj* **1** : involving or associated with a corporation • *corporate executives/debt* **2** : formed into a legal corporation • *The business is a corporate entity.*

cor·po·ra·tion /ˌkoəpəˈreiʃən/ *n* [C] : a large business or organization that under the law has the rights and duties of an individual and follows a specific purpose

cor·po·re·al /koəˈporijəl/ *adj, formal* : having or consisting of a physical body or form • *corporeal existence*

corps /koə/ *n, pl* **corps** /koəz/ [C] **1** : an organized part of the military • *the U.S. Marine Corps* **2** : a group of people who are involved in some activity • *members of the press corps* • *a corps of volunteers* — see also PEACE CORPS

corpse /koəps/ *n* [C] : a dead body

cor·pu·lent /ˈkoəpjələnt/ *adj, formal* : fat • *a corpulent man* — **cor·pu·lence** /ˈkoəpjələns/ *n* [U]

cor·pus /ˈkoəpəs/ *n, pl* **cor·po·ra** /ˈkoəpərə/ [C] : a collection of writings, conversations, speeches, etc., that people use to study and describe a language • *a computerized corpus of English*

cor·pus·cle /ˈkoəˌpʌsəl/ *n* [C] : a blood cell • *a red/white (blood) corpuscle*

[1]**cor·ral** /kəˈræl, *Brit* kəˈrɑːl/ *n* [C] : an area that is surrounded by a fence and used for holding animals on a farm or ranch

[2]**corral** *vb* **-ralled; -ral·ling** [T] : to gather and put (cows, horses, etc.) into a corral • *corralling cattle* • *(figurative) He corralled us into his office for a quick meeting.*

[1]**cor·rect** /kəˈrɛkt/ *adj* **1** : true or accurate : RIGHT • *the correct answer/response*

• *She is correct (in saying) that more money is needed.* **2** : having no errors or mistakes • *a grammatically correct sentence* • *correct pronunciation* **3** : proper or appropriate • *Did I give you the correct change?* • *He was correct to do what he did.* = *He did the correct thing.* **4** *sometimes disapproving* : considered proper by people with a strict set of beliefs or values • *We need to find a more environmentally correct way to dispose of these materials.* [=a way that does not damage the environment] — see also POLITICALLY CORRECT — **cor·rect·ly** *adv* — **cor·rect·ness** *n* [U]

[2]**correct** *vb* **1** [T] : to make (something) correct • *The computer program corrects spelling errors.* • *I hate it when she corrects my grammar.* ◇ To *correct someone* is to say that someone has made a mistake and to give the correct information. • *He quickly corrected himself and said that it cost two dollars, not four.* • *Correct me if I'm wrong, but I think you owe me another dollar.* ◇ The phrase *I stand corrected* is a somewhat formal way of saying that you have learned that you were wrong about something. • *I stand corrected. The meeting is on Monday, not Tuesday as I'd thought.* **2** [T] : to mark the errors on (something) • *correcting the students' tests* **3** [T] : to deal with or take care of (something) successfully • *correct a problem* • *surgery that will correct her vision* [=that will make her bad vision good/better] **4** [T/I] : to make an amount or number more accurate by considering other information • *The measurements are not accurate because I didn't correct for the change in temperature.* — **cor·rect·able** /kəˈrɛktəbəl/ *adj* • *a correctable error*

cor·rec·tion /kəˈrɛkʃən/ *n* **1** [C] : a change that makes something correct • *The teacher marked corrections on his students' tests.* • *Please make corrections before handing in your compositions.* **2** [U] : the act of correcting something • *the correction of your mistakes* • *people in need of vision correction* **3 a** [U] *old-fashioned* : the act or process of punishing and changing the behavior of criminals **b** [*plural*] *US* — used to refer to government systems and actions that relate to punishing and dealing with criminals • *the state Department of Corrections* • *a corrections officer* [=an official in a jail or prison] — **cor·rec·tion·al** /kəˈrɛkʃənl/ *adj, always before a noun, chiefly US* • *the state's correctional facilities/institutions* [=prisons or jails]

cor·rec·tive /kəˈrɛktɪv/ *adj* : meant to correct a problem : intended to make something better • *corrective surgery* • *corrective lenses, such as eyeglasses or contact lenses* — **corrective** *n* [C]

cor·re·late /ˈkorəˌleɪt/ *vb* **-lat·ed; -lat·ing** *formal* **1** [I] : to have a close connection with something ◇ If two things *correlate*, a change in one thing results in a change in the other thing. • *In general terms, brain size correlates with intelligence.* = *Generally, brain size is correlated with intelligence.* [=a larger brain generally suggests greater intelligence] **2** [T] : to show that a close connection exists between (two or more things) • There is no evidence correlating height and intelligence. — **cor·re·la·tion** /ˌkorəˈleɪʃən/ n [C/U] • a direct correlation between smoking and lung cancer

cor·re·spond /ˌkorəˈspɑːnd/ vb [I] **1** : to be similar or equal to something • The role of president corresponds to that of prime minister. **2** : to have a direct relationship to or with something • Each number corresponds to a location on the map. • His statements do not correspond with the facts. [=do not match the facts] **3** somewhat formal : to write to someone or to each other • We haven't corresponded (with each other) in years.

cor·re·spon·dence /ˌkorəˈspɑːndəns/ n **1** [U, singular] : the activity of writing letters or e-mails to someone • They communicated by telephone and correspondence. **2** [U] : the letters or e-mails that people write to each other • I have a pile of correspondence [=letters from people] on my desk. **3** [C/U] : a direct relationship to or with something or between two things • Note the correspondence of each number to a location on the map. • correspondences between spelling and pronunciation **4** [C/U] : the fact of being similar or equal to something • (a) close correspondence between the two texts

correspondence course n [C] : a class in which students receive lessons and assignments in the mail or by e-mail and then return completed assignments in order to receive a grade

cor·re·spon·dent /ˌkorəˈspɑːndənt/ n [C] **1** somewhat formal : someone who writes letters or e-mails to another person **2** : a person whose job is to send news to a newspaper, radio station, or television program • foreign correspondents [=reporters who send news from other countries]

cor·re·spond·ing /ˌkorəˈspɑːndɪŋ/ adj, always before a noun **1** : having the same characteristics as something else • The store earned more this month than it did in the corresponding [=same] month last year. **2** : directly related • As the cost of steel goes up, expect to see a corresponding increase in building costs. — **cor·re·spond·ing·ly** adv

cor·ri·dor /ˈkorədə, ˈkorəˌdoə/ n [C] **1** : a long, narrow passage inside a building or train with doors that lead to rooms on each side **2** : a long, narrow piece of land • A corridor of land lies between the two mountain ranges.

cor·rob·o·rate /kəˈrɑːrəˌbəˌreɪt/ vb -rat·ed; -rat·ing [T] formal : to support or help prove (a statement, theory, etc.) by providing information or evidence • Witnesses corroborated [=confirmed] his story. — **corroborating** adj • No corroborating evidence was found. — **cor·rob·o·ra·tion** /kəˌrɑːrəˈbeɪʃən/ n [U] — **cor·rob·o·ra·tive** /kəˈrɑːrəˌbeɪrɪv, kəˈrɑːbərətɪv/ adj

cor·rode /kəˈroud/ vb -rod·ed; -rod·ing [T/I] : to slowly break apart and destroy (something) through a chemical process

• Rainwater may corrode the steel containers. • The pipes began to corrode. • (figurative) Lies and secrets corroded their relationship. — **cor·ro·sion** /kəˈrouʒən/ n [U] — **cor·ro·sive** /kəˈrousɪv/ adj • highly corrosive chemicals

cor·ru·gat·ed /ˈkorəˌgeɪtəd/ adj : having a wavy surface • a corrugated metal roof • corrugated boxes = boxes made of corrugated cardboard

[1]**cor·rupt** /kəˈrʌpt/ vb **1** [T/I] : to cause (someone or something) to become dishonest, immoral, etc. • Violence on television may be corrupting our children. • a politician corrupted by greed • the corrupting influence/effects of power **2** [T] : to change (something) so that it is less pure or valuable • He's convinced that the Internet is corrupting the English language. **3** [T] : to change (a book, computer file, etc.) from the correct or original form • The file has been corrupted and no longer works properly. • a corrupted version of the ancient text — **cor·rupt·er** n [C] — **cor·rup·tion** /kəˈrʌpʃən/ n [C/U] • the corruption of public officials • corruption of the English language • computer file corruptions

[2]**corrupt** adj **1** : dishonest, evil, or immoral • corrupt judges who accept bribes **2** : changed or damaged • a corrupt version of the text • The document is corrupt. — **cor·rupt·ly** adv — **cor·rupt·ness** n [U]

cor·sage /koəˈsɑːʒ/ n [C] : a flower or small group of flowers that a woman wears on her clothing or wrist on special occasions

cor·set /ˈkoəsət/ n [C] : a tight, stiff piece of clothing worn by women under other clothing to make their waists appear smaller — **cor·set·ed** /ˈkoəsətəd/ adj • tightly corseted ladies

cor·tege also **cor·tège** /koəˈtɛʒ, Brit koˈteɪʒ/ n [C] : a line of people or cars moving slowly at a funeral

cor·tex /ˈkoəˌtɛks/ n, pl **cor·ti·ces** /ˈkoətəˌsiːz/ or **cor·tex·es** [C] medical : the outer layer of an organ in the body and especially of the brain • the cerebral cortex — **cor·ti·cal** /ˈkoətɪkəl/ adj

cor·ti·sone /ˈkoətəˌsoun/ n [U] medical : a hormone that is used to treat arthritis and other diseases

[1]**cosh** /ˈkɑːʃ/ n [C] Brit : a small, heavy weapon that is shaped like a stick

[2]**cosh** vb [T] Brit, informal : to hit (someone) with a cosh • He was coshed on the head.

co·sign /ˈkouˌsaɪn/ vb [T/I] : to sign a document saying that you agree to share the responsibility for a loan or contract with another person • She cosigned (the loan) for my car. — **co·sign·er** n [C]

[1]**cos·met·ic** /kazˈmɛtɪk/ n [C] : a substance (such as a cream, lotion, or powder) that you put on your face or body to improve your appearance • lipstick, nail polish, and other cosmetics

[2]**cosmetic** adj **1** always before a noun : used or done in order to improve a person's appearance • cosmetic creams • cosmetic surgery **2** : done in order to make something look better • The house

needs some cosmetic work. **3** : not important or meaningful • *They made a few cosmetic changes to the deal.*

cos·me·tol·o·gist /ˌkɑːzməˈtɑːlədʒɪst/ *n* [C] *US* : BEAUTICIAN — **cos·me·tol·o·gy** /ˌkɑːzməˈtɑːlədʒi/ *n* [U]

cos·mic /ˈkɑːzmɪk/ *adj* **1** *always before a noun* : of or relating to the universe or outer space • *cosmic theories/radiation* **2** : relating to spiritual matters • *cosmic beauty/wisdom* **3** : very large or important • *a cosmic shift in public opinion* — **cos·mi·cal·ly** *adv*

cosmic ray *n* [C] *technical* : a stream of energy that enters the Earth's atmosphere from outer space — usually plural

cos·mol·o·gy /kɑzˈmɑːlədʒi/ *n* [U] : the scientific study of the origin and structure of the universe — **cos·mo·log·i·cal** /ˌkɑːzməˈlɑːdʒɪkəl/ *adj* — **cos·mol·o·gist** /kɑzˈmɑːlədʒɪst/ *n* [C]

cos·mo·naut /ˈkɑːzmənɑːt/ *n* [C] : a Soviet or Russian astronaut

¹cos·mo·pol·i·tan /ˌkɑːzməˈpɑːlətən/ *adj* **1** : showing an interest in different cultures, ideas, etc. • *cosmopolitan writers* • *the cosmopolitan taste/sophistication of the store's customers* **2** : having people from many different parts of the world • *a cosmopolitan city*

²cosmopolitan *n* [C] : a person who has lived in and knows about many different parts of the world

cos·mos /ˈkɑːzməs, *Brit* ˈkɒz‚mɒs/ *n* — **the cosmos** : the universe especially when it is understood as an ordered system • *the origins of the cosmos*

¹cost /ˈkɑːst/ *n* **1** [C/U] : the amount of money that is needed to pay for or buy something • *The cost [=price] of the house was $200,000.* • *She attends college at a cost of $15,000 a year.* • *production costs* • *the hidden costs [=expenses] of owning a house* • *Everyone should have adequate medical care, regardless of cost.* • *The company needs to do some **cost cutting**.* [=needs to find ways to save money] **2** [C/U] : something that is lost, damaged, or given up in order to achieve or get something • *the costs of war* • *He had achieved fame, but **at a cost**; he'd lost most of his friends.* • *She is determined to win **at all costs**.* • *She is determined to win **at any cost**.* [=she will do whatever it takes to win] **3** [*plural*] : the money used to pay for a court case • *She was ordered to pay court costs.* — **at cost** *US* ✧ If you buy or sell something **at cost**, you buy or sell it for the amount of money that was needed to make it or get it. — **at no cost** — used to say that something is free • *Improvements have been made at no cost to taxpayers.* • *Club members can bring a friend at no extra cost.* — **to your cost** *chiefly Brit* : from your own bad experience • *I found out to my cost that he was a liar.*

²cost *vb* **cost; cost·ing** [T] **1 a** : to have (an amount of money) as a price • *Each ticket costs one dollar.* • *How much does it cost?* = *What does it cost?* • (*informal*) *New equipment **costs money**.* [=is expensive] • (*informal*) *a new car that doesn't **cost an arm and a leg*** [=that is not too expensive]

b : to cause (someone) to pay an amount of money • *The trip will cost you about $100 each way.* • (*informal*) *I can get the part you need, but it'll cost you.* [=you will have to pay a lot of money for it] ✧ If something does not **cost (you) a penny** or (*US*) **cost (you) a dime/nickel**, you do not need to pay any money for it; it is free. **2 a** : to cause (someone) to lose something • *Her mistake cost them the game.* • *His frequent absences ended up costing him his job.* • *Changing your mind now could **cost you dearly/dear.*** [=cause you to lose something or to suffer a lot] **b** : to cause (someone) to experience something unpleasant • *a blunder that has cost her considerable embarrassment* **3** *past tense* **cost·ed** *Brit, business* : to determine how much money will be needed to pay for (something) • *The project was costed (out) at 3 million pounds.*

co·star /ˈkoʊˌstɑɚ/ *n* [C] : one of two or more main actors in a movie, television show, or play • *the actress and her two costars* — **costar** *vb* **-starred; -star·ring** [T/I] • *The film costarred Katharine Hepburn and Spencer Tracy.* • *He costarred in her film.*

cost-ef·fec·tive /ˈkɑːstəˈfɛktɪv/ *adj* : producing good results without costing a lot of money • *a cost-effective way to store data* — **cost-ef·fec·tive·ness** [U]

cost-ef·fi·cient /ˈkɑːstɪˈfɪʃənt/ *adj* : COST-EFFECTIVE

cost·ly /ˈkɑːstli/ *adj* **cost·li·er; -est 1** : having a high price : EXPENSIVE • *costly jewelry* **2** : causing people to lose something or to suffer • *a costly mistake* — **cost·li·ness** *n* [U]

cost of living *n* [C] : the amount of money that is required in a particular area or society to pay for the basic things that people need (such as food, clothing, and housing) • *The cost of living is much higher in that area.*

cost price *n* [U] *Brit* : the amount of money that is needed to make or get something that you are going to sell • *The company sells the vaccine **at cost price**.* [=(*US*) *at cost*]

¹cos·tume /ˈkɑːˌstuːm, *Brit* ˈkɒˌstjuːm/ *n* [C] **1** : the clothes worn by someone (such as an actor) who is trying to look like a different person or thing • *a clown costume* **2** : the clothes worn by a group of people especially during a particular time in the past • *a formal 18th-century Japanese costume* **3** *Brit* : SWIMSUIT — **in costume** : wearing a costume • *The actors were all in costume.* — **cos·tumed** /ˈkɑːˌstuːmd, *Brit* ˈkɒˌstjuːmd/ *adj* • *costumed actors*

²costume *adj, always before a noun* : involving people wearing costumes • *a costume party* • **costume dramas** [=movies that are set in the past in which the actors are dressed like people from the past]

costume jewelry *n* [U] : fancy jewelry that is usually made of inexpensive materials

cosy *Brit spelling of* COZY

cot /ˈkɑːt/ *n* [C] **1** *US* : a narrow, light

bed often made of stretched cloth — called also (Brit) camp bed **2** Brit : ¹CRIB 1a

co·te·rie /ˈkoutəri/ n [C] formal : a small close group of people who usually do not allow other people to join the group ▪ her coterie of fellow musicians

cot·tage /ˈkɑːtɪdʒ/ n [C] : a small house especially in the country

cottage cheese n [U] : a type of soft, white, mild cheese

¹**cot·ton** /ˈkɑːtn̩/ **1** [U] : a soft, white material that grows on the seeds of a tall plant ▪ picking cotton; also : the plants on which this material grows ▪ fields of cotton **2** [C/U] : cloth or clothing that is made of cotton ▪ shirts/sheets made from cotton ▪ wearing cotton in the summer **3** [U] chiefly Brit : yarn that is made of cotton — **cotton** adj ▪ cotton fabrics/dresses — **cot·tony** /ˈkɑːtni/ adj ▪ a cottony material

²**cotton** vb -toned; -ton·ing — **cotton on** [phrasal vb] informal : to begin to understand something : to catch on ▪ She finally cottoned on to the fact that I like her. — **cotton to** [phrasal vb] US, informal : to begin to like someone or something ▪ We cottoned to our new neighbors right away.

cotton ball n [C] US : a small ball of cotton used to remove makeup, clean a wound, etc.

cotton candy n [U] US : candy made from sugar that is boiled and spun into a soft airy material — called also (Brit) candy floss

cotton swab n [C] : a short stick that has round pieces of cotton at both ends — called also (Brit) cotton bud; compare Q-TIPS

cot·ton·tail /ˈkɑːtn̩ˌteɪl/ n [C] : a small rabbit with a white tail

cot·ton·wood /ˈkɑːtn̩ˌwʊd/ n [C] : a type of tree that grows in the U.S. and has seeds with hairs that look like cotton

¹**couch** /ˈkaʊtʃ/ n [C] : a long piece of furniture on which a person can sit or lie down : SOFA

²**couch** vb [T] formal : to say or express (something) in a particular way ▪ The letter was couched in polite terms.

couch potato n [C] informal + disapproving : someone who spends a lot of time sitting and watching television

cou·gar /ˈkuːɡɚ/ n, pl **cou·gars** also **cougar** : a large brownish cat that was once common in North and South America

¹**cough** /ˈkɑːf/ vb [I] : to force air through your throat with a short, loud noise ▪ The dust made him cough. ▪ (figurative) The engine coughed and sputtered. — **cough up** [phrasal vb] **cough up (something)** or **cough (something) up 1** : to have (blood, mucus, etc.) come out of your mouth when you cough ▪ cough up blood **2** informal : to give (money, information, etc.) to someone especially when you do not want to ▪ We had to cough up an extra hundred dollars.

²**cough** n [C] **1** : a condition or illness that causes someone to cough ▪ He has a (bad) cough. **2** : an act of coughing or the sound made when someone coughs ▪

He gave a cough [=he coughed] to get my attention.

cough drop n [C] : a piece of candy that contains medicine to stop coughing

cough syrup n [U] : a thick liquid that contains medicine to stop coughing

could /ˈkʊd, kəd/ vb [modal vb] **1** — used as the past tense of can ▪ When I was younger I could run faster. ▪ She could be very rude at times. ▪ [=she was sometimes very rude] ▪ She said we could do whatever we wanted. **2 a** — used to say that something is possible ▪ You could [=might, may] be making a huge mistake! ▪ She could (very well) be right. ▪ It could happen to anyone. **b** — used with have to say that something was possible but did not actually happen ▪ You could have been hurt. ▪ The movie could have been better. [=the movie wasn't very good] **c** — used to talk about something that is not possible but that is hoped or wished for ▪ We would go if only we could! ▪ I wish I could fly! **3** — used in speech to make a polite request or suggestion ▪ Could you please pass the salt? ▪ Could I get you a cup of coffee? [=do you want a cup of coffee?] **4** — used to say that you are annoyed by something that was or was not done ▪ He could at least apologize! **5** — used in statements that express a strong emotional reaction ▪ I could just kill him! [=I am very angry at him] **6** — used in statements that describe something as very bad, good, etc. ▪ It could not be simpler. [=it is very simple] ▪ The situation couldn't be worse/better. [=the situation is as bad/good as it can be] ▪ I couldn't be happier. [=I'm very happy] — **could care less** see ²CARE — **could do with** ◆ If you could do with something, you need it or would be helped by it. ▪ I could do with something to eat.

couldn't /ˈkʊdnt/ — used as a contraction of could not ▪ I tried but I couldn't do it.

could've /ˈkʊdəv/ — used as a contraction of could have ▪ I could've done it if I had more time.

¹**coun·cil** /ˈkaʊnsəl/ n [C] **1** : a group of people who are chosen to make rules, laws, etc. ▪ the city/tribal council **2** : a group of people who provide advice or guidance ▪ the king's council — **coun·cil·lor** or US **coun·cil·or** /ˈkaʊnslɚ/ n [C] ▪ a city councillor [=council member] — **coun·cil·man** /-mən/ n, pl **-men** /-mən/ [C] US ▪ a city councilman — **coun·cil·wom·an** /ˈkaʊnsəlˌwʊmən/ n, pl **-wom·en** /-ˌwɪmən/ [C] US ▪ a town councilwoman

²**council** adj, always before a noun **1** : of or relating to a council ▪ a council member/meeting **2** Brit : provided by a local government council for people to live in for low rent ▪ council estates/houses/flats

¹**coun·sel** /ˈkaʊnsəl/ n, pl **counsel 1** [U] formal : advice given to someone ▪ They rejected my counsel. **2** [C/U] law : a lawyer who represents someone in a court of law ▪ On (the) advice of counsel, she refused to answer the question. ▪ the company's chief/general counsel

²**counsel** vb, US **-seled** or Brit **-selled**;

US **-sel·ing** *òr Brit* **-sel·ling** [T] *formal*
1 : to give advice to (someone) ▪ *She counseled* [=*advised*] *him not to accept the offer.* ▪ *He counsels* [=is a counselor for] *people who are trying to quit drinking.* **2** : to suggest or recommend (something) ▪ *The President's advisers counseled restraint.*

counseling (*US*) *or Brit* **counselling** *n* [U] : advice and support that is given to people to help them with problems, decisions, etc. ▪ *drug/debt/career counseling*

coun·sel·or (*US*) *or chiefly Brit* **coun·sel·lor** /ˈkaʊnslɚ/ *n* [C] **1** : a person who provides advice as a job ▪ *a marriage counselor* ▪ *The school guidance counselor helped me choose a college.* **2** *US* : a person who is in charge of young people at a summer camp ▪ *a camp counselor* **3** *US* : LAWYER ▪ *a counselor at law*

¹**count** /ˈkaʊnt/ *vb* **1 a** [T/I] : to add (people or things) together to find the total number ▪ *She made sure to count her change.* ▪ *He counted seven deer.* ▪ *Don't interrupt me. I'm counting.* ▪ *She was counting (up) the votes/money.* ▪ *When it comes to books, I have too many to count.* [=I have a lot] ▪ *She is counting calories.* [=being careful about how many calories she eats] ▪ *I'm 47 years old and counting.* [=with more to come] **b** [I] : to say numbers in order ▪ *count (up) to one hundred* **2** [T] : to include (someone or something) in a total ▪ *She counts several musicians among her friends.* [=her friends include musicians] ▪ *There will be 150 guests, not counting children.* **3** [I] : to be accepted or allowed officially ▪ *There was a penalty, so the goal does not count.* **4 a** [T] : to consider or regard (someone or something) in a specified way ▪ *I count myself lucky.* ▪ *She was counted as absent.* **b** [I] : to be considered or regarded as something ▪ *The job is so easy that it hardly counts as work.* **5** [I] : to have value or importance ▪ *Every vote counts.* ▪ *He played well when it really counted.* **6** [T/I] : to be considered in a specified way when a person or thing is being judged ▪ *count (something) for/against someone* ▪ *His experience counts in his favor.* — **count down** [phrasal vb] **1** : to count numbers in reverse order from higher to lower ▪ *He counted down from 10 (to 1).* **2** **count down (something)** *also* **count (something) down** : to pay close attention to the number of (days, miles, etc.) that remain ▪ *He is counting down the days left in the school year.* — **count heads** : to count how many people are present at a place — **count in** [phrasal vb] **count (someone) in** : to plan to include (someone) in an activity ▪ *If you're going to the beach, count me in!* — **count off** [phrasal vb] **1** : to count numbers that are spaced a certain number apart ▪ *He counted off by twos.* [=counted 2, 4, 6, 8, etc.] **2 count off (something)** *or* **count (something) off** : to list (something) out loud ▪ *She counted off all the things she wanted to do.* — **count on/upon** [phrasal vb] **1 a** : to rely or depend on (someone) to do something ▪ *I am counting on you to help me.*

b : to expect (someone) to do something ▪ *I wouldn't count on him to win the match.* **2** : to expect (something) to happen ▪ *Dad might loan me the money, but I can't count on it.* — **count out** [phrasal vb] **1 count (someone) out** : to not include (someone) in an activity ▪ *If you are looking for help cleaning, count me out.* **2 count (someone or something) out** *or* **count out (someone or something)** : to decide that (someone or something) cannot win or succeed ▪ *Don't count out our team just yet.* — **count toward/towards** [phrasal vb] **count toward/towards (something)** *or* **count (something) toward/towards (something)** : to have value as a credit or payment in relation to (something) ▪ *Fifty dollars will be counted toward your next bill.*

²**count** *n* **1** [C] **a** : an act or process of adding people or things together to find the total number ▪ *At (my) last count, I had 50 responses.* ▪ *The teacher took/did a quick count of the students.* **b** : the total number that is counted ▪ *The final count of people at the conference was over 200.* **2** [singular] : an act or process of saying numbers in order until a particular number is reached ▪ *I'll give you until the count of three to get out of here.* ▪ *If you're not out of here by the count of three, I'm calling the police.* **3** [C] law : one of the crimes that someone is charged with ▪ *She was charged with two counts of theft.* **4** [C] : an idea or opinion that is expressed in a statement, argument, etc. ▪ *I agree with you on both counts.* [=I agree with both the points you have made] **5** *the count baseball* : the number of balls and strikes that have been pitched to a batter ▪ *The count is two balls, two strikes.* ✧ A *full count* is a situation in baseball in which a batter has three balls and two strikes. — **down for the count** (*US*) *or* **out for the count** of a boxer : knocked down and unable to get up again while the referee counts to 10 ▪ *The boxer was down for the count.* — **keep count** : to remember or keep a record of a number or total ▪ *He has had so many different girlfriends that I no longer can keep count (of them all).* — **lose count** : to forget a number or total ▪ *I've lost count of how many girlfriends he's had.*

³**count** *n* [C] : a nobleman in some European countries who has a high rank similar to a British earl

count·down /ˈkaʊntˌdaʊn/ *n* [C] **1** : the act of counting down the number of seconds that remain before something happens ▪ *Begin the countdown to launch.* **2** : the period of time before an important or special event ▪ *the countdown to summer vacation*

¹**coun·te·nance** /ˈkaʊntn̩əns/ *n* [C] *formal + literary* : the appearance of a person's face ▪ *his somber countenance*

²**countenance** *vb* **-nanced; -nanc·ing** [T] *formal* : to accept, support, or approve of (something) ▪ *He did not officially countenance negotiations with the rebels.*

¹**count·er** /ˈkaʊntɚ/ *n* [C] **1** : a piece of

furniture with a flat surface that is used for doing business in a store, restaurant, etc. ▪ *the sales/checkout counter* ▪ *the man behind the counter* **2** *US* **a** : a long, flat surface on which food is prepared in a kitchen — called also *countertop*, (*Brit*) *worktop* **b** : a flat surface around a sink in a bathroom — called also *countertop* **3** : a person or device that counts something ▪ *The counter records how many people visit the Web site.* **4** : a small object that is used in some board games **5** *formal* : something that is made or done as a defense against or response to something else ▪ *The tax break is intended as a counter to rising fuel costs.* — **over the counter** : without a prescription from a doctor ▪ *The drug is available over the counter.* — **under the counter** : secretly and usually illegally ▪ *The workers were paid under the counter.*

²**coun·ter** /ˈkaʊntɚ/ *vb* **1 a** [*I*] : to do something in defense or in response to something ▪ *He countered with a punch to the other fighter's head.* **b** [*T*] : to make (something) less effective or ineffective ▪ *This pill will counter the side effects of the other one.* **2** [*T/I*] : to say (something) in response to something that another person has said ▪ *"I could say the same thing about you," she countered.*

³**coun·ter** /ˈkaʊntɚ/ *adv* : in a way that goes against or does not agree with something ▪ *The soldier acted counter to his orders.* ▪ *His theory ran counter to the beliefs of his time.*

coun·ter- /ˈkaʊntɚ/ *prefix* **1** : in a direction opposite to ▪ *counterclockwise* **2** : as a reaction against ▪ *counteroffensive*

coun·ter·act /ˌkaʊntɚˈækt/ *vb* [*T*] : to cause (something) to have less effect or no effect ▪ *The drug will counteract the poison.*

coun·ter·at·tack /ˈkaʊntɚˌtæk/ *n* [*C*] : an attack that is made in response to an attack by an enemy or opponent ▪ *launch/mount a counterattack* — **coun·ter·at·tack** *vb* [*T/I*] ▪ *The enemy counterattacked at dawn.*

coun·ter·bal·ance /ˈkaʊntɚˌbæləns/ *vb* -**anced**; -**anc·ing** [*T*] *formal* : to have an effect that is opposite but equal to (something) ▪ *Improved services have been counterbalanced by higher fees.* — **counterbalance** *n* [*C*] ▪ *The author's humor is a good counterbalance to the book's serious subject.*

coun·ter·clock·wise /ˌkaʊntɚˈklɑːkˌwaɪz/ *adv, US* : in the direction opposite to movement of a clock's hands ▪ *Turn the screw counterclockwise.* [=(*Brit*) *anticlockwise*] — **counterclockwise** *adj* ▪ *a counterclockwise direction*

coun·ter·cul·ture /ˈkaʊntɚˌkʌltʃɚ/ *n* [*C*] : a culture with values and customs that are very different from those accepted by most of society ▪ *the counterculture of the hippies*

coun·ter·es·pi·o·nage /ˌkaʊntɚˈɛspijəˌnɑːʒ/ *n* [*U*] *formal* : the activity of preventing or stopping enemies from spying

coun·ter·feit /ˈkaʊntɚˌfɪt/ *vb* [*T*] : to make an exact copy of (something) in order to trick people ▪ *They were counter-*

feiting money/documents. — **counterfeit** *adj* ▪ *counterfeit money/bills/tickets* — **counterfeit** *n* [*C*] ▪ *The 100-dollar bill was a counterfeit.* — **coun·ter·feit·er** *n* [*C*] — **coun·ter·feit·ing** *n* [*U*] ▪ *He was sent to jail for counterfeiting.*

coun·ter·foil /ˈkaʊntɚˌfojəl/ *n* [*C*] *chiefly Brit.* : ¹STUB 2, 3

coun·ter·in·tel·li·gence /ˌkaʊntɚɪnˈtɛlədʒəns/ *n* [*U*] *formal* : things a government does to hide secret information from an enemy ▪ *counterintelligence agents/operations*

coun·ter·in·tu·i·tive /ˌkaʊntɚɪnˈtuːwətɪv, *Brit* ˌkaʊntɚɪnˈtjuːətɪv/ *adj, formal* : different from what you would expect or what seems natural ▪ *an idea that seems counterintuitive*

coun·ter·mand /ˈkaʊntɚˌmænd, *Brit* ˈkaʊntɚˌmɑːnd/ *vb* [*T*] *formal* : to cancel (an order) especially by giving a new order ▪ *Orders to blow up the bridge were countermanded.*

coun·ter·mea·sure /ˈkaʊntɚˌmɛʒɚ/ *n* [*C*] : an action or device that is intended to stop or prevent something bad ▪ *new countermeasures against terrorism*

coun·ter·of·fen·sive /ˈkaʊntɚəˈfɛnsɪv/ *n* [*C*] : an attack made in order to defend against an enemy or opponent ▪ *mount/launch a counteroffensive*

coun·ter·of·fer /ˈkaʊntɚˌɑːfɚ/ *n* [*C*] : an offer that is made by someone in response to a previous offer ▪ *We made a counteroffer on the house.*

coun·ter·part /ˈkaʊntɚˌpɑɚt/ *n* [*C*] : someone or something that has the same job or purpose as another ▪ *The President met with his counterparts in Europe.* ▪ *Metal tools replaced their stone counterparts.*

coun·ter·pro·duc·tive /ˌkaʊntɚprəˈdʌktɪv/ *adj* : making the thing you want to happen less likely to happen ▪ *a counterproductive approach*

coun·ter·rev·o·lu·tion /ˌkaʊntɚˌrɛvəˈluːʃən/ *n* [*C/U*] : action by a group, army, etc., to overthrow a government that is in power because of an earlier revolution — **coun·ter·rev·o·lu·tion·ary** /ˌkaʊntɚˌrɛvəˈluːʃəˌneri, *Brit* ˈkaʊntɚˌrɛvəˈluːʃənri/ *adj* ▪ *counterrevolutionary forces* — **counterrevolutionary** *n, pl* -**ar·ies** [*C*]

coun·ter·sign /ˈkaʊntɚˌsaɪn/ *vb* [*T*] : to sign (a document) after another person has already signed it ▪ *The order has to be countersigned.*

coun·ter·top /ˈkaʊntɚˌtɑːp/ *n* [*C*] *US* : ¹COUNTER 2

coun·ter·vail·ing /ˌkaʊntɚˈveɪlɪŋ/ *adj, always before a noun, formal* : having an equal but opposite effect ▪ *countervailing influences*

coun·ter·weight /ˈkaʊntɚˌweɪt/ *n* [*C*] : a weight that provides a balance against something of equal weight ▪ *The crane has a counterweight on the back.*

count·ess /ˈkaʊntəs/ *n* [*C*] **1** : the wife of a count or an earl **2** : a woman who has the rank of count or earl

count·less /ˈkaʊntləs/ *adj* : too many to be counted : very many ▪ *countless reasons* ▪ *I've been there countless times.*

count noun n [C] *grammar* : a noun (such as *bean* or *ball*) that has both a singular and plural form and can be used after a numeral, after words such as *many* or *few*, or after the indefinite article *a* or *an* — compare NONCOUNT NOUN

¹**coun·try** /ˈkʌntri/ n, pl **-tries** **1 a** [C/U] : NATION ▪ *European/foreign countries* ▪ *They drove across the country from California to New York. = They drove across country.* **b the country** : the people who live in a country ▪ *The President has the support of most of the country.* **2** [U] : an area or region that is known for a particular activity, feature, etc. ▪ *We went camping in the hill country.* ▪ *They drove through miles of open country.* **3 the country** : land that is away from big towns and cities : COUNTRYSIDE ▪ *She lives somewhere out in the country.* **4** [U] : COUNTRY MUSIC

²**country** *adj, always before a noun* **1** : of, relating to, or characteristic of the country ▪ *a country town/road* ▪ *country living* ▪ *country folk* **2** : of or relating to country music ▪ *a country singer*

country and western n [U] : COUNTRY MUSIC

country club n [C] : a private club where people go for social events and to play golf, tennis, etc.

coun·try·man /ˈkʌntrimən/ n, pl **-men** /-mən/ [C] *formal* **1** : a person who lives in or comes from the same country as you ▪ *my fellow countrymen* **2** *Brit* : a person who lives in the countryside

country music n [U] : a style of music that developed in the southern and western U.S. and that often contains lyrics about life in the country

coun·try·side /ˈkʌntriˌsaɪd/ n [U] : land that is away from big towns and cities ▪ *a drive through the countryside*

coun·try·wide /ˌkʌntriˈwaɪd/ *adj* : happening or existing in all parts of a country ▪ *The murders attracted countrywide attention.* — **countrywide** *adv*

coun·ty /ˈkaʊnti/ n, pl **-ties** [C] : an area of a state or country that is larger than a city and has its own local government ▪ *the largest school district in the county* ▪ *the county sheriff*

coup /ˈkuː/ n [C] **1** : COUP D'ÉTAT ▪ *a military coup* **2** : an impressive victory or achievement ▪ *It was a major coup when they got an interview with the President.*

coup de grâce *or* **coup de grace** /ˌkuːdəˈgrɑːs/ n, pl **coups de grâce** *or* **coups de grace** /ˌkuːdəˈgrɑːs/ [C] *formal* : a hit or shot that kills a person or animal that is suffering; *also* : an action or event that ends or destroys something ▪ *The cut in funding has administered the coup de grâce to the program.*

coup d'état *or* **coup d'etat** /ˌkuːˌdeɪˈtɑː/ n, pl **coups d'état** *or* **coup d'etat** /ˌkuːˌdeɪˈtɑː/ [C] : a sudden violent attempt by a small group of people to take over the government

coupe (*US*) *or chiefly Brit* **cou·pé** /kuːˈpeɪ, ˈkuːp, *Brit* ˈkuːpeɪ/ n [C] : a car that has two doors and that has room for four

or sometimes only for two people

¹**cou·ple** /ˈkʌpəl/ n [C] **1** : two people who are married or who have a romantic or sexual relationship ▪ *a happily married couple* ▪ *Are they a couple?* **2** : PAIR ▪ *The people were lined up in couples.* — **a couple** *informal* : two or a few of something ▪ *Can you give me a couple more examples?* ▪ *"How many drinks have you had?" "Oh, just a couple."* ▪ (*US, informal*) *I took a couple* [=a couple of] *weeks off.* — **a couple of** : two of or a few of : two (things) or a few (things) ▪ *It happened a couple of days ago.* ▪ *Can you loan me a couple of dollars?*

²**couple** vb **cou·pled; cou·pling** [T] : CONNECT, JOIN ▪ *coupling the trailer to the truck* — **couple with** [*phrasal vb*] **couple (something) with** : to join or combine (something) with (something else) ▪ *The team's win, coupled with a loss by their rivals, put them in first place.*

cou·plet /ˈkʌplət/ n [C] : two lines of poetry that form a unit ▪ *a rhyming couplet*

cou·pling /ˈkʌplɪŋ/ n [C] **1** : a device that connects two parts or things **2** : the act of combining two things ▪ *a/the coupling of literature and science*

cou·pon /ˈkuːˌpɑːn, ˈkjuːˌpɑːn/ n [C] **1** : a usually small piece of printed paper that lets you get a service or product for free or at a lower price ▪ *The coupon is good for a free oil change.* **2** *chiefly Brit* : a section of an advertisement that you can cut out and mail to a company in order to request information or to order a product or service

cour·age /ˈkərɪdʒ/ n [U] : the ability to do something that you know is difficult or dangerous ▪ *It takes courage to stand up for your rights.* ▪ *I finally worked/got/summoned up the courage to confront him.* ▪ *He has the courage of his convictions.* [=he is not afraid to do what he believes is right]

cou·ra·geous /kəˈreɪdʒəs/ *adj* : very brave : having or showing courage ▪ *a courageous man/woman/soldier* ▪ *a courageous act/decision* — **cou·ra·geous·ly** *adv* — **cou·ra·geous·ness** n [U]

cou·ri·er /ˈkərijə/ n [C] **1** : a person whose job is to carry messages, packages, etc., from one person or place to another **2** : a business that is used to send messages, packages, etc. ▪ *an overnight courier* **3** *Brit* : a person whose job is to help people who are on holiday

¹**course** /ˈkoəs/ n **1 a** [C/U] : the path or direction that something or someone moves along ▪ *the course of a river* ▪ *The pilot brought the plane back on course.* ▪ *The ship was blown off course.* ▪ (*figurative*) *a battle that altered/changed the course of history* **b** [C] : a path or route that runners, skiers, bikers, etc., move along especially in a race ▪ *a cross-country/marathon/ski course* **2** [C] : a series of classes about a particular subject in a school ▪ *a writing/pottery course* ▪ *course materials/work/requirements* ▪ *I have a light/full course load this semester.* [=I am taking few/many classes this semester] **3** [U] : the normal or regular way that something happens over

time • *The treatment will slow the course of the disease.* • *the normal/ordinary course of events* [=the way things usually happen] • *the usual/normal/ordinary course of business* • *The disease usually runs its course* [=begins, gets worse, and ends] *in a few days.* **4** [*U*] — used to describe what happens during a period of time or when something is being done • *during/in/over the course of a year* • *facts discovered in the course of research* • *Things will get better in the course of time.* [=as time passes] **5** [*C*] : a way of behaving or proceeding that you choose • *Our wisest course is to retreat.* • *We're trying to determine the best course of action.* **6** [*C*] : a series of medical treatments that are given over a period of time • *a course of medication/therapy* **7** [*C*] : a part of a meal that is served separately from other parts • *We had salad for the first course.* • *the main course* • *a five-course dinner* **8** [*C*] : GOLF COURSE — **in due course** : after a normal or expected amount of time has passed • *The reasons will become apparent in due course.* — **of course 1** — used to show that what is being said is very obvious or already known • *Of course, it wasn't easy for me to admit I was wrong.* • *"Has the bus already left?" "Of course."* **2** — used informally to give permission or say yes in a way that shows you are very certain • *"May I borrow this book?" "Of course!"* • *"Are you angry with me?" "Of course not!"* [=I am not at all angry] **3** — used to stress that what you are saying is true and you feel no doubt about it • *Of course we'll come!* — **stay the course** see ¹STAY

²**course** *vb* **coursed; cours·ing** [*I*] : to move or flow quickly • *the blood coursing through my veins*

¹**court** /ˈkoət/ *n* **1 a** [*U*] : a formal legal meeting in which decisions about crimes, disagreements, etc., are made according to the law • *Court is now in session.* • *Court is adjourned.* • *a court battle/fight/case* **b** [*C/U*] : a place where legal cases are heard • *There were protesters outside the court.* • *take someone to court* [=to start a lawsuit against someone; to sue someone] • *The organization is prepared to go to court.* [=to start a lawsuit] • *The case was settled/resolved out of court.* [=without going to court] **c** [*C*] : an official group of people (such as a judge and jury) who make decisions about legal cases • *state/federal courts* • *The court ruled/declared the law unconstitutional.* **2** [*C*] : a large flat surface that is used for playing games like tennis and basketball • *a basketball/tennis court* **3 a** [*C/U*] : the place where the leader of a country and especially a king or queen lives and works • *the courts of Europe* • *He spent a lot of time at court.* **b** [*C*] : a king or queen and the people who live and work with him or her • *the king's/queen's court* — **hold court** : to talk to a group of people who listen to what you say because it is funny or interesting • *He was holding court at his usual table.* — **pay court to** *formal + old-fashioned* : ²COURT 1 • *He does not approve of the young man who*

has been paying court to his daughter. — **the ball is in your court** see ¹BALL

²**court** *vb* **1** [*T/I*] *somewhat old-fashioned* : to act in a way that shows that you want or intend to get married • *They courted for two years.* • *courting his college sweetheart* **2** [*T/I*] *of an animal* : to perform the actions that lead to sexual activity • *a pair of robins courting* **3** [*T*] : to give a lot of attention to (someone) in order to get approval, support, etc. • *The company is courting investors.* • *politicians courting middle-class voters* = *politicians courting favor with middle-class voters* = *politicians courting the favor of middle-class voters* **4** [*T*] : to act in a way that is likely to cause (something bad) to happen to you • *Anyone who refuses to evacuate is courting disaster.* • *They were courting danger/trouble.*

cour·te·ous /ˈkətijəs/ *adj* : very polite and respectful • *She was helpful and courteous.* — **cour·te·ous·ly** *adv*

cour·te·san /ˈkoətəzən, Brit ˌkɔːtəˈzæn/ *n* [*C*] *old-fashioned* : a prostitute who has sex with wealthy and powerful men

¹**cour·te·sy** /ˈkətəsi/ *n, pl* **-sies 1** [*U*] : behavior that is polite and respectful • *They treated us with courtesy.* • *He didn't have the common courtesy* [=the normal amount of politeness] *to say thank you.* **2 a** [*C*] : something that you do because it is polite, kind, etc. • *She did it as a courtesy.* **b** [*C*] : something that you say to be polite especially when you meet someone • *the usual courtesies* • *exchanging courtesies* **c** [*U*] : generosity in providing something • *The flowers were provided (by) courtesy of a local florist.* = *The flowers were provided through the courtesy of a local florist.* • (*informal*) *Photo courtesy* [=provided by] *Helen Jones.*

²**courtesy** *adj, always before a noun* **1** : done in order to be polite • *They paid a courtesy call* [=a visit to show politeness] *on the ambassador.* **2** : provided for free especially for temporary use by a customer, visitor, etc. • *a courtesy car/phone*

courtesy title *n* [*C*] : a polite and formal word (such as "sir," "ma'am," "Mr.," "Mrs.," "Ms.," "Miss," or "Dr.") that is used in place of or as part of someone's name

court·house /ˈkoətˌhaʊs/ *n* [*C*] *US* : a building in which legal cases are heard

court·ier /ˈkoətijə/ *n* [*C*] : a member of a royal court (sense 3b)

court·ly /ˈkoətli/ *adj* **court·li·er; -est** : polite and graceful in a formal way • *courtly manners* • *a courtly gentleman* — **court·li·ness** *n* [*U*]

court-mar·tial /ˈkoətˌmɑəʃəl/ *n, pl* **courts-martial** *also* **court-mar·tials 1** [*C/U*] : a military court • *tried/sentenced by court-martial* **2** [*C*] : a trial in a military court • *The sergeant is facing a court-martial.* — **court-martial** *vb, US* **-tialed** *or Brit* **-tialled;** *US* **-tial·ing** *or Brit* **-tial·ling** [*T*] • *He was court-martialed for failure to obey orders.*

court of appeals (*US*) *or chiefly Brit* **court of appeal** *n* [*C*] *law* : a court that studies the decisions made by a lower court and decides if they were correct

court of law n [C] : ¹COURT 1b

court order n [C/U] : a formal statement from a court that orders someone to do or stop doing something ▪ *He is barred by (a) court order from entering the building.*

court·room /ˈkoɚtˌruːm/ n [C] : a room in which legal cases are heard

court·ship /ˈkoɚtˌʃɪp/ n   1 [C/U] somewhat old-fashioned : the activities (such as dating) that could lead to marriage or the period of time when such activities occur ▪ *a two-year courtship*   2 [U] : the behavior of animals that leads to sexual activity or the period of time when such behavior occurs ▪ *courtship behavior*   3 [U] : an attempt to convince someone to support or choose you or your organization ▪ *the President's courtship of middle-class voters*

court·yard /ˈkoɚtˌjɑɚd/ n [C] : an open space surrounded by one or more buildings ▪ *the palace courtyards*

cous·in /ˈkʌzən/ n [C]   1 a : a child of your uncle or aunt — called also *first cousin*; see also SECOND COUSIN   b : a person who is related to you but not in a close or direct way ▪ *a distant cousin* [=*relative*]   2 : a person who is from another country but whose culture is similar to your own ▪ *our English cousins*   3 : something that is similar or related to something else ▪ *The cricket is a cousin of the grasshopper.*

cou·ture /kuˈtuɚ, Brit kuˈtjuə/ n [U] : the business of designing, making, or selling women's clothes; *also* : women's clothes in general

cove /ˈkoʊv/ n [C] : a small, sheltered inlet or bay

cov·en /ˈkʌvən/ n [C] : a group of witches

cov·e·nant /ˈkʌvənənt/ n [C]   1 formal : a formal and serious agreement or promise ▪ *the covenant of marriage*   2 law : a formal written agreement ▪ *an international covenant on human rights*

¹**cov·er** /ˈkʌvɚ/ vb   1 [T/I] : to put something over, on top of, or in front of (something else) ▪ *We covered the wall with paint.* ▪ *Please cover your mouth when you cough.* ▪ *Cover (the pot/pan) and simmer for one hour.*   2 [T] a : to be spread over or on top of (something) ▪ *Snow covered the hills.*   b : to be over much or all of the surface of (something) ▪ *Lakes cover much of the state.* ▪ *The wall is completely covered with graffiti.*   3 [T] : to pass over or through (an area, distance, etc.) ▪ *The hikers covered long distances every day.*   4 [T] a : to have (something) as a subject ▪ *This material was covered in the first chapter.* ▪ *We have a lot (of information) to cover in one hour.*   b : to relate to or have an effect on (something) ▪ *The patent covers* [=*applies to*] *both kinds of devices.*   5 [T] : to report news about (something) ▪ *She covers political news for the network.*   6 [T] of insurance : to agree to provide financial protection to (someone) or against (something) ▪ *The policy covers the traveler in any accident.* ▪ *The policy covers wa-*

ter damage. : to provide payment for (something) ▪ *My insurance doesn't cover this treatment/drug.*   7 [T] : to be or have enough money to pay for (something) ▪ *Your checking account balance will not cover the check.* ▪ *This money should cover the cost of repairs.*   8 [T] a : to guard or protect (something or someone) by being ready to fire a weapon ▪ *The ships were covering the harbor.* ▪ *The soldier yelled "Cover me!" and ran for the door.*   b : to protect (yourself or someone else) from possible trouble or danger ▪ *He was lying to cover himself.*   9 [T] a sports : to guard (an opponent) to prevent the other team from scoring ▪ *He covered the tight end.*   b baseball : to be in a position to receive a throw to (a base) ▪ *The shortstop was covering second base.* — see also *cover all the bases* at ¹BASE   10 [I] : to help you by doing your job when you are away or not able to do it ▪ *A coworker covered for me during my vacation.*   11 [T] a : to be responsible for selling or providing something to all the people in (an area) ▪ *One salesperson covers the whole state.*   b : to provide something to (a group of people) ▪ *There is enough vaccine to cover everyone.*   12 [T] : to record or perform (a song that was previously recorded by someone else) ▪ *The band covers hits from the 1980s.* — **cover up** [phrasal vb] **cover up** or **cover (something) up** or **cover up (something)**   1 : to cover yourself, part of your body, etc., with something (such as clothing) ▪ *She covered (herself) up with a robe.*   2 : to prevent people from learning the truth about (something) ▪ *They tried to cover up the crime/mistake.* — **have (got) someone or something covered** (informal) : to have done, gotten, or provided whatever is needed ▪ *Don't worry about a thing. We've got you covered.*

²**cover** n   1 [C] : something that is put around or on top of another thing ▪ *She put a cover* [=*lid*] *over/on the pan.* ▪ *the cover* [=*top, lid*] *of a box/jar*   2 [C] : a blanket or sheet on a bed ▪ *lying under the covers* ▪ *He threw off the covers.*   3 [C] a : the outer part of a book or magazine ▪ *the book's back/front cover* ▪ *She read the book from cover to cover.* [=she read all of the book]   b : the part of the case of a record album, CD, DVD, etc., that is seen from the outside ▪ *the picture on an album cover*   4 [U, singular] : something that covers the ground or the sky ▪ *a cover of snow* ▪ *The moon was hidden behind (a) thick cloud cover.*   5 [U] : a protected place or situation ▪ *The roof provided cover from the rain.* ▪ *The soldiers took/sought cover behind the wall.*   6 [U] : something that prevents actions, information, etc., from being seen or known ▪ *crimes committed under (the) cover of darkness/night*   7 [C] : something that is not what it seems to be but is used to hide something else ▪ *The business was a cover for a criminal gang.* ◆ A person who is **under cover** has his or her true identity hidden. The phrase usually describes a person (such as a police officer) who pretends to be someone else in or-

der to get information. ✧ To **blow some-one's cover** is to reveal someone's true identity. **8** [C] : a recording or performance of a song that was previously recorded by someone else ▪ *a cover (version) of a popular song* **9** [U] *Brit* : insurance coverage ▪ *a policy that provides cover for loss by fire* **10** [U] : protection from danger, an attack, etc. ▪ *Military planes provided air cover.*

cov·er·age /'kʌvərɪdʒ/ n **1** [U] : the activity of reporting about an event or subject in the news ▪ *The issue is not getting much (press/TV) coverage.* ▪ **live coverage** [=a broadcast of an event as it is happening] **2** [U] : discussion of a subject in a book, class, etc. ▪ *For more complete coverage of this issue, see Chapter Six.* **3** *US* **a** [U] : the financial protection that is provided by an insurance policy ▪ *insurance coverage* ▪ *affordable health/medical coverage* **b** [C] : something that an insurance company will pay for ▪ *optional/additional coverages* **4** [C/U] *chiefly US, sports* : the act of covering an opponent ▪ *He was responsible for coverage of the tight end.* **5** [U] — used to describe how much of an area or surface is covered by something ▪ *heavy cloud coverage* ▪ *There is no cell phone coverage* [=service] *in this valley.*

cov·er·all /'kʌvərˌɑːl/ n [C] *US* : a piece of clothing that is worn over other clothes to protect them — usually plural — called also (*Brit*) overalls

cover charge n [C] : an amount of money that must be paid to go into a nightclub or restaurant

cov·ered /'kʌvəd/ adj **1** : having a cover or lid ▪ *a covered dish/container* **2 a** : having a layer of something specified on top ▪ *snow-covered hills* **b** : having something specified over much or all of the surface ▪ *chocolate-covered pretzels* **3** : having a roof ▪ *a covered walkway/bridge*

covered wagon n [C] : a large wagon with a rounded top made of heavy cloth that was used in the past in North America

cover girl n [C] : an attractive young woman whose picture is on the front of a magazine

cov·er·ing /'kʌvərɪŋ/ n [C] : an object or substance that goes over or on top of something ▪ *a covering* [=*cover*] *of snow* ▪ *floor/wall/window coverings*

cov·er·let /'kʌvələt/ n [C] : BEDSPREAD

cover letter n [C] *US* : a letter that is sent with something (such as a résumé) to explain it — called also (*Brit*) covering letter

cover story n [C] : an important article that is the main subject shown on the cover of a magazine

co·vert /'koʊvət/ adj : secret or hidden ▪ *covert military operations* — **co·vert·ly** adv — **co·vert·ness** n [U]

cov·er-up /'kʌvəˌʌp/ n [C] **1** : a planned effort to hide a dishonest, immoral, or illegal act or situation ▪ *exposing an attempted cover-up* **2** : an action or a way of behaving that is meant to hide something ▪ *His brash manner is just a cover-up for his insecurity.*

cov·et /'kʌvət/ vb [T] : to want (something that you do not have) very much ▪ *coveting success*

cov·et·ous /'kʌvətəs/ adj, formal : feeling or showing a very strong desire for something that does not belong to you ▪ *They were covetous of his success.* — **cov·et·ous·ly** adv — **cov·et·ous·ness** n [U]

cov·ey /'kʌvi/ n, pl **-eys** [C] **1** : a small flock of birds ▪ *a covey of quail* **2** : a small group of people or things ▪ *a covey of schoolchildren*

¹**cow** /'kaʊ/ n [C] **1 a** : a large animal that is raised by people for milk or meat ▪ *horses and cows*; *especially* : the adult female of this animal ▪ *milk the cows* **b** : an adult female of some other large animals (such as elephants, whales, and seals) **2** *chiefly Brit slang, offensive* : a woman who is stupid or annoying — **have a cow** *slang* : to become very angry, upset, etc. ▪ *All right! Don't have a cow!* — **holy cow** *informal* — used to express surprise or excitement ▪ *Holy cow! That car almost hit us!* — **till/until the cows come home** *informal* : for a very long time ▪ *They'll be arguing about this till the cows come home.*

²**cow** vb [T] : to make (someone) too afraid to do something ▪ *I refuse to be cowed (into silence) by their threats.*

cow·ard /'kawəd/ n [C] : someone who is too afraid to do what is right or expected : a person who lacks courage

cow·ard·ice /'kawədəs/ n [U] : lack of courage ▪ *soldiers accused of cowardice*

cow·ard·ly /'kawədli/ adj : having or showing a lack of courage ▪ *a cowardly person/decision* — **cow·ard·li·ness** n [U]

cow·boy /'kaʊˌbɔɪ/ n [C] **1** : a man who rides a horse and whose job is to take care of cows or horses **2** : a man who performs in a rodeo **3** *usually disapproving* : someone who does things that other people consider foolish and dangerous ▪ *political cowboys* ▪ *cowboy diplomacy*

cow·er /'kawə/ vb [I] : to move back or bend your body down because you are afraid ▪ *They cowered at the sight of the gun.*

cow·girl /'kaʊˌgəl/ n [C] **1** : a woman who rides a horse and whose job is to take care of cows or horses **2** : a girl or woman who performs in a rodeo

cow·hand /'kaʊˌhænd/ n [C] : COWBOY 1

cow·herd /'kaʊˌhəd/ n [C] : a person whose job is to take care of cows

cow·hide /'kaʊˌhaɪd/ n [U] : the skin of a cow or leather made from it

cowl /'kawəl/ n [C] : a loose piece of clothing with a hood that a monk wears; *also* : the hood itself

cow·lick /'kaʊˌlɪk/ n [C] *chiefly US* : a small bunch of hair that will not lie flat

cowl·ing /'kaʊlɪŋ/ n [C] : a metal covering for the engine of an airplane

co·work·er /'koʊˌwəkə/ n [C] : someone you work with

cow·poke /'kaʊˌpoʊk/ n [C] *US, informal* : COWBOY 1

cox·swain /ˈkɑːksən/ n [C] : a person who is in charge of and usually steers a boat

coy /ˈkɔɪ/ adj **1** : seeming shy or innocent in order to be attractive or to get attention ▪ *her coy manner* ▪ *a coy glance/smile* **2** : not giving all the information that could be revealed ▪ *Both companies are being coy about the merger.* ▪ *a coy answer* — **coy·ly** adv — **coy·ness** n [U]

coy·ote /kaɪˈouti/ n, pl **coy·ot·es** or **coyote** [C] : a small wild animal of North America that is related to dogs and wolves

¹co·zy (US) or Brit **co·sy** /ˈkouzi/ adj **co·zi·er; -est 1** : small, comfortable, and warm ▪ *a cozy restaurant/cottage* **b** : friendly and pleasant ▪ *a cozy dinner/chat* ▪ *a cozy evening in front of the fire* **2** : very close especially in an improper way ▪ *They accused the senator of getting/being too cozy with powerful companies.* — **co·zi·ly** (US) or Brit **co·si·ly** /ˈkouzəli/ adv — **co·zi·ness** (US) or Brit **co·si·ness** n [U]

²cozy (US) or Brit **cosy** vb **-zies; -zied; -zy·ing** — **cozy up** [phrasal vb] informal : to try to become friendly with someone in order to get help or some advantage ▪ *He has been cozying up to the boss.*

CPA abbr certified public accountant

CPI abbr consumer price index

Cpl. abbr corporal ▪ *Cpl. Jones*

CPR /ˌsiːˌpiːˈɑɚ/ n [U] : a way of trying to save the life of someone who has stopped breathing and whose heart has stopped beating ▪ *They pulled her out of the swimming pool and began CPR.* ◆ *CPR* is an abbreviation of "cardiopulmonary resuscitation."

Cpt. abbr captain ▪ *Cpt. Smith*

CPU /ˌsiːˌpiːˈjuː/ n [C] : the part of a computer system that performs the computer's main functions — called also *processor* ◆ *CPU* is an abbreviation of "central processing unit."

¹crab /ˈkræb/ n **1 a** [C] : a sea animal that has a hard shell, eight legs, and two large claws **b** [U] : the meat of a crab eaten as food **2** [C] US, informal : an unhappy person who complains a lot : GROUCH

²crab vb **crabbed; crab·bing** [I] **1** : to catch or try to catch crabs **2** US, informal : to complain about something ▪ *He was crabbing about the weather.*

crab apple n [C] : a small, sour apple or the kind of tree that produces it

crab·bed /ˈkræbəd/ adj : difficult to read or understand ▪ *crabbed handwriting*

crab·by /ˈkræbi/ adj **crab·bi·er; -est** informal : unhappy and tending to complain a lot : GROUCHY ▪ *She gets crabby if she doesn't get enough sleep.*

crab·grass /ˈkræbˌgræs, Brit ˈkræbˌgrɑːs/ n [U] US : a type of grass that often spreads quickly in places where it is not wanted

crab·meat /ˈkræbˌmiːt/ n [U] : the meat of a crab eaten as food

¹crack /ˈkræk/ vb **1** [T/I] : to break (something) so that there are lines in its surface ▪ *crack a window* ▪ *The mirror/glass cracked.* ▪ *A piece of the statue cracked off.* [=broke off] **2** [T] : to hit or press (something) so that it breaks open suddenly ▪ *a tool for cracking nuts* ▪ *He cracked open the eggs.* **3** [T] : to hit (someone or something) hard and usually suddenly ▪ *Someone cracked him over the head with a bottle.* ▪ *He fell and cracked his elbow on/against the ice.* **4** [T] **a** : to open (a bottle or can) for drinking ▪ *He cracked open a beer.* **b** : to open (a book) for studying or reading ▪ *He hardly cracked (open) a book his whole first semester.* **5** [T] : to open (a safe) without having a key, combination, etc. ▪ *Any thief could crack this safe.* **6** [T] **a** : to find an answer or solution to (something) ▪ *crack* [=solve] *a mystery/puzzle* ▪ *The police cracked* [=broke] *the case.* **b** : to find the meaning of (a secret code) ▪ *He cracked* [=broke] *the enemy's code.* **7** [T] : to open (a door, window, etc.) a small amount ▪ *She cracked (open) the door and peeked inside.* **8** [T] : to cause (something) to make a sudden loud sound ▪ *his habit of cracking his knuckles* ▪ *She cracked the whip.* ▪ *The whip cracked.* **9** [I] : to change sharply in tone or pitch ▪ *Her voice cracked (with emotion) as she told them the news.* **10** [T] informal : to tell (a joke) ▪ *They're always cracking jokes.* **11** [I] : to lose strength or the ability to resist or fight ▪ *The suspect finally cracked and confessed.* ▪ *He cracked under the pressure/stress.* — **crack a smile** : to begin to smile — **crack down** [phrasal vb] : to enforce a law or rule more strictly ▪ *The police are cracking down on speeders.* — **crack the whip** : to force people to work very hard ▪ *a coach who isn't afraid to crack the whip* — **crack up** [phrasal vb] informal **1** **crack up** or **crack (someone) up** or **crack up (someone)** : to begin laughing or cause (someone) to begin laughing very much ▪ *When we saw the picture, we cracked up.* ▪ *That joke cracks me up.* [=I think it is very funny] **2** : to become mentally ill ▪ *She felt herself cracking up.* [=going crazy] **3** **crack up** or **crack up (something)** also **crack (something) up** US, informal : to damage (a vehicle) by crashing ▪ *I almost cracked up (the car) on a curve.* **4** ◆ Something that is **what/all/everything (etc.) it's cracked up to be** is as good as people say it is. ▪ *Is the movie really as good as it's cracked up to be?* — **get cracking** informal : to start doing something right away ▪ *You ought to get cracking on that assignment.* — **cracked** /ˈkrækt/ adj : a cracked windshield ▪ *His hands/lips were dry and cracked.* ▪ *cracked wheat/pepper/corn*

²crack n **1** [C] : a thin line where something is broken but not separated ▪ *There were cracks in the ice/glass/cement/vase.* **2** [C] : a very narrow space or opening between two things or two parts of something ▪ *looking through the cracks in the fence* ▪ *Could you please open the window a crack?* [=open it slightly] **3** [C] : a sudden loud, sharp sound ▪ *We heard a loud crack as the ice broke.* ▪ *the crack of the whip* **4** [C] : a brief change in the sound of a person's voice especially because of strong emotion • *There was a crack in her voice as she told her story.* **5** [C] : a weakness or problem • *Your theory/argument has a few cracks.* • *the cracks in their relationship* **6** [C] *informal* : a joke or rude remark • *They're always making cracks [=wisecracks] about their teacher.* **7** [C] : a hard and sudden hit • *Someone gave him a crack on the head.* **8** [C] *informal* : an effort or attempt to do something — usually + *at* • *her first crack at writing a novel* • *Let me **have/take a crack at it.*** **9** [U] : an illegal drug that is a form of cocaine • *smoking crack* — called also *crack cocaine* — **at the crack of dawn** : at dawn • *We got up at the crack of dawn to go fishing.* — **fall through/between the cracks** also **slip through/between the cracks** : to fail to be noticed or included with others • *children who fall through the cracks in the school system [=who don't get the help they need to succeed in school]*

³**crack** *adj, always before a noun* : of excellent quality or ability • *crack troops* • *a crack sales force* • *She's a crack shot.* [=she is very good at shooting a gun]

crack·down /ˈkrækˌdaʊn/ *n* [C] : an increased effort to enforce a law or rule • *a crackdown on speeding*

crack·er /ˈkrækɚ/ *n* [C] **1** : a dry, thin baked food that is made of flour and water and is often eaten with cheese **2** *Brit, informal* : a very good, amusing, or attractive person or thing • *The match should be real cracker.*

crack·le /ˈkrækəl/ *vb* **crack·led; crack·ling** [I] : to make a series of short, sharp noises • *a crackling fire* — **crackle** *n* [C] • *the crackle of distant gunfire* — **crack·ly** /ˈkrækəli/ *adj* • *the crackly sound of the old record*

crack·pot /ˈkrækˌpɑːt/ *n* [C] *informal* : a person who is crazy or very strange — **crackpot** *adj, always before a noun* • *a crackpot idea*

crack-up /ˈkrækˌʌp/ *n* [C] *US, informal* **1** : an accident in which a vehicle is badly damaged **2** : NERVOUS BREAKDOWN

¹**cra·dle** /ˈkreɪdl/ *n* [C] **1** : a bed for a baby that is usually designed to rock back and forth • *She rocked the cradle.* **2** *formal* : the place where something begins • *the cradle of civilization/liberty* **3** : something that is used to hold or support something else • *She placed the phone back on its cradle.* — **from (the) cradle to (the) grave** : from the beginning until the end of life • *He led a life of hardship from the cradle to the grave.* — **rob the cradle** *US, informal* : to date or marry someone who is much younger than you

²**cradle** *vb* **cra·dled; cra·dling** [T] : to hold (something or someone) gently • *cradle a baby* • *She cradled the injured man's head in her hands/arms.*

¹**craft** /ˈkræft, *Brit* ˈkrɑːft/ *n* **1** [C] : an activity that involves making something in a skillful way by using your hands : HANDICRAFT • *the craft of pottery* **2** [C] : a job or activity that requires special skill • *a photographer's craft* **3** [*plu-*

ral] : objects made by skillful use of the hands • *The store sells crafts [=handicrafts] from around the world.* • *a **crafts fair** [=an event at which crafts are sold]* — see also ARTS AND CRAFTS **4** *pl* **craft** [C] **a** : a usually small boat • *a fishing craft* • *fishing boats and **pleasure craft** [=boats used for pleasure rather than work]* **b** : an airplane, helicopter, or spacecraft

²**craft** *vb* [T] : to make or produce (something) with care or skill • *beautifully crafted wine/shoes/stories* • *crafting a strategy* — **craft·er** *n* [C]

crafts·man /ˈkræftsmən, *Brit* ˈkrɑːftsmən/ *n, pl* **-men** /-mən/ [C] **1** : a person (especially a man) who makes beautiful objects by hand • *Skilled craftsmen carved the mantel.* **2** : a person (especially a man) who is very skilled at doing something • *a writer who is a true craftsman*

crafts·man·ship /ˈkræftsmənˌʃɪp, *Brit* ˈkrɑːftsmənˌʃɪp/ *n* [U] **1** : skillful work • *The table is a fine piece of craftsmanship.* • *literary craftsmanship* **2** : the quality of something made with great skill • *the fine craftsmanship of the table/poetry*

crafts·per·son /ˈkræftsˌpɚsn, *Brit* ˈkrɑːftsˌpɜːsn/ *n* [C] : a craftsman or craftswoman

crafts·wom·an /ˈkræftsˌwʊmən, *Brit* ˈkrɑːftsˌwʊmən/ *n, pl* **-wom·en** /-ˌwɪmən/ [C] : a woman who makes beautiful objects by hand

crafty /ˈkræfti, *Brit* ˈkrɑːfti/ *adj* **craft·i·er; -est** : clever in usually a deceptive or dishonest way • *a crafty person/scheme* — **craft·i·ly** /ˈkræftəli, *Brit* ˈkrɑːftəli/ *adv* — **craft·i·ness** *n* [U]

crag /ˈkræg/ *n* [C] : a high and very steep area of rock on a mountain or cliff

crag·gy /ˈkrægi/ *adj* **crag·gi·er; -est 1** : having many crags • *a craggy island* **2** : rough in a way that suggests strength • *his craggy good looks*

cram /ˈkræm/ *vb* **crammed; cram·ming 1** [T] : to fill (something) completely • *Protesters crammed the streets.* • *His suitcase was crammed with clothes.* • *His suitcase was crammed full of clothes.* • *My schedule is crammed.* **2** [T/I] : to force (someone, something, or yourself) *in* or *into* a small space • *He crammed all his clothes in/into one suitcase.* • *We crammed everyone into my car.* = *We all crammed into my car.* • *She crammed a lot of activities into one week.* **3** [I] : to prepare for a test, exam, etc., by learning a lot of information quickly • *He's **cramming for** the exam.* — **cram in** [*phrasal vb*] **cram in (someone or something)** or **cram (someone or something) in** : to make time for (someone or something) although you are very busy • *I can cram you in this afternoon.* • *We crammed in as much sightseeing as possible.*

¹**cramp** /ˈkræmp/ *n* **1** [C/U] : a sudden painful tightening of muscle in a part of the body • *(US) I got a cramp in my leg.* • *(Brit) I got cramp in my leg.* **2** [*plural*] *chiefly US* : sharp pains in the stomach and the area near it especially because of menstruation

²**cramp** vb **1 a** [T] : to cause a cramp in (your hand, foot, etc.) • *Writing for a long time may cramp your hand.* **b** [I] : to experience a cramp or cramps • *His leg was cramping (up).* **2** [T] : to prevent (something) from developing or growing freely • *regulations that cramp business* **3** [T] : to prevent (someone) from behaving or expressing emotions freely • *She felt cramped by the strict regulations.* • *Having his kid brother with him was cramping his style.* [=preventing him from behaving the way he wanted]

cramped adj **1 a** : too small and crowded • *a cramped apartment* • *working in cramped conditions* **b** : feeling crowded and uncomfortable • *We were pretty cramped inside the tiny cabin.* **2** : small and having parts too close together • *his cramped handwriting* • *This keyboard is too cramped.*

cran·ber·ry /ˈkrænˌberi, Brit ˈkrænbəri/ n, pl **-ries** **1** [C] : a small, dark red berry or the plant that produces it **2** [U] : a dark red color

¹**crane** /ˈkreɪn/ n [C] **1** : a big machine with a long arm that is used for lifting and moving heavy things **2** : a type of tall waterbird that has a long neck and long legs

²**crane** vb **craned**; **cran·ing** [T/I] : to stretch out (your neck) in order to see better • *We craned our necks to see.*

cra·ni·um /ˈkreɪnijəm/ n, pl **-ni·ums** or **-nia** /-nijə/ [C] technical : SKULL — **cra·ni·al** /ˈkreɪnijəl/ adj • *cranial capacity/injuries*

¹**crank** /ˈkræŋk/ n [C] **1** : a machine part with a handle that can be turned in a circular motion to move something **2** informal **a** : a person who has strange ideas or thinks too much about one thing • *a harmless crank* **b** US : a person who is often angry or easily annoyed : GROUCH • *a bad-tempered old crank*

²**crank** vb [T] **1** : to move (something) by turning a crank • *Crank up/down* [=roll up/down] *the car window.* **2** informal : to increase (something) especially by a large amount • *He cranked the temperature (up) to 75 degrees.* • *Crank (up) the volume.* **3** : to start or try to start (an engine) • *Crank the engine to see if it will start.* — **crank out** [phrasal vb] **crank out (something)** or **crank (something) out** informal : to produce (something) quickly or carelessly • *He cranked out the report in less than an hour.*

³**crank** adj, always before a noun : made or sent as a joke or to cause harm • *a crank call/letter*

crank·case /ˈkræŋkˌkeɪs/ n [C] : the part of an engine that contains the crankshaft

crank·shaft /ˈkræŋkˌʃæft, Brit ˈkræŋkˌʃɑːft/ n [C] : a long metal piece that connects a vehicle's engine to the wheels

cranky /ˈkræŋki/ adj **crank·i·er; -est** informal, chiefly US : easily annoyed or angered • *I've been cranky all day.* • *a cranky baby* [=a baby that cries a lot] — **crank·i·ness** n [U]

cran·ny /ˈkræni/ n, pl **-nies** [C] : a small opening or space • *We explored every (nook and) cranny of the old castle.*

¹**crap** /ˈkræp/ n, informal + impolite **1** [U] : something that is worthless, unimportant, or of poor quality • *She treats him like (a piece of) crap.* • *the crap* [=junk] *in the garage* **2** [U] : foolish or untrue words or ideas : NONSENSE • *I think they're full of crap.* [=I think they're lying] • (US) *It's a bunch of crap.* **3** [U] : bad or unfair treatment • *Don't give me any crap.* • *He won't take crap from anyone.* **4 a** [U] : solid waste passed out of the body : FECES **b** [singular] : the act of passing solid waste from the body **5** — used for emphasis • *That movie scared/frightened the crap out of me.* [=scared me very badly] — **crap·py** /ˈkræpi/ adj **crap·pi·er; -est** • *crappy music/weather*

²**crap** vb **crapped; crap·ping** [I] informal + impolite : to pass solid waste from the body

craps /ˈkræps/ n [plural] : a game played for money with two dice • *playing/shooting craps* — **crap** adj • *a craps game/table*

¹**crash** /ˈkræʃ/ vb **1 a** [I] : to hit (the ground, a wall, etc.) hard enough to cause serious damage • *The airplane crashed.* • *The car crashed into the guardrail.* **b** [T] : to damage (a vehicle) by causing it to hit something • *She crashed her car (into a tree).* **2** [T/I] : to make or cause (something) to make a loud noise especially by falling, hitting something, etc. • *She crashed the cymbals together.* • *waves crashing (against the shore)* • *The books crashed to the floor.* • *The walls came crashing down (around them).* **3** [T/I] : to stop or cause (a computer) to stop working suddenly • *My computer keeps crashing.* • *This program crashes my computer.* **4** [I] informal **a** : to go to sleep • *I went straight home and crashed.* **b** : to stay or live for a short time with someone • *You can crash here tonight.* **5** [I] of a business, price, market, etc. : to go down in value very suddenly and quickly • *The stock market crashed.* **6** [T] informal : to go to (a party) without being invited • *He tried to crash the party.* — **crash and burn** US, informal : to fail completely • *The company crashed and burned after only two years.* — **crash·er** n [C] • *a party crasher*

²**crash** n [C] **1** : an accident in which a vehicle is seriously damaged or destroyed by hitting something • *He was injured in a car crash.* • *a train/airplane crash* • *the crash site/scene* **2** : a very loud noise • *The pot/glass fell to the floor with a crash.* • *a crash of thunder* **3** : an occurrence in which a computer suddenly stops working **4** : a sudden and extreme fall or drop in amount or value • *a stock market crash*

crash course n [C] : a class in which a lot of information is taught in a short period of time • *a crash course in Russian*

crash diet n [C] : a way of losing a lot of weight very quickly by eating very little • *go on a crash diet*

crash helmet n [C] : a very strong, hard hat that is worn to protect your head when you are riding a bicycle, motorcycle, etc.

crash–land /ˈkræʃˈlænd/ vb **-land·ed**; **-land·ing** [T/I] : to land (an airplane, helicopter, etc.) in an unusual way because of an emergency • *The pilot crash-landed (the plane) in the field.* — **crash land·ing** [C]

crass /ˈkræs/ adj, disapproving : rude and insensitive • *crass comments/jokes* — **crass·ly** adv — **crass·ness** n [U]

crate /ˈkreɪt/ n [C] **1** : a large wooden or plastic box used for moving things • *packing/shipping crates* • *a crate of apples* **2** : the amount of something contained in a crate • *They used a whole crate of oranges.* — **crate** vb **crat·ed**; **crat·ing** [T] • *The equipment was crated* [=put into a crate] *for shipping.*

cra·ter /ˈkreɪtɚ/ n [C] **1** : a large round hole in the ground • *The explosion/meteorite left a huge crater.* **2** : the area on top of a volcano that is shaped like a bowl

cra·vat /krəˈvæt/ n [C] : a piece of cloth that is worn around the neck and tucked inside the collar of a shirt or sweater

crave /ˈkreɪv/ vb **craved**; **crav·ing** [T] : to have a very strong desire for (something) • *He craves attention.* • *I was craving french fries.*

cra·ven /ˈkreɪvən/ adj, formal : very cowardly • *a craven decision/compromise* — **cra·ven·ly** adv

crav·ing /ˈkreɪvɪŋ/ n [C] : a very strong desire for something • *I had/felt a sudden craving for french fries.*

craw /ˈkrɑː/ n — **stick in your craw** informal ✧ If something *sticks in your craw* you cannot accept it because you think it is wrong or unfair. • *What really sticks in my craw is that he never apologized.*

craw·fish /ˈkrɑːˌfɪʃ/ n [C/U] US : CRAYFISH

¹**crawl** /ˈkrɑːl/ vb [I] **1 a** : to move on your hands and knees • *The baby crawled across the floor.* **b** : to move with the body close to or on the ground • *The soldiers crawled forward on their bellies.* **2** : to move slowly • *Traffic is crawling today.* • *I finally crawled into bed at 2 a.m.* • *The hours crawled by.* **3** : to be full of many people, insects, animals, etc. • *The courthouse is crawling with reporters.* • *The table was crawling with ants.* — **come/go crawling (back) to** informal : to beg for help, forgiveness, etc., in a way that shows you are sorry or weak • *Don't come crawling to me for help later.* • *He's gone crawling back to his old girlfriend.* — **crawl out of the woodwork** see WOODWORK — **make your skin/flesh crawl** : to cause you to feel fear or disgust • *Just thinking about snakes makes my skin crawl.*

²**crawl** n [singular] **1** : a very slow speed • *Traffic slowed to a crawl.* **2** : a way of swimming in which the swimmer lies facing down in the water and moves first one arm over the head and then the other while kicking the legs

cray·fish /ˈkreɪˌfɪʃ/ n [C] : an animal that looks like a small lobster and lives in rivers and streams

cray·on /ˈkreɪˌɑːn/ n [C/U] : a stick of colored wax that is used for drawing • *a box of crayons* • *The drawing is done in crayon.*

craze /ˈkreɪz/ n [C] : something that is very popular for a period of time • *the latest dance/fashion/music craze* • *the current craze for low-fat diets*

crazed /ˈkreɪzd/ adj : wild and uncontrolled • *a crazed killer* • *an addict crazed with drugs* [=made crazy by drugs]

¹**cra·zy** /ˈkreɪzi/ adj **cra·zi·er**; **-est** **1** : not sane: such as **a** *usually offensive* : having or showing severe mental illness • *a hospital for crazy people* ✧ This sense is now usually considered offensive. The phrase *mentally ill* is preferred. **b** : unable to think in a clear or sensible way • *She's crazy with jealousy.* • *He's been acting kind of crazy lately.* **c** — used in the phrase **drive/make (someone) crazy** to describe annoying or bothering someone very much • *That noise is driving me crazy.* **2** : wild and uncontrolled • *He had a crazy look in his eyes.* **3** : very foolish or unreasonable • *driving at crazy speeds* • *You'd be crazy not to accept their offer!* **4** : very strange or unusual • *How do you think of all these crazy ideas?* **5** : very fond of or enthusiastic about someone or something • *She's crazy for/about baseball.* • *They are crazy about each other.* [=they like each other a lot] • *teenagers who are girl/boy crazy* [=very interested in girls/boys] — **go crazy** **1** : to become mentally ill : to go insane — usually used in an exaggerated way • *I must be going crazy. I can't find my car keys anywhere.* **2** : to act in a wild or uncontrolled way • *He suddenly went crazy and started screaming.* • *The crowd went crazy.* [=became very excited] — **like crazy** informal **1** : with a lot of energy and speed • *They've been working like crazy.* [=very hard] **2** : very quickly • *Cars were selling like crazy.* **3** : very much • *When I broke my leg it hurt like crazy.* — **cra·zi·ly** /ˈkreɪzəli/ adv — **cra·zi·ness** n [U]

²**crazy** n, pl **-zies** [C] chiefly US, informal : a person who is crazy • *A bunch of crazies live there.*

creak /ˈkriːk/ vb [I] : to make a long, high sound • *The old floorboards creaked under our feet.* — **creak** n [C] • *the creak of the door opening*

creaky /ˈkriːki/ adj **creak·i·er**; **-est** **1** : making a creaking sound • *creaky floorboards* **2** : old and in bad condition • *the state's creaky economy*

¹**cream** /ˈkriːm/ n **1** [U] : the thick fatty part of milk that rises to the top • *Would you like some cream in your coffee?* • *whipped cream* **2** [C/U] : a food that is made with cream • *cream of tomato soup* • *a vanilla cream filling* **3** [C/U] : a very thick liquid or soft substance that is rubbed into the skin • *a bottle of hand cream* [=hand lotion] **4** **the cream** : the best part of something • *the cream of society* — see also *the cream of the crop* at ¹CROP **5** [C/U] : a pale yellowish color that is close to white

²**cream** vb [T] **1** : to stir or mix (ingredients) until they are soft and smooth • *Cream the butter and sugar.* **2** US, infor-

mal **a** : to defeat (a person or team) easily and completely ▪ *Our team was/got creamed in the play-offs.* **b** : to hit (someone) very hard ▪ *The surfer was/got creamed by a huge wave.* — **cream off** [*phrasal vb*] **cream off (someone or something)** *or* **cream (someone or something) off** *chiefly Brit* : to take (someone or something) away for yourself ▪ *Most of the profit was creamed off by the government.*

cream cheese *n* [*U*] : a soft white cheese made from milk and cream

cream·er /ˈkriːmɚ/ *n* **1** [*C*] *US* : a small container that is used for serving cream ▪ *a sugar bowl and creamer* **2** [*C/U*] : a liquid or powder that is used instead of cream in coffee or tea ▪ *nondairy creamer*

cream·ery /ˈkriːməri/ *n, pl* **-er·ies** [*C*] : a place where dairy products are made or sold

creamy /ˈkriːmi/ *adj* **cream·i·er; -est** **1** **a** : made with cream or tasting like cream ▪ *a rich, creamy flavor* **b** : thick and smooth ▪ *a creamy salad dressing* **2** : having a color like cream ▪ *a creamy yellow* ▪ *creamy skin* — **cream·i·ness** *n* [*U*]

¹**crease** /ˈkriːs/ *n* **1** [*C*] : a line or mark made by folding, pressing, or crushing something ▪ *He ironed his pants to make the creases sharp.* **2** [*C*] : a line or fold in someone's skin : WRINKLE ▪ *tiny creases at the corners of his eyes* **3** *the crease* : an area around or in front of a goal in some games (such as hockey) **4** [*singular*] *Brit* : the line where the batsman stands in cricket

²**crease** *vb* **creased; creas·ing** **1** [*T*] : to fold, press, or crush (cloth, paper, etc.) so that a line or mark is formed ▪ *a neatly creased pair of pants* **2** [*T/I*] : to make a line or fold in (someone's skin) ▪ *A frown creased [=wrinkled] his forehead.*

cre·ate /kriˈeɪt/ *vb* **-at·ed; -at·ing** [*T*] : to make, produce, or cause (something) ▪ *a plan to create jobs* ▪ *the scientists who created the atomic bomb* ▪ *The machine creates a lot of noise.* ▪ *working towards creating a better society* ▪ *He creates beautiful paintings/music.*

cre·a·tion /kriˈeɪʃən/ *n* **1** [*U*] : the act of creating something ▪ *25 years after the play's creation* ▪ *the creation of new jobs/businesses* **2** [*C*] : something that has been created ▪ *The company was the creation of one woman.* ▪ *his latest artistic creation* **3** [*U*] : everything in the world ▪ *the whole of creation* [=all of the world] ▪ *They've traveled all over creation.* [=everywhere] **4** *or* **Creation** [*U*] : the act of making the world ▪ *the biblical story of Creation*

cre·a·tive /kriˈeɪtɪv/ *adj* **1** : having or showing an ability to make new things or think of new ideas ▪ *a creative person/solution* ▪ *creative minds/thinking* **2** *always before a noun* : using the ability to make or think of new things ▪ *creative writing* ▪ *the creative process* **3** *always before a noun, usually disapproving* : done in an unusual and often dishonest way ▪ *Last year's record profits were due to some creative accounting.* — **cre·a·tive·ly** *adv*

— **cre·a·tive·ness** *n* [*U*]

cre·a·tiv·i·ty /ˌkriːˌeɪˈtɪvəti/ *n* [*U*] : the ability to make new things or think of new ideas ▪ *her artistic creativity*

cre·a·tor /kriˈeɪtɚ/ *n* **1** [*C*] : a person who makes something new ▪ *the creator of a television show* **2** *Creator* [*singular*] : GOD **1**

crea·ture /ˈkriːtʃɚ/ *n* [*C*] **1 a** : an animal of any type ▪ *furry/wild creatures* ▪ *all living creatures* **b** : an imaginary or very strange kind of animal ▪ *fantastic/mythical/legendary creatures* **2** : a person usually of a specified type ▪ *The poor creature had no way to get home.* **3** : a person or thing that is influenced or controlled by something specified — + *of* ▪ *She's a creature of politics.* ▪ *I'm a creature of habit.*

creature comfort *n* [*C*] : something that makes life easier or more pleasant ▪ *a hotel with all the creature comforts of home*

crèche /ˈkrɛʃ/ *n* [*C*] **1** *US* : a set of statues that represents the scene of Jesus Christ's birth and that is displayed during Christmas — called also (*chiefly Brit*) **crib** **2** *Brit* : a day care center

cre·dence /ˈkriːdns/ *n* [*U*] **1** : belief that something is true ▪ *I place/put little credence in statistics.* ▪ *Don't give credence to their gossip.* **2** : the quality of being believed or accepted as true or real ▪ *evidence that gives/adds/lends credence to their theory*

cre·den·tial /krɪˈdɛnʃəl/ *n* [*C*] **1** : a quality, skill, or experience that makes a person suited to do a job — usually plural ▪ *What are her academic/professional credentials?* [=qualifications] **2** : a document which shows that a person is qualified to do a particular job — usually plural ▪ *The doctor showed us her credentials.*

cred·i·bil·i·ty /ˌkrɛdəˈbɪləti/ *n* [*U*] : the quality of being believed or accepted as true, real, or honest ▪ *The new evidence lends credibility to their theory.* ▪ *They doubted the credibility of her story.*

cred·i·ble /ˈkrɛdəbəl/ *adj* **1** : able to be believed : reasonable to trust or believe ▪ *Their story seemed credible.* ▪ *credible information/witnesses* **2** : good enough to be effective ▪ *She does a credible job of playing the famous singer.* — **cred·i·bly** /ˈkrɛdəbli/ *adv*

¹**cred·it** /ˈkrɛdɪt/ *n* **1** [*U*] **a** : money that a bank or business will allow a person to use and then pay back ▪ *banks that extend credit to the public* ◇ If you buy something **on credit**, you take it and promise to pay for it later. **b** : a record of how well you have paid your bills in the past ▪ *Do you have good credit?* = *Do you have a good credit history?* **2** [*C*] **a** : an amount of money that is added to an account ▪ *received a credit of $50* — opposite DEBIT **b** : an amount of money that is subtracted from the amount that must be paid ▪ *a tax credit* **3** [*U*] : praise or special attention that is given to someone for doing something or for making something happen ▪ *She's finally getting the credit she deserves.* ▪ *You've got to give her credit: she knows what she's doing.* ▪ *He was given (full)*

credit for the discovery. ❖ If you **give credit where credit is due,** you praise someone who deserves to be praised. **4** [*U*] : a good opinion that people have about someone or something ▪ *Their excellent work does the company credit.* = *It brings credit to the company.* ▪ *He was rude but,* **to his credit,** *he later apologized.* **5** [*singular*] : a source of honor or pride for someone or something ▪ *You are a* **credit to** *your country.* **6** [*plural*] : a list of the names of the people who have worked on or performed in a movie, television program, etc. ▪ *the movie's opening/closing credits* **7** a [*C/U*] : a unit that measures a student's progress towards earning a degree ▪ *This course is worth 4 credits.* ▪ *earning academic credit* **b** [*U*] : the amount of points earned for work done on a test, exam, project, etc. ▪ *partial/full/extra credit*

²**credit** *vb* [*T*] **1** a : to add (an amount of money) to a total ▪ *Your payment of $38.50 has been credited to your account.* **b** : to add money to (an account) ▪ *The bank is crediting your account for the full amount.* **2** a : to give (someone or something) credit for something ▪ *They credit their coach for helping them succeed.* = *They credit their coach with their success.* **b** : to give credit for (something) *to* someone or something ▪ *She credits her success to her family's support.* **3** : to think of (someone) as having a particular quality or effect ▪ *She is credited as (being) the first woman to play the sport professionally.* **4** *chiefly Brit* : to believe that (something) is true ▪ *a story that's hard to credit*

cred·it·a·ble /ˈkrɛdətəbəl/ *adj* : good enough to be praised ▪ *a creditable performance* — **cred·it·a·bly** /ˈkrɛdətəbli/ *adv*

credit card *n* [*C*] : a small plastic card that is used to buy things that you agree to pay for later — called also *charge card*

cred·i·tor /ˈkrɛdətɚ/ *n* [*C*] : a person, bank, or company that lends money to someone

cre·do /ˈkriːdoʊ/ *n, pl* **-dos** [*C*] : an idea or set of beliefs that guides the actions of a person or group ▪ *My (personal) credo is "better safe than sorry."*

cre·du·li·ty /krɪˈduːləti, *Brit* krɪˈdjuːləti/ *n* [*U*] *formal* : ability or willingness to believe something ▪ *The book's ending tests/strains credulity.* [=its ending does not seem true or possible]

cred·u·lous /ˈkrɛdʒələs, *Brit* ˈkrɛdjʊləs/ *adj* : too ready to believe things : easily fooled or cheated ▪ *a credulous audience* — **cred·u·lous·ly** *adv* — **cred·u·lous·ness** *n* [*U*]

creed /ˈkriːd/ *n* [*C*] **1** : a statement of the basic beliefs of a religion ▪ *the religion's creed* ▪ *people of different races and creeds* [=religions] **2** : an idea or set of beliefs that guides the actions of a person or group ▪ *a political creed*

creek /ˈkriːk/ *n* [*C*] **1** *US* : a small stream **2** *Brit* : INLET — **up the creek** or **up the creek without a paddle** *informal* : in a very difficult situation that you cannot get out of

¹**creep** /ˈkriːp/ *vb* **crept** /ˈkrɛpt/; **creeping** [*I*] **1** : to move slowly with the body close to the ground ▪ *A spider was creeping* [=crawling] *along the floor.* **2** a : to move slowly and/quietly especially in order to not be noticed ▪ *She crept into bed.* **b** : to go or seem to go very slowly ▪ *The hours crept by.* **3** : to appear gradually and in a way that is difficult to notice ▪ *Prices are creeping up again.* ▪ *A few mistakes crept into the book.* **4** *of a plant* : to grow along the ground or up a surface (such as a tree or wall) ▪ *a creeping vine* — **creep out** [*phrasal vb*] **creep (someone) out** or **creep out (someone)** *US, informal* : to cause (someone) to feel nervous or afraid ▪ *That guy really creeps me out.* — **creep up on** [*phrasal vb*] *informal* : to slowly and quietly move closer to (someone) without being noticed ▪ *(figurative) Old age creeps up on us.* — **make your skin/flesh creep** : to cause you to feel fear or disgust ▪ *The thought of touching a cobweb makes my skin creep.*

²**creep** *n, informal* **1** [*C*] : a strange person who you strongly dislike ▪ *Leave me alone, you creep!* **2** **the creeps** : a feeling of nervousness or fear ▪ *I get the creeps every time he walks by.* ▪ *Snakes give me the creeps.*

creepy /ˈkriːpi/ *adj* **creep·i·er**, **-est** *informal* : causing people to feel nervous and afraid ▪ *a creepy movie/house* — **creep·i·ness** *n* [*U*]

cre·mate /ˈkriːˌmeɪt, krɪˈmeɪt/ *vb* **-mated**; **-mat·ing** [*T*] : to burn (the body of a person who has died) ▪ *He wants to be cremated when he dies.* — **cre·ma·tion** /krɪˈmeɪʃən/ *n* [*U*]

cre·ma·to·ri·um /ˌkriːməˈtoriːjəm, *Brit* ˌkrɛməˈtɔːriəm/ *n, pl* **-to·ria** /-ˈtoriːjə, *Brit* -ˈtɔːriə/ *or* **-to·ri·ums** [*C*] : CREMATORY

cre·ma·to·ry /ˈkriːməˌtori, *Brit* ˈkrɛməˌtri/ *n, pl* **-ries** [*C*] *chiefly US* : a place where the bodies of dead people are cremated

crème de la crème /ˈkrɛmdəlɑˈkrɛm/ *n* — **the crème de la crème** : the very best people or things in a group

Cre·ole /ˈkriːˌoʊl/ *n* **1** [*C*] : a person who has African and French or Spanish ancestors; *especially* : such a person who lives in the West Indies **2** [*C*] : a person whose ancestors were some of the first French or Spanish settlers in the southeastern U.S. **3** a [*U*] : a language that is based on French and that uses words from African languages ▪ *Some people in Louisiana speak Creole.* **b** **creole** [*C*] *linguistics* : a language that is based on one language but that has some words from another language

cre·ole *or* **Creole** /ˈkriːˌoʊl/ *adj* **1** : relating to people who are Creoles or to their language ▪ *Creole music/words* ▪ *a Creole woman* **2** — used to describe the traditional food of the Creoles from the southeastern U.S. ▪ *creole dishes such as gumbo*

crepe *or* **crêpe** /ˈkreɪp/ *n* **1** [*C*] : a very thin pancake **2** [*U*] : a kind of thin cloth with many small wrinkles

crepe paper *n* [*U*] : a type of colorful paper *that has a wrinkled surface*

crept *past tense and past participle of* ¹CREEP

cre·scen·do /krə'ʃɛndoʊ/ *n, pl* **-dos** *also* **-does** [C] **1** : a gradual increase in the loudness of a sound or section of music **2** : the highest or loudest point of something that increases gradually ▪ *The noise/excitement rose to a crescendo.* = *It reached a crescendo.*

cres·cent /'krɛsn̩t/ *n* **1** [*singular*] : the shape of the visible part of the moon when it is less than half full ▪ *the crescent moon* **2** [C] : a shape that is like a crescent moon

¹**crest** /'krɛst/ *n* [C] **1** : the highest part or point of something ▪ *the crest of the wave/hill/mountain* ▪ *He was at the crest of his fame when he died.* **2** : a bunch of decorative feathers at the top of a bird's head **3** : a special symbol used especially in the past to represent a family, group, or organization ▪ *her family's crest* — **crest·ed** /'krɛstəd/ *adj* ▪ *a crested bird*

²**crest** *vb* [T/I] : to reach the highest part, point, or level ▪ *We crested the hill/mountain/wave.* ▪ *The river crested at 10 feet above normal.* ▪ *His acting career crested in the 1940s.*

crest·fall·en /'krɛst,fɑːlən/ *adj* : very sad and disappointed ▪ *After losing its last game, the team was crestfallen.*

cre·tin /'kriːtn̩, Brit 'krɛtn̩/ *n* [C] *informal + offensive* : a very stupid or annoying person

cre·vasse /krɪ'væs/ *n* [C] : a deep, narrow opening or crack in an area of thick ice or rock

crev·ice /'krɛvəs/ *n* [C] : a narrow opening or crack in a hard surface and especially in rock

¹**crew** /'kruː/ *n* **1** [C] **a** : the group of people who operate a ship, airplane, or train ▪ *a ship's crew* ▪ *the passengers and crew* ▪ *crew members* **b** : the people who work on a ship except the captain and captain ▪ *the captain and crew* **2** [C] : a group of people who do a specified kind of work together ▪ *a construction crew* ▪ *television/news/film/camera crews* **3** [*singular*] *informal* : a group of people who are friends or who are doing something together ▪ *the crew* [=*gang*] *that hangs out at the diner* ▪ *We were a motley crew.* [=an unusual mixed group] **4 a** [C] : a team that rows a boat in a race against other boats **b** [U] *US* : the sport of racing in long, narrow boats that are moved by rowing with oars : ROWING

²**crew** *vb* [T/I] : to work as a member of a crew that operates a ship or airplane ▪ *The ship was crewed by 12 men.*

crew cut *n* [C] : a very short haircut usually for men or boys

crew·man /'kruːmən/ *n, pl* **-men** [C] : a member of a crew: such as **a** : a person who helps operate a ship, airplane, or train **b** : a person who is part of a group of people who work together ▪ *TV crewmen*

crew neck *n* [C] **1** : a plain, round neck on a T-shirt, sweater, etc. **2** *usually*

crew·neck /'kruː,nɛk/ : a sweater with a crew neck

¹**crib** /'krɪb/ *n* [C] **1 a** *US* : a small bed with high sides for a baby — called also (*Brit*) **cot b** *Brit* : ¹CRADLE 1 **2** *chiefly Brit* : CRÈCHE 1

²**crib** *vb* **cribbed; crib·bing** [T/I] : to copy an idea, a piece of writing, etc., from someone else ▪ *She cribbed a line from her favorite poet.* ▪ *students cribbing off each other's papers*

crib·bage /'krɪbɪdʒ/ *n* [U] : a card game for two players in which a special board is used to count each player's points

crick /'krɪk/ *n* [C] : a sudden pain especially in your neck or back ▪ *I got a crick in my neck from looking up for too long.*

crick·et /'krɪkət/ *n* **1** [C] : a small black insect that jumps high and that makes loud, high-pitched noises **2** [U] : a game played on a field by two teams of 11 players who try to score by hitting a ball with a bat and then running between two sets of sticks ▪ *a game of cricket* ▪ *a cricket match* — **not cricket** *Brit, old-fashioned* : not fair, polite, or proper

crick·et·er /'krɪkətə/ *n* [C] : a person who plays cricket

crime /'kraɪm/ *n* **1** [C] : an illegal act for which someone can be punished by the government ▪ *commit/solve a crime* **2** [U] : activity that is against the law : illegal acts in general ▪ *trying to prevent/deter/reduce/fight crime* ▪ *He turned to a life of crime.* [=he became a criminal] ▪ *He has links to organized crime.* [=a group of professional criminals] ▪ *the crime scene* [=the place where a crime happened] ▪ *a crime wave* [=a sudden increase in crime] ◆ Someone's **partner in crime** is a person who helps someone commit a crime. **3** [*singular*] : an act that is foolish or wrong ▪ *It's a crime* [=*sin*] *to let food go to waste.*

¹**crim·i·nal** /'krɪmənl̩/ *adj* **1** : involving illegal activity : relating to crime ▪ *criminal acts/activities/behavior* ▪ *a criminal organization* ▪ *He was accused of criminal negligence.* **2** *always before a noun* : relating to laws that describe crimes rather than to laws about a person's rights ▪ *a criminal court/case/trial/investigation* ▪ *criminal law/lawyers* **3** *not before a noun* : morally wrong ▪ *The way they're treated is criminal.* — **crim·i·nal·ly** *adv* ▪ *criminally liable/responsible*

²**criminal** *n* [C] : a person who is guilty of a crime ▪ *She's a convicted criminal.* ▪ *a violent/hardened criminal*

crim·i·nol·o·gy /,krɪmə'nɑːlədʒi/ *n* [U] : the study of crime, criminals, and the punishment of criminals — **crim·i·nol·o·gist** /,krɪmə'nɑːlədʒɪst/ *n* [C]

¹**crimp** /'krɪmp/ *vb* [T] **1** : to make the surface or edge of (hair, cloth, metal, etc.) have many small waves or folds ▪ *Crimp the edges of the pie crust with a fork.* **2** : to press or fold (parts or pieces) tightly together ▪ *Crimp the pieces of foil together.* **3** *US* : to prevent (something) from happening or proceeding in the usual or desired way ▪ *economic problems that have been crimping sales*

²**crimp** *n* [C] : a small wave or fold in the

surface of something (such as hair or cloth) — *put a crimp in US* : to prevent (something) from happening or proceeding in the usual or desired way ▪ *The storm put a crimp in our travel plans.*

crim·son /ˈkrɪmzən/ *n* [U] : a deep purplish-red color — **crimson** *adj*

cringe /ˈkrɪndʒ/ *vb* **cringed; cring·ing** [I] **1** : to feel disgust or embarrassment and often to show this feeling by a movement of your face or body ▪ *I always cringe when I hear that song.* **2** : to make a sudden movement from fear of being hit or hurt ▪ *The dog cringed at the noise.*

¹crin·kle /ˈkrɪŋkəl/ *vb* **crin·kled; crin·kling** [T/I] : to form small, thin lines on the surface ▪ *The corners of his eyes crinkle when he smiles.* ▪ *She crinkled (up) her nose in disgust.*

²crinkle *n* [C] : a small, thin line that appears on a surface ▪ *the crinkles at the corners of his eyes* — **crin·kly** /ˈkrɪŋkli/ *adj* **crin·kli·er; -est** ▪ *crinkly fabric*

¹crip·ple /ˈkrɪpəl/ *n* [C] **1** *old-fashioned + offensive* : a person who cannot move or walk normally because of a permanent physical problem **2** *informal* : a person who has emotional problems that prevent normal behavior with other people ▪ *social/emotional cripples*

²cripple *vb* **crip·pled; crip·pling** [T] **1** : to cause (a person or animal) to be unable to move or walk normally ▪ *Thousands of people have been crippled by the disease.* ▪ *The car accident left him crippled.* [=*disabled*] **2** : to make (something) unable to work normally ▪ *an economy crippled by inflation* — **crip·pling** *adj* ▪ *crippling diseases*

cri·sis /ˈkraɪsəs/ *n, pl* **-ses** /-ˌsiːz/ [C/U] : a difficult or dangerous situation that needs serious attention ▪ *She was dealing with a family crisis.* ▪ *an economic/financial/fiscal crisis* ▪ *an energy/fuel/water crisis* [=a time when there is not enough energy/fuel/water] ▪ *times of national crisis* ▪ *companies that are in crisis*

¹crisp /ˈkrɪsp/ *adj* **1 a** : dry, hard, and easily broken ▪ *crisp bacon* **b** : pleasantly firm and making a sharp sound when chewed or crushed ▪ *a crisp apple* **2** : clean, smooth, and somewhat stiff ▪ *a crisp $50 bill* **3** : having details that are easily seen or heard ▪ *crisp photographs* ▪ *a crisp recording* **4** : pleasantly cool, fresh, and dry ▪ *a crisp autumn day* **5** : moving or speaking quickly and directly ▪ *her crisp, businesslike manner* **6** : done in a very confident and skillful way ▪ *a crisp tennis serve* — **crisp·ly** *adv* — **crisp·ness** *n* [U]

²crisp *n* [C] **1** : a thin, hard, and usually salty piece of food; *especially, Brit* : POTATO CHIP **2** [C/U] *US* : a dessert made of cooked fruit with a sweet, dry topping ▪ *apple crisp* — **to a crisp** : to a state of being hard, dry, and easily broken ▪ *The toast is burned to a crisp.*

³crisp *vb* [T/I] : to make (something) crisp or to become crisp ▪ *The crust crisped (up) nicely in the oven.*

crispy /ˈkrɪspi/ *adj* **crisp·i·er; -est** : pleasantly thin, dry, and easily broken ▪ *crispy crackers* : having a pleasantly crisp

outer layer ▪ *crispy fried chicken* — **crisp·i·ness** *n* [U]

criss·cross /ˈkrɪsˌkrɑːs/ *vb* **1** [T/I] : to form a pattern on (something) with lines that cross each other ▪ *Several highways crisscross the state.* **2** [T] : to go from one side of (something) to the other side and come back again ▪ *Tourists crisscrossed the lake all day.* — **crisscross** *adj* ▪ *a crisscross pattern*

cri·te·ri·on /kraɪˈtɪrijən/ *n, pl* **-te·ria** /-ˈtɪrijə/ [C] : something that is used as a reason for making a judgment or decision ▪ *the university's criteria for admission*

crit·ic /ˈkrɪtɪk/ *n* [C] **1** : a person who gives opinions about books, movies, or other forms of art **2** : a person who criticizes someone or something ▪ *a fierce/loud/outspoken critic of tax reform*

crit·i·cal /ˈkrɪtɪkəl/ *adj* **1** : expressing criticism or disapproval ▪ *He's always so critical.* **2** : of or relating to the judgments of critics about books, movies, art, etc. ▪ *critical acclaim* ▪ *critical writings/theory* **3** : using or involving careful judgment about the good and bad parts of something ▪ *critical analysis/thinking* **4** : extremely important ▪ *a critical phase of the experiment* ▪ *a matter of critical importance* **5** *medical* : relating to or involving a great danger of death ▪ *critical injuries* ▪ *The patient is in critical condition.* = *The patient is critical.* — **crit·i·cal·ly** /ˈkrɪtɪkli/ *adv*

crit·i·cism /ˈkrɪtəˌsɪzəm/ *n* **1** [U] : the act of expressing disapproval and of noting the problems or faults of a person or thing ▪ *The idea attracted/drew widespread criticism.* ▪ *She gave me some constructive criticism of my essay.* **2** [C] : a remark or comment that expresses disapproval of someone or something ▪ *I had one minor criticism about her design.* **3** [U] : the activity of making careful judgments about the good and bad qualities of books, movies, etc. ▪ *literary criticism*

crit·i·cize *also Brit* **crit·i·cise** /ˈkrɪtəˌsaɪz/ *vb* **-cized; -ciz·ing 1** [T/I] : to express disapproval of (someone or something) ▪ *All he ever does is criticize (me).* **2** [T] : to look at and make judgments about (something) ▪ *He asked me to criticize* [=*critique*] *his drawings.*

cri·tique /krəˈtiːk/ *n* [C] : a careful judgment in which you give your opinion about the good and bad parts of something ▪ *a fair and honest critique of her work* — **critique** *vb* **-tiqued; -tiqu·ing** [T] ▪ *He critiqued my work.*

crit·ter /ˈkrɪtə/ *n* [C] *US, informal* : a usually small creature or animal

croak /ˈkroʊk/ *vb* **1** [I] : to make the deep, harsh sound that a frog makes **2** [T/I] : to say (something) in a rough, low voice that is hard to understand ▪ *He tried to speak but could barely croak (his name).* **3** [I] *slang* : to die ▪ *He had a heart attack and croaked.* — **croak** *n* [C] ▪ *the croaks of the frogs*

croc /ˈkrɑːk/ *n* [C] *informal* : CROCODILE

cro·chet /kroʊˈʃeɪ/ *n* [U] : a method of making cloth or clothing by using a nee dle with a hook at the end to form and weave loops in a thread — **crochet** vb [T/I]

crock /'krɑːk/ n **1** [C] : a pot or jar made of baked clay **2** [singular] US, informal : something that is impossible to believe because it is untrue or ridiculous ▪ She thinks horoscopes are a crock. **3** [C] Brit, informal : an old, ill, or unhappy person

crock·ery /'krɑːkəri/ n [U] **1** US : pots or jars made of baked clay used for cooking **2** chiefly Brit : plates, dishes, and cups used in dining

croc·o·dile /'krɑːkə،dajəl/ n [C] : a large reptile that has a long, thin mouth with sharp teeth and that lives in the water in regions with hot weather

crocodile tears n [plural] : a false expression of sadness or regret about something ▪ The company shed/cried crocodile tears for the workers who were laid off.

cro·cus /'kroukəs/ n [C] : a small purple, yellow, or white flower that blooms in the early spring

croft /'krɑːft/ n [C] Brit : a small farm usually with a house on it in Scotland

croft·er /'krɑːftər/ n [C] Brit : a person who owns or works on a croft

crois·sant /krə'sɑːnt, Brit 'kwɑːsɒŋ/ n [C] : a type of roll that has a curved shape and that is usually eaten at breakfast

crone /'kroun/ n [C] literary : a cruel or ugly old woman

cro·ny /'krouni/ n, pl **-nies** [C] disapproving : a friend of someone powerful (such as a politician) who is unfairly given special treatment or favors ▪ one of the mayor's cronies

cro·ny·ism /'krouni،ɪzəm/ n [U] disapproving : the unfair practice by a powerful person (such as a politician) of giving jobs and other favors to friends

¹**crook** /'kruk/ n [C] **1** informal **a** : a dishonest person **b** : a criminal ▪ a small-time crook **2 a** : the place where an arm, leg, or finger bends ▪ the crook of his arm **b** : a curved or hooked part of something ▪ a crook of the tree/cane **3** : a long stick with one end curved into a hook that is used by a shepherd — **by hook or by crook** see ¹HOOK

²**crook** vb [T] : to bend (your finger, neck, or arm) ▪ He crooked his finger at us and led us to the table.

crook·ed /'krukəd/ adj **1** : not straight ▪ a crooked smile/path ▪ a crooked tooth **2** informal **a** : not honest ▪ crooked politicians **b** : done to trick or deceive someone ▪ a crooked card game — **crook·ed·ly** adv — **crook·ed·ness** n [U]

croon /'kruːn/ vb [T/I] : to sing (a song) in a low soft voice ▪ She crooned (a lullaby) to the baby.

croon·er /'kruːnər/ n [C] : a male singer who sings slow, romantic songs in a soft, smooth voice

¹**crop** /'krɑːp/ n **1** [C] **a** : a plant or plant product that is grown by farmers ▪ corn crops **b** : the amount of a crop that is gathered at one time or in one season ▪ a bumper crop of tomatoes [=a very large

crop of tomatoes] **2** [singular] **a** : a group of people who begin to do something at the same time ▪ a new crop of students **b** : a group of things that happen or are produced at the same time ▪ a new crop of horror movies ✧ People or things that are **the cream of the crop** are the best of their kind or in their group. **3** [C] : a short whip used in horse riding ▪ a riding crop **4** [C] : a short and thick quantity of hair on a person's head ▪ a crop of red, curly hair **5** [C] : an area in the throat of a bird where food is stored for a time

²**crop** vb **cropped; crop·ping** [T] **1** : to cut off the upper or outer parts of (something) ▪ crop a dog's ears **2** : to cut off part of (a picture or photograph) ▪ I cropped the image to fit it into the frame. **3** : to cut (someone's hair) short ▪ closely cropped hair **4** : to bite off and eat the tops of (grass or plants) ▪ The cows were cropping the grass in the meadow. — **crop up** [phrasal vb] : to come or appear when not expected ▪ New problems crop up every day.

crop·per /'krɑːpər/ n — **come a cropper** informal : to fail completely in a sudden or unexpected way ▪ Her careful plan came a cropper.

cro·quet /krou'keɪ, Brit 'krəʊkeɪ/ n [U] : a game in which players use wooden mallets to hit balls through a series of curved wires that are stuck into the ground

¹**cross** /'krɑːs/ n [C] **1 a** : a long piece of wood with a shorter piece across it near the top that people were once fastened to and left to die on as a form of punishment **b** : an object or image in the shape of a cross **2** : a mark formed by two lines that cross each other **3** : a mixture of two different things, types, or qualities ▪ The dog is a cross of hunting dog and sheepdog. **4** boxing : a punch that goes over an opponent's punch ▪ a right cross **5** soccer : a kick or hit of the ball that goes across the field from one side to another or to the middle of the field — **cross to bear** : a problem that causes trouble or worry for someone over a long period of time ▪ We all have our crosses to bear.

²**cross** vb **1** [T/I] : to go from one side of (something) to the other ▪ We crossed the street. ▪ The train crosses through France. **2** [T/I] : to go or pass across each other ▪ the point at which two lines cross (each other) **3** [T] : to place one arm, leg, etc., over the other ▪ cross your arms/legs/fingers ✧ If you **cross your fingers** or **keep your fingers crossed**, you hope that you will be lucky and that something you want to happen will happen. **4** [I] : to pass in opposite directions ▪ Our letters crossed in the mail. **5** [T] : to turn (your eyes) inward toward your nose ▪ He crossed his eyes. **6** [T] : to act against the wishes, plans, or orders of (someone) ▪ She has a bad temper so you don't want to cross her. **7** [T] **a** : to make two different kinds of animals breed together ▪ The breeders crossed the bison with domestic cattle. **b** : to mix two kinds of

plants to form a new one • *cross two different types of corn* — **cross my heart (and hope to die)** *informal* — used in speech to stress that you are telling the truth and will do what you promise • **cross off** [*phrasal vb*] **cross (someone or something) off** *or* **cross off (someone or something)** : to draw a line through (a name or item on a list) • *They crossed off the names of the people who had already been invited.* — **cross out** [*phrasal vb*] **cross (something) out** *or* **cross out (something)** : to draw a line through (something) to show that it is wrong • *cross out a mistake* — **cross over** [*phrasal vb*] **1** : to move or go from one side of (something) to the other • *The bridge crosses over the river.* **2** : to change from one type of character or condition to another • *The singer crossed over from country to pop.* [=changed his style of music from country to pop] — **cross paths** ◆ When people **cross paths** or when their **paths cross,** they meet each other at a time that was not planned or expected. • *After they left college, it was many years before they crossed paths again.* — **cross someone's face** : to appear briefly on someone's face • *A smile crossed her face.* — **cross someone's mind** : to come into someone's thoughts • *Did it ever cross your mind that I could be right?* — **cross swords** : to fight or argue • *I didn't want to cross swords with him.* — **cross the line** : to go beyond what is proper or acceptable • *Her criticism crossed the line from helpful to just plain hurtful.* — **cross up** [*phrasal vb*] *US* **cross (someone or something) up** *or* **cross up (someone or something)** **1** : to make (someone) confused • *The team crossed up their opponent by throwing the ball instead of running it.* **2 cross (something) up** *or* **cross up (something)** : to ruin (something) completely • *His failure to meet the deadline crossed up the deal.* — **cross yourself** : to make the sign of the cross on your head and chest • *I crossed myself as I entered the church.* — **cross·er** [*C*]

³cross *adj* : annoyed or angry • *I was cross with her for being careless.* — **cross·ly** *adv*

cross·bar /ˈkrɑːˌbaɚ/ *n* [*C*] **1** : a bar that joins two posts (such as goalposts in soccer or hockey) **2** : the bar that goes between the seat and the handlebars of a bicycle

crossbones *see* SKULL AND CROSS-BONES

cross·bow /ˈkrɑːˌboʊ/ *n* [*C*] : a weapon that shoots arrows and that consists of a short bow attached to a longer piece of wood

cross–check /ˈkrɑːˌtʃɛk/ *vb* [*T*] : to use a different source or method to check information, calculations, etc. • *You should cross-check your answers with a calculator.* — **cross–check** *n* [*C*]

cross–coun·try /ˈkrɑːsˈkʌntri/ *adj,* always before a noun **1** : going or moving across a country • *a cross-country railroad/tour* **2** : going over the countryside rather than by roads or over a track • *a*

cross-country race **3** : relating to or used in a kind of skiing that is done over the countryside instead of down a mountain • *cross-country skiing/skis* — **cross–country** *adv*

cross–cul·tur·al /ˈkrɑːsˈkʌltʃərəl/ *adj* : relating to or involving two or more different cultures or countries • *a cross-cultural study*

cross–cur·rent /ˈkrɑːsˌkɚrənt/ *n* [*C*] : a current of water that flows against or across the main current • (*figurative*) *the political crosscurrents that interfere with the passing of laws*

cross–dress·ing /ˈkrɑːsˌdrɛsɪŋ/ *n* [*U*] : the act or practice of wearing clothes made for the opposite sex — **cross–dress·er** /ˈkrɑːsˌdrɛsɚ/ *n* [*C*]

cross–ex·am·ine /ˈkrɑːsɪɡˈzæmən/ *vb* **-ined; -in·ing** [*T*] *law* : to ask more questions of (a witness who has been questioned by another lawyer) • *The defendant's attorney cross-examined the witness.* — **cross–ex·am·i·na·tion** /ˈkrɑːsɪɡˌzæməˈneɪʃən/ *n* [*U*] — **cross–ex·am·in·er** /ˈkrɑːsɪɡˈzæmənɚ/ *n* [*C*]

cross–eyed /ˈkrɑːsˌaɪd/ *adj* : having one or both eyes turned inward toward the nose • *a cross-eyed person/look* — **cross–eyed** *adv*

cross·fire /ˈkrɑːsˌfajɚ/ *n* [*singular*] : shots that come from two or more places so that the bullets cross through the same area • (*figurative*) *She was caught in the crossfire when her parents argued.* [=she became involved in the quarrel between her parents and they became angry at her]

cross·ing /ˈkrɑːsɪŋ/ *n* [*C*] **1** : a place where two things (such as a street and a railroad track) cross each other • *a railroad crossing* **2** : a place where you can cross a street, stream, etc. • *a crossing for ferryboats* **3** : the act of going across something • *the crossing of a mountain range*

cross–legged /ˈkrɑːsˌlɛɡəd/ *adj* : having the legs crossed • *She sat in a cross-legged position.* — **cross–legged** *adv* • *He sat on the floor cross-legged.* [=with his legs crossed and her knees spread wide apart]

cross·over /ˈkrɑːsˌoʊvɚ/ *n* [*C*] : a change from one style or type of activity to another • *The actor made a smooth crossover to politics.* • *a successful crossover artist/star/celebrity*

cross·piece /ˈkrɑːsˌpiːs/ *n* [*C*] : something (such as a piece of wood) that is placed or that lies across something else

cross–pur·pos·es /ˈkrɑːsˈpɚpəsəz/ *n* — **at cross-purposes** : in a way that causes confusion or failure because people are working or talking with different goals or purposes • *They were talking/working at cross-purposes.*

cross–re·fer /ˌkrɑːsrɪˈfɚ/ *vb* **-ferred; -fer·ring** [*T/I*] : to direct a reader to more information that can be found in another place • *The entry cross-refers (you) to a table of weights.*

cross–ref·er·ence /ˈkrɑːsˈrɛfrəns/ *n* [*C*] : a note in a book (such as a dictionary) that tells you where to look for more information • *The almanac includes cross-*

references to a map for each country. — **cross–reference** vb **-enced; -enc·ing** [T] • *The book is heavily cross-referenced.* [=has many cross-references]

cross·road /'krɑːˌsroʊd/ n [C] **1** : a place where two or more roads cross • (*figurative*) *The industry is at a critical crossroad.* [=a time at which a decision must be made] **2** : a road that crosses a main road or that runs across land between main roads • *We turned onto a crossroad.*

cross section n **1** [C/U] : a view or drawing that shows what the inside of something looks like after a cut has been made across it • *a cross section of the human brain* • *The drawing showed the human brain in cross section.* **2** [C] : a small group that includes examples of the different types of people or things in a larger group • *a representative cross section of American society*

cross–town /'krɑːˌstaʊn/ adj, always before a noun **1** : located on different sides of a town or city • *The two schools were crosstown rivals in baseball.* **2** : going across a town or city • *crosstown traffic* — **crosstown** adv

cross–walk /'krɑːˌswɑːk/ n [C] US : a marked path where people can safely walk across a street or road

cross–wind /'krɑːˌswɪnd/ n [C] : a wind that blows across the direction that something (such as an airplane) is moving in

cross–wise /'krɑːˌswaɪz/ adj : going from one side or corner to another • *a crosswise cut* — **crosswise** adv

cross–word puzzle /'krɑːˌswɚd-/ n [C] : a puzzle in which words that are the answers to clues are written into a pattern of numbered squares that go across and down — called also *crossword*

crotch /'krɑːtʃ/ n [C] : the part of the body where the legs join together; *also* : the part of a piece of clothing that covers this part of the body • *the crotch of the pants/shorts/pajamas*

crotch·ety /'krɑːtʃəti/ adj : often annoyed and angry • *a crotchety old teacher*

crouch /'kraʊtʃ/ vb [I] **1** : to lower your body to the ground by bending your legs • *She crouched down to get a closer look at the spider.* **2** of an animal : to lie on the stomach close to the ground with the legs bent • *The lion crouched in the tall grass.* — **crouch** [C] — **crouched** /'kraʊtʃt/ adj • *a crouched position*

crou·ton /'kruːˌtɑːn/ n [C] : a small piece of bread that is toasted or fried until it is crisp

¹**crow** /'kroʊ/ n [C] **1** : a large black bird that has a loud and harsh cry **2** : the loud, high sound a rooster makes or a similar sound • *a crow of delight/triumph* — **as the crow flies** : measured in a straight line • *They live about three miles from here as the crow flies.* — **eat crow** see EAT

²**crow** vb **1** [I] : to make the loud, high sound that a rooster makes or a similar sound • *The boy crowed with delight.* **2** [T/I] : to talk in a way that shows too much pride about something you have

done • *"I've won three times in a row," he crowed.*

crow·bar /'kroʊˌbɑɚ/ n [C] : a metal bar that has a thin flat edge at one end and is used to open or lift things

¹**crowd** /'kraʊd/ vb **1 a** [T] : to fill (something) so that there is little or no room for anyone or anything else • *College students crowded* [=packed] *the bar.* **b** [T] : to push or force (something) *into* a small space • *They crowded too many people into the room.* • *The shoes are all crowded together in the closet.* **c** [I] : to move into a small space • *We crowded onto the bus.* **2** [T] chiefly US : to stand very close or too close to (someone or something) • *Please move back. You're crowding me.* — **crowd around/round** [phrasal vb] : to form a tight group around (something or someone) • *A group of people crowded around the car.* — **crowd in** [phrasal vb] **1** : to move as a group into a small space • *When we got to the elevator, everyone crowded in.* **2** of thoughts, memories, etc. : to come into your mind • *Memories of childhood crowded in on me.* — **crowd out** [phrasal vb] **crowd out (something or someone)** or **crowd (something or someone) out** : to push, move, or force (something or someone) out of a place or situation by filling its space • *Weeds are crowding out the flowers in our garden.*

²**crowd** n **1** [C] : a large group of people who are together in one place • *The crowd is restless.* = (*Brit*) *The crowd are restless.* • *a crowd of kids/reporters/shoppers* • *Crowds lined the street to watch the parade.* **2** *the crowd* : ordinary people • *She prefers to be one of the crowd.* [=she prefers not to be noticed or treated in any special way] ❖ Someone or something that **stands out from the crowd** is unusual in a good way. ❖ Someone who **follows the crowd** or **goes with the crowd** does whatever most other people are doing. **3** [singular] : a group of people who spend time together or have something in common • *She's been hanging out with the wrong crowd.* — **two's company, three's a crowd** see COMPANY

crowd·ed /'kraʊdəd/ adj : filled with too many people or things • *a crowded bar/lobby/waiting room* • *The room was crowded (with people).*

crowd–pleas·er /'kraʊdˌpliːzɚ/ n [C] : a person, performance, or food that most people like • *The play is a guaranteed crowd-pleaser.* — **crowd–pleas·ing** /'kraʊdˌpliːzɪŋ/ adj

¹**crown** /'kraʊn/ n **1** [C] : a decorative object that is shaped like a circle and worn on the head of a king or queen for special ceremonies **2 the crown** or **the Crown** : the government of a country that is officially ruled by a king or queen • *the blessing of the Spanish crown* **3 the crown** : the position of power that a king or queen has • *When the king died childless, his brother assumed the crown.* [=his brother became king] **4** [C] : something (such as a badge or decoration) in the shape of a king's or queen's crown **5**

[C] : the title or position held by the person who has won a particular competition ▪ *He won the heavyweight boxing crown.* **6** [C] : the part of a tooth that can be seen ▪ *an artificial crown made of porcelain* **7** [C] : the top of the head **8** [C] : the part of a hat that covers the top of the head **9** [C] : the highest point of something (such as a tree or mountain)

²**crown** *vb* [T] **1** : to give (someone) the power and title of a king or queen ▪ *She was crowned queen at the age of 18.* **2** : to officially or formally give (someone) the title or position of a champion, winner, etc. ▪ *The magazine crowned her the new queen of rock-and-roll music.* **3** : to end (something) in a successful and impressive way ▪ *She crowned her long career by designing the city's beautiful new bridge.* **4** *literary* : to be on top of (something) : to form the top of (something) ▪ *a hill crowned with yellow daffodils* ▪ *Her head is crowned by/with thick red hair.* **5** : to put an artificial crown on (a tooth) ▪ *I broke a tooth and I'll have to have it crowned.* **6** *informal* : to hit (someone) on the head ▪ *He got crowned with a beer bottle.*

crown·ing /ˈkraʊnɪŋ/ *adj, always before a noun* : greatest or most complete ▪ *the architect's crowning achievement* ▪ *The town's **crowning glory** is its old cathedral.*

crown jewel *n* **1 the crown jewels** : the crown, scepter, and other jeweled objects that a king or queen uses on formal occasions **2** [C] : the most valuable or attractive thing in a collection or group ▪ *The painting is the crown jewel of the museum's collection.*

crown prince *n* [C] : a prince who is expected to become king when the current king or queen dies

crown princess *n* [C] **1** : the wife of a crown prince **2** : a princess who is expected to become queen when the current king or queen dies

crow's-feet /ˈkroʊzˌfiːt/ *n* [*plural*] : wrinkles around the outer corners of a person's eyes

cru·cial /ˈkruːʃəl/ *adj* : extremely important ▪ *a crucial distinction/difference* ▪ *She played a crucial role in the meeting.* — **cru·cial·ly** *adv*

cru·ci·ble /ˈkruːsəbəl/ *n* [C] **1** : a pot in which metals or other substances are heated to a very high temperature or melted **2** *formal + literary* : a place or situation that forces people to change or make difficult decisions ▪ *His character was formed in the crucible of war.*

cru·ci·fix /ˈkruːsəˌfɪks/ *n* [C] : a model of a cross with a figure of Jesus Christ crucified on it

cru·ci·fix·ion /ˌkruːsəˈfɪkʃən/ *n* **1** [U] : an act of killing someone by nailing or tying his or her hands and feet to a cross ▪ *the crucifixion of the rebel Spartacus* **2 the Crucifixion** : the killing of Jesus Christ on a cross

cru·ci·fy /ˈkruːsəˌfaɪ/ *vb* **-fies; -fied; -fy·ing** [T] **1** : to kill (someone) by nailing or tying his or her hands and feet to a cross ▪ *Jesus Christ was crucified.* **2** *informal* : to criticize (someone or some-

thing) very harshly ▪ *They crucified her in the newspapers.*

crud /ˈkrʌd/ *n* [U] *informal* : a dirty or greasy substance ▪ *I scrubbed the crud off the old stove.*

crud·dy /ˈkrʌdi/ *adj* **crud·di·er; -est** *informal* **1** : dirty or greasy ▪ *a cruddy old stove* **2** *US* : not of good quality ▪ *They did a cruddy job.* **b** : not well or happy ▪ *I feel cruddy.*

¹**crude** /ˈkruːd/ *adj* **crud·er; crud·est** **1** : very simple and basic ▪ *a crude tool/drawing/shelter* **2** : talking about sexual matters in a rude way ▪ *crude* [=*vulgar*] *jokes* **3** : very simple and basic in a way that is true but not complete ▪ *a crude* [=*rough*] *estimate* — **crude·ly** *adv* — **crude·ness** *n* [U] — **cru·di·ty** /ˈkruːdəti/ *n, pl* **-ties** [C/U] ▪ *the crudity of the drawing*

²**crude** *n* [U] : oil as it exists in the ground — called also **crude oil**

cru·el /ˈkruːl/ *adj, US* **cru·el·er or Brit cru·el·ler; US cru·el·est or Brit cru·el·lest** **1** — used to describe people who hurt others and do not feel sorry about it ▪ *a cruel dictator/tyrant* **2** : causing or helping to cause suffering ▪ *a cruel joke* ▪ *Life has dealt them some **cruel blows** in recent years.* [=some very bad things have happened to them in recent years] — **cru·el·ly** *adv*

cru·el·ty /ˈkruːlti/ *n, pl* **-ties** **1** [U] : a desire to cause others to suffer ▪ *a dictator/tyrant known for his cruelty* **2 a** [U] : actions that cause suffering ▪ *cruelty to animals* **b** [C] : an act or occurrence that causes suffering ▪ *the cruelties of life/nature/war*

¹**cruise** /ˈkruːz/ *vb* **cruised; cruis·ing** **1** [T/I] : to travel on a boat or ship to a number of places as a vacation ▪ *We cruised for a week down the Yangtze River.* **2** [I] *of a car, airplane, etc.* : to move along at a steady speed ▪ *The plane was cruising at 30,000 feet.* **3** [T/I] : to drive or be driven slowly ▪ *Teenagers cruised (the main street) to show off their cars.* **4** [I] : to do something easily ▪ *The team cruised to victory.* **5** [T] : to move around in (a place) without a specific purpose but usually with the hope of finding something interesting ▪ *I cruised the mall for a couple hours on Saturday.* ▪ *(figurative) She spent hours cruising the Internet.* **6** [T/I] *slang* : to go (somewhere) in search of a sexual partner ▪ *They're out cruising (bars) for women.*

²**cruise** *n* [C] : a journey on a boat or ship to a number of places as a vacation ▪ *a Mediterranean cruise*

cruise control *n* [U] **1** : a device in a vehicle that a driver turns on to make the vehicle continue at whatever speed the driver has chosen **2** : a relaxed pace that does not require a lot of effort ▪ *She's been doing the job so long that she's **on cruise control**.* [=she does not put a lot of effort into the job]

cruis·er /ˈkruːzɚ/ *n* [C] **1** *US* : POLICE CAR **2** : a large and fast military ship **3** : a boat that has room to live on and that is used for pleasure — called also **cabin cruiser**

cruise ship n [C] : a large ship that takes many people on a cruise at one time — called also *cruise liner*

crumb /'krʌm/ n [C] **1** : a very small piece of food • *bread/cookie crumbs* **2** *informal* : a very small amount of something • *hoping for any crumb of affection*

crum·ble /'krʌmbəl/ vb **crum·bled; crum·bling 1** [T] : to break (something) into small pieces • *Crumble the cookies into small bits.* **2** [I] : to separate into many small pieces • *a crumbling building/monument/wall* **3** [I] : to break down completely • *Their marriage crumbled after five years.* — *that's the way the cookie crumbles* see COOKIE

crum·bly /'krʌmbali/ adj **crum·bli·er; -est** : easily broken into small pieces • *crumbly cheese/soil*

crum·my /'krʌmi/ adj **crum·mi·er; -est** *informal* **1** : not pleasant • *crummy weather* **2** : not of good quality • *a crummy job/movie/story* **3** *chiefly US* : not well or happy • *I feel crummy.*

crum·pet /'krʌmpət/ n [C] *Brit* : a small round bread that has a smooth bottom and holes in the top and that is eaten hot with butter

crum·ple /'krʌmpəl/ vb **crum·pled; crum·pling 1 a** [T] : to press or squeeze (something) so that it is no longer flat or smooth • *He crumpled (up) the note and threw it away.* **b** [I] : to become wrinkled or bent • *The fabric is stiff and does not crumple* [=*wrinkle*] *easily.* **2** [I] : to suddenly bend and fall • *He crumpled to the floor.*

¹**crunch** /'krʌntʃ/ vb **1** [I] **a** : to make the loud sound of something being crushed • *The snow crunched underfoot.* **b** : to move along a surface that makes the loud sound of something being crushed • *We could hear the truck's tires crunching along the gravel road.* **2** [T] : to examine and analyze (numbers, information, etc.) • *When she crunched the numbers, she found that she could not afford the trip.* — *crunch on* [*phrasal vb*] : to chew (a piece of food) in a way that makes a loud sound • *crunching on potato chips*

²**crunch** n **1** [C] : the sound made when something that is being chewed or crushed • *the crunch of someone eating a carrot* **2** *the crunch* : a very difficult point or situation • *The crunch came when the computer stopped working.* — see also CRUNCH TIME **3** [C] *US* : a situation in which there is not enough of something — usually singular • *a budget/energy/time crunch* **4** [C] : a stomach exercise in which you lie on your back, raise the top part of your body until your shoulders are off the floor, and then lower it — *crunchy* /'krʌntʃi/ adj **crunch·i·er; -est** • *crunchy chips/cereal/vegetables*

crunch time n [U] *informal* : the most important time in a game, event, etc. • *The end of the semester was crunch time for students.*

¹**cru·sade** /kru'seɪd/ n [C] **1** *Crusade* : any one of the wars that European Christian countries fought against Muslims in Palestine in the 11th, 12th, and 13th centuries — usually plural **2** : a major effort to change something • *a crusade for equal rights* • *a crusade against crime/pollution*

²**crusade** vb **-sad·ed; -sad·ing** [I] : to take part in a major effort to change something • *She crusaded for equal rights.* — **cru·sad·er** or **Crusader** n [C] • *human rights crusaders* • *the Crusaders of the Middle Ages*

¹**crush** /'krʌʃ/ vb [T] **1** : to press or squeeze (something) so hard that it breaks or loses its shape • *crushing grapes* **2** : to break (something) into a powder or very small pieces by pressing, pounding, or grinding it • *crushed herbs/ice/garlic* **3** : to defeat (a person or group that opposes you) by using a lot of force • *an attempt to crush the rebellion* **4** : to make (someone) feel very unhappy, upset, etc. • *She was crushed by the news.*

²**crush** n **1** [C] **a** : a strong feeling of romantic love for someone that is usually not expressed and does not last a long time • *I think he's got a crush on her.* • *a schoolgirl crush* [=romantic feelings felt by a schoolgirl or by someone who is being compared to a schoolgirl] **b** : the person on whom you have a crush • *my old high school crush* **2** [C] : a crowd of people who are pressed close together • *a crush of reporters* **3** [U] *chiefly Brit* : a drink made from fruit juice • *orange crush*

crush·ing /'krʌʃɪŋ/ adj : very bad, harmful, or severe • *The team suffered a crushing loss.* • *crushing poverty/sadness*

crust /'krʌst/ n [C/U] **1** : the hard outer surface of bread **2** : the outside part of a pie • *a pie with (a) flaky crust* **3** : the bread that is used to make a pizza **4** : a hard layer on the surface of something • *a thin crust of ice* • *the Earth's crust* — see also UPPER CRUST

crus·ta·cean /krə'steɪʃən/ n [C] *technical* : an animal (such as a crab or lobster) that has several pairs of legs and a body made up of sections that are covered in a hard outer shell — **crustacean** adj

crust·ed /'krʌstəd/ adj : having a hard surface layer • *mud-crusted shoes* [=mud-encrusted shoes] • *fish crusted with spices*

crusty /'krʌsti/ adj **crust·i·er; -est 1** : harsh and unfriendly • *a crusty old man* **2** *of food* : having a thick or crisp crust • *crusty bread* — **crust·i·ness** n [U]

crutch /'krʌtʃ/ n [C] **1** : a long stick with a padded piece at the top that fits under your arm and that you use to help you walk — usually plural • *I was on crutches for six weeks after I broke my leg.* **2** *usually disapproving* : something that a person uses too much for help or support • *Alcohol had become a/her crutch.* **3** *Brit* : CROTCH

crux /'krʌks/ n — *the crux* : the most important part of something (such as a problem, issue, puzzle, etc.) • *getting to the crux of the matter/problem*

¹**cry** /'kraɪ/ vb **cries; cried; cry·ing** [T/I] **1** : to produce tears from your eyes often while making loud sounds because of pain, sorrow, or other strong emotions •

The baby is crying. ▪ *Some people cry more easily than others.* ▪ *They cried tears of joy.* ❖ If you *cry your eyes/heart out,* you cry a lot. **2** : to shout or say something loudly ▪ *"Help!" he cried.* ▪ *I heard someone crying for help.* — **a shoulder to cry on** see ¹SHOULDER — **cry for** [*phrasal vb*] : to need or require (something) very much ▪ *The house is crying for a new coat of paint.* — **cry foul** *chiefly US* : to complain that someone has done something that is not fair ▪ *When he changed the rule, she cried foul.* — **cry off** [*phrasal vb*] *Brit* : to say that you will not do something you have promised to do ▪ *He said he'd help us but then he cried off* [=*begged off*] *at the last minute.* — **cry out** [*phrasal vb*] **1** : to make a loud sound because of pain, fear, surprise, etc. ▪ *She cried out in pain.* **2** : to speak in a loud voice ▪ *She cried out for help.* **3 cry out against** : to protest (something) ▪ *People cried out against civil rights abuses.* **4** — used to say that something clearly needs or should have a particular thing, person, use, etc. ▪ *The meal cried out to be eaten with a nice white wine.* = *The meal cried out for a nice white wine.* — **cry over spilled milk** (*US*) or *chiefly Brit* **cry over spilt milk** *informal* : to be upset about something that has happened and that cannot be changed ▪ *There's no use crying over spilled milk.* — **cry wolf** : to make people think there is danger when there is really none — **for crying out loud** *informal* — used to show anger, annoyance, etc. ▪ *For crying out loud, let's go already!*

²**cry** *n, pl* **cries 1** [*C*] : a loud sound that someone makes to express pain, hunger, sadness, etc. ▪ *cries of pain* **2** [*C*] : a shout or call ▪ *the children's happy cries* (*figurative*) *cries of outrage* **3** [*C*] : a loud sound made by an animal or bird ▪ *the wild cry of a coyote* **4** [*singular*] : an act of crying or a period of time spent crying ▪ *When they left I had a good cry.* **5** [*C*] : an act or way of behaving which shows that someone wants help, attention, etc. ▪ *His bad behavior could be a cry for help.* — **a far cry from** : very different from (something or someone) ▪ *The movie is a far cry from the book.*

cry·ba·by /ˈkraɪˌbeɪbi/ *n, pl* **-bies** [*C*] *informal* : a person who cries easily or complains often

cry·ing /ˈkraɪɪŋ/ *adj* — **a crying need** : a serious, important, and obvious need ▪ *There's a crying need for reform in this city.* — **a crying shame** : a situation that makes you feel sad or disappointed ▪ *It's a crying shame that he had to leave.*

crypt /ˈkrɪpt/ *n* [*C*] : a room under a church in which dead people are buried

cryp·tic /ˈkrɪptɪk/ *adj* : difficult to understand : having or seeming to have a hidden meaning ▪ *a cryptic message/title/remark* — **cryp·ti·cal·ly** /ˈkrɪptɪkli/ *adv*

cryp·tog·ra·phy /krɪpˈtɑːgrəfi/ *n* [*U*] : the process of writing or reading secret messages or codes — **cryp·tog·ra·pher** /krɪpˈtɑːgrəfə/ *n* [*C*]

crys·tal /ˈkrɪstl̩/ *n* **1** [*C*] : a small piece of a substance that has many sides and is formed when the substance turns into a solid ▪ *ice/salt crystals* ▪ *a crystal of quartz* **2** [*C/U*] : a clear hard mineral that is either colorless or very light in color and that is used in making jewelry ▪ *a necklace made of crystal* **3** [*U*] : a special type of glass that is very clear ▪ *a crystal chandelier/vase* **4** [*C*] *US* : the clear glass or plastic cover on a watch or clock

crystal ball *n* [*C*] : a clear glass ball in which some people say they can see the future by using magic

crystal clear *adj* **1** : perfectly clear ▪ *crystal clear water* **2** : perfectly easy to understand ▪ *Her intentions were crystal clear.*

crys·tal·line /ˈkrɪstələn, *Brit* ˈkrɪstəˌlaɪn/ *adj* **1** : clear and shining like crystal ▪ *the island's crystalline waters* **2** *technical* : made of or similar to crystal or crystals ▪ *a crystalline solid*

crys·tal·lize *also Brit* **crys·tal·lise** /ˈkrɪstəˌlaɪz/ *vb* **-lized; -liz·ing** [*T/I*] **1** *technical* : to change into a solid form that is made up of crystals ▪ *the conditions that crystallize carbon* **2** : to cause (something, such as an idea, belief, etc.) to become clear and fully formed ▪ *He tried to crystallize his thoughts.* ▪ *The plan crystallized slowly.* — **crys·tal·li·za·tion** *also Brit* **crys·tal·li·sa·tion** /ˌkrɪstələˈzeɪʃən, *Brit* ˌkrɪstəˌlaɪˈzeɪʃən/ *n* [*U*]

C–sec·tion /ˈsiːˌsɛkʃən/ *n* [*C*] : CESAREAN SECTION

ct. *abbr* carat

CT *abbr* Connecticut

CT scan /ˈsiːˈtiː-/ *n* [*C*] : CAT SCAN

cub /ˈkʌb/ *n* [*C*] **1** : a young animal that eats meat ▪ *a bear/fox/lion cub* **2 Cub** *Brit* : CUB SCOUT

cub·by·hole /ˈkʌbiˌhoʊl/ *n* [*C*] : a small space for storing things or a very small room

¹**cube** /ˈkjuːb/ *n* [*C*] **1** : an object that has six square sides ▪ *an ice cube* **2** *mathematics* : the number that results from multiplying a number by itself twice ▪ *The cube of 2 is 8.* [=2 × 2 × 2 = 8] **3** *US, informal + humorous* : CUBICLE 1

²**cube** *vb* **cubed; cub·ing** [*T*] **1** : to cut (food) into small cubes ▪ *Cube the carrots and potatoes.* **2** *mathematics* : to multiply (a number) by itself twice ▪ *2 cubed equals 8.* [=2 × 2 × 2 = 8]

cu·bic /ˈkjuːbɪk/ *adj* **1** — used to describe a measurement that is produced by multiplying something's length by its width and its height ▪ *one cubic centimeter* [=a measure that is one centimeter long, one centimeter wide, and one centimeter high] **2** : in the shape of a cube ▪ *cubic crystals/shapes*

cu·bi·cle /ˈkjuːbɪkəl/ *n* [*C*] **1** *chiefly US* : a work space in a large office with a desk that is usually surrounded by low walls ▪ *an office cubicle* **2** *Brit* : a small space in a public room (such as a bathroom) that has walls for privacy ▪ *a shower/toilet cubicle* [=(*US*) stall]

Cub·ism /ˈkjuːˌbɪzəm/ *n* [*U*] : a style of art that originated in the early 20th century in which objects are divided into and shown as a group of geometric shapes and from many different angles at the same time — **Cub·ist** /ˈkjuːbɪst/ *adj* — **Cubist** *n* [C]

Cub Scout *n* [C] : a member of an organization of Boy Scouts for boys ages 7 through 10

¹**cuck·oo** /ˈkuːku, *Brit* ˈkʊku/ *n* [C] : a type of bird that lays its eggs in the nests of other birds and that has a call that sounds like its name

²**cuckoo** *adj, informal + old-fashioned* : silly or crazy • *He's a little cuckoo.*

cuckoo clock *n* [C] : a clock that has a toy bird inside of it that comes out and makes a sound like a cuckoo to tell what time it is

cu·cum·ber /ˈkjuːˌkʌmbə/ *n* [C/U] : a long vegetable with dark green skin and crisp flesh that is often used in salads or for making pickles — **(as) cool as a cucumber** see ¹COOL

cud /ˈkʌd/ *n* [U] : the food that an animal (such as a cow) brings back up from its stomach into its mouth to be chewed again

cud·dle /ˈkʌdl/ *vb* **cud·dled; cud·dling** **1** [T] : to hold (someone or something) in your arms in order to show affection • *He cuddled the puppy.* **2** [I] : to lie or sit close together • *Let's cuddle (up) by the fire.* — **cuddle** *n* [C]

cud·dly /ˈkʌdli/ *adj* **cud·dli·er; -est** *informal* : having the soft or appealing quality of a thing or person that you would like to cuddle • *cuddly teddy bears*

cud·gel /ˈkʌdʒəl/ *n* [C] : a short heavy club

¹**cue** /ˈkjuː/ *n* [C] **1 a** : a word, phrase, or action in a play, movie, etc., that is a signal for a performer to say or do something **b** : a sign that tells a person to do something • *Their silence was a cue for him to speak.* • *We should take our cue from their example.* [=do what is suggested by their example] **c** : something that indicates the nature of what you are seeing, hearing, etc. • *auditory/visual cues* **2** ✧ When something happens **(right) on cue** or **as if on cue**, it happens at the exact moment you would expect it to. • *She arrived right on cue.* **3** : a long, thin stick that is used in playing pool, billiards, and snooker • *a pool cue*

²**cue** *vb* **cued; cu·ing** [T] : to give (someone) a signal to do something during a performance • *Cue the band.*

cue ball *n* [C] : the white ball that a player hits with the cue in pool, billiards, and snooker

¹**cuff** /ˈkʌf/ *n* **1** [C] : the part of a sleeve, glove, etc., that covers the wrist **2** [C] *US* : a piece of cloth at the bottom of a pant leg that is folded up **3** [C] : something that goes around a person's arm like the cuff of a sleeve • *a cuff bracelet* **4** [plural] : HANDCUFFS — **off the cuff** : without planning or preparation • *He talked/spoke off the cuff about the project.*

²**cuff** *vb* [T] **1** : to put (someone) in handcuffs • *He was cuffed and led away.* **2** : to hit (someone or something) with the palm of your hand • *She cuffed him on the head/ear.*

cuff link *n* [C] : a piece of jewelry that is

used to fasten the cuff of a sleeve on a man's shirt

cui·sine /kwɪˈziːn/ *n* **1** [C/U] : a style of cooking • *regional cuisines* • *gourmet/vegetarian/ethnic cuisine* **2** [U] : food that is cooked in a particular way • *spicy cuisine*

cul-de-sac /ˈkʌldɪˌsæk/ *n, pl* **cul-de-sacs** /ˈkʌldɪˌsæks/ *also* **culs-de-sac** /ˈkʌlzdɪˌsæk/ [C] : a street that is designed to connect to another street only at one end

cul·i·nary /ˈkʌləˌneri, *Brit* ˈkʌlənri/ *adj* : used in or relating to cooking • *culinary herbs* • *the culinary arts*

cull /ˈkʌl/ *vb* [T] **1** : to select or choose (someone or something) from a group • *She culled the information from newspapers.* **2** : to control the size of (a group of animals) by killing some animals • *culling the herd* — **cull** *n* [C]

cul·mi·nate /ˈkʌlməˌneɪt/ *vb* **-nat·ed; -nat·ing** **1** [I] : to reach the end or the final result of something • *The investigation culminated in/with several arrests.* **2** [T] *somewhat formal* : to be the end or final result of (something) • *A bitter feud culminated months of tension.*

cul·mi·na·tion /ˌkʌlməˈneɪʃən/ *n* [U] : the end or final result of something • *the culmination of years of research*

cul·pa·ble /ˈkʌlpəbəl/ *adj, formal* : guilty of doing something wrong • *Is she culpable for the accident?* — **cul·pa·bil·i·ty** /ˌkʌlpəˈbɪləti/ *n* [U] — **cul·pa·bly** /ˈkʌlpəbli/ *adv*

cul·prit /ˈkʌlprət/ *n* [C] : a person who has committed a crime or done something wrong • *The police located the culprits.* • *(figurative) Lack of exercise and poor diet are the chief/main/real culprits in heart disease.*

¹**cult** /ˈkʌlt/ *n* [C] **1** : a small religious group that is not part of a larger and more accepted religion and that has beliefs regarded by many people as extreme or dangerous • *a satanic cult* **2** : a situation in which people admire and care about something or someone very much or too much • *the cult of celebrity in modern America* [=the tendency of people to care too much about famous people] • *a cult of personality* = *a personality cult* **3** : a small group of very devoted supporters or fans • *a cult of admirers* • *a cult following* **4** *formal* : a system of religious beliefs and rituals • *an ancient fertility cult*

²**cult** *adj, always before a noun* : very popular among a group of people • *a cult film/classic/favorite*

cul·ti·vate /ˈkʌltəˌveɪt/ *vb* **-vat·ed; -vat·ing** [T] **1** : to prepare and use (soil) for growing plants • *farmers cultivating the land* **2** : to grow and care for (plants) • *a plant that is cultivated for its fruit* **3** : to improve or develop (something) by careful attention, training, or study • *She cultivated a taste for fine wines.* **4** : to try to become friendly with (someone) usually to get some advantage for yourself • *cultivating friends* — **cul·ti·va·tion** /ˌkʌltəˈveɪʃən/ *n* [U] — **cul·ti·va·tor** /ˈkʌltəˌveɪtə/ *n* [C]

cultivated adj **1 a** : raised or grown on a farm or under other controlled conditions ▪ *cultivated fruits/vegetables* **b** : prepared and used for growing crops ▪ *cultivated fields* **2** : having or showing good education, taste, and manners ▪ *a very cultivated gentleman*

cul·tur·al /ˈkʌltʃərəl/ adj **1** : of or relating to a particular group of people and their habits, beliefs, traditions, etc. ▪ *cultural differences/studies* **2** : of or relating to the fine arts (such as music, theater, painting, etc.) ▪ *cultural activities/events* — **cul·tur·al·ly** adv

¹**cul·ture** /ˈkʌltʃə/ n **1 a** [U] : the beliefs, customs, arts, etc., of a particular society, group, place, or time ▪ *Greek language and culture* **b** [C] : a particular society that has its own beliefs, ways of life, art, etc. ▪ *an ancient culture* **2** [C] : a way of thinking, behaving, or working that exists in a place or organization (such as a business) ▪ *their corporate/business culture* **3** [U] **a** : artistic activities (such as music, theater, painting, etc.) ▪ *the area's lack of culture* **b** : appreciation and knowledge of music, theater, painting, etc. ▪ *a person of culture* **4** *technical* **a** [U] : the act or process of growing living material (such as cells or bacteria) in controlled conditions for scientific study ▪ *the culture of living tissue* **b** [C] : a group of cells, bacteria, etc., grown in controlled conditions for scientific study ▪ *bacterial/tissue cultures*

²**culture** vb **-tured; -tur·ing** [T] *technical* : to grow (something) in controlled conditions ▪ *The virus is cultured in the laboratory.*

cultured adj **1** : having or showing good education, tastes, and manners ▪ *a cultured person* **2** : grown or made under controlled conditions ▪ *cultured cells/pearls*

culture shock n [C/U] : a feeling of confusion, doubt, or nervousness caused by being in a place that is very different from what you are used to

cul·vert /ˈkʌlvət/ n [C] : a drain or pipe that allows water to flow under a road or railroad

cum·ber·some /ˈkʌmbəsəm/ adj **1** : hard to handle or manage because of size or weight ▪ *a cumbersome package* **2** : complicated and hard to do ▪ *a cumbersome process*

cum·in /ˈkʌmən, ˈkjuːmən/ n [U] : dried seeds that are used as a spice in cooking

cu·mu·la·tive /ˈkjuːmjəlɑtɪv/ adj **1** : increasing or becoming better or worse over time through a series of additions ▪ *the cumulative effect(s) of smoking* **2** : including or adding together all of the things that came before ▪ *his cumulative scores* — **cu·mu·la·tive·ly** adv

¹**cun·ning** /ˈkʌnɪŋ/ adj : getting what is wanted in a clever and often deceptive way ▪ *a cunning criminal/plan* — **cun·ning·ly** adv

²**cunning** n [U] : cleverness or skill especially at tricking people in order to get something

¹**cup** /ˈkʌp/ n [C] **1 a** : a small round container that often has a handle and that is used for drinking liquids (such as tea and coffee) ▪ *a coffee cup* **b** : the liquid that is contained in a cup ▪ *Would you like another cup of tea?* **2** *US* : a unit of measurement that is used when you are cooking ▪ *two cups of flour/milk* **3** : a large gold or silver cup that is given as a prize for winning a competition or game **4** : something that is shaped like a cup ▪ *a custard cup* ▪ *He held the seeds in the cup of his hand.* **5** *chiefly US* : a food that is served in a cup or small bowl ▪ *a fruit cup* [=a mixture of chopped fruits that is served usually as a dessert] — **not your cup of tea** ◇ If something is *not your cup of tea*, you do not like it very much or you are not very good at it. ▪ *Camping just isn't my cup of tea.*

²**cup** vb **cupped; cup·ping** [T] : to curve your hand into the shape of a cup ▪ *He cupped his hands around his mouth.* = *He cupped his mouth with his hands.*

cup·board /ˈkʌbəd/ n [C] **1** : a piece of furniture used for storage that has doors and contains shelves ▪ *kitchen cupboards* **2** *US* : a small room with shelves where you keep cups, dishes, or food **3** *Brit* : CLOSET

cup·cake /ˈkʌpˌkeɪk/ n [C] : a very small cake that is baked in a pan shaped like a cup

cup·ful /ˈkʌpˌfʊl/ n, pl **cup·fuls** /ˈkʌpˌfʊlz/ also **cups·ful** /ˈkʌpsˌfʊl/ [C] : the amount held by a cup ▪ *a cupful of sugar*

cu·pid /ˈkjuːpəd/ n **1** *Cupid* [singular] : the god of sexual love in ancient Rome **2** [C] : a picture or statue of Cupid usually shown as a naked boy with wings who is holding a bow and arrow — **play Cupid** : to try to get two people to become romantically involved with each other ▪ *She was playing Cupid with her brother and her best friend.*

cu·pid·i·ty /kjuːˈpɪdəti/ n [U] *formal* : GREED

cu·po·la /ˈkjuːpələ/ n [C] **1** : a rounded roof or part of a roof **2** *US* : a small structure that is built on top of a roof

cur·able /ˈkjurəbəl/ adj : possible to cure ▪ *a curable disease*

cu·rate /ˈkjurət/ n [C] : a member of the clergy in certain churches (such as the Anglican church) who assists the priest in charge of a church or a group of churches

cu·ra·tive /ˈkjurətɪv/ adj : able to cure diseases or heal people ▪ *curative powers/properties*

cu·ra·tor /ˈkjurˌeɪtə, Brit kjuˈreɪtə/ n [C] : a person who is in charge of the things in a museum, zoo, etc.

¹**curb** /ˈkəb/ n [C] **1** *US* **curb** or Brit **kerb** : a short border along the edge of a street that is usually made of stone or concrete **2** : something that controls or limits something else ▪ *a curb on spending*

²**curb** vb [T] : to control or limit (something) ▪ *pills that curb your appetite*

curd /ˈkəd/ n [C/U] : a thick substance that forms when milk becomes sour and that is used to make cheese

cur·dle /ˈkədl/ vb **cur·dled; cur·dling** [T/I] : to thicken and separate into liquids and solids ▪ *Too much heat will cur-*

dle the custard. • *The milk has curdled.* — **make someone's blood curdle** see BLOOD

¹**cure** /ˈkjɚ/ n [C] **1** : something (such as a drug or medical treatment) that stops a disease and makes someone healthy again • *There is no cure for the common cold.* **2** : SOLUTION 1a • *a problem that has no easy cure*

²**cure** vb **cured; cur·ing 1** [T] : to make someone healthy again after an illness • *Doctors cured him of the disease.* = *Doctors cured his disease.* **2** [T] : to provide a solution for (something) • *Drinking won't cure your problems.* **3** [T] : to make (someone) free *of* something • *My wife cured me of most of my bad habits.* **4** [T/I] : to change something through a chemical or physical process so that it can be preserved for a long time • *cure bacon/meat*

cure-all /ˈkjɚˌɑːl/ n [C] : a cure or solution for any illness or problem • *The drug is effective, but it's not a cure-all.*

cur·few /ˈkɚfjuː/ n **1** [C/U] : an order or law that requires people to be indoors after a certain time at night or the time when such an order or law is in effect • *violating (a) curfew* **2** [C] chiefly US : the time set by a parent at which a child has to be back home after going out • *He has a 10 o'clock curfew.*

cu·rio /ˈkjɚrijoʊ/ n, pl **-ri·os** [C] : a small and unusual object that is considered interesting or attractive

cu·ri·os·i·ty /ˌkjɚriˈɑːsəti/ n, pl **-ties 1** [U] : the desire to learn or know more about something or someone ✧ The expression *curiosity killed the cat* is used to warn people that too much curiosity can be dangerous. **2** [C] : something that is interesting because it is unusual • *Tobacco was once a curiosity in Europe.*

cu·ri·ous /ˈkjɚrijəs/ adj **1** : having a desire to learn or know more about something or someone • *I'm curious about their reasons for leaving.* • *I'm curious to know more about her.* **2** : strange, unusual, or unexpected • *curious behavior* — **cu·ri·ous·ly** adv

¹**curl** /ˈkɚl/ vb **1** [T/I] : to twist or form (something) into a round or curved shape • *He curled the spaghetti around his fork.* • *She curls her hair every morning.* • *She curled (up) her legs under her.* • *My hair curls naturally.* **2** [I] : to become curved or rounded • *The old posters were curling (up) at the edges.* **3** [I] : to move in curves or circles • *Smoke curled from the chimney.* — **curl up** [phrasal vb] : to lie or sit with your back bent forward and with your legs pulled up close to your body • *She curled up on the couch.* — **curl your lip** : to move the corner of your lip up in an expression that usually shows disgust or disapproval

²**curl** n [C] **1** : a piece of hair that is formed into a round shape **2** : something that is curved or has a round shape • *a curl of smoke*

curl·er /ˈkɚlɚ/ n [C] : a small plastic or metal tube around which hair is wrapped to make it curl • *Her hair was in curlers.*

cur·li·cue /ˈkɚliˌkjuː/ n [C] : a decora-

tively curved line or shape

curly /ˈkɚli/ adj **curl·i·er; -est 1** : having curls • *curly hair* **2** : formed into a round shape • *The dog's tail is curly.*

cur·mud·geon /kɚˈmʌdʒən/ n [C] old-fashioned : a person (especially an old man) who is easily annoyed or angered and who often complains — **cur·mud·geon·ly** adj

cur·rant /ˈkɚrənt/ n [C] **1** : a small seedless raisin that is used in baking and cooking **2** : a small red, black, or white berry that is often used in making jams and jellies • *black/red currants*

cur·ren·cy /ˈkɚrənsi/ n, pl **-cies 1** [C/U] : the money that a country uses • *foreign currencies* • *U.S./paper currency* **2** [U] : the quality or state of being used or accepted by many people • *His ideas are gaining currency.* **3** [U] : the quality or state of being current • *the currency of the information*

¹**cur·rent** /ˈkɚrənt/ adj **1** always before a noun : happening or existing now • *the current crisis/month* • *current trends/fashions/ideas* **2** not before a noun, chiefly US : aware of what is happening in a particular area of activity • *We need to keep/stay current with the latest information.* — **cur·rent·ly** adv

²**current** n **1** [C] : a continuous movement of water or air in the same direction **2** [C/U] : a flow of electricity **3** [C] formal : an idea, feeling, opinion, etc., that is shared by many or most of the people in a group • *intellectual currents* • *the current of public opinion*

current account n [C] Brit : CHECKING ACCOUNT

current events n [plural] chiefly US : important events that are happening in the world — called also *current affairs*

cur·ric·u·lum /kəˈrɪkjələm/ n, pl **-la** /-lə/ also **-lums** [C] formal : the courses that are taught by a school, college, etc. • *the undergraduate/mathematics curriculum* — **cur·ric·u·lar** /kəˈrɪkjələ/ adj

cur·ric·u·lum vi·tae /kəˈrɪkjələmˈviːˌtaɪ/ n, pl ~ **vitae** [C] chiefly Brit : RÉSUMÉ — called also *CV*, (US) *vita*

cur·ried adj, always before a noun : cooked with curry powder • *curried chicken*

¹**cur·ry** /ˈkɚri/ n, pl **-ries 1** [C/U] : a food, dish, or sauce in Indian cooking that is seasoned with a mixture of spices • *We had (a) chicken curry for dinner.* • *curry sauce/paste* **2** [U] : CURRY POWDER

²**curry** vb **-ries; -ried; -ry·ing** — **curry favor** disapproving : to try to get the support or approval of a person or group in order to get some advantage for yourself • *He tried to curry favor with his boss.*

curry powder n [U] : a mixture of spices that are used in Indian cooking to give a hot flavor to food

¹**curse** /ˈkɚs/ n [C] **1** : an offensive word that people say when they are angry **2** : magical words that are said to cause trouble or bad luck for someone or the condition that results when such words are said • *There is a curse on that old house.* = *That old house is under a curse.*

3 : a cause of trouble or bad luck ▪ *His fame turned out to be a curse, not a blessing.*

²**curse** *vb* **cursed; curs·ing 1 a** [*I*] : to use offensive words when you speak ▪ *He was cursing at the police officer.* **b** [*T*] : to say offensive words to (someone) ▪ *She cursed him as he walked away.* **c** [*T*] : to say or think bad things about (someone or something) ▪ *He cursed himself for being so careless.* **2** [*T*] : to say words that are believed to have a magical power to cause trouble or bad luck for (someone or something) ▪ *In the book the witch curses the villagers.* — **curse out** [*phrasal vb*] **curse (someone) out** *or* **curse out (someone)** *US, informal* : to say angry and offensive words to (someone) ▪ *My boss cursed me out.*

cursed /ˈkɚst/ *adj* **1** : affected by a curse that causes bad things to happen ▪ *That old house is cursed.* **2** : affected by something bad ▪ *The team was cursed by injuries.*

cur·sor /ˈkɚsɚ/ *n* [*C*] : a mark on a computer screen that shows the place where information is being entered or read

cur·so·ry /ˈkɚsəri/ *adj, formal + often disapproving* : done or made quickly ▪ *a cursory glance/inspection/look*

curt /ˈkɚt/ *adj* : said or done in a quick and impolite way ▪ *a curt nod/reply* — **curt·ly** *adv* — **curt·ness** *n* [*U*]

cur·tail /kɚˈteɪl/ *vb* [*T*] *formal* : to reduce or limit (something) ▪ *efforts to curtail illegal drug use* — **cur·tail·ment** /kɚˈteɪlmənt/ *n* [*C/U*]

¹**cur·tain** /ˈkɚtn̩/ *n* [*C*] **1** : a piece of cloth that hangs down from above a window and can be used to cover the window **2** : a piece of cloth or other material that is hung to protect or hide something ▪ *a shower curtain* **3** : a very large piece of cloth that hangs at the front of a stage and that is raised when a performance begins and lowered when a performance ends ▪ *(figurative) The curtain came down on his film career.* [=his film career ended] ▪ *(figurative) His injury brought down the curtain on his baseball career.* [=his injury ended his career] **4** : something that covers or hides something else ▪ *a curtain of darkness/smoke* — **be curtains for** *informal* : to be the end, failure, or death of (someone or something) ▪ *It looks like it's curtains for the mayor after this election.* [=the mayor will not be elected again]

²**curtain** *vb* — **curtain off** [*phrasal vb*] **curtain (something) off** *or* **curtain off (something)** : to separate or cover (something) by using a curtain ▪ *The back of the room was curtained off.*

curtain call *n* [*C*] : the time when a performer returns to the stage at the end of a performance in response to the applause of the audience

cur·tained /ˈkɚtn̩d/ *adj, always before a noun* : decorated or covered with curtains ▪ *curtained windows*

curt·sy *also* **curt·sey** /ˈkɚtsi/ *n, pl* **curt·sies** *also* **curt·seys** [*C*] : a formal way of greeting an important person (such as a king or queen) in which a woman shows respect by placing one foot slightly behind the other and bending her knees — **curtsy** *also* **curtsey** *vb* **curt·sies** *also* **curt·seys; curt·sied** *also* **curt·seyed; curt·sy·ing** *also* **curt·sey·ing** [*I*] ▪ *She curtsied before the queen.*

cur·va·ceous /kɚˈveɪʃəs/ *adj, of a woman* : having an attractively curved body ▪ *a curvaceous figure/woman*

cur·va·ture /ˈkɚvətʃɚ/ *n* [*C/U*] *technical* : the amount that something is curved ▪ *the curvature of the Earth*

¹**curve** /ˈkɚv/ *n* [*C*] **1** : a smooth, rounded line, shape, path, etc. **2** *technical* : a curved line on a graph that shows how something changes or is affected by one or more conditions ▪ *the population growth curve* **3** : a curving line or shape of the human body and especially of a woman's body ▪ *her shapely curves* **4** *baseball* : CURVEBALL ▪ *(figurative) Life has thrown him some curves.* [=he has had some unexpected problems in his life] — **ahead of the curve** *chiefly US, approving* : faster about doing something than other people, companies, etc. ▪ *The company has been ahead of the curve in adopting new technologies.* — **behind the curve** *chiefly US, disapproving* : slower about doing something than other people, companies, etc. ▪ *We are behind the curve when it comes to advances in medicine.*

²**curve** *vb* **curved; curv·ing 1** [*I*] : to form a curve ▪ *The road curves to the left.* **2** [*T*] : to cause (something) to form a curve ▪ *He curved the wire slightly.*

curve·ball /ˈkɚvˌbɑːl/ *n* [*C*] *baseball* : a pitch that is thrown with spin so that the ball curves in the air — called also *curve*

curved *adj* : having a rounded shape ▪ *a curved wall/blade*

curvy /ˈkɚvi/ *adj* **curv·i·er; -est** : having many curves ▪ *a curvy line/road*

¹**cush·ion** /ˈkʊʃən/ *n* [*C*] **1** : a soft pillow, pad, etc. **2** : any one of the rubber parts that the ball bounces off along the inner edges of a billiard table **3** : something (such as an extra amount of money) that you can use to reduce the bad effect of something (such as an unexpected problem or expense) ▪ *a financial cushion*

²**cushion** *vb* [*T*] : to soften or reduce the bad effect of (something) ▪ *The pile of leaves cushioned his fall.* ▪ *The tax cut is meant to cushion the blow/impact of soaring gas prices.*

cushy /ˈkʊʃi/ *adj* **cush·i·er; -est** *informal* : very easy and pleasant ▪ *a cushy job*

cusp /ˈkʌsp/ *n* [*C*] *technical* : a pointed end or part where two curves meet ▪ *the cusp of a tooth* — **on the cusp** : at the point when something is about to change to something else ▪ *She is on the cusp of being a star.*

cuss /ˈkʌs/ *vb* [*I*] *US, informal* : CURSE 1 ▪ *She was cussing at him.* — **cuss out** [*phrasal vb*] **cuss (someone) out** *or* **cuss out (someone)** *US, informal* : to say angry and offensive words to (someone) ▪ *He cussed me out for crashing his car.*

cuss·word /ˈkʌsˌwɚd/ *n* [*C*] *US, informal* : CURSE, SWEARWORD

cus·tard /ˈkʌstəd/ n [C/U] : a type of sweet food that is made with eggs and milk — **cus·tardy** /ˈkʌstədi/ adj

cus·to·di·al /ˌkʌˈstoudijəl/ adj, always before a noun **1** law : having the responsibility for taking care of a child • the custodial parent **2** US : relating to the care of a building, equipment, or land • custodial duties **3** Brit, law : involving punishment that requires a criminal to spend time in a prison • a custodial sentence

cus·to·di·an /ˌkʌˈstoudijən/ n [C] **1** formal : someone who keeps and protects something valuable for another person **2** US : JANITOR

cus·to·dy /ˈkʌstədi/ n [U] **1** law : the legal right to take care of a child (such as a child whose parents are divorced) • She has sole custody of her daughter. **2** : the state of being kept in a prison or jail • Several suspects are in custody. • He was taken into custody.

¹**cus·tom** /ˈkʌstəm/ n **1** [C/U] : an action or way of behaving that is usual and traditional among the people in a particular group or place • tribal/local/family/ancient/social customs **2** [singular] : something that is done regularly by a person • She had breakfast in bed, as was her custom. **3** [plural] **a** : taxes or fees that are paid to the government when goods come into or go out of a country **b** : the place at an airport, border, etc., where government officers collect customs on goods and look for things that people are trying to bring into a country illegally • We went through customs at the airport. • a customs agent/officer/inspector **4** [U] Brit, formal : the practice of regularly going to the same shop or business to buy things or services • People have been taking their custom [=business] elsewhere.

²**custom** adj, always before a noun, chiefly US **1** : made to fit the needs or requirements of a particular person • custom cabinets/designs **2** : doing work that fits the needs or requirements of a particular person • a custom tailor

cus·tom·ary /ˈkʌstəˌmeri, Brit ˈkʌstəmri/ adj **1** : usually done in a particular situation or at a particular place or time • He forgot the customary "thank you." **2** always before a noun : usual or typical of a particular person • She dressed in her customary fashion. — **cus·tom·ar·i·ly** /ˌkʌstəˈmerəli, Brit ˈkʌstəmrəli/ adv

cus·tom–built /ˈkʌstəmˈbɪlt/ adj : built to fit the needs or requirements of a particular person • a custom-built home

cus·tom·er /ˈkʌstəmə/ n [C] **1** : someone who buys goods or services from a business • our best/regular customers • customer service/satisfaction **2** informal : a person who has a particular quality • a cool customer

cus·tom·ize also Brit **cus·tom·ise** /ˈkʌstəˌmaɪz/ vb **-ized; -iz·ing** [T] : to change (something) in order to fit the needs or requirements of a person, business, etc. • The program can be customized to serve different purposes. • a customized van — **cus·tom·i·za·tion** also Brit **cus·tom·i·sa·tion** /ˌkʌstəməˈzeɪʃən/ n [U]

cus·tom–made /ˈkʌstəmˈmeɪd/ adj : made to fit the needs or requirements of a particular person • custom-made curtains/furniture

¹**cut** /ˈkʌt/ vb **cut; cut·ting** **1 a** [T/I] : to use a sharp tool (such as a knife) to open or divide (something, such as paper or wood) • cutting paper/meat • She cut into the melon with a knife. **b** [T] : to make a hole or wound in (a person's skin) • I cut myself while shaving. **c** [T] : to make (a hole) in something by using a sharp tool • They cut a hole in the wall. **d** [T] : to divide or separate parts of (something) by using a sharp tool • It's time to cut [=slice] the cake! • The onion was cut into one-inch pieces. • pictures cut from magazines • She cut off a piece of string. **2** [I] **a** : to be able to cut something • This knife doesn't cut well. **b** : to be able to be cut • Aluminum foil cuts easily with scissors. **3** [T] : to make (hair, grass, etc.) shorter by using a sharp tool (such as scissors) • I cut my hair short for the summer. • cutting the grass **4** [T] : to give (hair or clothing) a certain style by cutting it • a dress that is cut low at the neck [=a low-cut dress] **5** [T] : to make or form (something) by cutting or removing material • builders cutting new roads in the forest **6** [T] : to make the amount of (something) smaller • cut costs • This route can cut five miles off the trip. **7** [T] **a** : to make (a book, film, etc.) shorter by removing parts • His article was cut by about 500 words. **b** : to remove (something) from a book, film, etc. • About 500 words were cut from his article. **8** [T] : to remove (something) from a computer document in a way that allows you to move it to another part of the document or to another document • After you select the text with your mouse, you can cut it and then paste it at the beginning of the paragraph. **9** [T] : to remove (someone) from a team, organization, etc. • The coach cut two players from the team. **10** [T/I] : to divide (a pack of cards) into two piles • You cut (the deck) and I'll deal. **11** [T] : to divide (an area of land) into two parts • The river cuts the city in half. **12** [I] : to move or go across or through something • We cut through the park on our way home. **13** [I] **a** : to move quickly • a fast ship cutting through the waves **b** : to move suddenly in a different direction • The driver cut across three lanes of traffic. **14** [I] : to move in front of other people in a line • She cut in front of us. **15** [T] chiefly US : to not go to (school or a class) when you should go to it • We cut school and went to the beach. **16** [T] informal : to record (a song, album, etc.) • He cut his first record in 1954. **17** [I] : to suddenly move from one image or scene to another in a movie, television program, etc. • The movie cuts quickly from one scene to the next. **18** [I] : to stop filming a scene in a movie or television show — usually used as a command • "Cut!" yelled the director. **19** [T] : to stop saying or doing (foolish or annoying things) • Let's cut the nonsense and get down to business. **20** [T] : to stop (a motor) by moving a

switch • *I parked and cut (off) the ignition.* **21** [*T/I*] : to cause painful feelings or emotions • *His words cut (me) deeply.* • *The disappointment cut like a knife.* **22** [*T*] *a US* : to make (alcohol) less strong by adding water or another liquid • *They cut the wine with water.* **b** : to make (a drug, such as heroin) less strong by mixing it with another substance • *The substance is used to cut cocaine.* **23** [*T*] : to cause (dirt, grease, etc.) to break apart and be removed • *soap that cuts grease and grime* — **cut a deal** : to make an agreement usually about business • *The band cut a deal with a recording company.* — **cut a figure** ✧ If you *cut a fine/dashing/heroic (etc.) figure*, you look very good and impressive. • *He cut a fine figure in his officer's uniform.* — **cut and run** : to leave quickly in order to avoid danger or trouble • *You can't just cut and run when your friends are in trouble.* — **cut a tooth** *of a baby* : to have a tooth begin to come through the gums — **cut away** [*phrasal vb*] **cut away (something)** or **cut (something) away** : to remove (something that is not needed) by cutting • *They cut away a few of the tree's lower branches.* — **cut back** [*phrasal vb*] **1** : to use less or do less of something • *We need to cut back on our spending.* **2 cut (something) back** or **cut back (something)** **a** : to make (a plant) smaller or shorter by cutting its branches • *Cut back the shrub in the late fall.* **b** : to reduce the size or amount of (something) • *They've cut back my hours at work.* — **cut both ways** : to have both good and bad results, effects, etc. • *These changes in the economy cut both ways.* — **cut corners** see ¹CORNER — **cut down** [*phrasal vb*] **1** : to use less or do less of something • *She suggested he cut down on his drinking.* **2 cut (something or someone) down** or **cut down (something or someone)** **a** : to remove (a tree or bush) by cutting through its trunk or base • *The tree was cut down for firewood.* **b** : to reduce the size or amount of (something) • *The shortcut cuts down our traveling time by 15 minutes.* **c** : to kill or wound (someone) • *She was cut down by a stray bullet.* — **cut in** [*phrasal vb*] **1** : INTERRUPT 1 • *We were trying to have a conversation, but she kept cutting in.* **2** : to stop two people who are dancing and take the place of one of them • *"May I cut in?"* **3** *of a machine* : to begin to work • *waiting for the heater to cut in* **4 cut (someone) in** : to include (someone) in a group of people who are receiving money or other benefits • *They'll help you if you cut them in on the profits.* — **cut into** [*phrasal vb*] : to reduce the amount of (something) • *Although it will cut into profits, we have to lower our prices.* — **cut it** *informal* **1** : to be able to do something well enough — usually used in negative statements • *She just couldn't cut it as an actress.* **2** : People use the informal phrase *any way you cut it* to say that something is true no matter how you look at it or think about it. • *Any way you cut it, it was a pretty good year for our company.* — **cut it**

close (*chiefly US*) or *chiefly Brit* **cut it fine** : to almost fail, lose, etc. • *It's cutting it a bit close to get to the station at 9:45 when the train leaves at 9:50!* — **cut off** [*phrasal vb*] **1** *of a machine* : to stop working suddenly • *The engine suddenly cut off.* **2 cut (something or someone) off** or **cut off (something or someone)** **a** : to remove (something) by cutting • *Cut off dead flowers to promote new growth.* **b** : to stop or end (something) • *They voted to cut off debate on the budget.* **c** : to stop people from seeing or using (something) • *Their fence cuts off our view of the ocean.* **d** : to stop the movement or supply of (something) • *The power was cut off to our apartment building.* **e** : to cause (someone or something) to be separate or alone • *She cut herself off from her family.* **f** : to stop (someone) from talking • *She cut me off to ask about dinner.* ✧ If you **get cut off** when you are using the telephone, the telephone connection suddenly ends and you can no longer hear the other person. **g** *US* : to drive in front of (someone in another vehicle) in a sudden and dangerous way • *He shouted at a driver who cut him off.* **h** : to decide not to give money or property to (someone) after your death • *In her will, she cut off her son without a cent/penny.* — **cut out** [*phrasal vb*] **1** *of a machine* : to stop working suddenly • *The plane's engines suddenly cut out.* **2** *chiefly US* : to leave quickly and suddenly • *We were tired, so we cut out before the concert ended.* **3 cut (something or someone) out** or **cut out (something or someone)** **a** : to form (something) by cutting with a sharp tool • *He cut a big heart out of a piece of red paper.* • (*figurative*) *She cut out a place for herself in history.* [=she caused herself to be important in history] **b** : to remove (something) by cutting • *I cut out the recipe from a magazine.* **c** : to remove (something) from something • *I focused on my work and cut out everything else in my life.* **d** : to stop doing (something) • *I finally cut out smoking altogether.* • *I told you to cut it/that out!* [=to stop it/that] **e** : to cause (someone) to no longer be included in something • *Don't cut me out of your life completely!* **f** ✧ If you are **cut out for (something)** or **cut out to do/be (something)**, you are naturally able or suited to do or be something. • *He's not cut out to be a teacher.* — **cut the mustard** see MUSTARD — **cut through** [*phrasal vb*] : to get through or past (something that blocks you or slows you down) quickly and directly • *It took some time to cut through the lies and get to the truth.* — **cut to the chase** see ¹CHASE — **cut up** [*phrasal vb*] *US, informal* : to behave in a silly or rude way • *He was always cutting up in class.* **2 cut (something or someone) up** or **cut up (something or someone)** **a** : to cut (something) into parts or pieces • *He cut up the apple into little pieces.* **b** : to hurt or damage (someone or something) by cutting • *His face and arms were all cut up.* **c** ✧ In informal British English, to be **cut up about** something is to be very sad or upset about something. — **cut your teeth** — used to describe the things that people do when they are starting their careers ▪ *He cut his teeth performing at local bars and nightclubs.*

²**cut** *n* [C] **1 a** : an opening or hole made with a sharp tool (such as a knife) **b** : a wound on a person's body that is made by something sharp ▪ *a deep/superficial cut* **2** : an act of making something smaller in amount ▪ *a cut in pay* = *a pay cut* ▪ *a tax cut* **3** : the act of removing something from a book, movie, etc. ▪ *We had to make some cuts in the manuscript.* **4** : a version of a movie at a particular stage of being edited ▪ *The scene didn't make the film's final cut.* ▪ *I saw a rough cut* [=a version that is not yet finished] *of the movie.* **5** : a song on a record, tape, or CD **6** : the shape and style of a piece of clothing ▪ *the cut of his pants* **7** : HAIRCUT ▪ *I had a shampoo and a cut.* **8** : a piece of meat that is cut from a particular part of an animal's body ▪ *a thick/ tender/expensive cut of meat* **9** : a part of something that is divided and shared among people ▪ *We each got a cut of the profits.* **10** : the act of reducing the size of a group (such as a group of competitors) by removing the ones that are not good enough or that have not done well enough ▪ *Only the best players are good enough to* **make the cut** *when the team is being chosen.* — **a cut above** : better than other people or things ▪ *All of his books are good, but this one is a cut above (the rest).* — **cut and thrust** *chiefly Brit* : the lively and exciting quality of an activity in which people compete or argue with each other ▪ *the cut and thrust of politics*

cut–and–dried /ˌkʌtnˈdraɪd/ *also US* **cut–and–dry** /ˌkʌtnˈdraɪ/ *adj* : having a clear and definite quality that does not allow doubt or that cannot be changed ▪ *a cut-and-dried decision/example*

cut·a·way /ˈkʌtəˌweɪ/ *adj* : having the top or outside removed so the inside parts can be seen ▪ *a cutaway view of an engine* — **cutaway** *n* [C]

cut·back /ˈkʌtˌbæk/ *n* [C] : the act of reducing the number or amount of something ▪ *cutbacks in spending*

cute /ˈkjuːt/ *adj* **cut·er**; **cut·est** **1** : having a pleasing and usually youthful appearance ▪ *cute babies/puppies* ▪ *She's* **as cute as a button!** [=she's very cute] **2** *chiefly US, informal* : attractive in a sexual way ▪ *Who's that cute guy?* **3** *chiefly US, informal* **a** : clever in an appealing way ▪ *a cute idea/trick* **b** : clever in a way that annoys people ▪ *Don't get cute with me!* **4** *chiefly US, informal* : trying too hard to be pleasant or likable ▪ *The movie's too cute to be taken seriously.* — **cute·ly** *adv* — **cute·ness** *n* [U]

cute·sy /ˈkjuːtsi/ *adj* **cute·si·er**; **-est** *informal + disapproving* : too cute in an annoying way ▪ *cutesy cartoon characters*

cu·ti·cle /ˈkjuːtɪkəl/ *n* [C] : the layer of dead or hard skin around the base of a fingernail or toenail

cut·ie /ˈkjuːti/ *n* [C] *informal* : a cute person

cut·lery /ˈkʌtləri/ *n* [U] **1** *US* : sharp tools made of metal (such as knives and scissors) that are used for cutting things **2** : SILVERWARE ▪ *plastic cutlery*

cut·let /ˈkʌtlət/ *n* [C] : a small, thin slice of meat ▪ *veal/chicken cutlets*

cut·off /ˈkʌtˌɑːf/ *n* **1** [C] : the act of stopping the movement or supply of something ▪ *a cutoff of the water supply* **2** [C] : the time when something must be done or completed ▪ *The cutoff (date) for new applications is next Wednesday.* **3** [*plural*] : short pants that are made from long pants by cutting off the legs at the knees or higher ▪ *a pair of cutoffs*

cut·out /ˈkʌtˌaʊt/ *n* [C] : a shape or picture that is cut from a piece of paper, cardboard, etc.

cut–price /ˈkʌtˈpraɪs/ *adj, chiefly Brit* : CUT-RATE

cut–rate /ˈkʌtˈreɪt/ *adj, chiefly US* **1** : selling goods or services at very low prices ▪ *a cut-rate airline/hotel/supermarket* **2** *of a price* : very low ▪ *cut-rate prices*

cut·ter /ˈkʌtɚ/ *n* [C] **1** : a person, machine, or tool that cuts something ▪ *a diamond/pizza cutter* **2** : a small military ship ▪ *a Coast Guard cutter*

cut–throat /ˈkʌtˌθroʊt/ *adj* — used to describe a situation in which people compete with each other in an unpleasant and often cruel and unfair way ▪ *a cut-throat business*

¹**cut·ting** /ˈkʌtɪŋ/ *n* [C] **1** : a stem, leaf, or root that is cut from a plant and used to grow a new plant **2** *Brit* : CLIPPING 1

²**cutting** *adj* **1** *always before a noun* : used for cutting things ▪ *a cutting blade* **2 a** : unpleasantly cold ▪ *a cutting wind* **b** : causing great physical pain ▪ *a sharp, cutting pain* **3** : very harsh and critical ▪ *a cutting remark*

cutting board *n* [C] *US* : a wooden or plastic board on which foods (such as meats and vegetables) are cut

cutting edge *n* **1** [C] : the sharp edge of something that is used to cut things ▪ *the knife's cutting edge* **2 the cutting edge** : the newest and most advanced area of activity in an art, science, etc. ▪ *His films are on the cutting edge.* — **cutting–edge** *adj* ▪ *cutting-edge technology*

cut–up /ˈkʌtˌʌp/ *n* [C] *US, informal* : a person who behaves in a silly way and makes other people laugh

CV /ˌsiːˈviː/ *n* [C] : CURRICULUM VITAE

cy·a·nide /ˈsajəˌnaɪd/ *n* [U] : a very poisonous chemical

cy·ber·net·ics /ˌsaɪbɚˈnɛtɪks/ *n* [U] : the scientific study of how people, animals, and machines control and communicate information — **cy·ber·net·ic** /ˌsaɪbɚ-ˈnɛtɪk/ *adj*

cy·ber·space /ˈsaɪbɚˌspeɪs/ *n* [U] : the online world of computer networks and the Internet

cy·borg /ˈsaɪˌbɔɚg/ *n* [C] *in stories* : a person whose body contains mechanical or electrical devices and whose abilities are greater than the abilities of normal humans

¹**cy·cle** /ˈsaɪkəl/ *n* [C] **1** : a repeating series of events or actions ▪ *a cycle of vio-*

lence • *These plants have a 2-year growth cycle.* [=the plants live and die within two years] **2** : a set of regular and repeated actions that are done by a machine as part of a longer process • *the spin cycle on a washing machine* **3** *chiefly Brit* : a bicycle or motorcycle

²**cycle** *vb* **cy·cled; cy·cling 1** [T/I] *US* : to go through a repeated process or to cause (something) to go through a repeated process • *The water (was) cycled back into/through the system.* **2** [I] : to ride a bicycle • *He cycled to the library.* — **cy·clist** /'saɪkləst/ *n* [C]

cy·clic /'saɪklɪk, 'sɪklɪk/ *or* **cy·cli·cal** /'saɪklɪkəl, 'sɪklɪkəl/ *adj* : happening again and again in the same order • *cyclic changes in the weather*

cycling *n* [U] : the sport or activity of riding a bicycle

cy·clone /'saɪˌkloʊn/ *n* [C] **1** : an extremely large, powerful, and destructive storm with very high winds **2** *chiefly US* : TORNADO — **cy·clon·ic** /saɪ'klɑːnɪk/ *adj*

Cy·clops /'saɪˌklɑːps/ *n* [*singular*] : a giant man in stories told by the ancient Greeks who had a single eye in the middle of his forehead

cyl·in·der /'sɪləndə/ *n* [C] **1** : a shape that has straight sides and two circular ends **2** : something that is shaped like a cylinder: such as **a** : a tube in which a piston of an engine moves • *a four-cylinder engine* **b** : the part of a gun that turns and that holds the bullets — *on all cylinders informal* : with the greatest possible amount of effort, power, or speed • *The economy is running/firing/hitting on all cylinders.*

cy·lin·dri·cal /sə'lɪndrɪkəl/ *adj* : shaped like a cylinder • *a cylindrical tank/tower*

cym·bal /'sɪmbəl/ *n* [C] : a musical instrument in the form of a slightly curved thin metal plate that is played by hitting it with a drumstick or with another cymbal

cyn·ic /'sɪnɪk/ *n* [C] : a person who has negative opinions about other people and about the things people do; *especially* : a person who believes that people are selfish and are only interested in helping themselves

cyn·i·cal /'sɪnɪkəl/ *adj* **1** : believing that people are generally selfish and dishonest • *He's cynical about marriage.* **2** : selfish and dishonest in a way that shows no concern about treating other people fairly • *a cynical attempt to win votes* — **cyn·i·cal·ly** /'sɪnɪkli/ *adv*

cyn·i·cism /'sɪnəˌsɪzəm/ *n* [U] : cynical beliefs

cypher *chiefly Brit spelling of* CIPHER

cy·press /'saɪprəs/ *n* [C/U] : a tall and narrow evergreen tree

cyst /'sɪst/ *n* [C] *medical* : a growth filled with liquid that forms in or on your body

cys·tic fi·bro·sis /'sɪstɪkfaɪ'broʊsəs/ *n* [U] : a very serious disease that usually appears in young children and that makes it hard to breathe and to digest food properly

czar *also* **tsar** *or* **tzar** /'zɑːr/ *n* [C] **1** : the title of the ruler of Russia before 1917 • *Russia's Czar Nicholas II* **2** *chiefly Brit* **a** : a very powerful person in a particular business or activity • *a banking czar* **b** — used as an unofficial title for the person who is in charge of a government office or department • *the education/housing/terrorism czar* — **czar·ist** *also* **tsar·ist** *or* **tzar·ist** /'zɑːrɪst/ *adj* • *czarist Russia*

cza·ri·na *also* **tsa·ri·na** *or* **tza·ri·na** /zɑ'riːnə/ *n* [C] : the wife of a Russian czar

Czech /'tʃɛk/ *n* **1** [C] : a person born, raised, or living in Czechoslovakia or the Czech Republic **2** [U] : the Slavic language of the Czechs — **Czech** *adj*

D

d *or* **D** /'diː/ *n, pl* **d's** *or* **ds** *or* **D's** *or* **Ds** **1** [C/U] : the fourth letter of the English alphabet • *names that start with (a) d* **2** [C/U] : a musical note or key referred to by the letter D • *play/sing a D* • *a song in the key of D* **3** [C] : a grade given to a student for doing poor work • *She got a D on her math test.* **4** [C] : the Roman numeral that means 500 • *CD* [=400]

d. *abbr* died • *Thomas Jefferson, d. 1826*

D *abbr* Democrat

'd /əd *after* t *or* d; d *elsewhere*/ — used as a contraction of *had, would,* and *did* • *We'd* [=we had] *better leave.* • *You can come if you'd* [=you would] *like to.* • *Where'd* [=where did] *he go?*

DA *abbr* district attorney

¹**dab** /'dæb/ *vb* **dabbed; dab·bing 1** [T/I] : to lightly touch (something) • *She dabbed (at) her eyes with a tissue.* **2** [T] : to put a small amount of something on something • *Dab a little paint on the canvas.*

²**dab** *n* [C] : a small amount of something • *a dab of butter/perfume*

dab·ble /'dæbəl/ *vb* **dab·bled; dab·bling 1** [I] : to participate in an activity in a way that is not serious — usually + *in* • *She dabbles in poetry.* **2** [T/I] : to play or move around in water • *The ducks dabbled in the stream.* • *She dabbled her feet in the water.* — **dab·bler** *n* [C]

dab hand *n* [C] *Brit, informal* : EXPERT • *She's a dab hand in the kitchen.*

dachs·hund /'dɑːksˌhʊnt, *Brit* 'dækˌsənd/ *n* [C] : a small type of dog that has a long body and very short legs

dad /'dæd/ *n* [C] *informal* : a person's father • *Dad, can I borrow the car?*

dad·dy /ˈdædi/ *n, pl* **-dies** [C] *informal* : DAD — used especially by young children ▪ *Where's your daddy?*

daf·fo·dil /ˈdæfəˌdɪl/ *n* [C] : a yellow flower that has a center shaped like a long tube

daf·fy /ˈdæfi/ *adj* **daf·fi·er; -est** *US, informal* : silly or strange in a funny way ▪ *a daffy comedy/character*

daft /ˈdæft, *Brit* ˈdɑːft/ *adj, Brit, informal* **1** : silly or strange ▪ *a daft sense of humor* **2** : crazy or foolish ▪ *Don't be daft!*

dag·ger /ˈdægɚ/ *n* [C] : a pointed knife that is used as a weapon ▪ *(figurative)* They **looked/shot/stared daggers at** [=they looked angrily at] *each other across the table.*

dahl·ia /ˈdæljə, *Brit* ˈdeɪljə/ *n* [C] : a type of garden plant that has large flowers

¹**dai·ly** /ˈdeɪli/ *adj, always before a noun* **1** : happening, done, made, used, or existing every day ▪ *TV is now a part of our daily lives.* ▪ *my daily routine/schedule* ▪ *He visits them on a daily basis.* [=every day] **2** : of or relating to one day ▪ *Their daily wage is only five dollars.* ▪ *daily lunch specials* [=lunch items offered on particular days of the week] — **daily** *adv* ▪ *The Web site is updated daily.* [=every day]

²**daily** *n, pl* **-lies** [C] : a newspaper that is published every day except Sunday

dain·ty /ˈdeɪnti/ *adj* **dain·ti·er; -est 1** : small and pretty ▪ *dainty pink flowers* ▪ *the girl's dainty little hands* **2** : done with small and careful movements ▪ *She took a dainty sip from her teacup.* **3** *of food* : attractive and served in small amounts ▪ *dainty portions/sandwiches* — **dain·ti·ly** *adv* — **dain·ti·ness** *n* [U]

dai·qui·ri /ˈdækəri, ˈdaɪkəri/ *n* [C] : an alcoholic drink that is usually made of rum, fruit, and sugar ▪ *frozen strawberry daiquiris*

¹**dairy** /ˈderi/ *n, pl* **dair·ies** [C] **1** : a farm that produces milk **2** : a company that sells milk, butter, cheese, etc.

²**dairy** *adj* **1** : made from milk ▪ *dairy products/foods* : relating to foods made from milk ▪ *the dairy section of the grocery store* **2** : of or relating to a type of farming that deals with the production of milk ▪ *dairy cows/farmers*

da·is /ˈdejəs/ *n* [C] : a raised platform in a large room or hall

dai·sy /ˈdeɪzi/ *n, pl* **-sies** [C] : a type of white flower that has a yellow center — **be pushing up daisies** *informal + humorous* : to be dead ▪ *We'll all be pushing up daisies by the time they balance the budget.*

dale /ˈdeɪl/ *n* [C] *old-fashioned* : VALLEY ▪ *hills and dales*

dal·li·ance /ˈdælijəns/ *n* [C] **1** : an action that is not serious ▪ *After a brief dalliance with acting, she pursued a law career.* **2** : a romantic or sexual relationship that is brief and not serious ▪ *sexual dalliances*

dal·ly /ˈdæli/ *vb* **-lies; -lied; -ly·ing** [I] **1** : to do something slowly or too slowly ▪ *Don't dally on the way home.* — **dally with** [*phrasal vb*] : to do or think about (something) in a way that is not serious ▪

He's been dallying with the idea of running for office.

dal·ma·tian *or* **Dal·ma·tian** /dælˈmeɪʃən/ *n* [C] : a type of dog that has short white fur with many small black spots

¹**dam** /ˈdæm/ *n* [C] : a structure that is built across a river or stream to stop water from flowing

²**dam** *vb* **dammed; dam·ming** [T] : to build a dam across (a river or stream) ▪ *Beavers dammed (up) the stream.*

¹**dam·age** /ˈdæmɪʤ/ *n* **1** [U] : physical harm ▪ *The items suffered some damage during shipping.* ▪ *The fall caused/did considerable damage to her knee.* ▪ *brain/liver/kidney damage* ▪ *Property damage after the storm was great.* [=many houses, cars, etc., were damaged or ruined by the storm] **2** [U] : emotional harm ▪ *Traumatic events can cause psychological damage.* **3** [U] : harmful effects on a situation, a person's reputation, etc. ▪ *The scandal caused significant damage to her career.* ▪ *He apologized, but the damage was already done.* **4** [*plural*] *law* : an amount of money that a court requires you to pay to someone you have treated unfairly or hurt in some way ▪ *She was awarded $5,000 in damages.* [=the people who hurt her had to pay her $5,000] **5** *the damage informal* : the amount of money that something costs ▪ *"What's the damage?" he asked the mechanic.* — **damage control** *or Brit* **damage limitation** : things that are done or said to limit the bad effect of something ▪ *The governor made an outrageous statement, forcing his staff to do damage control.*

²**damage** *vb* **dam·aged; dam·ag·ing** [T] : to cause damage to (something) ▪ *The items were damaged during shipping.* ▪ *The scandal damaged her reputation.* ▪ *a damaged reputation* — **damaging** *adj* ▪ *The evidence was very damaging to their case.*

dam·ask /ˈdæməsk/ *n* [C/U] : a thick usually shiny cloth ▪ *damask curtains*

dame /ˈdeɪm/ *n* [C] **1** *US slang, old-fashioned* : WOMAN ▪ *She's one classy dame.* **2** *Brit* : a woman who has been given a title for something she has done ▪ *She was made/created a dame.* ▪ *Dame Myra Hess*

¹**damn** /ˈdæm/ *interj, informal + impolite* — used to show that you are angry, annoyed, surprised, etc. ▪ *Damn! That really hurt!*

²**damn** *vb* [T] **1** *informal + impolite* — used to show that you are angry or annoyed at a person, thing, or situation ▪ *Damn them! They've ruined everything!* ▪ *Damn it! I forgot my keys!* **2** : to send (someone) to hell as punishment after death ▪ *He said that they would be damned (to hell).* [=that God would force them to be in hell] — **damn with faint praise** : to give praise without enthusiasm in a way that shows you really dislike someone or something — **I'll be damned** *informal + impolite* **1** — used to show that you are very surprised about something ▪ *Well, I'll be damned! We actually won!* **2** — used to say that

you cannot or will not do something • *I'll be damned if I can remember* [=I cannot remember] *where I left my keys.* — **the damned** : the people who have been sent to hell as punishment after their death • *the souls of the damned* — **(you're) damned if you do and damned if you don't** *informal* — used to say that you will be blamed or considered wrong no matter what you do —

damning *adj* • *A damning piece of evidence showed that he had been at the crime scene.*

³**damn** *n* [*singular*] *informal + impolite* : anything at all • *This computer's not worth a damn.* [=it is worthless] • *Her promises don't mean a damn.* [=don't mean anything] — **give/care a damn** : to care at all about someone or something • *He doesn't give a damn what people think about him.*

⁴**damn** *also* **damned** *adj, informal + impolite* **1** — used to show that you are angry, annoyed, surprised, etc. • *That's none of your damn business.* **2** — used to make a statement more forceful • *It's a damn shame.*

⁵**damn** *also* **damned** *adv, informal + impolite* : very or extremely • *That was a damn good movie.*

dam·na·tion /dæmˈneɪʃən/ *n* [*U*] : the state of being in hell as punishment after death • *eternal damnation*

¹**damned·est** /ˈdæmdəst/ *adj, informal + impolite* : most unusual or surprising • *He said the damnedest thing the other day.*

²**damnedest** *n* — **do/try your damnedest** *chiefly US, informal + impolite* : to try very hard to do something • *I'll try my damnedest to be there.*

¹**damp** /ˈdæmp/ *adj* : somewhat or slightly wet • *Wipe the table with a damp cloth.* • *a damp spring day* — **damp·ness** *n* [*U*]

²**damp** *n* [*U*] : slight wetness in the air • *the damp of the night*

³**damp** *vb* [*T*] : DAMPEN • *His hands were damped with sweat.* • *Nothing could damp his spirits.*

damp·en /ˈdæmpən/ *vb* [*T*] **1** : to make (something) somewhat or slightly wet • *The rain barely dampened the ground.* **2** : to make (something) less strong or active • *The bad weather didn't dampen our enthusiasm/spirits.*

damp·er /ˈdæmpɚ/ *n* [*C*] **1** : a flat piece of metal in a fireplace, furnace, etc., that controls the amount of air that can enter **2** : a small piece of wood inside a piano that stops the movement of a piano string — **put a damper on** : to make (something) less strong, active, or exciting • *His bad mood put a damper on the celebration.*

dam·sel /ˈdæmzəl/ *n* [*C*] *old-fashioned* : a young woman who is not married • (*humorous*) *She acted like a damsel in distress who needed to be rescued.*

¹**dance** /ˈdæns, *Brit* ˈdɑːns/ *vb* **danced; danc·ing** **1** [*I*] : to move your body in a way that follows the music being played • *She loves to dance.* • *Would you like to dance with me? =* (*more formally*) *Shall we dance?* • (*figurative*) *dancing to*

someone else's tune [=doing what someone else wants you to do] **2** [*T*] : to perform (a particular type of dance) • *dancing the waltz/polka/twist* **3** [*I*] : to move quickly and up and down, from side to side, etc. • *We danced for joy when we heard the news.* — **danc·er** *n* [*C*] • *ballet dancers* — **dancing** *n* [*U*] • *She loves dancing.* • *We're taking dancing lessons.*

²**dance** *n* **1** [*C*] : a way or style of dancing • *a slow dance* • *dance classes/moves* **2** [*C*] : an act of dancing • *May I have this dance?* [=will you dance with me?] • *He did a celebration dance after scoring the goal.* **3** [*U*] : the art or activity of dancing • *She studied dance in college.* **4** [*C*] : a social event at which people dance • *We met at a dance.* • *high school dances* **5** [*C*] : a song or piece of music (such as a waltz) to which people dance

dan·de·li·on /ˈdændəˌlajən/ *n* [*C*] : a common wild plant with bright yellow flowers

dan·druff /ˈdændrəf/ *n* [*U*] : very small white pieces of dead skin that form especially on a person's head

¹**dan·dy** /ˈdændi/ *adj* **dan·di·er; -est** *chiefly US, informal + old-fashioned* : very good • *Everything was fine and dandy.*

²**dandy** *n, pl* **-dies** [*C*] **1** *old-fashioned* : a man who cares too much about his appearance **2** *chiefly US, informal* : something that is very good • *That was a dandy of a game.*

Dane /ˈdeɪn/ *n* [*C*] : a person born, raised, or living in Denmark — see also GREAT DANE

dang /ˈdæŋ/ *interj, US, informal* — used as a more polite form of *damn* • *Dang! That hurt!*

dan·ger /ˈdeɪndʒɚ/ *n* **1 a** [*U*] : the possibility that you will be hurt or killed • *It was a journey fraught/filled with danger.* [=a very dangerous journey] • *The sign on the door read "Danger. Keep out."* • *Their lives are in* (*grave/great/serious*) *danger.* **b** [*U, singular*] : the possibility that something unpleasant or bad will happen • *There's a danger that you may be misunderstood.* • *We're all in danger of losing* [=we may all lose] *our jobs.* **2** [*C*] : a person or thing that is likely to cause injury, pain, harm, or loss • *the dangers of smoking* • *It poses a serious danger to our national security.* • *He is a danger to himself and others.*

dan·ger·ous /ˈdeɪndʒərəs/ *adj* **1** : involving possible injury, pain, or death • *a dangerous road/intersection* • *The city can be a dangerous place to live.* • *Smoking is dangerous to your health.* • (*figurative*) *The conversation was heading into dangerous territory.* [=a situation in which you may do or say something that will have a bad result, make people angry, etc.] **2** : able or likely to cause injury, pain, harm, etc. • *dangerous animals/drugs* • *The man is armed and might try to shoot someone*] — **dan·ger·ous·ly** *adv* • *dangerously high levels of pollution* • *living dangerously*

dan·gle /ˈdæŋɡəl/ *vb* **dan·gled; dan-**

gling 1 [T/I] : to hang down loosely ▪ *Wires were dangling from the ceiling.* ▪ *She sat dangling her feet in the pool.* 2 [T] *informal* : to offer (something) in order to persuade someone to do something ▪ *The money she dangled in front of him didn't convince him to sell.* — **leave/keep someone dangling** *informal* : to force someone to be in an uncertain position ▪ *We were kept dangling while they made their decision.*

¹**Dan·ish** /ˈdeɪnɪʃ/ *adj* : of or relating to Denmark, its people, or their language ▪ *Danish customs*

²**Danish** *n, pl* **Danish** *also* **Dan·ish·es** 1 [U] : the language of the Danes 2 [C/U] *US* : DANISH PASTRY ▪ *I had (a) cheese Danish for breakfast.*

Danish pastry *n* [C/U] : a sweet pastry that often has fruit, icing, etc., on top

dank /ˈdæŋk/ *adj* : wet and cold in a way that is unpleasant ▪ *a dark dank cave*

dap·per /ˈdæpɚ/ *adj, old-fashioned* : having a neat appearance ▪ *They looked dapper in their uniforms.* ▪ *a dapper suit*

dap·pled /ˈdæpəld/ *adj* : marked with many spots of color or light ▪ *a dappled gray horse*

¹**dare** /ˈdeɚ/ *vb* **dared; dar·ing** 1 [I] : to not be too afraid to do something ▪ *Try it if you dare.* ▪ *We wanted to laugh but didn't dare.* ▪ *No one dared (to) say anything.* 2 [T] : to tell (someone) to do something especially as a way of showing courage ▪ *She dared him to dive off the bridge.* — **don't you dare** — used to forcefully tell someone not to do something ▪ *Don't you dare do that again!* — **how dare you** — used to show that you are angry about what someone has done or said ▪ *How dare you treat me!* — **I dare say** *somewhat formal* + *old-fashioned* — used when you are stating your opinion about something ▪ *I dare say he's right.*

²**dare** *n* [C] : the act of telling someone to do something as a way of showing courage ▪ (*US*) *He jumped from the bridge on a* **dare**. ▪ (*Brit*) *He jumped from the bridge* **for a dare**. [=someone dared him to jump from the bridge]

dare·dev·il /ˈdeɚˌdɛvl/ *n* [C] : a person who does dangerous things especially in order to get attention ▪ *a daredevil driver/pilot*

daren't /ˈdeɚnt/ *chiefly Brit* — used as a contraction of **dare not** or **dared not** ▪ *I daren't tell her the truth.*

¹**daring** *adj* 1 : willing to do dangerous or difficult things ▪ *a daring reporter* 2 : showing a lack of fear ▪ *a daring rescue/plan* — **dar·ing·ly** /ˈderɪŋli/ *adv*

²**daring** *n* [U] : courage or fearlessness ▪ *Skydiving requires both skill and daring.*

¹**dark** /ˈdɑɚk/ *adj* 1 : having very little or no light ▪ *a dark room/closet* ▪ *It's getting darker outside.* ▪ *Suddenly the room went* **dark**. [=suddenly there was no light in the room] 2 : not light in color : of a color that is closer to black than white ▪ *dark clouds/clothing* ▪ *You've got dark circles under your eyes.* 3 *of a color* : having more black than white : not light ▪ *dark blue* ▪ *a dark green shirt* 4 *of a person's*

hair, eyes, skin, etc. : black or brown in color ▪ *a dark complexion* ▪ *He is tall, dark, and handsome.* [=he is a tall, handsome man with dark hair and eyes] 5 : lacking hope or happiness ▪ *a dark view of the future* ▪ *It was a dark time in my life.* 6 : bad or evil ▪ *her dark side = the dark side of her personality* 7 : dealing with unpleasant subjects such as crime, unhappy relationships, etc. ▪ *a dark comedy about drug abuse* 8 : full of mystery ▪ *the government's dark secrets* 9 *of a place* : not known or explored ▪ *the darkest regions of the continent* — **dark·ly** *adv* ▪ *darkly colored clothing* ▪ *He spoke darkly* [=in a way that shows a lack of hope] *of the coming war.* ▪ *She hinted darkly* [=in a threatening way] *that they might regret not helping her.* ▪ *a darkly humorous story* — **dark·ness** *n* [U] ▪ *We could barely see each other in the darkness.* ▪ *the darkness of his skin* ▪ *Their secret remained hidden/shrouded in darkness.* [=secrecy] ▪ *the forces/powers of darkness* [=evil]

²**dark** *n* 1 **the dark a** : a state in which no light can be seen ▪ *He's afraid of the dark.* **b** : a place where little or no light can be seen ▪ *The burglars hid in the dark behind the house.* ▪ (*figurative*) *Most of their deals were made* **in the dark**. [=in a hidden or secret way] ▪ (*figurative*) *The public was* **kept in the dark** [=was not told] *about the agreement.* 2 [U] : the time when the sky becomes dark for the night ▪ *We got home before/after dark.* 3 [*plural*] **a** : dark colors ▪ *He uses lots of darks in his decorating.* **b** : dark clothes ▪ *Wash the lights and the darks separately.*

Dark Ages *n* — **the Dark Ages** : the first 500 years of the Middle Ages ▪ (*figurative, humorous*) *In the Dark Ages before computers, we often wrote our letters by hand.*

dark·en /ˈdɑɚkən/ *vb* [T/I] 1 : to make (something) dark or to become dark or darker in color ▪ *Clouds darkened the sky.* ▪ *The wood darkens as it ages.* ▪ *He was sitting in a darkened corner of the room.* 2 : to make (something) less happy or to become less happy ▪ *The bad news darkened his mood.* ▪ *His mood darkened.* — **darken someone's door/doors** : to go to a place where you are not welcome ▪ *She told him to leave and to never darken her door again.* [=to never go to her home again]

dark horse *n* [C] 1 : a person (such as a politician), animal, or thing that competes in a race or other contest and is not expected to win ▪ *The movie is a dark horse for the award.* 2 *Brit* : a person who has interesting qualities or abilities that most people do not know about

dark·room /ˈdɑɚkˌruːm/ *n* [C] : a room that is used for making photographs

¹**dar·ling** /ˈdɑɚlɪŋ/ *n* [C] 1 **a** : a person you love very much ▪ *How was your day, darling?* **b** : a kind and helpful person ▪ *Be a darling and carry this inside for me.* 2 : someone who is liked very much by a person or group ▪ *a media darling* ▪ *a darling of the critics*

²**darling** *adj* 1 *always before a noun*

: greatly loved • *This is my darling daughter, Sara.* **2** *informal* : very pleasing or attractive • *That dress is just darling.*

¹darn /'dɑɚn/ *vb* [T] **1** : to fix (a piece of clothing, a hole, etc.) by sewing • *darning a pair of socks* **2** *chiefly US, informal* — used as a more polite form of *damn* • *Darn him! Why won't he call?* • *Be quiet, gosh darn it!*

²darn *interj, US, informal* — used as a more polite form of *damn* • *Darn! That hurt!* — **darn** *n* [*singular*] • *I don't give a darn* [=I don't care at all] *what people say about me.* — **darn** *or* **darned** /'dɑɚnd/ *adj* • *This darn computer isn't working right.*

darn·est /'dɑɚnəst/ *adj, chiefly US, informal* — used as a more polite form of *damnedest* • *Kids do and say the darnedest things.* — **darnedest** *n* [U] • *He was doing/trying his darnedest to please everyone.*

¹dart /'dɑɚt/ *n* **1** [C] : a small object that has a sharp point at one end and that is thrown in the game of darts or used as a weapon • *throwing darts* • *He was hit with a poisoned dart.* **2** **darts** [U] : a game in which darts are thrown at a board that is marked with circles • *Let's play darts.* **3** [*singular*] : a quick movement • *a quick dart to the left*

²dart *vb* [T/I] **1** : to run or move quickly or suddenly in a particular direction or to a particular place • *We saw a deer dart across the road.* • *The frog darted its tongue at a fly.* — **dart a glance/look at** : to look suddenly and briefly at (something or someone) • *She darted a suspicious glance at her sister.*

dart·board /'dɑɚt,boɚd/ *n* [C] : a round board that is used as a target in the game of darts

Dar·win·ian /dɑɚ'wɪnijən/ *adj* **1** : of or relating to the theories of Charles Darwin • *a Darwinian principle* **2** : of or relating to a situation in which only people, businesses, etc., with the greatest abilities are successful • *a Darwinian struggle to succeed*

Dar·win·ism /'dɑɚwə,nɪzəm/ *n* [U] : the theory of evolution — **Dar·win·ist** /'dɑɚwənɪst/ *adj* — **Darwinist** *n* [C]

¹dash /'dæʃ/ *vb* **1** [I] : to run or move quickly or suddenly • *The dog dashed across the street.* • *She dashed off* [=left suddenly and quickly] *after breakfast.* **2** **a** [I] : to hit something in a violent and forceful way • *The waves dashed* [=smashed] *against the rocks.* **b** [T] : to throw or hit (something) against something • *The waves dashed the boat against the rocks.* **3** [T] : to destroy or ruin a hope, expectation, etc. • *Her hopes of winning a medal were dashed after she broke her leg.* — **dash it (all)** *Brit, old-fashioned* — used in speech to express anger, frustration, etc. • *Dash it all! I'm late!* — **dash off** [*phrasal vb*] **dash off (something)** *or* **dash (something) off** : to write (something) in a very quick and hurried way • *I dashed off a short letter.*

²dash *n* **1** [C] : a punctuation mark — that is used especially to show a break in the structure of a sentence (as in "We don't know where—or how—the problem began.") **2** [C] : a small amount of something that is added to something else • *The soup needs a dash of salt.* • *She added a dash of humor to her essay.* **3** [*singular*] : the act of moving quickly or suddenly in a particular direction • *We made a (mad) dash for the exit.* **4** [C] : a short, fast race • *She ran in the 50-meter dash.* **5** [C] *informal* : DASHBOARD — **cut a dash** *Brit, old-fashioned* : to look attractive in your clothes • *He really cuts a dash in his new suit.*

dash·board /'dæʃ,boɚd/ *n* [C] : the part of the inside of a car, truck, etc., that is below the windshield and that has the controls on it — called also (*Brit*) *fascia*

dashed /'dæʃt/ *adj* : made up of a set of dashes (sense 1) • *a dashed line*

dash·ing /'dæʃɪŋ/ *adj, of a man* : attractive and impressive in a way that shows confidence • *She married a dashing young lawyer.* — **dash·ing·ly** /'dæʃɪŋli/ *adv*

das·tard·ly /'dæstɚdli/ *adj, old-fashioned* : very cruel : using tricks to hurt people • *dastardly villains/deeds*

da·ta /'deɪtə, 'dætə/ *n* **1** [*plural*] : facts or information used usually to calculate, analyze, or plan something • *She is reviewing the data from the experiment.* • *Data is plural in form but is used with both plural and singular verbs.* • *Is this data accurate?* • *Are these data reliable?* **2** [U] : information that is produced or stored by a computer • *data entry/retrieval* • *The computer is still processing the data.*

da·ta·base /'deɪtə,beɪs, 'dætə,beɪs/ *n* [C] : a collection of information that is organized and used on a computer • *an online database* — called also *data bank*

data processing *n* [U] : the process of putting information into a computer so that the computer can organize it, change its form, etc. • *data-processing software*

¹date /'deɪt/ *n* [C] **1 a** : a particular day of a month or year • *Today's date is March 1.* • *They have not yet set a date for the trial.* [=they have not decided what day the trial will start on] • *your date of birth* [=the day you were born] — see also DUE DATE **b** : writing that shows when something was done or made • *a coin with a date of 1902* **2** : an agreement to meet someone at a particular time or on a particular day • *"Let's meet for coffee next Tuesday." "Okay. It's a date."* [=I agree to meet you then] **3 a** : an occasion when two people who have or might have a romantic relationship do an activity together • *We went (out) on a few dates last year.* • *She asked him (out) on a date.* — see also BLIND DATE **b** *chiefly US* : a person you have a date with • *Are you bringing a date to the dance?* **4** : a small, sweet, brown fruit — **to date** : up to now : until the present time • *We've received no complaints to date.* — **up to date** — used to say that something or someone has or does not have the newest information • *These textbooks are not up to date.* • *We send out* these memos to **bring/keep** everyone **up to date**. [=give everyone the newest information] **2** — used to say that something is or is not modern or new ▪ *He wants to bring the kitchen up to date.* — **dateless** /ˈdeɪtləs/ *adj*

²**date** *vb* **dat·ed; dat·ing 1** [*T/I*] *chiefly US* : to go on a date or several dates with (someone) ▪ *She dated him twice.* [=she went on two dates with him] ▪ *They've been dating for six months.* **2** [*T*] : to write the date on (something) ▪ *Please sign and date the application.* ▪ *a memo dated July 12th, 2003* **3** [*T*] : to show or find out when (something) was made or produced ▪ *Historians date the document to the early 1700s.* **4** [*T*] : to make (someone or something) seem old-fashioned ▪ *The decor really dates the house.* **5** [*I*] : to appear for the first time ▪ *This bowl dates from* [=was made in] *the sixth century.* ▪ *a custom that dates back 400 years* [=that began 400 years ago] ▪ *jewelry dating back to* [=that was made in] *the 1700s*

dated *adj* : coming from or belonging to a time in the past : old-fashioned or out-of-date ▪ *dated decor/information*

date rape *n* [*U*] : the crime of raping someone you know especially while on a date ▪ *He was accused of date rape.*

da·tive /ˈdeɪtɪv/ *n* [*U*] *grammar* : the form of a noun or pronoun when it is the indirect object of a verb ▪ *words in the dative (case)*

da·tum /ˈdeɪtəm, ˈdætəm/ *n, pl* **da·ta** /ˈdeɪtə, ˈdætə/ *or* **da·tums** [*C*] *formal + technical* : a single piece of information ▪ *an important historical datum* [=fact]

¹**daub** /ˈdɑːb/ *vb* **1** [*T*] : to put something on something with quick, small motions : DAB ▪ *He daubed some cologne on his neck.* **2** [*T/I*] : to lightly touch (something) : DAB ▪ *He daubed (at) his eyes with a tissue.*

²**daub** *n* [*C*] : a small amount of something : DAB ▪ *a daub of paint*

daugh·ter /ˈdɑːtə/ *n* [*C*] : a female child ▪ *We have a daughter and two sons.*

daugh·ter–in–law /ˈdɑːtərɪnˌlɑː/ *n, pl* **-ters–in–law** /-təzɪnˌlɑː/ [*C*] : the wife of your son

daunt /ˈdɑːnt/ *vb* [*T*] *formal* : to make (someone) afraid or less confident ▪ *She was not daunted by the difficult task.* ▪ *The project was quite daunting.* [=it was very difficult to do or deal with] — **daunt·ing·ly** /ˈdɑːntɪŋli/ *adv* ▪ *a dauntingly complex system*

daunt·less /ˈdɑːntləs/ *adj, formal + literary* : very brave ▪ *dauntless heroes* — **daunt·less·ly** *adv*

daw·dle /ˈdɑːdl/ *vb* **daw·dled; daw·dling** [*I*] : to move or act too slowly ▪ *Come home right after school, and don't dawdle.* — **daw·dler** *n* [*C*]

¹**dawn** /ˈdɑːn/ *n* **1** [*C/U*] : the time of day when sunlight first begins to appear ▪ *We arrived at/before/after dawn.* ▪ *He woke up at the crack of dawn.* [=very early in the morning] ▪ *She drove from dawn to/until dusk.* [=from early morning until early evening] **2** [*C*] : the beginning of something ▪ *at the dawn of the 21st century* ▪ *since the dawn of time/civilization*

²**dawn** *vb* [*I*] **1** : to begin to become light as the sun rises ▪ *They waited for the day to dawn.* **2** : to start or begin ▪ *A new age/era is dawning.* — **dawn on** [*phrasal vb*] : to begin to be understood or realized by (someone) for the first time ▪ *It dawned on her* [=she realized] *that she was lost.* — **dawn·ing** *n* [*U*] ▪ *the dawning* [=beginning] *of a new day/age/era*

day /ˈdeɪ/ *n* **1** [*C*] : a period of 24 hours beginning at midnight ▪ *We're open seven days a week, 365 days a year.* ▪ *"What day is (it) today?" "(It's) Tuesday."* ▪ *It rained for a day and a half.* [=it rained for about 36 hours] ▪ *The office is closed for the day.* ▪ *Take one pill two times a day.* [=each day] ▪ *The party is the day after tomorrow.* = *The party is in two days.* ▪ *It happened the day before yesterday.* = *It happened two days ago.* ▪ *She studied for days on end.* [=several/many days] ▪ *You don't look a day over 40.* [=you don't look any older than 40 years old] **2** [*C/U*] : the time of light between one night and the next ▪ *What a beautiful summer day!* ▪ *June 22 is usually the longest day of the year.* ▪ *You can call me anytime, day or night.* ▪ *She's a student by day* [=during the day] *and a waitress by night.* ▪ *I woke at (the) break of day.* [=dawn, sunrise] **3** [*U, singular*] : the part of the day when people are usually most active and when most businesses are open ▪ *How was your day?* ▪ *We have an early day* [=we will get out of bed early] *tomorrow.* ▪ *I needed to relax after a long day at work.* [=after working for a long time] ▪ *"Thank you, ma'am. Have a nice day!"* ▪ *I'll be gone all day (long).* **4** [*C*] : the hours during a day when a person works or goes to school ▪ *I put in four twelve-hour days this week.* ▪ *his first day on the job* ▪ *Please allow 14 business days* [=weekdays that are not holidays] *for delivery.* ▪ *Solving crimes is all in a day's work for her.* [=it is part of her typical work] ▪ *He took the day off* [=he decided not to work on a particular day] *to go fishing.* **5** [*C*] : the day on which something specified happens or is expected to happen ▪ *It rained on their wedding day.* ▪ *the day of his birth* ▪ *If you've been waiting to buy a car, today's the day.* [=today is the perfect time] ▪ *So, when's the big day? When are you getting married?* ▪ *I never thought I would (live) to see the day when you would graduate from college.* [=I did not think I would live long enough to see you graduate] ▪ *This is your lucky day.* [=a day when something good happens to you] ▪ *You never know. Maybe today will be my day.* [=maybe I will succeed, win, etc., today] ▪ *"Do you think he'll ever apologize?" "That'll be the day!"* [=I don't think that will ever happen] **6** [*C*] : a particular period of time ▪ *his days as a soldier* ▪ *the olden days* ▪ *In those days many factory workers were children.* ▪ *In my day* [=when I was young], *boys asked girls out on dates, not the other way around.* ▪ *from 1875 to the present day* [=today] ▪ *When I was a kid, we spent our summers at the beach. Those were the* *(good old) days!* [=that period of time was pleasant and better than the present time] — *any day now* : within the next few days ▪ *We're expecting him any day now.* — *call it a day* see ¹CALL — *carry/win the day* : to win or be successful ▪ *Truth and justice will carry the day.* — *day after day* : for several days without stopping or changing ▪ *She wore the same pants day after day.* — *day and night* or *night and day* 1 : all the time : without stopping ▪ *We've been working on it day and night.* 2 — used to say that two things or people are completely different ▪ *The difference between them is (like) night and day.* — *day by day* : in small amounts every day ▪ *Day by day, he is growing stronger.* ▪ *After his surgery, he's just taking it/things day by day.* [=making progress in a slow and careful way by dealing with each day as it comes] — *day in, day out* or *day in and day out* : every day for many days ▪ *She does the same thing at her job day in, day out.* — *early days (yet)* see ²EARLY — *from day to day* : every day ▪ *His opinions seem to change from day to day.* — *from one day to the next* : as one day becomes another day ▪ *You never know from one day to the next what's going to happen.* — *give (someone) the time of day* chiefly US, informal : to pay attention to someone ▪ *No one would give us the time of day.* — *glory days* see ¹GLORY — *in all your born days* see BORN — *in the cold light of day* see ¹COLD — *in this day and age* : at the present time in history ▪ *Computers are essential in this day and age.* — *it is not every day* — used to say that something happens very rarely ▪ *It's not every day that I get to meet the President.* — *late in the day* see ¹LATE — *make someone's day* : to cause someone's day to be pleasant or happy ▪ *Thanks for the compliment. You've really made my day!* — *of the day* 1 : served in a restaurant as a special item on a particular day ▪ *What's the fish/vegetable of the day?* 2 : of a particular period of time ▪ *the important issues of the day* — *one day* 1 : at some time in the future ▪ *It'll happen one day. You'll see.* 2 : on a day in the past ▪ *One day, we had a bad argument.* — *save the day* see ¹SAVE — *some day* : SOMEDAY ▪ *I'd like to return there some day.* — *take each day as it comes* or *take (it/things) one day at a time* : to deal with each day's problems as they come instead of worrying about the future ▪ *Take things one day at a time so you don't feel too overwhelmed.* — *the other day* ¹OTHER — *these days* : at the present time ▪ *It seems everyone has a cell phone these days.* ✧ The phrase *one of these days* means at some time in the future. ▪ *One of these days, I'm going to buy a boat.* — *those days* : a period of time in the past ▪ *Remember when life was easy? Well, those days are gone.* ▪ *In those days, women couldn't own property.* — *to the day* : to exactly a specified number of years ▪ *It's been 100 years to the day since their great discovery.* — *to this day*

: continuing until today ▪ *The belief persists to this day.*

day·break /ˈdeɪˌbreɪk/ *n* [*U*] : the time of day when sunlight first begins to appear ▪ *She left at daybreak.* [=dawn]

day care *n* [*U*] : a place or organization that takes care of children or sick adults during the day ▪ *She left work early to pick up her son from day care.* ▪ *a day care center*

day·dream /ˈdeɪˌdriːm/ *n* [*C*] : pleasant thoughts about your life or future that you have while you are awake ▪ *I drifted off in a daydream during the class.*
  daydream *vb* [*I*] ▪ *He spent the hour daydreaming about his vacation.* — **daydream·er** [*C*]

day·light /ˈdeɪˌlaɪt/ *n* 1 [*U*] : the light of the sun during the day ▪ *Open up the curtains and let in some daylight.* ▪ *They stole my car in broad daylight.* [=during the day] 2 [*U*] : the time of day when the sky is light ▪ *It's almost daylight.* 3 [*U*] *informal* : distance or difference between people or things ▪ *There is no daylight between our positions.* 4 [*plural*] *informal* — used for emphasis ▪ *You scared/frightened the daylights out of me!* [=you frightened me very much] ▪ *They beat/kicked/knocked the (living) daylights out of that guy.* [=they hit/kicked him very badly]

daylight saving time *n* [*U*] *US* : a period of the year between spring and fall when clocks in the U.S. are set one hour ahead of standard time

day·long /ˈdeɪˌlɑːŋ/ *adj* : lasting an entire day ▪ *a daylong tour of the city*

day one *n* [*singular*] : the first day or very beginning of something ▪ *We've known this about the project since/from day one.*

days /ˈdeɪz/ *adv, chiefly US* : during the day ▪ *She works days and goes to school nights.*

day·time /ˈdeɪˌtaɪm/ *n* [*U*] 1 : the time of day when the sky is light ▪ *daytime hours* 2 : television that is shown during the day ▪ *daytime talk shows*

day-to-day /ˈdeɪtəˌdeɪ/ *adj* : done or happening every day ▪ *day-to-day life/activities/problems*

day trader *n* [*C*] : a person who buys stocks and then sells them very quickly — **day trading** *n* [*U*]

daze /ˈdeɪz/ *n* [*singular*] : a state in which someone is not able to think or act normally ▪ *I was in a daze after the test.*

dazed /ˈdeɪzd/ *adj* : not able to think or act normally because you have been surprised, injured, etc. ▪ *He had a dazed look on his face.*

daz·zle /ˈdæzəl/ *vb* **daz·zled; daz·zling** 1 [*T*] *of a bright light* : to cause (someone) to be unable to see for a short time ▪ *He was dazzled by the flash of a camera.* 2 [*T/I*] : to greatly impress or surprise (someone) by being very attractive or exciting ▪ *She dazzled us with her wit.* — **dazzle** *n* [*U*] — **dazzling** *adj* ▪ *her dazzling smile* — **daz·zling·ly** *adv* ▪ *dazzlingly white teeth*

dB *abbr* decibel

DC *abbr* **1** direct current **2** *or* **D.C.** District of Columbia

D-day *n* [*singular*] : a day on which something important is planned or expected to happen ◇ *D-day* is most commonly used to refer to June 6, 1944, when Allied forces began the invasion of France in World War II.

DDT /ˌdiːˌdiːˈtiː/ *n* [*U*] : a poisonous chemical that was used especially in the past to protect plants from insects and that is now banned in the U.S.

DE *abbr* Delaware

de- *prefix* **1** : do the opposite of ▪ *deactivate* **2** : remove someone or something from something ▪ *The king was dethroned.* ▪ *defrost a windshield*

dea·con /ˈdiːkən/ *n* [*C*] : a member of some Christian churches who has special duties

dea·con·ess /ˈdiːkənəs/ *n* [*C*] : a female deacon

de·ac·ti·vate /diˈæktəˌveɪt/ *vb* **-vat·ed;** **-vat·ing** [*T*] : to make (something) no longer active or effective ▪ *deactivate a bomb*

¹dead /ˈdɛd/ *adj* **1** : no longer alive or living ▪ *He is dead.* [=(more politely) *deceased*] *He died last year.* ▪ *dead insects/trees/leaves/skin* ▪ *the dead bodies of the soldiers* ▪ *She shot him dead.* [=she killed him by shooting him] ▪ *She's been dead and buried/gone for 50 years.* ▪ *He was as good as dead.* [=he was almost dead] ▪ *They beat him and left him for dead.* [=they knew/expected that he would die when they left him] ▪ *The patient was dead on arrival.* [=the patient died before arriving at the hospital] ▪ (*figurative*) *The proposal was dead on arrival.* [=it had no chance of being approved] **2 a** : ¹NUMB **1** ▪ *My hand was dead.* **b** : very tired ▪ *Our legs were dead after hiking all day.* **c** : feeling no emotions ▪ *After the war, I was emotionally dead.* [=unable to feel joy, sadness, etc.] **3** *informal* : to be punished or hurt ▪ *I'm dead if I come in late for work again.* **4** *of a machine or device* : no longer working especially because of not having electricity ▪ *dead batteries* ▪ *The phones went dead.* **5** : no longer active or operating ▪ *dead volcanoes* ▪ *a dead plan/deal* **6** : lacking in activity or excitement ▪ *The store's been dead all day.* **7** — used to describe a time when nothing is being said or done ▪ *We played cards to fill in the dead time between shows.* **8** : no longer performed or enjoyed ▪ *a dead art form* **9** *of a language* : no longer spoken ▪ *Latin is a dead language.* **10** *sports* — used to describe a situation in which play stops during a game ▪ *The ball is dead if it goes out of bounds.* **11 a** : complete, total, or absolute ▪ *dead silence* ▪ *She spoke with dead certainty.* ▪ *The camera is a dead giveaway* [=the camera clearly shows] *that you're a tourist.* ▪ *He's a dead ringer for* [=he looks exactly like] *his father.* **b** : sudden and complete ▪ *The bus came to a dead stop.* **12** : perfect or exact ▪ *the dead center of the target* — **(as) dead as a doornail/dodo** *informal* — used to stress that someone or something is dead

▪ (*figurative*) *The deal is as dead as a doornail.* — **beat/flog a dead horse** see ¹HORSE — **catch/see (someone) dead** *informal* ◇ If you **wouldn't be caught/seen dead** doing something, you refuse to let others see you doing it because it would cause you to be embarrassed. ▪ *I wouldn't be caught dead in/wearing that outfit.* — **dead in the water** *informal* : not having any chance of success ▪ *The peace talks were dead in the water.* — **dead men tell no tales** see TALE — **dead to rights** see ³RIGHT — **dead to the world** *informal* : sleeping very deeply ▪ *Two minutes after lying down in bed he was dead to the world.* — **drop dead** *informal* **1** : to fall to the ground and die very suddenly ▪ *She dropped dead while playing basketball.* **2** — used as a rude way to tell someone to leave you alone ▪ *Drop dead, you jerk!* — **knock (someone) dead** see ¹KNOCK — **over my dead body** see BODY

²dead *n, pl* **dead 1** [*plural*] : people who have died ▪ *There were over two million dead.* ▪ *His wife and son were among the dead.* **2** *the dead* : the state of being dead ▪ *For a moment, I thought Elvis had come back from the dead.* ▪ *I thought he had returned/risen from the dead.* **3** [*U*] : the time in the middle of the night or winter ▪ *He began his journey in the dead of night/winter.*

³dead *adv* **1** : completely or totally ▪ *You're dead wrong.* ▪ *I'm dead serious.* ▪ *She finished the race dead last.* ▪ *The mayor was dead set against* [=strongly opposed to] *the plan.* **2** : in a sudden and complete way ▪ *He stopped dead in his tracks.* [=stopped suddenly] **3** : directly or exactly ▪ *The island is dead ahead.* [=it is right in front of us]

dead·beat /ˈdɛdˌbiːt/ *n* [*C*] *disapproving* **1** : a lazy person ▪ *a bunch of deadbeats* **2** *chiefly US* : a person who does not pay money that is owed ▪ *a deadbeat dad* [=a father who owes money to his former wife to help raise their children but does not pay it]

dead bolt *n* [*C*] *chiefly US* : a lock with a heavy sliding bar — called also (*Brit*) **deadlock**

dead·en /ˈdɛdn/ *vb* [*T*] : to make (something) weaker or less noticeable ▪ *He took aspirin to deaden the pain.*

dead end *n* [*C*] **1** : a street that ends instead of joining with another street ▪ *We came to a dead end and had to turn around.* **2** : a situation that leads to nothing further ▪ *My career has hit a dead end.* — **dead-end** /ˈdɛdˌɛnd/ *adj* ▪ *dead-end streets* ▪ *He's stuck in a dead-end job.* [=a job that does not give you a chance to get a better job]

dead heat *n* [*C*] : a contest in which two or more competitors earn the same score or finish at the same time ▪ *They finished in a dead heat.*

dead·line /ˈdɛdˌlaɪn/ *n* [*C/U*] : a date or time when something must be finished ▪ *We had to hurry to meet/make the deadline.* ▪ *We missed the deadline.* ▪ *They're working under (a) deadline.*

dead·lock /ˈdɛdˌlɑːk/ *n* [*C*] **1** : a situation in which an agreement cannot be made ▪ *The jury was unable to break/end the deadlock.* [=to agree on a verdict] **2** *US* : a situation in which players, teams, etc., have the same score : TIE ▪ *His goal broke a 3–3 deadlock.* **3** *Brit* : DEAD BOLT — **deadlock** *vb* [T/I] ▪ *The jury deadlocked.* [=failed to agree on a verdict] ▪ *a deadlocked game*

¹**dead·ly** /ˈdɛdli/ *adj* **dead·li·er; -est 1** : causing or able to cause death ▪ *deadly weapons/snakes/diseases* ▪ *Officers are allowed to use deadly force if necessary.* **2** : extremely accurate and effective ▪ *She shoots with deadly accuracy.* **3** *always before a noun* : extreme or complete ▪ *He spoke with deadly seriousness.* — **dead·li·ness** *n* [U]

²**deadly** *adv* **deadlier; -est** : extremely or completely ▪ *He's deadly serious.*

dead-on /ˈdɛdˈɑːn/ *adj, informal* : exactly correct or accurate ▪ *His impersonation of the President was dead-on.*

dead·pan /ˈdɛdˌpæn/ *adj* : showing no feeling or emotion — used to describe humor that is said in a serious way ▪ *deadpan humor/jokes*

dead weight *n* [C/U] **1** : something heavy that is being carried ▪ *carrying 150 pounds of dead weight* **2** : someone or something that makes success more difficult ▪ *He was a dead weight on the team this year.*

dead·wood /ˈdɛdˌwʊd/ *n* [U] **1** : people or things that are not useful or helpful in achieving a goal ▪ *bureaucratic deadwood* **2** : dead wood on a tree

deaf /ˈdɛf/ *adj* **1** : not able to hear ▪ *a deaf child* ▪ *completely/partially deaf* ▪ *She's starting to go deaf.* [=become unable to hear] **2** : not willing to listen to or consider something — usually + *to* ▪ *They were deaf to reason.* — **fall on deaf ears** see EAR — **the deaf** : deaf people ▪ *a school for the deaf* — **turn a deaf ear** see EAR — **deaf·ness** *n* [U]

deaf·en /ˈdɛfən/ *vb* [T] : to make (someone) unable to hear ▪ *We were deafened by the explosion.* ▪ *the deafening roar of the planes* — **deaf·en·ing·ly** /ˈdɛfənɪŋli/ *adv*

¹**deal** /ˈdiːl/ *vb* **dealt** /ˈdɛlt/; **deal·ing 1** [T/I] : to give cards to the players in a card game ▪ *It's your turn to deal (the cards).* ▪ *(figurative) She was dealt a terrible hand in life.* [=many bad things happened to her] **2** [T] : to give (something) to someone ▪ *They were dealt another loss* [=they lost another game] *last night.* ▪ *(formal) He dealt his enemy a mighty blow.* [=he hit his enemy hard] ▪ *She deals out lots of good advice.* **3** [T/I] : to buy and sell (drugs, art, etc.) as a business ▪ *She got caught dealing (drugs) in school.* — **deal in** [*phrasal vb*] **1 a** : to buy and sell (something) as a business ▪ *He deals in rare books.* **b** : to use or be involved in (something) ▪ *We don't deal in gossip.* **2 deal (someone) in** : to include (someone) in a card game ▪ *I'd like to play, too. Deal me in.* — **deal with** [*phrasal vb*] **1** : to have (something) as a subject ▪ *The book deals with World War II.* **2** : to make business agreements

with (someone) ▪ *She deals fairly with all her customers.* **3** : to do something about (a person or thing that causes a problem or difficult situation) ▪ *The government dealt harshly with the rebels.* ▪ *I dealt with the problem myself.* **4** : to try to accept (something that is true and cannot be changed) ▪ *She's still trying to deal with his death.* — **deal·er** *n* [C] ▪ *a car/drug dealer*

²**deal** *n* **1** [C] : an agreement between two or more people or groups that helps each in some way ▪ *I'll make you a deal. If you help me, I'll help you.* ▪ *We are getting ready to close/seal the deal.* [=make the agreement official] ▪ *The two sides finally struck a deal* [=came to an agreement] *after weeks of negotiations.* ▪ *We think it's a fair/square deal.* [=a fair agreement] ▪ *The band got/landed/signed a record deal.* = *The band cut a deal with the record company.* ▪ *a package deal* [=a single price for a set of items or services that included plane tickets and hotel accommodations **2** [*singular*] : a way of treating someone ▪ *He was going to take the job, but another company offered him a better deal.* [=offered him more money, benefits, etc.] **3** [C] : a price that is fair or lower than the usual price ▪ *We got a (good) deal on a new car.* ▪ *Now that's a great deal!* **4** [*singular*] : a large number or amount ▪ *It costs a good deal* [=it costs a lot] *of money.* ▪ *The town has changed a great deal since we left.* **5** [C] : the act of giving cards to each player in a card game ▪ *It's your deal.* [=it's your turn to deal] **6 the deal** *informal* : basic information about a person, thing, or situation ▪ *What's the deal* [=story, situation] *with that guy?* — **one-shot deal** : something that happens only one time ▪ *This offer is a one-shot deal.* — **the real deal** *informal* : a thing or person that is not a copy or imitation ▪ *These diamonds aren't fake. They're the real deal.*

deal·er·ship /ˈdiːləˌʃɪp/ *n* [C] : a business that sells a specified kind of product ▪ *a car dealership*

deal·ing /ˈdiːlɪŋ/ *n* **1** [*plural*] : the actions that are a main part of the relationship between people, groups, organizations, etc. ▪ *her financial dealings with the company* **2** [U] : a way of behaving or of doing business ▪ *He has a reputation for fair dealing.*

dealt *past tense and past participle of* ¹DEAL

dean /ˈdiːn/ *n* [C] **1** : a person who is in charge of one of the parts of a university ▪ *She's the dean of the business school.* **2** : a person whose job is to make sure students obey the rules ▪ *the dean of students* **3** *US* : a person who has more experience in or knowledge about a particular profession, subject, etc., than anyone or almost anyone ▪ *She's considered the dean of American architecture.* **4** : a Christian priest who is in charge of several other priests or churches — **dean·ship** /ˈdiːnˌʃɪp/ *n* [C]

dean's list *n* [C] *US* : a list of college students who have earned high grades

¹**dear** /ˈdiə/ *adj* **1** : loved or valued very

much ▪ *He's a dear friend of mine.* ▪ *She is very dear to me.* **2** — used in writing to address someone ▪ *Dear Sir or Madam* ▪ *Dear Jane* **3** *chiefly Brit* : having a high price : EXPENSIVE ▪ *Peaches are dear this time of year.*

²**dear** *adv* : with love and respect ▪ *She lost everything you* **held dear.** [=loved and valued most]

³**dear** *n* [C] **1** — used to address someone you love ▪ *Hello, (my) dear.* **2** : a kind and helpful person ▪ *Be a dear and take this for me.*

⁴**dear** *interj* — used especially to express surprise, fear, or disappointment ▪ *Oh dear! We're late!* ▪ *Dear God! What happened?*

dear·ly /'diəli/ *adv* **1** : very much ▪ *She loved him dearly.* **2** : in a way that is difficult or severe ▪ *They paid dearly for their crimes.* [=they were punished severely]

dearth /'dəθ/ *n* [*singular*] *formal* : ²LACK — + *of* ▪ *a dearth of evidence*

death /'dɛθ/ *n* **1** [*C/U*] : the time when a person, animal, or plant dies ▪ *birth, life, and death* ▪ *We mourned his (tragic) death.* ▪ *The accident resulted in two deaths.* ▪ *death threats* ▪ *The* **cause of death** *is not known.* ▪ *She is close to death.* = *She is* **at death's door.** [=she will die soon] ▪ *a serial killer who was* **put to death** [=executed] *for the murder of 28 people* **2** [C] : the permanent end of something ▪ *the death of innocence/vaudeville* — *a matter of* **life and death** *see* LIFE — **be the death of** : to cause (someone) to die ▪ *The disease will be the death of him.* ▪ *(figurative) Those kids* **will be the death of me!** [=they worry and upset me very much] — **to death** **1** — used to say how someone died or was killed ▪ *He was shot/stabbed to death.* ▪ *They froze/starved to death.* **2** : very much ▪ *We were bored/scared to death.* [=extremely bored/scared] ▪ *I just love him to death.* ▪ *I'm* **sick to death** *of hearing* [=I've heard too much] *about the scandal.* — **to the death** **1** : until someone is dead ▪ *a battle/fight to the death* **2** : with all of your energy and effort ▪ *We'll fight to the death to keep the school open.* — **death·like** /'dɛθ,laɪk/ *adj*

death·bed /'dɛθ,bɛd/ *n* — **on your deathbed** : in the bed that you will soon die in ▪ *She made a startling confession on her deathbed.* [=just before she died] — **deathbed** *adj* ▪ *a deathbed confession*

death blow *n* [C] **1** : an act that kills a person or animal ▪ *The general received his death blow in battle.* **2** : an act or event that causes the end of something ▪ *events that dealt the ailing company its final death blow*

death camp *n* [C] : a place where many prisoners are taken to be killed during a war ▪ *Nazi death camps*

death certificate *n* [C] : an official document that gives information about a person's death

death–defying *adj* : very dangerous ▪ *death-defying stunts*

death grip *n* [*singular*] : a very tight hold on something ▪ *his death grip on the car's*

steering wheel ▪ *(figurative) Drugs have a death grip on their town.*

¹**death·ly** /'dɛθli/ *adj* : causing you to think of death ▪ *a deathly fear/silence*

²**deathly** *adv* **1** : in a way that is close to death or dying ▪ *He is deathly ill.* **2** : in a way that makes you think of death ▪ *She's deathly afraid of snakes.*

death penalty *n* — **the death penalty** : death as a punishment given by a court of law ▪ *If convicted, he could face the death penalty.* [=his punishment may be death]

death rate *n* [C] : a number that shows how many people died in a particular place or during a particular time ▪ *a decline in the country's death rate*

death row *n* [U] : the part of a prison where prisoners who will be executed live until they are killed ▪ *He's been on* **death row** *for 12 years.*

death sentence *n* [C] **1** : the decision by a court of law that the punishment for someone's crime will be death ▪ *She received a death sentence for the murders.* **2 a** : something that is sure to cause death ▪ *AIDS is no longer an automatic death sentence.* **b** : an act or event that ends something permanently ▪ *The cut in funding was a death sentence for the program.*

death throes *n* [*plural*] : the movements sometimes made by a person who is about to die ▪ *The opera ends with the hero in his death throes.* ▪ *(figurative) the death throes of a failing industry*

death toll *n* [C] : the number of people who die in an accident, war, etc. ▪ *The storm's death toll is expected to rise.*

death trap *n* [C] *informal* : a building, vehicle, etc., that is very dangerous and could cause someone's death ▪ *That old factory is a death trap.*

death warrant *n* [C] : an official document ordering a person to be killed as a punishment ▪ *(figurative) The company* **signed its own death warrant.** [=caused its own end]

death wish *n* [*singular*] : a desire to die ▪ *She drives like she has a death wish.*

de·ba·cle /dɪ'bɑːkəl, *Brit* deɪ'bɑːkəl/ *n* [C] : a great disaster or complete failure ▪ *a military/economic debacle*

de·bark /dɪ'bɑɚk/ *vb* [I] : DISEMBARK

de·base /dɪ'beɪs/ *vb* **-based; -bas·ing** [T] : to lower the value or reputation of (someone or something) ▪ *The governor debased himself by lying to the public.* ▪ *a debased coin* ▪ *a debasing comment* — **de·base·ment** /dɪ'beɪsmənt/ *n* [U]

¹**de·bate** /dɪ'beɪt/ *n* [C/U] : a discussion between people in which they express different opinions about something ◇ A debate can be an organized event, an informal discussion between two or more people, or a general discussion that involves many people. ▪ *presidential debates* ▪ *a heated debate* [=argument] ▪ *At the center/core/heart of the debate* [=controversy] *is the question of responsibility.* ▪ *The meaning of the text has been the subject of intense/lively debate for many years.* ▪ *The benefit of the tax cuts is a* **matter of debate.** = *It's* **open to debate.**

[=people have different ideas and opinions about it]

²**debate** vb -**bat·ed; -bat·ing** 1 [T] : to discuss (something) with people whose opinions are different from your own ▪ debating the meaning of a poem 2 [T/I] : to compete against (someone) in a debate ▪ The candidates debated (each other) for an hour. ▪ the school's **debating team** [=a group that competes against other teams in formal debates] 3 [T] : to think about (something) in order to decide what to do ▪ She is still debating (with herself) about whether to stay or go. — **de·bat·able** /dɪˈbeɪtəbəl/ adj ▪ The benefit of the tax cuts is debatable. [=it may or may not be true or real] — **de·bat·er** n [C]

de·bauched /dɪˈbɑːʧt/ adj, formal : behaving in an immoral way ▪ a debauched poet/society

de·bauch·ery /dɪˈbɑːʧəri/ n, pl -**er·ies** [C/U] formal : bad or immoral behavior that involves sex, drugs, alcohol, etc. ▪ drunken debauchery ▪ the evening's debaucheries

de·bil·i·tate /dɪˈbɪləˌteɪt/ vb -**tat·ed; -tat·ing** [T] formal + technical : to make (someone or something) weak ▪ an economy debilitated by years of civil war — **de·bil·i·ta·tion** /dɪˌbɪləˈteɪʃən/ n [U]

de·bil·i·ty /dɪˈbɪləti/ n, pl -**ties** [C/U] formal : physical weakness caused by illness or old age ▪ the debilities of elderly people

¹**deb·it** /ˈdɛbət/ n [C] : an amount of money that is taken from an account ▪ the account's credits and debits

²**debit** vb [T] : to take money from (an account) ▪ Your account will automatically be debited for the amount of your bill every month.

debit card n [C] : a card that is used to pay for things by having money taken directly from your bank account

deb·o·nair /ˌdɛbəˈneɚ/ adj, of a man : dressing and acting in an appealing and sophisticated way ▪ his handsome face and debonair manner

de·brief /diˈbriːf/ vb [T] formal : to officially question (someone) about a job that has been done ▪ The pilot was debriefed after his flight. — **de·brief·ing** n [C/U] ▪ a full debriefing

de·bris /dəˈbriː, Brit ˈdɛˌbriː/ n [U] : the pieces that are left after something has been destroyed or thrown away ▪ Workers cleared the debris after the earthquake. ▪ cigarette butts and other debris

debt /ˈdɛt/ n 1 [C] : an amount of money that you owe to a person, bank, company, etc. ▪ He is trying to pay off his credit card debts. ▪ the nation's **foreign debt** [=the amount of money a country owes other countries] 2 [U] : the state of owing money to someone or something ▪ a mountain/sea of debt ▪ He's been trying to get **out of debt**. ▪ **deep/heavily in debt** ▪ She went **into debt** to pay for college. 3 [C] : the fact that you have been helped or influenced by someone or something ▪ He owes a/his debt to Andy Warhol. ▪ He was influenced by Andy Warhol's work] ▪ I am forever **in your debt** [=I am very

thankful] for your help and support. ▪ The whole town **owes a debt of gratitude/ thanks to** [=has a good reason to be very grateful to] the parade organizers. — **debt to society** — used in phrases like **pay your debt to society** to refer to being punished for committing a crime ▪ After 10 years in prison, he has paid his debt to society.

debt·or /ˈdɛtɚ/ n [C] : a person, organization, government, etc., that owes money ▪ debtors and creditors

de·bug /diˈbʌg/ vb -**bugged; -bug·ging** [T] technical : to remove the mistakes from (something) ▪ debug computer programs

de·bunk /diˈbʌŋk/ vb [T] : to show that a belief, story, etc., is not true ▪ debunking myths

¹**de·but** /ˈdeɪˌbjuː/ n [C] : the first time an actor, musician, athlete, etc., does something in public or for the public ▪ He made his singing debut at a very young age. — sometimes used to refer to the first appearance of a product, sport, event, etc. ▪ the debut of a new car ▪ her debut album/film/novel

²**debut** vb 1 [I] : to appear in public for the first time ▪ The singer debuted at the age of 15. 2 [T] : to show or provide (something) to the public for the first time ▪ The network debuts a new TV show tonight.

deb·u·tante /ˈdɛbjʊˌtɑːnt/ n [C] : a young upper-class woman who has begun going to special parties

Dec. abbr December ▪ Dec. 1, 2004

de·cade /ˈdɛˌkeɪd/ n [C] : a period of 10 years ▪ The war lasted nearly a decade. ▪ the decade of the 1920s

dec·a·dence /ˈdɛkədəns/ n [U] disapproving : behavior that shows low morals and a great love of pleasure, money, fame, etc. ▪ the decadence of modern society

dec·a·dent /ˈdɛkədənt/ adj 1 disapproving a : having low morals and a great love of pleasure, money, fame, etc. ▪ a decadent aristocrat b : attractive to people of low morals ▪ decadent nightclubs 2 : extremely pleasing ▪ decadent lifestyles/desserts — **dec·a·dent·ly** adv

de·caf /ˈdiːˌkæf/ n [C/U] : coffee that does not contain caffeine ▪ Can I have (a) decaf, please?

de·caf·fein·at·ed /diˈkæfəˌneɪtəd/ adj : not containing caffeine ▪ decaffeinated coffee/tea/cola

de·cal /ˈdiːˌkæl/ n [C] US : a picture, design, or label that will stick to the surface on which it is placed

de·camp /dɪˈkæmp/ vb [I] : to leave a place suddenly and secretly ▪ She took the papers and decamped.

de·cant·er /dɪˈkæntɚ/ n [C] : a special glass bottle from which wine, whiskey, etc., is served

de·cap·i·tate /dɪˈkæpəˌteɪt/ vb -**tat·ed; -tat·ing** [T] : to cut off the head of (a person or animal) ▪ a decapitated body — **de·cap·i·ta·tion** /dɪˌkæpəˈteɪʃən/ n [C/U]

de·cath·lon /dɪˈkæθlən/ n [C] : a sports contest that consists of 10 different events • *the Olympic decathlon* — **de-cath-lete** /dɪˈkæθ,liːt/ *n* [C]

de-cay /dɪˈkeɪ/ *vb* **1** [T/I] : to be slowly destroyed by natural processes • *Fallen tomatoes decayed* [=rotted, decomposed] *on the ground.* **2** [I] : to slowly lose strength, health, etc. • *our decaying school system* **3** [I] *of a building, area, etc.* : to go slowly from a bad condition to a worse condition • *decaying neighborhoods* — **decay** *n* [U] • *tooth decay* • *the moral decay of our society* • *The old theater is falling into decay.*

de-ceased *adj* : no longer living • *My mother is deceased.* [=(less politely) dead] — **the deceased** *formal* : a dead person or dead people • *a relative of the deceased*

de-ceit /dɪˈsiːt/ *n* [C/U] : behavior that is meant to fool or trick someone • *a web of lies and deceit* • *Her excuse was really a deceit.* [=lie]

de-ceit-ful /dɪˈsiːtfəl/ *adj* : not honest • *a scheming, deceitful person* • *deceitful advertisements* — **de-ceit-ful-ly** *adv* — **de-ceit-ful-ness** *n* [U]

de-ceive /dɪˈsiːv/ *vb* -ceived; -ceiv-ing [T/I] : to make (someone) believe something that is not true • *He deceived the customer about the car's condition.* • *People who think they can easily quit smoking are deceiving themselves.* • *Unless my eyes deceive me* [=unless I am mistaken about what I am seeing], *everyone's gone.* • *Appearances can be deceiving.* [=deceptive] — **de-ceiv-er** *n* [C] — **de-ceiv-ing-ly** /dɪˈsiːvɪŋli/ *adv*

de-cel-er-ate /diːˈsɛlə,reɪt/ *vb* -at-ed; -at-ing [T/I] **1** : to move slower • *Slowly decelerate the car.* **2** : to cause (something) to happen more slowly • *decelerating economic growth* — **de-cel-er-a-tion** /diˌsɛləˈreɪʃən/ *n* [U]

De-cem-ber /dɪˈsɛmbɚ/ *n* [C/U] : the 12th and last month of the year • *Her birthday is in December.* • *the 10th of December* = (US) *December (the) 10th* • *They moved last December.* — abbr. **Dec.**

de-cen-cy /ˈdiːsn̩si/ *n, pl* -cies **1** [U] : polite, moral, and honest behavior that shows respect for other people • *If you're going to be late, please have the (common) decency to call and let me know.* • *Have you no sense of decency?* **2** [*plural*] *formal* : the behaviors that people in a society consider to be proper or acceptable • *observing the ordinary decencies*

de-cent /ˈdiːsn̩t/ *adj* **1** : polite, moral, and honest • *decent, hardworking people* • *I did the decent thing and told her the truth.* **2** : good enough but not the best • *She's a decent tennis player.* • *decent, affordable housing* • *He makes a decent living.* = *He has a job making/earning decent money.* • *a halfway decent* [=somewhat good] *movie* **3** : appropriate or suitable • *Try to get to bed at a decent hour.* [=at a time that is not too late at night] **4** : not using offensive language • *Please keep your jokes decent—there are children in the room.* **5** *informal* : wearing clothes that cover enough of your body • *Can I come in? Are you decent?* — **de-cent-ly** *adv*

de-cen-tral-ize *also Brit* **de-cen-tral-ise** /diːˈsɛntrəˌlaɪz/ *vb* -ized; -iz-ing [T/I] : to change (something) by taking control, power, etc., from one person or group and giving it to many people or groups • *They decentralized (the school system) and gave each district control over its own policies.* — **de-cen-tral-i-za-tion** *also Brit* **de-cen-tral-i-sa-tion** /diˌsɛntrələˈzeɪʃən/, *Brit* diˌsɛntrəˌlaɪˈzeɪʃən/ *n* [U, singular]

de-cep-tion /dɪˈsɛpʃən/ *n* **1** [U] : the act of deceiving someone • *a politician's use of deception to gain public support* **2** [C] : an act or statement intended to make people believe something that is not true • *a clever deception* [=trick] — **de-cep-tive** /dɪˈsɛptɪv/ *adj* • *The low price is deceptive since many fees are added to it.* — **de-cep-tive-ly** *adv* • *deceptively simple lyrics* • *deceptively low prices*

deci-bel /ˈdɛsə,bɛl/ *n* [C] *technical* : a unit for measuring how loud a sound is — abbr. **dB**

de-cide /dɪˈsaɪd/ *vb* -cid-ed; -cid-ing [T/I] **1 a** : to choose (something) after thinking about it • *I can't decide (what to do).* • *She decided that she would take the job.* = *She decided to take the job.* • *We are deciding if we should stay.* = *We are deciding whether or not to stay.* • *Voters must decide between the two candidates.* [=voters must choose one or the other candidate] • *I decided against telling her.* [=I decided not to tell her] **b** : to choose whether or not to believe (something) after thinking about it • *They decided that he was right.* **2** : to determine what the result of (something) will be • *This battle could very well decide the war.* • *The vice president will cast the deciding vote.* • *The deciding factor was cost.* [=the decision was based on cost] • *His home run was the deciding factor in the game.* [=his home run won the game] **3** *law* : to make a judgment in a court of law • *a case decided by the Supreme Court* • *The court decided in favor of the plaintiff.* [=the plaintiff won the case] • *The court decided against the defendant.* [=the defendant was found guilty] — **decide on/upon** [*phrasal vb*] : to choose (something) after thinking about the possible choices • *I am having trouble deciding on a gift for them.*

decided *adj* : obvious and definite • *a decided advantage* • *The new paint on the house is a decided improvement.* — **de-cid-ed-ly** /dɪˈsaɪdədli/ *adv* • *The phrases have decidedly different meanings.*

de-cid-u-ous /dɪˈsɪdʒəwəs/ *adj, of a tree, bush, etc.* : having leaves that fall off every year • *deciduous and coniferous trees*

¹**dec-i-mal** /ˈdɛsəməl/ *adj, mathematics* : based on the number 10 • *the decimal system* • *In the number 8.901, the 9 is in the first decimal place.* [=it is the first digit after the decimal point]

²**decimal** *n* [C] *mathematics* : a number that is written with a decimal point • *The decimal .2 is equal to the fraction* ²/₁₀.

decimal point *n* [C] *mathematics* : the dot (as in .678 or 3.678) that separates a whole number from tenths, hundredths, etc.

dec·i·mate /ˈdɛsəˌmeɪt/ vb **-mat·ed; -mat·ing** [T] **1** : to destroy a large number of (plants, animals, people, etc.) ▪ *The village/population was decimated by the disease.* **2** : to severely damage or destroy a large part of (something) ▪ *Budget cuts have decimated public services in small towns.* — **dec·i·ma·tion** /ˌdɛsəˈmeɪʃən/ n [U]

de·ci·pher /dɪˈsaɪfə/ vb [T] : to find the meaning of (something that is difficult to read or understand) ▪ *I couldn't decipher his sloppy handwriting.* — **de·ci·pher·able** /dɪˈsaɪfərəbəl/ adj

de·ci·sion /dɪˈsɪʒən/ n **1** [C] : a choice that you make about something after thinking about it ▪ *She announced her decision to go to medical school.* ▪ *He finally* **made/reached a decision.** = *He finally* **came to a decision.** ▪ *She made a* **conscious decision** *to leave the painting unfinished.* ▪ *an* **informed decision** [=a decision based on facts or information] **2** [U] formal : the ability to make choices quickly and confidently ▪ *a leader of courage and decision* [=decisiveness] **3** [C] : a legal or official judgment ▪ *the U.S. Supreme Court's 1954 decision that ended racial segregation in public schools* ▪ *The appeals court* **upheld/overturned the decision.** [=it agreed/disagreed with the decision made earlier by a lower court] **4** [U] : the act of deciding something ▪ *The moment of decision has come. You must decide.*

decision–making n [U] : the act or process of deciding something especially with a group of people ▪ *The project will require some difficult decision-making.* ▪ *their decision-making process*

de·ci·sive /dɪˈsaɪsɪv/ adj **1** : able to make choices quickly and confidently ▪ *a decisive leader* ▪ *taking decisive action* [=acting quickly and with confidence] **2** : determining what the result of something will be ▪ *She cast the decisive vote. The meeting is seen as a* **decisive step** *toward a peace treaty.* ▪ *His lack of experience was the* **decisive factor** *in my decision* [=the main reason I decided] *not to hire him.* **3** : very clear and obvious ▪ *a decisive win/advantage* — **de·ci·sive·ly** adv — **de·ci·sive·ness** n [U]

¹**deck** /ˈdɛk/ n **1** [C/U] : a flat surface that forms the main outside floor of a boat or ship ▪ *Some passengers had come* **on deck.** ▪ *We went below deck(s) to our cabin.* ❖ The phrase **all hands on deck** is used to call all people on a ship to the deck to do work that must be done. ▪ *The captain shouted "All hands on deck!"* **2** [C] **a** : one of the levels on a bus, ship, etc. ▪ *a cabin on B deck* **b** : one of the seating levels in a sports stadium ▪ *We sat in the lower/upper deck.* **3** [C] chiefly US : a wood structure that has a floor but no walls or roof, is attached to a building, and is used for relaxing ▪ *We ate out on the deck.* **4** [C] chiefly US : a complete set of playing cards ▪ *The dealer shuffled the deck (of cards).* ▪ (figurative, informal) *He's* **not playing with a full deck.** [=he is

not able to think or act in a normal way] — **clear the decks/deck** : to get rid of something to make room for something else ▪ *Firing the CEO will clear the decks for change within the company.* — **hit the deck** see ¹HIT — **on deck** US, baseball : waiting to bat next ▪ *Smith is batting and Jones is on deck.* ▪ (figurative) *The band's new song is on deck.* [=next]

²**deck** vb [T] **1 a** : to decorate (something) ▪ *We helped deck the chapel with flowers before the wedding.* ▪ *houses decked (out) in lights for the holidays* **b** : to dress (yourself or someone) in a particular way ▪ *sports fans decking themselves (out) in their team's colors* ▪ *We got* **(all) decked out** [=dressed in a very fancy way] *(in tuxedos) for the occasion.* **2** informal : to knock (someone) down by hitting very hard ▪ *He decked him with one punch.*

deck chair n [C] : a chair that can be folded up and that is used for sitting on a deck, beach, etc.

deck·hand /ˈdɛkˌhænd/ n [C] : a worker on a ship whose work does not require special training

de·claim /dɪˈkleɪm/ vb [T/I] formal : to say (something) in usually a loud and formal way ▪ *The actress declaimed her lines with passion.* — **dec·la·ma·tion** /ˌdɛkləˈmeɪʃən/ n [C/U] — **de·clam·a·to·ry** /dɪˈklæməˌtori, Brit dɪˈklæmətri/ adj ▪ *declamatory speeches*

dec·la·ra·tion /ˌdɛkləˈreɪʃən/ n **1** [C/U] : the act of declaring something ▪ *The government has made/issued a declaration of war on/against its enemies.* **2** [C] : something that is stated or made known in an official or public way ▪ *a declaration of love.* **3** [C] : a document that contains an official statement ▪ *The museum has a copy of the country's declaration of independence/sovereignty.*

de·clar·a·tive /dɪˈklerətɪv/ adj, grammar : having the form of a statement rather than a question or a command ▪ *"They went to school" is a declarative sentence.*

de·clare /dɪˈkleɚ/ vb **-clared; -clar·ing** [T] **1** : to say or state (something) in an official or public way ▪ *The government has just declared a state of emergency.* ▪ *He declared himself the winner.* = *He declared that he was the winner.* = *He declared victory.* ▪ *The company declared bankruptcy.* [=formally said in a legal document that it was bankrupt] **2** : to say (something) in a strong and confident way ▪ *He openly declared his love for her.* **3 a** : to tell the government about (money you have earned or received) in order to pay taxes ▪ *They failed to declare all of their earnings on their tax return.* **b** : to list the cost of (something bought in a different country) so that you can pay taxes on it ▪ *Large purchases must be declared at customs.* — **declare for** [phrasal vb] US : to officially say that you will take part in (something) ▪ *a basketball player who declared for the NBA draft* — **declare war** : to officially decide to fight or go to war ▪ *They declared war on/against their enemy.*

de·clas·si·fy /diˈklæsəˌfaɪ/ vb **-fies;**

-fied; -fy·ing [T] : to allow the public to see or learn about (something that has been a secret) • *That information has not yet been declassified.* — de·clas·si·fi·ca·tion /ˌdiˌklæsəfəˈkeɪʃən/ n

¹de·cline /dɪˈklaɪn/ vb -clined; -clin·ing 1 [I] : to become lower in amount or less in number • *Oil prices continue to decline.* • *the animal's declining numbers* 2 [I] : to become worse in condition or quality • *My grandmother's health/condition has been declining rapidly.* 3 a [T] : to say that you will not or cannot do something • *The company declined to comment on the scandal.* b [T/I] : to say no to something in a polite way • *He changed his mind and declined (the offer).*

²decline n [C/U] 1 : the process of becoming worse in condition or quality • *a period of economic decline* • *a decline in his health* • *His health is on the decline.* [=becoming worse] • *The country was in (a state of) decline.* [=becoming less powerful, wealthy, etc.] 2 : a change to a lower number or amount • *a sharp/ steep decline in sales* • *Sales are on the decline.* [=becoming less]

de·code /diˈkoʊd/ vb -cod·ed; -cod·ing [T] : to change (secret messages, documents, etc.) from a set of numbers, symbols, etc., into words you can understand • *Government agents decoded the message.* — de·cod·er /diˈkoʊdɚ/ n [C]

de·com·mis·sion /ˌdiːkəˈmɪʃən/ vb [T] : to officially stop using (a ship, weapon, dam, etc.) • *Several military bases are scheduled to be decommissioned.*

de·com·pose /ˌdiːkəmˈpoʊz/ vb -posed; -pos·ing [T/I] : to cause (dead plants, dead animals, etc.) to be slowly destroyed by natural processes, chemicals, etc. • *partially decomposed bodies* • *the smell of decomposing leaves* — de·com·po·si·tion /ˌdiˌkɑːmpəˈzɪʃən/ n [U]

de·com·press /ˌdiːkəmˈprɛs/ vb 1 [T/I] : to release or reduce the physical pressure on something • *Surgery decompressed the vertebrae.* 2 [T] computers : to change (a computer file that has been made smaller) back to its original size • *The file must be decompressed before it can be read.* 3 [I] US, informal : to rest and relax • *After their busy week, they needed some time to decompress.* — de·com·pres·sion /ˌdiːkəmˈprɛʃən/ n [U]

de·con·ges·tant /ˌdiːkənˈʤɛstənt/ n [C/U] : a medicine that helps stop thick fluid from building up in your nose, throat, or chest

de·con·tam·i·nate /ˌdiːkənˈtæməˌneɪt/ vb -nat·ed; -nat·ing [T] : to remove dirty or dangerous substances from (a person, thing, place, etc.) • *decontaminating an area after an oil spill* — de·con·tam·i·na·tion /ˌdiːkənˌtæməˈneɪʃən/ n [U]

de·cor or dé·cor /deɪˈkoɚ, ˈdeɪˌkoɚ/ n [C/U] : the way that the inside of a building is decorated • *the restaurant's elegant decor*

dec·o·rate /ˈdɛkəˌreɪt/ vb -rat·ed; -rat·ing 1 [T/I] : to make (something) more attractive usually by putting something on it • *I decorated my room in dark colors.* • *The gift was decorated with ribbons.* 2 [T] : to give a medal or award to (a soldier, police officer, etc.) • *He was decorated for bravery.* • *a decorated war veteran*

dec·o·ra·tion /ˌdɛkəˈreɪʃən/ n 1 [C/U] : something that is added to something else to make it more attractive • *Christmas decorations* • *The fruit on the table is for decoration.* [=it is used to make the table more attractive] 2 [U] : the act of decorating something • *a unique style of decoration* 3 [C] : an award that is given to someone for doing something brave or honorable • *He received a decoration from the President.*

dec·o·ra·tive /ˈdɛkrətɪv/ adj : used for decoration • *decorative elements/fruit/ shrubs* — dec·o·ra·tive·ly adv

dec·o·ra·tor /ˈdɛkəˌreɪtɚ/ n [C] : a person who decorates something especially as a job • *a cake decorator* • *She is an interior decorator.* [=interior designer]

dec·o·rous /ˈdɛkərəs/ adj, formal : correct and polite in a particular situation • *decorous behavior/conduct* — dec·o·rous·ly adv

de·co·rum /dɪˈkoɚəm/ n [U] formal : correct or proper behavior that shows respect and good manners • *He has no sense of decorum.*

de·coy /ˈdiːˌkoɪ/ n [C] 1 : a wooden or plastic bird that is used by hunters to attract live birds 2 : a person or thing that attracts people's attention so they will not notice someone or something else • *He had a decoy distract the guard while he stole the car.* — de·coy /dɪˈkoɪ/ vb [T] • *His partner decoyed the guard.*

¹de·crease /dɪˈkriːs/ vb -creased; -creas·ing [T/I] : to become smaller or to make (something) smaller in size, amount, etc. • *Sales have decreased.* • *The population is decreasing (in size).* • *ways to decrease* [=reduce, lower] *your chances of having a stroke* — decreased adj • *a decreased risk of heart disease* — de·creas·ing·ly /dɪˈkriːsɪŋli/ adv

²de·crease /ˈdiːˌkriːs/ n 1 [C/U] : the act of becoming smaller or of making something smaller in size, amount, number, etc. • *We've recently had a decrease in the number of accidents.* 2 [C] : the amount by which something is made smaller • *decreases of between 20 and 30 percent* • *on the decrease* : becoming less in size, amount, number, etc. • *decreasing* • *The number of students is on the decrease.*

de·cree /dɪˈkriː/ n [C/U] 1 : an official order given by a person with power or by a government • *The President issued a decree.* • *a royal decree* [=an order given by a king or queen] 2 : an official decision made by a court of law • *a court's decree* — decree vb -creed; -cree·ing [T/I] • *The government decreed a national holiday.*

de·crep·it /dɪˈkrɛpət/ adj : old and in bad condition or poor health • *a decrepit building* — de·crep·i·tude /dɪˈkrɛpəˌtuːd, Brit dɪˈkrɛpəˌtjuːd/ n [U] formal • *a state of decrepitude*

de·crim·i·nal·ize also Brit de·crim·i-

nal·ise /dɪˈkrɪmənəˌlaɪz/ vb **-ized; -iz-ing** [T] : to make (something that is illegal) legal by changing the law • *Should the government decriminalize marijuana?* — **de·crim·i·nal·i·za·tion** also Brit **de·crim·i·nal·i·sa·tion** /diˌkrɪmənələˈzeɪʃən, Brit diˌkrɪmənəˌlaɪˈzeɪʃən/ n [U]

de·cry /dɪˈkraɪ/ vb **-cries; -cried; -cry-ing** [T] formal : to say publicly and forcefully that you regard (something) as bad, wrong, etc. • *Parents decried the movie's emphasis on sex.*

ded·i·cate /ˈdɛdɪˌkeɪt/ vb **-cat·ed; -cat-ing** [T] : to officially make (something) a place for honoring or remembering a person, event, etc. • *a memorial dedicated to soldiers who died in the war* — **dedicate to** [phrasal vb] **1 dedicate (something) to** : to decide that (something) will be used for (a special purpose) • *He dedicated his life/time to helping the poor.* = *He dedicated himself to helping the poor.* [=he used his time, energy, etc., to help the poor] **2 dedicate (something) to** : to say that (a book, song, etc.) was written or is being performed to honor or express affection for (someone) • *She dedicated her first novel to her father.*

dedicated adj **1** : having very strong support for or loyalty to a person, group, cause, etc. • *dedicated teachers/fans* **2** always before a noun, technical : used only for one particular purpose • *a dedicated phone line*

ded·i·ca·tion /ˌdɛdɪˈkeɪʃən/ n **1** [U] : a feeling of very strong support for or loyalty to someone or something • *I admire her hard work and dedication.* **2** [C] : a message at the beginning of a book, song, etc., saying that it was written or is being performed in order to honor or express affection for someone **3** [C] : the act of officially saying that something (such as a new building) was created for a particular purpose (such as worship) or to remember or honor a particular person • *the dedication of a temple/building*

de·duce /dɪˈduːs, Brit dɪˈdjuːs/ vb **-duced; -duc·ing** [T] formal : to use logic or reason to form (a conclusion or opinion about something) • *A word's meaning can often be deduced from its context.*

de·duct /dɪˈdʌkt/ vb [T] : to take away (something, especially an amount of money) from a total • *The payment will be deducted from your account.*

¹de·duct·ible /dɪˈdʌktəbəl/ adj : able to be subtracted from an amount of money • *All donations to charities are deductible.* [=taxes do not have to be paid on money given to charities]

²deductible n [C] US : an amount of money that you have to pay for something (such as having your car fixed after an accident) before an insurance company pays for the remainder of the cost • *an insurance policy with a $1,000 deductible*

de·duc·tion /dɪˈdʌkʃən/ n **1 a** [C] : the act of taking away something (such as an amount of money) from a total • *automatic payroll deduction* [=money automatically taken out of someone's paycheck to pay for something] **b** [C]

: something (such as an amount of money) that is or can be subtracted from a total • *tax deductions for small businesses* **2 a** [U] : the act or process of using logic or reason to form a conclusion or opinion about something • *a guess based on intuition rather than deduction.* **b** [C] : a conclusion or opinion that is based on logic or reason • *a logical deduction* — **de·duc·tive** /dɪˈdʌktɪv/ adj

¹deed /ˈdiːd/ n [C/U] **1** : something that is done : an act or action • *good/evil/heroic deeds* • *We are judged by our deeds.* [=by what we do] **2** : a legal document that shows who owns a building or piece of land • *the deed to the property*

²deed vb [T] US : to give someone ownership of (a building or piece of land) by means of a deed • *She deeded the house to her children.*

deem /ˈdiːm/ vb [T] formal : to think of (someone or something) in a particular way • *The building was deemed unsafe.* • *Do whatever you deem (to be) necessary.*

¹deep /ˈdiːp/ adj **1 a** : having a large distance to the bottom from the surface or highest point • *a deep well/hole/valley* • *the plant's deep roots* **b** : going far inward from the outside or the front edge of something • *deep shelves/closets* **c** : located far inside something • *deep in/within the forest/jungle/mountains* (figurative) *I knew it deep in my heart.* [=I believed it very strongly] **2** not before a noun : having a specified measurement downward, inward, or backward • *The canyon is a mile deep.* • *The shelves are 10 inches deep.* • *knee-deep snow* [=snow as high as our knees] **3 a** : located near the outside edges of an area • *(baseball) a fly ball to deep right field* • *hit, thrown, or kicked a long distance* • *a deep* [=long] *pass* **4** : done by taking in or breathing out a large amount of air • *a deep breath/sigh* **5** : low in sound or musical pitch • *his deep voice* **6** : having a dark, strong color • *a deep blue sky* **7** : very intelligent and serious but complex or difficult to understand • *She's a deep* [=profound] *thinker.* • *deep thoughts* **8** : full of mystery • *a deep, dark secret* **9 a** : concentrating and giving all of your attention to something — + *in* • *deep in thought/conversation* **b** : affected by something in a very serious way • *I'm deep in debt* [=I have a lot of debt] **10** : very bad, serious, or severe • *a deep depression/recession* • *people living in deep poverty* • *I'm in deep trouble.* **11** : very strongly felt • *my deepest sympathy* • *the deep emotional bond between them* **12** : full, complete, or thorough • *a deep understanding of the issue* ✧ If you are in a **deep sleep**, you are thoroughly asleep and it is hard to wake you up. **13** US : going down to a very low price, level, etc. • *deep discounts* **14** US, sports : having many good players • *The team is very deep this year.* — **in deep water** : in a difficult situation : in trouble • *I thought I could handle it, but now I'm in deep water.* — **the deep end** informal **1** — used in phrases like *throw in (at) the deep end* and *jump in (at) the deep end* to describe starting a new and

difficult activity when you are not fully prepared or ready to do it ▪ *Teachers are thrown in the deep end when they first start teaching.* 2 ✧ To **go off the deep end** is to go crazy, such as by behaving foolishly or by becoming very angry or upset.
— **deep·ness** *n* [*U*] ▪ *the deepness [=depth] of the water*

²**deep** *adv* 1 a : far into or below the surface of something ▪ *The ship lies deep below/beneath the water's surface.* ▪ *a cavern deep underground* ▪ (*figurative*) *I stared deep into her eyes.* ▪ (*figurative*) *Her angry words hurt/cut him deep.* [=*deeply*] b : far into or inside something ▪ *We walked deep into the forest.* 2 *not before a noun* : at a specified measurement downward, inward, or backward ▪ *cars parked three deep* [=with three cars in a row] 3 : to a late time ▪ *dancing deep into the night* 4 *sports* : near the outside edges of a playing area ▪ *The outfielder was playing deep.* b : for a long distance ▪ *He threw/kicked the ball deep down the field.* 5 ✧ If you **breathe deep**, you take a large amount of air into your lungs. — **deep down** *(inside)* ✧ If you feel or believe something *deep down* or *deep down inside*, you feel or believe it completely even if you do not say it or show it to other people. ▪ *Deep down, I think we all felt the same way.* — **in** *(too)* **deep** *informal* : in a difficult situation that you cannot get out of ▪ *I want to get out of the deal, but I'm in too deep.* — **run deep** : to be felt very strongly ▪ *Fear runs deep in this small town.*

³**deep** *n* — **the deep** 1 *literary + formal* : the ocean ▪ *creatures of the deep* 2 *literary* : the middle part of something ▪ *awake in the deep of the night* — **the deeps** *literary + formal* : the deep parts of the ocean ▪ *the ocean deeps*

deep–dish /ˈdiːpˌdɪʃ/ *adj, always before a noun, US* : baked in a dish that has high sides ▪ *a deep-dish pie*

deep·en /ˈdiːpən/ *vb* [*T/I*] : to become or to cause (something) to become deep or deeper ▪ *Age had deepened the lines in his face.* ▪ *The water deepens toward the center of the river.* 2 [*T/I*] : to become or to cause (something, such as a feeling or emotion) to become stronger or more powerful ▪ *Their friendship deepened with time.* 3 [*T*] : to make (your knowledge, understanding, etc.) fuller or more complete ▪ *This class will deepen your understanding of economics.* 4 [*T/I*] : to become or to cause (something) to become worse or more severe ▪ *policies that have deepened the economic recession* 5 [*T/I*] : to become or to cause (something, such as a person's voice) to become lower in sound ▪ *His voice has deepened.* 6 [*I*] : to become darker or stronger in color ▪ *The sky deepened to a dark blue.* 7 ✧ To **deepen your breathing** is to take more air into your lungs when you breathe. — **deep·en·ing** /ˈdiːpənɪŋ/ *adj* ▪ *a deepening* [=*worsening*] *financial crisis* ▪ *deepening shadows* [=shadows that are becoming darker]

deep freeze *n* 1 [*C/U*] : a state of extreme cold ▪ *a (period of) deep freeze that*

lasted thousands of years 2 [*C*] *Brit* : FREEZER

deep–fry /ˈdiːpˈfraɪ/ *vb* **-fries; -fried; -fry·ing** [*T*] : to cook (food) in a deep layer of oil or fat ▪ *deep-fried chicken/potatoes*

deep·ly /ˈdiːpli/ *adv* 1 : in a way that is very complete, extreme, strongly felt, etc. ▪ *deeply in love* ▪ *I'm deeply* [=*very, extremely*] *sorry.* ▪ *a deeply religious family* 2 : far into or below the surface of something ▪ *designs carved deeply into the wood* ▪ (*figurative*) *digging/delving deeply into the history of the town* 3 ✧ If you **breathe deeply** or **sigh deeply**, you take a large amount of air into your lungs when you breathe or sigh. 4 ✧ If you are **sleeping deeply**, you are thoroughly asleep and it is hard to wake you up.

deep–root·ed /ˈdiːpˈruːtəd/ *adj* : existing for a long time and very difficult to change ▪ *deep-rooted beliefs*

deep–seat·ed /ˈdiːpˈsiːtəd/ *adj* : existing for a long time and very difficult to change ▪ *deep-seated problems*

deep–six /ˈdiːpˈsɪks/ *vb* [*T*] *US, informal* : to no longer use or consider (something) ▪ *The government deep-sixed* [=*eliminated*] *the program.*

Deep South *n* — **the Deep South** : the states in the most southern and eastern part of the U.S. and especially Georgia, Alabama, South Carolina, Louisiana, and Mississippi

deer /ˈdiɚ/ *n, pl* **deer** [*C*] : a large wild animal that has four long thin legs, brown fur, and antlers if male

de·face /dɪˈfeɪs/ *vb* **-faced; -fac·ing** [*T*] : to ruin the surface of (something) especially with writing or pictures ▪ *defacing public property with graffiti* — **de·face·ment** /dɪˈfeɪsmənt/ *n* [*U*]

de fac·to /dɪˈfæktoʊ, Brit ˌdeɪˈfæktoʊ/ *adj, always before a noun, formal* — used to describe something that exists but that is not officially accepted or recognized ▪ *the de facto leader of the group* [=the unofficial leader]

de·fame /dɪˈfeɪm/ *vb* **-famed; -fam·ing** [*T*] *formal* : to hurt the reputation of (someone or something) especially by saying things that are false or unfair ▪ *He says he was defamed by reports that falsely identified him as a former gangster.* — **def·a·ma·tion** /ˌdɛfəˈmeɪʃən/ *n* [*C/U*] ▪ *suing a newspaper for defamation (of character)* — **de·fam·a·to·ry** /dɪˈfæməˌtori, Brit dɪˈfæmətri/ *adj* ▪ *defamatory statements*

¹**de·fault** /dɪˈfɑːlt/ *n* 1 [*U*] — used to describe something that happens or is done when nothing else has been done or can be done ▪ *No one else wanted the job, so he became the club's president by default.* ▪ *a decision made by default* ▪ *the default winner* 2 [*C/U*] : a failure to make a payment (such as a payment on a loan) ▪ *She's in default on her loan.* [=she missed a payment on her loan] 3 [*C*] *computers* : a setting, option, etc., that a computer uses if you do not choose a different one ▪ *the computer's default settings*

²**default** *vb* [*I*] 1 : to fail to make the payments you must make on a loan, mort-

gage, etc. • *He defaulted on his loan (payments).* **2** *of a computer* : to automatically use a particular setting, option, etc., unless you choose a different one • *The program defaults to a standard font.* — **de·fault·er** *n* [C]

¹**de·feat** /dɪˈfiːt/ *vb* [T] **1** : to win a victory over (someone or something) in a war, game, etc. • *defeating an enemy in battle* • *Our candidate was defeated in the election.* **2 a** : to cause (someone or something) to fail • *The bill was defeated in the state Senate.* • *Working during your vacation defeats the purpose.* [=a vacation during which you work is not a real vacation] **b** : to control or overcome (something) • *efforts to defeat the disease* — see also DEFEATED

²**defeat** *n* **1** [C/U] : failure to succeed or to win • *his first defeat as a professional boxer* • *accept/admit/concede defeat* • *The bill suffered defeat.* = *The bill went down to defeat.* [=the bill was defeated] • *a hero even in defeat* [=even when not winning] **2** [C] : the act of winning a victory over someone or something • *the defeat of our enemy*

de·feat·ed /dɪˈfiːtəd/ *adj* **1** — used to describe someone or something that has lost a contest, game, etc. • *our defeated opponents* **2** : feeling unable to succeed or to achieve something • *She felt very/utterly defeated when she didn't get the job.*

de·feat·ism /dɪˈfiːˌtɪzəm/ *n* [U] *formal* : a way of thinking in which a person expects to lose or fail — **de·feat·ist** /dɪˈfiːtɪst/ *n* [C] — **defeatist** *adj* • *defeatist attitudes*

def·e·cate /ˈdɛfɪˌkeɪt/ *vb* -**cat·ed**; -**cat·ing** [I] *formal* : to pass solid waste from the body — **def·e·ca·tion** /ˌdɛfɪˈkeɪʃən/ *n* [C/U]

¹**de·fect** /ˈdiːˌfɛkt/ *n* [C] **1** : a physical problem that causes something to be less valuable, effective, healthy, etc. • *They examine their products for defects.* • *a heart defect* • *a birth defect* [=a physical problem that someone is born with] **2** : something that causes weakness or failure • *a defect* [=flaw] *in her logic* • *character defects*

²**de·fect** /dɪˈfɛkt/ *vb* [I] *formal* : to leave a country, political party, etc., and go to a different one that is a competitor or an enemy • *a Russian scholar who defected (to the West) in 1979* — **de·fec·tion** /dɪˈfɛkʃən/ *n* [C/U] — **de·fec·tor** /dɪˈfɛktɚ/ *n* [C]

de·fec·tive /dɪˈfɛktɪv/ *adj* : having a defect or flaw • *defective products/merchandise*

de·fend /dɪˈfɛnd/ *vb* **1** [T/I] : to not allow a person or thing to hurt, damage, or destroy (someone or something) • *defend a country against/from attackers* • *weapons used to defend against attack* **2** [T] : to fight or work hard in order to keep (a right, an interest, a cause, etc.) from being taken away • *defending the rights of the poor* **3** [T] : to speak or write in support of (someone or something that is being challenged or criticized) • *a cause worth defending* • *defending a friend's behavior* **4** [T/I] *sports* : to try to stop op-

ponents from scoring • *Defend the goal.* • *defending against a jump shot* **5** [T] : to compete in order to try to keep (a title, championship, etc.) • *hoping to defend a title/championship* [=to win a title/championship again] **6** [T] : to work as a lawyer for (someone who is being sued or accused of a crime) • *She defended herself during her trial.* — **de·fend·er** *n* [C] • *a staunch/tireless defender of human rights* — **de·fend·ing** /dɪˈfɛndɪŋ/ *adj* : *the defending world/national champions*

de·fend·ant /dɪˈfɛndənt/ *n* [C] : a person who is being sued or accused of a crime in a court of law — compare PLAINTIFF

de·fense (*US*) *or Brit* **de·fence** /dɪˈfɛns/ *n* **1** [C/U] : the act of defending someone or something from attack • *mounting a good defense* • *They fought in defense of their country.* [=to defend their country] • *the body's first line of defense* [=way of defending itself] *against illness* **2** [C] : something that is used to protect yourself, your country, etc. • *the nation's air defenses* • *the body's natural defenses against disease and infection* **3** [C/U] : the act of speaking or writing in support of someone or something that is being attacked or criticized • *a passionate defense of the mayor* • *His friends came/jumped to his defense.* [=his friends said that he was right or good] • *In her defense, I would have done the same thing that she did.* **4** [U] : the things that are done by a country to protect itself from enemies • *spending on defense* = *defense spending* • *the Secretary of Defense* = *the Defense Secretary* **5 a** [*singular*] : the lawyer or lawyers who represent the defendant in a court case • *defense attorneys/lawyers* • *The defense rests, Your Honor.* **b** [C] : the method that is used in a court case to prove that someone is innocent • *an insanity defense* [=an effort to prove that someone was not sane when committing a crime] **6** /ˈdiːˌfɛns/ **a** [C/U] : the group of players on a team who try to stop an opponent from scoring • *a talented defense* • *She's on defense.* [=she plays on the part of the team that defends the goal] **b** [U] : the way that players on a team try to stop an opponent from scoring • *They play good/strong/tough defense.*

de·fense·less (*US*) *or Brit* **de·fence·less** /dɪˈfɛnsləs/ *adj* : not able to defend yourself, your country, etc. • *The people of the town were completely defenseless.*

defense mechanism (*US*) *or Brit* **defence mechanism** *n* [C] *technical* **1** : a process in the brain that makes you forget or ignore painful or disturbing thoughts, situations, etc. **2** : a reaction in your body that protects against disease or danger • *defense mechanisms against infection*

de·fen·si·ble /dɪˈfɛnsəbəl/ *adj, formal* **1** : able to be thought of as good or acceptable • *a morally defensible position* **2** : able to be defended or protected • *a defensible bridge/location*

¹**de·fen·sive** /dɪˈfɛnsɪv/ *adj* **1** *always before a noun* : helping to keep a person or thing safe • *a defensive wall/alliance* • *de-*

fensive driving classes [=classes that teach you how to be a safe driver] **2** : behaving in a way that shows that you feel people are criticizing you ▪ *defensive behaviors/attitudes* ▪ *When we asked her about the mistakes, she became defensive.* **3** *always before a noun, sports* : of or relating to the way that players try to stop an opponent from scoring in a game or contest ▪ *a strong defensive strategy/player* — **de·fen·sive·ly** *adv* — **de·fen·sive·ness** *n* [U]

²**defensive** *n* — **on/onto the defensive**
1 : in or into a situation in which you are forced to defend or protect someone or something ▪ *We kept them on the defensive for most of the game.* **2** : in or into a position in which you have to argue that something (such as one of your actions or beliefs) is good or correct when others say that it is bad or wrong ▪ *The reporter's questions put her on the defensive.*

de·fer /dɪˈfɚ/ *vb* **-ferred; -fer·ring** [T] : to choose to do (something) at a later time ▪ *deferring a decision* — **defer to** [*phrasal vb*] **1** : to allow (someone else) to decide or choose something ▪ *deferring to the experts* **2** : to agree to follow (someone else's decision, a tradition, etc.) ▪ *He deferred to his parents' wishes.* — **de·fer·ral** /dɪˈfɚəl/ *n* [C/U] ▪ *a tax deferral*

def·er·ence /ˈdɛfərəns/ *n* [U] *formal* : a way of behaving that shows respect for someone or something ▪ *showing proper deference to our elders* — **in deference to** or **out of deference to** : in order to show respect for the opinions or influence of (someone or something) ▪ *The victim's name is being withheld out of deference to his family.* — **def·er·en·tial** /ˌdɛfəˈrɛnʃəl/ *adj* ▪ *listening with deferential attention* — **def·er·en·tial·ly** *adv*

de·fer·ment /dɪˈfɚmənt/ *n* [C/U] **1** : official permission to pay for something at a later time ▪ *requesting (a) deferment of a loan* **2** : official permission to not do required military service at a later time ▪ *a college/student deferment* [=permission to finish school before entering the military]

de·fi·ance /dɪˈfajəns/ *n* [U] : a refusal to obey something or someone ▪ *acts of defiance* ▪ *defiance of the law* — **in defiance of** : against or despite the wishes, rules, or laws of (someone or something) ▪ *acting in defiance of an order*

de·fi·ant /dɪˈfajənt/ *adj* : refusing to obey something or someone ▪ *defiant rebels* ▪ *a defiant act/stand* — **de·fi·ant·ly** *adv*

de·fi·cien·cy /dɪˈfɪʃənsi/ *n, pl* **-cies** [C/U] : a lack of something that is needed ▪ *The book's major deficiency is its plot.* ▪ *vitamin deficiency* **2** [C] : a problem in the way something is made or formed ▪ *There are several deficiencies in the plan.*

de·fi·cient /dɪˈfɪʃənt/ *adj* **1** : not having enough of something that is important or necessary ▪ *a nutritionally deficient diet* = *a diet deficient in nutrients* **2** : not good enough ▪ *mentally/structurally deficient*

def·i·cit /ˈdɛfəsət/ *n* [C] **1** : an amount (such as an amount of money) that is less

than the amount that is needed ▪ *the federal budget deficit* **2** : the amount by which a person or team is behind in a game or contest ▪ *a four-point deficit* **3** *chiefly US* : a problem that causes a decrease in some ability ▪ *a slight hearing deficit* — see also ATTENTION DEFICIT DISORDER

de·file /dɪˈfajəl/ *vb* **-filed; -fil·ing** [T] *formal* **1** : to make (something) dirty ▪ *a lake defiled by pollution* **2** : to take away or ruin the purity, honor, or goodness of (something or someone important) ▪ *Vandals defiled the church.* — **de·file·ment** /dɪˈfajəlmənt/ *n* [U]

de·fine /dɪˈfajn/ *vb* **-fined; -fin·ing** [T] **1** : to explain the meaning of (a word, phrase, etc.) ▪ *Define (the word) "grotesque."* **2** : to show or describe (someone or something) clearly and completely ▪ *The study seeks to define urban poverty.* ▪ *He was defined by his passions.* [=his passions showed what kind of person he was] ▪ *Tigers are broadly/loosely defined* [=described very generally] *as large cats.* **3** : to show the shape, outline, or edge of (something) very clearly ▪ *That fence defines the far edge of the property.* — **de·fin·able** /dɪˈfajnəbəl/ *adj* — **defined** *adj* ▪ *Her cheekbones are well-defined.* — **defining** *adj, always before a noun* ▪ *the campaign's defining moment* [=the moment that showed very clearly what kind of campaign it was]

def·i·nite /ˈdɛfənɪt/ *adj* **1** : said or done in a such way that others know exactly what you mean ▪ *I need a definite answer by noon.* **2** : already set or decided ▪ *Are her plans definite?* ▪ *I don't know anything definite yet.* **3** *not before a noun* : confident or certain about doing something or that something will happen ▪ *She seems pretty definite about leaving.*

definite article *n* [C] *grammar* : the word *the* used in English to refer to a person or thing that is identified or specified; *also* : a word that is used in a similar way in another language

def·i·nite·ly /ˈdɛfənɪtli/ *adv* : in a way that is certain or clear ▪ *The new model is definitely an improvement.* ▪ "*Will you come over on Saturday?*" "*Definitely!*" [=yes]

def·i·ni·tion /ˌdɛfəˈnɪʃən/ *n* **1** [C] **a** : an explanation of the meaning of a word, phrase, etc. ▪ *dictionary definitions* **b** : a statement that describes what something is ▪ *a definition of happiness* **2** [*singular*] : a clear or perfect example of a person or thing ▪ *A week of fishing is my definition of a vacation.* **3** [U] : the quality that makes it possible to see the shape, outline, and details of something clearly ▪ *muscle definition* ▪ *The picture lacks definition.* [=it is not sharp/clear] — **by definition** : according to the definition of a word that is being used to describe someone or something ▪ *A volunteer by definition is not paid.*

de·fin·i·tive /dɪˈfɪnətɪv/ *adj* **1** : not able to be argued about or changed ▪ *a definitive answer* **2** : complete, accurate, and considered to be the best of its kind ▪ *a* *definitive biography* — **de·fin·i·tive·ly** *adv*

de·flate /dɪˈfleɪt/ *vb* **-flat·ed; -flat·ing** **1 a** [*T*] : to release air or gas from (a tire, balloon, etc.) and make it smaller • *deflate the tires* **b** [*I*] : to lose air or gas from inside • *The balloons deflated after a few days.* **2** [*T*] **a** : to make (someone) lose confidence or pride • *The harsh criticism left him deflated.* **b** : to show that (something) is not important or true • *deflate an argument* **3** [*T*] : to cause (prices, costs, etc.) to decrease • *Deflated prices mean that farmers are getting less for their crops.*

de·fla·tion /dɪˈfleɪʃən/ *n* [*U*] **1** : a decrease in the amount of available money or credit in an economy that causes prices to go down **2** : the act or process of letting air or gas out of (something) • *deflation of a balloon* — **de·fla·tion·ary** /dɪˈfleɪʃəˌneri, *Brit* dɪˈfleɪʃənri/ *adj* • *a deflationary economic period*

de·flect /dɪˈflɛkt/ *vb* **1 a** [*T*] : to cause (something that is moving) to change direction • *armor that can deflect bullets* **b** [*I*] : to hit something and suddenly change direction • *The ball deflected off her shoulder.* **2** [*T*] : to keep (something, such as a question) from affecting or being directed at a person or thing • *trying to deflect attention from the troubled economy* — **de·flec·tion** /dɪˈflɛkʃən/ *n* [*C/U*] — **de·flec·tor** /dɪˈflɛktɚ/ *n* [*C*]

de·fog /diˈfɑːg/ *vb* **-fogged; -fog·ging** [*T*] *US* : to remove mist from (a window, mirror, etc.) by using dry heat • *defog the windshield* — **de·fog·ger** *n* [*C*]

de·for·es·ta·tion /diˌfoɚˈsteɪʃən/ *n* [*U*] : the act or result of cutting down or burning all the trees in an area — **de·for·est** /diˈfoɚəst/ *vb* [*T*] • *regions that have been deforested*

de·form /dɪˈfoɚm/ *vb* [*T/I*] : to change something so that it no longer has its normal or original shape • *The disease deforms the bones.* = *The disease causes the bones to deform.* — **de·formed** /dɪˈfoɚmd/ *adj* • *a deformed hand* — **de·for·ma·tion** /ˌdiːˌfoɚˈmeɪʃən/ *n* [*C/U*]

de·for·mi·ty /dɪˈfoɚməti/ *n, pl* **-ties** [*C/U*] : a condition in which part of the body does not have the normal or expected shape • *facial deformities* • *deformity of the spine*

de·fraud /dɪˈfrɑːd/ *vb* [*T/I*] : to trick or cheat someone or something in order to get money • *defrauding the public*

de·fray /dɪˈfreɪ/ *vb* [*T*] *somewhat formal* : to pay for (something) • *This will defray the costs/expenses.*

de·frock /dɪˈfrɑːk/ *vb* [*T*] : to officially remove (a priest) from his or her job as punishment for doing something wrong • *a defrocked priest*

de·frost /dɪˈfrɑːst/ *vb* **1** [*T/I*] : to warm something that is frozen until it is no longer frozen • *Defrost the soup in the microwave.* • *The meat is defrosting.* **2** [*T*] : to melt ice that has built up on the inside of a freezer or refrigerator • *defrost the freezer* **3** [*T*] : to melt ice on a car's

windows by using heat • *defrost the windshield*

de·frost·er /dɪˈfrɑːstɚ/ *n* [*C*] *US* : a device that uses heat or hot air to melt ice on or remove moisture from a surface

deft /ˈdɛft/ *adj* : skillful and clever • *a deft politician* — **deft·ly** *adv* — **deft·ness** /ˈdɛftnəs/ *n* [*U*]

de·funct /dɪˈfʌŋkt/ *adj, formal* : no longer existing or being used • *a defunct factory*

de·fuse /diˈfjuːz/ *vb* **-fused; -fus·ing** [*T*] **1** : to make (something) less serious, difficult, or tense • *Her joke diffused the tension.* **2** : to remove the part of (an explosive) that makes it explode • *defuse a bomb*

de·fy /dɪˈfaɪ/ *vb* **-fies; -fied; -fy·ing** [*T*] **1** : to refuse to obey (something or someone) • *She defied her parents and dropped out of school.* **2** : to make (something) very difficult or impossible • *The view defies description.* [=cannot be easily described] **3** : to go against (something) • *The team's win defied the odds.* [=was very unlikely] • *an explanation that defies all logic* [=that does not make sense] **4** : to tell (someone) to do something that you think cannot be done • *I defy you to prove it.*

deg. *abbr* degree

1de·gen·er·ate /dɪˈdʒɛnəˌreɪt/ *vb* **-at·ed; -at·ing** [*I*] : to become worse, weaker, less useful, etc. • *The patient's health degenerated rapidly.* • *The meeting degenerated into a shouting match.* — **de·gen·er·a·tion** /dɪˌdʒɛnəˈreɪʃən/ *n* [*U*]

2de·gen·er·ate /dɪˈdʒɛnərət/ *adj* : not honest, proper, or good • *a degenerate society* — **de·gen·er·a·cy** /dɪˈdʒɛnərəsi/ *n* [*U*]

3de·gen·er·ate /dɪˈdʒɛnərət/ *n* [*C*] : a person whose behavior is not morally right or socially acceptable • *a bunch of criminals and degenerates*

de·gen·er·a·tive /dɪˈdʒɛnərətɪv/ *adj* : causing the body or part of the body to become weaker or less able to function as time passes • *a degenerative disease*

de·grade /dɪˈgreɪd/ *vb* **-grad·ed; -grad·ing** **1** [*T*] : to treat (someone or something) poorly and without respect • *The ads degrade women.* • *I won't degrade myself by responding.* **2** [*T*] : to make the quality of (something) worse • *Scratches on a camera lens will degrade the image.* **3** [*T/I*] *technical* : to cause (something complex) to break down into simple substances or parts • *enzymes that degrade proteins* • *plastics that don't degrade easily* — **deg·ra·da·tion** /ˌdɛgrəˈdeɪʃən/ *n* [*C/U*] • *degradation of the environment* • *the degradations of poverty* — **degrad·ing** *adj* • *a degrading job/ad*

de·gree /dɪˈgriː/ *n* **1** [*C*] : a unit for measuring temperature • *20 degrees Fahrenheit/Celsius* [=20° F/C] — *abbr.* **deg.** **2** [*C*] : a unit for measuring the size of an angle • *a 15 degree angle* [=a 15° angle] — *abbr.* **deg.** **3** [*C/U*] : an amount or level that can be measured or compared to another amount or level • *We've had varying degrees of success.* • *a high degree of difficulty/skill* • *To what de-*

gree [=how much] *is she interested?* **4** [*U*] : a measure of how severe or serious something is • *murder in the first degree* = *first-degree murder* [=the most serious kind of murder] • *a second-degree burn* **5** [*C*] : an official document and title that is given to someone who has successfully completed a series of classes at a college or university • *She has a degree in engineering.* • *a bachelor's/master's degree* — **by degrees** : by a series of small changes • *changing by degrees from green to red* — **to some degree** *also* **to a (certain) degree** : not completely but partly • *To some degree, they're right.*

de·hu·man·ize *also Brit* **de·hu·man·ise** /diˈhjuːməˌnaɪz/ *vb* **-ized; -iz·ing** [*T*] : to treat (someone) as though he or she is not a person • *factory conditions that dehumanize workers* • *propaganda meant to dehumanize the enemy* [=to make the enemy seem less human]

de·hu·mid·i·fi·er /ˌdiːhjuˈmɪdəˌfajə/ *n* [*C*] : a machine that takes moisture out of the air

de·hy·drate /diˈhaɪˌdreɪt/ *vb* **-drat·ed; -drat·ing** *somewhat technical* **1** [*T*] : to remove water or moisture from (something, such as food) • *Salt dehydrates the meat and keeps it from spoiling.* — *dehydrated fruit* **2** [*T/I*] : to lose too much water • *Drink lots of water so you don't dehydrate.* — *dehydrated athletes* — **de·hy·dra·tion** /ˌdiːˌhaɪˈdreɪʃən/ *n* [*U*]

de·ice /diˈaɪs/ *vb* **-iced; -ic·ing** [*T*] : to remove ice from (something) • *deicing the plane before takeoff*

de·i·fy /ˈdijəˌfaɪ/ *vb* **-fies; -fied; -fy·ing** [*T*] : to treat (someone or something) like a god or goddess • *Our society deifies* [=worships] *money.* — **de·i·fi·ca·tion** /ˌdijəfəˈkeɪʃən, ˌdejəfəˈkeɪʃən/ *n* [*U*]

deign /ˈdeɪn/ *vb* [*I*] *formal + disapproving* : to do something that you think you should not have to do because you are too important • *She finally deigned to speak to me.*

de·i·ty /ˈdiːjəti, ˈdejəti/ *n, pl* **-ties** [*C*] : a god or goddess • *ancient Greek deities*

dé·jà vu /ˌdeɪˌʒɑːˈvuː/ *n* [*U*] : the feeling that you have already experienced something that is actually happening for the first time • *I entered the room and immediately felt a sense of déjà vu.*

de·ject·ed /dɪˈdʒɛktəd/ *adj* : sad because of failure, loss, etc. • *The dejected players left the field.* — **de·ject·ed·ly** *adv* — **de·jec·tion** /dɪˈdʒɛkʃən/ *n* [*U*]

Del. *abbr,* US Delaware

¹**de·lay** /dɪˈleɪ/ *n* **1** [*C/U*] : a situation in which something happens later than it should • *What's causing the delay?* • *flight delays* • *It must be repaired without delay.* [=immediately] **2** [*C*] : the amount of time that you must wait for something that is late • *We had/experienced a three-hour delay.*

²**delay** *vb* **1** [*T/I*] : to wait until later to do something : to make something happen later • *She's planning to delay her retirement.* • *"The sale ends soon, so don't delay!"* **2** [*T*] : to make (something or someone) late • *My flight was delayed.* — **de·layed** /dɪˈleɪd/ *adj* • *a delayed reac-*

tion [=a reaction that does not happen immediately]

de·lec·ta·ble /dɪˈlɛktəbəl/ *adj, somewhat formal* : very pleasant to taste or smell : DELICIOUS • *delectable food/meals* — **de·lec·ta·bly** /dɪˈlɛktəbli/ *adv*

¹**del·e·gate** /ˈdɛlɪgət/ *n* [*C*] : a person who is chosen or elected to vote or act for others : REPRESENTATIVE • *U.N. delegates*

²**del·e·gate** /ˈdɛlɪˌgeɪt/ *vb* **-gat·ed; -gat·ing** **1** [*T/I*] : to give (control, responsibility, authority, etc.) to someone • *A manager should delegate authority to the best employees.* • *He doesn't delegate very well.* **2** [*T*] : to choose (someone) to do something • *I've been delegated by the town to care for the monument.*

del·e·ga·tion /ˌdɛlɪˈgeɪʃən/ *n* **1** [*C*] : a group of people who are chosen to vote or act for someone else • *the state's congressional delegation* [=the group of officials elected to the U.S. Congress from a particular state] **2** [*U*] *formal* : the act of giving control, authority, a job, a duty, etc., to another person • *the delegation of authority*

de·lete /dɪˈliːt/ *vb* **-let·ed; -let·ing** [*T*] : to remove (words, pictures, computer files, etc.) from a document, recording, computer, etc. • *Delete this name from the list.* • *She deleted* [=erased] *the file/e-mail.* — **de·le·tion** /dɪˈliːʃən/ *n* [*C/U*]

del·e·te·ri·ous /ˌdɛləˈtirijəs/ *adj, formal* : damaging or harmful • *the deleterious effects of a drug*

deli /ˈdɛli/ *n* [*C*] : a store where you can buy foods (such as meats and sandwiches) that are already cooked or prepared — called also *delicatessen*

¹**de·lib·er·ate** /dɪˈlɪbərət/ *adj* **1** : done or said in a way that is planned or intended • *a deliberate attempt to trick people* **2** : done or decided after careful thought • *a deliberate choice/decision* **3** : slow and careful • *speaking in a clear, deliberate way* — **de·lib·er·ate·ly** /dɪˈlɪbərətli/ *adv* • *He deliberately tricked me.* • *She spoke clearly and deliberately.*

²**de·lib·er·ate** /dɪˈlɪbəˌreɪt/ *vb* **-at·ed; -at·ing** [*T/I*] : to think about or discuss something very carefully in order to make a decision • *The jury deliberated for two days before reaching a verdict.* • *He's deliberating whether or not to accept a job offer.*

de·lib·er·a·tion /dɪˌlɪbəˈreɪʃən/ *n* **1** [*C/U*] : careful thought or discussion done in order to make a decision • *Jury deliberations lasted two days.* • *hours of deliberation* **2** [*U*] : the quality of being slow and careful • *She spoke with clarity and deliberation.*

de·lib·er·a·tive /dɪˈlɪbəˌreɪtɪv, dɪˈlɪbərətɪv/ *adj, formal* : created or done in order to discuss and consider facts and reasons carefully • *Congress is a deliberative body.*

del·i·ca·cy /ˈdɛlɪkəsi/ *n, pl* **-cies** **1** [*C*] : a food that people like to eat because it is special or rare • *regional delicacies* **2** [*U*] **a** : the quality of being easily broken or damaged • *the delicacy of the glass* **b** : the quality of being easily injured, hurt, or made sick • *the delicacy of his* *health* **c** : the attractive quality of something that is formed from many small or fine parts ▪ *lace of great delicacy* **d** : the appealing quality of something that is not too strong ▪ *the delicacy of the wine* **3** [U] **a** : special care or skill that is needed to prevent people from becoming upset or angry ▪ *a difficult situation that requires delicacy* **b** : the quality of requiring special care or skill ▪ *the delicacy of the situation*

del·i·cate /ˈdɛlɪkət/ *adj* **1 a** : easily broken or damaged ▪ *The cup is very delicate.* **b** : easily injured, hurt, or made sick ▪ *her delicate health* **2 a** : attractive and made up of small or fine parts ▪ *delicate (facial) features* ▪ *delicate hands* [=small and attractive hands] **b** : very carefully and beautifully made ▪ *delicate lace curtains* **3** : attractive because of being soft, gentle, light, etc. ▪ *a delicate perfume/flavor* **4** : easily disturbed or upset ▪ *maintaining the delicate balance between work and family* **5** : requiring special care or skill ▪ *a delicate situation that needs to be handled carefully* — **del·i·cate·ly** *adv*

del·i·ca·tes·sen /ˌdɛlɪkəˈtɛsn̩/ *n* [C] : DELI

de·li·cious /dɪˈlɪʃəs/ *adj* **1 a** : very pleasant to taste ▪ *Dinner was delicious.* ▪ *a delicious cake* **b** : having a smell that suggests a very pleasant taste ▪ *delicious aromas* **2** *literary* : very pleasing or enjoyable ▪ *a delicious bit of gossip* — **de·li·cious·ly** *adv* ▪ *deliciously sweet* — **de·li·cious·ness** *n* [U]

¹de·light /dɪˈlaɪt/ *n* **1** [U] : a strong feeling of happiness ▪ *an expression of pure delight* [=joy] ▪ *kids squealing in delight* ▪ *To our delight, they loved the gift.* [=we were very happy that they loved the gift] ▪ *She takes delight in* [=very much enjoys] *her new job.* **2** [C] : something that makes you very happy ▪ *The trip was a delight.* ▪ *tasty delights*

²delight *vb* [T] : to make (someone) very happy ▪ *The toy delighted the children.* — **delight in** [*phrasal vb*] : to enjoy (something) very much ▪ *He delights in meeting new people.*

de·light·ed /dɪˈlaɪtəd/ *adj* : very happy ▪ *I'm delighted to meet you.* ▪ *the delighted expression on his face* — **de·light·ed·ly** *adv*

de·light·ful /dɪˈlaɪtfəl/ *adj* : very pleasant ▪ *It's delightful to meet you.* ▪ *a delightful party/person* — **de·light·ful·ly** *adv*

de·lin·eate /dɪˈlɪniˌeɪt/ *vb* **-eat·ed; -eat·ing** [T] *formal* : to clearly show or describe (something) ▪ *The report clearly delineates the process.* — **de·lin·ea·tion** /dɪˌlɪniˈeɪʃən/ *n* [U]

de·lin·quen·cy /dɪˈlɪŋkwənsi/ *n, pl* **-cies** [C/U] **1** : illegal or immoral behavior especially by young people ▪ *the prevention of crime and delinquency* ▪ *the problem of juvenile delinquency* **2** *US* : the condition of someone who owes money and is not making payments at the required or expected time ▪ *loan delinquencies*

¹de·lin·quent /dɪˈlɪŋkwənt/ *n* [C] : JUVENILE DELINQUENT

²delinquent *adj* **1** : doing things that are illegal or immoral ▪ *delinquent children/behavior* **2** *US* **a** : not paid at the required or expected time ▪ *delinquent taxes* **b** : failing to pay an amount of money that is owed ▪ *delinquent borrowers*

de·lir·i·ous /dɪˈlɪrijəs/ *adj* **1** : not able to think or speak clearly especially because of fever or other illness ▪ *The patient was delirious (with fever) and didn't know where he was.* **2** : very excited ▪ *delirious with happiness* — **de·lir·i·ous·ly** *adv* ▪ *deliriously happy*

de·lir·i·um /dɪˈlɪrijəm/ *n* **1** [C/U] : a mental state in which you cannot think or speak clearly usually because of fever or some other illness ▪ *a period of delirium* **2** [U] : a state of wild excitement and great happiness ▪ *fans in (a state of) delirium*

de·liv·er /dɪˈlɪvɚ/ *vb* **1** [T/I] : to take (something) to a person or place ▪ *The package/chair was delivered today.* ▪ *"Does the restaurant deliver?" "No, you have to pick up the food yourself."* **2** [T] : to say (something) officially or publicly ▪ *deliver a speech* ▪ *actors delivering their lines* ▪ *The jury delivered a verdict today.* **3 a** [I] : to do what you say you will do or what people expect you to do ▪ *failing to deliver on a promise* [=failing to do what you promise to do] **b** [T] : to provide or produce (something) ▪ *The company charges too much for what it delivers.* **4** [T] **a** : to give birth to (a baby) ▪ *She delivered twins this morning.* **b** : to help someone give birth to (a baby) ▪ *a doctor delivering a baby* **5** [T] : to give control of (someone or something) to another person or group ▪ *By letting children watch too much television, we are delivering them into the hands of advertisers.* ▪ *soldiers delivered up to* [=handed over to] *the enemy* **6** [T] : to cause (a punch, a thrown ball, etc.) to hit or go to a person or place ▪ *a boxer delivering a crushing blow to an opponent's head* ▪ *a country that can deliver* [=attack other countries with] *nuclear warheads* **7** [T] *chiefly US* : to get (votes) for a particular person or issue in an election ▪ *delivering the college student vote* [=convincing college students to vote a particular way] **8** [T] *formal + literary* : to free (someone) *from* something ▪ *those who long to be delivered from slavery/tyranny* — **de·liv·er·er** /dɪˈlɪvɚɚ/ *n* [C]

de·liv·er·ance /dɪˈlɪvərəns/ *n* [U] *formal* : the state of being saved from something dangerous or unpleasant ▪ *praying for deliverance from tyranny*

de·liv·ery /dɪˈlɪvəri/ *n, pl* **-er·ies** **1 a** [C/U] : the act of taking something to a person or place ▪ *The delivery is scheduled for today.* ▪ *a delivery truck/service* [=a truck/service that delivers something] ▪ *The company offers free delivery.* = *The company make deliveries for free.* ▪ *Payment is due on delivery of the goods.* [=when you receive the goods] — see also SPECIAL DELIVERY **b** [C] : something that is taken to a person or place ▪ *The store got a delivery of shirts yesterday.*

2 [C/U] : the act or process of giving birth • *a routine delivery* • *the* **delivery room** [=a special room in a hospital where women give birth to babies] **3** [*singular*] : the way someone says something officially or publicly • *I need to work on my delivery before I give the speech.* **4** [C] *sports* : the way a ball is thrown in baseball or cricket • *pitchers with similar deliveries* — **take delivery of** *formal* : to receive (something that is being delivered to you) • *taking delivery of a new car*

de·liv·ery·man /dɪˈlɪvəriˌmæn/ *n, pl* **-men** /-mən/ [C] : a man who delivers goods to customers

del·ta /ˈdɛltə/ *n* **1** [C] : the fourth letter of the Greek alphabet — Δ or δ **2** [C] : a piece of land shaped like a triangle that is formed when a river splits into smaller rivers before it flows into an ocean • *a river delta* **3** *or* **Delta** [*singular*] *US* : an area of low land along the Mississippi River that is mainly in the state of Mississippi • *the Mississippi Delta*

de·lude /dɪˈluːd/ *vb* **-lud·ed; -lud·ing** [T] : to cause (someone) to believe something that is not true • *They deluded themselves into believing they would win.* — **deluded** *adj* • *a deluded way of thinking*

¹**del·uge** /ˈdɛljuːdʒ/ *n* [C] **1** : a large amount of rain that suddenly falls in an area **2** : a large amount of things that come at the same time • *a deluge of mail*

²**deluge** *vb* **-uged; -ug·ing** [T] **1** : to give or send (someone) a large amount of things at the same time • *We were deluged with phone calls.* **2** : to flood (a place) with water • *Heavy rains deluged the region.*

de·lu·sion /dɪˈluːʒən/ *n* [C] **1** : a false idea • *delusions about how much it will cost* • *He is living/laboring* **under the delusion** *that he is incapable of making mistakes.* **2** : a false idea or belief that is caused by mental illness • *suffering from delusions* ✧ If you have **delusions of grandeur**, you believe that you are much more important than you really are. —
de·lu·sion·al /dɪˈluːʒənl/ *adj* • *delusional thinking* • *If you think we can afford a new car, you're delusional.*

de·luxe /dɪˈlʌks/ *adj* : of better quality and usually more expensive than the usual ones of its kind • *a deluxe* [=*fancy*] *hotel*

delve /ˈdɛlv/ *vb* **delved; delv·ing** [I] **1** : to search for information about something • *delving into the city's history* **2** *chiefly Brit* : to reach into a bag, container, etc., in order to find something • *delving into her handbag*

Dem. *abbr, US* Democrat

dem·a·gogue /ˈdɛməˌgɑːg/ *n* [C] *disapproving* : a political leader who tries to get support by making false claims and promises and using arguments based on emotion rather than reason • *a bigoted demagogue* — **dem·a·gog·ic** /ˌdɛməˈgɑːgɪk/ *adj* — **dem·a·gog·uery** /ˈdɛməˌgɑːgəri/ *also* **dem·a·gogy** /ˈdɛməˌgɑːgi/ *n* [U] • *political demagoguery*

¹**de·mand** /dɪˈmænd, *Brit* dɪˈmɑːnd/ *n* **1**

[C] : a forceful statement in which you say that something must be done or given to you • *The workers will not end the strike until their demands are met/satisfied.* • *a customer's demand for a refund* **2** [*singular*] : a strong need for something • *an increased demand for fuel* **3** [U, *singular*] : the ability and need or desire to buy goods and services • *They increased production to meet demand.* • *Demand for corn has surpassed supply.* [=people want to buy more corn than is available] — see also SUPPLY AND DEMAND **4** [*plural*] **a** : difficult things you have to do because someone requires you to do them or because they are part of a job, activity, etc. • *the demands of work/parenthood* **b** — used to describe something that requires a large amount of energy, time, etc. • *A full-time job in addition to school puts/places great demands on her time.* • *His novels make many demands on the reader.* [=his novels are difficult for people to read and understand] — **in demand** : needed or wanted by many people • *Plumbers are in demand.* — **on demand** : when needed or wanted • *a cable company that offers video on demand* — **popular demand** : a request made by or a desire shared by many people • *The circus is back by popular demand.* [=because many people wanted it to come back]

²**demand** *vb* [T] **1** : to say in a forceful way that something must be done or given to you • *The customer demanded a refund.* • *Parents have demanded that the teacher resign.* • *I demanded to see the manager.* **2** : to say or ask (something) in a very forceful way • *"Come here!" he demanded.* **3** : to require (something) • *The situation demands immediate action.* • *The job demands too much of me.* [=the job requires me to do too much]

de·mand·ing /dɪˈmændɪŋ, *Brit* dɪˈmɑːndɪŋ/ *adj* **1** : requiring much time, attention, or effort • *a demanding schedule/course* **2** : expecting much time, attention, effort, etc., from other people • *a demanding boss*

de·mean /dɪˈmiːn/ *vb* [T] : to cause (someone or something) to seem less important or less worthy of respect • *a talk show host who frequently demeans women* • *Her statement demeans their efforts.* — **de·mean·ing** /dɪˈmiːnɪŋ/ *adj* • *comments demeaning to women*

de·mean·or (*US*) *or Brit* **de·mean·our** /dɪˈmiːnɚ/ *n* [C] : a person's appearance and behavior • *She has a shy/friendly/warm demeanor.* [=*manner*]

de·ment·ed /dɪˈmɛntəd/ *adj* : not able to think clearly or to understand what is real and what is not real • *a demented person*

de·men·tia /dɪˈmɛnʃə/ *n* [C/U] *medical* : a mental illness that causes someone to be unable to think clearly or to understand what is real and what is not real

de·mer·it /dɪˈmerət/ *n* [C] **1** *US* : a mark that is made on the school record of a student who has done something wrong • *Students are given demerits if they arrive late for classes.* **2** *formal* : a feature or part of something or someone that is unpleasant • *considering the merits and demerits of the plan*

demi·god /ˈdɛmɪˌgɑːd/ n [C] **1** : an extremely impressive or important person • *the demigods of jazz* **2** : a being in mythology who is part god and part human • *the Greek demigod Triton*

de·mil·i·ta·rize *also Brit* **de·mil·i·ta·rise** /dɪˈmɪlətəˌraɪz/ vb **-rized; -riz·ing** [T] : to remove weapons and military forces from (an area) • *The area is now fully demilitarized.* • *the demilitarized zone [=DMZ] between North and South Korea* — **de·mil·i·ta·ri·za·tion** *also Brit* **de·mil·i·ta·ri·sa·tion** /dɪˌmɪlətərəˈzeɪʃən, Brit ˌdɪˌmɪlətəˌraɪˈzeɪʃən/ n [U]

de·mise /dɪˈmaɪz/ n [singular] formal **1** : DEATH • *the time of her demise* **2** : the end of something that is thought of as being like a death • *the company's imminent demise*

demo /ˈdɛmoʊ/ n, pl **dem·os** [C] **1** : an example of a product that is not yet ready to be sold • *a demo version of the software* **2** : DEMONSTRATION 1 • *The salesman gave us a demo of the vacuum cleaner.* **3** : a recording that musicians make in order to show what their music is like • *They sent the demo to a record company.* **4** Brit, informal : DEMONSTRATION 2 • *an antiwar demo*

de·moc·ra·cy /dɪˈmɑːkrəsi/ n, pl **-cies** **1 a** [U] : a form of government in which people choose leaders by voting **b** [C] : a country ruled by democracy • *In a democracy, every citizen should have the right to vote.* **2** [C/U] : an organization or situation in which everyone is treated equally and has equal rights • *The classroom is not a democracy; the teacher's decisions are final.*

dem·o·crat /ˈdɛməˌkræt/ n [C] **1** : a person who believes in or supports democracy **2** *Democrat* : a member of the Democratic Party of the U.S.

dem·o·crat·ic /ˌdɛməˈkrætɪk/ adj **1** : based on a form of government in which the people choose leaders by voting : of or relating to democracy • *a democratic (form of) government* • *a democratic election/constitution* **2** *Democratic* : of or relating to one of the two major political parties in the U.S. • *Democratic voters/candidates* • *the Democratic Party* — compare REPUBLICAN **3** : relating to the idea that all people should be treated equally • *promoting democratic principles/reforms/changes around the world* • *a more democratic society* — **dem·o·crat·i·cal·ly** /ˌdɛməˈkrætɪkli/ adv • *a democratically elected leader*

de·moc·ra·tize *also Brit* **de·moc·ra·tise** /dɪˈmɑːkrəˌtaɪz/ vb **-tized; -tiz·ing** **1** [C/U] : to make (a country or organization) more democratic • *efforts to democratize the organization* **2** [T] formal : to make it possible for all people to understand (something) • *The magazine's goal is to democratize art.* — **de·moc·ra·ti·za·tion** *also Brit* **de·moc·ra·ti·sa·tion** /dɪˌmɑːkrətəˈzeɪʃən, Brit dɪˌmɒkrəˌtaɪˈzeɪʃən/ n [U]

[superscript]1[/superscript]**de·mo·graph·ic** /ˌdɛməˈgræfɪk/ n **1** [plural] : the qualities (such as age, sex, and income) of a specific group of people • *The town's demographics suggest that the restaurant will do well there.* **2** [C] : a group of people that has a particular set of qualities — usually singular • *The magazine is trying to reach a younger/older demographic.*

[superscript]2[/superscript]**demographic** adj : of or relating to demography • *demographic trends/changes*

de·mog·ra·phy /dɪˈmɑːgrəfi/ n [U] : the study of changes (such as the number of births, deaths, marriages, and illnesses) that occur over a period of time in human populations; *also* : a set of such changes • *the shifting demography of Asia* — **de·mog·ra·pher** /dɪˈmɑːgrəfɚ/ n [C]

de·mol·ish /dɪˈmɑːlɪʃ/ vb [T] **1 a** : to destroy (a building, bridge, etc.) : to forcefully tear down or take apart (a structure) • *The old factory was demolished to make way for a new parking lot.* **b** : to damage (something) so that it cannot be repaired • *The car was demolished in the accident.* **2** (figurative) a demolished reputation **2** informal : to eat all of (something) quickly • *We demolished the pie.* **3** informal : to defeat (a person or team) easily or completely • *They demolished the other team 51–7.*

de·mo·li·tion /ˌdɛməˈlɪʃən/ n [C/U] : deliberate destruction of a building or other structure • *The factory is scheduled for demolition.* • *a demolition crew/team*

demolition derby n [C] chiefly US : a contest in which drivers in old cars crash into each other until only one car is still running

de·mon /ˈdiːmən/ n [C] **1** : an evil spirit • *angels and demons [=devils]* **2** informal : a person who has a lot of energy or enthusiasm • *She works like a demon.* [=she works very hard] — see also SPEED DEMON **3** : something that causes a lot of trouble or unhappiness — usually plural • *battling the demons of drug addiction*

de·mon·ic /dɪˈmɑːnɪk/ adj : caused or done by a demon • *demonic possession* : of, relating to, or like a demon • *demonic cruelty/laughter*

de·mon·stra·ble /dɪˈmɑːnstrəbəl/ adj, formal : able to be proven or shown • *a clearly demonstrable improvement* — **de·mon·stra·bly** /dɪˈmɑːnstrəbli/ adv

dem·on·strate /ˈdɛmənˌstreɪt/ vb **-strat·ed; -strat·ing** **1** [T] **a** : to prove (something) by showing examples of it • *Each student must demonstrate mastery of the subject matter in order to pass the class.* **b** : to prove (something) by being an example of it • *The latest test results clearly demonstrate that the vaccine works.* **2** [T] : to show (a quality, feeling, etc.) clearly to other people • *They've demonstrated a willingness to negotiate.* **3** [T] : to show or explain how something is used or done • *demonstrate a technique/procedure* • *Please demonstrate how the machine works.* **4** [I] : to take part in an event in which people gather together in order to show that they support or oppose something or someone • *Protesters demonstrated against the war.*

dem·on·stra·tion /ˌdɛmən'streɪʃən/ *n* [C/U] **1** : an act of showing someone how something is used or done ▪ *Please give us a demonstration so that we can see how the machine works.* **2** : an event in which people gather together in order to show that they support or oppose something or someone ▪ *demonstrations against the war = antiwar demonstrations* **3** : an act of showing or proving something ▪ *The latest tests are a clear demonstration that the vaccine works.* ▪ *a demonstration of grief/bravery* — **dem·on·stra·tion·al** /ˌdɛmən'streɪʃənl/ *adj* ▪ *a demonstrational video*

de·mon·stra·tive /dɪ'mɑːnstrətɪv/ *adj* **1** *formal* : freely and openly showing emotion or feelings ▪ *She is more demonstrative (about her feelings) than I am.* **2** *grammar* : showing who or what is being referred to ▪ *In the phrase "this is my hat," the word "this" is a demonstrative pronoun.* ▪ *In the phrase "give me that book," the word "that" is a demonstrative adjective.* — **demonstrative** *n* [C] ▪ *"This" and "that" are demonstratives.* [=words that tell you who or what is being referred to]

dem·on·stra·tor /'dɛmən,streɪtɚ/ *n* [C] **1** : a person who is part of an event in which people gather together in order to show that they support or oppose something or someone ▪ *antiwar demonstrators* **2** : a person who shows other people how something is used or done ▪ *a product demonstrator*

de·mor·al·ize *also Brit* **de·mor·al·ise** /dɪ'mɔrəˌlaɪz/ *vb* **-ized; -iz·ing** [T] : to cause (someone) to lose hope, courage, or confidence ▪ *a team demoralized by defeat* ▪ *The troops were completely demoralized.* ▪ *a series of demoralizing losses* — **de·mor·al·i·za·tion** /dɪˌmɔrələ'zeɪʃən, *Brit* dɪˌmɒrəˌlaɪ'zeɪʃən/ *n* [U]

de·mote /dɪ'moʊt/ *vb* **-mot·ed; -mot·ing** [T] : to change the rank or position of (someone) to a lower or less important one ▪ *The army major was demoted to captain.* — **de·mo·tion** /dɪ'moʊʃən/ *n* [C/U]

de·mur /dɪ'mɚ/ *vb* **-murred; -mur·ring** [I] *formal* **1** : to disagree politely with another person's statement or suggestion ▪ *She suggested that he would win easily, but he demurred.* **2** : to politely refuse to accept a request or suggestion ▪ *They wanted her to run for president, but she demurred.* [=declined]

de·mure /dɪ'mjuɚ/ *adj* **1** : quiet and polite — usually used to describe a woman or girl ▪ *a demure young lady* **2** : not showy or flashy ▪ *the demure charm of the cottage* — **de·mure·ly** *adv* — **de·mure·ness** *n* [U]

de·mys·ti·fy /di'mɪstəˌfaɪ/ *vb* **-fies; -fied; -fy·ing** [T] : to make (something) clear and easy to understand ▪ *a class that demystifies the Internet* — **de·mys·ti·fi·ca·tion** /dɪˌmɪstəfə'keɪʃən/ *n* [U]

den /'dɛn/ *n* [C] **1** : the home of some kinds of wild animals ▪ *a fox's/bear's den* **2 a** *US* : an informal room in a home ▪ *The TV is in the den.* **b** *chiefly Brit, informal + old-fashioned* : a small and quiet room in a home where someone goes to read, work, etc. **3** : a secret place where people meet especially to do things that are illegal or immoral ▪ *a gambling den* ▪ *a den of iniquity* [=a place where immoral or illegal things are done] **4** *Brit* : a small often secret structure that children play in **5** *US* : a group of Cub Scouts — see also DEN MOTHER

de·na·tion·al·ize *also* **de·na·tion·al·ise** /di'næʃənəˌlaɪz/ *vb* **-ized; -iz·ing** [T] *Brit* : PRIVATIZE

de·ni·able /dɪ'najəbəl/ *adj* : possible to deny ▪ *The failure of the policy is no longer deniable.*

de·ni·al /dɪ'najəl/ *n* **1** [C] : a statement saying that something is not true or real ▪ *a flat/absolute/outright denial of the charges* ▪ *her denial of responsibility* **2** [U] *psychology* : a condition in which someone will not admit that something sad, painful, etc., is true or real ▪ *She's in (a state of) denial about her husband's death.* [=she has not fully accepted that her husband is dead] **3** [C/U] : the act of not allowing someone to have something ▪ *the denial of voting rights to convicted felons* ▪ *Making false statements on a job application will result in a denial of employment.*

den·i·grate /'dɛnɪˌgreɪt/ *vb* **-grat·ed; -grat·ing** [T] *formal* **1** : to say very critical and often unfair things about (someone) ▪ *Her story denigrates him as a person and as a teacher.* **2** : to make (something) seem less important or valuable ▪ *Such behavior denigrates the value of honesty in the workplace.* — **den·i·gra·tion** /ˌdɛnɪ'greɪʃən/ *n* [U]

den·im /'dɛnəm/ *n* **1** [U] : a strong usually blue cotton cloth that is used especially to make jeans ▪ *a denim skirt/jacket* **2** [*plural*] : pants that are made of denim ▪ *faded denims*

den·i·zen /'dɛnəzən/ *n* [C] : a person, animal, or plant that lives in or often is found in a particular place or region ▪ *denizens of the deep* [=plants and animals that live in the deepest parts of the ocean]

den mother *n* [C] *US* : a woman who is the leader of a group of Cub Scouts

de·nom·i·na·tion /dɪˌnɑːmə'neɪʃən/ *n* [C] **1** : a religious group ▪ *Methodists, Baptists, and other Christian denominations* **2 a** : the value that a particular coin or bill has ▪ *coins of different denominations* [=pennies, nickels, dimes, etc.] **b** : an amount of money that something is worth ▪ *The gift certificates come in $5 and $10 denominations.* **3** *formal* : a general name for a group or kind ▪ *people of different political denominations* — **de·nom·i·na·tion·al** /dɪˌnɑːmə'neɪʃənl/ *adj*

de·nom·i·na·tor /dɪ'nɑːməˌneɪtɚ/ *n* [C] *mathematics* : the number in a fraction that is below the line and that divides the number above the line — compare NUMERATOR; see also COMMON DENOMINATOR

de·no·ta·tion /ˌdiːnoʊ'teɪʃən/ *n* [C] : the meaning of a word or phrase ▪ *The definition provides the word's denotation.*

de·note /dɪˈnoʊt/ vb **-not·ed; -not·ing** [T] formal **1** of a word : to have (something) as a meaning • The word "derby" can denote a horse race or a kind of hat. **2** : to show, mark, or be a sign of (something) • The symbol * next to a name denotes a contest finalist.

de·nounce /dɪˈnaʊns/ vb **-nounced; -nounc·ing** [T] **1** : to publicly state that someone or something is bad or wrong • The plan was denounced as risky and dangerous. **2** : to report (someone) to the police or other authorities for illegal or immoral acts • She was denounced as a spy to government authorities.

dense /ˈdɛns/ adj **dens·er; -est 1** : having parts that are close together • the dense jungle • dense bread **2** : crowded with people • the city's densest area **3** informal : not able to understand things easily • I'm sorry I'm so dense [=slow-witted] this morning. **4** : difficult to see through • dense [=thick] fog **5** : difficult to understand; especially : hard to read • the book's technical subject and dense language/prose **6** technical : heavier than most things of the same size • a dense substance like lead or mercury — **dense·ly** adv • a densely populated area [=an area in which many people live] • densely forested mountains — **dense·ness** n [U]

den·si·ty /ˈdɛnsəti/ n, pl **-ties 1** [U] : the quality or state of being dense • the density of the jungle • the fog's density • the density of her writing style **2** [C/U] : the amount of something in a particular space or area • The area has a high **population density**. [=many people live in the area] **3** [C/U] technical : the amount of matter in something that is shown by the relationship between its weight and size • the density of the atmosphere • bone density [=how solid and heavy someone's bones are]

¹dent /ˈdɛnt/ n [C] : an area on a surface that is lower than the rest of the surface especially because of being hit or pushed in • The accident left/made a dent in the car's fender. ✧ In figurative use, to **make a dent (in something)** or to **put a dent in something** is to decrease something slightly or to make it somewhat weaker. • The payment hardly makes a dent in the amount the company owes.

²dent vb **1** [T/I] : to make a dent in (something) • He dented his (car's) fender in the accident. • a metal that dents easily **2** [T] : to decrease (something) • losses that have dented the team's confidence

den·tal /ˈdɛntl̩/ adj : of or relating to teeth or to the work dentists do • dental decay • your **dental records** [=the information about your teeth that your dentist has] • **dental school** [=a school where you are trained to be a dentist]

dental floss n [U] : a special thread that is used to clean between your teeth

dental hygienist n [C] : a person who works with a dentist and whose job includes cleaning people's teeth

dente see AL DENTE

den·tist /ˈdɛntəst/ n **1** [C] : a person whose job is to care for people's teeth **2** the dentist or the dentist's : the place where a dentist works • I saw her at the dentist last week.

den·tist·ry /ˈdɛntəstri/ n [U] : the work that a dentist does • a career in dentistry

den·ture /ˈdɛntʃɚ/ n [C] : a set of artificial teeth • a pair of dentures [=false teeth] • partial dentures [=a partial set of artificial teeth]

de·nude /dɪˈnuːd, Brit dɪˈnjuːd/ vb **-nud·ed; -nud·ing** [T] : to remove all the trees from (an area) or all the leaves from (a tree) • a countryside denuded by wildfires

de·nun·ci·a·tion /dɪˌnʌnsiˈeɪʃən/ n [C/U] : a statement that denounces something or someone • The attack drew strong denunciations from around the world.

de·ny /dɪˈnaɪ/ vb **-nies; -nied; -ny·ing** [T] **1 a** : to say that something is not true • She denies the charges. • I don't deny that I made mistakes. [=I admit that I made mistakes] • Yes, I was there. I don't deny it. • **There's no denying** [=it is clearly true] that he knows how to sing. **b** : to refuse to accept or admit (something) • She denied responsibility [=she said that she was not responsible] for the error. **2** : to refuse to give (something) to someone • The banks denied them credit. • The judge denied their request. — **deny yourself** : to not allow yourself to enjoy things or to have the things that you want • On this diet, I don't feel like I'm denying myself.

de·odor·ant /dɪˈoʊdərənt/ n [C/U] : a substance that you put on your body and especially under your arms to prevent, remove, or hide unpleasant smells — **deodorant** adj, always before a noun • deodorant soap

de·odor·ize also Brit **de·odor·ise** /dɪˈoʊdəˌraɪz/ vb **-ized; -iz·ing** [T] : to remove an unpleasant smell from (something) • We had the carpet cleaned and deodorized. — **de·odor·iz·er** also Brit **de·odor·is·er** n [C]

de·oxy·ri·bo·nu·cle·ic acid /diˈɑːksiˌraɪboʊnuˈkliːjɪk-/ n [U] technical : DNA

dep. abbr depart; departure

de·part /dɪˈpɑɚt/ vb **1** somewhat formal **a** [T/I] : to leave a place especially to start a journey • The train departed (from the station) on time. = (US) The train departed the station on time. **b** [I] : to leave a job or position • She's replacing the departing manager. [=the manager who is leaving that job] **2** [I] : to change something or do something in a different way • The river departs from its original course here. • The actors were allowed to depart from the script. [=to say things that were not in the script]

de·part·ed /dɪˈpɑɚtəd/ adj **1** somewhat formal : no longer living — used as a polite way to say that someone is dead • our dear departed friend **2** literary : existing in the past • the elegance of a departed era — **the departed** : people who have died • the graves/spirits of the departed

de·part·ment /dɪˈpɑɚtmənt/ n [C] **1** : one of the major parts of a company, organization, government, or school •

the company's sales department ▪ the Department of Defense = the Defense Department ▪ the university's math and science departments ▪ our local police department — abbr. **dept.** **2** : an area in a store where a certain kind of product is sold ▪ the toy department **3** informal **a** : a subject or activity that a person is interested in or responsible for ▪ Taking care of the cat is not my department. [=responsibility] **b** often humorous — used to say that someone or something has or does not have a particular quality ▪ He does pretty well in the looks department. [=he is attractive] — **de·part·men·tal** /dɪˌpɑɚtˈmɛntl̩/ adj ▪ the departmental budget

de·part·men·tal·ize also Brit **de·part·men·tal·ise** /dɪˌpɑɚtˈmɛntəˌlaɪz/ vb **-ized; -iz·ing** [T] : to divide (something, such as a company) into departments ▪ The organization is highly departmentalized.

department store n [C] : a large store that has separate areas in which different kinds of products are sold

de·par·ture /dɪˈpɑɚtʃɚ/ n **1 a** [C/U] : the act of leaving a place especially to start a journey ▪ Our departure is scheduled for 5 p.m. = Our departure time is 5 p.m. ▪ a schedule of arrivals and departures **b** [C] : the act of leaving a job, an organization, etc. ▪ her sudden departure from the company **2** [C] : a new or different way of doing something ▪ His previous movies have all been comedies, so this dramatic role is a real departure for him. ▪ a departure from tradition

de·pend /dɪˈpɛnd/ vb [I] informal — used in speech in phrases like it depends and that depends to say that the answer to a question will be different in different situations ▪ "Are you going to the party?" "I might. It depends." [=there may be something that prevents me from going] ▪ (very informal) "How long does it take to get to the airport?" "Depends. If you don't hit traffic you can probably be there in 20 minutes." — **depend on/upon** [phrasal vb] **1** : to be determined or decided by (something) ▪ The stamp's value depends on how rare it is. ▪ It's not clear how many people were there. Reports vary between 10,000 and 20,000, depending on who's counting. [=some people report that there were 10,000 people there, others report that there were 20,000] — sometimes used informally without on or upon ▪ "Are you happy?" "It depends what you mean by 'happy.'" **2** : to need (someone or something) for support, help, etc. ▪ They depend solely/entirely on her income to pay the bills. [=without her income they would not be able to pay their bills] **3** : to trust (someone or something) ▪ She's someone you can always depend on. [=count on] ▪ (humorous) You can depend on him to disagree. [=you could always be sure that he would disagree]

de·pend·able /dɪˈpɛndəbəl/ adj : able to be trusted to do or provide what is needed ▪ The well is a dependable source of wa-

ter. [=there is always water in the well] — **de·pend·abil·i·ty** /dɪˌpɛndəˈbɪləti/ n [U] — **de·pend·ably** /dɪˈpɛndəbli/ adv

de·pen·dence /dɪˈpɛndəns/ n [U, singular] : the state of being dependent: such as **a** : the state of needing something or someone else for support, help, etc. — + on or upon ▪ the country's dependence on/upon foreign oil **b** : the state of being addicted to alcohol or a drug ▪ drug and alcohol dependence [=addiction, dependency]

de·pen·den·cy /dɪˈpɛndənsi/ n, pl **-cies** **1** [U, singular] : DEPENDENCE ▪ the country's dependency on foreign oil ▪ drug/chemical dependency **2** [C] : an area that is controlled by a country but that is not formally a part of it

¹**de·pen·dent** /dɪˈpɛndənt/ adj **1** : decided or controlled by something else ▪ The stamp's value is **dependent on/upon** how rare it is. ▪ I believe that success is dependent upon hard work. **2** : needing someone or something else for support, help, etc. ▪ soldiers with dependent children [=soldiers who have children whose food, clothing, etc., they are responsible for providing] ▪ They're entirely **dependent on/upon** her income to pay the bills. **3** : addicted to alcohol or a drug ▪ chemically dependent patients [=patients who are addicted to a drug]

²**dependent** also Brit **de·pen·dant** /dɪˈpɛndənt/ n : a person (such as a child) whose food, clothing, etc., you are responsible for providing ▪ insurance coverage for workers and their dependents

de·pict /dɪˈpɪkt/ vb [T] **1** : to show (someone or something) in a picture, painting, photograph, etc. ▪ a mural depicting famous scenes from American history **2** : to describe (someone or something) using words, a story, etc. ▪ The movie depicts the life of early settlers. ▪ His enemies depict [=portray] him as a cruel leader. — **de·pic·tion** /dɪˈpɪkʃən/ n [C/U] ▪ an honest depiction of life in the city

de·plane /dɪˈpleɪn/ vb **-planed; -plan·ing** [I] chiefly US : to get out of an airplane after it arrives at an airport ▪ We were the last passengers to deplane.

de·plete /dɪˈpliːt/ vb **-plet·ed; -plet·ing** [T] : to use most or all of (something important) ▪ activities that deplete our natural resources ▪ lakes that are depleted of fish — **de·ple·tion** /dɪˈpliːʃən/ n [C/U]

de·plor·able /dɪˈploʀəbəl/ adj : very bad in a way that causes shock, fear, or disgust ▪ children living in deplorable conditions — **de·plor·ably** /dɪˈploʀəbli/ adv

de·plore /dɪˈploɚ/ vb **-plored; -plor·ing** [T] : to hate or dislike (something) very much ▪ Many people deplored the change.

de·ploy /dɪˈploɪ/ vb **1** [T] : to organize and send out (people or things) to be used for a particular purpose ▪ The troops were deployed for battle. ▪ Supplies have been deployed across the country. **2** [T/I] : to open up and spread out the parts of (something, such as a parachute) ▪ The boat's sails were fully deployed. ▪ The parachute failed to deploy properly. — **de·ploy·ment** /dɪˈploɪmənt/ n [C/U] *additional troop deployments*

de·pop·u·late /dɪˈpɑːpjəˌleɪt/ *vb* **-lat·ed; -lat·ing** [*T*] : to greatly reduce the number of people living in (a city, region, etc.) • *areas depopulated by disease* — **de·pop·u·la·tion** /dɪˌpɑːpjəˈleɪʃən/ *n* [*U*]

de·port /dɪˈpoɚt/ *vb* [*T*] : to force (a person who is not a citizen) to leave a country • *immigrants who have been illegally deported* — **de·por·ta·tion** /ˌdiːˌpoɚˈteɪʃən/ *n* [*C/U*] • *She is facing deportation.* [=she may be forced to leave the country] • *illegal deportations* — **de·por·tee** /ˌdiːˌpoɚˈtiː/ *n* [*C*] • *thousands of deportees* [=people who have been deported]

de·port·ment /dɪˈpoɚtmənt/ *n* [*U*] *formal* : the way that a person behaves, stands, and moves especially in a formal situation • *proper dress and deportment*

de·pose /dɪˈpoʊz/ *vb* **-posed; -pos·ing** [*T*] : to remove (someone) from a powerful position • *a deposed military leader*

¹**de·pos·it** /dɪˈpɑːzɪt/ *vb* [*T*] **1** : to put (money) in a bank account • *My paycheck is automatically deposited into my account.* **2** *somewhat formal* : to put or leave (someone or something) in a particular place • *The taxi deposited us at the train station.* **3** : to leave an amount of (something, such as sand, snow, or mud) on a surface or area especially over a period of time • *layers of mud deposited by floodwaters* — **de·pos·i·tor** /dɪˈpɑːzətɚ/ *n* [*C*]

²**deposit** *n* [*C*] **1** : an amount of money that is put in a bank account • *a (bank) deposit of $300* • *savings deposits* [=money put into savings accounts] • *I made a deposit.* [=put some money in a bank account] **2 a** : money that you give someone when you agree to buy something (such as a house or car) ◇ *A deposit* shows that there is an agreement between a buyer and seller. When the sale is made final, the seller keeps the deposit as the first payment. • *We put a deposit on the house.* **b** : money that you pay when you buy or rent something and that you can get back if you return the thing or leave it in good condition • *The rental car company requires a deposit for drivers under the age of 25.* **3 a** : an amount of sand, snow, mud, etc., that has formed or been left on a surface or area over a period of time • *a deposit of mud left by the flood* • *fat/fatty deposits in the arteries* **b** : an amount of a substance (such as oil or coal) that exists naturally in the ground • *oil deposits below the ocean floor* — **on deposit** ◇ *Money that has been put in a bank is on deposit.* • *The company has millions of dollars on deposit with several foreign banks.*

deposit account *n* [*C*] *chiefly Brit* : SAVINGS ACCOUNT

de·po·si·tion /ˌdɛpəˈzɪʃən/ *n* [*C*] *law* : a formal statement that someone who has promised to tell the truth makes so that the statement can be used in court • *She gave a videotaped deposition about what she saw that night.*

de·pos·i·to·ry /dɪˈpɑːzəˌtori, *Brit* dɪ-

ˈpɒzətri/ *n, pl* **-ries** [*C*] : a place where something is put so that it can be kept safe • *a book/food depository*

de·pot /ˈdɛpoʊ, ˈdiːpoʊ/ *n* [*C*] **1** *US* : a train or bus station • *the train/bus depot* **2** : a place where military supplies are kept or where soldiers are trained • *supply/weapons depots* **3** : a place where goods are stored • *a storage depot*

de·praved /dɪˈpreɪvd/ *adj* : very evil • *a depraved criminal/mind*

de·prav·i·ty /dɪˈprævəti/ *n, pl* **-ties** **1** [*U*] : a very evil quality or way of behaving • *moral/sexual depravity* **2** [*C*] : an evil or immoral act • *the depravities of war*

dep·re·cate /ˈdɛprɪˌkeɪt/ *vb* **-cat·ed; -cat·ing** [*T*] *formal* : to criticize or express disapproval of (someone or something) • *I don't mean to deprecate his accomplishments.* — **deprecating** *adj* • *She made some deprecating remarks about her opponent.* — see also SELF-DEPRECATING — **dep·re·ca·tion** /ˌdɛprɪˈkeɪʃən/ *n* [*U*] — **dep·re·ca·to·ry** /ˈdɛprɪˌkeɪtəri, ˈdɛprɪkəˌtori, *Brit* ˈdɛprɪkeɪtri/ *adj* : deprecatory remarks

de·pre·ci·ate /dɪˈpriːʃiˌeɪt/ *vb* **-at·ed; -at·ing** **1** [*T/I*] : to decrease in value or to cause (something) to decrease in value • *New cars depreciate quickly.* • *The damage depreciated the value of the house.* **2** [*T*] *formal* : to describe (something) as having little value • *He often depreciates the importance of his work.* — **de·pre·ci·a·tion** /dɪˌpriːʃiˈeɪʃən/ *n* [*U*] • *the car's/currency's depreciation*

de·press /dɪˈprɛs/ *vb* [*T*] **1** : to make (someone) feel sad • *The news depressed me a little.* **2** : to decrease the activity or strength of (something) • *This medicine may depress your appetite.* [=may make you less hungry] • *Market conditions are likely to depress earnings in the next quarter.* **3** *formal* : to press (something) down • *Slowly depress the car's brake pedal.*

de·pres·sant /dɪˈprɛsnt/ *n* [*C*] : a chemical substance (such as a drug) that makes a body's systems less active • *alcohol and other depressants* — **depressant** *adj*

de·pressed /dɪˈprɛst/ *adj* **1 a** : feeling sad • *I've been feeling a little depressed lately.* • *He's depressed about the election.* **b** : having a serious medical condition that causes a person to feel very sad, hopeless, and unimportant : suffering from mental depression • *severely depressed patients* **2** : having little economic activity and few jobs • *a depressed economy* **3** : less strong, active, high, etc., than usual • *a depressed appetite*

de·press·ing /dɪˈprɛsɪŋ/ *adj* : causing someone to feel sad or without hope • *a very/deeply depressing movie* — **de·press·ing·ly** *adv*

de·pres·sion /dɪˈprɛʃən/ *n* **1** [*U*] **a** : a state of feeling sad • *anger, anxiety, and depression* **b** : a serious medical condition in which a person feels very sad, hopeless, and unimportant and is often unable to live in a normal way • *undergoing treatment for severe/deep/clinical de-*

pression **2** [C/U] : a period of time in which there is little economic activity and many people do not have jobs • *He grew up during the (Great) Depression.* [=the 1930s, when the U.S. and many other countries were in a very bad depression] • *periods of economic depression* **3** [C] : an area on a surface that is lower than other parts • *depressions in the moon's surface* **4** [C] *weather* : a large area where there is low pressure in the atmosphere with usually clouds and rain • *a tropical depression*

de·pres·sive /dɪˈprɛsɪv/ *adj, medical* : of or relating to the medical condition of depression • *a depressive illness* — **depressive** *n* [C] • *treatment of depressives* [=people who suffer from depression]

de·prive /dɪˈpraɪv/ *vb* **-prived; -priv·ing** — **deprive of** [*phrasal vb*] **deprive (someone or something) of** : to take something away from someone or something : to not allow (someone or something) to have or keep (something) • *The change in her status deprived her of access to classified information.* • *studying what happens to people when they are deprived of sleep* — **dep·ri·va·tion** /ˌdɛprəˈveɪʃən/ *n* [C/U] • *the effects of sleep deprivation*

deprived *adj* : not having the things that are needed for a good or healthy life • *Dieters who eat small amounts of their favorite foods don't feel deprived.* • *people who are sleep-deprived* [=people who do not get enough sleep]

dept. *abbr* department

depth /ˈdɛpθ/ *n* **1 a** [C/U] : a distance below a surface • *fish living at depths of 500 feet or more* • *shallow/great depths* • *the depth of a hole* • *The pool is 12 feet in depth.* [=12 feet deep] **b** [C] : the distance from the front of something to the back • *Measure the height, width, and depth of the cabinet.* **2** [C] : an area that exists far below a surface or far inside something : a deep place or area • *exploring the ocean depths* • *(figurative) the depths of sleep* • *(figurative) I knew it in the depths of my heart/soul/being.* [=I believed it very strongly] **3** [C] **a** : a very low or bad state or condition • *sinking into the depths of misery/despair/depression* • *I can't believe he lied. He's really sunk to new depths.* **b** : the worst part of something • *the depth/depths of the Great Depression* **4** [U] : the quality of being deep: such as **a** : the quality of being strongly felt • *the depth of her anger/love/pain/shame* • *expressing great depth of feeling/emotion* **b** : the quality of being very bad or serious • *the depth of the problem* **c** : the quality of being complete or thorough • *We were impressed by the depth of her experience.* • *Your essay lacks depth.* **d** : the quality of being strong in color, taste, etc. • *The wine has great depth of flavor.* **e** *US, sports* : the quality of having many good players on a team • *The team lacks depth this year.* — **in depth** : in a thorough or complete way • *The problem will be examined/explored/studied in depth.* — **out of your depth** *also* **beyond your depth**

1 : dealing with a situation or subject that is too difficult for you • *When the debate turned to physics, I knew that I was out of my depth.* **2** *chiefly Brit* : in water that is deeper than your height • *swimming in water that is out of my depth* [=over my head]

dep·u·ta·tion /ˌdɛpjəˈweɪʃən/ *n* [C] *formal* : a group of people who are sent to a place to represent other people • *Many countries sent deputations to the conference.*

dep·u·tize *also Brit* **dep·u·tise** /ˈdɛpjəˌtaɪz/ *vb* **-tized; -tiz·ing 1** [T] *chiefly US* : to give (someone) the power to do something in place of another person : to make (someone) a deputy • *deputizing nurses to perform some of the doctors' duties* **2** [I] *Brit* : to act *for* someone as a deputy • *I deputize for the newspaper's editor on the weekends.*

dep·u·ty /ˈdɛpjəti/ *n, pl* **-ties** [C] **1** : an important assistant who helps the leader of a government, organization, etc. • *(US) a sheriff's deputy* [=an assistant who helps a sheriff enforce the law] • *the department's deputy director* **2** : a member of Parliament in some countries

de·rail /dɪˈreɪl/ *vb* **1** [I] *of a train* : to leave its tracks • *The train derailed in heavy snow.* **2** [T] : to cause (a train) to leave its tracks • *The train was derailed by heavy snow.* • *(figurative) The incident threatened to derail her career.* — **de·rail·ment** /dɪˈreɪlmənt/ *n* [C/U]

de·ranged /dɪˈreɪndʒd/ *adj* : crazy or insane • *a deranged criminal/mind* — **de·range·ment** /dɪˈreɪndʒmənt/ *n* [U]

der·by /ˈdɚbi, Brit ˈdɑːbi/ *n, pl* **-bies** [C] **1** : a type of horse race that takes place every year — used especially in proper names • *the Kentucky Derby* **2** : a race or contest • *a fishing derby* **3** *Brit* : a game between local sports teams **4** *US* : a hard usually black cloth hat that has a round top — called also *(US)* **derby hat**, *(chiefly Brit)* **bowler**

de·reg·u·late /diˈrɛgjəˌleɪt/ *vb* **-lat·ed; lat·ing** [T] : to give up control of (something, such as an industry) by removing laws • *The government plans to further deregulate the oil industry.* — **de·reg·u·la·tion** /diˌrɛgjəˈleɪʃən/ *n* [U]

1der·e·lict /ˈdɛrəˌlɪkt/ *adj, formal* **1** : no longer cared for or used by anyone • *derelict warehouses* **2** *US, formal* : failing to do what should be done : NEGLIGENT • *The officer was charged with being derelict in his duty.*

2derelict *n* [C] : a person who has no money, job, home, etc. • *a drunken derelict*

der·e·lic·tion /ˌdɛrəˈlɪkʃən/ *n, formal* **1** [U] **a** : the act of no longer caring for, using, or doing something • *the dereliction of a cause* **b** : the bad condition of something that is not being cared for • *The house is in a state of dereliction.* **2** [singular] *law* : failure to do your job or duty • *The officer was formally charged with dereliction of duty.*

de·ride /dɪˈraɪd/ *vb* **-rid·ed; -rid·ing** [T] *formal* : to say that (someone or something) is ridiculous or has no value • *poli-*

ticians attempting to win votes by deriding their opponents

de·ri·sion /dɪˈrɪʒən/ *n [U] formal* : the feeling that people express when they criticize and laugh at someone or something in an insulting way ▪ *The governor's plan was greeted with derision by most journalists.* ▪ *"Nerd" is a* **term of derision.**
— **de·ri·sive** /dɪˈraɪsɪv/ *adj* ▪ *derisive laughter* — **de·ri·sive·ly** *adv*

der·i·va·tion /ˌderəˈveɪʃən/ *n* **1 a** [C/U] : the origin of a word ▪ *words of Latin derivation* **b** [U] : the act of forming a word *from* another word ▪ *"Childish" was formed by derivation from "child."* **2 a** [U] : the source or origin of something ▪ *foods of Indian derivation* **b** [C] : an act or process by which one thing is formed or created *from* another ▪ *the possible derivation of birds from dinosaurs*

¹de·riv·a·tive /dɪˈrɪvətɪv/ *n* [C] **1** : a word formed from another word ▪ *The word "childish" is a derivative of "child."* **2** : a substance that is made from another substance ▪ *Petroleum is a derivative of coal.*

²derivative *adj* **1** *usually disapproving* : made up of parts from something else : not new or original ▪ *A number of critics found the film derivative and predictable.* **2** : formed from another word ▪ *a derivative term*

de·rive /dɪˈraɪv/ *vb* **-rived; -riv·ing** **1** [T] : to take or get (something) *from* (something else) ▪ *I derive great satisfaction from our friendship.* ▪ *Many English words are derived from French.* **2** [I] : to come *from* something ▪ *Much of the book's appeal derives from the personality of its central character.* — **de·riv·able** /dɪˈraɪvəbəl/ *adj*

der·ma·tol·o·gy /ˌdɚməˈtɑːlədʒi/ *n* [U] : the scientific study of the skin and its diseases — **der·ma·tol·o·gist** /ˌdɚməˈtɑːlədʒɪst/ *n* [C]

de·rog·a·to·ry /dɪˈrɑːgəˌtori, *Brit* dɪˈrɒgətri/ *adj* : expressing a low opinion of someone or something ▪ *He made some derogatory remarks about her.* ▪ *a derogatory term/word*

der·rick /ˈderɪk/ *n* [C] **1** : a tall machine with a long part like an arm that is used to move or lift heavy things especially on ships **2** : a tall tower that is built over an oil well and used to support and guide the tool that is used to dig the hole and get oil out of the ground

der·ring–do /ˌderɪŋˈduː/ *n* [U] *old-fashioned + humorous* : brave acts : behavior that requires courage ▪ *spectacular feats of derring-do* [=*bravery*]

der·vish /ˈdɚvɪʃ/ *n* [C] : a member of a Muslim religious group that is known for its customs including a fast spinning dance that is done as part of worship ✧ In U.S. English, *dervish* is most common in figurative uses where it describes someone or something that is spinning or moving very fast.

de·scend /dɪˈsɛnd/ *vb, formal* **1** [T/I] : to go down : to go or move from a higher to a lower place or level ▪ *The workers descended into the hole.* ▪ *They descended from* [=got down from] *the*

platform. ▪ *an airplane descending to a lower altitude* ▪ *descend a ladder/staircase* **2** [I] : to slope or lead downward ▪ *The stairs descended into the tunnel.* **3** [I] : to go or change to a worse state or condition ▪ *He descended into a deep depression.* **4** [I] : to appear or happen like something that comes down from the sky ▪ *as night descended* ▪ *A crowd of people descended on/upon the town.* — **descend from** [*phrasal vb*] : to have (something or someone in the past) as an origin or source ▪ *The tradition descends from an ancient custom.* ▪ *They are descended from a noble British family.* — **descend to** [*phrasal vb*] : to lower yourself by doing (something) ▪ *She would not descend to asking her friends for help.* — **in descending order** : arranged in a series that begins with the greatest or largest and ends with the least or smallest ▪ *The states are listed in descending order of population size.*

de·scen·dant /dɪˈsɛndənt/ *n* [C] **1** : someone who is related to a person or group of people who lived in the past ▪ *Many people here are descendants of German immigrants.* **2** : a plant or animal that is related to a particular plant or animal that lived long ago ▪ *the theory that birds are the modern descendants of dinosaurs* **3** : something that developed from another thing that was made or existed earlier ▪ *The Italian language is one of Latin's descendants.*

de·scent /dɪˈsɛnt/ *n, formal* **1** [C] **a** : the act or process of going from a higher to a lower place or level ▪ *the submarine's descent* ▪ *The pilot announced our descent.* **b** : the act or process or changing to a worse state or condition ▪ *his descent into deep depression* **2** [C] : a downward slope, path, etc. ▪ *The path going down to the river is a rather steep descent.* **3** [U] : the people in your family who lived before you were born ▪ *Many people here are of German descent.* [=*ancestry*]

de·scribe /dɪˈskraɪb/ *vb* **-scribed; -scrib·ing** [T] : to tell someone the appearance, sound, smell, events, etc., of (something or someone) ▪ *He described the house in perfect detail.* ▪ *Reporters described the scene as a disaster area.* — **de·scrib·able** /dɪˈskraɪbəbəl/ *adj*

de·scrip·tion /dɪˈskrɪpʃən/ *n* **1** [C/U] : a statement that tells you how something or someone looks, sounds, etc. ▪ *Reporters called the scene a "disaster area," and I think that was an accurate description.* ▪ *a job description* ▪ *a brief/general description of the process* ▪ *beautiful beyond description* [=*extremely beautiful*] **2** [C] : type or kind — used after *of* ▪ *people of every description*

de·scrip·tive /dɪˈskrɪptɪv/ *adj* : using words to describe what something or someone is like ▪ *a descriptive account of the journey* ▪ *The black cat was given the descriptive name "Midnight."* ▪ *a name descriptive of the company's philosophy* — **de·scrip·tive·ly** *adv*

des·e·crate /ˈdɛsɪˌkreɪt/ *vb* **-crat·ed; -crat·ing** [T] : to damage (a holy place

or object) • *graves desecrated by vandals*
— **des·e·cra·tion** /ˌdɛsɪ'kreɪʃən/ *n* [U]

de·seg·re·gate /di'sɛgrəˌgeɪt/ *vb* -**gat·ed; -gat·ing** [T/I] : to end a policy that keeps people of different races apart : to end a policy of segregation • *The city's schools were finally desegregated in the 1960s.* — **de·seg·re·ga·tion** /diˌsɛgrɪ'geɪʃən/ *n* [U]

de·sen·si·tize *also Brit* **de·sen·si·tise** /di'sɛnsəˌtaɪz/ *vb* -**tized; -tiz·ing** [T] : to cause (someone or something) to react less to or be less affected by something : to cause (someone or something) to be less sensitive • *medicine to desensitize the nerve* • *People can become desensitized to violence by endless images of war.* — **de·sen·si·ti·za·tion** *also Brit* **de·sen·si·ti·sa·tion** /diˌsɛnsətə'zeɪʃən, Brit diˌsɛnsəˌtaɪ'zeɪʃən/ *n* [U]

¹**des·ert** /'dɛzɚt/ *n* 1 [C/U] : an area of very dry land that is usually covered with sand and is very hot • *Many settlers died while trying to cross the desert.* • *the shifting desert sands* • *a desert island* [=an island where no people live] 2 [C] : a place or area that does not have something interesting or important • *The city is a cultural desert.* — see also DESERTS

²**de·sert** /dɪ'zɚt/ *vb* 1 [T] : to go away from (a place) : to leave (a place) • *The inhabitants had deserted the town.* 2 [T] : to leave and stop helping or supporting (someone or something) • *Her husband deserted her.* • *They deserted the cause.* • *(figurative) Their courage deserted them.* [=they lost their courage] 3 [I] : to leave the military without permission and without intending to return • *Many soldiers deserted during the war.* — **de·sert·ed** /dɪ'zɚtəd/ *adj* • *The town was deserted.* [=there were no people in the town] • *deserted wives/husbands/children* — **de·sert·er** /dɪ'zɚtɚ/ *n* [C] — **de·ser·tion** /dɪ'zɚʃən/ *n* [C/U]

de·serts /dɪ'zɚts/ *n* [*plural*] : punishment that someone deserves • *We all want to see this criminal get/receive his just deserts.*

de·serve /dɪ'zɚv/ *vb* -**served; -serv·ing** [T] — used to say that someone or something should or should not have or be given something • *She deserves another chance.* • *He doesn't deserve the award.* • *They deserve a lot of credit for their efforts.* — often followed by *to* + *verb* • *They deserve to be punished.* — **de·served** /dɪ'zɚvd/ *adj* • *a well-deserved vacation* • *a deserved win/reputation* — **de·serv·ed·ly** /dɪ'zɚvədli/ *adv* • *She was deservedly praised.*

deserving *adj* 1 *always before a noun* : having good qualities that deserve praise, support, etc. • *He is a very deserving young man.* 2 *not before a noun* — used to say that someone or something should have or be given something • *She was deserving of praise.* [=she deserved praise]

¹**de·sign** /dɪ'zaɪn/ *vb* [T] 1 : to plan and make decisions about (something that is being built or created) • *A team of engineers designed the new engine.* • *a badly designed building* 2 : to plan and make

(something) for a specific use or purpose • *He designed the chair to adjust automatically.* • *The course is designed to teach beginners.* [=the purpose of the course is to teach beginners]

²**design** *n* 1 [C/U] : the way the parts of a building, machine, book, etc., are formed and arranged for a particular use or effect • *I like the design of the new stadium.* 2 [U] : the process of planning how something will look, happen, be made, etc. • *the design and development of new products* • *the design process* — see also INTERIOR DESIGN 3 [C] : a drawing of something that is being planned or created • *We reviewed the preliminary design for the new bridge.* 4 [C] : a decorative pattern that covers something • *The wallpaper has a floral design.* 5 [C/U] : something that you plan to do : INTENTION • *The meeting happened by accident, not by design.* [=on purpose] — **have designs on** : to have a secret desire and plan to get (something) • *She had designs on my job.*

¹**des·ig·nate** /'dɛzɪgˌneɪt/ *vb* -**nat·ed; -nat·ing** [T] 1 : to officially choose (someone or something) to do or be something • *We need to designate a new leader.* • *He was designated (as) team captain.* = *He was designated to be team captain.* 2 **a** : to call (something or someone) by a particular name or title • *The four parts were designated "A," "B," "C," and "D" in the diagram.* **b** : to be used as a name for (something or someone) • *The word eventually came to designate* [=refer to] *any kind of mistake.* 3 : to mark, show, or represent (something) • *Free items are designated by blue stickers.* — **designated** *adj* • *We all agreed to meet at a designated time.* [=a specific time that we agreed on] — **des·ig·na·tion** /ˌdɛzɪg'neɪʃən/ *n* [C/U]

²**designate** *adj, not before a noun, formal* : chosen for a particular job but not officially doing that job yet • *the governor designate*

designated driver *n* [C] : a person who agrees not to drink alcohol on a particular occasion so that he or she will be able to safely drive for other people who will be drinking alcohol

designated hitter *n* [C] *baseball* : a player who is chosen at the beginning of a game to bat in the place of the pitcher — called also *DH*

de·sign·er /dɪ'zaɪnɚ/ *n* [C] : a person who plans how something new will look and be made • *a fashion designer* • *She was the designer of the book's jacket.* — **designer** *adj, always before a noun* • *designer jeans/fashions* [=jeans/fashions created by a famous designer]

de·sir·able /dɪ'zaɪrəbəl/ *adj* 1 : having good or pleasing qualities • *a highly desirable location/neighborhood* • *desirable jobs/characteristics* 2 : sexually attractive • *a beautiful and desirable woman* — **de·sir·abil·i·ty** /dɪˌzaɪrə'bɪləti/ *n* [U] — **de·sir·ably** /dɪ'zaɪrəbli/ *adv*

¹**de·sire** /dɪ'zajɚ/ *vb* -**sired; -sir·ing** [T] 1 *somewhat formal* : to want or wish for (something) : to feel desire for (some-

thing • *Many people desire wealth.* • *He desired her approval more than anything.* • *I have always desired to go to France.* • *a desired effect/result* **2** : to want to have sex with (someone) • *She knew that men still desired her.* — **leave much to be desired** or **leave a lot to be desired** or **leave a great deal to be desired** — used to say that something is not very good at all or is not close to being good enough • *Your work leaves much to be desired.*

²**desire** *n* **1** a [U] : the feeling of wanting something • *an object of desire* [=something that people want to have] **b** [C] : a strong wish • *Both sides feel a real desire for peace.* • *They have a strong desire to have children.* **2** [C/U] : a feeling of wanting to have sex with someone • *sexual desire* **3** [C] : someone or something that you want or wish for • *He never achieved his desire.* [=never did the thing that he wanted to do] • *A good education was always her heart's desire.* [=something she wanted very much]

de-sir-ous /dɪˈzaɪrəs/ *adj, not before a noun, somewhat formal* : wanting or wishing for something very much • *consumers desirous of saving money* [=consumers who want to save money]

de-sist /dɪˈsɪst/ *vb* [I] *formal* : to stop doing something — often + *from* • *They were ordered to desist from using the symbol as a logo.* • *The court ordered the company to cease and desist from selling the photographs.*

desk /ˈdɛsk/ *n* [C] **1** : a piece of furniture that is like a table and often has drawers • *The people in the office were working quietly at their desks.* • *a desk lamp/calendar/chair* • *She left her desk job* [=the job that she did while sitting at a desk] *to become a farmer.* **2** : a place where people can get information or be served at an office, a hotel, etc. • *an information desk at an airport* • *the front desk at a hotel* **3** : the part of a company or organization that deals with a particular subject • *the television network's financial/foreign desk* [=department]

desk-top /ˈdɛskˌtɑːp/ *n* [C] **1** : the top surface of a desk **2** a : a computer that is designed to be used on a desk or table — called also *desktop computer* **b** : an area or window on a computer screen in which small pictures (called icons) are arranged like objects on top of a desk • *He created a new folder on his desktop.*

desktop publishing *n* [U] : the use of a computer to design and produce magazines, books, etc.

des-o-late /ˈdɛsələt/ *adj* **1** : lacking the people, plants, animals, etc., that make people feel welcome in a place • *a desolate landscape* **2** : very sad and lonely especially because someone you love has died or left • *desolate parents grieving over the death of their son* — **des-o-la-tion** /ˌdɛsəˈleɪʃən/ *n* [U] • *a scene of utter desolation* • *a state of desolation and despair*

¹**de-spair** /dɪˈspeɚ/ *n* [U] **1** : the feeling of no longer having any hope • *a cry of despair* • *She finally gave up in despair.* • *They were driven to despair.* **2** : some-

one or something that causes extreme sadness or worry • *He was the despair of his parents.*

²**despair** *vb* [I] : to no longer have any hope or belief that a situation will improve or change • *Don't despair.* • *a despairing cry/look* • *We had begun to despair of ever finding a house we could afford.* — **de-spair-ing-ly** /dɪˈsperŋli/ *adv*

despatch *Brit spelling of* DISPATCH

des-per-ate /ˈdɛspɚət/ *adj* **1** : very sad and upset because of having little or no hope • *As the supply of food ran out, people became desperate.* • *desperate cries for help* **2** : very bad or difficult to deal with • *a desperate situation* **3** : done with all of your strength or energy and with little hope of succeeding • *a desperate struggle to defeat the enemy* **4** : having a strong need or desire for something or to do something • *He is desperate for money.* • *She was desperate to prove that she was right.* **5** : very severe or strong • *They were in desperate need of food and water.* • *desperate measures* — **des-per-ate-ly** /ˈdɛspɚətli/ *adv* • *trying desperately to find a solution* • *desperately unhappy/poor*

des-per-a-tion /ˌdɛspəˈreɪʃən/ *n* [U] : a strong feeling of sadness, fear, and loss of hope • *She felt overcome by desperation.* • *They hired me out of desperation.* [=because they were desperate] • *Finally, in desperation, he tried to flee the country.*

de-spi-ca-ble /dɪˈspɪkəbəl/ *adj, somewhat formal* : causing strong feelings of dislike or hatred • *a despicable act of racism* — **de-spi-ca-bly** /dɪˈspɪkəbli/ *adv*

de-spise /dɪˈspaɪz/ *vb* -**spised**; -**spis-ing** [T] : to dislike or hate (something or someone) very much • *political enemies who truly despise each other*

de-spite /dɪˈspaɪt/ *prep* : without being prevented by (something) — used to say that something happens or is true even though there is something that might prevent it from happening or being true • *Despite* [=in spite of] *our objections, he insisted on driving.* • *She ran the race despite an injury.* — **despite yourself** : even though you do not want to • *Despite myself, I began to enjoy the movie.*

de-spon-dent /dɪˈspɑːndənt/ *adj, formal* : very sad and without hope • *She was despondent over/about losing her job.* — **de-spond-en-cy** /dɪˈspɑːndənsi/ *n* [U]

des-pot /ˈdɛspət/ *n* [C] : a ruler who has total power and who often uses that power in cruel and unfair ways — **des-pot-ic** /dɛˈspɑːtɪk/ *adj* • *a despotic ruler/government* — **des-po-tism** /ˈdɛspəˌtɪzəm/ *n* [U]

des-sert /dɪˈzɚt/ *n* [C/U] : sweet food eaten after the main part of a meal • *a chocolate dessert* • *We had ice cream and apple pie for dessert.*

de-sta-bi-lize *also Brit* **de-sta-bi-lise** /diˈsteɪbəˌlaɪz/ *vb* -**lized**; -**liz-ing** [T] : to cause (something, such as a government) to be unable to continue existing or working in the usual or desired way • *The economic crisis could destabilize the nation's currency.* — **de-sta-bi-li-za-**

tion also Brit **de·sta·bi·li·sa·tion** /diˌsteɪbələˈzeɪʃən, Brit diˌsteɪbəˌlaɪˈzeɪʃən/ n [U]

des·ti·na·tion /ˌdɛstəˈneɪʃən/ n [C] : a place to which a person is going or something is being sent ▪ a popular tourist destination ▪ The package reached its destination two days later.

des·tined /ˈdɛstənd/ adj, not before a noun **1 a** : certain to do or to be something ▪ The plan seems destined to fail. ▪ He was destined to be famous. **b** : certain to achieve or experience something ▪ a nation destined for greatness **2** : going or traveling to a particular place ▪ The ship was destined for New York.

des·ti·ny /ˈdɛstəni/ n, pl **-nies** **1** [C] : the things that someone or something will experience in the future ▪ He believed it was his destiny to be president. **2** [U] : a power that is believed to control what happens in the future ▪ She felt that destiny [=fate] had brought them together.

des·ti·tute /ˈdɛstəˌtuːt, Brit ˈdɛstəˌtjuːt/ adj **1** : extremely poor ▪ His business failures left him destitute. ▪ The charity provides food and clothing for the destitute. [=for very poor people] **2** formal + literary : without something that is needed or wanted ▪ a man destitute of wisdom — **des·ti·tu·tion** /ˌdɛstəˈtuːʃən, Brit ˌdɛstəˈtjuːʃən/ n [U]

de·stroy /dɪˈstrɔɪ/ vb [T] **1** : to cause (something) to end or no longer exist : to cause the destruction of (something) ▪ All the files were deliberately destroyed. **2** : to damage (something) so badly that it cannot be repaired ▪ The scandal destroyed [=ruined] his reputation.

de·stroy·er /dɪˈstrɔjɚ/ n [C] **1** : a small and fast military ship **2** : something that causes the destruction of something ▪ a destroyer of hope

de·struc·tion /dɪˈstrʌkʃən/ n [U] : the act or process of damaging something so badly that it no longer exists or cannot be repaired ▪ the destruction of documents/evidence ▪ **weapons of mass destruction** [=weapons that can destroy entire buildings, cities, etc.]

de·struc·tive /dɪˈstrʌktɪv/ adj : causing a very large amount of damage ▪ a very destructive storm ▪ destructive behavior ▪ destructive criticism [=harsh criticism that hurts someone] — **de·struc·tive·ly** adv — **de·struc·tive·ness** n [U]

des·ul·to·ry /ˈdɛsəlˌtori, Brit ˈdɛsəltri/ adj, formal **1** : not having a plan or purpose ▪ desultory conversation **2** : done without serious effort ▪ He made a desultory attempt to study.

de·tach /dɪˈtætʃ/ vb **1** [T/I] : to separate (something) from something larger ▪ Detach the upper part of the form and return it with your payment. ▪ The brush detaches from the vacuum cleaner for easy cleaning. **2** [T] : to separate (yourself) from someone or something ▪ It can be difficult to detach yourself from a bad relationship. — **de·tach·able** /dɪˈtætʃəbəl/ adj

de·tached /dɪˈtætʃt/ adj **1** : not influenced by emotions or personal interest ▪ a detached [=impartial] observer **2** : not

joined or connected ▪ The house has a detached garage.

de·tach·ment /dɪˈtætʃmənt/ n **1** [U] : lack of emotion or of personal interest ▪ She views the modern world with an air/sense of detachment. **2** [U] : the act, process, or result of separating something from a larger thing ▪ The form is perforated to make detachment of the bottom section easier. **3** [C] : a group of soldiers who have a special job or function ▪ A detachment of soldiers was called to assist the police.

¹de·tail /dɪˈteɪl, ˈdiːˌteɪl/ n **1 a** [C] : a small part of something ▪ Every/Each detail of the wedding was carefully planned. **b** [U] : the small parts of something ▪ the wooden box's fine carved detail ▪ The job requires attention to detail. ▪ She has a fine/good/keen eye for detail. [=she is good at noticing small but important things] **2 a** [C] : a particular fact or piece of information ▪ The article provides further details about the accident. **b** [U] : information about something or someone that is often specific or precise ▪ The book includes a wealth of detail on his early career. **3** [C/U] : a special job that is given to a soldier or group of soldiers ▪ They were assigned to (a) kitchen detail. — **go into detail** : to discuss or describe everything about something including the small or unimportant parts ▪ The newspaper reports went into (great) detail about his political background. — **in detail** : in a way that includes many details ▪ She explained in detail how they met.

²detail vb [T] **1** : to state particular facts or information about (something) ▪ She wrote a letter detailing her complaints. **2** US : to thoroughly clean (a car) in an attempt to make it look new ▪ He had his car detailed before he sold it. **3** formal : to choose (a person or group of people) to do a special job ▪ The officer was detailed to another unit.

de·tailed /dɪˈteɪld, ˈdiːˌteɪld/ adj : including many details : including a lot of information ▪ a detailed report/analysis/map

de·tain /dɪˈteɪn/ vb [T] **1** : to hold or keep (someone) in a prison or some other place ▪ They were detained by the police for questioning. **2** formal : to keep or prevent (someone) from leaving or arriving at the expected time ▪ We were detained [=delayed] for 15 minutes by a flat tire. — **de·tain·ment** /dɪˈteɪnmənt/ n [C/U]

de·tain·ee /dɪˌteɪˈniː/ n [C] : a person who is being kept in a prison especially for political reasons

de·tect /dɪˈtɛkt/ vb [T] : to discover or notice the presence of (something that is hidden or hard to see, hear, taste, etc.) ▪ The test is used to detect the presence of alcohol in the blood. — **de·tect·able** /dɪˈtɛktəbəl/ adj — **de·tec·tion** /dɪˈtɛkʃən/ n [U] ▪ methods of crime detection — **de·tec·tor** /dɪˈtɛktɚ/ n [C] ▪ a metal/smoke detector [=a device that detects the presence of metal/smoke]

de·tec·tive /dɪˈtɛktɪv/ n [C] **1** : a police officer whose job is to find information about crimes that have occurred and to catch criminals ▪ *a homicide detective* **2** : a person whose job is to find information about something or someone : PRIVATE INVESTIGATOR ▪ *She hired a detective to follow her husband.* — **detective** *adj, always before a noun* ▪ *detective work* ▪ *a detective novel/story*

dé·tente *or* **de·tente** /deɪˈtɑːnt/ *n [C/U] formal* : an ending of unfriendly or hostile relations between countries

de·ten·tion /dɪˈtɛnʃən/ *n [C/U]* **1** : the act of keeping someone in a prison or similar place ▪ *the detention of suspected terrorists* ▪ *detention camps/facilities/centers* ▪ *The protesters were held/kept in detention for six hours.* **2** : a punishment in which a student is required to stay at school after the rest of the students have left ▪ *He got (a) detention for being late to class.*

de·ter /dɪˈtɚ/ *vb* **-terred; -ter·ring** [T] **1** : to cause (someone) to decide not to do something ▪ *The new law should deter advertisers from making false claims.* **2** : to prevent (something) from happening ▪ *Painting the metal will deter rust.*

de·ter·gent /dɪˈtɚdʒənt/ *n [C/U]* : a powder or liquid that is used to clean clothes, dishes, etc. ▪ *laundry detergent*

de·te·ri·o·rate /dɪˈtɪrijəˌreɪt/ *vb* **-rat·ed; -rat·ing** [I] : to become worse as time passes ▪ *Her health continued to deteriorate.* ▪ *The disagreement deteriorated into a fight.* [=the disagreement got worse and eventually became a fight] — **deteriorated** *adj* ▪ *a badly deteriorated building* — **de·te·ri·o·ra·tion** /dɪˌtɪrijəˈreɪʃən/ *n [U, singular]* ▪ *(a) gradual deterioration of academic standards*

de·ter·mi·na·tion /dɪˌtɚməˈneɪʃən/ *n* **1** [U] : a quality that makes you continue trying to do or achieve something that is difficult ▪ *He has a lot of determination.* ▪ *We all respected her fierce determination to succeed.* **2** [C/U] *formal* : the act of finding out or calculating something ▪ *They were unable to make an accurate determination of the ship's position.* **3** [C/U] *formal* : the act of officially deciding something ▪ *determination of ownership*

de·ter·mine /dɪˈtɚmən/ *vb* **-mined; -min·ing** [T] **1 a** : to officially decide (something) especially because of evidence or facts ▪ *The new policy will be determined by a special committee.* **b** : to be the cause of or reason for (something) ▪ *The demand for a product determines its price.* ▪ *Cost was the determining factor in their decision.* [=was the reason for their decision] **2** : to learn or find out (something) by getting information ▪ *An autopsy will be performed to determine the cause of death.*

determined *adj* **1** *not before a noun* : having a strong feeling that you are going to do something and that you will not allow anyone or anything to stop you ▪ *She is very determined to succeed.* ▪ *We are determined that it will never happen again.* **2** : not weak or uncertain : having or showing determination to do something ▪ *a very determined opponent* ▪

a determined effort — **de·ter·mined·ly** *adv*

de·ter·mi·ner /dɪˈtɚmənɚ/ *n [C] grammar* : a word (such as "a," "the," "some," "any," "my," or "your") that comes before a noun and is used to show which thing is being referred to

de·ter·rence /dɪˈtɚrəns/ *n [U] formal* **1** : the act of preventing a particular act or behavior from happening ▪ *the deterrence of crime* **2** : the policy of developing a lot of military power so that other countries will not attack your country ▪ *nuclear deterrence*

de·ter·rent /dɪˈtɚrənt/ *n [C]* : something that makes someone decide not to do something ▪ *a crime deterrent* ▪ *They hope that the new law will be a deterrent against/to false advertising.* — **deterrent** *adj* ▪ *a deterrent effect*

de·test /dɪˈtɛst/ *vb [T] formal* : to dislike (someone or something) very strongly : HATE ▪ *Those two really seem to detest each other.* — **de·test·able** /dɪˈtɛstəbəl/ *adj* ▪ *a detestable* [=contemptible, despicable] *villain* — **de·test·ably** /dɪˈtɛstəbli/ *adv*

de·throne /dɪˈθroʊn/ *vb* **-throned; -thron·ing** [T] : to remove (a king or queen) from power ▪ *(figurative) Last year's champion was dethroned in the first round of the play-offs.*

det·o·nate /ˈdɛtnˌeɪt/ *vb* **-nat·ed; -nat·ing** [T/I] : to explode or to cause (something, such as a bomb) to explode ▪ *The first atomic bomb was detonated in 1945.* — **det·o·na·tion** /ˌdɛtnˈeɪʃən/ *n [C/U]*

det·o·na·tor /ˈdɛtnˌeɪtɚ/ *n [C]* : a device that is used to make a bomb explode

¹de·tour /ˈdiːˌtʊɚ/ *n [C]* **1** : the act of going or traveling to a place along a way that is different from the usual or planned way ▪ *an unexpected detour* ▪ *We had to make a detour around the heaviest traffic.* ▪ *We took a detour from the main streets.* ▪ *(figurative) After teaching for many years, he made a brief detour into professional cooking.* [=he worked as a cook for a short period of time] **2** *US* : a road, highway, etc., that you travel on when the usual way of traveling cannot be used ▪ *The road is closed ahead, so traffic will have to follow the detour.*

²detour *vb, US* **1** [I] : to go along a way that is different from and usually longer than the usual or planned way ▪ *We detoured around the heaviest traffic.* **2** [T] : to make (someone or something) go in a direction that is not planned or expected ▪ *Traffic was detoured to 72nd Street.* ▪ *(figurative) Her athletic career was detoured by a series of injuries.*

de·tox /ˈdiːˌtɑːks/ *n [C/U] informal* : special treatment that helps a person to stop using drugs or alcohol ▪ *He spent one week in detox.* ▪ *a detox center/clinic/program*

de·tract /dɪˈtrækt/ *vb* — **detract from** [*phrasal vb*] *formal* : to reduce the strength, value, or importance of (something) ▪ *The scandal could seriously detract from her chances for reelection.*

de·trac·tor /dɪˈtræktɚ/ *n [C] formal* : a person who criticizes something or someone ▪ *Even her detractors admit that she made the company successful.*

det·ri·ment /ˈdɛtrəmənt/ n [C/U] formal : something that will cause damage or injury to something or someone ▪ *The new regulations are a detriment to progress.* ▪ *He works long hours, to the detriment of* [=in a way that is harmful to] *his personal life.* — **det·ri·men·tal** /ˌdɛtrəˈmɛntl̩/ adj ▪ *the detrimental* [=harmful] *effects of overeating* — **det·ri·men·tal·ly** adv

deuce /ˈduːs, Brit ˈdjuːs/ n 1 [C] chiefly US, informal : a playing card that has the number two on it or two symbols on it ▪ *a pair of deuces* 2 [C/U] tennis : a situation in which each side has a score of 40 ▪ *The score is deuce.*

de·val·ue /diˈvælju/ vb -ued; -u·ing 1 [T/I] finance : to lower the value of a country's money so that it is worth less when it is traded with another country's money ▪ *Economic woes forced the government to devalue (its currency).* 2 [T] : to cause (something or someone) to seem or to be less valuable or important ▪ *a culture that devalues the importance of education* — **de·val·u·a·tion** /diˌvæljəˈweɪʃən/ n [C/U]

dev·as·tate /ˈdɛvəˌsteɪt/ vb -tat·ed; -tat·ing [T] 1 : to cause great damage or harm to (something) ▪ *The flood devastated the town.* 2 : to cause (someone) to feel extreme emotional pain ▪ *She was devastated by the breakup of her marriage.* — **devastating** adj ▪ *a devastating flood/loss* ▪ *The movie is a devastating satire of the current political scene.* — **dev·as·ta·tion** /ˌdɛvəˈsteɪʃən/ n [U]

de·vel·op /dɪˈvɛləp/ vb 1 [T/I] : to grow or to cause (something) to grow or become bigger or more advanced ▪ *She's exercising to develop her muscles.* ▪ *The course is designed to develop your writing skills.* ▪ *The town eventually developed into a city.* 2 [T] : to create (something) over a period of time ▪ *Scientists are developing a treatment for the disease.* 3 [T] : to make (an idea, argument, theory, etc.) easier to understand by giving more information ▪ *He develops the concept/theory more fully in his book.* 4 [I] : to gradually begin to exist ▪ *A dangerous situation is developing.* 5 [T] : to gradually begin to have (something) ▪ *She developed an interest in music when she was young.* 6 [T] : to begin to suffer from or be affected by (an illness, problem, etc.) ▪ *people who develop cancer late in life* ▪ *The pipe developed a leak.* 7 [I] chiefly US : to become known or understood ▪ *It eventually developed that he had forgotten to mail the package.* 8 [T] : to build houses or other buildings on (land) ▪ *A builder wants to develop the land along the river.* 9 [T] : to make a photograph from film by using special chemicals and a special process ▪ *Did you get the film/pictures developed yet?* — **de·vel·oped** /dɪˈvɛləpt/ adj ▪ *developed countries/nations* [=countries/nations that have many industries and relatively few poor people] ▪ *a highly developed sense of smell* [=a very strong sense of smell] — **de·vel-**

op·ing /dɪˈvɛləpɪŋ/ adj ▪ *international programs to assist developing countries/ nations* [=countries/nations that have few industries and many poor people]

de·vel·op·er /dɪˈvɛləpɚ/ n 1 [C] : a person or company that builds and sells houses or other buildings on a piece of land ▪ *a real estate developer* 2 [C] : a person or company that creates computer software ▪ *a software developer* 3 [U] : a chemical that is used to develop photographs

de·vel·op·ment /dɪˈvɛləpmənt/ n 1 [U] : the act or process of developing or of causing something to develop ▪ *Good nutrition is important for proper muscle development.* ▪ *economic development* [=growth] ▪ *The software is still in the early stages of development.* ▪ *The company is working on (the) development of a new method for recycling old tires.* ▪ *chemicals used for the development of film* ▪ *The new system is still under development.* [=being developed] ▪ *She has several projects in development.* 2 [C] : something that has happened or has become known ▪ *Have there been any new developments in the case?* 3 [C] : an area of land with buildings that were all built at around the same time ▪ *commercial and industrial developments* — see also HOUSING DEVELOPMENT — **de·vel·op·men·tal** /diˌvɛləpˈmɛntl̩/ adj ▪ *developmental processes/problems* — **de·vel·op·men·tal·ly** adv ▪ *a developmentally disabled child* [=a child who is not able to develop in the normal way because of a physical or mental problem]

de·vi·ant /ˈdiːvijənt/ adj : different from what is considered to be normal or morally correct ▪ *deviant behavior* — **de·vi·ance** /ˈdiːvijəns/ also **de·vi·an·cy** /ˈdiːvijənsi/ n [U] ▪ *sexual deviance* — **deviant** n [C] ▪ *a sexual deviant*

de·vi·ate /ˈdiːviˌeɪt/ vb -at·ed; -at·ing [I] : to do something that is different or to be different from what is usual or expected ▪ *He almost never deviates from his usual routine.*

de·vi·a·tion /ˌdiːviˈeɪʃən/ n 1 [C/U] : an action, behavior, or condition that is different from what is usual or expected ▪ *There have been slight deviations in the satellite's orbit.* ▪ *a deviation from his usual routine* 2 [C] technical : the difference between the average of a group of numbers and a particular number in that group

de·vice /dɪˈvaɪs/ n [C] 1 : an object, machine, or piece of equipment that has been made for some special purpose ▪ *mechanical/electronic devices* ▪ *a hidden recording device* 2 : a weapon that explodes ▪ *an explosive device* [=a bomb] 3 : something that is done or used in order to achieve a particular effect ▪ *a marketing device* ▪ *He is known for his use of irony and other literary devices.* — **leave you to your own devices** ◇ If someone **leaves you to your own devices** or you are **left to your own devices**, you are allowed to do what you want or what you are able to do without being controlled or helped by anyone else. ▪ *The* *students were left to their own devices when the teacher failed to appear on time.*

dev·il /'dɛvl/ *n* **1 a** *the Devil* : the most powerful spirit of evil in Christianity, Judaism, and Islam who is often represented as the ruler of hell **b** [C] : an evil spirit ▪ *an imaginary world haunted by ghosts and devils* **2** [C] *informal* **a** : a person who does bad things or causes trouble usually in a way that is not too serious ▪ *She is a tricky little devil, so be careful.* **b** : a person who is lucky, unlucky, etc. ▪ *The poor devil broke his leg.* ▪ *a lucky devil* **3** *the devil informal* — used to make a statement or question more forceful ▪ *Where the devil have you been?* **4** [*singular*] *informal* : something that is very difficult or that causes a lot of trouble ▪ *It's a devil of a problem.* [=a very difficult problem] ▪ *He had a devil of a time getting another job.* [=he found it very difficult to get another job] —
like the devil informal **1** : very much ▪ *It hurts like the devil.* **2** : with a lot of energy and speed ▪ *He ran like the devil.* [=very fast] — *speak/talk of the devil informal* — used in speech to say that someone you have been talking about has unexpectedly appeared ▪ *"Well, speak of the devil! We were just talking about you!"*

dev·iled (*US*) *or Brit* **dev·illed** /'dɛvld/ *adj, always before a noun* : spicy or highly seasoned ▪ *deviled eggs/ham*

dev·il·ish /'dɛvlɪʃ/ *adj* **1** : evil and cruel ▪ *a devilish villain* **2** : showing a desire to cause trouble but in a way that is not serious ▪ *She was attracted by his devilish charm.* — **dev·il·ish·ly** /'dɛvlɪʃli/ *adv* ▪ *a devilishly cruel villain* ▪ *a devilishly* [=very] *hard/difficult problem*

dev·il-may-care /ˌdɛvlˌmeɪˈkeə/ *adj* : relaxed and without worry ▪ *a devil-may-care attitude*

devil's advocate *n* [C] : a person who expresses an opinion that disagrees with others so that there will be an interesting discussion about some issue ▪ *Teachers often play devil's advocate in the classroom.*

de·vi·ous /'diːvijəs/ *adj* : willing to lie and trick people in order to get what is wanted ▪ *a dishonest and devious politician* ▪ *devious* [=dishonest, deceptive] *methods/tricks* — **de·vi·ous·ly** *adv* — **de·vi·ous·ness** *n* [U]

de·vise /dɪˈvaɪz/ *vb* **-vised; -vis·ing** [T] : to invent or plan (something that is difficult or complicated) ▪ *They have devised a new method for converting sunlight into electricity.*

de·void /dɪˈvɔɪd/ *adj* — **devoid of** : completely without (something) ▪ *He is devoid of (any) ambition.* [=he has no ambition]

de·volve /dɪˈvɑːlv/ *vb* **-volved; -volv·ing** *formal* **1** [I] *chiefly US* : to gradually go from an advanced state to a less advanced state ▪ *The debate quickly devolved into an angry argument.* **2** [T/I] : to pass (responsibility, power, etc.) from one person or group to another person or group at a lower level of authority ▪ *Responsibility has (been) de-*

volved to/on/upon the individual teachers. **3** [I] : to be given to someone after the owner has died ▪ *Upon his death, the estate devolved to/on/upon a distant cousin.* [=a distant cousin inherited the estate]

de·vote /dɪˈvoʊt/ *vb* **-vot·ed; -vot·ing** — **devote to** [*phrasal vb*] **devote (something) to** : to use (time, money, energy, attention, etc.) for (something) ▪ *They devote an hour every day to worship.* ▪ *Some of the money they raise will be devoted to repairing the church's roof.* = *He devoted his lifetime to helping the poor.* = *He devoted himself to helping the poor.* [=he used his time, energy, etc., to help the poor]

devoted *adj* : having strong love or loyalty for something or someone ▪ *devoted fans* ▪ *He remains devoted to his wife.* — **de·vot·ed·ly** *adv*

dev·o·tee /ˌdɛvəˈvoʊˈtiː/ *n* [C] : a person who enjoys or is interested in something very much ▪ *jazz devotees* ▪ *a devotee of the arts*

de·vo·tion /dɪˈvoʊʃən/ *n* **1** [*singular*] : a feeling of strong love or loyalty ▪ *I admire his devotion to his wife.* ▪ *devotion to duty* **2** [U] : the use of time, money, energy, etc., for a particular purpose ▪ *The project required the devotion of a great deal of time.* **3** [*plural*] : prayer, worship, or other religious activities that are done in private rather than in a religious service ▪ *daily devotions*

de·vo·tion·al /dɪˈvoʊʃənl/ *adj* : relating to or used in religious services ▪ *devotional music/literature*

de·vour /dɪˈvawə/ *vb* [T] **1** : to quickly eat all of (something) especially in a way that shows that you are very hungry ▪ *He devoured everything on his plate.* ▪ *(figurative) She devoured* [=eagerly read] *every golf magazine she could find.* **2** : to destroy (something) completely ▪ *The forest was devoured* [=consumed] *by fire.*

de·vout /dɪˈvaʊt/ *adj* **1** : deeply religious ▪ *They are devout Catholics.* **2** : very loyal to a particular belief, organization, etc. ▪ *I'm a devout believer in the value of a good education.* ▪ *devout fans* — **de·vout·ly** *adv*

dew /'duː, *Brit* 'djuː/ *n* [U] : drops of water that form outside at night on grass, trees, etc. — **dewy** /'duːwi, *Brit* 'djuːwi/ *adj* ▪ *a dewy meadow*

dex·ter·i·ty /dɛkˈsterəti/ *n* [U] **1 a** : the ability to use your hands skillfully ▪ *The job requires manual dexterity.* **b** : the ability to easily move in a way that is graceful ▪ *The amazing dexterity of the acrobat.* **2** *formal* : the ability to think and act quickly and cleverly ▪ *verbal/political dexterity*

dex·ter·ous *also* **dex·trous** /'dɛkstrəs/ *adj, formal* : having or showing great skill or cleverness ▪ *They praised her dexterous handling of the crisis.* ▪ *a dexterous maneuver* — **dex·ter·ous·ly** *also* **dex·trous·ly** *adv*

DH /ˌdiːˈeɪtʃ/ *n, pl* **DHs** [C] : **DESIGNATED HITTER**

di·a·be·tes /ˌdajəˈbiːtiz/ *n* [U] : a serious disease in which the body cannot properly control the amount of sugar in your blood because it does not have enough insulin

di·a·bet·ic /ˌdajəˈbɛtɪk/ adj : affected with diabetes or caused by diabetes ▪ diabetic patients ▪ a diabetic coma — **diabetic** n [C] ▪ He's a diabetic. [=a person who has diabetes]

di·a·bol·i·cal /ˌdajəˈbɑːlɪkəl/ also **di·a·bol·ic** /ˌdajəˈbɑːlɪk/ adj : extremely evil ▪ a diabolical plot to overthrow the government — **di·a·bol·i·cal·ly** /ˌdajəˈbɑːlɪkli/ adv ▪ a diabolically clever plan

di·ag·nose /ˈdajəɡˌnoʊs/ vb **-nosed; -nos·ing** [T] 1 : to recognize a disease, illness, etc., by examining someone ▪ The doctor was unable to diagnose her illness. ▪ The tumor was diagnosed as benign. ▪ She was diagnosed as having cancer. = She was diagnosed with cancer. 2 : to find the cause of (a problem) ▪ The mechanic diagnosed the problem as a faulty spark plug.

di·ag·no·sis /ˌdajəɡˈnoʊsəs/ n, pl **-no·ses** /ˌdajəɡˈnoʊˌsiːz/ 1 [U] : the act of identifying a disease, illness, or problem by examining someone or something ▪ The unusual symptoms made accurate diagnosis difficult. 2 [C] : a statement or conclusion that describes the reason for a disease, illness, or problem ▪ The diagnosis was a mild concussion. — **di·ag·nos·tic** /ˌdajəɡˈnɑːstɪk/ adj, technical ▪ a diagnostic test/tool

di·ag·o·nal /daɪˈæɡənl/ adj 1 of a straight line : joining two opposite corners of a shape (such as a square or rectangle) especially by crossing the center point of the shape ▪ a diagonal line 2 : not going straight across or up and down ▪ a diagonal pattern — **diagonal** n [C] ▪ Slice the vegetables on a/the diagonal. — **di·ag·o·nal·ly** adv

[1]**di·a·gram** /ˈdajəˌɡræm/ n [C] : a drawing that explains or shows the parts of something ▪ a diagram of the nervous system — **di·a·gram·mat·ic** /ˌdajəɡrəˈmætɪk/ adj

[2]**diagram** vb **-grammed** or **-gramed; -gram·ming** or **-gram·ing** [T] US : to show or explain (something) in a diagram ▪ The coach diagrammed the new play on the blackboard.

[1]**di·al** /ˈdajəl/ n [C] 1 a : the part of a clock or watch that has the numbers on it b : the part of a piece of equipment that shows the measurement of something with a moving piece (such as a needle) that points to a number ▪ the dial of a pressure gauge 2 : a round part that you turn on a piece of equipment: such as a : a round control on a radio or television that you use to select a station, change the volume, etc. ▪ a radio dial b : a round part of some telephones that you move to select numbers

[2]**dial** vb, US **di·aled** or Brit **di·alled;** US **di·al·ing** or Brit **di·al·ling** [T] 1 : to select (a series of numbers) on a telephone by turning a dial or pushing buttons ▪ I must have dialed the wrong number. 2 : to make a telephone call to (a person, business, etc.) ▪ She dialed her office when she got home.

di·a·lect /ˈdajəˌlɛkt/ n [C/U] : a form of a

language that is spoken in a particular area ▪ They speak a southern dialect of French. ▪ They were speaking in dialect. — **di·a·lec·tal** /ˌdajəˈlɛktl/ adj

dialling code n [C] Brit : AREA CODE

di·a·logue also US **di·a·log** /ˈdajəˌlɑːɡ/ n 1 [C/U] : the things that are said by the characters in a story, movie, play, etc. ▪ a book with clever dialogue 2 formal a [C/U] : a discussion or series of discussions that two groups or countries have in order to end a disagreement ▪ The two sides in the dispute are trying to establish a dialogue. b [C] : a conversation between two or more people ▪ They had a lengthy dialogue [=talk] about her plans.

dial tone n [C] US : the sound that comes from a telephone when it is ready for a call to be made — called also (Brit) dialling tone

di·al·y·sis /daɪˈæləsəs/ n [U] medical : the process of removing some of a person's blood, cleaning it, and then returning it to the person's body ◆ People usually receive dialysis when they have damaged kidneys.

di·am·e·ter /daɪˈæmətə/ n 1 [C] : a straight line from one side of something (such as a circle) to the other side that passes through the center point 2 [C/U] : the distance through the center of something from one side to the other ▪ a pipe with a diameter of two inches ▪ a hole that's two feet deep and three feet in diameter

di·a·met·ri·cal·ly /ˌdajəˈmɛtrɪkli/ adv : completely or entirely ▪ His position on the issue is diametrically opposed to mine. [=is the exact opposite of mine]

di·a·mond /ˈdaɪmənd/ n 1 [C/U] : a very hard usually colorless stone that is a form of carbon and is used especially in jewelry ▪ a necklace studded with diamonds and rubies ▪ a diamond mine/ring 2 [C] : a shape that is formed by four equal straight lines and that has two opposite angles that are smaller than a right angle and two opposite angles that are larger than a right angle 3 a [C] : a playing card that is marked with a red diamond shape b [plural] : the suit in a deck of playing cards that is marked by red diamond shapes ▪ the queen of diamonds 4 [C] a : the part of a baseball field that includes the area within and around the three bases and home plate : INFIELD b : the entire playing field in baseball ▪ It's sad to see the town's old baseball diamond deserted.

diamond in the rough n [C] US 1 : a person who has talent or other good qualities but who is not polite, educated, etc. 2 : something that is in poor condition but that is likely to become more valuable with appropriate care or attention

di·a·per /ˈdaɪpə/ n [C] US : a piece of cloth or other material that is placed between a baby's legs and fastened around the waist to hold body waste ▪ disposable diapers — called also (Brit) nappy — **diaper** vb [T] ▪ diaper a baby

di·aph·a·nous /daɪˈæfənəs/ adj, formal — used to describe cloth that is very thin and light ▪ diaphanous fabrics

di·a·phragm /ˈdajəˌfræm/ n [C] **1** *medical* : a large flat muscle that separates the lungs from the stomach area and that is used in breathing **2** *technical* : a device that controls the amount of light passing through the lens of a camera **3** : a device shaped like a cup that is placed in the vagina to prevent pregnancy — called also (*Brit*) **cap** **4** *technical* : a thin disk that is used in microphones, telephones, speakers, etc., to help reproduce sound or make sounds louder

di·ar·rhea (*US*) *or chiefly Brit* **di·ar·rhoea** /ˌdajəˈriːjə/ n [U] : an illness that causes you to pass waste from your body very frequently and in liquid rather than solid form

di·a·ry /ˈdajəri/ n, pl **-ries** [C] : a book in which you write down your personal experiences and thoughts each day ▪ *She* **kept a diary** [=wrote regularly in her diary] *while she was traveling in Europe.* — **di·a·rist** /ˈdajərəst/ n [C] ▪ *a famous diarist*

di·a·tribe /ˈdajəˌtraɪb/ n [C] *formal* : an angry and usually long speech or piece of writing that strongly criticizes someone or something ▪ *The article is a bitter diatribe against mainstream media.*

dibs /ˈdɪbz/ n [*plural*] *US, informal* : the right to have or choose something ▪ *We stood in line for hours to* **get/have dibs** *on the best seats in the theater.*

¹**dice** /ˈdaɪs/ n, pl **dice** **1** [C] : a small cube that is made of plastic, wood, etc., that has one to six dots on each side, and that is used usually in pairs in various games ▪ *He threw/rolled the dice.* **2** [U] : a gambling game played with dice ▪ *They were* **shooting dice***.* **3** [C] : a small cube ▪ *Chop the onions into ¼-inch dice.* — **no dice** *US, informal* — used to say that something hoped for or wanted was not possible to do or to get ▪ *We hoped that tickets would still be available, but no dice, they were all sold.* — **roll the dice** *informal* : to do something that may have a good result or a bad result ▪ *They decided to roll the dice and start their own business.*

²**dice** vb **diced; dic·ing** [T] : to cut (food) into small cubes ▪ *He diced the potatoes and added them to the soup.* ▪ *a cup of diced carrots*

dic·ey /ˈdaɪsi/ adj **dic·i·er; -est** *informal* : involving a chance that something bad or unpleasant could happen : RISKY ▪ *Starting a business can be quite a dicey proposition.*

di·chot·o·my /daɪˈkɑːtəmi/ n, pl **-mies** [C] *formal* : a difference between two opposite things ▪ *Her essay discusses the dichotomy between good and evil in the author's novels.*

dick /ˈdɪk/ n, *informal + offensive* [C] **1** : PENIS **2** : a cruel, stupid, or annoying man

dick·er /ˈdɪkə/ vb [I] *chiefly US* : to talk or argue with someone about the conditions of a purchase, agreement, or contract ▪ *They spent hours dickering over the car's price.*

dicta *plural of* DICTUM

¹**dic·tate** /ˈdɪkˌteɪt/ vb **-tat·ed; -tat·ing** [T]

1 : to speak or read (something) to a person who writes it down or to a machine that records it ▪ *She dictated a letter to her secretary.* **2** : to say or state (something) with authority or power ▪ *They insisted on being able to dictate the terms of surrender.* **3** : to make (something) necessary ▪ *Our choice of activities will likely be dictated by the weather.* ▪ *Tradition dictates that the youngest member should go first.* — **dictate to** [*phrasal vb*] : to give orders to (someone) ▪ *I resent being dictated to by someone with half my experience.*

²**dictate** n [C] *formal* **1** : an order or direction given with authority ▪ *the dictates of the ruling party* **2** : a rule or principle that guides an activity, a person's behavior, etc. ▪ *the dictates of fashion*

dic·ta·tion /dɪkˈteɪʃən/ n [U] : the act of speaking words that someone writes down or that a machine records ▪ *He used a tape recorder for dictation.* — **take dictation** : to write down the words that someone says so that they can be used in a letter, report, etc. ▪ *Her secretary's very good at taking dictation.*

dic·ta·tor /ˈdɪkˌteɪtə/ n [C] : a person who rules a country with total authority and often in a cruel or brutal way ▪ *a country ruled by a military dictator* — **dic·ta·to·ri·al** /ˌdɪktəˈtorijəl/ adj ▪ *a dictatorial ruler/government* ▪ *dictatorial powers* ▪ *a dictatorial boss* [=a boss who acts like a dictator]

dic·ta·tor·ship /dɪkˈteɪtəˌʃɪp/ n **1** [U] : rule by a dictator ▪ *The country suffered for many years under his dictatorship.* **2** [C] : a government or country in which total power is held by a dictator or a small group ▪ *a military dictatorship*

dic·tion /ˈdɪkʃən/ n [U] **1** : the clearness of a person's speech ▪ *an actor with poor diction* **2** : the way words are used in speech or writing ▪ *The essay was full of careless diction.*

dic·tio·nary /ˈdɪkʃəˌneri, Brit ˈdɪkʃənri/ n, pl **-nar·ies** [C] : a reference book that contains words listed in alphabetical order and that gives information about the words' meanings, forms, pronunciations, etc.

dic·tum /ˈdɪktəm/ n, pl **dic·ta** /ˈdɪktə/ also **dic·tums** [C] *formal* : a statement or well-known remark that expresses an important idea or rule ▪ *A doctor must follow the dictum of "First, do no harm."*

did *past tense of* DO

di·dac·tic /daɪˈdæktɪk/ adj, *formal* : designed or intended to teach people something ▪ *didactic poetry*

didn't /ˈdɪdn̩t/ — used as a contraction of *did not* ▪ *I didn't know you were coming.*

¹**die** /ˈdaɪ/ vb **died; dy·ing** [I] **1 a** [I] : to stop living ▪ *She claims she's not afraid to die.* ▪ *More than a hundred people died* [=were killed] *in the crash.* ▪ *He died happy/young.* [=he was happy/young when he died] ▪ *She died a hero.* [=she died in a heroic way] ▪ *My uncle* **died of** *cancer.* ▪ *I almost died of embarrassment.* [=I was extremely embarrassed] ▪ *(figurative) Would you like some water? You must be* **dying of** *thirst.* [=you must

be very thirsty] **b** [T] : to have or suffer (a specified kind of death) • *He died a violent death.* **2** [I] *informal* : to wish very strongly *for* something or *to do* something • *I'm dying for a cold drink.* • *They were dying to leave.* **3** [I] **a** : to stop existing • *Her secret died with her.* **b** : to disappear gradually or become less strong • *The wind gradually died.* • *The echo slowly died away.* **4** [I] : to stop working or running • *The motor died.* — **die down** [phrasal vb] : to gradually become less strong • *She waited for the noise/wind to die down.* — **die hard** : to take a long time to die or end : to continue for a long time • *That kind of determination dies hard.* — **die laughing** *informal* : to laugh very hard • *If the guys hear about this, they're going to die laughing.* — **die off** [phrasal vb] : to die one after another so that fewer and fewer are left • *The remaining members of his family gradually died off.* — **die out** [phrasal vb] : to disappear gradually • *Many more species could die out completely* [=become extinct] *unless we do something.* — **to die for** *informal* : extremely desirable or appealing • *The apartment has a view to die for.* [=has a great view]

²**die** /'daɪ/ *n* [C] **1** *pl* **dice** /'daɪs/ : ¹DICE 1 • *Each player throws/rolls one die.* **2** *pl* **dies** /'daɪz/ : a tool that is used for cutting, shaping, or stamping a material or an object — **the die is cast** — used to say that a process or course of action has been started and that it cannot be stopped or changed • *Once we signed the contract, the die was cast.*

die–hard /'daɪˌhɑɚd/ *adj* : very determined or loyal • *die-hard fans* • *a die-hard conservative* — **die-hard** *n* [C] • *a bunch of conservative diehards*

die·sel /'diːzəl/ *n* **1** [C] : a vehicle (such as a truck or bus) that has a diesel engine **2** [U] : DIESEL FUEL • *Does your car take diesel or gasoline?*

diesel engine *n* [C] : a type of engine that uses diesel fuel rather than gasoline and that is used especially in trucks, buses, etc.

diesel fuel *n* [U] : a type of fuel that is used in vehicles with diesel engines

¹**di·et** /'daɪjət/ *n* **1** [C/U] : the food that a person or animal usually eats • *a balanced diet* • *Many birds live on a diet of insects.* • *studying the association between diet and disease* **2** [C/U] : the kind and amount of food that a person eats for a certain reason (such as to improve health or to lose weight) • *She lost weight through diet and exercise.* • *a low-fat diet* • *He's on a diet* [=he is eating less food or only particular kinds of food in order to lose weight] • *He went on a diet and lost 30 pounds.* **3** [singular] : something that is provided or experienced repeatedly • *We've been given a steady diet of political scandals in recent months.* — **di·e·tary** /'daɪjəˌteri, *Brit* 'daɪjətri/ *adj* • *dietary needs/deficiencies*

²**diet** *vb* [I] : to eat less food or to eat only particular kinds of food in order to lose weight • *I've been dieting for two months.* — **di·et·er** /'daɪjətɚ/ *n* [C]

³**diet** *adj, always before a noun* **1** : having a smaller number of calories than usual • *a diet soda* **2** : intended to help people lose weight • *diet pills*

di·e·ti·tian *or* **di·e·ti·cian** /ˌdaɪjə'tɪʃən/ *n* [C] : a person whose job is to give people advice about what to eat in order to be healthy

dif·fer /'dɪfɚ/ *vb* [I] **1** : to be different • *Their styles differ.* • *The new version differs significantly from the old one.* • *widely differing* [=different] *views/opinions* **2** : to have opinions that do not agree • *We differ (with each other) on/about/over how best to raise the money.* — **beg to differ** see BEG

dif·fer·ence /'dɪfrəns/ *n* **1** [U, singular] : the quality that makes one person or thing unlike another • *She knows the difference between right and wrong.* • *There's no difference between the two cars. They're exactly the same.* • *There's a striking difference in the sisters' looks.* [=they look very different from each other] • *The new version is supposed to be much better than the old one, but I can't tell the difference (between them).* [=they seem the same to me] **2** [C] : something that people do not agree about • *They've always had their differences.* [=they have always disagreed about some things] • *We need to find a way to resolve/settle our differences.* [=to stop disagreeing, arguing, etc.] • *There seems to be a difference of opinion* [=people disagree] *about what we should do next.* **3** [C] : the degree or amount by which things differ • *There's a big difference in price.* — **make a difference** **1** : to be important in some way • *Cost can make a difference in deciding on a college.* • *"When would you like to leave?" "It makes no difference (to me)."* [=I don't care] • *It would make a lot of difference if you came.* • *Your help made a big difference.* • *It makes very little difference.* [=it matters very little] **2** : to do something important that helps people or makes the world a better place • *She got into politics because she wanted to make a difference.* — **what's the difference?** **1** — used to ask how one thing is different from another • *"I like this one more than that one." "Why? What's the difference (between them)?"* **2** *or* **what difference does it/that make?** — used to ask why something is important or to suggest that something is not important • *What's the difference whether I go or not?*

dif·fer·ent /'dɪfrənt/ *adj* **1** : not of the same kind : partly or totally unlike • *The students come from (very) different backgrounds.* • *We need to try an entirely different approach.* • *Our house is different from the others on our street.* • *(US) The movie was different than I expected.* • *(Brit) Her dress is different to mine.* **2** *always before a noun* : not the same • *They met on several different occasions.* **3** : not ordinary or common : UNUSUAL • *That movie certainly was different.* — **dif·fer·ent·ly** *adv*

¹**dif·fer·en·tial** /ˌdɪfə'renʃəl/ *adj, always before a noun, formal* : relating to or based on a difference • *differential treat-*

ment — **dif·fer·en·tial·ly** adv

²**differential** n [C] **1** : a difference between people or things • *a small price differential* [=a small difference in price] **2** technical : a part of a vehicle that allows one wheel to turn faster than another when the vehicle is going around a curve — called also *differential gear*

dif·fer·en·ti·ate /ˌdɪfəˈrɛnʃiˌeɪt/ vb **-ated; -at·ing 1** [T] : to make (someone or something) different in some way • *Our excellent customer service differentiates us from our competitors.* **2** [T/I] : to see or state the difference or differences between two or more things • *We learned how to differentiate between different types of plants.* • *It's sometimes hard to differentiate one action movie from the others.* — **dif·fer·en·ti·a·tion** /ˌdɪfəˌrɛnʃiˈeɪʃən/ n [U]

dif·fi·cult /ˈdɪfɪkəlt/ adj **1** : not easy : requiring much work or skill to do or make • *an extremely difficult* [=hard] *test* • *a very difficult decision/choice* • *It's difficult to imagine why she would do that.* **2** : not easy to deal with or manage • *I'm in a difficult position/situation.* • *These changes will* **make life/things difficult** *for everyone involved.* **3** : not willing to help others by changing your behavior • *He was a difficult child.* [=he did not obey his parents] • *Why do you have to be so difficult?*

dif·fi·cul·ty /ˈdɪfɪkəlti/ n, pl **-ties 1** [U] : the quality of something that makes it hard to do • *He has difficulty reading without his glasses.* [=it is difficult for him to read without his glasses] ◇ If something can be done **with difficulty,** it is difficult to do. • *It was only with (great/considerable) difficulty that we were able to continue.* ◇ To do something **without difficulty** is to do it easily or without problems. • *I couldn't breathe without difficulty.* **2** [C] : something that is not easy to do or to deal with — usually plural • *serious economic/financial difficulties* • *This television station is experiencing technical difficulties.* [=is having technical problems]

dif·fi·dent /ˈdɪfɪdənt/ adj : not feeling comfortable or confident around other people • *He becomes diffident* [=shy] *around girls.* • *a diffident manner* — **dif·fi·dence** /ˈdɪfədəns/ n [U] — **dif·fi·dent·ly** adv

dif·fract /dɪˈfrækt/ vb [T] technical : to cause (a beam of light) to bend or spread • *Light is diffracted when it passes through a prism.* — **dif·frac·tion** /dɪˈfrækʃən/ n [U]

¹**dif·fuse** /dɪˈfjuːs/ adj : spread out over a large space • *a soft, diffuse light* • *diffuse pain* — **dif·fuse·ly** adv — **dif·fuse·ness** n [U]

²**dif·fuse** /dɪˈfjuːz/ vb **-fused; -fus·ing** [T/I] : to spread out throughout an area • *The heat from the radiator (was) diffused throughout the room.* • *an area of soft, diffused light* — **dif·fu·sion** /dɪˈfjuːʒən/ n [U]

¹**dig** /ˈdɪg/ vb **dug** /ˈdʌg/; **dig·ging 1** [T/I] : to move soil, sand, snow, etc., in order to create a hole • *They dug into the* sand with their hands. • *He dug a hole three feet deep.* = *He dug down three feet.* • *The prisoners dug a tunnel.* **2** [I] : to look for information about something • *They won't stop digging until they find out what happened.* **3** slang **a** [T] : to like or admire (someone or something) • *I really dig this music.* **b** [T/I] : to understand (someone or something) • *You dig me?* **c** [T] : to pay attention to or look at (someone or something) • *Hey, dig that hat.* **4 a** [I] : to reach for something • *She dug (around) in her purse for her keys.* **b** [T] : to put (your hand) into something • *He dug his hands into his pockets.* — **dig for** [phrasal vb] : to search for (something) by digging • *miners digging for coal* • (figurative) *The police have been digging for clues to help solve this murder.* — **dig in** [phrasal vb] **1 dig in** or **dig (yourself) in** : to dig a trench and take position inside it • *The soldiers dug (themselves) in and waited for the enemy to approach.* **2** informal : to begin eating • *Just grab a plate and dig in.* **3 dig in your heels** or **dig your heels in** : to behave in a stubborn way • *The salesman dug in his heels and refused to lower the price.* — **dig into** [phrasal vb] **1 a** informal : to begin eating (something) • *They dug into their steaks.* **b** somewhat informal : to try to find information by studying (something) • *The detectives were digging into his past.* **2 dig (something) into (something)** or **dig into (something)** : to push against (a body part) in a sharp and painful way • *Her fingernails dug into my hand.* = *She dug her fingernails into my hand.* — **dig out** [phrasal vb] **dig (something) out** or **dig out (something)** : to get or uncover (something) by digging or searching • *We had to dig the car out (of the snow) after the storm.* • *I dug some old books out of the attic.* — **dig up** [phrasal vb] **dig up (something)** or **dig (something) up** : to uncover or find (something) by digging • *They dug up buried treasure.* • (figurative) *It took many months of research to dig up all the facts.*

²**dig** n **1** [C] : a push with a body part (such as your elbow) • *She gave me a dig* [=poke] *in the ribs to get my attention.* **2** [C] : a criticism or insult that is directed at a particular person or group • *Her comments were a sly dig at her former husband.* **3** [C] : a place where scientists try to find buried objects by digging • *archaeological digs* **4** [plural] US, informal : the place where someone lives • *her new digs in the city*

¹**di·gest** /daɪˈdʒɛst/ vb **1** [T/I] : to change (food that you have eaten) by a biological process into simpler forms that can be used by the body • *He has trouble digesting certain foods.* • *foods that digest easily* **2** [T] : to think over and try to understand (news, information, etc.) • *It will take me a while to digest this news.* — **di·gest·ible** /daɪˈdʒɛstəbəl/ adj

²**di·gest** /ˈdaɪˌdʒɛst/ n [C] : information or a piece of writing that has been made shorter • *a digest of the laws*

di·ges·tion /daɪˈdʒɛstʃən/ n [U] : the process by which food is changed to a simpler form after it is eaten • *She began to suffer from poor digestion as she grew older.* — **di·ges·tive** /daɪˈʤɛstɪv/ *adj* • *the digestive system of the body*

dig·it /ˈdɪʤət/ *n* [C] **1** : a written symbol for any of the numbers 0 to 9 • *a three-digit number like 507* **2** : a finger or toe • *She suffered several broken digits.*

dig·i·tal /ˈdɪʤətl̩/ *adj* **1** : showing the time with numbers instead of with hour and minute hands • *a digital watch/clock* **2** : of or relating to information that is stored in the form of the numbers 0 and 1 • *digital images/pictures* • *a digital recording* **3** : using or characterized by computer technology • *laptop computers and other digital devices* • *a digital camera* **4** : of or relating to the fingers or toes • *digital dexterity* — **dig·i·tal·ly** *adv*

dig·ni·fied /ˈdɪgnəˌfaɪd/ *adj* : serious and somewhat formal : having or showing dignity • *He looked very dignified in his new suit.* • *a dignified manner*

dig·ni·fy /ˈdɪgnəˌfaɪ/ *vb* **-fies; -fied; -fy·ing** [T] : to cause (something) to have a more serious and important quality • *She felt that formal clothing would help dignify the occasion.*

dig·ni·tary /ˈdɪgnəˌteri, *Brit* ˈdɪgnətri/ *n, pl* **-tar·ies** [C] : a person who has a high rank or an important position • *The dinner was attended by many foreign dignitaries.*

dig·ni·ty /ˈdɪgnəti/ *n* [U] **1** : a way of appearing or behaving that suggests seriousness and self-control • *She showed great dignity in defeat.* **2** : the quality of being worthy of honor or respect • *a country that cherishes freedom and human dignity* — **beneath your dignity** : not suitable for someone who is as important as you • *He thought washing dishes was beneath his dignity.*

di·gress /daɪˈgrɛs/ *vb* [I] : to speak or write about something that is different from the main subject being discussed • *If I can digress for a moment, I'd like to briefly mention her earlier films.* — **di·gres·sion** /daɪˈgrɛʃən/ *n* [C/U] • *The story is filled with humorous digressions.*

dike (*chiefly US*) *or chiefly Brit* **dyke** /ˈdaɪk/ *n* [C] **1** : a bank or mound of soil that is built to control water and especially to protect an area from flooding **2** : a long narrow hole that is dug in the ground to carry water : DITCH

di·lap·i·dat·ed /dəˈlæpəˌdeɪtəd/ *adj* : in very bad condition because of age or lack of care • *a dilapidated old building/neighborhood* — **di·lap·i·da·tion** /dəˌlæpəˈdeɪʃən/ *n* [U]

di·late /daɪˌleɪt/ *vb* **-lat·ed; -lat·ing** [T/I] : to become larger or wider • *The drug causes the blood vessels to dilate.* = *The drug dilates the blood vessels.* — **di·la·tion** /daɪˈleɪʃən/ *n* [U]

dil·a·to·ry /ˈdɪləˌtori, *Brit* ˈdɪlətri/ *adj, formal* **1** : causing a delay • *dilatory actions/tactics* **2** : slow to do something • *She tends to be dilatory about answering letters.*

di·lem·ma /dəˈlɛmə/ *n* [C] : a situation in which you have to make a difficult choice • *I don't know what to do; it's a real dilemma.* • *a moral dilemma* — **on the horns of a dilemma** see ¹HORN

dil·et·tante /ˈdɪləˌtɑːnt, ˌdɪləˈtænti/ *n* [C] : a person whose interest in an art or in an area of knowledge is not very deep or serious • *You can always tell a true expert from a dilettante.* — **dil·et·tant·ish** /ˈdɪləˌtɑːntɪʃ/ *adj* — **dil·et·tan·tism** /ˈdɪləˌtɑːnˌtɪzəm, *Brit* ˌdɪləˈtæntɪzəm/ *n* [U]

dil·i·gence /ˈdɪləʤəns/ *n* [U] : careful hard work : continued effort • *The reporter showed great diligence in tracking down the story.* — **dil·i·gent** /ˈdɪləʤənt/ *adj* • *a diligent worker* — **dil·i·gent·ly** *adv*

dill /ˈdɪl/ *n* [U] : an herb with leaves that are used in cooking and with seeds that are used in flavoring foods such as pickles — called also [U] *dill weed*

dill pickle *n* [C] : a pickle that is flavored with dill

dil·ly-dal·ly /ˈdɪliˌdæli/ *vb* **-dal·lies; -dal·lied; -dal·ly·ing** [I] *informal* : to move or act too slowly • *We need to stop dillydallying and get to work.*

di·lute /daɪˈluːt/ *vb* **-lut·ed; -lut·ing** [T] **1** : to make (a liquid) thinner or less strong by adding water or another liquid • *diluted wine* **2** : to lessen the strength of (something) • *The hiring of the new CEO diluted the power of the company's president.* — **dilute** *adj, technical* • *a dilute solution of acid* — **di·lu·tion** /daɪˈluːʃən/ *n* [C/U] • *lower dilutions of the medicine* • *There's been some dilution in the stock's value.*

¹**dim** /ˈdɪm/ *adj* **dim·mer; dim·mest 1** : not bright or clearly seen • *a dim [=dark] corner of the room* • *dim [=faint] lights/stars* • *a dim outline* **2** : not understood or remembered in a clear way • *a dim memory* **3** : not likely to be good or successful • *Prospects for a quick settlement of the strike appear dim.* • *(US) The industry faces a dim future.* **4** : not good or favorable • *She takes a dim view of human nature.* [=she believes that people are naturally bad] **5** *informal* : not intelligent : STUPID • *He can be pretty dim at times.* • *(US) He's a bit of a dim bulb* [=a stupid person] — **dim·ly** *adv* • *a dimly lit room* • *I dimly remember him.* — **dim·ness** *n* [U]

²**dim** *vb* **dimmed; dim·ming** [T/I] **1** : to make (a light) less bright or to become less bright • *Dim the lights.* • *The lights dimmed.* **2** : to make (something) less strong or clear or to become less strong or clear • *The latest setback has dimmed hopes of an early settlement.*

dime /ˈdaɪm/ *n* [C] : a U.S. or Canadian coin that is worth 10 cents — **a dime a dozen** *US, informal* : too common to be valuable or interesting • *Beautiful actresses are a dime a dozen.* — **on a dime** *informal* **1** : very quickly • *My new car can stop on a dime.* **2** : in a very small space • *turn on a dime*

di·men·sion /dəˈmɛnʃən/ *n* [C] **1** : the length, width, height, or depth of something • *She carefully measured each dimension of the room.* **2** : the amount or number of things that something affects or influences — usually plural ▪ *We underestimated the dimensions [=extent] of the problem.* **3** : a part of something ▪ *The social/political/religious dimensions of the problem must also be considered.*

dime store *n* [C] *US, old-fashioned* : a store that sells inexpensive goods — **dime–store** /ˈdaɪmˌstoɚ/ *adj, always before a noun, informal* ▪ *dime-store* [=cheap] *perfume*

di·min·ish /dəˈmɪnɪʃ/ *vb* **1** [T/I] : to become or to cause (something) to become less in size, strength, etc. ▪ *The passing years did nothing to diminish their friendship.* ▪ *The drug's side effects should diminish over time.* **2** [T] : to lessen the authority or reputation of (someone or something) ▪ *Nothing could diminish the importance of his contributions.* : to describe (something) as having little value or importance ▪ *I don't mean to diminish her accomplishments.* — **di·min·ish·ment** /dəˈmɪnɪʃmənt/ *n* [U]

di·min·u·tive /dəˈmɪnjətɪv/ *adj* **1** : very small ▪ *a diminutive actor* **2** *linguistics* : indicating small size ▪ *the diminutive noun "duckling".*

dim·mer /ˈdɪmɚ/ *n* [C] : a device that allows you to control the brightness of a light ▪ *a dimmer switch*

dim·ple /ˈdɪmpəl/ *n* [C] : a small area on a surface or a part of a person's body (such as the cheek or chin) that naturally curves in ▪ *She noticed his dimples when he smiled.* — **dim·pled** /ˈdɪmpəld/ *adj* ▪ *a dimpled chin*

dim·wit /ˈdɪmˌwɪt/ *n* [C] *informal* : a stupid person ▪ *a harmless dimwit* — **dim·wit·ted** /ˈdɪmˈwɪtəd/ *adj*

din /ˈdɪn/ *n* [*singular*] : a loud, confusing mixture of noises that lasts for a long time ▪ *It was hard to hear anything above/over the din in the restaurant.*

dine /ˈdaɪn/ *vb* **dined**; **din·ing** [I] *somewhat formal* : to eat dinner : to have the main meal of the day ▪ *We'll be dining at six o'clock.* ▪ *She likes to dine at/in expensive restaurants.* ▪ *We usually **dine in** [=have dinner at home] but sometimes on Saturday we **dine out**. [=have dinner in a restaurant]* — **dine on** [*phrasal vb*] : to eat (something) for dinner ▪ *We dined on pasta and fresh vegetables.* — **wine and dine** see ²WINE

din·er /ˈdaɪnɚ/ *n* [C] **1** : a person who is eating dinner in a restaurant ▪ *wealthy diners* **2** *chiefly US* : a small informal, and inexpensive restaurant that looks like a railroad car ▪ *a roadside diner*

di·nette /daɪˈnɛt/ *n* [C] : a small room or an area near a kitchen that is used for dining ▪ *The apartment includes a dinette.* ▪ *a cheap dinette set* [=a small dining table and chairs]

din·ghy /ˈdɪŋi/ *n, pl* **-ghies** [C] : a small boat that is often carried on or towed behind a larger boat

din·gy /ˈdɪndʒi/ *adj* **din·gi·er**; **-est** : dark and dirty : not fresh or clean ▪ *a dingy motel* ▪ *dingy colors* — **din·gi·ness** *n* [U]

dining room *n* [C] : a room that is used for eating meals

din·ky /ˈdɪŋki/ *adj* **din·ki·er**; **-est** *informal* **1** *US* : very small and not appealing ▪ *a dinky apartment* **2** *Brit* : small and appealing : CUTE ▪ *wearing nice shoes and dinky accessories*

din·ner /ˈdɪnɚ/ *n* **1** [C/U] : the main meal of the day ▪ *We had many pleasant dinners together.* ▪ *a steak/lobster dinner* ▪ *What's for dinner?* ▪ *dinner guests* ▪ *She hosted a **dinner party** [=a party at which dinner is served] at her apartment.* ▪ *the **dinner table** [=the table where people eat dinner]* ✧ *To go **out to dinner** is to have dinner at a restaurant.* ▪ *We haven't gone out to dinner in weeks.* **2** [C] : a usually large formal event at which dinner is eaten ▪ *Two hundred people attended his retirement dinner.* **3** [C] : a cooked and packaged meal that usually only needs to be heated before it is eaten ▪ *a frozen dinner*

dinner jacket *n* [C] : a jacket that is worn by men on formal occasions

dinner suit *n* [C] *Brit* : TUXEDO

din·ner·time /ˈdɪnɚˌtaɪm/ *n* [U] : the usual time for dinner ▪ *It's almost dinnertime.*

din·ner·ware /ˈdɪnɚˌweɚ/ *n* [U] *chiefly US* : plates, bowls, glasses, etc., that are used for serving and eating dinner

di·no·saur /ˈdaɪnəˌsoɚ/ *n* [C] **1** : one of many reptiles that lived on Earth millions of years ago **2** : someone or something that is no longer useful or current ▪ *The old factory is now a rusting dinosaur.*

dint /ˈdɪnt/ *n* — **by dint of** *formal* : because of (something) : by means of (something) ▪ *They succeeded by dint of hard work.*

di·o·cese /ˈdajəsəs/ *n* [C] : the area that is controlled by a bishop in a Christian church ▪ *a Catholic diocese* — **di·oc·e·san** /daɪˈɑːsəsən/ *adj*

di·ode /ˈdaɪˌoʊd/ *n* [C] *technical* : an electronic device that allows an electric current to flow in one direction only

¹**dip** /ˈdɪp/ *vb* **dipped**; **dip·ping 1** [T] **a** : to put (something) into a liquid and pull it out again quickly ▪ *He dipped the paintbrush into the paint.* ▪ *We dipped our toes in the water.* **b** : to move (something) into and out of something ▪ *He dipped his hand into his pocket and pulled out a key.* **2** [T] : to lift (liquid) out from a container ▪ *dipping water from a well* **3** [T/I] : to move downward ▪ *He dipped his head.* ▪ *The sun dipped below the horizon.* ▪ *The road dips over the hill.* **4** [I] : to decrease somewhat usually for a short time ▪ *The temperature could dip below freezing tonight.* **5** [T] *Brit* : to reduce the amount of light coming from (headlights) ▪ *Dip [=(US) dim] the car's headlights.* — **dip into** [*phrasal vb*] **1 a** : to take out an amount of money from (something) ▪ *They had to dip into their savings to pay for the repairs.* **b** : to use part of (something) ▪ *a company dipping into its pool of job applicants* **2** : to read parts of (something) in a casual or brief way ▪ *dip into a book of poetry*

²**dip** *n* **1** [C] : a brief swim ▪ *a quick dip in the pool* **2** [C] : a low place in a surface ▪ *a dip in the road* **3** [C] : a decrease that continues usually for a short time ▪ *a dip*

in prices **4** [C/U] : a sauce or soft mixture into which food (such as raw vegetables) may be dipped • *crackers and cheese dip* **5** [C] : an amount of something (such as food) that is taken by dipping into a container • *a dip of ice cream*

diph·the·ria /dɪfˈθɪrijə/ *n* [U] : a serious disease that makes breathing very difficult

diph·thong /ˈdɪfˌθɑːŋ/ *n* [C] *linguistics* : two vowel sounds joined in one syllable to form one speech sound • *The sounds of "ou" in "out" and of "oy" in "boy" are diphthongs.*

di·plo·ma /dəˈploʊmə/ *n* [C] : a document which shows that a person has finished a course of study or has graduated from a school • *a high school diploma*

di·plo·ma·cy /dəˈploʊməsi/ *n* [U] **1** : the work of maintaining good relations between the governments of different countries • *a career in diplomacy* • *international diplomacy* **2** : skill in dealing with others without causing bad feelings • *This is a situation that calls for tactful diplomacy.*

dip·lo·mat /ˈdɪpləˌmæt/ *n* [C] : a person who represents his or her country's government in a foreign country • *The President will be meeting with foreign diplomats.*

dip·lo·mat·ic /ˌdɪpləˈmætɪk/ *adj* **1** : involving the work of maintaining good relations between the governments of different countries • *Negotiators are working to restore full diplomatic relations.* • *a diplomatic career* **2** : having or showing an ability to deal with people politely • *We need to find a diplomatic way to say no.* — **dip·lo·mat·i·cal·ly** /ˌdɪpləˈmætɪkli/ *adv*

dip·per /ˈdɪpɚ/ *n* [C] : a large spoon with a long handle that is used for dipping liquids : LADLE — see also BIG DIPPER

dip·stick /ˈdɪpˌstɪk/ *n* [C] : a long, thin piece of metal with marks that are used to show how much of a fluid (such as motor oil) is in a container or an engine

dire /ˈdajɚ/ *adj* **dir·er; dir·est 1** : very bad : causing great fear or worry • *Even the smallest mistake could have dire consequences.* • *a dire emergency* • *The team found itself in dire straits.* [=in a very bad or difficult situation] **2** : describing or showing a very bad future • *a dire prediction/warning* **3 a** : requiring immediate action : very urgent • *dire necessity/need* **b** : very serious or extreme • *dire poverty*

¹di·rect /dəˈrɛkt/ *vb* **1** [T] : to cause (someone or something) to turn, move, or point in a particular way • *Lights were directed* [=aimed] *toward the paintings on the wall.* **2** [T] **a** : to cause (someone's attention, thoughts, emotions, etc.) to relate to a particular person, thing, goal, etc. • *Let me direct your attention to the book's second chapter.* • *He directed his anger at me.* **b** : to say (something) to a particular person or group • *I'd like to direct my opening comments to the younger members of the audience.* **3** [T] : to guide, control, or manage (someone or something) • *She's been chosen to direct the project.* • *We need someone to direct*

traffic. **4** [T/I] : to lead a group of people in performing or filming (a movie, play, etc.) • *She has directed over 20 films in her career.* • *She enjoys both acting and directing.* **5** [T] : to show or tell (someone) how to go to a place : to give (someone) directions • *Could you please direct me to the office?* **6** [T] *somewhat formal* **a** : to ask or tell (a person or group) *to do something* • *The judge directed the jury to disregard the attorney's comments.* **b** : to order (something) to be done — + *that* • *His will directed that the money be used to support local schools.* **7** [T] : to send (a letter, note, etc.) to a specified person or place • *The letter was directed to the company's president.*

²direct *adj* **1** : going the shortest distance from one place to another • *I found a more direct route to the city.* • *a direct* [=nonstop] *flight from New York to Los Angeles* **2** always before a noun : coming straight from a source • *direct sunlight* • *The coast was exposed to the direct force of the hurricane.* **3** always before a noun : connected or related to something in a clear way • *These problems are a direct result of poor planning.* • *The investigation began in direct response to the newspaper story.* **4** always before a noun : having no people or things in between that could have an effect • *This is a direct order from the General.* [=this order comes straight from the General] • *There's no direct evidence to support his claims.* • *direct knowledge/experience* **5** always before a noun : related in a line from your parent, grandparent, great-grandparent, etc. • *She's my direct ancestor.* • *a direct descendant of George Washington* **6** always before a noun : perfect or exact • *The word has no direct translation in English.* • *The building took a direct hit from an enemy plane.* **7 a** : said or done in a clear and honest way • *We need a direct answer. Are you coming or not?* **b** : speaking in a clear and honest way • *She has a very direct way of dealing with customers.* — **di·rect·ness** /dəˈrɛktnəs/ *n* [U]

³direct *adv* : in a direct way • *We flew direct* [=straight] *from Chicago to Paris.* • *It costs less if you buy it direct* [=directly] *from the manufacturer.*

direct current *n* [U] : an electric current that is flowing in one direction only — abbr. *DC*

di·rec·tion /dəˈrɛkʃən/ *n* **1** [C] : the course or path on which something is moving or pointing • *The army attacked from three different directions.* • *You're headed in the wrong direction.* • *The wind changed direction.* [=I've got a bad sense of direction.] [=I become lost frequently; I often don't know which way to go] • *The car was headed in the direction of* [=toward] *the stadium.* • *She started walking in my direction.* [=toward me] **2** [plural] **a** : a statement that tells a person what to do and how to do it • *Carefully read the directions* [=instructions] *before you begin the test.* **b** : instructions that tell you how to go to a place • *We had to stop to ask for directions to the beach.* **3** [U] **a** : control or management of someone or something ▪ *He was given overall direction of the program.* ▪ *Twenty-three employees work under her direction.* **b** : the act or process of directing a play, movie, etc. ▪ *The play's unusual direction demanded much from the actors.* **4 a** [*C*] : the way that something is progressing or developing ▪ *These discoveries have given a new direction to their research.* **b** [*U*] : a goal or purpose that guides your actions or decisions ▪ *Her life seemed to lack direction after she left school.* — **di·rec·tion·al** /də'rɛkʃ*ə*nl/ *adj* ▪ *directional signals* ▪ **di·rec·tion·less** *adj* ▪ *a talented but directionless musician*

di·rec·tive /də'rɛktɪv/ *n* [*C*] *formal* : an official order or instruction ▪ *They received a written directive instructing them to develop new security measures.*

¹di·rect·ly /də'rɛktli/ *adv* **1** : in a direct way ▪ *He refused to answer the question directly.* ▪ *The package will be sent directly to your home.* ▪ *The two accidents are directly related.* **2** : in a straight or direct line from a particular position ▪ *He sat directly across from me at the dinner table.* **3** : without delay ▪ *The second game followed directly* [=*immediately*] *after the first.* **4** *somewhat old-fashioned* : in a little while ▪ *We'll be leaving directly.* [=*soon*]

²directly *conj, Brit* : immediately after : as soon as ▪ *I came directly I received your message.*

direct object *n* [*C*] *grammar* : a noun, pronoun, or noun phrase which indicates the person or thing that receives the action of a verb ▪ *"Me" in "He likes me" is a direct object.* — compare INDIRECT OBJECT

di·rec·tor /də'rɛktɚ/ *n* [*C*] **1** : a person who manages an organized group of people or a part of an organization (such as a school or business) ▪ *the choir director* ▪ *The company will hire a new director of marketing.* **2** : one of a group of managers who control a company or corporation ▪ *executive/deputy/associate directors* ▪ *She's on the board of directors* [=a group of people who make decisions] *for a large corporation.* **3** : a person who directs a play, movie, etc. ▪ *She's considered one of the best young directors in Hollywood.* — **di·rec·to·ri·al** /də,rɛk'torijal/ *adj* ▪ *her directorial style/debut* — **di·rec·tor·ship** /də'rɛktɚ,ʃɪp/ *n* [*C/U*] ▪ *The company did well under her directorship.* [=while she was the company's director]

di·rec·to·ry /də'rɛktəri/ *n, pl* **-ries** [*C*] : a book that contains an alphabetical list of names of people, businesses, etc.; especially : PHONE BOOK

directory assistance *n* [*U*] *US* : a service that people can call to get the telephone number for a person or organization

dirge /'dɚdʒ/ *n* [*C*] : a slow song that expresses sadness or sorrow ▪ *a funeral dirge*

dirt /'dɚt/ *n* [*U*] **1** : earth or soil ▪ *mounds/piles of dirt* ▪ *a dirt road/floor* [=a road/floor with a hard dirt surface] **2** : a substance (such as mud or dust) that

makes things unclean ▪ *You've got some dirt on your face.* **3** *informal* : a person or thing that has no value ▪ *He treated me like dirt.* [=treated me very badly] **4** *informal* : information about someone that could harm the person's reputation ▪ *She's been spreading dirt about her ex-husband.* ▪ *He wrote his memoirs mainly to dish the dirt* [=spread harmful gossip] *on all his former lovers.* — **hit the dirt** see ¹HIT

dirt bike *n* [*C*] : a small motorcycle that is designed to be used on rough surfaces

dirt cheap *adj, informal* : very cheap or inexpensive ▪ *The tickets were dirt cheap.* — **dirt cheap** *adv* ▪ *I can get you a stereo system dirt cheap.*

dirt–poor /'dɚt'puɚ/ *adj, informal* : very poor ▪ *When I was growing up, my family was dirt-poor.*

¹dirty /'dɚti/ *adj* **dirt·i·er; -est** **1** : not clean ▪ *All my socks are dirty.* ▪ *dirty clothes/dishes* **2 a** : indecent and offensive ▪ *dirty language* — see also DIRTY WORD **b** : relating to sex in an indecent or offensive way ▪ *dirty movies/magazines/pictures* ▪ *dirty jokes* ▪ *He has a dirty mind.* [=he often thinks about sex] **3** : not fair or honest ▪ *He's a dirty player.* [=he cheats; he tries to hurt his opponents] ▪ *That was a dirty trick!* [=an unkind/unfair thing to do] **4 a** : very bad ▪ *War is a dirty business.* ▪ *a dirty lie/liar* **b** : likely to cause shame or disgrace ▪ *a dirty* [=*shameful*] *little secret* **5** : difficult or unpleasant ▪ *Why do I always get stuck doing the dirty work?* ▪ *Our boss isn't afraid to get her hands dirty.* [=do difficult or unpleasant work] **6** : showing dislike or anger ▪ *She gave me a dirty look.* — **dirt·i·ness** *n* [*U*]

²dirty *vb* **dirt·ies; dirt·ied; dirty·ing** [*T*] : to make (something) dirty ▪ *Take off your shoes to keep from dirtying the floor.* ▪ *Her fingers were dirtied with ink.*

³dirty *adv* **1** : in an unfair or dishonest way ▪ *He plays/fights dirty.* **2** : in an indecent or offensive way ▪ *talking dirty*

dirty laundry *n* [*U*] : private information that causes shame and embarrassment when it is made public ▪ *The company is trying to keep its dirty laundry from being aired/washed in public.* — called also **dirty linen**

dirty old man *n* [*C*] *disapproving* : an old man who is too interested in sex

dirty word *n* **1** [*C*] : an offensive word ▪ *a movie filled with dirty words* **2** [*singular*] : a word, subject, or idea that is disliked by some people ▪ *They regard "taxes" as a dirty word.*

dis *also* **diss** /'dɪs/ *vb* **dis·ses; dissed; dis·sing** [*T*] *US slang* **1** : to treat (someone) with disrespect ▪ *He got dissed by the other guys on the team.* **2** : to criticize (something) in a way that shows disrespect ▪ *Don't dis my car.*

dis- *prefix* **1** *in verbs* : to do the opposite of ▪ *disagree* **2** *in nouns* : opposite or absence of ▪ *disbelief* **3** *in adjectives* : not ▪ *disagreeable*

dis·abil·i·ty /ˌdɪsə'bɪləti/ *n, pl* **-ties** **1** [*C*] : a condition (such as an illness or an injury) that damages or limits a person's physical or mental abilities • *disabilities such as blindness and deafness* • *a program for children with disabilities* **2** [U] : the condition of being unable to do things in the normal way : the condition of being disabled • *It's a serious disease that can cause disability or death.* **3** [U] *US* : a program that provides financial support to a disabled person • *After he injured his back he had to quit his job and go* **on disability.**

dis·able /dɪsˈeɪbəl/ *vb* **-abled; -abling** [T] **1** : to cause (something) to be unable to work in the normal way • *disable an alarm* **2** : to make (someone) unable to do something (such as use part of the body) in the usual way • *He was disabled by the accident.* — **dis·able·ment** /dɪsˈeɪbəlmənt/ *n* [U] — **disabling** *adj* • *a disabling injury/condition*

disabled *adj* : having a physical or mental disability : unable to perform one or more natural activities (such as walking or seeing) because of illness, injury, etc. • *The organization is working to protect the rights of disabled veterans.* • *She's an effective spokesperson for the* **disabled.** [=for disabled people]

dis·abuse /ˌdɪsəˈbjuːz/ *vb* **-abused; -abus·ing** [T] *formal* : to show or convince (someone) that a belief is incorrect — *+ of* • *He offered to disabuse us of what he called our "cherished myths."*

dis·ad·van·tage /ˌdɪsədˈvæntɪdʒ/ *n* **1** [C] : something that makes someone or something worse or less likely to succeed than others • *This program has the disadvantage of being more expensive than the others.* • *She had the disadvantage of growing up in a poor community.* • *His lack of formal education* **put/placed him at a disadvantage.** [=made it harder for him to succeed] **b** : a bad or undesirable quality or feature • *There are advantages and disadvantages to the new system.* **2** [U] : loss, damage, or harm • *The deal worked to our disadvantage.* [=the deal was harmful to us in some way] — **dis·ad·van·ta·geous** /dɪsˌædˌvænˈteɪdʒəs/ *adj* • *They find themselves in a disadvantageous position.*

dis·ad·van·taged /ˌdɪsədˈvæntɪdʒd/ *adj* : lacking the things (such as money and education) that are considered necessary for an equal position in society • *economically disadvantaged groups/communities* • *protecting the rights of the* **disadvantaged** [=disadvantaged people]

dis·af·fect·ed /ˌdɪsəˈfɛktəd/ *adj, formal* : no longer happy and willing to support a leader, government, etc. • *disaffected voters* — **dis·af·fec·tion** /ˌdɪsəˈfɛkʃən/ *n* [U]

dis·agree /ˌdɪsəˈgriː/ *vb* **-agreed; -agree·ing** [I] **1** : to have a different opinion : to fail to agree • *I think that I should sell my car, but he disagrees.* • *They disagreed about the price.* • *We disagree on the best way to raise the money.* • *I strongly* **disagree with** *that statement.* *She disagrees with him on almost every subject.* **2** : to be different • *Two descriptions disagree.* [=they do not agree/match] **3** : to not be suitable for or

pleasing to someone • *Fried foods* **dis·agree with** *me.* [=make me feel unwell]

dis·agree·able /ˌdɪsəˈgriːjəbəl/ *adj* **1** : not pleasing : unpleasant or offensive • *a disagreeable taste/odor* • *Some of her duties are very disagreeable (to her).* **2** *of a person* : difficult to deal with : easily angered or annoyed • *I've never known her to be so disagreeable.* — **dis·agree·ably** /ˌdɪsəˈgriːjəbli/ *adv*

dis·agree·ment /ˌdɪsəˈgriːmənt/ *n* **1 a** [U] : failure to agree • *There's been a lot of disagreement about/on/over how best to spend the money.* • *He has expressed disagreement* [=he has said that he disagrees] *with the proposal.* **b** [C] : an argument caused by people having different opinions about something • *We've had a number of serious disagreements over the years.* **2** [U] : the state of being different or unalike • *There's considerable disagreement between the descriptions given by the two witnesses.*

dis·al·low /ˌdɪsəˈlaʊ/ *vb* [T] : to refuse to allow (something) • *The court disallowed* [=rejected] *their claim.* — **dis·al·low·ance** /ˌdɪsəˈlawəns/ *n* [U]

dis·ap·pear /ˌdɪsəˈpiɚ/ *vb* [I] **1** : to stop being visible • *The moon disappeared behind a cloud.* **2 a** : to stop existing • *These problems won't just disappear by themselves.* **b** : to become lost • *My car keys have disappeared.* [=I can't find them] • *He disappeared without a trace.* — **dis·ap·pear·ance** /ˌdɪsəˈpirəns/ *n* [C/U]

dis·ap·point /ˌdɪsəˈpɔɪnt/ *vb* [T/I] : to make (someone) unhappy by not being as good as expected or by not doing something that was hoped for or expected • *They disappointed their fans.* — **dis·ap·point·ed** /ˌdɪsəˈpɔɪntəd/ *adj* • *I am very disappointed that you didn't call.* — **dis·ap·point·ing** /ˌdɪsəˈpɔɪntɪŋ/ *adj* • *Dinner was disappointing.* — **dis·ap·point·ing·ly** /ˌdɪsəˈpɔɪntɪŋli/ *adv*

dis·ap·point·ment /ˌdɪsəˈpɔɪntmənt/ *n* **1** [U] : the state or feeling of being disappointed • *She couldn't hide her disappointment.* **2** [C] : someone or something that disappoints people • *The play was a (big) disappointment.*

dis·ap·prov·al /ˌdɪsəˈpruːvəl/ *n* [U] : the belief that someone or something is bad or wrong • *The plan met with disapproval.*

dis·ap·prove /ˌdɪsəˈpruːv/ *vb* **-proved; -prov·ing** [T/I] : to not approve of someone or something • *She married him even though her parents disapproved.* • *I disapproved of* [=I disagreed with] *their decision.* — **dis·ap·prov·ing** *adj* • *a disapproving look/frown* • *his disapproving parents* — **dis·ap·prov·ing·ly** *adv*

dis·arm /dɪsˈɑɚm/ *vb* **1 a** [T] : to take weapons from (someone or something) • *disarm a prisoner* **b** [I] : to give up weapons • *The terrorists have refused to disarm.* **2** [T] : to make (a bomb, mine, etc.) harmless • *disarm a bomb* **3** [T] : to make (someone) friendly or less suspicious • *He has a way of disarming his critics.*

dis·ar·ma·ment /dɪsˈɑɚməmənt/ *n* [U] : the process of reducing the number of weapons controlled by a country's military • *nuclear disarmament*

dis·arm·ing /dɪsˈɑɚmɪŋ/ *adj* : tending to remove any feelings of unfriendliness or distrust • *a disarming smile* — **dis·arm·ing·ly** *adv*

dis·ar·ray /ˌdɪsəˈreɪ/ *n* [*U*] : a confused or messy condition • *The room was in complete/total disarray.*

dis·as·sem·ble /ˌdɪsəˈsɛmbəl/ *vb* **-sem·bled; -sem·bling** [*T/I*] : to disconnect the pieces of (something) • *disassemble* [=*take apart*] *an engine* • *The bookshelf disassembles easily.*

dis·as·so·ci·ate /ˌdɪsəˈsoʊsiˌeɪt/ *vb* **-at·ed; -at·ing** [*T*] : DISSOCIATE

di·sas·ter /dɪˈzæstɚ, *Brit* dɪˈzɑːstə/ *n* 1 [*C*] : a flood, tornado, fire, etc., that happens suddenly and causes much suffering or loss to many people • *a natural disaster* [=a disaster (such as an earthquake) caused by natural forces] • *The new regulations could be a disaster for our business.* = *They could spell disaster for our business.* • *They're trying to find a way to avoid disaster.* **b** [*C*] : a complete or terrible failure • *The party was a disaster.*

disaster area *n* [*C*] 1 : an area where there has been a major disaster and where people can receive special help from the government (such as money to rebuild homes) • *The state was declared a disaster area after the hurricane.* 2 *informal* : a place that is very messy or dirty • *His office is a disaster area.*

di·sas·trous /dɪˈzæstrəs, *Brit* dɪˈzɑːstrəs/ *adj* 1 : causing great suffering or loss • *a disastrous fire* 2 : very bad or unfortunate • *The strike was economically disastrous.* — **di·sas·trous·ly** *adv*

dis·avow /ˌdɪsəˈvaʊ/ *vb* [*T*] *formal* : to deny that you know about, are responsible for, or are involved in (something) • *He disavowed the actions of his subordinates.* — **dis·avow·al** /ˌdɪsəˈvawəl/ *n* [*C/U*]

dis·band /dɪsˈbænd/ *vb* [*T/I*] : to end an organization or group (such as a club) • *They've decided to disband (the club).*

dis·be·lief /ˌdɪsbəˈliːf/ *n* [*U*] : a feeling that you do not or cannot believe or accept that something is true or real • *The reports were met with widespread disbelief.* [=many people did not believe the reports]

dis·burse /dɪsˈbɚs/ *vb* **-bursed; -burs·ing** [*T*] *formal* : to pay out (money) from a fund that has been created for a special purpose • *The government has disbursed millions of dollars in aid.* — **dis·burse·ment** /dɪsˈbɚsmənt/ *n* [*C/U*]

disc *or* **disk** /ˈdɪsk/ *n* 1 [*C*] : a flat, thin, round object • *a plastic disc* 2 **disk** [*C/U*] : a flat, thin, round object that is used to store large amounts of information (such as computer data) • *Insert the disk into the CD drive.* • *There isn't much disk space* [=room for storage on a computer disk] *left.* 3 **disc** [*C/U*] : CD • *I have that recording on disc.* 4 [*C*] *medical* : one of the flat, rubbery pieces that separate the bones of the backbone

dis·card /dɪsˈkɑɚd/ *vb* [*T*] : to throw (something) away because it is useless or unwanted • *Remove and discard the stems.* • *(figurative) Many of his theories have been discarded.* — **discard** *n* [*C*] • *a pile of discards*

disc brake *n* [*C*] : a brake that works by two plates pressing against the sides of a disc that is connected to the center of a wheel

dis·cern /dɪˈsɚn/ *vb* [*T*] 1 : to see, hear, or notice (something) with difficulty or effort • *We could just discern the ship through the fog.* 2 : to find out, recognize, or understand (something) • *The reasons for this change are difficult to discern.* — **dis·cern·ible** /dɪˈsɚnəbəl/ *adj* • *There is no discernible difference between them.* — **dis·cern·ibly** /dɪˈsɚnəbli/ *adv* — **dis·cern·ment** /dɪˈsɚnmənt/ *n* [*U*] • *His lack of discernment led to bad decisions.*

dis·cern·ing /dɪˈsɚnɪŋ/ *adj* : able to see and understand people, things, or situations clearly • *a discerning critic*

¹**dis·charge** /dɪsˈtʃɑɚdʒ/ *vb* **-charged; -charg·ing** 1 [*T*] : to allow (someone) to leave a hospital, prison, etc. • *She was discharged from the hospital today.* 2 [*T*] **a** : to end the employment of (someone) • *We had to discharge* [=*fire*] *several employees.* **b** : to end the service of (someone) in a formal or official way • *The judge discharged the jury.* 3 [*T/I*] : to shoot or fire (a weapon) • *discharging a firearm* • *The gun failed to discharge.* 4 [*T/I*] : to send out electricity, a liquid, gas, etc. • *discharging pollution into the lake* • *The electricity discharged safely.* • *discharge (electricity from) a battery* 5 [*T*] *formal* **a** : to do what is required by (something) • *discharge* [=*fulfill*] *an obligation* **b** : to pay (a debt) • *They failed to discharge their debts.*

²**dis·charge** /ˈdɪsˌtʃɑɚdʒ/ *n* 1 [*C/U*] : the release of someone from a hospital, prison, etc. • *The doctors approved her discharge.* 2 **a** [*C/U*] : the act of firing or dismissing someone from a job • *suing the company for wrongful discharge* **b** [*C*] : the act of ending a person's service to the military • *He was given a dishonorable discharge.* [=he did something wrong and was forced to leave the military] • *She received an honorable discharge.* 3 [*C/U*] : the act of firing a weapon • *(an) accidental discharge of a hunting rifle* 4 **a** [*C*] : a liquid or gas that flows out of something • *a clear discharge from the nose and eyes* **b** [*U*] : the movement of a liquid or gas from something • *the illegal discharge of pollution into a stream* 5 [*C*] : a flow of electricity • *an electrical discharge* 6 [*C/U*] *formal* : the act of doing what is required or of paying a debt • *the/a discharge of debts/obligations*

dis·ci·ple /dɪˈsaɪpəl/ *n* [*C*] 1 : someone who accepts and helps to spread the teachings of a famous person • *a disciple of Sigmund Freud* 2 : one of a group of 12 men who were sent out to spread the teachings of Jesus Christ

dis·ci·pli·nar·i·an /ˌdɪsəpləˈnerijən/ *n*

[C] : a person who is very strict about punishing bad behavior ▪ *a strict/rigid disciplinarian*

dis·ci·plin·ary /'dɪsəplə,neri, *Brit* 'dɪsəplənri/ *adj* : intended to correct or punish bad behavior ▪ *taking disciplinary action*

¹dis·ci·pline /'dɪsəplən/ *n* **1** [U] **a** : control that is gained by requiring that rules or orders be obeyed and punishing bad behavior ▪ *The teacher maintains discipline in the classroom.* **b** : a way of behaving that shows a willingness to obey rules or orders ▪ *The troops were praised for their dedication and discipline.* **c** : punishment for bad behavior ▪ *harsh discipline* **2** [U] : the ability to keep working at something that is difficult ▪ *It takes discipline to learn a musical instrument.* **3** [C] : an activity that is done regularly as a way of training yourself to do something or to improve your behavior ▪ *Keeping a journal is a good discipline for a writer.* **4** [C] : a field of study ▪ *academic disciplines*

²discipline *vb* **-plined; -plin·ing** [T] **1** : to punish (someone) as a way of making sure that rules or orders are obeyed ▪ *She was disciplined for misbehaving.* **2** : to train (yourself) to do something by controlling your behavior ▪ *I'm trying to discipline myself to eat less.* — **disciplined** *adj* ▪ *I'm not disciplined enough to exercise everyday.*

disc jockey *n* [C] : a person who plays popular recorded music on the radio or at a party or nightclub — called also *DJ*

dis·claim /dɪs'kleɪm/ *vb* [T] *formal* : to say that you do not have (something, such as knowledge, responsibility, etc.) ▪ *She disclaimed all responsibility for the accident.*

dis·claim·er /dɪs'kleɪmɚ/ *n* [C] : a statement that is meant to prevent an incorrect understanding of something ▪ *a disclaimer that the movie is not based on real events*

dis·close /dɪs'kloʊz/ *vb* **-closed; -closing** [T] : to make (something) known to the public ▪ *The victim's identity has not been disclosed.* — **dis·clo·sure** /dɪs'kloʊʒɚ/ *n* [C/U] ▪ *a series of shocking disclosures about his past* ▪ *full disclosure of the facts*

dis·co /'dɪskoʊ/ *n, pl* **-cos** **1** [C] : a nightclub where people dance to recorded popular music **2** [U] : a type of popular dance music

dis·col·or *(US)* or *Brit* **dis·col·our** /dɪs'kʌlɚ/ *vb* [T/I] : to change in color especially in a bad way ▪ *The stain discolored the rug.* — **dis·col·or·a·tion** /dɪs,kʌlə'reɪʃən/ *n* [C/U] ▪ *The medicine caused discoloration of his teeth.* — **dis·col·ored** /dɪs'kʌlɚd/ *adj* ▪ *discolored teeth*

dis·com·fit /dɪs'kʌmfət/ *vb* [T] *formal* : to make (someone) confused or upset ▪ *The governor was clearly discomfited* [=disconcerted] *by the question.* — **dis·com·fi·ture** /dɪs'kʌmfətʃɚ/ *n* [U]

dis·com·fort /dɪs'kʌmfɚt/ *n* **1** [C/U] : an uncomfortable or painful feeling in the body ▪ *The patient is experiencing discomfort.* **2** [U] : a feeling of being some-

what worried, unhappy, etc. ▪ *These developments are being watched with discomfort by many.*

dis·con·cert /,dɪskən'sɚt/ *vb* [T] : to make (someone) upset or embarrassed ▪ *I was disconcerted by her tone of voice.* — **dis·con·cert·ing** /,dɪskən'sɚtɪŋ/ *adj* ▪ *He has a disconcerting habit of answering a question with another question.* — **dis·con·cert·ing·ly** *adv*

dis·con·nect /,dɪskə'nɛkt/ *vb* [T] **1** : to separate (something) from something else ▪ *Disconnect the hose (from the faucet).* **2** : to stop or end the supply of electricity, water, gas, etc., to something ▪ *The alarm system had been disconnected.* ▪ *Before starting, disconnect the power supply.* **3** : to end the connection to a system, network, etc., through a telephone, computer, or other device ▪ *We were talking on the phone but got disconnected.* — **dis·con·nec·tion** /,dɪskə'nɛkʃən/ *n* [C/U]

dis·con·nect·ed /,dɪskə'nɛktəd/ *adj* **1** : not connected to something (such as a power source) ▪ *The phone lines are disconnected.* **2** : not having parts joined together in a logical way ▪ *a series of disconnected events/stories*

dis·con·so·late /dɪs'kɑːnsələt/ *adj, formal* : very unhappy or sad ▪ *Campaign workers grew increasingly disconsolate as the results came in.* — **dis·con·so·late·ly** *adv*

dis·con·tent /,dɪskən'tɛnt/ *n* [U] : a feeling of unhappiness or disapproval ▪ *public discontent with the current government* — **discontent** *adj* ▪ *Voters are growing increasingly discontent.* — **dis·con·tent·ed** /,dɪskən'tɛntəd/ *adj* ▪ *feeling discontented with work*

dis·con·tin·ue /,dɪskən'tɪnju/ *vb* **-tin·ued; -tin·u·ing** [T] **1** : STOP ▪ *The treatment has been discontinued.* **2** : to stop making or offering (a product, service, etc.) ▪ *They are planning to discontinue the current model.*

dis·cord /'dɪs,koɚd/ *n* [U] *formal* : lack of agreement between people, ideas, etc. ▪ *discord between political parties*

dis·cord·ant /dɪs'koɚdnt/ *adj* **1** : harsh or unpleasant in sound ▪ *discordant music* **2** : not agreeing or in harmony ▪ *bringing together a number of discordant elements*

dis·co·theque /,dɪskə'tɛk/ *n* [C] : DISCO 1

¹dis·count /'dɪs,kaʊnt/ *n* [C] : an amount taken off a price ▪ *a two percent discount* ▪ *We bought the tickets at a discount.* [=for less than the usual price]

²discount *adj, always before a noun* **1** : selling goods or services at reduced prices ▪ *a discount store/chain/retailer* **2** : offered or sold at a reduced price ▪ *discount tickets* **3** : cheaper than usual ▪ *discount prices/rates*

³discount *vb* [T] **1 a** : to lower the amount of (a bill, price, etc.) ▪ *a discounted price/rate* **b** : to lower the price of (a product) ▪ *They are discounting seasonal merchandise.* **2** : to think of (something) as having little importance or value • *You shouldn't discount the importance of studying.*

dis·cour·age /dɪˈskɚəʤ/ *vb* **-aged;** **-ag·ing** [*T*] **1** : to make (someone) less determined, hopeful, or confident • *Don't let him discourage you.* • *We were/got discouraged.* **2** : to make (something) less likely to happen or be done • *regulations that discourage investment* • *That type of behavior ought to be discouraged.* ❖ To **discourage (someone) from doing** (something) is to tell or advise someone not to do something. • *They discouraged her from going.* [=they told her why she should not go] — **discouraged** *adj* • *fans felt hopeless and discouraged* — **discouraging** *adj* • *another discouraging loss*

dis·cour·age·ment /dɪˈskɚəʤmənt/ *n* **1** [*U*] : the act of making something less likely to happen or of making people less likely to do something • *the discouragement of drug use among teenagers* **2** [*U*] : a feeling of having lost hope or confidence • *She expressed discouragement over the loss.* **3** [*C*] : something (such as a failure or difficulty) that discourages someone • *the discouragements of the past week*

dis·course /ˈdɪsˌkoɚs/ *n, formal* **1** [*U*] : the use of words to exchange thoughts and ideas • *public/political discourse* **2** [*C*] : a long talk or piece of writing about a subject • *an entertaining discourse on the film industry*

dis·cour·te·ous /dɪsˈkɚtijəs/ *adj, formal* : rude or impolite • *He was discourteous to me.*

dis·cov·er /dɪˈskʌvɚ/ *vb* [*T*] **1** : to see, find, or become aware of (something) for the first time • *Several new species have recently been discovered.* • *discover a solution* • *His life was never the same after he discovered sailing.* [=after he first went sailing; after he found how much he enjoyed sailing] **2** : to make (something) known • *The tests have discovered problems in the current design.* **3** : to learn or find out (something surprising or unexpected) • *I was surprised to discover that I had lost my keys.* **4** : to find out about and help (a talented new performer, writer, etc.) • *an agent who discovered many famous musicians* — **dis·cov·er·er** *n* [*C*]

dis·cov·ery /dɪˈskʌvəri/ *n, pl* **-er·ies** [*C/U*] : the act of finding or learning something for the first time • *Scientists announced the discovery of a new species of plant.* • *voyages of discovery* [=voyages done to discover and learn about new places, people, etc.] **2** [*C*] : something seen or learned for the first time • *recent archaeological discoveries*

dis·cred·it /dɪsˈkrɛdət/ *vb* [*T*] **1** : to cause (someone or something) to seem dishonest or untrue • *His theories have been discredited.* **2** : to damage the reputation of (someone) • *an attempt to discredit the governor* — **discredit** *n* [*U*] • *His crimes brought discredit upon/to/on his family.* — **dis·cred·it·able** /dɪsˈkrɛdətəbəl/ *adj* • *discreditable conduct*

dis·creet /dɪˈskriːt/ *adj* **1** — used to suggest that someone is being careful about not allowing something to be known or noticed by many people • *a discreet way to handle the problem* • *She is very discreet about her personal life.* **2** : not likely to be seen or noticed by many people • *I followed them at a discreet distance.* — **dis·creet·ly** *adv*

dis·crep·an·cy /dɪˈskrɛpənsi/ *n, pl* **-cies** [*C/U*] : a difference especially between things that should be the same • *There were discrepancies between their accounts of the accident.*

dis·crete /dɪˈskriːt/ *adj, formal* : separate and different from each other • *a number of discrete steps*

dis·cre·tion /dɪˈskrɛʃən/ *n* [*U*] **1** : the right to choose what should be done in a particular situation • *The coach used/exercised his own discretion to let the injured quarterback play.* • *Changes are left to the discretion of the individual.* = *Changes are made at the discretion of the individual.* [=each person will decide what changes to make] • *Parental discretion is advised.* **2** : the quality of being careful about what you do and say so that people will not be embarrassed or offended • *She handled the situation with discretion.* • *She is the soul of discretion.* [=she is very discreet]

dis·cre·tion·ary /dɪˈskrɛʃəˌneri, *Brit* dɪˈskrɛʃənri/ *adj* : available to be used when and how you decide • *discretionary income* [=income that is left after paying for things that are essential]

dis·crim·i·nate /dɪˈskrɪməˌneɪt/ *vb* **-nat·ed; -nat·ing** **1** [*I*] : to unfairly treat a person or group of people differently from other people or groups • *The school is not allowed to discriminate.* • *They discriminated against him because of his race.* **2** [*T/I*] *somewhat formal* : to recognize a difference between things • *discriminate right from wrong* • *I can discriminate (between) the individual voices in the choir.* — **dis·crim·i·na·tion** /dɪˌskrɪməˈneɪʃən/ *n* [*U*] • *unfair discrimination against minorities* — **dis·crim·i·na·tory** /dɪˈskrɪmənəˌtori, *Brit* dɪˈskrɪmənətri/ *adj* • *discriminatory treatment of women*

discriminating *adj, approving* : liking only things that are of good quality • *discriminating tastes/customers*

dis·cus /ˈdɪskəs/ *n* [*C*] : a heavy, flat, round object that people throw as far as they can as a sport

dis·cuss /dɪˈskʌs/ *vb* [*T*] **1** : to talk about (something) with another person or group • *She discussed the plan with several colleagues.* **2** : to give information, ideas, opinions, etc., about (something) in writing or speech • *The article discusses childcare issues.*

dis·cus·sion /dɪˈskʌʃən/ *n* **1** [*C/U*] : the act of talking about something with another person or a group of people • *They had a heated discussion about politics.* • *After much discussion, the plan was rejected.* • *The issue is under discussion.* [=being talked about] **2** [*C*] : a speech or piece of writing that gives information, ideas, opinions, etc., about something •

The article includes a discussion of his theories.

dis·dain /dɪsˈdeɪn/ *n* [*U, singular*] : a feeling of strong dislike or disapproval of someone or something you think does not deserve respect ▪ *He regarded them with disdain.* — **disdain** *vb* [*T*] ▪ *a critic who disdains* [=strongly dislikes] *modern art* — **dis·dain·ful** *adj* ▪ *disdainful of authority* — **dis·dain·ful·ly** *adv*

dis·ease /dɪˈziːz/ *n* **1** [*C/U*] : an illness that affects a person, animal, or plant ▪ *infectious/contagious diseases* ▪ *Thousands die of heart disease each year.* **2** [*C*] : a problem that a person, group, organization, or society has and cannot stop ▪ *the disease of poverty* — **dis·eased** /dɪˈziːzd/ *adj* ▪ *diseased cells/lungs/plants*

dis·em·bark /ˌdɪsəmˈbɑːrk/ *vb* [*I*] : to leave a ship or airplane ▪ *Passengers disembarked from the ship.*

dis·em·bod·ied /ˌdɪsəmˈbɑːdid/ *adj* **1** : not having or attached to a body ▪ *disembodied spirits* ▪ *a disembodied head* **2** : coming from a person who cannot be seen ▪ *disembodied voices*

dis·en·chant·ed /ˌdɪsɪnˈtʃæntəd, Brit ˌdɪsɪnˈtʃɑːntəd/ *adj* : no longer happy or satisfied with something ▪ *He was disenchanted with his job.* — **dis·en·chant·ment** /ˌdɪsɪnˈtʃæntmənt, Brit ˌdɪsɪnˈtʃɑːntmənt/ *n* [*U*]

dis·en·fran·chise /ˌdɪsɪnˈfræn.ʃaɪz/ *vb* -chised; -chis·ing [*T*] : to prevent (a person or group of people) from having the right to vote ▪ *disenfranchised minorities*

dis·en·gage /ˌdɪsɪnˈgeɪdʒ/ *vb* -gaged; -gag·ing [*T/I*] **1** : to move (a mechanism or part of a machine) so that it no longer fits into another part ▪ *She disengaged the clutch.* ▪ *The gears disengaged.* **2** *military* : to order (a group of soldiers) to stop fighting and move away from an area ▪ *The government will disengage soldiers from the region.* — **dis·en·gaged** /ˌdɪsɪnˈgeɪdʒd/ *adj* ▪ *She became disengaged* [=withdrawn] *as her depression worsened.* — **dis·en·gage·ment** /ˌdɪsɪnˈgeɪdʒmənt/ *n* [*U*]

dis·en·tan·gle /ˌdɪsɪnˈtæŋgəl/ *vb* -tangled; -tan·gling [*T*] : to separate (things that are twisted together or caught on one another) ▪ *She disentangled her hair from her necklace.* ▪ *(figurative) She disentangled herself from a bad relationship.*

dis·fa·vor (*US*) *or Brit* **dis·fa·vour** /dɪsˈfeɪvɚ/ *n* [*U*] *formal* **1** : a feeling of disapproval or dislike ▪ *He regarded the proposal with disfavor.* **2** : the condition of being disapproved of or disliked ▪ *The theory has long been in disfavor.* [=has been unpopular for a long time]

dis·fig·ure /dɪsˈfɪɡjɚ, Brit dɪsˈfɪɡə/ *vb* -ured; -ur·ing [*T*] : to spoil or damage the appearance of (something or someone) ▪ *His face was disfigured by a scar.* ▪ *The fire left her disfigured.* — **dis·fig·ure·ment** /dɪsˈfɪɡjɚmənt/ *n* [*C/U*]

dis·gorge /dɪsˈɡoɚdʒ/ *vb* -gorged; -gorg·ing [*T*] : to let out or release (someone or something) ▪ *an airplane disgorging its passengers*

¹dis·grace /dɪsˈɡreɪs/ *vb* -graced; -grac·ing [*T*] : to cause (someone or something) to lose or become unworthy of respect or approval ▪ *The governor has disgraced his office by accepting bribes.* ▪ *The administration was disgraced by the scandal.* ▪ *He disgraced himself.*

²disgrace *n* **1** [*U*] : the condition of feeling ashamed or of losing or becoming unworthy of respect or approval ▪ *political/personal disgrace* ▪ *She was forced to leave in disgrace.* **2** [*singular*] : something that you are or should be ashamed of ▪ *His manners are a disgrace.* ▪ *Those people are a disgrace to their country.* ▪ *It is no disgrace to be poor.* [=you should not feel ashamed because you are poor] — **dis·grace·ful** /dɪsˈɡreɪsfəl/ *adj* ▪ *disgraceful behavior* — **dis·grace·ful·ly** *adv*

dis·grun·tled /dɪsˈɡrʌntld/ *adj* : unhappy and annoyed ▪ *disgruntled employees/customers*

¹dis·guise /dəˈskaɪz/ *vb* -guised; -guis·ing [*T*] **1** : to change the usual appearance, sound, taste, etc., of (someone or something) so that people will not recognize that person or thing ▪ *He disguised his voice.* ▪ *She disguised herself in a wig and glasses.* **2** : to hide (something) so that it will not be seen or noticed ▪ *They disguised their true feelings.*

²disguise *n* **1** [*C/U*] : clothes or other things that you wear so that people will not recognize you ▪ *He wore a disguise.* ▪ *She went there in disguise.* [=wearing a disguise] ▪ *(figurative) a new fee that is just a tax increase in disguise* **2** [*U*] : the act of changing your appearance so that people will not recognize you ▪ *She is a master of disguise.* — **a blessing in disguise** see **BLESSING**

¹dis·gust /dɪsˈɡʌst/ *n* [*U*] **1** : a strong feeling of dislike for something that has a very unpleasant appearance, taste, smell, etc. ▪ *He eyed the food with/in disgust.* **2** : annoyance and anger that you feel toward something because it is not good, fair, etc. ▪ *He talked about his disgust with/at the media's focus on celebrities.* ▪ *She shook her head in disgust.*

²disgust *vb* [*T*] **1** : to cause (someone) to have a strong feeling of dislike for something especially because it has a very unpleasant appearance, taste, smell, etc. ▪ *The greasy food disgusted her.* **2** : to cause (someone) to feel very annoyed and angry because of unfairness, badness, etc. ▪ *His behavior disgusts me.* — **dis·gust·ed** /dɪsˈɡʌstəd/ *adj* ▪ *a disgusted look on her face* ▪ *He's disgusted with himself.* — **dis·gust·ing** /dɪsˈɡʌstɪŋ/ *adj* ▪ *The pizza/movie was disgusting.* — **dis·gust·ing·ly** *adv*

¹dish /ˈdɪʃ/ *n* **1** [*C*] **a** : a shallow container that you cook or serve food in ▪ *a baking/serving dish* [=a container used to bake/serve food] ▪ *a candy dish* [=a container used to serve candy] **b** : the food served in a dish ▪ *a small dish of ice cream* **2** [*C*] : food that is prepared in a particular way ▪ *The restaurant serves some of my favorite dishes.* **3** [*plural*] : all the things (such as plates, forks, glasses, pans, cooking utensils, etc.) that are used to prepare, serve, and eat a meal • *We piled all the dishes in the sink after dinner.* • *It's your turn to do the dishes.* [=wash the dishes] **4** [C] : something that is shaped like a shallow bowl • *a dish antenna* — see also SATELLITE DISH

²**dish** *vb* — **dish out** [*phrasal vb*] **dish out (something)** *also* **dish (something) out** *informal* **1** : to serve (food) • *The restaurant dishes out more than 500 meals every night.* **2** : to give (something) freely or in large amounts • *She's always dishing out advice/criticism.* — **dish up** [*phrasal vb*] **dish up (something)** *also* **dish (something) up** *informal* : to put (food) into a dish or dishes for serving or eating • *dish up some soup* • (*figurative*) *The movie dishes up a mix of comedy and drama.*

dis·har·mo·ny /dɪsˈhɑɚməni/ *n* [U] : lack of agreement that often causes unhappiness or trouble • *a period/source of marital disharmony*

dish·cloth /ˈdɪʃˌklɑːθ/ *n* [C] : a cloth that is used for washing dishes — called also (*US*) **dishrag**

dis·heart·en /dɪsˈhɑɚtn/ *vb* [T] : to cause (a person or group of people) to lose hope, enthusiasm, or courage • *I was/felt disheartened by the news.* — **dis·heart·en·ing** /dɪsˈhɑɚtnɪŋ/ *adj* • *a disheartening failure*

di·shev·eled (*US*) *also Brit* **di·shev·elled** /dɪˈʃɛvəld/ *adj* : not neat or tidy • *disheveled hair/clothes*

dis·hon·est /dɪsˈɑːnəst/ *adj* : saying or likely to say things that are untrue : not honest • *I think he is being dishonest.* • *a dishonest salesman* • *dishonest advertising/answers* • *dishonest business practices* — **dis·hon·est·ly** *adv* • *He answered the questions dishonestly.* — **dis·hon·es·ty** /dɪsˈɑːnəsti/ *n* [U] • *She accused me of dishonesty.*

¹**dis·hon·or** (*US*) *or Brit* **dis·hon·our** /dɪsˈɑːnɚ/ *n* [U] *somewhat formal* : damage to your reputation and loss of respect from other people • *His actions brought dishonor on/upon his family.* — **dis·hon·or·able** (*US*) *or Brit* **dis·hon·our·able** /dɪsˈɑːnərəbəl/ *adj* • *dishonorable behavior/conduct* — **dis·hon·or·ably** (*US*) *or Brit* **dis·hon·our·ably** /dɪsˈɑːnərəbli/ *adv*

²**dishonor** (*US*) *or Brit* **dishonour** *vb* [T] *somewhat formal* : to cause (someone or something) to no longer be respected • *His actions dishonored his family.*

dish·rag /ˈdɪʃˌræg/ *n* [C] *US* : DISHCLOTH

dish towel *n* [C] *US* : a cloth that is used for drying dishes — called also (*Brit*) **tea cloth**, (*chiefly Brit*) **tea towel**

dish·ware /ˈdɪʃˌweɚ/ *n* [U] *chiefly US* : plates, bowls, cups, etc., that are usually part of a set

dish·wash·er /ˈdɪʃˌwɑːʃɚ/ *n* [C] **1** : a person whose job is to wash dishes in a restaurant **2** : a machine that is used to wash dishes — **dish·wash·ing** /ˈdɪʃˌwɑːʃɪŋ/ *adj* • *dishwashing soap/detergent*

dish·wa·ter /ˈdɪʃˌwɑːtɚ/ *n* [U] : water in which dishes have been or are going to be washed • (*US, figurative*) *The conversa-tion was (as) dull as dishwater.* [=very dull; very boring]

dis·il·lu·sion /ˌdɪsəˈluːʒən/ *vb* [T] : to cause (someone) to stop believing that something is good, valuable, true, etc. • *The job disillusioned me about retail work.* • *a disillusioning experience* — **dis·il·lu·sion·ment** /ˌdɪsəˈluːʒənmənt/ *n* [U]

dis·il·lu·sioned /ˌdɪsəˈluːʒənd/ *adj* : having lost faith or trust in something • *a disillusioned journalist* • *She was disillusioned with politics.*

dis·in·cli·na·tion /dɪsˌɪnkləˈneɪʃən/ *n* [singular] *formal* : a feeling of not wanting to do something • *her disinclination* [=reluctance] *to talk about her past*

dis·in·clined /ˌdɪsənˈklaɪnd/ *adj, formal* : not wanting to do something • *He seemed disinclined to help us.*

dis·in·fect /ˌdɪsənˈfɛkt/ *vb* [T] **1** : to clean (something) especially by using a chemical substance that kills all germs and bacteria • *Chemicals were added to disinfect the water.* **2** *computers* : to remove a virus from (a computer) by using a special program

dis·in·fect·ant /ˌdɪsənˈfɛktənt/ *n* [C/U] : a chemical substance that is used to kill harmful germs and bacteria • *Clean the area with (a) disinfectant.*

dis·in·for·ma·tion /dɪsˌɪnfɚˈmeɪʃən/ *n* [U] : false information that is given to people in order to make them believe something or to hide the truth

dis·in·gen·u·ous /ˌdɪsɪnˈdʒɛnjəwəs/ *adj, formal* : not truly honest or sincere • *a disingenuous response* — **dis·in·gen·u·ous·ly** *adv*

dis·in·her·it /ˌdɪsənˈhɛrət/ *vb* [T] : to prevent (someone, such as your daughter or son) from having the legal right to receive your money or property after you die • *She threatened to disinherit her son.*

dis·in·te·grate /dɪsˈɪntəˌgreɪt/ *vb* -**grat·ed**; -**grat·ing** [T/I] **1** : to break apart into many small parts or pieces • *The paper will disintegrate if it gets wet.* • *The laser can disintegrate most kinds of rock.* • (*figurative*) *Their relationship gradually disintegrated.* — **dis·in·te·gra·tion** /dɪsˌɪntəˈgreɪʃən/ *n* [U]

dis·in·ter·est /dɪsˈɪntrəst/ *n* [U] : lack of interest • *His proposal was met with complete disinterest.*

dis·in·ter·est·ed /dɪsˈɪntrəstəd/ *adj* **1** : not influenced by personal feelings, opinions, or concerns • *a disinterested* [=unbiased, impartial] *third party* **2** : having no desire to know about a particular thing : not interested • *They are disinterested in politics.* ✧ This sense is common but some people consider it incorrect and say that "uninterested" should be used instead. — **dis·in·ter·est·ed·ly** *adv*

dis·joint·ed /dɪsˈdʒɔɪntəd/ *adj* : lacking order and organization • *a disjointed conversation/narrative/book*

disk *variant spelling of* DISC

disk drive *n* [C] : a computer part that holds a computer disk or set of disks and that reads data from and copies data to disks

dis·kette /ˈdɪˌskɛt/ n [C] : FLOPPY DISK

¹dis·like /dɪsˈlaɪk/ vb **-liked**; **-lik·ing** [T]
: to not like (something or someone) • I
dislike basketball. • He dislikes being interviewed.

²dislike n 1 [singular] : a feeling of not
liking or approving of something or
someone • His dislike of cats was obvious.
• They **took a dislike to** the new neighbors.
[=they disliked the new neighbors] 2
[C] : something that you do not like, approve of, or enjoy • She talked about her
likes and dislikes.

dis·lo·cate /ˈdɪsloʊˌkeɪt/ vb **-cat·ed**;
-cat·ing [T] 1 medical : to move (a
bone) out of its normal location or position in a joint • She fell and dislocated her
shoulder. • a dislocated finger/hip/wrist 2
chiefly US, formal : to force (someone or
something) to move from a place or position • The new hotel will dislocate several
businesses. • dislocated workers 3 formal
: to stop (something) from functioning
as it used to function • economies dislocated [=disrupted] by war — **dis·lo·ca·
tion** /ˌdɪsloʊˈkeɪʃən/ n [C/U]

dis·lodge /dɪsˈlɑːdʒ/ vb **-lodged**; **-lodg·
ing** [T] : to forcefully remove (something or someone) from a place or position • He kicked at the stone to dislodge it.

dis·loy·al /dɪsˈlɔjəl/ adj : not loyal or
faithful to your friends, family, country,
etc. • a traitor disloyal to his country • disloyal employees — **dis·loy·al·ty** /dɪs-
ˈlɔjəlti/ n [U]

dis·mal /ˈdɪzməl/ adj : 1 : showing or
causing unhappiness or sad feelings • dismal weather 2 : very bad or poor • a dismal performance • The team's record is
dismal. — **dis·mal·ly** adv

dis·man·tle /dɪsˈmæntl̩/ vb **-man·tled**;
-man·tling [T] 1 : to take (something,
such as a machine or structure) apart so
that it is in separate pieces • dismantle an
engine/bridge • the dismantling of old factories 2 : to gradually cause (something) to come to an end • The after-
school program was dismantled due to
lack of funding.

¹dis·may /dɪsˈmeɪ/ vb [T] : to cause
(someone) to feel very worried, disappointed, or upset • The news dismayed
me. — **dis·mayed** /dɪsˈmeɪd/ adj • I was
very dismayed by/at his indifference. —
dis·may·ing /dɪsˈmejɪŋ/ adj • dismaying
news

²dismay n [U] : a strong feeling of being
worried, disappointed, or upset • They
watched **in dismay** as the house burned. •
Much to the dismay of her fans, she announced her retirement.

dis·mem·ber /dɪsˈmɛmbɚ/ vb [T] : to cut
or tear (a body) into pieces • a dismem-
bered corpse • (figurative) dismembering a
corporate empire — **dis·mem·ber·
ment** /dɪsˈmɛmbɚmənt/ n [C/U]

dis·miss /dɪsˈmɪs/ vb [T] 1 : to decide
not to think about or consider (something or someone) • We dismissed his accusations. • Her idea was dismissed as impractical. 2 : to send (someone) away •
The students were dismissed early. • Class
is dismissed. [=the class is over and students are free to leave] 3 : to officially

make (someone) leave a job • He was dismissed [=fired] from his job. 4 law : to
officially end or stop (something, such as
a legal case) • The judge dismissed the
case/suit. — **dis·miss·al** /dɪsˈmɪsəl/ n
[C/U] • the dismissal of several employees
• the dismissal of the lawsuit

dis·mis·sive /dɪsˈmɪsɪv/ adj : showing
that you do not think something or
someone is worth thinking about or considering • a dismissive remark • He was
dismissive of my idea. — **dis·mis·sive·
ly** adv

dis·mount /dɪsˈmaʊnt/ vb [I] : to get
down from something (such as a horse
or bicycle) • The cyclist/gymnast/rider dis-
mounted. — **dismount** n [C] • the gymnast's dismount

dis·obe·di·ent /ˌdɪsəˈbiːdijənt/ adj : not
doing what someone or something with
authority tells you to do : refusing or
failing to obey rules, laws, etc. • a disobe-
dient child — **dis·obe·di·ence** /ˌdɪsə-
ˈbiːdijəns/ n [U]

dis·obey /ˌdɪsəˈbeɪ/ vb [T/I] : to not do
what someone or something with authority tells you to do • The patient dis-
obeyed the doctor's orders. • He was afraid
to disobey (his father).

dis·or·der /dɪsˈoɚdɚ/ n 1 [U] : a confused or messy state : a lack of order or
organization • The system was **thrown
into disorder** [=was disrupted or upset]
when the computer program malfunc-
tioned. • His papers were in complete disorder. [=were not organized at all] 2
[C/U] : a physical or mental condition
that is not normal or healthy • an eating
disorder • a form of personality/mental
disorder 3 [U] : a state or situation in
which there is a lot of noise, crime, violent behavior, etc. • public disorder

dis·or·dered /dɪsˈoɚdɚd/ adj 1 : having
a lack of order or organization • The
project was completely disordered. 2
medical : not working in a normal,
healthy way • a disordered mind

dis·or·der·ly /dɪsˈoɚdɚli/ adj 1 : causing a problem especially in a public place
by making a lot of noise, behaving violently, etc. • He was found guilty of **disorderly conduct**. 2 : not neat or orderly •
a disorderly pile of papers

dis·or·ga·nized also Brit **dis·or·ga·
nised** /dɪsˈoɚɡəˌnaɪzd/ adj 1 : not arranged or planned in a particular or effective way • The meeting was disorganized. • a disorganized essay/desk 2 : not
able to keep things arranged in a neat or
effective way • He is very disorganized. —
dis·or·ga·ni·za·tion also Brit **dis·or·
ga·ni·sa·tion** /dɪsˌoɚɡənəˈzeɪʃən/, Brit
dɪsˌɔːɡəˌnaɪˈzeɪʃən/ n [U]

dis·ori·ent /dɪsˈoɚrijənt/ vb [T] : to make
(someone) lost or confused • Fog can disorient even an experienced hiker. • The
patient became increasingly disoriented.
— **dis·ori·ent·ing** /dɪsˈoɚrijəntɪŋ/ adj • a
disorienting change

dis·ori·en·tate /dɪsˈoɚrijənˌteɪt/ vb **-tat·
ed**; **-tat·ing** [T] chiefly Brit : DISORIENT

dis·own /dɪsˈoʊn/ vb [T] : to say or decide that you will no longer be connected with, associated with, or responsible

for (someone or something) ▪ *Her parents threatened to disown her.*

dis·par·age /dɪˈsperɪdʒ/ *vb* **-aged;** **-ag·ing** [T] *formal* : to describe (someone or something) as unimportant, weak, bad, etc. ▪ *It's a mistake to disparage their achievements.* — **dis·par·age·ment** /dɪˈsperɪdʒmənt/ *n* [U] — **disparaging** *adj* ▪ *disparaging remarks/terms* — **dis·par·ag·ing·ly** *adv*

dis·par·ate /ˈdɪspərət/ *adj, formal* : different from each other ▪ *music that combines/blends disparate elements*

dis·par·i·ty /dɪˈsperəti/ *n, pl* **-ties** [C/U] *formal* : a noticeable and often unfair difference between people or things ▪ *There is (a) great disparity between (the) rich and (the) poor in this country.* ▪ *income disparity*

dis·pas·sion·ate /dɪsˈpæʃənət/ *adj* : not influenced or affected by emotions ▪ *dispassionate observers* — **dis·pas·sion·ate·ly** *adv*

¹**dis·patch** *also Brit* **des·patch** /dɪˈspætʃ/ *vb* [T] **1** : to send (someone or something) quickly to a particular place for a particular purpose ▪ *Rescue workers were dispatched to the area.* **2** : to defeat (a person or team) in a game, contest, etc. ▪ *She easily dispatched* [=(more commonly) *beat*] *her opponent.*

²**dispatch** *also Brit* **despatch** *n* **1** [C] : an important official message ▪ *The general sent a dispatch to headquarters.* ✧ In British English, a soldier who is *mentioned in dispatches* is noted for bravery. **2** [U] *somewhat formal* : the act of sending someone or something to a particular place for a particular purpose ▪ *the immediate dispatch of supplies/troops* **3** [C] : a news story that a reporter sends to a newspaper usually from a foreign country ▪ *dispatches from the war zone* — **with dispatch** *formal* : in a quick and efficient way ▪ *The problem was handled with dispatch.*

dis·patch·er /dɪˈspætʃɚ/ *n* [C] *US* **1** : someone whose job is to talk by radio with people in vehicles (such as police cars, ambulances, or taxis) in order to send them to a particular place **2** : someone who is in charge of the departure of trains, airplanes, buses, trucks, etc.

dis·pel /dɪˈspel/ *vb* **-pelled;** **-pel·ling** [T] : to make (something, such as a belief, feeling, or idea) go away or end ▪ *This report should dispel any doubts/fears/rumors.*

dis·pens·able /dɪˈspensəbəl/ *adj* : not necessary or required ▪ *Computers have made typewriters dispensable.*

dis·pen·sa·ry /dɪˈpensəri/ *n, pl* **-ries** [C] : a place where medicine or minor medical treatment is given ▪ *a hospital dispensary*

dis·pen·sa·tion /ˌdɪspənˈseɪʃən/ *n, formal* **1** [C/U] : permission to break a law or an official promise you have made ▪ *The state gave the town a special zoning dispensation.* **2** [*singular*] : an act of providing something to people ▪ *the dispensation* [=*distribution*] *of medicine*

dis·pense /dɪˈspens/ *vb* **-pensed;**

-pens·ing [T] : to give or provide (something) ▪ *a newspaper columnist who dispenses advice to readers* ▪ *Pharmacists are certified to dispense medication.* — **dispense with** [*phrasal vb*] *formal* : to no longer use or require (something) ▪ *Let's dispense with the chit-chat and get down to business.*

dis·pens·er /dɪˈspensɚ/ *n* [C] **1** : a machine or container that lets you take small amounts of something ▪ *a soap/tape dispenser* **2** : a person or organization that gives or provides something to people ▪ *hospitals and other health-care dispensers*

dis·perse /dɪˈspɚs/ *vb* **-persed;** **-pers·ing** [T/I] : to go or move in different directions : to spread apart ▪ *Police dispersed the protesters.* ▪ *Police ordered the crowd to disperse.* — **dis·per·sal** /dɪˈspɚsəl/ *n* [U] ▪ *crowd dispersal* — **dis·per·sion** /dɪˈspɚʒən/ *n* [U] *technical* ▪ *the dispersion of pollutants*

dis·pir·it·ed /dɪˈspirətəd/ *adj* : feeling unhappy and without hope or enthusiasm ▪ *The loss left the team dispirited.* — **dis·pir·it·ed·ly** *adv*

dis·pir·it·ing /dɪˈspirətɪŋ/ *adj* : causing a loss of hope or enthusiasm ▪ *a very dispiriting failure/loss*

dis·place /dɪˈspleɪs/ *vb* **-placed;** **-plac·ing** [T] **1** : to take the job or position of (someone or something) ▪ *Some say football has displaced baseball as America's national pastime.* **2 a** : to force (people or animals) to leave the area where they live ▪ *The war/hurricane has displaced thousands of people.* ▪ *a crisis involving thousands of displaced persons/people* **b** *chiefly US* : to remove (someone) from a job or position ▪ *The closing of the factory has displaced many workers.* **3** : to move (something) so that it is no longer in its original or regular location or position ▪ *(technical) The ship displaces 20,000 tons (of water).*

dis·place·ment /dɪˈspleɪsmənt/ *n* **1** [C/U] : the act of forcing people or animals to leave the area where they live ▪ *The war has caused the displacement of thousands of people.* **2 a** [C/U] : the movement of something from its original or regular position ▪ *displacement(s) in the Earth's crust* **b** [C] *technical* : the amount of water that is moved by an object when it is placed in water ▪ *The ship has a very large displacement.*

¹**dis·play** /dɪˈspleɪ/ *vb* [T] **1** : to put (something) where people can see it ▪ *The results are displayed* [=*shown*] *on the computer screen.* ▪ *Toys were displayed in the store window.* **2** : to show that you have (an emotion, quality, skill, etc.) ▪ *He displayed no emotion when I told him the news.* ▪ *The rookie player displayed great skill.*

²**display** *n* [C] **1** : an arrangement of objects intended to decorate, advertise, entertain, or inform people about something ▪ *a display of flowers = a flower display* ▪ *a display case/cabinet* ▪ *a store's window display* [=a display of products shown in a store's window] **2** : an event at which something is done or shown to

impress or entertain people ▪ *a spectacular fireworks display* **3** : an action, performance, etc., which shows very clearly that you have some ability, feeling, quality, etc. ▪ *a display of generosity/anger* **4** : an electronic device (such as a computer monitor) that shows information ▪ *The computer comes with a high-resolution color display.* **5** : a way of behaving that a bird or animal uses to show another bird or animal that it wants to show another fight, etc. ▪ *courtship/threat displays* — **on display** : put somewhere for people to see : in a display ▪ *Only a few of the artifacts will be on display.*

dis·please /dɪsˈpliːz/ *vb* **-pleased; -pleas·ing** [*T*] : to make (someone) feel unhappy or annoyed ▪ *She was/looked displeased by/with what I said.* — **displeasing** *adj* ▪ *visually displeasing buildings*

dis·plea·sure /dɪsˈplɛʒɚ/ *n* [*U*] : a feeling of unhappiness or annoyance ▪ *The fans showed/expressed their displeasure by booing loudly.*

dis·pos·able /dɪˈspoʊzəbəl/ *adj* **1** : made to be thrown away after one use or several uses ▪ *disposable diapers/razors* **2** *somewhat formal* : available to be used ▪ *disposable income* [=income that is left after paying taxes and for things that are essential, such as food and housing] — **disposable** *n* [*C*] ▪ *Do you use cloth diapers or disposables?* [=disposable diapers]

dis·pos·al /dɪˈspoʊzəl/ *n* **1** [*U*] **a** : the act of throwing something away ▪ *trash disposal* ▪ *the disposal of nuclear waste* **b** *law* : the act of giving control or ownership of land, possessions, etc., to someone ▪ *the disposal of property* **2** [*C*] *US* : GARBAGE DISPOSAL — **at someone's disposal** : available for someone to use ▪ *We had plenty of money at our disposal.*

dis·pose /dɪˈspoʊz/ *vb* **-posed; -pos·ing** [*T*] *formal* : to cause (someone) to be likely to do or have something ▪ *people whose genes dispose them to/toward a particular disease* — **dispose of** [*phrasal vb*] **1 a** : to throw (something) away : to get rid of (something) ▪ *Please dispose of your trash properly.* **b** *law* : to give control or ownership of (land, possessions, etc.) to someone ▪ *A will is a legal document that is used to dispose of property.* **2 a** : to defeat (a person or team) in a game, contest, etc. ▪ *She easily disposed of her opponent.* **b** : to kill (a person or animal) ▪ *weapons used to dispose of their enemies*

disposed *adj, not before a noun, formal* **1** : wanting to do something or likely to do something ▪ *dogs that are naturally disposed toward fighting* ▪ *She is disposed to distrust salespeople.* **2** : feeling or thinking in a specified way about something ▪ *They were favorably/unfavorably disposed to/toward the idea.* [=they liked/disliked the idea]

dis·po·si·tion /ˌdɪspəˈzɪʃən/ *n* **1** [*C*] : the usual attitude or mood of a person or animal ▪ *He always had a cheerful/nervous disposition.* **2** *formal* **a** [*singular*] : a tendency to act or think in a particular way ▪ *He has a disposition toward*

criminal behavior. **b** [*C*] : a tendency to develop a disease, condition, etc. ▪ *people with a genetic disposition toward a particular disease* **3** [*C/U*] *formal* : the act or power of officially or legally giving land, possessions, etc., to someone ▪ *the disposition of property*

dis·pos·sess /ˌdɪspəˈzɛs/ *vb* [*T*] *formal* : to take land, possessions, etc., from (someone) ▪ *They dispossessed many people of their land.* — **dis·pos·sessed** /ˌdɪspəˈzɛst/ *adj, always before a noun, formal* ▪ *dispossessed refugees* — **dis·pos·ses·sion** /ˌdɪspəˈzɛʃən/ *n* [*U*]

dis·pro·por·tion /ˌdɪsprəˈpoɚʃən/ *n* [*C/U*] *formal* : a difference that is not fair, reasonable, or expected ▪ *His salary is in disproportion to what people who have similar jobs earn.*

dis·pro·por·tion·ate /ˌdɪsprəˈpoɚʃənət/ *adj* : having or showing a difference that is not fair, reasonable, or expected : too large or too small in relation to something ▪ *A disproportionate number of the students are poor.* ▪ *The organization's influence is disproportionate to its size.* — **dis·pro·por·tion·ate·ly** *adv*

dis·prove /dɪsˈpruːv/ *vb* **-proved** *or chiefly US* **-prov·en** /-ˈpruːvən/; **-prov·ing** [*T*] : to show that (something) is false or wrong ▪ *The theory has been disproved.*

dis·put·able /dɪˈspjuːtəbəl/ *adj* : not yet proved or shown to be true : likely to be questioned or doubted ▪ *disputable claims/evidence*

¹**dis·pute** /dɪˈspjuːt/ *n* [*C/U*] : a disagreement or argument ▪ *legal/labor/land disputes* ▪ *a domestic dispute* [=an argument between people who live together] ▪ *There was (a) dispute over/about what to do with the extra money.* ▪ *How it happened is open to dispute.* [=people disagree about how it happened]

²**dispute** *vb* **-put·ed; -put·ing** **1** [*T*] : to say or show that (something) may not be true, correct, or legal ▪ *She disputed the claim.* ▪ *These theories are hotly/much disputed by scientists.* ▪ *There is no disputing the drug's effectiveness.* [=it is certain that the drug is effective] **2** [*T/I*] : to argue about (something) ▪ *The source of the text has been disputed for centuries.* **3** [*T*] *formal* : to fight in order to take control of (something) ▪ *Two warring gangs are disputing territory.*

dis·qual·i·fy /dɪsˈkwɑːləˌfaɪ/ *vb* **-fies; -fied; -fy·ing** [*T*] : to stop or prevent (someone) from doing, having, or being a part of something ▪ *His poor eyesight disqualified him from becoming a pilot.* ▪ *The winner was later disqualified for cheating.* — **dis·qual·i·fi·ca·tion** /dɪsˌkwɑːləfəˈkeɪʃən/ *n* [*C/U*]

dis·qui·et /dɪsˈkwajət/ *vb* [*T*] *formal* : to make (someone) worried or nervous ▪ *We were disquieted by the news.* — **dis·qui·et·ing** /dɪsˈkwajətɪŋ/ *adj* ▪ *disquieting news*

¹**dis·re·gard** /ˌdɪsrɪˈgɑɚd/ *vb* [*T*] : to ignore (something) or treat (something) as unimportant ▪ *Please disregard what I said before.*

²**disregard** *n* [*U, singular*] : the act of ig-

noring something or treating something as unimportant • *They treated the rules with complete/total disregard.* • *a reckless disregard for/of human life*

dis·re·pair /ˌdɪsrɪˈpeɚ/ *n* [U] : the state of needing to be repaired : bad condition • *The lighthouse was in (a state of) disrepair.* • *The house fell into disrepair.*

dis·rep·u·ta·ble /dɪsˈrɛpjətəbəl/ *adj, formal* : not respected or trusted by most people • *disreputable people* • *disreputable hiring practices*

dis·re·pute /ˌdɪsrɪˈpjuːt/ *n* [U] *formal* : a state of not being respected or trusted by most people • *The star player's drug use will bring the game into disrepute.* [=make people not respect the game]

dis·re·spect /ˌdɪsrɪˈspɛkt/ *n* [U, *singular*] : speech or behavior which shows that you do not think someone or something is valuable, important, etc. : lack of respect • *The student treated the teacher with disrespect.* • *He showed a shocking disrespect for authority.* — **disrespect** *vb* [T] • *She disrespected her employees.* [=treated her employees with disrespect] — **dis·re·spect·ful** /ˌdɪsrɪˈspɛktfəl/ *adj* • *She was very disrespectful to the teacher.* — **dis·re·spect·ful·ly** *adv*

dis·robe /dɪsˈroʊb/ *vb* -**robed**; -**rob·ing** [T/I] *formal* : UNDRESS • *She disrobed (herself) and stepped into the bathtub.*

dis·rupt /dɪsˈrʌpt/ *vb* [T] : to interrupt the normal progress or activity of (something) • *Protesters disrupted the conference.* • *a chemical that disrupts cell function* — **dis·rup·tion** /dɪsˈrʌpʃən/ *n* [C/U] • *The construction caused disruptions in bus service.* — **dis·rup·tive** /dɪsˈrʌptɪv/ *adj* • *disruptive behavior* — **dis·rup·tive·ly** *adv*

diss *variant spelling of* DIS

dis·sat·is·fac·tion /ˌdɪsˌsætəsˈfækʃən/ *n* [U] : a feeling of unhappiness or disapproval • *She expressed her dissatisfaction with the restaurant's service.*

dis·sat·is·fy /dɪsˈsætəsˌfaɪ/ *vb* -**fies**; -**fied**; -**fy·ing** [T] : to fail to make (someone) happy or pleased • *Their final decision dissatisfied everyone.* — **dis·sat·is·fied** *adj* • *She was dissatisfied with the service.* — **dis·sat·is·fy·ing** *adj* • *a dissatisfying experience*

dis·sect /daɪˈsɛkt, dɪˈsɛkt/ *vb* [T] **1** : to cut (a plant or dead animal) into separate parts in order to study it • *dissect a frog* **2** : to study or examine (something) closely and carefully : ANALYZE • *We dissected the poem in class.* **3** : to divide (something) into parts • *The city is dissected by a network of highways.* — **dis·sec·tion** /daɪˈsɛkʃən, dɪˈsɛkʃən/ *n* [C/U] • *The students performed a dissection.*

dis·sem·ble /dɪˈsɛmbəl/ *vb* -**sem·bled**; -**sem·bling** [I] *formal + literary* : to hide your true feelings, opinions, etc. • *He dissembled about the risks involved.* [=he did not tell the truth about the risks involved]

dis·sem·i·nate /dɪˈsɛməˌneɪt/ *vb* -**nat·ed**; -**nat·ing** [T] *formal* : to cause (something, such as information) to go to many people • *The findings were widely*

disseminated. — **dis·sem·i·na·tion** /dɪˌsɛməˈneɪʃən/ *n* [U]

dis·sen·sion /dɪˈsɛnʃən/ *n* [U] : disagreement that causes the people in a group to argue about something that is important to them • *religious/political dissension*

¹**dis·sent** /dɪˈsɛnt/ *vb* [I] *formal* : to publicly disagree with an official opinion, decision, or set of beliefs • *The Supreme Court, with two justices dissenting, ruled that the law was constitutional.* • *dissenting opinions/views/voices* — **dis·sent·er** /dɪˈsɛntɚ/ *n* [C]

²**dissent** *n* [C/U] *formal* : public disagreement with an official opinion, decision, or set of beliefs • *political dissent* **2** [C] *US, law* : a statement by a judge giving reasons why the judge does not agree with the decision made by the other judges in a court case

dis·ser·ta·tion /ˌdɪsɚˈteɪʃən/ *n* [C] : a long piece of writing about a particular subject that is done to earn an advanced degree at a university • *He wrote his dissertation on an obscure 16th-century poet.*

dis·ser·vice /dɪsˈsɚvɪs/ *n* [singular] : something that harms or damages someone or something • *Her comments were/did a disservice to those volunteers.*

dis·si·dent /ˈdɪsədənt/ *n* [C] : someone who strongly and publicly disagrees with and criticizes the government • *The dissidents were arrested.* — **dis·si·dence** /ˈdɪsədəns/ *n* [U] — **dissident** *adj, always before a noun* • *dissident scholars/students*

dis·sim·i·lar /dɪsˈsɪmələ/ *adj* : not the same : different or unalike • *The two movies are very dissimilar.* — **dis·sim·i·lar·i·ty** /dɪsˌsɪməˈlerəti/ *n* [C/U]

dis·si·pate /ˈdɪsəˌpeɪt/ *vb* -**pat·ed**; -**pat·ing** *formal* **1 a** [T] : to cause (something) to spread out and disappear • *The morning sun dissipated the fog.* **b** [I] : to separate into parts and disappear or go away • *By noon the crowd had dissipated.* • *(figurative) Her anger began to dissipate.* **2** [T] : to use all or a lot of (something, such as money or time) in a foolish way • *He dissipated his family's fortune in only a few years.*

dis·si·pa·tion /ˌdɪsəˈpeɪʃən/ *n, formal* **1** [U] : the process of slowly disappearing or becoming less • *the dissipation of heat* **2** [U] : the act of using all or a lot of money, time, etc., in a foolish way • *the dissipation of resources* **3** [C/U] *disapproving* : behavior that shows you are interested only in pleasure, money, etc. • *He lived a life of dissipation.* • *gambling and dissipations*

dis·so·ci·ate /dɪˈsoʊʃiˌeɪt/ *vb* -**at·ed**; -**at·ing** [T] : to end your relationship with or connection to someone or something • *The director has tried to dissociate himself from his earlier films.* — **dis·so·ci·a·tion** /dɪˌsoʊʃiˈeɪʃən/ *n* [U]

dis·so·lute /ˈdɪsəˌluːt/ *adj, formal + disapproving* — used to describe someone whose way of living is considered morally wrong • *a dissolute person/life*

dis·so·lu·tion /ˌdɪsəˈluːʃən/ *n* [U] *formal* : the act of officially ending a marriage,

organization, agreement, etc. ▪ *the disso-
lution of the marriage/business/contract*

dis·solve /dɪˈzɑːlv/ *vb* **-solved; -solv-
ing 1** [*T/I*] *of something solid* : to mix
with a liquid and become part of the liquid ▪ *Sugar/salt dissolves in water.* ▪ *Dissolve the tablet in water.* **2** [*T*] *formal* : to
officially end (something, such as a marriage, organization, or agreement) ▪ *The
company has been dissolved.* **3** [*T/I*]
somewhat formal : to end or disappear or
cause (something) to end or disappear ▪
His smile dissolved. ▪ *The treatment is
used to dissolve kidney stones.* ✧ If you
dissolve in/into tears/laughter (etc.), you
start to cry, laugh, etc., in an uncontrolled way.

dis·so·nant /ˈdɪsənənt/ *adj, formal* : not
in harmony ▪ *a song with dissonant
chords* ▪ (*figurative*) *groups with dissonant
views* [=views that do not agree] — **dis-
so·nance** /ˈdɪsənəns/ *n* [*C/U*]

dis·suade /dɪˈsweɪd/ *vb* **-suad·ed;
-suad·ing** [*T*] : to convince (someone)
not to do something ▪ *Our warnings did
not dissuade them from going.*

¹dis·tance /ˈdɪstəns/ *n* **1** [*C/U*] : the
amount of space between two places or
things ▪ *What is the distance between the
Earth and the Sun?* ▪ *The gas station is a
short distance away.* ▪ *Her house is within
walking/striking distance of the school.*
[=is close to the school] **2** [*singular*] : a
point or place that is far away from another point or place ▪ *The sign was hard
to read from a distance.* ▪ *We followed
them at a distance.* ▪ *He saw a light in the
distance.* [=a light that was far away] **3**
[*U, singular*] : a state in which people are
not involved with or friendly toward
each other ▪ *He wants to put distance between himself and his former boss.* — **go/
last the distance** : to complete something you have started ▪ *Don't volunteer
for the job if you can't go the distance.* —
keep (someone) at a distance : to be
unfriendly toward (someone) ▪ *She always kept me at a distance.* — **keep your
distance** : to avoid being close to someone or something ▪ *After their breakup,
she thought it was wise to keep her distance (from him).*

²distance *vb* **-tanced; -tanc·ing** [*T*] : to
end a connection to or relationship with
someone or something ▪ *She has tried to
distance herself from the scandal/situa-
tion.*

dis·tant /ˈdɪstənt/ *adj* **1** : existing or
happening far away in space ▪ *astrono-
mers studying distant galaxies* **2** *always
before a noun* : far away in time ▪ *in the
distant past* ▪ *a distant memory* ▪ *We're expecting changes in the not too distant future.* [=soon] **3** *always before a noun* —
used to describe a relative who is not
closely related to you ▪ *She's a distant
cousin of mine.* **4** : having to do with
something that is not related to what is
happening where you are or at the
present time ▪ *distant thoughts/possibili-
ties* **5** *somewhat formal* : not friendly or
showing emotion ▪ *He was cold and distant.* — **dis·tant·ly** *adv* ▪ *We are distant-
ly related to each other.*

dis·taste /dɪsˈteɪst/ *n* [*C/U*] : a strong
feeling of not liking someone or something ▪ *a distaste for paperwork*

dis·taste·ful /dɪsˈteɪstfəl/ *adj* **1** : not
pleasant or enjoyable ▪ *a distasteful subject* **2** : morally offensive ▪ *distasteful
jokes/behavior* — **dis·taste·ful·ly** *adv*

dis·tem·per /dɪsˈtɛmpɚ/ *n* [*U*] *medical*
: a serious disease of animals that is easily passed to other animals

dis·till (*US*) *or chiefly Brit* **dis·til** /dɪˈstɪl/
vb **-tilled; -till·ing** [*T*] **1 a** : to make (a
liquid) pure by heating it until it be-
comes a gas and then cooling it until it is
a liquid again ▪ *distilled water* **b** : to
make (a strong alcoholic drink) by using
this process ▪ *distill whiskey from barley*
2 : to take the most important parts of
something and put them in a different
and usually improved form ▪ *Her wisdom
is distilled from* [=her wisdom comes
from] *many years of experience.* — **dis-
til·la·tion** /ˌdɪstəˈleɪʃən/ *n* [*C/U*] ▪ *the
distillation of brandy from wine*

dis·till·er /dɪˈstɪlɚ/ *n* [*C*] : a person or
company that produces strong alcoholic
drinks by distilling them

dis·till·ery /dɪˈstɪləri/ *n, pl* **-er·ies** [*C*] : a
place where alcoholic drinks are pro-
duced

dis·tinct /dɪˈstɪŋkt/ *adj* **1** : different in a
way that you can see, hear, smell, feel,
etc. ▪ *three distinct categories/classes/
groups/types* ▪ *The class focuses on U.S.
English,* **as distinct from** *British English.*
[=the class focuses on U.S. English and
not on British English] **2** : easy to see,
hear, smell, feel, etc. ▪ *a distinct* [=notice-
able] *Southern accent* **3** : strong and
definite ▪ *a distinct possibility* — **dis-
tinct·ly** *adv* ▪ *I distinctly told you not to
call me.*

dis·tinc·tion /dɪˈstɪŋkʃən/ *n* **1** [*C*] : a
difference that you can see, hear, smell,
feel, etc. ▪ *distinctions between social
classes* ▪ *She* **made/drew a distinction between** *the words "less" and "fewer."* **2** [*U*]
: importance, excellence, or achieve-
ment ▪ *She was a politician of some distinction.* [=she was a distinguished politi-
cian] **3** [*C/U*] : a special honor,
recognition, or award ▪ *She's won many
distinctions.* ▪ *He graduated* **with distinction.** [=with special awards or recogni-
tion] **4** [*U*] : the quality that makes a
person or thing special or different ▪ *It
had the distinction of being the oldest
house in the city.*

dis·tinc·tive /dɪˈstɪŋktɪv/ *adj* : having a
quality or characteristic that makes a
person or thing different from others ▪ *a
distinctive walk/voice/haircut* — **dis-
tinc·tive·ly** *adv* — **dis·tinc·tive·ness**
n [*U*]

dis·tin·guish /dɪˈstɪŋgwɪʃ/ *vb* **1** [*T/I*]
: to notice or recognize a difference between people or things ▪ *I have trouble
distinguishing (between) them.* ▪ *distinguishing fact from fantasy* **2** [*T*] : to
make (someone or something) different
or special in some way ▪ *Our excellent
customer service distinguishes us from our
competitors.* ▪ *The law affects private property* **as distinguished from** *public proper-*

ty. [=the law affects private property and not public property] **3** [T] : to see or hear (someone or something) clearly • *You can't distinguish the detail from this distance.* — **distinguish yourself** : to do something very well or in a way that deserves special recognition • *He distinguished himself in the war.* — **dis·tin·guish·able** /dɪˈstɪŋgwɪʃəbəl/ *adj*

dis·tin·guished /dɪˈstɪŋgwɪʃt/ *adj* **1** : known by many people because of some quality or achievement • *a distinguished scientist/career* **2** : making someone seem important and worth respect • *He's a distinguished-looking gentleman.*

dis·tort /dɪˈstoɚt/ *vb* **1** [T/I] : to change the natural, normal, or original shape, appearance, or sound of (something) in a way that is usually not attractive or pleasing • *Her face was distorted by pain.* *The sound of the guitar was distorted.* **2** [T] : to change (something) so that it is no longer true or accurate • *She felt he was distorting the facts.* — **dis·tor·tion** /dɪˈstoɚʃən/ *n* [C/U]

dis·tract /dɪˈstrækt/ *vb* [T] **1** : to cause (someone) to stop thinking about or paying attention to someone or something and to think about or pay attention to someone or something else instead • *You sneak into his room while I distract him.* **2** : to take (attention) away from someone or something • *The local story distracted attention from news of the war.* — **dis·tract·ing** /dɪˈstræktɪŋ/ *adj* • *The music was very distracting.*

dis·trac·tion /dɪˈstrækʃən/ *n* **1** [C/U] : something that makes it difficult to think or pay attention • *It was hard to work with so many distractions.* **2** [C] : something that amuses or entertains you so that you do not think about problems, work, etc. • *A weekend at the beach was a good distraction from her troubles.* **3** [U] : a state in which you are very annoyed or upset • *Their endless chatter drove her to distraction.*

dis·traught /dɪˈstrɑːt/ *adj* : very upset • *She was distraught over the death of her partner.*

¹**dis·tress** /dɪˈstrɛs/ *n* [U] **1** : unhappiness or pain : suffering that affects the mind or body • *The patient showed no obvious signs of distress.* • *emotional/mental distress* • *He was clearly in distress.* [=very upset] **2** : a very difficult situation in which you do not have enough money, food, etc. • *Donations were given to families in (financial) distress.* **3** *of a boat, airplane, etc.* : a state of danger or desperate need • *The ship was in distress.* [=the ship was possibly going to sink]

²**distress** *vb* [T] : to worry or upset (someone) • *I was distressed to hear she left.* — **dis·tress·ing** /dɪˈstrɛsɪŋ/ *adj* • *some distressing news*

dis·tressed /dɪˈstrɛst/ *adj* **1** : feeling or showing extreme unhappiness or pain • *She felt emotionally distressed.* **2** : experiencing financial trouble • *a financially/economically distressed city/family*

dis·trib·ute /dɪˈstrɪbjuːt/ *vb* **-ut·ed; -ut·ing** [T] **1 a** : to give or deliver (something) to people • *The organization distributes food and clothing to needy families.* **b** : to deliver (something) to a store or business • *Copies of the CD were distributed to stores.* **2** : to divide (something) among the members of a group • *The profits were evenly distributed among/between them.* **3** : to spread or place (something) over an area • *Make sure the paint is/gets distributed evenly over the surface area.* • (figurative) *The plant is widely distributed throughout the world.* [=the plant grows throughout the world]

dis·tri·bu·tion /ˌdɪstrəˈbjuːʃən/ *n* **1** [U] **a** : the act of giving or delivering something to people • *The group collects food and clothing for distribution to needy families.* **b** : the act of delivering something to a store or business • *The company acquired U.S. distribution rights.* **2** [C/U] : the way that something is divided or spread out • *weight distribution*

dis·trib·u·tor /dɪˈstrɪbjətɚ/ *n* [C] **1** : a person or company that supplies stores or businesses with goods • *a software distributor* **2** *technical* : a device that sends electricity to the spark plugs of an engine

dis·trict /ˈdɪstrɪkt/ *n* [C] **1** : an area established by a government for official government business • *postal/election/congressional districts* **2** : an area or section that has some special characteristic or purpose • *the city's entertainment/shopping district*

district attorney *n* [C] : a lawyer who works for the U.S. government in a state, county, etc., and who is responsible for starting a criminal case against someone — *abbr. DA*

¹**dis·trust** /dɪsˈtrʌst/ *vb* [T] : to have no trust or confidence in (someone or something) • *He distrusts doctors.*

²**distrust** *n* [U, singular] : a feeling that someone or something is not honest and cannot be trusted • *He regards doctors with distrust.* — **dis·trust·ful** /dɪsˈtrʌstfəl/ *adj*

dis·turb /dɪˈstɚb/ *vb* [T] **1** : to interrupt or bother (someone or something) • *I'm sorry to disturb you at such a late hour.* • *They were arrested for disturbing the peace.* [=behaving in a violent or noisy manner in public] **2** : to worry or upset (someone) • *His behavior disturbs me.* • *She was disturbed to learn her son was failing class.* **3** : to change the position, arrangement, or order of (something) • *Don't disturb the crime scene.* [=don't touch or move anything] • *His visit disturbed our routine.* — **dis·turb·ing** /dɪˈstɚbɪŋ/ *adj* • *a deeply/very disturbing sight* — **dis·turb·ing·ly** *adv*

dis·turb·ance /dɪˈstɚbəns/ *n* [C/U] **1 a** : something that stops you from working, sleeping, etc. • *She suffered from frequent sleep disturbances.* **b** : a change in the position, arrangement, or order of something • *They noticed a slight disturbance in the water.* **2** : violent or noisy behavior especially in public • *They were arrested for creating/causing a disturbance.* **3** : an unhealthy physical or mental condition in which something is not normal ▪ *visual/emotional/mental disturbances*

dis·turbed /dɪˈstɚbd/ *adj* **1** : having or showing evidence of a mental or emotional illness ▪ *mentally/emotionally disturbed children* **2** : worried and unhappy ▪ *He seems disturbed about his work lately.*

dis·unit·ed /ˌdɪsjuˈnaɪtəd/ *adj, chiefly Brit* : not able to work or agree with other people within the same group, organization, etc. ▪ *a disunited political party*

dis·uni·ty /dɪsˈjuːnəti/ *n [U]* : the state of not being able to agree about important things ▪ *disunity within the party*

dis·use /dɪsˈjuːs/ *n [U]* : the state of not being used ▪ *The word fell into disuse.* [=people stopped using it] — **dis·used** /dɪsˈjuːzd/ *adj, always before a noun* ▪ *disused words/buildings*

¹**ditch** /ˈdɪtʃ/ *n [C]* : a long narrow hole that is dug along a road, field, etc., and used to hold or move water ▪ *irrigation ditches*

²**ditch** *vb* **1** *[T] informal* : to get rid of (something) ▪ *They ditched the car in a vacant lot.* **2** *[T] informal* : to end a relationship with (someone) ▪ *His girlfriend ditched him.* **3** *[T] US, informal* : to get away from (someone you do not want to be with) without saying that you are leaving ▪ *They ditched me at the concert.* **4** *[T/I]* : to land an aircraft on water because of an emergency ▪ *Engine trouble forced the pilot to ditch (the plane).*

¹**dith·er** /ˈdɪðɚ/ *n [singular] informal* : a very nervous, confused, or excited state ▪ *The news of his arrival had us (all) in a dither.*

²**dither** *vb [I] informal* : to delay taking action because you are not sure about what to do ▪ *We don't have time to dither.*

¹**dit·to** /ˈdɪtoʊ/ *adv, informal* — used to say that whatever you have said about one person or thing is also true of another person or thing ▪ *Boston is getting a lot of rain. Ditto New York.* [=New York is also getting a lot of rain] **2** — used in speech to show you agree with what someone has just said or have the same opinion ▪ *"I don't like spinach." "Ditto."* [=I don't like spinach either]

²**ditto** *n, pl* **-tos** *[C]* : a pair of marks " used underneath a word to save space and show that the word is repeated where the marks are — called also *ditto marks*

dit·ty /ˈdɪti/ *n, pl* **-ties** *[C]* : a short and simple song ▪ *Play us a little ditty.*

dit·zy *or* **dit·sy** /ˈdɪtsi/ *adj* **ditz·i·er** *or* **dits·i·er; -est** *chiefly US, informal* : silly and tending to forget things ▪ *She's a ditzy blonde.*

di·uret·ic /ˌdajəˈrɛtɪk/ *n [C] medical* : a substance that increases the amount of urine you pass from your body — **diuretic** *adj* ▪ *a diuretic drug/effect*

div. *also* **div** *abbr* division

di·va /ˈdiːvə/ *n [C]* **1** : the main female singer in an opera company **2** : an attractive and successful female performer or celebrity ▪ *pop/fashion divas*

di·van /dɪˈvæn/ *n [C]* **1** : a long, low seat that has no back or arms or only part of a back and one arm **2** *Brit* : a type of

bed that has a thick base

¹**dive** /ˈdaɪv/ *vb* **dived** /ˈdaɪvd/ *or chiefly US* **dove** /ˈdoʊv/; **div·ing** *[I]* **1** : to jump into water with your arms and head going in first ▪ *She dove into the pool.* **2** : to swim underwater usually while using special equipment to help you breathe ▪ *Many people enjoy diving on the island's coral reefs.* **3** : to go underwater or down to a deeper level underwater ▪ *The submarine can dive to 3,000 feet.* **4** : to move down through the air at a steep angle ▪ *The plane suddenly dove.* **5** : to fall suddenly and quickly in amount, value, etc. ▪ *The stock's value dove to an all-time low.* **6** : to suddenly jump toward something that is on or near the ground ▪ *He dove for the ball.* **7** *informal* : to start doing something with enthusiasm ▪ *They dove into their work.* ▪ *We have a lot of things to discuss, so let's dive (right) in.* [=let's get started immediately] **8** *informal* : to quickly reach *into* (a bag, pocket, etc.) ▪ *She dove into her purse to find some change.* — **div·er** /ˈdaɪvɚ/ *n [C]*

²**dive** *n [C]* **1** : a jump into water with your arms and head going in first ▪ *a perfect dive* **2** : an act of swimming underwater usually while using special equipment to help you breathe ▪ *This will be my first dive on a coral reef.* **3** : a usually steep downward movement of a submarine, airplane, bird, etc. ▪ *The jet rolled into a dive.* **4** : a sudden quick fall in amount, value, etc. ▪ *Temperatures across the region will take a dive tonight.* **5** *informal* : a bar, nightclub, etc., that is cheap and dirty ▪ *That bar is a real dive.* **6** : a sudden jump or movement toward something that is on or near the ground ▪ *He made a dive for the ditch/ball/gun.*

dive–bomb /ˈdaɪvˌbɑːm/ *vb [T]* : to drop a bomb from an airplane on (something) after approaching it at a sharp or steep angle ▪ *The pilots/planes dive-bombed the enemy ships.*

di·verge /dəˈvɚdʒ/ *vb* **-verged; -verging** *[I] formal* **1** : to split and move out in different directions from a single point ▪ *A prism causes rays of light to diverge.* **2** : to be or become different ▪ *When it comes to politics, their opinions/views diverge.* [=they have different opinions/views] — **di·ver·gence** /dəˈvɚdʒəns/ *n [C/U]* ▪ *a wide divergence of opinion* — **di·ver·gent** /dəˈvɚdʒənt/ *adj* ▪ *divergent lines/opinions*

di·verse /daɪˈvɚs/ *adj* **1** : different from each other ▪ *topics as diverse as chemistry and sculpture* **2** : made up of people or things that are different from each other ▪ *The group of students is very diverse.* [=the students are different ages, races, etc.] — **di·verse·ly** *adv*

di·ver·si·fy /dəˈvɚsəˌfaɪ/ *vb* **-fies; -fied; -fy·ing** *[T/I]* **1** : to change (something) so that it has more different kinds of people or things ▪ *You should diversify (your investments).* [=you should invest your money in several different ways instead of investing it all in one thing] ▪ *a diversified economy* [=an economy that has a variety of industries] **2** : to produce or sell more kinds of products ▪ *They want to diversify (the company).* — **di·ver·si·fi·ca·tion** /dəˌvəsəfəˈkeɪʃən/ *n* [U]

di·ver·sion /dəˈvəʒən/ *n* **1** [C/U] *formal* : the act of changing the direction or use of something ▪ *small diversions of river water for irrigation* ▪ *illegal diversion of public funds* [=illegal use of public money for some improper purpose] **2** [C/U] *formal* : something that people do because it is enjoyable, entertaining, or pleasant ▪ *Sports provide him with a welcome diversion from the pressures of his job.* **3** [C] : something that takes attention away from what is happening ▪ *He created a diversion while his partner stole her pocketbook.* **4** [C] *Brit* : ¹DETOUR 2

di·ver·sion·ary /dəˈvəʒəˌneri, Brit dəˈvəːʒənri/ *adj, formal* : tending or intended to take attention away from someone or something important ▪ *a diversionary tactic*

di·ver·si·ty /dəˈvəsəti/ *n, pl* **-ties** [C/U] **1** : the quality or state of having many different forms, types, ideas, etc. ▪ *biological/genetic/linguistic diversity* ▪ *She has a diversity of interests.* [=she has many different interests] **2** : the state of having people who are different races or who have different cultures in a group or organization ▪ *cultural/ethnic diversity* ▪ *The school aims for diversity in its student population.*

di·vert /dəˈvət/ *vb* [T] **1** : to change the direction or use of (something) ▪ *Police diverted traffic.* ▪ *They were charged with illegally diverting public funds.* **2 a** : to take (attention) away *from* someone or something ▪ *He lied to divert attention from the real situation.* **b** : to take the attention of (someone) away from something or someone ▪ *Nothing can divert me from my goal.*

di·vest /daɪˈvɛst/ *vb* [T] *finance* : to sell (something valuable, such as property or stocks) ▪ *We may have to divest assets to raise capital/money.* — **divest of** [*phrasal vb*] *formal* **1 divest (someone or something) of** : to take (something) away from (someone or something else) ▪ *He was divested of his title/power/property.* **2 divest (yourself) of** : to sell or give away (possessions, money, etc.) ▪ *She divested herself of most of her possessions.* — **di·vest·ment** /daɪˈvɛstmənt/ *n* [C/U]

¹**di·vide** /dəˈvaɪd/ *vb* **-vid·ed; -vid·ing** **1 a** [T/I] : to separate (something) into two or more parts or pieces ▪ *She divided the pie into eight pieces.* ▪ *The teacher divided the class (up) into four groups.* ▪ *The book is divided into three sections.* ▪ *The cells divide rapidly.* **b** [T] : to separate (something) into classes or categories ▪ *Animals can be divided into several major types.* **2** [T/I] **a** : to give (something) out in usually equal amounts ▪ *They divided (up) the profits/work between/among themselves.* **b** : to use (your time, energy, etc.) for two or more purposes or activities ▪ *Her time is divided between home, work, and school.* **3** [T] : to cause (something) to be separate or apart from something else ▪ *A tall fence divides the two yards.* **4** [T]

a : to separate (people) into groups that disagree ▪ *The nation was divided by war.* ▪ *The divorce divided the family.* **b** : to cause (opinions, views, etc.) to not agree ▪ *Opinions are divided.* [=people do not agree] **5** [T/I] *mathematics* : to calculate how many times one number contains another number ▪ *Eight divided by two is four.* [=8 ÷ 2 = 4; ⁸⁄₂ = 4]

²**divide** *n* [C] **1** *chiefly US* : a line of hills or mountains from which rivers drain **2** : a separation of people into two or more groups that is caused by different opinions or beliefs or by a disagreement ▪ *the divide between generations* ▪ *The argument created a divide within the group.*

divided *adj* **1** : separated by different opinions : in a state of disagreement ▪ *Experts are sharply divided on/over the issue.* **2** : given to two or more people or things rather than to just one person or thing ▪ *He has divided loyalties.* [=he is trying to be loyal to opposing groups, ideals, etc.]

divided highway *n* [C] *US* : a major road that has something (such as a guardrail or an area with grass and trees) that separates lanes of traffic moving in opposite directions — called also (*Brit*) *dual carriageway*

div·i·dend /ˈdɪvəˌdɛnd/ *n* [C] **1** *finance* : an amount of a company's profits that the company pays to people who own stock in the company **2** : an advantage or benefit that you get because of something you have done ▪ *Eating healthy and exercising yields big dividends.*

di·vid·er /dəˈvaɪdə/ *n* **1** [C] **a** : a thing that keeps two spaces or areas separate ▪ *Concrete barriers are used as highway dividers.* **b** : someone or something that causes people to disagree with one another ▪ *He's a uniter, not a divider.* **2** [*plural*] : a tool that consists of two pointed sticks joined at the top and that is used for measuring or marking lines and angles ▪ *a pair of dividers*

dividing line *n* [C] : a line or object that separates two areas ▪ (*figurative*) *the dividing line between right and wrong*

div·i·na·tion /ˌdɪvəˈneɪʃən/ *n* [U] : the art or practice of using signs (such as an arrangement of tea leaves or cards) or special powers to predict the future

¹**di·vine** /dəˈvaɪn/ *adj* **1** : relating to or coming from God or a god ▪ *divine will/law/love* ▪ *He ruled by divine right.* **2** *informal + somewhat old-fashioned* : very good ▪ *This pie is divine.* — **di·vine·ly** *adv*

²**divine** *vb* **-vined; -vin·ing** [T] *formal + literary* : to discover or understand (something) without having direct evidence ▪ *divine the truth*

diving *n* [U] **1** : a sport or activity in which people dive into water from a diving board or a platform ▪ *He won a gold medal in diving.* **2** : a sport or activity in which people swim underwater while using special equipment to breathe ▪ *We went diving on the coral reef.*

diving board *n* [C] : a board that people can jump off of to dive into water

di·vin·i·ty /dəˈvɪnəti/ *n, pl* **-ties** **1** [U]

: the state of being divine ▪ *Christians believe in the divinity of Jesus Christ.* **2** [C] : a god or goddess ▪ *the divinities of ancient Greece* **3** [U] : the formal study of religion, religious practices, and religious beliefs ▪ *a doctor of divinity*

di·vis·i·ble /dəˈvɪzəbəl/ *adj, not before a noun* : able to be divided ▪ *9 is divisible by 3*

di·vi·sion /dəˈvɪʒən/ *n* **1** [*U, singular*] : the act or process of dividing something into parts ▪ *the process of cell division* ▪ *a division of profits into equal shares* **2** [C] : something that physically divides or separates something else ▪ *A line of trees serves as a division between our property and theirs.* **3** [U] *mathematics* : the process of finding out how many times one number is contained in another **4** [C] : a group of people who do a particular job within a larger organization ▪ *the news division* [=*department*] *of a major television network* **5** [C] : a large military group ▪ *an infantry division* **6** [C] **a** : a group of teams that form one section of a sports league ▪ *There are five teams in the league's western division.* **b** : a group of people who are similar in age, size, etc., and who compete against each other ▪ *boxers competing in the heavyweight division* **7** [C/U] : a situation in which groups of people have different opinions, beliefs, or ways of life that separate them from each other ▪ *There were serious divisions within the party on a number of issues.* **8** [C] : any one of the parts or groups that form something : SECTION ▪ *a major division of the Earth's surface* — **di·vi·sion·al** /dəˈvɪʒənl/ *adj, always before a noun* ▪ *the divisional manager/commander/champion*

division sign *n* [C] *mathematics* : the symbol ÷ that is used to show that two numbers are to be divided into each other

di·vi·sive /dəˈvaɪsɪv/ *adj, formal* : causing people to disagree and separate into different groups ▪ *divisive issues like abortion* — **di·vi·sive·ness** *n* [U]

¹di·vorce /dəˈvoɚs/ *n* **1** [C/U] : the ending of a marriage by a legal process ▪ *They are getting a divorce.* ▪ *a divorce lawyer/court* **2** [C] *formal* : a complete separation ▪ *a divorce between theory and practice*

²divorce *vb* **-vorced; -vorc·ing 1** [T/I] : to legally end your marriage with (your husband or wife) ▪ *She wants to divorce him.* **2** [T] *formal* : to make or keep (something) separate ▪ *The constitution divorces church and/from state.* — **di·vorced** *adj* ▪ *They're getting divorced.* ▪ *a divorced man* ▪ *a theory that is divorced from reality* [=that shows no connection to reality]

di·vor·cé /dəˌvoɚˈseɪ/ *n* [C] *chiefly US* : a man who is divorced

di·vor·cée /dəˌvoɚˈseɪ/ *n* [C] : a divorced person; *especially* : a woman who is divorced

div·ot /ˈdɪvət/ *n* [C] : a loose piece of grass and dirt that is dug out of the ground when the ground is struck by

something (such as a golf club)

di·vulge /dəˈvʌldʒ/ *vb* **-vulged; -vulging** [T] *formal* : to give (information) to someone ▪ *The company will not divulge its sales figures.*

div·vy /ˈdɪvi/ *vb* **-vies; -vied; -vy·ing** — **divvy up** [*phrasal vb*] **divvy (something) up** *or* **divvy up (something)** *informal* : to divide or share (something) ▪ *We divvied up the money.*

diz·zy /ˈdɪzi/ *adj* **diz·zi·er; -est 1** : feeling that you are turning around in circles and are going to fall even though you are standing still ▪ *The children were dizzy after spinning in circles.* **2** : mentally or emotionally upset or confused ▪ *Complex math problems make me dizzy.* **3** *always before a noun* : causing you to feel dizzy: such as **a** : very high ▪ *dizzy heights* **b** : very fast ▪ *the dizzy pace of our lives* **4** *informal* : very silly and tending to forget things ▪ *an actress known for playing dizzy blondes* — **diz·zi·ly** /ˈdɪzəli/ *adv* — **diz·zi·ness** /ˈdɪzinəs/ *n* [U]

diz·zy·ing /ˈdɪzijɪŋ/ *adj, always before a noun* : causing or likely to cause dizziness ▪ *dizzying speeds/heights*

DJ /ˈdiːˌdʒeɪ/ *n* [C] : DISC JOCKEY

DMV *abbr, US* Department of Motor Vehicles

DMZ *abbr* demilitarized zone

DNA /ˌdiːˌɛnˈeɪ/ *n* [U] : a substance that carries genetic information in the cells of plants and animals ▪ *DNA testing* ◆ *DNA* is an abbreviation of "deoxyribonucleic acid."

¹do /ˈduː/ *vb* **does** /ˈdʌz/; **did** /ˈdɪd/; **done** /ˈdʌn/; **do·ing** /ˈduːwɪŋ/ **1 a** [T/I] : to perform (an action or activity) ▪ *This crime was done deliberately.* ▪ *I have to do some chores.* ▪ *I did a favor for him.* = *I did him a favor.* ▪ *"What are you doing this weekend?" "I'm just relaxing at home."* ▪ *What is the stock market doing now: rising or falling?* ▪ *She did nothing to help us.* ▪ *I did my best.* ▪ *I did as well as I could.* ▪ *Do as I say, not as I do.* [=do the things that I say you should do, not the things that I do myself] ▪ *What can I do to help you?* = *What can I do for you?* [=how can I help you?] ▪ *What have I done to you to make you so angry?* ▪ *Have you done something to/with this room?* [=have you changed this room in some way?] ▪ *It looks different.* ▪ *My knee is sore. I must have done something to it* [=I must have hurt it] *when I fell.* ▪ *I didn't do it!* = *I didn't do anything!* [=I didn't do what you said I did] ▪ *What have I done with my keys?* [=where did I put my keys?] **b** [T] — used with *what* to ask or talk about a person's job ▪ *"What does your husband do (for a living)?" "He's a writer."* **2** [T] : to finish working on (something) ▪ *Have you done your homework yet?* **3** [I] — used to describe the success or progress of someone or something ▪ *"How is she doing in school?" "She did badly/poorly at first, but now she's doing much better."* ▪ *The company is doing well.* ◆ *How are you doing?* *or* (*very informally*) *How you doing?* is used as a greeting. **4** [T] — used to describe the effect that something has ▪ *A few days off will do you* *(some) good.* [=will be good for you] • *We didn't mean to do him (any) harm.* [=to harm him] • *That hat does nothing for you.* [=that hat does not look good on you] **5** [T] : to create or produce (something) • *a painter who has done some beautiful landscapes* **6** [T] **a** : to play (a role or character) • *an actor who did Hamlet on Broadway* **b** : to pretend to be (someone, such as a famous person) • *a comedian who does a great George Bush* [=who does a very good and entertaining imitation of George Bush] **7** [T] **a** : to wash or clean (something) • *do the laundry/dishes* **b** : to decorate (a place) • *They did the bedroom in blue.* **c** : to make (someone's face, hair, etc.) more attractive by putting on makeup, styling, etc. • *She wanted to do her face before the party.* • *She had her hair done at the beauty parlor.* **8** [T] : to cook or prepare (food) • *I like my steak done rare.* **9** [T] *chiefly US, informal* : to participate in (an activity) with other people • *We should do dinner/lunch some time.* [=we should have dinner/lunch together] • *Let's do a movie.* [=go to a movie] **10** [T] : to go to (a place) when traveling • *a group of tourists who are doing 12 countries in 30 days* **11** [T] **a** : to move or travel (a distance) • *We did 500 miles yesterday.* **b** : to move at (a speed) • *They were doing 85 mph.* **12** [T] : to be in a place for (a period of time) • *He did two years in college before he dropped out.; especially* : to be in a prison for (a period of time) • *He did five years for robbery.* • *He's doing time in a federal penitentiary.* **13** [T/I] : to be enough or adequate for someone or something • *One piece of cake will do (me).* • *I'd prefer to use glue, but tape will/would do.* • *"Would you like anything else?" "No, that'll do it."* • *I have one more letter to sign and that should do it.* = *I have one more letter to sign and that does it.* [=and then I'll be finished] **14** [I] : to be proper — used in negative statements • *Such behavior will never do!* [=such behavior should not be allowed] • *This is a formal occasion, so jeans simply won't do.* ◇ In U.S. English, this sense of *do* is somewhat formal or old-fashioned. **15** [T] *informal* : to use (illegal drugs) • *He doesn't do drugs anymore.* **16** [I] *informal* **a** : to happen • *Let's find out what's doing downtown.* **b** ◇ People ask *what is something/someone doing . . . ?* when they are surprised or upset about where something or someone is. • *What are all my clothes doing on the floor?* [=why are all my clothes on the floor?] People ask *what is someone doing with (something)?* when they are surprised or upset because someone has something. • *What are you doing with my notebook?* [=why do you have my notebook?] — **be to do with** see HAVE TO DO WITH (below) — **do away with** [phrasal vb] **1** : to kill (someone) • *She planned to do away with her husband.* **2** : to get rid of (something) • *The company had to do away with a number of jobs.* — **do by** [phrasal vb] : to deal with or treat (someone) well or badly • *She feels that they did poorly/bad-*

ly by her. [=that they treated her poorly/badly] — see also *hard done by* at ²HARD — **do down** [phrasal vb] **do (someone) down** *Brit, informal* : to talk about (someone) in an insulting or critical way • *Stop doing yourself down: you've got a lot to offer!* — **do for** [phrasal vb] *Brit, informal* **1** : to cause the death or ruin of (someone) • *All that hard work nearly did for him.* **2** : to do the cleaning and cooking for (someone) • *Mrs. Jones does for the vicar.* — **do in** [phrasal vb] **do (someone) in** *informal* **1** : to cause the death or failure of (someone) • *They threatened to do him in.* • *a businessman who was done in by greed* **2** : to make (someone) very tired • *Working in the garden all day really did me in.* — **do out of** [phrasal vb] **do (someone) out of (something)** *informal* : to unfairly prevent (someone) from getting or having (something) • *I've been done out of what was rightfully mine!* — **do over** [phrasal vb] **1 do (something) over** *US* : to do (something) again • *I made a mistake and had to do the work over (again).* **2 do (something) over** or **do over (something)** : to decorate or change a room, house, etc., so that it looks very different • *We're doing over the kitchen.* **3 do (someone) over** or **do over (someone)** *Brit, informal* : to attack and beat (someone) • *He got done over by a gang of teenagers.* — **do up** [phrasal vb] **1 do up (something)** or **do (something) up** **a** : to decorate (something) • *They did up the room in bright colors.* **b** : to adjust (something) in a particular way • *She did up her hair in a ponytail.* **c** *chiefly Brit* : to wrap (something) • *packages done up in paper and ribbon* **d** *chiefly Brit* : to repair (something) • *do up an old house* **2 do (someone) up** : to dress (someone) up • *She did herself up for the party.* **3 do up (something)** or **do (something) up** or **do up (something)** : to be fastened or to fasten (something) with buttons, a zipper, etc. • *a dress that does up at the back* • *She did up her dress.* — **do well** ◇ If you *would do well* to do something, you should do it. • *You would do well to avoid him right now.* If you *did well* to do something, you were correct to do it. • *You did well to avoid him when he was in a bad mood.* If you *did well to escape, survive,* etc., you were lucky to escape, survive, etc. • *When the tornado hit, they did well to escape uninjured.* — **do with** [phrasal vb] : to be helped by having (something) • *I could (really) do with a cup of coffee right now!* [=I would really like a cup of coffee] — **do without** [phrasal vb] : to not have (something) : to live, work, etc., without having (something) • *If you can't afford a new car, you'll just have to do without (one).* • *I don't know how we ever did without computers.* • *I enjoy traveling, but I can/could do without having to wait around in airports.* [=I don't like having to wait around] — **have to do with 1** or *chiefly Brit* **be to do with** : to relate to or involve (someone or something) • *The problem has to do with fishing rights.* • *His job has something to do with computers.*

• *That's your problem: it has nothing to do with me!* = (*chiefly Brit*) *It's nothing to do with me!* • *You're wrong.* **It's got everything to do with you**: *you're legally responsible for what went wrong.* **2** : to be involved in or in some way responsible for (something) • *He claims that he had* **nothing to do with** *the accident.* [=that he was not involved in the accident] • *I know he* **had something to do with it.** **3** ◆ If you do not want to **have anything to do with** someone or if you **want nothing to do with** someone, you do not want to be involved with that person in any way. — compare ²DO — **do·able** /ˈduː·wə·bəl/ *adj*

²**do** *vb* **does; did; doing;** *negative forms* **do not** *or* **don't; did not** *or* **didn't; does not** *or* **doesn't** [*auxiliary vb*] **1 a** — used before the subject in a question • *Do you play the piano?* • *What did he say?* **b** — used to form brief questions that come at the end of a statement • *You play the piano, don't you?* • *Her husband works with computers, doesn't he?* **2 a** — used with *not* to form negative statements • *I do not know.* = *I don't know.* **b** — used with *not* to form commands • *Do not lie to me!* = *Don't lie to me!* **c** *somewhat formal* — used before the subject in a statement after words like *never, seldom,* and *rarely* • *Never did he see his native land again.* [=he never saw his native land again] **3** — used to replace another verb or verb phrase • *"May I come in?" "Yes, (please) do."* • (*informal*) *"Can you finish it today?" "Sure, boss, will do!"* [=I will finish it today] • (*informal*) *"Can you finish it today?" "Sorry, boss, no can do!"* [=I can't finish it today] • (*Brit*) *"Are you going to the party?" "I might do."* [=I might] **4 a** — used to make a statement stronger • *You really do look lovely today!* • *Oh, do be quiet!* **b** *somewhat formal* — used as a polite way to tell or urge someone to do something • *Do come in and have a seat.* — compare ¹DO

³**do** *n* [C] *informal* **1** : something that a person should do • *the* **dos and don'ts** *of dating* [=the things that you should and should not do when dating someone] **2** *US* : HAIRDO **3** : a party or social gathering • *We threw a big do for her.* — compare ⁴DO

⁴**do** /ˈdoʊ/ *or chiefly Brit* **doh** *n* [U] : the first note of a musical scale • *do, re, mi, fa, sol, la, ti* — compare ³DO

DOB *abbr* date of birth

Do·ber·man pin·scher /ˌdoʊbəmən-ˈpɪnʃɚ/ *n* [C] : a type of tall, thin, muscular dog with short hair that is usually black and tan — called also **Doberman**

doc /ˈdɑːk/ *n* [C] *informal* : DOCTOR • *Am I going to be OK, doc?*

doc. *abbr* document

doc·ile /ˈdɑːsəl, *Brit* ˈdəʊˌsaɪl/ *adj* : easily taught, led, or controlled • *a docile pet* — **doc·ile·ly** *adv* — **do·cil·i·ty** /dɑˈsɪləti, *Brit* dəʊˈsɪləti/ *n* [U]

¹**dock** /ˈdɑːk/ *n* **1** [C/U] : an area of water in a port where ships are loaded, unloaded, or repaired **2** [C] : a long structure that is built out into water and used as a place to get on, get off, or tie up a

boat **3** [C] *US* : a place for loading materials onto ships, trucks, trains, etc. • *a* **loading dock 4** [C] : the place in a court of law where a person who is accused of a crime stands or sits during a trial

²**dock** *vb* **1 a** [T/I] : to bring a ship or boat into a dock • *The captain was forced to dock the ship.* • *The ship docked in Miami.* **b** [T/I] : to join together (two spacecraft) while in space • *They docked the spaceship with the satellite.* **c** [T] : to connect an electronic device to another device • *You can dock the camera directly to the printer.* **2** [T] : to take away part of (the money that is paid to someone) • *Her boss docked her pay/wages for being late.*

dock·er /ˈdɑːkɚ/ *n* [C] *Brit* : DOCK-WORKER

dock·et /ˈdɑːkət/ *n* [C] *US* **1** : a list of the legal cases that will be tried in a court of law **2** : a list of things to do or discuss • *The new library will be the first* **item on the committee's** *docket.*

dock·land /ˈdɑːkˌlænd/ *n* [C/U] *Brit* : the part of a port where there are docks — called also **docklands**

dock·work·er /ˈdɑːkˌwɚkɚ/ *n* [C] *US* : a person who loads and unloads ships at a port

dock·yard /ˈdɑːkˌjɑɚd/ *n* [C] : SHIPYARD

¹**doc·tor** /ˈdɑːktɚ/ *n* [C] **1** : a person who is trained and licensed to treat sick and injured people • *I think you should see a doctor.* [=*physician*] **2** *US* **a** : a dentist — used chiefly as a title or as a form of address • *My dentist is Dr. Smith.* **b** : a person who is trained to treat sick and injured animals : VETERINARIAN • *an animal doctor* **3** : a person who has the highest degree (such as a PhD) given by a university • *a Doctor of Philosophy*

²**doctor** *vb* [T] **1** : to change (something) especially in order to trick or deceive people • *doctoring the company's financial records* • *a doctored photo* **2** : to add something (such as alcohol or drugs) to (a food or drink) • *Somebody doctored the punch.* **3** : to give medical treatment to (an injury, a person, etc.) • *He had time to doctor his wounds.*

doc·tor·al /ˈdɑːktərəl/ *adj, always before a noun* : of or relating to the highest degree that is given by a university • *a doctoral degree/dissertation*

doc·tor·ate /ˈdɑːktərət/ *n* [C] : the highest degree that is given by a university

doc·tri·naire /ˌdɑːktrəˈneɚ/ *adj, formal + disapproving* — used to describe a person who has very strong beliefs about what should be done and will not change them • *a doctrinaire socialist*

doc·trine /ˈdɑːktrən/ *n* **1** [C/U] : a set of ideas or beliefs that are taught or believed to be true • *a doctrine of equality for all people* • *religious doctrine* **2** [C] *US* : a statement of government policy especially in international relations • *the Truman/Monroe doctrine* — **doc·tri·nal** /ˈdɑːktrənl, *Brit* dɒkˈtraɪnl/ *adj*

do·cu·dra·ma /ˈdɑːkjəˌdrɑːmə/ *n* [C] : a movie that is usually made for television and that tells a story about recent events

¹**doc·u·ment** /ˈdɑːkjəmənt/ *n* [C] **1** : an official paper that gives information or is used as proof ▪ *legal/historical documents* **2** : a computer file that contains text that you have written

²**doc·u·ment** /ˈdɑːkjəˌment/ *vb* [T] **1** : to create a record of (something) through writing, film, etc. ▪ *He wrote a book documenting their struggle.* **2** : to prove (something) by using usually written evidence ▪ *The charges are well/fully documented.*

¹**doc·u·men·ta·ry** /ˌdɑːkjəˈmentri/ *n, pl* **-ries** [C] : a movie or television program that tells the facts about actual people and events ▪ *a documentary on the history of jazz*

²**documentary** *adj, always before a noun* : consisting of documents : written down ▪ *documentary evidence*

doc·u·men·ta·tion /ˌdɑːkjəmənˈteɪʃən/ *n* [U] **1** : the documents that are used to prove something or make something official ▪ *Can you provide documentation of the claims you're making?* **2** : written instructions for using a computer or computer program

dod·der·ing /ˈdɑːdərɪŋ/ *adj* : walking and moving in a slow and unsteady way because of old age ▪ *a doddering old man*

¹**dodge** /ˈdɑːdʒ/ *vb* **dodged; dodg·ing** **1 a** [T] : to move quickly to one side in order to avoid being hit by (someone or something) ▪ *He dodged the punch.* **b** [I] : to move quickly in order to avoid being hit, seen, stopped, etc. ▪ *He dodged behind the bushes.* **2** [T] : to get away from or avoid (someone or something) in a skillful or dishonest way ▪ *She dodged the question by changing the subject.* ▪ *They managed to dodge the reporters.* — **dodge a/the bullet** *chiefly US, informal* : to barely avoid being hit or affected by something harmful ▪ *The island dodged a bullet when the hurricane turned south.* — **dodg·er** /ˈdɑːdʒɚ/ *n* [C] ▪ *a draft dodger* [=a person who illegally avoids being drafted into the military]

²**dodge** *n* [C] : a trick done to avoid something ▪ *a tax dodge*

dodgy /ˈdɑːdʒi/ *adj* **dodg·i·er; -est** *chiefly Brit, informal* **1 a** : false or dishonest ▪ *dodgy business deals* **b** : causing a lack of trust or confidence ▪ *a dodgy reputation* **2** : in bad condition ▪ *a dodgy engine* **3** : difficult or risky ▪ *a dodgy situation*

do·do /ˈdoʊˌdoʊ/ *n, pl* **-does** *or* **-dos** [C] **1** : a type of large, heavy bird that lived in the past and was unable to fly **2** *US, informal + humorous* : a stupid or silly person

doe /ˈdoʊ/ *n, pl* **does** *or* **doe** [C] : a female animal (such as a deer, rabbit, or kangaroo)

do·er /ˈduːwɚ/ *n* [C] : a person who actively does things instead of just thinking or talking about them ▪ *I'm more of a thinker than a doer.*

does *see* DO

doesn't /ˈdʌznt/ — used as a contraction of *does not* ▪ *She doesn't like cake.*

doff /ˈdɑːf/ *vb* [T] *old-fashioned* : to take off or remove (a hat or a piece of cloth-

ing) ▪ *He doffed his cap.*

¹**dog** /ˈdɑːg/ *n* **1** [C] : a type of animal that is often kept as a pet or trained to work for people by guarding buildings, hunting, etc. **2** [C] *informal* **a** : a person who is regarded as lucky, unlucky, etc. ▪ *You lucky dog!* **b** : a person who is lazy or who is not liked ▪ *He's a worthless dog.* **c** *offensive* : an unattractive girl or woman **3** [C] *US, informal* : something that is poor in quality ▪ *a dog of a movie* **4** [C] *US, informal* : HOT DOG **5** [*plural*] *US, informal + old-fashioned* : FEET ▪ *My dogs were tired.* — **a dog's breakfast** *Brit, informal* : something that is messy or poorly done ▪ *a dog's life* : a difficult, boring, and unhappy life — **(as) sick as a dog** *informal* : very sick — **dog and pony show** *US, usually disapproving* : a very fancy and elaborate event that is done to sell something, to impress people, etc. ▪ *The sales presentation was a real dog and pony show.* — **every dog has his/its day** *informal* — used to say that every person has a successful moment in life — **go to the dogs** *informal* : to become ruined : to change to a much worse condition ▪ *The economy is going to the dogs.* — **let sleeping dogs lie** : to ignore a problem because trying to deal with it could cause an even more difficult situation — **rain cats and dogs** see ²RAIN — **you can't teach an old dog new tricks** — used to say that a person who is used to doing things in a certain way cannot learn or does not want to learn a new way

²**dog** *vb* **dogged; dog·ging** [T] **1** : to follow (someone) very closely ▪ *He dogged her every move.* **2** : to ask (someone) about or for something constantly or frequently ▪ *Reporters kept dogging her for information.* **3** : to cause problems for (someone) for a long time ▪ *an athlete who has been dogged by injuries*

dog·catch·er /ˈdɑːgˌkɛtʃɚ/ *n* [C] *US* : a public official who catches dogs that do not have homes — called also (*Brit*) **dog warden**

dog days *n* [*plural*] : the hottest time of the year ▪ *the dog days of summer*

dog-eared /ˈdɑːgˌiɚd/ *adj* : having pages with the top corners folded down ▪ *a dog-eared magazine*

dog-eat-dog /ˌdɑːgˌiːtˈdɑːg/ *adj* — used to describe a situation in which people compete with each other in a cruel, selfish way ▪ *a dog-eat-dog business*

dog·fight /ˈdɑːgˌfaɪt/ *n* [C] **1** : a fight between dogs **2** : a fight between fighter planes **3** : a fierce fight or struggle ▪ *The election has turned into a real dogfight.*

dog·ged /ˈdɑːgəd/ *adj* : stubborn and determined ▪ *a dogged pursuit of power* — **dog·ged·ly** *adv* — **dog·ged·ness** *n* [U]

dog·ger·el /ˈdɑːgərəl/ *n* [U] : poetry that is poorly written and that often is not meant to be taken seriously

doggie bag *also* **doggy bag** *n* [C] : a bag that is used for carrying home food that is left over from a meal eaten at a restaurant

dog·gy or **dog·gie** /ˈdɑːgi/ n, pl **-gies** [C] informal : a dog — used especially by children or when talking to children ▪ a cute little doggy

dog·house /ˈdɑːg.haʊs/ n [C] US : a shelter for a dog — **in the doghouse** informal : in a bad situation because someone is angry at you : in trouble ▪ He's in the doghouse with his wife. [=his wife is angry at him]

dog·leg /ˈdɑːg.lɛg/ n [C] : a sharp bend or turn in a road, golf course, etc. — **dogleg** vb **-legged; -leg·ging** [I] ▪ a fairway that doglegs to the left

dog·ma /ˈdɑːgmə/ n [C/U] formal 1 usually disapproving : a belief or set of beliefs that is accepted by the members of a group without being questioned or doubted ▪ These new findings challenge the current dogma in the field. 2 : a belief or set of beliefs taught by a religious organization

dog·mat·ic /dɑgˈmætɪk/ adj, disapproving : expressing opinions or beliefs as if they are certainly correct and cannot be doubted ▪ dogmatic critics/statements — **dog·mat·i·cal·ly** /dɑgˈmætɪkli/ adv — **dog·ma·tism** /ˈdɑːgmə,tɪzəm/ n [U] — **dog·ma·tist** /ˈdɑːgmətɪst/ n [C]

do-good·er /ˈduː,gʊdɚ/ n [C] disapproving : someone whose desire and effort to help people is regarded as wrong, annoying, useless, etc.

dog·sled /ˈdɑːg,slɛd/ n [C] chiefly US : a type of sled that is pulled by dogs — **dogsled** vb **-sled·ded; -sled·ding** [T/I] ▪ He dogsledded across the tundra.

dog tag n [C] : a piece of metal that is worn around the neck of an American soldier and lists the soldier's name, service number, and other information

dog warden n [C] Brit : DOGCATCHER

dog·wood /ˈdɑːg,wʊd/ n [C] : a type of bush or small tree with groups of small flowers

doh chiefly Brit spelling of ⁴DO

doi·ly /ˈdɔɪli/ n, pl **-lies** [C] : a usually round cloth or paper that has a decorative pattern made of many small holes ▪ She placed a lace doily under the vase.

do·ing /ˈduːwɪŋ/ n 1 [U] : the act of making something happen ▪ The doing of good deeds ▪ The party was not all our doing; we had lots of help. ▪ It will take some doing [=require a lot of effort] to win the game. 2 [plural] : things that are done or happen ▪ There have been some strange doings lately.

do-it-yourself adj, always before a noun : of or relating to work that you do yourself instead of hiring someone to do it ▪ do-it-yourself home repair ▪ do-it-yourself stores [=stores where you buy materials to fix or build things] — **do-it-yourself·er** n [C]

Dol·by /ˈdɑːlbi, ˈdoʊlbi/ trademark — used for an electronic device that removes unwanted noise from recorded or broadcast sound

dol·drums /ˈdoʊldrəmz/ n [plural] 1 : a state or period of sadness or depression ▪ the winter doldrums ▪ She's been in the doldrums lately. 2 : a state or period in which there is no activity or improve-

ment ▪ The stock market is in the doldrums.

¹**dole** /ˈdoʊl/ n [U] : money that a government (especially the British government) gives to people who do not have jobs or who are very poor ▪ They've been **on/off the dole** for a year.

²**dole** vb **doled; dol·ing** — **dole out** [phrasal vb] **dole out (something)** also **dole (something) out** : to give (something) to people ▪ doling out advice/money

dole·ful /ˈdoʊlfəl/ adj : very sad ▪ a doleful look/expression/manner — **dole·ful·ly** adv

¹**doll** /ˈdɑːl/ n [C] 1 : a child's toy in the form of a baby or small person — see also RAG DOLL 2 chiefly US, informal : a kind and helpful person ▪ Thanks for the help. You're a doll.

²**doll** vb — **doll up** [phrasal vb] **doll (yourself) up** informal : to make (yourself) attractive with makeup and fancy or stylish clothes ▪ She dolled herself up for the party. = She **got (all) dolled up** for the party.

dol·lar /ˈdɑːlɚ/ n [C] 1 a : a basic unit of money in the U.S., Canada, Australia, and other countries that is equal to 100 cents ▪ The property is worth a million dollars. b : a bill or coin that is worth one dollar 2 : money that is from a specified source or used for a specified purpose ▪ tax/taxpayer dollars [=money collected through taxes] ▪ advertising dollars — **look/feel like a million dollars** see MILLION

dollar sign n [C] : a symbol $ placed before a number to show that it represents an amount of dollars

doll·house /ˈdɑːl,haʊs/ n [C] US : a small toy house — called also (Brit) **doll's house**

dol·lop /ˈdɑːləp/ n [C] 1 : a small amount of soft food ▪ a dollop of ketchup 2 : a usually small amount of something ▪ dollops of wit and humor

dol·ly /ˈdɑːli/ n, pl **-lies** [C] 1 : a toy doll — usually used by children or when speaking to children 2 : a piece of equipment that has wheels and is used for moving heavy objects

dol·phin /ˈdɑːlfən/ n [C] : a small usually gray whale that has a pointed nose

dolt /ˈdoʊlt/ n [C] informal : a stupid person — **dolt·ish** /ˈdoʊltɪʃ/ adj : doltish people/behavior

do·main /doʊˈmeɪn/ n [C] 1 : the land that a ruler or government controls ▪ The forest is part of the king's domain. — see also EMINENT DOMAIN, PUBLIC DOMAIN 2 : an area of knowledge or activity ▪ Federal crimes are outside the domain of city police. 3 a : a section of the Internet that is made up of computers or sites that are related in some way (such as by use or source) b : DOMAIN NAME

domain name n [C] : the characters (such as Merriam-Webster.com) that form the main part of an Internet address

dome /ˈdoʊm/ n [C] 1 : a large rounded roof or ceiling ▪ the church's high dome 2 : a structure that looks like the dome of a building • *a dome of ice* **3** : a stadium that is covered by a roof — **domed** /'doumd/ *adj* • *a domed church*

¹do·mes·tic /də'mɛstɪk/ *adj* **1** : of, relating to, or made in your own country • *domestic affairs* • *The wine is domestic.* **2** *always before a noun* : relating to or involving someone's home or family • *domestic life/work/violence* • *a domestic worker/servant* [=a worker/servant who is hired to work in someone's home] **3** — used to describe a person who enjoys work and activities that are done at home • *She's not very domestic.* **4** *of an animal* : living with or under the care of people • *cattle and other domestic animals* — **do·mes·ti·cal·ly** /də'mɛstɪkli/ *adv*

²domestic *n* [C] *old-fashioned* : a servant who is hired to work in someone's home

do·mes·ti·cate /də'mɛstə,keɪt/ *vb* **-cat·ed; -cat·ing** [T] **1** : to breed or train (an animal) to need and accept the care of human beings • *Humans have domesticated dogs/cattle/chickens.* **2** : to grow (a plant) for human use • *Native Americans domesticated corn.* — **do·mes·ti·ca·tion** /də,mɛstə'keɪʃən/ *n* [U]

do·mes·tic·i·ty /,douˌmɛ'stɪsəti/ *n* [U] *formal* : the activities of a family or of the people who share a home • *a life of comfortable domesticity*

dom·i·cile /'dɑːmə,sajəl/ *n* [C/U] *law* : the place where you live : your home • *a change of domicile*

dom·i·nant /'dɑːmənənt/ *adj* **1** : more important, powerful, or successful than most or all others • *a dominant role/force* • *The company is dominant in its market.* **2** : most common • *the dominant language/religion of the country* **3** *biology* : causing or relating to a genetic characteristic or condition that prevents the expression of another • *dominant genes/traits* • *Brown eyes are dominant.* — **dom·i·nance** /'dɑːmənəns/ *n* [U, singular] • *the team's dominance over its rivals* — **dom·i·nant·ly** *adv*

dom·i·nate /'dɑːmə,neɪt/ *vb* **-nat·ed; -nat·ing** [T/I] **1** : to have control of or power over (someone or something) • *One company dominates the market.* • *Our team dominated (throughout) the game.* **2** : to be the most important, common, or noticeable part of (something) • *The business dominated her life.* • *The topic of her arrest dominated the conversation.* • *Pine trees dominate (in) the forest.* • *The room was dominated by a large table.* — **dominating** *adj* • *a dominating influence/team* — **dom·i·na·tion** /,dɑːmə'neɪʃən/ *n* [U] — **dom·i·na·tor** /'dɑːmə,neɪtə/ *n* [C]

dom·i·neer·ing /,dɑːmə'nɪrɪŋ/ *adj* : tending too often to tell people what to do • *a domineering parent*

do·min·ion /də'mɪnjən/ *n, formal* **1** [U] : control of a country, region, etc. • *The U.S. has/holds dominion over/of the island.* **2** [C] : the land that a ruler or government controls • *the dominions of the empire*

dom·i·no /'dɑːmə,nou/ *n, pl* **-noes** *or* **-nos 1** [C] : a small flat rectangular

block that has one or more dots on one side and is used in playing games **2 dominoes** [U] : a game played with dominoes

domino effect *n* [singular] : a situation in which one event causes a series of similar events to happen • *The delay created a domino effect, disrupting deliveries around the country.*

¹don /'dɑːn/ *n* [C] **1** *Brit* : a teacher in a college or university **2** *informal* : a powerful Mafia leader

²don *vb* **donned; don·ning** [T] *formal + old-fashioned* : to put on (a piece of clothing) • *She donned her jacket.*

do·nate /'dou,neɪt, dou'neɪt/ *vb* **-nat·ed; -nat·ing** [T/I] : to give (something) in order to help a person or organization • *We donated our old clothes to charity.* • *donating money/food/blood* — **do·na·tion** /dou'neɪʃən/ *n* [C/U] • *a generous donation* • *Would you like to make a donation?* — **do·na·tor** /'dou,neɪtə, dou'neɪtə/ *n* [C]

¹done *past participle of* **¹DO**

²done *adj, not before a noun* **1** — used to say that something has ended • *One more question and we're done.* • *The work is almost done.* [=finished, completed] • *Are you done with the scissors?* **2** : cooked completely or enough • *The cake/steak is done.* **3** : socially acceptable or fashionable • *Getting a divorce just wasn't done at the time.* — **done for** *informal* **1** : certain to fail, lose, be punished, etc. • *If she finds out we cheated, we're done for.* **2** : certain to die or be killed — **done in** *informal* : very tired • *I was/felt completely done in.* [=exhausted] — **over and done with** *see* **¹OVER**

done deal *n* [singular] *informal* : something that has been done and that cannot be changed • *The sale is a done deal.*

done·ness /'dʌnnəs/ *n* [U] : the state of being cooked completely or enough • *Cover the pan and cook to (the) desired doneness.*

don·key /'dɑːŋki/ *n, pl* **-keys** [C] : an animal that is like a small horse with large ears

don·ny·brook /'dɑːni,brʊk/ *n* [C] : a noisy or uncontrolled argument or fight • *a political donnybrook*

do·nor /'dounə/ *n* [C] : a person or group that donates something (such as money, food, or clothes) in order to help a person or organization • *The money was raised from individual donors.* • *blood/organ donors*

¹don't /'dount/ — used as a contraction of *do not* • *I don't like it.*

²don't *n* [C] *informal* : something that a person should not do • *the dos and don'ts of dating* [=the things that you should and should not do when dating someone]

donut *chiefly US spelling of* **DOUGHNUT**

doo·dad /'duː,dæd/ *n* [C] *US, informal* **1** : a small decorative object **2** : a small useful device : **GADGET** • *a clever doodad*

doo·dle /'duːdl̩/ *vb* **doo·dled; doo·dling** [I] : to draw something without thinking about what you are doing • *She doodled in her notebook.* — **doodle** *n* [C]

¹**doom** /ˈduːm/ n [U] **1** : very bad events or situations that cannot be avoided ▪ *We had a sense/feeling of (impending) doom as the storm approached.* [=we sensed or felt that something very bad was going to happen] ▪ *The papers are filled with stories of gloom and doom.* **2** : death or ruin ▪ *Prepare to meet your doom.* [=die] ▪ *The poor economy spelled doom for many small businesses.*

²**doom** vb [T] : to make (someone or something) certain to fail, suffer, die, etc. ▪ *a plan that is doomed to fail = a doomed plan* ▪ *If no one rescues us, we are doomed.*

doom·say·er /ˈduːmˌsejɚ/ n [C] : someone who predicts that bad things will happen

dooms·day /ˈduːmzˌdeɪ/ n [singular] : the day the world ends or is destroyed ▪ *It'll be like that from now until doomsday.* [=for a very long time; forever]

door /ˈdoɚ/ n [C] **1 a** : a movable piece of wood, glass, or metal that swings or slides open and shut so that people can enter or leave a room, building, vehicle, etc. ▪ *I heard a knock on/at the door.* ▪ *Can you answer the door?* [=open the door to see who is there] ▪ *(US) Can you get the door?* [=can you open or close the door for me?] **b** : a part of an object that swings or slides open and shut ▪ *the cupboard/oven door* **2** : the opening for a door : the entrance to a room or building ▪ *Please don't block the door.* ▪ *He greeted his guests as they came in/through the door. = He greeted his guests at the door.* ▪ *She walked out the door* [=left] *without saying goodbye.* **3** : a house, building, apartment, office, etc. ▪ *She lives in a house two doors down/up from me.* [=there is one house between our houses] ◆ If you do something *(from) door to door,* you do it at each of the houses, apartments, or buildings in an area. ▪ *Girl Scouts are selling cookies door to door. = Girl Scouts are going door to door selling cookies.* — see also NEXT DOOR, OUT OF DOORS **4** — used especially with *open* or *unlock* to describe an opportunity or possibility ▪ *A good education can open/unlock the door of success.* ▪ *The patent on the product has expired, which leaves the door open for* [=makes it possible for] *other companies to make it.* — **behind closed doors** see CLOSED — **close the door on** : to no longer think about, consider, or accept (something) ▪ *I'd like to close the door on that period in my life.* — **close your doors** **1** : to not allow someone to enter ▪ *The country has closed its doors to immigrants.* **2** : to close permanently : to stop operating ▪ *The store has closed its doors.* — **darken someone's door/doors** see DARKEN — **get your foot in the door** see ¹FOOT — **lay the blame for (something) at someone's door** : to blame someone for (something) ▪ *They laid the blame for the book's failure at my door.* — **open your doors** **1** : to allow someone to enter ▪ *The country has opened its doors to immigrants.* **2** : to open for business : to begin operating ▪

The store will be opening its doors next month. — **show (someone) the door** : to tell or force (someone) to leave ▪ *If the coach doesn't win this year, they'll show him the door.* [=fire him] — **show/see (someone) to the door** : to go to the door with (someone who is leaving) ▪ *My secretary will show you to the door.*

door·bell /ˈdoɚˌbɛl/ n [C] : a bell inside a house or building that is rung usually by pushing a button beside an outside door

do-or-die /ˈduːwɚˈdaɪ/ adj **1** always before a noun : very determined ▪ *a do-or-die attitude* **2** — used to describe a situation in which you have to do something or you will fail, lose, etc. ▪ *This is do-or-die for the team. If they don't score, the game is over.*

door·keep·er /ˈdoɚˌkiːpɚ/ n [C] : someone who guards a door and checks people to see if they are allowed to enter the building

door·knob /ˈdoɚˌnɑːb/ n [C] : a round handle that you turn to open a door

door·man /ˈdoɚˌmæn/ n, pl **-men** /-ˌmɛn/ [C] : a person whose job is to stand next to the main door of a building (such as a hotel) and help people by opening the door, calling taxis, etc.

door·mat /ˈdoɚˌmæt/ n [C] **1** : a mat placed on one side of a door so that people can wipe the bottoms of their shoes on it **2** informal : someone who is treated badly and does not complain ▪ *She was tired of being a doormat and decided it was time to stand up for herself.*

door·nail /ˈdoɚˌneɪl/ n — **(as) dead as a doornail** see ¹DEAD

door prize n [C] US : a prize that you get at a social event if you were given the winning ticket when you arrived

door·step /ˈdoɚˌstɛp/ n [C] : a step or series of steps leading up to a door that is used to enter or leave a building ▪ *The police were at my doorstep.* ▪ *(figurative) The beach is at your doorstep.* [=the beach is very close]

door·stop /ˈdoɚˌstɑːp/ n [C] **1** : an object that prevents a door from hitting and damaging the wall **2** : something that used to hold a door open

door-to-door /ˌdoɚtəˈdoɚ/ adj, always before a noun : going or made by going to each house, apartment, or building in an area ▪ *a door-to-door salesman/survey*

door·way /ˈdoɚˌweɪ/ n [C] : the opening where a door is ▪ *She stepped through the doorway.* ▪ *(figurative) We hope that these talks will be a doorway to peace.* [=will lead to peace]

doo·zy or **doo·zie** /ˈduːzi/ n, pl **-zies** [C] US, informal : something that is unusually good, bad, big, severe, etc. ▪ *They say the snowstorm tonight is going to be a doozy.*

¹**dope** /ˈdoup/ n, informal **1** [U] : an illegal drug (such as marijuana or heroin) ▪ *They were caught smoking dope.* **2** [C] : a stupid or annoying person **3** **the dope** : INFORMATION 1 ▪ *The magazine claims to have the inside dope* [=information known only by those involved] *on her new romance.* ▪ *Give me the*

straight dope on it. [=tell me the truth about it]

²**dope** *vb* **doped; dop·ing** [T] *informal* **1** : to give a drug to (a person or animal) especially to cause unconsciousness ▪ *They tried to dope him.* **2** : to put a drug in (something, such as food or a drink) to make a person or animal unconscious ▪ *They doped her food.* — **dope out** [*phrasal vb*] **dope out (something)** or **dope (something) out** *US* : to figure out (something) ▪ *trying to dope out what happened* — **dope up** [*phrasal vb*] **dope up (someone)** or **dope (someone) up** : to give (someone) a drug that affects the ability to think or behave normally ▪ *He was doped up on painkillers.*

dop·ey /ˈdoʊpi/ *adj* **dop·i·er; -est** *informal* **1 a** : feeling the effects of a drug ▪ *I'm still a little dopey from the painkillers.* **b** : slow because you are tired **2** : foolish or stupid ▪ *a dopey movie/movie*

doping *n* [U] : the illegal use of a drug (such as a steroid) to improve an athlete's performance ▪ *doping tests/scandals*

dork /ˈdoɚk/ *n* [C] *informal* : a person who behaves awkwardly around other people and usually has unstylish clothes, hair, etc. ▪ *I look like a complete dork in these clothes.* — **dorky** /ˈdoɚki/ *adj* **dork·i·er; -est** ▪ *a dorky guy with glasses*

dorm /ˈdoɚm/ *n* [C] *informal* : DORMITORY

dor·mant /ˈdoɚmənt/ *adj* : not active but able to become active ▪ *a dormant volcano* ▪ *The seeds remain/lie dormant until the spring.* — **dor·man·cy** /ˈdoɚmənsi/ *n* [U]

dor·mer /ˈdoɚmɚ/ *n* [C] **1** : a window that is in a part of a building that sticks out from a slanted roof — called also *dormer window* **2** : the part of a building that contains a dormer

dor·mi·to·ry /ˈdoɚmə₁tori, *Brit* ˈdɔːmətri/ *n, pl* **-ries** [C] **1** *US* : a building on a school campus that has rooms where students can live **2** : a large room with many beds where people can sleep

dor·mouse /ˈdoɚˌmaʊs/ *n, pl* **-mice** /-ˌmaɪs/ [C] : a European animal that looks like a small squirrel

dor·sal fin /ˈdoɚsəl-/ *n* [C] : a flat thin part on the back of some fish (such as sharks)

do·ry /ˈdori/ *n, pl* **-ries** [C] : a boat that has a flat bottom and high sides

dos·age /ˈdoʊsɪʤ/ *n* [C] : the amount of a medicine, drug, or vitamin that should be taken at one time or regularly during a period of time

¹**dose** /ˈdoʊs/ *n* [C] **1** : the amount of a medicine, drug, etc., that is taken at one time ▪ *a large dose of vitamin C* **2** : an amount of something that a person experiences or is affected by ▪ *a high dose of radiation* ▪ *a daily dose of hard work*

²**dose** *vb* **dosed; dos·ing** [T] : to give a dose of something to (someone or something) ▪ *She dosed herself with aspirin.* ▪ *The victims were dosed with poison.* ▪ *(US)* *The sauce was heavily dosed with garlic.* [=there was a lot of garlic in the sauce]

dos·sier /ˈdɑːˌsjeɪ/ *n* [C] : a group of papers that contain detailed information

about someone or something ▪ *the patient's medical dossier* = *a dossier on the patient*

¹**dot** /ˈdɑːt/ *n* [C] : a small round mark or spot ▪ *The dots on the map represent cities.* — **connect the dots** see CONNECT — **on the dot** *informal* : exactly at a particular time ▪ *She arrived at 3 o'clock on the dot.*

²**dot** *vb* **dot·ted; dot·ting** [T] **1** : to mark (something) with a dot ▪ *Don't forget to dot the i.* ✧ If you **dot the/your i's and cross the/your t's**, you make sure that all of the small details in something have been completed. **2** : to appear at many different places on the surface of (something) ▪ *Quaint cottages dot the countryside.* ▪ *The fields were dotted with wildflowers.*

dot·age /ˈdoʊtɪʤ/ *n* [U] : the time when a person is old and often less able to remember or do things ▪ *He has become friendlier in his dotage.*

dot-com /ˈdɑːˌkɑːm/ *n* [C] : a company that sells its products or services only on the Internet ▪ *a successful dot-com*

dote /ˈdoʊt/ *vb* **dot·ed; dot·ing** — **dote on/upon** [*phrasal vb*] : to give a lot of love or attention to (someone or something) ▪ *She doted on her grandchild.* — **doting** *adj* ▪ *the child's doting grandmother*

dot matrix *n* [C] : a pattern of dots that form letters, numbers, etc., on a computer screen or on something printed from a computer ▪ *a dot matrix printer*

dotted *adj* : covered with or made up of dots ▪ *the plant's dotted green and white leaves* ✧ *Dotted line* is often used to refer to the place at the bottom of a document where a person signs and agrees to the terms in the document.

dot·ty /ˈdɑːti/ *adj* **dot·ti·er; -est** *old-fashioned + informal* : somewhat crazy ▪ *my dotty old grandparents*

¹**dou·ble** /ˈdʌbəl/ *adj* **1** : made of two parts that are similar or the same ▪ *a double yellow line* ▪ *My name is "Allison," with a double "l."* ▪ *a double murder/album* **2** : having two very different parts or qualities ▪ *His statement has a double meaning.* [=it means two different things] ▪ *She was a newspaper reporter who lived/led a double life as a spy.* **3** : of a size that is twice as big as usual ▪ *a double espresso* ▪ *a double dose of medicine* : twice as great or as many ▪ *Our new car was double the price of our last one.* **4** : made for two people to use ▪ *a double room/bed*

²**double** *vb* **dou·bled; dou·bling** **1** [T/I] : to become two times as great or as many ▪ *The price of the house had doubled.* = *The house had doubled in price.* ▪ *They doubled their winnings.* **2** [I] : to have a second job or use ▪ *Our couch often doubles as a bed.* **3 a** [T] : to bend or fold (something) usually in the middle ▪ *I doubled over/up the paper.* **b** [T/I] : to bend forward at the waist ▪ *He doubled over/up in pain.* **4** [I] *baseball* : to hit a double ▪ *He doubled to left field.* — **double back** [*phrasal vb*] : to turn around and return on the same path — **double**

up [phrasal vb] : to share a place to live or sleep that is made for one person or one family ▪ *There was only one bed, so we had to double up.* — **double up on** [phrasal vb] : to use or do two times as many of (something) ▪ *I have to double up on classes this semester if I want to graduate this year.*

³**double** *n* **1** [singular] : something that is two times the usual size, strength, or amount ▪ *I'll have one more glass of vodka. Make it a double, please.* **2** [C] : someone who looks very much like another person ▪ *The actress's stunt double did all of the dangerous scenes.* **3** [C] *baseball* : a hit that allows a batter to reach second base **4** [plural] : a game of tennis or a similar sport that is played between two pairs of players **5** [C] : a room in a hotel, inn, etc., for two people — **double or nothing** (US) or Brit **double or quits** : a gambling bet in which you could win two times as much money as you have already won or you could lose all of the money — **on the double** (US) or Brit **at the double** informal : very quickly : as soon as possible ▪ *I need you back here on the double.*

⁴**double** *adv* : two times : two times as many or as much ▪ *I was charged/billed double.* — **bend double** : to fold in the middle ▪ *He bent double* [=doubled over] *in pain.* — **see double** : to see two things when only one thing is present ▪ *As her eyesight got worse, she began seeing double.* — **that goes double for** informal — used to say that something you have just said about one person or thing relates even more strongly to another ▪ *You're in trouble, Steven. And that goes double for you, John.* [=you, John, are in even more trouble than Steven]

double agent *n* [C] : a spy who pretends to spy for one government while actually spying for another

double bass *n* [C] : a very large musical instrument that is shaped like a violin

double bogey *n* [C] *golf* : a score of two strokes over par on a hole — **double bogey** *vb* [T] ▪ *He double bogeyed the fourth hole.*

double boiler *n* [C] : a pair of deep cooking pans that fit together so that the contents of the top pan can be cooked or heated by boiling water in the bottom pan

dou·ble–breast·ed /ˌdʌbəlˈbrɛstəd/ *adj* : having two rows of buttons ▪ *a double-breasted jacket*

dou·ble–check /ˌdʌbəlˈtʃɛk/ *vb* [T/I] : to check (something) again in order to be certain ▪ *Be sure to double-check your answers.* — **double check** *n* [C]

double chin *n* [C] : a fold of fat that some people have under their chin and that looks like a second chin

dou·ble–cross /ˌdʌbəlˈkrɑːs/ *vb* [T] : to cheat or deceive (someone) especially by doing something that is different from what you said you would do ▪ *I thought I could trust her, but she double-crossed me.* — **double cross** *n* [C] ▪ *lies and double crosses*

dou·ble–deal·ing /ˌdʌbəlˈdiːlɪŋ/ *n* [U]

: the practice of pretending to do or think one thing while really doing or thinking something different : dishonest or deceptive behavior ▪ *His double-dealing has caused many of his former friends to distrust him.*

dou·ble–deck·er /ˌdʌbəlˈdɛkə/ *n* [C] : something that has two levels or layers ▪ *a double-decker bus/sandwich*

double digits *n* [plural] chiefly US : a number or percentage that is 10 or greater ▪ *They won the game by double digits.* — called also *double figures* — **dou·ble–dig·it** /ˌdʌbəlˈdɪdʒɪt/ *adj, always before a noun* ▪ *the state's double-digit unemployment rate*

double dribble *n* [C] *basketball* : an illegal action that happens when a player dribbles the ball with two hands at the same time or starts to dribble again after stopping

dou·ble–edged /ˌdʌbəlˈɛdʒd/ *adj* **1** : having two sharp edges ▪ *a double-edged knife* **2** : having two different and opposite parts ▪ *a double-edged problem* **3** : able to be understood in two different ways ▪ *double-edged remarks*

double–edged sword *n* [C] `1 : a sword that has two sharp edges **2** : something that has both good and bad parts or results ▪ *Freedom of expression can be a double-edged sword.*

dou·ble en·ten·dre /ˈdʌbəlɑnˈtɑːndrə/ *n* [C] : a word or expression that can be understood in two different ways with one way usually referring to sex ▪ *The song's title is a double entendre.*

double fault *n* [C] *tennis* : two bad serves that result in the loss of a point

double figures *n* [plural] : DOUBLE DIGITS

dou·ble–head·er /ˌdʌbəlˈhɛdə/ *n* [C] chiefly US : two games (especially baseball games) that are played one after the other on the same day

double helix *n* [C] *technical* : the shape formed by two parallel lines that twist around each other ◇ The strands of DNA are arranged in a double helix.

double jeopardy *n* [U] US, law : the act of causing a person to be put on trial two times for the same crime

dou·ble–joint·ed /ˌdʌbəlˈdʒɔɪntəd/ *adj* : having a joint that allows body parts to move in ways that are not typical ▪ *double-jointed fingers*

double negative *n* [C] *grammar* : a clause that has two negative words (such as "nothing" and "don't") when only one is necessary ◇ Double negatives are usually considered incorrect in English. ▪ *"I didn't do nothing" is a double negative. If you want to be correct, you should say "I didn't do anything."*

dou·ble–park /ˌdʌbəlˈpɑːk/ *vb* [T/I] : to park a car or other vehicle beside a row of vehicles that are already parked on the side of the street ▪ *My truck is double-parked outside.*

double play *n* [C] *baseball* : a play in which the team in the field causes two runners to be put out

dou·ble–quick /ˈdʌbəlˌkwɪk/ *adj, always before a noun, chiefly Brit, informal* : extra fast or quick • *working in double-quick time* — **double–quick** *adv* • *get it done double-quick*

double–sided *adj* : having two sides that can be used • *double-sided tape*

dou·ble-space /ˌdʌbəlˈspeɪs/ *vb* **-spaced; -spac·ing** [*T/I*] : to write or type (a paper, letter, etc.) so that each line of words is followed by a line without words • *All essays must be typed and double spaced.*

dou·ble·speak /ˈdʌbəlˌspiːk/ *n* [*U*] : language that can be understood in more than one way and that is used to trick or deceive people • *political doublespeak*

double standard *n* [*C*] : a situation in which two people, groups, etc., are treated very differently from each other then in a way that is unfair to one of them • *She argued that society applies a double standard in dealing with women who commit adultery.*

double take *n* [*C*] : an act of quickly looking at something that is surprising or unusual a second time after looking at it a moment earlier • *His parents did a double take when he came home with a tattoo.*

dou·ble-talk /ˈdʌbəlˌtɔːk/ *n* [*U*] *disapproving* : language that uses many words but has very little meaning • *a bunch of meaningless double-talk*

double vision *n* [*U*] : a problem with the eyes that causes a person to see two objects when only one is present

double wham·my /-ˈwæmi/ *n* [*C*] *informal* : a situation that is bad in two different ways • *With the cold weather and the high cost of heating fuel, homeowners were hit with a double whammy this winter.*

dou·bly /ˈdʌbli/ *adv, always before an adjective* **1** : much more than usual or previously • *We did the test again because we wanted to be doubly sure the results were accurate.* **2** : in two ways : for two reasons • *Her grades and musical talent make her parents doubly proud of her.*

¹**doubt** /ˈdaʊt/ *vb* [*T*] **1** : to believe that (something) may not be true or is unlikely • *She began to doubt everything he said.* • *I doubt (that) my parents will let me go.* **2** : to have no confidence in (someone or something) • *She doubted his ability to succeed.* — **doubt·er** *n* [*C*]

²**doubt** *n* [*C/U*] : a feeling of being uncertain or unsure about something • *There is no doubt in my mind that he is the best candidate.* • *These mistakes cast/throw doubt on her ability.* • *Two separate studies have raised doubts about the car's safety.* — **beyond doubt** ✧ If something is *beyond doubt*, it is definitely true. • *The evidence proved her guilt beyond (all/any) doubt.* • *The charges against her were proved beyond a reasonable doubt.* • *I knew, beyond a shadow of a doubt, that he did it.* — **in doubt** : in a state of being uncertain or unsure • *The outcome was in doubt* [=not known with certainty] *until the final seconds of the game.* — **no doubt** : without doubt or with very little doubt • *No doubt many readers will find the book too long.* • *By now, you have no*

doubt heard the news. • *No doubt about it, the fans are disappointed in the team.* — **without (a) doubt** — used to stress that something is true • *They are, without doubt, the nicest people I've ever met.*

doubt·ful /ˈdaʊtfəl/ *adj* **1** : uncertain or unsure about something • *I tried to reassure them, but they remained doubtful.* • *I'm doubtful about his honesty.* **2** : not likely to be true • *a doubtful claim* • *It is doubtful that/if/whether she really meant what she said.* **3** : likely to be bad : not worthy of trust • *The water there is of doubtful quality.* **4** : not certain : unknown or undecided • *The outcome of the election remains doubtful.* — **doubt·ful·ly** *adv*

doubt·less /ˈdaʊtləs/ *adv* : without doubt or with very little doubt • *She was doubtless the smartest person in her class.*

douche /ˈduːʃ/ *n* [*C*] : a liquid that a woman squirts into her vagina to wash it; *also* : an object used to squirt such a liquid — **douche** *vb* **douched; douch·ing** [*I*]

dough /ˈdoʊ/ *n* **1** [*C/U*] : a mixture of flour, water, and other ingredients that is baked to make bread, cookies, etc. **2** [*U*] *informal* : MONEY • *I don't have much dough.* — **dough·y** /ˈdoʊi/ *adj*

dough·nut *or chiefly US* **do·nut** /ˈdoʊˌnʌt/ *n* [*C*] : a piece of sweet fried dough that is often shaped like a ring

dough·ty /ˈdaʊti/ *adj, always before a noun* **dough·ti·er; -est** *old-fashioned* : brave, strong, and determined • *a doughty fighter*

dour /ˈduːɚ, ˈdawɚ/ *adj, formal* : serious and unfriendly • *a dour politician/manner* — **dour·ly** *adv*

douse /ˈdaʊs/ *vb* **doused; dous·ing** [*T*] **1 a** : to cause (a fire) to stop burning by pouring or spraying water on it • *She managed to douse the flames with water.* **b** : to turn off (a light) • *Don't forget to douse the lights before coming to bed.* **2** : to cover (someone or something) with a liquid • *The books were doused in gasoline and set on fire.* • *She doused herself with perfume.*

¹**dove** /ˈdʌv/ *n* [*C*] **1** : a small bird that is related to pigeons ✧ Doves are often used as a symbol of peace. **2** : a person who wants peace — **dov·ish** /ˈdʌvɪʃ/ *adj* • *a dovish politician*

²**dove** *past tense and past participle of* ¹DIVE

¹**dove·tail** /ˈdʌvˌteɪl/ *n* [*C*] : a type of joint that is used to connect two pieces of wood together

²**dovetail** *vb* **1** [*T*] : to join (two pieces of wood) with dovetail joints • *The carpenter dovetailed (together) the corners of the boards).* **2** [*I*] *formal* : to fit together in a pleasing or satisfying way • *His research dovetails (nicely) with other similar studies.*

Dow /ˈdaʊ/ *n* — **the Dow** *US* : DOW JONES INDUSTRIAL AVERAGE

dow·a·ger /ˈdaʊwɪdʒɚ/ *n* [*C*] **1** : a woman who has inherited property or a title from her dead husband • *the dowager Duchess* **2** : an old woman who is very formal or serious • *a wealthy dowager*

dowdy /ˈdaʊdi/ adj **dowd·i·er; -est** : not attractive or stylish ▪ a dowdy old woman ▪ a dowdy dress

dow·el /ˈdawəl/ n [C] : a pin or peg that is used for joining together two pieces of wood, metal, plastic, etc.

Dow Jones Industrial Average /ˌdaʊˌdʒoʊnz-/ n — **the Dow Jones Industrial Average** : the daily average of the stock prices of a group of large American companies

¹**down** /ˈdaʊn/ adv **1 a** : from a higher to a lower place or position ▪ The land slopes down to the sea. ▪ Please pull down the window shade. ▪ She called down to her friends in the street below. ▪ We watched the sun go down. **b** : in a low position or place ▪ Keep your head down. **2** : to or toward the ground or floor ▪ fall/look down **3** : to a lying or sitting position ▪ sit/lie down **4 a** : to or toward the south ▪ They drove down (south) to Florida. **b** : to or toward a place that is thought of as below or away from another place ▪ She drove down to our house. ▪ Please move down so that we can sit here, too. **5** : on a piece of paper ▪ Write/Take down this number. **6** : to a lower or lesser degree, level, or amount ▪ slow/cool/calm down ▪ turn the volume down ▪ The team is 10 points down. [=has 10 fewer points than the other team] ▪ Gas prices are starting to go down. **7** : to a state of failure or defeat ▪ They voted the budget down. [=they voted not to pass the budget] **8** : from a past time ▪ This vase has been handed down in our family for generations. **9** : as a first payment : as a down payment ▪ We put 10 percent down [=we made a 10 percent down payment] on the house. ▪ She bought the car with no money down. [=without making a down payment] — **down to 1** : in a way that includes even (the smallest or least important part) ▪ accurate down to the last detail **2** : to the last person or thing that can be used ▪ It's down to you and me. [=we are the last two people that are available] ▪ I'm down to my last dollar. [=I have only one dollar left] — **down with** — used to say that you do not like something and want it to stop or fail ▪ Down with racism!

²**down** adj **1** : in a low place or position ▪ The window shades were down. **2** : going downward ▪ the down escalator **3** : lower in price or value ▪ Prices/Stocks are down today. **4** : less than an earlier or normal level ▪ Attendance has been down. **5** : having a lower level of activity ▪ a down market/economy **6** : having fewer points than an opponent ▪ His team was down by 10 points. [=trailed by 10 points] **7** : not operating properly : not able to function ▪ The system is down. **8** : sad or unhappy ▪ feeling down **9** : finished or completed ▪ I've got eight down and two more to go. [=I've finished eight and have two more to do] **10** : learned in a complete way ▪ Do you have your lines down? [=memorized] ▪ We have our routine down pat. **11** : having something written or recorded in an official way ▪ You are down for two tickets. [=you are signed up

to get two tickets] **12** US slang — used to say that you understand or approve of something ▪ I'm not down with lying to people. **13** baseball — used to say how many outs have been made in the inning by the team that is batting ▪ There are now two (men) down. **14** American football — used to say that the ball or the player who has the ball is on the ground and the play has ended ▪ The ball/runner was down. — **down on** informal : having a bad opinion of someone or something ▪ My coach has been down on me lately. — **down with** : affected by (an illness) ▪ down with the flu

³**down** prep **1** : from a higher to a lower part of (something) ▪ The children ran down the hill. ▪ She fell down the stairs. **2** : along the course or path of (something) ▪ Go down the road/hall and turn left. ▪ There's a bridge three miles down the river. ▪ pacing up and down [=back and forth in] the room

⁴**down** n **1** [C] : a period or state of failure, trouble, etc. ▪ We've had our **ups and downs**. **2** [C/U] American football : one of a series of four chances that a team has to move the ball forward 10 yards in order to keep the ball and begin a new series ▪ He caught the ball on second/third down. **3** [U] **a** : small, soft feathers ▪ goose down ▪ a down pillow **b** : small, soft hairs ▪ the down of a peach

⁵**down** vb [T] **1** : to cause (something) to fall to the ground ▪ The storm downed power lines. ▪ a downed plane **2** informal : to eat or drink (something) especially quickly ▪ She quickly downed the pills I gave her. **3** American football : to cause (a football) to be out of play ▪ The quarterback downed the ball. **4** informal : DEFEAT ▪ Smith downed Jones in the first round of the tournament.

down-and-out adj, informal : very poor and without hope : having no money, job, etc. ▪ No one would help him when he was down-and-out.

¹**down·beat** /ˈdaʊnˌbiːt/ n [C] music **1** : the downward movement that a conductor makes to show which note is played with the greatest stress or force **2** : the first beat of a measure of music

²**downbeat** adj : sad or depressing ▪ a movie with a downbeat ending

down·cast /ˈdaʊnˌkæst, Brit ˈdaʊnˌkɑːst/ adj **1** : not happy, confident, or hopeful ▪ I've never seen her looking so downcast. **2** : looking downward ▪ downcast eyes

down·court /ˈdaʊnˈkoət/ adv : into or toward the opposite end of a basketball court ▪ running downcourt

down·draft /ˈdaʊnˌdræft, Brit ˈdaʊnˌdrɑːft/ n [C] technical : a downward flow of air

down·er /ˈdaʊnə/ n [C] informal **1** : a drug that makes the body relax **2** : something that is unpleasant or depressing ▪ Our conversation about death was a bit of a downer.

down·fall /ˈdaʊnˌfɑːl/ n [C] **1** : a sudden loss of power, success, etc. ▪ She was blamed for the company's downfall. **2** : something that causes failure ▪ Bad decision-making was their downfall.

down·field /'daʊn'fiːld/ adv, sports : into or toward the part of the field toward which a team is headed ▪ kick the ball downfield — **downfield** adj

¹**down·grade** /'daʊnˌgreɪd/ vb **-grad·ed**; **-grad·ing** [T] **1** : to give (someone or something) a lower rank or grade ▪ The restaurant was downgraded from three to two stars. **2** : to cause (someone or something) to be thought of as less valuable, important, etc. ▪ She downgraded the importance of his work.

²**downgrade** n [C] chiefly US **1** : a downward slope ▪ a steep downgrade **2** : an occurrence in which something becomes worse, less valuable, etc. ▪ a downgrade in quality/prices

down·heart·ed /'daʊn'haɚtəd/ adj : not happy, confident, or hopeful ▪ Everyone was downhearted about the loss.

¹**down·hill** /ˌdaʊn'hɪl/ adv **1** : toward the bottom of a hill or mountain ▪ riding downhill **2** : toward a worse state ▪ Her health is heading downhill. ▪ After his divorce, he went **downhill.**

²**down·hill** /'daʊnˌhɪl/ adj **1** : going or sloping down toward the bottom of a hill or mountain ▪ a downhill path/slope **2** not before a noun **a** : not difficult : EASY ▪ The worst part is over. It's all downhill from here. **b** : becoming worse or less successful ▪ His career has been all downhill recently. **3** always before a noun : relating to or used in skiing that is done down a mountain or hill ▪ downhill skiing/skis

down–home /'daʊn'hoʊm/ adj, US : simple and informal in a way that reminds people of life in a small town or in the country ▪ down-home cooking

Dow·ning Street /'daʊnɪŋ-/ n [singular] : the British Prime Minister or the British government ✧ The term Downing Street comes from the address of the official home of the British Prime Minister at Number 10 Downing Street in London.

down·load /'daʊnˌloʊd/ vb [T/I] : to move or copy (a file, program, etc.) from a usually larger computer system to another computer ▪ He downloaded the files onto his computer. ▪ The software downloads quickly. — **download** n [C/U] ▪ a high-speed download — **down·load·able** /'daʊnˌloʊdəbəl/ adj

down–mar·ket /'daʊnˌmɑɚkət/ adj, chiefly Brit ▪ ²DOWNSCALE ▪ down-market stores/hotels/products

down payment n [C] : a first payment that you make when you buy something with an agreement to pay the rest later ▪ We put/made a down payment on the house.

down·play /'daʊnˌpleɪ/ vb [T] : to make (something) seem smaller or less important ▪ She tried to downplay the risk.

down·pour /'daʊnˌpoɚ/ n [C] : a sudden heavy rain ▪ a torrential downpour

down·right /'daʊnˌraɪt/ adv : to the fullest degree ▪ The movie was downright stupid/bad/scary. — **downright** adj, always before a noun ▪ a downright lie

down·riv·er /'daʊn'rɪvɚ/ adv : in the direction in which a river flows ▪ The raft drifted downriver.

downs /'daʊnz/ n [plural] : a high area of land that has low hills and no trees ▪ Sheep graze on the grassy downs.

¹**down·scale** /'daʊnˌskeɪl/ vb **-scaled**; **-scal·ing** [T] US : to make (something) smaller ▪ downscale production ▪ The festival will be downscaled this year.

²**downscale** adj, US : relating or appealing to people who do not have much money ▪ downscale products/stores

down·shift /'daʊnˌʃɪft/ vb [I] : to put the engine of a vehicle into a lower gear ▪ She downshifted to second gear.

down·side /'daʊnˌsaɪd/ n [C] : a part of something that you do not want or like ▪ The downside of the camera is that the batteries have to be replaced often.

down·size /'daʊnˌsaɪz/ vb **-sized**; **-siz·ing** [T/I] : to make (something) smaller ▪ They downsized the car's engine. ▪ downsize to a smaller apartment [=move to a smaller apartment] ▪ The company has downsized [=reduced] its staff.

down·slide /'daʊnˌslaɪd/ n [C] US : DOWNTURN ▪ an economic downslide

down·spout /'daʊnˌspaʊt/ n [C] US : a pipe that carries rainwater from the roof of a building to the ground — called also drainpipe

Down's syndrome /'daʊnz-/ n [U] : DOWN SYNDROME

down·stage /'daʊn'steɪdʒ/ adv : toward the front part of a stage ▪ The actress walked downstage.

¹**down·stairs** /'daʊn'steɚz/ adv : on or to a lower floor of a building ▪ He ran downstairs. — **downstairs** /'daʊnˌsteɚz/ adj ▪ the downstairs bathroom

²**down·stairs** /'daʊn'steɚz/ n — **the downstairs** : the lower and usually main floor of a building ▪ The downstairs needs to be cleaned.

down·state /'daʊn'steɪt/ n [U] US : the southern part of a state — **downstate** adj ▪ downstate New York — **downstate** /'daʊn'steɪt/ adv ▪ He lives downstate.

down·stream /'daʊn'striːm/ adv : in the direction in which a stream, river, etc., flows ▪ float downstream

down·swing /'daʊnˌswɪŋ/ n [C] **1** : DOWNTURN ▪ a financial downswing **2** golf : a forward and downward movement of a club

Down syndrome /'daʊn-/ n [U] medical : a condition that someone is born with and that causes below average mental abilities and problems in physical development — called also Down's syndrome

down·time /'daʊnˌtaɪm/ n [U] **1** US : time when you are not working or busy ▪ The kids napped during their downtime. **2** : time during which a computer or machine is not working ▪ network downtime

down–to–earth adj **1** : informal and easy to talk to ▪ a very down-to-earth person **2** : practical and sensible ▪ down-to-earth advice

down·town /'daʊn'taʊn/ n [C] chiefly US : the main or central part of a city or town ▪ I live close to downtown. — **down·town** /ˌdaʊn'taʊn/ adv ▪ shopping

downtown — **down·town** /ˌdaʊnˈtaʊn/
adj, always before a noun • *downtown offices and businesses* • *downtown Boston*

down·trod·den /ˈdaʊnˌtrɑːdn̩/ *adj,
somewhat formal* : without hope because
of being treated badly by powerful people, governments, etc. • *downtrodden
people*

down·turn /ˈdaʊnˌtɚn/ *n [C]* : a situation
in which something decreases or becomes worse • *an economic downturn* = *a
downturn in the economy*

¹**down·ward** (*chiefly US*) /ˈdaʊnwəd/ *or
chiefly Brit* **down·wards** /ˈdaʊnwədz/
adv **1** : from a higher place, amount, or
level to a lower one • *The stream flows
downward to the lake.* • *The temperature
is heading downward.* **2** : toward the
ground, floor, etc. • *The hawk flew downward.* **3** : toward people with less power, money, etc. • *everyone in the company,
from the president downward*

²**downward** *adj, always before a noun* **1**
: moving or going from a higher place,
amount, or level to a lower one • *a downward slope/trend* **2** : moving or going toward the ground, floor, etc. • *the hawk's
downward flight*

down·wind /ˈdaʊnˈwɪnd/ *adv* : in the direction that the wind is moving • *standing downwind off/from the campfire —
downwind adj* • *the downwind side*

downy /ˈdaʊni/ *adj* **down·i·er; -est 1**
— used to describe small, soft feathers
or something that resembles such feathers • *the downy feathers of a baby bird* •
downy hair **2** : covered or filled with
small, soft feathers or something like
them • *downy chicks/pillows*

dow·ry /ˈdaʊri/ *n, pl* **-ries** *[C]* : money or
property that a wife or wife's family
gives to her husband at the time of marriage in some cultures

dowse /ˈdaʊz/ *vb* **dowsed; dows·ing** *[I]*
: to search for an underground supply of
water by using a special stick that leads
you to it • *dowse for water —* **dows·er** *n
[C]*

doy·en /ˈdɔɪən/ *n [C] formal* : a person
who has a lot of experience in or knowledge about a particular profession, subject, etc. • *a fashion doyen*

doy·enne /dɔɪˈen/ *n [C]* : a woman who
has a lot of experience in or knowledge
about a particular profession, subject,
etc. • *the doyenne of the fashion industry*

doz. *abbr* dozen

doze /ˈdoʊz/ *vb* **dozed; doz·ing** *[I]* : to
sleep lightly especially for a short period
of time • *dozing on the sofa —* **doze off**
[phrasal vb] : to fall asleep especially for
a short period of time • *I dozed off during
the movie. —* **doze** *n [singular]*

doz·en /ˈdʌzn̩/ *n, pl* **doz·ens** *or* **dozen**
1 *pl* **dozen** *[C]* : a group of 12 people or
things • *a dozen eggs* [=12 eggs] **2** *dozens* [*plural*] : large numbers of people or
things • *dozens (and dozens) of hats*
[=many hats] — *a dime a dozen* see
DIME

dozy /ˈdoʊzi/ *adj* **doz·i·er; -est** *informal*
1 : tired or sleepy • *I feel dozy.* **2** *Brit*
: stupid or silly • *a dozy old chap*

Dr. (*US*) *or Brit* **Dr** *abbr* **1** doctor • *Dr.*

Jones **2** drive • *I live at 27 Chestnut Dr.*

drab /ˈdræb/ *adj* **drab·ber; drab·best**
: not bright or colorful • *drab clothes/
rooms —* **drab·ly** *adv —* **drab·ness** *n
[U]*

drabs /ˈdræbz/ *n —* **dribs and drabs** see
DRIBS

dra·co·ni·an /dreɪˈkoʊnijən/ *adj, formal
+ disapproving* : very severe or cruel •
draconian punishments

¹**draft** /ˈdræft, *Brit* ˈdrɑːft/ *n* **1** *[C]* : a version of something (such as a document)
that is made usually before the final version • *an early draft of the memo* • *a rough
draft* [=a first version that needs a lot of
editing and rewriting] • *a final draft* [=a final version] **2** *US* **draft** *or Brit* **draught**
[C] : cool air moving in a closed space
(such as a room) • *We sealed the windows
with plastic to stop drafts.* **3** *[C] US* **a** : a
system in which young people are re-
quired to join the armed forces for a period of service • *Congress reinstated the
draft.* • *a draft dodger* [=a person who illegally avoids joining the armed forces]
b : a system by which professional sports
teams choose new players • *He was chosen in the first round of the draft.* **4** *US*
draft *or Brit* **draught** *[C]* : a beer that is
stored in and poured from a large con-
tainer **5** *[C/U]* : an order for the payment of money from a person or bank to
another person or bank • *They issued a
draft.* • *a bank draft* **6** *US* **draft** *or Brit*
draught *technical* **a** *[C/U]* : the depth
of water that a boat needs in order to
float • *a boat with a deep/shallow draft* **b**
[U] : the depth of the water in a river,
channel, etc. • *The canal provides 60 feet
of draft.* **7** **draught** *[C] Brit* : CHECKER
3 — **on draft** (*US*) *or Brit* **on draught**
: stored in and poured from a large container instead of in individual bottles or
cans • *beer on draft*

²**draft** (*US*) *or Brit* **draught** *adj, always before a noun* **1** *of an animal* : used for
pulling heavy loads • *draft animals* **2**
: stored in and poured from a large container • *draft beer*

³**draft** *vb [T]* **1** : to make a version of
(something, such as a document or plan)
that will need more work in order to be
finished • *draft a speech/treaty* **2 a** : to
choose (someone) for a special purpose •
I was/got drafted to babysit. **b** *US* : to officially order (someone) to join the
armed forces • *He was/got drafted into the
army.* **c** *US* : to choose (someone) to
play on a professional sports team • *He
was/got drafted by the Jets.* — **draft·ee**
/ˈdræfˈtiː, *Brit* ˈdrɑːfˈtiː/ *n [C] US —* **draft-
er** *n [C]*

drafts·man /ˈdræftsmən, *Brit* ˈdrɑːfts-
mən/ *n, pl* **drafts·men** /ˈdræftsmən, *Brit*
ˈdrɑːftsmən/ *[C]* **1** *US* **draftsman** *or
Brit* **draughts·man** : a person whose job
is to make drawings that will be used to
make machines, buildings, etc. **2**
: someone who writes an official or legal
document (such as a law) based on the
ideas that have been officially discussed
3 *US* **draftsman** *or Brit* **draughtsman**
: an artist who draws well • *She is a first-
rate draftsman. —* **drafts·man·ship**

(US) or Brit draughts·man·ship /'dræftsmən,ʃɪp, Brit 'drɑːftsmən,ʃɪp/ n [U]

drafty (US) or Brit draughty /'dræfti, Brit 'drɑːfti/ adj draf·ti·er; -est : having cold air moving through in a way that is unpleasant or uncomfortable ▪ a drafty room/house — draft·i·ness (US) or Brit draught·i·ness /'dræftinəs, Brit 'drɑːftinəs/ n [U]

¹drag /'dræg/ vb dragged; drag·ging 1 [T] : to pull (someone or something that is heavy or difficult to move) ▪ Firefighters dragged the man to safety. ▪ (figurative) She was dragged kicking and screaming into the family business. [=she was forced to join the family business] 2 a [I] : to move along the ground, floor, etc., while being pulled ▪ The broken muffler dragged behind the car. b [T] : to cause (something) to move along the ground, floor, etc., by pulling it ▪ The dog was dragging her leash behind her. 3 a [T] : to force (yourself) to move or to go to a place when you are tired, busy, etc. ▪ I could barely drag myself out of bed. b [I] : to go or move more slowly than others ▪ Quit dragging—walk faster. 4 [T] : to bring (an unpleasant or complicated subject, fact, etc.) into a discussion or argument — + into or up ▪ Don't drag religion into this. ▪ dragging up the past 5 [I] : to go on for a long time in a way that seems slow and boring ▪ The movie dragged on for hours. ▪ The meeting dragged on for hours. 6 [T] : to pull a net or set of hooks through (a river, lake, pond, etc.) in order to search for or collect something ▪ Searchers dragged the river. 7 [T] computers : to move (items on a computer screen) by using a computer mouse ▪ Drag the file to this folder. — drag down [phrasal vb] drag (someone or something) down or drag down (someone or something) 1 : to bring (someone) into a bad situation or condition ▪ Stay away from him—he'll only drag you down. 2 : to make (someone) unhappy ▪ Don't let her bad moods drag you down. 3 : to make (something) lower in amount or quality ▪ High costs are dragging down profits. — drag into [phrasal vb] drag (someone) into : to involve (a person, group, etc.) in (a difficult or complicated situation) ▪ I'm sorry for dragging you into this. — drag out [phrasal vb] 1 drag out (something) or drag (something) out : to cause (something) to take more time than necessary ▪ Stop dragging the story out. 2 drag (something) out of : to force (something, such as a confession) from (someone) ▪ The teacher eventually dragged a confession out of him. — drag someone's name through the mud : to publicly say false or bad things that harm someone's reputation — drag your feet also drag your heels : to avoid doing something for a long time because you do not want to do it ▪ Quit dragging your feet and make a decision!

²drag n 1 [singular] informal : someone or something that is boring, annoying, or disappointing ▪ The meeting was a drag.

2 [singular] informal : someone or something that makes action or progress slower or more difficult ▪ High taxes have been a drag on the economy. 3 [C] informal : the act of breathing in smoke from a cigarette, cigar, etc. ▪ He took a (long/deep) drag on the cigarette. 4 [U] physics : the force of air that pushes against an airplane, a car, etc., as it moves forward ▪ The jet's design reduces drag. — in drag : wearing clothes that are usually worn by the opposite sex ▪ They went to the party dressed in drag. — see also MAIN DRAG

drag·on /'drægən/ n [C] : an imaginary animal that can breathe out fire and looks like a very large lizard with wings, a long tail, and large claws

drag·on·fly /'drægən,flaɪ/ n, pl -flies [C] : a large insect that has a long, thin body and four wings

drag race n [C] : a contest in which people race cars at very high speeds over a short distance — drag racer n [C] — drag racing n [U]

drag·ster /'drægstə/ n [C] : a car that is made for drag racing

drag strip n [C] : a place where drag races happen

¹drain /'dreɪn/ vb 1 a [T] : to remove liquid from something by letting it flow away or out ▪ Drain the canned tomatoes before using them. ▪ Drain the grease from the pan. ▪ They drained the pool/swamp. b [I] of a container : to become empty of a liquid ▪ waiting for the bathtub to drain c [I] of a liquid : to flow into, away from, or out of something ▪ The river drains into a lake. 2 a [T] : to cause (something) to lose something important — + of ▪ The war has drained the country of its resources. b [T/I] : to slowly be used up or to cause (something) to slowly be used up ▪ The war has drained the country's resources. ▪ She felt her anger drain away. 3 [T] : to make (someone) very physically or mentally tired ▪ The work drains me. ▪ Her work is draining. [=tiring] ▪ I feel totally drained. [=exhausted] 4 [T] : to drink all of the liquid in (something) ▪ He quickly drained the mug. — drain off [phrasal vb] drain off (something) or drain (something) off : to cause (a liquid) to flow away from something or to leave the surface of something ▪ Drain off the water and set the beans aside. b : to take (something important or valuable) from something ▪ An independent candidate could drain off votes from either party.

²drain n [C] 1 : something (such as a pipe) that is used for removing a liquid from a place or container ▪ The drain in the bathtub/sink is clogged. 2 : something that uses a lot of time, money, etc. ▪ Tuition costs are a drain on the family income. — down the drain informal 1 — used to describe something that is being wasted or lost ▪ All my hard work went down the drain. 2 — used to describe something that is getting much worse ▪ The public schools are going down the drain.

drain·age /'dreɪnɪdʒ/ n [U] : the act or

drainpipe • draw

process of removing water or liquid from a place or thing • *The soil has good drainage.* [=extra water does not stay in the soil] • *a drainage system*

drain·pipe /'dreɪnˌpaɪp/ *n* [C] **1** : a pipe that carries rainwater from the roof of a building to the ground : DOWNSPOUT **2** *US* : a pipe that carries liquid waste and water away from buildings

drake /'dreɪk/ *n* [C] : a male duck

dram /'dræm/ *n* [C] : a small amount of an alcoholic drink • *a dram of whiskey*

dra·ma /'drɑːmə/ *n* **1 a** [C] : a piece of writing that tells a story and is performed on a stage • *an ancient Greek drama* **b** [C/U] : a play, movie, television show, or radio show that is about a serious subject and is not meant to make the audience laugh • *a television/radio drama* • *I prefer drama to comedy.* **2** [U] : the art or activity of performing a role in a play, show, etc. : ACTING • *She studied drama in college.* • *a drama teacher/student* **3** [C/U] : a situation or series of events that is exciting and that affects people's emotions • *the dramas of teenage life* • *a moment of high drama* [=a very exciting and dramatic moment]

dra·mat·ic /drə'mætɪk/ *adj* **1 a** : sudden and extreme • *a dramatic increase/decrease/difference* **b** : greatly affecting people's emotions • *a dramatic victory/story* **c** : causing people to carefully listen, look, etc. • *a dramatic entrance/pause* • *dramatic colors/accents* **d** : tending to behave and react in an emotional and exaggerated way • *Don't be so dramatic.* [=melodramatic] **2** *always before a noun* : of or relating to plays and the performance of plays • *the local dramatic society* — **dra·mat·i·cal·ly** /drə'mætɪkli/ *adv*

dra·mat·ics /drə'mætɪks/ *n* **1** [*plural*] : behavior that is very emotional in a way that does not seem sincere • *a child prone to dramatics* **2** [U] : the study or practice of acting in or producing plays • *She is studying dramatics in school.*

dra·ma·tis per·so·nae /ˌdræmətəspə-'souni/ *n* [*plural*] *formal* : the characters or actors in a play, movie, etc.

dram·a·tist /'dræmətɪst/ *n* [C] : someone who writes plays, televison dramas, etc.

dram·a·tize *also Brit* **dram·a·tise** /'dræmə,taɪz/ *vb* **-tized; -tiz·ing** [T] **1** : to make (a book, an event, etc.) into a play, movie, television show, etc. • *The movie dramatizes his life.* **2** : to make a situation seem more important or serious than it really is • *I know I tend to dramatize things but it really was awful.* **3** : to show (something that might not be noticed) in a clear and effective way • *This tragedy dramatizes the need for improvements in highway safety.* — **dram·a·ti·za·tion** *also Brit* **dram·a·ti·sa·tion** /ˌdræmətə'zeɪʃən, Brit ˌdræmə,taɪ-'zeɪʃən/ *n* [C/U]

drank *past tense of* [1]DRINK

drape /'dreɪp/ *vb* **draped; drap·ing 1 a** [T] : to loosely place or hang (something) • *He had one leg draped over the arm of the sofa.* • *A scarf was draped around her neck.* **b** [I] *of cloth* : to hang

in a pleasing way • *This silk drapes beautifully.* **2** [T] : to cover (someone or something) with a cloth • *The tables were draped in linen.*

drap·ery /'dreɪpəri/ *n, pl* **-er·ies 1** [C/U] *US* : long, heavy curtains : DRAPES • *beautiful drapery/draperies* **2** [U] : a decorative cloth that is arranged or hung in loose folds

drapes /'dreɪps/ *n* [*plural*] *chiefly US* : long, heavy curtains • *This room needs new drapes.*

dras·tic /'dræstɪk/ *adj* : severe or serious • *drastic measures/action/cuts* — **dras·ti·cal·ly** /'dræstɪkli/ *adv*

[1]**draught** *Brit spelling of* DRAFT

[2]**draught** /'dræft, Brit 'drɑːft/ *n* [C] *Brit* : CHECKER **3**

draughts /'dræfts, Brit 'drɑːfts/ *n* [U] *Brit* : CHECKERS

draughtsman, draughty *Brit spellings of* DRAFTSMAN, DRAFTY

[1]**draw** /'drɑː/ *vb* **drew** /'druː/; **drawn** /'drɑːn/; **draw·ing 1** [T/I] : to make (a picture, image, etc.) by making lines on a surface especially with a pencil, pen, etc. • *draw a picture* • *He drew me a picture of the bike.* = *He drew a picture of the bike for me.* • *You draw very well.* **2** [T] : to cause (attention) to be given to someone or something • *I would like to draw your attention to the third line.* **3** [T] **a** : to cause (someone or something) to come • *The band always draws* [=attracts] *a large crowd.* • *She felt drawn* [=attracted] *to him.* • *My eye was drawn to the painting.* [=something about the painting made me want to look at it] **b** : to cause (someone) to become involved or interested — + *in, into,* or *to* • *What first drew you to teaching?* • *She was drawn in by his friendly manner.* • *I got drawn into the conversation.* **4** [T] : to get or receive (something) • *a television show that has drawn high ratings* • *The player drew a foul.* : to get (a particular response or reaction) • *His speech drew cheers.* • *Her remarks have drawn fire.* [=attracted angry criticism] **5 a** [I] : to move in a specified direction • *He drew back/away in horror.* • *The train drew* [=pulled] *into the station.* **b** [T] : to move (something) by pulling • *a carriage drawn by horses* • *a horse-drawn carriage* • *Draw the curtains.* [=open or close the curtains] • (*figurative*) *The tragedy drew us closer together.* [=made us emotionally closer] **6** [I] : to move gradually or steadily in time or space • *The lion drew closer to its prey.* • *The sun is setting and the day is drawing to a close.* [=ending] • *Spring is drawing near.* [=approaching] • *The car drew to a halt/stop.* [=slowed down and stopped] **7** [T] **a** : to form (something, such as an idea or conclusion) after thinking carefully about information you have • *You can draw your own conclusions.* • *We can draw lessons from past mistakes.* [=we can learn from past mistakes] **b** : to describe how two or more things are similar or different • *She drew comparisons/distinctions between the two methods.* **8 a** [T] : to take (something) out of a container, pocket, etc. • *One of the men drew*

[=*pulled*] *a gun.* ▪ *She drew water from the well.* **b** [*T*] : to get (something) *from* a source ▪ *She draws strength/inspiration from her family.* **c** [*T/I*] : to take (a card) from a group of cards ▪ *Draw four cards.* **9 a** [*T*] : to choose (a thing) from a group without knowing which one you are choosing ▪ *She drew the winning ticket.* ▪ *We drew names from a hat.* **b** [*I*] : to decide something by choosing something from a group ▪ *We'll draw to see who will drive.* **10** [*T*] : to make (something, such as a legal document) in a proper or legal form ▪ *We hired a lawyer to draw (up) a will.* **11** [*T*] : to take (air, smoke, etc.) into your lungs by breathing ▪ *She drew (in) a deep breath.* **12** [*T*] **a** : to take (money) from a bank account : WITHDRAW ▪ *He drew $100 from the bank.* ▪ *She drew out the money.* **b** : to receive (money) regularly from an employer, government, bank, etc. ▪ *She draws a pension.* **c** : to write (a check) and have money taken from a bank account ▪ *She is authorized to draw checks from the corporate account.* **13** [*T/I*] *Brit* : to finish a game, contest, etc., without having a winner ▪ *We drew [=(US) tied] the game 3-3.* **14** [*T*] *archery* : to bend (a bow) by pulling back the string ▪ *He drew his bow.* **15** [*T*] *Brit* : to cause (someone) to say more about something especially by questioning ▪ *She refused to be drawn on whether the company is considering a merger.* — **draw a bead on** see BEAD — **draw a blank** see ²BLANK — **draw a/the line** see ¹LINE — **draw blood** see BLOOD — **draw off** [*phrasal vb*] **draw off (something)** or **draw (something) off** : to take or remove (something) from a source or supply ▪ *They illegally drew off thousands of dollars from the charity.* — **draw on/upon** [*phrasal vb*] **1 draw on** *literary* : to come closer in time ▪ *It became colder as night drew on.* **2 a** : to use (something) as a source or supply ▪ *The family is drawing on/upon the community for support.* **b** : to use (information, experience, knowledge, etc.) to make something ▪ *Her new book draws on her personal experience.* **3 draw on** : to breathe in smoke from (a cigarette, cigar, pipe, etc.) — **draw out** [*phrasal vb*] **1 draw (something) out** or **draw out (something) a** : to cause (something) to leave a source or supply ▪ *Trees draw water out of the soil.* **b** : to cause (something) to last longer than the usual or expected amount of time ▪ *Questions drew the meeting out for another hour.* **2 draw (someone) out** or **draw out (someone)** : to cause (someone) to talk freely ▪ *The reporter was able to draw her out.* — **draw straws** ◆ If you *draw straws*, you choose a stick from a group of sticks, and whoever chooses the shortest stick or *gets/draws the short straw* will have to do a particular thing. ▪ *Let's draw straws to see who will drive.* — **draw the blinds/curtain/shades on** : to end (something that has been continuing for a long time) ▪ *Let's draw the curtain on this investigation.* — **draw up** [*phrasal vb*] **1** *of a vehicle* : to approach and stop

at a place ▪ *A car drew up in front of the house.* **2 draw (yourself) up** : to stand as straight and tall as you can ▪ *He drew himself up to (his) full height.*

²**draw** *n* [*C*] **1** : someone or something that causes a lot of people to come to a place ▪ *The festival is always a big draw.* **2** : the final result of a game, contest, etc., that does not have a winner : TIE ▪ *The game ended in a draw.* **3** *chiefly Brit* : DRAWING ▪ *The draw for the raffle will take place in one hour.* **4** : an act of breathing in smoke from a cigarette, cigar, pipe, etc. : DRAG ▪ *He took a long draw on/from his cigarette.* — **be quick on the draw** : to quickly take out a gun and be ready to shoot it ▪ *(figurative) Critics may have been a little too quick on the draw.* — **the luck of the draw** see ¹LUCK

draw·back /ˈdrɑːˌbæk/ *n* [*C*] : something that causes problems ▪ *There are several drawbacks to the plan.*

draw·bridge /ˈdrɑːˌbrɪʤ/ *n* [*C*] : a bridge that can be raised up so that people cannot cross it or so that boats can pass under it

draw·er /ˈdrɑːɚ/ *n* **1** [*C*] : a box that slides into and out of a piece of furniture (such as a desk) and that is used to store things ▪ *There are some pens in my desk drawer.* — see also CHEST OF DRAWERS **2** [*plural*] *old-fashioned* + *humorous* : underwear for the lower part of the body ▪ *He stood there in only his drawers.*

draw·ing /ˈdrɑːɪŋ/ *n* **1** [*C*] : a picture, image, etc., that is made by making lines on a surface with a pencil, pen, etc. ▪ *She made a drawing of my house.* **b** [*U*] : the act or art of making a picture, image, etc., with a pencil, pen, etc. ▪ *I've always loved drawing.* **2** [*C*] *US* : an act of choosing something (such as a winning ticket) from a group without knowing which one you are choosing ▪ *Who won the (prize) drawing?* ▪ *The drawing for the raffle will take place in one hour.*

drawing board *n* **1** [*C*] : a large flat board that is used for holding paper for drawing **2** [*U*] : the time during which something is being planned ▪ *Plans for the new stadium are on the drawing board.* [=are being created] ▪ *We need to go back to the drawing board.* [=to start over]

drawing pin *n* [*C*] *Brit* : THUMBTACK

drawing room *n* [*C*] *formal* + *old-fashioned* : a formal room that is used for spending time with guests or relaxing

drawl /ˈdrɑːl/ *vb* [*T/I*] : to speak slowly with vowel sounds that are longer than usual ▪ *He drawled his name in a Southern accent.* — **drawl** *n* [*C*] ▪ *She spoke with a drawl.*

¹**drawn** *past participle of* ¹DRAW

²**drawn** /ˈdrɑːn/ *adj* : looking very thin and tired ▪ *His illness left him looking very pale and drawn.*

drawn–out *adj* : continuing for or taking a long time ▪ *a drawn-out process*

draw·string /ˈdrɑːˌstrɪŋ/ *n* [*C*] : a string that can be pulled to close or tighten something (such as a bag or a piece of clothing)

¹**dread** /ˈdrɛd/ *vb* [*T*] : to fear something

that will or might happen • *I dread the thought of leaving.* • *I dread to think about what might happen.* — **dread·ed** /'drɛdəd/ *adj* • *a dreaded disease*

²dread *n* **1** [*U, singular*] : a strong feeling of fear about something that will or might happen • *She awaited her punishment with dread.* • *a dread of failure* • *They live in dread of another attack.* **2** [*C*] : a person or thing that causes fear • *Fire was a constant dread for her.* **3** [*plural*] *informal* : DREADLOCKS

³dread *adj, always before a noun, formal* : causing great fear • *a dread [=dreaded] disease*

dread·ful /'drɛdfəl/ *adj* : very bad or unpleasant • *a dreadful performance/mistake* • *dreadful manners/weather* — **dread·ful·ly** /'drɛdfəli/ *adv*

dread·locks /'drɛd,lɑːks/ *n* [*plural*] : hair that is twisted together into long pieces that hang down around your shoulders

¹dream /'driːm/ *n* **1** [*C*] : a series of thoughts, visions, or feelings that happen during sleep • *He had a dream about climbing a mountain.* • *Scary movies give me bad dreams.* [=*nightmares*] **2** [*C*] : an idea or vision that is created in your imagination and that is not real • *She indulged in dreams* [=*fantasies*] *of a life in a palace.* • *I've found the man/woman of my dreams.* • *They succeeded beyond their wildest dreams.* **3 a** [*C*] : something that you have wanted very much to do, be, or have for a long time • *a lifelong dream of becoming an actor* • *She followed/fulfilled her dreams.* • *Making it to the Olympics was a dream come true.* **b** [*singular*] : someone or something that has the qualities that a person wants most • *He's every woman's dream.* • *my dream home/job/husband/wife* **4** [*singular*] *informal* : something that is beautiful, excellent, or pleasing • *The car is a dream to drive.* = *The car drives like a dream.* [=*very well*] **5** [*singular*] : a state or condition in which you are not thinking about or aware of the real things that are around you • *He was walking around in a dream.* — **in your dreams** *informal* — used to say that you do not think something that another person wants or expects will ever happen • *"Maybe my parents will lend me the car tonight." "In your dreams."* — **dream·less** /'driːm-ləs/ *adj* — **dream·like** /'driːm,laɪk/ *adj*

²dream *vb* **dreamed** /'drɛmt, 'driːmd/ *or* **dreamt** /'drɛmt/; **dream·ing** [*T/I*] **1** : to have a dream while you are sleeping • *I dreamed (that) I could fly.* • *I dreamed about/of flying.* **2** : to think about something that you wish would happen or something that you want to do or be • *He dreamed of becoming an astronaut.* = *He dreamed (that) he would be an astronaut someday.* • *She dreams of romance/success.* • *You're dreaming* [=you're completely wrong] *if you think I'll agree to that.* • *I dreamed away the afternoon.* [=I spent the whole afternoon thinking and dreaming] • *I never dreamt that it would be so difficult.* [=it was much more diffi-

cult than I expected it to be] — **dream on** *informal* — used to say that you do not think something that another person wants or expects will ever happen • *"I'm sure we can win." "Dream on."* — **dream up** [*phrasal vb*] **dream up (something)** *also* **dream (something) up** : to think of or invent (something) in your mind • *a new recipe that she dreamed up herself* — **never/not dream of** — used to say that you would never do something • *I would never dream of asking for more money.*

dream·er *n* [*C*] **1** *disapproving* : a person whose ideas and plans are not practical • *I am a realist, but my sister is a dreamer.* **2** : a person who dreams while sleeping

dream·land /'driːm,lænd/ *n* [*U, singular*] *informal* : a pleasant place or situation that exists only in the mind • (*disapproving*) *He's living in (a) dreamland* [=he's dreaming] *if he thinks I'll agree.*

dreamt *past tense and past participle of* ²DREAM

dreamy /'driːmi/ *adj* **dream·i·er; -est 1** : tending to dream instead of thinking about what is real or practical • *a dreamy young idealist* **2** : having a quality which shows or suggests that you are not noticing or thinking about what is happening around you • *He had a dreamy look in his eyes.* **3** : pleasant, peaceful, and relaxing • *dreamy music* **4** *informal* + *old-fashioned* : very attractive • *Her boyfriend is dreamy.* — **dream·i·ly** /'driːməli/ *adv*

drea·ry /'driri/ *adj* **drea·ri·er; -ri·est** : causing sad feelings • *a gray, dreary morning* • *dreary economic times* — **drea·ri·ly** /'drirəli/ *adv* — **drea·ri·ness** *n* [*U*]

¹dredge /'drɛdʒ/ *vb* **dredged; dredg·ing 1 a** [*T/I*] : to remove mud from the bottom of (a lake, river, etc.) in order to deepen it or to search for something • *They dredged the river.* **b** [*T*] : to dig (something) out of the bottom of a lake, river, etc. • *dredging (up) sand from the river* **2** [*T*] : to lightly cover (food) with a dry substance (such as sugar or flour) • *Dredge the fish in/with flour before frying it.* — **dredge up** [*phrasal vb*] **dredge up (something)** *or* **dredge (something) up** : to start talking or thinking again about (something unpleasant that happened a long time ago) • *She didn't like to dredge up bad memories.*

²dredge *n* [*C*] : a machine or boat that removes mud, sand, etc., from the bottom of a lake, river, etc. — called also **dredg·er** /'drɛdʒɚ/

dregs /'drɛgz/ *n* [*plural*] **1** : solid materials that fall to the bottom of a container full of a liquid • *coffee dregs* **2** : the worst or most useless part of something • *people who were regarded as the dregs of society*

drench /'drɛntʃ/ *vb* [*T*] : to make (someone or something) completely wet • *She drenched him with cold water.* • *She was drenched in perfume.* [=wearing a lot of perfume] • (*figurative*) *a room drenched in sunlight*

¹dress /'drɛs/ *vb* **1 a** [*T*] : to put clothes

on (yourself or someone else) • *They dressed themselves in a hurry.* **b** [I] : to put clothes on yourself • *She showered, dressed, and ate breakfast.* **2** [I] **a** : to put on or wear a particular type or style of clothes • *dress warmly/fashionably* **b** : to put on or wear formal clothes • *They always dress for dinner.* **3** [T] : to clean, put medicine on, and cover (a wound) • *dress a cut* **4** [T] : to prepare (food) for cooking or eating • *dress the chicken/salad* **5** [T] : to decorate (something, especially a window) for display • *He dressed the store window for the holiday.* **6** [T] *technical* : to prepare (wood, stone, leather, etc.) for use — **dress down** [*phrasal vb*] **1** : to wear informal clothes • *On Fridays everyone in the office dresses down.* **2 dress (someone) down** or **dress down (someone)** : to speak angrily to (someone) for doing something wrong • *He was/got dressed down for failing to follow orders.* — **dress up** [*phrasal vb*] **1 a** : to put on or wear formal clothes • *We dressed up for the party.* **b** : to put on a costume • *We dressed up like/as ghosts for Halloween.* **2 dress (someone) up** or **dress up (someone)** : to put formal or fancy clothes or a costume on (someone) • *She dressed up the children for the wedding.* • *We dressed the baby up as a lion.* **3 dress up (something)** or **dress (something) up** : to make (something) more attractive, impressive, or fancy • *dress up a plain dessert with a rich sauce*

²**dress** *n* **1** [C] : a piece of clothing for a woman or a girl that has a top part that covers the upper body and a skirt that hangs down to cover the legs • *Her wedding dress was decorated with lace.* **2** [U] : a particular type of clothing • *The guests were clothed in traditional Indian dress.*

³**dress** *adj, always before a noun* : suitable or required for a formal event • *dress pants/shoes*

dress code *n* [C] : a set of rules about what clothing may and may not be worn at a school, office, restaurant, etc.

dressed *adj* : wearing clothes • *I'm not dressed yet.* • *It's time to get out of bed and get dressed.* [=put on clothes] : wearing clothes of a particular type • *She wasn't dressed for such hot weather.* • *dressed in black* • *a well-dressed young man*

dress·er /ˈdrɛsɚ/ *n* [C] **1** : a person who dresses in a particular way • *a stylish dresser* **2** *US* : a piece of furniture that has drawers for storing clothes : CHEST OF DRAWERS **3** *Brit* : HUTCH 1

dress·ing /ˈdrɛsɪŋ/ *n* **1** [C/U] : a usually seasoned mixture of liquids that is added to a salad — called also *salad dressing* **2** [C/U] *US* : STUFFING **2** • *turkey with dressing* **3** [C] : special material that is used to cover a wound • *The nurse applied a dressing.*

dressing gown *n* [C] : a loose piece of clothing that is worn indoors while relaxing, getting ready for bed, etc.

dressing room *n* [C] : a room where performers, actors, etc., can change their clothes

dress rehearsal *n* [C] : the final practice of a play that is done with all the costumes, scenery, etc., that will be used in the first real performance before an audience

dress shirt *n* [C] **1** *US* : a man's shirt that is usually worn with a necktie **2** : a man's formal white shirt that is worn with a bow tie

dressy /ˈdrɛsi/ *adj* **dress·i·er**; **-est** **1** : suitable for formal events • *dressy shoes/clothes* **2** : requiring fancy or formal clothes • *a dressy event*

drew *past tense of* ¹DRAW

¹**drib·ble** /ˈdrɪbəl/ *vb* **drib·bled**; **drib·bling** **1 a** [I] : to fall or flow in small drops • *Juice dribbled down his chin.* **b** [T] : to let (a liquid) fall in small drops • *She accidentally dribbled wine onto the rug.* **2** [I] : to let saliva or another liquid drip or trickle from your mouth • *The baby dribbled* [=drooled] *onto my shirt.* **3** [T/I] : to move a ball or puck forward by tapping, bouncing, or kicking it • *She dribbled (the ball) across the basketball court.*

²**dribble** *n* [C] **1** : a small flow of liquid • *He wiped a dribble of juice from the baby's chin.* **2** : an act of moving a ball or puck forward by tapping, bouncing, or kicking it • *She gave the ball a dribble before passing it.*

dribs /ˈdrɪbz/ *n* — **dribs and drabs** *informal* : small amounts that come or happen over a period of time • *They received donations in dribs and drabs.*

drier *variant spelling of* DRYER

¹**drift** /ˈdrɪft/ *n* **1** [*singular*] : a slow and gradual movement or change from one place, condition, etc., to another • *the slow drift of the clouds* **2** [C] : a large pile of snow or sand that has been blown by the wind **3** [*singular*] *informal* : the general or basic meaning of something said or written • *I get/catch your drift.* [=understand what you're saying] **4** [U] : movement of an airplane or a ship in a direction different from the one desired because of air or water currents

²**drift** *vb* [I] **1** : to move slowly on water, wind, etc. • *The boat slowly drifted out to sea.* **2** *of snow or sand* : to form a pile by being blown by the wind • *The snow drifted against the side of the house.* **3 a** : to move smoothly or easily in a way that is not planned or guided • *The party guests drifted from room to room.* • *The conversation drifted from topic to topic.* **b** : to behave or live in a way that is not guided by a definite purpose or plan • *She drifted from job to job.* **4** : to change slowly from one state or condition to another • *The patient drifted in and out of consciousness.* — **drift apart** [*phrasal vb*] : to stop having a close relationship • *They used to be friends, but they've gradually drifted apart.* — **drift off** [*phrasal vb*] *informal* : to fall asleep • *She drifted off (to sleep) while I was talking.*

drift·er /ˈdrɪftɚ/ *n* [C] : a person who moves from one place or job to another without a purpose or plan

drift·wood /ˈdrɪftˌwʊd/ *n* [U] : wood that

is floating in water or carried to the shore by water

¹drill /'drɪl/ n **1** [C] : a tool used for making holes in hard substances **2** [C/U] **a** : an exercise done to practice military skills or procedures • *recruits/soldiers doing drills* • *(chiefly Brit) soldiers doing drill* • *a drill sergeant* [=a sergeant who trains new soldiers] **b** : a physical or mental activity that is done repeatedly in order to learn something, become more skillful, etc. • *The students/players are doing their drills.* — see also FIRE DRILL — **know the drill** *informal* : to know how something is done • *You don't have to tell us what to do. We all know the drill.*

²drill vb **1** [T/I] : to make a hole in something with a drill • *The dentist drilled the tooth.* • *drill a hole* • *drilling for oil* **2** [T] **a** : to teach or train (someone) by repeating a lesson or exercise again and again • *We drilled the children on their multiplication tables.* **b** : to train (soldiers) by making them practice military procedures and exercises • *The commander drilled the troops.* — **drill into** [*phrasal vb*] **drill (something) into** : to force (something) to be learned very well by (someone) by repeating it again and again • *Our teacher drilled the lesson into our heads.* — **drill·er** n [C]

drily *variant spelling of* DRYLY

¹drink /'drɪŋk/ vb **drank** /'dræŋk/, **drunk** /'drʌŋk/; **drink·ing** **1** [T/I] : to take a liquid into your mouth and swallow it • *We drank orange juice with breakfast.* • *The baby still drinks from a bottle.* **2** [I] : to drink alcohol • *She drank too much at the party.* • *I don't drink.* [=I never drink alcohol] • *Drinking is not allowed in the park.* — **drink in** [*phrasal vb*] **drink in (something) or drink (something) in** : to stop and look at or listen to something in order to enjoy it fully • *drink in the view* — **drink to** [*phrasal vb*] : to speak words that honor or express good wishes for (someone or something) and then take a drink • *We drank (a toast) to their anniversary/health.* • *(figurative) "It will be the best vacation of our lives." "I'll drink to that!"* [=I completely agree] — **drink up** [*phrasal vb*] **drink up or drink up (something) or drink (something) up** : to drink all of (something) • *Here's a glass of wine. Drink up!* — **drink·able** /'drɪŋkəbəl/ *adj* — **drink·er** /'drɪŋkɚ/ n [C] • *a heavy drinker* • *a wine drinker*

²drink n **1** [C/U] : BEVERAGE • *coffee, tea, and other hot drinks* • *Food and drink will be provided.* — see also SOFT DRINK **2 a** [C] : an alcoholic beverage • *They went to the bar for a few drinks.* • *a stiff drink* [=a strong alcoholic drink] **b** [U] : the habit or practice of drinking a lot of alcohol • *She took to drink.* • *The stress drove him to drink.* **3** [*singular*] : an act of drinking • *He took a long drink from his glass.* **4** [C] : an amount of liquid for drinking • *Give the dog a drink of water.* — **the drink** *old-fashioned* : an area of water (such as a lake or pond) • *She fell into the drink.*

drip /'drɪp/ vb **dripped**; **drip·ping** **1** [I]

: to fall in drops • *Water dripped from a leak in the ceiling.* **2** [T/I] : to let drops of (a liquid) fall • *She dripped tea on her skirt.* • *The faucet is dripping.* • *His face was dripping with sweat.* [=sweat was dripping from his face] **3** [I] : to have or show a large amount of something • *Her voice dripped with contempt/charm.*

²drip n **1 a** [C] : a drop of liquid that falls from something • *Drips of water fell on the pavement.* **b** [*singular*] : the sound or action of liquid falling in drops • *the steady drip, drip, drip of the faucet* **2** [C] : a device used in hospitals to pass fluid slowly through a tube into a patient's blood • *a morphine drip*

drip–dry /'drɪpˌdraɪ/ *adj* : able to dry with few or no wrinkles when hung up while wet • *a drip-dry shirt*

¹drive /'draɪv/ vb **drove** /'droʊv/; **driv·en** /'drɪvən/; **driv·ing** **1 a** [T/I] : to direct the movement of (a car, truck, bus, etc.) • *He drove the car down the road.* • *She drives a taxi.* [=her job is driving a taxi] • *He is learning to drive.* **b** [I] *of a car, truck, etc.* : to move in a specified manner or direction • *The car drove away/off.* **c** [T/I] : to travel in a car • *We drove all night.* • *We drove (for) 160 miles.* • *I drive (on/along) this route every day.* **d** [T] : to take (someone or something) to a place in a car, truck, etc. • *I drove her to the station.* **e** [T] : to own and use (a vehicle of a specified kind) • *He drives a pickup.* **2** [T] : to move (people or animals) to or from a place by using force • *Cowboys drove the herds across the prairie.* • *They drove the invaders back.* **3** [T] : to push (something) with force • *He drove a nail into the wall.* **4** [T] : to make (a machine or vehicle) work or move • *Electricity drives the machinery.* • *(figurative) What drives the economy?* **5** [T] **a** : to cause (someone) to behave in a particular way • *Ambition drove her to succeed.* **b** : to force (someone) to work very hard • *The team was driven hard by the coach.* **6** [T] : to bring (someone) into a particular condition • *That noise is driving me crazy.* • *The new store drove him out of business.* **7** [T] : to cause (a price, number, etc.) to increase or decrease • *The news drove stock prices up/down.* **8** [I] *sports* : to move toward or through something with a lot of force or speed • *He drove to/toward the basket/net.* **9** [T] *sports* : to hit or kick (a ball or puck) with a lot of force or speed • *He drove the puck into the net.* **10** [I] *of rain, wind, etc.* : to fall or blow with great force • *The rain drove against the windows.* — **drive at** [*phrasal vb*] : to try to say (something) • *I think I see what you're driving at.* — **drive away** [*phrasal vb*] **drive (someone) away or drive away (someone)** : to cause or force (someone) to leave especially by making a situation unpleasant or unattractive • *The store's high prices are driving away customers.* — **drive in** [*phrasal vb*] **drive (someone or something) in or drive in (someone or something)** *baseball* : to cause (a run or runner) to score • *He drove in another run.* — **drive off** [*phrasal vb*] **drive (someone or something) off**

or **drive off (someone or something)** : to cause or force (someone or something) to leave ▪ *They drove off the invaders.* — **drive out** [*phrasal vb*] **drive (someone or something) out** or **drive out (someone or something)** : to cause or force (someone or something) to leave ▪ *The family was driven out of the neighborhood by rising property taxes.*

²**drive** *n* **1** [*C*] : a journey in a car ▪ *a two-hour drive* ▪ *Would you like to go for a drive?* **2** [*C*] : DRIVEWAY ▪ *My car is parked in the drive.* **3** — used in the name of some public roads ▪ *They live at 156 Woodland Drive.* — *abbr.* **Dr.** **4** [*C*] : an effort made by a group of people to achieve a goal, to collect money, etc. ▪ *a fund-raising drive* **5** [*C/U*] : a strong natural need or desire ▪ *The need for food and water are basic drives for all living things.* ▪ **sex drive** [=the desire to have sex] **6** [*U*] : a strong desire for success ▪ *She's full of drive and determination.* **7** [*C*] : a device in a computer that can read information off and copy information onto disks or tape ▪ *a CD-ROM drive* **8** [*U*] **a** : the way power from an engine controls and directs the movement of a vehicle ▪ *The car has rear-wheel drive.* **b** *chiefly US* : a condition in which the gears of a vehicle are working in a way that allows the vehicle to move forward ▪ *He put the car in/into drive.* **9** [*C*] **a** *sports* : a ball, puck, etc., that is hit very hard ▪ *He hit a hard/long drive down the left-field line.* **b** *golf* : a long shot that is hit from a tee ▪ *She hit her drive into the rough.* **10** [*C*] : a long or forceful military attack on an enemy ▪ *an armored drive into enemy territory* **11** [*C*] *American football* : a series of plays that move the ball down the field toward the opponent's end zone ▪ *a ten-play drive* **12** [*C*] : an act of leading cattle or sheep over land and keeping them in a group ▪ *a cattle drive*

drive–by /ˈdraɪvˌbaɪ/ *adj, always before a noun* : done from a moving vehicle ▪ *a drive-by shooting/killing*

drive–in /ˈdraɪvˌɪn/ *n* [*C*] **1** : a place where people can watch movies outdoors while sitting in their cars — called also *drive-in theater* **2** : a restaurant at which people are served in their cars — called also *drive-in restaurant*

¹**driv·el** /ˈdrɪvəl/ *n* [*U*] : foolish writing or speech ▪ *I'm not going to waste my time reading this drivel.*

²**drivel** *vb, US* -**eled** or *Brit* -**elled**; *US* -**el·ing** or *Brit* -**el·ling** [*I*] *informal* : to talk in a very foolish or silly way ▪ *What is he driveling about now?*

driven *past participle of* ¹DRIVE

driv·er /ˈdraɪvɚ/ *n* [*C*] **1** : a person who drives a car, truck, etc. ▪ *He's a good/careful/fast/bad driver.* **2** *technical* : a piece of computer software that controls a device (such as a mouse or printer) that is attached to the computer **3** *golf* : a club that is used for hitting long shots off a tee — **in the driver's seat** : in a position in which you are able to control what happens ▪ *When his boss went on va-*cation, he suddenly found himself in the driver's seat.

driver's license *n* [*C*] *US* : an official document or card which shows that you have the legal right to drive a vehicle — called also (*Brit*) *driving licence*

drive–shaft /ˈdraɪvˌʃæft, *Brit* ˈdraɪvˌʃɑːft/ *n* [*C*] *technical* : a part of a vehicle that carries power from the gears to the wheels

drive–through *also* **drive–thru** /ˈdraɪvˌθruː/ *n* [*C*] : a business that is designed so that customers can be served while remaining in their cars ▪ *a drive-through restaurant*

drive·way /ˈdraɪvˌweɪ/ *n* [*C*] : a short private road from a street to a house or other building where cars can usually be parked

¹**driz·zle** /ˈdrɪzəl/ *vb* **driz·zled; driz·zling** **1** [*I*] : to rain lightly ▪ *It's starting to drizzle.* **2** [*T*] : to pour a small amount of liquid on something ▪ *She drizzled syrup on her pancakes.* = *She drizzled her pancakes with syrup.*

²**drizzle** *n* [*singular*] : rain that falls lightly ▪ *Yes, it's raining, but it's only a drizzle.* — **driz·zly** /ˈdrɪzəli/ *adj* **driz·li·er; -est**

droll /ˈdroʊl/ *adj* : having an odd and amusing quality ▪ *a droll person/story*

¹**drone** /ˈdroʊn/ *n* [*C*] **1** : a deep continuous sound ▪ HUM ▪ *the drone of passing traffic* **2 a** : a type of male bee that does not gather honey **b** *chiefly US, informal* : a person who does work that is boring and not very important ▪ *one of many office drones*

²**drone** *vb* **droned; dron·ing** [*I*] : to make a continuous low humming sound ▪ *A plane droned overhead.* — **drone on** [*phrasal vb*] *informal* : to speak for a long time in a dull voice without saying anything interesting ▪ *The lecturer droned on.*

¹**drool** /ˈdruːl/ *vb* [*I*] **1** : to let saliva flow out from the mouth ▪ *a drooling baby* **2** : to show admiration or desire for something in an exaggerated way ▪ *Everyone was drooling over his new car.*

²**drool** *n* [*U*] *chiefly US* : saliva that drips from the mouth ▪ *He wiped the drool from the baby's face.*

droop /ˈdruːp/ *vb* [*I*] **1** : to sink, bend, or hang down ▪ *The flowers were drooping.* **2** : to become sad or weak ▪ *His spirits drooped.* — **droop** *n* [*singular*] ▪ *the droop of the flowers* — **droopy** /ˈdruːpi/ *adj* **droop·i·er; -est** ▪ *a droopy mustache*

¹**drop** /ˈdrɑːp/ *n* **1** [*C*] : a very small amount of liquid that falls in a rounded shape ▪ *a few drops of water/rain/blood* **2** [*C*] *informal* : a small amount of a drink ▪ *I'd just like a drop of brandy, please.* **3** [*singular*] : a small amount of something (such as a quality) ▪ *She doesn't have a drop of selfishness in her.* **4** [*plural*] : liquid medicine that is measured in drops and put into your eyes, ears, or nose ▪ *eye/ear drops* **5** [*C*] : a usually small, round piece of candy with a particular flavor ▪ *lemon drops* — see also COUGH DROP **6** [*C*] **a** : the distance from a higher to a lower level ▪ *a 50-foot drop* **b** : an area that goes downward suddenly ▪

a steep drop in the river **7** [C] : a decrease in amount or quality • *His income took a sudden drop.* • *a sharp drop in blood pressure* — **a drop in the bucket** (US) or Brit **a drop in the ocean** *informal* : an amount that is so small that it does not make an important difference or have much effect • *Our small donation is just a drop in the bucket.* — **at the drop of a hat** : very quickly and immediately • *She loses her temper at the drop of a hat.*

²**drop** *vb* **dropped; drop·ping** **1 a** [T] : to let (something) fall • *The player dropped the ball.* **b** [I] : to fall • *The pen dropped to the floor.* **2** [I] **a** : to lie down or fall down suddenly • *He dropped (down) to the floor and hid under the bed.* **b** : to lie down or become unconscious because you are sick or exhausted : COLLAPSE • *She was so tired she felt she would drop.* **3** [I] : to go down suddenly and form a steep slope • *The cliff drops almost vertically.* **4 a** [I] : to change to a lower level, amount, position, etc. • *The temperature/price dropped.* • *His voice dropped.* [=became quieter] • *The team has dropped* [=fallen] *to third place.* **b** [T] : to cause (something) to lessen or decrease in level or amount • *He dropped* [=lowered] *his voice.* **5** [T] : to send (someone) a letter, note, etc. • *I'll drop you an e-mail soon.* • *Drop me a line* [=write me a letter] *sometime.* **6 a** [T] : to stop talking or thinking about (something) • *You can drop that idea right now.* • *Let's just drop the subject.* • *Just drop it.* **b** [I] : to stop being talked about • *Please let the matter drop.* **7** [T] : to stop doing or continuing with (something) • *I'm going to drop my calculus class.* • *The prosecutors* **dropped the charges** *against her.* • *I dropped everything* [=stopped what I was doing] *and came right over.* **8** [T] : to not include (someone or something) • *He was dropped from the team.* **9** [T] : to suddenly end a relationship or connection with (someone) • *They dated for a while, but then she dropped him.* **10** [T] : to take (someone or something) to a place and then leave • *I dropped the kids (off) at school in the morning.* **11** [I] : to make a brief social visit • *His sister* **dropped by/in** *unexpectedly.* • **Drop over** *sometime!* **12** [T] : to say (something) in an informal or casual way • *He casually dropped the news that he got married.* • *She's always* **dropping names.** [=saying the names of famous people she knows] • *She has been* **dropping hints** *that she is looking for another job.* **13** [T] *informal* : to lose (a game) • *They dropped the first game.* **14** [T] *informal* : to spend (an amount of money) • *She dropped $300 on a new suit.* **15** [T] *informal* : to lose (an amount of weight) • *He dropped 20 pounds.* **16** [T/I] : to move down • *She* **dropped her eyes/head.** [=she looked down] • *His gaze dropped.* — **drop back** [*phrasal vb*] *American football* : to move straight back from the line of scrimmage • *The quarterback dropped back.* — **drop dead** see ¹DEAD — **drop off** [*phrasal vb*] **1** : to decrease in amount • *After the holi-*

days, business usually drops off. **2** : to fall asleep • *She quickly dropped off (to sleep).* — **drop out** [*phrasal vb*] **1** : to stop attending a school or university before you have completed your studies • *He dropped out (of school) after 10th grade.* **2** : to stop being part of a group • *She dropped out of the band.* **3** : to stop being involved in regular society because you do not agree with or support its rules, customs, and values • *Back in the sixties he dropped out and lived as a hippie.* — **drop out of sight** : to stop being seen • *a famous actor who suddenly dropped out of sight* — **drop the ball** see ¹BALL

drop–dead /'drɑːˈpˈdɛd/ *adj, informal* : very attractive or impressive • *a drop-dead evening gown* — **drop–dead** *adv* • *drop-dead beautiful/gorgeous*

drop–kick /'drɑːˌpˌkɪk/ *n* [C] : a kick that is made by dropping a ball to the ground and kicking it as it begins to bounce back up — **drop–kick** /'drɑːˌpˌkɪk/ *vb* [T]

drop·let /'drɑːplət/ *n* [C] : a very small drop • *droplets of water*

drop–off /'drɑːˌpˌɑːf/ *n* [C] **1** : a very steep downward slope • *The drop-off along the trail is very steep.* **2** : a very large decrease in level or amount • *a drop-off in attendance*

drop·out /'drɑːˌpˌaʊt/ *n* [C] **1** : a person who stops going to a school, college, etc., before finishing • *a high school dropout* **2** : a person who stops being involved in society because he or she does not believe in its rules, customs, and values

drop·per /'drɑːpɚ/ *n* [C] : a glass or plastic tube that is used to measure out liquids by drops — called also *eyedropper*

drop·ping /'drɑːpɪŋ/ *n* [C] : a piece of solid waste from an animal or bird • *bird droppings*

dross /'drɑːs/ *n* [U] **1** *technical* : unwanted material that is removed from a mineral (such as gold) to make it better **2** : something of low value or quality • *There's a lot of dross on TV these days.*

drought /'draʊt/ *n* [C/U] : a long period of time during which there is very little or no rain • *The drought caused serious damage to crops.*

¹**drove** /'droʊv/ *n* [C] : a large group of people or animals that move or act together • *droves of students* • *People came in droves.* [=many people came]

²**drove** *past tense of* ¹DRIVE

drown /'draʊn/ *vb* **1 a** [I] : to die by being underwater too long and unable to breathe • *She fell in the river and drowned.* **b** [T] : to hold (a person or animal) underwater until death occurs • *He tried to drown her/himself.* **2** [T] : to cover (something) completely with a liquid • *The food was drowned in sauce.* **3** [T] : to cause (something or someone) not to be heard by making a loud noise • *Noise drowned out our conversation.* **4** [T/I] : to experience or be affected by too much of something • *She is drowning in debt.* • *I'm being drowned in paperwork.* **5** [T] : to forget about (unpleasant feelings or thoughts) by getting drunk • *He*

went to the bar to **drown** *his* **sorrows.** —
drown·ing /ˈdraʊnɪŋ/ *n* [C/U]

drowsy /ˈdraʊzi/ *adj* **drows·i·er; -est** **1**
: tired and ready to fall asleep ▪ *I feel
drowsy.* [=*sleepy*] **2** : causing you to feel
relaxed and ready to sleep ▪ *a drowsy afternoon* — **drows·i·ly** /ˈdraʊzəli/ *adv* —
drows·i·ness *n* [U]

drub·bing /ˈdrʌbɪŋ/ *n* [C] *informal* : an
occurrence in which one person or team
easily beats another person or team ▪ *Our
team* **took a drubbing.** = *They* **gave us a
drubbing.** [=they beat us very easily]

drudge /ˈdrʌdʒ/ *n* [C] : a person who
does boring, difficult, or unpleasant
work ▪ *an office drudge* ▪ *drudge work*

drudg·ery /ˈdrʌdʒəri/ *n* [U] : boring, difficult, or unpleasant work ▪ *He hated the
drudgery of his job.*

¹**drug** /ˈdrʌg/ *n* [C] **1** : a substance that is
used as a medicine ▪ *an experimental
drug for the treatment of AIDS* ▪ *drug
treatment/therapy/companies* **2** : an illegal and often harmful substance (such as
heroin, cocaine, LSD, or marijuana) that
people take for pleasure ▪ *a drug over-
dose/addiction* ▪ *drug abuse* ▪ *He's* **hooked
on drugs.** [=addicted to drugs] ▪ *She's* **on
drugs.** [=she uses drugs or is high on a
drug]

²**drug** *vb* **drugged; drug·ging** [T] **1** : to
give a drug to (a person or animal) in order to make that person or animal very
sleepy or unconscious ▪ *He looks like he's
been drugged.* **2** : to add a drug to (a
food or drink) in order to make someone
sleepy or unconscious ▪ *Someone
drugged her drink.*

drug·gie /ˈdrʌgi/ *n* [C] *informal* : a person who often uses illegal drugs

drug·gist /ˈdrʌgɪst/ *n* [C] *US, somewhat
old-fashioned* : PHARMACIST

drug·store /ˈdrʌgˌstoɚ/ *n* [C] *US* : a store
that sells medicines and various other
products (such as newspapers, candy,
soap, etc.)

dru·id *or* **Druid** /ˈdruːwɪd/ *n* [C] : a member of a group of priests in an ancient
British religion

¹**drum** /ˈdrʌm/ *n* **1** [C] : a musical instrument that is made with a thin layer of
skin or plastic stretched over the end of a
round frame and that is played by hitting
the skin or plastic with sticks or with
your hands ▪ *a child beating (on) a drum* ▪
She plays the drums. **2** [U] : the sound
that is made when something hits a surface over and over again ▪ *the steady
drum of the rain on the roof* **3** [C] **a** : a
large usually metal container for liquids
▪ *oil drums* **b** : a machine or part of a
machine that is shaped like a cylinder ▪
the drum of a clothes dryer — **beat/bang
the drum for** : to say or write things that
strongly support (someone or something) ▪ *They came together to beat the
drum for their candidate.*

²**drum** *vb* **drummed; drum·ming** **1** [I]
: to beat or play a drum or set of drums ▪
She drummed while he played the guitar.
2 [T/I] : to make a sound by hitting a surface over and over again ▪ *Rain
drummed on the roof.* ▪ *She was drum-
ming her fingers on the table.* — **drum**

into [*phrasal vb*] **drum (something) into
(someone)** : to force (something) to be
learned by (someone) by repeating it
over and over again ▪ *Our teacher
drummed the lesson into our heads.* —
drum out of [*phrasal vb*] **drum (someone) out of (something)** : to force (someone) to leave (a place or organization) ▪
They drummed her out of the club. —
drum up [*phrasal vb*] **drum up (something)** *also* **drum (something) up** : to get
or create (support, business, etc.)
through hard work and a lot of effort ▪
We need to drum up some new business.

drum·beat /ˈdrʌmˌbiːt/ *n* [C] : the sound
made by beating a drum ▪ *a rock-and-roll
drumbeat* ▪ (*figurative*) *the drumbeat of
opposition*

drum major *n* [C] : the leader of a
marching band

drum majorette *n* [C] : MAJORETTE

drum·mer /ˈdrʌmɚ/ *n* [C] : a person who
plays a drum or a set of drums — **different drummer** *US* — used to describe a
person who thinks, lives, or behaves in
an unusual way ▪ *He has always* **marched
to (the beat of) a different drummer.**
[=done things differently from other
people]

drum roll *n* [C] : a continuous sound
made by a series of very quick hits on a
drum

drum·stick /ˈdrʌmˌstɪk/ *n* [C] **1** : the
lower part of the leg of a bird (such as a
chicken) that is eaten as food **2** : a stick
used for playing a drum

¹**drunk** *past participle of* ¹**DRINK**

²**drunk** /ˈdrʌŋk/ *adj* **1** : having drunk so
much alcohol that normal actions be-
come difficult to do ▪ *drunk drivers* ▪ *She
was so drunk that she could barely walk.* ▪
We **got drunk** *on wine.* **2** : behaving in
an unusual or improper way because of
excitement, anger, etc. ▪ *He was drunk
with power/anger/excitement.*

³**drunk** *n* [C] *disapproving* : a person who
is drunk or who often gets drunk ▪ *the
town drunk*

drunk·ard /ˈdrʌŋkəd/ *n* [C] *disapproving*
: a person who is drunk or who often
gets drunk ▪ *Her father was a drunkard.*

drunk·en /ˈdrʌŋkən/ *adj, always before a
noun* **1** : drunk or often becoming
drunk ▪ *drunken revelers* **2** : caused by
drinking too much alcohol ▪ *a drunken
stupor* **3** : involving people who are
drunk ▪ *a drunken brawl* — **drunk·en·ly**
adv — **drunk·en·ness** /ˈdrʌŋkənnəs/ *n*
[U]

druth·ers /ˈdrʌðəz/ *n* [*plural*] *US, informal* : the power or opportunity to
choose ▪ *If I had my druthers* [=if I could
choose what to do]*, I would travel all the
time.*

¹**dry** /ˈdraɪ/ *adj* **dri·er; -est** **1 a** : having
no or very little water or liquid ▪ *a cool,
dry place* ▪ *We tried to* **stay/keep dry** *in the
rain by standing under a tree.* **b** : no
longer wet ▪ *The paint should be dry in a
few hours.* **2** : having no rain or little
rain ▪ *dry weather* ▪ *a dry spell/season/cli-
mate* **3 a** : not having the usual or desired amount of moisture ▪ *My throat is
dry.* ▪ *dry hair/skin* **b** : having the mois-

ture removed by cooking or some other process ▪ *dry [=powdered] milk* **4** : not producing a wet substance ▪ *a dry cough* [=a cough that does not produce any phlegm] ▪ *His eyes were dry.* [=there were no tears in his eyes] **5** : no longer producing water, oil, etc. ▪ *a dry well* ▪ The well *went/ran dry.* ▪ *(figurative) The author went through a dry* [=unproductive] *period and couldn't write anything.* **6** : served or eaten without butter, jam, etc. ▪ *dry toast* **7** *of wine, sherry, etc.* : not sweet ▪ *a very dry red wine* **8** : not interesting, exciting, or emotional ▪ *His lectures were usually very dry.* **9** : funny or clever but expressed in a quiet or serious way ▪ *a dry sense of humor* **10 a** : not having or offering alcoholic beverages ▪ *a dry party* **b** : not allowing alcoholic beverages ▪ *a dry state/county* [=a state/county where alcoholic beverages cannot be sold] ▪ *c* : not drinking alcoholic beverages ▪ *He's been dry* [=sober] *for several years.* — **high and dry** see ²HIGH — **milk/bleed/suck (someone or something) dry** *informal* : to take or use up everything from (someone or something) ▪ *He married her for her money and then bled her dry.* — **dry·ness** *n* [U]

²**dry** *vb* **dries; dried; dry·ing 1 a** [*T*] : to remove water or moisture from (something or someone) ▪ *I'll dry the dishes.* ▪ *Dry your hands.* **b** [*I*] : to make plates, dishes, pots, etc., dry by rubbing them with a towel ▪ *I'll wash and you dry, okay?* **2** [*I*] : to become dry ▪ *The paint has dried.* — **dry off** [*phrasal vb*] **1 a** : to become dry ▪ *My umbrella's drying off in the hall.* **b** : to make your body dry ▪ *We got out of the pool and dried off.* **2 dry off (someone or something)** or **dry (someone or something) off** : to make (someone or something) dry ▪ *He dried off the bench and sat down.* — **dry out** [*phrasal vb*] **1** : to become dry ▪ *Don't allow the soil to dry out completely.* **2 dry out (something)** or **dry (something) out** : to make (something) dry ▪ *Baking at a high temperature will dry the meat out.* **3** *informal* : to stop using drugs or alcohol for a period of time especially by going to a special kind of hospital ▪ *He went to a clinic to dry out.* — **dry up** [*phrasal vb*] **1** : to become completely dry ▪ *The river/well is drying up.* **2 dry up (something)** or **dry (something) up** : to make (something) dry ▪ *The sun dried up the roads after the rain.* **3** *informal* : to go away or disappear completely ▪ *Interest in the project eventually dried up.* **4 dry up (something)** or **dry (something) up** : to cause the supply of (something) to go away or disappear ▪ *Closing the factory dried up local job opportunities.*

dry–clean /ˈdraɪˌkliːn/ *vb* [*T*] : to clean (clothing, curtains, etc.) by using special chemicals instead of water ▪ *His suit was dry-cleaned.* — **dry cleaner** *n* [*C*] ▪ *I take my clothes to a local dry cleaner.* [=a shop where things are dry-cleaned]

dry dock *n* [*C/U*] : a dock that can be kept dry and that is used for building or repairing boats or ships

dry·er *also* **dri·er** /ˈdraɪɚ/ *n* [*C*] : a device that is used for drying something (such as clothes) by using heat or air

dry–eyed /ˈdraɪˌaɪd/ *adj* : not crying ▪ *She was dry-eyed during the funeral but cried later.*

dry goods *n* [*plural*] : items (such as tobacco, tea, and coffee) that do not contain liquid

dry ice *n* [*U*] : solid carbon dioxide that is used mainly to keep food and other things cold and to create the appearance of smoke and fog in plays, movies, etc.

dry·ly *also* **dri·ly** /ˈdraɪli/ *adv* **1** : in a funny but quiet or serious way ▪ *"I love this store!" "I couldn't tell," she said dryly.* **2** : without excitement or emotion ▪ *"If that's the way it must be," he remarked dryly, "that's the way it will be."*

dry rot *n* [*U*] : a condition in which wood is destroyed by a type of fungus

dry run *n* [*C*] : a practice event that is done to prepare for the actual event that will happen in the future ▪ *After several dry runs, she was ready to give the speech.*

dry·wall /ˈdraɪˌwɑːl/ *n* [*U*] *US* : building material that is used for making walls and ceilings

DSL *abbr* digital subscriber line ▪ *high-speed DSL Internet access* ◆ **DSL** refers to a system that uses telephone lines to allow you to connect to the Internet at high speeds.

D.T.'s /ˌdiːˈtiːz/ *n* [*plural*] : a condition that is caused by drinking too much alcohol for a very long time and that causes a person to shake and see things that are not real ▪ *an alcoholic who has the D.T.'s*

du·al /ˈduːwəl, *Brit* ˈdjuːwəl/ *adj, always before a noun* **1** : having two different parts, uses, etc. ▪ *a dual purpose/function* ▪ *She held dual citizenship in France and the United States.* [=she was a citizen of both countries] **2** : having two of something ▪ *Our car has dual air bags.* [=has two air bags] — **du·al·ism** /ˈduːwəˌlɪzəm, *Brit* ˈdjuːwəˌlɪzəm/ *n* [*U*] ▪ *the dualism of good and evil* — **du·al·ly** *adv*

dual car·riage·way /-ˈkerɪʤˌweɪ/ *n* [*C*] *Brit* : DIVIDED HIGHWAY

du·al·i·ty /duːˈæləti, *Brit* djuːˈæləti/ *n, pl* -**ties** [*C/U*] *formal* : the quality or state of having two parts ▪ *the duality of human nature*

dub /ˈdʌb/ *vb* **dubbed; dub·bing** [*T*] **1** : to give (someone or something) a name or title ▪ *The actress was dubbed "America's sweetheart."* **2** : to replace the original recorded speech in a movie or television show with speech recorded in another language ▪ *The film was dubbed in/into Spanish.*

du·bi·ous /ˈduːbijəs, *Brit* ˈdjuːbijəs/ *adj* **1** *not before a noun* : unsure or uncertain : feeling doubt about something ▪ *I was dubious about our chances for success.* **2** : causing doubt, uncertainty, or suspicion ▪ *Her conclusions are dubious.* ▪ *a dubious claim* ▪ *a man of dubious character* **3** — used in phrases like **dubious honor** and **dubious distinction** to describe something bad or undesirable as if it were an honor or achievement ▪ *He is the* lawyer with the dubious honor of having lost the most cases in the firm. — **du·bi·ous·ly** adv — **du·bi·ous·ness** n [U]

du·cal /'du:kəl, Brit 'dju:kəl/ adj, always before a noun : of or relating to a duke • the ducal palace

duch·ess /'dʌtʃəs/ n [C] **1** : the wife or widow of a duke **2** : a woman who has the same rank as a duke

duchy /'dʌtʃi/ n, pl **duch·ies** [C] : an area of land that is controlled by a duke or duchess

¹**duck** /'dʌk/ n **1** [C] : any one of many different kinds of birds that swim and have a flat beak, a short neck, a heavy body, short legs, and webbed feet **2** [U] : the meat of a duck used as food • roast duck **3** [C] informal : a person who you think is lucky, unusual, etc. • He's a very odd/lucky duck. — **like a duck to water** informal : very quickly or easily • She took to dancing like a duck (takes) to water. — see also LAME DUCK, SITTING DUCK

²**duck** vb **1 a** [I] : to lower your head or body suddenly to avoid being seen or hit • The ceiling was so low I had to duck (down). **b** [T] : to lower (your head) suddenly • I had to duck my head. **c** [T] : to avoid (something, such as a punch) by lowering your head or body suddenly • He ducked the punch. **2** [T] : to avoid (something or someone you do not want to see or deal with) • He tried to duck the question. **3** [I] : to move quickly • She ducked into a store. — **duck out** [phrasal vb] informal : to leave suddenly and usually without telling anyone that you are leaving • I had to duck out of the meeting to take a phone call. • (figurative) He wants to duck out of the contract. [=to get out of the contract]

duck·ling /'dʌklɪŋ/ n [C] : a young duck — see also UGLY DUCKLING

ducky /'dʌki/ n, pl **duck·ies** [C] chiefly US, informal **1** : a duck — used especially by children or when talking to children • a cute little ducky **2** : a toy duck • a rubber ducky

duct /'dʌkt/ n [C] **1** : a pipe or tube for air, water, electric power lines, etc., to pass through • heating ducts **2** : a tube in the body that carries a particular liquid • tear ducts

duct tape n [U] : a wide, sticky, and usually silver tape that is made of cloth and that is used especially to repair things

dud /'dʌd/ n **1** [C] : something that does not do what it is supposed to do • The firework was a dud. [=it did not explode] **2** [plural] informal : clothes • wearing new duds

dude /'du:d, Brit 'dju:d/ n [C] chiefly US slang : a man — used especially by young people • Hey, dude, what's up?

dude ranch n [C] : a large farm especially in the western U.S. where people on vacation can ride horses and do other activities that cowboys typically do

dud·geon /'dʌdʒən/ n — **in high dudgeon** formal : feeling and usually showing that you are angry or offended • She walked out of the meeting in high dudgeon.

¹**due** /'du:, Brit 'dju:/ adj **1** not before a noun : required or expected to happen, appear, etc. • When is the assignment due? [=when are you supposed to give the completed assignment to your teacher?] • The movie is due out this summer. • They are due to arrive soon. **2** not before a noun **a** : expected to be born • The baby is due in three weeks. **b** : expected to give birth • My wife is due in three weeks. **3** not before a noun : having reached the date by which payment is required • The bill is due next week. • The bill is past due. [=it should have been paid before now] **4** not before a noun — used to say that someone should be given something or has earned something • He finally got the recognition he was due. • I give credit where credit is due. **5** always before a noun : appropriate or proper • due caution/care/modesty • I will answer your questions in due time. [=eventually at an appropriate time] — **due for** : needing, requiring, or expecting something to happen • I'm due for a dentist's appointment. [=I need to go to the dentist soon] — **due to** : because of (something) • The accident was due to her carelessness. • Due to the bad weather, the game was canceled. — **in due course** see COURSE

²**due** n **1** [plural] : a regular payment that you make to be a member of an organization • Membership dues are $45. **2** [U] : something that someone should be given • He deserves to be given his due. • (figurative) I can't say that I like him, but to give him his due [=to be fair to him], I trust him completely. — **pay your dues** : to work hard and have difficult experiences • You have to pay your dues if you want to succeed.

³**due** adv : directly or exactly — followed by north, south, east, or west • The road runs due south.

due date n [C] : the day when someone or something is due: such as **a** : the day by which something must be done, paid, etc. • The due date for the assignment is Friday. **b** : the day when a woman is expected to give birth

du·el /'du:wəl, Brit 'dju:wəl/ n [C] **1** : a fight between two people that includes the use of weapons (such as guns or swords) and that usually happens while other people watch • I challenge you to a duel. **2** : a situation in which two people or groups argue or compete with each other • a duel of wits — **duel** vb, US **du·eled** or Brit **du·elled**; US **du·el·ing** or Brit **du·el·ling** [I] • Legislators dueled over the taxes.

due process n [U] US, law : the official and proper way of doing things in a legal case

du·et /du'ɛt, Brit dju'ɛt/ n [C] : a piece of music that is performed by two singers or musicians • They sang/played a duet.

duf·fel bag or **duf·fle bag** /'dʌfəl-/ n [C] : a large, soft bag that is held by a strap or handles and is used to carry personal belongings

duf·fer /'dʌfə/ n [C] informal **1** chiefly US : a person who plays golf without much skill **2** Brit : a clumsy or awkward person ▪ *a lovable old duffer*

dug *past tense and past participle of* ¹DIG

dug-out /'dʌg,aʊt/ *n* [C] **1** : a low shelter that faces a baseball field and contains the bench where the players and coaches of a team sit **2** : a shelter that is made by digging a hole in the ground or into the side of a hill **3** : a small boat that is made by cutting out the center of a large tree trunk — called also *dugout canoe*

DUI /,di:,ju:'aɪ/ *n* [C/U] *US* : the crime of driving a vehicle while drunk ▪ *He was arrested for (a) DUI.*; *also* : a person who is arrested for driving a vehicle while drunk ▪ *a convicted DUI* ◇ *DUI* is an abbreviation of "driving under the influence."

du jour /du'ʒɚ/ *adj, not before a noun* : served in a restaurant as a special item on a particular day ▪ *Our soup du jour is chicken noodle.*

¹**duke** /'du:k, *Brit* 'dju:k/ *n* **1** [C] : a man of very high rank in the British nobility **2** [C] : the ruler of an independent area of land especially in some parts of Europe in the past **3** [*plural*] *US slang, old-fashioned* : fists or hands ▪ *Put up your dukes and fight!* — **duke-dom** /'du:kdəm, *Brit* 'dju:kdəm/ *n* [C]

²**duke** *vb* **duked; duk-ing** — **duke it out** *US, informal* : to fight with your fists ▪ *A couple of drunks were duking it out.* ▪ (*figurative*) *Scientists duked it out* [=argued] *over the causes of global warming.*

dul-cet /'dʌlsət/ *adj, formal* : pleasant to hear ▪ *dulcet sounds/tones*

¹**dull** /'dʌl/ *adj* **1** : BORING ▪ *a dull lecture/speaker* **2** : having an edge or point that is not sharp ▪ *a dull knife* **3** *of a sound* : not clear and loud ▪ *a dull thud* **4** : constant but not sharp or severe ▪ *a dull ache/pain* **5** : not shiny ▪ *a dull finish* **6** : not sunny ▪ CLOUDY ▪ *a dull winter sky* **7** : slightly grayish or dark : not bright ▪ *a dull light/blue* **8** *old-fashioned* : stupid or slow in understanding something ▪ *a dull student* — **dull-ness** *n* [U] — **dul-ly** *adv*

²**dull** *vb* [T/I] : to become dull or to make (something) dull ▪ *Earplugs dulled the sound.* ▪ *His hair dulled as he aged.* ▪ *She takes medicine to dull the pain.* ▪ *The knife was dulled from use.*

dull-ard /'dʌlɚd/ *n* [C] *old-fashioned* : a stupid and uninteresting person ▪ *The company is run by a bunch of dullards.*

du-ly /'du:li, *Brit* 'dju:li/ *adv, formal* : in the proper or expected way ▪ *We were duly impressed.* ▪ *The objections were duly noted.*

¹**dumb** /'dʌm/ *adj* **1** *informal* **a** : not showing or having good judgment or intelligence : stupid or foolish ▪ *a dumb person/idea/grin* ▪ *She played/acted dumb.* [=pretended to know or understand less than she really did] ▪ *not requiring or resulting from intelligence* ▪ *dumb luck* **2 a** : not able to speak especially after being shocked or surprised ▪ *I was struck dumb.* [=made speechless] **b** *old-fashioned* + *often offensive* : not having the ability to speak ▪ *He was born deaf and dumb.* — **dumb-ly** *adv* —

dumb-ness *n* [U] *informal*

²**dumb** *vb* — **dumb down** [*phrasal vb*] **dumb down (something)** *or* **dumb (something) down** *usually disapproving* **1** : to make (something) easier to understand ▪ *She refused to dumb down the language in her report.* **2** : to make (a group of people) less intelligent or educated ▪ *Cutting training programs will dumb down the workforce.*

dumb-bell /'dʌm,bɛl/ *n* [C] **1** : a short bar with weights at the ends that is used to make muscles stronger **2** *US, informal* : a stupid or foolish person

dumb-found-ed /,dʌm'faʊndəd/ *adj* : very shocked or surprised ▪ *We were dumbfounded at what we saw.* — **dumb-found** /,dʌm'faʊnd/ *vb* [T] ▪ *The news dumbfounded me.*

dumb-struck /'dʌm,strʌk/ *adj* : so shocked or surprised that you cannot speak ▪ *We were dumbstruck by his confession.*

¹**dum-my** /'dʌmi/ *n, pl* **-mies** [C] **1** *chiefly US, informal* : a stupid person ▪ *He's no dummy.* **2 a** : a doll that is shaped like and is as large as a person ▪ *They practiced CPR on a dummy.* **b** : a large doll with a movable mouth that is used by a performer ▪ *a ventriloquist's dummy* **3** : a copy of a finished object that is used during practice or training ▪ *The bomb was just a dummy.* **4** *Brit* : PACIFIER

²**dummy** *adj, always before a noun* : looking real but not functioning or able to be used ▪ *a dummy bomb/corporation*

dummy run *n* [C] *Brit* : DRY RUN

¹**dump** /'dʌmp/ *vb* [T] **1** : to put (something) somewhere in a quick and careless way ▪ *She dumped the coats on the bed.* ▪ (*figurative*) *The blizzard dumped three feet of snow in one night.* **2** : to leave or get rid of (something or someone) quickly or without concern ▪ *They had to dump* [=quickly sell] *most of their stock.* **3** *informal* : to end a romantic relationship with (someone) ▪ *My girlfriend dumped me.* **4** : to get rid of (waste or garbage) especially in a secret and illegal way ▪ *The factory has been dumping waste into the river.* **5** *computers* : to copy or move (data) from a computer's memory to a disk, another computer, etc. ▪ *Dump the file to a disk.* — **dump in your lap** *see* ¹LAP — **dump on** [*phrasal vb*] *informal* **1** *US* : to criticize (someone) severely ▪ *I get dumped on every time I make a mistake.* **2 dump (something) on (someone)** : to give (something) to (someone else) to do, deal with, or think about because you do not want to ▪ *I can't stand it when he dumps all his problems on me.*

²**dump** *n* [C] **1** : a place where waste (such as trash) is taken and left ▪ *the town dump* ▪ (*US*) *a garbage dump* **2** : a place where military supplies are stored ▪ *an ammunition dump* **3** *informal* : a messy, dirty, and unpleasant place ▪ *His house is a dump.* — **down in the dumps** *informal* : feeling very sad ▪ *I'm just down in the dumps.*

dump-er /'dʌmpɚ/ *n* [C] *chiefly US* : a person who leaves waste where it is not supposed to be left ▪ *illegal dumpers*

dumping ground n [C] : a place where people or things that are not wanted are sent • *The class became a dumping ground for students with behavioral problems.*

dump·ling /'dʌmplɪŋ/ n [C] **1** : a small lump of dough that is boiled or steamed • *chicken and dumplings* **2** : a piece of food that is wrapped in dough and cooked • *pork/apple dumplings*

Dump·ster /'dʌmpstə/ *trademark* — used for a large trash container

dump truck n [C] US : a large truck usually with a container on the back of it that is used for carrying and unloading loose material — called also (*Brit*) *dumper truck*

dumpy /'dʌmpi/ adj **dump·i·er; -est** *informal* **1** : short and fat • *a dumpy guy* **2** US : dirty and in bad condition • *dumpy hotel rooms*

dunce /'dʌns/ n [C] *old-fashioned* : someone who is stupid or slow at learning things

dune /'du:n, *Brit* 'dju:n/ n [C] : a hill of sand near an ocean or in a desert that is formed by the wind — called also *sand dune*

dune buggy n [C] : a small vehicle with very large tires for driving on sand — called also *beach buggy*

dung /'dʌŋ/ n [U] : solid waste from an animal • *cow/cattle dung*

dun·ga·rees /ˌdʌŋgə'ri:z/ n [plural] **1** US, old-fashioned : pants or work clothes made of usually blue denim **2** Brit : OVERALLS

dun·geon /'dʌndʒən/ n [C] : a dark underground prison in a castle

¹**dunk** /'dʌŋk/ vb **1** [T] **a** : to dip (food) quickly into a liquid (such as coffee or milk) while eating • *She dunked her doughnut in her coffee.* **b** *chiefly US* : to push (someone or something) under water or other liquid for a short amount of time • *She dunked him while they were swimming.* **2** [T/I] *basketball* : to jump high in the air and push (the ball) down through the basket • *He dunked the ball.*

²**dunk** n [C] *basketball* : a shot that is made by jumping high in the air and pushing the ball down through the basket — called also *dunk shot, slam dunk*

duo /'du:woʊ, *Brit* 'dju:wəʊ/ n, pl **du·os** [C] : two people who perform together, are usually seen together, or are associated with each other • *a comedy duo*

du·o·de·num /ˌdu:wə'di:nəm, *Brit* ˌdju:wə'di:nəm/ n, pl **-de·na** /-'di:nə/ or **-de·nums** [C] *medical* : the part of the small intestine that is right below your stomach — **du·o·de·nal** /ˌdu:wə'di:nl̩, *Brit* ˌdju:wə'di:nl̩/ adj

¹**dupe** /'du:p, *Brit* 'dju:p/ vb **duped; dup·ing** [T] : to deceive or trick (someone) into believing or doing something • *He was duped into coming.*

²**dupe** n [C] : a person who is easily deceived or tricked • *an unwitting dupe*

du·plex /'du:ˌplɛks, *Brit* 'dju:ˌplɛks/ n [C] US **1** : a building that is divided into two separate homes **2** : an apartment with two floors • *a duplex penthouse*

¹**du·pli·cate** /'du:plɪkət, *Brit* 'dju:plɪkət/ adj, always before a noun : exactly the same as something else • *duplicate copies of a magazine* : made as an exact copy of something else • *a duplicate key*

²**du·pli·cate** /'du:plɪˌkeɪt, *Brit* 'dju:plɪˌkeɪt/ vb **-cat·ed; -cat·ing** [T] **1** : to make an exact copy of (something) • *The results of the study could not be duplicated.* **2** : to produce (something) in another form • *If we both do the project, we'll just be duplicating the work.* [=doing the same work twice] — **du·pli·ca·tion** /ˌdu:plɪ'keɪʃən, *Brit* ˌdju:plɪ'keɪʃən/ n [C/U] • *He sent the manuscript out for duplication.* • *a needless duplication of effort/work*

³**du·pli·cate** /'du:plɪkət, *Brit* 'dju:plɪkət/ n [C] : an exact copy of something else • *He made an exact duplicate of the original model.* — **in duplicate 1** : two times so that there are two copies • *We filled out the paperwork in duplicate.* **2** : with an exact copy • *Please send the contract in duplicate.*

du·plic·i·ty /dʊ'plɪsəti, *Brit* djʊ'plɪsəti/ n [U] *formal* : dishonest behavior that is meant to trick someone • *He exposed her duplicity.* — **du·plic·i·tous** /dʊ'plɪsətəs, *Brit* djʊ'plɪsətəs/ adj

du·ra·ble /'dʊrəbəl, *Brit* 'djʊrəbəl/ adj : staying strong and in good condition over a long period of time • *durable fabric* • (*figurative*) *a durable athlete/myth* — **du·ra·bil·i·ty** /ˌdʊrə'bɪləti, *Brit* ˌdjʊrə'bɪləti/ n [U] — **du·ra·bly** /'dʊrəbli, *Brit* 'djʊrəbli/ adv

du·ra·tion /dʊ'reɪʃən, *Brit* djʊ'reɪʃən/ n [U] : the length of time that something exists or lasts • *Gradually increase the duration of your workout.* — **for the duration** : until the end of something • *The camera remained on the President for the duration of his speech.*

du·ress /dʊ'rɛs, *Brit* djʊ'rɛs/ n [U] *formal* : force or threats meant to make someone do something • *He gave the information under duress.*

dur·ing /'dʊrɪŋ, *Brit* 'djʊrɪŋ/ prep **1** : throughout the entire time of (an event, period, occurrence, etc.) • *We got along well during the trip.* **2** : at some time in the course of (something) • *The fire alarm went off during the ceremony.*

dusk /'dʌsk/ n [U] : the time when day changes into night and the sky begins to get darker • *The park closes at dusk.*

dusky /'dʌski/ adj **dusk·i·er; -est** : somewhat dark • *a dusky brown*

¹**dust** /'dʌst/ n [U] **1** : fine dry powder that builds up inside buildings on surfaces that have not recently been cleaned • *The floor was covered with dust.* • *The book was collecting/gathering dust on the shelf.* **2** : fine powder made up of very small pieces of earth or sand • *The car left a cloud of dust behind it.* **3** : fine powder made from a particular substance • *chalk/gold dust* — **bite the dust** see ¹BITE — **leave (someone) in the dust** US, informal : to go far ahead of (someone) : to be much more advanced than (someone) • *The company has left its competitors in the dust.* — **the dust settles** — used to talk about what happens

when things become clear or calm after a period of change or confusion • **When the dust settled** [=when the situation became less confusing], *our options became clear.* — **dusty** /ˈdʌsti/ *adj* **dust·i·er; -est** • *a dusty basement/shelf/road*

²**dust** *vb* **1** [*T/I*] : to make (something) clean by brushing or wiping dirt and dust from the surface • *He dusted (off) the furniture.* • *I dust at least once a week.* **2** [*T*] : to cover (something) with a fine powder • *The police dusted the table for fingerprints.* [=they put a fine powder on the table so that fingerprints could be seen] — **dust off** [*phrasal vb*] **dust (something) off** *or* **dust off (something)** : to use (something) again after not using it for a long time • *The comedian dusted off some of his old jokes.* — **dust·er** /ˈdʌstɚ/ *n* [*C*] • *a feather duster* [=a tool with feathers at one end used to remove dust]

dust·bin /ˈdʌstˌbɪn/ *n* [*C*] *Brit* : TRASH CAN

dust bowl *n* [*C*] : an area of land that was once used for farming but that has become a desert because of a lack of rain

dust bunny *n* [*C*] *US, informal* : a ball of dust that forms in places that are not swept or dusted often

dust jacket *n* [*C*] : a paper cover that protects a book and can be removed — called also **dust cover**

dust·man /ˈdʌstmən/ *n, pl* **-men** /-mən/ [*C*] *Brit* : GARBAGEMAN

dust·pan /ˈdʌstˌpæn/ *n* [*C*] : a flat pan that is open on one side and into which dirt from the floor is swept

dust storm *n* [*C*] : a very strong wind that carries clouds of dust across a large area

¹**Dutch** /ˈdʌtʃ/ *n* **1** [*U*] : the language of the Netherlands **2 the Dutch** : the people of the Netherlands • *learning about the Dutch* — **Dutch** *adj* • *Dutch history/people*

²**Dutch** *adv* — **go Dutch** : to go to a movie, restaurant, etc., as a group with each person paying for his or her own ticket, food, etc. • *When we go to the movies, we always go Dutch.*

Dutch oven *n* [*C*] *US* : a large covered pot

Dutch treat *n* [*U*] *chiefly US* : something (such as a dinner or movie) for which each person pays his or her own share of the cost • *It was Dutch treat—we each bought our own ticket.*

du·ti·ful /ˈduːtɪfəl, *Brit* ˈdjuːtɪfəl/ *adj* : doing what is expected of you • *a dutiful servant/daughter* — **du·ti·ful·ly** /ˈduːtɪfəli, *Brit* ˈdjuːtɪfli/ *adv*

du·ty /ˈduːti, *Brit* ˈdjuːti/ *n, pl* **-ties 1** [*C/U*] : something that is done as part of a job • *administrative duties* • *Please report for duty* [=show up for work] *at 7 a.m.* • *He was killed in the line of duty.* [=while doing his job] • *She went beyond the call of duty.* [=she did more than she was required or expected to do] **2** [*C/U*] : something that you must do because it is morally right or because the law requires it • *We felt it was our duty to help.* • *He was selected for jury duty.* [=to serve on a jury] **3** [*U*] : active military service

• *Her brother returned from duty overseas.* • *a twelve-month tour of duty* **4** [*C/U*] : a tax on goods that are being brought into a country • *We had to pay (a) duty.* — **do duty as 1** : to do the work of (someone or something) • *He did (double) duty as the star and director of the film.* **2** : to be used as (something) • *Her coat did duty as a pillow.* — **off duty** : not working at a particular time • *I go off duty in two hours.* — **on duty** : working at a particular time • *I'm still on duty.*

du·vet /duˈveɪ, ˈduːˌveɪ/ *n* [*C*] *chiefly Brit* : COMFORTER

DVD /ˌdiːˌviːˈdiː/ *n* [*C*] : a computer disk that contains a large amount of information (such as a movie) • *a DVD player; also* : a movie that is recorded on a DVD • *watching a DVD ◇ DVD* is an abbreviation of "digital video disc" or "digital versatile disc."

¹**dwarf** /ˈdwoɚf/ *n, pl* **dwarfs** /ˈdwoɚfs/ *also* **dwarves** /ˈdwoɚvz/ [*C*] **1** *in stories* : a creature that looks like a small man and that often lives underground and has magical powers **2** *sometimes offensive* : a person who is much smaller than most people because of a medical condition — **dwarf·ish** /ˈdwoɚfɪʃ/ *adj*

²**dwarf** *vb* [*T*] : to make (something) look very small or unimportant when compared with something else • *The small boat was dwarfed by the ship.*

³**dwarf** *adj, always before a noun, of a plant or animal* : smaller than normal size • *a dwarf evergreen/porcupine*

dwarf·ism /ˈdwoɚˌfizəm/ *n* [*U*] *medical* : a condition that causes a person to stop growing before reaching normal adult size

dweeb /ˈdwiːb/ *n* [*C*] *US, informal* : a person who behaves awkwardly around other people and usually has unstylish hair, clothes, etc. — **dweeby** /ˈdwiːbi/ *adj* • *a dweeby kid*

dwell /ˈdwɛl/ *vb* **dwelled** /ˈdwɛld, ˈdwɛlt/ *or* **dwelt** /ˈdwɛlt/; **dwell·ing** [*I*] *literary + formal* : to live in a particular place • *He dwelled in the same town for years.* • *the dwelling place of the gods* [=the place where the gods live] — **dwell on/upon** [*phrasal vb*] : to think or talk about (something) for a long time • *There is no need to dwell on the past.* — **dwell·er** /ˈdwɛlɚ/ *n* [*C*] • *a cave/city dweller*

dwelling *n* [*C*] *formal* : a place where a person lives • *a single-family dwelling* [=house]

DWI /ˌdiːˌdʌbəljuˈaɪ/ *n* [*C/U*] *US* : DUI ◇ *DWI* is an abbreviation of "driving while intoxicated."

dwin·dle /ˈdwɪndl̩/ *vb* **dwin·dled; dwin·dling** [*I*] : to gradually become smaller • *My interest dwindled.* • *dwindling resources*

¹**dye** /ˈdaɪ/ *n* [*C/U*] : a substance used for changing the color of hair, cloth, etc. • *purple dye*

²**dye** *vb* **dyed; dye·ing** [*T*] : to change the color of (hair, cloth, etc.) by using a dye • *She dyed her hair.*

dyed–in–the–wool /ˌdaɪdn̩ðəˈwʊl/ *adj, always before a noun, often disapproving* : having very strong beliefs, opinions, etc., that you are not willing to change ▪ *a dyed-in-the-wool conservative*

dying present participle of ¹DIE

dyke chiefly Brit spelling of DIKE

¹**dy·nam·ic** /daɪˈnæmɪk/ adj **1 a :** always active or changing ▪ *a dynamic city/relationship* **b :** having or showing a lot of energy ▪ *a dynamic speaker/performance* **2** technical **:** of or relating to energy, motion, or physical force ▪ *the dynamic theory of heat* — **dy·nam·i·cal·ly** /daɪˈnæmɪkli/ adv

²**dynamic** n [singular, plural] **:** the way that two or more people behave with each other because of a particular situation ▪ *the dynamic between a doctor and a patient* ▪ *The dynamics of this class are different from those of other classes.*

¹**dy·na·mite** /ˈdaɪnəˌmaɪt/ n [U] **1 :** a powerful explosive that is often used in the form of a stick ▪ *a stick of dynamite* **2 :** someone or something that may cause arguments or trouble ▪ *The issue is political dynamite.* — **dynamite** vb **-mit·ed; -mit·ing** [T] ▪ *They plan to dynamite the old bridge.*

²**dynamite** adj, informal **:** exciting and very impressive or pleasing ▪ *a dynamite performance*

dy·na·mo /ˈdaɪnəˌmoʊ/ n, pl **-mos** [C] **1 :** a machine that produces electricity **:** GENERATOR **2** informal **:** someone who has a lot of energy ▪ *He's a dynamo on-screen.*

dy·nas·ty /ˈdaɪnəsti, Brit ˈdɪnəsti/ n, pl **-ties** [C] **1 :** a family of rulers who rule over a country for a long period of time **2 :** a family, team, etc., that is very powerful or successful for a long period of time ▪ *a powerful political dynasty* — **dy·nas·tic** /daɪˈnæstɪk, Brit dɪˈnæstɪk/ adj

dys·en·tery /ˈdɪsnˌteri, Brit ˈdɪsn̩tri/ n [U] **:** a serious disease that causes severe diarrhea and a loss of blood

dys·func·tion /dɪsˈfʌŋkʃən/ n **1** [U] **:** the condition of having poor and unhealthy behaviors and attitudes within a group of people ▪ *family dysfunction* **2** [C/U] medical **:** the state of being unable to function in a normal way ▪ *sexual dysfunction* — **dys·func·tion·al** /dɪsˈfʌŋkʃənl̩/ adj ▪ *a dysfunctional family*

dys·lex·ia /dɪsˈlɛksijə/ n [U] medical **:** a condition in the brain that makes it hard for a person to read, write, and spell — **dys·lex·ic** /dɪsˈlɛksɪk/ adj ▪ *a dyslexic child* — **dyslexic** n [C] ▪ *a dyslexic* [=a person with dyslexia]

dys·pep·sia /dɪsˈpɛpʃə, dɪsˈpɛpsijə/ n [U] medical **:** INDIGESTION ▪ *suffering from dyspepsia* — **dys·pep·tic** /dɪsˈpɛptɪk/ adj

dystrophy see MUSCULAR DYSTROPHY

E

e or **E** /ˈiː/ n, pl **e's** or **es** or **E's** or **Es** [C/U] **1 :** the fifth letter of the English alphabet ▪ *a word that begins with (an) e* **2 :** the musical note or key referred to by the letter E ▪ *play/sing (an) E*

E abbr east, eastern

e- combining form **:** electronic ▪ *e-mail* ▪ *e-commerce* [=commerce on the Internet]

¹**each** /ˈiːtʃ/ adj **:** every one of two or more people or things considered separately ▪ *Each student has done his best.* = *Each student has done his or her best.* = (informal) *Each student has done their best.* ▪ *Each one of them costs 50 cents.* [=they each cost 50 cents] ▪ *I want to thank each and every person who helped us.*

²**each** pron **:** each one ▪ *Each (of us) took a turn.* = *We each took a turn.* — **to each his own** or **each to his own** — used to say that other people are free to like different things than you do ▪ *I don't care for football, but to each his own.*

³**each** adv **:** to or for each **:** APIECE ▪ *They cost 50 cents each.*

each other pron **:** each of two or more people, animals, etc., who are doing something together or in relationship to the other or others in the group ▪ *My brother and I looked at each other.* [=he looked at me and I looked at him]

ea·ger /ˈiːgə/ adj **:** very excited and interested ▪ *an eager student* ▪ *She was eager to* start. ▪ *They were eager for more.* — **ea·ger·ly** adv — **ea·ger·ness** n [U]

eager beaver n [C] informal **:** a person who is very enthusiastic about doing something

¹**ea·gle** /ˈiːgəl/ n **1** [C] **:** a large bird that has very good eyesight and that kills other birds and animals for food **2** [C/U] golf **:** a golf score of two strokes less than par on a hole ▪ *She made/scored an eagle.*

²**eagle** vb **ea·gled; ea·gling** [T] **:** to score an eagle on (a hole in golf) ▪ *She eagled the fourth hole.*

eagle eye n **1** [plural] **:** eyes that watch or look carefully ▪ *watching with eagle eyes* **2** [singular] **:** an unusually good ability to see or notice things ▪ *an editor with an eagle eye* **3** [singular] **:** close watch ▪ *The guard kept an eagle eye on the prisoner.* — **ea·gle–eyed** /ˈiːgəlˌaɪd/ adj ▪ *an eagle-eyed proofreader*

Eagle Scout n [C] **:** a Boy Scout who has reached the highest level of achievement in scouting

-ean see ¹-AN

ear /ˈiə/ n **1** [C] **:** the part of the body that you hear with ▪ *He whispered something in her ear.* ✧ To **lend an ear** or **lend someone your ears** is to listen to what someone has to say. **2** [singular] **a :** an ability to understand and appreciate something heard ▪ *He has a good ear for music.* **b** — used to describe the way something sounds to you • *The word sounds old-fashioned to my ear.* **3** [C] : the part of a corn plant on which the seeds grow • *an ear of corn* — **all ears** *informal* — used to say that someone is listening very closely • *As I told the story, my daughter was all ears.* — **bend someone's ear** see [1]**BEND** — **ears are burning** ◇ If **your ears are burning** or you **feel your ears burning**, you have the feeling that other people are talking about you. — **fall on deaf ears** : to fail to be heard : to be ignored • *Her pleas for mercy fell on deaf ears.* — **grin/smile from ear to ear** : to have a big smile on your face — **in one ear and out the other** : through someone's mind without being remembered or noticed • *Everything you say to him goes in one ear and out the other.* — **out on your ear** *informal* : forced out : thrown out • *If you're late again, you'll be out on your ear!* [=you'll be fired] — **play by ear** **1** ◇ To play a song or piece of music *by ear* is to play it after hearing it without looking at written music. **2** ◇ To *play it by ear* is to do something without special preparation. • *I don't know what they'll say, so we'll just have to play it by ear.* — **set (something) on its ear** *informal* : to cause (something) to be in a state of great excitement or shock • *She set the racing world on its ear by winning several major races.* — **turn a deaf ear** : to refuse to listen to what someone says • *He turned a deaf ear to my proposals.* — **up to your ears** : deeply involved in something • *They are up to their ears in debt/work.* — **wet behind the ears** see [1]**WET** — **eared** /ˈɪəd/ *adj* • *a long-eared dog*

ear‑ache /ˈɪəˌeɪk/ *n* [C/U] : an ache or pain in the ear

ear‑drum /ˈɪəˌdrʌm/ *n* [C] : a thin, tightly stretched piece of tissue in the ear that vibrates when sound waves hit it

ear‑ful /ˈɪəˌfʊl/ *n* [singular] *informal* : a lot of angry talk and criticism • *He gave me an earful.*

earl /ˈəl/ *n* [C] : a high-ranking member of the British nobility

ear‑lobe /ˈɪəˌloʊb/ *n* [C] : the soft part of the ear that hangs down

[1]**ear‑ly** /ˈəli/ *adv* **ear‑li‑er; -est** **1** : at or near the beginning of a period of time • *We left early in the day.* • *early next week* **2** : before the usual or expected time • *She arrived early.* • *I got up bright and early.* [=very early] — **early on** : at or during an early point or stage • *The problems were obvious early on in the experiment.*

[2]**early** *adj* **earlier; -est** **1** : existing or happening near the beginning of something • *early morning* • *the early 20th century* • *He is in his early thirties.* [=he is about 31 or 32 years old] • *It was still early (in the morning) when she got out of bed.* • *the early symptoms of the disease* • *The early part of the book is better than the later part.* **2 a** : coming or happening before the usual or expected time • *We had an early spring this year.* • *We're early. The show doesn't start for half an hour.* • *We'll get there by noon at the earli-*

est. = *The earliest time we'll get there is noon.* **b** : doing something before the usual time or before others usually do • *I'm an early riser.* ◇ The expression **the early bird catches/gets the worm** means that people who start or arrive before others are more likely to succeed. — **early days (yet)** *Brit* — used to say that it is too soon to know how something will turn out • *Things haven't gone so far, but it's early days yet.*

[1]**ear‑mark** /ˈɪəˌmɑək/ *n* [C] : a mark or quality that shows what something is or what it could be • *The plan had (all) the earmarks of success.* [=seemed likely to succeed]

[2]**earmark** *vb* [T] **1** : to say that something will be used or treated in a specified way • *The building has been earmarked for demolition.* **2** : to put (money) aside for a special purpose • *funds earmarked for education*

ear‑muff /ˈɪəˌmʌf/ *n* [C] : either one of a pair of connected pads that cover the ears to keep them warm • *a pair of earmuffs*

earn /ˈən/ *vb* [T] **1** : to get (money) for work that you have done • *She earns a good salary.* **2 a** : to deserve or get (something) because of something you have done • *He earned a promotion through hard work.* • *earn someone's trust/respect* **b** : to make (someone) worthy or deserving of (something) • *His hard work earned him a promotion.* — **earn‑er** *n* [C]

[1]**ear‑nest** /ˈənəst/ *adj* : serious and sincere • *an earnest plea/person* — **ear‑nest‑ly** *adv* — **ear‑nest‑ness** /ˈənəstnəs/ *n* [U]

[2]**earnest** *n* — **in earnest 1** : in an earnest or serious way • *The search began in earnest when the police arrived.* **2** : not fooling : serious and sincere • *We thought he was joking, but he was in earnest.*

earn‑ings /ˈənɪŋz/ *n* [plural] : money received as wages or gained as profit • *corporate earnings*

ear‑phone /ˈɪəˌfoʊn/ *n* [C] : a device that is worn over or inserted into the ear and is used for listening to music, a radio, etc., without having other people hear it

ear‑piece /ˈɪəˌpiːs/ *n* [C] : a part of a device that is placed in the ear for listening to something • *the earpiece of a stethoscope*

ear‑plug /ˈɪəˌplʌg/ *n* [C] : a piece of soft material put in your ear to keep out water, noise, etc.

ear‑ring /ˈɪrɪŋ/ *n* [C] : a piece of jewelry that is worn on the ear

ear‑shot /ˈɪəˌʃɑːt/ *n* [U] : the distance within which someone's voice can be heard • *They were within earshot of each other.* • *We waited until he was out of earshot before speaking again.*

ear‑split‑ting /ˈɪəˌsplɪtɪŋ/ *adj* : extremely loud or harsh • *an earsplitting noise*

earth /ˈəθ/ *n* **1 or Earth** [singular] : the planet on which we live **2** [U] : land as opposed to the sea, the air, etc. • *We could feel the earth shake.* **3** [U] : [1]**SOIL** **1** • *a mound of earth* **4** [C] *Brit* : [1]**GROUND 10** **5** [singular] *chiefly Brit, informal* : a large amount of money •

pay/cost the earth — **on earth 1** : in the world • *the tallest building on earth* • *Nothing on earth will change his mind.* **2** — used to make a question more forceful • *What on earth is he talking about?* — **the salt of the earth** see ¹SALT

earth·en /ˈɚθən/ *adj, always before a noun* : made of soil or of baked clay • *an earthen dam/floor/jar*

earth·en·ware /ˈɚθənˌweɚ/ *n* [U] : pottery, dishes, etc., made by baking clay

earth·ling /ˈɚθlɪŋ/ *n* [C] : a human being living on Earth — used in stories and movies that involve creatures from outer space

earth·ly /ˈɚθli/ *adj, always before a noun* **1** : having to do with life on the Earth • *earthly pleasures* • *our earthly existence* **2** : imaginable or possible • *What earthly good could it do?*

earth·quake /ˈɚθˌkweɪk/ *n* [C/U] : a shaking of a part of the Earth's surface that often causes great damage

earth·shak·ing /ˈɚθˌʃeɪkɪŋ/ *adj* : very important or shocking • *an earthshaking event*

earth·shat·ter·ing /ˈɚθˈʃætərɪŋ/ *adj* : very important or shocking • *earthshattering news*

earth·worm /ˈɚθˌwɚm/ *n* [C] : a long worm that lives in damp soil

earthy /ˈɚθi/ *adj* **earth·i·er; -est** **1** : suggesting earth or soil • *earthy aromas/colors* **2 a** : practical and straightforward : open and direct • *an earthy person* **b** *chiefly US* : plain and simple in style • *food made with simple, earthy ingredients* **c** : somewhat rude or crude • *earthy humor* — **earth·i·ness** *n* [U]

ear·wax /ˈiɚˌwæks/ *n* [U] : a waxlike substance produced inside the ear

ear·wig /ˈiɚˌwɪg/ *n* [C] : an insect that has long, thin feelers and two curved, pointed parts at the end of the body

¹**ease** /ˈiːz/ *n* [U] **1** : freedom from pain or trouble • *a life of ease* **2** : lack of difficulty • *ease of use* • *I did it with (the greatest of) ease.* [=(very) easily] **3** : a relaxed and informal way of behaving • *his charm and ease of manner* — **at ease 1** *also* **at your ease** : in a relaxed and comfortable state • *They no longer felt at ease with each other.* • *You can set/put your mind at ease.* — see also ILL AT EASE **2** : standing with the feet apart and one or both hands behind the back • *The troops stood at ease.* — **take your ease** : to rest or relax • *I found him taking his ease on the front porch.*

²**ease** *vb* **eased; eas·ing 1** [T] : to free (someone or something) from trouble or worry • *trying to ease my troubled mind* **2** [T] : to make (something) less painful • *unable to ease their suffering* **3** [T/I] : to make (something) less severe or to become less severe • *Tensions have eased.* • *The government has eased travel restrictions.* **4** [T/I] : to move slowly or carefully • *She eased herself into the driver's seat.* • *The car eased out into traffic.* — **ease off** *or* **ease up** [*phrasal vb*] : to become less severe • *The pressure should ease up soon.* — **ease up on** [*phrasal vb*] **1 a** : to treat (someone) in a less harsh or demanding way • *They'll do better if you ease up on them a little.* **b** : to apply less pressure to (something) • *ease up on the accelerator* **2** : to do or use less of (something) • *I should ease up on fatty foods.*

ea·sel /ˈiːzəl/ *n* [C] : a frame for supporting an artist's painting

eas·i·ly /ˈiːzəli/ *adv* **1** : in an easy manner : without difficulty • *We won easily.* **2** : by a great extent or degree : by far • *She's easily the best player on the team.*

¹**east** /ˈiːst/ *n* **1** [U] : the direction where the sun rises • *The wind blew from the east.* **2** *the east* or *the East* : regions or countries east of a certain point: such as **a** : the eastern part of the U.S. **b** : the countries of Asia (such as Japan, China, and Korea) — see also FAR EAST, MIDDLE EAST

²**east** *adj, always before a noun* **1** : lying toward or at the east • *the east side of town* **2** : coming from the east • *an east wind*

³**east** *adv* : to or toward the east • *The ships sailed east.*

east·bound /ˈiːstˌbaʊnd/ *adj* : going toward the east • *an eastbound train*

East·er /ˈiːstɚ/ *n* [C/U] : a Christian church festival that celebrates the return of Jesus Christ to life following his death; *also* : the Sunday in early spring on which this festival is observed • *Easter Sunday* • *an Easter egg* [=an egg that is specially decorated at Easter] • *an Easter basket* [=a basket of candy, toys, etc., that is given to children at Easter]

east·er·ly /ˈiːstɚli/ *adj* **1** : located or moving toward the east • *They sailed in an easterly direction.* **2** : blowing from the east • *an easterly wind*

east·ern /ˈiːstɚn/ *adj* **1** : located toward the east • *the eastern part of the state* • *Eastern Europe* **2** *Eastern* : of or relating to the countries of Asia : ASIAN • *Eastern philosophy* — **east·ern·most** /ˈiːstɚnˌmoʊst/ *adj*

East·ern·er /ˈiːstɚnɚ/ *n* [C] : a person born or living in the East; *especially* : a person born or living in the eastern U.S.

east·ward /ˈiːstwɚd/ *adv, also chiefly Brit* **east·wards** /ˈiːstwɚdz/ *adv* : toward the east • *We sailed eastward.* — **eastward** *adj*

¹**easy** /ˈiːzi/ *adj* **eas·i·er; -est 1** : not hard to do : not difficult • *an easy lesson/decision/goal* • *It's easy to use.* • *He's an easy person to like.* • *an easy life/mind* : free from pain, trouble, or worry • *an easy life/mind* **b** : not hurried • *an easy pace* **c** : not requiring much strength or energy • *easy, gentle movements* **3 a** : not harsh or severe in punishing or criticizing someone • *They're being too easy on him.* [=they're not criticizing/punishing him harshly enough] **b** : not hard to please • *an easy teacher* • (*informal*) *"Should we stay at home or go out?" "Whatever you like: I'm easy."* **4** : not steep • *easy slopes* **5** *informal* : not hard to get • *easy money* **6** : relaxed and informal • *an easy manner/smile* **7** — used to describe someone or something that is easy to attack, trick, criticize, etc. • *an easy target* **8** *informal*

: lightly pleasant and enjoyable ▪ *music for easy listening* — **easy on the eye** or US **easy on the eyes** *informal* : easy or pleasant to look at ▪ *She's very easy on the eyes.* [=good-looking] — **over easy** US, *of eggs* : fried on one side then turned and fried for a short time on the other side ▪ *two eggs over easy* — **eas·i·ness** *n [U]*

²**easy** *adv* **easier; -est** : without difficulty or stress ▪ *taking life easy* ▪ *The repairs will cost $100, easy.* [=will cost at least $100] ▪ *Success hasn't come easy for her.* — **easy come, easy go** *informal* — used to say that you are not bothered about losing something ▪ *His attitude toward money has always been easy come, easy go.* — **easy does it** *informal* — used to tell someone to move slowly and carefully ▪ *Easy does it! We don't want anyone to get hurt.* — **go easy** *informal* **1 go easy on** : to treat (someone) in a way that is not harsh or demanding ▪ *Go easy on him. He's got a lot to deal with right now.* **2 go easy on/with** : to use less of (something) ▪ *You should go easy on fatty foods.* — **nice and easy** see NICE — **rest easy** see ²REST — **take it easy** *informal* **1** : to relax and avoid hard work or strain ▪ *I just took it easy this weekend.* **2** : to stay or become calm ▪ *Take it easy, Joe. Calm down.*

easy chair *n [C]* : a chair that is large, soft, and very comfortable

easy·go·ing /ˌiːziˈgowɪŋ/ *adj* : relaxed and informal ▪ *an easygoing boss/manner*

eat /ˈiːt/ *vb* **ate** /ˈeɪt, Brit ˈɛt, ˈeɪt/; **eat·en** /ˈiːtn̩/; **eat·ing** **1** *[T/I]* : to take food into your mouth and swallow it ▪ *I ate a big breakfast.* ▪ *I'm hungry. Let's eat.* ✧ To **eat out** is to dine at a restaurant rather than at home. To **eat in** is to dine at home. **2** *[T/I]* : to gradually destroy, use, or take away something ▪ *Marketing costs ate into their profits.* ▪ *The acids were eating away at the metal.* **3** *[T]* *informal* : to bother or annoy (someone) ▪ *What's eating you?* — **be eating out of someone's hand** : to be completely controlled by someone ▪ *He had them eating out of his hand.* — **eat crow** (US) or **eat humble pie** *informal* : to admit that you were wrong or accept that you have been defeated ▪ *He was forced to eat crow when the company fired him.* — **eat (someone or something) alive 1** : to bite (someone or something) many times ▪ *The mosquitoes were eating us alive.* **2** : to badly defeat or harm (someone or something) ▪ *The press ate him alive.* — **eat up** [*phrasal vb*] **1** — used to tell someone to start or continue eating ▪ *Eat up! Your dinner is getting cold.* **2 eat up (something)** or **eat (something) up a** : to eat all of (something) ▪ *They ate up all the food.* **b** : to use up (time, resources, etc.) ▪ *The project has eaten up a lot of the budget.* **3** ✧ A person who is **eaten up** with or by jealousy, bitterness, etc., cannot escape that feeling and is made unhappy by it. ▪ *He was eaten up with envy of his brother's success.* **4 eat (something) up** *informal* : to enjoy (something) greatly ▪ *The audience ate up her speech.*

— **eat your heart out** : to be jealous of what someone else has — **eat your words** : to admit that what you said was wrong ▪ *She guaranteed victory and had to eat her words when she lost.* — **have your cake and eat it too** see ¹CAKE — **eat·er** *n [C]* ▪ *a big eater* [=someone who eats a lot]

eat·ery /ˈiːtəri/ *n, pl* **-er·ies** *[C]* *chiefly US, informal* : a usually small and informal restaurant

eats /ˈiːts/ *n [plural] informal* : FOOD ▪ *cheap/good eats*

eaves /ˈiːvz/ *n [plural]* : the lower edge of a roof that sticks out past the wall

eaves·drop /ˈiːvzˌdrɑːp/ *vb* **-dropped; -drop·ping** *[I]* : to listen secretly to what other people are saying ▪ *He was eavesdropping on his sister and her friends.* — **eaves·drop·per** *n [C]*

¹**ebb** /ˈɛb/ *n [C]* **1** : the time when the tide flows out from the land **2** : a low point or condition ▪ *Morale was at a low ebb.* — **ebb and flow** — used to describe something that changes in a regular and repeated way ▪ *the ebb and flow of fashion*

²**ebb** *vb [I]* **1** *of a tide* : to flow outward from the land **2** : to get worse ▪ *Their fortunes had begun to ebb.*

eb·o·ny /ˈɛbəni/ *n [U]* **1** : a hard, heavy wood that comes from tropical trees **2** : a very dark or black color — **ebony** *adj* ▪ *ebony skin*

e-book /ˈiːˌbʊk/ *n [C]* : a book that is read on a computer or other electronic device

ebul·lient /ɪˈbʊljənt/ *adj* : lively and enthusiastic ▪ *an ebullient entertainer* — **ebul·lience** /ɪˈbʊljəns/ *n [U]*

ec·cen·tric /ɪkˈsɛntrɪk/ *adj* **1 a** : tending to act in strange or unusual ways ▪ *an eccentric inventor* **b** : strange or unusual ▪ *eccentric ideas/clothes* **2** *technical* : not following a perfectly circular path ▪ *an eccentric orbit* — **eccentric** *n [C]* ▪ *a wealthy eccentric* — **ec·cen·tri·cal·ly** /ɪkˈsɛntrɪkəli/ *adv* — **ec·cen·tric·i·ty** /ˌɛksɛnˈtrɪsəti/ *n, pl* **-ties** *[C/U]*

ec·cle·si·as·ti·cal /ɪˌkliːziˈæstɪkəl/ *also* **ec·cle·si·as·tic** /ɪˌkliːziˈæstɪk/ *adj, formal* : of or relating to the Christian church or clergy ▪ *ecclesiastical history/authority*

ech·e·lon /ˈɛʃəˌlɑːn/ *n [C]* : a level in an organization : a level of authority or responsibility ▪ *the lower echelons of the firm*

echo /ˈɛkoʊ/ *n, pl* **ech·oes** *[C]* **1** : a sound that is a copy of another sound and that is produced when sound waves bounce off a surface (such as a wall) ▪ *the echo of footsteps in the hall* **2** : something (such as a feature or quality) that repeats or resembles something else ▪ *His work contains echoes of other writers.* — **echo** *vb* **echoes; ech·oed; ech·o·ing** *[T/I]* ▪ *The music echoed through the church.* ▪ *His words echoed in my head.* [=I kept thinking about what he had said] ▪ *(figurative)* Others have echoed [=repeated] *her criticisms.*

éclair /ɪˈkleə/ *n [C]* : a type of long pastry that is filled with whipped cream or a sweet cream filling and usually topped with chocolate

eclec·tic /ɪˈklɛktɪk/ adj : including things taken from many different sources • an eclectic mix • a person with eclectic tastes [=a person who likes many different kinds of things] — **eclec·ti·cism** /ɪˈklɛktəˌsɪzəm/ n [U]

¹**eclipse** /ɪˈklɪps/ n 1 [C] a : an occasion when the sun looks like it is completely or partially covered with a dark circle because the moon is between the sun and the Earth • a total/partial solar eclipse b : an occasion when the moon looks like it is completely or partially covered with a dark circle because the Earth's shadow is on it • a lunar eclipse 2 [U, singular] : a loss of power, success, popularity, etc. • an author who has fallen/gone into eclipse [=who has become much less popular] • Her acting career is in eclipse.

²**eclipse** vb eclipsed; eclips·ing [T] 1 : to cause an eclipse of (the sun or moon) • The sun was partially eclipsed by the moon. 2 a : to make (something) less important or popular • Train travel was eclipsed by air travel. b : to do or be much better than (someone or something) • Her sister's accomplishments eclipsed her own.

eco- combining form : ecology : ecological • eco-friendly technologies [=technologies that do not harm the environment]

E. coli /ˌiːˈkoʊˌlaɪ/ n [U] : a kind of bacteria that is sometimes in food and water and that can make people sick

ecol·o·gy /ɪˈkɑːlədʒi/ n, pl -gies 1 [U] : a science that deals with the relationships between groups of living things and their environments • plant/marine ecology 2 [C] : the relationships between a group of living things and their environment • the ecology of the desert — **eco·log·i·cal** /ˌiːkəˈlɑːdʒɪkəl/ adj • ecological awareness — **eco·log·i·cal·ly** /ˌiːkəˈlɑːdʒɪkli/ adv — **ecol·o·gist** /ɪˈkɑːlədʒɪst/ n [C]

e-com·merce /ˈiːˌkɑːmɚs/ n [U] : activities that relate to the buying and selling of goods and services over the Internet

ec·o·nom·ic /ˌɛkəˈnɑːmɪk/ adj 1 : relating to an economy • the country's economic growth 2 : ECONOMICAL • more economic ways of doing business

ec·o·nom·i·cal /ˌɛkəˈnɑːmɪkəl/ adj : using money, resources, etc., carefully • an economical way to heat your house • an economical writing style [=a writing style that uses few words] • economical cars [=cars that do not use a lot of fuel] • economical prices [=prices that many people can afford]

ec·o·nom·i·cal·ly /ˌɛkəˈnɑːmɪkli/ adv 1 : in a way that relates to an economy • An increase in tourism will help the city economically. 2 : in an economical way • a way to economically heat your house

ec·o·nom·ics /ˌɛkəˈnɑːmɪks/ n 1 [U] : a science concerned with the process or system by which goods and services are produced, sold, and bought • a professor of economics 2 [plural] : the part of something that relates to money • the

economics of buying a house — see also HOME ECONOMICS

econ·o·mist /ɪˈkɑːnəmɪst/ n [C] : a person who studies or specializes in economics (sense 1)

econ·o·mize also Brit **econ·o·mise** /ɪˈkɑːnəˌmaɪz/ vb -mized; -miz·ing [T/I] : to use money, resources, etc., carefully • finding ways to economize on fuel • (chiefly US) efforts to economize fuel/use

¹**econ·o·my** /ɪˈkɑːnəmi/ n, pl -mies 1 [C] : the process or system by which goods and services are produced, sold, and bought in a country or region • a strong/weak economy 2 [U] : careful use of money, resources, etc. • a writer known for her economy of language [=her use of only the words that are most necessary] • cars with better fuel economy [=cars that use less fuel] 3 [C/U] : something that makes it possible for you to spend less money • Mass production creates economies of scale. [=situations in which it costs less to produce something because you are producing a lot] • a false economy [=something that costs less at first but results in more money being spent later]

²**economy** adj, always before a noun : designed to cost less money • an economy car

eco·sys·tem /ˈiːkoʊˌsɪstəm/ n [C] : everything that exists in a particular environment • the forest's ecosystem

ec·sta·sy /ˈɛkstəsi/ n, pl -sies 1 [C/U] : a state of very great happiness • shouts of pure/sheer ecstasy 2 or **Ecstasy** [U] : an illegal drug that is used to produce a feeling of excitement and pleasure — **ec·stat·ic** /ɛkˈstætɪk/ adj • He was ecstatic [=very happy and excited] when he heard the news. — **ec·stat·i·cal·ly** /ɛkˈstætɪkli/ adv

ec·u·men·i·cal /ˌɛkjəˈmɛnɪkəl/ adj : involving people from different kinds of Christian churches • an ecumenical council/service

ec·ze·ma /ˈɛgzəmə/ n [U] : a disease that causes areas of the skin to become red, rough, and itchy

ed /ˈɛd/ n [U] informal : education • driver's ed [=classes or lessons that teach students to drive]

ed. abbr edited; edition; editor

-ed /əd, ɪd after t or d; t after p, k, tʃ, f, θ, s, or ʃ; d elsewhere; exceptions are pronounced at their entries/ vb suffix or adj suffix 1 — used to form the past tense and past participle of regular verbs • It ended. • It has ended. • tried 2 : having : characterized by • domed • two-legged

ed·dy /ˈɛdi/ n, pl ed·dies [C] : a circular movement of air or water — **eddy** vb ed·dies; ed·died; ed·dy·ing [I] • The wind gusted and eddied around us.

¹**edge** /ˈɛdʒ/ n [C] 1 : the line or part where an object or area begins or ends • the edge of the roof • The fabric was frayed at the edge. 2 : the part of a blade that cuts • the edge of an ax 3 a : a harsh or unkind quality • His voice had a sarcastic edge. b : force or effectiveness • Her writing has lost its edge. 4 : an advantage over others • Our experience gave us an/

the edge (on our competition). — see also CUTTING EDGE, LEADING EDGE — **close to the edge** *or* **on the edge** ✧ Someone who **lives (life) on the edge** *or* **lives close to the edge** often deals with dangerous situations and takes many risks. — **on edge** : feeling nervous ▪ *She was on edge before her exam.* — **on the edge of** : very close to (something) ▪ *a species on the edge of extinction* ▪ *They were poised on the edge of success.* — **on the edge of your seat** ✧ If you are *on the edge of your seat,* you are watching or listening to something with great interest especially because you do not know what is going to happen. — **over the edge** : into a mental or emotional state that makes someone completely lose control ▪ *His financial losses sent/drove/pushed him over the edge.* — **take the edge off** : to make (something) weaker or less severe ▪ *a medication that takes the edge off the pain*

²**edge** *vb* **edged; edg·ing** **1** [T] **a** : to give an edge to (something) ▪ *The sleeve was edged with/in lace.* [=it had a lace edge] **b** : to be on the edge of (something) ▪ *The garden is edged with/in/by flowers.* **2** [T/I] : to move slowly or with small movements in a specified direction ▪ *She edged away from him.* ▪ *Prices have been edging upward.* ▪ *I edged my chair closer to the table.* **3** [T] : to defeat (someone or something) by a small amount ▪ *She edged out her opponent.*

edge·wise (US) /ˈɛʤˌwaɪz/ *or chiefly Brit* **edge·ways** /ˈɛʤˌweɪz/ *adv* : SIDEWAYS ✧ If you can't **get a word in edgewise,** it means that someone else is talking so much that you are not able to say anything.

edg·ing /ˈɛʤɪŋ/ *n* [C/U] : something that forms an edge ▪ *sleeves with lace edging(s)*

edgy /ˈɛʤi/ *adj* **edg·i·er; -est** **1** : nervous and tense ▪ *Too much coffee makes me edgy.* **2** : somewhat harsh or unkind ▪ *edgy humor* **3** : new and unusual in a way that is likely to make some people uncomfortable ▪ *an edgy artist/film* — **edg·i·ness** /ˈɛʤinəs/ *n* [U, singular]

ed·i·ble /ˈɛdəbəl/ *adj* : suitable or safe to eat ▪ *edible fruit* — **ed·i·bil·i·ty** /ˌɛdə-ˈbɪləti/ *n* [U] — **edibles** *n* [plural] *informal* : cheese, crackers, and other edibles

edict /ˈiːˌdɪkt/ *n* [C] : an official order given by a person with power or by a government ▪ *an edict banning public demonstrations*

ed·i·fice /ˈɛdəfəs/ *n* [C] : a large and usually impressive building

ed·i·fy /ˈɛdəˌfaɪ/ *vb* **-fies; -fied; -fy·ing** [T] : to teach (someone) in a way that improves the mind or character ▪ *books that will entertain and edify readers* ▪ *an edifying sermon* — **ed·i·fi·ca·tion** /ˌɛdəfəˈkeɪʃən/ *n* [U]

ed·it /ˈɛdət/ *vb* [T] **1 a** : to make changes, correct mistakes, etc., in (something written) ▪ *edit a poem* ▪ *The book was poorly edited.* **b** : to change, move, or remove parts of (a film, recording, photo, etc.) ▪ *This film was edited for television.* **2** : to be in charge of the publica-

tion of (something) ▪ *edit a magazine* — **edit out** [*phrasal vb*] **edit out (something)** *or* **edit (something) out** : to remove an unwanted word, scene, etc.) while preparing something to be seen, used, published, etc. ▪ *They edited out the scene.*

edi·tion /ɪˈdɪʃən/ *n* [C] **1 a** : a particular version of a book, newspaper, or magazine ▪ *a hardcover/paperback edition* **b** : a particular version of a product ▪ *the latest edition of the software* **2** : all the copies of a book that are printed or published at one time ▪ *the book's second edition* **3** : something that is presented as one of a series ▪ *tonight's edition of the show*

ed·i·tor /ˈɛdətə/ *n* [C] **1** : a person whose job is to edit something ▪ *a magazine/film editor* **2** : a computer program that is used to create and make changes to data (such as words or pictures) ▪ *a text editor*

¹**ed·i·to·ri·al** /ˌɛdəˈtorijəl/ *adj* : of or relating to an editor ▪ *editorial jobs/offices* — **ed·i·to·ri·al·ly** *adv*

²**editorial** *n* [C] : an essay in a newspaper or magazine that gives the opinions of its editors or publishers

ed·u·cate /ˈɛʤəˌkeɪt/ *vb* **-cat·ed; -cat·ing** **1** [T/I] : to teach (someone) especially in a school, college, or university ▪ *She was educated at private schools.* **2** [T] : to give (someone) information about something ▪ *We need to educate the public about this issue.*

educated *adj* **1 a** : having an education and especially a good education ▪ *an educated person* **b** : having a particular kind of education ▪ *poorly/well educated* ▪ *college-educated people* **2** : showing education (sense 1b) ▪ *educated speech/ tastes*

ed·u·ca·tion /ˌɛʤəˈkeɪʃən/ *n* **1 a** [U] : the action or process of teaching someone especially in a school, college, or university ▪ *the education of children* **b** [C/U] : the knowledge, skill, and understanding that you get from a school, college, or university ▪ *college education* ▪ *She received her education at private schools.* **2** [U] : a field of study that deals with the methods and problems of teaching ▪ *a school of education* — **ed·u·ca·tion·al** /ˌɛʤəˈkeɪʃənl/ *adj* : *educational theories/experiences* ▪ *an educational film* [=a film that teaches something]

ed·u·ca·tion·ist /ˌɛʤəˈkeɪʃənɪst/ *or* **ed·u·ca·tion·al·ist** /ˌɛʤəˈkeɪʃənlɪst/ *n* [C] *Brit* : EDUCATOR

ed·u·ca·tor /ˈɛʤəˌkeɪtə/ *n* [C] *chiefly US* : a person (such as a teacher or a school administrator) who has a job in the field of education

-ee /i/ *n suffix* **1** : a person who gets or is affected by a specified action or thing ▪ *trainee* **2** : a person who does a specified action ▪ *escapee*

eel /ˈiːl/ *n* [C] : a long fish that looks like a snake

ee·rie /ˈiri/ *adj* **ee·ri·er; -est** : strange and mysterious ▪ *an eerie coincidence/ sound* — **ee·ri·ly** /ˈirəli/ *adv* — **ee·ri·ness** /ˈirinəs/ *n* [U, singular]

ef·face /ɪˈfeɪs/ vb **-faced; -fac·ing** [T] formal : to cause (something) to fade or disappear • *a memory effaced by time* — see also SELF-EFFACING

¹**ef·fect** /ɪˈfɛkt/ n **1** [C/U] : a change that results when something is done or happens • *The experience had a bad/adverse/negative effect on him.* • *a good/beneficial/positive effect* • *The effect of the drug soon wore off.* • *Adjustments were made to little/no effect.* **2** [C/U] : a particular feeling or mood created by something • *The total effect of the painting was one of gloom.* • *The movie exaggerates his odd habits for comic effect.* **3** [C] : an image or a sound that is created in television, radio, or movies to imitate something real • SPECIAL EFFECT • *sound/visual effects* **4** [U] : the state of something that is actually working or operating • *The policy will be in effect next year.* • *The law went/came into effect today.* • *The medication should take effect soon.* **5** [plural] : personal property or possessions • *household/personal effects* — **in effect** — used to say that one thing has the same effect or result as something else • *The suggestion was in effect an order.* — **to that effect** or **to the effect that** — used to indicate that the meaning of words is roughly correct even if the words themselves are not completely accurate • *He said more time was needed, or words to that effect.* = *He said something to the effect that more time was needed.*

²**effect** vb [T] formal : **1** : to make (something) happen • *She could not effect a change in policy.* **2** : to cause (something) to produce the desired result • *The duty of the legislature is to effect the will of the people.* — compare AFFECT

ef·fec·tive /ɪˈfɛktɪv/ adj **1** : producing a result that is wanted • *an effective method/speech* **2** : in use : ACTIVE • *The law becomes effective next year.* **3** : starting at a particular time • *Effective tomorrow, the store will be open until 8:00 p.m. every day.* **4** always before a noun — used to describe something that exists or has an effect but that is not officially stated or recognized • *the effective tax rate* — **ef·fec·tive·ly** /ɪˈfɛktɪvli/ adv • *communicating effectively* • *By turning down the permit they effectively ended the housing plans.* — **ef·fec·tive·ness** n [U]

ef·fec·tu·al /ɪˈfɛktʃəwəl/ adj, formal : producing a desired result or effect • *an effectual remedy* — **ef·fec·tu·al·ly** /ɪˈfɛktʃəwəli/ adv

ef·fem·i·nate /ɪˈfɛmənət/ adj : having or showing qualities that are considered more suited to women than to men • *an effeminate manner/voice* — **ef·fem·i·nate·ly** adv

ef·fer·ves·cence /ˌɛfərˈvɛsn̩s/ n [U] **1** : an exciting or lively quality • *Her effervescence was charming.* **2** : bubbles that form and rise in a liquid — **ef·fer·ves·cent** /ˌɛfərˈvɛsn̩t/ adj • *an effervescent personality/drink*

ef·fete /ɪˈfiːt/ adj, disapproving : lacking strength, courage, or spirit • *effete intellectuals*

ef·fi·ca·cious /ˌɛfəˈkeɪʃəs/ adj, formal : having the power to produce a desired result or effect • *an efficacious remedy* — **ef·fi·ca·cy** /ˈɛfɪkəsi/ n [U]

ef·fi·cient /ɪˈfɪʃənt/ adj : capable of producing desired results without wasting materials, time, or energy • *an efficient worker* • *efficient machinery* — **ef·fi·cien·cy** /ɪˈfɪʃənsi/ n [U] • *Because of her efficiency, the work was done quickly.* • *a car with greater fuel efficiency* [=a car that uses fuel more efficiently] — **ef·fi·cient·ly** adv • *working efficiently*

ef·fi·gy /ˈɛfədʒi/ n, pl **-gies** [C] : an image of a person that often has the form of a large doll • *He was hanged/burned in effigy by a mob of protesters.* [=a large doll that looked like him was hanged/burned]

ef·flu·ent /ˈɛˌfluːwənt/ n [C/U] formal : liquid (such as sewage or industrial chemicals) that is released as waste • *industrial effluent(s)*

ef·fort /ˈɛfət/ n **1** [C/U] : work done by the mind or body • *The job required/took a lot of effort.* • *the combined efforts of many people* • *She seems to do everything without effort.* [=effortlessly; very easily] ◇ If you get **an A for effort** or **an E for effort** or (Brit) **full marks for effort**, you are given credit for working hard to do something, even though the result of the work was not successful. **2** [C] : a serious attempt to do something • *They didn't win, but they made a good/valiant effort.* • *a determined effort to succeed* • *The school makes every effort* [=does all that it can] *to help students.* • *The project is a team effort.* [=is being done by a group of people] • *Despite my best efforts, I never found out who she was.* **3** [C] : something produced by work • *This painting was one of my best efforts.* **4** [singular] : something that is hard to do • *It was an effort (for me) to get out of bed this morning.*

ef·fort·less /ˈɛfətləs/ adj : showing or needing little or no effort : appearing very easy • *effortless grace* ◇ Effortless usually describes something that appears to be easy because of the skill of the person who is doing it. • *The skier made a series of effortless turns.* — **ef·fort·less·ly** adv

ef·fron·tery /ɪˈfrʌntəri/ n [U] formal : a very confident attitude or way of behaving that is shocking or rude • *He had the effrontery to deny doing what we all saw him do.*

ef·fu·sive /ɪˈfjuːsɪv/ adj : expressing a lot of emotion • *effusive praise/thanks* — **ef·fu·sive·ly** adv

EFL /ˌiːˌɛfˈɛl/ n [U] : the teaching of English as a foreign language

e.g. abbr for example • *products imported from many countries, e.g., France, Germany, and Japan*

egal·i·tar·i·an /ɪˌgæləˈterijən/ adj, formal : aiming for equal wealth, status, etc., for all people • *egalitarian policies/societies* — **egal·i·tar·i·an·ism** /ɪˌgæləˈterijəˌnɪzəm/ n [U]

¹**egg** /ˈɛg/ n **1** [C] : a hard-shelled oval thing from which a young bird is born; also : an oval or round thing from which

a snake, frog, insect, etc., is born **2** [C/U] : the egg of a bird (especially a chicken) eaten as food • *poached/fried/ boiled/scrambled eggs* • *egg white(s)/yolk* **3** [C] *biology* : a cell that is produced by the female sexual organs and that combines with the male's sperm in reproduction **4** [C] : something that is shaped like a bird's egg • *a chocolate egg* — **egg on your face** ✧ If you have *egg on your face*, you appear foolish, usually because something that you said would happen has not happened. — **lay an egg** *US, informal* : to fail completely • *The movie laid an egg.* — **put all your eggs in one basket** ✧ If you *put all your eggs in one basket*, you risk all you have on the success or failure of one thing. • *Investors should diversify their investments instead of putting all their eggs in one basket.* — **walk on eggs** see ¹WALK

²**egg** *vb* — **egg on** [*phrasal vb*] **egg (someone) on** : to urge or encourage (someone) to do something that is usually foolish or dangerous • *He continued to take off his clothes while the crowd egged him on.*

egg·head /ˈɛɡˌhɛd/ *n* [C] *informal + usually disapproving* : a highly educated person who may not know much about real life

egg·nog /ˈɛɡˌnɑːɡ/ *n* [C/U] : a drink made of eggs beaten with sugar, milk or cream, and often alcoholic liquor

egg·plant /ˈɛɡˌplænt/ *n* [C/U] *chiefly US* : a somewhat egg-shaped vegetable with usually purple skin — called also (*Brit*) *aubergine*

egg roll *n* [C] *US* : a very thin flat piece of dough that is wrapped around a mixture of chopped vegetables and often meat and then usually fried — called also *spring roll*

egg·shell /ˈɛɡˌʃɛl/ *n* [C] : the shell of an egg — **walk on eggshells** see ¹WALK

ego /ˈiːɡoʊ/ *n, pl* **egos** [C] **1** : the opinion that you have about yourself • *Winning was good for our egos.* [=winning made us proud of ourselves] • *He has a big/inflated/enormous ego.* [=an overly high opinion of himself] **2** *psychology* : a part of the mind that senses and adapts to the real world — see also ALTER EGO

ego·cen·tric /ˌiːɡoʊˈsɛntrɪk/ *adj* : caring too much about yourself and not about other people • *an egocentric actor*

ego·ism /ˈiːɡəˌwɪzəm/ *n* [U] : EGOTISM — **ego·ist** /ˈiːɡəˌwɪst/ *n* — **ego·is·tic** /ˌiːɡəˈwɪstɪk/ *adj*

ego·ma·ni·ac /ˌiːɡoʊˈmeɪniˌæk/ *n* [C] : someone who does not care about other people and thinks that their problems and concerns are not important — **ego·ma·nia** *n* [U]

ego·tism /ˈiːɡəˌtɪzəm/ *n* [U] : the feeling or belief that you are better, more important, more talented, etc., than other people — **ego·tist** /ˈiːɡəˌtɪst/ *n* [C] • *a selfish egotist* — **ego·tis·tic** /ˌiːɡəˈtɪstɪk/ *or* **ego·tis·ti·cal** /ˌiːɡəˈtɪstɪkəl/ *adj* • *an egotistical person/attitude*

ego trip *n* [C] *informal* : something that someone does to feel more important or better than other people • *Her latest movie is just an ego trip.*

egre·gious /ɪˈɡriːdʒəs/ *adj, formal* : very bad and easily noticed • *egregious misconduct/errors* — **egre·gious·ly** *adv*

egret /ˈiːɡrət/ *n* [C] : a large, long-legged bird that has a long neck and bill and usually white feathers

Egyp·tian /ɪˈdʒɪpʃən/ *n* **1** [C] : a person born or living in Egypt **2** [U] : the language spoken by ancient Egyptians — **Egyptian** *adj*

ei·der·down /ˈaɪdəˌdaʊn/ *n* **1** [U] : soft feathers that come from ducks and that are used in warm clothing and bed covers **2** [C] : a bed cover made with eiderdown

eight /ˈeɪt/ *n* **1** [C] : the number 8 **2** [C] : the eighth in a set or series • *the eight of hearts* **3** [U] : eight o'clock • *Dinner is at eight.* — **eight** *adj* • *eight cars* — **eight** *pron* • *Eight (of them) passed the test.*

eight ball *n* [C] : a black ball that is numbered 8 in the game of pool — **behind the eight ball** *informal* : in a bad position • *The loss of this contract puts the company behind the eight ball.*

eigh·teen /ˌeɪˈtiːn/ *n* [C] : the number 18 — **eighteen** *adj* • *eighteen years* — **eighteen** *pron* — **eigh·teenth** /ˌeɪˈtiːnθ/ *n* [C] — **eighteenth** *adj* — **eighteenth** *adv*

¹**eighth** /ˈeɪtθ/ *n* **1** [*singular*] : number eight in a series • *the eighth of June* **2** [C] : one of eight equal parts of something • *An eighth of a pound is two ounces.*

²**eighth** *adj* : occupying the number eight position in a series • *the eighth car in line* — **eighth** *adv* • *She finished eighth (in the race).*

eighty /ˈeɪti/ *n, pl* **eight·ies** **1** [C] : the number 80 **2** [*plural*] **a** : the numbers ranging from 80 to 89 • *The temperature rose to the high eighties.* **b** : a set of years ending in digits ranging from 80 to 89 • *She is in her mid-eighties.* • *a television show from the (nineteen) eighties* [=from 1980–1989] — **eight·i·eth** /ˈeɪtijəθ/ *n* [C] • *one eightieth of the total* — **eightieth** *adj* • *the eightieth day* — **eighty** *adj* • *eighty days* — **eighty** *pron* • *Eighty (of them) were rejected.*

¹**ei·ther** /ˈiːðə, *Brit* ˈaɪðə/ *adj* **1** : one and the other of two • *Either answer is correct.* [=both answers are correct] • *I don't like either book.* [=I like neither book] **2** : one or the other of two • *You may choose either answer.* • *It's fine with me either way.* [=both possibilities are acceptable to me]

²**either** *pron* : the one or the other • *Either (of the two answers) is correct.* [=both answers are correct] • *I don't like either of them.*

usage According to the rules of grammar, the pronoun *either* is singular and requires a singular verb. • *Either is correct.* However, in informal writing and speech, a plural verb is common when *either* is followed by *of*. • *Either of the answers is/are correct.*

³**either** *conj* — used with *or* to indicate choices or possibilities • *You can either go*

or stay. ▪ *He gave the money either to his son or his daughter.* ▪ *They can be either black, brown, or blue.* ✧ When *either* and *or* are used to join two subjects in a sentence, the verb should agree with the subject that is closer to it. ▪ *Either the professor or the students are wrong.*

⁴**either** *adv* : in addition — used after a negative statement ▪ *He is not wise or handsome either.* [=he is neither wise nor handsome] ▪ (*US, informal*) *"I didn't like the movie." "Me either."* [=I also didn't like the movie]

ejac·u·late /ɪˈdʒækjəˌleɪt/ *vb* -lat·ed; -lat·ing 1 [*T/I*] *medical* : to release semen from the penis 2 [*T*] *old-fashioned* : to say (something) suddenly and forcefully ▪ *"Good God!" he ejaculated.* — **ejac·u·la·tion** /ɪˌdʒækjəˈleɪʃən/ *n* [*C/U*]

eject /ɪˈdʒɛkt/ *vb* 1 [*T*] : to force (someone) to leave ▪ *She was ejected from the restaurant.* 2 [*T*] : to push (something) out ▪ *The player ejected the CD.* 3 [*I*] : to use a special device that throws you out and away from an airplane in an emergency ▪ *The pilot ejected when his plane caught fire.* — **ejec·tion** /ɪˈdʒɛkʃən/ *n* [*C/U*]

ejection seat (*US*) *or* **ejec·tor seat** /ɪˈdʒɛktɚ-/ *n* [*C*] : a special seat in an airplane that is used to throw you out and away from the plane when the plane is going to crash

eke /ˈiːk/ *vb* **eked**; **ek·ing** — *eke out* [*phrasal vb*] *eke out* (*something*) *also eke* (*something*) *out* 1 : to get or achieve (something) with great difficulty ▪ *They were barely able to eke out a living.* ▪ *He eked out a win in the election.* 2 : to increase (something) by a small amount ▪ *He eked out his small income by working for neighbors.* 3 : to make (a limited amount of something) last by using it carefully in small amounts ▪ *eke out food supplies*

EKG /ˌiːˌkeɪˈdʒiː/ *n* [*C*] *medical* 1 : a printed recording of the heart's electrical activity made by a special machine — called also *electrocardiogram* 2 : a machine that detects and records the electrical activity of the heart — called also *electrocardiograph*

¹**elab·o·rate** /ɪˈlæbərət/ *adj* : having many parts that are carefully arranged or planned ▪ *They made elaborate preparations for his visit.* ▪ *an elaborate plan/meal* — **elab·o·rate·ly** *adv* — **elab·o·rate·ness** *n* [*U*]

²**elab·o·rate** /ɪˈlæbəˌreɪt/ *vb* -rat·ed; -rat·ing 1 [*I*] : to give more details about something ▪ *She refused to elaborate on her earlier statements.* 2 [*T*] : to bring (something) to a more advanced or developed state ▪ *The philosopher spent years elaborating his ideas.* — **elab·o·ra·tion** /ɪˌlæbəˈreɪʃən/ *n* [*C/U*]

élan /eɪˈlɑːn/ *n* [*U*] *literary* : energy and enthusiasm ▪ *She performed with great élan.*

elapse /ɪˈlæps/ *vb* **elapsed**; **elaps·ing** [*I*] *of time* : to pass by ▪ *Weeks elapsed before he returned home.*

¹**elas·tic** /ɪˈlæstɪk/ *adj* 1 : able to return to an original shape or size after being stretched, squeezed, etc. ▪ *elastic fibers/bandages* 2 : able to be changed ▪ *an elastic* [=*flexible*] *plan* — **elas·tic·i·ty** /ɪˌlæˈstɪsəti/ *n* [*U*]

²**elastic** *n* 1 [*U*] : material that can be stretched ▪ *the elastic in socks* 2 [*C*] *US* : RUBBER BAND

elate /ɪˈleɪt/ *vb* **elat·ed**; **elat·ing** [*T*] : to make (someone) very happy and excited ▪ *The discovery has elated researchers.* ▪ *She was elated by/at/over the news.* — **ela·tion** /ɪˈleɪʃən/ *n* [*U*] ▪ *feelings of elation*

¹**el·bow** /ˈɛlˌboʊ/ *n* [*C*] 1 a : the joint where your arm bends b : the part of a piece of clothing that covers the elbow 2 : a pipe, piece of food, etc., that is bent like an elbow ▪ *elbow macaroni* — *rub elbows with* see ¹RUB

²**elbow** *vb* [*T/I*] : to push or shove (someone) with your elbow ▪ *I elbowed my friend to get his attention.* ▪ (*figurative*) *Older workers are being elbowed aside as the company tries to attract young employees.*

elbow grease *n* [*U*] *informal* : physical effort : hard work ▪ *It took some elbow grease to get the counter clean.*

elbow room *n* [*U*] : room or space to move or work freely ▪ *It's a small kitchen with very little elbow room.* ▪ (*figurative*) *The company provides its workers with elbow room to try new ideas.*

¹**el·der** /ˈɛldɚ/ *adj, always before a noun* : OLDER ▪ *my elder brother/sister* [=my brother/sister who is older than I am] ▪ *my elder son/daughter* [=the older one of my two sons/daughters] — *the elder* — used in comparing the ages of two people who are members of the same family ▪ *He's the elder of her two brothers.*

²**elder** *n* 1 [*C*] : a person who is older ▪ *He was told to respect his elders.* ▪ (*formal*) *He was my elder by 11 months.* [=he was 11 months older than I was] 2 [*C*] a : a person who has authority because of age and experience ▪ *a village elder* b : an official in some Christian churches 3 [*plural*] : old people ▪ *day care for elders* [=*the elderly*] 4 [*C*] : ELDERBERRY 2

el·der·ber·ry /ˈɛldɚˌberi/ *n, pl* -ries [*C*] 1 : a black or red berry that comes from a type of bush or tree with bunches of white or pink flowers 2 : a tree or bush that produces elderberries

el·der·ly /ˈɛldɚli/ *adj* : old or rather old ▪ *elderly people* — *the elderly* : elderly people ▪ *providing care for the elderly*

el·dest /ˈɛldəst/ *adj, always before a noun* : OLDEST ▪ *my eldest brother/sister/child* — *the eldest* — used in comparing the ages of people who are members of the same family ▪ *He's the eldest of her three brothers.*

¹**elect** /ɪˈlɛkt/ *vb* [*T*] 1 : to select (someone) for a position, job, etc., by voting ▪ *She was elected to the Senate.* ▪ *an elected official* 2 *somewhat formal* : to choose to do (something) ▪ *We elected to stay home.*

²**elect** *n* [*plural*] : people who belong to a special group and have privileges that other people do not have ▪ *His new status earned him a place among the city's elect.*

³**elect** *adj, always after a noun* : having been elected • *the governor elect* • *the president-elect*

elec·tion /ɪˈlɛkʃən/ *n* [C/U] **1** : the act or process of choosing someone for a public office by voting • *a presidential election* **2** : the fact of being elected • *Her election to the Senate was a surprise.*

¹**elec·tive** /ɪˈlɛktɪv/ *adj* **1** : held by a person who is elected • *an elective office* **2** : done or taken by choice : not necessary or required • *elective surgery*

²**elective** *n* [C] *US* : a class that is not required in a particular course of study

elec·tor /ɪˈlɛktər/ *n* [C] **1** : a member of the Electoral College in the U.S. **2** *formal* : someone who can vote in an election

elec·tor·al /ɪˈlɛktərəl, ˌiːˌlɛkˈtɔːrəl/ *adj, always before a noun* : of or relating to an election or to the process by which people are elected • *electoral politics/districts*

Electoral College *n* — **the Electoral College** : a group of people chosen from each U.S. state who meet to elect the President and Vice President of the U.S. based on the votes of all the people in each state

elec·tor·ate /ɪˈlɛktərət/ *n* [C] : the people who can vote in an election

elec·tric /ɪˈlɛktrɪk/ *adj* **1** *or* **elec·tri·cal** /ɪˈlɛktrɪkəl/ **a** : of or relating to electricity • *an electric/electrical current* **b** : operated by electricity • *an electric motor* **c** : providing electricity • *an electric socket/cord* **2** : producing sound by using electricity • *an electric piano/guitar* **3** : very exciting or thrilling • *an electric performance* • *The atmosphere in the room was electric.* — **elec·tri·cal·ly** /ɪˈlɛktrɪkli/ *adv*

electric chair *n* [*singular*] : a special chair in which a criminal who has been sentenced to death is killed by using a strong electric current

elec·tri·cian /ɪˌlɛkˈtrɪʃən/ *n* [C] : a person who works on and repairs electrical equipment

elec·tric·i·ty /ɪˌlɛkˈtrɪsəti/ *n* [U] **1** : a form of energy that is carried through wires and used to operate machines, lights, etc. **2** : electric current or power • *The electricity went off during the storm.* **3** : a feeling of excitement or tension • *You could feel the electricity in the room.*

elec·trics /ɪˈlɛktrɪks/ *n* [*plural*] *Brit* : the electrical parts of something

elec·tri·fy /ɪˈlɛktrəˌfaɪ/ *vb* **-fies; -fied; -fy·ing** [T] **1 a** : to pass electricity through (something) • *an electrified fence* [=a fence that has electricity running through it] **b** : to supply (an area, building, etc.) with electric power **2** : to cause (someone) to feel great excitement • *The news electrified the nation.* • *an electrifying performance* — **elec·tri·fi·ca·tion** /ɪˌlɛktrəfəˈkeɪʃən/ *n* [U]

elec·tro·car·dio·gram /ɪˌlɛktrouˈkɑːdiːəˌgræm/ *n* [C] : EKG

elec·tro·car·dio·graph /ɪˌlɛktrouˈkɑːdiːəˌgræf, *Brit* ɪˌlɛktrouˈkɑːdiːəˌgrɑːf/ *n* [C] : EKG

elec·tro·cute /ɪˈlɛktrəˌkjuːt/ *vb* **-cut·ed; -cut·ing** [T] : to kill (a person or animal) by electric shock • *He stepped on the power line and was nearly electrocuted.* — **elec·tro·cu·tion** /ɪˌlɛktrəˈkjuːʃən/ *n* [C/U]

elec·trode /ɪˈlɛkˌtroud/ *n* [C] : one of the two points through which electricity flows into or out of a battery or other device

elec·trol·y·sis /ɪˌlɛkˈtrɑːləsəs/ *n* [U] **1** : the process of removing unwanted hair by killing the hair root with an electric current **2** *chemistry* : the process of separating a liquid into its different chemical parts by passing an electric current through it

elec·tro·lyte /ɪˈlɛktrəˌlaɪt/ *n* [C] **1** *chemistry* : a liquid (such as the liquid in a battery) through which electricity can pass **2** *technical* : any one of various substances in the fluid of your body that control how your body processes waste and absorbs vitamins, minerals, etc.

elec·tro·mag·ne·tism /ɪˌlɛktrouˈmægnəˌtɪzəm/ *n* [U] *technical* : a magnetic field that is produced by a current of electricity — **elec·tro·mag·net·ic** /ɪˌlɛktroumægˈnɛtɪk/ *adj*

elec·tron /ɪˈlɛkˌtrɑːn/ *n* [C] *physics* : a very small particle of matter that has a negative charge of electricity and that travels around the nucleus of an atom

elec·tron·ic /ɪˌlɛkˈtrɑːnɪk/ *adj* **1** : operating through the use of many small electrical parts • *electronic devices such as televisions and computers* **2** : produced by the use of electronic equipment • *electronic music* **3** : operating or done by means of a computer • *an electronic dictionary* • *electronic banking* [=banking done over the Internet] • *electronic mail* [=e-mail] — **elec·tron·i·cal·ly** /ɪˌlɛkˈtrɑːnɪkli/ *adv*

elec·tron·ics /ɪˌlɛkˈtrɑːnɪks/ *n* **1** [*plural*] **a** *US* : electronic devices (such as televisions, radios, and computers) • *Sales of consumer electronics are up.* **b** : electronic parts • *There are problems with the system's electronics.* **2** [U] *technical* : a science that deals with the uses and effects of electrons

el·e·gant /ˈɛləgənt/ *adj* **1** : showing good taste : graceful and attractive • *elegant clothes* **2** : simple and clever • *an elegant solution* — **el·e·gance** /ˈɛləgəns/ *n* [U] — **el·e·gant·ly** *adv*

el·e·gy /ˈɛlədʒi/ *n, pl* **-gies** [C] *literary* : a sad poem or song especially for someone who is dead — **el·e·gi·ac** /ˌɛləˈdʒaɪək/ *adj* • *an elegiac poem/tone*

el·e·ment /ˈɛləmənt/ *n* **1** [C] *chemistry* : one of the basic substances that are made of atoms of only one kind and that cannot be separated by ordinary chemical means into simpler substances • *Water is composed of the elements hydrogen and oxygen.* **2** [C] : a particular part of something • *Self-confidence was a key element in her success.* • *There's always an element of risk in starting a new business.* • *The attackers were relying on the element of surprise.* [=they were relying on their attack being a surprise] **3** [*plural*] : the most basic parts of a subject of study • *the elements of grammar* **4** [C] : a group of people that form part of a larger group ▪ *the different elements of society* **5** [*plural*] : the weather and especially stormy or cold weather ▪ *The bare wood was exposed to the elements.* **6** [*singular*] : the state or place that is normal or suited to a person or thing ▪ *At school she was (really) in her element.* ▪ *I felt out of my element in the city.*

el·e·men·tal /ˌɛləˈmɛntl̩/ *adj* **1** *somewhat formal* : basic and important ▪ *elemental needs/differences* **2** *literary* : having the power of a force of nature ▪ *the elemental violence of the storm* **3** *technical* : of or relating to a chemical element ▪ *elemental components* — **el·e·men·tal·ly** *adv*

el·e·men·ta·ry /ˌɛləˈmɛntri/ *adj* **1** : basic and simple ▪ *an elementary principle/error* ▪ *elementary arithmetic* **2** *always before a noun, chiefly US* : of or relating to elementary school ▪ *elementary students/education*

elementary school *n* [*C/U*] : a school in the U.S. for young children ✧ Children in the U.S. attend elementary school for their first four to eight years of schooling. — called also *grade school, grammar school, primary school*

el·e·phant /ˈɛləfənt/ *n* [*C*] : a very large gray animal that has a long, flexible nose and two long tusks — see also WHITE ELEPHANT

el·e·vate /ˈɛləˌveɪt/ *vb* **-vat·ed; -vat·ing** [*T*] **1** : to lift (something) up ▪ *The doctor told her to elevate* [=*raise*] *her leg.* ▪ *an elevated highway* **2** : to increase the level of (something) ▪ *exercises that elevate the heart rate* **3** : to raise (someone) to a higher rank or level ▪ *He was elevated to (the position of) chairman.* **4** *somewhat formal* : to improve the mind or mood of (someone) ▪ *A great book can both elevate and entertain its readers.* ▪ *an elevated mind*

el·e·va·tion /ˌɛləˈveɪʃən/ *n* [*C*] **1** : the height of a place ▪ *a plant species found only at higher/lower elevations* **2** : an act or result of lifting or raising someone or something ▪ *elevations in temperature* **3** : a place (such as a hill) that is higher than the area around it

el·e·va·tor /ˈɛləˌveɪtɚ/ *n* [*C*] *US* **1** : a machine used for carrying people and things to different levels in a building — called also (*Brit*) **lift** **2** : a tall building for storing grain

elev·en /ɪˈlɛvən/ *n* **1** [*C*] : the number 11 **2** [*C*] : the eleventh in a set or series ▪ *page eleven* **3** [*U*] : eleven o'clock — **eleven** *adj* ▪ *eleven turtles* — **eleven** *pron* ▪ *Eleven (of them) were absent.* — **elev·enth** /ɪˈlɛvənθ/ *n* [*C*] ▪ *one eleventh of the total* — **eleventh** *adj* ▪ *the eleventh person in line* — **eleventh** *adv*

eleventh hour *n* [*singular*] : the latest possible time ▪ *The killer's life was spared at the eleventh hour.* [=*at the last minute*]

elf /ˈɛlf/ *n, pl* **elves** /ˈɛlvz/ [*C*] : a small creature in stories usually with pointed ears and magical powers — **elf·ish** /ˈɛlfɪʃ/ *adj*

elf·in /ˈɛlfən/ *adj* : of, relating to, or like an elf ▪ *the child's elfin charm/face*

elic·it /ɪˈlɪsət/ *vb* [*T*] *formal* : to get (a response, information, etc.) from someone ▪ *She's been trying to elicit their support.*

el·i·gi·ble /ˈɛlədʒəbəl/ *adj* **1** : able to be chosen for something : able to do or receive something ▪ *I'm not eligible to join yet.* ▪ *eligible voters* ▪ *eligible for a loan* **2** : suitable and desirable for marriage ▪ *an eligible bachelor* — **el·i·gi·bil·i·ty** /ˌɛlədʒəˈbɪləti/ *n* [*U*]

elim·i·nate /ɪˈlɪməˌneɪt/ *vb* **-nat·ed; -nat·ing** [*T*] **1** : to remove (something that is not wanted or needed) : to get rid of (something) ▪ *The company plans to eliminate more than 2,000 jobs.* ▪ *She's trying to eliminate fatty foods from her diet.* **2** : to defeat and remove (a team, player, etc.) from a competition ▪ *The team was eliminated in the first round of the playoffs.* — **elim·i·na·tion** /ɪˌlɪməˈneɪʃən/ *n* [*U*] ▪ *the elimination of waste from the body* ▪ *They arrived at their decision by a process of elimination.* [=by considering and rejecting each possible choice until only one was left]

elite /ɪˈliːt/ *n* [*C*] **1** : the people who have the most wealth and status in a society ▪ *the social/intellectual/political/academic elite* **2** *US* : a successful and powerful person ▪ *Many business elites oppose the new policy.* — **elite** *adj, always before a noun* ▪ *an elite club/university*

elit·ist /ɪˈliːtɪst/ *adj, disapproving* **1** : giving special treatment and advantages to wealthy and powerful people ▪ *elitist colleges/clubs* **2** : regarding other people as inferior because they lack power, wealth, etc. ▪ *She's an elitist snob.* — **elit·ism** /ɪˈliːˌtɪzəm/ *n* [*U*] — **elitist** *n* [*C*]

elix·ir /ɪˈlɪksɚ/ *n* [*C*] : a magical liquid that can cure illness or extend life

Eliz·a·be·than /ɪˌlɪzəˈbiːθən/ *adj* : relating to Queen Elizabeth I of England or the time when she ruled (1558 to 1603) ▪ *Elizabethan poetry* — **Elizabethan** *n*

elk /ˈɛlk/ *n, pl* **elk** *or* **elks** [*C*] **1** *US* : a large kind of North American deer with big antlers **2** *Brit* : a European or Asian moose

ELL *abbr* **1** English language learner **2** English language learning

el·lipse /ɪˈlɪps/ *n* [*C*] : a shape that resembles a flattened circle

el·lip·sis /ɪˈlɪpsəs/ *n, pl* **-lip·ses** /-ˈlɪpˌsiːz/ **1** [*U*] : the act of leaving out one or more words that are not necessary for a phrase to be understood ▪ *"Begin when ready" for "Begin when you are ready" is an example of ellipsis.* **2** [*C*] : a sign (such as ...) used in printed text to show that words have been left out

el·lip·ti·cal /ɪˈlɪptɪkəl/ *or* **el·lip·tic** /ɪˈlɪptɪk/ *adj* **1** : shaped like a flattened circle ▪ *an elliptical orbit* **2** : using few words and therefore hard to understand ▪ *a writer with an elliptical style* — **el·lip·ti·cal·ly** /ɪˈlɪptɪkli/ *adv*

elm /ˈɛlm/ *n* **1** [*C/U*] : a tall shade tree with spreading branches **2** [*U*] : the wood of an elm

el·o·cu·tion /ˌɛləˈkjuːʃən/ *n* [*U*] *formal*

: the study of how to speak clearly and in a way that is effective and socially acceptable

elon·gate /ɪˈlɑːˌŋɡeɪt, *Brit* ˈiːlɒŋɡeɪt/ *vb* **-gat·ed; -gat·ing** [T/I] : to make (something) longer or to grow longer • *exercising to elongate leg muscles* • *an elongating cell* — **elon·gat·ed** /ɪˈlɑːˌŋɡeɪtəd, *Brit* ˈiːlɒŋɡeɪtəd/ *adj* • *an elongated* [=long and thin] *figure* — **elon·ga·tion** /ˌiːlɑːŋˈɡeɪʃən/ *n* [U]

elope /ɪˈloʊp/ *vb* **eloped; elop·ing** [I] : to run away secretly to get married • *He eloped with his girlfriend.* — **elope·ment** /ɪˈloʊpmənt/ *n* [C/U]

el·o·quent /ˈɛləkwənt/ *adj* **1** : having or showing the ability to use language clearly and effectively • *an eloquent speech/speaker* **2** : clearly showing feeling or meaning • *His success is an eloquent reminder of the value of hard work.* — **el·o·quence** /ˈɛləkwəns/ *n* [U] — **el·o·quent·ly** *adv*

¹else /ˈɛls/ *adv* : in a different or additional manner or place • *How else could it be done?* [=in what other way could it be done?] • *Where else can we meet?* [=at what other place can we meet?] • *Let's go somewhere else.* : at a different or additional time • *I don't know when else we could go.* — **or else 1** — used to say what will happen if something is not done • *You have to leave or else you'll be arrested.* **2** — used to say what another possibility is • *He either thinks he can't do it or else he just isn't interested.* **3** *informal* — used in angry speech to express a threat without saying exactly what the threat is • *Do what I say or else!*

²else *adj* — used to refer to a different or additional person or thing • *He values friendship more than anything else.* • *That's somebody else's* [=some other person's] *problem.* • *What else did he say?* • *There was nothing else to be done.* • *The food was cheap, if nothing else.* [=the food was not very good, but at least it was cheap] — **something else** see **¹SOMETHING** — **what else is new?** *informal* — used to say that you are not surprised by something you have been told • *"They lost again." "So what else is new?"*

else·where /ˈɛlsˌweɚ/ *adv* : in or to another place • *He angrily said he would take his business elsewhere.*

elu·ci·date /ɪˈluːsəˌdeɪt/ *vb* **-dat·ed; -dat·ing** [T/I] *formal* : to make (something) clear or easy to understand • *She was asked to elucidate the government's policies (to/for us).* — **elu·ci·da·tion** /ɪˌluːsəˈdeɪʃən/ *n* [C/U]

elude /iˈluːd/ *vb* **elud·ed; elud·ing** [T] **1** : to avoid or escape (someone or something) by being quick, skillful, or clever • *The killer was able to elude the police.* • *He eluded capture.* **2 a** : to fail to be understood or remembered by (someone) • *Her name eludes me for the moment.* [=I don't remember her name] **b** : to fail to be achieved by (someone) • *Victory has eluded us.* **c** ◆ When something **eludes detection/discovery**, people try to find it but are unable to.

elu·sive /iˈluːsɪv/ *adj* **1** : hard to find or capture • *an elusive creature/solution* **2** : hard to understand, define, or remember • *an elusive concept/idea/name* — **elu·sive·ly** *adv* — **elu·sive·ness** *n* [U]

elves *plural of* ELF

em- see EN-

ema·ci·at·ed /ɪˈmeɪʃiˌeɪtəd/ *adj* : very thin because of hunger or disease • *The illness left her emaciated.* — **ema·ci·a·tion** /ɪˌmeɪʃiˈeɪʃən/ *n* [U]

e-mail /ˈiːˌmeɪl/ *n* **1** [U] : a system for sending messages from one computer to another computer • *They communicated by e-mail.* **2 a** [U] : messages that are sent by e-mail • *I get a lot of e-mail.* **b** [C] : an e-mail message • *She sent me an e-mail.* — **e-mail** *vb* [T] • *I'll e-mail my response to you tomorrow.*

em·a·nate /ˈɛməˌneɪt/ *vb* **-nat·ed; -nat·ing 1** [I] : to come out *from* a source • *Good smells emanated from the kitchen.* **2** [T] : to send or give (something) out • *substances emanating radiation* • *She seems to emanate happiness.* — **em·a·na·tion** /ˌɛməˈneɪʃən/ *n* [C/U]

eman·ci·pate /ɪˈmænsəˌpeɪt/ *vb* **-pat·ed; -pat·ing** [T] *formal* : to free (someone) from someone else's control or power • *emancipate a slave* • *He emancipated himself from his parents by moving away.* — **emancipated** *adj* • *an emancipated woman* [=a woman who is free from old social limitations and customs] — **eman·ci·pa·tion** /ɪˌmænsəˈpeɪʃən/ *n* [U] — **eman·ci·pa·tor** /ɪˈmænsəˌpeɪtɚ/ *n* [C] *chiefly US*

emas·cu·late /ɪˈmæskjəˌleɪt/ *vb* **-lat·ed; -lat·ing** [T] **1** : to deprive (a man) of his male strength, role, etc. • *a meek husband who has been emasculated by his domineering wife* **2** : to make (something) weaker or less effective • *The change will emasculate the law.* — **emas·cu·la·tion** /ɪˌmæskjəˈleɪʃən/ *n* [U]

em·balm /ɪmˈbɑːm/ *vb* [T] : to treat (a dead body) with special chemicals to keep it from decaying — **em·balm·er** *n* [C]

em·bank·ment /ɪmˈbæŋkmənt/ *n* [C] : a raised bank or wall that is built to carry a roadway or hold back water

em·bar·go /ɪmˈbɑːrɡoʊ/ *n, pl* **-goes** [C] : a government order that limits trade in some way • *an embargo on oil = an oil embargo* — **embargo** *vb* **-goes; -goed; -go·ing** [T] • *The government has embargoed all arms shipments.*

em·bark /ɪmˈbɑːrk/ *vb* [I] : to begin a journey especially on a ship or airplane • *The troops are waiting to embark.* — **embark on** *also* **embark upon** [*phrasal vb*] **1** : to begin (a journey) • *They embarked on their trip to America.* **2** : to begin (something that will take or happen for a long time) • *She's embarking on a new career.* — **em·bar·ka·tion** /ˌɛmˌbɑːrˈkeɪʃən/ *n* [U]

em·bar·rass /ɪmˈberəs/ *vb* **1** [T/I] : to make (someone) feel confused and foolish in front of other people • *Unexpected laughter embarrassed the speaker.* • *She's worried about embarrassing herself.* • *She* *doesn't embarrass easily.* **2** [*T*] : to make (a person, group, etc.) look foolish in public ▪ *He embarrassed his family.* — **em·bar·rassed** /ɪmˈberəst/ *adj* ▪ *I've never been more embarrassed in my life.* — **em·bar·rass·ing** /ɪmˈberəsɪŋ/ *adj* ▪ *a very embarrassing moment/situation/scandal* — **em·bar·rass·ing·ly** /ɪmˈberəsɪŋli/ *adv*

em·bar·rass·ment /ɪmˈberəsmənt/ *n* **1** [*U*] : the state of feeling foolish in front of others ▪ *She couldn't hide her embarrassment.* **2** [*C*] : something or someone that causes a person or group to look or feel foolish ▪ *He's an embarrassment to his family.* **3** [*C*] : a very large number of things from which to choose ▪ *an embarrassment of choices/riches*

em·bas·sy /ˈembəsi/ *n*, *pl* **-sies** [*C*] **1** : a group of people who work under an ambassador and represent their country in a foreign country **2** : the building where an ambassador lives and works

em·bat·tled /ɪmˈbætld/ *adj* **1** : engaged in battle or conflict ▪ *an embattled city* **2** : constantly criticized or attacked ▪ *an embattled coach*

em·bed /ɪmˈbed/ *vb* **-bed·ded; -bedding** [*T*] : to place or set (something) firmly in something else ▪ *embed a post in concrete* ▪ (*figurative*) *beliefs that are embedded in our culture*

em·bel·lish /ɪmˈbelɪʃ/ *vb* [*T*] : to decorate (something) by adding special details and features ▪ *a book embellished with illustrations* ▪ (*humorous*) *I didn't lie—I just embellished the story a little bit.* — **em·bel·lish·ment** /ɪmˈbelɪʃmənt/ *n* [*C/U*]

em·ber /ˈembɚ/ *n* [*C*] : a glowing piece of coal or wood from a fire

em·bez·zle /ɪmˈbezəl/ *vb* **-bez·zled; -bez·zling** [*T/I*] : to steal money that you have been trusted with ▪ *He embezzled money/funds from his clients.* — **em·bez·zle·ment** /ɪmˈbezəlmənt/ *n* [*U*] — **em·bez·zler** /ɪmˈbezlɚ/ *n* [*C*]

em·bit·ter /ɪmˈbɪtɚ/ *vb* [*T*] : to cause bitter feelings in (someone) ▪ *a man embittered by divorce*

em·bla·zon /ɪmˈbleɪzn/ *vb* [*T*] **1** : to write or draw (a name, picture, etc.) *on* a surface so that it can be seen very clearly ▪ *The team's name was emblazoned on their helmets.* **2** : to decorate (a surface) with a name, picture, etc. ▪ *banners emblazoned with slogans*

em·blem /ˈembləm/ *n* [*C*] **1** : an object or picture used to suggest a thing that cannot be shown ▪ *The flag is the emblem of our nation.* **2** : a person or thing that represents an idea ▪ *He is regarded as an emblem of conservatism.* — **em·blem·at·ic** /ˌemblə̱ˈmætɪk/ *adj* ▪ *The crown is emblematic of royalty.*

em·body /ɪmˈbɑːdi/ *vb* **-bod·ies; -bod·ied; -body·ing** [*T*] **1** : to represent (something) in a clear and obvious way ▪ *a leader who embodies courage* [=a very courageous leader] **2** *formal* : to include (something) as a part or feature ▪ *The new law embodies a revenue provi-*

sion. — **em·bod·i·ment** /ɪmˈbɑːdimənt/ *n* [*C*] ▪ *the embodiment of evil*

em·bold·en /ɪmˈboʊldən/ *vb* [*T*] : to make (someone) more confident ▪ *He was emboldened by his success.*

em·boss /ɪmˈbɑːs/ *vb* [*T*] : to decorate a surface with a raised pattern or design ▪ *His stationery is embossed with his initials.*

em·brace /ɪmˈbreɪs/ *vb* **-braced; -bracing** [*T/I*] **1** : to hold someone in your arms as a way of expressing love or friendship ▪ *They embraced (each other) warmly.* **2** [*T*] **a** : to accept (something or someone) readily or gladly ▪ *a politician who has been embraced by conservatives* ▪ *embrace a cause/religion* **b** : to use (something) eagerly ▪ *She gladly/eagerly embraced the opportunity/chance to study abroad.* **3** [*T*] *formal* : to contain or include (something) as a part of something larger ▪ *a subject that embraces many areas of learning* — **embrace** *n* [*C*] ▪ *He held her in a warm embrace.*

em·broi·der /ɪmˈbrɔɪdɚ/ *vb* [*T*] **1** : to sew a design on a piece of cloth ▪ *She embroidered flowers on the scarf.* ▪ *an embroidered scarf* **2** : to make (a story, the truth, etc.) more interesting by adding details that are not true or accurate ▪ *He embroidered the truth about his army career.* — **em·broi·der·er** /ɪmˈbrɔɪdərɚ/ *n* [*C*]

em·broi·dery /ɪmˈbrɔɪdəri/ *n*, *pl* **-der·ies** **1** [*U*] : the process or art of sewing a design on cloth **2** [*C/U*] : cloth decorated by sewing ▪ *her collection of embroidery*

em·broil /ɪmˈbrɔjəl/ *vb* [*T*] : to involve (someone or something) *in* conflict or difficulties ▪ *They were embroiled in a complicated lawsuit.* — **em·broil·ment** /ɪmˈbrɔjəlmənt/ *n* [*U*]

em·bryo /ˈembriˌoʊ/ *n*, *pl* **-bry·os** [*C*] : a human or animal in the early stages of development before it is born, hatched, etc. — **in embryo** *formal* : in an early or undeveloped stage ▪ *His ideas can be seen in embryo in his early books.* — **em·bry·on·ic** /ˌembriˈɑːnɪk/ *adj* : human embryonic development ▪ *embryonic tissue/cells* ▪ *an embryonic plan*

em·cee /ˌemˈsiː/ *n* [*C*] *US* : MASTER OF CEREMONIES — **emcee** *vb* **-ceed; -cee·ing** [*T/I*] ▪ *She emceed the awards dinner.*

emend /iˈmend/ *vb* [*T*] : to correct errors in (something written) ▪ *emend a text* — **emen·da·tion** /ˌiːˌmenˈdeɪʃən/ *n* [*C/U*]

em·er·ald /ˈemərəld/ *n* **1** [*C*] : a bright green stone that is used in jewelry **2** [*U*] : a bright or rich green color — called also *emerald green* — **emerald** /ˈemərəld/ *adj* ▪ *emerald eyes*

emerge /iˈmɚdʒ/ *vb* **emerged; emerging** [*I*] **1** : to become known or apparent ▪ *The facts emerged after a lengthy investigation.* ▪ *She has emerged as the leading contender.* **2** : to rise or appear *from* a hidden or unknown place or condition ▪ *The cat emerged from its hiding place behind the couch.* **3** — used to indicate the usually good state or condition of someone or something at the end of an event, process, etc. ▪ *They emerged victorious/triumphant.* [=they won] — **emergence** /ɪ'mɚdʒəns/ *n* [U]

emer·gen·cy /ɪ'mɚdʒənsi/ *n, pl* **-cies** [C/U] : an unexpected and usually dangerous situation that requires immediate action ▪ *Her quick thinking in an emergency saved the baby's life.* ▪ *emergency vehicles/procedures/exits* ◇ A **state of emergency** is declared to give the government special powers to deal with an emergency.

emergency medical technician *n* [C] *US* : EMT

emergency room *n* [C] *US* : a hospital room or area that is used for treating people who need immediate medical care — abbr. *ER* — called also (*Brit*) *casualty*

emer·gent /ɪ'mɚdʒənt/ *adj, always before a noun* : EMERGING ▪ *newly emergent nations*

emerging *adj, always before a noun* : newly created or noticed and growing in strength or popularity ▪ *an emerging breed/group of new filmmakers*

emer·i·tus /ɪ'mɛrətəs/ *adj* : retired with an honorary title from an office or position especially in a university ▪ *a professor emeritus = an emeritus professor*

em·ery board /'ɛməri-/ *n* [C] : a piece of cardboard that is covered with a rough material and used for smoothing and shaping fingernails

em·i·grant /'ɛmɪgrənt/ *n* [C] : a person who leaves a country or region to live in another one : a person who emigrates

em·i·grate /'ɛmɪˌgreɪt/ *vb* **-grat·ed; -grat·ing** [I] : to leave a country or region to live elsewhere ▪ *My grandparents emigrated to America from Hungary.* — **em·i·gra·tion** /ˌɛməˈgreɪʃən/ *n* [U]

émi·gré *also US* **emi·gre** /'ɛmɪˌgreɪ/ *n* [C] : EMIGRANT; *especially* : a person who is forced to leave a country for political reasons ▪ *a Soviet émigré*

em·i·nence /'ɛmɪnəns/ *n* **1** [U] : a condition of being well-known and successful ▪ *achieve literary/social eminence* **2** [C] *formal* : a person of high rank or achievements ▪ *a literary eminence*

em·i·nent /'ɛmɪnənt/ *adj* : successful, well-known and respected ▪ *an eminent physician*

eminent domain *n* [U] *law* : a right of a government to take private property for public use

em·i·nent·ly /'ɛmɪnəntli/ *adv, somewhat formal* : to a high degree ▪ *an eminently* [=extremely, very] *enjoyable evening*

emir /ə'miɚ/ *n* [C] : a ruler, chief, or commander in an Islamic country

emir·ate /'ɛmərət/ *n* [C] : the country or position of an emir

em·is·sary /'ɛməˌseri, Brit 'ɛmɛsri/ *n, pl* **-sar·ies** [C] : a person who is sent to represent someone else ▪ *government emissaries*

emis·sion /i'mɪʃən/ *n* **1** [U] : the act of producing or sending out something (such as energy or gas) from a source ▪ *emission of light* **2** [C] : something sent

out or given off ▪ *reducing auto emissions* [=harmful substances released into the air by automobiles]

emit /i'mɪt/ *vb* **emit·ted; emit·ting** [T] **1** : to send (light, energy, etc.) out from a source ▪ *light emitted by distant galaxies* ▪ *The flowers emit a powerful odor.* **2** : to make (a certain sound) ▪ *The brakes emitted a loud squeal.*

Em·my /'ɛmi/ *n, pl* **-mys** [C] : a small statue that is awarded each year to the best actors, programs, etc., in American television

emo·ti·con /i'moʊtɪˌkɑːn/ *n* [C] : a group of keyboard characters that are used to represent a facial expression (such as a smile or frown)

emo·tion /i'moʊʃən/ *n* [C/U] : a strong feeling (such as love, anger, joy, hate, or fear) ▪ *He found it hard to express (his) emotions.* ▪ *She showed/displayed no emotion when she heard the news.*

emo·tion·al /i'moʊʃənl/ *adj* **1** : relating to emotions ▪ *an emotional problem* **2 a** : easily upset, excited, etc. ▪ *He's a very emotional person.* **b** : showing emotion — used especially to describe someone who is crying because of strong emotion ▪ *He tends to get emotional at weddings.* **3** : causing a person to feel emotion ▪ *an emotional speech/experience/issue* — **emo·tion·al·ly** /i'moʊʃənəli/ *adv*

emo·tion·less /i'moʊʃənləs/ *adj* : showing, having, or expressing no emotion ▪ *She did her job with emotionless efficiency.*

emo·tive /i'moʊtɪv/ *adj* **1** : of or relating to emotions ▪ *emotive language* **2** *Brit* : causing strong emotions for or against something ▪ *Abortion is a very emotive* [=(US) *emotional*] *issue.*

em·pa·thize *also Brit* **em·pa·thise** /'ɛmpəˌθaɪz/ *vb* **-thized; -thiz·ing** [I] : to have the same feelings as another person ▪ *He learned to empathize with the poor.*

em·pa·thy /'ɛmpəθi/ *n* [U] : the feeling that you understand and share another person's experiences and emotions ▪ *He felt great empathy with/for/toward the poor.*

em·per·or /'ɛmpərɚ/ *n* [C] : a man who rules an empire

em·pha·sis /'ɛmfəsəs/ *n, pl* **-pha·ses** /-fəˌsiːz/ **1** [U] : a forceful quality in the way something is said or written ▪ *You need to state your arguments with greater emphasis.* **2** [U] : added force that is given to a spoken word or syllable ▪ *The emphasis* [=stress] *in the word "happiness" is on the first syllable.* **3** [C/U] : special importance or attention given to something ▪ *She puts/places/lays emphasis on developing good study habits.* ▪ *Each class has a different emphasis.*

em·pha·size *also Brit* **em·pha·sise** /'ɛmfəˌsaɪz/ *vb* **-sized; -siz·ing** [T] : to give special attention to (something) ▪ *Their father always emphasized* [=stressed] *the importance of honesty.*

em·phat·ic /ɪm'fætɪk/ *adj* **1** : said or done in a forceful or definite way ▪ *Her answer was an emphatic "Yes!"* ▪ *an emphatic victory* **2** : speaking or acting in a forceful way ▪ *They were emphatic about their opinions.* — **em·phat·i·cal·ly** /ɪm-ˈfætɪkli/ *adv* ▪ *He spoke emphatically.* ▪ *This is emphatically* [=definitely] *not the right thing to do.*

em·phy·se·ma /ˌɛmfəˈziːmə, Brit ˌɛmfəˈsiːmə/ *n* [U] : a disease in which the lungs become stretched and breathing becomes difficult

em·pire /ˈɛmˌpajɚ/ *n* [C] **1** : a group of countries or regions that are controlled by one ruler or one government ▪ *the Roman Empire* **2** : a very large business or group of businesses under the control of one person or company ▪ *a media/cattle empire*

em·pir·i·cal /ɪmˈpirɪkəl/ *also* **em·pir·ic** /ɪmˈpirɪk/ *adj* : based on testing or experience ▪ *empirical data/evidence/laws* — **em·pir·i·cal·ly** /ɪmˈpirɪkli/ *adv*

em·pir·i·cism /ɪmˈpirəˌsɪzəm/ *n* [U] : the practice of basing ideas and theories on testing and experience — **em·pir·i·cist** /ɪmˈpirəsɪst/ *n* [C]

em·place·ment /ɪmˈpleɪsmənt/ *n* **1** [C] : a position that is specially prepared for a weapon ▪ *machine-gun emplacements* **2** [U] : the act of putting something (such as a weapon) into position ▪ *secret emplacement of missiles on the island*

¹**em·ploy** /ɪmˈplɔɪ/ *vb* [T] **1** *somewhat formal* **a** : to use (something) for a particular purpose or to do something ▪ *She employed a pen for sketching wildlife.* ▪ *a method employed to improve garden soil* **b** : to use or direct (your time, effort, etc.) in order to achieve a particular goal ▪ *You should find better ways to employ your time.* **2 a** : to use or get the services of (someone) to do a particular job ▪ *I had to employ a lawyer to review the contract.* **b** : to provide (someone) with a job that pays wages or a salary ▪ *The company employs a staff of only 20.* ▪ *He's employed by the local drugstore.* [=he has a job at the local drugstore] — **em·ploy·able** /ɪmˈplɔɪjəbəl/ *adj*

²**employ** *n* — **in someone's employ** *formal* : employed by someone for wages or a salary ▪ *The company has been generous to people in their employ.* [=generous to their employees]

em·ploy·ee /ɪmˌplɔɪˈiː, ɪmˈplɔɪˌiː/ *n* [C] : a person who works for another person or for a company for wages or a salary ▪ *The company has about 200 employees.*

em·ploy·er /ɪmˈplɔɪɚ/ *n* [C] : a person or company that has people who do work for wages or a salary ▪ *My expenses were paid for by my employer.*

em·ploy·ment /ɪmˈplɔɪmənt/ *n* [U] **1** : the act of employing someone or something ▪ *laws that encourage the employment of women* ▪ *We object to the company's employment* [=use] *of pesticides.* **2 a** : work that a person is paid to do ▪ *The new factory should provide employment for hundreds of workers.* **b** : the number of people who have jobs in a particular place or area ▪ *Employment is at an all-time high.*

em·po·ri·um /ɪmˈporijəm/ *n, pl* **-po·ri·ums** *also* **-po·ria** /-ˈporijə/ [C] *old-fashioned* : a store or shop ▪ *a furniture emporium*

em·pow·er /ɪmˈpawɚ/ *vb* [T] : to give power or authority to (someone) ▪ *changes in the workplace that will empower women* ▪ *His attorney was empowered to act on his behalf.* — **em·pow·er·ment** /ɪmˈpawɚmənt/ *n* [U]

em·press /ˈɛmprəs/ *n* [C] **1** : the wife or widow of an emperor **2** : a woman who rules an empire

¹**emp·ty** /ˈɛmpti/ *adj* **1** : containing nothing ▪ *The box was empty.* ▪ *an empty can* **2** : having no people ▪ *an empty house/street/chair* **3** : having no real purpose or value ▪ *people leading empty lives* **4** : having no meaning or effect ▪ *an empty threat/promise* ▪ *empty talk/words* **5** : not showing emotion or life ▪ *a crowd of empty faces* — **come up empty** *see* COME — **empty of** (something) : completely without (something) ▪ *The arena was empty of spectators.* — **emp·ti·ly** /ˈɛmptəli/ *adv* — **emp·ti·ness** /ˈɛmptinəs/ *n* [U]

²**empty** *vb* **emp·ties; emp·tied; emp·ty·ing** **1** [T] : to make (something) empty ▪ *empty (out) a bag* ▪ *He emptied his glass.* [=he drank everything that was in his glass] ▪ *She tried to empty her mind (of thoughts).* **2** [I] : to become empty ▪ *The theater emptied (out) quickly after the show.* — **empty into** [*phrasal vb*] *of a river, stream, etc.* : to flow into (something) ▪ *The river empties into the Indian Ocean.*

³**empty** *n, pl* **empties** [C] : an empty bottle or can ▪ *Return your empties here.*

emp·ty-hand·ed /ˌɛmptiˈhændəd/ *adj* : without having, carrying, or bringing anything ▪ *She came back (from the store) empty-handed.*

emp·ty-head·ed /ˌɛmptiˈhɛdəd/ *adj* : STUPID ▪ *empty-headed people*

EMT /ˌiːˌɛmˈtiː/ *n* [C] : a person who provides emergency medical services to patients who are being taken to a hospital — called also *emergency medical technician*

emu /ˈiːmju, ˈiːmuː/ *n* [C] : a large Australian bird that does not fly

em·u·late /ˈɛmjəˌleɪt/ *vb* **-lat·ed; -lat·ing** [T] : to try to be like (someone or something you admire) ▪ *artists emulating (the style of) their teachers* — **em·u·la·tion** /ˌɛmjəˈleɪʃən/ *n* [U]

emul·si·fy /ɪˈmʌlsəˌfaɪ/ *vb* **-fies; -fied; -fy·ing** [T/I] *technical* : to mix liquids together to form an emulsion ▪ *emulsify oil and vinegar* — **emul·si·fi·ca·tion** /ɪˌmʌlsəfəˈkeɪʃən/ *n* [U] — **emul·si·fi·er** /ɪˈmʌlsəˌfajɚ/ *n* [C/U]

emul·sion /ɪˈmʌlʃən/ *n* [C] *technical* : a mixture in which small drops of one liquid are mixed throughout another liquid ▪ *an emulsion of oil in water*

en- /ɪn/ *also* **em-** /ɪm/ *prefix* ❖ In all senses *em-* is usually used before words starting with *b, m,* or *p.* **1** : to put into or onto ▪ *endanger* **2** : to cause to be ▪ *enslave* **3** : to provide with ▪ *empower* **4** : to cover with ▪ *enshroud* **5** : thoroughly ▪ *entangle*

en·able /ɪˈneɪbəl/ *vb* **-abled; -abling** [T]

1 a : to make (someone or something) able *to do* or *to be* something • *The system enables students to access class materials online.* • *What enabled the company to be successful?* **b :** to make (something) possible, practical, or easy • *The tax will enable the hiring of more teachers.* **2** *technical :* to cause (a feature or capability of a computer) to be active or available for use • *Enable the computer's firewall.*

en·act /ɪˈnækt/ *vb* [T] **1 :** to perform or act out (something) • *enacting a scene in a play* **2 :** to make (something) officially become part of the law • *The plan/bill/ legislation was enacted into law.* — **en·act·ment** /ɪˈnæktmənt/ *n* [C/U]

enam·el /ɪˈnæməl/ *n* **1 a** [C/U] **:** a material like colored glass that is used to decorate the surface of metal, glass, or pottery **b** [C] **:** something decorated with enamel • *fine enamels* **2** [U] **:** the very hard outer layer of a tooth **3** [C/U] **:** a kind of paint that is shiny and very hard when it dries

en·am·ored (*US*) *or Brit* **en·am·oured** /ɪˈnæmərd/ *adj* **:** in a state in which you love, admire, or are very interested in something or someone • *I became completely* **enamored** *of the island and its people.* • *He was enamored with her.* [=in love with her]

en·camp /ɪnˈkæmp/ *vb* [T/I] *formal :* to set up and use a camp • *Refugees are encamped along the border.* — **en·camp·ment** /ɪnˈkæmpmənt/ *n* [C] • *a military encampment*

en·cap·su·late /ɪnˈkæpsəˌleɪt/ *vb* **-lat·ed; -lat·ing** [T] **:** to show the main idea or quality of (something) in a brief way • *a phrase that encapsulates my feelings about the day* — **en·cap·su·la·tion** /ɪn-ˌkæpsəˈleɪʃən/ *n* [C/U]

en·case /ɪnˈkeɪs/ *vb* **-cased; -cas·ing** [T] **:** to completely cover (something) • *The package is encased in plastic.*

-ence /əns/ *n suffix* **1 :** the state of having a particular quality • *confidence* **2 :** the action or process of doing something • *emergence*

en·chant /ɪnˈtʃænt, *Brit* ɪnˈtʃɑːnt/ *vb* **1** [T/I] **:** to attract and hold the attention of (someone) by being interesting, pretty, etc. • *Visitors will be enchanted by the beauty of the place.* • *her enchanting smile* **2** [T] **:** to put a magic spell on (someone or something) • *a tale about a wizard who enchants a princess* — **en·chant·ing·ly** /ɪnˈtʃæntɪŋli, *Brit* ɪnˈtʃɑːntɪŋli/ *adv* — **en·chant·ment** /ɪnˈtʃæntmənt, *Brit* ɪnˈtʃɑːntmənt/ *n* [C/U] • *my enchantment with the place* • *the enchantments of sailing* • *stories about wizards and enchantments*

en·chant·ress /ɪnˈtʃæntrəs, *Brit* ɪnˈtʃɑːntrəs/ *n* [C] **1 :** a woman who uses spells or magic **2 :** a very interesting or beautiful woman

en·chi·la·da /ˌɛntʃəˈlɑːdə/ *n* [C] **:** a tortilla that is rolled around a meat, bean, or cheese filling and covered with a sauce — **the big enchilada** *US, informal :* the most important issue, person, etc. • *She's won many awards in the past, but this one*

is the big enchilada. — **the whole enchilada** *US, informal :* EVERYTHING • *There was music, food, fireworks—the whole enchilada.*

en·cir·cle /ɪnˈsɚkəl/ *vb* **-cir·cled; -cir·cling** [T] **:** to surround (someone or something) • *A crowd of reporters encircled the mayor.*

en·clave /ˈɛnˌkleɪv, ˈɑːnˌkleɪv/ *n* [C] **:** an area with people who are different in some way from the people in the areas around it • *a wealthy enclave* [=an area where only wealthy people live]

en·close /ɪnˈkloʊz/ *vb* **-closed; -clos·ing** [T] **1 a :** to surround (something) • *High walls enclose the courtyard.* **b :** to put something around (something) • *Enclose the fish in foil and bake.* **2 :** to include (something) with a letter or in a package • *Please enclose a check with your application.* • *The enclosed tickets are for you.* — **en·clo·sure** /ɪnˈkloʊʒɚ/ *n* [C/U] • *The horses are kept in an enclosure.* • *a letter with two enclosures*

en·code /ɪnˈkoʊd/ *vb* **-cod·ed; -cod·ing** [T] **1 :** to put (a message) into the form of a code **:** CODE • *an encoded message* **2 :** to put coded information on (something) • *Credit cards are encoded with cardholder information.* — **en·cod·er** *n* [C]

en·com·pass /ɪnˈkʌmpəs/ *vb* [T] **1 :** to include (something) as a part • *My interests encompass a broad range of topics.* **2 :** to cover or surround (an area) • *Fog encompassed the city.*

en·core /ˈɑːnˌkoɚ/ *n* [C] **1 :** an extra piece of music performed in response to a request from the audience • *The audience called for an encore.* **2 :** something that follows a success • *What will the novelist do for an encore?*

[1]en·coun·ter /ɪnˈkaʊntɚ/ *vb* [T] **1 :** to have or experience (problems, difficulties, etc.) • *Her plan has encountered a lot of opposition.* **2** *formal :* to meet (someone) without expecting to • *I encountered an old friend on a recent business trip.*

[2]encounter *n* [C] **1 a :** a meeting that is not planned or expected • *a chance encounter with a famous writer* **b :** a usually brief experience with another person • *sexual/romantic encounters* **c :** a violent or very unfriendly meeting • *a violent encounter between protesters and the police* **2 :** an occasion when you deal with or experience something • *her first encounter with drugs* • *The island has had several close encounters with hurricanes.* [=has almost been hit by hurricanes]

en·cour·age /ɪnˈkɚɪdʒ/ *vb* **-aged; -ag·ing** [T] **1 :** to make (someone) more determined, hopeful, or confident • *Encourage each other with kind words.* • *Researchers are encouraged by the findings.* • *We've just heard some encouraging news.* [=news that made us feel more hopeful] **2 a :** to make (something) more likely to happen • *The new regulations should encourage investment.* **b :** to make (someone) more likely *to do* something • *We want to encourage students to read more.* **:** to tell or advise (someone) *to do* something • *They encouraged her to go.* — **en-**

cour·age·ment /ɪnˈkɚrɪʤmənt/ *n* [C/U] ▪ *words of encouragement* — **en·cour·ag·ing·ly** /ɪnˈkɚrɪʤɪŋli/ *adv*

en·croach /ɪnˈkroʊtʃ/ *vb* [I] **1** : to gradually move or go into an area that is beyond the usual or desired limits ▪ *People are encroaching on/upon the animal's habitat.* **2** : to gradually take or affect something that belongs to someone else ▪ *The law would encroach on/upon states' authority.* — **en·croach·ment** /ɪnˈkroʊtʃmənt/ *n* [C/U]

en·crusted /ɪnˈkrʌstəd/ *adj* : coated or covered with something ▪ *a sword encrusted with jewels/blood*

en·crypt /ɪnˈkrɪpt/ *vb* [T] : to change (information) from one form to another especially to hide its meaning ▪ *The passwords are encrypted.*

en·cum·ber /ɪnˈkʌmbɚ/ *vb* [T] **1** : to make (someone or something) hold or carry something heavy ▪ *We were encumbered by our heavy coats and boots.* ▪ (*figurative*) *a company encumbered with debt* **2** : to cause problems or difficulties for (someone or something) ▪ *Lack of funding has encumbered the project.* — **en·cum·brance** /ɪnˈkʌmbrəns/ *n* [C] ▪ *These rules will only be an encumbrance.*

en·cy·clo·pe·dia *also* **en·cy·clo·pae·dia** /ɪnˌsaɪkləˈpiːdijə/ *n* [C] : a reference work (such as a series of books or a CD-ROM) that contains information about many different subjects or a lot of information about a particular subject ▪ *an encyclopedia of literature* — **en·cy·clo·pe·dic** *also* **en·cy·clo·pae·dic** /ɪnˌsaɪkləˈpiːdɪk/ *adj* ▪ *He has an encyclopedic knowledge of movies.* [=he knows a lot about movies]

¹end /ˈɛnd/ *n* **1** [*singular*] **a** : the point at which something no longer continues to happen or exist ▪ *The report is due at/by the end of the month.* ▪ *There is no end to their generosity.* [=they are extremely generous] ▪ (*figurative, informal*) *At the end of the day* [=when all things had been considered], *we knew we made the right choice.* ▪ (*figurative, informal*) *Losing your job is not the end of the world.* [=it is not as terrible or unpleasant as it seems to be] **b** : the last part of a story, movie, song, etc. ▪ *He read the entire book from beginning to end in one day.* **2** [C] **a** : the part at the edge or limit of an area ▪ *from one end of the island to the other* ▪ *the deep/shallow end of a swimming pool* ▪ *The house is at the end of the road.* ▪ (*figurative*) *A loss in the primary elections will mean the end of the road/line for her campaign.* [=will mean that her campaign has failed and is finished] **b** : the first or last part or section of something that is long ▪ *the car's front/rear/back end* ▪ *the pointed end of a knife* ▪ *Put the two tables end to end.* [=with their ends touching each other] ▪ (*figurative, informal*) *She was clearly at the end of her rope.* [=in a state in which she was no longer able to deal with a problem, difficult situation, etc.] **c** : either limit of a scale or range ▪ *The candidates are on opposite ends of the political spectrum.* **3** [C] : the stopping of a condition, activity,

or course of action ▪ *the end of the war* ▪ *The battle was at an end.* [=over] ▪ *bringing the concert to an end = bringing an end to the concert* [=stopping, finishing, or completing the concert] ▪ *The new mayor vowed to put an end to* [=stop] *the violence.* ▪ *The strike came to an end.* [=stopped] ▪ *Prices continue to go up with no end in sight.* [=it is not known when prices will stop going up] ▪ (*figurative*) *He promised to love her to/till/until the end of time.* [=always, forever] **4** [C] : DEATH ▪ *She came to a bad/tragic end.* [=she died in a bad/tragic way] ▪ *He met his end* [=died] *at a young age.* **5** [C] : a goal or purpose ▪ *ways to achieve/accomplish an end* ▪ *For him, taking classes is an end in itself.* [=it is something that he does because he wants to and not because it will help him accomplish something else] ▪ *They believe that the end justifies the means.* [=that a desired result is so good or important that any method, even a morally bad one, may be used to achieve it] ▪ *We want to save the building.* **To that/this end** [=as a way of dealing with or doing that/this], *we have hired people to renovate it.* **6** [C] *American football* : a player whose position is at the end of the line of scrimmage **7** [C] : the part of a project, activity, etc., that you are responsible for ▪ *Let me know if you have any problems at your end.* ▪ *He promised to keep/hold up his end of the agreement.* [=to do what he had agreed to do] **8** [C] : any one of the places connected by a telephone call ▪ *She heard an unfamiliar voice at the other end.* — **(a) light at the end of the tunnel** see ¹LIGHT — **at (your) wits'/wit's end** see WIT — **in the end 1** : finally or after a long time ▪ *We worked hard, and in the end, we achieved our goal.* **2** : when all things are considered ▪ *He thought about leaving, but in the end, decided to stay.* — **make ends meet** : to pay for the things that you need to live when you have little money ▪ *We had a hard time making ends meet.* — **never/not hear the end of it** see HEAR — **on end 1** : without interruption ▪ *For days on end* [=for many days] *she didn't answer the phone.* **2** : in an upright position ▪ *His skis stood on end in the corner.* — **the deep end** see ¹DEEP — **the ends of the earth** : the most remote places in the world — used figuratively ▪ *We will search the ends of the earth* [=everywhere] *if we have to.* — **(to) no end** : very much ▪ *It pleases me to no end to see you so happy.* — **to/till/until the bitter end** see ¹BITTER — see also ODDS AND ENDS

²end *vb* **1** [T/I] : to stop or finish ▪ *They ended the meeting an hour ago.* ▪ *The meeting ended an hour ago.* ▪ *The road ends at the top of the hill.* ▪ *She ended her career (as) a rich woman.* ▪ *She ended (up) a rich woman.* **2** [T] : to be the final part of (something) ▪ *Her speech will end the convention.* — **end in** [*phrasal vb*] : to have (something) at the end ▪ *words that end in "ing"* ▪ *Their marriage ended in divorce.* — **end up** [*phrasal vb*] **end up or end up (something) or end up (doing**

something) : to reach or come to a place, condition, or situation that was not planned or expected • *The book ended up ruined.* • *He ended up (living) in a nursing home.* • *We ended up seeing a different movie.* — **end with** [*phrasal vb*] **1** : to have (something) at the end • *The convention will end with her speech.* **2 end** (*something*) **with** : to cause (something) to have (something) at the end • *He ended the concert with a new song.* — **end your life** or **end it all** : to kill yourself • *He tried to end his life by cutting his wrists.*

³**end** *adj, always before a noun* : ¹FINAL • *the end result of the plan*

en·dan·ger /ɪnˈdeɪndʒɚ/ *vb* [*T*] : to cause (someone or something) to be in a dangerous place or situation • *The drought has endangered the area's crops.* • *The controversy endangered his chances for re-election.*

en·dan·gered /ɪnˈdeɪndʒɚd/ *adj* — used to describe a type of animal or plant that has become very rare and that could die out completely • *The bald eagle is no longer an* **endangered species.** • (*figurative*) *She says honest politicians are an endangered species.*

en·dear /ɪnˈdiɚ/ *vb* — **endear to** [*phrasal vb*] **endear** (*someone*) **to** : to cause (someone) to be loved or admired by (someone or something) • *They endeared themselves to the whole town.* — **en·dear·ing** /ɪnˈdɪrɪŋ/ *adj* • *Good humor is one of your most endearing traits.* — **en·dear·ing·ly** *adv*

en·dear·ment /ɪnˈdiɚmənt/ *n* [*C/U*] : a word or phrase that shows love or affection • *whispering endearments to your lover* • *"honey," "sweetie," and other* **terms of endearment**

¹**en·deav·or** (*US*) or *Brit* **en·deav·our** /ɪnˈdɛvɚ/ *vb* [*T*] *formal* : to seriously or continually try *to do* (something) • *The school endeavors to teach students to be good citizens.*

²**endeavor** (*US*) or *Brit* **endeavour** *n* [*C/U*] *formal* : a serious effort or attempt • *He failed despite his best endeavors.*

en·dem·ic /ɛnˈdɛmɪk/ *adj* **1** : growing or existing in a certain place or region • *endemic wildlife* • *The disease is endemic in/to this area.* **2** : common in a particular area or field • *A distrust of strangers is endemic in/to this community.*

end·ing /ˈɛndɪŋ/ *n* [*C*] **1** : the final part of something • *The movie has a happy ending.* **2** : a letter or group of letters added to the end of a word • *Many English adverbs have an "-ly" ending.*

en·dive /ˈɛnˌdaɪv, ˌɑːnˈdiːv/ *n* [*C/U*] : a plant with curly green leaves that are eaten raw

end·less /ˈɛndləs/ *adj* : lasting or taking a long time • *an endless meeting/line* — **end·less·ly** *adv*

en·dorse also **in·dorse** /ɪnˈdoɚs/ *vb* -**dorsed**; -**dors·ing** [*T*] **1** : to publicly or officially say that you support or approve of (someone or something) • *We do not endorse his position/candidacy.* **2** : to publicly say that you like or use (a product or service) in exchange for money • *She endorses a line of clothing.* **3** : to

write your name on the back of (a check) • *Endorse the check before you deposit it.* — **en·dorse·ment** also **in·dorse·ment** /ɪnˈdoɚsmənt/ *n* [*C/U*] • *political endorsements* • *athletes doing product endorsements* • *the endorsement of a check*

en·dow /ɪnˈdaʊ/ *vb* [*T*] **1** : to give a large amount of money to a school, hospital, etc., in order to pay for the creation or continuing support of (something) • *The wealthy couple endowed a new wing of the hospital.* **2** : to freely or naturally provide (someone or something) **with** something • *" . . . all men . . . are endowed . . . with certain unalienable rights . . . "* —*U.S. Declaration of Independence* (1776) — **en·dow·ment** /ɪnˈdaʊmənt/ *n* [*C/U*] • *a generous endowment to the hospital* • *an endowment fund* • *an athlete's physical endowments*

en·dur·ance /ɪnˈdɚəns, *Brit* ɪnˈdjʊərəns/ *n* [*U*] **1** : the ability to do something difficult for a long time • *a test of strength and endurance* • *physical/mental endurance* **2** : the quality of continuing for a long time • *the endurance of family traditions*

en·dure /ɪnˈdɚ, *Brit* ɪnˈdjʊə/ *vb* -**dured**; -**dur·ing 1** [*I*] : to continue to exist in the same state or condition • *This tradition has endured for centuries.* • *an enduring tradition/friendship* **2** [*T*] **a** : to experience (pain or suffering) for a long time • *He endured five years as a prisoner of war.* **b** : to deal with or accept (something unpleasant) • *We endured the lecture for as long as we could.* — **en·dur·able** /ɪnˈdɚəbəl, *Brit* ɪnˈdjʊərəbəl/ *adj* — **en·dur·ing·ly** *adv*

end zone *n* [*C*] : the area beyond the goal line at each end of the field in American football

en·e·ma /ˈɛnəmə/ *n* [*C*] *medical* : a procedure in which liquid is forced into the rectum in order to make solid waste pass from the body

en·e·my /ˈɛnəmi/ *n, pl* -**mies** [*C*] **1** : someone who hates or tries to harm another • *He made a lot of enemies during his life.* ◆ If you are *your own worst enemy,* you act in a way that causes harm to yourself or to the people or things that you care about. **2** : something that harms or threatens someone or something • *Tradition is the enemy of progress.* • *In our community, drug abuse is* **public enemy number one.** [=the most dangerous threat to society] **3** : a group of people against whom another group is fighting a war • *a soldier who went over to the enemy* • *He was behind enemy lines.* • *enemy fire*

en·er·get·ic /ˌɛnɚˈdʒɛtɪk/ *adj* **1** : having or showing a lot of energy • *I'm not feeling very energetic today.* **2** : involving a lot of effort • *an energetic campaign* — **en·er·get·i·cal·ly** /ˌɛnɚˈdʒɛtɪkli/ *adv*

en·er·gize also *Brit* **en·er·gise** /ˈɛnɚˌdʒaɪz/ *vb* -**gized**; -**giz·ing** [*T*] : to give energy or excitement to (someone or something) • *His speech energized the crowd.*

en·er·gy /ˈɛnɚdʒi/ n, pl **-gies** 1 [U, plural] : ability to be active ▪ The kids are full of energy. ▪ We devoted all our energies to the project. ▪ I have a lot of **nervous energy**. [=energy that comes from being nervous] 2 [U] : natural enthusiasm and effort ▪ She puts a lot of energy into her work. 3 [U] : usable power that comes from heat, electricity, etc. ▪ appliances that conserve energy ▪ renewable energy 4 [C/U] technical : the ability of heat, running water, etc., to be active or do work ▪ kinetic energy

en·er·vate /ˈɛnɚˌveɪt/ vb **-vat·ed; -vat·ing** [T] formal : to make (someone or something) very weak or tired ▪ a government enervated by corruption ▪ The heat was enervating. — **en·er·va·tion** /ˌɛnɚˈveɪʃən/ n [U]

en·fee·bled /ɪnˈfiːbəld/ adj, formal : made very weak or tired ▪ enfeebled by illness — **en·fee·ble·ment** /ɪnˈfiːbəlmənt/ n [U]

en·fold /ɪnˈfoʊld/ vb [T] formal : to cover (someone or something) completely ▪ Darkness enfolded the city. ▪ He enfolded the child in his arms. [=he hugged the child]

en·force /ɪnˈfoɚs/ vb **-forced; -forc·ing** [T] 1 : to make sure that people do what is required by (a law, rule, etc.) ▪ Police will be enforcing the curfew. 2 : to cause (something) to happen ▪ trying to enforce cooperation — **en·force·able** /ɪnˈfoɚsəbəl/ adj — **en·force·ment** /ɪnˈfoɚsmənt/ n [U] ▪ law enforcement — **en·forc·er** /ɪnˈfoɚsɚ/ n [C]

en·fran·chise /ɪnˈfræntʃaɪz/ vb **-chised; -chis·ing** [T] formal : to give (someone) the legal right to vote ▪ newly enfranchised voters — **en·fran·chise·ment** /ɪnˈfræntʃaɪzmənt/ n [U]

en·gage /ɪnˈgeɪdʒ/ vb **-gaged; -gag·ing** 1 [T] formal : to hire (someone) to perform a particular service ▪ He was engaged as a tutor. ▪ engage (the services of) a lawyer 2 [T] : to get and keep (someone's attention, interest, etc.) ▪ He sure can engage an audience. 3 [T/I] : to start fighting against (an opponent) ▪ The troops prepared to engage (with) the enemy. 4 [T/I] : to move (a part of a machine) so that it fits into another part ▪ She engaged the clutch and drove away. — **engage in** [phrasal vb] 1 : to do (something) ▪ We don't engage in that sort of behavior. 2 **engage (someone) in** : to cause (someone) to participate in (something) ▪ She engaged him in conversation. [=she started a conversation with him]

en·gaged /ɪnˈgeɪdʒd/ adj 1 : promised to be married ▪ They got engaged (to be married). ▪ She's engaged to him. 2 : busy with some activity ▪ (US) He is engaged in research. ▪ (Brit) He is engaged on research. 3 chiefly Brit, of a telephone line : being used ▪ The line is still engaged. [=(US) busy]

en·gage·ment /ɪnˈgeɪdʒmənt/ n 1 [C] : an agreement to be married ▪ We announced our engagement. ▪ an engagement ring 2 [C] : a promise to be somewhere at a particular time ▪ He declined the invitation due to a previous en-

gagement. **b** : a job as a performer ▪ She's had several speaking engagements. 3 [U, singular] : the act or state of being involved with something ▪ emotional engagement 4 [C/U] : a fight between military forces ▪ the rules of engagement 5 [U] formal : the act of hiring someone to perform a service ▪ engagement of a lawyer 6 [U] : the act or result of moving part of a machine so that it fits into another part ▪ engagement of the gears/clutch

engaging adj : very pleasing in a way that holds your attention ▪ an engaging smile/story — **en·gag·ing·ly** adv

en·gen·der /ɪnˈdʒɛndɚ/ vb [T] formal : to be the source or cause of (something) ▪ The issue has engendered much debate.

en·gine /ˈɛndʒən/ n [C] 1 : a machine that changes energy into mechanical motion ▪ a car's engine ▪ jet/diesel engines 2 : LOCOMOTIVE

¹**en·gi·neer** /ˌɛndʒəˈniɚ/ n [C] 1 : a person who is trained in engineering ▪ a mechanical/civil/electrical engineer 2 **a** : a person who is in charge of an engine in an airplane, a ship, etc. ▪ a flight engineer **b** US : a person who runs a train **c** Brit : REPAIRMAN ▪ the telephone engineer 3 : a soldier who builds roads, bridges, etc. ▪ Army engineers built the canal.

²**engineer** vb [T] 1 : to plan, build, or manage (something) by using scientific methods ▪ a well-engineered highway 2 : to produce or plan (something) in a clever and skillful way ▪ a brilliantly engineered plan 3 technical : to change the genetic structure of (a plant or animal) ▪ genetically engineered crops

en·gi·neer·ing /ˌɛndʒəˈniɚɪŋ/ n [U] : the work of designing and creating roads, bridges, etc., or new products or systems by using scientific methods ▪ mechanical/civil/chemical engineering

En·glish /ˈɪŋglɪʃ/ n 1 [U] **a** : the chief language of Great Britain, the U.S., etc. ▪ Do you speak English? **b** : a particular type of English ▪ British English **c** : English language or literature as a subject of study ▪ I teach high-school English. 2 **the English** : the people of England ▪ the customs of the English 3 [U] : normal English that is not difficult to understand ▪ I asked the doctor to tell me what was wrong in (plain) English. — **English** adj ▪ English customs ▪ English grammar/dictionaries — **En·glish·man** /ˈɪŋglɪʃmən/ n, pl **-men** /-mən/ — **English·wom·an** n, pl **-wom·en** /-ˌwɪmən/ [C]

English muffin n [C] US : a type of flat, round bread that is split and toasted just before it is eaten

en·grave /ɪnˈgreɪv/ vb **-graved; -grav·ing** [T] : to cut or carve letters, designs, etc., onto a hard surface ▪ a ring engraved with her initials ▪ (figurative) an incident that is engraved in my memory [=that I will never forget] — **en·grav·er** n [C]

engraving n [C] : a picture made from an engraved surface ▪ a wood engraving

en·gross /ɪnˈgroʊs/ vb [T] : to hold the complete interest or attention of (someone) ▪ They were engrossed in conversation. ▪ an engrossing story

en·gulf /ɪnˈgʌlf/ vb [T] : to flow over and cover (someone or something) • *Flames engulfed the building.* • (figurative) *a country engulfed by violence/fear*

en·hance /ɪnˈhæns, Brit ɪnˈhɑːns/ vb -hanced; -hanc·ing [T] : to increase or improve (something) • *Enhance the flavor of the dish by using fresh herbs.* • *a digitally enhanced image* — **en·hance·ment** /ɪnˈhænsmənt, Brit ɪnˈhɑːnsmənt/ n [C/U] — **en·hanc·er** n [C] • *flavor enhancers*

enig·ma /ɪˈnɪgmə/ n [C] : someone or something that is difficult to understand or explain • *The author was something of an enigma.*

en·ig·mat·ic /ˌɛnɪgˈmætɪk/ also **en·ig·mat·i·cal** /ˌɛnɪgˈmætɪkəl/ adj : mysterious and difficult to understand • *an enigmatic answer/smile* — **en·ig·mat·i·cal·ly** /ˌɛnɪgˈmætɪkli/ adv

en·join /ɪnˈdʒɔɪn/ vb [T] formal 1 : to direct or order (someone) to do something • *The court enjoined the debtors to pay.* 2 : to prevent (someone) from doing something • *The judge enjoined them from selling the property.*

en·joy /ɪnˈdʒɔɪ/ vb [T] 1 : to take pleasure in (something) • *Did you enjoy [=like] the movie?* • *No one enjoys being teased.* • *He really enjoyed himself* [=had a good time] *at the party.* 2 : to have or experience (something good) • *The show enjoyed great success.* — **en·joy·able** /ɪnˈdʒɔɪəbəl/ adj — **en·joy·ably** /ɪnˈdʒɔɪəbli/ adv — **en·joy·ment** /ɪnˈdʒɔɪmənt/ n [U, plural] • *I read the book for my own enjoyment.* • *This is land set aside for the public's enjoyment.* • *life's simple enjoyments*

en·large /ɪnˈlɑːdʒ/ vb -larged; -larg·ing [T/I] : to make (something) larger or to become larger • *We had the photograph enlarged.* — **enlarge on/upon** [phrasal vb] formal : to give more information about (something) • *Would you kindly enlarge on that point?* — **en·large·ment** /ɪnˈlɑːdʒmənt/ n [C/U] • *enlargement of the company's offices* • *I ordered several enlargements (of the photograph).*

en·light·en /ɪnˈlaɪtn̩/ vb [T] : to give knowledge or understanding to (someone) • *I don't understand; can you enlighten me?* — **en·light·en·ing** /ɪnˈlaɪtn̩ɪŋ/ adj • *We found the talk very enlightening.* [=informative]

en·light·ened /ɪnˈlaɪtn̩d/ adj : having or showing a good understanding of how people should be treated • *an enlightened society*

en·light·en·ment /ɪnˈlaɪtn̩mənt/ n [U] 1 : the state of having knowledge or understanding • *spiritual enlightenment* : the act of giving someone knowledge or understanding • *the enlightenment of the public* 2 **the Enlightenment** : a movement of the 18th century that promoted science and logic 3 Buddhism : a final spiritual state marked by the absence of desire or suffering

en·list /ɪnˈlɪst/ vb 1 [T] : to get help, support, etc., from someone or something • *We enlisted (the services of) a professional.* • *We'll need to enlist all available resources.* 2 **a** [T] : to sign up (a person) for duty in the army, navy, etc. • *They enlisted two new recruits.* **b** [T] : to become a member of the army, navy, etc. • *I enlisted in the navy.* — **en·list·ee** /ɪnˌlɪsˈtiː, ɪnˈlɪsti/ n [C] • *Army enlistees* — **en·list·ment** /ɪnˈlɪstmənt/ n [C/U] • *enlistments in the armed forces*

en·list·ed /ɪnˈlɪstəd/ adj, chiefly US : serving in the armed forces in a rank below the rank of officers • *enlisted personnel*

en·liv·en /ɪnˈlaɪvən/ vb [T] : to make (something) more lively or enjoyable • *A touch of color will enliven the room.*

en masse /ɑnˈmæs/ adv : as a single group • *Her supporters arrived en masse for the rally.*

en·mesh /ɪnˈmɛʃ/ vb [T] : to wrap (someone or something) in a net • *a dolphin enmeshed in/by a fishing net* • (figurative) *The committee was enmeshed in a dispute.*

en·mi·ty /ˈɛnməti/ n, pl -ties [C/U] formal : a very deep unfriendly feeling • *There's a long history of enmity between them.*

en·no·ble /ɪˈnoʊbəl/ vb -no·bled; -no·bling [T] formal : to make (someone or something) better or more admirable • *a life ennobled by suffering* — **en·no·ble·ment** /ɪˈnoʊbəlmənt/ n [U] — **en·no·bling** adj • *an ennobling experience*

en·nui /ˌɑːnˈwiː/ n [U] formal : a lack of spirit, enthusiasm, or interest • *a general sense of ennui* [=boredom]

enor·mi·ty /ɪˈnoəməti/ n, pl -ties 1 formal **a** [C] : a shocking, evil, or immoral act • *the enormities of war* **b** [U] : great evil or wickedness • *the enormity of the crime* 2 [U] : great size or importance • *the enormity of the project* • *They didn't fully grasp the enormity of their decision.*

enor·mous /ɪˈnoəməs/ adj : very great in size or amount • *enormous houses/costs* — **enor·mous·ly** adv • *an enormously popular album* — **enor·mous·ness** n [U]

¹enough /ɪˈnʌf/ adj : equal to what is needed • *Have you got enough money?* • *There's enough room for five people.*

²enough adv 1 : in the amount needed : to the necessary degree • *I couldn't run fast enough to catch up with her.* • *That's good enough for me.* • *Oddly/strangely enough, they've never actually met.* 2 : to a degree that is not very high or very low • *The solution seems simple enough.* [=seems fairly simple] — **sure enough** see ²SURE

³enough pron : an amount that provides what is needed or wanted • *There's enough for everyone.* • *Have you had enough to eat?* • *I've had (more than) enough of their foolishness.* [=I'm sick of their foolishness] • *That's enough, young lady!* [=stop behaving or talking in that way] • (informal) *"Is he in good condition?" "Well, he ran a marathon last month." "Enough said."* [=I understand completely and need no more information] • (informal) *I don't mind loaning her* *a bit of money now and then, but enough is enough!* [=I am tired/sick of loaning her money]

en·quire, en·quir·ing, en·quiry *chiefly Brit* spellings of INQUIRE, INQUIRING, INQUIRY

en·rage /ɪnˈreɪdʒ/ *vb* **-raged; -rag·ing** [T] : to make (someone) very angry • *People were enraged by/at/over the decision.*

en·rap·ture /ɪnˈræptʃɚ/ *vb* **-tured; -tur·ing** [T] *formal* : to fill (someone) with delight • *The children were enraptured by his stories.*

en·rich /ɪnˈrɪtʃ/ *vb* **-riched; -rich·ing** [T] **1** : to make (someone) rich or richer • *They enriched themselves at the expense of the poor.* **2** : to make (something) better • *Their lives were enriched by the experience.* **3** : to improve the usefulness or quality of (something) by adding something to it • *The drink is enriched with vitamin C.* — **en·rich·ment** /ɪnˈrɪtʃmənt/ *n* [U]

en·roll (*US*) *or chiefly Brit* **en·rol** /ɪnˈroʊl/ *vb* **1** [T/I] : to enter (someone) as a member of or participant in something — usually + *in* • *He enrolled (himself) in the army.* **2** [T] : to accept (someone) as a member or participant • *The college enrolls about 25,000 students.* — **en·roll·ment** (*US*) *or chiefly Brit* **en·rol·ment** /ɪnˈroʊlmənt/ *n* [C/U]

en route /ɑnˈruːt/ *adv* : while you are going to a place • *We stopped to eat en route to the museum.* — **en route** *adj* • *en route delays*

en·sconce /ɪnˈskɑːns/ *vb* **-sconced; -sconc·ing** [T] : to firmly place or hide (someone or something) • *He ensconced himself in front of the television.*

en·sem·ble /ɑnˈsɑːmbəl/ *n* [C] : a group of people or things that make up a complete unit • *a jazz ensemble* • *She wore a three-piece ensemble.*

en·shrine /ɪnˈfraɪn/ *vb* **-shrined; -shrin·ing** [T] *formal* : to remember and protect (someone or something that is valuable, admired, etc.) • *great players enshrined in the Hall of Fame* • *These rights are enshrined in the U.S. Constitution.*

en·shroud /ɪnˈfraʊd/ *vb* [T] *formal* : ²SHROUD • *Darkness enshrouded the earth.*

en·sign /ˈɛnsən, ˈɛnˌsaɪn/ *n* [C] **1** : an officer of the lowest rank in the U.S. Navy **2** : a flag that is flown on a ship to show what country the ship belongs to

en·slave /ɪnˈsleɪv/ *vb* **-slaved; -slav·ing** [T] : to make (someone) a slave • *They were enslaved during the war.* — **en·slave·ment** /ɪnˈsleɪvmənt/ *n* [U]

en·snare /ɪnˈsneɚ/ *vb* **-snared; -snar·ing** [T] : to catch (an animal or person) in a trap or in a place from which there is no escape • *The dolphin got ensnared in a net.* • (*figurative*) *ensnared in/by a web of lies*

en·sue /ɪnˈsuː, Brit ɪnˈsjuː/ *vb* **-sued; -su·ing** [I] : to happen as a result • *When the news broke, a long period of chaos ensued.* [=followed] • *In the ensuing weeks, her health gradually improved.*

en·sure /ɪnˈfʊɚ/ *vb* **-sured; -sur·ing** [T] : to make (something) sure, certain, or safe • *ensuring the safety of the passengers*

en·tail /ɪnˈteɪl/ *vb* [T] : to have (something) as a part, step, or result • *What does the job entail?* [=involve]

en·tan·gle /ɪnˈtæŋgəl/ *vb* **-tan·gled; -tan·gling** [T] : ¹TANGLE • *The kite got entangled in the tree.* • (*figurative*) *She's entangled in a messy lawsuit.* — **en·tan·gle·ment** /ɪnˈtæŋgəlmənt/ *n* [C/U] • *romantic/legal entanglements*

en·ter /ˈɛntɚ/ *vb* [T/I] **1** : to go or come into (something) • *Knock on the door before you enter (the room).* • *The medication will quickly enter the bloodstream.* **2** [T] **a** : to begin to be in (an organization, school, etc.) • *Our son will be entering college next year.* **b** : to cause (someone) to be in an organization, school, etc. • *enter a child in kindergarten* **3** [T] **a** : to start to do something • *She was a teacher before she entered politics.* [=before she began her political career] • *since she entered office* [=since she began her term in office] **b** : to begin to be in (a particular situation, period of time, etc.) • *entering middle age* • *The strike has now entered its second week.* **c** : to appear for the first time in (something) • *She entered the game in the fifth inning.* • *The idea of quitting never entered my mind/head.* [=I never thought of quitting] • *Once politics enters the picture/scene/equation* [=becomes involved in something; becomes something that must be considered or dealt with], *chances for a quick settlement are greatly reduced.* **4** [T/I] : to officially say that you will be in a race, competition, etc. • *She decided not to enter (the contest) this year.* • *She was entered* [=she was one of the people who was competing] *in the race.* • (*Brit*) *He entered for the tournament.* **5** [T] **a** : to include (something) in a book, list, etc. • *She entered my name on the roster.* • *words not yet entered in the dictionary* **b** : to type in (words, data, etc.) on a computer • *Enter your password.* **6** [T] : to make or state (something) in an official way • *enter a complaint* • *The defendant entered a guilty plea.* — **enter into** [*phrasal vb*] **1** : to begin to be in or to take part in (something) • *enter into a discussion/agreement* **2** : to be a part of or to influence (something) • *Don't allow your prejudices to enter into your decision.* — **enter on/upon** [*phrasal vb*] : to begin to be in or to take part in (something) • *entering on/upon a new career*

en·ter·prise /ˈɛntɚˌpraɪz/ *n* **1** [C] : a project or activity that involves many people and that is often difficult • *Moving the house was a costly enterprise.* • *economic/criminal enterprises* **2** [C] : a business organization • *a thriving commercial enterprise* **3** [U] : the ability or desire to do dangerous or difficult things or to solve problems in new ways • *He was criticized for his lack of enterprise in dealing with the crisis.* — see also FREE ENTERPRISE, PRIVATE ENTERPRISE

en·ter·pris·ing /ˈɛntɚˌpraɪzɪŋ/ *adj* : having or showing the ability or desire to do new and difficult things ▪ *an enterprising young reporter*

en·ter·tain /ˌɛntɚˈteɪn/ *vb* **1** [T/I] : to have people as guests in your home, in a restaurant, etc. ▪ *They like to entertain (their friends) at their summer home.* **2 a** [T] : to perform for (an audience) ▪ *Our father entertained us with stories.* **b** [T/I] : to provide or be entertainment for (someone) ▪ *His stories never fail to entertain (us).* [=they are always enjoyable] **3** [T] : to have (a thought, idea, etc.) in your mind ▪ *She entertained thoughts of* [=she thought about] *quitting her job.* — **en·ter·tain·ment** /ˌɛntɚˈteɪnmənt/ *n* [C/U] ▪ *plays, movies, and other entertainments* ▪ *They hired a band for the entertainment of* [=to entertain] *the guests.*

en·ter·tain·er /ˌɛntɚˈteɪnɚ/ *n* [C] : a professional performer ▪ *Elvis was one of the greatest entertainers of his time.*

en·ter·tain·ing /ˌɛntɚˈteɪnɪŋ/ *adj* : amusing and enjoyable ▪ *an entertaining book/speaker* — **en·ter·tain·ing·ly** *adv*

en·thrall (*chiefly US*) *or Brit* **en·thral** /ɪnˈθrɑːl/ *vb* [T] : to hold the attention of (someone) by being very exciting, interesting, or beautiful ▪ *I was enthralled by/with the beauty of the landscape.* — **en·thrall·ing** /ɪnˈθrɑːlɪŋ/ *adj* ▪ *an enthralling adventure story*

en·throne /ɪnˈθroʊn/ *vb* **-throned; -thron·ing** [T] : to make (someone) a king, queen, bishop, etc., in a formal ceremony ▪ *The archbishop was enthroned last year.* — **en·throne·ment** /ɪnˈθroʊnmənt/ *n* [C/U]

en·thuse /ɪnˈθuːz, Brit ɪnˈθjuːz/ *vb* **-thused; -thus·ing 1** [T/I] : to say (something) with enthusiasm ▪ *"This is wonderful!" he enthused.* ▪ *She enthused* [=expressed enthusiasm] *about/over the garden.* **2** [T] : to make (someone) enthusiastic ▪ *His idea failed to enthuse the group.* ▪ *They were not enthused* [=enthusiastic] *about the idea.*

en·thu·si·asm /ɪnˈθuːziˌæzəm, Brit ɪnˈθjuːziˌæzəm/ *n* **1** [U] : strong excitement about something ▪ *She spoke with enthusiasm about the election.* **2** [C] : something causing a feeling of excitement and active interest ▪ *His latest enthusiasm is sailing.* — **en·thu·si·ast** /ɪnˈθuːziˌæst, Brit ɪnˈθjuːziˌæst/ *n* [C] ▪ *a golf enthusiast* — **en·thu·si·as·tic** /ɪnˌθuːziˈæstɪk, Brit ɪnˌθjuːziˈæstɪk/ *adj* ▪ *her enthusiastic supporters* ▪ *They were enthusiastic about the idea.* — **en·thu·si·as·ti·cal·ly** /ɪnˌθuːziˈæstɪkli, Brit ɪnˌθjuːziˈæstɪkli/ *adv*

en·tice /ɪnˈtaɪs/ *vb* **-ticed; -tic·ing** [T] : to attract (someone) by offering or showing something that is appealing, interesting, etc. ▪ *enticing shoppers with attractive window displays* ▪ *an enticing display* — **en·tice·ment** /ɪnˈtaɪsmənt/ *n* [C/U] — **en·tic·ing·ly** /ɪnˈtaɪsɪŋli/ *adv*

en·tire /ɪnˈtajɚ/ *adj* : complete or full ▪ *We spent the entire day at the beach.* ▪ *the entire community* ▪ *I was listening the entire time.* — **en·tire·ly** *adv* ▪ *The decision is entirely yours.* ▪ *That's an entirely different issue.*

en·tire·ty /ɪnˈtajɚti/ *n* [U] : the whole or total amount of something ▪ *the entirety of an estate* ▪ *She played the song in its entirety.* [=she played the entire song]

en·ti·tle /ɪnˈtaɪtl/ *vb* **-ti·tled; -ti·tling** [T] **1** : to give a title to (something) ▪ *He entitled* [=titled] *his book "My Life on Mars."* **2** : to give a right to (someone) ▪ *The card entitles us to a discount.* [=we can get a discount because we have this card] ▪ *You're entitled to your opinion.* [=I don't agree with you, but you are free to think what you want]

en·ti·tle·ment /ɪnˈtaɪtlmənt/ *n* **1** [U] : the feeling that you deserve to be given something ▪ *celebrities with a sense of entitlement* **2** [C] *US* : a type of financial help provided by the government ▪ *social security and other entitlements*

en·ti·ty /ˈɛntəti/ *n, pl* **-ties** [C] *formal* : something that exists by itself ▪ *a government entity* ▪ *separate/independent entities*

en·tomb /ɪnˈtuːm/ *vb* [T] : to place (someone or something) in a tomb ▪ *The remains of former kings are entombed there.* — **en·tomb·ment** /ɪnˈtuːmmənt/ *n* [C/U]

en·to·mol·o·gy /ˌɛntəˈmɑːlədʒi/ *n* [U] : the scientific study of insects — **en·to·mo·log·i·cal** /ˌɛntəməˈlɑːdʒɪkəl/ *adj* — **en·to·mol·o·gist** /ˌɛntəˈmɑːlədʒɪst/ *n* [C]

en·tou·rage /ˌɑːntʊˈrɑːʒ/ *n* [C] : a group of people who go with and assist an important person ▪ *the President and his entourage*

en·trails /ˈɛnˌtreɪlz/ *n* [*plural*] : the internal organs of an animal ▪ *sheep entrails*

¹**en·trance** /ˈɛntrəns/ *n* **1** [C] : the act of entering something ▪ *the country's entrance into war* ▪ *Everyone noticed when she made her entrance.* [=when she entered] **2** [C] : something (such as a door) that is used for entering something ▪ *the theatre's main entrance* ▪ *There are two entrances to the park.* **3** [U] : the right to enter something ▪ *We gained entrance to the club.* ▪ *a college entrance exam*

²**en·trance** /ɪnˈtræns, Brit ɪnˈtrɑːns/ *vb* **-tranced; -tranc·ing** [T] : to fill (someone) with delight and wonder ▪ *We were entranced by/with the view.* ▪ *an entrancing view*

en·trant /ˈɛntrənt/ *n* [C] : a person who enters something (such as a contest) ▪ *Each entrant must agree to the rules.*

en·trap /ɪnˈtræp/ *vb* **-trapped; -trapping** [T] *formal* : to catch (someone or something) in a trap ▪ *We use nets to entrap fish.* ▪ *entrapped in an unhappy marriage* — **en·trap·ment** /ɪnˈtræpmənt/ *n* [U] ▪ *He was a victim of police entrapment.* [=the illegal act of tricking someone into committing a crime so that the person you have tricked can be arrested]

en·treat /ɪnˈtriːt/ *vb* [T] *formal* : to ask (someone) in a serious and emotional way ▪ *His parents entreated him to return to college.* — **en·treaty** /ɪnˈtriːti/ *n, pl* **-treat·ies** [C] ▪ *He succumbed to their entreaties.* [=he did what they asked]

en·trée or **en·tree** /ˈɑːnˌtreɪ/ n [C] : the main dish of a meal ▪ *We had steak as an entrée.*

en·trench /ɪnˈtrɛntʃ/ vb [T] : to place (someone or something) in a very strong position that cannot easily be changed ▪ *attitudes (deeply/firmly) entrenched in our culture* — **en·trench·ment** /ɪnˈtrɛntʃmənt/ n [U]

en·tre·pre·neur /ˌɑːntrəprəˈnɚ/ n [C] : a person who starts a business and is willing to risk loss in order to make money — **en·tre·pre·neur·i·al** /ˌɑːntrəprəˈnɚriəl/ adj — **en·tre·pre·neur·ship** /ˌɑːntrəprəˈnɚˌʃɪp/ n [U] ▪ *admired for her entrepreneurship*

en·trust /ɪnˈtrʌst/ vb [T] : to give someone the responsibility of doing or caring for something ▪ *She was entrusted with an important job.* ▪ *entrust your car to a friend = entrust a friend with your car*

en·try /ˈɛntri/ n, pl **-tries** 1 [U] : the act of entering something ▪ *The thieves gained entry through a back window.* ▪ *We were surprised by her entry into politics.* 2 [U] : the right to enter something ▪ *She was denied entry into the courtroom.* ▪ *students competing for entry into the college* ▪ *an entry fee/form* 3 [C] : ENTRYWAY ▪ *the south entry of the church* 4 a [U] : the act of entering something in a book, list, etc. ▪ *She was hired to do data entry.* [=to enter data on a computer] b [C] : something that is entered in a book, list, etc. ▪ *dictionary entries* 5 [C] : a person or thing that is entered in a contest ▪ *The race attracted a record number of entries.*

en·try·way /ˈɛntriˌweɪ/ n [C] : a place for entering something ▪ *A truck was blocking the entryway.*

en·twine /ɪnˈtwaɪn/ vb **-twined; -twin·ing** [T/I] : to twist together or around ▪ *The roses were entwined in the fence.* ▪ *(figurative) Their lives (were) tragically entwined.*

enu·mer·ate /ɪˈnuːməˌreɪt, Brit ɪˈnjuːməˌreɪt/ vb **-at·ed; -at·ing** [T] : to name (things) in a list ▪ *Let me enumerate my reasons for doing this.* — **enu·mer·a·tion** /ɪˌnuːməˈreɪʃən, Brit ɪˌnjuːməˈreɪʃən/ n [C/U]

enun·ci·ate /ɪˈnʌnsiˌeɪt/ vb **-at·ed; -at·ing** 1 [T] formal : to make a clear statement of (ideas, beliefs, etc.) ▪ *enunciating basic principles* 2 [T/I] : to pronounce words clearly ▪ *Enunciate (every syllable) clearly.* — **enun·ci·a·tion** /ɪˌnʌnsiˈeɪʃən/ n [U]

en·vel·op /ɪnˈvɛləp/ vb [T] : to completely cover or surround (someone or something) ▪ *The mountains were enveloped by/in mist.* — **en·vel·op·ment** /ɪnˈvɛləpmənt/ n [U]

en·ve·lope /ˈɛnvəˌloʊp, ˈɑːnvəˌloʊp/ n [C] : an enclosing cover for a letter, card, etc. — **push the envelope** : to go beyond the usual limits by doing something new, dangerous, etc. ▪ *a director who has pushed the envelope in his films*

en·vi·a·ble /ˈɛnvijəbəl/ adj : very desirable ▪ *She has an enviable reputation for honesty.* — **en·vi·a·bly** /ˈɛnvijəbli/ adv

en·vi·ous /ˈɛnvijəs/ adj : feeling or showing envy ▪ *They were envious of her success.* — **en·vi·ous·ly** adv

en·vi·ron·ment /ɪnˈvaɪrənmənt/ n 1 [C/U] : the conditions that affect the health, progress, etc., of someone or something ▪ *plants that can survive in harsh environments* ▪ *He grew up in a loving environment.* ▪ *a better business/learning environment* 2 **the environment** : the natural world ▪ *Pollution is bad for the environment.* — **en·vi·ron·men·tal** /ɪnˌvaɪrənˈmɛntl̩/ adj — **en·vi·ron·men·tal·ly** /ɪnˌvaɪrənˈmɛntl̩i/ adv

en·vi·ron·men·tal·ist /ɪnˌvaɪrənˈmɛntl̩ɪst/ n [C] : a person who works to protect the natural world — **en·vi·ron·men·tal·ism** /ɪnˌvaɪrənˈmɛntl̩ɪzm/ n [U]

en·vi·rons /ɪnˈvaɪrənz/ n [plural] : the area that is around a place ▪ *New York City and (its) environs*

en·vis·age /ɪnˈvɪzɪdʒ/ vb **-aged; -ag·ing** [T] : ENVISION

en·vi·sion /ɪnˈvɪʒən/ vb [T] chiefly US : to think of (something that you believe might exist or happen in the future) ▪ *She had envisioned a better life for herself.*

en·voy /ˈɛnˌvɔɪ, ˈɑːnˌvɔɪ/ n [C] : a person who is sent by one government to represent it in dealing with another government ▪ *diplomatic envoys*

¹**en·vy** /ˈɛnvi/ n [U] 1 : the feeling of wanting to have what someone else has ▪ *We watched with envy as he received the award.* ▪ *They were green with envy.* [=they were very envious] 2 : someone or something that causes envy ▪ *She was the envy of all her friends.* [=all her friends envied her]

²**envy** vb **-vies; -vied; -vy·ing** [T] : to feel a desire to have what someone else has ▪ *They envied his success.* = *They envied him for his success.* ▪ *I don't envy you your problems.* [=I'm glad that I don't have your problems]

en·zyme /ˈɛnˌzaɪm/ n [C] technical : a chemical substance in animals and plants that helps to cause natural processes (such as digestion) — **en·zy·mat·ic** /ˌɛnzəˈmætɪk/ adj

eon (US) or chiefly Brit **ae·on** /ˈiːˌɑːn/ n [C] : a very long period of time ▪ *The canyon developed over eons.* ▪ *(informal) How are you? I haven't seen you in eons!*

ephem·era /ɪˈfɛmərə/ n [plural] : things that are important or useful for only a short time ▪ *a collection of old menus and other ephemera*

ephem·er·al /ɪˈfɛmərəl/ adj : lasting a very short time ▪ *His fame was ephemeral.*

¹**ep·ic** /ˈɛpɪk/ n [C] 1 : a long poem that tells the story of a hero's adventures ▪ *Homer's epic "The Odyssey"* 2 : a long book, movie, etc., that tells a story about exciting adventures

²**epic** adj 1 : telling a story about a hero or exciting adventures ▪ *an epic poem/film/novel* 2 : very great or large and usually difficult or impressive ▪ *an epic achievement* = *an achievement of epic proportions* ▪ *an epic struggle for survival*

epi·cen·ter (US) or Brit **epi·cen·tre**

/ˈɛpɪˌsɛntə/ n [C] : the part of the Earth's surface where an earthquake starts

ep·i·cu·re·an /ˌɛpɪkjuˈriːjən, ˌɛpɪˈkjuriːjən/ adj : involving an appreciation of fine food and drink • *epicurean delights*

ep·i·dem·ic /ˌɛpəˈdɛmɪk/ n [C] medical : an occurrence in which a disease spreads very quickly and affects a large number of people • *a flu epidemic* • *(figurative) an epidemic of bankruptcies* — **epidemic** adj • *The violence has reached epidemic proportions.*

epi·du·ral /ˌɛpɪˈdʊrəl, Brit ˌɛpəˈdjuərəl/ n [C] medical : an injection that causes the lower part of the body to become unable to feel pain • *Many women undergoing childbirth are given epidurals.*

ep·i·gram /ˈɛpəˌgræm/ n [C] : a short and clever poem or saying — **ep·i·gram·mat·ic** /ˌɛpəgrəˈmætɪk/ adj

ep·i·lep·sy /ˈɛpəˌlɛpsi/ n [U] medical : a disorder of the nervous system that can cause people to have seizures — **ep·i·lep·tic** /ˌɛpəˈlɛptɪk/ adj • *an epileptic seizure/patient* — **epileptic** n [C] • *providing treatment for epileptics* [=people who have epilepsy]

ep·i·logue /ˈɛpəˌlɑːg/ n [C] : a final section after the main part of a book, play, or musical composition

epiph·a·ny /ɪˈpɪfəni/ n, pl -nies 1 **Epiphany** [singular] : a Christian festival on January 6 in honor of the coming of the three kings to the infant Jesus 2 [C] : a moment in which you suddenly see or understand something in a new or very clear way • *She had an epiphany about the kind of people her parents were.*

epis·co·pal /ɪˈpɪskəpəl/ adj 1 : of or relating to bishops • *an episcopal conference* 2 **Episcopal** : of or relating to the Protestant Episcopal Church • *an Episcopal church*

Epis·co·pa·lian /ɪˌpɪskəˈpeɪljən/ n [C] : a member of the Protestant Episcopal Church • *She is an Episcopalian.* — **Episcopalian** adj • *an Episcopalian church*

ep·i·sode /ˈɛpəˌsoʊd/ n [C] 1 : an event or a short period of time that is important or unusual • *a brief romantic episode* • *a painful episode from my childhood* 2 : a television show, radio show, etc., that is one part of a series • *the show's final episode* 3 : an occurrence of an illness • *a fainting episode* — **ep·i·sod·ic** /ˌɛpəˈsɑːdɪk/ adj, formal • *an episodic story* [=a story about many separate events] • *an episodic illness*

epis·tle /ɪˈpɪsəl/ n [C] formal : LETTER • *a lengthy epistle* — **epis·to·lary** /ɪˈpɪstəˌleri, Brit ɪˈpɪstələri/ adj • *an epistolary novel* [=a novel written in the form of a series of letters]

ep·i·taph /ˈɛpəˌtæf/ n [C] : words written on a gravestone

ep·i·thet /ˈɛpəˌθɛt/ n [C] 1 : a word or phrase that describes a person or thing • *He earned the epithet "Mr. Philanthropy."* 2 : an offensive word or name that is used to insult someone • *racial epithets*

epit·o·me /ɪˈpɪtəmi/ n [C] : a perfect example • *In his tailored suit, he was the*

(very) epitome of style. — **epit·o·mize** also Brit **epit·o·mise** /ɪˈpɪtəˌmaɪz/ vb -**mized**; -**miz·ing** [T] • *He epitomizes laziness.* [=he is the perfect example of laziness]

ep·och /ˈɛpək, Brit ˈiːˌpɒk/ n [C] : a period of time that is very important in history • *The Civil War era was an epoch in U.S. history.* — **ep·och·al** /ˈɛpəkəl, Brit ˈɛˌpɒkəl/ adj

ep·oxy /ɪˈpɑːksi/ n [U] : a type of glue

equa·ble /ˈɛkwəbəl/ adj, formal : tending to remain calm and free from sudden changes • *an equable man/temperament/climate* — **eq·ua·bly** /ˈɛkwəbli/ adv

¹**equal** /ˈiːkwəl/ adj 1 a : the same in number, amount, degree, rank, or quality • *an equal number of apples and oranges* • *issues of equal importance* • *We divided the profits into three equal shares.* • *I lost an amount equal to an entire month's salary.* b : having the same mathematical value — often + *to* • *½ is equal to ¾.* 2 : the same for each person • *equal rights* 3 formal : able to do what is needed • *I think I'm equal to* [=capable of completing] *the task.* — **all/other things being equal** see **THING** — **equal·i·ty** /ɪˈkwɑːləti/ n [U] : *racial/gender equality* — **equal·ly** /ˈiːkwəli/ adv • *sharing the work equally* • *The two projects are equally important.*

²**equal** n [C] : someone or something that is as good, skillful, valuable, etc., as another person or thing • *I consider him my equal.* • *She has no equal at chess.* = *She is without equal at chess.* [=no one plays chess as well as she does]

³**equal** vb, US **equaled** or chiefly Brit **equalled**; US **equal·ing** or chiefly Brit **equal·ling** 1 [linking vb] — used to say that one amount or number is the same as another • *His salary equals mine.* • *Three plus two equals five.* 2 [T] a : to be as good, strong, etc., as (something else) • *Nothing can ever equal that experience.* • *His arrogance is equaled only by his vanity.* [=he is both very arrogant and vain] b : to do something as well as someone else • *See if you can equal that!* • *No one can equal her in chess.*

equal·ize also Brit **equal·ise** /ˈiːkwəˌlaɪz/ vb -**ized**; -**iz·ing** 1 [T/I] : to make (something) equal or the same • *equalizing pay for workers with similar jobs* • *The pressure soon equalized.* 2 [I] Brit : to tie the score in a game (such as soccer) — **equal·i·za·tion** also Brit **equal·i·sa·tion** /ˌiːkwələˈzeɪʃən, Brit ˌiːkwəˌlaɪˈzeɪʃən/ n [U]

equal·iz·er also Brit **equal·is·er** /ˈiːkwəˌlaɪzɚ/ n [C] 1 : something that makes people or things equal • *Education can be the great equalizer.* [=it can give poor people an equal chance] 2 sports : a point, goal, etc., that ties a game • *He scored the equalizer.*

equal sign n [C] : a symbol = used to show that two numbers are equal • *½ = ¾* — called also **equals sign**

equa·nim·i·ty /ˌiːkwəˈnɪməti, ˌɛkwəˈnɪməti/ n [U] formal : calm emotions when dealing with problems or pressure

• *She accepted her misfortunes with equanimity.* [=she did not become upset]

equate /ɪˈkweɪt/ *vb* **equat·ed; equat·ing** [*T*] : to say or think that (two things) are equal or the same • *Don't equate wealth with/and happiness.* — **equate to** [*phrasal vb*] : to be the same as or similar to (something) • *Wealth doesn't equate to happiness.*

equa·tion /ɪˈkweɪʒən/ *n* **1** [*C*] *mathematics* : a statement that two expressions are equal • *Solve this equation: 2x − 3 = 7.* **2** [*C*] : a complicated situation or issue • *Were drugs part of the equation?* [=were drugs involved?] **3** [*U*] : the act of regarding two things as the same • *the equation of wealth with/and happiness*

equa·tor /ɪˈkweɪtə/ *n* — **the equator** : an imaginary circle around the middle of the Earth that is the same distance from the North Pole and the South Pole

equa·to·ri·al /ˌiːkwəˈtorijəl, ˌɛkwəˈtorijəl/ *adj* : located at or near the equator • *equatorial regions/Africa*

eques·tri·an /ɪˈkwestrijən/ *adj* : of or relating to the riding of horses • *equestrian sports* — **equestrian** *n* [*C*] : a talented equestrian [=person who rides horses]

equi·dis·tant /ˌiːkwəˈdɪstənt, ˌɛkwəˈdɪstənt/ *adj* : of equal distance • *Montreal is roughly equidistant from New York and Toronto.*

equi·lat·er·al triangle /ˌiːkwəˈlætərəl-, ˌɛkwəˈlætərəl-/ *n* [*C*] : a triangle in which all three sides are the same length

equi·lib·ri·um /ˌiːkwəˈlɪbrijəm, ˌɛkwəˈlɪbrijəm/ *n* [*U*] **1** : a state in which opposing forces or actions are balanced • *Supply and demand were in equilibrium.* **2** : a state of emotional balance or calmness • *It took me a minute to recover my equilibrium.*

equine /ˈiːˌkwaɪn, ˈɛˌkwaɪn/ *adj* : of or relating to horses • *an equine disease*

equi·nox /ˈiːkwəˌnɑːks, ˈɛkwəˌnɑːks/ *n* [*C*] : a day when day and night are the same length • *She was born March 21 on the spring/vernal equinox.* • *the autumn/autumnal equinox*

equip /ɪˈkwɪp/ *vb* **equipped; equip·ping** [*T*] **1 a** : to provide (someone) with necessary materials or supplies • *Money was needed to train and equip the troops.* **b** : to provide (something) with a particular feature or ability • *All of the buses are equipped with* [=all of the buses have] *air-conditioning.* **2** : to prepare (someone) for a particular activity or problem • *Those students are not equipped for college.*

equip·ment /ɪˈkwɪpmənt/ *n* [*U*] **1** : supplies or tools needed for a special purpose • *sports/stereo/medical equipment* **2** : the act of equipping someone or something • *the equipment of the troops*

eq·ui·ta·ble /ˈɛkwətəbəl/ *adj, formal* : dealing fairly and equally with everyone • *an equitable distribution of funds* — **eq·ui·ta·bly** /ˈɛkwətəbli/ *adv*

eq·ui·ty /ˈɛkwəti/ *n, pl* **-ties** **1** [*U*] *formal* : fairness or justice in the way people are treated • *equity and inequity* **2** *finance* **a** [*U*] : the value of a piece of property after any debts that remain to

be paid for it have been subtracted • *We've been paying off our mortgage and building up equity in our house.* **b** [*C*] : share of a company's stock — usually plural • *money invested in bonds and equities*

equiv·a·lent /ɪˈkwɪvələnt/ *adj* : having the same value, use, meaning, etc. • *Those companies manufacture equivalent products at cheaper prices.* • *two words that are equivalent in meaning* • *Letting him leave prison now would be* **equivalent to** [=would be the same as] *saying that his crime was not serious.* — **equiv·a·lence** /ɪˈkwɪvələns/ *n* [*U*] • *the equivalence of the two products* — **equiv·a·len·cy** /ɪˈkwɪvələnsi/ *n* [*U*] • (*chiefly US*) *He got his high school equivalency certificate.* [=a certificate that is equivalent to a high school degree] — **equivalent** *n* [*C*] • *a Chinese word for which English has no (exact) equivalent* — **equiv·a·lent·ly** *adv* • *equivalently priced products*

equiv·o·cal /ɪˈkwɪvəkəl/ *adj, formal* : having two or more possible meanings : AMBIGUOUS • *equivocal answers/results* — **equiv·o·cal·ly** /ɪˈkwɪvəkli/ *adv*

equiv·o·cate /ɪˈkwɪvəˌkeɪt/ *vb* **-cat·ed; -cat·ing** [*I*] *formal* : to use unclear language especially to deceive someone • *When asked about her tax plan, she didn't equivocate.* — **equiv·o·ca·tion** /ɪˌkwɪvəˈkeɪʃən/ *n* [*C/U*] • *evasions and equivocations*

er /ˈɚ:, ˈɚ: usually with a prolonged vowel/ *interj* — used when you are speaking and you are not sure what to say • *Well, er, I just don't know.*

ER *abbr* emergency room

¹**-er** /ə/ *adj suffix or adv suffix* — used to form the comparative form of many adjectives and adverbs • *faster* • *hotter* • *earlier*

²**-er** /ə/ *also* **-ier** /iə, jə/ *or* **-yer** /jə/ *n suffix* **1 a** : person having a particular job • *jailer* • *lawyer* **b** : person or thing belonging to or associated with something • *prisoner* **c** : native of : resident of • *New Yorker* **2** : person or thing that does or performs a specified action • *reporter* • *player* **3** : person who is • *foreigner* • *Westerner*

era /ˈɛrə, Brit ˈɪərə/ *n* [*C*] : a period of time that is associated with a particular quality, event, person, etc. • *the Victorian era* • *an era of prosperity* • *His death marks the end of an era.*

erad·i·cate /ɪˈrædəˌkeɪt/ *vb* **-cat·ed; -cat·ing** [*T*] *formal* : to destroy or remove (something) completely • *eradicating poverty/diseases* — **erad·i·ca·tion** /ɪˌrædəˈkeɪʃən/ *n* [*U*]

erase /ɪˈreɪs, Brit ɪˈreɪz/ *vb* **erased; erasing** **1** [*T*] : to remove something that has been recorded from a videotape, an audiotape, or a computer disk • *The file was accidentally erased.* • *You can erase the tape/disk and use it again.* **2** *chiefly US* **a** [*T/I*] : to remove (something written) by rubbing • *erase chalk/pencil marks* **b** [*T*] : to remove something written from (a surface) • *erase the blackboard* **3** [*T*] : to remove any thought or memory of (something) • *Time has* *erased the event from her memory.* [=she has completely forgotten the event] — **era·sure** /ɪˈreɪʒɚ, Brit ɪˈreɪʒə/ n [C/U] • *There were many erasures in her essay.*

eras·er /ɪˈreɪsɚ, Brit ɪˈreɪzə/ n [C] chiefly US : a small piece of rubber or other material that is used to erase something you have written or drawn — called also (Brit) **rubber**

ere /ˈeɚ/ prep or conj, literary : BEFORE • *ere long* [=soon]

¹**erect** /ɪˈrɛkt/ adj **1** : straight up and down • *erect trees* • *The soldiers stood erect.* **2** : swollen and stiff because of sexual excitement • *an erect penis* — **erect·ly** adv — **erect·ness** /ɪˈrɛktnəs/ n [U]

²**erect** vb [T] **1** : to build (something) by putting together materials • *They erected a stone wall/statue.* **2** : to set or place (something) so that it stands up • *erect a flagpole*

erec·tion /ɪˈrɛkʃən/ n **1** [C] : the state in which the penis becomes erect • *get/have an erection* **2** [U] : the act or process of building something • *the erection of a new building*

er·go /ˈeɚgoʊ, ˈəɚgoʊ/ adv, formal : THEREFORE • *The products are poorly constructed; ergo, they break easily.*

er·go·nom·ics /ˌəɚgəˈnɑːmɪks/ n [plural] : the parts or qualities of something's design that make it easy to use • *The chair's/car's/office's ergonomics are outstanding.* — **er·go·nom·ic** /ˌəɚgəˈnɑːmɪk/ adj • *ergonomic chairs* — **er·go·nom·i·cal·ly** /ˌəɚgəˈnɑːmɪkli/ adv

er·mine /ˈəɚmən/ n, pl **ermine** or **er·mines 1** [C] US : a small animal that has a long body and fur that turns white in winter **2** [U] : the white fur of an ermine • *an ermine coat*

erode /ɪˈroʊd/ vb **erod·ed; erod·ing** [T/I] : to be gradually destroyed by water, wind, etc. • *The shoreline was badly eroded by the storm.* • (figurative) *Support for the plan has been eroding steadily.* — **ero·sion** /ɪˈroʊʒən/ n [U] • *wind/soil erosion* • (figurative) *the erosion of moral standards* — **ero·sive** /ɪˈroʊsɪv/ adj, technical • *the erosive effect of water*

erog·e·nous /ɪˈrɑːdʒənəs/ adj : producing sexual pleasure when touched • *the body's erogenous zones*

erot·ic /ɪˈrɑːtɪk/ adj : relating to sex • *erotic feelings* : causing sexual feelings • *an erotic dance* — **erot·i·cal·ly** /ɪˈrɑːtɪkli/ adv — **erot·i·cism** /ɪˈrɑːtəˌsɪzəm/ n [U] • *the eroticism of his films*

err /ˈeɚ, ˈəɚ/ vb [I] formal : to make a mistake • *I may have erred in my calculations.* • *It's better to err on the side of generosity.* [=to be too generous so that you can be sure that you are being generous enough] • *We chose to err on the side of caution* [=to be very cautious] *when planning our investments.*

er·rand /ˈeɚənd/ n [C] : a short journey that you take to do or get something • *She had some errands to do before dinner.* • *I have to run some errands.* ◇ A *fool's errand* is an errand that does not need to be done or that cannot be done successfully.

er·rant /ˈeɚənt/ adj **1** always before a noun **a** : behaving wrongly • *an errant cop* [=a cop who has broken the law] **b** US : going outside the proper area • *an errant calf/motorboat* **c** US, sports : not going in the intended direction • *an errant throw* **2** : wandering in search of adventure • *an errant knight*

er·rat·ic /ɪˈrætɪk/ adj : acting, moving, or changing in ways that are not expected • *His behavior seemed erratic.* • *erratic oil prices* — **er·rat·i·cal·ly** /ɪˈrætɪkli/ adv

er·ro·ne·ous /ɪˈroʊnijəs/ adj, formal : not correct • *an erroneous diagnosis/theory* — **er·ro·ne·ous·ly** adv

er·ror /ˈeɚɚ/ n **1** [C/U] : a wrong action or statement : MISTAKE • *I made an error in my calculations.* • *spelling errors* • *It was an error in judgment.* [=a poor decision] • *The accident was caused by human error.* [=a mistake made by a person] • *The judge was in error* [=not correct] *when she made the decision.* • *The decision was made in error.* [=in an incorrect way] • *He acknowledged the error of his ways.* — see also **trial and error** at ¹**TRIAL 2** [C] : a mistake made by a person who is playing a sport (such as baseball or tennis) • *The shortstop was charged with an error.* — **er·ror·less** /ˈeɚələs/ adj

er·satz /ˈeɚˌsɑːts, Brit ˈeɚˌzæts/ adj : ¹FAKE • *an ersatz cowboy*

erst·while /ˈəɚstˌwaɪəl/ adj, always before a noun, formal : FORMER • *erstwhile friends/enemies* [=people who were friends/enemies in the past]

er·u·dite /ˈeɚəˌdaɪt/ adj : having or showing knowledge that is learned by studying • *an erudite professor/essay* — **er·u·di·tion** /ˌeɚəˈdɪʃən/ n [U] • *a professor of great erudition*

erupt /ɪˈrʌpt/ vb [I] **1** : to send out ash, lava, etc., in a sudden explosion • *The volcano began to erupt.*; also : to come out in a sudden explosion — + *from* • *Steam erupted from the geyser.* **2** : to begin suddenly and violently • *Riots/war erupted last summer.* **3** : to begin shouting, applauding, etc., suddenly • *The crowd erupted in applause.* • *The audience erupted into/with laughter.* — **erup·tion** /ɪˈrʌpʃən/ n [C/U] • *a volcanic eruption* • *the/an eruption of violence*

es·ca·late /ˈeskəˌleɪt/ vb **-lat·ed; -lat·ing** [T/I] **1** : to become worse or more severe • *The conflict has escalated into an all-out war.* • *escalating violence* **2** : to become greater or higher • *escalating costs/prices* — **es·ca·la·tion** /ˌeskəˈleɪʃən/ n [C/U]

es·ca·la·tor /ˈeskəˌleɪtɚ/ n [C] : a moving set of stairs that carries people up or down from one floor to another

es·ca·pade /ˈeskəˌpeɪd/ n [C] : an exciting, foolish, or dangerous experience or adventure • *a drunken/sexual escapade*

¹**es·cape** /ɪˈskeɪp/ vb **-caped; -cap·ing 1** [I] **a** : to get free by leaving a place where you are being held • *The prisoner escaped (from jail).* • *an escaped convict* [=a convict who has escaped from prison] **b** : to get away from a dangerous place or situation • *They managed to es-*

cape from the burning building. **2** [T/I] : to get away from something that is difficult or unpleasant ▪ *trying to escape (from) poverty* ▪ *A vacation will give us a chance to escape (from the routine of daily life).* **3** [T/I] : to avoid something ▪ *They escaped (without) injury/punishment.* = *They escaped (without) being injured/punished.* ▪ *escaping death/disaster* ▪ *She narrowly escaped with her life.* [=avoided dying] **4** [T] : to fail to be remembered or noticed by (someone) ▪ *His name escapes me.* [=I can't remember his name] ▪ *Nothing escapes her (notice).* **5** [I] : to come out or leak from somewhere ▪ *Gas is escaping from the tank.* — **there is no escaping** — used to say that something is certainly true, real, etc., and cannot be avoided or denied ▪ *There's no escaping the conclusion that he lied about his involvement.*

²**escape** *n* **1** [C] : an act of escaping from a place, situation, etc. ▪ *The prisoners attempted a daring escape.* **2** [C] : a way of escaping from a place, situation, etc. ▪ *The door was locked; there was no escape.* ▪ *Gardening offered an escape from her busy life.* **3** [C/U] : an occurrence in which an amount of liquid or gas passes out through a hole or crack in a container ▪ *an/the escape of poisonous gases*

es·cap·ee /ɪˌskeɪˈpiː/ *n* [C] : a prisoner who has escaped ▪ *an escapee from the local jail*

escape mechanism *n* [C] : a way of behaving that is used to avoid unpleasant facts or problems ▪ *She uses humor as an escape mechanism.*

es·cap·ism /ɪˈskeɪˌpɪzəm/ *n* [U] : something that allows people to forget about the real problems of life ▪ *Reading novels is for her a form of escapism.* — **es·cap·ist** /ɪˈskeɪpɪst/ *adj* ▪ *escapist fiction*

es·carp·ment /ɪˈskɑːrpmənt/ *n* [C] : a long cliff or steep slope

es·chew /ɛˈʃuː, ɛsˈtʃuː/ *vb* [T] *formal* : to avoid (something) because you do not think it is right, proper, etc. ▪ *They now eschew the violence of their past.*

¹**es·cort** /ˈɛsˌkoɚt/ *n* **1** : a person or group of people who go with someone to give protection or guidance ▪ *a police escort* **2** : a woman or a man who is hired to go with someone to a social event ▪ *an escort agency/service*

²**es·cort** /ɪˈskoɚt/ *vb* [T] : to go with (someone or something) to give protection or guidance ▪ *He escorted me to the door.*

Es·ki·mo /ˈɛskəˌmoʊ/ *n, pl* **Eskimo** or **Es·ki·mos** [C] : a member of a group of people of Alaska, northern Canada, Greenland, and northeastern Siberia ✧ The word *Eskimo* is now considered offensive by some people. — compare INUIT

ESL /ˌiːˌɛsˈɛl/ *n* [U] : the teaching of English in the U.S., Canada, England, etc., to people who speak a different language ✧ *ESL* is an abbreviation of "English as a second language."

esoph·a·gus (*US*) or Brit **oe·soph·a·gus** /ɪˈsɑːfəgəs/ *n, pl* **-a·gi** /-əˌgaɪ/ [C]

medical : the tube that leads from the mouth through the throat to the stomach

es·o·ter·ic /ˌɛsəˈtɛrɪk/ *adj* **1** : only understood by members of a special group ▪ *esoteric knowledge* : hard to understand ▪ *esoteric concepts* **2** : limited to a small number of people ▪ *esoteric religious sects* — **es·o·ter·i·cal·ly** /ˌɛsəˈtɛrɪkli/ *adv*

esp. *abbr* especially

ESP /ˌiːˌɛsˈpiː/ *n* [U] : EXTRASENSORY PERCEPTION

es·pe·cial·ly /ɪˈspɛʃəli/ *adv* **1** : VERY, EXTREMELY ▪ *an especially good meal* ▪ *There is nothing especially radical about that idea.* ▪ *(informal) "Would you like to go?" "No, not especially."* [=I am not interested in going] **2 a** — used to indicate something that deserves special mention ▪ *She had many doubts, especially in the beginning.* **b** : for a particular purpose or person ▪ *I made this pie especially for you.*

es·pi·o·nage /ˈɛspijəˌnɑːʒ/ *n* [U] : the activity of spying ▪ *He was charged with espionage.*

es·pla·nade /ˈɛspləˌnɑːd, Brit ˌɛspləˈneɪd/ *n* [C] : an area for walking or driving along a shore

es·pouse /ɪˈspaʊz/ *vb* **-poused; -pousing** [T] *formal* : to express support for (a cause, belief, etc.) ▪ *a new theory espoused by many physicists* — **es·pous·al** /ɪˈspaʊzəl/ *n* [singular] ▪ *her espousal of socialism* — **es·pous·er** *n* [C] ▪ *an espouser* [=supporter] *of liberal causes*

espres·so /ɛˈsprɛsoʊ/ *n, pl* **-sos** [C/U] : very strong coffee ▪ *an espresso = a cup of espresso*

Esq. *abbr* esquire

es·quire /ˈɛˌskwajɚ, Brit ɪˈskwajə/ *n* [C] — used as a title of courtesy after a name; in writing usually used in its abbreviated form *Esq.* ▪ *John Smith, Esq.* ✧ In U.S. English, *Esq.* is used in writing after the name of an attorney. ▪ *Sara Jones, Esq.*

¹**es·say** /ˈɛˌseɪ/ *n* [C] : a short piece of writing that tells a person's thoughts or opinions about a subject ▪ *Write a 500-word essay on/about the poem.* — **es·say·ist** /ˈɛˌsejɪst/ *n* [C] ▪ *a skillful essayist*

²**es·say** /ɛˈseɪ/ *vb* [T] *formal* : to try to do, perform, or deal with (something) ▪ *He at first essayed a career as a writer.*

es·sence /ˈɛsn̩s/ *n* **1** [singular] : the quality or qualities that make a thing what it is ▪ *The painting captures the essence of the story.* ▪ *Competition is the (very) essence of capitalism.* **2** [U] : a substance that contains in very strong form the taste, smell, etc., of the thing from which it is taken ▪ *essence of peppermint/lemon* — **in essence** : at the most basic level ▪ *She was in essence* [=basically] *an honest person.* — **of the essence** : of the greatest importance ▪ *Time/speed is of the essence.*

¹**es·sen·tial** /ɪˈsɛnʃəl/ *adj* **1** : extremely important and necessary ▪ *For a fighter pilot, good vision is essential.* ▪ *Food is essential for life.* ▪ *It's essential to arrive on time.* = *It's essential that we arrive on time.* **2** : very basic : FUNDAMENTAL ▪ *The es-*

sential problem with this plan is that it will cost too much. — **es·sen·tial·ly** /ɪ-'sɛnʃəli/ adv ▪ What he says is essentially true.

²**essential** n [C] : something that is basic or necessary — usually plural ▪ the essentials for success

-**est** /əst, ɪst/ adj suffix or adv suffix — used to form the superlative of many adjectives and adverbs ▪ sweetest ▪ fattest ▪ luckiest

es·tab·lish /ɪ'stæblɪʃ/ vb [T] **1 a** : to cause (someone or something) to be widely known and accepted ▪ The company has established itself as a leader in the industry. ▪ a well-established principle **b** : to put (someone or something) in a position, role, etc., that will last for a long time ▪ As a young doctor he worked hard to establish himself in the community. ▪ an established lawyer/artist **2 a** : to begin or create (something that is meant to last for a long time) ▪ The city/school was established in 1814. **b** : to succeed in making or creating (something) ▪ He never established a close relationship with his son. ▪ establish realistic goals **3 a** : to show that (something) is true or real ▪ He had to establish his innocence. ▪ establishing a link between diet and cancer **b** : to find out (something) ▪ I couldn't establish why it happened.

es·tab·lish·ment /ɪ'stæblɪʃmənt/ n **1** [C] : a place or organization where people live or do business ▪ a business establishment **2** [U] : the act of establishing something or someone ▪ the establishment of a school/town ▪ the establishment of a scientific fact **3 a** or **Establishment** [singular] often disapproving : the people in business, government, etc., who have power over the other people in a society ▪ a former hippie who became a member of the **Establishment b the establishment** : the part of a particular group that has power or control ▪ the medical/literary establishment

es·tate /ɪ'steɪt/ n [C] **1 a** : all of the things that a person owns ▪ His estate is worth millions of dollars. **b** : the things left by someone who has died ▪ He inherited the estate from his parents. **2** : a large piece of land with a large house on it ▪ a country estate **3** Brit : a group of buildings that were built for a particular purpose (such as housing or industry) on an area of land ▪ a council estate **4** Brit : ESTATE CAR, STATION WAGON

estate agent n [C] Brit : REAL ESTATE AGENT

estate car n [C] Brit : STATION WAGON

¹**es·teem** /ɪ'stiːm/ n [U] formal **1** : respect and affection ▪ Please accept this gift as a token of my esteem. **2** — used to say how much someone or something is admired and respected ▪ They hold him in high esteem. [=they respect and admire him]

²**esteem** vb [T] formal : to think very highly or favorably of (someone or something) ▪ an actress who is (highly) esteemed by her peers

esthetic variant spelling of AESTHETIC

es·ti·ma·ble /'ɛstəməbəl/ adj, formal : deserving respect ▪ We owe thanks to our estimable colleague.

¹**es·ti·mate** /'ɛstəmət/ n **1** [C] : a guess that you make based on the information you have about the size, amount, etc., of something ▪ One conservative estimate is that he stole five million dollars. ▪ a rough estimate **2** [C] : a statement about how much a job will cost ▪ The contractor's estimate for the job seemed high. **3** [U, singular] : an opinion or judgment about how good or bad something is ▪ He has a high estimate of his own abilities.

²**es·ti·mate** /'ɛstəˌmeɪt/ vb -**mat·ed**; -**mat·ing** [T] : to give or form a general idea about the value, size, or cost of (something) ▪ estimating distance/cost ▪ Damage from the storm is estimated (to be) in the billions of dollars. ▪ An estimated 50,000 people attended. — **es·ti·ma·tor** /'ɛstəˌmeɪtɚ/ n [C]

es·ti·ma·tion /ˌɛstə'meɪʃən/ n **1** [singular] formal : a judgment or opinion about something ▪ This is not, in my estimation, a good use of our resources. **2 a** [U] : the act of estimating something ▪ By his own estimation he had failed six times. **b** [C] : a guess about the size, amount, cost, etc., of something ▪ My estimation was wrong.

es·trange /ɪ'streɪndʒ/ vb -**tranged**; -**trang·ing** [T] formal **1** : to cause (someone) to be no longer friendly or close to another person or group ▪ They are estranged from their children. ▪ her estranged husband [=her husband who no longer lives with her] **2** : to cause (someone) to be no longer involved or connected with something ▪ He felt estranged from his past life. — **es·trange·ment** /ɪ'streɪndʒmənt/ n [U]

es·tro·gen (US) or Brit **oes·tro·gen** /'ɛstrədʒən, Brit 'iːstrədʒən/ n [U] medical : a hormone that occurs naturally in women

es·tu·ary /'ɛstʃəˌweri, Brit 'ɛstʃuəri/ n, pl -**ar·ies** [C] : an area where a river flows into the sea

ETA abbr estimated time of arrival ▪ The flight's ETA is 5:00 p.m. [=the flight is expected to arrive at around 5:00 p.m.]

et al. /ˌɛt'ɑːl, ˌɛt'æl/ abbr and others ▪ a paper written by Jones, Smith, et al.

etc. abbr et cetera

et cet·era /ɛt'sɛtərə/ : and other things of the same kind — usually written as etc. ▪ They said we were fat, stupid, lazy, etc.

etch /'ɛtʃ/ vb [T] : to cut a pattern, design, etc., on something by using an acid ▪ a set of etched wine glasses ▪ (figurative) That trip is etched in her memory. [=she will never forget it] — **etch·er** n [C]

etch·ing /'ɛtʃɪŋ/ n [C] : a picture made by putting ink on an etched piece of metal and then pressing paper against the metal

eter·nal /ɪ'tɚnl/ adj **1** : having no beginning and no end in time : lasting forever ▪ eternal life/damnation/bliss **2** : always true or valid ▪ eternal truths/wisdom **3**

: seeming to last forever • *Stop your eternal whining.* — **eter·nal·ly** *adv* • *I will be eternally grateful.*

eter·ni·ty /ɪˈtɚnəti/ *n* 1 [U] : time without an end • *I'll love him for all eternity.* [=I'll love him forever] 2 [U] : a state that comes after death and never ends • *They believe sinners spend eternity in hell.* 3 [*singular*] : time that seems to be without an end • *I waited (for) an eternity for my car to be fixed.*

-eth see -TH

eth·a·nol /ˈɛθəˌnɑːl/ *n* [U] *technical* : ALCOHOL 1 • *a mixture of ethanol and gasoline*

ether /ˈiːθɚ/ *n* [U] 1 : a liquid that was used in the past to prevent patients from feeling pain during operations 2 : the air or sky — used especially when describing electronic signals that travel through the air • *broadcasting radio signals into the ether*

ethe·re·al /ɪˈθirijəl/ *adj, formal* 1 : in heaven or seeming to come from heaven • *ethereal heights/music* 2 : very delicate • *an ethereal ballet dancer* • *ethereal poetry* — **ethe·re·al·ly** *adv*

Ether·net /ˈiːθɚˌnɛt/ *n* [U] *technical* : a system of wires and devices for connecting computers so that they can work together

eth·ic /ˈɛθɪk/ *n* 1 [C] : rules of behavior based on ideas about what is morally good and bad — usually plural • *legal/medical ethics* • *His ethics are questionable.* [=some of the things he does may be morally wrong] 2 *ethics* [U] : a branch of philosophy dealing with what is morally right or wrong 3 [C] : a belief that something is very important — usually singular • *a strong work ethic* [=a strong belief in the importance and value of work]

eth·i·cal /ˈɛθɪkəl/ *adj* 1 : involving questions of right and wrong behavior • *ethical principles/standards* 2 : morally right and good • *the ethical treatment of animals* — **eth·i·cal·ly** /ˈɛθɪkli/ *adv* • *behaving ethically* [=in a way that is right and good]

eth·nic /ˈɛθnɪk/ *adj* 1 : of or relating to races or large groups of people who have the same customs, religion, origin, etc. • *ethnic groups made up of immigrants or their descendants* • *ethnic violence* [=violence between different ethnic groups] 2 : associated with a particular group of people who have a culture that is different from the main culture of a country • *I love ethnic food/restaurants.* — **eth·ni·cal·ly** /ˈɛθnɪkli/ *adv* — **eth·nic·i·ty** /ɛθˈnɪsəti/ *n, pl* **-ties** [C/U] • *people of different ethnicities* [=people who belong to different ethnic groups]

ethos /ˈiːˌθɑːs/ *n* [*singular*] *formal* : the guiding beliefs of a person, group, or organization • *the company's business ethos*

et·i·quette /ˈɛtɪkət/ *n* [U] : the rules indicating the proper and polite way to behave • *telephone etiquette* [=the proper way to behave when speaking on the telephone]

-ette *n suffix* 1 : little one • *kitchenette* 2 : female • *majorette*

et·y·mol·o·gy /ˌɛtəˈmɑːlədʒi/ *n, pl* **-gies** 1 [C] : the history of a word • *According to its etymology, "dope" comes from the Dutch word "doop" (which means "sauce").* 2 [U] : the study of word histories • *an expert in etymology* — **et·y·mo·log·i·cal** /ˌɛtəˌməˈlɑːdʒɪkəl/ *adj* — **et·y·mol·o·gist** /ˌɛtəˈmɑːlədʒɪst/ *n* [C]

EU *abbr* European Union

eu·ca·lyp·tus /ˌjuːkəˈlɪptəs/ *n, pl* **-tus·es** *also* **-ti** /-ˌtaɪ/ [C] : a type of tree from western Australia

Eu·cha·rist /ˈjuːkərəst/ *n* — **the Eucharist** : COMMUNION 1 • *celebrate the Eucharist* — **Eu·cha·ris·tic** /ˌjuːkəˈrɪstɪk/ *adj*

eu·lo·gy /ˈjuːlədʒi/ *n, pl* **-gies** [C] : a speech that praises someone who has died • *He delivered a moving eulogy at his father's funeral.* — **eu·lo·gize** *also Brit* **eu·lo·gise** /ˈjuːləˌdʒaɪz/ *vb* **-gized; -gizing** [T] • *She was eulogized at her funeral as a great actress.*

eu·nuch /ˈjuːnək/ *n* [C] : a man who has had his sexual organs removed

eu·phe·mism /ˈjuːfəˌmɪzəm/ *n* [C] : a mild or pleasant word or phrase that is used instead of one that is unpleasant or offensive • *using "eliminate" as a euphemism for "kill"* — **eu·phe·mis·tic** /ˌjuːfəˈmɪstɪk/ *adj* — **eu·phe·mis·ti·cal·ly** /ˌjuːfəˈmɪstɪkli/ *adv*

eu·pho·ria /juˈforijə/ *n* [U] : a feeling of great happiness and excitement • *the euphoria following their victory* — **eu·phor·ic** /juˈforɪk/ *adj* — **eu·phor·i·cal·ly** /juˈforɪkli/ *adv*

Eur·asian /jʊˈreɪʒən/ *adj* 1 : of or relating to both Europe and Asia • *a Eurasian empire/species* 2 : having ancestors from both Europe and Asia • *a Eurasian child* — **Eurasian** *n* [C]

eu·re·ka /jʊˈriːkə/ *interj* — used to express excitement when a discovery has been made • *Eureka! I have found it!*

eu·ro /ˈjʊroʊ/ *n, pl* **-ros** *also* **-ro** [C] : a monetary unit used by countries of the European Union

Euro- *or* **Eur-** *combining form* : Europe : European : European and • *Euro-American relations*

Eu·ro·pe·an /ˌjʊrəˈpiːjən/ *n* [C] 1 : a person born, raised, or living in Europe 2 : a person who is descended from Europeans — **European** *adj* • *European history*

eu·tha·na·sia /ˌjuːθəˈneɪʒə/ *n* [U] : the act or practice of killing someone who is very sick or injured in order to prevent any more suffering

evac·u·ate /ɪˈvækjəˌweɪt/ *vb* **-at·ed; -at·ing** 1 [T] : to remove (someone) from a dangerous place • *People are being evacuated as the hurricane approaches.* 2 [T/I] : to leave (a dangerous place) • *Residents were ordered to evacuate (the building).* 3 [T] *medical* : to pass (solid waste) from your body • *evacuate your bowels* — **evac·u·a·tion** /ɪˌvækjəˈweɪʃən/ *n* [C]

evac·u·ee /ɪˌvækjəˈwiː/ *n* [C] : a person who has been evacuated from a dangerous place • *Fifty evacuees spent the night at the school.*

evade /ɪˈveɪd/ *vb* **evad·ed; evad·ing** [T]

1 a : to stay away from (someone or something) ▪ *The criminals have evaded the police.* ▪ *They have evaded arrest.* [=have avoided being arrested] **b** : to avoid dealing with or facing (something) ▪ *evading difficult questions* **c** : to avoid doing (something required) ▪ *evading taxes* [=failing to pay taxes] **2** : to not be understood by (someone) ▪ *Their purpose evades me.* [=I don't understand their purpose] — **evad·er** *n* [C] ▪ *tax evaders*

eval·u·ate /ɪˈvæljəˌweɪt/ *vb* **-at·ed; -at·ing** [T] : to judge the value or condition of (someone or something) in a careful and thoughtful way ▪ *We need to evaluate our options.* ▪ *evaluate a job candidate* — **eval·u·a·tion** /ɪˌvæljəˈweɪʃən/ *n* [C/U] ▪ *a psychiatric evaluation* ▪ *The program underwent careful evaluation.* — **eval·u·a·tive** /ɪˈvæljəˌweɪtɪv, Brit ɪˈvæljuətɪv/ *adj, formal* — **eval·u·a·tor** /ɪˈvæljəˌweɪtɚ/ *n* [C]

ev·a·nes·cent /ˌɛvəˈnɛsn̩t/ *adj, literary* : lasting a very short time ▪ *evanescent fame* — **ev·a·nes·cence** /ˌɛvəˈnɛsn̩s/ *n* [U]

evan·gel·i·cal /ˌiːˌvænˈdʒɛlɪkəl/ *adj* **1** : of or relating to some Christian groups that stress the authority of the Bible and the preaching of their beliefs to other people ▪ *evangelical Christians* **2** : having or showing very strong and enthusiastic feelings ▪ *He spoke about the project with evangelical zeal.* — **evangelical** or **Evangelical** *n* [C] ▪ *She is an Evangelical.* — **evan·gel·i·cal·ly** /ˌiːˌvænˈdʒɛlɪkli/ *adv*

evan·ge·list /ɪˈvændʒəlɪst/ *n* [C] **1** : a person who tries to convince people to become Christian **2** : someone who talks about something with great enthusiasm ▪ *an evangelist of space exploration* — **evan·ge·lism** /ɪˈvændʒəlɪzəm/ *n* [U] ▪ *television evangelism* — **evan·ge·lis·tic** /ɪˌvændʒəˈlɪstɪk/ *adj*

evan·ge·lize *also Brit* **evan·ge·lise** /ɪˈvændʒəˌlaɪz/ *vb* **-lized; -liz·ing** [T/I] : to try to convert (a group or area) to a different religion (especially Christianity) ▪ *The missionaries set out to evangelize the world.* ▪ (*figurative*) *They were evangelizing about the importance of saving energy.*

evap·o·rate /ɪˈvæpəˌreɪt/ *vb* **-rat·ed; -rat·ing 1** [T/I] : to change from a liquid into a gas ▪ *All the water evaporated.* **2** [I] : to disappear or vanish ▪ *The opportunity evaporated before we could act on it.* — **evap·o·ra·tion** /ɪˌvæpəˈreɪʃən/ *n* [U]

evaporated milk *n* [U] : canned milk from which most of the water has been removed

eva·sion /ɪˈveɪʒən/ *n* **1 a** [U] : the act of avoiding something that you do not want to do or deal with : the act of evading something ▪ *tax evasion* **b** [C] : a way of avoiding something ▪ *an illegal evasion of the law* **2** [C] : a statement or action that avoids directly dealing with something (such as a difficult question) ▪ *His reply was just an evasion.*

eva·sive /ɪˈveɪsɪv/ *adj* **1** : not honest or direct ▪ *an evasive answer* **2** : done to

avoid harm, an accident, etc. ▪ *an evasive maneuver* — **eva·sive·ly** *adv* — **eva·sive·ness** *n* [U]

eve /ˈiːv/ *n* [C] **1** *literary* : EVENING **2** : the evening or the day before a special day — usually singular ▪ *New Year's Eve* **3** : the period of time just before an important event ▪ *on the eve of their graduation*

¹**even** /ˈiːvən/ *adj* **1 a** : having a flat, smooth, or level surface ▪ *even ground* **b** : not having breaks or bumps ▪ *an even coastline* **2** : located next to someone or something else ▪ *The two runners were even with each other as they neared the finish.* **3** : not changing ▪ *a calm, even voice* ▪ *maintaining an even speed* **4 a** : equal and fair ▪ *an even trade* **b** : having nothing owed by either side ▪ *Here's the money I owe you. Now we're even.* **c** : not likely to be won easily by one side or another ▪ *an even match* **5 a** : able to be divided by two into two equal whole numbers ▪ *4, 6, and 8 are even numbers.* **b** : marked by an even number ▪ *even and odd pages* **c** *always before a noun* : not more or less than a stated amount ▪ *an even dozen* **6** — used to say that something is as likely to happen as to not happen ▪ *Our chances are about even.* — **break even** *see* ¹BREAK — **get even** : to do something bad to someone who has treated you badly ▪ *He vowed to get even (with them).* — **on an even keel** *see* ¹KEEL — **even·ly** *adv* ▪ *evenly divided/matched/applied* — **even·ness** /ˈiːvənnəs/ *n* [U]

²**even** *adv* **1** — used to stress something that is surprising or unlikely ▪ *Even a child can do it.* ▪ *We showed her proof, but even then, she wouldn't admit she was wrong.* ▪ *He is making plans even as we speak.* [=he is making plans right now] **2** — used to stress the difference between two things ▪ *His first book was good, but this one is even better.* **3** — used after a negative word (such as *not*) to stress the smallness of an amount or effort ▪ *They didn't even offer to help!* **4** — used to stress something that is worse, more specific, etc., than what has just been mentioned ▪ *The disease can cause blindness and even death.* — **even if** — used to stress that something will happen despite something else that might prevent it ▪ *I'm going to the party even if it rains.* — **even so** : NEVERTHELESS ▪ *"We don't like each other." "Even so, you must work together."* — **even though** — used as a stronger way to say "though" or "although" ▪ *I'm going even though it may rain.*

³**even** *vb* [T] : to make (something) equal ▪ *We evened the score in the first quarter.* — **even out** [*phrasal vb*] **even out** *or* **even out (something)** *out* *or* **even out (something) 1** : to make (something) even and smooth ▪ *Even out the rug.* **2** : to reach a middle state between extremes ▪ *Any variations will be evened out eventually.*

even·hand·ed /ˌiːvənˈhændəd/ *adj* : FAIR ▪ *an evenhanded assessment* — **even·hand·ed·ly** *adv* — **even·hand·ed·ness** *n* [U]

¹eve·ning /'iːvnɪŋ/ n [C] 1 : the last part of the day and early part of the night ▪ *We're going out this evening.* ▪ *Have a nice evening.* ▪ *an evening meal/walk* 2 : an event or activity that happens during an evening ▪ *an evening at the theater*

²evening present participle of ³EVEN

evening gown n [C] : a long, formal dress that is worn to evening parties or events — called also *evening dress*

eve·nings /'iːvnɪŋz/ adv, US : in the evening ▪ *He works evenings.*

event /ɪ'vɛnt/ n [C] 1 a : something (especially something important or notable) that happens ▪ *the (big/major) events of the past year* b : a planned occasion or activity ▪ *an upcoming sporting/social event* c — used to talk about a possible occurrence ▪ *In the event of rain* [=if it rains], *the party will be held indoors.* ▪ *The insurance will cover you in the (unlikely) event (that) you are injured.* [=if you are injured] 2 : any one of the contests in a sports program ▪ *track-and-field events* — **in any event** — used to say that something is true no matter what other things may or may not happen or be true ▪ *It's strange, in any event, that their decision bothers you so much.* — **in the event** *Brit* : when something that was planned or thought about actually happened ▪ *We thought we'd miss the bus, but, in the event, the bus was late, too.*

even–tempered adj : not easily upset or made angry ▪ *an even-tempered girl*

event·ful /ɪ'vɛntfəl/ adj : having many important things happening ▪ *an eventful day/life* — **event·ful·ly** adv — **eventful·ness** n [U]

even·tu·al /ɪ'vɛntʃəwəl/ adj : coming or happening at a later time ▪ *She lost to the eventual champion.* [=the person who would later become champion]

even·tu·al·i·ty /ɪˌvɛntʃəˈwæləti/ n, pl -ties [C] formal : something that might happen ▪ *ready for any eventuality*

even·tu·al·ly /ɪ'vɛntʃəwəli, ɪ'vɛntʃəli/ adv : at some later time ▪ *We'll win eventually.*

ev·er /'ɛvə/ adv 1 : at any time ▪ *Have you ever been to France?* ▪ *We need help now more than ever (before).* ▪ *That was the worst movie I ever saw.* ▪ *Don't ever do that again!* 2 formal : at all times ▪ *ever faithful* ▪ *The princess married the prince, and they all lived happily ever after.* [=they were happy from that time forward] 3 : to a greater degree ▪ *drawing ever closer* 4 — used to make a question more forceful ▪ *Where ever did I put my keys?* ▪ *"I can't do that." "Why ever not?"* 5 US, informal — used to give stress to what follows ▪ *Am I ever tired!* [=I am very tired] — **as ever** : as usual ▪ *The problem, as ever, is how to control spending.* — **ever since** 1 : continually or often from a past time until now ▪ *We met in college and have been together ever since.* 2 : continually from the time in the past when ▪ *She's wanted to be a chef ever since she was a child.* — **ever so** : VERY ▪ *Thank you ever so much.* — **ever such** chiefly Brit, informal — used as a more forceful way to say "such" ▪

He's ever such a nice person! — **for ever (and ever)** : FOREVER ▪ *I'll love you for ever and ever!* — **hardly/scarcely ever** : almost never ▪ *She hardly ever sings anymore.* — **never ever** informal — used as a more forceful way to say "never" ▪ *I promise to never ever do it again.* — **rarely/seldom ever** : almost never ▪ *She rarely ever drinks wine.* — **rarely/seldom if ever** — used as a more forceful way to say "rarely" or "seldom" ▪ *She rarely if ever sings anymore.* — **Yours ever or Ever yours** Brit — used as a way to end an informal letter ▪ *Yours ever, Robert*

ev·er·green /'ɛvəˌgriːn/ adj : having leaves that remain green all year long ▪ *evergreen trees/forests/leaves* — **evergreen** n [C]

ev·er·last·ing /ˌɛvəˈlæstɪŋ, Brit ˌɛvəˈlɑːstɪŋ/ adj : lasting forever ▪ *everlasting love* = *love everlasting* — **ev·er·last·ing·ly** adv

ev·ery /'ɛvri/ adj 1 : including each person or thing in a group or series ▪ *I heard every word you said.* ▪ *He took every last one* [=all] *of them.* ▪ *They question every little thing* [=everything] *she says.* ▪ *I'll support you every step of the way.* [=throughout the entire process] ▪ *Every time I go there I learn something new.* ▪ *We're making every effort* [=we're doing all that we can] *to solve the problem.* 2 a — used to describe how often a repeated activity, event, etc., happens or is done ▪ *She visits every few days.* ▪ *The fair is held every other/second year.* [=it is held one year, not held the next year, held the following year, and so on] b — used to describe how far apart things in a series are placed from each other ▪ *There's a post every 20 yards or so.* c — used in phrases to describe how common something is ▪ *problems that affect one in every two/three people* ▪ *I have every* [=complete, total] *confidence in you.* — **at every turn** see ²TURN — **every bit** see ¹BIT — **every man for himself** see ¹MAN — **every now and then/again or every once in a while or every so often** : sometimes but not often ▪ *We still see her every now and then.* — **every which way** US, informal 1 : in every direction ▪ *Bullets were flying every which way.* 2 : in a disorderly manner ▪ *books stacked every which way*

ev·ery·body /'ɛvriˌbɑdi, 'ɛvriˌbɑːdi, Brit 'ɛvriˌbɒdi/ pron 1 : EVERYONE 2 : every important person ▪ *Everybody will be there.*

ev·ery·day /'ɛvriˌdeɪ/ adj, always before a noun : used or seen every day ▪ *everyday clothes/objects* ▪ *everyday life*

ev·ery·one /'ɛvriˌwʌn/ pron : every person ▪ *Everyone agreed.*

ev·ery·place /'ɛvriˌpleɪs/ adv, US : EVERYWHERE

ev·ery·thing /'ɛvriˌθɪŋ/ pron 1 a : every thing there is ▪ *I agree with everything he said.* b : all that is related to a particular subject ▪ *Tell us everything that happened.* ◆ The phrase **everything from (something) to (something)** is used to show the wide range of things that are included in something. ▪ *They sell every-*

thing from golf tees to diapers. **2** : all that is important ▪ *She means everything to me.* **3** *informal* : the things that are happening in a person's life ▪ *Everything is fine.* ❖ Phrases like *How's everything?* and *How's everything going?* are used as informal ways to say "How are you?" — **and everything** : and other things like that ▪ *He's very busy, what with school and everything.*

ev·ery·where /ˈɛvriˌweɚ/ *adv* : in or to every place ▪ *Everywhere we went, people were friendly.* ▪ *People came from everywhere.* [=from many places]

evict /ɪˈvɪkt/ *vb* [*T*] : to force (someone) to leave a place ▪ *She was evicted from her apartment.* — **evic·tion** /ɪˈvɪkʃən/ *n* [*C/U*]

¹**ev·i·dence** /ˈɛvədəns/ *n* [*U*] **1** : something which shows that something else exists or is true ▪ *He found no evidence to support the theory.* **2** : material that is presented to a court of law to help find the truth about something ▪ *circumstantial evidence* ▪ *Anything you say may be used as/in evidence against you.* ▪ *They gave evidence* [=testified] *at the trial.* — **in evidence** : easily seen ▪ *Her charm is very much in evidence.*

²**evidence** *vb* **-denced; -denc·ing** [*T*] *formal* : to offer or show evidence of (something) ▪ *People once lived here,* **as (is) evidenced by** [=as is clearly shown by] *these remains.*

ev·i·dent /ˈɛvədənt/ *adj* : OBVIOUS ▪ *The problem has been evident for some time.*

ev·i·dent·ly /ˈɛvədəntli, ˌɛvəˈdɛntli/ *adv* **1** : in a way that can be easily seen or noticed ▪ *He was evidently angry.* **2** — used to describe something that appears to be true based on what is known ▪ *Evidently no one saw us.*

¹**evil** /ˈiːvəl/ *adj* **1** : morally bad ▪ *evil deeds/spirits* **2 a** : causing harm or injury ▪ *an evil curse* **b** : very unpleasant or offensive ▪ *an evil smell/temper* — **evil·ly** *adv* — **evil·ness** *n* [*U*]

²**evil** *n* **1** [*U*] : the force of things that are morally bad ▪ *the battle of good versus evil* **2** [*C*] : something that is harmful or bad ▪ *the evils of alcohol* ▪ *choosing the* **lesser of two evils** [=the better choice between two unpleasant choices] ▪ *Taxes are a* **necessary evil.** [=a bad or unwanted thing that has to be accepted to achieve some good result]

evil·do·er /ˌiːvəlˈduːwɚ/ *n* [*C*] : a person who does bad or evil things

evil eye *n* — **the evil eye** : a look that is thought to be able to harm someone ▪ *He gave her the evil eye.*

evil-mind·ed /ˌiːvəlˈmaɪndəd/ *adj* : thinking evil thoughts ▪ *an evil-minded villain*

evince /ɪˈvɪns/ *vb* **evinced; evinc·ing** [*T*] *formal* : to show (something) clearly ▪ *She evinced an early interest in art.*

evis·cer·ate /ɪˈvɪsəˌreɪt/ *vb* **-at·ed; -at·ing** [*T*] *formal* : to cause (someone or something) to lose power or effectiveness ▪ *The amendment eviscerated the law.*

evoke /ɪˈvoʊk/ *vb* **evoked; evok·ing** [*T*] **1** : to bring (a memory, feeling, image,

etc.) into the mind ▪ *The old house evoked memories of his childhood.* **2** : to cause (a particular reaction or response) to happen ▪ *Her remarks evoked an angry response.* — **evo·ca·tion** /ˌiːvoʊˈkeɪʃən/ *n* [*C/U*] ▪ *the evocation of a simpler time* — **evoc·a·tive** /ɪˈvɑːkətɪv/ *adj* ▪ *an evocative biography*

ev·o·lu·tion /ˌɛvəˈluːʃən/ *n* [*U*] **1** *biology* **a** : a theory that the differences between modern and ancient plants and animals are because of natural changes that happened over a very long time ▪ *the theory of evolution* **b** : the process by which changes in plants and animals happen over time ▪ *changes brought about by evolution* **2** : a process of slow change and development ▪ *the evolution of computers* — **ev·o·lu·tion·ary** /ˌɛvəˈluːʃəˌneri/ *adj* — **ev·o·lu·tion·ist** /ˌɛvəˈluːʃənɪst/ *n* [*C*]

evolve /ɪˈvɑːlv/ *vb* **evolved; evolv·ing** [*T/I*] : to change or develop slowly often into a more advanced state ▪ *Did birds evolve from dinosaurs? = Did some dinosaurs evolve into birds?* ▪ *Her hobby has evolved into a business.*

ewe /ˈjuː/ *n* [*C*] : a female sheep

ex /ˈɛks/ *n* [*C*] *informal* : a former husband, wife, boyfriend, or girlfriend ▪ *I saw my ex at the mall yesterday.*

ex- /ɛks/ *prefix* : former ▪ *ex-husband*

ex·ac·er·bate /ɪgˈzæsɚˌbeɪt/ *vb* **-bat·ed; -bat·ing** [*T*] : to make (a bad situation, a problem, etc.) worse ▪ *Running exacerbated his knee problems.* — **ex·ac·er·ba·tion** /ɪgˌzæsɚˈbeɪʃən/ *n* [*U*]

¹**exact** /ɪgˈzækt/ *adj* **1** : fully and completely correct or accurate ▪ *an exact copy* ▪ *his exact words* ▪ *The exact cause of the fire is unknown.* ▪ *He is the* **exact opposite** *of his father.* [=is completely different from his father] **2** : very careful and accurate ▪ *exact measurements* ▪ **exact same** *or US* **same exact** — used as a more forceful way to say "same" ▪ *They showed up in the same exact outfits.* — **to be exact** — used to indicate that a statement is accurate and specific ▪ *They had many children—nine, to be exact.* — **exact·ness** *n* [*U*]

²**exact** *vb* [*T*] *formal* **1** : to demand and get (something) especially by using force or threats ▪ *exact payment/revenge* **2** — used to say that something has caused a lot of suffering, loss, etc. ▪ *The war exacted a terrible toll.* ▪ *mistakes that exact a heavy price*

ex·act·ing /ɪgˈzæktɪŋ/ *adj* : very difficult or demanding ▪ *an exacting teacher/task/standard* — **ex·act·ing·ly** *adv*

ex·ac·ti·tude /ɪgˈzæktəˌtuːd, Brit ɪgˈzæktəˌtjuːd/ *n* [*U*] *formal* : the quality or state of being exact ▪ *recalling an event with exactitude*

ex·act·ly /ɪgˈzæktli/ *adv* **1** — used to stress that something is accurate, complete, or correct ▪ *They are exactly the same size.* ▪ *When exactly did they leave?* **2** *informal* — used in speech to say that you agree completely with what someone has said ▪ *"It's not worth the trouble." "Exactly."* **3** : in a way that agrees completely with what is needed ▪ *Do exactly* as you're told. **4** : in every way ▪ *That was exactly the wrong thing to do.* — **not exactly** *informal* **1** — used in speech to indicate that what someone has said is not completely correct ▪ *"He's your boss, isn't he?" "Not exactly."* **2** — used as a humorous or ironic way to say "not" ▪ *He's not exactly the smartest guy I've ever met.* [=he is not very smart]

ex·ag·ger·ate /ɪgˈzædʒəˌreɪt/ *vb* **-at·ed; -at·ing** [*T/I*] **1** : to think of or describe something as larger or greater than it really is ▪ *She exaggerated the importance of the discovery.* **2** [*T*] : to make (something) larger or greater than normal ▪ *exaggerated movements/gestures* — **ex·ag·ger·a·tion** /ɪgˌzædʒəˈreɪʃən/ *n* [*C/U*] — **ex·ag·ger·a·tor** /ɪgˈzædʒəˌreɪtə/ *n* [*C*]

ex·alt /ɪgˈzɑːlt/ *vb* [*T*] **1** *formal* : to raise (someone or something) to a higher level ▪ *He attained an exalted rank.* **2 a** *formal* : to praise (someone or something) highly ▪ *The essay exalts the country's beauty.* **b** : to present (something) in a very favorable way ▪ *The film exalts military power.*

ex·al·ta·tion /ˌɛgˌzɑːlˈteɪʃən/ *n* [*U*] *formal* **1** : the act of raising someone or something in importance ▪ *the exaltation of athletic skill* **2** : a strong sense of happiness, power, or importance ▪ *joy and exaltation*

ex·am /ɪgˈzæm/ *n* [*C*] **1** *US* : EXAMINATION 1b ▪ *an eye exam* **2** : EXAMINATION 2 ▪ *taking a final exam*

ex·am·i·na·tion /ɪgˌzæməˈneɪʃən/ *n* **1 a** [*C/U*] : the act of looking at something closely and carefully ▪ *the careful examination of evidence* ▪ *On closer/further examination, the painting appears to be a fake.* **b** [*C*] : a close study of a person or animal to find signs of illness or injury ▪ *a medical/eye/psychiatric examination* ▪ *an examination table* [=a table on which a patient lies to be examined] **2** [*C*] : a test to show a person's progress, knowledge, or ability ▪ *an examination in/on history* ▪ *I took an examination.* = (Brit) *I did/sat an examination.* ▪ *an entrance examination* [=a test to see if someone should be admitted to a school] **3** [*U*] *law* : the act of questioning a witness in a court of law ▪ *the examination of witnesses*

ex·am·ine /ɪgˈzæmən/ *vb* **-ined; -in·ing** [*T*] **1** : to look at (something) closely in order to learn more about it, to find problems, etc. ▪ *The police examined the evidence carefully.* **2** : to test or look carefully at (something or someone) for signs of illness or injury ▪ *She had her eyes examined.* ▪ *the examining room* [=a room in a doctor's office where the doctor examines patients] **3** *law* : to question (someone) closely ▪ *examine a witness* — **ex·am·in·er** *n* [*C*]

ex·am·ple /ɪgˈzæmpəl/ *n* **1** [*C/U*] : a person or way of behaving that is seen as a model that should be followed ▪ *We try to follow his example.* [=try to do as he does] ▪ *to set an example* [=to behave in a way that shows other people how to behave] ▪ *She leads by example.* [=leads by setting an example] ▪ *The judge decided*

to **make an example of him.** [=to punish him for doing something wrong as a way of warning other people not to do the same thing] **2** [*C*] **a** : someone or something that is mentioned to help explain what you are saying or to show that a statement is true ▪ *She gave/offered several examples to show that the program is effective.* **b** : something or someone chosen from a group in order to show what the whole group is like ▪ *an example of the artist's work* **3** [*C*] **a** : a phrase or sentence that shows how a word is used ▪ *a dictionary with lots of examples* **b** : something that is used to teach how a rule or process works ▪ *arithmetic examples* — **for example** — used when you are mentioning a specific person or thing that helps to explain what you are saying or to show that a general statement is true ▪ *A lot of my friends were there—John and Linda, for example.* [=for instance]

ex·as·per·ate /ɪgˈzæspəˌreɪt, Brit ɪgˈzɑːspəreɪt/ *vb* **-at·ed; -at·ing** [*T*] : to make (someone) very angry or annoyed ▪ *We were exasperated by the delays.* ▪ *Her behavior was exasperating.* — **ex·as·per·at·ing·ly** *adv* — **ex·as·per·a·tion** /ɪgˌzæspəˈreɪʃən, Brit ɪgˌzɑːspəˈreɪʃən/ *n* [*U*]

ex·ca·vate /ˈɛkskəˌveɪt/ *vb* **-vat·ed; -vat·ing** [*T*] **1** : to uncover (something) by removing the earth that covers it ▪ *excavating an ancient city* **2 a** : to form (something) by digging ▪ *excavate a hole/tunnel* **b** : to dig out and remove (dirt, soil, etc.) ▪ *The dirt was carefully excavated.* — **ex·ca·va·tion** /ˌɛkskəˈveɪʃən/ *n* [*C/U*]

ex·ca·va·tor /ˈɛkskəˌveɪtə/ *n* [*C*] **1** : a person who digs up things that have been buried for a long time **2** : STEAM SHOVEL

ex·ceed /ɪkˈsiːd/ *vb* [*T*] **1** : to be greater or more than (something) ▪ *The cost must not exceed 10 dollars.* : to be better than (something) ▪ *The show exceeded our expectations.* **2** : to go beyond the limit of (something) ▪ *The court exceeded its authority.*

ex·ceed·ing·ly /ɪkˈsiːdɪŋli/ *adv, formal* : EXTREMELY ▪ *an exceedingly fine job*

ex·cel /ɪkˈsɛl/ *vb* **-celled; -cel·ling** [*T/I*] : to be better than others ▪ *She excels at/in sports.* ▪ *She excels everyone else in sports.*

ex·cel·lence /ˈɛksələns/ *n* [*U*] : extremely high quality. ▪ *academic excellence*

Ex·cel·len·cy /ˈɛksələnsi/ *n, pl* **-cies** — used as a title for some high government and church officials ▪ *Yes, your Excellency.*

ex·cel·lent /ˈɛksələnt/ *adj* : very good ▪ *Dinner was excellent.* ▪ *The car is in excellent condition.* ▪ *"We're making a profit!" "(That's) Excellent!"* — **ex·cel·lent·ly** *adv*

¹**ex·cept** /ɪkˈsɛpt/ *also* **ex·cept·ing** /ɪkˈsɛptɪŋ/ *prep* : not including (or something) ▪ *The stores will be open daily except Sundays.* ▪ *Everyone was invited except (for) me.*

²**except** *conj* **1** — used to indicate the

only person or thing that is not included in or referred to by a previous statement ▪ *She didn't leave the house, except to go to church.* [=she only left the house to go to church] ▪ *He does nothing except complain.* [=all he does is complain] **2** — used to introduce a statement that explains the reason why something is not possible, will not happen, etc. ▪ *We'd go, except (that) it's too far.*

³**except** *vb* [T] *formal* : to leave out (someone or something) ▪ *I don't like lawyers—* *present company* *excepted!* [=I don't like lawyers, but I make an exception in your case]

ex·cep·tion /ɪkˈsɛpʃən/ *n* [C] **1** : someone or something that is different from others ▪ *I like all his books, with one exception.* [=I like all but one of his books] ▪ *It rains every day, and yesterday was no* *exception.* ▪ *Without exception, his books have been widely read and admired.* ▪ *Everyone should be there, with the exception of* [=*except for*] *my brother.* **2** : a case where a rule does not apply ▪ *We'll* *make an exception* [=allow the rule not to be followed] *this time.* — **take exception** : to feel or express disagreement with something ▪ *I take exception to* [=I am offended by] *the tone of her remarks.*

ex·cep·tion·al /ɪkˈsɛpʃənl/ *adj* **1** : not usual ▪ *an exceptional amount of rain* **2** : unusually good ▪ *exceptional students* **3** : mentally or physically disabled ▪ *a school for exceptional children* — **ex·cep·tion·al·ly** *adv* ▪ *exceptionally good*

ex·cerpt /ˈɛkˌsəpt, ˈɛgˌzəpt/ *n* [C] : a small part of a longer written work ▪ *an excerpt from the play*

ex·cess /ɪkˈsɛs, ˈɛkˌsɛs/ *n* **1** [U, singular] : an amount that is more than the usual or necessary amount ▪ *an excess of caution* ▪ *Eating anything in* *excess* [=in overly large amounts] *can be bad for you.* ▪ *speeds in* *excess* *of* [=more or greater than] *100 mph* ▪ *He often eats/drinks to* *excess.* [=more than is usual, normal, or proper] **2** [U, plural] : behavior that goes beyond what is usual, normal, or proper ▪ *a life of excess* ▪ *the violent excesses of the regime* — **excess** *adj* ▪ *excess baggage/energy* — **ex·ces·sive** /ɪkˈsɛsɪv/ *adj* ▪ *excessive sweating* ▪ *drinking excessive amounts of alcohol* — **ex·ces·sive·ly** *adv*

¹**ex·change** /ɪksˈtʃeɪndʒ/ *n* **1** [C/U] : an occurrence in which people give things of similar value to each other ▪ *the/an exchange of goods* ▪ *If I give you this, what will you give me in* *exchange?* [=what thing of similar value will you give to me?] ▪ *She bought me dinner in* *exchange* *for* [=as a way of paying me for] *my help.* **2** [C] **a** : an occurrence in which people direct something at each other ▪ *an exchange of insults/gunfire* **b** : an occurrence in which people give information to each other ▪ *an exchange of ideas* **3** [C] : a short and often angry conversation ▪ *a bitter/heated exchange* **4** [C] **a** : a place where things or services are traded ▪ *a book exchange* **b** : an office or building in which telephone calls are connected ▪ *a telephone exchange*

²**exchange** *vb* **-changed; -chang·ing** [T] **1** : to give something and receive something in return ▪ *We exchange gifts at the holidays.* **2** : to direct (words, looks, etc.) at each other ▪ *They exchanged glances/greetings/insults.* ▪ *They exchanged blows.* [=they hit each other] **3** : to return (a product) to a store and have it replaced by another product ▪ *exchange a sweater for a smaller one* — **exchange·able** /ɪksˈtʃeɪndʒəbəl/ *adj*

exchange rate *n* [C] : a number used to calculate the difference in value between money from two different countries — called also *rate of exchange*

exchange student *n* [C] : a student from one country who attends a school in another country

Ex·che·quer /ˈɛksˌtʃɛkɚ, ɪksˈtʃɛkɚ/ *n* [singular] : the treasury department of the British government ▪ *He was the* **Chancellor of the Exchequer.**

¹**ex·cise** /ˈɛkˌsaɪz/ *n* [C] : a tax on certain things that are made, sold, or used within a country — called also *excise tax*

²**ex·cise** /ɪkˈsaɪz/ *vb* **-cised; -cis·ing** [T] *formal* : to remove (something) by cutting it out ▪ *The passage was excised from the book.* — **ex·ci·sion** /ɪkˈsɪʒən/ *n* [C/U] ▪ *the excision of a tumor*

ex·cit·able /ɪkˈsaɪtəbəl/ *adj* : easily excited ▪ *an excitable dog/child*

ex·cite /ɪkˈsaɪt/ *vb* **-cit·ed; -cit·ing** [T] **1** : to make (someone) feel energetic and eager to do something ▪ *ideas that excite young people* **2** : to cause (a particular emotion or reaction) to be felt or to happen ▪ *excite anger/suspicion* **3** : to increase the activity of (something) ▪ *a chemical that excites nerve cells* — **exciting** *adj* ▪ *an exciting trip/book* — **ex·cit·ing·ly** *adv*

excited *adj* : very enthusiastic and eager about something ▪ *They were excited about/over the trip.* — **ex·cit·ed·ly** *adv* ▪ *He talked excitedly about visiting his old friends.*

ex·cite·ment /ɪkˈsaɪtmənt/ *n* **1** [U] : a feeling of eager enthusiasm and interest ▪ *Our excitement was building.* ▪ *She cried out in excitement.* **2 a** [C/U] : exciting activity ▪ *a trip filled with excitement and adventure* ▪ *the excitements of the day* **b** [singular] : a quality that causes feelings of eager enthusiasm ▪ *The job has lost its excitement.*

ex·claim /ɪkˈskleɪm/ *vb* **1** [T] : to say (something) in an enthusiastic or forceful way ▪ *"I won!" she exclaimed.* **2** [I] : to cry out or speak suddenly or with strong feeling ▪ *She exclaimed in delight.*

ex·cla·ma·tion /ˌɛkskləˈmeɪʃən/ *n* [C] : a sharp or sudden cry ▪ *an exclamation of surprise/pain/delight*

exclamation point *n* [C] *US* : a punctuation mark ! used to show a forceful way of speaking or a strong feeling ▪ *(figurative) ending his career with an exclamation point* [=in a very exciting way] — called also *(chiefly Brit)* exclamation mark

ex·clude /ɪkˈskluːd/ *vb* **-clud·ed; -clud·ing** [T] **1 a** : to prevent (someone) from doing something or being a part of a group • *Until 1920, women were excluded from voting in the U.S.* **b** : to not include (something) • *Prices exclude tax.* **2** : to think that (something) is not worth attention • *We can't exclude the possibility.* — **ex·clu·sion** /ɪkˈskluːʒən/ n [C/U]

excluding *prep* : not including (someone or something) • *The store is open all week, excluding Sundays.*

¹**ex·clu·sive** /ɪkˈskluːsɪv/ *adj* **1** : available to only one person or group • *The company has exclusive rights to (use) the logo.* • *an exclusive interview* **2 a** : only allowing in people from a high social class • *an exclusive club/party* **b** : available to only a few people because of high cost • *exclusive neighborhoods* — **exclusive of** *formal* : not including (something) • *a sale on all merchandise exclusive of jewelry* — **ex·clu·sive·ly** *adv* • *Our customers are almost exclusively [=all] male.* — **ex·clu·sive·ness** n [U] — **ex·clu·siv·i·ty** /ˌɛkˌskluːˈsɪvəti/ n [U] • *a symbol of wealth and exclusivity*

²**exclusive** *n* [C] : a news story that appears in only one newspaper or that is broadcast by only one TV or radio station

ex·com·mu·ni·cate /ˌɛkskəˈmjuːnəˌkeɪt/ *vb* **-cat·ed; -cat·ing** [T] : to not allow (someone) to continue being a member of the Roman Catholic church • *a priest who was excommunicated (from the church)* — **ex·com·mu·ni·ca·tion** /ˌɛkskəˌmjuːnəˈkeɪʃən/ n [C/U]

ex·co·ri·ate /ɛkˈskoriˌeɪt/ *vb* **-at·ed; -at·ing** [T] *formal* : to criticize (someone or something) very harshly • *He was excoriated as a racist.* — **ex·co·ri·a·tion** /ɛkˌskoriˈeɪʃən/ n [C/U]

ex·cre·ment /ˈɛkskrəmənt/ n [U] *formal* : solid waste passed out of the body : FECES

ex·crete /ɪkˈskriːt/ *vb* **-cret·ed; -cret·ing** [T] *formal* : to pass (waste matter) from the body • *excrete sweat/toxins* — **ex·cre·tion** /ɪkˈskriːʃən/ n [C/U] • *bodily excretions*

ex·cru·ci·at·ing /ɪkˈskruːʃiˌeɪtɪŋ/ *adj* **1** : very painful • *an excruciating headache* **2 a** : very severe • *excruciating shyness* **b** : extreme or excessive • *They described their day in excruciating detail.* — **ex·cru·ci·at·ing·ly** *adv*

ex·cur·sion /ɪkˈskɜːʒən/ n [C] : a short trip especially for pleasure • *a fishing excursion* • *(figurative)* *a brief excursion into politics*

¹**ex·cuse** /ɪkˈskjuːz/ *vb* **-cused; -cus·ing** [T] **1** : to forgive someone for making a mistake, doing something wrong, etc. • *Please excuse (me for) my clumsiness.* **2 a** : to say that (someone) is not required to do something • *I was excused from jury duty.* **b** : to allow (someone) to leave • *May I (please) be excused?* • *Please excuse yourself* [=say politely that you have to leave] *before leaving the table.* **3** : to be an acceptable reason for (something) : JUSTIFY • *Nothing can excuse her rudeness.* — **excuse me** ✧ *Excuse me* is a polite way of starting to say something. It can be used when you are interrupting someone, trying to get someone's attention, or disagreeing with someone. • *Excuse me, may I borrow your pen?* It is also used as a polite apology for a minor fault or offense, such as laughing, coughing, or burping, and, in U.S. English, for getting in someone's way or bumping into someone. • *Oh, excuse me. I didn't notice you there.* The phrase is also used to ask someone to repeat something. • *Excuse me? What did you say?* In informal use, *excuse me* is often used in an annoyed way when someone has suggested that you have done something wrong and you do not feel that you have. • *"You're late." "Well, excuse me! I had to fix a flat tire."* — **ex·cus·able** /ɪkˈskjuːzəbəl/ *adj* • *an excusable error*

²**ex·cuse** /ɪkˈskjuːs/ n [C] **1** : a reason that you give to explain a mistake, bad behavior, etc. • *Stop making excuses for him.* • *a lame/flimsy excuse* **2** : something that explains improper behavior and makes it acceptable • *There is no excuse for child abuse.* **3** : a reason for doing something • *a good excuse to have a party* **4** : a bad example • *He's a poor/sad/sorry excuse for a father.* [=he's a bad father]

ex·di·rec·to·ry /ˌɛksdəˈrɛktəri, *Brit* ˌɛksdaɪˈrɛktri/ *adj, Brit, of a telephone number* : UNLISTED

ex·e·cute /ˈɛksɪˌkjuːt/ *vb* **-cut·ed; -cut·ing** [T] **1** : to kill (someone) especially as punishment for a crime • *He was executed for murder.* **2 a** : to do (something that you have planned to do or been told to do) • *a carefully executed plan* **b** : to do or perform (an action that requires skill) • *The pilot executed an emergency landing.* **3** *law* : to do what is required by (a legal document or command) • *execute a decree/will* **4** : to make or produce (a work of art) • *a statue executed in bronze* — **ex·e·cu·tion** /ˌɛksɪˈkjuːʃən/ n [C/U] • *a prisoner awaiting execution* • *skillful execution of the dance steps* • *the execution of a will*

ex·e·cu·tion·er /ˌɛksɪˈkjuːʃənə/ n [C] : a person who executes people who have been sentenced to death

¹**ex·ec·u·tive** /ɪɡˈzɛkjətɪv/ n [C] : a person who manages or directs other people in a company or organization • *a sales executive*

²**executive** *adj, always before a noun* **1 a** : relating to the job of managing or directing other people in a company or organization • *executive positions/skills* **b** : of, relating to, or used by the people who manage or direct a company or organization • *executive offices* **2** : responsible for making sure laws are carried out and for managing the affairs of a nation • *In the U.S., the President is the head of the executive branch of government.*

executive order n [C] : an order that comes from the U.S. President or a government agency and must be obeyed like a law

ex·ec·u·tor /ɪɡˈzɛkjətə/ n [C] : someone who is named in a will as the person who will make sure that the will is properly followed

ex·em·pla·ry /ɪɡˈzɛmpləri/ *adj* **1** : extremely good and deserving to be admired and copied • *an exemplary citizen/ school* **2** *formal* : serving as an example of something • *a style exemplary of modernism*

ex·em·pli·fy /ɪgˈzɛmpləˌfaɪ/ *vb* **-fies; -fied; -fy·ing** [*T*] : to be a very good example of (something) • *works of art that exemplify the period* — **ex·em·pli·fi·ca·tion** /ɪgˌzɛmpləfəˈkeɪʃən/ *n* [*C/U*]

¹**ex·empt** /ɪgˈzɛmpt/ *adj* : not required to do something that others are required to do • *He was exempt from military service.*

²**exempt** *vb* [*T*] : to say that (someone or something) does not have to do something that others are required to do : to make (someone or something) exempt • *She was exempted from taking the test.*

ex·emp·tion /ɪgˈzɛmpʃən/ *n* **1** [*C/U*] : freedom from being required to do something that others are required to do • *They were granted (an) exemption from military service.* **2** [*C*] : a source or amount of income that is not taxed • *claiming tax exemptions for your dependents*

¹**ex·er·cise** /ˈɛksɚˌsaɪz/ *n* **1** [*C/U*] : physical activity that is done in order to become stronger and healthier • *You need to get more exercise.* • *knee exercises* **2** [*C*] : something that is done or practiced to develop a particular skill • *grammar exercises* **3** [*C*] : an activity that has a specified quality or result • *The negotiations were an exercise in futility.* [=they were not successful or worthwhile] **4** [*plural*] **a** *chiefly US* : a ceremony for students who have graduated from a school • *graduation/commencement exercises* **b** : military activities done for training • *naval exercises* **5** [*U*] : the use of an ability or power that you have • *the exercise of authority*

²**exercise** *vb* **-cised; -cis·ing 1** [*I*] : to do physical activities in order to make yourself stronger and healthier • *She eats right and exercises.* **2** [*T*] : to use (a body part) to make it stronger • *exercise a muscle* **b** : to cause (an animal) to walk, run, etc. • *They exercise the horses every day.* **3** [*T*] : to use (an ability, power, etc.) • *Exercise caution when using these chemicals.*

ex·ert /ɪgˈzɚt/ *vb* [*T*] **1.** : to use (strength, ability, etc.) • *exerting all of her authority/ strength* **2** : to cause (force, effort, etc.) to have an effect • *exerting influence/pressure on others* • *the force exerted by a machine* — **exert yourself** : to make an effort to do something • *Don't exert yourself too much.* — **ex·er·tion** /ɪgˈzɚʃən/ *n* [*C/U*] • *physical/mental exertion*

ex·hale /eksˈheɪl/ *vb* **-haled; -hal·ing** [*T/I*] : to breathe out • *He exhaled a sigh.* • *Exhale slowly.* — **ex·ha·la·tion** /ˌɛkshəˈleɪʃən/ *n* [*C/U*]

¹**ex·haust** /ɪgˈzɑːst/ *vb* [*T*] : to use all of someone's mental or physical energy • *Working so much will exhaust you.* • *Swimming exhausts me.* • *The hike was exhausting.* • *She was exhausted after the test.* **2 a** : to completely use up (something, such as supplies or money) • *They exhausted their savings.* **b** : to try all of

(something) • *They've exhausted (all) the possibilities.* **3** : to consider or talk about (something) thoroughly or completely • *We exhausted the subject/topic and went on to another one.* — **ex·haust·ing·ly** *adv*

²**exhaust** *n* **1** [*U*] : the gases produced by an engine • *exhaust fumes* **2** [*C*] : a pipe or system of pipes through which exhaust is released • *There's a problem with the car's exhaust.* — called also *exhaust pipe*

ex·haus·tion /ɪgˈzɑːstʃən/ *n* [*U*] **1** : the state of being extremely tired • *working to the point of exhaustion* **2** : the act of using all of something • *the exhaustion of our reserves*

ex·haus·tive /ɪgˈzɑːstɪv/ *adj* : very thorough • *an exhaustive study/search* — **ex·haus·tive·ly** *adv*

¹**ex·hib·it** /ɪgˈzɪbət/ *vb* [*T*] **1** : to make (something) available for people to see • *exhibiting artwork/trophies* **2** : to show or reveal (something) • *She exhibited no fear.* — **ex·hib·i·tor** /ɪgˈzɪbətɚ/ *n* [*C*]

²**exhibit** *n* [*C*] **1 a** : an object or a collection of objects that have been put out in a public space for people to look at • *The show includes some interesting exhibits.* **b** *chiefly US* : EXHIBITION 2a • *a photography exhibit* **2** : an object that is used as evidence in a court of law • *introduced the guns into evidence as exhibits A and B* • (*figurative*) *Small businesses have been hurt, and I offer my own company as exhibit A.* [=as evidence or proof] — **on exhibit** : being publicly shown in an exhibition • *The painting is on exhibit at a museum.*

ex·hi·bi·tion /ˌɛksəˈbɪʃən/ *n* **1** [*singular*] : an act of showing some quality or trait • *an exhibition of courage* **2 a** [*C*] : an event at which objects are put out in a public space for people to look at • *art/ science exhibitions* **b** [*U*] : the act of showing something in public • *the exhibition of paintings* • *The collection is now on exhibition.* [=being shown in an exhibition] **3** [*C*] : a public display of athletic skill • *a fencing exhibition*

ex·hi·bi·tion·ism /ˌɛksəˈbɪʃəˌnɪzəm/ *n* [*U*] *disapproving* : behavior that is meant to attract attention to yourself • *shameless exhibitionism* — **ex·hi·bi·tion·ist** /ˌɛksəˈbɪʃənɪst/ *n* [*C*] — **exhibitionist** *or* **ex·hi·bi·tion·ist·ic** /ˌɛksəˌbɪʃəˈnɪstɪk/ *adj*

ex·hil·a·rate /ɪgˈzɪləˌreɪt/ *vb* **-rat·ed; -rat·ing** [*T*] : to cause (someone) to feel very happy and excited • *We were exhilarated by the news.* • *exhilarating news* — **ex·hil·a·ra·tion** /ɪgˌzɪləˈreɪʃən/ *n* [*U*]

ex·hort /ɪgˈzoɚt/ *vb* [*T*] *formal* : to strongly urge (someone) *to do* something • *She exhorted them to support the ban.* — **ex·hor·ta·tion** /ˌɛkˌsoɚˈteɪʃən/ *n* [*C/U*]

ex·hume /ɪgˈzuːm, *Brit* ɪgˈzjuːm/ *vb* **-humed; -hum·ing** [*T*] *formal* : to remove (a body) from the place where it is buried • *The body was exhumed.* — **ex·hu·ma·tion** /ˌɛkshjuˈmeɪʃən/ *n* [*C/U*]

¹**ex·ile** /ˈɛgˌzajəl, ˈɛkˌsajəl/ *n* **1** [*U*] : a situation in which you are forced to leave your home and live in a foreign country •

He was forced into temporary exile. • *(figurative) She went into political exile after the election.* **2** [C] : a person who is in exile • *They were living as exiles.*

²**exile** *vb* **-iled; -il·ing** [T] : to force (someone) to go to live in a distant place or foreign country • *an exiled leader/writer*

ex·ist /ɪgˈzɪst/ *vb* [I] **1** : to be real • *Do ghosts really exist? • The Internet didn't exist then.* **2** : to continue to be or to live • *We cannot exist without oxygen.* • *ignore existing problems*

ex·is·tence /ɪgˈzɪstəns/ *n* **1** [U] : the state of existing • *the existence of God/ghosts • before the country had come into existence* [=begun to exist] • *The company has gone out of existence.* [=it no longer exists] **2** [C] : a particular way of living • *a comfortable/meager existence*

¹**exit** /ˈɛgzət, ˈɛksət/ *n* [C] **1** : a door, hall, etc., that is used as a way out of a place • *an emergency exit • The sign says "No Exit."* **2 a** : the act of going out or away from something • *She made a quick/graceful exit.* [=she left quickly/gracefully] **b** : the act of leaving a situation, competition, etc. • *the company's exit strategy* [=its plan for ending its involvement] **3** : a special road by which vehicles leave a highway • *exit ramps*

²**exit** *vb* **1** [T/I] : to leave a place or situation • *Exit (the building) through the back door.* **2** [T] : to cause (a computer program) to stop when you have finished using it • *Save your work and exit the program.*

ex·o·dus /ˈɛksədəs/ *n* [C] : a situation in which many people leave a place at the same time • *a mass exodus of refugees*

ex·on·er·ate /ɪgˈzɑːnəˌreɪt/ *vb* **-at·ed; -at·ing** [T] *formal* : to prove that someone is not guilty of a crime or responsible for a problem, bad situation, etc. • *The new evidence exonerates the defendant.* — **ex·on·er·a·tion** /ɪgˌzɑːnəˈreɪʃən/ *n* [U]

ex·or·bi·tant /ɪgˈzoəbətənt/ *adj* : too high, expensive, etc. • *exorbitant fees/prices* — **ex·or·bi·tant·ly** *adv*

ex·or·cise *also* **ex·or·cize** /ˈɛksəˌsaɪz/ *vb* **-cised** *also* **-cized; -cis·ing** *also* **-ciz·ing** [T] : to force (an evil spirit) to leave • *exorcise demons* • *(figurative) exorcising bad memories* — **ex·or·cism** /ˈɛksəˌsɪzəm/ *n* [C/U] — **ex·or·cist** /ˈɛksəˌsɪst/ *n* [C]

ex·ot·ic /ɪgˈzɑːtɪk/ *adj* **1** : very different, strange, or unusual • *exotic flavors/locations* **2** of a plant or animal : not living or growing naturally in a particular area • *exotic wildlife* — **ex·ot·i·cal·ly** /ɪgˈzɑːtɪkli/ *adv* — **ex·ot·i·cism** /ɪgˈzɑːtəˌsɪzəm/ *n* [U]

ex·pand /ɪkˈspænd/ *vb* **1 a** [I] : to become bigger • *Water expands when it is heated.* • *His business is expanding.* **b** [T] : to make (something) bigger • *There are plans to expand the school.* • *expand your knowledge* **2** [T] : to write (something) in full form • *Expand the abbreviation "deg." to "degree."* — **expand on/up·on** [phrasal vb] : to speak or write about (something) in a more complete or de-

tailed way • *She expanded on her earlier statement.* — **ex·pand·able** /ɪkˈspændəbəl/ *adj*

ex·panse /ɪkˈspæns/ *n* [C] : a large and usually flat open space or area • *the vast expanse of the ocean* • *an expanse of desert*

ex·pan·sion /ɪkˈspænʃən/ *n* **1** [U] : the act of becoming bigger or of making something bigger • *economic/territorial expansion* **2** [C] : a more complete and detailed written work or set of comments based on something shorter • *an expansion on her earlier statement*

ex·pan·sion·ism /ɪkˈspænʃəˌnɪzəm/ *n* [U] : the belief that a country should increase its territory — **ex·pan·sion·ist** /ɪkˈspænʃənɪst/ *adj* • *expansionist policies* — **expansionist** *n* [C]

ex·pan·sive /ɪkˈspænsɪv/ *adj* **1** *formal* : talking a lot • *She was in an expansive mood.* **2 a** : including many things • *The law is expansive in its scope.* **b** : covering a large space or area • *an expansive room/view* **3** : growing quickly or steadily • *an expansive economy* — **ex·pan·sive·ly** *adv*

ex·pat /ˈɛksˌpæt/ *n* [C] *informal* : EXPATRIATE

ex·pa·tri·ate /ɛkˈspeɪtriˌət, Brit ɛkˈspætriət/ *n* [C] : a person who lives in a foreign country • *American expatriates living in Paris*

ex·pect /ɪkˈspɛkt/ *vb* **1** [T] : to think that something will probably or certainly happen • *We expect (that) he will do well.* = *We expect him to do well.* • *Prices are expected to rise.* **2** [T] : to think that (someone or something) will arrive or that (something) will happen • *I'm expecting a phone call.* • *It's expected to rain today.* **3** [T] : to consider (something) to be reasonable, required, or necessary • *I expected more from/of you.* • *We expect to be paid on time.* • *We expect you to pay your debts.* **4** [T/I] : to be pregnant • *She's expecting (twins).* : to be due to give birth soon • *She's expecting next month.* **5** [T] *informal* : to suppose or think — usually used after *I* • *She feels the same way, I expect.* — **ex·pect·able** /ɪkˈspɛktəbəl/ *adj*

ex·pect·an·cy /ɪkˈspɛktənsi/ *n* [U] : a feeling that something is going to happen • *We were all in a state of (nervous) expectancy.* — see also LIFE EXPECTANCY

ex·pect·ant /ɪkˈspɛktənt/ *adj* **1** : feeling or thinking that something will happen • *an expectant crowd* **2** *always before a noun* : expecting the birth of a child • *expectant mothers* — **ex·pect·ant·ly** *adv*

ex·pec·ta·tion /ˌɛkˌspɛkˈteɪʃən/ *n* **1** [C/U] : a belief that something will happen or is likely to happen • *Their expectation was that the plan would succeed.* • *They have every expectation of success.* [=they believe they will succeed] **2** [C] : a feeling or belief about how successful, good, etc., someone or something will be — usually plural • *He couldn't live up to their expectations.* [=do as well as they expected him to do] • *The company failed to match/meet expectations.* = *It fell short of expectations.* [=it failed to be as successful as people thought it would be] ▪ *The restaurant has **exceeded** expectations*. [=it is more successful than people thought it would be]

ex·pe·di·ent /ɪkˈspiːdijənt/ *adj, often disapproving* : providing an easy and quick way to solve a problem or do something ▪ *a politically expedient solution* — **ex·pe·di·ence** /ɪkˈspiːdijəns/ *or* **ex·pe·di·en·cy** /ɪkˈspiːdijənsi/ *n* [*U*] — **expedient** *n* [*C*] ▪ *a simple expedient* [=an easy and quick way to do something] — **ex·pe·di·ent·ly** *adv*

ex·pe·dite /ˈɛkspəˌdaɪt/ *vb* **-dit·ed; -dit·ing** [*T*] *formal* : to cause (something) to happen faster ▪ *He asked the judge to expedite the lawsuits.*

ex·pe·di·tion /ˌɛkspəˈdɪʃən/ *n* [*C*] **1** : a journey especially by a group of people for a specific purpose (such as to explore a distant place or to do research) ▪ *a mountain-climbing expedition* **2** : a group of people on an expedition ▪ *The expedition discovered an ancient burial site.*

ex·pe·di·tion·ary /ˌɛkspəˈdɪʃəˌneri, *Brit* ˌɛkspəˈdɪʃənri/ *adj* : sent to fight in a foreign country ▪ *an expeditionary force*

ex·pe·di·tious /ˌɛkspəˈdɪʃəs/ *adj, formal* : acting or done in a quick and efficient way ▪ *an expeditious resolution* — **ex·pe·di·tious·ly** *adv*

ex·pel /ɪkˈspɛl/ *vb* **-pelled; -pel·ling** [*T*] **1** : to officially force (someone) to leave a place or organization ▪ *She was expelled from school.* **2** : to push or force (something) out ▪ *expel air from the lungs*

ex·pend /ɪkˈspɛnd/ *vb* [*T*] *formal* **1** : to use or spend (something) ▪ *expend funds/calories* **2** : to use (time, energy, effort, etc.) for a particular purpose ▪ *Can we expend the resources required to solve the problem?*

ex·pend·able /ɪkˈspɛndəbəl/ *adj* : easily replaced ▪ *employees whose jobs are considered expendable*

ex·pen·di·ture /ɪkˈspɛndɪtʃɚ/ *n, formal* **1** [*C/U*] **a** : an amount of money that is spent on something ▪ *an increase in military expenditure(s)* **b** : an amount of time, energy, effort, etc., that is used to do something ▪ *vast expenditures of time* **2 a** [*U*] : the act of spending money ▪ *the expenditure of funds* **b** [*C/U*] : the act of using something for a particular purpose ▪ *(a) greater expenditure of effort/time*

ex·pense /ɪkˈspɛns/ *n* **1** [*U*] : the amount of money that is needed to pay for or buy something ▪ *Is it worth the added expense? ▪ The repairs were made at **no expense** to us.* [=without costing us anything] ▪ *They built the house and **spared no expense**.* [=spent as much money as they needed to make the house as good as possible] ▪ *Why **go to the expense of** [=pay for] installing something that you'll never use?* **2** [*C*] : an amount of money that must be spent especially regularly to pay for something ▪ *legal/medical/household expenses ▪ an **all-expenses paid** trip* [=a trip for which all costs are already paid] **3** [*C*] : something on which money is spent ▪ *a business expense* [=something you need to buy in order to do

business] — **at someone's expense** **1** : paid for by someone ▪ *a stadium built at the taxpayers' expense* [=with money from taxes] **2** ✧ If someone makes a joke about you or laughs at you, the joke or laughter is said to be **at your expense**. ▪ *Everyone had a good laugh **at my expense**.* — **at the expense of** : in a way that harms (something or someone) ▪ *She acquired power at the expense of friendships.*

ex·pen·sive /ɪkˈspɛnsɪv/ *adj* : costing a lot of money ▪ *an expensive car/hobby/store* — **ex·pen·sive·ly** *adv*

¹**ex·pe·ri·ence** /ɪkˈspirijəns/ *n* **1** [*U*] **a** : skill or knowledge that you get by doing something ▪ *I know that from personal experience.* ▪ *I have little experience (dealing) with children.* **b** : the length of time that you have spent doing something ▪ *She has five years' experience as a nurse.* **2** [*C*] : something that you have done or seen or that has happened to you ▪ *frightening/memorable experiences*

²**experience** *vb* **-enced; -enc·ing** [*T*] : to do or see (something) or have (something) happen to you ▪ *I've never experienced an earthquake.* : to feel or be affected by (something) ▪ *He is experiencing pain in his arm.*

ex·pe·ri·enced /ɪkˈspirijənst/ *adj* : having skill or knowledge from experience ▪ *an experienced driver*

¹**ex·per·i·ment** /ɪkˈspɛrəmənt/ *n* [*C/U*] : a test in which you perform a series of actions and observe their effects in order to learn about something ▪ *perform/conduct/do an experiment* — **ex·per·i·men·tal** /ɪkˌspɛrəˈmɛntl/ *adj* ▪ *experimental data/evidence* ▪ *an experimental drug/treatment* — **ex·per·i·men·tal·ly** *adv*

²**ex·per·i·ment** /ɪkˈspɛrəˌmɛnt/ *vb* [*I*] : to make or do an experiment ▪ *scientists experimenting on rats ▪ teenagers experimenting with drugs* — **ex·per·i·men·ta·tion** /ɪkˌspɛrəmənˈteɪʃən/ *n* [*U*] — **ex·per·i·ment·er** /ɪkˈspɛrəˌmɛntɚ/ *n* [*C*]

¹**ex·pert** /ˈɛkˌspɚt/ *n* [*C*] : a person who has special skill or knowledge relating to a particular subject ▪ *an expert on/in child development*

²**expert** *adj* : having or showing special skill or knowledge ▪ *expert advice/testimony* — **ex·pert·ly** *adv* — **ex·pert·ness** *n* [*U*]

ex·per·tise /ˌɛkspɚˈtiːz/ *n* [*U*] : the special skill or knowledge of an expert ▪ *her expertise in legal matters ▪ my **area of expertise*** [=the subject area I know a lot about]

expiration date *n* [*C*] **1** : the date when something can no longer be officially be used ▪ *the expiration date on a credit card* **2** : the date when something (such as milk or medicine) can no longer be sold because it may no longer be good

ex·pire /ɪkˈspajɚ/ *vb* **-pired; -pir·ing** [*I*] **a** : to end ▪ *scoring before **time expires*** [=before the clock shows that there is no more time to play a game and play stops] **b** : to no longer be valid after a period of time ▪ *My driver's license has ex-*

pired. **2** [*I*] *formal* : to die ▪ *She expired after a long illness.* **3** /ɛkˈspaɪɚ/ [*T*] *medical* : EXHALE ▪ *air expired from the lungs* — **ex·pi·ra·tion** /ˌɛkspəˈreɪʃən/ *n* [*U*] ▪ *the expiration of a contract* ▪ *inhalation and expiration*

ex·pi·ry /ɪkˈspajəri/ *n* [*U*] *chiefly Brit* : the fact of expiring ▪ *the expiry* [=*expiration*] *of the waiting period*

ex·plain /ɪkˈspleɪn/ *vb* **1** [*T*] : to make (something) clear or easy to understand ▪ *She explained the contract to me.* ▪ *explaining how it works* **2** [*T/I*] : to tell, show, or be the reason for or cause of something ▪ *No one could explain the strange lights in the sky.* ▪ *Give me a chance to explain.* — **explain away** [*phrasal vb*] **explain away (something) or explain (something) away 1** : to make (something) seem less important by telling how it happened, what caused it, etc. ▪ *His lawyers couldn't explain away the new evidence.* **2** : to give a reason for (a fault, a mistake, etc.) so that you will not be blamed for it ▪ *They tried to explain away the delays.* — **explain yourself 1** : to give a reason for your behavior ▪ *I don't have to explain myself to you.* **2** : to say something clearly so that it can be understood ▪ *Let me try to explain myself.* — **ex·plain·able** /ɪkˈspleɪnəbəl/ *adj* — **ex·pla·na·tion** /ˌɛkspləˈneɪʃən/ *n* [*C/U*] ▪ *Some of the technical terms need explanation.* ▪ *They gave/offered no explanation for the delays.* — **ex·plan·a·to·ry** /ɪkˈsplænəˌtori, Brit ɪkˈsplænətri/ *adj* ▪ *explanatory notes* [=*notes included in order to explain something*]

ex·ple·tive /ˈɛksplətɪv, Brit ɪkˈspliːtɪv/ *n* [*C*] : an often offensive word or phrase (such as "Damn it!") that people sometimes say when they are angry or in pain

ex·pli·ca·ble /ˈɛkˈsplɪkəbəl, ˈɛksplɪkəbəl/ *adj, formal* : possible to explain ▪ *explicable mistakes*

ex·pli·cate /ˈɛkspləˌkeɪt/ *vb* **-cat·ed; -cat·ing** [*T*] *formal* : to explain or analyze (an idea, poem, etc.) ▪ *an essay explicating a story* — **ex·pli·ca·tion** /ˌɛkspləˈkeɪʃən/ *n* [*C/U*]

ex·plic·it /ɪkˈsplɪsət/ *adj* **1** : very clear and complete ▪ *explicit instructions* **2 a** : showing or referring openly to nudity, violence, or sexual activity ▪ *explicit lyrics/photos* **b** : openly shown ▪ *The movie contains explicit violence.* — **ex·plic·it·ly** *adv* ▪ *We explicitly asked for no sauce.* — **ex·plic·it·ness** *n* [*U*]

ex·plode /ɪkˈsploʊd/ *vb* **-plod·ed; -plod·ing** [*T/I*] : to suddenly break apart in a violent way with parts flying outward ▪ *The bomb could explode at any time.* **2** [*I*] **a** : to change in a very sudden and violent way ▪ *The situation exploded into all-out war.* **b** : to move with sudden speed and force ▪ *The horses exploded out of the gate.* **c** : to be affected by something very suddenly ▪ *The audience exploded with/in/into laughter.* **3** [*I*] : to express emotion in a sudden and violent way ▪ *She exploded with anger.* **4** [*T*] : to show that (a belief, theory, etc.) is false ▪

exploding old theories **5** [*I*] : to increase very quickly ▪ *The deer population has exploded.*

¹**ex·ploit** /ˈɛkˌsplɔɪt/ *n* [*C*] : an exciting act or action — usually plural ▪ *his youthful exploits* [=*adventures*]

²**ex·ploit** /ɪkˈsplɔɪt/ *vb* [*T*] **1** : to get value or use from (something) ▪ *exploiting weaknesses* ▪ *exploit natural resources* **2** : to use (someone or something) in a way that helps you unfairly ▪ *a tragedy exploited by the media* — **ex·ploit·able** /ɪkˈsplɔɪtəbəl/ *adj* — **ex·ploi·ta·tion** /ˌɛkˌsplɔɪˈteɪʃən/ *n* [*U*] — **ex·ploit·er** *n* [*C*]

ex·plore /ɪkˈsploɚ/ *vb* **-plored; -plor·ing 1** [*T*] **a** : to look at (something) in a careful way to learn more about it : to study or analyze (something) ▪ *exploring how language is acquired by children* **b** : to talk or think about (something) in a thoughtful way ▪ *explore your feelings* ▪ *We explored all possibilities.* **c** : to learn about (something) by trying it ▪ *exploring different activities* **2** [*T*] : to travel through (a place) in order to learn more about it or to find something ▪ *exploring Antarctica* **3** [*I*] : to search *for* something by traveling to different places ▪ *companies exploring for oil* — **ex·plo·ra·tion** /ˌɛksploˈreɪʃən/ *n* [*C/U*] ▪ *space exploration* — **ex·plor·a·to·ry** /ɪkˈsplorəˌtori, Brit ɪkˈsplɒrətri/ *adj* ▪ *exploratory surgery* [=*surgery done to find and identify a problem*] — **ex·plor·er** *n* [*C*]

ex·plo·sion /ɪkˈsploʊʒən/ *n* [*C*] : the act of exploding or an occurrence in which something explodes ▪ *The fire set off an explosion in the factory.* ▪ *a population explosion* [=*a sudden increase in a population*] ▪ *an explosion of anger/laughter*

¹**ex·plo·sive** /ɪkˈsploʊsɪv/ *adj* **1** : relating to or able to cause an explosion ▪ *a highly explosive substance* ▪ *an explosive device* **2 a** : tending to get angry very easily ▪ *He has an explosive temper.* **b** : likely to become violent very suddenly ▪ *an explosive situation* **c** : happening suddenly and quickly ▪ *explosive population growth*

²**explosive** *n* [*C*] : a substance (such as dynamite) that is used to cause an explosion ▪ *working with explosives*

ex·po·nent /ɪkˈspoʊnənt, ˈɛkˌspoʊnənt/ *n* [*C*] **1 a** : a supporter of something ▪ *a leading exponent* [=*proponent*] *of the civil rights movement* **b** : someone who is known for a particular method, style, etc. ▪ *an exponent of Romanticism* **2** *mathematics* : a symbol written to the right of a number to show how many times the number is to be multiplied by itself ▪ *The exponent 3 in 10^3 indicates $10 \times 10 \times 10$.*

ex·po·nen·tial /ˌɛkspəˈnɛnʃəl/ *adj* **1** : very fast ▪ *exponential growth* **2** *mathematics* : including or using an exponent ▪ *10^3 is an exponential expression.* — **ex·po·nen·tial·ly** /ˌɛkspəˈnɛnʃəli/ *adv*

ex·port /ɛkˈspoɚt/ *vb* [*T*] : to send a product to be sold in another country ▪ *oil exported to the U.S.* — **ex·port** /ˈɛkˌspoɚt/ *n* [*C*] ▪ *oil and other exports to the U.S.* ▪ *goods for export* — **ex·port·able** /ɛk-

'spoətəbəl/ adj — ex·por·ta·tion /ˌɛk-
ˌspoɚˈteɪʃən/ n [U] — ex·port·er /ɛk-
ˈspoɚtɚ/ n [C]

ex·pose /ɪkˈspouz/ vb -posed; -pos·ing
[T] **1 a** : to leave (something) without
covering or protection • *The colors will
fade if exposed to sunlight.* • *exposed wir-
ing/beams* **2** : to cause (someone) to experience or be affected by something •
*The workers were **exposed** to dangerous
chemicals.* **3 a** : to reveal (something
hidden, dishonest, etc.) • *expose a scam*
b : to reveal the crimes or faults of
(someone) • *She exposed him (as a fraud).*
4 : to let light fall on (film) in order to
create a photograph • *improperly exposed
film* — **expose yourself** : to show your
sexual organs in public

ex·po·sé /ˌɛkspouˈzeɪ, Brit ɛkˈspəuzeɪ/ n
[C] : a news report or broadcast that reveals something illegal or dishonest

ex·po·si·tion /ˌɛkspəˈzɪʃən/ n [C] : a
public show or exhibition • *the Paris Ex-
position of 1889*

ex·po·sure /ɪkˈspouʒɚ/ n **1** [U] : the
condition of being exposed *to* something
• *exposure to sunlight/danger/ridicule* **2**
[U] : the act of revealing crimes, secrets,
etc. • *the exposure of a scam* **3** [U] : public attention • *The candidates are competing for media exposure.* **4** [C] *photography* **a** : the amount of time that film is
exposed • *a three-second exposure* **b** : a
section of film used for one photograph •
a roll of film with 24 exposures **5** [U]
medical : a condition that results from
being in cold weather for a long time •
They died of exposure.

ex·pound /ɪkˈspaund/ vb [T/I] *formal* : to
explain or state (something) • *expound-
ing (on) the virtues of exercise*

¹**ex·press** /ɪkˈsprɛs/ vb [T] **1** : to make
(your thoughts and feelings) known usually by talking or writing • *He expressed
an interest in meeting her.* • *Her love of nature is expressed in her paintings.* • *Her anger **expresses** itself as/in/through tantrums.* [=her anger is seen in the form of
tantrums] • *He has a hard time expressing himself.* [=saying or showing his
thoughts and feelings] **2** : to show (an
amount, quantity, etc.) by a sign or a
symbol • *results expressed as a percentage*
3 *chiefly US* : to send (a package, letter,
etc.) so that it will be delivered more
quickly than usual • *He expressed the
package to us.* — **ex·press·ible** /ɪk-
ˈsprɛsəbəl/ adj

²**express** adj, *always before a noun* **1**
: said or given in a clear way • *express orders* **2** : of a particular kind • *I came for
that express purpose.* **3 a** : traveling at
high speed with few stops • *an express
train* **b** : delivered faster than usual • *an
express shipment* **c** : designed for fast
movement or travel • *express roads/lanes*
— **ex·press·ly** adv

³**express** n **1** [U] : a system for delivering
things (such as letters and packages)
quickly • *a package sent by express* **2** [C]
: a train or bus that travels quickly with
few stops • *taking the express*

⁴**express** adv : by a system that delivers
letters and packages quickly • *a package
sent express*

ex·pres·sion /ɪkˈsprɛʃən/ n **1** [C/U]
: the act of expressing something • *expressions of anger* • *artistic/creative expression* • *ways to **give** expression **to*** [=to
express] *an idea* **2** [C] : a word or
phrase • *The expression "to make fun of"
means "to ridicule."* **3** [C] : the way
someone's face looks that shows emotions and feelings • *Her (facial) expression showed that she was surprised.* **4** [U]
: a way of speaking, singing, etc., that
shows emotion • *reading aloud without
expression* **5** [C] : a mathematical symbol or combination of symbols • 10^3 *is an
exponential expression.* — **expres-
sion·less** /ɪkˈsprɛʃənləs/ adj — **ex-
pres·sion·less·ly** adv — **expres-
sion·less·ness** n [U]

ex·pres·sive /ɪkˈsprɛsɪv/ adj **1** : showing emotions and feelings clearly and
openly • *an expressive performance/face*
2 : showing or expressing something •
*His work is **expressive** of his personality.*
— **ex·pres·sive·ly** adv — **ex·pres-
sive·ness** n [U]

ex·press·way /ɪkˈsprɛsˌweɪ/ n [C] *US* : a
large highway that may be entered and
left only at certain places

ex·pro·pri·ate /ɪkˈsproupriˌeɪt/ vb -at-
ed; -at·ing *formal* : to take (someone's property) • *The land was expropri-
ated by the state/government.* — **ex·pro-
pri·a·tion** /ɪkˌsproupriˈeɪʃən/ n [C/U]

ex·pul·sion /ɪkˈspʌlʃən/ n **1** [C/U] : the
act of forcing someone to leave a country, school, etc. : the act of expelling
someone • *He was threatened with expulsion (from school).* **2** [U] : the act of
forcing something out • *the expulsion of
air from the lungs*

ex·punge /ɪkˈspʌndʒ/ vb -punged;
-pung·ing *formal* : to remove
(something) completely • *The criminal
charges were expunged from his record.*

ex·qui·site /ɛkˈskwɪzət, ˈɛkskwɪzət/ adj
1 : finely done or made • *exquisite workmanship* : very beautiful or delicate • *exquisite flowers/voices* **2** : very sensitive
or fine • *exquisite taste* **3** : extreme or
intense • *choosing words with exquisite
care* — **ex·qui·site·ly** adv — **ex·quis-
ite·ness** n [U]

ex·tant /ˈɛkstənt, Brit ɛkˈstænt/ adj, *formal* : still existing • *extant species* : not
destroyed or lost • *There are few extant
records from that period.*

ex·tem·po·ra·ne·ous /ɛkˌstɛmpəˈreɪ-
nijəs/ adj : made up or done without special preparation • *an extemporaneous
speech* — **ex·tem·po·ra·ne·ous·ly** adv

ex·tend /ɪkˈstɛnd/ vb **1 a** [T] : to cause
(your arm, leg, etc.) to stretch out • *extend a hand in greeting* **b** [I] : to be able
to become longer • *The table extends to
eight feet in length.* **2** [I] : to continue in
a specified direction or over a specified
distance, space, or time • *The woods extend for miles to the west.* • *His popularity
extends from coast to coast.* **3** [I] : to include a specified person or thing • *The offer **extends** to members only.* **4** [T] : to

make (something) longer or greater ▪ *She extended her visit by two weeks.* ▪ *an extended vacation* ▪ *extended warranties* [=warranties that cover more things or last for a longer period of time] **5** [*T*] **a** : to offer (an invitation, apology, etc.) to someone ▪ *extend a warm welcome to them* **b** : to make (something) available ▪ *The store extends credit to its regular customers.* — **extend yourself** : to work hard ▪ *She extends herself for others.*
ex·tend·able *or* **ex·tend·ible** /ɪk-ˈstɛndəbəl/ *adj* — **ex·tend·er** /ɪk-ˈstɛndə/ *n* [*C*]

extended family *n* [*C*] : a family that includes parents, children, and other relatives (such as grandparents and cousins)

ex·ten·sion /ɪkˈstɛnʃən/ *n* **1** [*C/U*] : the act of extending something ▪ *extension of the patient's life* ▪ *a contract extension* ▪ *He did some leg extensions.* **2** [*C*] : extra time allowed to do something ▪ *I was granted an extension.* **3** [*C/U*] : something that develops from something else ▪ *a natural extension of his career* ▪ *a benefit to taxpayers and, by extension, the economy* **4** [*C*] : a part that is added on to something to make it larger or longer ▪ *building an extension on a house* **5** [*C*] : an extra telephone that is connected to the main line; *also* : a phone number that connects to a particular extension ▪ *She gave me her extension.*

extension cord *n* [*C*] *US* : an electric cord that can be attached to another electric cord — called also (*Brit*) **extension lead**

ex·ten·sive /ɪkˈstɛnsɪv/ *adj* : large in size or amount ▪ *an extensive list* ▪ *extensive damage/repairs* — **ex·ten·sive·ly** *adv* ▪ *She has written extensively on the subject.* — **ex·ten·sive·ness** *n* [*U*]

ex·tent /ɪkˈstɛnt/ *n* [*U*] **1** : the range, distance, or space that is covered by or included in something ▪ *determine the extent of the damage/problem* **2** : the point or limit to which something extends or reaches ▪ *They will be prosecuted to the fullest extent of the law.* [=as fully as the law allows] ▪ *To what extent* [=how far, how much] *can we trust them?* **3** — used to indicate the degree to which something exists, happens, or is true ▪ *They're both right, to some/an extent.* [=they're both partly but not completely right] ▪ *She claims it's not her fault, and, to a certain extent, that's true.* [=that's partly true] ▪ *These traits are to a large/great extent inherited.* [=they are mostly inherited] ❖ The phrases *to the extent that*, *to that extent*, and *to a greater/lesser extent* are often used to describe the effect or importance of something in relation to something else. ▪ *She encouraged their bad behavior, and to that extent she's to blame for it.* *To the extent that* or *to such an extent that* can also be used to say that something is true to a very extreme degree. ▪ *He was fearful to the extent that he refused to leave his house.*

ex·ten·u·at·ing /ɪkˈstɛnjəˌweɪtɪŋ/ *adj* — used to describe something (such as an unusual situation) that makes something (such as a mistake) seem less serious or

deserving of blame ▪ *We were late due to bad weather and other* **extenuating circumstances.**

¹ex·te·ri·or /ɛkˈstiːrijə/ *adj* **1 a** : located on the outside of something ▪ *exterior walls* **b** : used on outside surfaces ▪ *exterior paint/lights* **2** : shown on the outside or surface ▪ *exterior beauty*

²exterior *n* [*C*] **1** : an outer part or surface ▪ *the building's plain exterior* **2** : a person's outward appearance — usually singular ▪ *his tough/calm exterior*

ex·ter·mi·nate /ɪkˈstɚməˌneɪt/ *vb* **-nat·ed; -nat·ing** [*T*] : to destroy or kill (a group of animals, people, etc.) completely ▪ *The insects were exterminated.* — **ex·ter·mi·na·tion** /ɪkˌstɚməˈneɪʃən/ *n* [*C/U*] — **ex·ter·mi·na·tor** /ɪkˈstɚməˌneɪtɚ/ *n* [*C*] ▪ *We hired an exterminator to get rid of the termites.*

ex·ter·nal /ɪkˈstɚnl/ *adj* **1** : located, seen, or used on the outside or surface of something ▪ *The medication is for external use only.* [=for use on the skin] **2** : coming from outside ▪ *external pressures* **3** : existing or occurring outside your mind ▪ *external reality* **4** : concerning relationships with foreign countries ▪ *external affairs* — **ex·ter·nal·ly** *adv*

ex·tinct /ɪkˈstɪŋkt/ *adj* : no longer existing or in use ▪ *an extinct species/language* — **ex·tinc·tion** /ɪkˈstɪŋkʃən/ *n* [*C/U*] ▪ *mass extinctions* ▪ *an animal threatened with extinction = an animal on the brink of extinction*

ex·tin·guish /ɪkˈstɪŋgwɪʃ/ *vb* [*T*] **1** : to cause (something) to stop burning ▪ *extinguish a fire/cigarette* **2** : to cause the end or death of (something) ▪ *extinguish all resistance* — **ex·tin·guish·er** *n* [*C*] — see also FIRE EXTINGUISHER

ex·tol *also US* **ex·toll** /ɪkˈstoʊl/ *vb* **-tolled; -tol·ling** [*T*] : to praise (someone or something) highly ▪ *She extols the benefits of exercise.*

ex·tort /ɪkˈstoɚt/ *vb* [*T*] : to get (something, such as money) from a person by using force or threats ▪ *extorting bribes* — **ex·tort·er** *n* [*C*] — **ex·tor·tion** /ɪkˈstoɚʃən/ *n* [*U*] ▪ *He was charged with extortion.* — **ex·tor·tion·ist** /ɪkˈstoɚʃənɪst/ *n* [*C*]

¹ex·tra /ˈɛkstrə/ *adj* *always before a noun* : more than is usual or necessary ▪ *a pizza with extra cheese* ▪ *earning some extra money* **2** : costing more ▪ *Lunch is included in the price, but drinks are/cost extra.* — **go the extra mile** see MILE

²extra *adv* **1** : beyond the usual size or amount ▪ *extra large/long* ▪ *We paid $5 extra for drinks.* **2** *informal* : very or unusually ▪ *She tried extra hard.*

³extra *n* [*C*] **1** : something added to make a product, service, etc., more appealing ▪ *The car has some nice extras.* **2** : a person hired to act in a group scene in a movie

extra- *prefix* : outside or beyond ▪ *an extramarital affair*

¹ex·tract /ɪkˈstrækt/ *vb* [*T*] **1** : to remove (something) by pulling or cutting it out ▪ *extract a tooth/tumor* **2 a** : to get (information, a response, etc.) from someone who does not want to give it ▪ *extract a* *confession* **b** : to get (information, data, etc.) *from* something ▪ *They extracted new insights from the test results.* **3** : to get (a substance) *from* something using a machine or chemicals ▪ *oil extracted from seeds* **4** : to quote (parts of a written work) ▪ *He extracted a few lines from a poem for use in his speech.* — **ex·tract·able** /ɪkˈstræktəbəl/ *adj* — **ex·trac·tor** /ɪkˈstræktɚ/ *n* [C]

²**ex·tract** /ˈɛkˌstrækt/ *n* **1** [C/U] : a substance that you get from something by using a machine or chemicals ▪ *vanilla extract* **2** [C] : a short piece of writing that is taken from a longer work (such as a book)

ex·trac·tion /ɪkˈstrækʃən/ *n* **1** [C/U] : the act of extracting something ▪ *tooth extractions* **2** [U] — used to describe the origin of a person or family ▪ *a family of Italian extraction*

ex·tra·cur·ric·u·lar /ˌɛkstrəkəˈrɪkjələ/ *adj* — used to describe extra school activities (such as sports) that are not part of regular classes ▪ *extracurricular activities* — **extracurricular** *n* [C]

ex·tra·dite /ˈɛkstrəˌdaɪt/ *vb* **-dit·ed; -dit·ing** [T] *law* : to send (a person who has been accused of a crime) to another state or country for trial ▪ *She was extradited across state lines.* — **ex·tra·di·tion** /ˌɛkstrəˈdɪʃən/ *n* [C/U] ▪ *a prisoner awaiting extradition*

ex·tra·mar·i·tal /ˌɛkstrəˈmerətl/ *adj* — used to describe sexual relations between a married person and someone who is not that person's husband or wife ▪ *an extramarital affair*

ex·tra·ne·ous /ɛkˈstreenijəs/ *adj* : not necessary or important ▪ *eliminating all extraneous steps* ▪ *extraneous details*

ex·traor·di·nary /ɪkˈstroɚdəˌneri, Brit ɪkˈstrɔːdənri/ *adj* **1** : very unusual ▪ *an extraordinary discovery/situation* ▪ *extraordinary rudeness* **2** : extremely good or impressive ▪ *a woman of extraordinary intelligence* — **ex·traor·di·nar·i·ly** /ɪkˌstrɔːdəˈnerəli, Brit ɪkˈstrɔːdənrəli/ *adv* ▪ *extraordinarily bad weather*

ex·trap·o·late /ɪkˈstræpəˌleɪt/ *vb* **-lat·ed; -lat·ing** [T/I] *formal* : to form an opinion or to make an estimate about something from known facts ▪ *They extrapolated these results from their research.* — **ex·trap·o·la·tion** /ɪkˌstræpəˈleɪʃən/ *n* [C/U]

ex·tra·sen·so·ry perception /ˌɛkstrəˈsɛnsəri-/ *n* [*singular*] : the ability to know things (such as what another person is thinking or what will happen in the future) that cannot be known by using the senses — called also *ESP*

ex·tra·ter·res·tri·al /ˌɛkstrətəˈrɛstrijəl/ *adj* : coming from or existing outside the planet Earth ▪ *extraterrestrial life* — **ex·traterrestrial** *n* [C]

ex·trav·a·gant /ɪkˈstrævɪgənt/ *adj* **1 a** : more than is usual, necessary, or proper ▪ *extravagant promises/praise* **b** : very fancy ▪ *an extravagant display* **2 a** : very expensive and not necessary ▪ *an extravagant purchase/vacation* **b** : spending a lot of money ▪ *extravagant spending* — **ex·trav·a·gance** /ɪkˈstrævɪgəns/ *n*

[C/U] ▪ *We can't afford such extravagances.* ▪ *the extravagance of their lifestyle* ▪ *his extravagance with money* — **ex·trav·a·gant·ly** *adv*

ex·trav·a·gan·za /ɪkˌstrævəˈgænzə/ *n* [C] : a very large and exciting show or event ▪ *a musical extravaganza*

extravert *variant spelling of* EXTROVERT

¹**ex·treme** /ɪkˈstriːm/ *adj* **1** : very great in degree ▪ *extreme cold* ▪ *living in extreme poverty* **2** : very serious or severe ▪ *an extreme punishment* ▪ *extreme weather conditions* **3** : not agreeing at all with the opinions of most people ▪ *extreme opinions* **4** *always before a noun* : in the farthest possible position ▪ *the extreme northern part of the state* **5** *sports* **a** : unusual and dangerous ▪ *extreme sports* **b** *always before a noun, US* : competing in an extreme sport ▪ *an extreme snowboarder/skier* — **go to extreme lengths** see LENGTH — **ex·treme·ly** *adv* ▪ *extremely slow/loud*

²**extreme** *n* [C] **1** : either one of two opposite conditions, feelings, positions, etc., that are thought of as being far from what is normal or reasonable ▪ *extremes of heat and cold* ▪ *His mood changed/swung from one extreme to the other.* **2** : an amount or degree that is far beyond what is normal or reasonable ▪ *The problems can be solved without going to (such) extremes.* ▪ *people who carry/take dieting to extremes* — **in the extreme** *formal* : to the greatest possible degree — used to make a statement more forceful ▪ *The work is difficult in the extreme.* [=very/extremely difficult]

ex·trem·ism /ɪkˈstriːˌmɪzəm/ *n* [U] : belief in and support for extreme ideas about politics, religion, etc. — **ex·trem·ist** /ɪkˈstriːmɪst/ *n* [C] ▪ *political extremists* — **extremist** *adj*

ex·trem·i·ty /ɪkˈstrɛməti/ *n, pl* **-ties** **1** [C] : a hand or foot — usually plural ▪ *your lower extremities* **2** [C] : the farthest limit, point, or part of something ▪ *the city's westernmost extremity* **3** [C/U] *formal* : an extreme degree or amount of emotion, pain, etc. ▪ *the extremity of her grief* ▪ *extremities of suffering*

ex·tri·cate /ˈɛkstrəˌkeɪt/ *vb* **-cat·ed; -cat·ing** [T] : to free or remove (someone or something) *from* a trap, situation, etc. ▪ *Two survivors were extricated from the wreckage.*

ex·trin·sic /ɛkˈstrɪnzɪk/ *adj, formal* : not part of something ▪ *extrinsic circumstances/factors*

ex·tro·vert *also* **ex·tra·vert** /ˈɛkstrəˌvɚt/ *n* [C] : a friendly person who likes being with and talking to other people — **ex·tro·vert·ed** *also* **ex·tra·vert·ed** /ˈɛkstrəˌvɚtəd/ *adj*

ex·u·ber·ant /ɪgˈzuːbərənt, Brit ɪgˈzjuːbərənt/ *adj* : very lively, happy, or energetic ▪ *exuberant people/music* — **ex·u·ber·ance** /ɪgˈzuːbərəns, Brit ɪgˈzjuːbərəns/ *n* [U] ▪ *her youthful exuberance* — **ex·u·ber·ant·ly** *adv*

ex·ude /ɪgˈzuːd/ *vb* **ex·ud·ed; ex·ud·ing** **1 a** [T] : to produce a liquid or smell that flows out slowly ▪ *Pine trees exude sap.* **b** [I] : to flow out slowly ▪ *Moisture exud-*

ed from the cave walls. **2** [*T*] : to show (a quality, emotion, etc.) very clearly ▪ *She exudes authority/elegance/confidence.*

ex·ult /ɪgˈzʌlt/ *vb* **1** [*I*] : to feel or show great happiness ▪ *They exulted in/over their victory.* **2** [*T*] : to say (something) in a very excited and happy way ▪ *"That was great!" he exulted.* — **ex·ul·tant** /ɪgˈzʌltənt/ *adj* ▪ *an exultant crowd/cheer* — **ex·ul·ta·tion** /ˌɛkˌsʌlˈteɪʃən, ˌɛgˌzʌlˈteɪʃən/ *n* [*U*] ▪ *cheering in exultation*

-ey see **-Y**

¹**eye** /ˈaɪ/ *n* **1** [*C*] : the part of the body that you see with ▪ *sad/sleepy eyes* ▪ *Her eyes lit up* [=she looked excited and happy] *when she saw him.* ▪ *She looked me (right) in the eye.* [=she looked directly at me] ▪ *pleasing to the eye* [=pleasing to look at] ▪ *She came home with tears in her eyes.* [=she was crying] ▪ *Seeing her again brought tears to my eyes.* [=made me shed tears] ▪ (*figurative*) *Our teacher has eyes in the back of her head.* [=she surprises us by seeing or noticing things that are behind her] **2** [*singular*] **a** : an ability to understand and appreciate something seen ▪ *an artist's eye for color* ▪ *He has a good/keen/sharp eye for detail.* [=he has a special ability to recognize details] **b** — used to describe the way something looks to you ▪ *It looks fine to my eye.* [=it looks fine to me] **c** : a way of looking at or judging something ▪ *a critical eye* **3** [*C*] — used to describe where someone is looking ▪ *My eye was attracted to the painting in the hall.* ▪ *All eyes were on her.* [=everyone was looking at her] ▪ *He averted his eyes* [=he looked away] *when she approached him.* ▪ *Her eyes fell* [=she looked down] *when he looked at her.* ▪ *Her eyes fell on* [=she saw] *a note on the table.* ▪ *She fixed her eyes on me.* [=she kept looking at me] ▪ *He'll be here soon, so have/keep an/your eye out for him.* [=look for him to arrive] ▪ *Will you keep an/your eye on* [=watch or care for] *my suitcase (for me) while I get a soda?* ▪ (*informal*) *They kept their eyes glued to the TV.* [=watched the TV very closely for a long time] ▪ (*informal*) *We kept our eyes open/peeled/skinned for* [=watched closely in order to find or see] *the hotel.* ▪ *I hope never to lay/set/clap eyes on* [=to see or look at] *him again!* ▪ *I saw it out of the corner of my eye.* [=to the side of where I was looking] ▪ *I never took my eyes off* [=stopped looking at] *the road.* ▪ *He couldn't take his eyes off her.* ▪ *Students work under the (watchful/vigilant) eye of* [=while being watched by] *their teacher.* **4** [*C*] : a way of looking at or thinking about something ▪ *looking at the problem with a fresh eye* [=in a new way] ▪ *In the eyes* [=opinion] *of many, he is the best person for the job.* ▪ *Beauty is in the eye of the beholder.* [=different people have different ideas about what is beautiful] **5** [*C*] : the hole through the top of a needle **6** [*C*] : a loop that a hook fits into **7** [*C*] : an area on a potato from which a new plant can grow **8** [*C*] : the center of a powerful storm — **all eyes** : watching something or someone closely ▪ *She was all eyes as I*

opened the box. — **an eye for an eye (and a tooth for a tooth)** — used to say that a person who has committed a crime should be given punishment that is as serious as the crime ▪ *At that time, punishment was an eye for an eye.* — **as far as the eye could see** : as far as could be seen ▪ *The crowd stretched away as far as the eye could see.* — **a sight for sore eyes** see ¹**SIGHT** — **before your eyes** or **in front of your eyes** : in a way that can be easily seen ▪ *Technology is changing (right) before our eyes.* — **close/shut your eyes to** : to ignore (something) ▪ *They have closed their eyes to the problem.* — **easy on the eyes** see ¹**EASY** — **for your eyes only** : intended to be seen only by you ▪ *This memo is for your eyes only.* — **give (someone) the eye** *informal* : to look at (someone) in a way that shows sexual attraction ▪ *He was giving her the eye across the bar.* — **have an eye to/toward** : to have (something) in your thoughts as a goal or purpose ▪ *She has an eye to going to college.* — **have your eye on** **1** : to watch (someone or something) closely ▪ *I'll have my eye on the kids while they're swimming.* **2** : to be thinking about buying (something) ▪ *He has his eye on a new car.* — **in the blink of an eye** see ²**BLINK** — **in the public eye** : in a position that receives a lot of public attention ▪ *She is used to being in the public eye.* — **in your mind's eye** ✧ If you see something in your mind's eye, you imagine or remember how it looks. ▪ *I can still see him in my mind's eye.* — **keep your eye on the ball** see ¹**BALL** — **make eyes at** *informal* : to look at (someone) in a way that shows sexual attraction ▪ *A man was making eyes at her from across the room.* — **more than meets the eye** : more importance, complexity, etc., than there appears to be at first ▪ *There is more to this proposal than meets the eye.* — **my eye** *informal* — used to express surprise or mild disagreement ▪ *A diamond, my eye! That's glass!* — **only have eyes for** : to have romantic feelings for only one person ▪ *He only has eyes for you.* — **open someone's eyes** : to cause someone to notice or be aware of something important ▪ *The film opened his eyes to the issue.* — **open your eyes** : to begin to notice or be aware of something important ▪ *Open your eyes and face the truth.* — **pull the wool over someone's eyes** see **WOOL** — **run your eye down** : to quickly read or look at (something) ▪ *She ran her eye down the list.* — **see eye to eye** : to have the same opinion : **AGREE** ▪ *They often don't see eye to eye (with each other).* — **the apple of someone's eye** see **APPLE** — **turn a blind eye** see ¹**BLIND** — **up to your eyes** : deeply involved in or affected by something ▪ *They're up to their eyes in debt.* — **with an eye to/toward** : with (something) in your thoughts as a goal or purpose ▪ *He took the job with an eye to the future.* [=because he felt it would help him in the future] — **with your/both eyes (wide) open** : fully aware of what could happen • *I went into the job with my eyes open.* — **with your eyes shut/closed** *informal* : very easily • *She could run that company with her eyes shut.*

²**eye** *vb* **eyed; eye·ing** *or* **ey·ing** [*T*] : to watch or look at (someone or something) in a very close or careful way • *She was eyeing me from across the street.*

¹**eye·ball** /'aɪˌbɑːl/ *n* [*C*] : the entire round part of the eye — **up to your eyeballs** *informal* : deeply involved in something • *We're up to our eyeballs in work.* [=we are very busy]

²**eyeball** *vb* [*T*] *informal* : to look at or stare at (someone or something) • *The police eyeballed the suspects.*

eye·brow /'aɪˌbrau/ *n* [*C*] : the line of hair that grows over your eye • (*figurative*) *No one raised an eyebrow* [=no one expressed surprise] *when she announced her plan to run for governor.* • (*figurative*) *His behavior has raised (a few) eyebrows.* [=people have reacted with surprise and disapproval to his behavior]

eye-catch·ing /'aɪˌkætʃɪŋ, 'aɪˌkɛtʃɪŋ/ *adj* : very noticeable because of being unusual or attractive • *an eye-catching ad/style*

eye chart *n* [*C*] : a chart that is used for testing someone's vision

eye contact *n* [*U*] : a situation in which two people are looking directly into each other's eyes • *He avoided/made/maintained eye contact with me.*

eyed /'aɪd/ *adj* : having eyes of a specified kind or number • *a brown-eyed boy*

eye-drop·per /'aɪˌdrɑːpə/ *n* [*C*] : DROPPER

eye·ful /'aɪˌfʊl/ *n* [*singular*] *informal* : something that is very surprising, attractive, etc., to look at • *We got quite an eyeful at the show.*

eye·glass·es /'aɪˌglæsəz, Brit 'aɪˌglɑːsəz/ *n* [*plural*] *chiefly US* : GLASSES • *wearing a pair of eyeglasses*

eye·lash /'aɪˌlæʃ/ *n* [*C*] : any one of the hairs that grow along the top of the eyelid • *false eyelashes*

eye level *n* [*singular*] : a level that is as high as a person's eyes • *Hang the picture at eye level.*

eye·lid /'aɪˌlɪd/ *n* [*C*] : either one of the two movable pieces of skin that cover your eye when it is closed

eye·lin·er /'aɪˌlaɪnə/ *n* [*C/U*] : a makeup used to put a dark line around the eyes

eye-open·er /'aɪˌoupənə/ *n* [*C*] *informal* : something that shows or teaches you something in a surprising way • *The speech was an eye-opener for us.* — **eye-open·ing** /'aɪˌoupənɪŋ/ *adj* • *an eye-opening experience*

eye·piece /'aɪˌpiːs/ *n* [*C*] : the part of a telescope or microscope that you look through

eye shadow *n* [*C/U*] : makeup that is put on the eyelids

eye·sight /'aɪˌsaɪt/ *n* [*U*] : the ability to see • *poor/failing eyesight*

eye socket *n* [*C*] : either one of the hollow places in the skull that hold the eyeballs

eye·sore /'aɪˌsoə/ *n* [*C*] : an ugly object or building • *The shack is a real eyesore.*

eye·tooth /'aɪˈtuːθ/ *n, pl* **-teeth** /-ˈtiːθ/ [*C*] : a pointed tooth : CANINE ✧ If you say you would **give your eyeteeth** for something, it means that you want to do or have it very much.

eye·wear /'aɪˌweə/ *n* [*U*] : glasses, sunglasses, etc. • *protective eyewear*

eye·wit·ness /'aɪˈwɪtnəs/ *n* [*C*] : a person who sees something happen and is able to describe it • *an eyewitness to the shooting* • *an eyewitness account*

F

¹**f** *or* **F** /'ɛf/ *n, pl* **f's** *or* **fs** *or* **F's** *or* **Fs** /'ɛfs/ **1** [*C/U*] : the sixth letter of the English alphabet • *The word "foot" begins with (an) f.* **2** [*C/U*] : a musical note or key referred to by the letter F • *play/sing (in) F* **3** [*C*] : a grade given to a student who is doing very poor work • *got an F on the test*

²**f** *abbr* **1** female **2** feminine

F *abbr* Fahrenheit

fa *or chiefly Brit* **fah** /'fɑː/ *n* [*U*] *music* : the fourth note of a musical scale • *do, re, mi, fa, sol, la, ti*

FAA *abbr* Federal Aviation Administration ✧ The Federal Aviation Administration is a part of the U.S. federal government that is responsible for controlling the use of aircraft.

fa·ble /'feɪbəl/ *n* **1** [*C*] : a short story that is intended to teach a lesson • *Aesop's fables* **2** [*C/U*] : a story or statement that is not true • *combining fact and fable*

fa·bled /'feɪbəld/ *adj* **1** : LEGENDARY • *a fabled underwater city* **2** : FAMOUS • *her fabled cherry pie*

fab·ric /'fæbrɪk/ *n* **1** [*C/U*] : CLOTH • *cotton fabric(s)* **2** [*singular*] : the basic structure of something • *the fabric of society*

fab·ri·cate /'fæbrɪˌkeɪt/ *vb* **-cat·ed; -cat·ing** [*T*] **1** : to make or build (something) • *a factory that fabricates car parts* **2** : to create or make up (something) in order to trick people • *a story fabricated to sell magazines* — **fab·ri·ca·tion** /ˌfæbrɪˈkeɪʃən/ *n* [*C/U*]

fab·u·lous /'fæbjələs/ *adj* **1** : very good • *I had a fabulous time.* • *The weather is fabulous.* **2** : very large in amount or size • *fabulous wealth/riches* — **fab·u·lous·ly** *adv* • *fabulously rich/successful*

fa·cade or **fa·çade** /fə'sɑːd/ n [C] **1** : the front of a building • *a brick facade* **2** : a way of appearing that hides your true feelings or situation • *her polite facade*

1face /feɪs/ n [C] **1** : the front part of the head that has the eyes, nose, and mouth on it • *a bearded/freckled/tanned face* • *His face is familiar.* [=I think I know him] • *the look/expression on her face* • *(US) He got in my face.* [=was criticizing me angrily] • *She laughed in his face.* [=in a very disrespectful way] • *If you have a problem with me, you should tell me to my face.* [=directly] • *Her guilt was written all over her face.* [=her face showed her guilt very clearly] **2** : a facial expression • *a happy/sad/smiling face* • *put on a brave face* [=appear brave] • *keep a straight face* [=avoid laughing] **3** : PERSON • *There are some new faces at the office.* • *a familiar face* [=a person that you know] **4 a** : the way something appears when it is first seen or thought about • *On the face of it, her proposal seems ridiculous.* [=when you first hear about her proposal it seems ridiculous, although it may not be ridiculous when you learn more about it] **b** : the way something is thought of by people • *the changing face of politics* • *put the best face on something* [=make something seem as good as possible] **5 a** : a front or outer surface of something • *the face of a cliff/building* • *the face of the earth* **b** : a surface or side that is marked or prepared • *the face of a document* **c** : a side of a coin **d** : the part of a clock or watch that shows the time **e** *mathematics* : any one of the flat surfaces of a solid shape • *A cube has six square faces.* — **face to face 1** : together and looking at each other • *sitting face to face* • *a face-to-face meeting* **2** : very close to something dangerous, difficult, etc. • *She came face to face with death.* — **in the face of** : while in a situation in which you have to deal with (something or someone that is dangerous, difficult, etc.) • *She showed great courage in the face of danger.* — **lose face** : to lose other people's respect — **make a face** or *chiefly Brit* **pull a face 1** : to make a facial expression that shows dislike or disgust • *He made a face when I mentioned her name.* **2** : to make a silly or amusing facial expression • *making (funny) faces at the children* — **save face** : to avoid having other people lose respect for you • *He tried to save face by working overtime.*

2face vb **faced; fac·ing 1** [T/I] **a** : to stand or sit with your face and body turned toward (something or someone) • *The teacher faced the class.* • *Turn and face to the east.* **b** : to have the front part toward (something) • *The house faces the park.* • *facing upward/downward* **2** [T] **a** : to deal with (something bad or unpleasant) in a direct way • *You must face your problems.* **b** : to admit that (something) is true or real • *face the truth* = *face reality* • *face (the) facts.* = *(Let's) face it. Our plan isn't working.* **3** [T] **a** : to have (something bad or un-

pleasant) as a problem or possibility • *He is facing criminal charges.* • *She faced a difficult choice.* **b** : to be a problem for (someone) • *There were many obstacles facing them.* **c** : to force (someone) to see and deal with something • *We are faced with two unpleasant options.* **4 a** [T] : to meet with (someone) despite shame, fear, or embarrassment • *I don't know if I can face him.* **b** [T/I] : to compete or fight against (someone) • *The team will face a tough opponent.* • *(US) two teams facing off in the play-offs* • *(US) protesters facing off against police* **5** [T] : to cover the front or the surface of (something) • *a chimney faced with brick* = *a brick-faced chimney* — **face the music** : to accept and deal with the unpleasant result of something you have said or done — **face up to** [phrasal vb] : to deal with (something bad or unpleasant) in a direct way • *She has to face up to her problems/fears.*

face·less /'feɪsləs/ adj, usually disapproving **1** : not having any unusual and interesting qualities • *a faceless corporation* **2** : not identified : ANONYMOUS • *a faceless accuser*

face-lift /'feɪsˌlɪft/ n [C] **1** : surgery to make a person's face look younger **2** : changes to make something more attractive or modern • *The hotel was given a face-lift.*

face mask n [C] : a mask or protective covering that goes over your face

face-off /'feɪsˌɑːf/ n [C] **1** *ice hockey* : a method of beginning play by dropping the puck between two players **2** *chiefly US* : a meeting of opponents : a conflict or fight • *a legal/diplomatic face-off*

face-sav·ing /'feɪsˌseɪvɪŋ/ adj, always before a noun : done to keep someone from looking foolish • *a face-saving gesture*

fac·et /'fæsət/ n [C] **1** : a part or element of something • *the different facets of our culture* **2** : a small, flat surface on a jewel

fa·ce·tious /fə'siːʃəs/ adj, of speech : meant to be funny but usually regarded as annoying, silly, or inappropriate • *I was just being facetious.* • *a facetious remark* — **fa·ce·tious·ly** adv

face value n [C] : the value that is shown on a coin, bill, etc. • *a face value of $50* • *bought the tickets at face value* • *(figurative) Nothing he says should be accepted/taken at face value.* [=accepted as true without being doubted]

1fa·cial /'feɪʃəl/ adj : of or relating to a person's face • *facial expressions/features/hair*

2facial n [C] : a beauty treatment for a person's face

fac·ile /'fæsəl, Brit 'fæsaɪl/ adj, formal **1** disapproving : too simple • *a facile explanation/solution* **2** always before a noun, disapproving : done or achieved too easily • *a facile victory*

fa·cil·i·tate /fə'sɪləˌteɪt/ vb **-tat·ed; -tat·ing** [T] formal : to make (something) happen more easily • *Tax cuts made facilitate economic recovery.* • *The moderator facilitates the discussion.* — **fa·cil·i·ta-**

tion /fəˌsɪləˈteɪʃən/ *n* [*U*] — **fa·cil·i·ta·tor** /fəˈsɪləˌteɪtə/ *n* [*C*]

fa·cil·i·ty /fəˈsɪləti/ *n, pl* **-ties 1 a** [*C*] : something (such as a building) that is built for a specific purpose ▪ *a manufacturing facility* ▪ *a medical facility* [=a hospital] ▪ *a correctional facility* [=a prison] **b** [*C*] : something that makes an action, operation, or activity easier ▪ *The resort offers a wide range of facilities.* **c** [*plural*] : BATHROOM ▪ *The facilities are at the end of the hall.* **2** [*U, singular*] : skill and ease in doing something ▪ *He had (a) great facility with words.*

fac·ing /ˈfeɪsɪŋ/ *n* [*C/U*] : a layer that is placed on the surface or front of something ▪ *a house with brick facing*

fac·sim·i·le /fækˈsɪməli/ *n* [*C*] **1** : an exact copy ▪ *a facsimile of the world's first computer* ▪ *a reasonable facsimile* [=a close but not exact copy] **2** *formal* : FAX 1

fact /ˈfækt/ *n* **1** [*C*] : something that truly exists or happens ▪ *Electronic communication is now a fact.* ▪ *It's hard to accept the fact that she's gone.* **2** [*C/U*] : a true piece of information ▪ *interesting facts and figures* ▪ *the (cold) hard facts of the case* ▪ *I know for a fact that he did it.* = *He did it, and that's a fact.* ▪ *separating fact from fiction* [=determining what is true and what is false] — used in various phrases to stress or question the truth of a statement ▪ *"Do you know her?" "As a matter of fact, I do."* [=I do indeed] ▪ *He is in fact* [=actually] *almost 60 years old.* ▪ *He said he told the truth, but in fact he lied.* = *In point of fact, he lied.* ▪ *Is that a fact?* [=I am surprised or doubtful about that] ▪ *He may not have meant to, but the fact is/remains that he lied.* — **after the fact** : after something has happened : AFTERWARD ▪ *They informed me of their decision only after the fact.*

fac·tion /ˈfækʃən/ *n* [*C*] : a part of a group that has different opinions from the rest of the group ▪ *The committee split into factions.* — **fac·tion·al** /ˈfækʃənl/ *adj* — **fac·tion·al·ism** /ˈfækʃənəˌlɪzəm/ *n* [*U*]

fact of life *n* **1** [*C*] : something that exists and that cannot be changed or ignored ▪ *Bills are a fact of life.* **2 the facts of life** : the facts about sex that are told to children

fac·toid /ˈfækˌtɔɪd/ *n* [*C*] : a brief and usually unimportant fact

¹fac·tor /ˈfæktə/ *n* [*C*] **1** : one of the things that cause something to happen ▪ *Several factors contributed to the decline.* ▪ *Cost was a major factor in their decision.* **2 a** *mathematics* : a number that evenly divides a larger number ▪ *6, 4, 3, and 2 are factors of 12.* **b** : an amount by which another amount is multiplied or divided ▪ *Costs increased/decreased by a factor of 10.* [=costs were 10 times higher/lower than they had been]

²factor *vb* [*T*] **1** : to consider or include (something) in making a judgment or calculation ▪ *We factored inflation into our calculations.* = *We factored in inflation.* **2** : to not consider or include (something) in making a judgment or

calculation ▪ *Even after factoring out inflation, costs have increased.*

fac·to·ry /ˈfæktəri/ *n, pl* **-ries** [*C*] : a building or group of buildings where products are made ▪ *an automobile factory* ▪ *factory workers*

fac·tu·al /ˈfækʃəwəl/ *adj* **1** : limited to, involving, or based on facts ▪ *factual information/errors* **2** : of or relating to facts ▪ *the factual aspects of the case* — **fac·tu·al·ly** *adv* ▪ *factually incorrect*

fac·ul·ty /ˈfækəlti/ *n, pl* **-ties 1 a** [*U*] : the group of teachers in a school or college ▪ *a member of the faculty* ▪ *a faculty meeting* **b faculty** [*plural*] *US* : faculty members or teachers ▪ *a meeting with students and faculty* **2 a** [*C*] : one of the powers of your mind or body ▪ *the faculty of hearing/speech* ▪ *your mental/critical faculties* [=your ability to think/judge] **b** [*singular*] : a natural talent for doing something ▪ *a faculty for making friends* **3** [*C*] : a department in a college or university ▪ *the Faculty of Law*

fad /ˈfæd/ *n* [*C*] : something that is very popular for a short time ▪ *the latest fads* ▪ *a fad diet* — **fad·dish** /ˈfædɪʃ/ *adj* [*J*]

fade /ˈfeɪd/ *vb* **fad·ed; fad·ing 1** [*J*] **a** : to lose strength or freshness ▪ *The flowers were fading.* ▪ *the fading light of day* ▪ *The cheers gradually faded (away).* **b** : to disappear gradually ▪ *The ship faded from view.* ▪ *The smile faded from his face.* ▪ *fading hopes/memories* ▪ *Their popularity has faded.* **2** [*T/I*] : to become less bright ▪ *fabrics that fade* ▪ *jeans faded by wear* ▪ *a faded photograph* **3** [*I*] : to change gradually in loudness, strength, or appearance ▪ *At the end of the movie, the screen fades to black.* ▪ *One scene fades out as the next fades in.* ▪ *The radio signal faded out.*

fae·ces *chiefly Brit* spelling of FECES

fah *chiefly Brit* spelling of FA

Fahr·en·heit /ˈferənˌhaɪt/ *adj* : relating to or having a scale for measuring temperature on which the boiling point of water is at 212 degrees above zero and the freezing point is at 32 degrees above zero ▪ *the Fahrenheit scale* ▪ *70 degrees Fahrenheit* — abbr. *F*; compare CELSIUS

¹fail /ˈfeɪl/ *vb* **1 a** [*T/I*] : to not succeed ▪ *He failed in his first attempt.* ▪ *She failed to finish.* ▪ *a failed experiment/marriage* ▪ *The crops failed.* [=did not grow successfully] ▪ *He only reads the directions if/when all else fails.* **b** [*I*] : to become bankrupt ▪ *The bank failed.* **2** [*T/I*] : to not do (something that is expected, that should be done, etc.) ▪ *He failed to act on their advice.* ▪ *The car failed to start.* ▪ *It never fails to rain* [=it always rains] *on my days off.* ▪ *I fail to see/understand why we need a new system.* **3** [*T*] : to not do or provide something that is needed by (someone) ▪ *He felt that he had failed her.* ▪ *His courage failed him.* [=he became afraid] ▪ *Words fail me.* [=I do not know what to say] **4 a** [*T/I*] : to be unsuccessful in passing (a test, class, etc.) ▪ *fail an exam* ▪ *He failed (in) chemistry.* **b** [*T*] : to decide that (someone) has not passed a test, class, etc. ▪ *The teacher failed several students.* ▪ *a failing grade/*

mark **5** [*I*] **a** : to stop working • *The power/engine failed.* • *His kidneys failed.* **b** : to become weak or weaker • *Her health/eyesight is starting to fail.*

²fail *n* — **without fail** — used to stress that something always happens or will definitely happen • *Every day, without fail, he gets up at dawn.* • *She said that she would be there without fail.*

¹fail·ing /ˈfeɪlɪŋ/ *n* [*C*] : WEAKNESS, FLAW • *He has some minor failings.*

²failing *prep, formal* : WITHOUT • *Failing more peace talks, war seems likely.* • *You can reach me by e-mail or,* **failing that** [=if that is not possible]*, by phone.*

fail–safe /ˈfeɪlˌseɪf/ *adj* : certain not to fail • *a fail-safe system* • *a fail-safe device/mechanism*

fail·ure /ˈfeɪljɚ/ *n* **1** [*C/U*] : the act or result of failing: such as **a** : a lack of success • *his repeated failures in business* • *her fear of failure* **b** : a situation in which something does not work as it should • *a power failure* • *a failure* [=*lapse*] *of memory* • *heart/kidney failure* **c** : an occurrence in which someone does not do something that should be done • *(a) failure to use proper procedures* **d** : an occurrence in which crops do not produce enough food • *The drought -caused (a) crop failure.* **2** [*C*] : a person or thing that has failed • *He felt like a failure when he lost his job.* • *The plan was a failure.*

¹faint /ˈfeɪnt/ *adj* **1** : not clearly seen, heard, etc. • *a faint noise/smell* • *a faint smile* • *a faint* [=*weak*] *radio signal* **2** : very slight or small • *a faint hope/possibility* • *I don't have the* **faintest idea** *what it means.* **3** *not before a noun* : weak and dizzy • *I feel faint.* • *faint from/with hunger* — **faint of heart** : lacking the courage to face something • *a climb that is* **not for the faint of heart** — **faint·ly** *adv* • *smiling faintly* • *smelled faintly of perfume* — **faint·ness** *n* [*U*]

²faint *vb* [*I*] : to suddenly become unconscious • *He faints at the sight of blood.* • *a fainting spell*

faint·heart·ed /ˈfeɪntˈhɑɚtəd/ *adj* : feeling or showing a lack of courage • *a fainthearted person/response* • *a job that is not for the fainthearted*

¹fair /ˈfeɚ/ *adj* **1** : agreeing with what is right or acceptable • *fair treatment/wages* • *a fair deal/price* • *That's a fair* [=*reasonable*] *question.* • *It's* **only fair**. [=it is the right thing to do] • *OK,* **fair enough**. [=that is reasonable] • *get/have your* **fair share** [=a reasonable amount] *of something* **2** : not favoring some people over others • *a fair and impartial jury* • *laws that are fair to/for everyone* • *Life isn't fair.* • *It's not fair that she gets to leave early.* • *All I want is a* **fair chance**. [=the same chance everyone else gets] **3** : not too harsh or critical • *I can't say I liked the movie, but,* **to be fair**, *parts of it are pretty funny.* **4 a** : of average or acceptable quality • *(The quality of) her work is fair.* • *did a fair job* • *The patient is in fair condition.* • *The food was* **fair to middling**. [=just average] **b** *approving* : good although usually not excellent • *a fair*

chance of winning • *a fair* [=pretty good] *bet/guess* **c** *always before a noun* : somewhat large • *He lives a fair distance from here.* • *a fair number of people* **5** : not stormy or cloudy • *fair skies/weather* **6** *of a person's hair, skin, etc.* : having a light color • *fair hair/skin* **7** *literary* : ATTRACTIVE • *Welcome to our fair city.* • *a fair maid/maiden* **8** *baseball* : in the area between the foul lines • *fair territory* • *a fair ball* — **all's fair in love and war** — used to describe a situation in which people do things that are normally considered unfair — **fair and square** : in an honest and fair manner • *He won fair and square.* — **fair's fair** *informal* — used to say that something was done or should be done because it is fair • *Fair's fair: I washed the dishes yesterday, so it's your turn to do them today.* — **fair warning** : enough warning to be able to avoid something bad • *(I'm giving you) fair warning: he's in a bad mood.* — **fair** *adv* • *His opponent wasn't playing fair.* — **fair·ness** *n* [*U*]

²fair *n* [*C*] **1** : a large public event at which there are competitions, games, rides, etc. • *the annual county/state fair* **2** : an event at which people gather to buy things or to get information • *a book/craft fair* **3** : an event at which crafts, food, etc., are sold usually for charity • *a church fair*

fair game *n* [*U*] : someone or something that can be chased, attacked, etc. • *Celebrities are fair game for the tabloids.*

fair·ground /ˈfeɚˌgraʊnd/ *n* [*C*] : an outdoor area where fairs, circuses, etc., are held

fair·ly /ˈfeɚli/ *adv* **1** : to a reasonable or moderate extent • *a fairly easy job* • *It's still fairly early.* **2** : in a way that is right or proper : in a fair way • *treating people fairly*

fair–mind·ed /ˈfeɚˈmaɪndəd/ *adj* : honest and fair • *a fair-minded man/review* — **fair–mind·ed·ness** *n* [*U*]

fair play *n* [*U*] : honesty and fairness • *in the spirit of fair play*

fair·way /ˈfeɚˌweɪ/ *n* [*C*] : the part of a golf course that has short grass and that lies between a tee and a green

fair–weath·er /ˈfeɚˌwɛðɚ/ *adj, always before a noun, disapproving* : loyal or helpful only during times of success and happiness • *fair-weather friends*

fairy /ˈferi/ *n, pl* **fair·ies** [*C*] *in stories* : a creature that looks like a very small person, has magic powers, and sometimes has wings — **fairy·like** /ˈferiˌlaɪk/ *adj*

fairy godmother *n* [*C*] *in stories* : a woman with magic powers who saves a person from trouble

fairy·land /ˈferiˌlænd/ *n* [*C*] *in stories* : a place where fairies live

fairy tale *n* [*C*] **1** : a simple children's story about magical creatures • *the fairy tale about the sleeping princess* • *(figurative) Their marriage is a fairy-tale romance.* **2** : a false story that is meant to trick people • *Everything he told us was a fairy tale.*

fait ac·com·pli /ˌfeɪtəˌkɑːmˈpliː/ *n, pl* **faits ac·com·plis** /ˌfeɪtəˌkɑːmˈpliː/ [*C*] *formal* : something that has been done and cannot be changed

faith /'feɪθ/ *n* **1** [*U*] : strong belief or trust sometimes without proof ▪ *blind/ unquestioning faith* ▪ *Our faith in them was shaken.* ▪ **have/lose faith in someone** ▪ *I put/have no/little faith in politicians.* ▪ *I'll accept/take it on faith that he's telling the truth.* ▪ *Lending him money was an act of faith.* ▪ *a leap of faith* [=a decision to believe without proof] ▪ *an article of faith* [=something you believe and do not question] **2 a** [*U*] : strong religious feelings or beliefs ▪ *religious faith* ▪ *her faith in God* **b** [*C*] : RELIGION ▪ *people of all faiths* — **break faith with** : to stop supporting or being loyal to (someone) ▪ *He broke faith with his supporters.* — **keep faith with** : to continue supporting or being loyal to (someone) ▪ *She kept faith with her old political allies.* — **keep the faith** : to continue to believe in, trust, or support someone or something ▪ *loyal fans who always keep the faith*

faith·ful /'feɪθfəl/ *adj* **1** : having or showing constant support or loyalty ▪ *a faithful friend/companion* ▪ *She has remained faithful to her values/beliefs.* **2** : deserving trust : loyal or reliable ▪ *her many years of faithful service* **3** : not having sex with someone who is not your wife, husband, girlfriend, or boyfriend ▪ *a faithful husband/wife* ▪ *He has always been faithful to her.* **4** : exact and accurate ▪ *The movie is a faithful adaptation of the book.* = *The movie is faithful to the book.* ▪ *a faithful copy* — **the faithful** **1** : members of a religion ▪ *bells that call the faithful to prayer* **2** : loyal members or supporters ▪ *the Republican/Democratic faithful* — **faith·ful·ly** /'feɪθfəli/ *adv* — **faith·ful·ness** *n* [*U*]

faith·less /'feɪθləs/ *adj* : not able to be trusted ▪ *a faithless friend*

¹**fake** /'feɪk/ *adj* : not true, real, or genuine ▪ *fake emotions* ▪ *a fake mustache*

²**fake** *n* [*C*] **1** : a copy of something that is meant to trick people ▪ *The painting/signature is a fake.* **2** : a person who pretends to have some special knowledge or ability or pretends to be someone else ▪ *Her lawyer turned out to be a fake.* **3** *US, sports* : a movement that is meant to trick an opponent ▪ *He made a fake to the left and then ran to the right.*

³**fake** *vb* **faked; fak·ing 1** [*T*] **a** : to make (something) seem real or true in order to trick someone ▪ *She faked a heart attack.* ▪ *He acts friendly, but he's just faking it.* **b** : to change or copy (something) in order to trick people ▪ *He faked* [=altered] *the test results.* ▪ *fake a signature* **2** [*T/I*] *US, sports* : to pretend to do something in order to trick an opponent ▪ *He faked a handoff and then threw a pass.* ▪ *He faked left and then ran to the right.* ▪ *He faked out the defender.* **3** [*T*] : to pretend to know or to be able to do (something) ▪ *I don't know the song, but I can fake it.* — **fake out** (*someone*) *or* **fake out** (*someone*) *chiefly US, informal* : to deliberately deceive (someone) : FOOL ▪ *Don't believe*

him. *He's just trying to fake you out.* — **fak·er** *n* [*C*]

fal·con /'fælkən, 'fɑːlkən/ *n* [*C*] : a type of hawk that can fly very fast and is sometimes trained to hunt

fal·con·ry /'fælkənri, 'fɑːlkənri/ *n* [*U*] : the sport of hunting with hawks — **fal·con·er** /'fælkənɚ, 'fɑːlkənɚ/ *n* [*C*]

¹**fall** /'fɑːl/ *vb* **fell** /'fɛl/; **fall·en** /'fɑːlən/; **fall·ing** [*I*] **1 a** : to come or go down quickly from a high place or position ▪ *A vase fell off the shelf.* ▪ *Rain fell from the sky.* ▪ *the falling rain* **b** : to come or go down suddenly from a standing position ▪ *She slipped and fell on the ice.* ▪ *fall down the stairs* ▪ *a fallen tree* — often + *down* or *over* ▪ *She fell down.* ▪ *The tree fell over.* **c** : to let yourself come or go down to a lower position ▪ *He fell to his knees.* **2 a** : to come down after moving through the air ▪ *The shot fell far from its target.* ▪ *A ray of light fell on the table.* **b** : to slope downward ▪ *The ground falls away* (*steeply*) *to the east.* **c** : to hang down ▪ *Her hair fell loosely over her shoulders.* **3 a** : to become lower or less ▪ *The tide rose and fell.* ▪ *falling temperatures* ▪ *Stock values have fallen* (*off*). **b** : to become less loud ▪ *The music rose and fell.* **4 a** : to become lowered ▪ *Her eyes fell.* [=she looked down] **b** : to begin to look ashamed or sad ▪ *His face fell when he heard the news.* **5** : to arrive or begin ▪ *Night/Darkness has fallen.* **6 a** : to be wounded or killed in battle ▪ *Many fell on the battlefield.* **b** : to be captured or defeated ▪ *The fortress fell.* **c** : to experience ruin or failure ▪ *great civilizations that have fallen* ▪ *a leader/party that fell from power* **7 a** : to happen at a specified time ▪ *Christmas falls on a Friday this year.* **b** : to pass to someone in a way that does not involve choice ▪ *The responsibility fell to me.* **c** : to have a specified proper place ▪ *The accent falls on the second syllable.* **8** : to belong in a particular category or range ▪ *This word falls within the class of verbs.* **9** : to pass to a specified state or condition ▪ *She fell ill/asleep/silent.* ▪ *This word has fallen out of use.* **10** : to start doing something in a very energetic way — + *to* ▪ *She fell immediately to work.* — **fall** (**all**) *over* **yourself** : to be very eager or too eager ▪ *Fans were falling all over themselves to meet her.* — **fall apart** [*phrasal vb*] **1** : to break into parts ▪ *The pie was falling apart as I served it.* ▪ (*figurative*) *My life is falling apart.* ▪ (*figurative*) *My old car is falling apart.* [=in very bad condition] **2** : to become unable to live in a normal way because of emotional pain, stress, etc. ▪ *She fell apart when her son got sick.* — **fall away** [*phrasal vb*] : to become gradually less ▪ *The sound of the parade fell away in the distance.* — **fall back** [*phrasal vb*] **1** : to move back : RETREAT ▪ *The guerrillas fell back across the border.* **2 fall back on/upon** : to use (something) for help in a bad situation ▪ *She had no savings to fall back on.* — **fall behind** [*phrasal vb*] **1** : to fail to move or go forward as quickly as others ▪ *The slower hikers kept falling behind.* **2** : to

fail to do something as quickly as planned or required • *We're falling behind with our work.* • *I fell behind on my payments.* — **fall down on the job** : to do a job badly • *Our city officials have been falling down on the job.* — **fall flat** : to produce no response or result • *All of his jokes fell flat.* — **fall for** [*phrasal vb*] **1** : to fall in love with (someone) • *He fell for her the moment he saw her.* **2** : to be fooled by (something) • *You fell for that old trick?* — **fall in** [*phrasal vb*] **1** : to fall down in an inward direction • *The roof fell in.* **2** : to take your place in a military formation • *The troops fell in.* — **fall in/into line** : to start to do what you are told to do • *They refused to fall in line (with the new regulations).* — **fall into** [*phrasal vb*] **1** : to be caught in (a trap) **2** : to begin to do or experience (something) without wanting or trying to • *He fell into debt.* • *She fell into the habit of snacking.* — **fall into place** : to fit together : to make sense • *The pieces of the puzzle/mystery are starting to fall into place.* — **fall into the hands of** : to come to be possessed by (someone) • *keeping weapons from falling into the hands of terrorists* — **fall into the wrong hands** : to come to be possessed by the wrong person or group • *These weapons must not fall into the wrong hands.* — **fall in with** [*phrasal vb*] **1** : to begin to spend time with (someone) • *She fell in with a bad crowd.* **2** : to accept and act in agreement with (something) • *They fell in with our plans.* — **fall off** [*phrasal vb*] : to stop being attached to something • *The handle fell off.* — **fall on/upon** [*phrasal vb*] **1 a** : to begin to experience (something) • *We fell on hard times.* **b** : to notice (something) especially without wanting or trying to • *Her eyes fell on the letter.* **2** : to attack (someone) suddenly • *They fell on the enemy soldiers.* — **fall out** [*phrasal vb*] **1** : to stop being attached to the body • *The treatments made her hair fall out.* **2** : to have an argument • *They fell out over money.* **3** : to leave your place in a military formation • *The soldiers were ordered to fall out.* — **fall short** **1** : to fail to be as good or successful as expected or hoped for • *Her new novel falls short (of her previous novel).* • *The cruise fell short of our expectations.* **2** : to fail to reach a goal • *Their efforts fell short (of their goal).* — **fall through** [*phrasal vb*] : to fail or stop in a sudden or final way • *Negotiations have fallen through.* — **fall under** [*phrasal vb*] : to be influenced or affected by (something) • *He fell under her influence.* • *He has fallen under suspicion.*

²**fall** *n* **1** [*C*] : the act of falling: such as **a** : the act of coming or going down from a high or standing position • *a fall from a horse* • *He used his arm to break his fall.* [=to stop himself from falling] **b** : the act of becoming lower • *the rise and fall of the tide* **2** [*C/U*] *US* : AUTUMN **1** • *She went to college in the fall.* • *fall colors/foliage* **3** [*C*] : DECREASE 1 • *a fall in the price of oil* **4** [*singular*] **a** : loss of power or greatness • *the rise and*

fall of an empire **b** : the surrender or capture of a place • *the fall of Troy* **c** : loss of innocence or goodness • *a fall from virtue* **5** [*C*] : WATERFALL — usually plural • *Niagara Falls*

fal·la·cy /ˈfæləsi/ *n, pl* **-cies** **1** [*C*] : a false or mistaken idea • *popular fallacies about medicine* **2** [*U*] : the quality of being false or wrong • *the fallacy of their ideas* — **fal·la·cious** /fəˈleɪʃəs/ *adj, formal* • *fallacious arguments*

fall guy *n* [*C*] *informal* : a person who is blamed for something done by others • *He was set up as a/the fall guy for crimes he had no part in.*

fal·li·ble /ˈfæləbəl/ *adj* : capable of making mistakes or being wrong • *fallible human beings* — **fal·li·bil·i·ty** /ˌfæləˈbɪləti/ *n* [*U*]

fall·ing-out /ˌfɑːlɪŋˈaʊt/ *n, pl* **fall·ings-out** [*C*] : a serious argument or disagreement • *He had a falling-out with his parents.*

falling star *n* [*C*] : METEOR

fall·out /ˈfɑːlˌaʊt/ *n* [*U*] **1** : the radioactive particles that are produced by a nuclear explosion and being wrong from the atmosphere **2** : a bad effect or result of something • *the political fallout from the scandal*

fal·low /ˈfæloʊ/ *adj* **1** : not used for growing crops • *fallow land/fields* • *allowing fields to lie fallow* **2** : not active or productive • *a writer going through a fallow period*

false /ˈfɑːls/ *adj* **1** : not real or genuine • *false documents/teeth* • *a trunk with a false bottom* **2** : not true or accurate • *a false statement; especially* : deliberately untrue • *false testimony/advertising* • *He used a false name.* **3 a** : based on mistaken ideas • *false [=incorrect] assumptions* • *false expectations/hopes* • *a false sense of security* **b** : not legally justified • *false arrest/imprisonment* **4 a** : not faithful or loyal • *a false friend* **b** : not sincere • *false modesty/sympathy* **5** : sudden or deceptive in a threatening way • *The police warned him not to make any false moves.* — **false·ly** *adv* • *He was falsely accused.* — **false·ness** *n* [*U*] — **fal·si·ty** /ˈfɑːlsəti/ *n, pl* **-ties** [*C/U*] • *(formal) the truth or falsity of the report* • *spreading falsities* [=(more commonly) falsehoods]

false alarm *n* [*C*] **1** : an alarm (such as a fire alarm) that is set off when it is not needed **2** : something that causes people to wrongly believe that something bad or dangerous is going to happen • *The report that the factory would be closing was a false alarm.*

false·hood /ˈfɑːlsˌhʊd/ *n* **1** [*C*] : an untrue statement : LIE • *spreading falsehoods* **2** [*U*] : the quality of not being true or accurate • *the line between truth and falsehood*

false start *n* [*C*] **1** : the mistake of starting too soon in a race • *make/commit a false start* **2** : an unsuccessful attempt to begin something • *After several false starts, the project went forward.*

fal·set·to /fɑlˈsɛtoʊ/ *n, pl* **-tos** [*C/U*] : a very high voice used by a man (such as a male singer) — **falsetto** adv • singing falsetto

fal·si·fy /'fɑːlsə,faɪ/ vb **-fies; -fied; -fy-ing** [T] : to change (something) in order to trick people • falsifying documents — **fal·si·fi·ca·tion** /,fɑːlsəfə'keɪʃən/ n [C/U]

fal·ter /'fɑːltɚ/ vb [I] **1** : to begin to fail or weaken • The business was faltering. • their faltering marriage **2** : to begin to walk or move in an unsteady way • Her steps faltered. **3** : to feel doubt about doing something • He never faltered in his determination. **4** of a voice : to sound unsteady because of doubt or emotion • Her voice faltered.

fame /'feɪm/ n [U] : the condition of being known or recognized by many people • her sudden rise to fame • achieved/gained fame as an actor

famed /'feɪmd/ adj : FAMOUS • a famed writer

fa·mil·ial /fə'mɪljəl/ adj : of, relating to, or suggesting a family • familial relationships • a familial atmosphere

fa·mil·iar /fə'mɪljɚ/ adj **1 a** : frequently seen, heard, or experienced • a familiar joke/sight/place • foods that are familiar to us **b** : easy to recognize because you have seen, heard, or experienced it many times • a familiar face/voice **c** : possibly known but not clearly remembered • He looked familiar (to me). • Her name is/sounds/seems familiar. **2 a** : relaxed and informal • written in a familiar style **b** : appropriate for use with people you know well • a familiar greeting **c** : too friendly • being too/overly familiar with the customers — **familiar with** : having some knowledge about (something) • We are familiar with the situation/area. — **fa·mil·iar·ly** adv

fa·mil·iar·i·ty /fə,mɪli'erəti/ n [U] **1** : the state of having knowledge about or something • his familiarity with local issues ◇ The expression **familiarity breeds contempt** means that knowing a lot about someone or something can cause you to like that person or thing less. **2** : a friendly and informal manner • spoke with an easy familiarity

fa·mil·iar·ize also Brit **fa·mil·iar·ise** /fə'mɪljə,raɪz/ vb **-ized; -iz·ing** [T] : to give (someone) knowledge about something — + with • familiarize students with the library • I'm familiarizing myself with the city. — **fa·mil·iar·i·za·tion** also Brit **fa·mil·iar·i·sa·tion** /fə,mɪljərə'zeɪʃən, Brit fə,mɪljə,raɪ'zeɪʃən/ n [U]

¹fam·i·ly /'fæmli/ n, pl **-lies 1 a** [C/U] : a group of people who are related to each other ◇ This sense of family can refer to a group that consists of parents and their children or to a bigger group of related people including grandparents, cousins, etc. It is often used specifically of a group of related people who live together in one house. • a happy family • a death in the family • his mother's side of the family • friends and family • He has family [=relatives] in Ohio. • my immediate family [=my parents, my brothers and sisters, and me] • a friend of the family • You're always welcome here because

you're family. • They treated me like (one of the) family. [=very warmly] • Musical talent runs in her family. [=is common in her family] **b** [C] : a person's children • his wife and family • They want to have a big/large family. [=to have many children] • raise a family [=to have children] • start a family [=to begin having children] **c** [C] : a group of related people including people who lived in the past • My family came to America from Italy. **2** [C] : a group of things that are alike in some way • a family of languages **3** [C] : a group of related plants or animals • a plant belonging to the cabbage family **4** [C] : a group of criminals who work together in an organized way • a crime family

²family adj, always before a noun **1** : of or relating to a family • a family picnic • He's a family man. [=he has a wife and children] • an old family friend **2** : designed or suitable for both children and adults • family entertainment • family [=wholesome] values

family doctor n [C] : a doctor who provides general medical care for people of all ages — called also **family practitioner**

family name n [C] : the name shared by the people in a family : SURNAME • Her family name is Smith.

family planning n [U] : the use of birth control to determine the number of children there will be in a family and when those children will be born

family room n [C] **1** US : an informal room in a family's house that is designed for playing and relaxing **2** Brit : a room in a pub in which children are allowed

family tree n [C] : a drawing or chart that shows how the members of a family are related

fam·ine /'fæmən/ n [C/U] : a situation in which many people do not have enough food to eat

fam·ished /'fæmɪʃt/ adj, informal : very hungry • I'm famished.

fa·mous /'feɪməs/ adj : known or recognized by very many people • a famous athlete • She became famous as a singer. • The hotel is famous for its luxury. — **fa·mous·ly** /'feɪməsli/ adv • the famously luxurious hotel • They get on/along famously. [=like each other very much]

¹fan /'fæn/ n [C] **1** : a machine or device that cools by moving the air: such as **a** : a flat device that you wave back and forth in front of your face **b** : a machine that has turning blades • an electric fan **2** : a person who likes and admires someone or something in a very enthusiastic way • I am a huge sports fan. • He's her biggest fan. • the singer's fan club • She gets lots of fan letters/mail.

²fan vb **fanned; fan·ning 1** [T] : to move air on or toward (someone or something) with a fan • He fanned himself with a newspaper. • (figurative) They are fanning the flames/fires of hate. [=they are making people become more angry, violent, etc.] **2** [T/I] baseball, informal : to strike out • The pitcher fanned six batters. • The batter fanned on a curveball. — **fan out** [phrasal vb] **fan out** or **fan out** (some-

thing) or fan (something) out : to spread apart or to cause (something) to spread apart • *The search party fanned out across the field.*

fa·nat·ic /fəˈnætɪk/ *n* [*C*] **1** : a person who is very enthusiastic about something • *a boating fanatic* **2** *disapproving* : someone who has extreme ideas about politics, religion, etc. • *a religious fanatic* — **fanatic** *or* **fa·nat·i·cal** /fəˈnætɪkəl/ *adj* • *a fanatical supporter* • *fanatical devotion* — **fa·nat·i·cal·ly** /fəˈnætɪkli/ *adv* — **fa·nat·i·cism** /fəˈnætəˌsɪzəm/ *n* [*U*] • *religious fanaticism*

fan·ci·ful /ˈfænsɪfəl/ *adj* **1** : coming from the imagination • *a fanciful tale* **2** : showing imagination : unusual and appealing • *fanciful architecture* — **fan·ci·ful·ly** /ˈfænsɪfli/ *adv*

¹**fan·cy** /ˈfænsi/ *adj* **fan·ci·er, -est 1** : not plain or ordinary • *a fancy dress/hairdo* **2** : very expensive and fashionable • *a fancy restaurant/car* **3** : done with great skill and grace • *fancy footwork* — **fan·ci·ly** /ˈfænsəli/ *adv*

²**fancy** *n, pl* **-cies 1** [*singular*] : the feeling of liking someone or something • *The movie really struck/caught/tickled/took their fancy.* • *She took a fancy to the stray dog.* • *a passing fancy* [=a liking that lasts only a short time] **2 a** [*U*] : IMAGINATION • *His plans are the product of pure fancy.* [=are not realistic] **b** [*C/U*] : FANTASY • *a mere fancy*

³**fancy** *vb* **-cied; -cy·ing** [*T*] **1** *informal* : to take pleasure in (something) • *She never fancied* [=liked, enjoyed] *parties.* **2** *chiefly Brit, informal* : to consider (someone or something) likely to win or succeed • *Which horse do you fancy?* **3** *chiefly Brit, informal* : to want to have or do (something) • *Do you fancy (having) another drink?* **4** *Brit, informal* : to feel sexually attracted to (someone) • *I think she fancies him.* **5** *Brit* : to imagine (something) • *I can't fancy you as a father.* • *Fancy that!* [=imagine that] **6** : to think or believe (something) without being certain • *I fancy (that) I've met him before.* — **fan·ci·er** /ˈfænsijɚ/ *n* [*C*] • *a cat/wine fancier* [=someone who likes cats/wine]

fan·fare /ˈfænˌfeɚ/ *n* **1** [*U*] : a lot of talk or activity showing that people are excited about something • *The new jet was introduced with great fanfare.* **2** [*C*] : a short piece of music played loudly with trumpets

fang /ˈfæŋ/ *n* [*C*] : a long, sharp tooth • *a tiger baring/showing its fangs* — **fanged** /ˈfæŋd/ *adj* • *a fanged monster*

fan·ny /ˈfæni/ *n, pl* **-nies** [*C*] *US, informal* : BUTTOCKS • *a kick in the fanny*

fan·ta·size *also Brit* **fan·ta·sise** /ˈfæntəˌsaɪz/ *vb* **-sized; -siz·ing** [*T/I*] : to imagine doing things that you are very unlikely to do • *He fantasized about becoming a painter.*

fan·tas·tic /fænˈtæstɪk/ *adj* **1** : extremely good • *That meal was fantastic!* **2** : extremely high or great • *fantastic speeds* **3** *also* **fan·tas·ti·cal** /fænˈtæstɪkəl/ : very strange, unusual, or unlikely • *a fantastic* [=wild] *scheme* • *fantastic creatures* —

fan·tas·ti·cal·ly /fænˈtæstɪkli/ *adv* • *fantastically high speeds* • *fantastically expensive clothes*

fan·ta·sy /ˈfæntəsi/ *n, pl* **-sies 1** [*C/U*] : an idea that is produced by the imagination and is not realistic • *His plans are pure fantasy.* • *Her fantasy is to be a film star.* • *romantic/sexual fantasies* **2** [*U*] : the act of imagining something • IMAGINATION • *His plans are the product of pure fantasy.* **3** [*C/U*] : a book, movie, etc., about things that happen in an imaginary world

FAQ /ˈfæk, ˌɛfˌeɪˈkjuː/ *abbr* frequently asked question, frequently asked questions — used to refer to a list of questions and answers that is shown on a Web site

¹**far** /ˈfɑɚ/ *adv* **far·ther** /ˈfɑɚðɚ/ *or* **fur·ther** /ˈfɚðɚ/; **far·thest** /ˈfɑɚðəst/ *or* **fur·thest** /ˈfɚðəst/ **1** : at or to a great distance in space or time • *She lives far out in the country.* • *looking far into the past* • *the far distant future* • *Her house isn't far (from here).* • *I don't like being so far (away) from home.* **2** : to a great extent • *far easier/greater/better* • *The car is far too expensive.* • *His views are far different from mine.* **3** : to or at a particular distance, point, or degree • *How far is it (from here) to the station?* • *Those birds aren't usually seen this far north.* • *as far away as China* • *as far back as the 17th century* • *She didn't know how far* [=to what extent] *she could trust him.* **4** : to an advanced point or extent • *These reforms don't go far enough.* • *He drove the stake far into the ground.* • *We still have far to go.* • *If she works hard, she'll go far.* [=be very successful] — **as far as 1** *also* **so far as a** — used in expressions like **as/so far as I know** to say that you think a statement is true but that there may be something you do not know which makes it untrue • *It's safe, as far as I know.* **b** — used in expressions like **as/so far as (something) goes** and **as/so far as (something) is concerned** to mean "about (something)" or "with regard to (something)" • *He has no worries as far as money is concerned.* [=he has no worries about money] **c** — used in expressions like **as/so far as (someone) is concerned** to mean "in someone's opinion" • *As far as she's concerned, he's perfect.* **2** *informal* : with regard to (something or someone) • *He's here. As far as* [=as for] *the others, they'll arrive later.* [=the others will arrive later] — **by far** : by a great extent or degree • *Frank was the best runner by far.* — **far and away** : by a great extent or degree : by far • *The college is far and away the best one in the area.* — **far and wide 1** : in every direction or in many different places • *We searched far and wide.* • *He's known far and wide for his skill as a cook.* **2** : distant places • *People came from far and wide to attend the fair.* — **far be it from me** : it is not appropriate for me — often used when giving advice or criticism • *Far be it from me to interfere* [=I should not interfere], *but I don't know why you keep dating that guy.* — **far from** : certainly not : not at all •

The trip was far from a failure. ▪ *The outcome is far from certain.* ▪ *Far from being friendly, he was openly rude to us.* — **far gone** *informal* : in a very bad, weak, or confused condition ▪ *He'd been drinking all day, so he was pretty far gone.* — **far off** : very wrong ▪ *He was not far off in his predictions.* — **from far and near** *or* **from near and far** : from distant places and from near places : from many different places ▪ *people came from far and near* — **so far 1** : until the present time : to this point ▪ *He has written two books so far.* ▪ *"How's the work going?" "So far, so good."* [=there have not yet been any problems] **2** : to a certain point, degree, or distance ▪ *Intelligence alone will only take you so far.* [=will only provide limited success] — **thus far** : until the present time : so far ▪ *Thus far the results have been disappointing.*

²**far** *adj, always before a noun* **farther** *or* **further**; **farthest** *or* **furthest 1** : very distant in space or time ▪ *the far corners of the world* ▪ *the far past* **2** — used to refer to the side, end, etc., that is more distant ▪ *on the far side of the lake* ▪ *the far end of the room* — **the far left** : the group of people whose political views are the most liberal — **the far right** : the group of people whose political views are the most conservative

far·a·way /ˈfɑrəˌweɪ/ *adj* : very distant ▪ *tales of faraway lands* ▪ *She had a faraway look in her eyes.* [=she seemed to be thinking about something far away]

farce /ˈfɑɚs/ *n* **1 a** [C] : a funny play or movie about ridiculous situations and events **b** [U] : the style of humor that occurs in a farce ▪ *an actor with a talent for farce* **2** [C] *disapproving* : something that is so bad that it seems ridiculous ▪ *This trial is a farce.* — **far·ci·cal** /ˈfɑɚsɪkəl/ *adj*

¹**fare** /ˈfeɚ/ *vb* **fared; far·ing** [I] : to do something well or badly ▪ *The team hasn't fared well recently.*

²**fare** *n* **1** [C] : the money a person pays to travel on a bus, train, etc. ▪ *I need cash for the taxi fare.* **2** [C] : a passenger who pays a fare ▪ *taxis picking up fares* **3** [U] : a specified kind of food ▪ *sampling the local fare* ▪ (*figurative*) *These kinds of shows are now standard fare* [=a very common thing] *on television.*

Far East *n* — **the Far East** : the countries of eastern and southeastern Asia (such as China, Japan, North Korea, South Korea, and Vietnam)

¹**fare·well** /ˌfeɚˈwɛl/ *interj, formal + literary* : ¹GOODBYE ▪ *Farewell until we meet again.*

²**farewell** *n* [C] *formal + literary* : ²GOODBYE ▪ *She bid/wished me farewell.* ▪ *a fond farewell*

³**farewell** /ˌfeɚˈwɛl/ *adj, always before a noun* : done when someone is leaving, ending a career, etc. ▪ *a farewell party/speech/concert*

far–fetched /ˈfɑɚˈfɛtʃt/ *adj* : not likely to happen or be true ▪ *a far-fetched story*

far–flung /ˈfɑɚˈflʌŋ/ *adj* **1** : covering a very large area ▪ *a far-flung* [=*vast*] *media empire* **2** : located in a very distant

place ▪ *a far-flung village*

¹**farm** /ˈfɑɚm/ *n* [C] : a piece of land used for growing crops or raising animals ▪ *a dairy/vegetable farm* — **buy the farm** see ¹BUY

²**farm** *vb* [T/I] : to use land for growing food or raising animals ▪ *He has been farming (on) this land for 30 years.* — **farm out** [*phrasal vb*] **farm (something) out** *or* **farm out (something)** : to send out (work) to be done by others ▪ *They decided to farm out the job.* — **farm·ing** /ˈfɑɚmɪŋ/ *n* [U]

farm·er /ˈfɑɚmɚ/ *n* [C] : a person who runs a farm ▪ *a cotton/hog farmer*

farm·hand /ˈfɑɚmˌhænd/ *n* [C] : a person who is hired to work on a farm

farm·house /ˈfɑɚmˌhaʊs/ *n* [C] : a house on a farm

farm·land /ˈfɑɚmˌlænd/ *n* [U] : land used or suitable for farming

farm·yard /ˈfɑɚmˌjɑɚd/ *n* [C] : BARNYARD

far–off /ˈfɑɚˌɑːf/ *adj* : very far away in time or space ▪ *tales of far-off lands*

far–out /ˈfɑɚˌaʊt/ *adj, informal* : very strange or unusual ▪ *some pretty far-out clothes*

far–reach·ing /ˈfɑɚˌriːtʃɪŋ/ *adj* : affecting many people or things ▪ *a far-reaching decision* = *a decision with far-reaching implications*

far·sight·ed /ˈfɑɚˌsaɪtəd/ *adj* **1** *chiefly US* : able to see things that are far away more clearly than things that are near ▪ *He wears glasses because he is farsighted.* [=(*Brit*) *longsighted*] **2** : wise with regard to planning or to the future ▪ *farsighted leaders* ▪ *a farsighted plan/approach* — **far·sight·ed·ness** *n* [U]

fart /ˈfɑɚt/ *vb* [I] *informal + impolite* : to release gas from the anus — **fart around** *informal + impolite* : to waste time doing things that are not important — **fart** *n* [C]

¹**far·ther** /ˈfɑɚðɚ/ *adv* : to or at a more distant place or time or a more advanced point : FURTHER ▪ *drive farther north* ▪ *It's farther away than I'd thought.* ▪ *Nothing could be farther from the truth.* [=that is not at all true]

²**farther** *adj, always before a noun* : more distant : FURTHER ▪ *the farther side of town*

¹**far·thest** /ˈfɑɚðəst/ *adv* **1** : to or at the greatest distance in space or time : FURTHEST ▪ *the seat farthest from the door* ▪ *Let's see who can jump the farthest.* **2** : to the most advanced point : FURTHEST ▪ *This plan goes farthest toward achieving our goal.* **3** *chiefly US* : by the greatest degree or extent : MOST, FURTHEST ▪ *Their research is the farthest advanced.*

²**farthest** *adj, always before a noun* : most distant in space or time : FURTHEST ▪ *the farthest reaches of space* ▪ (*figurative*) *Food is the farthest thing from my mind right now.*

fas·ci·nate /ˈfæsəˌneɪt/ *vb* **-nat·ed; -nat·ing** [T/I] : to cause (someone) to be very interested in something or someone ▪ *Her paintings fascinate me.* = *I'm fascinated by/with her paintings.* — **fas·ci·na·tion** /ˌfæsəˈneɪʃən/ *n* [U, singular] ▪ *I've stud-*

ied her paintings with fascination. ▪ *Her paintings have/hold a real fascination for me.* [=they interest me deeply] — **fas·ci·nat·ing** /ˈfæsəˌneɪtɪŋ/ *adj* ▪ *a fascinating book/painting*

fas·cism *or* **Fas·cism** /ˈfæˌʃɪzəm/ *n* [U] : a way of organizing a society in which a government is ruled by a dictator and in which people are not allowed to disagree with the government — **fas·cist** *or* **Fas·cist** /ˈfæʃɪst/ *n* [C] — **fascist** *or* **Fascist** *adj* ▪ *a Fascist state/dictator* — **fas·cis·tic** *or* **Fas·cis·tic** /fæˈʃɪstɪk/ *adj*

¹**fash·ion** /ˈfæʃən/ *n* **1 a** [C/U] : a popular way of dressing ▪ *jewelry/clothing fashions* ▪ *Long skirts were (all) the fashion then.* ▪ *Short skirts are in fashion.* [=popular] ▪ *come (back) into fashion* ▪ *fall/go out of fashion* **b** [U] : the business of creating and selling clothes in new styles ▪ *the world of fashion* ▪ *a fashion show* ▪ *c* [*plural*] : clothes that are popular ▪ *She always wears the latest fashions.* **2** [C/U] : a style, way of behaving, etc., that is popular ▪ *Literary fashions have changed.* ▪ *Action movies are (all) the fashion.* — *Her theories have fallen/gone out of fashion.* **3** [U, *singular*] : a specified way of acting or behaving ▪ *behaving in a strange fashion* [=behaving strangely] ▪ *We lined up in (an) orderly fashion.* — **after a fashion** : to a slight or minor degree — SOMEWHAT ▪ *I can play the piano after a fashion.*

²**fashion** *vb* [T] : to form (something) into something else ▪ *They fashioned the clay into bowls.* ▪ : to make (something) from something else ▪ *bowls fashioned from clay*

fash·ion·able /ˈfæʃənəbəl/ *adj* **1** : currently popular ▪ *fashionable* [=stylish] *clothes* **2** : dressing and acting in a way that is currently popular ▪ *fashionable people* — **fash·ion·ably** /ˈfæʃənəbli/ *adv* ▪ *She was fashionably dressed.*

¹**fast** /ˈfæst, *Brit* ˈfɑːst/ *adj* **1 a** : moving or able to move quickly ▪ *a fast runner/car/pitch* **b** : happening quickly ▪ *a fast race* ▪ *We're off to a fast start.* **c** : operating quickly ▪ *a fast computer* **d** : doing something or able to do something quickly ▪ *a fast learner* **e** : allowing movement at a great speed ▪ *a fast road/route* **2** *of a clock or watch* : showing a time that is later than the correct time ▪ *My watch is (ten minutes) fast.* **3** *informal* **a** : tricky and unfair ▪ *pull a fast one on someone* [=trick or deceive someone] **b** : earned or gotten quickly and often in a dishonest way ▪ *a fast buck* ▪ *fast money* **c** : quick and not safe to trust ▪ *The salesman gave us a lot of fast talk.* **4** *old-fashioned + humorous* : actively seeking excitement or pleasure ▪ *He runs with a fast crowd.* ▪ *fast living* **5 a** : placed, tied, attached, or closed securely ▪ *Make the rope fast to the anchor.* **b** : impossible to change ▪ *There are no hard and fast rules.* **c** : not likely to fade ▪ *fast colors* **6** : very loyal or faithful ▪ *They became fast friends.* — **fast and furious** : with one thing following an-

other very quickly ▪ *The action was fast and furious.*

²**fast** *adv* **1** : with great speed ▪ *We'd better work fast.* ▪ *You're driving too fast!* ▪ *a fast-paced story* : in a very short time : very quickly ▪ *This offer ends soon, so act fast!* ▪ *It all happened so fast.* **2 a** : in a quick and intelligent way ▪ *think fast* ▪ *You catch on fast.* **b** : quickly and persuasively ▪ *He'll have to talk fast to get himself out of this mess.* **3** : in a way that is not easily moved or changed ▪ *The window was stuck fast.* ▪ *She held fast to her beliefs.* ▪ *We must stand fast and not surrender!* — **going/getting nowhere fast** *informal* : failing to make progress ▪ *The plan for a new stadium is going nowhere fast.* — **not so fast** *informal* — used in speech to tell someone not to act, judge, etc., too quickly ▪ *"I'm leaving now." "Not so fast. Finish your dinner first."*

³**fast** *vb* [I] : to eat no food for a period of time ▪ *Patients must fast for six hours before having the procedure.* ▪ *periods of fasting* — **fast** *n* [C] ▪ *He went on a fast* [=he ate nothing] *for several days.*

fast·ball /ˈfæstˌbɑːl, *Brit* ˈfɑːstˌbɑːl/ *n* [C] *baseball* : a very fast pitch

fas·ten /ˈfæsn, *Brit* ˈfɑːsn/ *vb* **1 a** [T] : to attach (something) or join (two things or parts) with a pin, knot, etc. ▪ *fasten clothes on/onto/to a clothesline* ▪ *boards fastened together by/with nails* ▪ *fasten a cape* ▪ (*figurative*) *fasten your hopes on something* **b** [I] *of parts of something* : to become attached or joined ▪ *The dress fastens in the back.* **2 a** [T] : to put something in a position or location in such a way that it will not move ▪ *Fasten your seat belt.* ▪ *Is the lid tightly fastened?* **b** [T/I] : to close and lock (a window, door, etc.) ▪ *They fastened the shutters.* ▪ *The lock won't fasten.* **3** [T/I] : to grip and hold something ▪ *He fastened his hands on/around my arm.* ▪ *His hands fastened on/around my arm.* = *He fastened onto my arm.* — **fas·ten·er** /ˈfæsnə, *Brit* ˈfɑːsnə/ *n* [C] ▪ *window fasteners*

fas·ten·ing /ˈfæsnɪŋ, *Brit* ˈfɑːsnɪŋ/ *n* [C] : something that fastens one thing to another thing ▪ *a coat with button and loop fastenings*

fast food *n* [C/U] : food from a restaurant that makes and serves food very quickly ▪ *They eat a lot of fast food.* — **fast–food** *adj, always before a noun* ▪ *a fast-food restaurant*

fast–for·ward /ˌfæstˈfoəwəd, *Brit* ˌfɑːstˈfoːwəd/ *n* [U] : a function that causes a recording to go forward faster than normal ▪ *Hit the fast-forward button.* — **fast–forward** *vb* [T/I] ▪ *We fast-forwarded (the tape) to get to the last song.*

fas·tid·i·ous /fæˈstɪdijəs/ *adj* **1** : very careful about how you do something ▪ *a fastidious dresser/scholar* **2** : liking few things : hard to please ▪ *a fastidious eater* — **fas·tid·i·ous·ly** *adv* — **fas·tid·i·ous·ness** *n* [U]

fast lane *n* **1** [C] : a lane of a highway for cars that are traveling at high speeds **2** [*singular*] : a way of living that is exciting and often dangerous ▪ *living life in the fast lane*

fast–talk /ˈfæstˌtɔːk, *Brit* ˈfɑːstˌtɔːk/ *vb* [T] *informal* : to persuade (someone) by talking quickly and often in a dishonest way ▪ *The salesperson fast-talked him into buying the car.*

fast track *n* [*singular*] : a way of proceeding that produces a desired result quickly ▪ *The proposed law is on a fast track to/ for approval.* ▪ *She is on the fast track to success.*

¹**fat** /ˈfæt/ *adj* **fat·ter; fat·test** **1** : having a lot of body fat ▪ *The dog is getting fat.* ▪ *a cute, fat baby* **2** : having a full, rounded form ▪ *a fat belly* ▪ *a fat, juicy peach* ▪ *a fat* [=*swollen*] *lip* **3** : unusually wide or thick ▪ *a fat book/envelope* ▪ *fat tires* **4** *informal* : involving a large amount of money ▪ *a fat salary/contract/check* **5** *informal + disapproving* : successful or wealthy ▪ *The company grew fat on profits.* — **fat·ness** *n* [U]

²**fat** *n* **1** [U] : the soft flesh on the bodies of people and animals that helps keep the body warm and is used to store energy ▪ *excess body fat* ▪ *exercising to lose/ burn fat* **2** [C/U] : an oily solid or liquid substance in food ▪ *fats like butter and olive oil* ▪ *milk/bacon fat* ▪ *foods that are high/low in fat* ▪ *saturated fats* ▪ *(figurative) trim the fat off/from the budget* — **chew the fat** see CHEW — **live off/ on the fat of the land** : to live very well without having to work hard

fa·tal /ˈfeɪtl/ *adj* **1** : causing death ▪ *a fatal accident/disease/blow* ▪ *a chemical that is fatal to birds* **2** : causing ruin or failure ▪ *a fatal mistake/error* — **fa·tal·ly** *adv* ▪ *fatally shot/wounded*

fa·tal·ism /ˈfeɪtlˌɪzəm/ *n* [U] : the belief that what will happen has already been decided and cannot be changed ▪ *He has a sense of fatalism about the future.* — **fa·tal·ist** /ˈfeɪtlɪst/ *n* [C] — **fa·tal·is·tic** /ˌfeɪtlˈɪstɪk/ *adj*

fa·tal·i·ty /feɪˈtæləti/ *n, pl* **-ties** **1** [C] : a death that results from an accident, disaster, etc. ▪ *The car crash caused one fatality.* **2** [U] : a tendency to result in death ▪ *a disease with a high fatality rate*

fat cat *n* [C] *informal + disapproving* : an important, wealthy, or powerful person ▪ *political fat cats*

fate /ˈfeɪt/ *n* **1** [U] : a power that is believed to control what happens in the future ▪ *Fate brought us back together.* ▪ *a surprising turn/twist/quirk of fate* **2** [C] : the things that will happen to a person or thing ▪ *The lost boy's fate was unknown.* [=no one knew what happened to him] ▪ *Exile was his fate.* = *It was his fate to be exiled.* ▪ *her sad/unhappy/tragic fate* ▪ *Her fate was sealed.* [=her future could not be changed] ▪ *He met his fate* [=*died*] *on the battlefield.* — **tempt fate** see TEMPT — **fat·ed** /ˈfeɪtəd/ *adj* ▪ *They seemed fated* [=*destined*] *for each other.* ▪ *a character fated* [=*doomed*] *to die young*

fate·ful /ˈfeɪtfəl/ *adj* : having important or serious results ▪ *a fateful decision* ▪ *Hundreds perished on that fateful day.* — **fate·ful·ly** *adv*

fat–free *adj* : containing no fat ▪ *fat-free milk*

fat·head /ˈfætˌhɛd/ *n* [C] *informal* : a stupid person

¹**fa·ther** /ˈfɑːðɚ/ *n* [C] **1** : a male parent ▪ *become a father* ▪ *He's the father of three children.* ▪ *"He's very stubborn." "Well, like father, like son."* [=his father is also stubborn] **2** : a man who is thought of as being like a father ▪ *He was a father to me after my own father died.* **3** *Father* : GOD **1** ▪ *heavenly Father* **4** *formal* : ANCESTOR ▪ *the land on which her fathers toiled* **5** : a man who invents or begins something ▪ *George Washington is the father of our country.* **6** *old-fashioned* : an older man who is one of the leaders of a city, town, etc. ▪ *the city fathers* **7** : PRIEST — used especially as a title or a form of address ▪ *Father Fitzgerald* ▪ *Good morning, Father.* — **fa·ther·hood** /ˈfɑːðɚˌhʊd/ *n* [U] — **fa·ther·less** /ˈfɑːðɚləs/ *adj*

²**father** *vb* [T] **1** : to make a woman pregnant so that she gives birth to (a child) ▪ *He fathered three children.* **2** *of a man* : to invent, create, or produce (something) ▪ *He fathered a plan to improve the schools.*

Father Christmas *n* [*singular*] *Brit* : SANTA CLAUS

father figure *n* [C] : an older man who is respected and admired like a father

fa·ther–in–law /ˈfɑːðɚənˌlɑː/ *n, pl* **fathers–in–law** /ˈfɑːðɚzənˌlɑː/ [C] : the father of your husband or wife

fa·ther·land /ˈfɑːðɚˌlænd/ *n* [C] : the country where you were born or where your family came from ▪ *He fought to protect his fatherland.* ▪ *stories of the fatherland* ◇ *Fatherland* is often associated with Germany.

fa·ther·ly /ˈfɑːðɚli/ *adj* : of a father ▪ *fatherly responsibilities* : resembling a father ▪ *a fatherly old man* : showing the affection or concern of a father ▪ *fatherly advice*

Father's Day *n* [C/U] : the third Sunday in June treated as a special day for honoring fathers

¹**fath·om** /ˈfæðəm/ *n* [C] : a unit of length equal to six feet (about 1.8 meters) used especially for measuring the depth of water

²**fathom** *vb* [T] : to understand the reason for (something) ▪ *I couldn't fathom why she did that.* = *I couldn't fathom her reasons for doing that.*

¹**fa·tigue** /fəˈtiːg/ *n* **1** [U] : the state of being very tired ▪ *overcome by fatigue* **2** [*plural*] : the uniform that soldiers wear when they are doing physical work ▪ *dressed in (army) fatigues* **3** [U] *technical* : a tendency to break after being bent or moved many times ▪ *cracks caused by metal fatigue*

²**fatigue** *vb* **-tigued; -tigu·ing** [T] : to make (someone) tired ▪ *We were fatigued by the journey.* ▪ *feeling fatigued* ▪ *a very fatiguing* [=*tiring*] *journey*

fat·ten /ˈfætn/ *vb* **1** [T] : to make (someone or something) fat ▪ *fatten (up) pigs for slaughter* **2** [I] : to become fat ▪ *bears*

fattening up for the winter — **fattening**
adj • fattening foods

¹**fat·ty** /'fæti/ adj **fat·ti·er; -est** : containing fat and especially a large amount of fat • fatty tissue/foods — **fat·ti·ness** n [U]

²**fatty** n, pl **-ties** [C] informal + offensive : a fat person

fat·u·ous /'fætʃuwəs/ adj : foolish or stupid • fatuous remarks/notions — **fat·u·ous·ly** adv — **fat·u·ous·ness** n [U]

fau·cet /'fɑːsət/ n [C] US : a device that is used to control the flow of water from a pipe

¹**fault** /'fɑːlt/ n **1** [C] **a** : a bad quality or part of someone's character • In spite of her faults, she's a loyal friend. **b** : FLAW, DEFECT • the book's strengths and faults **2** [U] : responsibility for a problem, mistake, etc. • The accident was not her fault. • It's all my fault. • Through no fault of his own, he was delayed. **3** [C] tennis : a mistake that results in a bad serve • commit a fault — see also DOUBLE FAULT **4** [C] geology : a break in the Earth's crust • the San Andreas Fault — **at fault** : deserving blame for something bad : RESPONSIBLE • She's not at fault for the accident. — **find fault** see ¹FIND — **to a fault** : to a great or excessive degree • generous to a fault [=very/too generous] — **fault·less** /'fɑːltləs/ adj — **fault·less·ly** adv

²**fault** vb [T] **1** : to criticize (something) • She faulted the book as (being) too long. **2** : to blame or criticize (someone) • I can't fault him for protecting his family.

faulty /'fɑːlti/ adj **fault·i·er; -est** : having a mistake, fault, or weakness • a faulty argument/design • faulty statistics — **fault·i·ly** /'fɑːltəli/ adv — **fault·i·ness** /'fɑːltinəs/ n [U]

fau·na /'fɑːnə/ n, pl **fau·nas** also **fau·nae** /'fɑːˌniː/ [C/U] biology : all the animals that live in a particular area, time period, or environment • the fauna of the island — compare FLORA

faux pas /ˌfouˈpɑː/ n, pl **faux pas** /ˌfouˈpɑːz/ [C] : an embarrassing social mistake • making/committing a faux pas

fa·va bean /'fɑːvə-/ n [C] chiefly US : a large, flat, pale green seed that is eaten as a vegetable — called also (chiefly Brit) **broad bean**

fave /'feɪv/ n [C] informal : FAVORITE **1** • That show is my fave.

¹**fa·vor** (US) or Brit **fa·vour** /'feɪvɚ/ n **1** [C] : a kind or helpful act that you do for someone • do a favor for a friend = grant a favor to a friend • Can I ask you (for) a favor? • I owe her a favor. • **Do me a favor** [=do what I want you to do] and stop complaining! • Do yourself a favor and get there early. • He avoids her, and she returns the favor. [=she avoids him] • buying political favors **2** [U] **a** : approval, support, or popularity • He's trying to win her favor. • Her theories have found/gained/won favor (with scholars). • **come into favor** [=become popular] • An idea that is in favor [=popular] • **lose favor** = fall from favor = fall out of favor • **look with favor on something** [=approve of something] **b** : preference for one per-

son, group, etc., over another • show favor for/toward someone **3** [C] US : a small gift given to the people who come to a party • candies given out as (party) favors — curry favor see ²CURRY — **in favor of 1** : wanting or approving of (something) • All in favor of (having) a party, raise your hands. • Most voters are in favor of the tax cuts. **2** : in support of (something) • He argued in favor of [=for] the tax cuts. **3** : choosing (something) instead of something else • The idea was rejected in favor of a new plan. **4** : in support of (someone) • The judge ruled in favor of the defendant. — **in someone's favor 1** : in support of (someone) • The judge ruled in our favor. **2** : in a state of being liked or approved of by (someone) • trying to get back in her favor — **odds are in favor** ◇ If the odds are in your favor, you are likely to win or succeed. ◇ If the odds are in favor of something, that thing is likely to happen.

²**favor** (US) or Brit **favour** vb [T] **1 a** : to prefer (someone) especially in an unfair way • He claims that his parents favor his sister (over him). **b** : to approve of or support (something) • She favored (the idea of) cutting taxes. **c** : to regard (someone or something) as most likely to succeed or win • The team is favored to win this year. **2** formal : to do or give something as a kindness to (someone) — + with • She favored us with a song/smile. **3** : to treat (an injured leg, foot, etc.) gently • She was favoring her left leg (as she walked). **4** formal : to make (something) possible or easy • The weather favored our plans. **5** : to look like (a parent or other relative) • He favors his mother.

fa·vor·able (US) or Brit **fa·vour·able** /'feɪvɚrəbəl/ adj **1** : showing or expressing approval • favorable reviews • a favorable comparison = a comparison favorable to someone • They gave a favorable answer to our request. **2** : producing feelings of approval • She made a favorable [=good] impression on them. **3 a** : tending to produce a desired result • a favorable wind • plants growing under favorable conditions **b** : showing that a desired result is likely • Early test results were favorable. — **fa·vor·ably** (US) or Brit **fa·vour·ably** /'feɪvɚrəbli/ adv

¹**fa·vor·ite** (US) or Brit **fa·vour·ite** /'feɪvrət/ adj, always before a noun : most liked • Red is my favorite color.

²**favorite** (US) or Brit **favourite** n [C] **1** : a person or a thing that is liked more than others • She's the teacher's favorite. • That movie is my favorite. **2** : a person, team, etc., that is considered most likely to win • He's the (heavy/clear) favorite to win the election.

fa·vor·it·ism (US) or Brit **fa·vour·it·ism** /'feɪvrəˌtɪzəm/ n [U] : the unfair practice of treating some people better than others • showing favoritism • political favoritism

¹**fawn** /'fɑːn/ vb [I] disapproving : to try to get the approval of an important person by giving that person praise, attention, etc. • Her fans fawn (all) over her. = She is

fawned on by her fans.

²**fawn** *n* [C] : a young deer; *especially* : a deer that is less than a year old

fax /ˈfæks/ *n* **1 a** [U] : a system for sending and receiving documents, photographs, etc., using telephone lines ▪ *Send me a copy by fax.* **b** [C] : a machine used in this system — called also *fax machine* **2** [C] : something that is sent or received by fax ▪ *a fax of her report* ▪ *I received your fax.* — **fax** *vb* [T] ▪ *She faxed me a copy of her report. = She faxed a copy of her report to me.*

faze /ˈfeɪz/ *vb* **fazed; faz·ing** [T] : to cause (someone) to feel afraid or uncertain ▪ *Nothing fazes her.*

FBI *abbr* Federal Bureau of Investigation ▪ *The crime is being investigated by the FBI.* ▪ *an FBI agent/laboratory* ◇ The Federal Bureau of Investigation is a part of the U.S. federal government that is responsible for investigating crimes.

FCC *abbr* Federal Communications Commission ◇ The Federal Communications Commission is a part of the U.S. federal government that controls radio and television broadcasting.

FDA *abbr* Food and Drug Administration ◇ The Food and Drug Administration is a part of the U.S. federal government that tests, approves, and sets standards for foods, drugs, chemicals, and household products.

FDIC *abbr* Federal Deposit Insurance Corporation ◇ The Federal Deposit Insurance Corporation is a part of the U.S. federal government that provides insurance against loss of money that people have deposited in banks.

¹**fear** /ˈfiɚ/ *n* **1** [C/U] : a feeling of being afraid ▪ *We was trembling with fear.* ▪ *a story that inspires fear* ▪ *living without fear* ▪ *my fear of flying* ▪ *his hopes and fears* ▪ *They talked about their fears that the company would fail.* ▪ *allay/alleviate/ease fears of a recession* ▪ *She has a fear of cats.* ▪ *He won't speak out for fear of losing his job.* [=because he is afraid of losing his job] ▪ *She was in fear of her life. = (US) She was in fear for her life.* [=afraid she might be killed] ▪ *She lived in fear of being caught.* **2** [U] : a feeling of respect and wonder for something very powerful ▪ *fear of God* ▪ *The market crash put the fear of God into investors.* [=it frightened them very badly]

²**fear** *vb* **1** [T] : to be afraid of (something or someone) ▪ *She fears the water.* ▪ *a cruel king who was feared by all* **2** [T] : to expect or worry about (something bad or unpleasant) ▪ *They feared (that) he would fail.* ▪ *It wasn't as bad as he had feared (it might be).* ▪ *When we heard about the accident, we feared the worst.* ▪ *I fear that we're already too late.* ▪ *There is no easy solution, I fear.* [=*unfortunately*] **3** [I] : to be afraid and worried ▪ *There's no need to fear.* ▪ *Never fear* [=don't worry]— *help is available.* ▪ *Fear not* [=don't be afraid]—*I'll protect you.* ▪ *They feared for their lives.* [=they were afraid that they might be killed] ▪ *She feared for his safety.* **4** [T] : to feel respect and wonder for something very powerful ▪ *fear God*

fear·ful /ˈfiɚfəl/ *adj* **1** : feeling fear ▪ *a fearful flier* ▪ *He was fearful of losing. = He was fearful that he would lose.* ▪ *She was fearful for their safety.* **2** : showing or caused by fear ▪ *a fearful glance* **3** : very bad or extreme ▪ *fearful cold* ▪ *They won the war but at a fearful cost.* **4** : causing fear ▪ *a fearful night alone in the woods* — **fear·ful·ly** *adv*

fear·less /ˈfiɚləs/ *adj* : not afraid : very brave ▪ *a fearless warrior* — **fear·less·ly** *adv* — **fear·less·ness** *n* [U]

fear·some /ˈfiɚsəm/ *adj* : very frightening ▪ *a fearsome monster/opponent* — **fear·some·ly** *adv* ▪ *growling fearsomely* ▪ *fearsomely* [=*very, extremely*] *ambitious*

fea·si·ble /ˈfiːzəbəl/ *adj* : possible to do ▪ *This plan is not economically feasible.* — **fea·si·bil·i·ty** /ˌfiːzəˈbɪləti/ *n* [U] ▪ *She questions the feasibility of the plan.* ▪ *a feasibility study* — **fea·si·bly** /ˈfiːzəbli/ *adv*

¹**feast** /ˈfiːst/ *n* [C] **1** : a special meal with large amounts of food and drink ▪ *give/have a feast* ▪ *the royal wedding feast* [=*banquet*] ▪ *(figurative) The garden is a feast for the eyes.* [=is very beautiful] **2** : a religious festival ▪ *the feast of the Nativity*

²**feast** *vb* **feast·ed; feast·ing** [T/I] : to eat large amounts of food ▪ *We feasted on steak and potatoes.* ▪ *(figurative) We feasted our eyes on* [=looked with great pleasure at] *the beautiful view.*

feat /ˈfiːt/ *n* [C] : an act or achievement that shows courage, strength, or skill ▪ *acrobatic feats* ▪ *feats of strength*

¹**feath·er** /ˈfɛðɚ/ *n* [C] : any one of the light growths that cover a bird's body ▪ *duck feathers* ▪ *Her suitcase felt as light as a feather.* — **a feather in your cap** : an achievement or honor that you can be proud of ▪ *The promotion was a feather in his cap.* — **birds of a feather** : people or things that are the same or very similar ▪ *Those two guys are birds of a feather.* ◇ The expression **birds of a feather flock together** means that people who are alike tend to do things together. — **feath·ered** /ˈfɛðɚd/ *adj* ▪ *She likes to refer to birds as "our feathered friends."* — **feath·er·less** *adj* — **fea·thery** /ˈfɛðɚi/ *adj* ▪ *feathery leaves*

²**feather** *vb* [T] : to put a feather in or on (something) ▪ *feather an arrow* — **feather your (own) nest** : to make yourself richer in a dishonest way ▪ *She feathered her nest with the company's money.*

feath·er·brained /ˈfɛðɚˌbreɪnd/ *adj, informal* : very foolish or silly ▪ *a feather-brained idea/fool*

feath·er·weight /ˈfɛðɚˌweɪt/ *n* [C] : someone or something that weighs very little; *especially* : a boxer who weighs more than 118 pounds (53.5 kilograms) but less than 126 pounds (57 kilograms)

¹**fea·ture** /ˈfiːtʃɚ/ *n* [C] **1** : an interesting or important part, quality, etc. ▪ *a car with new safety/design features* ▪ *She explained the camera's features.* ▪ *combining the best features of the two plans* **2** : a part of the face (such as the eyes, nose, or mouth) ▪ *Her eyes are her best feature.* ▪ *attractive/handsome/delicate (facial) fea-*

tures **3** : a full-length movie • *tonight's feature • starring in his first* **feature film** • *a* **feature-length** *motion picture* **4** : a special story or section in a newspaper or magazine • *a feature on/about urban violence* — **fea·ture·less** /'fiːtʃələs/ *adj* • *a featureless plain*

²**feature** *vb* **-tured; -tur·ing** **1** [*T*] : to have or include (someone or something) as an important part • *The system features state-of-the-art technology.* • *The show now features a new singer.* **2** [*T*] : to give particular attention to (someone or something important) • *The newspaper featured the story on its front page.* • *She was featured in the article.* **3** [*I*] : to be a part of something — + *in* • *Health care features prominently in the new bill.* • *a character who features in many of his novels* — **featured** *adj* • *the featured* [=*main*] *speaker* • *She had a featured role in the movie.*

Feb. *abbr* February

fe·brile /'fɛˌbrajəl, *Brit* 'fiːˌbraɪl/ *adj, medical* : FEVERISH • *a febrile illness* • (*figurative*) *a febrile* [=very active] *imagination*

Feb·ru·ary /'fɛbjəˌweri, 'fɛbrəˌweri/ *n, pl* **-ar·ies** *or* **-ar·ys** [*C/U*] : the second month of the year • *in (early/middle/mid-/late) February* • *early/late in February* • *on February the fourth* = (*US*) *on February fourth* = *on the fourth of February* • *the previous two Februaries* — *abbr.* Feb.

fe·ces (*US*) *or Brit* **fae·ces** /'fiːˌsiːz/ *n* [*plural*] : EXCREMENT — **fe·cal** (*US*) *or Brit* **fae·cal** /'fiːkəl/ *adj* : *fecal matter*

feck·less /'fɛkləs/ *adj* : having or resulting from a weak character or nature • *her feckless son* • *feckless behavior* — **feck·less·ness** *n* [*U*]

fe·cund /'fɛkənd/ *adj, formal* : FERTILE • *fecund fields* • *a fecund breed of cattle* — **fe·cun·di·ty** /fɪ'kʌndəti/ *n* [*U*]

¹**fed** *past tense and past participle of* ¹FEED

²**fed** *or* **Fed** /'fɛd/ *n* [*C*] *US, informal* : a U.S. federal agent, officer, or official • *He was investigated by the feds.* — **the Fed** *US, informal* : the group of officials (**the Federal Reserve Board**) who control the U.S. government's central banking system (**the Federal Reserve System**) • *The Fed has cut interest rates.*

fed·er·al /'fɛdərəl/ *adj* **1 a** : of or relating to a form of government in which power is shared between a central government and individual states, provinces, etc. • *a federal government/system* **b** : of or relating to the central government • *federal laws/employees* • *a federal district/court* **2** *or* **Federal** : of, relating to, or loyal to the federal government during the American Civil War • *a Federal soldier/stronghold* — **fed·er·al·ly** *adv*

federal case *n* [*C*] *US* **1** *law* : a legal case that will be decided in a U.S. federal court **2** *informal* : something that is given too much importance • *Do you have to* **make a federal case out of it**? [=get so upset, angry, etc.]

fed·er·al·ist /'fɛdərəlɪst/ *n* [*C*] **1** *or* **Federalist** : a supporter of federal government; *especially, US* : a supporter of the U.S. Constitution **2** *Federalist US* : a member of a major political party in the early years of the U.S. that wanted a strong central government — **fed·er·al·ism** *or* **Federalism** /'fɛdərəˌlɪzəm/ *n* [*U*] — **federalist** *or* **Federalist** *adj* • *the Federalist period*

fed·er·al·ize *also Brit* **fed·er·al·ise** /'fɛdərəˌlaɪz/ *vb* **-ized; -iz·ing** [*T*] *chiefly US* **1** : to join (states, nations, etc.) together in or under a federal government • *a federalized government* **2** : to cause (something) to be under the control of a federal government • *federalizing several state programs*

fed·er·ate /'fɛdəˌreɪt/ *vb* **-at·ed; -at·ing** [*T*] : to join (organizations, states, etc.) in a federation • *The provinces were federated to form a nation.*

fed·er·a·tion /ˌfɛdə'reɪʃən/ *n* **1** [*C*] **a** : a country formed by separate states that have given certain powers to a central government while keeping control over local matters **b** : an organization that is made by joining together smaller organizations • *a federation of labor unions* **2** [*U*] : the act of joining together separate organizations or states

fe·do·ra /fɪ'dorə/ *n* [*C*] : a type of soft hat for men that has a wide brim

fed up *adj, informal* : angry about something that has continued for a long time • *I'm fed up with all these delays.* • *getting/feeling fed up*

fee·ble /'fiːbəl/ *adj* **fee·bler** /'fiːbələr/; **-blest** /'fiːbələst/ **1** : very weak • *feeble from illness* • *a feeble cry for help* • *a feeble economy* **2** : not good enough : not successful or effective • *a feeble joke/excuse* • *a feeble attempt/effort* — **fee·ble·ness** /'fiːbəlnəs/ *n* [*U*] — **fee·bly** /'fiːbli/ *adv*

fee·ble·mind·ed /ˌfiːbəl'maɪndəd/ *adj* **1** *often offensive* : having less than normal intelligence • *a feebleminded person* **2** : foolish or stupid • *a feebleminded approach/solution* — **fee·ble·mind·ed·ness** *n* [*U*]

¹**feed** /'fiːd/ *vb* **fed** /'fɛd/; **feed·ing** **1 a** [*T*] : to give food to (someone or something) • *Don't feed the animals.* • *feed plants with fertilizer* • *We fed the horses with/on hay.* **b** [*T*] : to give (something) as food • *They fed* [=*gave, served*] *us breakfast.* • *We fed apples to the horses.* • (*figurative*) *He was feeding* [=*giving*] *information to the enemy.* **c** [*T*] : to produce or provide food for (someone or something) • *enough supplies to feed an army* • *He has a family to feed.* • *helping to feed the poor* **d** [*I*] : EAT — *usually used of animals* • *ducks feeding in a pond* • *the feeding habits of sharks* • *a favorite* **feeding ground** [=an area where animals feed] **2** [*T*] : to provide fuel, material, etc., to be used by something • *using wood to feed the fire* • *The streams feed the creek.* • *The motor is fed by a current.* • *The logs are fed into the mill.* • *She fed the*

data into the computer. **3** [T] : to give support or strength to (a feeling, belief, etc.) ▪ *He fed their hopes with false promises.* ▪ *fears fed by ignorance* **4** [T] : to make (something) move through an opening ▪ *She fed more coins into the slot.* — **feed off** [*phrasal vb*] : to gain strength, energy, or support from (something) ▪ *She fed off the crowd's enthusiasm.* ▪ *His anger fed off his jealousy.* — **feed on/upon** [*phrasal vb*] : to eat (something) as food — usually used of animals ▪ *birds that feed on insects* — **feed your face** *slang* : to eat a lot of food ▪ *He sat there feeding his face.*

²feed *n* **1 a** [U] : food for animals ▪ *cattle feed* — see also CHICKEN FEED **b** [C] *informal* : a large meal ▪ *a good feed* **c** [C] *Brit* : FEEDING ▪ *the baby's last feed* **2** [C] : a part that sends material or electricity into a machine or system ▪ *There's a jam in the paper feed.* ▪ *the main power feed* **3** [C] : a television program that is sent to a station for broadcasting ▪ *a live satellite feed*

feed·back /ˈfiːdˌbæk/ *n* [U] **1** : helpful information or criticism that is given to someone to say what can be done to improve a performance, product, etc. ▪ *He asked for feedback from his boss.* **2** *technical* **a** : something (such as information) that is returned to a machine, system, or process ▪ *The system responds to feedback from the sensors.* **b** : an unwanted sound caused by signals being returned to an electronic sound system ▪ *getting feedback from the microphone*

feed·er /ˈfiːdɚ/ *n* [C] **1** : a person or device that supplies food to animals ▪ *a wooden bird feeder* ▪ *pigeon feeders holding bags of bread* **2** : a road, railway, etc., that connects to a larger road, railway, etc. ▪ *a feeder road/route/line* **3** : a part that sends materials into a machine or system **4** : a person or thing that feeds in a specified way or on a specified kind of food ▪ *a messy/heavy feeder* ▪ *a carrion feeder*

feeding *n* [C] *US* : the act of giving food to a person or an animal ▪ *the baby's last feeding* [=(*Brit*) *feed*]

feeding frenzy *n* [C] : a state of wild activity in which many animals are all trying to eat something ▪ *sharks in a feeding frenzy* ▪ (*figurative*) *a media feeding frenzy*

¹feel /ˈfiːl/ *vb* **felt** /ˈfɛlt/; **feel·ing** **1** [T] : to be aware of (something that affects your body) ▪ *He felt a pain in his leg.* ▪ *feel the warmth of the sun* ▪ *I felt someone tap/tapping my shoulder.* ▪ *Do you feel a draft?* **2** [*linking vb*] — used to describe or ask about someone's physical or mental state ▪ *How are you feeling today?* = *How do you feel today?* ▪ *I feel bad/good/sick/well/fine.* ▪ *I hope you feel better soon.* ▪ *feel happy/sad (about something)* ▪ *I feel confident/certain/sure that we'll win.* ▪ *I feel a fool.* = (*chiefly Brit*) *I feel a fool.* ▪ *I feel as if/though I'm falling.* = (*informal*) *I feel like I'm falling.* ▪ **Feel free** *to visit anytime.* [=you are welcome to visit anytime] ✧ If you **feel like** doing something, you want to do it. ▪ *Do you feel like (taking) a walk?* ▪ *I feel like crying.* ▪ *He does whatever he*

feels like (doing). **3 a** [T] : to touch (something) with your fingers to see what it is like ▪ *She felt the fabric.* **b** [T] : to find (something) by touching with your fingers ▪ *feel a small lump* **c** [I] : to search for something by reaching or touching usually with your fingers ▪ *He felt (around) for the switch.* **d** [*linking vb*] — used to describe the quality that something has when it is touched ▪ *This feels like wool (to me).* ▪ *It feels soft/smooth.* **4** [T] : to believe or think (something) ▪ *He feels (that) they behaved badly.* ▪ *I felt it necessary* [=thought that it was necessary] *to explain.* **5** [T] : to have an opinion ▪ *How do you feel about* [=what do you think of] *this proposal?* ▪ *We feel (very) strongly that the law is unfair.* **6** [T] : to be aware of (something) in your mind or emotions ▪ *He felt her disapproval.* ▪ *She could feel* [=sense] *his presence.* ▪ *I feel the urge/need to speak.* ▪ *I feel your pain.* [=I am aware that you have suffered] **7** [T] **a** : to experience the effect of (something) ▪ *He felt the medicine starting to work.* **b** : to experience (something) ▪ *We will all feel the impact of this decision.* ▪ *feel pleasure/anger* ▪ *feel contempt for someone* ▪ *He felt no remorse for his crime.* **c** : to be hurt by (something) ▪ *They felt the insult deeply.* **8** [*linking vb*] **a** : SEEM ▪ *It doesn't feel right to be doing this.* ▪ *This place really feels like home.* ▪ *It feels as if it's going to rain.* = (*chiefly US*) *It feels like rain.* **b** : to have a specified physical quality ▪ *My eyes feel dry.* — **feel for** [*phrasal vb*] : to have sympathy or pity for (someone) ▪ *I feel (deeply) for you.* — **feel no pain** *chiefly US, informal* : to be drunk ▪ *He was clearly feeling no pain.* — **feel out** [*phrasal vb*] **feel (someone) out** : to question (someone) in an indirect way to find out if something you want will be possible ▪ *He was feeling us out to see if we'd loan him money.* — **feel up** [*phrasal vb*] **feel (someone) up** or **feel up (someone)** *informal* : to touch (someone who does not want to be touched) for sexual pleasure — **feel your way 1** : to move forward carefully by putting your hands in front of you so that you can feel anything that blocks you ▪ *He felt his way through the darkened room.* **2** : to move toward a goal very slowly and carefully ▪ *They were just feeling their way (along), trying not to make mistakes.*

²feel *n* [*singular*] **1 a** : the quality of a thing that is experienced by touching it ▪ *It had a greasy feel.* ▪ *the feel of leather* **b** : a particular quality ▪ *The decor has an Asian feel (to/about it).* **2 a** : an understanding of something ▪ *trying to get the feel of the town* = *trying to get a feel for the town* ▪ *She has a feel for how they think.* **b** : an ability to use or do something in a skillful way ▪ *He's starting to get a feel for the instrument.* ▪ *She has a feel for language.* **3** : a feeling or sensation ▪ *the feel of the sun on my face* — **by feel 1** : by feeling with your hands when you cannot see ▪ *It was dark, so she had to find the door by feel.* **2** : by being guided by feelings, senses, etc., instead of by rules or directions ▪ *an athlete who plays by feel*

feel·er /'fiːlɚ/ *n* [C] **1** : a movable part (such as an antenna) of an animal or insect that is used for touching things **2** : a suggestion or question to find out the opinions of other people ▪ *The companies have been putting out feelers* [=asking quietly] *about a merger.*

feel–good /'fiːlˌgʊd/ *adj, always before a noun* : producing good or happy feelings ▪ *a feel-good movie*

feel·ing /'fiːlɪŋ/ *n* **1** [C/U] : an awareness by your body of something in it or on it : SENSATION ▪ *a feeling of pain/nausea* ▪ *I had a queasy feeling (in my stomach).* ▪ *He had no feeling in his right leg.* **2** [C/U] : an emotional state or reaction ▪ *feelings of joy/sorrow/anger/love/guilt* ▪ *bad/ill feelings* [=feelings of anger, dislike, etc.] ▪ *I have a good feeling about this project.* [=I expect it to go well] ▪ *He has ambivalent/mixed feelings* [=both good and bad feelings] *about his job.* ▪ *warm feelings* [=good, pleasant, or friendly feelings] ▪ *I know the feeling.* [=I know how you feel] ▪ *No hard feelings, right?* [=you're not angry, are you?] ▪ *You hurt my feelings.* [=you hurt me emotionally] ▪ *trying to spare his feelings* [=avoid hurting his feelings] ▪ *speak with feeling* [=with strong emotion] **3** a [C] : an opinion or belief ▪ *What's your feeling on/about this?* = *What are your feelings on/about this?* ▪ *I get the feeling* [=impression] *that you don't like me.* ▪ *My feeling is that we need more staff.* ▪ *She shared her feelings with us.* ❖ If you *have a/the feeling* that something might happen or be true, you think it might happen or be true even though you have no definite reason to think so. ▪ *He had the feeling (that) he was being watched.* ▪ *I had a feeling you'd say that.* ▪ *I have a nagging/funny feeling that I've forgotten something.* **b** [U] : an opinion that is shared by many people ▪ *Anti-war feeling has reached an all-time high.* **4** [*singular*] : the general quality of something : FEEL ▪ *The story has an eerie feeling.* ▪ *a big city with a small-town feeling* **5** [U] : the quality of a song, painting, etc., that shows the emotion of the artist or performer ▪ *You need to play it with more feeling.* **6** [*singular*] : an ability to understand the nature of something : ²FEEL 2 ▪ *a painter with a good feeling for color* — **have feelings for** : to feel love or affection for (someone) ▪ *They still have feelings for each other.*

feet *plural of* ¹FOOT

feign /'feɪn/ *vb* [T] : to pretend to feel or be affected by (something) ▪ *He feigned being ill.* = *He feigned illness.* ▪ *feign surprise/sleep/ignorance*

feint /'feɪnt/ *vb* [I] *sports* : to pretend to make an attack as a trick to fool your opponent ▪ *He feinted with his right, then followed with a left hook.* — **feint** *n* [C] ▪ *make a feint*

feisty /'faɪsti/ *adj* **feist·i·er; -est** : not afraid to fight or argue : very lively and aggressive ▪ *a feisty heroine* ▪ *her feisty spirit* — **feist·i·ness** *n* [U]

fe·lic·i·tous /fɪ'lɪsətəs/ *adj, formal* : very suitable or appropriate ▪ *a felicitous phrase* — **fe·lic·i·tous·ly** *adv*

fe·lic·i·ty /fɪ'lɪsəti/ *n, pl* **-ties** *formal* **1** [U] : great happiness ▪ *domestic/marital felicity* **2** [C] : something that is pleasing and well chosen ▪ *felicities of phrasing* **3** [U] : a talent for speaking or writing ▪ *his felicity with words*

fe·line /'fiːˌlaɪn/ *adj* **1** : of or relating to the cat family ▪ *feline diseases* **2** : resembling a cat ▪ *feline agility/grace* — **feline** *n* [C] ▪ *domesticated felines* [=cats]

¹**fell** *past tense of* ¹FALL

²**fell** /'fɛl/ *vb* [T] **1** : to cut down (a tree) ▪ *using an ax to fell a tree* **2** : to beat or knock down (someone or something) ▪ *strong enough to fell an ox* ▪ (*figurative*) *felled* [=killed] *by a heart attack*

³**fell** *adj* — **in one fell swoop** *also* **at one fell swoop** : with a single, quick action or effort ▪ *Her decision solved all our problems in one fell swoop.*

fel·la /'fɛlə/ *n* [C] *informal* : a male person : FELLOW ▪ *He's not a bad fella.*

¹**fel·low** /'fɛloʊ/ *n* [C] **1** *informal + somewhat old-fashioned* : a boy or man ▪ *He's a nice fellow.* [=guy] **2** *or* **Fellow** : a member of a literary, artistic, or scientific organization ▪ *a fellow of the American College of Surgeons* **b** : a senior member of some British colleges and universities **3** *chiefly US* : a graduate student who has been granted a fellowship ▪ *a postdoctoral fellow*

²**fellow** *adj, always before a noun* — used to describe people who belong to the same group or class or who share a situation, experience, etc. ▪ *my fellow students* [=people who are students, as I am] ▪ *learning to love your fellow man* [=other people]

fel·low·ship /'fɛloʊˌʃɪp/ *n* **1** [U] : a friendly relationship among people ▪ *sharing good food and fellowship* **2** [U] : the relationship of people who share interests or feelings ▪ *traditions that bind us together in fellowship* **3** [C] : a group of people who have similar interests ▪ *a youth fellowship* **4** [C] **a** : an amount of money to pay for food, housing, etc., that is given to a graduate student who teaches or does research at a university ▪ *a teaching/research fellowship* **b** : the position of a fellow at a university or college ▪ *He holds a fellowship at the university.*

fel·on /'fɛlən/ *n* [C] : a criminal who has committed a felony ▪ *a convicted felon*

fel·o·ny /'fɛləni/ *n, pl* **-nies** [C] *law* : a serious crime (such as murder or rape) — compare MISDEMEANOR — **fe·lo·ni·ous** /fə'loʊnijəs/ *adj* ▪ *felonious assault*

¹**felt** *past tense and past participle of* ¹FEEL

²**felt** /'fɛlt/ *n* [U] : a soft, heavy cloth made by pressing together fibers of wool, cotton, or other materials ▪ *a felt hat*

felt–tip /'fɛltˌtɪp/ *n* [C] : a pen that has a writing point made of felt — called also *felt-tip pen*

fem *abbr* female; feminine

¹**fe·male** /'fiːˌmeɪl/ *adj* **1 a** : of or relating to the sex that can produce young or lay eggs ▪ *a female bird/mammal* ▪ *a study of*

female [=women's] *sexuality*   **b** : characteristic of girls or women ▪ *a female* [=*feminine*] *voice/name*   **c** : having members who are all girls or women ▪ *a female choir*   **2** *of a plant* : having only seed-producing flowers — **fe·male·ness** *n* [U]

²**female** *n* [C]   **1** : a woman or a girl ▪ *According to the study, males scored about the same as females.*   **2** : an animal that can produce young or lay eggs ▪ *Females of this species weigh 8 to 10 pounds.*   **3** : a plant that can produce seed or fruit

fem·i·nine /ˈfɛmənən/ *adj*   **1** : of, relating to, or suited to women or girls ▪ *a feminine look/appearance* ▪ *feminine hygiene* ▪ *a feminine perspective*   **2** *grammar, in some languages* : of or belonging to the class of words (called a *gender*) that ordinarily includes most of the words referring to females ▪ *a feminine noun/pronoun* ▪ *the feminine gender* — **fem·i·nin·i·ty** /ˌfɛməˈnɪnəti/ *n* [U]

fem·i·nism /ˈfɛməˌnɪzəm/ *n* [U]   **1** : the belief that men and women should have equal rights and opportunities   **2** : organized activity in support of women's rights and interests — **fem·i·nist** /ˈfɛmənɪst/ *n* [C] ▪ *liberal feminists* — **feminist** *adj* ▪ *the feminist movement*

femme fa·tale /ˌfɛmfəˈtæl/ *n, pl* **femmes fa·tales** /ˌfɛmfəˈtælz/ [C] : a very attractive woman who causes trouble or unhappiness for the men who become involved with her

¹**fence** /ˈfɛns/ *n* [C] : a structure like a wall built outdoors usually of wood or metal that separates two areas or prevents people or animals from entering or leaving — **mend fences** see ¹MEND — **on the fence** : unable to decide about something ▪ *trying to persuade those still (sitting) on the fence*

²**fence** *vb* **fenced; fenc·ing**   **1** [T]   **a** : to put a fence around (a place or area) ▪ *I fenced (in) the yard.*   **b** : to keep (something or someone) in or out with a fence ▪ *He fenced (in) the sheep.*   **2** [I] : to practice the art or sport of fencing — **fenc·er** *n* [C] ▪ *a skilled fencer*

fencing *n* [U]   **1** : the art or sport of fighting with swords   **2** : material that is used for making fences ▪ *barbed-wire fencing*

fend /ˈfɛnd/ *vb* — **fend for yourself** : to do things without help ▪ *They had to fend for themselves while their mother was away.* — **fend off** [*phrasal vb*] **fend off (someone or something)** or **fend (someone or something) off** : to defend yourself against (someone or something) ▪ *fending off attackers/allegations*

fend·er /ˈfɛndɚ/ *n* [C] *US*   **1** : a part of a vehicle that covers a wheel — called also (*Brit*) **wing**   **2** : a curved piece of metal that covers a wheel of a motorcycle or bicycle

fender bender *n* [C] *US, informal* : a minor car accident

fen·nel /ˈfɛnl/ *n* [U] : a garden plant that is grown for its seeds, stems, and leaves

fe·ral /ˈfɛrəl/ *adj*   **1** : of, relating to, or resembling a wild beast ▪ *feral instincts*   **2** — used to describe a cat or dog that has

escaped and become wild ▪ *feral cats*

¹**fer·ment** /fɚˈmɛnt/ *vb* [T/I] : to go through a chemical change that results in the production of alcohol ▪ *The wine ferments in oak barrels.* ▪ *Yeast ferments the sugar in the juice.* ▪ (*figurative*) *letting the plan ferment* [=*develop*] *in my mind* — **fer·men·ta·tion** /ˌfɚmənˈteɪʃən/ *n* [U]

²**fer·ment** /ˈfɚˌmɛnt/ *n* [U] : a situation in which there is much excitement and confusion caused by change ▪ *social/religious ferment*

fern /ˈfɚn/ *n* [C] : a type of plant that has large, delicate leaves and no flowers

fe·ro·cious /fəˈroʊʃəs/ *adj*   **1** : very fierce or violent ▪ *ferocious animals*   **2** : very great or extreme ▪ *a ferocious appetite* — **fe·ro·cious·ly** *adv* — **fe·ro·cious·ness** *n* [U]

fe·roc·i·ty /fəˈrɑːsəti/ *n* [U] : a very fierce or violent quality ▪ *the ferocity of the lion/storm*

¹**fer·ret** /ˈfɛrət/ *n* [C] : a small animal that is used for hunting rodents

²**ferret** *vb* — **ferret out** [*phrasal vb*] **ferret out (something)** or **ferret (something) out** : to find (something, such as information) by careful searching ▪ *ferret out answers/problems/facts*

Fer·ris wheel /ˈfɛrəs-/ *n* [C] *chiefly US* : a very large upright wheel that has seats around its edge where people sit while the wheel turns ✧ Ferris wheels are rides that are found at amusement parks.

¹**fer·ry** /ˈfɛri/ *vb* **-ries; -ried; -ry·ing** [T] : to carry or move (someone or something) on a vehicle (such as a boat or a car) usually for a short distance between two places ▪ *A bus ferries visitors from the parking lot to the entrance gate.*

²**ferry** *n, pl* **-ries** [C] : FERRYBOAT ▪ *a ferry service/ride*

fer·ry·boat /ˈfɛriˌboʊt/ *n* [C] : a boat that is used to carry people and things for a short distance between two places

fer·tile /ˈfɚtl/ *adj*   **1** : able to support the growth of many plants ▪ *fertile farmland/soil*   **2 a** : producing a large amount of something ▪ *The area is a fertile breeding ground for political extremism.*   **b** : producing many ideas ▪ *a fertile mind/imagination*   **3 a** : able to produce children, young animals, etc. ▪ *healthy, fertile women/men*   **b** : able to grow or develop ▪ *a fertile egg* — **fer·til·i·ty** /fɚˈtɪləti/ *n* [U] ▪ *a fertility test/drug* ▪ *soil fertility*

fer·til·ize *also Brit* **fer·til·ise** /ˈfɚtəˌlaɪz/ *vb* **-ized; -iz·ing**   **1** [T]   **a** : to make (an egg) able to grow and develop ▪ *sperm fertilizing an egg*   **b** : to make (a plant or flower) able to produce seeds ▪ *bees fertilizing plants*   **2** [T/I] : to make (soil, land, etc.) richer and better able to support plant growth by adding chemicals or a natural substance (such as manure) ▪ *fertilizing the lawn* — **fer·til·i·za·tion** *also Brit* **fer·til·i·sa·tion** /ˌfɚtələˈzeɪʃən/ *n* [U]

fer·til·iz·er *also Brit* **fer·til·is·er** /ˈfɚtəˌlaɪzɚ/ *n* [C/U] : a substance (such as manure or a special chemical) that is added to soil to help the growth of plants

fer·vent /ˈfɚvənt/ *adj* : felt very strongly ▪ *fervent nationalism* : having or showing very strong feelings • *a fervent admirer/ opponent* — **fer·vent·ly** *adv*

fer·vor *(US) or Brit* **fer·vour** /ˈfɔrvɚ/ *n [U]* : a strong feeling of excitement and enthusiasm • *religious fervor*

fess /ˈfɛs/ *vb* — **fess up** [*phrasal vb*] *chiefly US, informal* : CONFESS • *He finally fessed up about his involvement.*

fes·ter /ˈfɛstɚ/ *vb [I]* **1** : to become painful and infected • *a festering sore/wound* **2** : to become worse as time passes • *feelings of resentment that festered for years*

fes·ti·val /ˈfɛstəvəl/ *n [C]* **1** : a special time or event when people gather to celebrate something • *a festival to celebrate the harvest* **2** : an organized series of performances • *a film/jazz festival*

fes·tive /ˈfɛstɪv/ *adj* : cheerful and exciting : suited to a celebration or holiday • *a festive mood/occasion*

fes·tiv·i·ty /fɛˈstɪvəti/ *n, pl* **-ties 1** *[U]* : celebration and enjoyment • *The decorations give the hall an air of festivity.* **2** *[plural]* : enjoyable activities at the time of a holiday or other special occasion • *New Year's Eve festivities*

fes·toon /fɛˈstuːn/ *vb [T]* : to cover or decorate (something) with many small objects, pieces of paper, etc. • *We festooned the halls with leaves and white lights.*

fe·tal *(US) or Brit* **foe·tal** /ˈfiːtl̩/ *adj* : of or relating to a fetus • *a fetal heartbeat*

fetal position *(US) or Brit* **foetal position** *n [singular]* : a position in which you lie on your side with both legs and both arms bent and pulled up to your chest and with your head bowed forward

fetch /ˈfɛtʃ/ *vb* **1** *[T/I]* : to go after and bring back (someone or something) • *I'll fetch [=get] the doctor.* • *dogs trained to fetch* **2** *[T]* : to be sold for (an amount of money) • *This table should fetch quite a bit at auction.* — **fetch up** [*phrasal vb*] *chiefly Brit, informal* : to reach or come to a place, condition, or situation that was not planned or expected • *She eventually fetched up [=ended up] in Italy.*

fetch·ing /ˈfɛtʃɪŋ/ *adj* : attractive or pleasing • *a fetching smile* — **fetch·ing·ly** *adv*

¹**fete** *or* **fête** /ˈfeɪt, ˈfɛt/ *n [C]* **1** *US* : a large party or celebration **2** *Brit* : an outdoor event for raising money that usually includes competitions and things for sale

²**fete** *or* **fête** *vb* **fet·ed** *or* **fêt·ed; fet·ing** *or* **fêt·ing** *[T]* : to honor (a person) or celebrate (something) with a large party or public celebration • *She was feted for her contributions to science.*

fet·id /ˈfɛtəd/ *adj* : having a strong, unpleasant smell • *a fetid pool of water*

fe·tish /ˈfɛtɪʃ/ *n [C]* **1** : a strong and unusual need or desire for something • *a fetish for secrecy* **2** : a need or desire for an object, body part, or activity for sexual excitement • *a foot/leather fetish* **3** : an object that is believed to have magical powers — **fe·tish·ism** /ˈfɛtɪˌɪzəm/ *n [U]* — **fe·tish·ist** /ˈfɛtɪʃɪst/ *n [C]*

fet·ter /ˈfɛtɚ/ *vb [T] formal* : to prevent (someone or something) from moving or

acting freely • *restrictions that fetter creativity*

fet·ters /ˈfɛtɚz/ *n [plural]* **1** *formal* : something that prevents someone or something from moving or acting freely • *free of the fetters of family obligations* **2** : chains placed around a person's feet to restrict motion • *a prisoner in fetters*

fe·tus *or chiefly Brit* **foe·tus** /ˈfiːtəs/ *n [C]* : a human being or animal in the later stages of development before it is born

feud /ˈfjuːd/ *n [C]* : a long and angry fight or quarrel between two people or two groups • *a family feud* — **feud** *vb [I]* • *a family feuding over a will*

feu·dal·ism /ˈfjuːdəˌlɪzəm/ *n [U]* : a social system that existed in Europe during the Middle Ages in which people worked and fought for nobles who gave them protection and the use of land in return — **feu·dal** /ˈfjuːdl̩/ *adj* • *a feudal law/lord*

fe·ver /ˈfiːvɚ/ *n* **1** *[C/U]* **a** : a body temperature that is higher than normal • *He has a fever.* **b** : a disease that causes an increase in body temperature **2** *[singular]* **a** : a state of excited emotion or activity • *a fever of anticipation* **b** : a state of great enthusiasm or interest • *The town has football fever.* [=everyone in the town is very excited about football]

fe·vered /ˈfiːvɚd/ *adj* **1** : having or affected by a fever • *the sick child's fevered brow* **2** : very excited or active • *fevered activity/experimentation*

fe·ver·ish /ˈfiːvərɪʃ/ *adj* **1** : having or relating to a fever • *feeling tired and feverish* **2** : feeling or showing great or extreme excitement • *feverish activity/anticipation* — **fe·ver·ish·ly** *adv*

fever pitch *n [U, singular]* : a state of extreme excitement or activity • *New allegations brought interest in the scandal to (a) fever pitch.*

¹**few** /ˈfjuː/ *adj* **1** : not many • *Few people came.* • *the next/last/past few weeks* • *He caught fewer fish than I did.* **2** : not many but some — used in the phrase **a few** • *Only/Just a few people came.* • *I'm leaving in a few minutes.* ✧ The phrases **quite a few** and, less commonly, **not a few** or *(chiefly Brit)* **a good few** all mean "fairly many." • *Quite a few people were there.* — **as few as** — used to suggest that a number or amount is surprisingly small • *As few as half the students passed the test.* — **few and far between** : not common or frequent • *Opportunities like that are few and far between.* — **no fewer than** : at least — used to suggest that a number or amount is surprisingly large • *No fewer than 1,000 people attended.* — **of few words** ✧ A person *of few words* is someone who does not talk very much.

²**few** *pron* **1** : not many people or things • *His stories may be entertaining, but few (if any) are true.* — used in the phrase **a few** • *I bought several magazines and read a few (of them).* **2** : some people or things that are chosen or regarded as special or unusual in some way • *A select few will receive advance tickets.* — **have a few** *or* **have a few too many** *informal* : to have

too many alcoholic drinks

few·er /ˈfjuːwə/ adj : not so many : a smaller number of • I take fewer (and fewer) vacations every year. **usage** see ¹LESS — **fewer** pron • Fewer came than were expected.

fi·an·cé /ˌfiˌɑːnˈseɪ, fiˈɑːnˌseɪ/ n [C] : a man that a woman is engaged to be married to • her/my fiancé

fi·an·cée /ˌfiˌɑːnˈseɪ, fiˈɑːnˌseɪ/ n [C] : a woman that a man is engaged to be married to • his/my fiancée

fi·as·co /fiˈæskoʊ/ n, pl **-coes** [C] : a complete failure or disaster • The party was a complete/utter fiasco.

fi·at /ˈfiːət, ˈfaɪˌæt/ n [C/U] formal : an official order given by someone who has power • a judicial fiat • government by fiat

fib /ˈfɪb/ n [C] informal : an untrue statement about something minor or unimportant • I told a fib when I said I liked the movie. — **fib** vb **fibbed; fib·bing** [I] • I fibbed when I said I liked the movie.

fi·ber (US) or Brit **fi·bre** /ˈfaɪbə/ n 1 [U] : plant material that cannot be digested but that helps you to digest other food • foods that are high in fiber 2 [C/U] : a thin thread of material that can be used to make cloth, paper, etc. • a mix of synthetic and natural fibers; also : material (such as cloth) that is made from thin threads • bits of fiber 3 [C/U] : a long, thin piece of material that forms a type of tissue in your body • muscle/nerve fibers/fiber 4 [U] formal : strength or toughness of character • the moral fiber of the nation's youth — **with every fiber of your being** : with all of your effort or desire • She wanted it with every fiber of her being.

fi·ber·glass (US) or Brit **fi·bre·glass** /ˈfaɪbəˌglæs, Brit ˈfaɪbəˌglɑːs/ n [U] : a light and strong material that is made from thin threads of glass and that is used in making various products

fiber optics (US) or Brit **fibre optics** n [U] technical : the use of thin threads of glass or plastic to carry very large amounts of information in the form of light signals — **fi·ber-op·tic** (US) or Brit **fi·bre-op·tic** /ˈfaɪbəˌɑːptɪk/ adj

fi·brous /ˈfaɪbrəs/ adj : containing, made of, or resembling fibers • a fibrous texture/material

fick·le /ˈfɪkəl/ adj 1 : changing often • fickle weather 2 disapproving : changing opinions often • fickle friends — **fick·le·ness** n [U]

fic·tion /ˈfɪkʃən/ n 1 [U] : literature that tells stories which are imagined by the writer • great works of fiction 2 [C/U] : something that is not true • an explanation that is pure fiction [=completely untrue] — **fic·tion·al** /ˈfɪkʃənl/ adj • a fictional character/place/account

fic·tion·al·ize also Brit **fic·tion·al·ise** /ˈfɪkʃənəˌlaɪz/ vb **-ized; -iz·ing** [T] : to change (a true story) into fiction by changing or adding details • a fictionalized account of her travels

fic·ti·tious /fɪkˈtɪʃəs/ adj : not true or real • fictitious stories/characters

¹**fid·dle** /ˈfɪdl/ n [C] informal : VIOLIN — **fit as a fiddle** see ¹FIT — **play second**

fiddle : to have a less important position or status than someone or something else • a former star athlete who is not happy to play second fiddle to the younger players on the team

²**fiddle** vb **fid·dled; fid·dling** /ˈfɪdlɪŋ/ [I] informal : to play a violin • a fiddling competition — **fiddle around** or chiefly Brit **fiddle about** [phrasal vb] : to spend time in activity that does not have a real purpose • Stop fiddling [=fooling] around. — **fiddle with** [phrasal vb] 1 : to move or handle (something) with your hands or fingers in a nervous way • nervously fiddling with her pen 2 : to change or handle (something) in a way that shows you are not sure what to do • fiddling with the controls of the television 3 : to change (something) in a harmful or foolish way • Someone had fiddled with the equipment. — **fid·dler** /ˈfɪdlə/ n [C] • an expert/champion fiddler

fi·del·i·ty /fəˈdɛləti/ n [U] 1 a : the quality of being faithful to your husband, wife, or sexual partner • sexual fidelity b : the quality of being faithful or loyal to a country, organization, etc. • fidelity to one's country 2 : the degree to which something matches or copies something else • The movie's director insisted on total fidelity to the book. [=insisted that the story told in the movie should accurately copy the story told in the book] 3 : the degree to which a device (such as a CD player, radio, or television) correctly reproduces sounds, pictures, etc. — see also HIGH FIDELITY

fidg·et /ˈfɪdʒət/ vb [I] : to make a lot of small movements because you are nervous, bored, etc. • children fidgeting in their chairs — **fidget with** [phrasal vb] : to move or handle (something) with your hands and fingers in a nervous way • fidgeting with his ring — **fidg·ety** /ˈfɪdʒəti/ adj • Coffee makes me fidgety.

¹**field** /ˈfiːld/ n [C] 1 a : an open area of land without trees or buildings • a grassy/muddy field b : an area of land that has a special use • a field of wheat = a wheat field 2 : an area of work, study, etc. • the field of genetic research • fields of learning/interest/study 3 a : an area of land that is used for sports • football/athletic/baseball/soccer fields • Spectators are not allowed on the field of play. [=playing field] ◇ In a baseball or cricket game, when one team is batting the other team is **in the field**. b ◇ In basketball a shot taken **from the field** is a shot taken during ordinary play rather than a free throw. 4 : the area where work is done away from a laboratory, office, etc. • archaeologists/salesmen working in the field • doing field research in Alaska 5 : the group of people, horses, teams, etc., that are in a race or other competition • a large field of candidates • She's leading/trailing the field by a wide margin. • (figurative) The company is working hard to stay/keep ahead of the field. [=to continue to be more successful than its competitors] 6 : a place where battles and other military activities happen • the field of battle 7 : a region or space in which

an effect or force (such as gravity, electricity, or magnetism) exists • *an electric/magnetic field* **8** : an area in which a particular type of information is placed • *You must complete all fields before submitting the form.* **9** : FIELD OF VISION — see also FIELD OF VIEW — **play the field** see ¹PLAY

²**field** *vb* [T] **1** *baseball or cricket* : to catch or stop and throw a ball • *fielding a ground ball*; *also* : to play (a position) on a baseball team • *a shortstop who fields his position flawlessly* **2 a** : to deal with or respond to (something, such as a telephone call or a request) • *fielding offers on the house* **b** : to give an answer to (a question) • *fielding reporters' questions* **3** : to put (a team, army, etc.) into the field to compete or fight • *the greatest fighting force the nation has ever fielded* — **field-er** /ˈfiːldə/ *n* [C]

field day *n* [C] : a day of outdoor sports and athletic competition for school children — **have a field day** : to get a lot of pleasure and enjoyment from doing something — used especially to describe getting enjoyment from criticizing someone, making fun of someone, etc. • *Journalists had a field day with the scandal.*

field event *n* [C] : an event in a track meet that is not a race

field goal *n* [C] **1** *American football* : a score of three points made by kicking the ball between the goalposts **2** *basketball* : BASKET 2b

field guide *n* [C] : a book that helps you to identify birds, plants, animals, rocks, etc. • *a field guide to the birds*

field hockey *n* [U] *US + Canada* : a game that is played on a field in which each team uses curved sticks to try to hit the ball into the opponent's goal — called also (*chiefly Brit*) *hockey*

field house *n* [C] *US* : a large building that is used for athletic events and that usually has seats for spectators

field marshal *n* [C] : the highest ranking military officer in the British Army

field mouse *n* [C] : a type of mouse that lives in open fields

field of view *n* [C] **1** : the area that can be seen when you look through a telescope, a pair of binoculars, etc. **2** : FIELD OF VISION

field of vision *n* [C] : the area that you can see without moving your eyes

field–test /ˈfiːldˌtɛst/ *vb* [T] : to test (something, such as a product) by using it in the actual conditions it was designed for • *These products need to be field-tested before we can begin using them.* — **field test** *n* [C]

field trip *n* [C] : a visit to a place (such as a museum or zoo) that is made by students to learn about something • *The class went on a field trip.*

field-work /ˈfiːldˌwɚk/ *n* [U] : the work of gathering information by going into the field (sense 4) • *doing fieldwork in Alaska*

fiend /ˈfiːnd/ *n* [C] **1 a** : an evil spirit : a demon or devil **b** : a very evil or cruel person • *a murderous fiend* **2** *informal* **a** : a person who is very enthusiastic about something • *a golf fiend* **b** : a person who is addicted to a drug or to a kind of behavior • *a dope/sex fiend* — **like a fiend** *chiefly US, informal* — used to say that someone does a lot of something • *working like a fiend* [=working very hard]

fiend-ish /ˈfiːndɪʃ/ *adj* **1** : very evil or cruel • *a fiendish plot* **2** : extremely bad, unpleasant, or difficult • *a fiendish problem* — **fiend-ish-ly** *adv*

fierce /ˈfiɚs/ *adj* **fierc-er; -est 1 a** : very violent • *fierce combat/fighting* **b** : eager to fight or kill • *a fierce tiger/warrior* **2** : having or showing a lot of strong emotion • *a fierce argument/struggle/rivalry* • *fierce determination* **3** : very harsh or powerful • *a fierce storm/squall* — **something fierce** *US, informal* : very much • *I miss her something fierce.* — **fierce-ly** *adv*

fi-ery /ˈfajəri/ *adj* **fi-er-i-er; -est 1** : having or producing fire • *a fiery crash/explosion* **2** *of food* : tasting very hot and spicy • *a fiery sauce* **3 a** : having or showing a lot of strong and angry emotion • *a fiery speech/politician* **b** : easily made angry • *a fiery temper* **4** : having the color of fire • *a fiery red/orange*

fi-es-ta /fiˈɛstə/ *n* [C] : a public celebration in Spain and Latin America with parades and dances in honor of a saint

fife /ˈfaɪf/ *n* [C] : a musical instrument that looks like a small flute

fif-teen /ˌfɪfˈtiːn/ *n* [C] : the number 15 — **fifteen** *adj* • *fifteen dollars* — **fifteen** *pron* • *Only fifteen (of them) showed up on time.* — **fif-teenth** /ˌfɪfˈtiːnθ/ *n* [C] — **fifteenth** *adj* — **fifteenth** *adv*

¹**fifth** /ˈfɪfθ, ˈfɪfθ/ *n* **1** [*singular*] : number five in a series • *the fifth of the month* **2** [C] : one of five equal parts of something • *a fifth of her income* **3** [C] : a unit of measure for alcoholic liquor that is equal to one fifth of a U.S. gallon (approximately 750 ml); *also* : a bottle that holds this amount of liquor • *a fifth of whiskey* — **take/plead the Fifth** *chiefly US* : to refuse to answer questions in a court of law because your answers might be harmful to you or might show that you have committed a crime ✧ The phrase *take/plead the Fifth* refers to the Fifth Amendment of the U.S. Constitution.

²**fifth** *adj* : occupying the number five position in a series • *the fifth dancer* — **fifth** *adv* • *She finished fifth in the race.*

fif-ty /ˈfɪfti/ *n, pl* **-ties 1** [C] : the number 50 **2** [*plural*] **a** : the numbers ranging from 50 to 59 **b** : a set of years ending in digits ranging from 50 to 59 • *She's in her fifties.* • *growing up in the fifties* [=1950–1959] **3** [C] *US* : a fifty-dollar bill — **fif-ti-eth** /ˈfɪftiəθ/ *adj* • *their fiftieth wedding anniversary* — **fiftieth** *n* [C] — **fifty** *adj* • *fifty cats* — **fifty** *pron*

fif-ty–fif-ty /ˌfɪftiˈfɪfti/ *adj* **1** : shared equally • *a fifty-fifty split* [=an equal split] **2** : equally good and bad • *a fifty-fifty chance of succeeding* — **fifty–fifty** *adv* • *They divide/split expenses fifty-fifty.* [=equally]

fig /ˈfɪg/ *n* [C] : a sweet fruit that grows on

fig. *abbr* figure

¹fight /ˈfaɪt/ *vb* **fought** /ˈfɑːt/; **fight·ing 1 a** [*T/I*] : to use weapons or physical force to try to hurt someone, to defeat an enemy, etc. ▪ *The soldiers fought bravely.* ▪ *The U.S. fought (against) Germany in World Wars I and II.* **b** [*T*] : to be involved in (a battle, struggle, etc.) ▪ *fight a war for independence* ▪ *You're fighting a losing battle.* [=trying to do something that you will not be able to do] **2** [*I*] : to argue in an angry way ▪ *They're always fighting (with each other) over/about money.* **3** [*I*] : to try hard *to* do something that is difficult ▪ *fighting to stay awake/alive* **4 a** [*T/I*] : to work hard to defeat, end, or prevent something ▪ *fighting (against) poverty/AIDS* ▪ *fight crime* **b** [*T*] : to struggle against (something) ▪ *I'm fighting a cold.* ▪ *fight traffic* [=drive through a lot of traffic] **5** [*T*] : to try not to be affected by (a feeling, urge, etc.) ▪ *fighting the urge/impulse to laugh* [=trying not to laugh] **6** [*T/I*] : to participate in the sport of boxing ▪ *fighting for the heavyweight title* — **fight back** [*phrasal vb*] **1** : to attack or try to defeat someone who is attacking or trying to defeat you ▪ *responding to their accusations by fighting back* **2** : to make a new effort against an opponent ▪ *They fought back and tied the score in the second half.* **3** ◆ Someone who is **fighting back tears** is trying very hard not to cry. — **fight fire with fire** : to fight against an opponent by using the same methods or weapons that the opponent uses — **fight for** [*phrasal vb*] **1** : to fight in support of (something) ▪ *soldiers fighting for their country* **2** : to fight or struggle to get, keep, or achieve (something) ▪ *fighting for our rights as citizens* ▪ *a patient fighting for breath* [=struggling to breathe] ▪ *She's fighting for her life.* [=she is struggling to survive; she is in danger of dying] — **fight it out** : to be in a fight ▪ *people fighting it out over parking spaces* **2** : to end a dispute by fighting or arguing ▪ *This matter won't be settled until the lawyers fight it out in court.* — **fight like cats and dogs** (*chiefly US*) *or Brit* **fight like cat and dog** *informal* : to fight or argue a lot or in a very forceful and angry way — **fight off** [*phrasal vb*] **fight (someone or something) off** *or* **fight off (someone or something)** : to defend yourself against (someone or something) by fighting or struggling ▪ *They fought off the attack/attackers.* — **fight on** [*phrasal vb*] : to continue fighting ▪ *He vowed to fight on alone.* — **fight the good fight** : to try very hard to do what is right ▪ *fighting the good fight against oppression* — **fight with** [*phrasal vb*] **1** : to fight against (someone or something) ▪ *He fought with his wife over/about money.* **2** : to fight on the same side as (someone or something) ▪ *The U.S. fought (together) with the Soviet Union in World War II.* **3** : to fight by using (something, such as a weapon) ▪ *fighting with knives/fists* — **fight your way** : to move forward or make progress by pushing, fighting, or struggling ▪ *fight-*

ing our way through the crowd — **fight·ing** *adj* ▪ *a powerful fighting force* ◆ **Fighting words** are angry or insulting words that are likely to cause a fight. ◆ In U.S. English, someone who is **fighting mad** is angry enough to fight. — **fight·ing** *n* [*U*] ▪ *Fighting has broken out along the border.*

²fight *n* **1** [*C*] : a violent physical struggle between opponents ▪ *A fight broke out in the bar.* ▪ *He's always getting into fights.* ▪ *Don't pick a fight* [=start a fight] *with them.* **2** [*C*] : an argument or quarrel ▪ *They got into another fight about/over money.* **3** [*C*] : a boxing match ▪ *a fight for the heavyweight title* **4** [*C*] : a struggle to achieve a goal or to defeat something or someone ▪ *leading/joining the fight against cancer* **5** [*U*] : a willingness to fight ▪ *full of fight*

fight·back /ˈfaɪtˌbæk/ *n* [*C*] *Brit* : COME-BACK ▪ *The team staged a fightback in the second half.*

fight·er /ˈfaɪtɚ/ *n* [*C*] **1** : a warrior or soldier ▪ *nationalist fighters* **2** : BOXER 1 ▪ *a championship fighter* **3** : someone who continues fighting or trying ▪ *She'll succeed because she's a (real) fighter.* **4** : a fast airplane that has weapons for destroying enemy aircraft ▪ *a fighter plane/pilot*

fig·ment /ˈfɪgmənt/ *n* [*C*] : something produced by the imagination ▪ *I thought I heard her voice, but I guess it was just a* **figment** *of my imagination.*

fig·u·ra·tive /ˈfɪgjərətɪv/ *adj* **1** of words, language, etc. : used with a meaning that is different from the basic meaning and that expresses an idea in an interesting way by using language that usually describes something else : not literal ▪ *The phrase "know your ropes" means literally "to know a lot about ropes," while its figurative meaning is "to know a lot about how to do something."* **2** : showing people and things in a way that resembles how they really look : not abstract ▪ *figurative art* — **fig·u·ra·tive·ly** /ˈfɪgjərətɪvli/ *adv* ▪ *In the phrase "know your ropes," the word "ropes" is being used figuratively.*

¹fig·ure /ˈfɪgjɚ, *Brit* ˈfɪgə/ *n* [*C*] **1 a** : a symbol that represents a number : DIGIT ▪ *a six-figure salary* [=a salary of at least $100,000] **b** : a value that is expressed in numbers ▪ *The company had yearly sales figures of half a million units.* **2 a** : a person or animal that can be seen only as a shape or outline ▪ *I saw some figures moving in the mist.* **b** : the shape or form of a person's body ▪ *the human/male/female figure* ◆ *Figure* in this sense usually refers to women rather than men. ▪ *a slim, youthful figure* **c** ◆ The phrase *a fine figure of a man/woman* describes someone who is tall and has a strong and well-formed body. **3** : a drawing, sculpture, etc., that represents the form of a person or animal ▪ *a collection of bronze/carved figures* — see also STICK FIGURE **4** : a person who has a specified status or who is regarded in a specified way ▪ *a popular sports figure* ▪ *She's a key figure in the organization.* ▪ *a figure of authority = an authority figure*

[=a person who has authority over other people] **5 a** : a diagram or picture ▪ *Look at the figure on page 15.* — abbr. *fig.* **b** *mathematics* : a combination of points, lines, or surfaces in geometry ▪ *geometric figures like squares and cones*

²**figure** *vb* **-ured; -ur·ing 1** [*T*] : to expect or think (something) ▪ *I figured (that) they would lose.* ▪ *(US)* *He figured [=expected] to lose money in the deal.* **2** *US, informal* **a** [*T*] : to understand or find (something, such as a reason) by thinking ▪ *I've finally figured [=figured out] a way to manage my time better.* **b** [*I*] : to appear likely to do something ▪ *She figures to finish by noon.* **3** [*I*] : to have an important part in something ▪ *The economy figured prominently in the last election.* **4** [*T*] : to calculate (an amount, cost, etc.) ▪ *He figured the cost at about $100.* **5** [*I*] *chiefly US, informal* : to seem reasonable, normal, or expected ▪ *Her explanation just doesn't figure.* [=add up] ▪ **It figures** [=it is not surprising] *that he would be late today.* ▪ *That figures.* [=that doesn't surprise me] — **figure in** [*phrasal vb*] **1 figure (something) in** or **figure in (something)** *US* : to include (something) while making calculations ▪ *They forgot to figure in occasional travel expenses.* **2** : to be involved in (something, such as an activity) ▪ *persons who figured in the robbery* — **figure into** [*phrasal vb*] *US* : to be included as a part of (something) ▪ *Age may figure into the equation.* — **figure on** [*phrasal vb*] *US, informal* **1** : to expect to get or have (something) ▪ *They weren't figuring on the extra income.* **2** : to plan to do (something) ▪ *I figure on going.* [=I plan to go] — **figure out** [*phrasal vb*] **figure out (something or someone)** or **figure (something or someone) out 1 a** : to understand or find (something, such as a reason or a solution) by thinking ▪ *I'm trying to figure out a way to do it.* **b** : to find an answer or solution for (something, such as a problem) ▪ *figure out [=solve] a math problem* **2** : to understand the behavior of (someone) ▪ *I just can't figure him out.* — **go figure** *US, informal* — used to say that something is surprising or hard to understand ▪ *After losing their first six games, they won the next ten. Go figure.*

figure eight *n* [*C*] *US* : something that is shaped like the numeral 8 ▪ *tracing a figure eight in the sand* — called also (*Brit*) **figure-of-eight**

fig·ure·head /ˈfɪgjəˌhɛd, *Brit* ˈfɪgəˌhɛd/ *n* [*C*] **1** : a carved figure on a ship's bow **2** : a person who is called the head or chief of something but who has no real power ▪ *The king is merely a figurehead.*

figure of speech *n* [*C*] : a phrase or expression that uses words in a figurative way rather than in a plain or literal way ▪ *"You are the apple of my eye" is a figure of speech.*

figure skate *n* [*C*] : a special skate that is used for figure skating

figure skating *n* [*U*] : ice-skating in which the skaters perform various jumps, spins, and dance movements —

figure skater *n* [*C*]

fig·u·rine /ˌfɪgjəˈriːn/ *n* [*C*] : a small figure or model of a person made of wood, plastic, etc.

fil·a·ment /ˈfɪləmənt/ *n* [*C*] **1** : a thin thread or hair **2** : a thin wire in a light bulb that glows when electricity passes through it

filch /ˈfɪltʃ/ *vb* [*T*] *informal* : to steal (something that is small or that has little value) ▪ *filch a pen*

¹**file** /ˈfajəl/ *n* [*C*] **1 a** : a device (such as a box, folder, or cabinet) in which documents that you want to keep are stored so that they can be found easily **b** : a collection of documents that have information you want to keep and that are stored so that they can be found easily ▪ *The FBI has a large file on her.* ✧ Something that is **on file** is stored in a file. **2** : a collection of computer data that forms a single unit and that is given a particular name ▪ *You should save the file frequently as you do your work.* **3** : a metal tool that has sharp ridges and that is used to make rough surfaces smooth — see also NAIL FILE **4** : a row of people, animals, or things that form a line ▪ *a file of soldiers* ▪ *marching in file* [=in a line]

²**file** *vb* **filed; fil·ing 1** [*T*] : to put (a document) in a place where it can be found easily ▪ *She filed (away) the letters.* **2** [*T/I*] : to give (something, such as a legal document) to someone so that it can be considered, dealt with, approved, etc. ▪ *file a form/lawsuit* ▪ *filing for divorce/bankruptcy* **3** [*T*] : to send (a story or report) to a newspaper ▪ *reporters filing their stories* **4** [*T*] : to make something smooth by using a file (sense 3) ▪ *He filed away/down the metal box's rough edges.* **5** [*I*] : to walk in a line ▪ *The customers filed out slowly.* — **fil·er** /ˈfajlə/ *n* [*C*]

file cabinet *n* [*C*] *US* : a piece of furniture that is used for storing documents so that they can be found easily — called also **filing cabinet**

fil·i·al /ˈfɪlijəl/ *adj, formal* : of, relating to, or appropriate for a son or daughter ▪ *filial duties/obedience/devotion*

fil·i·bus·ter /ˈfɪləˌbʌstə/ *n* [*C*] *chiefly US* : an effort to prevent action in a legislature by making a long speech or series of speeches — **filibuster** *vb* [*T/I*] ▪ *They are filibustering to delay the vote.*

fil·i·gree /ˈfɪləˌgriː/ *n* [*U*] : decoration that consists of delicate and complicated designs made of fine gold or silver wire

fil·ing /ˈfajlɪŋ/ *n* [*C*] : a small piece that is removed when something is smoothed or rubbed with a file ▪ *iron filings*

filing cabinet *n* [*C*] : FILE CABINET

¹**fill** /ˈfɪl/ *vb* **1** [*T/I*] : to become full or to make (something) full ▪ *fill (up) a glass with water* ▪ *enough books to fill a library* ▪ *Two hundred people filled the room.* ▪ *Her eyes filled with tears.* = *Tears filled her eyes.* [=she began to cry] ▪ *a theater filled to capacity* [=completely full] ✧ If something **fills you** or **fills your heart** with an emotion, it makes you feel that emotion very strongly. ▪ *The thought of leaving fills me with sadness.* [=makes me very sad]

2 [T] : to spread all through (an area, the air, etc.) ▪ *Smoke filled the room.* ▪ *Laughter filled the air.* **3** [T] : to spend or use (time) ▪ *She filled (up) her day with small chores.* ▪ *a fun-filled afternoon* [=a very enjoyable afternoon] **4** [T/I] : to make (someone) full with food and drink — usually + *up* ▪ *foods that won't fill you up* ▪ *We filled up on sandwiches.* **5** [T] : to place material inside of (a hole, crack, etc.) in order to repair a surface ▪ *fill (a cavity in) a tooth* [=put filling in a cavity/tooth] ▪ *(figurative) trying to fill the gaps in my record collection* [=getting more records in order to make my record collection complete] ▪ *(figurative) efforts to fill the void left by her retirement* **6** [T] : to do or provide what is needed for (something) ▪ *fill a requirement/need* **7** [T] **a** : to perform the work of (an office, position, etc.) ▪ *fill the office of president* **b** : to hire a person for a job that has become available ▪ *fill a job opening* **8** [T] : to provide the things that are asked for in (something, such as an order) ▪ *fill an order* — **fill in** [*phrasal vb*] **1 fill (something) in or fill in (something) a** : to complete (a document) by providing necessary information ▪ *fill in an application* ▪ *Please fill in the blanks.* [=put information in the blank spaces] **b** : to provide (more information) ▪ *filling in the details* **2 fill (someone) in or fill in (someone)** : to provide information to (someone) ▪ *She filled us in on the details.* **3** : to take the place of someone who is away for a time ▪ *He can't be here, so he asked me to fill in (for him).* — **fill out** [*phrasal vb*] **1** : to become larger and heavier ▪ *The tree should fill out in a few years.* **2 fill (something) out or fill out (something)** *chiefly US* : to complete (something, such as a form) by providing necessary information ▪ *fill out an application* — **fill someone's shoes** : to take someone's place or position ▪ *Who will fill her shoes after she retires?* — **fill the bill** see ¹BILL

²**fill** *n* [U] **1** : a full amount ◆ If you have **eaten/drunk your fill**, you have eaten/drunk all that you want. ◆ If you **had your fill** of something, you do not want to do or have any more of it. ▪ *We've had our fill of dance music for one night.* **2** : material that is used to fill something ▪ *a load of fill for the trench*

fill·er /ˈfɪlɚ/ *n* [C/U] **1 a** : a substance that is added to a product to increase its size or weight **b** : material that is used to fill holes and cracks in a surface **2** : extra material that is added to a newspaper page, a recording, etc., to fill space that would otherwise be empty ▪ *extra songs used as filler(s) to make the CD longer*

¹**fil·let** *also US* **fi·let** /ˈfɪlət, fɪˈleɪ/ *n* [C] : a piece or slice of boneless meat or fish

²**fillet** *vb* **fil·leted** /ˈfɪlətəd, fɪˈleɪd/; **fil·let·ing** [T] : to cut (meat or fish) into fillets ▪ *filleting the fish with a sharp knife*

¹**fill·ing** /ˈfɪlɪŋ/ *adj, of food* : causing you to feel full ▪ *a filling soup*

²**filling** *n* **1** [C] : material that is used to fill something ▪ *a filling for a tooth* **2** [C/U] : a food mixture that is used to fill something (such as pastry or a sandwich) ▪ *pies with fruit fillings*

filling station *n* [C] : GAS STATION

fil·ly /ˈfɪli/ *n, pl* **-lies** [C] : a young female horse

¹**film** /ˈfɪlm/ *n* **1** [U] : a special material that is used for taking photographs **2 a** [C/U] : MOVIE ▪ *a film about war* ▪ *film critics/reviewers/criticism* ▪ *an event captured on film* [=recorded by a movie or video camera] **b** [U] : the process, art, or business of making movies ▪ *a career in film* **3** [C] : a thin layer on or over the surface of something ▪ *a film of ice*

²**film** *vb* **1** [T] : to photograph (an event, scene, etc.) with a movie or video camera ▪ *She filmed the children playing.* **2** [I] : to make a movie ▪ *We'll begin filming next week.*

film-mak·er /ˈfɪlmˌmeɪkɚ/ *n* [C] : a person (such as a director or producer) who makes movies

filmy /ˈfɪlmi/ *adj* **film·i·er**; **-est** : very thin and light ▪ *filmy fabric*

¹**fil·ter** /ˈfɪltɚ/ *n* [C] **1** : a device that is used to remove something unwanted from a liquid or gas that passes through it ▪ *a water filter* **2** : a device that prevents some kinds of light, sound, electronic noises, etc., from passing through **3** *computers* : software that prevents someone from looking at or receiving particular kinds of material through the Internet ▪ *a spam filter*

²**filter** *vb* **1** [T] : to pass something (such as a gas or liquid) through a filter to remove something unwanted ▪ *filtering the water to remove impurities* ▪ *a device that filters impurities from water* ▪ *sunglasses that filter (out) ultraviolet light* ▪ *(figurative) an interview to filter out people who are not good candidates for the job* **2** [I] **a** : to move through or into something in small amounts or in a gradual way ▪ *Sunlight filtered through the leaves.* ▪ *ideas filtering down to our children* **b** : to come or go slowly in small groups or amounts ▪ *Early election returns have begun to filter in.* — **fil·tra·tion** /fɪlˈtreɪʃən/ *n* [U] ▪ *water filtration*

filth /ˈfɪlθ/ *n* [U] **1** : a large and very unpleasant amount of dirt ▪ *covered in filth* : very dirty conditions ▪ *living in filth and squalor* **2** : something that is very offensive or disgusting and often is about sex ▪ *magazines full of filth*

¹**filthy** /ˈfɪlθi/ *adj* **filth·i·er**; **-est** **1** : very dirty ▪ *filthy clothes/streets* **2 a** : very offensive or disgusting and usually about sex ▪ *a filthy movie/joke* **b** : very evil ▪ *That's a filthy lie!* **c** : very bad ▪ *a filthy mood/temper* ▪ *(chiefly Brit) filthy weather* — **filth·i·ness** /ˈfɪlθinəs/ *n* [U]

²**filthy** *adv, informal* : VERY ▪ *He's filthy rich.*

fin /ˈfɪn/ *n* [C] **1** : a thin flat part that sticks out from the body of a fish and is used in moving or guiding the fish through water ▪ *a shark fin* **2** : a part on a car, airplane, etc., that is shaped like a fish's fin — **finned** /ˈfɪnd/ *adj*

fi·na·gle /fəˈneɪgəl/ *vb* **-na·gled**; **-na·gling** [T] *informal* : to get (something) in a clever or dishonest way ▪ *He finagled an invitation to the conference.*

¹**fi·nal** /ˈfaɪnl̩/ *adj* **1** *always before a noun* : happening or coming at the end ▪ *the final act of the play* ▪ *Our final destination is Tokyo.* ▪ *final exams* [=exams at the end of a class or term] ▪ *the final score/product/result* **2** — used to say that something will not be changed or done again ▪ *This is my final offer.* ▪ *You can't go, and that's final!*

²**final** *n* **1** [C] : the last competition (such as a game or race) or set of competitions in a series ▪ *I won in the semifinals but was defeated in the finals.* **2 a** [*plural*] : the examinations that happen at the end of a class, term, or course of study ▪ *I passed my finals.* **b** [C] *US* : an examination at the end of a class ▪ *a history final*

fi·na·le /fəˈnæli, fəˈnɑːli/ *n* [C] : the last part of a musical performance, play, etc. ▪ *the TV show's season finale* [=the last program of the season] — see also GRAND FINALE

fi·nal·ist /ˈfaɪnl̩ɪst/ *n* [C] : a person who competes in the last part of a competition ▪ *a finalist in the tennis tournament*

fi·nal·i·ty /faɪˈnæləti/ *n* [U] : the quality or state of being final or finished and not able to be changed ▪ *the finality of death*

fi·nal·ize *also Brit* **fi·nal·ise** /ˈfaɪnəˌlaɪz/ *vb* **-ized; -iz·ing** [T] : to put (a plan, an agreement, etc.) in a final or finished form ▪ *We've finalized our plans.*

fi·nal·ly /ˈfaɪnl̩i/ *adv* **1** : at the end of a long period of time ▪ *They're finally here.* ▪ *"They're here." "Finally!"* **2 a** — used to describe the last action or event in a series of actions or events ▪ *He stood up, cleared his throat, and finally began to speak.* **b** — used to introduce a final statement or series of statements ▪ *Finally, I'd like to thank my parents.* **3** : in a way that cannot be changed ▪ *The dispute has not yet been finally settled.*

¹**fi·nance** /ˈfaɪˌnæns, fəˈnæns/ *n* **1** [U] : the way in which money is used and handled ▪ *a course on personal finance*; *especially* : the way in which large amounts of money are used and handled by governments and companies ▪ *an expert in corporate finance* — see also HIGH FINANCE **2** [*plural*] **a** : money available to a government, business, or person ▪ *handling the library's finances* **b** : matters relating to money and how it is spent or saved ▪ *His finances were in bad shape.* [=he did not have enough money]

²**fi·nance** /fəˈnæns, ˈfaɪˌnæns/ *vb* **-nanced; -nanc·ing** [T] **1** : to provide money for (something or someone) ▪ *The study was financed by a government grant.* **2** : to buy (something) by borrowing money that will be paid back over a period of time ▪ *finance a new car*

fi·nan·cial /fəˈnænʃəl/ *adj* : relating to money ▪ *financial problems/advice* ▪ *a financial institution* [=a company that deals with money; a bank] — **fi·nan·cial·ly** *adv*

financial year *n* [C] *Brit* : FISCAL YEAR

fin·an·cier /ˌfɪnənˈsɪɚ, *Brit* fəˈnænsɪɚ/ *n* [C] : a person who controls the use and lending of large amounts of money

finch /ˈfɪntʃ/ *n* [C] : a small bird with a short, thick beak

¹**find** /ˈfaɪnd/ *vb* **found** /ˈfaʊnd/; **find·ing** **1** [T] **a** : to discover (something or someone) without planning or trying to ▪ *I found a dollar on the ground.* **b** ◇ Something or someone that *is found* in a specified place exists there or lives there. ▪ *Many artifacts can be found in this area.* [=there are many artifacts in this area] **2** [T] : to get or discover (something or someone that you are looking for) ▪ *find a missing person* ▪ *My glasses are nowhere to be found.* = *I can't find my glasses.* **3** [T] **a** : to discover or learn (something) by studying about it ▪ *find the answer/cure* **b** : to get (something needed or wanted) by effort ▪ *find the time/courage to do something* **4** [T] **a** : to regard (someone or something you have met, seen, experienced, etc.) in a specified way ▪ *I found the book (to be) useful.* ▪ *I'm finding it hard to concentrate.* [=it is hard for me to concentrate] **b** : to be affected by (something) in a specified way ▪ *He finds laughing/laughter painful.* **c** : to feel (a pleasing emotion) ▪ *We found some satisfaction in having played well.* **5** [T] **a** : to discover (someone) in a specified state ▪ *I found her relaxing by the pool.* **b** : to become aware that you are doing something or that you are in a particular place or situation ▪ *I often find myself thinking about her.* **6** [T] : to begin to have (something) ▪ *The product found few buyers.* [=few people bought it] ▪ *ideas that have found approval/favor* **7** [T/I] *law* : to make a decision about the guilt or innocence of someone ▪ *The jury found her guilty/innocent.* — **find fault** : to criticize someone or something ▪ *He found fault with everything she did.* — **find its mark/target** : to hit a target that was aimed for ▪ *The bullet found its mark.* — **find out** [*phrasal vb*] **1** : to learn (something) by making an effort ▪ *Can you find out where the meeting is?* **2 find out about** : to become aware of (something) ▪ *I found out about the error.* **3 find (someone) out** : to learn the unpleasant truth about (someone) ▪ *He was found out before he could do any harm.* — **find yourself** : to learn what you truly value and want in life ▪ *I traveled for a while, trying to find myself.* — **find your voice** : to be able to speak or to express yourself as a writer ▪ *a young novelist who has found her voice* — **find your way 1** : to look for and find where you need to go in order to get somewhere ▪ *I easily found my way home.* ▪ (*figurative*) *He's still finding his way as a teacher.* [=learning what he needs to do to succeed as a teacher] **2** : to go or arrive somewhere by chance or after a time of wandering ▪ *settlers who found their way to California* — **find·er** /ˈfaɪndɚ/ *n* [C]

²**find** *n* [C] : something or someone that has been found; *especially* : a valuable person or thing that has been found or discovered ▪ *That assistant of yours is a real find!*

find·ing /ˈfaɪndɪŋ/ *n* [C] **1** : a legal decision : VERDICT **2** : the results of an investigation • *publish findings*

¹**fine** /ˈfaɪn/ *adj* **fin·er; -est** **1** *not before a noun* : good, acceptable, or satisfactory • *"Is there anything wrong?" "No, everything's fine."* ✧ *Fine* is often used as a response to show acceptance or approval. • *"I have to leave early, all right?" "Fine."* **2 a** *always before a noun* : very good • *That's a fine idea.* **b** *always before a noun* : deserving praise, admiration, or respect • *a fine person/musician/mind* **3** *not before a noun* : well or healthy : not sick or injured • *"Did you hurt yourself?" "No, I'm fine."* **4** *of weather* : sunny and pleasant • *a fine spring day* **5 a** : very thin • *fine thread/wire/yarn* **b** : very sharp or narrow • *a pen/brush with a fine tip* : having a sharp point • *a fine pen/brush* **c** : made up of very small pieces, drops, etc. • *fine sand/dust/powder* **d** : very small • *The print was so fine that I could barely read it.* • *She has fine features.* [=her eyes, nose, and mouth are small and delicate] — see also FINE PRINT **6 a** : small and done with a lot of care and accuracy • *fine measurements/movements* **b** : small and difficult to see or understand : SUBTLE • *a fine distinction* • *There's a fine line* [=a very small difference] *between being helpful and being intrusive.* **7** *always before a noun* : expensive and of high quality • *fine china/dining* — **fine·ly** /ˈfaɪnli/ *adv* • *finely chopped* [=chopped into small pieces] • *a finely judged response that was just right* — **fine·ness** /ˈfaɪnnəs/ *n* [U]

²**fine** *adv, somewhat informal* **1** : not badly or poorly : well enough • *She did fine on the test.* **2** *always after a verb* : in small pieces • *The onions were chopped fine.* [=finely]

³**fine** *n* [C] : an amount of money that you pay as a punishment for breaking a law or rule • *a fine for speeding*

⁴**fine** *vb* **fined; fin·ing** [T] : to require (someone) to pay a fine as a punishment • *He was fined for speeding.*

fine art *n* **1** : [C/U] : a type of art (such as painting, sculpture, or music) that is done to create beautiful things • *a collector of fine art* • *She's in the department of fine arts.* **2** [*singular*] : an activity that requires skill and care • *the fine art of gourmet cooking*

fine print *n* [U] : the part of an agreement or document that contains important details and that is sometimes written in small letters

fin·ery /ˈfaɪnəri/ *n* [U] *somewhat formal* : clothes, jewels, etc., that are expensive and beautiful • *wedding finery*

¹**fi·nesse** /fəˈnɛs/ *n* [U] : skill and cleverness that is shown in the way someone deals with a situation, problem, etc. • *She handled the questions with finesse.*

²**finesse** *vb* **-nessed; -ness·ing** [T] : to handle, deal with, or do (something) in an indirect and skillful or clever way • *trying to finesse the issue*

fine–tune /ˈfaɪnˈtuːn/ *vb* [T] : to make small changes to (something) in order to improve the way it works or to make it exactly right • *fine-tune a TV set*

¹**fin·ger** /ˈfɪŋɡə/ *n* **1** [C] : one of the five

long parts of the hand that are used for holding things; *especially* : one of the four that are not the thumb • *He put the ring on her finger.* **2** [C] **a** : something that is long and thin and looks like a finger • *a finger of land extending into the sea* **b** : the part of a glove into which a finger is placed **3** **the finger** *US, informal* : an obscene gesture made by pointing the middle finger up, keeping the other fingers down, and turning the palm towards you • *Some angry driver **gave/flipped me the finger**.* — **cross your fingers** see ²CROSS — **finger on the pulse** ✧ If you **have/keep your finger on the pulse** of something, you know about the latest things that are happening. — **have a finger in a/the pie** : to have an interest or share in something • *a talent agent who has a finger in nearly every pie in show business* — **keep your fingers crossed** see ²CROSS — **lay a finger on** *informal* : to touch or hit (someone) • *I never laid a finger on him!* — **lift a finger** : to make an effort to do something • *She won't lift a finger to help me.* — **point an accusing finger at** or **point a/the finger at** : to accuse or blame (someone) • *Let's stop pointing fingers at each other and just solve the problem!* — **put your finger on** : to find out the exact nature of (something) • *I can't quite put my finger on the problem.* — **the finger of blame/suspicion** — used to say that someone is being blamed or suspected • *He realized that the finger of suspicion was now pointed at him.* [=that he was now suspected] — **work your fingers to the bone** : to work very hard — **wrap (someone) around your (little) finger** see ¹WRAP

²**finger** *vb* [T] **1** : to touch (something) with your fingers • *fingering the fabric* **2** *chiefly US, informal* : to identify (someone) as the person who has committed a crime • *He was fingered as a suspect.*

finger food *n* [C/U] *US* : a piece of food that is meant to be picked up with the fingers and eaten

fin·ger·ing /ˈfɪŋɡərɪŋ/ *n* [U] : the way in which the fingers are used and positioned in order to play a musical instrument

fin·ger·nail /ˈfɪŋɡəˌneɪl/ *n* [C] : the hard covering at the end of your fingers

fin·ger·print /ˈfɪŋɡəˌprɪnt/ *n* [C] **1** : the mark that is made by pressing the tip of a finger on a surface • *The suspect's fingerprints were on the gun.* **2** : something (such as genetic material) that can be used to identify a person • *a DNA fingerprint* — **fingerprint** *vb* [T] • *The suspect was fingerprinted by the police.*

fin·ger·tip /ˈfɪŋɡəˌtɪp/ *n* [C] : the very end of a finger — **at your fingertips** : easily available : easy to find or use • *She had the information at her fingertips.*

fin·icky /ˈfɪnɪki/ *adj* **1** : very hard to please • *a finicky eater* **2** : requiring a lot of care or attention • *a finicky machine*

¹**fin·ish** /ˈfɪnɪʃ/ *vb* **1** [T/I] **a** : to stop doing (something) because it is completed : *finish (giving) a speech* • *He hasn't finished his work.* = *He hasn't finished working.* • *I'll wait until you finish.* **b** : to be done

with building or creating (something) • *We're building a new home and hope to finish (it) by winter.* **c** : to cause something to end or stop • *finish a meeting* • *The meeting finished* [=ended] *at noon.* **2** [*T*] **a** : to cause the ruin or failure of (someone or something) • *The allegations could finish her (career).* **b** : to kill (someone or something already wounded) — usually + *off* • *The crowd shouted for the gladiator to finish off his opponent.* • *(figurative)* Climbing the stairs just about *finished me off.* [=climbing the stairs exhausted me] **3** [*T*] : to use, eat, or drink all that is left of (something) • *They finished (off/up) the pie.* **4** [*T/I*] : to end a race, competition, etc., in a specified position or manner • *The horse finished third.* = *The horse finished (the race) in third place.* **5** [*T*] : to put a final coat or surface on (something) • *finish a table with varnish* — **finishing touch** : one of the last things done to make something complete • *They're putting the finishing touches on their new home.* — **finish with** [*phrasal vb*] **1** : to stop using (something) • *Can I see the newspaper when you finish with it?* **2** : to end a romantic relationship with (someone) • *She says she's going to finish with him once and for all.* **3** : to stop dealing with, working on, or punishing (someone or something) • *I haven't finished with you yet!* — see also FINISHED

²**finish** *n* **1** [*singular*] : the last part of something • *a close race from start to finish* [=from the beginning to the end] • *a fight to the finish* [=a fight that goes on until one side is completely defeated] **2** [*C*] : the final coating on a surface or the appearance produced by such a coating • *the table's shiny finish*

fin·ished /ˈfɪnɪʃt/ *adj* **1** *not before a noun* : having reached the end of an activity, job, etc. • *I started an hour ago and I'm still not finished.* **b** : not requiring more work : entirely done or completed • *The job is finally finished.* • *a finished basement/attic* [=a basement/attic that has floors, ceilings, and walls like the rooms in the main part of the house] **2** *not before a noun* **a** : having reached the end of a romantic relationship • *We're finished! I never want to see you again!* **b** : completely ruined or defeated • *This scandal means that his career is finished.*

finish line *n* [*C*] *US* : a line that marks the end of a race — called also *(Brit)* **finishing line**

fi·nite /ˈfaɪˌnaɪt/ *adj* **1** : having limits • *a finite number of possibilities* **2** *grammar* : of or relating to a verb form that shows action that takes place at a particular time (such as the past) • *a finite verb such as "is" or "are"* — **fi·nite·ly** *adv*

fink /ˈfɪŋk/ *n* [*C*] *chiefly US, informal* **1** : a person who is strongly disliked • *He's a rotten fink.* **2** : a person who gives information to the police or to some other authority about the bad behavior or criminal activity of someone else

fiord *variant spelling of* FJORD

fir /ˈfɚ/ *n* [*C*] : a tall evergreen tree

¹**fire** /ˈfajɚ/ *n* **1** [*U*] : the light and heat and especially the flame produced by burning • *Stay away from the fire.* **2** [*C/U*] : the destruction of something (such as a building or a forest) by fire • *They died in that terrible fire.* • *The shack caught (on) fire* [=began to burn] *when it was struck by lightning.* • *Someone set a fire* [=deliberately started a fire] *in the shack.* • *Someone set fire to the shack.* **3** [*C*] : a controlled occurrence of fire created by burning something (such as wood or gas) in a fireplace, stove, etc. • *We warmed our hands over the fire.* **4** [*U*] : the shooting of weapons • *heavy rifle fire* • *They exchanged fire.* [=shot at each other] • *He was caught in the line of fire and killed.* • *The troops opened fire on* [=began shooting at] *the enemy.* • *Hold your fire!* [=don't shoot] • *Cease fire!* [=stop shooting] **5** [*U*] : very heavy or harsh criticism • *The company has drawn/taken (heavy) fire for its policies.* **6** [*U*] : strong emotion, anger, enthusiasm, etc. • *hearts full of fire* [=passion] **7** [*C*] *Brit* : a small device that uses gas or electricity to heat a room — **fight fire with fire** see ¹FIGHT — **hang fire** see ¹HANG — **on fire 1** : in the process of burning • *a house on fire* **2** : feeling very strong enthusiasm, love, etc. • *hearts on fire* **3** : very successful • *The team is on fire, winning 10 of its last 11 games.* — **play with fire** see ¹PLAY — **under fire 1** : being shot at by the enemy • *a soldier showing courage under fire* **2** : exposed to criticism • *The company has come under fire* [=has been criticized] *for its policies.*

²**fire** *vb* **fired; fir·ing 1 a** [*T/I*] : to shoot a weapon • *fire a bullet/gun* • *The gun failed to fire.* • *(figurative)* Reporters fired questions at her. **b** [*T*] : to throw (something) with speed and force • *The shortstop fired the ball to first base.* **2** [*T*] : to give life or energy to (something or someone) • *The story fired his imagination.* **3** [*T*] : to dismiss (someone) from a job • *I got/was fired (from my job).* **4** [*I*] : to begin working • *The engine/cylinders failed to fire.* • *(figurative)* a team that's *firing on all cylinders.* [=playing very well] **5** [*T*] *technical* : to heat (a clay pot, dish, etc.) in an oven in order to make it very hard — **fire away** *informal* — used in speech to tell someone to begin asking you questions • *"I have some questions." "OK. Fire away."* — **fire back** [*phrasal vb*] : to answer someone quickly and usually angrily • *"It's true," he said. "Prove it," she fired back.* — **fire off** [*phrasal vb*] **fire (something) off** or **fire off (something)** : to write and send (a letter, memo, etc.) in a quick and often angry way • *fire off a letter of complaint* — **fire up** [*phrasal vb*] **1 fire (something) up** or **fire up (something)** : to start (something) by lighting a fire • *Fire up the grill for the barbecue.* • *(figurative)* I fired up my computer and got to work. **2 fire (someone) up** or **fire up (someone)** : to fill (someone) with energy or enthusiasm • *We were fired up for the concert.*

fire alarm *n* [*C*] : a device that makes a

loud sound to warn people when there is a fire

fire·arm /'faja,ɑəm/ n [C] : a small gun

fire·ball /'faja,bɑːl/ n [C] : a huge mass of fire • *The house erupted into a fireball.*

fire·bomb /'faja,bɑːm/ n [C] : a bomb that causes a fire when it explodes — **firebomb** vb [T] • *Rioters firebombed the courthouse.*

fire·brand /'faja,brænd/ n [C] : a person who tries to get people to become angry and to do things for a political or social cause • *a political firebrand*

fire brigade n [C] **1** US : a group of people who work to put out a fire **2** Brit : FIRE DEPARTMENT

fire·crack·er /'faja,krækə/ n [C] : a small paper cylinder that is filled with an explosive and that produces a loud noise when it explodes

fire department n [C] US : an organization for preventing and putting out fires

fire drill n [C] : an activity in which people practice leaving a place quickly so that they will know what to do if there is a fire

fire engine n [C] : a truck with equipment for putting out fires — called also (US) *fire truck*

fire escape n [C] : a stairway or ladder that can be used to escape from a burning building

fire extinguisher n [C] : a metal container filled with chemicals that is used to put out a fire

fire·fight /'faja,faɪt/ n [C] : a battle in which people shoot guns

fire·fight·er /'faja,faɪtə/ n [C] : a member of a group that works to put out fires — **fire·fight·ing** n [U] • *firefighting equipment*

fire·fly /'faja,flaɪ/ n, pl **-flies** [C] : a small flying insect that produces a soft light — called also (US) *lightning bug*

fire·house /'faja,haʊs/ n [C] US : FIRE STATION

fire hydrant n [C] : a pipe usually in the street that provides water especially for putting out fires — called also *hydrant*, (US) *fireplug*

fire·light /'faja,laɪt/ n [U] : the light produced by a fire in a fireplace, stove, etc.

fire·man /'faja,mən/ n, pl **-men** /-mən/ [C] : a man who is a member of group that works to put out fires

fire·place /'faja,pleɪs/ n [C] : a specially built place in a room where a fire can be built

fire·plug /'faja,plʌg/ n [C] US : FIRE HYDRANT

fire·pow·er /'faja,pawə/ n [U] **1** : the amount or strength of military weapons that can be used against an enemy • *having the/enough firepower to defeat the invaders* **2** : effective power or force • *intellectual firepower*

fire·proof /'faja,pruːf/ adj : not easily burned • *fireproof suits* — **fireproof** vb [T] • *fireproof a building*

fire sale n [C] **1** : a sale of products that have been damaged by fire **2** : a sale at very low prices

¹fire·side /'faja,saɪd/ n [C] : an area close to a fireplace, campfire, etc.

²fireside adj, always before a noun : having an informal or friendly quality • *a fireside chat*

fire station n [C] : a building in which the members of a fire department and the equipment used to put out fires are located

fire·storm /'faja,stoəm/ n [C] **1** : a very large fire that destroys everything in its path and produces powerful winds **2** : a large amount of anger and criticism • *a firestorm of public protest*

fire·trap /'faja,træp/ n [C] : a building that is difficult to get out of and is likely to have a deadly fire

fire truck n [C] US : FIRE ENGINE

fire wall n [C] **1** : a very thick wall that keeps fire from spreading **2** usually **firewall** : a computer program or piece of equipment that keeps people from using or connecting to a computer or a computer network without permission

fire·wood /'faja,wʊd/ n [U] : wood used to make a fire

fire·work /'faja,wək/ n **1 a** [C] : a small device that explodes to make a display of light and noise • *setting off fireworks* **b** [plural] : a display where fireworks are exploded • *Are you going to stay for the fireworks?* **2** [plural] : a display of anger • *We expect a few fireworks during the debate.*

firing line n **1** [C] : a line of soldiers who are shooting at an enemy **2** [singular] : a place or position in which someone is not protected from attack or criticism • *School administrators are not on the firing line every day like the teachers are.*

firing squad n [C/U] : a group of soldiers whose job is to shoot a prisoner who has been sentenced to death

¹firm /'fəm/ adj **1** : fairly hard or solid : not soft • *a firm mattress/cheese* **2** : set, placed, or attached in a way that is not easily moved • *a firm base/foundation* **3** : not weak or uncertain • *a firm grip/voice* • *taking a firm stand on the issue* **4 a** : not likely to change or be changed • *a firm price/estimate/offer* **b** : having or showing true and constant support for something or someone • *I'm a firm believer in the value of exercise.* • *firm friends* — **hold firm** see ¹HOLD — **stand firm** see ¹STAND — **firm·ly** adv • *We stand firmly behind our boss.* • *He pulled the hat down firmly over his ears.* • *I firmly believe in the value of exercise.* — **firm·ness** n [U]

²firm vb **1** [T] : to put (something, such as a plan) into a final form • *firming up plans* **2** [T] : to make (something) harder or stronger • *exercises to firm (up) and strengthen stomach muscles* • *It's only firmed her resolve.* **3** [I] : to become less likely to change or become weaker • *The market is firming (up).*

³firm n [C] : a business organization • *a law firm*

¹first /'fəst/ adj **1** : coming before all others in time, order, or importance • *first prize* • *his first wife* • *her first book/child/attempt* **2** : having or playing the main part in a group of instruments • *first violin* — **at first blush** or **at first glance**

also **at first sight** : when first seen or considered • *At first blush, the proposal seems ridiculous.* — **at first hand** : in a direct way : FIRSTHAND • *verifying his claims at first hand* • **first among equals** ✧ A person who is *first among equals* is the leader of a group of people but is officially considered equal in rights and status to the other members of the group. — **first thing 1 the first thing** : anything at all • *I don't know/understand the first thing about it.* **2** : before anything else : very early • *I'll call first thing (on) Monday morning.* — **first things first** — used to say that you should do the things that are most important before doing other things • *You must set priorities and learn how to put first things first.*

²**first** *adv* **1 a** : before any other in time, order, or importance • *She finished first in the race.* • *You go first.* **b** : for the first time • *We first met at a party.* **c** : before doing other things • *We'll start soon, but first let's make sure everyone is here.* **2** — used to introduce a statement that is the first in a series of statements • *First, let me explain why I called this meeting.* = *First of all, let me explain why I called this meeting.* • **First off,** *there's some confusion we have to clear up.* — **come first** : to be more important than other things • *My family comes first.* — **first and foremost** : at the most basic level • *He is first and foremost a teacher.* — **first come, first served** or **first come, first serve** — used to say that the people who arrive earliest get served or treated before the people who arrive later • *The campsites are first come, first served, so we'd better get there early.*

³**first** *n* **1** : something that is first: such as **a** [C] : an occurrence, achievement, etc., that happens or exists before any other of that kind • *engineering firsts* **b** [U] : the position of the winner in a competition or contest • *He took first in the contest.* **c** [C] : a degree of the highest level from a British university • *take/get a first in English* **2** [U] *baseball* : FIRST BASE • *a runner on first* — **at first** : when something first happens or begins to happen • *We didn't like each other at first. [=when we met]* • *At first [=initially] the book bored me.* — **from the first** : from the beginning • *I've loved her from the first.*

⁴**first** *pron* : the first one or ones • *the first of many delays* • *the first of May* [=May 1]

first aid *n* [U] : emergency treatment given to a sick or injured person ✧ A **first aid kit** is a set of materials and tools used for giving first aid.

first base *n* [*singular*] *baseball* : the base that must be touched first by a base runner — **get to first base** *chiefly US, informal* : to make the first step in a course or process that you hope will lead further • *Her proposal never got to first base.* [=never had any success at all] — **first baseman** [C] */*'beɪsmən/ *n* [C]

first-born /'fəst'boən/ *adj* : born first • *their firstborn child* — **firstborn** *n* [C] • *She's our firstborn.*

first class *n* [U] : the best or highest group or class: such as **a** : the best of usually three kinds of service you can have when you travel • *flying in first class* **b** : a class of mail in the U.S. that includes letters and postcards **c** : a class of mail in the U.K. that includes letters and packages which are delivered sooner than ordinary second-class mail but cost more to send

first–class /'fəst'klæs, *Brit* 'fəːst'klɑːs/ *adj* **1** : of or relating to first class • *passengers in the first-class cabin* • *first-class mail* **2** : of the best quality • *a first-class meal* — **first–class** *adv* • *flying first-class*

first cousin *n* [C] : a child of your aunt or uncle : COUSIN 1a — compare SECOND COUSIN

first–de·gree /'fəstdɪ'griː/ *adj, always before a noun* **1** *US* : of the most serious type • *first-degree murder/theft/arson* **2** : of the least harmful or mildest type • *a first-degree burn*

first down *n* [U] *American football* : the first of a series of usually four downs in which a team must gain 10 yards to keep the ball

first floor *n* [C] **1** *US* : the floor of a building that is at ground level : GROUND FLOOR **2** *Brit* : the floor of a building that is immediately above the ground floor

first-hand /'fəst'hænd/ *adj* : coming directly from actually experiencing or seeing something • *a firsthand description* — **firsthand** *adv* • *I know firsthand how hard it can be.*

first lady *n* [C] **1** or **First Lady** : the wife of the U.S. president **2** : a woman who has great importance, influence, or success in a specified activity or profession • *the first lady of American dance*

first lieutenant *n* [C] **1** : an officer in the U.S. Army, Air Force, or Marine Corps who ranks below a captain **2** : a naval officer who is responsible for keeping a ship in good condition

first-ly /'fəstli/ *adv* — used to introduce a statement that is the first in a series of statements • *I have several concerns. Firstly [=first], I see a serious lack of funding. Secondly, ...*

first name *n* [C] : the name that comes first in someone's full name • *Her first name is Susan.* ✧ People who are on a **first-name basis** (*US*) or on **first-name terms** (*Brit*) know each other well and address each other by their first names.

first person *n* [U] **1** : a set of words or word forms (such as pronouns or verb forms) that refer to the person who is speaking or writing • *"Me" is the objective case of the first person singular pronoun "I," and "us" is the objective case of the first person plural pronoun "we."* **2** : a writing style that uses first person pronouns and verbs • *The sentence "I was born in Maine" is (written) in the first person.*

first–rate /'fəst'reɪt/ *adj* : of the best quality : EXCELLENT • *a first-rate chef/education*

first–string /'fəst'strɪŋ/ *adj, US, sports* : most skillful : used as one of the regular players on a team • *the first-string quarterback/catcher*

fis·cal /ˈfɪskəl/ *adj* : of or relating to money and especially to the money. a government, business, or organization earns, spends, and owes • *fiscal policy/responsibility* — **fis·cal·ly** *adv*

fiscal year *n* [*C*] *chiefly US* : a 12-month period used by a government, business, or organization to calculate how much money is being earned, spent, etc. • *Our fiscal year runs from October 1 to September 30.* — called also (*Brit*) *financial year*

¹**fish** /ˈfɪʃ/ *n, pl* **fish** *or* **fish·es** 1 [*C*] : a cold-blooded animal that lives in water, breathes with gills, and usually has fins and scales

---

usage When you are talking about more than one fish, the plural *fish* is more commonly used than *fishes*. • *We caught several fish.* When you are talking about more than one kind or species of fish, both *fishes* and *fish* are used. • *all the fish/fishes of the sea*

---

2 [*U*] : the meat of a fish eaten as food • *We're having fish for dinner.* — **a big fish in a small pond** (*chiefly US*) *or Brit* **a big fish in a little pond** : a person who is very well known or important in a small group of people but who is not known or important outside that group — **a fish out of water** : a person who is in a place or situation that seems unnatural or uncomfortable • *I feel like a fish out of water here in the big city.* — **fish to fry** *informal* : things to do or deal with • *Right now we've got other/bigger fish to fry.* [=we've got other/bigger problems to deal with]

²**fish** *vb* [*I*] 1 : to catch or try to catch fish • *He was fishing for trout.* 2 : to use your hand to try to find something • *I fished around in my purse for my keys.* — **fish for** [*phrasal vb*] : to ask for or try to get (something, such as praise or attention) in an indirect way • *fishing for answers/compliments* — **fish out** [*phrasal vb*] **fish (something) out** *or* **fish out (something)** 1 : to pull (something) out of water or some other liquid • *Police fished the car out of the harbor.* 2 : to pull (something) out from a container, bag, etc. • *She reached into her purse and fished out her keys.*

fish and chips *n* [*U*] : a meal that consists of fried fish and french-fried potatoes

fish·bowl /ˈfɪʃˌboʊl/ *n* [*C*] 1 : a bowl used for keeping live fish 2 *chiefly US* : a place or condition in which there is no privacy • *Politicians live in a fishbowl—every part of their lives is open to public view.*

fish·er·man /ˈfɪʃəmən/ *n, pl* **-men** /-mən/ [*C*] : a person (especially a man) who catches fish

fish·ery /ˈfɪʃəri/ *n, pl* **-er·ies** [*C*] 1 : a part of the ocean where fish and other sea creatures are caught • *a salmon fishery* 2 : a business that catches and sells fish • *commercial fisheries*

fish·hook /ˈfɪʃˌhʊk/ *n* [*C*] : a small

curved piece of metal that is attached to the end of a piece of fishing line and used to catch fish

fish·ing /ˈfɪʃɪŋ/ *n* [*U*] : the sport or business of catching fish • *The fishing was pretty good today.* • *I'm going fishing this weekend.*

fish·mong·er /ˈfɪʃˌmɑːŋɡə, ˈfɪʃˌmʌŋɡə/ *n* [*C*] *chiefly Brit* : a person or shop that sells fish

fish·net /ˈfɪʃˌnɛt/ *n* 1 [*C*] : a net for catching fish 2 [*U*] : a type of fabric that has many small holes like a net • *fishnet stockings*

fish·tail /ˈfɪʃˌteɪl/ *vb* [*I*] *chiefly US, of a car, truck, etc.* : to slide in an uncontrolled way with the rear end going from side to side • *The car fishtailed on the ice.*

fishy /ˈfɪʃi/ *adj* **fish·i·er; -est** 1 : of or relating to fish • *a fishy odor/taste* 2 *informal* : likely to be bad, untrue, dishonest, etc. • *That story sounds/smells fishy.* [=suspicious, dubious]

fis·sion /ˈfɪʃn/ *n* [*U*] *physics* : a process in which the nucleus of a heavy atom is split apart ◇ A large amount of energy is released when fission occurs. — called also *nuclear fission*

fis·sure /ˈfɪʃə/ *n* [*C*] : a narrow opening or crack • *a fissure in the Earth's crust*

fist /ˈfɪst/ *n* [*C*] : the hand with its fingers bent down into the palm • *pounding on the door with both fists* • *a clenched fist* • *make a fist* — **hand over fist** see ¹**HAND**

fist·fight /ˈfɪstˌfaɪt/ *n* [*C*] : a fight in which people hit each other with their fists

fist·ful /ˈfɪstˌfʊl/ *n* [*C*] : an amount that can be held in one hand : HANDFUL • *a fistful of coins*

fist·i·cuffs /ˈfɪstɪˌkʌfs/ *n* [*plural*] *old-fashioned* : a fight with fists • *an argument that ended in fisticuffs*

¹**fit** /ˈfɪt/ *adj* **fit·ter; -test** 1 a : proper or acceptable : morally or socially correct • *a movie fit for the whole family* • *a subject not fit for discussion* = *a subject not fit to be discussed* b : suitable for a specified purpose • *water not fit for drinking* = *water not fit to drink* 2 : physically healthy and strong • *physically fit* • *Try to get/keep fit.* 3 : having the necessary skills • *He's not fit for the job.* — **fit as a fiddle** *also Brit* **fit as a flea** *informal* : very healthy and strong • *I feel (as) fit as a fiddle this morning.* — **fit for a king** : good enough even for a king : very good • *a meal (that is) fit for a king* — **fit to be tied** *informal* : very angry or upset • *She was fit to be tied when she found out.* — **see/think fit** ◇ To *see fit* or *think fit* to do something is to choose to do it because you think it is right or appropriate. • *You can spend your money as you see fit.* [=as you choose] — **fit·ness** *n* [*U*] • *her fitness for the job* • *physical fitness* [=being healthy through exercise]

²**fit** *vb* **fit·ted** *or chiefly US* **fit; fit·ting** 1 [*T/I*] : to be the right size and shape for (someone or something) • *The suit fits (me) perfectly.* • *I hope this key fits the lock.* • *the way the pieces fit together* ◇ Something that *fits (you) like a glove* fits (you) very well. 2 [*T/I*] : to go into or

through or to cause (something) to go into or through a particular space • *All these groceries won't fit in the trunk of my car.* • *I couldn't fit the box through the door.* **3** *past tense and past participle* **fitted** [T] : to measure (someone) in order to choose clothes that are the right size and shape for that person • *I got fitted for a new suit.* **4** [T] : to find time to meet with (someone) or do (something) • *I'll try to fit you into my schedule.* **5** [I] : to belong in a particular situation, place, or group • *I just don't fit (in) at this school.* **6** [T] **a** : to be suitable or appropriate for (someone or something) • *The punishment should fit the crime.* **b** : to make (someone or something) suitable or appropriate for or to something • *Her experience fitted her for the job.* **7** [T] : to be in agreement with (something or someone) • *He fits the description perfectly.* **8** *past tense and past participle* **fitted** [T] : to supply equipment for (something) • *a lab fitted with the latest equipment* • **fit out** *an expedition* — **fit the bill** see ¹BILL — **fit·ter** /ˈfɪtɚ/ n [C]

³**fit** n [C] : the way something suits the size and shape of your body or goes into or through a particular space • *a loose/snug/comfortable fit* • *It was a tight fit but we got the box through the door.*

⁴**fit** n [C] **1** : an uncontrolled expression of strong emotion • *He had/threw a fit.* [=he became very angry and upset] **2** : a sudden occurrence of some activity, emotion, etc. • *a fit of anger* **3** : an abnormal state in which you become unconscious and your body moves in an uncontrolled and violent way • *an epileptic fit* — **by/in fits and starts** : by stopping and starting again • *Progress came only in fits and starts.* — **in fits** *Brit, informal* : laughing very much • *The audience was in fits.* [=in stitches]

fit·ful /ˈfɪtfəl/ adj : not regular or steady • *a few fitful hours of sleep* — **fit·ful·ly** adv

fit·ted /ˈfɪtəd/ adj : shaped for a precise fit • *a fitted sheet/shirt*

¹**fit·ting** /ˈfɪtɪŋ/ adj : of a kind that is appropriate for the situation or purpose • *It seemed only fitting* [=proper, right] *that she should win.* • *a fitting memorial/tribute* — **fit·ting·ly** adv

²**fitting** n [C] **1** : the act of putting on clothes to see if they fit properly • *a fitting for a suit/dress* **2** : a small part • *a pipe fitting* **3** *Brit* : something (such as a refrigerator or a bookcase) that is in a house or building but can be removed if the house or building is sold • *pay extra for fixtures and fittings*

five /ˈfaɪv/ n **1** [C] : the number 5 **2** [C] : the fifth in a set or series • *the five of clubs* • *page five* **3** [U] : five o'clock • *I left at five.* **4** [C] **a** *US* : a five-dollar bill **b** *Brit* : a five-pound note : FIVER — **five** adj • *five years* — **five** pron • *Five (of them) are missing.*

fiv·er /ˈfaɪvɚ/ n [C] *Brit, informal* : a five-pound note

¹**fix** /ˈfɪks/ vb [T] **1 a** : to make (something) whole or able to work properly again • *fix a leaky faucet* **b** : to deal with or correct (a problem) • *People expect the*

schools *to fix whatever is wrong with their kids.* **2** : to attach (something) in such a way that it will not move • *The table was fixed to the floor.* • *(figurative) I want to fix this moment in my mind.* [=I want to remember this moment] **3 a** : to set or place (something) definitely • *They haven't yet fixed the date of their wedding.* • *illegal price fixing* **b** : to find out (something) with certainty • *We're trying to fix the ship's location.* **c** : to arrange the details of something • *My lawyer fixed it* [=made arrangements] *so I wouldn't have to go to court.* **4** *chiefly US* **a** : to make (something, such as a meal) ready • *fix dinner* • *Can I fix you a drink?* **b** *informal* : to make (someone's hair, makeup, etc.) neat or attractive • *fixing her lipstick/makeup* **5** : to control or affect (something, such as a game or election) in a dishonest way • *The election was fixed.* **6** : to change the appearance of (someone's face, nose, etc.) through surgery • *getting her nose fixed* **7** *informal* : to do something to punish (someone who has treated you badly or unfairly) • *I'll fix you!* **8** *US* : to make (an animal) unable to reproduce • *You should have your dog/cat fixed.* **9** *US, informal* + *old-fashioned* : to be or get ready to do something • *We're fixing to leave.* — **fix on/upon** [phrasal vb] **1** : to direct your attention or thoughts toward (something) • *All eyes fixed on the door.* [=everyone looked at the door] **2** : to make a decision about or choose (something) • *They finally fixed on a solution.* — **fix (someone) with a stare/look (etc.)** : to look directly at (someone) usually in an angry way • *She fixed him with an angry stare.* — **fix up** [phrasal vb] **1** *fix up (something)* or *fix (something) up* : to improve the appearance or condition of (something, such as a building) • *We're fixing up our house.* **2** *fix (someone or something) up* *chiefly US* : to make (someone or something) more attractive or fancy • *She got herself all fixed up for the party.* **3** *fix (someone) up* **a** : to provide (someone) with something that is needed or wanted • *We'll fix you up with a bicycle.* **b** : to arrange a date for (someone) • *She tried to fix me up with her cousin.* — **fix your eyes/gaze (etc.) on/upon** : to look at (someone or something) steadily • *Everyone fixed their eyes on the door.* — **fix your hopes/sights (etc.) on/upon** : to direct your hopes, efforts, etc., toward (something) • *They fixed their sights on winning the championship.*

²**fix** n [C] **1** : a difficult or embarrassing situation • *I'm in an awful fix.* **2** : SOLUTION • *a quick fix* **3** : the act of dishonestly controlling or affecting something (such as a game or election) • *(US) It was obvious early in the game that the fix was in.* [=the outcome of the game was being controlled in a dishonest way] **4** : an amount of an illegal drug that someone wants or needs to have • *an addict in search of his next fix* • *(figurative) an ice-cream fix* **5 a** : the exact position of something (such as a ship or an airplane)

▪ *We're trying to get a fix on the ship's location.* [=trying to find the ship's exact location] **b** : an accurate understanding of something ▪ *Analysts are reading reports to get a fix on how the market will perform.*

fix•ate /ˈfɪkˌseɪt/ *vb* -at•ed; -at•ing [*I*] : to look at or think about something constantly ▪ *Why do people fixate on scandals?* — **fixated** *adj* ▪ *Why are people so fixated on scandals?* — **fix•a•tion** /fɪkˈseɪʃən/ *n* [*C*] ▪ *our fixation on scandals*

fixed /ˈfɪkst/ *adj* **1 a** — used to describe something that does not change ▪ *living on a fixed income* ▪ *a fixed stare/expression/smile* **b** : placed or attached in a way that does not move easily ▪ *a mirror fixed to the wall* **2** *informal* : having something needed ▪ *We're well fixed for food.* [=we have a good supply of food] ▪ *He's fixed for life.* [=he has enough money to live comfortably for the rest of his life] — **fix•ed•ly** /ˈfɪksədli/ *adv*

fix•ings /ˈfɪksənz/ *n* [*plural*] *US, informal* : foods that are traditionally served with the main dish of a particular meal ▪ *a Thanksgiving dinner with turkey and all the fixings* [=potatoes, vegetables, etc.]

fix•i•ty /ˈfɪksəti/ *n* [*U, singular*] *formal* : the state or quality of not changing ▪ *with (a) fixity of purpose*

fix•ture /ˈfɪkstʃɚ/ *n* [*C*] **1** : something (such as a light, toilet, sink, etc.) that is attached to a house or building and that is not removed when the house or building is sold ▪ *bathroom/lighting fixtures* **2** : a person or thing that has been part of something or involved in something for a long time ▪ *He's been a fixture in the parade for many years.* **3** *Brit, sports* : a game played at a particular time and place ▪ *all the team's home fixtures*

fizz /ˈfɪz/ *n* **1** [*U*] : a sound like many small bubbles popping ▪ *the fizz of soda* **2** [*U*] : energy and liveliness ▪ *All the fizz was gone from their relationship.* **3 a** [*C*] : a drink with many small bubbles ▪ *a gin fizz* **b** [*U*] *Brit, informal* : CHAMPAGNE — **fizz** *vb* [*I*] ▪ *The soda fizzed.* — **fizzy** /ˈfɪzi/ *adj* **fizz•i•er; -est** ▪ *a fizzy drink*

fiz•zle /ˈfɪzəl/ *vb* **fiz•zled; fiz•zling** [*I*] *informal* : to gradually fail or end ▪ *The project ended up fizzling (out).* — **fizzle** *n* [*C*] ▪ *the team's recent fizzle* [=failure, flop]

fjord *also* **fiord** /fiˈoɚd/ *n* [*C*] : a narrow part of the ocean between cliffs or steep hills or mountains ▪ *the fjords of Norway*

FL *abbr* Florida

Fla *abbr* Florida

flab /ˈflæb/ *n* [*U*] *informal* : extra soft flesh on a person's body ▪ *stomach/arm flab* — **flab•bi•ness** /ˈflæbinəs/ *n* [*U*] — **flab•by** /ˈflæbi/ *adj* **flab•bi•er; -est** ▪ *flabby arms*

flab•ber•gast /ˈflæbɚˌgæst, *Brit* ˈflæbəˌgɑːst/ *vb* [*T*] : to shock or surprise (someone) very much ▪ *I'm flabbergasted by the number of people who still support them.*

flac•cid /ˈflæsəd/ *adj* : not hard or solid ▪ *flaccid muscles/tissue*

¹**flack** /ˈflæk/ *n* [*C*] *US, informal + disapproving* : a person whose job is to make

people like or be interested in someone or something ▪ *a public relations flack*

²**flack** *variant spelling of* FLAK

¹**flag** /ˈflæg/ *n* [*C*] **1** : a piece of cloth with a special design that is used as a symbol of a nation or group ▪ *raise/lower the flag* **2** : a piece of cloth used as a signal or to attract attention ▪ *a penalty flag*

²**flag** *vb* **flagged; flag•ging** **1** [*T*] : to signal (someone or something that is moving past you) to stop especially by raising or waving your hand ▪ *flag a taxi* ▪ *We should flag someone down and ask for directions.* **2** [*T*] : to mark (something, such as a page or section of a book) so that it can be easily seen or found ▪ *She flagged several pages for me to review.* **3** [*T*] *American football* : to signal that you are giving a penalty to (a player) by throwing a penalty flag ▪ *He was flagged for holding.* **4** [*I*] **a** : to become weak ▪ *Our interest flagged as the speaker droned on.* **b** : to become less interesting, attractive, or valuable ▪ *my flagging career*

flag•el•late /ˈflæʤəˌleɪt/ *vb* **-lat•ed; -lat•ing** [*T*] *formal* : to hit (yourself or another person) with a whip as punishment or as part of a religious ritual — **flag•el•la•tion** /ˌflæʤəˈleɪʃən/ *n* [*U*]

flag•pole /ˈflægˌpoʊl/ *n* [*C*] : a tall pole from which a flag hangs

fla•grant /ˈfleɪgrənt/ *adj* : too bad to be ignored ▪ *a flagrant violation/error* — **fla•grant•ly** *adv*

flag•ship /ˈflægˌʃɪp/ *n* [*C*] **1** : the ship that carries the commander of a group of ships **2** : the best, largest, or most important one of a group of products, stores, etc. ▪ *the company's flagship store*

flag•staff /ˈflægˌstæf, *Brit* ˈflægˌstɑːf/ *n* [*C*] : FLAGPOLE

flag•stone /ˈflægˌstoʊn/ *n* [*C*] : a hard, flat piece of stone that is used for making paths

flail /ˈfleɪl/ *vb* **1** [*T/I*] : to move or swing your arms or legs in a wild and uncontrolled way ▪ *flailing our arms to drive away the insects* **2** [*T*] : to strike or hit (something or someone) in a wild and uncontrolled way ▪ *The bird's wings flailed the water.*

flair /ˈfleɚ/ *n* [*singular*] **1** : a natural ability to do something — usually + *for* ▪ *a flair for storytelling* **2** : an unusual and appealing quality or style ▪ *a restaurant with a European flair*

flak *also* **flack** /ˈflæk/ *n* [*U*] **1** : exploding shells that are shot at enemy aircraft from guns on the ground **2** *informal* : harsh criticism ▪ *He caught/drew heavy flak for his decision.*

¹**flake** /ˈfleɪk/ *n* [*C*] **1** : a small, thin piece of something ▪ *white flakes of dandruff* ▪ *soap flakes* **2** *chiefly US, informal* : a strange or unusual person ▪ *He's a bit of a flake.* — **flaky** /ˈfleɪki/ *adj* **flak•i•er; -est** ▪ *pie with a crisp, flaky crust* ▪ *He's a little flaky.* [=strange]

²**flake** *vb* **flaked; flak•ing** [*I*] **1** : to break apart into small, thin pieces ▪ *Bake the fish until it flakes easily when tested with a fork.* **2** : to form loose, thin pieces that fall off ▪ *The paint is flaking (off).*

flam•boy•ant /flæmˈbojənt/ *adj* : having

a very noticeable quality that attracts a lot of attention • *flamboyant performers/ clothes* — **flam·boy·ance** /flæm-ˈbojəns/ *n* [U] — **flam·boy·ant·ly** *adv*

¹**flame** /ˈfleɪm/ *n* **1** [C] : the hot, glowing gas that can be seen when a fire is burning • *the flame of a candle* **2** [C/U] : a state of burning brightly • *The engine suddenly **burst/exploded** into flames/ flame.* [=the engine suddenly began burning] • *The entire building was in flames.* [=was on fire; was burning] **3** [C] : strongly felt emotion • *the flames of passion* **4** [C] *informal* : SWEETHEART • *He's an old flame from her high-school days.* **5** [C] : an angry or insulting e-mail message

²**flame** *vb* **flamed; flam·ing 1** [I] : to burn with a flame : to produce a flame • *The pan flamed up suddenly.* **2** [T] : to send an angry or insulting e-mail message to (someone) on the Internet. — **flame out** [*phrasal vb*] **1** *of a jet engine* : to stop working suddenly **2** *US, informal* : to fail or end in a very sudden way • *His career flamed out after the failure of his last movie.*

fla·men·co /fləˈmɛŋkoʊ/ *n, pl* **-cos** [C/U] : a fast and lively Spanish dance or the music played for this dance

flame·proof /ˈfleɪmˌpruːf/ *adj* : FIRE-PROOF

flame·throw·er /ˈfleɪmˌθroʊwɚ/ *n* [C] : a weapon that shoots a stream of burning liquid

flam·ing /ˈfleɪmɪŋ/ *adj* **1** : having a bright or glowing red or orange color • *flaming red hair* **2** : burning with bright flames • *a flaming torch* **3** : very intense or strongly felt • *flaming passion* **4** *informal* — used to make an angry or critical statement more forceful • *She's a flaming idiot.*

fla·min·go /fləˈmɪŋgoʊ/ *n, pl* **-gos** *also* **-goes** [C] : a large tropical bird that has pink or red wings and a very long neck and legs

flam·ma·ble /ˈflæməbəl/ *adj* : capable of being set on fire and of burning quickly • *a flammable liquid*

flange /ˈflændʒ/ *n* [C] : an edge that sticks out from something (such as a wheel) and is used for strength, for guiding, or for attachment to another object

¹**flank** /ˈflæŋk/ *n* [C] **1** : the area on the side of an animal (such as a horse) between the ribs and the hip **2** : the right or left side of a military formation • *They attacked the enemy on both flanks.* **3** : the side of something • *the eastern flank of a volcano*

²**flank** *vb* [T] : to be located on both sides of (something or someone) • *Guards flanked the entrance.* • *The bed was flanked by two small tables.*

flan·nel /ˈflænl/ *n* **1** [U] : a soft cloth made of wool or cotton • *a flannel shirt* **2** [*plural*] : pants made of flannel • *a dark blazer and gray flannels* **3** [C] *Brit* : WASHCLOTH **4** [U] *Brit, informal* : foolish or meaningless words

¹**flap** /ˈflæp/ *n* [C] **1** : a flat piece of material that is attached to something on one side and that can be easily moved • *the*

inside flap of a book's cover **2** : the movement or sound of something that is moving up and down or back and forth • *the steady flap of the bird's wings* **3** *informal* **a** : a state or situation in which many people are excited or upset • *the recent flap about the new book* **b** *chiefly Brit* : a state in which someone is very upset • *She's in a flap* [=upset] *over the delays.* **4** : a movable part of an airplane wing that can be raised or lowered and that is used to increase lift

²**flap** *vb* **flapped; flap·ping** [T/I] : to move (something) up and down or back and forth • *birds flapping their wings* • *The flag flapped in the breeze.*

flap·jack /ˈflæpˌdʒæk/ *n* [C] **1** *US* : PANCAKE **2** *Brit* : a thick, sweet cake made of oatmeal usually with molasses or honey

¹**flare** /ˈfleɚ/ *vb* **flared; flar·ing 1** [I] : to shine or burn suddenly and briefly • *A match flared (up) in the darkness.* **2** [I] : to become suddenly excited, angry, or active • *Tempers flared* [=people became angry] *during the debate.* • *Her asthma has flared up again.* [=has become suddenly active or worse again] **3** [T/I] : to open or spread outward • *pants that flare (out) at the bottom* • *The bull flared its nostrils.*

²**flare** *n* **1** [C] : a light that shines brightly and briefly • *the sudden flare of the match* **2** [C] : a very bright light that is used to give a signal, to light up something, or to attract attention; *also* : a device that produces such a light **3** [C] : a shape or part that spreads outward • *the flare at the bottom of the vase* **4** [*plural*] : BELL-BOTTOMS

flare–up /ˈfleɚˌʌp/ *n* [C] **1** : a sudden occurrence of flame **2** : a sudden occurrence or expression of anger • *a flare-up of temper* **3** : an occurrence in which something suddenly begins or becomes worse • *a flare-up of asthma/violence*

¹**flash** /ˈflæʃ/ *vb* [T/I] **1** : to shine or give off bright light suddenly or repeatedly • *Cameras flashed as the celebrities passed.* • *She flashed her car's headlights (at us).* **2** : to move or appear quickly or suddenly • *A car flashed by.* • *A message flashed on the screen.* **3** : to show something briefly • *The officer flashed his badge.* • *Her eyes flashed with anger.*

²**flash** *n* **1** [C] : a sudden bright light • *a flash of lightning* **2** [C] : a sudden appearance or occurrence of something • *a flash of color/wit/anger* — see also HOT FLASH **3** [U] *usually disapproving* : a fancy or exciting quality or appearance that is meant to attract attention and that is usually not very good or interesting • *a show with a lot of flash but little substance* **4** [C/U] : a device that is used to produce a flash of light for taking photographs • *a picture taken using (a) flash* **5** [C] : NEWSFLASH — **(as) quick as a flash** *informal* : very quickly • *The waitress brought our order as quick as a flash.* — **flash in the pan** : a person or thing that fails after being very popular or successful for a brief time — **in a**

flash *informal* : very quickly or suddenly ▪ *I'll be back in a flash.*

³**flash** *adj* **1** *always before a noun* : beginning suddenly and lasting only a short time ▪ *a flash fire/flood* **2** *always before a noun, US, informal* : very talented ▪ *a flash athlete* **3** *Brit, informal + disapproving* : FLASHY, SHOWY ▪ *a flash car*

flash·back /ˈflæʃˌbæk/ *n* **1** [C/U] : a part of a story or movie that describes or shows something that happened in the past **2** [C] : a strong memory of a past event that comes suddenly into a person's mind ▪ *He's having flashbacks off/to his days in the war.*

flash·bulb /ˈflæʃˌbʌlb/ *n* [C] : an electric bulb that produces a flash of light for taking photographs

flash card *n* [C] : a card that has words, numbers, or pictures on it and that is used to help students learn about a subject

flash·er /ˈflæʃɚ/ *n* [C] **1** : a light that shines briefly and repeatedly ▪ *The car had its flashers on.* **2** *informal* : a man who shows his sexual organs in public

flash·light /ˈflæʃˌlaɪt/ *n* [C] *US* : a small electric light that can be carried in your hand and that runs on batteries — called also (*Brit*) *torch*

flashy /ˈflæʃi/ *adj* **flash·i·er; -est** *usually disapproving* : bright or fancy in a way that is meant to attract attention ▪ *flashy colors/cars/ads* ▪ *a flashy dresser* — **flash·i·ly** /ˈflæʃəli/ *adv* — **flash·i·ness** /ˈflæʃinəs/ *n* [U]

flask /ˈflæsk, *Brit* ˈflɑːsk/ *n* [C] **1** : a container that is shaped like a flattened bottle and that is used to carry alcohol **2** : a glass bottle used in scientific laboratories **3** *Brit* : THERMOS

¹**flat** /ˈflæt/ *adj* **flat·ter; flat·test 1** : having a smooth, level, or even surface ▪ *flat ground* ▪ *a flat stomach* **2** : having a wide, smooth surface and little thickness ▪ *Coins are usually round and flat.* ▪ *shoes with flat heels* **3** : having a flat heel or no heel ▪ *flat shoes* **4** : spread out on or along a surface ▪ *He was (lying) flat on his back.* **5** : very clear and definite ▪ *a flat refusal* ▪ (*Brit*) *I'm not going to do it and that's flat!* **6 a** : not changing in amount ▪ *a flat [=fixed] fee/tax* **b** : not having much business activity ▪ *The market is very flat.* **7** : not having much interest or energy ▪ *a flat performance* **8** : no longer having bubbles ▪ *flat beer/champagne* **9** : not having enough air ▪ *a flat tire* **10** *music* **a** : lower than the true pitch ▪ *Her singing was flat.* **b** : lower than a specified note by a semitone ▪ *B flat* [=a note that is a semitone lower than B] **11** : not shiny ▪ *flat paint* **12** *Brit* : no longer producing electricity : DEAD ▪ *The battery has gone flat.* — (*as*) *flat as a pancake informal* : very flat ▪ *The land/tire is as flat as a pancake.* — **flat·ly** *adv* ▪ *He flatly refuses to talk about it.* ▪ *Lay the map flatly on the desk.* — **flat·ness** *n* [U]

²**flat** *n* [C] **1** : a level area of land ▪ *salt/tidal flats* **2** : a flat part or surface ▪ *the flat of a sword* **3 a** : a musical note that is one semitone lower than a specified note

▪ *B flat* **b** : a written symbol ♭ that is placed before a note to show that it should be played a semitone lower **4** *US* : a shallow box in which young plants are grown **5** *chiefly US* : a shoe or slipper that has a flat heel or no heel **6** *chiefly Brit* : an apartment typically on one floor ▪ *They moved out of their old flat.* **7** : a tire that does not have enough air

³**flat** *adv* **1 a** : on or against a flat surface ▪ *Lay the map flat on the desk.* **b** : in the position of someone or something that is lying spread out on the ground or another surface ▪ *He slipped and landed/fell flat on his back/face.* **2** : exactly or precisely — used to describe something that happens quickly ▪ *He got there in two minutes flat.* ▪ *She finished her homework in nothing flat.* [=very quickly] **3** *informal* : completely or absolutely ▪ *We asked for more time but they turned us down flat.* ▪ (*US*) *What they're doing is flat wrong.* ▪ *I'm flat broke.* [=I have no money] **4** : below the correct musical pitch ▪ *He sang flat.* — **fall flat** see ¹FALL

flat foot *n* [C] : a foot that is flat on the bottom so that the entire sole rests upon the ground ▪ *He has flat feet.*

flat–foot·ed /ˈflætˌfʊtəd/ *adj* **1** : having flat feet ▪ *a flat-footed man* **2** *chiefly US, informal* : not ready or prepared — usually used in the phrase **catch flat-footed** ▪ *The fastball caught the batter flat-footed.* [=he was not prepared for the fastball]

flat·mate /ˈflætˌmeɪt/ *n* [C] *chiefly Brit* : a person who shares a flat (sense 6) with someone

flat out *adv, informal* **1** *chiefly US* : in a very clear and direct way ▪ *They refused us flat out.* **2** : at the fastest possible speed ▪ *The car does 180 mph flat out.* ▪ *running/working flat out* **3** *usually* **flat-out** *US, informal* — used to make a statement more forceful ▪ *The movie was flat-out awful.* — **flat–out** /ˈflætˌaʊt/ *adj, always before a noun* ▪ *a flat-out* [=complete] *lie/refusal* ▪ *a flat-out* [=total] *effort*

flat–pan·el /ˈflætˌpænl/ *adj, always before a noun* : FLAT-SCREEN

flat–screen /ˈflætˌskriːn/ *adj, always before a noun* — used to describe a television, computer monitor, etc., that has a thin, flat screen ▪ *We bought a new flat-screen TV.*

flat·ten /ˈflætn̩/ *vb* **1** [T/I] : to make (something) flat or to become flat or flatter ▪ *He opened the map and flattened it (out) against the tabletop.* ▪ *The dough flattened smoothly.* **2** [T] : to knock down (something or someone) ▪ *The houses were flattened by the tornado.* **3** [I] : to go to and stay at a lower level ▪ *Prices have flattened (out).*

flat·ter /ˈflætɚ/ *vb* [T] **1** : to praise (someone) in a way that is not sincere ▪ *He flattered her with comments about her youthful appearance.* **2** : to cause (someone) to feel pleased by showing respect, affection, or admiration ▪ *It flattered her to be asked to sing at their wedding.* ▪ *I'm flattered that he asked me out.* **3** : to show or describe (someone or something) in a way that is very favorable or too favorable ▪ *That portrait/dress flatters her.* [=makes her look attractive] — **flatter yourself** : to believe something about yourself that makes you feel pleased or proud ▪ *I flatter myself on my skill in dancing.* — **flat·ter·er** /ˈflætərɚ/ *n* [C] — **flat·ter·ing** /ˈflætərɪŋ/ *adj* ▪ *a flattering comment/dress* — **flat·ter·ing·ly** /ˈflætərɪŋli/ *adv*

flat·tery /ˈflætəri/ *n* [U] : praise that is not sincere ▪ *He tried to win his teacher's favor with flattery.*

flat·u·lence /ˈflætʃələns, *Brit* ˈflætjələns/ *n* [U] : the presence of too much gas or air in the stomach or intestines — **flat·u·lent** /ˈflætʃələnt, *Brit* ˈflætjələnt/ *adj*

flat·ware /ˈflætˌweɚ/ *n* [U] *US* : forks, spoons, and knives used for serving and eating food

flaunt /ˈflɑːnt/ *vb* [T] : to show (something) in a very open way so that other people will notice ▪ *She flaunts her wealth by wearing furs and jewelry.* ▪ *If you've got it, flaunt it!* [=you should not be afraid to show your good features and talents]

flau·tist /ˈflɑːtɪst/ *n* [C] : FLUTIST

¹**fla·vor** (*US*) *or Brit* **fla·vour** /ˈfleɪvɚ/ *n* 1 a [C/U] : the quality of something that you can taste ▪ *the hot, spicy flavor(s) of Mexican food* b [C] : a particular type of taste ▪ *different flavors of ice cream* c [U] : a good or appealing taste ▪ *The food lacks flavor.* 2 [C/U] *chiefly US* : a substance that is added to food or drink to give it a desired taste : FLAVORING ▪ *artificial flavors* 3 a [C] : a particular quality that something has ▪ *I like the Italian flavor of the neighborhood.* b [U] : an appealing quality ▪ *Her performance adds flavor to the show.* 4 [C] *informal* : a type or version of something ▪ *different flavors of software* — **fla·vor·ful** (*US*) *or Brit* **fla·vour·ful** /ˈfleɪvɚfəl/ *adj* ▪ *flavorful recipes* — **fla·vor·less** (*US*) *or Brit* **fla·vour·less** /ˈfleɪvɚləs/ *adj* ▪ *flavorless food*

²**flavor** (*US*) *or Brit* **flavour** *vb* [T] : to give or add flavor to (something) ▪ *We flavored the cookies with cinnamon.*

fla·vor·ing (*US*) *or Brit* **fla·vour·ing** /ˈfleɪvərɪŋ/ *n* [C/U] : a substance that is added to a food or drink to give it a desired taste ▪ *ginger and other natural flavorings*

flaw /ˈflɑː/ *n* [C] 1 : a small physical problem (such as a crack) that makes something less valuable : DEFECT ▪ *There was a flaw in the vase.* 2 : a small fault or weakness ▪ *Vanity was the one flaw in his character.* ▪ *There are a few flaws in your argument.* — **flawed** /ˈflɑːd/ *adj* ▪ *badly flawed reasoning* ▪ *a flawed but powerful performance* — **flaw·less** /ˈflɑːləs/ *adj* ▪ *a flawless* [=perfect] *performance* — **flaw·less·ly** *adv*

flax /ˈflæks/ *n* [U] 1 : a plant that has blue flowers and that is grown for its fiber and its seed 2 : the fiber of the flax plant

flax·en /ˈflæksən/ *adj, literary* : having a pale yellow color ▪ *flaxen hair*

flea /ˈfliː/ *n* [C] : a very small insect that lives on animals and that has strong legs used for jumping

flea market *n* [C] : a usually outdoor market in which old and used goods are sold

fleck /ˈflɛk/ *n* [C] : a small spot or mark ▪ *a brown cloth with flecks of yellow* — **fleck** *vb* [T] ▪ *a brown beard flecked with gray* [=a brown beard that has many small areas or spots of gray]

fled *past tense and past participle of* FLEE

fledg·ling /ˈflɛdʒlɪŋ/ *n* [C] 1 : a young bird that has just become able to fly 2 : someone or something that is getting started in a new activity ▪ *a fledgling novelist*

¹**flee** /ˈfliː/ *vb* **fled** /ˈflɛd/; **flee·ing** 1 [I] : to run away from danger ▪ *They fled for their lives.* 2 [T] : to run away from (a place) ▪ *He fled the scene of the accident.*

¹**fleece** /ˈfliːs/ *n* 1 [C] : the woolly coat of a sheep 2 a [U] : a soft cloth that is used to make warm clothes b [C] *chiefly Brit* : a jacket made from this cloth — **fleecy** /ˈfliːsi/ *adj* **fleec·i·er**, **-est** ▪ *fleecy clouds/fabric*

²**fleece** *vb* **fleeced**; **fleec·ing** [T] *informal* : to deceive and take money from (someone) ▪ *tourists fleeced by a scam artist*

¹**fleet** /ˈfliːt/ *n* [C] 1 a : a group of military ships that are controlled by one leader ▪ *the commander of the Pacific fleet* b : all of a country's military ships ▪ *the British fleet* 2 : a group of ships or vehicles that move or work together or that are controlled or owned by one company ▪ *a fishing fleet* ▪ *a fleet of taxis*

²**fleet** *adj, literary* : very fast ▪ *a fleet runner* ▪ *She is fleet of foot.* [=she runs very fast] — **fleet·ly** *adv* — **fleet·ness** *n* [U]

fleet–foot·ed /ˈfliːtˌfʊtəd/ *adj* : able to run fast ▪ *a fleet-footed runner*

fleet·ing /ˈfliːtɪŋ/ *adj* : lasting for only a short time ▪ *autumn's fleeting beauty* ▪ *Her fame was fleeting.*

Flem·ish /ˈflɛmɪʃ/ *n* [U] : the Germanic language that is spoken by people in northern Belgium and that is now called Dutch — **Flemish** *adj*

¹**flesh** /ˈflɛʃ/ *n* [U] 1 : the soft parts of the body of an animal or person ▪ *the flabby white flesh of his belly* 2 : the skin of a person ▪ *sun-tanned flesh* ▪ *The memory of all that blood was enough to make my flesh crawl/creep.* [=to make me feel disgusted, afraid, etc.] 3 : parts of an animal used as food : MEAT ▪ *flesh-eating mammals* 4 : the soft part of a fruit that is eaten ▪ *the sweet flesh of a peach* 5 : the physical nature of a person rather than the mind or spirit ▪ *pleasures of the flesh* [=physical pleasures, such as eating, drinking, and having sex] — **flesh and blood** 1 : a human being ▪ *It was more than flesh and blood can bear.* 2 : a person in your family ▪ *How could you do something so cruel to your own flesh and blood?* — **in the flesh** ◇ If you see someone in the flesh, you see that person directly rather than in a picture, on television, etc. — **pound of flesh** see ¹POUND — **press the flesh** see ²PRESS

²**flesh** *vb* — **flesh out** [*phrasal vb*] **flesh**

(something) out or **flesh out (something)** : to provide more information about (something) ▪ *You need to flesh out your plan with more details.*

flesh wound *n* [C] : a wound that injures the skin and flesh but does not go deep into the body

fleshy /'flɛʃi/ *adj* **flesh·i·er; -est** : having a large amount of flesh ▪ *fleshy arms* 2 : soft and thick ▪ *fleshy fruit* — **flesh·i·ness** *n* [U]

flew *past tense of* ¹FLY

¹**flex** /'flɛks/ *vb* 1 [T/I] : BEND ▪ *flex your legs/finger* ▪ *The material flexes easily.* 2 [T] : to move or tighten (a muscle) ▪ *He flexed the muscles of his right arm.* ▪ (figurative) *The election will give us a chance to flex our political muscles.* [=to show our political strength]

²**flex** *n* [C] *Brit* : CORD 2

flex·i·ble /'flɛksəbəl/ *adj* 1 : capable of bending or being bent ▪ *flexible plastic* ▪ *exercising to become stronger and more flexible* 2 : easily changed ▪ *Our schedule for the weekend is flexible.* : able or willing to change or to do different things ▪ *Whatever you want to do is fine with me. I'm flexible.* — **flex·i·bil·i·ty** /ˌflɛksə'bɪləti/ *n* [U]

¹**flick** /'flɪk/ *n* [C] 1 : a short, quick movement ▪ *a flick of his thumb/wrist* 2 *informal* : MOVIE ▪ *the new action flick*

²**flick** *vb* 1 [T/I] : to move (something) with a short, quick movement ▪ *flick a switch* ▪ *The snake's tongue flicked in and out.* b [T] : to cause (something) to fly through the air by making a quick movement with your hand, finger, or thumb ▪ *He flicked his cigarette butt out the window.* 2 [T] : to turn (something) *on* or *off* with a switch ▪ *flick on/off the lights*

¹**flick·er** /'flɪkɚ/ *vb* [I] 1 : to burn or glow in an unsteady way ▪ *The light kept flickering off and on.* ▪ *a flickering flame* 2 : to appear or pass briefly or quickly ▪ *Thoughts flickered through his mind.*

²**flicker** *n* [C] 1 : a quick, unsteady movement of light ▪ *the flicker of candlelight* 2 : a sudden, quick movement ▪ *the flicker of an eyelash* 3 : a very small amount of something ▪ *a flicker of interest/hope*

flick–knife /'flɪkˌnaɪf/ *n* [C] *Brit* : SWITCHBLADE

fli·er or **fly·er** /'flajɚ/ *n* [C] 1 : a person or animal that flies ▪ *These birds are graceful fliers.* ▪ *a frequent flier* [=a person who flies often on a particular airline] 2 *usually flyer* : a piece of paper that has an advertisement, announcement, etc., printed on it and that is given to many people ▪ *They distributed flyers announcing the concert throughout the city.* — **take a flier** *US, informal* : to do something risky ▪ *Investors have been unwilling to take a flier on* [=to invest money in] *such a small company.*

flight /'flaɪt/ *n* 1 [U] a : the act of moving through the air by the use of wings ▪ *the flight of a bee* ▪ *a bird in flight* [=a bird that is flying] b : the act of moving through the air or through outer space ▪ *the flight of a bullet/rocket* 2 [C/U] : the act of running away in order to escape from danger ▪ *the flight of refugees* 3 [C]

a : a journey on an airplane ▪ *a direct/ nonstop flight* b : the airplane that is making a journey ▪ *Our flight leaves at noon.* ▪ *They boarded Flight 101.* 4 [C] : a group of similar birds, airplanes, etc., that are flying through the air together ▪ *a flight of geese* 5 [C] : a series of stairs going from one level or floor to another ▪ *He fell down a flight of stairs.* — **flight of fancy** also **flight of imagination/fantasy** : an idea, story, etc., that shows great imagination but is very unlikely to be true or practical — **take flight** 1 : to leave or run away from danger ▪ *Fearing arrest, they took flight and hid in the mountains.* 2 *US* : to begin flying ▪ *The bird took flight when we approached it.* 3 *US* : to begin a period of rapid activity, development, or growth ▪ *The idea really took flight and soon it seemed everyone was copying it.*

flight attendant *n* [C] : a person whose job is to help passengers who are traveling in an airplane

flight deck *n* [C] 1 : the top deck of an aircraft carrier 2 : the area where the pilots sit in a large airplane

flight·less /'flaɪtləs/ *adj* : unable to fly ▪ *flightless birds*

flight lieutenant *n* [C] : an officer in the British Air Force

flighty /'flaɪti/ *adj* **flight·i·er; -est** 1 : likely to forget things or to change opinions, plans, etc., without reason ▪ *a flighty person* 2 : easily excited or frightened ▪ *flighty* [=skittish] *horses/investors*

flim·sy /'flɪmzi/ *adj* **flim·si·er; -est** 1 : not strong or solid ▪ *flimsy construction/ material* 2 : not likely to be true or to be believed ▪ *a flimsy* [=weak] *excuse* ▪ *flimsy evidence* — **flim·si·ness** /'flɪmzinəs/ *n* [U]

flinch /'flɪntʃ/ *vb* [I] 1 : to move suddenly because you are afraid of being hit or hurt ▪ *He flinched when I tapped him on the shoulder.* 2 : to hesitate from doing something unpleasant or dangerous ▪ *She met danger without flinching.*

¹**fling** /'flɪŋ/ *vb* **flung** /'flʌŋ/; **fling·ing** [T] 1 : to throw or push (something) in a sudden and forceful way ▪ *She flung the door open and stormed into the room.* ▪ *They flung their hats into the air.* ▪ (figurative) *They were flinging insults at each other.* 2 : to forcefully move (yourself or a part of your body) in a specified way ▪ *She flung herself into his arms.* ▪ *He flung his arms around her.* — **fling yourself into** : to begin doing or working on (something) with great energy and enthusiasm ▪ *He flung himself into (composing/performing) his music.*

²**fling** *n* [C] 1 : a brief sexual relationship ▪ *She had a fling with her boss.* 2 : a short period of time spent doing enjoyable and exciting things ▪ *They had time for one last fling before going back to school.* — **give (something) a fling** or **have a fling at (something)** : to try something without being very serious about it ▪ *He had always thought about starting his own business, and he decided to give it a fling.*

flint /'flɪnt/ n 1 [C/U] : a hard rock that produces a spark when it is hit by steel 2 [C] : a piece of metal used for producing a spark ▪ the flint in a cigarette lighter

flinty /'flɪnti/ adj flint·i·er; -est : not soft or gentle : having a very serious quality or manner ▪ flinty determination ▪ a flinty-eyed man

¹**flip** /'flɪp/ vb flipped; flip·ping 1 [T] : to turn (something) over by throwing it up in the air with a quick movement ▪ flip a coin 2 [T/I] : to cause (something) to turn or turn over quickly ▪ flip (through) the pages of a magazine ▪ flip a pancake ▪ (informal) He got a job flipping burgers. [=working as a cook in a fast-food restaurant] ▪ His car flipped over on the interstate. 3 [T] a : to move (something) with a quick, light movement : FLICK ▪ flip a switch b : to turn (something) on or off with a switch ▪ flip on/off the radio/TV 4 [T] : to throw (something) with a quick movement ▪ Flip the ball to me. 5 [I] informal : to become very excited or angry ▪ You'll flip (out) when you hear this! 6 [T/I] : to change or move through (channels, stations, etc.) quickly ▪ He flipped the channel back to the golf tournament. — flip open [phrasal vb] flip open or flip open (something) or flip (something) open : to open or to cause (something) to open with a quick movement ▪ Her notebook flipped open. ▪ She flipped open her notebook. — flip your lid also chiefly US flip your wig informal : to become crazy or very angry

²**flip** n [C] 1 : the act of flipping something : a quick turn, toss, or movement ▪ the flip of a coin/switch 2 : an athletic movement in which someone jumps in the air and rolls forward or backward ▪ a back flip

³**flip** adj, informal : not serious : FLIPPANT ▪ a flip answer/attitude

flip–flop /'flɪp,flɑːp/ n [C] 1 : a type of loose rubber sandal 2 chiefly US, informal : a sudden change of opinion ▪ a politician accused of doing flip-flops on important issues — flip–flop vb -flopped; -flop·ping [I] chiefly US, informal ▪ a politician accused of flip-flopping on important issues

flip·pant /'flɪpənt/ adj : lacking proper respect or seriousness ▪ a flippant response to a serious question — flip·pan·cy /'flɪpənsi/ n [U] — flip·pant·ly adv

flip·per /'flɪpɚ/ n [C] 1 : one of two flat body parts that stick out from the side of a seal, whale, etc., and are used for swimming 2 : a flat rubber shoe that has a very wide front and is used for swimming

flip side n [C] 1 : the side of a record that has a song which is not as popular and well known as the one on the other side 2 : the bad or unpleasant part or result of something ▪ Loss of privacy is the flip side of fame. — the flip side of the coin see ¹COIN

¹**flirt** /'flɚt/ vb [I] 1 : to behave in a way that shows a sexual attraction for someone but is not meant to be taken seriously ▪ He flirts with the women in his office. 2 : to think about something or become involved in something in a way that is usually not very serious ▪ She's been flirting with the idea of going back to school. 3 : to come close to reaching or experiencing something ▪ The temperature flirted with 100 yesterday. ▪ They were flirting with death/disaster. — flir·ta·tion /flɚ-'teɪʃən/ n [C] ▪ They had a brief flirtation.

²**flirt** n [C] : a person who enjoys flirting with other people ▪ He admits that he's a terrible flirt. [=that he flirts a lot]

flir·ta·tious /flɚ'teɪʃəs/ adj : feeling or showing a sexual attraction for someone that is usually not meant to be taken seriously ▪ a flirtatious person/smile — flir·ta·tious·ly adv

flit /'flɪt/ vb flit·ted; flit·ting [I] : to move or fly quickly from one place or thing to another ▪ butterflies flitting around the garden ▪ writers who flit from topic to topic

¹**float** /'floʊt/ vb 1 [T/I] a : to rest or cause (something) to rest on top of a liquid ▪ She was floating on her back. ▪ Will this material sink or float? ▪ The tide floated the ship off the reef. b : to rest or cause (something) to be carried along by moving water or air ▪ The raft floated downstream. ▪ They floated the logs down the river. 2 [I] : to move or go in a gentle, graceful, or quiet way ▪ She floated gracefully across the stage. 3 [I] : to live without having any serious purpose or goal ▪ He floated through life without ever settling down. 4 [T] : to suggest (an idea, plan, etc.) for acceptance ▪ Someone floated this idea for a new book. 5 [T] US : to make arrangements for (a loan) ▪ Could you float me a loan? [=could you lend money to me?] 6 [T] finance : to sell (shares in a company) in the market ▪ The company will be floating a new issue of securities next month. 7 [T/I] of a government : to allow the value of a currency when it is exchanged to change freely ▪ float a currency

²**float** n [C] 1 : something that floats: such as a : a light object that is attached to a fishing line b : a floating platform near a shore for use by swimmers or boats c : a structure that holds up an airplane on water 2 : a vehicle with a platform used to carry an exhibit in a parade 3 US : a soft drink with ice cream floating in it ▪ a root beer float 4 Brit : an amount of money that is kept available for making change in a shop

¹**flock** /'flɑːk/ n [C] 1 : a group of birds or animals ▪ a flock of birds/sheep 2 : a large number of people ▪ a flock of tourists 3 : the members of a church ▪ a priest caring for his flock

²**flock** vb [I] : to gather or move in a crowd ▪ Thousands of people flock to the beach each weekend.

floe /'floʊ/ n [C] : a sheet or mass of floating ice ▪ an ice floe

flog /'flɑːg/ vb flogged; flog·ging [T] : to beat or whip (someone) severely ▪ The sailors were flogged for attempting a mutiny. — flog a dead horse see ¹HORSE — flogging n [C/U] ▪ They gave him a good flogging. [=they beat/whipped him severely]

¹**flood** /'flʌd/ n 1 [C] : a large amount of

water covering an area of land that is usually dry ▪ *the devastating flood of 1936* **2** [*singular*] : a large amount of things that come or happen at the same time ▪ *a flood of mail/criticism/memories* — **in flood** ◆ A river that is *in flood* has so much water in it that it may flow over its banks and flood the land next to it. ▪ *(figurative) The revolt was in full flood.* [=was in a fully active state throughout the area]

²**flood** *vb* **1 a** [*T/I*] : to cover (land) with a flood ▪ *Heavy rains flooded the valley.* ▪ *The rivers are flooding.* **b** [*I*] : to become filled or covered by a flood ▪ *The valley flooded after the heavy rains.* **2** [*T*] **a** : to fill (something) completely ▪ *Light flooded the room.* **b** : to cause (something) to receive or take in a large amount of things at the same time ▪ *The company flooded the market with its new product.* ▪ *The office has been flooded with phone calls.* **3** [*I*] : to go or come in large numbers or as a large amount ▪ *The phone calls have been flooding in.* ▪ *Memories came flooding into my mind.* **4** [*T/I*] : to cause too much fuel to go into (an engine) ▪ *The car wouldn't start because the engine was flooded.*

flood·gate /ˈflʌdˌgeɪt/ *n* [*C*] : a gate for controlling the flow of water from a lake, river, etc. ▪ *(figurative) The court's ruling opened the floodgates for/to many more lawsuits.* [=caused a large number of new lawsuits]

flood·light /ˈflʌdˌlaɪt/ *n* [*C*] : a light that shines brightly over a wide area ▪ *The yard was lit by floodlights.* — **flood·lit** /ˈflʌdˌlɪt/ *adj* ▪ *a floodlit stadium*

flood·plain /ˈflʌdˌpleɪn/ *n* [*C*] : an area of low, flat land along a stream or river that may flood

flood tide *n* [*C*] **1** : a rising tide **2** : a very large amount of something ▪ *a flood tide of criticism*

flood·wa·ter /ˈflʌdˌwɑːtɚ/ *n* [*C*] : the water of a flood ▪ *The floodwaters have started to recede.*

¹**floor** /ˈfloɚ/ *n* **1** [*C*] : the part of a room on which you stand **2** [*C*] **a** : the lower inside surface of something (such as a vehicle) ▪ *the floor of a car* **b** : the area of ground at the bottom of something ▪ *the ocean/forest floor* **3** [*C*] : a level in a building ▪ *She lives on the second floor of a five-story building.* **4** [*C*] : a large indoor space where people gather for some activity ▪ *the factory/dance floor* **5 the floor** : the people who are gathered in a place for a public meeting ▪ *He will now take questions from the floor.* **6** [*C*] : a lower limit ▪ *a floor for wages and prices* ▪ *The stock's value has dropped/gone/fallen through the floor.* [=to a very low level] — **have the floor** : to have the right to speak at a public meeting — **hold the floor** : to be the person who is speaking at a public meeting — **take the floor** **1** : to begin speaking at a public meeting **2** : to go out onto a dance floor to begin dancing — **wipe the floor with** see ¹**WIPE**

²**floor** *vb* [*T*] **1** : to cover (a surface) with material to make a floor ▪ *The lobby is*

floored with marble. **2 a** : to knock (someone) to the floor or ground ▪ *He floored me with his first punch.* **b** *informal* : to surprise, shock or amaze (someone) very much ▪ *I was floored by the news.* **3** *US, informal* : to press (the accelerator of a vehicle) to the floor ▪ *When the light turned green, he floored it.* [=he pressed the accelerator all the way down and sped away]

floor·board /ˈfloɚˌboɚd/ *n* [*C*] **1** : a board in a floor **2** *US* : the floor of a vehicle

floor·ing /ˈflorɪŋ/ *n* [*U*] : material used for floors ▪ *marble/tile/hardwood flooring*

floor plan *n* [*C*] : a plan that shows the position of the rooms in a building

floo·zy *or* **floo·zie** /ˈfluːzi/ *n, pl* **-zies** [*C*] *informal + old-fashioned* : a usually young woman whose behavior is not morally correct or proper

flop /ˈflɑːp/ *vb* **flopped; flop·ping** [*I*] **1** : to fall, lie, or sit down in a sudden, awkward, or relaxed way ▪ *He flopped down onto the bed.* **2** *informal* : to fail completely ▪ *The play flopped.* **3** : to swing or move in a loose, awkward, or uncontrolled way ▪ *The curtains were flopping around in the breeze.* — **flop** *n* [*C*] ▪ *The movie was a flop.* [=failure]

¹**flop·py** /ˈflɑːpi/ *adj* **flop·pi·er; -est** : soft and flexible ▪ *a floppy hat*

²**floppy** *n, pl* **-pies** [*C*] : FLOPPY DISK

floppy disk *n* [*C*] : a small, thin, square case with a flexible disk inside on which data for a computer can be stored

flo·ra /ˈflorə/ *n* [*C/U*] *biology* : all the plants that live in a particular area, time, period, or environment ▪ *aquatic flora* — compare FAUNA

flo·ral /ˈflorəl/ *adj* : of or relating to flowers ▪ *a floral display/design*

flor·id /ˈflorəd/ *adj* **1** : very fancy or too fancy ▪ *florid writing* **2** : having a red or reddish color ▪ *a florid complexion*

flo·rist /ˈflorɪst/ *n* [*C*] : a person whose job or business is to sell flowers and plants

¹**floss** /ˈflɑːs/ *n* [*U*] : DENTAL FLOSS

²**floss** *vb* [*T/I*] : to use dental floss to clean your teeth

flo·ta·tion /floʊˈteɪʃən/ *n* [*U*] : the act, process, or state of floating or of causing or allowing something to float ▪ *fills the tanks with air for flotation* ▪ *the flotation of a currency*

flo·til·la /floʊˈtɪlə/ *n* [*C*] : a group of small ships

flot·sam /ˈflɑːtsəm/ *n* [*U*] : floating pieces, parts, etc., from a ship that has been wrecked ▪ *(figurative) bits of flotsam gathered from yard sales* ▪ *(figurative) He spends a lot of time sorting through the flotsam and jetsam that come(s) across his desk each day.*

flounce /ˈflaʊns/ *vb* **flounced; flounc·ing** [*I*] **1** : to move with exaggerated motions ▪ *She flounced around on the stage.* **2** *chiefly Brit* : to walk or move quickly in a way that shows anger or annoyance ▪ *He flounced out of the room.*

¹**floun·der** /ˈflaʊndɚ/ *n, pl* **flounder** *or* **floun·ders** [*C/U*] : a type of fish that has a flat body and is eaten as food

²**flounder** vb [I] **1** : to move in an awkward way with a lot of difficulty and effort ▪ *floundering through the deep snow* **2 a** : to be unsure about what to do or say ▪ *After watching me flounder for a few minutes, my instructor took over.* **b** : to have a lot of problems and difficulties ▪ *The team has been floundering lately.*

flour /ˈflawɚ/ n [C/U] : powder made from a grain (especially wheat) that is used in making bread, cakes, etc. — **flour** vb [T] ▪ *The fish was lightly floured* [=covered with flour] *and then fried.* — **floury** /ˈflawɚri/ adj ▪ *floury hands*

¹**flour·ish** /ˈflərɪʃ/ vb **1** [I] : to grow well ▪ *plants and animals that flourish on the island* **2** [I] : to be very successful : to do very well ▪ *The business is flourishing.* ▪ *a style that flourished in the 1920s* **3** [T] : to hold up and show (something) in an excited or proud way ▪ *He flourished his sword.*

²**flourish** n [C] **1** : something that is added as a detail or decoration ▪ *a simple writing style without unnecessary flourishes* **2 a** : a dramatic or fancy way of doing something ▪ *Dinner was served with a flourish.* **b** : a sudden smooth movement that is likely to be noticed ▪ *With a flourish of her pen, she signed the contract.*

flout /ˈflaʊt/ vb [T] : to break or ignore (a law, rule, etc.) without showing fear or shame ▪ *Despite repeated warnings, they continued to flout the law.*

¹**flow** /ˈfloʊ/ vb [I] **1** : to move in a steady, continuous way ▪ *rivers flowing into the sea* ▪ *a gently flowing stream* ▪ *electricity flowing through a circuit* ▪ *Traffic has been flowing smoothly/steadily.* ▪ *Money has continued to flow in.* ▪ (figurative) *Excitement was flowing through the crowd.* **2** : to hang down in a loose, graceful way ▪ *Her gown flowed around her.* ▪ *her flowing hair* **3** : to come from something ▪ *the wealth that flows from trade* **4** of a tide : to move in toward the land : RISE ▪ *The tide ebbs and flows twice every 24 hours.*

²**flow** n **1** [U, singular] : an act of flowing ▪ *a sudden flow of tears* : the movement of something that is flowing ▪ *a steady/smooth flow of traffic* ▪ *the free flow of ideas* **2** [C] : an area of mud, lava, etc., that is flowing or that was formed by flowing ▪ *an ancient lava flow* **3** [U] : the amount of something that flows in a certain time ▪ *measuring blood flow to the brain* — see also CASH FLOW — **ebb and flow** see ¹EBB — **go against the flow** : to do things that do not agree with what most other people are doing — **go with the flow** : to relax and accept what is happening ▪ *When I'm on vacation, I just like to take it easy and go with the flow.* — **in full flow** chiefly Brit **1** — used to describe someone who is talking continuously and enthusiastically ▪ *He can talk for hours when he's in full flow.* **2** — used to describe the time when something is most active, successful, etc. ▪ *The party was already in full flow.*

flow chart n [C] : a chart that shows each step of a process using special symbols that are connected by lines

¹**flow·er** /ˈflawɚ/ n **1 a** [C/U] : the part of a plant that is often brightly colored, that usually lasts a short time, and from which the seed or fruit develops ▪ *a tree with large white flowers* ▪ *a bouquet of flowers* ▪ *The tree came into flower early.* [=the flowers on the tree bloomed early] ▪ *a bush that is in flower* [=that has blooming flowers] **b** [C] : a small plant that is grown for its beautiful flowers ▪ *We planted flowers in the garden.* **2** [singular] literary : the best part of something ▪ *in the flower of his youth*

²**flower** vb [I] **1** : to produce flowers ▪ *The tree flowers in early spring.* ▪ *flowering plants* **2** : to develop or grow in a successful way ▪ *His genius flowered at the university.*

flow·ered /ˈflawɚd/ adj : decorated with flowers or with pictures of flowers ▪ *flowered wallpaper*

flower girl n [C] US : a young girl who carries flowers at a wedding

flow·er·pot /ˈflawɚˌpɑːt/ n [C] : a container (such as a clay or plastic pot) in which plants are grown

flow·ery /ˈflawɚri/ adj **1 a** : filled with flowers ▪ *flowery fields* **b** : decorated with pictures of flowers ▪ *a flowery dress* **c** : smelling like a flower ▪ *flowery perfume* **2** of language : very fancy or too fancy or elaborate ▪ *flowery prose*

flown past participle of ¹FLY

fl. oz. abbr fluid ounce(s)

flu /ˈfluː/ n [U] : a common disease that is caused by a virus : INFLUENZA ▪ *She has the flu.* = (Brit) *She has flu.*

flub /ˈflʌb/ vb **flubbed; flub·bing** [T] US, informal : to fail to do (something) correctly ▪ *The actress flubbed several lines.* — **flub** n [C] ▪ *a verbal flub* [=blunder]

fluc·tu·ate /ˈflʌktʃəˌweɪt/ vb **-at·ed; -at·ing** [I] : to change level, strength, or value frequently ▪ *fluctuating prices* — **fluc·tu·a·tion** /ˌflʌktʃəˈweɪʃən/ n [C/U]

flue /ˈfluː/ n [C] : a channel or pipe in a chimney for carrying flame and smoke to the outer air

flu·ent /ˈfluːwənt/ adj **1** : able to speak a language easily and well ▪ *a fluent speaker* ▪ *He is fluent in Chinese.* **2** : done in a smooth and easy way ▪ *a fluent performance* — **flu·en·cy** /ˈfluːwənsi/ n [U] ▪ *Students must demonstrate fluency in a foreign language.* ▪ *He plays the piano with speed and fluency.* — **flu·ent·ly** adv

¹**fluff** /ˈflʌf/ n [U] **1** : light and soft material ▪ *fluff from a pillow* **2** chiefly US, informal : something that has little importance or interest ▪ *The movie was pure fluff.* — **fluffy** /ˈflʌfi/ adj **fluff·i·er; -est** ▪ *a fluffy cloud/cushion*

²**fluff** vb [T] **1** : to shake or move (a pillow, feathers, etc.) so that it is fuller, lighter, or softer ▪ *The bird fluffed (up) its feathers.* **2** informal : to do (something) badly : FLUB ▪ *The golfer fluffed the shot.*

¹**flu·id** /ˈfluːwəd/ adj **1** : capable of flowing freely like water ▪ *fluid lava* **2** : changing easily or often ▪ *a fluid situation* **3** : having or showing a smooth, easy style ▪ *a dancer's fluid movements* — **flu·id·i·ty** /fluˈɪdəti/ n [U] — **flu·id·ly** adv

²**fluid** n [C/U] : a substance that is able to flow freely : a liquid substance ▪ *She needs to drink plenty of fluids.*

fluid ounce n [C] **1** *US* : a unit of liquid measurement equal to ¹⁄₁₆ of a U.S. pint or about 29.6 milliliters **2** *Brit* : a unit of liquid measurement equal to ¹⁄₂₀ of a British pint or about 28.4 milliliters

fluke /ˈfluːk/ n [C] *informal* : something that happens because of luck ▪ *Her second championship shows that the first one was no mere fluke.*

flung past tense and past participle of ¹FLING

flunk /ˈflʌŋk/ vb, US, informal **1** [T/I] : to get a failing grade in (something) ▪ *flunk a test/class* **2** [T] : to give a failing grade to (someone) ▪ *The teacher flunked two students.* — **flunk out** [phrasal vb] US, informal : to be required to leave a school because you have failed your courses ▪ *He flunked out (of college).*

flun·ky or **flun·key** /ˈflʌŋki/ n, pl **-kies** or **-keys** [C] informal + disapproving : a person who does small jobs for someone powerful or important

flu·o·res·cent /fluˈrɛsn̩t/ adj **1** : producing light when electricity flows through a tube that is filled with a type of gas ▪ *a fluorescent light/lamp* **2** : very bright ▪ *fluorescent colors/paint* — **flu·o·res·cence** /fluˈrɛsn̩s/ n [U]

flu·o·ri·date /ˈflurəˌdeɪt/ vb **-dat·ed; -dat·ing** [T] : to add fluoride to (water or toothpaste) ▪ *The drinking water here is fluoridated.* — **flu·o·ri·da·tion** /ˌflurəˈdeɪʃən/ n [U]

flu·o·ride /ˈfloʊˌaɪd/ n [U] : a chemical that is sometimes added to drinking water and toothpaste to help keep teeth healthy

flur·ry /ˈfləri/ n, pl **-ries** [C] **1** : a brief, light snowfall **2** : a brief period of excitement or activity ▪ *a flurry of trading/requests*

¹**flush** /ˈflʌʃ/ n [C] **1** : redness on a person's face because of emotion, heat, etc. — see also HOT FLUSH **2** : the act of cleaning a toilet with a flow of water ▪ *the flush of a toilet* **3** : a sudden feeling or strong emotion ▪ *a flush of pride* **4** : a set of cards that a player has in a card game (such as poker) that are all of the same suit — see also ROYAL FLUSH — **in the (first) flush of** : in the early and exciting time of (something) ▪ *Everyone felt hopeful in the first flush of victory.*

²**flush** vb **1** [T/I] : to cause a strong flow of water to clean (a toilet) ▪ *flush the toilet* ▪ *The toilet flushes automatically.* ✧ If you **flush something down the toilet**, you get rid of it by putting it in the toilet bowl and flushing it down. **2** [T] : to clean or remove (something) with a flow of water or some other liquid ▪ *Flush the wound with water.* ▪ *He flushed out the car's radiator.* ▪ *He used a hose to flush the leaves from the gutters.* **3** [I] : to become red in the face because of heat, emotion, etc. ▪ *She flushed with anger.* **4** [T] : to cause or force (someone or something) to leave a hiding place ▪ *The police flushed (out) the suspects from the building.*

³**flush** adj, not before a noun **1** : even or level with another surface ▪ *The paneling and the wall should be flush (with each other).* **2** informal : having a large amount of money ▪ *She is flush with money.*

⁴**flush** adv **1** : in order to be level or even with another surface ▪ *He arranged the books flush with the edge of the shelf.* **2** : in a way that makes very solid contact ▪ *He landed a punch flush on my chin.*

flushed /ˈflʌʃt/ adj : red because of heat or emotion ▪ *a flushed face* ▪ *He was flushed with pride/success.*

flus·ter /ˈflʌstɚ/ vb [T/I] : to make (someone) nervous and confused ▪ *The interruption flustered the speaker.* ▪ *He was too flustered to speak.*

flute /ˈfluːt/ n [C] : a musical instrument that is shaped like a thin pipe and played by blowing across a hole near one end

flut·ed /ˈfluːtəd/ adj : decorated with long, rounded lines that are cut into the surface ▪ *fluted columns*

flut·ist /ˈfluːtɪst/ n [C] US : a flute player

¹**flut·ter** /ˈflʌtɚ/ vb **1** [T/I] : to move or flap the wings quickly ▪ *The bird was fluttering its wings.* ▪ *Butterflies fluttering in the garden.* **2** [T/I] : to move with quick, light movements ▪ *The breeze made the curtains flutter.* ▪ *She fluttered her eyelashes.* **3** [I] : to move or behave in a nervous and excited way ▪ *She nervously fluttered around the office.* ✧ If your **heart/stomach flutters**, you become very nervous or excited.

²**flutter** n **1** [C] : a quick, light movement ▪ *With a flutter of wings, the birds settled into the nest.* **2** [singular] : a state of excitement or confusion ▪ *He was in a flutter until he found his keys.*

flux /ˈflʌks/ n [U] **1** : a series of changes : continuous change ▪ *a state of constant flux* **2** technical : a substance used for helping to melt or join metals

¹**fly** /ˈflaɪ/ vb **flies**; **flew** /ˈfluː/; **flown** /ˈfloʊn/; **fly·ing** [I/T] **1** [I/T] : to move through the air with wings ▪ *insects/birds flying over the water* **2** [I] : to move through the air especially at a high speed ▪ *Clouds flew across the sky.* ▪ *Bullets were flying in all directions.* ▪ *He tripped and went flying (through the air).* ▪ *(figurative)* *Rumors are flying everywhere.* **3** [T/I] : to control (an airplane, helicopter, etc., as it moves through the air ▪ *learning to fly (a plane)* **4 a** [T/I] : to travel in an aircraft or spacecraft ▪ *They flew to California.* ▪ *He always flies (on) the same airline.* **b** [T] : to carry (someone or something) to a place in an aircraft ▪ *Supplies/Volunteers were flown to the disaster area.* **5 a** [T/I] : to show (something, such as a flag) by putting it in a high place ▪ *fly your country's flag* ▪ *Banners fly in front of the building.* **b** [T] : to cause (something, such as a kite) to fly in the air ▪ *Children were flying kites in the park.* **6** [I] : to move, go, or pass quickly ▪ *The door flew open.* ▪ *Cars were flying past us.* ▪ *Time flies.* ▪ *Our vacation flew by.* ▪ *He flew into a rage.* **7** [I] *chiefly US, informal* : to be approved or accepted ▪ *This plan will never fly.* — **as the crow flies** see ¹CROW — **fly at**

[phrasal vb] : to attack (someone) with sudden violence ▪ *He flew at me in a rage.* — **fly high** *informal* **1** : to be very happy and excited ▪ *She was flying high after her excellent exam results.* **2** : to be very successful ▪ *The company is flying high again.* — **fly in the face of** *also US* **fly in the teeth of** : to oppose or contradict (something) directly ▪ *a theory that flies in the face of logic* — **fly off the handle** *informal* : to become very angry ▪ *He suddenly flew off the handle and started yelling.* — **fly the coop** *informal* : to leave suddenly or secretly : to escape or go away ▪ *The suspect had flown the coop.* — **let fly (with)** *informal* : to throw (something) in a forceful way ▪ *The quarterback let fly a long pass.* ▪ *(figurative) She let fly with a few angry words.* — compare ²FLY

²**fly** *vb* **flies; flied; fly·ing** *[I]* *baseball* : to hit a fly ball ▪ *The batter flied (out) to left field.* — compare ¹FLY

³**fly** *n, pl* **flies** *[C]* **1** : a small insect that has two wings **2** : a hook that looks like an insect and is used for catching fish ▪ *an artificial fly* **3** : an opening in a piece of clothing that is closed by a zipper or a row of buttons ▪ *He zipped/buttoned his fly.* **4** *baseball* : FLY BALL — **drop like flies** *also* **die like flies** *informal* ◇ If people or animals are **dropping/dying like flies**, they are dropping or dying very quickly in large numbers. ▪ *(figurative) Candidates were dropping like flies during the campaign.* — **fly in the ointment** : someone or something that causes problems ▪ *We're almost ready to start work. Getting the permit is the only fly in the ointment.* — **on the fly 1** : quickly and often without preparation ▪ *making decisions on the fly* **2** : through the air ▪ *The home run went 450 feet on the fly.* **3** : while something else is also being done on a computer ▪ *software that handles formatting on the fly* — **wouldn't hurt a fly** ◇ Someone who *wouldn't hurt a fly* is too gentle to want to hurt anyone.

fly ball *n* *[C]* *baseball* : a baseball that is hit high into the air ▪ *He hit a long fly ball to left field.*

fly-by-night /ˈflaɪbaɪˌnaɪt/ *adj, always before a noun, informal* : trying to make money quickly by using dishonest or illegal methods ▪ *a fly-by-night insurance company*

flyer *variant spelling of* FLIER

fly-fish·ing /ˈflaɪˌfɪʃɪŋ/ *n* *[U]* : the activity of catching fish by using artificial flies

¹**fly·ing** /ˈflaɪɪŋ/ *adj* : moving or able to move in the air ▪ *flying insects* — **with flying colors** : with complete or great success ▪ *She passed the exam with flying colors.*

²**flying** *n* *[U]* : the activity of traveling in an aircraft

flying saucer *n* *[C]* : a flying object that people say they have seen in the sky, that is usually round like a saucer or disc, and that is believed by some people to be a spaceship from another world

flying start *n* *[singular]* : a good or fast start ▪ *The meeting got off to a flying start.*

fly·leaf /ˈflaɪˌliːf/ *n, pl* **-leaves** /-ˌliːvz/ *[C]* : an empty page at the beginning or end of a book

fly·pa·per /ˈflaɪˌpeɪpə/ *n* *[U]* : a long piece of sticky paper that is used for catching and killing flies

fly-swat·ter /ˈflaɪˌswɑːtə/ *n* *[C]* : a device used for killing flies and other insects that consists of a flat piece of material attached to a handle

fly·wheel /ˈflaɪˌwiːl/ *n* *[C]* : a heavy wheel that is part of a machine and that controls the speed of machinery

FM /ˈɛfˌɛm/ *n* *[U]* : a system for sending radio signals ▪ *a show broadcast on FM* ▪ *FM radios/stations* ◇ **FM** is an abbreviation of "frequency modulation."

foal /ˈfoʊl/ *n* *[C]* : a young horse; *especially* : a horse that is less than one year old

¹**foam** /ˈfoʊm/ *n* *[U]* **1** : a mass of small bubbles that are formed in or on a liquid ▪ *the foam in a glass of beer* **2** : a substance that is like a thick liquid made of many small bubbles ▪ *shaving foam* **3** : FOAM RUBBER — **foamy** /ˈfoʊmi/ *adj* **foam·i·er; -est** ▪ *a foamy glass of beer*

²**foam** *vb* *[I]* : to produce foam ▪ *The soda foamed in the glass.* — **foam at the mouth 1** : to produce foam from the mouth because of illness or excitement ▪ *The dog was foaming at the mouth.* **2** *informal* : to be very angry about something ▪ *He was foaming at the mouth with rage.*

foam rubber *n* *[U]* : a soft, light rubber material that has many small holes throughout it ▪ *The pad is (made of) foam rubber.* ▪ *a foam-rubber pad*

¹**fob** /ˈfɑːb/ *n* *[C]* **1** : a short chain attached especially to a pocket watch **2** : a small object that is a decoration on a watch chain or a key ring

²**fob** *vb* **fobbed; fob·bing** — **fob off** **[phrasal vb]** **fob (someone or something) off** *or* **fob off (someone or something)** *informal* **1** : to cause (someone) to accept something that is false, badly made, etc. ▪ *He tried to fob me off with some excuse about being too busy.* **2** : to present or offer (something fake or false) *as* genuine or true ▪ *fob off science fiction as truth* **3** *US* : to give (someone or something not wanted) to someone else ▪ *fobbing the child off on relatives and babysitters*

fo·cal /ˈfoʊkəl/ *adj, always before a noun* : having central or great importance ▪ *a focal character*

focal point *n* *[C]* **1** : a center of activity, interest, or attention ▪ *The new law was the focal point of the debate.* **2** *technical* : ¹FOCUS 3

¹**fo·cus** /ˈfoʊkəs/ *n, pl* **fo·ci** /ˈfoʊˌsaɪ/ *also* **fo·cus·es** **1** *[C]* : a subject that is being discussed or studied ▪ *the focus of the discussion* **2** *[U, singular]* : a main purpose or interest ▪ *His life lacks (a) focus.* **3** *[C]* *technical* : a point at which rays of light, heat, or sound meet or separate; *especially* : the point at which an image is formed by a mirror, lens, etc. ▪ *[U]* **a** : a state in which a camera, telescope, etc., produces a clear picture or image ▪ *bringing the binoculars into focus* ▪ *the binoculars were not in focus.* = *The binoc-*

*ulars were **out of focus**.* **b** : a state in which the small details of a picture or image can be clearly seen ▪ *The picture is not in focus. = The picture is out of focus.* **c** : a state or condition in which something can be clearly understood ▪ *She brought the important issues into focus.*

²**focus** *vb* -**cus·es** *also* -**cus·ses**; -**cused** *also* -**cussed**; -**cus·ing** *also* -**cus·sing** [*T/I*] **1** : to direct your attention, effort, or eyes at something specific ▪ *We need to focus (our attention) on the major issues.* ▪ *His eyes were focused on the road.* **2** : to adjust (a lens, camera, etc.) to make an image clear ▪ *He focused his binoculars on a distant ship.* **3** *technical* : to cause (light) to come together at a point ▪ *focus rays of light*

focused *also* **focussed** *adj* **1** : giving attention and effort to a specific task or goal ▪ *a focused effort to reach our goal* **2** : having very clear and definite goals and ambitions ▪ *a very focused woman*

fod·der /ˈfɑːdɚ/ *n* [*U*] **1** : food given to horses, cows, etc. **2** : material that is used for a particular purpose ▪ *good fodder for stories* — see also CANNON FODDER

foe /ˈfoʊ/ *n* [*C*] : an enemy ▪ *political foes*

foetal, foetus *chiefly Brit spellings of* FETAL, FETUS

¹**fog** /ˈfɑːg/ *n* **1** [*C/U*] : many small drops of water floating in the air above the ground, sea, etc. ▪ *Heavy fog made it difficult to see the road.* **2** [*singular*] : a state of mental confusion ▪ *This problem has me in a fog.*

²**fog** *vb* **fogged; fog·ging** **1** [*T/I*] : to make (something) foggy or to become foggy ▪ *The steam fogged (up) the window.* ▪ *His glasses were fogging (up).* **2** [*T*] : to make (someone or something) confused ▪ *drugs that fog your mind/judgment*

fogey *chiefly Brit spelling of* FOGY

fog·gy /ˈfɑːgi/ *adj* **fog·gi·er**; -**est** **1** : covered or filled with fog ▪ *a foggy morning/valley/mirror* **2** : not clear : vague or confused ▪ *My memory of that day is a little foggy.* ▪ *"Where did I put my keys?" "I haven't the foggiest (idea)."* [=I don't know]

fog·horn /ˈfɑːgˌhoɚn/ *n* [*C*] : a loud horn on a boat, ship, etc., that is used in foggy weather to warn nearby ships

fo·gy (*chiefly US*) *or chiefly Brit* **fo·gey** /ˈfoʊgi/ *n, pl* **fo·gies** [*C*] : a person with old-fashioned ideas ▪ *He's just an old fogy.*

foi·ble /ˈfoɪbəl/ *n* [*C*] : a minor fault in someone's character or behavior ▪ *We all have our little foibles.*

¹**foil** /ˈfojəl/ *vb* [*T*] **1** : to prevent (someone) from doing something or achieving a goal ▪ *Police managed to foil the burglars.* **2** : to prevent (something) from happening or being successful ▪ *Police foiled an attempted robbery.*

²**foil** *n* **1** [*U*] : a very thin, light sheet of metal ▪ *Cover the dish with aluminum foil.* **2** [*C*] : someone or something that is different from another person or thing in a useful or appealing way ▪ *His reserved manner was a perfect foil to her bubbly*

personality. **3** [*C*] : a sword that has a light, thin blade and is used in the sport of fencing

foist /ˈfoɪst/ *vb* [*T*] : to force someone to accept (something that is not good or not wanted) ▪ *He foisted his prejudices on/upon his young students.*

¹**fold** /ˈfoʊld/ *vb* **1** [*T/I*] : to bend one part of (something) over or against another part ▪ *He folded the paper in half.* ▪ *The map folds up neatly.* **2** [*T/I*] : to reduce the length or size of something by moving parts of it so that they lie close together ▪ *fold (up) a lawn chair* ▪ *The bed folds (away) into a space in the wall.* **3** [*T*] **a** : to put your arm or hand over your other arm or hand in a way that keeps them together ▪ *He folded his arms around her. = He folded her in his arms.* ▪ *hands folded in prayer* **b** : to bend (a leg, a knee, an elbow, etc.) ▪ *He sat with his legs folded under him.* **4** [*T*] : to add (a food ingredient) to a mixture by gently and repeatedly lifting one part over another ▪ *Fold the egg whites into the chocolate mixture.* **5** [*I*] : to fail completely ▪ *The business folded.* **6** [*I*] : to accept defeat in a card game (such as poker) by removing your cards from the game

²**fold** *n* **1** [*C*] **a** : a line or mark made by folding something ▪ *the folds of a map* **b** : a part of something that lies or hangs over another part ▪ *the folds of the curtain* ▪ *folds of fat* **c** : the act of folding something ▪ *She made a paper airplane by using a simple series of folds.* **2** [*C*] : an enclosed area for sheep **b the fold** : a group of people who have a shared faith or interest ▪ *His former colleagues welcomed him back into the fold.*

-**fold** /ˌfoʊld/ *suffix* **1** : multiplied by (a specified number) : times ▪ *a twelvefold increase* **2** : having (so many) parts ▪ *a threefold problem*

fold·er /ˈfoʊldɚ/ *n* [*C*] **1** : a folded cover or large envelope for holding documents **2** : a collection of files or documents that are stored together on a computer

fold·out /ˈfoʊldˌaʊt/ *n* [*C*] : a large folded page in a book or magazine ▪ *The book includes foldout maps.*

fo·liage /ˈfoʊlijɪʤ/ *n* [*U*] : the leaves of a plant or of many plants ▪ *autumn/green foliage*

¹**folk** /ˈfoʊk/ *n, informal* **1 folks** [*plural*] *chiefly US* : people ▪ *Folks say that house is haunted.* ▪ *Do you folks need any help?* **2** *or chiefly US* **folks** [*plural*] : a certain kind of people ▪ *city folk* [=people who live in a city] ▪ *old folks* **3 folks** [*plural*] *chiefly US* : family members; *especially* : PARENTS ▪ *His folks gave him everything a kid could want.* **4** [*U*] : FOLK MUSIC ▪ *My favorite type of music is folk.*

²**folk** *adj, always before a noun* : of or relating to the common people of a country or region ▪ *folk customs/art* ▪ *a folk hero* [=someone who is greatly admired by many people]

folk·lore /ˈfoʊkˌloɚ/ *n* [*U*] : traditional customs, beliefs, stories, and sayings ▪ *Native American folklore*

folk music *n* [*U*] : the traditional music of the people in a country or region ▪

Irish folk music; also : a type of popular music that is based on traditional music and that does not use electric instruments

folk·sing·er /ˈfoʊkˌsɪŋər/ *n [C]* : a person who sings folk songs

folk song *n [C]* : a song created by the people of a country or region : a song sung in folk music

folk·sy /ˈfoʊksi/ *adj* **folks·i·er; -est** *informal* : friendly or informal • *folksy politicians/charm* — **folks·i·ness** /ˈfoʊksinəs/ *n [U]*

fol·li·cle /ˈfɑːlɪkəl/ *n [C]* : a tiny hole in the skin from which a hair grows

fol·low /ˈfɑːloʊ/ *vb* **1 a** *[T/I]* : to go or come after or behind (someone or something) • *The dog followed the children around.* • *If one sheep goes through the gate, the rest will follow.* • *Winter is followed by spring.* • *The number 15 follows 14.* • *First came the speeches, and the presentation of awards followed.* **b** *[T]* : to go after or behind (someone) secretly and watch to find out what happens • *I think that someone is following us.* = *I think we're being followed.* **2** *[T]* : to have or do something after (something else) • *We followed our dinner with dessert.* **3 a** *[T/I]* : to happen after and as a result of (something) • *Rioting followed the unjust verdict.* • *If you work hard, success will follow.* **b** *[I]* : to be true or seem to be true because of something • *Several conclusions follow from the evidence given.* • *From the evidence given, it follows that the accused is guilty.* **4** *[T]* **a** : to be guided by (something) • *follow my advice/instructions* • *You should follow her example.* [=do what she did] **b** : to do the same thing as (someone) • *She followed her father (by going) into medicine.* **5** *[T]* : to move forward on or along (a road, path, etc.) • *Follow that path, and you will come to a log cabin.* • *The path follows the river.* • *(figurative) Her friends went to college, but she followed a different path.* **6** *[T]* **a** : to keep your eyes or attention on (something) • *Follow the bouncing ball.* **b** : to give close attention to (something) • *He followed her career with interest.* **7** *[T/I]* : to understand (something or someone) • *I found it hard to follow the movie's plot.* — **as follows** — used to introduce a list, a statement, instructions, etc. • *The names of the finalists are as follows: Mary, James, and George.* • *Proceed as follows: go straight ahead to Martin Street and then turn left.* — **follow in someone's footsteps** see FOOTSTEP — **follow suit 1** *in card games* : to play a card of the same suit (such as hearts) as the card that was played just before **2** : to do the same thing that someone else has just done • *His brother went to medical school, and he followed suit.* — **follow through** [*phrasal vb*] **1 follow through** *or* **follow (something) through** : to complete an activity or process that has been started • *We feared they would follow through on/with their threat.* [=that they would do what they threatened to do] **2** *sports* : to keep your arms, legs, etc., moving after you hit or kick a ball • *fol-

low through on your backhand* — **follow up** [*phrasal vb*] **follow up (something)** *or* **follow (something) up** *or* **follow up 1** : to follow (something) with something similar, related, or additional • *She followed up the novel with another best seller.* **2 a** : to try to get more information about (something) • *The police followed up (on) the leads.* **b** : to take appropriate action about (something) • *Police followed up (on) the complaints with several arrests.* — **follow your nose** *informal* : to do what seems right or best without careful planning • *You don't need my advice—just follow your nose.*

fol·low·er /ˈfɑːloʊwər/ *n [C]* **1 a** : someone who supports and is guided by another person or by a group, religion, etc. • *loyal/faithful followers of Islam* **b** : a person who likes and admires (someone or something) very much : FAN • *followers of the band* **2** : someone who does what other people say to do • *He's a follower, not a leader.*

¹fol·low·ing /ˈfɑːloʊwɪŋ/ *adj* **1** : coming next • *We met again the following day.* **2** : listed or shown next • *Trains will leave at the following times: 2 p.m., 4 p.m., and 8 p.m.*

²following *n [C]* : a group of followers or fans • *The band has a large following in Japan.* — **the following** : the following one or ones • *The following are the finalists: Mary, James, and George.*

³following *prep* : immediately after (something) • *Following the lecture, refreshments were served.*

fol·low–through /ˈfɑːloʊˌθruː/ *n* **1** *[C]* *sports* : the part of a stroke, swing, or kick that happens after a ball is hit **2** *[singular]* : the act of completing an action or process • *He makes a lot of promises, but there's no follow-through.* [=he does not do what he promises to do]

fol·low–up /ˈfɑːloʊˌʌp/ *n [C]* : something that continues or completes a process or activity • *a follow-up to the study done five years ago* — **follow–up** *adj, always before a noun* • *a follow-up appointment a week after his surgery*

fol·ly /ˈfɑːli/ *n, pl* **-lies 1** *[U]* : the lack of good sense or judgment : FOOLISHNESS • *his folly in thinking that he would not be noticed* **2** *[C/U]* : a foolish act or idea • *youthful follies*

fo·ment /ˈfoʊˌment/ *vb [T]* *formal* : to cause or try to cause (something bad or harmful) : INCITE • *foment rebellion*

fond /ˈfɑːnd/ *adj* **1** : feeling or showing love or friendship • *a fond admirer* • *fond memories* • *He wished them a fond farewell.* **2** : strongly felt • *their fondest wishes* — **fond of** : having a liking for or love of (someone or something) • *She is fond of him.* — **fond·ly** /ˈfɑːndli/ *adv* • *She speaks fondly of you.* • *I fondly remember those days.* — **fond·ness** /ˈfɑːndnəs/ *n [U, singular]*

fon·dle /ˈfɑːndl̩/ *vb* **fon·dled; fon·dling** *[T]* **1** : to touch or handle (something) in a gentle way • *She fondled the dog's ear.* **2** : to touch (someone) in a sexual way • *She claims that her boss tried to fondle her.*

fon·due /fɑn'du:, Brit 'fɒnˌdju:/ n [C/U] : a dish that people prepare for themselves at the table by putting small pieces of bread, meat, etc., into a hot liquid (such as melted cheese)

font /'fɑ:nt/ n [C] **1** : a set of letters, numbers, and punctuation marks that are all one size and style • printed in a boldface/small font **2** : a container that holds the water which is used for baptizing a child **3** US : a source from which something comes : FOUNT • a font of knowledge

food /'fu:d/ n **1** [C/U] : the things that people and animals eat • buy/grow food • healthy/frozen foods **2** [U] : substances taken in by plants and used for growth • plant food — **food for thought** : something that should be thought about or considered carefully • The unexpected test results have given us food for thought.

food chain n [C] : a series of types of living things in which each one uses the next lower member of the series as a source of food • Sharks eat fish that are lower in the food chain. • (figurative) directors at the top of the Hollywood food chain [=very powerful and successful directors]

food court n [C] : an area within a building (such as a shopping mall) where there are many small restaurants

food·ie /'fu:di/ n [C] informal : a person who enjoys and cares about food very much

food poisoning n [U] : sickness caused by bacteria or chemicals in food

food processor n [C] : an electric kitchen device that is used for cutting and mixing food

food stamp n [C] US : a small document that is given by the government to poor people and that can be used to buy food

food·stuff /'fu:dˌstʌf/ n [C] technical : a substance that is used as food • grain and other foodstuffs

¹fool /'fu:l/ n [C] **1** : a person who lacks good sense or judgment : a stupid or silly person • Only a fool would ask such a silly question. ✧ A smart or clever person can be described as **no fool** or as **nobody's fool**. • Don't try to trick me—I'm nobody's fool. **2** US, informal : a person who enjoys something very much • He's a dancing fool. [=he loves to dance] • She's a fool for candy. [=she loves to eat candy] **3** : JESTER — **act/play the fool** : to behave in a silly or foolish way — **make a fool of yourself** : to behave in a very foolish or silly way • He got drunk and made a fool of himself. — **make a fool (out) of** : to cause (someone) to look stupid or foolish • She made a fool of me by insulting me in front of my friends.

²fool vb **1** [I] : to speak or act in a way that is not serious • I was only fooling. [=kidding] **2** [T] : to trick or deceive (someone) • He fooled me into thinking I could trust him. • "He's an expert." "Well, you sure could have fooled me!" [=I doubt that he is really an expert] • He really had me fooled. • Stop fooling yourself—she doesn't really love you. — **fool around** also Brit **fool about** [phras-

al vb] informal **1** : to do things that are not useful or serious • It's time to stop fooling around and get to work. **2** : to have sex with someone who is not your husband, wife, or regular partner • His wife discovered that he was fooling around (on her). **3 fool around/about with** a : to use or do (something) in a way that is not very serious • I'm not really a painter; I just like to fool around with paints. b : to handle or play with (something) in a careless or foolish way • Stop fooling around with the stereo. — **fool with** [phrasal vb] informal **1** : to handle, deal with, or play with (something) in a foolish or careless way • Don't fool with that gun. **2** : to deal with (someone) in a way that may cause anger or violence • I wouldn't want to fool with that guy.

fool·har·dy /'fu:lˌhɑɚdi/ adj : foolishly doing things that are too dangerous or risky • foolhardy investors

fool·ish /'fu:lɪʃ/ adj : having or showing a lack of good sense or judgment • a foolish person/decision/mistake — **fool·ish·ly** adv — **fool·ish·ness** n [U]

fool·proof /'fu:lˌpruːf/ adj : done, made, or planned so well that nothing can go wrong • a foolproof plan

¹foot /'fʊt/ n, pl **feet** /'fiːt/ **1** [C/U] : the part of the leg on which an animal or person stands and moves • He was wearing boots on his feet. • The dog was lying near/at his feet. — see also ATHLETE'S FOOT, COLD FEET **2** pl also **foot** [C] : a unit of measurement equal to ⅓ yard (0.3048 meter) or 12 inches • a 10-foot pole = a pole 10 feet long • He's six feet, three inches tall. = He's six foot three. **3** [singular] a : the lowest part of something : BOTTOM • at the foot of the stairs/mountain b : the end of something that is opposite to the end that is called the head • the foot of the bed [=the end where your feet are when you are lying on the bed] **4** [C] : a group of syllables forming a basic unit of rhythm in a line of poetry • Each line of the poem has five feet. — **drag your feet** see ¹DRAG — **get/start off on the right/wrong foot** : to begin a relationship well/badly • I want to get off on the right foot with your parents. — **get your feet wet** see ¹WET — **get your foot in the door** : to make the first step toward a goal by gaining entry into an organization, a career, etc. • He took a job as a secretary to get his foot in the door. — **have one foot in the grave** : to be close to dying because of old age or illness — **have/keep your feet on the ground** : to be a sensible and practical person — **off your feet** : in or into a sitting or lying position • The doctor suggested that he stay off his feet. [=avoid standing and walking] — **on foot** : by walking • We traveled on foot. — **on your feet** **1** : in a standing position • I've been on my feet all day. • He landed on his feet. **2** : in a healthy or good condition • She'll be out of the hospital and (back) on her feet again soon. • The business is finally/back on its feet. **3** : quickly and while actively doing something • Good debaters can think on their feet. — **put a foot *wrong* : to make a mistake • *He never put a foot wrong during the campaign.* — **put your best foot forward 1** *US* : to behave very well so that someone will like you and approve of you **2** *Brit* : to try as hard as possible to do something difficult — **put your feet up** *informal* : to sit and relax • *I'm going to go home and put my feet up.* — **put your foot down 1** : to deal with someone in a harsh or strict way **2** *Brit* : to make a car go faster — **put your foot in your mouth** (*chiefly US*) **or put your foot in it** *informal* : to say something that causes someone to be embarrassed, upset, or hurt especially when you did not expect that reaction — **set foot in** : to enter (a place) • *That was the last time she ever set foot in this house.* — **stand on your own two feet** : to support yourself without help from other people — **sweep (someone) off his/her feet** see ¹SWEEP — **the shoe is on the other foot or** *Brit* **the boot is on the other foot** — used to say that a situation has changed to the opposite of what it was before • *I used to boss her around. Now the shoe is on the other foot.* [=now she bosses me around] — **to your feet** : to a standing position • *His speech brought the crowd to its feet.* — **two left feet** ◇ A person who dances badly can be described as having *two left feet.* — **under your feet** *chiefly Brit* : in the way : UNDERFOOT • *I can't get any work done with those kids under my feet.* — **wait on (someone) hand and foot** see ¹HAND

²**foot** *vb* — **foot the bill** : to pay for something • *His parents footed the bill for his college education.*

foot·age /ˈfʊtɪʤ/ *n* [*U*] **1** : scenes or action recorded on film or video • *disturbing footage of the war* **2** : the size of something measured in feet • *calculating the square footage of the room*

foot–and–mouth disease *n* [*U*] : a serious and often deadly disease of animals (such as cows and sheep)

foot·ball /ˈfʊtˌbɑːl/ *n* **1** [*U*] : any one of several games in which two teams try to get a ball to the goals at each end of a large field: such as **a** *US* : an American game that is played between two teams of 11 players each and in which the ball is moved forward by running or passing **b** : a similar Canadian game between two teams of 12 players each **c** *Brit* : SOCCER **2** [*C*] : a ball filled with air that is used in the game of football

foot·ball·er /ˈfʊtˌbɑːlɚ/ *n* [*C*] *chiefly Brit* : a person who plays soccer

foot·bridge /ˈfʊtˌbrɪʤ/ *n* [*C*] : a bridge for people who are walking

foot·ed /ˈfʊtəd/ *adj* : having a foot or feet of a specified kind or number • *a four-footed animal* • *flat-footed*

foot·er /ˈfʊtɚ/ *n* [*C*] **1** : someone or something that is a specified number of feet tall or long • *The putt was a six-footer.* **2** : a word, phrase, etc., that is placed at the bottom of every page of a document — compare HEADER

foot·hill /ˈfʊtˌhɪl/ *n* [*C*] : a hill next to a

higher mountain or group of mountains • *the foothills of the Rockies*

foot·hold /ˈfʊtˌhoʊld/ *n* [*C*] **1** : a place where your foot may be placed when you are climbing a cliff, a mountain, etc. **2** : a position that makes it possible to begin an activity or effort • *The company has gained a foothold in the market.*

foot·ing /ˈfʊtɪŋ/ *n* **1** [*singular*] **a** : the ability of your feet to stay where you put them as you walk, run, etc. • *He lost his footing and fell.* **b** : the condition of the ground that makes it easy or hard for your feet to stay where you put them as you walk or run • *The footing here is slippery.* **2** [*singular*] — used to describe the kind of relationship that exists between people, countries, etc. • *a nation that is on a friendly footing with its neighbors* • *They all started on an equal footing (with one another).* **3** [*C*] : the base or foundation on which something is established or built • *The business is on a firm financial footing.* • *the steel footings of the bridge*

foot·lights /ˈfʊtˌlaɪts/ *n* [*plural*] : a row of lights across the front of a stage floor that shine on the performers

foot·lock·er /ˈfʊtˌlɑːkɚ/ *n* [*C*] *US* : a strong box that is kept at the foot of a soldier's bed and used for storing personal property

foot·loose /ˈfʊtˌluːs/ *adj* : able to act or move freely • *footloose bachelors*

foot·man /ˈfʊtmən/ *n, pl* **-men** /-mən/ [*C*] : a male servant who lets visitors into a house and serves food at the dinner table

foot·note /ˈfʊtˌnoʊt/ *n* [*C*] **1** : a note with added information that is placed below the text on a printed page **2** : someone or something that is remembered or regarded as minor or unimportant • *a movement now regarded as a footnote in history*

foot·path /ˈfʊtˌpæθ, *Brit* ˈfʊtˌpɑːθ/ *n* [*C*] : a narrow path that people walk on

foot·print /ˈfʊtˌprɪnt/ *n* [*C*] **1** : a track or mark left by a foot or shoe **2** : the amount of space that is covered on a surface by something • *The computer has a small footprint.*

foot·race /ˈfʊtˌreɪs/ *n* [*C*] : a running race

foot·rest /ˈfʊtˌrest/ *n* [*C*] : something that you put your feet on to raise them off the ground when you are sitting

foot·step /ˈfʊtˌstɛp/ *n* [*C*] **1** : a movement made by your foot as you walk or run • *She took one footstep toward him.* **2** : the sound of a foot making a step • *We could hear the approaching footsteps.* — **follow in someone's footsteps** : to do the same things that another person has done before • *She followed in her father's footsteps by becoming a doctor.*

foot·stool /ˈfʊtˌstuːl/ *n* [*C*] : a low, small piece of furniture that you can put your feet on when you are sitting

foot·wear /ˈfʊtˌweɚ/ *n* [*U*] : things (such as shoes and boots) that are worn on your feet

foot·work /ˈfʊtˌwɚk/ *n* [*U*] **1** : the activity of moving or walking from place to place • *The job requires a lot of footwork.*

2 : movement of the feet in a sport, dance, etc. ▪ *He used quick/fancy footwork to dodge his opponent.*

¹for /ˈfoɚ, fə/ *prep* **1 a** — used to indicate the place someone or something is going to or toward ▪ *heading for home* **b** — used to indicate the person or thing that something is sent or given to ▪ *This present is for you.* **2 a** — used to indicate the thing that something is meant to be used with ▪ *This food is for the party.* **b** — used to indicate the person who should use or have something ▪ *suits for tall men* **3 a** — used to indicate the use of something ▪ *an instrument for measuring speed* **b** — used to indicate why something is done ▪ *studying for examinations* ▪ *This is for your own good.* [=to help you] ▪ *For more information, call our main office.* ▪ *He shouted for joy.* **4** — used to indicate the person that a statement refers to ▪ *Seeing her again must be difficult for him.* ▪ *It's time for us to leave.* ▪ *It is not for you to say* [=it is not appropriate for you to say] *that she can't go.* **5** : in favor of (someone or something) ▪ *Which candidate are you for?* ▪ *You're either for or against me.* ▪ *I am all for* [=completely in favor of] *freedom of speech.* **6** — used to indicate the person or thing toward which feelings, thoughts, etc., are directed ▪ *I feel sorry for him.* **7** — used to indicate time or space ▪ *You can see for miles from here.* ▪ *We're staying there for the summer.* ▪ *The wedding is planned for next April.* ▪ *That's all for now/today.* **8 a** : instead of (someone or something else) ▪ *Johnson is batting for Smith.* **b** : as a representative of (someone) ▪ *His lawyer will act for him.* **c** : in order to help or serve (someone or something) ▪ *What else can I do for you?* ▪ *They fought and died for their country.* **9** : in order to cure or treat (an illness, injury, disease, etc.) ▪ *You should take something for that cough.* **10** — used to indicate an amount or value ▪ *a check for $100* **11** : as an employee, member, player, etc., of (something) ▪ *She works for the government.* **12** *chiefly US* : with the name of (someone) ▪ *He was named for* [=after] *his grandfather.* **13** — used to indicate the parts of a list or series ▪ *For one thing, we have no money; for another, we have no time.* **14** — used to refer to something that is surprising or unexpected when compared to something else ▪ *He's tall for his age.* **15** — used to indicate the relationship between numbers or amounts that are being compared ▪ *For every good writer there are a dozen bad ones.* **16** — used in various emphatic phrases ▪ *I for one will vote for him.* ▪ *For the last time, will you stop that noise!* ▪ *I wish you'd be sensible for once.* — **for all 1** : in spite of (something) ▪ *You don't convince me for all your clever arguments.* **2** — used in phrases like *for all someone knows* and *for all someone cares* to say that someone does not know, care, etc., about something ▪ *For all I know, she's still there.* [=she may still be there, but I don't know] — **in for** *informal* : certain to experience (something) ▪ *She's in for a* big surprise. — **in for it or** Brit **for it** *informal* : certain to be punished ▪ *If his parents find out what he's done, he'll be in for it.* — **once and for all** see ¹ONCE — **that's/there's . . . for you** *informal* — used to say that something is very good, very disappointing, or very common ▪ *They didn't even thank me! There's gratitude for you!* [=they were very ungrateful not to thank me]

²for *conj, formal + literary* : BECAUSE ▪ *They were certainly there, for I saw them.*

fora *plural of* FORUM

for·age /ˈforɪdʒ/ *vb* **-aged; -ag·ing** [*I*] **1** *of an animal* : to eat growing grass or other plants ▪ *The cows were foraging in the pasture.* **2** : to search for something (such as food or supplies) ▪ *He had to forage for firewood.* — **for·ag·er** *n* [*C*]

for·ay /ˈforeɪ/ *n* [*C*] **1** : a sudden invasion or attack ▪ *a foray into enemy territory* **2** : an attempt to do something ▪ *her first foray into politics* **3** : a short journey ▪ *a quick foray into town for supplies*

¹for·bear /foɚˈbeɚ/ *vb* **-bore** /-ˈboɚ/; **-borne** /-ˈboɚn/; **-bear·ing** [*T/I*] *formal* : to choose not to do (something that you could do) ▪ *He forbore any mention of her name.* = *He forebore to mention her name.*

²forbear *variant spelling of* FOREBEAR

for·bear·ance /foɚˈberəns/ *n* [*U*] *formal* : the quality of someone who is very patient with a difficult person or situation ▪ *He showed great forbearance in his dealings with them.*

for·bid /fɚˈbɪd/ *vb* **-bade** /-ˈbæd, -ˈbeɪd/ *or* **-bad** /-ˈbæd/; **-bid·den** /-ˈbɪdn/; **-bid·ding** [*T*] **1** : to order (someone) not to do something ▪ *I forbid you to go!* ▪ *She was forbidden from marrying him.* **2** *formal* : to say that (something) is not allowed ▪ *The museum forbids flash photography.* ▪ *Smoking is forbidden.* [=not allowed/permitted] — **God/heaven forbid** — used in speech to say that you hope a bad thing will not happen ▪ *Heaven forbid that something bad should happen.*

forbidding *adj* : having a frightening or threatening appearance ▪ *a forbidding landscape/scowl* — **for·bid·ding·ly** *adv*

¹force /ˈfoɚs/ *n* **1** [*U*] : physical strength, power, or effect ▪ *the force of the collision/wind* **2** [*U*] : power or violence used on a person or thing ▪ *He used brute force to open the door.* ▪ *He took the purse from her by force.* **3** [*U*] : strength or power that is not physical ▪ *These regulations do not have the force of law.* ▪ *She succeeded by/through sheer force of will.* [=because she was determined to succeed] **4** [*C/U*] *technical* : a natural power or effect that is able to change the speed or direction of something ▪ *the force of gravity* **5** [*C*] : something (such as rain or wind) that occurs in nature and that can be very powerful ▪ *a cliff eroded by the forces of nature* **6** [*C*] : a group of people who do a particular job or are available for a particular purpose ▪ *a force of 20,000 soldiers* ▪ *enemy forces* ▪ *our country's labor/work force* ▪ *the company's sales force* — see also AIR FORCE,

ARMED FORCES, POLICE FORCE, TASK FORCE **7** [C] : a person or group that has the power to do something or make something happen • *The organization has been a strong force for good.* [=has done a lot of good things] • *the driving/motivating force behind the changes* • *a force to be reckoned with* [=a person who has a lot of power and influence] — *in force* **1** : in large numbers • *Picnickers were out in force today.* [=there were many picnickers out today] **2** *of a law, rule, etc.* : actually working or operating • *The ban remains in force.* [=in effect] — *into force* : into the condition of actually working or operating • *The law came/went into force* [=into effect] *last year.* — *join forces* also *combine forces* : to begin working together in order to achieve something • *The company has joined forces with local environmental groups.* — see also TOUR DE FORCE

²**force** *vb* forced; forc·ing [T] **1** : to make (someone) do something • *They forced us to work long hours.* • *After seeing the evidence, I was forced to admit my error.* • *The pilot was forced to land when the plane's engine caught fire.* • *I forced myself to get up and go to work.* **2** : to make (something) necessary • *The scandal forced his resignation.* **3** : to move (someone or something) by physical effort • *Their car was forced off the road.* • *A pump forces air into the chamber.* • *They forced (open) the door.* • *The door/lock had been forced.* • *If the key doesn't fit the lock, don't force it.* **4** : to produce (something, such as a smile) by making an effort • *She forced a smile.* — *force on/upon* [*phrasal vb*] *force (someone or something) on/upon* : to cause (someone or something that is not wanted) to be accepted by (someone) • *They resent having these decisions forced on them.* — *force someone's hand* : to make it necessary for someone to do something • *She wanted to wait, but events forced her hand.* — *force the issue* see ¹ISSUE — *force your way* : to move ahead by pushing and making people move out of your way • *They forced their way into the room.*

forced /ˈfoɚst/ *adj* **1** : caused by force or necessity • *The plane made a forced landing.* • *a forced confession* **2** : done with effort • *forced laughter*

force·ful /ˈfoɚsfəl/ *adj* **1** : strong and confident • *a forceful personality/leader* **2** : expressed in a way that is effective and that influences people • *a forceful argument* **3** : done with military or physical force • *a forceful kick* — **force·ful·ly** *adv* — **force·ful·ness** *n* [U]

for·ceps /ˈfoɚˌsɛps/ *n, pl* **forceps** [C] : a medical tool that is used for grasping or holding things

forc·i·ble /ˈfoɚsəbəl/ *adj* : made or done by physical force or violence • *the forcible removal of the rioters* — **forc·i·bly** /ˈfoɚsəbli/ *adv*

¹**ford** /ˈfoɚd/ *vb* [T] : to cross (an area of water) by walking or riding across a shallow part • *ford the river*

²**ford** *n* [C] : a shallow part of a river, stream, etc., that may be crossed by walking or driving

¹**fore** /ˈfoɚ/ *n* — *to the fore* : in or into a place of importance • *The issue has come to the fore.*

²**fore** *adv* : toward or at the front part of a boat, ship, or airplane • *The plane's exits are located fore and aft.* — **fore** *adj*

fore·arm /ˈfoɚˌɑɚm/ *n* [C] : the part of the arm between the elbow and the wrist

fore·bear also **for·bear** /ˈfoɚˌbeɚ/ *n* [C] *formal* : ANCESTOR

fore·bod·ing /foɚˈboudɪŋ/ *n* [C/U] : a feeling that something bad is going to happen • *She was filled with a sense of foreboding.*

¹**fore·cast** /ˈfoɚˌkæst, *Brit* ˈfɔːˌkɑːst/ *vb* **-cast** also **-cast·ed**; **-cast·ing** [T] : to say that (something) will happen in the future • *They're forecasting rain for this weekend.* — **fore·cast·er** *n* [C]

²**forecast** *n* [C] : a statement about what you think is going to happen in the future • *weather/economic forecasts*

fore·close /foɚˈkloʊz/ *vb* **-closed; -clos·ing** [T/I] : to take back property because the money owed for it has not been paid • *The bank foreclosed (on) their mortgage/property.* — **fore·clo·sure** /foɚˈkloʊʒɚ/ *n* [C/U]

fore·fa·ther /ˈfoɚˌfɑːðɚ/ *n* [C] : a person (especially a man) who was in your family in past times : ANCESTOR

fore·fin·ger /ˈfoɚˌfɪŋɡɚ/ *n* [C] : the finger that is next to the thumb — called also *index finger*

fore·front /ˈfoɚˌfrʌnt/ *n* [C] : the most important part or position • *Their company is at/in the forefront of research in this area.* • *The issue has been brought to the forefront.*

forego variant spelling of FORGO

fore·go·ing /foɚˈɡoʊɪŋ/ *adj, formal* : listed, mentioned, or occurring before • *the foregoing examples/discussion*

fore·gone /ˈfoɚˌɡɑːn/ *adj* — *a foregone conclusion* : something in the future that is certain to happen or be true • *It was a foregone conclusion that he would take over the business after his father retired.*

fore·ground /ˈfoɚˌɡraʊnd/ *n* **1** [C] : the part of a scene or picture that is nearest to and in front of the viewer **2** [*singular*] : an important position • *The issue is in the foreground.*

fore·hand /ˈfoɚˌhænd/ *n* [C] *sports* : a way of hitting a ball in tennis and similar games in which the palm of the hand is turned in the direction of the ball • *She hit a forehand across the court.* • *a forehand stroke/shot*

fore·head /ˈfoɚˌhɛd, ˈfɑrəd/ *n* [C] : the part of the face above the eyes

for·eign /ˈforən/ *adj* **1** : located outside a particular place or country and especially outside your own country • *foreign countries* • *a foreign correspondent* [=a journalist who reports from a foreign country] **2** : coming from or belonging to a different place or country • *foreign visitors/languages* **3** : relating to or dealing with other nations • *foreign policy/af-*

fairs/trade　**4** : not normally found in the place or part where it is located ▪ *Dust and other foreign bodies can irritate the eyes.*　**5** : not known or familiar ▪ *That concept is completely foreign to me.* —
for·eign·ness /ˈforənnəs/ *n* [U]

for·eign·er /ˈforənə/ *n* [C] : a person who is from a country that is not your own

foreign exchange *n* [U] *finance* **1** : the process by which people in different countries pay each other by exchanging different types of money　**2** : money from foreign countries

fore·know·ledge /ˌfoəˈnɑːlɪʤ/ *n* [U] *formal* : knowledge of something before it happens or exists ▪ *He denied any fore-knowledge of the crime.*

fore·leg /ˈfoəˌlɛg/ *n* [C] : a front leg of an animal

fore·lock /ˈfoəˌlɑːk/ *n* [C] : a piece of hair growing from the front of the head

fore·man /ˈfoəmən/ *n* [C] **1** : the member of a jury who is the leader　**2** : a person who is in charge of a group of workers

¹**fore·most** /ˈfoəˌmoʊst/ *adj* : most important ▪ *Safety is their foremost concern.*

²**foremost** *adv* **1** : in the first or most important position ▪ *The building's designers put safety foremost.*　**2** : at the most basic or important level ▪ *He is foremost [=primarily] an authority on the American Civil War.* — **first and foremost** see ²FIRST

fore·name /ˈfoəˌneɪm/ *n* [C] *chiefly Brit, formal* : FIRST NAME

fo·ren·sic /fəˈrɛnsɪk/ *adj, law* **1** : relating to the use of scientific knowledge or methods in solving crimes ▪ *forensic science/experts*　**2** *somewhat formal* : relating to, used in, or suitable to a court of law ▪ *a lawyer's forensic skills*

fo·ren·sics /fəˈrɛnsɪks/ *n* [U] **1** : the study or science of solving crimes by using scientific knowledge or methods　**2** : the results of a scientific test done to help solve a crime ▪ *The forensics showed he was at the scene of the crime.*

fore·play /ˈfoəˌpleɪ/ *n* [U] : sexual actions (such as kissing and touching) that people do with each other before they have sex

fore·run·ner /ˈfoəˌrʌnə/ *n* [C] : someone or something that comes before another ▪ *a simple machine that was the forerunner of today's computers*

fore·see /foəˈsiː/ *vb* **-saw** /-ˈsɑː/; **-seen** /-ˈsiːn/; **-see·ing** [T] *somewhat formal* : to see or become aware of (something that has not yet happened) ▪ *She foresaw the company's potential.* — **fore·see·able** /foəˈsiːjəbəl/ *adj* ▪ *We have no plans to sell our house in/for the foreseeable future.* [=soon]

fore·shad·ow /foəˈʃædoʊ/ *vb* [T] : to give a suggestion of (something that has not yet happened) ▪ *His death is foreshadowed in the novel's first chapter.*

fore·short·en /foəˈʃoətn/ *vb* [T] **1** : to cause (something) to appear shorter than it really is because it is in the foreground of a drawing, painting, etc.　**2** *somewhat*

formal : to make (something) shorter ▪ *His athletic career was foreshortened by injuries.*

fore·sight /ˈfoəˌsaɪt/ *n* [U] : the ability to see what will or might happen in the future ▪ *His choice shows a lack of foresight.* — **fore·sight·ed** /ˈfoəˌsaɪtəd/ *adj* ▪ *foresighted investors/investments*

fore·skin /ˈfoəˌskɪn/ *n* [C] : a fold of skin that covers the end of the penis

for·est /ˈforəst/ *n* [C/U] : a thick growth of trees and bushes that covers a large area — **not see the forest for the trees** see TREE — **for·est·ed** /ˈforəstəd/ *adj*

fore·stall /foəˈstɑːl/ *vb* [T] **1** : to stop (something) from happening or to cause (something) to happen at a later time ▪ *forestall the deal*　**2** : to act before (someone else) in order to prevent something ▪ *He forestalled critics by offering a defense of the project.*

for·est·er /ˈforəstə/ *n* [C] : a person whose job is to take care of forests

forest ranger *n* [C] *US* : RANGER 1

for·est·ry /ˈforəstri/ *n* [U] : the science and practice of caring for forests

fore·taste /ˈfoəˌteɪst/ *n* [C] *somewhat formal* : a small experience of something that will not be fully experienced until later ▪ *a foretaste of winter*

fore·tell /foəˈtɛl/ *vb* **-told** /-ˈtoʊld/; **-tell·ing** [T] *formal + literary* : to describe (something) before it happens : PREDICT ▪ *foretell the future*

fore·thought /ˈfoəˌθɑːt/ *n* [U] : careful thinking or planning about the future ▪ *Her decision showed a lack of forethought.*

for·ev·er /fəˈrɛvə/ *adv* **1 a** : for an endless time ▪ *He promised he'd love her forever.*　**b** : for a very long time ▪ *I waited forever for their decision.*　**2** : at all times : CONSTANTLY ▪ *a dog that was forever chasing cars* — **forever** [U] ▪ *It took forever* [=took an extremely long time] *to find his keys.*

fore·warn /foəˈwoən/ *vb* [T] : to warn (someone) before something happens ▪ *They had been forewarned of the danger.*

fore·wo·man /ˈfoəˌwʊmən/ *n* [C] : a woman who is the leader of a jury

fore·word /ˈfoəˌwəd/ *n* [C] : a section at the beginning of a book that introduces the book

¹**for·feit** /ˈfoəfət/ *vb* [T/I] : to lose or give up (something) as a punishment or because of a rule or law ▪ *He forfeited his right to a trial by jury.* ▪ *They had to forfeit (the game).* — **for·fei·ture** /ˈfoəfəʧə/ *n* [C/U] ▪ *forfeiture of assets*

²**forfeit** *n* [C/U] : something that is lost or given up as punishment or because of a rule or law ▪ *They were required to pay a forfeit.* ▪ *We won the game by forfeit.* [=we won because the other team forfeited the game]

forgave *past tense of* FORGIVE

¹**forge** /ˈfoəʤ/ *vb* **forged**; **forg·ing** **1** [T] : to form or create (an agreement, relationship, etc.) through great effort ▪ *The countries forged a strong alliance.*　**2** [T] : to make or copy (something) falsely in order to deceive someone ▪ *forge a check/ signature*　**3** [T] : to form something by

heating and shaping metal ▪ *forging hooks out of pieces of iron* **4** [*I*] **a** : to move forward slowly and steadily ▪ *The ship forged (ahead) through heavy seas.* **b** : to move with a sudden increase of speed and power ▪ *He forged into the lead.* ▪ *The company has forged ahead of its competitors.* — **forg·er** *n* [*C*] ▪ *a check forger*

²forge *n* [*C*] : a place where objects are made by heating and shaping metal

forg·ery /ˈfoɚdʒəri/ *n, pl* **-er·ies** **1** [*U*] : the crime of forging a document ▪ *check forgery* **2** [*C*] : something that is forged ▪ *These paintings are forgeries.* [=*fakes*]

for·get /fɚˈgɛt/ *vb* **-got** /-ˈgɑːt/; **-got·ten** /-ˈgɑːtn̩/ *or* **-got**; **-get·ting** **1** [*T/I*] : to be unable to think of or remember (something) ▪ *I keep forgetting her name.* ▪ *I forgot to pay the bill.* ▪ *I forgot (all) about paying the bill.* **2** [*T*] : to fail to remember to bring or take (something) ▪ *He forgot his wallet.* **3** *or* **forget about** [*T/I*] : to stop thinking or caring about (someone or something) ▪ *He was once a famous actor, but now most people have forgotten (about) him.* ▪ *We need to forget (about) our differences and learn to get along.* ▪ *If you're hoping he'll apologize, forget it, it's not going to happen.* ▪ *a forgotten hero* ▪ *We've argued in the past, but now it's time to forgive and forget.* — **forget yourself** : to lose control of your emotions because of anger, excitement, etc. ▪ *She forgot herself and said some things that she later regretted.*

for·get·ful /fɚˈgɛtfəl/ *adj* : forgetting things often or easily ▪ *He became forgetful in his old age.* ▪ *She has been forgetful of her duties.* — **for·get·ful·ly** *adv* — **for·get·ful·ness** *n* [*U*]

for·get-me-not /fɚˈgɛtminɑːt/ *n* [*C*] : a type of small plant that has bright blue flowers

for·get·ta·ble /fɚˈgɛtəbəl/ *adj* : likely to be forgotten : not worth remembering ▪ *a forgettable performance*

for·giv·able /fɚˈgɪvəbəl/ *adj* : able to be forgiven ▪ *a forgivable mistake*

for·give /fɚˈgɪv/ *vb* **-gave** /-ˈgeɪv/; **-giv·en** /-ˈgɪvən/; **-giv·ing** **1** [*T/I*] : to stop feeling anger toward (someone who has done something wrong) : to stop blaming (someone) ▪ *forgive your enemies* ▪ *I've never forgiven myself for the way I treated her.* **2** [*T*] : to stop feeling anger about (something) ▪ *forgive an insult* **3** [*T*] : to stop requiring payment of (money that is owed) ▪ *He forgave some of the debt.* — **forgive me** — used as a polite way of starting to say something that may seem rude or unpleasant ▪ *Forgive me (for saying so), but I don't think you understood my point.* — **for·give·ness** /fɚˈgɪvnəs/ *n* [*U*] — **for·giv·er** *n* [*C*]

forgiving *adj* **1** : able or willing to forgive someone or something ▪ *a person with a forgiving nature* ▪ *She was forgiving of their mistakes.* **2** — used to describe something that produces good results even when it is not used perfectly ▪ *a forgiving tennis racket* [=a racket designed to produce good shots even when the ball is not hit perfectly]

for·go *or* **fore·go** /foɚˈgou/ *vb* **-went** /-ˈwɛnt/; **-gone** /-ˈgɑːn/; **-go·ing** [*T*] : to give up the use or enjoyment of (something) ▪ *forgo an opportunity*

forgot *past tense of* FORGET

forgotten *past participle of* FORGET

¹fork /ˈfoɚk/ *n* [*C*] **1 a** : a small tool with two or more pointed parts used for picking up and eating food **b** : a garden tool with two or more pointed parts used for lifting and digging soil **2 a** : a place where a road, river, etc., divides into two parts ▪ *a fork in the road* **b** : either one of the parts that a road, river, etc., divides into ▪ *take the left fork* **3** : a part or tool that divides into two parts ▪ *the front fork of a bicycle* — see also TUNING FORK

²fork *vb* **1** [*I*] *of a road, river, etc.* : to divide into two parts ▪ *The road forks to the north and south.* **2** [*T*] *informal* : to pay or give (money) ▪ *He forked over/up the money.* ▪ *The company has already forked out thousands of dollars.* **3** [*T*] : to lift or throw (something) with a fork ▪ *They forked the hay into the loft.*

forked /ˈfoɚkt/ *adj* : divided into two parts at one end ▪ *a bird with a forked tail* — **speak/talk with (a) forked tongue** : to speak in a dishonest way that is meant to deceive people

fork·lift /ˈfoɚkˌlɪft/ *n* [*C*] : a machine that is used for lifting and moving heavy objects

for·lorn /fɚˈloɚn/ *adj* **1** : sad and lonely ▪ *a forlorn old widow* **2** : empty and in poor condition ▪ *a forlorn factory* **3** : not having much chance of success ▪ *a forlorn cause/hope* — **for·lorn·ly** *adv*

¹form /ˈfoɚm/ *n* **1** [*C*] **a** : a type or kind of something ▪ *a rare/deadly form of cancer* ▪ *forms of entertainment* **b** : one of several different ways in which something is seen, experienced, or produced ▪ *medicine in the form of liquids or pills* ▪ *The essays are available in book form.* **2 a** [*C/U*] : the shape of something ▪ *the building's massive form* **b** [*C*] : bodily shape ▪ *the human form* **3** [*C*] : a document with blank spaces for filling in information ▪ *application/tax forms* **4** [*U*] : a way of behaving that is judged as proper or improper ▪ *It's bad form* [=it is not proper] *to arrive so early.* **5** [*U*] **a** : a manner or style of performing ▪ *a swimmer with good form* **b** : condition for performing ▪ *an athlete in top form* **c** — used to describe how well or badly someone is performing ▪ *The comedians were in great form tonight.* **6** [*C*] : any one of the different ways in which a word may be written or spoken ▪ *the plural/possessive form of a noun* **7** [*U*] : a grade in a British secondary school ▪ *students in the sixth form* — **as a matter of form** — used to say that something is done because it is polite, usual, or required ▪ *He was invited only as a matter of form.* — **form of address** see ²ADDRESS — **in any way, shape, or form** see ¹WAY — **take form** : to begin to develop : to start to exist or be seen ▪ *a movement that took form in the 1960s* — **true to form** ◇ Something or someone that is (or runs, holds, etc.) **true to form** behaves or proceeds in the usual and expected way. ▪ *True to form, he was 20 minutes late for the meeting.* — **form·less** /ˈfoɚmləs/ *adj* ▪ *a formless* [=shapeless] *pile*

²**form** *vb* **1** [*T*] : to cause (something) to have a particular shape or form ▪ *Form the dough into balls.* **2** [*T*] : to get, create, or develop (something) over a period of time ▪ *form an idea/opinion/habit* **3 a** [*T/I*] : to begin to exist or to be seen ▪ *Beads of sweat formed on his forehead.* ▪ *A plan formed (itself) in my mind.* **b** [*I*] : to gather together in a group ▪ *An angry crowd began to form.* **4** [*T*] : to make or create (something) ▪ *Mix the flour and water to form a paste.* **5** [linking *vb*] : to be something ▪ *These products form* [=constitute] *the foundation of the company's success.* **6** [*T*] : to be arranged in (a shape) ▪ *The chairs formed a circle.* : to move or be moved into (a shape) ▪ *The dancers formed (themselves into) a line.*

¹**for·mal** /ˈfoɚməl/ *adj* **1** : requiring or using serious and proper clothes and manners ▪ *a formal dinner/event*; *also* : suitable for a formal occasion ▪ *a formal dress* **2** of language : suitable for serious or official speech and writing ▪ *formal Spanish* ▪ *a formal word* **3 a** : made or done in an official and usually public way ▪ *a formal announcement/statement* ▪ *formal recognition* **b** : done in a proper way according to the law ▪ *a formal contract/offer* **4** : arranged in a very orderly way ▪ *a formal garden* **5** : showing great concern for behaving in a proper and serious way ▪ *a formal manner* **6** : received in a school ▪ *a formal education* — **for·mal·ly** *adv*

²**formal** *n* [*C*] *US* : a formal social gathering (such as a dance)

form·al·de·hyde /foɚˈmældəˌhaɪd/ *n* [*U*] : a chemical that is used to prevent decay in dead bodies

for·mal·i·ty /foɚˈmæləti/ *n*, *pl* **-ties** **1** [*U*, *singular*] : a formal quality ▪ *the formality of the occasion* **2** [*C*] : something that is required or usual but that has little true meaning ▪ *The interview is just a formality.* **3** [*C*] : a formal part, activity, etc. — usually plural ▪ *Let's skip the formalities and get down to business.*

for·mal·ize *also Brit* **for·mal·ise** /ˈfoɚməˌlaɪz/ *vb* **-ized**; **-iz·ing** [*T*] : to give proper or official form to (something) ▪ *formalizing an agreement* — **for·mal·i·za·tion** *also Brit* **for·mal·i·sa·tion** /ˌfoɚmələˈzeɪʃən, *Brit* ˌfoɚməˌlaɪˈzeɪʃən/ *n* [*U*]

¹**for·mat** /ˈfoɚˌmæt/ *n* [*C/U*] **1** : the form, design, or arrangement of a magazine, TV program, etc. ▪ *the book's large-print format* ▪ *The radio station has a jazz format.* [=it plays jazz music] **2** : the way in which information is stored on a computer disk ▪ *The file is saved in (an) MP3 format.*

²**format** *vb* **-mat·ted**; **-mat·ting** [*T*] **1** : to arrange (something) in a particular format ▪ *The data was improperly formatted.* **2** : to prepare (a computer disk) so

that it can store information in a particular format ▪ *format a floppy disk*

for·ma·tion /foɚˈmeɪʃən/ *n* **1** [*U*] : the act of forming or creating something ▪ *the formation of new ideas* **2** [*C*] : something that is formed or created ▪ *cloud/rock/word formations* **3** [*C/U*] : an orderly arrangement or group of people, ships, or airplanes ▪ *jets flying in formation* ▪ *The team lined up in a punt formation.*

for·ma·tive /ˈfoɚmətɪv/ *adj* **1** — used to describe the time when someone or something is growing or being formed ▪ *The project is in its formative stages.* ▪ *his formative years* [=his childhood] **2** : helping to develop something ▪ *a formative influence*

for·mer /ˈfoɚmɚ/ *adj*, *always before a noun* **1** — used to say what someone or something was in the past ▪ *a former judge/friend* **2** : existing in the past ▪ *restoring an old hotel to its former glory* ▪ *my former self* — **the former** : the first of two things or people that were mentioned ▪ *Of these two options, the former is cheaper than the latter.*

for·mer·ly /ˈfoɚmɚli/ *adv* : in the past ▪ *She was formerly employed as a nanny.*

form-fit·ting /ˈfoɚmˌfɪtɪŋ/ *adj* : fitting tightly or closely ▪ *a form-fitting dress*

for·mi·da·ble /ˈfoɚmədəbəl, foɚˈmɪdəbəl/ *adj* **1** : very powerful or strong ▪ *a formidable opponent* **2** : very difficult to deal with ▪ *a formidable task* **3** : large or impressive in size or amount ▪ *a formidable amount of planning* — **for·mi·da·bly** /ˈfoɚmədəbli, foɚˈmɪdəbli/ *adv*

form letter *n* [*C*] : a letter that has a standard form and is sent to many people

for·mu·la /ˈfoɚmjələ/ *n*, *pl* **-las** *also* **-lae** /-ˌliː/ **1** [*C*] **a** : a plan or method for doing, making, or achieving something ▪ *a formula for success* **b** : a list of the ingredients used for making a medicine, drink, etc. ▪ *the company's secret cola formula* **2** [*C*] **a** *mathematics* : a general rule expressed in letters and symbols ▪ *The formula for the area of a rectangle is l X w.* [=length times width] **b** *chemistry* : a series of letters, numbers, and symbols showing the chemicals in a compound ▪ *The formula for water is H_2O.* **3** [*U*] *US* : a liquid that is used for feeding a baby ▪ *infant formula* **4** [*C*] : a common way of saying something or telling a story ▪ *Politicians use a familiar formula when discussing the issue.*

for·mu·la·ic /ˌfoɚmjəˈleɪjɪk/ *adj* **1** : produced according to a formula : not new or original ▪ *a formulaic movie/novel/plot* **2** : commonly used ▪ *a formulaic phrase such as "Sincerely yours"*

for·mu·late /ˈfoɚmjəˌleɪt/ *vb* **-lat·ed**; **-lat·ing** [*T*] : to create, invent, or produce (something) by careful thought and effort ▪ *formulate a plan/theory* ▪ *a specially formulated shampoo* — **for·mu·la·tion** /ˌfoɚmjəˈleɪʃən/ *n* [*C/U*]

for·ni·cate /ˈfoɚnəˌkeɪt/ *vb* **-cat·ed**; **-cat·ing** [*I*] *formal + disapproving* : to have sex with someone you are not married to — **for·ni·ca·tion** /ˌfoɚnə-ˈkeɪʃən/ n [U] — **for·ni·ca·tor** /ˈfoɚnəˌkeɪtɚ/ n [C]

for·sake /fɚˈseɪk/ vb **-sook** /-ˈsʊk/; **-saken** /-ˈseɪkən/; **-sak·ing** [T] : to give up or leave (someone or something) entirely ▪ *forsaking one's family*

for·swear /foɚˈsweɚ/ vb **-swore** /-ˈswoɚ/; **-sworn** /-ˈswoɚn/; **-swear·ing** [T] formal : to promise to give up (something) or to stop doing (something) ▪ *She forswore her allegiance to the old regime.*

for·syth·ia /fɚˈsɪθijə, Brit fəˈsaɪθiə/ n, pl **-ias** also **-ia** [C/U] : a type of bush that has yellow flowers in the spring

fort /ˈfoɚt/ n [C] : a strong building or group of buildings where soldiers live ▪ *The enemy captured the fort.* — **hold (down) the fort** : to be in charge of a place while someone else is away ▪ *Hold the fort while I'm gone.*

forte /ˈfoɚt, ˈfoɚˌteɪ/ n [C] : something that a person does well ▪ *Drawing is not her forte.*

forth /ˈfoɚθ/ adv, literary **1** : out into notice or view : OUT ▪ *Go forth and spread the news.* **2** : forward in time or place ▪ *She stretched forth her hands.* ▪ *from that day forth* [=from that time onward] — **and so forth** see [1]SO — **bring forth** see BRING — **call forth** see [1]CALL — **hold forth** see [1]HOLD — **put forth** see [1]PUT — **sally forth** see [2]SALLY — **set forth** see [1]SET — see also BACK AND FORTH

forth·com·ing /foɚθˈkʌmɪŋ/ adj **1** always before a noun : appearing, happening, or arriving soon ▪ *her forthcoming novel* **2** not before a noun : readily available ▪ *No help has been forthcoming from the state.* [=the state has not provided any help] **3** not before a noun : honest and open ▪ *He was forthcoming about his past.*

forth·right /ˈfoɚθˌraɪt/ adj : honest and direct ▪ *a forthright answer/person* — **forth·right·ly** adv — **forth·right·ness** n [U]

forth·with /foɚθˈwɪθ/ adv, formal : IMMEDIATELY ▪ *The company will cease operations forthwith.*

for·ti·fy /ˈfoɚtəˌfaɪ/ vb **-fies**; **-fied**; **-fy·ing** [T] **1** : to strengthen (a place) by building military defenses (such as walls, trenches, etc.) ▪ *a border/city fortified by high walls* **2** : to make (someone or something) stronger ▪ *fortify the body against illness* **3** : ENRICH **3** ▪ *fortify soil with fertilizer* ▪ *milk fortified with vitamin D* — **for·ti·fi·ca·tion** /ˌfoɚtəfəˈkeɪʃən/ n [C/U] ▪ *the fortification of the city* ▪ *The city was protected by massive fortifications.* [=protective walls, towers, etc.]

for·ti·tude /ˈfoɚtəˌtuːd, Brit ˈfɔːtəˌtjuːd/ n [U] formal : mental strength and courage ▪ *She endured her illness with fortitude and patience.*

fort·night /ˈfoɚtˌnaɪt/ n [C] chiefly Brit : two weeks ▪ *They stayed for a fortnight.* — **fort·night·ly** /ˈfoɚtˌnaɪtli/ adj ▪ *a fortnightly* [=biweekly] *magazine* — **fortnightly** adv

for·tress /ˈfoɚtrəs/ n [C] : a place that is protected against attack ▪ *a mountaintop fortress*

for·tu·i·tous /foɚˈtuːwətəs, Brit fɔː-ˈtjuːətəs/ adj, formal **1** : happening by chance ▪ *a fortuitous circumstance* **2** : fortunate or lucky ▪ *You arrived at a fortuitous time.* — **for·tu·i·tous·ly** adv ▪ *Fortunately, no one was hurt.*

for·tu·nate /ˈfoɚtʃənət/ adj **1** : having good luck : LUCKY ▪ *They were fortunate to have his help.* ▪ *people who are less fortunate than us* **2** : coming or happening because of good luck ▪ *a fortunate outcome*

for·tu·nate·ly /ˈfoɚtʃənətli/ adv — used to say that something good or lucky has happened ▪ *Fortunately, no one was hurt.*

for·tune /ˈfoɚtʃən/ n **1** [C] : a very large amount of money — usually singular ▪ *Their house is worth a fortune.* ▪ *She spent a small fortune* [=a surprisingly large amount of money] *on that dress.* ▪ *She made her/a fortune in real estate.* **2** [U] : something that happens by chance : LUCK ▪ *They had the good fortune to escape harm.* **3** [C] : the future that someone or something will have ▪ *She told me my fortune.* [=told me what would happen to me in the future]

fortune cookie n [C] : a thin cookie served in Chinese restaurants that contains a slip of paper on which a message (such as a prediction about your future) is printed

for·tune—tell·er /ˈfoɚtʃənˌtɛlɚ/ n [C] : a person who tells people their fortunes — **for·tune—tell·ing** /ˈfoɚtʃənˌtɛlɪŋ/ n [U]

for·ty /ˈfoɚti/ n, pl **-ties** [C] : the number 40 **2** [plural] **a** : the numbers ranging from 40 to 49 ▪ *The temperature is in the high forties.* **b** : a set of years ending in digits ranging from 40 to 49 ▪ *She is in her forties.* ▪ *songs from the (nineteen) forties* [=from 1940–1949] — **for·ti·eth** /ˈfoɚtijəθ/ n [U] — **fortieth** adj — **forty** adj ▪ *forty days* — **forty** pron — **for·ty·ish** /ˈfoɚtijɪʃ/ adj ▪ *He looks fortyish.* [=about 40 years old]

fo·rum /ˈfoɚəm/ n, pl **fo·rums** also **fo·ra** /ˈfoɚə/ [C] **1** : a meeting at which a subject can be discussed ▪ *The town held a public forum.* **2** : a place or opportunity for discussing a subject ▪ *an online forum*

[1]**for·ward** /ˈfoɚwəd/ also chiefly Brit **for·wards** /ˈfoɚwədz/ adv **1** : toward the front ▪ *She took a step forward.* **2** : toward the future ▪ *Set the clock forward one hour.* ▪ *from that time forward* **3** : to or toward a more advanced state or condition ▪ *The technology has taken a big step/leap forward.* ▪ *We're going forward* [=proceeding] *with the sale of the house.* — **bring forward** see BRING — **come forward** see COME — **know (something) backward and forward** see [1]KNOW — **look forward to** see [1]LOOK — **put forward** see [1]PUT — **put your best foot forward** see [1]FOOT

[2]**forward** adj **1** always before a noun **a** : moving or directed ahead or toward the front ▪ *a forward movement/somersault* **b** : moving toward the future or toward a more advanced state or condition ▪ *the forward movement of history/technology* **2** : too confident or direct in social situations ▪ *a forward man/question* — **for·ward·ness** n [U]

[3]**forward** vb [T] **1 a** : to send (something

you have received, such as a letter) to someone else ▪ *Forward the e-mail to me.* = *Forward me the e-mail.* **b** : to send (something) to a different place ▪ *Please forward my mail to my new address.* **2** : to help (something) continue to a more advanced state ▪ *He helped forward her career.*

⁴forward *n* [*C*] *sports* : a player who plays near the opponent's goal

forwarding address *n* [*C*] : an address that you give to someone so that any mail that comes to your old address can be sent to your new one

for·ward–look·ing /ˈfoɚwəd,lʊkɪŋ/ *adj, approving* : relating to the future ▪ *forward-looking ideas/products* : planning for the future ▪ *forward-looking politicians*

for·ward–think·ing /ˈfoɚwəd,θɪŋkɪŋ/ *adj* : FORWARD-LOOKING

fos·sil /ˈfɑːsəl/ *n* [*C*] **1** : an extremely old leaf, bone, footprint, etc., that you can see in some rocks ▪ *a dinosaur fossil* **2** *informal* : a person whose ideas are very out-of-date ▪ *He says the directors are a bunch of fossils.*

fossil fuel *n* [*C/U*] : a fuel (such as coal or oil) that is formed in the earth from dead plants or animals

fos·sil·ize *also Brit* **fos·sil·ise** /ˈfɑːsə,laɪz/ *vb* **-ized; -iz·ing** [*T/I*] : to become a fossil or to cause (something) to become a fossil ▪ *The wood fossilized in the mud.* ▪ *fossilized wood/bones* — **fos·sil·i·za·tion** *also Brit* **fos·sil·i·sa·tion** /,fɑːsələˈzeɪʃən, Brit ,fɒsə,laɪˈzeɪʃən/ *n* [*U*]

¹fos·ter /ˈfɑːstɚ/ *vb* **1** [*T*] : to help (something) grow or develop ▪ *foster a sense of community* **2** [*T/I*] : to become or be the foster parent of a child ▪ *Would you foster a child?*

²foster *adj, always before a noun* — used to describe a situation in which for a period of time a child lives with people who are not the child's parents ▪ *They are foster parents to three foster children.* ▪ *She's in foster care.* = *She's in a foster home.*

fought *past tense and past participle of* ¹FIGHT

¹foul /ˈfawəl/ *adj* **1** : very unpleasant to taste or smell ▪ *foul odors/air/breath* **2** : morally bad ▪ *a foul crime* **3** : very bad or unpleasant ▪ *a foul mood* ▪ *foul weather* **4** : indecent and offensive ▪ *foul language* ▪ *She has a foul mouth.* [=she uses foul language] **5** : very unfair ▪ *He won by foul means.* — see also FOUL PLAY **6** *baseball* : outside the area between the foul lines ▪ *He hit a foul ball.* [=a batted ball that lands in the area outside the foul lines] — **fall foul of** : to get into trouble because of (the law, a rule, etc.) ▪ *She fell foul of the law.* — **foul·ly** *adv* — **foul·ness** *n* [*U*]

²foul *n* [*C*] **1** *sports* : an action that is against the rules and for which a player is given a penalty ▪ *She committed a foul.* = *She was charged with a foul.* **2** *baseball* : a batted ball that lands outside the foul lines ▪ *He hit a foul.* — **cry foul** see ¹CRY

³foul *vb* **1** [*T*] : to make (a substance, place, etc.) dirty ▪ *pollutants that foul the*

air **2** *sports* **a** [*I*] : to commit a foul ▪ *She fouled on her first jump.* **b** [*T*] : to commit a foul against (another player) ▪ *He was fouled as he attempted the shot.* **3** [*T*] *baseball* : to hit (a pitched ball) so that it lands outside the foul lines ▪ *fouling pitches/balls into the stands* — **foul out** [*phrasal vb*] *basketball* : to be forced to leave a game for making too many fouls ▪ *She fouled out in the fourth quarter.* — **foul up** [*phrasal vb*] *informal* ▪ **foul (something) up** : to ruin or spoil (something) ▪ *The weather fouled up our plans.* **2** : to make mistakes ▪ *Whenever I try to be clever, I usually foul up.*

foul line *n* [*C*] **1** *baseball* : either one of two straight lines that go from home plate through first and third base on to the edge of the outfield **2** *basketball* : a line from which a player shoots free throws

foul–mouthed /ˈfawl,mauθt/ *adj* : using indecent or offensive language ▪ *foul-mouthed kids*

foul play *n* [*U*] : criminal violence or murder ▪ *There is no evidence of foul play in his death.*

foul shot *n* [*C*] *basketball* : FREE THROW

foul–up /ˈfawl,ʌp/ *n* [*C*] *informal* : a problem caused by someone making a mistake ▪ *an administrative foul-up*

¹found *past tense and past participle of* ¹FIND

²found /ˈfaund/ *vb* [*T*] **1** : to begin or create (something that is meant to last for a long time) ▪ *The college was founded in 1793.* ▪ *Thomas Jefferson and the other* **Founding Fathers** [=a man who had an important part in creating the government of the U.S.] **2** : to provide support for something ▪ *His suspicions were founded on rumors.* — **found·er** /ˈfaundɚ/ *n* [*C*] ▪ *the company's founder*

foun·da·tion /faunˈdeɪʃən/ *n* **1** [*C*] **a** : a usually concrete structure that supports a building from underneath ▪ *dig/lay/pour the house's foundation* **b** : an idea, a principle, a fact, etc., that provides support for something ▪ *the moral foundations on which her political career was built* ▪ *Her research laid the foundation* [=provided the basis] *for many important medical discoveries.* **2** [*C*] : an organization that is supported with money that people give in order to do something that helps society ▪ *a foundation to help orphans* ▪ *a charitable foundation* **3** [*C/U*] : makeup that is the color of your skin and that you use before putting on other makeup **4** [*U*] : the act of founding something ▪ *the foundation of a new school*

foun·der /ˈfaundɚ/ *vb* [*I*] **1** : to be unsuccessful : FAIL ▪ *a foundering career/marriage* **2** : to fill with water and sink ▪ *a foundering boat/ship*

founding member *n* [*C*] : an original member of a group (such as a club or corporation)

found·ling /ˈfaundlɪŋ/ *n* [*C*] : a baby that is found after being left by its parents

found·ry /ˈfaundri/ *n, pl* **-ries** [*C*] : a factory where metals are produced

fount /ˈfaunt/ *n* [*C*] **1** *literary* : the

source of something ▪ *a fount of knowl-edge/justice* **2** *Brit* : FONT 1

foun·tain /ˈfaʊntn̩/ *n* [C] **1** : a device or structure that sends a stream of water into the air ▪ *a garden with a marble foun-tain*; *also* : the water that rises from a fountain ▪ *a fountain of water* — see also SODA FOUNTAIN, WATER FOUNTAIN **2** : the source of something : FOUNT 1 ▪ *a fountain of wisdom*

fountain pen *n* [C] : a pen with ink in-side that flows to a special metal tip (called a nib)

four /ˈfoɚ/ *n* **1** [C] : the number 4 **2** [C] : the fourth in a set or series ▪ *the four of hearts* **3** [U] : four o'clock ▪ *It's almost four.* — **four** *adj* ▪ *four hours* — **four** *pron* ▪ *Four (of them) are broken.*

four–letter word *n* **1** [C] : DIRTY WORD 1 ▪ *a book that contains a lot of four-letter words* **2** [*singular*] : DIRTY WORD 2 ▪ *"Tax" is a four-letter word as far as he's concerned.*

401(k) /ˌfoɚˌoʊˌwʌnˈkeɪ/ *n* [C] *US* : a method of saving money for retirement

four·score /ˈfoɚˈskoɚ/ *adj, old-fashioned* : EIGHTY ▪ *"Fourscore and seven [=87] years ago . . ."* —Abraham Lincoln, Gettysburg Address (1863)

four·some /ˈfoɚsəm/ *n* [C] : a group of four people or things ▪ *a foursome of golf-ers*

four–star /ˈfoɚˈstaɚ/ *adj, always before a noun* : of very high quality ▪ *a four-star hotel*

four·teen /foɚˈtiːn/ *n* [C] : the number 14 — **fourteen** *adj* ▪ *fourteen days* — **four-teen** *pron* — **four·teenth** /foɚˈtiːnθ/ *n* [C] — **fourteenth** *adj* — **fourteenth** *adv*

fourth /ˈfoɚθ/ *n* **1** [*singular*] : number four in a series ▪ *I'll be there on May the fourth.* **2** [C] : one of four equal parts of something ▪ *Cut the cake into fourths.* **3 the Fourth** : INDEPENDENCE DAY ▪ *watching fireworks on the Fourth* — **fourth** *adj* ▪ *the fourth day* — **fourth** *adv* ▪ *the fourth highest mountain*

Fourth of July *n* [*singular*] : INDEPEN-DENCE DAY

four–wheel drive *n* [U] : a system that applies engine power directly to all four wheels of a vehicle ▪ *My car has four-wheel drive.*

fowl /ˈfawəl/ *n, pl* **fowl** *also* **fowls** **1** [C] : a bird that is raised for food — usually plural ▪ *chickens, ducks, and other fowl* **2** [U] : the meat of such a bird used as food ▪ *roasted fowl*

fox /ˈfɑːks/ *n* **1 a** [C] : a small wild ani-mal that is related to dogs and that has a long pointed nose and a bushy tail **b** [U] : the fur of a fox ▪ *a fox coat* **2** [C] : a clever person ▪ *He's a wily/sly old fox.* **3** [C], *US, informal* : an attractive person ▪ *She's a real fox.*

fox·glove /ˈfɑːksˌglʌv/ *n* [C] : a tall plant with bell-shaped flowers

fox·hole /ˈfɑːksˌhoʊl/ *n* [C] : a hole dug for a soldier to sit or lie in for protection from the enemy

foxy /ˈfɑːksi/ *adj* **fox·i·er**, **-est 1** : very clever ▪ *a foxy strategy* **2** *US, informal* : physically attractive : SEXY ▪ *a foxy lady*

foy·er /ˈfojɚ, ˈfoɪˌeɪ/ *n* [C] **1** : an open area in a hotel, theater, etc., near the en-trance **2** *US* : an open area near the en-trance in someone's home

fr. *abbr* **1** father **2** franc **3** from

Fr. *abbr* **1** France; French **2** Friday

fra·cas /ˈfreɪkəs, *Brit* ˈfraˌkɑː/ *n, pl* **fra-cas·es** (*US*) *or Brit* **fracas** : a noisy argument or fight ▪ *a drunken fracas*

frac·tion /ˈfrækʃən/ *n* [C] **1** *mathemat-ics* : a number (such as ½ or ¾) which indicates that one number is being divid-ed by another; *also* : a number (such as 3.323) that consists of a whole number and a decimal **2** : a part or amount of something ▪ *a fraction of an inch/second* ▪ *This car is a fraction of the cost of* [=much less expensive than] *that one.* — **frac-tion·al** /ˈfrækʃənl/ *adj* ▪ *fractional num-bers* ▪ *a fractional* [=very small] *amount* — **frac·tion·al·ly** *adv*

frac·tious /ˈfrækʃəs/ *adj* **1** : hard to manage or control ▪ *a fractious crowd* **2** : full of anger and disagreement ▪ *frac-tious relationships/negotiations* — **frac-tious·ness** *n* [U]

frac·ture /ˈfræktʃɚ/ *n* [C] : a crack or break ▪ *a fracture in the Earth's crust; es-pecially* : a broken bone ▪ *a wrist fracture* — **fracture** *vb* **-tured**; **-tur·ing** [T/I] ▪ *She fractured* [=broke] *her wrist.* ▪ *a frac-tured skull*

frag·ile /ˈfrædʒəl, ˈfræˌdʒaɪəl/ *adj* : easily broken or damaged ▪ *fragile bones* ▪ *Her health is fragile.* : not strong ▪ *a fragile agreement* — **fra·gil·i·ty** /frəˈdʒɪləti/ *n* [U]

¹**frag·ment** /ˈfrægmənt/ *n* [C] **1** : a bro-ken part or piece of something ▪ *bone/pottery fragments* **2** : an incomplete part ▪ *I could only hear fragments of their con-versation.* — see also SENTENCE FRAG-MENT

²**frag·ment** /ˈfrægˌment, *Brit* frægˈment/ *vb* [T/I] : to break or to cause (some-thing) to break into parts or pieces ▪ *The issue is fragmenting our society.* ▪ *a frag-mented society* — **frag·men·ta·tion** /ˌfrægmənˈteɪʃən/ *n* [U]

frag·men·tary /ˈfrægmənˌteri, *Brit* ˈfrægməntri/ *adj* : made up of fragments ▪ *fragmentary evidence/fossils/memories*

fra·grance /ˈfreɪgrəns/ *n* [C] **1** : a pleas-ant and usually sweet smell ▪ *a lemony fragrance* **2** : a perfume or cologne ▪ *a new fragrance* — **fra·grant** /ˈfreɪgrənt/ *adj* ▪ *a fragrant flower*

frail /ˈfreɪl/ *adj* **1** : very weak ▪ *a frail old man* ▪ *His health is frail.* **2** : easily dam-aged or destroyed ▪ *a frail ship* — **frail-ness** *n* [U]

frail·ty /ˈfreɪlti/ *n, pl* **-ties 1** [U] : physi-cal weakness ▪ *the frailty of her health* **2** [C/U] : weakness of character that caus-es a person to do things that are morally wrong ▪ *the (human) frailties of our lead-ers*

¹**frame** /ˈfreɪm/ *n* **1** [C] : the basic shape of the body of a person or animal ▪ *her petite/thin/wiry frame* **2** [C] : the parts that support and form the basic shape of

something • *the frame of a house* • *a bicycle frame* **3 a** [C] : an open structure that holds something (such as glass) • *a picture/window frame.* **b** [*plural*] : the plastic or metal structure that holds the lenses of eyeglasses • *thick, black frames* **4** [C] : one of the pictures in the series of pictures that make up a film • *The film runs at eight frames per second.*

²**frame** *vb* **framed; fram·ing** [T] **1 a** : to put (something) in a frame • *frame a picture* • *wire-framed glasses* **b** : to be around the edge of (something) • *Her face was framed by brown curls.* **2** : to produce (something written or spoken) • *It was the first state to frame a constitution.* : to express (a question, answer, etc.) in words • *She framed her questions carefully.* **3** : to make (an innocent person) appear to be guilty of a crime • *She says she was framed.* — **fram·er** *n* [C]

frame of mind *n* [C] : a person's emotional state : MOOD • *Wait until he's in a better frame of mind.*

frame of reference *n* [C] : a set of ideas, experiences, etc., that affect how something is thought about or understood • *the reader's frame of reference*

frame·work /ˈfreɪmˌwɚk/ *n* [C] **1** : the basic structure of something • *the framework of our society* : a set of ideas or facts that provide support for something • *a framework for understanding politics* **2** : a supporting structure • *the building's steel framework*

franc /ˈfræŋk/ *n* [C] : a basic unit of money that is used in some countries where French is spoken; *also* : a coin or bill representing one franc

fran·chise /ˈfrænˌtʃaɪz/ *n* [C] **1** : the right to sell a company's goods or services in a particular area; *also* : a business that is given such a right • *a fast-food franchise* **2** *US, sports* : a team that is a member of a professional sports league • *He's the best player in the history of the franchise.*

fran·chi·see /ˌfrænˌtʃaɪˈziː/ *n* [C] : a person who has been granted a franchise

Fran·co- /ˌfræŋkoʊ/ *combining form* : French • *Franco-American diplomacy*

¹**frank** /ˈfræŋk/ *adj* : very honest and direct • *a frank discussion* • *To be very frank (with you), I don't think you're good enough.* — **frank·ness** *n* [U]

²**frank** *n* [C] *US, informal* : HOT DOG 1

frank·furt·er /ˈfræŋkˌfɚtɚ/ *n* [C] : HOT DOG 1

frank·in·cense /ˈfræŋkənˌsɛns/ *n* [U] : a substance that is burned for its sweet smell

frank·ly /ˈfræŋkli/ *adv* : in an honest and direct way • *Let me speak frankly.* — often used to introduce a statement that tells your true opinion, reason, etc. • *Frankly, I think you're wrong.*

fran·tic /ˈfræntɪk/ *adj* **1** : feeling or showing a lot of fear and worry • *frantic cries for help* • *a frantic search* • *I was frantic with worry.* **2** : having a lot of wild and hurried activity • *frantic preparations* • *a frantic effort to finish on schedule* — **fran·ti·cal·ly** /ˈfræntɪkli/ *adv*

frat /ˈfræt/ *n* [C] *US, informal* : FRATERNITY 1 • *a frat party* • *a frat boy* [=a member of a fraternity]

fra·ter·nal /frəˈtɚnl̩/ *adj* **1** : of or relating to brothers • *fraternal love* **2** : made up of members who share an interest or purpose • *a fraternal organization* **3** : friendly or brotherly • *a fraternal feeling* — **fra·ter·nal·ly** *adv*

fraternal twin *n* [C] : either member of a pair of twins that are produced from different eggs

fra·ter·ni·ty /frəˈtɚnəti/ *n, pl* **-ties 1** [C] : an organization of male students at a U.S. college **2** [C] : a group of people who have the same job, interests, etc. • *the legal fraternity* **3** [U] *formal* : the feeling of friendship that exists between people in a group • *an atmosphere of fraternity*

frat·er·nize *also Brit* **frat·er·nise** /ˈfrætɚˌnaɪz/ *vb* **-nized; -niz·ing** [I] : to spend time with someone in a friendly way • *The soldiers were caught fraternizing (with the enemy).* — **frat·er·ni·za·tion** *also Brit* **frat·er·ni·sa·tion** /ˌfrætɚnəˈzeɪʃən, *Brit* ˌfrætɚnaɪˈzeɪʃən/ *n* [U] — **frat·er·niz·er** *also Brit* **frat·er·nis·er** /ˈfrætɚˌnaɪzɚ/ *n* [C]

frat·ri·cide /ˈfrætrəˌsaɪd/ *n* [C] : the crime of murdering your own brother or sister

fraud /ˈfrɑːd/ *n* **1** [C/U] : the crime of using dishonest methods to take something valuable from another person • *bank fraud* • *an elaborate credit card fraud* **2** [C] **a** : a person who pretends to be what he or she is not in order to trick people • *He said he was a doctor, but he turned out to be a fraud.* **b** : a copy of something that is meant to look like the real thing in order to trick people • *The painting was a fraud.*

fraud·u·lent /ˈfrɑːdʒələnt/ *adj* : done to trick someone for the purpose of getting something valuable • *a fraudulent election/scheme* — **fraud·u·lence** /ˈfrɑːdʒələns/ *n* [U] — **fraud·u·lent·ly** *adv*

fraught /ˈfrɑːt/ *adj* : causing or having a lot of emotional stress or worry • *a fraught silence/atmosphere* — **fraught with** : full of (something bad or unwanted) • *The situation was fraught with danger.* [=very dangerous]

¹**fray** /ˈfreɪ/ *n* [C] : a fight, struggle, or disagreement that involves many people • *He joined/entered the fray.* • *She remained above the fray.* [=not directly involved in an angry struggle or disagreement]

²**fray** *vb* [T/I] : to separate the threads of (a material) • *The bottoms of her jeans were fraying.* • *(figurative)* *His nerves were starting to fray.* [=he was becoming angry]

fraz·zle /ˈfræzəl/ *vb* **fraz·zled; fraz·zling** [T] *informal* : to make (someone) very nervous or upset • *frazzle someone's nerves* • *I was feeling tired and frazzled.*

¹**freak** /ˈfriːk/ *n* [C] **1 a** *disapproving* : a very strange person • *Who's that freak with the green hair?* **b** *old-fashioned* : a person or animal that is physically abnormal • *a circus freak* • *a freak show* **2** *informal* : a person who is very interested or active in something • *a fitness/mov-*

ie/computer freak **3** : something that is very unusual or unexpected ▪ *That storm was a freak of nature.* — **freak** *adj, always before a noun* ▪ *a freak accident* [=an accident that was not typical or normal] — **freak·ish** /ˈfriːkɪʃ/ *adj* ▪ *freakish* [=*unusual*] *weather* — **freak·ish·ly** *adv* — **freaky** /ˈfriːki/ *adj* **freak·i·er; -est** ▪ *a freaky* [=*strange, weird*] *day/kid*

²**freak** *vb, informal* **1** [*T*] : to make (someone) very upset ▪ *He was a little freaked by the accident.* — usually + *out* ▪ *She was freaked out by what you said.* **2** [*I*] : to become very upset ▪ *She really freaked (out) when she said that.*

freck·le /ˈfrɛkəl/ *n* [*C*] : a small, brownish spot on someone's skin ▪ *a redheaded girl with freckles* ▪ *a freckle-faced girl* — **freckle** *vb* **freck·led; freck·ling** [*T/I*] ▪ *a freckled face* ▪ *His skin freckles but doesn't tan.*

¹**free** /ˈfriː/ *adj* **fre·er; fre·est 1** : not costing any money ▪ *free tickets/drinks/ advice* ▪ *The tickets are free for the taking.* [=anyone who wants one can take one] ▪ *We got in for free.* [=without paying any money] **2 a** : not held as a slave or prisoner ▪ *After 10 years in jail, he was finally a free man.* ▪ *He was finally set free.* **b** : not physically held by something ▪ *The animal struggled to get (itself) free off/from the trap.* **3** : able to do what you want to do without being stopped ▪ *You are free to leave.* ▪ *Feel free to call me* [=there is no reason to hesitate calling me] *if you have questions.* ▪ (*figurative*) *I was as free as a bird.* [=completely free] **4 a** : not controlled by a harsh ruler or laws ▪ *a free country/society* **b** : not limited by government control ▪ *free speech/elections* **5 a** : not limited by fear, uncertainty, etc. ▪ *a free exchange of ideas* **b** : not limited in any way ▪ *The ships were allowed free passage into the port.* — see also *free rein* at ¹REIN **6** : not having, including, or suffering from something unpleasant, painful, or unwanted ▪ *sugar-free chewing gum* ▪ *free from/of disease* **7 a** : available to do something ▪ *I'm free tonight.* **b** *of time* : not being used for work or other activities ▪ *Monday is her only free day.* ▪ *I need more free time.* **8 a** : not being used ▪ *"Is this seat free?" "No, it's taken."* **b** : not holding anything ▪ *He waved with his free hand.* **c** : not attached to anything ▪ *the free end of the rope* **9** : not covered or filled with things ▪ *The floor was free of clutter.* **10** : giving, doing, or saying something very often ▪ *She's very free with her money.* [=she spends a lot of money without worrying about trying to save it] — **free·ly** *adv* ▪ *We passed freely through the gate.*

²**free** *adv* **1** : in a free way ▪ *The animals roam free in this zoo.* **2** : without paying money ▪ *We got in free.* [=*for free*] ▪ *Buy one, get one free.* — **break free** see ¹BREAK — **free and clear** : without owing any more money ▪ *I own the property free and clear.* — **free of charge** : without receiving money ▪ *He fixed our car free of charge.* — **home free** see ²HOME

³**free** *vb* **freed; free·ing** [*T*] : to cause (someone or something) to be free ▪ *The*

government freed the prisoners. ▪ *The animal freed itself from the trap.* ▪ *freeing yourself from debt* ▪ *I'll free (up) some time on my schedule.* ▪ *Working from home frees him to spend more time with his family.* ▪ *Free your imagination.*

free agent *n* [*C*] **1** : a person who is not controlled by someone else **2** : a professional athlete who is free to sign a contract to play for any team — **free agen·cy** *n* [*U*]

free·bie *or* **free·bee** /ˈfriːbi/ *n* [*C*] *informal* : something that is given for free

free·dom /ˈfriːdəm/ *n* **1** [*U*] : the state of being free: such as **a** : the power to do what you want to do ▪ *religious/academic freedom* ▪ **freedom of speech/expression** [=the right to express your opinions freely] **b** : the state of not being a slave, prisoner, etc. ▪ *a struggle to win one's freedom* **c** : the state of not having or being affected by something unpleasant or unwanted ▪ **freedom from care/pain/fear 2** [*C*] : a political right ▪ *basic human freedoms*

freedom fighter *n* [*C*] : a person who is part of an organized group fighting against an unfair government or system

free enterprise *n* [*U*] : a system in which private businesses compete with each other with little control by the government — called also *private enterprise*

free fall *n* **1** [*U*] : the state or condition of falling through the air toward the ground ▪ *a skydiver in free fall* **2** [*C/U*] : the state of something that is quickly becoming lower, less, or fewer ▪ *Stock prices went into (a) free fall.*

free-float·ing /ˈfriːˈfloʊtɪŋ/ *adj* : not connected to or caused by anything specific ▪ *free-floating ideas/anxiety*

free-for-all /ˈfriːfɔɚˌɑːl/ *n* [*C*] : an uncontrolled fight or competition that involves many people ▪ *A fight between two players quickly turned into a free-for-all.* ▪ (*figurative*) *The press conference became a free-for-all.*

free-form /ˈfriːˈfoɚm/ *adj* : created or done in any way you choose ▪ *free-form dancing*

free·hand /ˈfriːˌhænd/ *adj, always before a noun* : done without special tools ▪ *a freehand drawing* — **freehand** *adv* ▪ *drawing freehand*

free hand *n* — **a free hand** : the freedom to do things and make decisions without being controlled by another ▪ *She was given a free hand in running the business.*

free kick *n* [*C*] *soccer* : a kick that is allowed because of a foul by an opponent

free·lance /ˈfriːˌlæns/ *adj* : earning money by being hired to work on different jobs for short periods of time ▪ *a freelance writer* — **freelance** *vb* **-lanced; -lanc·ing** [*I*] ▪ *a writer who freelances*

free·load /ˈfriːˌloʊd/ *vb* [*I*] *informal + disapproving* : to get or ask for food, money, etc., from people without paying for them ▪ *their freeloading adult son* — **free·load·er** *n* [*C*]

free·man /ˈfriːmən/ *n, pl* **-men** /-mən/ [*C*] : a man who is not a slave

free market n [C] : an economic system in which prices are based on competition among private businesses — **free-market** adj, always before a noun ▪ a free-market economy

Free·ma·son /ˈfriːˌmeɪsn/ n [C] : a member of a large organization of men who have secret rituals — **Free·ma·son·ry** /ˈfriːˌmeɪsn̩ri/ n [U]

free–range /ˈfriːˌreɪndʒ/ adj : not kept in cages ▪ free-range chickens; also : coming from free-range animals ▪ free-range eggs

free spirit n [C] approving : a person who thinks and acts without worrying about normal social rules

free·stand·ing /ˈfriːˈstændɪŋ/ adj : standing alone without being attached to or supported by something else ▪ a freestanding wall

free·style /ˈfriːˌstajəl/ n [singular] **1** : a competition in which the competitors can use different styles or methods ▪ freestyle skating **2** : ²CRAWL 2

free·think·er /ˈfriːˈθɪŋkɚ/ n [C] : a person who forms his or her own opinions instead of accepting what other people say — **free·think·ing** /ˈfriːˈθɪŋkɪŋ/ adj

free throw n [C] : a basketball shot that is given because of a foul by an opponent — called also foul shot

free trade n [U] : a system of trade between nations in which there are no special taxes placed on imports

free·way /ˈfriːˌweɪ/ n [C] US : a wide highway built for fast travel

free·wheel·ing /ˌfriːˈwiːlɪŋ/ adj : not held back by rules, duties, or worries ▪ a freewheeling adventurer ▪ a freewheeling discussion

free will n [U] **1** : the ability to choose how to act ▪ I do this of my own free will. [=because I want to do it] **2** : the ability to make choices that are not controlled by fate or God ▪ He says we all have free will.

¹**freeze** /ˈfriːz/ vb froze /ˈfrouz/; fro·zen /ˈfrouzn̩/; freez·ing **1** [T/I] : to become hard because of cold ▪ Water freezes (in)to ice. ▪ The pond froze (over). **2** [I] : to be very cold ▪ You'll freeze out there without a coat. ▪ I nearly froze to death. [=nearly died from the cold] **3** [T/I] : to become blocked because of ice ▪ The water pipes froze. **4** [T/I] : to preserve (food) by storing it in a very cold place ▪ We froze the leftovers. ▪ Lettuce doesn't freeze well. **5** [I] **a** : to stop moving : to become completely still ▪ The guard told him to freeze. **b** : to become unable to do or say anything ▪ She froze (up) when the teacher asked her a question. **c** : to stop working ▪ My computer froze (up). **6** [T] **a** : to stop (something) from changing or increasing ▪ freeze prices/wages **b** : to stop (money or property) from being used, spent, etc. ▪ freeze assets — **freezing** adj or adv ▪ I'm freezing! [=I'm very cold] ▪ freezing weather ▪ It's freezing cold [=very cold] in here!

²**freeze** n [C] **1** : a period in which the weather is very cold ▪ The freeze destroyed many oranges. **2** : a stop in the change of prices or wages ▪ a price freeze ▪ a freeze on wages

freeze–dry /ˈfriːzˈdraɪ/ vb -dries; -dried; -dry·ing [T] : to preserve (something) by a process that both dries and freezes it ▪ freeze-drying food — **freeze–dried** adj ▪ freeze-dried fruit/coffee

freez·er /ˈfriːzɚ/ n [C] : a device or room for keeping food frozen

freezing point n [C] : the temperature at which a liquid freezes ▪ The freezing point of water is 32 degrees Fahrenheit.

¹**freight** /ˈfreɪt/ n [U] **1 a** : goods that are carried by ships, trains, trucks, or airplanes ▪ a truck carrying freight ▪ (US) a freight car [=a railroad car that carries freight] ▪ a freight train [=a train that carries freight] **b** : the system by which goods are carried from one place to another ▪ items shipped by freight **2** : the amount of money paid for carrying goods ▪ paid the full freight

²**freight** vb [T] **1** : to send (goods) from one place to another ▪ cargo freighted by airplane **2** : to cause (something) to have or carry too many things ▪ an essay freighted with complex arguments

freight·er /ˈfreɪtɚ/ n [C] : a large ship used to carry goods

French /ˈfrɛntʃ/ n **1** [U] : the language of the French people ▪ speaking French **2** the French : the people of France ▪ the customs of the French — **French** adj ▪ French cuisine — **French·man** /ˈfrɛntʃmən/ n, pl -men /-mən/ [C] — **French·wom·an** /ˈfrɛntʃˌwʊmən/ n, pl -wom·en /-ˌwɪmən/ [C]

French bean n [C] Brit : GREEN BEAN

French door n [C] chiefly US : a pair of windows that reach to the floor and open like doors

French dressing n [U] **1** US : a creamy salad dressing that is made with tomatoes **2** Brit : a salad dressing made of vinegar, oil, and spices

french fry or **French fry** n, pl ~ **fries** [C] chiefly US : a long, thin piece of potato that is deep-fried — called also (Brit) chip, (US) fry — **french–fried** adj, chiefly US ▪ french-fried potatoes

French horn n [C] : a brass musical instrument that has a long tube which forms a circle and has a wide opening at one end

French kiss n [C] : a kiss made with the mouths open and the tongues touching

French toast n [U] : bread that is covered in a mixture of eggs and milk and fried ▪ a slice of French toast

fre·net·ic /frɪˈnɛtɪk/ adj : filled with excitement, activity, or confusion ▪ frenetic activity — **fre·net·i·cal·ly** /frɪˈnɛtɪkli/ adv

fren·zied /ˈfrɛnzid/ adj : very excited or upset ▪ frenzied fans/dancing

fren·zy /ˈfrɛnzi/ n, pl -zies [C] : great and often wild or uncontrolled activity ▪ He worked himself (up) into a frenzy. ▪ a frenzy of shopping

fre·quen·cy /ˈfriːkwənsi/ n, pl -cies **1** [U] : the fact or condition of happening often ▪ I am concerned about the frequency of errors. **2** [U] : the number of times that something happens during a particular period ▪ The frequency of our visits decreased. [=we visited less often] **3**

[C/U] *technical* : the number of times that a wave (such as a radio wave) is repeated in a period of time • *high/low radio frequencies*

¹**fre·quent** /ˈfriːkwənt/ *adj* **1** : happening often • *We made frequent trips to town.* • *a frequent occurrence* **2** : acting or returning often • *a frequent visitor/customer* — **fre·quent·ly** *adv*

²**fre·quent** /friˈkwɛnt/ *vb* [T] : to visit or go to (a place) often • *He began frequenting cheap bars.* — **fre·quent·er** *n* [C] • *a frequenter of cheap bars*

fres·co /ˈfrɛskoʊ/ *n, pl* **-coes** **1** [U] : the art of painting on wet plaster • *scenes done in fresco* **2** [C] : a painting done on wet plaster • *a ceiling fresco*

¹**fresh** /ˈfrɛʃ/ *adj* **1 a** : recently picked, caught, made, etc. : not frozen, canned, etc. • *fresh vegetables/herbs/fish/bread* **b** : not old, spoiled, etc. • *The meat was kept fresh in the refrigerator.* **2 a** : clean and pure • *fresh air* **b** : not having an unpleasant smell, taste, etc. • *fresh breath* **c** : not worn or dirty • *He changed into a fresh shirt.* **3** : not containing salt • *fresh water* **4 a** : newly made, experienced, or received • *a fresh wound* **b** : replacing something old or used • *a fresh piece of paper* • *Let's make a fresh start.* [=let's start again] **c** : clearly remembered • *Her words are still fresh in my mind.* **d** : new and original • *a fresh idea/approach* **5 a** : RUDE, IMPOLITE • *Don't be/get fresh (with me)!* **b** *old-fashioned* : behaving or talking in a way that shows sexual attraction to someone • *He got fresh with me.* — **a breath of fresh air** see BREATH — **fresh from** or **fresh out of** : having recently left or come from (a place) • *We hired him fresh out of college.* — **fresh·ly** *adv* • *freshly baked pie* — **fresh·ness** *n* [C/U]

²**fresh** *adv* : just recently : FRESHLY • *fresh-baked bread* — **fresh out (of something)** *US, informal* — used to say that you have no more of something • *We're fresh out of bagels/ideas.*

fresh·en /ˈfrɛʃən/ *vb* [T] **1** : to cause (something) to be more pleasant • *We freshened (up) the room with some new color.* • *gum that freshens the breath* **2** *chiefly US* : to pour more of a drink into someone's glass • *Can I freshen your drink?* — **freshen up** [*phrasal vb*] : to wash yourself • *I freshened up after the game.* — **fresh·en·er** /ˈfrɛʃənɚ/ *n* [C] • *an air/room freshener* [=something used to make a room smell more pleasant]

fresh·er /ˈfrɛʃɚ/ *n* [C] *Brit, informal* : a university freshman

fresh–faced /ˈfrɛʃˈfeɪst/ *adj* : having a young, healthy, and innocent appearance • *fresh-faced students*

fresh·man /ˈfrɛʃmən/ *n, pl* **-men** /-mən/ [C] : a student in the first year of high school or college • *a college freshman* • *my freshman year* **2** *chiefly US* : someone who is starting a job or activity • *a freshman senator*

fresh·wa·ter /ˈfrɛʃˈwɑːtɚ/ *adj, always before a noun* : of, relating to, or living in water that is not salty • *a freshwater fish/stream*

¹**fret** /ˈfrɛt/ *vb* **fret·ted; fret·ting** [I] : to worry or be concerned • *She told me not to fret (about/over it).*

²**fret** *n* [C] : any one of a series of ridges on the neck of a guitar, banjo, etc.

fret·ful /ˈfrɛtfəl/ *adj* : upset and worried • *a fretful child* — **fret·ful·ly** *adv* — **fret·ful·ness** *n* [U]

Freud·i·an /ˈfrɔɪdijən/ *adj* **1** : of, relating to, or following the theories of Sigmund Freud • *Freudian psychology* **2** : relating to or coming from hidden desires or feelings • *a Freudian slip* [=a mistake in speech that shows what the speaker is truly thinking] — **Freudian** *n* [C]

Fri. *abbr* Friday

fri·ar /ˈfrajɚ/ *n* [C] : a member of a men's Roman Catholic group who is poor and studies or teaches about Christianity

fric·tion /ˈfrɪkʃən/ *n* [U] **1 a** : the act of rubbing one thing against another • *the friction of sandpaper on wood* **b** : the force that causes a moving object to slow down when it is touching another object • *Oil in a car engine reduces friction.* **2** : disagreement or tension between people or groups • *There's some friction between us.*

Fri·day /ˈfraɪˌdeɪ/ *n* [C/U] : the day of the week between Thursday and Saturday • *I'll arrive (on) Friday.* = (*Brit*) *I'll arrive on the Friday.* • *She was here last Friday.* — *abbr.* **Fri.** — **Fridays** *adv* • *He works late Fridays.* [=every Friday]

fridge /ˈfrɪdʒ/ *n* [C] : REFRIGERATOR

fried /ˈfraɪd/ *adj* **1** : cooked in hot oil • *fried fish* **2** *US, informal* : not able to think clearly because you are tired • *My brain is fried.*

friend /ˈfrɛnd/ *n* [C] **1** : a person who you like and enjoy being with • *She's a good/close/dear friend (of mine).* • *my best friend* [=my closest friend] • *childhood/old friends* [=people who have been friends since childhood or for a long time] • *We are just friends.* [=we are not in a romantic relationship] • *It was hard for him to make friends* [=to become someone's friend] *(with other kids).* • *She has friends in high places.* [=she knows people with social or political influence or power] **2** : a person who helps or supports someone or something • *She is a friend of the environment.* [=she supports environmental causes] — **man's best friend** see ¹MAN — **friend·less** /ˈfrɛndləs/ *adj* • *He was friendless and alone.*

friend·ly /ˈfrɛndli/ *adj* **friend·li·er; -est** **1 a** : kind and helpful • *friendly neighbors* **b** : having or showing the feelings that friends have for each other • *a friendly smile* **2** : showing support or approval • *a politician who is overly friendly to/toward special interests* **3** : cheerful or pleasant • *the friendly glow of the fire* **4** : not an enemy : not hostile • *a friendly rivalry*; *specifically* : involving or coming from your own military forces • *soldiers killed by friendly fire* [=accidentally killed by weapons fired from their own side] **5** : not harmful • *environmentally friendly products* **6** : done for enjoyment instead of for money or prizes ▪ *a friendly game of tennis/poker* — **friend·li·ness** *n* [U]

friend·ship /ˈfrɛndˌʃɪp/ *n* 1 [C/U] : the state of being friends : the relationship between friends ▪ *They have enjoyed many years of friendship.* ▪ *a lasting friendship* 2 [U] : kindness or help given to someone ▪ *I'm grateful for the friendship you have shown me.*

frieze /ˈfriːz/ *n* [C] : a decorative border on the top of a building or wall

frig·ate /ˈfrɪɡət/ *n* [C] : a small and fast military ship

fright /ˈfraɪt/ *n* 1 a [U] : fear caused by sudden danger ▪ *I almost died of fright.* [=I was very afraid] ▪ *The deer took fright* [=became afraid] *and ran away.* b [C] : a feeling of sudden fear — usually singular ▪ *The sudden noise gave me a fright!* 2 [C] *old-fashioned* : something that looks strange, shocking, ugly, etc. ▪ *Your hair looks a fright!* [=it looks very messy or unattractive]

fright·en /ˈfraɪtn̩/ *vb* 1 [T] : to cause (someone) to become afraid ▪ *Stop frightening the children.* ▪ *a frightened child* ▪ *a frightening story* ▪ *He nearly frightened me to death.* [=he scared me badly] 2 [I] : to become afraid ▪ *She doesn't frighten easily.* — **frighten away/off** [*phrasal vb*] **frighten** (*someone or something*) **away/off** : to cause (someone or something) to go away or stay away because of fear ▪ *The dog frightened the prowler away.* — **frighten into** [*phrasal vb*] **frighten** (*someone*) **into** (*doing something*) : to cause (someone) to do (something) because of fear ▪ *They frightened the boy into confessing.* — **frighten out of** [*phrasal vb*] **frighten** (*someone*) **out of** (*doing something*) : to keep (someone) from (doing something) because of fear ▪ *They frightened me out of going.* — **fright·en·ing·ly** *adv* ▪ *The car came frighteningly close to the cliff's edge.*

fright·ful /ˈfraɪtfəl/ *adj, old-fashioned* 1 : causing fear ▪ *a frightful scream/illness* 2 : very bad or shocking ▪ *a frightful mess* — **fright·ful·ly** /ˈfraɪtfəli/ *adv* ▪ *frightfully expensive*

frig·id /ˈfrɪdʒəd/ *adj* 1 : very cold ▪ *frigid wind/water* 2 : not friendly or loving ▪ *a frigid family* 3 *of a woman* : not wanting or enjoying sex — **fri·gid·i·ty** /frɪˈdʒɪdəti/ *n* [U]

frill /ˈfrɪl/ *n* [C] 1 : a strip of cloth that is gathered into folds and attached to clothing, curtains, etc., as a decoration 2 : something that is added but is not necessary ▪ *plain food with no frills* — **frilly** /ˈfrɪli/ *adj* **frill·i·er; -est** ▪ *a frilly dress*

fringe /ˈfrɪndʒ/ *n* 1 [C/U] : a decorative border made of hanging threads ▪ *a skirt/rug/curtain with (a) fringe* 2 [*singular*] : an area of activity that is outside of whatever is most widely accepted ▪ *a party on the political fringe* : a group of people with extreme views or unpopular opinions ▪ *the conservative/liberal fringe* ▪ *fringe activists* 3 [C] *Brit* : BANGS ▪ *She wears her hair in a fringe.* [=(US) she has bangs] — **on the fringe(s)** : on the outer edge of something ▪ *They lived on the*

fringe of the forest. ▪ *(figurative) working on the fringes of the entertainment industry* — **fringe** *vb* [T] ▪ *a skirt fringed with lace*

fringe benefit *n* [C] : something extra (such as vacation time) that is given to workers in addition to their regular pay

Fris·bee /ˈfrɪzbi/ *trademark* — used for a plastic disc that you throw to someone who tries to catch it

frisk /ˈfrɪsk/ *vb* [T] : to pass your hands over (someone) to search for something that may be hidden in clothing ▪ *We were frisked (for weapons) at the border.*

frisky /ˈfrɪski/ *adj* **frisk·i·er; -est** 1 : very playful or lively ▪ *frisky kittens* 2 *informal* : sexually playful or excited ▪ *feeling frisky* — **frisk·i·ly** /ˈfrɪskəli/ *adv* — **frisk·i·ness** *n* [U]

¹**frit·ter** /ˈfrɪtɚ/ *n* [C] : a small piece of food that has been coated in flour and egg and fried ▪ *apple/corn fritters*

²**fritter** *vb* — **fritter away** [*phrasal vb*] **fritter away** (*something*) or **fritter** (*something*) **away** : to spend or use up (something) in a slow and foolish way ▪ *He frittered his time/money away.*

fritz /ˈfrɪts/ *n* — **on the fritz** *US, informal* : not working properly ▪ *The stereo is on the fritz.*

friv·o·lous /ˈfrɪvələs/ *adj* 1 : not important or worthwhile ▪ *a frivolous activity/ lawsuit* 2 : silly and not serious ▪ *a frivolous conversation* — **fri·vol·i·ty** /frɪˈvɑːləti/ *n, pl* **-ties** [C/U] ▪ *He has no patience for frivolity.* ▪ *wasting money on frivolities* — **friv·o·lous·ly** *adv*

frizz /ˈfrɪz/ *n* [U] : very tightly curled hair ▪ *Hair gel helps control the frizz.* — **frizz** *vb* [I] ▪ *Humidity makes my hair frizz.* — **frizzy** /ˈfrɪzi/ *adj* **frizz·i·er; -est**

fro /ˈfroʊ/ *adv* see TO AND FRO

frock /ˈfrɑːk/ *n* [C] 1 *old-fashioned* : a woman's or girl's dress ▪ *a party frock* 2 : a long outer garment worn by some Christian monks and friars

frog /ˈfrɑːɡ/ *n* [C] : a small animal that spends much of the time in water and has smooth skin, webbed feet, and long back legs for jumping — *a frog in your throat* ◆ If you have *a frog in your throat*, you are unable to speak normally because your throat is dry.

¹**frol·ic** /ˈfrɑːlɪk/ *vb* **-icked; -ick·ing** [I] : to play and move about happily : ROMP ▪ *children frolicking in the yard*

²**frolic** *n* [C/U] : an enjoyable time or activity ▪ *a frolic in the sun* — **frol·ic·some** /ˈfrɑːlɪksəm/ *adj* ▪ *frolicsome children*

from /ˈfrʌm, ˈfrɑːm, frəm/ *prep* 1 — used to indicate the starting point of a physical movement or action ▪ *He drove here from the city.* ▪ *She fell from a tree.* 2 — used to indicate the place that something comes out of ▪ *He took a dime from his pocket.* 3 — used to indicate the place where someone lives or was born ▪ *Where are you from?* 4 — used to indicate the starting or central point of any activity ▪ *She watched them from her car.* ▪ *He spoke from the heart.* 5 — used to indicate the starting point in measuring something ▪ *a week from today* ▪ *I live 20 miles from here.* 6 — used to indicate a physical separation between two things ▪ *An ocean separates America from Europe.* **7** — used to indicate something that is blocked or removed ▪ *This lotion protects you from the sun.* ▪ *Please refrain from talking.* ▪ *They excluded her from the club.* ▪ *subtract 3 from 9* **8** — used to indicate change to a different state or condition ▪ *Things have gone from bad to worse.* **9** — used to indicate the material that is used to make something ▪ *wine made from red grapes* **10** — used to indicate the source of something ▪ *I got a call from my lawyer.* ▪ *I bought a book from him.* [=he sold a book to me] **11** — used to indicate the basis or cause of something ▪ *suffering from a bad cold* ▪ *I knew she was angry from the look on her face.* **12** — used to indicate the lowest point, amount, etc., in a range ▪ *These parts cost from $5 to $10.* **13** — used to indicate the group out of which someone or something is chosen ▪ *She was chosen from over 200 competitors.* — **as from** see ²AS

frond /ˈfrɑːnd/ *n* [C] : a large, long leaf ▪ *palm fronds*

¹**front** /ˈfrʌnt/ *n* **1** [C] : the forward part or surface of something — usually singular ▪ *the front of the box/house/shirt* **2** [C] : a place, position, or area that is most forward or is directly ahead — usually singular ▪ *He stood at the front of the classroom.* **3** [C] : the part of your body that faces forward — usually singular ▪ *The baby rolled from his back onto his front.* **4** [C] : the first few pages of a book, magazine, etc. — usually singular ▪ *the introduction at the front of the book* **5** [singular] : a way of behaving that is meant to hide your true feelings, thoughts, etc. ▪ *Her anger was just a front!* [=she was pretending to be angry] ▪ *Though sad, she* **put up a good/brave front.** [=she acted as if she was not sad] **6** [C] : someone or something that hides or protects an illegal activity ▪ *The business is a front for organized crime.* **7** [C] **a** : an area where military forces are fighting ▪ *sending troops to the front* **b** : an area or field of activity ▪ *We are making progress on the educational front.* **8** [C] *weather* : the place where two large areas of air that are of different temperatures come together — **in front 1** : in an area at the front of something ▪ *There is a free seat in front.* **2** : in the leading position in a race or competition ▪ *She's (out) in front, but the other runners are catching up to her.* — **in front of 1** : directly before or ahead of (something or someone) ▪ *There's a tree in front of the house.* ▪ *A deer ran (out) in front of the car.* **2** : in the presence of (someone) ▪ *Don't argue in front of the children.* — **out front** : in the area directly before or ahead of something (such as a building) ▪ *They put a new sign out front.* — **united front** : a group of people or organizations that join together to achieve a shared goal ▪ *presenting a united front against the proposal* — **up front 1** : in or at the most forward position ▪ *We sat up front.* **2** *informal* : before beginning

to do something ▪ *He insisted on being paid up front.* **3** *informal* : in a direct and honest way ▪ *They told me up front that my chances weren't good.*

²**front** *adj, always before a noun* **1** : located at the front ▪ *my front pocket* ▪ *the front entrance/door* ▪ *the front page of the newspaper* ▪ *the hotel's* **front desk** [=the desk where visitors are greeted] **2** *golf* — used to refer to the first 9 holes of an 18-hole golf course ▪ *the front nine* — **front and center** *US* : in the most important position or area ▪ *issues that are front and center in voters' minds*

³**front** *vb* **1** [T/I] : to have the front toward (something) ▪ *The house fronts (on/onto) Main Street.* **2** [T] **a** : to be the lead singer of (a musical group) ▪ *He fronts the band.* **b** *Brit* : to host or present (a radio or TV show) ▪ *He fronts a talk show.*

front·age /ˈfrʌntɪdʒ/ *n* [U] : the part of a building or of the land that a building is on that runs along a river, road, etc. ▪ *We have frontage on Main Street.*

front·al /ˈfrʌntl̩/ *adj, always before a noun* **1** : directed at the front ▪ *a frontal attack* **2** : relating to or showing the front of the human body ▪ *(full) frontal nudity* — **fron·tal·ly** *adv*

front burner *n* — **on the front burner** *chiefly US* : in the position that will receive immediate attention and action ▪ *The President put tax cuts on the front burner.*

front–end loader *n* [C] *chiefly US* : a vehicle with a large scoop in front that is used for digging

fron·tier /ˌfrʌnˈtiɚ, *Brit* ˈfrʌntiə/ *n* [C] **1** : a border between two countries ▪ *the frontier between Canada and the U.S.* **2** : a distant area where few people live ▪ *They settled in the western frontier.* ▪ *frontier life* **3** : the limits of knowledge in a particular field — usually plural ▪ *the frontiers of science* — **fron·tiers·man** /ˌfrʌnˈtiɚzmən, *Brit* ˈfrʌntiɚzmən/ *n, pl* **-men** /-mən/ [C] ▪ *fur traders and frontiersmen*

front line *n* [C] **1** : an area where soldiers are fighting ▪ ¹FRONT 7a ▪ *troops on the front line* **2** : the most important and active position in a job or field of activity ▪ *She's on/at the front line of cancer research.*

front–page /ˈfrʌntˈpeɪdʒ/ *adj, always before a noun* **1** : printed on the front page of a newspaper ▪ *a front-page story* **2** : very important ▪ *front-page news*

front–run·ner /ˈfrʌntˌrʌnɚ/ *n* [C] : the person or thing that is most likely to win a race or competition ▪ *the two presidential front-runners*

front–wheel drive *n* [U] : a system that applies engine power to a vehicle's front wheels ▪ *a car with front-wheel drive*

¹**frost** /ˈfrɑːst/ *n* **1** [U] : a thin layer of ice that forms on the ground, on grass, etc. ▪ *grass/windows covered with frost* **2** [C] : the occurrence of weather in which frost forms ▪ *an early/late frost*

²**frost** *vb* **1** [T/I] : to cover (something) with frost or to become covered with frost ▪ *frosted windows* **2** [T] *chiefly US*

: to cover (something) with frosting •
frost a cake **3** [T] *chiefly US* : to lighten
the top layer of your hair • *She had frosted hair.*

frost·bite /ˈfrɑːstˌbaɪt/ *n* [U] : a condition
in which part of your body (such as your
fingers or toes) freezes or almost freezes
• *He wore gloves to prevent frostbite.*

frost·ing /ˈfrɑːstɪŋ/ *n* [C/U] *chiefly US* : a
sweet, creamy mixture used to cover
cakes • *cupcakes with chocolate frosting*

frosty /ˈfrɑːsti/ *adj* **frost·i·er; -est** **1**
: cold enough to produce frost • *a frosty
night* **2** : covered with frost • *frosty windows* **3** : unfriendly or cold • *a frosty
welcome* — **frost·i·ly** /ˈfrɑːstəli/ *adv* —
frost·i·ness *n* [U]

¹**froth** /ˈfrɑːθ/ *n* [U] : small bubbles that
form in or on a liquid • *froth on the waves*
— **frothy** /ˈfrɑːθi/ *adj* **froth·i·er; -est**

²**froth** *vb* [I] : to produce or form froth • *a
frothing mug of beer* — **froth at the
mouth** **1** : to produce froth from the
mouth because of illness or excitement •
The dog was frothing at the mouth. **2** *informal* : to be very angry • *She was frothing at the mouth with rage.*

¹**frown** /ˈfraʊn/ *n* [C] : a serious facial expression that usually shows anger, displeasure, or concentration • *She was
wearing a frown.*

²**frown** *vb* [I] : to make a frown in anger,
concentration, etc. • *She frowned when I
told her the news.* — **frown on/upon**
[*phrasal vb*] : to disapprove of (something) • *The company frowns on dating
among employees.*

froze *past tense of* ¹FREEZE

frozen *past participle of* ¹FREEZE

fruc·tose /ˈfrʌkˌtoʊs/ *n* [U] : a kind of
sugar that is in fruit juices and honey

fru·gal /ˈfruːgəl/ *adj* : careful about
spending money or using things when
you do not need to • *a frugal shopper* —
fru·gal·i·ty /fruˈgæləti/ *n* [U] — **fru·
gal·ly** /ˈfruːgəli/ *adv*

fruit /ˈfruːt/ *n* **1 a** [C/U] : a usually sweet
food (such as a blueberry or apple) that
grows on a tree or bush • *a bowl/piece of
fruit* • *fruit juice/trees* **b** [C] *technical*
: the part of a plant that has the seeds in
it (such as the pod of a pea or a nut) **2**
[C] : a result or reward that comes from
some action or activity — usually plural
• *the fruits of our labors*

fruit·cake /ˈfruːtˌkeɪk/ *n* [C] **1** : a cake
that contains nuts, fruits, and spices **2**
informal : a foolish, strange, or crazy
person

fruit fly *n* [C] : a very small fly

fruit·ful /ˈfruːtfəl/ *adj* : producing a good
result : very productive • *a fruitful discus-
sion/meeting* — **fruit·ful·ly** *adv* — **fruit·
ful·ness** *n* [U]

fru·i·tion /fruˈɪʃən/ *n* [U] : the state of being real or complete • *His plans have
come to fruition.* [=he has done the
things he planned to do] • *She couldn't
bring her dreams to fruition.* [=she
couldn't achieve her dreams]

fruit·less /ˈfruːtləs/ *adj* : producing no
good results • *a fruitless argument* —
fruit·less·ly *adv*

fruit machine *n* [C] *Brit* : SLOT MA-
CHINE

fruity /ˈfruːti/ *adj* **fruit·i·er; -est** **1** : tasting or smelling like fruit • *a fruity cereal/
wine* **2** *US, informal* : strange or crazy •
She's a little fruity. **3** *Brit, of a voice*
: rich and deep

frumpy /ˈfrʌmpi/ *adj* **frump·i·er; -est**
: dressed in an unattractive way • *a
frumpy housewife*; *also, of clothing* : old
and unattractive • *a frumpy dress*

frus·trate /ˈfrʌˌstreɪt/ *vb* **-trat·ed; -trat·
ing** [T] **1** : to cause (someone) to feel
angry, discouraged, or upset because of
not being able to do something • *We were
frustrated by/at/with all the delays.* **2** : to
prevent (efforts, plans, etc.) from succeeding • *Bureaucratic delays frustrated
our efforts to resolve this problem.* —
frus·trat·ing /ˈfrʌˌstreɪtɪŋ/ *adj* • *The delays were frustrating.* — **frus·trat·ing·ly**
adv — **frus·tra·tion** /ˌfrʌˈstreɪʃən/ *n*
[C/U] • *He shook his head in frustration.* •
The delays were a major frustration. • *He
was angry about the frustration of his
plans.*

¹**fry** /ˈfraɪ/ *vb* **fries; fried; fry·ing** [T/I] : to
cook (food) in fat or oil • *They fried (up)
some chicken.* • *bacon and fried eggs* • *onions frying in a pan* — **fish to fry** see
¹FISH

²**fry** *n, pl* **fries** [C] *US* : FRENCH FRY • *an
order of fries*

fry·er /ˈfraɪɚ/ *n* [C] : a device or deep pan
for frying foods

frying pan *n* [C] : a metal pan that has a
long handle and is used for frying

ft. *abbr* **1** feet; foot **2** fort

FTC *abbr* Federal Trade Commission ✧
The Federal Trade Commission is a part
of the U.S. government that is responsible for preventing unfair or deceptive
business practices.

fuch·sia /ˈfjuːʃə/ *n* [C/U] **1** : a type of
bush with pink, red, purple, or white
flowers **2** : a bright reddish-purple col-
or

fud·dy–dud·dy /ˈfʌdiˌdʌdi/ *n, pl* **-dies**
[C] *informal + disapproving* : a person
with old-fashioned or conservative ideas
and attitudes • *an old fuddy-duddy* •

¹**fudge** /ˈfʌʤ/ *vb* **fudged; fudg·ing** **1**
[T/I] : to fail to deal with (something) in
an open and direct way • *She tried to
fudge the issue.* **2** [T] : to change (something) in order to trick people • *They
fudged the data/facts/figures.*

²**fudge** *n* [U] : a soft, sweet candy • *chocolate fudge* — **hot fudge** *US* : a hot, thick
chocolate sauce • *a hot-fudge sundae*
[=ice-cream topped with hot fudge] —
fudgy /ˈfʌʤi/ *adj* **fudg·i·er; -est** *chiefly
US* • *fudgy brownies*

¹**fu·el** /ˈfjuːwəl/ *n* **1** [C/U] : a material
(such as coal, oil, or gas) that is burned
to produce heat or power • *The truck/fire
needs more fuel.* **2** [U] : something that
gives support or strength to something
(such as an argument or angry feelings) •
*The controversy continues, and these new
accusations will only add fuel to the fire.*

²**fuel** *vb, US* **fueled** *or Brit* **fuelled;** *US*
fuel·ing *or Brit* **fuel·ling** **1** [T/I] : to
take in fuel or supply (something) with

fuel ▪ *The airplane (was) fueled in midair.*
2 [T] **a :** to give support or strength to (something) ▪ *The criticism has only fueled her determination to succeed.* **b :** to provide the necessary conditions for (something) ▪ *Inflation was fueled by high prices.* — **fuel up** [*phrasal vb*] **:** to put fuel into a car, airplane, etc. ▪ *We stopped to fuel up.*

fu·gi·tive /ˈfjuːdʒətɪv/ *n* [C] **:** a person who is running away to avoid being captured ▪ *He's a fugitive from the law.* [=he is trying to escape being arrested by the police] ▪ *a fugitive slave*

¹-ful /fəl/ *adj suffix* **1 :** full of ▪ *prideful* **2 :** characterized by ▪ *peaceful* **3 :** having the qualities of ▪ *masterful* **4 :** tending or likely to ▪ *forgetful*

²-ful /fʊl/ *n suffix* **:** the number or amount that fills or would fill ▪ *a roomful* ▪ *a cupful*

ful·crum /ˈfʊlkrəm, ˈfʌlkrəm/ *n, pl* **ful·crums** *also* **ful·cra** /ˈfʊlkrə, ˈfʌlkrə/ [C] *technical* **:** the support on which a lever moves when it is used to lift something

ful·fill (*US*) *or Brit* **ful·fil** /fʊlˈfɪl/ *vb* **ful·filled; ful·fill·ing** [T] **1 :** to do what is required by (something) ▪ *fulfill a promise/obligation/contract* **2 a :** to succeed in doing or providing (something) ▪ *You haven't fulfilled the requirements to graduate.* **b :** to succeed in achieving (something) ▪ *He fulfilled his childhood wish/dream/ambition to become an astronaut.* **3 :** to make (someone or yourself) happy by achieving or doing something that was wished for ▪ *Her work fulfills her.* ▪ *She feels fulfilled.* ▪ *fulfilling work* — **ful·fill·ment** (*US*) *or Brit* **ful·fil·ment** /fʊlˈfɪlmənt/ *n* [U] ▪ *the fulfillment of a dream* ▪ *She found fulfillment by starting her own business.*

¹full /ˈfʊl/ *adj* **1 :** containing or holding as much or as many as possible ▪ *a full cup/disk/theater* ▪ *a cup full of milk* **2** *always before a noun* **a :** not lacking anything **:** COMPLETE ▪ *a full set of dishes* ▪ *They waited for three full months.* ◇ The phrase *a full* is often used to stress the large size of an amount. ▪ *It was a full three months before they decided.* **b :** not limited in any way ▪ *We need your full attention/cooperation.* ▪ *taking full advantage of an opportunity* ▪ *make a full recovery* ▪ *We're waiting to hear the full story.* **c :** not reduced or shortened ▪ *He paid full price.* ▪ *What is your full name?* **d :** existing or working at the highest or greatest degree ▪ *full power/speed/size/volume* ▪ *a fuller understanding* ▪ *The campaign is going* **full speed/steam ahead**. [=with as much speed and power as possible] **3 a** *always before a noun* **:** including many things ▪ *a full range of interests* **b :** involving many activities ▪ *a full schedule/day* **:** very active ▪ *She lived a full life.* **4 :** having a rounded shape **:** not thin ▪ *a full face/figure* ▪ *full lips* **5 :** having or containing a great number or amount of something ▪ *The room was full of pictures.* ▪ *full of hope* **6 a :** having eaten all that is wanted ▪ *No more for me, thanks. I'm full.* **b** *always before a noun*

: large enough to satisfy hunger ▪ *a full meal* **7 a :** having a large amount of material ▪ *a full skirt* **b :** having a large amount of hair ▪ *a full head of hair* ▪ *a full beard* **8 :** thinking of something all the time ▪ *full of worries* ▪ *She is so full of herself.* [=she thinks about herself more than she should] **9 :** having a strong and pleasing quality ▪ *the food's full flavors* **10** *of the moon* **:** appearing as a bright circle ▪ *The moon is full.* — **full blast** see ¹BLAST — **full count** see ²COUNT — **full of beans** see BEAN — **full of it** *informal* + *sometimes offensive* **:** saying things that are not true ▪ *You're so full of it.* — **have your hands full** see ¹HAND — **to the fullest :** in a very active and energetic way ▪ *She lives life to the fullest.* — **full·ness** *also* **ful·ness** *n* [U] ▪ *The gel added fullness to her hair.*

²full *adv* **1 :** entirely or completely ▪ *a full-grown man* **2 :** directly or squarely ▪ *He kissed her full on the lips.* — **full out :** with as much effort as possible ▪ *She was running full out.* — **full well :** very well ▪ *I knew full well who they were.*

³full *n* — **in full :** entirely or completely ▪ *The bill has been paid in full.*

full·back /ˈfʊlˌbæk/ *n* [C] **1** *American football* **:** a player on offense who lines up behind the line of scrimmage and who runs with the ball and blocks **2 :** a defensive player in soccer, field hockey, etc., who is positioned near the goal

full beam *n* [U] *Brit* **:** HIGH BEAM

full-blood·ed /ˈfʊlˌblʌdəd/ *adj, always before a noun* **:** having parents who are of the same race or origin ▪ *a full-blooded Aborigine/Irishman*

full-blown /ˈfʊlˈbloʊn/ *adj* **:** fully developed ▪ *a full-blown recession* ▪ *full-blown AIDS*

full circle *adv* **:** through a series of changes that lead back to an original position or situation ▪ *The movie star began acting in the theater, and now her career has* **come/gone full circle**. [=she has returned to acting in the theater]

full-court press *n* [C] **1** *basketball* **:** a very aggressive way of playing defense **2** *US* **:** a very aggressive effort or attack usually involving many people ▪ *The bill's supporters are mounting/launching a full-court press.*

full dress *n* [U] **:** special clothes that are worn for a ceremony or for important social occasions ▪ *The officers were in full dress.*

full-fledged /ˈfʊlˈflɛdʒd/ *adj, always before a noun, chiefly US* **1 :** fully developed ▪ *a full-fledged recession/war* **2 :** meeting all the requirements to be something ▪ *a full-fledged member*

full house *n* [C] **1 :** a theater or concert hall that is filled with spectators ▪ *performing before a full house* **2** *poker* **:** a set of cards containing three cards of one value and two cards of another value

full-length /ˈfʊlˈlɛŋθ/ *adj* **1 :** showing all of a person's body from the head to the feet ▪ *a full-length mirror* **2 :** reaching to the end of your legs or arms ▪ *full-*

length dresses/sleeves **3** : having the normal length ▪ *a full-length version of the play*

full marks *n* [*plural*] *Brit* **1** : praise given for an achievement ▪ *Full marks to Mary for her suggestion!* [=Mary should be praised for her suggestion] **2** : the highest score that you can get on a test

full moon *n* [*singular*] : the moon when it appears as a bright circle

full-on /ˈfʊlˌɑːn/ *adj, always before a noun* : not limited in any way : fully developed ▪ *a full-on brawl*

full-out /ˈfʊlˈaʊt/ *adj, always before a noun* **1** : made or done with as much effort as possible : ALL-OUT ▪ *a full-out sprint* **2** : fully developed : ALL-OUT ▪ *a full-out war*

full-scale /ˈfʊlˈskeɪl/ *adj* **1** : having the same size as the original ▪ *a full-scale model/replica* **2** : not limited in any way ▪ *a full-scale war/attack*

full-ser·vice /ˈfʊlˈsɚvəs/ *adj, always before a noun* : offering all the expected services ▪ *a full-service bank/resort*

full-size /ˈfʊlˈsaɪz/ *adj* : FULL-SCALE 1 ▪ *a full-size model*

full stop *n* [*C*] *Brit* : ¹PERIOD 4a

full-time *adj* **1** : working or done during the full number of hours considered normal ▪ *full-time employees* ▪ *a full-time job* **2** : requiring a large amount of your time ▪ *Caring for children is a full-time job.* — **full–time** *adv* ▪ *She worked full-time at the office.*

ful·ly /ˈfʊli/ *adv* **1** : in every way or detail : COMPLETELY ▪ *He fully recovered from the operation.* ▪ *We need to understand the situation more fully.* ▪ *the novel's fully developed characters* **2** : AT LEAST — used to stress the large size of a number or amount ▪ *Fully 90 percent voted for her.*

ful·ly–fledged /ˌfʊliˈfledʒd/ *adj, Brit* : FULL-FLEDGED

ful·mi·nate /ˈfʊlməˌneɪt, ˈfʌlməˌnert/ *vb* **-nat·ed; -nat·ing** [*I*] *formal* : to complain loudly or angrily ▪ *She was fulminating about/over/at the slow service.* — **ful·mi·na·tion** /ˌfʊlməˈneɪʃən, ˌfʌlmə-ˈneɪʃən/ *n* [*C/U*]

ful·some /ˈfʊlsəm/ *adj, formal, often disapproving* : expressing something in a very enthusiastic or emotional way that often seems excessive or insincere ▪ *fulsome praise/apologies* — **ful·some·ly** *adv*

fum·ble /ˈfʌmbəl/ *vb* **fum·bled; fum·bling** **1** [*I*] : to search for something by reaching or touching with your fingers in an awkward or clumsy way ▪ *She fumbled (around) in her pocket for her keys.* ▪ *(figurative) fumbling for an answer* **2** [*T/I*] : to handle something in an awkward or clumsy way ▪ *She fumbled with her keys as she tried to unlock the door.* ▪ *He made a fumbling attempt to explain his behavior.* **3** [*T/I*] *sports* : to fail to catch or hold the ball ▪ *He fumbled (the ball) on the 20-yard line.* — **fumble** *n* [*C*] ▪ *(American football)* He had one fumble during the game. — **fum·bler** *n* [*C*]

¹**fume** /ˈfjuːm/ *n* [*C*] : smoke or gas that smells unpleasant — usually plural ▪ *car exhaust fumes*

²**fume** *vb* **fumed; fum·ing** **1 a** [*I*] : to show or feel anger ▪ *She's still fuming about/over/at not being invited to the party.* **b** [*T*] : to say (something) in an angry way ▪ *"That's not fair," she fumed.* **2** [*T/I*] : to produce or give off (smoke, fumes, etc.) ▪ *The volcano was fuming (thick black smoke).*

fu·mi·gate /ˈfjuːməˌgeɪt/ *vb* **-gat·ed; -gat·ing** [*T*] : to kill germs, insects, etc., in (a room or building) with smoke or gas ▪ *All the rooms had to be fumigated.* — **fu·mi·ga·tion** /ˌfjuːməˈgeɪʃən/ *n* [*C/U*] — **fu·mi·ga·tor** /ˈfjuːməˌgeɪtɚ/ *n* [*C*]

¹**fun** /ˈfʌn/ *n* [*U*] **1** : someone or something that is amusing or enjoyable ▪ *The game was a lot of fun.* [=it was very enjoyable] ▪ *She's fun to be with.* = *It's fun to be with her.* **2** : an enjoyable or amusing time ▪ *We had fun at the movie.* ▪ *a fun-loving couple* [=a couple who love to have fun] **3** : the feeling of being amused or entertained ▪ *He plays cards just for fun.* — **in fun** : said or done in a joking way that is not serious ▪ *Her remark had been all in (good) fun.* — **make fun of** : to laugh at and make jokes about (someone or something) in an unkind way ▪ *The other kids made fun of me.* — **poke fun at** : to make a joke about (someone or something) usually in a friendly way ▪ *I poke fun at my boss, but he's really a good guy.*

²**fun** *adj, sometimes* **fun·ner;** *sometimes* **fun·nest** *informal* : amusing or enjoyable ▪ *a fun time/place/person*

fun and games *n* [*plural*] : activity that is meant to be enjoyable rather than serious — often used in a disapproving way to describe activity that is considered silly and not useful ▪ *There's no time for fun and games.*

¹**func·tion** /ˈfʌŋkʃən/ *n* **1** [*C/U*] : the special purpose or activity for which a thing exists or is used ▪ *The heart's function is to pump blood through the body.* ▪ *bodily functions* ▪ *The design achieves a perfect blend of form and function.* **2** [*C*] : the job or duty of a person ▪ *Her main/primary function is to provide legal advice.* **3** [*C*] : a large ceremony or social event ▪ *school/social functions* **4** [*C*] **a** : something (such as a quality or measurement) that is related to and changes with something else ▪ *Height is a function of age in children.* [=the height of children increases as their age increases] **b** : a result of something else ▪ *His problems are a function of his drinking.*

²**function** *vb* [*I*] **1** : to work or operate ▪ *The machine functions well/properly.* **2** : to have a specified function, role, or purpose : SERVE ▪ *The couch also functions as a bed.* — **func·tion·al** /ˈfʌŋkʃənl/ *adj* ▪ *The camera is still functional.* [=it still works properly] ▪ *a functional* [=practical] *design* — **func·tion·al·i·ty** /ˌfʌŋkʃəˈnæləti/ *n* [*U*] ▪ *the beauty and functionality of the design* — **func·tion·al·ly** *adv*

func·tion·ary /ˈfʌŋkʃəˌneri, Brit ˈfʌŋk-*

ʃənri/ n, pl **-ar·ies** [C] : a person who works for a government or political party ▪ *a party functionary*

¹**fund** /ˈfʌnd/ n 1 [C] : an amount of money that is used for a special purpose ▪ *a fund to aid the poor* ▪ *a pension fund* 2 [plural] : available money ▪ *His funds were getting low.* ▪ *campaign funds*

²**fund** vb [T] : to provide money for (something) ▪ *The program is funded by the state.* = *The program is state-funded.* ▪ *The plan is fully funded.* [=it has all the money it needs] — **fund·ing** n [U] ▪ *The program gets funding from the state.*

¹**fun·da·men·tal** /ˌfʌndəˈmɛntl̩/ adj 1 : forming or relating to the most important part of something : BASIC ▪ *a fundamental difference/right* ▪ *beliefs that are fundamental to our society* 2 : of or relating to the basic structure or function of something ▪ *making fundamental changes in the way we do business*

²**fundamental** n [C] : one of the basic and important parts of something : a fundamental part — usually plural ▪ *the fundamentals of algebra*

fun·da·men·tal·ist /ˌfʌndəˈmɛntlɪst/ n [C] : a person who strictly and literally follows a set of rules and laws ▪ *a religious fundamentalist* — **fun·da·men·tal·ism** /ˌfʌndəˈmɛntəˌlɪzəm/ n [U] — **fundamentalist** adj

fun·da·men·tal·ly /ˌfʌndəˈmɛntl̩i/ adv : at the most basic level ▪ *Our plan is fundamentally different.*

fund–rais·er /ˈfʌndˌreɪzɚ/ n [C] 1 : a person who collects money for a charity, school, etc. 2 : a social event held to collect money for a charity, school, etc. — **fund–rais·ing** /ˈfʌndˌreɪzɪŋ/ n [U] ▪ *political fund-raising*

fu·ner·al /ˈfjuːnərəl/ n [C] : a ceremony held for a dead person ▪ *His funeral will be held on Friday.* ▪ *a funeral procession/service/director* ▪ *a funeral home* = (US) *a funeral parlor* [=a place where dead people are prepared for burial or cremation and where wakes and funerals are held]

funeral director n [C] : a person whose job is to arrange and manage funerals : UNDERTAKER

fu·ne·re·al /fjuːˈnɪrijəl/ adj : very sad and serious ▪ *funereal silence/music*

fungi plural of FUNGUS

fun·gi·cide /ˈfʌndʒəˌsaɪd, ˈfʌŋɡəˌsaɪd/ n [C/U] : a substance that kills fungi

fun·gus /ˈfʌŋɡəs/ n, pl **fun·gi** /ˈfʌnˌdʒaɪ, ˈfʌŋˌɡaɪ/ also **fun·gus·es** [C] : any one of a group of related plants (such as molds, mushrooms, or yeasts) that live on decaying things — **fun·gal** /ˈfʌŋɡəl/ adj ▪ *a fungal infection*

fun house n [C] US : a building in an amusement park with features that amuse and surprise people as they walk or ride through it

funk /ˈfʌŋk/ n 1 [C] chiefly US, informal : a sad or depressed condition — usually singular ▪ *He has been in a funk lately.* ▪ (figurative) *The economy is in a funk.* [=it is doing poorly] 2 [U] : a type of popular music that has a strong beat and combines blues, gospel, soul, etc.

funky /ˈfʌŋki/ adj **funk·i·er; -est** 1

: having the style or feeling of funk music ▪ *a funky beat/song* 2 informal : stylish or appealing in an unusual way ▪ *a funky bar/outfit* 3 US : having a strange or unpleasant odor ▪ *These shoes smell a little funky.*

¹**fun·nel** /ˈfʌnl̩/ n [C] 1 : a device that is shaped like a hollow cone and that is used for pouring something into a narrow opening 2 : something that is shaped like a funnel ▪ *the funnel cloud of a tornado* 3 : a large pipe on a ship through which smoke or steam comes out

²**funnel** vb, US **-neled** or Brit **-nelled**; US **-nel·ing** or Brit **-nel·ling** 1 [T/I] : to pass through a funnel or a narrow opening ▪ *Smoke funneled up the chimney.* ▪ *The crowd funneled through the doors.* 2 [T] : to send (something) to someone or something in usually an indirect or secret way ▪ *funneling money into a campaign*

fun·nies /ˈfʌniz/ n — **the funnies** US, informal : the comic strips in a newspaper ▪ *Did you read the funnies today?*

¹**fun·ny** /ˈfʌni/ adj **fun·ni·er; -est** 1 : causing laughter ▪ *He's a very funny guy.* ▪ *What's so funny?* ▪ *a funny story/movie* 2 informal : odd or strange ▪ *a funny-looking hat* ▪ *My car started making a funny noise.* ▪ *"I can't find my keys." "That's funny—they were here a minute ago."* ▪ *It's funny you should say that—I was just thinking the same thing myself.* 3 not before a noun, informal : somewhat ill ▪ *My stomach feels funny.* ▪ *I feel a little funny.* 4 informal : meant to deceive someone ▪ *He told the prisoner not to try anything funny.* ▪ *We won't put up with any funny business.* [=dishonest activity] — **fun·ni·ly** /ˈfʌnl̩i/ adv

²**funny** adv, informal : in an odd or strange way ▪ *He's been acting funny lately.*

funny bone n [C] : a place at the back of your elbow where you feel a painful tingling sensation when it is hit ▪ (figurative) *The movie really tickled my funny bone.* [=it was amusing to me]

fur /ˈfɚ/ n 1 [U] : the hairy coat of an animal ▪ *a rabbit's soft fur* 2 [C/U] : the fur of an animal used for clothing ▪ *a fur coat* b [U] : a material that looks and feels like the fur of an animal ▪ *a teddy bear with soft fur* — **furred** /ˈfɚd/ adj

fu·ri·ous /ˈfjʊrijəs/ adj 1 : very angry ▪ *I am furious with/at them.* 2 a : very powerful or violent ▪ *a furious storm* b : very active or fast ▪ *a furious pace* — **fast and furious** see ¹FAST — **fu·ri·ous·ly** adv ▪ *working furiously* [=very quickly]

furl /ˈfɚl/ vb [T] : to wrap or roll (something) close to or around something ▪ *They furled the sails.*

fur·lough /ˈfɚˌloʊ/ n [C] 1 : a period of time when a soldier is allowed to leave his or her station ▪ *a four-week furlough* 2 US : a period of time when an employee is told not to come to work and is not paid ▪ *a one-day furlough for federal employees* 3 US : a period of time when a prisoner is allowed to leave prison — **on furlough** : having a furlough ▪ *workers/*

prisoners/soldiers on furlough — **fur-lough** vb [T] • **furloughing** [=granting furloughs to] soldiers/inmates

fur·nace /ˈfɚnəs/ n [C] : an enclosed container in which heat is produced: such as **a** : one for melting metals **b** chiefly US : one for heating a building or apartment

fur·nish /ˈfɚnɪʃ/ vb [T] **1** : to provide (a room or building) with furniture • a room furnished with antiques • a beautifully furnished inn **2** : PROVIDE 1 • We'll furnish the food for the party. • We were furnished with all the necessary information/materials.

fur·nish·ings /ˈfɚnɪʃɪŋz/ n [plural] : furniture, curtains, rugs, and decorations for a room or building • the room's furnishings

fur·ni·ture /ˈfɚnɪʧɚ/ n [U] : chairs, tables, beds, etc., that make a room ready for use • office furniture • a large piece of furniture

fu·ror (US) /ˈfjʊɚˌoɚ, ˈfjʊrɚ/ also chiefly Brit **fu·rore** /ˈfjʊɚˌoɚ, Brit fjuˈrɔːri/ n [singular] : a situation in which many people are very angry and upset • The senator resigned amid a public furor.

fur·ri·er /ˈfɚrijɚ/ n [C] : a person who sells or makes fur clothing

fur·row /ˈfɚroʊ/ n [C] **1** : a long and narrow cut in the ground • plowing furrows in a field **2** : a narrow line or wrinkle in the skin of a person's face • He has deep furrows in his brow. — **furrow** vb [T/I] • plows furrowing the fields • His forehead furrows when he frowns. • a furrowed field/forehead

fur·ry /ˈfɚri/ adj **fur·ri·er; -est 1** : covered with fur • furry animals **2** : covered with something that looks or feels like fur • furry slippers

¹**fur·ther** /ˈfɚðɚ/ adv **1** : to or at a more distant place or time : FARTHER • We couldn't go any further. [=we couldn't go beyond that point] **2** : to a greater degree or extent • I will look into this matter further. • They wanted to question me further. • She says that he is arrogant, but nothing could be further from the truth. [=that is a completely untrue thing to say] • They expect me to retire, but nothing could be further from my mind. [=I have no intention of retiring] **3** formal : in addition to what has been said : FURTHERMORE • I had enough money to invest. I realized, further, that the risk was small.

²**further** adj : ADDITIONAL, MORE • Further study/research/information is needed. • I have nothing further to say. • We will be closed until further notice. [=until some time in the future which has not yet been decided or stated]

³**further** vb [T] : to cause (something) to become more successful or advanced • furthering the cause • What can I do to further my career? — **fur·ther·ance** /ˈfɚðərəns/ n [U] formal • the furtherance of your career

further education n [U] Brit : CONTINUING EDUCATION

fur·ther·more /ˈfɚðɚˌmoɚ/ adv, formal : in addition to what has been said

: MOREOVER • She always arrives on time. Her work, furthermore, is excellent.

¹**furth·est** /ˈfɚðəst/ adv **1** : to or at the greatest distance in space or time : FARTHEST • Who can run (the) furthest in five minutes? **2** : to the most advanced point : FARTHEST • She went the furthest [=she made the greatest effort] to research the issue. **3** : by the greatest degree or extent : MOST • Of all his paintings, this one is the furthest removed from reality.

²**furthest** adj, always before a noun : most distant in space or time : FARTHEST • the furthest extremes of the political spectrum • Retiring is the furthest thing from my mind. [=I am not thinking at all about retiring]

fur·tive /ˈfɚtɪv/ adj : done in a quiet and secret way to avoid being noticed • a furtive glance/smile — **fur·tive·ly** adv — **fur·tive·ness** n [U]

fu·ry /ˈfjuri/ n **1** [U, singular] : violent anger : RAGE • I could see the fury in her eyes. • Nothing could contain his fury. • She is in a fury. [=she is very angry] • He flew into a fury. [=he became very angry] **2** [U] : wild and dangerous force • The hurricane unleashed its fury.

¹**fuse** /ˈfjuːz/ n [C] **1** : a device that causes electricity to stop flowing when a current becomes too strong • The lights went out when the fuse blew. • (figurative, informal) She blew a fuse [=became very angry] when I came home late. • a fuse box [=a box that contains the fuses for the electrical system in a building] **2** : a string that is connected to a bomb, firecracker, etc., and that is set on fire to cause the device to explode • light a fuse • (figurative, informal) She has a short fuse. [=becomes angry very quickly]

²**fuse** vb **fused; fus·ing** [T/I] **1** : to join or become joined because of heat or a chemical reaction • She fused the wires (together). **2** : to join or combine (different things) together • His songs fuse jazz and blues elements. • Dreams fuse with reality in her latest film.

fu·se·lage /ˈfjuːsəˌlɑːʒ, Brit ˈfjuːzəˌlɑːʒ/ n [C] : the part of an airplane that holds the crew, passengers, and cargo

fu·sil·lade /ˈfjuːsəˌlɑːd, Brit ˌfjuːzəˈleɪd/ n [singular] : a large number of shots that are fired very quickly • a fusillade of bullets • (figurative) a fusillade of obscenities

fu·sion /ˈfjuːʒn/ n **1** [C/U] : a combination or mixture of things • a fusion of different methods/styles • the fusion of news and entertainment **2** [U] physics : a process in which the nuclei of atoms are joined • a fusion reactor/reaction — called also nuclear fusion **3** [U] : a type of popular music that combines different styles (such as jazz and rock) **4** [U] : food prepared by combining methods and ingredients from different areas of the world — called also fusion cuisine

¹**fuss** /ˈfʌs/ n [U, singular] **1** : activity or excitement that is unusual and that often is not wanted or necessary • What is all the fuss about? • We'd love to come to dinner, but please don't make a fuss. [=don't do a lot of extra work] • (US) They made a fuss over the baby. = (Brit) They made a

fuss of the baby. [=they paid a lot of excited attention to the baby] **2** : an expression of anger or complaint ▪ *She accepted the task without any fuss.* [=she did not complain about the task] ▪ *I don't want to make a fuss, but this soup is cold.*

²**fuss** *vb* [*I*] **1** : to be or become upset or worried ▪ (*Brit*) *I'm not fussed about which restaurant we eat at.* **2** *US* : to show that you are annoyed or unhappy ▪ *The baby fussed all day.* ▪ *Stop fussing and get to work!* — **fuss over** [*phrasal vb*] : to pay a lot of attention to (someone or something) in a nervous or excited way ▪ *They fussed over the baby.* ▪ *Please don't fuss over me.* — **fuss with** [*phrasal vb*] : to move or handle (something) in a nervous or uncertain way ▪ *Stop fussing with your hair.*

fussy /ˈfʌsi/ *adj* **fuss·i·er; -est 1** : very careful about choosing or accepting things ; hard to please ▪ *a fussy shopper/eater* ▪ *I'm not fussy about where we eat.* **2** *US* : often upset or unhappy ▪ *a fussy baby* **3** *disapproving* : too fancy or complicated ▪ *fussy dresses/furniture* — **fuss·i·ly** /ˈfʌsəli/ *adv* — **fuss·i·ness** *n* [*U*]

fus·ty /ˈfʌsti/ *adj* **fus·ti·er; -est 1** : full of dust and unpleasant smells : MUSTY ▪ *a trunk full of fusty clothing* **2** : very old-fashioned ▪ *fusty ideas about art*

fu·tile /ˈfjuːtl̩, ˈfjuːˌtajəl/ *adj* : having no result or effect : pointless or useless ▪ *Our efforts were futile.* ▪ *They made a futile attempt to control the flooding.* — **fu·tile·ly** *adv* — **fu·til·i·ty** /fjuˈtɪləti/ *n* [*U*] ▪ *an exercise in futility*

fu·ton /ˈfuːˌtɑːn/ *n* [*C*] : a mattress that is used on the floor or in a frame as a bed, couch, or chair

¹**fu·ture** /ˈfjuːtʃɚ/ *n* **1 a** [*U*] : the period of time that will come after the present time ▪ *We're making plans for the future.* ▪ (*US*) *I will do better in the future.* = (*Brit*) *I will do better in future.* ▪ *Changes are expected in the not too distant future.* [=soon] **b the future** : the events that will happen after the present time ▪ *trying to predict the future* **2** [*C*] : the condition or situation of someone or something in the time that will come ▪ *He has a promising future (ahead of him).* ▪ *The company faces an uncertain future.* ▪ *There is no future for you* [=there is no chance you will succeed] *in this business.* **3 the future** *grammar* : FUTURE TENSE **4** [*plural*] *finance* : goods or shares that

are bought at prices which are agreed to now but that are delivered at a later time ▪ *trading in oil futures* — **mortgage the/your future** see ²MORTGAGE

²**future** *adj*, *always before a noun* **1** : coming after the present time ▪ *future events/generations* ▪ *Keep these instructions for future reference.* [=so that you can use them when you need to in the future] **2** — used to say what someone or something will be ▪ *his future wife* [=the woman who will become his wife]

future perfect *n* — **the future perfect** *grammar* : a verb tense that is used to refer to an action that will be completed by a specified time in the future ✧ The *future perfect* in English is formed with "will have" and "shall have," as in "They will have left by the time we arrive."

future tense *n* [*C*] *grammar* : a verb tense that is used to refer to the future

fu·tur·ist /ˈfjuːtʃərɪst/ *n* [*C*] : a person who tries to tell what the future will be like

fu·tur·is·tic /ˌfjuːtʃəˈrɪstɪk/ *adj* **1** : very modern ▪ *futuristic furniture/designs* **2 a** : relating to or telling about events in the future ▪ *a futuristic novel* **b** : existing in the future ▪ *The film depicts a futuristic society.*

fuzz /ˈfʌz/ *n* **1** [*U*] : short, soft hairs ▪ *the fuzz on a peach* **2 the fuzz** *old-fashioned slang* : the police ▪ *He was arrested by the fuzz.*

fuzzy /ˈfʌzi/ *adj* **fuzz·i·er; -est 1** : covered with short, soft hairs, fur, etc. ▪ *a fuzzy sweater/blanket* ▪ *fuzzy leaves* **2 a** : not clear : not sharp or distinct ▪ *a fuzzy* [=blurry] *photo* ▪ *The line between our areas of responsibility is fuzzy.* **b** : not clear in thought ▪ *His reasoning is a little fuzzy.* **3** *US, informal* : pleasant or comforting ▪ *The movie leaves you with a warm, fuzzy feeling.* ▪ *a warm and fuzzy personality* — **fuzz·i·ly** /ˈfʌzəli/ *adv* — **fuzz·i·ness** *n* [*U*]

fuzzy logic *n* [*U*] *technical* : a system of logic in which statements do not have to be entirely true or false

fwd. *abbr* forward

-fy /faɪ/ *vb suffix* : cause to become ▪ *beautify* ▪ *purify*

FYI *abbr* for your information — used when you are giving someone interesting or useful information in a note, an e-mail, etc. ▪ *FYI, the meeting has been canceled.*

G

g *or* **G** /ˈdʒiː/ *n, pl* **g's** *or* **gs** *or* **G's** *or* **Gs**
1 [C/U] : the seventh letter of the English alphabet ▪ *words that end in (a) g* **2** [C/U] : a musical note or key referred to by the letter G ▪ *play/sing (a) G* ▪ *a song in the key of G* **3** [C] : the force of gravity at the Earth's surface ▪ *three g's* [=an amount of force equal to three times the normal force of gravity]

g *abbr* gram

G — used as a special mark to indicate that people of all ages may see a particular movie in a movie theater ▪ *The movie is rated G.*

GA *abbr* Georgia

gab /ˈgæb/ *vb* **gabbed; gab·bing** [*I*] *informal* : to talk a lot in an informal way usually about things that are not important or serious ▪ *They were gabbing (away) on the phone.* — **gab** *n* [U] ▪ *(US) a salesman with the gift of gab* (*Brit*) *a salesman with the gift of the gab* [=a salesman who is good at talking to people] — **gab·by** /ˈgæbi/ *adj* **gab·bi·er; -est** *informal* ▪ *a gabby talk show host*

ga·ble /ˈgeɪbəl/ *n* [C] : a section of a building's outside wall that is shaped like a triangle and that is formed by two sections of the roof sloping down — **gabled** /ˈgeɪbəld/ *adj* ▪ *a gabled house/roof*

gad·get /ˈgædʒət/ *n* [C] : a small, useful device ▪ *cell phones, pagers, and other gadgets* — **gad·get·ry** /ˈgædʒətri/ *n* [U] ▪ *a kitchen equipped with the latest gadgetry* [=gadgets]

gaffe /ˈgæf/ *n* [C] : a mistake made in a social situation ▪ *a verbal/diplomatic gaffe*

¹**gag** /ˈgæg/ *vb* **gagged; gag·ging** **1** [*T*] : to put something (such as a piece of cloth) into or over a person's mouth in order to prevent that person from speaking, calling for help, etc. ▪ *The hostages were bound and gagged.* [=their hands and feet were tied and their mouths were gagged] ▪ (*figurative*) *The government is trying to gag the press.* **2** [*I*] : to vomit or feel as if you are about to vomit ▪ *The smell (almost) made me gag.* ▪ *gagging on the fumes*

²**gag** *n* [C] **1** : something said or done to make people laugh ▪ JOKE ▪ *a typical sitcom gag* ▪ *The movie is full of sight gags.* [=jokes that do not involve speaking] **2** : something (such as a piece of cloth) that is put into or over someone's mouth in order to prevent speech ▪ (*figurative*) *The government has put a gag on the press.*

ga·ga /ˈgɑːˌgɑː/ *adj, informal* : extremely enthusiastic about or interested in something or someone ▪ *He was gaga over/about golf.* ▪ *She's gone gaga over her boss's nephew.*

gage *variant spelling of* GAUGE

gag·gle /ˈgægəl/ *n* [C] **1** : a group of geese **2** : a group of people ▪ *a gaggle of photographers/tourists*

gag order *n* [C] *chiefly US, law* : an order by a judge or court saying that the people involved in a legal case cannot talk about the case or anything related to it in public — called also (*Brit*) **gagging order**

gai·ety /ˈgeɪjəti/ *n* [U] *old-fashioned* : a happy and lively quality ▪ *the gaiety of the carnival*

gai·ly /ˈgeɪli/ *adv, old-fashioned* **1** : in a happy and lively way ▪ *chatting/playing/laughing gaily* **2** : in a bright and colorful way ▪ *gaily dressed crowds*

¹**gain** /ˈgeɪn/ *vb* **1** [T] **a** : to get (something wanted or valued) ▪ *gain an advantage* ▪ *gaining control of/over the territory* ▪ *She's gaining confidence in herself.* [=becoming more confident] **b** : to win (something) in a competition, battle, etc. ▪ *gain a victory* **c** : to gradually get (something) or more of (something) as time passes ▪ *gain weight* ▪ *The movement is gaining strength.* **2** [T] : to cause (someone) to have (something) ▪ *Her work gained her their respect.* [=she has gained their respect through her work] **3** [*T/I*] **a** : to increase in (something) ▪ *Some stocks are gaining (in) value.* **b** : to increase in value by (a specified amount) or when compared to something else ▪ *The stocks gained three percent last month.* ▪ *The dollar gained against the pound last month.* **4** [T] *American football* : to move the ball (a specified distance) down the field ▪ *They gained five yards on the last play.* — **gain ground** *see* ¹GROUND — **gain on** [*phrasal vb*] : to come nearer to (someone or something that is ahead of you in a race or competition) ▪ *The other runners were gaining on her.* — **gain time** : to cause something to be delayed so that more time is available to do what is needed ▪ *His lawyers are trying to gain time to prepare their defense.* — **gain·er** *n* [C]

²**gain** *n* **1** [C] : something wanted or valued that is gotten ▪ *ill-gotten gains* [=money and other valuable things gotten through dishonest methods]; *especially* : money gotten through some activity or process ▪ *financial/stock-market gains* **2** [U] : something that is helpful ▪ *He acted only for his own personal/political gain.* [=he acted only to benefit himself] **3** [C/U] : an increase in amount, size, or number ▪ *They hope to make big gains in Congress in the coming election.* ▪ *The medication can cause weight gain.* **4** [C] *American football* : the distance the ball is moved down the field during a play ▪ *a five-yard gain*

gain·ful /ˈgeɪnfəl/ *adj* : paying money ▪ *gainful employment* — **gain·ful·ly** *adv*

gain·say /ˌgeɪnˈseɪ/ *vb* **-says** /-ˈseɪz, -sɛz/; **-said** /-ˈseɪd, -sɛd/; **-say·ing** [T] *formal* : to show or say that (something) is not true ▪ *There is no gainsaying such* *evidence.* [=the truth of such evidence cannot be denied]

gait /'geɪt/ *n* [C] : a particular way of walking ▪ *an easy/unsteady/awkward gait*

gal /'gæl/ *n* [C] *chiefly US, informal* : a girl or woman ▪ *She's a fun gal.*

gal. *abbr* gallon

ga·la /'geɪlə, *Brit* 'gɑːlə/ *n* [C] : a public party or celebration ▪ *a grand gala celebrating the town's centennial* ▪ *a gala event*

gal·axy /'gæləksi/ *n, pl* **-ax·ies** 1 *astronomy* **a** [C] : any one of the very large groups of stars that make up the universe ▪ *a giant/spiral galaxy* **b** *the Galaxy* : the galaxy in which we live : MILKY WAY 2 [C] : a large group of important or well-known people or things ▪ *a galaxy of artists/celebrities* — **ga·lac·tic** /gə'læktɪk/ *adj* : galactic objects

gale /'geɪl/ *n* [C] 1 : a very strong wind ▪ *a fierce gale* ▪ *gale-force winds* 2 : a sudden occurrence of laughter, tears, etc. ▪ *The audience erupted in gales of laughter.*

¹**gall** /'gɑːl/ *n* [U] : extreme confidence expressed in a way that is impolite ▪ *He had the gall that he could replace me!*

²**gall** *vb* [T] : to make (someone) feel annoyed or angry ▪ *It galls me that he said that.* — **gall·ing** /'gɑːlɪŋ/ *adj* ▪ *a galling defeat*

gal·lant *adj* /'gælənt/ 1 : showing courage : very brave ▪ *a gallant knight* ▪ *a gallant attempt* /'gælənt/ 2 : large and impressive ▪ *a gallant ship* 3 /gə'lænt, gə-'lɑːnt/ : having or showing politeness and respect for women ▪ *He greeted her with a gallant bow.* — **gal·lant·ly** *adv* — **gal·lant·ry** /'gæləntri/ *n* [U] ▪ *a medal for gallantry* [=courage, heroism] *in battle* ▪ *She was charmed by his old-fashioned gallantry.*

gall·blad·der /'gɑːlˌblædɚ/ *n* [C] *medical* : the organ in the body in which bile from the liver is stored

gal·lery /'gæləri/ *n, pl* **-ler·ies** [C] 1 **a** : a room or building in which people look at paintings, sculptures, etc. ▪ *an art gallery* **b** : a business that sells paintings, sculptures, etc. 2 : a group or collection of people or things ▪ *a gallery of weird characters* 3 **a** : the highest section of seats in a theater or the people sitting in those seats **b** : the people who watch a tennis or golf match — **play to the gallery** : to do things that you think will be popular among many people instead of doing what you think is right ▪ *a governor who refuses to play to the gallery*

gal·ley /'gæli/ *n, pl* **-leys** [C] 1 : the kitchen of a ship or airplane 2 : a long, low ship that was moved by oars and sails and that was used in ancient times by the Egyptians, Greeks, and others ▪ *a slave galley* [=a galley rowed by slaves]

gal·li·vant /'gæləˌvænt/ *vb* [U] *somewhat informal + often disapproving* : to go or travel to many different places for pleasure ▪ *gallivanting all over town*

gal·lon /'gælən/ *n* [C] 1 *US* : a unit of liquid measurement equal to four U.S. quarts or 3.785 liters 2 *Brit* : a unit of liquid measurement equal to four British

quarts or 4.546 liters

gal·lop /'gæləp/ *vb* 1 **a** [I] *of a horse or similar animal* : to run very fast and in such a way that all four feet leave the ground at the same time ▪ *The horse galloped toward us.* **b** [T/I] : to ride on a galloping horse ▪ *She galloped (her horse) toward us.* 2 [I] : to run or move quickly ▪ *I galloped out the door.* ▪ *The program gallops through early American history.* — **gallop** *n* [C/U] ▪ *The horse took off at a/full gallop.*

gal·lows /'gælouz/ *n* [C] : a structure on which a criminal who has been sentenced to death is killed by being hanged ▪ *She was sent to the gallows.* [=sentenced to death]

gallows humor *n* [U] : humor that relates to very serious or frightening things (such as death and illness)

gall·stone /'gɑːlˌstoʊn/ *n* [C] *medical* : a hard object like a small stone that sometimes forms in the gallbladder and that can cause great pain

ga·lore /gə'loɚ/ *adj, always after a noun, informal* : in large numbers or amounts ▪ *bargains galore* [=lots of bargains]

ga·losh·es /gə'lɑːʃəz/ *n* [*plural*] 1 *old-fashioned* : tall rubber shoes that are worn over other shoes in wet weather to keep your feet dry 2 : rubber boots worn in wet weather to keep the feet dry

gal·va·nize *also Brit* **gal·va·nise** /'gælvəˌnaɪz/ *vb* **-nized; -niz·ing** [T] 1 **a** : to cause (people) to become so excited or concerned about an issue, idea, etc., that they want to do something about it ▪ *an issue that galvanized the public (to take action)* **b** : to cause (a force that is capable of causing change) to become active ▪ *trying to galvanize public opinion against the proposed law* 2 *technical* : to cover (steel or iron) with a layer of zinc to prevent it from rusting — **galvanized** *adj* ▪ *galvanized nails/steel*

gam·bit /'gæmbət/ *n* [C] : something done or said in order to gain an advantage or to produce a desired result ▪ *their opening gambit* [=their first move] *in the negotiations*

¹**gam·ble** /'gæmbəl/ *vb* **gam·bled; gam·bling** 1 [I] : to play a game in which you can win or lose money or possessions : to bet money or other valuable things ▪ *I like to gamble (on football).* 2 [T] : to risk losing (an amount of money) in a game or bet ▪ *He would often gamble hundreds of dollars on a hand of poker.* ▪ *(figurative) She gambled* [=risked] *everything to start the business.* 3 [T/I] : to do something that could have the good result that you want or a bad result that you cannot control ▪ *The mayor is gambling that the new policies will help the city.* ▪ *They're willing to gamble on the new treatment.* — **gamble away** [*phrasal vb*] **gamble away (something)** or **gamble (something) away** : to lose (something, such as money) by gambling ▪ *She gambled away her inheritance.* — **gam·bler** /'gæmblɚ/ *n* [C]

²**gamble** *n* [C] : something that could produce a desired result or a bad or unpleasant result : RISK ▪ *Starting a business right*

now is too much of a *gamble*. ▪ *She took a gamble on the new treatment.* [=tried the new treatment]

gam·bling *n* [*U*] : the activity of risking money in a game or bet ▪ *illegal gambling* ▪ *a gambling casino/resort/problem*

¹**game** /ˈgeɪm/ *n* **1** [*C*] **a** : a physical or mental activity or contest that has rules and that people do for pleasure ▪ *a card/computer game* ▪ *Baseball is my favorite game.* [=sport] **b** : a particular occurrence of a game ▪ *I won/lost the game.* **c** : one of the games that are part of a larger contest (such as a tennis match) ▪ *She won the first two games, but lost the match.* **2** [*plural*] **a** : playful activities ▪ *children playing at their games* **b** or **Games** : an organized series of athletic contests ▪ *the 23rd Winter (Olympic) Games* **3** a [*singular*] : the way someone plays in a sport ▪ *They play a rough/strong game.* ▪ *She needs to improve her game if she wants to win.* **b** [*C*] : a skill that is used in playing a particular game or sport ▪ *a football team with a strong running/passing game* **4** [*C*] : an activity, business, etc., that is being compared to a game or contest ▪ *the game of love/life* ▪ *the newspaper game* [=profession] **5** [*C*] : something that is not meant to be taken seriously ▪ *Politics for her is just a game.* **6** [*C*] : a usually dishonest or unfair plan for doing something ▪ *The game is up.* [=the plan has been discovered and will not be allowed to continue] **7** [*U*] : animals that are hunted ▪ *wild/small game* ▪ *a game preserve* [=an area of land in which hunting and fishing are carefully controlled] ▪ (*figurative*) *The police aren't interested in small-time crooks; they're after much bigger game.* — **ahead of the game** : in a position or situation in which you are likely to succeed, win, etc. ▪ *The company has stayed ahead of the game.* — **early/late in the game** : at an early/late time in a game or sport ▪ *She scored a goal early in the game.* [=near the beginning of the game] ▪ (*figurative*) *It's too late in the game* [=it's too late] *to change the date of the meeting.* — **got game** ✧ In informal U.S. English, someone who has *got game* is very good at playing a particular game or sport, such as basketball. — **head/mind games** : actions that are meant to confuse or upset someone in order to get an advantage — **on/off your game** ✧ If you are *on your game*, you are playing a sport or game well; if you are *off your game*, you are playing poorly. — **play games** **1** : to treat someone in a dishonest or unfair way in order to get an advantage ▪ *Stop playing games (with me) and tell me what really happened!* **2** : to behave in a way that is not serious ▪ *Let's stop playing games and get down to business.* — **the only game in town** : the only available, desirable, or valuable thing ▪ *Our company is no longer the only game in town.* [=we now have competition]

²**game** *adj* **gam·er; -est 1** : willing or ready to do something ▪ *They were game for anything.* = *They were game to try any-*

thing. **2** : showing a willingness to work hard, keep trying, etc. ▪ *a game effort* — **game·ly** *adv*

game·keep·er /ˈgeɪmˌkiːpɚ/ *n* [*C*] : a person who is in charge of the breeding and protection of animals that are hunted on private land

game plan *n* [*C*] **1** : a plan for playing a game (such as American football or soccer) **2** : a plan for doing or achieving something ▪ *developing a game plan to lure businesses to the region*

gam·er /ˈgeɪmɚ/ *n* [*C*] *US* : a person who plays games and especially video or computer games

game show *n* [*C*] : a television program in which people try to win prizes in a game

games·man·ship /ˈgeɪmzmənˌʃɪp/ *n* [*U*] *usually disapproving* **1** : the practice of winning a game or contest by doing things that seem unfair but that are not actually against the rules **2** : the clever use of skills or tricks to succeed or do something ▪ *corporate/political gamesmanship*

gamey *variant spelling of* GAMY

gam·ing /ˈgeɪmɪŋ/ *n* [*U*] **1** : the activity of playing computer games ▪ *He does a lot of gaming online.* **2** : the act or activity of gambling ▪ *casino gaming*

gamma rays *n* [*plural*] : powerful invisible rays that are sent out from some radioactive substances — called also *gamma radiation*

gam·ut /ˈgæmət/ *n* [*singular*] : a range or series of related things ▪ *the full gamut of human emotions* ▪ *Her emotions ran the gamut from joy to despair.* [=she felt emotions ranging from joy to despair]

gamy *or* **gam·ey** /ˈgeɪmi/ *adj* **gam·i·er; -est** : having the flavor of meat from wild animals especially when it is slightly spoiled ▪ *The meat tasted gamy.*

gan·der /ˈgændɚ/ *n* **1** [*C*] : a male goose **2** [*singular*] : a look at something ▪ *I'll take/have a gander at your new car.* — **what's good for the goose is good for the gander** *see* ¹GOOSE

¹**gang** /ˈgæŋ/ *n* [*C*] **1** : a group of criminals ▪ *a gang of thieves* **2** : a group of young people who do illegal things together and who often fight against other gangs ▪ *He is in a gang.* ▪ *gang violence* **3** *informal* : a group of people who are friends and who do things together ▪ *the gang at the office*

²**gang** *vb* — **gang up** [*phrasal vb*] *informal* : to form a group to attack, oppose, or criticize someone ▪ *They all ganged up on/against him.*

gang·bust·ers /ˈgæŋˌbʌstɚz/ *n* — **like gangbusters** *US, informal* **1** : very well or successfully ▪ *The team has been coming on like gangbusters.* [=has been doing very well] **2** : very quickly ▪ *The company has been growing like gangbusters.*

gang·land /ˈgæŋˌlænd/ *n* [*singular*] : the violent world of organized crime ▪ *a gangland shooting*

gan·gling /ˈgæŋglɪŋ/ *adj* : GANGLY ▪ *a gangling teenager*

gan·gly /ˈgæŋgli/ *adj* **gan·gli·er; -est 1**

: tall, thin, and awkward • *a gangly teen-ager* **2** : long and thin • *gangly legs*

gang·plank /'gæŋ,plæŋk/ n [C] : a board or other structure that people walk on to get on or off a ship

gan·grene /'gæŋ,griːn/ n [U] *medical* : the decay of flesh that occurs in a part of the body that no longer has blood flowing to it — **gan·gre·nous** /'gæŋgrənəs/ adj • *a gangrenous foot*

gang·sta rap /'gæŋstə-/ n [U] : a type of rap music with lyrics about the violence and drug use of street gangs — **gangsta rapper** n [C]

gang·ster /'gæŋstə/ n [C] : a member of a group of violent criminals

gang·way /'gæŋ,weɪ/ n **1** [C] : GANG-PLANK **2** — used to tell people in a crowd to move aside so that someone can pass through • *"Gangway!" the man shouted.*

gantlet *variant spelling of* GAUNTLET 1

gaol, gaol·break, gaol·er *Brit spellings of* JAIL, JAILBREAK, JAILER

gap /'gæp/ n [C] **1 a** : a space between two people or things • *She had a gap between her two front teeth.* • *the gap between the lead runner and the other racers* **b** : a hole or space where something is missing • *a gap in the fence* **2** : a missing part • *gaps in his story/knowledge* **3** : a part or period in which nothing happens • *She waited for a gap in the conversation.* **4** : a difference between two people, groups, or things • *a gap between the rich and the poor* • *We hope to **close/bridge the gap** between well-funded suburban schools and the struggling schools in poor-er communities.* — see also GENERA-TION GAP

gape /'geɪp/ vb **gaped; gap·ing** [I] **1** : to open widely • *Her mouth gaped (open).* **2** : to look at someone or some-thing with your mouth open in surprise or wonder • *They gaped at the celebrity.*

gap·ing /'geɪpɪŋ/ adj : wide open : very large • *a gaping wound/hole*

¹ga·rage /gə'rɑːʒ, *Brit* 'gærɪʤ/ n [C] **1** : a building or part of a building in which a car, truck, etc., is kept • *a two-car garage* **2** : a shop where vehicles are repaired • *I brought my car to the garage.*

²garage vb **-raged; -rag·ing** [T] : to put or keep (a car, truck, etc.) in a garage • *He garaged the car for the winter.*

garage sale n [C] *chiefly US* : a sale of used furniture, clothing, etc., held at the seller's home — called also (*US*) *tag sale*, (*US*) *yard sale*

garb /'gɑːb/ n [U] : a particular style or type of clothing • *dressed in ceremonial garb* — **garb** vb [T] • *He was garbed* [=*dressed*] *in a black robe.*

gar·bage /'gɑːbɪʤ/ n [U] **1** *chiefly US* : TRASH • *The park was littered with gar-bage.* — often used to refer specifically to food waste that is being thrown out • *the smell of rotting garbage* **2** *informal* : something that is worthless, unimpor-tant, or of poor quality • *watching gar-bage on TV* **3** *informal* : NONSENSE • *That's a bunch/load of garbage.*

garbage can n [C] *US* : a container for garbage — called also (*US*) *garbage pail*

garbage disposal n [C] *US* : a device in a kitchen sink that grinds up food waste so it can be washed down the drain

gar·bage·man /'gɑːbɪʤ,mæn/ n, pl **-men** [C] *US* : a person whose job is to collect and remove garbage

gar·ble /'gɑːbəl/ vb **gar·bled; gar·bling** [T] : to cause (a word, name, message, etc.) to be unclear or confusing • *He gar-bled her name.* [=he said her name incor-rectly] • *a garbled phone message*

¹gar·den /'gɑːdn/ n [C] **1** *US* : an area of ground where plants (such as flowers or vegetables) are grown • *a vegetable/rose garden* • *a garden hose/cart/rake/path* **2** *Brit* : YARD 1 **3** : a public area with many plants and trees • *a botanical/pub-lic garden* • *Kew Gardens* **4** *US* : a large stadium or building for sports or enter-tainment • *Madison Square Garden*

²garden vb [I] : to take care of the plants in a garden • *He likes to garden.* — **gar·den·er** /'gɑːdənə/ n [C] • *He hired a gardener.* — **gar·den·ing** /'gɑːdnɪŋ/ n [U] • *She enjoys gardening.*

gar·de·nia /gɑː'diːnjə/ n [C] : a large white or yellowish flower that has a pleasant smell

garden-variety adj, *always before a noun, US* : ordinary or common • *It's just a garden-variety cold.*

gar·gan·tuan /gɑː'gæntʃəwən/ adj : very large in size or amount • *a gargan-tuan appetite*

gar·gle /'gɑːgəl/ vb **gar·gled; gar·gling** [T/I] : to clean your throat and mouth with a liquid that you move around in your mouth and then spit out • *He gar-gled (with) salt water.* — **gargle** n [C/U] • *a gargle* [=a liquid for gargling] *used for sore throats*

gar·goyle /'gɑːgɔjəl/ n [C] : a strange or ugly human or animal figure that sticks out from the roof of a building (such as a church)

gar·ish /'gerɪʃ/ adj : too bright or color-ful • *garish clothes/colors* — **gar·ish·ly** adv

gar·land /'gɑːlənd/ n [C] : a ring or rope that is made of leaves, flowers, or some other material and that is used as a deco-ration • *They placed a garland of flowers around the winner's neck.* — **garland** vb [T] • *The winner was garlanded with flow-ers.*

gar·lic /'gɑːlɪk/ n [U] : a plant that is re-lated to the onion and that has small sec-tions (called cloves) that have a strong taste and smell and are used for flavoring foods — **gar·licky** /'gɑːlɪki/ adj • *a gar-licky flavor*

gar·ment /'gɑːmənt/ n [C] *somewhat for-mal* : a piece of clothing • *silk garments*

gar·ner /'gɑːnə/ vb [T] *formal* **1** : to collect or gather (something) • *garnered evidence/support for the theory* **2** : to get or receive (something wanted or valued) • *The novel has garnered much praise.*

gar·net /'gɑːnət/ n [C] : a dark red stone that is used in jewelry

gar·nish /'gɑːnɪʃ/ vb [T] : to put some-thing on (food) as a decoration • *Garnish the cake with chocolate curls.* • *The fish was garnished with parsley.* — **garnish**

[C] • *a parsley garnish*

gar·ret /ˈgerət/ n [C] : a usually small and unpleasant room or space just below the roof of a building

gar·ri·son /ˈgerəsən/ n [C] **1** : a military camp, fort, or base **2** : a group of soldiers who are living at a garrison • *a garrison of 5,000 men* — **garrison** vb [T] • *garrison a town* [=send soldiers to a town to defend it]

gar·ru·lous /ˈgerələs/ adj : tending to talk a lot • *a garrulous host*

gar·ter /ˈgɑɚtɚ/ n [C] **1** : an elastic band of material that is worn around the leg to hold up a stocking or sock **2** US : a piece of material that hangs down from a woman's underwear and that is used to hold up a stocking

garter belt n [C] US : a piece of underwear that is worn around a woman's waist and hips and that has garters (sense 2) attached to it

garter snake n [C] : a harmless American snake that has stripes along its back

¹**gas** /ˈgæs/ n, pl **gas·es** also **gas·ses 1 a** [C/U] : a substance (such as oxygen or hydrogen) that is like air and has no fixed shape • *Carbon monoxide is a poisonous gas.* **b** [U] : a gas or mixture of gases that is burned as a fuel • *We heat our house with gas.* • *a gas stove* **2** [U] US : gas in your stomach and intestines that causes pain or discomfort • *Certain foods give me gas.* [=(Brit) wind] **3** US [U] : GASOLINE • *We need to stop for gas.* [=(Brit) petrol] **b the gas** informal : the accelerator pedal of a vehicle • *He was driving with one foot on the gas and one foot on the brake.* ✧ If you **step on the gas**, **hit the gas**, or **give it the gas**, you suddenly press down on the accelerator to drive at a higher speed.

²**gas** vb **gasses**; **gassed**; **gas·sing 1** [T] : to poison or kill (someone) with gas • *soldiers gassed on the battlefield* **2** [T/I] US : to put gasoline in (a car, truck, etc.) • *We need to stop and gas up (the car).*

gas chamber n [C] : a room in which prisoners are killed by poisonous gas

gas·eous /ˈgæʃəs/ adj : having the form of gas • *changing from a liquid to a gaseous state*

gas·guz·zler /ˈgæsˌgʌzlɚ/ n [C] US, informal : a usually large vehicle that uses a lot of gasoline

gash /ˈgæʃ/ n [C] : a long, deep cut • *He had a gash in his leg.* — **gash** vb [T] • *The knife slipped and gashed his finger.* [=made a deep cut in his finger]

gas·ket /ˈgæskət/ n [C] : a piece of rubber or some other material that is used to make a tight seal between two parts that are joined together — **blow a gasket 1** of a car, engine, etc. : to develop a very bad leak in a gasket **2** informal, of a person : to become very angry • *When he heard the news, he blew a gasket.*

gas mask n [C] : a mask used to protect the face and lungs against poisonous gases

gas·o·line /ˈgæsəˌliːn/ n [U] US : a liquid made from petroleum and used especially as a fuel for engines — called also (US) gas, (Brit) petrol

gasp /ˈgæsp, Brit ˈgɑːsp/ vb **1** [I] : to breathe in suddenly and loudly with your mouth open because of surprise, shock, or pain • *She gasped in/with surprise.* **2** [I] : to breathe with difficulty • *a dying man gasping for breath/air* **3** [T] : to say (something) with quick, difficult breaths • *"Have mercy!" he gasped.* — **gasp** n [C] • *She let out a gasp of surprise.*

gas pedal n [C] US : ACCELERATOR

gas station n [C] US : a place where gasoline is sold for vehicles — called also filling station, service station

gas·sy /ˈgæsi/ adj **gas·si·er**; **-est 1** : of or containing gas • *a gassy odor/liquid* **2** US : having gas in your stomach • *He felt gassy.*

gas·tric /ˈgæstrɪk/ adj, medical : of, relating to, or located near the stomach • *gastric ulcers*

gas·tro·in·tes·ti·nal /ˌgæstroʊɪnˈtɛstən̩/ adj, medical : of or relating to both the stomach and the intestines • *gastrointestinal disorders*

gas·tron·o·my /gæˈstrɑːnəmi/ n [U] formal : the art or activity of cooking and eating fine food — **gas·tro·nom·ic** /ˌgæstrəˈnɑːmɪk/ also **gas·tro·nom·i·cal** /ˌgæstrəˈnɑːmɪkəl/ adj

gate /ˈgeɪt/ n [C] **1** : a place in a wall or a fence that has a movable part which can be opened or closed like a door • *He pushed the gate open.* **2** : a device that can be opened and closed to control the flow of water or other liquids • *canal gates* **3** : an area at an airport where passengers arrive and leave • *Flight 213 is now boarding at Gate 6.* **4** : the number of people who buy tickets for a sports event • *The game drew/attracted a large gate.* — **gat·ed** /ˈgeɪtəd/ adj • *a gated entrance* • *a gated community* [=a group of expensive homes that are surrounded by a gated wall or fence]

gate·keep·er /ˈgeɪtˌkiːpɚ/ n [C] : a person who guards a gate • *the palace gatekeeper*

gate·way /ˈgeɪtˌweɪ/ n [C] : an opening in a wall or fence that can be closed by a gate • *(figurative) Studying is the gateway to success.* [=studying leads to success]

gath·er /ˈgæðɚ/ vb **1** [T] **a** : to bring (things or people) together into a group • *Let me gather my things.* • *The coach gathered her players together.* **b** : to choose and collect (things) • *We gathered (up) wood for the fire.* **c** : to get or take (things) from different people or places and bring them together • *gathering evidence/contributions/donations* **2** [I] : to come together to form a group • *A crowd began to gather.* • *He asked us to gather around/round the table.* **3** [T] : to get more of (something) gradually • *gather speed* • *The campaign has begun to gather momentum/strength.* [=has begun to be more popular and effective] **4** [I] : to increase in amount or strength • *the gathering storm* **5** [T] **a** : to prepare yourself to use (your courage, strength, etc.) in order to do something difficult • *He gathered his courage and finally spoke up.* **b** : to prepare (yourself, your thoughts, etc.) before doing something difficult •

*He paused to **gather** himself.* ▪ *I barely had time to **gather** my thoughts/wits before replying.* **6** [*T*] : to believe that something is probably true because of what you have heard or learned ▪ *I **gather** (from her comments) that she's read a great deal about this topic.* **7** [*T*] : to pull (someone or something) close to your body ▪ *He **gathered** the child (up) in his arms.* — **gath·er·er** /ˈgæðərər/ *n* [*C*]

gath·er·ing /ˈgæðərɪŋ/ *n* [*C*] : an occasion when people come together as a group ▪ *social/family **gatherings*** ▪ *a gathering of political leaders*

ga·tor /ˈgeɪtər/ *n* [*C*] *US, informal* : ALLIGATOR

gauche /ˈgoʊʃ/ *adj* **gauch·er; -est** : socially awkward ▪ *Would it be **gauche** of me to ask her how old she is?*

gaudy /ˈgɑːdi/ *adj* **gaud·i·er; -est** **1** : too bright and heavily decorated ▪ *gaudy jewelry/colors/costumes* **2** *informal* : very large or impressive ▪ *a gaudy sum of money* ▪ *(disapproving) He collected fancy cars and other gaudy symbols of wealth.* — **gaud·i·ly** /ˈgɑːdəli/ *adv* — **gaud·i·ness** /ˈgɑːdinəs/ *n* [*U*]

¹**gauge** *also US* **gage** /ˈgeɪdʒ/ *n* **1** [*C*] : an instrument that is used for measuring something ▪ *a fuel/gas gauge* **2** [*C*] : something that can be used to measure or judge something else ▪ *These tests are not an accurate gauge of intelligence.* **3** [*U*] : the distance between the rails of a railroad ▪ *a broad/narrow gauge railroad* **4** [*U*] : the thickness of something (such as a sheet of metal) or the diameter of wire or a screw ▪ *20-gauge wire* **5** [*U*] : the size of a shotgun based on how big the inside of the barrel is ▪ *a 12-gauge shotgun*

²**gauge** *also US* **gage** *vb* **gauged** *also* **gaged; gaug·ing** *also* **gag·ing** [*T*] **1** : to make a judgment about (something) ▪ *gauging the overall state of the economy* **2** : to measure (something) exactly ▪ *instruments for gauging temperature and humidity*

gaunt /ˈgɑːnt/ *adj* : very thin usually because of illness or suffering ▪ *He left the hospital looking tired and gaunt.*

gaunt·let /ˈgɑːntlət/ *n* [*C*] **1** *also US* **gant·let** : a situation in which someone is attacked, criticized, questioned, etc., by many people ▪ *He had to run the gauntlet of reporters waiting outside the court.* **2** : a long, heavy glove worn to protect the hand — **pick/take up the gauntlet** : to accept or respond to a challenge ▪ *Will they pick up the gauntlet and do something about this problem?* — **throw down the gauntlet** : to say or show that you are ready to fight, argue, or compete with someone : to challenge someone ▪ *The company threw down the gauntlet and told the union that this offer for a contract was final.*

gauze /ˈgɑːz/ *n* [*U*] : loosely woven cotton that is used as a bandage ▪ *He wrapped the wound in gauze.*

gauzy /ˈgɑːzi/ *adj* **gauz·i·er; -est** **1** : light and thin ▪ *gauzy curtains/dresses* **2** *US* : not clear : HAZY ▪ *gauzy images/memories*

gave *past tense of* ¹GIVE

gav·el /ˈgævəl/ *n* [*C*] : a small hammer that someone (such as a judge) bangs on a table to get people's attention in a meeting or in a court of law

gawk /ˈgɑːk/ *vb* [*I*] *informal* : to stare at someone or something in a rude or stupid way ▪ *tourists gawking at celebrities* — **gawk·er** *n* [*C*]

gawky /ˈgɑːki/ *adj* **gawk·i·er; -est** *informal* : awkward and clumsy ▪ *a tall, gawky teenager*

¹**gay** /ˈgeɪ/ *adj* **1 a** : HOMOSEXUAL ▪ *My uncle is gay.* **b** *always before a noun* : of, relating to, or used by homosexuals ▪ *the gay rights movement* **2** *old-fashioned* : happy, cheerful, and lively ▪ *a gay festival/reception* **3** *old-fashioned* : COLORFUL ▪ *the gayest of the spring flowers* — **gay·ness** *n* [*U*]

²**gay** *n* [*C*] : a person and especially a man who is homosexual ▪ *gays and lesbians*

gaze /ˈgeɪz/ *vb* **gazed; gaz·ing** [*I*] : to look at someone or something in a steady way and usually for a long time ▪ *He gazed out the window.* ▪ *She gazed into his eyes.* — **gaze** *n* [*C*] ▪ *a calm, steady gaze* ▪ *I met his gaze.* [=looked back at him when he looked at me] ▪ *He dropped/lifted his gaze.* [=looked down/up]

ga·ze·bo /gəˈziːˌboʊ/ *n, pl* **-bos** [*C*] : a small building in a garden or park that is open on all sides

ga·zelle /gəˈzɛl/ *n, pl* **ga·zelles** *also* **gazelle** [*C*] : a small animal that is very graceful and fast

ga·zette /gəˈzɛt/ *n* [*C*] : NEWSPAPER ▪ *The Daily Gazette*

GB *abbr* **1** gigabyte **2** Great Britain

¹**gear** /ˈgiɚ/ *n* **1** [*U*] : supplies, tools, or clothes needed for a special purpose ▪ *fishing gear* ▪ *rain gear* [=waterproof clothes worn in the rain] **2** [*C/U*] : a part that connects the engine of a vehicle or the pedals of a bicycle to the wheels and controls the speed at which the wheels turn ▪ *a car with four forward gears* ▪ *Halfway up the hill, my bike slipped out of gear.* ▪ *He put the car in/into gear* [=he moved the lever that controls the car's gears into the position that allows the car to begin moving] *and drove away.* — **change/shift/switch gears** (*US*) *or Brit* **change gear** : to move from one level or area of activity to another ▪ *She's decided to shift gears, quit her job, and go back to school.* — **get in gear** *or* **get (something) in gear** *informal* : to start working or doing something in a more energetic and effective way ▪ *We need to get in gear if we want to finish on time.* — **in/into high gear** *see* HIGH GEAR

²**gear** *vb* [*T*] : to make (something) suitable for a particular use or type of person ▪ *The book is geared toward children.* [=is intended to be used by children] — **gear up** [*phrasal vb*] **gear up** *or* **gear (someone) up** *or* **gear up (someone)** : to get ready or to cause (someone) to get ready for something or to do something ▪ *The team is gearing up for a comeback.* ▪ *The*

coach is gearing up the team for a comeback.

gear·box /'gɪɚˌbɑːks/ *n* [C] : a box in a car, truck, etc., that contains the gears

gear·shift /'gɪɚˌʃɪft/ *n* [C] *US* : a lever or other device that is moved to change gears in a car, on a bicycle, etc.

GED /ˌdʒiːˌiːˈdiː/ *n* [C] *US* **1** : a test that is taken by an adult who did not finish high school to show that the person being tested has as much knowledge of basic math, science, English, etc., as a high school graduate ◇ *GED* in this sense is an abbreviation of "General Educational Development." **2** : an official document that is given to a person who has taken and passed the GED ◇ *GED* in this sense is an abbreviation of "general equivalency diploma."

gee /'dʒiː/ *interj, chiefly US* — used especially to show surprise, enthusiasm, or disappointment ▪ *Gee, that sounds like fun.*

geek /'giːk/ *n* [C] *chiefly US, informal* **1** : a usually intelligent person who does not fit in with other people ▪ *He was a real geek in high school.* **2** : a person who is very interested in and knows a lot about a particular field or activity ▪ *She's a computer geek.* — **geeky** /'giːki/ *adj* **geek·i·er; -est** ▪ *I was a geeky kid.*

geese *plural of* GOOSE

gee·zer /'giːzɚ/ *n* [C] *informal* **1** *US* : an old man ▪ *a group of old geezers* **2** *Brit* : GUY

Gei·ger counter /'gaɪɡɚ-/ *n* [C] : an instrument used for finding and measuring radioactivity

¹**gel** /'dʒɛl/ *n* [C/U] : a thick substance that is like jelly and that is used in various products ▪ *hair gels* [=gels used for styling hair]

²**gel** *vb* **gelled; gel·ling 1** [I] : to change into a thick substance that is like jelly ▪ *The mixture will gel as it cools.* **2** [I] : to become clear and definite ▪ *Our plans are finally starting to gel.* **3** [T] : to style (hair) with gel ▪ *She gelled her hair.*

gel·a·tin (*chiefly US*) *or chiefly Brit* **gel·a·tine** /'dʒɛlətən/ *n* [U] **1** : a clear substance that is made by boiling animal bones or tissues and that is used in making jelly **2** : a food made with gelatin ▪ *a gelatin dessert* — **ge·lat·i·nous** /dʒə-'lætənəs/ *adj* ▪ *a gelatinous mass*

gem /'dʒɛm/ *n* [C] **1** : a valuable stone that has been cut and polished for use in jewelry **2** : something that is admired for its beauty or excellence ▪ *That house is a real gem.*

Gem·i·ni /'dʒɛməni, 'dʒɛməˌnaɪ/ *n* **1** [U] : the third sign of the zodiac that comes between Taurus and Cancer and has a pair of twins as its symbol **2** [C] : a person born between May 21st and June 21st ▪ *His girlfriend is a Gemini.*

gem·stone /'dʒɛmˌstoʊn/ *n* [C] : a stone that can be used in jewelry when it is cut and polished

Gen. *abbr* General ▪ *Gen. Smith*

gen·der /'dʒɛndɚ/ *n* **1** [C] : the state of being male or female : SEX ▪ *Please state your name, birth date, and gender.* **2** [C/U] *grammar* : one of the categories (masculine, feminine, and neuter) into which words (such as nouns, adjectives, and pronouns) are divided in many languages ▪ *The adjective and noun must agree in number and gender.*

gene /'dʒiːn/ *n* [C] *biology* : a part of a cell that controls or influences the appearance, growth, etc., of a living thing ▪ *She inherited a good set of genes from her parents.*

ge·ne·al·o·gy /ˌdʒiːniˈɑːlədʒi, ˌdʒiːni-'ælədʒi/ *n, pl* **-gies** [C] : the history of a particular family showing how the different members of the family are related to each other — **ge·ne·a·log·i·cal** /ˌdʒiːnijəˈlɑːdʒɪkəl/ *adj* — **ge·ne·al·o·gist** /ˌdʒiːniˈɑːlədʒɪst, ˌdʒiːniˈælədʒɪst/ *n* [C]

genera *plural of* GENUS

¹**gen·er·al** /'dʒɛnrəl/ *adj* **1** *always before a noun* : of, relating to, or affecting all the people or things in a group ▪ *a general warning/order/alarm* : involving or including many or most people ▪ *The general mood is optimistic.* [=most people are optimistic] **2 a** : relating to the main or major parts of something rather than the details : not specific ▪ *a general observation/discussion/idea* **b** *always before a noun* — used to indicate that a description relates to an entire person or thing rather than a particular part ▪ *The building was in good general shape.* **3** *always before a noun* : not exact : APPROXIMATE ▪ *I'm going in the general direction of the store.* **4** *always before a noun* : ordinary, normal, or usual ▪ *As a general rule, they offer a deal in such cases.* [=they usually/generally offer a deal in such cases] **5** : of the basic or usual kind ▪ *a science book for the general reader* [=the reader who is not a scientist] ▪ *general medicine* [=basic health care that is not specialized] **6** *always before a noun* : of high rank : having wide authority or responsibility ▪ *a general manager*

²**general** *n* [C] : a military officer of very high rank — **in general 1** — used to say that a statement describes your general feeling or opinion ▪ *In general, I like the way things have gone.* **2** — used to say that a statement refers to most or all the people or things in a group ▪ *It doesn't matter much to people in general.* [=all or most people] **3** : in most cases : USUALLY ▪ *In general, it takes about a month for the shipment to arrive.*

gen·er·al·i·ty /ˌdʒɛnəˈræləti/ *n, pl* **-ties** *formal* **1** [C] : a statement that is not specific or detailed ▪ *He spoke in generalities.* **2** [U] : the quality or state of being general rather than specific or detailed ▪ *the generality of her ideas* **3** [U] *Brit* : MAJORITY ▪ *the generality of the students* [=most of the students]

gen·er·al·ize *also Brit* **gen·er·al·ise** /'dʒɛnrəˌlaɪz/ *vb* **-ized; -iz·ing** [I] : to make a general statement or form a general opinion; *especially* : to state an opinion about a larger group that is based on a smaller number of people or things within that group ▪ *generalizing about men* — **gen·er·al·i·za·tion** *also Brit* **gen·er·al·i·sa·tion** /ˌdʒɛnrələˈzeɪʃən,

Brit /ˌdʒenrəˌlaɪˈzeɪʃən/ *n* [C/U] • *sweeping/broad generalizations about men*

gen·er·al·ly /ˈdʒenrəli/ *adv* **1** : in a way that is not detailed or specific • *He talked generally about his plans.* **2** : USUALLY • *It generally takes about a month for the shipment to arrive.* • *Generally (speaking), writers oppose censorship.* **3** : by or to most people • *a generally used phrase*

general practitioner *n* [C] : a person (especially a doctor) whose work is not limited to a special area — *abbr. G.P.*

general public *n* — **the general public** : all the people of an area, country, etc. • *The park is open to the general public.*

general store *n* [C] : a store usually in a small town that sells many different things

gen·er·ate /ˈdʒenəˌreɪt/ *vb* **-at·ed; -at·ing** [T] **1** : to produce (something) or cause (something) to be produced • *windmills used to generate electricity* • *a computer-generated list* [=a list that was made by a computer program] **2** : to be the cause of or reason for (something, such as interest or excitement) • *Her comments generated a lot of excitement/controversy.*

gen·er·a·tion /ˌdʒenəˈreɪʃən/ *n* **1** [C] **a** : a group of people born and living during the same time • *She was worshipped by a generation of fans.* • *saved for future generations* **b** : the people in a family born and living during the same time • *That family has lived in the same house for four generations.* **2** [C] : the average length of time between the birth of parents and the birth of their children • *She's a generation* [=around 20–30 years] *older than most of her colleagues.* **3** [C] : a group of things that are developed from an earlier type • *the next generation of portable computers* **4** [U] : the act or process of making or producing something • *the generation of heat* — **gen·er·a·tion·al** /ˌdʒenəˈreɪʃənəl/ *adj* • *generational differences/problems*

generation gap *n* [singular] : the differences in opinions, values, etc., between younger people and older people

Generation X *n* [U] : the group of people in the U.S. who were born during the late 1960s and the 1970s

gen·er·a·tor /ˈdʒenəˌreɪtɚ/ *n* [C] : something that produces something; *especially* : a machine that produces electricity • *a backup generator for the store*

ge·ner·ic /dʒəˈnerɪk/ *adj* **1** : of or relating to a whole group or class • *a generic term/name* **2** : not sold or made under a particular brand name • *generic drugs* — **generic** *n* [C] • *You can substitute generics* [=generic drugs] *for brand-name drugs.* — **ge·ner·i·cal·ly** /dʒəˈnerɪkli/ *adv*

gen·er·ous /ˈdʒenərəs/ *adj* **1** : freely giving or sharing money and other valuable things • *He was generous with his time and money.* • *She is very generous toward/to the poor.* **2** : providing more than the amount that is needed or normal • *a generous supply/portion* **3** : showing kindness and concern for others • *She has a generous heart/spirit.* —

gen·er·os·i·ty /ˌdʒenəˈrɑːsəti/ *n* [U] • *her generosity to/toward the poor* — **gen·er·ous·ly** *adv* • *She tipped the waiter generously.*

gen·e·sis /ˈdʒenəsəs/ *n* [U] *somewhat formal* : the beginning of something - ORIGIN • *a book about the genesis of the civil rights movement*

ge·net·ic /dʒəˈnetɪk/ *adj* : of, relating to, or involving genes • *a genetic disease* • **genetic fingerprinting** [=using genes or parts of genes to identify a person, such as a criminal] — **ge·net·i·cal·ly** /dʒəˈnetɪkli/ *adv*

genetic engineering *n* [U] : the science of making changes to the genes of a plant or animal to produce a desired result — **genetic engineer** *n* [C]

ge·net·ics /dʒəˈnetɪks/ *n* [U] : the scientific study of how genes control the characteristics of plants and animals — **ge·net·i·cist** /dʒəˈnetəsɪst/ *n* [C]

ge·nial /ˈdʒiːnijəl/ *adj* : cheerful and pleasant • *a genial host/manner* — **ge·nial·i·ty** /ˌdʒiːniˈæləti/ *n* [U] — **ge·nial·ly** /ˈdʒiːnjəli/ *adv*

ge·nie /ˈdʒiːni/ *n* [C] *in stories* : a magic spirit that looks like a person, often lives in a lamp or bottle, and serves the person who calls it

gen·i·tal /ˈdʒenətl/ *adj, always before a noun* : of or relating to the sexual organs • *a genital disease*

gen·i·ta·lia /ˌdʒenəˈteɪljə/ *n* [plural] : GENITALS

gen·i·tals /ˈdʒenətlz/ *n* [plural] : sexual organs; *especially* : the sexual organs on the outside of the body • *male/female genitals*

gen·i·tive /ˈdʒenətɪv/ *n* [U] *grammar* : the form of a noun or pronoun when it is used to show that someone or something owns, controls, or is associated with someone or something else — **genitive** *adj* • *the genitive case*

ge·nius /ˈdʒiːnjəs/ *n* **1** [C] **a** : a person who has a level of talent or intelligence that is very rare or remarkable • *a musical/artistic/creative genius* **b** : a person who is very good at doing something • *a genius at handling the press* **2 a** [U] : great natural ability : remarkable talent or intelligence • *He's admired for his comic/artistic/scientific genius.* **b** [singular] : a great or unusual talent or ability • *She has a genius for knowing what will sell.* **3** [singular] : a part of something that makes it unusually good or valuable • *My plan is simple—that's the genius of it.* — **a stroke of genius** : a brilliant and successful idea or decision • *Deciding to relocate the company was a stroke of genius.*

geno·cide /ˈdʒenəˌsaɪd/ *n* [U] : the deliberate killing of people who belong to a particular racial, political, or cultural group — **geno·cid·al** /ˌdʒenəˈsaɪdl/ *adj*

genre /ˈʒɑːnrə/ *n* [C] : a particular type or category of literature or art • *a literary/film/musical genre*

gent /ˈdʒent/ *n* [C] *informal + old-fashioned* : GENTLEMAN • *ladies and gents*

gen·teel /dʒenˈtiːl/ *adj* **1** *somewhat old-fashioned* : of, relating to, or having the qualities of people who have high social status • *a genteel family* • *speaking in a genteel accent* **2** : having a quietly appealing or polite quality • *genteel manners*

gen·tile *or* **Gen·tile** /ˈdʒɛnˌtajəl/ *n [C]* : a person who is not Jewish — **gentile** *or* **Gentile** *adj*

gen·til·i·ty /dʒɛnˈtɪləti/ *n [U]* **1** : high social status • *Education was considered a mark of gentility.* **2** : a quietly appealing and polite quality or manner • *He's a model of gentility.* [=courtesy]

gen·tle /ˈdʒɛntl̩/ *adj* **gen·tler** /ˈdʒɛntl̩ɚ/; **gen·tlest** /ˈdʒɛntl̩əst/ **1** : having or showing a kind and quiet nature : not harsh or violent • *a very gentle man/dog* • *gentle eyes* **2 a** : not hard or forceful • *a gentle rain/breeze/push* **b** : not strong or harsh in effect or quality • *a soap that is gentle on the skin* • *a gentle reminder* **3** : not steep or sharp • *a gentle slope/hill/curve* — **gen·tle·ness** /ˈdʒɛntl̩nəs/ *n [U]* — **gent·ly** /ˈdʒɛntl̩/ *adv* • *She spoke to him gently.*

gen·tle·man /ˈdʒɛntl̩mən/ *n, pl* **-men** /-mən/ *[C]* **1** : a man who treats other people in a proper and polite way • *A gentleman would never do that.* **2** : MAN — used especially in polite speech or when speaking to a group of men • *Good evening, ladies and gentlemen.* **3** *old-fashioned* : a man of high social status — **gen·tle·man·ly** /ˈdʒɛntl̩mənli/ *adj* • *gentlemanly conduct*

gentleman's agreement *or* **gentlemen's agreement** *n [C]* : an informal agreement based on trust rather than on a legal document

gen·tri·fy /ˈdʒɛntrəˌfaɪ/ *vb* **-fies**; **-fied**; **-fy·ing** *[T]* : to change (a place, such as an old neighborhood) by improving it and making it more appealing to people who have money • *The neighborhood was/became gentrified.* — **gen·tri·fi·ca·tion** /ˌdʒɛntrəfəˈkeɪʃən/ *n [U]*

gen·try /ˈdʒɛntri/ *n* — **the gentry** *old-fashioned* : people of high social status • *the landed gentry* [=wealthy people who own land]

gents /ˈdʒɛnts/ *n [singular] Brit, informal* : MEN'S ROOM

gen·u·flect /ˈdʒɛnjəˌflɛkt/ *vb* [*I*] : to kneel on one knee and then rise again as an act of respect • *They genuflected before the altar.*

gen·u·ine /ˈdʒɛnjəwən/ *adj* **1** : actual, real, or true : not false or fake • *genuine leather* • *This painting is the genuine article.* [=not a copy] **2** : sincere and honest • *genuine emotions/interest* • *a genuine interest/concern/desire* • *a very genuine person* — **gen·u·ine·ly** *adv* — **gen·u·ine·ness** *n [U]*

ge·nus /ˈdʒiːnəs/ *n, pl* **gen·era** /ˈdʒɛnərə/ *[C] biology* : a group of related animals or plants that includes several or many different species

ge·og·ra·phy /dʒiˈɑːgrəfi/ *n, pl* **-phies** **1** [*U*] : an area of study that deals with the location of countries, cities, rivers, mountains, lakes, etc. **2** [*C/U*] : the natural features (such as rivers, mountains, etc.) of a place • *studying the geography of the western United States* — **ge·og·ra·**

pher /dʒiˈɑːgrəfɚ/ *n* [*C*] — **geo·graph·ic** *(chiefly US)* /ˌdʒiːjəˈgræfɪk/ *or* **geo·graph·i·cal** /ˌdʒiːjəˈgræfɪkəl/ *adj* • *a large geographic area* • *geographical names* — **geo·graph·i·cal·ly** /ˌdʒiːjəˈgræfɪkli/ *adv*

ge·ol·o·gy /dʒiˈɑːlədʒi/ *n* [*U*] **1** : a science that studies rocks, layers of soil, etc., in order to learn about the history of the Earth and its life **2** : the rocks, land, processes of land formation, etc., of a particular area • *the geology of Hawaii* — **geo·log·ic** *(chiefly US)* /ˌdʒiːjəˈlɑːdʒɪk/ *or* **geo·log·i·cal** /ˌdʒiːjəˈlɑːdʒɪkəl/ *adj* — **ge·ol·o·gist** /dʒiˈɑːlədʒɪst/ *n* [*C*]

ge·om·e·try /dʒiˈɑːmətri/ *n* [*U*] : a branch of mathematics that deals with points, lines, angles, surfaces, and solids — **geo·met·ric** /ˌdʒiːjəˈmɛtrɪk/ *also* **geo·met·ri·cal** /ˌdʒiːjəˈmɛtrɪkəl/ *adj* • *geometric shapes/patterns*

geo·pol·i·tics /ˌdʒiːjouˈpɑːləˌtɪks/ *n* **1** [*U*] : the study of how geography and economics have an influence on politics and on the relations between nations **2** [*plural*] : the political and geographic parts of something • *the geopolitics of war* — **geo·po·lit·i·cal** /ˌdʒiːjoupəˈlɪtɪkəl/ *adj*

ge·ra·ni·um /dʒəˈreɪnijəm/ *n* [*C*] : a plant that is grown for its red, white, pink, or purple flowers

ger·bil /ˈdʒɚbəl/ *n* [*C*] : a small animal that is often kept as a pet

ge·ri·at·ric /ˌdʒɛriˈætrɪk/ *adj* **1** *always before a noun, medical* : of or relating to the process of growing old and the medical care of old people • *geriatric patients/medicine* **2** *informal* : OLD — *a geriatric* [=old and outdated] *computer* — **geriat·ric** *n* [*C*] : providing medical care for geriatrics [=old people] — **ge·ri·at·rics** /ˌdʒɛriˈætrɪks/ *n* [*U*] : a doctor who specializes in geriatrics [=medicine relating to old people]

germ /ˈdʒɚm/ *n* [*C*] **1** *biology* : a very small living thing that causes disease **2 a** : the origin or basis of something • *the germ of an idea* **b** : a very small amount of something • *a germ of truth*

Ger·man /ˈdʒɚmən/ *n* **1** [*C*] : a person who is from Germany **2** [*U*] : the language of Germany that is also spoken in Austria, parts of Switzerland, and other places — **German** *adj* • *German food/literature*

ger·mane /dʒɚˈmeɪn/ *adj, formal* : relating to a subject in an appropriate way • *Her comments were not germane (to the discussion).*

Ger·man·ic /dʒɚˈmænɪk/ *adj* **1** : of or relating to Germans • *Germanic music/influence/tribes* **2** : of or relating to the German language or to other closely related languages

German measles *n* [*U*] : a disease that is less severe than typical measles but that can harm an unborn child if the mother gets the disease when she is pregnant — called also *rubella*

German shepherd *n* [*C*] : a large dog that is often used in police work and as a guide dog for blind people

ger·mi·nate /ˈʤɚməˌneɪt/ vb **-nat·ed;**
-nat·ing [T/I] : to begin to grow or to
cause (a seed) to begin to grow • *The
seeds germinated quickly.* • (figurative)
*The idea has been germinating for some
time.* — **ger·mi·na·tion** /ˌʤɚmə-
ˈneɪʃən/ n [U]

ger·on·tol·o·gy /ˌʤerənˈtɑːləʤi/ n [U]
: the scientific study of old age and of the
process of becoming old

ger·und /ˈʤerənd/ n [C] grammar : an
English noun formed from a verb by
adding *-ing* • *In the sentence "Learning
can be fun," "learning" is a gerund.*

ges·ta·tion /ʤeˈsteɪʃən/ n [U] : the time
when a person or animal is developing
inside its mother before it is born • *the
last month of gestation* • (figurative) *the
gestation of new ideas*

ges·tic·u·late /ʤeˈstɪkjəˌleɪt/ vb **-lat·ed;**
-lat·ing [I] : to move your arms and
hands especially when speaking in an angry or emotional way • *gesticulating wildly* — **ges·tic·u·la·tion** /ʤeˌstɪkjə-
ˈleɪʃən/ n [C/U]

ges·ture /ˈʤesʧɚ/ n [C] **1** : a movement
of your body (especially of your hands
and arms) that shows or emphasizes an
idea or a feeling • *an angry gesture* **2**
: something said or done to show a particular feeling or attitude — *a thoughtful/
polite/friendly gesture* — **gesture** vb
-tured; -tur·ing [I] • *He gestured at/to-
ward the door.*

get /ˈgɛt/ or US **got** /ˈgɑːt/; **got** or US **gotten** /ˈgɑːtn/; **get·ting 1** [T] **a** : to receive or be given (something) • *Did you
get my message?* **b** : to obtain (something) through effort, chance, etc. • *get a
job* • *She got a look at the thief.* [=she saw
the thief] **c** : to obtain the use or services of (something) • *get a taxi* **d** : to earn
or gain (something) • *I got $50 for my old
bicycle.* • *I got an "A" on my exam!* **2** [T]
: to buy or pay for (something) • *He got a
necklace for his wife.* **3** [T] : to go somewhere and come back with (something
or someone) • *I'll get a pencil from the
desk.* **4** [T] : to send or take (something
or someone) *to* a person or place • *We
have to get him to the hospital.* **5 a** [T]
: to cause (someone or something) to
move or to go • *She got the car out of the garage.* **b** [I] : to move or go • *He got on/
off the horse.* **c** [I] : to arrive at a place •
He got home last night. **6** [T] : to begin
to have (a feeling, an idea, etc.) • *He got
the idea/impression that I was lying to
him.* **7** [T] : to become affected by (a
disease) • *get a bad cold/infection* **b** : to
suffer (an injury) • *Where/how did you get
that bruise?* **8** [T] : to have or experience (something) • *We've been getting a
lot of rain recently.* **9** [T] : to cause (a
particular reaction) • *That joke always
gets a laugh.* **10** [I] : to make progress
in some activity • *He hasn't gotten far with
the essay.* • *At last we're getting somewhere (with our work)!* **b** [T] : to cause
or help (someone) to make progress • *All
that effort didn't really get us very far.* **11**
[T] : to cause (someone or something) to
be in a specified position or condition •
He got his feet wet. • *I need to get my hair*

cut. **12** [T] : to cause (someone or
something) to do something • *I can't get
the children to behave.* • *He got the computer working again.* **13** [I] : to start doing something • *We got talking about old
times.* **14** [I] : to have or be given the
chance *to do* something • *She never got to
go to college.* **15** [T] : to deal with
(something that needs attention) • *Would
somebody please get* [=*answer*] *the phone?*
• *get* [=open or close] *the door* **16** [T] **a**
: to understand (something or someone) •
I don't get the point/joke. • *Oh, now I get
it.* • *Don't get me wrong.* [=don't misunderstand what I am saying] **b** : to hear
and understand (something) • *I didn't
quite get his name.* **17 a** [linking vb]
: BECOME 1 • *My hands got dirty.* • *I got
sick last week.* • *It's getting late.* • *We'd better get busy.* [=begin to work] ✧ People
say *how stupid/lucky (etc.) can you get*
to mean that someone or something is
unusually stupid, lucky, etc. **b** [I] : to
change in a specified way as time passes •
She is getting to be [=*becoming*] *quite a
big girl now!* **18** [I] : to do something
specified • *Once you get to know him,
you'll like him.* **19** [auxiliary vb] — used
like *be* with the past participle of some
verbs to form passive constructions •
They got [=were] *married.* • *He got* [=was]
paid. **20** [T] : to grip and hold (something or someone) • *He got* [=grabbed] *me
around/by the neck.* **21** [T] : to hit
(someone) • *The bullet got him in the leg.*
22 [T] : to hurt or cause trouble for
(someone) • *His enemies are out to get
him.* • *I'll get you if it's the last thing I do!*
23 [T] informal **a** : to bother or annoy
(someone) • *It really gets me that such a
foolish man has so much influence.*
b : to make (someone) sad • *The end of that
movie always gets me.* **c** : to cause
(someone) to be fooled or unable to
think of an answer • *That's a good question. You've got me (there).* [=I don't
know the answer] **24** [T] : to make a
phone call and hear or speak to (a person
or answering machine) • *trying to get him
(on the phone)* **25** [T] : to produce or
provide (a level of performance) • *Our
new car gets excellent gas mileage.* — **get
across** [phrasal vb] **get (something)
across** or **get across (something)** : to express (something) clearly so that it is understood • *I don't know if I was able to get
my point across.* — **get after** [phrasal vb]
US, informal : to tell (someone) repeatedly to do something • *His parents are always getting after him about (doing) his
homework.* — **get ahead** [phrasal vb]
: to become more successful • *how to get
ahead in the business world* — **get (a)
hold of** see ²HOLD — **get along** [phras-
al vb] **1** : to be or remain friendly • *They
don't really get along (with each other).* **2**
: to make progress while doing something • *How are you getting along with
your work?* **3** : to leave a place • *I must
be getting along.* [=going] **4** : to become
old • *Her parents are getting along in
years.* — **get around/round** [phrasal vb]
1 : to go,
walk, or travel to different places • *He's*

having trouble getting around because of his sore knee. **2** : to become known by many people ▪ *Word got around that he was resigning.* **3** : to avoid having to deal with (something) ▪ *finding a way to get around these problems* **4 get around to** or chiefly Brit **get round to** : to do or deal with (something that you have not yet done or dealt with) ▪ *I've been meaning to call her, but I just haven't gotten around to it.* — **get at** [phrasal vb] **1** : to reach (something or someone) ▪ *An angry mob tried to get at him.* **2** : to find out (information that is hidden or hard to know) ▪ *How can we ever get at the truth?* **3** : to say or suggest (something) in an indirect way ▪ *What are you getting at?* **4** Brit : to criticize (someone) repeatedly ▪ *His teachers are always getting at him.* **5 get at it** US, informal : to start doing something ▪ *I have a lot of work so I'd better get at it.* — **get away** [phrasal vb] **1** : to go away from a place ▪ *I can't get away (from work) until tonight.* ▪ (figurative) *They've gotten away from* [=have stopped doing] *the things they do best.* **2** : to go away from your home for a vacation ▪ *I really need to get away (from it all) for a few days.* **3** : to escape ▪ *The robbers got away (from the police).* **4 get away with** : to not be criticized or punished for (something) ▪ *I don't know how she gets away with her rude behavior.* — **get back** [phrasal vb] **1** : to return to a place after going away ▪ *When did you get back from your vacation?* **2** : to return to an activity, condition, etc. ▪ *Things are finally getting back to normal.* ▪ *It's time to get back to work.* **3 get (something) back** or **get back (something)** : to get or obtain (something you have lost) again ▪ *He got his old job back.* **4 get (someone) back** or **get back at (someone)** or Brit **get your own back** informal : to do something bad or unpleasant to someone who has treated you badly or unfairly ▪ *I'll get you back!* ▪ *trying to get back at his old boss* **5 get back to** : to talk to or write to (someone) at a later time in order to give more information, answer a question, etc. ▪ *He got back to me (by e-mail).* — **get by** [phrasal vb] **1** : to do enough or to do well enough to avoid failure ▪ *He's barely getting by in math.* **2** : to be able to live or to do what is needed by using what you have even though you do not have much ▪ *How can you get by on/with such a small salary?* — **get down** [phrasal vb] **1 get (someone) down** : to cause (someone) to become sad or depressed ▪ *The weather was getting her down.* **2 get (something) down** or **get down (something)** **a** : to eat or drink (something) ▪ *You'll feel better once you get this medicine down.* **b** : to write (something) down ▪ *You should get your ideas down (in writing).* **3** informal : to play music or dance with skill and enthusiasm ▪ *She likes to get down on the dance floor.* **4 get down to** : to start to do (something) ▪ *Let's get down to work/business.* — **get going 1** : to leave ▪ *We ought to get going soon.* **2** : to start doing something ▪ *You should get going*

on that assignment. **3** : to start talking or cause (someone) to start talking ▪ *Once he gets going you can't shut him up.* ▪ *Don't get him going.* — **get in** [phrasal vb] **1 a** : to enter a place ▪ *The burglar got in through an open window.* **b** : to arrive at a place ▪ *The train got in late.* **c** : to arrive home ▪ *He didn't get in until almost midnight.* **2** : to become involved in an activity ▪ *They got in at the beginning of the business.* **3 get in** or **get (someone) in** : to be accepted or to cause (someone) to be accepted as a student, member, etc. ▪ *It's a very good school. I hope your daughter gets in.* **4 get (something) in** or **get in (something)** **a** : to do or say (something) by making an effort ▪ *May I get a word in here?* [=may I say something here?] **b** : to send or deliver (something) to the proper person or place ▪ *Did you get your assignment in?* **c** : to do (something) in the amount of time that is available ▪ *get in a few hours of reading* **5 get in on** : to become involved in (something) ▪ *I'd like to get in on the project.* **6 get in with** : to become friends with (someone) ▪ *He managed to get in good with the boss.* [=he got the boss to like him] — **get into** [phrasal vb] **1 a** : to enter (a place) ▪ *A dog got into the house.* **b** : to arrive at (a place) ▪ *I got into New York late last night.* **2 a** : to become involved in (an activity) ▪ *people who got into the project at the beginning* **b** : to begin to be interested in and to enjoy (something) ▪ *I tried reading the book, but I just couldn't get into it.* **3 get into** or **get (someone) into** **a** : to be accepted or to cause (someone) to be accepted as a student, member, etc. ▪ *I hope your daughter gets into college.* **b** : to become involved or to cause (someone) to become involved in (something bad, such as trouble or a fight) ▪ *They got into an argument.* ▪ *His friends got him into trouble.* **4** : to talk about (something) ▪ *I don't want to get into it.* **5** — used to say that someone is behaving in an unusual way and you don't know why ▪ *I don't know what has gotten into him lately.* — **get off** [phrasal vb] **1** : to leave at the start of a journey ▪ (figurative) *He and I got off to a bad/slow/good start.* [=he and I began our relationship poorly/slowly/well] **2 get off** or **get (someone) off** **a** : to not be punished for a crime : to help (someone) to be judged not guilty ▪ *He was arrested, but he got off.* ▪ *His lawyer got him off.* **b** : to be given or to help (someone) to be given only a slight punishment for a crime ▪ *He got off with a light sentence.* **3** : to stop being on or against someone or something ▪ *I took the subway and got off at the downtown station.* **4** : to finish working and leave the place where you work ▪ *I get off (work) at 5:00.* **5 get (something) off** or **get off (something)** **a** : to write and send (a letter, an e-mail message, etc.) ▪ *I'll get the letter off tomorrow.* **b** : to shoot (something) from a gun ▪ *He got off* [=fired] *several shots.* **6 get off** or **get (someone) off** chiefly Brit : to fall asleep or to help (someone, such as a baby) to fall asleep • *I just got the baby off to sleep.* **7 get off** or **get (someone) off** *US, informal* : to have an orgasm or to cause (someone) to have an orgasm **8 get off on** *informal + sometimes disapproving* : to enjoy or be excited by (something) especially in a sexual way • *He gets off on making other people feel guilty.* **9** *informal* ◇ To **tell someone where to get off** is to criticize or disagree with someone in a very direct and angry way. **10** *US* ◇ If you **don't know where someone gets off** (doing something), you are angry because someone has done something that is not right. — **get on** [*phrasal vb*] **1 get on with** : to continue doing (something) • *I'll let you get on with your work.* **2** *chiefly Brit* : to be or remain friendly • *We get on well enough.* **3** *chiefly Brit* **a** : to make progress while doing something • *How is your daughter getting on in/at school?* **b** : to achieve greater success • *trying to get on in business* **4** *US* : to start to do or deal with (something) • *"These files need to be organized." "I'll get on it."* **5** *US* : to criticize (someone) repeatedly • *His boss has been getting on him lately.* **6 get it on** *US slang* : to have sex **7 get on** or **get on in years** *informal* : to grow old • *He's getting on (in years), but he's still very active.* — **get onto** or **get on to** [*phrasal vb*] **1** : to start to do or deal with (something) • *"We need to send these out." "I'll get onto it right away."* : to start to talk about something • *How did we get onto this topic?* **2** *Brit* : to speak to or write to (someone) about a particular problem, job, etc. • *I'll get onto the doctor straightaway.* — **get out** [*phrasal vb*] **1** : to go to places outside your home for social occasions, events, etc. • *You need to get out more.* **2** : to become known • *Their secret got out.* **3** *US, informal* — used in speech to show that you are surprised by something or do not believe it • *"They gave the job to Jane." "Get out!"* = **"Get out of here!"** **4 get out of** or **get (someone or something) out of a** : to avoid doing (something) or to help (someone) to avoid doing (something) • *He tried to get out of doing his homework.* **b** : to stop having (a habit) or to cause (someone) to stop having (a habit) • *My illness has gotten me out of the habit of exercising.* **5 get (something) out of a** : to take (something) from (something or someone) • *The police officer got a confession out of him.* **b** : to gain (something) from (something) • *What do you hope to get out of this experience?* — **get over** [*phrasal vb*] **1 a** : to stop being controlled or bothered by (something) • *You need to get over your fear.* **b** : to stop feeling unhappy about (something) • *She'll get over it eventually.* **c** *informal* — used to say that you are very surprised or impressed by something • *I can't get over how much weight you've lost!* **2** : to become healthy again after (an illness) • *He still hasn't gotten over his cold.* **3** : to stop feeling unhappy after ending a relationship with (someone) • *He still hasn't gotten over her.* **4 get (something) over a** or **get (some-**

thing) over with : to finish (something) • *I just want to get this ordeal over!* **b** *chiefly Brit* : to express (something) clearly so that it is understood • *trying to get my message over to them* — **get there** : to reach a goal : to do what you are trying to do • *We haven't made a profit yet, but we'll get there.* : to come closer to reaching a goal • *We haven't made a profit, but we're getting there.* — **get through** [*phrasal vb*] **1 a** *chiefly Brit* : to finish a job or activity • *When you get through (with that job), I've got something else for you to do.* **b** : to do or finish (something, such as an amount of work) • *There's still a lot of paperwork to get through.* **2 get through** or **get through (something)** or **get (something) through** : to pass or cause (something) to pass through or beyond something that blocks you or slows you down • *Traffic was very heavy, but we managed to get through (it).* • *getting supplies through to flood victims* **3 get through** or **get (someone) through** : to have the experience of living through (something) • *They managed to get through* [=survive] *the winter.* : to help (someone) to live through (something) • *Hope got them through that crisis.* **4** *chiefly Brit* : to spend or use all of (something) • *He got through all the money he inherited.* **5 a** : to be clearly expressed to and understood by someone • *I think my message finally got through (to them).* **b get through to** or **get (something) through to** : to express something clearly so that it is understood by (someone) • *I just can't seem to get (my message) through to him.* **6** : to make a successful telephone call to someone • *I tried to call but I couldn't get through (to you).* — **get to** [*phrasal vb*] **1 a** : to start (doing something) • *We got to talking about old times.* **b** : to deal with (something) • *I'll get to it as soon as I can.* **2 a** : to bother or annoy (someone) • *All these delays are starting to get to me.* **b** : to make (someone) feel sad • *The movie's sad ending really got to me.* **c** *chiefly US* : to change or influence the behavior of (someone) wrongly or illegally by making threats, paying money, etc. • *The witness changed his story. Someone must have gotten to him.* **3** : to go to or reach (somewhere) • *We got to the station/airport just in time.* — **get together** [*phrasal vb*] **1 a** : to meet and spend time together • *I'd like to get together with you soon.* **b** : to begin to have a sexual or romantic relationship • *He and his wife got together in college.* **2** : to agree to do or accept something • *They were unable to get together on a new contract.* **3 get together (things or people)** or **get (things or people) together** : to collect (things) or gather (people) into one place or group • *The government got together a group of experts to study the problem.* **4 get your act together** or **get yourself together** or **get it together** *informal* **a** : to begin to live in a good and sensible way • *He stopped drinking and got his act together.* **b** : to begin to function in a skillful or effective way • *The company* *got its act together and started making a profit.* — **get to sleep** : to fall asleep ▪ *She got to sleep after midnight.* — **get to work** : to start working ▪ *We need to get to work.* — **get up** [*phrasal vb*] **1 get up** *or* **get (someone) up** : to rise or to cause (someone) to rise after lying or sleeping in a bed ▪ *I got up early/late.* **2** : to stand up ▪ *He got up to greet her.* **3 get (something) up** *or* **get up (something) a** : to produce (something, such as courage) in yourself by trying or making an effort ▪ *getting up the courage to ask them out* **b** : to prepare or organize (something that involves a group of people) ▪ *trying to get up a petition* — **have got** see HAVE

get·away /ˈgɛtəˌweɪ/ *n* [*C*] **1** : the act of getting away or escaping ▪ *The robbers made a clean getaway.* **2 a** : a short vacation ▪ *a weekend getaway* **b** : a place where people go for a short vacation ▪ *the perfect island getaway*

get-go /ˈgɪtˌgoʊ, ˈgɛtˌgoʊ/ *n* — **from the get-go** *US, informal* : from the very beginning ▪ *She didn't like me from the get-go.*

get·ter /ˈgɛtə/ *n* [*C*] : someone or something that receives, gets, or is given something ▪ *the top vote getter*

get–to·geth·er /ˈgɛttəˌgɛðə/ *n* [*C*] : an informal social gathering ▪ *a family get-together*

get·up /ˈgɛtˌʌp/ *n* [*C*] *informal* : an unusual outfit or costume ▪ *a cowboy getup*

get–up–and–go /ˌgɛtˌʌpnˈgoʊ/ *n* [*U*] *informal* : energy and enthusiasm ▪ *full of get-up-and-go*

gey·ser /ˈgaɪˌzə, *Brit* ˈgiːzə/ *n* [*C*] : a hole in the ground that shoots out hot water and steam; *also* : the column of water and steam that comes from a geyser

ghast·ly /ˈgæstli, *Brit* ˈgɑːstli/ *adj* **ghast·li·er; -est 1** : very shocking or horrible ▪ *a ghastly crime* **2** : very bad : TERRIBLE ▪ *a ghastly mistake* ▪ *I feel ghastly.* [=very unwell]

ghet·to /ˈgɛtoʊ/ *n, pl* **-tos** *also* **-toes** [*C*] **1** : a part of a city in which members of a particular group or race live usually in poor conditions ▪ *a Jewish ghetto* **2** : the poorest part of a city ▪ *He grew up in the ghetto.*

ghost /ˈgoʊst/ *n* **1** [*C*] : the soul of a dead person thought of as living in an unseen world or as appearing to living people ▪ *a house haunted by ghosts* ▪ (*figurative*) *the ghosts of the past* [=memories of the past] **2** [*singular*] : a very small amount or trace ▪ *the ghost of a smile* ▪ *He doesn't have/stand a ghost of a chance* [=any chance] *of winning.* — **give up the ghost** *informal* : to die ▪ (*figurative*) *My car finally gave up the ghost.*

ghost·ly /ˈgoʊstli/ *adj* **ghost·li·er; -est** : of or relating to a ghost ▪ *A ghostly figure appeared.* : suggesting a ghost ▪ *a ghostly fog* — **ghostly** *adv* ▪ *Her face was ghostly pale/white.*

ghost town *n* [*C*] : a town that no longer has any people living in it

ghost·write /ˈgoʊstˌraɪt/ *vb* **-wrote** /-ˌroʊt/; **-writ·ten** /-ˌrɪtn/; **-writ·ing** [*T*] : to write (something, such as a book) for

someone else using that person's name ▪ *She was hired to ghostwrite the mayor's autobiography.* — **ghost·writ·er** *n* [*C*]

ghoul /ˈguːl/ *n* [*C*] : an evil creature in frightening stories that robs graves and eats dead bodies — **ghoul·ish** /ˈguːlɪʃ/ *adj* ▪ *a ghoulish laugh* — **ghoul·ish·ly** *adv*

GI /ˌʤiːˈaɪ/ *n, pl* **GI's** *or* **GIs** [*C*] : a member or former member of the U.S. armed forces

¹**gi·ant** /ˈʤaɪənt/ *adj* : very large : much larger or more powerful than normal ▪ *a giant photograph/machine/corporation* ▪ *a giant-size/giant-sized box of detergent*

²**giant** *n* [*C*] **1** : a legendary creature usually thought of as being an extremely large and powerful person **2** : a person or thing that is very large, powerful, or successful ▪ *a giant of the automotive industry* ▪ *an American literary giant*

giant panda *n* [*C*] : PANDA

gib·ber /ˈʤɪbə/ *vb* [*I*] : to talk in a fast or foolish way ▪ *What are they gibbering about?*

gib·ber·ish /ˈʤɪbərɪʃ/ *n* [*U*] : foolish, confused, or meaningless words ▪ *She was talking gibberish in her sleep.*

gibe *or* **jibe** /ˈʤaɪb/ *n* [*C*] : an insulting or critical remark that is meant to hurt someone or make someone appear foolish ▪ *cruel gibes about his weight*

gib·let /ˈʤɪblət/ *n* [*C*] : an organ (such as the heart or liver) of a bird that is cooked and eaten as food ▪ *gravy with giblets*

gid·dy /ˈgɪdi/ *adj* **gid·di·er; -est 1** : playful and silly ▪ *giddy children/antics* **2** : feeling or showing great happiness and joy ▪ *He was giddy with delight.* ▪ *giddy laughter* **3** *always before a noun* : causing dizziness ▪ *giddy heights* ▪ (*figurative*) *the giddy heights of fame* — **gid·di·ly** /ˈgɪdəli/ *adv* — **gid·di·ness** /ˈgɪdinəs/ *n* [*U*]

gift /ˈgɪft/ *n* [*C*] **1** : something that is given to another person or to a group or organization ▪ *a birthday/Christmas/anniversary/wedding gift* [=present] **2** : a special ability ▪ *an actor with a gift for comedy* ▪ *She claimed to have the gift of prophecy.* — **God's gift** *informal* + *disapproving* — used to describe the attitude of people who think that they are very talented, attractive, etc. ▪ *He thinks he's God's gift to the world.* [=he is very vain or conceited] — **look a gift horse in the mouth** see ¹HORSE

gift certificate *n* [*C*] *US* : a piece of paper that is worth a certain amount of money and is given to someone to be used like money to pay for things (such as the products or services of a particular business) ▪ *a $10 gift certificate* — called also (*Brit*) **gift token**, (*Brit*) **gift voucher**

gift·ed /ˈgɪftəd/ *adj* : having great natural ability : TALENTED ▪ *a school for gifted children* — **gifted with** : having (something) as a special ability or quality ▪ *He is gifted with a good sense of humor.*

gift wrap *n* [*U*] : decorative paper that is used for wrapping gifts ▪ *a roll of gift wrap* — **gift wrap** *vb* ~ **wrapped**; ~ **wrapping** [*T*] ▪ *The store will gift wrap your purchases.* ▪ *a gift-wrapped box*

gig /ˈgɪg/ *n* [C] *informal* : a job for a musician, an actor, etc. ▪ *her last acting gig*

giga·byte /ˈgɪgəˌbaɪt/ *n* [C] : a unit of computer information that is equal to 1,073,741,824 bytes ▪ *a twenty-gigabyte hard drive* — abbr. *GB*

gi·gan·tic /dʒaɪˈgæntɪk/ *adj* : extremely large ▪ *a gigantic corporation* ▪ *a gigantic* [=*huge*] *mistake*

gig·gle /ˈgɪgəl/ *vb* **gig·gled; gig·gling** [*I*] : to laugh in a nervous or childlike way ▪ *She giggled like a little kid.* — **gig·gle** *n* [C] ▪ *trying to suppress a giggle* ▪ (*Brit*) *That would be a bit of a giggle.* [=*would be amusing or enjoyable*] — **gig·gly** /ˈgɪgəli/ *adj* ▪ *giggly children*

gig·o·lo /ˈdʒɪgəˌloʊ/ *n, pl* **-los** [C] : a man who is paid by a woman to be her lover and companion

gild /ˈgɪld/ *vb* **gild·ed** /ˈgɪldəd/ *or* **gilt** /ˈgɪlt/; **gild·ing** [*T*] : to cover (something) with a thin layer of gold ▪ *gild a statue* — **gild the lily** : to try to improve something that does not need to be improved ▪ *Putting ice cream on the cake is just gilding the lily.* — **gilded** *adj* ▪ *a gilded sculpture/mask/design* ♢ A **gilded age** is a time of great success and wealth.

gill /ˈgɪl/ *n* [C] : the body part that a fish uses for breathing — **to the gills** *informal* **1** : as full as possible ▪ *The car was packed to the gills.* **2** : very thoroughly or completely ▪ *a theater equipped to the gills with new sound equipment*

¹gilt /ˈgɪlt/ *n* **1** [U] : a thin layer of gold or of something like gold ▪ *She covered the frame with gilt.* **2** [C] *Brit* : a stock or bond that is considered to be a very safe investment ▪ *She keeps her money in gilts.*

²gilt *past tense and past participle of* GILD

gilt–edged /ˈgɪltˌedʒd/ *adj* : having the best quality or rating ▪ *gilt-edged securities* [=stocks and bonds that are the safest kind of investment]

¹gim·me /ˈgɪmi/ — used in writing to represent the sound of the phrase *give me* when it is spoken quickly ▪ *Gimme the money.*

²gimme *n* [C] *US, informal* : something that is easily done, achieved, won, etc. ▪ (*golf*) *This putt is no gimme.* [=this is not an easy putt]

gim·mick /ˈgɪmɪk/ *n* [C] *often disapproving* : a method or trick that is used to get people's attention or to sell something ▪ *a marketing gimmick* — **gim·micky** /ˈgɪmɪki/ *adj* ▪ *a gimmicky movie*

gimpy /ˈgɪmpi/ *adj* **gimp·i·er; -est** *US, informal* : having an injury that makes walking difficult or painful ▪ *a gimpy football player* ▪ *a gimpy leg/foot*

gin /ˈdʒɪn/ *n* [C/U] : a clear alcoholic drink that is flavored with juniper berries

gin·ger /ˈdʒɪndʒə/ *n* [U] **1 a** : the strongly flavored root of a tropical plant that is used in cooking **b** : a spice made from ginger ▪ *a teaspoon of ginger* **2** *chiefly Brit* : a light reddish or reddish-brown color — **ginger** *adj, chiefly Brit* ▪ *ginger* [=reddish-brown] *hair*

ginger ale *n* [C/U] : a soft drink that is flavored with ginger

gin·ger·bread /ˈdʒɪndʒəˌbred/ *n* [U] : a cake or cookie made with molasses and ginger ▪ ***gingerbread men*** [=gingerbread cookies shaped like people]

gin·ger·ly /ˈdʒɪndʒəli/ *adv* : very carefully ▪ *She gingerly put the glass down.*

gin·ger·snap /ˈdʒɪndʒəˌsnæp/ *n* [C] : a hard cookie that is flavored with ginger — called also (*Brit*) **ginger nut**

ging·ham /ˈgɪŋəm/ *n* [U] : a cotton cloth that often is marked with a pattern of colored squares

gin·gi·vi·tis /ˌdʒɪndʒəˈvaɪtəs/ *n* [U] : a disease in which the gums become red, swollen, and sore

gin·seng /ˈdʒɪnˌsɛŋ/ *n* [U] : a Chinese herb that is used as a medicine

gi·raffe /dʒəˈræf, *Brit* dʒəˈrɑːf/ *n, pl* **giraffes** *or* **giraffe** [C] : a very tall African animal that has an extremely long neck and legs

gird /ˈgəd/ *vb* [T/I] : to prepare yourself to fight or to do something difficult ▪ *Both sides are girding (themselves) for battle.*

gird·er /ˈgədə/ *n* [C] : a strong beam used to build buildings, bridges, etc.

¹gir·dle /ˈgədl/ *n* [C] : something that wraps or circles around something else; *specifically* : a tight piece of clothing worn especially in the past by women under other clothes to make the area around the waist look thinner

²girdle *vb* **gir·dled; gir·dling** [T] *formal* : to form a circle around (something) or to surround (something) ▪ *the rings that girdle the planet Saturn*

girl /ˈgəl/ *n* **1** [C] **a** : a female child ▪ *a baby/little girl* **b** : DAUGHTER ▪ *Is this your little girl?* **2** [C] **a** : a young woman ▪ *teenage girls* ▪ *a* ***party girl*** [=a young woman who enjoys parties] ▪ *the* ***girl next door*** [=a wholesome young woman from a middle-class family] **b** : a usually young woman from a specified kind of place ▪ *a city/country girl* **3** *informal* ***the girls*** : the female friends or work partners of a woman viewed as a group ▪ *She went out dancing with the girls.* **b** [C] : a woman of any age — often used as a friendly way for one woman to address another woman ▪ *Girl, you will not believe what just happened to me!* **c** [C] : a woman or girl who does a particular job or activity ▪ *a shop girl* ♢ The use of *girl* to refer to an adult woman is often considered offensive, especially when it is used this way by a man. **4** [C] *informal + old-fashioned* : GIRLFRIEND ▪ *I took my girl out to the movies last night.* — **girl·hood** /ˈgəlˌhʊd/ *n* [U] ▪ *her girlhood friends* — **girl·ish** /ˈgəlɪʃ/ *adj* ▪ *a girlish voice* — **girl·ish·ly** *adv* — **girl·ish·ness** *n* [U]

girl·friend /ˈgəlˌfrend/ *n* [C] **1** : a woman that someone has a romantic or sexual relationship with ▪ *My girlfriend and I have only been dating for a couple of months.* **2** : a female friend ▪ *talking with her girlfriends*

Girl Guide *n* [C] : a member of a worldwide organization for girls ages 7 through 18 that is similar to the Girl Scouts in the United States — called also **Guide**

girl·ie also **girly** /ˈgɚli/ adj **1** always before a noun : featuring attractive young women who are wearing little or no clothing ▪ a girlie show/magazine **2** : having a quality that is considered suitable for girls or women and not suitable for men or boys ▪ a girlie voice

Girl Scout n [C] : a member of a U.S. organization for girls ages 5 through 17 ✧ Girl Scouts participate in group activities, learn skills, and are encouraged to have good morals and be good citizens. — called also **Scout**

girth /ˈgɚθ/ n [C/U] : the size of someone or something measured around the middle ▪ The tree is about two meters in girth.

gist /ˈdʒɪst/ n — the **gist** : the general or basic meaning of something said or written ▪ I got the gist of the speech. [=I understood the main points of the speech]

¹**give** /ˈgɪv/ vb **gave** /ˈgeɪv/; **giv·en** /ˈgɪvən/; **giv·ing 1** a [T] : to cause or allow someone to have (something) as a present ▪ She gave him a camera for Christmas. **b** [T/I] : to cause or allow (something valued or needed) to go to another person, group, etc. ▪ She gives money to many worthy causes. ▪ give blood ▪ It is better to give than to receive. **2** [T] : to put (something) into someone's hand ▪ He gave [=handed] me the letter. **3** [T] **a** : to provide someone with (something wanted or needed) ▪ They gave me a job/ride/chance. **b** : to allow someone to have or take (an amount of time) ▪ Just give me a few more minutes and I'll be ready. **4** [T] **a** : to treat or regard someone or something with (a particular attitude, feeling, etc.) ▪ You should give them some respect. [=you should respect them] **b** : to direct (something) toward someone ▪ He gave her a smile. [=he smiled at her] **5** [T] **a** : to tell (information) to someone ▪ Just give me the facts. ▪ The drawing gives [=shows] the dimensions of the room. **b** : to express or say (something) to someone ▪ They gave him careful instructions. ▪ Give them my regards. ▪ I give you my word [=I swear; I promise], I knew nothing about their plans. **c** : to show (something) ▪ She gave (us) no hint/indication that she was upset. **d** : to offer (something) for consideration or acceptance ▪ He gave no reason for his absence. **6** [T] : to say that someone has or deserves (something) ▪ He gives the credit for his success to his wife. **7** [T] **a** : to cause someone to have or experience (an emotion, a problem, etc.) ▪ Spicy food gives me indigestion. ▪ All that noise is giving me a headache. **b** : to cause someone to become affected by (something, such as an illness) ▪ His sister gave him the measles. **c** : to cause someone or something to have (a quality) ▪ The large windows give the room an open feeling. **8** [T] : to cause someone to get or take (a medicine) ▪ The doctor gave him an injection. **9** [T] **a** : to present (a show, speech, etc.) in public ▪ give a concert/lecture/talk/speech/performance **b** : to provide (something) as entertainment or as a social gathering ▪ give [=throw] a party **10**

[T] : to do (an action) ▪ She gave the door a push. [=she pushed the door] ▪ He gave her a hug. **11** [T] **a** : to cause someone to experience or suffer (a form of punishment) ▪ The judge gave him life (imprisonment) for murder. **b** : to cause someone to undergo or do (something) ▪ The teacher gave us a test. **12** ✧ To **give something thought/consideration** (etc.) is to think about it. ▪ We've given your proposal a lot of consideration. **13** ✧ To **give someone a call/ring/buzz/bell** is to make a telephone call to someone. ▪ I'll give you a call later. **14** ✧ If you try to do something, you **give it a try** or (informally) **give it a go/shot/stab**. **15** ✧ If you would **give anything** or **give your right hand/arm** to do or to have something, you want to do or have it very much. ▪ I'd give anything to be able to sing like that! **16** [T] : to make (something, such as your hand) available for someone ▪ She gave him her arm. [=she linked her arm in his arm] ✧ When a woman **gives her hand in marriage** to a man, she marries him. **17** [T] **a** : PAY ▪ I wouldn't give a penny for that old bike! **b** : SELL ▪ I'll give you the ticket for $20. **18** [T] : to say or judge that someone or something will last for (an amount of time) ▪ The doctor gave him only a few weeks to live. [=said that he would live for only a few weeks] **19** [T] informal : to admit (something) to or about someone ▪ He made an effort, I'll give him that (much). **20** [T] : to have or produce (something) as a product, result, or effect ▪ Cows give milk. **21** [T] formal : to cause someone to believe or think (something) ▪ He gave me to understand that he was there. ✧ To **give someone an idea/impression** (etc.) is to cause someone to believe or think something. ▪ Whatever gave you the idea (that) he was there?! **22** [I] **a** : to bend because of force, pressure, or strain ▪ The branch gave a bit under his weight. **b** : to break because of force, pressure, or strain ▪ The branch suddenly gave under his weight, and he fell to the ground. **23** [I] : to stop trying to resist or oppose someone ▪ Both sides refuse to give in this dispute. ▪ For the strike to be settled, **something has (got) to give!** [=one side or the other has to give in] — **give away** [phrasal vb] **give (something or someone) away** or **give away (something or someone) 1** a : to make a present of (something) ▪ The store is giving away free samples. **b** : to lose (something) in a careless way ▪ He gave the election away when he made a racist remark. **c** : to allow (something hidden or secret) to become known ▪ The way she looked at him gave away her real feelings for him. **2** a : to bring (the bride) to the groom at a wedding ▪ Traditionally, it's the father of the bride who gives his daughter away at the wedding. **b** : to reveal the truth about (someone) ▪ His accent gave him away as a northerner. — **give back** [phrasal vb] **give (something) back** or **give back (something)** : to cause someone to have (something) again ▪ He gave back the tools he borrowed. — **give birth** see BIRTH — **give ground** see ¹GROUND — **give in** [*phrasal vb*] : to stop trying to fight or resist something • *The strike continued because neither side would give in.* • *He refused to give in to their demands.* — **give of** [*phrasal vb*] **give of yourself** or **give of your time** *formal* : to use your time and effort to help others • *They freely gave of their time when their help was needed.* — **give off** [*phrasal vb*] : to send (light, a smell, etc.) out from a source • *The garbage gave off a terrible smell.* — **give or take** — used to indicate that the stated amount is approximate and might be increased or decreased by a specified amount • *He ran a mile, give or take a few yards.* — **give out** [*phrasal vb*] **1** : to stop working • *The engine gave out.* • *His voice gave out.* [=he was unable to talk] **2** : to become used up • *Our supply of fuel had almost given out.* **3** : to produce (noise, light, etc.) • *The stove gives out a lot of heat.* **4 give (something) out** or **give out (something)** : to give (something) to many people • *They gave out copies of the newsletter.* — **give over** [*phrasal vb*] *Brit, informal* : to stop doing something that is annoying or unpleasant • *Oh, give over! I'm tired of your complaints!* — **give over to** [*phrasal vb*] **give (something) over to 1** : to give (something) to (someone) to have, use, do, etc. • *She gave most of her work over to me.* **2 give (yourself) over to** : to allow (yourself) to be fully affected by, controlled by, or involved in (something) • *He gave himself over to despair.* **3** ◆ Something that is **given over to** a specified purpose is used for that purpose. • *One of the upstairs rooms is given over to storage.* — **give place to** see ¹PLACE — **give rise to** see ²RISE — **give up** [*phrasal vb*] **1** : to stop an activity or effort • *He vowed that he would never give up.* **2 give (something) up** or **give up (something) a** : to stop having, doing, or using (something) • *I tried to give up smoking/cigarettes.* • *They never gave up hope.* **b** : to stop trying to do (something) • *We tried to fix the engine, but in the end we had to give it up as impossible.* **c** *sports* : to allow (a score, a hit, etc.) by an opposing team or player • *The pitcher didn't give up a hit till the ninth inning.* **3 give (yourself) up** : to surrender (yourself) as a prisoner • *He gave himself up (to the police/authorities).* **4 give (yourself) up to** : to allow (yourself) to be fully affected by, controlled by, or involved in (something) • *She gave herself up to her work.* **5 give up on a** : to stop trying to improve the condition or behavior of (someone) • *His parents have never given up on him.* **b** : to stop having hope of seeing (someone) • *We'd given up on you hours ago!* **c** : to stop trying to do or achieve (something) • *They gave up on their plan.* — **give way** see ¹WAY — **What gives?** *informal* — used to ask the reason for something • *You've been acting weird all week. What gives?* [=why are you acting weird?]

²**give** *n* [*U*] : the ability of a material to

bend or stretch • *fabric with a lot of give*

give–and–take /ˌgrvənˈteɪk/ *n* [*U*] **1** : the process by which people reach an agreement with each other by giving up something that was wanted and agreeing to some of the things wanted by the other person • *A successful marriage requires a lot of give-and-take.* **2** *US* : the act or process of exchanging ideas or comments • *She enjoys a lot of friendly give-and-take with her customers.*

give·a·way /ˈgrvəˌweɪ/ *n* **1** [*singular*] : a movement, facial expression, etc., that clearly shows something that had not been known • *The way she looked at me was a dead giveaway that she was lying.* **2** [*C*] **a** : something that is given away free • *The store is offering coffee mugs as free giveaways.* **b** : an event at which things are given away • *staging a promotional giveaway*

¹**giv·en** /ˈgrvən/ *adj* — used to refer to a particular time, place, etc., that has been, will be, or might be specified • *They agreed to meet again at a given location/time.* — **given to** — used to say that a person often behaves in a specified way • *a man (very) much given to swearing/profanity* — **take (something) as given** : to regard or accept (something) as true or real • *We can take their support as given.* [=we can assume that they will support us]

²**given** *n* [*C*] : a basic fact or assumption • *In our system it is a given that all are equal before the law.*

³**given** *prep* — used to indicate something that is being assumed or considered • *Given the bad conditions under which the work was done, she did it very well.* • *Even given that the house is not perfect, it's still a great buy!*

given name *n* [*C*] *US* : FIRST NAME

giv·er /ˈgrvə/ *n* [*C*] : someone who gives something to another person • *a giver of orders* — often used in combination • *caregivers*

giz·mo /ˈgrzˌmoʊ/ *n, pl* **-mos** [*C*] *informal* : GADGET • *a clever gizmo*

giz·zard /ˈgrzəd/ *n* [*C*] : a part in a bird's stomach in which food is broken down into small pieces

gla·cial /ˈgleɪʃəl/ *adj* **1** : of, relating to, or caused by glaciers • *glacial flow/ice* • *a glacial lake* **2** : very cold • *a glacial wind* • *(figurative) a glacial stare* **3** : very slow • *a glacial pace* — **gla·cial·ly** *adv*

gla·cier /ˈgleɪʃə, Brit ˈglæsiə/ *n* [*C*] : a very large area of ice that moves slowly down a slope or valley or over a wide area of land

glad /ˈglæd/ *adj* **glad·der; -dest 1** *not before a noun* : feeling pleasure, joy, or delight • *We're glad (that) you could come.* • *I'm so glad to see you!* • *She was glad of his help.* **2** *not before a noun* : very willing *to do something* • *I'll be glad to answer your questions.* **3** *always before a noun, old-fashioned* : causing happiness and joy • *glad news/tidings* — **glad·ly** *adv* — **glad·ness** *n* [*U*]

glad·den /ˈglædn̩/ *vb* [*T*] *old-fashioned* : to make (someone) glad • *I was gladdened by the news.*

glade /ˈgleɪd/ n [C] : a grassy open space in a forest

glad·i·a·tor /ˈglædiˌeɪtɚ/ n [C] : a man in ancient Rome who fought against another man or animal for public entertainment

glam·or·ize also Brit **glam·or·ise** /ˈglæməˌraɪz/ vb **-ized**; **-iz·ing** [T] : to make (something) seem exciting and attractive • a movie that glamorizes violence/war

glam·or·ous /ˈglæmərəs/ adj : very exciting and attractive • She looked glamorous in her formal black gown. • glamorous movie stars — **glam·or·ous·ly** adv

glam·our also US **glam·or** /ˈglæmɚ/ n [U] : a very exciting and attractive quality • the glamour of the movie business

¹**glance** /ˈglæns, Brit ˈglɑːns/ vb **glanced**; **glanc·ing** [I] **1** : to look at someone or something very quickly • I glanced at my watch. **2** : to hit something and bounce off at an angle • A rock glanced off the windshield. — **glanc·ing** /ˈglænsɪŋ, Brit ˈglɑːnsɪŋ/ adj, always before a noun • A rock struck the windshield with a glancing blow.

²**glance** n [C] : a quick look • They exchanged glances. [=looked at each other quickly] — **at a glance** : with a quick look • She identified the problem at a glance. — **at first glance** see ¹FIRST

gland /ˈglænd/ n [C] : an organ in the body that makes a substance (such as saliva, sweat, or bile) which is used by the body • sweat glands — **glan·du·lar** /ˈglændʒələ/ adj

glandular fever n [U] chiefly Brit : MONONUCLEOSIS

¹**glare** /ˈgleɚ/ vb **glared**; **glar·ing** [I] **1** : to shine with a harsh, bright light • The sun glared down on us. **2** : to look directly at someone in an angry way • He glared at me from across the table.

²**glare** n **1** [C/U] : a harsh, bright light • the glare of the headlights/sun — sometimes used figuratively to suggest the idea of a very bright light shining on someone who is being given a lot of public attention • (figurative) She could not escape the glare of publicity. **2** [C] : an angry look • an angry/icy glare

glar·ing /ˈglerɪŋ/ adj **1** : very obvious or noticeable • a glaring mistake/omission **2** : shining with a harsh, bright light • the glaring sun — **glar·ing·ly** adv

glass /ˈglæs, Brit ˈglɑːs/ n **1** [U] : a hard usually transparent material that is used for making windows and other products • a glass bowl/bottle **2** [C] **a** : a drinking container made out of glass • a wine glass **b** : the amount held by a glass container • She drank two glasses of water. **3** [plural] : a pair of glass or plastic lenses set into a frame and worn over the eyes to help a person see • I have to wear glasses [=spectacles, (US) eyeglasses] for reading. — **under glass** : in a glass container • Most of the articles in the museum are preserved under glass.

glass ceiling n [C] : an unfair system or set of attitudes that prevents some people (such as women) from getting the most powerful jobs • women executives trying to break through the glass ceiling

glass·ware /ˈglæsˌweɚ, Brit ˈglɑːsˌweə/ n [U] : things made of glass

glassy /ˈglæsi, Brit ˈglɑːsi/ adj **glass·i·er**; **-est** **1** : smooth and shiny • the glassy surface of the lake **2** : not shiny or bright • glassy eyes

glau·co·ma /glaʊˈkoʊmə, glɑːˈkoʊmə/ n [U] : a disease in which pressure inside the eye causes gradual loss of vision

¹**glaze** /ˈgleɪz/ vb **glazed**; **glaz·ing** **1** [T] : to give a smooth and shiny coating to (something) • glazed ceramic pots **2** [I] : to become dull and lifeless • His eyes **glazed over**. [=he began to look very bored and tired]

²**glaze** n [C/U] : a liquid mixture that is put on the surface of something and that becomes shiny and smooth when it is dry • doughnuts with a chocolate glaze

gla·zier /ˈgleɪʒɚ, Brit ˈgleɪzɪə/ n [C] : a person who puts glass in window frames

gleam /ˈgliːm/ n **1** [C] : a small, bright light • the gleam of a flashlight **2** [singular] : a bright or shining quality • the gleam of the polished wood **3** [C] : a small amount or sign of something • a gleam of hope **4** [C] : a small amount or sign of happiness or excitement that can be seen in someone's eyes • He had a gleam (of delight) in his eyes. — **gleam** vb [I] • The sun gleamed on the water. • His eyes were gleaming with delight.

glean /ˈgliːn/ vb [T] **1** : to gather or collect (something) in a gradual way • She gleaned her data from various studies. **2** : to search (something) carefully • gleaning the files for information — **glean·ings** /ˈgliːnɪŋz/ n [plural] • the gleanings of long hours of research

glee /ˈgliː/ n [U] : a strong feeling of happiness • They were dancing with/in glee. — **glee·ful** /ˈgliːfəl/ adj — **glee·ful·ly** /ˈgliːfəli/ adv

glen /ˈglɛn/ n [C] : a narrow valley

glib /ˈglɪb/ adj **glib·ber**; **-best** disapproving **1** : said or done too easily or carelessly • glib answers **2** : speaking in a smooth, easy way that is not sincere • glib politicians — **glib·ly** adv — **glib·ness** n [U]

glide /ˈglaɪd/ vb **glid·ed**; **glid·ing** **1** [I] : to move in a smooth way • The boat glided through the water. **2** [T/I] of an airplane : to fly without engine power • The pilot glided (the plane) to a safe landing. — **glide** n [singular]

glid·er /ˈglaɪdɚ/ n [C] : an aircraft that is similar to an airplane but without an engine

glim·mer /ˈglɪmɚ/ n [C] **1** : a weak, unsteady light • the glimmer of a distant star **2** : a small amount or sign of something • a glimmer of hope — **glimmer** vb [I] • a glimmering candle

glim·mer·ing /ˈglɪmərɪŋ/ n [C] : GLIMMER • glimmerings of hope

glimpse /ˈglɪmps/ vb **glimpsed**; **glimps·ing** [T] : to look at or see (something or someone) for a very short time • We glimpsed him through the window. • (figurative) The book allows us to glimpse the future of the industry. — **glimpse** n [C] • We caught/got/had a glimpse of him. [=saw him briefly] • (figurative) The book *offers a glimpse into the future of the industry.*

glint /ˈglɪnt/ *n* [C] **1** : a small flash of light • *glints of sunlight* **2** : a small amount of emotion seen in a person's eyes • *He had a playful glint in his eyes.* — **glint** *vb* [I] • *The sun glinted off the waves.*

glis·ten /ˈglɪsn̩/ *vb* [I] : to shine with light reflected off a wet surface • *Her eyes glistened with tears.*

glitch /ˈglɪtʃ/ *n* [C] *informal* : an unexpected and usually minor problem • *computer/software/technical glitches*

¹**glit·ter** /ˈglɪtər/ *vb* [I] : to shine brightly • *Her eyes glittered with amusement.*

²**glitter** *n* [U] **1** : light that shines in small, bright points • *the glitter of diamonds* **2** : an appealing, fancy, and exciting quality • *the glitter of the city's nightlife* **3** : small, shiny objects used to decorate a surface — **glit·tery** /ˈglɪtəri/ *adj*

glitz /ˈglɪts/ *n* [U] *often disapproving* : a very fancy and attractive quality that is associated with rich or famous people • *the glitz and glamour of Hollywood life* — **glitzy** /ˈglɪtsi/ *adj* **glitz·i·er**; **-est** • *a glitzy casino*

gloat /ˈgloʊt/ *vb* [I] : to show in an improper or selfish way that you are happy with your own success or another person's failure • *He gloated over his victory.* • *a gloating remark/look*

glob /ˈglɑːb/ *n* [C] *informal* : a large, round drop of something soft or wet • *globs of whipped cream*

glob·al /ˈgloʊbəl/ *adj* **1** : involving the entire world • *the global economy* **2** : involving all of something and especially a computer system, file, etc. • *global database searches* — **glob·al·ly** /ˈgloʊbəli/ *adv*

global warming *n* [U] : the recent increase in the world's temperature that is believed to be caused by the increase of certain gases (such as carbon dioxide) in the atmosphere

globe /ˈgloʊb/ *n* **1** [C] : an object that is shaped like a large ball with a map of the world on it **2** *the globe* : the Earth • *satellites circling the globe* **3** [C] : a round object • *colorful glass globes* — **glob·u·lar** /ˈglɑːbjələr/ *adj* • *globular [=round] fruit*

globe–trot·ter /ˈgloʊbˌtrɑːtər/ *n* [C] : a person who frequently travels to different places around the world — **globe–trot·ting** /ˈgloʊbˌtrɑːtɪŋ/ *n* [U] • *globe-trotting adj* • *a globe-trotting diplomat*

glob·ule /ˈglɑːbjuːl/ *n* [C] : a tiny ball of something (such as a thick liquid) • *globules of fat/mercury*

gloom /ˈgluːm/ *n* [U] **1** : partial or total darkness • *the gloom of the forest* **2** : a feeling of sadness • *stories of gloom and doom* [=sad and tragic stories]

gloomy /ˈgluːmi/ *adj* **gloom·i·er**; **-est** **1** : somewhat dark • *a gloomy hallway* : not bright or sunny • *gloomy weather* **2** : causing feelings of sadness • *a gloomy landscape* : not hopeful or promising • *gloomy economic forecasts* **3** : sad or depressed • *feeling a little gloomy* — **gloom·i·ness** /ˈgluːminəs/ *n* [U]

glo·ri·fied *adj, always before a noun* — used to say that someone or something that seems to be impressive is actually not very important, powerful, etc. • *His title sounds good, but he's really just a glorified errand boy.*

glo·ri·fy /ˈglorəˌfaɪ/ *vb* **-fies**; **-fied**; **-fy·ing** [T] **1** : to honor or praise (a god or goddess) • *Glorify and give thanks to God.* **2** : to make (something) seem much better or more important than it really is • *The film glorifies violence.* — **glo·ri·fi·ca·tion** /ˌglorəfəˈkeɪʃən/ *n* [U]

glo·ri·ous /ˈgloriəs/ *adj* **1** : having or deserving glory, fame, or honor • *a glorious career/past/victory* **2** : very beautiful or delightful • *a glorious sunset/view* — **glo·ri·ous·ly** *adv*

¹**glo·ry** /ˈglori/ *n, pl* **-ries** **1** [U] : public praise, honor, and fame • *As a young soldier he dreamed of winning military glory.* • *the glory of his athletic career* • *Everything he did was for the greater glory of his country.* [=to bring honor to his country] • *They are basking in the glory of their success.* **2** [C] : something that is a source of great pride • *the glories of ancient civilizations* • *The movie was the crowning glory* [=the final, most successful achievement] *of his career.* **3** [U] : a state of great success or beauty • *the building's former glory* • *The autumn leaves are in their glory now.* [=are at their most beautiful stage now] — **glory days/years** : a time in the past that is remembered for great success or happiness • *The team's glory days are long gone.*

²**glory** *vb* **-ries**; **-ried**; **-ry·ing** — **glory in** [*phrasal vb*] : to feel or show great joy or pleasure because of (something) • *They gloried in their team's success.*

¹**gloss** /ˈglɑːs/ *n* **1** [*singular*] : the brightness of a smooth and shiny surface **2** [U, *singular*] : an attractive quality or appearance that hides the way a person or thing really is • *Her ambition was covered by a thin gloss of good manners.* **3** [U] : a type of makeup that is used to add shine and often color to the lips • *lip gloss* **4** [C] : a brief explanation of the meaning of a word used in a text

²**gloss** *vb* [T] : to give the meaning of (a word or phrase used in a text) • *Many unfamiliar terms are glossed in the book's introduction.* — **gloss over** [*phrasal vb*] : to treat or describe (something, such as a serious problem or error) as if it were not important • *He glossed over the accident.*

glos·sa·ry /ˈglɑːsəri/ *n, pl* **-ries** [C] **1** : a list that gives definitions of the hard or unusual words found in a book **2** : a dictionary of the special terms in a particular field or job

¹**glossy** /ˈglɑːsi/ *adj* **gloss·i·er**; **-est** : having a shiny, smooth surface • *glossy leaves/paint*

²**glossy** *n, pl* **gloss·ies** [C] **1** : a photograph with a shiny surface • *an 8x10* [=8-inch by 10-inch] *glossy* **2** *chiefly Brit* : a popular magazine that is printed on smooth and shiny paper

glove /ˈglʌv/ *n* [C] **1** : a covering for the hand that has separate parts for each finger • *a pair of gloves* **2 a** *baseball* : a padded leather covering for the hand that is used to catch the ball and has individual thumb and finger sections **b** : a very thick, padded covering for the hand that is worn in the sport of boxing • *a boxing glove* — often used figuratively in the phrases *take off the gloves* and *the gloves are off* to say that people are beginning to criticize or attack each other in a very harsh and direct way • *The candidates have taken off the gloves and started to make personal attacks against each other.* — **fit (you) like a glove** see ²FIT — **hand in glove** see ¹HAND — **gloved** /ˈɡlʌvd/ *adj* • *a gloved hand*

glove compartment *n* [C] : a small storage area in front of the front seat of a car, truck, etc. — called also *glove box*

¹**glow** /ˈɡloʊ/ *vb* [I] **1 a** : to shine with low light and heat but usually without flame • *The coals glowed in the fireplace.* **b** : to shine with a steady light • *The lamp glowed (brightly/softly) in the window.* **2 a** : to have a warm, reddish color from exercise, emotion, etc. • *Her face was glowing with embarrassment.* **b** : to look happy, excited, or healthy • *The children were glowing with pleasure/excitement.*

²**glow** *n* [singular] **1** : a soft and steady light • *the glow of the lamp* **2** : a pink color in your face from exercising, being excited, etc. • *the rosy glow of health* **3** : a pleasant feeling • *the glow of victory*

glow·er /ˈɡlaʊ̯ɚ/ *vb* [I] : to look at someone or something in an angry way • *He glowered at us when he heard us laughing.* — **glower** *n* [C]

glowing *adj* : full of praise • *a glowing recommendation/review* — **glow·ing·ly** /ˈɡloʊɪŋli/ *adv*

glow·worm /ˈɡloʊ̯ˌwɚm/ *n* [C] : a type of insect that produces a small amount of light from its body

glu·cose /ˈɡluːˌkoʊs/ *n* [U] *technical* : a type of sugar that is found in plants and fruits

¹**glue** /ˈɡluː/ *n* [C/U] : a substance used to stick things tightly together — **stick like glue** see ²STICK — **glu·ey** /ˈɡluːwi/ *adj* **glu·i·er; -est**

²**glue** *vb* **glued; glu·ing** also **glue·ing** [T] **1** : to make (something) stick to something else by using glue • *I glued the pieces of the cup back together.* **2** : to stay in one place because of interest, shock, excitement, etc. • *I was glued to the phone, waiting for her to call.* • *a thriller that will keep you glued to your seat*

glum /ˈɡlʌm/ *adj* **glum·mer; -mest** : sad or depressed • *feeling glum* • *a glum silence* — **glum·ly** *adv*

glut /ˈɡlʌt/ *n* [C] : too much of something • *There's a glut of oil on the market.* — **glut** *vb* **glut·ted; glut·ting** [T] • *The market is glutted with oil.*

glu·ten /ˈɡluːtn̩/ *n* [U] : a substance in wheat and flour that holds dough together

glu·ti·nous /ˈɡluːtn̩əs/ *adj* : STICKY • *glutinous rice*

glut·ton /ˈɡlʌtn̩/ *n* [C] **1** : a person who eats too much **2** : someone who wants a large amount of something — + *for* • *a*

glutton for gossip • *He's a real glutton for punishment.* [=he seems to enjoy things that other people dislike] — **glut·ton·ous** /ˈɡlʌtən̩əs/ *adj* • *a gluttonous person/appetite* — **glut·tony** /ˈɡlʌtən̩i/ *n* [U]

gm *abbr* gram

GMT *abbr* Greenwich Mean Time

gnarled /ˈnɑɚld/ *adj* **1** *of wood* : having many twists and hard bumps or knots • *gnarled branches/trees* **2** : bumpy or twisted • *the old man's gnarled fingers/hands*

gnash /ˈnæʃ/ *vb* — **gnash your teeth 1** : to grind your teeth together • *He gnashed his teeth in his sleep.* **2** : to show you are angry, upset, etc. • *His opponents have been gnashing their teeth in/with frustration.*

gnat /ˈnæt/ *n* [C] : a small fly that bites people and animals

gnaw /ˈnɑː/ *vb* [T/I] : to bite or chew (something) repeatedly • *The dog was gnawing (at/on) a bone.* — **gnaw at** [phrasal vb] : to be a source of worry or concern to (someone) • *This problem has been gnawing at me lately.*

gnome /ˈnoʊm/ *n* [C] **1** *in stories* : a small creature who lives inside the earth and guards treasure ✧ A gnome looks like a little man and is often shown wearing a pointed hat. **2** : a statue that looks like a gnome and is often used outside in a garden • *a garden gnome*

gno·mic /ˈnoʊmɪk/ *adj, formal* : said or written using few words that are difficult to understand • *gnomic writing/wisdom*

GNP *abbr* gross national product

¹**go** /ˈɡoʊ/ *vb* **goes** /ˈɡoʊz/; **went** /ˈwɛnt/; **gone** /ˈɡɑːn/; **go·ing** /ˈɡoʊɪŋ/ **1** [I] **a** : to move or travel to a place • *Let's go home/outside/downstairs.* • *a train going to Chicago* **b** : to travel to and stay in a place for a particular amount of time • *I went to Rome last year.* **c** : to move or travel in a particular way or for a particular distance • *The car was going too fast.* • *Go straight for two blocks.* • *(figurative) Their relationship doesn't seem to be going anywhere.* [=doesn't seem to be making any progress] • *(figurative) Where do we go from here?* [=what do we do now?] • *(figurative) We still have a long way to go.* [=much more to do] • *(figurative) She could go far.* [=be very successful] • *(figurative) These changes will go a long way toward solving the dispute.* • *(figurative) Would you go so far as to call them dishonest?* [=would you say that they are dishonest?] • *(figurative) This time you've gone too far!* [=done something that cannot be allowed] **2** [I] **a** : to move to or be at a place (such as an office or school) for work, study, etc. — + *to* • *She goes to church/work at 9 a.m.* • *He went to prison.* **b** : to do something that involves moving or traveling to a place • *We're going on vacation next week.* • *I like to go walking/swimming/shopping.* [=I like to walk/swim/shop] **c** : to move or travel to a place for a particular purpose • *We went to see a movie last night.* • *Are you going to the wedding?* • *I may go to see them next week.* = *I may go and see them next week.* = *(US) I may go see them*

next week. **3** [I] : to leave a place ▪ *It's getting late. I should go.* **4** [T/I] : to lie or move along a particular route or in a particular direction ▪ *The road goes from the town to the lake.* ▪ *Are you going my way?* [=are you going in the same direction that I'm going in?] ▪ (figurative) *He always goes his own way.* [=does the things he wants to do] **5** [I] : to provide a way to get to a place ▪ *That door goes to the cellar.* **6** [I] : to be lost, used, or spent ▪ *I don't know where the money goes.* ▪ *I put my keys here a few minutes ago, and now they're gone.* ▪ *The money was all gone by Friday.* **7** [I] : to die ▪ *She went peacefully last night.* **8** [I] **a** *of time* : to pass ▪ *The time/day seemed to go very quickly.* **b** : to happen in a particular way ▪ *The evening went well/badly.* ▪ **The way things are going** [=if things keep happening this way], *I may get laid off.* **9** [I] *informal* — used to talk or ask about how you are feeling ▪ *"How are things going? = How's it going?" "Everything's going well/fine/great."* **10** [I] : to be given up, thrown away, etc. ▪ *I want to keep these, but that one can go.* **11** [I] : to be sold ▪ *The cabinets go for about $400.* **12** [I] : to fail or become weak because of use, age, etc. ▪ *His hearing has started to go.* **13** [I] : to break because of force or pressure ▪ *The dam/roof could go at any time.* **14** [I] : to start doing something ▪ *Everyone's here, so I think we're ready to go.* = (US, informal) *I think we're good to go.* [=ready to start] **15** [I] — used to describe the result of a contest, election, decision, etc. ▪ *The election went in her favor.* **16** [I] : to work in the usual or expected way ▪ *I finally got the engine going.* **17 a** [linking vb] : to become — used to describe a change ▪ *The building has gone condo.* [=the building has become a condominium] — used especially to describe a change that is not wanted ▪ *The tire went flat.* ▪ *The company went bankrupt.* **b** [I] : to change ▪ *The situation went from bad to worse.* **18** [linking vb] — used to describe someone's or something's condition ▪ *There was no food, so we had to go hungry.* **19** [I] — used to talk about a story, song, etc. ▪ *I can't remember how the story goes.* [=what happens in the story] **20** [I] **a** : to be able to fit in or through a space ▪ *The box was too big to go through the door.* **b** : BELONG 1 ▪ *These books go on the top shelf.* **21** [I] : to require you to do what is said or demanded ▪ *What she says goes!* [=you have to do what she tells you to do] **22** [I] *informal* : to use the toilet ▪ *The boy said he had to go.* **23** [T/I] : to make a sound ▪ *The cow went "moo."* **24** [T] *informal* : to say (something) — used in describing what people said in a conversation ▪ *So she goes, "Did you write this?" and I go, "Mind your own business!"* **25** [I] *of a sports team or player* : to have a specified record ▪ *The team went 11–2 last season.* [=the team won 11 games and lost 2 games last year] — **anything goes** : anything is acceptable ▪ *She dresses conservatively at work, but on the weekends, anything goes.* — **as**

(someone or something) goes — used to compare someone or something with someone or something else of the same kind ▪ *As lectures go, it was very interesting.* — **be going to** — used to talk about what will happen or could happen ▪ *It's going to rain.* ▪ *I was just going to call him.* — **go about** [phrasal vb] **1** : to start to do (something) ▪ *I don't know how to go about (doing) it.* **2** : to do (something) ▪ *People are just quietly going about their business.* [=doing the things that they usually do] — **go after** [phrasal vb] **1 a** : to follow and try to stop or catch (someone) ▪ *The police went after the suspect.* **b** : to try to find and punish (someone) ▪ *The government is going after him.* **2** : to try to get (something or someone) ▪ *If you want the job, you should just go after it.* — **go against** [phrasal vb] **1** : to not agree with (something) ▪ *values that go against those of society* **2 a** : to oppose (someone or something) ▪ *He went against their wishes.* **b** : to compete against (a player or team) in a contest or game ▪ *The Red Sox will go against the Yankees today.* **3** : to not be good for (someone) ▪ *Everything seemed to be going against her.* — **go ahead** [phrasal vb] **1** : to do or begin to do something ▪ *They went ahead and started working without my approval.* ▪ *Despite the bad weather, they went ahead with the party.* ▪ *"Could I sit here?" "Sure, go (right) ahead."* **2** : to happen or proceed ▪ *The party went ahead as planned.* — **go all out** : to do something with as much effort as possible ▪ *When he has a party, he likes to go all out.* [=have a big and expensive party] — **go along** [phrasal vb] **1** : to continue or proceed ▪ *The project is going along smoothly.* **2** : to go or travel with someone ▪ *I asked whether I could go along (with them).* **3** : to agree to do or accept what other people want ▪ *He refused to go along (with our plan).* **4** : to be part of something — + with ▪ *You have to accept the stress that goes along with the job.* — **go around** or chiefly Brit **go round** [phrasal vb] **1 a** : to go to different places ▪ *She goes around with her friends to lots of clubs.* **b** chiefly Brit : to travel to a place that is nearby ▪ *I went round to his flat.* **c** — used to describe the way a person often dresses or behaves ▪ *You can't go around treating people so rudely.* **2** : to go or pass from one person to another person ▪ *There's a rumor going around (the office) that she's about to get fired.* **3** ✧ If people want something and there is **enough/plenty to go around**, there is enough for all of the people who want it or need it. **4 what goes around comes around** *informal* — used to say that if you treat other people badly you will eventually be treated badly by someone else — **go at** [phrasal vb] **1 a** : to attack (someone) ▪ *They went at each other viciously.* **b** : to fight or argue ▪ *They went at it for almost an hour.* **2** : to make an effort to do or deal with (something) ▪ *trying to go at the problem from a different angle* — **go away** [phrasal vb] **1 a** : to leave a place or person ▪ *She told him to go away.* **b** : to leave your home for a period of time ▪ *He went away to college.* **2** : to stop or end ▪ *I wish there was some way to make the pain go away.* — **go back** [*phrasal vb*] **1 a** : to return to a place ▪ *After college she went back home.* **b** : to begin doing something again — + *to* ▪ *I turned off the alarm and went back to sleep.* ✧ The phrase **there's no going back** means that you have done or decided something and cannot change it. **2 a** : to have existed for a particular amount of time or since a particular period ▪ *a tradition that goes back to colonial times* **b** : to have known each other for a particular amount of time ▪ *We go back 30 years.* **c** : to think or talk about something from the past ▪ *I'd like to go back to your earlier comment.* **3 go back on** : to not do what is required by (something, such as a promise) ▪ *She went back on her promise.* — **go before** [*phrasal vb*] **1** : to happen or exist at an earlier time than (someone) ▪ *remembering the people who went before us* **2** : to be considered by (someone or something) for an official decision or judgment ▪ *The case went before the court.* — **go by** [*phrasal vb*] **1** *of time* : to pass ▪ *Many years have gone by since then.* ▪ *happy memories of days gone by* [=days/times in the past] **2 a** : to be guided or directed by (something) ▪ *That's a good rule to go by.* **b** : to form an opinion from (something) ▪ *You can't always go by appearances.* **3** : to be known by (a name) ▪ *His name is Edwin but he goes by Ed.* [=people call him Ed] **4** : to go somewhere in order to visit someone ▪ *I went by (her house) to see her.* — **go down** [*phrasal vb*] **1** : to fall or crash to the ground ▪ *The airplane went down in a field.* **2** : to sink into the water ▪ *The ship went down after hitting an iceberg.* **3 a** : to drop to a lower level ▪ *Prices should go down soon.* **b** : to become less or smaller ▪ *The swelling has gone down.* **4** : to become less bright ▪ *The lights went down as the movie started.* **5 a** — used to say how easy or hard it is to eat or drink something ▪ *The medicine went down easily.* **b** — used to say how easy or hard it is to accept or agree to something ▪ *His suggestion didn't go down very well with his boss.* **6** : to lose or fail ▪ *She went down in the first round of the tournament.* **7** *of a computer, system, etc.* : to stop working ▪ *The network went down this morning.* **8** : to be remembered or talked about as an important person, event, etc. ▪ *He will go down (in history) as a great leader.* **9** *slang* : to happen ▪ *We need to find out what's going down.* **10 go down with** *Brit* : to begin to have or suffer from (an illness) ▪ *He went down with measles.* — **go for** [*phrasal vb*] **1 a** : to attack (someone) ▪ *My dog went for the intruder.* **b** : to try to get (something) ▪ *go for the prize* **2** : to accept or agree to (something, such as a plan or suggestion) ▪ *I asked her to lend us some money, but she wouldn't go for it.* **3** *informal* **a** : to like or be attracted to (someone or something) ▪ *I*

don't really go for modern art. **b** : to relate to or apply to (someone or something) ▪ *The rule goes for you, too.* **4** : to be sold for (a particular price) ▪ *The painting went for more than a million dollars.* **5** : to do an activity (such as walking or driving a car) that usually involves going somewhere ▪ *She went for a walk/stroll/drive/swim.* **6** ✧ If you **have something going for you**, you have a talent, skill, etc., that helps you. ▪ *You have a lot going for you!* [=you have many talents, abilities, etc.] — **go in** [*phrasal vb*] **1 go in for** : to like or be interested in (something) ▪ *She doesn't go in for sports.* **2 go in on** *US, informal* : to help pay for (something, such as a present) ▪ *We all went in on the gift together.* **3 go in with** : to join (someone) in a business, project, etc. ▪ *She went in with him on his new business.* — **go into** [*phrasal vb*] **1 a** : to start to be in (a different state or condition) ▪ *She went into a deep depression.* ▪ *He went into hiding.* **b** : to start to move in (a different and usually bad way) ▪ *The car went into a skid.* **2** : to start to do (something) as a job or career ▪ *She wants to go into medicine.* ▪ *His dream is to go into business for himself.* [=to start his own business] **3** : to talk about (something) ▪ *I told the story without going into too many details.* : to talk about the details of (something) ▪ *I don't feel like going into what happened right now.* **4** : to be used for (something) ▪ *Lots of time went into (completing) the project.* — **go off** [*phrasal vb*] **1 a** : to explode ▪ *The building was evacuated before the bomb went off.* **b** : to shoot ▪ *The gun went off accidentally.* **c** : to begin to make a sudden loud noise ▪ *I woke up when the alarm went off.* **2** *of lights, electricity, etc.* : to stop working ▪ *The lights in the building suddenly went off.* **3 a** : to occur or happen ▪ *The meeting went off as scheduled.* **b** : to happen a particular way ▪ *The party went off well.* **4** *US, informal* : to begin shouting at someone in an angry way ▪ *Her boss went off (on her) because she was late.* **5** *Brit* : to stop liking (someone or something) ▪ *My boss has gone off the idea.* **6 go off with** *chiefly Brit* **a** : to leave (a spouse, partner, etc.) for someone else ▪ *He left his wife and went off with another woman.* **b** : to steal (something) ▪ *Someone went off with my pencil.* — **go on** [*phrasal vb*] **1 a** : to continue ▪ *We stopped briefly in Detroit, and then went on to Chicago.* ▪ *Life goes on.* ▪ *She went on working.* [=continued to work] ▪ *We can't go on like this.* **b** : to continue talking ▪ *He went on (and on) about how unfairly he had been treated.* **2** : to go or travel to a place before another person or group that is with you ▪ *You go on (ahead). I'll come later.* **3** : to do or say something else after you have finished doing or saying something ▪ *He accepted the nomination and went on to win the election.* ▪ *She went on to say that more changes would be necessary.* **4** : to happen ▪ *What's going on?* **5** *of lights, electricity, etc.* : to begin to work or function ▪ *The lights went on briefly and then* *went out again.* **6** : to form an opinion or conclusion from something ▪ *There's very little evidence* **to go on**. [=very little evidence that can be used to form an opinion] **7** — used in speech to urge someone to do something ▪ *Go on (and try it): you might actually like it!* **8 go on at** *chiefly Brit, informal* : to criticize (someone) often or repeatedly ▪ *Quit going on at me all the time!* — **go out** [*phrasal vb*] **1** : to leave your home for an activity ▪ *I'm going out for a walk.* ▪ *He went out drinking with his friends.* **2** : to be sent from a person or place ▪ *The message went out by e-mail.* **3** : to stop being popular or fashionable ▪ *That hairstyle went out (of fashion) years ago.* **4 a** : to go on a date with someone ▪ *They went out a couple of times.* **b** : to have a continuing romantic relationship with someone ▪ *I've been going out with her for quite a while.* **5** : to stop working, shining, or burning ▪ *The electricity suddenly went out.* ▪ *The fire/candle/lights went out.* **6** *chiefly US* : to try to become a member of a team, group, etc. ▪ *He went out for football last year.* **7** : to be broadcast on the radio, television, etc. ▪ *A distress call went out three hours ago.* — **go over** [*phrasal vb*] **1** *US* : to be accepted or received in a particular way ▪ *Her proposal/joke didn't go over very well.* **2 a** : to talk about or think about (something) carefully ▪ *He went over all the arguments before making up his mind.* **b** : to look at or study (something) again in order to correct it, learn it, etc. ▪ *Let's go over the instructions.* — **go the distance** see ¹DISTANCE — **go there** *informal* : to start to talk or think about something — usually used in negative statements ▪ *"Do you remember when we were dating?" "Let's not go there."* [=I don't want to talk about that] — **go through** [*phrasal vb*] **1 a** : to study or look at (something) in a careful way ▪ *Let's go through the plan one more time.* **b** : to look in or at (something) in order to find something ▪ *I found him going through my closet.* **c** : to experience (something) ▪ *He's going through a painful divorce.* **d** : to spend or use all of (something) ▪ *He went through all the money he inherited.* **e** : to occur throughout (something) ▪ *A note of despair goes through the narrative.* ◆ If an idea, song, etc., is **going through your head/mind**, you are thinking about or remembering it. **f** : to do (something) ▪ *It took me an hour to go through my morning routine.* **2** ◆ Something (such as a law or contract) that **goes through** is officially accepted and approved. ▪ *The bill is expected to go through (Congress) easily.* **3 go through with** : to do (something that you have thought or talked about) ▪ *I never thought he'd actually go through with it.* — **go to** [*phrasal vb*] **1** : to begin to be in (a particular state, condition, or situation) ▪ *You need to go to sleep.* ▪ *The countries went to war.* **2** : to be given to (someone or something) ▪ *First prize went to the team from Chicago.* **3** *chiefly US* : to do something that causes you (trouble or expense) ▪ *You*

shouldn't go to all this trouble just for me. — **go together** [*phrasal vb*] **1** : to be suited to or appropriate for each other ▪ *The tie and his suit go together well.* **2** : to have a continuing romantic relationship ▪ *They've been going together for several years.* — **go to show/prove** : to help show or prove something ▪ *Her success goes to show that hard work pays off.* — **go toward(s)** [*phrasal vb*] : to help pay for (something) ▪ *My extra income is going towards a new car.* — **go under** [*phrasal vb*] **1** : to sink below the surface of the water ▪ *The ship went under.* **2** : to fail ▪ *The company is in danger of going under.* — **go up** [*phrasal vb*] **1** : to rise to a higher level ▪ *Prices have gone up.* **2** : to become brighter ▪ *The lights went up when the movie ended.* **3** : to be built ▪ *A new store is going up downtown.* — **go with** [*phrasal vb*] **1** : to date (someone) ▪ *I've been going with her for a while now.* **2 a** : to be suitable for or appropriate with (something) ▪ *Her skirt doesn't really go with her blouse.* **b** : to exist or occur as a necessary part of (something) ▪ *the stress that goes with the job.* **3** : to choose or use (someone or something) ▪ *She didn't get the job because they decided to go with someone else.* — **go without** [*phrasal vb*] : to not have (something) ▪ *go without sleeping/sleep* — **here goes (nothing)** see ¹HERE — **to go** **1** : still remaining ▪ *There are only three days to go until my birthday!* **2** *US, of food* : sold to be taken away and eaten somewhere else ▪ *I'd like a hamburger to go.*

²**go** *n, pl* **goes** **1** [*C*] : an attempt to do something ▪ *Let me have a go (at it).* [=let me try to do it] ▪ *I had never tried skiing but I decided to give it a go.* **2** [*singular*] *US, informal* : permission to do something ▪ *She gave the project a go.* [=she gave permission for the project to go ahead] ◆ In informal U.S. English, if you say that something **is a go**, you mean that it will or can happen in the way that was planned or hoped for. ▪ *The project is a go.* If you say **all systems (are) go**, you mean that everything is working correctly so that something can continue or proceed in the planned or expected way. ▪ *NASA officials have declared all systems go for the rocket launch.* **3** [*C*] *Brit* : a turn in a game or other activity ▪ *It's your go.* — **make a go of** : to succeed in doing (something) ▪ *He started a business, but he wasn't able to make a go of it.* — **no go** *US, informal* — used to say that something will not be allowed or cannot be done ▪ *I asked my boss for more time, but she said no go.* — **on the go** **1** : very active or busy ▪ *She's always on the go.* **2** *chiefly Brit* : happening or going ▪ *I have several projects on the go.*

goad /ˈɡoʊd/ *vb* [*T*] : to urge or force (someone) to do something ▪ *He was goaded (on) by a sense of duty.* — **goad** *n* [*C*] ▪ *The threat of legal action is a powerful goad to companies that ignore the rules.*

¹**go-ahead** /ˈɡoʊəˌhɛd/ *n* — **the go-ahead** : permission to do something ▪

We were given the go-ahead for the project.
²go–ahead *adj, always before a noun* **1** *US, sports* : allowing a team to take the lead in a game • *the go-ahead run/touchdown/goal* **2** *Brit* : having a lot of energy and desire to try new ideas and methods • *a vigorous go-ahead company*

goal /'goʊl/ *n* [C] **1** : something that you are trying to do or achieve • *achieve/accomplish/reach/realize a goal* **2 a** : an area or object into which a ball or puck must be hit, kicked, etc., to score points in various games (such as soccer and hockey) **b** : the act of hitting, kicking, etc., a ball or puck into a goal or the score that results from doing this • *She scored the winning goal.*

goal·ie /'goʊli/ *n* [C] : a player who defends the goal in soccer, hockey, etc.

goal·keep·er /'goʊlˌkiːpɚ/ *n* [C] : a player who defends the goal in various games (especially soccer) — **goal·keep·ing** /'goʊlˌkiːpɪŋ/ *n* [U]

goal line *n* [C] : a line that must be crossed to score a goal in soccer, hockey, football, etc.

goal·post /'goʊlˌpoʊst/ *n* [C] : one of two upright posts that form part of the goal in various games (such as soccer, hockey, and football) — **move/shift the goalposts** *Brit* : to change the rules or requirements in a way that makes success more difficult

goal·tend·er /'goʊlˌtɛndɚ/ *n* [C] *US* : a player who defends the goal in various games (especially hockey) — **goal·tend·ing** /'goʊlˌtɛndɪŋ/ *n* [U]

goat /'goʊt/ *n* [C] **1** : a small animal that is related to the sheep **2** *the goat US* : a person who is blamed for a loss or failure — **get your goat** *informal* ✧ If something *gets your goat*, it upsets you or irritates you.

goa·tee /goʊ'tiː/ *n* [C] : a small pointed beard on a man's chin

gob /'gɑːb/ *n* **1** [C] : a lump of something • *a gob of gum* **2** [*plural*] *US, informal* : a large amount of something • *gobs of money*

gob·ble /'gɑːbəl/ *vb* **gob·bled; gob·bling** **1** [T] : to swallow or eat (something) quickly • *He gobbled (down/up) his food.* **2** [T] : to take (something) quickly or suddenly • *The local bank was gobbled up by a national conglomerate.* **3** [I] : to make the sound that a male turkey makes

go–be·tween /'goʊbəˌtwiːn/ *n* [C] : a person who talks to people or groups who disagree in order to help deal with or end the disagreement • *He'll act/serve as a go-between during the negotiations.*

gob·let /'gɑːblət/ *n* [C] : a container used for drinking liquids that has a round bowl on top of a stem attached to a flat base

gob·lin /'gɑːblən/ *n* [C] *in stories* : an ugly and sometimes evil creature that likes to cause trouble

gob·smacked /'gɑːbˌsmækt/ *adj, Brit, informal* : very surprised or shocked • *I was (really) gobsmacked by the news!*

god /'gɑːd/ *n* **1** **God** [*singular*] **a** : the perfect and all-powerful spirit or being

that is worshipped especially by Christians, Jews, and Muslims as the one who created and rules the universe **b** ✧ **God** is used informally by itself and in phrases to make a statement or question more forceful or to express surprise, anger, etc. These uses are common but are considered offensive by some people. • *God, it's hot out today.* • *Good God, that's a lot of food!* • *Oh my God! I can't believe it!* • *I wish to God you would stop complaining.* **2** [C] : one of various spirits or beings worshipped in some religions • *the gods and goddesses of ancient Egypt* — often used informally to suggest that what happens to someone is controlled by gods or by luck • *The gods smiled/frowned on us.* [=we had good/bad luck] **3** [C] : a person and especially a man who is greatly loved or admired • *a guitar god like Jimi Hendrix* — **God bless you** see BLESS — **God forbid** see FORBID — **God help (someone)** see ¹HELP — **God knows** see ¹KNOW — **God's gift** see GIFT — **God willing** — used to say what you hope and expect to do or happen if no problems occur • *God willing, I'll finish my degree this year.* — **play God** see ¹PLAY — **so help me God** see ¹HELP — **thank God** see THANK —

god·like /'gɑːdˌlaɪk/ *adj*

god–aw·ful /gɑdˈɑːfəl/ *adj, informal + sometimes offensive* : very bad or unpleasant • *god-awful weather*

god·child /'gɑːdˌtʃaɪəld/ *n, pl* **-chil·ren** /-ˌtʃɪldrən/ [C] : a child that you promise to help teach and guide in religious matters when you become the child's godparent in a Christian baptism ceremony

god·damn *also* **god·dam** /ˌgɑːdˈdæm/ *or* **god·damned** /ˌgɑːdˈdæmd/ *adj, always before a noun, informal + impolite* : DAMN • *a goddamn fool/lie*

> *usage* **Goddamn** is an angry word that many people find offensive.

god·daugh·ter /'gɑːdˌdɑːtɚ/ *n* [C] : a female godchild

god·dess /'gɑːdəs/ *n* [C] **1** : a female god (sense 2) **2** : a woman who is greatly loved or admired

god·fa·ther /'gɑːdˌfɑːðɚ/ *n* [C] **1** : a man who is a godparent **2 a** : a man who invents or begins something • *the godfather of rock and roll* **b** *usually* **Godfather** : the leader of a group of criminals who belong to a secret criminal organization (such as the Mafia)

God–fear·ing /'gɑːdˌfiːrɪŋ/ *adj* — used to describe religious people who try to obey the rules of their religion and to live in a way that is considered morally right • *hardworking, God-fearing people*

god·for·sak·en /'gɑːdfɚˌseɪkən/ *adj, always before a noun, of a place* : not at all interesting or appealing and usually located far from interesting people and places • *a godforsaken little town*

God–giv·en /'gɑːdˈgɪvən/ *adj* : received as a gift from God • *a God-given talent*

god·less /'gɑːdləs/ *adj, disapproving* : not believing in God • *a godless people/society*

god·ly /ˈgɑːdli/ *adj* **god·li·er; -est** *old-fashioned* : believing in God and in the importance of living a moral life ▪ *a godly person/life* — **god·li·ness** *n* [U] ▪ *Cleanliness is next to godliness.* [=it is almost as important to be clean as it is to be good]

god·moth·er /ˈgɑːdˌmʌðɚ/ *n* [C] : a woman who is a godparent — see also FAIRY GODMOTHER

god·par·ent /ˈgɑːdˌperənt/ *n* [C] : a person who promises to help teach and guide someone in religious matters as part of a Christian baptism ceremony : a godfather or godmother

god·send /ˈgɑːdˌsɛnd/ *n* [C] : something or someone that provides great and usually unexpected help when it is needed ▪ *The new drug is a godsend for many people.*

god·son /ˈgɑːdˌsʌn/ *n* [C] : a male godchild

goes see GO

go·fer /ˈgoʊfɚ/ *n* [C] *informal* : a person whose job is to do various small and usually boring jobs for other people

go–get·ter /ˈgoʊˌgɛtɚ/ *n* [C] *informal* : a person who works very hard and who wants very much to succeed

gog·gle–eyed /ˈgɑːgl̩ˌaɪd/ *adj, informal* : with the eyes very open in a way that shows surprise, amazement, etc. ▪ *He stared at me goggle-eyed.*

gog·gles /ˈgɑːgl̩z/ *n* [*plural*] : special eyeglasses that fit close to your face and that are worn to protect your eyes ▪ *swimming/ski/safety goggles*

¹**go·ing** /ˈgoʊɪŋ/ *n* **1** [C] : the act of leaving a place ▪ *We were sad to learn of her going.* [=departure] ▪ *watching the comings and goings of museum visitors* **2** [U] **a** : the condition of the ground for walking, running, etc. ▪ *Debris in the street made the going difficult.* **b** — used to describe a situation in which you are trying to make progress or do something ▪ *It's been slow going so far.* [=progress has been slow so far] ▪ *The report is pretty hard/heavy going.* [=it is quite difficult to understand] ▪ *rough/tough going* ▪ *What will you do when the going gets tough?* [=when it becomes difficult to continue or to make progress]

²**going** *adj* **1** *always after a noun, informal* : living or existing ▪ *He's the best novelist going.* **2** *always before a noun* : current or usual — used to describe an amount of money (such as a price or salary) ▪ *What's the going price/rate?* — **going on** : coming closer to (something, such as an age) ▪ *Their daughter is six years old going on seven.*

go·ing–over /ˌgoʊɪŋˈoʊvɚ/ *n* [*singular*] **1** : a careful examination ▪ *I gave the documents a (thorough) going-over.* **2** *informal* : a severe beating ▪ *They threatened to give him a (good) going-over if he didn't cooperate.*

go·ings–on /ˌgoʊɪŋzˈɑːn/ *n* [*plural*] : things that are happening ▪ *We heard about all the goings-on at the office.*

goi·ter (*US*) *or chiefly Brit* **goi·tre** /ˈgoɪtɚ/

n [C/U] : a swelling on the front of the neck caused by the thyroid gland becoming too large

go–kart /ˈgoʊˌkɑːɚt/ *n* [C] : a small car that has one or two seats and an open top and that is used especially for racing

gold /ˈgoʊld/ *n* **1** [U] : a soft yellow metal that is very valuable and that is used especially in jewelry **2** [U] : gold coins ▪ *a bag of gold* ▪ (*figurative*) *All the gold* [=money, wealth] *in the world won't make you happy.* ▪ *She's chasing after a pot of gold* (at the end of the rainbow). [=something impossible to get or achieve] **3** [C/U] : a deep yellow color **4** [C] : GOLD MEDAL — **(as) good as gold** : very good ▪ *The children were as good as gold this morning.* — **worth your weight in gold** : very useful, valuable, or important ▪ *Good teachers are worth their weight in gold.* — **gold** *adj* ▪ *gold jewelry/bullion* ▪ *gold paint*

gold·en /ˈgoʊldən/ *adj* **1** : made of gold ▪ *a golden idol* **2** : having the deep yellow color of gold ▪ *golden hair/wheat* **3** : very happy and successful ▪ *a golden era* **4** : very excellent ▪ *This is a golden opportunity.* [=an excellent chance to do or get something] **5** : very talented, popular, and successful — used in the phrases **golden boy** and **golden girl** ▪ *He was once the golden boy of tennis.* **6** : having a rich and smooth sound ▪ *a smooth golden voice* **7** *not before a noun, informal* : in a very good or fortunate position or situation ▪ *If the bank approves the loan, we're golden.* **8** *always before a noun* : of or relating to the 50th anniversary of an important event (such as a marriage) ▪ *They will celebrate their golden (wedding) anniversary this year.* = (*Brit*) *They will celebrate their golden wedding this year.* — **silence is golden** see ¹SILENCE — **the golden goose** *or* **the goose that lays the golden egg** see ¹GOOSE

golden age *n* [C] : a time of great happiness, success, and achievement ▪ *the golden age of art/literature*

golden oldie *n* [C] *informal* : a song, recording, or television show that was very popular in the past

golden retriever *n* [C] : a type of dog that has long yellowish-brown fur

gold·en·rod /ˈgoʊldənˌrɑːd/ *n* [U] : a type of wild plant that has large groups of yellow flowers

golden rule *n* **1** *the Golden Rule* : a general rule for how to behave that says that you should treat people the way you would like other people to treat you **2** [C] : an important rule to follow when you do something ▪ *The golden rule in sales is to know your customer.*

golden years *n* [*plural*] : the time of life when someone is old ▪ *They were active well into their golden years.* [=old age]

gold·finch /ˈgoʊldˌfɪntʃ/ *n* [C] **1** : a small mostly yellow American bird **2** : a small European bird that has red on its head and yellow and black wings

gold·fish /ˈgoʊldˌfɪʃ/ *n, pl* **goldfish** [C]

: a small usually orange fish that people often keep in ponds or in fishbowls or tanks as a pet

goldfish bowl n [C] : a place or condition in which there is no privacy • *celebrities living in the goldfish bowl of constant publicity*

gold leaf n [U] : a very thin sheet of gold used especially to decorate a surface • *a frame covered with gold leaf*

gold medal n [C] : a medal made of gold that is awarded as the prize for first place in a sports competition

gold mine n [C] **1** : a place where gold is dug from the ground **2** : something that has or produces a lot of something desired (such as money) • *The library is a gold mine of information.*

gold–plat·ed /ˈgoʊldˈpleɪtəd/ adj : covered with a thin layer of gold • *a gold-plated tray*

gold record n [C] : an award that is given to a singer or musical group for selling a lot of recordings

gold rush n [C] : a situation in which many people go quickly to a place where gold has been discovered because they hope to find more gold and become rich • *the California gold rush of 1849*

gold·smith /ˈgoʊldˌsmɪθ/ n [C] : a person who makes gold jewelry and other gold items

gold standard n — **the gold standard 1** : a system in which a unit of money (such as the dollar) is equal to a particular amount of gold **2** : something that is considered to be the best and that is used to judge the quality or level of other, similar things • *This car is the gold standard for luxury automobiles.*

golf /ˈgɑːlf/ n [U] : an outdoor game in which players use special sticks (called golf clubs) to try to hit a small ball with as few strokes as possible into each of 9 or 18 holes • *playing a round of golf* — **golf** vb [I] • *He likes to golf.* [=to play golf] — **golf·er** n [C]

golf ball n [C] : a small ball used in the game of golf

golf cart n [C] : a small car that is used to carry golfers and their equipment around a golf course

golf club n [C] **1** : a special long stick with a larger part at the bottom that is used to hit the ball in golf **2** : an organization whose members play golf • *He joined a golf club last year.*

golf course n [C] : a large area of land set up for the game of golf

gol·ly /ˈgɑːli/ interj, old-fashioned — used to express mild surprise • *Golly, I never thought I'd see YOU here!*

gon·do·la /ˈgɑːndələ/ n [C] **1** : a long narrow boat used on the canals of Venice **2 a** : the part of a balloon in which passengers are carried **b** : a vehicle that hangs from a cable and is used for carrying passengers (such as skiers) especially up a mountain

gon·do·lier /ˌgɑːndəˈliɚ/ n [C] : a person who operates a gondola (sense 1)

¹**gone** past participle of ¹GO

²**gone** /ˈgɑːn/ adj, not before a noun **1** : no longer at a place • *How long was he*

gone? [=away, absent] **2** : no longer existing • *Those days are (long) gone.* — **far gone** see ¹FAR

³**gone** prep, Brit, informal : AFTER, PAST • *It was (just) gone six when he got back.*

gon·er /ˈgɑːnɚ/ n [C] informal : someone or something that is going to die or that can no longer be used • *This old computer is a goner. We'll have to get a new one.*

gong /ˈgɑːŋ/ n [C] **1** : a large metal disc that makes a deep ringing sound when it is struck with a padded hammer **2** Brit, informal : a medal or award

gon·na /ˈgʌnə, gənə/ — used in writing to represent the sound of the phrase *going to* when it is spoken quickly • *I'm gonna* [=going to] *leave now.*

gon·or·rhea (US) or Brit **gon·or·rhoea** /ˌgɑːnəˈriːjə/ n [U] : a disease of the sex organs that is spread by sexual contact

gon·zo /ˈgɑːnzoʊ/ adj, always before a noun, chiefly US, informal : having a very strange or unusual quality • *gonzo humor*

goo /ˈguː/ n [U] informal : a wet and sticky substance • *What's this goo all over the stove?* • (figurative) *The movie is a lot of sentimental goo.* [=the movie is too sentimental]

¹**good** /ˈgʊd/ adj **bet·ter** /ˈbɛtɚ/; **best** /ˈbɛst/ **1 a** : of high quality • *The food was good.* • *Keep up the good work.* • *The movie is no good.* [=it is boring, poorly made, etc.] **b** : of somewhat high but not excellent quality • *The food was good but not great.* **2** : correct or proper • *good grammar/manners* **3 a** : pleasant, pleasing, or enjoyable • *I had a good time at the party.* • *good weather* • *You look good in that dress.* = *That dress looks good on you.* **b** : not having, marked by, or relating to problems, troubles, etc. • *good and bad news* • *good luck/fortune* **c** : adequate or suitable • *He's a good person to contact if you need help.* • *I need tires that are good (for driving) in snow.* • *These tires aren't any good.* = *These tires are no good.* **d** : sensible or reasonable • *good judgment/advice* • *a very good question/point* **e** : producing or likely to produce a pleasant or favorable result • *a good deal/plan* • *"The plane arrived on time." "That's good."* **f** : having a desired quality • *Did you get good grades in school?* • *She has good taste.* **g** : expressing approval or praise • *a movie that has been getting good reviews* **h** — used in speech as a response • *"I'm ready." "Good. Let's go." • She's in good health.* **4 a** : HEALTHY • *not feeling very well* • *She's in good health.* **b** : not causing harm or trouble • *good nutrition* • *Regular exercise is good for you.* **5 a** : morally proper or correct • *a good person* • *good conduct/behavior* • *It's hard to tell the good guys* [=morally correct people/characters] *from the bad guys in this movie.* • *Her ex-husband is no good.* [=he's a bad person] • *kind or helpful* • *You've always been so good to me.* — sometimes used to formally make a request • *Would you be good enough to show me the way?* [=would you please show me the way?] **c** : behaving properly • *a good dog* **6 a** : doing or able to do something well • *She's a very good*

golfer/musician/cook. • *Those children are in good hands.* [=with people who are able to take care of them well] • *He's not very/any good at sports.* = *He's no good at sports.* **b** : able to use something or to deal with something or someone well • *He's very good with his hands.* [=he can easily make/do things with his hands] **c** : having a tendency to do something • *She's good about exercising.* [=she exercises often] **7 a** : happy or pleased • *I feel good about what happened.* **b** : cheerful or calm • *She's in a good mood.* **8** *not before a noun* **a** — used to say how long something will continue or be valid • *This offer is good until the end of the month.* **b** : still suitable to eat or drink • *Is the milk still good or has it gone bad?* **9** — used in phrases like *good heavens* and *good God* to express surprise or anger or to make a statement or question more forceful • *Good heavens! You startled me!* **10** : ¹FUNNY 1 • *I heard a good joke the other day.* **11 a** : large in size, amount, or quantity • *The store has a good selection of products.* • *He makes good money.* = *He makes a good living.* [=he earns a lot of money] • *They couldn't have succeeded without a good deal of luck.* [=a lot of luck] • *Things could be a good deal worse.* [=much worse] • *Tourists have been coming to the area in good numbers.* [=many tourists have been coming to the area] **b** : at least — used in the phrase *a good* • *He weighs a good 200 pounds.* **12** *always before a noun* : forceful or thorough • *Take a good look at this.* **13** : having a high social position or status • *a good family/neighborhood* **14** *always before a noun* **a** — used to describe people who know each other well and care about each other very much • *She's a good friend of mine.* **b** : belonging to and having loyalty to a group or organization • *a good Catholic* **15** *not before a noun, sports* **a** *of a serve or shot* : landing in the proper area of the court in tennis and similar games • *The serve was good.* **b** *of a shot or kick* : successfully done • *(basketball) Both free throws were good.* • *(American football) The field goal was no good.* [=was missed] **16** *not before a noun, informal* : not wanting or needing anything more • *"Would you like more coffee?" "No, thanks. I'm good."* — **as good as** : almost or nearly • *The plan is as good as dead.* — **as good as it gets** *informal* **1** — used to say that nothing better is possible or available • *It's not a great restaurant, but in this part of the city, it's as good as it gets.* **2** — used to say that something is very good and cannot be improved • *There's nothing I enjoy more than spending time at home with my family. That's as good as it gets.* — **as good as new** see ¹NEW — **fight the good fight** see ¹FIGHT — **for good measure** see ¹MEASURE — **good and** /ˌgʊdn̩/ *chiefly US, informal* **1** : VERY • *I like my coffee good and hot.* **2** : completely or entirely • *We'll leave when I'm good and ready.* — **good for** *somewhat informal* : able to provide or produce (something)

• *I'm good for a hundred dollars if you need a loan.* — **good for it** *informal* : able to pay back a loan • *Why won't you lend me the money? You know I'm good for it.* — **good old** *informal* — used before a noun to describe a familiar person or thing with affection or approval • *They were talking about the good old days.* [=happy times in the past] — **good riddance** see RIDDANCE — **good to go** *US, informal* : ready to leave or to start doing something • *We have what we need, so we're good to go.* — **good word** see ¹WORD — **have it good** : to be in a favorable position or situation • *She really has it (pretty) good.* • *He's never had it so good.* [=has never been in such a good situation] — **hold good** : to be true • *The advice she gave us 10 years ago still holds good today.* — **if you know what's good for you** : if you want to avoid trouble, problems, etc. • *You'll take my advice if you know what's good for you.* — **in good part** see ¹PART — **make good 1** : to become successful • *a kid from a small town trying to make good in the big city* ✧ If you **make good your escape**, you escape successfully. **2** : to do something that you have promised or threatened to do • *He made good his promise.* — usually + *on* in U.S. English • *He made good on his promise.* **3 a** : to pay for (something) • *The insurance company was required to make good on the loss.* **b** *chiefly Brit* : to repair (something) • *The contract obliges you to make good any damaged windows.* — **too good to be true** — used to say that something cannot be as good as it seems to be • *The price of the car is too good to be true. There must be something wrong with it.* — **very good** *formal* — used as a response to say you will do something that you have been told or asked to do • *"Show the ambassador in." "Very good, sir."*

²**good** *n* **1 a** [U] : morally good forces or influences • *the battle of good versus evil* **b** [C] : something that is right or good • *What is life's highest/greatest good?* **2 the good** [*singular*] : the pleasant things that happen to people • *You have to take the good with the bad.* [=you have to accept both the good things and the bad things that happen to you] **b** [*singular*] : things that are morally proper or correct • *the difference between the good and the bad* **c** [*plural*] : morally good people • *She believes that the good go to heaven when they die.* **3** [U] : the part of someone that is kind, honest, generous, helpful, etc. • *She believes there is some good in everyone.* **4** [U] **a** : something that helps someone or something to be better, stronger, etc. • *She did it for the good of the community.* [=to help the community] • *citizens working together for the common/public good* • *This is for your own good.* [=it will make you stronger, better, etc.] **b** : a useful or favorable result • *What good can possibly come of that?* **5** [*plural*] **a** : things for sale • *baked/canned goods* • *goods and services* • *a store that sells sporting goods* [=prod-

ucts that are used for playing sports] **b** : things that are owned by a person • *He sold all of his worldly goods.* [=all of his possessions] — **be any good** : to be useful or helpful • *Would an apology be any good?* — **deliver the goods** or chiefly *Brit* **come up with the goods** *informal* : to do what is wanted or expected • *We knew we could count on him to deliver the goods.* — **do good** 1 : to do kind or helpful things • *She has done a lot of good in the community.* **2 a** : to be useful or helpful • *You can try, but it probably won't do any/much good.* **b** : to be useful or helpful for someone or something • *Exercising more would do you (some) good.* ✧ If you do not think that something is helpful, useful, or worth doing, you can ask *What good does it do?, What good is it?, What's the good of it?,* etc. • *What's the good of working hard if you don't get any credit for it?* — **for good** also **for good and all** : forever • *She's gone for good.* — **have/get the goods on** *informal* ✧ To have/get the goods on someone is to have/get evidence showing that someone has done something wrong. • *We can't arrest her until we get the goods on her.* — **in good with** US, *informal* : in a favored position with (someone) • *She's in good with the boss.* — **no good** or **not any good** : not effective or useful • *It's no good* [=*no use*] *talking to him.* — **to the good** 1 — used to say that a particular result or effect is good or would be good • *If it saves us money, that's all to the good.* [=that's a good thing] 2 — used to indicate an amount of gain or profit • *In the end, we were $100 to the good.* [=we gained $100] — **up to no good** *informal* : doing bad things or planning to do bad things • *She was clearly up to no good.*

³**good** *adv, informal* 1 chiefly US : ¹**WELL** 1 • *The team is doing good this year.* ✧ The use of *good* to mean "well" is considered wrong by many people. It occurs mainly in very informal speech. 2 chiefly US : completely and thoroughly • *The other team whipped us good.* 3 — used for emphasis before words like *long* and *many* • *I haven't seen her for a good long time.* [=a very long time]

good afternoon *interj, somewhat formal* — used to say hello to someone in the afternoon • *Good afternoon! Thanks for calling.*

Good Book *n* — **the Good Book** : BIBLE 1a • *As the Good Book says . . .*

¹**good·bye** also **good·by** /ˌgʊdˈbaɪ/ *interj* — used to express good wishes when someone is leaving • *Goodbye! See you later!*

²**goodbye** also **goodby** *n [C]* 1 : a remark or gesture made when someone is leaving • *He said his goodbyes and left.* • *They said/waved/kissed goodbye.* • *(figurative) She said goodbye to her old job.* [=she left her old job] 2 : a time or occasion when someone leaves • *a tearful/long goodbye* — **kiss (something) goodbye** see KISS

good day *interj, somewhat formal + old-fashioned* — used to say hello or

goodbye to someone in the daytime • *Welcome and good day.*

good evening *interj, somewhat formal* — used to say hello to someone in the evening • *Good evening, everyone.*

good faith *n [U]* : honesty in dealing with other people • *They questioned my good faith.* • *a good-faith effort* — **in good faith** : in an honest and proper way • *Both parties acted in good faith.*

good–for–noth·ing /ˈgʊdfɚˌnʌθɪŋ/ *adj, informal* : of no use or value • *her good-for-nothing brother* — **good–for–nothing** *n [C]* • *Her brother is a lazy good-for-nothing.*

Good Friday *n [C/U]* : the Friday before Easter that is observed by Christians as the anniversary of the death of Jesus Christ

good–heart·ed /ˈgʊdˈhɑɚtəd/ *adj* : kind and generous • *a good-hearted person*

good–hu·mored (*US*) or *Brit* **good–hu·moured** /ˈgʊdˈhjuːməd/ *adj* : pleasant and cheerful • *She was still good-humored at the end of a tiring day.*

goodie *variant spelling of* GOODY

good–look·ing /ˈgʊdˈlʊkɪŋ/ *adj* : having a pleasing or attractive appearance • *a very good-looking woman/man*

good·ly /ˈgʊdli/ *adj, always before a noun* **good·li·er; -est** *somewhat old-fashioned* : large in size or amount • *a goodly sum*

good morning *interj* — used to say hello to someone in the morning • *Good morning. How are you today?*

good name *n [C]* : a person's good reputation • *The scandal could ruin my good name.*

good–na·tured /ˈgʊdˈneɪtʃɚd/ *adj* : friendly, pleasant, or cheerful • *a good-natured person/competition*

good·ness /ˈgʊdnəs/ *n [U]* 1 : the quality or state of being good • *I believe there is (some) goodness in everyone.* • *She helped him out of the goodness of her heart.* [=because she is a kind and generous person] 2 — used to express mild surprise or shock • *Goodness, it's hot out today!* • *Oh, my goodness!* ✧ People use **I swear to goodness, I hope to goodness,** or **I wish to goodness** to add force to a statement. • *I wish to goodness that you would hurry up!* — **for goodness' sake** — used to express surprise or annoyance • *Will you hurry up, for goodness' sake?* — **goodness knows** see ¹KNOW

good night *interj* — used to express good wishes in the evening especially when someone is leaving or going to sleep • *Good night. I'll see you in the morning.*

good old boy or **good ol' boy** or **good ole boy** /ˈgʊdoʊlˌbɔɪ/ *n [C] US, informal* : a white man from the southern U.S. who has interests, beliefs, etc., that are commonly associated with white southern men

Good Sa·mar·i·tan /-səˈmerətən/ *n* : a person who helps other people and especially strangers when they have trouble

good–sized /ˈgʊdˈsaɪzd/ *adj* : somewhat large • *a good-sized crowd/house*

good–tem·pered /'gʊd'tɛmpəd/ adj
: usually calm and cheerful ▪ a good-
tempered baby/dog

good·will /'gʊd'wɪl/ n [U] 1 or good
will : a kind, helpful, or friendly feeling
or attitude ▪ They allowed him to keep the
extra money as a gesture of goodwill. ▪ a
goodwill ambassador/gesture 2 business
: the amount of value that a company's
good reputation adds to its overall value

goody or **good·ie** /'gʊdi/ n, pl **good·ies**
[C] informal 1 : something that tastes
good ▪ The store sells cakes, pies and other
goodies. 2 : something that people want
or like ▪ This song is an oldie but a goodie.
3 — used in speech especially by children to show excitement and pleasure ▪
"Are we going to the circus? Goody!" 4
Brit : a good person in a book, movie,
etc. ▪ He plays one of the goodies in his latest film.

goody–goody /,gʊdi'gʊdi/ n, pl -good-
ies [C] informal + disapproving : a person (such as a child) whose good behavior and politeness are annoying because
they seem to be excessive or not sincere

goo·ey /'gu:wi/ adj goo·i·er; -est informal : wet and sticky ▪ a gooey mess ▪
(figurative) a gooey romantic comedy [=a
very sentimental romantic comedy]

¹goof /'gu:f/ vb [T/I] chiefly US, informal
: to make a careless or stupid mistake ▪ It
was clear that I had goofed (up). ▪ He
goofed up his lines. — **goof around**
[phrasal vb] chiefly US, informal : to
spend time doing silly or playful things ▪
The kids are goofing around downstairs.
— **goof off** [phrasal vb] chiefly US, informal : to spend time doing things that are
not useful or serious ▪ He spent the day
goofing off instead of working.

²goof n [C] chiefly US, informal 1 : a silly
or stupid person ▪ Don't be such a goof.
2 : a careless or stupid mistake ▪ I made a
major goof.

goof·ball /'gu:f,bɑːl/ n [C] US, informal
: a silly or stupid person : GOOF

goof–off /'gu:f,ɑːf/ n [C] chiefly US, informal : a person who avoids work or responsibility ▪ a lazy goof-off

goofy /'gu:fi/ adj goof·i·er; -est informal : crazy or silly ▪ a goofy guy/grin —
goof·i·ness /'gu:finəs/ n [U]

goon /'gu:n/ n [C] informal 1 chiefly US
: a person who is hired to threaten, beat
up, or kill someone 2 chiefly Brit : a stupid person

goop /'gu:p/ n [U] informal : a sticky or
greasy substance ▪ I stepped in some goop.

¹goose /'gu:s/ n, pl **geese** /'gi:s/ 1 [C]
: any one of many different kinds of
birds that swim, that are larger than
ducks, and that have a long neck and
webbed feet ▪ a flock/gaggle of geese 2
[C] : a female goose 3 [U] : the meat of
a goose used as food ▪ roast goose 4 [C]
informal + old-fashioned : a foolish or silly person — **cook someone's goose**
see ²COOK — **the golden goose** or **the
goose that lays the golden egg**
: something that is a very good source of
money or business ▪ The city's leaders
don't want to do anything that could kill
the golden goose of tourism. — **what's**

**good for the goose is good for the
gander** (US) or chiefly Brit **what's
sauce for the goose is sauce for the
gander** — used to say that one person
or situation should be treated the same
way that another person or situation is
treated ▪ If he can go out with his friends
at night, then she should be able to, too.
What's good for the goose is good for the
gander.

²goose vb goosed; goos·ing [T] US, informal 1 : to touch or pinch (someone)
on the buttocks 2 : to increase the activity or amount of (something) ▪ trying
to goose (up) profits

goose bumps n [plural] chiefly US, informal : small bumps on your skin that
are caused by cold, fear, or a sudden
feeling of excitement ▪ I get goose bumps
every time I think about it. — called also
goose flesh, (chiefly Brit) goose pimples

goose step n [singular] : a way of
marching by kicking your legs forward
very high and not bending your knees —
goose–step /'gu:s,stɛp/ vb -stepped;
-step·ping [I]

GOP /,dʒi:,oʊ'pi:/ n — the GOP : the Republican Party of the U.S. ▪ members of
the GOP — often used as GOP before another noun ▪ a GOP governor ◇ GOP is
an abbreviation of "Grand Old Party."

go·pher /'goʊfə/ n [C] : an American animal that is similar to a large rat and that
lives in the ground

¹gore /'goə/ n [U] 1 : thick blood from a
wound 2 : violent images or scenes that
show a lot of blood ▪ a movie that has a
lot of blood and gore

²gore vb gored; gor·ing [T] of an animal
: to wound (a person or another animal)
with a horn or tusk ▪ He was gored by a
bull.

¹gorge /'goədʒ/ n [C] 1 : a deep, narrow
area between hills or mountains 2 ◇ If
your gorge rises or something makes
your gorge rise, you feel sick, disgusted,
or angry. ▪ My gorge rises when I think of
children living in such bad conditions.

²gorge vb gorged; gorg·ing 1 [T/I] : to
eat large amounts of food ▪ We gorged
(ourselves) on chips and cookies. 2 [T]
: to fill (something) completely ▪ tissue
gorged with blood

gor·geous /'goədʒəs/ adj 1 : very beautiful or attractive ▪ Your baby is absolutely gorgeous! ▪ a gorgeous young man/
woman 2 : very enjoyable or pleasant ▪
a gorgeous day — **gor·geous·ly** adv —
gor·geous·ness n [U]

go·ril·la /gə'rɪlə/ n [C] 1 : a type of very
large ape that has black fur and that
comes from Africa 2 informal : a large,
strong, and usually ugly or frightening
man ▪ She hired some gorilla as her bodyguard. — **800-pound gorilla** US, informal : someone or something that is very
powerful and difficult to control or ignore ▪ Their company is the 800-pound
gorilla of the computer industry.

gorm·less /'goəmləs/ adj, Brit, informal
: very stupid or foolish ▪ a gormless fool

gory /'gori/ adj gor·i·er; -est : having or
showing a lot of violence and blood ▪ a
gory crime scene ▪ They described the

murder in gory detail. ▪ *(figurative) Please, spare us the gory details.* [=do not tell us all the unpleasant facts]

gosh /'gɑːʃ/ *interj, informal* — used to express surprise or mild anger ▪ *"Gosh, is she OK?"*

gos·ling /'gɑːzlɪŋ/ *n* [C] : a young goose

gos·pel /'gɑːspəl/ *n* **1** *or* **Gospel** [*singular*] : the teachings of the Christian religion ▪ *spreading the Gospel* [=telling people about Christianity] **2** *Gospel* [C] : any one of the first four books of the Christian Bible ▪ *the Gospel of St. John* **3** [*singular*] : a set of ideas that someone believes and often tries to make other people believe ▪ *preaching the gospel of good health* **4** [*U*] : something that is believed to be definitely true ▪ *myths accepted/taken as gospel* [=believed to be true] **5** [*U*] : a type of Christian music that was created by African-Americans in the southern U.S. ▪ *a gospel choir* — called also *gospel music*

gos·sa·mer /'gɑːsəmə/ *n* [U] *literary* : a very light or delicate material ▪ *gossamer wings/petals*

gos·sip /'gɑːsəp/ *n* **1** [U] **a** : information about the behavior and personal lives of other people ▪ *He spreads gossip about his coworkers.* **b** : information about the lives of famous people ▪ *the latest Hollywood gossip* ▪ *a gossip columnist* **2** [C] : a person who often talks about the private details of other people's lives ▪ *He's a terrible gossip.* — **gossip** *vb* [I] ▪ *They were gossiping about their neighbors.* [=talking about their neighbors' personal lives] — **gos·sip·er** *n* [C] — **gos·sipy** /'gɑːsəpi/ *adj, informal* ▪ *a gossipy magazine/writer*

got *past tense and past participle of* GET

Goth·ic /'gɑːθɪk/ *adj* : of or relating to a style of architecture used in Europe between the 12th and 16th centuries ▪ *a Gothic cathedral*

go-to /'goʊˌtuː/ *adj, always before a noun, US, informal* : always helpful ▪ *He's the go-to guy* [=he's the guy to ask] *in the office for tax information.*

got·ta /'gɑːtə/ — used in writing to represent the sound of the phrase *got to* when it is spoken quickly in informal English ▪ *"We('ve) gotta go."* [=we have got to go]

gotten *past participle of* GET

gouge /'gaʊdʒ/ *vb* **gouged**; **goug·ing** [T] **1** : to make a deep hole in something ▪ *The lamp fell and gouged (a hole in) the table.* **2** *US, informal* : to make (someone) pay too much money for something ▪ *The gas station has been gouging its customers.* ▪ *accused of price gouging* [=making customers pay too much money] — **gouge out** [*phrasal vb*] **gouge out (something)** *or* **gouge (something) out** **1** : to remove (something) by digging or cutting ▪ *He threatened to gouge my eyes out.* **2** : to cut or dig (a hole or path) ▪ *The river gouged out a path between the mountains.* — **gouge** *n* [C] ▪ *The lamp fell and made a gouge in the table.*

gou·lash /'guːˌlɑːʃ, *Brit* 'guːˌlæʃ/ *n* [U] : a dish of meat, vegetables, and paprika that is slowly cooked in liquid

gourd /'goʊəd, 'guəd/ *n* [C] : any one of several types of fruits that have a hard shell and that are used for decoration and not for eating — **out of your gourd** *US, informal* : CRAZY ▪ *That guy is completely out of his gourd.*

gour·met /'guəˌmeɪ, guə'meɪ/ *n* [C] : a person who enjoys and knows a lot about good food and wine — **gourmet** *adj* ▪ *a gourmet meal* [=a meal of very high quality]

gout /'gaʊt/ *n* [U] : a disease that causes painful swelling of the joints

gov *abbr* **1** *gov.* government **2** *Gov.* governor ▪ *Gov. Jerry Brown* **3** government institution — used in Internet addresses ▪ *http://www.whitehouse.gov*

gov·ern /'gʌvən/ *vb* **1** [T/I] : to officially control and lead (a group of people) : to make decisions about laws, taxes, etc., for (a country, state, etc.) ▪ *How would he govern (the country) if he were elected president?* ▪ *a governing council/body* **2** [T] : to control the way that (something) is done ▪ *laws governing the sale of alcohol* **3** [T] : to control or guide the actions of (someone or something) ▪ *Tradition governs their lives.* = *Tradition is the governing factor in their lives.*

gov·er·nance /'gʌvənəns/ *n* [U] *formal* : the way that a city, company, etc., is controlled by the people who run it ▪ *different styles of governance*

gov·ern·ess /'gʌvənəs/ *n* [C] : a woman who is paid to care for and teach a child in the child's house

gov·ern·ment /'gʌvəmənt/ *n* **1** [C] : the group of people who control and make decisions for a country, state, etc. ▪ *She works for the federal/state government.* ▪ *the British government* ▪ *a government agency/official/program* **2** [U] **a** : a particular system used for controlling a country, state, etc. ▪ *democratic/representative government* **b** : the process or manner of controlling a country, state, etc. ▪ *different methods/systems of government* — **gov·ern·men·tal** /ˌgʌvən'mɛntl̩/ *adj*

gov·er·nor /'gʌvnə/ *n* [C] **1** *or* **Governor** : a person who is the leader of the government of a state, province, etc. ▪ *the governor of the state of Florida* ▪ *Governor Jones* — *abbr.* **Gov.** **2 a** : a member of a group that controls a large organization, school, etc. ▪ *the school's board of governors* **b** *chiefly Brit* : a person who is in charge of a school, prison, etc. ▪ *the governor of the Bank of England* **3** *Brit, informal* : BOSS ▪ *Wait here while I get the governor.* — **gov·er·nor·ship** /'gʌvnəˌʃɪp/ *n* [C/U] ▪ *a candidate for the governorship*

govt. *(chiefly US) or Brit* **govt** *abbr* government

gown /'gaʊn/ *n* [C] **1** : a long, formal dress that a woman wears especially during a special event ▪ *the bride's wedding gown* ▪ *a red evening gown* [=a gown worn to events in the evening] **2** : a loose piece of clothing that covers most of the body ▪ *a hospital gown* [=a robe worn by a patient in a hospital] **3** : a loose piece of clothing that is worn over other clothes during an official event by a judge, priest, student, etc.

G.P. *(chiefly US)* or *Brit* **GP** *abbr* general practitioner

GPA *abbr, US* grade point average

GPS /ˌdʒiːˌpiːˈɛs/ *n* [*U*] : a radio system that uses signals from satellites to tell you where you are and give you directions to other places ▪ *The car comes with GPS.* ◇ *GPS* is an abbreviation of "Global Positioning System."

¹**grab** /ˈgræb/ *vb* **grabbed; grab·bing** **1** [*T/I*] : to quickly take and hold (someone or something) with your hand or arms ▪ *She grabbed his wrist.* = *She grabbed him by the wrist.* ▪ *He grabbed hold of a tree branch.* ▪ *The little boy grabbed onto his mother's leg.* **2** [*T*] : to take or get (something) in a quick and informal way ▪ *Grab me a pen, please.* ▪ *Let's grab a bite to eat.* **3** [*T*] *informal* : to get or be given (something) ▪ *She has been grabbing a lot of attention lately.* ▪ *The trial grabbed (the) headlines.* [=it was given much attention in the news] **4** [*T*] : to take (something) usually in an unfair way ▪ *They tried to grab the money for themselves.* — **grab at/for** [*phrasal vb*] : to quickly stretch out your hand and try to touch or hold (something or someone) ▪ *People grabbed at her as she walked through the crowd.* ▪ *(figurative) politicians grabbing for power* — **grab·ber** *n* [*C*] ▪ *That outfit is a real attention grabber.*

²**grab** *n* [*C*] **1** : a quick attempt to take or get something — often + *for* ▪ *a grab for attention/power* ▪ *She made a grab for* [=tried to grab] *the last cookie.* **2** : the act of taking something in a forceful or illegal way ▪ *an illegal land grab* — **up for grabs** : available for anyone to try to get ▪ *The job is still up for grabs.*

grab·by /ˈgræbi/ *adj* **grab·bi·er; -est** *informal* : tending to take things in a quick and selfish way ▪ *a grabby corporation*

¹**grace** /ˈgreɪs/ *n* **1** [*U*] : a way of moving that is smooth and attractive ▪ *She danced with effortless grace.* **2 a** [*U*] : a controlled, polite, and pleasant way of behaving ▪ *showing remarkable grace during a crisis* ▪ *She has the (good) grace* [=she is polite/nice enough] *to listen to our complaints.* **b** [*plural*] : skills needed for behaving in a polite way in social situations ▪ *her lack of social graces* **3** [*U*] : help or kindness that God gives or shows to people ▪ *By the grace of God, no one was seriously hurt.* **4** [*U*] : a short prayer that was said before a meal ▪ *They asked her to say grace at dinner.* **5** *Grace* [*U*] — used as a title for a duke, a duchess, or an archbishop; used with *his, her,* or *your* ▪ *His Grace the Duke* ▪ *Yes, Your Grace.* — **fall from grace** ◇ If you *fall from grace* or experience a *fall from grace,* you no longer enjoy the success or good reputation that you once had, usually because you have done something wrong. ▪ *The governor fell from grace after the scandal.* — **in someone's good graces** ◇ If you are in *someone's good graces,* that person likes you and has a

good opinion of you. ▪ *He works late to stay in his boss's good graces.* — see also SAVING GRACE — **grace·ful** /ˈgreɪsfəl/ *adj* ▪ *a graceful dancer/shape* ▪ *There was no graceful way to tell her no.* — **grace·ful·ly** *adv* ▪ *She has aged gracefully.* [=she has continued to be young looking as she has gotten older] — **grace·ful·ness** *n* [*U*] — **grace·less** /ˈgreɪsləs/ *adj* ▪ *graceless movements* — **grace·less·ly** *adv* — **grace·less·ness** *n* [*U*]

²**grace** *vb* **graced; grac·ing** [*T*] *formal* : to add beauty to (something) ▪ *Her face has graced* [=appeared on] *the cover of many magazines.* — **grace (a person, group, etc.) with your presence** : to come to a place to be with (a person, group, etc.) ▪ *(humorous) I see you decided to grace us with your presence.* [=to show up]

grace period *n* [*C*] : an amount of extra time that someone is given to pay a bill, finish a project, etc. ▪ *a ten-day grace period*

gra·cious /ˈgreɪʃəs/ *adj* **1** : very polite in a way that shows respect ▪ *a gracious hostess* **2** : having or showing the attractive things that are associated with having a lot of money ▪ *a guide to gracious living* **3** *old-fashioned* — used as an interjection to express mild surprise or for emphasis ▪ *Good gracious, No.* — **gra·cious·ly** *adv* — **gra·cious·ness** *n* [*U*]

grad /ˈgræd/ *n* [*C*] *US, informal* : GRADUATE ▪ *college grads* — **grad** *adj* ▪ *He's still in grad school.*

gra·da·tion /greɪˈdeɪʃən/ *n* [*C*] : a small difference between two points or parts ▪ *subtle gradations of color/meaning*

¹**grade** /ˈgreɪd/ *n* [*C*] **1** *US* **a** : a level of study that is completed by a student during one year ▪ *Our son is in (the) twelfth grade.* **b** : the students in the same year of study at a school ▪ *The fifth grade will take a field trip today.* **2** : a number or letter that indicates how a student performed in a class or on a test ▪ *a grade of 90 percent or better* ▪ *Her grades are up/better this year.* **3 a** : a particular level of quality ▪ *a higher grade of beef* **b** : a particular position or rank in an organization ▪ *junior grade officers* **4** *US* : GRADIENT ▪ *a steep grade* — **make the grade** : to be good enough to succeed ▪ *Only a few applicants make the grade.*

²**grade** *vb* **grad·ed; grad·ing** [*T*] **1** *chiefly US* : to give a grade to (a student or a student's work) ▪ *She finished grading the exams.* **2** : to give a rating to (something) ▪ *How would you grade your meal on a scale from one to five?* **3** : to separate (things) into groups or classes according to a particular quality ▪ *The eggs are graded according to size.* **4** : to give (a surface) a desired slope ▪ *They graded the new highway.*

grade A *adj* : of the highest quality ▪ *a grade A performance*

grade point average *n* [*C*] *US* : a number that indicates a student's average grade — abbr. *GPA*

grad·er /ˈgreɪdɚ/ *n* [*C*] **1** *US* : a student in a particular grade in school ▪ *a sixth* *grader* [=a student in the sixth grade] **2** : a person who grades students or their work ▪ *She's a tough/easy grader.* **3** : a machine used for grading a surface ▪ *a road grader*

grade school *n* [C/U] *US* : ELEMENTARY SCHOOL — **grade–school·er** /ˈgreɪdˌskuːlə/ *n* [C]

gra·di·ent /ˈgreɪdijənt/ *n* [C] : a place where the ground slopes up or down : SLOPE ▪ *a steep gradient*

grad·u·al /ˈgrædʒəwəl/ *adj* **1** : moving or changing in small amounts : happening in a slow way over a long period of time ▪ *a gradual change in temperature* **2** : not steep ▪ *a gradual slope* — **grad·u·al·ly** *adv* ▪ *The population gradually increased.*

¹**grad·u·ate** /ˈgrædʒəˌweɪt/ *vb* **-at·ed; -at·ing** **1** [T/I] : to earn a degree or diploma from a school, college, or university ▪ *She graduated (from college) with a degree in history.* ▪ *a graduating class of 300 students* ▪ (*US, informal*) *He joined the navy after graduating high school.* **b** [T] *US, of a school, college, or university* : to award a degree or diploma to (a student) ▪ *We graduated 300 students last year.* **2** [I] : to move *from* one level *to* another usually higher level ▪ *She has graduated from baby food to solid food.*

²**grad·u·ate** /ˈgrædʒəwət/ *n* [C] : a person who has earned a degree or diploma from a school, college, or university ▪ *a college graduate* ▪ *a Harvard graduate* = *a graduate of Harvard*

³**graduate** *adj, always before a noun, US* : of or relating to a course of studies taken after earning a bachelor's degree or other first degree ▪ *He is taking graduate classes at the university.* ▪ *graduate students/school*

grad·u·at·ed /ˈgrædʒəˌweɪtəd/ *adj, always before a noun* : gradually increasing ▪ *graduated payments* ▪ *a graduated income tax* [=a tax that increases in rate as income increases]

grad·u·a·tion /ˌgrædʒəˈweɪʃən/ *n* **1** [U] : the act of graduating from a school, college, or university ▪ *She joined the navy after graduation.* **2** [C] : a ceremony at which degrees or diplomas are given out ▪ *They went to their grandson's graduation.*

graf·fi·ti /grəˈfiːti/ *n* [U] : pictures or words painted or drawn on a wall, building, etc. ▪ *Vandals covered the walls with graffiti.*

¹**graft** /ˈgræft, *Brit* ˈgrɑːft/ *n* **1** [U] *chiefly US* : dishonest activity in which people (such as political leaders) use their position and influence to get money and advantages ▪ *exposing graft in the city government* **2** [C] **a** *technical* : a part of a plant that is attached to another plant in such a way that it grows with the plant **b** *medical* : a piece of skin, muscle, or bone that is attached to a part of the body to repair a damaged area ▪ *a skin graft; also* : an operation that is done to attach a graft ▪ *perform a bone graft* **3** [U] *Brit, informal* : hard work or effort ▪ *years of hard graft*

²**graft** *vb* [T] **1** *technical* : to attach (a part

of a plant) to another plant **2** *medical* : to attach (a piece of skin, muscle, or bone) to a part of the body ▪ *The surgeon grafted skin over the scar.*

gra·ham cracker /ˈgræm-/ *n* [C] *US* : a slightly sweet type of cracker

grail /ˈgreɪl/ *n* [C] : HOLY GRAIL

grain /ˈgreɪn/ *n* **1 a** [U] : the seeds of plants (such as wheat, corn, and rice) that are used for food ▪ *grinding grain into flour; also* [C] : a seed of wheat, corn, etc. ▪ *a grain of rice* **b** [C/U] : a plant that produces grain ▪ *fields planted with grain(s)* **2** [C] **a** : a small, hard piece of something ▪ *a grain of sand/salt* — see also *take (something) with a grain of salt* at ¹SALT **b** : a very small amount of something ▪ *There is not a grain of truth in that.* **3** [*singular*] : the way the lines or fibers in something (such as wood) are arranged ▪ *Sand the wood with/against the grain.* ▪ (*figurative*) *It takes courage to go against the grain.* [=to act in a way that is different from what is normal or usual] — **grained** /ˈgreɪnd/ *adj* ▪ *beautifully grained wood*

grainy /ˈgreɪni/ *adj* **grain·i·er; -est** **1** : not smooth or fine ▪ *The mustard has a grainy texture.* **2** : not clear or sharp ▪ *a grainy photograph* — **grain·i·ness** *n* [U]

gram *also Brit* **gramme** /ˈgræm/ *n* [C] : a unit of weight in the metric system that is equal to 1/1000 kilogram

gram·mar /ˈgræmə/ *n* **1** [C/U] : the set of rules that explain how words are used in a language ▪ *the rules of (English/Japanese) grammar* **2** [U] : speech or writing judged by how well it follows the rules of grammar ▪ *"Him and I went" is bad/poor grammar.* **3** [C] : a book that explains the grammar rules of a language ▪ *an English grammar* — **gram·mar·i·an** /grəˈmerijən/ *n* [C] — **gram·mat·i·cal** /grəˈmætɪkəl/ *adj* : *grammatical rules/errors* ▪ *That sentence is not grammatical.* [=it does not follow the rules of grammar] — **gram·mat·i·cal·ly** /grəˈmætɪkli/ *adv*

grammar school *n* [C/U] **1** : ELEMENTARY SCHOOL **2** : a school in Britain for children over age 11

gramme *Brit spelling of* GRAM

gra·na·ry /ˈgreɪnəri, *Brit* ˈgrænəri/ *n, pl* **-ries** [C] : a building in which grain is stored

¹**grand** /ˈgrænd/ *adj* **1** : involving or including many people or things ▪ *He thinks the event was part of some grand conspiracy.* ▪ *They had grand plans for renovating the house.* ▪ *Pollution affects nature on a grand scale.* [=in a way that involves a great amount of money, effort, space, people, or things] **2 a** : impressive because of size, importance, etc. ▪ *grand Victorian homes* ▪ *She lived to the grand old age of 103.* **b** : intended to impress people ▪ *Despite its grand name, the hotel is small and seedy.* ▪ *He planned to make a grand entrance, arriving in a fancy red sports car.* **3** *always before a noun* : having higher rank than others of the same kind ▪ *We won the grand prize.* ▪

a Grand Duchess **4** *informal* : very good • *We had a grand time at the picnic.* — **grand·ly** *adv*

²**grand** *n, pl* **grand** [C] *informal* : a thousand dollars or pounds • *The car cost about five grand.*

grand·child /ˈgrænd₁tʃaɪld/ *n, pl* **-children** /-ˈtʃɪldrən/ [C] : a child of your son or daughter

grand·dad *also* **gran·dad** /ˈgrænˌdæd/ *n* [C] *informal* : GRANDFATHER

grand·dad·dy *also* **gran·dad·dy** /ˈgrænˌdædi/ *n, pl* **-dies** [C] *informal* **1** : GRANDFATHER **2** : someone or something that is the first or oldest one in a particular area or field • *the granddaddy of computer manufacturers*

grand·daugh·ter /ˈgrænˌdɑːtɚ/ *n* [C] : a daughter of your son or daughter

grande dame /ˈgrɑːnˈdɑːm/ *n, pl* **grandes dames** /ˈgrɑːnˈdɑːm/ [C] : an old woman who is highly respected • *She is the grande dame of American theater.*

gran·deur /ˈgrændʒɚ/ *n* [U] : a great and impressive quality • *They restored the hotel to its original grandeur.* — see also *delusions of grandeur* at DELUSION

grand·fa·ther /ˈgrænˌfɑːðɚ/ *n* [C] : the father of your father or mother

grandfather clock *n* [C] : a tall clock that stands on the floor

grand finale *n* [C] : a very exciting or impressive ending of a performance or show • *the grand finale of the fireworks display*

gran·dil·o·quent /grænˈdɪləkwənt/ *adj, formal* : using words that are intended to sound very impressive and important • *a grandiloquent speaker* — **gran·dil·o·quence** /grænˈdɪləkwəns/ *n* [U]

gran·di·ose /ˈgrændiˌoʊs/ *adj, disapproving* : seeming to be impressive but not really possible or practical • *grandiose ideas/plans/schemes* — **gran·di·ose·ly** *adv*

grand jury *n* [C] *US, law* : a group of people who look at the evidence against someone in order to decide if they should be a trial

grand·kid /ˈgrænd₁kɪd/ *n* [C] *US, informal* : GRANDCHILD

grand larceny *n* [U] *US, law* : the crime of stealing something very valuable

grand·ma /ˈgræˌmɑː/ *n* [C] *informal* : GRANDMOTHER

grand marshal *n* [C] *chiefly US* : a person who is honored by being made the leader of a parade

grand·moth·er /ˈgrændˌmʌðɚ/ *n* [C] : the mother of your father or mother

grand opening *n* [C] : a celebration held for the opening of a new business, stadium, etc.

grand·pa /ˈgræmˌpɑː/ *n* [C] *informal* : GRANDFATHER

grand·par·ent /ˈgrændˌperənt/ *n* [C] : a parent of your father or mother

grand piano *n* [C] : a very large piano

Grand Prix /ˈgrɑːnˈpriː/ *n, pl* **Grand Prix** [C] : one of a series of international car races

grand slam *n* [C] **1** *baseball* : a home run that is hit with three runners on base **2** *or* **Grand Slam** : the achievement of

winning all of the major events of a sport (such as tennis or golf) in one season

grand·son /ˈgrændˌsʌn/ *n* [C] : a son of your son or daughter

¹**grand·stand** /ˈgrændˌstænd/ *n* [C] : a usually roofed structure with seats for people to sit on while they are watching a sporting event

²**grandstand** *vb* [I] *US, disapproving* : to behave or speak in a way that is intended to impress people • *a grandstanding ball player* • *political grandstanding*

grand theft *n* [U] *US, law* : GRAND LARCENY

grand total *n* [C] : a final total reached by adding together other total amounts • *They raised a grand total of $15 million in the past five years.* • *(humorous) A grand total of two people signed up for the class.*

gran·ite /ˈgrænət/ *n* [U] : a very hard type of rock that is used in buildings and monuments

gran·ny *also* **gran·nie** /ˈgræni/ *n, pl* **-nies** [C] *informal* : GRANDMOTHER

gra·no·la /grəˈnoʊlə/ *n* [C/U] *chiefly US* : a mixture of oats, nuts, raisins, etc. • *a granola bar* [=a bar of granola that is eaten as a snack]

¹**grant** /ˈgrænt, *Brit* ˈgrɑːnt/ *vb* [T] **1 a** : to agree to do, allow, or allow (something asked for or hoped for) • *The mayor granted my request for an interview.* • *She granted me an interview.* [=she agreed to let me interview her] **b** : to give (something) legally or formally • *We were not granted access to the archive.* • *The judge granted custody of the children to their mother.* **2** : to admit (something) although it does not support your opinion • *The house is not perfect, I grant you (that)* [=I admit that the house is not perfect], *but it's still a great deal.* • *Granted, the house is not perfect, but it's still a great deal.* • *Even granting that you may be right* [=even if you are right], *I still think we need to consider other solutions.* — **take for granted 1 take (something) for granted** : to believe or assume that (something) is true or probably true without knowing that it is true • *We took our invitation for granted.* = *We took it for granted that we'd be invited.* [=we did not think about the possibility that we wouldn't be invited] **2 take (someone or something) for granted** : to fail to appreciate (someone or something that is helpful or important to you) • *We often take our freedom for granted.* • *I'm tired of being taken for granted.*

²**grant** *n* [C] **1** : an amount of money that is given to someone by a government, a company, etc., to be used for a particular purpose (such as scientific research) • *a federal grant* **2** : an area of land that is given to someone by a government • *a land grant*

gran·u·lar /ˈgrænjələ/ *adj* : made of or appearing to be made of small pieces or granules • *granular rock* • *a granular texture*

gran·u·lat·ed /ˈgrænjəˌleɪtəd/ *adj* : formed into small grains or pieces • *granulated sugar*

gran·ule /'græn,juːl/ *n* [C] : a small grain or piece of something ▪ *salt/sugar/coffee granules*

grape /'greɪp/ *n* [C] : a green, red, or purple berry that is eaten or used to make wine ▪ *a bunch of grapes* — see also SOUR GRAPES

grape·fruit /'greɪp,fruːt/ *n, pl* **grapefruit** *or* **grape·fruits** [C/U] : a large, yellow citrus fruit

grape·vine /'greɪp,vaɪn/ *n* [C] **1** : a climbing plant on which grapes grow **2** : an informal way of spreading information or rumors through conversation — usually singular ▪ *the office grapevine* ▪ *I heard about it through the grapevine.*

graph /'græf/ *Brit* 'grɑːf/ *n* [C] : a drawing that uses a series of dots, lines, etc., to show how much or how quickly something changes ▪ *She drew/plotted a graph showing the changes in temperature.*

¹**graph·ic** /'græfɪk/ *adj* **1** : shown or described in a very clear way — used especially to refer to things that are unpleasant or shocking ▪ *The reporter gave a graphic account of the car crash.* ▪ *graphic language/violence* **2** *always before a noun* : relating to the artistic use of pictures, shapes, etc., especially in books and magazines ▪ *a graphic artist/designer* — **graph·i·cal·ly** /'græfɪkli/ *adv* ▪ *He graphically described the crash.* ▪ *information presented graphically* [=in a graph]

²**graphic** *n* **1** [*plural*] : images on the screen of a computer, TV, etc. ▪ *computer graphics* **2** [C] : a picture, drawing, or graph used to make something easier to understand ▪ *magazine articles illustrated with graphics*

graphic novel *n* [C] : cartoon drawings that tell a story and are published in a book

graph·ite /'græ,faɪt/ *n* [U] : a black substance used in pencils

graph paper *n* [U] : paper that is covered with vertical and horizontal lines that form squares

grap·ple /'græpəl/ *vb* **grap·pled; grap·pling** [I] **1** : to hold and fight with another person ▪ *The wrestlers grappled (with each other) on the mat.* **2** : to try to solve a problem : to deal with a problem — + *with* ▪ *The company has been grappling with supply problems.* — **grap·pler** /'græpələ/ *n* [C]

¹**grasp** /'græsp, *Brit* 'grɑːsp/ *vb* [T] **1** : to take and hold (something) with your fingers, hands, etc. ▪ *I grasped the rope and pulled.* ▪ (*figurative*) *We need to grasp* [=seize] *this opportunity while we can.* ▪ (*figurative*) *They were ready to* **grasp at** *any possible solution.* [=to try to take or get any possible solution] ▪ (*figurative*) *He was grasping for attention.* **2** : to understand (something that is complicated or difficult) ▪ *We failed to grasp the logic of their decision.* — **grasp at straws** see STRAW

²**grasp** *n* [*singular*] **1** : a usually strong hold ▪ *Keep a firm grasp on the rope.* [=hold the rope firmly with your hand] ▪ *The ball slipped/fell from her grasp.* [=she dropped the ball] **2** : an understanding of something ▪ *She has a good/firm/thor-*

ough grasp of mathematics. [=she understands mathematics well] **3 a** : the distance that can be reached by your arms and hands : REACH ▪ *The top shelf is just beyond my grasp.* **b** : the ability to get or find something ▪ *Success seemed to be beyond our grasp.* [=we seemed unable to succeed] ▪ *The solution is within her grasp.* [=she can find the solution] **4** : power or control ▪ *He had the country in his grasp.*

grasp·ing /'græspɪŋ, *Brit* 'grɑːspɪŋ/ *adj* : GREEDY ▪ *her grasping relatives*

grass /'græs, *Brit* 'grɑːs/ *n* **1 a** [U] : plants that have narrow green leaves and are commonly grown on lawns ▪ *a field/tuft/blade of grass* ▪ *mow/cut the grass* [=mow/cut the lawn] **b** [C] : a particular type of grass ▪ *wild/ornamental grasses* **2** [U] *slang* : MARIJUANA — **put (someone) out to grass** *Brit* : to force (someone) to leave a job because of old age ▪ *I'm not ready to be put out to grass* [=put out to pasture] *just yet.* — **the grass is always greener on the other side (of the fence)** — used to say that the things you do not have always seem more appealing than the things you do have — **grass-like** /'græs,laɪk, *Brit* 'grɑːs,laɪk/ *adj* — **grassy** /'græsi, *Brit* 'grɑːsi/ *adj* **grass·i·er; -est** ▪ *a grassy field*

grass·hop·per /'græs,hɑːpə, *Brit* 'grɑːs-,hɒpə/ *n* [C] : an insect that has long legs used for jumping

grass·land /'græs,lænd, *Brit* 'grɑːs,lænd/ *n* [C/U] : land covered with grasses but not with bushes and trees

grass roots *n* [*plural*] : the people in a society or organization who do not have a lot of money and power ▪ *He has lost touch with the party's grass roots.* — **grass·roots** /'græs,ruːts, *Brit* 'grɑːs-,ruːts/ *adj, always before a noun* ▪ *A grassroots environmental movement has sprung up.*

¹**grate** /'greɪt/ *n* [C] : a metal frame with bars across it that is used in a fireplace or to cover an opening

²**grate** *vb* **grat·ed; grat·ing** **1** [T] : to cut (food) into very small pieces by rubbing it against a special tool (called a grater) ▪ *grated cheese/carrots* **2** [I] : to make a harsh, unpleasant noise by rubbing against something ▪ *I hear a grating sound whenever I step on the brake.* **3** [I] : to have an annoying effect ▪ *Her shrill voice can really grate (on your nerves/ear).* ▪ *She has a grating voice.*

grate·ful /'greɪtfəl/ *adj* : feeling or showing thanks ▪ *I'm grateful (that) I don't have to work today.* : feeling or showing thanks to someone for some helpful act ▪ *I'm grateful (to you) for your help.* — **grate·ful·ly** *adv* — **grate·ful·ness** *n* [U]

grat·er /'greɪtə/ *n* [C] : a tool that has a rough metal surface with small holes and is used to cut food into small pieces

grat·i·fy /'grætə,faɪ/ *vb* **-fies; -fied; -fy·ing** [T] *formal* **1** : to make (someone) happy or satisfied ▪ *He's gratified by the response his new book has been getting.* ▪ *The response has been gratifying.* ▪ *a grati-*

fying victory **2** : to do or give whatever is wanted or demanded by (someone or something) • *gratify a whim/desire* — **grat·i·fi·ca·tion** /ˌɡrætəfəˈkeɪʃən/ *n* [C/U] • *the selfish gratification of his own desires*

grat·ing /ˈɡreɪtɪŋ/ *n* [C] : a grate that is used to cover an opening

gra·tis /ˈɡrætəs/ *adj* : FREE • *The food was gratis.* — **gratis** *adv* • *The food was supplied gratis.*

grat·i·tude /ˈɡrætəˌtuːd, *Brit* ˈɡrætəˌtjuːd/ *n* [U] : a feeling of appreciation or thanks • *Let me express my sincere gratitude for all your help.* • *We owe them a debt of gratitude.* [=we should be grateful to them]

gra·tu·i·tous /ɡrəˈtuːwətəs, *Brit* ɡrəˈtjuːətəs/ *adj, formal* : not necessary or appropriate • *the film's gratuitous violence* — **gra·tu·i·tous·ly** *adv*

gra·tu·i·ty /ɡrəˈtuːwəti, *Brit* ɡrəˈtjuːˈəti/ *n, pl* **-ties** [C] *formal* : an amount of money given to a waiter, waitress, etc., for performing a service : TIP • *a 15 percent gratuity*

¹**grave** /ˈɡreɪv/ *n* [C] **1** : a hole in the ground for burying a dead body • *He was buried in a shallow grave.* • *(figurative) The company founder must be turning/rolling (over) in his grave.* [=the company founder, who is dead, would be very shocked or upset to see something that is happening now] **2** — used to talk about death • *She took her secrets with her to the grave.* [=she died without telling anyone her secrets] • *A hard life drove him to an early grave.* [=caused him to die when he was fairly young] • *She went to her grave* [=she died] *a bitter woman.* — **from (the) cradle to (the) grave** see ¹CRADLE — **have one foot in the grave** see ¹FOOT

²**grave** *adj* **grav·er; -est** *1 formal* : very serious : requiring or causing serious thought or concern • *grave danger* • *a grave illness* **2** : serious and formal in appearance or manner • *The judge had a grave expression on his face.* — **grave·ly** *adv* • *gravely ill*

grav·el /ˈɡrævəl/ *n* [U] : small pieces of rock • *a gravel road* [=a road with a top surface made of gravel]

grav·el·ly /ˈɡrævəli/ *adj* **1** : containing gravel • *gravelly soil* **2** : having a rough sound • *a gravelly voice*

grave·stone /ˈɡreɪvˌstoʊn/ *n* [C] : a stone that marks the place where a dead person is buried

grave·yard /ˈɡreɪvˌjɑːd/ *n* [C] : a place where people are buried : CEMETERY

graveyard shift *n* [C] *chiefly US* : a period of work that begins late at night and ends in the morning

grav·i·tas /ˈɡrævəˌtɑːs/ *n* [U, *singular*] *formal* : a very serious quality or manner • *a comic actress who lacks the gravitas for dramatic roles*

grav·i·tate /ˈɡrævəˌteɪt/ *vb* **-tat·ed; -tat·ing** [I] **1** : to move or tend to move *to* or *toward* someone or something • *The conversation gravitated toward politics.* **2** : to be attracted *to* or *toward* something

or someone • *Many young people now gravitate to careers in the computer industry.*

grav·i·ta·tion /ˌɡrævəˈteɪʃən/ *n* [U] **1** *technical* : GRAVITY 2 **2** : movement to or toward someone or something • *the gravitation of young people to/toward computer careers* — **grav·i·ta·tion·al** /ˌɡrævəˈteɪʃənl/ *adj, technical*

grav·i·ty /ˈɡrævəti/ *n* [U] **1** : the condition of being grave or serious • *They didn't understand the gravity of the situation.* **2** *technical* : the force that causes things to fall towards the Earth • *attempting to defy gravity* — see also CENTER OF GRAVITY

gra·vy /ˈɡreɪvi/ *n, pl* **-vies** **1** [C/U] : a sauce made from the juices of cooked meat **2** [U] *chiefly US, informal* : something valuable or pleasing that is more than what is earned or expected • *The bonus he receives every year is pure gravy.*

¹**gray** (*US*) *or chiefly Brit* **grey** /ˈɡreɪ/ *adj* **1** : having a color between black and white • *gray hair/socks* **2** : having gray hair • *He's gone gray.* **3** : not bright or cheerful • *a cold, gray day* • *the gray faces of the people in the crowd* — **gray** (*US*) *or chiefly Brit* **grey** [C/U] • *shades of gray* — **gray·ish** (*US*) *or chiefly Brit* **grey·ish** /ˈɡreɪɪʃ/ *adj* — **gray·ness** (*US*) *or chiefly Brit* **grey·ness** *n* [U]

²**gray** (*US*) *or chiefly Brit* **grey** *vb* [I] **1** : to become gray • *His hair is graying.* = *He has graying hair.* **2** : to become older • *The population is graying.*

gray area *n* [C] : an area or situation in which it is difficult to judge what is right and what is wrong • *a legal gray area*

gray matter *n* [U] : the tissue that makes up the brain • *(figurative) His books don't challenge the reader's gray matter.* [=intelligence]

graze /ˈɡreɪz/ *vb* **grazed; graz·ing** **1** [T] **a** : to touch or hit (something) while moving past it • *He was grazed by a bullet.* **b** : to injure (the skin, a body part, etc.) by scraping against something • *She grazed her knee when she fell.* **2 a** [T/I] *of an animal* : to eat grass growing in a field • *grazing cattle* • *Fields grazed by cattle.* **b** [T] : to cause (animals) to graze • *We grazed cattle on that pasture.*

¹**grease** /ˈɡriːs/ *n* [U] **1** : melted animal fat • *bacon grease* **2** : an oily substance • *axle grease* — see also ELBOW GREASE — **greasy** /ˈɡriːsi/ *adj* **greas·i·er; -est** • *greasy hair/food*

²**grease** *vb* **greased; greas·ing** [T] : to put grease or oil on (something) • *Grease the pan then pour in the cake batter.*

greasy spoon *n* [C] *informal* : a small and cheap restaurant

¹**great** /ˈɡreɪt/ *adj* **1** : very big or large in size • *a great cloud of smoke* • *the Great Wall of China* • *(informal) They live in a great big house.* [=a very large house] **2** : very large in amount or extent • *The project required a great amount of time and money.* • *The show was a great success.* • *Our speed gradually became greater.* • *She made a great deal of* [=a large amount of] *money.* • *Things could be a great deal worse.* [=much worse] **3 a**

: very strong • *products with great appeal* • *We're in no great hurry.* • *great sadness/ admiration/love* • *The matter must be treated with great care.* [=very carefully] **b** — used for emphasis • *I'm a great admirer of his work.* [=I admire his work very much] **c** : very bad, extreme, or severe • *The storm caused great damage/destruction.* • *a great disaster* • *in great pain* **4** : better than good: such as **a** : of the highest quality • *great art/music* **b** : very important and admired • *great leaders/ scientists* • *a great discovery/achievement* **c** : very talented or successful • *She's a great judge of character.* • *My brother is great at (playing) golf.* [=he plays golf very well] **d** *informal* : very enjoyable, favorable, etc. • *The movie was (really) great!* • *The food tastes great!* • *a great party/show/meal* • *Have a great time!* • *It was great to see you.* • *Great work, everybody!* • *"I passed the exam!" "That's great!"* • *That hat looks great on you.* • *I don't feel too great.* [=I don't feel well] **5** *always before a noun* : more distant in a family relationship by one generation • *My father's/mother's uncle is my great uncle.* • *My great-great-grandmother is my great-grandfather's mother.* — **great** *adv, informal* • *Keep up the good work. You're doing great!* — **great·ness** *n* [U]

²**great** *n* [C] : a very successful or admired person — usually plural • *He is one of the all-time greats in baseball.*

Great Dane *n* [C] : a very large type of dog

Great·er /ˈɡreɪtɚ/ *adj* : consisting of a central city and the surrounding areas that are connected with it — always before the name of a place • *Greater London/Tokyo*

great·ly /ˈɡreɪtli/ *adv* : very much • *She contributes greatly to our success.* • *I greatly admire his work.*

Gre·cian /ˈɡriːʃən/ *adj* : of or relating to ancient Greece • *a Grecian sculpture*

greed /ˈɡriːd/ *n* [U] : a selfish desire to have more of something (especially money) • *a businessman motivated by ambition and greed* • *corporate greed*

greedy /ˈɡriːdi/ *adj* **greed·i·er; -est** : having or showing greed • *a greedy businessman* • *Don't get greedy—there's plenty for everyone.* **2** : very eager to have something — + *for* • *The company is greedy for publicity.* — **greed·i·ly** /ˈɡriːdəli/ *adv* — **greed·i·ness** /ˈɡriːdinəs/ *n* [U]

Greek /ˈɡriːk/ *n* **1** [C] : a person who is from Greece **2** [U] : the language of the Greeks ✧ In informal English you can describe something that you do not understand by saying *It's (all) Greek to me.* — **Greek** *adj* • *Greek mythology*

¹**green** /ˈɡriːn/ *adj* **1** : having the color of growing grass • *green leaves/pants* **2 a** : covered by green grass • *green fields* **b** : consisting of green leaves • *a green salad* **3** : feeling envy • *His sister's success made him green with envy.* **4 a** : not ripe yet • *green tomatoes* **b** : not having training, knowledge, or experience • *She is still very green but eager to learn.* **5** : concerned with protecting the environ-

ment • *green companies/products* — **green·ish** /ˈɡriːnɪʃ/ *adj* — **green·ness** /ˈɡriːnnəs/ *n* [U]

²**green** *n* **1** [C/U] : a color that is like the color of growing grass • *shades of green* **2** [*plural*] : the leaves of plants used for food • *salad/turnip greens* **3** [C] **a** : a large area of grass in the center of a town • *the village green* **b** golf : an area around the hole into which the ball must be played — called also *putting green* **4** or **Green** [C] : a person who tries to protect the natural world : ENVIRONMENTALIST

green·back /ˈɡriːnˌbæk/ *n* [C] *informal* : a piece of U.S. paper money

green bean *n* [C] : a type of bean whose long green seed cases are eaten as a vegetable

green card *n* [C] : a card indicating that a person from a foreign country can live and work in the U.S.

green·ery /ˈɡriːnəri/ *n* [U] : green leaves or plants • *the lush greenery of the islands*

green fingers *n* [*plural*] *Brit* : GREEN THUMB

green·gro·cer /ˈɡriːnˌɡroʊsɚ/ *n* [C] *chiefly Brit* : a person who works in a store that sells fresh vegetables and fruit

green·horn /ˈɡriːnˌhoɚn/ *n* [C] *informal* : a person who lacks experience and knowledge

green·house /ˈɡriːnˌhaʊs/ *n* [C] : a glass building or room that is used for growing plants

greenhouse effect *n* — **the greenhouse effect** : the warming of the Earth's atmosphere that is caused by air pollution

green light *n* — **the green light** : permission to start or continue something • *We finally got the green light to start the new project.*

green onion *n* [C] *US* : a very young, small onion — called also (*US*) *scallion*, (*chiefly Brit*) *spring onion*

green pepper *n* [C] : a sweet pepper that is green and that is eaten raw or cooked

green·room /ˈɡriːnˌruːm/ *n* [C] : a room in a theater or studio where performers can relax before or after they perform

green thumb *n* [*singular*] *US* : an unusual ability to make plants grow • *I wish I had my mother's green thumb.*

Green·wich mean time /ˈɡrɪnɪdʒ-, ˈɡrɛnɪtʃ-/ *n* [*singular*] : the time in Greenwich, England, that is used as the basis of standard time throughout the world — called also (*US*) *Greenwich time*

greet /ˈɡriːt/ *vb* [T] **1** : to meet (someone who has just arrived) with usually friendly and polite words and actions • *We greeted our guests at the door.* **2** : to react to (someone or something) in a specified way • *Her idea was greeted with enthusiasm.* **3** : to be seen or experienced by (someone) • *We were greeted by a snowstorm at the airport.* — **greet·er** *n* [C] • *He was hired as a greeter, welcoming customers to the store.*

greet·ing /ˈɡriːtɪŋ/ *n* **1** [C/U] : something that is said or done to show people that you are happy to meet or see them • *a formal/friendly greeting* **2** [C] : a message that expresses good wishes to someone • *a birthday greeting* • *season's greetings*

greeting card *n* [C] *US* : a decorated card with a message of good wishes that is given to someone on a special occasion

greetings *interj* — used to greet someone who has just arrived • *Greetings! I'm glad you came.*

gre·gar·i·ous /grɪˈgerijəs/ *adj* : enjoying the company of other people • *a gregarious person/personality* — **gre·gar·i·ous·ly** *adv* — **gre·gar·i·ous·ness** *n* [U]

grem·lin /ˈgrɛmlən/ *n* [C] : a small imaginary creature that is blamed when something does not work properly • *The new computer had some gremlins.* [=there were some problems with the new computer]

gre·nade /grəˈneɪd/ *n* [C] : a small bomb that is shot from a rifle or thrown • *a hand grenade* • *a grenade-launcher*

grew past tense of GROW

grey *chiefly Brit* spelling of GRAY

grey·hound /ˈgreɪˌhaʊnd/ *n* [C] : a tall, thin dog that runs very fast

grid /ˈgrɪd/ *n* [C] **1** : GRILLE **2** : a pattern of lines that cross each other to form squares on a piece of paper, a map, etc. • *The city streets form a grid.* **3** : a network of electrical wires and equipment that supplies electricity to a large area

grid·dle /ˈgrɪdl̩/ *n* [C] : a flat surface or pan on which food is cooked

grid·iron /ˈgrɪdˌaɪən/ *n* [C] *US, informal* : the field on which American football is played • *his many moments of glory on the gridiron*

grid·lock /ˈgrɪdˌlɑːk/ *n* [U, singular] **1** : a situation in which streets are so full that vehicles cannot move **2** : a situation in which no progress can be made • *(a) legislative gridlock* — **grid·locked** /ˈgrɪdˌlɑːkt/ *adj* • *Congress remains gridlocked.*

grief /ˈgriːf/ *n* **1 a** [U] : deep sadness caused especially by someone's death • *She was overcome with/by grief.* **b** [C] : a cause of deep sadness • *joys and griefs* **2** [U] *informal* **a** : trouble or annoyance • *Trying to fix the computer isn't worth the grief.* **b** : annoying or playful criticism • *He's taken/gotten/had a lot of grief from his friends.* — **come to grief** : to experience failure, disaster, etc. • *The boat came to grief on the rocks.* — **good grief** *informal* — used to express surprise or annoyance • *Good grief! You're not ready yet?*

grief–strick·en /ˈgriːfˌstrɪkən/ *adj* : very sad • *The death of her son has left her grief-stricken.*

griev·ance /ˈgriːvəns/ *n* **1** [C/U] : a feeling of having been treated unfairly • *He has a deep sense of grievance against his former employer.* **2** [C] : a reason for complaining or being unhappy with a situation • *The students listed their grievances against the university.* **3** [C] : a statement in which you say you are unhappy or not satisfied with something • *filing a*

formal grievance • *Several customers came to air their grievances.*

grieve /ˈgriːv/ *vb* **grieved; griev·ing** **1** [T] : to cause (someone) to feel sad or unhappy • *It grieves me to see them suffering.* **2** [T/I] : to feel or show grief or sadness • *They are grieving (over) their mother's death.* • *a grieving widow*

griev·ous /ˈgriːvəs/ *adj, formal* : very serious or severe • *the grievous cost of war* • *a grievous error/mistake/loss* — **griev·ous·ly** *adv* • *She was grievously injured.*

grif·fin *also* **grif·fon** *or* **gryph·on** /ˈgrɪfən/ *n* [C] *in stories* : an animal that is half eagle and half lion

¹**grill** /ˈgrɪl/ *n* [C] **1** : a metal frame that is used to cook food over hot coals or a fire **2** : a restaurant that serves grilled foods • *a local bar and grill* **3** : a dish of grilled or broiled food • *a mixed grill* [=a dish of various grilled meats] **4** *Brit* : BROILER 1

²**grill** *vb* [T] **1** *chiefly US* **a** : to cook (food) on a metal frame over fire • *Let's grill some chicken.* **b** : to fry or toast (something) on a hot surface • *a grilled cheese sandwich* **2** *Brit* : BROIL **3** *informal* : to ask (someone) difficult and unpleasant questions • *Her parents grilled her when she came home late.* — **grill·ing** /ˈgrɪlɪŋ/ *n* [C/U] • *The police gave him a grilling about the robbery.*

grille *also* **grill** /ˈgrɪl/ *n* [C] : a metal frame with bars running across it that is used to cover or protect something • *a vent covered with a grille*

grim /ˈgrɪm/ *adj* **grim·mer; -mest** **1** : unpleasant or shocking to see or think about • *The accident serves as a grim reminder of the dangers of drinking and driving.* **2** : causing feelings of sadness or worry • *a grim winter* • *The prognosis is grim—she is expected to live less than six months.* **3** : having a very serious appearance or manner • *His face looked grim.* **4** : strongly felt and serious • *grim determination* — **grim·ly** *adv* — **grim·ness** *n* [U]

grim·ace /ˈgrɪməs/ *n* [C] : a facial expression in which you show disgust, disapproval, or pain — **grimace** *vb* **-aced; -ac·ing** [I] • *The patient grimaced in pain.*

grime /ˈgraɪm/ *n* [U] : dirt that covers a surface — **grimy** /ˈgraɪmi/ *adj* **grim·i·er; -est** • *grimy windows*

Grim Reaper *n* — **the Grim Reaper** : death thought of as a skeleton holding a scythe and wearing a dark cloak with a hood

grin /ˈgrɪn/ *vb* **grinned; grin·ning** [I] : to smile widely • *He was grinning from ear to ear.* • *(figurative) I don't agree with their decision, but all I can do is grin and bear it.* [=accept it because I have no choice] — **grin** *n* [C] • *He had/wore a foolish grin on his face.*

¹**grind** /ˈgraɪnd/ *vb* **ground** /ˈgraʊnd/; **grind·ing** **1** [T] **a** : to crush (something) into very small pieces • *They grind the corn into meal.* • *ground coffee beans* **b** : to cut (meat) into small pieces by putting it through a special machine • *(US) a pound of ground beef* [=(US) hamburger,

(*Brit* mince] **2** [*T/I*] : to make (something) sharp or smooth by rubbing it against a hard surface ▪ *grind an ax* — see also *ax to grind* at ¹AX **3** [*T/I*] : to rub against each other in a noisy way ▪ *I heard a car's gears grinding.* **4** [*T*] : to rub or press (something) against a surface ▪ *Dirt was ground into the carpet.* — **grind along** [*phrasal vb*] : to continue in a slow and steady way ▪ *The traffic ground along (through) the city streets.* — **grind away** [*phrasal vb*] : to work or study in a steady, determined way ▪ *She was grinding away at her studies.* — **grind down** [*phrasal vb*] **1 grind (something) down** *or* **grind (something) down** : to make (something hard) smaller and smoother by rubbing ▪ *His teeth were ground down by use.* **2 grind down (someone or something)** *or* **grind (someone or something) down** : to weaken or destroy (someone or something) gradually ▪ *Poverty ground their spirit down.* — **grind on** [*phrasal vb*] : to continue for a long time — used to describe something unpleasant ▪ *The war ground on for many more months.* — **grind out** [*phrasal vb*] **grind out (something)** *or* **grind (something) out** : to produce (something) quickly as part of a continuous process ▪ *He grinds out a new novel every year.* — **grind to a halt** *or* **come to a grinding halt** *of a machine* : to stop working or moving forward ▪ *The machine ground to a halt.* ▪ (*figurative*) *The project came to a grinding halt.*

²**grind** *n* **1** [*singular*] : boring or difficult work ▪ *a break from the daily grind* **2** [*C*] *US* : a person who works or studies too much

grind·er /'graɪndɚ/ *n* [*C*] **1** : a person or thing that grinds something ▪ *a coffee grinder* **2** *US* : SUBMARINE SANDWICH

grinding *adj* : very harsh or difficult ▪ *grinding poverty*

grind·stone /'graɪnˌstoʊn/ *n* [*C*] : a stone disc that is used for sharpening tools ▪ (*figurative*) *You'll do well at school if you just* **keep your nose to the grindstone.** [=do hard, continuous work]

¹**grip** /'grɪp/ *vb* **gripped**; **grip·ping** [*T*] **1** : to grab or hold (something) tightly ▪ *She gripped her mother's hand tightly.* **2** : to get and hold the interest or attention of (someone) ▪ *The scandal has gripped the nation.*

²**grip** *n* **1** [*C*] **a** : the act of grabbing or holding something — often + *on* ▪ *He lost his grip on the rope.* **b** : a way or style of holding something ▪ *a loose/tight grip* **2** [*singular*] **a** : power or control ▪ *He's trying to maintain/tighten his grip on the company's finances.* ▪ *We're still* **in the grip of** *winter.* **b** : an understanding of something — often + *on* ▪ *She has a good grip on local politics.* [=she understands local politics well] **3** [*C*] : a part for holding something ▪ *I need new grips for my golf clubs.* — **come to grips with** *or Brit* **get to grips with** : to begin to understand or deal with (something) in a direct or effective way ▪ *The government needs to come to grips with the problem.* — **get a grip (on yourself)** *informal* : to get control of your thoughts and emotions and stop behaving in an uncontrolled way — **lose your grip** *informal* : to lose control of your thoughts and emotions ▪ *He seems to be* **losing his grip on reality.** [=confusing what is real and what is not real]

gripe /'graɪp/ *vb* **griped**; **grip·ing** [*T/I*] *informal* : COMPLAIN ▪ *The students griped that they had too much homework.* — **gripe** [*C*] ▪ *I'm sick of their gripes.* [=complaints]

gripping *adj* : very interesting and exciting ▪ *a gripping story/novel*

gris·ly /'grɪzli/ *adj* **gris·li·er; -est** : causing horror or fear ▪ *a grisly murder/discovery/scene*

grist /'grɪst/ *n* — **grist for your/the mill** (*US*) *or Brit* **grist to your/the mill** : something that can be used for a particular purpose ▪ *As a writer, he regards his difficult childhood experiences as grist for the mill.* [=material that he can use as a writer]

gris·tle /'grɪsəl/ *n* [*U*] : tough matter in meat that is difficult to eat — **gris·tly** /'grɪsəli/ *adj* **gris·tli·er; -est**

grit /'grɪt/ *n* [*U*] **1** : very small pieces of sand or stone **2** *informal* : mental toughness and courage ▪ *the resourcefulness and grit of pioneers*

²**grit** *vb* **grit·ted; grit·ting** — **grit your teeth 1** : to press or rub your teeth together ▪ *He gritted his teeth in anger/pain.* **2** : to show courage and determination when dealing with challenges ▪ *The work is hard, but we have to just grit our teeth and keep at it.*

grits /'grɪts/ *n* [*plural*] : a type of ground corn that is eaten especially in the southern U.S.

grit·ty /'grɪti/ *adj* **grit·ti·er; -est 1** : containing very small pieces of sand or stone ▪ *gritty vegetables* **2** *informal* : having or showing a lot of courage and determination ▪ *the story's gritty heroine* **3** : harsh and unpleasant ▪ *the gritty realities of life on the streets*

griz·zled /'grɪzəld/ *adj* : having gray hair ▪ *a grizzled man/beard*

grizzly bear *n* [*C*] : a very large bear of western North America

groan /'groʊn/ *vb* **1 a** [*I*] : to make a deep sound because of pain, grief, disappointment, etc. ▪ *She groaned when she saw the bill.* **b** [*T*] : to say (something that expresses annoyance or unhappiness) ▪ *"Oh, no," she groaned, "I have to start all over."* **2** [*I*] : to complain about something ▪ *He's always moaning and groaning about his salary.* **3** [*I*] : to make a deep sound caused especially by weight or pressure ▪ *The chair groaned under his weight.* — **groan** *n* [*C*] ▪ *the groans of the wounded men*

gro·cer /'groʊsɚ/ *n* [*C*] : a person who sells food and household supplies

gro·cery /'groʊsri/ *n, pl* **-cer·ies 1** [*C*] *chiefly US* : GROCERY STORE **2** [*plural*] : food bought at a store ▪ *He picked up some groceries for supper.* — **grocery** *adj, always before a noun* ▪ *grocery bags/shopping*

grocery store n [C] chiefly US : a store that sells food and household supplies : SUPERMARKET

grog·gy /'grɑːgi/ adj **grog·gi·er; -est** : not able to think or move normally because of being tired, sick, etc. • The medicine can make patients groggy. — **grog·gi·ness** /'grɑːginəs/ n [U]

groin /'groɪn/ n [C] : the area of the body where your legs come together

¹**groom** /'gruːm/ n [C] **1** : a man who has just married or is about to be married **2** : a person who takes care of horses

²**groom** vb [T] **1** : to clean and care for (an animal) • They have their dog groomed professionally. **2 a** : to make (someone) neat and attractive • She spent hours grooming herself. **b** : to make (something) neat, smooth, or attractive • a carefully groomed lawn **3** : to prepare (someone) for a particular job or position • He is being groomed to take over the company. — **groom·ing** n [U]

groom·er /'gruːmə/ n [C] : a person who cleans and cares for an animal • a dog groomer

grooms·man /'gruːmzmən/ n, pl **-men** /-mən/ [C] chiefly US : a male friend or relative who helps a groom at his wedding

¹**groove** /'gruːv/ n **1** [C] : a long, narrow cut in a surface • the grooves on a vinyl record **2** [singular] informal **a** US : a state in which you are able to do something well and easily because you are doing it often • It's not hard to do a little studying each day once you get into a/the groove. **b** chiefly Brit : ¹RUT **2** • She's stuck in a groove in her job. **3** [C] informal : an enjoyable pattern of sound in music • dance grooves — **grooved** /'gruːvd/ adj • a grooved surface

²**groove** vb **grooved; groov·ing** [I] informal : to enjoy listening to or dancing to music • We grooved to the beat.

groovy /'gruːvi/ adj **groov·i·er; -est** informal + old-fashioned : very good and enjoyable • groovy music

grope /'groʊp/ vb **groped; grop·ing 1** [I] : to search for something by reaching in an awkward way • I groped for the light switch. **2** [T/I] : to move forward carefully by putting your hands in front of you • We groped (our way) along the dark passage. **3** [T] : to touch (someone) in an unwanted sexual way • He tried to grope her.

¹**gross** /'groʊs/ adj **1** always before a noun : very obvious or noticeable • a gross exaggeration/injustice **2 a** : rude or offensive • gross language **b** informal : very disgusting • That soup looks gross. **3** always before a noun : including everything • the shipment's gross weight • gross earnings [=the total amount of money earned before anything (such as taxes or expenses) is taken away] — **gross·ly** adv • She is grossly overweight. — **gross·ness** n [U]

²**gross** vb [T] : to earn (an amount of money) before taxes, expenses, etc., are taken away • They grossed $50,000 before taxes. — **gross out** [phrasal vb] **gross (someone) out** also **gross out (someone)**

chiefly US, informal : to cause (someone) to feel disgusted • Horror movies gross me out.

³**gross** n [C] **1** : the amount of money earned before taxes, expenses, etc., are taken away • They donate five percent of their gross to charity every year. **2** pl **gross** : 12 dozen • selling pencils by the gross

gross national product n [C/U] : the total value of the goods and services produced by the people of a nation during a year — abbr. GNP

gro·tesque /groʊ'tɛsk/ adj **1** : very strange or ugly in a way that is not normal or natural • animals with grotesque deformities **2** : extremely different from what is expected or usual • a grotesque distortion of the facts — **gro·tesque·ly** adv — **gro·tesque·ness** n [U]

grot·to /'grɑːtoʊ/ n, pl **-toes** also **-tos** [C] : a small cave

¹**grouch** /'graʊtʃ/ n [C] : a person who complains frequently

²**grouch** vb [T/I] informal : to complain in an annoyed way • He's always grouching about work.

grouchy /'graʊtʃi/ adj **grouch·i·er; -est** informal : having a bad temper • I get grouchy when I'm tired. — **grouch·i·ness** /'graʊtʃinəs/ n [U]

¹**ground** /'graʊnd/ n **1** [U] : the surface of the earth • lying/sitting on the ground • close/low to the ground • a ground war [=a war fought by soldiers on the ground] • The bird's nest is located high above ground. [=on top of the earth's surface] • The seeds should be planted a few inches below ground. [=below the earth's surface] **2** [U] : the soil that is on or under the surface of the earth • solid/firm/dry ground **3 a** [U] : an area of land • They built their house on high/level ground. • hallowed/sacred ground **b** [C] : an area of land or water that is used for a particular purpose • a camping ground • (Brit) a football ground [=(US) a soccer field] • the fish's spawning ground • an ancient burial ground [=a place where people were buried in ancient times] **c** [plural] : the land around a building • trespassing on school grounds • the grounds of the estate **4** [U] : the bottom of the ocean, a lake, etc. • The boat struck ground. **5** [U] : an area of knowledge or interest • We have a lot of ground to cover. [=a lot of information to discuss] **6** [singular] : a place or situation in which someone or something is developed or tested • The laboratory has become a **testing ground** for ideas about the universe's origins. **7** [U, singular] : a set of beliefs, opinions, or attitudes • They are trying to find some **common ground**. [=an area in which they can agree with each other] • looking for a **middle ground** between two extremes • He's on dangerous ground. [=he is doing or saying something that may cause anger or criticism] — see also HIGH GROUND **8** [C] : a reason for doing or thinking something — usually plural • Her husband's infidelity was grounds for divorce. **9** [plural] : very small pieces of crushed coffee beans • coffee grounds

10 [C] *US* : a wire or metal object that makes an electrical connection with the earth — called also (*Brit*) **earth** — **break ground 1** : to dig into the ground at the start of building something ▪ *Workers broke ground on the new stadium last week.* **2** *or* **break new ground** : to make new discoveries ▪ *The study does not break (any) new ground in the search for a cure for cancer.* — **from the ground up 1** : completely or thoroughly ▪ *The car has been redesigned from the ground up.* **2** : from the very beginning ▪ *They built the resort from the ground up.* — **gain ground** *or* **make up ground** : to move faster so that you come closer to someone or something that is in front of you ▪ *She started to gain ground (on the lead runners).* ▪ (*figurative*) *The campaign is trying to make up ground by advertising heavily in key states.* — **get (something) off the ground** : to begin to operate in a successful way ▪ *The project never got off the ground.* ▪ *We couldn't get the project off the ground.* — **give ground** : to move backward when you are being attacked ▪ *The troops had to give ground.* ▪ (*figurative*) *Both parties are refusing to give ground on the issue.* — **hit the ground running** see ¹HIT — **hold/stand your ground** : to not change your position when you are being attacked ▪ *The troops held their ground.* ▪ (*figurative*) *The president continues to stand his ground despite criticism.* — **into the ground 1** : to the point of being very tired or exhausted ▪ *She's been working herself into the ground.* **2** : to the point of complete failure or ruin ▪ *He ran that company into the ground.* [=he destroyed that company] — **lose ground** : to move slower so that you are farther away from someone or something that is in front of you ▪ *She was losing ground (to the leaders) in the race.* ▪ (*figurative*) *The company is losing ground to* [=not doing as well as] *its competitors.*

²**ground** *vb* **1** [T] : to provide a basis or reason for (something) ▪ *Our fears were well grounded.* [=there was a good reason for our fears] — often + *in* ▪ *a theory grounded in fact* **2** [T/I] : to cause a ship or boat to hit the ground below the water so that it cannot move ▪ *The ship was grounded on a sandbar.* **3** [T] : to prevent (an aircraft or a pilot) from flying ▪ *Bad weather grounded his flight.* **4** [T] : to stop (a child) from leaving the house to spend time with friends as a form of punishment ▪ *Her parents threatened to ground her for a week.* ▪ *I can't go out because I'm grounded.* **5** [T] *US* : to connect (a wire, a device, etc.) electrically to the ground for safety ▪ *The wire was not properly grounded.* — **ground in** [*phrasal vb*] **ground (someone) in** : to give (someone) basic knowledge about (something) ▪ *She is well/solidly grounded in* [=she has a good knowledge of] *mathematics.*

³**ground** *past tense and past participle of* ¹GRIND

ground ball *n* [C] *baseball* : a ball that is hit by the batter and rolls or bounces along the ground ▪ *He hit a ground ball to the shortstop.*

ground·break·ing /ˈɡraʊndˌbreɪkɪŋ/ *adj* : introducing new ideas or methods ▪ *a groundbreaking new book*

ground cover *n* [C/U] : a low garden plant that covers the ground

ground crew *n* [C] : a group of people at an airport who take care of and repair aircraft

ground·ed /ˈɡraʊndəd/ *adj* : sensible and having an understanding of what is really important in life ▪ *He has stayed grounded despite all the fame.*

ground·er /ˈɡraʊndɚ/ *n* [C] : GROUND BALL

ground floor *n* [C] : the floor of a building that is at ground level ▪ (*figurative*) *She was able to get in on the ground floor* [=become involved at the very beginning] *of the computer industry.*

ground·hog /ˈɡraʊndˌhɑːɡ/ *n* [C] : WOODCHUCK

Groundhog Day *n* [*singular*] : February 2 observed in the U.S. as a day that indicates whether winter will end soon ❖ Tradition says that if a groundhog sees its shadow on February 2, the winter will last six more weeks, and if it does not see its shadow because of cloudy weather, the winter will end soon.

ground·ing /ˈɡraʊndɪŋ/ *n* [*singular*] : training or instruction that gives someone basic knowledge of a particular subject ▪ *He has a solid grounding in* [=he knows about and understands] *the issues.*

ground·less /ˈɡraʊndləs/ *adj* : not based on facts ▪ *The charges against him were groundless.*

ground rule *n* [C] : a basic rule about what should be done in a particular situation, event, etc. — usually plural ▪ *We laid out the ground rules for the meeting.*

grounds·keep·er /ˈɡraʊndzˌkiːpɚ/ *n* [C] *US* : a person who takes care of a large area of land (such as a park) — called also (*chiefly Brit*) **groundsman**

ground·swell /ˈɡraʊndˌswɛl/ *n* [C] : a fast increase in the amount of public support for something ▪ *a groundswell of enthusiasm for the candidate*

ground·wa·ter /ˈɡraʊndˌwɑːtɚ/ *n* [U] : water that is underground

ground·work /ˈɡraʊndˌwɚk/ *n* [U] : something that is done at an early stage and that makes later work or progress possible ▪ *He did/laid the groundwork for further research.*

ground zero *n* [U] **1** : the point on the earth's surface where an explosion occurs **2** : the central point in an area of fast change or intense activity ▪ *ground zero in the battle over immigration laws* **3** : the beginning state or starting point ▪ *We'll need to start again at ground zero.*

¹**group** /ˈɡruːp/ *n* [C] **1 a** : two or more people or things that are together or in the same place ▪ *a small group of islands* ▪ *We went there as a group.* ▪ *They worked (together) in groups.* **b** : a number of people who are connected by some shared activity, interest, or quality ▪ *ethnic/religious groups* ▪ *She joined a discus-*

sion groups. ▪ *The disease was seen in all age groups.* [=groups made up of people who are the same age] ▪ *a group discussion* [=a discussion involving a group of people] **c** : a number of things that are related in some way ▪ *the four food groups* **2** : a number of musicians who play together regularly ▪ *a rock/musical group* [=band]

²**group** *vb* **1** [*T*] : to put (people or things) in a group ▪ *English and Dutch can be grouped (together) as Germanic languages.* **2** [*I*] : to form a group ▪ *The children grouped (together) around the table.*

group·ie /ˈgruːpi/ *n* [*C*] *informal* **1** : a fan of a music group who follows the group on concert tours **2** : an enthusiastic supporter or follower of something ▪ *a political groupie*

group·ing /ˈgruːpɪŋ/ *n* [*C*] : a set of people or things combined in a group ▪ *a grouping of stars/islands*

group therapy *n* [*U*] : a method for helping people by having them discuss their problems together in a group

¹**grouse** /ˈgraʊs/ *n, pl* **grouse** [*C*] : a small bird that is often hunted

²**grouse** *vb* **groused; grous·ing** [*T/I*] *informal* : COMPLAIN ▪ *She was grousing about her job.*

grout /ˈgraʊt/ *n* [*U*] : material used for filling spaces between tiles — **grout** *vb* [*T*] ▪ *grouting the bathroom tiles*

grove /ˈgroʊv/ *n* [*C*] : a small group of trees ▪ *a grove of oaks* ▪ *an orange/pecan grove*

grov·el /ˈgrɑːvəl, ˈgrʌvəl/ *vb, US* **grov·eled** *or Brit* **grov·elled;** *US* **grov·el·ing** *or Brit* **grov·el·ling** [*I*] **1** : to kneel, lie, or crawl on the ground ▪ *They groveled before the king.* **2** : to treat someone with too much respect or fear in order to be forgiven or to gain approval ▪ *He had to grovel to get her to accept his apology.* — **grov·el·er** (*US*) *or Brit* **grov·el·ler** *n* [*C*]

grow /ˈgroʊ/ *vb* **grew** /ˈgruː/; **grown** /ˈgroʊn/; **grow·ing** **1** [*I*] : to become larger : to increase in size, amount, etc. ▪ *a rapidly growing city* ▪ *The sport is growing in popularity.* [=is becoming more popular] **2** [*I*] : to be improved in some way ▪ *She has grown as a person since going to college.* **3** [*I*] : to become larger and change from being a child to being an adult ▪ *He's still a growing boy.* ▪ *She's grown (by) an inch since last year.* **4 a** [*I*] *of a plant* : to exist and develop ▪ *These trees grow two feet a year.* ▪ *The flowers grow wild* [=grow without being planted by people] *here.* **b** [*T*] : to cause (a plant) to grow ▪ *She grows tomatoes in her garden.* **5** [*T/I*] *of hair, fingernails, etc.* : to become longer ▪ *She's letting her hair grow.* ▪ *He tried to grow a beard/mustache.* **6 a** [*linking vb*] : BECOME ▪ *She suddenly grew pale/tired.* ▪ *He's worried about growing old.* **b** [*I*] : to have or form an opinion, attitude, etc., after time passes ▪ *I grew to admire her.* **7** [*T*] : to cause (something) to develop ▪ *He claims that his plan will help grow the economy.* — **grow apart** [*phrasal vb*] : to become less emotionally close ▪ *My wife and I*

have grown apart over the years. — **grow from** [*phrasal vb*] : to originate from (something) ▪ *The company grew from an idea he had in college.* — **grow into** [*phrasal vb*] **1** : to become (something) as time passes ▪ *Her small company has grown into a huge corporation.* **2** : to become large enough for (a certain size of clothing) ▪ *Ben will grow into Billy's shoes in a year or two.* — **grow on** [*phrasal vb*] : to become more appealing to (someone) as time passes ▪ *I didn't like him at first, but he's starting to grow on me.* — **grow on trees** *informal* : to exist in large amounts and be easy to get ▪ *Good jobs don't grow on trees.* — **grow out** [*phrasal vb*] **1 grow (something) out** *or* **grow out (something)** : to allow (something) to get longer ▪ *She's growing out her hair.* **2 grow out of a** : to develop or come from (a source) ▪ *This new theory grew out of their earlier research.* **b** : to become too large for (a certain size of clothing) ▪ *He quickly grew out of his clothes.* **c** : to stop doing or having (something) because you are more mature ▪ *He's wild now, but he'll grow out of it.* — **grow up** [*phrasal vb*] **1 a** : to become an adult ▪ *She wants to be a firefighter when she grows up.* — used to describe your life when you were a child ▪ *I grew up in the city.* ▪ *We grew up poor.* **b** : to stop thinking and behaving in a childish way ▪ *It's time for them to grow up.* **2** : to begin to exist and develop ▪ *A rivalry grew up between the villages.* — **grow·er** /ˈgroʊɚ/ *n* [*C*] ▪ *corn/fruit growers* ▪ *This plant is a fast grower.*

growing pains *n* [*plural*] : the problems that are experienced as something grows larger or more successful ▪ *a young company/city dealing with growing pains*

growl /ˈgraʊl/ *vb* **1** [*I*] **a** *of an animal* : to make a deep threatening sound ▪ *The dog growled at me.* **b** : to make a low sound like the sound of a growling animal ▪ *My stomach's been growling all morning.* **2** [*T/I*] : to say (something) in an angry way ▪ *"What do you want?" he growled.* — **growl** *n* [*C*] ▪ *a menacing growl*

¹**grown** *past participle of* GROW

²**grown** /ˈgroʊn/ *adj, always before a noun* : ²ADULT ▪ *She has two grown children.* [=two children who are now adults]

grown–up /ˈgroʊnˌʌp/ *adj* **1** : fully grown ▪ *Their kids are all grown-up.* [=are adults] **2** *informal* : suitable for adults ▪ *a grown-up movie/party* **b** : like an adult ▪ *How grown-up you look!* — **grown–up** *n* [*C*] *informal* ▪ *kids and grown-ups* [=adults]

growth /ˈgroʊθ/ *n* **1** [*U*] : the process of growing: such as **a** : natural increase in size ▪ *The medication could slow/stunt a child's growth.* **b** : the process of forming or developing something ▪ *a substance that promotes the growth of new blood vessels* **c** : an increase in the number, amount, or size of something ▪ *population/economic growth* **d** : the development of a person's mind, emotions, etc. ▪ *personal growth* [*U, singular*] : a result or product of growing ▪ *Prune the bush to* encourage new growth. **3** [C] medical : an abnormal mass of tissue • *a cancerous growth*

¹**grub** /ˈgrʌb/ n **1** [C] : the young, wormlike form of an insect **2** [U] informal : FOOD **1** • *Let's go get some grub.*

²**grub** vb **grubbed; grub·bing** [I] **1** : to dig in the ground for something • *animals grubbing for roots* **2** informal : to try hard to get or find something • *grubbing for attention*

grub·by /ˈgrʌbi/ adj **grub·bi·er; -est** informal : dirty or messy • *grubby clothes/ hands* — **grub·bi·ness** /ˈgrʌbinəs/ n [U]

¹**grudge** /ˈgrʌdʒ/ n [C] : a feeling of anger toward someone that lasts for a long time • *She still has/holds/bears a grudge against him for the way he treated her in school.* • *The race had turned into a grudge match.* [=a contest or fight between players, teams, etc., who dislike each other]

²**grudge** vb **grudged; grudg·ing** [T] : BEGRUDGE • *I don't grudge paying my share.*

grudg·ing /ˈgrʌdʒɪŋ/ adj : said, done, or given in an unwilling or doubtful way • *He has earned the grudging admiration/ respect of his rivals.* — **grudg·ing·ly** adv

gru·el /ˈgruːwəl/ n [U] : oatmeal or some other grain boiled in water or milk • *a bowl of gruel*

gru·el·ing (US) or Brit **gru·el·ling** /ˈgruːwəlɪŋ/ adj : requiring great effort • *a grueling schedule*

grue·some /ˈgruːsəm/ adj : causing horror or disgust • *a gruesome murder* — **grue·some·ly** adv — **grue·some·ness** n [U]

gruff /ˈgrʌf/ adj **1** : rough or very serious in manner or speech • *a gruff old man* **2** : low and rough • *He spoke in a gruff voice.* — **gruff·ly** adv — **gruff·ness** n [U]

grum·ble /ˈgrʌmbəl/ vb **grum·bled; grum·bling** [T/I] **1** : to complain quietly about something • *Customers grumbled about the poor service.* • *"When are we going to leave?" he grumbled.* **2** [I] : to make a low, heavy sound • *Her stomach was grumbling.* — **grum·bler** /ˈgrʌmbələ/ n [C] — **grum·bling** n [C/U] • *Stop your grumbling.*

grumpy /ˈgrʌmpi/ adj **grump·i·er; -est** informal : having a bad temper or complaining often • *He's a grumpy old man.* — **grump** /ˈgrʌmp/ n [C] • *He's an old grump.* — **grump·i·ly** /ˈgrʌmpəli/ adv — **grump·i·ness** /ˈgrʌmpinəs/ n [U]

grunge /ˈgrʌndʒ/ n [U] : a type of loud rock music • *a grunge band*

grun·gy /ˈgrʌndʒi/ adj **grun·gi·er; -est** chiefly US, informal : ¹DIRTY • *a grungy pair of jeans*

¹**grunt** /ˈgrʌnt/ n [C] **1** : a short, low sound from the throat • *the grunt of a pig* **2** US, informal : a person who does ordinary and boring work • *She does all the grunt work for her boss.*

²**grunt** vb **1** [I] : to make a short, low sound • *They grunted with effort as they lifted the sofa.* **2** [T] : to say (something) with a grunt • *"I don't know," she grunted.*

gryphon variant spelling of GRIFFIN

gua·ca·mo·le /ˌgwɑːkəˈmouli/ n [U] : a Mexican food made of mashed avocado and usually chopped tomatoes and onion

¹**guar·an·tee** /ˌgerənˈtiː/ n [C] **1** : a usually written promise: such as **a** : a promise that the quality of something will be as good as expected • *The washer comes with a guarantee against major defects.* • *a money-back guarantee* [=a promise that the money you spend on a product will be returned if the product is not good enough] **b** : a promise that something is true or real • *a guarantee that the document is authentic* **2** : a promise that something will happen or be done • *a guarantee of job security* **3** : a thing that makes something sure to happen or exist • *There is no guarantee* [=no way to be sure] *that they will agree.*

²**guarantee** vb **-teed; -tee·ing** [T] **1 a** : to make a usually written promise that whatever you are selling, doing, etc., is what you say it is • *The washer is guaranteed against defects.* **b** : to promise to pay for (something) if another person fails to pay for it • *He personally guaranteed the loan.* **2 a** : to say (something) with great confidence • *I guarantee that you'll like it.* **b** : to make (something) certain • *We can't guarantee your safety.* • *a guaranteed annual wage* • *It's guaranteed to rain today.* [=it will certainly rain today] **c** : to say that (something) will certainly happen • *He guaranteed a victory.*

guar·an·tor /ˌgerənˈtoɚ/ n [C] finance : a person who promises to guarantee a loan

guar·an·ty /ˈgerənti/ n, pl **-ties** [C] **1** law : a formal promise to pay a debt • *a loan guaranty* **2** : a promise that something will be protected or maintained • *the guaranty of free speech*

¹**guard** /ˈgɑːd/ n **1** [U] : a state in which someone is carefully looking for possible danger, threats, problems, etc. • *Police officers were standing/keeping guard along the parade route.* • *Soldiers were on guard* [=watching and ready to respond if needed] *at the gate.* • *The soldiers were on their guard.* [=watching and ready to respond] • *He always has/keeps his guard up.* [=is careful and alert] • *He never lets his guard down.* **2** [C] **a** : a person whose job or duty is to watch and protect someone or something • *There were several (armed) guards at the gate.* **b** : a group of people (such as soldiers) who protect a person or place • *the palace guard* **3** [C] **a** : something that keeps an unwanted result or effect from happening — often + *against* • *Clean the wound as a guard against infection.* **b** : a special part or device that protects someone or something from injury or damage • *a mouth/shin guard* **4** [C] a American football : either one of two players who play in positions on either side of the center **b** basketball : either one of two players who control their team's play when they are trying to score points **5** [C] Brit : CONDUCTOR **2** — off guard : in an unprepared state • *Her angry response caught/threw me off guard.* [=sur-

prised me] — **under guard** : in the position of someone (such as a prisoner) who is being watched by a guard • *He was arrested and placed under guard.* [=he was arrested and watched carefully so he would not escape]

²**guard** *vb* [T] **1** : to watch (someone) in order to prevent escape • *Two policemen guarded the prisoner.* **2** : to protect (someone or something) from danger or attack • *Soldiers guarded the entrance/president.* **3** : to be careful about not telling or talking about (something) • *a tightly/closely guarded secret* **4** *sports* : to try to keep (an opponent) from scoring • *She will guard their best player.* — **guard against** [*phrasal vb*] : to try to keep (something) from happening • *Clean the wound to guard against infection.*

guard dog *n* [C] : a dog that is trained to protect a place

guard·ed /ˈgɑɚdəd/ *adj* : very careful about giving information, showing feelings, etc. • *a guarded answer* • *guarded optimism* — **guard·ed·ly** *adv*

guard·house /ˈgɑɚdˌhaʊs/ *n* [C] : a building for soldiers who are watching something (such as an entrance)

guard·i·an /ˈgɑɚdijən/ *n* [C] **1** : someone or something that watches or protects something • *She is the guardian of our family's traditions.* **2** *law* : someone who takes care of another person or of another person's property • *After her parents died, her uncle became her legal guardian.* — **guard·i·an·ship** /ˈgɑɚdijənˌʃɪp/ *n* [U]

guard·rail /ˈgɑɚdˌreɪl/ *n* [C] **1** *US* : a strong metal bar along the side of a road that prevents vehicles from driving off the road **2** : a strong bar or fence that prevents people from falling off a deck, bridge, etc.

gua·va /ˈgwɑːvə/ *n* **1** [C/U] : a sweet, yellow, tropical fruit **2** [C] : a tree that produces guavas

gu·ber·na·to·ri·al /ˌguːbɚnəˈtorijəl/ *adj* : of or relating to the governor of a U.S. state or to the position of governor • *a gubernatorial candidate/election*

guer·ril·la *also* **gue·ril·la** /gəˈrɪlə/ *n* [C] : a member of a group of soldiers who do not belong to a regular army and who fight in a war as an independent unit • *guerrilla warfare/attacks*

¹**guess** /ˈgɛs/ *vb* **1 a** [T/I] : to form an opinion or give an answer about something when you do not know much or anything about it • *If you can't think of an answer, guess.* • *We can only guess (at) what really happened.* • *I'm guessing that she won't come.* [=I don't think she'll come] ✧ Phrases like **guess what** or **guess who** are used as informal ways of saying that you have surprising news. • *"Guess what!" "What?" "I bought a new car."* • *Guess where I'm going on my vacation!* **b** [T] : to guess (something) correctly • *She guessed my age on her first try.* **2** [T] *chiefly US, informal* : to suppose or think (something) • *I guess you're right.* • *I guess this means that we can't go.* ✧ The phrase **I guess (so)** is used as an informal

way of agreeing or saying "yes" when you are not certain or not very excited or interested. • *"Are you hungry?" "I guess."* ✧ The phrase **I guess not** is used as an informal way of agreeing with a negative statement or of saying "no." • *"That wasn't a smart thing to do, was it?" "I guess not."* — **keep/leave (someone) guessing** : to make it impossible for someone to know what will happen next • *He likes to keep us guessing about his plans.* — **guess·er** *n* [C]

²**guess** *n* [C] : an attempt to give an opinion or answer about something when you do not know much about it or are not sure about it • *My guess is that he's about 40 years old.* • *"I don't know the answer." "Make a guess."* = (*US*) *"Take a guess."* = (*chiefly Brit*) *"Have a guess."* • *Your guess is as good as mine.* [=I don't know any more than you do] • *a wild guess* [=a guess based on no knowledge or information] • *an educated guess* [=a guess that is probably close to being correct because it is based on some amount of knowledge] • *It's anybody's/anyone's guess* [=no one knows] *what his next book will be about.*

guess·work /ˈgɛsˌwɚk/ *n* [U] : the act or process of finding an answer by guessing • *This book takes the guesswork out of buying a home.* [=it gives you the information you need so that you can be sure about what to do]

guest /ˈgɛst/ *n* [C] **1** : a person who is invited to visit or stay in someone's home • *Our guests have arrived.* **2** : a person who is invited to a place or an event as a special honor • *Only members and their guests are allowed to use the pool.* • *She will be the guest of honor* [=the person who is being specially honored] *at the banquet.* • *a guest speaker* [=a person invited to a gathering to give a speech] **3** : a customer at a hotel, restaurant, etc. • *Frequent guests receive a discount.* **4** : a usually well-known person who is invited to appear or perform on a program, at an event, etc. • *He made a guest appearance on the show.* — **be my guest** — used to say that someone is welcome to do or take something • *"Could I borrow your pen?" "Sure, be my guest."*

guest·house /ˈgɛstˌhaʊs/ *n* [C] **1** *chiefly US* : a building that is separate from the main house of a property and that is used for guests **2** *chiefly Brit* : a small hotel

guest room *n* [C] : a bedroom for guests

guff /ˈgʌf/ *n* [U] *informal* : foolish nonsense • *The book has a lot of guff about conspiracies.*

guf·faw /gəˈfɑː/ *vb* [I] : to laugh loudly • *The reporters guffawed at his jokes.* — **guffaw** *n* [C] • *She let out a loud guffaw.*

guid·ance /ˈgaɪdns/ *n* [U] : help or advice that tells you what to do • *I couldn't have done it without her guidance.*

guidance counselor *n* [C] *US* : a person who gives advice to students about educational and personal decisions

¹**guide** /ˈgaɪd/ *n* [C] **1 a** : a person who leads or directs other people on a journey • *We hired a guide for our trip to the*

mountains. **b** : a person who shows and explains the interesting things in a place • *a tour guide* **2** : a person who helps to direct another person's behavior, life, career, etc. • *He was my spiritual guide.* **3** : something that helps to direct a person's actions, thoughts, etc. • *They sailed using the stars as their guide.* **4** : a book, magazine, etc., that provides information about a particular subject • *a guide for new parents* • *a guide to New York restaurants*

²**guide** *vb* **guid·ed; guid·ing** [*T*] **1** : to direct or lead (someone) • *He guided us around the city.* • *We were guided to our seats by an usher.* • *You'll need an experienced lawyer to guide you through the legal system.* • *a guided tour of the factory* **2 a** : to direct or control the path or course of (something) • *She guided her team to victory.* **b** : to direct or influence the thoughts or behavior of (someone) • *Let your conscience guide you.* • *She helped guide me toward a career in medicine.*

guide·book /ˈgaɪdˌbʊk/ *n* [*C*] : a book of information for travelers

guided missile *n* [*C*] : a missile whose course may be changed during flight

guide dog *n* [*C*] : a dog that is trained to lead blind people

guide·line /ˈgaɪdˌlaɪn/ *n* [*C*] : a rule or instruction that shows or tells how something should be done • *some guidelines for following a balanced diet*

guild /ˈgɪld/ *n* [*C*] : an organized group of people who have joined together because they share the same job or interest • *the local artists' guild*

guile /ˈgajəl/ *n* [*U*] : the use of clever and usually dishonest methods to achieve something • *They resorted to guile in order to win.*

guile·less /ˈgajələs/ *adj* : very innocent : NAIVE • *a guileless person/smile*

guil·lo·tine /ˈgɪləˌtiːn/ *n* [*C*] : a machine with a heavy blade that was used in the past to cut off people's heads — **guillotine** *vb* **-tined; -tin·ing** [*T*] • *She was guillotined during the French Revolution.*

guilt /ˈgɪlt/ *n* **1** [*U*] : responsibility for a crime or for doing something bad or wrong • *The jury determines the defendant's guilt or innocence.* **2** [*C/U*] : a bad feeling caused by knowing or thinking that you have done something bad or wrong • *I was overwhelmed by feelings of guilt.* • *I was guilt-ridden.* • *our secret guilts and insecurities* — **guilt·less** /ˈgɪltləs/ *adj* • *a guiltless pleasure* [=a pleasure that does not make you feel guilty]

guilt trip *n* [*C*] *informal* : a bad feeling you get when someone suggests that you have done something wrong or that you are not doing something that you should • *"I guess you're just too busy to call."* *"Mom, I don't need you to lay/put a (big) guilt trip on me."* [=make me feel guilty]

guilty /ˈgɪlti/ *adj* **guilt·i·er; -est** **1** : responsible for committing a crime or doing something bad or wrong • *Is he innocent or guilty?* • *The jury found her guilty of robbery.* • *(humorous)* *"Did you plan this party?"* *"Guilty as charged."* [=yes, I

did] **2 a** : showing that you know you have done something bad or wrong • *The boys exchanged guilty looks.* • *He has a guilty conscience.* **b** : having a feeling of guilt • *I feel guilty about what happened.* • *Chocolate is one of my guilty pleasures.* [=something that I enjoy even though eating it causes feelings of guilt] — **guilt·i·ly** /ˈgɪltəli/ *adv*

guinea pig *n* [*C*] **1** : a small animal that is often kept as a pet **2** : a person or thing used for testing something • *He volunteered to act as a guinea pig in the experiment.*

guise /ˈgaɪz/ *n* **1** [*C*] : one of several ways in which something is seen, experienced, or produced • *They serve the same basic dish in various guises.* **2** [*singular*] : a way of seeming or looking that is not true or real • *She swindles people under the guise of friendship.* [=by pretending to be their friend] • *a demon in the guise of* [=a demon disguised as] *an angel*

gui·tar /gɪˈtɑɚ/ *n* [*C*] : a musical instrument that has usually six strings which are played with your fingers or with a pick • *an acoustic/electric guitar* — **gui·tar·ist** /gɪˈtɑrɪst/ *n* [*C*]

gulch /ˈgʌltʃ/ *n* [*C*] *chiefly US* : a small, narrow valley with steep sides : RAVINE

gulf /ˈgʌlf/ *n* [*C*] **1** : a large area of ocean that is partly surrounded by land • *the Gulf of Mexico* • *the Persian Gulf* **2** : a difference between two people, groups, or things • *The program is intended to help bridge the gulf between younger and older generations.*

gull /ˈgʌl/ *n* [*C*] : SEAGULL

gul·let /ˈgʌlət/ *n* [*C*] : ESOPHAGUS

gull·ible /ˈgʌləbəl/ *adj* : quick to believe something that is not true • *I'm not gullible enough to believe that.* • *gullible tourists* — **gull·ibil·i·ty** /ˌgʌləˈbɪləti/ *n* [*U*]

gul·ly /ˈgʌli/ *n, pl* **-lies** [*C*] : a long, narrow, low area in the ground that water moves through when it rains

gulp /ˈgʌlp/ *vb* **1** [*T*] : to eat or swallow (something) quickly or in large amounts • *They gulped (down) their beers and left.* **2** [*T/I*] : to take (air) into your lungs quickly • *The runners were gulping (for) air.* **3** [*T/I*] : to swallow because of fear, shock, etc. • *I gulped nervously before beginning my speech.* — **gulp** *n* [*C*] • *a quick gulp of coffee*

¹**gum** /ˈgʌm/ *n* **1** [*C*] : the flesh that surrounds the roots of your teeth • *swollen gums* **2 a** [*U*] : CHEWING GUM • *a pack/ stick/piece of gum* **b** [*C*] *Brit* : GUMDROP **3** [*C/U*] : a sticky substance in some kinds of plants

²**gum** *vb* **gummed; gum·ming** [*T*] *US* : to chew (something) with the gums because you do not have teeth • *The baby gummed her food.* — **gum up** [*phrasal vb*] **gum (something) up** *or* **gum up (something)** *informal* : to prevent (something) from working or flowing properly • *The road construction will gum up traffic.* • *Some dirt got inside the gears and gummed up the works.*

gum·bo /ˈgʌmboʊ/ *n* [*U*] : a thick soup made with meat or seafood and usually okra • *a bowl of real Cajun gumbo*

gum·drop /'gʌm,drɑːp/ n [C] US : a sweet, chewy candy

gum·my /'gʌmi/ adj **gum·mi·er**; **-est** : made of, containing, or covered with a sticky or chewy substance ▪ *gummy candy* — **gum·mi·ness** n [U]

gump·tion /'gʌmpʃən/ n [U] informal : courage and confidence ▪ *It took a lot of gumption to say that.*

¹**gun** /'gʌn/ n [C] **1** : a weapon that shoots bullets or shells ▪ *fire/shoot a gun* ▪ *He pulled/drew a gun on us.* [=he took out a gun and pointed it at us] ▪ *a loaded gun* [=a gun that has bullets in it] **2** : a device that looks like a gun ▪ *a spray gun* — **jump the gun** : to start or do something too soon ▪ *Several racers jumped the gun.* [=started to run before a gun was fired to start the race]* ▪ (figurative) *The newspaper jumped the gun* [=acted too soon] *and announced the wrong winner.* — **stick to your guns** : to continue to have a particular opinion, plan, etc., when other people say that you are wrong ▪ *The governor is sticking to her guns on this issue.* — **under the gun** chiefly US : in a situation in which you have only a short amount of time to do something ▪ *We were under the gun to finish the project on time.*

²**gun** vb **gunned**; **gun·ning** [T] informal **1** US : to cause (a car or a car's engine) to go very fast ▪ *She gunned the engine.* **2** US : to throw (something) very hard ▪ *He gunned the ball to first base.* — **gun down** [phrasal vb] **gun down (someone)** or **gun (someone) down** : to shoot (someone) with a gun ▪ *He was gunned down in the street.* — **gun for** [phrasal vb] **1** : to try to get or achieve (something) in a very determined way ▪ *He's gunning for my job.* **2** : to try to hurt or defeat (someone) ▪ *Her political enemies are gunning for her.*

gun·boat /'gʌn,boʊt/ n [C] : a small ship with guns — **gunboat diplomacy** : the threat to use military force as a way of forcing a country to do something

gun control n [U] : laws that control how guns are sold and used

gun·fight /'gʌn,faɪt/ n [C] : a fight in which people use guns

gun·fire /'gʌn,fajɚ/ n [U] : the firing of guns ▪ *We heard gunfire.*

gunge /'gʌndʒ/ n [U] Brit, informal : ¹GUNK — **gun·gy** /'gʌndʒi/ adj **gun·gi·er**; **-est**

gung ho /'gʌŋ'hoʊ/ adj : extremely excited and enthusiastic about doing something ▪ *They were a little too gung ho about leaving.*

¹**gunk** /'gʌŋk/ n [U] chiefly US, informal : material that is dirty, sticky, or greasy ▪ *I wiped the gunk off my hands.* — **gunky** /'gʌŋki/ adj **gunk·i·er**; **-est** ▪ *a gunky residue*

²**gunk** vb — **gunk up** [phrasal vb] **gunk up (something)** or **gunk (something) up** US, informal : to cause (something) to be dirty, sticky, or greasy ▪ *Don't gunk up your hair with a lot of styling products.*

gun·man /'gʌnmən/ n, pl **-men** /-mən/

[C] : a man who uses a gun to shoot or try to shoot someone ▪ *shot by an unknown gunman*

gun·ner /'gʌnɚ/ n [C] **1** : a soldier who operates a large gun **2** Brit : a soldier in the British artillery

gun·nery /'gʌnɚi/ n [U] : the use of large military guns ▪ *gunnery practice*

gun·ny·sack /'gʌni,sæk/ n [C] US : a large bag made of rough, heavy cloth

gun·point /'gʌn,pɔɪnt/ n — **at gunpoint** — used to describe being threatened by a person with a gun ▪ *They were robbed/held at gunpoint.*

gun·pow·der /'gʌn,paʊdɚ/ n [U] : a dry explosive substance

gun·shot /'gʌn,ʃɑːt/ n **1** [C/U] : bullets fired from a gun ▪ *gunshot wounds/victims* **2** [C] : the firing of a gun ▪ *We heard several gunshots.*

gun·sling·er /'gʌn,slɪŋɚ/ n [C] : someone who is able to shoot a gun extremely well ▪ *a gunslinger in the Wild West*

gup·py /'gʌpi/ n, pl **-pies** [C] : a small tropical fish

gur·gle /'gɚgəl/ vb **gur·gled**; **gur·gling** [I] **1** : to make the quiet sound of water moving over rocks, through a pipe, etc. ▪ *a gurgling stream* **2** : to make a sound like a liquid boiling ▪ *You could hear my stomach gurgling.* **3** of a baby : to make happy and quiet sounds ▪ *She gurgled contentedly.* — **gurgle** n [C/U]

gur·ney /'gɚni/ n, pl **-neys** [C] US : a bed on a frame with wheels that is used for moving sick or injured people ▪ *a hospital gurney*

gu·ru /'guru/ n, pl **-rus** [C] **1** : a religious and spiritual guide in Hinduism **2** : a person who has a lot of experience in or knowledge about a particular subject ▪ *financial/fitness gurus*

¹**gush** /'gʌʃ/ vb [T/I] **1** : to flow out very quickly and in large amounts ▪ *Oil gushed from the well.* ▪ *The wound gushed blood.* **2** : to speak in an extremely enthusiastic way ▪ *She was gushing over/about the baby.* ▪ *"Oh, your baby is so cute!" she gushed.*

²**gush** n [C] : a sudden outward flow of liquid ▪ (figurative) *a sudden gush of emotion*

gush·er /'gʌʃɚ/ n [C] : someone or something that gushes; especially : an oil well that produces a large flow of oil

gushy /'gʌʃi/ adj **gush·i·er**; **-est** informal + usually disapproving : very emotional or enthusiastic ▪ *gushy praise*

gus·sy /'gʌsi/ vb **gus·sies**; **gus·sied**; **gus·sy·ing** — **gussy up** [phrasal vb] **gussy (someone or something) up** or **gussy up (someone or something)** US, informal : to make (someone or something) more attractive, impressive, or fancy ▪ *She was all gussied up for the party.* ▪ *I gussied up the soup with fresh herbs.*

gust /'gʌst/ n [C] : a sudden strong wind ▪ *a gust of wind* ▪ *Today will be windy, with gusts of up to 40 miles per hour.* — **gust** vb [I] ▪ *The winds were gusting up to 40 miles per hour.* — **gusty** /'gʌsti/ adj **gust·i·er**; **-est**

gus·to /'gʌstoʊ/ n [U] : great enjoyment,

energy, and enthusiasm ▪ *She ate her dinner with (great) gusto.*

¹**gut** /ˈgʌt/ *n* **1** [*plural*] **a** : the internal organs of an animal ▪ *fish guts* **b** *informal* : the inside parts of something ▪ *the guts of a machine* **c** *informal* : the most important parts of something ▪ *the guts of a business deal* **2** [*plural*] *informal* : COURAGE ▪ *That decision took a lot of guts.* **3** [*C*] *informal* — used to talk about feelings, ideas, etc., that come from what seems true or right rather than from logic or reason ▪ *She knew in her gut that he was lying.* ▪ *a gut feeling/reaction* **4** [*C*] *informal* : a person's belly ▪ *Her cruel remark was like a kick in the gut.* **5** [*C*] : INTESTINE — **blood and guts** : violent acts or images ▪ *a movie with lots of blood and guts* — **hate someone's guts** *informal* : to dislike someone very much ▪ *He really hates my guts.* — **spill your guts** *informal* : to tell your secrets or private feelings to another person

²**gut** *vb* **gut·ted**; **gut·ting** [*T*] **1** : to remove the internal organs from (a fish or an animal) ▪ *The salmon was gutted and filleted.* **2 a** : to destroy the inside of (a structure) ▪ *The building was gutted by fire.* **b** : to make (something) no longer effective ▪ *These changes will gut the law.*

gut·less /ˈgʌtləs/ *adj, informal* : lacking courage ▪ *a gutless coward*

gutsy /ˈgʌtsi/ *adj* **guts·i·er**; **-est** *informal* : very tough or brave ▪ *the book's gutsy heroine* ▪ *a very gutsy decision*

gut·ter /ˈgʌtɚ/ *n* **1** [*C*] **a** : a long, hollow device that is attached to the edges of a roof to catch rain and carry it away from a building **b** : a low area at the side of a road that catches water and carries it away from the road **2** [*C*] : a long, narrow low section along the sides of a bowling lane **3** *the gutter* **a** : the lowest or poorest conditions of human life ▪ *He lost all his money and wound up in the gutter.* [=a state of severe poverty] **b** *US, informal* — used to refer to thoughts that relate to sex ▪ *Get your mind out of the gutter.* [=stop thinking that everything relates to sex]

gut·tur·al /ˈgʌtərəl/ *adj* : formed or pronounced in the throat ▪ *guttural sounds* — **gut·tur·al·ly** *adv*

gut–wrench·ing /ˈgʌtˌrɛntʃɪŋ/ *adj, informal* : causing great mental or emotional pain ▪ *gut-wrenching decisions*

guv /ˈgʌv/ *n* [*singular*] *Brit, informal* — used by a man to address another man ▪ *"Where to, guv?" asked the taxi driver.*

guy /ˈgaɪ/ *n, informal* **1** [*C*] : a man ▪ *He seems like a nice guy.* ▪ *It's hard to tell the good guys* [=the heroes] *from the bad guys* [=the villains] *in this movie.* **2** [*plural*] *chiefly US* — used to refer to two or

more people ▪ *Quiet down, guys.* ▪ *Would you guys like anything else?*

guz·zle /ˈgʌzəl/ *vb* **guz·zled**; **guz·zling** /ˈgʌzlɪŋ/ [*T/I*] *informal* : to drink (something) quickly or in large amounts ▪ *She spends her days guzzling (down) coffee.* ▪ *(figurative) cars that guzzle gasoline* — **guz·zler** /ˈgʌzələr/ *n* [*C*] ▪ *beer guzzlers*

gym /ˈdʒɪm/ *n* **1** [*C*] : GYMNASIUM, HEALTH CLUB ▪ *He works out at the gym.* ▪ *a gym membership* **2** [*U*] : PHYSICAL EDUCATION ▪ *Students are required to take gym.* ▪ *gym class* ▪ *gym shoes* [=sneakers]

gym·na·si·um /dʒɪmˈneɪzijəm/ *n* [*C*] : a room or building that has equipment for sports activities or exercise

gym·nas·tics /dʒɪmˈnæstɪks/ *n* **1** [*U*] : a sport in which athletes perform various exercises on a mat or on special equipment ▪ *She swims and does gymnastics.* **2** [*plural*] : an activity that requires unusual ability or effort ▪ *mental/vocal gymnastics* — **gym·nast** /ˈdʒɪmˌnæst/ *n* [*C*] ▪ *an Olympic gymnast* — **gym·nas·tic** /dʒɪmˈnæstɪk/ *adj* ▪ *gymnastic moves*

gy·ne·col·o·gy (*US*) *or chiefly Brit* **gy·nae·col·o·gy** /ˌgaɪnəˈkɑːlədʒi/ *n* [*U*] *medical* : the scientific study of the reproductive system of women and its diseases — **gy·ne·co·log·i·cal** (*US*) *or chiefly Brit* **gy·nae·co·log·i·cal** /ˌgaɪnɪkəˈlɑːdʒɪkəl/ *adj* — **gy·ne·col·o·gist** (*US*) *or chiefly Brit* **gy·nae·col·o·gist** /ˌgaɪnəˈkɑːlədʒɪst/ *n* [*C*]

¹**gyp** /ˈdʒɪp/ *n* [*singular*] *chiefly US, informal* : an act of cheating someone ▪ *Is that all they give you? What a gyp!*

²**gyp** *vb* **gypped**; **gyp·ping** [*T*] *chiefly US, informal* : to cheat (someone) ▪ *You paid $100? You got/were gypped.* ▪ *She got gypped out of a big promotion.*

gyp·sum /ˈdʒɪpsəm/ *n* [*U*] : a white mineral that is used to make plaster of paris

Gyp·sy /ˈdʒɪpsi/ *n, pl* **-sies** [*C*] : a member of a group of people who are known for moving from place to place and who live mostly in Asia, Europe, and North America

gypsy moth *n* [*C*] : a type of moth whose caterpillar damages trees

gy·rate /ˈdʒaɪˌreɪt, Brit dʒaɪˈreɪt/ *vb* **-rat·ed**; **-rat·ing** [*I*] : to move back and forth with a circular motion ▪ *They gyrated to the music.* — **gy·ra·tion** /dʒaɪˈreɪʃən/ *n* [*C/U*]

gy·ro /ˈjiːˌroʊ/ *n, pl* **-ros** [*C*] : a pita wrapped around a filling of usually lamb, onion, tomato, and a yogurt sauce

gy·ro·scope /ˈdʒaɪrəˌskoʊp/ *n* [*C*] : a wheel that spins in a frame that allows it to tilt in any direction and that is used in steering devices on ships, airplanes, etc. — **gy·ro·scop·ic** /ˌdʒaɪrəˈskɑːpɪk/ *adj*

H

h *or* **H** /'eɪtʃ/ *n, pl* **h's** *or* **hs** *or* **H's** *or* **Hs**
/'eɪtʃəz/ [C/U] : the eighth letter of the
English alphabet ▪ *The word "hand" begins with (an) h.*

ha /'hɑ:/ *interj* — used especially to express surprise or pleasure when you do
something or find out about something ▪
Ha! I did it!

hab·it /'hæbət/ *n* **1** [C/U] : something
that a person does often in a regular and
repeated way ▪ *good study/eating habits*
▪ *He has a habit of coughing when he's nervous.* ▪ *I locked the door out of habit.* ▪ *I did
it by/from force of habit.* [=without
thinking because it is what I usually do] ▪
*She got in/into the habit of reading before
bed.* ▪ *I'm not in the habit of getting involved* [=I usually do not get involved] *in
other people's arguments.* ▪ *You can leave
work early today, but don't make a habit
of it.* [=don't do it often] **2** [C] : a strong
need to use a drug, to smoke cigarettes,
etc. ▪ *trying to kick a cocaine/cigarette
habit* **3** [C] : a piece of clothing worn by
members of a religious group ▪ *a nun's
habit*

hab·it·able /'hæbətəbəl/ *adj* : suitable to
live in ▪ *The house is not habitable.*

hab·i·tat /'hæbə,tæt/ *n* [C] : the place or
type of place where a plant or animal
normally lives or grows ▪ *a bear's natural
habitat*

hab·i·ta·tion /,hæbə'teɪʃən/ *n* [U] : the
act of living in a place ▪ *The house is not
fit for human habitation.*

hab·it–form·ing /'hæbət,foɚmɪŋ/ *adj*
: causing a strong need to regularly have
or do something ▪ *habit-forming drugs*

ha·bit·u·al /hə'bɪtʃəwəl/ *adj* **1** : done
regularly or repeatedly ▪ *habitual drug
use* **2** *always before a noun* : doing
something regularly or repeatedly ▪ *She's
a habitual liar.* [=she often tells lies] —
ha·bit·u·al·ly *adv*

¹hack /'hæk/ *vb* **1** [T/I] : to cut (something) many times in a rough and often
violent way ▪ *The table had been hacked
to pieces.* ▪ *hacking (away) at a tree with
an ax* **2** [T] : to make (a path) by cutting plants ▪ *We hacked our way through
the jungle.* **3** [T] *informal* : to manage or
deal with (something) successfully ▪ *I
couldn't hack the new job.* ▪ *I just couldn't
hack it.* **4** [I] : to cough loudly ▪ *a hacking cough* [=a loud, dry cough] **5** [T/I]
computers : to secretly access the files on
a computer system in order to get information, cause damage, etc. ▪ *hacking into
the network* ▪ *The Web site had been
hacked.* — **hack off** [*phrasal vb*] **hack
(something) off** *or* **hack off (something)**
: to cut (something) off in a rough and
violent way ▪ *hacking a branch off (a tree)*

²hack *n* [C] **1** : the act of hitting something roughly with an ax, knife, etc. ▪
Take a hack at the branch. **2** : a loud,
dry cough ▪ *a smoker's hack* **3** *disap-

proving* : someone who does work that is
not important or original ▪ *a political
hack*

hack·er /'hækɚ/ *n* [C] **1** *computers* : a
person who hacks into a computer sys-
tem **2** *US, informal* : a person who
plays a sport badly ▪ *I play golf but I'm
just a hacker.* ▪ *a tennis hacker*

hack·les /'hækəlz/ *n* [*plural*] : hairs
along the neck and back of an animal ▪
(*figurative*) *The ruling is sure to raise
hackles.* [=to upset some people]

hack·neyed /'hæknid/ *adj* : not fresh or
original ▪ *hackneyed phrases/jokes*

hack·saw /'hæk,sɑ:/ *n* [C] : a saw used
for cutting metal

had *past tense and past participle of* HAVE

had·dock /'hædək/ *n* [C/U] : a fish that
lives in the Atlantic Ocean and that is often eaten as food

Ha·des /'heɪ,di:z/ *n* [*singular*] : the home
of the dead in Greek mythology

hadn't /'hædnt/ — used as a contraction
of *had not* ▪ *They hadn't arrived yet.*

**haemoglobin, haemophilia, haem-
orrhage, haemorrhoid** *Brit spellings
of* HEMOGLOBIN, HEMOPHILIA, HEMOR-
RHAGE, HEMORRHOID

hag /'hæg/ *n* [C] *offensive* : an ugly, evil,
or unpleasant old woman

hag·gard /'hægɚd/ *adj* : looking very
thin and tired ▪ *his haggard appearance*

hag·gle /'hægəl/ *vb* **hag·gled; haggling** [I] : to talk or argue with someone
in order to agree on a price ▪ *haggling
(with a salesman) over/about the price of a
new car* ▪ *We haggled over the price.*

ha ha *or* **ha–ha** /'hɑː'hɑː/ *interj* — used
to represent laughter ▪ *"Ha ha! That's a
good one!"* — often used in an ironic way
▪ *Oh, ha ha. Very funny.* [=that's not funny at all]

¹hail /'heɪl/ *n* **1** [U] : pieces of ice that fall
from clouds like rain ▪ *cars damaged by
hail* **2** [*singular*] : a large number of
small hard objects flying or falling together ▪ *a hail of bullets* ▪ (*figurative*) *Her
decision was met with a hail of criticism.*
[=was criticized by many people]

²hail *vb* **1** [T] : to speak of or welcome
(someone or something) with praise or
enthusiasm ▪ *The town hailed him as a
hero.* ▪ *They hailed* [=strongly praised] *her
decision to run for reelection.* ▪ *a drug
hailed as a breakthrough* **2** [T] : to call
out in order to stop or get the attention
of (someone or something) ▪ *hail a taxi*
3 [I] — used with *it* to say that hail is falling ▪ *It's hailing.* — **hail from** [*phrasal
vb*] : to have been born or raised in (a
place) ▪ *He hails from New York.*

hail·stone /'heɪl,stoʊn/ *n* [C] : a piece of
hail

hail·storm /'heɪl,stoɚm/ *n* [C] : a storm
that produces hail

hair /'heɚ/ *n* **1 a** [C] : a thin growth
from the skin of a person or animal ▪

dog/cat/human hairs **b** [*U*] : a covering or growth of hairs ▪ *the dark hair on his arms* ▪ *facial hair* **c** [*U*] : the hair on a person's head ▪ *I just got my hair cut.* ▪ *She has long/black/straight hair.* ▪ *a thick/ full head of hair* ▪ *a lock/strand of hair* ▪ *I'm having a bad hair day.* [=my hair does not look nice today] ▪ (*figurative*) *The sound made my hair stand on end.* [=it frightened me] ▪ (*figurative*) *The kids have been in my hair* [=they have been annoying or bothering me] *all day.* ▪ (*figurative*) *I can't wait to get these kids out of my hair.* ▪ (*figurative*) *Come dancing with us and let your hair down.* [=relax and enjoy yourself] ▪ (*figurative*) *We've been pulling/ tearing our hair out about it.* [=very worried or upset about it] **2** [*singular*] *informal* : a very small distance or amount ▪ *He won the race by a hair.* — **split hairs** : to argue about small details or differences that are not important ▪ *His lawyers are splitting hairs over the wording of his contract.* — **haired** /ˈheɚd/ *adj* ▪ *a long-haired cat* ▪ *a dark-haired person* — **hair‧less** /ˈheɚləs/ *adj*

hair‧brush /ˈheɚˌbrʌʃ/ *n* [*C*] : a brush for the hair on your head

hair‧cut /ˈheɚˌkʌt/ *n* [*C*] : the act or result of cutting and shaping someone's hair ▪ *getting a haircut* ▪ *Do you like my haircut?*

hair‧do /ˈheɚˌduː/ *n, pl* **-dos** [*C*] : a way of cutting and arranging someone's hair ▪ *a stylish hairdo*

hair‧dress‧er /ˈheɚˌdresɚ/ *n* [*C*] : a person who cuts and arranges hair — **hair‧dress‧ing** /ˈheɚˌdresɪŋ/ *n* [*U*]

hair‧grip /ˈheɚˌɡrɪp/ *n* [*C*] *Brit* : BOBBY PIN

hair‧line /ˈheɚˌlaɪn/ *n* [*C*] **1** : a thin line or crack ▪ *a hairline bone fracture* **2** : the line where your hair starts on your forehead ▪ *a receding hairline*

hair‧net /ˈheɚˌnɛt/ *n* [*C*] : a net worn over someone's hair to keep it in place

hair‧piece /ˈheɚˌpiːs/ *n* [*C*] : a section of real or false hair that is worn to cover a bald spot or to make your hair look longer or thicker

hair‧pin /ˈheɚˌpɪn/ *n* [*C*] **1** : a pin that is worn to hold your hair in place **2** : an extremely sharp turn in a road that is shaped like a U ▪ *a hairpin turn/curve*

hair–rais‧ing /ˈheɚˌreɪzɪŋ/ *adj* : very frightening or exciting ▪ *a hair-raising story* — **hair‧rais‧ing‧ly** *adv*

hair's breadth *or US* **hair‧breadth** /ˈheɚˌbrɛθ/ *n* [*singular*] : a very small distance or amount ▪ *He came within a hair's breadth of winning the race.* [=he almost won the race]

hair slide *n* [*C*] *Brit* : BARRETTE

hair‧split‧ting /ˈheɚˌsplɪtɪŋ/ *n* [*U*] : the act of arguing about differences that are too small to be important ▪ *legalistic hair-splitting*

hair‧style /ˈheɚˌstajəl/ *n* [*C*] : HAIRDO

hair‧styl‧ing /ˈheɚˌstaɪlɪŋ/ *n* [*U*] : the act or job of cutting and arranging people's hair ▪ *trends in hairstyling* — **hair‧styl‧ist** /ˈheɚˌstaɪlɪst/ *n* [*C*]

hair‧trig‧ger /ˈheɚˌtrɪɡɚ/ *adj, always before a noun* : reacting to something in a

very quick way ▪ *a hair-trigger temper/response*

hairy /ˈheri/ *adj* **hair‧i‧er; -est** **1** : covered with a lot of hair ▪ *hairy arms* **2** *informal* : dangerous or stressful ▪ *The taxi ride got a little hairy.* — **hair‧i‧ness** /ˈherinəs/ *n* [*U*]

hal‧cy‧on /ˈhælsijən/ *adj, always before a noun, literary* : very happy and successful — used to refer to a time in the past that is remembered as being better than today ▪ *the halcyon days/years of her career*

hale /ˈheɪl/ *adj* **hal‧er; hal‧est** : healthy and strong ▪ *a hale and hearty old man*

¹half /ˈhæf, *Brit* ˈhɑːf/ *n, pl* **halves** /ˈhævz, *Brit* ˈhɑːvz/ **1** [*C/U*] : one of two equal or nearly equal parts into which something can be divided ▪ *"Which half do you want?" "I'll take the smaller half."* ▪ *The price was reduced by half.* [=by 50 percent] ▪ *Cut the apple in half.* [=into two equal halves] **2 a** [*C*] : either of the two equal periods of playing time in sports like football and basketball ▪ *the first half of the game* **b** **the half** : HALFTIME ▪ *The score was tied at the half.* — **and a half** **1** — used to indicate one half of a unit of measurement ▪ *She's two and a half (years old).* [=two years and six months old] ▪ *a foot and a half* [=one foot and six inches] ▪ *ten and a half pounds* [=ten pounds and eight ounces] **2** *informal* — used to say that something is very good, large, difficult, etc. ▪ *Renovating a house is a job and a half.* [=it is a very difficult job] — **go halves** : to share the cost of something equally ▪ *We went halves (with each other) on the expenses.* — **the half of it** *informal* — used to say that a situation is even worse than it seems to be ▪ *Sales are down, but that's only the half of it—the company is closing five stores.* — **too . . . by half** *chiefly Brit, informal* — used to say that someone or something has too much of a particular quality usually in an annoying way ▪ *She's too clever by half.*

²half *pron* : a number or amount that is equal to one half of a total ▪ *Ten students took the exam; half (that number) passed.* [=5 students passed] ▪ *Half of 10 is/equals 5.* ▪ *She gave half (of) her money to charity.* ▪ *half a million people* ▪ *half (of) a sandwich* ▪ *Getting there is half the fun.* ▪ *Half the problem is that we do not have enough employees.* ▪ **half an hour** [=30 minutes] ▪ *Wait (for) half a minute/second.* [=for a moment] ▪ **half a dozen** [=six] *eggs* ▪ *women half his age* [=women who are much younger than he is] — **half the battle** see ¹BATTLE — **have half a mind** see ¹MIND

³half *adj, always before a noun* **1** : equal or nearly equal in size, value, amount, etc., to one half of something ▪ *a half circle* ▪ *a half pound of cheese* ▪ *a half million people* ▪ *a half dozen* [=six] *eggs* **2** : not complete : PARTIAL ▪ *a shy half smile* ▪ *We need real action, not timid half-measures.*

⁴half *adv* **1** : to an extent that is equal or nearly equal to half of something ▪ *The glass is half full/empty.* ▪ *The crowd was*

half cheering and half jeering. • *The meeting began at **half** past two.* [=at 2:30] = (*Brit*) *The meeting began at half two.* • *We left at noon and arrived at half past.* [=at 12:30] **2** : not completely : PARTIALLY • *The door was half open.* • *I am only half sure.* • *He was **half** asleep* [=not completely awake] *when I called.* — **half as big/much/good (etc.) as** — used to say that the size, amount, or quality of one thing is half or nearly half that of another • *This dress costs half as much as that one.* • *Only half as many people came as were expected.* • *The sequel isn't half as good as the original movie.* [=the original movie was much better than the sequel] — **half off** — used to say that something is being sold at half the original price • *Peaches are half off today.* — **not half 1** : not nearly • *He's not half the fool you think he is.* [=he is much smarter than you think he is] **2** *Brit, informal* — used to emphasize a statement or description • *"Is it cold out?" "Not half!"* [=yes, it is very cold] — **not half bad** *informal* : surprisingly good • *The food there is not half bad.* [=not bad at all]

half-and-half /ˌhæfn̩ˈhæf, *Brit* ˌhɑːfn̩ˈhɑːf/ *n* [U] *US* : a mixture of cream and whole milk • *coffee with half-and-half*

half·back /ˈhæfˌbæk, *Brit* ˈhɑːfˌbæk/ *n* [C] **1** *American football* : a player on offense who lines up next to the fullback and who runs with the ball and blocks **2** : a defensive player in soccer, field hockey, etc., who is positioned in front of the fullback

half-baked /ˈhæfˈbeɪkt, *Brit* ˈhɑːfˈbeɪkt/ *adj, informal* : not well planned • *a half-baked idea*

half brother *n* [C] : a brother with the same father but a different mother or the same mother but a different father • *He's my half brother.*

half-dol·lar /ˈhæfˈdɑːlɚ, *Brit* ˈhɑːfˈdɒlə/ *n* [C] *US* : a coin that is worth 50 cents

half-heart·ed /ˈhæfˈhɑɚtəd, *Brit* ˈhɑːfˈhɑːtəd/ *adj* : feeling or showing a lack of interest or enthusiasm • *a halfhearted smile/attempt* — **half·heart·ed·ly** *adv*

half hour *n* [*singular*] **1** : 30 minutes • *Trains depart every half hour.* • *I waited a half hour.* **2** : the middle point of an hour • *Tours start on the half hour.* [=at 12:30, 1:30, 2:30, etc.]

half-mast /ˈhæfˈmæst, *Brit* ˈhɑːfˈmɑːst/ *n* [U] : the position in the middle of a mast or pole ◇ *A flag is flown **at half-mast** or lowered **to half-mast** to show respect for a person who has died.*

half note *n* [C] *US* : a musical note equal in time to half of a whole note

half price *n* [U] : half of the original price • *I paid half price for these shoes.* — **half-price** *adj* • *All coats are half-price.*

half sister *n* [C] : a sister with the same father but a different mother or the same mother but a different father • *She's my half sister.*

half-staff /ˈhæfˈstæf, *Brit* ˈhɑːfˈstɑːf/ *n* [U] *US* : HALF-MAST

half step *n* [C] *US, music* : SEMITONE

half-time /ˈhæfˌtaɪm, *Brit* ˈhɑːfˌtaɪm/ *n* [U] : the period of rest between the first

and second halves in games like football and basketball • *The score was tied at halftime.*

half–truth /ˈhæfˌtruːθ, *Brit* ˈhɑːfˌtruːθ/ *n* [C] : a statement that is only partly true and that is intended to deceive people • *Her story was full of lies and half-truths.*

half·way /ˈhæfˈweɪ, *Brit* ˈhɑːfˈweɪ/ *adj* : in the middle between two points • *the halfway mark/point of a race* — **meet (someone) halfway** see ¹MEET — **halfway** *adv* • *I was already halfway home/finished.* • (*informal*) *I'll eat anywhere as long as the food is **halfway** decent.* [=fairly good]

halfway house *n* **1** [C] : a place where people who have recently left a prison, mental hospital, etc., are considered ready to live until they can live by themselves **2** [*singular*] *chiefly Brit* : something that combines the qualities of two different things • *The car is a halfway house between a family caravan and a sedan.*

half–wit /ˈhæfˌwɪt, *Brit* ˈhɑːfˌwɪt/ *n* [C] *informal* : a foolish or stupid person — **half-wit·ted** /ˈhæfˈwɪtəd, *Brit* ˈhɑːfˈwɪtəd/ *adj*

hal·i·but /ˈhæləbət/ *n, pl* **halibut** [C/U] : a large fish that is often eaten as food

hal·i·to·sis /ˌhæləˈtoʊsəs/ *n* [U] *medical* : the condition of having breath that smells bad : bad breath

hall /ˈhɑːl/ *n* [C] **1** : a usually long, narrow passage inside a building with doors that lead to rooms on the sides • *The bathroom is down the hall.* • *It's at the end of the hall.* **2** : the area inside the entrance of a building • *the front hall* **3 a** : a large room or building for meetings, entertainment, etc. • *We rented a hall for the party.* • *a concert/dining/dance hall* • *a **lecture hall*** [=*auditorium*] **b** : DORMITORY • (*US*) *a **residence hall** = (Brit) a **hall of residence*** **4** *Brit* : a large, impressive house • *The family owns Locksley Hall.*

hal·le·lu·jah /ˌhæləˈluːjə/ *interj* — used to express praise, joy, or thanks especially to God • *She's alive! Hallelujah!*

hall·mark /ˈhɑːlˌmɑɚk/ *n* [C] **1** : a quality, ability, etc., that is typical of a particular person or thing • *He had all the hallmarks of a great actor.* **2** : a mark that is put on gold and silver objects in Britain to indicate their purity

Hall of Fame *n* [C] *chiefly US* : a place that is like a museum with exhibits honoring the famous people and events related to a sport, a kind of music, etc.; *also* : the people who are honored in such a place • *a member of the Baseball Hall of Fame* — **Hall of Fam·er** /ˌhɑːləˈfeɪmɚ/ *n* [C]

hal·lowed /ˈhæloʊd/ *adj* **1** : holy or blessed • *hallowed ground* **2** : highly respected • *hallowed traditions*

Hal·low·een /ˌhæləˈwiːn, ˌhɑːləˈwiːn/ *n* [C/U] : the night of October 31 when children wear costumes and go to houses to ask for candy

hal·lu·ci·nate /həˈluːsəˌneɪt/ *vb* **-nat·ed; -nat·ing** [T/I] : to see or sense something that is not really there : to have hallucinations • *Her thirst made her hallucinate.*

hal·lu·ci·na·tion /həˌluːsəˈneɪʃən/ *n* [C] : something (such as an image, a sound, or a smell) that seems real but does not really exist • *The medication caused him to have hallucinations.* — **hal·lu·ci·na·to·ry** /həˈluːsənəˌtori, *Brit* həˈluːsənətri/ *adj* • *hallucinatory drugs* [=drugs that cause hallucinations] • *hallucinatory images*

hal·lu·ci·no·gen /həˈluːsənədʒən/ *n* [C] : a substance (such as a drug) that causes hallucinations — **hal·lu·ci·no·gen·ic** /həˌluːsənəˈdʒɛnɪk/ *adj*

hall·way /ˈhɑːlˌweɪ/ *n* [C] 1 : HALL 1 • *a room at the end of the hallway* 2 : HALL 2 • *the front hallway*

ha·lo /ˈheɪloʊ/ *n, pl* **-los** *or* **-loes** [C] 1 : a circle of light that is shown in art around the head of an angel, saint, etc. 2 : a bright circle seen around the sun or the moon

¹**halt** /ˈhɑːlt/ *vb* 1 [T] : to stop (something or someone) from moving or continuing • *The project had to be halted due to lack of funds.* 2 [I] : to stop moving or happening • *The troops halted outside the city.* • *Halt! Who goes there?*

²**halt** *n* [*singular*] : ²STOP 1 • *The contract put/brought a halt to* [=ended] *the strike.* • *The project came to a (grinding) halt.* • *The project ground to a halt.* [=it stopped completely]

hal·ter /ˈhɑːltɚ/ *n* [C] 1 : a set of straps placed around a horse's head 2 : a kind of shirt worn by a woman that is held in place by straps around the neck and back — called also *halter top*

halt·ing /ˈhɑːltɪŋ/ *adj* : stopping often because of not being sure about what to say or do • *a halting voice/step* — **halt·ing·ly** *adv*

halve /ˈhæv, *Brit* ˈhɑːv/ *vb* **halved; halv·ing** [T] 1 : to divide (something) into two equal parts • *He halved the sandwich.* 2 : to reduce (something) to one half of the original amount or size • *halving prices*

halves plural of ¹HALF

¹**ham** /ˈhæm/ *n* 1 [C/U] : meat from the leg of a hog that is often prepared by smoking or salting • *a juicy (piece/slice of) ham* • *a ham sandwich* 2 [C] *informal* : someone who tends to behave in an exaggerated or playful way when people are watching • *She's a ham in front of the camera.* 3 [C] : someone who operates an amateur radio station • *ham radio*

²**ham** *vb* **hammed; ham·ming** — **ham it up** *informal* : to act or behave in an exaggerated or playful way • *hamming it up for the camera*

ham·burg /ˈhæmˌbɚg/ *n* [C] *US, informal* : HAMBURGER

ham·burg·er /ˈhæmˌbɚgɚ/ *n* 1 [C] : a flat, usually round cake of finely chopped beef that is cooked and served usually in a roll or bun • *hot dogs and hamburgers* 2 [U] : ground beef • *a pound of hamburger* — called also (*Brit*) *mince*

ham-fist·ed /ˈhæmˌfɪstəd/ *adj* : awkward or clumsy : HAM-HANDED

ham-hand·ed /ˈhæmˌhændəd/ *adj*

: awkward or clumsy • *a ham-handed attempt at humor*

ham·let /ˈhæmlət/ *n* [C] : a small village

¹**ham·mer** /ˈhæmɚ/ *n* [C] 1 a : a tool that has a heavy metal head attached to a handle and that is used for hitting nails b : a similar wooden tool used to make a loud noise • *an auctioneer's hammer* 2 : the part of a gun that strikes a charge causing the gun to shoot 3 : a piece inside a piano that strikes a string to produce a sound

²**hammer** *vb* 1 a [T/I] : to force (something) into a particular place or shape by hitting it with a hammer • *He hammered the dent out of the fender.* • *hammering nails into a wall* b [T] : to attach (something) with a hammer and nails • *hammering studs to a frame* 2 *informal* a [T] : to hit (something or someone) in a very forceful way • *The batter hammered the ball over the fence.* • *towns hammered by the storm* b [T/I] : to hit (something) hard and repeatedly • *The typist was hammering (away) at the keys.* 3 [T] *informal* : to defeat (an opponent) very easily • *We got hammered 9-0.* 4 [T] *informal* : to harm or criticize (someone or something) severely • *Local businesses are being hammered by the new mall.* 5 [I] : to keep talking about something or trying to do something • *keep hammering (away) at a problem* — **hammer into** [*phrasal vb*] **hammer (something) into** : to force (something) to be learned very well by (someone) by repeating it again and again • *hammering good manners into the children* — **hammer out** [*phrasal vb*] **hammer out (something)** or **hammer (something) out** : to produce (something) by a lot of discussion or argument • *hammering out an agreement/deal* • *We'll hammer the details out later.*

ham·mer·ing /ˈhæmɚrɪŋ/ *n* 1 [*U, singular*] : the sound made when something is being hit by a hammer, by rain, etc. • *We could hear the hammering of the rain on the roof.* 2 [*singular*] *informal* — used to say that someone or something has been very forcefully hit, damaged, criticized, etc. • *The governor is taking/getting (quite) a hammering from the media.*

ham·mock /ˈhæmək/ *n* [C] : a type of bed that consists of a piece of cloth hung between two trees, poles, etc.

¹**ham·per** /ˈhæmpɚ/ *vb* [T] : to slow the movement, progress, or action of (someone or something) • *Bad weather hampered (us in) our search efforts.*

²**hamper** *n* [C] 1 : a basket for food that usually has a cover • *a picnic hamper* 2 *US* : a basket for holding dirty clothes until they can be washed • *a clothes hamper*

ham·ster /ˈhæmstɚ/ *n* [C] : a small, furry animal that is often kept as a pet

¹**ham·string** /ˈhæmˌstrɪŋ/ *n* [C] 1 : a tendon at the back of a person's knee 2 : a muscle at the back of a person's upper leg • *stretching your hamstrings*

²**hamstring** *vb* **-strung** /-ˌstrʌŋ/; **-string·ing** [T] : to damage or ruin the force or effectiveness of (something or someone)

▪ *regulations that hamstring certain companies*

¹**hand** /ˈhænd/ *n* **1** [*C*] **a** : the body part at the end of your arm that includes your fingers and thumb ▪ *She put her hands over his eyes.* ▪ *I took him* **by the hand** [=I held his hand] *and led him outside.* ▪ *She's* **good with her hands.** [=skillful at things that require the use of your hands] ▪ *Get/* **Keep your hands off (of)** [=do not touch] *the cookies!* ▪ **Hands off** [=do not touch] *my property!* ▪ *I never* **laid a hand on** [=touched or harmed] *him.* ▪ *crawling on* **your hands and knees** [=with your hands and knees on the ground] ▪ *He killed the bird* **with his bare hands.** [=using only his hands and no tools or weapons] **b** — used in some phrases to refer to a person ▪ *We need* **more than one pair of hands** [=more than one person] *to do it.* ▪ (*Brit*) *She would be a* **safe pair of hands.** [=someone who can be trusted with responsibility or a job] **2 a** [*plural*] : power, possession, or control ▪ *The maps are in the hands of the enemy.* [=the enemy has the maps] ▪ *The land is in private hands.* [=is privately owned] ▪ *He wants to* **get/lay his hands on** [=to get or control] *her money.* ▪ *Wait until I* **get my hands on** *you.* [=you will be in trouble when I catch you] ▪ *I'd like to help you, but my* **hands are tied.** [=I do not have the power to act freely] ▪ *With her in charge, the office is* **in good/safe hands.** [=she will take care of the office very well] ▪ *If you don't want it anymore, I'll be glad to* **take it off your hands.** [=to take possession of it] ▪ *The decision is* **out of my hands.** [=I cannot control it] **b** [*C*] — used to say that someone is responsible for doing something ▪ *They lost their freedom* **at the hand(s) of** [=by or through the action of] *a cruel dictator.* ▪ *She suffered* **by her own hand.** [=by her own actions] ▪ *She* **had a hand in** [=was involved in] *designing the new bridge.* **3** [*singular*] : assistance in doing something ▪ *Do you need a hand (with that)?* ▪ *I'm happy to* **lend a hand.** [=help] ▪ *Can you* **give/lend me a hand** [=help me] *with this box?* **4** [*C*] : a long, thin part that points to a number on a clock or dial ▪ *a clock with a second hand, a minute hand, and an hour hand* **5** [*U*] : a promise of marriage ▪ *He asked for her* **hand (in marriage).** [=he asked her to marry him] **6** [*singular*] : the act of hitting your hands together to show approval, appreciation, etc. ▪ *Let's give him a big hand!* [=a big round of applause] **7** [*C*] **a** : the cards that are held by a player in a card game ▪ *a hand with two pairs* ▪ (*figurative*) *She was dealt a cruel hand in life.* [=she suffered or had bad things happen to her] **b** : a single round of play in a card game ▪ *I lost the first hand.* **8** [*C*] **a** : a hired worker ▪ *factory hands* ▪ *They're* **hired hands** *with no ownership rights.* **b** : a member of a ship's crew ▪ *All hands on deck!* **9** [*C*] : someone who performs or produces something (such as a work of art) ▪ *The portraits are by the same hand.* [=the same artist] **10** [*singular*] : a particular way or style of doing or handling something ▪ *He runs the busi-*

ness with a *firm hand.* ▪ *He has a* **heavy hand** *with the salt.* [=he uses too much salt] **11** [*singular*] *old-fashioned* : the way a person's writing looks ▪ *a note written in an elegant hand* — **a bird in the hand is worth two in the bush** see BIRD — **a show of hands** see ²SHOW — **at first hand** see ¹FIRST — **at hand** : close in distance or time ▪ *Keep the phone (close) at hand.* ▪ *the problem at hand* [=the problem we are dealing with] — **be eating out of someone's hand** see EAT — **by hand** **1** : with the hands ▪ *a stone carved by hand* **2** : from one person directly to another ▪ *I delivered the letter by hand.* — **change hands** see ¹CHANGE — **fall into the hands of** see ¹FALL — **fall into the wrong hands** see ¹FALL — **force someone's hand** see ²FORCE — **give your right hand** see ¹GIVE — **hand in glove** : very closely ▪ *working hand in glove with the police* — **hand in hand** **1** : holding hands ▪ *walking hand in hand* **2** — used to say that two people or things are very closely connected or related ▪ *The images and sounds go hand in hand.* — **hand over fist** *informal* — used to say that someone is earning or losing money very quickly or in large amounts ▪ *making/earning money hand over fist* — **hand to mouth** : with little money ▪ *We've been living hand to mouth since I lost my job.* = *It's been hand to mouth since I lost my job.* — **hat/cap in hand** : asking or begging for something in a respectful way ▪ *He came to me, hat in hand, asking if I could help him.* — **have someone in the palm of your hand** see ¹PALM — **have your hands full** : to be very busy ▪ *She has her hands full with the new baby.* — **hold hands** *or* **hold someone's hand** **1** : to hold a person's hand in one of your hands ▪ *two people walking and holding hands (with each other)* **2** : to guide someone through a process by carefully explaining each step ▪ *I don't need you to hold my hand.* — **in hand** **1** : in your possession or control ▪ *setting off with compass and map in hand* ▪ *He has the situation well in hand.* [=he is in control of the situation] **2** *chiefly Brit* : available for use ▪ *We have a month in hand before our deadline.* — **join hands** see JOIN — **know (something) like the back of your hand** see ¹KNOW — **on hand** **1** : available for use ▪ *Have plenty of water on hand.* **2** : present and available to do something ▪ *A priest was on hand to console them.* — **on the one hand . . . on the other (hand)** — used to introduce statements that describe two different or opposite ideas, people, etc. ▪ *On the one hand, the price is fair, but on the other hand, I really can't afford it.* — **on your hands** — used to say that you have something or are responsible for something ▪ *We had a little extra time on our hands.* [=free time] — **out of hand** **1** : very quickly without serious thought ▪ *He rejected the plan out of hand.* **2** : not controlled ▪ *The kids were (getting) out of hand.* [=behaving in a wild and uncontrolled way] — **play into someone's** *hands* see ¹PLAY — **take (something) into your (own) hands** : to take control of something • *She took matters into her own hands.* • *people who insist on taking the law into their own hands* [=trying to punish criminals themselves] — **try your hand** : to try to do something • *She wanted to try her hand at photography.* — **turn your hand to** : to start (a new activity, field of study, etc.) • *She has turned her hand to directing.* — **wait on (someone) hand and foot** : to provide everything that someone needs or wants • *They waited on the princess hand and foot.* — **wash your hands of** see ¹WASH

²**hand** *vb* [T] : to give (something) to someone using your hands • *She handed a note to him.* • *Hand me that pen.* — **hand back** [*phrasal vb*] **hand (something) back** *or* **hand back (something)** : to return (something) by handing it to someone • *He handed the note back (to her).* — **hand down** [*phrasal vb*] **hand (something) down** *or* **hand down (something)** **1** : to pass (something) to a person who is younger • *The farm was handed down from generation to generation.* **2** *chiefly US, law* : to form and express (a decision or opinion) in writing • *The Supreme Court handed down its decision.* — **hand in** [*phrasal vb*] **hand (something) in** *or* **hand in (something)** : to give (something) to a person who will review or accept it • *He handed in his assignment/resignation.* — **hand it to** : to give credit to (someone) for doing something • *I've got to hand it to you. You did a great job.* — **hand off** [*phrasal vb*] **hand (something) off** *or* **hand off (something)** *US* : to give (something) to another person • *She handed the job off to her assistant.* — **hand out** [*phrasal vb*] **hand (something) out** *or* **hand out (something)** : to give (something) to several or many people • *handing out flyers* — **hand over** [*phrasal vb*] **hand (someone or something) over** *or* **hand over (someone or something)** : to give up control or possession of (something or someone) • *They handed over their hostages.*

hand·bag /ˈhænd₁bæg/ *n* [C] : a woman's small bag or purse used for carrying personal things and money

hand·ball /ˈhænd₁bɑːl/ *n* **1** [U] : a game for two or four players who use their hands to hit a ball against a wall **2** [C] : the ball used in handball

hand·bas·ket /ˈhænd₁bæskət/ *n* — **go to hell in a handbasket** *US, informal* : to become completely ruined • *The country is going to hell in a handbasket.*

hand·book /ˈhænd₁bʊk/ *n* [C] : a small book that gives useful information about a particular subject • *a grammar handbook*

hand·craft /ˈhænd₁kræft, *Brit* ˈhænd₁krɑːft/ *vb* [T] : to make (something) by using your hands • *a handcrafted vase*

hand·cuff /ˈhænd₁kʌf/ *vb* [T] : to put handcuffs on (someone) • *handcuff a prisoner*

hand·cuffs /ˈhænd₁kʌfs/ *n* [*plural*] : a set of two metal rings that are joined together and locked around a person's wrists

hand·ful /ˈhænd₁fʊl/ *n* **1** [C] : an amount that you can hold in your hand • *a handful of berries* **2** [*singular*] : a small amount or number • *Only a handful of people came.* **3** [*singular*] *informal* : someone or something that is difficult to control • *Our dog is a real handful.*

hand·gun /ˈhænd₁gʌn/ *n* [C] : a small gun (such as a revolver or a pistol) designed to be held and shot with one hand

¹**hand·held** /ˈhænd₁hɛld/ *adj, always before a noun* : designed to be used while being held in your hands • *a handheld movie camera*

²**handheld** *n* [C] : a small electronic device or computer that fits in your hand

hand—hold·ing /ˈhænd₁hoʊldɪŋ/ *n* [U] : patient attention, support, or instruction • *New computer users often require a lot of hand-holding.*

¹**hand·i·cap** /ˈhændi₁kæp/ *n* [C] **1** *sometimes offensive* : a physical or mental condition that may limit what a person can do • *a physical handicap* ◆ Some people prefer the word *disability.* **2** : a problem, situation, or event that makes progress or success difficult • *Shyness is a handicap in this job.* **3** *golf* : a number that shows a golfer's level of skill • *She has a low handicap.* [=she is a skillful golfer]

²**handicap** *vb* **-capped; -cap·ping** [T] **1** : to make success or progress difficult for (someone) • *He is handicapped by his shyness.* **2** *US* : to make a judgment about the likely winner of a race or contest • *handicap (the horses in) a race* —

hand·i·cap·per /ˈhændi₁kæpɚ/ *n* [C]

hand·i·capped /ˈhændi₁kæpt/ *adj* **1** *sometimes offensive* : having a physical or mental handicap • *mentally handicapped* ◆ Some people prefer the word *disabled.* **2** : designed or reserved for disabled people • *handicapped parking spaces*

hand·i·craft /ˈhændi₁kræft, *Brit* ˈhændi₁krɑːft/ *n* [C] **1** : an activity that involves making something in a skillful way by using your hands • *sewing and other handicrafts* **2** : an object made by skillful use of your hands • *vendors selling handicrafts*

hand·i·ly /ˈhændəli/ *adv* : very easily • *He won handily.*

hand·i·work /ˈhændi₁wɚk/ *n* [U] **1** : work that is done by using your hands • *the potter's beautiful handiwork* **2** : something done by a particular person or group • *These problems are her handiwork.*

hand·ker·chief /ˈhæŋkɚtʃəf/ *n, pl* **-chiefs** *also* **-chieves** /-tʃɑfs/ [C] : a small cloth used for wiping your face, nose, or eyes

¹**han·dle** /ˈhændl/ *n* [C] : a part of something that is designed to be held by your hand • *the shovel's wooden handle* • *The handles on the bag tore.* • *a door handle* [=the part that you turn with your hand to open a door] — **fly off the handle** see ¹FLY — **get/have a handle on** *informal* : to understand and be able to deal with (something) • *She has a good handle on the situation.* — **han·dled** /ˈhændld/ • *a wooden-handled basket*

²**handle** vb **han·dled; han·dling 1** [T]
a : to touch, feel, hold, or move (something) with your hand • *The plates were
too hot to handle with our bare hands.* **b**
: to manage or control (something) with
your hands • *He knows how to handle a
motorcycle.* **2** [T] : to do the work required for (something) • *She handles all
the bookkeeping.* **3** [T] : to deal with (a
person, situation, etc.) successfully • *A
good politician knows how to handle the
press.* • *Can you handle the pressure/truth?*
4 [T] : to express thoughts about (something) in a piece of music, writing, or art
• *the way the author handles her subject
matter* **5** [T] : to be involved with the
buying or selling of (something) • *a store
that handles rugs* **6** [I] — used to describe how easy or difficult it is to control a vehicle • *a car that handles well in
the snow* — **handle yourself** : to behave
• *She handled herself well under the circumstances.*

han·dle·bar /ˈhændl̩ˌbɑɚ/ n [C] : a bar
with a handle at each end that is used to
steer a bicycle, motorcycle, etc. • *a bike
with straight handlebars*

han·dler /ˈhændlə/ n [C] **1** : a person
who trains or controls an animal • *a dog
handler* **2** : a person who carries or
handles something • *baggage handlers* **3**
chiefly US : a person who guides, helps,
or manages a political or public figure • *a
politician's handlers*

han·dling /ˈhændlɪŋ/ n [U] **1 a** : the act
of touching, feeling, holding, or moving
something • *These dishes require careful
handling.* **b** : the way that someone
deals with a person, situation, etc. • *the
media's handling of the tragedy* **2** : the
act or process of packing and shipping
something to someone (such as a customer) • *Pay $8.99 plus shipping and handling.* **3** : the way a vehicle moves when
it is driven or ridden • *the car's smooth
handling*

hand luggage n [U] : small pieces of
luggage that a passenger can carry onto
an airplane • *one piece of hand luggage*

hand·made /ˈhændˈmeɪd/ adj : made
with the hands or by using hand tools •
handmade furniture/rugs

hand·maid·en /ˈhændˌmeɪdn̩/ n [C] : a
female servant or maid • *(figurative) a
government that is the handmaiden of* [=a
government that only serves] *corporate
interests*

hand–me–down /ˈhændmiˌdaʊn/ adj
: owned or used by someone else before
you — used especially of clothing • *an
old, hand-me-down jacket* — **hand–
me–down** n [C] • *a closet full of hand-
me-downs*

hand·off /ˈhændˌɑːf/ n [C] *American football* : an act of handing the ball to another player • *He fumbled the ball while attempting a handoff.*

hand·out /ˈhændˌaʊt/ n [C] **1** : something (such as food, clothing, or money)
that is given to someone who is poor •
government handouts **2** : a document
that is given to people • *The handouts listed the major points of his speech.*

hand·over /ˈhændˌoʊvə/ n [singular]

: the act or process of giving control of
someone or something to another person, country, etc. • *the handover of power
between the old and new governments*

hand·pick /ˈhændˈpɪk/ vb [T] **1** : to
pick (something, such as a fruit) by using
your hand • *handpicked strawberries* **2**
: to choose (something or someone) by
yourself instead of letting someone else
do it • *She handpicked her successor.*

hand·rail /ˈhændˌreɪl/ n [C] : a bar on the
side of a walkway or a flight of stairs that
you can hold as you walk

hand·saw /ˈhændˌsɑː/ n [C] : a saw designed to be used with one hand

hands down /ˈhændzˈdaʊn/ adv, *informal* **1** : very easily • *She won hands
down.* **2** : without any doubt • *It's hands
down the best movie of the year.* —
hands–down /ˈhændzˌdaʊn/ adj • *the
hands-down favorite to win*

hand·set /ˈhændˌsɛt/ n [C] : the part of a
telephone that you hold near your ear
and mouth

hands–free adj : designed to be used
without being held in your hands • *a
hands-free cell phone*

hand·shake /ˈhændˌʃeɪk/ n [C] : the act
of shaking someone's hand as a way of
greeting someone or as a sign that you
have made an agreement • *She greeted
him with a handshake.* • *a deal sealed with
a handshake; also* : the manner in which
a person shakes hands • *a firm/weak
handshake*

hands–off /ˈhændzˈɑːf/ adj : allowing
people to do what they want to do without bothering or stopping them • *a
hands-off approach to teaching*

hand·some /ˈhænsəm/ adj **hand·som·er; -est 1** : pleasing to look at • *a handsome house* — used especially to describe a man • *Her husband is tall, dark,
and handsome.* • *his handsome face* **2**
always before a noun : large in size or
amount • *a handsome profit* — **hand·some·ly** adv • *a handsomely illustrated
book* • *He was handsomely rewarded for
his loyalty.* — **hand·some·ness** n [U]

hands–on /ˈhændzˈɑːn/ adj **1** *always
before a noun* : gained by actually doing something rather than learning about
it from books, lectures, etc. • *hands-on
training/experience* **b** : involving or allowing the use of your hands or touching
with your hands • *a children's museum
with hands-on displays* **2** : actively and
personally involved in something (such
as running a business) • *She has a hands-
on management style.*

hand·spring /ˈhændˌsprɪŋ/ n [C] : a fast
movement in which you jump onto your
hands, swing your legs up and over your
body, and then land on your feet • *doing
a front/back handspring*

hand·stand /ˈhændˌstænd/ n [C] : the
act of balancing on your hands with the
body and legs straight up in the air

hand–to–hand /ˈhændtəˈhænd/ adj, *always before a noun* — used to describe
fighting that is done with knives, clubs,
etc., instead of guns, arrows, etc. • *hand-
to-hand combat*

hand–to–mouth /ˈhændtəˈmaʊθ/ adj

: having only enough money to survive ▪ *living a hand-to-mouth existence*

hand tool *n [C]* : a small tool (such as a hammer or wrench) that does not use electricity

hand towel *n [C]* : a small towel for drying your hands

hand·wring·ing /ˈhændˌrɪŋɪŋ/ *n [U]* *disapproving* : worried talk or behavior ▪ *There was a lot of hand-wringing over the economy.*

hand·writ·ing /ˈhændˌraɪtɪŋ/ *n [C/U]* : the way a person's writing looks ▪ *Her handwriting is hard to read.* — **handwriting (is) on the wall** see ¹WALL

hand·writ·ten /ˈhændˌrɪtn̩/ *adj* : written with a pen or pencil and not with a computer or typewriter ▪ *a handwritten note*

handy /ˈhændi/ *adj* **hand·i·er; -est** **1 a** : very useful or helpful ▪ *a handy tool/gadget* ▪ *The flashlight came in handy* [=was useful] *when we lost electricity.* **b** : near or close ▪ *I keep a dictionary handy.* ▪ *(Brit) My flat is handy for* [=near to] *the underground.* **2** : clever or skillful in using your hands, doing small jobs, etc. ▪ *She's handy with a needle and thread.* ▪ *He's handy around the house.*

handy·man /ˈhændiˌmæn/ *n, pl* **-men** /-ˌmɛn/ *[C]* : a person who is skillful at doing small jobs (such as household repairs)

¹**hang** /ˈhæŋ/ *vb* **hung** /ˈhʌŋ/ *or in sense 3* **hanged; hang·ing** **1** *[T/I]* : to attach or place something so that it is held up without support from below ▪ *hang a painting on the wall* ▪ *hanging laundry on a clothesline* ▪ *Your coat is hanging in the closet.* ▪ *hang wallpaper* [=put wallpaper on a wall] **2** *[T/I]* : to be in a lowered position ▪ *Her hair hung loose/limply.* ▪ *He hung his head* [=turned his head downward] *in shame/embarrassment.* **3** *past tense and past participle usually* **hanged** *[T/I]* : to kill (someone) by using a rope that goes around the neck and holds the person's body in the air ▪ *He (was) hanged for his crimes.* ▪ *She hanged herself.* **4** *[I]* : to float over a place or object for a long time ▪ *Smoke hung over the city.* ▪ *Her perfume hung in the air.* ▪ *(figurative) The design of the new school is still hanging in the air.* [=it is still incomplete or uncertain] **5** *[I] US, informal* **a** : to be or stay somewhere for a period of time without doing much ▪ *We were hanging* [=hanging around/out] *at the bar.* **b** : to continue doing what you are doing and not make any changes ▪ *I'll hang in* [=keep working or trying] *until I make the business work.* ▪ **Hang in there, kid!** *Don't quit!* ▪ *Investors are being advised to* **hang tight** [=wait before doing anything] ▪ *If we just* **hang together** [=stay with each other], *I know we can work out our problems.* ▪ *The team* **hung tough** [=kept working or trying] *through the whole game.* **6** *[T] chiefly US, informal* : to make (a turn) especially while driving ▪ *Hang a right at the stoplight.* — **hang around** *or Brit* **hang about/round** [*phrasal vb*] *informal* **1** : to be or stay in a place for a period of time without doing much ▪ *hanging around, listening to music* ▪ *We hung around the theater after the play.* **2** **hang around/about/round with** : to spend time relaxing, talking, or doing things with (someone) ▪ *She hangs around with older kids.* — **hang back** [*phrasal vb*] : to stay behind others ▪ *She followed them but hung back a little.* ▪ *He hung back and let the others give their answers first.* — **hang by a thread** : to be in a very dangerous situation or state ▪ *My life was hanging by a thread.* [=I was very close to dying] — **hang fire** *chiefly Brit* : to be delayed ▪ *The project has been hanging fire for several years.* — **hang on** [*phrasal vb*] **1** : to keep happening or continuing ▪ *Her cold hung on all spring.* **2** : to wait or stop briefly ▪ *"Can we go now?" "Hang on, I'm almost ready."* **3** **hang on (to)** : to hold or grip someone or something tightly ▪ *Hang on (tight) or you'll fall!* ▪ *The children hung on (to) his arm.* ▪ *Hang on to your purse.* **4** **hang on to** : to keep (something) ▪ *You should hang on to your receipt.* **5 a** : to be determined or decided by (something) ▪ *The decision hangs on one vote.* **b** **hang (something) on** : to base (a story, theory, etc.) on (something) ▪ *You can't hang your case on her testimony.* **6** **hang on someone's every word** : to listen very carefully or closely to (someone) ▪ *They hung on her every word.* — **hang out** [*phrasal vb*] **1** *informal* : to be or stay somewhere for a period of time without doing much ▪ *They hang out at the bar.* **2** **hang out with** *informal* : to spend time relaxing, talking, or doing something with (someone) ▪ *I was hanging out with friends.* **3** **hang (something) out** *or* **hang out (something)** : to hang (something wet) outside to dry ▪ *I hung the laundry out on the clothesline.* **4** **hang (someone or something) out to dry** *informal* : to leave (someone or something) in a helpless or unprotected state ▪ *The company hung us out to dry.* — **hang over** [*phrasal vb*] : to cause (someone) to feel worried or guilty ▪ *I can't relax with that test hanging over my head.* [=I can't relax until after I take that test] — **hang up** [*phrasal vb*] **1** **hang up** *or* **hang up (something)** *or* **hang (something) up** : to end a telephone connection ▪ *"Is he still on the phone?" "No, he hung up."* ▪ *I can't believe he hung up on me!* [=that he suddenly hung up the phone while I was talking to him] **2** **hang (something) up** *or* **hang up (something)** : to put (something) on a hook or hanger ▪ *I'll hang up your coat.* **3** **hang up (something)** *or* **hang (something) up** *informal* : to stop doing (something) : to finish using (something) for the last time ▪ *She decided to hang up her tennis racket.* [=to quit playing tennis] ▪ *(US) After all this time, you're just going to hang it up?* [=quit] — **hang with** [*phrasal vb*] *US, informal* **1** : to spend time with (someone) ▪ *hanging with his friends* **2** : to stay close to (someone) ▪ *He hung with the leaders for the first half of the race but then fell behind.* — **let it all hang out** see LET

²**hang** *n* — **get the hang of** *informal* : to learn the skills that are needed to do

(something) • *I'm finally getting the hang of this job.* — **give a hang** *informal* : to care about something • *I don't give a hang what they say.*

hang·ar /'hæŋɚ/ *n* [C] : a building where aircraft are kept

hang·dog /'hæŋˌdɑːg/ *adj* : sad or depressed • *a hangdog expression/look*

hang·er /'hæŋɚ/ *n* [C] : a curved piece of metal, plastic, or wood that is used for hanging clothing

hang·er-on /ˌhæŋɚˈɑːn/ *n, pl* **hangers-on** [C] : someone who spends a lot of time around a person, place, or group in order to gain fame, money, etc. • *a celebrity and her hangers-on*

hang glider *n* [C] : a metal frame covered with strong cloth that is flown by a person who hangs beneath it — **hang gliding** *n* [U]

hang·ing /'hæŋɪŋ/ *n* **1** [C/U] : the act of killing someone by hanging that person from a rope tied around the neck • *a public hanging* • *death by hanging* **2** [C] : something (such as a curtain) that is hung for decoration • *antique wall hangings*

hang·man /'hæŋmən/ *n, pl* **-men** /-mən/ [C] : a person whose job is to hang criminals

hang·nail /'hæŋˌneɪl/ *n* [C] : a small piece of skin hanging loose at the side of a fingernail

hang·out /'hæŋˌaʊt/ *n* [C] *informal* : a place where a person spends a lot of time • *The park was their favorite hangout.*

hang·over /'hæŋˌoʊvɚ/ *n* [C] : a sick feeling that comes after drinking too much alcohol at an earlier time • *She woke up with a hangover.*

hang-up /'hæŋˌʌp/ *n* [C] *informal* : something that causes you to feel worried, afraid, embarrassed, etc. • *We all have our hang-ups.* • *hang-ups about money*

han·ker /'hæŋkɚ/ *vb* [I] *informal + old-fashioned* : to have a strong or constant desire for something • *hankering for* [=*longing for*] *a return to the good old days* — **han·ker·ing** /'hæŋkərɪŋ/ *n* [*singular*] • *I have a hankering for ice cream.*

han·kie *or* **han·ky** /'hæŋki/ *n, pl* **-kies** [C] *informal* : HANDKERCHIEF

han·ky-pan·ky /ˌhæŋkiˈpæŋki/ *n* [U] *informal* **1** : sexual activity • *I think there's some hanky-panky going on between them.* **2** : dishonest or suspicious activity • *financial hanky-panky*

Ha·nuk·kah *also* **Cha·nu·kah** /'hɑːnəkə/ *n* [C/U] : an eight-day Jewish holiday that is celebrated in November or December

hap·haz·ard /ˌhæpˈhæzɚd/ *adj* : having no plan, order, or direction • *a haphazard procedure/tour* — **hap·haz·ard·ly** *adv*

hap·less /'hæpləs/ *adj* : having no luck : very unfortunate • *a hapless heroine who is unlucky in love* — **hap·less·ly** *adv*

hap·pen /'hæpən/ *vb* [I] **1** : to take place especially without being planned : OCCUR • *Mistakes/Accidents will happen.* • *It was bound to happen sooner or later.* • *What happened at school today?* • *"What's happening?" "They're leaving."* **2** : to affect or involve someone or something as the result of an event or action • *An odd thing happened to me last week.* • *Whatever happened to him?* [=where has he gone and what has he been doing?]; *especially* : to affect someone or something in a bad or harmful way • *I promise nothing (bad) will happen to you.* **3 a** : to do or be something by chance • *I happened to be asleep when she called.* = *It (so) happened that I was asleep when she called.* • *"Do you happen to know him?" "It (just so) happens that I do."* **b** — used to make an angry or forceful statement • *The woman you're staring at happens to be my wife!* • *I happen to think (that) you're wrong.* — **happen along/by** [*phrasal vb*] *US, literary* : to come to or by a place by chance • *I was about to leave when they happened by.* — **happen on/upon** [*phrasal vb*] *literary* : to find or meet (someone or something) by chance • *She happened on a cottage in the woods.*

¹hap·pen·ing /'hæpənɪŋ/ *n* [C] : an event or occurrence • *strange happenings*

²happening *adj, informal* : fashionable or popular • *a happening place*

hap·pen·stance /'hæpənˌstæns/ *n* [C/U] *literary* : something that happens by chance • *Our meeting was (a) happenstance.*

hap·pi·ly /'hæpəli/ *adv* **1** : in a happy way or state • *The story ended happily.* **2** — used to say that something good or lucky has happened • *Happily, no one was hurt.* **3** : in a very willing way • *I'll happily wait for you.*

hap·py /'hæpi/ *adj* **hap·pi·er; -est 1 a** : feeling pleasure and enjoyment because of your life, situation, etc. • *She's a very happy child.* • *one big, happy family* • *trying to make/keep someone happy* • *She's happiest (when she's) playing outside.* **b** : showing or causing feelings of pleasure and enjoyment • *the children's happy laughter* • *a very happy childhood/marriage* • *a happy occasion* • *a movie with a happy ending* **c** *not before a noun* : pleased or glad about a particular situation, event, etc. • *I'm so happy that you came.* • *We're not at all happy about/with the changes.* • *I'm happy for him.* [=I'm glad something good happened to him] **d** : very willing to do something • *I'm happy to help.* **2** — used as part of a greeting or wish for someone on a special holiday or occasion • *Happy birthday, Mom!* • *Happy Holidays!* **3** *always before a noun* : lucky or fortunate • *a series of happy coincidences* — **happy returns** see **²RETURN** — **hap·pi·ness** /'hæpinəs/ *n* [C/U] : finding happiness [=*joy*] • *I wish you every happiness.* • *=many experiences that will make you happy*

happy camper *n* [C] *chiefly US, informal* : someone who is pleased or happy • *She's not a happy camper today.*

hap·py-go-lucky /ˌhæpigoʊˈlʌki/ *adj* : not worried about anything • *a happy-go-lucky guy*

happy hour *n* [C/U] : a time at a bar

when drinks are sold at a lower price than usual ▪ *Happy hour is from 5:00 to 7:00.*

ha·rangue /həˈræŋ/ *vb* **-rangued; -rangu·ing** [*T*] : to speak to (someone) in a forceful or angry way ▪ *He harangued us about the evils of alcohol.* — **harangue** *n* [*C*] ▪ *listening to his angry harangues*

ha·rass /həˈræs, ˈherəs/ *vb* [*T*] : to annoy or bother (someone) in a constant or repeated way ▪ *She was harassed by the other students.* ▪ *He's accused of* **sexually harassing** [=making unwanted sexual comments to] *his secretary.* — **ha·rass·ment** /həˈræsmənt, ˈherəsmənt/ *n* [*U*] ▪ *He's accused of* **sexual harassment**.

har·bin·ger /ˈhɑɚbəndʒɚ/ *n* [*C*] : something that shows what is coming ▪ *The warm weather is a harbinger of spring.*

¹har·bor (*US*) *or Brit* **har·bour** /ˈhɑɚbɚ/ *n* [*C*] **1** : a part of the ocean, a lake, etc., that is next to land and that is protected and deep enough for ships **2** : a place of safety and comfort ▪ *He found (a)* **safe harbor** *with them.*

²harbor (*US*) *or Brit* **harbour** *vb* [*T*] **1** : to hide and protect (someone) ▪ *harboring an escaped convict* **2** : to have (a thought, feeling, etc.) in your mind for a long time ▪ *harboring doubts/bitterness/ grudges* **3** : to hold or contain (something) ▪ *animals that harbor diseases*

¹hard /ˈhɑɚd/ *adj* **1** : very firm or solid : not easy to bend, cut, etc. : not soft ▪ *hard chairs/rubber* ▪ *This bread is (as)* **hard as a rock**. [=very hard] **2** : physically or mentally difficult : not easy ▪ *That test was hard.* ▪ *hard work* ▪ *asking hard questions* ▪ *making some hard choices/decisions* ▪ *It's hard to solve this problem.* = *This is a hard problem (to solve).* ▪ *five years of* **hard labor** [=five years in prison doing intense physical work] ▪ *She had a hard time writing/with her essay.* [=it was hard for her to write her essay] **3 a** : difficult to experience : severe or harsh ▪ *learning hard lessons* ▪ *a very cold winter with harsh weather* : having a lot of pain, trouble, or worries ▪ *She had a hard life.* = *Life was hard for her.* ▪ *She promised to stick with him through the* **hard times**. [=the times when there is a lot of trouble, poverty, worry, or failure] ▪ *The business has* **fallen on hard times**. ▪ *He found out* **the hard way** [=in a way that involves difficult or painful experiences] *that crime doesn't pay.* **b** : having a harmful or destructive effect ▪ *years of hard living* ▪ *a bicycle that's gotten some hard use* **4** : working or doing something with a lot of energy ▪ *a hard worker* **5** : very forceful ▪ *a hard rain* : quick and forceful ▪ *a hard left turn* **6** : done with a lot of careful thought and attention ▪ *They are taking a long hard look at how the company is run.* **7** : not able to be questioned or doubted ▪ *the (cold) hard facts of the case* ▪ *hard data/evidence* **8** : not seeming to care about other people or to feel kindness or affection ▪ *her hard heart* ▪ *He's* **as hard as nails**. [=he's very hard or tough] **9** : holding extreme po-

litical views ▪ *the hard right/left* **10** : relating to serious matters ▪ *hard news* **11 a** : containing a large amount of alcohol ▪ *hard liquor* **b** : containing alcohol ▪ *hard cider/lemonade* **12** : powerful and extremely harmful to the health ▪ *cocaine and other hard drugs* **13** *of water* : containing many minerals and unable to make bubbles with soap **14** : having clear, sharp lines ▪ *the hard edges of the image* **15** : very bright and unpleasant ▪ *the cold, hard light of day* **16** : sounding like the "c" in "cold" or the "g" in "geese" ▪ *The "g" in "gorilla" is hard, but the "g" in "giant" is soft.* **17** *informal* : strong and muscular ▪ *hard bodies* — **between a rock and a hard place** *see* ²ROCK — **give (someone) a hard time** : to criticize or annoy (someone) ▪ *They gave him a hard time about quitting.* — **hard feelings** ✧ If you have *hard feelings*, you feel dislike or anger toward someone who you think has mistreated you. ▪ *The argument caused a lot of hard feelings.* ▪ *"I didn't mean to insult you.* **No hard feelings**?" [=are you upset?] *"No hard feelings."* [=I'm not upset] — **hard of hearing** : not able to hear well ▪ *I'm a little hard of hearing.* — **hard on 1 a** : causing damage or strain to (something) ▪ *This kind of work can be hard on your back.* **b** : causing stress or worry to (someone) ▪ *Yesterday was hard on everyone.* **2** : treating or judging (someone) in a harsh or critical way ▪ *Don't be so hard on yourself—you did the best you could.* — **hard up** *informal* **1** : lacking money ▪ *We're hard up these days.* **2** : having not enough of something ▪ *hard up for cash/friends* — **play hard to get** *see* ¹PLAY — **hard·ness** /ˈhɑɚdnəs/ *n* [*U, singular*]

²hard *adv* **1** : with a lot of effort or energy ▪ *She tried really hard.* ▪ *working/studying/running hard* ▪ *I thought long and hard about it.* ▪ *We're hard at work* [=working with a lot of effort and energy] *on the new project.* **2** : in a very forceful way ▪ *He hit the ball hard.* ▪ *She pushed hard against the door.* ▪ *It's snowing/raining hard.* : in a loud and forceful way ▪ *breathing/laughing/crying hard* ✧ If you are **hit hard** or **hard hit** by something or if something **hits you hard**, it affects you powerfully in a very painful or shocking way. ▪ *His business was hit hard by the recession.* ▪ *When he left, she took it hard.* [=she was very upset about it] **3 a** : in a very direct and intense way ▪ *He looked hard at us.* **b** : in an extreme or complete way ▪ *He fell hard for her.* — **die hard** *see* ¹DIE — **hard done by** *Brit* : treated harshly or unfairly ▪ *He felt hard done by when he was laid off.*

hard–and–fast /ˈhɑɚdnˈfæst, *Brit* ˌhɑːdnˈfɑːst/ *adj* — used to say that something cannot be changed ▪ *a hard-and-fast rule*

hard·back /ˈhɑɚdˌbæk/ *n* [*C/U*] : HARDCOVER

hard·ball /ˈhɑɚdˌbɑːl/ *n* [*U*] *chiefly US, informal* **1** : BASEBALL **2** : forceful and sometimes dishonest methods used to get something you want ▪ *playing*

hardball [=using tough methods] *in politics* • *hardball tactics/politics*

hard·bit·ten /ˈhɑəˈbɪtn̩/ *adj* : tough and experienced • *hard-bitten journalists*

hard–boiled /ˈhɑəˈbɔjəld/ *adj* **1** *of an egg* : boiled until the inside parts are solid **2** : not feeling or showing affection, kindness, etc. • *a hard-boiled detective*

hard·bound /ˈhɑəˌbaʊnd/ *adj, chiefly US, of a book* : having a stiff or hard cover

hard cash *n* [U] : money in the form of bills and coins rather than checks or credit cards • *paying in (cold) hard cash*

hard–charging *adj, US* : very aggressive, determined, or ambitious : HARD-DRIVING

hard copy *n* [C] *computers* : a printed copy of a document • *print a hard copy of the report*

hard–core /ˈhɑəˈkoə/ *adj* **1** : very active and enthusiastic • *a hard-core supporter/fan* **2** : showing sex acts very openly • *hard-core pornography*

hard·cov·er /ˈhɑəˈkʌvɚ/ *n* [C/U] *US* : a book that has stiff or hard covers • *new hardcovers* • *a book published in hardcover* • *hardcover editions*

hard currency *n* [C/U] : money that comes from a country with a strong government and economy and that is not likely to lose its value

hard disk *n* [C] *computers* : a disk that is not flexible and that is used to store computer data

hard–drinking *adj* — used to describe a person who often drinks a lot of alcohol • *their violent, hard-drinking father*

hard drive *n* [C] *computers* : a device that is used for storing computer data • *a removable hard drive*

hard–driv·ing /ˈhɑəˈdraɪvɪŋ/ *adj* : very aggressive, determined, or ambitious • *a hard-driving businesswoman*

hard–earned *adj* : achieved or acquired through a lot of effort or hard work • *hard-earned money/victories*

hard–edged /ˈhɑəˈɛdʒd/ *adj* : having a tough or sharp quality • *hard-edged satire/realism*

hard·en /ˈhɑədn̩/ *vb* **1** [T/I] : to become hard or firm or to make (something) hard or firm • *The glue hardens quickly.* • *substances that can harden the arteries* **2** [T/I] : to become or to make (something) become more definite and strongly felt • *Opposition to the government has hardened.* • *The news has hardened opposition to the government.* **3** [T] : to make (someone) less emotional and less likely to care about or feel sorry for other people • *soldiers hardened by combat* • *a hardened criminal* [=a criminal who does not feel fear, sorrow, etc.] • *She* **hardened** *her heart against him.* [=stopped having kind feelings for him] ◇ If you become **hardened to** something, you are no longer saddened or shocked when you see or experience it. • *New doctors quickly become hardened to the terrible injuries suffered by accident victims.* **4** [I] : to begin to be or seem harsh, angry, serious, etc. • *Her voice/manner hardened as she spoke.*
— **hard·en·er** /ˈhɑədnɚ/ *n* [C] —

hard·en·ing /ˈhɑədnɪŋ/ *n* [U] • *hardening of the arteries*

hard–eyed /ˈhɑəˌaɪd/ *adj* : looking at things in a very critical way without emotion • *a hard-eyed realist*

hard–fought *adj* : requiring a lot of effort or hard work • *a hard-fought campaign* **2** : achieved or acquired through a lot of effort or hard work • *a hard-fought victory*

hard hat *n* [C] : a hat that workers wear at a building site to protect their heads

hard·head·ed /ˈhɑəˈhɛdəd/ *adj* **1** : not willing to change ideas or opinions : very stubborn • *a hardheaded old man* **2** : having or involving careful and practical thoughts and ideas that are not influenced by emotions • *hardheaded advice/judgments* — **hard·head·ed·ness** *n* [U]

hard–heart·ed /ˈhɑəˈhɑətəd/ *adj* : having or showing no kindness or sympathy for other people • *a hard-hearted woman* — **hard–heart·ed·ness** *n* [U]

hard–hit·ting /ˈhɑəˈhɪtɪŋ/ *adj* : very effective or forceful • *a hard-hitting interview/reporter*

hard line *n* [singular] : a strict and forceful way of behaving when you are dealing with other people • *taking a hard line with terrorists* [=dealing with terrorists in a forceful way] — **hard–line** /ˈhɑəˈlaɪn/ *adj* • *a hard-line* [=very strict] *conservative* — **hard–lin·er** /ˈhɑəˈlaɪnɚ/ *n* [C] • *liberal hard-liners*

hard–luck /ˈhɑəˌlʌk/ *adj, always before a noun* : of or relating to bad luck • *a hard-luck story*

hard·ly /ˈhɑədli/ *adv* **1 a** : BARELY, SCARCELY — used to say that something was almost not possible or almost did not happen • *She was hardly able to control her excitement.* • *I could hardly believe my eyes.* [=it was difficult to believe what I was seeing] **b** : almost not at all • *We hardly knew them.* **c** : almost not • *Hardly anyone showed up.* • *Hardly a day goes by when I don't think about him.* **d** — used to say that something happened only a short time before • *I had hardly* [=barely] *arrived when the phone rang.* **2** : certainly not • *The news is hardly surprising.* = *The news is hardly a surprise.* [=it is not surprising at all] • *"Is this a new movie?" "Hardly! It was made ten years ago."* — **hardly ever** see EVER

hard–nosed /ˈhɑəˈnoʊzd/ *adj* **1** : very tough • *a hard-nosed cop* **2** : practical and realistic • *hard-nosed realism*

hard–pressed /ˈhɑəˈprɛst/ *adj* **1** — used to say that it is difficult to do something • *You'd be hard-pressed* [=it would be difficult] *to find a better car.* **2** : in a bad situation because you do not have enough of something • *families that are hard-pressed for time/money*

hard put *adj* : HARD-PRESSED • *I would be hard put* [=it would be difficult for me] *to find an explanation.*

hard rock *n* [U] : loud rock music that has a heavy beat

hard science *n* [C/U] : a science (such as chemistry, physics, or astronomy) that deals with things that can be observed and measured — **hard scientist** n [C]

hard·scrab·ble /'haɔd,skræbəl/ adj, US 1 : having poor soil ▪ *hardscrabble farms/ prairies* 2 : having harsh and difficult conditions because of poverty ▪ *a hardscrabble childhood/town*

hard sell n [singular] 1 : an aggressive way of selling something ▪ *giving customers* **the hard sell** 2 US : something that others are not willing or likely to accept ▪ *Such an expensive project will be a hard sell during a budget crisis.*

hard·ship /'haɔd,ʃɪp/ n 1 [U] : pain and suffering ▪ *financial/economic hardship* 2 [C] : something that causes pain, suffering, or loss ▪ *the hardships of life on the frontier*

hard shoulder n [C] Brit : ¹SHOULDER 5

hard·top /'haɔd,taːp/ n [C] : a car that has a metal top which cannot be removed

hard·ware /'haɔd,weə/ n [U] 1 : things (such as tools or parts of machines) that are made of metal ▪ *a hardware store* 2 : equipment used for a particular purpose ▪ *military hardware* [=guns, tanks, etc.]; *especially* : computer equipment — compare SOFTWARE

hard–wearing adj, Brit : lasting for a long time : DURABLE ▪ *hard-wearing boots*

hard–wired /'haɔd,wajəd/ adj : having permanent electronic circuits and connections ▪ *a hardwired network* ▪ (figurative) *Humans are hardwired for speech.* = *Speech is hardwired in/into the human brain.*

hard–won /'haɔd'wʌn/ adj : HARD-EARNED ▪ *a hard-won victory*

hard·wood /'haɔd,wud/ n 1 [C/U] : the heavy and hard wood of an oak tree, a maple tree, etc. ▪ *floors made of hardwood* = *hardwood floors* 2 [C] : a tree that produces hardwood ▪ *oaks, maples, and other hardwoods*

hard·work·ing /'haɔd'wəkɪŋ/ adj : working very hard : not lazy ▪ *a hardworking waitress*

har·dy /'haɔdi/ adj **har·di·er; -est** 1 : able to live through difficult weather conditions ▪ *a hardy rose* 2 : strong and able to accept difficult or unpleasant conditions ▪ *Only the hardiest pilgrims made the journey.* — **har·di·ness** /'haɔdinəs/ n [U]

hare /'heə/ n, pl **hares** also **hare** [C] : a fast animal that resembles a rabbit

hare·brained /'heə'breɪnd/ adj, informal : very silly or foolish ▪ *a harebrained scheme/idea/plan*

har·em /'herəm/ n [C] 1 : a house or part of a house in which the women of a Muslim household live 2 : the women who live in a harem

hark /'haɔk/ vb [I] literary : LISTEN — usually used as a command ▪ *"Hark, she speaks!"* —Shakespeare, *Macbeth* (1605–06) — **hark back to** [phrasal vb] 1 : to return to or remember (something in the past) ▪ *harking back to the days of our youth* 2 : to look or seem like (something in the past) ▪ *a style that harks back to the 1930s*

har·le·quin /'haɔlɪkwən/ n [C] : a pattern of diamond-shaped figures of different colors ▪ *fabric with a harlequin pattern*

har·lot /'haɔlət/ n [C] old-fashioned + disapproving : ¹PROSTITUTE

¹**harm** /'haɔm/ n [U] : physical or mental damage or injury ▪ *I never meant (to do/ cause you) any harm.* [=I never meant to harm/hurt you in any way] ▪ *They threatened him with bodily harm.* ▪ *The scandal did irreparable/lasting/great harm to his reputation.* ▪ *No harm will come to her.* [=she won't be hurt in any way] ▪ *What's the harm in it?* = *I don't see any harm in it.* = *There's no harm in it.* [=it will not hurt anyone or cause a bad result] ▪ *The treatment may* **do more harm than good**. [=be more harmful than helpful] ▪ (informal) *"I'm sorry I forgot to call." "That's OK.* **No harm done.**" [=no apology or concern is necessary because no damage has been done] — **harm's way** : a dangerous place or situation ▪ *soldiers sent into harm's way* — **harm·ful** /'haɔmfəl/ adj ▪ *harmful* [=dangerous] *bacteria* — **harm·ful·ly** adv — **harm·ful·ness** n [U] — **harm·less** /'haɔmləs/ adj ▪ *That snake is harmless.* ▪ *a harmless joke* [=a joke that is not meant to cause harm or offense] — **harm·less·ly** adv — **harm·less·ness** n [U]

²**harm** vb [T] : to cause hurt, injury, or damage to (someone or something) : to cause harm to (someone or something) ▪ *I never meant to harm you.* ▪ *killing weeds without harming crops* ▪ *The scandal harmed his reputation.*

har·mon·i·ca /haɔˈmaːnɪkə/ n [C] : a small musical instrument with many small openings that is played with your mouth

har·mo·ni·ous /haɔˈmoʊnijəs/ adj 1 music : having a pleasing mixture or combination of notes ▪ *harmonious voices* 2 : having parts that are related or combined in a pleasing way ▪ *harmonious colors/flavors* 3 : not experiencing disagreement or fighting ▪ *harmonious relations between two countries* — **har·mo·ni·ous·ly** adv ▪ *voices/flavors blending (together) harmoniously* — **har·mo·ni·ous·ness** n [U]

har·mo·nize also Brit **har·mo·nise** /'haɔmə,naɪz/ vb -nized; -niz·ing 1 [I] : to play or sing in harmony ▪ *The four singers harmonize beautifully.* 2 [T/I] : to be combined or to cause (two or more things) to be combined in a pleasing way ▪ *The voices harmonize (with one another) nicely.* ▪ *a recipe that harmonizes flavors from different parts of the world* — **har·mo·ni·za·tion** also Brit **har·mo·ni·sa·tion** /,haɔmənəˈzeɪʃən, Brit ,haːmə ,naɪˈzeɪʃən/ n [U]

har·mo·ny /'haɔməni/ n, pl -nies 1 [C/U] : the combination of different musical notes played or sung at the same time to produce a pleasing sound ▪ *the song's complex harmonies and rhythms* ▪ *singing in harmony* [=singing notes that combine with other notes in a pleasing way] 2 [singular] : a pleasing combination or arrangement of different things ▪ *a harmony of flavors/colors* ✧ When things are *in harmony* or *in harmony with* each other, they go together well or they agree with each other very well. ▪ *parts moving in perfect harmony* ▪ *actions that are not in harmony with our ideals* ◇ When people are *in harmony* or *in harmony with* each other, they live together in a peaceful and friendly way. ▪ *living in harmony with our neighbors* ◇ To bring something *into harmony with* something else is to change it so that it agrees with or matches something else. ▪ *We revised our proposal to bring it into harmony with their requirements.* ◇ When things are *out of harmony* or *out of harmony with* each other, they do not agree or combine well. ▪ *The furnishings seem out of harmony with the architecture.*

¹har·ness /ˈhɑɚnəs/ *n* [C] **1** : a set of straps that are placed on a horse, bull, etc., so that it can pull something heavy **2** : a set of straps that are used to connect a person to a parachute, seat, etc. ▪ *a safety harness* — **in harness** *Brit* : working at a job ▪ *I was back in harness on Monday.*

²harness *vb* [T] **1** : to put a harness on (an animal) ▪ *harness the horses* **b** : to attach (an animal) to something with a harness ▪ *The horses were harnessed to the wagon.* **2** : to use (something) for a particular purpose ▪ *new ways to harness the sun's energy* ▪ *harness anger to fight injustice* **3** : to connect or join (things) together ▪ *harnessing two computers to work together*

¹harp /hɑɚp/ *n* [C] : a musical instrument that has strings stretched across a large open frame and that you play with your fingers — **harp·ist** /ˈhɑɚpɪst/ *n* [C]

²harp *vb* — **harp at** [phrasal vb] *US, informal* : to tell (someone) repeatedly to do something ▪ *She's always harping at me to clean my room.* — **harp on** (*US*) or *Brit* **harp on about** [phrasal vb] *informal* : to talk about (a subject) repeatedly in an annoying way ▪ *He seems to enjoy harping on my shortcomings.*

har·poon /hɑɚˈpuːn/ *n* [C] : a long weapon used especially for hunting large fish or whales — **harpoon** *vb* [T] ▪ *harpoon a whale* [=kill a whale with a harpoon] — **har·poon·er** *n* [C]

harp·si·chord /ˈhɑɚpsɪˌkoɚd/ *n* [C] : an instrument that is like a piano but with strings that are plucked rather than struck

har·ried /ˈherid/ *adj* : very worried or anxious ▪ *harried shoppers/travelers*

har·row·ing /ˈherowɪŋ/ *adj* : very painful or upsetting ▪ *a harrowing ordeal/experience/account* — **har·row·ing·ly** *adv*

harsh /hɑɚʃ/ *adj* **1 a** : unpleasant and difficult to accept or experience ▪ *a harsh climate/environment/winter* ▪ *the harsh realities of the situation* **b** : too intense or powerful ▪ *The lighting in the room was very harsh.* ▪ *harsh detergents* **2 a** : severe or cruel ▪ *a harsh disciplinarian* ▪ *her harsh treatment of the students* **b** : very critical : strongly negative ▪ *harsh language/criticism* ▪ *He's one of her harshest critics.* — **harsh·ly** *adv* — **harsh·ness** *n* [U]

¹har·vest /ˈhɑɚvəst/ *n* [C] **1** : the season when crops are gathered from the fields or the activity of gathering crops ▪ *the end of the harvest* ▪ *harvest time* **2** : the amount of crops that are gathered ▪ *a bountiful harvest*

²harvest *vb* [T] **1** : to gather (a crop) ▪ *It is time to harvest the wheat.* **2** : to gather or collect (something) for use ▪ *harvesting timber* ▪ (*figurative*) *harvesting the rewards/fruits of our labors*

har·vest·er /ˈhɑɚvəstɚ/ *n* [C] **1** : a person who gathers crops or other natural products **2** : a large machine that is used for harvesting crops

has *see* HAVE

has–been /ˈhæzˌbɪn/ *n* [C] *informal* : a person who is no longer popular or successful ▪ *a washed-up old has-been*

¹hash /ˈhæʃ/ *vb* — **hash out** [phrasal verb] *US, informal* **hash out (something)** or **hash (something) out** : to find a solution by talking about (something) ▪ *Let's sit down and hash things out.* [=talk about things; discuss the situation] ▪ *Their lawyers hashed out a resolution.* ▪ *trying to hash out our differences*

²hash *n* **1** [C/U] : a dish of chopped meat and potatoes ▪ *corned beef hash* **2** [U] *informal* : HASHISH — **make a hash of** *informal* : to ruin (something) by making many mistakes ▪ *He made a hash of the whole project!*

hash browns *n* [plural] : boiled potatoes that have been cut up and fried until brown — called also *hashed browns*

hash·ish /ˈhæˌʃiːʃ, hæˈʃiːʃ/ *n* [U] : an illegal drug that comes from hemp

hasn't /ˈhæznt/ — used as a contraction of *has not* ▪ *She hasn't called yet.*

has·sle /ˈhæsəl/ *vb* **has·sled; has·sling** *informal* **1** [T] : to bother or annoy (someone) constantly or repeatedly ▪ *Other kids hassle her about her weight.* **2** [I] *US* : to argue or fight ▪ *I don't have time to hassle with you about this!*

hassle *n* [C] *informal* **1** : something that is annoying or that causes trouble ▪ *flight delays and other travel hassles* ▪ *Cooking is too much of a hassle tonight.* [=it is too much trouble to do] **2** *US* : a fight or argument ▪ *He got into a hassle with his landlord.*

haste /ˈheɪst/ *n* [U] : quickness or eagerness that can result in mistakes ▪ *In their haste to leave, they forgot their passports.* ▪ *leaving in haste* — **make haste** *old-fashioned* : HURRY ▪ *Come, we must make haste.*

has·ten /ˈheɪsn/ *vb* **1** [T] : to cause (something) to happen more quickly ▪ *a death hastened by alcoholism* **2** [T/I] *old-fashioned* : to move or act quickly ▪ *She hastened up the stairs.* — **hasten to add/say/explain (etc.)** : to immediately say something in order to prevent confusion or misunderstanding ▪ *They hastened to mention that more testing needs to be done.*

hasty /ˈheɪsti/ *adj* **hast·i·er; -est** **1 a** : done or made very quickly ▪ *a hasty sketch* ▪ *The cat made a hasty retreat up a tree.* **b** : done or made too quickly ▪ *Don't make any hasty decisions.* **2** : acting too quickly • *He was too hasty in his decision to quit.* — **hast·i·ly** /ˈheɪstəli/ *adv* — **hast·i·ness** *n* [U]

hat /ˈhæt/ *n* [C] : a covering for the head that often has a brim • *a straw hat* • *(figurative)* *a new place to* **hang my hat** [=a new place to live or stay] • *(figurative)* *I'll tell you, but you have to* **keep it under your hat** [=keep it a secret] • *(figurative)* *I (have to)* **take my hat off to her.** [=give her praise or credit] *She did a great job.* • *(figurative) Another competitor has* **thrown his hat into the ring.** [=announced that he is going to try to win a contest] • *(figurative) She* **wears many hats** [=has many jobs or roles]: *she's a doctor, a musician, and a writer.* — **at the drop of a hat** see ¹DROP — **hat in hand** see ¹HAND — **hats off to** *informal* — used to give praise or credit to someone • *Hats off to Susan for doing such a great job.* — **tip your hat** see ¹TIP — see also OLD HAT

¹**hatch** /ˈhætʃ/ *n* [C] **1 a** : an opening in the deck of a ship or in the floor, wall, or roof of a building **b** : the covering of such an opening • *Lift/open the hatch.* **2** : a small door or opening in an airplane or spaceship — **batten down the hatches** see BATTEN — **down the hatch** *informal* ✧ If something goes *down the hatch*, you swallow it.

²**hatch** *vb* **1** [T/I] *of a bird, insect, fish, etc.* : to be born or to cause (something) to be born by coming out of an egg • *watching chicks hatch* • *newly hatched turtles* **2 a** [T] *of an egg* : to break open as a bird, insect, etc., is born • *The eggs hatched.* **b** [T] : to cause (an egg) to hatch • *a hen hatching her eggs* **3** [T] : to create (an idea, plan, etc.) usually in a secret way • *hatching (up) a scheme*

hatch·back /ˈhætʃˌbæk/ *n* [C] : a door that opens upward on the back of a car; *also* : a car that has such a door

hatch·ery /ˈhætʃəri/ *n, pl* **-er·ies** [C] : a place where people raise young chicken, fish, etc., from eggs • *a salmon hatchery*

hatch·et /ˈhætʃət/ *n* [C] : a small ax with a short handle — **bury the hatchet** : to agree to stop arguing or fighting and become friendly • *After all these years, they've finally buried the hatchet.*

hatchet job *n* [C] *informal* : a very harsh and unfair spoken or written attack • *Reviewers did a hatchet job on their latest book.* [=they criticized it very harshly]

hatchet man *n* [C] : a person whose job is to do harsh and unpleasant things that other people do not want to do • *She lets her hatchet men criticize her opponent's character for her.*

hatch·ling /ˈhætʃlɪŋ/ *n* [C] : a very young animal that has just hatched from an egg

¹**hate** /ˈheɪt/ *n* [C/U] : a very strong feeling of dislike • *I saw the hate* [=hatred] *in his eyes.* • *politicians who get* **hate mail** [=extremely angry letters, e-mail, etc.] • *a* **hate crime** [=a crime done against someone because of the person's race, religion, etc.]

²**hate** *vb* **hat·ed; hat·ing 1** [T/I] : to feel hate for (someone) • *He was hated and feared by his people.* • *She hated them for*

betraying her. • *a hated enemy* • *children who have been taught to hate* **2** [T] : to find (something) very unpleasant • *I hate spinach.* • *I hate the idea of leaving.* • *She hates cooking.* = *She hates to cook.* • *I hate it when he lies to me.* **3** [T] — used to apologize for doing something or to express regret or guilt • *I hate to* [=I'm sorry to] *bother you, but could you move your car?* • *I'd hate it if they got the wrong idea.* = *I'd hate (for) them to get the wrong idea.* [=I would feel regret if they misunderstood] • *I hate to say it, but we're not going to win.* — **hat·er** *n* [C] • *a cat hater* [=a person who hates cats]

hate·ful /ˈheɪtfəl/ *adj* **1** : causing or deserving hate • *a hateful crime* **2** : full of hate • *hateful people* : showing hate • *hateful words* — **hate·ful·ly** *adv* — **hate·ful·ness** *n* [U]

ha·tred /ˈheɪtrəd/ *n* [C/U] : a very strong feeling of dislike : HATE • *an irrational hatred of foreigners*

hat·ter /ˈhætɚ/ *n* [C] : a person who makes, sells, or repairs hats

hat trick *n* [C] : three goals scored by one player in a game of ice hockey, soccer, etc. • *score a hat trick* • *(figurative) She scored a hat trick by winning prizes for all three of her novels.*

haugh·ty /ˈhɑːti/ *adj* **haugh·ti·er; -est** : having or showing the insulting attitude of people who think that they are better, smarter, or more important than other people • *haughty* [=arrogant] *aristocrats* — **haugh·ti·ly** /ˈhɑːtəli/ *adv* — **haugh·ti·ness** /ˈhɑːtinəs/ *n* [U]

¹**haul** /ˈhɑːl/ *vb* [T] **1 a** : to pull or drag (something) with effort • *Haul (in) the ropes.* • *The car was hauled away/off to the junkyard.* **b** : to move or carry (something) with effort • *hauling water in buckets* • *hauling a heavy bag around with me* **2** : to force (someone) to go or come to a place • *They hauled her off to court/jail.* • *The prisoner was hauled away in handcuffs.* **3** : to carry (someone or something) in a vehicle • *trucks that haul freight* — **haul off and** US, *informal* : to suddenly do (something specified) • *She hauled off and punched him in the face.* — **haul over the coals** see COAL — **haul·er** (US) /ˈhɑːlɚ/ *or Brit* **haul·i·er** /ˈhɑːljɚ/ *n* [C] • *freight haulers*

²**haul** *n* [C] **1** : the act of pulling or dragging something with effort • *each haul of the rope* **2** : a large amount of something that has been stolen, collected, or won • *a burglar's haul* • *The kids collected quite a haul of candy on Halloween.* **3** : a distance to be traveled • *It's a short haul from the cabin to the beach.* — see also LONG HAUL

haunch /ˈhɑːntʃ/ *n* [C] : the upper part of a person's or animal's leg — **on your haunches** : sitting on your heels with your knees bent • *She sat/squatted on her haunches to tend the flowers.*

¹**haunt** /ˈhɑːnt/ *vb* [T] **1** : to visit or live in (a place) as a ghost • *They say a ghost haunts the inn.* • *a haunted house* **2** : to eventually cause problems for (someone) as time passes • *Their failure to plan ahead is now* **coming back to haunt**

them. 3 : to keep coming back to the mind of (someone) especially in a way that makes the person sad or upset ▪ *He was haunted by his memories of the war.* **4 :** to visit (a place) often ▪ *someone who haunts antique shops*

²**haunt** *n* [*C*] : a place that you go to often ▪ *The café was one of her favorite haunts.*

haunting *adj* : sad or beautiful in a way that is difficult to forget ▪ *a haunting reminder* ▪ *the haunting beauty of her voice* — **haunt·ing·ly** *adv*

haute cou·ture /ˌoutkuˈtuɚ, Brit ˌoutkuˈtjuɚ/ *n* [*U*] *somewhat formal* : the people and companies that create clothes that are very expensive and fashionable; *also* : the clothes they create ▪ *haute couture fashions/designers*

haute cui·sine /ˌoutkwɪˈziːn/ *n* [*singular*] : skillful and complicated cooking

have /ˈhæv, əv; *in "have to" meaning "must" usually* ˈhæf/ *vb* **has** /ˈhæz, əz; *in "has to" meaning "must" usually* ˈhæs/; **had** /ˈhæd, əd/; **hav·ing** /ˈhævɪŋ/ ◆ *For many senses of* **have**, *the phrase* **have got** *can also be used.*

1 [*T*] **a :** to own, use, or hold (something) ▪ *She has a red bike.* ▪ *Do you have the newspaper?* ▪ *He has his own room.* ▪ *I have enough tickets for everyone.* — *also* used for things that cannot be seen or touched ▪ *Do you have an appointment?* ▪ *We had no choice/alternative.* — *also* **have got** ▪ *Have they got a new car?* **b** ◆ If you **have (something) to do, finish** *(etc.)*, there is something that you must do or want to do in order to complete a task. ▪ *We have things to do.* ▪ *I have several more pages to read.* — *also* **have got** ▪ *We've got things to do.* **2** [*T*] — used to describe a quality, skill, feature, etc., of a person or thing ▪ *The children have red hair.* ▪ *The museum has interesting exhibits.* — *also* **have got** ▪ *The car's got power brakes.* **3** [*T*] : to include or contain (something or someone) ▪ *The list has my name on it.* ▪ *April has 30 days.* — *also* **have got** ▪ *The club's got 100 members.* **4** [*T*] : to give birth to (a child) ▪ *She had a baby.* **5** [*T*] — used to describe a relationship between people ▪ *They have a son.* ▪ *I have two sisters.* ▪ *She has many friends.* ▪ *Does he have a girlfriend?* — *also* **have got** ▪ *I've got two sisters and a brother.* **6** [*T*] : to receive or be given (something) ▪ *We had some bad/good news.* ▪ *Waiter, can I have the check, please?* **7** [*T*] — used to describe the position of a person or thing ▪ *He had his hands behind his back.* [=his hands were behind his back] — *also* **have got** ▪ *The house has got a large tree next to it.* **8** [*T*] : to cause or produce (something) ▪ *Her decision had serious consequences.* **9** [*T*] **a :** to experience (something) ▪ *Are you having fun?* ▪ *Everyone had a good time at the party.* ▪ *I'm having trouble with my car.* ▪ *She had a heart attack.* **b :** to be affected by (an illness or injury) ▪ *My uncle has diabetes.* — *also* **have got** ▪ *I've got a cold.* **c :** to experience (an emotion or feeling) ▪ *I have complete confidence in your abilities.* — *also* **have got** ▪ *I've got many regrets.* **10** [*T*] — used to describe a per-

son's thoughts, ideas, etc. ▪ *I have a few thoughts on the matter.* ▪ *"What time is it?" "I have no idea."* [=I don't know] — *also* **have got** ▪ *Everyone's got a different opinion.* **11** [*T*] : to perform (an action) : to do or participate in (an activity) ▪ *Did you have a good nap?* ▪ *We need to have a talk.* ▪ *Let me have a try/look.* [=let me try/look] **12** [*T*] : to provide (something) as entertainment or as a social gathering ▪ *We're having a party on Saturday.* ▪ *The museum is having an exhibition of her work.* **13** [*T*] **a :** to cause, tell, or ask (someone) to do something ▪ *You should have someone check that.* ▪ *He had the barber cut his hair short.* **b :** to cause (something) to be changed, removed, added, or affected in a specified way ▪ *I had new tires put on the car.* **c** — used when you hire someone to do something or when you go to a hospital, a mechanic's shop, etc., so that something can be done ▪ *She's having surgery.* ▪ *We're having work done on the house.* **14** [*T*] — used to say that someone is at your home or is coming to your home ▪ *We're having guests this weekend.* **15** [*T*] **a :** to cause (something) to be in a specified state or condition ▪ *He had dinner ready when she came home.* — *also* **have got** ▪ *She's got the radio on loud.* **b** — used when something that belongs to someone or something is changed, destroyed, or taken ▪ *She had her car stolen.* [=her car was stolen] **16** [*T*] : to allow (something) ▪ *We'll have no more of that behavior!* = *We can't have that sort of behavior!* **17** [*T*] : to accept (someone) ▪ *I'll marry her if she'll have me (as her husband)!* **18** [*T*] **a :** to be able to control, capture, or defeat (someone) ▪ *We have him now!* — *also* **have got** ▪ *We've got him now!* **b** ◆ The phrases **You have me there**, **There you have me**, and (more commonly) **You've/You got me (there)** are used in speech to mean "I don't know." The phrase **You got me** is sometimes shortened to **Got me** in very informal speech. ▪ *"Why did she leave?" "You got me."* **19** [*T*] **a :** to eat or drink (something) ▪ *We had steak for dinner.* ▪ *We'll be having dinner at six.* ▪ *I have* [=take] *my coffee black.* **b :** to smoke (something) ▪ *She had a cigarette while she was waiting.* **20** [*auxiliary vb*] — used with the past participle to form the perfect tenses of verbs ▪ *I have not seen that movie.* ▪ *Has the rain stopped?* ▪ *I have never been so embarrassed!*

---

usage When *have* is used as an auxiliary verb, the shortened forms *'ve* for *have*, *'s* for *has*, and *'d* for *had* are common in informal writing and usual in speech. ▪ *We've been friends for years.* ▪ *She's bought a new car.* ▪ *They'd already left by the time we arrived.* The negative forms *haven't*, *hasn't*, and *hadn't* are also common in informal writing and usual in speech. ▪ *I haven't seen that movie.* ▪ *Hasn't the rain stopped?* ▪ *We hadn't arrived yet when they left.*

— **be had** : to be tricked or fooled by someone ▪ *I don't trust them. I think we've been had.* — **have against** [*phrasal vb*] **have (something) against** : to have (something) as a reason for not liking (someone or something) ▪ *She has a grudge against her former boss.* ▪ *What do you have against him?* [=why do you dislike him?] ▪ *I have nothing against her.* — also **have got** ▪ *What have you got against him?* — **have back** [*phrasal vb*] **1 have (something) back** : to receive (something that is returned to you) ▪ *Can I have my book back?* **2 have (someone) back a** : to be with (someone who has returned) again ▪ *We would love to have you back for another visit.* **b** : to allow (someone) to return ▪ *His wife won't have him back and she's filing for divorce.* — **have got** : HAVE

> **usage** Examples of *have got* are shown above and below for each sense, idiom, and phrasal verb in which it occurs. Note that *have got* is used only in the present tense. It is common in place of *have* in informal writing, and it is usual in ordinary speech. The contracted forms **'s** for *has* and **'ve** for *have* are commonly used for the first part of this phrase. The usual negative forms of *have got* are **haven't got** and **hasn't got**.

— **have had it** *informal* **1 a** : to be too old or damaged to be used ▪ *We need a new stove. This one has had it.* **b** : to be so tired or annoyed that you will no longer allow or accept something ▪ *I've been working all day and I've had it.* **2** : to be completely ruined or defeated ▪ *His political career has had it.* — **have it 1** — used to say that what is being reported is a rumor, a story, etc. ▪ *Rumor/Word has it* [=a rumor says] *that the company will be going out of business.* ▪ *Legend has it* [=according to legend] *George Washington slept here.* **2** — used to describe a person's condition or situation ▪ *He's had it pretty tough* [=his life has been difficult] *since his wife died.* — also **have got** ▪ *We've got it pretty good right now.* — **have it in for** : to want to hurt or cause problems for (someone you do not like) — also **have got** ▪ *She's got it in for me.* — **have it in you** : to have the ability to do something ▪ *His last performance was wonderful; I didn't know he had it in him!* — also **have got** ▪ *I don't think she's got it in her to be cruel.* — **have it out** : to settle a disagreement by talking or arguing ▪ *If you don't like the way he's treated you, you should have it out with him.* — **have on** [*phrasal vb*] **1 have (something) on** or **have on (something)** : to be wearing (something) ▪ *He had nothing on.* [=he was naked] — also **have got** ▪ *She's got on a new suit.* **2 have (something) on (you)** *informal* : to be carrying (something) ▪ *I don't have my wallet on me.* — also **have got** ▪ *Have you got any money on you?* **3 have (something) on** *chiefly Brit* : to have plans for (something) ▪ *What do you have on for to-*

morrow? — also **have got** ▪ *Have you got anything on for tomorrow?* **4 have (someone) on** *Brit, informal* : to trick or fool (someone) in a joking way ▪ *He was just having you on.* **5 have nothing on** or **not have anything on** : to have no evidence showing that someone has committed a crime or done something bad ▪ *The police were suspicious, but they had nothing on her.* — also **have got** ▪ *They haven't got anything on me.* — **have over** [*phrasal vb*] **have (someone) over** — used to say that someone is coming to your home as a guest ▪ *We're having some friends over for dinner.* — **have to 1** : to be forced or required to do something : MUST ▪ *You have to follow the rules.* ▪ *I have to remember to stop at the store.* ▪ *If you have to go, at least wait until the storm is over.* ▪ *I didn't want to do it but I had to.* ▪ *All passengers have to exit at the next stop.* — also **have got to** ▪ *You've got to stop.* **2** — used to say that something is desired or should be done ▪ *You have to read this book. It's fantastic!* — also **have got to** ▪ *You've got to come visit us soon.* **3** — used to say that something is very likely ▪ *There has to be some mistake.* — also **have got to** ▪ *It's got to be close to noon.* **4** — used in various spoken phrases to emphasize a statement ▪ *I have to say, I was surprised to hear from him.* ▪ *I have to warn you, this will not be easy.* — also **have got to** ▪ *She's a talented actress, you've got to admit.* — **have to do with** see ¹DO — **have with** [*phrasal vb*] **have (someone or something) with (you)** — used to indicate the person or thing that is with you or that you are carrying ▪ *They had their grandchildren with them.* ▪ *I don't have my wallet with me.* — **there you have it** — used to say that something has just been shown, described, or stated in a very clear and definite way ▪ *"But we can't spend more money unless we have more money to spend!" "Precisely. There you have it."* — **what have you** see ¹WHAT

ha·ven /ˈheɪvən/ *n* [C] : a place where you are protected from danger, trouble, etc. ▪ *The inn is a haven for weary travelers.*

have–nots /ˈhæv͵nɑːts/ *n* — **the have-nots** : people who have little money and few possessions : poor people ▪ *the gap between the haves and the have-nots*

haven't /ˈhævənt/ — used as a contraction of *have not* ▪ *I haven't been there.*

haves /ˈhævz/ *n* — **the haves** : people who have a lot of money and possessions : wealthy people ▪ *the gap between the haves and the have-nots*

hav·oc /ˈhævək/ *n* [U] : a situation in which there is much destruction or confusion ▪ *A tornado wreaked havoc on* [=caused great destruction to] *the village.* ▪ *The children created/caused havoc in the house.*

haw /ˈhɑː/ *vb* — **hem and haw** see ²HEM

¹**hawk** /ˈhɑːk/ *n* [C] **1 a** : a bird that kills other birds and animals for food ▪ **2** : a person who supports war or the use of military force — **watch (someone or something) like a hawk** : to watch

(someone or something) very carefully — **hawk·ish** /'hɑːkɪʃ/ *adj* ▪ *a hawkish politician*

²hawk *vb* [*T*] **1** : to offer (something) for sale especially by calling out or by going from one person to another ▪ *Vendors were hawking soda and hot dogs.* **2** : to clear (material) from your throat by coughing, making a noise with your voice, etc. ▪ *hawking up phlegm* — **hawk·er** *n* [*C*]

haw·thorn /'hɑːˌθoən/ *n* [*C*] : a type of bush or small tree with white or pink flowers and small red fruits

hay /'heɪ/ *n* [*U*] : grass that has been cut and dried to be used as food for animals ▪ *a bale of hay* — **hit the hay** see ¹HIT — **make hay (while the sun shines)** : to get value or use from an opportunity while it exists ▪ *These good economic conditions won't last forever, so investors need to make hay while the sun shines.*

hay fever *n* [*singular*] : a sickness that is like a cold and that is caused by breathing in plant pollen

hay·ride /'heɪˌraɪd/ *n* [*C*] *US* : an informal event in which people ride in a wagon, sleigh, or open truck that is partly filled with straw or hay

hay·stack /'heɪˌstæk/ *n* [*C*] : a large pile of hay — **a needle in a haystack** see ¹NEEDLE

hay·wire /'heɪˌwajə/ *adj, informal* : not working properly ▪ *The radio went haywire.*

¹haz·ard /'hæzəd/ *n* [*C*] **1** : a source of danger ▪ *the hazards of excessive drinking* ▪ *That old staircase is a safety hazard.* [=is dangerous] ▪ *a fire hazard* [=something that could cause a fire] ▪ *a hazard to your health* [=something that could make you sick] **2** : something on a golf course (such as a pond or an area of sand) that makes hitting the ball into the hole more difficult

²hazard *vb* [*T*] **1** : to risk losing (something, such as money) in an attempt to get, win, or achieve something ▪ *hazard a small sum in a business venture* **2** : to offer (a guess, an opinion, etc.) even though you may be wrong ▪ *hazard a guess as to the outcome of the election*

haz·ard·ous /'hæzədəs/ *adj* : involving risk or danger ▪ DANGEROUS ▪ *a hazardous voyage/chemical* ▪ *Smoking is hazardous to your health.*

haze /'heɪz/ *n* [*singular*] **1** : dust, smoke, or mist that has filled the air so that you cannot see clearly ▪ *a haze of smoke* **2** : a state of confusion ▪ *a drug-induced haze*

ha·zel /'heɪzəl/ *n* **1** [*C*] : a kind of bush or small tree that produces nuts **2** [*C/U*] : a color that combines light brown with green and gray — **hazel** *adj* ▪ *hazel eyes*

ha·zel·nut /'heɪzəlˌnʌt/ *n* [*C*] : the nut of a hazel

haz·ing /'heɪzɪŋ/ *n* [*U*] *US* : the practice of playing unpleasant tricks on someone or forcing someone to do unpleasant things ✧ *Hazing* is done as part of a ritual that people must go through before they are allowed to become members of a group (such as a college fraternity).

hazy /'heɪzi/ *adj* **haz·i·er**; **-est** **1** : partly hidden, darkened, or clouded by dust, smoke, or mist ▪ *a hazy view of the mountain* **2 a** : not clear in thought or expression : VAGUE ▪ *She has only hazy memories of the accident.* **b** : not certain ▪ *I'm a little hazy on/about the details.* — **haz·i·ly** /'heɪzəli/ *adv* — **haz·i·ness** /'heɪzinəs/ *n* [*U*]

H–bomb /'eɪtʃˌbɑːm/ *n* [*C*] : HYDROGEN BOMB

HDTV *abbr* high-definition television

¹he /'hiː, i/ *pron* **1** : that male ▪ *He is my father.* **2** : that person — used in a general sense or when the sex of the person is unknown ▪ *Everyone should do the best he can.* ✧ This use of *he* was common in the past but is now often avoided because it is considered sexist.

²he /'hiː/ *n* [*singular*] : a boy, man, or male animal ▪ *"Somebody called when you were out." "Was it a he or a she?"*

¹head /'hɛd/ *n, pl* **heads** *or in sense 5* **head** **1** [*C*] : the part of the body containing the brain, eyes, ears, nose, and mouth ▪ *He nodded his head.* ▪ *head injuries* ▪ *They were covered from head to foot/toe in mud.* [=they were completely covered in mud] **2** [*C*] : a person's mental ability : MIND ▪ *She's always had a (good) head for business.* ▪ *She did some quick calculations in her head.* [=without writing anything; mentally] ▪ *That song keeps running through my head.* = *I can't get that song out of my head.* ▪ *The problem is all in his head.* [=the problem is not real; he's just imagining it] ▪ *Don't go putting ideas in/into his head.* [=don't cause him to have ideas that he would not have himself] ▪ *He should have his head examined.* = *He's not right in the head.* [=he's crazy] ▪ *a cool/calm/clear head* ✧ If you have *a good head on your shoulders,* you are intelligent and have good judgment. ✧ When you *get/take it into your head* to do something, you suddenly decide to do it in a way that seems foolish or surprising. ▪ *He's taken it into his head to try skydiving.* ✧ If you *get it into your head* that something is true, you begin to believe something even though there is no good reason for believing it. ▪ *She's gotten it into her head that I don't like her.* **3** [*singular*] : a distance equal to the length of a head ▪ *The horse won the race by a head.* **4** [*C*] : the front side of a coin : the side of a coin that shows a picture of a person's head — *the head of a penny* — usually used in the plural to refer to one of the two choices you can make when a coin is thrown in the air to decide something ▪ *Is it heads or tails?* [=did the coin land with heads or tails facing up?] **5** *head* [*plural*] : individual animals ▪ *100 head of cattle* **6** [*C*] **a** : an end of something that is like a head in shape or position ▪ *the head of the bed/table* ▪ *the head* [=*front*] *of the line* ▪ *the head* [=*top*] *of a nail* **b** : the part of an object that hits or touches something else ▪ *the hammer's head* **7** [*U*] : the position of being a leader ▪ *She's at the head of her class.* [=she is the best student in her class] **8** [*C*] : a person who leads or directs a group or organization ▪ *the head of the department* ▪ **heads of state** [=leaders of countries] ▪ *the head coach/chef* **9** [*C*] : a tight mass of leaves or flowers on a plant ▪ *a head of lettuce* **10** [*C*] : the place where a stream or river begins ▪ *the head of the Nile* **11** [*singular*] : pressure caused by the water or steam in a machine ✧ When an engine has a *full head of steam*, it has a full amount of power. This phrase is often used figuratively to describe something that is moving forward in a fast and powerful way. ▪ *The project started slowly, but now we have a full head of steam.* **12** [*C*] : the bubbles that form on the top of some liquids (such as beer) ▪ *the foamy head on a beer* **13** [*singular*] : the point at which a situation becomes very serious or when action is required ▪ *Things came to a head when the workers threatened to go on strike.* — **a big/swelled head** *informal* : an overly high opinion of yourself ▪ *Their compliments gave him a big head.* — **butt heads** see ³BUTT — **get it through someone's head** : to cause someone to learn and remember something ▪ *She's finally gotten it through their heads that she doesn't eat meat.* — **get it through your head** : to accept or understand (something) ▪ *He can't seem to get it through his head that I'm not interested.* — **go over someone's head** : to discuss something with a person who is higher in rank than someone else ▪ *He went over his supervisor's head to complain about the policy to the company's president.* — **go to your head** **1** *of an alcoholic drink* : to make you feel drunk ▪ *The wine went straight to my head.* **2** : to make you believe that you are better than other people ▪ *He has never let his fame go to his head.* — **head and shoulders above** — used to say that someone or something is much better than others ▪ *They are/stand head and shoulders above the competition.* — **head in the sand** ✧ If you *bury/have/hide (etc.) your head in the sand*, you ignore something unpleasant that you should be dealing with. — **head over heels** : very deeply in love ▪ *We were head over heels (in love).* — **heads roll** *informal* ✧ If you say that *heads will roll*, you mean that people will be severely punished or will lose their jobs because of something that has happened. — **hit the nail on the head** see ¹HIT — **hold up your head** or **hold your head (up) high** : to be proud : to not feel ashamed ▪ *They lost, but they can still hold their heads high because they tried their best.* — **keep your head** : to remain calm ▪ *She can keep her head in a crisis.* — **keep your head above water** : to avoid financial failure while having money problems ▪ *We can barely keep our heads above water these days.* — **keep your head down** *informal* : to behave in a quiet way that does not attract attention — **lose your head** : to become very upset or angry ▪ *He lost his head and said some things he regrets.* — **not make head or/nor tail of** *or US* **not make heads or/nor tails (out) of** *infor-*

mal : to be unable to understand (something) ▪ *I couldn't make heads or tails of her reaction.* — **off the top of your head** see ¹TOP — **off your head** *Brit, informal* : crazy or foolish — **on your head** **1** : with the upper and lower parts of your body reversed in position ▪ *Can you stand on your head?* **2** : in or into great disorder ▪ *News of the discovery turned the scientific world on its head.* **3** — used to say that you will be blamed for something ▪ *If we miss our deadline, it will be on your head.* [=it will be your fault] — **out of your head** *informal* : unable to act or think in a reasonable and controlled way because of drunkenness or strong emotion ▪ *He was (drunk) out of his head.* [=he was extremely drunk] — **over your head** : beyond your understanding or ability ▪ *The technical details were over my head.* [=too complicated for me to understand] — **put your heads together** : to think of a solution to a problem with another person ▪ *We can solve this problem if we just put our heads together.* — **rear/raise its ugly head** ✧ If something bad *rears/raises its ugly head*, it suddenly becomes obvious or causes trouble. ▪ *Inflation threatened to rear its ugly head.* — **scratch your head** *informal* : to be unable to understand the reason for something ▪ *His odd behavior left us all scratching our heads.* — **scream/shout/yell/laugh (etc.) your head off** *informal* : to scream/shout/yell/laugh (etc.) very loudly or for a long time — **shake your head** see ¹SHAKE — **turn heads** : to attract attention or notice ▪ *The car's design is bound to turn heads.* — **headless** /ˈhɛdləs/ *adj* ▪ *a headless body*

²**head** *vb* **1** [*T*] **a** : to be the leader of (something) ▪ *She heads (up) the committee.* **b** : to be first on (a list) ▪ *He heads the list of job candidates.* **2** [*I*] : to go in a specified direction or toward a specified place ▪ *She headed (for) home.* ▪ *Where are you heading/headed?* [=where are you going?] ▪ *He headed off to work.* (*figurative*) *If you keep acting like this, you'll be heading/headed for trouble!* **3** [*T*] *soccer* : to hit (the ball) with your head — **head off** [*phrasal vb*] **head (someone or something) off** or **head off (someone or something)** : to stop (someone or something) from moving forward ▪ *We can head them off at the pass.* (*figurative*) *They tried to head off* [=prevent] *the crisis by raising interest rates.*

head·ache /ˈhɛdˌeɪk/ *n* **1** [*C/U*] : an ache or pain in the head ▪ *I'm starting to get a headache.* **2** [*C*] : a difficult or annoying situation or problem ▪ *The city's biggest headache is traffic.*

head·band /ˈhɛdˌbænd/ *n* [*C*] : a band of cloth or some other material worn on or around your head

head·board /ˈhɛdˌboɚd/ *n* [*C*] : an upright board at the end of a bed where you rest your head

head count *n* [*C*] : an act of counting the number of people at a place, event, etc. ▪ *She did a head count to make sure all the students were on the bus.*

head·dress /'hɛd,drɛs/ n [C] : a decorative covering for your head • a ceremonial headdress

head·ed /'hɛdəd/ adj : having a head or heads of a specified type or number • a curly-headed child [=a child with curly hair] • a two-headed ax

head·er /'hɛdə/ n [C] 1 : a word, phrase, etc., that is placed at the beginning of a document, passage, etc. — compare FOOTER 2 informal : a fall in which your head hits the ground • She tripped on the rock and took a header. 3 soccer : a shot or pass made by hitting the ball with your head

head·first /'hɛd'fəst/ adv 1 : with the head leading • She dove into the water headfirst. 2 : without taking time to think about your actions • She rushed into the relationship headfirst. — **headfirst** adj • a headfirst dive

head·gear /'hɛd,giə/ n [U] : things (such as hats and helmets) that are worn on your head • protective headgear

head·hunt·ing /'hɛd,hʌntɪŋ/ n [U] : the activity of finding people who are suited for a particular job • They retained a head-hunting firm to fill the position of chief executive officer. — **head·hunt·er** /'hɛd,hʌntə/ n [C] • They used a head-hunter to find candidates for the job.

head·ing /'hɛdɪŋ/ n [C] 1 : the direction in which a ship or aircraft points • What is your current heading? 2 : a word, phrase, etc., that is placed at the beginning of a document, passage, etc. • chapter headings

head·lamp /'hɛd,læmp/ n [C] : HEADLIGHT

head·land /'hɛdlənd/ n : a narrow area of land that sticks out into the sea

head·light /'hɛd,laɪt/ n [C] : a light on the front of a vehicle

¹**head·line** /'hɛd,laɪn/ n 1 [C] : the title written in large letters over a story in a newspaper 2 [plural] : the major news stories reported in newspapers, magazines, or television news programs • He made/grabbed (the) headlines [=became the subject of major news] with his anti-smoking campaign. • The murder investigation has been in the headlines lately.

²**headline** vb -lined; -lin·ing [T] 1 : to provide (a newspaper story) with a headline • The story of his arrest was headlined "Caught!" 2 US : to be the main performer in (a show or concert) • The band is headlining the music festival.

head·lin·er /'hɛd,laɪnə/ n [C] : the main performer in a show or concert

head·long /'hɛd'lɑːŋ/ adv 1 : with the head leading • I dove headlong to the floor. 2 : without taking time to think about your actions • We rushed headlong into marriage. — **head·long** /'hɛd,lɑːŋ/ adj, always before a noun • a headlong rush for the door

head·mas·ter /'hɛd'mæstə, Brit 'hɛd'mɑːstə/ n [C] 1 : a man who is the head of a U.S. private school 2 : a man who is the head of a British school

head·mis·tress /'hɛd'mɪstrəs/ n [C] 1 : a woman who is the head of a U.S. private school 2 : a woman who is the head of a British school

head–on /'hɛd'ɑːn/ adv 1 : with the head or front hitting first • The cars collided head-on. 2 : in a very direct way • confront/meet a challenge head-on — **head–on** adj, always before a noun • a head-on collision

head·phones /'hɛd,foʊnz/ n [plural] : a device that is worn over your ears and used for listening to music, the radio, etc. • a pair/set of headphones

head·quar·ters /'hɛd,kwɔətəz/ n [plural] : a place from which something (such as a business or a military action) is controlled or directed • The company's headquarters is/are in Atlanta. — **head·quar·tered** /'hɛd,kwɔətəd/ adj, not before a noun • The company is headquartered in Atlanta.

head·rest /'hɛd,rɛst/ n [C] : the part of a seat or chair that supports your head

head·room /'hɛd,ruːm/ n [U] : the space between the top of your head and a ceiling or roof when you are standing or sitting • a car with a lot of headroom

head·set /'hɛd,sɛt/ n [C] 1 : a pair of headphones 2 : a device that holds an earphone and a microphone in place on a person's head

head start n [C] 1 : an advantage given to someone at the beginning of a race • They gave me a five-minute head start. 2 : an advantage that you have or get when you are starting to do something • She took some extra classes to get a head start in/on her career.

head·stone /'hɛd,stoʊn/ n [C] : a stone that marks the place where a dead person is buried and that usually has the person's name and birth and death dates on it

head·strong /'hɛd,strɑːŋ/ adj : very stubborn • The child is very headstrong.

¹**heads–up** /'hɛdz'ʌp/ n [singular] US, informal : a message that tells or warns someone about something that is going to happen • She gave him a heads-up that the company's president will be visiting the office.

²**heads–up** adj, always before a noun, US, informal : showing that you are very aware of what is happening around you • a heads-up play by the first baseman

head–to–head adv : in a direct competition or contest • The two teams will compete/go head-to-head for the championship. — **head–to–head** adj • a head-to-head competition

head·wait·er /'hɛd'weɪtə/ n [C] : a waiter who is in charge of other waiters in a restaurant

head·wa·ters /'hɛd,wɑːtəz/ n [plural] : the beginning and upper part of a stream or river • the headwaters of the Amazon

head·way /'hɛd,weɪ/ n — **make headway** : to move forward or make progress • They've recently made some headway in their search for a cure.

head·wind /'hɛd,wɪnd/ n [C] : a wind that is blowing toward something (such as a ship or an airplane) as it moves forward

head·word /'hɛd,wɚd/ n [C] : a word placed at the beginning of an entry in a dictionary, encyclopedia, etc.

heady /'hɛdi/ adj **head·i·er; -est** : causing feelings of excitement or dizziness • a heady aroma • The plane soared to heady heights.

heal /'hi:l/ vb **1** [I] : to become healthy or well again • The cut healed slowly. • After the divorce, he needed time to heal. **2** [T] : to make (someone or something) healthy or well again • The ointment will help heal the wound. — **heal·er** /'hi:lɚ/ n [C]

health /'hɛlθ/ n [U] **1 a** : the condition of being well or free from disease • We nursed him back to health. **b** : the overall condition of someone's body or mind • He's in good/poor health these days. • Smoking is bad for your health. **2** : the condition or state of something • Investors are worried about the company's health. — **health** adj, always before a noun • health insurance/services

health care n [U] : the prevention or treatment of illness by doctors, dentists, psychologists, etc. — **health–care** adj, always before a noun • health-care workers

health club n [C] : a private club where people go to exercise

health food n [C/U] : a food that is believed to be good for your health

health·ful /'hɛlθfəl/ adj : good for your health : HEALTHY • a healthful lifestyle/diet

healthy /'hɛlθi/ adj **health·i·er; -est 1** : having or showing good health • healthy babies • tips for staying healthy • a healthy complexion/appetite **2** : good for your health : HEALTHFUL • healthy living/food **3** : doing well : successful or growing • a healthy economy/company **4** : large in size or amount • a healthy bank account **5** : sensible or natural • a healthy curiosity about the world • a healthy respect for dangerous animals — **health·i·ly** /'hɛlθəli/ adv — **health·i·ness** /'hɛlθinəs/ n [U] — **healthy** adv, informal • He eats healthy.

¹**heap** /'hi:p/ n [C] **1** : a large, disordered pile of things • a heap of old newspapers — see also SCRAP HEAP **2** informal : a great number or large amount of something • He's in a heap of trouble! • heaps of money — **collapse/fall (etc.) in a heap** : to fall very suddenly to the ground and lie there • Overcome by exhaustion, he collapsed in a heap.

²**heap** vb [T] **1 a** : to put (something) in a large pile • They heaped food on our plates. [=they put a lot of food on our plates] • Bags of flour were heaped (up) on the counter. **b** : to put a pile or heap on or in (something) • They heaped our plates with food. • a basket heaped with fruit **2** : to give (praise, blame, etc.) in large amounts • The critics heaped scorn on/upon our efforts.

heap·ing /'hi:pɪŋ/ adj, US **1** : holding a large pile of something • a heaping plateful of rice and beans **2** : holding as much as can be held • one heaping tablespoon of sugar

hear /'hiɚ/ vb **heard** /'hɚd/; **hear·ing 1 a** [T/I] : to be aware of (sound) through the ear • Do you hear that music? • I can't hear you. • She doesn't hear well. [=her hearing is poor] **b** [T] : to listen to (someone or something) • I heard that song on the radio. • The committee will hear witnesses today. **2** [T/I] : to be told (something) • I hear he's leaving town. • He heard the news on the radio. • Didn't you hear? There's a storm heading our way. • I'm sick of hearing about his problems. **3** [T] law : to listen to and make a judgment about (a court case) • The judge will hear the case. — **hear from** [phrasal vb] : to receive a letter, a telephone call, etc., from (someone) • We heard from them yesterday. — **hear of** [phrasal vb] : to be or become aware of the existence of (someone or something) • This is the first time I've ever (even) heard of the singer. • If I hear of a job opening, I'll let you know. — **hear out** [phrasal vb] **hear (someone) out** : to listen to (someone who wants to tell you something) • I know you don't agree but hear me out. — **hear yourself think** informal — used to say that you cannot think clearly because of loud talking, music, etc. • That music is so loud I can't hear myself think. — **never/not hear the end of it** informal — used to say that someone will keep talking about something for a long time • If it turns out that he's right, we'll never hear the end of it. — **not hear of** : to not allow (something) • We tried to pay him for his help, but he wouldn't hear of it. — **hear·er** /'hirɚ/ n [C]

hear·ing /'hirɪŋ/ n **1** [U] : the sense through which a person or animal is aware of sound : the ability to hear • Her hearing is good/poor. • She is hearing-impaired. [=not able to hear well] — see also hard of hearing at ¹HARD **2** [U] : the distance within which someone's voice can be heard • She stayed within hearing of her mother's voice. [=she stayed close enough to her mother to hear her voice] **3** [C] : an opportunity to explain why you did, said, or believe something • They agreed to give both sides a fair hearing. **4** [C] : a meeting or session at which evidence and arguments about a crime, complaint, etc., are presented to a person or group • The committee held public hearings on the bill.

hearing aid n [C] : an electronic device worn in or on the ear to help a person who has hearing problems to hear better

hear·say /'hiɚ,seɪ/ n [U] : something heard from another person • They're supposedly getting married soon, but that's just hearsay.

hearse /'hɚs/ n [C] : a large car that is used for carrying a coffin to a grave

heart /'hɑɚt/ n **1** [C] : the organ in your chest that pumps blood through your veins and arteries • I could feel my heart pounding/racing. • heart failure/disease **2** [C/U] **a** : the heart thought of as the place where emotions are felt • When she heard the news, her heart filled with joy/sorrow. • You're a man **after my own heart**. [=we have similar likes and dislikes] • *He offered to help us out of the goodness of his heart.* [=because he is a good person] • *I didn't have the heart to tell her that I didn't like her singing.* [=I couldn't tell her because I knew that she would be hurt by what I said] • *I decided to follow my heart* [=to do what I truly wanted to do] *and take up acting.* • *Her heart's desire* [=greatest wish] *was to become a movie star.* • *They did the work, but their hearts (just) weren't in it.* [=they did not really feel much interest or enthusiasm about doing it] • *This topic is very close to my heart.* [=I care very much about this subject] • *She's 81 years old, but she's still young at heart.* [=she behaves and thinks like a younger person] **b** : a kind or generous feeling for other people • *a ruler without (a) heart* • *a kind/cold heart* • *She has a big heart.* [=she is a very kind person] — see also CHANGE OF HEART **3** [U] : feelings of love or affection • *It's best not to interfere in matters/affairs of the heart.* • *He was determined to win/steal/capture her heart.* **4** [U] : emotional strength that allows you to continue in a difficult situation • *The team has shown a lot of heart.* • *They never lost heart.* **5** [C] : the central or most important part of something • *the heart of the matter/forest* **6** [C] : a shape that looks like a simple drawing of a heart and that is used as a symbol of love and affection **7 a** [C] : a playing card that is marked with a red heart **b** [plural] : the suit in a deck of playing cards that consists of cards marked by hearts — **break someone's heart** : to cause someone to feel great sorrow or sadness • *He broke her heart when he left her for another woman.* • *He left her with a broken heart.* — **by heart** : from memory • *She knows/learned the entire poem by heart.* [=she learned the poem and can recite it from memory] — **cross my heart (and hope to die)** see ²CROSS — **do your heart good** : to make you feel very happy • *It does his heart good to know that his daughters have become friends.* — **eat your heart out** see EAT — **faint of heart** see ¹FAINT — **from the bottom of your heart** or **from your heart** : in a very sincere way • *He thanked us from the bottom of his heart.* — **have your heart set on (something)** or **set your heart on (something)** ✧ When you *have your heart set on something* or when you *set your heart on something,* you want it very much. • *She has her heart set on a new bicycle.* — **heavy heart** : a feeling of sadness • *She spoke with a heavy heart.* — **light heart** : a feeling of happiness • *He left for home with a light heart.* — **open your heart** **1** : to talk in a very open and honest way about your feelings **2** : to begin to be generous and kind • *We should all open our hearts and do something to help those poor children.* — **sing/dance/play (etc.) your heart out** : to sing/dance/play (etc.) with great energy or effort — **take (something) to heart** : to be deeply affected or hurt by something • *He took their criticism (very much) to heart.* — **to**

your heart's content : as long or as much as you want • *They let him eat and drink to his heart's content.* — **your heart bleeds for** ✧ If *your heart bleeds for* someone, you feel great sadness or pity for that person. — **your heart leaps** ✧ When *your heart leaps,* you become very happy or joyful about something. — **your heart sinks** ✧ When *your heart sinks,* you become sad or disappointed about something.

heart·ache /ˈhɑɚtˌeɪk/ *n* [C/U] : a strong feeling of sadness • *She's had a lot of heartache(s) in her life.*

heart attack *n* [C] : a sudden painful and dangerous condition in which your heart stops beating properly • *a minor/massive heart attack*

heart·beat /ˈhɑɚtˌbiːt/ *n* [C] : the action or sound of the heart as it pumps blood • *irregular/rapid heartbeats* — **in a heartbeat** *US, informal* : without any delay or hesitation • *I'd agree to do it again in a heartbeat.*

heart·break /ˈhɑɚtˌbreɪk/ *n* [C/U] : a very strong feeling of sadness, disappointment, etc. • *He recently suffered a string of romantic heartbreaks.*

heart·break·er /ˈhɑɚtˌbreɪkɚ/ *n* [C] : someone or something that causes you to feel very sad, disappointed, etc. • *The team's loss was a real heartbreaker.*

heart·break·ing /ˈhɑɚtˌbreɪkɪŋ/ *adj* : causing great sadness, disappointment, etc. • *a heartbreaking story/defeat* — **heart·break·ing·ly** *adv*

heart·bro·ken /ˈhɑɚtˌbroʊkən/ *adj* : filled with great sadness • *She was heartbroken when he left her.*

heart·burn /ˈhɑɚtˌbɚn/ *n* [U] : an unpleasant hot feeling in your chest caused by something that you ate

heart·en /ˈhɑɚtn̩/ *vb* [T] : to cause (someone) to feel more cheerful or hopeful • *The team's fans were heartened by the victory.* — **hear·ten·ing** /ˈhɑɚtnɪŋ/ *adj* • *heartening news*

heart·felt /ˈhɑɚtˌfɛlt/ *adj* : deeply felt : very sincere • *heartfelt thanks/sympathy/congratulations*

hearth /ˈhɑɚθ/ *n* [C] : the floor in front of or inside a fireplace • (*literary*) *the comforts of hearth and home* [=the comforts of home]

heart·land /ˈhɑɚtˌlænd/ *n* [C] **1 a** : a central area of land • *Scotland's heartland* **b** : the central area of the U.S. which is known for traditional values • *a politician who is popular in the American heartland* **2** : an area that is the center of an industry or activity • *the heartland of high technology*

heart·less /ˈhɑɚtləs/ *adj* : very cruel • *a heartless person/act*

heart·rend·ing /ˈhɑɚtˌrɛndɪŋ/ *adj* : causing great sadness or sorrow • *a heart-rending story*

heart·sick /ˈhɑɚtˌsɪk/ *adj* : very sad or disappointed • *I was heartsick to learn of their divorce.*

heart·strings /ˈhɑɚtˌstrɪŋz/ *n* [plural] : deep emotions • *That movie really tugs/pulls at your heartstrings.* [=makes you emotional]

heart·throb /ˈhɑɚtˌθrɑːb/ n [C] : an attractive and usually famous man

heart-to-heart /ˈhɑɚtəˈhɑɚt/ adj : very sincere and honest • a heart-to-heart talk

heart·warm·ing /ˈhɑɚtˌwoɚmɪŋ/ adj : causing feelings of happiness • a heart-warming story

heart·y /ˈhɑɚti/ adj **heart·i·er; -est 1** : done or expressed in a very open, cheerful, and energetic way • a hearty welcome/laugh/handshake **2** : strong, healthy, and active • hearty young men • She has a **hearty appetite**. = She's a **hearty eater**. **3** : large enough to satisfy hunger • a hearty meal/soup — **heart·i·ly** /ˈhɑɚtəli/ adv • They ate/laughed heartily. • I'll be heartily [=very] glad when this job is done. — **heart·i·ness** n [U]

¹**heat** /ˈhiːt/ n **1** [U] : energy that causes things to become warmer • the intense heat of a fire **2** [U] : hot weather or temperatures • The crops were damaged by drought and extreme heat. • the 90-degree/midday heat **3** [C/U] : the level of temperature that is used to cook something • The meat was cooked at a high/low heat. **4** [U] chiefly US : a system that is used to provide warmth to a room or building • electric/gas/oil/solar heat [=heating] **5** [U] : the time when emotions are most strongly felt • The crime was committed in the heat of passion. [=when the criminal was very angry] • She said some harsh things in the heat of the moment. [=when she was angry for a short period of time] — see also in the heat of (the) battle at ¹BATTLE **6** chiefly US, informal **a the heat** : pressure to do something • The administration is putting the heat on legislators to approve the tax bill. • She's at her best when the heat is on. **b** [U] : criticism or abuse • He took/got a lot of heat for his decision. **7** [C] : one of several races or contests that are held in order to decide who will be in the final race or contest • The top two runners in each heat will move on to the finals. — see also DEAD HEAT — **in heat** (US) or Brit **on heat** — used to describe a female animal that is ready to have sex and is able to become pregnant • a dog in heat

²**heat** vb [T] : to cause (something) to become warm or hot • I heated the vegetables in the microwave. • They heat their house with a wood stove. — **heat up** [phrasal vb] **1** : to become warm or hot • The day heated up quickly. **2** : to become more active, intense, or angry • Their conversation started to heat up. **3** **heat (something) up** or **heat up (something)** : to cause (something) to become warm or hot • I'll heat up the vegetables.

heat·ed /ˈhiːtəd/ adj **1** : including a system that provides warmth • a heated pool/cabin **2** : marked by excited or angry feelings • a heated argument — **heat·ed·ly** adv

heat·er /ˈhiːtɚ/ n [C] : a machine that heats water or air • a water heater

heath /ˈhiːθ/ n [C] : an area of land that is covered with grass and small shrubs

hea·then /ˈhiːðən/ n, pl **hea·thens** or **heathen** [C] old-fashioned + often offensive : a person who is not religious or who does not practice Christianity, Judaism, or Islam — **heathen** adj • heathen gods/practices

heath·er /ˈhɛðɚ/ n [C] : a low-growing plant of northern areas that has small leaves and tiny white or purplish-pink flowers

heat·ing /ˈhiːtɪŋ/ n [U] : a system that is used to provide warmth to a room or building • a house with electric heating

heat·stroke /ˈhiːtˌstroʊk/ n [U] medical : a serious condition that happens when someone has been in high temperatures for a long time and that causes a person to stop sweating, have a very high body temperature, and become exhausted or unconscious

heat wave n [C] : a period of unusually hot weather

¹**heave** /ˈhiːv/ vb **heaved; heav·ing 1** [T/I] : to lift or pull (something) with effort • We heaved the box (up) onto the table. • The sailors started heaving on the rope. **2** [T] US : to throw (something) with effort • heave a rock **3** [T] : to breathe in and breathe out (a sigh) in a slow or loud way • She heaved a sigh of relief. **4** [I] : to move up and down repeatedly • He stopped running and stood there with his chest heaving. **5** [I] informal : VOMIT

²**heave** n [C] **1** : an act of lifting or pulling something with effort • He gave the rope a heave. **2** : a forceful throw • a long heave down the field

heav·en /ˈhɛvən/ n **1** or **Heaven** [singular] : the place where God lives and where good people go after they die according to some religions **2** [U] : something that is very pleasant or good • The week at the beach was (sheer/pure) heaven. • (chiefly US) The cake tastes like heaven. [=it is delicious] **3 the heavens** : the sky • the brightest star in the heavens **4** — used informally by itself and in phrases to make a statement or question more forceful or to express surprise, anger, etc. • "Have you ever committed a crime?" "Heavens, no!" • **Good heavens!** You startled me. • Who **in heaven's name** could that be? • Who **in heaven's name** could that be? • Turn down that music! — **(a) heaven on earth** : a very pleasant or enjoyable place or situation — **heaven forbid** see FORBID — **heaven help (someone)** see ¹HELP — **heaven knows** see ¹KNOW — **made in heaven** : very good and successful • Theirs was a marriage/match made in heaven. — **move heaven and earth** see ¹MOVE — **thank heaven/heavens** see THANK — see also SEVENTH HEAVEN

heav·en·ly /ˈhɛvənli/ adj **1** always before a noun : appearing or occurring in the sky • the moon, stars, and other heavenly bodies **2** always before a noun : of or relating to heaven • heavenly angels/grace **3** informal : very pleasant or good • The weather was heavenly.

heav·en·ward /ˈhɛvənwɚd/ also chiefly Brit **heav·en·wards** /ˈhɛvənwɚdz/ adv : toward the sky • Lift your eyes heavenward.

heav·i·ly /ˈhɛvəli/ adv **1** : to a great degree : very much ▪ *heavily salted foods* ▪ *He relies heavily on his wife for advice.* ▪ *She drank and smoked heavily.* **2** : in a slow or heavy way ▪ *He sat down heavily on the couch.*

¹**heavy** /ˈhɛvi/ *adj* **heavi·er; -est 1 a** : having great weight : difficult to lift or move ▪ *The box is too heavy.* ▪ *a heavy load* **b** : large in size and weight ▪ *a tall, heavy man* **2** : having a particular weight ▪ *How heavy is it?* [=how much does it weigh?] **3** : unusually great in amount, force, or effect ▪ *Traffic was heavy.* ▪ *heavy winds/bleeding/damage/ penalties* ▪ *She was wearing heavy make-up.* ▪ *She is the heavy favorite to win.* ▪ *the heavy breathing of a tired runner* ▪ *a heavy eater/drinker/smoker* ▪ *heavy drinking/ smoking* **4** : involving a lot of physical effort ▪ *doing the heavy lifting/work* ▪ (figurative) *He does all the heavy lifting.* [=difficult work] **5** : very loud or forceful ▪ *The song has a heavy beat.* ▪ *heavy footsteps* **6** : important and serious ▪ *doing some heavy reading/thinking* **7** : dense and thick ▪ *a heavy beard* ▪ *heavy fog* **8** : made of thick material ▪ *a heavy coat/blanket* **9 a** : showing signs of rain or snow ▪ *heavy weather/clouds* **b** : having large waves ▪ *heavy seas* **10** : large and powerful ▪ *heavy machinery/artillery* **11** *of a person's accent* : very easy to notice ▪ *She spoke German with a heavy* [=thick] *accent.* — **go heavy on** : to use a lot of (something) ▪ *Go heavy on the sauce, please.* — **heavy heart** ✧ If you have a *heavy heart*, you are sad. ▪ *I announced my decision to leave with a heavy heart.* — **heavy on** : having or using a large amount of (something) ▪ *His movies are heavy on action.* — **heavy sleeper** : someone who does not wake up easily — **heavy with** : carrying or having a large amount of (something) ▪ *Her comments were heavy with irony.* — **hot and heavy** see HOT — **make heavy weather of** *Brit, informal* : to treat (something) in a way that makes it seem more important or difficult than it really is ▪ *an actor who makes heavy weather of what should be a simple scene* — **heavi·ness** *n* [*U, singular*] — **heavy** *adv* ▪ *The smoke hung/lay heavy in the air.*

²**heavy** *n, pl* **heav·ies** [*C*] **1** : a bad person in a movie or play : VILLAIN ▪ *He played the heavy in that movie.* **2** *US, informal* : a person or thing that is serious, important, or powerful : HEAVYWEIGHT ▪ *an industry heavy*

heavy–du·ty /ˈhɛviˈduːti, *Brit* ˈhɛviˈdjuːti/ *adj* **1** : designed to do difficult work without breaking ▪ *heavy-duty vehicles/machines* **2** *US* : very intense or serious ▪ *Her plan is facing some heavy-duty opposition.*

heavy–hand·ed /ˈhɛviˈhændəd/ *adj* **1** : dealing with people or problems in a severe or harsh way ▪ *heavy-handed tactics/ measures* **2** : awkward or clumsy ▪ *a writer with a heavy-handed style*

heavy industry *n* [*U*] : the production of goods (such as coal or steel) that are used to make other goods — compare LIGHT INDUSTRY

heavy metal *n* **1** [*U*] : a type of loud rock music that has a strong beat **2** [*C/U*] *technical* : a metal that is very dense and heavy ▪ *lead, gold, and other heavy metals*

heavy–set /ˈhɛviˈsɛt/ *adj* : having a heavy and often somewhat fat body ▪ *a short, heavyset man*

heavy·weight /ˈhɛviˌweɪt/ *n* [*C*] **1** : a fighter in the heaviest class of boxers ▪ *the heavyweight champion* **2** : a person or thing that is very important and powerful ▪ *Their company is one of the industry's heavyweights.* **3** : something that is heavy ▪ *heavyweight cotton/paper*

He·brew /ˈhiːbruː/ *n* **1** [*C*] : a member of an ancient group of people who lived mostly in the kingdom of Israel and practiced Judaism **2** [*U*] **a** : the language of the ancient Hebrews **b** : the language of modern Israel — **Hebrew** *adj* ▪ *the Hebrew people/Bible*

heck /ˈhɛk/ *n* [*U*] *informal* — used as a more polite form of *hell* ▪ *"Did you give her any money?" "Heck, no!"* ▪ *I decided to go just for the heck of it.* ▪ *Let's get the heck out of here.* ▪ *What the heck was that?*

heck·le /ˈhɛkəl/ *vb* **heck·led; heck·ling** [*T/I*] : to shout annoying or rude comments or questions at (someone) ▪ *The players were being heckled by the fans.* — **heck·ler** /ˈhɛklɚ/ *n* [*C*]

hect·are /ˈhɛkˌteɚ/ *n* [*C*] : a unit of area in the metric system that is equal to 10,000 square meters or 2.47 acres

hec·tic /ˈhɛktɪk/ *adj* : very busy and filled with activity ▪ *a hectic schedule/day*

hec·tor /ˈhɛktɚ/ *vb* [*T*] : to criticize or question (someone) in a threatening way ▪ *The attorney was hectoring the witness.*

he'd /ˈhiːd, id/ — used as a contraction of *he had* or *he would* ▪ *He'd* [=he had] *never been there before.* ▪ *He'd* [=he would] *do it if he could.*

¹**hedge** /ˈhɛdʒ/ *n* [*C*] **1** : a row of shrubs or small trees that are planted close to each other in order to form a boundary **2** : something that provides protection or defense ▪ *She invests her money as a hedge against inflation.*

²**hedge** *vb* **hedged; hedg·ing 1** [*T*] : to surround (an area) with a hedge ▪ *The garden is hedged by shrubs.* **2** [*T/I*] : to avoid giving a promise or direct answer ▪ *She hedged when she was asked to support the campaign.* — **hedge against** [*phrasal vb*] : to protect yourself from (something) ▪ *They hedge against inflation by investing their money.* — **hedge around/ about** [*phrasal vb*] **hedge (something) around/about** *Brit* : to limit or restrict (something) ▪ *a rule that is hedged around by/with exceptions* — **hedge in** [*phrasal vb*] **hedge in (something or someone) or hedge (something or someone) in 1** : to form a boundary around (something) ▪ *a field hedged in by trees* **2** : to surround or restrict (someone) in a way that prevents free movement or action ▪ *We were hedged in by their regulations.* — **hedge your bets** : to do things that will prevent great loss or failure if future events do not happen as you plan or

hope • *They decided to hedge their bets by putting half their money in stocks and the other half in bonds.*

hedge fund *n* [C] *finance* : a group of investors who take financial risks together in order to try to earn a lot of money

hedge·hog /'hɛdʒ,hɑːg/ *n* [C] : a small, brown animal of Europe, Asia, and Africa that has sharp spines on its back

hedge·row /'hɛdʒ,rou/ *n* [C] : a row of shrubs or trees that form the boundary of an area

he·do·nism /'hiːdə,nɪzəm/ *n* [U] : the belief that pleasure or happiness is the most important goal in life — **he·do·nist** /'hiːdənɪst/ *n* [C] — **he·do·nis·tic** /,hiːdə'nɪstɪk/ *adj* • *a hedonistic lifestyle*

¹**heed** /'hiːd/ *vb* [T] : to pay attention to (advice, a warning, etc.) • *She failed to heed the warnings.*

²**heed** *n* [U] : attention or notice • *He failed to **take heed** of our advice.* = *He failed to **pay heed** to our advice.* [=he failed to follow our advice] — **heed·less** /'hiːdləs/ *adj* • *They remain heedless of their own safety.* • *the heedless use of natural resources* — **heed·less·ly** *adv*

¹**heel** /'hiːl/ *n*   **1** [C] : the back part of your foot that is below the ankle   **2** a [C] : the part of a shoe or sock that covers the heel of your foot   **b** [C] : the part of the bottom of a shoe or boot that is under the heel of your foot • *shoes with low/high heels*   **c** [*plural*] *informal* : shoes with high heels • *She was wearing heels.*   **3** [C] : the part of the inside of your hand that is closest to your wrist   **4** [C] : the end of a loaf of bread   **5** [C] *old-fashioned* : a bad or selfish man • *He acted like a heel.* — **at someone's heels** : following someone very closely • *The dog was (nipping) at my heels.* — **cool your heels** *informal* : to wait for someone or something • *We had to sit and cool our heels when our flight was delayed.* — **dig in your heels** see ¹DIG — **drag your heels** see ¹DRAG — **head over heels** see ¹HEAD — **kick up your heels** see ¹KICK — **on someone's or something's heels** **1** ✧ If you are *(close/hard/hot)* on someone's or something's heels, you are chasing or following that person or thing very closely. **2** ✧ If something comes or follows *close/hard/hot* on something's heels, it happens very soon afterward. • *Her second movie followed close on the heels of her first one.* — **to heel** **1** : to a position that is close behind • *She called the dog to heel.* **2** : into a controlled or obedient condition • *We hope these measures will help to **bring inflation to heel**.* [=will help to control inflation] — **under heel** ✧ If you are *under the heel* of someone, *under someone's heel*, or (*US*) *under heel*, you are completely controlled by another person, group, etc. — see also ACHILLES' HEEL

²**heel** *vb* [I]   **1** — used as a command to tell a dog to walk next to you   **2** *of a boat or ship* : to lean to one side • *The boat heeled (over).*

¹**heft** /'hɛft/ *n* [U] : weight or heaviness • *the heft of a good hammer*

²**heft** *vb* [T] *chiefly US* : to lift (something) up • *He hefted the suitcase (up) onto the bed.*

hefty /'hɛfti/ *adj* **heft·i·er; -est** **1** : large and heavy • *a hefty book* : big and strong • *hefty football players* **2** : very large • *a hefty amount/fee* **3** : very forceful • *a hefty kick/shove*

heif·er /'hɛfə/ *n* [C] : a young female cow that has not had a calf

height /'haɪt/ *n*   **1** [C/U] : a measurement of how tall a person or thing is • *What's the height of the building?* • *a woman of average height* • *He is six feet in height.* **2** [C] : the distance above a level or surface • *The height of the ceiling is eight feet.* [=the ceiling is eight feet above the floor] **3** [C] : a great distance above the ground • *I'm afraid of heights.* **4** [*singular*] : the most advanced or extreme point of something • *During the height of the violence, dozens of people lost their lives.* • *He was **at the height of** his fame when he died.* **5** [*plural*] : very good or successful levels • *Her popularity rose to great heights.* **6** *the height of* — used to say that something is an extreme example of something • *It was the height of stupidity to quit the team.*

height·en /'haɪtn/ *vb* [T/I] : to increase the amount, degree, or extent of (something) • *This tragedy has heightened our awareness of the need for improved safety measures.* • *Tensions between the two groups have heightened.*

hei·nous /'heɪnəs/ *adj* : very bad or evil • *heinous crimes*

heir /'eə/ *n* [C] **1** : a person who has the legal right to receive the property of someone who dies • *She is the sole heir to her family's fortune.* **2** : a person who has the right to become a king or queen or to claim a title when the person holding it dies

heir apparent *n, pl* **heirs apparent** [C] **1** : an heir whose right to receive money, property, or a title cannot be taken away **2** : a person who is very likely to have a job or position after the person who has it now leaves • *The coach named her as his assistant as her heir apparent.*

heir·ess /'erəs/ *n* [C] : a girl or woman who inherits a large amount of money

heir·loom /'eə,luːm/ *n* [C] : a valuable object that is owned by a family for many years and passed from one generation to another

heist /'haɪst/ *n* [C] *chiefly US, informal* : an act of stealing something from a bank or store • *a bank/jewel heist*

held *past tense of* ¹HOLD

helices *plural of* HELIX

he·li·cop·ter /'hɛlə,kɑːptə/ *n* [C] : an aircraft that can stay in the air without moving forward and that has metal blades that turn around on its top

he·li·pad /'hɛlə,pæd/ *n* [C] : a special area where a helicopter can take off and land

he·li·port /'hɛlə,poət/ *n* [C] : a small airport that is designed for use by helicopters

he·li·um /'hiːljəm/ *n* [U] : a chemical element that is a colorless gas, that is lighter than air, and that is often used to fill balloons

he·lix /ˈhiːlɪks/ *n, pl* **-li·ces** /ˈhɛlə₁siːz/ *also* **-lix·es** [C] : the shape formed by a line that curves around and along a central line : SPIRAL — see also DOUBLE HELIX — **he·li·cal** /ˈhɛlɪkəl/ *adj*

hell /ˈhɛl/ *n* **1** *or* **Hell** [*singular*] : the place where the devil lives and where evil people go after they die according to some religions **2** [*U, singular*] : a very difficult or unpleasant situation or experience ▪ *He went through hell during his divorce.* ▪ *The pain has made her life a living hell.* **3** *informal + impolite* — used to express anger, annoyance, etc. ▪ *Hell, I don't know why he did it!* — **all hell breaks loose** *informal* — used to describe what happens when violent, destructive, and confused activity suddenly begins ▪ *All hell broke loose when they announced the decision.* — **as hell** *informal + somewhat impolite* — used to make a statement more forceful ▪ *It was (as) funny as hell.* [=it was very funny] — **catch hell** *chiefly US, informal + somewhat impolite* : to be yelled at or criticized in a very angry and severe way ▪ *She caught hell (from her boss) for coming in late.* — **for the hell of it** *informal + somewhat impolite* : for the fun of doing something without a particular reason ▪ *Just for the hell of it, I decided to go.* — **give (someone) hell** *informal + somewhat impolite* : to yell at or criticize (someone) in an angry way ▪ *Her boss gave her hell for being late.* — **go to hell** *informal + impolite* **1** — used to show that you are very angry with someone ▪ *He told his boss to go to hell.* **2** : to fail completely ▪ *The economy is going to hell.* — **hell of a** *informal + somewhat impolite* **1** — used to make a statement more forceful ▪ *It was one hell of a good fight.* [=it was a very good fight] **2** : very good ▪ *She's a hell of a player.* **3** : very bad or difficult ▪ *This is a hell of a mess.* — **hell on** *US, informal + somewhat impolite* — used to describe something that causes a lot of damage or trouble ▪ *Running can be hell on your knees.* [=can do a lot of harm to your knees] — **hell to pay** see ¹PAY — **in hell** *informal + impolite* — used to make a statement more forceful ▪ *There is no way in hell I'm going!* **2** *or* **in the hell** *US* — used to make a question more forceful ▪ *What in (the) hell is wrong now?* — **like a bat out of hell** see ¹BAT — **like hell** *informal + impolite* **1** : very much ▪ *My back hurts like hell.* **2** : with a lot of energy and speed ▪ *run like hell* **3** : very bad ▪ *This place looks like hell.* **4** — used to say in an angry and forceful way that you will not do something, do not agree, etc. ▪ *"You're coming with me!" "Like hell I am!"* — **raise hell** *informal + somewhat impolite* **1** : to complain in a loud or angry way **2** : to behave wildly and make a lot of noise ▪ *getting drunk and raising hell* — **the hell** *informal + impolite* **1** — used to make a statement or question more forceful ▪ *What the hell is going on?* **2** — used to say in an angry and forceful

way that you will not do something, do not agree, etc. ▪ *"It's your fault!" "The hell it is!"* — **the hell out of** *informal + impolite* — used for emphasis after words like *scare, frighten,* and *beat* ▪ *That movie scared the hell out of me.* [=scared me very badly] — **to hell with** *or* **the hell with** *informal + impolite* — used to say in a forceful and angry way that you do not care about someone or something ▪ *To hell with them! I'll do what I want to do!* — **what the hell** *informal + impolite* **1** — used to express anger, surprise, etc. ▪ *What the hell! Just what do you think you're doing!?* **2** — used to say that you are not worried about or bothered by something ▪ *We lost a little money, but what the hell, it's not a big deal.*

he'll /ˈhiːl, hɪl/ — used as a contraction of *he will*

hell–bent /ˈhɛlˌbɛnt/ *adj* : very determined to do something especially when the results might be bad — usually + *on* ▪ *He's hell-bent on (getting) revenge.*

Hel·len·ic /hɛˈlɛnɪk/ *adj* : of or relating to ancient Greek culture

hell·hole /ˈhɛlˌhoʊl/ *n* [C] *informal* : a very dirty or unpleasant place

hell·ish /ˈhɛlɪʃ/ *adj* : very bad, unpleasant, or shocking ▪ *hellish living conditions*

hel·lo /həˈloʊ/ *n, pl* **-los 1** — used as a greeting ▪ *Hello, my name is Linda.* **2** [C] : the act of saying the word *hello* to someone as a greeting ▪ *They welcomed us with a warm hello.* **3** — used when you are answering the telephone ▪ *Hello. Who's this?* [=who is calling?] **4** — used to get someone's attention ▪ *Hello? Is anybody here?* **5** — used to express surprise ▪ *Well, hello! What do we have here?*

helm /ˈhɛlm/ *n* **1** [C] : a handle or wheel that is used to steer a ship or boat **2** [*singular*] : a position of full control or authority in an organization ▪ *She took the helm of the university.* ▪ *He left after only a year at the helm of the corporation.*

hel·met /ˈhɛlmət/ *n* [C] : a hard hat that is worn to protect your head — **hel·met·ed** /ˈhɛlmətəd/ *adj* ▪ *helmeted warriors*

helms·man /ˈhɛlmzmən/ *n, pl* **-men** /-mən/ [C] : a person who steers a ship or boat

¹**help** /ˈhɛlp/ *vb* **1** [*T/I*] : to do something that makes it easier for someone to do a job, to deal with a problem, etc. ▪ *Let me help you with that box.* ▪ *help a child with her homework* = *help a child (to) do her homework* ▪ *Help (me)! I'm drowning!* **2** [*T/I*] : to make something more pleasant or easier to deal with ▪ *She took an aspirin to help her headache.* ▪ *It helps to know you care.* **3** [*T*] **a** : to give (yourself or another person) food or drink ▪ *There's plenty of food, so help yourself.* — often + *to* ▪ *He helped his guest to a glass of wine.* **b** *informal* : to take something for (yourself) without permission ▪ *He helped himself to the money.* — **can help** ✧ If you **can help something**, you can prevent it from happening. ▪ *It won't happen again. At least not if I can help it.* [=if I can prevent it] — **cannot help** ✧ If you *cannot help* something, you cannot

stop or prevent yourself from doing something. ▪ *I can't help loving you.* ▪ *We couldn't help laughing.* = *We couldn't help but laugh.* ▪ *I know I shouldn't eat any more, but I can't help myself.* ▪ *I know I shouldn't be angry, but I can't help it—it's just the way I feel.* ▪ *It's too bad that we have to leave, but it can't be helped.* — **God/Lord/heaven help (someone)** — used to express strong feelings of worry or concern about what is happening or could happen ▪ *If he ever gets control of the country, Lord help us!* — **help out** [*phrasal vb*] **help out** or **help (someone) out** or **help out (someone)** : to do something so another person's job or task is easier ▪ *I can't do this myself. Won't someone please help me out?* ▪ *I sometimes help out in the kitchen.* — **so help me (God)** — used to stress that a statement is serious and truthful ▪ *I'm going on a diet and, so help me, this time I'll stick to it!* — **help·er** /ˈhɛlpɚ/ *n* [C]

²**help** *n*, *pl* **help** **1** [U] **a** : activities or efforts that make it easier to do a job, deal with a problem, etc. ▪ *He thanked us for our help.* ▪ *The situation is beyond help.* [=nothing can be done to improve the situation] **b** : something (such as money or advice) that is given to someone who needs it ▪ *I couldn't have bought this house without financial help.* **2** [*singular*] : someone or something that makes it easier to do a job, deal with a problem, etc. ▪ *You haven't been a help to me.* = *You've been (of) no help to me.* [=you haven't helped me] **3** [*plural*] : servants or paid workers ▪ *The help have already left for the day.* ▪ (*US*) *the help wanted ads* [=the part of the newspaper in which jobs are advertised] — **help·ful** /ˈhɛlpfəl/ *adj* : a helpful person/suggestion [=a person/suggestion that gives help to someone] — **help·ful·ly** *adv* — **help·ful·ness** *n* [U]

help·ing /ˈhɛlpɪŋ/ *n* [C] : an amount of food that is put on a plate at one time : SERVING ▪ *two helpings of carrots*

helping hand *n* [C] : help or assistance ▪ *She offered to lend/give a helping hand.* [=to help]

helping verb *n* [C] *grammar* : AUXILIARY VERB

help·less /ˈhɛlpləs/ *adj* **1** : not able to defend yourself ▪ *a helpless baby* **2** : unable to do something to make a situation, task, etc., better or easier ▪ *I feel helpless. Isn't there anything I can do?* **3** : not able to control something or to be controlled ▪ *helpless rage* ▪ *The crowd was helpless with laughter.* — **help·less·ly** *adv* — **help·less·ness** *n* [U]

help·mate /ˈhɛlpˌmeɪt/ *n* [C] *old-fashioned* : a person who is a companion and helper; *especially* : WIFE

hel·ter-skel·ter /ˌhɛltɚˈskɛltɚ/ *adv* : in a confused and careless way ▪ *The children raced helter-skelter through the house.* — **helter-skelter** *adj*

¹**hem** /ˈhɛm/ *n* [C] : the edge of a piece of cloth that is folded back and sewn down ▪ *the hem of a dress*

²**hem** *vb* **hemmed; hem·ming** [T] : to sew down a folded edge of cloth on (some-

thing) ▪ *The curtains need to be hemmed.* — **hem and haw** *chiefly US, informal* : to stop often and change what you are saying ▪ *She hemmed and hawed as she before answering the question.* — **hem in** [*phrasal vb*] **hem (someone or something) in** or **hem in (someone or something)** : to surround (someone or something) very closely ▪ *He was hemmed in by reporters.* ▪ (*figurative*) *He felt hemmed in by the school's rules.* [=he felt that the rules prevented him from acting freely]

he-man /ˈhiːˌmæn/ *n*, *pl* **-men** /-ˌmɛn/ [C] *informal* : a man who is very strong and masculine

hemi·sphere /ˈhɛməˌsfiɚ/ *n* [C] **1** : a half of the Earth ▪ *the Northern/Southern Hemisphere* ▪ *the Eastern/Western Hemisphere* **2** : half of a round object **3** *technical* : either of the two halves of the brain ▪ *the right/left cerebral hemisphere* — **hemi·spher·ic** /ˌhɛməˈsfɪrɪk/ or **hemi·spher·i·cal** /ˌhɛməˈsferɪkəl/ *adj*

hem·line /ˈhɛmˌlaɪn/ *n* [C] : the bottom edge of a dress, skirt, or coat

hem·lock /ˈhɛmˌlɑːk/ *n* **1** [C/U] : an evergreen tree with soft wood **2** [U] : a type of poisonous plant that has small white flowers

he·mo·glo·bin (*US*) or *Brit* **hae·mo·glo·bin** /ˈhiːməˌɡloʊbən/ *n* [U] *technical* : the part of blood that contains iron, carries oxygen through the body, and gives blood its red color

he·mo·phil·ia (*US*) or *Brit* **hae·mo·phil·ia** /ˌhiːməˈfɪljə/ *n* [U] : a serious disease that causes a person who has been cut or injured to keep bleeding for a very long time — **he·mo·phil·i·ac** (*US*) or *Brit* **hae·mo·phil·i·ac** /ˌhiːməˈfɪliˌæk/ *n* [C] ▪ *He's a hemophiliac.* [=a person with hemophilia]

¹**hem·or·rhage** (*US*) or *Brit* **haem·or·rhage** /ˈhɛmərɪdʒ/ *n* [C/U] *medical* : a condition in which a person bleeds too much and cannot stop the flow of blood ▪ *The patient suffered a cerebral hemorrhage.* — **hem·or·rhag·ic** (*US*) or *Brit* **haem·or·rhag·ic** /ˌhɛməˈrædʒɪk/ *adj*

²**hemorrhage** (*US*) or *Brit* **haemorrhage** *vb* **-rhaged; -rhag·ing** **1** [I] *medical* : to bleed in a very fast and uncontrolled way **2** [T] : to lose (people, money, etc.) in a very fast and uncontrolled way ▪ *The company is hemorrhaging money.*

hem·or·rhoid (*US*) or *Brit* **haem·or·rhoid** /ˈhɛmˌrɔɪd/ *n* [C] : a swollen and painful area located at or near the anus

hemp /ˈhɛmp/ *n* [U] : a plant that is used to make thick ropes and some drugs (such as hashish and marijuana)

hen /ˈhɛn/ *n* [C] **1** : an adult female chicken **2** : a female bird of any kind

hence /ˈhɛns/ *adv*, *formal* **1** : for this reason ▪ *He knew he could not win the election—hence his decision to withdraw.* **2** : later than the present time ▪ *What will life be like a century hence?*

hence·forth /ˈhɛnsˌfoɚθ/ *adv*, *formal* : from this time forward ▪ *Henceforth, supervisors will report directly to the manager.*

hench·man /ˈhɛntʃmən/ *n*, *pl* **-men** /-mən/ [C] *disapproving* : a trusted follower or supporter who does unpleasant, wrong, or illegal things for a powerful person • *a gangster surrounded by his henchmen*

hen·pecked /ˈhɛnˌpɛkt/ *adj, informal* — used to describe a man who is constantly controlled and criticized by his wife • *a henpecked husband*

hep·a·ti·tis /ˌhɛpəˈtaɪtəs/ *n* [U] : a serious disease of the liver that causes fever and makes your skin and eyes yellow

¹her /ˈhɚ, ə/ *adj, always before a noun, possessive form of* SHE : relating to or belonging to a certain woman, girl, or female animal • *She bought her own house.* • *her parents/name* : made or done by a certain woman, girl, or female animal • *She was jailed for her crime.* — sometimes used figuratively to refer to something thought of as female • *The ship had her hull repaired.* • *the United States and her allies*

²her *pron, objective form of* SHE — used to refer to a certain woman, girl, or female animal as the object of a verb or a preposition • *Tell her I said hello.* • *I gave the book to her.*

¹her·ald /ˈhɛrəld/ *vb* [T] **1** : to be a sign of (something that is beginning to happen or will happen soon) • *Rain heralds the arrival of spring.* **2** : to greet (someone or something) with enthusiasm • *She is being heralded as the year's best new author.*

²herald *n* [C] *formal* **1** : a sign that something will happen • *The early flowers are heralds of spring.* **2** : an official messenger in the past

her·ald·ry /ˈhɛrəldri/ *n* [U] *formal* : the activity of creating or studying coats of arms and of tracing and recording family histories — **he·ral·dic** /hɛˈrældɪk/ *adj*

herb /ˈɚb, *Brit* ˈhɑːb/ *n* [C] : a plant or a part of a plant that is used as medicine or to give flavor to food

her·ba·ceous /ɚˈbeɪʃəs/ *adj* **1** : relating to herbs • *herbaceous flavors/aromas* **2** : relating to a type of plant that has a soft stem • *herbaceous plants/perennials*

herb·al /ˈɚbəl, *Brit* ˈhɑːbəl/ *adj, always before a noun* : made of or relating to herbs • *herbal tea/supplements/medicine*

herb·al·ist /ˈɚbəlɪst, *Brit* ˈhɑːbəlɪst/ *n* [C] : a person who grows, sells, or uses herbs to treat illness

her·bi·cide /ˈhɚbəˌsaɪd/ *n* [C/U] : a chemical used to destroy plants or stop plant growth

her·bi·vore /ˈhɚbəˌvoɚ/ *n* [C] : an animal that only eats plants — **her·biv·o·rous** /hɚˈbɪvərəs/ *adj*

¹herd /ˈhɚd/ *n* **1** [C] : a group of animals that live or are kept together • *herds of cattle/horses/elephants* **2** [C] : a large group of people • *a herd of shoppers* **the herd** : common people • *I refuse to follow the herd.* [=do what other people do] — **ride herd on** see ¹RIDE

²herd *vb* [T/I] : to gather and move (a group of animals or people) • *herd cattle* •

We were herded onto a bus. • *The commuters herded onto the train.* — **herd·er** /ˈhɚdɚ/ *n* [C]

herds·man /ˈhɚdzmən/ *n, pl* **-men** /-mən/ [C] : a person who watches over a herd of cows, sheep, etc.

¹here /ˈhiɚ/ *adv* **1 a** : in this place : at this location • *I like it here.* • *Turn here.* • *At last we're here! = Here we are at last!* • *Have you seen my glasses? Oh, here they are.* **b** : to or into this place • *Come here.* • *Here comes the bus.* [=the bus is coming right now] **2 a** : at this point in a process, activity, story, etc. • *Here the author introduces a new character.* **b** : appearing or happening now • *Winter is here.* **3** — used when you are giving something to someone • *Here's my phone number.* • *"Could you pass the salt?" "Sure, here you are/go."* = *"Sure, here it is."* — **here and now** : at the present time • *problems that exist here and now = problems that exist in the here and now* — **here goes** *or chiefly US* **here goes nothing** *informal* — used when you are about to try doing something new, difficult, or unpleasant • *I've never skied before, so here goes nothing.* — **here is** — used in speech and informal writing to introduce a person, subject, or action • *Here is what I think we should do.* • *Here's how you should hold the golf club.* — **here's to** — used to express good wishes for someone, to say that you are pleased about something, etc., before you drink something; used for making a toast to someone or something • *Here's to the new couple. May they find great happiness together.* — **neither here nor there** : not important or interesting • *What I think is really neither here nor there.*

²here *interj* **1** — used to say that you are present • *When he calls your name, say "here."* **2** — used for emphasis or to attract someone's attention • *Here, let me help you with that.* **3** — used in calling a pet to you • *Here, boy! Good dog!*

³here *n* [U] **1** : this place • *get away from here* **2** : this point • *I've done my part. You take it from here.* [=you are responsible from now on] — **from here on (out)** *US, informal* : from this time forward • *From here on out, I'm making all the decisions.* — **up to here** see ²UP

here·abouts /ˈhiɚəˌbaʊts/ *also US* **here·about** /ˈhiɚəˌbaʊt/ *adv, informal* : near or around this place : in this area • *We don't see a lot of snow hereabouts.*

here·af·ter /hiɚˈæftɚ, *Brit* hiɚˈɑːftɚ/ *adv, formal* : after this : from now on • *Hereafter the two companies will operate in full partnership.* — **the hereafter** : life after death • *belief in the hereafter*

here·by /hiɚˈbaɪ/ *adv, formal* : by means of this act, these words, this document, etc. • *I hereby declare the Olympic Games officially open.*

he·red·i·tary /həˈrɛdəˌteri, *Brit* həˈrɛdətri/ *adj* **1** : passed or able to be passed from parent to child before birth • *hereditary traits/diseases* **2** *formal* **a** : passing from a person who has died to that person's child or younger relative • *hereditary monarchy* **b** : holding a position or title that was passed on from your parent or an older relative ▪ *a hereditary ruler/monarch*

he·red·i·ty /həˈrɛdəti/ *n* [U] *formal* : the natural process by which physical and mental qualities are passed from a parent to a child

here·in /hiəˈrɪn/ *adv, formal* **1** : in this book, document, etc. ▪ *a list of the abbreviations used herein* **2** : in this statement, fact, or detail ▪ *The company faces more competition every year. Herein lies the challenge.*

her·e·sy /ˈhɛrəsi/ *n, pl* **-sies** [C/U] : a belief or opinion that does not agree with the official belief or opinion of a particular religion ▪ *They were accused of heresy.* ▪ *He was preaching dangerous heresies.* ▪ *(figurative) To disagree with the party leadership was heresy.*

her·e·tic /ˈhɛrəˌtɪk/ *n* [C] : someone who believes or teaches something that goes against accepted or official beliefs — **he·ret·i·cal** /həˈrɛtɪkəl/ *adj* ▪ *heretical ideas/writings*

here·to·fore /ˈhiətəˌfoɚ/ *adv, formal* : until this time : before now ▪ *This technology has created heretofore unimaginable possibilities.*

here·with /hiəˈwɪθ, hiəˈwɪð/ *adv, formal* : with this note, letter, document, etc. ▪ *You will find my check herewith.*

her·i·ta·ble /ˈhɛrətəbəl/ *adj, formal* **1** : able to be passed from parent to child before birth ▪ *a heritable disease* **2** *law* : able to be passed from a parent or older relative to a child ▪ *a heritable title*

her·i·tage /ˈhɛrətɪdʒ/ *n* [C] : the traditions, achievements, beliefs, etc., that are part of the history of a group or nation — usually singular ▪ *He's proud of his Polish heritage.*

her·maph·ro·dite /həˈmæfrəˌdaɪt/ *n* [C] : a person, plant, or animal that has both male and female parts

her·met·ic /həˈmɛtɪk/ *adj, formal* : AIRTIGHT 1 ▪ *hermetic seals* — **her·met·i·cal·ly** /həˈmɛtɪkli/ *adv* ▪ *hermetically sealed*

her·mit /ˈhɚmət/ *n* [C] : a person who lives in a simple way apart from others especially for religious reasons

her·mit·age /ˈhɚmətɪdʒ/ *n* [C] : a place where a hermit lives

hermit crab *n* [C] : a type of small crab that lives in the empty shell of another animal

her·nia /ˈhɚnijə/ *n* [C/U] *medical* : a painful condition in which an organ (such as the intestine) pushes through the muscles that are around it ▪ *He was treated for (a) hernia.*

he·ro /ˈhiroʊ/ *n, pl* **he·roes** *or in sense 3* **he·ros** [C] **1 a** : a person who is admired for great or brave acts ▪ *He returned from the war a hero.* **b** : a person and especially a man who is greatly admired ▪ *a football hero* ▪ *My father is my hero.* **2** : the chief male character in a story, movie, etc. **3** *pl usually* **heros** *US* : SUBMARINE SANDWICH

he·ro·ic /hɪˈroʊɪk/ *adj* **1** : of or relating to heroes ▪ *heroic legends* **2** : having or showing great courage ▪ *the soldier's he-*

roic actions **3** : very large or great in size, amount, etc. ▪ *heroic efforts/proportions* — **he·ro·i·cal·ly** /hɪˈroʊɪkli/ *adv*

he·ro·ics /hɪˈroʊɪks/ *n* [*plural*] : actions that show courage ▪ *his heroics on the football field* — often used to describe heroic actions that are regarded as foolish ▪ *This is no time for heroics.*

her·o·in /ˈhɛrəwən/ *n* [U] : a powerful illegal drug that is made from morphine

her·o·ine /ˈhɛrəwən/ *n* [C] **1** : a woman who is admired for great or brave acts or fine qualities ▪ *a national heroine* **2** : the chief female character in a story, play, movie, etc.

her·o·ism /ˈhɛrəˌwɪzəm/ *n* [U] : great courage ▪ *acts of heroism*

her·on /ˈhɛrən/ *n* [C] : a large bird that has long legs and a long neck and bill

hero worship *n* [U] : foolish or excessive admiration of someone

her·pes /ˈhɚpiːz/ *n* [U] : a disease that causes painful spots on the skin

her·ring /ˈhɛrɪŋ/ *n, pl* **herring** *or* **herrings** [C/U] : a fish that lives in the Atlantic Ocean and is often eaten as food — see also RED HERRING

her·ring·bone /ˈhɛrɪŋˌboʊn/ *n* [U] : a pattern used on cloth that consists of rows of parallel lines that slant in opposite directions to form V shapes ▪ *a herringbone design/jacket*

hers /ˈhɚz/ *pron* : that which belongs to or is connected with her ▪ *This book is hers.* [=this book belongs to her] ▪ *Hers is the red book.* [=her book is the red one] ▪ *a friend of hers*

her·self /həˈsɛlf/ *pron* **1** — used as the object of a verb or preposition to refer to a woman, girl, or female animal that has already been mentioned ▪ *She considers herself lucky.* ▪ *She is proud of herself for winning.* ▪ *She wrapped the blanket around herself.* ▪ *"What did he mean?" she said/thought to herself.* ▪ *She had the house (all) to herself.* [=she was alone in the house] ▪ *She wanted to see it for herself.* [=rather than have someone tell her about it] — often used for emphasis ▪ *She told me herself that she would be here.* **2** : her normal or healthy self ▪ *She's not herself today.* — **by herself** **1** : without any help from other people ▪ *She fixed it (all) by herself.* **2** : ALONE ▪ *She lives by herself.*

hertz /ˈhɚts/ *n, pl* **hertz** [C] *technical* : a unit used for measuring the frequency of sound waves — abbr. *Hz*

he's /ˈhiːz, iz/ — used as a contraction of *he is* or *he has* ▪ *He's* [=*he is*] *tall.* ▪ *He's* [=*he has*] *won.*

hes·i·tant /ˈhɛzətənt/ *adj* : slow to act or speak especially because you are nervous or unsure about what to do ▪ *He was hesitant about taking the job.* — **hes·i·tan·cy** /ˈhɛzətənsi/ *n* [U] — **hes·i·tant·ly** *adv*

hes·i·tate /ˈhɛzəˌteɪt/ *vb* **-tat·ed; -tat·ing** **1** [*I*] : to stop briefly before you do something especially because you are nervous or unsure about what to do ▪ *She hesitated and waited for him to say something.* **2** [*T*] : to be unwilling *to do* something because of doubt or uncertainty • *Don't hesitate to call if there is a problem.* — **hes·i·ta·tion** /ˌhɛzəˈteɪʃən/ *n [C/U]* • *I would do it again **without hesitation.** [=with no delay or doubts]

hes·sian /ˈhɛʃən, Brit ˈhesiən/ *n [U] Brit* : BURLAP

het·er·o·ge·neous /ˌhɛtərəˈdʒiːnijəs/ *adj, formal* : made up of parts that are different • *a heterogeneous population* — **het·er·o·ge·ne·i·ty** /ˌhɛtəroʊdʒəˈniːjəti/ *n [U]*

het·ero·sex·u·al /ˌhɛtəroʊˈsɛkʃəwəl/ *adj* : sexually attracted to people of the opposite sex • *He's heterosexual.* — **heterosexual** *n [C]* • *male heterosexuals* — **het·ero·sex·u·al·i·ty** /ˌhɛtəroʊˌsɛkʃəˈwæləti/ *n [U]*

hew /ˈhjuː/ *vb* **hewed**; **hewed** *or* **hewn** /ˈhjuːn/; **hew·ing** *[T]* : to shape (something) by cutting with a sharp tool • *roughly hewn logs/stones* — **hew to** *[phrasal vb] US* : to follow or obey (something) • *a politician who always hews to the party line*

hex /ˈhɛks/ *n [C] chiefly US* : a magical spell that is meant to cause bad luck for someone • *She put a hex on me.* — **hex** *vb [T]* • *She hexed me.*

hexa·gon /ˈhɛksəˌgɑːn, Brit ˈhɛksəgən/ *n [C] mathematics* : a flat shape that has six equal sides — **hex·ag·o·nal** /hɛkˈsægən̩l/ *adj*

hey /ˈheɪ/ *interj* **1** — used to attract someone's attention or to express surprise, joy, or anger • *Hey, wait for me!* **2** — used to indicate that something is not important, that you are not upset about something, etc. • *"We lost." "Hey, you can't win them all."*

hey·day /ˈheɪˌdeɪ/ *n [C]* : the time when someone or something is most successful, popular, etc. — usually singular • *in the heyday of disco*

hi /ˈhaɪ/ *interj* — used as an informal way of saying "hello" • *Hi, how are you?* • *I just called to say hi.*

HI *abbr* Hawaii

hi·a·tus /haɪˈeɪtəs/ *n [C/U]* : a period of time when an activity, program, etc., is stopped • *She is teaching again after a five-year hiatus.* • *(US) She went on hiatus for five years.*

hi·ba·chi /hɪˈbɑːtʃi/ *n [C] chiefly US* : a small grill (sense 1) for cooking food over charcoal

hi·ber·nate /ˈhaɪbɚˌneɪt/ *vb* **-nat·ed; -nat·ing** *[I]* : to spend the winter sleeping or resting • *hibernating bears* — **hi·ber·na·tion** /ˌhaɪbɚˈneɪʃən/ *n [U]*

hi·bis·cus /haɪˈbɪskəs/ *n, pl* **hibiscus** *or* **hi·bis·cus·es** *[C/U]* : a type of shrub that has large colorful flowers

hic·cup *also* **hic·cough** /ˈhɪˌkʌp/ *n* **1 a** *[C]* : a sound in your throat that is caused by a sudden, uncontrolled movement of muscles in your chest **b** *[plural]* : a condition in which you make hiccups repeatedly • *I have (the) hiccups.* **2** *[C] informal* : a small problem, change, or delay • *a hiccup in the power supply* — **hiccup** *vb* **-cuped** *also* **-cupped; -cup·ing** *also* **-cup·ping** *[I]* • *Someone in the audience started hiccuping.*

hick /ˈhɪk/ *n [C] US, informal + disapprov-*

ing : an uneducated person from a small town or the country • *a bunch of hicks* • *a hick town* [=a town where the people are hicks]

hick·o·ry /ˈhɪkəri/ *n, pl* **-ries** **1** *[C]* : a type of tree that has very hard wood **2** *[U]* : the wood of a hickory

¹**hide** /ˈhaɪd/ *vb* **hid** /ˈhɪd/; **hid·den** /ˈhɪdn̩/ *or* **hid; hid·ing** /ˈhaɪdɪŋ/ **1** *[T]* **a** : to put (something) in a place where it cannot be seen or found • *The gifts were hidden (away) under the bed.* • *a hidden microphone/camera* **b** : to prevent (something) from being seen • *Clouds hid the sun all day.* **2 a** *[I]* : to go to or stay at a place where you cannot be seen or found • *She hid under the bed.* • *criminals hiding (out) from the police* • *(figurative) He tried to hide from* [=he tried to avoid] *his responsibilities.* • *The kids' favorite **hiding place** [=their favorite place to hide] is in the attic.* **b** *[T]* : to put (someone or yourself) in a place that cannot be seen or found • *She hid him from the police.* **3** *[T]* : to keep (something) from being known • *He tried to hide his anger.* • *the hidden costs in buying a house* • *hidden agendas/motives*

²**hide** *n [C]* **1** : the skin of a usually large animal **2** *informal* — used to talk about protecting or saving yourself or someone else from harm • *He was protecting his own hide.* [=protecting himself] **3** *chiefly Brit* : ³BLIND **2** — **hide or/nor hair** *informal* : any sign of a particular person or thing • *I haven't seen hide or hair of him.*

hide–and–seek *n [U]* : a children's game in which everyone hides from one player who tries to find them • *play hide-and-seek* — called also *(US)* **hide-and-go-seek**

hide·away /ˈhaɪdəˌweɪ/ *n [C]* : a hidden place • *a romantic hideaway*

hide·bound /ˈhaɪdˌbaʊnd/ *adj, disapproving* : not willing to accept new or different ideas • *hidebound conservatives/traditions*

hid·eous /ˈhɪdijəs/ *adj* : very ugly or disgusting • *hideous furniture* • *a hideous crime* — **hid·eous·ly** *adv* — **hid·eous·ness** *n [U]*

hide·out /ˈhaɪdˌaʊt/ *n [C]* : a place where someone (such as a criminal) hides to avoid being found or captured

hid·ing /ˈhaɪdɪŋ/ *n* **1** *[U]* : the state of being in a place where you cannot be seen or found • *He went into hiding to avoid reporters.* • *He has been in hiding for years.* • *He **came out of hiding** to answer the rumors.* **2** *[C] Brit, informal* : a severe beating • *gave him a good hiding* — **on a hiding to nothing** *Brit, informal* : certain to fail

hi·er·ar·chy /ˈhajəˌrɑːrki/ *n, pl* **-chies** *[C]* **1** : a group that controls an organization and is divided into different levels • *decisions made by the church hierarchy* **2** : a system in which people or things are placed in a series of levels with different importance or status • *She was high/low in the corporate hierarchy.* — **hi·er·ar·chi·cal** /ˌhajəˈrɑːkɪkəl/ *also* **hi·er·ar·chic** /ˌhajəˈrɑːkɪk/ *adj*

hi·ero·glyph·ics /ˌhajərəˈglɪfɪks/ n [plural] : a system of writing that uses characters that look like pictures ▪ Egyptian hieroglyphics — **hi·ero·glyph·ic** /ˌhajərəˈglɪfɪk/ adj

hi–fi /ˈhaɪˈfaɪ/ n 1 [U] : HIGH FIDELITY 2 [C] somewhat old-fashioned : a piece of electronic equipment for reproducing sound in a clear and accurate way ▪ We bought a hi-fi for the bedroom. — **hi–fi** adj

¹high /ˈhaɪ/ adj 1 a : rising or extending upward a great distance ▪ high mountains/buildings b : extending or reaching upward more than other things of the same kind ▪ a high collar/fence ▪ high grass ▪ higher elevations c : located far above the ground or another surface ▪ high altitudes/ceilings ▪ high above the clouds d : having a specified height ▪ a building 100 stories high ▪ The grass was knee-high. [=the grass reached a person's knees] e always before a noun : rising above surrounding land ▪ a house built on high ground 2 a : greater than usual in amount, number, or degree ▪ traveling at a high (rate of) speed ▪ high cholesterol/fevers ▪ high heat/humidity/temperatures ▪ a high salary ▪ The price is too high. ▪ His books are in high demand. b : near or at the top of a range ▪ Temperatures were in the high 80s. [=were around 87–89] 3 a : very favorable ▪ He holds you in high regard/esteem. = He has a high opinion of you. ▪ We were in high spirits. [=very happy and excited] b : very good ▪ products of high quality ▪ high marks/grades ▪ My trip ended on a high note. [=in a pleasant or enjoyable way] ▪ The museum was the high point [=the best part] of our vacation. c : morally good ▪ high ideals/principles 4 : above others in power, importance, etc. ▪ high officials = officials of high rank = high-ranking officials ▪ a high priority ▪ He has friends in high places. [=he has friends who have power and influence] ▪ She is high on the list of candidates for the job. [=she is considered to be a good choice for the job] 5 : not low in sound ▪ a high voice/note 6 always before a noun : very strong or forceful ▪ high winds 7 : having qualities that appeal to intelligent people ▪ high art/comedy 8 always before a noun : of or relating to people who have a lot of money and spend it on travel, good food, etc. ▪ high society/living ▪ high fashion ▪ the high life 9 : very exciting or intense ▪ high adventure ▪ moments of high drama [=very dramatic moments] 10 : having more water than usual ▪ The river is high. 11 not before a noun, informal : intoxicated by alcohol or drugs ▪ He wanted to get high. ▪ high on cocaine ▪ He was as high as a kite. [=very intoxicated] — **in-high** in : containing a large amount of (something) ▪ a diet high in fiber ▪ high on US, informal : excited or enthusiastic about (someone or something) ▪ The coach is very high on this new player. — **it's high time** informal ✧ If it's high time to do something, it is time to do some-

thing that should have been done a long time ago. ▪ It's high time we made some changes.

²high adv 1 : at or to a high place or level ▪ The letters were stacked high on the table. ▪ a high-flying airplane ▪ She aims high. [=she is ambitious] 2 : at a high rate ▪ a high-paid lawyer 3 : at a high price ▪ buy low and sell high 4 informal : in a rich or luxurious manner ▪ He lives pretty high. = He lives pretty high off/on the hog. — **be riding high** see ¹RIDE — **fly high** see ¹FLY — **high and dry** : without help or protection ▪ He left his family high and dry. — **high and low** : EVERYWHERE ▪ They searched/looked high and low for the receipts.

³high n [C] 1 : a high point or level ▪ an all-time/record high ▪ The high [=the highest temperature] today was 75. ▪ the highs and lows [=the good parts and bad parts] of his career 2 informal : a state of intoxication produced by a drug ▪ The high only lasted a few minutes. 3 weather : an area of high atmospheric pressure — **on high** : in the sky ▪ the clouds on high ▪ She heard a voice from on high. [=from God or heaven]

high beam n [U, plural] US : the setting of a vehicle's headlights that makes the brightest light ▪ Turn off/on your high beams. — called also (Brit) full beam

high–born /ˈhaɪˈboən/ adj, formal : born into a family with very high social status ▪ a highborn lady

high·brow /ˈhaɪˌbraʊ/ adj : interested in serious art, literature, ideas, etc. ▪ highbrow literary critics : relating to or intended for highbrow people ▪ highbrow theaters — **highbrow** n [C] ▪ literary highbrows

high chair n [C] : a child's chair with long legs

high–class /ˈhaɪˈklæs, Brit ˈhaɪˈklɑːs/ adj **high·er–class; high·est–class** : very fancy, wealthy, or expensive ▪ a high-class party/neighborhood/clientele

High Court n [singular] : SUPREME COURT

high–definition adj, of a television : having a very clear picture and a wide screen ▪ a new high-definition TV

high–end /ˈhaɪˈɛnd/ adj **high·er–end; high·est–end** US : higher in price and of better quality than most others ▪ high-end stores/clothing

higher learning n [U] : education or learning at a college or university ▪ an institution of higher learning [=a college or university] — called also higher education

higher power n [C] : a spirit or being (such as God) that has great power, knowledge, etc., and that can affect nature and the lives of people ▪ belief in a higher power

high·er–up /ˌhajəˈʌp/ n [C] informal : a person in an organization who has a lot of power and authority ▪ Her hard work impressed the higher-ups.

high·fa·lu·tin /ˌhaɪfəˈluːtn̩/ adj, informal : seeming or trying to seem great or important ▪ highfalutin language

high fidelity n [U] : the very good quality that some recorded sounds or copied images have — **high–fidelity** *adj* • *high-fidelity recordings/speakers*

high finance *n* [U] : activities (such as investing in stocks) that involve large amounts of money

high five *n* [C] *chiefly US, informal* : a gesture in which you slap the palm of your hand against the palm of someone else's hand in the air usually to show that you are happy about an accomplishment • *He gave me a high five.* — **high–five** *vb* **-fived; -fiv·ing** [T/I] *US, informal* • *They high-fived each other.*

high–flown /'haɪ'floʊn/ *adj, disapproving* : using fancy words that are meant to sound important and impressive • *high-flown language*

high–fly·ing /'haɪ'flajɪŋ/ *adj* **1** : flying far above the ground • *high-flying air-planes* **2** : very successful or determined to succeed • *a high-flying young executive* — **high–fli·er** or **high–fly·er** /'haɪ'flajə/ *n* [C] • *young high-fliers in the industry*

high gear *n* [U] *US* : a gear that is used for faster speeds in a vehicle • *She shifted the car into high gear.* — **in/into high gear** : in or into a state of great or intense activity • *The project is now in high gear.* • *The summer travel season will soon kick/move into high gear.*

high ground *n* — **the high ground** : a position in which you have an advantage over others • *She believes she has the moral high ground* [=she believes her position is the morally correct one] *on this issue.*

high–hand·ed /'haɪ'hændəd/ *adj* : not having or showing any interest in the rights, opinions, or feelings of other people • *her high-handed treatment of employees* — **high–hand·ed·ness** *n* [U]

high–heeled *adj, always before a noun* : having a tall heel • *high-heeled shoes/ boots*

high heels *n* [*plural*] : women's shoes that have tall heels

high horse *n* [*singular*] *informal* ✧ If you are on **a/your high horse**, you are talking or behaving in a way that shows that you think you are better than other people or that you know more about something than other people do. • *Oh, climb/get (down) off your high horse.*

high jinks /'haɪˌʤɪŋks/ *n* [*plural*] : wild or playful behavior • *adolescent high jinks*

high jump *n* — **the high jump** : an athletic event in which people compete by trying to jump over a bar that is high above the ground — **high jumper** *n* [C]

high·land /'haɪlənd/ *n* [C] : an area where there are many mountains — usually plural • *the Scottish Highlands* — **highland** *adj* — **high·land·er** /'haɪləndə/ *n* [C]

high–lev·el /'haɪ'lɛvəl/ *adj, always before a noun* : of great importance or high rank • *high-level officials*

¹**high·light** /'haɪˌlaɪt/ *n* [C] **1** : a very interesting, exciting, or important part of

something • *the highlights of our trip* **2** : a light spot or area • *brown hair with gold highlights*

²**highlight** *vb* [T] **1 a** : to make people notice or be aware of (someone or something) • *highlight a problem* **b** : to be a highlight of (something) • *Our trip was highlighted by a day at the beach.* **2** : to mark (something, such as text) with a bright color • *highlight important dates in the book* • (*computers*) *Use your mouse to highlight the text that you want to revise.*

high·light·er /'haɪˌlaɪtə/ *n* [C] : a special pen with brightly colored ink that you can see through

high·ly /'haɪli/ *adv* **1 a** : to a great degree : VERY • *a highly sensitive matter* • *highly respected/successful* **b** : in an amount or number that is greater than usual • *a highly paid executive* **2** : in an approving way • *He speaks highly of you.*

highly strung *adj, Brit* : HIGH-STRUNG

high–mind·ed /'haɪ'maɪndəd/ *adj* : having or showing intelligence and a strong moral character • *high-minded people/intentions* — **high–mind·ed·ly** *adv* — **high–mind·ed·ness** *n* [U]

High·ness /'haɪnəs/ *n* [C] — used as a title for a member of a royal family; used with *his, her,* or *your* • *Her (Royal) Highness the Queen* • *Yes, your Highness.*

high noon *n* [U] *old-fashioned* : exactly noon • *a duel at high noon*

high performance *adj, always before a noun* : better, faster, or more efficient than others • *high performance cars*

high–pitched /'haɪ'pɪtʃt/ *adj* : making a high sound • *a high-pitched squeal/voice*

high–pow·ered /'haɪ'pawəd/ *also* **high-pow·er** /'haɪ'pawə/ *adj* **1** *of a person* : very successful, important, and powerful • *a high-powered executive* **2** : very energetic or forceful • *a high-powered performance* **3** *of a machine or device* : very powerful • *high-powered computers*

high–pressure *adj, always before a noun* **1** : using or involving forceful methods to sell something • *high-pressure salesmen/tactics* **2** : very stressful • *a high-pressure job* **3** : having or using a lot of force or pressure from air, water, etc. • *a high-pressure hose*

high priest *n* [C] **1** *informal* : a person (especially a man) who is a leader in a particular profession, subject, etc. • *the high priest of tennis* **2** : an important priest in some religions

high priestess *n* [C] **1** *informal* : a woman who is a leader in a particular profession, subject, etc. • *a high priestess of jazz* **2** : an important priestess in some religions

high–profile *adj* : attracting a lot of attention in newspapers, on TV, etc. • *a high-profile athlete/job*

high–ranking *adj* : having a high rank or position • *high-ranking officials*

high–rise /'haɪ'raɪz/ *adj, always before a noun* : having many floors or stories • *a high-rise building* — **high rise** *n* [C] • *a fifty-story high rise*

high–risk *adj* **1** : likely to result in failure, harm, or injury • *a high-risk activity/ investment* **2** : more likely than others to get a particular disease, condition, or injury • *high-risk patients*

high road *n* — **the high road** **1** *chiefly US* : a morally proper way of doing something • *She took the high road and refused to spread the rumor.* **2** : an easy way to do something • *the high road to financial success*

high roller *n* [C] *informal* : a person who gambles large amounts of money

high school *n* **1** [C/U] : a school in the U.S. and Canada for older children ✧ Children attend high school for their last three or usually four years of schooling before possibly going to college. **2** [*singular*] — used in the U.K. in the names of secondary schools • *a student at Slough High School for Girls*

high school·er /-'skuːlə/ *n* [C] *US* : a high-school student

high seas *n* [*plural*] : the part of a sea or ocean that is away from land • *The ship was attacked on the high seas.*

high–security *adj, always before a noun* : carefully protected or guarded • *a high-security prison/facility*

High Sheriff *n* [C] *Brit* : SHERIFF 2

high–sound·ing /'haɪ'saʊndɪŋ/ *adj, disapproving* : using words that are meant to sound important and impressive • *high-sounding rhetoric/language*

high–speed /'haɪ'spiːd/ *adj* **1** : designed to go or move very fast • *high-speed trains* **2** : going or moving very fast • *a high-speed chase* • *a high-speed Internet connection*

high–spir·it·ed /'haɪ'spɪrɪtəd/ *adj* : full of energy or enthusiasm • *a high-spirited performance* — **high–spir·it·ed·ness** *n* [U]

high street *n* [C] *Brit* : a town's main street where there are many shops, banks, etc. • *74 High Street*

high–strung /'haɪ'strʌŋ/ *adj, chiefly US* : very nervous or easily upset • *high-strung dogs*

high·tail /'haɪˌteɪl/ *vb* — **hightail it** *US, informal* : to leave a place as quickly as possible • *We hightailed it out of there as quick as we could.*

high tea *n* [C/U] *Brit* : an early evening meal at which tea and often sandwiches are usually served

high tech *also* **hi–tech** /'haɪ'tɛk/ *n* [U] : HIGH TECHNOLOGY — **high–tech** *also* **hi–tech** *adj* • *high-tech devices/methods/businesses*

high technology *n* [U] : the use or creation of new scientific methods or materials especially when they involve computers or electronic devices • *advances in high technology*

high–tension *adj, always before a noun* : HIGH-VOLTAGE 1

high tide *n* [C/U] : the tide when the water is at its highest level • *At high tide the water covers the rocks completely.*

high–toned /'haɪˌtoʊnd/ *adj, chiefly US* **1** : having a high moral or intellectual tone or quality • *a high-toned play* **2** : HIGH-SOUNDING • *high-toned rhetoric*

high treason *n* [U] : TREASON

high–up *n* [C] *Brit* : HIGHER-UP

high–volt·age /'haɪ'voʊltɪdʒ/ *adj* **1** : having or using a very powerful flow of electricity • *high-voltage wires* **2** : having or showing a lot of energy • *a high-voltage performer*

high–water mark *n* [C] **1** : the time when something is most active, successful, etc. • *the high-water mark of her career* **2** : the highest level that water from a river, lake, etc., reaches

high·way /'haɪˌweɪ/ *n* [C] *chiefly US* : a main road that connects cities, towns, etc.

highway robbery *n* [U] *US, informal* : the practice of charging a price that is very high and usually unfair for something • *Charging that much for water is highway robbery!*

high wire *n* [C] : TIGHTROPE • *a high-wire act* [=a circus performance on a high wire]

hi·jack /'haɪˌdʒæk/ *vb* [T] **1 a** : to stop and steal (a moving vehicle) • *He hijacked a truck.* **b** : to steal (something) from a moving vehicle that you have stopped • *They hijacked the load of furs from the truck.* **2** : to take control of (an aircraft) by force • *Terrorists hijacked the plane.* **3** : to take or take control of (something) for your own purposes • *The organization has been hijacked by radicals.* — **hijack** *n* [C] — **hi·jack·er** *n* [C] — **hi·jack·ing** /'haɪˌdʒækɪŋ/ *n* [C]

¹**hike** /'haɪk/ *vb* **hiked; hik·ing** **1** [T/I] : to walk a long distance especially for pleasure or exercise • *We hiked (up) to the camp.* • *hike a trail* **2** [T] : to suddenly increase the cost, amount, or level of (something) • *They hiked the tax on cigarettes.* **3** [T] : to pull or lift (something) with a quick movement • *She hiked up her long skirt and stepped over the curb.* **4** [T] *American football* : to pass (the ball) back to the quarterback at the start of a play • *The center hiked the ball to the quarterback.* — **hik·er** *n* [C] — **hiking** *adj, always before a noun* • *hiking boots* — **hiking** *n* [U] • *We like to go hiking.*

²**hike** *n* [C] **1** : a usually long walk especially for pleasure or exercise • *We went for a hike around the lake.* **2** : a usually sudden increase in the cost, level, or amount of something • *a price/tax/wage hike* — **take a hike** *US, informal + impolite* — used in speech as an angry way of telling someone to leave

hi·lar·i·ous /hɪ'lerijəs/ *adj* : very funny • *a hilarious story* — **hi·lar·i·ous·ly** *adv* — **hi·lar·i·ty** /hɪ'lerəti/ *n* [U] • *a source of great hilarity*

hill /'hɪl/ *n* **1** [C] : a usually rounded area of land that is higher than the land around it but that is not as high as a mountain • *driving down a hill* **2** [C] : a pile of something • *a hill of snow* **3 the Hill** *US, informal* — used to refer to the U.S. Congress • *a new law being debated on the Hill* [=on Capitol Hill] — **a hill of beans** *chiefly US, informal* : something that has little or no value • *These proposals don't amount to a hill of beans.* [=these proposals have no value] — **over the hill** *informal* : old and no longer successful, attractive, etc. ▪ *an over-the-hill ath-lete* — **hilly** /'hɪli/ *adj* **hill·i·er; -est** ▪ *hilly roads/terrain*

hill·bil·ly /'hɪl,bɪli/ *n, pl* **-lies** [C] *US, usually disapproving* : a person who lives in the country and who is often regarded as lacking education

hill·ock /'hɪlək/ *n* [C] : a small hill

hill·side /'hɪl,saɪd/ *n* [C] : the side of a hill ▪ *a hillside town*

hill·top /'hɪl,tɑ:p/ *n* [C] : the top of a hill ▪ *a hilltop view*

hilt /'hɪlt/ *n* [C] : the handle of a sword or dagger — **to the hilt** : as much as possible ▪ *The farm was mortgaged (up) to the hilt.*

him /'hɪm, ɪm/ *pron, objective form of* HE **1** — used to refer to a certain man, boy, or male animal as the object of a verb or preposition ▪ *Do you know him?* ▪ *I'll give him a call.* **2** — used to indicate either a male or female object of a verb or preposition when the sex of the person is unknown ▪ *If any student misbehaves, send him to the office.* ✧ This use of *him* is now often avoided because it is considered sexist.

him·self /hɪm'sɛlf/ *pron* **1** — used as the object of a verb or preposition to refer to a man, boy, or male animal that has already been mentioned ▪ *He accidentally cut himself while shaving.* ▪ *He doesn't consider himself old.* = *He doesn't think of himself as (being) old.* ▪ *He had the house (all) to himself.* [=he was alone in the house] ▪ *"It's almost morning," he said to himself.* ▪ *He wanted to see it for himself.* [=he wanted to see it rather than have someone tell him about it, describe it to him, etc.] — often used for emphasis ▪ *He told me himself that he had lied.* **2** : that same person — used to indicate either a male or female object of a verb or preposition ▪ *Everyone must fend for himself.* ✧ This use of *himself* is now often avoided because it is considered sexist. **3** : his normal or healthy self ▪ *He's not (feeling) himself today.* ▪ *He should just be himself.* [=behave like he normally does] — **by himself 1** : without any help from other people ▪ *He did it (all) by himself.* **2** : ALONE ▪ *He lives by himself.* — **every man for himself** see [1]MAN

[1]**hind** /'haɪnd/ *adj, always before a noun* : at or near the back of something ▪ *the dog's hind legs*

[2]**hind** *n* [C] *chiefly Brit* : a female deer

hin·der /'hɪndɚ/ *vb* [T] : to make (something, such as a task or action) slow or difficult ▪ *The snowstorm hindered the search efforts.*

Hin·di /'hɪndi/ *n* [*singular*] : an official language of India — **Hindi** *adj*

hind·quar·ter /'haɪnd,kwoɚtɚ/ *n* [C] : the back left or right part of the body of an animal with four feet — usually plural ▪ *the horse's hindquarters*

hin·drance /'hɪndrəns/ *n* **1** [C] : a person or thing that makes a situation difficult ▪ *He is more of a hindrance (to me) than a help.* **2** [U] : the act of making it difficult for someone to act or for some-

thing to be done ▪ *She is allowed to do as she chooses without hindrance.* [=without being hindered]

hind·sight /'haɪnd,saɪt/ *n* [U] : the knowledge and understanding that you have about an event only after it has happened ▪ *In hindsight, it's clear we had alternatives.*

Hin·du·ism /'hɪn,du:,ɪzəm/ *n* [U] : the main religion of India which includes the worship of many gods and the belief in reincarnation — **Hin·du** /'hɪn,du:/ *n* [C] ▪ *devout Hindus* — **Hindu** *adj* ▪ *Hindu philosophy*

[1]**hinge** /'hɪndʒ/ *n* [C] : a usually metal piece that attaches a door or cover to something and allows it to open and close

[2]**hinge** *vb* **hinged; hing·ing** [T] : to attach (a door, gate, or cover) by hinges ▪ *a trunk with a hinged lid* — **hinge on/upon** [*phrasal vb*] : to be determined or decided by (something) ▪ *The outcome of the election hinges on this debate.*

[1]**hint** /'hɪnt/ *n* [C] **1** : a small piece of information that helps you guess an answer or do something more easily ▪ *I'll give you a hint.* [=clue] ▪ *helpful hints* [=tips] *for grilling* **2** : a statement that suggests something that you do not want to say in a direct way ▪ *She's been dropping hints* [=she's been saying things that show] *that she'd like to be invited.* ▪ *"I have a lot of work to do." "OK, I'll leave. I can take a hint."* **3** : a very small amount of something ▪ *tea with a hint of lemon*

[2]**hint** *vb* [T/I] : to say (something) or give information about (something) in an indirect way ▪ *He's been hinting that he might quit.* ▪ *The boss hinted about possible layoffs.* — **hint at** [*phrasal vb*] : to talk about (something) in an indirect way ▪ *He's been hinting at the possibility of quitting.* ▪ *What is she hinting at?*

hin·ter·land /'hɪntɚ,lænd/ *n* [C] : an area that is not close to any cities or towns ▪ *She grew up in the hinterlands.*

[1]**hip** /'hɪp/ *n* [C] : the part of your body between your waist and legs on each side ▪ *She stood with her hands on her hips."*— **shoot from the hip** see [1]SHOOT

[2]**hip** *adj* **hip·per; hip·pest** *informal* **1** : knowing about and following the newest styles, fashions, etc. ▪ *his hip new friends* **2** : very popular or fashionable ▪ *the hippest music/restaurants* — **hip to** *informal* : aware of (something) ▪ *He's hip to all the latest trends.* — **hip·ness** /'hɪpnəs/ *n* [U]

[3]**hip** *interj* — used in a cheer ▪ *Hip, hip, hooray!*

hip bone *n* [C] : the large bone between your waist and your legs that forms the hips

hip–hop /'hɪp,hɑ:p/ *n* [U] : rap music ▪ *hip-hop and R & B; also* : the culture associated with rap music

hip·pie *also* **hip·py** /'hɪpi/ *n, pl* **-pies** [C] : a usually young person who rejects established social customs (such as by dressing in an unusual way or living in a commune) and who opposes violence and war; *especially* : a young person of this kind in the 1960s and 1970s ▪ *long-haired hippies*

hip·po /ˈhɪpoʊ/ *n, pl* **-pos** [C] : HIPPOPOTAMUS

hip·po·pot·a·mus /ˌhɪpəˈpɑːtəməs/ *n, pl* **-mus·es** *or* **-mi** /-ˌmaɪ/ [C] : a large African animal that has a large head and mouth and short legs and that spends most of its time in water

hip·ster /ˈhɪpstɚ/ *n* [C] *informal* : a person who follows the latest styles, fashions, etc.

¹**hire** /ˈhajɚ/ *vb* **hired; hir·ing** **1 a** [T/I] *chiefly US* : to give work or a job to (someone) in exchange for wages or a salary ▪ *a hired hand* ▪ *We hired someone to clean the office.* ▪ *We're not hiring right now.* ▪ *the company's hiring practices* **b** [T] : to use or get the services of (someone) to do a particular job ▪ *She hired a divorce lawyer.* **2** [T] *chiefly Brit* : RENT ▪ *a hired car* — **hire out** [*phrasal vb*] **1 hire out (something)** *or* **hire (something) out** *chiefly Brit* : to allow someone to use (something) in exchange for money ▪ *The hotel hires out [=rents] boats to guests.* **2 hire out** *or* **hire out (yourself)** *US, informal* : to take a job ▪ *She hired (herself) out as a cook.*

²**hire** *n* **1** [C] *US, informal* : someone who has been hired for a job ▪ *the company's new hires* **2** [U] *Brit* : RENTAL ▪ *a car-hire firm* — **for hire** **1** : available to be used or to do work in exchange for money ▪ *We have boats (available) for hire.* ▪ *a gardener for hire* **2** : in exchange for money ▪ *He does farm work for hire.*

hired gun *n* [C] *chiefly US* **1** : a person who is paid to kill someone **2** : a person who is hired to do a specific job that some people consider to be morally wrong ▪ *politicians and their hired guns*

hire·ling /ˈhajɚlɪŋ/ *n* [C] *disapproving* : a person who is paid for doing a job that is not respected or that is considered morally wrong ▪ *political hirelings*

¹**his** /ˈhɪz, ɪz/ *adj, always before a noun, possessive form of* HE **1** : relating to or belonging to a certain man, boy, or male animal ▪ *His house is nearby.* ▪ *What is his name?* : made or done by a certain man, boy, or male animal ▪ *It's his turn to play.* **2** — used to refer to a person of either sex when the sex of the person is unknown ▪ *Each student has his own computer.* ◇ This use of *his* is now often avoided because it is considered sexist.

²**his** /ˈhɪz/ *pron* : that which belongs to or is connected with him ▪ *The book is his.* [=it belongs to him] ▪ *My eyes are blue and his are brown.* ▪ *a friend of his*

His·pan·ic /hɪˈspænɪk/ *adj* : coming originally from Latin America ▪ *Hispanic people*; *also* : of or relating to Hispanic people ▪ *Hispanic culture* — **Hispanic** *n* [C]

hiss /ˈhɪs/ *vb* **1** [I] : to produce a sound like a long "s" ▪ *The snake hissed.* ▪ *a hissing noise* **2** [T/I] : to show that you dislike or disapprove of someone by making a hiss ▪ *The audience booed and hissed (at him).* **3** [T] : to say (something) in a loud or angry whisper ▪ *"Leave me alone!" she hissed.* — **hiss** *n* [C] ▪ *the hiss of a snake*

his·to·ri·an /hɪˈstorijən/ *n* [C] : a person who studies or writes about history

his·tor·ic /hɪˈstorɪk/ *adj* **1 a** : famous or important in history ▪ *a/an historic event/landmark* **b** : having great and lasting importance ▪ *a historic court decision* **c** : considered in comparison with the past ▪ *The unemployment rate is at a historic low.* [=it is lower than it has ever been] **2** : of or relating to history or the past ▪ *historic artifacts/relics*

his·tor·i·cal /hɪˈstorɪkəl/ *adj* **1** : of or relating to history ▪ *historical accuracy/research/facts* **2** : based on history ▪ *historical fiction* **3** : arranged in the order that things happened or came to be : CHRONOLOGICAL ▪ *The kings are listed in historical order.* — **his·tor·i·cal·ly** /hɪˈstorɪkli/ *adv* ▪ *historically significant events*

his·to·ry /ˈhɪstəri/ *n, pl* **-ries** **1** [U] : the study of past events ▪ *a history professor* **2** [U] **a** : events of the past ▪ *one of the greatest teams in history* ▪ *throughout (human) history* ▪ *History has shown that such attempts have always failed.* ▪ *You can't rewrite history.* [=you can't change the past] ▪ *A talent scout spotted her and the rest is history.* [=the rest of the story about her success is well-known] ▪ *They won last year. Will history repeat itself?* [=will they win again?] ▪ *This day will go down in history.* [=it will be remembered as a very important day] ▪ *We made history that day.* [=did something that will be remembered as part of history] **b** : past events that relate to a particular subject, place, organization, etc. ▪ *throughout the company's history* [=throughout the time the company has existed] ▪ *There's a lot of history* [=much has happened] *in this old house.* ▪ *The school can trace its history back to* [=the school has existed since] *the early 19th century.* **3** [C] : a written record of important events that have happened since the beginning of something ▪ *He wrote a history of the British Empire.* **4** [C] : an established record of past events, actions, etc. — *usually singular* ▪ *She has no (prior) history of heart problems.* [=she has not had heart problems in the past] ▪ *a patient's medical history* [=a record of past medical problems and treatments] ▪ *a worker's employment history* [=a record of jobs that a worker has had] **5** [U] *informal* : someone or something that is finished ▪ *Their winning streak is history.* ▪ *Those problems are ancient history.* [=they happened long ago and are no longer important]

his·tri·on·ic /ˌhɪstriˈɑːnɪk/ *adj, disapproving* : too emotional or dramatic ▪ *histrionic gestures* — **his·tri·on·i·cal·ly** /ˌhɪstriˈɑːnɪkli/ *adv*

his·tri·on·ics /ˌhɪstriˈɑːnɪks/ *n* [*plural*] *disapproving* : behavior that is too emotional or dramatic ▪ *He told the story without any histrionics.*

¹**hit** /ˈhɪt/ *vb* **hit; hit·ting** **1 a** [T/I] : to move your hand, a bat, etc., quickly so

that it touches someone or something in a forceful or violent way ▪ *She hit him with her purse.* **b** [*T*] : to cause (a ball, puck, etc.) to move by hitting it forcefully with a bat, racket, etc. ▪ *She hit the ball right to the shortstop.* **c** [*T/I*] : to touch (something or someone) in a forceful or violent way after moving at a high speed ▪ *The ball hit the house.* ▪ *He was hit by a car.* **d** [*T*] : to cause or allow (your head, knee, etc.) to touch something in a forceful or violent way ▪ *She hit her elbow on/against the edge of the table.* **2 a** [*T*] : to attack (something or someone) ▪ *We will hit the enemy before they can hit us.* **b** [*T/I*] : to affect (something or someone) in a harmful or damaging way ▪ *They were unprepared when the storm hit (the city).* ▪ *When the factory closed, many families were hit hard.* = *Many families were hard hit.* [=many families were badly affected] **3** [*T*] **a** : to come to (something) by chance or accident while you are moving ▪ *I hit a traffic jam on the way over.* **b** : to begin to have or experience (problems, trouble, etc.) ▪ *We hit some problems early on in the project.* **4** [*T*] *informal* : to become suddenly or completely clear to (someone) ▪ *It suddenly hit me* [=I suddenly realized] *that I was wrong.* ▪ *The smell hit me* [=I noticed the smell] *as soon as I opened the door.* **5** [*T*] : to get or come to (a goal, level, etc.) ▪ *The temperature hit 90 today.* ▪ *a singer who can hit the high notes* ▪ *The stock market hit bottom.* [=reached an extremely low point] **6** [*T*] *informal* : to arrive or appear at, in, or on (a place) ▪ *We decided to hit the beach.* ▪ *The magazine's new issue hits newsstands today.* **7** [*T*] *informal* **a** : to turn (something) on or off with a switch ▪ *Could you please hit the lights?* **b** : to move (a switch) to an on or off position ▪ *I hit the switch and the lights came on.* **c** : to push down on (the brake pedal or accelerator in a vehicle) in a sudden and forceful way ▪ *I had to hit the brakes hard to avoid an accident.* ▪ *(US) She hit the gas and sped away.* **8 a** [*T/I*] : to succeed in hitting (something aimed at) with a shot, throw, etc. ▪ *The first shot hit (the target) but the second shot missed.* ▪ *(figurative) Her criticism hit the mark.* [=it was very accurate] **b** [*T*] : to succeed in making (a shot) ▪ *She hit all of her baskets/shots.* **c** [*T*] : to succeed in making a pass to (another player) ▪ *The quarterback hit the wide receiver for a touchdown.* **9 a** [*I*] : to try to hit the ball with a bat in baseball or cricket ▪ *It's your turn to hit.* [=bat] **b** [*T*] : to produce (a home run, a ground ball, etc.) by batting ▪ *He hit 30 home runs last year.* **c** [*I*] : to have a specified batting average ▪ *He's hitting .300.* [=his batting average is .300] — **hit a nerve** see NERVE — **hit a/the wall** see ¹WALL — **hit back** [*phrasal vb*] : to attack or criticize someone who has attacked or criticized you ▪ *The Senator hit back at his critics.* — **hit home** see ²HOME — **hit it** *informal* — used to tell a group of musicians to begin playing ▪ *Hit it, boys!* — **hit (it) big** see ²BIG — **hit it off** *informal* : to

become friends ▪ *They hit it off (with each other) immediately.* — **hit on/upon** [*phrasal vb*] **1 hit on** *US, informal* : to talk to (someone) in order to try to start a sexual relationship ▪ *A guy at the bar was hitting on her.* **2** : to succeed in finding (a solution, answer, etc.) ▪ *We hit on/upon the answer accidentally.* — **hit the books** see ¹BOOK — **hit the deck/dirt/ground** : to drop down to the ground or floor suddenly ▪ *She hit the deck when the gunfire started.* — **hit the ground running** : to begin an effort or activity in a quick, energetic, and effective way ▪ *The new president hit the ground running.* — **hit the hay/sack** *informal* : to go to bed ▪ *It's time to hit the hay.* — **hit the jackpot** see JACKPOT — **hit the nail on the head** *informal* : to be exactly right ▪ *He hit the nail on the head with that analysis.* — **hit the road** see ROAD — **hit the roof/ceiling** *informal* : to become very angry or upset ▪ *She hit the roof when she found out he had lied.* — **hit the skids** see ²SKID — **hit the spot** see ¹SPOT — **hit the streets/pavement** *informal* : to go out in search of something or for a specific purpose ▪ *We hit the streets to interview passersby.* — **hit the trail** see ²TRAIL — **hit up** [*phrasal vb*] **hit (someone) up** or **hit up (someone)** *US, informal* : to ask (someone) for something (such as money) ▪ *She hit up her father for a loan.* — **hit your stride** see ²STRIDE — **know what hit you** see ¹KNOW — **hit·ter** /ˈhɪtɚ/ *n* [*C*]

²**hit** *n* [*C*] **1** : an act of hitting or being hit by someone or something ▪ *The bunker took a direct hit from the bombers.* ▪ *(figurative) She took a big financial hit* [=she lost a lot of money] *when the stock market fell.* **2 a** : something that is very successful ▪ *The show was a (smash/big) hit.* ▪ *a hit record/song* **b** : someone or something that is liked by someone very much ▪ *The pony ride was a big hit (with the kids) at the party.* **3** : a successful effort to reach a desired goal or result ▪ *His business ventures were a mix of hits and misses.* [=some were successful and some failed] **4** *baseball* : BASE HIT **5** *computers* **a** : an act of connecting to a particular Web site ▪ *The site had/got a million hits* [=people connected to the site a million times] *last month.* **b** : a successful attempt to find something in a search of a computer database or the Internet ▪ *A search for his name produced/found more than 30 hits.* **6** *informal* : a single dose of an illegal drug ▪ *He took a hit of LSD.* **7** *informal* : a planned murder done by a paid killer ▪ *an attempted hit on the gang's leader* — **hit·less** /ˈhɪtləs/ *adj*

hit–and–miss /ˌhɪtn̩ˈmɪs/ *adj* : HIT-OR-MISS

hit–and–run /ˌhɪtn̩ˈrʌn/ *adj, always before a noun* : involving a driver who does not stop after causing an accident ▪ *a hit-and-run accident/driver*

¹**hitch** /ˈhɪtʃ/ *vb* **1** [*T*] : to attach, fasten, or connect (something) with a hook, knot, etc. ▪ *hitch a trailer to a car* **2** [*I*] *informal* : HITCHHIKE ▪ *She hitched a ride/lift back to town.* ▪ *He hitched (his*

way) *across the country.* — **get hitched**
informal : to get married ▪ *He's getting
hitched tomorrow.*

²hitch *n* [C] **1** : a hidden problem that
makes something more complicated or
difficult to do ▪ *The plan went off without
a hitch.* **2** : a device that is used to connect one thing to another ▪ *a trailer hitch*

hitch·hike /ˈhɪtʃˌhaɪk/ *vb* -**hiked**; -**hiking** [T/I] : to get a ride in a passing vehicle by standing on the side of the road ▪
*He hitchhiked (his way) across the coun-
try.* — **hitch·hik·er** *n* [C]

hi-tech *variant spelling of* HIGH TECH

hith·er /ˈhɪðɚ/ *adv, old-fashioned + literary* : to this place ▪ *come hither* [=come
here]

hith·er·to /ˈhɪðɚˌtuː/ *adv, formal* : until
now : before this time ▪ *The biography reveals some hitherto unknown facts about
him.*

hit list *n* [C] : a list of people, groups, etc.,
that someone plans to oppose or elimi-
nate ▪ *the gunman's/governor's hit list*

hit man *n* [C] : a person who is paid to
kill someone

hit-or-miss /ˌhɪtɚˈmɪs/ *adj* : not carefully planned or directed ▪ *a hit-or-miss
method of finding answers*

HIV /ˌeɪtʃˌaɪˈviː/ *n* [U] *medical* : a virus
that causes AIDS ▪ *He is HIV positive/
negative.*

¹hive /ˈhaɪv/ *n* [C] **1 a** : a nest for bees **b**
: the bees living in a hive **2** : a place
filled with busy activity ▪ *The house was a
hive of activity before the party.*

²hive *vb* **hived**; **hiv·ing** — **hive off**
[*phrasal vb*] *chiefly Brit* **hive off (something)** *or* **hive (something) off** : to give
control of (something) to another person
or group ▪ *The new owners hived off the
best parts of the company.*

hives /ˈhaɪvz/ *n* [U] *medical* : a condition
in which an area of your skin becomes
red and itchy ▪ *I broke out in hives.*

HM *abbr* Her Majesty, Her Majesty's, His
Majesty, His Majesty's

hmm *also* **hm** /ˈm, ˈhm/ *interj* — used to
represent a sound made by someone
who is thinking about what to say or do ▪
Hmm, I'm not sure.

HMO /ˌeɪtʃˌɛmˈoʊ/ *n* [C] *US* : an organization that provides health care to people
who make regular payments to it and
who agree to use the doctors, hospitals,
etc., that belong to the organization ◆
*HMO is an abbreviation of "health main-
tenance organization."*

HMS *abbr* Her Majesty's ship; His Majesty's ship

ho /ˈhoʊ/ *interj* **1** — used to attract attention ▪ *"Land ho!"* [= I see land] **2** *ho
ho (ho)* — used to represent laughter ▪
Ho ho ho! Merry Christmas!

hoa·gie /ˈhoʊgi/ *n* [C] *US* : SUBMARINE
SANDWICH

hoard /ˈhoɚd/ *vb* [T] : to collect and hide
a large amount of (something valuable) ▪
hoarding money/food — **hoard** *n* [C] ▪ *a
hoard of jewels* — **hoard·er** *n* [C]

hoard·ing /ˈhoɚdɪŋ/ *n* [C] *Brit* : BILL-
BOARD

hoarse /ˈhoɚs/ *adj* **hoars·er**; -**est** : having a harsh or rough sound or voice ▪ *You

sound a little hoarse.* — **hoarse·ly** *adv*
— **hoarse·ness** *n* [U]

hoary /ˈhori/ *adj* **hoar·i·er**; -**est**
: very old ▪ *hoary legends* **2** : not fresh
or original ▪ *a hoary cliché*

hoax /ˈhoʊks/ *n* [C] : an act that is meant
to trick or deceive people ▪ *The bomb
threat was just a hoax.* — **hoax** *vb* [T] ▪
He was hoaxed by the Web site. — **hoax-
er** *n* [C]

hob /ˈhɑːb/ *n* [C] *Brit* : COOKTOP

hob·ble /ˈhɑːbəl/ *vb* **hob·bled**; **hob-
bling 1** [I] : to walk with difficulty because of injury or weakness ▪ *She hobbled across the room.* **2** [T] : to slow the
movement, progress, or action of (someone or something) ▪ *She was hobbled by
self-doubt.* ▪ *hobbled by a knee injury*

hob·by /ˈhɑːbi/ *n, pl* -**bies** [C] : an activity that a person does for pleasure when
not working ▪ *His hobbies include fishing
and hiking.* — **hob·by·ist** /ˈhɑːbijɪst/ *n*
[C]

hob·gob·lin /ˈhɑːbˌgɑːblən/ *n* [C] : something that causes fear or worry ▪ *the hob-
goblins of etiquette*

hob·nob /ˈhɑːbˌnɑːb/ *vb* -**nobbed**; -**nob-
bing** [I] : to spend time with a famous or
wealthy person in a friendly way ▪ *hob-
nob with celebrities*

ho·bo /ˈhoʊboʊ/ *n, pl* -**boes** *also* -**bos**
[C] *US* : ²TRAMP 1

¹hock /ˈhɑːk/ *n* **1** [U] : the state of being
in a pawnbroker's possession ▪ *His gold
watch is in hock, but he'll get it out of
hock once he has the money to buy it
back.* **2** [C] : the part of the rear leg of a
four-footed animal that is like the human ankle ▪ *ham hocks* [=meat from the
lower leg of a pig] **3** [C/U] *Brit* : a type
of German white wine

²hock *vb* [T] : to give (something that you
own) to a pawnbroker in exchange for
money ▪ *He hocked* [=pawned] *his gold
watch.*

hock·ey /ˈhɑːki/ *n* [U] **1** *chiefly US* : ICE
HOCKEY **2** *chiefly Brit* : FIELD HOCKEY

ho·cus-po·cus /ˌhoʊkəsˈpoʊkəs/ *n* [U]
: language or activity that is meant to
trick or confuse people ▪ *political hocus-
pocus*

hodge·podge /ˈhɑːdʒˌpɑːdʒ/ *n* [*singular*]
chiefly US : a mixture of different things
▪ *a hodgepodge of styles*

hoe /ˈhoʊ/ *n* [C] : a garden tool that has a
flat blade on a long handle — **hoe** *vb*
hoed; **hoe·ing** [T/I] ▪ *The garden has to
be hoed.* [=worked on with a hoe]

hoe·down /ˈhoʊˌdaʊn/ *n* [C] *US* : a country party where people do square dances

¹hog /ˈhɑːg/ *n, pl* **hogs** *also* **hog** [C] **1 a**
chiefly US : a pig **b** *Brit* : a male pig that
is raised for meat **2** *informal* : a selfish or greedy person ▪ *Don't be such a
hog!* **b** : something that uses a large
amount of something ▪ *This car is a gas
hog.* [=it uses a lot of gasoline]

²hog *vb* **hogged**; **hog·ging** [T] *informal*
: to take, keep, or use (something) in a
selfish way ▪ *He always hogs the remote
control.*

hog·wash /ˈhɑːgˌwɑːʃ/ *n* [U] *informal*
: NONSENSE ▪ *His argument is hogwash.*

ho–hum /ˈhoʊˈhʌm/ *adj, informal* : having or showing no excitement or enthusiasm ▪ *a very ho-hum* [=dull, boring] *existence*

hoi pol·loi /ˌhɔɪpəˈlɔɪ/ *n* [*plural*] : ordinary people ▪ *aristocrats who treated the hoi polloi with contempt*

¹hoist /ˈhɔɪst/ *vb* [T] **1** : to raise (something) especially by using ropes or machinery ▪ *hoist the sail/flag* **2** *chiefly US, informal* : ¹DRINK ▪ *hoisting a few beers*

²hoist *n* [C] : a machine used for lifting heavy loads

hok·ey /ˈhoʊki/ *adj* **hok·i·er; -est** *US, informal + disapproving* : very silly, old-fashioned, or sentimental ▪ *a hokey melodrama*

ho·kum /ˈhoʊkəm/ *n* [U] *informal* **1** *chiefly US* : NONSENSE ▪ *That story is pure hokum.* **2** : writing, music, etc., that is too dramatic or sentimental and not very original ▪ *Hollywood hokum*

¹hold /ˈhoʊld/ *vb* **held** /ˈhɛld/; **hold·ing 1** [T] **a** : to have or keep (something) in your hand, arms, etc. ▪ *Hold the rail so you won't fall.* ▪ *He was holding a cat (in his arms).* ▪ *She held his hand.* = *She held him by the hand.* **b** : to put your arms around (someone) ▪ *He held her close/tight.* **2 a** [T] : to put or keep (something or someone) in a specified place or position ▪ *She held the trophy over her head.* ▪ *I held the door (open) for her.* **b** [T] : to keep (something or someone) in the same place or position ▪ *It took six people to hold him (down/back).* ▪ *The boards are held in place with nails.* ▪ *The lid was held on by some tape.* **c** [I] : to remain in the same place or position ▪ *The tape didn't hold.* ▪ *Hold still for a moment.* ▪ *His weight has held steady for a year.* **3** [I] : to continue to be good ▪ *We hope the weather holds through the weekend.* **4** [T] **a** : to own or possess (something) ▪ *The bank holds (the) title to the car.* ▪ *holding shares/stock in a company* **b** : to have or keep (a job, a position, etc.) ▪ *He can't hold a job.* ▪ *She has never held public office.* ▪ *President Clinton held office for 8 years.* **c** : to succeed in keeping (something that is being attacked) ▪ *The troops were able to hold the bridge.* ▪ *The soldiers held their position/ground.* **d** : to have (something that you have achieved or earned) ▪ *She holds a degree in chemistry.* ▪ *He holds two world records.* **5** [T] : to support the pressure or weight of (something or someone) ▪ *The floor will hold 10 tons.* **6** [T] **a** : to have or keep (a belief, a feeling, etc.) in your mind ▪ *holding a grudge* ▪ *a belief held by many* = *a widely held belief* **b** : to consider or judge (someone or something) in a specified way ▪ *They held me responsible (for the damage).* ▪ *This book is widely held to be his best.* ▪ *"We hold these truths to be self-evident . . ."* —U.S. *Declaration of Independence* (1776) ▪ *somewhat formal* : to have or express (an opinion, belief, etc.) ▪ *The court held that she was not at fault.* **7** [T] : to cause (a meeting, class, sale, etc.) to take place ▪ *Elections will be held next month.* ▪ *holding a press conference* **8** [T] **a** : to contain (something) ▪ *The box holds a bunch of old pho-*

tos. **b** : to have enough room for (an amount) ▪ *The disk can hold 1.44 megabytes of data.* ▪ *The dining room holds 500 people.* **9** [T] : to continue to have (someone's interest or attention) ▪ *The movie didn't hold their attention.* **10** [T] : to have (a specified quality, feature, etc.) ▪ *She holds a special place in my heart.* [=I have special feelings for her] ▪ *What will the future hold (for us)?* [=what will happen (to us) in the future] **11** [T] : to stop doing (something) or wait to do (something) ▪ *Hold everything.* [=wait, stop] *We're not doing this right.* ▪ *Hold it right there.* [=stop right there] ▪ *Tell them to hold their fire.* [=not shoot] **12** [T] **a** : to keep (something) available for later use ▪ *We will hold a table for you until six o'clock.* **b** : to delay the handling of (something) for a time ▪ *Please hold all my calls while I'm in the meeting.* **13** [T] : to prevent (something, such as a vehicle) from leaving ▪ *Would you hold the elevator for me?* ▪ *Hold that taxi!* **14** [T] *chiefly US* : to not use or include (something) in preparing food ▪ *I'd like a tuna sandwich on rye, and hold the pickles.* [=do not put pickles on the sandwich] **15** [T] : to force (someone) to stay in a place (such as a prison) ▪ *The police held him for questioning.* ▪ *They were held hostage/captive/prisoner.* ▪ (*figurative*) *He was held captive by his own fears.* **16** [T] : to continue moving on (a course) without change ▪ *The ship held its course.* **17** [I] : to remain true or valid ▪ *The general rule holds in most cases.* ▪ *Her advice still holds true today.* **18** [T/I] : to wait to speak to someone on the phone ▪ *All operators are busy. Please hold.* = *Please hold the line.* — **hold a candle to** see CANDLE — **hold against** [*phrasal vb*] **hold (something) against** : to use (something) as a reason to have a bad opinion of (someone) ▪ *He lied to her once, and she still holds it against him.* — **hold back** [*phrasal vb*] **1 a** : to stop yourself from doing something ▪ *She wanted to speak to him but she held back.* **b** : to make a less than complete effort ▪ *Don't hold back. Give it all you've got.* [=try as hard as you can] **c hold (someone) back** : to stop (someone) from doing something ▪ *Once he starts talking, there's no holding him back.* [=it's very hard to make him stop talking] **2 hold (something or someone) back or hold back (something or someone) a** : to not allow (something) to be seen or known by someone ▪ *He couldn't hold back his tears.* [=keep from crying] ▪ *Don't hold anything back (from me).* [=tell me everything] **b** : to keep (something) ▪ *He held some money back in case of an emergency.* **c** : to delay (something) ▪ *The company held back the first shipment of the new product.* **d** : to stop (someone or something) from advancing to the next level, grade, or stage ▪ *Bad health held her back from competing.* ▪ *He was held back in first grade.* — **hold court** see ¹COURT — **hold down** [*phrasal vb*] **hold (something or someone) down or hold down (something or someone) 1 a** : to stop (something) from being or becoming too high ▪ *Hold the noise down. I'm trying to read.* **b** : to continue to have (a job) ▪ *He struggled to hold down a job.* **2** : to stop (someone) from doing something or advancing to a higher level, position, etc. ▪ *These restrictions are holding us down.* — **hold (down) the fort** see FORT — **hold firm** : to refuse to change what you have been doing or believing ▪ *Despite opposition, she has held firm to/on her decision.* — **hold forth** [*phrasal vb*] *formal* : to speak about something for a long time ▪ *He held forth about/on the need for reform.* — **hold in** [*phrasal vb*] **hold (something) in** or **hold in (something)** : to stop (an emotion) from being expressed ▪ *Don't hold your feelings in. Let them out.* — **hold off** [*phrasal vb*] **1 a** : to wait to do something ▪ *He held off as long as he could.* ▪ *She held off on her vacation.* ▪ *He held off (on) announcing his decision.* **b** : to not happen until later ▪ *The rain held off* [=it didn't rain] *until we got home.* **2 hold (someone or something) off** or **hold off (someone or something)** **a** : to stop (someone) from coming near someone or something ▪ *Her bodyguard held off the crowd.* **b** : to defend against (something) successfully ▪ *The soldiers held off the attack.* — **hold on** [*phrasal vb*] **1** : to have or keep your hand, arms, etc., tightly around something ▪ *I held on for dear life.* ▪ *Hold on (tight). It's going to get bumpy.* ▪ *Hold on to the railing.* **2** : to succeed in keeping a position, condition, etc. ▪ *Hold on until help arrives.* **3** : to wait or stop briefly ▪ *"Can we go now?" "Hold on, I'll be ready in a minute."* **4 hold on to** : to keep possession of (something) ▪ *He is holding on to his lead in the polls.* — **hold out** [*phrasal vb*] **1 a** : to continue to exist or be available ▪ *How much longer will our food supply hold out?* **b** : to continue to work ▪ *My old car is still holding out.* **2** : to continue to oppose someone or defend against something ▪ *Many strikers are holding out.* **3 hold out (something)** or **hold (something) out** **a** : to reach outward with (something) ▪ *He held out his hand to greet us.* **b** : to say that there is a good reason to have (something) ▪ *The doctor didn't hold out much hope for her recovery.* **c** : to say that (a possibility) exists ▪ *The mayor has held out the possibility* [=has said that it is possible] *that the library will be expanded.* **4 hold out for** : to refuse to accept or agree to something in order to get (something) ▪ *The workers are holding out for higher pay.* **5 hold out on** *informal* : to keep something (such as information) from (someone) ▪ *She didn't tell me she was rich; she's been holding out on me.* — **hold over** [*phrasal vb*] **1 hold over (something)** or **hold (something) over** **a** : to cause (something) to happen later ▪ *A decision has been held over until Monday.* **b** *US* : to cause (something) to continue beyond a normal or planned time ▪ *The movie is being held over* [=it will continue to be shown] *for two more weeks.* **2 hold (something) over** : to use your knowl-

edge of (something) to influence or control the behavior of (someone) ▪ *She knows about his past and has been holding it over him.* [=she has been threatening to tell other people about his past] — **hold the bag** (*US*) or *Brit* **hold the baby** *informal* : to be given all of the blame or responsibility that should be shared with others ▪ *His friends ran away and he was stuck/left holding the bag.* — **hold the line** see ¹LINE — **hold to** [*phrasal vb*] **1 a** : to continue to have or follow (a plan, purpose, belief, etc.) ▪ *She has held to her decision.* **b hold (someone) to** : to force (someone) to do what is required by (a promise, standard, etc.) ▪ *I'm going to hold you to your promise.* **2 hold (someone) to** : to prevent (an opponent) from getting more than (a specified number of scores or shots) ▪ *We held the other team to just three runs.* — **hold together** [*phrasal vb*] **1** : to stay joined together or in one piece ▪ *The empire held together for many decades.* **2 hold (something) together** or **hold together (something)** : to cause (something) to stay joined together or in one piece ▪ *The box was held together with glue.* — **hold up** [*phrasal vb*] **1** : to continue in the same condition without failing or losing effectiveness or force ▪ *They were holding up well under the stress.* ▪ *The nurse came to see how I was holding up.* **2 hold (something) up** or **hold up (something)** : to raise (something) ▪ *He held up his hand.* **3 hold up (something or someone)** or **hold (something or someone) up** **a** : DELAY ▪ *Their decision was held up for months.* ▪ *I got held up in traffic.* **b** : to use a gun to rob (a person, store, etc.) ▪ *Someone held up the gas station.* **c** : to cause (someone or something) to be noticed for a particular reason ▪ *Critics held the program up as an example of government waste.* — **hold water** see ¹WATER — **hold with** [*phrasal vb*] : to agree with or approve of (something) ▪ *I don't hold with your views.* — **hold your breath** see BREATH — **hold your ground** see ¹GROUND — **hold your horses** see ¹HORSE — **hold your liquor** see LIQUOR — **hold your own** : to do well in a difficult situation ▪ *She held her own at the press conference.* — **hold your tongue/peace** : to not say anything about something ▪ *He somehow managed to hold his tongue.*

²hold *n* **1** [*C/U*] : the act of holding or gripping something — usually singular ▪ *He had/kept a tight hold on the rope.* ▪ *He grabbed/took hold of the rope.* [=he grabbed/took the rope and held it] ▪ *(figurative) Jealousy took hold of her.* [=she began to feel very jealous] **2** [*C*] : a way of holding your opponent in wrestling ▪ *He used an illegal hold.* **3** [*singular*] **a** : power that is used to control something or someone ▪ *tightening her hold on the company's finances* ▪ *He has a hold on her.* [=he has power over her] **b** : an understanding of something ▪ *It's hard to get a hold on* [=understand] *the problem.* **4** [*singular*] : an order that something is to be kept for a particular person or time • *I asked the library to put a hold on the book for me.* **5** [C] : an area on a ship or airplane where cargo is stored — **get (a) hold of** **1** : to succeed in getting (something) • *She got hold of tickets to the concert.* **2** : to find and talk to (someone) • *Were you able to get a hold of him?* **3 get (a) hold of yourself** : to get control of your thoughts and emotions and stop behaving in a foolish or uncontrolled way • *Get a hold of yourself and tell me what happened.* — **no holds barred** ✧ If there are *no holds barred*, there are no limits or rules for what can and cannot be done in a particular situation. — **on hold** **1** : in the state of waiting to speak to someone on the phone • *The operator put my call on hold.* • *They kept me on hold for hours!* **2** : in the state of being delayed for a time • *Our vacation plans were (put) on hold.* — **take (a) hold** : to become effective, established, or popular • *The change in the law has not yet taken hold.*

hold·er /ˈhoʊldɚ/ *n* [C] **1** : a person who holds or owns something • *ticket holders* • *a world record holder* **2** : a device that holds something • *a cup holder*

¹hold·ing /ˈhoʊldɪŋ/ *n* **1** [C] : property that is owned by someone • *land/stock holdings* **2** [U] *sports* : the illegal act of using your hands or arms to slow or stop the movement of an opponent in ice hockey, American football, etc.

²holding *adj, always before a noun* **1** : causing or intended to cause a temporary stop or delay • *a holding operation* **2** — used to describe a place where someone or something is kept for a time before being moved somewhere else • *a holding tank* • *a holding cell for prisoners*

holding pattern *n* [C] : a course flown by an aircraft while waiting for permission to land • *Our plane was in a holding pattern for an hour.*

hold·out /ˈhoʊldˌaʊt/ *n* [C] **1 a** : a person who refuses to reach an agreement until certain terms are met • *He was a holdout in the negotiations.* **b** : an act of holding out for something • *He ended his holdout.* **2** : a person who continues to do or use something after others have stopped doing or using it • *Only a few holdouts still use typewriters.*

hold·over /ˈhoʊldˌoʊvɚ/ *n* [C] *US* : someone or something that remains or is kept from an earlier time • *a holdover from the last administration*

hold·up /ˈhoʊldˌʌp/ *n* [C] **1** : a usually brief delay • *Hey, what's the holdup?* [=what is the reason for the delay?] **2** : a robbery that is done using a gun • *a holdup at a bank*

¹hole /ˈhoʊl/ *n* **1** [C] : an opening in or through something • *There's a hole in my sock/roof.* • *a bullet hole* • *(figurative) Lawyers tried to punch holes in her argument.* [=they tried to weaken it by proving that parts of it were wrong] • *(figurative, informal) I need your advice like a hole in the head.* [=I don't need your advice at all] **2** [C] **a** : a hollow place in the ground • *The dog dug a hole.* **b** : a place in the ground where an animal

lives • *a rabbit hole* **3** [C] *golf* **a** : the cup into which the ball is hit **b** : one of the separate parts of a golf course that includes a tee and a green • *The course has 18 holes.* **4** [C] : a flaw or weakness • *There are many holes in her theory/defense.* **5** [*singular*] *informal* : a difficult or embarrassing situation • *a financial hole* • *(US) He is hundreds of dollars in the hole* [=he owes hundreds of dollars] **6** [C] — used to describe a situation in which someone or something is gone or missing • *She left/made a big hole in their lives.* [=they missed her very much]

²hole *vb* : holed; hol·ing [T/I] *golf* : to hit (the ball) into the hole • *She holed a long putt for a birdie.* — **hole up** [*phrasal vb*] *informal* : to stay in a place hidden or apart from other people • *The band (was/ stayed) holed up in the recording studio.*

hole in one *n* [C] *golf* : a score of one on a hole in golf • *She got/made/had a hole in one on the eighth hole.*

hole–in–the–wall *n* [C] *informal chiefly US* : a small bar, restaurant, etc., that is not fancy or expensive • *We ate at some hole-in-the-wall.* **2** *Brit* : ATM

hol·ey /ˈhoʊli/ *adj, informal* : having holes • *holey socks*

hol·i·day /ˈhɑːləˌdeɪ, *Brit* ˈhɒlədi/ *n* **1** [C] : a special day of celebration • *a religious holiday* : a day when most people do not have to work • *July 4 is a national holiday in the U.S.* • *(US) celebrating the holiday season* = *celebrating the holidays* [=the time from November until the beginning of January during which many holidays are celebrated] **2** [C/U] *Brit* : VACATION • *taking a holiday in the Alps* • *She's on holiday.* — **holiday** *vb* [I] *Brit* : holidaying in the Alps

holiday–maker *n* [C] *Brit* : VACATIONER

ho·li·er–than–thou /ˌhoʊlijɚðən̩ˈðaʊ/ *adj, disapproving* : having or showing the annoying attitude of people who believe that they are morally better than other people • *a holier-than-thou attitude*

ho·li·ness /ˈhoʊlinəs/ *n* **1** [U] : the quality or state of being holy • *the holiness of this sacred place* **2 Holiness** [C] — used in the titles of high religious officials • *His Holiness the pope*

hol·is·tic /hoʊˈlɪstɪk/ *adj* : relating to or concerned with complete systems rather than with individual parts • *holistic medicine* • *a holistic approach to improving our schools*

hol·ler /ˈhɑːlɚ/ *vb, chiefly US, informal* [T/I] : SHOUT • *He hollered (out orders) to his workers.* • *screaming and hollering at each other* **2** [I] : to make loud or angry complaints • *hollering about taxes* — **holler** *n* [C] • *If you need help, give (me) a holler.* [=tell me that you need help]

¹hol·low /ˈhɑːloʊ/ *adj* **1** : having nothing inside • *a hollow log* **2** : curved inward • *hollow cheeks* **3** : not having real value or meaning • *a hollow victory/promise* • *Their threats ring hollow.* [=do not seem truthful or sincere] **4** : weak and without any emotion • *a hollow voice* — **hol·low·ness** *n* [U]

²hollow *n* [C] **1** : an area that is lower

than the area around it • *a grassy hollow*
2 : an empty space inside of something •
a nest in the hollow of a tree
³**hollow** *vb* [*T*] **1** : to remove the inside of
(something) • *a hollowed log* — **hollow
out** [*phrasal vb*] **hollow (something) out
or hollow out (something) 1** : to remove the inside of (something) • *a
hollowed-out pumpkin* **2** : to form
(something) by digging or cutting the inside of something • *hollowing out a tunnel*
hol·ly /'hɑːli/ *n, pl* **-lies** [*C/U*] : a tree or
bush with dark green leaves and bright
red berries
Hol·ly·wood /'hɑːli,wʊd/ *n* [*singular*]
: the American movie industry • *She had
a long career in Hollywood.* ✧ Hollywood
is a part of Los Angeles, California. —
Hollywood *adj, always before a noun* •
the Hollywood lifestyle
ho·lo·caust /'houlə,kɑːst, 'hɑːlə,kɑːst/ *n,
formal* **1** *the Holocaust* : the killing of
millions of Jews and other people by the
Nazis during World War II • *survivors of
the Holocaust = Holocaust survivors* **2**
[*C*] : an event in which many people are
killed and many things are destroyed especially by fire • *a nuclear holocaust*
ho·lo·gram /'houlə,græm, 'hɑːlə,græm/
n [*C*] : a picture that is produced by a laser and that looks three-dimensional
hol·ster /'houlstɚ/ *n* [*C*] : a case that you
wear on your body to hold a small gun
ho·ly /'houli/ *adj* **ho·li·er; -est 1 a**
: connected to a god or a religion • *a holy
relic/temple* • *the Holy Bible* **b** : religious
and morally good • *a holy man* **2** *informal* — used in phrases that show surprise or excitement • *Holy cow/mackerel/
smoke!* [=*Wow!*] **3** *informal* — used for
emphasis • *That boy is a holy terror.* [=he
is very difficult to control]
holy day *n* [*C*] : a day when a religious
festival or holiday is observed
Holy Father *n* [*singular*] — used to refer
to the Pope
Holy Ghost *n* — *the Holy Ghost* : HO-
LY SPIRIT
Holy Grail *or* **holy grail** *n* [*C*] : something that you want very much but that
is very hard to get or achieve • *Finding a
cure for cancer is the holy grail of medical
researchers.*
Holy Land *n* — *the Holy Land* : the
area in the Middle East where the events
of the Bible happened
Holy Spirit *n* — *the Holy Spirit* : God in
the form of a spirit in Christianity • *the
Father, the Son, and the Holy Spirit* —
called also *the Holy Ghost*
Holy Trinity *n* — *the Holy Trinity*
: TRINITY 1
holy war *n* [*C*] : a war that is fought to
defend or spread one group's religious
beliefs
holy water *n* [*U*] : water that has been
blessed by a priest
hom·age /'ɑːmɪdʒ, *Brit* 'hɑːmɪdʒ/ *n* **1**
[*U*] : respect or honor • *Her paintings pay
homage to mothers.* **2** [*singular*] : something that is done to honor someone or
something • *Her book is a/an homage to
Paris.*
¹**home** /'houm/ *n* **1** [*C/U*] : the house,

apartment, etc., where a person lives •
The fire destroyed their home. • *There's no
place like home.* • *Let's stay (at) home tonight.* [=let's not go out tonight] • *I will be
away from home* [=I will not be at my
house] *for two weeks.* • *He has no place to
call home.* [=he has no place to live] • *He
works at/from home.* [=he does his work
in his house and not in an office build-
ing] **2** [*C*] : a family living together in
one building, house, etc. • *She made a
good home for her children.* • *She came
from a troubled home.* [=a family with
many problems] • *a broken home* [=a
family in which the parents have di-
vorced] • *He left home* [=left his parent's
house and lived in his own house] *after
graduation.* **3** [*C/U*] : a place where
something normally or naturally lives or
is located • *Australia is the home of the
kangaroo.* • *The islands are home to many
species of birds.* **4** [*C/U*] : the place
where someone lives or originally comes
from • *visiting his boyhood home* • *New
York will always be home to me.* • *He misses his friends back home.* [=in his home-
town] • *They made their home* [=they set-
tled] *in Ohio.* **5** [*C*] : the place where an
organization, a company, etc., is located
and operates • *This building will be the orchestra's new home.* **6** [*C*] : a place
where people who are unable to care for
themselves live and are cared for • *an old
people's home* • *She put her mother in a
home.* **7** [*U*] : a place that you try to
reach in some games (such as baseball) •
He was tagged out at home. — **at home
1** : in your own country and not a foreign country • *both at home and abroad*
2 *sports* : in a team's own stadium, park,
etc. • *The team's next game is at home.* **3**
: relaxed and comfortable • *She feels at
home on the stage.* • *They made me feel
(right) at home.* • *Come on in and make
yourself at home.* [=do what you need to
do to feel relaxed and comfortable] —
home away from home (*US*) *or Brit*
home from home : a place that is as
comfortable as your own home • *His
brother's house was like a home away
from home.* — **home sweet home** ✧
You say *home sweet home* to show that
you are happy when you return to your
home.
²**home** *adv* **1** : to or at the place where
you live • *She called home to say she
would be late.* • (*chiefly US*) *They're never
home when I call.* • *I can't wait to* **come/
go/get** *home.* • *He brings/takes home*
[=the amount of money he gets after
paying taxes, health insurance, etc., is]
about $750 a week. **2** *sports* : to, toward,
or into a goal • *He fired the puck home.* —
bring (something) home : to make
(something) very clear and obvious in a
usually a forceful or unpleasant way •
*The importance of exercise was brought
home (to him) when his friend had a heart
attack.* — **drive your point home** : to
say something in a very strong or forceful way • *She drove her point home in the
debate.* — **hit/strike home** : to become
very clear and obvious in usually a forceful or unpleasant way • *The importance*

of exercise finally hit home. — **home free** (US) *or Brit* **home and dry** *informal* : sure to succeed ▪ *If we meet this next deadline, we'll be home free.*

³**home** *adj, always before a noun* **1** : of or relating to a home or family ▪ *a happy home life* ▪ *my home address* **2** : designed to be used in your home ▪ *a home entertainment system* : done or made in your home ▪ *home cooking* ▪ *a home-cooked meal* **3** *sports* : at a team's own field, stadium, arena, etc. ▪ *the home team* **4** *chiefly Brit* : ¹DOMESTIC 1 ▪ *the home market*

⁴**home** *vb* **homed; hom·ing** — **home in on** [*phrasal vb*] : to find and move directly toward (someone or something) ▪ *The missile homed in on its target.* ▪ *(figurative)* Researchers are homing in on a cure.*

home base *n* **1** [*C*] : the place in which someone or something lives or operates ▪ *the company's home base* **2** [*U*] *baseball* : HOME PLATE

home·body /ˈhoʊmˌbɑːdi/ *n, pl* **-bod·ies** [*C*] *informal* : a person who likes to stay home

home·bound /ˈhoʊmˌbaʊnd/ *adj* **1** : unable to leave your house because of age, injury, etc. ▪ *They deliver meals to homebound people.* **2** : going home ▪ *homebound traffic/travelers*

home·boy /ˈhoʊmˌbɔɪ/ *n* [*C*] *US slang* : a boy or man who is one of your friends ▪ *hanging out with his homeboys*

home·com·ing /ˈhoʊmˌkʌmɪŋ/ *n* **1** [*C*] : the act of returning to your home ▪ *the soldiers' homecoming* **2** *or* **Homecoming** [*C/U*] *US* **a** : an annual celebration for people who attended a college or university ▪ *Homecoming weekend* **b** : a celebration for high-school students that includes sports games and a formal dance ▪ *Who are you taking to Homecoming?*

home economics *n* [*U*] : a class that teaches cooking, sewing, etc. — called also (US, *informal*) **home ec**

home fries *n* [*plural*] *US* : potatoes that have been cut into small pieces and fried

home front *n* — **the home front** : the people who stay in a country and work while that country's soldiers are fighting in a war in a foreign country ▪ *keeping up morale on the home front*

home·girl /ˈhoʊmˌgɜːrl/ *n* [*C*] *US slang* : a girl or woman who is one of your friends

home·grown /ˈhoʊmˈgroʊn/ *adj* **1** : grown or made at home ▪ *homegrown vegetables* **2** : raised in or coming from your local area ▪ *homegrown musical talent*

home help *n* [*C*] *Brit* : a person whose job is to help ill or elderly people in their homes with cooking, cleaning, etc.

home·land /ˈhoʊmˌlænd/ *n* [*C*] **1** : the country where someone was born or grew up ▪ *He returned to his homeland.* **2** : a usually large area where a particular group of people can live ▪ *an independent homeland*

home·less /ˈhoʊmləs/ *adj* : having no place to live ▪ *homeless people* ▪ *a homeless shelter* [=a building where homeless

people can sleep and get food] — **the homeless** : people who have no place to live — **home·less·ness** *n* [*U*]

home loan *n* [*C*] : ¹MORTGAGE

home·ly /ˈhoʊmli/ *adj* **home·li·er; -est** **1** *US* : not pretty or handsome ▪ *He's a bit homely.* **2** *Brit* : ¹HOMEY ▪ *a homely atmosphere* — **home·li·ness** *n* [*U*]

home·made /ˈhoʊmˈmeɪd/ *adj* : made in the home and not in a factory, store, etc. ▪ *homemade bread*

home·mak·er /ˈhoʊmˌmeɪkɚ/ *n* [*C*] *chiefly US* : HOUSEWIFE — **home·mak·ing** /ˈhoʊmˌmeɪkɪŋ/ *n* [*U*]

home movie *n* [*C*] : a movie that you make usually of your family

home office *n* **1** [*C*] : a room or space in your house where you do office work **2** *the Home Office* *Brit* : the department in the British government that deals with the law, the police, etc.

ho·me·op·a·thy *also Brit* **ho·moe·op·a·thy** /ˌhoʊmiˈɑːpəθi/ *n* [*U*] : a way of treating illnesses by using small amounts of substances that would in larger amounts produce symptoms of the illnesses in healthy people — **ho·meo·path·ic** *also Brit* **ho·moeo·path·ic** /ˌhoʊmijəˈpæθɪk/ *adj* ▪ *homeopathic medicine/remedies*

home·own·er /ˈhoʊmˌoʊnɚ/ *n* [*C*] : a person who owns a home, apartment, etc.

home page *n* [*C*] : the part of a Web site that is seen first and that contains links to other parts of the site

home plate *n* [*U*] *baseball* : the base that a runner must touch in order to score

hom·er /ˈhoʊmɚ/ *n* [*C*] *baseball, informal* : HOME RUN — **homer** *vb* [*I*] ▪ *He homered twice in today's game.*

home·room /ˈhoʊmˌruːm/ *n* [*C/U*] *US* : a classroom where students go at the beginning of each school day ▪ *He was late for homeroom.*

home rule *n* [*U*] : government of a place by the people who live there

home run *n* [*C*] *baseball* : a hit that allows the batter to go around all the bases and score a run ▪ *He hit three home runs.*

home·school /ˈhoʊmˌskuːl/ *vb* [*T/I*] *US* : to teach your children at home instead of sending them to a school ▪ *They homeschool their son.* — **home·school·er** /ˈhoʊmˌskuːlɚ/ *n* [*C*] — **home·school·ing** /ˈhoʊmˌskuːlɪŋ/ *n* [*U*]

home·sick /ˈhoʊmˌsɪk/ *adj* : sad because you are away from your family and home ▪ *He was/got homesick at college.* — **home·sick·ness** *n* [*U*]

home·spun /ˈhoʊmˌspʌn/ *adj* : plain and simple ▪ *her folksy, homespun manner*

¹**home·stead** /ˈhoʊmˌstɛd/ *n* [*C*] : a house and the farmland it is on

²**homestead** *vb* [*T/I*] *US* : to settle on government land and farm it ▪ *They homesteaded the territory in the 1860s.* — **home·stead·er** /ˈhoʊmˌstɛdɚ/ *n* [*C*]

home·stretch /ˈhoʊmˈstrɛtʃ/ *n* [*C*] : the part of a racetrack between the last turn and the finish line ▪ *The horses are in the homestretch.* ▪ *(figurative)* The campaign is nearing the homestretch.* [=it is almost over] — called also (*Brit*) **home straight**

home·town /ˈhoʊmˌtaʊn/ *n* [C] : the city or town where you were born or grew up

home video *n* **1** [U] *US* : movies that are sold on videotapes or DVDs ▪ *new releases in home video* **2** [C] : a home movie that is recorded with a video camera

home visit *n* [C] *Brit* : HOUSE CALL

home·ward /ˈhoʊmwəd/ *also* **home·wards** /ˈhoʊmwədz/ *adv* : in the direction of home ▪ *I am homeward bound.* [=going home] — **homeward** *adj*

home·work /ˈhoʊmˌwɝk/ *n* [U] **1** : school work that a student is given to do at home ▪ *I did/finished my homework.* **2** : research or reading done in order to prepare for something ▪ *He did his homework before the debate.*

¹**hom·ey** /ˈhoʊmi/ *adj* **hom·i·er**; **-est** *chiefly US* : comfortable or familiar like home ▪ *a homey* [=(*Brit*) *homely*] *atmosphere* — **hom·ey·ness** *or* **hom·i·ness** *n* [U]

²**homey** *n, pl* **-ies** [C] *US slang* : HOMEBOY

ho·mi·ci·dal /ˌhɑːməˈsaɪdl̩/ *adj* **1** : likely to kill someone ▪ *a homicidal maniac* **2** : of or relating to murder ▪ *homicidal thoughts*

ho·mi·cide /ˈhɑːməˌsaɪd/ *n* [C/U] *chiefly US* : the act of killing another person : MURDER

hom·i·ly /ˈhɑːməli/ *n, pl* **-lies** [C] *formal* : a usually short talk on a religious or moral topic ▪ *The priest gave a homily on sin.*

hom·ing /ˈhoʊmɪŋ/ *adj, always before a noun, technical* : able to find and follow a target ▪ *a homing device/torpedo*

ho·mo·ge·neous /ˌhoʊməˈdʒiːnjəs/ *adj* : made up of the same kind of people or things ▪ *a racially homogeneous town* [=a town in which all people are the same race] — **ho·mo·ge·ne·ity** /ˌhoʊmədʒəˈniːjəti/ *n* [U] *formal*

ho·mog·e·nize *also Brit* **ho·mog·e·nise** /hoʊˈmɑːdʒəˌnaɪz/ *vb* **-nized; -niz·ing** [T] *formal* **1** : to treat (milk) so that the fat is mixed throughout instead of floating on top ▪ *homogenized milk* **2** : to change (something) so that its parts are similar ▪ *homogenizing education across the country* — **ho·mo·ge·ni·za·tion** *also Brit* **ho·mog·e·ni·sa·tion** /hoʊˌmɑːdʒənəˈzeɪʃən, *Brit* həʊˌmɒdʒəˌnaɪˈzeɪʃən/ *n* [U]

ho·mog·e·nous /hoʊˈmɑːdʒənəs/ *adj* : HOMOGENEOUS

ho·mo·graph /ˈhɑːməˌgræf, *Brit* ˈhɒməˌgrɑːf/ *n* [C] : a word that is spelled like another word but that is different in origin, meaning, or pronunciation ▪ *The words "bow" for a part of a ship and "bow" for a weapon that shoots arrows are homographs.*

hom·onym /ˈhɑːməˌnɪm/ *n* [C] : a word that is spelled and pronounced like another word but is different in meaning ▪ *The noun "bear" and the verb "bear" are homonyms.*

ho·mo·phobe /ˈhoʊməˌfoʊb/ *n* [C] : a person who hates or is afraid of homosexuals — **ho·mo·pho·bia** /ˌhoʊmə-

ˈfoʊbijə/ *n* [U] — **ho·mo·pho·bic** /ˌhoʊməˈfoʊbɪk/ *adj* ▪ *homophobic remarks*

ho·mo·phone /ˈhɑːməˌfoʊn/ *n* [C] : a word that is pronounced like another word but is different in meaning, origin, or spelling ▪ *"To," "too," and "two" are homophones.*

Ho·mo sa·pi·ens /ˌhoʊmoʊˈseɪpijənz, *Brit* ˌhəʊməʊˈsæpiənz/ *n, pl* **Homo sapiens** [C/U] *technical* : the species of human beings that exist today

ho·mo·sex·u·al /ˌhoʊməˈsɛkʃəwəl/ *adj* : sexually attracted to people of the same sex ▪ *She's homosexual.* — **homosexual** *n* [C] — **ho·mo·sex·u·al·i·ty** /ˌhoʊməˌsɛkʃəˈwæləti/ *n* [U]

Hon. *also Brit* **Hon** *abbr* honorable — used in titles ▪ *the Hon. Judge Smith presiding*

hon·cho /ˈhɑːntʃoʊ/ *n, pl* **-chos** [C] *chiefly US, informal* : a person who is in charge of other people ▪ *He's the head honcho.* [=the person with the most authority]

hone /ˈhoʊn/ *vb* **honed; hon·ing** [T] : to make (something) better or more effective ▪ *She's honing her language skills.* — **hone in on** *[phrasal vb] US* : to find and go directly toward (someone or something) ▪ *The missile honed in on its target.* ▪ *(figurative) Researchers are honing in on a cure.*

¹**hon·est** /ˈɑːnəst/ *adj* **1 a** : not lying, stealing, or cheating ▪ *honest people/citizens/politicians* **b** : showing or suggesting a good and truthful character ▪ *He has an honest face.* **2** : not hiding the truth about someone or something ▪ *I want an honest answer.* ▪ *In my honest opinion, you were great!* ▪ *To be perfectly/quite honest, I don't like it.* ▪ *Be honest with me.* [=tell me the truth] **3 a** : not deserving blame ▪ *It was an honest mistake.* **b** : done using your own work or effort ▪ *an honest day's work* : not gotten by cheating, lying, etc. ▪ *He's just trying to earn an honest living.* [=to earn a good amount of money for his hard work] — **make an honest woman of (someone)** *old-fashioned + humorous* : to marry (a woman, especially a woman you have had sex with) ▪ *He finally made an honest woman of her.* — **hon·es·ty** /ˈɑːnəsti/ *n* [U] ▪ *In all honesty, I don't know what you're talking about.* ▪ *He believes that honesty is the best policy.* [=telling the truth is better than lying even when it is hard to do]

²**honest** *adv, informal* — used to stress that a statement is true ▪ *I didn't do it, honest!* ▪ *Honest to God/goodness, I wasn't there that night.*

hon·est·ly /ˈɑːnəstli/ *adv* **1 a** : without cheating or lying ▪ *He spoke honestly about the situation.* ▪ *I can honestly say that I've never met him.* **b** : in a genuine way ▪ *She honestly believes that he is innocent.* **2** — used to stress that a statement is true ▪ *I honestly don't know.* **3** *informal* — used to express annoyance or disapproval ▪ *Honestly! Is that the best you can do?!*

honest–to–goodness *adj, always be-*

fore a noun, chiefly US, informal : REAL ▪ an honest-to-goodness hero

hon·ey /'hʌni/ n **1** [U] : a thick, sweet substance made by bees **2** informal — used to address someone you love ▪ Honey, I'm home! **3** [singular] chiefly US, informal : something that is very good ▪ a real honey of a car — **a land of milk and honey** see ¹LAND

hon·ey·bee /'hʌni,bi:/ n [C] : a bee that makes honey

hon·ey·comb /'hʌni,koʊm/ n [C/U] : a group of wax cells that are built by honeybees in their hive

hon·ey·moon /'hʌni,mu:n/ n [C] **1** : a trip or vacation taken by a newly married couple **2** : a pleasant period of time at the start of something (such as a relationship or a politician's term in office) when people are happy, cooperative, etc. ▪ The governor's honeymoon (period) was brief. — **honeymoon** vb [I] ▪ They honeymooned in Mexico. — **hon·ey·moon·er** n [C]

hon·ey·suck·le /'hʌni,sʌkəl/ n [C/U] : a type of shrub that has fragrant flowers

honk /'hɑːŋk/ n [C] : the loud sound made by a goose; also : a similar loud sound ▪ the honk of a horn — **honk** vb [T/I] ▪ I heard a goose honk. ▪ a honking horn ▪ They kept honking (their horns) at us.

hon·ky-tonk /'hɑːŋki,tɑːŋk/ n **1** [U] US : a type of country music with a heavy beat **2** [C] US : a cheap nightclub that often features country music

¹**hon·or** (US) or Brit **hon·our** /'ɑːnə/ n **1** [U] : respect that is given to someone who is admired ▪ They should be treated with honor. ▪ She was the **guest of honor**. [=the person who was being honored] ▪ He was given a **place of honor** at the table. [=a seat for someone who is being specially honored] ▪ There was a dinner in honor of the coach. [=in order to show respect and admiration for the coach] **2** [U] **a** : good reputation ▪ He fought to defend/protect/uphold his family's honor. **b** : high moral standards of behavior ▪ a code/matter/man/woman of honor **3** [singular] formal **a** : a special opportunity to do something that makes you proud ▪ She was given/granted the honor of christening the ship. **b** : something that shows that other people have respect for you ▪ It was an honor to be invited. **4** [C] : something (such as a title or medal) that is given to a person as a sign of respect and admiration ▪ She has received/won many honors and awards. **5** [singular] : an admired person who is a source of pride and respect for the other members of a group, organization, etc. ▪ She was an honor to her profession. **6** Honor [C] — used as a title for a judge or mayor ▪ Please welcome His Honor, the mayor. **7** [plural] **a** : special credit or recognition given to students who have successfully done work at a high level ▪ She graduated with (top/high) honors. **b** : a special course of study for students who want to take classes at a high level ▪ honors classes/courses — **do the honors** : to do the actions performed by a host

or hostess ▪ The Ambassador did the honors by introducing the guest speaker. — **on your honor** formal — used to say that you promise to do something ▪ On my honor, I will do my duty. — **word of honor** see ¹WORD

²**honor** (US) or Brit **honour** vb [T] **1 a** : to regard or treat (someone) with respect and admiration ▪ We were honored with/by his presence. ▪ an honored guest **b** : to show admiration for (someone or something) in a public way ▪ She has been honored for her charitable works. ▪ a way to honor his memory/achievements **2 a** : to do what is required by (something, such as a promise) ▪ The company failed to honor the contract/warranty. **b** : to accept (something) as payment ▪ honor a check **c** : to repay (a debt) ▪ failing to honor their debts

hon·or·able (US) or Brit **hon·our·able** /'ɑːnərəbəl/ adj **1 a** : deserving honor and respect ▪ an honorable profession **b** : having or showing honesty and good moral character ▪ an honorable man **c** : fair and proper ▪ His intentions were honorable. **2** Honorable — used as a title for some government officials and members of the nobility ▪ the Honorable Senator/Judge — abbr. Hon. — **hon·or·ably** (US) or Brit **hon·our·ably** /'ɑːnərəbli/ adv

honorable mention n [C] : an award or special praise given to someone who has done something extremely well but who has not won any of the official prizes

hon·or·ary /'ɑːnəˌreri, Brit 'ɑːnərəri/ adj **1** : given as a sign of honor or achievement ▪ an honorary degree/title **2** always before a noun **a** : regarded as one of a group although not officially elected or included ▪ an honorary member of the club **b** : holding a position for which no payment is given : not paid ▪ the honorary president/chairman

honor guard n [C] chiefly US : a person or group that is the guard at a formal or ceremonial event (such as a military funeral or a parade)

hon·or·if·ic /ˌɑːnəˈrɪfɪk/ adj : giving or expressing honor or respect ▪ an honorific name/title

honor roll n [C] US : a list of people who deserve to be honored; especially : a list of students who have received good grades in school

honour, honourable Brit spellings of HONOR, HONORABLE

hood /'hʊd/ n [C] **1 a** : a soft covering for the head and neck often attached to a coat or cape **b** : a cloth covering worn over the entire head to hide a person's face **2 a** : a cover that is used to protect or shield something ▪ a lens hood **b** US : the movable metal covering over the engine of an automobile — called also (Brit) bonnet **3** US, informal : HOODLUM **4** US slang : a poor neighborhood in a large city ▪ his friends in the hood

-hood /-ˌhʊd/ n suffix **1** : state : condition : quality ▪ falsehood ▪ childhood **2** : people sharing a condition or character ▪ brotherhood

hood·ed /'hʊdəd/ adj **1** : having or

wearing a hood • *a hooded jacket/ sweatshirt* • *a hooded figure* **2** — used to describe eyes that are half closed • *He looked at us with hooded eyes.*

hood·lum /ˈhuːdləm, ˈhʊdləm/ *n* [C] : a tough and violent criminal : THUG • *a small-time hoodlum*

hood·wink /ˈhʊdˌwɪŋk/ *vb* [T] *informal* : to deceive or trick (someone) • *He hoodwinked us into believing him.*

¹hoof /ˈhʊf/ *n, pl* **hooves** /ˈhuːvz, ˈhʊvz/ *also* **hoofs** [C] : the hard covering on the foot of an animal (such as a horse or pig) — **hoofed** /ˈhʊft/ *adj* • *hoofed animals*

²hoof *vb* — **hoof it** *US, informal* : to walk or run • *We hoofed it down to the subway station.* — **hoof·er** /ˈhʊfə/ *n* [C] • *a talented hoofer* [=*dancer*] *on Broadway*

¹hook /ˈhʊk/ *n* [C] **1** : a curved or bent tool for catching, holding, or pulling something **2** : a ball or shot in golf and other games that curves to the side instead of going straight • *She hit a hook into the left rough.* **3** *boxing* : a punch coming from the side of the body instead of going straight forward • *a right/left hook* **4** *basketball* : HOOK SHOT **5** : something (such as part of a song) that attracts people's attention • *The song has a catchy hook.* — **by hook or by crook** *informal* : by any possible means • *She was determined to succeed by hook or by crook.* — **hook, line and sinker** *informal* : COMPLETELY • *They fell for the story hook, line and sinker.* [=they believed the story completely] — **off the hook 1** *informal* — used to describe someone who has avoided trouble or punishment • *I'm not going to let her off the hook so easily.* **2** *of a telephone* : with the receiver not resting in its usual position — **on the hook for** *US, informal* : owing money for (something) • *He's still on the hook for the cost of the repairs.*

²hook *vb* **1 a** [T] : to connect or attach (something) with a hook • *The train cars were hooked together.* **b** [I] : to be attached by hooks • *The dress hooks in the back.* **2** [T] : to catch (something, such as a fish) with a hook • *He hooked a large fish.* **3** [T] : to bend (a part of your body, such as an arm) and place it around something • *He hooked his arm around my neck.* **4** [I] : to curve like a hook • *The bird's beak hooks downward.* **5** [T/I] *sports* : to hit or kick (a ball or shot) in a way that causes it to curve to the side • *(golf)* *She hooked her drive into the rough.* — **hook into** [*phrasal vb*] *informal* : to become connected to (something, such as a computer network or a source of electrical power) • *How do I hook into the network?* — **hook up** [*phrasal vb*] **1** *informal* : to join together to do something • *The two men hooked up to form a new company.* **2** *chiefly US, informal* : to meet at a place • *We plan to hook up after the game.* **3** **hook (someone) up** *chiefly US, informal* **a** : to cause (someone) to have a friendly or romantic relationship with someone • *She tried to hook him up with one of her friends.* **b** : to provide (someone) with something that

is needed or wanted • *She hooked me up with some great tickets.* **4** **hook up (something or someone) or hook (something or someone) up** : to attach (something or someone) to a device by means of electrical connections • *hook up the wires/speakers*

hooked /ˈhʊkt/ *adj* **1** : shaped like a hook • *the bird's hooked beak* **2** *not before a noun, informal* **a** : addicted to a drug • *He was hooked on cocaine.* **b** : very interested in and enthusiastic about something • *She got hooked (on golf) after one lesson.*

hook·er /ˈhʊkə/ *n* [C] *informal* : ¹PROSTITUTE

hook shot *n* [C] *basketball* : a shot made by swinging the ball up and over your head with a long movement of your arm

hook·up /ˈhʊkˌʌp/ *n* [C] : an arrangement or part by which pieces of equipment can be connected • *telephone/computer/Internet hookups*

hooky *also* **hook·ey** /ˈhʊki/ *n* — **play hooky** *US, informal* : to be away from school without permission • *He was playing hooky with his friends.*

hoo·li·gan /ˈhuːlɪgən/ *n* [C] : a usually young man who does noisy and violent things as part of a group or gang — **hoo·li·gan·ism** /ˈhuːlɪgəˌnɪzəm/ *n* [U]

hoop /ˈhuːp/ *n* [C] **1 a** : a circular object : a large ring **b** : a large metal ring used for holding together the sides of a barrel **2** *basketball* **a** : a metal ring that the ball must go through in order to score points **b** *informal* : a successful shot • *They scored a quick hoop.* [=basket, bucket] **c** *US, informal* : BASKETBALL — usually plural • *hoops fans* • *Let's play/ shoot some hoops.* — **jump through hoops** see ¹JUMP

hoop·la /ˈhuːˌplɑː/ *n* [U] *chiefly US, informal + usually disapproving* : talk or writing that is designed to get people excited about and interested in something • *There's been a lot of hoopla surrounding the new theater.*

hooray *variant spelling of* HURRAH

¹hoot /ˈhuːt/ *n* [C] **1** : the loud, deep sound made by an owl; *also* : a similar loud, deep sound • *(Brit) the hoot of a car's horn* **2** : a loud laugh or call made by a person • *hoots of laughter* **3** *informal* : an amusing person or thing • *Your brother's a hoot!* — **give a hoot** *also* **care a hoot** *informal* : to care at all about someone or something • *I don't care a hoot about that.*

²hoot *vb* **1** [I] *of an owl* : to make a hoot • *an owl hooting in the woods* **2** [T/I] *Brit* : HONK • *They kept hooting (their horns) at us.* • *a hooting horn* **3** [T/I] : to call out or laugh loudly • *The crowd booed and hooted (its disapproval) when he stood up to speak.*

hoot·er /ˈhuːtə/ *n* [C] **1** : a person or device that hoots **2** *Brit slang* : ¹NOSE 1

hoo·ver /ˈhuːvə/ *vb* [T/I] *Brit* : VACUUM • *I spent the morning hoovering (the carpet).*

hooves *plural of* ¹HOOF

¹hop /ˈhɑːp/ *vb* **hopped; hop·ping 1** [I] : to move by a quick jump or series of jumps • *A frog was hopping along the edge* *of the pond.* **2** [T] : to jump over (something) ▪ *hop a puddle/fence* **3** [I] *informal* **a** : to move or go quickly ▪ *He hopped in the car and drove off.* **b** : to go from place to place without staying long at any one place ▪ *She's been hopping from job to job for years.* **4** *informal* **a** [T] *US* : to ride on (an airplane, train, etc.) ▪ *She hopped a flight to New York.* **b** [I] : to make a short trip especially in an airplane ▪ *They plan to hop down/over to the conference.* — **hop it** *Brit, informal* : to go away ▪ *She angrily told him to hop it.* — **hop to it** *informal* : to act or move quickly ▪ *You better hop to it.*

²**hop** *n* [C] **1 a** : a short, quick jump **b** : the bounce of a ball ▪ *He fielded the ball on the second hop.* **2** *old-fashioned* : a social event with dancing **3** *informal* **a** : a short flight in an airplane ▪ *a hop down to Philadelphia* **b** *chiefly US* : a short trip ▪ *a quick hop to the grocery store* — **a hop, skip, and (a) jump** *informal* : a short distance ▪ *Her house is just a hop, skip, and jump from mine.*

¹**hope** /ˈhoʊp/ *vb* **hoped**; **hop·ing** [T/I] : to want something to happen or be true and think that it could happen or be true ▪ *She hoped (that) she would be invited.* = *She hoped to receive an invitation.* ▪ *He's hoping for a promotion.* ▪ *Everyone in your family is well, I hope.* ▪ *"Will you be at the party?" "I hope so."* [=I hope that I will be there] ▪ *"Will you have to miss the party?" "I hope not."* — **here's hoping** *informal* — used to say that you hope something will happen ▪ *Here's hoping (that) it doesn't rain.* — **hope against hope** : to hope for something when you know that it will probably not happen or be true ▪ *We're hoping against hope that they are all right.*

²**hope** *n* **1** [C/U] : a feeling that something good will happen or be true ▪ *The drug has brought/given hope to thousands of sufferers.* ▪ *Our hopes are fading/dwindling.* ▪ *We had high hopes of winning.* [=we felt we had a very good chance of winning] ▪ *You shouldn't get your hopes up.* [=feel so hopeful] **2** [U] : the chance that something good will happen ▪ *She believes there's hope of/for a cure.* [=that a cure is possible] ▪ *His condition is beyond hope.* [=his condition is hopeless] **3** [singular] : someone or something that may be able to provide help ▪ *He's our last/best hope.* **4** [C] : something that is hoped for ▪ *We all have hopes and dreams for the future.* — **in (the) hope of/that** or **in hopes of/that** : with the hope that something will happen or could happen ▪ *He waited in hopes that she would show up.* — **live in hope** *chiefly Brit* : to hope for something when you know that it will probably not happen or be true ▪ *We live in hope that there will be some survivors of the crash.* — **pin (all) your hopes on** see *pin on* at ²PIN

¹**hope·ful** /ˈhoʊpfəl/ *adj* **1** : full of hope ▪ *a hopeful message/mood* : feeling or showing hope ▪ *I'm hopeful about the future.* **2** : giving someone feelings of

hope ▪ *There are hopeful signs that the crisis may end soon.* — **hope·ful·ness** *n* [U]

²**hopeful** *n* [C] : a person who hopes to do something ▪ *a presidential hopeful* [=a person who hopes to become president]

hope·ful·ly /ˈhoʊpfəli/ *adv* **1** : in a hopeful manner ▪ *They gazed up at us hopefully.* **2** : it is hoped : I hope : we hope ▪ *Hopefully, it won't rain tomorrow.* [=I hope that it won't rain tomorrow]

hope·less /ˈhoʊpləs/ *adj* **1** : having or feeling no hope ▪ *He felt confused and hopeless after losing his job.* **2 a** *always before a noun* : unable to be changed ▪ *She's a hopeless romantic.* **b** *informal* : very bad ▪ *We were hopeless at (playing) golf.* **3** : giving no reason for hope ▪ *a hopeless situation* **4** : IMPOSSIBLE ▪ *a hopeless problem/task* — **hope·less·ly** /ˈhoʊpləsli/ *adv* ▪ *staring hopelessly out the window* — used especially to add force to a statement ▪ *They fell hopelessly in love.* — **hope·less·ness** *n* [U]

hop·per /ˈhɑːpɚ/ *n* **1** [C] : someone or something that hops **2** [C] : a container that is used for pouring material (such as grain or coal) into a machine or opening **3** *the hopper US* **a** : a box that bills are put into before they are considered by a legislature **b** : a mix of things to be considered or done ▪ *The company has several new product ideas in the hopper.*

hop·ping /ˈhɑːpɪŋ/ *adj, informal* : very busy or active ▪ *The boss kept me hopping all day.* — **hopping mad** *informal* : very angry ▪ *Workers are hopping mad over the new contract.*

hops /ˈhɑːps/ *n* [plural] : the dried flowers of a plant that are used to give a bitter flavor to beer and ale

¹**hop·scotch** /ˈhɑːpˌskɑːtʃ/ *n* [U] : a child's game in which players hop through a series of squares drawn on the ground

²**hopscotch** *vb* [I] *chiefly US, informal* : to move from one place to another ▪ *The tour hopscotched from city to city.*

horde /ˈhoɚd/ *n* [C] *usually disapproving* : a large group of people ▪ *a horde of tourists*

ho·ri·zon /həˈraɪzn/ *n* **1** *the horizon* : the line where the earth or sea seems to meet the sky **2** [C] **a** : the limit or range of a person's knowledge, understanding, or experience ▪ *Reading broadens/expands our horizons.* **b** : the limit of what is possible in a particular field or activity ▪ *opening up new horizons in the field of cancer research* — **on the horizon** : coming in the near future ▪ *A major breakthrough is on the horizon.*

hor·i·zon·tal /ˌhorəˈzɑːntl̩/ *adj* : parallel to the ground ▪ *a horizontal line/beam* — compare VERTICAL — **horizontal** *n* [C] — **hor·i·zon·tal·ly** /ˌhorəˈzɑːntl̩i/ *adv*

hor·mone /ˈhoɚˌmoʊn/ *n* [C] : a natural substance that is produced in the body and that influences the way the body grows or develops ▪ *sex hormones* — **hor·mon·al** /hoɚˈmoʊnl̩/ *adj*

¹**horn** /ˈhoɚn/ *n* **1 a** [C] : one of the hard pointed parts that grows on the head of cattle, goats, sheep, etc. **b** [C] : a hard

pointed part that grows on the nose of a rhinoceros **c** [U] : the hard material of which horns are made ▪ *utensils made of horn* **2** [C] : something that is shaped like an animal's horn ▪ *a saddle horn* **3** [C] **a** : a brass musical instrument (such as a trumpet or trombone) **b** : an instrument made from an animal's horn that is used for music or for producing loud signals **4** [C] : a device that makes a loud noise ▪ *Drivers were blowing/honking their horns.* **5 the horn** *US slang* : [1]TELEPHONE ▪ *He got on the horn to the police.* [=he phoned the police] — **blow your own horn or toot your own horn** *US, informal* : to talk about yourself or your achievements especially in a way that shows that you are proud or too proud ▪ *We had a very good year, and I think we have a right to blow our own horn.* — **lock horns** see [2]LOCK — **on the horns of a dilemma** : in a situation in which you have to choose between things that are unpleasant or undesirable — **take the bull by the horns** see BULL

[2]**horn** *vb* — **horn in** [phrasal vb] *US, informal + usually disapproving* : to add your comment or opinion to a conversation or discussion that you have been listening to ▪ *He always horns in on the conversation.*

hor·net /ˈhoɚnət/ *n* [C] : a flying insect that has a powerful sting

hornet's nest *n* [singular] : an angry reaction ▪ *His comments stirred up a hornet's nest of opposition/criticism.*

horn-rimmed glasses *n* [plural] : eyeglasses with frames made of a plastic that resembles horn (sense 1c)

horny /ˈhoɚni/ *adj* **horn·i·er; -est 1** : made of horn (sense 1c) or a similar substance ▪ *a horny growth* **2** : hard and tough ▪ *horny skin* **3** *informal* : sexually excited ▪ *horny teenagers*

horo·scope /ˈhorəˌskoʊp/ *n* [C] : advice and future predictions based on the date of a person's birth and the positions of the stars and planets

hor·ren·dous /həˈrɛndəs/ *adj* : very bad or unpleasant ▪ *horrendous crimes* ▪ *Her taste in clothes is horrendous.* — **hor·ren·dous·ly** *adv*

hor·ri·ble /ˈhorəbəl/ *adj* **1** : very shocking and upsetting ▪ *a horrible accident* **2** : very bad or unpleasant ▪ *a horrible smell/mistake* — **hor·ri·bly** /ˈhorəbli/ *adv*

hor·rid /ˈhorəd/ *adj* **1** : very shocking or bad ▪ *horrid living conditions* **2** : very unpleasant ▪ *a horrid little man* — **hor·rid·ly** *adv*

hor·rif·ic /hoˈrɪfɪk/ *adj* : causing horror or shock ▪ *a horrific crime* — **hor·rif·i·cal·ly** *adv*

hor·ri·fy /ˈhorəˌfaɪ/ *vb* **-fies; -fied; -fy·ing** [T] : to greatly upset and shock (someone) ▪ *The crime horrified the nation.* — **horrifying** *adj* ▪ *a horrifying experience* — **hor·ri·fy·ing·ly** *adv*

[1]**hor·ror** /ˈhorɚ/ *n* **1** [U] : a very strong feeling of fear, dread, and shock ▪ *There was a look of horror on her face.* ▪ *The crowd watched in horror as the fire*

spread. **2** [U] : the quality of something that causes feelings of fear, dread, and shock ▪ *the horror of war* **3** [C/U] : something that causes feelings of fear, dread, and shock ▪ *the horrors of the war* ▪ *tales of horror* — **have a horror of** : to have a strong dislike for or fear of (something) ▪ *Like many teenagers, she has a horror of being seen in public with her parents.*

[2]**horror** *adj, always before a noun* : intended to cause feelings of fear or horror ▪ *a horror movie/novel*

horror story *n* [C] *informal* **1** : a story about an actual event or experience that is very unpleasant **2** : an experience that is very unpleasant ▪ *Her childhood was a horror story.*

hors d'oeuvre /ˌoɚˈdɚv/ *n* [C] : a food served in small portions before the main part of a meal

[1]**horse** /ˈhoɚs/ *n* **1** [C] : a large animal that is used for riding and for carrying and pulling things ▪ *ride/mount a horse* **2** [C] : SAWHORSE **3** [plural] *US, informal* : HORSEPOWER ▪ *a car with 275 horses* **4 the horses** [plural] *informal* : horse races ▪ *betting on the horses* **5** [C] *US, informal* : an athlete who is strong and who helps a team to win — usually plural ▪ *a team with the horses to win the pennant* [=a team with the good players needed to win the pennant] — **a horse of a different color** *chiefly US, informal* : a very different thing or issue ▪ *That's what we'll do. But if he doesn't show up . . . well, that's a horse of a different color.* — **beat a dead horse** (*chiefly US*) or **flog a dead horse** *informal* : to keep talking about a subject that has already been discussed or decided — **change horses in midstream** : to choose a different leader or policy during a time when serious problems are being dealt with — **eat a horse** *informal* ♦ Someone who is very hungry can be described as being hungry enough to *eat a horse.* ▪ *I'm so hungry I could eat a horse.* — **from the horse's mouth** *informal, of information* : from the original source or person and therefore thought to be true ▪ *I know it's hard to believe but I heard it (straight) from the horse's mouth.* — **hold your horses** *informal* — used to tell someone to slow down, stop, or wait for a short time ▪ *"Hurry up. We need to get going." "Hold your horses. I'll be ready in a minute."* — **look a gift horse in the mouth** : to look in a critical way at something that has been given to you — **put the cart before the horse** see [1]CART

[2]**horse** *vb* **horsed; hors·ing** — **horse around** or *Brit* **horse about** [phrasal vb] *informal* : to play in a rough or loud way ▪ *They were horsing around instead of studying.*

horse·back /ˈhoɚsˌbæk/ *n* — **on horseback** : on the back of a horse ▪ *traveling on horseback* — **horseback** *adj, always before a noun* ▪ *a horseback rider* [=a person riding on a horse] ▪ *I enjoy horseback riding.* — **horseback** *adv, chiefly US* ▪ *riding horseback*

horse chestnut *n* [C] : a tree with large

bunches of flowers and large brown seeds; *also* : the seed of a horse chestnut tree

horse–drawn *adj* : pulled by a horse or by a group of horses ▪ *a horse-drawn carriage*

horse·fly /ˈhoɚsˌflaɪ/ *n, pl* **-flies** [C] : a type of large biting fly

horse·hair /ˈhoɚsˌheɚ/ *n* [U] : hair from the mane or tail of a horse — **horsehair** *adj* ▪ *horsehair fabric*

horse·man /ˈhoɚsmən/ *n, pl* **-men** /-mən/ [C] : a person (especially a man) who rides horses or who breeds or raises horses — **horse·man·ship** /ˈhoɚsmənˌʃɪp/ *n* [U]

horse·play /ˈhoɚsˌpleɪ/ *n* [U] : rough or loud play : energetic and noisy playful activity ▪ *kids engaging in horseplay*

horse·pow·er /ˈhoɚsˌpawɚ/ *n, pl* **horsepower** [C/U] : a unit used to measure the power of engines ▪ *an engine with 200 horsepower* ▪ (*figurative*) *intellectual horsepower*

horse·rad·ish /ˈhoɚsˌrædɪʃ/ *n* **1** [C] : a tall plant whose root is used for making a sauce **2** [U] : a strong sauce made from the root of the horseradish plant

horse·shoe /ˈhoɚsˌʃuː/ *n* **1** [C] : a U-shaped band of iron nailed to the bottom of a horse's hoof as a shoe **2** [*plural*] *US* : a game in which players try to get horseshoes around a stake in the ground by throwing them at the stake from a certain distance

horse·whip /ˈhoɚsˌwɪp/ *vb* **-whipped;** **-whip·ping** [T] : to hit (someone) with a whip ▪ *He thinks government officials who steal public money should be horsewhipped.*

horse·wom·an /ˈhoɚsˌwʊmən/ *n, pl* **-wom·en** /-ˌwɪmən/ [C] : a woman who rides horses or who breeds or manages horses

hors·ey *or* **horsy** /ˈhoɚsi/ *adj* **hors·i·er;** **-est** **1** : of, relating to, or involved with horses ▪ *horsey people* **2** : suggesting a horse or horses ▪ *a horsey face*

hor·ti·cul·ture /ˈhoɚtəˌkʌltʃɚ/ *n* [U] : the science of growing fruits, vegetables, and flowers — **hor·ti·cul·tur·al** /ˌhoɚtəˈkʌltʃərəl/ *adj* — **hor·ti·cul·tur·ist** /ˌhoɚtəˈkʌltʃərɪst/ *or chiefly Brit* **hor·ti·cul·tur·al·ist** /ˌhoɚtəˈkʌltʃrəlɪst/ *n* [C]

ho·san·na /hoʊˈzænə, moʊˈzɑːnə/ *n* [C] : an expression of enthusiastic praise ▪ *The book was met with hearty hosannas from literary critics.* [=literary critics praised the book enthusiastically]

¹hose /ˈhoʊz/ *n* **1** *pl* **hos·es** [C/U] : a long, usually rubber tube that liquids or gases can flow through ▪ *a fire hose* [=a hose used to spray water on a fire] ▪ *a garden hose* [=a hose used to water a garden] **2** [*plural*] : clothes (such as stockings, socks, and pantyhose) that are worn on the legs and feet ▪ *women's hose* — called also *hosiery*

²hose *vb* **hosed; hos·ing** [T] **1** : to spray or wash (something) with water from a hose ▪ *He hosed down/off the sidewalk.* **2** *US slang* : to cheat or trick (someone) ▪ *We got hosed.*

hose·pipe /ˈhoʊzˌpaɪp/ *n* [C] *Brit* : ¹HOSE 1

ho·siery /ˈhoʊʒəri, *Brit* ˈhəʊzjəri/ *n* [U] : ¹HOSE 2

hos·pice /ˈhɑːspəs/ *n* [C] : a place that provides care for people who are dying

hos·pi·ta·ble /hɑːˈspɪtəbəl, ˈhɑːspɪtəbəl/ *adj* **1** : generous and friendly to guests or visitors ▪ *The people there were very hospitable (to us).* **2** : having an environment where plants, animals, or people can live or grow easily ▪ *a hospitable climate* ▪ *The climate here is hospitable to many species.* **3** : ready or willing to accept or consider something ▪ *a person/company known for being hospitable to new ideas* — **hos·pi·ta·bly** /hɑːˈspɪtəbli, ˈhɑːspɪtəbli/ *adv*

hos·pi·tal /ˈhɑːspɪtl/ *n* [C] : a place where sick or injured people are given care or treatment and where babies are often born ▪ (*US*) *She's in the hospital.* = (*Brit*) *She's in hospital.* ▪ *a hospital bed/gown*

hos·pi·tal·i·ty /ˌhɑːspəˈtæləti/ *n* [U] **1** : generous and friendly treatment of visitors and guests ▪ *We were grateful for their kindness and hospitality.* **2** : the activity of providing food, drinks, etc., for people who are the guests or customers of an organization ▪ *a job in the hospitality business/industry*

hos·pi·tal·ize *also Brit* **hos·pi·tal·ise** /ˈhɑːspɪtəˌlaɪz/ *vb* **-ized; -iz·ing** [T] : to place (someone) in a hospital for care or treatment ▪ *He was hospitalized after the accident.* — **hos·pi·tal·i·za·tion** *also Brit* **hos·pi·tal·i·sa·tion** /ˌhɑːspɪtələˈzeɪʃən, *Brit* ˌhɑːspɪtəˌlaɪˈzeɪʃən/ *n* [C/U]

¹host /ˈhoʊst/ *n* [C] **1** : a person (especially a man) who is entertaining guests socially or as a job **2** : a person who talks to guests on a television or radio show ▪ *a game-show host* **3** : an animal or plant in which another animal or plant lives and gets its food or protection **4** : a great amount or number ▪ *a (whole) host of options* **5** *the Host* : a round, thin piece of bread used in the Christian Communion ceremony — **play host to** ◆ A place or organization that *plays host to* an event (such as a meeting or convention) provides the things that are needed for that event. ▪ *The city played host to the Olympic Games.*

²host *vb* [T] : to be the host for (a social event, a group of people, etc.) ▪ *They hosted a dinner party.*

hos·tage /ˈhɑːstɪdʒ/ *n* [C] : a person who is captured by someone who demands that certain things be done before the captured person is freed ▪ *The terrorists released the hostages.* ▪ *a hostage crisis* ▪ *The passengers were held/taken hostage.*

hos·tel /ˈhɑːstl/ *n* [C] : an inexpensive place for usually young travelers to stay overnight — called also *youth hostel*

hos·tel·ry /ˈhɑːstlri/ *n, pl* **-ries** [C] *old-fashioned* : an inn, pub, or hotel

host·ess /ˈhoʊstəs/ *n* [C] **1** : a woman who is entertaining guests socially or as a job **2** : a woman whose job it is to greet and help people in a restaurant or on an airplane or ship **3** : a woman who talks to guests on a television or radio show

hos·tile /ˈhɑːstl, ˈhɑːˌstajəl/ *adj* **1** : of or relating to an enemy ▪ *hostile territories/troops* **2** : not friendly ▪ *a hostile atmosphere/expression* ▪ *hostile behavior* ▪ *a hostile witness* [=a witness in a legal case who supports the opposing side] **3** : unpleasant or harsh ▪ *a hostile climate/workplace* **4** *business* : involving an attempt to buy a company from people who do not want to sell it ▪ *a hostile takeover*

hos·til·i·ty /hɑːˈstɪləti/ *n, pl* **-ties** **1** [*U*] : an unfriendly or hostile state, attitude, or action ▪ *They showed open hostility to/toward outsiders.* **2** [*plural*] *formal* : acts of fighting in a war ▪ *Both sides were calling for a cessation of hostilities.*

hot /ˈhɑːt/ *adj* **hot·ter; hot·test** **1 a** : having a high temperature ▪ *hot weather* ▪ *a hot climate/country* **b** : having a feeling of high body heat ▪ *I was hot and tired.* **c** *of food or drink* : heated to a hot or warm temperature ▪ *hot cereal* ▪ *a hot beverage/meal* **2** *informal* **a** : currently liked or wanted by many people ▪ *a hot new restaurant* : currently very active or strong ▪ *hot trends/fashions* : currently causing a lot of interest or discussion ▪ *a hot concept/idea/topic* ✧ Something or someone that is a **hot commodity/item/property** is currently very valuable or popular. ▪ *Computer games are a hot item in stores this year.* **b** : very good — usually used in negative statements ▪ *That's not such a hot idea.* [=that's not a good idea] ▪ *He wasn't feeling too hot.* [=wasn't feeling well] **c** : having a period of unusual success or good luck ▪ *The team has been hot recently.* = *The team has recently been on a hot streak.* ▪ *When you're hot, you're hot.* [=when you are having good luck, you keep winning or succeeding repeatedly] **3 a** : marked by anger or strong feelings ▪ *a hot argument/debate/dispute* **b** *always before a noun* : easily excited or angered ▪ *He has a hot temper.* **c** : ANGRY ▪ *He was getting pretty hot about the delays.* ▪ *The delays got him all hot and bothered.* **4** *of food* : having a spicy or peppery flavor ▪ *hot sauce/mustard* **5** *informal* **a** : sexually excited by or interested in someone — + *for* ▪ *She's hot for the new guy in her office.* **b** : sexually attractive ▪ *The girl he's dating is really hot.* **c** : exciting in a sexual or romantic way ▪ *He has a hot date tonight.* **d** *of sex* : very intense or exciting ▪ *hot sex* ▪ **e** : EAGER ▪ *She's hot to party.* **6** *music* : having an exciting rhythm ▪ *hot jazz* **7** *informal* : very strong or determined ▪ *We faced some hot competition.* **8** : newly made : fresh and warm ▪ *bread hot from the oven* ✧ Something, such as a story or book, that is **hot off the press** has just recently been completed, published, or printed. **9** : following closely ▪ *The police are in hot pursuit of the suspect.* [=the police are chasing the suspect] ✧ To be **hot on the heels/trail** of someone is to be chasing someone very closely. To be/follow/come **hot on the heels** of something is to come or happen immediately or very soon after something. ▪

Their second album is coming hot on the heels of the first. To be **hot on the trail** of something is to be very close to doing, finding, or getting something. ▪ *The company says it is hot on the trail of a new cancer treatment.* **10** : very bright ▪ *hot pink* **11** : carrying electric current ▪ *The black wire is hot.* **12** *informal* : recently stolen ▪ *hot jewels* — **hot and heavy** *informal* : sexually intense, active, or exciting ▪ *They have a very hot and heavy relationship.* — **hot on** *informal* : strongly favoring or liking (something) ▪ *The company president is very hot on the idea of developing new products.* — **hot under the collar** *informal* : angry or upset — **hot·ly** *adv* ▪ *a hotly contested election* ▪ *a hotly debated issue* ▪ *He hotly denied any involvement in the controversy.* — **hot·ness** *n* [*U*] ▪ *the hotness* [=*spiciness*] *of the pepper*

hot air *n* [*U*] *informal* : talk that is meant to sound important but does not mean very much ▪ *He's full of hot air.*

hot–air balloon *n* [*C*] : a large balloon that is filled with heated air and that floats in the sky with a basket underneath for people to ride in

hot·bed /ˈhɑːtˌbɛd/ *n* [*C*] : a place where something grows or develops easily ▪ *a hotbed of political unrest*

hot–blood·ed /ˈhɑːtˈblʌdəd/ *adj* : becoming angry or excited very easily ▪ *a hot-blooded young man*

hot·cake /ˈhɑːtˌkeɪk/ *n* [*C*] *chiefly US* : PANCAKE — **like hotcakes** *informal* : very quickly ▪ *The book is selling like hotcakes.*

hot chocolate *n* [*C/U*] : a hot drink that is chocolate-flavored — called also *hot cocoa*

hotch·potch /ˈhɑːtʃˌpɑːtʃ/ *n* [*singular*] *Brit* : HODGEPODGE

hot dog /ˈhɑːtˌdɑːg/ *n* [*C*] **1** : a small cooked sausage that is mild in flavor and is usually served in a long roll (called a hot dog bun) **2** *US, informal* : a person (such as an athlete) who performs or plays in a way that is meant to attract attention ▪ *The other players don't like him because he's such a hot dog.*

hot·dog /ˈhɑːtˌdɑːg/ *vb* **-dogged; -dogging** [*I*] *US, informal* : to perform or play in a way that is meant to attract attention ▪ *hotdogging skiers*

ho·tel /hoʊˈtɛl/ *n* [*C*] : a building that has rooms for people to stay in especially when they are traveling

ho·tel·i·er /hoʊˈtɛljə/ *n* [*C*] : a person who owns or operates a hotel

hot flash *n* [*C*] *US* : a sudden brief hot feeling experienced especially by women during menopause

hot flush *n* [*C*] *Brit* : HOT FLASH

hot·head /ˈhɑːtˌhɛd/ *n* [*C*] *informal* : a person who gets angry easily

hot·head·ed /ˈhɑːtˈhɛdəd/ *adj, informal* : easily angered ▪ *a hotheaded boss; also* : very angry ▪ *He wrote a hot-headed letter.*

hot·house /ˈhɑːtˌhaʊs/ *n* [*C*] : a heated building used for growing plants

hot line *n* [*C*] **1** : a telephone service for the public to use to get help in emergencies **2** : a telephone connection that allows leaders of different countries to talk to each other directly and that is always kept ready for use ▪ *They set up a hot line between Washington and Moscow.*

hot plate *n* [*C*] : a small portable device with a metal plate used for cooking or heating food

hot pot *n* [*C/U*] *chiefly Brit* : a mixture of meat and vegetables cooked together with liquid in a single pot

hot potato *n* [*C*] *informal* : an issue or question about which people have different opinions and feel very strongly ▪ *political hot potatoes like abortion*

hot rod *n* [*C*] *informal* : a car that has been changed so that it can be driven and raced at very fast speeds

hots /'hɑːts/ *n* — **the hots** *informal* : strong feelings of sexual attraction *for* someone ▪ *She has the hots for him.* [=she is very attracted to him]

hot seat *n* — **the hot seat** : the position of someone who is in trouble or is being asked many difficult or embarrassing questions ▪ *The company's president is in the hot seat.*

hot-shot /'hɑːt,ʃɑːt/ *n* [*C*] *informal* : a talented and successful person ▪ *a young hotshot* ▪ *a hotshot*

hot spot *n* [*C*] *informal* **1** : a very popular or active place ▪ *a vacation hot spot* **2** : a place where there is much danger or fighting ▪ *a global hot spot* [=an area in the world where war is possible or likely]

hot stuff *n* [*U*] *informal* **1** : someone or something that is unusually good or popular ▪ *His music was hot stuff in those days.* **2** : a sexually attractive person ▪ *Her new boyfriend is hot stuff.*

hot-tem-pered /'hɑːt'tɛmpəd/ *adj* : becoming angry very easily : having or showing a hot temper ▪ *a hot-tempered boss/reply*

hot tub *n* [*C*] : a large tub of hot water in which people sit to relax or spend time together

hot water *n* [*U*] *informal* : a difficult situation : TROUBLE ▪ *He's in hot water with the IRS.*

hot-water bottle *n* [*C*] : a rubber container that is filled with hot water and used to warm a bed or a part of your body

hot-wire /'hɑːt,wajə/ *vb* **-wired; -wiring** [*T*] *informal* : to start (a car or the engine of a car) by connecting wires in the electrical system without using a key

¹**hound** /'haʊnd/ *n* [*C*] **1** : a dog; *especially* : a type of dog that has a very good sense of smell and is trained to hunt **2** : a person who is very determined to get something especially for a collection ▪ *autograph hounds*

²**hound** *vb* [*T*] : to chase or bother (someone or something) in a constant or determined way ▪ *He is being hounded by the press.*

hour /'awə/ *n* **1** [*C*] : 60 minutes ▪ *We've been waiting (for) an hour.* ▪ *They arrived a few hours later.* **2** [*C*] **a** : the time shown on a clock or watch ▪ *The hour is half past ten.* [=10:30] ▪ *(US) The movie starts at the top of the hour.* [=at the be

ginning of the hour; at 12:00, 1:00, 2:00, etc.] ▪ *The next train will leave on the hour.* [=at the beginning of the next hour] ▪ *Trains leave the station every hour on the hour.* [=at the beginning of each hour; at 12:00, 1:00, 2:00, etc.] **b** : a particular time during the day ▪ *What are you doing here at this hour (of the night)?* [=at such a late time?] ▪ *at the midnight hour* [=at midnight] ▪ *We arrived at the appointed hour.* [=at the time that had been agreed upon] ▪ *They serve breakfast at all hours.* = *They serve breakfast at any hour.* [=at any time of day] ▪ *They were up till/until all hours.* [=they were up very late] ▪ *The store is open twenty-four hours a day.* [=all day and night] ▪ *They studied into the wee hours.* [=until early in the morning] **3 a** [*C*] : the time of a specified activity ▪ *during her lunch hour* ▪ *the cocktail/dinner hour* **b** [*C*] : a particular time or period of time ▪ *They helped us in our hour of need.* [=when we needed help] ▪ *our country's finest hour* [=a time of great success, courage, or heroism] ◇ The *man/woman (etc.) of the hour* is a person who is being honored or praised or who is enjoying success at a particular time. **c** [*plural*] : a time scheduled or used for a particular purpose or activity ▪ *Business hours are from 8 a.m. to 5 p.m.* ▪ *She works long hours.* [=works for more hours than usual each day] ▪ *Hospital visiting hours are between 2 p.m. and 6 p.m.* ▪ *He enjoys reading in his off hours.* [=when he is not working] ▪ *She keeps late hours at the office.* [=she works until late at night] **4** [*C*] : the distance that can be traveled in an hour ▪ *She lives two hours away.* — **after hours** or *Brit* **out of hours** : after the regular hours of work or operation ▪ *The professor gave out his phone number so students could reach him after hours.* — **an/per hour** — used in measurements that describe the speed of something ▪ *The speed limit is 65 miles per hour.*

hour-glass /'awə,glæs, *Brit* 'awə,glɑːs/ *n* [*C*] : a device for measuring time ◇ An hourglass is a glass container with an upper part and a lower part connected by a narrow opening. The upper part contains sand which flows into the lower part in a specified amount of time (such as an hour). — **hourglass** *adj, always before a noun* ▪ *an hourglass figure/shape*

hour-ly /'awəli/ *adj* **1** : happening every hour ▪ *hourly bus service* **2 a** : paid for one hour of work ▪ *an hourly wage* **b** : paid by the hour ▪ *hourly workers* — **hourly** *adv*

¹**house** /'haʊs/ *n* **1 a** [*C*] : a building in which a person, family, etc., lives ▪ *Would you like to come to my house for dinner?* **b** [*singular*] : the people who live in a house ▪ *The noise woke the whole house.* **2** [*C*] **a** : a structure or shelter in which animals are kept **b** : a building in which something is stored ▪ *a carriage house* **3** [*C*] : a building where students or members of a religious group live ▪ *a fraternity house* **4 a** [*C*] : a group of people who meet to discuss and make the laws of a country ▪ *The bill has been

approved by both houses of Congress. **b** **the House** : HOUSE OF REPRESENTA-TIVES **5** [C] **a** : a specified kind of business ▪ *a publishing/fashion/brokerage house* **b** : a place or building where a specified kind of activity or entertainment occurs ▪ *an auction house* ▪ *a house of God/worship* [=a place, such as a church, where people go for religious services] : a place where an illegal activity occurs ▪ *a house of prostitution* ▪ a particular kind of restaurant ▪ *a seafood house* ▪ *Oyster stew is a specialty of the house.* [=a special dish that is featured in a restaurant] ✧ A *house wine* is a basic wine that is always available in a restaurant. A *house salad* and a *house (salad) dressing* are the regular salad and dressing in a U.S. restaurant. **6** [C] : the audience in a theater or concert hall ▪ *They had a full/packed house on opening night.* ✧ To **bring down the house** or to **bring the house down** is to get great approval and applause or laughter from an audience. **7** *House* [C] : a royal or noble family including ancestors and all the people who are related to them ▪ *the House of Tudor* — **clean house** US **1** : to clean the floors, furniture, etc., inside a house ▪ *He cleans house on Tuesdays.* **2** : to make important basic changes in an organization, business, etc., in order to correct problems ▪ *The mayor decided it was time to clean house.* — **house in order** ✧ To put/get/set (etc.) your *house in order* is to improve or correct the way you do things. ▪ *We should get our (own) house in order before we criticize others.* — **keep house** : to do the work that is needed to take care of a house ▪ *You need someone to keep house for you.* — **like a house on fire** *informal* : extremely well ▪ *They got on/along like a house on fire.* [=they liked each other very much] — **on the house** : FREE ▪ *The drinks are on the house.* — **play house** ✧ When children *play house* they pretend that they are adults and that they are doing the things that adults do in a house, such as cooking and serving food. — **set up house** : to become settled in a house where you are going to live ▪ *They set up house in Los Angeles.*

²**house** /ˈhaʊz/ *vb* **housed; hous·ing** [T] **1** : to provide shelter or a living space for (someone) ▪ *The students were housed with local families.* **2** : to store or contain (something) ▪ *The paintings are housed in the National Gallery.* **3** : to surround or enclose (something) in order to protect it ▪ *He built casing to house the pipes.*

house arrest *n* [U] *law* : the condition of being forced to stay in your home rather than in prison as a form of punishment ▪ *He was placed under house arrest.*

house·boat /ˈhaʊsˌboʊt/ *n* [C] : a boat that is also used as a house

house·bound /ˈhaʊsˌbaʊnd/ *adj* : unable to leave your home ▪ *She has been housebound since she fell.*

house·break /ˈhaʊsˌbreɪk/ *vb* **-broke** /-ˌbroʊk/; **-bro·ken** /-ˌbroʊkən/; **-break·ing** [T] US : to train (an animal)

to urinate or defecate outside the home or in an acceptable place indoors ▪ *housebreak a puppy* — **housebroken** *adj* ▪ *Is the dog housebroken?*

house·break·ing /ˈhaʊsˌbreɪkɪŋ/ *n* [U] : the act of forcefully entering someone's house in order to commit a crime (such as robbery) — **house·break·er** /ˈhaʊsˌbreɪkɚ/ *n* [C]

house call *n* [C] *chiefly US* : a visit by a doctor to someone's house

house cat *n* [C] : a cat that is kept as a pet

house·clean·ing /ˈhaʊsˌkliːnɪŋ/ *n* [*singular*] : the act or activity of cleaning the inside of a house or apartment and its furniture, appliances, etc.

house·coat /ˈhaʊsˌkoʊt/ *n* [C] : an informal and often long and loose piece of clothing that is worn by a woman at home

house·dress /ˈhaʊsˌdrɛs/ *n* [C] *chiefly US* : an informal dress that is usually worn only while cleaning or doing other housework

house·fly /ˈhaʊsˌflaɪ/ *n, pl* **-flies** [C] : a common fly that lives in or near people's houses

house·guest /ˈhaʊsˌgɛst/ *n* [C] : a person who visits and usually stays in someone's home overnight

¹**house·hold** /ˈhaʊsˌhoʊld/ *n* [C] : the people in a family or other group that are living together in one house

²**household** *adj, always before a noun* **1** : of or relating to a house or to the people living in a house ▪ *household appliances/chores* **2** : familiar or common ▪ *a famous actor who has become a household name* [=a person or thing whose name is very well-known]

house·hus·band /ˈhaʊsˌhʌzbənd/ *n* [C] : a married man who stays at home, does cleaning, cooking, etc., and does not have another job outside the home

house·keep·er /ˈhaʊsˌkiːpɚ/ *n* [C] : a person whose job is to manage the cooking, cleaning, etc., in a house

house·keep·ing /ˈhaʊsˌkiːpɪŋ/ *n* [U] **1** : HOUSEWORK **2** : the things that must be done regularly to keep something working properly ▪ *We took the computer offline to do some basic housekeeping.*

house·mate /ˈhaʊsˌmeɪt/ *n* [C] : a person who lives in the same house with another person but is not a part of that person's family

House of Commons *n* — **the House of Commons** : the part of the British or Canadian Parliament whose members are elected by voters

House of Lords *n* — **the House of Lords** : the part of the British Parliament whose members are not elected by voters

House of Representatives *n* — **the House of Representatives** : the larger part of the U.S. Congress or of the Parliament of Australia or New Zealand

house·plant /ˈhaʊsˌplænt, *Brit* ˈhaʊsˌplɑːnt/ *n* [C] : a plant that is grown or kept indoors

house—sit /ˈhaʊsˌsɪt/ *vb* **-sat; -sit·ting** [T/I] : to stay in and take care of some-

one's house or apartment while that person is away • *They will house-sit for us while we're away.* • *He house-sat our apartment while we were on vacation.* —
house·sit·ter /ˈhaʊsˌsɪtə/ *n* [C]

house–to–house /ˌhaʊstəˈhaʊs/ *adj, always before a noun* : going or made by going to each house, apartment, or building in an area • *a house-to-house search*

house·wares /ˈhaʊsˌweəz/ *n* [*plural*] : small things (such as cooking utensils or lamps) that are used in a house

house·warm·ing /ˈhaʊsˌwoəmɪŋ/ *n* [C] : a party to celebrate moving into a new home

house·wife /ˈhaʊsˌwaɪf/ *n, pl* **-wives** /-ˌwaɪvz/ [C] : a married woman who stays at home, does cleaning, cooking, etc., and does not have another job outside the home

house·work /ˈhaʊsˌwək/ *n* [U] : work (such as cleaning, cooking, or laundry) that is done to keep a house clean and running properly

hous·ing /ˈhaʊzɪŋ/ *n* **1** [U] : the houses, apartments, etc., in which people live • *low-income housing* • *housing costs* **2** [C] : something that covers or protects something else (such as a mechanical part) • *I removed the housing to inspect the vent.*

housing development *n* [C] *US* : a group of houses that are built near each other and sold or rented by one owner — called also (*Brit*) *housing estate*

housing project *n* [C] *US* : a group of houses or apartments that are built for poor people — called also (*US*) *project*

hov·el /ˈhʌvəl, ˈhɑːvəl/ *n* [C] : a small, poorly built and often dirty house

hov·er /ˈhʌvə, *Brit* ˈhɒvə/ *vb* [I] **1** : to float in the air without moving in any direction • *Helicopters hovered above us.* **2** : to stay very close to a person or place • *Waiters hovered near our table.* **3 a** : to stay near a specified point or level • *Temperatures will continue to hover around freezing.* **b** : to be or remain in a specified state or condition • *The country hovers on the brink of famine.*

¹how /ˈhaʊ/ *adv* **1** : in what manner or way • *How did you meet him?* : by what means • *"How did she die?"* **2** : for what reason • WHY • *How did you happen to move here?* **3** : to what degree, extent, or amount — used before an adjective or adverb • *How tall is he?* • *How often do you see them?* **4** — used for emphasis before an adjective • *How wonderful/strange/awful!* • (*informal*) *How cool is that!* [=that is really cool] **5 a** — used to ask if someone feels good, bad, happy, sad, etc. • *"How are you?" "Very well, thank you."* • *How do you feel?* = *How are you feeling?* **b** — used to ask if something is good, bad, etc. • *How's the new job?* [=do you like your new job?] • *How are things at home?* • **How do you like the soup?** = *How is the soup?* [=do you like the soup?] — **and how** *chiefly US, informal* — used for emphasis • *"Will you be glad when it's over?" "And how!"* [=I will be very glad] — **as how** *informal* : ²THAT •

I don't know as how your plan would be any better than mine. • **Seeing as how** *things were getting worse* [=because things were getting worse]*, she decided to do something.* — **how about 1** : does that include (someone) • *"We're all going." "How about Kenny?"* **2** *informal* **a** — used to show that you are very impressed by someone or something • *He won again! How about that guy!* **b** **how about that** *chiefly US* — used to show that you are surprised or pleased by something • *He won again! How about that!* **3** *also US* (*informal*) **how's about** — used to make a suggestion about what could be done • *What should we do tonight? How about (seeing) a movie?* **4** — used to ask someone to tell you something in response to what you have just said • *I'm ready to go. How about you?* [=are you ready, too?] — **how can/could 1** — used to show you think that someone has done or said something shocking or wrong • *How could she just walk away from her children like that?* **2** — used to express doubt that something will happen, is possible, etc. • *How can I ever thank you?* [=I am extremely grateful to you] **3 how could you** *informal* — used to show disappointment in someone's actions, thoughts, words, etc. • *You told him? Oh, how could you!* — **how come** *chiefly US, informal* — used to ask why something has happened, is true, etc. • *"He said he's not going." "How come?"* [=why isn't he going?] • *How come you're here so early?* [=why are you here so early?] — **how do you do** *formal* : HELLO — used especially when you are first introduced to someone • *How do you do, Miss Smith?* — **how do you like that** — used for emphasis or to show surprise or disapproval • *She canceled at the last minute. How do you like that?* — **how so** : in what way : why do you think that • *"This room looks different." "How so?"* — **how's that (again)** *informal* : WHAT — used to request that something be repeated or explained again • *I don't understand. How's that again?*

²how *conj* **1** : in what manner or way • *I asked how I could help.* • *She explained how she knew them.* • *And that's how it is.* [=that is the state of the situation] **2** : THAT • *It's amazing how they completed the bridge so quickly.*

how'd /ˈhaʊd/ — used as a contraction of *how would* or *how did* • *How'd* [=how did] *he do that?* • *How'd* [=how would] *you like to go to the beach?*

how·dy /ˈhaʊdi/ *interj, US* — used as an informal greeting • *Howdy, folks.*

¹how·ev·er /haʊˈevə/ *adv* **1** — used when you are saying something that is different from or contrasts with a previous statement • *Sales are up this quarter. However, expenses have increased as well.* **2** : to whatever degree or extent : no matter how — used before an adjective or adverb • *She couldn't convince him, however hard* [=no matter how hard] *she tried.* **3** — used as a more forceful way of saying *how* ▪ *However did you do that?* [=how did you ever do that?]

²**however** *conj* : in whatever manner or way ▪ *I will help however I can.*

how·it·zer /ˈhawətsə/ *n* [*C*] : a large gun that is used to fire shells high into the air for a short distance

howl /ˈhawəl/ *vb* **1** [*I*] *of a dog, wolf, etc.* : to make a long, loud cry that sounds sad **2** [*I*] *of the wind* : to make a long, loud sound ▪ *The wind was howling.* **3** [*I*] : to cry out loudly in pain, anger, amusement, etc. ▪ *The audience howled with laughter.* **4** [*T/I*] : to say something in a loud and angry way ▪ *"I can't take it!" she howled.* ▪ *protesters howling for change* — **howl** *n* [*C*]

howl·er /ˈhawlə/ *n* [*C*] *informal* : a stupid but funny mistake or error

how's /ˈhawz/ — used as a contraction of *how is* ▪ *How's your meal?*

how-to /ˈhawˈtu/ *adj, always before a noun, chiefly US* : giving practical instruction or advice on how to do something yourself ▪ *how-to books*

hp *abbr* horsepower ▪ *a 200-hp engine*

HQ *abbr* headquarters ▪ *Check in at camp HQ by 8:00.*

hr *abbr* hour ▪ *a 35-hr workweek*

HRH *abbr* Her Royal Highness; His Royal Highness

ht. *abbr* height

HTML /ˌeɪtʃˌtiˌemˈel/ *n* [*U*] : a computer language that is used to create documents or Web sites on the Internet

http *abbr* hypertext transfer protocol; hypertext transport protocol — used in Internet addresses ▪ *http://www.Merriam-Webster.com*

hub /ˈhʌb/ *n* [*C*] **1** : the central and most active part or place ▪ *the hub of the city* ▪ *a major tourist hub* [=a place where many tourists go] **2** : the airport or the city through which an airline sends most of its flights **3** : the center of a wheel, propeller, fan, etc.

hub·bub /ˈhʌˌbʌb/ *n* [*U*] **1** : a loud mixture of sound or voices **2** : a situation in which there is much noise, confusion, excitement, and activity ▪ *What's all the hubbub about?*

hub·by /ˈhʌbi/ *n, pl* **-bies** [*C*] *informal* : HUSBAND

hub·cap /ˈhʌbˌkæp/ *n* [*C*] : a removable plastic or metal cover on the center of a car or truck wheel

huck·ster /ˈhʌkstə/ *n* [*C*] *US, disapproving* : someone who sells or advertises something in an aggressive, dishonest, or annoying way

HUD /ˈhʌd/ *abbr, US* (Department of) Housing and Urban Development ▪ *an official at HUD* ✧ *The Department of Housing and Urban Development is a part of the U.S. federal government that is responsible for policies that relate to providing housing for U.S. citizens.*

¹**hud·dle** /ˈhʌdl/ *vb* **hud·dled; hud·dling** [*I*] **1** : to come close together in a group ▪ *We huddled around the campfire.* **2** : to sit or lie in a curled or bent position ▪ *The students huddled over their desks.* **3 a** : to come together to talk about something privately ▪ *Union representatives are*

huddling to discuss the proposal. **b** *American football* : to gather in a huddle ▪ *The players huddled (up).*

²**huddle** *n* [*C*] **1** : a group of people or things that are close to each other **2 a** : a private discussion or meeting ▪ *The boss is in a huddle with the marketing director.* **b** *American football* : a group of players who have gathered away from the line of scrimmage for a short time to hear instructions for the next play

hue /ˈhju/ *n* [*C*] **1** : a color or a shade of a color ▪ *hues of blue and green* **2** : kind or type ▪ *politicians of every hue* — **hued** /ˈhjuːd/ *adj* ▪ *brightly/richly hued cloth*

hue and cry *n* [*singular*] : an angry protest about something ▪ *There was a hue and cry in opposition to the film.*

¹**huff** /ˈhʌf/ *vb* [*T*] : to say (something) in a way that shows you are annoyed or angry ▪ *"This is a complete waste of time," she huffed.* — **huff and puff** : to breathe in a loud and heavy way because of physical effort ▪ *He was huffing and puffing when he got to the top of the stairs.*

²**huff** *n* — **in a huff** : in an angry or annoyed state ▪ *They argued and she left in a huff.*

huffy /ˈhʌfi/ *adj* **huff·i·er; -est** *informal* : angry or annoyed ▪ *Now, don't get huffy—I was only teasing.*

hug /ˈhʌg/ *vb* **hugged; hug·ging** **1** [*T/I*] : to put your arms around someone especially as a way of showing love or friendship ▪ *She hugged her son.* **2** [*T*] : to hold (something) tightly with your arms ▪ *I hugged my knees to my chest.* **3** [*T*] : to stay close to (something) ▪ *The road hugs the river.* — **hug** *n* [*C*] ▪ *He gave me a hug.* [=he hugged me]

huge /ˈhjuːdʒ/ *adj* : very large ▪ *a huge building/truck/crowd* — **huge·ly** *adv* ▪ *a hugely popular movie*

huh /ˈhʌ/ *interj, informal* **1** *chiefly US* — used at the end of a statement to ask whether someone agrees with you ▪ *It's pretty good, huh?* **2** — used when you have not heard or understood something that was said ▪ *"His name is Cholmondely." "Huh?"* [=what?] **3** — used to show surprise, disbelief, or disapproval ▪ *"His wife left him." "Huh! I thought they had a happy marriage."*

hu·la /ˈhuːlə/ *n* [*singular*] : a Hawaiian dance that has flowing hand and hip movements

hulk /ˈhʌlk/ *n* [*C*] **1** : the main part of something (such as a ship, car, or building) that has been ruined and is no longer used ▪ *the burned out hulk of the factory* **2** *informal* : a large person ▪ *He's a (great) hulk of a man.*

hulk·ing /ˈhʌlkɪŋ/ *adj, always before a noun* : very large or heavy ▪ *a hulking figure*

¹**hull** /ˈhʌl/ *n* [*C*] **1** : the deck, sides, and bottom of a ship or boat **2** : the outer covering of a fruit, grain, or seed

²**hull** *vb* [*T*] : to remove the outer covering of (a fruit or seed) ▪ *hulling seeds*

hul·la·ba·loo /ˈhʌləbəˌluː/ *n* [*U, singular*] *informal* **1** : a very noisy and confused situation ▪ *quite a hullabaloo* ▪ *The announcement caused a lot of hullabaloo.*

2 : a situation in which many people are upset and angry about something ▪ *There was a hullabaloo over his comments.*

hum /ˈhʌm/ *vb* **hummed; hum·ming** 1 [*I*] : to make a low continuous sound ▪ *The refrigerator hummed in the background.* 2 [*T/I*] : to sing the notes of a song while keeping your lips closed ▪ *hum a tune* ▪ *We hummed along to the music.* 3 [*I*] : to be very active or busy ▪ *The office was really humming.* — **hum** *n* [*singular*] ▪ *the hum of insects/conversation*

¹**hu·man** /ˈhjuːmən/ *adj* 1 : of, relating to, or affecting people ▪ *the human body* ▪ *human history* ▪ *The accident was blamed on human error.* [=was blamed on a person's mistake] 2 a : typical of people ▪ *human kindness/emotions/weaknesses* b : having good or bad qualities that people usually have ▪ *I'm not perfect. I'm (only) human, like everyone else.* c : looking or acting like a person ▪ *The dog's expression was almost human.* 3 *always before a noun* : made up of or consisting of people ▪ *We held hands and formed a human chain.*

²**human** *n* [*C*] : a person ▪ *a disease that affects both humans and animals*

human being *n* [*C*] : a person ▪ *We should do more to help our fellow human beings.*

hu·mane /hjuˈmeɪn/ *adj* : kind or gentle to people or animals ▪ *the humane treatment of animals/prisoners* — **hu·mane·ly** *adv*

hu·man·ism /ˈhjuːməˌnɪzəm/ *n* [*U*] : a system of values and beliefs that is based on the idea that people are basically good and that problems can be solved using reason instead of religion — **hu·man·ist** /ˈhjuːmənɪst/ *n* [*C*] — **hu·man·is·tic** /ˌhjuːməˈnɪstɪk/ *adj*

hu·man·i·tar·i·an /hjuˌmænəˈterijən/ *n* [*C*] : a person who works to make other people's lives better — **humanitarian** *adj, always before a noun* ▪ *humanitarian aid/efforts* — **hu·man·i·tar·i·an·ism** /hjuˌmænəˈterijəˌnɪzəm/ *n* [*U*]

hu·man·i·ty /hjuˈmænəti/ *n, pl* **-ties** 1 [*U*] a : the quality or state of being human ▪ *our shared/common humanity* b : the quality or state of being kind to other people or to animals ▪ *We appealed to his sense of humanity.* 2 [*U*] : HUMANKIND ▪ *She was cut off from the rest of humanity.* 3 [*plural*] : areas of study (such as history, language, and literature) that relate to human life and ideas ▪ *the college of arts and humanities*

hu·man·ize *also Brit* **hu·man·ise** /ˈhjuːməˌnaɪz/ *vb* **-ized; -iz·ing** [*T*] : to make (someone or something) seem gentler, kinder, or more appealing to people ▪ *humanizing the corporation's image*

hu·man·kind /ˈhjuːmənˌkaɪnd/ *n* [*U*] : all people as a group

hu·man·ly /ˈhjuːmənli/ *adv* : within the range of human ability ▪ *We'll do everything humanly possible* [=everything we can do] *to help.*

human nature *n* [*U*] : the ways of thinking, feeling, and acting that are common to most people ▪ *You can't change human nature.*

hu·man·oid /ˈhjuːməˌnɔɪd/ *adj, always before a noun* : looking or acting like a human ▪ *humanoid robots* — **humanoid** *n* [*C*]

human race *n* — **the human race** : all people ▪ *the history of the human race*

human resources *n* [*U*] : a department within an organization that deals with the people who work for that organization

human right *n* [*C*] : a basic right (such as the right to be treated well or the right to vote) that many societies believe every person should have ▪ *The defendant was deprived of his human rights.*

¹**hum·ble** /ˈhʌmbəl/ *adj* **hum·bler; hum·blest** 1 : not thinking of yourself as better than other people ▪ *He is very humble (about his achievements).* 2 a *always before a noun* : given or said in a way that shows you do not think you are better than other people ▪ *a humble request/apology* ▪ (*sometimes humorous*) *In my humble opinion* [=in my opinion], *this one is best.* b : showing that you do not think of yourself as better than other people ▪ *a humble attitude/manner* 3 : not high in rank or status ▪ *his humble background/beginnings* 4 : not special, fancy, or expensive ▪ *a meal made of humble ingredients* ▪ *Welcome to our humble home/abode.* — **eat humble pie** see EAT — **hum·bly** /ˈhʌmbli/ *adv*

²**humble** *vb* **hum·bled; hum·bling** [*T*] 1 : to make (someone) feel less important or proud ▪ *The experience humbled him.* 2 : to easily defeat (someone or something) in a way that is surprising or not expected ▪ *Last year's champion was humbled by an unknown newcomer.* — **humbling** *adj* ▪ *a humbling experience*

hum·bug /ˈhʌmˌbʌg/ *n* [*U*] : language or behavior that is false or meant to deceive people ▪ *Their claims are humbug.*

hum·ding·er /ˈhʌmˈdɪŋɚ/ *n* [*C*] *informal* : something that is very impressive or exciting ▪ *a humdinger of a storm*

hum·drum /ˈhʌmˌdrʌm/ *adj* : dull, boring, and ordinary ▪ *humdrum chores*

hu·mid /ˈhjuːməd/ *adj* : having a lot of moisture in the air ▪ *a humid climate/day/season* — **hu·mid·i·ty** /hjuˈmɪdəti/ *n* [*U*] ▪ *an area of low/high humidity*

hu·mid·i·fi·er /hjuˈmɪdəˌfajɚ/ *n* [*C*] : a machine that adds moisture to the air in a room

hu·mil·i·ate /hjuˈmɪliˌeɪt/ *vb* **-at·ed; -at·ing** [*T*] : to make (someone) feel very ashamed or foolish ▪ *She was hurt and deeply humiliated by their lies.* — **humiliating** *adj* ▪ *a humiliating defeat* — **hu·mil·i·a·tion** /hjuˌmɪliˈeɪʃən/ *n* [*C/U*]

hu·mil·i·ty /hjuˈmɪləti/ *n* [*U*] : the quality or state of not thinking you are better than other people ▪ *He accepted the honor with humility.*

hum·ming·bird /ˈhʌmɪŋˌbɚd/ *n* [*C*] : a very small, brightly colored American bird that has wings which beat very fast

hum·mock /ˈhʌmək/ *n* [*C*] : a small hill

hum·mus /ˈhʊməs/ *n* [*U*] : a soft food made of ground chickpeas, garlic, and oil

hu·mon·gous *also* **hu·mun·gous** /hjuˈmʌŋɡəs/ *adj, informal* : very large ▪ *a humongous meal*

¹**hu·mor** (*US*) *or Brit* **hu·mour** /ˈhjuːmɚ/ *n* 1 [*U*] a : a funny or amusing quality ▪ *the humor of the situation* b : jokes, funny stories, etc., of a particular kind ▪ *ethnic humor* 2 [*U*] : the ability to be funny or to be amused by things that are funny ▪ *His humor is one of his most attractive qualities.* ▪ *She has a great* **sense of humor.** 3 [*U, singular*] *formal* : the way someone feels emotionally ▪ *She was in a good/bad humor all day.* ▪ *his charm and* **good humor** — **hu·mor·less** (*US*) *or Brit* **hu·mour·less** /ˈhjuːmɚləs/ *adj*

²**humor** (*US*) *or Brit* **humour** *vb* [*T*] : to try to please or satisfy (someone) by doing what is wanted ▪ *I know you don't agree, but just humor me.* [=listen to me]

hu·mor·ist /ˈhjuːmərɪst/ *n* [*C*] : someone (such as a writer) who tells funny stories

hu·mor·ous /ˈhjuːmərəs/ *adj* : FUNNY ▪ *a humorous story/writer* — **hu·mor·ous·ly** *adv*

humour *Brit spelling of* HUMOR

¹**hump** /ˈhʌmp/ *n* [*C*] : a rounded lump on the surface of something ▪ *a hump in the road* ▪ *a camel's hump* — **over the hump** *informal* : past the most difficult part of something ▪ *We are finally over the hump on this project.*

²**hump** *vb* [*T*] *chiefly Brit* : to carry (something heavy) ▪ *They humped the supplies upstairs.*

hump·back whale /ˈhʌmpˌbæk-/ *n* [*C*] : a type of large whale that has a curved back and very long flippers — called also *humpback*

humungous *variant spelling of* HU-MONGOUS

hu·mus /ˈhjuːməs/ *n* [*U*] : a brown or black material in soil that is formed when plants and animals decay

¹**hunch** /ˈhʌntʃ/ *vb* 1 [*I*] : to bend your body forward and down so that your back is rounded ▪ *She hunched over her desk.* 2 [*T*] : to raise (your shoulders or back) while bending your head forward especially to hide or protect your face ▪ *He hunched his shoulders as he headed out into the storm.*

²**hunch** *n* [*C*] : a belief or idea about something (especially a future event) that is not based on facts or evidence ▪ *My hunch is that the stock is going to go up in value.* ▪ *I had a hunch (that) I'd see you here.*

hunch·back /ˈhʌntʃˌbæk/ *n* [*C*] 1 : a back in which the spine is curved in an abnormal way 2 *offensive* : a person with a hunchback — **hunch·backed** /ˈhʌntʃˌbækt/ *adj*

hun·dred /ˈhʌndrəd/ *n* 1 *pl* **hundred** [*C*] : the number 100 2 [*plural*] a : an amount that is more than 200 ▪ *Hundreds (and hundreds) (of them) came.* b — used to refer to a specified century ▪ *in the sixteen-hundreds* [=the 1600s; the 17th century] 3 [*C*] : a very large number — usually plural ▪ *I've seen that mov-*

ie *hundreds of times.* 4 [*C*] *US* : a hundred-dollar bill — **hundred** *adj, always before a noun* ▪ *several hundred people* — **hun·dredth** /ˈhʌndrədθ/ *n* [*C*] : one hundredth of a second [=¹⁄₁₀₀ second] — **hundredth** *adj* ▪ *the hundredth person to join*

hung *past tense and past participle of* ¹HANG

Hun·gar·i·an /ˌhʌnˈɡerijən/ *n* 1 [*C*] : a person who is from Hungary 2 [*U*] : the language of the Hungarian people — **Hungarian** *adj*

¹**hun·ger** /ˈhʌŋɡɚ/ *n* 1 [*U*] a : a very great need for food ▪ *the fight against world hunger* ▪ *Thousands of people are dying from/of hunger.* b : an uncomfortable feeling in your stomach that is caused by the need for food ▪ *hunger pangs* 2 [*C*] : a strong desire ▪ *spiritual/sexual hungers* ▪ *a hunger for success* = *a hunger to succeed*

²**hunger** *vb* [*I*] *literary* : to have or feel a strong desire ▪ *He hungered for/after success.*

hunger strike *n* [*C*] : the act of refusing to eat as a way of showing that you strongly disagree with or disapprove of something ▪ *She went on a hunger strike.* [=refused to eat]

hung jury *n* [*C*] *law* : a jury whose members cannot agree about what the verdict should be

hung over *adj* : sick because you drank too much alcohol at an earlier time

hun·gry /ˈhʌŋɡri/ *adj* **hun·gri·er; -est** 1 a : suffering because of a lack of food ▪ *millions of hungry people* ▪ *Many people* **go hungry** *every day.* [=suffer because they do not have enough food] b : feeling hunger ▪ *I'm hungry. When's dinner?* 2 *not before a noun* : feeling a strong desire or need *for* something or *to* do something ▪ *They were hungry to learn more.* ▪ *hungry for success/attention/power* ▪ *power-hungry politicians* 3 *always before a noun* : showing hunger or desire ▪ *hungry eyes* — **hun·gri·ly** /ˈhʌŋɡrəli/ *adv*

hung up *adj, informal* 1 *US* : delayed for a time ▪ *She got hung up at the airport.* 2 : thinking or worrying too much about something or someone ▪ *He's still hung up on his ex-wife.*

hunk /ˈhʌŋk/ *n* [*C*] 1 : a large lump or piece of something ▪ *a hunk of cheese/bread/meat* 2 *informal* : an attractive man ▪ *He is such a hunk!* — **hunk·y** /ˈhʌŋki/ *adj* **hunk·i·er; -est** *informal*

hun·ker /ˈhʌŋkɚ/ *vb* [*I*] *chiefly US* : to lower your body to the ground by bending your legs ▪ *The hikers hunkered (down) under a cliff until the storm passed.* — **hunker down** [*phrasal vb*] : to stay in a place for a period of time ▪ *They hunkered down for the negotiations.*

¹**hunt** /ˈhʌnt/ *vb* [*T/I*] 1 : to chase and kill (wild animals) for food or pleasure ▪ *The wolf was hunting its prey.* ▪ *He likes to hunt and fish.* 2 : to search for something or someone very carefully and thoroughly ▪ *She hunted (around) for her shoes.* — **hunt down** [*phrasal vb*] **hunt (something or someone) down** *or* **hunt down (something or someone)** 1 : to succeed

in finding (something) ▪ *trying to hunt down a phone number* **2** : to find and capture (someone) — *Police hunted down the killer.* — **hunt out** [*phrasal vb*] **hunt (something) out** or **hunt out (something)** : to find (something) after searching for it ▪ *It took a while to hunt out the papers.* — **hunt up** [*phrasal vb*] **hunt (someone or something) up** or **hunt up (someone or something)** : to succeed in finding (someone or something) ▪ *She hunted up a good used car.*

²**hunt** *n* [*C*] **1** : an occasion when people hunt wild animals ▪ *a fox hunt* **2** : an act of searching for something or someone ▪ *We finally found a good restaurant after a long hunt.*

hunt·er /ˈhʌntɚ/ *n* [*C*] **1** : a person who hunts wild animals **2** : a person who searches for something ▪ *bargain-hunters* ▪ *job-hunters*

hunt·ing /ˈhʌntɪŋ/ *n* [*U*] **1** : the activity or sport of chasing and killing wild animals ▪ *big-game hunting* ▪ *She likes to go hunting.* **2** : the activity of searching for something ▪ *bargain-hunting* ▪ *job-hunting*

hur·dle /ˈhɚdl/ *n* [*C*] **1** : one of a series of barriers to be jumped over in a race **2** : something that makes an achievement difficult ▪ *financial hurdles* — **hur·dle** *vb* **hur·dled; hur·dling** [*T*] ▪ *The horse hurdled* [=jumped over] *the fence.* — **hur·dler** /ˈhɚdlɚ/ *n* [*C*]

hurl /ˈhɚrəl/ *vb* **1** [*T*] : to throw (something) with force ▪ *He hurled a rock at me.* **2** [*T*] : to say or shout (something) in a loud and forceful way ▪ *She hurled insults at us.* **3** [*I*] *US slang* : VOMIT — **hurl·er** /ˈhɚlɚ/ *n* [*C*]

hur·ly-bur·ly /ˌhɚliˈbɚli/ *n* [*U*] : a very active or confused state or situation ▪ *the hurly-burly of city life*

hur·rah /huˈrɑː/ *or* **hoo·ray** /huˈreɪ/ *also* **hur·ray** /huˈreɪ/ *interj* — used to express joy, approval, or encouragement ▪ *Hurrah! I got the job!* ▪ *Hip, hip, hooray!*

hur·ri·cane /ˈhɚrəˌkeɪn, *Brit* ˈhʌrəkən/ *n* [*C*] : an extremely large, powerful, and destructive storm with very strong winds

hur·ried /ˈhɚrid/ *adj* **1** : happening or done very quickly or too quickly ▪ *a hurried decision/meeting/meal/departure* **2** : working very quickly or too quickly ▪ *a hurried waitress* — **hur·ried·ly** /ˈhɚrədli/ *adv*

¹**hur·ry** /ˈhɚri/ *vb* **-ries; -ried; -ry·ing** **1** [*I*] : to move, act, or go quickly ▪ *She hurried (off) to her class.* ▪ *We'll be late if we don't hurry.* ▪ **Hurry up!** *We're going to be late!* **2** [*T*] **a** : to make (someone) move, act, or go quickly ▪ *The teacher hurried us through the lesson.* ▪ *Could you hurry it up please?* [=could you please do what you are doing more quickly?] **b** : to carry or send (someone or something) more quickly than usual ▪ *They hurried the children off to bed.* **3** [*T*] **a** : to increase the speed of (something) ▪ *He hurried his pace.* **b** : to do (something) quickly or too quickly ▪ *Don't hurry your homework.*

²**hurry** *n* [*U*] : a need to do something more quickly than usual ▪ *Take your*

time. There's no (great) hurry. — **in a hurry 1** : very quickly ▪ *The weather got worse in a hurry.* **2** : feeling a strong need to move, act, or go quickly ▪ *He was in too much of a hurry to stop and say hello.* ▪ *We're* **not in a/any hurry.** = *We're in no hurry.* — sometimes used to say that someone does not want to do something ▪ *He was not in a/any hurry to leave.* [=he did not seem to want to leave]

¹**hurt** /ˈhɚt/ *vb* **hurt; hurt·ing** **1 a** [*T*] : to cause pain or injury to (yourself, someone else, or a part of your body) ▪ *Be careful with that knife or you could hurt yourself.* ▪ *She was badly/seriously hurt in a car accident.* **b** [*I*] : to be a source or cause of pain ▪ *My tooth/back hurts (a lot/ little).* ▪ *Ouch! That hurts!* **c** [*I*] : to feel physical pain ▪ *When I woke up this morning I hurt all over.* **2 a** [*T*] : to make (someone) sad or upset ▪ *Her comments hurt me deeply.* ▪ *I don't want to hurt his* **feelings.** [=make him sad or upset] **b** [*I*] : to feel emotional pain or distress ▪ *She has really* **been** *hurting since her husband left her.* **3** [*T/I*] : to do harm to (someone or something) ▪ *These new regulations will hurt sales/profits.* ▪ *The scandal hurt her image.* ▪ *We may not finish on time, but it* **won't** *hurt to try.* [=we should try] ▪ *"Should I ask her for a job?" "It* **couldn't/can't** *hurt (to ask)."* [=she may give you a job if you ask] **4** [*I*] : to have many problems ▪ *The local economy is* **hurting** *right now.* [=it is doing poorly] — **hurt for** [*phrasal vb*] *US, informal* : to lack (something needed) ▪ *Those children* **are hurting** *for attention.* [=they need to be given more attention]

²**hurt** *adj* **1** : having a physical injury ▪ *She has a hurt back.* **2** : feeling or showing emotional pain ▪ *hurt pride* ▪ *His behavior caused some hurt* **feelings.** [=it made people upset or sad]

³**hurt** *n* [*C/U*] : mental or emotional pain ▪ *Her sympathy eased the hurt she felt.* — **put the/a hurt on** *US, informal* : to injure or damage (someone or something) ▪ *They really put a hurt on him.* [=hurt/injured him very badly]

hurt·ful /ˈhɚtfəl/ *adj* : causing emotional pain : cruel or unkind ▪ *She said some very hurtful things.*

hur·tle /ˈhɚtl/ *vb* **hur·tled; hur·tling** **1** [*I*] : to move or fall with great speed and force ▪ *comets hurtling through space* ▪ *(figurative) a country hurtling toward disaster* **2** [*T*] : HURL ▪ *He hurtled himself into the crowd.*

¹**hus·band** /ˈhʌzbənd/ *n* [*C*] : a married man : the man someone is married to ▪ *Have you met her husband?*

²**husband** *vb* [*T*] *formal* : to carefully use or manage (something, such as a resource) ▪ *The country has husbanded its resources well.*

hus·band·ry /ˈhʌzbəndri/ *n* [*singular*] *formal* : FARMING ▪ *crop/animal husbandry*

¹**hush** /ˈhʌʃ/ *vb* **1** [*T*] : to make (someone) quiet, calm, or still ▪ *She tried to hush her baby.* ▪ *speaking in hushed tones* **2** [*I*] : to become quiet — usually used to tell someone to be quiet ▪ *Hush, children.*

I'm going to tell you a story. — **hush up** [*phrasal vb*] **hush (something) up** or **hush up (something)** : to prevent people from knowing the truth about (something, such as a crime) ▪ *hush up a crime/scandal*

²**hush** *n* [*singular*] : a time of silence, stillness, or calm especially after noise ▪ *A hush fell/came over the room.*

hush-hush /ˈhʌʃˌhʌʃ/ *adj* : known only to a few people ▪ *They kept their relationship hush-hush.*

hush money *n* [*U*] : money paid so that someone will keep information secret

husk /ˈhʌsk/ *n* [*C*] : a usually thin, dry layer that covers some seeds and fruits

¹**hus·ky** /ˈhʌski/ *adj* **hus·ki·er**; **-est** **1** : sounding somewhat rough ▪ *a husky voice* **2** : large and strong ▪ *a husky man*

²**husky** *n, pl* **-kies** [*C*] : a large dog that has thick fur and that is used for pulling sleds

hus·sy /ˈhʌsi/ *n, pl* **-sies** [*C*] *old-fashioned* + *offensive* : a girl or woman who does things that people consider immoral, improper, etc.

¹**hus·tle** /ˈhʌsəl/ *vb* **hus·tled**; **hus·tling** /ˈhʌsəlɪŋ/ **1** [*T*] : to quickly move or push (someone) often in a rough way ▪ *She hustled the children (off) to school.* **2** [*I*] *chiefly US* **a** : to move or work in a quick and energetic way ▪ *If we want to catch that bus, we'll have to hustle.* **b** : to play a sport with a lot of energy and effort ▪ *He's not the best player on the team, but he always hustles.* **3** *US, informal* **a** [*T/I*] : to get (something, such as money) in an illegal or improper way ▪ *hustling change* [=asking people for money] *on the sidewalk* **b** [*T*] : to sell (something illegal, such as drugs) ▪ *He hustled drugs for a few years.* **4** [*T*] *informal* **a** : to swindle or cheat (someone) ▪ *a scam to hustle elderly people* **b** *chiefly US* : to earn money by playing (a gambling game) and especially by playing against people who are less skillful than you are ▪ *He made a living by hustling pool.* **5** [*I*] *US, informal* : to work as a prostitute — **hus·tler** /ˈhʌslɚ/ *n* [*C*]

²**hustle** *n* **1** [*U*] **a** : energetic activity ▪ *the hustle and bustle of the city* **b** *chiefly US* : effort and energy in playing a sport ▪ *The fans admire him for his hustle.* **2** [*C*] *informal* : a dishonest plan for getting money

hut /ˈhʌt/ *n* [*C*] : a small and simple house or building

hutch /ˈhʌtʃ/ *n* [*C*] **1** *US* : a piece of furniture that is used for displaying and storing dishes **2** : an enclosed area or cage for an animal ▪ *a rabbit hutch*

hy·a·cinth /ˈhajəsɪnθ/ *n* [*C*] : a type of plant that is grown in gardens and has flowers that smell sweet

hy·brid /ˈhaɪbrəd/ *n* [*C*] **1** : an animal or plant that is produced from two animals or plants of different kinds **2** : something that is formed by combining two or more things ▪ *a hybrid of jazz and rock* **3** : a vehicle that runs on both electricity and gasoline — **hybrid** *adj, always before a noun* ▪ *a hybrid car*

hy·drant /ˈhaɪdrənt/ *n* [*C*] : FIRE HYDRANT

¹**hy·drate** /ˈhaɪˌdreɪt/ *n* [*C*] *technical* : a substance that is formed when water combines with another substance

²**hydrate** *vb* **-drat·ed**; **-drat·ing** [*T*] *somewhat technical* : to add water or moisture to (something) ▪ *lotions and creams that hydrate the skin* — **hy·dra·tion** /haɪˈdreɪʃən/ *n* [*U*]

hy·drau·lic /haɪˈdrɑːlɪk/ *adj* **1** : operated by the pressure of a fluid ▪ *hydraulic brakes/systems* **2** : occurring or used in a hydraulic system ▪ *hydraulic fluid/pressure* — **hy·drau·li·cal·ly** /haɪˈdrɑːlɪkli/ *adv*

hy·drau·lics /haɪˈdrɑːlɪks/ *n* [*U*] : the science that deals with ways to use liquid (such as water) when it is moving

hy·dro·car·bon /ˈhaɪdroʊˌkɑɚbən/ *n* [*C*] *technical* : a substance (such as coal or natural gas) that contains only carbon and hydrogen

hy·dro·chlo·ric acid /ˌhaɪdrəˈklorɪk-/ *n* [*U*] *chemistry* : a strong acid that is used especially in scientific experiments and in manufacturing

hy·dro·elec·tric /ˌhaɪdroʊɪˈlɛktrɪk/ *adj, technical* : of or relating to the production of electricity by using machines that are powered by moving water ▪ *hydroelectric power* — **hy·dro·elec·tric·i·ty** /ˌhaɪdroʊɪˌlɛkˈtrɪsəti/ *n* [*U*]

hy·dro·foil /ˈhaɪdrəˌfojəl/ *n* [*C*] : a very fast boat that rises partly out of the water when moving at high speeds

hy·dro·gen /ˈhaɪdrədʒən/ *n* [*U*] : a chemical element that has no color or smell and that is the simplest, lightest, and most common element

hydrogen bomb *n* [*C*] : a bomb that produces an extremely powerful and destructive explosion when hydrogen atoms unite — called also *H-bomb*

hydrogen peroxide *n* [*U*] : a liquid that is used to make things lighter in color or to kill bacteria

hy·dro·plane /ˈhaɪdrəˌpleɪn/ *vb* **-planed**; **-plan·ing** [*I*] *US, of a vehicle* : to slide on a wet road because a thin layer of water on the road causes the tires to lose contact with it ▪ *The car started hydroplaning and skidded off the road.*

hy·e·na /haɪˈiːnə/ *n* [*C*] : a large animal of Asia and Africa that has a call which sounds like very loud laughter ▪ *She was laughing like a hyena.* [=laughing very loudly]

hy·giene /ˈhaɪˌdʒiːn/ *n* [*U*] : the things that you do to keep yourself and your surroundings clean in order to maintain good health ▪ *Poor sanitation and hygiene caused many of the soldiers to get sick.*

hy·gien·ic /haɪˈdʒiːnɪk, haɪˈdʒɛnɪk/ *adj* **1** : relating to being clean and to the things that are done to maintain good health ▪ *It was done for hygienic reasons.* **2** : clean and likely to maintain good health ▪ *hygienic conditions* — **hy·gien·i·cal·ly** /haɪˈdʒiːnɪkli/ *adv*

hy·gien·ist /haɪˈdʒiːnɪst, haɪˈdʒɛnɪst/ *n* [*C*] : DENTAL HYGIENIST

hy·men /ˈhaɪmən/ n [C] : a fold of tissue that partly covers the opening of the vagina

hymn /ˈhɪm/ n [C] : a religious song ▪ *a book of hymns = a hymn book* ▪ (figurative) *The novel is a hymn to childhood innocence.* [=the novel praises childhood innocence]

hym·nal /ˈhɪmnəl/ n [C] : a book of hymns

¹**hype** /ˈhaɪp/ n [U] *informal + often disapproving* : talk or writing that is intended to make people excited about or interested in something or someone ▪ *There was a lot of media hype about the movie.*

²**hype** vb **hyped; hyp·ing** [T] *informal + often disapproving* : to talk or write about (something or someone) in a way that is intended to make people excited or interested ▪ *He's being hyped (up) as the next big star.* — **hype up** [phrasal vb] **hype (someone) up or hype up (someone)** *informal* : to make (someone) very excited ▪ *The announcer was trying to hype the crowd up.* ▪ *I was so hyped up, I couldn't sleep.*

hy·per /ˈhaɪpɚ/ adj, *informal* : very excited, nervous, or active ▪ *a hyper kid*

hyper- /ˈhaɪpɚ/ prefix **1** : excessively or extremely ▪ *hyperactive* ▪ *hypersensitive* **2** : excessive or extreme ▪ *hypertension*

hy·per·ac·tive /ˌhaɪpɚˈæktɪv/ adj : extremely active or too active ▪ *hyperactive children* — **hy·per·ac·tiv·i·ty** /ˌhaɪpɚˌæk'tɪvəti/ n [U]

hy·per·bo·le /haɪˈpɚbəli/ n [C/U] : language that describes something as better or worse than it really is ▪ *He's somewhat given to hyperbole.* [=he tends to exaggerate] — **hy·per·bol·ic** /ˌhaɪpɚˈbɑːlɪk/ adj

hy·per·drive /ˈhaɪpɚˌdraɪv/ n [U] *chiefly US, informal* : a state of extremely fast activity ▪ *The campaign has shifted into hyperdrive.*

hy·per·link /ˈhaɪpɚˌlɪŋk/ n [C] *computers* : a highlighted word or picture in a document or Web page that you can click on with a computer mouse to go to another place in the same or a different document or Web page

hy·per·sen·si·tive /ˌhaɪpɚˈsɛnsətɪv/ adj : very sensitive ▪ *a hypersensitive child* ▪ *She is hypersensitive to the chemical.*

hy·per·ten·sion /ˌhaɪpɚˈtɛnʃən/ n [U] *medical* : high blood pressure — **hy·per·ten·sive** /ˌhaɪpɚˈtɛnsɪv/ adj ▪ *hypertensive patients*

hy·per·text /ˈhaɪpɚˌtɛkst/ n [U] *computers* : an arrangement of the information in a computer database that allows a user to get information and to go from one document to another by clicking on highlighted words or pictures

hy·per·ven·ti·late /ˌhaɪpɚˈvɛntəˌleɪt/ vb **-lat·ed; -lat·ing** [I] : to breathe very quickly and deeply ▪ *He panicked and began hyperventilating.* — **hy·per·ven·ti·la·tion** /ˌhaɪpɚˌvɛntəˈleɪʃən/ n [U]

hy·phen /ˈhaɪfən/ n [C] : a punctuation mark - that is used to connect words or parts of words

hy·phen·ate /ˈhaɪfəˌneɪt/ vb **-at·ed; -at·ing** [T] : to connect (words or parts of words) with a hyphen ▪ *In English, we hyphenate some compounds but not others.* — **hyphenated** adj ▪ *"Runner-up" is a hyphenated term.*

hyp·no·sis /hɪpˈnoʊsəs/ n [U] : a state that resembles sleep but in which you can hear and respond to questions or suggestions ▪ *He underwent hypnosis.* ▪ *While under hypnosis, she described the accident in detail.*

hyp·no·ther·a·py /ˌhɪpnoʊˈθerəpi/ n [U] *medical* : the use of hypnosis to help people with emotional and psychological problems

hyp·not·ic /hɪpˈnɑːtɪk/ adj **1** *always before a noun* : of or relating to hypnosis ▪ *a hypnotic state* **2** : having an effect like hypnosis: such as **a** : tending to cause sleep or relaxation ▪ *the steady, hypnotic rhythm of the train* **b** : attractive or interesting in a powerful or mysterious way ▪ *a hypnotic personality* — **hyp·not·i·cal·ly** /hɪpˈnɑːtɪkli/ adv

hyp·no·tize also Brit **hyp·no·tise** /ˈhɪpnəˌtaɪz/ vb **-tized; -tiz·ing** [T] **1** : to put (a person) into a state of hypnosis ▪ *The therapist hypnotized him.* **2** : to hold the attention of (someone) ▪ *He can hypnotize people with his stare.* ▪ *I was hypnotized by her beauty.* — **hyp·no·tism** /ˈhɪpnəˌtɪzəm/ n [U] ▪ *a therapist who employs hypnotism* — **hyp·no·tist** /ˈhɪpnətɪst/ n [C]

hy·po·chon·dri·ac /ˌhaɪpəˈkɑːndriˌæk/ n [C] : a person who is often or always worried about being ill — **hy·po·chon·dria** /ˌhaɪpəˈkɑːndrijə/ n [U]

hy·poc·ri·sy /hɪˈpɑːkrəsi/ n, pl **-sies** [C/U] *disapproving* : the behavior of people who do things that they tell other people not to do ▪ *the hypocrisy of people who say one thing but do another* ▪ *an awareness of their hypocrisies*

hyp·o·crite /ˈhɪpəˌkrɪt/ n [C] *disapproving* : a person who claims or pretends to have certain beliefs about what is right but who behaves in a way that disagrees with those beliefs — **hyp·o·crit·i·cal** /ˌhɪpəˈkrɪtɪkəl/ adj ▪ *hypocritical remarks/people* — **hyp·o·crit·i·cal·ly** /ˌhɪpəˈkrɪtɪkli/ adv

¹**hy·po·der·mic** /ˌhaɪpəˈdɚmɪk/ adj, *medical* **1** : going under the skin ▪ *a hypodermic injection* **2** : used for putting fluids into or taking fluids out of the body by going under the skin ▪ *a hypodermic needle/syringe*

²**hypodermic** n [C] *medical* : SYRINGE

hy·pot·e·nuse /haɪˈpɑːtəˌnuːs, Brit ˌhaɪˈpɒtəˌnjuːz/ n [C] *mathematics* : the long side opposite the right angle of a triangle

hy·po·ther·mia /ˌhaɪpoʊˈθɚmijə/ n [U] *medical* : a condition in which the temperature of your body is very low

hy·poth·e·sis /haɪˈpɑːθəsəs/ n, pl **-e·ses** /-əˌsiːz/ [C] : an idea or theory that is not proven but that leads to further study or discussion ▪ *The experiment did not support/confirm his hypothesis.*

hy·poth·e·size also Brit **hy·poth·e·sise** /haɪˈpɑːθəˌsaɪz/ vb **-sized; -siz·ing** [T] : to suggest (an idea or theory) ▪ *Biolo-*

gists have hypothesized *(that there is) a relationship between the two species.*

hy·po·thet·i·cal /ˌhaɪpəˈθɛtɪkəl/ *adj* **1** : involving or based on a suggested idea or theory • *a hypothetical argument/discussion* **2** : not real : imagined as an example • *a hypothetical question/situation/example* — **hy·po·thet·i·cal·ly** /ˌhaɪpəˈθɛtɪkli/ *adv*

hys·ter·ec·to·my /ˌhɪstəˈrɛktəmi/ *n, pl* **-mies** [C/U] *medical* : an operation to remove a woman's uterus

hys·te·ria /hɪˈstɛrijə, hɪˈstɪrijə/ *n* [U] **1** : a state in which your emotions (such as fear) are so strong that you behave in an uncontrolled way • *fits/attacks of hysteria* **2** : a situation in which many people behave or react in an extreme or uncon-

trolled way because of fear, anger, etc. • *A disease outbreak could cause* **mass hysteria.**

hys·ter·i·cal /hɪˈstɛrɪkəl/ *also* **hys·ter·ic** /hɪˈstɛrɪk/ *adj* **1** : feeling or showing extreme and uncontrolled emotion • *crowds of hysterical fans* • *By the time we arrived, he had become hysterical.* **2** *informal* : very funny • *His movies are hysterical.* — **hys·ter·i·cal·ly** /hɪˈstɛrɪkli/ *adv*

hys·ter·ics /hɪˈstɛrɪks/ *n* [*plural*] : uncontrolled laughter, crying, or extreme emotion • *My mother* **went into hysterics** *when she saw my tattoo.* • *The audience was* **in hysterics.** [=was laughing very hard]

Hz *abbr* hertz

I

i *or* **I** /ˈaɪ/ *n, pl* **i's** *or* **is** *or* **I's** *or* **Is** /ˈaɪz/ **1** [C/U] : the ninth letter of the English alphabet • *The word "ice" begins with (an) i.* **2** [C] : the number one in Roman numerals

¹I /ˈaɪ/ *pron* : the person who is speaking or writing — used as the subject of a verb • *I feel fine.* • *My brother and I are five years apart in age.* • *Here I am.* **usage** see ¹ME

²I *abbr* **1** island, isle **2** intransitive

IA *abbr* Iowa

-ian see -AN

ibid *abbr* — used in formal writing to indicate that a reference is from the same source as a previous reference

-ible see -ABLE

ibu·pro·fen /ˌaɪbjuˈproufən/ *n* [U] *medical* : a medicine that reduces pain and fever

¹ice /ˈaɪs/ *n* [U] **1** : frozen water • *The steps were coated with ice.* • *ice cubes* **2** : a sheet of frozen water • *She skated out onto the ice.* **3** : cubes or pieces of ice • *Fill the glass with ice.* — **break the ice** *informal* : to say or do something that helps people to relax and begin talking at a meeting, party, etc. • *He told a joke to break the ice.* — **cut ice** *informal* : to have importance to someone • *His opinion doesn't cut any ice with me.* [=is not important to me] — **on ice** **1** : on top of pieces of ice in order to be kept cool • *champagne on ice* **2** *informal* : in the state of being delayed for a time • *We'll have to put/keep the project on ice.* [=stop working on the project] **3** *US, informal* : in a condition that makes victory certain • *With that last goal they put the game on ice.* — **on thin ice** : in a situation that may cause you to get into trouble • *In going against his father's wishes, he was (skating/walking) on thin ice.*

²ice *vb* **iced; ic·ing** [T] **1** : to make (something) cold with ice • *ice* [=put ice on] *a twisted ankle* **2** : to cover (something) with icing • *ice a cake* **3** *US, informal* : to make winning or getting (some-

thing) certain • *The last goal iced* [=clinched] *the game/win.* — **ice over/up** [*phrasal vb*] : to become covered with ice • *As the weather grew colder, the pond iced over.*

ice age *or* **Ice Age** *n* [C] : a time in the distant past when a large part of the world was covered with ice • *a valley formed during the* **Ice Age**

ice·berg /ˈaɪsˌbɚg/ *n* [C] : a very large piece of ice floating in the ocean — **the tip of the iceberg** : a small part of a problem, story, etc., that is seen or known about when there is a much larger part that is not seen or known about • *The stories we've heard so far are just the tip of the iceberg.*

iceberg lettuce *n* [U] : a type of light green lettuce that is often eaten in salads

ice·box /ˈaɪsˌbɑːks/ *n* [C] *US, old-fashioned* : REFRIGERATOR

ice·break·er /ˈaɪsˌbreɪkɚ/ *n* [C] **1** : a ship designed to clear a passage through ice **2** : something done or said to help people to relax and begin talking at a meeting, party, etc. • *The joke was a good icebreaker.*

ice cap *n* [C] : a very large and thick sheet of ice that covers the North Pole, the South Pole, or another region • *the polar ice cap*

ice–cold /ˈaɪsˈkould/ *adj* : very cold • *ice-cold beer*

ice cream /ˌaɪsˈkriːm/ *n* [C/U] : a frozen food containing sweetened and flavored cream • *chocolate/vanilla ice cream*

iced *adj* : containing small pieces of ice or ice cubes • *iced coffee/tea*

ice hockey *n* [U] : a game played on an ice rink in which two teams of six players on skates use curved sticks to try to shoot a puck into the opponent's goal — called also (*US*) hockey

ice pack *n* [C] **1** : a container or bag filled with ice that is used to cool part of your body   **2** : a large area of ice on the ocean

ice pick *n* [C] : a sharp tool used for breaking off small pieces of ice

ice rink *n* [C] : an often enclosed area that has a sheet of ice for ice-skating

ice skate *n* [C] : a shoe with a special blade on the bottom that is used for skating on ice

ice–skate /ˈaɪsˌskeɪt/ *vb* **-skat·ed; -skat·ing** [*I*] : to skate on ice ▪ *I had never ice-skated before.* — **ice–skat·er** /ˈaɪsˌskeɪtə/ *n* [C] — **ice–skating** [U] ▪ *Let's go ice-skating.*

ice water *n* [U] *US* : water that has ice in it ▪ *a glass of ice water* [=(*Brit*) *iced water*]

ici·cle /ˈaɪˌsɪkəl/ *n* [C] : a hanging piece of ice formed when water freezes as it drips down from something

ic·ing /ˈaɪsɪŋ/ *n* [U] : FROSTING ▪ *a cake with chocolate icing* — **icing on the cake** : something extra that makes a good thing even better ▪ *The concert was great, and getting to meet the band was (the) icing on the cake.*

icky /ˈɪki/ *adj* **ick·i·er; -est** *informal* : having a very unpleasant quality ▪ *an icky taste*

icon /ˈaɪˌkɑːn/ *n* [C]   **1** *computers* : a small picture on a computer screen that represents a program or function ▪ *Click on the icon.*   **2 a** : a person who is very successful and admired ▪ *a pop/Hollywood icon*   **b** : a widely known symbol ▪ *The Statue of Liberty has become an American cultural icon.*   **3** : a religious image in the Orthodox Christian church — **icon·ic** /aɪˈkɑːnɪk/ *adj* ▪ *He has achieved iconic status in the movie business.*

icon·o·clast /aɪˈkɑːnəˌklæst/ *n* [C] *formal* : a person who criticizes or opposes beliefs and practices that are widely accepted — **icon·o·clast·ic** /aɪˌkɑːnəˈklæstɪk/ *adj* ▪ *iconoclastic theories*

ico·nog·ra·phy /ˌaɪkəˈnɑːgrəfi/ *n* [U] : the images or symbols related to something ▪ *Christian iconography*

ICU *abbr* intensive care unit ▪ *She spent several days in the ICU after the surgery.*

icy /ˈaɪsi/ *adj* **ic·i·er; -est**   **1** : covered with ice ▪ *icy roads/sidewalks*   **2** : very cold ▪ *an icy cold wind*   **3** : not friendly or kind ▪ *an icy stare* — **ic·i·ness** /ˈaɪsinəs/ *n* [U]

id /ˈɪd/ *n* [C] *psychology* : a part of a person's unconscious mind that relates to basic needs and desires

¹ID /ˈaɪˈdiː/ *n, pl* **ID's** *or* **IDs** [C/U] : a document, card, etc., that has your name and other information about you and that often includes your photograph ▪ *You must show (your) ID.* ▪ *an ID card*

²ID *vb* **ID's** *or* **IDs; ID'd** *or* **IDed; ID'ing** *or* **IDing** [*T*] *informal* : IDENTIFY ▪ *The police have not ID'd the victim.*

³ID *abbr* Idaho

I'd /ˈaɪd/ — used as a contraction of *I had* or *I would* ▪ *I'd* [=I had] *already read the book.* ▪ *I'd* [=I would] *rather do it myself.*

idea /aɪˈdiːjə/ *n*   **1** [C] : a thought, plan, or suggestion about what to do ▪ *Buying the car was a good/bad idea.* ▪ *I'm not sure*

what to do next. *Do you have any ideas?*   **2** [C] : an opinion or belief ▪ *He has some pretty strange ideas.* ▪ *"I thought she'd help us." "What gave you that idea?"* ▪ *I thought I'd handle it, but he had other ideas.* [=he did not agree]   **3** [C/U] : something that you imagine or picture in your mind ▪ *A quiet night at home is my idea of a good time.*   **4** [*singular*] : an understanding of something ▪ *He has a clear idea of his responsibilities.* [=he knows what his responsibilities are] ▪ *I have no idea what you're talking about.* [=I do not know/understand at all what you're talking about] ▪ *I get the idea.* [=I understand] ▪ *Don't get the wrong idea.* [=don't misunderstand me]   **5 the idea** : the central meaning or purpose of something ▪ *The idea is to raise money.* ▪ (*informal*) *Hey! What's the big idea!?* [=why are you doing that?] — **give someone ideas** *or* **put ideas in/into someone's head** : to cause someone to think about doing something that probably should not be done

¹ide·al /aɪˈdiːl/ *adj* : PERFECT ▪ *ideal weather* ▪ *She is an ideal candidate for the job.*

²ideal *n* [C]   **1** : an idea or standard of perfection or excellence ▪ *an ideal of romantic love* ▪ *She remained true to her ideals.* [=she continued to work for the things she considered worthwhile and important]   **2** : someone or something that you admire and want to imitate ▪ *She considers the actress her ideal.*

ide·al·ism /aɪˈdiːjəˌlɪzəm/ *n* [U] : the attitude of a person who believes that it is possible to live according to very high standards of behavior and honesty ▪ *youthful idealism* — **ide·al·ist** /aɪˈdiːjəlɪst/ *n* [C] ▪ *The group was a mix of realists and idealists.* — **ide·al·is·tic** /aɪˌdiːjəˈlɪstɪk/ *adj* ▪ *idealistic young people*

ide·al·ize *also* **Brit ide·al·ise** /aɪˈdiːjəˌlaɪz/ *vb* **-ized; -iz·ing** [*T*] : to think of or represent (someone or something) as being perfect ▪ *She tends to idealize her job.* ▪ *an idealized view of the American life* — **ide·al·i·za·tion** *also* **Brit ide·al·i·sa·tion** /aɪˌdiːjələˈzeɪʃən, Brit aɪˌdɪəˌlaɪˈzeɪʃən/ *n* [C/U]

ide·al·ly /aɪˈdiːli/ *adv*   **1** : PERFECTLY ▪ *His skills made him ideally suited for the job.*   **2** — used to say what should happen or be done to produce the best results ▪ *Ideally, you should do these exercises daily.*

iden·ti·cal /aɪˈdɛntɪkəl/ *adj*   **1** : exactly the same ▪ *We visited the identical place we stopped at last year.*   **2** : exactly alike or equal ▪ *identical coats/cars* ▪ *The results were identical to/with those of the first test.* — **iden·ti·cal·ly** /aɪˈdɛntɪkli/ *adv*

identical twin *n* [C] : either member of a pair of twins that are produced from a single egg and who look exactly alike

iden·ti·fi·ca·tion /aɪˌdɛntəfəˈkeɪʃən/ *n*   **1** [C/U] : the act of finding out who someone is or what something is ▪ *The police have made a positive identification of the suspect.*   **2** [U] : a document, card, etc., that has your name and other information about you and that often includes your photograph ▪ *I had to show (my) identification before they would cash the check.* **3** [*U*] : a feeling that you share and understand the problems or experiences of another person ▪ *They had/felt a (strong) sense of identification with their neighbors.*

iden·ti·fy /aɪˈdɛntəˌfaɪ/ *vb* **-fies**; **-fied**; **-fy·ing** [*T*] **1** : to know and say who someone is or what something is ▪ *He correctly identified the mushroom.* ▪ *The witness identified the suspect.* **2** : to find out who someone is or what something is ▪ *They had no difficulty in identifying the problem.* **3** : to show who someone is or what something is ▪ *His clothes identified him as a clerk.* ▪ *an identifying mark/feature* [=a mark/feature that shows who someone is or what something is] — **identify with** [*phrasal vb*] **1** *identify (something) with* : to think of (something) as being the same as (something else) ▪ *It is a mistake to identify being healthy with being thin.* **2** *identify (someone) with* : to think of (someone) as being very closely associated with (something) ▪ *She has always been identified with the civil rights movement.* **3** : to think of yourself as having the same problems and feelings as someone ▪ *Many readers identify with the characters in her novels.* ▪ *He could identify with her problems.* — **identify yourself** : to say who you are ▪ *He refused to identify himself (to the police).* — **iden·ti·fi·able** /aɪˌdɛntəˈfaɪəbəl/ *adj* — **iden·ti·fi·ably** /aɪˌdɛntəˈfaɪəbli/ *adv*

iden·ti·ty /aɪˈdɛntəti/ *n, pl* **-ties** [*C/U*] **1** : who someone is : the name of a person ▪ *The identity of the criminal/victim is not known.* ▪ *Her face was hidden in order to protect her identity.* [=to keep her name from being known] **2** : the qualities, beliefs, etc., that make a particular person or group different from others ▪ *As children grow, they establish their own identities.* ▪ *His art reflects his cultural/racial identity.*

identity crisis *n* [*C*] : a feeling of unhappiness and confusion caused by not being sure about what type of person you really are or what the true purpose of your life is

identity theft *n* [*U*] : the illegal use of someone else's personal identifying information (such as a Social Security number) in order to get money or credit

ideo·logue /ˈaɪdijəˌlɑːg/ *n* [*C*] *formal + often disapproving* : someone who very strongly supports and is guided by the ideology of a particular group ▪ *conservative/liberal ideologues*

ide·ol·o·gy /ˌaɪdiˈɑːlədʒi/ *n, pl* **-gies** [*C/U*] : the set of ideas and beliefs of a group or political party ▪ *progressive/liberal/conservative ideologies* — **ideo·log·i·cal** /ˌaɪdijəˈlɑːdʒɪkəl/ *adj* ▪ *ideological conflicts* — **ideo·log·i·cal·ly** /ˌaɪdijəˈlɑːdʒɪkli/ *adv*

id·i·o·cy /ˈɪdijəsi/ *n, pl* **-cies** **1** [*U*] : extreme stupidity ▪ *an act of sheer idiocy* **2** [*C*] : something that is extremely stupid

or foolish ▪ *the idiocies of the people he works for*

id·i·om /ˈɪdijəm/ *n* **1** [*C*] : an expression that cannot be understood from the meanings of its separate words but that has a separate meaning of its own ▪ *The expression "give way," meaning "retreat," is an idiom.* **2** [*C/U*] : a form of a language that is spoken in a particular area and that uses some of its own words, grammar, and pronunciations **3** [*C/U*] : a style or form of expression that is characteristic of a particular person, type of art, etc. ▪ *a poet's idiom* ▪ *a feature of modern jazz idiom* — **id·i·om·at·ic** /ˌɪdijəˈmætɪk/ *adj* ▪ *an idiomatic expression/phrase* [=an expression/phrase that is an idiom] ▪ *a use of language that is not idiomatic* [=that does not sound natural or correct] — **id·i·om·at·i·cal·ly** /ˌɪdijəˈmætɪkli/ *adv*

id·io·syn·cra·sy /ˌɪdijəˈsɪŋkrəsi/ *n, pl* **-sies** [*C*] **1** : an unusual way in which a particular person behaves or thinks ▪ *Her habit of pulling at her shirt was just one of her idiosyncrasies.* **2** : an unusual part or feature of something ▪ *The current system has a few idiosyncracies.* — **id·io·syn·crat·ic** /ˌɪdijouˌsɪnˈkrætɪk/ *adj* ▪ *His taste in music was very idiosyncratic.*

id·i·ot /ˈɪdijət/ *n* [*C*] : a very stupid or foolish person ▪ *I really made an idiot of myself.* [=I acted very stupidly] — **id·i·ot·ic** /ˌɪdiˈɑːtɪk/ *adj* ▪ *idiotic people/behavior*

¹idle /ˈaɪdl̩/ *adj* **1** : not working, active, or being used ▪ *They have not been idle.* [=they have been active/busy] ▪ *The factory has been lying/sitting/standing idle.* [=not used] ▪ *the idle rich* [=rich people who do not have to work] **2** : not having any real purpose or value ▪ *idle rumors/gossip/speculation* ▪ *an idle threat* [=a threat that is not really. meant] **3** : not having much activity ▪ *the idle days of summer* — **idle·ness** /ˈaɪdl̩nəs/ *n* [*U*]

²idle *vb* **idled**; **idling** **1** [*T/I*] *of an engine or vehicle* : to run without being connected for doing useful work ▪ *She left the engine idling for a few seconds before she turned it off.* ▪ *idle an engine* **2** [*T/I*] : to spend time doing nothing or nothing useful ▪ *A group of boys were idling in the doorway.* ▪ *We idled away the evening playing cards.* **3** [*T*] *US* : to cause (someone or something) to stop working ▪ *The workers have been idled by the bad economy.* — **idler** /ˈaɪdl̩ə/ *n* [*C*] ▪ *a lazy idler*

idly /ˈaɪdli/ *adv* : without much thought, effort, or concern ▪ *We sat idly, waiting for something to happen.* ▪ *I idly wondered what they were doing.*

idol /ˈaɪdl̩/ *n* [*C*] **1** : a greatly loved or admired person ▪ *a sports/teen/pop idol* ▪ *a fallen idol* [=a person who is no longer greatly admired] **2** : a picture or object that is worshipped as a god

idol·a·try /aɪˈdɑːlətri/ *n* [*U*] : the worship of a picture or object as a god — **idol·a·trous** /aɪˈdɑːlətrəs/ *adj*

idol·ize *also Brit* **idol·ise** /ˈaɪdəˌlaɪz/ *vb* **-ized**; **-iz·ing** [*T*] : to love or admire (someone) very much or too much ▪ *The* boy idolizes his father. [=he thinks his father is perfect]

idyll /ˈaɪdl̩/ n [C] literary : a happy and enjoyable scene or experience ▪ a pastoral/romantic idyll

idyl·lic /aɪˈdɪlɪk/ adj : very peaceful, happy, and enjoyable ▪ an idyllic scene/childhood

i.e. abbr that is — used to introduce something that explains a preceding statement more fully or exactly ▪ The medicine needs be taken for a short period of time; i.e., three to five days.

-ier see ²-ER

¹**if** /ˈɪf/ conj **1** — used to talk about the result or effect of something that may happen or be true ▪ If it rains, (then) we won't go to the park. ▪ What will happen if I fail the test? ▪ You should study. **If not**, you won't pass the test. ▪ If you don't (study), you won't pass the test. ▪ Please arrive early **if possible**. ▪ I'll do the work myself **if necessary**. **2** — used to discuss the imaginary result or effect of something that did not happen or that is or was not true ▪ If you had studied, you would have passed the test. **3** — used to say that something must happen before another thing can happen ▪ He said he'll come to the party if she comes too. **4** — used to indicate a result that always occurs when something happens ▪ The engine stalls if [=when] you let it get too hot. **5** : even though : ALTHOUGH ▪ He had to perform an annoying, if necessary, task. **6** — used to introduce a statement or question about something that is not certain ▪ I'll see if [=whether] I can come. ▪ I wonder if it's true (or not). **7 a** — used to make a polite request or suggestion ▪ Would you mind if I sat here? [=may I sit here?] ▪ I'd like to stay a little longer, **if you don't mind**. **b** — used to state an opinion in a polite way ▪ You're looking lovely today, **if I may say so**. **8** — used in statements that describe feelings (such as regret) about a possible situation ▪ I don't care if we're late. **9** — used in statements and questions that express doubt ▪ If you're so smart, why didn't you think of that? **10** — used to introduce an even stronger alternative to what has just been said ▪ These changes will have little **if any** impact on the problem. ▪ Rarely, **if ever**, does that happen. ▪ saving thousands, **if not** millions, of lives — **as if** see ²AS — **even if** see ²EVEN — **if anything** — used to make a statement that strongly disagrees or contrasts with a preceding statement ▪ The economy has not improved—if anything, it has gotten worse. — **if I were you** — used when giving advice to people about how they should behave ▪ I'd study more if I were you. [=I think you should study more] — **if not for** : WITHOUT ▪ If (it were) not for modern medicine, fewer babies would survive. ▪ **If it hadn't been for** him, I wouldn't be where I am today. — **if nothing else** : at least — used to stress that an approving statement is true even though a stronger statement might not be ▪ If nothing else, he's polite! — **if only** — used to talk about something that you want to happen or be true ▪ If only it would stop raining. — **if you ask me** — used in statements that express an opinion ▪ If you ask me [=in my opinion], he's a liar. — **what if** see ¹WHAT

²**if** n [C] : something that could either happen or not happen ▪ They could win if they get lucky, but **that's a big if**. [=it is not likely that they will get lucky] ▪ (US) There are no **ifs, ands, or buts** about it! = (Brit) There are no **ifs and buts** about it! [=it is certain; there is no doubt about it]

if·fy /ˈɪfi/ adj **if·fi·er; -est** informal **1** : having many uncertain or unknown qualities or conditions ▪ an iffy situation/proposal/decision **2** : not certain to be good ▪ The weather looks a bit iffy.

ig·loo /ˈɪˌgluː/ n, pl **-loos** [C] : a house made of blocks of snow or ice in the form of a dome

ig·ne·ous /ˈɪgniːjəs/ adj, technical : formed when hot, liquid rock cools and becomes hard ▪ igneous rock

ig·nite /ɪgˈnaɪt/ vb **-nit·ed; -nit·ing 1 a** [T] : to set (something) on fire : to cause (a fire) to start ▪ The fire was ignited by sparks. **b** [I] : to begin burning : to catch fire ▪ a material that ignites easily **2** [T] **a** : to give life or energy to (someone or something) ▪ The story ignited her imagination. **b** : to cause the sudden occurrence of (something) ▪ Her comments have ignited a controversy. ▪ igniting opposition

ig·ni·tion /ɪgˈnɪʃən/ n **1** [C] **a** : the electrical system in an engine that causes the fuel to burn so that the engine begins working **b** : the device that is used to start a car's engine ▪ Put the key in the ignition. **2** [U] : the act of causing something to start burning ▪ ignition of the fire

ig·no·ble /ɪgˈnoʊbəl/ adj, formal : not deserving respect ▪ an ignoble past ▪ ignoble thoughts — **ig·no·bly** /ɪgˈnoʊbli/ adv

ig·no·min·i·ous /ˌɪgnəˈmɪnijəs/ adj, formal : causing disgrace or shame ▪ an ignominious defeat — **ig·no·min·i·ous·ly** adv

ig·no·min·y /ˈɪgnəˌmɪni/ n, pl **-nies** [C/U] formal : a situation or event that causes you to feel ashamed or embarrassed ▪ the ignominy of being forced to resign

ig·no·ra·mus /ˌɪgnəˈreɪməs/ n [C] : an ignorant or stupid person

ig·no·rance /ˈɪgnərəns/ n [U, singular] : a lack of knowledge, understanding, or education ▪ His racist attitudes showed his ignorance. ▪ an appalling ignorance about/of other cultures ▪ Their decisions were made **in ignorance of** [=without knowing] the true nature of the situation. ▪ When asked about their reasons, she **pleaded/pled ignorance**. [=she said that she did not know] — **ignorance is bliss** — used to say that a person who does not know about a problem does not worry about it

ig·no·rant /ˈɪgnərənt/ adj **1** : lacking knowledge or information ▪ an ignorant racist ▪ ignorant about the dangers of the drug ▪ He remains ignorant of the changes. **2** : resulting from or showing a lack of knowledge ▪ *an ignorant mistake* — **ig·no·rant·ly** *adv*

ig·nore /ɪgˈnoɚ/ *vb* **-nored; -nor·ing** [T] **1** : to refuse to show that you hear or see (something or someone) ▪ *Just try to ignore him.* **2** : to do nothing about or in response to (something or someone) ▪ *They ignored the warning signs.* ▪ *ignoring the poor*

igua·na /ɪˈgwɑːnə/ *n* [C] : a large lizard that lives in the tropical regions of Central and South America

IL *abbr* Illinois

ilk /ˈɪlk/ *n* [*singular*] : sort or kind ▪ *punk rockers and others of that ilk*

¹**ill** /ˈɪl/ *adj* **1 a** : sick or unhealthy ▪ *a chronically/critically/terminally ill patient* ▪ *mentally ill adults* — usually used after a verb ▪ *What's wrong? You look ill.* ▪ *She was suddenly taken ill.* = (US) *She suddenly took ill.* ▪ (US) *The sight made her physically ill.* [=made her nauseated] ▪ (US) *He became violently ill.* [=he vomited] ▪ *her ill health* : not normal or good ▪ *her ill* [=*poor*] *health* **2** always before a noun : harmful or damaging ▪ *no ill effects* ▪ *ill treatment* **3** always before a noun : not helpful or lucky ▪ *an ill omen* **4** always before a noun : not kind or friendly ▪ *ill humor/temper* ▪ *Her comment caused some ill feeling(s).* [=feelings of anger or resentment] — **ill repute** see **REPUTE**

²**ill** *adv* **1** : BADLY, POORLY — often hyphenated ▪ *He is ill-equipped/-prepared.* [=he does not have the experience or preparation that is needed] ▪ *Her arrival was ill-timed.* [=she arrived at a bad time] **2** : in an unfavorable or unkind way ▪ *She never spoke ill of anyone.* — **ill afford** ✧ If you can *ill afford* something, you should not do it or get it because it will cause problems. ▪ *We can ill afford more bad publicity.*

³**ill** *n* **1** [U] : bad or unlucky things ▪ *She does not wish anyone ill.* **2 a** [C] : a sickness or disease ▪ *a cure for every ill* [=*ailment*] ▪ *childhood ills* **b** [*plural*] : troubles or problems ▪ *the ills of society*

I'll /ˈajəl/ — used as a contraction of *I will* ▪ *I'll call you.*

ill–ad·vised /ˌɪləd'vaɪzd/ *adj* : FOOLISH ▪ *an ill-advised decision*

ill at ease *adj* : not comfortable or relaxed ▪ *He seemed ill at ease when we spoke with him.*

il·le·gal /ɪˈliːgəl/ *adj* **1** : not allowed by the law ▪ *illegal drugs* ▪ *an illegal alien/immigrant* [=a foreign person who is living in a country without having official permission to live there] **2** : not allowed by the rules in a game ▪ *an illegal pass* — **il·le·gal·i·ty** /ˌɪlɪˈgæləti/ *n, pl* **-ties** [C/U] : *the illegality of these activities* ▪ *fundraising illegalities* [=illegal activities] — **il·le·gal·ly** /ɪˈliːgəli/ *adv*

il·leg·i·ble /ɪˈlɛdʒəbəl/ *adj* : not clear enough to read ▪ *illegible handwriting* — **il·leg·i·bly** /ɪˈlɛdʒəbli/ *adv*

il·le·git·i·mate /ˌɪlɪˈdʒɪtəmət/ *adj* **1** : born to a father and mother who are not married ▪ *an illegitimate child* **2** : not allowed according to rules or laws ▪ *an illegitimate government* **3** : not reasonable or fair ▪ *fired for illegitimate rea-*

sons — **il·le·git·i·ma·cy** /ˌɪlɪˈdʒɪtəməsi/ *n* [U] — **il·le·git·i·mate·ly** *adv*

ill–fat·ed /ˈɪlˈfeɪtəd/ *adj* : ending in disaster ▪ *an ill-fated decision*

ill–got·ten /ˈɪlˈgɑːtn̩/ *adj* : obtained in a dishonest or illegal way ▪ *ill-gotten gains* [=money and other valuable things gotten through dishonest methods]

il·lic·it /ɪˈlɪsət/ *adj* **1** : not allowed by law ▪ *illicit drugs* **2** : involving activities that are not considered morally acceptable ▪ *She had an illicit affair with her boss.* — **il·lic·it·ly** *adv*

il·lit·er·ate /ɪˈlɪtərət/ *adj* **1** : not knowing how to read or write ▪ *an illiterate person* **2** : having or showing a lack of knowledge about a particular subject ▪ *He's illiterate when it comes to computers.* — **il·lit·er·a·cy** /ɪˈlɪtərəsi/ *n* [U] — **illiterate** *n* [C] ▪ *a class for computer illiterates*

ill–man·nered /ˈɪlˈmænɚd/ *adj, formal* : having or showing bad manners ▪ *an ill-mannered child/remark*

ill·ness /ˈɪlnəs/ *n* **1** [U] : a condition of being unhealthy in your body or mind ▪ *He showed no signs of illness.* ▪ *mental illness* **2** [C] : a sickness or disease ▪ *cancer, diabetes, and other illnesses*

il·log·i·cal /ɪˈlɑːdʒɪkəl/ *adj* : not showing good judgment : not thinking about things in a reasonable or sensible way ▪ *an illogical argument* ▪ *You're being completely illogical.* — **il·log·i·cal·ly** /ɪˈlɑːdʒɪkli/ *adv*

ill–tem·pered /ˈɪlˈtɛmpɚd/ *adj* : easily annoyed or angered : BAD-TEMPERED ▪ *an ill-tempered neighbor*

il·lu·mi·nate /ɪˈluːməˌneɪt/ *vb* **-nat·ed; -nat·ing** [T] **1** : to shine light on (something) ▪ *Candles illuminate* [=*light*] *the church.* **2** : to make (something) clear and easier to understand ▪ *A university study has illuminated the problem.* — **il·luminating** *adj* ▪ *an illuminating discussion*

illuminated *adj* **1** : lit by bright lights ▪ *an illuminated entrance* **2** of an old book, document, etc. : decorated with gold or colored designs and pictures ▪ *an illuminated manuscript from the Middle Ages*

il·lu·mi·na·tion /ɪˌluːməˈneɪʃən/ *n* **1** [U] : light that comes into a room, that shines on something, etc. ▪ *When taking photographs indoors, use a flash for illumination.* **2** [U] *formal* : knowledge or understanding ▪ *in search of spiritual illumination* **3** [C] : a gold or colored decoration in an old book ▪ *an old manuscript with beautiful illuminations* **4** [*plural*] *Brit* : lights used as decorations ▪ *Illuminations were hung throughout the city.*

il·lu·sion /ɪˈluːʒən/ *n* [C] **1** : something that is false or not real but that seems to be true or real ▪ *They used paint to create the illusion of metal.* **2** : an idea that is based on something that is not true ▪ *She had/harbored no illusions about the expense.* [=she knew it would be expensive] ▪ *He was under the illusion* [=he mistakenly believed] *that he was a good player.*

il·lu·so·ry /ɪˈluːsəri/ *adj, formal* : based

on something that is not true or real • *an illusory hope*

il·lus·trate /ˈɪləˌstreɪt/ *vb* -trat·ed; -trat·ing [T] 1 : to give examples in order to make (something) easier to understand • *He illustrated his lecture with stories of his own experiences.* 2 : to be proof or evidence of (something) • *Recent events illustrate the need for change.* 3 : to explain or decorate a story, book, etc., with pictures • *She wrote and illustrated the book.* • *The book is illustrated.* — il·lus·tra·tor /ˈɪləˌstreɪtɚ/ *n* [C] • *an illustrator of children's books*

il·lus·tra·tion /ˌɪləˈstreɪʃən/ *n* 1 [C] : a picture or drawing in a book, magazine, etc. • *a book with many photographs and illustrations* 2 [C] : an example or story that is used to make something easier to understand • *The illustrations that he provided in his speech were very effective.* 3 [U] a : the act or process of producing or providing pictures for a book, magazine, etc. • *selecting photos for the illustration of the book* b : the act or process of giving examples to make something easier to understand • *By way of illustration* [=as an example], *let us examine this poem.*

il·lus·tra·tive /ɪˈlʌstrətɪv, *Brit* ˈɪləstrətɪv/ *adj, formal* : used to explain something or as an example of something • *illustrative examples/stories* • *Her struggle is illustrative of* [=a good example of] *the difficulties facing women today.*

il·lus·tri·ous /ɪˈlʌstrijəs/ *adj, formal* : admired and respected very much because a lot was achieved • *an illustrious history/past/career*

ill will *n* [U] : a feeling of hatred or dislike • *We bear/feel/harbor/have/hold no ill will toward each other.*

I'm /ˈaɪm/ — used as a contraction of *I am* • *I'm happy to meet you.*

im·age /ˈɪmɪdʒ/ *n* 1 [C] : a picture that is produced by a camera, artist, mirror, etc. • *She studied her image in the mirror.* • *black-and-white images of the city* 2 [C] : the thought of how something looks or might look • *His poem evokes images of the sea and warm summer days.* 3 [C/U] : the idea that people have about someone or something • *He's trying to improve/protect his image.* • *the company's public image* • *a politician who cares more about image than about telling the truth* 4 [*singular*] : someone who looks very much like another person or kind of person • *He's the (very/living) image of his father.* [=he looks like his father] • *She was the (very) image of a successful businesswoman.* [=she looked like a successful businesswoman] 5 [C] : an interesting or memorable way of showing or describing something in a book, movie, etc. • *The book contains many striking/startling images.* 6 [C] : a statue or picture that is made to look like a person or thing • *images carved in stone* • *religious images*

im·ag·ery /ˈɪmɪdʒri/ *n* [U] 1 *technical* : pictures or photographs • *satellite imagery* [=pictures taken from satellites] 2 a : language that causes people to imagine pictures in their mind • *The book contains a great deal of sexual imagery.* b : pictures of people or things in a work of art • *biblical/religious imagery*

imag·in·able /ɪˈmædʒənəbəl/ *adj* : possible for people to imagine • *We tried every imaginable therapy.* — often used to give emphasis • *the worst imaginable weather* = *the worst weather imaginable*

imag·i·nary /ɪˈmædʒəˌneri, *Brit* ɪˈmædʒənri/ *adj* : not real : existing only in your mind or imagination • *an imaginary line/friend/monster/world*

imag·i·na·tion /ɪˌmædʒəˈneɪʃən/ *n* 1 a [C/U] : the ability to form a picture in your mind of something that you have not seen or experienced • *You can find a solution if you use some/your imagination.* • *children with vivid/fertile imaginations* • *It was a figment of his imagination.* [=something that he imagined] b [U] : the ability to think of new things • *He's an okay writer, but he lacks imagination.* 2 [U] : something that only exists or happens in your mind • *Is it just my imagination, or is it getting warm in here?* — capture/catch someone's imagination : to make someone very interested or excited • *Her books have captured the imaginations of children around the world.* — leave (something) to the imagination : to not show or describe all of the parts or details of (something) • *The movie's sex scenes leave nothing to the imagination.* [=they show everything]

imag·i·na·tive /ɪˈmædʒənətɪv/ *adj* : having or showing an ability to think of new and interesting ideas • *an imaginative filmmaker* • *imaginative thinking/writing* — imag·i·na·tive·ly *adv*

imag·ine /ɪˈmædʒən/ *vb* -ined; -in·ing [T] 1 a : to think of or create (something that is not real) in your mind • *a writer who has imagined an entire world of amazing creatures* b : to form a picture or idea in your mind of (something that is not real or present) • *Imagine a world without poverty or war.* • *It's hard to imagine what it would be like to be so wealthy.* • *I can't imagine why she would be late.* [=I do not understand why she is late] 2 : to have or form (an idea or opinion that is not accurate or based on reality) • *She imagines herself to be very charming.* [=she thinks that she is charming but actually she is not] • *He was imagining all sorts of terrible things happening.* • *You're just imagining things.* 3 : to think or believe (something) • *The company will do better next year, I imagine.* • *It was worse than they had imagined.*

im·ag·ing /ˈɪmədʒɪŋ/ *n* [U] : the process of creating and showing images on a computer • *digital imaging technology*

imag·in·ings /ɪˈmædʒənɪŋz/ *n* [*plural*] : ideas, stories, etc., that are thought of in your mind but that are not true or real • *a level of success beyond his wildest imaginings*

imam /ɪˈmɑːm/ *n* [C] : a Muslim religious leader

im·bal·ance /ɪmˈbæləns/ *n* [C] : a state or condition in which different things do not occur in equal or proper amounts • *a chemical imbalance in the brain*

im·be·cile /ˈɪmbəsəl, Brit ˈɪmbəˌsiːl/ n [C] : a very stupid person • *acting like a complete imbecile*

im·bibe /ɪmˈbaɪb/ vb **-bibed**; **-bib·ing** [T/I] *formal + often humorous* : to drink (something, such as alcohol) • *She imbibed vast quantities of coffee.* • *He never imbibes.* [=drinks alcohol]

im·bro·glio /ɪmˈbroʊlˌjoʊ/ n, pl **-glios** [C] *formal* : a complex dispute or argument • *a political/legal imbroglio*

im·bue /ɪmˈbjuː/ vb **-bued**; **-bu·ing** [T] : to cause (someone or something) to be deeply affected by a feeling or to have a certain quality • *His experiences imbued in him a strong sense of patriotism.* = *His experiences imbued him with a strong sense of patriotism.*

im·i·tate /ˈɪməˌteɪt/ vb **-tat·ed**; **-tat·ing** [T] **1** : to make or do something the same way as (something else) • *Her style has been imitated by many other writers.* **2 a** : to do the same thing as (someone) • *She's always imitating* [=copying] *her older sister.* **b** : to copy (someone's or something's behavior, sound, appearance, etc.) • *She can imitate the calls of many different birds.* — **im·i·ta·tive** /ˈɪməˌteɪtɪv, Brit ˈɪmətətɪv/ adj • *imitative behavior* — **im·i·ta·tor** /ˈɪməˌteɪtə/ n [C]

im·i·ta·tion /ˌɪməˈteɪʃən/ n **1** [C/U] : the act of copying or imitating someone or something • *Children learn by imitation.* • *He did a hilarious imitation of his father.* • *designed in imitation of a Japanese temple* **2** [C] : something that is made or produced as a copy • *These are imitations of the real paintings.* — **imitation** adj, always before a noun • *imitation pearls/leather*

im·mac·u·late /ɪˈmækjələt/ adj **1** : perfectly clean • *The house was immaculate.* **2** : PERFECT • *an immaculate record of service* — **im·mac·u·late·ly** adv

im·ma·te·ri·al /ˌɪməˈtiriəl/ adj : not important or significant • *Whether or not he intended to cause problems is immaterial.* • *The judge ruled the evidence was immaterial.*

im·ma·ture /ˌɪməˈtuɚ, ˌɪməˈtʃɚ/ adj **1** : not fully developed or grown • *adult and immature birds* **2** : acting in a childish way • *immature behavior* • *He's so immature.* — **im·ma·tu·ri·ty** /ˌɪməˈturəti, ˌɪməˈtʃɚəti/ n [U] • *His tantrums are a sign of immaturity.*

im·mea·sur·able /ɪˈmɛʒərəbəl/ adj, formal : very great in size or amount : impossible to measure • *The war has caused immeasurable damage.* — **im·mea·sur·ably** /ɪˈmɛʒərəbli/ adv

im·me·di·a·cy /ɪˈmiːdijəsi/ n [U, singular] : the quality that makes something seem important or interesting because it is or seems to be happening now • *Television coverage gave the war (a) great immediacy that it had ever before had.*

im·me·di·ate /ɪˈmiːdijət/ adj **1 a** : happening or done without delay • *immediate action* • *The response to the crisis was immediate.* **b** : happening or existing now • *no immediate threat/danger* **c** always before a noun : important now • *Our (most) immediate concern is to provide aid to the victims.* **2** always before a noun : close to a particular place, time, or event • *everyone in the immediate area/vicinity* • *outside the immediate neighborhood/surroundings* • *the war's immediate aftermath* • *the immediate future* **3** always before a noun : having no other person or thing in between • *He was sitting to my immediate right.* • *Hospital visits are limited to immediate family.* [=a person's parents, brothers and sisters, husband or wife, and children] **4** always before a noun : coming straight from a cause or reason • *There is an immediate connection between the two events.*

¹**im·me·di·ate·ly** /ɪˈmiːdijətli/ adv **1** : with no person or thing in between • *the house immediately* [=directly] *behind this one* • *the person immediately to my left* • *Dinner was served immediately after the ceremony.* **2** : without any delay • *We need to leave immediately.*

²**immediately** conj, Brit, formal : as soon as • *Immediately you fill in this form, we will process your request.*

im·me·mo·ri·al /ˌɪməˈmɔrijəl/ adj, formal + literary : from a time so long ago that it cannot be remembered • *People have been creating art since/from time immemorial.* [=a very long time ago]

im·mense /ɪˈmɛns/ adj : very great in size or amount • *an immense fortune* • *immense power/wealth/talent* — **im·mense·ly** adv • *immensely popular* • *We enjoyed ourselves immensely.* [=very much] — **im·men·si·ty** /ɪˈmɛnsəti/ n [U] • *the immensity of the universe/ocean*

im·merse /ɪˈmɚs/ vb **-mersed**; **-mers·ing** [T] **1** : to put (something) in a liquid so that all parts are completely covered • *Immerse the fabric completely in the dye.* **2** : to make (yourself) fully involved in some activity or interest • *She had immersed herself in writing short stories.* • *He became completely/totally immersed in their culture.* — **im·mer·sion** /ɪˈmɚʒən/ n [U] • *immersion in hot water* • *complete immersion in a foreign culture/language*

im·mi·grant /ˈɪməgrənt/ n [C] : a person who comes to a country to live there • *Millions of immigrants came to America from Europe.* • *an illegal immigrant* [=a person who enters and lives in a country without official permission]

im·mi·grate /ˈɪməˌgreɪt/ vb **-grat·ed**; **-grat·ing** [I] : to come to a country to live there • *My grandparents immigrated to America.* — **im·mi·gra·tion** /ˌɪməˈgreɪʃən/ n [U]

im·mi·nent /ˈɪmənənt/ adj : happening very soon • *Their arrival is imminent.* • *a species in imminent danger of extinction* [=very close to becoming extinct] — **im·mi·nence** /ˈɪmənəns/ n [U] — **im·mi·nent·ly** adv

im·mo·bile /ɪˈmoʊbəl, ɪˈmoʊˌbajəl/ adj **1** : unable to move • *The tranquilizer made the animal immobile.* **2** : not moving • *She stood immobile.* [=motionless] — **im·mo·bil·i·ty** /ˌɪmoʊˈbɪləti/ n [U]

im·mo·bi·lize also Brit **im·mo·bi·lise** /ɪ-ˈmoʊbəˌlaɪz/ vb **-lized; -liz·ing** [T] : to keep (something or someone) from moving or working ▪ Doctors immobilized her wrist by putting it in a cast. ▪ I was immobilized by fear.

im·mod·er·ate /ɪˈmɑːdərət/ adj, formal : going beyond reasonable limits : not moderate ▪ the dangers of immoderate [=excessive] drinking — **im·mod·er·ate·ly** adv

im·mod·est /ɪˈmɑːdəst/ adj **1** : having or showing a high or too high opinion of yourself or your worth ▪ an immodest person/boast **2** of clothing : showing a lot of your body in a way that is considered improper ▪ a rather immodest outfit — **im·mod·est·ly** adv

im·mor·al /ɪˈmorəl/ adj : morally evil or wrong ▪ immoral people/behavior/acts — **im·mo·ral·i·ty** /ˌɪˌmoʊˈræləti/ n [U] ▪ the immorality of their behavior

¹**im·mor·tal** /ɪˈmoʊtl̩/ adj **1** : not capable of dying : living forever ▪ immortal gods **2** — used to say that something will last or be remembered forever ▪ immortal fame — **im·mor·tal·i·ty** /ˌɪˌmoʊˈtæləti/ n [U] ▪ He found/achieved immortality through his films.

²**immortal** n [C] **1** : an immortal being (such as a god or goddess) **2** : a famous person who will never be forgotten ▪ baseball immortals

im·mor·tal·ize also Brit **im·mor·tal·ise** /ɪˈmoʊtl̩ˌaɪz/ vb **-ized; -iz·ing** [T] : to cause (someone or something) to be remembered forever ▪ The battle/captain was immortalized in a famous poem.

im·mov·able /ɪˈmuːvəbəl/ adj : not able to be moved ▪ an immovable object

im·mune /ɪˈmjuːn/ adj **1** not before a noun : not capable of being affected by a disease ▪ Some people are immune to the disease. ▪ (figurative) He's immune to [=not affected or influenced by] persuasion/criticism. **2** not before a noun : having special protection from something that is required for most people by law ▪ He was immune from prosecution. [=he could not be prosecuted] **3** always before a noun : of or relating to the body's immune system ▪ an immune response/reaction — **im·mu·ni·ty** /ɪˈmjuːnəti/ n [U, singular] ▪ They developed (an) immunity to the virus. ▪ He was granted immunity from prosecution.

immune system n [C] : the system that protects your body from diseases and infections ▪ a strong/healthy immune system

im·mu·nize also Brit **im·mu·nise** /ˈɪmjəˌnaɪz/ vb **-nized; -niz·ing** [T] : to give (someone) a vaccine to prevent infection by a disease ▪ The children were immunized against polio. — **im·mu·ni·za·tion** also Brit **im·mu·ni·sa·tion** /ˌɪmjənəˈzeɪʃən, Brit ˌɪmjəˌnaɪˈzeɪʃən/ n [C/U]

im·mu·ta·ble /ɪˈmjuːtəbəl/ adj, formal : unable to be changed ▪ the immutable laws of nature

imp /ˈɪmp/ n [C] **1** : a small creature that plays harmful tricks in children's stories **2** : a child who causes trouble in a playful way

¹**im·pact** /ˈɪmˌpækt/ n **1** [C/U] : the act or force of one thing hitting another ▪ The wall could not withstand the impact. ▪ The bomb exploded **on/upon impact**. [=when it hit] **2** [C] : a powerful or major influence or effect ▪ The book had a huge impact when it first came out. ▪ The policy has a negative/positive impact on the community. [=harms/helps the community]

²**im·pact** /ˌɪmˈpækt/ vb **1** [T/I] : to have a strong and often bad effect on (something or someone) ▪ Both events (negatively) impacted her life. ▪ The bad economy is impacting **on/upon** small businesses. **2** [T] formal : to hit (something) with great force ▪ The meteor impacted the planet's surface.

im·pact·ed /ɪmˈpæktəd/ adj, of a tooth : growing under another tooth ▪ impacted wisdom teeth

im·pair /ɪmˈpeɚ/ vb [T] : to make (something) weaker or worse ▪ Drinking impairs a person's ability to think clearly. — **im·paired** /ɪmˈpeɚd/ adj ▪ impaired vision/hearing ▪ hearing-impaired people [=people with impaired hearing] — **im·pair·ment** /ɪmˈpeɚmənt/ n [C/U] ▪ (a) hearing/vision/memory impairment

im·pale /ɪmˈpeɪl/ vb **-paled; -pal·ing** [T] : to cause a pointed object to go into or through (someone or something) ▪ The matador was impaled by/on the bull's horns.

im·part /ɪmˈpɑɚt/ vb [T] formal **1** : to give (something, such as a quality) to a thing ▪ The oil imparts a distinctive flavor to the sauce. **2** : to make (something) known to someone ▪ imparting knowledge to the students

im·par·tial /ɪmˈpɑɚʃəl/ adj : treating all people and groups equally ▪ an impartial judge/observer/decision — **im·par·tial·i·ty** /ˌɪmˌpɑɚʃiˈæləti/ n [U] — **im·par·tial·ly** /ɪmˈpɑɚʃəli/ adv

im·pass·able /ɪmˈpæsəbəl/ adj : impossible to pass, cross, or travel over ▪ The roads were impassable.

im·passe /ˈɪmˌpæs, Brit æmˈpɑːs/ n [C] : a situation in which no progress seems possible ▪ Negotations are at an impasse. = Negotations have reached/hit an impasse.

im·pas·sioned /ɪmˈpæʃənd/ adj : showing or feeling very strong emotions ▪ an impassioned speech/plea/supporter

im·pas·sive /ɪmˈpæsɪv/ adj : not showing emotion ▪ Her face/expression remained impassive. — **im·pas·sive·ly** adv

im·pa·tient /ɪmˈpeɪʃənt/ adj **1 a** : not willing to wait for something or someone ▪ Customers have grown impatient with/at the repeated delays. ▪ He was impatient for the departure of his flight. **b** : wanting or eager to do something without waiting ▪ She was impatient to leave. **2** : showing that you do not want to wait : showing a lack of patience ▪ an impatient answer/gesture/look — **im·pa·tience** /ɪmˈpeɪʃəns/ n [U] ▪ He sighed with impatience. — **im·pa·tient·ly** adv

im·peach /ɪmˈpiːtʃ/ vb [T] law **1** : to charge (a public official) with a crime done while in office ▪ impeach a judge/

President **2** *formal* : to cause doubts about the truthfulness of (a witness, testimony, etc.) • *Lawyers tried to impeach the witness's testimony.* — **im·peach·able** /ɪmˈpiːtʃəbəl/ *adj* • *an impeachable offense/crime* — **im·peach·ment** /ɪmˈpiːtʃmənt/ *n [C/U]*

im·pec·ca·ble /ɪmˈpɛkəbəl/ *adj* : free from fault or error • *impeccable manners/taste/timing* — **im·pec·ca·bly** /ɪmˈpɛkəbli/ *adv* • *impeccably dressed*

im·pede /ɪmˈpiːd/ *vb* -**ped·ed**; -**ped·ing** [*T*] : to slow the movement, progress, or action of (someone or something) • *Economic growth is being impeded by government regulations.*

im·ped·i·ment /ɪmˈpɛdəmənt/ *n [C]* **1** : something that makes it difficult to do or complete something • *There were no legal impediments to the deal.* **2** : a condition that makes it difficult to speak normally • *a speech impediment*

im·pel /ɪmˈpɛl/ *vb* -**pelled**; -**pel·ling** [*T*] : to cause (someone) to feel a strong need or desire to do something • *She was impelled by a sense of adventure.*

im·pend·ing /ɪmˈpɛndɪŋ/ *adj, always before a noun* : happening or likely to happen soon • *an impending arrival/disaster*

im·pen·e·tra·ble /ɪmˈpɛnətrəbəl/ *adj* **1** : impossible to pass or see through • *an impenetrable wall/barrier/jungle* • *impenetrable darkness/fog* **2** : impossible to understand • *an impenetrable mystery*

[1]**im·per·a·tive** /ɪmˈpɛrətɪv/ *adj* **1** *formal* : very important • *an imperative duty* **2** *grammar* : having the form that expresses a command rather than a statement or a question • *"Help" in the sentence "Help me!" is an imperative verb.* • *a verb in the imperative mood*

[2]**imperative** *n* **1** [*C*] *formal* : a command, rule, duty, etc., that is very important or necessary • *a moral/legal imperative* **2** *grammar* **a the imperative** : the form that a verb or sentence has when it is expressing a command • *"Eat your spinach!" is in the imperative.* **b** [*C*] : an imperative verb or sentence • *"Go" and "buy" are imperatives in the sentence "Please go to the store and buy some milk."*

im·per·cep·ti·ble /ˌɪmpəˈsɛptəbəl/ *adj* : impossible to see or notice • *imperceptible changes/differences* — **im·per·cep·ti·bly** /ˌɪmpəˈsɛptəbli/ *adv*

[1]**im·per·fect** /ɪmˈpəfɪkt/ *adj* **1** : having mistakes or problems : not perfect • *an imperfect society/solution* **2** *grammar* : of or relating to a verb tense used to express an incomplete action in the past or a state that continued for a period of time in the past • *In "He was singing," "was singing" is in the imperfect tense.* — **im·per·fect·ly** *adv*

[2]**imperfect** *n* — **the imperfect** *grammar* : the imperfect tense of a verb • *a verb in the imperfect*

im·per·fec·tion /ˌɪmpəˈfɛkʃən/ *n* [*C*] : a small flaw or bad part • *imperfections in the cloth/jewel* **2** [*U*] : the state of being imperfect • *human imperfection*

im·pe·ri·al /ɪmˈpɪriəl/ *adj, always before a noun* : of or relating to an empire or an

emperor • *the imperial family/army/palace*

im·pe·ri·al·ism /ɪmˈpɪriəˌlɪzəm/ *n* [*U*] **1** : a policy or practice by which a country increases its power by gaining control over other areas of the world **2** : the effect that a powerful country or group of countries has in changing or influencing the way people live in other, poorer countries • *economic/cultural imperialism* — **im·pe·ri·al·ist** /ɪmˈpɪriəlɪst/ *n* [*C*] — **imperialist** *adj* • *imperialist power/expansion* — **im·pe·ri·al·is·tic** /ɪmˌpɪriəˈlɪstɪk/ *adj* • *imperialistic aims/goals*

im·per·il /ɪmˈpɛrəl/ *vb, US* -**iled** *or Brit* -**illed**; *US* -**il·ing** *or Brit* -**il·ling** [*T*] *formal* : to put (something or someone) in a dangerous situation • *The fumes imperiled the lives of the trapped miners.*

im·pe·ri·ous /ɪmˈpɪriəs/ *adj, formal* : having or showing the proud and unpleasant attitude of someone who gives orders and expects other people to obey them • *an imperious leader/manner/tone* — **im·pe·ri·ous·ly** *adv*

im·per·me·able /ɪmˈpəmijəbəl/ *adj, technical* : not allowing something (such as a liquid) to pass through • *an impermeable layer of rock*

im·per·son·al /ɪmˈpəsənəl/ *adj* **1 a** : having or showing no interest in individual people or their feelings • *a giant impersonal corporation* **b** : not relating to or influenced by personal feelings • *We discussed the weather and other impersonal topics.* **2** *grammar* : having no specified subject or no subject other than "it" • *"Rained" in "it rained" is an impersonal verb.* • *an impersonal sentence/construction* — **im·per·son·al·ly** /ɪmˈpəsənəli/ *adv*

im·per·son·ate /ɪmˈpəsəˌneɪt/ *vb* -**at·ed**; -**at·ing** [*T*] : to pretend to be (another person) • *He was arrested for impersonating a police officer.* — **im·per·son·a·tion** /ɪmˌpəsəˈneɪʃən/ *n* [*C/U*] • *He does a great impersonation of the President.* — **im·per·son·a·tor** /ɪmˈpəsəˌneɪtə/ *n* [*C*] • *an Elvis impersonator* [=an entertainer who pretends to be Elvis Presley]

im·per·ti·nent /ɪmˈpətnənt/ *adj, formal* : rude and showing a lack of respect • *an impertinent person/question* — **im·per·ti·nence** /ɪmˈpətnəns/ *n* [*U*]

im·per·turb·a·ble /ˌɪmpəˈtəbəbəl/ *adj, formal* : very calm : very hard to disturb or upset • *an imperturbable person/disposition*

im·per·vi·ous /ɪmˈpəvijəs/ *adj* **1** *technical* : not allowing something (such as water or light) to enter or pass through • *a substance impervious to light* **2** *formal* : not bothered or affected by something • *He seems impervious to criticism.* — **im·per·vi·ous·ness** *n* [*U*]

im·pet·u·ous /ɪmˈpɛtʃəwəs/ *adj* : acting or done quickly and without thought • *an impetuous young man* • *an impetuous decision* — **im·pet·u·ous·ly** *adv*

im·pe·tus /ˈɪmpətəs/ *n* [*U, singular*] : a force that causes something (such as a process or activity) to be done or to become more active • *The movement is now gaining/losing impetus.* • *Her work provid-*

ed the major impetus behind the movement.

im·pinge /ɪmˈpɪndʒ/ *vb* **-pinged; -pinging** — **impinge on/upon** [*phrasal vb*] *formal* : to affect (something) in a way that is unwanted ▪ *The publicity could impinge on the defendant's right to a fair trial.*

imp·ish /ˈɪmpɪʃ/ *adj* : having or showing a playful desire to cause trouble ▪ *an impish grin/smile*

im·pla·ca·ble /ɪmˈplækəbəl/ *adj* : opposed to someone or something in a very angry or determined way that cannot be changed ▪ *an implacable hatred for his opponents* — **im·pla·ca·bly** /ɪmˈplækəbli/ *adv*

im·plant /ɪmˈplænt/ *vb* [*T*] **1** *medical* : to place (something) in a person's body by means of surgery ▪ *a hearing aid that is surgically implanted in the ear* **2** : to cause (something) to become a part of the way a person thinks or feels ▪ *She implanted a love of reading in her students.* [=she taught her students to love reading] — **implant** *n* [*C*] *medical* ▪ *silicone breast implants*

im·plau·si·ble /ɪmˈplɑːzəbəl/ *adj* : not believable or realistic ▪ *implausible claims/excuses* — **im·plau·si·bly** /ɪmˈplɑːzəbli/ *adv* ▪ *an implausibly happy ending*

¹**im·ple·ment** /ˈɪmpləmənt/ *n* [*C*] : TOOL ▪ *farming implements*

²**im·ple·ment** /ˈɪmpləˌmɛnt/ *vb* [*T*] : to begin to do or use (something, such as a plan) ▪ *The government implemented a series of reforms.* ▪ *Our plan was never fully implemented.* — **im·ple·men·ta·tion** /ˌɪmpləmənˈteɪʃən/ *n* [*U*]

im·pli·cate /ˈɪmpləˌkeɪt/ *vb* **-cat·ed; -cat·ing** [*T*] : to show that someone or something is closely connected to or involved in something (such as a crime) ▪ *His business partner was implicated in the theft.*

im·pli·ca·tion /ˌɪmpləˈkeɪʃən/ *n* **1** [*C*] : a possible future effect or result ▪ *What are the long-term implications of the new policy?* ▪ *economic/political implications* **2** [*C/U*] : something that is suggested without being said directly ▪ *I'm offended by his/the implication that women can't do math.* ▪ *He condemned the court and, by implication, the entire legal system.* **3** [*U*] : the fact or state of being involved in or connected to something (such as a crime) ▪ *the implication of his partner in the crime*

im·plic·it /ɪmˈplɪsət/ *adj* **1** : understood though not clearly or directly stated ▪ *an implicit agreement/warning/assumption* **2** : ABSOLUTE, COMPLETE ▪ *I have implicit trust/confidence/faith in her honesty.* — **im·plic·it·ly** *adv*

im·plode /ɪmˈploʊd/ *vb* **-plod·ed; -plod·ing** [*I*] : to collapse inward in a very sudden and violent way ▪ *an imploding star* ▪ *(figurative) The economy is about to implode.* — **im·plo·sion** /ɪmˈploʊʒən/ *n* [*C/U*]

im·plore /ɪmˈploɚ/ *vb* **-plored; -plor·ing** [*T*] *formal* : BEG ▪ *She implored her son not to go.* ▪ *"Think of the children!" he im-*

plored. — **imploring** *adj* ▪ *an imploring look*

im·ply /ɪmˈplaɪ/ *vb* **-plies; -plied; -ply·ing** [*T*] : to suggest (something) without saying or showing it plainly ▪ *Early reports implied that his death was not an accident.* ▪ *Are you implying that I stole it?*

im·po·lite /ˌɪmpəˈlaɪt/ *adj* : not polite : RUDE ▪ *It's impolite to talk during the performance.* ▪ *an impolite child* — **im·po·lite·ly** *adv*

¹**im·port** /ɪmˈpoɚt/ *vb* [*T*] **1** : to bring a product into a country to be sold ▪ *He imports German cars to/into the U.S.* **2** *computers* : to bring (something, such as data) into a file, system, etc., from another source ▪ *import photographs/files* — **im·port·ed** /ɪmˈpoɚtəd/ *adj* ▪ *imported cars/coffee* — **im·port·er** *n* [*C*]

²**im·port** /ˈɪmpoɚt/ *n* **1 a** [*C*] : a product brought into a country to be sold there ▪ *They sell luxury imports from around the world.* **b** [*U*] : the act of importing something ▪ *laws affecting the import of foreign goods* **2** [*U*] *formal* : IMPORTANCE ▪ *a matter of great import*

im·por·tance /ɪmˈpoɚtns/ *n* [*U*] : value or significance ▪ *a medical discovery of great/major importance* [=a very important medical discovery] ▪ *Nothing of importance* [=nothing important] *was decided.*

im·por·tant /ɪmˈpoɚtnt/ *adj* **1** : having serious meaning or worth ▪ *She's an important member of the team.* : deserving or requiring serious attention ▪ *an important problem/discovery* ▪ *It's important to send these forms on time.* **2** : having power, authority, or influence ▪ *an important artist/scholar* — **im·por·tant·ly** /ɪmˈpoɚtntli/ *adv* ▪ *The treatment is unpleasant and, more importantly, ineffective.* [=it is more important that it is ineffective] ▪ *She contributed importantly to our understanding of the disease.*

im·por·ta·tion /ˌɪmˌpoɚˈteɪʃən/ *n* [*U*] : the act of importing products ▪ *illegal importation of weapons*

im·pose /ɪmˈpoʊz/ *vb* **-posed; -pos·ing** **1** [*T*] **a** : to cause (a tax, fine, rule, punishment, etc.) to affect someone or something by using your authority ▪ *The judge imposed a life sentence.* ▪ *A curfew has been imposed on/upon the city's youth.* **b** : to establish or create (something unwanted) in a forceful or harmful way ▪ *the limits imposed by my own fear of failure* **2** [*T*] : to force someone to accept (something or yourself) ▪ *He imposed his will on/upon his subjects.* [=he forced his subjects to do what he wanted them to do] ▪ *I don't want to impose myself on other people.* **3** [*I*] : to ask for or expect more than is fair or reasonable ▪ *I didn't want to impose on (her).*

im·pos·ing /ɪmˈpoʊzɪŋ/ *adj* : very large or impressive ▪ *an imposing man/building*

im·po·si·tion /ˌɪmpəˈzɪʃən/ *n* **1** [*C*] : a demand or request that is not reasonable or that causes trouble for someone ▪ *You can stay with me—it's no imposition.* **2** [*U*] : the act of establishing or creating something in an official way ▪ *the imposition of a tax on liquor*

im·pos·si·ble /ɪmˈpɑːsəbəl/ *adj* **1 a** : unable to be done or to happen ▪ *It's impossible to predict the future.* ▪ *The heavy rain made it impossible to see the road.* ▪ *physically/logically/almost impossible* ▪ *It's virtually/nearly/almost impossible to book a flight just before the holiday.* ▪ *I find it impossible to believe* [=I cannot believe] *he's telling the truth.* ▪ *an impossible dream* **b** : very difficult ▪ *an impossible* [=hopeless] *situation* ▪ *These math problems are impossible!* **2** *of a person* : very difficult to deal with : very irritating or annoying ▪ *You're impossible!* ▪ *My boss is just an impossible manager.* — **the impossible** : something that cannot be done or that is very difficult ▪ *You are asking the impossible.* [=what you want is not possible] — **im·pos·si·bil·i·ty** /ˌɪmˌpɑːsəˈbɪləti/ *n, pl* **-ties** [C/U] ▪ *the impossibility of knowing the future* ▪ *a logical impossibility* [=something that is logically impossible] — **im·pos·si·bly** /ɪmˈpɑːsəbli/ *adv* ▪ *impossibly high standards*

im·pos·tor *or* **im·pos·ter** /ɪmˈpɑːstɚ/ *n* [C] : a person who deceives others by pretending to be someone else

im·po·tent /ˈɪmpətənt/ *adj* **1** : lacking power or strength ▪ *an impotent political party* **2** *of a man* : unable to get or keep an erection — **im·po·tence** /ˈɪmpətəns/ *n* [U]

im·pound /ɪmˈpaʊnd/ *vb* [T] : to use legal powers to get and hold (something) ▪ *The police impounded her car.*

im·pov·er·ish /ɪmˈpɑːvərɪʃ/ *vb* [T] **1** : to make (someone) poor ▪ *The dictator impoverished his people.* **2** : to use up the strength or richness of (something, such as land) ▪ *Poor farming practices impoverished the soil.* — **im·pov·er·ished** /ɪmˈpɑːvərɪʃt/ *adj* ▪ *the most impoverished areas* [=the poorest areas] *of the country* ▪ *impoverished soil* — **im·pov·er·ish·ment** /ɪmˈpɑːvərɪʃmənt/ *n* [U]

im·prac·ti·cal /ɪmˈpræktɪkəl/ *adj* **1** : not easy to do or use ▪ *Little cars are impractical for large families.* ▪ *an impractical plan/solution* **2** *of a person* : not sensible : not able to deal with practical matters effectively ▪ *a dreamy and impractical young man* — **im·prac·ti·cal·i·ty** /ɪmˌpræktɪˈkæləti/ *n, pl* **-ties** [C/U]

im·pre·cise /ˌɪmprɪˈsaɪs/ *adj* : not clear or exact ▪ *imprecise language/measurements* — **im·pre·ci·sion** /ˌɪmprɪˈsɪʒən/ *n* [U]

im·preg·na·ble /ɪmˈprɛɡnəbəl/ *adj* : not able to be captured by attack : very strong ▪ *an impregnable fortress/defense*

im·preg·nate /ˈɪmprɛɡˌneɪt/ *vb* **-nat·ed; -nat·ing** [T] **1** : to cause (a material) to be filled or soaked with something ▪ *a cake impregnated with brandy* **2** *technical* : to make (a woman or a female animal) pregnant

im·pre·sa·rio /ˌɪmprəˈsɑːriˌoʊ/ *n, pl* **-ri·os** [C] : a person who manages a performance (such as a concert or play)

im·press /ɪmˈprɛs/ *vb* [T/I] : to cause (someone) to feel admiration or interest ▪ *He's trying to impress her.* ▪ *We were impressed by/with his credentials.* **2** [T] : to produce a clear idea or image of (some-

thing) ▪ *She tried to impress on/upon him how important this was.* [=tried to make him understand how important this was]

im·pres·sion /ɪmˈprɛʃən/ *n* [C] **1** : the effect or influence that something or someone has on a person's thoughts or feelings ▪ *Her words made a strong/favorable/good/positive impression (on us).* ▪ *First impressions are important but can be misleading.* ▪ *He's trying to avoid (giving) the impression that he's insensitive.* **2** : an idea or belief that is usually not clear or certain ▪ *It was my impression* [=I thought] *that admission was free.* = *I was under the impression that admission was free.* ▪ *I'm sorry if I gave you the wrong impression.* **3** : an appearance or suggestion of something ▪ *His lifestyle conveyed the impression of great wealth.* **4** : something (such as a design or a footprint) made by pressing or stamping a surface ▪ *an impression in the mud* **5** : an imitation of a famous person that is done for entertainment ▪ *He does a good impression of Elvis Presley.*

im·pres·sion·able /ɪmˈprɛʃənəbəl/ *adj* : easy to influence ▪ *impressionable children/minds*

im·pres·sion·ism *or* **Im·pres·sion·ism** /ɪmˈprɛʃəˌnɪzəm/ *n* [U] : a style of painting that began in France around 1870, that uses spots of color to show the effects of different kinds of light, and that attempts to capture the feeling of a scene rather than specific details — **im·pres·sion·is·tic** /ɪmˌprɛʃəˈnɪstɪk/ *adj*

im·pres·sion·ist /ɪmˈprɛʃənɪst/ *n* [C] **1** *or* **Impressionist** : a painter who practices impressionism **2** : an entertainer who does impressions (sense 5)

im·pres·sive /ɪmˈprɛsɪv/ *adj* : deserving attention, admiration, or respect ▪ *an impressive vocabulary/performance* — **im·pres·sive·ly** *adv*

¹**im·print** /ɪmˈprɪnt/ *vb* [T] **1** : to create a mark by pressing against a surface ▪ *a T-shirt imprinted with the company logo* **2** : to cause (something) to stay in your mind or memory ▪ *a picture imprinted in my memory*

²**im·print** /ˈɪmˌprɪnt/ *n* [C] **1** : a mark created by pressing against a surface ▪ *a fossil imprint of a dinosaur's foot* **2** : a strong effect or influence ▪ *She was determined to put/leave her imprint on the company.*

im·pris·on /ɪmˈprɪzn/ *vb* [T] : to put (someone) in prison ▪ *He was imprisoned for murder.* ▪ *He imprisoned his political opponents.* — **im·pris·on·ment** /ɪmˈprɪznmənt/ *n* [U]

im·prob·a·ble /ɪmˈprɑːbəbəl/ *adj* : not likely to be true or to happen : UNLIKELY ▪ *It's (highly) improbable that he'll be convicted.* ▪ *an improbable story* — **im·prob·a·bil·i·ty** /ɪmˌprɑːbəˈbɪləti/ *n, pl* **-ties** [C/U] — **im·prob·a·bly** /ɪmˈprɑːbəbli/ *adv*

im·promp·tu /ɪmˈprɑːmptuː, *Brit* ˈprɒmptjuː/ *adj* : not prepared ahead of time : made or done without preparation ▪ *an impromptu speech about honor and responsibility* — **impromptu** *adv* ▪ *speaking impromptu*

im·prop·er /ɪmˈprɑːpɚ/ *adj* **1** : not correct • *improper grammar* **2** : not following legal or moral rules of acceptable behavior • *evidence of improper police conduct* **3** : not suitable or appropriate for the situation • *improper dress/clothes* **4** : not polite • *improper remarks/behavior* — **im·prop·er·ly** *adv*

im·pro·pri·e·ty /ˌɪmprəˈprajəti/ *n, pl* **-ties** *formal* **1** [U] **a** : rude, improper, or immoral behavior • *She was shocked by the young man's impropriety.* **b** : a rude or improper quality • *the impropriety of his behavior/language* **2** [C] : a wrong, improper, or immoral act • *accused of financial/sexual improprieties*

im·prove /ɪmˈpruːv/ *vb* **-proved; -proving** [T/I] : to become better or make (something) better • *Her writing has improved.* • *This operation will greatly/dramatically/significantly improve her chances of survival.* • *The ad has resulted in greatly improved sales.* — **improve on/upon** [*phrasal vb*] : to do better than (something previously done) • *It'll be hard to improve on the success they had last year.*

im·prove·ment /ɪmˈpruːvmənt/ *n* **1** [U] : the act or process of making something better • *His cooking needs improvement.* = *There's room for improvement in his cooking.* **2** [C] **a** : the quality of being better than before • *I've noticed a significant improvement in your work recently.* **b** : an addition or change that makes something better or more valuable • *She made some improvements to/in the article.* • **home improvements** [=changes made to your house that make it more valuable] • *The food is an improvement on/over* [=is better than] *what we're usually served.*

im·pro·vise /ˈɪmprəˌvaɪz/ *vb* **-vised; -vis·ing** [T/I] **1** : to speak or perform without preparation • *Good jazz musicians know how to improvise.* • *He had to improvise his speech.* **2** : to make or create (something) by using whatever is available • *I improvised (a meal) with what I had in my refrigerator.* — **im·pro·vi·sa·tion** /ɪmˌprɑːvəˈzeɪʃən/ *n* [C/U] • *an actor who is good at improvisation* — **im·pro·vi·sa·tion·al** /ɪmˌprɑːvəˈzeɪʃənl/ *adj* — **im·pro·vis·er** *also chiefly US* **im·pro·vi·sor** /ˈɪmprəˌvaɪzɚ/ *n* [C]

im·pru·dent /ɪmˈpruːdn̩t/ *adj, formal* : not wise or sensible • *an imprudent investment/decision* — **im·pru·dent·ly** *adv*

im·pu·dent /ˈɪmpjədənt/ *adj, formal* : failing to show proper respect and courtesy • *impudent behavior* • *an impudent soldier* — **im·pu·dence** /ˈɪmpjədəns/ *n* [U]

im·pugn /ɪmˈpjuːn/ *vb* [T] *formal* : to criticize (a person's character, intentions, etc.) by suggesting that someone is not honest and should not be trusted • *She impugned his character.*

im·pulse /ˈɪmˌpʌls/ *n* **1** [C/U] : a sudden strong desire to do something • *He has to learn to control his impulses.* • *She quit her job on impulse.* [=quickly and without thinking about it first] • *The camera was an impulse buy/purchase.* [=something that is usually not needed and is bought quickly without much thought] **2** [C] *technical* : a small amount of energy that moves from one area to another • *an electrical impulse*

im·pul·sive /ɪmˈpʌlsɪv/ *adj* **1** : doing things or tending to do things suddenly and without careful thought • *She's impulsive and does things that she later regrets.* **2** : done suddenly and without planning • *impulsive behavior/decisions* — **im·pul·sive·ly** *adv* — **im·pul·sive·ness** *n* [U]

im·pu·ni·ty /ɪmˈpjuːnəti/ *n* [U] : freedom from punishment, harm, or loss • *The rioters set fires and looted with impunity.*

im·pure /ɪmˈpjuɚ/ *adj* **1** : DIRTY • *impure water* **2** : mixed with something else that is usually not as good • *an impure chemical* **3** : sexual in a way that is considered morally wrong • *impure thoughts*

im·pu·ri·ty /ɪmˈpjuɚəti/ *n, pl* **-ties** **1** [U] : the quality or state of being impure • *moral impurity* **2** [C] : an unwanted substance that is found in something else and that prevents it from being pure • *The water is free of impurities.*

im·pute /ɪmˈpjuːt/ *vb* **-put·ed; -put·ing** [T] *formal* : to say or suggest that someone or something has or is guilty of (something) • *imputing selfish motives to my actions* [=saying my actions were motivated by selfishness]

¹in /ˈɪn, ən/ *prep* **1** — used to indicate location or position within something • *a house in the country* • *Albuquerque is in New Mexico.* **2** : to the inside of (a room, container, etc.) • *I threw it in* [=*into*] *the garbage.* **3 a** — used to indicate that someone or something belongs to or is included as part of something • *She used to play in* [=as a member of] *a band.* **b** — used to indicate the existence of something or someone within a story, movie, etc. • *He saw it in a dream.* **4 a** : during (a period of time, a season, etc.) • *It happened in the 1930s.* • *We haven't seen them in a long time.* **b** : at the end of (a period of time) • *I'll be there in a minute.* **c** — used to indicate an approximate age or number • *a woman in her thirties* [=a woman who is between 30 and 39 years old] **5** — used to indicate the method, materials, or form of something • *a note written in French* • *a symphony in (the key of) C* • *50 dollars in cash* **6 a** — used to indicate the state or condition of someone or something • *She was in danger.* • *Are you in pain?* **b** : to a specified state, condition, or form • *They were always getting in* [=*into*] *trouble.* **7** — used to indicate how people or things are arranged • *They stood in a circle/row.* **8** — used to indicate the conditions that are around someone or something • *I found her sitting in the dark.* **9** : while or as a result of (doing something) • *Many mistakes were made in planning the project.* **10** — used to indicate the manner or purpose of something • *They left in a hurry.* • *a banquet in his honor* [=to honor him] ▪ *She moved here in hopes of finding a better job.* **11** — used to make a statement or description more limited or specific in meaning ▪ *They are alike in some ways/respects.* ▪ *It measures two feet in length.* [=it is two feet long] **12** — used to indicate the person who is being described ▪ *In her, you have a true friend.* **13** — used to indicate the object of a belief, opinion, or feeling ▪ *I have no interest in sports.* [=sports do not interest me] **14** — used to indicate a job or area of activity ▪ *She has a job in marketing.* **15** : wearing (something) as clothes ▪ *He showed up in his best suit.*

²**in** /ˈɪn/ *adv* **1** : to or toward the inside of something (such as a building) ▪ *She went in and closed the door.* ▪ *Please come in!* **2 a** : to or toward a place ▪ *They flew in yesterday.* ▪ *The tide is coming in.* [=towards shore] **b** : at the place where someone or something arrives after traveling ▪ *We expect to get in* [=to arrive] *around noon.* **3** : at or inside a home, office, etc. ▪ *The doctor is in.* [=the doctor is in his/her office] **4** : at or to a location that is near to something or that seems near to something ▪ *Pull the car further in.* [=closer to the curb, house, etc.] **5 a** : in a way that will blend into or join with something ▪ *Gradually mix in the flour.* **b** : to or at a proper or indicated place ▪ *Please fill in your name and address on the application.* **6** : in a way that surrounds something or someone or prevents something or someone from leaving ▪ *They fenced in the property.* [=they put a fence around the property] **7** : in the position of someone who is involved or participating in something ▪ *Count me in.* [=include me in your plans] **8** : in or into a position or job ▪ *They voted him in.* [=they elected him] **9** : in a friendly relationship *with* someone ▪ *She was in with the city's most powerful people.* **10** : present or in your possession and available for use ▪ *Are all the votes/results in?* **11** *sports* : inside the area where players or the ball must stay in sports like tennis, basketball, and American football ▪ *Her serve was just barely in.* — **all in** *informal* : very tired ▪ *I'm all in. I'm going to bed.* — **in for** *informal* : sure to experience (something) ▪ *Boy, is she in for a surprise!* — **in on** ✧ If you are *in on* something you have knowledge about it or are involved in it. ▪ *They were all in on the scheme/secret.* — **in that** — used to introduce a statement that explains or gives more specific information about what you have just said ▪ *The book is good, in that it's well written, but I didn't actually like reading it.*

³**in** /ˈɪn/ *adj* **1** : popular or fashionable ▪ *the in thing to do* **2** : aware of and strongly influenced by what is new and fashionable ▪ *It's what the in crowd is wearing this season.*

⁴**in** /ˈɪn/ *n* [C] *chiefly US, informal* : a way of becoming involved in something or of influencing someone ▪ *They must have an in with the boss.* — see also INS AND OUTS

in. *abbr* inch, inches

IN *abbr* Indiana

in·abil·i·ty /ˌɪnəˈbɪləti/ *n* [U, singular] : the condition of not being able to do something ▪ *an inability to concentrate*

in·ac·ces·si·ble /ˌɪnɪkˈsɛsəbəl/ *adj* : difficult or impossible to reach ▪ *The area is inaccessible by road.*

in·ac·cu·rate /ɪnˈækjərət/ *adj* : not correct or exact : having a mistake or error ▪ *an inaccurate statement/quotation* — **in·ac·cu·ra·cy** /ɪnˈækjərəsi/ *n* [C/U] ▪ *The article is filled with inaccuracies.* [=incorrect statements; errors or mistakes] — **in·ac·cu·rate·ly** *adv*

in·ac·tion /ɪnˈækʃən/ *n* [U] : failure to do something that should be done ▪ *They criticized the administration's inaction on environmental issues.*

in·ac·tive /ɪnˈæktɪv/ *adj* **1** : not doing things that require physical movement and energy ▪ *Inactive people suffer higher rates of heart disease.* **2** : not involved in the activities of a group or organization ▪ *an inactive club member* **3** : no longer being used ▪ *the bank's inactive accounts* **4** *of a volcano* : not capable of erupting **5** : not having a chemical effect ▪ *inactive ingredients* — **in·ac·tiv·i·ty** /ˌɪnækˈtɪvəti/ *n* [U]

in·ad·e·quate /ɪnˈædɪkwət/ *adj* : not enough or not good enough ▪ *inadequate information/supplies* ▪ *He made her feel inadequate.* — **in·ad·e·qua·cy** /ɪnˈædɪkwəsi/ *n* [C/U] — **in·ad·e·quate·ly** *adv*

in·ad·mis·si·ble /ˌɪnədˈmɪsəbəl/ *adj* : not able to be allowed or considered in a legal case ▪ *The evidence was inadmissible.*

in·ad·ver·tent /ˌɪnədˈvɚtənt/ *adj* : not intended or planned : ACCIDENTAL ▪ *an advertent error/omission* — **in·ad·ver·tent·ly** *adv* ▪ *I inadvertently dialed the wrong number.*

in·ad·vis·able /ˌɪnədˈvaɪzəbəl/ *adj* : not wise, sensible, or reasonable ▪ *It would be highly/very inadvisable to do this ourselves.*

in·alien·able /ɪnˈeɪljənəbəl/ *adj, formal* : impossible to take away or give up ▪ *inalienable rights*

in·ane /ɪˈneɪn/ *adj* : very silly or stupid ▪ *inane comments/questions/chatter*

in·an·i·mate /ɪnˈænəmət/ *adj* : not living ▪ *an inanimate object*

in·ap·pli·ca·ble /ɪnˈæplɪkəbəl, ˌɪnəˈplɪkəbəl/ *adj, formal* : not able to be used in a particular situation ▪ *That information is inapplicable in this instance.*

in·ap·pro·pri·ate /ˌɪnəˈproʊprijət/ *adj* : not right or suited for some purpose or situation ▪ *inappropriate behavior/conduct/language* — **in·ap·pro·pri·ate·ly** *adv* — **in·ap·pro·pri·ate·ness** *n* [U]

in·ar·tic·u·late /ˌɪnɑɚˈtɪkjələt/ *adj* **1** : not able to express ideas clearly and effectively in speech or writing ▪ *He's smart, but somewhat inarticulate.* **2 a** : not expressed clearly or easily understood ▪ *an inarticulate explanation* **b** : not able to be expressed ▪ *inarticulate longings* — **in·ar·tic·u·late·ly** *adv*

in·as·much as /ˌɪnəzˈmʌtʃəz/ *conj, formal* — used to introduce a statement that explains, limits, or gives more specific information about what you have just said ▪ *They were lucky inasmuch as no one was hurt in the fire.*

in·at·ten·tion /ˌɪnəˈtɛnʃən/ *n* [*U*] : failure to carefully think about, listen to, or watch someone or something : lack of attention ▪ *his inattention to detail* — **in·at·ten·tive** /ˌɪnəˈtɛntɪv/ *adj* ▪ *inattentive drivers*

in·au·di·ble /ɪnˈɑːdəbəl/ *adj* : impossible to hear ▪ *The sound is almost inaudible to humans.* — **in·au·di·bly** /ɪnˈɑːdəbli/ *adv*

in·au·gu·ral /ɪnˈɑːgjərəl/ *adj, always before a noun* **1** : happening as part of an official ceremony or celebration when someone (such as a newly elected official) begins an important job ▪ *the President's inaugural address* **2** : happening as the first one in a series of similar events ▪ *The new train will make its inaugural* [=*first*] *run next week.* — **inaugural** *n* [*C*] *chiefly US* ▪ *President Franklin D. Roosevelt's first inaugural* [=*inauguration*]

in·au·gu·rate /ɪnˈɑːgjəˌreɪt/ *vb* **-rat·ed; -rat·ing** [*T*] **1** : to introduce (someone, such as a newly elected official) into a job or position with a formal ceremony ▪ *He was inaugurated (as President) on the 20th of January.* **2** : to celebrate the fact that (something) is officially ready to be used ▪ *They inaugurated the new headquarters with a brief ceremony.* — **in·au·gu·ra·tion** /ɪnˌɑːgjəˈreɪʃən/ *n* [*C/U*] ▪ *presidential inaugurations*

in·aus·pi·cious /ˌɪnɑːˈspɪʃəs/ *adj, formal* : not showing or suggesting that future success is likely ▪ *an inauspicious start/beginning* — **in·aus·pi·cious·ly** *adv*

in·au·then·tic /ˌɪnɑːˈθɛntɪk/ *adj* : not real, accurate, or sincere ▪ *Their Mexican dishes are inauthentic.* [=*they are not like real Mexican food*]

in·born /ˈɪnˈboən/ *adj* : existing from the time someone is born ▪ *an inborn talent/ability*

in·bound /ˈɪnˌbaʊnd/ *adj* : traveling into a place ▪ *inbound flights* [=*flights coming to an airport*]

in–box /ˈɪnˌbɑːks/ *n* [*C*] **1** *US* : a box or other container on a desk in which letters, notes, etc., that are sent to the desk are placed **2** *computers* : a computer folder that holds new e-mail messages

in·bred /ˈɪnˈbrɛd/ *adj* **1** : existing as a basic part of a person's nature or character ▪ *They have an inbred love of freedom.* **2** : born from or produced by animals, plants, or people that are closely related ▪ *inbred mice*

in·breed·ing /ˈɪnˈbriːdɪŋ/ *n* [*U*] : a process by which animals, plants, or people are born from or produced by closely related parents ▪ *genetic defects caused by inbreeding*

in·built /ˈɪnˈbɪlt/ *adj, Brit* : BUILT-IN ▪ *It comes with several inbuilt features.*

Inc. *abbr* incorporated ▪ *Merriam-Webster Inc.*

in·cal·cu·la·ble /ɪnˈkælkjələbəl/ *adj, formal* **1** : very large or great ▪ *incalculable*

damage **2** : not able to be predicted ▪ *The consequences of their decision are incalculable.*

in·can·des·cent /ˌɪnkənˈdɛsnt/ *adj* **1 a** : white or glowing because of great heat ▪ *incandescent gas* **b** : producing bright light when heated ▪ *an incandescent light bulb* **2** : very impressive, successful, or intelligent ▪ *an incandescent performance* — **in·can·des·cence** /ˌɪnkənˈdɛsns/ *n* [*U*]

in·ca·pa·ble /ɪnˈkeɪpəbəl/ *adj* : not able to do something ▪ *He seemed incapable of happiness.*

in·ca·pac·i·tate /ˌɪnkəˈpæsəˌteɪt/ *vb* **-tat·ed; -tat·ing** [*T*] : to make (someone or something) unable to work, move, or function in the usual way ▪ *He was incapacitated by the pain.* ▪ *an incapacitating illness/injury* ▪ *a computer system incapacitated by software problems*

in·ca·pac·i·ty /ˌɪnkəˈpæsəti/ *n, pl* **-ties** [*C/U*] *formal* : a lack or loss of the ability to do something in the usual or desired way ▪ *I'm aware of my weaknesses and incapacities.*

in·car·cer·ate /ɪnˈkɑɚsəˌreɪt/ *vb* **-at·ed; -at·ing** [*T*] *formal* : to put (someone) in prison ▪ *She was incarcerated for robbery.* — **in·car·cer·a·tion** /ɪnˌkɑɚsəˈreɪʃən/ *n* [*U*]

in·car·nate /ɪnˈkɑɚnət/ *adj, formal* : having a human body ▪ *acts as though she's the devil incarnate* [=*a very evil person*]

in·car·na·tion /ˌɪnkɑɚˈneɪʃən/ *n* [*C*] **1** : one of a series of lives that a person is believed to have had in the past in some religions ▪ *He claims that he was a Greek soldier in a previous incarnation.* ▪ *(figurative) The software's latest incarnation* [=*version*] *includes many new features.* **2** : a person who represents a quality or idea ▪ *She is the incarnation of goodness.* [=*she is a very good person*]

in·cen·di·ary /ɪnˈsɛndiˌeri, *Brit* ɪnˈsɛndiəri/ *adj* **1** : containing chemicals that explode into flame ▪ *an incendiary bomb/device* **2** : causing anger ▪ *incendiary words/language*

¹in·cense /ˈɪnˌsɛns/ *n* [*U*] : a substance that is used often in religious ceremonies to produce a strong and pleasant smell when it is burned

²in·cense /ɪnˈsɛns/ *vb* **-censed; -cens·ing** [*T*] : to make (someone) very angry ▪ *We were incensed by her arrogance.*

in·cen·tive /ɪnˈsɛntɪv/ *n* [*C/U*] : something that encourages a person to do something or to work harder ▪ *providing a strong/powerful incentive to conserve energy* ▪ *special tax/financial incentives*

in·cep·tion /ɪnˈsɛpʃən/ *n* [*U, singular*] *formal* : BEGINNING, START ▪ *The project has been in trouble from/since its inception.*

in·ces·sant /ɪnˈsɛsnt/ *adj* : continuing without stopping — used to describe something that is unpleasant or annoying ▪ *Their incessant talking distracts the other students.* — **in·ces·sant·ly** *adv*

in·cest /ˈɪnˌsɛst/ *n* [*U*] : sexual intercourse between people who are very closely related ▪ *commit incest*

in·ces·tu·ous /ɪnˈsɛstʃəwəs/ *adj* : involving sexual intercourse between closely related people ▪ *an incestuous relationship* ▪ *(figurative) lobbyists who have an incestuous relationship* [=an excessively close relationship] *with politicians* — **in-ces-tu-ous-ly** *adv*

¹inch /ˈɪnʧ/ *n* [C] **1** : a unit of measurement equal to ¹⁄₃₆ yard or ¹⁄₁₂ of a foot (2.54 centimeters) **2** : a small amount, distance, or degree ▪ *The ball missed my head by inches.* ▪ *I begged him to reconsider, but he wouldn't give/budge an inch.* [=he wouldn't make even a slight change in his opinion or attitude] ▪ *She opposed me every inch of the way.* [=she opposed everything that I tried to do] ✦ The expression **(if you) give them an inch, (and) they'll take a mile** means that if you allow people to have a small amount of something that they want, they will take much more of it. — **every inch** : to the highest degree ▪ *He's every inch a winner.* [=he's a winner in every way] — **inch by inch** : by moving very slowly ▪ *We made our way inch by inch through the crowd.* — **within an inch of** : almost to the point of (something) ▪ *She came within an inch of death/dying.* [=she came very close to dying]

²inch *vb* [T/I] : to move very slowly or by a small amount in a specified direction or manner ▪ *We inched along in heavy traffic.* ▪ *I inched the car into the garage.*

in-ci-dence /ˈɪnsədəns/ *n* [C] : the number of times something happens or develops ▪ *The drug has been linked with a higher incidence of certain cancers.* [=people who take the drug seem to be more likely to get certain cancers]

in-ci-dent /ˈɪnsədənt/ *n* [C/U] : an unexpected and usually unpleasant thing that happens ▪ *an embarrassing incident* ▪ *a shooting incident.* *The suspects were arrested without incident.* [=without any unexpected trouble]

in-ci-den-tal /ˌɪnsəˈdɛntl̩/ *adj* : happening as a minor part or result of something else ▪ *You may incur some incidental expenses on the trip.* ▪ *This chapter is incidental to the plot.*

in-ci-den-tal-ly /ˌɪnsəˈdɛntl̩i/ *adv* **1** : as something that is less interesting or important ▪ *They discussed the problem only incidentally.* [=in passing] **2** — used to introduce a statement that provides added information or that mentions another subject ▪ *I recently met his wife who, incidentally* [=by the way]*, is a well-known author.*

in-cin-er-ate /ɪnˈsɪnəˌreɪt/ *vb* **-at-ed; -at-ing** [T] : to burn (something) completely ▪ *The waste is incinerated in a large furnace.* — **in-cin-er-a-tor** *n* [C] ▪ *a trash/garbage incinerator* [=a machine that burns trash/garbage]

in-cip-i-ent /ɪnˈsɪpijənt/ *adj, always before a noun, formal* : beginning to develop or exist ▪ *an incipient romance*

in-ci-sion /ɪnˈsɪʒən/ *n* [C] : a cut made in something; *especially, medical* : a cut made into the body during surgery ▪ *an abdominal incision*

in-ci-sive /ɪnˈsaɪsɪv/ *adj* : very clear and direct ▪ *an incisive analysis/commentary/*

observation : able to explain difficult ideas clearly and confidently ▪ *She's known for her incisive mind.*

in-ci-sor /ɪnˈsaɪzɚ/ *n* [C] : one of the four front teeth of the upper or lower jaw

in-cite /ɪnˈsaɪt/ *vb* **-cit-ed; -cit-ing** [T] **1** : to cause (someone) to act in an angry, harmful, or violent way ▪ *inciting a crowd to violence* ▪ *inciting students to riot* **2** : to cause (an angry, harmful, or violent action or feeling) ▪ *inciting* [=*provoking*] *a riot* — **in-cite-ment** /ɪnˈsaɪtmənt/ *n* [C/U]

incl. *abbr* include; included; including; inclusive

in-clem-ent /ɪnˈklɛmənt, ˈɪnkləmənt/ *adj, formal* : STORMY ▪ *inclement weather*

in-cli-na-tion /ˌɪnkləˈneɪʃən/ *n* **1** [C/U] : a feeling of wanting to do something : a tendency to do something ▪ *She shows no/little inclination to give in to their demands.* ▪ *My first/initial/natural inclination was to say no.* ▪ *a person with artistic inclinations* [=a person who wants to do artistic things] **2** [C] : SLOPE ▪ *a steep inclination* **3** [C] : the act of bending your head or body forward ▪ *a slight inclination of the head*

¹in-cline /ɪnˈklaɪn/ *vb* **-clined; -clin-ing** **1** [T/I] : to bend forward or to cause (something) to bend forward ▪ *Her head inclined forward.* ▪ *He inclined his head slightly.* **2** [I] : to lean or slope ▪ *The road inclines at an angle of about 12 degrees.* **3** [T] *formal* : to think or to cause (someone) to think that something is probably true or correct ▪ *The evidence inclines me to think that she isn't guilty.* [=makes me think that she probably isn't guilty]

²in-cline /ˈɪnˌklaɪn/ *n* [C] : SLOPE ▪ *You can adjust the incline of the ramp.*

in-clined /ɪnˈklaɪnd/ *adj* **1** *not before a noun* : wanting to do something or likely to do something ▪ *I'm inclined* [=I would like] *to wait a while longer.* ▪ *Feel free to leave early if you're so inclined.* [=if you want to] **2** — used with verbs like agree, think, believe, suppose, etc., to express a thought or opinion that is not strong or certain ▪ *I'm inclined to agree with you.* [=I think you are probably correct] **3** : having an interest in or a talent for something ▪ *She's artistically inclined.* [=she has a talent for art] **4** : having a slope ▪ *an inclined surface*

in-clude /ɪnˈkluːd/ *vb* **-clud-ed; -clud-ing** [T] **1** : to have (someone or something) as part of a group or total ▪ *The speakers will include several experts on the subject.* ▪ *The price of dinner includes dessert.* ▪ *Everyone, myself/me included, liked the movie.* = *Everyone, including me, liked the movie.* **2** : to make (someone or something) a part of something ▪ *He wants to be included in the project.* — **in-clu-sion** /ɪnˈkluːʒən/ *n* [C/U] ▪ *The collection has some surprising inclusions.* [=it includes some surprising things]

in-clu-sive /ɪnˈkluːsɪv/ *adj* **1** : covering or including everything ▪ *an inclusive fee* ▪ *an inclusive insurance policy* **2** : open to everyone : not limited to certain people ▪ *an inclusive club* **3** *not before a* *noun* : including the stated limits and everything in between ▪ *a program for children seven to ten years of age inclusive* [=for children seven, eight, nine, and ten years of age] — *inclusive of formal* : including (something) ▪ *The price is inclusive of tax.* — **in·clu·sive·ness** *n* [U]

in·cog·ni·to /ˌɪnˌkɑːgˈniːtoʊ/ *adv* : with your true identity kept secret (as by using a different name or a disguise) ▪ *He travels incognito.* — **incognito** *adj*

in·co·her·ent /ˌɪnkoʊˈhɪrənt/ *adj* **1** : not able to talk or express yourself in a clear way ▪ *He was very upset and incoherent after the accident.* **2** : not logical or well-organized ▪ *an incoherent story* — **in·co·her·ence** /ˌɪnkoʊˈhɪrəns/ *n* [U] — **in·co·her·ent·ly** *adv*

in·come /ˈɪnˌkʌm/ *n* [C/U] : money that is earned from work, investments, business, etc. ▪ *taxable income* ▪ *families with low/high incomes*

income tax *n* [C/U] : a tax paid on the money that a person or business receives as income

in·com·ing /ˈɪnˌkʌmɪŋ/ *adj, always before a noun* **1** : arriving at or coming to a place ▪ *incoming mail/flights* **2** : taking a place or position that is being left by another person or group ▪ *the incoming president*

in·com·mu·ni·ca·do /ˌɪnkəˌmjuːnəˈkɑːdoʊ/ *adj, not before a noun, formal* : in a situation or state that does not allow communication with other people ▪ *The prisoner was held/kept incommunicado.*

in·com·pa·ra·ble /ɪnˈkɑːmpərəbəl/ *adj* : better than any other ▪ *an incomparable musician* — **in·com·pa·ra·bly** /ɪnˈkɑːmpərəbli/ *adv*

in·com·pat·i·ble /ˌɪnkəmˈpætəbəl/ *adj* **1** : not able to exist together without trouble or conflict ▪ *incompatible people/colors* **2** : not able to be used together ▪ *incompatible computer systems* — **in·com·pat·i·bil·i·ty** /ˌɪnkəmˌpætəˈbɪləti/ *n, pl* **-ties** [C/U]

in·com·pe·tent /ɪnˈkɑːmpətənt/ *adj* : lacking necessary ability or skills ▪ *an incompetent worker* — **in·com·pe·tence** /ɪnˈkɑːmpətəns/ *n* [U] — **in·com·pe·ten·cy** *n* [U] — **incompetent** *n* [C] ▪ *That department is full of incompetents.* [=incompetent people] — **in·com·pe·tent·ly** *adv*

in·com·plete /ˌɪnkəmˈpliːt/ *adj* **1** : lacking some part : not finished or complete ▪ *an incomplete set of encyclopedias* ▪ *an incomplete sentence* **2** *American football* : not caught by the player the ball was thrown to ▪ *an incomplete pass* — **in·com·plete·ly** *adv*

in·com·pre·hen·si·ble /ˌɪnˌkɑːmprɪˈhensəbəl/ *adj* : impossible to understand ▪ *an incomprehensible theory/decision*

in·con·ceiv·able /ˌɪnkənˈsiːvəbəl/ *adj* : impossible to imagine or believe ▪ *an inconceivable amount of damage*

in·con·clu·sive /ˌɪnkənˈkluːsɪv/ *adj* : not showing that something is certainly true ▪ *The results of the test were inconclusive.* — **in·con·clu·sive·ly** *adv*

in·con·gru·ous /ɪnˈkɑːŋgrəwəs/ *adj* : strange because of not agreeing with what is usual or expected ▪ *The modern sculpture seems incongruous among all the antiques.* — **in·con·gru·i·ty** /ˌɪnkɑːnˈgruːwəti/ *n, pl* **-ties** [C/U] — **in·con·gru·ous·ly** *adv*

in·con·se·quen·tial /ˌɪnˌkɑːnsəˈkwenʃəl/ *adj, formal* : not important ▪ *inconsequential evidence*

in·con·sid·er·able /ˌɪnkənˈsɪdərəbəl/ *adj, formal* : not large enough in size or amount to be considered important ▪ *a woman of not inconsiderable wealth* [=a wealthy woman]

in·con·sid·er·ate /ˌɪnkənˈsɪdərət/ *adj* : not thinking about the rights and feelings of other people ▪ *an inconsiderate remark/person* — **in·con·sid·er·ate·ly** *adv*

in·con·sis·tent /ˌɪnkənˈsɪstənt/ *adj* **1** : not always acting or behaving in the same way ▪ *His pitching has been inconsistent.* ▪ *inconsistent customer service* **2** : not continuing to happen or develop in the same way ▪ *Her grades have been inconsistent.* **3** : having parts that disagree ▪ *The results of the experiments were inconsistent.* ▪ *His statements were inconsistent with the truth.* — **in·con·sis·ten·cy** *n, pl* **-cies** [C/U] ▪ *Police noted inconsistencies in his statements.* — **in·con·sis·tent·ly** *adv*

in·con·sol·able /ˌɪnkənˈsoʊləbəl/ *adj* : extremely sad and not able to be comforted ▪ *She was inconsolable when she learned that he had died.* — **in·con·sol·ably** /ˌɪnkənˈsoʊləbli/ *adv*

in·con·spic·u·ous /ˌɪnkənˈspɪkjəwəs/ *adj* : not very easy to see or notice ▪ *an inconspicuous brick building* — **in·con·spic·u·ous·ly** *adv*

in·con·test·able /ˌɪnkənˈtestəbəl/ *adj, formal* : not able to be doubted or questioned ▪ *an incontestable fact* — **in·con·test·ably** /ˌɪnkənˈtestəbli/ *adv*

in·con·ti·nent /ɪnˈkɑːntənənt/ *adj, medical* : not having control of your bladder or bowels — **in·con·ti·nence** /ɪnˈkɑːntənəns/ *n* [U]

in·con·tro·vert·ible /ɪnˌkɑːntrəˈvɜːtəbəl/ *adj, formal* : not able to be doubted or questioned ▪ *incontrovertible evidence* — **in·con·tro·vert·ibly** /ɪnˌkɑːntrəˈvɜːtəbli/ *adv*

¹**in·con·ve·nience** /ˌɪnkənˈviːnjəns/ *n* **1** [U] : trouble or problems ▪ *I hope this delay doesn't cause you any inconvenience.* **2** [C] : something that causes trouble or problems ▪ *The delay was an inconvenience.*

²**inconvenience** *vb* **-nienced; -nienc·ing** [T] : to cause trouble or problems for (someone) ▪ *We were inconvenienced by the bad weather.*

in·con·ve·nient /ˌɪnkənˈviːnjənt/ *adj* : causing trouble or problems ▪ *I can call back if this is an inconvenient time to talk.* ▪ *an inconvenient location/delay* — **in·con·ve·nient·ly** *adv*

in·cor·po·rate /ɪnˈkoɚpəˌreɪt/ *vb* **-rat·ed; -rat·ing** **1** [T] : to include (something) as part of something else ▪ *a diet that incorporates many different fruits and vegetables* ▪ *The results of the study were incorporated in/into the final report.* **2**

[T/I] : to form into a corporation • *The company (was) incorporated in 1981.* — **in·cor·po·ra·tion** /ɪnˌkoɚpəˈreɪʃən/ n [U]

in·cor·po·rat·ed /ɪnˈkoɚpəˌreɪtəd/ adj : formed into a legal corporation in the U.S. — often used in the names of corporations • *Merriam-Webster, Incorporated* — abbr. *Inc.*

in·cor·rect /ˌɪnkəˈrɛkt/ adj 1 : not true or accurate : WRONG • *an incorrect answer* 2 : having errors or mistakes • *a grammatically incorrect sentence* 3 : not proper or appropriate • *incorrect behavior* — see also POLITICALLY INCORRECT — **in·cor·rect·ly** adv

in·cor·ri·gi·ble /ɪnˈkorədʒəbəl/ adj : not able to be corrected or changed • *an incorrigible gambler/habit*

in·cor·rupt·ible /ˌɪnkəˈrʌptəbəl/ adj : very honest : incapable of being corrupted • *the town's incorruptible mayor*

¹**in·crease** /ɪnˈkriːs/ vb **-creased; -creasing** 1 [I] : to become larger or greater in size, amount, number, etc. • *Sales increased this year.* • *The house increased in value.* • *Her policies have faced increasing criticism.* 2 [T] : to make (something) larger or greater in size, amount, number, etc. • *They increased [=raised] the price.* • *an increased heart rate*

²**in·crease** /ˈɪnˌkriːs/ n 1 [C/U] : the act of becoming larger or of making something larger or greater in size, amount, number, etc. • *a tax increase* • *an increase in wages* 2 [C] : the amount by which something is made larger or greater • *an increase of three dollars* — **on the increase** : becoming more in size, amount, number, etc. • *The population is on the increase.*

in·creas·ing·ly /ɪnˈkriːsɪŋli/ adv : more and more • *The situation grew increasingly hopeless.*

in·cred·i·ble /ɪnˈkrɛdəbəl/ adj 1 : difficult or impossible to believe • *an incredible story of survival* • *It's incredible to me that such a lazy person could be so successful.* 2 : extremely good, great, or large • *a person of incredible skill/intelligence* • *We did an incredible amount of work.* — **in·cred·i·bly** /ɪnˈkrɛdəbli/ adv

in·cred·u·lous /ɪnˈkrɛdʒələs/ adj : not able or willing to believe something : feeling or showing a lack of belief • *She listened to his explanation with an incredulous smile.* — **in·cre·du·li·ty** /ˌɪnkrɪˈduːləti, Brit ˌɪnkrɪˈdjuːləti/ n [U] — **in·cred·u·lous·ly** adv

in·cre·ment /ˈɪnkrəmənt/ n [C] : a usually small amount or degree by which something is made larger or greater • *They increased the dosage of the drug in small increments.* • *(Brit) an annual increment* [=an annual salary increase] *of three percent* — **in·cre·men·tal** /ˌɪnkrəˈmɛntl̟/ adj : *incremental changes* [=changes that occur in small amounts or very gradually] — **in·cre·men·tal·ly** /ˌɪnkrəˈmɛntl̟i/ adv

in·crim·i·nate /ɪnˈkrɪməˌneɪt/ vb **-nated; -nating** [T] : to cause (someone) to appear guilty of or responsible for something (such as a crime) • *Material found at the crime scene incriminates the defendant.* — **in·crim·i·nat·ing** /ɪnˈkrɪməˌneɪtɪŋ/ adj • *incriminating evidence* — **in·crim·i·na·tion** /ɪnˌkrɪməˈneɪʃən/ n [U]

in·cu·bate /ˈɪŋkjəˌbeɪt/ vb **-bated; -bating** 1 a [T] *of a bird* : to sit on eggs so that they will be kept warm and will hatch b [I] *of an egg* : to be kept warm before hatching • *The eggs need to incubate for two weeks.* 2 [T/I] *technical* : to keep (something) in the proper conditions for development • *The virus will incubate in the body for several days.* — **in·cu·ba·tion** /ˌɪŋkjəˈbeɪʃən/ n [C/U]

in·cu·ba·tor /ˈɪŋkjəˌbeɪtɚ/ n [C] 1 : a device that is used to keep eggs warm before they hatch 2 *medical* : a piece of equipment in which very weak or sick babies are placed for special care and protection after their birth

in·cul·cate /ɪnˈkʌlˌkeɪt, ˈɪnˌkʌlˌkeɪt/ vb **-cated; -cating** [T] *formal* : to cause (something) to be learned by (someone) by repeating it again and again • *A sense of responsibility was inculcated in the students.* = *The students were inculcated with a sense of responsibility.*

¹**in·cum·bent** /ɪnˈkʌmbənt/ n [C] : a person who holds a particular office or position — **in·cum·ben·cy** /ɪnˈkʌmbənsi/ n, pl **-cies** [C/U] • *during her incumbency* [=during the time when she held her office]

²**incumbent** adj, always before a noun, formal : holding an office or position • *the incumbent president* — **incumbent on/upon** formal : necessary as a duty for (someone) • *It is incumbent on us to help.* [=it is our duty to help]

in·cur /ɪnˈkɚ/ vb **-curred; -curring** [T] formal : to cause yourself to have or experience (something unpleasant or unwanted) • *incur expenses/debt*

in·cur·able /ɪnˈkjɚəbəl/ adj 1 : impossible to cure • *an incurable disease* 2 : not likely to be changed • *an incurable optimist* — **in·cur·ably** /ɪnˈkjɚəbli/ adv

in·cur·sion /ɪnˈkɚʒən/ n [C] formal : a sudden invasion or attack • *an incursion into enemy airspace*

in·debt·ed /ɪnˈdɛtəd/ adj : owing money, thanks, etc., to someone or something : in debt • *heavily/deeply indebted countries* • *I'm indebted to you for your help.* — **in·debt·ed·ness** n [U]

in·de·cent /ɪnˈdiːsnt/ adj 1 : sexually offensive or shocking • *indecent photos* 2 : not covering enough of your body • *indecent clothing* 3 : not appropriate or proper • *indecent* [=offensive] *language* — **in·de·cen·cy** /ɪnˈdiːsnsi/ n, pl **-cies** [C/U] — **in·de·cent·ly** adv

in·de·ci·pher·able /ˌɪndɪˈsaɪfərəbəl/ adj : impossible to read or understand • *an indecipherable code/message*

in·de·ci·sion /ˌɪndɪˈsɪʒən/ n [U] : difficulty in making a decision • *They were paralyzed by indecision.*

in·de·ci·sive /ˌɪndɪˈsaɪsɪv/ adj 1 : not able to make choices quickly and confidently • *an indecisive person* 2 : not settling something or making something final or certain • *an indecisive battle* — **in-**

de·ci·sive·ness n [U]

in·deed /ɪnˈdiːd/ adv **1** : without any question — used to stress the truth of a statement • *Indeed, he is a great poet.* = *He is indeed a great poet.* • *The problem is a very serious one indeed.* • *"Do you know him?" "Yes, indeed!"* [=I certainly do] • *"Did you do your best." "I did my best."* "Did you indeed?"* **3** — used in a question that repeats and emphasizes a preceding question to show that you do not know the answer • *"How can we help them?" "How, indeed?"*

in·de·fat·i·ga·ble /ˌɪndɪˈfætɪɡəbəl/ adj, formal : able to work or continue for a very long time without becoming tired • *an indefatigable campaigner*

in·de·fen·si·ble /ˌɪndɪˈfɛnsəbəl/ adj **1** : not able to be thought of as good or acceptable • *Slavery is morally indefensible.* **2** : not able to be kept safe from damage or harm • *an indefensible location*

in·de·fin·able /ˌɪndɪˈfaɪnəbəl/ adj : impossible to describe or explain • *an indefinable quality*

in·def·i·nite /ɪnˈdɛfənət/ adj **1** : not certain in amount or length • *an indefinite period of time* **2** : not clear or certain in meaning or details • *She is indefinite about her plans.*

indefinite article n [C] : the word *a* or *an* used in English to refer to a person or thing that is not identified or specified; *also* : a word that has a similar use in another language

in·def·i·nite·ly /ɪnˈdɛfənətli/ adv : for a period of time that might not end • *Economic growth will not continue indefinitely.* [=forever]

indefinite pronoun n [C] : a pronoun that does not refer to a specific person or thing • *"Anyone," "something," and "few" are indefinite pronouns.*

in·del·i·ble /ɪnˈdɛləbəl/ adj **1** : impossible to remove or forget • *an indelible image* **2** : producing marks that cannot be erased • *an indelible pencil* — **in·del·i·bly** /ɪnˈdɛləbli/ adv • *images indelibly captured on film*

in·del·i·cate /ɪnˈdɛlɪkət/ adj, formal : not polite or proper • *an indelicate question*

in·dem·ni·fy /ɪnˈdɛmnəˌfaɪ/ vb **-fies; -fied; -fy·ing** [T] law **1** : to protect (someone) by promising to pay for the cost of possible future damage, loss, or injury • *The policy indemnifies* [=insures] *you against/for any losses caused by fire.* **2** : to give (someone) money or another kind of payment for some damage, loss, or injury • *He was required to indemnify his neighbor for the damage.*

in·dem·ni·ty /ɪnˈdɛmnəti/ n, pl **-ties** law **1** [U] : a promise to pay for the cost of possible damage, loss, or injury • *an agreement providing indemnity against prosecution/loss* **2** [C] : a payment made to someone because of damage, loss, or injury • *$2 million in indemnities*

¹**in·dent** /ɪnˈdɛnt/ vb [T/I] : to start (one or more lines of text) farther to the right than other lines of text • *The first line of each paragraph should be indented.*

²**in·dent** /ˈɪnˌdɛnt/ n [C] : a space at the beginning of a written line or paragraph • *Start each paragraph with an indent.*

in·den·ta·tion /ˌɪnˌdɛnˈteɪʃən/ n **1 a** [C] : a space at the beginning of a written line or paragraph : INDENT **b** [U] : the act of indenting a line or paragraph **2** [C] : a cut in or into the edge of something • *A slight indentation was cut into the wood.* **3** [C] : a small hole or inward curve made by pressure : DENT • *small indentations in the surface of the table*

in·den·tured /ɪnˈdɛntʃəd/ adj : required by a contract to work for a certain period of time • *indentured servants*

Independence Day n [U] : July 4 celebrated as a legal holiday in the U.S. in honor of the day when the Declaration of Independence was signed in 1776

in·de·pen·dent /ˌɪndəˈpɛndənt/ adj **1 a** : not controlled or ruled by another country • *an independent nation* **b** : not requiring or relying on other people for help or support • *an independent income* • *a woman of independent means* **c** : not associated with or owned by a larger business • *an independent bookstore; also* : produced by an independent company • *an independent film* **2** : separate from and not connected to other people, things, etc. • *an independent study* [=a course of study done by a student that is not part of an organized class] • *The speed of the particle is independent of its wavelength.* [=is not connected/related to its wavelength] **3** : acting or thinking freely instead of being guided by other people • *an independent person/thinker/mind* **4** : not belonging to a political party • *independent voters/candidates* — **in·de·pen·dence** /ˌɪndəˈpɛndəns/ n [U, singular] • *fighting for independence from colonial rule* • *financial independence* — **independent** n [C] • *She registered to vote as an independent.* — **in·de·pen·dent·ly** adv

in-depth /ɪnˈdɛpθ/ adj : covering many or all important points of a subject • *an in-depth investigation/analysis*

in·de·scrib·able /ˌɪndɪˈskraɪbəbəl/ adj : impossible to describe : very great or extreme • *indescribable beauty/joy/pain* — **in·de·scrib·ably** /ˌɪndɪˈskraɪbəbli/ adv

in·de·struc·ti·ble /ˌɪndɪˈstrʌktəbəl/ adj : impossible to break or destroy • *indestructible toys*

in·de·ter·mi·nate /ˌɪndɪˈtɚmənət/ adj, formal : not able to be stated or described in an exact way • *an indeterminate number of people*

¹**in·dex** /ˈɪnˌdɛks/ n, pl **in·dex·es** or **in·di·ces** /ˈɪndəˌsiːz/ [C] **1** pl usually **indexes a** : an alphabetical list at the end of a book that shows the page where each thing in the list can be found **b** : a group of related things that are in alphabetical or numerical order • *The card catalog is an index to the materials in the library.* **2** : a sign or number that shows how something is changing or performing • *The price of goods is an index* [=indication] *of business conditions.* • *a stock index* **3** : a device used to point to

something (such as a number) • *the index on a scale*

²**index** *vb* [T] **1** : to provide an index for (something, such as a book) • *an indexed book* [=a book that has an index] **2** : to list or include (something) in an index • *Each term in the book is indexed.* **3** : to link wages, benefits, etc., to a measurement of changes in the price of goods and services so that they increase at the same rate • *Social security benefits are indexed to inflation.* [=they increase when inflation occurs]

index card *n* [C] : a thin paper card used especially for creating an alphabetical index

index finger *n* [C] : the finger next to the thumb

In·di·an /ˈɪndijən/ *n* [C] **1** : a person from India **2** *often offensive* : NATIVE AMERICAN *usage* see NATIVE AMERICAN — **Indian** *adj* • *Indian culture/food*

Indian summer *n* [C] : a period of warm weather in late autumn or early winter

in·di·cate /ˈɪndəˌkeɪt/ *vb* -**cat·ed**; -**cat·ing** **1** [T] : to show (something) • *Studies indicate (that) this chemical could cause cancer.* • *The map indicates where the treasure is buried.* **2** [T] : to point out or to (someone or something) • *The general indicated on the map exactly where the troops would land.* **3** [T] : to represent or be a symbol of (something or someone) • *The markers indicate a distance of 50 yards.* **4** [T] : to say or express (something) briefly • *He nodded his head to indicate his approval.* **5** [I] *Brit* : to make a signal which shows that you are going to turn when you are driving a vehicle

in·di·ca·tion /ˌɪndəˈkeɪʃən/ *n* [C/U] : something that points out or shows something • *She gave no indication that she was angry.* = *She gave no indication of her anger.* • *There's every indication* [=it appears to be very likely] *that the strike will end soon.*

¹**in·dic·a·tive** /ɪnˈdɪkətɪv/ *adj* **1** *not before a noun, formal* : showing or indicating something • *His bitter remarks are indicative of the resentment he still feels.* **2** *grammar* : of or relating to the verb form that is used to state a fact that can be known or proved • *In "I walked to school," the verb "walked" is in the indicative mood.*

²**indicative** *n* — **the indicative** *grammar* : the form that a verb or sentence has when it is stating a fact that can be known or proved • *a verb in the indicative*

in·di·ca·tor /ˈɪndəˌkeɪtɚ/ *n* [C] **1** : a sign that shows the condition or existence of something • *Economic indicators suggest that prices will go up.* • *Her smile is a good indicator of how she's feeling.* **2 a** : a pointer or light that shows the state or condition of something **b** : a device that shows a measurement • *an airspeed indicator* **c** *Brit* : TURN SIGNAL

indices *plural of* ¹INDEX

in·dict /ɪnˈdaɪt/ *vb* [T] *chiefly US, law* : to formally decide that someone should be put on trial for a crime • *A grand jury indicted him for murder.* — **in·dict·able** /ɪnˈdaɪtəbəl/ *adj* • *an indictable crime*

in·dict·ment /ɪnˈdaɪtmənt/ *n* **1** *chiefly US, law* **a** [C] : an official written statement charging a person with a crime **b** [U] : the act of officially charging someone with a crime • *He is under indictment* [=he has been indicted] *for perjury.* **2** [C] : an expression or statement of strong disapproval • *The book is an indictment of the media.*

in·die /ˈɪndi/ *adj, always before a noun, informal* : not connected with or created by a major producer of music or movies • *indie bands/films*

in·dif·fer·ent /ɪnˈdɪfərənt/ *adj* **1** : not interested in or concerned about something • *People were indifferent about the trial.* • *She seems indifferent to our problems.* **2** : neither good nor bad : not very good • *an indifferent performance* — **in·dif·fer·ence** /ɪnˈdɪfərəns/ *n* [U, singular] • *She watched them with (a) cool indifference.* — **in·dif·fer·ent·ly** *adv*

in·dig·e·nous /ɪnˈdɪdʒənəs/ *adj* : produced, living, or existing naturally in a particular region or environment • *an indigenous culture/language/plant* — **in·dig·e·nous·ly** *adv*

in·di·gent /ˈɪndɪdʒənt/ *adj, formal* : lacking money : very poor • *indigent people*

in·di·gest·ible /ˌɪndaɪˈdʒɛstəbəl/ *adj* : not capable of being used in the body as food • *indigestible carbohydrates*

in·di·ges·tion /ˌɪndaɪˈdʒɛstʃən/ *n* [U] : an unpleasant feeling in your stomach or chest that is caused by difficulty in digesting food

in·dig·nant /ɪnˈdɪgnənt/ *adj* : feeling or showing anger because of something that is unfair or wrong • *He got very indignant about/over the changes.* — **in·dig·nant·ly** *adv*

in·dig·na·tion /ˌɪndɪgˈneɪʃən/ *n* [U] : anger caused by something that is unfair or wrong • *a tone of moral/righteous indignation*

in·dig·ni·ty /ɪnˈdɪgnəti/ *n, pl* -**ties** [C/U] : an act or occurrence that hurts someone's dignity or pride • *He suffered the indignity of being forced to leave the courtroom.*

in·di·rect /ˌɪndəˈrɛkt/ *adj* **1** : not going straight from one point to another • *We took an indirect route.* **2** : not said or done in a clear and direct way • *vague, indirect answers* **3** : not having a clear and direct connection • *an indirect cause of the disease* — **in·di·rect·ly** *adv*

indirect object *n* [C] *grammar* : a noun, pronoun, or noun phrase that occurs in addition to a direct object after some verbs and indicates the person or thing that receives what is being given or done • *In "He gave me the book," the indirect object is "me."*

in·dis·creet /ˌɪndɪˈskriːt/ *adj* : revealing things that should not be revealed • *He was indiscreet about his love affairs.* • *an indiscreet question*

in·dis·cre·tion /ˌɪndɪˈskrɛʃən/ *n* **1** [U] : lack of good judgment or care in behavior and especially in speech • *He showed indiscretion in his remarks.* **2** [C] : an act or remark that shows a lack of good judgment • *She committed a few minor indiscretions.*

in·dis·crim·i·nate /ˌɪndɪˈskrɪmənət/ *adj, disapproving* **1** : affecting or harming many people or things in a careless or unfair way • *the indiscriminate use of pesticides* **2** : not careful in making choices • *She was indiscriminate in choosing her friends.* — **in·dis·crim·i·nate·ly** *adv*

in·dis·pens·able /ˌɪndɪˈspɛnsəbəl/ *adj* : extremely important and necessary • *She is indispensable to the team.* • *an indispensable tool*

in·dis·posed /ˌɪndɪˈspoʊzd/ *adj, formal* **1** : slightly ill • *He was (somewhat) indisposed by/with a cold.* **2** : not willing or likely to do something • *Officials are indisposed to grant their request.*

in·dis·put·able /ˌɪndɪˈspjuːtəbəl/ *adj* : impossible to question or doubt • *indisputable proof* — **in·dis·put·ably** /ˌɪndɪˈspjuːtəbli/ *adv*

in·dis·tinct /ˌɪndɪˈstɪŋkt/ *adj* : not easily seen, heard, or recognized • *indistinct figures in the fog* — **in·dis·tinct·ly** *adv*

in·dis·tin·guish·able /ˌɪndɪˈstɪŋgwɪʃəbəl/ *adj* : unable to be recognized as different • *The copy and the original are indistinguishable (from each other).*

¹in·di·vid·u·al /ˌɪndəˈvɪdʒəwəl/ *adj* **1** *always before a noun* : of, relating to, or existing as just one part of a larger group • *the individual needs of patients* • *Students receive individual attention.* **2** : having a special and unusual quality that is easily seen • *She has a very individual style.* **3** *always before a noun* : intended or designed for one person • *individual servings of dessert* — **in·di·vid·u·al·ly** *adv* • *Each student met individually with the teacher.*

²individual *n* [C] **1** : a single person • *the rights of the individual* **2** : a particular person • *She's a very talented individual.* **3** : a single member or part of a group • *The markings on tigers are unique to each individual.*

in·di·vid·u·al·ism /ˌɪndəˈvɪdʒəwəˌlɪzəm/ *n* [U] **1** : the belief that the needs of each person are more important than the needs of the whole society or group **2** : the actions or attitudes of a person who does things without being concerned about what other people will think

in·di·vid·u·al·ist /ˌɪndəˈvɪdʒəwəlɪst/ *n* [C] : a person who does things without being concerned about what other people will think — **in·di·vid·u·al·is·tic** /ˌɪndəˌvɪdʒəwəˈlɪstɪk/ *also* **individualist** *adj* • *an individualistic approach to jazz music*

in·di·vid·u·al·i·ty /ˌɪndəˌvɪdʒəˈwæləti/ *n* [U] : the quality that makes one person or thing different from all others • *She uses her clothing to express her individuality.*

in·di·vid·u·al·ize *also Brit* **in·di·vid·u·al·ise** /ˌɪndəˈvɪdʒəwəˌlaɪz/ *vb* **-ized; -iz·ing** [T] : to change (something) so that it fits each person's needs • *Teachers should individualize their lessons.* • *individualized computer programs*

individual retirement account *n* [C] : IRA

in·di·vis·i·ble /ˌɪndəˈvɪzəbəl/ *adj, formal + literary* : impossible to divide or separate • *an indivisible nation* — **in·di·vis·i·bil·i·ty** /ˌɪndəˌvɪzəˈbɪləti/ *n* [U]

in·doc·tri·nate /ɪnˈdɑːktrəˌneɪt/ *vb* **-nat·ed; -nat·ing** [T] *disapproving* : to teach (someone) to fully accept the ideas, opinions, and beliefs of a particular group and to not consider other ideas, opinions, and beliefs • *indoctrinating new members in/with the group's philosophy* — **in·doc·tri·na·tion** /ɪnˌdɑːktrəˈneɪʃən/ *n* [U]

in·do·lent /ˈɪndələnt/ *adj, formal* : not liking to work or be active : LAZY • *an indolent young man* — **in·do·lence** /ˈɪndələns/ *n* [U]

in·dom·i·ta·ble /ɪnˈdɑːmətəbəl/ *adj, formal* : impossible to defeat or discourage • *her indomitable strength/will*

in·door /ˈɪnˌdoɚ/ *adj, always before a noun* : done, living, located, or used inside a building • *an indoor sport/pet/pool*

in·doors /ˈɪnˈdoɚz/ *adv* : in, inside, or into a building • *The game was played indoors.* • *We went indoors when it began to rain.*

indorse *variant spelling of* ENDORSE

in·du·bi·ta·ble /ɪnˈduːbətəbəl, *Brit* ɪnˈdjuːbətəbəl/ *adj, formal* : certainly true : not able to be doubted • *an indubitable truth* — **in·du·bi·ta·bly** /ɪnˈduːbətəbli, *Brit* ɪnˈdjuːbətəbli/ *adv* • *He was indubitably the best.*

in·duce /ɪnˈduːs, *Brit* ɪnˈdjuːs/ *vb* **-duced; -duc·ing** [T] **1** *somewhat formal* : to cause (someone or something) to do something • *The ad is meant to induce people to eat more fruit.* **2** : to cause (something) to happen or exist • *medication to induce vomiting* • *drug-induced sleep* **3** *medical* : to give a pregnant woman special medicine in order to make her give birth • *The mother was induced.* • *They induced labor.*

in·duce·ment /ɪnˈduːsmənt, *Brit* ɪnˈdjuːsmənt/ *n* [C/U] *formal* : something that gives you a reason for doing something and makes you want to do it • *The large salary was an inducement to take the job.*

in·duct /ɪnˈdʌkt/ *vb* [T] **1** : to have (someone) officially begin a new job, position, etc. • *The new president was inducted into office last year.* **2 a** : to officially make (someone) a member of a group or organization • *She was inducted into the Basketball Hall of Fame.* **b** *US* : to enroll (someone) for military training or service • *He was inducted into the army.* — **in·duct·ee** /ɪnˌdʌkˈtiː/ *n* [C] *chiefly US* • *After the ceremony, we met the new inductees.* [=the people who had just been inducted]

in·duc·tion /ɪnˈdʌkʃən/ *n* **1** [C] **a** : the formal act or process of placing someone into a new job, position, etc. **b** *US* : the formal act of making someone a member of the military • *the registration and induction of draftees* **2** [U] *medical* : the act of giving a pregnant woman special drugs so that she will give birth • *induction of labor* **3** [U] *technical* : a kind of reasoning that uses particular examples in order to reach a general conclusion about something • **4** [U] *technical* : the process by which an electric current, an electric charge, or magnetism is produced in objects by being close to an electric or magnetic field

in·duc·tive /ɪnˈdʌktɪv/ *adj, technical* : using particular examples to reach a general conclusion about something • *inductive reasoning*

in·dulge /ɪnˈdʌldʒ/ *vb* **-dulged; -dulg·ing 1** [T/I] : to allow (yourself) to have or do something as a special pleasure • *It's my birthday so I'm going to indulge myself and eat whatever I want.* • *We indulged in an expensive dinner.* **2** [T] **a** : to allow (someone) to have or do something even though it may not be proper, healthy, appropriate, etc. • *His aunt always indulges* [=*spoils*] *him.* **b** : to patiently allow (someone) to do or say something • *Please indulge me while I review the topics we covered yesterday.* **3** [T] : to do the things that you want to do because of (a feeling, interest, desire, etc.) • *At the museum, children can indulge their curiosity about dinosaurs.*

in·dul·gence /ɪnˈdʌldʒəns/ *n* **1** [U] : the behavior or attitude of people who allow themselves to do what they want or who allow other people to do what they want • *She lived a life of selfish indulgence.* • *They showed great indulgence toward the sick boy.* **2** [U] : the act of doing something that you enjoy but that is usually thought of as wrong or unhealthy • *his indulgence in forbidden pleasures* **3** [C] : something that is done or enjoyed as a special pleasure • *We allowed ourselves the indulgence of an elegant dinner at our favorite restaurant.*

in·dul·gent /ɪnˈdʌldʒənt/ *adj* **1** *sometimes disapproving* : willing to allow someone to have or enjoy something even though it may not be proper, healthy, appropriate, etc. • *These children are being spoiled by (overly) indulgent parents.* **2** : done or enjoyed as a special pleasure • *an indulgent dessert* — **in·dul·gent·ly** *adv*

in·dus·tri·al /ɪnˈdʌstrijəl/ *adj* **1** : of or relating to factories, the people who work in factories, or the things made in factories • *industrial development* • *an industrial engineer* • *an industrial accident* [=an accident at work] **2** : having factories that actively make a product • *an industrial nation/city* **3** : made or used in factories • *industrial diamonds/chemicals; also* : stronger than most other products of its kind • *an industrial cleaner* — **in·dus·tri·al·ly** *adv*

in·dus·tri·al·ist /ɪnˈdʌstrijəlɪst/ *n* [C] : someone who owns or manages an industry

in·dus·tri·al·ize *also Brit* **in·dus·tri·al·ise** /ɪnˈdʌstrijəˌlaɪz/ *vb* **-ized; -iz·ing** [T/I] : to build and operate factories and businesses in a city, region, country, etc. • *This region industrialized* [=gained in industry] *before the rest of the country.* • *industrialized nations* — **in·dus·tri·al·i·za·tion** *also Brit* **in·dus·tri·al·i·sa·tion**

/ɪnˌdʌstrijələˈzeɪʃən, *Brit* ɪnˌdʌstrijəˌlaɪˈzeɪʃən/ *n* [U]

industrial–strength *adj, often humorous* : stronger, more powerful, or more intense than others of its kind • *industrial-strength coffee* [=very strong coffee]

in·dus·tri·ous /ɪnˈdʌstrijəs/ *adj* : working very hard : not lazy • *an industrious worker* — **in·dus·tri·ous·ly** *adv* — **in·dus·tri·ous·ness** *n* [U]

in·dus·try /ˈɪndəstri/ *n, pl* **-tries 1 a** [U] : the process of making products by using machinery and factories • *He favors policies that promote industry.* **b** [C] : a group of businesses that provide a particular product or service • *the automobile/oil/computer industry* — see also **CAPTAIN OF INDUSTRY 2** [U] : the habit of working hard and steadily • *She is admired for her industry.*

in·ebri·at·ed /ɪˈniːbriˌeɪtəd/ *adj, formal* : DRUNK • *He was obviously inebriated.* — **in·ebri·a·tion** /ɪˌniːbriˈeɪʃən/ *n* [U]

in·ed·i·ble /ɪnˈɛdəbəl/ *adj* : not suitable or safe to eat • *inedible mushrooms*

in·ef·fa·ble /ɪnˈɛfəbəl/ *adj, formal* : too great, powerful, beautiful, etc., to be described or expressed • *ineffable joy/beauty* — **in·ef·fa·bly** /ɪnˈɛfəbli/ *adv*

in·ef·fec·tive /ˌɪnəˈfɛktɪv/ *adj* : not producing or having the effect you want • *The treatment was ineffective against the disease.* • *an ineffective law/leader* — **in·ef·fec·tive·ly** *adv* — **in·ef·fec·tive·ness** *n* [U]

in·ef·fec·tu·al /ˌɪnəˈfɛktʃəwəl/ *adj* : not producing or able to produce the effect you want • *an ineffectual politician/attempt* — **in·ef·fec·tu·al·ly** /ˌɪnəˈfɛktʃəwəli/ *adv*

in·ef·fi·cient /ˌɪnəˈfɪʃənt/ *adj* : not capable of producing desired results without wasting materials, time, or energy • *an inefficient worker/system* — **in·ef·fi·cien·cy** /ˌɪnəˈfɪʃənsi/ *n, pl* **-cies** [C/U] — **in·ef·fi·cient·ly** *adv*

in·el·e·gant /ɪnˈɛləgənt/ *adj, somewhat formal* : not graceful, attractive, or polite • *an inelegant dancer* • *inelegant language* — **in·el·e·gant·ly** *adv*

in·el·i·gi·ble /ɪnˈɛlədʒəbəl/ *adj* : not allowed to do or be something • *She was ineligible to participate in the contest.*

in·ept /ɪˈnɛpt/ *adj* : lacking skill or ability • *inept mechanics/planning* • *a socially inept teenager* [=a teenager who is shy or awkward around other people] — **in·ept·ly** *adv* — **in·ept·ness** *n* [U]

in·ep·ti·tude /ɪˈnɛptəˌtuːd, *Brit* ɪˈnɛptəˌtjuːd/ *n* [U] : a lack of skill or ability • *The team's poor play is being blamed on the ineptitude of the coaching staff.*

in·equal·i·ty /ˌɪnɪˈkwɑːləti/ *n, pl* **-ties** [C/U] : an unfair situation in which some people have more rights or better opportunities than other people • *social/sexual/racial inequality* • *inequalities of education/income*

in·eq·ui·ta·ble /ɪnˈɛkwətəbəl/ *adj, formal* : not fair or equal • *the inequitable treatment of employees* — **in·eq·ui·ta·bly** /ɪnˈɛkwətəbli/ *adv*

in·eq·ui·ty /ɪnˈɛkwəti/ *n, pl* **-ties** *formal*

1 [U] : lack of fairness : unfair treatment • *racial inequity* [=*injustice*] **2** [C] : something that is unfair • *the inequities in wages paid to men and women*

in·ert /ɪˈnət/ *adj* **1** : unable to move • *an inert body* **2** : moving or acting very slowly • *an inert economy* **3** *chemistry* : not able to affect other chemicals when in contact with them • *an inert gas* — **in·ert·ness** *n* [U]

in·er·tia /ɪˈnəʃə/ *n* [U] **1 a** : lack of movement or activity especially when movement or activity is wanted or needed • *governmental inertia* **b** : a feeling of not having the energy or desire that is needed to move, change, etc. • *She finally overcame her inertia and went back to school.* **2** *physics* : a property of matter by which something that is not moving remains still and something that is moving goes at the same speed and in the same direction until another thing or force affects it

in·es·cap·able /ˌɪnəˈskeɪpəbəl/ *adj* : impossible to deny or avoid • *an inescapable truth/conclusion* — **in·es·cap·ably** /ˌɪnəˈskeɪpəbli/ *adv* • *an inescapably obvious truth*

in·es·ti·ma·ble /ɪnˈɛstəməbəl/ *adj, formal* : too great, valuable, or excellent to be measured • *inestimable value/worth*

in·ev·i·ta·ble /ɪnˈɛvətəbəl/ *adj* : sure to happen • *the inevitable result* — **the inevitable** : something that is sure to happen • *They're just trying to delay/postpone the inevitable.* — **in·ev·i·ta·bil·i·ty** /ɪˌnɛvətəˈbɪləti/ *n* [U] — **in·ev·i·ta·bly** /ɪnˈɛvətəbli/ *adv* • *The changes inevitably resulted in criticism.*

in·ex·act /ˌɪnɪɡˈzækt/ *adj* : not completely correct or precise • *an inexact calculation/description*

in·ex·cus·able /ˌɪnɪkˈskjuːzəbəl/ *adj* : too bad or wrong to be excused or ignored • *an inexcusable mistake* — **in·ex·cus·ably** /ˌɪnɪkˈskjuːzəbli/ *adv*

in·ex·haust·ible /ˌɪnɪɡˈzɑːstəbəl/ *adj* : impossible to use up completely • *an inexhaustible supply*

in·ex·o·ra·ble /ɪnˈɛksərəbəl/ *adj, formal* : not able to be stopped or changed • *an inexorable conclusion* — **in·ex·o·ra·bly** /ɪnˈɛksərəbli/ *adv*

in·ex·pen·sive /ˌɪnɪkˈspɛnsɪv/ *adj* : low in price • *an inexpensive meal* — **in·ex·pen·sive·ly** *adv*

in·ex·pe·ri·ence /ˌɪnɪkˈspiːrijəns/ *n* [U] : lack of experience • *He blames his mistakes on inexperience.* — **in·ex·pe·ri·enced** /ˌɪnɪkˈspiːrijənst/ *adj* • *an inexperienced driver*

in·ex·pli·ca·ble /ˌɪnɪkˈsplɪkəbəl, ɪnˈɛksplɪkəbəl/ *adj* : not able to be explained or understood • *an inexplicable mystery/accident* — **in·ex·pli·ca·bly** /ˌɪnɪkˈsplɪkəbli, ɪnˈɛksplɪkəbli/ *adv*

in·ex·press·ible /ˌɪnɪkˈsprɛsəbəl/ *adj, somewhat formal* : too strong or great to be expressed or described • *inexpressible joy/pain*

in·ex·tri·ca·ble /ˌɪnɪkˈstrɪkəbəl, ɪnˈɛkstrɪkəbəl/ *adj, formal* : impossible to separate : closely joined or related • *an inextricable link between poverty and*

poor health — **in·ex·tri·ca·bly** /ˌɪnɪkˈstrɪkəbli, ɪnˈɛkstrɪkəbli/ *adv*

in·fal·li·ble /ɪnˈfæləbəl/ *adj* : not capable of being wrong or failing • *an infallible memory* — **in·fal·li·bil·i·ty** /ɪnˌfælə-ˈbɪləti/ *n* [U] — **in·fal·li·bly** /ɪnˈfæləbli/ *adv*

in·fa·mous /ˈɪnfəməs/ *adj* : well-known for being bad or evil • *an infamous traitor/crime* • *a city infamous for poverty and crime* • (*humorous*) *We experienced some of the city's infamous weather.* — **in·fa·mous·ly** *adv*

in·fa·my /ˈɪnfəmi/ *n* [U] : the condition of being known for having done bad things or for being evil • *a day of infamy* [=a day on which something very bad happened]

in·fan·cy /ˈɪnfənsi/ *n* [U] **1** : the time in your life when you are a baby • *She was often sick during her infancy.* • *a skill developed in infancy* **2** : a beginning : an early stage of development • *when the Internet was still in its infancy* [=very new]

¹**in·fant** /ˈɪnfənt/ *n* [C] : a very young child : BABY • *He showed us a picture of his infant daughter.*

²**infant** *adj, always before a noun* **1** : made or suitable for babies • *an infant bathtub* **2** *Brit* : of, relating to, or for children between the ages of about four and seven • *infant school/teachers* **3** : very new and still developing • *our infant steel industry*

in·fan·tile /ˈɪnfənˌtajəl/ *adj* **1** *disapproving* : annoying and childish • *infantile jokes/behavior* **2** *always before a noun, medical* : affecting babies or very young children • *infantile diseases*

in·fan·try /ˈɪnfəntri/ *n* [U, *plural*] : the part of an army that has soldiers who fight on foot • *The infantry is/are coming.*

in·fan·try·man /ˈɪnfəntrimən/ *n, pl* **-men** /-mən/ [C] : a soldier who is in the infantry

in·fat·u·at·ed /ɪnˈfæʧəˌweɪtəd/ *adj* : filled with foolish or very strong love or admiration • *He was infatuated with his teacher.* — **in·fat·u·a·tion** /ɪnˌfæʧəˈweɪʃən/ *n* [C/U] • *The attraction he felt for her was just (an) infatuation, not true love.*

in·fect /ɪnˈfɛkt/ *vb* [T] **1** : to cause (someone or something) to become sick or affected by disease • *The virus infected many people.* • *preventing bacteria from infecting the wound* • *He was infected by a coworker.* **2** : to cause (someone) to feel a particular emotion • *She has infected everyone with her enthusiasm.* [=has made everyone enthusiastic] **3** *of a computer virus* : to cause (a computer or computer file) to stop working as it should • *The virus has infected many computers.*

in·fec·tion /ɪnˈfɛkʃən/ *n* **1** [U] : the act or process of infecting someone or something : the state of being infected • *Poor hygiene can increase the danger of infection.* **2** [C] : a disease caused by germs that enter the body • *viral/bacterial/ear infections*

in·fec·tious /ɪnˈfɛkʃəs/ *adj* **1 a** : capable of causing infection • *viruses and other infectious agents* **b** : capable of being passed to someone else by germs that enter the body • *a highly infectious disease*

c : suffering from a disease that can be spread to other people by germs ▪ *an infectious patient* **2** : capable of being easily spread to other people ▪ *Their enthusiasm was infectious.* ▪ *infectious laughter* — **in·fec·tious·ly** *adv*

in·fer /ɪnˈfɚ/ *vb* **-ferred; -fer·ring** [T] **1** : to form (an opinion) from evidence ▪ *I inferred from his silence that he was angry about my decision.* **2** *informal* : to hint or suggest (something) : IMPLY ▪ *Are you inferring that I'm wrong?* ✧ Many people regard this use of *infer* as an error, but it occurs commonly in spoken English.

in·fer·ence /ˈɪnfərəns/ *n* **1** [U] : the act or process of reaching a conclusion about something from known facts or evidence ▪ *Its existence is only known by inference.* **2** [C] : a conclusion or opinion that is formed because of known facts or evidence ▪ *Past purchases can be used to make/draw inferences about what customers will buy in the future.*

¹**in·fe·ri·or** /ɪnˈfirijɚ/ *adj* **1** : of poor quality : low or lower in quality ▪ *inferior materials/products* ▪ *an inferior performer/performance* ▪ *These pearls are inferior (in quality) to those.* **2** : of little or less importance or value ▪ *a socially inferior group* ▪ *He felt inferior to his brother.* — **in·fe·ri·or·i·ty** /ɪnˌfiriˈorəti/ *n* [U]

²**inferior** *n* [C] : a person of low rank or status ▪ *She treated us as social inferiors.*

inferiority complex *n* [C] : a belief that you are less worthy or important than other people ▪ *His shyness is the result of an inferiority complex.*

in·fer·nal /ɪnˈfɚnl/ *adj, always before a noun* **1** *literary* : of or relating to hell ▪ *the infernal regions of the dead* **2** *informal + old-fashioned* : very bad or unpleasant ▪ *Stop making that infernal racket!*

in·fer·no /ɪnˈfɚnoʊ/ *n, pl* **-nos** [C] : a very large and dangerous fire ▪ *a raging inferno*

in·fer·tile /ɪnˈfɚtl/ *adj* **1** : not able to produce children, young animals, etc. ▪ *an infertile man/woman* **2** : unable to support the growth of plants ▪ *infertile soil* — **in·fer·til·i·ty** /ɪnˌfɚˈtɪləti/ *n* [U]

in·fest /ɪnˈfɛst/ *vb* [T] *of something harmful or unwanted* : to be in or over (a place, an animal, etc.) in large numbers ▪ *The trees were infested by/with caterpillars.* ▪ *shark-infested waters* — **in·fes·ta·tion** /ˌɪnfɛˈsteɪʃən/ *n* [C/U] ▪ *an infestation of caterpillars*

in·fi·del /ˈɪnfədl/ *n* [C] *disapproving* : a person who does not believe in a religion that someone regards as the true religion

in·fi·del·i·ty /ˌɪnfəˈdɛləti/ *n, pl* **-ties** [C/U] : the act or fact of having a romantic or sexual relationship with someone other than your husband, wife, or partner ▪ *She accused her husband of infidelity.*

in·field /ˈɪnˌfiːld/ *n* [C] **1 a** : the part of a baseball field that includes the area within and around the three bases and home plate **b** : the part of a cricket field that is close to the wickets **2** *chiefly US* : the area that a racetrack or running track goes around — **in·field·er** /ˈɪnˌfiːldɚ/ *n*

[C] *US* ▪ *a skillful infielder* [=a baseball player who plays in the infield]

in·fight·ing /ˈɪnˌfaɪtɪŋ/ *n* [U] : fighting or disagreement among the members of a group or organization ▪ *political infighting*

in·fil·trate /ɪnˈfɪlˌtreɪt, ˈɪnfɪlˌtreɪt/ *vb* **-trat·ed; -trat·ing** [T] : to secretly enter or join a group, organization, etc., in order to get information or do harm ▪ *The gang was infiltrated by undercover agents.* — **in·fil·tra·tion** /ˌɪnfɪlˈtreɪʃən/ *n* [U] — **in·fil·tra·tor** /ˈɪnfɪlˌtreɪtɚ, ˈɪnfɪlˌtreɪtɚ/ *n* [C]

in·fi·nite /ˈɪnfənət/ *adj* : having or seeming to have no limits ▪ *infinite space* ▪ *infinite patience/choices* — **in·fi·nite·ly** *adv*

in·fin·i·tes·i·mal /ˌɪnˌfɪnəˈtɛsəməl/ *adj* : extremely small ▪ *an infinitesimal difference* — **in·fin·i·tes·i·mal·ly** /ˌɪnˌfɪnəˈtɛsəməli/ *adv*

in·fin·i·tive /ɪnˈfɪnətɪv/ *n* [C] *grammar* : the basic form of a verb ✧ In English the infinitive form of a verb is usually used with *to* ("I asked him *to go*") except with modal verbs like *should* and *could* ("He should *go*") and certain other verbs like *see* and *hear* ("I saw him *go*").

in·fin·i·ty /ɪnˈfɪnəti/ *n* **1** [U] **a** : the quality of having no limits or end ▪ *the infinity of space* **b** : a space, amount, or period of time that has no limits or end ▪ *numbers that continue to infinity* **2** [*singular*] : a very great number or amount ▪ *an infinity of choices*

in·firm /ɪnˈfɚm/ *adj* : having a condition of weakness or illness that usually lasts for a long time and is caused especially by old age ▪ *mentally and physically infirm people*

in·fir·ma·ry /ɪnˈfɚməri/ *n, pl* **-ries** [C] **1** : a place where sick people stay and are cared for in a school, prison, summer camp, etc. **2** *Brit* : HOSPITAL

in·fir·mi·ty /ɪnˈfɚməti/ *n, pl* **-ties** **1** [U] : the quality or state of being weak or ill especially because of old age **2** [C] : a disease or illness that usually lasts for a long time ▪ *the infirmities of old age*

in·flame /ɪnˈfleɪm/ *vb* **-flamed; -flam·ing** [T] **1 a** : to cause (a person or group) to become angry or violent ▪ *His angry speech inflamed the mob.* **b** : to make (something) more active, angry, or violent ▪ *ideas that inflame the imagination* **2** : to cause (a part of your body) to grow sore, red, and swollen ▪ *a chemical that can inflame the skin*

inflamed *adj* : sore, red, and swollen from disease, injury, etc. ▪ *an inflamed appendix*

in·flam·ma·ble /ɪnˈflæməbəl/ *adj* : capable of being set on fire and burning quickly ▪ *inflammable chemicals*

in·flam·ma·tion /ˌɪnfləˈmeɪʃən/ *n* [C/U] : a condition in which a part of your body becomes red, swollen, and painful ▪ *(an) inflammation of the throat and ears*

in·flam·ma·to·ry /ɪnˈflæməˌtori, Brit ɪnˈflæmətri/ *adj* **1** *medical* : causing or having inflammation ▪ *inflammatory diseases* **2** : causing anger ▪ *inflammatory remarks*

in·flate /ɪnˈfleɪt/ *vb* **-flat·ed; -flat·ing** **1**

a [T] : to add air or gas to (a tire, balloon, etc.) and make it larger ▪ *an inflated balloon* **b** [I] : to become larger by being filled with air or gas ▪ *The balloon slowly inflated.* **2** [T] **a** : to think or say that (something) is larger or more important than it really is ▪ *His memoirs inflate his contributions to the war effort.* **b** : to cause (a person's ego, reputation, etc.) to become too large ▪ *The publicity inflated his ego.* [=made him too proud and conceited] **3** [T/I] : to increase prices, costs, etc., in a way that is not normal or expected ▪ *Rapid economic growth may cause prices to inflate.* — **in·flat·able** /ɪnˈfleɪtəbəl/ *adj* ▪ *an inflatable raft*

in·fla·tion /ɪnˈfleɪʃən/ *n* [U] **1** : an act of inflating something or the state of being inflated ▪ *the inflation of a balloon* ▪ *tire inflation* **2** : a continual increase in the price of goods and services ▪ *trying to control/reduce/curb (economic) inflation*

in·fla·tion·ary /ɪnˈfleɪʃəˌneri, *Brit* ɪnˈfleɪʃənri/ *adj* : of or relating to economic inflation ▪ *an inflationary increase/period*

in·flect /ɪnˈflɛkt/ *vb* [T/I] *grammar* : to change the form of a word when using it in a particular way ▪ *Most nouns in English are inflected for plural use by adding "-s" or "-es."* — **in·flect·ed** /ɪnˈflɛktəd/ *adj* ▪ *"Gone" and "went" are inflected forms of the verb "go."*

in·flec·tion *also Brit* **in·flex·ion** /ɪnˈflɛkʃən/ *n* **1** [C/U] : a rise or fall in the sound of a person's voice ▪ *She spoke with no inflection.* **2** *grammar* **a** [U] : a change in the form of a word that occurs when it has a particular use **b** [C] : a form of a word that occurs when it has a particular use ▪ *"Gone" and "went" are inflections of the verb "go."*

in·flex·i·ble /ɪnˈflɛksəbəl/ *adj* **1** : not easily influenced or persuaded ▪ *an inflexible judge* **2** : not easily bent or twisted ▪ *inflexible plastic* **3** : not easily changed ▪ *an inflexible deadline/rule* — **in·flex·i·bil·i·ty** /ɪnˌflɛksəˈbɪləti/ *n* [U]

in·flict /ɪnˈflɪkt/ *vb* [T] : to cause someone to experience or be affected by (something unpleasant or harmful) ▪ *inflict pain/injury/punishment* ▪ *the suffering he has inflicted on/upon innocent people* — **in·flic·tion** /ɪnˈflɪkʃən/ *n* [U]

in–flight /ɪnˈflaɪt/ *adj, always before a noun* : made, done, or provided while you are flying in an airplane ▪ *an in-flight meal/movie*

in·flow /ˈɪnˌfloʊ/ *n* [C/U] : a flow or movement of something into a place, organization, etc. ▪ *(an) inflow of water/money*

¹in·flu·ence /ˈɪnˌfluːwəns/ *n* **1** [U, *singular*] : the power to cause changes without directly forcing them to happen ▪ *He used his influence to reform the company's policies.* ▪ *Health concerns had some influence on/upon his decision.* ▪ *She was under the influence of drugs.* [=she was affected by drugs] ▪ *She has remained under the influence of her parents.* **2** [C] : a person or thing that affects someone or something in an important way ▪ *My parents have been major influences in my*

life. — **in·flu·en·tial** /ˌɪnfluˈɛnʃəl/ *adj* ▪ *an influential book/person*

²influence *vb* **-enced; -enc·ing** [T] : to affect or change (someone or something) in an indirect but usually important way ▪ *I was deeply/greatly influenced by my parents.* ▪ *No one knows what may have influenced them to commit these crimes.*

in·flu·en·za /ˌɪnfluˈɛnzə/ *n* [U] *medical* : a common illness that is caused by a virus and that causes fever, weakness, severe aches and pains, and breathing problems ▪ *patients suffering from influenza* [=the flu]

in·flux /ˈɪnˌflʌks/ *n* [C] : the arrival or inward flow of a large amount of things or people ▪ *an influx of capital/tourists*

in·fo /ˈɪnfoʊ/ *n* [U] *informal* : INFORMATION

in·fo·mer·cial /ˈɪnfoʊˌmɚʃəl/ *n* [C] *chiefly US* : a television program that is a long advertisement and that usually includes people talking about and using the product that is being sold

in·form /ɪnˈfoɚm/ *vb* [T/I] : to give information to (someone) ▪ *We haven't yet been informed of/about her decision.* ▪ *They informed us that our flight was delayed.* — **inform on** *also* **inform against** [*phrasal vb*] : to give information about the secret or criminal activity of (someone) to the police ▪ *He refused to inform on the other conspirators.*

in·for·mal /ɪnˈfoɚməl/ *adj* **1** : having a friendly and relaxed quality ▪ *an informal party/conversation* **2** : suited for ordinary use when you are relaxing ▪ *informal clothes* **3** *of language* : not suited for serious or official speech and writing ▪ *informal English/writing/words* — **in·for·mal·i·ty** /ˌɪnfoɚˈmæləti/ *n* [U] — **in·for·mal·ly** /ɪnˈfoɚməli/ *adv*

in·for·mant /ɪnˈfoɚmənt/ *n* [C] : INFORMER

in·for·ma·tion /ˌɪnfɚˈmeɪʃən/ *n* [U] **1** : knowledge that you get about someone or something ▪ *We need more information on/about/concerning their plans.* ▪ *We enclose a price list for your information.* [=to provide you with information that we think will interest you] **2** *US* : a service that telephone users can call to find out the telephone number for a specified person or organization — **in·for·ma·tion·al** /ˌɪnfɚˈmeɪʃənl/ *adj* ▪ *an informational brochure*

in·for·ma·tive /ɪnˈfoɚmətɪv/ *adj* : providing information ▪ *an informative book*

in·formed /ɪnˈfoɚmd/ *adj* **1** : having information ▪ *informed voters* ▪ *Please keep me informed on any changes.* [=please tell me about any changes] **2** : based on information ▪ *an informed choice/decision*

in·form·er /ɪnˈfoɚmɚ/ *n* [C] : a person who gives information especially to the police about secret or criminal activities

in·fo·tain·ment /ˌɪnfoʊˈteɪnmənt/ *n* [U] : television programs that present information (such as news) in a way that is meant to be entertaining

in·frac·tion /ɪnˈfrækʃən/ *n* [C] *formal* : an act that breaks a rule or law ▪ *a minor traffic infraction*

in·fra·red /ˌɪnfrəˈrɛd/ *adj, technical* : producing or using rays of light that cannot be seen and that are longer than rays that produce red light • *infrared radiation/ beams*

in·fra·struc·ture /ˈɪnfrəˌstrʌktʃɚ/ n [C/U] : the basic equipment and structures (such as roads and bridges) that are needed for a country, region, or organization to function properly — **in·fra·struc·tur·al** /ˈɪnfrəˌstrʌktʃərəl/ adj

in·fre·quent /ɪnˈfriːkwənt/ adj : not happening often • *an infrequent event* — **in·fre·quen·cy** /ɪnˈfriːkwənsi/ n [U] — **in·fre·quent·ly** adv

in·fringe /ɪnˈfrɪndʒ/ vb **-fringed; -fring·ing** [T/I] **1** : to do something that does not obey or follow (a rule, law, etc.) • *in-fringe a treaty/patent* • (*chiefly US*) *His use of the name infringes on/upon their copyright.* **2** : to wrongly limit or restrict (something, such as another person's rights) • *infringing on/upon the right of free speech* — **in·fringe·ment** /ɪnˈfrɪndʒmənt/ n [C/U] • *infringements of our rights* • *copyright infringement*

in·fu·ri·ate /ɪnˈfjɔriˌeɪt/ vb **-at·ed; -at·ing** [T] : to make (someone) very angry • *His arrogance infuriates me!* • *He has an infuriating habit of ignoring me.* — **in·fu·ri·at·ing·ly** /ɪnˈfjɔriˌeɪtɪŋli/ adv

in·fuse /ɪnˈfjuːz/ vb **-fused; -fus·ing 1** [T] : to cause a person or thing to be filled with something • *She has infused her followers with confidence.* = *She has infused confidence into her followers.* **2** [T/I] : to allow something (such as tea or herbs) to stay in a liquid (such as hot water) in order to flavor the liquid • *The tea should be allowed to infuse for several minutes.* — **in·fu·sion** /ɪnˈfjuːʒən/ n [C/U] • *an infusion of cash into the company* • *infusion of herbs*

¹-ing /ɪŋ, ɪn/ vb suffix or adj suffix — used to form the present participle of a verb • *sailing*

²-ing n suffix **1** : action or process • *running* **2** : product or result of an action or process • *a painting*

in·ge·nious /ɪnˈdʒiːnjəs/ adj : very smart or clever • *an ingenious plan/person* — **in·ge·nious·ly** adv

in·ge·nue (*US*) or **in·gé·nue** /ˈændʒəˌnuː, ˈɑːndʒəˌnuː, ˈænʒəˌnjuː/ n [C] : an innocent girl or young woman

in·ge·nu·i·ty /ˌɪndʒəˈnuːwəti, *Brit* ˌɪndʒəˈnjuːwəti/ n [U] : skill or cleverness that allows someone to solve problems, invent things, etc. • *It will take some ingenuity to fix these problems.*

in·gen·u·ous /ɪnˈdʒɛnjəwəs/ adj : having or showing the innocence, trust, and honesty that young people often have • *an ingenuous man/smile*

in·gest /ɪnˈdʒɛst/ vb [T] : to take (something, such as food) into your body • *The drug is more easily ingested in pill form.* • (*figurative*) *She ingested large amounts of information.* — **in·ges·tion** /ɪnˈdʒɛstʃən/ n [U]

in·glo·ri·ous /ɪnˈgloːrijəs/ adj, literary : causing shame or disgrace • *an inglorious defeat*

in·got /ˈɪŋgət/ n [C] : a solid piece of metal that has been formed into a particular shape (such as a brick) so that it is easy to handle or store • *gold ingots*

in·grained /ˈɪnˌgreɪnd/ adj : existing for a long time and very difficult to change • *an ingrained habit/tradition*

in·grate /ˈɪnˌgreɪt/ n [C] formal : a person who does not show proper appreciation or thanks for something

in·gra·ti·ate /ɪnˈgreɪʃiˌeɪt/ vb **-at·ed; -at·ing** [T] often disapproving : to gain favor or approval for (yourself) by doing or saying things that people like • *She tried to ingratiate herself with voters by promising a tax cut.*

ingratiating adj, often disapproving : intended to gain someone's favor or approval • *an ingratiating smile*

in·grat·i·tude /ɪnˈgrætəˌtuːd, *Brit* ɪnˈgrætəˌtjuːd/ n [U] : lack of proper appreciation or thanks for something • *He was hurt by their ingratitude.*

in·gre·di·ent /ɪnˈgriːdijənt/ n [C] **1** : one of the things that are used to make a food, product, etc. • *the ingredients in/ of the soap/soup* **2** : a quality or characteristic that makes something possible • *Honesty is an essential ingredient of/for a successful marriage.*

in·ground /ˈɪnˌgraʊnd/ adj, US : built into the ground • *an inground swimming pool*

in·grow·ing /ˈɪnˌgroʊɪŋ/ adj, Brit : INGROWN

in·grown /ˈɪnˌgroʊn/ adj : having a tip or edge that has grown back into the flesh • *an ingrown toenail/hair*

in·hab·it /ɪnˈhæbət/ vb [T] **1** : to live in (a place) • *Several hundred species of birds inhabit the island.* • *The island is no longer inhabited.* [=no people live there] **2** : to be present in (something) • *There is a romantic quality that inhabits all her paintings.* — **in·hab·it·able** /ɪnˈhæbətəbəl/ adj

in·hab·it·ant /ɪnˈhæbətənt/ n [C] : a person or animal that lives in a particular place • *The city has more than a million inhabitants.* [=residents]

in·hale /ɪnˈheɪl/ vb **-haled; -hal·ing** [T/I] : to breathe in • *He inhaled (the air) deeply and exhaled slowly, trying to relax.* — **in·ha·la·tion** /ˌɪnhəˈleɪʃən/ n [C/U] • *(an) inhalation of chemical fumes*

in·hal·er /ɪnˈheɪlɚ/ n [C] medical : a device used for inhaling a medicine

in·her·ent /ɪnˈhɪrənt, ɪnˈhɛrənt/ adj, formal : belonging to the basic nature of someone or something • *He has an inherent sense of fairness.* • *problems inherent in the design* — **in·her·ent·ly** adv

in·her·it /ɪnˈhɛrət/ vb [T] **1** : to receive (money, property, etc.) from someone when that person dies • *She inherited the business from her father.* **2 a** biology : to have (a characteristic, disease, etc.) because of the genes that you get from your parents when you are born • *He inherited his father's blue eyes.* **b** : to get (a personal quality, interest, etc.) because of the influence or example of your parents or other relatives • *She inherited a love of baseball from her dad.* **3 a** : to receive (something) from someone who had it previously • *When my brother left*

for college, I inherited his old computer.
b : to have to deal with (a situation, problem, etc.) when you take a job or position that someone else had before you ▪ *The company's new president will inherit some complicated legal problems.*
— **in·her·it·able** /ɪnˈherətəbəl/ *adj* ▪ *an inheritable disease* — **in·her·i·tance** /ɪnˈherətəns/ *n [C/U]* ▪ *He left sizable inheritances to his children.* ▪ *the inheritance of a genetic trait* — **in·her·it·ed** /ɪnˈherətəd/ *adj* ▪ *an inherited disease/estate* — **in·her·i·tor** /ɪnˈherətɚ/ *n [C]*

in·hib·it /ɪnˈhɪbət/ *vb [T]* **1** : to keep (someone) from doing what he or she wants to do ▪ *You shouldn't allow fear of failure to inhibit you.* ▪ *a shy, inhibited child* **2** : to prevent or slow down the activity or occurrence of (something) ▪ *Strict laws are inhibiting economic growth.* — **in·hib·i·tor** /ɪnˈhɪbətɚ/ *n [C]*

in·hi·bi·tion /ˌɪnhəˈbɪʃən/ *n* **1** *[C/U]* : a nervous feeling that prevents you from expressing your thoughts, emotions, or desires ▪ *She has no inhibitions about stating her opinion.* **2** *[U]* : the act of preventing or slowing the activity or occurrence of something ▪ *inhibition of muscle growth*

in·hos·pi·ta·ble /ˌɪnhɑˈspɪtəbəl, ɪnˈhɑːspɪtəbəl/ *adj* **1** : not generous and friendly to guests or visitors ▪ *He was inhospitable to his guests.* **2** : having an environment where plants, animals, or people cannot live or grow easily ▪ *an inhospitable desert/habitat*

in-house /ˈɪnˌhaʊs/ *adj* : created, done, or existing within a company or organization ▪ *in-house testing* — **in-house** *adv* ▪ *All the testing was done in-house.*

in·hu·man /ɪnˈhjuːmən/ *adj* **1** : very fierce or cruel ▪ *inhuman punishment/crimes* ▪ *an inhuman tyrant* **2** : extremely poor, dirty, or unhealthy ▪ *inhuman living conditions* **3** : unlike what might be expected from a human being ▪ *He let out an inhuman moan.* — **in·hu·man·ly** *adv*

in·hu·mane /ˌɪnhjuˈmeɪn/ *adj* : not kind or gentle to people or animals ▪ *the inhumane treatment of prisoners* — **in·hu·mane·ly** *adv*

in·hu·man·i·ty /ˌɪnhjuˈmænəti/ *n [U]* : the quality or state of being cruel to other people or to animals ▪ *the inhumanity [=brutality] of war*

in·im·i·ta·ble /ɪˈnɪmətəbəl/ *adj* : impossible to copy or imitate ▪ *an inimitable style*

in·iq·ui·ty /ɪˈnɪkwəti/ *n, pl* **-ties** *formal* **1** *[U]* : the quality of being unfair or evil ▪ *a notorious den of iniquity* [=a place where immoral things are done] **2** *[C]* : something that is unfair or evil ▪ *the iniquities of slavery*

¹**ini·tial** /ɪˈnɪʃəl/ *adj, always before a noun* : occurring at the beginning of something ▪ *the initial stages of the disease* ▪ *Her initial* [=first] *reaction was to say no.* — **ini·tial·ly** /ɪˈnɪʃəli/ *adv*

²**initial** *n [C]* : the first letter of a name ▪ *The initials F.D.R. stand for "Franklin Delano Roosevelt."*

³**initial** *vb, US* **-tialed** *or Brit* **-tialled**; *US* **-tial·ing** *or Brit* **-tial·ling** *[T]* : to mark

(something) with your initials ▪ *She initialed each page of the contract.*

¹**ini·ti·ate** /ɪˈnɪʃiˌeɪt/ *vb* **-at·ed; -at·ing** *[T]* **1** *formal* : to start or begin (something) ▪ *initiate a new project* **2** : to formally accept (someone) as a member of a group or organization usually in a special ceremony ▪ *He was initiated into a secret society.* **3** : to teach (someone) the basic facts or ideas about something ▪ *They initiated her into the ways of the corporate world.* — **ini·ti·a·tion** /ɪˌnɪʃiˈeɪʃən/ *n [C/U]* ▪ *the initiation* [=start] *of therapy* ▪ *her initiation into the sorority* — **ini·ti·a·tor** /ɪˈnɪʃiˌeɪtɚ/ *n [C]*

²**ini·tiate** /ɪˈnɪʃijət/ *n [C]* : a person who is being formally accepted or who has been formally accepted as a member of a group or organization

ini·tia·tive /ɪˈnɪʃətɪv/ *n* **1** *the initiative* : the power or opportunity to do something before others do ▪ *If you want to meet her, you're going to have to take the initiative and introduce yourself.* **2** *[U]* : the energy and desire that is needed to do something ▪ *She has ability but lacks initiative.* ▪ *I'm doing this on my own initiative.* [=because I want to] ▪ *You should use your own initiative to come up with a solution.* **3** *[C]* : a plan or program that is intended to solve a problem ▪ *anti-poverty initiatives*

in·ject /ɪnˈdʒɛkt/ *vb [T]* **1 a** : to force a liquid medicine or drug into someone or something by using a special needle ▪ *The medicine is injected into the muscle.* ▪ *The patients were injected with the vaccine.* **b** : to force (a liquid) into something ▪ *inject fuel into an engine* ▪ *a fuel-injected engine* **2** : to introduce (something needed or additional) *into* something ▪ *She told a few jokes to inject a little humor into her speech.* — **in·jec·tion** /ɪnˈdʒɛkʃən/ *n [C/U]* ▪ *an injection of a painkiller* ▪ *The medicine was given/administered by injection.* — **in·jec·tor** /ɪnˈdʒɛktɚ/ *n [C]* ▪ *a fuel injector*

in·ju·di·cious /ˌɪndʒuˈdɪʃəs/ *adj, formal* : not having or showing good judgment ▪ *an injudicious comment*

in·junc·tion /ɪnˈdʒʌŋkʃən/ *n [C] law* : an order from a court of law that says something must be done or must not be done ▪ *The court has issued/granted an injunction against the strike.*

in·jure /ˈɪndʒɚ/ *vb* **-jured; -jur·ing** *[T]* : to harm or damage (someone or something) ▪ *She fell and injured herself.* ▪ *She fell and injured her arm.* ▪ *The criticism injured his pride.* ▪ *One of the players is injured.*

in·ju·ri·ous /ɪnˈdʒurijəs/ *adj, formal* : causing injury : HARMFUL ▪ *injurious behavior*

in·ju·ry /ˈɪndʒəri/ *n, pl* **-ries** *[C/U]* : harm or damage : an act or event that causes someone or something to no longer be fully healthy or in good condition ▪ *trying to prevent injury* ▪ *She survived the accident without injury.* ▪ *She fell and suffered an injury to her arm.* — **add insult to injury** see ²INSULT

injury time *n [U] Brit* : time that is added at the end of a game of hockey, soccer, etc., because of time lost when players are injured

in·jus·tice /ɪnˈdʒʌstəs/ n [C/U] : unfair treatment : a situation in which the rights of a person or a group of people are ignored • *economic/racial/social injustice* • *the injustices of apartheid* — **do (someone or something) an injustice** : to treat (someone or something) in an unfair way • *I think you do the book an injustice when you call it "trash."*

¹ink /ɪŋk/ n [C/U] : colored liquid that is used for writing or printing

²ink vb [T] **1** : to put ink on (something) • *ink the printing block* **2** US, informal **a** : to sign (a document) to show that you accept or agree with what is written on it • *He inked a new deal.* **b** : to hire (someone) to do something by having that person sign a contract • *The team inked [=signed] him to a new contract.*

ink–jet printer n [C] computers : a printer that works by spraying small drops of ink onto paper

ink·ling /ˈɪŋklɪŋ/ n [C] : a slight, uncertain idea about something • *I didn't have an inkling of what it all meant.*

ink·well /ˈɪŋkˌwɛl/ n [C] : a small container in the surface of a desk that was used in the past for holding ink

inky /ˈɪŋki/ adj **1** literary : very dark or black like ink • *inky blackness/darkness* **2** : made dirty by ink • *inky hands*

in·laid /ˈɪnˈleɪd/ adj **1** : set into the surface of something in a decorative pattern • *inlaid designs/marble* **2** : decorated with an inlaid design • *an inlaid box*

in·land /ˈɪnˌlænd/ adv : in, into, or toward the middle of a country • *They traveled/live inland.* — **inland** adj • *an inland sea*

Inland Revenue n — **the Inland Revenue** : the department of the British government that is responsible for collecting taxes

in–law /ˈɪnˌlɑː/ n [C] : a person you are related to because of your marriage; *especially* : the father or mother of your husband or wife • *She was nervous when she met her in-laws for the first time.*

¹in·lay /ɪnˈleɪ/ vb -**laid** /-ˈleɪd/; -**lay·ing** [T] : to set pieces of wood, metal, etc., into the surface of (something) for decoration • *The desk is inlaid with ivory.*

²in·lay /ˈɪnˌleɪ/ n [C/U] : material that is set into the surface of something for decoration • *decorative/marble inlay*

in·let /ˈɪnˌlɛt/ n [C] **1** : a narrow area of water that goes into the land from a sea or lake **2** : an opening through which air, gas, or liquid can enter something • *a gas/air inlet*

in·mate /ˈɪnˌmeɪt/ n [C] : a person who is kept in a prison or mental hospital

in me·mo·ri·am /ˌɪnməˈmorijəm/ prep, formal : in memory of (someone who has died)

in·most /ˈɪnˌmoʊst/ adj, always before a noun : INNERMOST • *her inmost thoughts and feelings*

inn /ˈɪn/ n [C] **1** : a house usually in the country where people can eat and rent a room to sleep in **2** chiefly Brit : a pub

in·nards /ˈɪnədz/ n [plural] informal **1** : the internal organs of a person or an animal **2** : the inside parts of something • *the car's innards*

in·nate /ɪˈneɪt/ adj **1** : existing from the time a person or animal is born • *an innate ability/talent* **2** : existing as part of the basic nature of something • *the innate problems of wireless communication* — **in·nate·ly** adv

in·ner /ˈɪnə/ adj, always before a noun **1** : located toward the inside of something • *an inner room* **2** : not known to or seen by most people • *the poem's inner meaning* • *the inner workings of the political campaign* [=the parts of the campaign that are only known by the people who work on it] **3** : of or relating to a person's mind or spirit • *inner peace/conflict* • *his inner self*

inner circle n [C] : a small group of people who lead a government or an organization or who are close to its leader • *The President has an inner circle of advisers.*

inner city n [C] : the central section of a large city where mostly poor people live — **inner–city** adj, always before a noun • *an inner-city neighborhood*

in·ner·most /ˈɪnəˌmoʊst/ adj **1** always before a noun : most private and personal • *her innermost feelings/secrets* **2** : closest to the center or inside of something • *the innermost part of the cave*

inner sanctum n [C] somewhat formal : a very private room or place • *She was admitted to the building's inner sanctum.* • (figurative) *the inner sanctum of the CIA*

inner tube n [C] : a round tube that holds air inside a tire

in·ning /ˈɪnɪŋ/ n [C] baseball : one of the usually nine parts of a game in which each team bats until three outs are made

in·nings /ˈɪnɪŋz/ n, pl **innings** [C] cricket : one of the parts of a game in which a team or player bats

inn·keep·er /ˈɪnˌkiːpə/ n [C] old-fashioned : a person who owns or manages an inn

in·no·cence /ˈɪnəsəns/ n [U] **1** : the state of being not guilty of a crime or other wrong act • *He vows that he will prove his innocence in court.* **2** : lack of experience with the world and with the bad things that happen in life • *the innocence of childhood*

in·no·cent /ˈɪnəsənt/ adj **1** : not guilty of a crime or other wrong act • *I am innocent of the crime.* • *A person accused of a crime is innocent until proven guilty.* **2** always before a noun : not deserving to be harmed • *an innocent victim* **3** : lacking experience with the world and the bad things that happen in life • *an innocent child* **4** : not intended to cause harm or trouble • *an innocent question/mistake* — **innocent** n [C] • *She was an innocent when it came to romance.* — **in·no·cent·ly** adv • *I innocently mentioned what turned out to be a very painful topic.* • *She smiled innocently.*

in·noc·u·ous /ɪˈnɑːkjəwəs/ adj **1** : not likely to bother or offend anyone • *innocuous jokes* **2** : causing no injury : HARMLESS • *an innocuous gas* — **in·noc·u·ous·ly** adv

in·no·vate /ˈɪnəˌveɪt/ *vb* **-vat·ed; -vat·ing** [*T/I*] : to do something in a new way : to have new ideas about how something can be done • *The company plans to continue innovating and experimenting.* — **in·no·va·tor** /ˈɪnəˌveɪtɚ/ *n* [*C*]

in·no·va·tion /ˌɪnəˈveɪʃən/ *n* **1** [*C*] : a new idea, device, or method • *the latest innovation in computer technology* **2** [*U*] : the act or process of introducing new ideas, devices, or methods • *the rapid pace of technological innovation*

in·no·va·tive /ˈɪnəˌveɪtɪv/ *adj* **1** : introducing or using new ideas or methods • *an innovative approach/solution/design* **2** : having new ideas about how something can be done • *an innovative young designer* — **in·no·va·tive·ly** *adv*

in·nu·en·do /ˌɪnjəˈwɛndoʊ/ *n, pl* **-dos** *or* **-does** [*C/U*] : a statement which indirectly suggests that someone has done something immoral, improper, etc. • *His reputation was damaged by innuendos about his drinking and gambling.*

Innuit *variant spelling of* INUIT

in·nu·mer·a·ble /ɪˈnuːmərəbəl, *Brit* ɪˈnjuːmərəbəl/ *adj* : too many to be counted : very many • *the innumerable stars in the sky*

in·oc·u·late /ɪˈnɑːkjəˌleɪt/ *vb* **-lat·ed; -lat·ing** [*T*] *medical* : to give (a person or animal) a weakened form of a disease in order to prevent infection by the disease • *The children were inoculated against smallpox.* — **in·oc·u·la·tion** /ɪˌnɑːkjəˈleɪʃən/ *n* [*C/U*]

in·of·fen·sive /ˌɪnəˈfɛnsɪv/ *adj* : not likely to offend or bother anyone • *an inoffensive person/remark*

in·op·er·a·ble /ɪnˈɑːpərəbəl/ *adj* **1** *medical* : not able to be corrected or removed by surgery • *an inoperable tumor* **2** *formal* : not capable of being used • *an inoperable machine*

in·op·er·a·tive /ɪnˈɑːpərətɪv/ *adj, formal* **1** : not capable of being used • *The accident rendered the car inoperative.* **2** : having no force or effect • *The law has become inoperative.*

in·op·por·tune /ˌɪnˌɑːpəˈtuːn, *Brit* ɪnˈɒpəˌtjuːn/ *adj* **1** : not suitable or right for a particular situation • *He arrived at an inopportune time.* **2** : done or happening at the wrong time • *an inopportune sale of stocks*

in·or·di·nate /ɪnˈɔɚdnət/ *adj* : going beyond what is usual, normal, or proper • *an inordinate amount of time* — **in·or·di·nate·ly** *adv*

in·or·gan·ic /ˌɪnɔɚˈgænɪk/ *adj* : made from or containing material that does not come from plants or animals • *inorganic fertilizer*

in·pa·tient /ˈɪnˌpeɪʃənt/ *n* [*C*] : a patient who stays for one or more nights in a hospital for treatment • *inpatient surgery* [=surgery performed on inpatients]

¹in·put /ˈɪnˌpʊt/ *n* **1** [*U*] : advice or opinions that help someone make a decision • *She provided some valuable input at the start of the project.* **2** *technical* **a** [*U*] : information that is put into a computer • *The computer gets its input from a keyboard or mouse.* **b** [*U*] : something (such as power or energy) that is put into a machine or system • *electrical input* **c** [*C*] : the place at which information, power, etc., enters a computer, machine, or system • *audio/video inputs* **3** [*U*, *singular*] : the act or process of putting something in or into something else • *The job will require a considerable input of money.*

²input *vb* **-put·ted** *or* **-put; -put·ting** [*T*] : to enter (information) into a computer • *She inputted the sales figures into the spreadsheet.*

in·quest /ˈɪnˌkwɛst/ *n* [*C*] *law* : an official investigation to find the reason for something (such as a person's death)

in·quire *or chiefly Brit* **en·quire** /ɪnˈkwajɚ/ *vb* **-quired; -quir·ing** [*T/I*] *somewhat formal* : to ask for information • *He was inquiring about a friend who used to work here.* • *We inquired the way to the station.* • *"So, what do you want?" he inquired.* — **inquire after** [*phrasal vb*] : to ask for information about (someone or something) • *She inquired after my wife's health.* — **inquire into** [*phrasal vb*] : to gather or collect information about (something) • *A panel has been appointed to inquire into their activities.* — **in·quir·er** *n* [*C*]

inquiring *or chiefly Brit* **enquiring** *adj, always before a noun* **1** : asking questions : wanting to learn more • *an inquiring reporter/mind* **2** : showing a desire to ask a question or learn more • *an inquiring look*

in·qui·ry *or chiefly Brit* **en·qui·ry** /ɪnˈkwaɪri, ˈɪnkwəri/ *n, pl* **-ries 1** [*C*] : a request for information • *She refused to answer inquiries from the media about her marriage.* **2** [*C/U*] : a careful investigation • *judicial/legislative inquiries* — often + *into* • *an inquiry into the circumstances of his death* **3** [*U*] : the act of asking questions in order to get information • *The police are pursuing a new line of inquiry.*

in·qui·si·tion /ˌɪnkwəˈzɪʃən/ *n* **1 the Inquisition** : an organization in the Roman Catholic Church in the past that was responsible for finding and punishing people who did not accept its beliefs and practices **2** [*C*] : a harsh and unfair investigation or series of questions • *conducting an inquisition into the details of his personal life*

in·quis·i·tive /ɪnˈkwɪzətɪv/ *adj* **1** : having a desire to know or learn more • *an inquisitive mind/child* **2** *disapproving* : asking too many questions about other people's lives • *an overly inquisitive neighbor* — **in·quis·i·tive·ly** *adv*

in·quis·i·tor /ɪnˈkwɪzətɚ/ *n* [*C*] : a person who asks many difficult questions in a harsh or unkind way — **in·quis·i·to·ri·al** /ɪnˌkwɪzəˈtorijəl/ *adj*

in·road /ˈɪnˌroʊd/ *n* [*C*] — used to describe a situation in which someone or something becomes more successful or important often by making someone or something else less successful • *The sport is making inroads in the U.S.* [=becoming more popular in the U.S.]

in·rush /ˈɪnˌrʌʃ/ *n* [*singular*] : a fast flow

or movement into a place ▪ *an inrush of water/air*

ins and outs /ˌɪnzənˈaʊts/ *n* — **the ins and outs** : the details about how something works or is done ▪ *learning all the ins and outs of American politics*

in·sane /ɪnˈseɪn/ *adj* **1 a** : having or showing severe mental illness ▪ *an insane person* — now usually used in such legal phrases as *criminally insane* and *temporarily insane* **b** : unable to think in a clear or sensible way ▪ *She was insane with jealousy/anger.* **c** — used in the phrase **drive/make (someone) insane** to describe annoying or bothering someone very much ▪ *That noise is driving me insane.* **2** : very foolish or unreasonable : CRAZY ▪ *driving at insane speeds* ▪ *an insane idea* **3** : used for people who have severe mental illnesses ▪ *an insane asylum* [=(now more commonly) a mental hospital] — **go insane** : to become mentally ill : to go crazy — usually used in an exaggerated way ▪ *I must be going insane. I can't find my car keys anywhere.* — **in·sane·ly** *adv* ▪ *Her boyfriend was insanely jealous.*

in·san·i·tary /ɪnˈsænəˌteri/ *adj, chiefly Brit* : dirty and likely to cause disease : UNSANITARY

in·san·i·ty /ɪnˈsænəti/ *n, pl* **-ties 1** [U] : severe mental illness : the condition of being insane ▪ *temporary insanity* **2** [C/U] : something that is very foolish or unreasonable ▪ *His friends thought his decision to quit his job was pure insanity.*

in·sa·tia·ble /ɪnˈseɪʃəbəl/ *adj* : not able to be satisfied ▪ *an insatiable appetite/thirst* — **in·sa·tia·bly** /ɪnˈseɪʃəbli/ *adv*

in·scribe /ɪnˈskraɪb/ *vb* **-scribed;** **-scrib·ing** [T] : to write or cut words, a name, etc., in or on something ▪ *The winner's name is inscribed on the trophy.* ▪ *They inscribed the monument with the soldiers' names.* ▪ *(figurative) The image is inscribed in my memory.* [=I remember the image very clearly]

in·scrip·tion /ɪnˈskrɪpʃən/ *n* [C] : words that are written on or cut into a surface ▪ *The painting had an inscription that read, "To my loving wife."*

in·scru·ta·ble /ɪnˈskruːtəbəl/ *adj, formal* : difficult to understand ▪ *an inscrutable* [=mysterious] *smile/man* — **in·scru·ta·bly** /ɪnˈskruːtəbli/ *adv*

in·sect /ˈɪnˌsɛkt/ *n* [C] **1** : a small animal that has six legs and a body formed of three parts and that may have wings ▪ *flies, bees, and other insects* **2** : an animal (such as a spider) that is similar to an insect

in·sec·ti·cide /ɪnˈsɛktəˌsaɪd/ *n* [C/U] : a chemical substance that is used to kill insects — **in·sec·ti·cid·al** /ɪnˌsɛktəˈsaɪdl̩/ *adj*

in·se·cure /ˌɪnsɪˈkjɚ/ *adj* **1** : not confident about yourself or your ability to do things well ▪ *I feel shy and insecure around strangers.* ▪ *She is insecure about her height.* **2** : not certain to continue or be successful for a long time ▪ *an insecure investment/job* **3** : not locked or well protected ▪ *The country's borders remain insecure.* — **in·se·cu·ri·ty** /ˌɪnsɪˈkjɚəti/ *n, pl* **-ties** [C/U] ▪ *job/economic insecurity* ▪ *the insecurities of teenagers*

in·sem·i·nate /ɪnˈsɛməˌneɪt/ *vb* **-nat·ed;** **-nat·ing** [T] *technical* : to put semen into (a woman or a female animal) in order to cause pregnancy ▪ *She was artificially inseminated.* — **in·sem·i·na·tion** /ɪnˌsɛməˈneɪʃən/ *n* [U]

in·sen·si·ble /ɪnˈsɛnsəbəl/ *adj, formal* **1** : not able to feel pain, emotions, etc. ▪ *insensible to fear/pain* **2** : not aware of something ▪ *insensible of the danger ahead* **3** : not conscious ▪ *She was knocked insensible by the collision.*

in·sen·si·tive /ɪnˈsɛnsətɪv/ *adj* **1** : showing that you do not know or care about the feelings, needs, problems, etc., of other people ▪ *He's just a rude, insensitive jerk.* ▪ *a racially insensitive comment* ▪ *The government has been insensitive to the public's demands.* **2** *not before a noun* : not greatly affected by something ▪ *insensitive to pain* — **in·sen·si·tive·ly** *adv* — **in·sen·si·tiv·i·ty** /ɪnˌsɛnsəˈtɪvəti/ *n* [U]

in·sep·a·ra·ble /ɪnˈsɛpərəbəl/ *adj* : not able to be separated ▪ *One problem is inseparable from the other.* ▪ *inseparable friends* — **in·sep·a·ra·bly** /ɪnˈsɛpərəbli/ *adv*

¹in·sert /ɪnˈsɚt/ *vb* [T] : to put (something) in or into something ▪ *He inserted the key in/into the lock.* ▪ *insert a comma/space*

²in·sert /ˈɪnˌsɚt/ *n* [C] : something that is put into something else ▪ *shoe inserts; especially* : a small section or piece of paper with information that is placed inside something ▪ *advertising inserts in the Sunday paper*

in·ser·tion /ɪnˈsɚʃən/ *n* **1** [U] : the act or process of putting something into something else ▪ *Treatment may include the insertion of a tube in his ear.* **2** [C] : something (such as a comment) that is added to a piece of writing ▪ *The report contains a number of insertions.*

¹in·set /ˈɪnˌsɛt/ *n* [C] : a small map or picture that is shown on or next to a larger map or picture in order to show more detail

²inset *vb* **-set; -set·ting** [T] **1** : to put (something) in something larger for decoration, to give information, etc. ▪ *inset a map in a larger map* **2** : to put something into (something) often for decoration ▪ *The ring is inset with diamonds.* — **inset** *adj* ▪ *a table with an inset glass top* ▪ *an inset map*

in·shore /ˈɪnˈʃoɚ/ *adj* **1** : moving toward the shore away from the water ▪ *an inshore breeze* **2** : located near the shore ▪ *inshore waters* — **inshore** *adv* ▪ *The animals move inshore to feed.*

¹in·side /ɪnˈsaɪd, ˈɪnˌsaɪd/ *n* [C] **1** : an inner side, edge, or surface of something ▪ *The door can only be locked from the inside.* ▪ *the inside of my mouth* **2** : an inner part of a building, machine, etc. ▪ *the inside of the church* ▪ *the insides of a computer* ▪ *I felt like my insides were tied up in knots.* [=I felt nervous, anxious, etc.] — **on the inside 1** : on the inner side, edge, or surface of something ▪ *The other car tried to pass the leader on the inside (of* the track). **2** — used to describe how someone is feeling • *She looked happy, but she was sad on the inside.* **3** : in a position within an organization or group • *The bank robbers had help from someone on the inside.* [=someone working for the bank]

²inside *adj, always before a noun* **1** : located on or near the inner side, edge, or surface of something • *an inside wall* • *the inside edge of her foot* • (*baseball*) *He struck out on an inside pitch.* **2 a** : coming from someone within a group or organization • *inside sources/information* • *an inside joke* [=a joke that is understood only by people with special knowledge about something] **b** : done by someone within a group or organization • *The police suspect that the bank robbery was an inside job.*

³inside *prep* **1** : in or into the inner part of (something or someone) • *We waited inside the store.* • *She kept her hands inside her pockets.* **2 a** : within the borders or limits of (something) • *He lives inside the city limits.* **b** : before the end of (a period of time) • *We should hear the results inside* [=in less than] *an hour.* **3** : belonging to (a group or organization) • *sources inside the company* — **inside of** *chiefly US* : INSIDE • *We waited inside of the store.*

⁴inside *adv* **1** : in the inner part of something • *I cleaned my car inside and out.* • *He keeps his feelings locked up inside.* [=he does not express his feelings] **2** : in or into the inner part of a building, room, etc. • *We went/stayed inside during the storm.* — **inside out 1** : so that the inner surface becomes the outer surface • *He was wearing his socks inside out.* **2** *informal* : very well and thoroughly • *She knows this area inside out.* — **turn (something) inside out** *informal* **1** : to cause (a place) to become disorganized while you are trying to find something • *I turned the closet inside out and still couldn't find those shoes.* **2** : to change (something) completely • *Her life was turned inside out after the accident.*

in·sid·er /ɪnˈsaɪdɚ, ˈɪnˌsaɪdɚ/ *n* [C] : a person who belongs to a group or organization and has special knowledge about it • *political insiders* • *an insider's view of Hollywood*

insider trading *n* [U] *finance* : the illegal activity of buying and selling a company's stocks while using secret information from a person who works for the company

in·sid·i·ous /ɪnˈsɪdijəs/ *adj, formal* : causing harm in a way that is gradual or not easily noticed • *an insidious enemy/disease* — **in·sid·i·ous·ly** *adv*

in·sight /ˈɪnˌsaɪt/ *n* **1** [U] : the ability to understand people and situations in a very clear way • *a leader of great insight* **2** [C/U] : an understanding of the true nature of something • *I had a sudden insight.* • *The author analyzes the problem with remarkable insight.* • *new insights into brain development* — **in·sight·ful** /ˈɪnˌsaɪtfəl/ *adj* • *an insightful comment/leader* — **in·sight·ful·ly** *adv*

— **in·sight·ful·ness** *n* [U]

in·sig·nia /ɪnˈsɪgnijə/ *n, pl* **insignia** *or US* **in·sig·ni·as** [C] : a badge or sign which shows that a person is a member of a particular group or has a particular rank

in·sig·nif·i·cant /ˌɪnsɪgˈnɪfɪkənt/ *adj* : small or unimportant • *insignificant details* — **in·sig·nif·i·cant·ly** *adv* — **in·sig·nif·i·cance** /ˌɪnsɪgˈnɪfɪkəns/ *n* [U]

in·sin·cere /ˌɪnsɪnˈsiɚ/ *adj* : not expressing or showing true feelings • *insincere flattery* • *an insincere apology/person* — **in·sin·cere·ly** *adv* — **in·sin·cer·i·ty** /ˌɪnsɪnˈserəti/ *n* [U]

in·sin·u·ate /ɪnˈsɪnjəˌweɪt/ *vb* **-at·ed; -at·ing** [T] **1** : to say (something, especially something bad or insulting) in an indirect way • *Are you insinuating that I cheated!?* **2** *formal* : to gradually make (yourself) a part of a group, a person's life, etc., often by behaving in a dishonest way • *He insinuated himself into her life.* — **insinuating** *adj* • *He made an insinuating remark about my weight.* — **in·sin·u·a·tion** /ɪnˌsɪnjəˈweɪʃən/ *n* [C/U] • *I resent your/the insinuation that I cheated.*

in·sip·id /ɪnˈsɪpəd/ *adj, formal* **1** : not interesting or exciting • *an insipid novel* **2** : lacking strong flavor : BLAND • *insipid food/flavors*

in·sist /ɪnˈsɪst/ *vb* **1** [T/I] : to demand that something happen or that someone do something • *She insisted that I (should) go.* • *"Come on, let's go." "Oh, all right, if/since you insist."* **2** [T] : to say (something) in a way that is very forceful and does not allow disagreement • *She kept insisting (that) she was right.* — **insist on/upon** *[phrasal vb]* **1** : to say or show that you believe that something is necessary or very important • *She insists on doing everything her own way.* **2** *informal* : to continue doing (something that other people think is annoying or unimportant) • *The people sitting next to us insisted on talking during the entire movie.*

in·sis·tence /ɪnˈsɪstəns/ *n* [U] **1** : the act of demanding something or saying something in a way that does not allow disagreement • *I was surprised by their insistence on privacy.* • *He enrolled in the army at his father's insistence.* [=because his father insisted that he should enroll] **2** : the quality or state of being insistent • *He spoke with great insistence of the need for reform.*

in·sis·tent /ɪnˈsɪstənt/ *adj* **1** : demanding that something happen or that someone do something • *My friends were insistent that I go. = They were insistent on my going.* [=they insisted that I go] **2** : happening for a long time and very difficult to ignore • *an insistent drumbeat* — **in·sis·tent·ly** *adv*

in·so·far as /ˌɪnsəˈfɑɚ/ *also* **in so far as** *conj, formal* : to the extent or degree that • *She helped us insofar as she was able.* [=as much as she could]

in·sole /ˈɪnˌsoʊl/ *n* [C] **1** : the bottom of the inside of a shoe **2** : a thin piece of material that you put at the bottom of the inside of a shoe for comfort

in·so·lent /ˈɪnsələnt/ *adj, somewhat for-*

mal : rude, impolite, or disrespectful ▪ *insolent children/behavior* — **in·so·lence** /ˈɪnsələns/ *n* [U] — **in·so·lent·ly** *adv*

in·sol·u·ble /ɪnˈsɑːljəbəl/ *adj* **1** *formal* : not able to be solved or explained ▪ *an insoluble mystery* **2** *technical* : not able to be dissolved in a liquid ▪ *a substance insoluble in water*

in·sol·vent /ɪnˈsɑːlvənt/ *adj* : not having enough money to pay debts ▪ *insolvent debtors* — **in·sol·ven·cy** /ɪnˈsɑːlvənsi/ *n* [U]

in·som·nia /ɪnˈsɑːmnijə/ *n* [U] : the condition of not being able to sleep

in·som·ni·ac /ɪnˈsɑːmniˌæk/ *n* [C] : a person who is not able to sleep

in·spect /ɪnˈspɛkt/ *vb* [T] **1** : to look at (something) carefully in order to learn more about it, to find problems, etc. ▪ *The guard inspected their passports.* ▪ *After the storm, we went outside to inspect the damage.* **2** : to officially visit a school, hospital, etc., in order to see if rules are being followed and things are in their proper condition ▪ *inspecting a restaurant for health code violations* — **in·spec·tion** /ɪnˈspɛkʃən/ *n* [C/U] ▪ *an inspection of the car/restaurant* ▪ *On closer inspection* [=when it was examined more closely], *the painting proved to be a fake.*

in·spec·tor /ɪnˈspɛktɚ/ *n* [C] **1** : a person whose job is to inspect something ▪ *a building inspector* ▪ *safety/health inspectors* [=people who make sure that a place or thing is safe/healthy] **2** : a police officer who is in charge of several police departments

inspector general *n* [C] : a person who is in charge of a group of inspectors or a system of inspection

in·spi·ra·tion /ˌɪnspəˈreɪʃən/ *n* **1 a** [U] : something that makes someone want to do something or that gives someone an idea about what to do or create ▪ *His paintings take/draw their inspiration from nature.* ▪ *Her early childhood provided (the) inspiration for her first novel.* ▪ *Her courage is a source of inspiration to us all.* **b** [C] : a person, place, experience, etc., that makes someone want to do or create something ▪ *Her courage is an inspiration to us all.* ▪ *She truly is an inspiration.* **2** [U, *singular*] : a good idea ▪ *Deciding to have the party outdoors was (a) sheer inspiration.* — **in·spi·ra·tion·al** /ˌɪnspəˈreɪʃənl/ *adj* ▪ *an inspirational speaker* ▪ *Her courage is inspirational.*

in·spire /ɪnˈspajɚ/ *vb* **-spired; -spir·ing** [T] **1** : to make (someone) want to do something : to give (someone) an idea about what to do or create ▪ *Her courage has inspired us.* ▪ *Her early childhood inspired her to write her first novel.* **2** : to cause (something) to happen or to be created or felt ▪ *His discoveries inspired a whole new line of scientific research.* ▪ *Her first novel was inspired by her early childhood.* ▪ *The news inspired hope.* — **in·spiring** *adj* ▪ *an inspiring leader/story*

inspired *adj* **1** : very good or clever ▪ *an inspired performance* **2** : having a particular cause or influence ▪ *Her comments were politically inspired.* [=were

made for political reasons] ▪ *Italian-inspired architecture*

in·sta·bil·i·ty /ˌɪnstəˈbɪləti/ *n* [U] **1** : the state of being likely to change ▪ *Investors are worried about the instability of the stock market.* **2** : the tendency to change your behavior very quickly or to react to things in an extremely emotional way ▪ *emotional/mental instability*

in·stall /ɪnˈstɑːl/ *vb* **1** [T/I] : to make (a machine, a service, etc.) ready to be used in a certain place ▪ *New locks were installed on the doors.* ▪ *installing a new phone system* ▪ *The software installs easily on your hard drive.* **2** [T] : to put (someone) in an official or important job ▪ *The college recently installed its first woman president.* — **in·stal·la·tion** /ˌɪnstəˈleɪʃən/ *n* [C/U] ▪ *easy software installation* ▪ *Her installation as president will take place tomorrow.* — **in·stall·er** *n* [C] ▪ *a professional carpet installer*

in·stall·ment (*US*) or chiefly *Brit* **in·stal·ment** /ɪnˈstɑːlmənt/ *n* **1** [C/U] : any one of a series of small payments that you make over a long time until you have paid the total cost of something ▪ *the last installment of a $20,000 loan* ▪ *pay for the computer in installments* ▪ (*US*) *We are paying on installment.* **2** [C] : any one of several parts of a long book, television program, etc., that are published or shown over a period of time ▪ *the first installment of a five-part series*

installment plan *n* [C] *US* : a way of paying for something by making a series of small payments over a long time

in·stance /ˈɪnstəns/ *n* [C] : an example of a particular type of action or situation ▪ *an instance of great courage* ▪ *In most instances the disease can be controlled by medication.* — **for instance** : as an example : for example ▪ *Lack of insurance is a problem for a lot of older people, like my grandmother, for instance.* ▪ *Now, take this car, for instance.*

¹**in·stant** /ˈɪnstənt/ *n* [C] : a very short period of time ▪ *For an instant, I forgot where I was.* ▪ *The ride was over in an instant.* ▪ *I knew it was him the instant (that)* [=as soon as] *I heard his voice.* ▪ *Come in the house, this instant!* [=immediately]

²**instant** *adj* **1** : becoming something very quickly ▪ *The movie was an instant hit/success.* ▪ *He became an instant celebrity.* **2** : happening or done without delay ▪ *an instant response* ▪ *The Internet provides instant access to information.* **3** *of food* : able to be made very quickly : partially prepared by the manufacturer so that final preparation is quick and easy ▪ *instant coffee/pudding/rice*

in·stan·ta·neous /ˌɪnstənˈteɪnijəs/ *adj* : happening very quickly ▪ *an instantaneous response* — **in·stan·ta·neous·ly** *adv*

in·stant·ly /ˈɪnstəntli/ *adv* : without delay : IMMEDIATELY ▪ *They instantly fell in love.* ▪ *She was killed instantly when her car hit a tree.*

instant messaging *n* [U] : a system for sending messages quickly over the Internet from one computer to another computer — **instant message** n [C]

in·stant replay n [C/U] US : a recording of an action in a sports event that can be shown on television immediately after the original play happens ▪ *We watched the goal again on instant replay.* — called also (Brit) **action replay**

in·stead /ɪnˈstɛd/ adv — used to say that one thing is done or that one thing or person is chosen when another is not chosen, cannot be done, etc. ▪ *I was going to write you an e-mail, but I decided to call instead.* ▪ *They didn't choose me: they chose her instead.* = *They chose her instead of me.* ▪ *Instead of buying a new car, I bought a used one.*

in·step /ˈɪnˌstɛp/ n [C] **1** : the raised middle part of the top of your foot between the toes and the ankle **2** : the part of a shoe, sock, etc., that fits over the instep

in·sti·gate /ˈɪnstəˌgeɪt/ vb **-gat·ed; -gat·ing** [T] : to cause (something) to happen or begin ▪ *an increase in the amount of violence instigated by gangs* — **in·sti·ga·tion** /ˌɪnstəˈgeɪʃən/ n [U] ▪ *the instigation of divorce proceedings* ▪ *It was done at the instigation of the company's president.* [=the company's president caused it to be done] — **in·sti·ga·tor** /ˈɪnstəˌgeɪtɚ/ n [C]

in·still (US) or Brit **in·stil** /ɪnˈstɪl/ vb [T] : to gradually cause someone to have (an attitude, feeling, etc.) ▪ *instill character/discipline* ▪ *They have instilled a love of music in/into their children.*

in·stinct /ˈɪnˌstɪŋkt/ n **1** [C/U] **a** : a natural desire or tendency that makes you want to act in a particular way ▪ *Cats possess a natural hunting instinct.* ▪ *a decision based on (gut) instinct* **b** : something you know without learning it or thinking about it ▪ *You have to learn to trust/follow your instincts.* [=to trust your feelings about what is right or true] ▪ *He knew by instinct what not to say.* **2** [C] : a natural ability ▪ *a strong survival instinct* = *a strong instinct for survival* — **in·stinc·tive** /ɪnˈstɪŋktɪv/ adj ▪ *instinctive reactions/behaviors* — **in·stinc·tive·ly** adv

¹**in·sti·tute** /ˈɪnstəˌtuːt, Brit ˈɪnstəˌtjuːt/ n [C] : an organization created for a particular purpose (such as research or education) ▪ *an institute for research into the causes of mental illness* ▪ *an art institute*

²**institute** vb **-tut·ed; -tut·ing** [T] formal : to begin or create (a new law, rule, system, etc.) ▪ *They have instituted a new policy.*

in·sti·tu·tion /ˌɪnstəˈtuːʃən, Brit ˌɪnstəˈtjuːʃən/ n **1** [C] **a** : an established organization ▪ *educational/academic/financial institutions* **b** : a place where an organization takes care of people for a usually long period of time ▪ *a mental institution* [=a hospital for people with mental or emotional problems] ▪ *a correctional institution* [=a prison] **2** [C] **a** : a custom, practice, or law that is accepted and used by many people ▪ *the institution of marriage/slavery* **b** : someone or something that is very well known and established in a particular field or

place ▪ *He is an institution in local politics.* [=people consider him to be a regular part of local politics] **3** [U] : the act of beginning or creating a new law, rule, system, etc. ▪ *the institution of new rules* — **in·sti·tu·tion·al** /ˌɪnstəˈtuːʃənl̩, Brit ˌɪnstəˈtjuːʃənl̩/ adj ▪ *institutional power/funds/care*

in·sti·tu·tion·al·ize also Brit **in·sti·tu·tion·al·ise** /ˌɪnstəˈtuːʃənəˌlaɪz, Brit ˌɪnstəˈtjuːʃənəˌlaɪz/ vb **-ized; -iz·ing** [T] **1** : to cause (a custom, practice, law, etc.) to become accepted and used by many people ▪ *It will take time to institutionalize these reforms.* **2** : to put (someone, such as a mentally ill person) in an institution (sense 1b) ▪ *They had to institutionalize their youngest son.* — **in·sti·tu·tion·al·i·za·tion** also Brit **in·sti·tu·tion·al·i·sa·tion** /ˌɪnstəˌtuːʃənəlaɪˈzeɪʃən, Brit ˌɪnstəˌtjuːʃənəˌlaɪˈzeɪʃən/ n [U]

institutionalized also Brit **institutionalised** adj **1** : created and controlled by an established organization ▪ *institutionalized religion* **2** : established as a common and accepted part of a system or culture ▪ *an institutionalized practice* ▪ *institutionalized beliefs*

in·struct /ɪnˈstrʌkt/ vb [T] formal **1** : to teach (someone) a subject, skill, etc. ▪ *His friend instructed him in English.* ▪ *She instructed us on what to do.* **2** : to give (someone) an order or command ▪ *She instructed us to remain in our seats.* = *She instructed us that we were to remain in our seats.*

in·struc·tion /ɪnˈstrʌkʃən/ n **1** [C] **a** : a statement that describes how to do something ▪ *She gave us instructions.* [=directions] ▪ *an instruction manual* **b** : an order or command ▪ *I gave you explicit instructions to be here by six o'clock.* ▪ *Don't you know how to follow instructions?* **2** [U] : the action or process of teaching : the act of instructing someone ▪ *The students are receiving instruction in algebra.*

in·struc·tion·al /ɪnˈstrʌkʃənl̩/ adj : giving information about how to do or use something ▪ *instructional materials/videos*

in·struc·tive /ɪnˈstrʌktɪv/ adj : providing knowledge or information ▪ *an instructive lesson/experience*

in·struc·tor /ɪnˈstrʌktɚ/ n [C] **1** : a person who teaches a subject or skill ▪ *a swimming/driving instructor* **2** US : a teacher in a college or university who is not a professor

in·stru·ment /ˈɪnstrəmənt/ n [C] **1** : a tool or device used for a particular purpose ▪ *surgical/laboratory instruments* **2** : a device that measures something (such as temperature or distance) ▪ *The pilot knows how to read the plane's instruments.* **3** : a device that is used to make music ▪ *Do you play any (musical) instruments?* **4** : someone or something that can be used to do or achieve something ▪ *an instrument of social change* [=something that causes social change]

in·stru·men·tal /ˌɪnstrəˈmɛntl̩/ adj **1** : very important in helping or causing something to happen or be done ▪ *He was instrumental in organizing the club.* **2**

music : written for or performed on musical instruments without singing ▪ *instrumental music* — **in·stru·men·tal·ly** /ˌɪnstrəˈmɛntl̩i/ *adv*

in·stru·men·tal·ist /ˌɪnstrəˈmɛntlɪst/ *n* [C] : a person who plays a musical instrument

in·stru·men·ta·tion /ˌɪnstrəmənˈteɪʃən/ *n* [U] **1** : a way of writing or arranging music so that it can be performed in a particular style or by particular instruments ▪ *jazz instrumentation* **2** : a set of instruments ▪ *the airplane's instrumentation*

in·sub·or·di·nate /ˌɪnsəˈboɚdənət/ *adj, formal* : refusing to follow orders ▪ *insubordinate soldiers/behavior/attitudes* — **in·sub·or·di·na·tion** /ˌɪnsəˌboɚdəˈneɪʃən/ *n* [U] ▪ *She was fired for insubordination.*

in·sub·stan·tial /ˌɪnsəbˈstænʃəl/ *adj* **1** : not large or important ▪ *an insubstantial amount of money* **2** : not strong or solid ▪ *a thin and insubstantial material* — **in·sub·stan·ti·al·i·ty** /ˌɪnsəbˌstænʃiˈæləti/ *n* [U]

in·suf·fer·able /ɪnˈsʌfrəbəl/ *adj* : too unpleasant to deal with or accept ▪ *insufferable arrogance* ▪ *an insufferable bore* — **in·suf·fer·ably** /ɪnˈsʌfrəbli/ *adv*

in·suf·fi·cient /ˌɪnsəˈfɪʃənt/ *adj, somewhat formal* : not having or providing enough of what is needed ▪ *There was insufficient evidence to prove their case.* — **in·suf·fi·cien·cy** /ˌɪnsəˈfɪʃənsi/ *n, pl* **-cies** [C/U] — **in·suf·fi·cient·ly** *adv*

in·su·lar /ˈɪnsʊlɚ, Brit ˈɪnsjʊlə/ *adj* : not connected to or interested in new or different ideas, other cultures, etc. ▪ *an insular group* ▪ *an insular way of thinking* — **in·su·lar·i·ty** /ˌɪnsʊˈlerəti, Brit ˌɪnsjʊˈlærəti/ *n* [U]

in·su·late /ˈɪnsəˌleɪt, Brit ˈɪnsjʊˌleɪt/ *vb* **-lat·ed; -lat·ing** **1** [T/I] : to add a material or substance to (something) in order to stop heat, electricity, or sound from going into or out of it ▪ *They insulated the attic.* ▪ *an insulated ceiling* **2** [T] : to prevent (someone or something) from dealing with or experiencing something ▪ *I wish I could insulate my children from/against painful experiences.* — **in·su·la·tor** /ˈɪnsəˌleɪtɚ, Brit ˈɪnsjʊˌleɪtə/ *n* [C] ▪ *Fiberglass is a good insulator.*

in·su·la·tion /ˌɪnsəˈleɪʃən, Brit ˌɪnsjʊˈleɪʃən/ *n* [U] **1** : a material or substance that is used to stop heat, electricity, or sound from going into or out of something ▪ *fiberglass insulation* **2** : the quality or state of being insulated ▪ *materials used to provide insulation* **b** : the act of insulating something ▪ *I hired them to do the insulation of the attic.*

in·su·lin /ˈɪnsəl(ə)n, Brit ˈɪnsjʊlən/ *n* [U] : a substance that your body makes and uses to turn sugar into energy ◆ *If your body does not produce enough insulin, you will develop diabetes.*

¹in·sult /ɪnˈsʌlt/ *vb* [T] : to do or say something offensive that shows a lack of respect for (someone) ▪ *We were greatly insulted by his rudeness.* ▪ *Don't insult my intelligence.* [=don't treat me as though I am stupid] — **in·sult·ing** /ɪnˈsʌltɪŋ/ *adj* ▪ *an insulting remark*

²in·sult /ˈɪnˌsʌlt/ *n* [C] : a rude or offensive act or statement ▪ *We could hear them angrily trading/exchanging insults (with each other).* ▪ *The assignment was an insult to our intelligence.* [=the assignment was too simple] — **add insult to injury** : to do or say something that makes a bad situation even worse for someone ▪ *We were forced to work longer hours each week, and to add insult to injury, the company cut our pay.*

in·sur·ance /ɪnˈʃɚəns/ *n* [U] **1** : an agreement in which a person makes regular payments to a company and the company promises to pay money if the person is injured or dies, or to pay money equal to the value of something (such as a house or car) if it is damaged, lost, or stolen ▪ *health/medical/auto/life insurance* ▪ *an insurance policy* ▪ *We took out insurance on* [=insured] *the boat.* **2 a** : the amount of money a person regularly pays an insurance company as part of an insurance agreement ▪ *What's the monthly insurance on your car?* **b** : the amount of money that a person receives from an insurance company ▪ *We used the insurance (money) to buy a new house.* **3** : the business of providing insurance ▪ *a job in insurance* ▪ *an insurance company* **4** : protection from bad things that may happen in the future ▪ *Education provides insurance against instability in the job market.*

in·sure /ɪnˈʃɚ/ *vb* **-sured; -sur·ing** [T] **1 a** : to buy insurance for (something, such as property or health) ▪ *We insured our house/boat.* **b** : to provide insurance for (something) ▪ *the company that insures my car; also* : to provide (someone) with insurance ▪ *She can't find a company to insure her.* **2** *US* : to make (something) sure, certain, or safe : ENSURE ▪ *Careful planning will insure success.* — **insure against** [*phrasal vb*] **1** : to make (something bad) less likely to happen usually by planning and preparing ▪ *exercising to insure against health problems* **2 insure (someone) against** : to protect (someone) from (something bad) ▪ *We can't always insure our children against harm.* — **in·sur·er** /ɪnˈʃɚɚ/ *n* [C]

in·sur·gent /ɪnˈsɚdʒənt/ *n* [C] : a person who fights against an established government or authority — **in·sur·gen·cy** /ɪnˈsɚdʒənsi/ *n, pl* **-cies** [C/U] ▪ *The insurgency* [=rebellion] *has continued for three years.*

in·sur·mount·able /ˌɪnsɚˈmaʊntəbəl/ *adj* : impossible to solve or get control of ▪ *insurmountable obstacles/problems*

in·sur·rec·tion /ˌɪnsɚˈrɛkʃən/ *n* [C/U] : a usually violent attempt to take control of a government ▪ *an armed insurrection* — **in·sur·rec·tion·ist** /ˌɪnsɚˈrɛkʃənɪst/ *n* [C] ▪ *a group of armed insurrectionists*

in·tact /ɪnˈtækt/ *adj* : not broken or damaged ▪ *The house survived the war intact.* ▪ *Their friendship remains intact.*

in·take /ˈɪnˌteɪk/ *n* **1** [C/U] : the amount of something (such as food or drink) that is taken into your body ▪ *your daily intake of sugar* **2** [C] : the act of taking something (such as air) into your body ▪ *a sudden intake of breath* **3** [C] : a place or part where liquid or air enters something (such as an engine) ▪ *the fuel intake* **4** [C/U] *Brit* : the number of things or people that are taken into something (such as an organization) ▪ *the school's intake of students*

in·tan·gi·ble /ɪnˈtændʒəbəl/ *adj* : not made of a physical substance ▪ *Leadership is an intangible asset to a company.* — **intangible** *n* [C] ▪ *intangibles such as talent and experience*

in·te·ger /ˈɪntɪdʒɚ/ *n* [C] *mathematics* : any number that is not a fraction or decimal ▪ *positive and negative integers*

in·te·gral /ˈɪntɪgrəl/ *adj* : very important and necessary ▪ *She is an integral part of their lives.* ▪ *His character is integral to the story.* — **in·te·gral·ly** /ˈɪntɪgrəli/ *adv*

in·te·grate /ˈɪntəˌgreɪt/ *vb* **-grat·ed; -grat·ing 1** [T] **a** : to combine (two or more things) to form or create something ▪ *a design that integrates art and/with technology* **b** : to make (something) a part of another larger thing ▪ *These books should be integrated into the curriculum.* **2** [T/I] **a** : to make (a person or group) part of a larger group or organization ▪ *efforts to integrate women into the military* ▪ *immigrants who have integrated into American culture* **b** : to end a policy that keeps people of different races apart in (a place, such as a school) ▪ *efforts to integrate* [=desegregate] *public schools* — **integrated** *adj* ▪ *integrated schools/neighborhoods* — **in·te·gra·tion** /ˌɪntəˈgreɪʃən/ *n* [U] ▪ *racial/social integration*

integrated circuit *n* [C] *computers* : MICROCHIP

in·te·gra·tion·ist /ˌɪntəˈgreɪʃənɪst/ *n* [C] : a person who supports racial integration

in·teg·ri·ty /ɪnˈtɛgrəti/ *n* [U] **1** : the quality of being honest and fair ▪ *I admire his integrity.* **2** : the state of being complete or whole ▪ *the cultural integrity of the community* ▪ *The earthquake damaged the building's structural integrity.*

in·tel·lect /ˈɪntəˌlɛkt/ *n* **1** [C/U] : the ability to think in a logical way ▪ *a woman of superior intellect* ▪ *a sharp/keen intellect* **2** [C] : a very smart person ▪ *He was one of the greatest intellects of his time.*

¹in·tel·lec·tu·al /ˌɪntəˈlɛktʃəwəl/ *adj* **1** : of or relating to the ability to think in a logical way ▪ *intellectual challenges/activities/development* **2 a** : involving serious study and thought ▪ *the social and intellectual life of the campus* **b** *of a person* : smart and enjoying serious study and thought ▪ *a rather intellectual poet* — **in·tel·lec·tu·al·ly** /ˌɪntəˈlɛktʃəwəli/ *adv*

²intellectual *n* [C] : a smart person who enjoys serious study and thought ▪ *She's a hard worker but she's no great intellectual.*

in·tel·li·gence /ɪnˈtɛlədʒəns/ *n* [U] **1** : the ability to learn or understand things or to deal with new or difficult situations ▪ *a person of average/normal/high/low intelligence* **2** : secret information that a

government collects about an enemy or possible enemy ▪ *military intelligence* ▪ *intelligence sources/operations; also* : a government organization that collects such information ▪ *He was the head of army intelligence.*

intelligence quotient *n* [C] : IQ

in·tel·li·gent /ɪnˈtɛlədʒənt/ *adj* **1** : having or showing the ability to easily learn or understand things or to deal with new or difficult situations ▪ *highly/very intelligent* [=*smart*] *people* ▪ *an intelligent decision/question* **2** : able to learn and understand things ▪ *Dogs are intelligent animals.* ▪ *They are looking for signs of intelligent life* [=creatures that can learn and understand things] *on other planets.* **3** : having an ability to deal with problems or situations that resembles or suggests the ability of an intelligent person ▪ *intelligent software* — **in·tel·li·gent·ly** *adv*

in·tel·li·gen·tsia /ɪnˌtɛləˈdʒɛntsijə, -ˌtɛləˈgɛntsijə/ *n* [*singular*] : a group of intelligent and well-educated people who guide or try to guide the political, artistic, or social development of their society ▪ *Her new book has been embraced by the intelligentsia.*

in·tel·li·gi·ble /ɪnˈtɛlədʒəbəl/ *adj* : able to be understood ▪ *an intelligible plan; especially* : clear enough to be heard, read, etc. ▪ *Very little of the passage/recording was intelligible.* — **in·tel·li·gi·bil·i·ty** /ɪnˌtɛlədʒəˈbɪləti/ *n* [U] — **in·tel·li·gi·bly** /ɪnˈtɛlədʒəbli/ *adv*

in·tem·per·ate /ɪnˈtɛmpərət/ *adj, formal* **1** : having extreme conditions ▪ *an intemperate* [=extremely *hot/cold*] *climate/zone* **2** : having or showing a lack of emotional calmness or control ▪ *an intemperate discussion* — **in·tem·per·ance** /ɪnˈtɛmpərəns/ *n* [U]

in·tend /ɪnˈtɛnd/ *vb* [T] **1 a** : to have (something) in your mind as a purpose or goal ▪ *He didn't intend to hurt anybody.* ▪ *She clearly intends to stay here.* ▪ *I didn't intend any disrespect.* **b** : to plan for or want (someone or something) to do or be something ▪ *They intended the wedding to be formal.* ▪ *He will graduate this spring if everything goes as intended.* **2 a** : to want (something that you control, provide, or have made) to be used for a particular purpose or by a particular person ▪ *The film was intended to educate people.* ▪ *The author intended the book to be read by adults.* = *The book was intended for adults.* **b** : to want (something) to express a particular meaning ▪ *What was intended by the author?* [=what meaning was the author trying to express?] — **in·tend·ed** /ɪnˈtɛndəd/ *adj* ▪ *The book failed to reach its intended audience.*

in·tense /ɪnˈtɛns/ *adj* **1** : very strong or extreme ▪ *intense heat/cold/pain/anger* **2 a** : done with or showing great energy, enthusiasm, or effort ▪ *many years of intense study* ▪ *an intense effort* **b** *of a person* : very serious ▪ *an intense young man* — **in·tense·ly** *adv*

in·ten·si·fi·er /ɪnˈtɛnsəˌfajɚ/ *n* [C] *grammar* : a word (such as *really* or *very*) that gives force or emphasis to a statement — called also *intensive*

in·ten·si·fy /ɪnˈtɛnsəˌfaɪ/ *vb* **-fies; -fied; -fy·ing** **1** [*I*] : to become stronger or more extreme • *The fighting/storm has intensified.* **2** [*T*] : to make (something) stronger or more extreme • *They intensified their efforts.* — **in·ten·si·fi·ca·tion** /ɪnˌtɛnsəfəˈkeɪʃən/ *n* [*U, singular*]

in·ten·si·ty /ɪnˈtɛnsəti/ *n, pl* **-ties** **1** [*U*] : extreme strength or force • *the intensity of the heat/argument* **2** [*C/U*] : the degree or amount of strength or force that something has • *hurricanes of different intensities* • *The noise grew in intensity.* [=became louder]

¹in·ten·sive /ɪnˈtɛnsɪv/ *adj* **1** : involving very great effort or work • *an intensive effort* **2** *grammar* : giving force or emphasis to a statement • *an intensive pronoun/adverb* **3** : designed to increase production without using more land • *intensive farming/agriculture* — **in·ten·sive·ly** *adv*

²intensive *n* [*C*] *grammar* : INTENSIFIER

intensive care *n* [*U*] : a section of a hospital where special medical equipment and services are provided for patients who are seriously injured or ill • *patients in intensive care = patients in the intensive care unit* [=*ICU*]

¹in·tent /ɪnˈtɛnt/ *n* [*C*] : the thing that you plan to do or achieve • *She thinks I'm trying to oppose her, but that's not my intent.* • *What was the writer's intent?* — **to all intents and purposes** *also US* **for all intents and purposes** — used to say that one thing has the same effect or result as something else • *Their decision to begin bombing was, to all intents and purposes, a declaration of war.*

²intent *adj* : showing concentration or great attention • *an intent gaze* — **intent on/upon (something)** : giving all of your attention and effort to a specific task or goal • *They were intent on their work.* • *She seems intent on destroying our credibility.* — **in·tent·ly** *adv* • *She listened intently to the news report.*

in·ten·tion /ɪnˈtɛnʃən/ *n* [*C*] : the thing that you plan to do or achieve • *She announced her intention to run for governor.* • *He has no intention of marrying her.* [=he does not intend to marry her] • *He has good intentions, but his suggestions aren't really helpful.*

in·ten·tion·al /ɪnˈtɛnʃənl/ *adj* : done in a way that is planned or intended : DELIBERATE • *an intentional act of defiance* • *I apologize for the error. It was not intentional.* — **in·ten·tion·al·ly** *adv*

in·ter /ɪnˈtɚ/ *vb* **-terred; -ter·ring** [*T*] *formal* : to bury (a dead body)

inter- /ɪntɚ/ *prefix* **1** : between : among • *together* • *interlock* • *interrelation* **2** : involving two or more • *international*

in·ter·act /ɪntɚˈækt/ *vb* [*I*] **1** : to talk or do things with other people • *a quiet child who doesn't interact much (with other children)* **2** : to come together and have an effect on each other • *When these two drugs interact (with each other), the results can be deadly.* — **in·ter·ac·tion** /ɪntɚˈækʃən/ *n* [*C/U*] • *social interactions*

in·ter·ac·tive /ɪntɚˈæktɪv/ *adj* **1** : designed to respond to the actions, commands, etc., of a user • *an interactive Web site* **2** : requiring people to talk with each other or do things together • *interactive learning* — **in·ter·ac·tive·ly** *adv*

in·ter·cede /ɪntɚˈsiːd/ *vb* **-ced·ed; -ced·ing** [*I*] *formal* : to try to help settle an argument or disagreement between two or more people or groups • *I interceded in their argument.* : to speak to someone in order to defend or help another person • *Several other employees interceded (with the boss) on her behalf.* — **in·ter·ces·sion** /ɪntɚˈsɛʃən/ *n* [*C/U*]

in·ter·cept /ɪntɚˈsɛpt/ *vb* [*T*] **1** : to stop and take someone or something that is going from one place to another place before that person or thing gets there • *intercept a secret message* **2** *sports* : to catch or receive (a pass made by an opponent) • *He intercepted the pass/ball.* • *(American football) The quarterback was intercepted twice.* [=two passes thrown by the quarterback were intercepted] — **in·ter·cep·tion** /ɪntɚˈsɛpʃən/ *n* [*C/U*]

¹in·ter·change /ɪntɚˌtʃeɪndʒ/ *n* **1** [*C/U*] : the act of sharing or exchanging things • *a friendly interchange of ideas* **2** [*C*] : an area where two or more highways meet that is designed to allow traffic to move from one highway to another without stopping

²in·ter·change /ɪntɚˈtʃeɪndʒ/ *vb* **-changed; -chang·ing** [*T*] : to put each of two or more things in the place of the other • *We interchanged the two tires.* — **in·ter·change·able** /ɪntɚˈtʃeɪndʒəbəl/ *adj* • *These words are similar but not interchangeable (with each other).* — **in·ter·change·ably** /ɪntɚˈtʃeɪndʒəbli/ *adv*

in·ter·col·le·giate /ɪntɚkəˈliːdʒət/ *adj*, *always before a noun, chiefly US* : involving or involved in competition between colleges • *intercollegiate sports/athletics*

in·ter·com /ɪntɚˌkɑːm/ *n* [*C*] : a system which allows a person speaking into a microphone to be heard on a speaker by people in a different room or area • *I heard my name called on/over the intercom.*

in·ter·con·nect /ɪntɚkəˈnɛkt/ *vb* [*T/I*] : to connect (two or more things) with each other • *The systems are interconnected with/by wires.* • *a group of interconnecting stories/rooms* — **in·ter·con·nec·tion** /ɪntɚkəˈnɛkʃən/ *n* [*C/U*]

in·ter·con·ti·nen·tal /ɪntɚˌkɑːntəˈnɛntl/ *adj* : traveling or occurring between continents • *intercontinental flights/trade/travel*

in·ter·course /ɪntɚˌkoɚs/ *n* [*U*] **1** : SEXUAL INTERCOURSE **2** *formal* : communication and actions between people • *the unspoken rules of social intercourse*

in·ter·de·pen·dent /ɪntɚdɪˈpɛndənt/ *adj* : related in such a way that each needs or depends on the other • *The two nations are economically interdependent.* — **in·ter·de·pen·den·tly** *adv*

in·ter·dis·ci·plin·ary /ɪntɚˈdɪsəpləˌneri/ *adj* : involving two or more academic, scientific, or artistic areas of knowledge •

interdisciplinary studies

¹in·ter·est /ˈɪntrəst/ *n* **1 a** [*U, singular*] : a feeling of wanting to learn more about something or to be involved in something ▪ *She took/had an interest in the debate.* ▪ *He expressed/showed an interest in learning more.* ▪ *She has had a lifelong interest in music.* ▪ *I have no interest in politics.* [=I am not interested in politics] ▪ *The kids soon lost interest in the toy.* ▪ *The topic held/kept our interest.* ▪ *I've been following his career with (great) interest.* **b** [*U*] : a quality that attracts your attention and makes you want to learn more about something or to be involved in something ▪ *The stories about his personal life add interest to the book.* ▪ *I thought this article might be of interest* [=interesting] *to you.* ▪ *a story that has human interest* = *a human-interest story* [=a story that is interesting because it involves the experiences of real people] **2** [*C*] : something (such as a hobby) that a person enjoys learning about or doing ▪ *Music is one of her many interests.* **3** [*C*] — used when discussing what is the best or most helpful thing for someone ▪ *It's in your (own) interest to keep silent.* ▪ *We are thinking of the child's best interests.* [=of what is best for the child] ▪ *We did it in the interest of* [=for the sake of] *fairness.* **4** [*U*] **a** : the money paid by a borrower for the use of borrowed money ▪ *We pay six percent interest on the loan.* **b** : money paid to you by a bank for the money you have in a bank account ▪ *He made about $500 in interest last year.* **5** [*C*] : a legal share in a business or property ▪ *They offered to buy his interest in the company.* **6** [*plural*] : a group financially involved in an industry or business ▪ *This law is opposed by the oil interests.* — see also SPECIAL INTEREST

²interest *vb* [*T*] **1** : to cause (someone) to want to learn more about something or to become involved in something ▪ *Military history doesn't really interest me.* ▪ *It interested me to learn that she had once lived in California.* **2** : to persuade (someone) to have, take, or participate in (something) ▪ *Can I interest you in a game of tennis?* [=would you like to play tennis?]

in·ter·est·ed /ˈɪntrəstəd/ *adj* **1 a** : wanting to learn more about something or to become involved in something ▪ *students who are interested in archaeology* **b** : having the desire to do or have something ▪ *Are you interested in playing tennis?* [=would you like to play tennis?] **2** : having a direct or personal involvement in something ▪ *The plan will have to be approved by all interested parties.*

in·ter·est·ing /ˈɪntrəstɪŋ/ *adj* : attracting your attention and making you want to learn more about something or to be involved in something : not dull or boring ▪ *an interesting book/movie* ▪ *It will be interesting to see what she does.* ▪ *This building has an interesting history.* — **in·ter·est·ing·ly** *adv* ▪ *Interestingly (enough), these animals rarely fight.* [=it is interesting that these animals rarely fight]

¹in·ter·face /ˈɪntɚˌfeɪs/ *n* [*C*] **1** : the place or area at which different things meet and communicate with or affect each other ▪ *the interface between engineering and science* **2** : a system that is used for operating a computer ▪ *The software has a user interface that's easy to operate.*

²interface *vb* **-faced; -fac·ing** [*T/I*] : to connect or become connected ▪ *the point at which the two machines interface*

in·ter·fere /ˌɪntɚˈfiɚ/ *vb* **-fered; -fer·ing** [*I*] : to become involved in the activities and concerns of other people when your involvement is not wanted ▪ *He's always interfering in my life.* — **interfere with** [*phrasal vb*] : to stop or slow (something) ▪ *The drug might interfere with a child's physical development.*

in·ter·fer·ence /ˌɪntɚˈfiɚəns/ *n* [*U*] **1** : involvement in the activities and concerns of other people when your involvement is not wanted ▪ *We had to put up with constant interference from the neighbors.* **2** : additional signals that weaken or block the main signal in a radio or television broadcast ▪ *It was hard to hear the radio program because of all the interference.* **3** *sports* : the act of illegally hitting or getting in the way of an opponent ▪ *a hockey player receiving a penalty for interference* — **run interference** *American football* : to run in front of the player who is carrying the ball in order to block opponents ▪ *(figurative) He was able to survive the scandal only because his assistants ran interference for him.*

in·ter·im /ˈɪntərəm/ *n* [*singular*] : a period of time between events : INTERVAL ▪ *The regulations will change next winter, and in the interim* [=meanwhile]*, we'll be working hard to prepare.* — **interim** *adj, always before a noun* ▪ *an interim solution*

¹in·te·ri·or /ɪnˈtɪrijɚ/ *adj, always before a noun* : located on the inside of something ▪ *a large car with lots of interior room* ▪ *interior walls* ▪ *interior paint/lights*

²interior *n* [*C*] **1** : an inner part, area, or surface ▪ *a black car with gray leather interior* ▪ *the interior of the house* **2** : the part of a country that is far from the coast ▪ *the interior of Australia* **3** : the events and activities of a country that involve the country itself rather than foreign countries ▪ *Secretary of the Interior*

interior design *n* [*U*] : the art or job of planning how the rooms of a building should be furnished and decorated — called also *interior decoration* — **interior designer** *n* [*C*]

interj *abbr* interjection

in·ter·ject /ˌɪntɚˈdʒɛkt/ *vb* [*T/I*] *formal* : to interrupt that someone else is saying with a comment, remark, etc. ▪ *If I may interject, I have something to add.*

in·ter·jec·tion /ˌɪntɚˈdʒɛkʃən/ *n* [*C*] *grammar* : a spoken word, phrase, or sound that expresses sudden or strong feeling ▪ *interjections such as "oh," "alas," and "wow"*

in·ter·lace /ˌɪntɚˈleɪs/ *vb* **-laced; -lac·ing** [*T/I*] : to join together (narrow things, such as strings or branches) by crossing them over and under each other

- *Interlace the branches and bend them into a circle.*

in·ter·link /ˌɪntə'lɪŋk/ *vb* [T/I] : to connect (two or more things) together : LINK ▪ *interlink Web sites*

in·ter·lock /ˌɪntə'lɑːk/ *vb* [T/I] : to connect or lock (two or more things) together ▪ *The pieces of the puzzle interlock (with each other).*

in·ter·lop·er /ˌɪntə'loʊpə/ *n* [C] : a person who is not wanted or welcome by the other people in a situation or place ▪ *The older kids regarded her as an interloper.*

in·ter·lude /ˈɪntə,luːd/ *n* [C] : a period of time between events or activities ▪ *They met again after a two-year interlude.*

in·ter·mar·ry /ˌɪntə'meri/ *vb* -ries; -ried; -ry·ing [I] : to marry a member of a different racial, social, or religious group ▪ *The settlers and the native people seldom intermarried.* — **in·ter·mar·riage** /ˌɪntə'merɪdʒ/ *n* [C/U]

in·ter·me·di·ary /ˌɪntə'miːdiˌeri/ *n, pl* -ar·ies [C] : a person who works with opposing sides in an argument or dispute in order to bring about an agreement

in·ter·me·di·ate /ˌɪntə'miːdijət/ *adj* **1** : occurring in the middle of a process or series ▪ *an intermediate stage of growth* **2** : relating to or having the knowledge or skill of someone who is more advanced than a beginner but not yet an expert ▪ *an intermediate swimming class* ▪ *an intermediate swimmer* — **intermediate** *n* [C] ▪ *a swimming class for intermediates*

in·ter·ment /ɪn'tɚmənt/ *n* [C/U] *formal* : the act of burying a dead person

in·ter·mi·na·ble /ɪn'tɚmənəbəl/ *adj, disapproving* : continuing for a very long time ▪ *an interminable wait/war* — **in·ter·mi·na·bly** /ɪn'tɚmənəbli/ *adv*

in·ter·min·gle /ˌɪntə'mɪŋgəl/ *vb* -min·gled; -min·gling [T/I] : to mix together ▪ *In her stories, science fiction and romance are intermingled.* ▪ *The colors intermingle perfectly (with each other) in the painting.*

in·ter·mis·sion /ˌɪntə'mɪʃən/ *n* [C] : a short break between the parts of a play, movie, concert, etc. ▪ *We'll return after a brief intermission.*

in·ter·mit·tent /ˌɪntə'mɪtnt/ *adj* : starting, stopping, and starting again ▪ *The forecast is for intermittent rain.* — **in·ter·mit·tent·ly** *adv*

¹**in·tern** /ˈɪn,tɚn/ *n* [C] *US* **1** : a student or recent graduate who works for a period of time at a job in order to get experience ▪ *a teaching intern* **2** : a person who works in a hospital in order to complete training as a doctor — **intern** *vb* [I] ▪ *He interned* [=worked as an intern] *at the university hospital.* — **in·tern·ship** /ˈɪn,tɚn,ʃɪp/ *n* [C] ▪ *He will finish his internship in April.*

²**in·tern** /ˈɪn,tɚn, ɪn'tɚn/ *vb* [T] : to put (someone who has not been accused of a crime) in prison for political reasons especially during a war ▪ *protesting the government's decision to intern citizens without evidence of wrongdoing* — **in·tern·ment** /ɪn'tɚnmənt/ *n* [U] ▪ *internment camps*

in·ter·nal /ɪn'tɚnl/ *adj* **1** : existing or located on the inside of something ▪ *the internal structure of the planet* **2** : coming from inside ▪ *internal pressures* **3 a** : existing or occurring within your body ▪ *internal bleeding/organs* **b** : existing or occurring within your mind ▪ *internal doubts/thoughts* **4 a** : existing or occurring within a country ▪ *internal affairs* **b** : existing or occurring within an organization (such as a company or business) ▪ *an internal memo* — **in·ter·nal·ly** *adv*

internal combustion engine *n* [C] : a type of engine that is used for most vehicles : an engine in which the fuel is burned within engine cylinders

in·ter·nal·ize *also Brit* **in·ter·nal·ise** /ɪn'tɚnə,laɪz/ *vb* -ized; -iz·ing [T] : to make (something, such as an idea or an attitude) an important part of the kind of person you are ▪ *They have internalized their parents' values.*

internal medicine *n* [U] *US* : the work of a doctor who treats diseases that do not require surgery

Internal Revenue Service *n* — **the Internal Revenue Service** : the department of the U.S. federal government that is responsible for collecting taxes — *abbr.* IRS

in·ter·na·tion·al /ˌɪntə'næʃənl/ *adj* **1** : involving two or more countries : occurring between countries ▪ *international trade/relations/agreements/flights* **2** : made up of people or groups from different countries ▪ *an international association of chemists* **3** : active or known in many countries ▪ *an international star* ▪ *international fame* — **in·ter·na·tion·al·ly** *adv*

international date line *n* — **the international date line** : an imaginary line that runs through the Pacific Ocean from the North Pole to the South Pole and that marks the place where each day officially begins

in·ter·ne·cine /ˌɪntə'ne,siːn, *Brit* ˌɪntə'niːˌsaɪn/ *adj, always before a noun, formal* : occurring between members of the same country, group, or organization ▪ *a brutal internecine war/battle*

In·ter·net /ˈɪntə,net/ *n* — **the Internet** : a system that connects computers throughout the world ▪ *She spent hours surfing the Internet.* — **Internet** *adj, always before a noun* ▪ *an Internet connection/site*

in·ter·nist /ˈɪn,tɚnɪst/ *n* [C] *US, medical* : a doctor who specializes in diseases that do not require surgery

in·ter·of·fice /ˌɪntə'ɑːfəs/ *adj, always before a noun, chiefly US* : going or happening between people who are part of the same company or organization ▪ *an interoffice memo*

in·ter·per·son·al /ˌɪntə'pɚsənəl/ *adj, always before a noun* : relating to or involving relations between people ▪ *interpersonal skills/relationships*

in·ter·play /ˈɪntə,pleɪ/ *n* [U, singular] : the ways in which two or more things, groups, etc., affect each other when they happen or exist together ▪ *the interplay between the old and the new* ▪ *a complex* *interplay of light and color*

in·ter·pose /ˌɪntə'pouz/ *vb* **-posed**; **-pos·ing** [*T*] *formal* : to place (someone or something) *between* two or more things or people ▪ *The new system has interposed a bureaucratic barrier between doctors and patients.*

in·ter·pret /ɪn'təprət/ *vb* **1** [*T*] : to explain the meaning of (something) ▪ *interpret a dream/law/result* **2** [*T*] : to understand (something) in a specified way ▪ *Her comment was meant to be interpreted as sarcasm.* **3** [*T*] : to perform (something, such as a song or a role) in a way that shows your own thoughts and feelings about it ▪ *Every actor interprets the role of Hamlet a little differently.* **4** [*I*] : to translate the words that someone is speaking into a different language ▪ *I'll need someone to interpret for me when I travel to China.* — **in·ter·pret·er** /ɪn'təprətə/ *n* [*C*]

in·ter·pre·ta·tion /ɪnˌtəprə'teɪʃən/ *n* **1** [*C/U*] : the way something is explained or understood ▪ *careful interpretation of the evidence* ▪ *a literal/loose interpretation of the law* ◇ If something is **open/subject to interpretation**, it can be understood in different ways. **2** [*C*] : a particular way of performing something ▪ *an actor's interpretation of the role of Hamlet* — **in·ter·pre·tive** /ɪn'təprətɪv/ *or* **in·ter·pre·ta·tive** /ɪn'təprə,teɪtɪv/ *adj*

in·ter·re·late /ɪn'təri'leɪt/ *vb* **-lat·ed**; **-lat·ing** [*I*] : to have a close or shared relationship ▪ *Linguists have found that language interrelates closely with culture.* — **interrelated** *adj* ▪ *interrelated topics* — **in·ter·re·la·tion** /ɪnˌtəri'leɪʃən/ *n* [*C/U*] — **in·ter·re·la·tion·ship** /ˌɪntəri'leɪʃən,ʃɪp/ *n* [*C/U*]

in·ter·ro·gate /ɪn'terə,geɪt/ *vb* **-gat·ed**; **-gat·ing** [*T*] : to ask (someone) questions in a thorough and often forceful way ▪ *interrogate a prisoner* — **in·ter·ro·ga·tion** /ɪn,terə'geɪʃən/ *n* [*C/U*] — **in·ter·ro·ga·tor** /ɪn'terə,geɪtə/ *n* [*C*]

¹in·ter·rog·a·tive /ˌɪntə'rɑ:gətɪv/ *adj* **1** *grammar* **a** : having the form of a question rather than a statement or command ▪ *"Did you go to school today?" is an interrogative sentence.* **b** : used to ask a question ▪ *an interrogative pronoun such as "who"* **2** *formal* : asking or suggesting a question ▪ *an interrogative tone of voice*

²interrogative *n* [*C*] *grammar* : a word (such as *who, what,* or *which*) that is used in asking a question — **the interrogative** : the form that a phrase or sentence has when it is asking a question ▪ *a sentence in the interrogative*

in·ter·rupt /ˌɪntə'rʌpt/ *vb* **1** [*T/I*] : to ask questions or say things while another person is speaking ▪ *It's not polite to interrupt (people).* **2** [*T*] : to cause (something) to stop happening for a time ▪ *His dinner was interrupted by a phone call.* **3** [*T*] : to change or stop the sameness or smoothness of (something) ▪ *The intense heat is occasionally interrupted by periods of cool weather.* — **in·ter·rup·tion** /ˌɪntə'rʌpʃən/ *n* [*C/U*] ▪ *frequent/annoying interruptions* ▪ *She spoke for an hour without interruption.*

in·ter·scho·las·tic /ˌɪntəskə'læstɪk/ *adj,* always before a noun, *US* : existing or done between schools ▪ *interscholastic sports/athletics*

in·ter·sect /ˌɪntə'sɛkt/ *vb* **1 a** [*T*] : to divide (something) by passing through or across it : CROSS ▪ *Line A intersects line B.* **b** [*I*] : to meet and cross at one or more points ▪ *The two roads intersect.* ▪ *intersecting lines/paths/streets* **2** [*I*] : to share some common area ▪ *the place where politics and business intersect*

in·ter·sec·tion /ˌɪntə'sɛkʃən/ *n* [*C*] : the place or point where two or more things come together; *especially* : the place where two or more streets meet or cross each other ▪ *The accident occurred at a busy intersection.*

in·ter·sperse /ˌɪntə'spəs/ *vb* **-spersed**; **-spers·ing** [*T*] **1** : to put (something) at different places among other things ▪ *The pictures were interspersed throughout the book.* **2** : to put things at different places within (something) ▪ *The forecast calls for scattered showers interspersed with sunny periods.* [=scattered showers with sunny periods between the showers]

¹in·ter·state /ˌɪntə'steɪt/ *adj,* always before a noun : relating to or connecting different states especially in the U.S. ▪ *an interstate highway* ▪ *interstate commerce*

²in·ter·state /'ɪntə,steɪt/ *n* [*C*] *US* : a major highway that connects two or more states ▪ *You'll get there quicker if you take the interstate.*

in·ter·twine /ˌɪntə'twaɪn/ *vb* **-twined**; **-twin·ing** [*T/I*] **1** : to twist (things) together ▪ *The branches are intertwined (with each other).* = *The branches intertwine (with each other).* ▪ *intertwining branches* **2** : to be or become very closely involved with each other ▪ *In the story, past and present intertwine.* ▪ *His fate is intertwined with hers.*

in·ter·val /'ɪntəvəl/ *n* [*C*] **1** : a period of time between events ▪ *a three-month interval between jobs* **2** *music* : the difference in pitch between two notes **3** *Brit* : INTERMISSION — **at intervals 1** : with an amount of space in between ▪ *There are signs at regular intervals along the outside wall.* **2** : with an amount of time in between ▪ *It recurs at (regular) intervals of every six months.*

in·ter·vene /ˌɪntə'vi:n/ *vb* **-vened**; **-ven·ing** [*I*] **1** : to come or occur between two times or events ▪ *Twenty years intervened between their first and last meetings.* **2** : to become involved in something (such as a conflict) in order to influence or stop it ▪ *When two children began to argue, the teacher quickly intervened.* **3** : to happen as an unrelated event that causes a delay or problem ▪ *We will leave on time unless some crisis intervenes.* — **in·ter·ven·tion** /ˌɪntə'vɛnʃən/ *n* [*C/U*] ▪ *praying for divine intervention* ▪ *military intervention(s)*

¹in·ter·view /'ɪntə,vju:/ *n* [*C*] : a meeting at which people talk to each other in order to ask questions and get information: such as **a** : a formal meeting with someone who is being considered for a job or other position ▪ *The company is holding* *interviews for several new jobs.* ◇ If you **have an interview**, you have an appointment to speak to someone who could hire you. **b** : a meeting between a reporter and another person in order to get information for a news story ▪ *a journalist conducting/doing interviews with political leaders* ▪ *an actor who has stopped giving/granting/doing interviews*

²**interview** /ˈɪntɚˌvjuː/ *vb* **1** [*T*] : to question or talk with (someone) in order to get information or learn about that person ▪ *interviewing candidates for a job* ▪ *She was interviewed on television.* **2** [*I*] *US* : to participate in an interview for a position (such as a job) ▪ *Several people have interviewed for the position.* — **in·ter·view·ee** /ˌɪntɚˌvjuːˈiː/ *n* [*C*] ▪ *He asked the interviewee some very personal questions.* — **in·ter·view·er** *n* [*C*]

in·ter·weave /ˌɪntɚˈwiːv/ *vb* **-wove** /-wouv/; **-woven** /-wouvən/; **-weav·ing** [*T*] : to twist or weave (threads, fibers, etc.) together ▪ *The long strands of ribbon are interwoven (together).* ▪ *(figurative) The two themes are interwoven throughout the poem.*

in·tes·tate /ɪnˈtɛˌsteɪt/ *adj, law* : not having made a will ▪ *He died intestate.* [=he did not have a will when he died]

in·tes·tine /ɪnˈtɛstən/ *n* [*C*] : a long tube in the body that helps digest food after it leaves the stomach — see also LARGE INTESTINE, SMALL INTESTINE — **in·tes·ti·nal** /ɪnˈtɛstənl/ *adj* ▪ *the intestinal tract/wall*

in·ti·ma·cy /ˈɪntəməsi/ *n, pl* **-cies** **1** [*U, singular*] : emotional warmth and closeness ▪ *the intimacy of old friends* **2** [*U*] : sexual relations ▪ *sexual/physical intimacy* **3** [*C*] : something that is very personal and private ▪ *They shared intimacies about their private lives.*

¹**in·ti·mate** /ˈɪntəmət/ *adj* **1** : having a very close relationship ▪ *intimate friends* **2** : very personal or private ▪ *intimate thoughts/feelings* ▪ *(chiefly US)* intimate apparel [=women's underwear and clothes for sleeping] **3** : involving sex or sexual relations ▪ *They are in an intimate relationship.* **4** *of a place* : private and pleasant in a way that allows people to feel relaxed and comfortable ▪ *an intimate nightclub* **5** : very closely related or connected ▪ *There is an intimate connection/relationship between diet and health.* **6** : very complete ▪ *She has an intimate* [=very detailed] *knowledge of the company.* — **in·ti·mate·ly** *adv*

²**in·ti·mate** /ˈɪntəmət/ *n* [*C*] *somewhat formal* : a very close and trusted friend ▪ *an intimate of the mayor*

³**in·ti·mate** /ˈɪntəˌmeɪt/ *vb* **-mat·ed; -mat·ing** [*T*] : to say or suggest (something) in an indirect way ▪ *He intimated that we should leave soon.* — **in·ti·ma·tion** /ˌɪntəˈmeɪʃən/ *n* [*C/U*] ▪ *There were intimations* [=suggestions] *that the project was in trouble.*

in·tim·i·date /ɪnˈtɪməˌdeɪt/ *vb* **-dat·ed; -dat·ing** [*T*] : to make (someone) afraid ▪ *He tries to intimidate his opponents.* ▪ *Many people are/feel intimidated by new technology.* — **intimidating** *adj* ▪ *an in-*

timidating person/experience — **in·tim·i·da·tion** /ɪnˌtɪməˈdeɪʃən/ *n* [*U*]

intl. *or* **intnl.** *abbr* international

in·to /ˈɪntu, ˈɪntə/ *prep* **1** : to or toward the inside of (something) ▪ *She came into the room/house.* ▪ *He jumped into the pool.* **2** : in the direction of (something) ▪ *She was just staring into space.* **3** — used to describe hitting or touching something or someone ▪ *He ran/bumped into a wall.* **4** : to the state, condition, or form of (something) ▪ *as day turns into night* ▪ *I got into trouble again.* ▪ *change dollars into euros* **5 a** — used to say that something or someone has become a part of something ▪ *He was born into a wealthy family.* **b** — used to say that someone has become involved in something (such as a profession) ▪ *She wants to get into politics.* **c** — used to say that someone has been forced or persuaded to do something ▪ *He was pressured into doing this.* **6** *informal* — used to say that someone is interested in and excited about (something) ▪ *He was never into sports.* **7** — used to say how long something lasts ▪ *The party continued well/far/long/late into the night.* **8** : relating to or concerning (something) ▪ *an investigation into the causes of the accident* **9** — used to describe dividing one number by another number ▪ *Six goes into 18 three times.*

in·tol·er·a·ble /ɪnˈtɑːlərəbəl/ *adj* : too bad, harsh, or severe to be accepted or tolerated ▪ *intolerable pain/behavior* — **in·tol·er·a·bly** /ɪnˈtɑːlərəbli/ *adv*

in·tol·er·ant /ɪnˈtɑːlərənt/ *adj* **1 a** : not willing to allow or accept something ▪ *They were intolerant of his lifestyle.* **b** *disapproving* : not willing to allow some people to have equality, freedom, or other social rights ▪ *an intolerant racist* **2** *medical* : unable to take a certain substance into the body without becoming sick ▪ *She is lactose intolerant.* [=she is unable to eat foods that contain lactose] — **in·tol·er·ance** /ɪnˈtɑːlərəns/ *n* [*U*] ▪ *a campaign against religious intolerance*

in·to·na·tion /ˌɪntouˈneɪʃən/ *n* [*C/U*] : the rise and fall in the sound of your voice when you speak

in·tone /ɪnˈtoun/ *vb* **-toned; -ton·ing** [*T*] **1** : to speak (a prayer, poem, etc.) in a way that sounds like music or chanting ▪ *intone a prayer* **2** : to say (something) in a slow and even voice ▪ *"Coming soon to a theater near you," the announcer intoned.*

in·tox·i·cate /ɪnˈtɑːksɪˌkeɪt/ *vb* **-cat·ed; -cat·ing** [*T*] *somewhat formal* **1** *of alcohol, a drug, etc.* : to make (someone) unable to think and behave normally ▪ *The beer I drank was not enough to intoxicate me.* **2** : to excite or please (someone) in a way that suggests the effect of alcohol or a drug ▪ *He was intoxicated by her beauty.* — **intoxicated** *adj* ▪ *He was intoxicated.* [=drunk] — **intoxicating** *adj* ▪ *the intoxicating effects of alcohol* ▪ *her intoxicating beauty* — **in·tox·i·ca·tion** /ɪnˌtɑːksəˈkeɪʃən/ *n* [*U*]

in·trac·ta·ble /ɪnˈtræktəbəl/ *adj, formal* **1** : not easily managed, controlled, or solved ▪ *an intractable problem* **2** : not easily relieved or cured • *an intractable infection/disease* — **in·trac·ta·bly** /ɪn-'træktəbli/ *adv*

in·tra·mu·ral /ˌɪntrə'mjɜrəl/ *adj, US* : existing or occurring within a particular group or organization (such as a school) • *intramural sports* [=sports in which the students of a school compete against each other]

in·tran·si·gent /ɪn'trænsədʒənt/ *adj, formal* : completely unwilling to change : very stubborn • *intransigent enemies/opponents* — **in·tran·si·gence** /ɪn-'trænsədʒəns/ *n* [U]

in·tran·si·tive /ɪn'trænsətɪv/ *adj, grammar, of a verb* : not having a direct object • *an intransitive verb* — **in·tran·si·tive·ly** *adv* • *a verb being used intransitively*

in·tra·uter·ine device /ˌɪntrə'juːtərən-, ˌɪntrə'juːtəˌraɪn-/ *n* [C] *medical* : a device that is inserted in the uterus and left there to prevent pregnancy — called also *IUD*

in·tra·ve·nous /ˌɪntrə'viːnəs/ *adj, always before a noun* : entering the body through a vein • *intravenous feedings/drugs* — **in·tra·ve·nous·ly** *adv*

in·trep·id /ɪn'trɛpəd/ *adj, literary • often humorous* : very bold or brave • *an intrepid explorer*

in·tri·cate /'ɪntrəkət/ *adj* : having many parts • *intricate machinery* • *an intricate* [=*complex*] *design/pattern/plot* — **in·tri·ca·cy** /'ɪntrəkəsi/ *n, pl* **-cies** [C/U] — **in·tri·cate·ly** *adv*

¹**in·trigue** /ɪn'triːg/ *vb* **-trigued; -trigu·ing** [T] : to make (someone) want to know more about something • *Your idea intrigues me.* • *She was intrigued with/by what he said.* — **in·trigu·ing** *adj* • *an intriguing* [=*interesting*] *idea/person/question* — **in·trigu·ing·ly** *adv*

²**in·trigue** /'ɪnˌtriːg/ *n* **1** [U] : the activity of making secret plans • *a novel of intrigue and romance* **2** [C] : a secret plan • *political intrigues*

in·trin·sic /ɪn'trɪnzɪk/ *adj* : occurring as a natural part of something • *intrinsic beauty/value* • *Creativity is intrinsic to her nature.* — **in·trin·si·cal·ly** /ɪn'trɪnzɪkli/ *adv*

in·tro /'ɪnˌtroʊ/ *n, pl* **-tros** [C] *informal* : a short introduction to a performance, musical work, etc.

in·tro·duce /ˌɪntrə'duːs, Brit ˌɪntrə'djuːs/ *vb* **-duced; -duc·ing** [T] **1** : to make (someone) known to someone else by name • *He introduced his guest.* • *She introduced herself to the class.* **2 a** : to cause (something) to begin to be used for the first time • *introduce a change in procedure* **b** : to make (something) available for sale for the first time • *introduce a new line of clothes* **c** : to present (something) for discussion or consideration • *New evidence was introduced at the trial.* **3** : to bring a type of plant, animal, etc., to a place for the first time • *an Asian plant that has been introduced to America* **4** : to speak briefly to an audience about (the next performance, performer, etc.) • *She introduced the speaker.* **5** : to mention or refer to (something) for the first time • *The main topics are intro-* duced in the first chapter. **6** : to cause (someone) to learn about or try (something) for the first time — + *to* • *The program introduces children to different sports.* **7** : to put or insert (something) into something else • *The new carpet introduces some color into* [=adds some color to] *the room.*

in·tro·duc·tion /ˌɪntrə'dʌkʃən/ *n* **1** [C] : the act of making a person known to others by name • *I'll make the introductions.* [=I'll introduce everyone] **2** [U] : the act of introducing something • *the introduction of telephone service to the area* • *the introduction of a new product* • *the introduction of an Asian plant species to America* **3** [C] : a statement made to an audience about the next performer, performance, etc. • *After a brief introduction, the performer took the stage.* ◇ A person who **needs no introduction** is well-known to the audience. **4** [C] **a** : the beginning part of a book, essay, speech, etc., that explains what will follow in the main part • *Did you read the introduction?* **b** : the beginning part of a piece of music **5** [C] : something (such as a book or a course of study) that provides basic information about a subject • *The course is an introduction to computer programming.* **6** [*singular*] : a person's first experience with something • *That concert was my introduction to her music.* **7** [C] : something that is added or introduced to something else • *The plant is a recent introduction from Asia.*

in·tro·duc·to·ry /ˌɪntrə'dʌktəri/ *adj* **1** : providing information about someone who is about to speak, perform, etc., or something that is about to begin • *introductory remarks* **2** : providing basic information about a subject • *an introductory class/text* **3** : intended to attract customers when a new product, service, etc., is introduced • *an introductory offer/price*

in·tro·spec·tion /ˌɪntrə'spɛkʃən/ *n* [U] : the process of examining your own thoughts or feelings • *a moment of quiet introspection* — **in·tro·spec·tive** /ˌɪntrə'spɛktɪv/ *adj* • *a quiet and introspective person*

in·tro·vert /'ɪntrəˌvɜt/ *n* [C] : a quiet person who does not find it easy to talk to other people — **in·tro·vert·ed** /'ɪntrəˌvɜtəd/ *adj* • *an introverted person/personality*

in·trude /ɪn'truːd/ *vb* **-trud·ed; -trud·ing** [I] **1** : to come or go into a place where you are not wanted or welcome • *Would I be intruding if I came along with you?* **2** : to become involved with something private in an annoying way • *Reporters constantly intruded into her private life.* — **in·tru·sion** /ɪn'truːʒən/ *n* [C/U] • *The phone call was an unwelcome intrusion.* • *protection from unwanted intrusion* — **in·tru·sive** /ɪn'truːsɪv/ *adj* : *intrusive reporters/questions*

in·trud·er /ɪn'truːdə/ *n* [C] **1** : a person who is not welcome or wanted in a place • *The other children regarded him as an intruder.* **2** : a person who enters a place illegally • *The police arrested the intruder.*

in·tu·it /ɪn'tu:wət, Brit ɪn'tju:ət/ vb [T] formal : to know or understand (something) because of what you feel or sense rather than because of evidence ▪ He was able to intuit the answer immediately.

in·tu·i·tion /ˌɪntu'ɪʃən, Brit ˌɪntju'ɪʃən/ n 1 [U] : a feeling that guides a person to act a certain way without fully understanding why ▪ Intuition was telling her that something was very wrong. 2 [C] : something that is known or understood without proof or evidence ▪ I had an intuition that you would drop by.

in·tu·i·tive /ɪn'tu:wətɪv, Brit ɪn'tju:ətɪv/ adj 1 : having the ability to know or understand things without any proof or evidence ▪ an intuitive mind/person 2 : based on or agreeing with what is known or understood without any proof or evidence ▪ an intuitive awareness/understanding 3 a : agreeing with what seems naturally right ▪ The argument makes intuitive sense. b : easily and quickly learned or understood ▪ The software has an intuitive interface. — **in·tu·i·tive·ly** adv

In·u·it /'ɪnjuwət, 'ɪnuwət/ n, pl **Inuit** or **In·u·its** also **Innuit** or **In·nu·its** 1 [C] : a member of a group of native people of northern North America and Greenland 2 [U] : the language of the Inuit people

in·un·date /'ɪnən,deɪt/ vb -dat·ed; -dat·ing [T] 1 : to cause (someone or something) to receive or take in a large amount of things at the same time ▪ The office was inundated with calls/letters. 2 formal : ²FLOOD 1a ▪ Low-lying areas were inundated by rising rivers. — **in·un·da·tion** /ˌɪnən'deɪʃən/ n [C/U]

in·ure /ɪ'nuɚ, ɪ'njuɚ/ vb -ured; -ur·ing [T] formal : to cause (someone) to be less affected by something unpleasant ▪ Does violence on television inure children to violence in real life?

in·vade /ɪn'veɪd/ vb -vad·ed; -vad·ing 1 [T/I] : to enter (a place, such as a foreign country) in order to take control by military force ▪ invade a country ▪ The troops invaded at dawn. 2 a [T/I] : to enter (a place) in large numbers ▪ Tourists invaded the town. b [T] : to enter or be in (a place where you are not wanted) ▪ She was invading my space. [=she was too close to me] 3 [T/I] : to spread over or into (something) in a harmful way ▪ Weeds had invaded the garden. 4 [T] : to affect (something) in an unwanted way ▪ Photographers **invaded** her privacy. — **in·vad·er** n [C]

¹in·val·id /ɪn'væləd/ adj 1 : having no force or effect ▪ an invalid contract 2 : not based on truth or fact ▪ an invalid argument — **in·val·id·i·ty** /ˌɪnvə'lɪdəti/ n [U]

²in·va·lid /'ɪnvələd, Brit 'ɪnvə,li:d/ n [C] : a person who needs to be cared for because of injury or illness ▪ Her husband has become an invalid.

in·val·i·date /ɪn'vælə,deɪt/ vb -dat·ed; -da·ting [T] 1 : to weaken or destroy the effect of (something) ▪ invalidate a contract/marriage 2 : to show or prove (something) to be false or incorrect ▪ factors that may invalidate the test results

in·valu·able /ɪn'væljəbəl/ adj : extremely valuable or useful ▪ an invaluable experience

in·vari·able /ɪn'verijəbəl/ adj : not changing or capable of change ▪ an invariable routine — **in·vari·ably** /ɪn'verijəbli/ adv ▪ He is invariably [=always] courteous.

in·va·sion /ɪn'veɪʒən/ n [C/U] 1 : the act of entering a place in an attempt to take control of it ▪ The enemy launched/mounted an invasion. 2 : the act of entering a place in large numbers especially in a way that is harmful or unwanted ▪ an invasion of/by insects/tourists — **invasion of privacy** : a situation in which someone tries to get information about a person's private life in an unwanted and usually improper way ▪ I consider these questions to be an invasion of (my) privacy.

in·va·sive /ɪn'veɪsɪv/ adj 1 : tending to spread ▪ invasive plants 2 medical : involving entry into the body by cutting or by inserting an instrument ▪ an invasive medical procedure

in·vec·tive /ɪn'vɛktɪv/ n [U] formal : rude and angry language ▪ a barrage/stream of racist invective

in·veigh /ɪn'veɪ/ vb — **inveigh against** [phrasal vb] formal : to protest or complain about (something or someone) very strongly ▪ Employees inveighed against mandatory overtime.

in·vei·gle /ɪn'veɪgəl/ vb -gled; -vei·gling [T] formal 1 : to persuade (someone) to do something in a clever or deceptive way ▪ They tried to inveigle her into taking the job. 2 : to get (something) in a clever or deceptive way ▪ We inveigled the information from him.

in·vent /ɪn'vɛnt/ vb [T] 1 : to create or produce (something useful) for the first time ▪ Thomas Edison invented the phonograph. 2 : to create or make up (something) in order to trick someone ▪ She invented a clever excuse/story. — **in·ven·tor** /ɪn'vɛntɚ/ n [C]

in·ven·tion /ɪn'vɛnʃən/ n 1 a [C] : a useful new device or process ▪ an amazing invention 2 b [C/U] : something (such as a false story) that is made up ▪ The stories he told about his military service were just inventions. 2 [U] : the act of inventing something ▪ the invention of a product/excuse 3 [U] : the ability to think of new ideas ▪ an artist with exceptional powers of invention

in·ven·tive /ɪn'vɛntɪv/ adj : having or showing an ability to think of new ideas and methods ▪ an inventive child/artist — **in·ven·tive·ness** n [U]

in·ven·to·ry /'ɪnvən,tori, Brit 'ɪnvəntri/ n, pl -ries 1 [C] : a complete list of the things that are in a place ▪ an inventory of supplies 2 [C/U] chiefly US : a supply of goods that are stored in a place ▪ a large inventory of used cars and trucks 3 [U] chiefly US : the act or process of making a complete list of the things that are in a place ▪ We'll be doing inventory on the collection soon. — **inventory** vb -ries;

-ried; -ry·ing [T] ▪ *We inventoried the collection.*

¹in·verse /ɪnˈvɚs, ˈɪnˌvɚs/ *adj, always before a noun* — used to describe two things that are related in such a way that as one becomes larger the other becomes smaller ▪ *The study indicates an inverse relationship between the unemployment rate and inflation.* [=as the unemployment rate drops, inflation rises] — in·verse·ly *adv*

²inverse *n [singular] formal + technical* : something that is the opposite of something else ▪ *the inverse of your argument*

in·vert /ɪnˈvɚt/ *vb [T] formal* **1** : to turn (something) upside down ▪ *The lens inverts the image.* **2** : to change the position, order, or relationship of things so that they are the opposite of what they had been ▪ *invert the order of two words in a sentence*

in·ver·te·brate /ɪnˈvɚtəbrət/ *n [C]* : a type of animal that does not have a backbone ▪ *Worms are invertebrates.*

inverted comma *n [C] Brit* : QUOTATION MARK

in·vest /ɪnˈvɛst/ *vb* **1** [T/I] : to use your money to purchase stock in a company, to buy property, etc., in order to make future profit ▪ *He invested (his money) in real estate.* **2 a** [T/I] : to spend (money) on building or improving something ▪ *The city invested heavily in its educational system.* **b** [T] : to give your time or effort in order to do something or make something better ▪ *We need to invest more time in educating our children.* ▪ *(chiefly US) She is deeply invested in this project.* [=she has given a lot of time and effort to this project] **3** [T] *formal* : to provide (someone or something) *with* (something) ▪ *The United States Constitution invests the President with certain powers.* — **invest in** [*phrasal vb*] *informal* : to spend money on (something useful or helpful to yourself) ▪ *I am planning to invest in* [=*buy*] *a good coat.* — in·ves·tor /ɪnˈvɛstɚ/ *n [C]*

in·ves·ti·gate /ɪnˈvɛstəˌgeɪt/ *vb* -gat·ed; -gat·ing **1** [T/I] : to try to find out the facts about (a crime, accident, etc.) ▪ *The police are still investigating (the murder).* **2** [T] : to try to get information about (someone who may have done something illegal) ▪ *He was investigated for his involvement in the incident.* — in·ves·ti·ga·tion /ɪnˌvɛstəˈgeɪʃən/ *n [C/U]* ▪ *Police began an investigation into/of the incident.* ▪ *The accident is under investigation.* [=being investigated] — in·ves·ti·ga·tive /ɪnˈvɛstəˌgeɪtɪv/ *adj, always before a noun* ▪ *investigative methods/journalism* — in·ves·ti·ga·tor /ɪnˈvɛstəˌgeɪtɚ/ *n [C]*

in·vest·ment /ɪnˈvɛstmənt/ *n* **1 a** [C/U] : the act of using money to earn more money ▪ *She got a good return on her investment.* [=her investment earned a good profit] **b** [C] : an amount of money that is invested in something ▪ *Her initial investment was $2,000.* **2** [C] : something that you buy with the idea that it will increase in value, usefulness, etc. ▪ *The house turned out to be a good investment.*

3 [C/U] **a** : the act of spending money on something that is valuable or expected to be useful or helpful ▪ *The government has set aside money for investment in public transportation.* **b** : the act of giving your time or effort in order to accomplish something or make something better ▪ *The project required (a) substantial investment of time and energy.*

in·vet·er·ate /ɪnˈvɛtərət/ *adj, formal + often disapproving* : always or often doing something specified ▪ *an inveterate liar*

in·vig·o·rate /ɪnˈvɪgəˌreɪt/ *vb* -rat·ed; -rat·ing [T] : to give life and energy to (someone or something) ▪ *A brisk walk in the cool morning air always invigorates me.* — in·vig·o·rat·ing *adj* ▪ *an invigorating walk*

in·vin·ci·ble /ɪnˈvɪnsəbəl/ *adj* : impossible to defeat or overcome ▪ *an invincible army* — in·vin·ci·bil·i·ty /ɪnˌvɪnsəˈbɪləti/ *n [U]*

in·vi·o·la·ble /ɪnˈvajələbəl/ *adj, formal* : too important to be ignored or treated with disrespect ▪ *an inviolable oath/law/right*

in·vi·o·late /ɪnˈvajələt/ *adj, formal* : not harmed or changed ▪ *inviolate rights*

in·vis·i·ble /ɪnˈvɪzəbəl/ *adj* : impossible to see ▪ *Sound waves are invisible.* — in·vis·i·bil·i·ty /ɪnˌvɪzəˈbɪləti/ *n [U]* — in·vis·i·bly /ɪnˈvɪzəbli/ *adv*

in·vi·ta·tion /ˌɪnvəˈteɪʃən/ *n* **1** [C] : a written or spoken request for someone to go somewhere or to do something ▪ *We sent out more than 100 invitations for the party/wedding.* ▪ *an invitation to lunch/dinner* **2** [U] : the act of inviting someone ▪ *She attended the fund-raiser at the invitation of the chairperson.* [=because she was invited by the chairperson] **3** [singular] : something that encourages someone to do something or that makes something more likely to happen ▪ *Speeding is an invitation to disaster/trouble.*

in·vite /ɪnˈvaɪt/ *vb* -vit·ed; -vit·ing [T] **1 a** : to ask (someone) to go somewhere or do something ▪ *She invited me (to go) out to dinner.* **b** : to ask (someone) formally or politely to do something ▪ *Employees are invited to apply for the new position.* **c** : to request (something) formally or politely ▪ *The company invites suggestions from customers.* **2** : to make (something unwanted) more likely to happen ▪ *invite disaster by speeding*

in·vit·ing /ɪnˈvaɪtɪŋ/ *adj* : attractive in a way that makes you want to do something, go somewhere, be near someone, etc. ▪ *The room is very inviting.* ▪ *an inviting smile* — in·vit·ing·ly *adv*

in·vo·ca·tion /ˌɪnvəˈkeɪʃən/ *n* **1** [C/U] *formal* : the act of mentioning or referring to someone or something in support of your ideas — + *of* ▪ *his repeated invocations of the ancient philosophers* **2** [C/U] *literary* : the act of asking for help or support especially from a god ▪ *by invocation of God* **3** [C] *US* : a prayer for blessing or guidance at the beginning of a service, ceremony, etc.

in·voice /ˈɪnˌvoɪs/ *n [C]* : a document that shows a list of goods or services and

the prices to be paid for them : BILL —
invoice *vb* **-voiced; -voic·ing** [*T*] •
They will invoice you [=send you an invoice] *directly.*

in·voke /ɪn'voʊk/ *vb* **-voked; -vok·ing**
[*T*] *formal* **1 a** : to mention (someone
or something) in an attempt to make
people feel a certain way or have a certain idea in their mind • *He invoked the
memory/name of his predecessor.* **b** : to
refer to (something) in support of your
ideas • *She invoked history to prove her
point.* **2** : to make use of (a law, a right,
etc.) • *He invoked his Fifth Amendment
privileges.* **3** : to ask for help or protection from (someone or something) • *They
invoked God's mercy.*

in·vol·un·tary /ɪn'vɑːlən,teri, Brit ɪn-
'vɒləntri/ *adj* **1** : not done or made consciously • *involuntary bodily movements*
2 : not done by choice • *involuntary*
[=*forced*] *labor* • *an involuntary confession* — **in·vol·un·tari·ly** /ɪn,vɑːlən'terəli,
Brit ɪn'vɒləntrəli/ *adv*

in·volve /ɪn'vɑːlv/ *vb* **-volved; -volv·ing**
[*T*] **1 a** : to have or include (someone
or something) as a part of something •
Does this involve me? • *Three cars were involved in the accident.* **b** : to cause
(someone) to be included in some activity, situation, etc. • *I didn't intend to involve you in this mess.* **c** : to cause
(someone) to be associated *with* someone
or something • *She remained involved
with the organization for many years.* **2**
: to require (something) as a necessary
part • *The job involves a lot of traveling.* —
in·volve·ment /ɪn'vɑːlvmənt/ *n* [*U*] •
He denied any involvement in the crime. •
their romantic involvement [=*relationship*]

in·volved /ɪn'vɑːlvd/ *adj* **1** : very complicated • *an involved story/process* **2** *not
before a noun* **a** : having a part in something • *I don't want to become involved in
this argument.* **b** : actively participating
in something • *She was so involved in her
work that she didn't hear the phone ring.*
c : having a romantic or sexual relationship • *They quickly became romantically
involved.*

in·vul·ner·a·ble /ɪn'vʌlnərəbəl/ *adj* : impossible to harm, damage, or defeat •
teenagers who think they are invulnerable
— **in·vul·ner·a·bil·i·ty** /ɪn,vʌlnərə-
'bɪləti/ *n* [*U*]

¹in·ward /'ɪnwəd/ *adj* **1** *always before a
noun* : of or relating to a person's mind
or spirit • *inward feelings* **2** : directed or
moving toward the inside of something •
an inward flow/curve

²inward *also chiefly Brit* **in·wards**
/'ɪnwədz/ *adv* **1** : toward the inside of
something • *The door opens inward.* **2**
: toward the mind or spirit • *He turned
his attention inward.*

in·ward·ly /'ɪnwədli/ *adv* : in a way that
is not openly shown or stated • *She was
outwardly calm but inwardly nervous.*

io·dine /'ajə,daɪn, Brit 'ajə,diːn/ *n* [*U*] : a
chemical element that is used especially
in medicine and photography

ion /'aɪ,ɑːn, 'ajən/ *n* [*C*] *technical* : an
atom or group of atoms that has a positive or negative electric charge from los-

ing or gaining one or more electrons

io·ta /aɪ'oʊtə/ *n* [*singular*] : a very small
amount — usually used in negative
statements • *There isn't an iota of truth in
what he says.*

IOU /,aɪ,oʊ'juː/ *n* [*C*] *informal* : a usually
written promise to pay a debt • *I don't
have any cash, so I'll have to give you an
IOU.* ◇ *IOU is from the pronunciation of
the phrase "I owe you."*

IPA /,aɪ,piː'eɪ/ *n* [*U*] : a system of symbols
that represent all of the sounds made in
speech ◇ *IPA is an abbreviation of "International Phonetic Alphabet."*

IQ /,aɪ'kjuː/ *n* [*C*] : a number that represents your intelligence and that is based
on your score on a special test • *children
with high IQs* • *an IQ test* ◇ *IQ is an abbreviation of "intelligence quotient."*

¹IRA /,aɪ,aə'reɪ/ *n* [*C*] *US* : a special account in which you can save and invest
money for your retirement without having to pay taxes on the money until a later time ◇ *IRA is an abbreviation of "individual retirement account."*

²IRA *abbr* Irish Republican Army

iras·ci·ble /ɪ'ræsəbəl/ *adj* : becoming angry very easily • *an irascible old football
coach*

irate /aɪ'reɪt/ *adj* : very angry • *an irate
neighbor*

ire /'ajə/ *n* [*U*] : intense anger • *He directed his ire at his coworkers.*

ir·i·des·cent /,ɪrə'dɛsnt/ *adj* : shining
with many different colors when seen
from different angles • *an iridescent gemstone* — **ir·i·des·cence** /,ɪrə'dɛsn̩s/ *n*
[*U*]

iris /'aɪrəs/ *n* [*C*] **1** : the colored part of
your eye **2** : a plant with long pointed
leaves and large blue or yellow flowers

Irish /'aɪrɪʃ/ *n, pl* **Irish** **1** [*plural*] : the
people of Ireland : Irish people • *the Irish
in America* [*U*] : the language of Ireland • *Do you speak Irish?* — **Irish** *adj* •
Irish culture — **Irish·man** /'aɪrɪʃmən/ *n,
pl* **-men** /-mən/ [*C*] — **Irish·wom·an**
/'aɪrɪʃ,wʊmən/ *n, pl* **-wom·en** /-,wɪmən/
[*C*]

irk /'ək/ *vb* [*T*] : to bother or annoy
(someone) • *I was irked by her comment.*

irk·some /'əksəm/ *adj* : annoying or irritating • *an irksome task*

¹iron /'ajən/ *n* **1** [*U*] : a heavy type of
metal that is very common, occurs naturally in blood, and is used to make steel
and in many products • *iron bars/chains* •
(figurative) She has a will of iron. = *She
has an iron will.* [=a very strong will] • *an
iron man* [=a very strong man] **2** [*C*] : a
device with a flat metal base that is heated and is used to press wrinkles out of
clothing — see also WAFFLE IRON **3**
[*C*] : a golf club that has a metal head
and is identified by a number • *a five-iron*
4 [*plural*] : chains placed on a prisoner's
arms or legs • *They clapped/put the prisoner in irons.* — **irons in the fire** : activities or projects that someone is involved
in • *an artist who has quite a few irons in
the fire* — **pump iron** see ²PUMP —
strike while the iron is hot see
¹STRIKE

²iron *vb* [*T/I*] : to use a heated iron to

make clothing or fabric smooth • *I ironed (clothes) all morning.* — **iron out** [*phrasal vb*] **iron (something) out** or **iron out (something)** 1 : to remove (wrinkles) in cloth by using a heated iron • *iron out the creases in the curtains* 2 a : to find a solution to (something) • *We're trying to iron out our differences.* b : to reach an agreement about (something) • *The final details of the contract still have to be ironed out.*

Iron Age *n* — **the Iron Age** : a period of time between about 3000 B.C. and 1000 B.C. in which people used iron to make weapons and tools

iron·clad /ˈajənˌklæd/ *adj* 1 : not able to be changed • *an ironclad policy/promise* 2 : too strong to be doubted or questioned • *an ironclad alibi*

Iron Curtain *n* — **the Iron Curtain** : the political and military barrier in the past that separated the communist countries of Europe from the rest of Europe

iron·ic /aɪˈrɑːnɪk/ *also* **iron·i·cal** /aɪˈrɑːnɪkəl/ *adj* 1 : using words that mean the opposite of what you really think especially in order to be funny • *an ironic remark* 2 : strange or funny because something (such as a situation) is different from what you expected • *It's ironic that computers break down so often, since they're meant to save people time.* — **iron·i·cal·ly** /aɪˈrɑːnɪkli/ *adv* • *Ironically* [=it is ironic that], *her work includes the same mistakes she criticizes.*

iron·ing /ˈajənɪŋ/ *n* [*U*] 1 : the activity of using an iron to smooth out clothes or fabric 2 : clothes that need to be ironed • *a pile of ironing*

ironing board *n* [*C*] : a flat, padded surface on which clothes are ironed

iro·ny /ˈaɪrəni/ *n, pl* **-nies** 1 [*U*] : the use of words that mean the opposite of what you really think especially in order to be funny • *"What a beautiful view," he said, his voice dripping with irony.* 2 [*C/U*] : a situation that is strange or funny because things happen in a way that seems to be the opposite of what you expected • *The (awful/bitter) irony is that in trying to forget her, he thought of her even more.*

ir·ra·tio·nal /ɪˈræʃənəl/ *adj* 1 : not thinking clearly : not able to use reason or good judgment • *He became irrational as the fever got worse.* 2 : not based on reason, good judgment, or clear thinking • *an irrational fear of cats* — **ir·ra·tio·nal·i·ty** /ɪˌræʃəˈnæləti/ *n* [*U*] — **ir·ra·tio·nal·ly** /ɪˈræʃənəli/ *adv*

ir·rec·on·cil·able /ɪˌrɛkənˈsaɪləbəl/ *adj, formal* : so different that agreement is not possible • *They are filing for divorce, citing irreconcilable differences.* — **ir·rec·on·cil·ably** /ɪˌrɛkənˈsaɪləbli/ *adv*

ir·re·deem·able /ˌɪrɪˈdiːməbəl/ *adj, formal* : not able to be saved, helped, or made better : HOPELESS • *an irredeemable racist*

ir·re·fut·able /ˌɪrɪˈfjuːtəbəl, ɪˈrɛfjətəbəl/ *adj, formal* : not able to be proved wrong • *irrefutable evidence*

ir·reg·u·lar /ɪˈrɛgjələ/ *adj* 1 : not normal or usual • *highly irregular behavior* 2 : not even or smooth • *an irregular out-*

line/shape/surface 3 a : happening or done at different times that change often • *an irregular schedule* b : not happening at times that are equally separated • *an irregular heartbeat* 4 *grammar* : not following the normal patterns by which word forms (such as the past tenses of verbs) are usually created • *"Sell" is an irregular verb because its past tense is "sold."* 5 *US* : not able to have normal bowel movements : CONSTIPATED — **ir·reg·u·lar·ly** *adv*

ir·reg·u·lar·i·ty /ɪˌrɛgjəˈlerəti/ *n, pl* **-ties** 1 [*U*] : the quality or state of being irregular • *the irregularity of his behavior* • *(US) He is suffering from irregularity.* [=*constipation*] 2 [*C*] a : something that is irregular • *an irregularity* [=a raised or rough area] *on the surface of the jewel* b : something that is not usual or proper • *We uncovered irregularities in the town's finances.*

ir·rel·e·vant /ɪˈrɛləvənt/ *adj* : not important or relating to what is being discussed right now • *His comment was irrelevant (to the discussion).* — **ir·rel·e·vance** /ɪˈrɛləvəns/ *also* **ir·rel·e·van·cy** /ɪˈrɛləvənsi/ *n, pl* **-vanc·es** *also* **-van·cies** [*C/U*] • *He talked about the weather and other irrelevancies.* — **ir·rel·e·vant·ly** *adv*

ir·rep·a·ra·ble /ɪˈrɛprəbəl/ *adj, formal* : too bad to be corrected or repaired • *irreparable harm* — **ir·rep·a·ra·bly** /ɪˈrɛprəbli/ *adv*

ir·re·place·able /ˌɪrɪˈpleɪsəbəl/ *adj* : too valuable or rare to be replaced • *irreplaceable works of art*

ir·re·press·ible /ˌɪrɪˈprɛsəbəl/ *adj* 1 : impossible to hold back, stop, or control • *irrepressible curiosity* 2 : very lively and cheerful • *an irrepressible sense of humor* — **ir·re·press·ibly** /ˌɪrɪˈprɛsəbli/ *adv*

ir·re·proach·able /ˌɪrɪˈproʊtʃəbəl/ *adj, formal* : not deserving criticism or blame • *irreproachable manners* — **ir·re·proach·ably** /ˌɪrɪˈproʊtʃəbli/ *adv*

ir·re·sist·ible /ˌɪrɪˈzɪstəbəl/ *adj* : impossible to resist especially because of strength or attractiveness • *Women find him irresistible.* [=*women think he is very attractive*] — **ir·re·sist·ibly** /ˌɪrɪˈzɪstəbli/ *adv*

ir·res·o·lute /ɪˈrɛsəˌluːt/ *adj, formal* : not certain about what to do • *an irresolute leader*

ir·re·spec·tive of /ˌɪrɪˈspɛktɪv-/ *prep, formal* : without thinking about or considering (something) • *They are protected by the law, irrespective of race.* [=*regardless of race*]

ir·re·spon·si·ble /ˌɪrɪˈspɑːnsəbəl/ *adj* : not having or showing maturity or good judgment • *an irresponsible person/decision* — **ir·re·spon·si·bil·i·ty** /ˌɪrɪˌspɑːnsəˈbɪləti/ *n* [*U*] — **ir·re·spon·si·bly** /ˌɪrɪˈspɑːnsəbli/ *adv*

ir·re·triev·able /ˌɪrɪˈtriːvəbəl/ *adj, somewhat formal* : impossible to recover or get back • *The data was irretrievable after the computer crashed.* — **ir·re·triev·ably** /ˌɪrɪˈtriːvəbli/ *adv*

ir·rev·er·ent /ɪˈrɛvərənt/ *adj* : having or

showing a lack of respect for someone or something that is usually treated with respect • *an irreverent sense of humor* • *an irreverent comedian* — **ir·rev·er·ence** /ɪˈrɛvərəns/ *n* [U] — **ir·rev·er·ent·ly** *adv*

ir·re·vers·ible /ˌɪrɪˈvəsəbəl/ *adj*, *somewhat formal* : impossible to change back to a previous condition or state • *irreversible harm*

ir·rev·o·ca·ble /ɪˈrɛvəkəbəl/ *adj*, *formal* : not capable of being changed : impossible to revoke • *an irrevocable change/decision* — **ir·rev·o·ca·bly** /ɪˈrɛvəkəbli/ *adv*

ir·ri·gate /ˈɪrəˌgeɪt/ *vb* -gat·ed; -gat·ing [T] **1** : to supply (something) with water by using artificial means (such as pipes) • *irrigate fields/crops* **2** *medical* : to clean (a wound or a part of the body) with flowing liquid (such as water) • *The surgeon irrigated the wound.* — **ir·ri·ga·tion** /ˌɪrəˈgeɪʃən/ *n* [U]

ir·ri·ta·ble /ˈɪrətəbəl/ *adj* : becoming angry or annoyed easily • *I felt tired and irritable.* — **ir·ri·ta·bil·i·ty** /ˌɪrətəˈbɪləti/ *n* [U] — **ir·ri·ta·bly** /ˈɪrətəbli/ *adv*

ir·ri·tant /ˈɪrətənt/ *n* [C] **1** : something that makes part of your body sore and painful • *lung/skin irritants* **2** : something that is unpleasant or annoying • *The delay was a minor irritant.*

ir·ri·tate /ˈɪrəˌteɪt/ *vb* -tat·ed; -tat·ing [T] **1** : to make (someone) impatient, angry, or annoyed • *I was irritated by her rudeness.* **2** : to make (part of your body) sore or painful • *Harsh soaps can irritate the skin.* — **irritating** *adj* • *an irritating question* — **ir·ri·tat·ing·ly** /ˈɪrəˌteɪtɪŋli/ *adv* — **ir·ri·ta·tion** /ˌɪrəˈteɪʃən/ *n* [C/U]

IRS *abbr* Internal Revenue Service

is see BE

Is. *abbr* island

-ise *Brit spelling of* - IZE

-ish *adj suffix* : almost or approximately • *The car is greenish.* • *She looks to be about fiftyish.*

Is·lam /ɪˈslɑːm, ˈɪzˌlɑːm/ *n* [U] **1** : the religion which teaches that there is only one God and that Muhammad is God's prophet : the religion of Muslims **2** : the modern nations in which Islam is the main religion — **Is·lam·ic** /ɪˈslɑːmɪk, ɪzˈlɑːmɪk/ *adj* • *Islamic faith/law*

is·land /ˈaɪlənd/ *n* [C] **1** : an area of land that is surrounded by water • *an island in the Caribbean* **2** : an area or object that is separated from other things: such as **a** : a raised area within a road, parking lot, or driveway that is used to separate or direct traffic • *a traffic island* **b** *chiefly US* : a separate raised area with a flat surface on which food is prepared in a kitchen

is·land·er /ˈaɪləndɚ/ *n* [C] : a person born or living on an island • *Pacific islanders*

isle /ˈajəl/ *n* [C] *literary* : ISLAND 1 • *a tropical isle*

-ism /ɪzəm/ *n suffix* **1 a** : the act, practice, or process of doing something — used to form nouns from verbs that end in *-ize* • *criticism* **b** : behavior like that of a specified kind of person or thing •

heroism **c** : unfair treatment of a group of people who have a particular quality • *sexism* **2** : the state or fact of being a specified kind of person or thing • *skepticism* **3** *medical* : abnormal state or condition • *alcoholism* **4** : teachings or beliefs • *Buddhism* • *socialism*

isn't /ˈɪznt/ — used as a contraction of *is not* • *This isn't what I expected.*

iso·late /ˈaɪsəˌleɪt/ *vb* -lat·ed; -lat·ing [T] **1** : to put or keep (someone or something) in a place or situation that is separate from others • *Certain patients must be isolated (from others) in a separate ward.* **2 a** : to find and deal with (something, such as a problem) by removing other possibilities • *We need to isolate the problem.* [=to find out exactly what the problem is] **b** *technical* : to separate (something) from another substance • *Scientists have isolated the gene/virus that causes the disease.*

iso·lat·ed *adj* **1** : separate from others • *an isolated area/community/place* • *She felt isolated in her new school.* **2** : happening just once • *an isolated incident/case* **3** : happening in different places and at different times • *a few isolated cases of vandalism*

iso·la·tion /ˌaɪsəˈleɪʃən/ *n* [U] **1** : the state of being in a place or situation that is separate from others • *a feeling of isolation* [=loneliness] **2** : the act of separating something from other things • *isolation of the gene/virus* — **in isolation** : apart from others • *The researchers work in isolation.*

iso·la·tion·ism /ˌaɪsəˈleɪʃəˌnɪzəm/ *n* [U] : the belief that a country should not be involved with other countries — **iso·la·tion·ist** /ˌaɪsəˈleɪʃənɪst/ *adj* — **isolationist** *n* [C]

iso·met·rics /ˌaɪsəˈmɛtrɪks/ *n* [*plural*] : exercises in which muscles are made stronger by pushing against other muscles or against something that does not move — **iso·met·ric** /ˌaɪsəˈmɛtrɪk/ *adj*

isos·ce·les triangle /aɪˈsɑːsəˌliːz-/ *n* [C] *mathematics* : a triangle in which two sides have the same length

Is·rae·li /ɪzˈreɪli/ *n* [C] : a person from modern Israel — **Israeli** *adj*

Is·ra·el·ite /ˈɪzriːjəˌlaɪt, ˈɪzrəˌlaɪt/ *n* [C] : a person who was born in or who lived in the ancient kingdom of Israel

¹is·sue /ˈɪˌʃuː/ *n* **1** [C] : something that people are talking about, thinking about, etc. • *The President's speech addressed a number of important issues.* **2** [C] : the version of a newspaper, magazine, etc., that is published at a particular time • *the current/latest issue* **3** [*singular*] : the act of officially making something available or giving something to people to be used • *a government-issue gun* [=a gun that the government has officially given to someone] **4** [*plural*] : problems or concerns • *health issues* — **at issue** : being discussed or considered • *At issue is the city's budget plan.* — **force the issue** : to force someone to do something or to make a decision about something • *They would never have addressed the problem if we hadn't forced the issue.* — **have is-**

sues *informal* **1** : to have problems that make you unhappy and difficult to deal with ▪ *Her boyfriend has (a lot of) issues.* **2** : to have reasons for disliking someone or something — *+ with* ▪ *I have some issues with his behavior.* — **make an issue of** : to argue about (something) or insist that (something) be treated as an important problem ▪ *I knew they'd made a mistake, but I was too tired to make an issue of it.* — **take issue with** : to disagree with (someone or something) ▪ *She took issue with their decision.*

²**issue** *vb* **-sued; -su·ing** **1** [*T*] **a** : to give (something) to someone in an official way ▪ *The police have issued numerous tickets for speeding in recent days.* ▪ *Each employee is issued an identification card.* **b** : to make (something) available to be sold or used ▪ *the bank's newly issued credit card* **2** [*T*] : to announce (something) in a public and official way ▪ *The police have issued a warrant for her arrest.* **3** [*I*] *formal* : to go, come, or flow out *from* some source ▪ *A flow of lava issued from a crack in the rock.* — **is·su·er** *n* [*C*]

-ist /ɪst/ *n suffix* **1 a** : a person who does a specified action or activity ▪ *typist* **b** : a person who makes or produces something specified ▪ *novelist* **c** : a person who plays a specified musical instrument ▪ *pianist* **d** : a person who operates a specified machine or vehicle ▪ *machinist* **2** : a person who has a specified job or skill ▪ *geologist* **3** : a person who has particular beliefs or a particular quality — used to form nouns from related nouns that end in *-ism* ▪ *socialist* ▪ *idealist*

isth·mus /ˈɪsməs/ *n* [*C*] : a narrow area of land that connects two larger land areas

¹**it** /ɪt, ət/ *pron* **1** : that one just mentioned — used to refer to an object or substance ▪ *I caught the ball and threw it back.* — used to refer to a living thing whose sex is unknown or is being ignored ▪ *"Who is it?" "It's only me."* — used to refer to an idea, quality, emotion, etc. ▪ *Beauty is everywhere, and it is a source of great joy.* **2** — used as the subject of a verb that describes a condition or occurrence ▪ *It is cold/hot/raining/snowing outside.* ▪ *It will soon be summer.* ▪ *It is ten (minutes) after four (o'clock).* **3** — used in the place of a noun, phrase, or clause that usually comes later ▪ *It makes me happy just to think about her.* ▪ *They made it clear that they needed our help.* ▪ *It was in this city that the treaty was signed.* **4** — used to refer to something that has been done or is being done or is going to be done ▪ *We're going to have to do it again.* ▪ *Quit it!* [=stop doing what you are doing] **5** — used as a direct object with little or no meaning ▪ *living it up* [=doing exciting and enjoyable things] ▪ *I decided to go it alone.* [=to go by myself; to go alone] **6** : the general situation ▪ *How's it going?* ▪ *It hasn't been the same since you left.* **7** : something previously discussed or known ▪ *When the bell rings, it means that class is over.* — **that is it** or **that's it** *informal* **1** — used to say that

something is finished or completed ▪ *Okay, that's it. You can go now.* **2** — used to say that something is all that is needed or wanted ▪ *I came here to see you and that's it.* [=that is all I wanted to do here] **3** — used to say that something is correct ▪ *"I think his name was Brian Johnson." "Yes, that's it."* **4** — used in an angry or annoyed way to say that you will not accept any more of something ▪ *That's it! I'm leaving!* — **this is it** *informal* — used to say that this is the most important or final point ▪ *Well, this is it—the day we've been waiting for.*

²**it** /ɪt/ *n* [*C*] : the player in some children's games who performs the main action of the game (such as finding or catching other players) ▪ *You're it!*

Ital·ian /ɪˈtæljən/ *n* **1** [*C*] : a person from Italy **2** [*U*] : the language of the Italians — **Italian** *adj*

Italian dressing *n* [*U*] *US* : a salad dressing that is made of oil, vinegar, and herbs

¹**ital·ic** /ɪˈtælɪk/ *adj* : having letters, numbers, etc., that slant upward to the right ▪ *These words are italic.* ▪ *italic type*

²**italic** *n* [*U, plural*] : letters, numbers, etc., that slant upward to the right : italic type ▪ *These words are printed in italic(s).*

ital·i·cize *also Brit* **ital·i·cise** /ɪˈtæləˌsaɪz/ *vb* **-cized; -ciz·ing** [*T*] : to put letters, numbers, etc., in italics ▪ *italicize a word*

¹**itch** /ɪtʃ/ *vb* [*I*] **1** : to have or produce an unpleasant feeling on your skin or inside your mouth, nose, etc., that makes you want to scratch ▪ *My back really itches.* ▪ *This sweater makes me itch.* **2** *informal* : to have a strong desire *to do* something or *for* something — always used as *(be) itching* ▪ *I'm itching to get started.* [=I'm very eager to begin] ▪ *She was itching for a fight.* — **itching** *n* [*U*] ▪ *Symptoms include minor itching and redness.*

²**itch** *n* [*C*] **1** : an uncomfortable or unpleasant feeling on your skin or inside your mouth, nose, etc., that makes you want to scratch ▪ *I had a slight itch on my back.* **2** *somewhat informal* : a constant and strong desire *for* something or *to do* something ▪ *an itch for adventure* ▪ *an itch to travel* — **itch·i·ness** /ˈɪtʃinəs/ *n* [*U*] — **itchy** /ˈɪtʃi/ *adj* **itch·i·er; -est** ▪ *itchy skin* ▪ *an itchy sweater/rash* ◆ If you have **itchy feet**, you have a strong desire to leave a place, job, etc., and go somewhere else. ◆ If you have an **itchy finger** or **itchy fingers**, you have a strong desire to do or get something, especially something that other people think is wrong or dangerous. ▪ *a gunman with an itchy (trigger) finger* [=who is eager or likely to shoot someone]

item /ˈaɪtəm/ *n* **1** [*C*] : an individual thing ▪ *household items* ▪ *He always orders the most expensive item on the menu.* ▪ *There are a lot of items on our agenda.* **2** [*C*] : a separate piece of news or information ▪ *I saw an item in the paper about the mayor's plans.* **3** [*singular*] *informal* : two people who are in a romantic or sexual relationship ▪ *They were rumored to be an item.*

item·ize *also Brit* **item·ise** /ˈaɪtəˌmaɪz/ *vb* **-ized; -iz·ing** [*T*] : to create a detailed list of (things) ▪ *You'll need to itemize all of your expenses.* — **item·i·za·tion** also Brit **item·i·sa·tion** /ˌaɪtəmə'zeɪʃən, Brit ˌaɪtəˌmaɪ'zeɪʃən/ *n* [U]

itin·er·ant /aɪ'tɪnərənt/ *adj, always before a noun* : traveling from place to place ▪ *an itinerant preacher/lecturer/performer*

itin·er·ary /aɪ'tɪnəˌreri, Brit aɪ'tɪnərəri/ *n, pl* **-ar·ies** [C] : the places you go to or plan to go to on a journey ▪ *Our itinerary included stops at several cathedrals.*

it'll /'ɪtl/ — used as a contraction of *it will* ▪ *It'll be dark soon.*

its /'ɪts, əts/ *adj, always before a noun, possessive form of* IT : relating to or belonging to a certain thing, animal, etc. ▪ *the dog in its kennel* ▪ *Each region has its own customs.* — compare IT'S

it's /'ɪts, əts/ — used as a contraction of *it is* and *it has* ▪ *It's* [=*it is*] *going to rain.* ▪ *It's* [=*it has*] *been fun.* — compare ITS

it·self /ɪt'sɛlf/ *pron* **1 a** — used as the object of a verb or preposition to refer to something that has already been mentioned ▪ *The cat washed itself.* **b** — used for emphasis to refer to something that has already been mentioned ▪ *I found the envelope, but the letter itself was missing.* **2** — used after a noun to say that someone or something has a lot of a particular quality ▪ *She was/seemed kindness itself.* [=she was extremely kind] — **by itself 1** : on its own : without being directly controlled by a person ▪ *The computer shuts off by itself if you don't use it.* **2** : with nothing nearby : ALONE ▪ *The house stands by itself at the end of the street.* — **in itself** : when considered as something separate from other things ▪ *The idea was not in itself bad.* : without anything else added ▪ *That's a story in itself.*

it·sy-bit·sy /'ɪtsi'bɪtsi/ *or* **it·ty-bit·ty** /'ɪti'bɪti/ *adj, informal* : TINY ▪ *itsy-bitsy steps*

IUD /ˌaɪˌju:'di:/ *n* [C] *medical* : INTRA-UTERINE DEVICE

IV /ˌaɪ'vi:/ *n* [C] *US, medical* : a device that is used to allow a fluid (such as blood or a liquid medication) to flow directly into a patient's veins ✧ *IV* is an abbreviation of *intravenous*.

I've /'aɪv, əv/ — used as a contraction of *I have* ▪ *It was the best movie I've ever seen.*

ivo·ry /'aɪvəri/ *n, pl* **-ries** **1** [U] : a hard white substance that forms the tusks of elephants and other animals ▪ *a carved piece of ivory* **2** [U] : a slightly yellowish white color **3** [C] *informal* : a piano key ✧ To **tickle the ivories** is to play the piano.

ivory tower *n* [C] *disapproving* : a place or situation in which people make and discuss theories about problems (such as poverty and racism) without having any experience with those problems ▪ *a college professor who's spent her entire career in an ivory tower* ▪ *an ivory-tower intellectual*

ivy /'aɪvi/ *n, pl* **ivies** [C/U] : a plant that has long stems and that often grows on the outsides of buildings ▪ *walls covered with ivy = ivy-covered walls* — see also POISON IVY

Ivy League *n* [*singular*] : a group of eight colleges and universities in the eastern U.S. that have been respected for providing an excellent education for a long time ▪ *an Ivy League degree/university*

-ize also Brit **-ise** /aɪz/ *vb suffix* **1 a** : to cause to become or become like something specified ▪ *Americanize* : to become or become like something specified ▪ *crystallize* **b** : to treat like something specified ▪ *idolize* **2** : to talk or write about someone or something in a specified way ▪ *romanticize* **3** : to make or suggest something specified ▪ *theorize* **4** : to place someone in something specified ▪ *hospitalize*

J

j *or* **J** /'dʒeɪ/ *n, pl* **j's** *or* **js** *or* **J's** *or* **Js** [C/U] : the 10th letter of the English alphabet ▪ *a word that begins with (a) j*

¹jab /'dʒæb/ *vb* **jabbed; jab·bing** [T/I] : to push something sharp or hard quickly into or toward someone or something ▪ *The nurse jabbed the needle into his arm.* ▪ *He jabbed (at) me with his fist.*

²jab *n* [C] **1** : a quick or sudden hit with something sharp or hard ▪ *She gave him a jab in the ribs.* **2** : a short, straight punch ▪ *throw a jab* **3** *Brit, informal* : an injection of something (such as medicine) into your body with a needle ▪ *a flu jab* [=(*chiefly US*) *shot*]

jab·ber /'dʒæbər/ *vb* [T/I] *informal* : to talk in a fast, unclear, or foolish way ▪ *jabbering away for hours*

¹jack /'dʒæk/ *n* **1** [C] : a device used for

lifting something heavy (such as a car) **2** [C] : a playing card that is worth more than a ten and less than a queen ▪ *the jack of spades* **3** [C] : a small opening where something connects with a wire to something else ▪ *a phone/stereo jack* **4 a** [C] : a small object with six points that is used in the game of jacks **b** [*plural*] : a child's game in which jacks are picked up while bouncing and catching a small ball

²jack *vb* — **jack in** [*phrasal vb*] **jack in (something)** *or* **jack (something) in** *Brit, informal* : to stop doing (something) ▪ *He was building a new shed but jacked it in.* — **jack up** [*phrasal vb*] **jack up (something)** *or* **jack (something) up** **1** : to lift (something) with a jack ▪ *Jack up the car and change the tire.* **2** *informal* : to increase (something) by a large amount • *The store jacked up its prices.*

jack·al /ˈdʒækəl/ *n* [C] : a wild dog found in Africa and Asia

jack·ass /ˈdʒækˌæs/ *n* [C] **1** : a male donkey **2** *chiefly US, informal + impolite* : a stupid person

jack·et /ˈdʒækət/ *n* [C] **1** : a short and light coat **2** : an outer covering: such as **a** : DUST JACKET **b** *chiefly US* : a paper, cardboard, or plastic envelope for holding a record, CD, or DVD

jack·ham·mer /ˈdʒækˌhæmɚ/ *n* [C] *chiefly US* : a heavy, electric tool used to break asphalt, concrete, etc.

jack-in-the-box /ˈdʒækɪnðəˌbɑːks/ *n* [C] : a toy that is a small box containing a figure which jumps up when the box is opened

¹**jack·knife** /ˈdʒækˌnaɪf/ *n, pl* **-knives** [C] : POCKETKNIFE

²**jackknife** *vb* **-knifed; -knif·ing** [I] *of a large vehicle* : to have the back part slide out of control toward the front part • *The truck jackknifed on the icy road.*

jack-of-all-trades /ˌdʒækəvˌɑːlˈtreɪdz/ *n* [C] : a person who can do many different jobs

jack-o'-lan·tern /ˈdʒækəˌlæntɚn/ *n* [C] : a pumpkin that has had its insides removed, a face cut into it, and often a light placed inside it for Halloween

jack·pot /ˈdʒækˌpɑːt/ *n* [C] **1** : a usually large amount of money won in a game of chance — **hit the jackpot 1** : to win all the money that can be won in a game of chance **2** : to have unexpected success or good luck • *They hit the jackpot when they hired her.* [=she is a very valuable employee]

jack·rab·bit /ˈdʒækˌræbət/ *n* [C] : an animal that is like a large rabbit

Ja·cuz·zi /dʒəˈkuːzi/ *trademark* — used for a bathtub that causes water and air bubbles to move around your body

jade /ˈdʒeɪd/ *n* [U] : a usually green stone that is used for jewelry

jad·ed /ˈdʒeɪdəd/ *adj* : feeling or showing a lack of interest caused by having experienced too much of something • *a public jaded by political scandals*

jag·ged /ˈdʒægəd/ *adj* : having a sharp, uneven edge or surface • *jagged pieces of glass*

jag·uar /ˈdʒægˌwɑɚ, *Brit* ˈdʒægjəwə/ *n* [C] : a large wild cat with black spots that lives in Central and South America

jail *also Brit* **gaol** /ˈdʒeɪl/ *n* [C/U] : a place where people are kept when they have been arrested and are being punished for a crime • *He's in jail.* • *He went to jail for his crimes.* • *She just got out of jail.* — **jail** *also Brit* **gaol** *vb* [T] • *He was jailed* [=put in jail] *for assault.*

jail·break *also Brit* **gaol·break** /ˈdʒeɪlˌbreɪk/ *n* [C] : an escape from jail

jail·er *also* **jail·or** *or Brit* **gaol·er** /ˈdʒeɪlɚ/ *n* [C] : a person who is in charge of a jail

jail·house /ˈdʒeɪlˌhaʊs/ *n* [C] *US* : JAIL

ja·la·pe·ño /ˌhɑːləˈpeɪnjoʊ/ *n, pl* **-ños** [C] : a small green pepper that is very hot

ja·lopy /dʒəˈlɑːpi/ *n, pl* **-lop·ies** [C] *informal* : an old car that is in poor condition

¹**jam** /ˈdʒæm/ *vb* **jammed; jam·ming 1 a** [T/I] : to fill (a place) completely • *Thousands of people jammed (into) the hall.* **b** [T] : to fill (something) so that movement is slow or stopped • *Traffic jammed the roads.* • *(figurative) The phone lines were jammed with calls from angry customers.* **2 a** [T] : to push (an object) into a tight place • *He jammed the book into the bookcase.* **b** [T/I] : to push (something) suddenly and forcefully • *She jammed (her foot down) on the brakes.* **c** [T] : to cause (a part of your body) to be painfully crushed, squeezed, etc. • *My finger got jammed in the car door.* **3** [T/I] : to stop or cause something to stop working properly because something inside prevents movement • *The gun jammed.* **4** [T] : to weaken or block (a radio signal) • *jam a radio broadcast* **5** [I] : to play music informally together without preparation • *Let's jam.*

²**jam** *n* **1** [C] : a situation in which something slows or stops the movement of a machine, traffic, etc. • *There's a paper jam in the printer.* • *stuck in a traffic jam* **2** [C] *informal* : a difficult situation • *They helped her out of a jam.* **3** [C/U] : a food made of fruit and sugar • *eating toast with jam*

jamb /ˈdʒæm/ *n* [C] : a board that forms the side of a door or window

jam·bo·ree /ˌdʒæmbəˈriː/ *n* [C] : a kind of large party • *a country music jamboree*

jam-packed /ˈdʒæmˈpækt/ *adj* : filled completely • *The theater was jam-packed (with people).*

Jan. *abbr* January

Jane Doe /ˈdʒeɪnˈdoʊ/ *n* [C] *US, law* — used as a name for a woman whose true name is not known or is being kept secret

jan·gle /ˈdʒæŋgəl/ *vb* **jan·gled; jan·gling** [T/I] : to make or cause something to make a harsh ringing sound • *She jangled her keys.* — **jangle** *n* [C]

jan·i·tor /ˈdʒænətɚ/ *n* [C] *chiefly US* : a person who cleans a building — **jan·i·to·ri·al** /ˌdʒænəˈtorijəl/ *adj*

Jan·u·ary /ˈdʒænjəˌweri/ *n, pl* **-ar·ies** [C/U] : the first month of the year • *Her birthday is in January.* • *on January the fourth* = (*US*) *on January fourth* = *on the fourth of January* — abbr. *Jan.*

¹**Jap·a·nese** /ˌdʒæpəˈniːz/ *n* **1 the Japanese** : the people of Japan • *the customs of the Japanese* **2** [U] : the language of the Japanese

²**Japanese** *adj* : of or relating to Japan, its people, or their language • *Japanese history* • *She is Japanese.*

Japanese beetle *n* [C] : a small beetle that damages plants

¹**jar** /ˈdʒɑɚ/ *n* [C] **1** : a glass container with a wide opening and usually a lid • *a pickle jar* **2** : the amount of something inside a jar • *We ate a jar of pickles.*

²**jar** *vb* **jarred; jar·ring 1** [T/I] : to have a harsh or unpleasant effect on someone or something • *The loud music jarred (on) my ears.* **2** [T/I] : to hit or shake (something) • *The earthquake jarred the tiles loose.* **3** [T] : to make (someone) feel

uneasy • *It was jarring to see how sick she was.*

jar·gon /ˈdʒɑɚgən/ *n* [U] *usually disapproving* : the language used for a particular activity or by a particular group of people • *legal/medical/sports jargon*

jas·mine /ˈdʒæzmən/ *n* [U] : a plant that has flowers with a very sweet smell

jaun·dice /ˈdʒɑːndəs/ *n* [U] *medical* : a disease that causes a person's skin to turn yellow

jaun·diced /ˈdʒɑːndəst/ *adj* **1** *medical* : affected with jaundice • *jaundiced patients* **2** : feeling or showing dislike, distrust, or anger because of past experiences • *She has a jaundiced view of politics.*

jaunt /ˈdʒɑːnt/ *n* [C] : a brief trip taken for pleasure • *a jaunt to the coast*

jaun·ty /ˈdʒɑːnti/ *adj* **jaun·ti·er; -est** : lively in manner or appearance • *a jaunty tune/greeting* — **jaunt·i·ly** /ˈdʒɑːntəli/ *adv*

ja·va /ˈdʒɑːvə, ˈdʒɑːvə/ *n* [U] *US, informal* : COFFEE • *a cup of java*

jave·lin /ˈdʒævələn/ *n* **1** [C] : a long spear **2** *the javelin* : an event in which people compete by throwing a javelin as far as they can • *winner of the javelin*

¹**jaw** /ˈdʒɑː/ *n* **1** [C] : either one of the two bones of the face where teeth grow • *the jaws of a tiger/shark* • (*figurative*) *He barely escaped from the jaws of death.* [=he almost died] • (*figurative*) *The team snatched victory from the jaws of defeat.* [=they won after almost losing] ✧ *If your jaw drops*, you open your mouth in a way that shows you are very surprised or shocked. **2** [*plural*] : two parts of a tool that close to hold or crush something • *the jaws of a vise*

²**jaw** *vb* [I] *informal* : to talk in an angry way or for a long time • *The coach was jawing with/at the referee.*

jaw·bone /ˈdʒɑːˌboʊn/ *n* [C] : MANDIBLE

jaw·line /ˈdʒɑːˌlaɪn/ *n* [C] : the bottom edge of a person's face • *He has a strong jawline.*

jay /ˈdʒeɪ/ *n* [C] : a noisy bird that is often brightly colored — see also BLUE JAY

jay·walk /ˈdʒeɪˌwɑːk/ *vb* [I] : to cross a street at an illegal or dangerous place • *She was fined for jaywalking.* — **jay·walk·er** *n* [C]

¹**jazz** /ˈdʒæz/ *n* [U] : a type of American music with lively rhythms and melodies that are often made up by musicians as they play • *a jazz musician*

²**jazz** *vb* — **jazz up** [*phrasal vb*] **jazz up** (*something*) *or* **jazz** (*something*) **up** *informal* : to make (something) more interesting, exciting, or attractive • *The company jazzed up its image.*

jazzy /ˈdʒæzi/ *adj* **jazz·i·er; -est** **1** : having the qualities of jazz music • *jazzy tunes* **2** *informal* : lively or fancy • *a jazzy suit*

jeal·ous /ˈdʒɛləs/ *adj* **1 a** : feeling or showing an unhappy or angry desire to have what someone else has • *His success made his friends jealous (of him).* **b** : feeling or showing unhappiness or anger because you think that someone you love likes or is liked by someone else • *a jealous husband* • *She became jealous*

when he talked to other women. • *in a jealous rage* **2** *formal* : very concerned about protecting or keeping something • *He is jealous of his privacy.* — **jeal·ous·ly** *adv* — **jeal·ou·sy** /ˈdʒɛləsi/ *n, pl* **-sies** [C/U]

jeans /ˈdʒiːnz/ *n* [*plural*] : pants made of denim • *He wore (a pair of) jeans.*

Jeep /ˈdʒiːp/ *trademark* — used for a kind of small truck

jeer /ˈdʒiɚ/ *vb* [T/I] : to laugh at or criticize someone in a loud and angry way • *The prisoner was jeered by the crowd.* — **jeer** *n* [C] • *He drew jeers from the crowd.*

Je·ho·vah /dʒɪˈhoʊvə/ *n* [*singular*] : GOD 1

jell /ˈdʒɛl/ *vb* [I] **1** : to become clear and definite • *Our plans are starting to jell.* **2** : to change into a thick substance • *Boil the jam until it jells.*

Jell-O /ˈdʒɛloʊ/ *trademark* — used for a dessert made with gelatin

jel·ly /ˈdʒɛli/ *n, pl* **-lies** **1** [C/U] : a soft food made by boiling sugar and fruit juice until it is thick • *a peanut butter and jelly sandwich* **2** [U] *Brit* : a dessert made with gelatin

jelly bean *n* [C] : a candy that is shaped like a bean

jel·ly·fish /ˈdʒɛliˌfɪʃ/ *n, pl* **jellyfish** [C] : a sea animal that has a very soft body and that can sting

jeop·ar·dize *also Brit* **jeop·ar·dise** /ˈdʒɛpɚˌdaɪz/ *vb* **-dized; -diz·ing** [T] : to put (something or someone) in danger • *The decision (seriously) jeopardized her career/health.*

jeop·ar·dy /ˈdʒɛpɚdi/ *n* — **in jeopardy** : in danger • *The decision put her career in (serious) jeopardy.*

¹**jerk** /ˈdʒɚk/ *n* [C] **1** *informal* : a person who is stupid or not well-liked or who treats other people badly • *Her boyfriend's a real jerk.* **2 a** : a quick pull or twist • *I gave the door a jerk, but it was stuck.* **b** : a sudden sharp movement • *The car started with a jerk.*

²**jerk** *vb* **1** [T] : to push, pull, or twist (something) with a quick movement • *She jerked the phone out of my hand.* **2** [T/I] **a** : to move with a sharp, quick motion • *The car jerked forward.* **b** : to cause (someone) to move suddenly • *He was jerked awake when the baby started crying.* — **jerk around** [*phrasal vb*] **jerk** (*someone*) **around** *chiefly US, informal* : to lie to or cheat (someone) • *I felt like I was getting jerked around by that salesman.*

¹**jer·ky** /ˈdʒɚki/ *n* [U] *US* : strips of dried meat • *beef jerky*

²**jerky** /ˈdʒɚki/ *adj* **jerk·i·er; -est** **1** : marked by quick rough motions or sudden starts and stops • *The movie was jerky and hard to watch.* **2** *informal* : foolish, stupid, or rude • *jerky behavior* — **jerk·i·ness** /ˈdʒɚkinəs/ *n* [U]

jer·ry-built /ˈdʒɛriˌbɪlt/ *adj, informal* : built cheaply and quickly • *jerry-built houses*

jer·ry-rigged /ˈdʒɛriˌrɪgd/ *adj, chiefly US* : made in a quick or careless way : not built or designed well • *a jerry-rigged heating system*

jer·sey /ˈdʒɚzi/ n, pl -seys 1 [C] : a loose shirt worn by a member of a sports team • a football jersey 2 [C] Brit : SWEATER a 3 [U] : a soft knitted cloth • a dress made of cotton jersey 4 Jersey [C] : a type of small, light brown cow

jest /ˈdʒɛst/ n [C/U] formal + old-fashioned : JOKE • a harmless jest • I said it in jest. [=I was joking] — jest vb [I] • You voted for him? Surely you jest. [=you must be joking]

jest·er /ˈdʒɛstɚ/ n [C] : a man who in the past was kept by a ruler to amuse people • the court jester

Je·sus Christ /ˈdʒiːzəsˈkraɪst/ n [singular] : the man who is the basis of the Christian religion — called also Christ, Jesus

¹**jet** /ˈdʒɛt/ n [C] 1 : a fast airplane that has one or more jet engines • a private/corporate jet 2 : a strong stream of liquid or gas that comes out through a narrow opening • jets of air

²**jet** vb jet·ted; jet·ting [T/I] 1 : to travel by jet airplane • She jetted (off) to London for a meeting. 2 : to come through a narrow opening with great force • Steam jetted from the kettle's spout.

jet black n [U] : a very dark black color — jet-black /ˈdʒɛtˈblæk/ adj • jet-black hair

jet engine n [C] : an engine in which heated air and gases shoot out and push the engine forward

jet lag n [U] : a tired feeling that you can get when you travel by airplane to a place that is far away • I still have jet lag after my flight. — jet-lagged /ˈdʒɛt-ˌlægd/ adj • jet-lagged tourists

jet-pro·pelled /ˈdʒɛtprəˈpɛld/ adj : moved forward by a jet engine • a jet-propelled missile — jet propulsion n [U]

jet·sam /ˈdʒɛtsəm/ n [U] : objects that are thrown into the water from a ship • (figurative) She was sorting through the flotsam and jetsam that had accumulated on her desk.

jet set n — the jet set : wealthy people who often travel to different parts of the world — jet-set·ter /ˈdʒɛtˌsɛtɚ/ n [C] • a hotel popular among jet-setters — jet-set·ting /ˈdʒɛtˌsɛtɪŋ/ adj • jet-setting film stars

jet stream n [C] technical : a current of fast winds high above the Earth's surface

jet·ti·son /ˈdʒɛtəsən/ vb [T] 1 : to drop (something) from a moving ship, airplane, etc. • jettison cargo/fuel 2 : to get rid of (something) • They jettisoned the plan/idea.

jet·ty /ˈdʒɛti/ n, pl -ties [C] : a long structure that is built out into water and used as a place to get on and off a boat

Jew /ˈdʒuː/ n [C] : someone whose religion is Judaism, who is descended from Jewish people, or who participates in Jewish culture — Jew·ish /ˈdʒuːwɪʃ/ adj • Are you Jewish? — Jew·ish·ness n [U]

jew·el /ˈdʒuːl/ n [C] 1 : a valuable stone that has been cut and polished • diamonds, rubies, and other jewels 2 : someone or something that is highly valued or admired • The building is one of the jewels of modern architecture. — see also CROWN JEWEL — jew·eled (US) or Brit jew·elled /ˈdʒuːld/ adj • a jeweled sword [=a sword decorated with jewels]

jew·el·er (US) or Brit jew·el·ler /ˈdʒuːlɚ/ n [C] : a person who makes, repairs, or sells jewelry and watches

jew·el·ry (US) or Brit jew·el·lery /ˈdʒuːl-ri/ n [U] : decorative objects (such as rings, necklaces, and earrings) that people wear on their body • silver jewelry • jewelry stores

Jew·ry /ˈdʒuːri/ n [U] formal : Jewish people as a group

¹**jibe** /ˈdʒaɪb/ vb jibed; jib·ing [I] US, informal : to agree with someone or something • His story didn't jibe with the testimony of other witnesses.

²**jibe** variant spelling of GIBE

jif·fy /ˈdʒɪfi/ n [singular] informal : a very brief time • I'll be there in a jiffy.

jig /ˈdʒɪg/ n [C] : a type of lively dance • She did/danced a little jig. — the jig is up US, informal + old-fashioned — used to say that a dishonest activity has been discovered and will be stopped

jig·ger /ˈdʒɪgɚ/ n [C] : a small glass used to measure alcohol • a jigger of rum

jig·gle /ˈdʒɪgəl/ vb jig·gled; jig·gling [T/I] : to move or cause (something) to move with quick, short movements up and down or side to side • He jiggled the doorknob. — jiggle n [C] • He gave the doorknob a jiggle.

jig·saw /ˈdʒɪgˌsɑː/ n [C] : a machine with a narrow blade for cutting curved lines

jigsaw puzzle n [C] : a picture that has been cut into many small pieces that can be fit back together • a jigsaw puzzle of Mount Fuji

ji·had /dʒɪˈhɑːd/ n [C] : a war fought by Muslims to spread or defend their beliefs

jilt /ˈdʒɪlt/ vb [T] : to end a romantic relationship with (someone) in a sudden and painful way • a jilted lover

jim·my /ˈdʒɪmi/ vb -mies; -mied; -my·ing [T] US : to force (something) open with a metal bar or a similar tool • The burglar jimmied the lock/door/window (open).

¹**jin·gle** /ˈdʒɪŋgəl/ n [C] 1 : a light ringing sound • I heard the jingle of bells. 2 : a short song that helps sell a product on TV or radio • an advertising jingle

²**jingle** vb jin·gled; jin·gling [T/I] : to make or cause (something) to make a light ringing sound • jingling bracelets/bells/coins

jin·go·ism /ˈdʒɪŋgoʊˌɪzəm/ n [U] disapproving : the beliefs of people who think that their country is always right and who are in favor of aggressive acts against other countries — jin·go·is·tic /ˌdʒɪŋgoʊˈɪstɪk/ adj

¹**jinx** /ˈdʒɪŋks/ n [C] informal : someone or something that causes bad luck • That guy is a jinx.

²**jinx** vb [T] informal : to bring bad luck to (someone or something) • She feels (like she has been) jinxed.

jit·ters /ˈdʒɪtɚz/ n — the jitters informal : a very nervous feeling • I always get the jitters before I give a speech. — jit·tery

/ˈdʒɪtəri/ *adj* • *jittery* [=*nervous*] *investors*

¹**jive** /ˈdʒaɪv/ *n* [*U*] *informal* + *old-fashioned* **1** *US* **a** : informal language that includes many slang terms • *talking jive* **b** : deceptive or foolish talk • *I'm tired of listening to your jive.* **2** : a type of fast, lively music

²**jive** *vb* **jived; jiv•ing** *informal* + *old-fashioned* **1** [*T/I*] *US* : to say foolish or deceptive things to (someone) • *He's just jiving (you).* **2** [*I*] : to dance to or play jive music • *jiving to the beat*

Jnr *abbr, Brit* junior • *Dave Smith Jnr*

job /ˈdʒɑːb/ *n* [*C*] **1** : the work that a person does regularly in order to earn money • *He took/got a job as a waiter.* • *The factory created thousands of jobs.* • *They offered him the job.* • *a part-time/full-time job* • *I could lose my job. = I could be out of a job.* • *He was injured on the job.* [=while working on a job] • *New employees are given on-the-job training.* **2** : a duty, task, or function that someone or something has • *It's your job to mow the lawn.* • *He does odd jobs* [=small tasks of different kinds that are not planned and do not happen regularly] *around the farm.* **3** — used to describe how well or badly something has been done • *Whoever planned the party did a good/great job.* [=that person planned the party very well] • *"I finished ahead of schedule." "Good job!"* **4** *informal* : a thing of some kind • *I bought one of those little quilted jobs at the craft fair.* **5** *informal* : a criminal act such as robbery • *They pulled the bank job.* [=they robbed the bank] • *The bank robbery was an inside job.* [=it was done by or with the help of someone who works in the bank] — **do a job on** *US, informal* : to damage (something or someone) badly • *Moving that sofa did a job on my back.* — **do the job** *informal* : to achieve a desired result • *A few more adjustments ought to do the job.* — **job•less** /ˈdʒɑːbləs/ *adj* — **job•less•ness** *n* [*U*]

jock /ˈdʒɑːk/ *n* [*C*] *chiefly US, informal* + *sometimes disapproving* : ATHLETE • *She was a jock in high school.* • *He's just a dumb jock.*

¹**jock•ey** /ˈdʒɑːki/ *n, pl* **-eys** [*C*] : someone who rides horses in races — see also DISC JOCKEY

²**jockey** *vb* **-eyed; -ey•ing** [*I*] : to do something in an effort to get an advantage • *political jockeying* • *Several companies are jockeying for position* [=are trying to get a better position or situation] *in the market.*

jock•strap /ˈdʒɑːkˌstræp/ *n* [*C*] : a piece of underwear worn by men and boys while playing sports

joc•u•lar /ˈdʒɑːkjələr/ *adj, formal* : playful and not serious • *a jocular man/conversation* — **joc•u•lar•i•ty** /ˌdʒɑːkjəˈlerəti/ *n* [*U*] — **joc•u•lar•ly** *adv*

jodh•purs /ˈdʒɑːdpərz/ *n* [*plural*] : pants worn for horseback riding

joe /ˈdʒoʊ/ *n, US, informal* **1** *or* **Joe** [*C*] : an ordinary man • *an average Joe* **2** [*singular*] : COFFEE • *I need a cup of joe.*

¹**jog** /ˈdʒɑːg/ *vb* **jogged; jog•ging** **1** [*I*] : to run slowly • *She jogs three miles a*

day. • *She goes jogging every day.* **2** [*T*] : to push or bump (someone or something) lightly • *She jogged him with her elbow.* — **jog someone's memory** : to cause or help someone to remember something • *Maybe this photo will jog your memory.* — **jog•ger** /ˈdʒɑːgər/ *n* [*C*]

²**jog** *n* [*C*] : a slow run done for exercise • *We're going for a jog around the park.*

john /ˈdʒɑːn/ *n* [*C*] *chiefly US, informal* **1** : BATHROOM • *He's in the john.* **2** : a man who pays money to a prostitute for sex

John Doe /ˈdʒɑːnˈdoʊ/ *n* [*C*] *US, law* — used as a name for a man whose true name is not known or is being kept secret

John Han•cock /ˈdʒɑːnˈhænˌkɑːk/ *n* [*C*] *US* : a person's signature • *He put his John Hancock on the contract.* [=he signed the contract]

john•ny /ˈdʒɑːni/ *n, pl* **-nies** [*C*] *US* : a loose piece of clothing that is worn by someone who is being examined or treated by a doctor

join /ˈdʒɔɪn/ *vb* **1 a** [*T*] : to put or bring (two or more things) together • *She joined the pieces (together) with glue.* : to connect (two or more things) • *The islands are joined by a bridge.* **b** [*T/I*] : to come together with (something) • *The roads/rivers join (each other) near here.* • *The paths eventually join up (with each other).* **2 a** [*T*] : to go somewhere in order to be with (a person or group) • *Would you like to join us for lunch?* • *May I join you?* **b** [*T/I*] : to do something with (a person or group) • *They joined (me) in congratulating her on a job well done.* • *The singer asked the whole audience to join in.* **c** [*T/I*] : to become involved in (something) • *Please join the line and wait your turn.* • *He joined (in) the conversation/debate.* **3** [*T/I*] : to become a member of (a group or organization) • *She joined the band/club.* • *joining the Navy* • *More than 100 people have joined up.* — **if you can't beat them, join them** see ¹BEAT — **join forces** see ¹FORCE — **join hands** : to hold the hand of another person • *(figurative) We can do it if we all join hands and work together.* — **join (someone) in marriage/ matrimony** *formal* : to marry (someone) • *They were joined in marriage this morning.* — **join the club** see ¹CLUB — **join up** [*phrasal vb*] : to meet each other at a particular place • *Let's join up (with each other) after the game.*

join•er /ˈdʒɔɪnər/ *n* [*C*] **1** *US* : a person who joins many organizations **2** *chiefly Brit* : a person whose job is to build things (such as door or window frames) by joining pieces of wood

join•ery /ˈdʒɔɪnəri/ *n* [*U*] : the work done by a joiner (sense 2)

¹**joint** /ˈdʒɔɪnt/ *n* **1** [*C*] **a** : a point where two bones meet in the body • *the elbow/ knee joint* **b** : a place where two things or parts are joined • *seal the joints of the pipes* **2** [*C*] *informal* **a** : a particular place • *People were running all over the joint.* [=*everywhere*] • *(US, informal) The team is really stinking up the joint.* [=per-

forming badly] **b** : a cheap bar or club ▪ *Let's get out of this joint.* **c** : an informal restaurant ▪ *a burger/pizza joint* **3** [*C*] *informal* : a marijuana cigarette ▪ *smoking a joint* **4** *the joint US slang* : PRISON ▪ *five years in the joint* **5** [*C*] *chiefly Brit* : a large piece of meat ▪ *a roasting joint* — **out of joint 1** *of a bone* : out of its socket ▪ *His shoulder kept slipping out of joint.* **2** *informal* : not in agreement or order ▪ *My plans have gotten a little out of joint.*

²**joint** *adj, always before a noun* **1** : done by or involving two or more people or groups ▪ *a joint session of (both houses of) Congress* ▪ *a joint venture/effort* ▪ *filing a joint tax return* ▪ *divorced parents who have joint custody of their child* **2** : doing something together ▪ *joint owners* — **joint·ly** *adv* ▪ *jointly owned property*

Joint Chiefs of Staff *n* [*plural*] : a group made up of the leaders of the U.S. Army, Navy, Air Force, and Marines that advises the President

joist /ˈdʒoɪst/ *n* [*C*] : a strong, heavy board that supports a floor or ceiling

¹**joke** /ˈdʒoʊk/ *n* [*C*] **1** : something said or done to cause laughter ▪ *She meant it as a joke, but he took her seriously.* ▪ *They are always making jokes about his car.* ▪ *He thought he could embarrass us, but now the joke is on him.* [=he is the one who looks foolish] ▪ *He just can't take a joke.* [=he gets upset when other people make jokes about him] **b** : a brief story with a surprising and funny ending ▪ *She's always cracking/telling jokes.* ▪ *I didn't get/understand the joke.* ▪ *an inside joke* [=a joke that is understood only by people with special knowledge about something] **2** *disapproving* : someone or something that is not worth taking seriously ▪ *That exam was a joke.* ▪ *Being lost in the woods is no joke.* [=it is a serious situation]

²**joke** *vb* **joked; jok·ing** [*T/I*] : to tell or make jokes ▪ *My friends would joke about my work uniform.* ▪ *She joked that she might quit her job.* ▪ *Don't take it seriously: I was only joking.* ▪ *"The report is due today." "You're joking."* = *"You must be joking."* [=that is very surprising or hard to believe] ▪ *It's no joking matter.* [=it is a serious matter] — **joking aside** or Brit **joking apart** — used to introduce a serious statement that follows a humorous statement ▪ *This looks like a job for Superman! But joking aside, this is a serious problem and we're going to need help.* — **jok·ing·ly** /ˈdʒoʊkɪŋli/ *adv* ▪ *She spoke jokingly about quitting her job.*

jok·er /ˈdʒoʊkɚ/ *n* [*C*] **1** : a person who tells or makes many jokes ▪ *a constant joker* **2** : an extra playing card used in some card games ▪ *Jokers are wild in this game.* **3** *informal* : an annoying, stupid, or offensive person ▪ *I can't believe that joker beat me.*

joke·ster /ˈdʒoʊkstɚ/ *n* [*C*] : JOKER 1 ▪ *the family jokester*

jok·ey /ˈdʒoʊki/ *adj, informal* : tending or intended to make people laugh ▪ *a jokey movie*

¹**jol·ly** /ˈdʒɑːli/ *adj* **jol·li·er; -est 1** : hap-

py and cheerful ▪ *He's a very jolly man.* **2** *old-fashioned* : very pleasant or enjoyable ▪ *She had a jolly time at the party.*

²**jolly** *adv, Brit, informal + old-fashioned* : very or extremely ▪ *a jolly good time/fellow/book* — **jolly well** — used to emphasize anger, annoyance, or disapproval ▪ *You'll jolly well do as you're told!*

¹**jolt** /ˈdʒoʊlt/ *vb* **1** [*T/I*] : to move or cause (something or someone) to move in a quick and sudden way ▪ *He (was) jolted forward when the bus stopped suddenly.* ▪ *The loud bang jolted me awake.* **2** [*T*] : to surprise or shock (someone) ▪ *She jolted the medical world with her announcement.* ▪ *a jolting experience*

²**jolt** *n* [*C*] **1** : a sudden, rough movement ▪ *The car stopped with a jolt.* **2** : a sudden shock or surprise ▪ *I got/had quite a jolt when I heard the door slam.* **3** : a small but powerful amount of something ▪ *a jolt of electricity* ▪ *The praise gave him a jolt of confidence.*

josh /ˈdʒɑːʃ/ *vb* [*T/I*] *informal* : to talk to someone in a friendly and joking way ▪ *He's just joshing (you).*

jos·tle /ˈdʒɑːsəl/ *vb* **jos·tled; jos·tling** [*T/I*] : to push against (someone) while moving against in a crowd of people ▪ *Everyone was jostling (each other) for a better view.*

¹**jot** /ˈdʒɑːt/ *vb* **jot·ted; jot·ting** [*T*] : to write down (something) quickly ▪ *He jotted (down) a few notes on a slip of paper.*

²**jot** *n* [*singular*] *informal + old-fashioned* : the smallest amount ▪ *It doesn't make a jot of difference.*

jot·tings /ˈdʒɑːtɪŋz/ *n* [*plural*] : notes that are written down quickly ▪ *the jottings in his notebooks*

joule /ˈdʒuːl/ *n* [*C*] *physics* : a unit of work or energy

jour·nal /ˈdʒɚnl/ *n* [*C*] **1** : DIARY ▪ *She keeps a journal.* **2 a** : a newspaper — usually used in titles ▪ *the Wall Street Journal* **b** : a serious magazine that reports on things of special interest to a particular group of people ▪ *a medical/scholarly journal*

jour·nal·ism /ˈdʒɚnəˌlɪzəm/ *n* [*U*] : the activity or job of collecting, writing, and editing news stories ▪ *investigative/broadcast journalism* — **jour·nal·ist** /ˈdʒɚnəlɪst/ *n* [*C*] ▪ *She is a respected journalist.* — **jour·nal·is·tic** /ˌdʒɚnəˈlɪstɪk/ *adj*

¹**jour·ney** /ˈdʒɚni/ *n, pl* **-neys** [*C*] : an act of traveling from one place to another : TRIP ▪ *a long journey across the country* ▪ *We wished her a safe journey.* ▪ *(figurative) a spiritual journey*

²**journey** *vb* **-neyed; -ney·ing** [*I*] : to go on a journey : TRAVEL ▪ *the first woman to journey into space*

jour·ney·man /ˈdʒɚnimən/ *n, pl* **-men** [*C*] **1** : a worker who learns a skill and then works for another person ▪ *a journeyman carpenter* **2** : a worker, performer, or athlete who is experienced and good but not excellent ▪ *a journeyman ball player*

joust /ˈdʒaʊst/ *vb* [*I*] *of knights in the Middle Ages* : to fight on horseback with lances • (*figurative*) verbal jousting — **joust** n [C]

jo·vi·al /ˈdʒouvijəl/ adj : CHEERFUL 1 • *They were in a jovial mood.* • *a jovial woman* • *a jovial party* /ˌdʒouviˈælæti/ n [U] — **jo·vi·al·ly** adv

jowl /ˈdʒawəl/ n [C] : loose flesh on the cheeks, lower jaw, or throat — usually plural • *a man with heavy jowls* — **cheek by jowl** see CHEEK — **jowly** /ˈdʒauli/ adj • *a jowly face/man*

joy /ˈdʒoi/ n 1 [U] : a feeling of great happiness • *tears of joy* • *He found great joy in (doing) his work.* • *They were shouting/jumping for joy.* [=they shouted/jumped because they were very happy] 2 [C] : a source or cause of great happiness • *What a joy it was to see her again.* • *the joys of parenthood* • *Her son is her pride and joy.* [=her son makes her very proud and happy] 3 [U] Brit, informal : success in doing, finding, or getting something • *"You've spent hours looking for it. Any joy?" "No joy whatsoever, I'm afraid. I can't find it."* — **joy·less** /ˈdʒoiləs/ adj • *a joyless occasion/person/look* — **joy·less·ly** adv

joy·ful /ˈdʒoifəl/ adj : feeling, causing, or showing great happiness • *the children's joyful faces* • *joyful news* — **joy·ful·ly** adv — **joy·ful·ness** n [U]

joy·ous /ˈdʒojəs/ adj : JOYFUL • *a joyous day/celebration* — **joy·ous·ly** adv — **joy·ous·ness** n [U]

joy·ride /ˈdʒoiˌraid/ n [C] : a fast car ride taken for pleasure • *Some teenager stole my car and took it for a joyride.* — **joy·rid·er** /ˈdʒoiˌraidɚ/ n [C] — **joy·rid·ing** /ˈdʒoiˌraidiŋ/ n [U] • *He went joyriding in my car.*

joy·stick /ˈdʒoiˌstik/ n [C] 1 : an upright lever used to control an airplane 2 : a lever used to control the movement of images on the screen in a computer or video game

J.P. abbr justice of the peace

Jr. abbr junior • *John Smith, Jr.*

ju·bi·lant /ˈdʒuːbələnt/ adj : very happy • *a jubilant crowd/celebration* — **ju·bi·lant·ly** adv — **ju·bi·la·tion** /ˌdʒuːbəˈleiʃən/ n [U] • *the jubilation of the crowd*

ju·bi·lee /ˈdʒuːbəˌliː, ˌdʒuːbəˈliː/ n [C] : a special anniversary • *a silver/golden jubilee*

Ju·da·ism /ˈdʒuːdəˌizəm/ n [U] : the religion that stresses belief in God and faithfulness to the laws of the Torah : the religion of the Jewish people — **Ju·da·ic** /dʒuˈdejik/ adj • *Judaic tradition*

¹judge /ˈdʒʌdʒ/ vb **judged; judg·ing 1** [T/I] : to form an opinion about (something or someone) after careful thought • *You shouldn't judge people by their appearance.* • *Her pie was judged (to be) the best.* • *Judging by/from its smell, I'd say the milk is spoiled.* **2** [T] : to regard (someone) as either good or bad • *Who are you to judge me?* • *Don't judge her too severely/harshly.* **3** [T] law : to make a decision about a legal case or about the guilt or innocence of someone • *The jury will be asked to judge the defendant's guilt.* **4** [T] : to decide the winner of (a competition) • *judge a contest*

²judge n [C] **1 a** law : a person who has the power to make decisions on cases brought before a court of law • *a federal judge* — often used as a title • *The case is being heard by Judge Smith.* **b** : a person who decides the winner in a contest or competition • *a panel of judges* **2 a** : a person who makes a decision or judgment • *"These problems don't concern you." "I'll be the judge of that!"* [=I'll decide if they concern me] **b** : a person who is good, bad, etc., at making judgments • *She is a good judge of character.*

judge·ship /ˈdʒʌdʒˌʃip/ n [C] chiefly US, law : the position of being a judge • *She was appointed to a federal judgeship.*

judg·ment or chiefly Brit **judge·ment** /ˈdʒʌdʒmənt/ n **1 a** [C] : an opinion or decision that is based on careful thought • *In my judgment, the stock has performed badly.* • *The judgment of the editors is final.* • *I stayed, even though it was against my better judgment.* [=even though I did not think it was the best thing to do] • *value judgments* [=opinions about the worth or value of something] **b** [U] : the act or process of forming an opinion or making a decision after careful thought • *She rushed to judgment without examining the evidence.* • *Don't pass judgment on me* [=don't criticize me] *until you know all the facts.* **2** [U] : the ability to make good decisions about what should be done • *He showed bad judgment.* = *He showed a lack of judgment.* **3** [C] law : a decision made by a court • *a judgment in favor of the plaintiffs* — **sit in judgment** : to say whether or not someone or something is morally good, proper, etc. • *He has no right to sit in judgment on/of/over me.* [=he has no right to judge me]

judg·men·tal or chiefly Brit **judge·men·tal** /ˌdʒʌdʒˈmɛntl̩/ adj **1** disapproving : tending to judge people too quickly and critically • *He's judgmental of everyone except himself.* **2** : of, relating to, or involving judgment • *a judgmental error*

judgment call n [C] : a decision that is based on your opinion • *The rules aren't clear, so officials must make a judgment call.*

Judgment Day n [U] : the day when according to some religions all people will be judged by God

ju·di·cial /dʒuˈdiʃəl/ adj, always before a noun **1** : of or relating to courts of law or judges • *the judicial system* • *the judicial branch of government* **2** : ordered or done by a court • *a judicial decision*

ju·di·cia·ry /dʒuˈdiʃiˌeri, dʒuˈdiʃɚi/ n [U] : the courts of law and judges in a country • *the federal judiciary*

ju·di·cious /dʒuˈdiʃəs/ adj, formal : having or showing good judgment : WISE • *judicious use of our resources* • *a judicious decision* — **ju·di·cious·ly** adv — **ju·di·cious·ness** n [U]

ju·do /ˈdʒuːˌdou/ n [U] : a sport developed in Japan in which opponents try to throw each other to the ground

jug /ˈdʒʌg/ n [C] **1** chiefly US : a large, deep container with a narrow opening and a handle ▪ *a jug of cider* **2** *chiefly Brit* : ²PITCHER

jug·ger·naut /ˈdʒʌɡɚˌnɑːt/ *n* [*C*] **1** : an extremely large and powerful force, campaign, etc., that cannot be stopped ▪ *an advertising/political juggernaut* **2** *Brit* : a very large, heavy truck

jug·gle /ˈdʒʌɡəl/ *vb* **jug·gled; jug·gling** **1** [*T/I*] : to keep several objects in motion in the air at the same time by repeatedly throwing and catching them ▪ *He can juggle four balls at once.* **2** [*T*] : to do (several things) at the same time ▪ *It can be hard to juggle family responsibilities and/with the demands of a full-time job.* — **jug·gler** /ˈdʒʌɡlɚ/ *n* [*C*]

jug·u·lar /ˈdʒʌɡjələ/ *n* [*C*] : JUGULAR VEIN — **go for the jugular** *informal* : to attack an opponent in a very aggressive way ▪ *He went for the jugular in the debate.*

jugular vein *n* [*C*] : a large vein in the neck

¹juice /ˈdʒuːs/ *n* **1 a** [*C/U*] : liquid that can be squeezed out of vegetables and fruits ▪ *a glass of apple/orange/carrot juice* **b** [*U, plural*] : the liquid part of meat ▪ *beef juices* **2** [*U*] *informal* : ELECTRICITY **1** ▪ *The battery ran out of juice.* **3** [*C*] : the natural fluids in your stomach — usually plural ▪ *digestive juices* **4** [*plural*] *informal* : energy that gives you the ability to do something in a very effective way — used with *flow* ▪ *Her creative juices have started flowing again.*

²juice *vb* **juiced; juic·ing** [*T*] : to remove juice from (a fruit or vegetable) ▪ *juice a lemon* — **juic·er** /ˈdʒuːsɚ/ *n* [*C*]

juicy /ˈdʒuːsi/ *adj* **juic·i·er; -est** **1** : containing a lot of juice ▪ *juicy oranges* **2** *informal* : very interesting and exciting especially because of shocking or sexual elements ▪ *juicy news/gossip* — **juic·i·ness** /ˈdʒuːsinəs/ *n* [*U*]

juke·box /ˈdʒuːkˌbɑːks/ *n* [*C*] : a machine that plays music when money is put into it

Jul. *abbr* July

Ju·ly /dʒʊˈlaɪ/ *n* [*C/U*] : the seventh month of the year ▪ *The wedding is in (early/late) July.* ▪ *On July the first = (US) on July first = on the first of July* ▪ *It happens every July.* — abbr. **Jul.**

¹jum·ble /ˈdʒʌmbəl/ *vb* **jum·bled; jumbling** [*T*] : to cause (things) to be mixed together in a disorderly way ▪ *He jumbled (up) the wires when he moved the TV.* ▪ *The necklaces were all jumbled together in the box.* ▪ *jumbled thoughts*

²jumble *n* **1** [*C*] : a group of things that are not arranged in a neat or orderly way ▪ *a jumble of wires* **2** [*U*] *Brit* : unwanted things (such as old clothes) that are being sold in an informal sale ▪ *a bag/box of jumble*

jumble sale *n* [*C*] *Brit* : RUMMAGE SALE

jum·bo /ˈdʒʌmboʊ/ *adj, always before a noun* : very large ▪ *jumbo shrimp*

jumbo jet *n* [*C*] : a very large airplane

¹jump /ˈdʒʌmp/ *vb* **1 a** [*I*] : to move your body upward from the ground by pushing with your legs ▪ *The cat jumped (up) onto the table.* ▪ *The fans were jumping up and down with excitement.* ▪ *We jumped*

for joy *when we won the award.* **b** [*I*] : to cause your body to drop from something by pushing with your legs ▪ *The cat jumped down off/from the table.* ▪ *jump off a bridge* **c** [*T/I*] : to move forward through the air and over (something) ▪ *a runner jumping (over) a hurdle* **2** [*I*] **a** : to move quickly ▪ *He jumped into/in his truck and drove away.* ▪ *She jumped up [=she stood up quickly] and ran out the door.* ▪ *(figurative) The team jumped from last place to first place.* ▪ *(figurative) She always jumps to his defense.* [=quickly defends him] ▪ *(figurative) They jumped into action.* [=acted immediately] **b** : to make a sudden movement because of surprise or shock ▪ *She jumped when she heard a loud knock late at night.* ▪ *I almost jumped out of my skin.* [=I was very surprised] **3** [*I*] : to start or go forward quickly ▪ *She jumped (off) to an early lead in the race.* **4** [*I*] : to suddenly increase in value or amount ▪ *The price of gasoline jumped (by) 10 percent.* **5** [*I*] **a** : to go in a sudden and unexpected way ▪ *jumping from job to job* **b** : to suddenly go forward to a later point ▪ *He jumped (ahead) to the end of the book.* **6** [*I*] : to be lively with activity ▪ *The place was jumping.* **7** [*T*] : to attack (a person) especially in a robbery ▪ *He was jumped by a mugger.* **8** [*I*] : to behave in an energetic way especially to please another person ▪ *When the boss walks in, everybody jumps.* **9** [*T*] *chiefly US* : to get onto (a moving train) ▪ *jump a train* **10** [*T*] : to begin moving before (a signal to begin) ▪ *The car ahead of me jumped the light.* [=started moving before the traffic light turned green] — **jump all over** *informal* : to angrily criticize or shout at (someone) ▪ *His mother jumped all over him for being late.* — **jump at** [*phrasal vb*] : to eagerly take (a chance, offer, etc.) ▪ *She jumped at the chance/opportunity to go sailing.* — **jump down someone's throat** see THROAT — **jump in** [*phrasal vb*] *informal* : to join a conversation ▪ *Jump in if you have any questions.* — **jump on** [*phrasal vb*] *informal* **1** : to angrily criticize or shout at (someone) ▪ *The coach jumped on him for not playing hard enough.* **2 a** : to strongly attack or criticize (something) ▪ *She was quick to jump on his mistakes.* **b** : to get on (a train, bus, etc.) ▪ *She jumped on a bus to Denver.* — **jump out at** [*phrasal vb*] **1** : to suddenly come at (someone) from a hiding place ▪ *The assailant jumped out at them.* **2** : to immediately get the attention of (someone) ▪ *I checked for errors, but nothing jumped out at me.* [=I did not notice any errors] — **jump rope** see ¹ROPE — **jump ship** see ¹SHIP — **jump the queue** see QUEUE — **jump the track(s)/rails** : to come off the track ▪ *The train jumped the track.* — **jump through hoops** *informal* : to do a complicated or annoying series of things in order to get or achieve something ▪ *We had to jump through a lot of hoops to get a loan from the bank.*

²jump *n* **1** [*C*] : an act of jumping ▪ *He made a running jump over the fence.* **2**

[*singular*] : a sudden movement because of surprise or shock ▪ *He gave a jump when she entered the room.* **3** [C] **a** : something to be jumped over ▪ *The horse took/cleared the first jump easily.* **b** : something that you ride over in order to jump through the air ▪ *a motorcycle jump* **4** [C] : a sudden increase ▪ *a jump in the price of gasoline* ▪ *a jump in sales* — **a hop, skip, and (a) jump** see ²HOP — **get/have/gain a/the jump on** : to get or have an early advantage over (someone) by acting quickly or doing something first ▪ *We need to get the jump on our competitors.* — **one jump ahead** ✧ If you are/keep/stay *one jump ahead* of someone, you have or keep an advantage over someone by learning about or doing something new.

jump·er /ˈdʒʌmpɚ/ *n* [C] **1** : a person or animal that jumps ▪ *a good jumper* **2** *US* : a type of dress with no sleeves that is worn with a blouse **3** *Brit* : SWEATER a **4** *basketball* : JUMP SHOT

jumper cables *n* [*plural*] *US* : cables used to jump-start a vehicle

jumping jack *n* [C] *US* : an exercise in which a standing person jumps to a position with the legs and arms spread out and then jumps back to the original position

jumping–off point *n* [C] : a place or point from which something begins ▪ *a jumping-off point for a discussion* — called also *jumping-off place*

jump rope *n, US* **1** [C] : a rope used in exercise or a children's game that involves jumping over it when it is swung near the ground **2** [U] : the game of jumping over a jump rope ▪ *children playing jump rope*

jump shot *n* [C] : a basketball shot made while jumping

jump–start /ˈdʒʌmpˈstɑɚt/ *vb* [T] **1** : to start (a vehicle whose battery is not working) by connecting its battery to another source of power (such as the battery of another vehicle) ▪ *I used his truck to jump-start my car.* **2 a** : to cause (something) to start quickly ▪ *jump-starting a political campaign* **b** : to give new energy to (something) ▪ *a plan to jump-start the economy* — **jump–start** *n* [C] ▪ *give the car a jump-start*

jump·suit /ˈdʒʌmpˌsuːt/ *n* [C] : a piece of clothing that consists of a shirt with attached pants

jumpy /ˈdʒʌmpi/ *adj* **jump·i·er**; **-est** *informal* : nervous or easily frightened ▪ *trying to calm jumpy passengers*

Jun. *abbr* June

junc·tion /ˈdʒʌŋkʃən/ *n* [C] **1** : a place where two things join ▪ *a junction of nerves and muscle* **2** : a place where roads or railroad lines come together ▪ *the junction of Route 12 and Route 87*

junc·ture /ˈdʒʌŋktʃɚ/ *n* [C] **1** : an important point in a process or activity ▪ *Negotiations reached a critical juncture.* **2** : a place where things join : JUNCTION ▪ *the juncture of two rivers*

June /ˈdʒuːn/ *n* [C/U] : the sixth month of the year ▪ *Her birthday is in June.* ▪ *on June the first* = (*US*) *on June first* = *on the*

first of June ▪ *It happens every June.* — abbr. *Jun.*

jun·gle /ˈdʒʌŋgəl/ *n* [C] **1** : a tropical forest where plants and trees grow very thickly ▪ *a dense jungle* **2** : a harsh or dangerous place or situation in which people struggle for survival or success ▪ *the corporate jungle* ▪ *It's a jungle out there.* — **the law of the jungle** see LAW

jungle gym *n* [C] *US* : a structure of metal bars for children to climb on

¹**ju·nior** /ˈdʒuːnjɚ/ *adj* **1** *not before a noun, US* — used in the form *Jr.* to identify a son who has the same name as his father ▪ *John Smith Jr. and John Smith Sr.* **2** *always before a noun* : lower in standing or rank ▪ *a junior partner in the law firm* ▪ *a junior officer* **3** *always before a noun* : designed for or done by young people ▪ *junior hockey/tennis*

²**junior** *n* [C] **1** : a person who is younger or of lower rank than another person ▪ *He is six years my junior.* [=he is six years younger than I am] **2 a** *US* : a student in the third year in a high school or college ▪ *She's a junior at a state college.* ▪ *the junior class/prom* **b** *Brit* : a student at a junior school **3** *US, informal* — used like a name for a male child or son ▪ *They brought junior to the park.*

junior college *n* [C] *US* : a school that has two years of studies similar to those in the first two years of a four-year college

junior high school *n* [C] *US* : a school usually including the seventh, eighth, and sometimes ninth grades

junior school *n* [C] *Brit* : a school for children aged 7 to 11

ju·ni·per /ˈdʒuːnəpɚ/ *n* [C/U] : an evergreen shrub or tree that has tiny fruits that look like berries

¹**junk** /ˈdʒʌŋk/ *n* [U] **1** : old things that have been thrown away or that have little value ▪ *The yard was cluttered with junk.* **2** : something that is in very poor condition ▪ *That car is (a piece of) junk.* **3** : material that has no real value or interest ▪ *There's nothing but junk on TV tonight.* — **junky** /ˈdʒʌŋki/ *adj, chiefly US, informal* ▪ *junky old furniture*

²**junk** *vb* [T] *informal* : to get rid of (something) because it is worthless, damaged, etc. ▪ *We junked our old computer.*

junk bond *n* [C] *business* : a type of bond that pays high interest but also has a high risk

jun·ket /ˈdʒʌŋkət/ *n* [C] *chiefly US* : a trip or journey that is paid for by someone else ▪ *the senator's junkets to foreign countries*

junk food *n* [C/U] *informal* : food that contains high amounts of fat or sugar ▪ *eating too much junk food*

junk·ie *also* **junky** /ˈdʒʌŋki/ *n, pl* **junk·ies** [C] *informal* **1** : a person who uses illegal drugs ▪ *a heroin junkie* **2** : a person who has an unusual amount of interest in something ▪ *a news/political junkie*

junk mail *n* [U] : mail that is not wanted and consists mostly of advertising

junk·yard /ˈdʒʌŋkˌjɑɚd/ *n* [C] : a place where you can leave junk ▪ *The car was hauled off to the junkyard.*

jun·ta /ˈhʊntə/ n [C] : a military group controlling a government after taking control of it by force

Ju·pi·ter /ˈdʒuːpətər/ n [singular] : the large planet that is fifth in order from the sun

ju·ris·dic·tion /ˌdʒərəsˈdɪkʃən/ n 1 [U] : the power or right to make judgments about the law, to punish criminals, etc. • The matter falls outside/within the jurisdiction of this court. 2 [U] : the right to govern an area • territory under the jurisdiction of the U.S. government 3 [C] : an area within which a particular system of laws is used • He was arrested in another jurisdiction. — **ju·ris·dic·tion·al** /ˌdʒərəsˈdɪkʃənl/ adj

ju·ris·pru·dence /ˌdʒərəsˈpruːdəns/ n [U] formal : the study of law • American jurisprudence

ju·rist /ˈdʒərɪst/ n [C] : a person who has a thorough knowledge of law; especially : ²JUDGE 1

ju·ror /ˈdʒərər/ n [C] : a member of a jury

ju·ry /ˈdʒəri/ n, pl **-ries** [C] 1 : a group of citizens who are chosen to make a decision in a legal case • The jury found the defendant guilty/innocent. • (figurative) The jury is still out on [=no one knows yet] whether the new company will succeed. 2 : a group of people who decide the winners in a contest • The jury judged her pie to be the best.

ju·ry-rig /ˈdʒəriˌrɪg/ vb **-rigged**; **-rig·ging** [T] chiefly US : to build (something) using the materials that you have available • He jury-rigged a new antenna out of coat hangers.

¹**just** /ˈdʒʌst/ adj, formal 1 : morally right or good : FAIR • a just decision/person/society 2 : deserved and appropriate • a just punishment/reward • The criminal got his just deserts. [=the punishment he deserved] — **just·ly** adv • She is justly admired. — **just·ness** /ˈdʒʌstnəs/ n [U]

²**just** adv 1 : to an exact degree or in an exact manner • You look just like your father. • He was just like all the other men she'd dated. • I have just the thing [=the best or perfect thing] for your hair. 2 a : very recently • The bell just rang. • She had just returned when he entered. b : at this or that exact moment or time • I was just going to call you! c — used to say that events are happening at the same time or with very little time between them • He confessed just before he died. The phone rang just as/when we were leaving. • I came just as soon as I heard the news. d — used to emphasize that a moment or time is not far from the present moment • I saw her just yesterday. 3 a : by a small amount • I arrived just in time to see him win. • We should be there in just under an hour. b : by a small distance • The café is just down the street. 4 a : nothing more than : ONLY • He is just an assistant to the manager. • She was just a baby during the war. • We have just two more miles to go. • I've met him just (the) once. [=only one time] • She's just somebody I work with. • He's just another guy trying to get rich. • She's not just my friend, she's my lawyer. [=she's my friend

and my lawyer] b — used to stress the simple truth of a description or statement • We'd like to buy a new car. We just don't have the money. • You'll just have to wait. • I feel just great! • They camped in the backyard, just for fun. [=simply to have fun] c — used in polite requests • Could I just borrow that pen for a minute? Thanks! d — used for emphasis when you give an order or make a suggestion • Don't argue with me: just do it! • Just look at the size of that thing! e — used to describe what someone does instead of doing what is necessary or expected • Don't just stand there: do something! 5 — used to refer to something that is possible • You don't expect him to succeed, but he might/may/could just surprise you. [=he might/may/could succeed] • It's a crazy idea, but it just might work! — **just about** : almost or nearly • The work is just about done. • That's just about the stupidest thing I've ever heard. — **just a minute/second/moment** 1 — used to ask someone to wait or stop briefly • Just a second and I'll get that book for you. 2 — used to demand that someone stop or listen • Just a minute! You can't park there! — **just anyone** : any person at all • I don't lend money to just anyone. — **just as** : to an equal degree as • Our house is just as nice as theirs. : in the same way as • Just as I thought, the door is locked. [=I thought the door would be locked, and it is] — **just as soon** ◇ If you would just as soon do something, you would prefer to do it. • We asked him to come with us, but he said he'd just as soon stay home. — **just as well** ◇ If it is just as well that something happens, then it is a good thing, even if it was not expected or intended. • It's just as well she didn't get that job, since she'll now be closer to home. — **just like that** : very suddenly • She vanished just like that. — **just now or just this minute/second** 1 : a moment ago • I saw him just now. 2 : at this moment • They are leaving just this minute. — **just so** : in a particular way • Everything has to be arranged just so [=exactly as she likes it] or she gets upset. — **just the same** see ²SAME — **just yet** : right now — used in negative statements to say that something is not done yet or true yet but will be soon • I haven't finished just yet. • "Are you ready?" "Not just yet."

jus·tice /ˈdʒʌstəs/ n 1 [U] : the process or result of using laws to fairly judge and punish crimes and criminals • the justice system • criminals attempting to escape justice • The killer was brought to justice. [=arrested and punished for a crime in a court of law] 2 Justice — used as a title for a judge (such as a judge of the U.S. Supreme Court) • Justice Marshall 3 [U] a : the quality of being fair or just • a sense of justice b : fair treatment • striving to achieve justice for all people • (figurative) Words could never do justice to [=could not adequately describe] her beauty. • The movie does not do the book justice. [=the movie is not as good as the book]

justice of the peace n [C] : a local official who decides minor legal cases and in the U.S. performs marriages — abbr. *J.P.*

jus·ti·fy /'dʒʌstə,faɪ/ vb **-fies**; **-fied**; **-fy·ing** [T] **1** : to provide or be a good reason for (something) • *He tried to justify his behavior by saying he was pressured by his boss.* • *It's hard to justify spending money on a new car right now.* **2** : to provide a good reason for the actions of (someone) • *She was (perfectly/fully) justified in* [=she had a good reason for] *complaining to her boss.* • *Why should I have to justify myself?* [=to provide an explanation for my actions] — **jus·ti·fi·able** /'dʒʌstə,faɪəbəl/ adj — **jus·ti·fi·ably** /'dʒʌstə,faɪəbli/ adv • *They were justifiably proud of their son.* — **jus·ti·fi·ca·tion** /,dʒʌstəfə'keɪʃən/ n [C/U] • *There's no justification for what she did.* • *His behavior is without justification.*

jut /'dʒʌt/ vb **jut·ted**; **jut·ting** [T/I] : to stick out, up, or forward • *mountains jutting (up) into the sky* • *He jutted out his jaw in defiance.*

jute /'dʒuːt/ n [U] : a fiber used for making rope and cloth

¹**ju·ve·nile** /'dʒuː və,najəl/ adj **1** *disapproving* : unpleasantly childish and immature • *juvenile pranks* **2** *always before a noun* **a** : relating to or meant for young people • *juvenile fiction* **b** : of or relating to young people who have committed crimes • *a juvenile court* **3** : not yet fully grown • *juvenile animals*

²**juvenile** n [C] **1** : a young person • *crimes committed by juveniles* **2** : a young bird or animal

juvenile delinquent n [C] : a young person who has committed a crime — **juvenile delinquency** n [U]

jux·ta·pose /'dʒʌkstə,poʊz/ vb **-posed**; **-pos·ing** [T] *formal* : to place (different things) together in order to create an interesting effect or to show how they are the same or different • *juxtaposing modern art with classical art* — **jux·ta·po·si·tion** /,dʒʌkstəpə'zɪʃən/ n [C/U] • *an interesting juxtaposition of colors*

K

k or **K** /'keɪ/ n, pl **k's** or **ks** or **K's** or **Ks** **1** [C/U] : the 11th letter of the English alphabet • *The word begins with (a) k.* **2** pl **K** [C] **a** *informal* : THOUSAND • *The car costs $35K.* **b** *computers* : KILOBYTE • *350K of disk space*

K abbr **1** Kelvin • *200 degrees K* **2** kilometer • *a 5K run* **3** or *k* karat

kabob *variant spelling of* KEBAB

kai·ser /'kaɪzɚ/ n [C] : the title of the ruler of Germany from 1871 to 1918 • *Kaiser Wilhelm*

kale /'keɪl/ n [C/U] : a type of cabbage that has wrinkled leaves

ka·lei·do·scope /kə'laɪdə,skoʊp/ n **1** [C] : a tube that contains mirrors and loose pieces of colored glass or plastic so that you see patterns when you look inside [singular] : a mixture of many different things • *a kaleidoscope of colors/ flavors* — **ka·lei·do·scop·ic** /kə,laɪdə-'skɑːpɪk/ adj

ka·mi·ka·ze /,kɑːmɪ'kɑːzi, Brit ,kæmɪ-'kɑːzi/ n [C] : one of the Japanese pilots in World War II who were assigned to crash their planes into their targets • *(figurative) kamikaze drivers* [=reckless drivers]

kan·ga·roo /,kæŋgə'ruː/ n, pl **-roos** [C] : an Australian animal that hops on its rear legs ✧ The female kangaroo has a pouch in which the young are carried.

ka·put /kə'pʊt/ adj, not before a noun, informal **1** : no longer working • *Our TV is kaput.* [=broken] **2** : completely ruined or defeated • *His career is kaput.*

kar·a·oke /,keri'oʊki/ n [U] : a form of entertainment in which a device plays the music of popular songs and people sing the words

kar·at (US) or chiefly Brit **car·at** /'kerət/ n [C] : a unit for measuring how pure a piece of gold is • *an 18 karat gold ring* • *Pure gold is 24 karats.* — abbr. *K* or *k*

ka·ra·te /kə'rɑːti/ n [U] : a form of fighting in which your feet and hands are used to kick and hit an opponent

kar·ma /'kɑːrmə/ n [U] **1** *often* **Karma** : the force created by a person's actions that is believed in Hinduism and Buddhism to determine what that person's next life will be like **2** *informal* : the force created by a person's actions that some people believe causes good or bad things to happen to that person • *good/ bad karma*

kay·ak /'kaɪ,æk/ n [C] : a long narrow boat that is moved by a paddle with two blades

ka·zoo /kə'zuː/ n, pl **-zoos** [C] : a toy musical instrument that is shaped like a short tube

KB abbr kilobyte

ke·bab /kə'bɑːb, Brit kə'bæb/ also chiefly US **ka·bob** /kə'bɑːb/ n [C] : a dish made by pushing a long, thin stick through pieces of meat and vegetables and cooking them on a grill

¹**keel** /'kiːl/ n [C] : a long piece of wood or metal along the center of the bottom of a boat — **on an even keel** : strong and not likely to fail or get worse • *They kept the company on an even keel.*

²**keel** vb — **keel over** [phrasal vb] informal : to fall down suddenly • *He just keeled over and died.*

keen /'kiːn/ adj **1** : having or showing an ability to think clearly and to understand what is not obvious about something • *a keen intellect/mind/observer*

2 : very strong and sensitive • *The dog has a keen sense of smell.* • *He has a keen eye for details.* **3 a** : strong or intense • *a keen sense of loss* • *a keen interest in art* **b** : feeling a strong and impatient desire to do something • *He is keen to learn about art.* — **keen on 1** : very excited about and interested in (something) • *She's keen on tennis.* • *I'm not keen on* [=I don't like] *that idea.* **2** *chiefly Brit* : interested in or attracted to (someone) • *He's keen on her.* — **keen·ly** *adv* — **keen·ness** /ˈkiːnnəs/ *n* [C/U]

¹**keep** /ˈkiːp/ *vb* **kept** /ˈkɛpt/; **keep·ing 1** [*T*] : to not return, lose, sell, give away, or throw away (something) • *She kept the money she found.* • *Should I sell my old car or keep it?* • *She got to keep her job.* [=she didn't lose her job] • *"The fare is $4." "Here's $5. Keep the change."* • *He kept his cool/composure.* [=did not become upset or angry] • *He vowed to keep his silence* [=to not tell anyone] *about what he saw.* **2 a** [*linking vb*] : to continue in a specified state, condition, or position • *Please keep quiet/still.* • *trying to keep warm* • *She likes to keep busy.* • *Do you keep in touch with him?* [=do you continue to talk to or write to him?] • (*Brit*) *"How are you keeping* [=how are you doing], *Jill?" "Fine, thanks."* **b** [*T*] : to cause (someone or something) to continue in a specified state, condition, or position • *how to keep kids safe near water* • *keeping costs under control* • *This scarf keeps me warm.* • *Keep both hands on the steering wheel.* • *I kept my hat on all day.* **3** [*T*] : to cause or force (someone) to stay in a place • *I won't keep you (here) much longer.* • *If you're in a hurry, don't let me keep you.* • *You're late. What kept you?* [=why are you late?] **4** [*T*] **a** : to do (something) continuously or again and again — + -*ing verb* • *The dog keeps falling all afternoon.* • *The dog keeps running away.* • *The band's music just keeps on getting better (and better).* **b** : to cause (someone or something) to do something continuously or again and again • *His boss kept him waiting for an hour.* **5** [*T*] **a** : to do what is required by (something) • *She always keeps her promises/word.* [=does what she says she will do] • *He failed to keep* [=he did not go to] *his appointment.* **b** : to not tell (a secret) • *I can keep a secret.* • *a well-kept secret* [=a secret that has not been told to people] **c** : to act properly in relation to (something) • *He keeps the Sabbath. They keep kosher.* **6** [*T*] **a** : to store (something) in a specified place • *Where do you keep the towels?* • *He keeps his wallet in his pocket.* **b** : to have or hold (something) for later use instead of using it now • *We ate two cookies and kept the rest for later.* • (*Brit*) *I'll keep a seat for you.* **7** [*I*] *of food* : to continue to be in a good condition • *The meat will keep well in the freezer for a few months.* **8** [*T*] *formal* : to protect (someone) • *May the Lord bless you and keep you (from harm).* **9** [*T*] : to produce (a journal, record, etc.) by writing information over a period of time • *She kept a diary.* • *He kept a*

detailed *record of his expenses.* **10** [*T*] : to take care of (something) • *keep a garden* — **keep after** [*phrasal vb*] **1** *informal* : to tell (someone) again and again to do something • *She kept after me to quit smoking.* **2** *keep (someone) after US* : to require (a student) to stay at school after classes have ended • *The teacher kept him after (school) for misbehaving.* — **keep at** [*phrasal vb*] **1** *keep at it* : to continue doing or trying to do something • *If you keep at it long enough, you'll succeed.* **2** *keep (someone) at it* : to force or cause (someone) to continue doing something • *The coach kept us (hard) at it all morning.* — **keep back** [*phrasal vb*] **1** : to not go near something • *The police asked us to keep back.* **2** *keep (someone) back* or *keep back (someone)* **a** : to not allow (someone) to go near something • *The police kept us back.* **b** *US* : to not allow (a student) to advance to the next grade level • *He was kept back a year.* **3** *keep (something) back* or *keep back (something)* : to not allow (something) to appear or be known • *He tried to keep back his tears.* [=not to cry] • *They kept back the information from the media.* — **keep company** [*phrasal vb*] **1** *keep company with* : to spend time with (someone) • (*figurative*) *In her garden, roses keep company with lilies.* **2** *keep (someone) company* : to spend time with (someone who would be alone if you were not there) • *I'll keep you company for a while.* — **keep down** [*phrasal vb*] **1** *keep (someone) down* : to prevent (someone) from succeeding, winning, etc. • *You can't keep a good man down.* **2** *keep (something) down* or *keep down (something)* **a** : to prevent (something) from increasing or rising • *keeping down costs/expenses/prices* **b** : to prevent (food, water, etc.) from coming up from your stomach • *He's so sick that he can't keep anything down.* **3** *keep it down* — used to ask someone to be quiet • *Keep it down. I'm trying to study.* — **keep from** [*phrasal vb*] **1** *keep from (doing something)* or *keep (someone or something) from (doing something)* : to not do or experience (something) • *She tried to keep from laughing.* [=she tried not to laugh] • *My hat kept me from getting wet.* • *I don't want to keep you from (doing) your work.* **2** *keep (something) from* : to not tell (something) to (someone) • *What are you keeping from me?* [=what are you not telling me?] • *They are keeping the truth from us.* — **keep going** [*phrasal vb*] **1** : to continue moving forward • *He walked past me and just kept going.* **2** : to continue doing something • *I wanted to give up, but I kept going.* **3** *keep (someone) going* : to make (someone) able to continue doing something at a difficult time • *What keeps her going after all these years?* **4** *keep (something) going* : to cause (something) to continue to exist or function • *He kept the business/conversation going.* — see also ¹**HOUSE** — **keep in** [*phrasal vb*] **1** *keep (something) in* : to not show or express (something) ▪ *Don't keep your emotions in.* **2 keep (someone) in** : to continue to provide (someone) with (something needed or wanted) ▪ *It's expensive keeping my children in clothes that fit.* **3 keep in with** *chiefly Brit* : to remain friendly with (someone) ▪ *keeping in with the people with power* — **keep off** [*phrasal vb*] **1 keep off** or **keep (someone or something) off** : to stop (someone or something) from being on (something) ▪ *Keep off the grass.* [=do not walk on the grass] ▪ *Keep the dog off the sofa.* **2 keep (weight) off** : to not regain weight that you have lost ▪ *He lost 20 pounds and has kept it off for a year.* **3 a** : to not talk about (something) ▪ *Let's keep off that subject.* **b keep (someone) off** : to prevent (someone) from talking about (something) ▪ *We tried to keep them off (the subject of) the war.* — **keep on** [*phrasal vb*] **1** *informal* : to continue happening, working, etc. ▪ *The rain kept on all night.* **2 keep (someone) on** : to continue to have (someone) as an employee ▪ *The chef was kept on even after the restaurant was sold.* **3 keep on at** *chiefly Brit, informal* : to say the same thing to (someone) again and again in a way that is annoying ▪ *My parents kept on at me to go back to college.* — **keep out** [*phrasal vb*] **1** : to not enter a place ▪ *The sign said "Keep out!"* **2 keep out of a** : to not enter (a place) ▪ *He told us to keep out of his office.* **b** : to not become involved in (something) ▪ *This argument doesn't involve you, so keep out of it.* **3 keep out** or **keep (someone or something) out (of a place)** : to stop (someone or something) from entering (a place) ▪ *The curtains help keep out the drafts.* — **keep pace with** see ¹PACE — **keep score** see ¹SCORE — **keep tabs on** see ¹TAB — **keep the faith** see FAITH — **keep time** see ¹TIME — **keep to** [*phrasal vb*] **1 a** : to stay in or on (something) : to not leave (something) ▪ *She kept to the main roads.* **b** : to not go beyond (something) ▪ *We try to keep to our budget.* **c** : to act or behave in the way required by (something) ▪ *keep to the rules of the game* **d** : to not move away from or change (something) ▪ *They kept to their alibi.* **2 keep to yourself a** or *chiefly Brit* **keep yourself to yourself** : to stay apart from other people ▪ *She was shy and kept mostly to herself.* **b keep (something) to yourself** : to not tell (something) to others ▪ *She likes to keep things to herself.* — **keep track** see ¹TRACK — **keep up** [*phrasal vb*] **1** : to go or make progress at the same rate as others ▪ *He couldn't keep up (with the rest of the class/runners).* **2** : to continue to know the newest information about something ▪ *I try to keep up on/with the news.* **3** : to continue happening ▪ *The rain kept up all night.* **4 keep (someone) up** : to prevent (someone) from sleeping ▪ *The sirens kept me up all night!* **5 keep (something) up** or **keep up (something) a** : to continue doing (something) ▪ *Keep up the good work.* **b** : to prevent (something) from getting worse, weaker, etc. ▪

Keep your spirits up! ▪ *The house had been kept up nicely.* **c** ✧ If you **keep up your end** of a bargain, agreement, etc., you do what you have promised or agreed to do. ▪ *Will she keep up her end of the deal?* — **keep your chin up** see CHIN — **keep your distance** see ¹DISTANCE — **keep your head** see ¹HEAD

²**keep** *n* — **for keeps** *informal* **1** : forever or permanently ▪ *He moved back to the city for keeps.* **2** : with the understanding that you may keep what you win ▪ *playing marbles for keeps* — **your keep** : the amount of money you need to pay for food, clothing, a place to live, etc. ▪ *It's time for our son to get a job and start earning his keep.*

keep·er /ˈkiːpɚ/ *n* [C] **1 a** : a person whose job is to guard or take care of something or someone ▪ *a lion keeper* **b** *Brit* : CURATOR **2** *US, informal* : something or someone that is good, valuable, etc. ▪ *Hold on to that boyfriend of yours—he's a keeper!* **3** : GOALKEEPER

keep·ing /ˈkiːpɪŋ/ *n* [U] **1** : the state of agreeing with or sharing important qualities with (something) ▪ *In keeping with* [=in a way that agrees with, obeys, or matches] *the needs of modern travelers, the hotel offers wireless Internet access.* ▪ *Her clothes are in (perfect) keeping with her personality.* ▪ *The modern décor was out of keeping with* [=did not agree with] *the church's architecture.* **2** : ¹CARE 2 ▪ *The car/child had been left in his keeping.* [=he was expected to protect or take care of the car/child]

keep·sake /ˈkiːpˌseɪk/ *n* [C] : something that you keep to help you remember a person, place, or event

keg /ˈkɛɡ/ *n* [C] : a barrel for holding or serving something ▪ *a keg of beer*

kelp /ˈkɛlp/ *n* [U] : a type of seaweed

Kel·vin /ˈkɛlvən/ *adj, technical* : relating to or having a scale for measuring temperature on which the boiling point of water is at 373.1 degrees above zero and the freezing point is at 273.15 degrees above zero ▪ *200 degrees Kelvin* — abbr. *K*

ken·nel /ˈkɛnl̩/ *n* [C] **1** : a place where dogs are kept while their owners are away — called also (*Brit*) **kennels 2** : a container for a dog or cat to stay in

kept *past tense and past participle of* ¹KEEP

kerb *Brit spelling of* ¹CURB 1

ker·chief /ˈkɚtʃəf/ *n* [C] : a square piece of cloth that is worn around your neck or on your head

ker·nel /ˈkɚnl̩/ *n* [C] **1 a** : the small part inside a seed or nut **b** : a whole seed; *especially* : one of the seeds on an ear of corn ▪ *corn kernels* **2** : a very small amount of something ▪ *a kernel of truth*

ker·o·sene /ˈkɛrəˌsiːn/ *n* [U] *chiefly US* : a type of oil that is burned as a fuel ▪ *a kerosene heater/lamp* — called also (*Brit*) **paraffin**

ketch·up /ˈkɛtʃəp/ *n* [C/U] : a thick sauce made with tomatoes

ket·tle /ˈkɛtl̩/ *n* [C] : a container used for heating or boiling liquid ▪ *a soup kettle; especially* : TEAKETTLE

ket·tle·drum /ˈkɛtlˌdrʌm/ n [C] : a large drum with a rounded bottom

¹**key** /ˈkiː/ n [C] **1 a** : a device that is used to open a lock or start an automobile ◇ The usual type of key is a small metal object that you insert into a narrow opening and turn. ▪ *She turned the key and opened the door.* ▪ *house/car keys* **2** : something that is necessary in order to do or achieve something ▪ *Hard work is the key to success.* **3 a** : something that provides an explanation or solution ▪ *the key to a riddle* **b** : a list of words or phrases that explain the meaning of symbols or abbreviations ▪ *a pronunciation key* **4 a** : any one of the buttons of a computer or typewriter that you push with your fingers **b** : any one of the parts that you push with your fingers to play a piano **5** *music* : a system of musical tones based on a scale beginning on the note for which the system is named ▪ *the key of C* **6** : a low island or reef ▪ *the Florida Keys* — **under lock and key** see ¹LOCK

²**key** adj : extremely important ▪ *a key player/person in the organization* ▪ *Underline key words as you read.*

³**key** vb [T] : ²TYPE 1 ▪ *The typist keyed (in) the changes.* — **key to** [phrasal vb] *chiefly US* **key (something) to** : to make (something) suitable for (a particular use or type of person) ▪ *The program is keyed to the needs of working women.*

¹**key·board** /ˈkiːˌboɚd/ n [C] **1 a** : a row or set of keys that are pushed to play a musical instrument (such as a piano) **b** : a musical instrument that has a keyboard and that produces sounds electronically **2** : the set of keys that are used for a computer or typewriter

²**keyboard** vb [T/I] : to type (information) into a computer ▪ *keyboarding a manuscript*

key·board·ist /ˈkiːˌboɚdɪst/ n [C] : a musician who plays a keyboard (sense 1b)

key chain n [C] : a metal ring that is used to hold keys — called also *key ring*

keyed up adj, informal : excited or nervous ▪ *I was too keyed up to sleep.*

key·hole /ˈkiːˌhoʊl/ n [C] : the opening in a lock into which a key is placed

key·note /ˈkiːˌnoʊt/ n [C] : the most important idea or part of something ▪ *Humor is the keynote of the play.*

keynote address n [C] : the main speech given at a gathering (such as a political convention) — called also *keynote speech*

key·pad /ˈkiːˌpæd/ n [C] : a set of keys for entering information into a calculator, telephone, etc.

key ring n [C] : KEY CHAIN

key·stone /ˈkiːˌstoʊn/ n [C] : something on which other things depend for support ▪ *the keystone of her faith*

key·stroke /ˈkiːˌstroʊk/ n [C] : the act of pushing down a key on a keyboard ▪ *a single keystroke*

key·word /ˈkiːˌwɚd/ n [C] : a word that is used to find information in a piece of writing, in a computer document, or on the Internet ▪ *a keyword search of the database*

kg abbr kilogram

KGB abbr the former Soviet organization responsible for national security ▪ *a member of the KGB*

kha·ki /ˈkæki, ˈkɑːki/ n **1** [U] : a yellowish-brown cloth **2** [plural] : pants made of khaki ▪ *a pair of khakis*

kHz abbr kilohertz

ki·bosh /ˈkaɪˌbɑːʃ/ n — **put the kibosh on** informal : to stop or end (something) ▪ *She put the kibosh on his smoking habit.* [=she forced him to stop smoking]

¹**kick** /ˈkɪk/ vb **1 a** [T] : to hit (someone or something) with your foot ▪ *He kicked me in the stomach.* ▪ *Kick the ball to me.* ▪ *She kicked the door open.* **b** [T/I] : to move your leg or legs in the air or in water especially in a strong or forceful way ▪ *He told the child to kick her legs as she swam.* ▪ *The boy was carried out of the store kicking and screaming.* **2** [T] *sports* : to score (a goal) by kicking a ball ▪ *She kicked the winning field goal.* **3** [T] *informal* : to completely stop doing (something harmful to yourself) ▪ *He kicked his cocaine habit.* ▪ *I smoked for years before I finally kicked the habit.* **4** [I] *informal* : to be full of life and energy ▪ *The company is still alive and kicking.* — **kick around** [phrasal vb] *informal* **1** : to spend time in (a place) without having a goal or purpose ▪ *After graduation, he kicked around (Boston) for a while.* **2** : to be lying somewhere within a general area or place ▪ *I have a copy of that book kicking around somewhere.* **3** **kick around (something) or kick (something) around** : to consider or talk about (ideas, plans, etc.) in an informal way ▪ *We kicked around some ideas about a new movie plot.* **4** **kick (someone) around or kick around (someone)** : to treat (someone) in a very bad or unfair way ▪ *He gets kicked around by his older brother.* — **kick back** [phrasal vb] *chiefly US, informal* : to relax and enjoy yourself ▪ *I wanted to kick back and watch TV.* — **kick in** [phrasal vb] *informal* **1** : to begin to work or to have an effect ▪ *waiting for the new law to kick in* **2** **kick in (something) or kick (something) in** *US* : CONTRIBUTE ▪ *We each kicked in a few dollars for her gift.* — **kick off** [phrasal vb] **1** : to start play in a game (such as American football or soccer) by kicking the ball ▪ *They kicked off from the 30-yard line.* **2 a** **kick off (something) or kick (something) off** : to begin (something, such as a performance, an event, or a discussion) ▪ *Her speech will kick off the conference.* **b** : BEGIN ▪ *The game/concert kicks off at 1:00.* **3** **kick (someone) off** : to force (someone) to leave (a team or group) ▪ *The coach kicked him off the team.* **4** **kick off (your shoes) or kick (your shoes) off** : to remove (your shoes) by making a kicking motion ▪ *She kicked off her shoes and started to dance.* — **kick out** [phrasal vb] **kick (someone) out or kick out (someone)** : to force (someone) to leave a place, group, school, etc. ▪ *He was/got kicked out of school for cheating.* ▪ *She kicked her husband out (of the house).* — **kick the bucket** informal : to die

His uncle kicked the bucket. — **kick up**
[*phrasal vb*] **kick up (something) or kick
(something) up** **1** : to cause (something) to rise upward • *The cars were
kicking up dirt.* **2** *informal* : to cause
(something) to become stronger • *The
praise kicked her confidence up a notch.*
3 *informal* : to cause (something) to happen • *The high winds kicked up huge
waves.* — **kick up your heels** *US, informal* : to have a good and lively time • *The
students had some time to kick up their
heels.* — **kick yourself** *informal* : to
blame or criticize yourself for something
you have done • *He was kicking himself
for having forgotten the meeting.*

²**kick** *n* [C] **1 a** : an act of hitting someone or something with your foot • *She
gave the car's tire a little kick.* : a sudden
forceful movement with your foot • *a karate kick* **b** : an act of hitting a ball with
your foot • *a long kick in football* **2 a** : a
sudden forceful movement • *The rifle has
a powerful kick.* **b** *informal* : a quality
that produces a powerful effect •
chili with a kick [=a very spicy flavor] **3**
informal : a feeling or source of pleasure
• *I got a kick out of seeing her again.* • *We
play for kicks.* [=for enjoyment] • *He gets
his kicks from* [=he enjoys] *embarrassing
his teammates.* **4** *informal* — used with
on to say that someone is doing a lot of
something for usually a brief period of
time • *He's been on a sushi kick lately.*
[=he has been eating a lot of sushi lately]
5 : an increase in speed at the end of the
race • *a runner with a strong kick*

kick·back /ˈkɪkˌbæk/ *n* [C] : an amount
of money that is given to someone in return for providing help in a secret and
dishonest business deal • *He had been accepting kickbacks.*

kick·box·ing /ˈkɪkˌbɑːksɪŋ/ *n* [U] : a
form of boxing in which fighters are allowed to kick each other

kick·er /ˈkɪkɚ/ *n* **1** [C] : a person who
kicks something **2** [*singular*] *US, informal* : a sudden and surprising occurrence, remark, etc. • *The kicker came
when she said that she was quitting.*

kick·off /ˈkɪkˌɑːf/ *n* [C] **1** : a kick that
starts play in a game (such as American
football or soccer) • *Kickoff is at 1:00.*
[=the game begins at 1:00] **2** : the start
of something • *the kickoff of his campaign*

kick·stand /ˈkɪkˌstænd/ *n* [C] : a metal
bar on a bicycle or motorcycle that
swings down to hold it upright when it is
not in use

kick-start /ˈkɪkˌstɑɚt/ *vb* [T] **1** : to start
(a motorcycle) by pushing down on a
lever with your foot **2** : JUMP-START 2 •
kick-starting a campaign • *a plan to kick-
start the economy* — **kick-start** *n* [C]

¹**kid** /ˈkɪd/ *n* [C] **1** *informal* **a** : a son or
daughter : CHILD • *He has a wife and two
kids.* **b** : a young person • *a bunch of
college kids* • *Hey, kid! Get off my yard!* •
(*figurative*) *a lawyer who is the new kid on
the block* [=who has recently joined a
particular group] **2** : a young goat

²**kid** *adj, always before a noun, chiefly US,
informal* : younger • *my kid sister* [=my
sister who is younger than I am]

³**kid** *vb* **kid·ded; kid·ding** [T/I] *informal*
: to say things that are not true to (someone) in a joking way • *Don't be offended.
He was just/only kidding (around).* • *The
test is today.* **You must be kidding (me)!** •
"The test is today." "Are you kidding me?!"
"I kid you not." [=I am not kidding you]
— **kid yourself** : to fail to admit the
truth to yourself • *If you think he'll help
us, you're just kidding yourself.* — **no kidding** *informal* **1** — used to emphasize
the truth of a statement • *No kidding, the
test is today.* **2** — used to show that you
are surprised by or interested in what has
been said • *"My brother just got engaged."
"No kidding! That's great news!"* — often
used in an ironic way in response to a
statement that is regarded as very obvious • *"You're going to be late." "Gee, no
kidding."* — **kid·der** *n* [C]

kid·die *also* **kid·dy** /ˈkɪdi/ *n, pl* **-dies** [C]
informal : a young child • *a kiddie pool
for toddlers*

kid·do /ˈkɪdoʊ/ *n, pl* **-dos** [C] *chiefly US,
informal* — used by an adult to speak to
a young person • *See you later, kiddo!*

kid gloves *n* — **with kid gloves** : with
special care in order to avoid causing
damage or offense • *The issue was treated
with kid gloves.*

kid·nap /ˈkɪdˌnæp/ *vb* **-napped** *also US*
-naped *also US* **-nap·ping** *also US* **-nap·ing**
[T] : to take away (someone) by force
usually in order to demand money for
returning the person • *She was kidnapped
(from her home).* — **kid·nap·per** *also
US* **kid·nap·er** *n* [C] • *The kidnapper demanded a large ransom.* — **kidnapping**
also US **kidnaping** *n* [C/U]

kid·ney /ˈkɪdni/ *n, pl* **-neys** [C] **1** : either of two organs in your body that
make urine • *a patient with a damaged
kidney* **2** : an animal kidney used as
food • *steak and kidney pie*

kidney bean *n* [C] : a type of large, dark
red bean

kidney stone *n* [C] *medical* : a hard object that can form in a kidney and cause
great pain

¹**kill** /ˈkɪl/ *vb* **1** [T/I] : to cause the death
of (a person, animal, or plant) • *The flu
kills thousands of people every year.* • *a
chemical that kills weeds* • *a disease that
can kill* • (*figurative*) *I'd kill for* [=I wish I
had] *hair like hers!* **2** [T] : to cause the
end of (something) • *Her injury killed her
chances of winning.* • *The committee
killed the bill.* **3** [T] *informal* : to turn
(something) off with a switch • *Kill the
lights.* **4** [T] *informal* : to spend (time)
doing something while you are waiting •
We killed time by watching TV. **5** [T] *informal* **a** : to cause (someone) to feel
pain or to suffer • *My feet are killing me.*
[=they hurt a lot] **b** : to make (someone) nervous or unhappy • *The suspense
is killing me.* • *It kills me to think of how
much money I wasted.* **6** [T] *informal*
: to amuse or entertain (someone) very
much • *That guy kills me.* — **kill off**
[*phrasal vb*] **kill off (something) or kill
(something) off** **1** : to kill every one of
(a group) • *What killed off the dinosaurs?*
2 : to remove (something) completely •

The company has killed off its competition. — **kill the clock** see ¹CLOCK — **kill two birds with one stone** : to achieve two things by doing a single action ▪ *We can kill two birds with one stone by dropping off the mail when we go to the store.*

²**kill** n [C] **1** : an act of killing someone or something ▪ *The tiger made a kill in this area.* ▪ (*figurative*) *Her political opponents are moving in for the kill.* **2** : an animal that has been killed ▪ *a lion eating its kill*

¹**kill·er** /ˈkɪlɚ/ n [C] **1** : a person or thing that kills someone or something ▪ *The police found the killer.* [=*murderer*] ▪ *a weed killer* **2** *informal* : something that is very difficult ▪ *That was a killer of an exam.*

²**killer** *adj, always before a noun, chiefly US* **1** : causing death or destruction ▪ *a killer tornado* **2** *informal* : very impressive or appealing ▪ *a killer smile* **3** *informal* : very difficult ▪ *a killer exam*

killer instinct n [C] : a very strong desire to succeed or win

killer whale n [C] : a black-and-white whale that kills and eats other animals (such as seals)

kill·ing /ˈkɪlɪŋ/ n [C] **1** : an act of killing someone or something ▪ *the killing of two civilians* **2** *informal* : a large amount of money ▪ *He made a killing in the stock market.*

kill·joy /ˈkɪlˌdʒɔɪ/ n [C] *disapproving* : a person who spoils other people's fun or enjoyment

kiln /ˈkɪln/ n [C] : an oven or furnace that is used in making pottery, glass, etc.

ki·lo /ˈkiːloʊ/ n, pl **-los** [C] : KILOGRAM

ki·lo·byte /ˈkɪləˌbaɪt/ n [C] : a unit of computer information equal to 1,024 bytes — abbr. **KB**

ki·lo·gram /ˈkɪləˌgræm/ n [C] : a unit of weight equal to 1,000 grams — abbr. **kg**

ki·lo·hertz /ˈkɪləˌhɚts/ n, pl **-hertz** [C] *technical* : a unit of frequency equal to 1,000 hertz — abbr. **kHz**

kilo·li·ter (*US*) or Brit **kilo·li·tre** /ˈkɪləˌliːtɚ/ n [C] : a unit for measuring the volume of a liquid or gas that is equal to 1,000 liters — abbr. **kl**

ki·lo·me·ter (*US*) or Brit **ki·lo·me·tre** /kəˈlɑːmətɚ, ˈkɪləˌmiːtɚ/ n [C] : a unit of length equal to 1,000 meters — abbr. **km**

kilo·watt /ˈkɪləˌwɑːt/ n [C] : a unit of electrical power equal to 1,000 watts — abbr. **kW**

kilowatt–hour n [C] *technical* : a unit of work or energy equal to the amount produced by one kilowatt in one hour — abbr. **kWh**

kilt /ˈkɪlt/ n [C] : a type of skirt traditionally worn by men in Scotland

kil·ter /ˈkɪltɚ/ n — **out of kilter** or **off kilter** — used to describe something that is not in the exactly right condition ▪ *Our schedule has been knocked off kilter.*

ki·mo·no /kəˈmoʊnoʊ/ n, pl **-nos** [C] : a loose piece of clothing with wide sleeves that is traditionally worn in Japan

kin /ˈkɪn/ n [plural] *old-fashioned* : a person's relatives ▪ *She and I are kin.* [=we are related to each other] ▪ *He's no kin to me.* [=he is not related to me]

¹**kind** /ˈkaɪnd/ n [C] : a particular type or variety of person or thing ▪ *hawks and other birds of that kind* ▪ *"What kind of (a) car do you drive?" "The same kind you drive."* ▪ *different kinds of food/people/restaurants* ▪ *What kind of fool do you think I am?* [=do you think that I am a fool?] ▪ *I like all kinds of* [=a large number or variety of] *movies/sports.* ▪ *Boston is my kind of (a) town.* [=I like Boston] ▪ *He said I hung up on him, but I did nothing of the kind!* [=I never hung up on him] ▪ *She's/ It's one of a kind.* [=not like any other person/thing] ▪ *John and his dad are two of a kind.* [=they are very much alike] — **in kind 1** : in a way that is equal or very similar to what someone else has done for you ▪ *If you help me, I'll help you in kind.* **2** *business* : in goods or services rather than in money ▪ *payment in kind rather than in cash* — **kind of** *informal* : SOMEWHAT ▪ *It's kind of cold in here.*

²**kind** *adj* **1** : having or showing a gentle nature and a desire to help others ▪ *a kind old woman* ▪ *It was very kind of you to help.* ▪ *He was kind to us.* ▪ *a kind smile* **2** — used to say that something does not cause harm, is not harsh, etc. ▪ *Old age has been kind to her: she still looks great at 84.* ▪ *Years of sunbathing have not been kind to her skin.* **3** — used to make a formal request ▪ *Would you be kind enough to show me the way? = Would you be so kind as to show me the way?*

kinda /ˈkaɪndə/ — used in writing to represent the sound of the phrase *kind of* when it is spoken quickly ▪ *I'm kinda* [=*kind of*] *tired.*

kin·der·gar·ten /ˈkɪndɚˌgɑːtn/ n [C/U] : a school or class for children who are about five years old — **kin·der·gart·ner** /ˈkɪndɚˌgɑːtnɚ/ or **kin·der·gar·ten·er** /ˈkɪndɚˌgɑːtənɚ/ n [C] *US*

kind·heart·ed /ˌkaɪndˈhɑːtəd/ *adj* : having or showing a kind and gentle nature ▪ *a kindhearted gesture/person* — **kind·heart·ed·ness** n [U]

kin·dle /ˈkɪndl/ vb **kin·dled**; **kin·dling** [T] **1** : to cause (a fire) to start burning ▪ *using twigs to kindle a fire* **2** : to cause the start of (something) ▪ *The event kindled a national debate.*

kin·dling /ˈkɪndlɪŋ/ n [U] : dry twigs, pieces of paper, etc., that are used to start a fire

¹**kind·ly** /ˈkaɪndli/ *adj* **kind·li·er; -est** : KIND ▪ *a kindly smile/woman* — **kind·li·ness** /ˈkaɪndlinəs/ n [U]

²**kindly** *adv* **1** : in a kind way ▪ *She always treats us kindly.* ▪ *He kindly offered to help.* **2** — used to make a formal request ▪ *Would you kindly pass the salt?* — **look kindly on/upon** : to approve of (something or someone) ▪ *He does not look kindly on such behavior.* — **take kindly to** : to willingly accept or approve of (someone or something) ▪ *She does not take kindly to criticism.* [=she does not like to be criticized]

kind·ness /ˈkaɪndnəs/ n **1** [U] : the quality or state of being kind **2** [C] : a kind act

kin·dred /ˈkɪndrəd/ *adj, formal* **1** : alike or similar ▪ *She and I are kindred spirits/*

souls.   **2** : closely related • *kindred tribes/languages*

ki·net·ic /kəˈnɛtɪk/ *adj* : of or relating to the movement of objects • *kinetic energy*

kin·folk /ˈkɪnˌfoʊk/ *n* [*plural*] *old-fashioned* : KIN

king /ˈkɪŋ/ *n* **1** [*C/U*] : a male ruler of a country who usually inherits his position and rules for life • *He became (the) king.* **2 a** [*C*] : a boy or man who is very successful or popular • *the king of soul music* **b** [*C*] : a boy or man who is awarded the highest honor for an event or contest • *He was voted prom king.* **c** [*C/U*] : something that is powerful or considered better than all others • *The lion is the king of the jungle.* • *when coal was king* [=when coal was the most important source of fuel] **3** [*C*] : the most important piece in the game of chess **4** [*C*] : a playing card that has a picture of a king and that is worth more than a queen • *the king of hearts* — **fit for a king** see ¹FIT — **king·ly** /ˈkɪŋli/ *adj* **king·li·er; -est** • *kingly authority* • *a kingly feast/price/fortune* — **king·ship** /ˈkɪŋˌʃɪp/ *n* [*U*]

king·dom /ˈkɪŋdəm/ *n* **1** [*C*] : a country whose ruler is a king or queen • *the Kingdom of Jordan* **2** [*U*] : the spiritual world of which God is king • *the kingdom of heaven* **3** [*C*] : one of the three main divisions into which natural objects are classified • *the animal/mineral/plant kingdom* — **to kingdom come** *informal* : to a state of complete destruction • *an explosion that could blast/blow them all to kingdom come*

king·fish·er /ˈkɪŋˌfɪʃɚ/ *n* [*C*] : a type of brightly colored bird that catches fish by diving into water

king·pin /ˈkɪŋˌpɪn/ *n* [*C*] : a person who controls an organization or activity • *a mob kingpin* [=a man who controls a gang of criminals]

king–size /ˈkɪŋˌsaɪz/ *or* **king–sized** /ˈkɪŋˌsaɪzd/ *adj* : extremely large • *a king-size sandwich/appetite*

king's ransom *n* [*singular*] : a very large amount of money • *We paid a king's ransom for that car.*

kink /ˈkɪŋk/ *n* [*C*] **1** : a tight bend and curl in a rope, hose, etc. • *a kink in the chain* **2** *chiefly US* : a pain in your neck or back caused by tight muscles **3** : a small problem or flaw • *We're still working/ironing out the kinks* [=trying to fix the problems] *with the program.* — **kink** *vb* [*T/I*] • *My hair kinks when it rains.*

kinky /ˈkɪŋki/ *adj* **kink·i·er; -est 1** *of hair* : having many tight bends or curls **2** *informal* : involving or liking unusual sexual behavior • *kinky sex toys* — **kink·i·ness** *n* [*U*]

kin·ship /ˈkɪnˌʃɪp/ *n* **1** [*U*] : the state of being related to the people in your family • *the bonds of kinship* **2** [*U*, *singular*] : a feeling of being connected to other people • *He feels a kinship with the other survivors.*

kins·man /ˈkɪnzmən/ *n, pl* **-men** /-mən/ [*C*] *old-fashioned* : a male relative

kins·wom·an /ˈkɪnzˌwʊmən/ *n, pl* **-wom·en** /-ˌwɪmən/ [*C*] *old-fashioned* : a female relative

ki·osk /ˈkiːˌɑsk/ *n* [*C*] **1** : a very small store with open sides • *a kiosk in the mall* **2** : a structure that provides information and services on a computer screen

kip /ˈkɪp/ *n* [*U*, *singular*] *Brit, informal* : ²SLEEP • *Try to get a bit of kip.*

kip·per /ˈkɪpɚ/ *n* [*C*] *chiefly Brit* : a herring that has been preserved with salt and then smoked — **kip·pered** /ˈkɪpɚd/ *adj* • *a kippered herring*

kiss /ˈkɪs/ *vb* **1 a** [*T/I*] : to touch (someone) with your lips as a greeting or as a way of showing love or sexual attraction • *He kissed her (on the) cheek.* • *the night we first kissed (each other)* • (*figurative, informal*) *It's time for them to kiss and make up.* [=to become friendly again after a fight or disagreement] **b** [*T*] : to touch (something) with your lips • *He knelt down and kissed the ground.* **2** [*T*] : to touch (something) gently or lightly • *The tree's branches kissed the ground below.* — **kiss and tell** : to tell people about the private details of your romantic relationships • *I never kiss and tell.* — **kiss off** [*phrasal vb*] *informal + impolite* — used in angry speech to tell someone to leave and stop bothering you • *She told him to kiss off.* — **kiss (something) goodbye** *informal* : to accept the fact that you have lost or will never get something • *They can kiss their vacation plans goodbye now.* — **kiss up to** [*phrasal vb*] *US, informal + disapproving* : to try to make (someone) like you • *kissing up to the boss* — **kiss** *n* [*C*] • *He gave her a kiss on the cheek.* • *She blew me a kiss.* [=kissed the palm of her hand, put her hand flat in front of her mouth, and then blew on it toward me]

kiss·er /ˈkɪsɚ/ *n* [*C*] **1** : a person who kisses • *He's a good kisser.* [=he is good at kissing] **2** *old-fashioned slang* : MOUTH • *Punch him in the kisser.*

kiss of death *n* [*singular*] : something that causes something to fail or be ruined • *Bad reviews can be the kiss of death for a new movie.*

kiss of life *n* — **the kiss of life** *Brit* : MOUTH-TO-MOUTH RESUSCITATION

¹**kit** /ˈkɪt/ *n* **1** [*C*] : a set of tools or supplies that a person uses for a particular purpose or activity • *a shaving/sewing/tool kit* **2** [*C*] : a set of parts that are put together to build something • *an aquarium starter kit* [=a set of things needed to set up an aquarium] **3** [*C*] : a collection of written materials about a particular subject • *a tourist information kit* **4** [*U*] *Brit* : clothing or equipment used for a particular purpose • *cricket kit* • (*informal*) *She got her kit off* [=took off her clothes] *for the photos.* — **first aid kit** see FIRST AID — **the whole (kit and) caboodle** see CABOODLE

²**kit** *vb* **kit·ted; kit·ting** — **kit out/up** [*phrasal vb*] **kit out/up (someone or something)** *or* **kit (someone or something) out/up** *Brit* : to give (someone or something) the clothing or equipment needed for a particular activity • *The team was kitted out in new uniforms.*

kitch·en /ˈkɪtʃən/ *n* [*C*] : a room in which

food is cooked ▪ *a house with a large kitchen* ▪ *kitchen cabinets* ▪ *He brought everything but the kitchen sink.* [=an extremely large number of things]

kitch·en·ette /ˌkɪtʃəˈnɛt/ *n* [C] : a small kitchen or a part of a room where food is cooked

kite /ˈkaɪt/ *n* [C] **1** : a light frame covered with cloth, paper, or plastic that is flown in the air at the end of a long string ▪ *flying kites* **2** : a type of hawk — **as high as a kite** *informal* : greatly affected by alcohol or drugs : very drunk or intoxicated

kith /ˈkɪθ/ *n* — **kith and kin** *old-fashioned* : friends and relatives ▪ *They invited all their kith and kin to their new home.*

kitsch /ˈkɪtʃ/ *n* [U] : things (such as movies or works of art) that are of low quality and that many people find enjoyable — **kitschy** /ˈkɪtʃi/ *adj* **kitsch·i·er; -est** ▪ *kitschy horror films*

kit·ten /ˈkɪtn̩/ *n* [C] : a young cat

kit·ten·ish /ˈkɪtn̩ɪʃ/ *adj* : cute and playful in a way that attracts attention ▪ *a kittenish actress*

kit·ty /ˈkɪti/ *n, pl* **-ties** [C] **1** *informal* : a cat or kitten **2** : the amount of money that can be won in a card game **3** : an amount of money that has been collected from many people for some purpose ▪ *She had a $10 million kitty for her campaign.*

kit·ty–cor·ner /ˈkɪtiˌkoɚnɚ/ *adv, US* — used to describe two things that are located across from each other on opposite corners ▪ *The store is kitty-corner from the park.*

ki·wi /ˈkiːˌwiː/ *n* [C] **1** *Kiwi informal* : a person who lives in or is from New Zealand **2** : a bird from New Zealand that cannot fly **3** : KIWIFRUIT

ki·wi·fruit /ˈkiːˌwiːˌfruːt/ *n, pl* **kiwifruit** *or* **ki·wi·fruits** [C/U] : a small fruit that has green flesh, black seeds, and brown, hairy skin

KJV *abbr* King James Version ✧ The King James Version is the version of the Christian Bible that is used for quotations in this dictionary.

kl *abbr* kiloliter

Klee·nex /ˈkliːˌnɛks/ *trademark* — used for a paper tissue (sense 1)

klep·to·ma·nia /ˌklɛptəˈmeɪnijə/ *n* [U] : a strong desire to steal things — **klep·to·ma·ni·ac** /ˌklɛptəˈmeɪniˌæk/ *n* [C]

klutz /ˈklʌts/ *n* [C] *chiefly US, informal* : a person who often drops things, falls down, etc. : a clumsy person ▪ *I'm a complete klutz on the dance floor.* — **klutzy** /ˈklʌtsi/ *adj* **klutz·i·er; -est**

km *abbr* kilometer

knack /ˈnæk/ *n* [*singular*] : an ability, talent, or special skill needed to do something ▪ *He has a knack for cooking.*

knack·ered /ˈnækɚd/ *adj, Brit, informal* : very tired or exhausted

knap·sack /ˈnæpˌsæk/ *n* [C] *chiefly US* : BACKPACK

knave /ˈneɪv/ *n* [C] *old-fashioned* : a dishonest man ▪ *fools and knaves*

knead /ˈniːd/ *vb* [T] **1** : to prepare (dough) by pressing a mixture of flour,

water, etc., with your hands ▪ *Knead the dough until it is smooth.* **2** : to press and squeeze (a person's muscles) with your hands ▪ *kneading the muscles in my neck*

¹**knee** /ˈniː/ *n* [C] **1** : the joint that bends at the middle of your leg ▪ *I fell and hurt my knee.* ▪ *She dropped/fell/sank to her knees and begged for forgiveness.* = *She got down on her knees and begged for forgiveness.* ▪ *He got/went down on one knee and proposed to her.* **2** : the upper part of your leg when you are sitting ▪ *My little grandson sat on my knee.* **3** : the part that covers the knee on a pair of pants ▪ *Her jeans had holes at the knees.* **4** : a forceful hit with a bent knee ▪ *She gave him a knee to the stomach.* — **bring (someone) to his/her knees** : to completely defeat or overwhelm (someone) ▪ *He vowed to bring the enemy to their knees.* ▪ *(figurative) The economy was brought to its knees.* — **on bended knee/knees** see ¹BEND — **weak at/in the knees** see WEAK

²**knee** *vb* **kneed; knee·ing** [T] : to hit (a person) with your knee ▪ *He kneed me in the stomach.*

knee·cap /ˈniːˌkæp/ *n* [C] : a flat bone on the front of your knee

knee–deep /ˈniːˈdiːp/ *adj* **1** : reaching as high as your knees ▪ *knee-deep snow* **2** : standing in something that reaches your knees ▪ *We were knee-deep in snow/water.* ▪ *(figurative) knee-deep in work* [=very busy] — **knee–deep** *adv*

knee–high /ˈniːˈhaɪ/ *adj* : reaching as high as your knees ▪ *The grass is knee-high.*

knee–jerk /ˈniːˌdʒɚk/ *adj, always before a noun* **1** : occurring quickly and without thought ▪ *a knee-jerk reaction* **2** *disapproving* : often reacting quickly and without thought ▪ *knee-jerk politicians*

kneel /ˈniːl/ *vb* **knelt** /ˈnɛlt/ *also chiefly US* **kneeled; kneel·ing** [I] : to put one or both of your knees on the floor ▪ *He knelt (down) before the king.* : to have both of your knees on the floor ▪ *She was kneeling on the floor.*

knee–length /ˈniːˌlɛŋkθ/ *adj, of clothing* : reaching the knees ▪ *a knee-length skirt*

knee sock *n* [C] *chiefly US* : a sock that reaches your knee

knees–up /ˈniːˌzʌp/ *n* [C] *Brit, informal* : a noisy party usually with dancing

knell /ˈnɛl/ *n* [C] *literary* : a sound of a bell when it is rung slowly because someone has died ▪ *(figurative) The mistake was the death knell for his campaign.* [=it was the sign or indication that his campaign would fail or end soon]

knelt *past tense and past participle of* KNEEL

knew *past tense of* ¹KNOW

knick·er·bock·ers /ˈnɪkɚˌbɑːkɚz/ *n* [*plural*] *Brit* : KNICKERS

knick·ers /ˈnɪkɚz/ *n* [*plural*] **1** *US* : loose-fitting pants that reach just below the knee **2** *Brit* : PANTIES

knick·knack /ˈnɪkˌnæk/ *n* [C] : a small object used for decoration ▪ *shelves filled with knickknacks*

¹**knife** /ˈnaɪf/ *n, pl* **knives** /ˈnaɪvz/ [C] : a usually sharp blade attached to a handle

that is used for cutting or as a weapon • *knives, forks, and spoons* — *under the knife informal* : having surgery • *I'm going under the knife tomorrow.*

²**knife** *vb* **knifed; knif·ing** **1** [*T*] : to injure (someone) with a knife • *He was knifed in the chest.* **2** [*I*] : to move easily and quickly through something • *The ship knifes through the waves.*

knife—edge /ˈnaɪfˌɛdʒ/ *n* — *on a/the knife-edge* : in a dangerous or important situation in which two very different results are possible • *living on the knife-edge of poverty*

knife·point /ˈnaɪfˌpɔɪnt/ *n* — *at knifepoint* : while someone is threatening you with a knife • *They were robbed at knifepoint.*

¹**knight** /ˈnaɪt/ *n* [*C*] **1** : a soldier in the past who had a high social rank and who fought while riding a horse and usually wearing armor • (*figurative*) *The firefighter who rescued us was our* **knight in shining armor.** [=a brave man] • *She is still waiting for her knight in shining armor.* [=her perfect romantic partner] **2** : a man who is given the title of *Sir* by the king or queen of England **3** : a chess piece shaped like a horse's head — **knight·ly** /ˈnaɪtli/ *adj*

²**knight** *vb* [*T*] : to give (a man) the rank of a knight • *He was knighted by the Queen.*

knight·hood /ˈnaɪtˌhʊd/ *n* [*C/U*] : the rank or title of a knight

¹**knit** /ˈnɪt/ *vb* **knit** *or* **knit·ted; knit·ting** **1** [*T/I*] : to make (a piece of clothing) from yarn or thread by using long needles or a special machine • *She knit/knitted a sweater for me.* • *a red knit shirt* • *a knitted cap* **2** [*T*] **a** : to closely join or combine (things or people) • *a style that knits together material from many different sources* **b** : to form (something) by bringing people or things together • *a town knit/knitted together by farming* — **knit your brow/brows** : to move your eyebrows together in a way that shows that you are thinking about something or are worried, angry, etc. • *She knit her brow and asked what I was doing.* — **knit·ter** *n* [*C*]

²**knit** *n* [*C*] : a piece of clothing that has been made by knitting • *cotton knits*

knitting needle *n* [*C*] : one of two or more long, thin sticks that are used for knitting

knit·wear /ˈnɪtˌweə/ *n* [*U*] : knitted clothing

knives *plural of* ¹KNIFE

knob /ˈnɑːb/ *n* [*C*] **1** : a round switch on a television, radio, etc. **2** : a round handle on a door, drawer, etc. **3** *chiefly Brit* : a small lump or piece of something • *a knob of butter/coal*

knob·bly /ˈnɑːbli/ *adj* **knob·bli·er; -est** *chiefly Brit* : KNOBBY

knob·by /ˈnɑːbi/ *adj* **knob·bi·er; -est** *chiefly US* **1** : covered with small bumps • *knobby tires* **2** : forming hard rounded lumps • *knobby knees*

¹**knock** /ˈnɑːk/ *vb* **1** [*I*] : to hit something (such as a door) with the knuckles of your hand or with a hard object in order to get people's attention • *Someone is*

knocking (at/on the door). **2** [*T*] : to hit (something or someone) in a forceful way • *She knocked the glass from my hand.* • *The ball knocked out one of his teeth.* • *The wind knocked him off his feet.* [=the wind hit him so hard that he fell to the ground] • *The collision knocked her unconscious/senseless.* [=caused her to become unconscious] **3** [*T/I*] : to touch or hit someone or something in a way that is not planned or intended • *I knocked my knee against the table.* **4** [*T*] : to make (a hole) by hitting something • *He used a hammer to knock a hole in the wall.* **5** [*T*] *informal* : to criticize (someone or something) • *Don't knock it until you've tried it.* [=wait until you try something before criticizing it] **6** [*I*] : to produce a repeated loud noise • *The engine was knocking.* — **knees are knocking** *informal* ◇ If your **knees are knocking** they are shaking because you are nervous or afraid. — **knock around/about** [*phrasal vb*] *informal* **1 a** : to spend time in (a place) without having a goal or purpose • *He spent the year knocking around (in) Europe.* **b knock around/about** *with Brit* : to spend time with (another person) • *I was knocking around with my brother.* **2 knock around (something)** *or* **knock (something) around** : to consider or talk about (ideas, plans, etc.) in an informal way • *We knocked the idea around for a while.* **3 knock (someone) around/about** : to beat or hit (someone) badly or repeatedly • *The boy was getting knocked around by bullies.* • (*figurative*) *I got knocked around at the meeting.* — **knock back** *informal* **knock (something) back** *or* **knock back (something)** : to drink or swallow (an alcoholic drink) quickly • *He knocked back a few beers.* — **knock down** [*phrasal vb*] **1 knock (someone or something) down** *or* **knock down (someone or something)** **a** : to cause (someone or something) to fall to the ground • *He knocked me down.* • *knocking down a wall* **b** *Brit* : to hit and injure or kill (a person or animal) with a vehicle • *She was knocked down by a car.* **2** *informal* **a knock (something) down** *or* **knock down (something)** : to reduce or lower (a price, an amount, etc.) • *They knocked down the price by 10 percent.* **b knock (someone) down** : to cause or persuade (someone) to reduce a price • *I managed to knock him down from $50 to $45.* **3 knock (something) down** *or* **knock down (something)** *chiefly US, informal* : to say no to (an idea, plan, proposal, etc.) • *My boss knocked down all of my ideas.* — **knock off** [*phrasal vb*] *informal* **1 knock off** *or* **knock (something) off** *or* **knock off (something)** : to stop doing something (such as work) • *The boss says we can knock off (work) early today.* • *I told you kids to knock it off!* [=stop doing something immediately] **2 knock (something) off** *or* **knock off (something)** **a** : to take (an amount) away from something • *He knocked off 10 dollars from the price.* [=reduced the price by 10 dollars] **b** *US* : to steal money or things from (a bank or store) • *They* *knocked off a jewelry store.* **c** *chiefly Brit* : to steal (something) • *They knocked off a lot of valuables.* **d** *US* : to make a cheaper copy of (something) • *Other companies knocked off our design.* **3 knock (someone) off** or **knock off (someone)** **a** : to kill (someone) • *She tried to knock off her husband.* **b** *US* : to defeat (someone) • *They knocked off the best team in the league.* — **knock on wood** see WOOD — **knock out** [*phrasal vb*] **1 knock (someone or something) out** or **knock out (someone or something) a** : to make (a person or animal) unconscious • *The drug knocked her out cold.* **b** *boxing* : to defeat (an opponent) with a knockout • *He was knocked out in the third round.* **c** : to defeat (an opponent) in a competition so that the opponent cannot continue • *My team was knocked out (of the competition) in the third round.* **2 knock (something) out** or **knock out (something) a** : to cause (something) to stop working • *The storm knocked out the town's electricity.* **b** : to produce (something) very quickly • *knocking out hit records* **3 knock (yourself) out** *informal* **a** : to make (yourself) very tired by doing work • *We knocked ourselves out trying to finish on time.* **b** *US* — used to tell someone that he or she has permission to do something • *"Do you mind if I try to fix it?" "Knock yourself out."* **4 knock (someone) out** *informal* : to make a very strong and good impression on (someone) • *His suggestion knocked us out.* [=we liked his suggestion very much] — **knock over** [*phrasal vb*] **1 knock (someone or something) over** or **knock over (someone or something) a** : to cause (someone or something) to fall to the ground • *The dog knocked over the lamp.* **b** *Brit* : to hit and injure or kill (a person or animal) with a vehicle • *The dog was knocked over by a car.* **2 knock (someone) over** or **knock over (someone) i** *informal* : to greatly surprise or shock (someone) • *I was knocked over by the news.* • *I was so surprised that you could have knocked me over with a feather.* **3 knock (something) over** or **knock over (something)** *US, informal* : to steal money or things from (a bank or store) • *The men knocked over a bank.* — **knock (someone) dead** *informal* : to make a very strong and good impression on (someone) • *She told the dancers to go out there and knock 'em/them dead.* — **knock someone's head/block off** *informal* : to hit someone very hard • *I'd like to knock his block off.* — **knock (someone) sideways** *Brit* : to upset, confuse, or shock (someone) very much • *The news about the accident really knocked him sideways.* — **knock (something) on the head** *Brit, informal* : to cause the end or failure of (something) • *The hurricane knocked our holiday plans on the head.* — **knock the stuffing out of** see STUFFING — **knock up** [*phrasal vb*] **knock (someone or something) up** or **knock up (someone or something) 1** *informal, chiefly US, impolite* : to make (someone) pregnant • *She got knocked*

up. [=she got pregnant] **b** *Brit* : to wake (someone) by knocking on a door • *knocked him up at 6 a.m.* **2** *Brit* : to make or produce (something) quickly • *knock up a quick meal*

²**knock** *n* [*C*] **a** : a hard, sharp hit • *I got a knock on the head.* **b** : the sound made by a hard hit • *I heard a loud knock at the door.* **2** [*C*] *informal* : a difficult or painful experience • *She took some hard knocks early in her career.* **3** [*C*] *informal* : a critical or negative comment • *One of the knocks against TV is that there are too many commercials.* **4** [*C/U*] : a loud noise produced by an engine when it is not working properly • *a type of fuel that reduces engine knock*

knock-down /ˈnɑːkˌdaʊn/ *adj, always before a noun, chiefly Brit, informal, of a price* : greatly reduced from the original price • *buying items at knockdown prices*

knock–down, drag–out or **knock–down–drag–out** *adj, always before a noun, US, informal* : very angry or violent • *a knock-down-drag-out fight/argument*

knock·er /ˈnɑːkɚ/ *n* [*C*] : a small metal device on a door that you move in order to make a knocking sound

knock–kneed /ˈnɑːkˈniːd/ *adj* : having legs that curve inward at the knees • *a knock-kneed kid*

knock–off /ˈnɑːkˌɑːf/ *n* [*C*] : a cheap or inferior copy of something • *That purse is a knockoff.*

¹**knock·out** /ˈnɑːkˌaʊt/ *n* [*C*] **1** : a punch that causes a boxer to fall down and be unable to start fighting again before 10 seconds have passed • *He won the match by a knockout.* **2** *informal* : a very attractive or appealing person or thing • *She's a knockout in that dress.*

²**knockout** *adj, always before a noun* **1** : causing someone to become unconscious • *a knockout punch/blow* **2** *informal* : extremely attractive or appealing • *a knockout actress/movie* **3** *Brit, of a contest or competition* : designed so that winning teams or players continue to play and losing teams or players do not

knoll /ˈnoʊl/ *n* [*C*] : a small hill • *a grassy knoll*

¹**knot** /ˈnɑːt/ *n* [*C*] **1 a** : a part that forms when you tie a piece of rope, string, fabric, etc., to itself or to something else • *tie/tighten/untie/loosen a knot* **b** : a part where something has become twisted or wrapped around itself • *Her hair was tangled in knots.* **2** : an uncomfortable feeling of tightness in part of your body • *a knot in a muscle* • *I was so nervous that my stomach was (tied up) in knots.* [=I had a tight feeling in my stomach] **3** : a dark round mark on a piece of wood • *a board full of knots* **4** : a unit of speed equal to one nautical mile per hour • *Wind is from the north at 12 knots.* — **tie the knot** *informal* : to get married • *When are they going to tie the knot?*

²**knot** *vb* **knot·ted; knot·ting 1** [*T*] : to make a knot in (something) • *a knotted rope; also* : to connect (two or more parts or things) with a knot • *Knot the threads together.* **2** [*I*] : to develop an

uncomfortable feeling of tightness ▪ *My stomach knotted up as I waited to speak.*

knot·ty /'nɑ:ti/ *adj* **knot·ti·er; -est** **1** *of wood* : having many knots ▪ *knotty pine/wood* **2** : difficult or complicated ▪ *a knotty problem/situation*

¹**know** /'noʊ/ *vb* **knew** /'nu:, Brit 'nju:/; **known** /'noʊn/; **know·ing** **1 a** [*T/I*] : to have (information of some kind) in your mind ▪ *I know the answer.* ▪ *Do you know what time it is?* ▪ *"What time is it?" "I don't know."* ▪ *She knows the rules of the game.* ▪ *He knows (all) about horses.* ▪ *Do you know where she went? ▪ No one knows (for sure) how long it will take.* ▪ *He knows perfectly/full well how to do it.* **b** [*T/I*] : to understand (something) : to have a clear and complete idea of (something) ▪ *We don't know why it happened.* ▪ *I don't know what to do.* ▪ *"How could she do that?" "How should/would I know?!"* [=I don't know, and you should not expect me to know] **c** [*T*] : to have learned (something, such as a skill or a language) ▪ *She knows karate/CPR/Spanish.* ▪ *Do you know how to swim?* ▪ *I'd love to go swimming, but I don't know how.* [=I never learned to swim] **2** [*T/I*] : to be aware of (something) ▪ *She knows that the job will not be easy.* ▪ *I knew about the problem.* ▪ *Do you know of a good lawyer?* ▪ *It's wrong and you know it!* [=you are aware that it is wrong] ▪ *There was no way for me to know that he was your brother.* ▪ *How was I to know that he was your brother?* ▪ *"I'm sorry I threw out the bag." "It's okay: you couldn't have known that I needed it."* = *"It's okay: you had no way of knowing that I needed it."* = (*Brit*) *"It's okay: you weren't to know that I needed it."* ▪ *You ought to know by now that she is always late.* ▪ *If you've never been there, you don't know what you're missing.* [=you would enjoy going there very much] ▪ *You know as well as I do that he's wrong.* ▪ *You don't know how happy I am* [=I am extremely happy] *to see you.* ▪ *As far as I know, they haven't left yet.* [=I believe they have not left yet, but I am not sure] ▪ *As you know, he is retiring next month.* ▪ *"Is he married?" "Not that I know of."* [=I don't think he is married] **3** [*T/I*] : to be certain of (something) ▪ *I knew he'd forget.* ▪ *"She says she's not coming." "I knew it!"* [=I was sure that she wouldn't come] ▪ *I knew it all along.* [=I was always sure of it] ▪ *"They're coming." "Do you know for sure/certain?"* [=are you certain], *or are you just guessing?"* **4** [*T*] **a** : to have met and talked to (someone) : to be acquainted or familiar with (a person) ▪ *"Do you know Clara?" "Yes, we've met."* ▪ *"Do you know Clara?" "We've met but I don't really know her."* [=I don't know much about her] ▪ *Knowing you, you'll be the first one there.* [=because I know you so well, I expect you to be the first one there] ▪ *She's the kindest person I know.* ▪ *We're still getting to know* [=we're still meeting] *our neighbors.* **b** : to have experience with (something) ▪ *She knows the city very well.* ▪ *Do you know any good restaurants in this area?* ▪ *We're still getting to know the neighborhood.* ▪ *life as*

we know it [=as it exists now] **c** : to have experienced (something) ▪ *I've known failure.* [=I have failed] ▪ : to recognize or identify (someone or something) ▪ *I would know that voice anywhere.* ▪ *I know his face* [=his face is familiar to me] *but I don't remember his name.* **b** : to be able to distinguish (one thing) *from* another ▪ *know right from wrong* **6** [*T*] **a** : to be sure that (someone or something) has a particular quality, character, etc., because of your experiences with that person or thing ▪ *I know him to be honest.* **b** : to think of (someone or something) as having a particular quality, character, etc. — + *as* ▪ *His neighbors knew him as a friendly person.* ▪ *She is known as an expert in the field.* — used to indicate the name that people know or use for someone or something; + *as* ▪ *The writer Samuel L. Clemens was better known as* [=most people called him] *Mark Twain.* **d** — used to say that someone or something has a particular quality, feature, ability, etc., that people know about; + *for* ▪ *The restaurant is known for its desserts.* [=the restaurant's desserts are popular] **e** — used to say that someone has been or done something in the past ▪ *I've never known her to be wrong.* [=I do not know of any time when she has been wrong] ▪ *We've known him to study all night.* = *He's been known to study all night.* — **before you know it** : very quickly or soon ▪ *We'll be there before you know it.* — **don't I know it** *informal* — used to say that you agree with what has just been said ▪ *"It's freezing in here!" "Don't I know it."* [=I agree] — **for all I know** *informal* — used to say that you have little or no knowledge of something ▪ *For all I know, he left last night.* [=I don't know when he left; it's possible that he left last night] — **God/good-ness/heaven/Lord knows** *informal* **1** — used to stress that something is not known ▪ *God (only) knows if the reports are true.* **2** — used to make a statement more forceful ▪ *She didn't win, but Lord knows she tried.* — **I don't know 1** — used to say that you do not have the information someone is asking for ▪ *"Where is the library?" "I don't know."* **2** *informal* — used to express disagreement, doubt, or uncertainty ▪ *She thinks we should go now, but I don't know.* [=I'm not sure] *Maybe we should wait.* **3** — used to say that you are uncertain *about* someone or something ▪ *I don't know about you* [=you may feel differently than I do about this], *but I'm leaving.* ▪ *I don't know about him*—he's hard to figure out. — **if you must know** — used when you are answering a question that you do not want to answer because the information is personal, embarrassing, etc. ▪ *"Why did you leave that job?" "If you must know, I was fired."* — **I know (it) 1** — used to express agreement ▪ *"This place is a mess." "I know."* [=I agree] **2** — used to introduce a suggestion ▪ *"What should we do tonight?" "I know* [=I have an idea]—*how about a movie?"* — **I wouldn't know** — used to say that you have not experienced something • *"Their house is huge!" "I wouldn't know. I've never seen it."* — **know better 1** : to be smart or sensible enough not to do something • *You walked home alone? Don't you know better (than that)?* • *She'll know better than to* [=she will not] *trust them again.* • *He's just a child and he doesn't know (any) better.* [=he is too young to be expected to behave properly] • *He's old enough to know better.* **2** : to know or understand the truth about something • *She said it wasn't her fault, but I know better.* [=I know it was her fault] **3** : to know or understand more than other people • *He always thinks he knows better.* — **know different/otherwise** : to know that something that people think or say is true is not really true • *She says she has no money but I know otherwise.* [=I know that she does have money] — **know no boundaries** see BOUNDARY — **know no bounds** see ³BOUND — **know (something) backward and forward or know (something) inside (and) out or know (something) like the back of your hand** : to know something completely • *She knows the business inside and out.* — **know (something or someone) for what it/he/she is** : to understand what something or someone truly is • *Now I know them for what they are—liars.* — **know (something) when you see it/one** : to be able to recognize or identify something immediately • *She knows a bargain when she sees it.* • *I'm not sure what I want, but I'll know it when I see it.* — **know the drill** see ¹DRILL — **know the score** see ¹SCORE — **know what hit you** — used to say that something you did not expect surprised you very much • *I didn't know what hit me—suddenly I just felt so dizzy.* — **know what it is or to know what it's like** : to have experience with a situation, activity, or condition • *He knows what it is to be poor.* [=he has been poor] — **know (what's) best** : to know or understand better than someone else what should be done • *I'll do whatever you say. You know best.* — **know what you are talking about** : to have knowledge or experience with something and to deserve to be listened to • *Don't listen to him. He doesn't know what he's talking about.* [=he is wrong] — **know which side your bread is buttered on** see ¹BREAD — **know your way around** : to be very familiar with • *He knows his way around Boston.* • *They know their way around computers.* [=they are good at using computers] — **let (someone) know** : to tell something to someone • *Let me know* [=tell me] *if you need help.* — **let (something) be known or make (something) known** *formal* : to tell people something • *He let it be known* [=he announced] *that he will run for mayor.* — **make yourself known** *formal* : to introduce yourself • *The candidate needs to make herself known to voters.* — **might/should have known** — used to say that you are not surprised to learn of something • *I should have known he would be late.* — **not**

know someone from Adam *informal* : to not know someone at all • *She doesn't know me from Adam.* — **not know the first thing about** : to have little or no knowledge about (something or someone) • *I don't know the first thing about sports.* — **what do you know** *informal* **1** — used to express surprise • *She's an astronaut? Well, what do you know!* • *"He's in law school." "Well what do you know about that?"* [=I am surprised about that] **2** — used to say that someone is wrong about something • *"She thinks I should quit." "What does she know? You should do what you want."* — **wouldn't you know (it)?** *informal* — used to say that something annoying is the kind of thing that often happens • *Wouldn't you know?—I left my purse at home.* — **you know** *informal* **1** — used when you are trying to help someone remember something • *They live on the other side of town. You know—near the golf course.* **2** — used for emphasis • *You know, we really have to go.* **3** — used when you are not sure of what to say or how to say it • *Would you like to, you know, go out sometime?* — **you know something/what?** *informal* **1** — used to emphasize the statement that comes after it • *You know something? I never trusted her.* **2** — used to get someone's attention • *Hey, you know what? I'm hungry.* — **you know what I mean** *informal* — used to ask if the hearer agrees with and understands what has been said • *He's kind of strange. Do you know what I mean? = He's kind of strange—know what I mean?* • *He's kind of strange, if you know what I mean.* — **you know what they say** *informal* — used to introduce a common saying that expresses a common belief • *You know what they say: if at first you don't succeed, try, try again.* — **you never know** — used to say that it is impossible to be sure about what will happen • *You never know—you might win the lottery.*

²**know** *n* — **in the know** : having information that most people do not have • *people who are in the know*

know·able /ˈnoʊəbəl/ *adj* : able to be known • *information that is not easily knowable*

know–all /ˈnoʊˌɑːl/ *n [C] Brit, informal* : KNOW-IT-ALL

know–how /ˈnoʊˌhaʊ/ *n [U]* : knowledge of how to do something well • EXPERTISE • *technical know-how*

know·ing /ˈnoʊɪŋ/ *adj, always before a noun* : showing that you have special knowledge • *a knowing glance/smile*

know·ing·ly /ˈnoʊɪŋli/ *adv* **1** : in a way that shows that you have special knowledge • *She looked at us knowingly.* **2** : with knowledge of what is being done • *Did he knowingly withhold information?*

know–it–all /ˈnoʊwətˌɑːl/ *n [C] informal + disapproving* : a person who talks and behaves like someone who knows everything • *She's a real know-it-all, always telling me what to do.*

knowl·edge /ˈnɑːlɪdʒ/ *n* **1** [*U, singular*] : information, understanding, or skill that you get from experience or education • *a thirst/quest for knowledge* • *a knowledge of carpentry* **2** [U] : awareness of something • *I had no knowledge of their plans.* • *The decision was made* ***without my knowledge.*** [=I did not know about the decision] • *They went on vacation,* ***safe/secure in the knowledge*** [=feeling safe or secure because they knew] *that the farm would be well cared for.* — ***common knowledge*** : something that many or most people know • *It's common knowledge that she plans to run for mayor.* — ***public knowledge*** : something that people know because it has been reported in the news • *His legal problems are a matter of public knowledge.* — ***to someone's knowledge*** : according to what someone knows • *"Did anyone arrive late?" "Not to my knowledge."* — ***to the best of my knowledge*** — used to say that you think a statement is true but that there may be something you do not know which makes it untrue • *I answered their questions to the best of my knowledge.* [=I gave the best answers I could based on what I knew]

knowl·edge·able /ˈnɑːlɪdʒəbəl/ *adj* : having a lot of knowledge • *a knowledgeable person* — **knowl·edge·ably** /ˈnɑːlɪdʒəbli/ *adv*

¹known *past participle of* ¹KNOW

²known /ˈnoʊn/ *adj* **1** *always before a noun* **a** : generally accepted as something specified • *a known criminal* **b** : included in the knowledge that all people have • *There is no known cure for the disease.* **2** : familiar to people • *a little/widely known story*

know–noth·ing /ˈnoʊˌnʌθɪŋ/ *n* [C] : a stupid or ignorant person • *a know-nothing politician*

¹knuck·le /ˈnʌkəl/ *n* [C] **1** : any one of the joints in your fingers **2** : a piece of meat that includes a joint from the leg of an animal

²knuckle *vb* **knuck·led; knuck·ling** — ***knuckle down*** [*phrasal vb*] *informal* : to begin to work hard • *It's time to knuckle down and get to work.* — ***knuckle under*** [*phrasal vb*] *informal* : to stop trying to fight or resist something • *He refused to knuckle under (to anyone).*

knuck·le·ball /ˈnʌkəlˌbɑːl/ *n* [C] *baseball* : a pitch that is thrown with very little spin by holding the ball with the knuckles or fingertips

knuck·le·head /ˈnʌkəlˌhɛd/ *n* [C] *US, informal* : a stupid person

¹KO /ˌkeɪˈoʊ/ *n* [C] *boxing* : ¹KNOCKOUT 1

²KO *vb* **KO'd** /ˌkeɪˈoʊd/; **KO'·ing** /ˌkeɪˈoʊɪŋ/ [T] *boxing* : to knock (an opponent) out • *He was KO'd in the second round.*

ko·ala /koʊˈwɑːlə/ *n* [C] : an Australian animal that has thick gray fur and no tail — called also *koala bear*

kook /ˈkuːk/ *n* [C] *informal* : a person whose ideas or actions are very strange or foolish — **kooky** /ˈkuːki/ *adj* **kook·i·er; -est** • *a kooky idea/outfit/person*

Ko·ran *also* **Qur·an** *or* **Qur·'an** /kəˈræn, kəˈrɑːn/ *n* [*singular*] : the book of sacred writings used in the Muslim religion — **Ko·ran·ic** *also* **Qu·ran·ic** *or* **Qur·'an·ic** /kəˈrænɪk/ *adj*

Ko·re·an /kəˈriːjən/ *n* **1** [C] : a person who is from Korea **2** [U] : the language of the Korean people — **Korean** *adj*

ko·sher /ˈkoʊʃər/ *adj* **1 a** : accepted by Jewish law as fit for eating or drinking • *kosher foods/salt/meat* • *They* ***keep kosher.*** [=they obey Jewish laws about eating and drinking] **b** : selling or serving kosher food • *a kosher butcher/deli* **2** *informal* : proper or acceptable • *The deal doesn't seem kosher.*

kow·tow /ˈkaʊˌtaʊ/ *vb* [I] *informal + disapproving* : to obey someone in a way that seems weak • *I refuse to kowtow to his demands.*

kph *abbr* kilometers per hour

Krem·lin /ˈkrɛmlən/ *n* — **the Kremlin** : the government of Russia and the former Soviet Union; *also* : the buildings of the Russian government in Moscow

kryp·ton /ˈkrɪpˌtɑːn/ *n* [U] : a chemical element that is a colorless gas

KS *abbr* Kansas

ku·dos /ˈkuːˌdoʊz, *Brit* ˈkjuːˌdɒs/ *n* [U] *informal* : praise or respect that you get because of something you have done or achieved • *Kudos to everyone who helped.*

kum·quat /ˈkʌmˌkwɑːt/ *n* [C] : a fruit that looks like a small orange

kung fu /ˌkʌŋˈfuː/ *n* [U] : a form of fighting without weapons that was developed in China

Kurd /ˈkʊəd, ˈkəd/ *n* [C] : a member of a group of people who live in a region that includes parts of Turkey, Iran, and Iraq — **Kurd·ish** /ˈkʊədɪʃ, ˈkədɪʃ/ *adj*

kW *abbr* kilowatt

Kwan·zaa *also* **Kwan·za** /ˈkwɑːnzə/ *n* [C/U] : an African-American cultural festival held from December 26 to January 1

kWh *abbr* kilowatt-hour

KY *abbr* Kentucky

L

¹l or L /ˈɛl/ n, pl l's or ls or L's or Ls /ˈɛlz/
1 [C/U] : the twelfth letter of the English
alphabet ▪ a word that starts with (an) l 2
[C] : the Roman numeral that means 50 ▪
LV [=55]

²l or L abbr 1 large — usually used for a
clothing size ▪ The shirt comes in S, M, L,
and XL. 2 left 3 length ▪ The area of a
rectangle is L x W. 4 line — used to refer to a line of poetry or of a play ▪ act
one, scene two, l 25 ◆ The abbreviation
for "lines" is ll. ▪ ll 15–25 5 liter

la /ˈlɑː/ n [U] music : the sixth note of a
musical scale ▪ do, re, mi, fa, sol, la, ti

LA abbr 1 Los Angeles 2 Louisiana

lab /ˈlæb/ n [C] informal : LABORATORY ▪
a chemistry/computer/crime lab ▪ a lab
coat

Lab abbr, Brit Labour (Party) ▪ Jane Smith
MP (Lab)

¹la·bel /ˈleɪbəl/ n [C] 1 : a piece of paper,
cloth, or similar material that is attached
to something to identify or describe it ▪
Read the warning label before you take
the medicine. 2 : a word or phrase that
describes or identifies something or
someone ▪ a word with the label "obsolete"
3 : a company that produces musical recordings ▪ a major/independent record label 4 : a name shown on clothes that
indicates the store, company, or person
who sold, produced, or designed the
clothes ▪ a designer label

²label vb, US -beled or -belled; US -bel-
ing or -bel·ling [T] 1 : to put a word or
name on something to describe or identify it ▪ Label the switches so that you don't
confuse them. 2 : to name or describe
(someone or something) in a specified
way ▪ words that are labeled "obsolete"

¹la·bor (US) or Brit la·bour /ˈleɪbə/ n
1 [C/U] : physical or mental effort : WORK
▪ The job required hours of difficult labor.
▪ menial/manual labor ◆ A labor of love
is a task that you do for enjoyment rather than pay. ◆ When you enjoy the fruits
of your labor/labors, you enjoy the
things that you have gained by working.
2 [U] a : workers considered as a group
▪ a shortage of skilled labor ▪ poor labor
relations [=poor relations between the
workers and the managers of a compa-
ny] ▪ the labor force [=the total number
of people available for working] b : the
organizations or officials that represent
groups of workers ▪ a law opposed to organized labor 3 [U, singular] : the process by which a woman gives birth to a
baby ▪ a difficult labor ▪ She went into labor this morning. ▪ She is in labor. ▪ She's
having labor pains. 4 Labour [singular]
Brit, politics : the Labour Party of the
United Kingdom or another part of the
Commonwealth of Nations

²labor (US) or Brit la·bour vb [I] 1 a : to
do work ▪ Workers labored in the vine-
yard. b : to work hard in order to

achieve something ▪ She labored in vain
to convince them. ◆ If you continue to
believe something that is not true, you
are laboring under a delusion/misappre-
hension/misconception. 2 : to move or
proceed with effort ▪ The truck labored
up the hill. 3 : to repeat or stress something too much or too often ▪ I don't want
to labor the point, but I want to mention
again that it's late.

lab·o·ra·to·ry /ˈlæbrəˌtori, Brit ləˈbɒrə-
tri/ n, pl -ries [C] : a room or building
with special equipment for doing scientific experiments and tests ▪ a research
laboratory ▪ laboratory experiments

labor camp n [C] : a place where prisoners are kept and forced to do hard physical labor

Labor Day n [C/U] : the first Monday in
September celebrated in the U.S. as a
holiday in honor of working people

la·bored (US) or Brit la·boured /ˈleɪbəd/
adj 1 : produced or done with great effort ▪ labored breathing 2 : not having
an easy or natural quality ▪ labored writ-
ing/speech

la·bor·er (US) or Brit la·bour·er /ˈleɪbər-
ə/ n [C] : a person who does hard physical work for money ▪ a farm laborer

la·bor–in·ten·sive (US) or Brit la·bour–
in·ten·sive /ˈleɪbərɪnˌtɛnsɪv/ adj : requiring a lot of work or workers to produce ▪ an expensive and labor-intensive
process

la·bo·ri·ous /ləˈborijəs/ adj : requiring a
lot of time and effort ▪ a slow and labori-
ous process/procedure — la·bo·ri·ous-
ly adv

la·bor–sav·ing (US) or Brit la·bour–
sav·ing /ˈleɪbəˌseɪvɪŋ/ adj : designed to
make a job or task easier to do ▪ a labor-
saving device such as a dishwasher

labor union n [C] US : an organization
of workers formed to protect the rights
and interests of its members

Lab·ra·dor retriever /ˈlæbrəˌdoɚ-/ n [C]
: a medium to large short-haired dog
that is black, yellow, or brown in color
— called also Labrador

lab·y·rinth /ˈlæbəˌrɪnθ/ n [C] 1 : a place
that has many confusing paths or passages ▪ a complex labyrinth of tunnels and
chambers 2 : something that is extremely complicated or difficult to understand ▪ a labyrinth of customs and
rules

¹lace /ˈleɪs/ n 1 [C] : a cord or string used
for tying or holding things together; especially : SHOELACE 2 [U] : a very thin
and light cloth made with patterns of
holes ▪ lace curtains

²lace vb laced; lac·ing [T] 1 : to pull a
lace through the holes of (a shoe, boot,
etc.) ▪ lacing (up) her shoes 2 a : to add a
small amount of alcohol, a drug, a poison, etc., to (something, such as a drink)
▪ punch laced with brandy ▪ pills laced

with poison　**b** : to add something that gives flavor or interest to (something) ▪ *conversation laced with sarcasm*

lac·er·ate /ˈlæsəˌreɪt/ *vb* **-at·ed; -at·ing** [*T*] : to cut or tear (someone's flesh) deeply or roughly ▪ *The patient's hand was severely lacerated.* — **lac·er·a·tion** /ˌlæsəˈreɪʃən/ *n* [*C*] ▪ *deep lacerations on the patient's legs*

¹**lack** /ˈlæk/ *vb* [*T/I*] : to not have (something) ▪ *His book lacks any coherent structure.* : to not have enough of (something) ▪ *someone who lacks confidence* ▪ *(chiefly US)* *The area does not lack for good restaurants.* [=the area has many good restaurants]

²**lack** *n* [*U, singular*] : the state or condition of not having any or enough of something ▪ *a lack of experience/money/sleep* ▪ *There's no lack of interest in the proposal.* [=there's much interest in the proposal] ▪ *They called it a comet,* **for lack of** *a better term/word.* [=because they could not think of a better term/word for it]

lack·a·dai·si·cal /ˌlækəˈdeɪzɪkəl/ *adj* : feeling or showing a lack of interest or enthusiasm ▪ *a lackadaisical student* — **lack·a·dai·si·cal·ly** /ˌlækəˈdeɪzɪkli/ *adv*

lack·ey /ˈlæki/ *n, pl* **-eys** [*C*] *disapproving* : a person who is or acts like a weak servant of someone powerful ▪ *a celebrity surrounded by his lackeys*

lack·ing /ˈlækɪŋ/ *adj* **1** : not having any or enough of something that is needed or wanted ▪ *He is lacking in experience.* [=he lacks experience] **2** : needed, wanted, or expected but not present or available ▪ *There was something lacking in her performance.*

lack·lus·ter *(US)* or *Brit* **lack·lus·tre** /ˈlækˌlʌstɚ/ *adj* : lacking excitement or interest ▪ *a lackluster performance*

la·con·ic /ləˈkɑːnɪk/ *adj* : using few words in speech or writing ▪ *a laconic reply/response* — **la·con·i·cal·ly** /ləˈkɑːnɪkli/ *adv*

lac·quer /ˈlækɚ/ *n* [*C/U*] : a liquid that is spread on wood or metal and that dries to form a hard and shiny surface — **lacquered** /ˈlækɚd/ *adj* ▪ *a lacquered table*

la·crosse /ləˈkrɑːs/ *n* [*U*] : an outdoor game in which players use long-handled sticks with nets for catching, throwing, and carrying the ball

lac·tose /ˈlækˌtoʊs/ *n* [*U*] *chemistry* : a type of sugar that is present in milk ▪ *She's lactose intolerant.* [=unable to digest lactose]

lacy /ˈleɪsi/ *adj* **lac·i·er; -est** : made of lace or resembling lace ▪ *a lacy veil/border* ▪ *a flower with lacy petals*

lad /ˈlæd/ *n* [*C*] *informal* **1** *chiefly Brit* : a boy or young man **2** *Brit* : a man with whom you are friendly ▪ *He's out with the lads.*

lad·der /ˈlædɚ/ *n* [*C*] **1** : a device used for climbing that has two long pieces of wood, metal, or rope with a series of steps or rungs between them **2** : a series of steps or stages by which someone moves up to a higher or better position ▪ *moving up the corporate/social ladder* **3**

Brit : a long hole in a stocking : RUN

lad·en /ˈleɪdn/ *adj* : having or carrying a large amount of something ▪ *branches laden with fruit* ▪ *(figurative) a voice laden with sarcasm* [=a very sarcastic voice]

ladies' man *n* [*C*] *informal* : a man who enjoys being with and giving attention to women

ladies' room *n* [*C*] *US* : a public bathroom for use by women and girls

la·dle /ˈleɪdl/ *n* [*C*] : a large and deep spoon with a long handle that is used for serving a liquid ▪ *a soup ladle* — **ladle** *vb* **la·dled; la·dling** [*T*] ▪ *The soup was ladled into the bowls.*

la·dy /ˈleɪdi/ *n, pl* **-dies** [*C*] **1** : a woman who behaves in a polite way ▪ *taught to act like a lady* **2** : WOMAN — used especially in polite speech or when speaking to a group of women ▪ *The lady behind the counter will take your order.* ▪ *Good evening, ladies and gentlemen!* — sometimes used informally before another noun ▪ *a lady doctor* [=(more commonly and politely) a female/woman doctor] **3 Lady** : a woman who is a member of the nobility — used as a title ▪ *Lady Margaret*

la·dy·bug /ˈleɪdiˌbʌg/ *n* [*C*] *US* : a type of small flying insect that has a round red back with dark spots — called also *(Brit)* **la·dy·bird** /ˈleɪdiˌbɚd/

la·dy·like /ˈleɪdiˌlaɪk/ *adj* : polite and quiet in a way that has traditionally been considered suited to a woman ▪ *ladylike behavior*

¹**lag** /ˈlæg/ *vb* **lagged; lag·ging** [*I*] **1 a** : to move more slowly than others ▪ *One of the hikers was lagging behind the rest of the group.* **b** : to be in a position that is behind others ▪ *The company lags behind its competitors in developing new products.* **2** : to happen or develop more slowly than expected or wanted ▪ *Production has continued to lag (far/well/way) behind schedule/demand.*

²**lag** *n* [*singular*] : a space of time between two events ▪ *Work has resumed after a lag of several months.* — called also *time lag*

la·ger /ˈlɑːgɚ/ *n* [*C/U*] : a type of beer that is light in color and is aged at cool temperatures

la·goon /ləˈguːn/ *n* [*C*] : an area of sea water that is separated from the ocean by a reef or sandbar

laid *past tense and past participle of* ¹LAY

laid–back /ˈleɪdˈbæk/ *adj, informal* : relaxed and calm ▪ *She's pretty laid-back about it.* ▪ *a laid-back attitude*

lain *past participle of* ¹LIE

lair /ˈleɚ/ *n* [*C*] **1** : the place where a wild animal sleeps ▪ *a bear's lair* **2** : a place where someone hides or where someone goes to be alone and to feel safe or comfortable ▪ *the villain's lair*

lais·sez–faire /ˌleˌseɪˈfeɚ/ *n* [*U*] *economics* : a policy that allows businesses to operate with very little interference from the government — **laissez–faire** *adj* ▪ *laissez-faire capitalism/economics*

la·ity /ˈlejəti/ *n* [*U*] : the people of a religion who are not priests, ministers, etc.

lake /ˈleɪk/ *n* [*C*] : a large area of water that is surrounded by land ▪ *a cottage at/*

by/on the lake — often used in names ▪ *Lake Erie*

lake·front /'leɪk,frʌnt/ *n [C] chiefly US* : the land beside a lake ▪ *lakefront property*

lake·side /'leɪk,saɪd/ *n [C]* : LAKEFRONT ▪ *a lakeside cottage/community*

lam /'læm/ *n* — **on the lam** *US, informal* : trying to avoid being caught by the police ▪ *two escaped convicts on the lam*

lamb /'læm/ *n* **1 a** [C] : a young sheep **b** [U] : the meat of a lamb ▪ *leg of lamb* **2** [C] *informal* : an innocent, weak, or gentle person ▪ *You poor lamb.*

lam·baste *or* **lam·bast** /,læm'beɪst, ,læm'bæst/ *vb* **-bast·ed; -bast·ing** [T] : to criticize (someone or something) very harshly ▪ *The coach lambasted the team for its poor play.*

lame /'leɪm/ *adj* **lam·er; -est** **1** : having an injured leg or foot that makes walking difficult or painful ▪ *a lame horse* ▪ *caring for the sick and the lame* [=people who are lame] **2** *informal* : not strong, good, or effective ▪ *a lame excuse/joke* **3** *US, informal* : not smart or impressive ▪ *She's really lame.* — **lame·ly** *adv* — **lame·ness** *n [U]*

lame duck *n [C]* **1** *chiefly US* : an elected official whose time in an office or position will soon end ▪ *a president who's a lame duck* = *a lame-duck president* **2** *chiefly Brit* : a person, company, etc., that is weak or unsuccessful and needs help

¹la·ment /lə'mɛnt/ *vb [T/I] formal* : to express sorrow, regret, or unhappiness about something ▪ *She lamented (the fact) that she had lost the ring.* = *She lamented (over) the loss of the ring.* ▪ *her late lamented husband* [=her husband who has died and who is deeply missed]

²lament *n [C] formal* : an expression of sorrow; *especially* : a song or poem that expresses sorrow for someone who has died or something that is gone

la·men·ta·ble /lə'mɛntəbəl, 'læməntə-bəl/ *adj, formal* : deserving to be criticized or regretted ▪ *a lamentable consequence of the war* — **la·men·ta·bly** /lə-'mɛntəbli, 'læməntəbli/ *adv*

lam·en·ta·tion /,læmən'teɪʃən/ *n [C/U] formal* : an expression of great sorrow or deep sadness ▪ *bitter lamentations for the dead*

¹lam·i·nate /'læmə,neɪt/ *vb* **-nat·ed; -nat·ing** [T] : to cover (something) with a thin layer of clear plastic for protection

²lam·i·nate /'læmənət/ *n [C/U]* : a product made by pressing together thin layers of material ▪ *kitchen counters made of plastic laminate*

lam·i·nat·ed /'læmə,neɪtəd/ *adj* **1** : made by pressing together thin layers of material ▪ *laminated wood* **2** : covered with a thin layer of clear plastic for protection ▪ *a laminated photograph*

lamp /'læmp/ *n [C]* **1** : a device that produces light ▪ *turn on/off the lamp* ◆ : LIGHT BULB

lamp·light /'læmp,laɪt/ *n [U]* : the light of a lamp

lam·poon /læm'puːn/ *vb [T]* : to publicly criticize (someone or something) in a

way that causes laughter ▪ *a politician lampooned in cartoons*

lamp·post /'læmp,poʊst/ *n [C]* : a post with an outdoor lamp on top

lamp·shade /'læmp,ʃeɪd/ *n [C]* : a cover that softens or directs the light of a lamp

¹lance /'læns, Brit 'lɑːns/ *n [C]* : a long, pointed weapon used in the past by knights riding on horses

²lance *vb* **lanced; lanc·ing** [T] *medical* : to cut (an infected area on a person's skin) with a sharp tool so that pus will flow out ▪ *have a boil/blister lanced*

lance corporal *n [C]* : a person in the U.S. Marines, the Royal Marines, or the British Army with a rank just below that of corporal

¹land /'lænd/ *n* **1** [U] : an area of ground ▪ *arid/fertile/flat land* ▪ *clearing land to grow crops* ▪ *land animals* [=animals that live on land] **2** [U, plural] : an area of the earth's solid surface that is owned by someone ▪ *They own land in Alaska.* ▪ *a piece/plot of land* **3** [C] : a country or nation ▪ *foreign lands* ▪ *my native land* [=the country in which I was born] **4** **the land** : land in the countryside that is thought of as providing a simple and good way of living ▪ *people who are living off the land* [=getting food by farming, hunting, etc.] ▪ *farmers working the land* [=planting and growing crops] — **a land of milk and honey** : a place or country where there is plenty of food and money and life is very easy

²land *vb* **1 a** [I] : to return to the ground or another surface after a flight ▪ *The plane landed (safely) on the runway.* ▪ *The bird landed in a tree.* ▪ *a flight scheduled to land in Paris at 4:00* **b** [T] : to cause (an airplane, helicopter, etc.) to return to the ground or another surface after a flight ▪ *The pilot landed the plane in a field.* **2** [I] : to hit or come to a surface after falling or moving through the air ▪ *I fell and landed on my shoulder.* [=my shoulder hit the ground when I fell] ▪ *The ball landed in the trees.* **3 a** [T] : to cause (someone) to be in a specified place or situation ▪ *The injury landed her in the hospital.* **b** [I] : to reach or come to a place or situation that was not planned or expected ▪ *She took the wrong subway and landed (up) on the other side of town.* **4** [T] : to succeed in getting (something) ▪ *He landed the job.* **5** [I] **a** : to go onto the shore from a ship or boat ▪ *The troops landed on the island.* **b** *of a ship or boat or its passengers* : to reach the shore ▪ *The boat landed at dusk.* **6** [T] : to catch and bring in (a fish) ▪ *landing a trout* **7** [T] : to hit someone with (a punch, blow, etc.) ▪ *land a punch* — **land with** [*phrasal vb*] **land (someone) with** *Brit, informal* : to force (someone) to deal with (something or someone unpleasant) ▪ *I always get landed with the washing-up.*

land·fall /'lænd,fɑːl/ *n [C/U]* : the land that is first seen or reached after a journey by sea or air ▪ *They made landfall* [=they reached land] *their next day.*

land·fill /'lænd,fɪl/ *n* **1** [U] : a system in which waste materials are buried under the ground • *using landfill to dispose of trash* **2** [C/U] : an area where waste is buried under the ground • *a park built on (a) landfill*

land·ing /ˈlændɪŋ/ *n* **1** [C/U] : an act of returning to the ground or another surface after a flight • *The plane made a smooth landing.* • *a plane cleared for landing* **2** [C] : a level area at the top of stairs or between two sets of stairs **3** [C] : a place where boats and ships load and unload passengers and cargo • *the ferry landing* **4** [C] : a military action in which soldiers are brought by boat, airplane, helicopter, etc., to land at a place controlled by the enemy

landing gear *n* [U] : the wheels and other parts of an aircraft that support its weight when it is on the ground

landing strip *n* [C] : AIRSTRIP

land·la·dy /ˈlændˌleɪdi/ *n, pl* **-dies** [C] **1** : a woman who owns a house, apartment, etc., and rents it to other people **2** : a woman who runs an inn, pub, or rooming house

land·locked /ˈlændˌlɑːkt/ *adj* : surrounded by land • *a landlocked country*

land·lord /ˈlændˌloɚd/ *n* [C] **1** : a person who owns a house, apartment, etc., and rents it to other people **2** : a man who runs an inn, pub, or rooming house

land·mark /ˈlændˌmaɚk/ *n* [C] **1 a** : an object or structure on land that is easy to see and recognize • *The Golden Gate Bridge is a famous/familiar landmark in San Francisco.* **b** *US* : a building or place that was important in history • *The battlefield is a national historical landmark.* **2** : a very important event or achievement • *a landmark court decision*

land·mass /ˈlændˌmæs/ *n* [C] : a very large area of land (such as a continent) • *continental landmasses*

land mine *n* [C] : a bomb that is buried in the ground and that explodes when someone steps on it or drives over it • *(figurative) The issue is an emotional/political land mine.* [=it could cause great emotional/political damage]

land·own·er /ˈlændˌoʊnɚ/ *n* [C] : a person who owns land • *a large landowner* [=a person who owns a large amount of land]

¹**land·scape** /ˈlændˌskeɪp/ *n* **1** [C] : a picture that shows a natural scene of land or the countryside • *a landscape painter/artist* **2** [C] : an area of land that has a particular quality or appearance • *a desert/rural/urban landscape* **3** [C] : a particular area of activity • *changes in the political landscape* [=scene] **4** [U] : a way of printing a page so that the shorter sides are on the left and right and the longer sides are at the top and bottom — compare PORTRAIT

²**landscape** *vb* **-scaped; -scap·ing** [T] : to make changes to improve the appearance of (an area of land) • *a beautifully landscaped campus* — **land·scap·er** *n* [C] • *He hired professional landscapers to plan a garden.* — **landscaping** *n* [U] • *the beautiful landscaping of the campus/yard*

land·slide /ˈlændˌslaɪd/ *n* [C] **1** : a large

mass of rocks and earth that suddenly and quickly moves down the side of a mountain or hill • *The earthquake triggered a landslide.* **2** : an election in which the winner gets a much greater number of votes than the loser • *She won the election by/in a landslide.*

land·slip /ˈlændˌslɪp/ *n* [C] *Brit* : LANDSLIDE 1

lane /ˈleɪn/ *n* [C] **1** : a narrow road or path • *a country lane* — often used in the names of streets • *I live on Maple Lane.* **2** : a part of a road that is marked by painted lines and that is for a single line of vehicles • *a highway with three (traffic) lanes = a three-lane highway* • *a driver changing lanes* **3** : a narrow part of a track or swimming pool that is used by a single runner or swimmer in a race **4** : an ocean route used by ships • *shipping lanes* **5** : a long narrow surface that is used for bowling **6** *US* : an area in a store (such as a supermarket) where customers form a line while waiting to pay for the things they are buying — *memory lane* see MEMORY

lan·guage /ˈlæŋgwɪdʒ/ *n* **1 a** [U] : the system of words or signs that people use to express thoughts and feelings to each other • *spoken and written language* • *the origin of language* — see also BODY LANGUAGE **b** [C] : any one of the systems of human language that are used and understood by a particular group of people • *How many languages do you speak?* • *a foreign language* • *a language instructor/teacher* — see also SIGN LANGUAGE **2** [U] : words of a particular kind • *the formal language of the report* • *bad/foul/obscene/strong/vulgar language* • *You'd better watch your language.* [=be careful about the words you use] **3** [U] : the words and expressions used in a particular activity or by a particular group of people • *legal/military language* **4** [C] : a system of signs and symbols that is used to control a computer • *a programming language*

lan·guid /ˈlæŋgwəd/ *adj, formal + literary* : showing or having very little strength, energy, or activity • *a languid pace* • *a hot, languid summer day* — **lan·guid·ly** *adv*

lan·guish /ˈlæŋgwɪʃ/ *vb* [I] *formal* : to continue for a long time without activity or progress in an unpleasant or unwanted situation • *The bill languished in the Senate for months.*

lan·guor /ˈlæŋgɚ/ *n* [U, singular] *literary* : a state of feeling tired and relaxed • *the languor of a hot summer afternoon* — **lan·guor·ous** /ˈlæŋgɚəs/ *adj* • *a long languorous afternoon*

lank /ˈlæŋk/ *adj, of hair* : hanging straight down in an unattractive way • *long, lank hair*

lanky /ˈlæŋki/ *adj* **lank·i·er; -est** : tall and thin with usually an awkward quality • *a lanky teenager*

lan·tern /ˈlæntɚn/ *n* [C] : a light that has usually a glass covering and that can be carried by a handle

¹**lap** /ˈlæp/ *n* [C] **1** : the area between the knees and the hips of a person who is sit-

ting down • *She held the baby in/on her lap.* **2** : an act of going completely around a track or over a course when you are running, swimming, etc. • *the last/final lap of the race* — **drop/fall into your lap** or **land in your lap** *informal* ✧ If something good *drops/falls into your lap* or *lands in your lap*, it comes to you suddenly in an unexpected way even though you did not try to get it. — **drop/dump (something) in/into/on your lap** *informal* ✧ If something is *dropped/dumped in/into/on your lap*, it is given to you suddenly even though you did not want it or expect it. — **in the lap of luxury** : in a situation of great ease, comfort, and wealth • *living in the lap of luxury*

²**lap** *vb* **lapped; lap·ping 1** [*T*] : to cause (something) to partly cover something else • *lap one shingle over another* **2** [*T*] : to go past (another racer who is one or more laps behind you) • *The slower runners got lapped by the winner.* **3** [*T/I*] : to drink by licking with the tongue • *a dog lapping (at/up) water* • *(figurative) The crowd lapped up* [=eagerly listened to and accepted] *every word he said.* **4** [*T/I*] *of water* : to move repeatedly over or against something in gentle waves • *Waves gently lapped (at/against) the dock.*

la·pel /ləˈpɛl/ *n* [*C*] : either one of the two folds of fabric that are below the collar on the front of a coat or jacket

¹**lapse** /ˈlæps/ *n* [*C*] **1 a** : an occurrence in which you fail to think or act in the usual or proper way for a brief time and make a mistake • *He blamed the error on a minor mental lapse.* • *a lapse in judgment/security* • *memory lapses* [=times when you forget things that you should remember] **b** : an occurrence in which someone behaves badly for usually a short period of time • *moral/ethical lapses* **c** : a change that results in worse behavior • *a lapse into bad habits* **2** : a period of time between events • *She returned to college after a lapse of several years.* **3** : the ending of something that happens when the payments necessary for it to continue are not made • *the lapse of an insurance policy*

²**lapse** *vb* **lapsed; laps·ing** [*I*] **1** : to stop for usually a brief time • *After a few polite words the conversation lapsed.* **2** : to become no longer effective or valid • *My insurance policy lapsed.* — **lapse into** [*phrasal vb*] **1** : to begin using or doing (something that should be avoided) for a short period of time • *a good writer who occasionally lapses into jargon* **2** : to begin to be in (a worse or less active state or condition) • *The patient lapsed into a coma.*

lap·top /ˈlæpˌtɑːp/ *n* [*C*] : a small computer that is designed to be easily carried — called also *laptop computer*

lar·ce·ny /ˈlɑːrsəni/ *n, pl* **-nies** [*C/U*] *law* : the act of stealing something : THEFT • *commit (a) larceny* — see also GRAND LARCENY, PETIT LARCENY

larch /ˈlɑːrtʃ/ *n* [*C/U*] : a type of tree that is related to the pines and that drops its needles in the winter

lard /ˈlɑːrd/ *n* [*U*] : a soft white substance that is made from the fat of pigs and used in cooking

lar·der /ˈlɑːrdɚ/ *n* [*C*] : a small room or area where food is kept

large /ˈlɑːrdʒ/ *adj* **larg·er; -est 1** : great in size or amount : BIG • *a large bowl/room/company* • *A large part/portion/percentage of the population is literate.* • *a very large man* **2** : not limited in importance, range, etc. • *She played a larger* [=more active] *role in the negotiations.* — **at large 1** : not having been captured • *The criminal is still at large.* **2** : as a group : as a whole • *the beliefs of the public at large* [=the beliefs of most people] **3** *US* : not having a specific subject • *a critic at large* [=a critic who writes about many different things] — **by and large** see ²BY — **in large part/measure** : not entirely but mostly • LARGELY • *The economy is based in large part on farming.* — **larger than life 1** : bigger than the size of an actual person or thing • *The statue is larger than life.* **2** *of a person* : having an unusually exciting, impressive, or appealing quality • *a larger-than-life hero* — **writ large** see ²WRIT — **large·ness** *n* [*U*]

large intestine *n* [*C*] : the end part of the intestine that is wider and shorter than the small intestine

large·ly /ˈlɑːrdʒli/ *adv* : not completely but mostly • *The economy is based largely on farming.*

large–scale *adj* **1** : involving many people or things • *large-scale production* **2** : covering or involving a large area • *a large-scale map/network*

lar·gesse *also* **lar·gess** /lɑːrˈʒɛs/ *n* [*U*] *somewhat formal* : the act of giving away money or the quality of a person who gives away money • *a philanthropist known for his largesse* [=generosity]

larg·ish /ˈlɑːrdʒɪʃ/ *adj* : fairly large • *a largish nose*

¹**lark** /ˈlɑːrk/ *n* [*C*] **1** : any one of several birds that usually have pleasant songs **2** *informal* : something done for enjoyment or adventure • *(US) She entered the race* **on/as a lark.** = *(chiefly Brit) She entered the race for a lark.* [=she entered the race just as a way to have fun]

²**lark** *vb* — **lark about/around** [*phrasal vb*] *Brit, informal* : to behave in a silly and enjoyable way • *girls larking about in the garden*

lar·va /ˈlɑːrvə/ *n, pl* **lar·vae** /ˈlɑːrˌviː/ [*C*] : a very young form of an insect that looks like a worm • *The larva of a butterfly is called a caterpillar.* — **lar·val** /ˈlɑːrvəl/ *adj* • *the larval stage of an insect*

lar·yn·gi·tis /ˌlerənˈdʒaɪtəs/ *n* [*U*] *medical* : a disease in which your throat and larynx become sore so that it is difficult to talk

lar·ynx /ˈlerɪŋks/ *n, pl* **la·ryn·ges** /ləˈrɪnˌdʒiːz/ *or* **lar·ynx·es** [*C*] *medical* : the part of your throat that contains the vocal cords

la·sa·gna (*chiefly US*) *or chiefly Brit* **la·sa·gne** /ləˈzɑːnjə, *Brit* ləˈsænjə/ *n* [*C/U*] : a type of Italian food that has layers of flat noodles baked with a sauce usually of tomatoes, cheese, and meat

las·civ·i·ous /ləˈsɪrvijəs/ *adj, disapproving* : filled with or showing sexual desire ▪ *He was arrested for lewd and lascivious behavior.* — **las·civ·i·ous·ly** *adv*

la·ser /ˈleɪzɚ/ *n* [*C*] : a device that produces a narrow and powerful beam of light that has many special uses in medicine, industry, etc. ▪ *laser surgery*

laser beam *n* [*C*] : the narrow beam of light produced by a laser

laser disc *n* [*C*] : OPTICAL DISK

laser printer *n* [*C*] : a computer printer that prints an image formed by a laser beam

¹**lash** /ˈlæʃ/ *vb* **1** [*T/I*] : to hit (a person or animal) with a whip, stick, or something similar ▪ *The sailor was lashed for disobeying the captain.* **2** [*T/I*] : to hit (something) with force ▪ *Waves lashed (at) the shore.* **3** [*T/I*] : to make a sudden and angry attack against (someone) ▪ *He sometimes lashes out at people when he's upset.* **4** [*T/I*] *of an animal* : to move (the tail) from side to side in a forceful way ▪ *a tiger lashing its tail* **5** [*T*] : to tie (something) to an object with a rope, cord, or chain ▪ *They lashed the canoe to the top of the car.*

²**lash** *n* **1** **a** [*C*] : a hit with a whip ▪ *50 lashes* **b** **the lash** : the punishment of being hit with a whip ▪ *The sailors were threatened with the lash.* **c** [*C*] : the thin piece on the end of a whip **2** [*C*] : EYELASH ▪ *long lashes*

lass /ˈlæs/ *n* [*C*] *chiefly Brit, informal* : a girl or young woman

las·so /ˈlæsou, læˈsuː/ *n, pl* **-sos** *or* **-soes** [*C*] : a rope with a loop that is used for catching animals (such as cattle or horses) — **lasso** *vb* **-sos** *or* **-soes**; **-soed**; **-so·ing** [*T*] ▪ *The cowboy lassoed the horse.*

¹**last** /ˈlæst, *Brit* ˈlɑːst/ *vb* **1** **a** [*I*] : to continue in time ▪ *The movie lasts (for) about two hours.* [=the movie is about two hours long] ▪ *The conference starts on Monday and it lasts until Friday.* **b** [*I*] : to continue in good condition ▪ *The car should last 10 years.* **c** [*I*] : to continue to be available ▪ *These oranges are on sale while they/supplies last.* [=until they have all been sold] **d** [*T/I*] : to continue to be enough for the needs of someone ▪ *We have enough food to last (us) (for) a week.* **2** [*I*] : to be able to continue in a particular situation or condition ▪ *Can you last a whole day without cigarettes?* **b** : to continue to live ▪ *She's very ill and may not last much longer.* ▪ *(chiefly Brit) He may not last out the night.* — **last the distance** see ¹DISTANCE

²**last** *adj* **1** **a** : coming after all others in time, order, or importance : FINAL ▪ *He was the last person out of the building.* ▪ *the last week of the summer* **b** : remaining after the rest are gone ▪ *I'm down to my last dollar.* [=I have one dollar left] **2** : belonging to the final part of something ▪ *the last hours of her life* **3** : most recent ▪ *I liked her last [=previous] novel better than this new one.* — used to identify a preceding period of time ▪ *We saw them last week.* **4** **a** : least likely ▪ *You are the*

last person I would expect to see here. [=I never expected to see you here] **b** : least desirable ▪ *Another bill is the last thing I need right now!* **c** : least important ▪ *Work is the last thing on my mind.* [=I am not thinking about work at all] — **every last** — used as a more forceful way of saying *every* ▪ *Every last soldier was captured.* — **last thing** : after everything else ▪ *Heat the vegetables last thing so that they don't get cold.* ▪ *very late ▪ I'll be back last thing (on) Monday night.* — **on your/its last legs** see ¹LEG — **the last laugh** see ²LAUGH — **the last straw** see STRAW — **the last word** see ¹WORD

³**last** *adv* **1** : after any others in time, order, or importance ▪ *My horse was/finished last in the race.* ▪ *She was first to arrive and last to leave.* : at the end ▪ *The best part of the book comes last.* **2** : most recently : on the most recent occasion ▪ *I last saw him in the supermarket.* **3** — used to introduce a final statement or subject ▪ *Last, I'd like to talk about the company's future.* — **last but not least** — used to say that a final statement is not less important than previous statements ▪ *Last but not least, I would like to introduce our new vice president.*

⁴**last** *pron* **1** **the last** : the last person or thing in a group or series ▪ *She was the last to leave.* **2** **a** **the last** : the last time someone is seen, something is mentioned, etc. ▪ *I hope we've finally seen the last of them.* [=I hope we won't see them again] ▪ *I know I haven't heard the last of my mistake.* [=I know people will continue to talk about my mistake] **b** *informal* — used to describe the most recent information you have about someone or something ▪ *"Do you know where my keys are?" "(The) Last I saw* [=the last time I saw them], *they were in the kitchen."* **3** **the last** **a** : the end of something ▪ *They fought hard to the last.* **b** : the end of someone's life ▪ *He was cheerful to the last.* [=until he died] **4** **a** : the final thing or things that have been mentioned previously ▪ *They had cats, dogs, and a horse. This last* [=the horse] *was kept in an old barn.* **b** : the most recent one of something ▪ *the night/week before last* [=the night/week before last night/week]

⁵**last** *n* — **at last** *or* **at long last** : after a delay or long period of time ▪ *We're finished at last.* ▪ *It appears that this problem will soon be solved, at long last.*

last-ditch /ˈlæstˈdɪtʃ, *Brit* ˈlɑːstˈdɪtʃ/ *adj, always before a noun* : made as a final effort to keep something bad from happening ▪ *a last-ditch effort/attempt*

last hurrah *n* [*C*] : a last effort, production, or appearance ▪ *the game show's last hurrah* [=its last episode]

last·ing /ˈlæstɪŋ, *Brit* ˈlɑːstɪŋ/ *adj* : existing or continuing for a long time ▪ *The trip had a lasting effect on her.*

Last Judgment *n* — **the Last Judgment** : the time when according to some religions all people will be judged by God : JUDGMENT DAY

last·ly /ˈlæstli, *Brit* ˈlɑːstli/ *adv* : at the end ▪ *He worked for the company as trea-*

surer, vice president, and lastly, as president. — used to introduce the last things you are going to say ▪ *Lastly, I would like to discuss the company's future plans.*

last minute *n* — **the last minute** : the last possible time when something can be done ▪ *They were making changes right up to the last minute.* — **last-minute** *adj, always before a noun* ▪ *last-minute changes*

last name *n* [C] : the name that comes at the end of someone's full name ▪ *His first name is John and his last name is Smith.*

last rites *n* — **the last rites** : a religious ceremony that is performed for a Catholic priest for someone who is dying

¹**latch** /ˈlætʃ/ *n* [C] **1** : a device that holds a door, gate, or window closed and that consists of a bar that falls into a holder when it is closed and that is lifted when it is open **2** *chiefly Brit* : a type of door lock that can be opened from the inside by turning a lever or knob but can only be opened from the outside with a key

²**latch** *vb* [T] : to close or fasten (something, such as a door) with a latch ▪ *latch the gate* — **latch on** [*phrasal vb*] *informal* **1** *Brit* : to begin to understand something ▪ *Her explanation was complicated, so it took me a while to latch on.* [=*catch on*] **2** *latch on to* or *latch onto* **a** : to grab and hold (something) ▪ *He latched onto her arm and wouldn't let go.* ▪ *(figurative) The news media has latched on to the scandal.* **b** : to begin using or doing (something) in an enthusiastic way ▪ *companies that have latched onto the trend* **c** : to stay close to (something or someone) ▪ *He latched on to her* [=started talking to her] *at the party and wouldn't go away.*

latch·key /ˈlætʃˌkiː/ *n, pl* **-keys** [C] : a key for opening an outside door

latchkey child *n* [C] : a young child who is alone at home after school because the child's parents are working — called also *latchkey kid*

¹**late** /ˈleɪt/ *adj* **lat·er**; **-est 1** : existing or happening near the end of a period of time ▪ *It happened in late spring.* ▪ *He's in his late thirties.* [=he is about 38 or 39 years old] ▪ *in the late 1930s* [=in about 1938 or 1939] ▪ *It was late (in the evening) when I went to bed.* **2** : coming or happening after the usual, expected, or desired time ▪ *The train is (a half hour) late.* ▪ *I'm sorry I'm late.* ▪ *He made a late payment.* ▪ *Their warning was too late to help us.* **3** *always before a noun* : living until recently : not now living ▪ *the late Jane Smith* — **it's getting late** — used to say that time is passing and especially that evening or late evening is coming ▪ *It's getting late. I should leave.* — **late in the day** : after the expected or proper time ▪ *It's rather late in the day for an apology now.* [=*you should have apologized sooner*] — **late night** : a night when you stay awake until a late hour ▪ *I had a late night* [=stayed up late] *last night.* — **late·ness** *n* [U]

²**late** *adv* **later; -est 1** : at or near the end of a period of time or a process, activity, series, etc. ▪ *late in the day/year* ▪ *She*

wrote it late in her career. ▪ *It'll arrive late next week.* **2** : after the usual or expected time ▪ *She arrived (a half hour) late.* ▪ *I like getting up late.* — **late of** *formal* : having recently lived or worked in (a place, a company, etc.) ▪ *Mark Jones, late of Chicago* — **of late** *formal* : during a recent period ▪ *I haven't seen her of late.* [=*lately, recently*]

late·com·er /ˈleɪtˌkʌmɚ/ *n* [C] **1** : a person who arrives late ▪ *Latecomers had nowhere to park.* **2** : someone or something that has recently arrived or become involved in something : NEWCOMER ▪ *The company is a latecomer to the industry.*

late·ly /ˈleɪtli/ *adv* : in the recent period of time : RECENTLY ▪ *I've been tired lately.*

la·tent /ˈleɪtn̩t/ *adj* — used to describe something (such as a disease) that exists but is not active or cannot be seen ▪ *a latent infection* — **la·ten·cy** /ˈleɪtn̩si/ *n* [U]

¹**lat·er** /ˈleɪtɚ/ *adj, always before a noun* **1** : happening near the end of a process, activity, series, life, etc. ▪ *the composer's later works* ▪ *comparing the early sections of the book with the later sections* **2** : coming or happening after a certain time or at a future time ▪ *a later occasion*

²**later** *adv* **1** : at a time in the future ▪ *We'll talk later.* ▪ *at a time following an earlier time* ▪ *She returned several weeks later.* ▪ *We need to know no/not later than next week.* ✧ In informal spoken English, *later* is used especially by young people as a shortened form of the phrase (*I'll*) *see you later* to say goodbye to someone. ▪ *Later, dudes!* — **later on** : at a time in the future or following an earlier time ▪ *They regretted their decision later on.* — **sooner or later** see SOON

lat·er·al /ˈlætərəl/ *adj* : toward, on, or coming from the side ▪ *a lateral view of the human body* [=*a view from the side*] — **lat·er·al·ly** *adv*

lateral thinking *n* [U] *chiefly Brit* : a method for solving problems by making unusual or unexpected connections between ideas — **lateral thinker** *n* [C]

lat·est /ˈleɪtəst/ *n* [U] : the last possible or acceptable time — usually used in the phrase **at the latest** ▪ *The job will be finished by next year at the (very) latest.* — **the latest** *informal* **1** : the most recent news or information about something ▪ *Have you heard the latest?* **2** : the most recent or modern version of something ▪ *The store carries the latest in cameras.*

la·tex /ˈleɪˌtɛks/ *n* [U] : a white fluid produced by certain plants that is used for making rubber; *also* : a similar material that is used for making various products (such as paint and glue) ▪ *latex paint/gloves*

lathe /ˈleɪð/ *n* [C] : a machine in which a piece of wood or metal is held and turned while being shaped by a sharp tool

¹**lath·er** /ˈlæðɚ, *Brit* ˈlɑːðə/ *n* **1** [U, *singular*] : tiny bubbles formed from soap mixed with water **2** [*singular*] *informal* : a very upset, angry, or worried condition ▪ *He worked himself into a lather.*

[=he became very upset]

²lath·er vb **1** [T] : to spread lather over (something) ▪ *He lathered his face before shaving.* **2** [I] : to form lather ▪ *The soap lathers easily.*

¹Lat·in /ˈlætn̩/ n **1** [U] : the language of ancient Rome **2** [C] : a person born or living in Latin America or in a country (such as Spain or Italy) where a language that comes from Latin is spoken

²Latin adj **1** : based on, relating to, or written in Latin ▪ *Latin grammar* **2** : of or relating to the people of Central America and South America ▪ *Latin music* **3** : of or relating to the people of European countries (such as Spain and Italy) in which languages that come from Latin are spoken ▪ *a Latin lover*

La·ti·na /ləˈtiːnə/ n [C] : a woman or girl who was born in or lives in South America, Central America, or Mexico or a woman or girl in the U.S. whose family is originally from South America, Central America, or Mexico — **Latina** adj ▪ *a famous Latina singer*

Latin–American adj : based in or relating to the American countries south of the U.S. where people speak Spanish and Portuguese ▪ *Latin-American literature/leaders*

La·ti·no /ləˈtiːnoʊ/ n, pl **-nos** [C] : a person who was born or lives in South America, Central America, or Mexico or a person in the U.S. whose family is originally from South America, Central America, or Mexico ✧ The singular form *Latino* usually refers to a man. The plural form *Latinos* often refers to men and women as a group. — **Latino** adj ▪ *Latino children*

lat·i·tude /ˈlætəˌtuːd, Brit ˈlætəˌtjuːd/ n **1 a** [C/U] : distance north or south of the equator measured in degrees up to 90 degrees ▪ *an island located at 40 degrees north latitude* [=at a point 40 degrees north of the equator] **b** [C] : an imaginary line that circles the Earth at a particular latitude and that is parallel to the equator ▪ *Madrid and New York City are on nearly the same latitude.* ▪ *the northern latitudes* [=the northern parts of the world] — compare LONGITUDE **2** [U] somewhat formal : freedom to choose how to act or what to do ▪ *We weren't given much latitude in deciding how to do the job.*

la·trine /ləˈtriːn/ n [C] : an outdoor toilet that is usually a hole dug in the ground

lat·ter /ˈlætɚ/ adj, always before a noun : coming or happening near the end of a process, activity, series, life, etc. : LATER ▪ *the latter stages of the process* — **the latter 1** : the second of two things or people that were mentioned ▪ *Of these two options, the former is less expensive, while the latter is less risky.* **2** : the last thing or person mentioned ▪ *Of chicken, fish, and beef, I like the latter best.* [=I like beef the most]

lat·ter–day /ˈlætɚˌdeɪ/ adj, always before a noun : regarded as a modern version of someone or something from the past ▪ *He thinks he's some sort of latter-day Moses.*

lat·ter·ly /ˈlætɚli/ adv, chiefly Brit, formal **1** : at a later time ▪ *I devoted my free time to painting, sculpture, and, latterly, to gardening.* **2** : during a recent period ▪ *a business that's grown latterly* [=lately]

lat·tice /ˈlætəs/ n [C] : a frame or structure made of crossed wood or metal strips — **lat·ticed** /ˈlætəst/ adj ▪ *a latticed door*

lat·tice·work /ˈlætəsˌwɚk/ n [C/U] : a frame or structure made of crossed wood or metal strips ▪ *the intricate latticework of the fence*

laud /ˈlɑːd/ vb [T] somewhat formal : to praise (someone or something) ▪ *Many people lauded (her for) her efforts to help the poor.*

laud·able /ˈlɑːdəbəl/ adj, somewhat formal : deserving praise ▪ *a laudable goal* — **laud·ably** /ˈlɑːdəbli/ adv

¹laugh /ˈlæf, Brit ˈlɑːf/ vb **1** [I] : to show that you are happy or that you think something is funny by smiling and making a sound from your throat ▪ *What are you laughing about?* ▪ *Everyone laughed at the joke.* ▪ *Why is everyone laughing at me?* ▪ *I laughed out loud when I saw him.* ▪ *I burst out laughing.* [=I suddenly started laughing] ▪ *The movie was hilarious. We laughed our heads off.* ▪ *It's no laughing matter when you lose your job.* [=it's a serious and important thing that people should not joke about] **2** [T] : to say (something) in an amused way ▪ *"I've never seen anything so ridiculous," he laughed.* — **don't make me laugh** informal — used as a response to a statement that you think is very wrong or foolish ▪ *"I could beat you at chess easily." "Don't make me laugh."* — **he who laughs last, laughs best** or **he laughs best that laughs last** — used to say that even if you are not successful now you still succeed or win in the end — **laugh all the way to the bank** : to make a lot of money especially by doing something that other people thought was foolish or amusing — **laugh in someone's face** : to laugh directly at someone in a way that shows disrespect ▪ *When I asked for her help she laughed in my face.* — **laugh off** [phrasal vb] **laugh (something) off** or **laugh off (something)** : to laugh about or make jokes about (something) in order to make people think it is not serious or important ▪ *The injury was serious, but he laughed it off.* — **laugh·er** /ˈlæfɚ, Brit ˈlɑːfɚ/ n [C]

²laugh n **1** [C] : the act or sound of laughing ▪ *a loud/nervous laugh* ▪ *a joke that always gets a (big) laugh.* ▪ *He'll do anything for a laugh.* [=to make people laugh] ▪ *She's always good for a laugh.* [=she's a funny person] ▪ *We had a (good) laugh about it.* [=we laughed about it] **2** informal **a** [C] : something funny or foolish ▪ *You're going to be a movie star? That's a laugh.* **b** [singular] chiefly Brit : a funny person ▪ *He's a real laugh.* — **a barrel of laughs** see ¹BARREL — **a laugh a minute** informal : someone or something that is very funny ▪ *That movie/guy is a laugh a minute.* — **for laughs** or chiefly Brit **for a laugh** informal : for amusement ▪ *They were saying every word backward, just for laughs.* — **the last laugh** ✧ If you *have/get the last laugh*, you finally succeed or win after people laughed at or doubted you.

laugh·able /ˈlæfəbəl, *Brit* ˈlɑːfəbəl/ *adj* : bad in a way that seems foolish or silly ▪ *a laughable attempt to hide the truth* — **laugh·ably** /ˈlæfəbli, *Brit* ˈlɑːfəbli/ *adv*

laugh·ing·ly /ˈlæfɪŋli, *Brit* ˈlɑːfɪŋli/ *adv* **1** : with laughter : in an amused way ▪ *He laughingly recalled his friends in college.* **2** : in a way that is a joke or that you think is silly, foolish, etc. ▪ *a difficult time that some people now laughingly call "the good old days"*

laugh·ing·stock /ˈlæfɪŋˌstɑːk, *Brit* ˈlɑːfɪŋˌstɒk/ *n* [*C*] : a person or thing that is regarded as very foolish or ridiculous ▪ *The mayor became a laughingstock.*

laugh·ter /ˈlæftɚ, *Brit* ˈlɑːftə/ *n* [*U*] : the action or sound of laughing ▪ *Laughter filled the air.* ▪ *peals/gales/shrieks of laughter* ▪ *The audience* **erupted in laughter.** [=suddenly began laughing]

¹**launch** /ˈlɑːntʃ/ *vb* [*T*] **1 a** : to send or shoot (something) into the air or water or into outer space ▪ *launch a rocket/satellite* **b** : to put (a boat or ship) on the water ▪ *launch a battleship* **c** : to throw (something) forward in a forceful way ▪ *launch* [=*hurl*] *a spear* **2 a** : to begin (something that requires much effort) ▪ *launch a business* ▪ *launch an attack* **b** : to cause (a person or group) to start to be successful in a career, business, etc. ▪ *He helped launch her in her career as a singer.* **c** : to offer or sell (something) for the first time ▪ *The company launched several new products last year.* **3** *computers* : to cause (a program) to start operating ▪ *Launch the program by clicking on the icon.* — **launch into** [*phrasal vb*] **1** : to suddenly begin doing or saying (something) in an energetic way ▪ *He launched into a speech about taxes.* **2** *launch (yourself) into* : to become involved in (something) in an energetic way ▪ *She launched herself into the campaign.* — **launch out** [*phrasal vb*] : to begin doing something that is new and very different from what you have been doing ▪ *It's time to launch out and expand my horizons.* — **launch·er** *n* [*C*] ▪ *a rocket launcher*

²**launch** *n* [*C*] **1** : an act of launching something ▪ *a rocket launch* ▪ *the launch of an attack* ▪ *a party to celebrate the launch of a new product/book* **2** : a boat that carries passengers to the shore from a larger boat that is in a harbor

launch·pad /ˈlɑːntʃˌpæd/ *n* [*C*] : an area from which a rocket is launched ▪ (*figurative*) *Her radio show was the launchpad for her television career.* [=it was the first step that led to her television career] — called also *launching pad*

laun·der /ˈlɑːndɚ/ *vb* [*T*] **1** : to make (clothes, towels, sheets, etc.) ready for use by washing, drying, and ironing them ▪ *a freshly laundered shirt* **2** : to put (money that you got by doing something illegal) into a business or bank account in order to hide where it really came

from ▪ *laundering money from drug dealing* — **laun·der·er** /ˈlɑːndərɚ/ *n* [*C*] ▪ *a money launderer*

laun·der·ette /ˌlɑːndəˈrɛt/ *n* [*C*] *chiefly Brit* : a place that has machines to use for washing and drying clothes, towels, sheets, etc.

Laun·dro·mat /ˈlɑːndrəˌmæt/ *service mark* — used for a place that has machines for washing and drying clothes, towels, sheets, etc.

laun·dry /ˈlɑːndri/ *n, pl* **-dries 1** [*U*] : clothes, towels, sheets, etc., that need to be washed or that have been washed ▪ *clean/dirty laundry* ▪ *I have to do the laundry today.* [=to wash the dirty clothes, towels, etc.] — see also DIRTY LAUNDRY **2** [*C*] : a business or place where clothes, towels, sheets, etc., are washed and dried ▪ *work at/in a laundry*

laundry list *n* [*C*] *informal* : a long list of related things ▪ *a laundry list of goals/ problems*

lau·re·ate /ˈlorijət/ *n* [*C*] **1** : someone who has won an important prize or honor or for achievement in an art or science ▪ *a Nobel laureate* **2** : POET LAUREATE

lau·rel /ˈlorəl/ *n* [*C/U*] **1** : an evergreen tree or bush with shiny pointed leaves **2** [*plural*] : honor or fame given for some achievement ▪ *the laurels of victory* ▪ **rest/sit on your laurels** : to be satisfied with past success and do nothing to achieve further success

la·va /ˈlɑːvə/ *n* [*U*] : melted rock from a volcano ▪ *molten lava*

lav·a·to·ry /ˈlævəˌtori, *Brit* ˈlævətri/ *n, pl* **-ries** [*C*] **1** *formal* : a room with a toilet and sink **2** *Brit* : TOILET 1 **3** *US, technical* : a bathroom sink

lav·en·der /ˈlævəndɚ/ *n* [*C/U*] **1** : a plant with narrow leaves and small purple flowers that have a sweet smell **2** : a pale purple color

¹**lav·ish** /ˈlævɪʃ/ *adj* **1** : giving or using a large amount of something ▪ *She's lavish in giving praise to her employees.* [=she praises her employees a lot] ▪ *a cook who is lavish with spices* **2** : given in large amounts ▪ *She has drawn/gained lavish praise* [=a great amount of praise] *for her charitable works.* **3** : having a very rich and expensive quality ▪ *a lavish home/ feast* — **lav·ish·ly** *adv* ▪ *a lavishly illustrated book* — **lav·ish·ness** [*U*]

²**lavish** *vb* — **lavish on/upon** [*phrasal vb*] **lavish (something) on/upon (someone)** : to give a large amount of (something) to (someone) ▪ *They lavished gifts on us.* [=they gave us many gifts] — **lavish with** [*phrasal vb*] **lavish (someone or something) with (something)** : to give (someone or something) a large amount of (something) ▪ *They lavished us with gifts.*

law /ˈlɑː/ *n* **1** [*U*] **a** : the whole system or set of rules made by the government of a town, state, country, etc. ▪ *state/federal law* ▪ *Stealing is* **against the law.** [=is illegal] ▪ *He denied that he had* **broken/violated the law.** ▪ *The job of the police is to* **enforce the law.** [=make sure that people obey the law] ▪ *a career in law enforcement* [=a career as a police officer] — see also MARTIAL LAW   **b** : a particular kind of law • *criminal/contract/immigration law* — see also COMMON LAW   **2** [*C/U*] : a rule made by the government of a town, state, country, etc. • *a new law to protect people from being evicted unfairly* • *laws against discrimination* • *Schools are required by law to provide a safe learning environment.* • *The bill was signed into law by the governor.* [=the proposed law became officially active when the governor signed it]   **3** *the law* : the people and organizations (such as the police and the courts) whose job is to find or punish people who do not obey laws • *He's in trouble with the law.*   **4** [*U*]   **a** : the job of a lawyer : the legal profession • *a career in law* • *a law firm* • *She practices law.* [=she works as a lawyer]   **b** : the area of study that relates to laws and how they are used • *a professor of law* • *law school* [=a school that trains you to become a lawyer]   **5** [*C/U*] : a religious rule • *the body of Islamic laws* • *according to Jewish law*   **6** [*C*]   **a** : a rule stating that something (such as an art or profession) should be done in a certain way • *Balance is the first law of architecture.* [=the most important principle in architecture]   **b** *Brit* : a rule in a sport or game • *the laws of tennis*   **7** [*C*] : a statement that describes how something works in the natural world • *the law of gravity* • *the laws of nature/physics* — **above the law** : not required to obey the law • *No one is above the law.* — **law and order** : a state or situation in which people obey the law • *The police work to preserve law and order.* — **lay down the law** see *lay down* at ¹LAY — **outside the law**   **1** : not agreeing with the law • *actions that may have been outside the law* [=illegal]   **2** : in an illegal way • *a business operating outside the law* — **take the law into your own hands** : to try to punish someone for breaking a law even though you do not have the right to do that — **the law of averages** : the idea or principle that something which can produce different results will produce those results in a regular or predictable way over a period of time — **the law of the jungle** — used to describe a situation in which people do whatever they want to or whatever is necessary to survive or succeed • *an industry governed by the law of the jungle* — **within the law**   **1** : agreeing with the law • *Everything I did was within the law.* [=legal]   **2** : in a legal way • *working/operating within the law* — **your word is law** ❖ If *your word is law*, other people must do what you say.

law-abid-ing /ˈlɑːˌbaɪdɪŋ/ *adj* : obeying the law • *a law-abiding citizen*

law-break-er /ˈlɑːˌbreɪkɚ/ *n* [*C*] : a person who does something that is not legal — **law-break-ing** /ˈlɑːˌbreɪkɪŋ/ *n* [*U*]

law court *n* [*C*]   **1** *US* : a court of law : COURT 1c   **2** : a building or room where legal decisions are made : COURT 1b

law-ful /ˈlɑːfəl/ *adj, formal*   **1** : allowed by the law • *a lawful search of the property*

2 : according to the law • *the property's lawful owner* — **law-ful-ly** /ˈlɑːfəli/ *adv*

law-less /ˈlɑːləs/ *adj*   **1** : having no laws • *the lawless society of the frontier*   **2** : not obeying the law • *a lawless mob* — **law-less-ness** *n* [*U*]

law-mak-er /ˈlɑːˌmeɪkɚ/ *n* [*C*] : someone who makes laws : LEGISLATOR — **law-mak-ing** /ˈlɑːˌmeɪkɪŋ/ *n* [*U*]

lawn /ˈlɑːn/ *n* [*C/U*] : an area of ground (such as the ground around a house or in a garden or park) that is covered with short grass • *a neighborhood with well-kept lawns*

lawn bowling *n* [*U*] *US* : a game in which wooden balls are rolled across an area of grass so that they stop close to a smaller ball

lawn chair *n* [*C*] *US* : a light chair made to be used outside

lawn mower *n* [*C*] : a machine used for cutting the grass on lawns

law-suit /ˈlɑːˌsuːt/ *n* [*C*] : a process by which a court of law makes a decision to end a disagreement between people or organizations • *win/lose a lawsuit* • *He filed/initiated a lawsuit against them.* [=he sued them]

law-yer /ˈlɑːjɚ, ˈlojɚ/ *n* [*C*] : a person whose job is to guide and assist people in matters relating to the law

lax /ˈlæks/ *adj, disapproving* : not careful or strict enough • *Security has been lax.* — **lax-i-ty** /ˈlæksəti/ *n* [*U*] • *moral laxity* — **lax-ly** *adv*

lax-a-tive /ˈlæksətɪv/ *n* [*C/U*] : a medicine or food that makes it easier for solid waste to pass through the body — **laxative** *adj* • *an herb with a mild laxative effect*

¹**lay** /ˈleɪ/ *vb* **laid** /ˈleɪd/; **lay-ing**   **1** [*T*] : to place (someone or something) down gently in a flat position • *She laid the baby (down) in his crib for a nap.* • *I never laid a finger/hand on her.* [=I never touched her]   **2** [*T*]   **a** : to build or set (something) on or in the ground or an-other surface • *lay (down) tracks for the new railroad* • *lay pipe/cable/lines*   **b** *chiefly US* : to spread (something) over a surface • *lay plaster/paint*   **3** [*T*] : BURY 1 • *They laid him in his grave.*   **4** [*I*] *informal* : to be in a flat position on a surface : LIE • *The book was laying on the table.* ❖ The use of *lay* to mean "lie" occurs commonly in informal speech, but it is regarded as an error by many people.   **5** [*T*]   **a** : to beat or strike (something) down with force • *wheat laid flat by the wind*   **b** : to change the condition of something in a specified way • *The mountainside was laid bare by loggers.* [=all the trees on the mountainside were cut down by loggers] • *He laid himself open to criticism.* [=he did or said something that made it possible/easy for people to criticize him]   **6** [*T/I*] *of a bird, insect, etc.* : to produce (an egg) outside of the body • *old chickens that no longer lay (eggs)*   **7** [*T*] — used like *make, place*, or *put* in various phrases • *Even the best-laid plans* [=the most carefully made plans] *sometimes go wrong.* • *The author lays the blame/responsibility for the problem on*

the government. [=the author blames the government for the problem] **8** [T] : to prepare (something) • *lay a fire in the fireplace* • (*Brit*) *lay* [=*set*] *the table for a meal* — **lay aside** [*phrasal vb*] **lay (something) aside** *or* **lay aside (something)** **1** : to place (something) to one side • *She laid aside her book.* • (*figurative*) *a time to lay aside old prejudices* **2** : to keep (something) for special or future use • *We're trying to lay aside a few dollars each week.* — **lay by** [*phrasal vb*] **lay (something) by** *or* **lay by (something)** : to keep (something) for special or future use • *trying to lay by a few dollars each week* — **lay charges** *Brit* : to accuse someone officially of doing something illegal • *Police may lay charges (against her).* — **lay down** [*phrasal vb*] **1** **lay (something) down** *or* **lay down (something)** **a** : to clearly state (a rule, standard, guideline, etc.) • *The company has laid down strict new safety standards.* **b** : to stop using (something) • *The strikers laid down their tools.* **2 lay down your life** *formal* : to die for a good cause • *heroes who laid down their lives to preserve our nation* **3 lay down the law** : to make a strong statement about what someone is or is not allowed to do • *The agreement lays down the law (to everyone) on what the group allows.* — see also ¹LAY 1 (above) — **lay in** [*phrasal vb*] **lay (something) in** *or* **lay in (something)** : to get and store (a supply of something) for future use • *They laid in canned goods for the winter.* — **lay into** [*phrasal vb*] *informal* : to angrily attack or criticize (someone or something) • *The coach laid into us for playing badly.* — **lay it on the line** see ¹LINE — **lay off** [*phrasal vb*] **1 lay (someone) off** *or* **lay off (someone)** : to stop employing (someone) because there is not enough work • *The company laid off most of the staff.* **2** *informal* : to stop doing, using, eating, or drinking (something) • *My doctor advised me to lay off caffeine.* **3** *informal* : to stop annoying someone • *Lay off (me)!* — **lay on** [*phrasal vb*] **lay (something) on** *or* **lay on (something)** **1** : to spread (something) over a surface • *Lay the grout on the surface evenly.* • (*figurative*) *He was laying on the flattery.* [=using a lot of flattery] • (*figurative*) *Compliment her cooking but don't lay it on too thick or she'll think you don't mean it.* **2** *Brit* : to provide (something) for someone • *If more people want to come, more coaches will be laid on for them.* — **lay out** [*phrasal vb*] **lay (something) out** *or* **lay out (something)** **1** : to place (something) on a surface in a carefully arranged way • *Brochures were laid out on a table.* **2** : to arrange (something) in a particular pattern or design • *The city is laid out in the form of a grid.* **3** : to plan the details of (something) • *The work for tomorrow is all laid out.* **4** *informal* : to spend (money) • *The city laid out millions of dollars on the new stadium.* — **lay over** [*phrasal vb*] *US* **1** : to make a stop in the middle of a journey • *Our flight to Italy laid over in Madrid for several hours.* **2 lay (someone) over** : to

cause (someone) to stop in the middle of a journey • *We were laid over in Madrid for several hours.* — **lay siege to** see SIEGE — **lay to rest** see ¹REST — **lay up** [*phrasal vb*] **lay (something or someone) up** *or* **lay up (something or someone)** **1 a** *old-fashioned* : to store (something) • *lay up grain for the winter* **b** : to take (something) out of active use or service • *We laid up the boat for the winter.* **2** : to cause (someone) to stay at home or in bed because of illness or injury • *I was laid up for a week with the flu.* — **lay waste to** : to cause very bad damage to (something) • *The fire laid waste to the land.*

²lay *past tense of* ¹LIE

³lay *adj, always before a noun* **1** : not trained in a certain profession • *a magazine for lay and professional readers* **2** : belonging to a religion but not officially a priest, minister, etc. • *lay preachers*

lay·about /ˈleɪəˌbaʊt/ *n* [C] *informal* : a lazy person

lay·away /ˈleɪəˌweɪ/ *n* [*singular*] *US* : a way of buying something in which you do not receive the thing you are buying until you have paid the full price by making small payments over a period of time • *buying furniture on layaway*

lay·by /ˈleɪˌbaɪ/ *n, pl* **-bys** [C] *Brit* : an area next to a road where vehicles can stop : TURNOUT

¹lay·er /ˈleɪə/ *n* [C] **1** : an amount of something that is spread over an area • *Everything was covered by a thin layer of sand/dust.* **2** : a covering piece of material or a part that lies over or under another • *Wear several layers of clothing.* • (*figurative*) *a novel with layers* [=*levels*] *of meaning* **3** : a bird that lays eggs **4** : a worker who lays something (such as bricks) • *a brick layer*

²layer *vb* [T] : to form or arrange parts or pieces of something on top of each other • *Layer the pasta and the sauce in the pan.* [=place a layer of pasta in the pan, then a layer of sauce, then another layer of pasta, and so on] • *hair that has been layered* [=cut in sections that are different lengths]

layer cake *n* [C] *chiefly US* : a cake made of more than one layer

lay·man /ˈleɪmən/ *n, pl* **-men** /-mən/ [C] **1** : a person who is not a member of a particular profession • *explaining the process in layman's terms* [=in simple language that anyone can understand] **2** : a person who belongs to a religion but is not a priest, minister, etc.

lay·off /ˈleɪˌɑːf/ *n* [C] **1** : the act of ending the employment of a worker or group of workers • *More layoffs are expected at the factory later this year.* **2** : a period of time during which there is no activity • *The band has a new album after a three year layoff.*

lay·out /ˈleɪˌaʊt/ *n* [C] : the design or arrangement of something • *the layout of an apartment*

lay·over /ˈleɪˌoʊvə/ *n* [C] *US* : a period of time when you are not traveling in the middle of a journey • *a two-hour layover*

lay·per·son /ˈleɪˌpɚsn̩/ *n* [C] : LAYMAN

laze /ˈleɪz/ *vb* **lazed; laz·ing** [*I*] : to spend time relaxing • *lazing in the sun* — **laze away** [*phrasal vb*] **laze (something) away** *or* **laze away (something)** : to relax and do very little for (a period of time) • *She lazed away the afternoon lying in the sun.*

la·zy /ˈleɪzi/ *adj* **la·zi·er; -est 1** *disapproving* : not liking to work hard or to be active • *a lazy child* • *I should have cleaned this weekend, but I was feeling lazy.* **2** *always before a noun* : causing people to feel that they do not want to be active • *a lazy summer day* **3** *always before a noun* : moving slowly • *a hawk flying in lazy circles* — **la·zi·ly** /ˈleɪzəli/ *adv* — **la·zi·ness** /ˈleɪzinəs/ *n* [*U*]

lb. *abbr* pound • *a 5-lb. bag of flour*

LCD /ˌɛlˌsiːˈdiː/ *n* [*C*] : a screen (such as a television screen or the screen on a watch) that works by passing a small amount of electricity through a special liquid ◆ *LCD* is an abbreviation for "liquid crystal display."

¹**lead** /ˈliːd/ *vb* **led** /ˈlɛd/; **lead·ing 1 a** [*T/I*] : to guide someone to a place especially by going in front • *You lead (us) and we'll follow right behind you.* • *The teacher led the boy by the hand to his seat.* • *The prisoner was led off to jail* [=was taken to jail] *in handcuffs.* • *(figurative) This leads me to my next point, which is that the building needs a new roof.* **b** [*T*] : to go or be at the front part of (something) • *lead a march/parade* **2** [*I*] : to lie or go in a specified direction • *This road leads to the village.* • *stairs that lead down to the basement* • *(figurative) a relationship that will never lead to marriage* • *(figurative) The investigation was leading nowhere.* [=was not making any progress] **3** [*T/I*] : to be in charge of a person, group, activity, etc. • *She led a successful boycott of the store.* • *We need someone who can lead.* • *lead an expedition/orchestra* • *She led the children in a song.* [=she sang a song and the children sang with her] **4** [*T*] : to cause (a person, group, etc.) to do something or to follow some course of action • *Her interest in art led her into the field of art history.* • *His volunteer work led him to a career in nursing.* = *His volunteer work led him to become a nurse.* • *The evidence leads me to believe* [=makes me believe] *that this disease is curable.* **5** [*T/I*] : to be first, best, or ahead in a race or competition • *At the end of the fourth inning, the Red Sox led by two runs.* • *a runner who is leading the pack/field* [=who is ahead of the group of other runners] • *(figurative) The company leads the world* [=is the most successful company in the world] *in developing this kind of technology.* **6** [*T*] : to have (a specified kind of life) • *leading a quiet/peaceful life* • *He led a charmed life.* [=he was lucky] • *She needs to lead her own life.* [=to make her own decisions about her life] — **lead off** [*phrasal vb*] **lead off** *or* **lead (something) off** *or* **lead off (something) 1** : to start something (such as an activity or performance) in a specified way • *She led off (the presentation) with a brief overview of the project.* **2** *baseball* : to be the first

batter in an inning • *He led off (the inning) with a home run.* — **lead on** [*phrasal vb*] **lead (someone) on** : to cause (someone) to wrongly continue believing or doing something • *He didn't really love her. He had only been leading her on.* — **lead the way** : to be the first person to go somewhere • *You lead the way, and we'll follow.* • *(figurative) a company that led the way in developing new technologies* — **lead to** [*phrasal vb*] : to result in (something) • *a course of study leading to a degree in agriculture* — **lead up to** [*phrasal vb*] **1** : to occur in the time that comes before (something) • *the days leading up to the election* **2** : to come before and help to cause (something) • *a series of errors leading up to the accident* **3** : to come before and help to introduce (something) • *a chapter leading up to the main topic of the book*

²**lead** *n* **1 the lead a** : a position that is ahead of others • *They walked single file, with the oldest boy in the lead.* • *You take the lead.* [=go first] **b** : a position that is ahead of others in a race or competition • *A runner from Kenya is in the lead in the race.* [=is leading the race] • *He has/holds the lead.* **2** [*C*] : the amount or distance by which someone or something is ahead in a race or competition • *a narrow/slim/comfortable lead* **3** [*C*] : a piece of information that could help produce a desired result • *I'm a good salesman, but I need more leads.* [=names of potential customers]; *especially* : a piece of information that might help in solving a crime • *The police have no leads in the case.* **4** [*C*] **a** : the main role in a movie or play • *She got/played the lead in a major Hollywood movie.* • *She got the lead role.*; *also* : someone who plays the main role in a movie or play • *She's the lead.* **b** : the main performer in a group • *He sang/played lead* [=sang/played as the main performer] *in the band.* • *the lead singer/guitarist* **5** [*C*] : the beginning part of a news story • *A story's lead should grab the reader's attention.* **b** : the most important news story in a newspaper or broadcast • *The story of his arrest was the lead in newspapers across the country.* • *the lead story* **6** [*C*] *baseball* : a position taken by a runner at a distance from a base before a pitch is thrown • *The runner took a big lead.* **7** [*C*] *chiefly Brit* : LEASH **8** [*C*] *chiefly Brit* : a wire that carries electricity from a source to an electrical device (such as a lamp or radio) — **follow someone's lead** : to do the same thing that someone else has done • *He followed her lead and voted in favor of the proposal.*

³**lead** /ˈlɛd/ *n* **1** [*U*] : a heavy and soft metal that has a gray color • *a pipe made of lead* = *a lead pipe* **2** [*C/U*] : a thin stick of dark material used in pencils to make marks • *a lead pencil* **3** [*U*] *chiefly US, informal* : bullets • *They shot him full of lead.* — **get the lead out** *US, informal* : to begin going or moving more quickly • *Get the lead out! We don't want to be late!*

lead·ed /ˈlɛdəd/ *adj* **1** : containing lead •

leaded gasoline 2 : having pieces of glass separated by narrow pieces of lead ▪ *leaded glass*

lead·en /ˈlɛdn/ *adj* 1 : having a dull gray color ▪ *a leaden sky/sea* 2 : feeling heavy and difficult to move ▪ *walked with leaden feet* 3 : not lively or exciting ▪ *leaden [=dull] conversation*

lead·er /ˈliːdɚ/ *n* [C] 1 : someone or something that leads others ▪ *a tour leader [=guide]* ▪ *She was the leader for most of the race.* ▪ *religious/political leaders* ▪ *a leader of the antiwar movement* ▪ *a market leader* [=a product or company that is more successful than all competing products or companies] 2 : a person who leads a musical group ▪ *the leader of a big band*; specifically, *US* : the conductor of an orchestra ▪ *the orchestra leader* 3 *Brit* : ²EDITORIAL — see also LOSS LEADER — **lead·er·less** *adj*

lead·er·ship /ˈliːdɚˌʃɪp/ *n* 1 [U] a : a position as a leader of a group, organization, etc. ▪ *She assumed (the) leadership of the company.* b : the time when a person holds the position of leader ▪ *The company did well under her leadership.* [=while she was its leader] 2 [U] : the power or ability to lead other people ▪ *a politician who lacks leadership* ▪ *leadership skills* 3 [C] : the leaders of a group, organization, or country ▪ *The party leadership is uncertain about what to do next.*

lead·ing /ˈliːdɪŋ/ *adj*, always before a noun 1 : having great importance, influence, or success ▪ *a leading topic of conversation* ▪ *a leading citizen of the town* 2 : most important ▪ *the leading cause of death*

leading article *n* [C] *Brit* : ²EDITORIAL

leading edge *n* 1 [C] : the front edge of something that moves ▪ *the leading edge of an airplane's wing* 2 [singular] : the most important or advanced area of activity in a particular field ▪ *the leading edge [=cutting edge] of technology*

leading lady *n* [C] : an actress who plays the most important female role in a play or movie

leading light *n* [C] : a person who is a very important member of a group, organization, or community ▪ *He is one of the leading lights of the labor movement.*

leading man *n* [C] : an actor who plays the most important male role in a play or movie

leading question *n* [C] : a question asked in a way that is intended to produce a desired answer

lead–up /ˈliːdˌʌp/ *n* [singular] : something that comes before or prepares for something else ▪ *the lead-up to the war*

¹**leaf** /ˈliːf/ *n, pl* **leaves** /ˈliːvz/ 1 [C] : one of the flat and typically green parts of a plant that grow from a stem or twig ▪ *a maple/tobacco leaf* ▪ *a pile of dead leaves* ▪ *By the end of April, most trees are in leaf.* [=most trees have grown their new leaves] 2 [C] : a sheet of paper in a book : PAGE ▪ *(figurative) I may take/borrow a leaf out of his book* [=do the same thing that he did] *and start biking to work.* 3 [C] : a part that can be added to or removed from a table to change the size of

its top surface 4 [U] : a very thin sheet of metal (such as gold or silver) that is used to decorate something ▪ *silver leaf* — **turn over a new leaf** : to start behaving or living in a different and better way ▪ *I decided to turn over a new leaf and stop worrying so much.* — **leaf·less** /ˈliːfləs/ *adj* ▪ *leafless trees*

²**leaf** *vb* — **leaf out** [phrasal vb] *US, of a tree* : to produce leaves ▪ *The tree will leaf out in the spring.* — **leaf through** [phrasal vb] : to turn the pages of (a book, a magazine, etc.) ▪ *She was leafing through the magazine.*

leaf·let /ˈliːflət/ *n* [C] : a printed and often folded sheet of paper that is usually given to people for no cost ▪ *an advertising leaflet*

leafy /ˈliːfi/ *adj* **leaf·i·er; -est** 1 : having many leaves or trees ▪ *leafy trees* ▪ *a leafy suburb* [=a suburb in which there are many trees] 2 : consisting mostly of leaves ▪ *leafy vegetables/greens*

league /ˈliːg/ *n* [C] 1 : a group of sports teams that play against each other ▪ *a softball/bowling league* ▪ *(figurative) I'm out of my league playing chess with Kim.* [=Kim plays chess much better than I do] ▪ *He's a good writer, but he's not in the same league as she is.* [=she is a much better writer than he is] ▪ *a cook who's in a league of his own* [=who is a much better cook than anyone else] 2 : a group or organization of nations or people united for a purpose ▪ *the League of Nations* — **in league (with)** : working with someone especially to do something dishonest ▪ *She's in league with corrupt officials.*

¹**leak** /ˈliːk/ *vb* 1 a [T/I] : to let something (such as a liquid or gas) in or out through a hole in a surface ▪ *The roof leaks.* [=rainwater comes into the building through the roof] ▪ *The boat leaked (water) badly.* ▪ *a leaking boat/roof* b [I] of a liquid, gas, etc. : to come in or go out through a hole in a surface ▪ *Air leaked out of the tire.* ▪ *Water leaked through a hole in the roof.* 2 a [T] : to give (secret information) to someone so that it becomes known to the public ▪ *Someone leaked the story to the press.* b [I] : to become known to the public ▪ *Eventually, news of the accident leaked out.*

²**leak** *n* [C] 1 a : a hole in a surface that lets something (such as a liquid or gas) pass in or out ▪ *The boat has a leak.* ▪ *a tire with a slow leak* [=a small hole through which air escapes slowly] ▪ *The pipe sprung a leak.* [=began to leak] b : an occurrence in which something (such as a liquid or gas) passes through a hole in a surface ▪ *a gas leak* 2 : a situation in which people learn about information that is supposed to be secret ▪ *a security leak* — **take a leak** or *Brit* **have a leak** *informal + impolite* : URINATE — **leak·proof** /ˈliːkˌpruːf/ *adj* ▪ *a leakproof container*

leak·age /ˈliːkɪʤ/ *n* [C/U] 1 : an occurrence in which something (such as a liquid or gas) passes through a hole in a surface ▪ *preventing accidental leakage(s)* 2 : an occurrence in which secret information becomes known • *leakage of confidential information*

leaky /ˈliːki/ *adj* **leak·i·er**; **-est** : having a hole that allows something (such as a liquid or gas) to pass in or out : having a leak • *a leaky boat/pipe*

¹**lean** /ˈliːn/ *vb* **leaned** *or Brit* **leant** /ˈlɛnt/; **lean·ing** 1 [*T/I*] : to bend or move or to cause (something) to bend or move from a straight position • *The tree leans to one side.* • *I leaned my chair back.* = *I leaned back in my chair.* • *leaning over the table* 2 [*T/I*] : to rest or to cause (something) to rest *on* or *against* something or someone for support • *The ladder was leaning against the house.* • *He leaned the ladder against the house.* • *She leaned her head on my shoulder.* 3 [*I*] **a** — used to describe what someone wants to do, tends to do, or is likely to do • *She's leaning toward a career in medicine.* [=she is probably going to choose a career in medicine] **b** — used to say that someone supports one group or set of beliefs more than another • *an independent candidate who leans toward the Democrats and their views* **c** — used to say that something is more like one thing than another • *The album leans more toward rock than country.* — **lean on** [*phrasal vb*] 1 : to depend on (someone or something) for support • *She's someone you can lean on.* 2 *informal* : to force or try to force (someone) to do something especially by making threats • *They were leaning on the governor to pass the law.*

²**lean** *adj* 1 : having little fat on the body • *a lean, athletic body* 2 : containing little or no fat • *lean meat* 3 : not having or producing much money, food, etc. • *Those were lean years for the company.* [=years in which the company earned little money] • *a lean budget/profit/harvest* 4 *usually approving* : not using a lot of something (such as words or money) • *a lean writing style* : not wasteful • *We want our business to be lean and mean.* — **lean·ness** /ˈliːnnəs/ *n* [*U*]

lean·ing /ˈliːnɪŋ/ *n* [*C*] : a preference for something or tendency to do something • *His political leanings are unknown.*

lean–to /ˈliːnˌtuː/ *n, pl* **-tos** [*C*] : a small and usually roughly made building that is built on the side of a larger building

¹**leap** /ˈliːp/ *vb* **leaped** /ˈliːpt, ˈlɛpt/ *or* **leapt** /ˈlɛpt, ˈliːpt/; **leap·ing** 1 **a** [*I*] : to jump from a surface • *The cat leaped into the air.* • *He leapt off the bridge.* **b** [*T*] : to jump over (something) • *The horse leaped the stone wall.* 2 [*I*] : to move quickly • *She leapt up* [=she stood up quickly] *and ran out the door.* • *The crowd leapt to its feet.* [=stood up quickly in excitement] • *(figurative) He leaped to her defense.* [=he quickly began to defend her] 3 [*I*] : to suddenly increase by a large amount • *The price of gasoline leaped (by) 10 percent.* — **leap at** [*phrasal vb*] : to eagerly take (a chance, opportunity, etc.) • *She leaped at the chance to try out for the team.* — **leap out at** [*phrasal vb*] 1 : to suddenly come at (someone) from a hiding place • *The assailant leaped out at them.* 2 : to immediately get the attention of (someone) • *The picture on the magazine's cover leaps out at you.* • ***your heart leaps*** see HEART — **leap·er** /ˈliːpɚ/ *n* [*C*]

²**leap** *n* 1 [*C*] : a long or high jump • *She made a graceful leap into the air.* 2 [*C*] : a great and sudden change, increase, or improvement • *She made the difficult leap from college to the workplace.* • *Technology has taken a great leap forward.* — see also QUANTUM LEAP 3 [*singular*] : a serious attempt to do or understand something new • *It required a **leap of the imagination** to picture how the finished project would look.* • *He took/made a **leap of faith** in starting his own business.* — **by/in leaps and bounds** : very quickly and greatly • *The company grew by leaps and bounds.*

leap·frog /ˈliːpˌfrɑːg/ *n* [*U*] : a children's game in which one player bends down so that another player can leap over the back of the first player — **leapfrog** *vb* **-frogged**; **-frog·ging** [*T/I*] • *(figurative) Skipping his last two years of high school, he leapfrogged (over) his classmates and went to college.*

leap year *n* [*C*] : a year of 366 days instead of 365 with February having 29 days instead of 28 ✧ A leap year occurs every four years.

learn /ˈlɚn/ *vb* **learned** *also chiefly Brit* **learnt** /ˈlɚnt/; **learn·ing** 1 [*T/I*] : to gain knowledge or skill by studying, practicing, being taught, or experiencing something • *I can't swim yet, but I'm learning.* • *We learned about the war in our history class.* • *He's learning French.* • *learn to play the guitar* 2 [*T*] : to cause (something) to be in your memory by studying it : MEMORIZE • *learn the alphabet* 3 [*T/I*] : to hear or be told (something) : to find out (something) • *I was surprised when I learned (that) he wasn't coming.* • *We were shocked to learn of her death.* 4 [*T/I*] : to become able to understand (something) through experience • *learn the difference between right and wrong* • *It's important to learn to respect other people.* • *He learned the hard way that crime doesn't pay.* [=he found out by being punished for his crimes] • *It's a bad situation, but we'll just have to **learn to live with it**.* [=we will have to accept it and deal with it] — **learn·er** /ˈlɚnɚ/ *n* [*C*]

learned *adj* 1 /ˈlɚnəd/ *formal* : having or showing a lot of learning, education, or knowledge • *a learned scholar/discussion* 2 /ˈlɚnd/ — used to describe something that people get or have because of learning or experience • *a learned behavior/response*

learn·ing /ˈlɚnɪŋ/ *n* [*U*] : knowledge or skill gained from learning something • *a person of considerable/great learning* • *book learning* [=knowledge gained from reading books]

learning curve *n* [*C*] : the rate at which someone learns something new • *The job has a very steep learning curve.* [=there is a large amount that has to be learned quickly in order to do the job]

learnt *chiefly Brit past tense and past participle of* LEARN

¹**lease** /ˈliːs/ *n [C]* : a legal agreement that lets someone use a car, house, etc., for a period of time in return for payment — *a new lease on life* (*US*) *or Brit a new lease of life* : a chance to continue living or to become successful or popular again • *This medicine gives patients a new lease on life.*

²**lease** *vb* **leased; leas·ing** [*T*] **1** : to use (something) for a period of time in return for payment • *She could either buy or lease the car.* **2** : to allow someone to use (something) for a period of time in return for payment • *We leased the house to them.*

leash /ˈliːʃ/ *n [C] chiefly US* : a long, thin piece of rope, chain, etc., that is used for holding a dog or other animal • (*figurative*) *The coach kept her players on a (short/tight) leash.* [=closely watched and controlled her players] — called also (*chiefly Brit*) **lead** — **leash** *vb* [*T*] • *leash a dog* [=put a dog on a leash]

¹**least** /ˈliːst/ *adj, superlative form of* ¹LITTLE : smallest in amount or degree • *The least noise would startle her.*

²**least** *n* — **the least** : something of the lowest importance, strength, value, etc. • *That's the least of my worries/problems.* — **at least 1** : not less than a specified amount, level, etc. • *At least once a year, we visit our grandparents.* • *You must be at least 21 years of age to enter.* **2** — used to say that something (such as a bad situation) could be or have been worse • *The weather was cold, but at least it didn't rain.* **3** — used to indicate the smallest or easiest thing that someone can or should do • *He could have at least apologized.* **4** — used to indicate that the truth of a statement is uncertain, might change, etc. • *We're going to have a picnic, at least if it doesn't rain.* • *Her name is Sue, or at least I think it is.* — **at the (very) least** — used to indicate the least thing that is true, acceptable, desirable, or certain to happen • *He wanted to win the race, or at the least, to finish second.* — **not (in) the least** : not at all : not in any way or respect • *It did not interest me in the least.* — **the least (someone) can do** : the smallest or easiest thing that someone can or should do • *The least he could do is tell me what happened.* — **to say the least** — used to emphasize a statement • *She was not happy, to say the least.* [=she was very unhappy]

³**least** *adv, superlative form of* ²LITTLE : in or to the smallest degree • *That was the least important of her reasons.* — **last but not least** see ³LAST — **least of all** : especially not • *No one, least of all the children, wanted to go home early.* — **not least** *formal* : especially or particularly • *We had many things to consider, not least the safety of our children.*

least common denominator *n [U] US* : LOWEST COMMON DENOMINATOR

leath·er /ˈlɛðɚ/ *n [U]* : animal skin that is chemically treated to preserve it and that is used in making clothes, shoes, furniture, etc. — **leather** *adj* • *a leather jacket*

— **leath·ery** /ˈlɛðəri/ *adj* • *leathery skin*

¹**leave** /ˈliːv/ *vb* **left** /ˈlɛft/; **leav·ing 1** [*T/I*] : to go away from (a place or person) • *What time did you leave the office?* • *We left him doing his work.* [=he was doing his work when we left him] • *We'll have to leave soon.* • *We're leaving for the game in an hour.* • *He left home* [=left his parents' house and lived somewhere else] *after graduating from high school.* **2** [*T/I*] : to stop living with and having a close personal relationship with (someone) • *His wife left him for another man.* **3 a** [*T*] : to give up or stop having (a job, position, etc.) • *He left* [=quit] *his job and went back to school.* **b** [*T/I*] : to stop attending, belonging to, or working for (a school, a group, an organization, etc.) • *She left school and got a job.* **c** [*T*] : to stop participating in (something, such as a game) • *He had to leave the game because of an injury.* **4** [*T*] **a** : to go away and allow or cause (something or someone) to remain • *You may leave your things in this room.* • *They went out to dinner and left their children (home) with a babysitter.* : to put or bring (something or someone) somewhere and go away • *Please leave the package by the door.* **b** : to go away and forget or neglect to take (something) • *He left his wallet at the restaurant.* **c** : to go away permanently without taking (something or someone) • *He left nothing in his old apartment.* • *They left behind everything they owned.* • *I wanted to leave the past behind.* [=forget about the past] **5** [*T*] : to put (something) in a place for another person to take or have • *We left a good tip for our waitress.* = *We left our waitress a good tip.* • *I left a message (for you) on your answering machine.* **6** [*T*] **a** : to allow someone else to deal with or do (something) • *"It's a complicated problem." "Leave it with me: I'll see what I can do."* • *You don't have to wash the dishes. Just leave them for me (to do).* • *Just leave it (up) to me. I'll handle it.* **b** ✧ In informal U.S. English, you can say **leave it to someone** (to do something), when someone has acted in a way that is typical or expected. • *Leave it to my mom to make everyone feel comfortable.* [=my mom always makes everyone feel comfortable] **c** ✧ If people **leave you to do** something, they do not help you do it. • *He left me to find my own way home.* **7** [*T*] : to cause (something or someone) to be or remain in a specified condition or position • *The accident left him paralyzed.* • *She left the door/window open.* • *It left them wondering when it would all end.* • *Let's just leave it at that.* [=let's not change it or discuss it further] • *I don't want to punish you, but your actions leave me (with) no/little choice.* [=your actions make it necessary for me to punish you] **8** [*T*] **a** : to allow (something) to remain available or unused • *Please leave space/room for another chair.* **b** ✧ An amount that *is left (over)* or that you *have left (over)* is an amount that remains after the rest has been used or taken away. • *There is only one piece of bread left.* [=remaining] • *Do*

we have any pizza left over from last night?
9 [*T*] : to cause (something) to remain as a result, mark, or sign ▪ *The cut left an ugly scar.* ▪ *The grape juice left a stain on the carpet.* ▪ *His visit left a lasting impression on our family.* **10** [*T*] **a** : to have (family members) living after your death ▪ *He left (behind) a widow and two children.* **b** : to give (money, property, etc.) to (someone) after your death ▪ *She left a fortune to her husband.* — **leave no stone unturned** see ¹STONE — **leave off** [*phrasal vb*] **1** : to stop before finishing a story, conversation, etc. ▪ *Where did we leave off in our conversation?* **2** *informal* : to stop (doing something) ▪ *They finally left off trying to reach an agreement.* — **leave out** [*phrasal vb*] **leave out (someone or something) or leave (someone or something) out** : to not include or mention (someone or something) ▪ *The movie leaves a lot out of the story.* ▪ *He always feels left out when his friends talk about sports.* — **leave (someone or something) alone** also **leave (someone or something) be** : to not bother or touch (someone or something) ▪ *Please leave the baby alone. She needs to sleep.* — **leave well enough alone** or *Brit* **leave well alone** : to stop changing something that is already good enough ▪ *He just doesn't know when to leave well enough alone.*
²**leave** *n* **1** [*U, singular*] : a period of time when someone has special permission to be away from a job or from military service ▪ *The soldiers were given a two-month leave.* ▪ *The company granted her maternity leave.* [=time off to take care of a newborn child] ▪ *The professor is on leave this semester.* — called also *leave of absence* **2** [*U*] *formal* : permission to do something ▪ *The soldier was guilty of being absent without (official) leave.* — **take leave of someone** or **take your leave** *formal* : to say goodbye to someone ▪ *It was late when they finally took leave of their friends and headed home.* — **take leave of your senses** : to begin acting or thinking in a very foolish way

leav·en /ˈlɛvən/ *n* [*U*] : a substance (such as yeast) that makes dough rise and become light before it is baked — called also *leavening* — **leaven** *vb* [*T*] ▪ *using yeast to leaven the dough/bread*

leave of absence *n* [*C/U*] : a period of time when someone has special permission to be away from a job : LEAVE ▪ *He was granted/given (a) leave of absence.* ▪ *She has been on leave of absence for two months.*

leaves *plural of* ¹LEAF

lech·er /ˈlɛtʃɚ/ *n* [*C*] *disapproving* : a man who shows an excessive or disgusting interest in sex ▪ *a dirty lecher* — **lech·er·ous** /ˈlɛtʃərəs/ *adj* ▪ *a lecherous old man* — **lech·ery** /ˈlɛtʃəri/ *n* [*U*]

lec·tern /ˈlɛktɚn/ *n* [*C*] : a stand that holds a book, notes, etc., for someone who is reading, speaking, or teaching

¹**lec·ture** /ˈlɛktʃɚ/ *n* [*C*] **1** : a talk or speech given to a group of people to teach them about a particular subject ▪ *a lecture about/on politics* **2** : a talk that

criticizes someone's behavior in an angry or serious way ▪ *I gave her a lecture about doing better in school.*

²**lecture** *vb* **-tured; -tur·ing** **1** [*I*] : to give a talk or a series of talks to a group of people to teach them about a particular subject ▪ *She lectures (to undergraduates) on modern art at the local college.* **2** [*T*] : to talk to (someone) in an angry or serious way ▪ *They lectured their children about/on the importance of honesty.* — **lec·tur·er** /ˈlɛktʃərɚ/ *n* [*C*]

led *past tense and past participle of* ¹LEAD

LED /ˌɛlˌiːˈdiː/ *n* [*C*] *technical* : a device that lights up and displays information when electricity passes through it ◆ *LED* is an abbreviation of "light-emitting diode."

ledge /ˈlɛdʒ/ *n* [*C*] **1** : a narrow, flat surface that sticks out from a wall ▪ *a window ledge* **2** : a flat rock surface that sticks out from a cliff

led·ger /ˈlɛdʒɚ/ *n* [*C*] : a book that a company uses to record information about the money it has paid and received

leech /ˈliːtʃ/ *n* [*C*] **1** : a type of worm that attaches itself to the skin of animals and sucks their blood **2** *disapproving* : a person who uses other people for personal gain

leek /ˈliːk/ *n* [*C*] : a vegetable that has long green leaves rising from a thick white base and that tastes like a mild onion

leer /ˈliɚ/ *vb* [*I*] : to look at someone in an evil or unpleasantly sexual way ▪ *Some disgusting man was leering at her.* — **leer** *n* [*C*]

leery /ˈliri/ *adj* : feeling or showing a lack of trust in someone or something ▪ *They were leery of their neighbors.*

lee·way /ˈliːˌweɪ/ *n* [*U*] : freedom to do something the way you want to do it ▪ *They give/allow their students leeway to try new things.*

¹**left** /ˈlɛft/ *adj, always before a noun* **1 a** : located on the same side of your body as your heart ▪ *her left hand/leg* **b** : done with your left hand ▪ *He hit him with a left hook to the jaw.* **2** : located nearer to the left side of your body than to the right ▪ *the left side of the street* ▪ *a left turn* — **two left feet** see ¹FOOT

²**left** *adv* **1 a** : toward the left ▪ *move left* **b** : toward the political Left ▪ *a political party that has shifted left* **2** *US* : using the left hand ▪ *He bats/throws left.* [=left-handed]

³**left** *n* **1** [*U*] : a location closer to the left side of your body than to the right ▪ *We read from left to right.* ▪ *My house will be on your/the left.* ▪ *Move the picture to the left.* **2** [*C*] : a turn or movement toward the left ▪ *Go to the next intersection and take a left.* **3** [*C*] : a punch made with the left hand ▪ *a left to the jaw* **4 a the Left** : political groups who favor sharing money and property more equally among the members of a society : political groups who support liberal or socialist policies ▪ *The new law is disliked by the Left.* **b the left** : the position of people who support the beliefs and policies of the political Left ▪ *The party has shifted to*

the left. [=has become more liberal]

⁴**left** past tense and past participle of ¹LEAVE

left field n [U] : the part of a baseball outfield that is to the left when you are looking out from home plate; also : the position of the player defending left field ▪ He plays left field. — **come out of left field** US, informal : to be very surprising and unexpected ▪ That question came out of left field. — **out in left field** US, informal : very strange or unusual ▪ ideas that are out in left field — **left fielder** n [C]

left-hand /ˈlɛftˈhænd/ adj, always before a noun : located closer to your left hand : located on the left side ▪ Our building will be on the left-hand side. ▪ a left-hand turn

left-hand-ed /ˈlɛftˈhændəd/ adj 1 : using the left hand more easily than the right hand ▪ My sister is right-handed but I'm left-handed. 2 a : made for the left hand ▪ a left-handed glove b : using or done with the left hand ▪ a left-handed catch/punch 3 : swinging from the left side of the body to the right side in sports like baseball and golf ▪ a left-handed batter/hitter — **left-handed** adv ▪ She bats left-handed.

left-hand-er /ˈlɛftˈhændɚ/ n [C] : a left-handed person; especially : a left-handed pitcher in baseball

left-ist /ˈlɛftɪst/ n [C] : a person who belongs to or supports the political Left — **leftist** adj ▪ a leftist government

left-over /ˈlɛftˌoʊvɚ/ n 1 [plural] : food that has not been finished at a meal and that is often served at another meal 2 [C] : a thing that remains after something is finished or ended ▪ The law is a leftover from earlier times. — **leftover** adj ▪ leftover pizza

left-ward (chiefly US) /ˈlɛftwɚd/ or chiefly Brit **left-wards** /ˈlɛftwɚdz/ adv : toward the left ▪ moving leftward — **leftward** adj ▪ a leftward turn

left wing n [singular] : the part of a political group that consists of people who support liberal or socialist ideas and policies — **left-wing** /ˈlɛftˈwɪŋ/ adj ▪ left-wing politics/politicians — **left-wing-er** /ˈlɛftˈwɪŋɚ/ n [C]

lefty /ˈlɛfti/ n, pl **left-ies** [C] informal 1 chiefly US : LEFT-HANDER 2 chiefly Brit, disapproving : a person who supports liberal or socialist political policies : LEFTIST

¹**leg** /ˈlɛg/ n 1 [C] : one of the long body parts that are used especially for standing, walking, and running ▪ He sat on a chair with his legs crossed. 2 [C/U] : an animal's leg when it is used as food ▪ (a) leg of lamb 3 [C] : any one of the long thin parts that support a table, chair, etc. 4 [C] : the part of a pair of pants that covers the leg 5 [C] : a part of a journey or race ▪ the last leg of the race 6 [plural] US, informal : lasting appeal or interest ▪ a news story with legs — **a leg up** informal 1 **give someone a leg up a** : to hold your hands together so that someone can step into them while climbing up onto something **b** : to give someone an advantage over others ▪ These skills will give you a leg up in the job market. 2

have a leg up : to have an advantage over others ▪ The company has a leg up on the competition. — **an arm and a leg** see ¹ARM — **break a leg** informal — used in speech to wish good luck to someone (such as a performer) ▪ **not have a leg to stand on** : to have no support for what you think, say, or do — **on your/its last legs** informal : very close to failure, exhaustion, or death ▪ The company is on its last legs. — **pull someone's leg** informal : to trick or lie to someone in a playful way ▪ I got upset, but then I saw that she was just pulling my leg. — **shake a leg** informal : to go or move quickly ▪ Shake a leg! You're going to be late! — **stretch your legs** informal : to stand up and walk especially after sitting for a long period of time — **legged** /ˈlɛgəd/ adj ▪ a four-legged animal [=an animal with four legs] ▪ a long-legged bird

²**leg** vb **legged; leg-ging** — **leg it** chiefly Brit, informal : to run fast especially in order to get away from someone or something ▪ When they saw the police car, they legged it.

leg-a-cy /ˈlɛgəsi/ n, pl **-cies** [C] 1 : property, money, etc., that is received from someone who has died ▪ a substantial legacy 2 : something that happened in the past or that comes from someone in the past ▪ Her artistic legacy lives on through her children.

le-gal /ˈliːgəl/ adj 1 : of or relating to the law ▪ legal problems/action ▪ a legal adviser ▪ a country's legal system 2 : allowed by the law or by the rules in a game ▪ Is it legal to fish in this river? — **le-gal-i-ty** /lɪˈgæləti/ n, pl **-ties** [C/U] ▪ We questioned the legality of the testing. — **le-gal-ly** /ˈliːgəli/ adv ▪ The drug is legally sold in many countries. ▪ This agreement is legally binding. ▪ He was legally drunk. [=he was drunk according to the law]

legal holiday n [C] US : a public holiday recognized by law — called also (Brit) bank holiday

le-gal-is-tic /ˌliːgəˈlɪstɪk/ adj, disapproving : too concerned with legal rules and details ▪ a legalistic argument

le-gal-ize also Brit **le-gal-ise** /ˈliːgəˌlaɪz/ vb **-ized; -iz-ing** [T] : to make (something) legal ▪ They wanted to legalize gambling. — **le-gal-i-za-tion** also Brit **le-gal-i-sa-tion** /ˌliːgələˈzeɪʃən, Brit ˌliːgəˌlaɪˈzeɪʃən/ n [U]

le-ga-tion /lɪˈgeɪʃən/ n [C] : a group of government officials sent to work in a foreign country; also : the building where such a group works

leg-end /ˈlɛdʒənd/ n 1 [C/U] : a story from the past that is believed by many people but cannot be proved to be true ▪ the legend of a lost continent ▪ According to legend, the city was destroyed by a great flood. = Legend has it that the city was destroyed by a great flood. — see also URBAN LEGEND 2 [C] : a famous or important person who is known for doing something extremely well ▪ a baseball legend ▪ She is a legend in her own time. = She is a living legend. [=she has become a legend while still living] 3 [C]

: a list that explains the symbols on a map

leg·end·ary /ˈlɛdʒənˌderi, Brit ˈlɛdʒəndri/ adj **1** always before a noun : told about in a legend • legendary tales/creatures **2** : very famous or well-known • legendary musicians

leg·gings /ˈlɛgɪŋz/ n [plural] **1** : pants for women that are made of a material that stretches to fit tightly around the legs **2** : coverings for the legs that are usually made of cloth or leather and worn over pants

leg·gy /ˈlɛgi/ adj **leg·gi·er**; **-est** : having long legs • a leggy actress

leg·i·ble /ˈlɛdʒəbəl/ adj : clear enough to be read • legible handwriting — **leg·i·bil·i·ty** /ˌlɛdʒəˈbɪləti/ n [U] — **leg·i·bly** /ˈlɛdʒəbli/ adv

le·gion /ˈliːdʒən/ n [C] **1** : a large group of soldiers • a Roman legion • the French Foreign Legion **2** : a national organization for former soldiers • the American Legion **3** : a very large number of people • She has a legion of admirers/fans. — **legion** adj, not before a noun • Her admirers are legion. [=she has many admirers]

le·gion·naire /ˌliːdʒəˈneɚ/ n [C] : a member of a legion

leg·is·late /ˈlɛdʒəˌsleɪt/ vb **-lat·ed**; **-lat·ing** **1** [T/I] : to make laws • The state legislated against hunting certain animals. **2** [T] : to control, create, or cause (something) by making laws • the need to better legislate foreign trade

leg·is·la·tion /ˌlɛdʒəˈsleɪʃən/ n [U] **1** : a law or set of laws made by a government • She introduced/proposed legislation for protecting the environment. **2** : the action or process of making laws

leg·is·la·tive /ˈlɛdʒəˌsleɪtɪv, Brit ˈlɛdʒəslətɪv/ adj, always before a noun **1** : having the power to make laws • the state legislative body/assembly • the **legislative branch** of the government **2** : relating to the making of laws • the legislative process • legislative power — **leg·is·la·tive·ly** adv

leg·is·la·tor /ˈlɛdʒəˌsleɪˌtoɚ, ˈlɛdʒəˌsleɪtɚ/ n [C] : a person who makes laws : a member of a legislature • your state legislator

leg·is·la·ture /ˈlɛdʒəˌsleɪtʃɚ/ n [C] : a group of people with the power to make or change laws • Each state has its own legislature.

le·git /lɪˈdʒɪt/ adj, informal : LEGITIMATE • What she's doing is perfectly legit.

le·git·i·mate /lɪˈdʒɪtəmət/ adj **1 a** : allowed according to rules or laws • a legitimate heir/business **b** : real, accepted, or official • Is the letter legitimate? [=genuine] **2** : fair or reasonable • a legitimate excuse/claim **3** : born to a father and mother who are married • legitimate children — **le·git·i·ma·cy** /lɪˈdʒɪtəməsi/ n [U] — **le·git·i·mate·ly** adv

le·git·i·mize /lɪˈdʒɪtəˌmaɪz/ also Brit **le·git·i·mise** vb **-mized**; **-miz·ing** [T] : to make (something or someone) legitimate • a new government trying to legitimize its power

leg·room /ˈlɛgˌruːm/ n [U] : space in which you can extend your legs when you are sitting • airplane seats that offer little legroom

le·gume /ˈlɛˌgjuːm/ n [C] : a type of plant (such as a pea or a bean plant) with seeds that grow in long cases (called pods); also : these seeds eaten as food — **le·gu·mi·nous** /lɪˈgjuːmənəs/ adj • leguminous plants

lei·sure /ˈliːʒɚ, Brit ˈlɛʒə/ n [U] **1** : enjoyable activities that you do when you are not working • I don't have much time for leisure. • leisure activities/pursuits • Now that she's retired, she has more **leisure time.** • She leads a life of leisure. [=she does not have to work] **2** : time when you are not working • In his leisure, he paints and gardens. — **at leisure** or **at your leisure 1** : in a slow and relaxed way • We were able to study the menu at leisure. **2** : when you have free time available • You can look over the contract at your leisure.

lei·sured /ˈliːʒɚd, Brit ˈlɛʒəd/ adj, always before a noun **1** : not having to work : having leisure • the leisured class **2** : not hurried • We set off at a leisured pace.

lei·sure·ly /ˈliːʒɚli, Brit ˈlɛʒəli/ adj : not hurried : slow and relaxed • They strolled along at a leisurely pace. • a leisurely lunch — **leisurely** adv

lem·ming /ˈlɛmɪŋ/ n [C] : a small animal that lives in northern areas of North America, Europe, and Asia ◇ According to legend, large groups of lemmings sometimes march into the sea and drown. Because of this, people are sometimes said to be acting **like lemmings** when they do something that is harmful or stupid because other people are doing it.

lem·on /ˈlɛmən/ n **1** [C/U] : a yellow citrus fruit that has a sour taste **2** [U] : a bright yellow color — called also **lemon yellow 3** [C] chiefly US, informal : a product that is not made well or does not work well • The car is a lemon. — **lem·ony** /ˈlɛməni/ adj • a lemony flavor/color

lem·on·ade /ˌlɛməˈneɪd/ n [C/U] **1** : a drink made usually of lemon juice, sugar, and water **2** Brit : a sweet lemon-flavored drink that contains many bubbles

le·mur /ˈliːmɚ/ n [C] : an animal that is related to monkeys and that lives in trees mostly in Madagascar

lend /ˈlɛnd/ vb **lent** /ˈlɛnt/; **lend·ing 1 a** [T] : to give (something) to (someone) to be used for a period of time and then returned • She lent me the book. = She lent the book to me. **b** [T/I] : to give (money) to someone who agrees to pay it back in the future • Can you lend me 50 cents? • Many banks won't lend to people with bad credit. **2** [T] : to make (something) available to (someone or something) • They are glad to lend their support to worthy causes. • She's always there to **lend a (helping) hand**. [=she's always there to help] **3** [T] : to add (something that is needed or wanted) to (something) • A bit of grated carrot lends some color to the dish. — **lend itself to** ◇ Something that *lends itself to* a purpose is good or suitable for that purpose. • *Her voice lends itself well to (singing) opera.* — **lend·er** *n* [C]

length /ˈlɛŋθ/ *n* **1 a** [C/U] : the distance from one end of something to the other end : a measurement of how long something is • *"What is its length?" "It measures 10 inches in length."* [=it is 10 inches long] • *We walked the entire length of the beach.* **b** [U] : the size or extent of a piece of writing • *Your essay should be no more than 250 words in length.* **2** [U] : the amount of time something lasts • *the length of a movie* **3** [C] : a piece of something that is long and thin or narrow • *a length of pipe/yarn* **4** [U] : a measure of how far down on your body your hair, a piece of clothing, etc., reaches • *the length of a skirt* • *a waist-length jacket* [=a jacket that reaches only to your waist] — *at arm's length* see ¹ARM — *at length* **1** : for a long time • *We talked at length about the ceremony.* • *The speaker went on at considerable/great/ some length.* **2** : in a full or complete way • *The topic will be treated at length in the next chapter.* **3** *literary* : after a long time • *At length, we decided to return home.* — *go to any length or go to any/extreme/great (etc.) lengths* : to make a great or extreme effort to do something • *She'll go to any length to avoid doing work.* — **the length and breadth of** : through all parts of (a place) • *I've been/traveled the length and breadth of the canyon.*

length·en /ˈlɛŋθən/ *vb* [T/I] : to make (something) longer or to become longer • *lengthen a pair of trousers* • *The days lengthened with the approach of spring.*

length·ways /ˈlɛŋθˌweɪz/ *adv, chiefly Brit* : LENGTHWISE — **lengthways** *adj*

length·wise /ˈlɛŋθˌwaɪz/ *adv* : in the direction of the long side of something • *a piece of paper folded lengthwise* — **lengthwise** *adj* • *a lengthwise cut*

lengthy /ˈlɛŋθi/ *adj* **length·i·er; -est** **1** : lasting for a long time • *a lengthy discussion/trip/delay* **2** : having many pages, items, etc. • *lengthy lists*

le·nient /ˈliːnjənt/ *adj* : allowing a lot of freedom and not punishing bad behavior in a strong way • *a lenient teacher/punishment/policy* — **le·nien·cy** /ˈliːnjənsi/ *also* **le·nience** /ˈliːnjəns/ *n* [U] — **le·nient·ly** *adv*

lens /ˈlɛnz/ *n* [C] **1** : a clear curved piece of glass or plastic that is used in eyeglasses, cameras, etc., to make things look clearer, smaller, or bigger • *glasses with thick lenses* • *a camera lens* **2** : the clear part of the eye that focuses light to form clear images

lent *past tense and past participle of* LEND

Lent /ˈlɛnt/ *n* [U] : a period of 40 days before Easter during which many Christians do not eat certain foods or do certain pleasurable activities as a way of remembering the suffering of Jesus Christ — **Lent·en** /ˈlɛntn̩/ *adj, always before a noun* • *the Lenten season*

len·til /ˈlɛntl̩/ *n* [C] : a type of flat, round seed that is eaten as a vegetable

Leo /ˈliːˌoʊ/ *n, pl* **Leos** **1** [U] : the fifth sign of the zodiac that comes between Cancer and Virgo and has a lion as its symbol **2** [C] : a person born between July 23rd and August 22nd

leop·ard /ˈlɛpəd/ *n* [C] : a large brownish-yellow cat with black spots that lives in Asia and Africa

le·o·tard /ˈliːjəˌtɑəd/ *n* [C] : a piece of clothing that fits tightly and covers the body except for the legs and sometimes the arms and that is worn especially by a dancer, gymnast, or acrobat — often plural in U.S. English • *She was wearing leotards.*

lep·er /ˈlɛpə/ *n* [C] **1** : a person who has leprosy **2** : someone who is disliked and avoided by other people • *They treated him like a (social) leper.*

lep·re·chaun /ˈlɛprəˌkɑːn/ *n* [C] : a creature in old Irish stories that looks like a very small man

lep·ro·sy /ˈlɛprəsi/ *n* [U] : a serious disease that causes painful rough areas on the skin and that badly damages nerves and flesh — **leprous** *adj*

les·bi·an /ˈlɛzbijən/ *n* [C] : a woman who is a homosexual — **lesbian** *adj, always before a noun* • *a lesbian relationship* — **les·bi·an·ism** /ˈlɛzbijəˌnɪzəm/ *n* [U]

le·sion /ˈliːʒən/ *n* [C] *medical* : an injured or diseased spot or area on or in the body • *skin lesions*

¹**less** /ˈlɛs/ *adj, comparative form of* ¹LITTLE : not so much : smaller in amount or number • *She finished in less time than I did.* • *We made it there in less than six hours.* — **no less** — used to suggest that something is surprising or impressive • *She was contacted by the president, no less!* — **no less than** : at least — used to suggest that a number or amount is surprisingly large • *No less than half the students failed the test.*

usage The adjectives *less* and *fewer* have similar meanings but are used in slightly different ways. *Fewer* is used with nouns that can be counted. • *We had fewer problems than expected.* *Less* is usually used with nouns that cannot be counted. • *He makes less money than she does.* But *less* is also more likely than *fewer* to be used with count nouns that refer to distances and amounts of money. • *an investment of less than $2,000* • *It's less than 100 miles away.* *Less* is also used in mathematical expressions and in certain phrases. • *an angle of less than 180 degrees* • *Write it in 25 words or less.* It is also used instead of *fewer* with other sorts of plural nouns, although many people still consider this use incorrect. • *Less than 10 people showed up.* = *Fewer than 10 people showed up.*

²**less** *adv, comparative form of* ²LITTLE : not so much : to a smaller extent or degree • *This test seemed much/far less difficult than the last one.* • *I like this one (a little) less than the other.* — **in less than no time** *informal* : very soon • *If we start now, we'll be finished in less than no time.* — **less and less** : in a way that is grad-

ually smaller, weaker, or less common • *The medicine becomes less and less effective over time.* • *We see them less and less (often/frequently) each year.* — **less than** : not completely or not at all • *She was less than happy with the results.* — **more or less** see ²MORE — **much less** or chiefly Brit **still less** — used after a negative statement to say that something is even less likely or possible than the thing previously mentioned • *I don't eat eggs, much less (eat) meat.*

³**less** *pron* : a smaller number or amount • *He's trying to save more and spend less.* • *I read much/far/even less of the second book than of the first.* • *Regarding his recent behavior, perhaps* **the less said, the better.** • [=his recent behavior has been so bad that it is better to not say anything about it] — **could/couldn't care less** see ²CARE — **less and less** : an amount that becomes gradually smaller • *I seem to save less and less each year.* — **nothing less than** see ²NOTHING — **think less of** see THINK

⁴**less** *prep* : after taking away or subtracting (something) • *We earned two hundred dollars, less* [=minus] *travel expenses.*

-less /ləs/ *adj suffix* **1** : not having something specified : without something • *childless* • *painless* **2** : never doing or becoming something specified • *tireless workers* [=workers who never become tired]

les·see /lɛˈsiː/ *n* [C] *law* : a person who has a lease on something

less·en /ˈlɛsn/ *vb* [T/I] : to become less or to cause (something) to become less • *The pain will lessen over time.* • *The drug will lessen the pain.*

¹**less·er** /ˈlɛsɚ/ *adj, always before a noun* **1** : of smaller size • *a lesser amount* **2** : of less strength, quality, or importance • *A lesser man than he might have given up.* • *the artist's lesser works* • *She agreed to plead guilty to a lesser charge.* • *Traffic congestion is a problem in the city and,* **to a lesser extent,** *the suburbs.*

²**lesser** *adv* : ²LESS • *lesser-known writers*

les·son /ˈlɛsn/ *n* [C] **1 a** : an activity that you do in order to learn something • *You can't go out to play until you've finished your lessons.*; *also* : something that is taught • *They studied the lessons of the great philosophers.* **b** : a single class or part of a course of instruction • *The book is divided into 12 lessons.* • *She took/gave piano lessons for years.* **2** : something learned through experience • *the lessons of history* • *I've* **learned my lesson**—*I'll never do that again!* • *I'm glad they got caught. That will* **teach them a lesson!** [=they will learn that they should not do that again] • **Let that be a lesson to you** —*if you don't take better care of your toys, they'll get broken!*

les·sor /ˈlɛˌsoɚ/ *n* [C] *law* : a person or company that leases property (such as a car or house) to someone

lest /ˈlɛst/ *conj, formal + literary* : for fear that • *He was concerned lest anyone think that he was guilty.* [=he was concerned that people would think he was guilty] • *She's a talented singer and,* **lest we forget,** *a fine musician as well.* [=we should not forget that she is also a fine musician]

let /ˈlɛt/ *vb* **let; let·ting 1** [T] : to allow or permit (someone or something) to do something • *I'll be happy to help you if you'll let me (help you).* • *Don't let this opportunity slip away!* • *She lets the children do whatever they want to do.* • *Please let me do that for you.* • *Let them enter at once.* • *(figurative) Let it rain all day—I don't care.* [=I don't care if it rains all day] • *My philosophy is* **"Live and let live."** [=live your life as you choose and let other people do the same]

> **usage** Let is never used as *be let*; use *be allowed* or *be permitted* instead. • *They let him speak.* [=he was allowed/permitted (by them) to speak]

2 [T] — used to express a warning • *Just let her try to do it again!* [=she will be in trouble if she tries to do it again] **3 a ◇ Let's** and (more formally) **let us** are used to introduce statements that express a wish, request, suggestion, or command. • *Let's hope for the best.* [=we should hope for the best] • *Let us suppose that he's right. What then?* • *Let's get out of here!* • *Let's see what's on the menu.* = *Let's have a look at the menu.* • *"Let's go." "No, let's not (go)."* **b ◇** The phrase **let's go** is used in speech to tell someone to go or work faster. • *Are you still getting dressed? Let's go! We need to leave in five minutes!* **c ◇** The phrases **let's face it** and **let's be honest** are used to say that something is true and cannot be denied. • *Let's face it: we need more time.* **4 a** [T] : to allow someone to use (something) in return for payment • *They have rooms to let.* [=to rent] **b** [I] *chiefly Brit* : to be rented or leased for a specified amount of money • *The flat lets* [=rents] *for 350 pounds a month.* **5** [T] : to allow (someone or something) to go, pass by, etc. • *Let me out/in/through!* — **let alone 1** — used to refer to something that is even less likely or possible than the thing previously mentioned • *I can barely understand it, let alone explain it.* **2 let (someone or something) alone** : to not bother or touch (someone or something) • *Let* [=(more commonly) *leave*] *your sister alone.* • *I never did learn to* **let well enough alone.** [=to stop changing something that is already good enough] — **let down** [*phrasal vb*] **1 let (someone) down a** : to fail to give help or support to (someone who needs or expects it) : DISAPPOINT • *I promised Mary that I'd help her, and I can't let her down.* **b** : to make (someone) unhappy or displeased by not being as good as expected • *The end of the story really let me down.* **2 ◇** To **let someone down easy/gently** is to give someone unpleasant news in a gentle or kind way. • *She tried to let him down gently when she told him he didn't get the job.* **3 let (something) down** or **let down (something) a** : to cause or allow (something) to move down gradually • *Let down the bucket into the well.* **b** : to make (a skirt, a pair of pants, etc.) longer • *The pants were too short and needed to* be let down. — **let fly (with)** see ¹FLY — **let go** 1 or **let (something or someone) go** or **let go of (something or someone)** or **let go (something or someone)** : to stop holding or gripping something or someone • *I tried to take the ball from him, but he wouldn't let go.* • *He let the rope go.* = *He let go of the rope.* • (figurative) *When a child grows up and moves away from home, it can be hard for parents to let go.* 2 or **let (yourself) go** : to behave in a very free and open way • *She has a hard time relaxing and letting herself go.* 3 **let (someone) go** a : to allow (someone) to be free • *They let the prisoner go.* b : to officially make (someone) leave a job • *The company let him go at the end of the month.* 4 **let (yourself) go** : to fail to take care of (yourself) • *I was very depressed back then and had really let myself go.* — **let it all hang out** *informal* : to show your true feelings : to behave in a very free and open way • *When I'm with my friends, I let it all hang out.* — **let loose** see ¹LOOSE — **let me see** or **let's see** or **let me think** — used in speech by someone who is trying to remember something • *Let me see, where did I put my keys?* — **let off** [phrasal vb] 1 **let (someone) off** or **let off (someone)** : to allow (someone) to get off a bus, an airplane, etc. • *The bus stopped to let off a few passengers.* 2 **let (someone) off** : to allow (someone who has been caught doing something wrong or illegal) to go without being punished • *The police officer let her off with just a warning.* 3 : to cause (something) to explode or to be released in a forceful way • *let off pressure* — **let on** [phrasal vb] 1 **let (someone) on** or **let on (someone)** : to allow (someone) to get on a bus, an airplane, etc. • *The bus stopped to let on a few more passengers.* 2 *informal* : to tell, admit, or show that you know something • *Don't let on that I told you!* 3 *US, informal* : to pretend or seem • *She's not as happy as she lets on.* — **let out** [phrasal vb] 1 **let (something or someone) out** or **let out (something or someone)** a : to release (something or someone) • *She let out a scream.* [=she screamed] • *They let the prisoner out (of prison) for the weekend.* b : to make (a skirt, a pair of pants, etc.) larger • *The skirt is too tight and needs to be let out.* 2 *US, of a school* : to end a semester, year, or session • *School lets out in June.* — **let rip** see ¹RIP — **let (someone) have it** *informal* : to attack, punish, or criticize (someone) in a violent or angry way • *When she found out what they'd been doing, she really let them have it.* — **let (someone) in on (something)** : to allow (someone) to know (a secret) • *He let me in on his plans.* — **let (someone) know** see ¹KNOW — **let (someone or something) be** : to not bother or touch (someone or something) • *Please let* [=leave] *me be.* — **let (something) be known** see ¹KNOW — **let up** [phrasal vb] 1 : to stop or become slower • *Won't this rain ever let up?* 2 **let up on (someone)** : to treat (someone) in a less harsh or de-

manding way • *The students might respond better if the teacher let up on them a little.* 3 **let up on (something)** : to apply less pressure to (something) • *I let up on the gas pedal.* — **let (yourself) in for** : to cause (yourself) to have or experience (something bad or unpleasant) • *When I agreed to help, I didn't know what I was letting myself in for.*

let·down /ˈlɛtˌdaʊn/ n [C] : something that is not as good as it was expected to be • *The news was a letdown.* [=disappointment]

le·thal /ˈliːθəl/ adj : causing or able to cause death • *lethal chemicals/weapons* • *The disease can be lethal.* — **le·thal·ly** adv

leth·ar·gy /ˈlɛθɚdʒi/ n [U] : a lack of energy or a lack of interest in doing things • *Symptoms of the disease include loss of appetite and lethargy.* — **le·thar·gic** /lǝˈθɑɚdʒɪk/ adj • *The patient is weak and lethargic.*

let's /ˈlɛts/ — used as a contraction of *let us* • *Let's do our best.*

¹**let·ter** /ˈlɛtɚ/ n 1 [C] : any one of the marks that are symbols for speech sounds in written language and that form an alphabet • *the letter "a"* • *I wrote my name in capital letters.* 2 [C] : a written or printed message to someone • *write/send/mail/answer a letter* • *a letter of recommendation/introduction* 3 [plural] *formal* : LITERATURE • *the field of English letters* • *a man/woman of letters* [=a man/woman who writes or knows a lot about literature] 4 [singular] : the exact meaning of something (such as a law) that is stated in writing • *obeying the letter of the law* [=doing exactly what the law says] — **to the letter** : exactly or precisely • *obey the law to the letter*

²**letter** vb [T] : to write or print letters on (something) : to mark (something) with letters • *a sign lettered by hand* = *a hand-lettered sign*

letter box n [C] Brit : MAILBOX

letter carrier n [C] US : a person who delivers mail

let·ter·head /ˈlɛtɚˌhɛd/ n [C] : the name and address of an organization that is printed at the top of a piece of paper used for writing official letters; *also* [U] US : paper that has the name and address of an organization printed at the top • *They sent her a letter printed on company letterhead.*

let·ter·ing /ˈlɛtɚɪŋ/ n [U] : letters written or printed on something • *a sign with gold lettering*

let·tuce /ˈlɛtǝs/ n [C/U] : a plant that has large leaves which are eaten especially in salads • *a head of lettuce*

let·up /ˈlɛtˌʌp/ n [U, singular] : a time during which something stops or slows down • *It rained three days without (a) letup.*

leu·ke·mia or chiefly Brit **leu·kae·mia** /luˈkiːmijǝ/ n [U] : a very serious disease in which the body forms too many white blood cells — **leu·ke·mic** or chiefly Brit **leu·kae·mic** /luˈkiːmɪk/ adj • *leukemic cells/patients*

lev·ee /ˈlɛvi/ n [C] US : a long wall of soil built along a river to prevent flooding

¹**lev·el** /ˈlɛvəl/ n **1 a** [C/U] : a specific height ▪ The pictures were hung on the wall at eye level. ▪ at street/ground level [C] : a part of a building that is at a specific height ▪ the upper level [=floor] of the restaurant **2** [C/U] : an amount of something ▪ a normal level of intelligence ▪ a rise in water level **3** [C] : a position or rank in a scale : a position that is high or low when compared to others ▪ She rose to the level of manager. ▪ people at all levels of society **4** [C] : a way of thinking about, talking about, or dealing with something ▪ The argument appeals to me on an intellectual level but not on an emotional level. **5** [C] : a device used to see when something is exactly flat — **descend/sink/stoop to someone's level** : to behave as badly as someone who has treated you wrongly — **on the level** informal : not false or dishonest ▪ Is this guy on the level? [=is he honest?]

²**level** adj **1** : having a flat or even surface ▪ level ground **2** : not going up or down ▪ Interest rates have remained level. **3 a** : having the same height as something else — usually + with ▪ The water was level with my waist. **b** : not in front of or behind something or someone else ▪ The boards are level (with each other). ▪ They drew level with the rest of the runners. **4** chiefly Brit : having the same position, score, or rank : EVEN ▪ The teams are level (with each other) in the standings. **5** : steady and calm ▪ It's important to **keep a level head**. [=to remain calm] — **your level best** : your best effort at doing something ▪ He tried/did his level best to win the race. [=he tried as hard as he could to win the race.]

³**level** vb, US -**eled** or chiefly Brit -**elled**; US -**el·ing** or chiefly Brit -**el·ling** [T] **1** : to make (something) flat or level ▪ level (off) a field **2** : to knock (someone or something) down ▪ He leveled him with a right hook. **3 a** : to point (a weapon) at someone ▪ The robber leveled a gun at his head. **b** : to direct (something) at or against someone ▪ Several complaints have been leveled at/against the store. **4** chiefly Brit : to make (something) equal : TIE ▪ Her goal leveled the score at 3–3. — **level off/out** [phrasal vb] : to stop going up or down ▪ The plane leveled off at 30,000 feet. — **level the playing field** : to make a situation fair for everyone ▪ He wants the government to level the playing field by breaking up large corporations so that smaller companies can compete. — **level with** [phrasal vb] informal : to speak honestly to (someone) ▪ Level with me. Why did you do it? — **lev·el·er** (US) or chiefly Brit **lev·el·ler** /ˈlɛvələr/ n [C]

lev·el·head·ed /ˌlɛvəlˈhɛdəd/ adj : having or showing an ability to think clearly and to make good decisions ▪ a levelheaded person/assessment

lev·el-peg·ging /ˌlɛvəlˈpɛgɪŋ/ adj, Brit : even with one another in a contest or competition ▪ The candidates are level-pegging in all the opinion polls.

level playing field n [singular] : a situation that is fair for everyone ▪ The government should break up large corporations so that there is a level playing field for smaller companies.

le·ver /ˈlɛvər, ˈliːvə/ n [C] **1** : a bar that is used to lift and move something heavy **2** : a bar or rod that is used to operate or adjust something on a machine, vehicle, etc. **3** : something used to achieve a desired result ▪ They used their money as a lever to gain power. — **lever** vb [T] ▪ He levered the rock out of the hole.

le·ver·age /ˈlɛvərɪdʒ, ˈliːvərɪdʒ/ n [U] **1** : influence or power used to achieve a desired result ▪ The union's size gave it leverage in the labor contract negotiations. **2** : the increase in force gained by using a lever

lev·i·tate /ˈlɛvəˌteɪt/ vb -**tat·ed**; -**tat·ing** [T/I] : to rise or make (something) rise into the air in a way that appears to be magical ▪ The magician claimed he could levitate a car. — **lev·i·ta·tion** /ˌlɛvəˈteɪʃən/ n [U]

lev·i·ty /ˈlɛvəti/ n [U] somewhat formal : a lack of seriousness ▪ She would not tolerate any levity in the classroom.

¹**levy** /ˈlɛvi/ n, pl **lev·ies** [C] : an amount of money that must be paid and that is collected by a government or other authority ▪ a levy [=tax] on gasoline

²**levy** vb **levies**; **lev·ied**; **levy·ing** [T] : to use legal authority to demand and collect (a fine, a tax, etc.) ▪ They levied a tax on imports.

lewd /ˈluːd/ adj : sexual in an offensive or rude way ▪ lewd behavior — **lewd·ly** adv — **lewd·ness** n [U]

lex·i·con /ˈlɛksəˌkɑːn, Brit ˈlɛksəkən/ n [C] : the words used in a language or by a person or group of people ▪ a computer term that has entered the general lexicon

lg. abbr large

li·a·bil·i·ty /ˌlajəˈbɪləti/ n, pl -**ties** **1** [U] : the state of being legally responsible for something ▪ The judge cleared me of any/all liability for the accident. **2** [C] : something (such as the payment of money) for which a person or business is legally responsible ▪ business assets and liabilities [=debts] **3** [C] : someone or something that causes problems ▪ His small size was a liability (to him) as a football player.

li·a·ble /ˈlajəbəl/ adj **1** : legally responsible for something ▪ They are liable for any damage. **2** : likely to be affected or harmed by something — + to ▪ liable to injury **3** : likely to do something — + to ▪ You're liable to fall if you're not more careful.

li·ai·son /ˈliːəˌzɑːn, liˈeɪˌzɑːn/ n **1 a** [U, singular] : a relationship that allows different organizations or groups to work together and provide information to each other ▪ Administrators need to establish a close liaison with employees. **b** [C] : a person who helps organizations or groups to work together ▪ She acts as a liaison between the police department and city schools. **2** [C] : a secret sexual relationship ▪ sexual liaisons

li·ar /ˈlajər/ n [C] : a person who tells lies

lib /ˈlɪb/ n [U] informal : LIBERATION ▪ women's lib

li·bel /ˈlaɪbəl/ n [C/U] : the act of publishing a false statement that causes people to have a bad opinion of someone ▪ He sued the newspaper for libel. — **libel** vb, US **-beled** or chiefly Brit **-belled**; US **-bel·ing** or chiefly Brit **-bel·ling** [T] ▪ He was libeled by the newspaper. — **li·bel·ous** (US) or chiefly Brit **li·bel·lous** /ˈlaɪbələs/ adj ▪ a libelous magazine article

¹**lib·er·al** /ˈlɪbərəl, ˈlɪbrəl/ adj **1 a** : believing that government should be active in supporting social and political change ▪ liberal politicians/policies **b** Liberal Brit : of or belonging to the liberal political party in countries like Canada and the United Kingdom ▪ Liberal voters/policies **2** : not opposed to new ideas or ways of behaving ▪ a liberal attitude toward sex **3** : GENEROUS ▪ She has been liberal with her donations. ▪ a liberal donation **4** : not strict or exact ▪ a liberal interpretation of the law — **lib·er·al·ly** /ˈlɪbərəli, ˈlɪbrəli/ adv

²**liberal** n [C] **1** : a person who believes that government should be active in supporting social and political change ▪ a policy that is supported both by liberals and conservatives **2** Liberal Brit : a member or supporter of a liberal political party in countries like the United Kingdom and Canada

liberal arts n [plural] : areas of study (such as history, language, and literature) that are intended to give you general knowledge rather than to develop specific skills needed for a profession

lib·er·al·ism /ˈlɪbərəˌlɪzəm, ˈlɪbrəˌlɪzəm/ n [U] formal : belief in the value of social and political change in order to achieve progress ▪ political liberalism

lib·er·al·ize also Brit **lib·er·al·ise** /ˈlɪbrəˌlaɪz/ vb **-ized; -iz·ing** [T/I] : to make (something) less strict or to become less strict ▪ trying to liberalize immigration policies — **lib·er·al·i·za·tion** also Brit **lib·er·al·i·sa·tion** /ˌlɪbrələˈzeɪʃən, Brit ˌlɪbrəˌlaɪˈzeɪʃən/ n [U]

lib·er·ate /ˈlɪbəˌreɪt/ vb **-at·ed; -at·ing** [T] **1** : to free (someone or something) from the control of another person, group, etc. ▪ Rebels fought to liberate the country. **2** : to give freedom or more freedom to (someone) ▪ Laptop computers liberate workers from their desks. ▪ a liberating experience — **lib·er·a·tor** /ˈlɪbəˌreɪtə/ n [C]

liberated adj : freed from or opposed to traditional social and sexual attitudes or ways of behaving ▪ a liberated woman

lib·er·a·tion /ˌlɪbəˈreɪʃən/ n [U] **1** : the act of liberating someone or something ▪ their liberation from slavery **2** : the removal of traditional social or sexual rules, attitudes, etc. ▪ women's liberation

lib·er·tar·i·an /ˌlɪbəˈterijən/ n [C] : a person who believes that people should be allowed to do and say what they want without any interference from the government — **libertarian** adj ▪ libertarian theories

lib·er·ty /ˈlɪbəti/ n, pl **-ties 1** [U] : the state or condition of being able to act and speak freely : FREEDOM ▪ soldiers willing to die in defense of liberty **2** [C] : a political right ▪ personal liberties — **at liberty** formal : able to act or speak freely ▪ You are at liberty to go. — **take liberties** disapproving : to make important changes to something — usually + with ▪ The movie takes too many liberties with the original story. — **take the liberty of** ◇ If you take the liberty of doing something, you do something without asking for permission to do it. ▪ I took the liberty of making a reservation for us.

li·bi·do /ləˈbiːdoʊ/ n, pl **-dos** [C/U] technical : a person's desire to have sex

Li·bra /ˈliːbrə/ n **1** [U] : the seventh sign of the zodiac that comes between Virgo and Scorpio and has a pair of scales as its symbol **2** [C] : a person born between September 22nd and October 23rd

li·brar·i·an /laɪˈbrerijən/ n [C] : a person who works in a library

li·brary /ˈlaɪˌbreri, Brit ˈlaɪbrəri/ n, pl **-brar·ies** [C] **1** : a place where books, magazines, videos, etc., are available for people to use or borrow **2** : a room in a person's house where books are kept **3** : a collection of similar things ▪ He has an impressive library of jazz records.

lice plural of ¹LOUSE 1

¹**li·cense** (US) or chiefly Brit **li·cence** /ˈlaɪsns/ n **1** [C] : an official document, card, etc., that gives you permission to do, use, or have something ▪ a license to sell liquor ▪ a fishing license ▪ He showed his (driver's) license to prove his age. **2** [U, singular] : freedom to act however you want to ▪ His job as a reporter gives him (a) license to go anywhere and ask anything. **3** [U] : the freedom of an artist, writer, etc., to change the way something is described or shown in order to produce a work of art ▪ artistic/poetic/creative license

²**license** also Brit **licence** vb **-censed; -cens·ing** [T] : to give official permission to someone or something to do, use, or have something ▪ The restaurant is licensed to sell liquor. ▪ The gun is licensed to him. [=he has a license to own the gun] ▪ licensed drivers

li·cens·ee /ˌlaɪsnˈsiː/ n [C] business : a person or company that has a license to have, make, do, or use something

license number n [C] US : the numbers and letters on a vehicle's license plate

license plate n [C] US : a metal plate on a vehicle that shows a series of numbers and letters that are used to identify the vehicle — called also (chiefly Brit) number plate

li·cen·tious /laɪˈsɛnʃəs/ adj, formal : sexually immoral or offensive ▪ licentious behavior — **li·cen·tious·ness** n [U]

li·chen /ˈlaɪkən/ n [U] : a type of small plant that grows on rocks and walls

¹**lick** /ˈlɪk/ vb **1** [T/I] : to pass the tongue over (a surface, an object, etc.) ▪ The dog licked my cheek. = The dog licked me on the cheek. **2** [T] : to take (something) into your mouth with your tongue ▪ She licked the sauce off her finger. **3** [T/I] : to lightly touch or go over (a surface) ▪

Flames were already licking (at/against) the ceiling. **4** [T] *informal* **a** : to defeat (someone) in a fight or contest • *I think I can lick him.* **b** : to solve (a problem) • *They think they've licked the problem.* — **lick your lips** or *US* **lick your chops** : to feel or show excitement because something good is expected to happen • *The players were licking their chops as they waited for the game to start.* — **lick your wounds** : to recover from defeat or disappointment • *He went home to lick his wounds after losing the election.*

²**lick** *n* [C] **1** : the act of passing your tongue over something • *He gave the bowl a lick.* **2** *informal* : a small amount : BIT • *He hasn't done a lick of work.* **3** *informal* : a hard hit • *(figurative)* *The movie has* ***taken its licks*** *from the critics.* [=has been harshly reviewed by the critics] **4** *informal* : a very short part of a piece of music • *guitar licks*

lick·ing /ˈlɪkɪŋ/ *n* [*singular*] *informal* : a severe beating or defeat • *His father threatened to give him a licking.* • *The team got/took a licking.*

lic·o·rice or *chiefly Brit* **li·quor·ice** /ˈlɪkərɪʃ/ *n* [U] : a candy made from the dried root of a European plant

lid /ˈlɪd/ *n* [C] **1** : a cover on a box, can, jar, etc., that can be lifted or removed • **2** : EYELID — **blow the lid off** (*chiefly US*) or *chiefly Brit* **lift the lid on** : to reveal the truth about (something) • *The investigation blew the lid off corruption in city hall.* — **flip your lid** see ¹FLIP — **keep a lid on** **1** : to keep (something secret) from being known • *She tried to keep a lid on the news.* **2** : to control (something) : to keep (something) from becoming worse • *trying to keep a lid on inflation* — **put a lid on** : to stop (something) from growing or becoming worse • *putting a lid on rising medical costs*

¹**lie** /ˈlaɪ/ *vb* **lay** /ˈleɪ/; **lain** /ˈleɪn/; **ly·ing** /ˈlajɪŋ/ [I] **1** *of a person or animal* : to be in or move to a flat position on a surface • *She lay asleep on the bed.* • *The doctor asked him to lie (down/back) on the table.* • *(figurative)* *He vowed that he would not take the court's decision lying down.* [=that he would fight against the court's decision] **2** *of things* : to be in a flat position on a surface • *snow lying on the ground* • *to be or remain in a specified state or condition* • *The book was lying open.* • *dishes lying dirty in the sink* **4** : to be located in a particular place • *Ohio lies (to the) east of Indiana.* • *(figurative)* *I don't know where the answer lies.* — **lie ahead** : to be in the future • *No one knows what lies ahead (of us).* — **lie around** or *Brit* **lie about** [*phrasal vb*] **1** **a** : to be lying in a disordered way • *clothes lying around the house* **b** : to be somewhere within a general area or place • *I know that pen is lying around here somewhere.* **2** : to spend time resting in a lazy way • *We were lying around by the pool.* — **lie behind** [*phrasal vb*] : to be the cause of (something) • *Greed lies behind the higher prices.* — **lie in wait** see ²WAIT — **lie low** : to stay hidden or inactive in order to avoid being

noticed or found • *The prisoners had to lie low after their escape.* — **lie with** [*phrasal vb*] — used to say who has the blame or responsibility for something • *Responsibility for the accident lies with the company.* — **make your bed and lie in it** see ¹BED — compare ³LIE

²**lie** *n* [C] : something untrue that is said or written to deceive someone • *She told a lie to her parents.* — **give the lie to** *formal* : to show that (something) is not true • *Her success has given the lie to the notion that women cannot compete with men.* — **live a lie** : to live in a way that does not show who you truly are or what your feelings truly are

³**lie** *vb* **lied**; **ly·ing** [I] : to say or write something that is not true in order to deceive someone : to tell a lie • *She lied to me.* • *He has been accused of lying about his military record.* — compare ¹LIE

lie detector *n* [C] : a device used to measure the heart rate, breathing, etc., in order to find out if someone is being honest

lie–down /ˈlaɪˌdaʊn/ *n* [*singular*] *Brit* : a brief rest : NAP • *They often have a lie-down in the afternoon.*

lien /ˈliːn/ *n* [C] *law* : a legal claim that someone or something has on the property of another person until a debt has been paid back • *The bank has a lien on our house.*

lieu /ˈluː, *Brit* ˈljuː/ *n* — **in lieu of** : in place of : instead of • *You can use your ATM card in lieu of cash.*

lieut. *abbr* lieutenant

lieu·ten·ant /luˈtɛnənt, *Brit* lɛfˈtɛnənt/ *n* [C] **1** : an officer in the army, navy, or air force with a fairly low rank **2** *US* : an officer in a fire or police department who has a rank below a captain **3** : a person who represents and works for someone who is more powerful • *one of the boss's most loyal lieutenants*

life /ˈlaɪf/ *n, pl* **lives** /ˈlaɪvz/ **1** [U] : the ability to grow, change, etc., that separates plants and animals from things like water or rocks • *the miracle of life* **2** [C/U] **a** : the period of time when a person is alive • *I've known her all my life.* • *He is nearing the end of his life.* • *a long/ short life* • *He became famous late in life.* [=at a relatively old age] **b** : the experience of being alive • *life in the city* = *city life* • *She has dedicated her life to helping other people.* • *She told us her* ***life story.*** [=she told us about many of the things that had happened to her in her life] **3** [C] **a** : a specified part of a person's life • *the social lives of college students* **b** : a specified way or manner of living • *He lived/led a life of crime.* • *a traditional* ***way of life*** **4** [C] : the state or condition of being alive • *Her life was in danger.* • *She* ***risked her life.*** [=did something very dangerous that could have caused her death] • *(figurative)* *They brought the restaurant back to life with a new menu.* **5** [U] : living things of a specified kind or in a specified place • *animal/plant/ocean life* **6** [C/U] : the period when something exists or is useful or effective • *battery life* • *the life of an insurance policy* **7** [U] **a** : energy and spirit ▪ *eyes full of life* ▪ *She breathed (new) life into those old songs.* **b** : activity and movement ▪ *There were no signs of life in the deserted village.* **8** [U] : the punishment of being kept in a prison for the rest of your life ▪ *He was sentenced to life.* — *a life of its own* ✧ Something that *takes on a life of its own* becomes very large, important, or hard to control. — *all walks of life* or *every walk of life* see ²WALK — *a matter of life and death* : something that is extremely important and often involves decisions that will determine whether someone lives or dies — *a new lease on/of life* see ¹LEASE — *(as) big as life* (US) or chiefly Brit *(as) large as life* informal : in person ▪ *There she was, as big as life.* — *bet/stake your life on* ✧ If you would *bet/stake your life on* something, you are very sure that it will happen. — *come to life* **1** : to become very interesting, appealing, or exciting ▪ *The movie really comes to life when she appears on the screen.* **2** *of a place* : to become filled with the energy and excitement of active people ▪ *Downtown comes to life when the clubs open.* **3** *or sputter/roar (etc.) to life of a machine* : to begin working ▪ *The engine suddenly roared to life.* — *for dear life* : very tightly or quickly because of fear or danger ▪ *hanging on for dear life* — *for life* : for the whole of your life ▪ *We remained friends for life.* — *for the life of me* informal : in any way at all ▪ *I couldn't for the life of me remember her name.* — *frighten/scare the life out of* informal : to frighten (someone) very badly ▪ *larger than life* see LARGE — *lose your life* : to die ▪ *She nearly lost her life in a car accident.* — *not on your life* informal — used as a very forceful way of saying "no" or "never" ▪ *Do the government's policies really help the average worker? Not on your life.* — *risk life and limb* : to do something that is very dangerous ▪ *They risked life and limb to pull the child from the river.* — *take/claim someone's life* : to cause someone's death ▪ *The illness took his life.* — *take your own life* : to kill yourself — *the life of the party* (US) or chiefly Brit *the life and soul of the party* : someone who is very lively and amusing at a party or other social gathering — *the light of your life* see ¹LIGHT — *true to life* see ¹TRUE

life-and-death adj : extremely important and serious especially because your survival or life may depend on success ▪ *a life-and-death struggle*

life assurance n [U] Brit : LIFE INSURANCE

life-blood /ˈlaɪfˌblʌd/ n [U] : the most important part of something ▪ *The town's lifeblood is its fishing industry.*

life-boat /ˈlaɪfˌboʊt/ n [C] : a small boat that is carried on a ship and that is used for saving people's lives if the ship sinks

life expectancy n [C/U] : the average number of years that a person or animal can expect to live ▪ *improvements in diet that have resulted in greater life expectancy for many people*

life form n [C] : a living thing of any kind ▪ *primitive/simple life forms*

life-guard /ˈlaɪfˌgɑɹd/ n [C] : a person whose job is to protect swimmers from drowning

life imprisonment n [U] : the punishment of being kept in a prison for the rest of your life

life insurance n [U] : a type of insurance that pays money to the family of someone who has died

life jacket n [C] : something that is worn over your upper body and that is designed to save you from drowning — called also (US) *life vest*

life-less /ˈlaɪfləs/ adj **1** : having no living things ▪ *a lifeless landscape* **2** : dead or appearing to be dead ▪ *a lifeless body* **3** : lacking spirit, interest, or energy ▪ *the book's lifeless plot*

life-like /ˈlaɪfˌlaɪk/ adj : looking like a real person or thing ▪ *a lifelike doll*

life-line /ˈlaɪfˌlaɪn/ n [C] **1** : something which provides help or support that is needed for success or survival ▪ *The new jobs were an economic lifeline for the city.* **2** : a rope used for saving the life of someone (such as someone who has fallen into water)

life-long /ˈlaɪfˌlɑːŋ/ adj, always before a noun : continuing or lasting through a person's life ▪ *a lifelong friendship*

life preserver n [C] chiefly US : a floating device that is designed to save you from drowning

lif-er /ˈlaɪfɚ/ n [C] informal **1** US : a person who spends an entire career in the same job **2** : a criminal who has been sentenced to spend the rest of his or her life in prison

life raft n [C] : a small rubber boat designed for saving the lives of people when a larger boat or ship sinks

life-sav-er /ˈlaɪfˌseɪvɚ/ n [C] **1** : something that saves a person's life ▪ *a drug that has been a lifesaver for many people* **2** : something or someone which provides help that is badly needed ▪ *Thanks for your help. You're a real lifesaver!* — **life-sav-ing** /ˈlaɪfˌseɪvɪŋ/ adj, always before a noun ▪ *a lifesaving surgical procedure*

life-size /ˈlaɪfˌsaɪz/ also **life-sized** /ˈlaɪfˌsaɪzd/ adj : having the same size as a real person or thing ▪ *a life-size model of a dinosaur*

life span n [C] : the amount of time that a person or animal actually lives ▪ *the average human lifespan* ▪ *(figurative) the life span of a battery*

life-style /ˈlaɪfˌstaɪl/ n [C] : the way a person lives or a group of people live ▪ *a healthy lifestyle*

life support n [U] **1** medical : the equipment, material, and treatment needed to keep a very sick or hurt patient alive ▪ *She was put/kept on life support.* **2** : the things that are needed to keep someone alive in a place (such as outer space) where life is usually not possible ▪ *a life-support system*

life-time /ˈlaɪfˌtaɪm/ n [C] **1** : the time during which a person is alive ▪ *I don't think it will happen in our lifetime.* ▪ *the* *thrill of a lifetime* [=a great thrill] • *a lifetime achievement award* • *(figurative) It will take me a lifetime to read all those books.* **2** : the time during which something lasts or is useful • *the lifetime of a planet/star/comet*

life vest *n* [C] *US* : LIFE JACKET

¹lift /ˈlɪft/ *vb* **1** [T/I] : to move to a higher position • *lift a bucket of water* • *He lifted his head (up) and looked at us.* • *The balloon lifted into the sky.* **2** [T] : to move (someone or something) to a higher condition or position • *The story lifted him to national recognition.* • *lifting people from poverty* ✧ If your **spirits lift** or your **mood lifts** or if something **lifts your spirits/mood**, you become happier or less sad. • *The beauty of the sunrise lifted her spirits.* **4** [T] *informal* **a** : to take (an idea, plan, etc.) *from* another source often in a way that is wrong • *an idea lifted from another novel* **b** : to steal (something) • *Somebody lifted her purse.* **5** [T] : to stop or remove (something) often for only a short time • *lift a blockade/ban* **6** [I] *of fog, clouds, or smoke* : to move up and disappear so that it is possible to see • *when the clouds/smoke/fog finally lifted* — **lift a finger** see ¹FINGER — **lift off** [*phrasal vb*] *of an airplane, rocket, etc.* : to rise up from the ground or another surface • *planes lifting off from the runway* — **lift·er** *n* [C]

²lift *n* **1** [C] : the act of raising or lifting something • *a slight lift of his eyebrows* **2** [C] : a free ride in a vehicle • *I need a lift to the bus station.* **3** [C] **a** *Brit* : ELEVATOR 1 **b** : SKI LIFT **4** [*singular*] : an improved mood or condition • *The coach's speech gave the team a lift.* • *A tax cut could give the economy a lift.* [=improve the economy] **5** [U] *technical* : an upward force that makes it possible for aircraft to fly • *a wing design that generates more lift*

lift-off /ˈlɪftˌɑːf/ *n* [C/U] : the upward movement from the ground by a rocket, helicopter, or space vehicle as it begins flight

lig·a·ment /ˈlɪgəmənt/ *n* [C] : a tough piece of tissue in your body that holds bones together or keeps an organ in place

¹light /ˈlaɪt/ *n* **1** [U] : the brightness produced by the sun, by fire, by a lamp, etc., that makes it possible to see things • *a ray/shaft/beam of light* • *a source of light* • *the light of the moon* • **natural light** [=sunlight] • **artificial light** [=light produced by electric lamps] **2** [C] **a** : a source of light (such as an electric lamp) • *turn/switch on/off the light* • *The lights suddenly went out.* **b** : a light on a vehicle • *His car's battery died because he left his lights on.* **3** [*singular*] : a way of showing or understanding something or someone • *I see things in a different light now.* [=I see/understand things differently now] • *The lawyer depicted him in a bad/good light* [=in a way that made him seem bad/good] **4** [C] : TRAFFIC LIGHT • *Turn left at the next light.* **5** [*singular*] *informal* : a flame for lighting a cigarette • *Do you have a light?* **6** [U] *formal* : DAYLIGHT 1

• *Things look different by the light of day.* **7** [*singular*] : a quality in a person's eyes that shows emotion • *I saw the light of recognition in her eye.* **8** [*plural*] : light colors • *the composition of lights and darks in the painting* • *light-colored clothes* • *Wash the lights and the darks separately.* — **(a) light at the end of the tunnel** : a reason to believe that a bad situation will end soon or that a long and difficult job will be finished soon • *The work has been going on for months, but we're starting to see a light at the end of the tunnel.* — **bring (something) to light** : to tell people about (something) • *Many new facts were brought to light during the investigation.* — **cast/throw light on** : to help to explain (something) • *I hope my theory throws light on the situation.* — **come to light** : to become known • *It has come to light that he was promoted unfairly.* — **in the light of** or *US* **in light of** **1** : while thinking about (something that affects the way you see or understand things) • *You should think about his advice in light of your own needs.* **2** : because of (something) • *It's an important topic in light of recent events.* — **out like a light** *informal* : asleep or unconscious • *As soon as my head hit the pillow, I was out like a light.* — **punch someone's lights out** see ¹PUNCH — **see the light** *informal* : to suddenly understand or realize the truth of something • *They doubted his theory, but now they've seen the light.* [=they now realize that his theory is correct] — **set light to** *chiefly Brit* : to cause (something) to begin burning • *using a match to set light to paper* — **the light of your life** : a person you love very much and who makes you happy • *His daughter is the light of his life.*

²light *adj* **1** : not dark or deep in color • *light blue* **2 a** : having a lot of light : BRIGHT • *a light and airy room* **b** : having the light of the day • *Let's go while it's still light (out).* [=before night has fallen] • *In summer it gets light early.* **3** : not heavy : having little weight or less than usual weight • *This suitcase is light enough for a child to carry.* **4 a** : less in amount or degree than usual • *Traffic was light this morning.* • *light rain/snow* **b** : not strong or violent • *a light breeze* **c** : not great or large • *The storm caused light damage.* **d** : not difficult to accept or bear • *a light responsibility* • *light punishment* **e** : slight or minor in degree or effect • *She has a light cold.* **5** : not involving a lot of physical effort • *light exercise/housework* **6** : not loud or forceful • *a light touch/tap* **7** : not important or serious • *doing some light reading* **8** : not dense and thick • *a light beard* • *light fog/smoke* **9** : made with thin cloth and not very warm • *a light coat/blanket* **10** : eating, drinking, or using a small amount of something • *He's a light eater/smoker.* **11 a** : not having a large amount of food • *a light lunch/snack* **b** : made with fewer calories or with less of some ingredient than usual • *light beer* **c** : not rich, dense, or thick • *light cream/*

syrup **12 a** : designed to carry a small load or few passengers ▪ *a light truck* **b** : not as large and powerful as other weapons, machines, etc. ▪ *light artillery* — **light on** : having or using a small amount of (something) ▪ *an essay that is light on facts but heavy on speculation* — **light on your feet** : capable of moving in a quick and graceful way ▪ *He's very light on his feet for such a big person.* — **light sleeper** : someone who wakes up easily — **make light of** : to treat (something, such as a problem) in a joking way ▪ *I don't mean to make light of this very serious issue.* — **light·ness** /ˈlaɪtnəs/ *n* [U]

³**light** *vb* **light·ed** *or* **lit** /ˈlɪt/; **light·ing 1** [T] : to provide light for (something) ▪ *a dimly/poorly/brightly lit room* ▪ *We used a candle to light the way.* **2 a** [T] : to cause (something) to burn ▪ *light a match/candle* ▪ *I lit (up) a cigarette for him.* = *I lit him a cigarette.* **b** [I] : to begin to burn ▪ *waiting for the wood to light* — **light into** [*phrasal vb*] *US, informal* : to attack or criticize (someone) forcefully ▪ *He lit into his employees for their sloppy work.* — **light on/upon** [*phrasal vb*] : to find or see (something) by chance ▪ *His eye lit on a story in the newspaper.* — **light out** [*phrasal vb*] *US, informal* : to leave in a hurry for someplace ▪ *He suddenly lit out for home.* — **light up** [*phrasal vb*] **1** *of a light* : to become lit : to begin shining ▪ *All of the lights on the display suddenly lit up.* ▪ *(figurative) His eyes/face lit up.* [=he looked very happy and pleased] **2 light (something) up** *or* **light up (something)** : to provide light for (something) ▪ *light up a room* ▪ *Fireworks lit up the sky.* ▪ *(figurative) Her smile lights up the room.* [=she has an extremely bright and attractive smile] **3** *informal* : to light a cigarette ▪ *I can't wait to light up* [=smoke a cigarette] *after work.*

⁴**light** *adv* — **eat light** *US* : to eat foods that will not cause you to gain weight ▪ *She eats light and exercises often.* — **trav·el light** : to travel with little luggage ▪ *She always travels light.*

light bulb *n* [C] : a glass bulb or tube that produces light when it is supplied with electricity

light·en /ˈlaɪtn̩/ *vb* **1** [T/I] : to make (something) brighter or lighter or to become brighter or lighter ▪ *She lightens her hair.* ▪ *He turned on a lamp to lighten (up) the room.* ▪ *The sky lightened as the clouds began to move away.* **2** [T/I] : to make (something) less heavy or difficult or to become less heavy or difficult ▪ *lighten a burden/load* ▪ *His workload has lightened in recent weeks.* **3** [T] : to make (something) less sad or serious or to become less sad or serious ▪ *He told a joke to lighten the atmosphere/conversation/mood.* ▪ *Her somber mood lightened* [=brightened] *as the weather improved.* **4** [I] : to become less forceful ▪ *The wind lightened a bit.* — **lighten up** [*phrasal vb*] *informal* : to become more relaxed and informal ▪ *Lighten up (a bit) and enjoy yourself!* — **light·en·er** /ˈlaɪtn̩ɚ/ *n* [C]

light·er /ˈlaɪtɚ/ *n* [C] : a small device that

produces a flame used for lighting something (such as a cigarette) ▪ *a cigarette lighter*

light–head·ed /ˈlaɪtˌhɛdəd/ *adj* : unable to think and move in a normal way because of a weak and dizzy feeling ▪ *Standing up too quickly usually makes her light-headed.* — **light–head·ed·ness** *n* [U]

light–heart·ed /ˈlaɪtˌhɑɚtəd/ *adj* **1** : having or showing a cheerful and happy nature ▪ *a lighthearted person/mood* **2** : not serious ▪ *a lighthearted comedy* — **light–heart·ed·ly** *adv* — **light–heart·ed·ness** *n* [U]

light heavyweight *n* [C] : a fighter who is in a class of boxers with an upper weight limit of 175 pounds (79.5 kilograms)

light·house /ˈlaɪtˌhaʊs/ *n* [C] : a tower with a powerful light that is built on or near the shore to guide ships away from danger

light industry *n* [U] : the production of small goods that will be sold to the people who use them rather than to another manufacturer

light·ing /ˈlaɪtɪŋ/ *n* [U] **1 a** : light that is of a particular kind or that has a particular quality ▪ *artificial/natural lighting* **b** : the equipment used to provide light ▪ *There was a problem with the lighting.* **2** : the use of light for a particular purpose in a movie, play, etc. ▪ *He's in charge of the lighting for the show.*

light·ly /ˈlaɪtli/ *adv* : in a light manner; such as **a** : with little weight or force ▪ *The rain fell lightly on the roof.* **b** : in a way that is not serious ▪ *a problem should not be taken lightly* [=that should be treated seriously] **c** : in a quick and graceful way ▪ *She moved lightly across the room.* **d** : to a small degree or extent ▪ *lightly salted/roasted peanuts* ▪ *a lightly populated area* **e** : in a way that is not as harsh or severe as it could or should be ▪ *Considering the harm she did, he's gotten off lightly with only a warning.*

¹**light·ning** /ˈlaɪtnɪŋ/ *n* [U] : the flashes of light that are produced in the sky during a storm ▪ *a bolt/flash of lightning* = *a lightning bolt/flash* — **catch/capture lightning in a bottle** *chiefly US* : to succeed in a way that is very lucky or unlikely — **like (greased) lightning** *informal* : very quickly ▪ *moving like greased lightning*

²**lightning** *adj, always before a noun* : moving or done very quickly ▪ *moving at lightning speed*

lightning bug *n* [C] *US* : FIREFLY

lightning rod *n* [C] *US* **1** : a metal rod that is placed on a building and connected with the ground below to protect the building from being damaged by lightning — called also (*Brit*) **lightning conductor** **2** : someone or something that attracts criticism or gets blamed when things go wrong ▪ *He became a lightning rod for controversy/criticism.*

light·weight /ˈlaɪtˌweɪt/ *n* [C] **1** : a fighter who is in a class of boxers weighing from 125 to 132 pounds (57 to 60 kilograms) **2** : someone or something that does not weigh as much as others ▪ *a* lightweight jacket **3** : someone or something that has little importance or power ▪ *an intellectual lightweight*

light—year /'laɪt,jɪə/ *n* **1** [C] *technical* : a unit of distance equal to the distance that light travels in one year ▪ *a star about 10 light-years away* **2** [*plural*] **a** — used to say that someone or something is much better or more advanced than others ▪ *This new technology puts us light-years ahead of our competitors.* **b** — used to refer to a time that is or seems very far away ▪ *A cure for the disease is still probably light-years away.*

lik•able *or* **like•able** /'laɪkəbəl/ *adj* : easy to like ▪ *a friendly, likable person* — **lik•abil•i•ty** *or* **like•abil•i•ty** /,laɪkə'bɪləti/ *n* [U]

¹**like** /'laɪk/ *vb* **liked; lik•ing 1** [T] **a** : to enjoy (something) ▪ *My son likes (watching/playing) baseball.* ▪ *I like to play the guitar.* ▪ *Do you like Mexican food?* **b** : to regard (something) in a favorable way ▪ *I don't like the idea of leaving her alone all week.* **2** [T] : to feel affection for (someone) ▪ *I think she likes you.* [=I think she is attracted to you] ▪ *What do you like or dislike about him most?* **3** [T] — used to ask about someone's feelings or opinion about something ▪ *So how do you like sailing?* [=do you like or dislike sailing?] **4** [T] **a** : to want to have (something) — used with *would* to make a polite suggestion, offer, or request ▪ *Would you like some coffee?* ▪ *I'd like (a chance) to reply to the last speaker.* **b** : to want or prefer *to do* something ▪ *Would you like to go outside?* [=do you want to go outside?] **c** — used in various spoken phrases that typically express anger or surprise ▪ *She left without saying a word to me.* **How would you like it** *if someone ignored you that way?* ▪ *"She left without saying a word.* **How do you like that**?" **5** [T] : to choose or prefer to have (something) in a specified way or condition ▪ *"How do you like your steaks cooked?" "I like my steaks medium rare."* **6** [I] : to make a choice about what to do, have, etc. ▪ *You can leave any time you like.* ▪ *There are plenty of cookies, so take as many as you like.* **7** [T] : to do well in (certain conditions) ▪ *This plant likes dry soil.* — **if you like 1 a** — used to say that you can do something if you want to do it ▪ *Have another drink, if you like.* **b** — used to agree politely to a suggestion or request ▪ *"Could we stay a little longer?" "Yes, if you like."* [=if that's what you want to do] **2** *chiefly Brit* — used to suggest a possible way of describing or thinking about something ▪ *The experience was, if you like, a glimpse of the future.*

²**like** *prep* **1** : similar to (something or someone) ▪ *The house looks like a barn.* ▪ *The baby is/looks more like his mother than his father.* ▪ *I used to be selfish, but I'm not like that anymore.* [=I'm not selfish anymore] — used with *what* in phrases that ask about or refer to the qualities of a person or thing ▪ *"What's he like?"* [=how would you describe him?] *"He's very nice."* ▪ *She knows what it's like to be*

lonely. = *She knows what it feels like to be lonely.* **2** : typical of (someone) ▪ *It's just/not like him to be late.* **3** : comparable to or close to (something) ▪ *It costs* **something like** *five dollars.* [=it costs about five dollars.] ▪ *He said it would only take a few minutes, but it ended up taking* **more like** *half an hour.* [=it took about half an hour] **4** : in a way that is similar to (someone or something) ▪ *Quit acting like a fool.* **5** — used to introduce an example or series of examples ▪ *They studied subjects like* [=such as] *physics and chemistry.* — **just like that** see ²JUST — **like new** see ¹NEW — **like so** : in the manner shown — used in speech when you are showing someone how to do something ▪ *Fold the cloth like so.* — **like that/this 1** : of that/this kind ▪ *I love books like that.* **2** : in that/this manner ▪ *I hate it when it rains like this.* — **more like it** *informal* — used to say that something is better or more pleasing ▪ *"I've done twice as much today as yesterday!" "Well,* **that's more like it!** *Congratulations!"*

³**like** *adj* : having the same or similar qualities ▪ *They have like* [=(more commonly) *similar*] *dispositions.*

⁴**like** *n* [C] **1** : a person or thing that is similar to another person or thing ▪ *We may never see his like* [=another person like him] *again.; also* : a group of similar people or things ▪ *comparing like with like* [=comparing similar people or things] **2** : something that you like, approve of, or enjoy — usually plural ▪ *my likes and dislikes* — **and the like** : and others of a similar kind ▪ *ghosts, vampires and the like* — **the likes of** *also* **the like of 1** : such people as ▪ *many great writers, including the likes of Jane Austen and Robert Browning* **2** *disapproving* : such a person as ▪ *We have no use for the likes of you.* **3** : the kind or sort of ▪ *It was a beautiful sunset, the likes of which I've never seen before.*

⁵**like** *adv* — **as like as not** *or* **like as not 1** : PROBABLY ▪ *Like as not the crime will never be solved.*

---

usage Like has many uses in informal speech, especially in the speech of young people. It is commonly used to emphasize a word or phrase. ▪ *He was, like, gorgeous.* ▪ (*chiefly Brit*) *He was gorgeous, like.* It is used in a way that shows you are not sure or confident about what you are saying. ▪ *I think it costs, like, 20 dollars.* In very informal speech in U.S. English, it is used with the verb *be* to say what someone thinks, says, etc. ▪ *She was telling me what to do and I was like* [=I was thinking], *"Mind your own business."* ▪ *He's always criticizing everyone but it's like, "Who cares what he thinks?"* [=he's always criticizing everyone but no one cares what he thinks]

---

⁶**like** *conj, informal* **1 a** : the way it would be if ▪ *It seemed like* [=as if] *he'd never been away.* **b** : the way someone would do if ▪ *She acts like* [=as if] *she's better than us.* **2** : the same as ▪ *You sound just*

like he does. • *Does it look now like (it did) before?* • **Like I said** [=*as I said*] *before, I just don't know.* **3** : in the way or manner that • *I did it like you told me.* **4** : such as • *a bag like a doctor carries*

> **usage** The use of *like* as a conjunction is regarded by some people as an error. It occurs mainly in speech and informal writing.

likeable *variant spelling of* LIKABLE

like·li·hood /ˈlaɪkliˌhʊd/ *n* [*U, singular*] : the chance that something will happen • *A poor diet increases the likelihood of (developing) serious health problems.* • **In all likelihood** *it will rain tomorrow.* [=it is very likely that it will rain tomorrow]

¹**like·ly** /ˈlaɪkli/ *adj* **like·li·er; -est 1** : used to indicate the chance that something will happen • *It is/seems highly/very likely that it will rain tomorrow.* • *She may get the job, but it isn't likely.* • *"Will she get the job?" "Not likely."* [=she probably will not get the job] • *It's more than likely* [=very probable] *that this problem will occur again.* **2** : seeming to be true • *the most likely explanation* ◆ The phrase *a likely story* is often used in an informal way to say that you do not believe what someone has said. • *He says he forgot. A likely story!* **3** *always before a noun* : seeming to be right or suited for a purpose • *a likely candidate for the job*

²**likely** *adv* : without much doubt : PROBABLY • *They're very likely be late.* • *It will most likely rain tomorrow.* • *She will more than likely get the job.*

like–mind·ed /ˈlaɪkˈmaɪndəd/ *adj* : having similar opinions and interests • *like-minded people*

lik·en /ˈlaɪkən/ *vb* — **liken to** [*phrasal vb*] **liken** (someone or something) **to** : to describe (someone or something) as similar to (someone or something else) • *She likened their house to a museum.*

like·ness /ˈlaɪknəs/ *n* **1** [*C*] : a picture of a person • *The painting is a good likeness of her.* [=the painting looks very much like her] **2** [*C/U*] : the quality or state of being alike or similar especially in appearance • *There's some likeness between them.*

like·wise /ˈlaɪkˌwaɪz/ *adv* **1** : in the same way • *He left already, and you should do likewise.* [=you should also leave] • *a painter who is likewise a sculptor* — often used to introduce a statement that adds to and is related to a previous statement • *Homelessness is increasing. Likewise, unemployment is up.* **3** — used in informal speech to say that you share the feelings that someone else has just expressed • *"I'm pleased to meet you." "Likewise."*

lik·ing /ˈlaɪkɪŋ/ *n* [*singular*] : the feeling of liking or enjoying something or someone • *a (strong) liking for spicy foods* • *The colors are too bright for my liking.* [=I like colors that are less bright] • *I took a liking to him* [=I started to like him] *immediately.* • *She reads poetry, but fiction is more to her liking.* [=she likes fiction more than poetry]

li·lac /ˈlaɪˌlæk, *Brit* ˈlaɪlək/ *n* **1** [*C*] : a

type of bush with purple or white flowers that bloom in the spring **2** [*U*] : a light purple color

lilt /ˈlɪlt/ *n* [*singular*] : the attractive quality of speech or music that rises and falls in a pleasing pattern — **lilt·ing** /ˈlɪltɪŋ/ *adj* • *a lilting melody/voice*

lily /ˈlɪli/ *n, pl* **lil·ies** [*C*] : a type of plant that has large white or colorful bell-shaped flowers; *also* : the flower — see also WATER LILY — **gild the lily** see GILD

lily–white /ˈlɪliˈwaɪt/ *adj* **1** : very white • *lily-white skin* **2** : morally pure • *She's not as lily-white as you might think.* **3** *chiefly US, disapproving* : consisting entirely or mostly of white people • *a lily-white suburb*

li·ma bean /ˈlaɪmə-, *Brit* ˈliːmə-/ *n* [*C*] : a type of flat and pale green or white bean

limb /ˈlɪm/ *n* [*C*] **1** : a leg or arm • *an artificial limb* **2** : a large branch of a tree • **out on a limb** : in or into a risky or dangerous position or situation • *She went out on a limb to help you.* — **risk life and limb** see LIFE — **tear (someone) limb from limb** : to attack or kill (someone) in a very violent way — **limbed** /ˈlɪmd/ *adj* • *long-limbed*

¹**lim·ber** /ˈlɪmbə/ *adj* : bending easily — used of people or their bodies • *a limber gymnast*

²**limber** *vb* — **limber up** [*phrasal vb*] : to prepare for physical activity by doing exercises so that your body can move and bend more easily • *She limbered up for a few minutes before starting to run.*

lim·bo /ˈlɪmboʊ/ *n* **1** or **Limbo** [*singular*] *in the Roman Catholic religion* : a place where the souls of people who have not been baptized go after death **2** [*U*] : a dance or contest in which you have to bend backward and go under a bar which is lowered after each time you go under it • *do/dance the limbo* — **in limbo 1** : in a forgotten or ignored place, state, or situation • *orphaned children left in limbo in foster homes* **2** : in an uncertain or undecided state or condition • *The project is in limbo while we look for financing.*

lime /ˈlaɪm/ *n* **1** [*C/U*] : a small green fruit that is related to the lemon and orange and has a sour taste **2** [*U*] : LIME GREEN **3** [*U*] : a white substance that is made by heating limestone or shells and that is used in various products (such as plaster and cement) and in farming — **lime** *vb* **limed; lim·ing** [*T*] • *lime a garden* [=spread lime (sense 3) on a garden]

lime green *n* [*U*] : a bright, light yellowish-green color — **lime–green** *adj*

lime·light /ˈlaɪmˌlaɪt/ *n* — **the limelight** : public attention or notice thought of as a bright light that shines on someone • *She shuns the limelight.* • *The controversy thrust him into the limelight.* • *an actor who loves being in the limelight*

lim·er·ick /ˈlɪmərɪk/ *n* [*C*] : a humorous rhyming poem of five lines

lime·stone /ˈlaɪmˌstoʊn/ *n* [*U*] : a type of white stone that is commonly used in building

¹**lim·it** /ˈlɪmət/ n [C] **1** : a point beyond which it is not possible to go • *He has reached the limit of his endurance.* • *In training, she pushed her body to its physical limits.* **2** : a point beyond which someone is not allowed to go • *Parents need to set limits for their children.* **3** : an amount or number that is the highest or lowest allowed • *Two drinks is my limit.* [=I stop after having two drinks] — see also SPEED LIMIT **4** : an area or line that is at the outer edge of something — usually plural • *within the city limits* [=within the city] — **over the limit** *Brit* : having more alcohol in the blood than is legally allowed for someone who is driving • *He was arrested for driving over the limit.* — **the sky's the limit** — used to say that there are no limits and that anything is possible • *You can achieve anything if you really want to. The sky's the limit.* — **to the limit** : as much as possible • *My schedule is filled to the limit.* — **within limits** : without going beyond what is considered reasonable or allowable • *We can do whatever we want, within (certain) limits.* — **without limit** : without being controlled or stopped • *allowing costs to increase without limit*

²**limit** vb [T] **1** : to stop or prevent an increase in (something) • *limiting expenses/damage* **2** : to prevent (something) from being larger, longer, more, etc. • *The hospital limits visits to 30 minutes.* • *The damage was limited to the rear of the building.* **3** : to stop (someone) from having or doing more • *Our lack of money limits us to fewer options.* • *We had to limit ourselves to fewer options.*

lim·i·ta·tion /ˌlɪməˈteɪʃən/ n **1** [U] : the act of controlling the size or extent of something • *a law aimed at the limitation of federal power* **2** [C] : something that controls how much of something is possible or allowed • *They have placed a limitation on the amount of time we have available.* **3** [C] : something (such as a lack of ability or strength) that controls what a person is able to do • *physical limitations*

lim·it·ed /ˈlɪmətəd/ adj : not high or great in number, amount, etc. • *limited resources/time* • *The company has had limited success.*

lim·it·less /ˈlɪmətləs/ adj : very great or large : having no limit • *seemingly limitless possibilities*

limo /ˈlɪmoʊ/ n, pl **lim·os** [C] informal : LIMOUSINE

lim·ou·sine /ˌlɪməˈziːn/ n [C] **1** : a very large and comfortable car usually driven by a professional driver (called a chauffeur) **2** chiefly US : a vehicle (such as a bus or van) that carries passengers to and from an airport

¹**limp** /ˈlɪmp/ vb [I] **1** : to walk in a slow and awkward way because of an injury to a leg or foot • *The dog was limping slightly.* **2** : to go or continue slowly or with difficulty • *The damaged ship limped back to port.*

²**limp** n [C] : a slow and awkward way of walking caused by an injury to a leg or foot • *He was walking with a slight limp.*

³**limp** adj **1** : not firm or stiff • *a limp handshake* • *Her hair hung limp around her shoulders.* **2** : feeling very tired • *He was limp with fatigue.* — **limp·ly** adv — **limp·ness** n [U]

lim·pid /ˈlɪmpəd/ adj, literary **1** : perfectly clear • *the limpid waters of the stream* **2** : clear and simple in style • *limpid prose*

linch·pin also **lynch·pin** /ˈlɪntʃˌpɪn/ n [C] : the most important part of a complex situation or system • *This witness is the linchpin of the defense's case.*

¹**line** /ˈlaɪn/ n **1** [C] **a** : a long narrow mark on a surface • *a horizontal/vertical/diagonal line* **b** : a mark on the ground that shows the edge of the playing area in a sport • *a tennis serve that was over the line* **2** [C] : an area or border that separates two places • *property lines* • *the town line* **3** [C] **a** : a group of people or things that are next to each other in a row • *a line of trees* **b** US : a group of people, vehicles, etc., that are in front of and behind each other in a row while they wait to move forward • *The line* [=(chiefly Brit) queue] *of fans moved slowly.* • *Everybody had to get in line and wait their turn.* **4** [C] : the outline of a figure, body, or surface • *the car's sleek lines* **5** [C] : a long and thin rope, string, etc. • *a fishing line* **6** [C] **a** : a pipe for carrying something (such as steam, water, or oil) • *a break in the water line* **b** : a wire or set of wires that carries electricity or a telephone signal • *a telephone line* **7** [C] : a telephone connection • *I'm sorry, the line is busy/engaged.* • *There's a call for you on line 2.* • *Please hold the line.* [=please do not hang up the phone] **8 a** [C] : a row of words, letters, numbers, or symbols written across a page • *a line of poetry; also* : a space on a page where such a line could be placed • *a blank line* **b** [plural] : the words that an actor speaks in a play, movie, etc. • *The actors had to memorize their lines.* **c** [C] : a short note or message • *Drop me a line* [=send me a brief message] *while you're away.* **d** [C] : a spoken or written comment • *a funny/clever line* **9** [C] : a wrinkle on a person's skin • *the deep lines on his face* **10** [C] : the path along which something moves or is directed • *a bullet's line of flight* • *caught in the line of fire* [=in the place where bullets were being shot] **11** [C] : a railroad track **12 a** [singular] : a series of similar things • *a long line of problems* **b** [C] : the series of people who are born in a family as years pass • *She comes from a long line of farmers.* **13** [C] **a** : a way of behaving, thinking, etc. • *I don't follow your line of reasoning.* [=I don't understand the reasoning behind what you are saying] • *The police pursued a new line of inquiry/investigation.* • *trying a different line of attack* [=a different approach] **b** : an official or public position or opinion • *adhering to the party line* [=supporting the position taken by a political party] **14** [C] : an area of activity or interest • *a job in the retail line* • *a dangerous line of work* [=a dangerous job] • *a soldier/po-*

liceman/fireman *who was killed* **in the line of duty** [=was killed while doing his job] **15** [C] : the position of military forces who are facing the enemy ▪ *The enemy soldiers broke through the line.* ▪ *caught behind enemy lines* [=in an area controlled by the enemy] **16** [C] : a group of related products that are sold by one company ▪ *a line of clothing* **17** [C] **a** : a system used for moving people or things from one place to another ▪ *a bus line* ▪ *military supply lines; also* : a company that owns or controls such a system **b** : a system that allows people to share information ▪ *keeping the* **lines of communication** *open* **18** [plural] — used in phrases like **along the lines of** to refer to something that is similar or close to the thing being mentioned ▪ *He said he was too busy to help, or something along those lines.* **19** [C] *American football* **a** : LINE OF SCRIMMAGE **b** : the players who are positioned on the line of scrimmage ▪ *the defensive/offensive line* — **along the line** *informal* : during a process or series of events ▪ *He lost interest in music somewhere along the line.* [=at some time in the past] — **cross the line** see ²CROSS — **down the line** *informal* : in the future ▪ *We'll have to fix this further down the line.* — **draw a/the line** : to refuse to do or allow something : to set a limit ▪ *He helps out a lot but draws the line at cleaning the bathroom.* — **fall in/into line** see ¹FALL — **get/have a line on** *US, informal* : to get or have information about (someone or something that you are trying to find) ▪ *She says she has a line on a new car.* — **hold the line** : to not allow any more changes or increases ▪ *The President vowed to hold the line on tax increases.* — **hook, line and sinker** see ¹HOOK — **in line** **1** — used to say that someone should get something or is likely to get something ▪ *He's in line for a promotion.* **2** — used to refer to a person or thing that follows or could follow another person or thing ▪ *The Vice President is* **first in line** *to succeed the President.* **3** : doing what other people want or expect ▪ *keeping him in line* — **in line with** : in agreement with ▪ *My thinking is in line with yours.* — **into line** : into a state of agreement or cooperation ▪ *It was difficult to get/bring everyone into line.* — **lay it on the line** *informal* : to speak very honestly and directly to someone ▪ *Let me lay it on the line (to/for you): if your work doesn't improve, you'll be fired.* — **on line** : in or into operation ▪ *The new system will be coming on line next month.* — **on the line** : in danger of being lost or harmed ▪ *My job is on the line.* ▪ *He put/laid his life on the line.* — **out of line** *informal* : not right or appropriate ▪ *Your behavior is out of line.* — **read between the lines** see ¹READ — **toe the line** see ²TOE

²**line** *vb* **lined; lin·ing** **1** [T] : to place or form a line along (something) ▪ *Shops line the street.* ▪ *a street lined with trees = a tree-lined street* **2** [T/I] *baseball* : to hit a line drive ▪ *She lined a single to left field.* **3** [T] : to cover the inner surface of

(something) ▪ *I lined the box with paper.* ▪ *Her gloves were lined with fur.* — **line up** [*phrasal vb*] **1** : to form a line ▪ *(US) People lined up* [=(chiefly Brit) queued up] *to buy tickets.* **2 line (people or things) up** or **line up (people or things)** : to put (people or things) into a line ▪ *The teacher lined up the children.* **3 line (things) up** or **line up (things)** : ALIGN ▪ *line up (the edges of) two pieces of paper* **4 line (something) up** or **line up (something)** : to succeed in getting (something) ▪ *She managed to line up a summer job.* — **line your pockets** *informal* : to take or get a lot of money by doing something illegal or dishonest ▪ *corrupt officials who have been lining their pockets at the public's expense* [=have been stealing public money]

lin·e·age /ˈlɪnijɪʤ/ *n* [C/U] : the people who were in someone's family in past times ▪ *a person of unknown lineage*

lin·e·ar /ˈlɪnijɚ/ *adj* **1 a** : formed by lines ▪ *a linear design* **b** : forming a line ▪ *a flat, almost linear horizon* **2** : of or relating to the length of something ▪ *linear measurements* **3** : going from one thing to the next thing in a direct and logical way ▪ *a linear narrative*

line·back·er /ˈlaɪnˌbækɚ/ *n* [C] *American football* : a player on the defending team whose usual position is a short distance in back of the line of scrimmage

lined /ˈlaɪnd/ *adj* **1** : marked with lines ▪ *lined paper* **2** : having many wrinkles ▪ *a deeply lined face* **3** *of clothing* : having a lining ▪ *a lined jacket/skirt*

line drive *n* [C] *baseball* : a ball that is hit by the batter and goes in a nearly straight line not far above the ground

line·man /ˈlaɪnmən/ *n, pl* **-men** /-mən/ [C] **1** *American football* : a player whose position is on the line of scrimmage ▪ *a defensive lineman* **2** *US* : a person whose job is to set up and repair power lines or telephone lines

lin·en /ˈlɪnən/ *n* **1** [U] : a smooth, strong cloth made from flax ▪ *a linen tablecloth* **2** [U, singular] : tablecloths, sheets, etc., made of linen or a similar cloth ▪ *She washes the linen(s) every week.*

line of scrimmage *n* [singular] *American football* : an imaginary line that goes across the field at the place where the football is put before each play begins

lin·er /ˈlaɪnɚ/ *n* [C] **1** : a large ship used for carrying passengers ▪ *an ocean liner* **2** *baseball* : LINE DRIVE **3** : something that covers the inner surface of another thing ▪ *the liner of a jacket*

liner notes *n* [plural] *chiefly US* : information about a record, CD, or tape that is printed on its cover or on a piece of paper placed inside its cover

lines·man /ˈlaɪnzmən/ *n, pl* **-men** [C] : an official in a sport such as football, tennis, or hockey who decides if a ball, puck, or player has gone out of the proper playing area

line·up /ˈlaɪnˌʌp/ *n* [C] **1 a** : a list of the players who are playing in a game (such as baseball) **b** : the players on such a list ▪ *The team has a powerful lineup.* **2 a** : a group of people who are going to perform at an event • *the show's star-studded lineup (of performers)* **b** : a group of television programs that are shown one after another • *tonight's lineup of shows* **3** *US* : a line of people who stand next to each other while someone tries to identify one of them as the person who has committed a crime • *a police lineup*

lin·ger /ˈlɪŋgə/ *vb* [*I*] **1** : to stay somewhere beyond the usual or expected time • *They lingered over coffee after dinner.* **2 a** : to continue to exist as time passes • *The idea lingered in their minds.* • *His unhappiness lingered on.* **b** : to remain alive while becoming weaker • *He was very ill, but he lingered on for several more months.* — **lin·ger·er** /ˈlɪŋgərə/ *n* [*C*] — **lin·ger·ing** /ˈlɪŋgərɪŋ/ *adj* • *lingering doubts/questions*

lin·ge·rie /ˌlɑːndʒəˈreɪ, Brit ˈlænʒəri/ *n* [*U*] : women's underwear and clothing that is worn in bed

lin·go /ˈlɪŋgoʊ/ *n, pl* **-goes** *informal* **1** [*C*] : a language • *a foreign lingo* **2** [*C/U*] : the special language used for a particular activity or by a particular group of people • *The book has a lot of computer lingo that I don't understand.*

lin·guist /ˈlɪŋgwɪst/ *n* [*C*] **1** : a person who speaks several languages **2** : a person who studies linguistics

lin·guis·tic /lɪŋˈgwɪstɪk/ *adj* : of or relating to language or linguistics • *linguistic differences/development/theories* — **lin·guis·ti·cal·ly** /lɪŋˈgwɪstɪkli/ *adv*

lin·guis·tics /lɪŋˈgwɪstɪks/ *n* [*U*] : the study of language and of the way languages work

lin·i·ment /ˈlɪnəmənt/ *n* [*C/U*] : a liquid that is rubbed on your skin to relieve pain or stiffness in your muscles

lin·ing /ˈlaɪnɪŋ/ *n* [*C*] : material that covers the inner surface of something • *gloves with silk linings* • *brake linings*

¹link /ˈlɪŋk/ *vb* **1** [*T/I*] **a** : to join or connect (two or more things, places, etc.) together • *A bridge links the island to the mainland.* • *The pipe links (up) to/with the main gas line.* **b** : to connect (someone or something) to a system, network, etc. • *The computer is linked with/to the fax machine.* • *Hotel guests can link (up) to the Internet from their rooms.* **2 a** [*T*] : to show or prove that a person or thing is related to or involved with something • *The evidence links him to the crime.* ◆ A thing or person that *is linked to/with* something is connected or related to it in some way. • *High cholesterol is linked to an increased risk of heart attacks.* **3** [*T/I*] : to cause (different groups, countries, etc.) to be joined together • *The marriage of their children has linked the two families.* • *The companies linked (up) to form a multinational association.*

²link *n* [*C*] **1 a** : a relationship or connection between things • *Police have discovered a direct link between the two murders.* **b** : a relationship between people, groups, nations, etc. • *She felt a strong link with/to her ancestors.* **2 a** : something that allows movement from one place to another • *The bridge was the island's link to the mainland.* **b** : some-

thing that allows two or more people or things to communicate with each other • *a satellite/video link* **c** : HYPERLINK • *His Web site includes links to other sites.* **3** : a single part of a chain • *The chain broke at its weakest link.* • *(figurative) an important link in the chain of events* [=an important event in a series of related events] • *(figurative) It is the weak link* [=the least strong or successful part] *in the company's line of products.*

link·age /ˈlɪŋkɪdʒ/ *n* **1** [*C/U*] : a connection or relationship between two or more things • *linkages between population growth and disease* **2** [*C*] : a part that connects two or more things • *repairing a broken linkage*

linking verb *n* [*C*] *grammar* : a verb (such as *appear, be, become, feel, grow,* or *seem*) that connects a subject with an adjective or noun that describes or identifies the subject • *"Look" in "you look happy" is a linking verb.*

links /ˈlɪŋks/ *n, pl* **links** [*C*] : a golf course; *especially* : a golf course that is next to the ocean • *a seaside links*

li·no·leum /ləˈnoʊlijəm/ *n* [*U*] : a type of material that is produced in thin sheets, has a shiny surface, and is used to cover floors and counters

lin·seed oil /ˈlɪnˌsiːd-/ *n* [*U*] : a yellowish oil from the seeds of the flax plant that is used in paint, printing ink, etc.

lint /ˈlɪnt/ *n* [*U*] *chiefly US* : tiny pieces of cloth or another soft material • *The clothes dryer was clogged with lint.*

lin·tel /ˈlɪntl/ *n* [*C*] : a piece of wood or stone that lies across the top of a door or window and holds the weight of the structure above it

li·on /ˈlajən/ *n* [*C*] : a large wild cat that has golden brown fur and that lives mainly in Africa

li·on·ess /ˈlajənəs/ *n* [*C*] : a female lion

li·on·ize *also Brit* **li·on·ise** /ˈlajəˌnaɪz/ *vb* **-ized; -iz·ing** [*T*] : to treat (someone) as a very important and famous person • *She was lionized everywhere after her novel became a best seller.*

lion's share *n* [*U*] : the largest part of something • *She claimed the lion's share of the credit for the show's success.*

lip /ˈlɪp/ *n* **1** [*C*] : either one of the two soft parts that surround the mouth • *the lower/upper lip* • *She was nervously biting her lip.* • *She had a smile on her lips.* [=she was smiling] **2** [*C*] : the edge of a cut, hole, or container • *the lip of a crater/pitcher* **3** [*U*] *informal* : rude speech in reply to someone who should be spoken to with respect • *Don't give me any of your lip!* [=don't talk to me in that disrespectful way] — **lick your lips** see ¹LICK — **my lips are sealed** *informal* — used to say that you will not tell secret information to anyone • *Your secret is safe with me: my lips are sealed.* — **on everyone's/everybody's lips** *informal* : being said or discussed by many people • *The murder trial was on everyone's lips.* — **on the lips of** *informal* : being said or discussed by (people) • *a topic that is on the lips of many people* — **read lips** see

¹**READ** — **lipped** /ˈlɪpt/ *adj* • *a thin-lipped man* [=a man with thin lips]

li·po·suc·tion /ˈlaɪpəˌsʌkʃən/ *n* [U] : a kind of surgery that removes fat from a person's body

lip–read /ˈlɪpˌriːd/ *vb* **lip–read** /-ˌrɛd/; **-read·ing** /-ˌriːdɪŋ/ [T/I] : to understand what people are saying by watching the movement of their lips • *She can lip-read.* [=*read lips*] — **lip–read·er** /ˈlɪpˌriːdə/ *n* [C] — **lip–reading** *n* [U]

lip service *n* [U] : support for someone or something that is expressed by someone in words but that is not shown in that person's actions • *So far all we've gotten from him is lip service.*

lip·stick /ˈlɪpˌstɪk/ *n* [C/U] : a type of makeup that is spread on the lips and that comes in the form of a stick

lip–synch *or* **lip–sync** /ˈlɪpˌsɪŋk/ *vb* [T/I] : to pretend to sing or say (recorded words) • *It was obvious that he was lip-synching (the song).*

liq·ue·fy *also* **liq·ui·fy** /ˈlɪkwəˌfaɪ/ *vb* **-fies; -fied; -fy·ing** [T/I] : to become liquid or to cause (something) to become liquid • *The intense heat liquefied the plastic.*

li·queur /lɪˈkɚ, *Brit* lɪˈkjʊə/ *n* [C/U] : a sweet, strong alcoholic drink that is usually flavored with fruits or spices and drunk in small glasses after a meal

¹**liq·uid** /ˈlɪkwəd/ *n* [C/U] : a substance that is able to flow freely : FLUID • *Water and milk are liquids.*

²**liquid** *adj* **1** : capable of flowing freely like water • *Water and milk are liquid substances.* **2** *literary* **a** : shining and clear • *She had large liquid eyes.* **b** : clear, smooth, and pleasant in sound • *the liquid notes of a bird* **c** : having or showing a smooth and easy style • *the liquid grace of the dancer's movements* **3** *business* : made up of money or easily changed into money • *liquid assets/funds/investments* — **li·quid·i·ty** /lɪˈkwɪdəti/ *n* [U]

liq·ui·date /ˈlɪkwəˌdeɪt/ *vb* **-dat·ed; -dat·ing 1** *business* **a** [T/I] : to sell (a business, property, etc.) especially to pay off debt • *The company is liquidating its assets.* **b** [T] : to pay all the money owed for (a debt) • *liquidate a debt/loan* **2** [T] *informal* : to destroy (something) or kill (someone) • *He liquidated his enemies.* — **liq·ui·da·tion** /ˌlɪkwəˈdeɪʃən/ *n* [C/U]

liquid crystal display *n* [C] : LCD

liq·uid·iz·er /ˈlɪkwəˌdaɪzə/ *n* [C] *Brit* : BLENDER

liquify *variant spelling of* LIQUEFY

li·quor /ˈlɪkɚ/ *n* [C/U] : an alcoholic drink; *especially* : a strong alcoholic drink • *vodka, whiskey, and other liquors* • *a liquor bottle/store* • *He drinks beer and wine, but he doesn't drink any hard liquor.* — **hold your liquor** *informal* : to be able to drink alcoholic beverages without becoming too drunk • *He can't hold his liquor at all.*

liquorice *chiefly Brit spelling of* LICORICE

lisp /ˈlɪsp/ *n* [*singular*] : a speech problem that causes someone to pronounce the letters "s" and "z" like "th" — **lisp** *vb* [T/I] • *a child who lisps* — **lisp·er** *n* [C]

¹**list** /ˈlɪst/ *n* [C] : a series of names, words, numbers, etc., that are usually written down with each new one appearing below the previous one • *a long/short list of names* • *She made a list of the things she needed to buy.* • *I like all of his books, but this one is at the top of the list.* [=this is the best one]

²**list** *vb* **1** [T] : to make a list of (names, things, etc.) • *He listed the requirements for the job.* **2** [T] **a** : to include (something) in a list • *Her name is listed* [=*entered*] *in the directory.* **b** : to enter information about (someone or something) in a list • *The animal has been listed as endangered/threatened.* **3** [I] *US* : to have a specified list price • *The car lists at/for $30,000.* **4** [I] *of a ship* : to lean to one side • *The ship was listing to port/starboard.*

lis·ten /ˈlɪsn/ *vb* [I] **1 a** : to pay attention to someone or something in order to hear what is being said, sung, played, etc. • *She listened politely as he talked about his work.* • *listening to music* **b** — used to tell a person to listen to what you are saying • *Listen, no one is more concerned about this than I am.* **2** : to hear what someone has said and understand that it is serious, important, or true • *She tried to warn him, but he wouldn't listen (to her).* — **listen for** *or Brit* **listen out for** [*phrasal vb*] : to pay attention to sounds in order to hear (something expected) • *We listened for (the sound of) his footsteps.* — **listen in** [*phrasal vb*] : to·listen to a conversation without being part of it • *They let me listen in when the plans were presented.*; *especially* : to listen secretly to a private conversation • *He was listening in on our conversation.* — **listen up** [*phrasal vb*] *chiefly US, informal* : to listen closely to what is being said — usually used as a command • *Everybody listen up! I have something to say.* — **lis·ten·er** /ˈlɪsnə/ *n* [C] • *She's a good listener.* [=she is good at listening to other people and understanding what they are saying] • *a radio program that has many listeners*

list·ing /ˈlɪstɪŋ/ *n* [C] : a printed list • *a listing of local restaurants* • *movie/TV listings*

list·less /ˈlɪstləs/ *adj* : lacking energy or spirit • *Everyone was tired and listless.* • *a listless economy* — **list·less·ly** *adv* — **list·less·ness** *n* [C/U]

list price *n* [C] : the price of a product that is shown in a catalog, advertisement, etc.

¹**lit** /ˈlɪt/ *past tense and past participle of* ³LIGHT

²**lit** *n* [U] *informal* : LITERATURE • *taking a course in English lit*

lit·a·ny /ˈlɪtni/ *n, pl* **-nies** [C] **1** : a prayer in a Christian church service in which the people at the service respond to lines spoken by the person who is leading the service **2** : a long list of complaints, problems, etc. • *He has a litany of grievances against his former employer.*

li·ter (*US*) *or chiefly Brit* **li·tre** /ˈliːtə/ *n* [C]

: a metric unit for measuring the volume of a liquid or gas that is equal to 1.057 quarts

lit·er·a·cy /ˈlɪtərəsi/ n [U] **1** : the ability to read and write ▪ *literacy programs/skills/tests* **2** : knowledge that relates to a specified subject ▪ *computer literacy*

lit·er·al /ˈlɪtərəl/ adj **1** : involving the ordinary or usual meaning of a word ▪ *the word's literal sense/meaning* **2** : giving the meaning of each individual word ▪ *a literal translation of a book* **3** : completely true and accurate ▪ *The story he told was basically true, even if it wasn't the literal truth.*

lit·er·al·ly /ˈlɪtərəli/ adv **1** : in a literal way: such as **a** : in a way that uses the ordinary and usual meaning of a word ▪ *Many words can be used both literally and figuratively.* ▪ *He took her comments literally.* **b** — used to stress that a statement or description is true and accurate even though it may be surprising ▪ *There were literally hundreds of people involved.* **c** : with the meaning of each individual word given exactly ▪ *The term "Mardi Gras" literally means "Fat Tuesday" in French.* **d** : in a completely accurate way ▪ *The story he told was basically true, even if it wasn't literally true.* **2** informal — used in an exaggerated way to emphasize a statement or description that is not literally true or possible ▪ *Steam was literally coming out of his ears.* [=he was very angry]

lit·er·ary /ˈlɪtəˌreri, Brit ˈlɪtrəri/ adj **1** : of or relating to literature ▪ *a literary magazine* ▪ *literary criticism/theory* **b** : used in literature ▪ *a literary word/style/device* **2** always before a noun : having a lot of knowledge about literature ▪ *a literary man* **3** always before a noun : relating to the writing and publishing of literature ▪ *a literary agent*

lit·er·ate /ˈlɪtərət/ adj **1** : able to read and write ▪ *He was barely literate.* **2** : having or showing knowledge about a particular subject ▪ *The job requires you to be computer literate.* — **literate** n [C] ▪ *computer literates* [=people who know how to use computers]

li·te·ra·ti /ˌlɪtəˈrɑːˌti/ n — the literati : educated people who know about and are interested in literature

lit·er·a·ture /ˈlɪtərəʧɚ/ n **1** [C/U] : written works (such as poems, plays, and novels) that are considered to be very good and to have lasting importance ▪ *She took courses in history and literature.* ▪ *American/German literature* **2** [U] **a** : books, articles, etc., about a particular subject ▪ *medical/scientific literature* **b** : printed materials (such as booklets, leaflets, and brochures) that provide information about something ▪ *promotional/sales literature*

lithe /ˈlaɪð/ adj : moving in an easy and graceful way ▪ *a lithe athlete/dancer/body*

lit·i·gant /ˈlɪtɪgənt/ n [C] law : a person who is involved in a lawsuit

lit·i·gate /ˈlɪtəˌgeɪt/ vb **-gat·ed; -gat·ing** [T/I] law : to make (something) the subject of a lawsuit ▪ *litigating the dispute* — **lit·i·ga·tion** /ˌlɪtəˈgeɪʃən/ n [U] ▪ *The*

case is still in litigation. [=being decided in a court of law] — **lit·i·ga·tor** /ˈlɪtəˌgeɪtɚ/ n [C] ▪ *a famous/successful litigator* [=lawyer]

li·ti·gious /ləˈtɪʤəs/ adj, formal : too ready or eager to sue someone or something in a court of law ▪ *a very litigious group of people*

lit·mus paper /ˈlɪtməs-/ n [U] technical : special paper that is used to test how much acid is in a solution

litmus test n [C] : something (such as an opinion about a political or moral issue) that is used to make a judgment about whether someone or something is acceptable ▪ *The party is using attitudes about gun control as a litmus test for political candidates.*

litre chiefly Brit spelling of LITER

¹**lit·ter** /ˈlɪtɚ/ n **1** [U] : things that have been thrown away and that are lying on the ground in a public place ▪ *roadside litter* **2** [U] : dry material that is spread in a container and used as a toilet by animals (especially cats) while they are indoors ▪ *cat/kitty litter* **3** [C] : a group of young animals that are born at a single time ▪ *a litter of puppies/piglets* ▪ (figurative) *Of all the cars on the market, this one is clearly the pick of the litter.* [=the best one]

²**litter** vb **1** [T] : to cover (a surface) with many things in an untidy way ▪ *Paper and popcorn littered the streets after the parade.* ▪ *a desk littered with old letters and bills* ▪ (figurative) *The book is littered with errors.* [=the book contains many errors] **2** [I] : to throw or leave trash on the ground in a public place ▪ *It is illegal to litter.* — **lit·ter·er** /ˈlɪtərɚ/ n [C]

litter bin n [C] Brit : TRASH CAN

lit·ter·bug /ˈlɪtɚˌbʌg/ n [C] informal : a person who throws or leaves trash in a public place — called also (Brit) litter lout

¹**lit·tle** /ˈlɪtl/ adj less /ˈlɛs/ or less·er /ˈlɛsɚ/ also lit·tler /ˈlɪtlɚ/; least /ˈliːst/ also lit·tlest /ˈlɪtləst/ **1 a** : small in size ▪ *a little cat/house/room/window* ▪ *a tiny little fish* **b** : not tall : SHORT ▪ *a little man* **c** : small in amount ▪ *I got very little sleep last night.* ▪ *There has been little if any improvement.* [=there has been almost no improvement] ▪ *These items have little or no value.* **d** : not having many things or people included ▪ *We're having a little party this weekend.* **2** : young or younger ▪ *a little boy/girl* ▪ *my little brother/sister* [=my brother/sister who is younger than I am] **3** : not lasting for a long time ▪ *We talked for a little while.* **4** : not very important ▪ *a few little problems* **5** : not easily seen, heard, etc. ▪ *He gave her a little smile.* — **lit·tle·ness** /ˈlɪtlnəs/ n [U]

²**little** adv less; least **1 a** : in a very small amount or degree ▪ *She works very little and sleeps even less.* **b** : not very much ▪ *She cared little (about) what he thought.* ▪ *a little-known fact* ▪ *Little did she know* [=she did not know] *what fate had in store for her.* **2** : not very often ▪ *She travels little.* — **little by little** : by small steps or amounts : GRADUALLY ▪ *Little by little,*

he got better. ▪ *I got to know them little by little.* — **little more than** or **little better than** : not much more or better than (something) ▪ *They ate little more than ice cream and hot dogs all day.*

³**little** *pron* : a small amount or quantity ▪ *There is little we can do to help.* ▪ *I understood little of what was going on.* — **a little** **1** : not much but some ▪ *I like a little cream in my coffee.* ▪ *I have a little money left.* ▪ *They brought him a little something.* [=they brought him something] ▪ *I was more than a little upset.* [=I was very upset] **2** : not much but somewhat or slightly ▪ *I'm feeling a little better today.* ▪ *Her behavior was more than a little upsetting.* [=was very upsetting] **3** : for a brief time ▪ *We can walk a little and then catch a cab.* **4** : a small amount or quantity ▪ *They don't understand much but they do understand a little.* — **a little bit** **1** : to some extent ▪ SOMEWHAT ▪ *It bothered me a little bit.* **2** *chiefly US* : a short time ▪ *We talked for a little bit.* **3** : a small amount of something ▪ *The buffet had a little bit of everything.*

little finger *n* [*C*] : the finger that is farthest from your thumb — called also (*chiefly US + Scotland*) *pinkie*

Little League *n* [*singular*] *US* : a baseball league for boys and girls from 8 to 12 years old — **Little Leagu·er** [*C*]

little toe *n* [*C*] : the smallest toe on the outside of your foot

lit·ur·gy /ˈlɪtədʒi/ *n, pl* **-gies** [*C/U*] : a fixed set of ceremonies, words, etc., that are used during public worship in a religion ▪ *studying Christian liturgy* — **li·tur·gi·cal** /ləˈtədʒɪkəl/ *adj*

liv·able or *chiefly Brit* **live·able** /ˈlɪvəbəl/ *adj* **1** : suitable or enjoyable to live in ▪ *a livable city* ▪ *The house was barely livable.* **2** *US* : making it possible to live or to have the things that people need to live properly ▪ *livable conditions/wages*

¹**live** /ˈlɪv/ *vb* **lived; liv·ing** **1** [*I*] **a** : to be alive ▪ *the people who lived during colonial times* **b** : to continue to be alive ▪ *He lived to the age of 92.* ▪ *I'll remember that day for as long as I live.* **2** [*I*] **a** : to have a home in a specified place ▪ *He lives next door.* ▪ *We live in the city/suburbs/country.* **b** *of a plant or animal* : to grow naturally in a specified place or area ▪ *the plants and animals that live in this area* **3** [*T/I*] : to spend your life in a certain way or condition ▪ *They live well/simply/dangerously/peacefully.* ▪ *They are living a dream.* [=they are doing what they dreamed of doing] ▪ *They lived happily ever after.* [=they lived happily for the rest of their lives] **4** [*I*] : to have an enjoyable and exciting life ▪ *Now that he's retired he just wants to live a little.* [=to spend time doing enjoyable things] ▪ *You haven't lived until you've had a piece of my mom's apple pie!* [=you would greatly enjoy my mom's apple pie] **5** [*T*] **a** : to spend (your life or part of your life) in a specified way ▪ *She lived her final years in seclusion.* **b** : to have (a particular kind of life) ▪ *They live a normal life.* **6** [*I*] : to continue to exist ▪ *That day will always live in my memory.* [=I will always re-

member that day] — **live a lie** see ²LIE — **live and breathe** see BREATHE — **live and let live** : to let others live the way they want to ▪ *His philosophy was to live and let live.* — **live by** [*phrasal vb*] **1** : to agree with and follow (something, such as a set of beliefs) ▪ *a principle I try to live by* **2 a** : to survive by (doing something) ▪ *They were an ancient people who lived by hunting and gathering.* **b** : to survive by doing ▪ **live by your wits** : to survive by doing clever and sometimes dishonest things ▪ *a young thief who lives by her wits* — **live down** [*phrasal vb*] **live down (something)** or **(live (something) down** : to stop being blamed or laughed at for (something, such as a foolish or embarrassing error) ▪ *I can't believe I forgot my wife's birthday! I'll never live this down.* — **live for** [*phrasal vb*] **1** : to wait or hope for (something) very eagerly ▪ *I live for the day when we'll be together!* **2** : to think of (something) as the most important or enjoyable part of your life ▪ *She lives for her work.* : to think of (something) as a reason for being alive ▪ *He feels as if he has nothing left to live for.* — **live in** [*phrasal vb*] *chiefly Brit* : to live in the place where you work ▪ *a maid who lives in* — **live in hope** see ²HOPE — **live in sin** *old-fashioned* : to live together and have sex without being married ▪ *living in sin with his girlfriend* — **live in the past** : to think too much about something that happened in the past ▪ *You have to stop living in the past.* — **live it up** *informal* : to do exciting and enjoyable things ▪ *He's been living it up with his friends.* — **live off** [*phrasal vb*] : to use (someone or something) as a source of the money or other things you need to live ▪ *He has been living off his inheritance/girlfriend.* — **live on** [*phrasal vb*] **1** : to continue to exist ▪ *His legend lives on.* **2 a** : to have or use (an amount of money) to pay for the things that you need to live ▪ *You can't live on this salary.* **b** : to have (a particular food) as the only or main food that you eat ▪ *They lived mainly/mostly on fruits and berries.* — **live out** [*phrasal vb*] **1** *Brit* : to live away from the place where you work ▪ *a servant who lives out* **2 live out (something)** or **(live (something) out** **a** : to spend the rest of (your life) in a specified way ▪ *He lived out (the final years of) his life in quiet retirement.* **b** : to do (the things you have dreamed of doing) ▪ *a chance to live out his dreams/fantasies* — **live through** [*phrasal vb*] **1** : to survive (an experience, a troubling time, etc.) ▪ *If I can live through this, I can live through anything.* **2** *US, sometimes disapproving* : to enjoy the experiences and achievements of (another person) instead of your own experiences and achievements ▪ *She can't live through her daughter.* — **live together** [*phrasal vb*] : to live with another person and have sex without being married ▪ *They lived together before getting married.* — **live up to** [*phrasal vb*] **1** : to do what is required by (something) ▪ *She lived up to her promises.* [=she kept her promises] **2** : to be good enough for (something) ▪

Our vacation didn't live up to our expectations. [=wasn't as good as we expected it to be] — **live with** [*phrasal vb*] **1 :** to accept and deal with (something unpleasant) • *I don't agree with his decision, but I'll have to live with it.* **2 :** to live together and usually have sex with (someone) • *She's been living with him since college.*

²**live** /'laɪv/ *adj* **1 a** *always before a noun* **:** living or alive • *live animals* • *a live birth* [=a birth of a living child or animal] **b** *informal* **:** not imaginary — used in the phrase *real live* • *a real live celebrity* [=an actual celebrity] **2 a :** of or involving a play, concert, etc., that is performed in front of people • *live music/entertainment* • *a live album* [=an album made by recording a performance before an audience] **b :** watching a performance as it happens • *a live (studio) audience* **c :** broadcast while a performance, event, etc., is happening • *a live television/radio program* **3 :** carrying an electric current • *live electrical wires* • *a live microphone* **4 :** carrying a charge and capable of exploding or being shot • *live ammunition/bullets* **5 :** not yet decided or settled • *a live controversy/issue* **6** *US, sports* **:** still in play • *The ball is live until it goes out of bounds.*

³**live** /'laɪv/ *adv* **:** during, from, or at the actual time that something (such as a performance or event) happens • *The program was shown live.* • *We are broadcasting live from downtown.* — **go live :** to begin operating or to become available for use • *Our new Web site will be going live next month.*

liveable *chiefly Brit spelling of* LIVABLE

live–in /'lɪv,ɪn/ *adj, always before a noun* **1 :** living in the place where you work • *a live-in maid* [=a maid who lives in the house where she works] **2 :** living with someone else (especially a boyfriend or girlfriend) • *her live-in boyfriend*

live·li·hood /'laɪvli,hʊd/ *n* [*C/U*] **:** a way of earning money in order to live • *Many fishermen believe that the new regulations threaten their livelihood(s).*

live·ly /'laɪvli/ *adj* **live·li·er; -est ;** very active and energetic • *lively children/puppies* • *She has a lively imagination.* [=she imagines many things] **2 :** full of energy, excitement, or feeling • *a very lively writing style* • *She takes a lively interest in politics.* [=she is very interested in politics] **3 :** full of movement or activity • *lively streets* • *a lively dance/atmosphere* — **live·li·ness** *n* [*U, singular*]

liv·en /'laɪvən/ *vb* **1** [*T*] **:** to make (something) more lively, interesting, or exciting • *He played some music to liven the atmosphere.* • *She tried to liven up her speech with a few jokes.* **2** [*I*] **:** to become more lively, interesting, or exciting • *The party really livened up after she arrived.*

liv·er /'lɪvə/ *n* **1** [*C*] **:** a large organ of the body that produces bile and cleans the blood **2** [*C/U*] **:** the liver of an animal that is eaten as food • *We had liver and onions for dinner.*

liv·er·wurst /'lɪvə,wəst/ *n* [*U*] *chiefly US* **:** a type of soft sausage made chiefly of cooked liver

liv·ery /'lɪvəri/ *n, pl* **-eries 1** [*U*] **:** the business of keeping vehicles that people can hire • *livery service* **2** [*C/U*] *Brit* **:** the colors or designs that are used on a company's products, vehicles, etc. • *cars with similar livery/liveries* **3** [*C/U*] **:** a special uniform worn by servants especially in the past

lives *plural of* LIFE

live·stock /'laɪv,stɑːk/ *n* [*U, plural*] **:** farm animals (such as cows, horses, and pigs) that are kept, raised, and used by people • *a market where livestock is/are bought and sold*

live wire *n* [*C*] *informal* **:** a very lively and energetic person

liv·id /'lɪvɪd/ *adj* **1 :** very angry • *He was livid (with rage) when I came home late.* **2** *literary* **:** having a dark purplish color • *a livid bruise*

¹**liv·ing** /'lɪvɪŋ/ *adj* **1 :** not dead • *living beings/creatures/animals/plants/things* **2** *always before a noun* **:** currently active or being used • *a living faith/culture* • *a living language* [=a language that is still being used and spoken by people] **3** *always before a noun* **:** having the form of a person who is alive • *I'm living proof that success is possible.* [=my success shows that other people can succeed as well] **4** *always before a noun* **:** of or relating to the place, conditions, or manner in which people live • *They have an unusual living arrangement; they work in different cities and only see each other on weekends.* • *Their yard is an outdoor living area.* • *a home with more living space* • *children in terrible living conditions* • *He gave me a tour of his living quarters.* [=the rooms where he lives] **5** *informal* — used to emphasize a noun • *You scared the living daylights out of me!* — **in living color :** in the bright colors of real life • *a television program shown in living color* — **in/within living memory :** during a time that can be remembered by people who are still alive • *These events occurred within living memory.*

²**living** *n* **1** [*C*] **:** a way of earning money • *His investments provide him with a good living.* • *What do you do for a living?* [=what is your job?] • *He earned a/his living as a cook.* = *He made a living by working as a cook.* **2** [*U*] **:** a way of living • *city/outdoor/healthy living* — **the living :** people who are alive • *the living and the dead*

living room *n* [*C*] **:** a room in a house for general family use

living standard *n* [*C*] **:** STANDARD OF LIVING

liz·ard /'lɪzəd/ *n* [*C*] **:** a type of reptile that has four legs and a long body and tail

'll — used as a contraction of *will* • *That'll be enough.*

lla·ma /'lɑːmə/ *n* [*C*] **:** a South American animal that has a long neck and thick fur and that is used for its wool and for carrying things

lo /'loʊ/ *interj, old-fashioned + literary* —

used to call attention to something or to show wonder or surprise • *Lo, the king approaches!* — **lo and behold** — used to express wonder or surprise; often used in a humorous or ironic way • *We opened the door, and lo and behold, the delivery man had arrived.*

¹**load** /'loʊd/ n [C] **1 a** : something that is lifted and carried • *carrying a heavy/light load* **b** : an amount that can be carried at one time • *a load of firewood/sand* • *a load of laundry* [=the amount of laundry that can fit into a washing machine] — often used in combination • *an armload of firewood* • *a truckload of sand* **2** *somewhat technical* : the weight that is carried or supported by something • *Losing weight will lessen the load on your knees.* **3** : something that causes worry or sadness • *His death is a heavy load to bear.* • *The good news has taken a load off my mind.* [=has allowed me to stop worrying] **4** *informal* **a** : a large amount of something • *a load of trouble* • *We had loads of fun.* **b** — used in phrases like *a load of garbage, a load of trash,* etc., to say that something is worthless • *I think his idea is a load of garbage!* **5 a** : the amount of work done or expected to be done • *She's taking a full/heavy course load this semester.* **b** *technical* : the amount of work done by a machine • *the load on an engine* **c** *technical* : the amount of power used by an electrical device or produced by a power source — **get a load of** *informal* : to look at (someone or something) • *Get a load of that car!* — **take a load off (your feet)** *chiefly US, informal* : to sit down and relax • *You look tired. Come in and take a load off.*

²**load** vb **1 a** [T/I] : to put an amount of something in or on (something) • *We loaded (up) the car and drove off.* • *We loaded up and drove off.* **b** [T] : to put (an amount of something) into or onto something • *load packages on/onto a truck* **c** [T] : to supply (someone or something) *with* a large amount of something • *Mom loaded me (up) with supplies for the hike.* **2** [T/I] : to put something necessary into a machine or device so that it can be used • *load a camera with film* • *load film into a camera* • *The film didn't load properly.* **3 a** [T] *of a boat, vehicle, etc.* : to be boarded by (passengers) • *The bus stopped to load more passengers.* **b** [I] : to go onto something (such as a boat or vehicle) • *Passengers loaded on/onto the bus.* **4** [T/I] *computers* : to cause (a program, file, etc.) to begin being used or displayed by a computer • *load a new Web page* • *The program loads quickly.* **5** [T] *baseball* : to put runners on (first, second, and third base) • *The bases are loaded.* — **load down with** [phrasal vb] **load (someone or something) down with** : to cause or force (someone or something) to accept or deal with (something difficult) • *They are loaded down with debt.* [=have a lot of debt] — **load up on** [phrasal vb] *informal* **1** : to drink or eat a large amount of (something) • *people loading up on fat-*

ty foods **2** : to get a large amount of (something) • *Investors were loading up on hot stocks.* — **load·er** n [C]

load·ed /'loʊdəd/ adj **1** *not before a noun, informal* : very rich • *His parents are loaded.* **2 a** *of a gun* : having bullets inside • *a loaded rifle/pistol* **b** *of a camera* : having film inside • *Is this camera loaded?* **3** — used to describe dice that can be used for cheating because they have weights inside so that particular numbers always result when the dice are thrown • *a pair of loaded dice* **4** : capable of causing harm or trouble because of a hidden or extra meaning • *a loaded term/expression/question* **5** *chiefly US, informal* : having a good amount of what is needed or wanted • *a fully loaded car* [=a car that has many extra features] **6** *chiefly US slang* : very drunk • *He went to a bar and got loaded.* — **loaded with** : having or carrying a large amount of (something) • *Her arms were loaded with books.*

loading dock n [C] *chiefly US* : an area at the side of a building where goods are loaded onto and unloaded from vehicles — called also (*chiefly Brit*) **loading bay**

¹**loaf** /'loʊf/ n, pl **loaves** /'loʊvz/ [C] : an amount of bread that has been baked in a long, round, or square shape • *a loaf of bread* — see also MEAT LOAF

²**loaf** vb [I] : to spend time relaxing instead of working • *I spent most of the weekend just loafing around the house.*

loaf·er /'loʊfə/ n [C] **1** : a low shoe with no laces • *a pair of loafers* **2** : a person who does not work hard • *a lazy loafer*

loam /'loʊm/ n [U] : a type of soil that is good for growing plants — **loamy** /'loʊmi/ adj **loam·i·er; -est** • *loamy soil*

¹**loan** /'loʊn/ n **1** [C] : an amount of money that is borrowed • *He took out a loan (from the bank) to pay for the car.* • *She asked her friend for a loan.* **2** [U] *somewhat formal* : permission to use something for a period of time • *Can I have the loan of your car?* [=can I borrow your car?] — **on loan** : borrowed from someone or something for a period of time • *This painting is on loan from the National Gallery.*

²**loan** vb [T] **1** : to give (something) to (someone) for a period of time : LEND • *He loaned his car to me.* • *He loaned me his car.* [=I borrowed his car] **2** *chiefly US* : to give (money) to (someone) who agrees to pay it back in the future : LEND • *Can you loan me $20?*

loan·er /'loʊnə/ n [C] *US* : something (such as a car) that is loaned to someone as a replacement for something that is being repaired

loan shark n [C] *disapproving* : someone who lends money to people and charges a very high rate of interest — **loan-shark·ing** /'loʊnˌʃɑːkɪŋ/ n [U]

loath /'loʊθ/ also **loathe** /'loʊð/ or **loth** /'loʊθ/ adj : not wanting or willing to do something • *She was loath to admit her mistakes.*

loathe /'loʊð/ vb **loathed; loath·ing** [T] : to hate (someone or something) very much • *She loathed him.*

loathing n [U] : a very strong feeling of hatred or disgust ▪ *She regarded them with loathing.*

loath·some /'loʊθsəm/ adj : causing feelings of hatred or disgust ▪ *loathsome behavior*

loaves plural of ¹LOAF

lob /'lɑːb/ vb **lobbed; lob·bing** [T] : to hit, throw, or kick (something, such as a ball) so that it goes through the air in a high curving path ▪ *He lobbed the ball over his opponent's head.* — **lob** n [C] ▪ *He hit a lob over my head.*

¹**lob·by** /'lɑːbi/ n, pl **-bies** [C] **1** : a large open area inside and near the entrance of a public building (such as a hotel or theater) ▪ *a hotel lobby* **2** : an organized group of people who work together to influence government decisions that relate to a particular industry, issue, etc. ▪ *the gun/tobacco/oil lobby*

²**lobby** vb **-bies; -bied; -by·ing** [T/I] **1** : to try to influence government officials to make decisions for or against something ▪ *an organization that has been lobbying (Congress) for reform* **2** : to try to get something you want by talking to the people who make decisions ▪ *She lobbyied (her boss) for a raise.* — **lob·by·ist** /'lɑːbiɪst/ n [C]

lobe /'loʊb/ n [C] **1** : a curved or rounded part of something (such as a leaf or a part of the body) ▪ *the frontal lobe of the brain* **2** : EARLOBE

lo·bot·o·my /loʊ'bɑːtəmi/ n, pl **-mies** [C] medical : an operation in which part of the brain is cut in order to treat some mental disorders

¹**lob·ster** /'lɑːbstər/ n **1** [C] : an ocean animal that has a long body, a hard shell, and a pair of large claws and that is caught for food **2** [U] : the meat of the lobster eaten as food

¹**lo·cal** /'loʊkəl/ adj **1 a** : relating to or occurring in a particular area, city, or town ▪ *local news* ▪ *a local custom/newspaper/road* **b** : located or living nearby ▪ *a local man/restaurant* **2** of a bus or train : making all the stops on a route ▪ *She took the local bus.* **3** : involving or affecting only a small area of the body ▪ *a local infection* ▪ *local anesthesia* — **lo·cal·ly** adv

²**local** n [C] **1** : a person who lives in a particular area, city, or town ▪ *The restaurant is popular with (the) locals.* **2** : a train or bus that makes all of the stops along its route **3** US : a local part of a labor union ▪ *He's the president of the union local at the factory.* **4** Brit, informal : a pub that is near the place where you live

local color (US) or Brit **local colour** n [U] : interesting information about a particular place and about the people who live there that is included in a story, movie, etc.

lo·cale /loʊ'kæl, Brit ləʊ'kɑːl/ n [C] : the place where something happens ▪ *They chose a tropical island as the locale for their wedding.* ▪ *a movie's/story's locale*

lo·cal·i·ty /loʊ'kæləti/ n, pl **-ties** [C] : a particular place or area ▪ *The plant has only been found in one locality.*

lo·cal·ize also Brit **lo·cal·ise** /'loʊkə-,laɪz/ vb **-ized; -iz·ing** [T] **1** : to keep (something) within a limited area ▪ *Doctors are trying to localize the infection.* **2** : to find or identify the location of (something) ▪ *They were able to localize the fault quickly.*

localized also Brit **localised** adj : occurring only within a small area ▪ *localized flooding* ▪ *a localized infection*

lo·cate /'loʊˌkeɪt, loʊˈkeɪt/ vb **-cat·ed; -cat·ing 1** [T] : to find the place or position of (something or someone) ▪ *Can you locate your town on the map?* ▪ *The missing boy was located by police in the woods.* **2 a** [T] : to put (something or someone) in a particular place ▪ *The company chose to locate its factory near the airport.* **b** [I] US : to make an area, city, etc., your home or the place where your business operates ▪ *The company located near the airport.* **c** ◇ Something or someone that *is located* in a specified place is in or at that place. ▪ *The factory is located near the airport.*

lo·ca·tion /loʊˈkeɪʃən/ n **1** [C] : a place or position ▪ *This is a lovely location for a house.* **2** [C/U] : a place outside a studio where a movie is filmed ▪ *movies filmed in exotic locations* ▪ *The movie was filmed on location in the desert.* **3** [U] : the act of finding where something or someone is ▪ *Fog made location of the harbor difficult.*

loch /'lɑːk/ n [C] Scotland : a lake or a part of the sea that is almost surrounded by land — used in names ▪ *Loch Ness*

¹**lock** /'lɑːk/ n **1** [C] : a device that keeps something (such as a door, window, or box) from being opened and that is usually opened by using a key **2** [C] : an area in a canal or river that has gates at each end which are opened and closed to control the level of the water in different sections of the canal or river as boats move through it **3** [C] : a method of holding someone so that the person being held cannot move ▪ *a leg lock* **4** US, informal **a** [singular] : complete control of something ▪ *He appears to have a lock on the nomination.* [=he appears to be sure of getting the nomination] ▪ *He was able to get a lock on the nomination.* **b** [C] : someone or something that is certain to have or do something ▪ *The team is a lock to win the championship.* **c** [C] : something that is certain to happen ▪ *It looks like his nomination is a lock.* **5 a** [C] : a small bunch of hair **b** [plural] literary + humorous : a person's hair ▪ *her long, flowing locks* ▪ *golden locks* — **lock, stock, and barrel** : including everything ▪ *He gave us control of the business, lock, stock, and barrel.* — **under lock and key** : in a room, box, etc., that is locked ▪ *The jewels are kept under lock and key.*

²**lock** vb **1 a** [T] : to fasten (something) with a lock ▪ *They locked the door.* ▪ *The door was locked.* **b** [T] : to fasten the door, lid, etc., of (something) with a lock ▪ *He locked the car.* **c** [I] : to become fastened with a lock ▪ *The door locked behind him.* **2 a** [I] : to become fixed in

one position • *The wheels/brakes locked and the car skidded off the road.* • *Their eyes locked.* [=they looked directly at each other without looking away] **b** [*T*] : to hold (someone or something) in a fixed position • *They were locked in each other's arms.* • *His eyes were locked on her.* [=he was looking at her and at nothing else] • *(figurative)* *They were locked in a contract dispute.* **3** [*T*] *computers* : to make (a file, database, etc.) impossible for others to open or change • *The file is locked for editing.* — **lock away** [*phrasal vb*] **lock (something or someone) away** or **lock away (something or someone)** **1** : to put (something) in a locked container, place, etc. • *The jewelry was locked away in a cabinet.* **2** : to put (someone) in a locked place (such as a prison) for a long period of time • *The state locked her away in a psychiatric hospital.* **3** *lock (yourself) away* : to stay in a room or place by yourself for a long period of time • *He locked himself away in his room while he studied.* = *He was locked away in his room while he studied.* — **lock horns** : to fight or argue • *They've locked horns (with each other) many times.* — **lock in** [*phrasal vb*] **1** *lock (someone or something) in* : to put or keep (someone or something) in a locked place, room, etc. • *She locked herself in the bathroom.* **2** *lock (something) in or lock in (something)* : to do something that makes you sure to get (something that could change, such as a good price, an interest rate, etc.) • *If you sign the contract today, you can lock in this low interest rate before it goes any higher.* — **lock on/onto** [*phrasal vb*] : to use electronic methods to find (a target) • *The missile locked on the target.* — **lock out** [*phrasal vb*] **lock (someone or something) out or lock out (someone)** **1** : to prevent (someone) from entering a place, car, etc., by locking it • *I locked myself out (of the house) accidentally.* **2** : to prevent (workers) from going to work in order to force an agreement • *The company threatened to lock out its factory workers unless they agree to a new contract.* — **lock up** [*phrasal vb*] **1** : to lock all of the doors of a building before leaving it • *Don't forget to lock up.* **2** *lock (something or someone) up or lock up (something or someone)* **a** : to put (something) in a locked container, room, etc. • *The money is locked up in a safe.* • *(figurative)* *Most of his money is locked up in real estate.* [=most of his money is not easily available because it is invested in real estate] **b** : to put (someone) in a locked place (such as a prison) for a long period of time • *The police should lock him up.* **c** *chiefly US* : to make control or achievement of (something) certain • *The team has first place locked up.* [=the team is certain of getting first place]

lock·er /ˈlɑːkɚ/ *n* [*C*] **1** : a cupboard or cabinet that has a door which can be locked and that is used to store personal items (such as books, clothes, shoes, etc.) **2** *US* : a cold room in which fresh or frozen foods are stored • *a meat locker*

locker room *n* [*C*] : a room in a school, sports stadium, etc., for changing clothes and for storing clothes and equipment in lockers

lock·et /ˈlɑːkət/ *n* [*C*] : a small case that is usually worn on a chain around a person's neck

lock·jaw /ˈlɑːkˌdʒɑː/ *n* [*U*] *informal* : TETANUS

lock·out /ˈlɑːkˌaʊt/ *n* [*C*] : a situation in which an employer tries to force workers to accept certain conditions by refusing to let them come to work until those conditions are accepted

lock·smith /ˈlɑːkˌsmɪθ/ *n* [*C*] : a person whose job is to make and repair locks

lock·step /ˈlɑːkˌstɛp/ *n* [*U*] : a way of marching in which people follow each other very closely — **in lockstep** *chiefly US* : in a way that very closely matches someone or something else • *He refused to march in lockstep with* [=to conform with] *others in the party.*

lock·up /ˈlɑːkˌʌp/ *n* [*C*] **1** : JAIL • *a police station lockup* **2** *Brit* : a garage (sense 1) that is rented out — called also *lockup garage*

lo·co·mo·tion /ˌloʊkəˈmoʊʃən/ *n* [*U*] *technical* : the act or power of moving from place to place • *Walking is a form of locomotion.*

¹lo·co·mo·tive /ˌloʊkəˈmoʊtɪv/ *n* [*C*] : the vehicle that pulls a train

²locomotive *adj, technical* : of or relating to locomotion • *locomotive power*

lo·cust /ˈloʊkəst/ *n* [*C*] : a type of grasshopper that can cause great destruction by eating crops • *a swarm of locusts*

lode /ˈloʊd/ *n* [*C*] : an amount of a mineral (such as gold or silver) that fills a space in rock — see also MOTHER LODE

¹lodge /ˈlɑːdʒ/ *vb* **lodged; lodg·ing** **1 a** [*T*] : to provide (someone) with a place to stay for a short period of time • *The workers were lodged in camps.* **b** [*I*] : to stay at a place for a short period of time • *We lodged at the resort.* **2** [*T/I*] : to become stuck or fixed in a specified place or position • *The bullet lodged (itself) in his brain.* • *A bone got/became lodged in her throat.* **3** [*T*] : to present (something) to someone so that it can be considered, dealt with, etc. • *lodge a complaint/grievance (against someone)*

²lodge *n* [*C*] **1** : a house or hotel for people who are doing some outdoor activity • *a hunting/ski lodge* **2** : the place where a beaver lives **3** : a local group that is part of a larger organization • *a Masonic lodge; also* : a meeting place for such a group **4** *chiefly Brit* : a small house, room, or shelter used by a worker • *the gamekeeper's/janitor's/porter's lodge*

lodg·er /ˈlɑːdʒɚ/ *n* [*C*] : a person who rents a room in another person's house

lodg·ing *n* [*C/U*] : a place where a person (such as a traveler) can sleep • *find inexpensive lodging(s)* • *(Brit) working for board and lodging* [=(US) room and board]

¹loft /ˈlɑːft/ *n* [*C*] **1** : a room or space that is just below the roof of a building • *a bedroom with a loft* **2** : a high section of seats in a church or hall • *the choir loft* **3** *chiefly US* : an upper floor of a warehouse or business building especially when it is not divided by walls ▪ *He lives in a converted loft.*

²loft /ˈlɑːft/ *vb* [T] : to hit or throw (something) so that it rises high in the air ▪ *He lofted a home run into the stands.*

lofty /ˈlɑːfti/ *adj* **loft·i·er; -est** **1** *literary* : very tall and impressive ▪ *lofty redwood trees* **2** : very high and good ▪ *lofty goals/ideals/standards* **3** : showing the insulting attitude of people who think that they are better than other people ▪ *She showed a lofty disregard for their objections.* — **loft·i·ly** /ˈlɑːftəli/ *adv* ▪ *loftily dismissed their objections*

¹log /ˈlɑːg/ *n* [C] **1 a** : a long, heavy section of a tree that has fallen or been cut down ▪ *a log cabin* **b** : a thick piece of wood ▪ *Throw another log on the fire.* **2** : a record of performance, activities, etc. ▪ *the captain's/pilot's log* [=record of travel] ▪ *a computer/repair log* — **sleep like a log** see **¹SLEEP**

²log *vb* **logged; log·ging** **1** [T/I] : to cut down trees in an area for wood ▪ *a company that logs (trees) in this area* **2** [T] : to make an official record of (something) ▪ *logging deliveries/calls* **3** [T] **a** : to do something for (a specified distance or time) ▪ *She logs hundreds of miles/hours of driving every month.* **b** *chiefly US* : to succeed in achieving (a record of something) ▪ *He has logged more than a hundred wins.* — **log off/out** [*phrasal vb*] *computers* : to end the connection of a computer to a network or system ▪ *Log off when you're finished.* — **log on/in** [*phrasal vb*] *computers* : to start the connection of a computer to a network or system ▪ *I logged on (to the Internet).* — **log·ger** /ˈlɑːgɚ/ *n* [C] ▪ *trees felled by loggers*

log·a·rithm /ˈlɑːgəˌrɪðəm/ *n* [C] *mathematics* : a number that shows how many times a base number (such as ten) is multiplied by itself to produce a third number (such as 100) — **log·a·rith·mic** /ˌlɑːgəˈrɪðmɪk/ *adj*

log·book /ˈlɑːgˌbʊk/ *n* [C] : ¹LOG 2 ▪ *a pilot's logbook*

log·ger·heads /ˈlɑːgɚˌhɛdz/ *n* — **at loggerheads** : in a state of strong disagreement ▪ *The two nations are at loggerheads (with each other).*

log·ic /ˈlɑːdʒɪk/ *n* **1 a** [U, *singular*] : a proper or reasonable way of thinking about something ▪ *the rules of logic* ▪ *There's some/no logic to/in what he says.* ▪ *Her decision defies logic.* = *Her decision is against all logic.* [=is not logical] **b** [U] : a particular way of thinking about something ▪ *the logic behind/of your reasoning* ▪ *faulty logic* **2** [U] : the science that studies the formal processes used in thinking and reasoning — **lo·gi·cian** /loʊˈdʒɪʃən/ *n* [C] ▪ *a trained logician*

log·i·cal /ˈlɑːdʒɪkəl/ *adj* **1** : sensible or reasonable ▪ *a logical argument/conclusion/explanation* ▪ *He is a logical choice for the job.* ▪ *a logical thinker* **2** : of or relating to the formal processes used in thinking and reasoning ▪ *logical principles* — **log·i·cal·ly** /ˈlɑːdʒɪkli/ *adv*

lo·gis·tics /loʊˈdʒɪstɪks/ *n* [*plural*] : the

things that must be done to plan and organize a complicated activity or event that involves many people ▪ *the logistics of (planning) the trip* ▪ *Logistics is/are the key to a successful campaign.* — **lo·gis·tic** /loʊˈdʒɪstɪk/ *or* **lo·gis·ti·cal** /loʊˈdʒɪstɪkəl/ *adj*

log·jam /ˈlɑːgˌdʒæm/ *n* [C] **1** : a situation in which many logs floating down a river become tangled and stop moving **2** : a situation in which no progress seems possible ▪ *trying to break the logjam in the negotiations*

logo /ˈloʊgoʊ/ *n, pl* **log·os** [C] : a symbol that is used to identify a company ▪ *corporate logos*

loin /ˈloɪn/ *n* **1 a** [C] : an area on the back of an animal's body near the tail **b** [C/U] : meat from this area ▪ *pork loin* **2** [*plural*] : the area of a person's body that includes the sexual organs ▪ *There was a towel wrapped around his loins.* ▪ *(figurative) They girded (up) their loins* [=prepared] *for a long court battle.*

loin·cloth /ˈloɪnˌklɑːθ/ *n* [C] : a piece of cloth worn to cover the sexual organs especially by men in very hot parts of the world

loi·ter /ˈloɪtɚ/ *vb* [I] : to remain in an area when you do not have a particular reason to be there ▪ *A group of teenagers was loitering (around) in the parking lot.* — **loi·ter·er** /ˈloɪtɚɚ/ *n* [C]

loll /ˈlɑːl/ *vb* [I] **1** : to hang or bend loosely ▪ *a dog with its tongue lolling out* **2** : to lie or sit in a relaxed or lazy manner ▪ *He lolled about/around in his pajamas all day.*

lol·li·pop *or* **lol·ly·pop** /ˈlɑːliˌpɑːp/ *n* [C] : a round piece of hard candy on the end of a stick

lol·ly·gag /ˈlɑːliˌgæg/ *vb* **-gagged; -gagging** [I] *US, informal* : to fool around and waste time ▪ *Stop lollygagging around/about and get to work!* — **lol·ly·gag·ger** *n* [C]

lone /ˈloʊn/ *adj, always before a noun* **1** : standing, acting, or being alone ▪ *a lone traveler/gunman* **2** *Brit* : ¹SINGLE 2 ▪ *a lone parent/father/mother*

lone·ly /ˈloʊnli/ *adj* **lone·li·er; -est** **1** : sad from being apart from other people ▪ *He was/felt lonely without her.* **2** : causing sad feelings that come from being apart from other people ▪ *a lonely night* ▪ *It's lonely at the top.* [=powerful and successful people often have few friends] **3** : not visited by or traveled on by many people ▪ *a lonely stretch of road* — **lone·li·ness** /ˈloʊnlinəs/ *n* [U]

lon·er /ˈloʊnɚ/ *n* [C] : a person who is often alone or who likes to be alone

lone·some /ˈloʊnsəm/ *adj, chiefly US* : LONELY ▪ *He was/felt lonesome (for her).* ▪ *a lonesome highway* — **(all) by your lonesome** *informal* : entirely alone ▪ *He sat by his lonesome.* [=by himself] ▪ *She did it all by her lonesome.* [=without help]

¹long /ˈlɑːŋ/ *adj* **lon·ger** /ˈlɑːŋgɚ/; **longest** /ˈlɑːŋgəst/ **1** : extending a great distance : not short ▪ *long hair/legs* ▪ *a long corridor* ▪ *the longest bridge in the world* **b** : having a specified length ▪ *one meter long* **2 a** : lasting or continuing for a great amount of time ▪ *a long pause/wait/marriage* ▪ *I've known her for a long time.* ▪ *It happened a long time ago.* [=far in the past] ▪ *working long hours* [=many hours at a time] ▪ *It's been a long day.* [=a difficult day] ▪ *We took a long weekend.* [=a weekend plus an extra day] **b** : lasting or continuing for a specified amount of time ▪ *The movie is three hours long.* **3 a** : having many pages, items, etc. ▪ *a long book/essay/list* **b** : having a specified number of pages, items, etc. ▪ *The book is 300 pages long.* **4** *of clothing* : covering all or most of the arms or legs ▪ *long sleeves/pants* ▪ *a long skirt* **5** *sports* : going beyond the area of play ▪ *His serve was long.* **6** *linguistics, of a vowel* — used to identify certain vowel sounds in English (such as the "a" in "make," the "e" in "sweet," the "i" in "ice," and the "u" in "use") ▪ *a long "a"* — compare ¹SHORT 8 **7** *of someone's face* : showing sadness ▪ *Why the long face?* — **a long way** : a great distance, amount, or length of time ▪ *Their house is a long way (away) from here.* ▪ *We've come a long way on the project, but we still have a long way to go.* ▪ *We go back a long way.* [=we have known each other for a long time] — **long in the tooth** see TOOTH — **long on** : having or providing a lot of (something) ▪ *He was long on criticism but short on advice.* — **long time no see** *informal* — used to greet someone you have not seen for a long time ▪ *Hello! Long time no see!* — **not long for this world** see WORLD

²**long** *adv* **1** : for many years, days, hours, etc. ▪ *wait/last long* ▪ *Wait a bit longer.* ▪ *Will he be away (very) long?* ▪ *It has long been a subject of debate.* ▪ *It's been so long since I've seen him.* ▪ *That meeting was way too long.* ▪ *She's been away so long.* [=very long] ▪ *her long-awaited new novel* **2** : for a specified period of time ▪ *They played/talked all day long.* ▪ *all summer/week long* **3** : at a time far before or after a specified moment or event ▪ *It happened long before/after we were married.* ▪ *Not long after/afterward, the phone rang.* **4** : for a great distance ▪ *threw the ball long* — **as long as** *or* **so long as 1** : SINCE ▪ *As long as I'm here, we may as well begin.* **2** : IF ▪ *I'll go with you as long as you'll drive.* **3** : during the time that ▪ WHILE ▪ *As long as you live here, you'll follow my rules.* — **be long** : to last, use, or require a lot of time ▪ *I won't be long. = I won't be much longer.* [=I will return, finish, etc., soon] ▪ *It won't be long now.* [=it will happen/come soon] — **long ago** : at a time in the distant past ▪ *events that happened (not) long ago* ▪ *It wasn't so/very long ago.* — **long gone** : having ended, died, etc., at a distant time in the past ▪ *Those buildings are long gone now.* — **long since** : at a time in the distant past : long ago ▪ *I have long since given up trying to change her mind.* — **no longer** *or* **not any longer** — used to say that something that was once true or possible is not now true or possible ▪ *They could wait no longer. = They couldn't wait any longer.* ▪ *I can*

no longer afford the car.* — **so long** *informal* : ¹GOODBYE ▪ *So long (for now)!* — **take long** : to require a large amount of time ▪ *It won't take long to make dinner.*

³**long** *n* — **before long** : in a short amount of time : SOON ▪ *They'll arrive before long.* — **for long** : for many years, days, hours, etc. : for a long time ▪ *I haven't known him for long.* ▪ *He won't be away for (very) long.* — **the long and (the) short of it** : the most basic explanation ▪ *It's complicated, but the long and short of it is that I need a change.*

⁴**long** *vb* [*I*] : to feel a strong desire *for* something or *to* do something ▪ *We all long for peace.* ▪ *How I long to see you again!* ▪ *that longed-for day*

long-dis·tance /ˈlɑːŋˈdɪstəns/ *adj* **1** always before a noun : going or covering a great distance ▪ *long-distance travel* ▪ *a long-distance runner* ▪ involving people who are far apart ▪ *a long-distance relationship* **2** *of a telephone call* : connecting to a place that is far away ▪ *long-distance (phone/telephone) calls* — **long-distance** *adv* ▪ *She called us long-distance.*

long-drawn-out *adj* : continuing for a long time or for too long ▪ *a long-drawn-out investigation*

lon·gev·i·ty /lɑnˈdʒɛvəti/ *n* [*U*] **1 a** : long life ▪ *a people famous for their longevity* [=for living to be very old] **b** : length of life ▪ *an increase in human longevity* **2** : the length of time that something or someone lasts ▪ *the longevity of a car's tires*

long-haired /ˈlɑːŋˈheəd/ *adj* : having long fur or hair ▪ *a long-haired cat/girl*

long-hand /ˈlɑːŋˌhænd/ *n* [*U*] : writing that is done by using a pen or pencil ▪ *wrote it (out) in longhand*

long haul *n* [*U*] **1** : a long journey or distance **2** *chiefly US* : a long period of time ▪ *We're in this job for the long haul.* [=we are prepared to work on it until it is completed] ▪ *Will they succeed over the long haul?*

¹**long·ing** /ˈlɑːŋɪŋ/ *n* [*C/U*] : a strong desire for something or someone ▪ *a look of longing* ▪ *secret longings* ▪ *They felt a deep longing for peace.* ▪ *He had a longing to be with her.*

²**longing** *adj, always before a noun* : showing a strong desire for something or someone ▪ *a longing gaze* — **long·ing·ly** /ˈlɑːŋɪŋli/ *adv*

lon·gi·tude /ˈlɑːndʒəˌtuːd, *Brit* ˈlɒndʒə-ˌtjuːd/ *n* [*C/U*] : distance measured in degrees east or west from an imaginary line (called the prime meridian) that goes from the North Pole to the South Pole and that passes through Greenwich, England ▪ *lines of latitude and longitude* ▪ *calculating the longitudes of different places*; *also* [*C*] : an imaginary line that circles the Earth at a particular longitude ▪ *two places on the same longitude* — compare LATITUDE

lon·gi·tu·di·nal /ˌlɑːndʒəˈtuːdənəl, *Brit* ˌlɒndʒəˈtjuːdənəl/ *adj, always before a noun* **1** : placed or going along the long side of something ▪ *longitudinal stripes* **2**

: of or relating to longitude ▪ *the longitudinal position of a ship*

long johns /ˈlɑːŋˌdʒɑːnz/ *n* [*plural*] : underwear that covers your legs — called also (*US*) **long underwear**

long jump *n* — **the long jump** : an athletic event in which people compete by trying to jump as far as they can ▪ *won a gold medal in the long jump*

long-last-ing /ˈlɑːŋˈlæstɪŋ, *Brit* ˈlɒŋˈlɑːstɪŋ/ *adj* **long-er-last-ing**; **long-est-last-ing** : existing or continuing for a long time ▪ *a long-lasting effect*

long-lived /ˈlɑːŋˈlɪvd/ *adj* **long-er-lived**; **long-est-lived** : living or lasting for a long time ▪ *long-lived people/traditions*

long-lost /ˈlɑːŋˈlɑːst/ *adj, always before a noun* : not seen or found for many years ▪ *a long-lost masterpiece* ▪ *They greeted him like a long-lost brother.*

long-range /ˈlɑːŋˈreɪndʒ/ *adj, always before a noun* **1** : able to travel or be used over great distances ▪ *long-range missiles/weapons* **2** : involving a long period of time ▪ *long-range goals/trends/plans*

long run *n* — **the long run** : a long period of time after the beginning of something ▪ *investing for the long run* ▪ *This deal will cost you more in/over the long run.*

long·shore·man /ˈlɑːŋˌʃoɚmən/ *n, pl* **-men** /-mən/ [*C*] *US* : a person whose job is to load and unload ships at a port

long shot *n* [*C*] **1** : an attempt or effort that is not likely to be successful ▪ *I hope to double my profits, but I know that's a long shot.* **2** *chiefly US* : a person or thing that is not likely to win a contest, race, etc. ▪ *betting on a long shot* — **by a long shot** : by a great extent or degree : by far ▪ *It was our biggest problem by a long shot.* — **not by a long shot** : not at all ▪ *We're not done yet, not by a long shot.*

long-sight-ed /ˈlɑːŋˌsaɪtəd/ *adj, Brit* : FARSIGHTED

long-stand-ing /ˈlɑːŋˈstændɪŋ/ *adj* : lasting or existing for a long time ▪ *a long-standing tradition/problem*

long-suf-fer-ing /ˈlɑːŋˌsʌfərɪŋ/ *adj* : suffering for a long time without complaining ▪ *his forgiving and long-suffering wife*

long term *n* — **the long term** : a long period of time after the beginning of something ▪ *investing for the long term* [=*the long run*] ▪ *I think it's the better choice in/over the long term.*

long–term /ˈlɑːŋˈtɚm/ *adj* : lasting for, relating to, or involving a long period of time ▪ *the long-term effects of the medication* ▪ *a long-term strategy/investment* ▪ *long-term memory*

long-time /ˈlɑːŋˈtaɪm/ *adj, always before a noun* : having been something specified for many years ▪ *the committee's longtime chairman* ▪ *her longtime boyfriend*

long underwear *n* [*U*] *US* : LONG JOHNS

long-wind-ed /ˈlɑːŋˈwɪndəd/ *adj* : using too many words in speaking or writing ▪ *a long-winded speaker/speech/expansion*

loo /ˈluː/ *n, pl* **loos** [*C*] *Brit, informal* : TOILET

¹look /ˈlʊk/ *vb* **1** [*I*] : to direct your eyes

in a particular direction ▪ *He looked straight ahead.* ▪ **look around/away/back/down** ▪ *Look both ways before you cross the street.* — often + *at* ▪ *What are you looking at?* ▪ *looking at the stars* ▪ *The house isn't much to look at.* [=is not very attractive] ▪ (*figurative*) *She looks down her nose at us.* [=she does not respect us] **2 a** [*linking vb*] : to seem to be something especially because of appearance ▪ *He looks angry.* ▪ *That haircut makes you look younger.* ▪ *The cake looks delicious.* ▪ *The situation looks pretty bad/good.* ▪ *a kind-looking woman* ▪ *She looked to be about thirty years old.* — often used in the phrases **look as if/though** and **look like** ▪ *It looks like it will be a rough week.* ▪ *It looks to me like an error.* = *It looks like an error to me.* ▪ *It/He looked as though he was ill.* **b** [*T*] : to have an appearance that is suitable for (something) ▪ *She looks her age.* ▪ *an actor who really looks the part* **3** [*I*] : to try to find something or someone ▪ *"I can't find my keys." "Look in the drawer."* ▪ *I've looked high and low.* = *I've looked everywhere.* = *I've looked all over.* ▪ *Keep looking (for them).* ▪ **Look no further**—*here they are.* **4** [*I*] : to pay attention by directing your eyes at something ▪ *I wasn't looking and almost missed it.* ▪ (*in a store*) *"Do you need help?" "No, I'm just looking."* ▪ (*figurative*) *If you're planning to invest,* **look before you leap.** [=find out about possible problems before you invest] **5** [*I*] **a** — used to direct someone's attention to something or someone ▪ *Look! Over there!* ▪ *Look at the time! I'd better go.* ▪ **Look what** *I found.* ▪ **Look who's** *here.* ▪ **Look how** *easy it is.* **b** — used to warn someone or to express anger or disappointment ▪ *Careful!* **Look where** *you're going.* ▪ **Look what** *you did!* = *Look what you've done! You broke it.* **c** — used to get someone to notice what you are saying ▪ *Look, this isn't going to work.* ▪ **Look here**, *you need to change your ways.* **6** [*T*] **a** : to want or try to do something ▪ *a company looking to become a leader in the industry* **b** : EXPECT ▪ *We are looking to have a good year.* **7** [*I*] : to have a specified direction : FACE ▪ *The house looks east.* — **don't look now** — used to tell someone to be aware of something without looking ▪ *Don't look now, but they're coming our way.* — **look after** [*phrasal vb*] : to take care of (someone or something) ▪ *They hired a babysitter to look after the children.* ▪ *He looks after the house.* — **look ahead** [*phrasal vb*] : to think about what will happen in the future ▪ *looking ahead to the coming year* — **look around** or *Brit* **look round** [*phrasal vb*] **1** : to explore a place ▪ *The kids looked around (the hotel) while we unpacked.* **2 look around/round for** : to search for (something) ▪ *I looked around for my keys.* — **look at** [*phrasal vb*] **1 a** : to think about or consider (something or someone) ▪ *They're looking at the possibility of moving.* ▪ *That's not the way I look at* [=see] *it.* ▪ *We're looking at her as a possible candidate.* **b** : to examine or study (someone or something) ▪ *You should* have a doctor look at that bruise. **2 a** : to have (something bad) as a problem or possibility ▪ *He could be looking at [=facing] prison.* **b** : to read (something) ▪ *Did you look at that fax?* — **look back** [*phrasal vb*] : to think about something in the past ▪ *Looking back (to/at that time), I can see how foolish I was.* ▪ *I look back at/on that time with fondness.* ▪ *She left home and* **never looked back.** — **look down on** [*phrasal vb*] : to think of or treat (someone or something) as unimportant ▪ *They looked down on me because I was poor.* — **look for** [*phrasal vb*] **1** : to search for (someone or something) ▪ *She's looking for a job.* ▪ *The police are looking for him.* ▪ *Are you* **looking for** trouble? [=trying to cause problems or get in a fight] **2** : to expect (something or someone) ▪ *You can look for me (to arrive) around noon.* ▪ *looking for the economy to improve* — **look forward to** [*phrasal vb*] : to expect (something) with pleasure ▪ *We're looking forward to our vacation.* — **look in on** [*phrasal vb*] : to make a brief social visit to (someone) ▪ *look in on a friend* — **look into** [*phrasal vb*] : to try to get information about (something) ▪ *Investigators are looking into the cause of the accident.* — **look like** : to resemble (someone or something) ▪ *You look just like your mother! That sugar looks like snow.* — **look on/upon** [*phrasal vb*] **1 look on** : to watch something as it happens without becoming involved ▪ *A crowd of people looked on as the house burned.* **2** : to think of or consider (someone or something) in a specified way ▪ *I've always looked on her as a friend.* ▪ *He looked upon his son's accomplishments with pride.* — **look out** [*phrasal vb*] **1** — used to tell someone to be aware of something dangerous ▪ *Look out* [=watch out]*—the walk is icy.* — **look (something) out** or **look out (something)** *Brit* : to succeed in finding (something) ▪ *I'll look out his phone number for you.* — **look out for** [*phrasal vb*] **1** : to be aware of and try to avoid (something) ▪ *problems (that) you should look out for* ▪ *Look out for that pothole!* **2** : to take care of or protect (someone or something) ▪ *I can look out for myself.* ▪ *She's looking out for our interests.* — **look over** [*phrasal vb*] **look (something) over** or **look over (something)** : to read or examine (something) quickly ▪ *look a proposal over* — **look (someone) in the eye** also **look (someone) in the face** : to look directly at (someone who is also looking at you) ▪ *I looked him (right) in the eye and told him the truth.* — **look the other way** : to ignore something that should be noticed or dealt with ▪ *We can't just look the other way while others are suffering.* — **look through** [*phrasal vb*] **1 a** : to read some of the pages of (something) ▪ *look through a magazine* **b** : to look at the different parts of (something) ▪ *I looked through his letters.* **2** : to pretend to not see or recognize (someone) ▪ *When she passed me on the street she looked (right/ straight) through me!* — **look to** [*phrasal vb*] **1** : to think about or examine

(something) ▪ *They look to the future with hope.* ▪ **look to nature for inspiration** **2** : to depend or rely on (someone) ▪ *She looks to you for help/advice.* — **look up** [*phrasal vb*] **1** : IMPROVE ▪ *Things are starting to look up for me.* **2 look (something or someone) up** or **look up (something or someone)** **a** : to search for (something) in a book, on the Internet, etc. ▪ *look up an address* ▪ *look a word up (in the dictionary)* **b** : to call or go to see (someone) when you are in the area where that person lives ▪ *Look me up when you're in town.* — **look up to** [*phrasal vb*] : to respect and admire (someone) ▪ *I've always looked up to him.*

²**look** *n* **1** [*C*] : the act of looking at something ▪ *Feel free to* **have/take a look** around. ▪ *Take/Have a look at this!* ▪ *She didn't* **get a (good) look** *at his face.* ▪ *We* **took one look** *at the weather and decided to stay home.* **2** [*C*] : the act of examining or considering something ▪ *We need to take a hard/close look at these issues.* **3** [*singular*] : the act of trying to find something or someone ▪ *I took a quick look (around), but he wasn't there.* **4** [*C*] : the emotions seen in a person's face or eyes ▪ *You should have seen the look on her face!* ▪ *the look in her eyes* ▪ *He gave me an angry/dirty look.* **5 a** [*C*] : the way that something looks ▪ *The house has an old-fashioned look (to it).* ▪ *I don't like the look of those storm clouds.* ▪ **From the look of things,** *that car won't last much longer.* [=that car seems unlikely to last much longer] **b** [*plural*] : physical appearance ▪ *his boyish* **good looks.** ▪ *She's worried about* **losing her looks** [=becoming less attractive] *as she grows older.* **c** [*C*] : a style or fashion ▪ *a new look in women's fashion* ▪ *That's a good look for you.*

look–alike /ˈlʊkəˌlaɪk/ *n* [*C*] : someone or something that looks like another person or thing ▪ *She and her cousin are look-alikes.* [=they look like each other]

look·er /ˈlʊkɚ/ *n* [*C*] *informal* : a person (especially a woman) who is very attractive ▪ *She's a real looker.*

looking glass *n* [*C*] *old-fashioned* : ¹MIRROR 1

look·out /ˈlʊkˌaʊt/ *n* [*C*] **1** : a person who watches for danger ▪ *The troops posted a lookout.* **2** : a high place from which you can see a wide area ▪ *scenic lookouts* ▪ *a lookout tower* **3** : an act or state of watching or searching ▪ *The guard kept a lookout for* [=watched for] *suspicious activity.* ▪ *She's always* **on the lookout for** *sales.*

¹**loom** /ˈluːm/ *vb* [*I*] **1** : to appear in a large, strange, or frightening form ▪ *A ship loomed (up) out of the fog.* ▪ *Storm clouds loomed on the horizon.* **2** : to be close to happening — used especially of unpleasant or frightening things ▪ *A workers' strike is looming.* ▪ *a looming battle/conflict/problem/storm* — **loom large** : to have great importance or influence ▪ *The economy looms large in the minds of many people.*

²**loom** n [C] : a frame or machine that is used to weave threads or yarns to produce cloth

loon /ˈluːn/ n [C] **1** : a large bird that eats fish and has a strange cry **2** informal : a crazy person ▪ He's a complete loon.

loo·ny /ˈluːni/ adj **loo·ni·er; -est** informal : crazy or foolish ▪ loony extremists ▪ He's a little loony. — **loony** n, pl **-nies** [C] ▪ a bunch of loonies

¹**loop** /ˈluːp/ n **1** [C] **a** : a curved shape made when a rope, thread, etc., bends so that it touches or crosses over itself ▪ a loop of wire/string **b** : something that is shaped like a loop ▪ The road formed a loop around the pond. ▪ draw a loop **c** : a ring or curved piece used for holding something ▪ a belt loop **2** [C] : an action in which an airplane flies in an upright circle perpendicular to the ground ▪ The pilot did/performed a loop. **3** the loop : a group of people who know about or have influence over a process, decision, etc. ▪ She wants to stay in the loop. ▪ He was kept out of the loop. — **knock/throw (someone) for a loop** US, informal : to cause (someone) to be very amazed, confused, or shocked ▪ The news of her death really knocked me for a loop. — **knock (something) for a loop** US, informal : to damage or ruin (something) ▪ The town's economy was knocked for a loop by the factory's closing.

²**loop** vb [T/I] **1** : to form or cause (something) to form a loop ▪ The road loops around the pond. ▪ She looped a string around her finger. **2** : to move or cause (something) to move in a high curving path ▪ The ball looped over the shortstop's head. ▪ The batter looped a single to left field.

loop·hole /ˈluːpˌhoʊl/ n [C] : an error in the way a law, rule, etc., is written that makes it possible for some people to legally avoid obeying it ▪ a tax loophole

¹**loose** /ˈluːs/ adj **loos·er; -est 1** : not tightly fastened, attached, or held ▪ a loose tooth/knot ▪ A shingle had come/worked loose. ▪ The boat came loose from its moorings. **2 a** : not pulled or stretched tight ▪ a loose belt ▪ loose skin **b** of clothing : not fitting close to your body : not tight ▪ a loose dress/skirt/sweater **3** : not physically held or contained ▪ The dog was wandering loose. The lion got/broke loose from its cage. **4 a** : not held together in a solid or tight mass ▪ loose dirt/rocks/soil **b** : not held together in a bundle, container, etc. ▪ loose sheets of paper ▪ She let her hair hang down loose. **5** : not stiff or tense ▪ a loose stride ▪ loose muscles **6** : not closely joined or united ▪ a loose alliance/association/coalition **7 a** : not exact or precise ▪ a loose translation/interpretation **b** : talking too freely ▪ Loose talk spread the rumor. ▪ She has a loose tongue and can't keep a secret. **8** sports : not controlled or held ▪ a loose ball/puck **9** old-fashioned : not respectable sexually : not decent or moral ▪ a loose woman ▪ loose morals — **cut loose 1 cut (someone) loose** : to stop supporting or employing (someone) ▪ He didn't do a good job, so we had to cut him loose. **2** chiefly US, informal : to act in a free and relaxed way ▪ She enjoys cutting loose on weekends. — **let loose 1 let (someone or something) loose** or **set/turn (someone or something) loose** : to allow (someone or something) to move or go freely ▪ He let/set the dogs loose. ▪ (figurative) the violence that has been let loose on the city **2** : to produce (a cry, yell, etc.) in a sudden and forceful way ▪ She let loose (with) a scream. — **loose·ly** adv ▪ The clothes fit loosely. ▪ He held the reins loosely. — **loose·ness** n [U] ▪ moral looseness ▪ the looseness of the translation/clothes

²**loose** vb **loosed; loos·ing** [T] **1** : to release or untie (an animal or person) ▪ They loosed the dogs on the prowlers. **2** : LOOSEN ▪ He loosed his grip. **3** : to shoot or fire (an arrow, bullet, etc.) ▪ loose a volley of rifle fire

³**loose** n — **on the loose** : not controlled or held in a prison, cage, etc. ▪ A killer is on the loose.

loose cannon n [C] : a person who cannot be controlled and who causes problems, embarrassment, etc., for others

loose change n [U] : coins that a person is carrying ▪ He had a few dollars in loose change in his pockets.

loose end n [C] : a part of a job, story, etc., that has not been completed ▪ There are still a few loose ends to wrap/tie up. — **at loose ends** (US) or Brit **at a loose end** : not knowing what to do ▪ With everyone away she was at loose ends.

loose–leaf /ˈluːsˈliːf/ adj : designed so that sheets of paper can be added or removed by opening or closing a locking device ▪ a loose-leaf notebook/binder/folder

loos·en /ˈluːsn̩/ vb [T/I] **1** : to make (something) loose or looser or to become loose or looser ▪ loosen a screw/belt/tie ▪ She loosened her grip/hold on the rope. ▪ Her grip loosened. **2** : to become or to cause (something) to become less strict ▪ loosening (up) the restrictions ▪ Standards of behavior seem to be loosening. — **loosen someone's tongue** : to cause someone to talk more freely ▪ A few drinks loosened his tongue. — **loosen up** [phrasal vb] **1** : RELAX ▪ loosen up by exercising ▪ After a couple of drinks she loosened up. **2 loosen (someone or something) up** or **loosen up (someone or something)** : to cause (someone or something) to relax ▪ stretching to loosen up your muscles ▪ I tried to loosen her up by telling a few jokes.

¹**loot** /ˈluːt/ n [U] **1** : something that is stolen or taken by force in a war, robbery, etc. ▪ The thieves took the loot and ran. **2** informal : MONEY ▪ He made/earned a lot of loot.

²**loot** vb [T/I] : to steal things from (a store, house, etc.) during or after a war, riot, etc. ▪ Rioters looted the stores. ▪ supplies looted from a warehouse — **loot·er** n [C] — **looting** n [U] ▪ There was widespread looting throughout the city.

lop /ˈlɑːp/ vb **lopped; lop·ping** [T] **1** : to cut branches from (a tree, bush, etc.)

• *trees that were heavily lopped* **2** : to cut or cut off (something) • *lop off a branch* • *(figurative) They lopped $20 off the price.*

lope /ˈloʊp/ *vb* **loped; lop·ing** [*I*] *of a person or animal* : to run in a relaxed way with long strides • *The horses loped across/over the fields.* — **lope** *n* [*singular*] • *She ran with an easy lope.*

lop·sid·ed /ˈlɑːpˌsaɪdəd/ *adj* **1** : having one side that is lower or smaller than the other • *a lopsided grin/smile* • *a lopsided roof* **2** : uneven or unequal • *a lopsided vote of 99 to 1*

lo·qua·cious /loʊˈkweɪʃəs/ *adj* : liking to talk and talking smoothly and easily • *a loquacious politician/host* — **lo·qua·cious·ness** *n* [*U*] — **lo·quac·i·ty** /loʊˈkwæsəti/ *n* [*U*] *formal* • *a politician known for her loquacity*

¹**lord** /ˈloɚd/ *n* **1** [*C*] : a man who has power and authority • *feudal lords in the Middle Ages* • *a crime/drug/gang lord* **2 Lord** [*singular*] **a** — used as a name for God or Jesus Christ • *Praise the Lord.* • *Oh Lord, hear our prayers.* **b** — used informally for emphasis or to express surprise, anger, etc. • *Lord, it's hot today.* • *(Oh) My Lord! = Lord almighty! = Good Lord! What have you done?!* **3** [*C*] : a man who is British nobleman or male official of high rank • *a British lord* — often used as a title • *Lord Churchill* **4 the Lords** *Brit* : HOUSE OF LORDS

²**lord** *vb* — **lord it over someone** : to show that you think you are better or more important than someone • *He won and was lording it over us.*

lord·ly /ˈloɚdli/ *adj* **lord·li·er; -est** **1** : suitable for or resembling a lord • *a lordly and dignified man* • *a lordly estate* **2** : having or showing a feeling of being better than other people • *He regarded them with lordly disdain.*

lord·ship /ˈloɚdˌʃɪp/ *n* [*C*] *chiefly Brit* **1 Lordship** — used as a title when addressing or referring to a British lord • *His Lordship is not at home.* • *Can I get your Lordship anything else?* **2** : the authority, power, or territory of a lord • *He inherited a lordship.*

Lord's Prayer *n* — **the Lord's Prayer** : a prayer that Jesus Christ taught to his followers

lore /ˈloɚ/ *n* [*U*] : traditional knowledge, beliefs, and stories that relate to a particular place, subject, or group • *an event that has become part of local lore* • *the lore of sailing*

lor·ry /ˈlori/ *n, pl* **-ries** [*C*] *Brit* : ¹TRUCK 1a

lose /ˈluːz/ *vb* **lost** /ˈlɑːst/; **los·ing** **1** [*T*] : to be unable to find (something or someone) • *She lost her gloves/keys.* • *The airline lost my luggage.* **2** [*T/I*] : to fail to win (a game, contest, etc.) • *We lost the battle/game.* • *She lost the lawsuit.* • *The team lost in the finals.* • *He hates to lose.* • *The Yankees lost to the Red Sox.* **3 a** [*T*] : to fail to keep or hold (something wanted or valued) • *lose an advantage* • *losing power/influence* • *She lost control of the car.* • *She lost her job.* • *He hasn't lost his sense of humor.* • *I've lost my appetite.* • *The patient was losing blood.* • *I'm sorry I'm late. I lost track of the time.* • *She lost her balance and fell.* • *You might as well try. You have nothing (else/left) to lose and everything to gain.* • *I can't quit now. I have too much to lose. = I have a lot to lose.* **b** [*T/I*] : to fail to earn or keep (money) • *They lost all their savings in a poor investment.* • *The company has been losing money.* **c** [*T*] : to have (something) taken from you or destroyed • *We lost (electrical) power during the storm.* • *He lost an arm in the war.* • *They lost everything in the fire.* • *He yelled so much that he lost his voice.* **d** [*T*] : to gradually have less of (something) as time passes • *lose weight by dieting* • *He was gradually losing his eyesight/hair.* • *lose interest in something* **4** [*T*] : to cause the loss of (something) for (someone) • *A careless comment lost the election for her. = A careless comment lost her the election.* **5 a** [*T/I*] : to decrease in (something) • *The plane was losing altitude.* • *Some stocks are losing (value) while others are gaining.* **b** [*T*] : to decrease in value by (a specified amount) or when compared to something else • *The pound lost three percent last quarter.* • *The dollar lost against the pound last week.* **6** [*T*] **a** : to experience or suffer the death of (a relative, friend, etc.) • *She lost her husband in the war.* [=her husband was killed in the war] • *soldiers who were lost* [=killed] *in/during the war* = *soldiers who lost their lives in/during the war* • *a surgeon who has never lost a patient* • *a sailor who was lost at sea* **b** : to no longer have or be with (someone who leaves) • *I love you and I couldn't bear to lose you.* **7** [*T*] : to fail to keep control of (something) • *He lost his temper/cool/composure.* [=he became angry] • *She felt like she was losing her mind/sanity.* [=becoming insane] • *He seems to be losing his nerve.* [=becoming afraid] **8** [*T*] : to fail to use (something) : WASTE • *Don't lose this chance/opportunity.* • *We lost (a lot of) time in traffic.* • *She lost no time in getting started.* [=she got started immediately] • *We need to get started. There's no time to lose.* **9** [*T*] : to explain something in a way that is not clear to (someone) • *I'm sorry. You've lost me.* [=I don't understand what you're telling me] **10** [*T*] : to succeed in getting away from (someone) • *She tried to lose her pursuers.* **11** [*T*] *informal* : to get rid of (something unwanted) • *I can't seem to lose this cold.* • *Lose the attitude, okay?* [=stop having a bad attitude] — **lose it** *informal* **1** : to become insane • *I think he's completely lost it.* **2** : to start behaving in an uncontrolled way • *I was so angry that I almost lost it.* — **lose out** [*phrasal vb*] : to fail to keep or get something valued or desired • *Don't lose out on a great opportunity!* • *She lost out to a better-known actress for the role.* — **lose yourself** : to give all of your attention or thought to something • *He lost himself in his work.* — **los·ing** *adj* • *the losing candidate* • *a losing record/season/streak*

los·er /ˈluːzɚ/ *n* [*C*] **1** : someone or something that loses a game, contest, etc. • *The loser of the bet has to buy drinks for* *the winner.* ▪ *She's a good loser.* [=she does not become upset or angry when she loses] ▪ *She's a bad/poor loser.* = (US) *She's a sore loser.* **2** : someone who is harmed or put in a worse position as the result of something ▪ *Whoever benefits from the new government programs, the real loser will be the taxpayer.* **3** *informal* + *disapproving* : a person who is not successful, attractive, etc. ▪ *She's a (total, complete) loser.* ▪ *a born loser*

loss /ˈlɑːs/ *n* **1 a** [C/U] : failure to keep or to continue to have something ▪ *There have been heavy job losses.* — usually + *of* ▪ *his loss of support/influence/control* ▪ *(a) loss of blood/appetite* ▪ *The war caused enormous loss of life.* [=many people died in the war] **b** [U] : the experience of having something taken from you or destroyed ▪ *He suffered the loss of an arm.* **2** [C] : money that is spent and that is more than the amount earned or received ▪ *profits and losses* ▪ *They took a loss on the deal.* [=they lost money on the deal] ▪ *The business is operating at a loss.* [=is spending more money than it is earning] **3** [C/U] : failure to win a game, contest, etc. ▪ *wins and losses* ▪ *the loss of the game* **4 a** [U, singular] : a decrease in something or in the amount of something ▪ *The plane experienced a loss of altitude.* ▪ *a loss in value* ▪ *Side effects include memory/weight/hair loss.* **b** [singular] : a decrease in value by a specified amount ▪ *a loss of four percent* **5** [U] **a** : the death of a relative, friend, etc. ▪ *mourning the loss of a friend to cancer* **b** : the experience of having someone leave ▪ *The company has had to deal with the loss of several employees.* **c** : a feeling of sadness that you have when someone dies, leaves, etc. ▪ *a sense/feeling of loss* **6** [singular] : something that causes harm, sadness, etc., *to* a group or organization ▪ *His death was a great loss to the community.* **7** [singular] : something that is completely destroyed ▪ *No one was injured, but the car was a complete/total loss.* **8** [plural] : soldiers killed, wounded, or captured in battle ▪ *The allies suffered heavy losses.* — **at a loss** : not knowing what should be done or said ▪ *I don't know what to do. I'm at a (complete) loss.* ▪ *They were at a loss to explain* [=they were unable to explain] *what had happened.* ▪ (*chiefly US*) *I was at a loss for words.* [=I did not know what to say] — **cut your losses** : to stop an activity, business, etc., that is failing ▪ *Many investors have decided to cut their losses and sell their stocks.* — **it's your loss** — used to say that someone has made a poor choice in deciding not to do something ▪ *If she doesn't want to come to the party, it's her loss.*

loss leader *n* [C] : a product that is sold for less than it is worth in order to attract customers

¹lost *past participle of* LOSE

²lost /ˈlɑːst/ *adj* **1** : unable to be found ▪ *lost baggage/luggage* **2** : not knowing where you are or how to get to where you want to go ▪ *The child was lost.* ▪ *We took a wrong turn and got lost.* ▪ *a lost pup-*

py **3 a** : no longer held, owned, or possessed ▪ *He was trying to regain his lost youth.* **b** : no longer known ▪ *a lost civilization/art* **c** : no longer available ▪ *a lost* [=missed] *opportunity/chance* ▪ *The strike has cost us millions in lost sales.* ▪ *working faster to* **make up for lost time 4 a** : not won or able to be won ▪ *a lost battle* ▪ *The game was already lost by halftime.* **b** : not capable of succeeding ▪ *They gave the project up as a* **lost cause. 5 a** *not before a noun* : feeling unsure of what to do ▪ *She felt a bit lost in the big city.* ▪ *I'd be lost without my computer.* **b** : very unhappy ▪ *a lost soul* [=a lonely and unhappy person] **6** *not before a noun* : so interested in something that you do not notice other things ▪ *He was lost in a book.* ▪ *She was lost in thought.* — **get lost** *informal + impolite* : to go away : LEAVE ▪ *Get lost, you jerk!* — **lost for words** *chiefly Brit* : unable to think of anything to say ▪ *I was so surprised that I was lost for words.* — **lost on** : not appreciated or understood by (someone) ▪ *The meaning of her remark wasn't lost on him.*

lot /ˈlɑːt/ *n* **1** [C] *chiefly US* : a small piece of land; *especially* : one that is or could be used for building something ▪ *a vacant/empty lot* ▪ *the house on the corner lot* ▪ *a building lot* **2** [C] : a small object used to choose someone ◇ When someone is **chosen by lot** or when people **draw lots** to choose someone, each person takes a small object from a container. The person whose object is different from the others is chosen. **3** [singular] : a person's situation in life especially as decided by chance ▪ *trying to improve the lot of underprivileged youth* ▪ *She was unhappy with her lot in life.* **4** *informal* **a** [C] *chiefly Brit* : all the members of a group of people ▪ *Pipe down, the (whole) lot of you.* = *Pipe down, you lot.* **b the lot** : all the things of a group ▪ *This one's the best of the lot.* — **a lot 1** *also (informal)* **lots** : a large amount ▪ *She has done a lot to help us.* ▪ *We did quite a lot this morning.* ▪ *We still have a lot to do.* = *We still have lots (and lots) to do.* **2** : very often ▪ *Do they hike a lot?* **3** *also (informal)* **lots** : to a large degree or extent : MUCH ▪ *This is a lot nicer.* ▪ *I'm feeling lots better.* ▪ *Thanks a lot.* [=very much] ▪ *I liked it a lot.* — **a lot of** *also (informal)* **lots of** : a large number or amount of (things, people, etc.) ▪ *a lot of people/money* ▪ *We had lots of fun.* ▪ *We don't have an awful lot of* [=much] *money/time.* ▪ *It doesn't make a whole lot of difference.* ▪ *Not a lot of people* [=not many people] *know that.*

loth *variant spelling of* LOATH

lo·tion /ˈloʊʃən/ *n* [C/U] : a liquid that is rubbed onto your skin or hair ▪ *a bottle of suntan lotion*

lot·tery /ˈlɑːtəri/ *n, pl* **-ter·ies 1** [C] : a way of raising money in which tickets are sold and a few are chosen by chance to win prizes ▪ *a state/national lottery* ▪ *a lottery ticket* ▪ *win/play the lottery* **2** [C/U] : a system used to decide by chance who will get or be given something • *Room assignments are determined by lottery.*

lo·tus /ˈloʊtəs/ *n* [*C*] : a type of flowering plant that grows on the surface of water

loud /ˈlaʊd/ *adj* 1 : making or causing a lot of noise • *a loud noise/party* • *loud music/laughter/applause* 2 a : noisy in a way that bothers other people • *a loud and aggressive person* b : expressing ideas or opinions in a very forceful way • *He was loud in (his) praise of their efforts.* [=he strongly praised their efforts] 3 : very bright or too bright in color • *loud clothes/colors/jewelry* — **out loud** : in a way that is loud enough to be clearly heard : ALOUD • *reading out loud* — **loud** *adv, not before a verb* • *Don't talk so loud!* • *They complained loud and long.* • *I can hear you loud and clear.* — **loud·ly** *adv* • *loudly singing* • *complain loudly* — **loud·ness** *n* [*U*]

loud·hail·er /ˌlaʊdˈheɪlə/ *n* [*C*] *Brit* : BULLHORN

loud·mouth /ˈlaʊdˌmaʊθ/ *n* [*C*] *informal* + *disapproving* : a loud and annoying person — **loud·mouthed** /ˈlaʊdˌmaʊθt/ *adj*

loud·speak·er /ˈlaʊdˌspiːkə/ *n* [*C*] : a device that is used to make music, speech, etc., louder so that many people can hear it • *He made an announcement over/on the loudspeaker.*

¹**lounge** /ˈlaʊndʒ/ *vb* **lounged; loung·ing** [*I*] : to sit or lie in a relaxed way • *lounging on the sofa* : to spend time resting or relaxing • *He was lounging by the pool.* • *We spent our vacation just lounging around.* = (*Brit*) *We spent our vacation just lounging about.*

²**lounge** *n* 1 [*C*] a : a public room with comfortable furniture for relaxing • *an airport lounge* • (*US*) *the faculty/student lounge* b *Brit* : LIVING ROOM 2 [*C*] *chiefly US* : a long chair or couch • *She sat/reclined on the lounge.* 3 [*singular*] : an act or period of relaxing • *They had a leisurely lounge by the pool.*

lounge chair *n* [*C*] *chiefly US* : CHAISE LONGUE

¹**louse** /ˈlaʊs/ *n* [*C*] 1 *pl* **lice** /ˈlaɪs/ : a type of small insect that lives on the bodies of people or animals • *a problem with head lice* 2 *pl* **lous·es** *informal* : a bad or cruel person • *He's a real louse.*

²**louse** *vb* **loused; lous·ing** — **louse up** [*phrasal vb*] **louse (something) up** *or* **louse up (something)** *informal* : to do (something) badly • *The waitress loused up our order.* : to cause (something) to be ruined or spoiled • *The weather loused up our plans.*

lousy /ˈlaʊzi/ *adj* **lous·i·er; -est** *informal* : bad or poor • *She got lousy grades in school.* • *lousy weather* • *He was a lousy husband.* • *They did a lousy job.* • *He's lousy at sports.* • *I woke up feeling lousy.* [=feeling ill] • *I feel lousy* [=sorry, bad] *about what happened.* — **lousy with** *informal* : having too much or too many of (something) • *That area is lousy with tourists.* — **lous·i·ness** /ˈlaʊzinəs/ *n* [*U*]

lout /ˈlaʊt/ *n* [*C*] : a stupid, rude, or awk-

ward man • *a dumb/drunken lout* — **lout·ish** /ˈlaʊtɪʃ/ *adj* — **lout·ish·ly** *adv*

lou·ver (*US*) *or Brit* **lou·vre** /ˈluːvə/ *n* [*C*] 1 : an opening in a door or window that has one or more slanted strips to allow air in and out while keeping out rain and sun 2 : one of the slanted strips of a louver — **lou·vered** (*US*) *or Brit* **lou·vred** /ˈluːvəd/ *adj* • *a louvered door/window*

lov·able *also* **love·able** /ˈlʌvəbəl/ *adj* : easy to love : having attractive or appealing qualities • *a lovable person*

¹**love** /ˈlʌv/ *n* 1 [*U*] : a feeling of strong or constant affection for a person • *motherly/maternal love* • *fatherly/paternal love* • *brotherly/sisterly love* • *her love for her family* 2 [*U*] : the strong affection felt by people who have a romantic relationship • *He was just a lonely man looking for love.* • *a love song/story* • *They're still very much in love (with each other).* [=they still love each other] • *madly/passionately in love* • *They fell in love (with each other).* • *When he met her it was love at first sight.* 3 [*C*] : a person you love in a romantic way • *a lost love* • *your first love* • *He was her one true love.* = *He was the love of her life.* 4 [*singular*] *chiefly Brit* a : a kind or helpful person : DEAR • *Be a love and carry this inside, would you?* b — used to address someone in a loving or friendly way • *Would you bring me a drink, (my) love?* 5 [*U*] : an expression of love and affection • *When you see them, please give them my love.* • *Mike and Meg send their love, too.* — used to express affection at the end of a written message • *Hope to see you soon. Love, Mike* 6 a [*singular*] : a feeling of great interest, affection, or enthusiasm for something • *his love for/of baseball* • *a love of good food* • *I paint just for the love of it.* • *She's in love with the idea.* b [*C*] : something about which a person feels great interest or enthusiasm • *Baseball was his first love.* 7 [*singular*] : a score of zero in tennis • *The score was 40–love.* — **for love or money** *or chiefly Brit* **for love nor money** *informal* — used to emphasize a negative statement • *We couldn't convince him for love or money.* — **for the love of God** *informal* — used to emphasize an angry statement • *For the love of God, quiet down!* — **love is blind** — used to say that people do not see the faults of the people that they love — **make love** : to have sex with someone • *the first time they made love (to/with each other)* — **no love lost** ◇ When there is *no love lost* or *very little love lost* between people, they dislike each other. — **love·less** /ˈlʌvləs/ *adj* • *a loveless marriage*

²**love** *vb* **loved; lov·ing** 1 [*T/I*] : to feel love for (someone) • *She loves her family.* 2 [*T*] : to feel sexual or romantic love for (someone) • *He loves her (madly), but she doesn't love him back.* • *I couldn't marry a man I didn't love.* 3 [*T*] : to like or desire (something) very much • *He loves good food.* • *a much-loved song* • *I would love it if you came.* = *I would love you to come.* = (*US*) *I would love for you to come.*

• *She loved to play the violin.* = *She loved playing the violin.* **4** [*T*] : to do very well in (certain conditions) • *This plant loves dry soil.* — **loved one** ◇ Your *loved ones* are the people you love, especially members of your family. • *her friends and loved ones*

love affair *n* **1** [*C*] : a romantic or sexual relationship especially between two people who are not married to each other • *Theirs was a great love affair.* [=they were very much in love] **2** [*singular*] : a feeling of great interest in and enthusiasm for something • *America's love affair with baseball*

love·birds /ˈlʌvˌbɚdz/ *n* [*plural*] *informal + humorous* : people who are lovers • *I'll leave you two lovebirds alone.*

love life *n* [*C*] : a person's romantic and sexual activities and relationships • *She doesn't like to talk about her love life.*

love·lorn /ˈlʌvˌloɚn/ *adj* : LOVESICK • *a lovelorn young suitor*

love·ly /ˈlʌvli/ *adj* **love·li·er; -est 1** : attractive or beautiful especially in a graceful way • *a lovely dress/woman* • *She looks lovely in that dress!* = *That dress looks lovely on her!* **2** : very good or likable • *He's a lovely man.* **3** : very pleasing : FINE • *a lovely view/dinner* • *a singer with a lovely voice* — **love·li·ness** *n* [*U*]

lov·er /ˈlʌvɚ/ *n* [*C*] **1 a** : a partner in a romantic or sexual relationship • *They became lovers.* **b** : someone with whom a married person is having a love affair • *She left her husband and ran away with her lover.* **2** : a person who loves something • *a lover of music* = *a music lover*

love seat *n* [*C*] *US* : a seat or sofa for two people

love·sick /ˈlʌvˌsɪk/ *adj* : feeling foolish, unhappy, etc., because someone you love does not love you • *a lovesick teenager* — **love·sick·ness** *n* [*U*]

lovey-dovey /ˌlʌviˈdʌvi/ *adj, informal* : showing a lot of love or affection • *lovey-dovey newlyweds*

lov·ing /ˈlʌvɪŋ/ *adj* **1** : feeling or showing love • *a loving home/family* • *a loving husband/wife* **2** : very careful and thorough • *The house needs some tender loving care.* [=the house needs many repairs] — **lov·ing·ly** *adv* • *He gazed at her lovingly.* • *The house was lovingly restored.*

¹**low** /ˈloʊ/ *adj* **1 a** : not rising or extending upward a great distance • *low mountains/peaks/hills* • *a low building* **b** : extending or reaching upward less than other things of the same kind • *low boots* • *a low fence* **c** : not located far above the ground, floor, etc. • *low clouds/altitudes/ceilings* **d** *always before a noun* : not rising above surrounding land • *The houses are built on low ground.* **2 a** : less than usual in amount, number, or degree • *a low (rate of) speed* • *low blood pressure* • *a low dose of medicine* • *low rates/prices* • *Demand for his books has remained low.* **b** : near or at the bottom of a range • *Temperatures were in the low eighties.* [=were around 81–83] **c** : not having enough or the amount needed • *Our supplies are getting/running low.* = *We're get-*

ting/running low on supplies. **d** : having less than the usual or average amount of something — often used in combination • *a low-calorie diet* **3 a** : not favorable • *He holds them in low regard/esteem.* = *He has a low opinion of them.* • *low hopes/expectations* • *Everyone was in low spirits.* [=*unhappy*] **b** : sad or unhappy • *She's been feeling low.* • *a low mood* **c** : not good • *low quality/standards* • *low marks/grades* • *low morale* • *Our vacation ended on a low note.* [=in an unpleasant way] • *the low point* [=the least enjoyable part] *of our vacation* **d** : morally bad • *a person of low character* • *a low trick* **4** : below others in power, importance, etc. • *a low priority* • *officials of low rank* **5 a** : not loud : SOFT • *a low whisper/moan* • *speaking in a low voice* **b** : near the bottom of a range of sounds • *a singer with a low* [=*deep*] *voice* **6 a** : not strong or forceful • *low winds* **b** : not bright • *plants that grow well in low light* **c** : not hot • *cooking over low heat* **7** : having qualities that do not appeal to intelligent people • *low art/humor* **8** : having less water than usual • *The river is low.* — **low in** : containing a small amount of (something) • *foods that are low in sodium/fat/calories* — **low·ness** *n* [*U*]

²**low** *adv* **1** : at or to a low place or level • *a village nestled low in the hills* • *The plane circled low over the airport.* • *a low-flying plane* **2 a** : in or to a low or poor condition • *a family brought low by misfortune* **b** : at a low rate • *a low-paid worker* **3** : at a low price • *buy low and sell high* **4** : with a quiet voice : not loudly • *speaking low* [=*softly*] — **high and low** see ²HIGH — **lie low** see ¹LIE

³**low** *n* [*C*] **1** : a low point or level • *Stocks fell to an all-time/record low.* • *The low* [=lowest temperature] *last night was 25.* • *the highs and lows* [=the good parts and bad parts] *of his career* **2** *weather* : an area of low atmospheric pressure

low beam *n* [*U, plural*] *US* : the setting of a vehicle's headlights that makes the least bright light • *Turn on/off your low beams.*

low blow *n* [*C*] **1** *boxing* : an illegal punch that hits a boxer below the waist **2** : an action or comment that is very hurtful and unfair • *Firing her on her birthday was really a low blow.*

low·brow /ˈloʊˌbraʊ/ *adj, often disapproving* : not interested in serious art, literature, etc. • *a lowbrow audience* : relating to or intended for a lowbrow audience • *lowbrow humor* • *a lowbrow comedy* — **lowbrow** *n* [*C*] • *Critics have dismissed him as a lowbrow.*

low-cut *adj* : having a neck opening that shows the top of the chest • *a low-cut blouse*

low·down /ˈloʊˌdaʊn/ *n* — **the lowdown** : important information or facts about something • *trying to get the lowdown on what happened* • *He gave me the lowdown about the situation.*

low–down /ˈloʊˌdaʊn/ *adj, always before a noun, informal* : morally bad : dishonest and unfair • *a low-down, good-for-nothing liar*

low-end /'loʊˌɛnd/ adj **low-er-end;**
low-est-end US : lower in price and
quality than most others ▪ a low-end
camera

¹low-er /'loʊɚ/ adj **1** always before a
noun : located below another or others
of the same kind ▪ her lower jaw/lip ▪ the
ship's upper and lower decks **2** : located
toward the bottom part of something ▪
her lower leg/back

²low-er /'loʊɚ/ vb **1** [T] : to make (something or someone) lower: such as **a** : to
cause (someone or something) to move
to a lower position ▪ He slowly lowered
himself into the chair. ▪ lower a flag/win-
dow ▪ She lowered her eyes. [=she looked
down] **b** : to reduce the loudness of
(something) ▪ Please lower your voice. **c**
: to reduce the value or amount of
(something) ▪ Prices have been lowered. ▪
lower your cholesterol **2** [I] : to become
lower : DECREASE ▪ The property has
lowered [=fallen] in value. — **lower yourself** : to do something that causes people
to have less respect for you ▪ I won't lower
myself to respond to these accusations.

low-er-case /ˌloʊɚˈkeɪs/ adj : having as
its typical form a, b, c rather than A, B, C
: not capital ▪ lowercase letters
— compare UPPERCASE — **lowercase**
n [U] ▪ letters written in lowercase

lower class n [C] : a social class that is
below the middle class and that has the
lowest status in a society ▪ a member of
the lower class/classes — **low-er-class**
/ˌloʊɚˈklæs, Brit ˌloʊɚˈklɑːs/ adj ▪ lower-
class families

lowest common denominator n [U]
1 mathematics : the smallest number
that can be divided exactly by all the
numbers below the lines in a group of
two or more fractions **2** disapproving —
used to say that the quality of something
is poor because it is intended to appeal to
the largest possible number of people ▪
The movie appeals to the lowest common
denominator.

low-fat adj : containing or having less fat
than usual ▪ a low-fat diet/food

low gear n [U] US : a gear that is used for
slower speeds in a vehicle ▪ She shifted
the car into low gear.

low-key /'loʊˈkiː/ also **low-keyed** /'loʊ-
ˈkiːd/ adj : quiet and relaxed ▪ a politician with a low-key style ▪ The party was a
low-key affair.

low-land /'loʊlənd/ n [C] : an area where
the land is at, near, or below the level of
the sea and is usually flat — usually plural ▪ a village in the lowlands — **lowland**
adj, always before a noun ▪ a lowland re-
gion/village — **low-land-er** /'loʊləndɚ/
n [C]

low-lev-el /'loʊˈlɛvəl/ adj : of low importance or rank ▪ low-level jobs/workers

low-life /'loʊˌlaɪf/ n, pl **-lifes** [C] US, informal : a bad person : a person of low
moral character ▪ a bunch of lowlifes

low-light /'loʊˌlaɪt/ n [C] US : a very unpleasant or dull part of something ▪ one
of the lowlights of our vacation

low-ly /'loʊli/ adj **low-li-er; -est** : low in
rank, position, or importance : HUMBLE
▪ a lowly clerk ▪ her lowly origins — **low-
li-ness** n [U]

low-ly-ing /'loʊˈlaɪɪŋ/ adj **1** : not far
above the level of the sea ▪ low-lying land/
hills **2** : close to the ground ▪ low-lying
clouds

low-pitched /'loʊˈpɪtʃt/ adj **low-er-
pitched; low-est-pitched** : making a
low sound : LOW ▪ a low-pitched hum/
voice

low-rank-ing adj, always before a noun
low-er-rank-ing; low-est-rank-ing
: having a low rank or position ▪ low-
ranking officials

low-rise /'loʊˈraɪz/ adj : not tall : having
few floors or stories ▪ a low-rise building

low-risk adj **1** : not likely to result in
failure, harm, or injury ▪ low-risk investments **2** : less likely than others to get a
particular disease, condition, or injury ▪
low-risk patients

low-spir-it-ed /'loʊˈspɪrətəd/ adj : feeling sad or depressed ▪ I've never seen her
looking so low-spirited.

low-tech /'loʊˈtɛk/ adj : not using new
electronic devices and technology : tech-
nologically simple ▪ a low-tech industry/
solution

low tide n [C/U] : the tide when the water
is at its lowest point ▪ You can walk across
the sandbar at low tide.

lox /'lɑːks/ n [U] chiefly US : smoked
salmon ▪ bagels and lox

loy-al /'lojəl/ adj : having or showing
complete and constant support for
someone or something : FAITHFUL ▪ the
team's loyal fans ▪ a loyal customer/sup-
porter/friend ▪ She remained loyal to her
friends. — **loy-al-ly** adv

loy-al-ist /'lojəlɪst/ n [C] : a person who is
loyal to a political cause, government, or
leader ▪ a group of party loyalists

loy-al-ty /'lojəlti/ n, pl **-ties 1** [U] : the
quality or state of being loyal ▪ the loyalty
of the team's fans ▪ his loyalty to the cause
2 [C] : a loyal feeling ▪ He was torn by
conflicting/divided loyalties.

loz-enge /'lɑːzɪndʒ/ n [C] : a small candy
that usually contains medicine ▪ a throat/
cough lozenge

LP /ˌɛlˈpiː/ n, pl **LP's** or **LPs** [C] : a phonograph record designed to be played at
33⅓ revolutions per minute ◆ **LP** is an
abbreviation of "long-playing record."

LSD /ˌɛlˌɛsˈdiː/ n [U] : an illegal drug that
causes people to see and hear things that
do not really exist

Lt. abbr lieutenant

Ltd. abbr limited — used in business
names ▪ Roundy & Son Ltd.

lu-au /'luːˌaʊ/ n [C] : a Hawaiian feast

lu-bri-cant /'luːbrɪkənt/ n [C/U] : a substance (such as grease or oil) that causes
something (such as a machine part) to be
slippery and to move more smoothly

lu-bri-cate /'luːbrəˌkeɪt/ vb **-cat-ed;
-cat-ing** [T] : to apply a lubricant to (a
machine, gear, etc.) ▪ lubricate an engine
— **lu-bri-ca-tion** /ˌluːbrəˈkeɪʃən/ n
[C/U]

lu-cid /'luːsəd/ adj **1** : very clear and
easy to understand ▪ a lucid explanation
2 : able to think clearly ▪ The patient has

remained lucid throughout his illness. — **lu·cid·i·ty** /luˈsɪdəti/ *n* [*U*] — **lu·cid·ly** *adv*

lu·cerne /luˈsən/ *n* [*U*] *Brit* : ALFALFA

Lu·ci·fer /ˈluːsəfə/ *n* [*singular*] — used as a name of the Devil

¹luck /ˈlʌk/ *n* [*U*] **1** : the things that happen to a person because of chance ▪ *We met by (pure) luck.* ▪ *She's hoping that her luck will change.* [=hoping that she will begin to have success] ▪ *have good/bad luck* ▪ *As luck would have it* [=because of good/bad luck], *I caught/missed the bus.* ▪ *(I wish you the) Best of luck in your new job!* = *Good luck (to you) in your new job!* ▪ *I'm sorry you lost. Better luck next time.* ▪ *She's been down on her luck* [=having bad luck] ▪ *"The bus already left." "(That's) Just my luck!"* [=I am often unlucky] ▪ *Luck was on my side.* = *Luck was with me.* [=I was lucky] ▪ *Luck was against me.* [=I was unlucky] ▪ *I have a job interview today. Wish me luck!* ▪ *(ironic) "I need more money." "Tough luck. I'm not giving you any more."* **2 a** : good fortune : good luck ▪ *We need a bit of luck.* = *We need a little luck.* ▪ *She gave him a kiss for luck.* ▪ *Some people/guys have all the luck.* [=some people are very lucky] ▪ *"I won!" "That's just beginner's luck."* ▪ *With (any) luck we'll arrive on time.* ▪ *You're in luck. The bus hasn't left yet.* ▪ *I had hoped to catch the last bus, but no such luck.* ▪ *I was out of luck: the bus had already left.* ▪ *He's trying his luck* [=hoping to succeed] *at starting his own restaurant.* **b** : success in doing or getting something ▪ *Have you had any luck (in) finding a job?* ▪ *"I'm looking for a job." "Any luck?" "No, not yet."* — **Lady Luck** *or* **lady luck** — used to refer to luck as if it were a woman ▪ *He blamed his problems on lady luck.* — **push your luck** *or US* **press your luck** : to take more risks or ask for more favors than you should ▪ *"Can you loan me more money?" "Don't press/push your luck."* — **the luck of the draw** — used to say that the result of something cannot be controlled and depends on chance ▪ *We might win or lose—it all depends on the luck of the draw.* — **luck·less** /ˈlʌkləs/ *adj* ▪ *a luckless loser*

²luck *vb* — **luck into** [*phrasal vb*] *US, informal* : to find or get (something) because of good luck ▪ *She lucked into a good job.* — **luck out** [*phrasal vb*] *US, informal* : to have good luck ▪ *We arrived late but we lucked out—the bus hadn't left yet.*

luck·i·ly /ˈlʌkəli/ *adv* — used to say that something good or lucky has happened ▪ *Luckily* [=fortunately] *no one was hurt.*

lucky /ˈlʌki/ *adj* **luck·i·er; -est 1** : having good luck : FORTUNATE ▪ *We're lucky that no one was hurt.* ▪ *He's lucky to be alive.* ▪ *Lucky you!* = *Aren't you the lucky one!* [=you are lucky] ▪ *I was lucky enough to get a ticket.* ▪ *the lucky few who got tickets* ▪ *the lucky winner* ▪ *(chiefly US) He's a lucky stiff.* [=lucky person] ▪ *He was always lucky in love.* [=lucky in his romantic relationships] **2** : resulting from or causing good luck ▪ *He scored on*

a lucky shot. ▪ *We got a lucky break.* ▪ *a lucky accident/coincidence* ▪ *a lucky coin/charm* ▪ *It's lucky for us that the weather is good.* ▪ *This must be your lucky day.* ▪ *You should thank your lucky stars* [=be very grateful] *that you have a friend like her.* — **get lucky** : to have good luck ▪ *We got lucky—there were still some tickets left.*

lu·cra·tive /ˈluːkrətɪv/ *adj* : producing money or wealth : PROFITABLE ▪ *a lucrative career/investment* — **lu·cra·tive·ly** *adv*

lu·di·crous /ˈluːdəkrəs/ *adj* : very foolish : RIDICULOUS ▪ *a ludicrous idea/suggestion* — **lu·di·crous·ly** *adv*

¹lug /ˈlʌg/ *vb* **lugged; lug·ging** [*T*] : to pull or carry (something) with great effort ▪ *She had to lug her suitcases out to the car.*

²lug *n* [*C*] **1** : a part (such as a handle) that sticks out like an ear **2** *US, informal + humorous* : a large and awkward or stupid man — often used to show affection ▪ *It's great to see you again, you big lug.*

lug·gage /ˈlʌgɪdʒ/ *n* [*U*] : the bags and suitcases that a person carries when traveling : BAGGAGE

lug nut *n* [*C*] *US* : a heavy piece of metal that is screwed on to the bolts that hold a wheel on a vehicle

lu·gu·bri·ous /luˈguːbrijəs/ *adj, formal* : very sad especially in an exaggerated way ▪ *wearing a lugubrious expression* — **lu·gu·bri·ous·ly** *adv*

luke·warm /ˈluːkˈwoəm/ *adj* **1** : slightly warm ▪ *a lukewarm bath* ▪ *I hate lukewarm coffee.* **2** : not enthusiastic ▪ *Our plan got a lukewarm reception.* ▪ *He was lukewarm about the idea.* — **luke·warm·ly** *adv*

¹lull /ˈlʌl/ *vb* [*T*] **1** : to cause (someone) to fall asleep or become sleepy ▪ *The music lulled him to sleep.* = *He was lulled to sleep by the music.* **2** : to cause (someone) to feel safe and relaxed instead of careful and alert ▪ *She was lulled into a false sense of security.*

²lull *n* [*C*] : a brief time when an action or activity stops ▪ *There was a lull in the conversation/action/storm.*

lul·la·by /ˈlʌləˌbaɪ/ *n, pl* **-bies** [*C*] : a song used to help a child fall asleep

lum·ba·go /ˌlʌmˈbeɪgoʊ/ *n* [*U*] : pain in the lower back ▪ *an attack of lumbago*

lum·bar /ˈlʌmbə/ *adj, always before a noun, medical* : relating to or lying near the lower back ▪ *the lumbar region*

¹lum·ber /ˈlʌmbə/ *vb* [*I*] : to move in a slow or awkward way ▪ *an elephant lumbering along* ▪ *trucks lumbering down the street* — **lumber with** [*phrasal vb*] **lumber (someone) with** *Brit, informal* : to cause (someone) to have (something unwanted or unpleasant) ▪ *His classmates lumbered him with an unfortunate nickname.*

²lumber *n* [*U*] *US* : wooden boards or logs that have been sawed and cut for use ▪ *trees turned into lumber* [=timber]

lum·ber·ing /ˈlʌmbərɪŋ/ *n* [*U*] *US* : the activity or business of making lumber from logs

lum·ber·jack /ˈlʌmbɚˌdʒæk/ n [C] : a person whose job is to cut down trees for wood

lum·ber·yard /ˈlʌmbɚˌjɑɚd/ n [C] US : a place where wooden boards are kept for sale

lu·mi·nary /ˈluːməˌneri, Brit ˈluːmənəri/ n, pl **-nar·ies** [C] : a very famous or successful person ▪ luminaries of the art world

lu·mi·nes·cence /ˌluːməˈnɛsn̩s/ n [U] technical : the creation of light by processes that do not involve heat; also : the light created ▪ the luminescence of the watch — **lu·mi·nes·cent** /ˌluːməˈnɛsn̩t/ adj ▪ a luminescent watch dial

lu·mi·nous /ˈluːmənəs/ adj 1 : producing or seeming to produce light ▪ luminous stars/galaxies ▪ a watch with a luminous dial 2 a : filled with light ▪ The room was luminous with sunlight. b : very bright in color ▪ a luminous blue — **lu·mi·nos·i·ty** /ˌluːməˈnɑːsəti/ n [singular] ▪ measuring a star's luminosity — **lu·mi·nous·ly** adv

¹**lump** /ˈlʌmp/ n [C] 1 : a small piece or mass of something ▪ a lump of coal/clay/sugar 2 : an area of swelling or growth on your body ▪ The blow left a lump on his head. — **a lump in your throat** : a tight feeling in your throat that you get when you are about to start crying or when you are trying not to cry ▪ I got a lump in my throat when he said goodbye. — **take your lumps** or **take a lot of lumps** US, informal : to be badly beaten or hurt ▪ He took a lot of lumps growing up in the city. ▪ (figurative) Their first album took its lumps from the critics.

²**lump** vb 1 [T] : to put (people or things) together or in the same group ▪ She often gets lumped in/together with other modern artists. 2 [I] : to form lumps : to become lumpy ▪ Stir the mixture to keep it from lumping. — **lump it** informal : to accept or allow something unpleasant or unwanted ▪ Like it or lump it [=whether you like it or not], the decision is final.

lump sum n [C] : an amount of money that is paid at one time ▪ The bonus is paid in a lump sum. ▪ a lump-sum payment

lumpy /ˈlʌmpi/ adj **lump·i·er**; **-est** : having lumps : full of lumps ▪ a lumpy mattress

lu·na·cy /ˈluːnəsi/ n [U] 1 a : extreme foolishness ▪ an act of sheer/pure lunacy b : something that is very foolish ▪ Quitting her job was lunacy. 2 old-fashioned : INSANITY

lu·nar /ˈluːnɚ/ adj, always before a noun : of or relating to the moon ▪ a lunar rock/eclipse

¹**lu·na·tic** /ˈluːnəˌtɪk/ n [C] informal 1 old-fashioned + sometimes offensive : an insane person ▪ He was raving like a lunatic. 2 : a person who behaves in a very foolish way ▪ My boss is a complete lunatic.

²**lunatic** adj, always before a noun 1 a old-fashioned + sometimes offensive : designed for insane people ▪ a lunatic asylum b : not sane ▪ a lunatic genius 2 : wildly foolish ▪ lunatic ideas/behavior

¹**lunch** /ˈlʌntʃ/ n [C/U] : a light meal eaten in the middle of the day ▪ eat/have (a healthy) lunch ▪ a picnic lunch ▪ What's for lunch? ▪ I bought her lunch. ▪ We discussed the idea over lunch. ▪ (informal) Let's **do lunch** [=have lunch and discuss business] sometime. ▪ He took her **out to lunch**. [=to a restaurant for lunch] — **lose your lunch** US slang : to throw up : VOMIT ▪ I felt like I was about to lose my lunch. — **no free lunch** ✧ The expression **there is no free lunch** or **there is no such thing as a free lunch** means that it is not possible to get something that is desired or valuable without having to pay for it in some way. — **out to lunch** informal : not aware of what is really happening ▪ That guy acts like he's out to lunch.

²**lunch** vb [I] : to eat lunch ▪ She often lunches in the park. — **lunch·er** n [C]

lunch box n [C] : a box in which a lunch can be kept and carried

lunch break n [C] : LUNCH HOUR

lunch counter n [C] US 1 : a long counter at which lunches are sold 2 : LUNCHEONETTE

lun·cheon /ˈlʌntʃən/ n [C] : a usually formal lunch that occurs as part of a meeting or for entertaining a guest ▪ a company luncheon

lun·cheon·ette /ˌlʌntʃəˈnɛt/ n [C] US : a small restaurant where lunches are served

luncheon meat n [C/U] : cooked meat (such as sliced meat or canned meat) that is usually eaten cold — called also (US) lunch meat

lunch hour n [C] : the time when people stop working or studying to have lunch ▪ She often runs errands during her lunch hour.

lunch·room /ˈlʌntʃˌruːm/ n [C] US 1 : a large room in a school or business where people eat lunch 2 : LUNCHEONETTE

lunch·time /ˈlʌntʃˌtaɪm/ n [C/U] : the time in the middle of the day when people usually eat lunch ▪ It was nearly lunchtime when we got there.

lung /ˈlʌŋ/ n [C] : either one of the two organs that people and animals use to breathe air ▪ He filled his lungs with fresh air. ▪ lung disease/cancer ▪ She shouted **at the top of her lungs**. [=as loudly as possible]

¹**lunge** /ˈlʌndʒ/ n [C] : a sudden forward movement ▪ He made a lunge at me.

²**lunge** vb **lunged**; **lung·ing** [I] : to move or reach forward in a sudden, forceful way ▪ He lunged at me.

lu·pus /ˈluːpəs/ n [U] : a disease that affects the nervous system, joints, and skin

¹**lurch** /ˈlɚtʃ/ vb [I] 1 : to make a sudden sideways or forward motion ▪ The bus lurched along/down the highway. ▪ The Jeep lurched to a stop. 2 : to move or walk in an awkward or unsteady way ▪ She tripped and lurched into the counter. ▪ He lurched to his feet. ▪ (figurative) lurching from one crisis to another

²**lurch** n [C] : a sudden sideways or forward movement ▪ The train gave a lurch as it left the station. — **leave (someone) in the lurch** : to leave someone without

help or protection when it is needed • *His advisers left him in the lurch when he needed them the most.*

¹**lure** /ˈlʊɚ/ *vb* **lured; lur·ing** [*T*] : to cause or persuade (a person or an animal) to go somewhere or to do something by offering some pleasure or gain • *They lured the bear out of its den.* • *luring shoppers into the store*

²**lure** *n* [*C*] **1** : an appealing or attractive quality • *the lure of easy money* **2** : a device used for attracting and catching animals • *a fishing lure*

lu·rid /ˈlʊrəd/ *adj, disapproving* **1** : causing shock or disgust • *lurid tabloid headlines* • *a lurid tale* **2** : shining or glowing with a bright and unpleasant color • *a lurid neon sign* — **lu·rid·ly** *adv*

lurk /ˈlɚk/ *vb* [*I*] : to wait in a hidden place especially in order to do something wrong • *She sensed someone lurking in the shadows.* • *(figurative)* Trouble lurks around every corner. — **lurk·er** *n* [*C*]

lus·cious /ˈlʌʃəs/ *adj* **1** : having a very appealing taste or smell : DELICIOUS • *luscious desserts* **2 a** : richly appealing • *a luscious singing voice* **b** *informal* : very physically attractive • *an incredibly luscious actress* — **lus·cious·ly** *adv* — **lus·cious·ness** *n* [*U*]

¹**lush** /ˈlʌʃ/ *adj* **1 a** : having a lot of full and healthy growth • *lush grass/growth* **b** : covered with healthy green plants • *lush green pastures* • *hills lush with grass* **2** : having a pleasingly rich quality • *lush photos* • *a lush carpet* — **lush·ly** *adv* — **lush·ness** *n* [*U*]

²**lush** *n* [*C*] *informal* : a person who is often drunk : DRUNK • *He's just an old lush.*

¹**lust** /ˈlʌst/ *n* **1** [*C/U*] : a strong feeling of sexual desire • *He was consumed by lust.* • *satisfying their lusts* **2** [*U, singular*] : a strong desire for something • *(a) lust for money/power/adventure* • *a lust for life* [=a strong desire to live a full and rich life] — **lust·ful** /ˈlʌstfəl/ *adj* • *He looked at her with lustful eyes.* • *lustful thoughts*

²**lust** *vb* [*I*] **1** : to have a strong sexual desire for someone • *He lusted after her.* = (*less commonly*) *He lusted for her.* **2** : to have a strong desire for something • *She's been lusting after that job.* • *lusting for profits* • *a general who lusted to command*

lus·ter (*US*) *or Brit* **lus·tre** /ˈlʌstɚ/ *n* [*singular*] **1** : the shiny quality of a surface that reflects light • *He polished the silver to restore its luster.* **2** : an appealing, exciting, or admired quality • *The job loses some of its luster after a while.* — **lus·trous** /ˈlʌstrəs/ *adj* • *lustrous silk* • *a lustrous surface*

lusty /ˈlʌsti/ *adj* **lust·i·er; -est** : full of strength and energy • *a lusty shout/cry* • *lusty singing* — **lust·i·ly** /ˈlʌstəli/ *adv* • *singing/cheering lustily*

lute /ˈluːt/ *n* [*C*] : a musical instrument with strings that was played especially in past centuries

Lu·ther·an /ˈluːθərən/ *n* [*C*] : a member of one of the Protestant churches that follow the teachings of Martin Luther — **Lutheran** *adj*

lux·u·ri·ant /ˌlʌɡˈʒɚrijənt, *Brit* ˌlʌɡ-

ˈzjʊəriənt/ *adj* **1** : having heavy and thick growth : LUSH • *a luxuriant beard* • *luxuriant vegetation* **2** : having an appealingly rich quality • *luxuriant music/colors* — **lux·u·ri·ance** /ˌlʌɡˈʒɚrijəns, *Brit* ˌlʌɡˈzjʊəriəns/ *n* [*U*] — **lux·u·ri·ant·ly** *adv*

lux·u·ri·ate /ˌlʌɡˈʒɚriˌeɪt, *Brit* ˌlʌɡˈzjʊəriˌeɪt/ *vb* **-at·ed; -at·ing** [*I*] : to enjoy something that is appealingly rich or relaxing • *He spent the morning luxuriating in his bed.*

lux·u·ri·ous /ˌlʌɡˈʒɚrijəs, *Brit* ˌlʌɡ-ˈzjʊəriəs/ *adj* **1** : very comfortable and expensive • *a luxurious apartment/hotel* • *luxurious fabrics/furs* **2** : feeling or showing a desire for expensive things • *luxurious tastes* — **lux·u·ri·ous·ly** *adv*

lux·u·ry /ˈlʌkʃəri/ *n, pl* **-ries** **1** [*U*] : a condition or situation of great comfort, ease, and wealth • *living in luxury* • *a luxury apartment* **2 a** [*C*] : something that is expensive and not necessary • *expensive wines and other luxuries* • *A new car is a luxury that I can't afford.* **b** [*singular*] : something that is helpful or welcome and that is not usually or always available • *We can't afford the luxury of waiting any longer.*

¹**-ly** /li/ *adv suffix* **1** : in a (specified) manner • *sadly* • *slowly* **2 a** : in a (specified) period of time • *weekly* **b** : to a (specified) degree or extent • *extremely good* **c** : in a (specified) place in a series • *secondly* • *lastly*

²**-ly** *adj suffix* : similar in appearance, manner, or nature to a (specified) person • *queenly* • *fatherly*

Ly·cra /ˈlaɪkrə/ *trademark* — used for a type of cloth that stretches

lye /ˈlaɪ/ *n* [*U*] : a strong chemical that is used especially in making soap

lying *present participle of* LIE

lymph /ˈlɪmf/ *n* [*U*] *medical* : a pale fluid that contains white blood cells and that passes through channels in the body and helps to keep bodily tissues healthy — **lym·phat·ic** /lɪmˈfætɪk/ *adj*

lymph node *n* [*C*] *medical* : any one of many rounded masses of tissue in the body through which lymph passes to be filtered and cleaned

lynch /ˈlɪntʃ/ *vb* [*T*] : to kill (someone) illegally as punishment for a crime • *He was lynched by an angry mob.*

lynch mob *n* [*C*] : a crowd of people who lynch or try to lynch someone

lynchpin *variant spelling of* LINCHPIN

lynx /ˈlɪŋks/ *n, pl* **lynx** *or* **lynx·es** [*C*] : a large wild cat of North America

lyre /ˈlajɚ/ *n* [*C*] : a musical instrument with strings that was used especially in ancient Greece

lyr·ic /ˈlɪrɪk/ *n* [*C*] **1** : the words of a song — usually plural • *She knows the lyrics to all her favorite songs.* **2** : a poem that expresses deep personal feelings in a way that is like a song • *a poet admired for his lyrics* — **lyric** *adj* • *Greek lyric poetry*

lyr·i·cal /ˈlɪrɪkəl/ *adj* : having an artistically beautiful or expressive quality • *a painter known for his lyrical landscapes*

— **lyr·i·cal·ly** /ˈlɪrɪkli/ adv • *lyrically beautiful writing* — **lyr·i·cism** /ˈlɪrəˌsɪzəm/ n [U] • *poetic lyricism*

lyr·i·cist /ˈlɪrəsɪst/ n [C] : a person who writes the words of a song : a writer of lyrics

M

¹**m** or **M** /ˈɛm/ n, pl **m's** or **ms** or **M's** or **Ms** 1 [C/U] : the 13th letter of the English alphabet • *a word that starts with (an) m* 2 [C] : the Roman numeral that means 1,000 • *MM* [=2,000]

²**m** abbr 1 male 2 married 3 meter 4 mile

M abbr 1 medium • *The shirt comes in S, M, L, and XL.* 2 million

ma /ˈmɑː/ n [C] informal : a person's mother • *When's supper, Ma?*

MA abbr 1 master of arts • *She has an MA in English.* 2 Massachusetts

ma'am /ˈmæm/ n [U] 1 US : MADAM 1 • *May I help you, ma'am?* 2 Brit — used to speak to the Queen or to a woman of high rank in the police or military

ma·ca·bre /məˈkɑːb, məˈkɑːbrə/ adj : involving death or violence in a way that is strange or frightening • *a macabre crime scene*

mac·a·ro·ni /ˌmækəˈrouni/ n [U] : a type of pasta in the shape of small curved tubes • *macaroni and cheese* [=macaroni in a cheese sauce]

mac·a·roon /ˌmækəˈruːn/ n [C] : a cookie made of egg, sugar, and almonds or coconut

ma·caw /məˈkɑː/ n [C] : a type of large, colorful parrot

¹**mace** /ˈmeɪs/ n [U] : a spice made from the covering of nutmeg

²**mace** vb **maced; mac·ing** [T] : to spray (a person) with Mace • *She maced her attacker.*

Mace /ˈmeɪs/ trademark — used for a spray that stings the eyes and skin and that is used against an attacker

Mach /ˈmɑːk, Brit ˈmæk/ n [U] technical — used to indicate the high speed of something • *a jet flying at Mach 2* [=twice the speed of sound]

ma·chete /məˈʃɛti/ n [C] : a large, heavy knife that is used for cutting plants and as a weapon

Ma·chi·a·vel·lian /ˌmækijəˈvɛlijən/ adj : clever and dishonest • *Machiavellian tactics*

mach·i·na·tions /ˌmækəˈneɪʃənz/ n [plural] formal : deceptive actions or methods that are used to get or achieve something • *the machinations of his enemies*

¹**ma·chine** /məˈʃiːn/ n 1 [C/U] : a piece of equipment with moving parts that does work when it is given power from electricity, gasoline, etc. • *How do you operate/use/run this machine?* • *The machine is working/running properly.* • *a fax machine* • *a soda/ice machine* [=a machine from which you can get soda/ice] • *(informal) I have a load of laundry in the*

machine. [=in the washing machine] • *The mail is sorted by machine.* [=with a machine] 2 [C] a : a person or group that does something efficiently or quickly like a machine • *He's an eating machine.* • *a publicity machine* b : a powerful and well-organized group • *Their army is a well-oiled machine.* — **ma·chine·like** /məˈʃiːnˌlaɪk/ adj • *working with machinelike efficiency*

²**machine** vb **-chined; -chin·ing** [T] : to shape (something) by using a machine • *machining the parts of an engine*

machine gun n [C] : a gun that is able to shoot many bullets very quickly — **machine–gun** vb **-gunned; -gun·ning** [T] • *machine-gun a target*

ma·chin·ery /məˈʃiːnəri/ n [U] 1 : machines of a particular kind or machines in general • *the factory's machinery* • *a piece of farm machinery* 2 : the working parts of a machine • *The machinery is clogged.* 3 : an organization or system by which something is done • *the machinery of government*

ma·chin·ist /məˈʃiːnɪst/ n [C] : a person who makes or operates machines

ma·cho /ˈmɑːtʃou, Brit ˈmætʃou/ adj, often disapproving : masculine in a very noticeable or exaggerated way • *a macho attitude*

mack·er·el /ˈmækərəl/ n, pl **mackerel** or **mack·er·els** [C/U] : a large fish that is often eaten as food

mack·in·tosh /ˈmækənˌtɑːʃ/ n [C] Brit, old-fashioned : RAINCOAT

mac·ra·mé /ˈmækrəˌmeɪ/ n [U] : the art of tying knots in string to make decorative things

mac·ro·bi·ot·ic /ˌmækroubaɪˈɑːtɪk/ adj : consisting of mainly whole grains and vegetables • *a macrobiotic diet*

mac·ro·cosm /ˈmækrəˌkɑːzəm/ n [singular] : a large system (such as the entire universe) that contains many smaller systems

mac·ro·eco·nom·ics /ˌmækrouˌɛkəˈnɑːmɪks, ˌmækrouˌiːkəˈnɑːmɪks/ n [U] : the study of large economic systems — **mac·ro·eco·nom·ic** /ˌmækrouˌɛkəˈnɑːmɪk, ˌmækrouˌiːkəˈnɑːmɪk/ adj

mad /ˈmæd/ adj **mad·der; mad·dest** 1 not before a noun, chiefly US, informal : very angry • *Don't make/get him mad.* • *She was mad at me for being late.* • *She was mad with jealousy/anger.* 2 a : having or showing severe mental illness • *He was stark raving mad.* [=completely insane] • *a movie about a mad scientist* b : unable to think in a clear or sensible way • *She was mad with jealousy/anger.* 3 chiefly Brit, informal : liking someone or something very much • *He's mad* *about her.* **4** *always before a noun* : wild and uncontrolled • *a mad rush/scramble* — **drive (someone) mad 1** : to cause (someone) to become mentally ill • *Years alone in the jungle had driven him mad.* **2** : to annoy or bother (someone) very much • *That noise is driving me mad!* — **go mad 1** : to become mentally ill • *He had gone mad after years alone in the jungle.* **2** : to act wildly • *The crowd went mad when the team won.* — **like mad** *informal* **1** : with a lot of energy and speed • *We've been working like mad.* **2** : very quickly • *spending money like mad* **3** : very much • *shivering like mad* — **mad·ly** /ˈmædli/ *adv* • *grinning madly* • *She fell madly in love with him.* — **mad·ness** /ˈmædnəs/ *n* [U] • *The tragedy nearly drove him to madness.* • *The idea was pure madness.*

mad·am /ˈmædəm/ *n* [C] **1** *pl* **mes·dames** /meɪˈdɑːm, meɪˈdæm/ *formal* — used to politely speak to a woman who you do not know • *Would you like a drink, madam?* **2 Madam** — used at the start of a formal letter to a woman whose name you do not know • *Dear Sir or Madam* **3 Madam** — used when you are speaking to a woman who has a high rank or position • *Madam President* **4** : a woman who is in charge of a brothel **5** *Brit, informal + disapproving* : a girl who expects other people to do things for her • *a bossy little madam*

mad·cap /ˈmædˌkæp/ *adj* : very foolish or silly • *madcap antics/schemes*

mad cow disease *n* [U] : a fatal disease that affects the brain and nervous system of cattle

mad·den /ˈmædn̩/ *vb* [T] : to make (someone) angry • *She was maddened by the delays.* • *her husband's maddening* [=very annoying] *habits* — **mad·den·ing·ly** /ˈmædn̩ɪŋli/ *adv* • *maddeningly slow service*

¹**made** *past tense and past participle of* ¹MAKE

²**made** /ˈmeɪd/ *adj* **1** *not before a noun* **a** — used to say that someone has the right qualities *to be* or *to do* something • *He was made to be an actor.* = *He was made to act.* **b** — used to say that something has the right qualities *for* or *to do* something • *She has a body made for running.* • *The furniture was made to last.* [=it will last a long time] **2** : built, formed, or shaped in a specified way • *American-made cars* — **have it made** *informal* : to be in a very good position or situation • *My brother has it made with a good job and a beautiful family.* — **made for each other** *informal* : perfectly suited to each other • *My parents were made for each other.* — **what you're made of** ◊ If people want to find out *what you're made of,* they want to see if you have the necessary courage, skill, etc., to succeed.

made-to-mea·sure *adj* : CUSTOM-MADE • *a made-to-measure suit*

made-to-or·der *adj* : CUSTOM-MADE • *made-to-order furniture*

made-up /ˈmeɪdˈʌp/ *adj* **1** : created from the imagination • *a made-up story/*

name **2** : wearing makeup • *She was nicely made-up.*

mad·house /ˈmædˌhaʊs/ *n* [C] *informal* : a place where there is a lot of excitement or confusion • *The stadium was a madhouse.*

mad·man /ˈmædˌmæn/ *n, pl* **-men** /-ˌmɛn/ [C] : an insane man • *(figurative, informal)* *He drives like a madman.* [=very recklessly]

Ma·don·na /məˈdɑːnə/ *n* **1 the Madonna** : the Virgin Mary : the mother of Jesus Christ **2** [C] : a painting or statue of the Virgin Mary

mad·ri·gal /ˈmædrɪgəl/ *n* [C] : a type of song for several singers without instruments

mad·wom·an /ˈmædˌwʊmən/ *n, pl* **-wom·en** /-ˌwɪmən/ [C] : an insane woman • *a story about a madwoman* *(figurative, informal)* *She's a madwoman on the dance floor.* [=she dances in a wild way]

mael·strom /ˈmeɪlstrəm/ *n* [C] *literary* : a situation in which there are many confused activities, emotions, etc. • *a maelstrom of emotions/activity*

mae·stro /ˈmaɪstroʊ/ *n, pl* **-stros** *also* **-stri** /ˈmaɪˌstriː/ [C] : an expert at writing, conducting, or teaching music • *Maestro Bernstein*

Ma·fia /ˈmɑːfijə, *Brit* ˈmæfiə/ *n* **1** : a secret criminal organization in Italy or a similar organization in the U.S. • *a member of the Mafia* = *a Mafia member* **2** *or* **mafia** [C] : a group of closely connected people who have great power or influence in a particular field or business • *He's an important figure in the television mafia.*

ma·fi·o·so /ˌmɑːfiˈoʊsoʊ, *Brit* ˌmæfiˈəʊsəʊ/ *n, pl* **-si** /-siː/ [C] : a member of the Mafia

mag·a·zine /ˈmægəˌziːn, ˌmægəˈziːn/ *n* [C] **1** : a type of thin book that is usually published every week or month • *literary/fashion/gardening magazines* • *a magazine article* **2** : a part of a gun that holds bullets

ma·gen·ta /məˈdʒɛntə/ *n* [C/U] : a deep purplish-red color

mag·got /ˈmægət/ *n* [C] : a wormlike insect that is a young form of a fly • *rotten meat infested with maggots*

mag·ic /ˈmædʒɪk/ *n* [U] **1 a** : a power that allows people to do impossible things by saying special words or performing special actions • *witches performing magic* • *She believes in magic.* • *(figurative) a mop that gets rid of dirt as if by magic* [=by the power of magic] • *(figurative) a mop that works like magic* [=that works very well] **2** : tricks that seem to be impossible and that are done to entertain people • *a book on how to do magic* **3** : special power, influence, or skill • *Their star pitcher seems to have lost his magic.* • *the kitchen where the cook works her magic* [=where she cooks very well] • *waiting for the medication to work its magic* [=to have its desired effect] **4** : a very pleasant, attractive, or exciting quality • *the magic of their singing* — **magic** *adj* • *a magic* *charm/potion/spell/wand* ▪ *a magic trick/ show/act* ▪ These problems haves no magic solution. [=there is no way to solve these problems quickly and easily] — **mag·i·cal** /ˈmædʒɪkəl/ *adj* ▪ *magical potions/ powers* ▪ *a magical* [=very pleasant or exciting] *evening* — **mag·i·cal·ly** /ˈmædʒɪkli/ *adv*

ma·gi·cian /məˈdʒɪʃən/ *n* [C] **1** : a person who is skilled in magic ▪ *The magician pulled a rabbit out of a hat.* **2** : a person who has amazing skills ▪ *She's a magician in the kitchen.*

Magic Marker *trademark* — used for a felt-tip pen

mag·is·te·ri·al /ˌmædʒəˈstirijəl/ *adj* **1** *formal* : showing impressive knowledge about a subject ▪ *Her book is a magisterial study of the artist.* **2** *formal* : having the confident quality of someone who expects to be obeyed by other people ▪ *He spoke with a magisterial tone.* **3** : of or relating to a magistrate ▪ *magisterial duties*

mag·is·trate /ˈmædʒəˌstreɪt/ *n* [C] : a local official who has some of the powers of a judge

mag·ma /ˈmægmə/ *n* [U] *technical* : hot liquid rock below Earth's surface

mag·nan·i·mous /mægˈnænəməs/ *adj, formal* : having or showing a generous and kind nature — *a magnanimous gesture/person* — **mag·na·nim·i·ty** /ˌmægnəˈnɪməti/ *n* [U] ▪ *He had the magnanimity to forgive her.* — **mag·nan·i·mous·ly** *adv*

mag·nate /ˈmægˌneɪt/ *n* [C] : a person who has great wealth and power in a particular business or industry ▪ *a railroad magnate*

magnesia see MILK OF MAGNESIA

mag·ne·sium /mægˈniːzijəm/ *n* [U] : a silver-white metallic element

mag·net /ˈmægnət/ *n* [C] **1** : a piece of material that can attract iron **2** : something or someone that attracts people or things ▪ *The town is a tourist magnet.* = *The town is a magnet for tourists.*

mag·net·ic /mægˈnɛtɪk/ *adj* **1** : of or relating to a magnet or magnetism ▪ *a strong magnetic field* **2** : having great power to attract the interest of other people ▪ *a magnetic personality/performer* — **mag·net·i·cal·ly** /mægˈnɛtɪkli/ *adv*

magnetic resonance im·ag·ing /-ˈɪmɪdʒɪŋ/ *n* [U] *medical* : a method used to produce images of the inside of a person's body — called also *MRI*

magnetic tape *n* [U] : a thin plastic tape on which sound, TV images, etc., may be stored

mag·ne·tism /ˈmægnəˌtɪzəm/ *n* [U] **1** : the power of a magnet to attract iron **2** : a quality that makes someone able to attract the interest of other people ▪ *his personal magnetism*

mag·ne·tize *also Brit* **mag·ne·tise** /ˈmægnəˌtaɪz/ *vb* -**tized**; -**tiz·ing** [T] : to cause (something) to become magnetic ▪ *a magnetized particle*

mag·nif·i·cent /mægˈnɪfəsənt/ *adj* : very beautiful or impressive ▪ *magnificent cathedrals/performances* — **mag·nif·i-**

cence /mægˈnɪfəsəns/ *n* [U] — **mag·nif·i·cent·ly** *adv*

mag·ni·fy /ˈmægnəˌfaɪ/ *vb* -**fies**; -**fied**; -**fy·ing** [T] **1 a** : to make (something) greater ▪ *The sound was magnified by the calm air.* **b** : to make (something) seem greater or more important than it is ▪ *His failures were magnified by his sister's success.* **2** : to make (something) appear larger ▪ *The lens magnifies images 100 times.* — **mag·ni·fi·ca·tion** /ˌmægnəfəˈkeɪʃən/ *n* [C/U] ▪ *magnification of an image* ▪ *examining cells under magnification* — **mag·ni·fi·er** /ˈmægnəˌfajɚ/ *n* [C]

magnifying glass *n* [C] : a specially shaped piece of glass that is used to make an object look larger than it is ▪ *She examined the diamond with a magnifying glass.*

mag·ni·tude /ˈmægnəˌtuːd, Brit ˈmægnəˌtjuːd/ *n* **1** [U] : the size, extent, or importance of something ▪ *No one knows the real magnitude of the problem.* **2** [C/U] *technical* : a number that shows the power of an earthquake ▪ *a magnitude 6.7 earthquake*

mag·no·lia /mægˈnoʊljə/ *n* [C] : a tree that has large, usually white flowers

mag·pie /ˈmægˌpaɪ/ *n* [C] : a noisy black-and-white bird

ma·hog·a·ny /məˈhɑːgəni/ *n* [U] : a strong reddish-brown wood that is used especially for making furniture

maid /ˈmeɪd/ *n* [C] **1** : a female servant ▪ *She hired a maid to clean the house.* ▪ *a hotel maid* **2** *literary* : MAIDEN ▪ *a young maid* — see also OLD MAID

¹**maid·en** /ˈmeɪdn/ *n* [C] *literary* : a young girl or woman who is not married ▪ *a knight who rescues a fair maiden* ▪ *a maiden in distress*

²**maiden** *adj, always before a noun* : first or earliest ▪ *the ship's maiden voyage*

maiden name *n* [C] : a woman's family name before she is married ▪ *my mother's maiden name*

maid of honor (*US*) *or Brit* **maid of honour** *n* [C] *chiefly US* : an unmarried woman who is the main bridesmaid at a wedding ▪ *Her sister was her maid of honor.*

¹**mail** /ˈmeɪl/ *n* [U] **1** : the system used for sending letters and packages from one person to another ▪ *They do business by mail.* ▪ *The check is in the mail.* [=it has been sent and will be delivered by mail] — called also (*chiefly Brit*) *post* **2** : letters or packages sent from one person to another ▪ *Did we get any mail today?* ▪ *Has the mail arrived yet?* ▪ *a pile of mail* ▪ *They get a lot of hate mail.* [=angry letters, e-mail, etc.] — called also (*chiefly Brit*) *post* **3** : E-MAIL

²**mail** *vb* [T] *chiefly US* : to send (something) by mail ▪ *We just mailed (out) the invitations.* ▪ *She mailed me a letter.*

mail·box /ˈmeɪlˌbɑːks/ *n* [C] *chiefly US* **1** : a public box in which letters are placed to be collected and sent out **2** : a private box on or near a house in which mail is placed when it is delivered **3** : a computer folder that holds e-mail ▪ *an electronic mailbox*

mail carrier *n* [C] *US* : LETTER CARRIER

mail·er /ˈmeɪlɚ/ n [C] chiefly US : something (such as an advertisement) that is sent by mail

mail·ing /ˈmeɪlɪŋ/ n **1** [U] : the act of mailing something ▪ The letters are ready for mailing. **2** [C] : a letter, advertisement, etc., that is mailed to many people at one time ▪ mass mailings

mailing list n [C] : a list of names and addresses to which mail is sent ▪ The charity sent out letters to everyone on its mailing list.

mail·man /ˈmeɪlˌmæn/ n, pl -men /-ˌmɛn/ [C] US : a man who delivers mail

mail order n [C/U] : an order for products that are sent and received by mail ▪ She purchased the books by mail order. ▪ a mail-order catalog [=a catalog of products that can be ordered through the mail]

mail·shot /ˈmeɪlˌʃɑːt/ n [C] Brit : MAILING

maim /ˈmeɪm/ vb [T] : to injure (someone) very badly by violence ▪ The bomb maimed several people.

¹main /ˈmeɪn/ adj, always before a noun : most important ▪ the main idea/purpose ▪ The company's main office is in New York. ▪ the novel's main character ▪ the main road/entrance ▪ the appetizer and main course ▪ the evening's main event — **main·ly** adv ▪ I don't like the plan, mainly because it's too expensive. ▪ They depend mainly upon fish for food.

²main n **1** [C] : the largest pipe in a system of connected pipes ▪ a gas/water main **2** [plural] Brit **a** : the system of pipes or wires for electricity, gas, or water ▪ We lost mains water/electricity during the storm. **b** : the place where electricity, gas, or water enters a building or room ▪ Turn off the water at the mains. — **in the main** : in general — used to say that a statement is true in most cases or at most times ▪ The workers are in the main very capable. [=most of the workers are very capable]

main drag n [C] US, informal : the main street in a town or city ▪ cruising down the main drag

main·frame /ˈmeɪnˌfreɪm/ n [C] : a large and very fast computer

main·land /ˈmeɪnˌlænd/ n [singular] : a large area of land that forms a country or a continent and that does not include islands ▪ the Chinese mainland = mainland of China = mainland China ▪ returning to the mainland

¹main·line /ˈmeɪnˌlaɪn/ adj, chiefly US : belonging to an established and widely accepted group or system ▪ mainline [=mainstream] churches

²mainline vb -lined; -lin·ing [T/I] slang : to inject (a drug) directly into a vein ▪ He began mainlining (heroin).

main·spring /ˈmeɪnˌsprɪŋ/ n [C] **1** : the most important spring in a watch or clock **2** : the most important or powerful cause or part of something ▪ Agriculture is the mainspring of their economy.

main·stay /ˈmeɪnˌsteɪ/ n [C] : a very important part of something ▪ Fish is a mainstay of their diet.

main·stream /ˈmeɪnˌstriːm/ n — the

mainstream : the thoughts, beliefs, and choices that are accepted by the largest number of people ▪ His ideas are well outside the mainstream. — **mainstream** adj ▪ mainstream medicine [=the type of medicine that is most widely practiced]

main·tain /meɪnˈteɪn/ vb [T] **1** : to cause (something) to exist or continue without changing ▪ trying to maintain a healthy weight **2** : to keep (something) in good condition by making repairs, correcting problems, etc. ▪ The house has been poorly maintained. **3** : to continue having or doing (something) ▪ She still maintains a close relationship with her college roommate. ▪ maintain control/balance/order ▪ He struggled to maintain his composure. [=to remain calm and not become upset] **4** : to say that (something) is true ▪ He maintains his innocence. = He maintains that he is innocent. **5** : to provide support for (someone or something) ▪ He has a family to maintain. — **main·te·nance** /ˈmeɪntənəns/ n [U] ▪ car maintenance ▪ maintenance of law and order ▪ a maintenance worker [=a worker whose job is to keep property or equipment in good condition]

maize /ˈmeɪz/ n [U] : CORN 1a

maj·es·ty /ˈmædʒəsti/ n, pl -ties **1** [U] : a great and impressively beautiful quality ▪ the majesty of the mountains **2 Majesty** [C] — used as a title for a king, queen, emperor, or empress; used with his, her, your, or their ▪ Yes, your Majesty. ▪ Her Majesty's Government — **ma·jes·tic** /məˈdʒɛstɪk/ adj ▪ majestic mountains — **ma·jes·ti·cal·ly** /məˈdʒɛstɪkli/ adv

¹ma·jor /ˈmeɪdʒɚ/ adj **1 a** : very important ▪ a major event/artist/city ▪ She played a major role in the negotiations. ▪ No major changes are expected. **b** always before a noun : large in number, amount, or extent ▪ Butter is a major ingredient in the recipe. **2** : very serious or bad ▪ None of the problems are major. ▪ a major accident/illness **3** music : having semitones between the third and fourth and the seventh and eighth notes ▪ a major scale/key

²major n [C] **1** : a military officer in the army, air force, or marines who ranks above a captain ▪ an Army major **2** US **a** : the main subject studied by a college student ▪ He chose history as his major and French as his minor. **b** : a student who has a specified main subject of study ▪ He was a history major.

³major vb — **major in** [phrasal vb] US : to have (something) as your main subject of study in college ▪ He majored in history.

ma·jor·ette /ˌmeɪdʒəˈrɛt/ n [C] : a girl or woman who marches with a band and spins a baton

ma·jor·i·ty /məˈdʒɑːrəti/ n, pl -ties **1** [singular] : a number that is greater than half of a total ▪ a policy supported by the vast/overwhelming majority of (the) voters ▪ the majority opinion [=the opinion of most of the people] **2 a** [C] : a number of votes that is more than half of the total number ▪ The bill failed to win a majority in the Senate. [=fewer than half of the senators voted for the bill] **b** [*singular*] : the group or party that is the greater part of a large group • *The Republicans are currently the majority in the Senate.* • *Supporters of the law are* **in the majority.** [=most people support the law]

major leagues *n* — **the major leagues** : the two highest U.S. baseball leagues — *playing in the major leagues* — **major-league** *adj* • *major-league baseball/players* — **major leagu·er** *n* [C]

¹**make** /ˈmeɪk/ *vb* **made** /ˈmeɪd/; **mak·ing**
1 [*T*] **a** : to build, create, or produce (something) by work or effort • *He works in a factory that makes jet engines.* • *She made the dress herself.* • *make a fire* • *a salad dressing made with oil and vinegar* • *Cheese is made from milk.* • *a box made of wood* [=a wooden box] **b** : to use (something) to create a product — + *into* • *She made the material into a dress.* **2** [*T*] : to cause (something) to exist, happen, or appear • *The car started making a strange noise.* • *I try not to make trouble/mistakes.* • *make a doctor's appointment* • *They moved over and made room for them.* **3** [*T*] : to create or write (something) in an official or legal way • *I'm not the one who makes the rules.* **4** [*T*] : to produce, direct, or act in (something) • *That actor/director has made many films.* **5** [*T*] : to cause (something or someone) to be changed in a specified way • *The experience made him (into) a cynic.* **6** [*T*] : to cause (something or someone) to have a specified quality, feeling, etc. • *A good teacher makes learning fun.* • *She made us really angry.* • *Do these pants make me look fat?* • *He made it clear that he expected us to help.* • *The experience made him cynical.* • *Why don't you make yourself useful* [=do something useful] *by washing the dishes?* **7** [*T*] : to cause (something) to be or become something • *Yes, you can leave work early today, but don't make it a habit.* **8** [*T*] **a** : to cause (someone) to do something • *He made her cry.* • *How can I make you understand that I love you?!* **b** : to force (someone) to do something • *They made me wait for an hour.* • *If he doesn't want to do it, we can't make him (do it).* **9** [*T*] : to give a particular job, title, status, etc., to (someone) • *They made him (the) Emperor.* • *They made her a member of their club.* **10** [*T*] : to perform (a particular action) • *I have to make a phone call.* [=I have to call someone] • *May I make a suggestion?* [=may I suggest something?] • *Make a decision.* *"Make love, not war!" he shouted.* • *She made a promise to him.* = *She made him a promise.* **11** [*T*] : to form (a plan) in your mind • *Have you made any plans for your vacation?* **12** [*T*] : to arrange the blankets and sheets on (a bed) so that the mattress is covered • *She made the bed and got dressed.* **13** [*T*] : to prepare (food or drink) • *She helped me make dinner.* • *Can I make you a drink?* **14 a** [*linking vb*] — used to indicate a total • *I've lost again! That makes $3 I owe you.* "*I'm hungry." "That makes two of us."* [=I'm hungry too] **b** [*T*] : to be equal to (an amount) • *Three plus two make/*

makes *five.* **c** [*T*] : to calculate (an amount, total, etc.) • *What time do you make it?"* [=what do you think the time is?] **15** [*linking vb*] : to be suited for use as (something) • *This building would make a fine school.* **b** : to be or become (something) • *They make a lovely couple.* • *She will make a fine judge one day.* **16** [*T*] : to earn or gain (money, a profit, etc.) • *He makes $50,000 a year.* • *She made $100 on the deal.* • *He* **makes a/his living** *by doing small jobs.* • *He* **made a/his fortune** *in the stock market.* **17** [*T*] **a** : to be accepted as a member of (a group) • *She made the team.* **b** : to appear on or in (a newspaper, a headline, etc.) • *The story made the front page of the paper.* • *making headlines* **18** [*T*] *sports* **a** : to succeed in doing (something that you attempt) • *I missed the first shot but made the second one.* **b** : to produce (a particular score) • *He made a birdie/bogey.* **19** [*T*] **a** : to not be too late for (something) • *They (just/barely) made the train/deadline.* **b** : to reach or go to (a place) • *We made Atlanta in under two hours.* **c** : to succeed in reaching or going to (something) • *The team made the play-offs.* • *I can't make that meeting.* **20** [*T*] : to act in a way that causes someone to be your friend, enemy, etc. • *She makes friends easily.* **21** [*T*] : to cause the success of (someone or something) • *This film could make or break her career.* [=her career could depend on the success or failure of this film] **22** [*T*] : to cause (something) to be enjoyable, attractive, etc. • *His compliment really made my day!* — **make a face** see ¹FACE — **make believe** see BELIEVE — **make do** : to do what you can with the things that you have • *We don't have much money, but we somehow make do.* • *If we don't have carrots for the soup, we'll have to make do (without them).* — **make eyes at** see ¹EYE — **make for** [*phrasal vb*] **1** : to go toward (a place) quickly • *Everyone made for the exits.* **2** : to cause (something) to happen or to be more likely • *Courtesy makes for safer driving.* — **make it 1** : to reach a particular place, goal, etc. • *We finally made it to the top of the mountain.* • *Welcome! I'm glad you could make it (to the party)!* • *trying to make it home before dark* **2** : to not fail, die, etc. : SURVIVE • *Many new businesses don't make it through their first year.* **3** : to become successful • *I know you'll make it eventually.* • *He made it big* [=became very successful] *in real estate.* — **make like** *US, informal* **1** : to pretend to be (someone or something) • *making like a rooster* **2** : to act in a way that does not show your true feelings • *He made like he didn't care.* — **make love** see ¹LOVE — **make much of** : to treat (something) as very important • *Don't make too much of what he said—he was only joking.* — **make nice** see NICE — **make of** [*phrasal vb*] **1** **make (something) of** : to have an opinion about (something or someone) • *I don't know what to make of her behavior.* [=I don't understand her behavior] **2** **make (a** *day, night, etc.) of it* : to continue doing an activity during all of (a day, night, etc.) ▪ *Let's make an evening of it and go to a movie after dinner.* **3 make something of (yourself or your life)** : to become successful ▪ *She has worked very hard to make something of herself.* — **make off** [*phrasal vb*] **1** *chiefly Brit* : to leave quickly especially in order to escape ▪ *The thieves made off toward the highway.* **2 make off with** : to take or steal (something) and go away ▪ *They made off with thousands of dollars.* — **make out** [*phrasal vb*] **1 make (something or someone) out** or **make out (something or someone) a** : to write down the required information on (something) ▪ *He made out a check for $100.* ▪ *make out a shopping list* **b** : to see and identify (something) ▪ *We could just make out a ship on the horizon.* **c** : to hear and understand (something) ▪ *I couldn't make out what she said.* **d** : to learn or understand (something) by studying, searching, etc. ▪ *We're still trying to make out what really happened.* **e** *informal* : to understand the behavior of (someone) ▪ *I can't make him out.* [=figure him out] **f** : to describe (someone or something) in a specified and usually false way ▪ *He's not as bad as he's made out (to be).* = *He's not as bad as people make him out (to be).* **2** *informal* — used to ask about or describe the success or progress of someone or something ▪ *"How are you making out in your new job?" "Just fine, thanks!"* **3** *chiefly US, informal* : to kiss and touch for a long time in a sexual way ▪ *They were making out in his car.* — **make over** [*phrasal vb*] **make (something or someone) over** or **make over (something or someone)** : to change the appearance of (something or someone) ▪ *making a room over* — **make up** [*phrasal vb*] **1 make (something or someone) up** or **make up (something or someone) a** : to create or invent (a story, a lie, etc.) ▪ *Stop making up excuses.* ▪ *It never happened: you made it all up!* **b** : to combine to produce (something) ▪ *This book is made up of 10 chapters.* **c** : to produce or create (something) by putting together different parts ▪ *make up a shopping list* **d** : to prepare (something) so that it is ready to be used ▪ *I'll make up a bed for you.* [=I'll prepare a bed for you to use] **e** *Brit* : to supply (something) according to directions ▪ *make up* [=(US) *fill*] *a prescription* **f** : to provide an amount of time, money, etc., that is needed ▪ *If you pay half, I'll make up the rest/difference.* ▪ *I have to leave work early today, but I'll make up the time tomorrow.* **g** : to put makeup on (someone or someone's face) ▪ *She made herself up for the party.* **h** : to change the appearance of (someone or something) by using costumes, decorations, etc. ▪ *The room was made up to look like a disco.* **2** *informal* : to become friendly again after being angry ▪ *He made up with his girlfriend.* **3 make up for** : to do or have something as a way of correcting or improving (something else) ▪ *She tried*

to make up for lost time by working extra hard. **4 make it up to** : to do something helpful or good for (someone you have hurt or treated wrongly) ▪ *I'm sorry. Let me make it up to you by buying you dinner.* — **make up your mind** see ¹MIND — **make your way, make way** see ¹WAY — see also ²MADE

²make *n* [*C*] : a group of products that are all made by a particular company and given a particular name ▪ *different makes and models* ▪ *"What make of car is that?" "It's a Ford."* — **on the make** *informal* : trying to get money, power, or sex ▪ *a man who is always on the make*

make‑be‑lieve /ˈmeɪkbəˌliːv/ *n* [*U*] : things that are imagined or pretended to be true or real ▪ *He has been living in a world of make-believe.* [=he has been believing things that are not true] ▪ *living in a make-believe world*

make‑or‑break /ˈmeɪkəˈbreɪk/ *adj, always before a noun* : resulting in either definite success or definite failure ▪ *a make-or-break decision*

make‑over /ˈmeɪkˌoʊvə/ *n* [*C*] : the act or process of making changes to improve the appearance or effectiveness of someone or something ▪ *She's in need of a fashion makeover.* ▪ *They gave their store a makeover.*

mak‑er /ˈmeɪkə/ *n* [*C*] : a person, company, or machine that makes something ▪ *a maker of action films* ▪ *government policymakers* ▪ *one of the nation's leading makers* [=manufacturers] *of fine cars* ▪ *an ice-cream maker* ▪ *a coffeemaker* — **meet your maker** or **meet your Maker** : to die ▪ *He says he's not afraid to meet his maker.*

make‑shift /ˈmeɪkˌʃɪft/ *adj* : used as a rough replacement for something ▪ *A large box served as a makeshift table.*

make‑up /ˈmeɪkˌʌp/ *n* **1** [*singular*] : the way in which something is put together or arranged ▪ *the makeup of the Earth's atmosphere* **2** [*U*] **a** : substances (such as lipstick or powder) used to make someone's face look more attractive ▪ *She put on some makeup before the party.* **b** : materials (such as wigs or cosmetics) that are used to change the appearance of an actor ▪ *theatrical/stage makeup* **3** [*C*] *US* : a special test for a student who has missed or failed a previous test ▪ *He'll have to pass the makeup (test/exam) to graduate.*

mak‑ing /ˈmeɪkɪŋ/ *n* **1** [*U*] : the action or process of making something ▪ *policymaking* ▪ *The film was three years in the making.* [=it took three years to make the film] ▪ *We were watching history in the making.* [=watching an important historical event as it happened] ▪ *The problem was entirely of your own making.* [=it was caused by your own actions] **2** [*plural*] **a** *US* : the people or things that are needed for making something ▪ *With beans, cheese, and tortillas, you have (all) the makings of/for a burrito.* **b** : the qualities that are needed to become something ▪ *He has (all) the makings of* [=he has the talent needed to become] *a great quarterback.*

mal·ad·just·ed /ˌmælə'dʒʌstəd/ adj : not able to deal with other people in a normal or healthy way ▪ a maladjusted teenager — **mal·ad·just·ment** /ˌmælə'dʒʌstmənt/ n [U]

mal·adroit /ˌmælə'drɔɪt/ adj, formal : very awkward : not skillful or adroit ▪ the governor's maladroit handling of the budget crisis — **mal·adroit·ly** adv

mal·a·dy /'mælədi/ n, pl -dies [C] formal : a disease or illness ▪ a mysterious malady ▪ (figurative) crime and other social maladies

ma·laise /mə'leɪz/ n [U, singular] 1 medical : a general feeling of not being healthy or happy ▪ (a) physical/spiritual malaise 2 : a problem or condition that harms or weakens a group, society, etc. ▪ (a) deep economic malaise

ma·lar·ia /mə'lerijə/ n [U] : a serious disease that is passed between people by mosquitoes — **ma·lar·i·al** /mə'lerijəl/ adj

mal·con·tent /ˌmælkən'tɛnt, Brit 'mælkən'tɛnt/ n [C] disapproving : a person who is usually unhappy or angry about something ▪ Her boss is a malcontent.

¹**male** /'meɪl/ adj 1 a : of or relating to the sex that cannot produce young or lay eggs ▪ a male bird/mammal ▪ male and female athletes b : characteristic of boys or men ▪ a male [=masculine] voice/name c : having members who are all boys or men ▪ a male choir 2 of a plant : not producing fruit or seeds — **male·ness** n [U]

²**male** n [C] 1 : a man or a boy ▪ The school has more males than females. 2 : a male animal ▪ the male of the species 3 : a plant that does not produce seed or fruit

male·fac·tor /'mælə'fæktə/ n [C] formal : someone who is guilty of a crime or offense ▪ chronic malefactors [=criminals]

ma·lev·o·lent /mə'lɛvələnt/ adj, formal : having or showing a desire to cause harm to another person ▪ a malevolent lie/smile — **ma·lev·o·lence** /mə'lɛvələns/ n [U] — **ma·lev·o·lent·ly** adv

mal·fea·sance /ˌmæl'fiːzn̩s/ n [U] law : illegal or dishonest activity ▪ corporate malfeasance

mal·for·ma·tion /ˌmælfoɚ'meɪʃən/ n [C/U] medical : a condition in which part of the body does not have the normal shape ▪ (a) malformation of the spine

mal·formed /ˌmæl'foɚmd/ adj, medical : not having the normal or expected shape ▪ a malformed foot

mal·func·tion /ˌmæl'fʌŋkʃən/ n [I] : to fail to function or work properly ▪ a problem that caused the system to malfunction — **malfunction** n [C/U] ▪ a system malfunction

mal·ice /'mæləs/ n [U] : a desire to cause harm to another person ▪ Her criticisms were without malice. — **ma·li·cious** /mə'lɪʃəs/ adj : malicious gossip/liars — **ma·li·cious·ly** adv — **ma·li·cious·ness** n [U]

ma·lign /mə'laɪn/ vb [T] formal : to criticize (someone or something) publicly in a harsh or unfair way ▪ He was unfairly maligned in the press. ▪ They have given

up their much-maligned [=widely criticized] attempt to reform tax policy.

ma·lig·nant /mə'lɪgnənt/ adj 1 medical : likely to grow and spread in an uncontrolled way that can cause death : CANCEROUS ▪ a malignant tumor/growth 2 formal : very evil ▪ a powerful and malignant influence — **ma·lig·nan·cy** /mə'lɪgnənsi/ n, pl -cies [C/U] ▪ The test revealed a malignancy in her chest. — **ma·lig·nant·ly** adv

ma·lin·ger /mə'lɪŋgə/ vb [I] : to pretend to be sick or injured in order to avoid doing work ▪ His boss suspected him of malingering. — **ma·lin·ger·er** /mə'lɪŋgɚə/ n [C]

mall /'mɑːl/ n [C] 1 : a large building that contains many different kinds of stores ▪ They spent the afternoon shopping at the mall. 2 : a public area where people walk ▪ a pedestrian mall

mal·lard /'mæləd/ n, pl mallard or mallards [C] : a common wild duck

mal·lea·ble /'mælijəbəl/ adj 1 technical : able to be stretched or bent ▪ a malleable metal 2 formal : able to be easily changed or influenced ▪ malleable young minds — **mal·lea·bil·i·ty** /ˌmælijə'bɪləti/ n [U]

mal·let /'mælət/ n [C] 1 : a hammer with a large usually wooden head 2 sports : a club used for hitting the ball in croquet or polo

mal·nour·ished /ˌmæl'nɚɪʃt/ adj : not eating enough food or not eating enough healthy food : suffering from malnutrition ▪ malnourished children

mal·nu·tri·tion /ˌmælnu'trɪʃən, Brit ˌmælnju'trɪʃən/ n [U] : the unhealthy condition that results from not eating enough food or not eating enough healthy food ▪ a program to prevent malnutrition

mal·odor·ous /ˌmæl'oudərəs/ adj, formal : having a bad smell ▪ malodorous chemicals

mal·prac·tice /ˌmæl'præktəs/ n [U] law : careless, wrong, or illegal actions by someone who is performing a professional duty ▪ a doctor/surgeon accused of malpractice

malt /'mɑːlt/ n 1 [U] : grain and especially barley that is used in making beer, whiskey, etc. 2 [C] US, informal : MALTED MILK ▪ a chocolate malt 3 [C/U] : liquor made with malt

malted milk n [C/U] US : a drink made by mixing a special powder into a liquid (such as milk) and usually adding ice cream and flavoring

mal·treat /ˌmæl'triːt/ vb [T] : to treat (someone) in a rough or cruel way ▪ maltreating prisoners — **mal·treat·ment** /ˌmæl'triːtmənt/ n [U] ▪ the maltreatment of prisoners

ma·ma or **mam·ma** also **mom·ma** /'mɑːmə/ n [C] informal : a person's mother

mama's boy n [C] US, disapproving : a boy or man who is seen as weak because he is controlled or protected too much by his mother

mam·mal /'mæməl/ n [C] : a type of animal that has hair or fur and that feeds milk to its young • *Humans, dogs, and cats are all mammals.* — **mam·ma·li·an** /məˈmeɪlijən/ *adj, technical* • *mammalian species*

mam·ma·ry /ˈmæməri/ *adj, technical* : of or relating to the breasts • **mammary glands** [=glands that produce milk in the breasts]

mam·mo·gram /ˈmæməˌgræm/ *n* [C] *medical* : a photograph of a woman's breasts made by X-rays — **mam·mog·ra·phy** /mæˈmɑːgrəfi/ *n* [U]

¹**mam·moth** /ˈmæməθ/ *n* [C] : a large, hairy elephant that lived in ancient times

²**mammoth** *adj* : very large • *a mammoth building/undertaking*

¹**man** /ˈmæn/ *n, pl* **men** /ˈmɛn/ **1** [C] : an adult male human being • *boys, girls, men, and women* • *a good/talented/handsome man* **2** [C/U] : a man or boy who shows the qualities (such as strength and courage) that men are traditionally supposed to have • *Don't cry, little boy:* **be a man!** • *Are you* **man enough** *to fight?* **3** [C/U] : a woman's husband or boyfriend • *Who's her new man?* **4 a** [C] : PERSON • *the belief that all men are created equal* **b** [U] : the human race • *prehistoric man* ✧ Senses 4a and 4b are now sometimes avoided because they are considered sexist. **5** [C] — used when you are talking to a man • *(US, informal)* *Hey,* **(my) man,** *how are you?* **6** [C] : a male worker who goes to people's homes • *The furnace man came to repair the heater.* **7** [*plural*] : a group of male workers, soldiers, etc. • *He led his men into battle.* **8** [C] : a man who does a particular kind of work or has a specified job or position • *a medical/military man* • *a shrewd businessman* **9** [*singular*] **a** : a person who can do what is needed • *If you need someone to organize the files,* **he's/she's your man!** [=he's/she's the person you need for the job] **b** : the person someone (such as a police officer) is looking for • *He matches the description, but he's not our man.* **10** [C] : one of the pieces in a game like chess or checkers — **every man for himself** — used to describe a situation in which people do not help each other and each person has to take care of himself or herself • *As soon as there was a crisis, it was every man for himself.* — **man's best friend** — used to refer to a dog or to dogs as a group • *The fund helps man's best friend.* — **the man** *US, informal* **1** or **the Man** : the police • *running from the Man* **2** or **the Man** *also* **The Man** : the white people who are seen as having power in the U.S. • *He got a job working for the Man.* **3** : a man who is admired or respected as the best man in a particular field, sport, etc. • *His teammates know that he's the man.* • *You're the man! = (very informal)* *You the man!* — **the man in the street** : the ordinary and average person • *What does the man in the street think about it?* — **the odd man out** see ODD — **to the last man** : until all the men in a group are killed, defeated, etc. • *They vowed to fight to the last man.*

²**man** *interj, chiefly US, informal* — used to express excitement, surprise, etc. • *Man, what a game!* • *Oh man, I can't believe she said that!*

³**man** *vb* **manned; man·ning** [T] **1** : to be the person who controls or is in charge of (something) • *He/She mans the cash register.* **2** : to place people at or on (something) to do work • *man the sails/lifeboats*

man·a·cle /ˈmænɪkəl/ *n* [C] : either one of a set of two metal rings that lock around a person's wrists or ankles • *The prisoner was in manacles.* — **manacle** *vb* **-cled; -cling** [T] • *a manacled prisoner*

man·age /ˈmænɪdʒ/ *vb* **-aged; -ag·ing 1** [T] **a** : to have control of (a business, department, sports team, etc.) • *She manages her family's bakery.* • *a badly managed company* **b** : to take care of and make decisions about (someone's time, money, etc.) • *You need to manage your time more wisely.* **c** : to direct the professional career of (an entertainer, athlete, etc.) • *an agency that manages entertainers* **2** [T] **a** : to control the movements or actions of (something) • *She manages her skis well.* : to keep (something) under your control • *This form of diabetes can be managed by eating a proper diet.* **b** : to control the behavior of (a child, animal, etc.) • *They'll have difficulty managing her students.* **3** [T] : to use (something) carefully and without waste • *managing the country's natural resources* **4 a** [I] : to be able to live or to do what is needed by using what you have even though you do not have much — often + *on*, *with*, or *without* • *We can manage on just my salary.* • *We'll have to manage with just one car.* • *They'll have to manage without our help.* **b** [T/I] : to succeed in doing (something) • *He could only manage (taking) a few steps at a time.* • *She never studies but always manages to pass her tests.* • *I don't know how we ever managed without you.* — **man·age·able** /ˈmænɪdʒəbəl/ *adj* • *The problem was manageable.* [=easy to control or deal with]

man·age·ment /ˈmænɪdʒmənt/ *n* **1 a** [U] : the act or skill of controlling and making decisions about a business, department, etc. • *a career in (business) management* • *Business improved under the management of new owners.* **b** [C/U] : the people who make decisions about a business, department, etc. • *Management and labor could not agree.* • *senior/top management* • *The restaurant is now* **under new management**. [=is now controlled by different people] **2** [U] : the act or process of deciding how to use something • *time/money management* **3** [U] : the act or process of controlling and dealing with something • *anger/crisis management*

man·ag·er /ˈmænɪdʒɚ/ *n* [C] **1** : someone who is in charge of a business, department, etc. • *I'd like to speak to the manager, please.* • *He was promoted to manager.* **2** : someone who directs the training and performance of a sports team • *The manager changed pitchers in* *the eighth inning.* **3** : someone who directs the career of an entertainer or athlete ▪ *The actress fired her manager.* — **man·a·ge·ri·al** /ˌmænəˈdʒirijəl/ *adj* ▪ *managerial positions/experience*

managing director *n* [C] : someone who is in charge of a large company or organization

man·a·tee /ˈmænəˌti/ *n* [C] : a large animal that lives in warm waters and eats plants

man·da·rin /ˈmændərən/ *n* **1** [C] : a small type of orange **2** [C] : official in China in the past **3** *Mandarin* [U] : the official language of China

¹man·date /ˈmænˌdeɪt/ *n* [C] *formal* **1** : an official order to do something ▪ *They carried out the governor's mandate to build more roads.* **2** : the power to act that voters give to their elected leaders ▪ *He has been given a mandate (from the people) for change/reform.*

²mandate *vb* **-dat·ed; -dat·ing** [T] *chiefly US, formal* : to officially demand or require (something) ▪ *The law mandates that every car have seat belts.* ▪ *drug tests mandated by the government*

man·da·to·ry /ˈmændəˌtori, Brit ˈmændətri/ *adj* : required by a law or rule ▪ *This meeting is mandatory for all employees.* [=all employees must go to this meeting] ▪ *a mandatory drug test*

man·di·ble /ˈmændəbəl/ *n* [C] : the bone that forms the lower jaw

man·do·lin /ˌmændəˈlɪn/ *n* [C] : a small musical instrument that has a long neck, a body that is shaped like a pear, and usually eight strings

mane /ˈmeɪn/ *n* [C] **1** : long, thick hair growing from the neck of a horse or around the neck of a lion **2** *informal* : long, thick hair on a person's head ▪ *an actor with a thick mane of silver hair*

man·eat·er /ˈmænˌiːtɚ/ *n* [C] : an animal that kills and eats people — **man-eat·ing** /ˈmænˌiːtɪŋ/ *adj* ▪ *man-eating tigers/sharks*

¹ma·neu·ver (*US*) *or Brit* **ma·noeu·vre** /məˈnuːvɚ/ *n* **1** [C/U] : a clever or skillful action or movement ▪ *acrobats performing dangerous maneuvers* ▪ *A series of legal maneuvers kept him out of jail.* **2 a** [C] : a planned movement of soldiers or ships ▪ *a well-planned maneuver* **b** [*plural*] : military activities that are done for training ▪ *The navy is performing/conducting maneuvers off the coast.*

²maneuver (*US*) *or Brit* **manoeuvre** *vb* [T/I] **1** : to move (something or someone) in a careful and usually skillful way ▪ *She maneuvered her car into the tiny garage.* ▪ *The vehicle easily maneuvered through rocky terrain.* **2** : to do something in an effort to get an advantage, get out of a difficult situation, etc. ▪ *The companies are maneuvering (themselves) for position in the limited market.* ▪ *The strict requirements left us very little room to maneuver.* [=opportunity to make changes or to do things differently] — **ma·neu·ver·ing** /məˈnuːvərɪŋ/ *n* [C/U] ▪ *legal/political maneuverings*

ma·neu·ver·able (*US*) *or Brit* **ma·noeu·vra·ble** /məˈnuːvərəbəl/ *adj* : able to be

moved quickly, easily, or in small spaces ▪ *The new ships are faster and more maneuverable.* — **ma·neu·ver·abil·i·ty** (*US*) *or Brit* **ma·noeu·vra·bil·i·ty** /məˌnuːvərəˈbɪləti/ *n* [U]

man·ful·ly /ˈmænfəli/ *adv* : in a brave and strong way ▪ *He manfully accepted the challenge.*

man·ga·nese /ˈmæŋgəˌniːz/ *n* [U] : a grayish-white metal

mange /ˈmeɪndʒ/ *n* [U] : a skin disease of cats, dogs, etc., that causes itching and loss of hair

man·ger /ˈmeɪndʒɚ/ *n* [C] : an open box that holds food for farm animals

man·gle /ˈmæŋgəl/ *vb* **man·gled; man·gling** [T] **1** : to injure or damage (something or someone) severely by cutting, tearing, or crushing ▪ *a mangled piece of metal* **2** : to ruin (something) because of carelessness or a lack of skill ▪ *The newspaper mangled the story.* [=it did not report the story correctly]

man·go /ˈmæŋgoʊ/ *n, pl* **-goes** *also* **-gos** [C] : a juicy tropical fruit that has firm yellow and red skin and a large seed at its center

man·grove /ˈmænˌgroʊv/ *n* [C] : a tropical tree that grows in swamps

man·gy /ˈmeɪndʒi/ *adj* **mang·i·er; -est** **1** *of an animal* : suffering from mange ▪ *a mangy dog* **2** : having thin or bare spots ▪ *a mangy beard/rug*

man·han·dle /ˈmænˌhændl̩/ *vb* **-han·dled; -han·dling** [T] **1** : to move (something) by using rough force ▪ *They manhandled the heavy boxes onto the truck.* **2** : to treat (someone) in a rough way ▪ *He says he was manhandled by the police.*

man·hole /ˈmænˌhoʊl/ *n* [C] : a covered hole in a street that a person can go down into to do work under the street

man·hood /ˈmænˌhʊd/ *n* [U] **1** : the qualities (such as strength and courage) that are expected in a man ▪ *He took the comment as a challenge to his manhood.* **2** : the state or condition of being an adult man ▪ *growing from boyhood to manhood*

man–hour /ˈmænˌawɚ/ *n* [C] : an hour of work done by one worker ▪ *The job will take at least 300 man-hours.*

man·hunt /ˈmænˌhʌnt/ *n* [C] : an organized search for a person and especially for a criminal ▪ *The FBI launched a manhunt to find the kidnappers.*

ma·nia /ˈmeɪnijə/ *n* [C/U] **1** : mental illness in which a person becomes very emotional or excited ▪ *periods of mania followed by severe depression* **2** : extreme enthusiasm for something ▪ *The city's sports mania is well-known.* ▪ *He had a mania for cleanliness.*

ma·ni·ac /ˈmeɪniˌæk/ *n* [C] **1** : someone who is violent and mentally ill ▪ *a homicidal maniac* **2** *informal* : a person who behaves in a very wild way ▪ *She drives like a maniac.* [=in a very reckless way] **3** *informal* : a person who is extremely enthusiastic about something ▪ *sports maniacs* — **ma·ni·a·cal** /məˈnajəkəl/ *adj* ▪ *maniacal killers/fans* ▪ *a maniacal* *laugh* — **ma·ni·a·cal·ly** /məˈnajəkli/ *adv*

man·ic /ˈmænɪk/ *adj* **1** : having or relating to a mental illness that causes someone to become very excited or emotional • *She has a* manic *personality.* **2** : very excited, energetic, or emotional • *a manic sense of humor* • manic *behavior* — **man·i·cal·ly** /ˈmænɪkli/ *adv*

manic depression *n* [*U*] : a mental illness in which a person experiences periods of strong excitement followed by periods of sadness

man·ic-de·press·ive /ˌmænɪkdɪˈprɛsɪv/ *n* [*C*] : someone who has manic depression • *He's a* manic-depressive. — **manic-depressive** *adj* • *manic-depressive behavior/patients*

¹man·i·cure /ˈmænəˌkjɚ/ *n* [*C*] : a beauty treatment for the hands and fingernails • *She just got a* manicure.

²manicure *vb* -**cured**; -**cur·ing** [*T*] **1** : to give a beauty treatment to (someone's hands and fingernails) • *She* manicured *her nails.* **2** : to make a lawn, garden, etc., look neat, smooth, and attractive • *a well-manicured lawn*

man·i·cur·ist /ˈmænəˌkjɚɪst/ *n* [*C*] : a person who gives manicures

¹man·i·fest /ˈmænəˌfɛst/ *adj, formal* : easy to see or understand • *Their sadness was* manifest *in their faces.* • *a* manifest *injustice* — **man·i·fest·ly** *adv*

²manifest *vb* [*T*] *formal* : to show (something) clearly • *Their religious beliefs are* manifested *in every aspect of their lives.* • *Her behavior problems began* manifesting *themselves soon after she left home.*

man·i·fes·ta·tion /ˌmænəfəˈsteɪʃən/ *n* [*C*] *formal* **1** : a sign that shows something clearly • *the first* manifestations *of her behavior problems* **2** : one of the forms that something has when it appears or occurs • *hate in all its* manifestations

man·i·fes·to /ˌmænəˈfɛstoʊ/ *n, pl* -**tos** *or* -**toes** [*C*] : a written statement that describes the policies, goals, and opinions of a person or group • *a political party's* manifesto

man·i·fold /ˈmænəˌfoʊld/ *adj, formal* : many and various • *the country's* manifold *problems* • *The benefits are* manifold.

ma·ni·la /məˈnɪlə/ *adj* : made of strong, light brown paper • manila *folders/envelopes*

ma·nip·u·late /məˈnɪpjəˌleɪt/ *vb* -**lat·ed**; -**lat·ing** [*T*] **1 a** : to move or control (something) with your hands or by using a machine • manipulate *a pencil* • *The mechanical arms are* manipulated *by a computer.* **b** *medical* : to move (muscles and bones) with your hands as a form of treatment • *The doctor* manipulated *my spine.* **2** : to use or change (numbers, information, etc.) in a skillful way or for a particular purpose • *The program was designed to organize and* manipulate *large amounts of data.* **3 a** : to deal with or control (someone or something) in a clever and usually unfair or selfish way • *She knows how to* manipulate *her parents to get what she wants.* **b** : to change (something) in an unfair or selfish way •

He manipulated *the price of the stock.* — **ma·nip·u·la·tion** /məˌnɪpjəˈleɪʃən/ *n* [*C/U*] • *(a) blatant* manipulation *of public opinion* — **ma·nip·u·la·tive** /məˈnɪpjəˌleɪtɪv, məˈnɪpjələtɪv/ *adj* • *their daughter's* manipulative *behavior* — **ma·nip·u·la·tor** /məˈnɪpjəˌleɪtɚ/ *n* [*C*] • *He's a clever political* manipulator.

man·kind /ˈmænˈkaɪnd/ *n* [*U*] : all people thought of as one group : HUMANKIND • *the history of* mankind

man·ly /ˈmænli/ *adj* **man·li·er**; -**est** : having or showing qualities (such as strength or courage) that are expected in a man • *a* manly *competitor* • *a deep, manly voice* — **man·li·ness** *n* [*U*]

man-made /ˈmænˈmeɪd/ *adj* : made by people rather than by nature • *a man-made lake* • *She prefers cotton to man-made fabrics.*

manned /ˈmænd/ *adj* : carrying or done by a person • *a* manned *mission to the moon*

man·ne·quin /ˈmænɪkən/ *n* [*C*] : a figure shaped like a human body that is used for making or displaying clothes

man·ner /ˈmænɚ/ *n* **1** [*singular*] *somewhat formal* : the way that something is done or happens • *He has a very forceful* manner *of speaking.* — often used after *in* • *She taught her class in an informal* manner. • *His retirement was the beginning of his real career,* **in a manner of speaking.** [=in a way that is true even if it is not literally or completely true] **2 a** [*C*] : the way that a person normally behaves — usually singular • *It was her friendly* manner *that got her the job.* **b** [*plural*] : behavior while with other people • *His children have excellent* manners. [=they behave very well] • *It's bad* manners *to talk with your mouth full.* **c** [*plural*] : knowledge of how to behave politely while with other people • *Someone should teach you some* manners! • *Don't forget to* **mind your manners.** [=behave in a polite and proper way] **3** [*singular*] : an artistic style or method • *This church was built* **in/after the manner of** *the English Gothic style.* — **all manner of** : all kinds of (things or people) • *All* manner *of people come to the city.* — **not by any manner of means** *see* MEANS

man·nered /ˈmænɚd/ *adj* **1** : behaving in a certain way • *a mild-mannered man who rarely becomes angry* • *well-mannered children* **2** *disapproving* : formal in a way that is intended to impress other people • *He had a very* mannered [=unnatural] *way of speaking.*

man·ner·ism /ˈmænəˌrɪzəm/ *n* [*C*] : a person's particular way of talking or moving • *He can mimic the President's* mannerisms *perfectly.*

man·nish /ˈmænɪʃ/ *adj* : suitable for or typical of a man rather than a woman • *She wears* mannish *clothing.*

manoeuvre, manoeuvrable *Brit spellings of* MANEUVER, MANEUVERABLE

man of the house *n* — **the man of the house** : the male family member who has the most responsibility for taking care of the household • *When my hus-*

band died, my son became the man of the house.

man of the people *n — a man of the people* : a man (such as a politician) who understands and is liked by ordinary people

man of the world *n [C]* : a man who has had many experiences and who is not shocked by things that may be shocking to other people

man·or /ˈmænə/ *n [C]* : a large house on a large piece of land — **ma·no·ri·al** /məˈnorijəl/ *adj* • *manorial estates*

man·pow·er /ˈmænˌpawə/ *n [U]* : the number of people who are available to work • *a shortage of manpower*

man·ser·vant /ˈmænˌsəvənt/ *n, pl* **men·ser·vants** /ˈmɛnˌsəvənts/ *[C]* old-fashioned : a male servant

man·sion /ˈmænʃən/ *n [C]* : a large and impressive house • *a mansion with 10 bedrooms*

man·slaugh·ter /ˈmænˌslɔːtə/ *n [U]* law : the crime of killing a person without intending to do so • *a drunk driver who was convicted of manslaughter*

man's man *n [singular]* : a man who is liked and admired by other men

man·tel /ˈmæntl̩/ *n [C]* chiefly US : the shelf above a fireplace

man·tel·piece /ˈmæntl̩ˌpiːs/ *n [C]* **1** : the shelf above a fireplace and the decorative pieces on the sides of the fireplace **2** : MANTEL

man·tle /ˈmæntl̩/ *n [C]* **1** : ¹CLOAK 1 **2** *literary* : something that covers or surrounds something else — + *of* • *mountains blanketed/wrapped in a mantle of snow* • *A mantle of secrecy surrounded her past.* [=her past was kept secret] **3** *formal* : the position of someone who has responsibility or authority • *She accepted/assumed the mantle of leadership.* **4** *technical* : the layer of the Earth that is between the top crust and the inner core

man–to–man /ˈmæntəˈmæn/ *adj, always before a noun* — used to describe speech between men that is honest, open, and informal • *We need to have a man-to-man talk.* — **man–to–man** *adv* • *talking man-to-man*

man·tra /ˈmɑːntrə, Brit ˈmæntrə/ *n [C]* **1** : a sound, word, or phrase that is repeated by someone who is praying or meditating **2** : a word or phrase that expresses someone's basic beliefs • *a businessman whose mantra is "bigger is better"*

¹**man·u·al** /ˈmænjəwəl/ *adj, always before a noun* **1** : doing or involving hard physical work • *low-paid manual laborers* **2** : of or relating to using the hands • *manual skill/dexterity* **3** : operated or controlled with the hands or by a person • *a car with a manual transmission* [=with a system for changing gears that has to be operated by the driver] : operated without electric power • *manual typewriters* — **man·u·al·ly** *adv*

²**manual** *n [C]* **1** : a small book that gives useful information about something : HANDBOOK • *Check the owner's manual of your car.* • *a computer program's user's manual* • *We used the instruction manual to put our bikes together.* **2** : a car with a

manual transmission • *Is your car a manual or an automatic?*

¹**man·u·fac·ture** /ˌmænjəˈfækʧə/ *vb* **-tured; -tur·ing** *[T]* **1** : to make (something) usually in large amounts by using machines • *a company that manufactures cars/computers/clothing* **2** : to create (a false story, explanation, etc.) often in order to trick or deceive someone • *He manufactured a lie in order to get out of trouble.* — **man·u·fac·tur·er** /ˌmænjəˈfækʧərə/ *n [C]* • *a leading manufacturer of men's clothing*

²**manufacture** *n [U]* : the process of making products with machines in factories • *materials used in the manufacture of cars*

man·u·fac·tur·ing /ˌmænjəˈfækʧərɪŋ/ *n [U]* : the industry of making products with machines in factories • *creating new jobs in manufacturing*

ma·nure /məˈnuə, Brit məˈnjuə/ *n [C/U]* : solid waste from farm animals that is used as fertilizer

man·u·script /ˈmænjəˌskrɪpt/ *n [C/U]* : the original copy of a play, book, etc., before it has been printed • *the author's original manuscript*

¹**many** /ˈmɛni/ *adj* — used to refer to a large number of things or people • *She worked there for many years.* • *the many benefits of learning English* • *You can never have too many friends.* • *There weren't many* [=there was a small number of] *people at the party.* • *Some people will come, but many more people will not.* — *as many* — used to talk about or compare amounts • *He invited as many people as he could.* [=he invited the largest number of people possible] • *She read three times as many books as he did.* [=three times more books than he did] — *how many* — used to ask or talk about an amount • *How many people were there?* • *I was surprised by how many people were there.* • *How many times* [=how often] *do I have to tell you?*

²**many** *pron* : a large number of people or things • *Many of his friends never went to college.* • *Too many have died in this war.* • *A lot of people have tried to climb the mountain, but a great/good many of them have failed.* — *as many as* — used to suggest that a number or amount is surprisingly large • *As many as 60 students competed for the prize.* — *many a/an* formal + literary — used with a singular noun to refer to a large number of things or people • *Many a man has tried.* [=many men have tried] — *the many* : the great majority of people • *policies that help the privileged few at the expense of the many*

¹**map** /ˈmæp/ *n [C]* : a picture or chart that shows the rivers, streets, etc., in a particular area • *a map of the country/world* • *a road/street map* [=a map showing the roads/streets of an area] • *Can you find where we are on the map?* • *(figurative) The story has put the little town on the map.* [=made the town well-known] — *all over the map* US, informal : not staying the same : characterized by frequent and extreme changes • *Prices have been all over the map.*

²**map** *vb* **mapped; map·ping** [T] **1** : to make a map of (something) ▪ *mapping the stars* **2** *US* : to plan the details of (something) ▪ *We mapped* [=mapped out] *a plan of action.* — **map out** [*phrasal vb*] **map** (something) **out** or **map out** (something) : to plan the details of (a program, your future, etc.) ▪ *She has her future all mapped out.*

ma·ple /'meɪpəl/ *n* **1** [C] : a type of tree that grows in northern parts of the world ▪ *The maple leaf is an emblem of Canada.* **2** [U] : the hard wood of a maple tree ▪ *maple cabinets*

maple sugar *n* [U] : a sugar made from maple syrup

maple syrup *n* [U] : a sweet liquid made from the sap of maple trees ▪ *pancakes served with maple syrup*

mar /'mɑɚ/ *vb* **marred; mar·ring** [T] : to ruin the perfection of (something) ▪ *a car marred by scratches* ▪ *Numerous errors mar the report.*

Mar. *abbr* March

¹**mar·a·thon** /'merə,θɑːn/ *n* [C] **1** : a running race that is about 26 miles (42 kilometers) long ▪ *He ran (in) a marathon.* **2** : something (such as an event or activity) that lasts an extremely long time ▪ *a movie/shopping marathon* ▪ *a dance marathon* [=a contest in which people compete to see who can dance for the longest amount of time]

²**marathon** *adj, always before a noun* : lasting an unusually long time ▪ *a marathon negotiating session*

mar·a·thon·er /'merə,θɑːnɚ/ *n* [C] : a runner who competes in a marathon

ma·raud·ing /mə'rɑːdɪŋ/ *adj, always before a noun* : traveling from place to place to attack others ▪ *a marauding gang of thieves* — **ma·raud·er** /mə'rɑːdɚ/ *n* [C] ▪ *a gang of marauders*

mar·ble /'mɑɚbəl/ *n* **1** [U] : a kind of stone that is often polished and used in buildings and statues ▪ *the museum's marble floor* ▪ *marble countertops* **2 a** [C] : a little glass ball used as a toy or in some games ▪ *playing with marbles* **b** [*plural*] : a children's game played with little glass balls ▪ *playing (a game of) marbles* — **lose your marbles** *informal + humorous* : to become insane ▪ *He hasn't completely lost his marbles yet.*

mar·bled /'mɑɚbəld/ *adj* **1** : made from or decorated with marble ▪ *marbled columns/halls* **2** : having markings or colors similar to marble ▪ *marbled paper* **3** *of meat* : having lines of fat mixed throughout ▪ *meat marbled with fat*

¹**march** /'mɑɚtʃ/ *vb* **1** [I] **a** : to walk in the regular and organized way of soldiers ▪ *The band marched onto the field.* ▪ *Hundreds of people marched in the parade.* **b** : to go into, out of, or through a place as an army ▪ *The army marched south.* **2** [I] : to walk with a large group of people who are protesting or supporting something ▪ *marching for/against new elections* ▪ *Demonstrators marched on City Hall to protest the war.* **3** [I] : to walk somewhere quickly in a direct and forceful way ▪ *I marched into the office and demanded an answer.* **4** [T] : to cause or force (a person) to walk somewhere ▪ *We marched the children off to bed.* [=made them go to bed] — **march on** [*phrasal vb*] : to go or continue onward ▪ *Time marches on.* — **march·er** /'mɑɚtʃɚ/ *n* [C] ▪ *She was a marcher in the parade.*

²**march** *n* **1** [C/U] : an act of marching ▪ *The soldiers began their march.* ▪ *a protest march* ▪ *The soldiers were on the march.* [=marching toward a place] **2** [*singular*] : forward movement or progress ▪ *the march of time* **3** [C] : a piece of music that is written to be played while people are marching ▪ *The band was playing a march.* — **steal a march on** *chiefly Brit* : to gain an advantage over (someone) in an unexpected and clever way ▪ *He stole a march on his rivals/competitors.*

March /'mɑɚtʃ/ *n* [C/U] : the third month of the year ▪ *She was born in (early/late) March.* ▪ *on March the fourth = (US) on March fourth = on the fourth of March* ▪ *Sales are up this March.* — abbr. **Mar.**

marching band *n* [C] : a group of musicians who play instruments while marching together at a parade or sports event

marching orders *n* [*plural*] **1** *US* : orders that tell you what to do ▪ *The boss gave the new employees their marching orders.* **2** *Brit* — used to say that someone has been ordered to leave a place, job, etc. ▪ *I was given my marching orders.* [=I was fired from my job]

Mar·di Gras /'mɑːdi,grɑː/ *n* [U, singular] : the Tuesday before the beginning of Lent that is often celebrated with parades and parties ▪ *celebrating Mardi Gras in New Orleans*

mare /'meɚ/ *n* [C] : an adult female horse

mar·ga·rine /'mɑɚdʒərən, Brit ˌmɑː·dʒə·'riːn/ *n* [C/U] : a food that resembles butter and is made from vegetable oils ▪ *a stick of margarine*

mar·ga·ri·ta /ˌmɑɚɡə'riːtə/ *n* [C] : a drink made of tequila, lime or lemon juice, and an orange-flavored liqueur

mar·gin /'mɑɚdʒən/ *n* [C] **1** : the part of a page that is above, below, or to the side of the printed part ▪ *a book with wide/narrow margins* **2** : the edge of something ▪ *Mountains lie at the city's northern margins.* ▪ *people who live on/at the margins of the city* ▪ (*figurative*) *poor families who are living on the margins of society* [=who are often forgotten or ignored by society] ▪ (*figurative*) *The business has been operating on the margins of respectability.* [=in a way that is not truly respectable] **3** : an extra amount of time, space, etc., that can be used if it is needed ▪ *a safety margin* ▪ *The schedule allows us little/no margin for/of error.* [=we need to be very careful not to make mistakes or take too much time in order to stay on schedule] **4** : a measurement of difference ▪ *The bullet missed his heart by a narrow/slim margin.* [=the bullet almost hit his heart] ▪ *We lost the election by a one-vote margin.* [=we lost the election by one vote] ◆ A **margin of error** is a number or percentage that shows how accurate a measurement is. ▪ *She is supported by 54 percent of the voters, with a margin of error of 3 percent.* [=as few as 51 percent or as many as 57 percent of the voters support her]

mar·gin·al /ˈmɑɚʤənl/ *adj* **1 a** : not very significant • *a marginal problem* **b** : very slight or small • *There was only a marginal improvement in her condition.* **2** : not included in the main part of society or of a group • *marginal voters* **3** *chiefly US* : not very good • *She's a marginal athlete.* **4** *always before a noun* : written or printed in the margin of a page • *marginal notes* **5** *Brit* : able to be won or lost by changing only a few votes • *marginal seats in Parliament* — **mar·gin·al·ly** /ˈmɑɚʤənəli/ *adv* • *The plan was marginally* [=slightly] *successful.* • (*US*) *He is only marginally* [=barely] *qualified for the job.*

mar·gin·al·ize *also Brit* **mar·gin·al·ise** /ˈmɑɚʤənəˌlaɪz/ *vb* **-ized; -iz·ing** [T] : to put or keep (someone) in a powerless or unimportant position within a society or group • *policies that marginalize women* [=that do not allow women to have important or powerful positions in a society] — **mar·gin·al·i·za·tion** *also Brit* **mar·gin·al·i·sa·tion** /ˌmɑɚʤənələˈzeɪʃən, Brit ˌmɑːʤənəˌlaɪˈzeɪʃən/ *n* [U]

ma·ri·a·chi /ˌmɑriˈɑːʧi, ˌmeriˈɑːʧi/ *n* [U] *US* : a type of lively Mexican street music • *a mariachi band*

mari·gold /ˈmerəˌgoʊld/ *n* [C] : a plant with bright yellow or orange flowers

mar·i·jua·na /ˌmerəˈwɑːnə/ *n* [U] : the dried leaves and flowers of the hemp plant that are smoked as a drug

ma·ri·na /məˈriːnə/ *n* [C] : an area of water where privately owned boats are kept

¹mar·i·nade /ˌmerəˈneɪd/ *n* [C/U] : a sauce in which meat or fish is soaked to add flavor

²marinade *vb* **-nad·ed; -nad·ing** [T] : MARINATE

mar·i·nate /ˈmerəˌneɪt/ *vb* **-nat·ed; -nat·ing** [T/I] : to soak meat or fish in a marinade • *Marinate the chicken overnight.* • *The chicken should marinate overnight.*

¹ma·rine /məˈriːn/ *adj, always before a noun* : of or relating to the sea or the plants and animals that live in the sea • *marine life/animals* • **marine biologists** [=scientists who study life in the sea]

²marine *or* **Marine** *n* [C] : a member of the U.S. Marine Corps or the British Royal Marines • *He is a former U.S. Marine.* • *marine barracks* — **the Marines** : the U.S. Marine Corps or the British Royal Marines • *an officer in the Marines*

Marine Corps *n* — **the Marine Corps** : the part of the U.S. military that consists of soldiers who serve at sea and also on land

mar·i·ner /ˈmerənɚ/ *n* [C] *literary* : SAILOR

mar·i·o·nette /ˌmerijəˈnɛt/ *n* [C] : a puppet that is moved by pulling strings or wires that are attached to its body

mar·i·tal /ˈmerətl/ *adj, always before a noun* : of or relating to marriage • *marital problems/vows*

marital status *n* [U] : the state of being married or not married — used on forms to ask if a person is married, single, divorced, or widowed • *What is your marital status?*

mar·i·time /ˈmerəˌtaɪm/ *adj* **1** : of or relating to sailing on the sea or doing business by sea • *the country's maritime industry* • *a maritime museum* **2** : located near or next to the sea • *maritime nations/regions*

mar·jo·ram /ˈmɑɚʤərəm/ *n* [U] : an herb that is often used in cooking

¹mark /ˈmɑɚk/ *n* **1** [C] **a** : a small area on the surface of something that is dirty, damaged, etc. • *a burn/scratch mark* **b** : an area that is a different color from the area around it • *a white cat with black marks on its head* **2** [C] : a written or printed shape or symbol • *proofreading marks* **3** [C] : a sign or indication of something • *They removed their hats as a mark of respect.* • *Asking tough questions is the mark of* [=the trait that is typical of] *a good journalist.* **4** [C] : ¹GRADE 2 • *getting passing/failing marks in school* • *(figurative) I give them high/top marks for honesty.* **5** [*singular*] : a specified point or level • *at the halfway mark of our climb* • *The population topped the 1,000,000 mark.* **6** [C] : something that is aimed at or shot at : TARGET • *The arrow hit/missed the mark.* • *(figurative) Their estimate was close to the mark* [=almost correct] • *(figurative) The ad was supposed to appeal to young people but it missed its/the mark.* [=it failed] • *(figurative) His efforts were off the mark. His efforts fell/were short of the mark.* [=they were not successful] **7** [C] : the line or place where a race starts • *Runners, take your marks.* [=get into position for the start of the race] • *On your mark, get set, go!* • *(figurative) I was slow off the mark* [=slow to act] *and missed my chance.* — **leave/make a/your mark** : to do something that causes you to be remembered • *He worked at several jobs, but he didn't make much of a mark in any of them.* • *Her kindness left its mark on her students.*

²mark *vb* **1** [T/I] : to make or leave a mark on something • *Her shoes marked the floor.* **2** [T] **a** : to write a note about (something) • *I'll mark the event on my calendar.* **b** : to write or make a mark on (something) • *She marked the box with an "X." • Mark that page.* **3** [T] **a** : to indicate (something) with a mark, symbol, etc. • *X marks the spot where the suspect was last seen.* • *I have marked (out) the best route on the map.* **b** : to put something on or near (a particular place) in order to find it later • *Use a bookmark to mark your place.* **4** [T] : to be a typical feature or quality of (someone or something) : CHARACTERIZE • *His artwork is marked by unusual uses of color.* **5** [T/I] : to give a mark to (a student or a student's work) : GRADE • *She was marking her students' exams/papers.* **6** [T] **a** : to be or occur at (a particular time) • *This year marks her 10th year with the company.* **b** : to celebrate (an important event or time) • *a big party to mark our 50th anniversary* — **mark down** [*phrasal vb*] **1 mark down or**

mark (someone or something) **down** or **mark down** (someone or something) : to give a lower grade to (a student or a student's work) ▪ *He was marked down for poor grammar.* **2 mark** (something) **down** or **mark down** (something) : to give (something) a lower price ▪ *Everything in the store is marked down.* — **mark my words** — used to tell someone to listen to and remember what you are saying ▪ *Mark my words: nothing good will come of this!* — **mark off** [phrasal vb] **mark** (something) **off** or **mark off** (something) : to make (an area) separate with a line, fence, etc. ▪ *We marked off an area for a new garden.* — **mark out** [phrasal vb] **mark** (something) **out** or **mark out** (something) **1** : to draw lines around (something) so that it can be clearly seen ▪ *He marked out his mining claim.* **2** : to plan the details of (a course of action) ▪ *the course the country has marked out for itself* — **mark up** [phrasal vb] **mark** (something) **up** or **mark up** (something) **1** : to make marks and write comments in or on (something) ▪ *mark up a manuscript* **2** : to give (something) a higher price ▪ *marking up dairy products*

mark·down /ˈmɑɚkˌdaʊn/ n [C] : a reduction in price ▪ *a markdown of 10 percent*

marked /ˈmɑɚkt/ adj **1** : having a mark or a particular kind of mark ▪ *The bird's wings are marked with white.* ▪ *The streets are well-marked.* [=they have signs showing their names] **2** always before a noun : very noticeable ▪ *marked changes* ▪ *His friendliness is in marked contrast to his usual behavior.* — **a marked man/woman** : someone who is not liked or trusted or who is in danger of being harmed ▪ *Her unpopular ideas made her a marked woman at work.* — **mark·ed·ly** /ˈmɑɚkədli/ adv ▪ *markedly different opinions*

mark·er /ˈmɑɚkɚ/ n [C] **1** : something that shows the location, presence, or existence of something ▪ *a grave marker* ▪ *A person's accent can be a marker of social class.* **2** : a type of pen that makes wide lines

¹**mar·ket** /ˈmɑɚkət/ n **1** [C] **a** : a place where products are bought and sold ▪ *a fish market* **b** *US* : SUPERMARKET **2** [C] **a** : an area where a product or service can be sold ▪ *foreign markets for American cotton* **b** : a particular type of people who might buy something ▪ *the educational/youth market* **3** [singular] : the available supply of workers or jobs ▪ *the labor/job market* **4** [C] : the activity of buying and selling a particular product ▪ *the software market* ▪ *a good/growing market for new homes* ▪ *prices determined by the market without government interference* ▪ *a market-driven industry/economy* **5** [singular] : STOCK MARKET ▪ *The market was down today.* — **in the market** : interested in buying or finding something ▪ *She is in the market for a new job/house.* ▪ *He's in the market for a wife.* — **on the market** : available to be bought ▪ *New software is on the market.* ▪ *They are putting their house on*

the market. [=they are selling their house]

²**market** vb [T] **1** : to do things that cause people to know about and want to buy (something) ▪ *products marketed to kids through TV ads* **2** : SELL 1 ▪ *He markets his wares at craft shows.* — **mar·ket·er** n [C] ▪ *a marketer of software* — **mar·ket·ing** /ˈmɑɚkətɪŋ/ n [U] ▪ *She runs the company's marketing department.*

mar·ket·able /ˈmɑɚkətəbəl/ adj : wanted by buyers or employers ▪ *marketable products/skills*

mar·ke·teer /ˌmɑɚkəˈtiɚ/ n [C] : a person or company that sells or promotes a product or service : MARKETER ▪ *a black marketeer* [=a person who sells things on the black market]

mar·ket·place /ˈmɑɚkətˌpleɪs/ n **1** [singular] : the economic system through which different companies compete with each other to sell their products **2** [C] : a place in a town where products are bought and sold

market value n [C/U] : the price that buyers are willing to pay for something ▪ *The house sold below (its) market value.*

mark·ing /ˈmɑɚkɪŋ/ n [C] **1** : a mark, shape, or word that is written or drawn on something ▪ *reading the markings on a label* **2** : a mark or pattern of marks on the body of an animal ▪ *a black cat with white markings* — **have (all) the markings** of chiefly US : to have the qualities or features of (something) ▪ *They have all the markings of a great team.*

marks·man /ˈmɑɚksmən/ n, pl **-men** /-mən/ [C] : a person who is skilled in shooting a gun at a target — **marks·man·ship** /ˈmɑɚksmənˌʃɪp/ n [U]

mark·up /ˈmɑɚkˌʌp/ n [C] : the difference between the cost of producing something and its selling price ▪ *selling cars at high markups*

mar·lin /ˈmɑɚlən/ n, pl **marlin** or **marlins** [C] : a large fish that lives in the sea and that people catch for sport

mar·ma·lade /ˈmɑɚməˌleɪd/ n [C/U] : a sweet jelly that contains pieces of fruit ▪ *orange marmalade*

¹**ma·roon** /məˈruːn/ n [U] : a dark red color — **maroon** adj

²**maroon** vb [T] : to leave (someone) in a place that is difficult or impossible to get away from ▪ *The sailors were marooned on the island.*

¹**mar·quee** /mɑɚˈkiː/ n [C] **1** *US* **a** : a covered structure over the entrance to a hotel, theater, etc. **b** : a sign over the entrance to a theater that shows the name of the show, movie, etc., and the names of the main performers **2** *Brit* : a large tent that is set up for an outdoor event

²**marquee** adj, always before a noun, US, informal : very popular and well known ▪ *marquee athletes/events*

mar·quess /ˈmɑɚkwəs/ n [C] : a British nobleman who has a rank that is below a duke and above an earl

mar·quis /ˈmɑɚkwəs/ n [C] : MARQUESS

mar·riage /ˈmerɪdʒ/ n [C/U] **a** : the relationship that exists between a husband and a wife ▪ *They have a very happy* *marriage.* **b** : a similar relationship between people of the same sex • *gay marriage* **2** [C] : WEDDING • *Many friends and relatives were present at their marriage.* **3** [*singular*] : a close union of or between two things • *a marriage of science and art* — **mar·riage·able** /ˈmerɪdʒəbəl/ *adj* • *a woman of marriageable age*

mar·ried /ˈmerɪd/ *adj* : united in marriage • *a married couple/man/woman* • *enjoying married life* • *They're getting married.* • *He is married to her.* • *(figurative) She's married to her work.* [=she gives all of her attention to her work]

married name *n* [C] : a married woman's last name if she uses her husband's last name as her own

mar·row /ˈmeroʊ/ *n* **1** [U] : BONE MARROW **2** [C/U] *Brit* : a large, long vegetable with usually dark green skin

mar·ry /ˈmeri/ *vb* **-ries; -ried; -ry·ing** **1** [T/I] : to become the husband or wife of (someone) • *He asked her to marry him.* • *She married young.* [=she was young when she married] **2** [T] : to perform a ceremony in which two people get married • *A priest married them.* **3** [T] : to find a husband or wife for (your child) • *They married off their children.* **4** [T] : to join or combine (two things) closely • *The design marries traditional and modern elements.* — **marry into** [*phrasal vb*] : to become a member of (a family, group, etc.) by marrying someone • *He married into a wealthy family.* [=his wife's family is wealthy]

Mars /ˈmɑɚz/ *n* [*singular*] : the planet that is fourth in order from the sun

marsh /ˈmɑɚʃ/ *n* [C/U] : an area of soft, wet land that has many grasses and other plants — **marshy** /ˈmɑɚʃi/ *adj* **marsh·i·er; -est** • *marshy land*

¹**mar·shal** /ˈmɑɚʃəl/ *n* [C] **1** : an officer of the highest rank in some military forces **2** *US* : a federal official who is responsible for enforcing the law **3** *US* : the head of a division of a police or fire department • *a fire marshal*

²**marshal** *vb, US* **-shaled** *or chiefly Brit* **-shalled;** *US* **-shal·ing** *or chiefly Brit* **-shal·ling** [T] : to arrange (people or things) in an orderly way • *marshal the troops* • *marshal an argument*

marsh·land /ˈmɑɚʃˌlænd/ *n* [C/U] : MARSH

marsh-mal·low /ˈmɑɚʃˌmeloʊ, *Brit* ˌmɑːʃˈmæloʊ/ *n* [C/U] : a soft, white, sweet food made of sugar and eggs

mar·su·pi·al /mɑɚˈsuːpijəl/ *n* [C] : a type of animal (such as a kangaroo or an opossum) that carries its babies in a pocket of skin on the mother's stomach

mart /ˈmɑɚt/ *n* [C] *chiefly US* : a place where things are bought and sold : MARKET • *an antiques mart*

mar·tial /ˈmɑɚʃəl/ *adj, always before a noun* : of or relating to war or soldiers • *martial discipline*

martial art *n* [C] : any one of several forms of fighting and self-defense (such as karate and judo) that are widely practiced as sports — **martial artist** *n* [C]

martial law *n* [U] : control of an area by military forces rather than by the police • *an area placed under martial law*

¹**Mar·tian** /ˈmɑɚʃən/ *adj, always before a noun* : of or relating to the planet Mars • *the Martian landscape*

²**Martian** *n* [C] : an imaginary creature that comes from the planet Mars

mar·ti·net /ˌmɑɚtəˈnɛt/ *n* [C] *formal* : a person who is very strict and demands obedience from others

mar·ti·ni /mɑɚˈtiːni/ *n* [C] : an alcoholic drink made with gin or vodka and vermouth

¹**mar·tyr** /ˈmɑɚtɚ/ *n* [C] : a person who is killed or who suffers greatly rather than give up his or her religion, cause, etc. • *a Christian martyr* • *She was a martyr to* [=she died or suffered for] *a noble cause.*

²**martyr** *vb* [T] : to kill (someone) for refusing to give up a belief or cause • *He was martyred for his religious beliefs.*

mar·tyr·dom /ˈmɑɚtɚdəm/ *n* [C/U] : the suffering and death of a martyr • *religious martyrdom*

¹**mar·vel** /ˈmɑɚvəl/ *n* [C] : someone or something that is extremely good, skillful, etc. • *The bridge is a marvel of engineering.*

²**marvel** *vb, US* **-veled** *or chiefly Brit* **-velled;** *US* **-vel·ing** *or chiefly Brit* **-vel·ling** [T/I] : to feel great surprise, wonder, or admiration • *The audience marveled at/over the magician's skill.*

mar·vel·ous (*US*) *or chiefly Brit* **mar·vel·lous** /ˈmɑɚvələs/ *adj* : extremely good or enjoyable • *a marvelous writer/book/idea* — **mar·vel·ous·ly** (*US*) *or chiefly Brit* **mar·vel·lous·ly** *adv*

Marx·ism /ˈmɑɚkˌsɪzəm/ *n* [U] : the political, economic, and social theories of Karl Marx — **Marx·ist** /ˈmɑɚksɪst/ *adj* — **Marxist** *n* [C]

mas·cara /mæˈskerə, *Brit* mæˈskɑːrə/ *n* [C/U] : a type of makeup used on the eyelashes

mas·cot /ˈmæˌskɑːt/ *n* [C] : a person, animal, or object used as a symbol to represent a school, sports team, etc.

mas·cu·line /ˈmæskjələn/ *adj* **1** : of, relating to, or suited to men or boys • *a masculine name/voice/perspective* **2** *grammar, in some languages* : of or belonging to the class of words (called a gender) that ordinarily includes most of the words referring to males • *a masculine noun/pronoun* — **mas·cu·lin·i·ty** /ˌmæskjəˈlɪnəti/ *n* [U]

¹**mash** /ˈmæʃ/ *vb* [T] : to make (something) into a soft mass by beating or crushing it • *mashed potatoes*

²**mash** *n* [U] *Brit, informal* : mashed potatoes • *bangers and mash*

mash·er /ˈmæʃɚ/ *n* [C] : a tool that is used for mashing food

¹**mask** /ˈmæsk, *Brit* ˈmɑːsk/ *n* [C] **1** : a covering for your face or part of your face that is worn usually to disguise or protect it • *Halloween masks* • *a (baseball) catcher's mask* • *a doctor's surgical mask* **2** : a way of appearing or behaving that is not true or real • *She hid behind a mask of friendship.* [=she pretended to be friendly]

²**mask** vb [T] **1** : to hide (something) from sight • *The house was masked by trees.* **2** : to keep (something) from being known or noticed • *They tried to mask their real purpose.*

masked /'mæskt, Brit 'mɑːskt/ adj : wearing a mask • *masked robbers*

masking tape n [U] : a type of tape that is sticky on one side and that has many different uses (such as to cover an area when you are painting near it)

mas·och·ism /'mæsə,kızəm/ n [U] : enjoyment from being hurt or punished — **mas·och·ist** /'mæsəkıst/ n [C] — **mas·och·is·tic** /,mæsə'kıstık/ adj

ma·son /'meısn/ n [C] **1** : a person who builds or works with stone, brick, or concrete **2** *Mason* : FREEMASON

Ma·son·ic /mə'sɑnık/ adj : of or relating to Freemasons or Freemasonry • *a Masonic temple*

ma·son jar or **Ma·son jar** /'meısn-/ n [C] US : a glass jar usually used in preserving fruits or vegetables

ma·son·ry /'meısnri/ n [U] **1** : the stone, brick, or concrete used to build things **2** : work done using stone, brick, or concrete

¹**mas·quer·ade** /,mæskə'reıd/ n [C] **1** : a party at which people wear masks and often costumes **2** : a way of appearing or behaving that is not true or real • *Their happy marriage was a masquerade.*

²**masquerade** vb -ad·ed; -ad·ing [I] : to pretend to be someone or something else • *a man masquerading as a woman* — **mas·quer·ad·er** n [C]

¹**mass** /'mæs/ n **1** [C] : an amount of a substance that has no particular shape • *a mass of clay* • *a cold air mass* **2** [C] : a large number or amount of something • *a mass of information/people* **3** *the masses* [plural] : the ordinary or common people • *His films appeal to the masses.* **4** [U] physics : the quantity of matter in something • *a star's mass* **5** *Mass* [C] : a Christian ceremony in which people celebrate Communion

²**mass** vb [T/I] : to form or gather into a large group • *A large crowd massed outside the courthouse.*

³**mass** adj, always before a noun : involving, affecting, or designed for many people • *mass demonstrations* • *mass destruction*

¹**mas·sa·cre** /'mæsıkə/ n [C/U] : the violent killing of many people • *(figurative, informal) The game was a complete massacre.* [=one team easily defeated the other]

²**massacre** vb -sa·cred; -sa·cring [T] **1** : to violently kill (a group of people) • *Hundreds were massacred in the uprising.* **2** : to do (something) very badly • *She massacred that song.*

mas·sage /mə'sɑːʒ, Brit 'mæ,sɑːʒ/ vb -saged; -sag·ing [T] : to rub or press someone's body in a way that helps muscles to relax • *She massaged his back.* — **massage** n [C/U] • *a neck massage* • *a massage therapist*

mas·seur /mæ'sə/ n [C] : a man whose job is to give massages

mas·seuse /mæ'səz/ n [C] : a woman whose job is to give massages

mas·sive /'mæsıv/ adj **1** : very large and heavy • *a massive ship* **2 a** : large in amount or degree • *a massive amount of data* **b** : very severe • *a massive heart attack* — **mas·sive·ly** adv — **mas·sive·ness** n [U]

mass media n [plural] : ²MEDIA 1

mass noun n [C] grammar : NONCOUNT NOUN

mass–pro·duce /,mæsprə'duːs, Brit ,mæsprə'djuːs/ vb -duced; -duc·ing [T] : to produce very large amounts of (something) usually by using machinery • *mass-producing computer chips* — **mass–produced** adj • *mass-produced foods* — **mass production** n [U]

mass transit n [U] chiefly US : the system that moves large numbers of people on buses, trains, etc. • *commuters using mass transit*

mast /'mæst, Brit 'mɑːst/ n [C] **1** : a long pole that supports the sails of a boat or ship **2** : a tall pole that supports something (such as a flag)

¹**mas·ter** /'mæstə, Brit 'mɑːstə/ n **1** [C] : someone who has control or power over another person, an animal, or a thing • *the slave's/dog's/ship's master* • *We are the masters of our own destiny.* **2** [C] : a person who has become very skilled at doing something • *a chess master = a master at/of chess* **3** [C] old-fashioned : a male teacher **4** [C] : an original version of something (such as a recording) from which copies can be made **5** *Master* formal + old-fashioned — used as a title for a boy who is too young to be called *Mister* • *Master Timothy*

²**master** adj, always before a noun **1** : highly skilled • *a master chef/carpenter* **2** : largest or most important • *the master bedroom* **3** — used to describe an original version from which other copies can be made • *a master recording*

³**master** vb [T] **1** : to succeed in controlling (something) • *He mastered his fear.* **2** : to learn (something) completely • *mastering French/chess* — **mas·tery** /'mæstəri, 'mɑːstəri/ n [U, singular] • *mastery of/over his fears* • *(a) mastery of French*

mas·ter·ful /'mæstəfəl, Brit 'mɑːstəfəl/ adj : very skillful • *a masterful performance* — **mas·ter·ful·ly** adv

master key n [C] : a key that can be used to open many locks

mas·ter·ly /'mæstəli, Brit 'mɑːstəli/ adj : very skillful • *a masterly performance*

mas·ter·mind /'mæstə,maınd, Brit 'mɑːstə,maınd/ n [C] : a person who plans and organizes something • *the mastermind behind the terrorist plot* — **mastermind** vb [T] • *He masterminded the bank robbery.*

master of ceremonies n [C] : a person who introduces guests, speakers, or performers at a formal event

mas·ter·piece /'mæstə,piːs, Brit 'mɑːstə,piːs/ n [C] : something done or made with great skill • *a literary/cinematic masterpiece*

master plan n [C] : a plan for doing something that will require a lot of time and effort • *He has a master plan for becoming a millionaire.*

master's *n, pl* **master's** [C] *informal* : MASTER'S DEGREE • *She has a master's in biology.*

master's degree *n* [C] : a degree that is given to a student usually after two more years of study following a bachelor's degree

mas·ter·work /'mæstəˌwəːk, *Brit* 'maːstəˌwəːk/ *n* [C] : MASTERPIECE

mast·head /'mæstˌhɛd, *Brit* 'maːstˌhɛd/ *n* [C] **1** : the top of a ship's mast **2** : the name of a newspaper shown on the top of the first page

mas·tiff /'mæstəf/ *n* [C] : a type of large, powerful dog

mas·to·don /'mæstəˌdaːn/ *n* [C] : a type of extinct animal that was related to the mammoth

mas·tur·bate /'mæstəˌbeɪt/ *vb* **-bat·ed; -bat·ing** [I] : to touch your own sexual organs for pleasure — **mas·tur·ba·tion** /ˌmæstəˈbeɪʃən/ *n* [U]

mat /'mæt/ *n* [C] **1 a** : a small piece of material used to cover the floor or to protect the surface of a table : a thick pad that is used as a soft surface for wrestling, gymnastics, etc. **2** : a thick mass of something that is stuck or twisted together • *a mat of hair*

mat·a·dor /'mætəˌdoəʳ/ *n* [C] : the person who kills the bull in a bullfight

¹match /'mætʃ/ *n* **1** [*singular*] : someone or something that is equal to or as good as another person or thing • *He was no match for his opponent.* [=his opponent was able to defeat him easily] • *She knew after the first game that she had met her match.* [=that her opponent could defeat her] **2** [*singular*] **a** : two people or things that are suited to each other • *The curtains and carpet are a good/perfect match (for each other).* • *Jill and Brad are a match made in heaven.* [=perfectly suited to each other] **b** : someone or something that is suited to another person or thing • *The sweater was a nice match for her skirt.* **3** [C] : a contest between two or more players or teams • *a tennis/boxing/chess match* • *(figurative) He got into a shouting match with his neighbor.* [=he and his neighbor were angrily shouting at each other] **4** [C] : a thin piece of wood or thick paper with a special tip that produces fire when it is scratched against something else

²match *vb* **1** [T/I] **a** : to be suited to (someone or something) : to go well with (someone or something) • *The curtains match the carpet.* • *She wore a blue sweater with a matching skirt.* • *He's a large man with hands to match.* [=a large man with large hands] **b** : to have the same appearance, color, etc. • *Your socks don't match (each other).* **2** [T] : to make or see a connection or relationship between (two people or things) • *The children matched (up) the names of the animals to/ with the correct pictures.* **3** [T/I] : to be in agreement with (something) • *His story doesn't match (up) with the facts.* **4 a** [T/I] : to be as good as (something or someone) • *Nothing will ever match the*

excitement of that game. • *Nobody can match him at golf.* • *The teams are evenly matched.* [=they are equally good] • *The concert didn't match up to* [=equal, meet] *our expectations.* **b** [T] : to provide, produce, or do something that is equal to (something else) • *We matched their offer.* **5** [T] : to place (someone or something) in competition against another • *They were matched against/with each other in the play-offs.* **6** [T] : to compare (something) with something else • *The fingerprints were matched against those in the database.*

match·book /'mætʃˌbʊk/ *n* [C] : a small folder that contains rows of matches

match·box /'mætʃˌbaːks/ *n* [C] : a small box for matches

match·less /'mætʃləs/ *adj* : better than all others • *a matchless art collection* • *matchless beauty*

match·mak·er /'mætʃˌmeɪkə/ *n* [C] : a person who tries to bring two people together so that they will marry each other — **match·mak·ing** /'mætʃˌmeɪkɪŋ/ *n* [U]

¹mate /'meɪt/ *n* **1** [C] : a person who lives with you, works in the same place as you, etc. • *She and I are office mates.* [=we work in the same office] **2** [C] : either one of a pair of animals that are breeding • *a nesting bird and its mate* **3** [C] *chiefly US* : a person's husband, wife, or romantic or sexual partner • *an ideal mate* **4** [C] *chiefly US, informal* : either one of a pair of objects • *I can't find this glove's mate.* **5** [C] : an officer on a ship who has a rank below the captain • *a first mate* **6** [C] *chiefly Brit, informal* : a friend • *Got a light, mate?* **7** [C] *chiefly Brit* : an assistant or helper • *a plumber's mate* **8** [C] : CHECKMATE

²mate *vb* **mat·ed; mat·ing** *of animals* **1** [I] : to have sex in order to produce young • *a mating call/ritual* • *the mating season* [=the time of year when an animal mates] • *These birds mate for life.* [=they form pairs and stay together throughout their lives] **2** [T] : to bring (animals) together so that they will breed and produce young • *mating pandas in captivity*

¹ma·te·ri·al /məˈtirijəl/ *n* **1** [C/U] : a substance from which something is made or can be made • *building materials* **2** [C/U] : something used in doing a particular activity • *writing materials* **3** [U] : cloth or fabric **4** [U] : information or ideas • *The comedian gets her material from current events.* **5** [U] : a person who is suited to a particular position, job, or activity • *I was never college material.* [=a person who should go to college]

²material *adj* **1** *always before a noun* **a** : relating to or made of matter : PHYSICAL • *the material world* • *material objects* **b** : physical rather than spiritual or intellectual • *material comforts/goods/wealth* **2** *formal* : having real importance • *The evidence is not material to the case.* — **ma·te·ri·al·ly** *adv*

ma·te·ri·al·ism /məˈtirijəˌlɪzəm/ *n* [U] **1** : a way of thinking that gives too much importance to material possessions • *the* *materialism of our society* **2** *philosophy* : the belief that only material things exist — **ma·te·ri·al·ist** /məˈtirijəlɪst/ *n* [C] — **ma·te·ri·al·is·tic** /məˌtirijəˈlɪstɪk/ *adj* • *a materialistic society*

ma·te·ri·al·ize *also Brit* **ma·te·ri·al·ise** /məˈtirijəˌlaɪz/ *vb* -**ized;** -**iz·ing** [I] : to appear, occur, or become real • *Rain clouds materialized on the horizon.* • *The money they promised never materialized.* — **ma·te·ri·al·i·za·tion** /məˌtirijələˈzeɪʃən, Brit məˌtɪəriəˌlaɪˈzeɪʃən/ *n* [U]

ma·ter·nal /məˈtɚnəl/ *adj* **1** : of or relating to a mother • *maternal instincts* **2** *always before a noun* : related through the mother • *his maternal grandparents* [=the parents of his mother] — compare PATERNAL — **ma·ter·nal·ly** *adv*

¹**ma·ter·ni·ty** /məˈtɚnəti/ *n* [U] : the state of being a mother — compare PATERNITY

²**maternity** *adj, always before a noun* **1** : designed to be worn by a woman who is pregnant • *maternity clothes* **2** : relating to the time when a woman gives birth to a baby • *the hospital's maternity unit/ward* • *She was granted maternity leave.* [=time off to take care of a newborn child]

¹**mat·ey** /ˈmeɪti/ *adj* **mat·i·er;** -**est** *Brit, informal* : FRIENDLY • *a boss who is matey with his staff*

²**mat·ey** /ˈmeɪti/ *n* [*singular*] *Brit, informal* + *sometimes impolite* — used as a way for one man to address another man • *Listen, matey, I've had enough!*

math /ˈmæθ/ *n* [U] *US* : MATHEMATICS • *She's always been good at math.* [=(Brit) maths]

math·e·mat·i·cal /ˌmæθəˈmætɪkəl/ *adj* **1** : of, relating to, or involving mathematics • *a mathematical problem/equation* **2** : very exact or complete • *mathematical precision* **3** : possible but very unlikely • *The team has only a mathematical chance of making the play-offs.* — **math·e·mat·i·cal·ly** /ˌmæθəˈmætɪkli/ *adv*

math·e·ma·ti·cian /ˌmæθəməˈtɪʃən/ *n* [C] : a person who is an expert in mathematics

math·e·mat·ics /ˌmæθəˈmætɪks/ *n* [U] : the science of numbers, quantities, and shapes and the relations between them • *a professor of mathematics*

maths /ˈmæθs/ *n* [U] *Brit* : MATHEMATICS

mat·i·nee *or* **mat·i·née** /ˌmætnˈneɪ, Brit ˈmætɪˌneɪ/ *n* [C] : a play, movie, etc., that is performed or shown in the afternoon

ma·tri·arch /ˈmeɪtriˌɑɚk/ *n* [C] : a woman who controls a family, group, or government • *a tribe ruled by a matriarch* — **ma·tri·ar·chal** /ˌmeɪtriˈɑɚkəl/ *adj* • *matriarchal societies* [=societies that are controlled by women]

ma·tri·ar·chy /ˈmeɪtriˌɑɚki/ *n, pl* -**chies** **1** [C] : a family, group, or government controlled by women or a woman **2** [U] : a social system in which family members are related to each other through their mothers

matrices *plural of* MATRIX

ma·tri·cide /ˈmætrəˌsaɪd/ *n* [C] : the act of murdering your own mother

ma·tric·u·late /məˈtrɪkjəˌleɪt/ *vb* -**lat·ed;** -**lat·ing** [I] *formal* : to become a student at a school • *She matriculated in/at the college.* — **ma·tric·u·la·tion** /məˌtrɪkjəˈleɪʃən/ *n* [U]

mat·ri·mo·ny /ˈmætrəˌmoʊni/ *n* [U] *formal* : MARRIAGE • *two people joined in matrimony* — **mat·ri·mo·ni·al** /ˌmætrəˈmoʊnijəl/ *adj* • *matrimonial vows*

ma·trix /ˈmeɪtrɪks/ *n, pl* -**tri·ces** /-trəˌsiːz/ *also* -**trix·es** /-trɪksəz/ [C] *technical* **1** : something within or from which something else develops or forms • *complex social matrices* **2** *mathematics* : a set of numbers that are listed in rows and columns and that can be added or multiplied according to special rules — see also DOT MATRIX

ma·tron /ˈmeɪtrən/ *n* [C] **1** : an older married woman • *society matrons* **2** *US* : a woman whose job is to be in charge of children or other women • *the matron of a school for girls*

ma·tron·ly /ˈmeɪtrənli/ *adj* : like or suitable for an older married woman • *a matronly woman/dress*

matron of honor (*US*) *or Brit* **matron of honour** *n* [C] : a married woman who is the main bridesmaid at a wedding

matte (*US*) *or Brit* **matt** /ˈmæt/ *adj* : having a surface that is not shiny • *photos with a matte finish*

mat·ted /ˈmætəd/ *adj* : twisted together in an untidy way • *matted fur*

¹**mat·ter** /ˈmætɚ/ *n* **1** [C] : something that is being done, dealt with, talked about, or thought about • *personal/financial matters* • *She brought the matter to our attention.* [=she told us about the problem or issue] • *That's a matter for a jury (to decide).* • *This is no joking/laughing matter. = This is no small matter.* • *Finishing this project is no small matter.* [=is not an easy thing to do] • *He laughed at her and then, to make matters worse, he accused her of lying!* • *The budget is tight this year. The fact/truth of the matter is, we have to lay off a few employees.* • *He decided to take matters into his own hands.* [=to do something himself instead of waiting for other people to do something] **2** [U] **a** *physics* : the thing that forms physical objects and occupies space • *matter and energy* **b** : material of a particular kind • *organic matter* • *printed/reading matter* [=books, magazines, etc.] **3** *the matter* — used to ask if there is a problem or to say that there is or is not a problem • *What's the matter?* [=what's the problem?] • *"Is anything the matter?"* [=is anything wrong?] *"No, nothing's the matter."* • *There's something the matter* [=there's something wrong] *with the car.* • *(disapproving) You keep making stupid mistakes. What's the matter with you?* [=why do you keep making stupid mistakes?] — *a matter of* **1** — used to refer to a small amount • *It cooks in a matter of (a few) minutes.* [=in just a few minutes] **2** — used to say that one thing results from or requires another • *Learning to ski is a matter of practice.* [=learning to ski requires practice] • *It's only a*

matter of time before/until we catch him. [=we will catch him eventually] **3** — used to say that something is based on something • *Ties must be worn as a matter of policy.* [=because our policy requires it] • *"He's doing a bad job." "That's a matter of opinion."* • *"Do you have a pen?" "As a matter of fact, I do."* **4** — used to say that something is important, interesting, etc. • *The trial is a matter of interest* [=it is interesting] *to many people.* — **as a matter of course** — used to say that something will or should happen because it is natural, usual, or logical • *You should take proper precautions as a matter of course.* — **for that matter** — used with a statement that adds to a previous statement • *I haven't seen him for years—or her either, for that matter.* — **no matter 1** *informal* — used to say that something is not important • *"I may be late." "No matter.* [=it doesn't matter] *We will still have time."* **2** — used with *what, how, when,* etc., to say that something does not, will not, or should not affect something else • *I'm going to do it, no matter what (you say).*

²**matter** *vb* [*I*] : to be important • *the people who matter most to us* [=the people we care about most] • *"Which would you prefer?" "Either one is fine. It really doesn't matter (to me)."* • *All that matters is that you're safe.* • *It doesn't matter how old you are.* • *What does it matter?* = *It doesn't matter.* [=it's not important] • *She's late again. Not that it matters (to me).* [=it is not important to me]

mat·ter-of-fact /ˌmætərəˈfækt/ *adj* : not showing emotion • *His tone was calm and matter-of-fact.* — **mat·ter-of-fact·ly** /ˌmætərəˈfæktli/ *adv*

mat·tress /ˈmætrəs/ *n* [*C*] : a cloth case that is filled with material and used as a bed

¹**ma·ture** /məˈtuɚ, məˈtʃuɚ/ *adj* **ma·tur·er; -est 1** : having or showing the mental and emotional qualities of an adult • *She's very mature for her age.* • *a mature outlook on life* **2 a** : grown to full size • *mature trees/animals* **b** : having reached a final or desired state • *a mature wine* **3** *finance* : having reached the time when an amount of money must be paid • *The bond becomes mature in 10 years.* — **ma·ture·ly** *adv* • *They acted maturely.*

²**mature** *vb* **-tured; -tur·ing** [*I*] : to become mature • *Girls mature earlier than boys.* • *He matured into a kind young man.* • *Wine matures with age.* • *The bond matures in 10 years.* — **mat·u·ra·tion** /ˌmætʃəˈreɪʃən/ *n* [*U*] *formal*

mature student *n* [*C*] *Brit* : a student at a college or university who starts studying there at a later age than usual

ma·tu·ri·ty /məˈturəti, məˈtʃurəti/ *n, pl* **-ties 1** [*U*] **a** : the state of being fully developed in the body or the mind • *His behavior shows a lack of maturity.* **b** *finance* : the state of being due for payment • *The bond will reach maturity in 10 years.* **2** [*C*] *finance* : the amount of time that must pass before something becomes due for payment • *Maturities on*

these bonds can be as long as 10 years.

maud·lin /ˈmɑːdlən/ *adj* : showing or expressing too much emotion especially in a foolish or annoying way • *maudlin poetry*

maul /ˈmɑːl/ *vb* [*T*] : to attack and injure (someone) in a way that cuts or tears skin • *He was mauled by a dog.* • *(figurative) The movie was mauled by the critics.*

mau·so·le·um /ˌmɑːsəˈliːjəm/ *n* [*C*] : a stone building for the dead bodies of several people or the body of an important person

mauve /ˈmɑːv, ˈmoʊv/ *n* [*C/U*] : a light or medium purple color — **mauve** *adj*

ma·ven /ˈmeɪvən/ *n* [*C*] *US* : ¹EXPERT • *wine/marketing mavens*

mav·er·ick /ˈmævrɪk/ *n* [*C*] : a person who refuses to follow the customs or rules of a group • *a maverick in the world of fashion* • *a maverick director*

maw /ˈmɑː/ *n* [*C*] *literary* : the mouth, jaws, or throat of an animal • *(figurative) the dark maw of the cave*

mawk·ish /ˈmɑːkɪʃ/ *adj* : sad or romantic in a foolish or exaggerated way • *mawkish poetry* — **mawk·ish·ly** *adv*

¹**max** /ˈmæks/ *n* [*singular*] *chiefly US, informal* : ¹MAXIMUM • *(informal) The theater was filled to the max.* [=as much as possible]

²**max** *adv, informal* : at the most : MAXIMUM • *You'll need to wait two weeks max.* [=you will not have to wait longer than two weeks]

³**max** *vb* — **max out** [*phrasal vb*] *informal* **1** : to come to the highest level possible • *Most athletes max out before the age of 30.* • *The car maxed out at* [=could go no faster than] *100 mph.* **2** *max (something) out* or *max out (something)* **a** : to spend all of the money that your credit card allows you to borrow • *She maxed out her credit card.* **b** : to use or fill (something) as much as possible • *maxing out the city's resources/schools*

max·im /ˈmæksəm/ *n* [*C*] : a well-known phrase (such as "Don't count your chickens before they hatch") that expresses a general truth about life or a rule about behavior

max·i·mal /ˈmæksəməl/ *adj, technical* : greatest or highest possible • *a maximal heart rate* — **max·i·mal·ly** *adv*

max·i·mize *also Brit* **max·i·mise** /ˈmæksəˌmaɪz/ *vb* **-mized; -miz·ing** [*T*] **1** : to increase (something) as much as possible • *The company is trying to maximize its profits.* [=to make the most money possible] **2** : to use (something) in a way that will get the best result • *ways to maximize your time* **3** *computers* : to make (a program's window) fill the screen of a computer — **max·i·mi·za·tion** *also Brit* **max·i·mi·sa·tion** /ˌmæksəməˈzeɪʃən, *Brit* ˌmæksəˌmaɪˈzeɪʃən/ *n* [*U*]

¹**max·i·mum** /ˈmæksəməm/ *n, pl* **-mums** *or technical* **-ma** /-mə/ [*C*] : the highest number or amount that is possible or allowed • *She will serve a maximum of 20 years in jail.*

²**maximum** *adj, always before a noun*

: greatest possible in amount or degree ▪ *The maximum number of points is 100.* ▪ *maximum-strength medicine*

³**maximum** *adv* : at the most ▪ *She will serve 20 years maximum in jail.*

may /ˈmeɪ/ *vb* [*modal vb*] **1** — used to indicate that something is possible or probable ▪ *They may still succeed.* ▪ *You may be right.* ▪ *What you see may (well/very well) surprise you.* ▪ *There may be trouble ahead.* ▪ *As you **may or may not** know, we won!* **2** — used to say that one thing is true but something else is also true ▪ *It may be cold, but it's still a beautiful day.* **3** *formal* — used to indicate that something is allowed ▪ *You may* [=you have permission to] *go now.* **4** *formal* — used to ask a question or make a request or suggestion in a polite way ▪ *"May I borrow your pen?" "Of course you may!"* ▪ *May I ask who is calling?* ▪ *It may be wise to proceed cautiously.* ▪ *I'd like to ask a question, **if I may**.* ▪ ***May I just say*** [=I would like to say] *how pleased I am to be here.* **5** *formal* — used to express a wish ▪ *May the best man win!* **6** *formal + old-fashioned* — used to indicate the reason for or the purpose of something ▪ *We exercise so that we may be healthy.* — **be that as it may** *formal* — used to introduce a statement that is somehow different from what has just been said ▪ *There has been some improvement in the economy in recent months, but, be that as it may, many people are still looking for work.* — **come what may** *see* COME

May /ˈmeɪ/ *n* [C/U] : the fifth month of the year ▪ *in (early/mid/late) May* ▪ *We left on May the fourth.* = (US) *We left on May fourth.* = *We left on the fourth of May.*

may·be /ˈmeɪbi/ *adv* **1** : possibly but not certainly ▪ *Maybe we'll meet again.* ▪ *"Will you go?" "Maybe, maybe not."* ▪ *You should hear from them soon, maybe even by next week.* ▪ *There were maybe 10,000 fans at the game.* ▪ *Did you ever think that maybe, just maybe, it wasn't his fault?* **2** — used to say that one thing is true but that something else is also true ▪ *Maybe at first I didn't like her, but now she's my best friend.*

May·day /ˈmeɪˌdeɪ/ — a word used to call for help when an airplane or ship is in danger ▪ *The pilot shouted "Mayday! Mayday!" over the radio.*

May Day /ˈmeɪˌdeɪ/ *n* [*singular*] : May 1 celebrated in many countries as a holiday

may·hem /ˈmeɪˌhɛm/ *n* [U] : a scene or situation that involves a lot of violence ▪ *murder and mayhem* ▪ *There was mayhem* [=a lot of excited activity] *after the championship.*

mayo /ˈmeɪoʊ/ *n* [U] *informal* : MAYONNAISE

may·on·naise /ˈmeɪjəˌneɪz/ *n* [U] : a thick, white sauce used especially in salads and on sandwiches and made chiefly of eggs, oil, and vinegar or lemon juice

may·or /ˈmeɪjɚ/ *n* [C] **1** : an official who is elected to be the head of the government of a city or town ▪ *the mayor of New York* **2** : a British official who repre-

sents a city or borough at public events — **may·or·al** /ˈmeɪjərəl/ *adj* ▪ *mayoral elections* — **may·or·al·ty** /ˈmeɪjərəlti/ *n, pl* **-ties** [C/U] *formal* ▪ *during her mayoralty* [=the time when she was mayor]

maze /ˈmeɪz/ *n* [C] **1** : a complicated and confusing system of connected passages ▪ *The mouse finds its way through a maze to get its reward of cheese.* **2** : a confusing collection or mixture of things ▪ *a maze of rules*

MB *abbr* **1** megabyte **2** *chiefly Brit* Bachelor of Medicine

M.B.A. *or* **MBA** *abbr* Master of Business Administration ▪ *She earned/has an M.B.A. from Harvard.*

MC /ˌɛmˈsiː/ *n* [C] : MASTER OF CEREMONIES

McCoy /məˈkɔɪ/ *n* — **the real McCoy** *informal* : something or someone that is real or genuine ▪ *These diamonds look like the real McCoy, but they could be fake.*

MD *abbr* **1** *or US* **M.D.** Doctor of Medicine **2** Maryland **3** *Brit* Managing Director

¹**me** /ˈmiː/ *pron, objective case of* I — used to refer to the speaker as the indirect object or direct object of a verb ▪ *She gave me a book.* ▪ *Can you help me?* — used to refer to the speaker as the object of a preposition ▪ *Are you talking to me?*

> **usage** In ordinary speech *me* is used instead of *I* after the verb *to be.* ▪ *"Who's there?" "It's me." [="I am."]* ▪ *This dress is pretty, but it's not really me.* [=it doesn't look right for me] *Me* is also used alone without a verb in spoken questions, answers, etc. ▪ *"Who's there?" "Me."* ▪ *"Come here!" "Who? Me?"* ▪ *"I'm hungry." "Me too."* *Me* is also sometimes used in very informal speech in place of *I* if the subject of a sentence has two parts that are connected by *and.* ▪ *My brother and me were there.* = *Me and my brother were there.* But in ordinary polite use, *I* is required in such sentences. ▪ *My brother and I were there.*

²**me** *chiefly Brit spelling of* MI

ME *abbr* Maine

mead /ˈmiːd/ *n* [U] : an alcoholic drink made from honey

mead·ow /ˈmɛdoʊ/ *n* [C] : an area of land that is covered with tall grass

mead·ow·lark /ˈmɛdoʊˌlɑɚk/ *n* [C] : a North American songbird

mea·ger (*US*) *or Brit* **mea·gre** /ˈmiːgɚ/ *adj* **1** : very small or too small in amount ▪ *a meager wage/harvest* **2** : not having enough money, food, etc., for comfort or happiness ▪ *a meager existence*

meal /ˈmiːl/ *n* [C] **1** : the foods eaten or prepared for eating at one time ▪ *He eats/has three meals a day.* ▪ *a meal of chicken and rice* ▪ *This soup is a meal in itself.* [=all that is needed for a meal] **2** : a time or occasion when food is eaten ▪ *Breakfast is her favorite meal.* ▪ *a big holiday meal* ▪ *He doesn't eat between meals.*

meal ticket n [C] informal : a person or thing that is depended on as a source of money, success, etc.

meal·time /ˈmiːlˌtaɪm/ n [C/U] : the usual time when a meal is eaten ▪ Take one pill at mealtime.

mealy /ˈmiːli/ adj **meal·i·er; -est** : feeling rough and dry in your mouth ▪ a mealy potato

mealy-mouthed /ˈmiːliˌmaʊðd/ adj, informal : not willing to tell the truth in clear and simple language ▪ a mealy-mouthed politician

¹**mean** /ˈmiːn/ vb **meant** /ˈmɛnt/; **meaning** 1 [T] a : to have (a particular meaning) ▪ "What does the French word 'bonjour' mean?" "It means 'hello.'" ▪ "Bonjour" is a French word meaning "hello." ▪ The abbreviation "U.S." means "United States." ▪ Red means "stop." 2 [T] : to want or intend to express (a particular idea or meaning) ▪ I meant what I said. ▪ When she says the play was "interesting," she means (that) it wasn't very good. ▪ He's ambitious, and I mean that as a compliment. ▪ "He can be a little difficult. (Do you) Know what I mean?" "Yeah, I know what you mean." [=I agree] ▪ "He can be a little difficult." "What's that supposed to mean?" [=I don't agree with that] 3 [T] : to have (something) in your mind as a purpose or goal ▪ Just what do you mean (by) coming into my room without knocking? ▪ She meant (you) no harm. [=she did not intend to cause any harm (to you)] ▪ He never meant to hurt her. ▪ I keep meaning to visit you, but I never seem to have the time. 4 a [T/I] : to plan for or want (someone or something) to do or to be something ▪ She meant her remarks to be funny. ▪ It was meant as a joke. ▪ (chiefly US) We meant for her to come with us. b [T] : to want (something) to be used for a particular purpose or by or for a particular person ▪ They meant the book to be a present. 5 [T] : to make a statement to or about (someone) ▪ "Hey, you!" "Do you mean me?" [=are you talking to me?] 6 [T] a : to indicate or show (something) ▪ Those clouds mean rain. = Those clouds mean (that) it's going to rain. b : to cause or result in (something) ▪ The bad weather could mean further delays. c : to involve or require (something) ▪ I'll finish today even if it means working late. 7 [T] — used to say or ask how important something is to someone ▪ Your opinion means a lot to us. ▪ Money means nothing to him. ▪ She means the world to me. [=I love her very much] — **I mean** informal 1 — used to correct a previous statement ▪ We met in Toronto—I mean Montreal. 2 — used when you are unsure of what to say or how to say it ▪ I'm not mad. It's just that, I mean, I think you've been acting a little selfishly. — **know what it means** : to understand what it is like to do or be something ▪ I know what it means to be poor. ▪ I know what it means to quit! [=I never quit] — **mean business** see BUSINESS — **meant for (someone)** informal : perfectly suited for (someone) ▪ We were meant for each other. — **meant to be/**

do something 1 : intended to do or be something ▪ I was never meant to teach. ▪ I wanted to be friends, but I guess it wasn't meant to be. 2 Brit : supposed to be or do something ▪ The bus is meant to arrive soon. — **mean well** : to want to do good or helpful things ▪ He means well, but he's not helping anyone.

²**mean** adj 1 somewhat informal a : not kind to people : cruel or harsh ▪ a mean boss/trick ▪ Why are you being so mean to me? ▪ It was mean of them not to invite her to the party. b chiefly US : dangerous or vicious ▪ a mean dog 2 always before a noun : occurring exactly between the highest and lowest number : AVERAGE ▪ the mean temperature 3 chiefly Brit : STINGY 1 ▪ He's mean with his money. 4 literary : of poor quality or status ▪ mean city streets ▪ (informal) Finishing on time will be no mean feat. [=will be an impressive accomplishment] 5 chiefly US, informal : excellent or impressive ▪ He plays a mean trumpet. [=he plays the trumpet very well] ▪ an athlete who describes himself as a lean, mean scoring machine — **mean·ly** /ˈmiːnli/ adv — **mean·ness** /ˈmiːnnəs/ n [U]

³**mean** n [C] : ¹AVERAGE 1 ▪ Take all these temperatures and calculate/find their mean. — see also MEANS

me·an·der /miˈændə/ vb [I] 1 : to have curves instead of going in a straight line ▪ a meandering stream 2 : to walk slowly without a specific goal, purpose, or direction ▪ We meandered around/through the village. 3 : to go from one topic to another without any clear direction ▪ a meandering speech

mean·ie /ˈmiːni/ n [C] informal : a mean or unkind person — used especially by children ▪ He's just a big meanie!

mean·ing /ˈmiːnɪŋ/ n 1 [C/U] : the idea that is represented by a word, phrase, etc. ▪ The word has more than one meaning. ▪ (figurative) I don't know the meaning of the word "failure." [=I am determined not to fail] 2 [C/U] : the idea that a person wants to express by using words, signs, etc. ▪ the meaning of his remark ▪ the poem's meaning 3 [U] a : the true purpose of something ▪ What is the meaning of life? b : the value and importance of something ▪ Becoming a mother has given her life new meaning. c : the reason or explanation for something ▪ What is the meaning of this intrusion?

mean·ing·ful /ˈmiːnɪŋfəl/ adj 1 : having a clear meaning ▪ meaningful results 2 : expressing an emotion or idea without words ▪ a meaningful pause 3 : having real importance or value ▪ meaningful work — **mean·ing·ful·ly** adv ▪ She paused meaningfully.

mean·ing·less /ˈmiːnɪŋləs/ adj 1 : having no meaning ▪ a meaningless phrase 2 : having no real importance or value ▪ meaningless work — **mean·ing·less·ly** adv

means /ˈmiːnz/ n, pl **means** 1 [C] : a way of doing something or of achieving a desired result ▪ trains, buses, and other means of transportation ▪ The property was obtained by illegal means. • *succeeding by any means necessary* [=by doing whatever is needed] • *For her, marrying a rich man was just a means to an end.* [=something done only to produce a desired result] • *having no means of support* [=no way to pay for the things that you need to live] **2** [*plural*] : the money that someone has • *a woman of means* [=a wealthy woman] • *She was living beyond her means.* [=spending more money than she could afford to spend] — *by all means* : of course : CERTAINLY • *"May I come in?" "By all means!"* — *by means of* : through the use of (something) • *He got out of trouble by means of a clever trick.* — *by no means* or *by any (manner of) means* : in no way : not at all • *It's by no means certain that he'll come.*

mean–spir·it·ed /ˈmiːnˈspirətəd/ *adj* : feeling or showing a desire to cause harm or pain • *a mean-spirited book review*

meant past tense and past participle of ¹MEAN

mean·time /ˈmiːnˌtaɪm/ *n* — *for the meantime* : for the present time : until some time in the future • *Continue to take the medicine for the meantime.* — *in the meantime* **1** : during the time before something happens or before a specified period ends • *The wedding is in three months, and there's a lot to be done in the meantime.* **2** : while something else is or was being done • *She is studying for her law degree. In the meantime, she continues to work at the bank.*

¹**mean·while** /ˈmiːnˌwajəl/ *adv* : at or during the same time • *You can set the table. Meanwhile, I'll finish making dinner.*

²**meanwhile** *n* — *in the meanwhile* : at or during the same time : in the meantime • *The new computers won't arrive until next week, but we can keep using the old ones in the meanwhile.*

mea·sles /ˈmiːzəlz/ *n* [*U*] : a disease that causes a fever and red spots on the skin

mea·sly /ˈmiːzli/ *adj, informal + disapproving* : very small or too small in size or amount • *a measly pay raise*

mea·sur·able /ˈmɛʒərəbəl/ *adj* : large enough to be measured or noticed • *measurable improvements in performance* — **mea·sur·ably** /ˈmɛʒərəbli/ *adv*

¹**mea·sure** /ˈmɛʒɚ/ *n* **1** [*C/U*] : an amount or degree of something • *The show mixes comedy and drama in equal measure.* **2** [*C*] : a unit used in measuring something • *The meter is a measure of length.* **3** [*C*] : an action planned or taken to achieve a desired result • *cost-cutting measures* • *resorting to desperate/extreme measures* **4** [*C*] : a sign or indication of something • *Wealth is not a measure of happiness.* **5** [*C*] : a way of judging something • *The company is a success by any measure.* • *Are IQ tests the best measure of intelligence?* **6** [*C*] *chiefly US, music* : a part of a line of written music that is between two vertical lines or the group of beats between these lines — *beyond measure* *formal* : to a very great degree • *Her joy was beyond mea-*

sure. [=she was very happy] — *for good measure* : as something added or extra • *He performed a couple of his old songs for good measure.* — *have/take/get the measure of (someone)* or *have/take/get someone's measure* *chiefly Brit* : to have or get a good understanding about what is needed to defeat or deal with (someone) • *She failed to take the measure of her opponent.* — *in no small measure* see SMALL

²**measure** *vb* **-sured; -sur·ing** **1** [*T*] **a** : to find out the size, length, or amount of (something) • *measure the line with a ruler* • *mental abilities measured by IQ testing* **b** : to find out the size of (someone) for clothing • *He's being measured for a new suit.* **2** [*T*] : to judge the importance, value, or extent of (something) • *measuring the importance of the event* • *Her accomplishments were measured against* [=compared with] *those of her predecessor.* **3** [*linking vb*] : to have a specified size • *The cloth measures 3 meters.* — *measure off* [*phrasal vb*] *measure off (something)* also *measure (something) off* : to measure (something) and mark its edges or its beginning and ending • *He measured off three yards of cloth.* — *measure out* [*phrasal vb*] *measure out (something)* also *measure (something) out* : to measure and remove (something) from a larger amount • *She measured out three cups of flour.* — *measure up* [*phrasal vb*] : to be as good as expected or needed • *His recent films haven't measured up to his earlier works.* — **mea·sur·er** /ˈmɛʒərɚ/ *n* [*C*]

mea·sured /ˈmɛʒəd/ *adj* : done with thought and care • *a measured response*

mea·sure·ment /ˈmɛʒəmənt/ *n* **1** [*U*] : the act or process of measuring something **2** [*C*] : a size, length, or amount known by measuring something • *The room's measurements are 30 by 15 feet.* • *The tailor took my measurements.*

measuring cup *n* [*C*] *US* : a cup that has markings for measuring ingredients when cooking; *also* : a cup that holds a particular amount of an ingredient

measuring jug *n* [*C*] *Brit* : a cup that has markings for measuring liquids when cooking

measuring tape *n* [*C*] : TAPE MEASURE

meat /ˈmiːt/ *n* **1 a** [*U*] : the flesh of an animal used as food • *She doesn't eat meat.* • *raw meat* • *pasta with meat sauce* [=sauce that contains meat] ◇ *Meat* often refers specifically to the flesh of mammals or birds instead of the flesh of fish. It can also sometimes refer only to the flesh of mammals. • *She eats fish but not meat.* • *The soup can be made with meat, chicken, or fish.* **b** [*C*] : a type of meat • *sandwich meats* **2** [*U*] : the part of something (such as a nut) that can be eaten • *coconut meat* **3** [*U*] : the most important or interesting part of something • *the meat of the story*

meat and potatoes *n* [*U*] *US, informal* : the most basic or important part of something • *the meat and potatoes of the argument*

meat·ball /ˈmiːtˌbɑːl/ n [C] : a small ball of ground meat ▪ *spaghetti and meatballs*

meat loaf n, pl ~ **loaves** also ~ **loafs** [C/U] : ground meat that is mixed with spices, onions, etc., and baked in the form of a loaf

meaty /ˈmiːti/ adj **meat·i·er; -est** **1 a** : of, relating to, or resembling meat ▪ *a meaty flavor/texture* **b** : having or including a large amount of meat ▪ *a meaty stew* **2** : having a lot of interesting ideas or information ▪ *a meaty novel* — **meat·i·ness** n [U]

mec·ca /ˈmɛkə/ n **1** **Mecca** [singular] : a city in Saudi Arabia that was the birthplace of Muhammad and is the holiest city of Islam **2** [C] : a place that attracts many people ▪ *The valley is a mecca for wine lovers.*

me·chan·ic /mɪˈkænɪk/ n [C] : a person who repairs machines (such as cars) and keeps them running properly

me·chan·i·cal /mɪˈkænɪkəl/ adj **1 a** : of or relating to machinery ▪ *mechanical problems/parts* **b** : having or using machinery ▪ *a mechanical toy* **2** disapproving : happening or done without thought or without any effort to be different or interesting ▪ *a mechanical reply* — **me·chan·i·cal·ly** /mɪˈkænɪkli/ adv

mechanical drawing n [C/U] US : drawing in a very precise and accurate way by using special instruments

me·chan·ics /mɪˈkænɪks/ n **1** [U] : a science that deals with physical energy and forces and their effect on objects **2** [plural] : the details about how something works or is done ▪ *the mechanics of running*

mech·a·nism /ˈmɛkəˌnɪzəm/ n [C] **1** : a mechanical part or group of parts having a particular function ▪ *The camera's shutter mechanism is broken.* ▪ *a locking mechanism* **2** : a process or system that is used to produce a particular result ▪ *the body's mechanisms for controlling weight* ▪ *a mechanism to enforce the new law* **3** : a way of acting, thinking, or behaving that helps or protects a person in a specified way ▪ *a coping/survival mechanism*

mech·a·nize also Brit **mech·a·nise** /ˈmɛkəˌnaɪz/ vb **-nized; -niz·ing** [T] : to change (a process or an activity) so that it is done with machines instead of by people or animals ▪ *mechanizing agriculture* ▪ *a highly mechanized industry* — **mech·a·ni·za·tion** also Brit **mech·a·ni·sa·tion** /ˌmɛkənəˈzeɪʃən, Brit ˌmɛkəˌnaɪˈzeɪʃən/ n [U]

¹med /ˈmɛd/ adj, always before a noun, chiefly US, informal : ¹MEDICAL ▪ *med school*

²med n [C] chiefly US, informal : MEDICATION **1** — usually plural ▪ *He took his meds.*

³med abbr medium

¹med·al /ˈmɛdl̩/ n [C] : a piece of metal often in the form of a coin in honor of a special event, achievement, etc. ▪ *He was awarded a medal for his heroism.*

²medal vb, US **-aled** or chiefly Brit **-alled**; US **-al·ing** or chiefly Brit **-al·ling** [I] : to win a medal ▪ *She medaled in diving in the Olympics.*

med·al·ist (US) or chiefly Brit **med·al·list** /ˈmɛdl̩ɪst/ n [C] : a person who receives or wins a medal ▪ *an Olympic medalist*

me·dal·lion /məˈdæljən/ n [C] **1** : a large medal **2** : something that is shaped like a large medal

med·dle /ˈmɛdl̩/ vb **med·dled; med·dling** [I] **1** : to become involved in the activities and concerns of other people when your involvement is not wanted : INTERFERE ▪ *Stop meddling in other people's lives.* **2** : to handle something in an unwanted or harmful way ▪ *Don't meddle with my stuff.* — **med·dler** /ˈmɛdlə/ n [C]

med·dle·some /ˈmɛdl̩səm/ adj : inclined to meddle or interfere ▪ *meddlesome neighbors*

¹media plural of **¹MEDIUM**

²me·dia /ˈmiːdijə/ n [plural] **1** : the radio stations, TV stations, and newspapers through which information is communicated to the public ▪ *He feels that the media are/is ignoring this issue.* **2** chiefly US : people who work as news reporters, publishers, and broadcasters ▪ *The event attracted a lot of media.* ▪ *a major media event* [=an event that attracts attention from the news media]

mediaeval variant spelling of MEDIEVAL

¹me·di·an /ˈmiːdijən/ n [C] **1** mathematics : the middle value in a series of values arranged from smallest to largest **2** US : MEDIAN STRIP

²median adj, always before a noun, mathematics : having a value that is in the middle of a series of values arranged from smallest to largest ▪ *the median price of homes in the area*

median strip n [C] US : an area that divides a highway so that traffic going in one direction is kept separate from traffic going in the opposite direction

me·di·ate /ˈmiːdiˌeɪt/ vb **-at·ed; -at·ing** [T/I] : to work with opposing sides to get an agreement ▪ *He was appointed to mediate (in the dispute) between the company and the striking workers.* ▪ *mediate a settlement* — **me·di·a·tion** /ˌmiːdiˈeɪʃən/ n [U] — **me·di·a·tor** /ˈmiːdiˌeɪtə/ n [C]

med·ic /ˈmɛdɪk/ n [C] **1** US : a member of the military whose job is to provide emergency medical care to soldiers who have been wounded in battle **2** Brit, informal : a medical student or doctor

Med·ic·aid /ˈmɛdɪˌkeɪd/ n [singular] US : a government program that provides medical care for poor people

¹med·i·cal /ˈmɛdɪkəl/ adj : of or relating to the science of medicine ▪ *medical care/problems/bills/school* — **med·i·cal·ly** /ˈmɛdɪkli/ adv

²medical n [C] Brit : ²PHYSICAL

medical examiner n [C] US : a public official who examines the bodies of dead people to find the cause of death

medical practitioner n [C] formal : ¹DOCTOR 1

Medi·care /ˈmɛdɪˌkeə/ n [singular] US : a

government program that provides medical care especially for old people

med·i·cate /'mɛdɪ,keɪt/ *vb* **-cat·ed; -cat·ing** [*T*] : to treat (a person or disease) with medicine ▪ *The patient was heavily medicated.*

med·i·cat·ed *adj* : containing a substance that helps to keep your skin or hair healthy ▪ *medicated shampoo*

med·i·ca·tion /,mɛdɪ'keɪʃən/ *n* **1** [*C/U*] : MEDICINE 1 ▪ *She's taking medication for diabetes.* = *She's on medication for diabetes.* **2** [*U*] : the act or process of treating a person or disease with medicine ▪ *The patient/condition requires medication.*

me·dic·i·nal /məˈdɪsənəl/ *adj* : used to prevent or cure disease or to relieve pain ▪ *medicinal herbs/properties/purposes* — **me·dic·i·nal·ly** *adv*

med·i·cine /'mɛdəsən, *Brit* 'mɛdsən/ *n* **1** [*C/U*] : a substance that is used in treating disease or relieving pain ▪ *cough medicine* ▪ *He took his/some medicine.* **2** [*U*] : the science that deals with preventing, curing, and treating diseases ▪ *She's interested in a career in medicine.* ▪ *preventive medicine*

medicine man *n* [*C*] : a person in Native American cultures who is believed to have magic powers that can cure illnesses and keep away evil spirits

me·di·eval *also* **me·di·ae·val** /,miːdiˈiːvəl, *Brit* ˌmɛdiˈiːvəl/ *adj* : of or relating to the Middle Ages ▪ *medieval history*

me·di·o·cre /ˌmiːdiˈoʊkɚ/ *adj* : not very good ▪ *a mediocre wine/actor* — **me·di·oc·ri·ty** /ˌmiːdiˈɑːkrəti/ *n* [*U*]

med·i·tate /'mɛdə,teɪt/ *vb* **-tat·ed; -tat·ing** [*I*] : to spend time in quiet thought for religious purposes or relaxation — **meditate on/upon** [*phrasal vb*] : to think about (something) carefully ▪ *meditating on the meaning of life* — **med·i·ta·tion** /ˌmɛdəˈteɪʃən/ *n* [*C/U*] ▪ *(a) daily meditation* — **med·i·ta·tive** /'mɛdə,teɪtɪv/ *adj* ▪ *She was in a meditative* [=very thoughtful] *mood.*

Med·i·ter·ra·nean /ˌmɛdətəˈreɪnijən/ *adj* : of or relating to the Mediterranean Sea or to the lands that surround it ▪ *Mediterranean cuisine*

¹**me·di·um** /'miːdijəm/ *n, pl* **me·di·ums** *or* **me·dia** /'miːdijə/ [*C*] **1** *pl* **mediums** : something that is in the middle size, position, etc. ▪ *These shirts are all mediums and I take a large.* **2** *pl usually* **media** : a particular form or system of communication (such as newspapers, radio, or TV) ▪ *an effective medium for advertising* **3** : the materials or methods used by an artist ▪ *Her preferred medium is sculpture/watercolor.* **4** : the thing by which or through which something is done ▪ *Money is a medium of exchange.* **5** *pl* **mediums** : a person who claims to be able to communicate with the spirits of dead people **6** *formal* : a surrounding condition or environment ▪ *a medium of salt water* — **happy medium** : a good choice or condition that avoids any extremes ▪ *They are looking for a happy medium: a house that is not too big but that has lots of storage space.*

²**medium** *adj* **1** : in the middle of a range of possible sizes, amounts, degrees, etc. ▪ *a medium shirt* ▪ *a person of medium height* ▪ *a medium blue* **2** *of meat* : cooked to a point that is between rare and well-done — **medium** *adv* ▪ *a steak cooked medium*

med·ley /'mɛdli/ *n, pl* **-leys** [*C*] **1** : a song made up of parts of other songs ▪ *a medley of show tunes* **2** : a mixture of different things ▪ *a vegetable medley*

meek /'miːk/ *adj* : having or showing a quiet and gentle nature ▪ *a meek child/reply* — **meek·ly** *adv* — **meek·ness** *n* [*U*]

¹**meet** /'miːt/ *vb* **met** /'mɛt/; **meet·ing** **1** [*T/I*] : to see and speak to (someone) for the first time ▪ *She met him in college.* ▪ *Have we met (before)? You look familiar.* ▪ *I'd like you to meet my friend Bob.* ▪ *I'm pleased to meet you.* ▪ *It was nice meeting you.* **2 a** [*T/I*] : to go to a place to be with someone ▪ *Let's meet at the park.* ▪ *We met (each other) for lunch.* = (*informal*) *We met up with each other for lunch.* **b** [*I*] : to have a meeting ▪ *The club meets every Monday.* ▪ *We are meeting today to discuss the plans.* ▪ *Can you meet with us later today?* **3** [*T*] : to see and talk to (someone) by chance ▪ *I met an old friend at the store.* **4** [*T/I*] : to face each other in a game, war, etc. ▪ *The teams met in the finals last year.* ▪ *The army advanced to meet the enemy.* **5** [*T/I*] : to touch and join with or cross something else ▪ *where the river meets the sea* **6** [*T*] **a** : to be equal to (something) : to match (something) ▪ *The store promises to meet the price of any competitor.* **b** : to succeed in doing, accomplishing, or providing (something) ▪ *meeting requirements/goals* ▪ *We met a deadline.* ▪ *We have enough money to meet our needs.* ▪ *It didn't meet (our) expectations.* [=it was not as good as we expected it to be] ▪ *They met the challenge.* **7** [*T*] **a** : to experience or be affected by (something bad or unpleasant) ▪ *The idea has met (with) some opposition.* [=there has been some opposition to the idea] ▪ *the place where he met his death* [=where he was killed] **b** : to deal with or face (something) directly ▪ *She met his gaze without looking away.* ▪ *Their eyes met.* [=they looked at each other] **8** [*T*] : to be sensed by (the eyes, ears, etc.) ▪ *They were met by/with a shocking sight.* [=they saw something shocking] — **make ends meet** *see* ¹END — **meet (someone) halfway** : to reach an agreement with (someone) by compromising ▪ *We can't give you everything you want, but we can meet you halfway.*

²**meet** *n* [*C*] : a large gathering of people for a sports competition or hunt ▪ *a track/swim meet*

meet·ing /'miːtɪŋ/ *n* [*C*] **1** : a gathering of people for a particular purpose ▪ *Let's have/hold/call/convene a meeting to discuss the issue.* ▪ *business/staff meetings* ▪ *a prayer meeting* ▪ *She was in a meeting with her boss.* **2 a** : a situation or occasion when two people see and talk to each other ▪ *We started dating soon after our first meeting.* **b** : an occasion when athletes compete against each other • *The game will be their first meeting of the season.* — **a meeting of (the) minds** : an understanding or agreement between two people or groups • *coming to a meeting of the minds* [=reaching an agreement]

meet·ing·house /'mi:tɪŋ,haʊs/ *n* [*C*] : a building used for public gatherings and especially for Christian worship in the past

mega- /mɛgə/ *combining form* **1 a** : great : large • *a megastore* **b** *informal* : extremely • *mega-rich* **2** *technical* : million : multiplied by one million • *megahertz*

mega·bucks /'mɛgə,bʌks/ *n* [*plural*] *informal* : an extremely large amount of money • *athletes who earn megabucks*

mega·byte /'mɛgə,baɪt/ *n* [*C*] *computers* : a unit of computer information equal to 1,048,576 bytes — abbr. *MB*

mega·hertz /'mɛgə,həts/ *n*, *pl* **-hertz** [*C*] *technical* : a unit of radio frequency equal to one million hertz — abbr. *MHz*

meg·a·lo·ma·nia /,mɛgəloʊ'meɪnijə/ *n* [*U*] : a condition that causes people to think that they have great power or importance — **meg·a·lo·ma·ni·ac** /,mɛgəloʊ'meɪni,æk/ *n* [*C*] • *My boss is a real megalomaniac.* — **meg·a·lo·ma·ni·a·cal** /,mɛgəloʊmə'najəkəl/ *adj*

mega·phone /'mɛgə,foʊn/ *n* [*C*] : a cone-shaped device used to make your voice louder when you speak through it

mega·plex /'mɛgə,plɛks/ *n* [*C*] *US* : a building that contains many movie theaters

mega·star /'mɛgə,stɑɚ/ *n* [*C*] *informal* : a very famous and successful actor, athlete, etc.

mega·store /'mɛgə,stoɚ/ *n* [*C*] : a very large store

mega·ton /'mɛgə,tʌn/ *n* [*C*] : an explosive force that is equal to one million tons of TNT

mega·watt /'mɛgə,wɑ:t/ *n* [*C*] : a unit of electrical power equal to one million watts

mel·an·chol·ic /,mɛlən'kɑ:lɪk/ *adj*, *old-fashioned + literary* : very sad • *a melancholic outlook* • *melancholic music*

mel·an·choly /'mɛlən,kɑ:li/ *n* [*U*] : a sad mood or feeling • *a time of melancholy* — **melancholy** *adj* • *He was quiet and melancholy.*

mé·lange /meɪ'lɑ:nʤ/ *n* [*C*] : a mixture of different things • *a mélange of styles*

mel·a·nin /'mɛlənən/ *n* [*U*] : a dark brown or black substance that is a natural part of people's skin, hair, and eyes

mel·a·no·ma /,mɛlə'noʊmə/ *n* [*C/U*] *medical* : a type of cancer or tumor that begins as a dark area on the skin

meld /'mɛld/ *vb* [*T/I*] : to blend or mix together • *Simmer the sauce to let the flavors meld (together).*

me·lee /'meɪ,leɪ, Brit 'mɛ,leɪ/ *n* [*C*] : a confused struggle or fight involving many people • *He was injured in the melee.*

mel·lif·lu·ous /mɛ'lɪfləwəs/ *adj*, *formal* : having a smooth, flowing sound • *a mellifluous voice*

¹**mel·low** /'mɛloʊ/ *adj* **1** : pleasantly soft : not harsh, bright, or irritating • *mellow music/colors* **2** : having a pleasing rich flavor that develops over time • *a mellow wine* **3** : very calm and relaxed • *a mellow mood/crowd*

²**mellow** *vb* [*T/I*] : to become or to cause (someone or something) to become less harsh, irritating, nervous, etc. • *The wine needs time to mellow.* • *Old age has mellowed her.* — **mellow out** [*phrasal vb*] *US*, *informal* : to become relaxed and calm • *She mellowed out as she grew older.* — **mel·low·ness** *n* [*U*]

me·lod·ic /mə'lɑ:dɪk/ *adj* **1** : of or relating to melody • *the melodic flow of the music* • *a pleasing melodic line/pattern* **2** : having a pleasant musical sound or melody • *a melodic tune/voice* — **me·lod·i·cal·ly** /mə'lɑ:dɪkli/ *adv*

me·lo·di·ous /mə'loʊdijəs/ *adj* : having or making a pleasant musical sound • *a melodious song/voice/bird* — **me·lo·di·ous·ly** *adv*

melo·dra·ma /'mɛlə,drɑːmə/ *n* [*C/U*] **1** : drama in which many exciting events happen and the characters have very strong or exaggerated emotions • *an actor with a talent for melodrama* **2** : a situation in which people have very strong emotions • *The trial turned into a melodrama.*

melo·dra·mat·ic /,mɛlədrə'mætɪk/ *adj*, *often disapproving* : emotional or dramatic in a way that is extreme or exaggerated • *melodramatic movies/music* — **melo·dra·mat·i·cal·ly** /,mɛlədrə'mætɪkli/ *adv*

mel·o·dy /'mɛlədi/ *n*, *pl* **-dies** **1** [*C/U*] : a pleasing series of musical notes that form the main part of a song or piece of music • *a beautiful/haunting melody* **2** [*C*] : a song or tune • *He sang a few old-fashioned melodies.*

mel·on /'mɛlən/ *n* [*C/U*] : a large, round fruit that has a hard skin and sweet, juicy flesh

¹**melt** /'mɛlt/ *vb* **1** [*T/I*] : to change or to cause (something) to change from a solid to a liquid usually because of heat • *The snow is melting.* • *Melt the butter in the pan.* • *melted cheese* • (*figurative*) *The fish practically melts in your mouth.* [=it is delicious and becomes soft when you put it in your mouth] **2** [*I*] : to gradually become less or go away : DISAPPEAR • *Their determination melted in the face of opposition.* • *Her anger melted away when she saw that he was sorry.* **3** [*T/I*] : to begin to have feelings of love, kindness, sympathy, etc. • *Her heart melted with compassion.* • *His apology melted her heart.* [=filled her with compassion, sympathy, etc.] — **melt down** [*phrasal vb*] **1 a** *of a nuclear reactor* : to heat up accidentally, melt, and release radiation **b** : to experience a very fast collapse or failure • *The stock market has melted down.* **2 melt (something) down or melt down (something)** : to melt (something) so that it can be used for another pur-

pose • *melt down a coin — melt into* [*phrasal vb*] : to become difficult or impossible to see by changing into or becoming combined with (something else) • *The colors in the painting melt into one another.* • *She melted into* [=disappeared into] *the crowd.*

²**melt** *n* [C] *US* : a sandwich made with melted cheese • *a tuna melt*

melt·down /'mɛlt,daʊn/ *n* 1 [C/U] : an accident in which the core of a nuclear reactor melts and releases radiation • *a nuclear meltdown* 2 a [C/U] : a very fast collapse or failure • *(a) financial meltdown* b [C] *chiefly US, somewhat informal* : a very fast loss of emotional self-control • *The toddler had a major meltdown.*

melting point *n* [C/U] : the temperature at which something melts

melting pot *n* [C] : a place where different types of people live together and gradually create one community • *The city is a melting pot of cultures. — in the melting pot Brit* : not yet certain or finally decided • *Our plans are still in the melting pot.*

mem·ber /'mɛmbə/ *n* [C] : someone or something that belongs to a group or an organization • *team/family members* • *a member of the audience*

mem·ber·ship /'mɛmbə,ʃɪp/ *n* [C/U] 1 : the state of belonging to a group or an organization • *a one-year membership* 2 : all the people or things that belong to an organization or a group • *clubs that are hoping to increase (their) membership*

mem·brane /'mɛm,breɪn/ *n* [C] : a thin sheet or layer; *especially* : a thin sheet or layer of tissue that is part of a plant or an animal's body • *a cell membrane —* **mem·bran·ous** /'mɛmbrənəs/ *adj*

me·men·to /mə'mɛntoʊ/ *n, pl* **-tos** *or* **-toes** [C] : something that is kept as a reminder of a person, place, or thing

memo /'mɛmoʊ/ *n, pl* **mem·os** [C] : MEMORANDUM

mem·oirs /'mɛm,wɑɚz/ *n* [*plural*] : a written account in which someone describes past experiences • *a retired politician who is writing his memoirs*

mem·o·ra·bil·ia /,mɛmərə'bɪlijə/ *n* [*plural*] : objects or materials that are collected because they are related to a particular event, person, etc. • *sports memorabilia*

mem·o·ra·ble /'mɛmərəbəl/ *adj* : very good or interesting and worth remembering • *a memorable vacation/performance —* **mem·o·ra·bly** /'mɛmərəbli/ *adv*

mem·o·ran·dum /,mɛmə'rændəm/ *n, pl* **-dums** *or* **-da** /-də/ [C] : a usually brief written message or report from one person or department in a company or organization to another • *He sent a memorandum* [=memo] *to each employee.*

me·mo·ri·al /mə'morijəl/ *n* [C] : a monument, ceremony, etc., that honors a person who has died or serves as a reminder of an event in which many people died • *The new hospital is a fitting memorial to her. —* **memorial** *adj, always before a noun* • *a memorial service/monument*

me·mo·ri·al·ize *also* **me·mo·ri·al·ise** /mə'morijə,laɪz/ *vb* **-ized; -iz·ing** [T] *formal* : to do or create something that causes people to remember (a person, thing, or event) • *a period in history that has been memorialized in many popular books*

memoriam SEE IN MEMORIAM

mem·o·rize *also Brit* **mem·o·rise** /'mɛmə,raɪz/ *vb* **-rized; -riz·ing** [T] : to learn (something) so well that you are able to remember it perfectly • *memorize a speech —* **mem·o·ri·za·tion** *also Brit* **mem·o·ri·sa·tion** /,mɛmərə'zeɪʃən, Brit ,mɛmə,raɪ'zeɪʃən/ *n* [U]

mem·o·ry /'mɛməri/ *n, pl* **-ries** 1 [C/U] : the power or process of remembering what has been learned • *She has an excellent memory.* • *He committed the speech to memory.* [=he memorized the speech] • *If memory serves (me correctly)* [=if I remember accurately], *his name is John.* 2 a [C] : something that is remembered • *childhood memories* b [U] : the things learned and kept in the mind • *The happiness of those times is vivid in my memory.* • *Could you refresh my memory?* [=remind me] 3 [C] : the things that are remembered about a person who has died • *He is no longer with us, but his memory lives on.* [=we still remember him] 4 [C/U] : the period of time that a person can remember • *The harbor froze over for the first time in (modern/recent) memory.* 5 [U] *computers* a : capacity for storing information • *512MB of memory* b : the part of a computer in which information is stored • *information stored in memory — from memory* : without reading or looking at notes • *She delivered the speech from memory. — in memory of or in someone's memory* : made or done to honor someone who has died • *a monument in memory of Civil War soldiers — memory lane* ✧ If you *take a stroll/trip/walk (etc.) down memory lane,* you think or talk about pleasant things from the past.

men *plural of* ¹MAN

men·ace /'mɛnəs/ *n* 1 [C] a : a dangerous or possibly harmful person or thing • *a criminal who is a menace to society* b : someone who causes trouble or annoyance • *That kid is a menace.* 2 [U] : a dangerous or threatening quality • *There was a hint of menace in his voice.*

²**menace** *vb* **-aced; -ac·ing** [T] *somewhat formal* : to threaten harm to (someone or something) • *a country menaced by war —* **menacing** *adj* • *a menacing look —* **men·ac·ing·ly** /'mɛnəsɪŋli/ *adv*

me·nag·er·ie /mə'nædʒəri/ *n* [C] : a collection of animals • *(figurative) a menagerie of criminals*

¹**mend** /'mɛnd/ *vb* 1 [T] : to make (something broken or damaged) usable again • *mending a roof* • *mending (the holes in) socks* • *(figurative) He's trying to mend his reputation.* 2 [T/I] : to heal or cure (something) • *Only time can mend a broken heart.* [=make someone stop being sad] • *Her arm mended slowly after surgery. — mend fences or mend your fences* : to improve or repair a relation-

ship that has been damaged by an argument or disagreement • *She mended fences with her father.* — **mend your ways** : to change or improve your bad behavior • *It's time (for you) to mend your ways.*

²mend *n* [*singular*] : a place where something has been repaired • *a mend in a sleeve* — **on the mend** : becoming better • *Her health is on the mend.* • *The economy is on the mend.*

me·ni·al /ˈmiːnijəl/ *adj* — used to describe boring or unpleasant work that does not require much special skill and usually does not pay much money • *a menial job* • *menial labor*

men·in·gi·tis /ˌmɛnənˈdʒaɪtəs/ *n* [*U*] : a serious and often deadly disease in which an outside layer of the brain or spinal cord becomes infected and swollen

men·o·pause /ˈmɛnəˌpɑːz/ *n* [*U*] : the time near the age of 50 when a woman stops menstruating • (*US*) *a woman going through menopause* = (*Brit*) *a woman going through the menopause* — **men·o·paus·al** /ˌmɛnəˈpɑːzəl/ *adj*

me·no·rah /məˈnorə/ *n* [*C*] : an object that holds seven or nine candles and that is used in Jewish worship

men's room *n* [*C*] *US* : a public bathroom for use by men and boys

men·stru·al /ˈmɛnstruwəl/ *adj* : of or relating to the flow of blood that comes from a woman's body each month • *menstrual blood/pain*

menstrual period *n* [*C*] : the time when a woman menstruates each month — called also *period*

men·stru·ate /ˈmɛnstruˌeɪt/ *vb* **-at·ed; -at·ing** [*I*] *of a woman* : to have blood flow from your body as part of a process that happens each month • *She began menstruating at the age of 12.* — **men·stru·a·tion** /ˌmɛnstruˈeɪʃən/ *n* [*U*]

mens·wear /ˈmɛnzˌweə/ *n* [*U*] : clothes for men

-ment /mənt/ *n suffix* **1** : the action or process of doing something • *improvement* **2** : the product or result of an action • *entertainment* **3** : the state or condition caused by an action • *amazement*

men·tal /ˈmɛntl̩/ *adj* **1 a** : of or relating to the mind • *mental abilities/health* **b** : existing or happening in the mind • *a mental image/note* **2** *always before a noun* : relating to an illness of the mind • *mental patients/hospitals* **3** *informal* : CRAZY • *She looked at me as if I had gone mental.* • *That guy is a mental case.* [=he is crazy] — **men·tal·ly** *adv* • *mentally ill*

men·tal·i·ty /mɛnˈtæləti/ *n, pl* **-ties** [*C*] : a particular way of thinking • *a military mentality*

men·thol /ˈmɛnˌθɑːl/ *n* [*U*] : an oil made from mint that has a strong smell and that is used in candies, cigarettes, and medicines — **men·tho·lat·ed** /ˈmɛnθəˌleɪtəd/ *adj*

¹men·tion /ˈmɛnʃən/ *vb* [*T*] **1** : to talk about, write about, or refer to (something or someone) especially in a brief way • *I mentioned the problem to you last week.* • *She mentioned that she would be late.* • *She helped me in ways too numer-*

ous to mention. [=in very many ways] **2** : to refer to or suggest (someone) as having a possible role or status • *He's being mentioned as a possible candidate.* — **don't mention it** — used to answer someone who has just thanked you for something • *"Thank you for your help." "Don't mention it. It was the least I could do."* — **not to mention** — used when referring to another thing that relates to what you have just said • *We were cold and hungry, not to mention* [=and also] *tired.*

²mention *n* [*C/U*] : a short statement about something or someone • *She carefully avoided any mention of her sister.* • *Her contributions deserve a/some mention.* = *Her contributions are worthy of mention.* • *She made mention of* [=mentioned] *their contributions.*

men·tor /ˈmɛnˌtoə/ *n* [*C*] : someone who teaches or gives help and advice to a less experienced and often younger person • *The professor became her mentor.* • *young boys in need of mentors* — **mentor** *vb* [*T*] • *Our program focuses on mentoring teenagers.*

menu /ˈmɛnˌjuː/ *n* [*C*] **1 a** : a list of the foods that may be ordered at a restaurant • *I'd like to see a menu, please.* **b** : the foods that are served at a meal • *planning the menu for a dinner party* **2** : a list of things that you can choose from; *especially, computers* : a list shown on a computer from which you make choices to control what the computer does • *Choose "Save" from the "File" menu.*

me·ow (*chiefly US*) *or Brit* **mi·aow** /miˈaʊ/ *n* [*C*] : the crying sound made by a cat — **meow** (*chiefly US*) *or Brit* **miaow** *vb* [*I*] • *The cat meowed at the door.*

mer·can·tile /ˈməkənˌtiːl, ˈməkənˌtajəl/ *adj, always before a noun, formal* : of or relating to the business of buying and selling products to earn money • *a mercantile family/town*

¹mer·ce·nary /ˈməsəˌneri, Brit ˈməːsənəri/ *n, pl* **-nar·ies** [*C*] : a soldier who is paid by a foreign country to fight in its army

²mercenary *adj* **1** *always before a noun* : hired to fight • *a mercenary army/soldier* **2** *disapproving* : caring only about making money • *a mercenary businesswoman*

¹mer·chan·dise /ˈmətʃənˌdaɪz/ *n* [*U*] *somewhat formal* : goods that are bought and sold • *We sell quality merchandise.*

²merchandise *vb* **-dised; -dis·ing** [*T*] **1** : to make the public aware of (a product being offered for sale) by using advertising and other methods • *merchandising women's shoes* **2** : to present (someone) to the public like a product being offered for sale • *merchandise a movie star* — **mer·chan·dis·er** *n* [*C*] — **mer·chan·dis·ing** /ˈmətʃənˌdaɪzɪŋ/ *n* [*U*]

¹mer·chant /ˈmətʃənt/ *n* [*C*] **1** : someone who buys and sells goods especially in large amounts • *a wine merchant* **2** *chiefly US or Scotland* : the owner or manager of a store • *The town's merchants were opening their shops.*

²**mer·chant** *adj, always before a noun* : used for or involved in trading goods ▪ *merchant ships*

merchant marine *n* [*singular*] *chiefly US* : all of a country's ships that are used for trading goods rather than for war; *also* : the people who work such ships — called also (*Brit*) **merchant navy**

mer·ci·ful /ˈməsɪfəl/ *adj* **1** : treating people with kindness and forgiveness : not cruel or harsh ▪ *a merciful ruler/decision* **2** : giving relief from suffering ▪ *He died a quick and merciful death.* — **mer·ci·ful·ly** /ˈməsɪfəli/ *adv* ▪ *He was dealt with mercifully.* ▪ *The lecture was mercifully brief.* [=I was glad that the lecture was so brief]

mer·cu·ri·al /məˈkjərijəl/ *adj* **1** : likely to suddenly change from happy to angry or upset ▪ *a mercurial movie star* **2** : changing often ▪ *mercurial weather*

mer·cu·ry /ˈməkjəri/ *n* **1** [*U*] **a** : a silver metal that is liquid at normal temperatures **b** : the mercury in a thermometer that shows the air's temperature ▪ *The mercury reached 100 degrees Fahrenheit.* **2** *Mercury* [*singular*] : the planet that is closest to the sun

mer·cy /ˈməsi/ *n, pl* **-cies** **1** [*U*] : kind or forgiving treatment ▪ *She begged/pleaded for mercy.* ▪ *May God have mercy on us all.* [=may God treat us all with kindness and forgiveness] ▪ *He took mercy on us.* [=he treated us kindly] **2** [*U*] : kindness or help given to people who are in a very bad or desperate situation ▪ *a mission/errand of mercy* **3** [*C*] : a good or lucky fact or situation ▪ *We should be grateful/thankful for small mercies.* [=grateful that our situation is not worse] **4** *old-fashioned + informal* — used as an interjection to show surprise ▪ *Mercy (me)! That wind is cold!* — **at the mercy of** *or* **at someone's or something's mercy** : in a position or situation in which you can be harmed by (someone or something you cannot control) ▪ *The ship was at the mercy of the sea.* — **mer·ci·less** /ˈməsiləs/ *adj* ▪ *a merciless* [=very cruel] *killer* — **mer·ci·less·ly** *adv*

mercy killing *n* [*C/U*] : the killing of someone who is very sick or injured in order to prevent any further suffering

mere /ˈmiɚ/ *adj, always before a noun* **mer·est** **1** — used to say that something or someone is small, unimportant, etc. ▪ *a mere child* ▪ *The trip takes a mere two hours.* [=takes only two hours] **2** — used to say that something small is important or has a big effect or influence ▪ *The mere thought of going makes me nervous.*

mere·ly /ˈmiɚli/ *adv* : ONLY, JUST — used to say that someone or something is small, unimportant, etc. ▪ *It was merely a suggestion.* — used to describe the only reason for something or the only effect of something ▪ *I'm not criticizing you. I'm merely asking a question.*

merge /ˈməʤ/ *vb* **merged; merg·ing** **1 a** [*T*] : to cause (two or more things) to come together and become one thing ▪ *They merged* [=combined] *the two companies.* : to join or unite (one thing) with another ▪ *She agreed to merge her company with mine.* **b** [*I*] : to become joined or united ▪ *The two banks merged* (with each other). ▪ *Three lanes of traffic all merged* (into one). **2** [*I*] : to change into or become part of something else in a very gradual way ▪ *Day slowly merged into night.*

merg·er /ˈməʤɚ/ *n* [*C*] : the act or process of combining two or more businesses into one business ▪ *a merger of two companies*

me·rid·i·an /məˈrɪdijən/ *n* [*C*] : any one of the lines that go from the North Pole to the South Pole on maps of the world

me·ringue /məˈræŋ/ *n* [*C/U*] : a light, sweet mixture of egg whites and sugar that is baked and used as a topping for pies and cakes ▪ *lemon meringue pie*

¹**mer·it** /ˈmerət/ *n* **1** [*C*] : a good quality or feature that deserves to be praised ▪ *The plan has many merits.* ▪ *The contestants will be judged on their own merits.* [=by looking at their skills and their good and bad qualities] **2** [*U*] *formal* : the quality of being good, important, or useful ▪ *His ideas have (some) merit.*

²**merit** *vb* [*T*] : to deserve (something, such as attention or good treatment) by being important or good ▪ *Both ideas merit further consideration.*

mer·i·to·ri·ous /ˌmerəˈtorijəs/ *adj, formal* : deserving honor or praise ▪ *meritorious conduct/service*

mer·maid /ˈməˌmeɪd/ *n* [*C*] : an imaginary sea creature that has a woman's head and body and a fish's tail instead of legs

mer·ri·ment /ˈmerimənt/ *n* [*U*] : laughter and enjoyment ▪ *a time of joy and merriment*

mer·ry /ˈmeri/ *adj* **mer·ri·er; -est** *somewhat old-fashioned* **1** : very happy and cheerful ▪ *Let's eat, drink, and be merry!* ▪ *merry laughter* **2** : causing joy and happiness ▪ *a merry occasion* — **go on your merry way 1** *or* **be on your merry way** : to leave a place ▪ *Soon I'll be on my merry way.* **2** *often disapproving* : to continue doing what you have been doing ▪ *She just goes on her merry way, breaking men's hearts.* — **make merry** *old-fashioned* : to have fun and enjoy yourself by eating, drinking, dancing, etc. ▪ *They made merry throughout the night.* — **Merry Christmas** — used to wish someone an enjoyable Christmas holiday — **the more the merrier** — used to say that more people are welcome or invited to do something ▪ *"Can I bring a friend?" "Of course, the more the merrier!"* — **mer·ri·ly** /ˈmerəli/ *adv* — **mer·ri·ness** /ˈmerinəs/ *n* [*U*]

mer·ry-go-round /ˈmerigouˌraʊnd/ *n* [*C*] **1** : a large round platform that turns around in a circle and has seats and figures of animals (such as horses) on which children sit for a ride — called also (*US*) **carousel**, (*Brit*) **roundabout** **2** : a set or series of repeated activities that are quick, confusing, or difficult to leave ▪ *a legal merry-go-round*

mer·ry·mak·ing /ˈmeriˌmeɪkɪŋ/ *n* [*U*]

: joyful celebration that includes eating, drinking, singing, and dancing ▪ *a night of merrymaking* — **mer·ry·mak·er** /'meri-,meɪkɚ/ *n* [C]

me·sa /'meɪsə/ *n* [C] : a hill in the southwestern U.S. that has a flat top and steep sides

mesdames *plural of* MADAM 1

¹**mesh** /'mɛʃ/ *n* [C/U] : a material made from threads or wires with evenly spaced holes that allow air or water to pass through ▪ *(a) nylon/wire mesh*

²**mesh** *vb* **1** [T] : to cause (things) to fit together or work together successfully ▪ *The ceremony meshed traditions from several cultures.* **2** [I] : to fit or work together successfully ▪ *The movie's score meshes well with its story line.*

mes·mer·ize *also Brit* **mes·mer·ise** /'mɛzmə,raɪz/ *vb* -**ized**; -**iz·ing** [T] : to hold the attention of (someone) entirely ▪ *He was mesmerized by her smile.* — **mesmerizing** *also Brit* **mesmerising** *adj*

¹**mess** /'mɛs/ *n* **1 a** [C] : a very dirty or untidy state or condition ▪ *It took hours to clean up the mess.* ▪ *The kids* **made a mess** of/in *the kitchen.* **b** [*singular*] : something or someone that looks very dirty or untidy ▪ *The apartment is a mess.* **2** [C] **a** : a situation that is very complicated or difficult to deal with ▪ *This is a fine mess you've gotten me into!* **b** : something that is not organized well or working correctly ▪ *The economy is a mess.* **3** [*singular*] *informal* **a** : someone who is very unhappy, confused, etc. ▪ *She was a real mess after her divorce.* **b** *US* : someone who is showing a lot of emotion especially by crying ▪ *I was a mess during the wedding ceremony.* **4** [C] : the place where people in the military eat — called also *mess hall* **5** [*singular*] *US, informal* : a large amount of something ▪ *a mess of cash/trouble* — **make a mess of** : to ruin (something) ▪ *The weather made a mess of our plans.* — **messy** /'mɛsi/ *adj* **mess·i·er**; -**est** ▪ *a messy* [=untidy] *room* ▪ *a messy* [=difficult and complicated] *divorce* — **mess·i·ness** /'mɛsinəs/ *n* [U]

²**mess** *vb* — **mess around** *or Brit* **mess about** [*phrasal vb*] *informal* **1** : to spend time doing things that are not useful or serious ▪ *She spent the day messing around on the computer.* **2** : to have sex with someone who is not your regular partner ▪ *He was caught messing around (on his wife).* **3 mess (someone) around/about** *Brit* : to cause problems or trouble for (someone) especially by making unexpected changes ▪ *I don't like being messed about this way!* **4 mess around/about with a** : to use or do (something) in a way that is not very serious ▪ *I enjoy messing around with paints.* **b** : to handle or play with (something) in a careless or foolish way ▪ *Stop messing around with the stereo.* — **mess up** [*phrasal vb*] *informal* **1** : to make a mistake ▪ *She's afraid she'll mess up on the test.* **2 mess (something) up** *or* **mess up (something) a** : to make mistakes when you are doing or making (something) ▪ *I*

messed up the recipe. **b** : to make (something) dirty or untidy ▪ *Don't mess up my room.* **c** : to damage or ruin (something) ▪ *She's really messed up her life.* : to damage or change (something) so that it does not work properly ▪ *I messed up the computer somehow.* **3 mess (someone) up** *or* **mess up (someone) a** *US* : to beat and injure (someone) ▪ *They messed him up pretty badly.* **b** : to make (someone) very upset and unhappy ▪ *Breaking up with her boyfriend really messed her up.* — **mess with** [*phrasal vb*] *informal* **1** : to deal with (someone) in a way that may cause anger or violence ▪ *You'd better not be messing with me.* **2 a** *chiefly US* : to deal with or be involved with (something that causes or that could cause trouble) ▪ *Don't mess with cocaine.* **b** : to handle or play with (something) in a careless way ▪ *Don't mess with the camera.* **3** *informal* ◇ Something that **messes with your mind/head** causes you to feel confused.

mes·sage /'mɛsɪdʒ/ *n* **1** [C] : a piece of information that is sent or given to someone ▪ *a short phone/e-mail message* ▪ *Did anyone leave a message for me?* ▪ *He's not here right now. Can I take a message?* **2** [*singular*] : an important idea that someone is trying to express in a book, movie, speech, etc. ▪ *I agree with the book's message.* ▪ *I'm just trying to get the/my message across.* — **get the message** *informal* : to understand something that is not being said directly ▪ *When they didn't return my phone calls, I finally got the message.* [=finally realized that they did not want to talk to me]

message board *n* [C] : a public computer system on the Internet that allows people to read and leave messages for other users

mes·sag·ing /'mɛsɪdʒɪŋ/ *n* [U] : a system used for sending messages electronically ▪ *wireless messaging*

mes·sen·ger /'mɛsn̩dʒɚ/ *n* [C] : someone who delivers a message or does other small jobs that involve going somewhere — **blame/shoot the messenger** : to become angry at someone who has told you bad news

mess hall *n* [C] : ¹MESS 4

mes·si·ah /mə'sajə/ *n* **1 the Messiah a** *Judaism* : a king who will be sent by God to save the Jews **b** *Christianity* : Jesus Christ **2** [C] : a person who is expected to save people from a very bad situation ▪ *a political messiah*

mes·si·an·ic /,mɛsi'ænɪk/ *adj* **1** : relating to or having the qualities of a messiah ▪ *a messianic leader* **2** : enthusiastically supporting a social, political, or religious cause or set of beliefs ▪ *messianic zeal*

Messrs. (*US*) *or Brit* **Messrs** /'mɛsɚz/ — used as a formal plural of *Mr.* ▪ *Messrs. Lowry and Jones*

met *past tense and past participle of* ¹MEET

me·tab·o·lism /mə'tæbə,lɪzəm/ *n* [C/U] *biology* : the chemical processes by which a plant or an animal uses food, water, etc., to grow and heal and to make energy ▪ *Regular exercise can in-*

crease your metabolism. [=increase the rate at which your body turns food into energy] — **met·a·bol·ic** /ˌmɛtəˈbɑːlɪk/ adj — **me·tab·o·lize** also Brit **me·tab·o·lise** /məˈtæbəˌlaɪz/ vb -**lized**; -**liz·ing** [T] • Food is metabolized by the body.

met·al /ˈmɛtl/ n [C/U] : a substance (such as gold, tin, or copper) that usually has a shiny appearance, is a good conductor of electricity and heat, can be melted, and is usually capable of being shaped • a piece of metal • a metal roof

me·tal·lic /məˈtælɪk/ adj **1 a** : shiny like metal • metallic blue **b** : tasting like metal • a metallic taste **2** : made of metal or containing metal • a metallic element **3** : having a harsh sound • a metallic screech

met·al·lur·gy /ˈmɛtlˌɚʤi, Brit məˈtælərʤi/ n [U] : a science that deals with the nature and uses of metal — **met·al·lur·gi·cal** /ˌmɛtlˈɚʤɪkəl/ adj — **met·al·lur·gist** /ˈmɛtlˌɚʤɪst, Brit məˈtælərʤɪst/ n [C]

met·al·work /ˈmɛtlˌwɚk/ n [U] : things that are made out of metal; especially : metal objects that are made in an artistic and skillful way • a beautiful piece of metalwork

meta·mor·pho·sis /ˌmɛtəˈmoɚfəsəs/ n, pl -**pho·ses** /-fəˌsiːz/ [C/U] **1** : a major change in the appearance or character of someone or something • her metamorphosis from a shy girl into a self-confident woman **2** biology : a major change in the form or structure of some animals or insects that happens as the animal or insect becomes an adult • the metamorphosis of tadpoles into frogs • caterpillars undergoing metamorphoses — **meta·mor·phose** /ˌmɛtəˈmoɚˌfouz/ vb -**phosed**; -**phos·ing** [I] • caterpillars metamorphosing into butterflies

met·a·phor /ˈmɛtəˌfoɚ, Brit ˈmɛtəfə/ n **1** [C/U] : a word or phrase for one thing that is used to refer to another thing in order to show or suggest that they are similar • "He was drowning in paperwork" is a metaphor in which having to deal with a lot of paperwork is compared to drowning. **2** [C] : an object, activity, or idea that is used as a symbol of something else • The author uses flight as a metaphor for freedom. — **met·a·phor·i·cal** /ˌmɛtəˈfoɚɪkəl/ adj — **met·a·phor·i·cal·ly** /ˌmɛtəˈfoɚɪkli/ adv

meta·phys·i·cal /ˌmɛtəˈfɪzɪkəl/ adj **1** : of, relating to, or based on metaphysics • metaphysical questions **2** : of or relating to things that are thought to exist but that cannot be seen • a metaphysical world of spirits — **meta·phys·i·cal·ly** /ˌmɛtəˈfɪzɪkli/ adv

meta·phys·ics /ˌmɛtəˈfɪzɪks/ n [U] : the part of philosophy that is concerned with the basic causes and nature of things

mete /ˈmiːt/ vb **met·ed**; **met·ing** — **mete out** [phrasal vb] **mete** (something) **out** or **mete out** (something) : to give (something) to the people who you decide should get it • Fines were meted out as punishment.

me·te·or /ˈmiːtijɚ/ n [C] : a piece of rock or metal that burns and glows brightly in the sky as it falls from outer space into the Earth's atmosphere • a meteor shower [=a large number of meteors seen in a short time]

me·te·or·ic /ˌmiːtiˈorɪk/ adj **1** : very sudden or fast • a meteoric rise/fall **2** : marked by very quick success • a meteoric career

me·te·or·ite /ˈmiːtijəˌraɪt/ n [C] : a piece of rock or metal that has fallen to the ground from outer space

me·te·o·rol·o·gy /ˌmiːtijəˈrɑːləʤi/ n [U] : a science that deals with the atmosphere and with weather — **me·te·o·ro·log·i·cal** /ˌmiːtijərəˈlɑːʤɪkəl/ adj • meteorological conditions/forecasts — **me·te·o·rol·o·gist** /ˌmiːtiəˈrɑːləʤɪst/ n [C] • a storm forecast by meteorologists

me·ter /ˈmiːtɚ/ n **1** [C] **a** : a device that measures and records the amount of something that has been used • a gas/water meter **b** : PARKING METER • He went out to feed the meter. [=put more money in the parking meter] **2** or Brit **me·tre** [C] : the basic metric unit of length equal to about 39.37 inches **3** or Brit **me·tre** [C/U] : a way of arranging the sounds or beats in poetry • the poet's use of meter

meter maid n [C] chiefly US, somewhat old-fashioned : a woman whose job is to find vehicles that are parked illegally

meth·a·done /ˈmɛθəˌdoun/ n [U] : a drug that people take to help them stop taking heroin

meth·ane /ˈmɛˌθein, Brit ˈmiːˌθein/ n [U] : a colorless gas that has no smell and that can be burned for fuel

meth·a·nol /ˈmɛθəˌnɑːl/ n [U] technical : a poisonous alcohol that is used to keep liquids from freezing, as a fuel, etc.

meth·od /ˈmɛθəd/ n **1** [C] : a way of doing something • a new method for/of growing tomatoes • a teaching method **2** [U] formal : a careful or organized plan • The book lacks method. [=it is not arranged in an orderly way] — **(a) method in/to your madness** ✧ If there is method in your madness or (US) (a) method to your madness, there are good reasons for your actions even though they may seem foolish.

me·thod·i·cal /məˈθɑːdɪkəl/ adj **1** : done by using a careful and organized procedure • a methodical search **2** : working in a very careful and organized way • a methodical worker — **me·thod·i·cal·ly** /məˈθɑːdɪkli/ adv

Meth·od·ist /ˈmɛθədɪst/ adj : of or relating to any one of several Christian churches that follow the teachings of John Wesley • a Methodist church/preacher — **Meth·od·ism** /ˈmɛθəˌdɪzəm/ n [U] — **Methodist** [C]

meth·od·ol·o·gy /ˌmɛθəˈdɑːləʤi/ n, pl -**gies** [C/U] : a set of methods, rules, or ideas that are important in a science or art • scientific theories and methodologies

me·tic·u·lous /məˈtɪkjələs/ adj : very careful about doing something in an extremely accurate way • a meticulous researcher • meticulous work/records — **me·tic·u·lous·ly** adv — **me·tic·u·lous·ness** /məˈtɪkjələsnəs/ n [U]

metre *Brit spelling of* METER 2, 3

met·ric /ˈmɛtrɪk/ *adj* : of, relating to, or based on the metric system ▪ *a metric unit*

metric system *n* — **the metric system** : a system of weights and measures that is based on the meter and on the kilogram

metric ton *n* [C] : a unit of mass and weight equal to one million grams

¹**met·ro** /ˈmɛtroʊ/ *n, pl* **-ros** [C] : an underground railway system in some cities ▪ *the Paris Metro*

²**metro** *adj, always before a noun, US, informal* : of or relating to a large city and sometimes to the area around it ▪ *the metro* [=*metropolitan*] *area*

met·ro·nome /ˈmɛtrəˌnoʊm/ *n* [C] : a device that makes a regular, repeated sound to show a musician how fast a piece of music should be played — **met·ro·nom·ic** /ˌmɛtrəˈnɑːmɪk/ *adj*

me·trop·o·lis /məˈtrɑːpələs/ *n* [C] : a very large or important city ▪ *a bustling metropolis*

met·ro·pol·i·tan /ˌmɛtrəˈpɑːlətən/ *adj* : of or relating to a large city and the surrounding cities and towns ▪ *metropolitan Los Angeles* ▪ *a metropolitan newspaper*

met·tle /ˈmɛtl̩/ *n* [U] : ability to continue despite difficulties ▪ *He proved/showed his mettle.* [=*toughness*] ▪ *The competition will test her mettle.*

Mex·i·can /ˈmɛksɪkən/ *n* [C] : a person who is from Mexico — **Mexican** *adj*

mez·za·nine /ˈmɛzəˌniːn/ *n* [C] **1** : a small floor that is between two main levels of a building **2** *US* : the lowest balcony in a theater

mez·zo–so·pra·no /ˌmɛtsoʊsəˈprænoʊ, ˌmɛtsoʊsəˈprɑːnoʊ/ *n, pl* **-nos** [C] *music* : a female singing voice that is higher than the contralto and lower than the soprano; *also* : a female singer with such a voice

mg *abbr* milligram

MHz *abbr* megahertz

mi *or chiefly Brit* **me** /ˈmiː/ *n* [U] *music* : the third note of a musical scale ▪ *do, re, mi, fa, sol, la, ti*

mi. *abbr* mile

MI *abbr* Michigan

miaow *Brit spelling of* MEOW

mi·as·ma /maɪˈæzmə/ *n* [C] *formal + literary* : a heavy cloud of something unpleasant or unhealthy ▪ *a miasma of smog/odors*

mi·ca /ˈmaɪkə/ *n* [U] : a mineral that separates easily into thin sheets

mice *plural of* MOUSE

mick·ey /ˈmɪki/ *n, pl* **-eys** [C] *informal + old-fashioned* : a drink of alcohol to which a drug has been added to cause the person who drinks it to become unconscious ▪ *Someone slipped him a mickey.* [=*gave him a drugged drink*] — **take the mickey (out of someone)** *Brit, informal* : to make fun of someone

Mickey Mouse *adj, informal + disapproving* : not deserving to be taken seriously ▪ *a Mickey Mouse* [=*very easy*] *course*

micro- *combining form* **1** : very small ▪

microcomputer 2 : making a sound louder or an image larger ▪ *microphone* ▪ *microscope*

mi·crobe /ˈmaɪˌkroʊb/ *n* [C] : MICROORGANISM ▪ *a disease-causing microbe* — **mi·cro·bi·al** /maɪˈkroʊbijəl/ *adj*

mi·cro·bi·ol·o·gy /ˌmaɪkroʊbaɪˈɑːlədʒi/ *n* [U] : a science that studies extremely small forms of life (such as bacteria and viruses) — **mi·cro·bi·o·log·i·cal** /ˌmaɪkroʊˌbajəˈlɑːdʒɪkəl/ *adj* — **mi·cro·bi·ol·o·gist** /ˌmaɪkroʊbaɪˈɑːlədʒɪst/ *n* [C]

mi·cro·brew·ery /ˌmaɪkroʊˈbruːwəri/ *n, pl* **-er·ies** [C] *chiefly US* : a small brewery that makes beer in small amounts

mi·cro·chip /ˈmaɪkroʊˌtʃɪp/ *n* [C] *computers* : a group of tiny electronic circuits that work together on a very small piece of hard material (such as silicon)

mi·cro·com·put·er /ˈmaɪkroʊkəmˌpjuːtə/ *n* [C] : PERSONAL COMPUTER

mi·cro·cosm /ˈmaɪkroʊˌkɑːzəm/ *n* [C] : something that is seen as a small version of something much larger ▪ *The village is a microcosm of the whole country.*

mi·cro·fiche /ˈmaɪkroʊˌfiːʃ/ *n* [C/U] : MICROFILM

mi·cro·film /ˈmaɪkroʊˌfɪlm/ *n* [C/U] : film on which very small photographs of the printed pages of a newspaper, magazine, etc., are stored ▪ *newspapers available on microfilm*

mi·cro·man·age /ˌmaɪkroʊˈmænɪdʒ/ *vb* **-aged; -ag·ing** [T] *chiefly US* : to try to control or manage all the small parts of (something) in a way that is usually not wanted ▪ *He micromanaged every detail of the budget.*

mi·cro·or·gan·ism /ˌmaɪkroʊˈoɚgəˌnɪzəm/ *n* [C] *biology* : an extremely small living thing that can only be seen with a microscope

mi·cro·phone /ˈmaɪkrəˌfoʊn/ *n* [C] : a device into which people speak or sing in order to record their voices or to make them sound louder — called also (*informal*) *mike*

mi·cro·pro·ces·sor /ˈmaɪkroʊˈprɑːˌsɛsɚ, *Brit* ˈmaɪkrəʊˈprəʊˌsɛsə/ *n* [C] *computers* : the device in a computer that manages information and controls what the computer does

mi·cro·scope /ˈmaɪkrəˌskoʊp/ *n* [C] : a device used for producing a much larger view of very small objects so that they can be seen clearly — **under a/the microscope** : in a state of being watched very closely ▪ *celebrities living under the microscope*

mi·cro·scop·ic /ˌmaɪkrəˈskɑːpɪk/ *adj* **1** : able to be seen only through a microscope ▪ *a microscopic clump of cells* : extremely small ▪ *a microscopic crack* **2** : much smaller than what is usual, normal, or expected ▪ *He has a microscopic attention span.* — **mi·cro·scop·i·cal·ly** /ˌmaɪkrəˈskɑːpɪkli/ *adv*

mi·cro·sec·ond /ˈmaɪkroʊˌsɛkənd/ *n* [C] : one millionth of a second

¹**mi·cro·wave** /ˈmaɪkroʊˌweɪv/ *n* [C] **1** : MICROWAVE OVEN ▪ *The apartment came with a microwave.* ▪ *a microwave*

dinner **2** *physics* : a very short wave of electromagnetic energy

²**microwave** *vb* **-waved; -wav·ing** [*T*] : to cook or heat (food) in a microwave oven • *microwave a bowl of soup* — **mi·cro·wav·able** *or* **mi·cro·wave·able** /ˌmaɪkrəˈweɪvəbəl/ *adj* • *a microwavable plate/pizza*

microwave oven *n* [*C*] : an oven in which food is cooked or heated quickly by very short waves of electromagnetic energy — called also *microwave*

mid /ˈmɪd/ *adj, always before a noun* : in or near the middle of something • *the mid to late 1700s* • *the mid-18th century*

mid-air /ˈmɪdˈeə/ *n* [*U*] : a region in the air not close to the ground • *The planes collided in midair.*

mid·day /ˈmɪdˌdeɪ/ *n* [*U*] : the middle of the day • *They arrived around midday.* • *the midday meal* [=lunch]

¹**mid·dle** /ˈmɪdl/ *adj, always before a noun* **1** : equally distant from the ends or sides • *the middle* [=center] *aisle* : halfway between two points • *temperatures in the middle 80s* **2** : in a state or place between two things or people • *She sat in the middle seat.*

²**middle** *n* [*C*] **1** : a middle part, point, or position • *the middle of the room* • *We plan to move by the middle of next summer.* • *Slice the banana right down the* **middle.** [=into two equal parts] **2** : the middle part of a person's body • *She put her arms around his middle.* — **in the middle** : in a difficult or unpleasant position • *He was caught in the middle of his parents' divorce.* — **in the middle of** **1** : during (something) • *He interrupted her in the middle of a sentence.* • *I woke up in the middle of the night.* **2** : in the process of (doing something) • *I was in the middle of (eating) dinner when the phone rang.* — **in the middle of nowhere** : in a place that is far away from other people, houses, or cities

middle age *n* [*U*] : the period in a person's life from about age 40 to about age 60 • *a man approaching middle age* — **mid·dle-aged** /ˌmɪdlˈeɪdʒd/ *adj* • *a middle-aged man*

Middle Ages *n* — **the Middle Ages** : the period of European history from about A.D. 500 to about 1500

Middle America *n* [*U*] : the usually traditional or conservative people of the middle class in the U.S. • *a politician who understands the needs of Middle America* — **Middle American** *n* [*C*] — **middle–American** *also* **Middle-American** *adj*

mid·dle·brow /ˈmɪdlˌbraʊ/ *adj* : interested in art, literature, etc., that is not very serious and that is easy to understand • *middlebrow readers* : relating to or intended for middlebrow people • *a middlebrow magazine/movie*

middle class *n* [*C*] : the social class that is between the upper class and the lower class and that includes mainly business and professional people, government officials, and skilled workers — **middle-class** *adj* • *middle-class values* • *a middle-class family*

Middle East *n* — **the Middle East** : the countries of northern Africa and southwestern Asia that are on or near the eastern edge of the Mediterranean Sea — **Middle Eastern** *adj* — **Middle Easterner** *n* [*C*]

Middle English *n* [*U*] : the English language between about 1100 and 1400

middle finger *n* [*C*] : the long finger that is the middle one of the five fingers of the hand

middle ground *n* [*U, singular*] : a position or set of opinions that is acceptable to many different people • *a middle ground between harshness and leniency*

mid·dle·man /ˈmɪdlˌmæn/ *n, pl* **-men** /-ˌmɛn/ [*C*] **1** : a person or company that buys goods from a producer and sells them to someone else • *We keep our prices low by eliminating/bypassing the middleman.* **2** : a person who helps two people or groups to deal with and communicate with each other • *He acted as the middleman in the talks between labor and management.*

middle name *n* **1** [*C*] : a name between a person's first name and family name • *John F. Kennedy's middle name was "Fitzgerald."* **2** [*singular*] *informal* : a word that accurately describes a person's qualities • *Patience is her middle name.* [=she is very patient]

middle school *n* [*C/U*] **1** *US* : a school for children that usually includes grades five to eight or six to eight **2** *Brit* : a school for children between the ages of 8 and 12 or 9 and 13 — **middle schooler** /-ˈskuːlə/ *n* [*C*] *US*

mid·dle·weight /ˈmɪdlˌweɪt/ *n* [*C*] *sports* : a fighter who is in a class of boxers with an upper weight limit of 160 pounds (72 kilograms) • *a middleweight boxer/champion*

mid·dling /ˈmɪdlɪŋ/ *adj* : of average size or quality • *a middling performance* • *The food was fair to middling.* [=not especially good]

Mid·east /ˌmɪdˈiːst/ *n* — **the Mideast** *US* : the Middle East — **Mid·east·ern** /ˌmɪdˈiːstən/ *adj*

mid·field /ˈmɪdˌfiːld/ *n* [*U*] : the area of a playing field in sports like American football and soccer that is in the middle between the two goals — **mid·field·er** /ˈmɪdˌfiːldə/ *n* [*C*] • *a talented midfielder*

midge /ˈmɪdʒ/ *n* [*C*] : a very small flying insect that bites people and animals

midg·et /ˈmɪdʒət/ *n* [*C*] *often offensive* : a very small person

mid·land /ˈmɪdlənd/ *n* [*C*] : the central region of a country — usually plural • *I left the midlands for the coast.*

mid-life /ˈmɪdˈlaɪf/ *n* [*U*] : MIDDLE AGE • *changes that occur at midlife*

midlife crisis *n* [*C*] : a time in middle age when a person feels a strong desire for change • *He is going through a midlife crisis.*

mid·night /ˈmɪdˌnaɪt/ *n* [*U*] : 12 o'clock at night • *We arrived home at (12) midnight.* • *a midnight snack* • *at the midnight hour* [=at midnight] — **burn the midnight oil** see ¹BURN

mid·point /ˈmɪdˌpɔɪnt/ *n* [*C*] : a point at

the middle of something ▪ *the midpoint of the season* : a point halfway between two places ▪ *the midpoint between New York and Chicago*

mid·riff /ˈmɪˌdrɪf/ *n* [C] : the front of a person's body between the chest and the waist ▪ *She wore an outfit that showed her bare midriff.*

mid·sec·tion /ˈmɪdˌsɛkʃən/ *n* [C] *chiefly US* : a middle section, part, or area ▪ *the midsection of a boat/bridge; especially* : the area around a person's middle ▪ *He threw a hard punch to my midsection.*

mid·ship·man /ˈmɪdˌʃɪpmən/ *n, pl* **-men** /-mən/ [C] 1 : someone who is being trained to become an officer in the U.S. Navy 2 : an officer who is of the lowest rank in the British Navy

midst /ˈmɪdst/ *n* [U] 1 a : the middle area or part of something ▪ *a bustling city in the midst of the desert* b : the period of time when something is happening or being done ▪ *We are in the midst of re-modeling our house.* 2 — used to say that someone is among the people in a group ▪ *There is a traitor in our midst.* [=someone in our group is a traitor]

mid·stream /ˈmɪdˈstriːm/ *n* — **in midstream** 1 : in the middle of a river or stream ▪ *The boat sunk in midstream.* 2 : while in the process of doing something ▪ *She began talking about the party but changed topics in midstream.* — see also *change horses in midstream* at [1]HORSE

mid·sum·mer /ˈmɪdˈsʌmə/ *n* [U] : the middle of summer ▪ *The product should be in stores by midsummer.*

mid·term /ˈmɪdˌtəm/ *n, US* 1 a [C] : an examination given at the middle of a school term ▪ *The students have midterms next week.* ▪ *a midterm exam* b [U] : the middle of a school term ▪ *He dropped the course before midterm.* 2 [U] : the middle of a term of office ▪ *midterm Congressional elections* [=elections that occur halfway through a President's term of office]

mid·town /ˈmɪdˌtaʊn/ *n* [U] *chiefly US* : the part of a city or town between its downtown and uptown ▪ *Rents are high in midtown.* ▪ *midtown restaurants*

[1]**mid·way** /ˈmɪdˌweɪ/ *adv* 1 : in the middle between two places or points ▪ *We stopped for lunch midway* [=halfway] *between New York and Philadelphia.* 2 : in the middle of an act, process, or period of time ▪ *I left midway* [=halfway] *through her speech.* — **midway** *adj* ▪ *the midway point*

[2]**midway** *n* [C] *US* : an area at a fair, carnival, or amusement park for food stands, games, and rides

mid·week /ˈmɪdˌwiːk/ *n* [U] : the middle of the week ▪ *The report is due by midweek.* — **midweek** *adj, always before a noun* ▪ *a midweek deadline* — **midweek** *adv* ▪ *They'll be arriving midweek.*

Mid·west /ˌmɪdˈwɛst/ *n* — **the Midwest** : the northern central part of the U.S. : the Middle West ▪ *farmlands of the Mid-west* — **Midwest** *adj, always before a noun* ▪ *Midwest cities* — **Mid·west·ern** /ˌmɪdˈwɛstən/ *adj* ▪ *Midwestern cities* — **Mid·west·ern·er** /ˌmɪdˈwɛstənə/ *n* [C]

mid·wife /ˈmɪdˌwaɪf/ *n, pl* **-wives** /-ˌwaɪvz/ [C] : a person (usually a woman) who helps a woman when she is giving birth to a child ▪ *a certified midwife* — **mid·wife·ry** /ˌmɪdˈwɪfəri/ *n* [U]

mid·win·ter /ˈmɪdˈwɪntə/ *n* [U] : the middle of winter ▪ *the short days of midwinter* ▪ *a midwinter day*

mid·year /ˈmɪdˌjiə/ *n* [U] : the middle of a year ▪ *a midyear review*

mien /ˈmiːn/ *n* [singular] *old-fashioned + literary* : a person's appearance or facial expression ▪ *a kindly mien*

miffed /ˈmɪft/ *adj, informal* : slightly angry or annoyed ▪ *She was miffed at me for not inviting her.*

[1]**might** /ˈmaɪt/ *vb* [modal vb] 1 — used to say that something is possible ▪ *The test might include some questions about geography.* ▪ *The answer might (very well) surprise you.* 2 — used to say that one thing is true but something else is also true ▪ *He might* [=may] *be slow, but he does good work.* [=although he's slow, he does good work] 3 — used to talk about a possible condition that does not or did not actually exist ▪ *If she had been given a chance, she might have succeeded.* 4 *formal* — used as the past tense of *may* ▪ *He asked if he might* [=could] *leave.* [=he asked, "May I leave?"] 5 a — used in speech to ask a question or make a request in a polite way ▪ *Might* [=may] *I ask who is calling?* b — used to make a polite suggestion ▪ *It might be wise to proceed cautiously.* c — used to politely say something about someone or something ▪ *He is her husband and, I might add, one of her biggest fans.* 6 — used to say that you are annoyed by something that was or was not done ▪ *You might have called!* [=I am upset because you didn't call] 7 — used to indicate what is or was expected ▪ *I might* [=should] *have known you'd forget!* 8 — used in speech when asking a question about someone or something that surprises or annoys you ▪ *"I have a request to make." "And what might that be?"* [=what is your request?]

[2]**might** *n* [U] : force or strength ▪ *a display of military might* ▪ *He swung the bat with all his might.* [=as hard as he could] — **might makes right or might is right** — used to say that people who have power are able to do what they want because no one can stop them

might·i·ly /ˈmaɪtəli/ *adv* 1 : to a great degree ▪ *They contributed mightily to the cause.* 2 : with great force or strength ▪ *The soldiers fought mightily.*

mightn't /ˈmaɪtnt/ — used as a contraction of *might not* ▪ *They mightn't have heard the news yet.*

might've /ˈmaɪtəv/ — used as a contraction of *might have* ▪ *I think we might've had different goals.*

[1]**mighty** /ˈmaɪti/ *adj* **might·i·er; -est** 1 : having or showing great strength or power ▪ *a mighty army/empire* 2 : very great ▪ *a mighty effort*

[2]**mighty** *adv, chiefly US, informal* : VERY ▪ *mighty proud/tasty*

mi·graine /'maɪˌgreɪn, Brit 'miːˌgreɪn/ n [C/U] : a very bad headache

mi·grant /'maɪgrənt/ n [C] **1** : a person who goes from one place to another especially to find work • *migrant workers* **2** : a bird or animal that moves from one area to another at different times of the year

mi·grate /'maɪˌgreɪt/ vb **-grat·ed; -grat·ing** [I] **1** : to move from one country or place to live or work in another • *Thousands of workers migrate to this area each summer.* **2** *of a bird or animal* : to move from one area to another at different times of the year • *The whales are migrating to their breeding ground.* • *migrating birds* — **mi·gra·tion** /maɪˈgreɪʃən/ n [C/U] • *bird migration* • *mass migrations of workers* — **mi·gra·to·ry** /'maɪgrəˌtori, Brit maɪˈgreɪtəri/ adj • *migratory birds*

¹**mike** /'maɪk/ n [C] informal : MICROPHONE

²**mike** vb **miked; mik·ing** [T] informal : to put a microphone on (someone) • *The announcer was miked.*

mild /'maɪld/ adj **1** : gentle in nature or behavior • *a mild person/disposition* • *a mild-mannered young man* **2 a** : not strong in action or effect • *a mild drug/detergent* **b** : not strong or harsh in taste • *mild flavors* **c** : not strongly felt • *a mild [=slight] interest* **3 a** : not harsh or severe • *a mild headache* **b** : not too hot or too cold : pleasantly warm • *a mild climate/winter* — **mild·ly** adv • *mildly amusing* • *She was upset, to put it mildly.* [=she was very upset] — **mild·ness** n [U]

mil·dew /'mɪlˌduː, Brit 'mɪlˌdjuː/ n [U] : a substance that grows on the surface of things in wet, warm conditions • *The damp walls were covered with mildew.* — **mil·dewed** /'mɪlˌduːd, Brit 'mɪlˌdjuːd/ adj • *mildewed walls* — **mil·dewy** /'mɪlˌduːwi, Brit 'mɪlˌdjuːwi/ adj

mile /'maɪl/ n **1** [C] : a unit of measurement equal to 5,280 feet (about 1,609 meters) • *How many miles is it from here to New York?* • *The car was traveling at 70 miles per/an hour.* • *(figurative)* *He won the election by a mile.* [=by a very large margin] • *(figurative)* *She talks a mile a minute.* [=very fast] **2** [plural] : a great distance • *They walked for miles.* • *There was no one (to be seen) for miles around.* • *(figurative)* *He was miles ahead of the other students in his class.* • *His house is miles from anywhere/nowhere.* [=very far from other people and places] — **go the extra mile** : to do more than you are required to do • *She's always willing to go the extra mile to help a friend.*

mile·age /'maɪlɪdʒ/ n [U] **1 a** : distance in miles • *What's the mileage* [=how many miles is it] *from here to New York?* **b** : distance traveled in miles by a vehicle • *The car has a lot of mileage.* [=it has been driven many miles since it was new] **2** : the average number of miles a vehicle will travel on a gallon of gasoline • *My new car gets better (gas) mileage than my old one did.* **3** : benefit or use over a period of time • *We've gotten a lot of mileage out of this couch.*

miles /'maɪlz/ adv, chiefly Brit, informal : very much • *This one is miles worse/better than that one.*

mile·stone /'maɪlˌstoʊn/ n [C] **1** : a stone by the side of a road that shows the distance in miles to a place **2** : an important point in the progress or development of something • *The birth of her first child was a (major) milestone in her life.*

mi·lieu /miːˈljuː/ n, pl **mi·lieus** or **mi·lieux** /miːˈljuːz/ [C] formal : the physical or social setting in which people live or in which something happens or develops • *They come from different cultural milieus.* [=backgrounds, environments]

mil·i·tant /'mɪlətənt/ adj : having or showing a desire or willingness to use strong, extreme, and sometimes forceful methods to achieve something • *militant protesters/speech* — **mil·i·tan·cy** /'mɪlətənsi/ n [U] — **militant** n [C] • *a protest by angry militants*

mil·i·ta·rism /'mɪlətəˌrɪzəm/ n [U] : the opinions or actions of people who believe that a country should use military methods, forces, etc., to gain power and to achieve its goals • *the militarism of the government's foreign policy* — **mil·i·ta·rist** /'mɪlətərɪst/ adj — **militarist** n [C] — **mil·i·ta·ris·tic** /ˌmɪlətəˈrɪstɪk/ adj

mil·i·ta·rize also Brit **mil·i·ta·rise** /'mɪlətəˌraɪz/ vb **-rized; -riz·ing** [T] **1** : to put weapons and military forces in (an area) • *The area is fully militarized.* • *a militarized zone* **2** : to give a military quality or character to (something) • *an increasingly militarized society*

¹**mil·i·tary** /'mɪləˌteri/ adj **1** : of or relating to soldiers or the armed forces (such as the army, navy, marines, and air force) • *military aircraft/personnel/bases/hospitals* • *He avoided military service.* [=avoided becoming a member of the military] **2** : controlled or supported by armed forces • *a military regime/coup* — **mil·i·tar·i·ly** /ˌmɪləˈterəli/ adv

²**military** n [plural] : members of the armed forces • *There were many military present but only a few civilians.* — **the military** : the armed forces • *a career in the military*

mil·i·tate /'mɪləˌteɪt/ vb **-tat·ed; -tat·ing** — **militate against** [phrasal vb] formal : to make (something) unlikely to happen • *His inexperience militates against his getting a promotion.*

mi·li·tia /məˈlɪʃə/ n [C] : a group of people who are not part of the armed forces of a country but are trained like soldiers — **mi·li·tia·man** /məˈlɪʃəmən/ n, pl **-men** /-mən/ [C]

¹**milk** /'mɪlk/ n [U] **1** : a white liquid produced by a woman to feed her baby or by female animals to feed their young • *mother's/breast milk; especially* : milk from cows or goats that is used as food by people • *a glass of milk* • *whole milk* [=milk from which no fat has been removed] **2** : a white liquid produced by a plant • *coconut milk* — **a land of milk and honey** see ¹LAND — **cry over**

spilled/spilt milk see ¹CRY — *the milk of human kindness* literary : kind feelings or behavior toward other people • *He was filled with the milk of human kindness.*

²**milk** *vb* [T] **1** : to get milk from (an animal) • *milk a cow* **2** : to use (something or someone) in a way that helps you unfairly • *They milked* [=*exploited*] *their advantage.*

milk·man /ˈmɪlkˌmæn/ *n, pl* **-men** /-ˌmɛn/ [C] : a man who sells or delivers milk

milk of mag·ne·sia /-mægˈniːʒə/ *n* [U] : a thick, white liquid that contains magnesium and is used as a medicine for stomach problems (such as indigestion)

milk·shake /ˈmɪlkˌʃeɪk/ *n* [C] : a thick drink made of milk, a flavoring syrup, and often ice cream • *a chocolate milkshake*

milk·weed /ˈmɪlkˌwiːd/ *n* [C/U] : a type of North American plant that has white juice

milky /ˈmɪlki/ *adj* **milk·i·er; -est 1 a** : looking or tasting like milk • *a milky taste* • *milky (white) skin* **b** : not clear • *a milky* [=*cloudy*] *liquid* **2** : containing a large amount of milk • *milky coffee* — **milk·i·ness** *n* [U]

Milky Way *n* — **the Milky Way 1** : a broad band of light that can be seen in the night sky and that is caused by the light of a very large number of faint stars **2** : the galaxy in which we live that contains the stars that make up the Milky Way

¹**mill** /ˈmɪl/ *n* [C] **1 a** : a building with machinery for grinding grain into flour **b** : a machine for grinding grain **2 a** : a small machine for grinding or crushing pepper, coffee, etc. **3** : a building in which a particular product is made • *a paper/steel mill* • *mill workers* **4** : something that is compared to a factory because it produces things in large numbers or in a mechanical way • *a diploma mill* [=a school where students can obtain diplomas very easily] • *The rumor mill has been churning out stories about their marriage.* — *through the mill* : through a very difficult experience • *They've been (put) through the mill.*

²**mill** *vb* **1** [T] : to produce (something) in a mill especially by grinding, crushing, or cutting it • *milled wheat/lumber* **2** [I] *of a group of people* : to walk around in a general area without any particular aim or purpose — usually + *around* or (*chiefly Brit*) *about* • *People were milling around while they waited.*

mil·len·ni·um /məˈlɛniəm/ *n, pl* **-nia** /-niə/ *or* **-ni·ums** [C] **1** : a period of 1,000 years • *Changes have occurred in the landscape over many millennia.* **2** : a period of a thousand years counted from the beginning of the Christian era • *the third millennium* — **mil·len·ni·al** /məˈlɛniəl/ *adj*

mill·er /ˈmɪlɚ/ *n* [C] : a person who works in or is in charge of a flour mill

mil·let /ˈmɪlət/ *n* [U] : a type of grass that is grown for its seeds which are used as food; *also* : the seeds

mil·li·gram *also Brit* **mil·li·gramme** /ˈmɪləˌgræm/ *n* [C] : a weight equal to 1/1000 gram

mil·li·li·ter (*US*) *or Brit* **mil·li·li·tre** /ˈmɪləˌliːtɚ/ *n* [C] : a measure of capacity equal to 1/1000 liter

mil·li·me·ter (*US*) *or Brit* **mil·li·me·tre** /ˈmɪləˌmiːtɚ/ *n* [C] : a length equal to 1/1000 meter

mil·li·ner /ˈmɪlənɚ/ *n* [C] : a person who designs, makes, or sells women's hats

mil·li·nery /ˈmɪləˌnɛri/ *n* [U] **1** : women's hats • *a shop that sells millinery* **2** : the business of making or selling women's hats

mil·lion /ˈmɪljən/ *n, pl* **mil·lions** *or* **million** [C] **1** : the number 1,000,000 • *a/one/two million (of them)* • *The company is worth millions.* [=millions of dollars, pounds, euros, etc.] • *a million dollars* **2** : a very large amount or number • *I've heard that excuse a million times.* • *The drug could save millions of lives.* — *look/feel like a million dollars/bucks* informal : to look/feel very good — *one in a million* informal : a person or thing that is very unusual, special, or admired • *Thanks! You're one in a million.* — *thanks a million* informal : thank you very much • *Hey, thanks a million for your help.* — **mil·lionth** /ˈmɪljənθ/ *adj* • *our (one) millionth customer* — **millionth** *n* [C] • *one millionth of a second*

mil·lion·aire /ˌmɪljəˈneɚ/ *n* [C] : a rich person who has at least a million dollars, pounds, etc.

mil·li·pede /ˈmɪləˌpiːd/ *n* [C] : a small creature that is like an insect and that has a long, thin body with many legs

mil·li·sec·ond /ˈmɪləˌsɛkənd/ *n* [C] : one thousandth of a second

¹**mime** /ˈmaɪm/ *n* **1** [U] : a form of entertainment in which a performer plays a character or tells a story without words by using body movements and facial expressions • *an actor with a gift for mime* **2** [C] **a** : a performance done without speaking **b** : a performer who uses mime • *He's a talented mime.*

²**mime** *vb* **mimed; mim·ing** [T] : to make the movements of someone who is doing (something) without actually doing it • *He mimed playing a guitar.*

¹**mim·ic** /ˈmɪmɪk/ *vb* **-icked; -ick·ing** [T] **1** : to copy (someone or something) especially for humor • *He mimicked her accent.* • *a talent for mimicking people* **2** : to create the appearance or effect of (something) • *The lamp mimics natural sunlight.* **3** : to naturally look like (something) • *a butterfly that mimics a leaf* — **mim·ic·ry** /ˈmɪmɪkri/ *n* [U] • *a talent for mimicry*

²**mimic** *n* [C] : a person who copies the behavior or speech of other people • *She's a talented mimic.*

min·a·ret /ˌmɪnəˈrɛt/ *n* [C] : a tall, thin tower of a mosque with a balcony from which the people are called to prayer

¹**mince** /ˈmɪns/ *vb* **minced; minc·ing 1** [T] : to cut (food) into very small pieces • *Mince the onions.* • *minced parsley* • (*chiefly Brit*) *minced beef* [=(*US*) *ground beef, hamburger*] **2** [I] : to walk with

quick, short steps in a way that does not seem natural and that is often meant to be funny • *He minced across the stage.* • *mincing steps* — **not mince (your) words** or US **mince no words** : to speak in a very direct and honest way without worrying that you may be offending someone • *He doesn't mince words when discussing politics.*

²**mince** *n* [U] **1** *Brit* : HAMBURGER 2 • *a pound of mince* [=(US) ground beef]; *also* : ground meat of a specified kind • *lamb mince* **2** : MINCEMEAT 2 • *mince pie*

mince·meat /'mɪns,miːt/ *n* [U] **1** : meat that has been cut into very small pieces **2** : a mixture of raisins, apples, spices, etc., that is used especially in pies — **make mincemeat out of** *informal* : to destroy, ruin, or defeat (someone or something) • *They've been making mincemeat of the competition.*

¹**mind** /'maɪnd/ *n* **1** [C/U] : the part of a person that thinks, reasons, feels, and remembers • *He read great literature to develop his mind.* • *She went for a walk to help clear her mind.* • **Put that out of your mind.** [=stop thinking about that] • *Is there something on your mind?* [=are you worried about something?] • *I wish I could ease your (troubled) mind.* [=make you stop worrying] • *These problems have been preying/weighing on his mind.* [=he has been worrying about these problems] • *Losing was the furthest thing from my mind.* [=I never thought about losing] • *She says that getting married is the last thing on her mind.* [=she is not thinking at all about getting married] • *What was going/running through your mind?* [=what were you thinking?] • *His name slips/escapes my mind.* [=I can't remember his name] • *He's in a bad/good state of mind.* [=mood] • *peace of mind* [=a feeling of being safe or protected] ✧ If something (such as an illness) is *all in your/the mind,* you are imagining it. ✧ If *your mind is set on* something or you *have your mind set on* something, you are very determined to do or to get something. **2** [C] — used to describe the way a person thinks or the intelligence of a person • *She has a brilliant mind.* **3** — used in phrases that describe someone as mentally ill or crazy • *He's not in his right mind.* [=he is mentally ill] • *(law) He was not of sound mind* [=was not sane or rational] *when he changed his will.* — usually used informally in an exaggerated way • *You must be out of your mind!* [=crazy] • *I feel like I'm losing my mind.* [=going crazy] ✧ The phrase *out of your mind* is also used informally to make a statement stronger. • *I was bored out of my mind.* [=I was very bored] **4** [C] : a very intelligent person • *Many of the world's greatest minds will be attending the convention.* **5** [U] : a particular way of thinking about a situation • *Everyone was of like mind.* [=everyone agreed] • *She is of the same mind as me.* [=she agrees with me] • *We're all of one mind.* [=we all agree] • *To/In my mind, that's wrong.* **6** [U] : attention that is given to a person or thing • *Try to take/get/*

keep your mind off your problems. [=stop thinking about your problems] • *I'm finding it hard to keep my mind on* [=concentrate on] *my work.* • *She was finally able to turn her mind to other matters.* • *Don't pay him any mind.* [=don't pay attention to him] — **a meeting of (the) minds** see MEETING — **at/in the back of your mind** see ¹BACK — **blow someone's mind** *informal* : to amaze or overwhelm someone • *The music really blew my mind.* — **call/bring (something) to mind** : to cause (something) to be remembered or thought of • *Seeing her again brought to mind happy times from years ago.* — **change someone's mind** : to cause someone to change an opinion or decision • *I couldn't change her mind.* — **change your mind** : to change your decision or opinion about something • *He was going to go, but he changed his mind.* — **come/spring/leap to mind** : to be remembered or thought of • *What comes to mind when you hear his name?* — **cross someone's mind** see ²CROSS — **give someone a piece of your mind** : to speak to someone in an angry way — **have a good mind** or **have half a mind** ✧ If you *have a good mind* or *have half a mind* to do something, you have a feeling that you want to do it, especially because you are angry or annoyed, but you will probably not do it. • *I have half a mind to quit this job.* — **have a mind of your own** : to have your own ideas and make your own choices about what should be done • *Her parents want her to go to college, but she has a mind of her own.* — **have (someone or something) in mind** **1** : to be thinking of choosing (someone) for a job, position, etc. • *They have you in mind for the job.* **2** : to be thinking of doing (something) • *"I'd like to do something fun tonight." "What sort of thing do you have in mind?"* • *He had it in mind* [=intended] *to write a letter.* — **in mind** : in your thoughts • *We designed this product with people like you in mind.* [=we designed it for people like you] • *Keep/bear in mind* [=remember] *that she already paid us.* — **in your mind's eye** see ¹EYE — **make up your mind** : to make a decision • *He's thinking about going, but he still hasn't made up his mind.* • *His mind is made up.* [=he has made a decision and will not change it] — **of two minds** (US) or Brit **in two minds** : not decided or certain about something • *I'm of two minds about (hiring) him: he seems capable, but he doesn't have much experience.* — **open your mind** see ²OPEN — **put (someone) in mind of (something)** : to cause (someone) to remember or think of (something) • *That story puts me in mind of* [=reminds me of] *what happened to me last week.* — **put/set your mind to (something)** : to give your attention to (something) and try very hard to do it • *We can solve this problem if we put our minds to it.* — **speak your mind** : to say what you think • *Don't be afraid to speak your mind.* — **take a load/weight off your mind** : to make you stop worrying about something ▪ *Hearing that she's safe has really taken a load off my mind!*

²**mind** *vb* **1** [T/I] : to object to or dislike (something) ▪ *I don't mind the rain. — It is raining, but I don't mind.* [=the rain doesn't bother me] ▪ *I don't mind making dinner.* [=I am willing to make dinner] ▪ *She served me a huge piece of pie—not that I minded!* [=I was happy to get a large piece] ▪ *I'll come early, if you don't mind.* [=if it is all right with you] **2** [T] : to care about or worry about (something or someone) ▪ *They don't seem to mind where they sit.* ▪ *Don't mind him—he's always complaining about something!* **3** [T] **a** — used to make a polite request ▪ *Do you mind if I smoke? = Would you mind if I smoked?* ▪ *Would you mind closing the door?* **b** — used in phrases with *if* when you have said something that might bother or upset someone ▪ *How old are you, if you don't mind my/me asking?* ▪ *You look a bit old for this job, if you don't mind my/me saying so.* **c** — used in informal phrases with *I* ▪ *"Would you like a cup of coffee?" "Thank you: I don't mind if I do!"* [=yes, I'd like a cup] ▪ *I was shocked by the news, I don't mind telling you!* [=I must say/admit that I was shocked by the news] **d** — used in informal phrases that show anger or annoyance ▪ *"That woman's a real pain!" "Do you MIND!? That's my mother you're talking about!"* **4** [T] *US* : OBEY ▪ *Mind your parents!* **5** [T] : to take care of or be in charge of (something or someone) ▪ *Who's minding the children/office?* **6** [T] **a** : to be careful about (something) ▪ *Mind your language!* [=stop saying offensive things] ▪ *Mind your manners.* [=behave in a polite way] **b** *chiefly Brit* — used to tell someone to be aware of something that could be a problem or danger ▪ *Mind the broken glass!* **c** *chiefly Brit* — used to tell someone to be sure to do something or to be careful to prevent something from happening ▪ *Mind he doesn't lose his ticket!* — **mind the store** (*US*) *or Brit* **mind the shop** : to be in charge of a place when the person who is usually in charge is not there ▪ *Who's minding the store while the boss is away?* — **mind you** *informal* — used in speech to give stress to a statement that you are making ▪ *I'm not criticizing him, mind you.* — often used in British English without *you* ▪ *I'm not criticizing him, mind!* — **mind your own business** see BUSINESS — **mind your step** see ¹STEP — **never mind 1** — used to tell someone not to worry about something ▪ *Have you seen my keys? Oh, never mind. Here they are.* **2** — used to refer to something that is even less likely or possible than the thing previously mentioned ▪ *I can barely understand it, never mind* [=let alone, much less] *explain it.* — **never you mind** *informal* — used to tell someone that you will not be answering a question ▪ *"How old are you?" "Never you mind!"*

mind–al·ter·ing /'maɪnd,ɑːltərɪŋ/ *adj* : causing changes to the mind or to behavior ▪ *mind-altering drugs*

mind–blow·ing /'maɪnd,bloʊɪŋ/ *adj, informal* : very confusing, exciting, or shocking ▪ *a mind-blowing performance* — **mind–blow·ing·ly** *adv*

mind–bog·gling /'maɪnd,bɑːglɪŋ/ *adj, informal* : having a very powerful or overwhelming effect on the mind ▪ *a mind-boggling performance* : amazingly or confusingly large, great, etc. ▪ *The vastness of space is mind-boggling.* — **mind–bog·gling·ly** *adv*

mind·ed /'maɪndəd/ *adj* **1** : having a particular kind of mind — used in combination ▪ *open-minded* **2** : interested in or concerned about a particular subject — used in combination ▪ *She's very health-minded.* [=she is very concerned about doing things that promote good health]

mind·ful /'maɪndfəl/ *adj* : AWARE ▪ *Investors should be mindful of current political trends.* ▪ *We should be mindful that political trends may influence the market.*

mind·less /'maɪndləs/ *adj* **1 a** : having or showing no ability to think, feel, or respond ▪ *a mindless bureaucracy* **b** : showing no use of intelligence or thought ▪ *mindless devotion to fashion* : having no purpose ▪ *mindless violence* **c** : requiring very little attention or thought ▪ *mindless activity/work* **2** : not aware of something ▪ *She was mindless of her appearance.* ▪ *mindless of danger* — **mind·less·ly** *adv*

mind–numb·ing /'maɪnd,nʌmɪŋ/ *adj, informal* : very dull or boring ▪ *mind-numbing work*

mind reader *n* [C] : someone who is able to know another person's thoughts without being told what they are ▪ *How was I supposed to know that? I'm no mind reader.* — **mind reading** *n* [U]

mind–set /'maɪnd,sɛt/ *n* [C] : a person's attitude or set of opinions about something ▪ *a conservative/liberal mind-set*

¹**mine** /'maɪn/ *pron* : that which belongs to me ▪ *The book is mine.* [=it is my book] ▪ *Those books are mine.* [=those are my books] ▪ *His eyes are blue and mine are brown.* ▪ *a friend of mine* [=one of my friends]

²**mine** *n* [C] **1** : a pit or tunnel from which coal, gold, diamonds, etc., are taken **2** : a bomb that is placed in the ground or in water and that explodes when it is touched

³**mine** *vb* **mined; min·ing 1 a** [T/I] : to dig a mine in order to find and take away coal, gold, diamonds, etc. ▪ *They mined (the area) for gold.* **b** [T] : to find and take away (something) from a mine ▪ *mining coal/gold* **2** [T] : to search for something valuable in (something) ▪ *They mined the tapes for information.* [=they listened to the tapes in order to get information] **3** [T] : to put mines (sense 2) in or under (something) ▪ *The road was mined.* — **min·er** /'maɪnɚ/ *n* [C] ▪ *coal miners*

mine·field /'maɪn,fiːld/ *n* [C] **1** : an area of land or water that contains mines (sense 2) **2** : something that has many dangers or risks ▪ *a political minefield*

min·er·al /'mɪnərəl/ *n* [C] **1** : a substance (such as quartz, coal, salt, etc.) that is naturally formed under the ground **2** : a chemical substance (such as iron or zinc) that occurs naturally in certain foods and that is important for good health

min·er·al·o·gy /ˌmɪnəˈrælədʒi/ n [U] : the scientific study of minerals — **min·er·al·o·gist** /ˌmɪnəˈrælədʒɪst/ n [C]

mineral water n [C/U] : water that contains mineral salts and gases (such as carbon dioxide)

min·e·stro·ne /ˌmɪnəˈstrouni/ n [U] : a thick Italian soup that is usually made with beans, vegetables, and pasta

min·gle /ˈmɪŋgəl/ vb **min·gled; min·gling** **1** [T/I] : to combine or bring together two or more things • *The story mingles fact and/with fiction.* • *Several flavors mingle in the stew.* **2** [I] : to move around during a party, meeting, etc., and talk informally with different people • *The host mingled with his guests.*

mini- *combining form* : smaller or shorter than usual or normal • *miniskirt*

[1]**min·i·a·ture** /ˈmɪnijəˌtʃuɹ/ adj, always before a noun : very small • *a miniature camera*

[2]**miniature** n [C] : a very small sculpture, portrait, or painting • *porcelain miniatures* — **in miniature** : in a very small form • *The model depicts the project in miniature.*

min·i·a·tur·ize also Brit **min·i·a·tur·ise** /ˈmɪnijətʃəˌraɪz/ vb **-ized; -iz·ing** [T] : to design or make (something) in a very small size • *a miniaturized radio* — **min·i·a·tur·i·za·tion** also Brit **min·i·a·tur·i·sa·tion** /ˌmɪnijətʃuɹəˈzeɪʃən/ n [U]

minima plural of MINIMUM

min·i·mal /ˈmɪnəməl/ adj : very small or slight in size or amount • *minimal damage/costs* — **min·i·mal·ly** adv

min·i·mal·ist /ˈmɪnəməlɪst/ adj : of, relating to, or following a style in art, literature, or music that is very simple and uses a small number of colors, parts, materials, etc. • *minimalist art/artists* — **min·i·mal·ism** /ˈmɪnəməˌlɪzəm/ n [U] — **minimalist** n [C]

min·i·mize also Brit **min·i·mise** /ˈmɪnəˌmaɪz/ vb **-mized; -miz·ing** [T] **1** : to make (something bad or not wanted) as small as possible • *Try to minimize the chance of error.* **2** : to treat or describe (something) as smaller or less important than it is • *They minimized her contributions.* **3** *computers* : to make (a program's window) change to a very small form that takes almost no room on a computer's screen • *Please minimize all open windows.*

min·i·mum /ˈmɪnəməm/ n, pl **-mums** or technical **-ma** /-mə/ [C] : the lowest number or amount that is possible or allowed • *She will serve a minimum of* [=at least] *10 years in jail.* • *We'll need a year at a/the minimum.* [=we'll need at least a year] • *We need to keep expenses to a (bare) minimum.* [=as low as possible] — **minimum** adj, always before a noun • *The minimum sentence is 10 years.* — **minimum** adv • *She will serve 10 years minimum.*

minimum wage n [*singular*] : an amount of money that is the least amount of money per hour that workers must be paid according to the law

min·ion /ˈmɪnjən/ n [C] : someone who is not powerful or important and who obeys the orders of a powerful leader or boss • *the boss's minions*

mini·se·ries /ˈmɪniˌsɪriz/ n, pl **miniseries** [C] : a story on television that is shown in two or more parts on different days

mini·skirt /ˈmɪniˌskət/ n [C] : a very short skirt

[1]**min·is·ter** /ˈmɪnəstə/ n [C] **1** : a person whose job involves leading church services, performing religious ceremonies, and providing spiritual or religious guidance **2** : an official who heads a government department or a major section of a department in some countries (such as Britain) • *(Brit) the Minister of Defence* [=(US) *the Secretary of Defense*] — see also PRIME MINISTER **3** : a person who represents his or her own government while living in a foreign country — **min·is·te·ri·al** /ˌmɪnəˈstirijəl/ adj, always before a noun • *ministerial duties*

[2]**minister** vb — **minister to** [*phrasal vb*] : to help or care for (someone or something) • *The nurse ministered to his wounds.*

min·is·tra·tions /ˌmɪnəˈstreɪʃənz/ n [*plural*] formal + humorous : actions done to help someone • *She recovered quickly despite the ministrations of her doctor.*

min·is·try /ˈmɪnəstri/ n, pl **-tries** **1 a** : the ministry : religious leaders as a group • *a member of the ministry* **b** [C/U] : the office, duties, or work of a religious minister • *His ministry is among the city's poor.* • *She is drawn to the ministry.* [=she is interested in becoming a minister] **2** [C] : a government department or the building in which it is located • *(Brit) the Ministry of Defence* [=(US) *Department of Defense*]

mini·van /ˈmɪniˌvæn/ n [C] : a small van

mink /ˈmɪŋk/ n, pl **mink** or **minks** [C] **1** : a small animal that has a thin body and soft, dark brown fur **2 a** [U] : the skin and fur of a mink used for making clothing • *a mink coat* **b** [C] : a piece of clothing (such as a coat) made of mink • *women wearing minks*

min·now /ˈmɪnoʊ/ n, pl **min·nows** also **minnow** [C] : a very small fish that is often used as bait to catch larger fish

[1]**mi·nor** /ˈmaɪnə/ adj **1 a** : not very important or valuable • *a minor artist/celebrity* • *a minor news story* **b** always before a noun : small in number, quantity, or extent • *Tuition is only a minor part of the cost.* **2** : not causing much trouble or damage • *a minor annoyance/injury* **3** *music* : having semitones between the second and third, the fifth and sixth, and sometimes the seventh and eighth notes in a scale • *a minor scale/key* **4** always before a noun : not yet old enough to have the rights of an adult • *He has minor children living in the house.*

[2]**minor** n [C] **1** : a person who is not yet old enough to have the rights of an adult

▪ *It is illegal to sell alcohol to minors.* **2** *US* : a second subject studied by a college or university student in addition to a main subject ▪ *She majored in chemistry with a minor in biology.* — **the minors** *US, informal* : the minor leagues of baseball ▪ *He spent his entire career in the minors.*

³**minor** *vb* — **minor in** [*phrasal vb*] *US* : to have (a specified second subject of study) in addition to your main subject ▪ *She minored in biology.*

mi·nor·i·ty /məˈnorəti/ *n, pl* **-ties** **1** [*singular*] : a number or amount that is less than half of a total ▪ *A minority of voters oppose the proposal.* **2** [*singular*] : the group that is the smaller part of a larger group ▪ *The Republicans/Democrats are now the minority in the Senate.* ▪ *a minority party* ▪ *Opponents of the new law appear to be in the minority.* [=fewer people oppose the new law than support it] **3** [*C*] **a** : a group of people who are different from the larger group in a country, area, etc. ▪ *ethnic/racial/religious minorities* **b** *chiefly US* : a member of such a group — usually plural ▪ *scholarships for minorities*

minor league *n* [*C*] : a professional baseball league that is not one of the major leagues — usually plural ▪ *He spent many years in the minor leagues.* — **minor-league** *adj* ▪ *minor-league baseball* — **minor leagu·er** *n* [*C*]

min·strel /ˈmɪnstrəl/ *n* [*C*] **1** : a musical entertainer in the Middle Ages ▪ *a wandering minstrel* **2** *US* : a member of a group of entertainers who performed black American songs and jokes usually with blackened faces in the 19th and early 20th centuries ▪ *a minstrel show*

¹**mint** /ˈmɪnt/ *n* **1 a** [*U*] : an herb that has a strong pleasant smell and taste and that is used in medicine and food **b** [*C*] : a piece of candy that tastes like mint **2 a** [*C*] : a place where coins are made ▪ *coins shipped from the mint* **b** [*singular*] *informal* : a large amount of money ▪ *Her family is worth a mint.* [=is very wealthy] — **in mint condition** : in perfect condition ▪ *He kept the car in mint condition.* — **minty** /ˈmɪnti/ *adj* **mint·i·er; -est** ▪ *a minty flavor*

²**mint** *vb* [*T*] : to make (coins) out of metal ▪ *coins that were minted before 1965*

min·u·et /ˌmɪnjəˈwɛt/ *n* [*C*] **1** : a slow, graceful dance that was popular in the 17th and 18th centuries **2** : the music for a minuet

¹**mi·nus** /ˈmaɪnəs/ *prep* **1** — used to indicate that one number or amount is being subtracted from another ▪ *10 minus 5 equals/is 5.* ▪ *We earned 600 dollars minus travel expenses.* **2** *informal* : WITHOUT ▪ *He looks like Joe, minus the mustache.* — **plus or minus** see ³PLUS

²**minus** *n* [*C*] *informal* : a problem or disadvantage ▪ *The pluses of the job outweigh the minuses.*

³**minus** *adj* *always before a noun* **1** : having a value that is below zero ▪ *The temperature was minus 10.* [=10 degrees below zero] **2** — used following a grade to show that the work is slightly worse than

the letter by itself would indicate ▪ *I got a B minus on the exam.* — **on the minus side** — used to describe the less appealing or attractive part of something ▪ *On the minus side, the job doesn't pay well.*

mi·nus·cule /ˈmɪnəˌskjuːl/ *adj* : very small ▪ *a minuscule* [=tiny] *amount*

minus sign *n* [*C*] *mathematics* : the symbol − used to show that a number is being subtracted from another number or that a quantity is less than zero

¹**min·ute** /ˈmɪnət/ *n* **1** [*C*] **a** : a unit of time equal to 60 seconds ▪ *Bake the cake for 25–30 minutes.* **b** : a brief period of time ▪ *I saw him a minute ago.* ▪ *Could I have a minute of your time? = Do you have a minute?* [=could I speak to you briefly?] ▪ *I'll be back in a minute.* [=soon] ✧ If something could happen (at) any minute (now), it could happen very soon. **2** [*C*] : the distance that can be traveled in a minute ▪ *My house is just a few minutes from here.* **3** [*plural*] : an official record of what was said and done in a meeting ▪ *The secretary read the minutes of the last meeting.* **4** [*C*] *technical* : one of 60 equal parts into which a degree can be divided for measuring angles ▪ *42 degrees and 30 minutes* — **from minute to minute** or **from one minute to the next** or **minute by minute** : very quickly as time passes ▪ *Things kept changing from minute to minute.* — **hold/hang on a minute** or **wait/just a minute** *informal* **1** — used to tell someone to wait or to stop for a brief time ▪ *Hold on a minute. I'm almost done.* **2** — used to express surprise or disbelief ▪ *Hey, wait a minute! That's not what you said yesterday!* — **not for a/one minute** : at no time ▪ *I did not believe her for one minute.* [=I never believed her] — **the minute** : as soon as ▪ *Call me the minute you get home.* — **this minute** : IMMEDIATELY ▪ *Stop it this minute!* — **to the minute** : exactly or precisely ▪ *The buses were on time to the minute.* — **within minutes** : within a very short amount of time ▪ *The ambulance arrived within minutes.*

²**mi·nute** /maɪˈnuːt, *Brit* maɪˈnjuːt/ *adj* **mi·nut·er; -est** **1** : very small : TINY ▪ *minute particles* **2** : very complete and precise ▪ *minute detail* — **mi·nute·ly** *adv*

min·ute·man /ˈmɪnətˌmæn/ *n, pl* **-men** /-ˌmɛn/ [*C*] : a member of a group of men who fought on the side of the American colonies and who were ready to go quickly into battle during the American Revolution

mi·nu·ti·ae /məˈnuːʃiˌiː, *Brit* məˈnjuːʃiˌiː/ *n* [*plural*] : small or minor details ▪ *the minutiae of daily life*

mir·a·cle /ˈmɪrɪkəl/ *n* [*C*] **1** : an unusual or wonderful event that is believed to be caused by the power of God ▪ *a divine miracle* **2** : a very amazing or unusual event, thing, or achievement ▪ *It would take a miracle for this team to win.* ▪ *She worked miracles* [=accomplished wonderful things] *with those kids.* ▪ *a miracle drug/cure* [=a drug/cure that is extremely or amazingly effective] ▪ *By some mir-*

acle, I arrived on time. [=it is surprising/amazing that I arrived on time]

mi·rac·u·lous /məˈrækjələs/ *adj* : very wonderful or amazing like a miracle • *a miraculous recovery* — **mi·rac·u·lous·ly** *adv*

mi·rage /məˈrɑːʒ, *Brit* ˈmɪrɑːʒ/ *n* [C] 1 : something (such as a pool of water in the middle of a desert) that is seen and appears to be real but that is not actually there 2 : something that you hope for or want but that is not possible or real • *A peaceful solution proved to be a mirage.*

mire /ˈmajɚ/ *n* [C/U] : thick and deep mud • *She walked through the muck and the mire.* • *(figurative)* *We found ourselves in a mire of debt.* [=we could not get out of debt]

mired /ˈmajɚd/ *adj, not before a noun* 1 : stuck in a very difficult situation • *We are mired in debt.* 2 : stuck in deep mud • *The car was mired in the muck.*

¹mir·ror /ˈmirɚ/ *n* [C] 1 : a piece of glass that reflects images • *She saw her reflection in the mirror.* 2 : something that shows what another thing is like in a very clear and accurate way — usually singular • *Her art is a mirror of modern American culture.*

²mirror *vb* [T] 1 : to be very similar to (something) • *Her mood mirrored the gloomy weather.* [=her mood was gloomy like the weather] : to show (something) in a very clear and accurate way • *Her art mirrors modern American culture.* 2 : REFLECT 2 • *The building was mirrored in the lake.*

mirth /ˈmɚθ/ *n* [U] *formal + literary* : happiness and laughter • *Her silly jokes were the cause of much mirth.* — **mirth·ful** /ˈmɚθfəl/ *adj* — **mirth·less** /ˈmɚθləs/ *adj, formal + literary* • *a mirthless smile*

mis·ad·ven·ture /ˌmɪsədˈvɛntʃɚ/ *n* [C] : a bad experience or accident that is usually minor • *a series of misadventures*

mis·an·thrope /ˈmɪsn̩ˌθroʊp/ *n* [C] *formal* : a person who does not like other people — **mis·an·throp·ic** /ˌmɪsn̩ˈθrɑːpɪk/ *adj* • *a misanthropic woman*

mis·ap·pli·ca·tion /ˌmɪsˌæpləˈkeɪʃən/ *n* [C/U] : the act of using (something) incorrectly or in a way that was not intended • *the misapplication of public funds*

mis·ap·pre·hen·sion /ˌmɪsˌæprəˈhɛnʃən/ *n* [C/U] *formal* : an incorrect understanding of something • *(a) misapprehension of the facts*

mis·ap·pro·pri·ate /ˌmɪsəˈproʊpriˌeɪt/ *vb* -**at·ed**; -**at·ing** [T] *formal* : to take (something) dishonestly for your own use • *He was accused of misappropriating town funds.* — **mis·ap·pro·pri·a·tion** /ˌmɪsəˌproʊpriˈeɪʃən/ *n* [U]

mis·be·have /ˌmɪsbɪˈheɪv/ *vb* -**haved**; -**hav·ing** [I/I] : to behave badly • *The children were misbehaving.* — **mis·be·hav·ior** (*US*) *or Brit* **mis·be·hav·iour** /ˌmɪsbɪˈheɪvjɚ/ *n* [U]

misc. *abbr* miscellaneous

mis·cal·cu·late /mɪsˈkælkjəˌleɪt/ *vb* -**lat·ed**; -**lat·ing** [T/I] 1 : to make an error about the size or amount of something • *Unless I miscalculated, we have about $500 left.* 2 : to make an error in judg-

ing a situation • *She miscalculated the effect of her decision.* — **mis·cal·cu·la·tion** /ˌmɪsˌkælkjəˈleɪʃən/ *n* [C/U] • *a slight miscalculation*

mis·car·riage /ˈmɪsˌkerɪʤ/ *n* 1 [C] *medical* : a condition in which a pregnancy ends too early and does not result in the birth of a live baby • *She had a miscarriage.* 2 [C] *law* : an unjust legal decision • *His conviction was a tragic miscarriage of justice.*

mis·car·ry /ˌmɪsˈkeri/ *vb* -**ries**; -**ried**; -**ry·ing** [I] 1 *medical* : to experience the early and unexpected end of a pregnancy • *She miscarried when she was 13 weeks pregnant.* 2 *formal* : to fail or go wrong • *The plan miscarried.*

mis·cel·la·neous /ˌmɪsəˈleɪnijəs/ *adj* : including many things of different kinds • *miscellaneous expenses/tools*

mis·cel·la·ny /ˈmɪsəˌleɪni, *Brit* mɪˈsɛləni/ *n, pl* -**nies** [C] : a collection of different things • *a miscellany of toys*

mis·chief /ˈmɪstʃəf/ *n* [U] 1 : behavior or activity that is annoying but that is not meant to cause serious harm or damage • *He's always up to some mischief.* = *He's always getting into mischief.* • *keeping him out of mischief* 2 : a playful desire to cause trouble • *(a hint of) mischief in her eyes/smile* 3 : harmful behavior • *criminal/malicious mischief*

mis·chie·vous /ˈmɪstʃəvəs/ *adj* 1 : causing or tending to cause annoyance or minor harm or damage • *a mischievous puppy/child* 2 : showing a playful desire to cause trouble • *a mischievous smile* 3 : intended to harm someone or someone's reputation • *mischievous gossip/lies* — **mis·chie·vous·ly** *adv*

mis·con·ceived /ˌmɪskənˈsiːvd/ *adj* : poorly planned or thought out • *a misconceived notion/attempt*

mis·con·cep·tion /ˌmɪskənˈsɛpʃən/ *n* [C] : a wrong or mistaken idea • *a common misconception*

mis·con·duct /mɪsˈkɑːndəkt/ *n* [U] : behavior or activity that is illegal or morally wrong • *employee/sexual misconduct*

mis·con·strue /ˌmɪskənˈstruː/ *vb* -**strued**; -**stru·ing** [T] *formal* : to understand (something) incorrectly • *My words/intentions were misconstrued.*

mis·cre·ant /ˈmɪskrijənt/ *n* [C] *formal* : a person who does something illegal or morally wrong • *jail time for miscreants*

mis·deed /ˌmɪsˈdiːd/ *n* [C] *formal* : a morally wrong or illegal act • *committing misdeeds*

mis·de·mean·or (*US*) *or Brit* **mis·de·mean·our** /ˌmɪsdɪˈmiːnɚ/ *n* [C] *law* : a crime that is less serious than a felony • *He was charged with (committing) a misdemeanor.*

mis·di·ag·nose /mɪsˈdajɪgˌnoʊs/ *vb* -**nosed**; -**nos·ing** [T] : to form an incorrect opinion about the cause of (a disease or problem) • *Her condition was misdiagnosed.* — **mis·di·ag·no·sis** /ˌmɪsˌdajɪgˈnoʊsəs/ *n, pl* -**no·ses** /-noʊˌsiːz/ [C/U]

mis·di·rect /ˌmɪsdəˈrɛkt/ *vb* [T] 1 : to use or direct (something) in a way that is not correct or appropriate • *misdirected* *energy/efforts* **2 a** : to send (someone or something) to the wrong place ▪ *Their mail was misdirected.* **b** : to give (someone) incorrect information ▪ *He's trying to misdirect you.* — **mis·di·rec·tion** /ˌmɪsdəˈrɛkʃən/ *n* [U]

mi·ser /ˈmaɪzɚ/ *n* [C] *disapproving* : a person who hates to spend money

mis·er·a·ble /ˈmɪzərəbəl/ *adj* **1 a** : very unhappy ▪ *a miserable person/childhood* ▪ *My boss is making my life miserable.* **b** : very sick or unwell ▪ *I feel miserable.* **2** : very severe or unpleasant ▪ *The weather was miserable.* **3** *always before a noun* : very poor in condition or quality ▪ *miserable living conditions* ▪ *She did a miserable job making the sign.* [=she made the sign very poorly] **4** *always before a noun* : deserving to be hated ▪ *Their boss is a miserable tyrant.* — **mis·er·a·bly** /ˈmɪzərəbli/ *adv* ▪ *We failed miserably.*

mi·ser·ly /ˈmaɪzɚli/ *adj, disapproving* **1** : hating to spend money ▪ *a miserly woman* **2** : very small or too small ▪ *a miserly raise/salary*

mis·ery /ˈmɪzəri/ *n, pl* **-er·ies** **1** [U] : suffering or unhappiness ▪ *The war brought misery to thousands of refugees.* **2 a** [C] : something that causes suffering or unhappiness ▪ *the joys and miseries of life* ▪ [*singular*] : a very unhappy or painful time or experience ▪ *He made my life a misery.* ▪ ***putting** a sick dog **out of its misery*** [=killing a sick dog because it is suffering too much] ▪ *(figurative, humorous) I'll put you out of your misery* [=end your suffering] *and tell you the secret.*

mis·fire /ˌmɪsˈfajɚ/ *vb* **-fired**; **-fir·ing** [I] **1** *of an engine or gun* : to fail to work or fire properly **2** : to fail to have an intended effect ▪ *The plan/joke misfired.* — **misfire** *n* [C] ▪ *an engine misfire* ▪ *The joke was a misfire.*

mis·fit /ˈmɪsˌfɪt/ *n* [C] : a person who does not seem to belong in a particular group or situation ▪ *a social misfit*

mis·for·tune /ˌmɪsˈfoɚtʃən/ *n* **1** [U] : bad luck ▪ *a victim of misfortune* **2** [C] : an unlucky condition or event ▪ *Her injury was a great misfortune.*

mis·giv·ing /ˌmɪsˈgɪvɪŋ/ *n* [C/U] : a feeling of doubt about something ▪ *I had some misgivings about the plan.* ▪ *They regarded the plan with misgiving.*

mis·guid·ed /ˌmɪsˈgaɪdəd/ *adj* : resulting from or having wrong or improper goals or values ▪ *misguided friends* ▪ *a misguided idea/effort*

mis·han·dle /ˌmɪsˈhændl/ *vb* **-han·dled**; **-han·dling** [T] **1** : to deal with or manage (something) badly or incorrectly ▪ *They mishandled the investigation.* **2** : to touch or treat (something) in a way that causes damage ▪ *Apples bruise when mishandled.* — **mis·han·dling** *n* [U] ▪ *their mishandling of the investigation*

mis·hap /ˈmɪsˌhæp/ *n* [C/U] : a mistake, accident, or occurrence of bad luck ▪ *a tragic mishap* ▪ *The ceremony proceeded* ***without mishap.***

mish-mash /ˈmɪʃˌmæʃ/ *n* [*singular*] *informal* : a confused mixture of things ▪ *a mishmash of different styles*

mis·in·form /ˌmɪsɪnˈfoɚm/ *vb* [T] : to give (someone) false or incorrect information ▪ *I was badly misinformed about the risks.* — **mis·in·for·ma·tion** /ˌmɪsˌɪnfɚˈmeɪʃən/ *n* [U] ▪ *providing misinformation*

mis·in·ter·pret /ˌmɪsɪnˈtɚprət/ *vb* [T] : to understand or explain (something) incorrectly ▪ *His statements were misinterpreted.* — **mis·in·ter·pre·ta·tion** /ˌmɪsɪnˌtɚprəˈteɪʃən/ *n* [C/U]

mis·judge /ˌmɪsˈdʒʌdʒ/ *vb* **-judged**; **-judg·ing** [T] **1** : to have an unfair opinion about (someone) ▪ *I see that I've misjudged you.* **2** : to estimate (an amount, distance, etc.) incorrectly ▪ *The pilot misjudged the landing.* — **mis·judg·ment** *also chiefly Brit* **mis·judge·ment** /ˌmɪsˈdʒʌdʒmənt/ *n* [C/U]

mis·lead /ˌmɪsˈliːd/ *vb* **-led** /-lɛd/; **-lead·ing** [T/I] : to cause (someone) to believe something that is not true ▪ *She deliberately mislead the public.* ▪ *misleading comments* — **mis·lead·ing·ly** /ˌmɪsˈliːdɪŋli/ *adv*

mis·man·age /ˌmɪsˈmænɪdʒ/ *vb* **-aged**; **-ag·ing** [T] : to manage or control (something) badly ▪ *mismanage a company* — **mis·man·age·ment** /ˌmɪsˈmænɪdʒmənt/ *n* [U]

mis·match /ˈmɪsˌmætʃ/ *vb* [T] : to put (people or things that are not suited to each other) together ▪ *mismatched colors/socks* — **mismatch** *n* [C] ▪ *a mismatch between supply and demand* [=a situation in which supply and demand are not equal or suited to each other]

mis·name /ˌmɪsˈneɪm/ *vb* **-named**; **-nam·ing** [T] : to give (someone or something) a name that is not correct or appropriate ▪ *She was misnamed in the article.*

mis·no·mer /ˌmɪsˈnoʊmɚ/ *n* [C] : a name that is wrong or not appropriate ▪ *His title of Chief Officer is a misnomer, since the board makes all the decisions.*

mi·sog·y·nist /məˈsɑːdʒənɪst/ *n* [C] : a man who hates women ▪ *a misogynist joke/boss* — **mi·sog·y·ny** /məˈsɑːdʒəni/ *n* [U]

mis·place /ˌmɪsˈpleɪs/ *vb* **-placed**; **-plac·ing** [T] **1** : to put (something) in the wrong place ▪ *misplace a comma* **2** : to lose (something) for a short time by forgetting where you put it ▪ *He misplaced his keys.* **3** : to direct (trust, confidence, etc.) toward someone or something that does not deserve it ▪ *Her trust had been misplaced.* ▪ *misplaced loyalty/faith* — **mis·place·ment** /ˌmɪsˈpleɪsmənt/ *n* [U]

mis·print /ˈmɪsˌprɪnt/ *n* [C] : a mistake in something printed ▪ *a book with many misprints*

mis·pro·nounce /ˌmɪsprəˈnaʊns/ *vb* **-nounced**; **-nounc·ing** [T] : to pronounce (a word or name) incorrectly ▪ *His name is often mispronounced.* — **mis·pro·nun·ci·a·tion** /ˌmɪsprəˌnʌnsiˈeɪʃən/ *n* [C/U]

mis·quote /ˌmɪsˈkwoʊt/ *vb* **-quot·ed**; **-quot·ing** [T] : to repeat (something spoken or written) in a way that is not correct ▪ *She was misquoted by the press.* — **misquote** *n* [C]

mis·read /ˌmɪsˈriːd/ *vb* **-read** /-ˈrɛd/;

-read·ing [T] **1** : to read (something) incorrectly • *I misread the note.* **2** : to understand (something) incorrectly • *He misread her mood.* — **mis·read·ing** [C]

mis·rep·re·sent /ˌmɪsˌrɛprɪˈzɛnt/ *vb* [T] : to describe (someone or something) in a false way • *The company misrepresented its earnings.* • *He misrepresented himself as a writer.* [=he said he was a writer but he wasn't one] — **mis·rep·re·sen·ta·tion** /ˌmɪsˌrɛprɪˌzɛnˈteɪʃən/ *n* [C/U]

¹**miss** /ˈmɪs/ *vb* **1** [T/I] : to fail to hit, catch, reach, or get (something) • *miss a target* • *He swung and missed (the ball).* • *They (just/barely) missed the deadline.* • *The team missed* [=failed to qualify for] *the play-offs.* **2** [T] **a** : to fail to use (something, such as an opportunity) • *She missed her chance to join the club.* **b** : to fail to do, take, make, or have (something) • *The driver missed the/his turn.* [=failed to turn when he should have] • *They missed a payment on their car loan.* • *I missed lunch.* **3** [T] : to be without (something) • *He was missing two teeth.* [=he did not have two of his teeth] **4** [T] **a** : to fail to be present for (something) • *She missed a day of school.* • *an event that is not to be missed* [=that you should experience] • *I wouldn't miss it for the world.* [=I will definitely go] **b** : to arrive too late for (something or someone) • *He missed his train/flight/connection.* • *You just missed her.* **5** [T] : to notice or feel the absence of (someone or something) • *We miss* [=we feel sad because we are not near] *our old friends.* • *I miss being* [=I am sad not to be] *home at Christmas.* **6** [T] **a** : to fail to understand (something) • *You're missing my point.* • *Am I missing something?* **b** : to fail to hear or learn about (something) • *I'm sorry, but I missed what you said.* **c** : to fail to see or notice (something or someone) • *It's a big building on the corner—you can't miss it.* [=it is impossible not to notice it] **7** [T] : to avoid (something) • *Her car barely missed (hitting) a tree.* **8** [I] : to fail to succeed • *With a cast like this, the movie can't miss.* [=it will definitely succeed] — **miss a beat** see ²BEAT — **miss out** [*phrasal vb*] **1** : to be unable to have or enjoy something • *You really missed out (on a great opportunity).* **2 miss out (someone or something, thing) or miss (someone or something) out** *Brit* : to leave (someone or something) out : OMIT • *You've missed out the most important fact!* — **miss the boat** see BOAT — **miss the forest for the trees** see TREE

²**miss** *n* **1** [C] : a failure to hit something • *She hit the target five times without a miss.* • *(figurative) Was the movie a hit or a miss?* [=was it a success or a failure?] **2 Miss a** — used as a title before the name of an unmarried woman or girl • *Miss Jones* — compare MRS., MS. **b** *Brit* — used by children as a way to address a female teacher **3** — used as a polite way to address a girl or young woman • *Can I help you, miss?* **4** [*plural*] *US* : a clothing size for women of average

height and weight • *misses dresses* — **give (something) a miss** *chiefly Brit, informal* : to choose not to do (something) or go (somewhere) • *I decided to give the party a miss.*

mis·shap·en /ˌmɪsˈʃeɪpən/ *adj* : badly shaped • *a misshapen hand*

mis·sile /ˈmɪsəl, *Brit* ˈmɪˌsaɪl/ *n* [C] : an object that is thrown, shot, or launched as a weapon; *especially* : a rocket that explodes when it hits a distant target • *a nuclear missile*

miss·ing /ˈmɪsɪŋ/ *adj* **1** : unable to be found : not in a usual or expected place • *My keys are missing.* [=I can't find my keys] • *One of his front teeth is missing.* [=he does not have one of his front teeth] • *missing children* • *Some papers are missing from her desk.* • *My keys have gone missing again.* [=I can't find my keys again] • *The new evidence may provide the crime's missing links.* [=the evidence that is needed to solve the crime] **2** : needed or expected but not included • *It's a good sauce, but there's something missing.* [=it lacks something that would make it better] • *Something was missing from his life.* — **missing in action** — used to say that a soldier cannot be found after a battle

missing person *n* [C] : a person whose location is not known and whose absence has been reported to the police • *They've filed a missing persons report.* [=a document that officially reports that someone is missing]

mis·sion /ˈmɪʃən/ *n* [C] **1 a** : a task or job that someone is given to do • *a fact-finding mission* = *a mission to gather information* • *go on a rescue mission* [=go somewhere to rescue someone] **b** : a specific military task • *a combat/training/peacekeeping mission* **c** : a flight by an aircraft or spacecraft to perform a specific task • *a mission to the moon* **2** : a task that you consider to be a very important duty • *He has made it his mission in life to help poor children.* • *She's on a mission* [=she is very determined] *to locate her lost sister.* **3 a** : a group of missionaries **b** : a place where missionaries work • *touring a Spanish mission in California*

mis·sion·ary /ˈmɪʃəˌneri, *Brit* ˈmɪʃənri/ *n, pl* **-ar·ies** [C] : a person who is sent to a foreign country to do religious work (such as to help poor people or to convince people to join a religion) • *a Christian missionary* • *missionary work*

mis·sive /ˈmɪsɪv/ *n* [C] *formal* : ¹LETTER 2 • *a lengthy missive from my father*

mis·spell /ˌmɪsˈspɛl/ *vb* **-spelled** *or chiefly Brit* **-spelt** /-ˈspɛlt/; **-spell·ing** [T] : to spell (a word or name) incorrectly • *He misspelled my name.* — **mis·spell·ing** /ˌmɪsˈspɛlɪŋ/ *n* [C] • *a few misspellings*

mis·spend /ˌmɪsˈspɛnd/ *vb* **-spent** /-ˈspɛnt/; **-spend·ing** [T] : to spend or use (time, money, etc.) in a way that is not legal, careful, or wise • *misspending public money* • *misspent time*

mis·state /ˌmɪsˈsteɪt/ *vb* **-stat·ed**; **-stat·ing** [T] : to state or report (something) incorrectly • *The company misstated its profits.* — **mis·state·ment** /ˌmɪs-ˈsteɪtmənt/ *n* [C/U]

mis·step /ˌmɪsˈstɛp/ *n* [C] *chiefly US* : an action or decision that is a mistake • *They made a strategic misstep.*

mis·sus /ˈmɪsəz/ *n* **1** [C] *informal + old-fashioned* : WIFE • *How's the missus?* **2** *Brit, informal* — used to address a woman whose name is not known • *Need a hand, missus?*

¹mist /ˈmɪst/ *n* [C/U] : water in the form of very small drops floating in the air or falling as rain • *The hills were veiled/shrouded in (a) fine mist.*

²mist *vb* **1** [I] **a** : to become covered with very small drops of water • *My glasses misted up when I came in from the cold.* **b** *of a person's eyes* : to fill with tears • *Her eyes misted over/up.* **2** [T] : to spray (something) with very small drops of water • *Mist the plants regularly.* **3** [I] : to rain very lightly • *It was misting when we arrived.*

¹mis·take /məˈsteɪk/ *n* [C] : an action, statement, judgment, etc., that is wrong or not correct • ERROR • *There must be some mistake.* • *There's a mistake in the schedule.* • *a stupid/careless/costly/fatal mistake* • *spelling mistakes* • *Everybody makes mistakes from time to time.* • *It was an honest mistake.* [=a mistake that anyone could make] — **by mistake** : without intending to • *I got on the wrong train by mistake.* [=accidentally] — **make no mistake** — used to stress the truth of a statement • *Make no mistake (about it), we must address these problems now.*

²mistake *vb* **mis·took** /məˈstʊk/; **mis·tak·en** /məˈsteɪkən/; **mis·tak·ing** [T] **1** : to understand (something or someone) incorrectly • *They mistook my meaning. If you think we're done, you are sadly/badly/sorely mistaken.* [=you are wrong; we are not done] • *If I'm not mistaken* [=if I am not wrong], *the bus leaves at 7:00.* **2** : to make a wrong judgment about (something) • *There was no mistaking his intention.* [=his intention was very clear] **3** : to identify (someone or something) incorrectly • *I mistook him for* [=I thought he was] *his brother.* • *Her arrest was a case of mistaken identity.* [=she was arrested because the police thought she was someone else] — **mis·tak·en·ly** *adv* • *He mistakenly believed that he was safe.*

mis·ter /ˈmɪstər/ *n* **1** *Mister* — used sometimes in writing instead of *Mr.* **2** *informal* — used in speech especially by children to address a man whose name is not known • *Hey mister, is that your dog?*

mis·tle·toe /ˈmɪsəlˌtoʊ/ *n* [U] : a plant with white berries that is traditionally used as a Christmas decoration

mistook *past tense of* ²MISTAKE

mis·treat /ˌmɪsˈtriːt/ *vb* [T] : to treat (someone or something) badly • ABUSE • *mistreating prisoners* — **mis·treat·ment** /ˌmɪsˈtriːtmənt/ *n* [U]

mis·tress /ˈmɪstrəs/ *n* [C] **1** : a woman who has control or power over (someone or something) • *the master and mistress of the house* • *(Brit) the Mistress of* [=the

woman who is in charge of] *Girton College* **2** : a woman who has a sexual relationship with a married man • *He has a mistress.* **3** *Mistress* *old-fashioned* — used as a title before the name of a woman • *Mistress Jones*

mis·tri·al /ˈmɪsˌtraɪəl/ *n* [C] *law* : a trial that is not valid because of an error or because the jury is unable to decide a verdict • *The judge declared a mistrial.*

mis·trust /ˌmɪsˈtrʌst/ *n* [U, *singular*] : a feeling that someone is not honest and cannot be trusted • DISTRUST • *She has a strong mistrust of politicians.* — **mistrust** *vb* [T] • *She mistrusts politicians.* — **mis·trust·ful** /ˌmɪsˈtrʌstfəl/ *adj* • *She is mistrustful of politicians.*

misty /ˈmɪsti/ *adj* **mist·i·er; -est** **1** : full of mist • *misty weather* **2** : not clearly seen or remembered • *misty memories* **3** *informal* : TEARFUL • *misty eyes* • *I get (all) misty when I hear that song.*

mis·un·der·stand /ˌmɪsˌʌndərˈstænd/ *vb* **-stood** /-ˈstʊd/; **-stand·ing** [T] : to fail to understand (someone or something) correctly • *You misunderstood my question.* • *a misunderstood person/genius*

misunderstanding *n* **1** [C/U] : a failure to understand something • *Use clear language to avoid/prevent misunderstandings.* **2** [C] : a usually minor argument or disagreement • *an unfortunate misunderstanding between old friends*

¹mis·use /ˌmɪsˈjuːz/ *vb* [T] : to use (something) incorrectly • *a word that is frequently misused*

²mis·use /ˌmɪsˈjuːs/ *n* [C/U] : the act of using something in an illegal, improper, incorrect, or unfair way • *the misuse of company funds*

mite /ˈmaɪt/ *n* [C] : a very small creature that often lives on plants, animals, and foods — **a mite** : to a small degree : somewhat or slightly • *The movie's plot is a mite* [=a bit, a little] *confusing.*

mit·i·gate /ˈmɪtəˌgeɪt/ *vb* **-gat·ed; -gat·ing** [T] *formal* : to make (something) less severe, harmful, or painful • *helping to mitigate the effects of the disaster* • *medicines used to mitigate pain* • *His sentence was reduced because of mitigating circumstances.* [=things that make a crime seem less serious] — **mit·i·ga·tion** /ˌmɪtəˈgeɪʃən/ *n* [U]

mitt /ˈmɪt/ *n* [C] **1** : MITTEN **2** : a special type of glove worn by certain players on a baseball team • *a catcher's mitt* • *a first baseman's mitt* **3** *informal* : HAND • *Get your mitts off me!*

mit·ten /ˈmɪtn/ *n* [C] : a covering for the hand that has a separate part for the thumb only

¹mix /ˈmɪks/ *vb* **1 a** [T/I] : to combine (two or more things) to make one thing that is the same throughout • *Mix the powdered sugar with a little milk and vanilla.* • *You can make purple by mixing red and blue.* • *Add the ingredients and mix (them) well.* • *Oil and water don't mix.* **b** [T] : to add (something) to something else • *Mix some water with the flour to make a paste.* • *I mixed in a little more sugar.* **2** [T] : to make or prepare (something) by combining different things • *mixing alcoholic drinks* **3** [*T*] : to make (a recording of music) by electronically putting sounds together from more than one source • *mixing a CD of dance music* **4** [*T*] : to bring (different things) together • *She buys pieces of clothing that she can* **mix and match.** [=that she can put together in different ways] • *Playing golf with clients is a way to* **mix business with pleasure.** [=to do something enjoyable that is related to your work] **5** [*I*] : to be able to be combined or put together in a way that has good results • *Drinking (alcohol) and driving* **don't mix.** [=you should not drive after you have been drinking alcohol] — **mix it up** (*US*) or Brit **mix it** *informal* : to fight or argue • *He loves to mix it up with his brothers.* — **mix up** [*phrasal vb*] *informal* **mix (someone or something) up** or **mix up (someone or something) 1** : to mistakenly think that (someone or something) is someone or something else • *He got the days mixed up* [=confused] *and thought the meeting was today.* • *I always mix up their names.* **2** : to mistakenly put (something) in a place where something else should be • *I mixed up the two files.* • *Did my homework get mixed up with your papers?* **3** : to cause (someone) to be involved with someone or something that is dangerous, improper, etc. • *She got mixed up with the wrong crowd.* • *He got mixed up in* [=he became involved in] *a plan to steal the money.*

²**mix** *n* **1** [*C/U*] : a dry mixture of ingredients that is sold in one package and used for making something • *a cake mix* • *a bag of cement mix* **2** [*singular*] : MIXTURE 2 • *a snack mix containing pretzels, nuts, and raisins* • *an attractive mix of red, orange, and yellow*

mixed /'mɪkst/ *adj* **1** *always before a noun* : made of different kinds of things combined together • *mixed nuts/candy* • *a mixed drink* [=an alcoholic drink made with two or more ingredients] **2 a** : including or involving people of different races or religions • *She's of mixed African and European ancestry.* • *a mixed marriage* [=a marriage between two people of different races or religions] **b** : including or involving people of both sexes • *a mixed chorus* • *Don't tell lewd jokes in* **mixed company.** [=when both women and men are present] **3** : both good and bad, favorable and unfavorable, etc. • *The play received mixed reviews.* [=some critics liked the play, while other critics did not] • *I'm having mixed feelings/emotions* [=both good and bad thoughts or feelings] *about this decision.* • *He keeps giving me mixed messages/signals.* [=he keeps doing things that make me think one thing and then doing things that make me think a different thing] • *Living near your in-laws is a mixed blessing.* [=something that is good in some ways and bad in other ways]

mixed bag *n* [*singular*] **1** : a collection of different kinds of things • *a mixed bag of ideas* **2** : something that has both good and bad qualities or parts • *His performance was a mixed bag.*

mixed–up /'mɪkst'ʌp/ *adj, informal* **1** : confused and usually emotionally troubled • *crazy, mixed-up kids* **2** : confusing and filled with problems • *He has mixed-up ideas about our past.* — often written as two separate words when used following a verb • *Her life is mixed up.*

mix·er /'mɪksə/ *n* [*C*] **1** : a machine used for mixing things • *Use a handheld/electric mixer for the cake batter.* • *a cement mixer* **2** : a beverage that does not contain alcohol and that is used in a mixed drink **3** *chiefly US* : a social gathering to help people in a group meet each other • *an informal mixer*

mix·ture /'mɪkstʃə/ *n* **1** [*C*] : something made by combining two or more ingredients • *Add eggs to the mixture.* • *The horses are fed a mixture of grass and oats.* **2** [*C*] : a combination of different things • *a mixture of red and white roses* • *a mixture of English and Spanish* **3** [*U*] : the act of mixing two or more things together • *the mixture of different cultures*

mix–up /'mɪks.ʌp/ *n* [*C*] : a mistake caused by confusion about something • *I thought you were someone else. Sorry for the mix-up.*

ml *abbr* milliliter

mm *abbr* millimeter

MN *abbr* Minnesota

Mo. *abbr* Monday

¹**MO** /'ɛm'oʊ/ *n* [*C*] : MODUS OPERANDI • *two thieves with very different MOs*

²**MO** *abbr* Missouri

moan /'moʊn/ *vb* **1** [*I*] : to make a long, low sound because of pain, physical pleasure, etc. • *The patient moaned in/with pain.* **2 a** [*I*] : to express unhappiness about something • *He's always moaning and groaning about his salary.* **b** [*T*] : to say (something) in a way that shows pain or unhappiness • *"But I don't want to go," he moaned.* **3** [*I*] : to make a long, low sound • *the moaning of the wind* — **moan** *n* [*C*] • *a moan of despair/pleasure* • *the moan of the wind*

moat /'moʊt/ *n* [*C*] : a deep ditch that surrounds a castle and that is usually filled with water

¹**mob** /'mɑːb/ *n* **1** [*C*] : a large group or crowd of people who are angry, violent, or difficult to control • *an angry mob* • (*US*) *The protest turned into a* **mob scene.** [=a place or situation where a crowd of people behave in a violent or uncontrolled way] **2** [*C*] *informal* : a large number of people • *Mobs of teenagers filled the room.* **3** or **Mob** *informal* : MAFIA • *Their family had mob connections.* • *a mob boss* • *The Mob controlled most businesses in the city.*

²**mob** *vb* **mobbed; mob·bing** [*T*] **1** *of a group of people* : to crowd around (someone) in an aggressive, excited, or annoying way • *The actor's fans mobbed him wherever he went.* **2** : to come together in (a place) with many other people • *The stores were mobbed by/with customers.*

¹**mo·bile** /'moʊbəl, 'moʊˌbajəl/ *adj* **1 a** : able to move from one place to another • *when babies become mobile* [=able to crawl or walk] **b** : able to move with the use of trucks, planes, etc. • *The army*

is fully mobile. **2** : able to be moved • *a mobile crime lab* **3** : able to move from one level of a society to another • *socially mobile people*

²**mo·bile** /ˈmoʊˌbiːl, *Brit* ˈməʊbaɪl/ *n* [C]
1 : a decoration that is hung from above and that has attached figures that move easily in the air • *They hung a mobile over the baby's bed.* **2** *Brit, informal* : CELL PHONE

mobile home *n* [C] : a house that is built in a factory and then moved to the place where people will live in it

mobile phone *n* [C] : CELL PHONE

mo·bil·i·ty /moʊˈbɪləti/ *n* [U] **1** : the ability or tendency to move from one position or situation to another usually better one • *social/economic/career mobility* **2** : ability to move quickly and easily • *elderly people with limited mobility*

mo·bi·lize *also Brit* **mo·bi·lise** /ˈmoʊbəˌlaɪz/ *vb* **-lized; -liz·ing** **1** [T/I] : to come together or bring (people) together for action • *He mobilized* [=*rallied*] *his supporters.* **2** [T] : to make (soldiers, an army, etc.) ready for war • *Troops were mobilized for war.* — **mo·bi·li·za·tion** *also Brit* **mo·bi·li·sa·tion** /ˌmoʊbələˈzeɪʃən, *Brit* ˌməʊbəˌlaɪˈzeɪʃən/ *n* [C/U]

mob·ster /ˈmɑːbstɚ/ *n* [C] : someone who is part of a secret organized group of criminals : a member of the Mob

moc·ca·sin /ˈmɑːkəsən/ *n* [C] : a kind of flat leather shoe — see also WATER MOCCASIN

mo·cha /ˈmoʊkə, *Brit* ˈmɒkə/ *n* [C/U] : a drink or flavor that is a mixture of coffee and chocolate

¹**mock** /ˈmɑːk/ *vb* [T] **1** : to laugh at or make fun of (someone or something) especially by copying an action or a way of behaving or speaking • *They mocked her accent.* [=made fun of her accent by copying it in an exaggerated way] **2** : to criticize and laugh at (someone or something) for being bad, worthless, or unimportant • *We were mocked for our beliefs.*
— **mocking** *adj* • *mocking words* — **mock·ing·ly** /ˈmɑːkɪŋli/ *adv*

²**mock** *adj, always before a noun* **1** : not based on real or honest feelings • *mock anger/surprise* **2** : done or performed to look like the real thing • *a mock trial* [=a fake legal trial used for education and practice]

mock·ery /ˈmɑːkəri/ *n* **1** [U] : behavior or speech that makes fun of someone or something in a hurtful way • *the children's cruel mockery of each other* **2** [*singular*] : a bad or useless copy of something • *The judge's decisions have made a mockery of the legal system.* [=made the legal system seem ridiculous or useless]

mock·ing·bird /ˈmɑːkɪŋˌbɚd/ *n* [C] : a North American bird that sings the songs of other birds

mock–up /ˈmɑːkˌʌp/ *n* [C] : a full-sized model of something (such as a car) that is used for studying, testing, or showing its features

mod·al /ˈmoʊdl̩/ *n* [C] *grammar* : MODAL VERB

modal verb *n* [C] *grammar* : a verb

(such as *can, could, shall, should, ought to, will,* or *would*) that is usually used with another verb to express ideas such as possibility, necessity, and permission — called also *modal, modal auxiliary, modal auxiliary verb*

mod cons /ˌmɑːdˈkɑːnz/ *n* [*plural*] *Brit, informal* : the equipment and features that are found in a modern home and that make life easier and more comfortable • *a flat with all the mod cons you'd expect: a dishwasher, central heating . . .*

mode /ˈmoʊd/ *n* [C] **1** *formal* **a** : a particular form or type of something (such as communication or behavior) • *buses, trains, airplanes, and other modes of transportation* **b** : a particular way of doing something • *a different mode of teaching/living* **2** : the state in which a machine does a particular function • *I put the camera in flash mode.* **3** *informal* : a specified way of thinking, feeling, or acting • *Get into work mode.* [=get ready to work] • *He went into attack mode.* [=he became very hostile and aggressive]

¹**mod·el** /ˈmɑːdl̩/ *n* [C] **1** : a usually small copy of something • *a plastic model of the human heart* • *a scale model* [=a small but exact copy] *of a ship* **2** : a particular type or version of a product (such as a car or computer) • *We've improved on last year's model.* **3** : a set of ideas and numbers that describe the past, present, or future state of an economy, business, etc. • *a mathematical/computer model* **4** **a** : something or someone that is a very good example of something • *The city is a model of safety and cleanliness.* [=it is very safe and clean] **b** : something or someone that deserves to be copied by others • *Her work has become a model to/for other writers.* **5** : someone who is paid to model clothing, jewelry, etc. • *a fashion model* **6** : someone whose image is painted, photographed, etc., by an artist • *drawings of nude models*

²**model** *adj, always before a noun* **1** : deserving to be copied by others • *a model husband/student* **2** — used to describe something that is a small copy of something larger • *a model airplane/train*

³**model** *vb, US* **-eled** *or Brit* **-elled;** *US* **-el·ing** *or Brit* **-el·ling** **1** [T] : to design (something) so that it is similar to something else • *Their system was modeled on our system.* [=our system was used as a model for their system] • *(chiefly US) The church was modeled after an earlier French design.* • *She models herself on/after* [=tries to be like or behave like] *the leaders that came before her.* **2** [T] : to make something by forming or shaping clay or some other material • *modeling figures in/from clay* **3** [T/I] : to wear clothing, jewelry, etc., in photographs, fashion shows, etc., so that people will see and want to buy what you are wearing • *They're modeling this year's new spring fashions.* • *She models* [=she works as a fashion model] *for a modeling agency.* **4** [I] : to be painted or photographed by an artist • *She modeled for him.*

mo·dem /ˈmoʊdəm/ *n* [C] : a device that

allows information to be sent through phone lines from one computer to another

¹mod·er·ate /ˈmɑːdərət/ adj **1 a** : average in size or amount ▪ drinking moderate amounts of coffee ▪ mild to moderate pain **b** : neither very good nor very bad ▪ They had only moderate success. **2** : not too expensive ▪ The hotel offers rooms at moderate prices. **3** : having or expressing political beliefs that are neither very liberal nor very conservative ▪ moderate Democrats/Republicans ▪ The group needs more moderate voices. [=more members who do not express extreme ideas] **4 a** : avoiding behavior that goes beyond what is normal, healthy, or acceptable ▪ a moderate diet ▪ moderate drinking **b** : not showing strong emotions or excitement ▪ moderate language — **mod·er·ate·ly** /ˈmɑːdərətli/ adv ▪ The medicine is only moderately effective. ▪ moderately priced hotels

²mod·er·ate /ˈmɑːdərət/ n [C] : a person whose political ideas are not extreme ▪ moderates from both parties

³mod·er·ate /ˈmɑːdəˌreɪt/ vb **-at·ed; -at·ing** [T/I] **1** : to become or make (something) become less harsh, strong, or severe ▪ They will not moderate their demands. ▪ The wind moderated after the storm. **2** : to guide a discussion or direct a meeting ▪ moderate (at) a debate

mod·er·a·tion /ˌmɑːdəˈreɪʃən/ n **1** [U] : the quality or state of avoiding behavior that goes beyond what is normal or acceptable ▪ The organization is encouraging moderation among the world's leaders. **2** [U, singular] : a decrease in something that is strong or severe ▪ There will be a slight moderation in temperature. [=the temperature will become slightly cooler] — **in moderation** : in a way that is reasonable and not excessive ▪ Is drinking alcohol in moderation good for you?

mod·er·a·tor /ˈmɑːdəˌreɪtə/ n [C] : someone who leads a discussion in a group and tells each person when to speak ▪ She acts as the moderator in our office meetings.

¹mod·ern /ˈmɑːdən/ adj **1** always before a noun **a** : happening, existing, or developing at a time near the present time ▪ ancient and modern history ▪ the father of modern medicine ▪ the modern American family [=the typical American family living today] **b** or **Modern** : of or relating to the current period of a language ▪ Modern Greek/English. **2** : based on or using the newest information, methods, or technology ▪ a very modern city ▪ modern methods of communication including e-mail and the Internet **3** : of or relating to a style or way of thinking that is new and different ▪ He decorated his house to look less old-fashioned and more modern. ▪ a modern version of a classic story **4** : of or relating to forms of art in which the styles used are very different from the more traditional styles ▪ modern dance/music/art/architecture

²modern n [C] : a modern artist or writer ▪ the ancients and the moderns

mod·ern–day /ˈmɑːdənˌdeɪ/ adj, always before a noun : existing today ▪ modern-day China ▪ The two lovers are a modern-day Romeo and Juliet.

mod·ern·ism /ˈmɑːdəˌnɪzm/ n [U] : a style of art, literature, etc., that uses ideas and methods which are very different from those used in the past — **mod·ern·ist** /ˈmɑːdənɪst/ n [C] — **modernist** adj

mo·der·ni·ty /məˈdənəti/ n [U] formal : a modern way of living or thinking ▪ a town that has resisted modernity

mod·ern·ize also Brit **mod·ern·ise** /ˈmɑːdəˌnaɪz/ vb **-ized; -iz·ing 1** [T] : to make (something) modern and more suited to present styles or needs ▪ The school needs modernized classrooms. **2** [I] : to begin using the newest information, methods, or technology ▪ older companies that need to modernize — **mod·ern·i·za·tion** also Brit **mod·ern·i·sa·tion** /ˌmɑːdənəˈzeɪʃən, Brit ˌmɒdəˌnaɪˈzeɪʃən/ n [U]

mod·est /ˈmɑːdəst/ adj **1** : not very large in size or amount ▪ She enjoyed modest success with her singing career. ▪ a modest home/income **2** approving : not too proud or confident about yourself or your abilities ▪ She's very modest about her achievements. ▪ Don't be so modest. You were wonderful! **3 a** of clothing : not showing too much of a person's body ▪ modest swimsuits **b** : shy about showing your body especially in a sexual way ▪ a modest young woman — **mod·est·ly** adv ▪ modestly successful ▪ modestly dressed

mod·es·ty /ˈmɑːdəsti/ n [U] : the quality of being modest ▪ the modesty of her clothing ▪ He is known for his modesty. ▪ There was no false modesty in her victory speech. ▪ I'll admit in/with all modesty [=in a way that is true even if it sounds like something said because of pride] that I am very good at golf.

mo·di·cum /ˈmɑːdɪkəm/ n [singular] formal : a small amount ▪ a modicum of success/truth/sense/intelligence

mod·i·fi·er /ˈmɑːdəˌfajə/ n [C] grammar : a word (such as an adjective or adverb) or phrase that describes another word or group of words ▪ In "a red hat," "red" is a modifier describing "hat."

mod·i·fy /ˈmɑːdəˌfaɪ/ vb **-fies; -fied; -fy·ing** [T] **1** : to change some parts of (something) while not changing other parts ▪ He modified the recipe by using oil instead of butter. ▪ modify a plan ▪ We played a modified version of the game. **2** grammar : to limit or describe the meaning of (a word or group of words) ▪ Adjectives usually modify nouns, and adverbs usually modify verbs, adjectives, and other adverbs. — **mod·i·fi·ca·tion** /ˌmɑːdəfəˈkeɪʃən/ n [C/U] ▪ We made a few minor modifications to our plan.

mod·u·lar /ˈmɑːdʒələ/ adj : having parts that can be connected or combined in different ways ▪ a factory that produces modular homes ▪ modular buildings/walls ▪ (chiefly Brit) This is a modular course of three components.

mod·u·late /ˈmɑːdʒəˌleɪt/ vb **-lat·ed; -lat-**

ing [T] *formal* : to change (something) so that it exists in a proper amount • *These organs modulate* [=regulate] *the amount of salt in the body.* — **mod·u·la·tion** /ˌmɑːdʒəˈleɪʃən/ *n* [C/U]

mod·ule /ˈmɑːˌdʒuːl, *Brit* ˈmɒdjuːl/ *n* [C] **1** : one of a set of parts that can be connected or combined to build or complete something • *engines, transmissions, brakes, and other modules for cars* • (*chiefly Brit*) *This is a modular course of three components, and students can take those three modules in any order.* **2** : a part of a computer or computer program that does a particular job • *special software/memory modules* **3** : a part of a space vehicle that can work alone • *a lunar module* [=a space vehicle used to land on the moon]

mo·dus ope·ran·di /ˌmoʊdəsˌɑːpəˈrændi/ *n* [*singular*] *formal* : a usual way of doing something; *especially* : the usual way that a particular criminal performs a crime • *the murderer's modus operandi* — called also *MO*

mo·gul /ˈmoʊgəl/ *n* [C] : a powerful and important person • *TV/ad moguls*

mo·hair /ˈmoʊˌheɚ/ *n* [U] : an expensive fabric or wool made from the hair of a goat from Asia • *a mohair sweater*

moist /ˈmɔɪst/ *adj* **1** : slightly or barely wet • *moist eyes/soil/cake* **2** : having a lot of moisture in the air : HUMID • *moist tropical heat*

moist·en /ˈmɔɪsn/ *vb* [T/I] : to make (something) slightly wet or to become slightly wet • *moisten a stamp/envelope* • *His eyes moistened* [=became tearful] *at the memory.*

mois·ture /ˈmɔɪstʃɚ/ *n* [U] : a small amount of a liquid (such as water) that makes something wet • *the moisture in the air*

mois·tur·ize *also Brit* **mois·tur·ise** /ˈmɔɪstʃəˌraɪz/ *vb* -**ized**; -**iz·ing** [T] : to add moisture to (something, such as a person's skin) • *a cream that moisturizes dry skin* • *a moisturizing cream/lotion* — **mois·tur·iz·er** *also Brit* **mois·tur·is·er** *n* [C/U] • *She uses a moisturizer on her skin.*

mo·jo /ˈmoʊdʒoʊ/ *n* [C/U] *chiefly US, informal* : a power that may seem magical and that allows someone to be very effective, successful, etc. • *The team has lost its mojo.*

mo·lar /ˈmoʊlɚ/ *n* [C] : a large tooth near the back of the jaw

mo·las·ses /məˈlæsəz/ *n* [U] *chiefly US* : a thick, brown, sweet liquid that is made from raw sugar — called also (*Brit*) *treacle* — **slow as molasses** or **slower than molasses** *US, informal* : very slow or slowly • *They're moving/working slower than molasses.*

¹**mold** (*US*) or *Brit* **mould** /ˈmoʊld/ *n* **1** [C] **a** : a container that is used to give its shape to something that is poured on or pressed into it • *wax/gelatin poured into a mold* **b** : something made in a mold • *a plaster mold of a foot* **2** [C] : a pattern or type of something that is an example to be followed • *She does not fit (into/in) the mold of a typical college professor.* [=she is

not a typical college professor] **3** [C/U] : a soft substance that grows on the surface of damp or rotting things • *She's allergic to mold.* — **break the mold 1** : to do something in a completely new way • *candidates who will break the mold and give honest answers* **2** *informal* — used to describe a very unusual or admired person • *They broke the mold when they made that guy.* [=there will never be another person like him]

²**mold** (*US*) or *Brit* **mould** *vb* **1** [T] **a** : to form or press (wax, plastic, dough, etc.) into a particular shape • *molding clay into shapes* **b** : to make (something) from a material that has been formed, pressed, or poured into a mold • *a tiny statue that she molded from clay* • *a molded plastic chair* **2** [T] : to create, influence, or affect the character of (someone or something) • *teaching and molding young children/minds* **3** [I] : to fit to the shape of something • *a mattress that molds to* [=that changes its shape to fit] *your body* — **mold·er** (*US*) or *Brit* **mould·er** /ˈmoʊldɚ/ *n* [C] • *a molder of young minds*

mold·ing (*US*) or *Brit* **mould·ing** /ˈmoʊldɪŋ/ *n* [C/U] : a strip of wood or other material with some design or pattern that is used as a decoration on a wall, around a window, etc. • *a house with beautiful moldings around its doors*

moldy (*US*) or *Brit* **mouldy** /ˈmoʊldi/ *adj* **mold·i·er**; -**est** : covered with mold • *moldy bread/fruit*

mole /ˈmoʊl/ *n* [C] **1** : a small animal with soft fur that digs tunnels in the ground and eats insects **2** : a spy who works inside an organization **3** : a small, brown spot on a person's skin

mol·e·cule /ˈmɑːlɪˌkjuːl/ *n* [C] : the smallest possible amount of a particular substance that has all the characteristics of that substance • *a molecule of water/oxygen* — **mo·lec·u·lar** /məˈlɛkjələ/ *adj* • *molecular structure/weight* • *molecular biology*

mole·hill /ˈmoʊlˌhɪl/ *n* [C] : a small pile of dirt that is pushed up by a mole • (*figurative*) *You're making a mountain out of a molehill.* [=making something seem much more difficult or important than it really is]

mo·lest /məˈlɛst/ *vb* [T] **1** : to touch (someone) in a sexual and improper way • *sent to jail for molesting children* **2** *old-fashioned* : to bother or annoy (a person or animal) • *It was illegal to molest, capture, or kill any of the animals.* — **mo·les·ta·tion** /ˌmoʊˌlɛˈsteɪʃən/ *n* [U] • *a victim of molestation* — **mo·lest·er** /məˈlɛstɚ/ *n* [C] • *child molesters*

mol·li·fy /ˈmɑːlɪˌfaɪ/ *vb* -**fies**; -**fied**; -**fy·ing** [T] : to make (someone) less angry • *He tried to mollify his critics with an apology.*

mol·lusk (*US*) or *Brit* **mol·lusc** /ˈmɑːləsk/ *n* [C] *biology* : any one of a large group of animals (such as snails and clams) that have a soft body and that usually live in a shell

mol·ly·cod·dle /ˈmɑːliˌkɑːdl̩/ *vb* -**cod·dled**; -**cod·dling** [T] : to treat (someone) too nicely or gently ▪ *The coach has been mollycoddling the team's star players.*

Mo·lo·tov cocktail /'mɑːlə,tɑːf-/ n [C] : a bomb made from a bottle filled with gasoline and stuffed with a piece of cloth

molt (*US*) or *Brit* **moult** /'moʊlt/ vb [I] *biology* : to lose a covering of hair, feathers, etc., and replace it with new growth in the same place ▪ *a molting bird*

mol·ten /'moʊltən/ *adj, always before a noun* : melted by heat ▪ *molten metal/glass/lava*

mom /'mɑːm/ n [C] *US, informal* : a person's mother ▪ *Mom, do you know where my keys are?*

mom–and–pop /'mɑːmən'pɑːp/ *adj, always before a noun, chiefly US* : owned and run by a married couple or by a small number of people ▪ *a mom-and-pop business*

mo·ment /'moʊmənt/ n **1** [C] : a very short period of time ▪ *The sun was shining. Moments later, it began to rain.* ▪ *Let's stop for a moment to rest.* ▪ *Do you have a moment?* [=do you have some free time to talk with me?] ▪ *The crowd observed a moment of silence* [=a short period of silent thought or prayer] *for those who died.* ▪ *The doctor arrived not a moment too soon.* [=just in time to help] ▪ *I'll explain that in a moment.* [=shortly, soon] **2** [C] : a particular time ▪ *She waited for the right moment to ask for a raise.* ▪ *We enjoyed every moment of the play.* [=we enjoyed all of the play] ▪ *There was never a dull moment at the party.* **3 a** [U] : the present time ▪ *At the moment* [=right now] *she is working on a novel.* ▪ *As of this moment* [=right now], *there's nothing you can do.* ▪ *It is the world's largest city, for the moment.* [=that is true now, but that may not be true much longer] **b** [C] : a time of importance or success ▪ *her moment of triumph* ▪ *He's not the best player, but he has his moments.* [=he has times when he is very good] ▪ *It was a defining/crowning moment in his presidency.* —

(at) any moment (now) : very soon ▪ *He could lose his temper at any moment.* ▪ *The movie will start any moment now.* —

at/on a moment's notice see ¹NOTICE — **from moment to moment** or **from one moment to the next** or **moment by moment** : very quickly as time passes ▪ *The weather kept changing from one moment to the next.* — **hold/hang on a moment** or **wait/just a moment** *informal* — used to tell someone to wait or to stop for a brief time ▪ *Hang on a moment—I'm almost done.* — **moment of truth** : the time when you have to do or decide something ▪ *The moment of truth came early, when we had to decide whether to stay or go.* — **not for a/one moment** : not at all ▪ *I did not believe her for one moment.* [=I never believed her] — **on/at the spur of the moment** see ¹SPUR — **the last moment** : the latest possible time ▪ *Our flight was canceled at the last moment.* — **the moment** : as soon as ▪ *Everything stops the moment she walks in the room.* — **within moments**

: very quickly ▪ *Within moments, dozens of people had gathered.*

mo·men·tar·i·ly /,moʊmən'terəli, *Brit* 'məʊməntərəli/ *adv* **1** : for a short time : BRIEFLY ▪ *He paused momentarily before finishing his speech.* **2** *US* : very soon ▪ *We will be landing momentarily.*

mo·men·tary /'moʊmən,teri, *Brit* 'məʊməntri/ *adj* : lasting a very short time ▪ *a momentary loss of consciousness*

mo·men·tous /moʊ'mɛntəs/ *adj* : very important ▪ *a momentous decision/occasion*

mo·men·tum /moʊ'mɛntəm/ n [U] **1 a** : the strength or force that something has when it is moving ▪ *The wagon gathered/gained momentum.* [=it moved faster] ▪ *The wagon lost momentum.* [=it slowed down] **b** : the strength or force that allows something to continue or to grow stronger or faster as time passes ▪ *The campaign slowly gained momentum.* [=became more popular and successful] **2** *physics* : the property that a moving object has due to its mass and its motion

mom·ma *variant spelling of* MAMA

mom·my /'mɑːmi/ n, pl **-mies** [C] *chiefly US, informal* : a person's mother — used by children ▪ *Mommy, can I go out to play?*

Mon. *abbr* Monday

mon·arch /'mɑː,nɑɚk/ n [C] : a person (such as a king or queen) who rules a kingdom or empire ▪ *French monarchs*

monarch butterfly n [C] : a large orange and black American butterfly

mon·ar·chist /'mɑnəkɪst/ n [C] : a person who supports a monarch or monarchy

mon·ar·chy /'mɑnəki/ n, pl **-chies** **1** [C] : a country that is ruled by a monarch **2** [C/U] : a form of government in which a country is ruled by a monarch ▪ *the 18th-century French monarchy*

mon·as·tery /'mɑːnə,steri, *Brit* 'mɑːnəstri/ n, pl **-ter·ies** [C] : a place where monks live and work together ▪ *a Catholic/Buddhist monastery*

mo·nas·tic /mə'næstɪk/ *adj* **1** : of or relating to monks or monasteries ▪ *a monastic community* **2** : resembling or suggesting a monk ▪ *a quiet, monastic existence*

Mon·day /'mʌn,deɪ/ n [C/U] : the day of the week between Sunday and Tuesday ▪ *next/last Monday* ▪ *The paper is due (on) Monday.* — abbr. **Mon.** or **Mo.** — **Mon·days** *adv* ▪ *He works late Mondays.* [=every Monday]

mon·e·tary /'mɑːnə,teri, *Brit* 'mʌnətri/ *adj* **1** : of or relating to money ▪ *a crime committed for monetary gain* **2** : of or relating to the money in a country's economy ▪ *the U.S. monetary system* — **mon·e·tar·i·ly** /,mɑːnə'terəli, *Brit* 'mʌnətrəli/ *adv* ▪ *They will benefit/gain monetarily.*

mon·ey /'mʌni/ n, pl **mon·ies** or **mon·eys** /'mʌniz/ **1** [U] : coins, bills, etc., used as a way to pay for goods and services and to pay people for their work ▪ *Dinner cost a lot of money.* ▪ *a sum of money* ▪ *save money for a new car* ▪ *raise money for charity* ▪ *He asked her for* *(some) money.* ▪ *She makes a lot of money in her job.* = *(informal) She makes big/good money in her job.* ▪ *The club* **made money** [=earned money; made a profit] *by selling ads in the newsletter.* ▪ *For them,* **money is no object.** [=they are not concerned about the price of things] ▪ *(informal) They were poor but now they're* **in the money.** [=they have lots of money] ▪ *(informal) Do I look like I'm* **made of money?** [=rich] ▪ *(figurative)* **Money talks** [=money has a powerful influence on people's actions and decisions] *in politics.* ▪ *(figurative, informal) cars for people with* **money to burn** [=a large amount of money to spend] ▪ *(figurative, informal) It's time for the mayor to* **put her money where her mouth is** [=to do something to support what she has been talking about] *and increase funding for schools.* ▪ *(figurative) He really* **throws (his) money around.** [=spends money in a careless way] ▪ *(figurative)* **throwing money at** *a problem* [=trying to solve a problem by spending a large amount of money on it without giving enough thought to exactly what should be done] **2** [*U*] : a person's wealth ▪ *He made his money in the movie business.* ▪ *We didn't have much money when I was growing up.* ▪ *She* **comes from money.** [=her family is rich] ▪ *She married into money.* [=she married a wealthy man] **3** [*plural*] *formal* : amounts of money ▪ *All monies received will be deposited in a special account.* — **a run for your money** see ²RUN — **for love or money** see ¹LOVE — **for my money** *informal* : in my opinion ▪ *This book is, for my money, her best novel yet.* [=I think this is her best novel yet] — **on the money** *US, informal* : exactly right or accurate ▪ *His prediction was (right) on the money.* — **put (your) money on** : to bet on (something or someone) ▪ *They put their money on the underdog.* ▪ *It's going to rain tomorrow. I'd put money on it.* [=I'm almost positive it will rain] — **time is money** — used to say that a person's time is as valuable as money — **your money's worth** : as much as you deserve because of the money you paid or the effort you made ▪ *He stayed until the end of the show to* **get his money's worth.**

mon·ey-back /ˈmʌniˌbæk/ *adj, always before a noun* : allowing buyers to have their money returned if the product breaks, does not work, or is not what the buyer wanted ▪ *a money-back guarantee*

mon·eyed /ˈmʌnid/ *adj, formal* : very rich ▪ *the moneyed classes*

mon·ey-grub·bing /ˈmʌniˌgrʌbɪŋ/ *adj, informal* : wanting or caring about getting money too much ▪ *a money-grubbing miser* — **money-grubbing** *n* [*U*]

mon·ey·lend·er /ˈmʌniˌlɛndɚ/ *n* [*C*] : a person who lends money as a business

mon·ey·mak·er /ˈmʌniˌmeɪkɚ/ *n* [*C*] **1** : something (such as a product) that earns a profit ▪ *This movie was a big money-maker.* **2** : a person who earns or wins a large amount of money ▪ *the top money-makers in pro tennis*

money order *n* [*C*] : a written order to pay an amount of money to a specified person or company that can be bought from a bank or post office and sent by mail like a check ▪ *a payment made by money order* — called also *(Brit)* **postal order**

mon·ey-spin·ner /ˈmʌniˌspɪnɚ/ *n* [*C*] *Brit, informal* : MONEY-MAKER 1 — **mon·ey-spin·ning** /ˈmʌniˌspɪnɪŋ/ *adj, Brit*

mon·goose /ˈmɑːnˌguːs/ *n* [*C*] : a small, fast animal from India that eats snakes and rodents

mon·grel /ˈmɑːŋgrəl/ *n* [*C*] : a dog with parents of different breeds

monies *plural of* MONEY

mon·i·ker /ˈmɑːnɪkɚ/ *n* [*C*] *informal* : a name or nickname ▪ *He earned the moniker "Happy."*

¹**mon·i·tor** /ˈmɑːnətɚ/ *n* [*C*] **1** : a device that is used for showing, watching, or listening to something ▪ *a TV/computer monitor* [=a device used to see images on a screen] ▪ *a baby monitor* [=a device for listening to sounds in another room] ▪ *a heart monitor* [=a device used to watch and record heartbeats] **2** : a student who helps the teacher at a school ▪ *(US) a hall monitor* [=a student who watches the hallways for bad behavior] **3** : a person who has the job of checking or watching some activity or behavior ▪ *U.N. weapons monitors and inspectors*

²**monitor** *vb* [*T*] : to watch, observe, listen to, or check (something) for a special purpose over a period of time ▪ *Nurses monitored the patient's heart rate.* ▪ *monitor* [=keep track of] *a student's progress*

monk /ˈmʌŋk/ *n* [*C*] : a member of a religious community of men who usually promise to remain poor, unmarried, and separated from the rest of society ▪ *Catholic/Buddhist monks*

¹**mon·key** /ˈmʌŋki/ *n, pl* **-keys** [*C*] : a type of animal that is related to apes and that has a long tail — **make a monkey out of** *informal* : to cause (someone) to look very foolish : to make a fool out of (someone) ▪ *I'm not going to let that salesman make a monkey out of me!*

²**monkey** *vb* **-keys; -keyed; -key·ing** — **monkey around** *or Brit* **monkey about** [*phrasal vb*] *informal* **1** : to do things that are not useful or serious ▪ *We were just monkeying around.* **2 monkey around/about with** *informal* : to handle or play with (something) in a careless or foolish way ▪ *monkeying around with dangerous chemicals* — **monkey with** [*phrasal vb*] *informal* : to monkey around with (something) ▪ *Don't monkey with the lawn mower.*

monkey bars *n* [*plural*] *US* : a frame of bars that children can play on

monkey business *n* [*U*] *informal* **1** : playful tricks or jokes ▪ *Don't try any monkey business while I'm gone.* **2** : illegal or improper activity or behavior ▪ *political monkey business*

monkey wrench *n* [*C*] : a wrench that can be adjusted to grip things of different sizes — **throw/hurl/toss a monkey wrench into** *US, informal* : to damage or change (something) in a way that ruins it or prevents it from working properly ▪ *The storm threw a monkey wrench into their plans.*

mono /ˈmɑːnoʊ/ *n* [U] *informal* : MONONUCLEOSIS

mono·chro·mat·ic /ˌmɑːnəkroʊˈmætɪk/ *adj* : having or made up of one color or shades of one color ▪ *a monochromatic room*

mono·chrome /ˈmɑːnəˌkroʊm/ *adj* **1** : MONOCHROMATIC ▪ *a monochrome paint scheme* **2** : using or showing only black and white and shades of gray ▪ *a monochrome film/photo*

mon·o·cle /ˈmɑːnɪkəl/ *n* [C] : a single round lens for one eye to help you see

mo·nog·a·my /məˈnɑːɡəmi/ *n* [U] : the state or practice of being married to only one person at a time or of having only one sexual partner during a period of time ▪ *couples who practice monogamy* — **mo·nog·a·mous** /məˈnɑːɡəməs/ *adj* ▪ *a monogamous relationship*

mono·gram /ˈmɑːnəˌɡræm/ *n* [C] : a symbol that has the first letters of a person's first, middle, and last names — **mono·grammed** /ˈmɑːnəˌɡræmd/ *adj* ▪ *monogrammed towels*

mono·lin·gual /ˌmɑːnəˈlɪŋɡwəl/ *adj* : using or expressed in only one language ▪ *a monolingual dictionary*

mono·lith /ˈmɑːnəˌlɪθ/ *n* [C] **1** : a very large building or other structure ▪ *a massive steel monolith* **2** *often disapproving* : a very large and powerful organization that acts as a single unit ▪ *a media monolith* — **mono·lith·ic** /ˌmɑːnəˈlɪθɪk/ *adj* ▪ *a monolithic building/organization*

mono·logue /ˈmɑːnəˌlɑːɡ/ *n* [C] : a long speech given by a character in a movie, play, etc., or by a performer ▪ *a comedian's famous monologue*

mono·nu·cle·o·sis /ˌmɑːnəˌnuːkliˈoʊsəs, *Brit* ˌmɒnəˌnjuːkliˈəʊsəs/ *n* [U] *medical* : a disease that makes people very tired and weak for a long time

mo·nop·o·lize *also Brit* **mo·nop·o·lise** /məˈnɑːpəˌlaɪz/ *vb* **-lized; -liz·ing** [T] **1** : to take over and control (something or someone) completely ▪ *monopolizing a conversation* ▪ *The company has monopolized the market.* **:** to use (something) in a way that prevents others from using it ▪ *One group monopolized the camping area.* — **mo·nop·o·li·za·tion** *also Brit* **mo·nop·o·li·sa·tion** /məˌnɑːpələˈzeɪʃən, *Brit* məˌnɒpəˌlaɪˈzeɪʃən/ *n* [U]

mo·nop·o·ly /məˈnɑːpəli/ *n, pl* **-lies** **1** [C] **a** : complete control of the entire supply of goods or of a service in a certain area or market ▪ *a monopoly on/on/over the logging industry* **b** : a large company that has a monopoly ▪ *laws that break up monopolies* **2** [*singular*] : complete ownership or control of something ▪ *She thinks she has a monopoly on the truth.* [=that she is the only person who knows what is true]

mono·rail /ˈmɑːnəˌreɪl/ *n* [C/U] : a type of railroad that uses a single track which is usually high off the ground ▪ *traveling by monorail*

mono·syl·lab·ic /ˌmɑːnəsəˈlæbɪk/ *adj* **1** : having only one syllable ▪ *a monosyl-*

labic word/reply **2** : saying very little ▪ *The movie star was monosyllabic with reporters.*

mono·the·ism /ˈmɑːnəˌθiːˌjɪzəm/ *n* [U] : the belief that there is only one God — **mono·the·ist** /ˈmɑːnəˌθiːjɪst/ *n* [C] — **mono·the·is·tic** /ˌmɑːnəˌθiˈɪstɪk/ *adj* ▪ *a monotheistic religion*

mono·tone /ˈmɑːnəˌtoʊn/ *n* [*singular*] : a way of talking or singing without raising or lowering the sound of your voice ▪ *She spoke in a dull monotone.* ▪ *a monotone voice*

mo·not·o·nous /məˈnɑːtn̩əs/ *adj* — used to describe something that is boring because it is always the same ▪ *a monotonous task* — **mo·not·o·nous·ly** *adv* — **mo·not·o·ny** /məˈnɑːtn̩i/ *n* [U] ▪ *the monotony of the job*

mono·un·sat·u·rat·ed /ˌmɑːnoʊˌʌnˈsætʃəreɪtəd/ *adj, technical* — used to describe a type of healthful oil or fat that is found in olives, almonds, etc. ▪ *monounsaturated fats*

monoxide see CARBON MONOXIDE

mon·soon /mɑːnˈsuːn/ *n* [C] **1** : the rainy season that occurs in southern Asia in the summer ▪ *the end of the monsoon (season)* **2** : the rain that falls during this season — sometimes used in an exaggerated way to refer to a heavy rainstorm ▪ *The game was played in a monsoon.*

¹**mon·ster** /ˈmɑːnstɚ/ *n* [C] **1** : a strange or horrible imaginary creature ▪ *a sea monster* **2** *informal* : something that is extremely or unusually large ▪ *It's a monster of a house.* [=a very large house] **3 a** : a very cruel or evil person ▪ *That man is a monster.* **b** : a person who behaves very badly ▪ *My nephew is a little monster.*

²**monster** *adj, always before a noun, informal* : very popular and successful ▪ *The movie was a monster hit.*

mon·stros·i·ty /mɑːnˈstrɑːsəti/ *n, pl* **-ties** [C] : something that is very large and ugly ▪ *The new mall is a monstrosity.*

mon·strous /ˈmɑːnstrəs/ *adj* **1** : extremely or unusually large ▪ *a monstrous billboard* **2** : very wrong or unfair ▪ *a monstrous injustice* **3** : very ugly, cruel, or vicious ▪ *a monstrous crime/criminal* — **mon·strous·ly** *adv* ▪ *monstrously large*

mon·tage /mɑːnˈtɑːʒ/ *n* [C/U] : a work of art that is made up of several different kinds of things ▪ *a photographic/literary/musical montage*

Mon·te·rey jack /ˌmɑːntəˌreɪˈdʒæk/ *n* [U] *US* : a mild kind of cheese

month /ˈmʌnθ/ *n* **1** [C] : any one of the 12 parts into which the year is divided ▪ *July is my favorite month.* ▪ *the winter/summer months* ▪ *Payments are due on/by the third of the month.* [=on the third day of every month] ▪ *It changes from month to month.* = *It changes from one month to the next.* [=every month] **2** [C] : a period of time that lasts about four weeks or 30 days ▪ *The baby is four months old.* [=a four-month-old baby] ▪ *He was gone for a month.* **3** [*plural*] : a long period of time that is less than a year ▪ *He's been gone for months.*

month·long /ˈmʌnθˈlɑːŋ/ adj : lasting an entire month • *a monthlong vacation*

¹**month·ly** /ˈmʌnθli/ adj 1 : happening, done, or made every month • *a monthly meeting* • *She visits us on a monthly basis.* 2 : published once every month • *a monthly column/magazine* 3 : of or relating to one month • *her monthly salary* [=the salary she receives every month] — **monthly** adv • *She visits us monthly.*

²**monthly** n [C] : a magazine that is published once every month • *one of the travel monthlies*

mon·u·ment /ˈmɑːnjəmənt/ n [C] 1 a : a building, statue, etc., that honors a person or event • *a monument in honor of war veterans* b : a building or place that is historically important • *ancient monuments* c : NATIONAL MONUMENT 2 : an example of something • *That is a monument to* [=it is a perfect example of] *bad taste.*

mon·u·men·tal /ˌmɑːnjəˈmɛntl̩/ adj 1 : very important • *a monumental discovery/achievement* 2 : very great or extreme • *a monumental task/job* — **mon·u·men·tal·ly** adv • *monumentally important*

moo /ˈmuː/ n, pl **moos** [C] : the sound made by a cow — **moo** vb [I] • *We heard the cows mooing.*

mooch /ˈmuːtʃ/ vb [T/I] US, informal + disapproving : to ask for and get things from other people without paying for them or doing anything for them • *She's been mooching (money) off her friends.* — **mooch around/about** [phrasal verb] Brit, informal : to walk around with no particular purpose • *I've just been mooching about all afternoon.*

mood /ˈmuːd/ n 1 [C] : the way someone feels • *The music lifted/lightened her mood.* • *The news put me in a good mood.* [=made me happy] • *He's in a bad mood.* = *He's in one of his moods.* [=he's unhappy] • *She's in no mood for joking.* • *She can be sociable when/if the mood takes her.* [=when/if she has the feeling of wanting to be sociable] • *He put on some mood music.* [=music that is meant to create a relaxed or romantic feeling] • *a mood swing* [=a very fast change in mood] • *(medical) mood disorders such as severe depression or anxiety* [singular] : an attitude or feeling shared by many people • *The mood of the city was grim.* 3 [C] grammar : a set of forms of a verb that shows whether the action or state expressed by the verb is thought of as a fact, a command, or a wish or possibility • *the indicative/imperative/subjunctive mood* — **in the mood** : feeling a desire to have or do something • *I'm in the mood for sushi.* • *"Do you want to see a movie?" "No, I'm not in the mood (to see a movie)."*

moody /ˈmuːdi/ adj **mood·i·er**; **-est** : often unhappy or unfriendly • *He can be moody sometimes.* • *He's a moody guy.* — **mood·i·ly** /ˈmuːdəli/ adv — **mood·i·ness** /ˈmuːdinəs/ n [U]

¹**moon** /ˈmuːn/ n 1 **the moon** or **the Moon** : the large round object that circles the Earth and that shines at night • *the surface of the moon* • *The moon isn't out tonight.* = *There's no moon tonight.* [=the moon cannot be seen tonight] • *the orbit of the Moon around the Earth* 2 [C] : an object like the moon that circles around a planet • *the moons of Jupiter* — **ask for the moon or cry for the moon** informal : to ask for something that is very difficult or impossible to get • *They just want to be paid what they're worth. They're not asking for the moon.* — **many moons** informal : a very long time • *But that was many moons ago.* — **over the moon** informal : very happy or pleased about something • *She's over the moon at being chosen for the award.* — **reach/shoot for the moon** : to try to do or get something that is very difficult to do or get • *an ambitious businessman who is always shooting for the moon* — **moon·less** /ˈmuːnləs/ adj • *a moonless night* [=a night during which the moon cannot be seen]

²**moon** vb [T/I] informal : to show your bare buttocks to someone as a rude joke or insult • *One of the boys mooned (at) the crowd.* — **moon around/about** [phrasal vb] Brit, informal : to move around slowly because you are unhappy • *I mooned about all day.* — **moon over** also US **moon after** [phrasal vb] : to spend too much time thinking about or looking at (someone or something that you admire or want very much) • *fans mooning over movie stars*

¹**moon·light** /ˈmuːnˌlaɪt/ n [U] : the light of the moon • *A figure appeared in the moonlight.* • *a moonlight cruise* [=a cruise at night]

²**moonlight** vb [I] : to work at a second job in addition to your regular job • *a secretary who moonlights as a waitress*

moon·lit /ˈmuːnˌlɪt/ adj : lighted by the moon • *a moonlit night/room*

moon·shine /ˈmuːnˌʃaɪn/ n [U] informal 1 chiefly US : a kind of alcohol that people make illegally • *a jug of moonshine* 2 Brit : NONSENSE • *That's a load of moonshine.*

¹**moor** /ˈmuɚ/ n [C] : a broad area of open land especially in Great Britain that is not good for farming • *the sun setting over the moors*

²**moor** vb [T/I] : to hold (a boat or ship) in place with ropes, cables, or an anchor • *We moored (the boat) for the night.*

Moor /ˈmuɚ/ n [C] : a member of a group of North African Arab people who ruled parts of Spain in the past — **Moor·ish** /ˈmuɚɪʃ/ adj • *Moorish architecture*

moor·ing /ˈmurɪŋ/ n 1 [C] : a place where a boat or ship can be moored • *a private mooring* 2 [plural] : the anchors, ropes, and cables that are used to hold a boat or ship in place • *The wind tore the boat from its moorings.*

moose /ˈmuːs/ n, pl **moose** [C] : a large animal with large, flat antlers that lives in northern America, Europe, and Asia

moot /ˈmuːt/ adj 1 : argued about but not possible for people to prove • *He says they could have foreseen the accident, but that point is moot.* [=debatable] 2 US

: no longer important or worth discussing • *Whether you agree or not, it's a moot point.*

¹**mop** /'mɑːp/ *n* [C] **1** : a tool for cleaning floors that has a bundle of cloth or yarn or a sponge attached to a long handle **2** : a large amount of untidy hair on a person's head • *a mop of hair*

²**mop** *vb* **mopped; mop·ping** **1** [T/I] : to clean (a floor) with a mop • *I just mopped (the floor).* **2** [T] **a** : to wipe (something that is wet) • *He mopped his brow.* **b** : to wipe (a liquid) from something • *He mopped the sweat from/off his brow.* — **mop up** [*phrasal vb*] **1 mop (something) up** *or* **mop up (something)** : to remove (a liquid) from a surface by using a mop, towel, etc. • *mop up the spill* **2 mop up** *or* **mop (something) up** *or* **mop up (something)** *informal* : to do the final things that are needed to complete a job or task • *Just let me mop up* [=*finish*] *a few things and I'll be done.*

mope /'moʊp/ *vb* **moped; mop·ing** [I] *disapproving* **1** : to behave in a way that shows you are unhappy and depressed • *He mopes when he doesn't get what he wants.* **2** : to move around slowly because you are unhappy • *I was moping around the house.*

mo·ped /'moʊˌpɛd/ *n* [C] : a kind of small motorcycle

¹**mor·al** /'mɔrəl/ *adj* **1** *always before a noun* : concerning, based on, or relating to what is right and wrong in human behavior • *moral* [=*ethical*] *issues* • *We have a moral obligation/duty to help the poor.* • *a woman with strong moral convictions* [=*who firmly believes that some things are right and others are wrong*] **2** : considered right and good by most people • *moral conduct* • *a moral man* = *a man who behaves in a moral way* — **moral support** : help that is given in the form of support or encouragement rather than money or practical help • *Her sisters gave her moral support.* — **moral victory** ◇ If you achieve a *moral victory* you do not win anything but you achieve something that is important and good. • *Although they lost, the minority claimed the vote as a moral victory since they had won the support of so many former opponents.*

²**moral** *n* **1** [C] : a lesson that is learned from a story or an experience • *The moral of the story is to be kind to strangers.* **2** [*plural*] : proper ideas and beliefs about how to behave in a way that is considered right and good by most people • *No one questions her morals.* [=no one doubts that she is a good and moral person] • *He has no morals.* [=he is not a good or honest person]

mo·rale /məˈræl/ *n* [U] : the feelings of enthusiasm that a person or group has about a task or job • *Employee morale is low.* [=employees do not feel happy about their work] • *boost/raise/improve the morale of the troops*

mor·al·ist /'mɔrəlɪst/ *n* [C] *usually disapproving* : a person who has strong opinions about what is right and who tries to control the moral behavior of other peo-

ple — **mor·al·is·tic** /ˌmɔrəˈlɪstɪk/ *adj* • *a moralistic speech/tone/attitude*

mo·ral·i·ty /məˈræləti/ *n, pl* **-ties** **1** [C/U] : beliefs about what is right behavior and what is wrong behavior • *a return to traditional morality* **2** [U] : the degree to which something is right and good • *The decision may be legally justified, but I question its morality.*

mor·al·ize *also Brit* **mor·al·ise** /'mɔrəˌlaɪz/ *vb* **-ized; -iz·ing** [I] *usually disapproving* : to express beliefs about what is good behavior and what is bad behavior • *moralizing about the evils of alcohol*

mor·al·ly /'mɔrəli/ *adv* : according to what is considered right and good by most people • *morally wrong/right* • *He acted morally.* [=in a moral way]

mo·rass /məˈræs/ *n* [C] : an area of soft, wet ground • *a morass of mud* • (*figurative*) *a legal morass*

mor·a·to·ri·um /ˌmɔrəˈtorijəm/ *n, pl* **-to·ri·ums** *or* **-to·ria** /-ˈtorijə/ [C] : a time when a particular activity is not allowed • *a moratorium on nuclear testing*

mor·bid /'mɔəbəd/ *adj* **1** : relating to unpleasant subjects (such as death) • *He has a morbid sense of humor.* • *a morbid fascination with death* **2** *technical* : not healthy or normal • *morbid obesity* — **mor·bid·ly** *adv*

¹**more** /'mɔə/ *adj* **1** : greater in amount, number, or size • *causing more pain/problems* • *Would you like more sugar?* • *More and more people* [=an increasingly large number of people] *are using e-mail.* • *The company has more than* [=*over*] *2,000 employees.* • *Choose no/not more than three options.* [=choose three options or fewer] **2** : extra or additional • *I bought more apples.* • *I offered him some more coffee.*

²**more** *adv* **1** : to a greater degree or extent • *The shot hurt more than I expected.* • *It happens more often than it used to.* • *a more comfortable position* • *It's the same product—they've done nothing more than change the label.* • *She is more an acquaintance than a friend.* • *It's getting more and more difficult* [=increasingly difficult] *to distinguish fake diamonds from real ones.* • *The fact that they'd written the play themselves made it all the more impressive.* **2** : more often or for a longer period of time • *She's a better piano player than I am because she practices more (than I do).* **3** : in addition • *wait one day more* — **more or less** **1** : not completely but to a great degree • *The clothes are more or less dry.* **2** — used to indicate that a number, amount, time, etc., is not exact or certain • *It should take you 20 minutes, more or less.* • *six more or less equal parts* — **more than** : to a great degree • *I am more than* [=*very*] *happy to help you.* • *He was more than a little* [=*very*] *surprised by her decision.* — **once more** see ¹**ONCE** — **what's more** see ¹**WHAT**

³**more** *pron* : a greater number or amount • *I need to spend less and save more.* • *You have more than everyone else.* • *It costs a little/much more for work with it.* • *We need 22 boxes—no more, no less.* • *more*

of — used to say that one way of describing a person or thing is better or more accurate than another ▪ *It's more of a guess than an estimate.* — **more's the pity** see ¹PITY — **more than meets the eye** see ¹EYE — **the more the merrier** see MERRY

more-over /moɚˈoʊvɚ/ *adv, somewhat formal* : in addition to what has been said ▪ *It probably wouldn't work. Moreover, it would be very expensive to try it.*

mo-res /ˈmoɚˌeɪz/ *n* [*plural*] : the customs, values, and behaviors that are accepted by a particular group, culture, etc. ▪ *social mores*

morgue /ˈmoɚg/ *n* [C] : a place where the bodies of dead people are kept until they are buried or cremated

mor-i-bund /ˈmoɚəˌbʌnd/ *adj, formal* : close to death ▪ *The patient was moribund.* ▪ *(figurative) a moribund economy*

Mor-mon /ˈmoɚmən/ *n* [C] : a member of the Church of Jesus Christ of Latter-day Saints — **Mor-mon-ism** /ˈmoɚməˌnɪzəm/ *n* [U]

morn /ˈmoɚn/ *n* [C/U] *literary* : MORNING

morn-ing /ˈmoɚnɪŋ/ *n* **1** [C/U] : the early part of the day : the time of day from sunrise until noon ▪ *I saw him this morning, and I'll be meeting with him again tomorrow morning.* ▪ *We have a meeting at 10 o'clock Wednesday morning.* ▪ *On Sunday mornings I like to relax and read the newspaper.* ▪ *the morning sun* ▪ *I'm a morning person.* [=a person who likes the early part of the day] **2** [U] : the part of the day between midnight and noon ▪ *The phone rang at 2 o'clock in the morning.* — **morning, noon, and night** : during all times of the day : all the time ▪ *We've been working morning, noon, and night.*

morning glory *n* [C] : a plant that has many brightly colored flowers that open in the morning

morning sickness *n* [U] : a feeling of sickness that a pregnant woman may feel especially early in the morning

mo-ron /ˈmoɚˌɑːn/ *n* [C] *informal* : a very stupid or foolish person ▪ *They were acting like a bunch of morons.* — **mo-ron-ic** /məˈrɑːnɪk/ *adj* ▪ *moronic behavior/humor*

mo-rose /məˈrous/ *adj* **1** *of a person* : very serious, unhappy, and quiet ▪ *He became morose and withdrawn.* **2** : very sad or unhappy ▪ *morose thoughts* — **mo-rose-ly** *adv*

morph /ˈmoɚf/ *vb* [T/I] : to change gradually and completely from one thing into another thing ▪ *a shy girl who has morphed into a glamorous actress*

mor-phine /ˈmoɚˌfiːn/ *n* [U] : a drug made from opium that is used to reduce pain

mor-phol-o-gy /moɚˈfɑːlədʒi/ *n, pl* **-gies 1** [U] *linguistics* : the study and description of how words are formed in language **2** *biology* **a** [U] : the study of the form and structure of animals and plants **b** [C/U] : the form and structure of a plant or animal or any of its parts ▪

plants with unusual morphologies — **mor-pho-log-i-cal** /ˌmoɚfəˈlɑːdʒɪkəl/ *adj*

Morse code /ˈmoɚs-/ *n* [U] : a system of sending messages that use long and short sounds, flashes of light, or marks to represent letters and numbers

mor-sel /ˈmoɚsəl/ *n* [C] : a small piece of food ▪ *tender morsels of beef* ▪ *(figurative) a juicy morsel of gossip*

¹**mor-tal** /ˈmoɚtl̩/ *adj* **1** : certain to die ▪ *mortal creatures* **2 a** : causing death ▪ *a mortal wound/injury* **b** : possibly causing death ▪ *facing mortal danger* **c** : relating to or connected with death ▪ *mortal agony* **3** *always before a noun* : very great or severe ▪ *She lived in mortal fear/terror/dread of being betrayed.* — **mortal enemy** *also* **mortal foe/rival** : someone you hate very much and for a long time — **mor-tal-ly** /ˈmoɚtl̩i/ *adv* ▪ *He was mortally* [=*fatally*] *wounded in the battle.*

²**mortal** *n* [C] : a human being ▪ *gods and mortals* ▪ *(humorous) He's a big star now. He doesn't waste his time talking to mere/lesser mortals like you and me.*

mor-tal-i-ty /moɚˈtæləti/ *n, pl* **-ties 1** [U] : the quality or state of being a person or thing that is alive and therefore certain to die ▪ *The news of her cousin's death reminded her of her own mortality.* **2** [C/U] : the death of a person, animal, etc. ▪ *cancer mortalities* [=*deaths caused by cancer*] **3** [U] : the number of deaths that occur in a particular time or place ▪ *efforts to reduce infant mortality* = *efforts to reduce the mortality rate among infants* [=to reduce the number of infants who die each year]

mor-tar /ˈmoɚtɚ/ *n* **1** [C] : a heavy, deep bowl in which seeds, spices, etc., are pounded or crushed with a heavy tool (called a pestle) **2** [C] : a military weapon used to fire shells into the air **3** [U] : a wet substance that is spread between bricks or stones and that holds them together when it hardens — **mortar** *vb* [T] ▪ *bricks mortared together*

mor-tar-board /ˈmoɚtɚˌboɚd/ *n* [C] : a hat with a flat square top that is worn for special ceremonies (such as graduations) at some schools

¹**mort-gage** /ˈmoɚgɪdʒ/ *n* [C] : a legal agreement in which a person borrows money to buy property (such as a house) and pays back the money over a period of years ▪ *They took out a mortgage to buy the house.*

²**mortgage** *vb* **-gaged; -gag-ing** [T] : to give someone a legal claim on (property that you own) in exchange for money that you will pay back over a period of years ▪ *She mortgaged her house in order to buy the restaurant.* — **mortgage the/your future** *chiefly US, disapproving* : to borrow a large amount of money that will have to be paid back in the future or to do something that may cause problems for you in the future ▪ *The city has mortgaged its future to pay for the new stadium.*

mort-gag-ee /ˌmoɚgɪˈdʒiː/ *n* [C] *law* : a

person or organization (such as a bank) that lends money to someone for buying property

mort·gag·or /ˌmɔɚgɪˈdʒoɚ/ n [C] law : a person who borrows money for buying property

mor·ti·cian /mɔɚˈtɪʃən/ n [C] US, formal : a person whose job is to prepare dead people to be buried and to arrange and manage funerals

mor·ti·fy /ˈmɔɚtəˌfaɪ/ vb **-fies**; **-fied**; **-fy·ing** [T] : to cause (someone) to feel very embarrassed and foolish ▪ Her behavior mortified her parents. = Her parents were mortified by her behavior. ▪ a mortifying experience — **mor·ti·fi·ca·tion** /ˌmɔɚtəfəˈkeɪʃən/ n [U] ▪ Imagine my mortification when I realized who she was!

mor·tu·ary /ˈmɔɚtʃəˌweri, Brit ˈmɔːtʃuəri/ n, pl **-ar·ies** [C] 1 US : FUNERAL HOME 2 chiefly Brit : MORGUE

mo·sa·ic /mouˈzejɪk/ n [C/U] : a decoration on a surface made by pressing small pieces of colored glass or stone into a soft material that then hardens

mo·sey /ˈmouzi/ vb [I] US, informal : to walk or move in a slow and relaxed way ▪ He moseyed up to the bar. ▪ I'm finished here, so I'll just mosey along [=leave] now.

Mos·lem /ˈmɑːzləm/ variant spelling of MUSLIM ◊ The spelling Moslem is old-fashioned and is sometimes considered offensive.

mosque /ˈmɑːsk/ n [C] : a building that is used for Muslim religious services

mos·qui·to /məˈskiːtou/ n, pl **-toes** also **-tos** [C] : a small flying insect that bites the skin of people and animals and sucks their blood

moss /ˈmɑːs/ n [C/U] : a type of green plant that has very small leaves and no flowers and that grows on rocks, bark, or wet ground — **mossy** /ˈmɑːsi/ adj **moss·i·er**; **-est** ▪ mossy rocks

¹**most** /ˈmoust/ adj 1 : almost all : the majority of ▪ Most people believe this. ▪ I like most foods. 2 : greatest in amount or degree ▪ Choosing a color took the most time. ▪ His science project got the most attention. — **for the most part** 1 : almost all or almost completely ▪ Menu items are, for the most part, under $5. 2 — used to describe a condition or situation that usually exists or is true ▪ Streets fill with people during the festival, but for the most part [=most of the time] it's a quiet town.

²**most** adv 1 : in or to the greatest degree ▪ Of all the gifts he received, the book pleased him most. ▪ What matters most to you? ▪ The island is the most southern in the chain. ▪ the most common/popular kind 2 somewhat formal : to a great extent : VERY ▪ He is a most careful driver. 3 US, informal : ALMOST ▪ The cost of most everything is higher. ▪ They most always skip lunch.

³**most** n — **at (the) most** : not more than a specified amount, level, etc. ▪ It took an hour at most. [=it took an hour or less than an hour] ▪ It costs, at the most, only a few dollars. — **make the most of** : to use (something) in a way that will get the best result ▪ She made the most of the op-

portunity. — **the most** : something of the greatest importance, strength, value, etc. ▪ The most I can give you is $10. [=I can give you $10, but I can't give you more than $10] ▪ A second chance is the most we can hope for.

⁴**most** pron 1 : the largest number of people or things ▪ Some of the chairs were broken, but most were in good condition. ▪ Most (of them) will appreciate the offer. 2 : the largest part of something ▪ Most of it is hidden from view.

most·ly /ˈmoustli/ adv 1 — used to say that a statement you are making is true or correct at most times or that it describes a usual situation or condition ▪ He gets around mostly by car. ▪ Today I worked in the yard, mostly. 2 : almost all or almost completely ▪ The story was mostly accurate. ▪ The people at the concert were mostly older people.

mo·tel /mouˈtɛl/ n [C] : a place that has rooms for people to stay in especially when they are traveling by car

moth /ˈmɑːθ/ n, pl **moths** /ˈmɑːðz/ [C] : a kind of insect that is similar to a butterfly but that flies mostly at night and is usually less colorful

¹**moth·ball** /ˈmɑːθˌbɑːl/ n 1 [C] : a small ball that contains a strong-smelling chemical and that is used to keep moths away from stored clothing 2 [plural] : the state of being stored somewhere for a long time ▪ The ship was put in/into mothballs after the war. ▪ The old ship is being taken out of mothballs.

²**mothball** vb [T] : to stop using (something) while keeping it to be possibly used in the future ▪ Many ships were mothballed after the war.

moth-eat·en /ˈmɑːθˌiːtn/ adj : having holes caused by moths : eaten into by moths ▪ a moth-eaten sweater/sofa ▪ (figurative) a moth-eaten [=outdated] computer system

¹**moth·er** /ˈmʌðɚ/ n [C] 1 : a female parent ▪ She became a mother when she was in her 20s. ▪ She's the mother of three small children. 2 : a woman who is thought of as being like a mother ▪ She was a mother to me after my own mother died. 3 : a woman who invents or begins something ▪ the mother of an important social movement 4 : MOTHER SUPERIOR — used especially as a title or as a form of address ▪ Mother Teresa — **necessity is the mother of invention** — used to say that new ways to do things are found or created when there is a strong and special need for them — **moth·er·hood** /ˈmʌðɚˌhud/ n [U] — **moth·er·less** /ˈmʌðɚləs/ adj

²**mother** vb [T] 1 : to give birth to (a child) ▪ She mothered two sons but no daughters. 2 : to be or act as mother to (someone) ▪ He says he's old enough to care for himself and he doesn't want to be mothered.

moth·er·board /ˈmʌðɚˌboɚd/ n [C] : the main circuit board of a computer

mother figure n [C] : an older woman who is respected and admired like a mother

mother hen n [C] : a person who cares

moth·er-in-law /ˈmʌðərənˌlɑː/ n, pl **moth·ers-in-law** /ˈmʌðəzənˌlɑː/ [C] : the mother of your husband or wife

moth·er·land /ˈmʌðərˌlænd/ n [C] : the country where you were born or where your family came from ▪ She still spoke the language of her motherland. ▪ They wanted to return to the motherland. ✧ Motherland is often associated with Russia.

mother lode n [C] chiefly US : the place where the largest amount of gold, silver, etc., in a particular area can be found ▪ The miners struck/hit the mother lode. ▪ (figurative) The book is a mother lode of information.

moth·er·ly /ˈmʌðəli/ adj : of a mother ▪ motherly duties/instincts : resembling a mother ▪ a motherly nurse : showing the affection or concern of a mother ▪ motherly advice

Mother Nature n [singular] — used to refer to the natural world as if it were a woman ▪ the forces of Mother Nature

moth·er-of-pearl /ˌmʌðərəvˈpɚl/ n [U] : a hard, shiny, smooth substance that is on the insides of the shells of some shellfish

Mother's Day n [C/U] : the second Sunday in May in the U.S. and the fourth Sunday in Lent in Britain treated as a special day for honoring mothers

mother ship n [C] : a large ship or spaceship that sends out boats or smaller spaceships to explore, do scientific research, etc.

Mother Superior n [C] : a woman who is the head of a convent

mother tongue n [C] : the language that a person learns to speak first

mo·tif /moʊˈtiːf/ n [C] **1** : an idea, subject, etc., that is repeated throughout a book, story, etc. **2** : a single or repeated design or pattern ▪ The wallpaper has a flower motif.

¹mo·tion /ˈmoʊʃən/ n **1 a** [C/U] : an act or process of moving : MOVEMENT ▪ the rhythmic motion(s) of the waves **b** [C] : a movement of your body or of a part of your body ▪ He made hand motions to get our attention. **2** [C] : a formal suggestion, proposal, or request that is made at a meeting for something to be done or happen ▪ She made a motion that the meeting (should) be adjourned. ▪ The judge denied a motion to delay the hearing. **3** [C] Brit, medical **a** : an act of passing solid waste from the body ▪ a bowel motion **b** : the solid waste that is passed from the body — **go through the motions** : to do something without making much effort to do it well ▪ He claimed that he was looking for a job, but he was really just going through the motions. — **in motion 1** : moving ▪ photographs of people in motion **2** ✧ When a plan, process, etc., is in motion or has been set in motion or put in/into motion, it has begun and is proceeding. — **mo·tion·less** /ˈmoʊʃənləs/ adj

²motion vb [T/I] : to make a movement of your hand, head, etc., that tells someone to move or act in a certain way ▪ They motioned me to come forward. ▪ She motioned to her assistant.

motion picture n [C] US : MOVIE, FILM ▪ a major motion picture ▪ the motion-picture industry

motion sickness n [U] : a feeling of sickness caused by the motion of a car, airplane, boat, etc.

mo·ti·vate /ˈmoʊtəˌveɪt/ vb **-vat·ed; -vat·ing** [T] : to give someone a reason for doing something ▪ methods to motivate employees to work harder ▪ Political pressures motivated his decision to resign. ▪ a crime motivated by racism = a racially motivated crime — **motivated** adj ▪ a highly motivated employee — **mo·ti·va·tion** /ˌmoʊtəˈveɪʃən/ n [C/U] ▪ employees who lack motivation ▪ There seemed to be no motivation [=reason] for his behavior. — **mo·ti·va·tion·al** /ˌmoʊtəˈveɪʃənl/ adj ▪ a motivational speech [=a speech made to motivate people] — **mo·ti·va·tor** /ˈmoʊtəˌveɪtɚ/ n [C]

¹mo·tive /ˈmoʊtɪv/ n [C] : a reason for doing something ▪ the motive for the crime ▪ Her offer to help was based on selfish motives. — **mo·tive·less** /ˈmoʊtɪvləs/ adj

²motive adj, always before a noun, technical : of, relating to, or causing motion ▪ motive power

mot·ley /ˈmɑːtli/ adj, usually disapproving : made up of many different people or things ▪ a motley group of musicians

¹mo·tor /ˈmoʊtɚ/ n [C] **1** : a machine that produces motion or power for doing work ▪ electric/gasoline motors **2** chiefly Brit, informal + old-fashioned : CAR — **mo·tor·less** /ˈmoʊtɚləs/ adj

²motor adj, always before a noun **1 a** : of, relating to, used in, or involving a vehicle that is powered by a motor (such as a car or motorcycle) ▪ a motor trip/accident ▪ motor oil/sports **b** : having a motor ▪ a motor cart **2** technical : of or relating to the part of the nervous system that controls the movement of muscles ▪ motor nerves/activities

³motor vb [I] : to travel in a car : DRIVE ▪ We motored through the countryside. ▪ The car motored slowly up the hill.

mo·tor·bike /ˈmoʊtɚˌbaɪk/ n [C] **1** US : a small motorcycle **2** Brit : MOTORCYCLE

mo·tor·boat /ˈmoʊtɚˌboʊt/ n [C] : a boat with a motor

mo·tor·cade /ˈmoʊtɚˌkeɪd/ n [C] : a group or line of cars or other vehicles that travel together

mo·tor·car /ˈmoʊtɚˌkɑɚ/ n [C] old-fashioned : CAR

mo·tor·cy·cle /ˈmoʊtɚˌsaɪkəl/ n [C] : a vehicle with two wheels that is powered by a motor and that can carry one or two people — **mo·tor·cy·clist** /ˈmoʊtɚˌsaɪkəlɪst/ n [C]

motor home n [C] : a type of vehicle that people can live and sleep in when they are traveling

mo·tor·ist /ˈmoʊtərɪst/ n [C] : a person who drives a car ▪ When our car broke down, we were helped by a passing motorist.

mo·tor·ized also Brit **mo·tor·ised**

/ˈmoʊtəˌraɪzd/ adj **1** : having a motor • motorized vehicles **2** : using motorized vehicles • motorized troops

mo·tor·mouth /ˈmoʊtəˌmaʊθ/ n [C] informal : a person who talks too much

motor scooter n [C] : a small vehicle with two wheels that is powered by a motor and that has a low seat and a flat area for resting your feet — called also scooter

motor vehicle n [C] : a vehicle (such as a car, truck, or motorcycle) that is powered by a motor

mo·tor·way /ˈmoʊtəˌweɪ/ n [C] Brit : a large highway

mot·tled /ˈmɑːtld/ adj : marked with colored spots or areas • mottled leaves/skin

mot·to /ˈmɑːtoʊ/ n, pl -toes also -tos [C] : a short sentence or phrase that expresses a rule guiding the behavior of a particular person or group • The Boy Scout motto is "Be prepared."

mould, moulding, mouldy Brit spellings of MOLD, MOLDING, MOLDY

mound /ˈmaʊnd/ n [C] **1** : a small hill or pile of dirt or stones • the burial mounds of an ancient people **2** : the slightly raised area of ground on which a baseball pitcher stands **3** : a heap or pile of something • a mound of dirty laundry

¹**mount** /ˈmaʊnt/ vb **1** [T] : to go or climb up (something) • mount a ladder **2** [I] : to increase in amount • Their troubles have continued to mount. • Costs can mount (up) quickly. **3** [T/I] : to seat yourself on a horse, bicycle, etc. • The cowboy mounted his horse and rode off. = The cowboy mounted (up) and rode off. **4** [T] : to attach (something) to something for support or use • The jeweler mounted the pearl in a ring. • The speakers were mounted on the walls. **5** [T] : to organize and do (something) • The soldiers mounted an attack.

²**mount** n [C] **1** : something onto which something else is or can be attached • a lens mount [=the part of a camera where a lens is attached] **2** old-fashioned + literary : a horse that is being ridden • The cowboy got down slowly from his mount. **3** : MOUNTAIN 1 • Mount Everest

moun·tain /ˈmaʊntn/ n [C] **1** : an area of land that rises very high above the land around it and that is higher than a hill • a cabin in the mountains • mountain climbing **2** : a very large amount of something • a mountain of mail/data

mountain bike n [C] : a type of bicycle that has a strong frame, thick tires, and straight handlebars and that is used for riding over rough ground

moun·tain·eer /ˌmaʊntəˈnɪə/ n [C] : a person who climbs mountains — **moun·tain·eer·ing** /ˌmaʊntəˈnɪrɪŋ/ n [U] • the sport of mountaineering

mountain goat n [C] : an animal that has horns and a thick white coat and that lives in the mountains of western North America

mountain lion n [C] : COUGAR

moun·tain·ous /ˈmaʊntənəs/ adj **1** : having many mountains • a mountainous area **2** : extremely large • mountainous waves

moun·tain·side /ˈmaʊntnˌsaɪd/ n [C] : the side of a mountain • a steep mountainside

moun·tain·top /ˈmaʊntnˌtɑːp/ n [C] : the top of a mountain • a snowy mountaintop

mount·ed /ˈmaʊntəd/ adj : having a horse or horses for riding • a mounted policeman

Mount·ie /ˈmaʊnti/ n [C] : a member of the Royal Canadian Mounted Police

mourn /ˈmoən/ vb [T/I] : to feel or show great sadness especially because someone has died • Thousands of people mourned his death. = Thousands mourned for him. • She mourned for her lost youth. — **mourn·er** /ˈmoənə/ n [C]

mourn·ful /ˈmoənfəl/ adj : full of sorrow : very sad • a mournful face/occasion — **mourn·ful·ly** /ˈmoənfəli/ adv

mourn·ing /ˈmoənɪŋ/ n [U] **1** : the act of mourning for someone who has died • a day of national mourning • She is still in mourning for her dead husband. **2** : great sadness felt because someone has died • a period of deep mourning **3** : black clothing that is worn to show that you are mourning for someone who has died • His widow was dressed in mourning.

mouse /ˈmaʊs/ n, pl mice /ˈmaɪs/ [C] **1** : a very small animal that has a pointed nose and a long, thin tail **2** pl also **mous·es** : a small device that is connected to a computer and that you move with your hand to control the movement of a pointer on the computer screen

mouse·trap /ˈmaʊsˌtræp/ n [C] : a small trap for catching mice

mousse /ˈmuːs/ n [C/U] **1** : a cold and sweet food made with whipped cream or egg whites and usually fruit or chocolate • chocolate mousse **2** : a foamy substance that is used in styling a person's hair

moustache chiefly Brit spelling of MUSTACHE

mousy also **mous·ey** /ˈmaʊsi/ adj **mous·i·er; -est 1** : shy and quiet • a mousy young woman **2** : dull brown in color • mousy brown hair

¹**mouth** /ˈmaʊθ/ n, pl mouths /ˈmaʊðz/ **1** [C/U] : the opening through which food passes into the body • He threatened to punch me in the mouth. • The candy melts in your mouth. **2** [C] : an opening in something • the mouth of a cave/bottle **3** [C] : the place where a river enters the ocean • the mouth of the river = the river's mouth **4** [singular] informal : an unpleasant or offensive way of talking • That guy has quite a mouth on him. • He cursed and his mother angrily told him to **watch his mouth**. [=to not use offensive language] — **by word of mouth** see ¹WORD — **down in the mouth**: unhappy or depressed — **from the horse's mouth** see ¹HORSE — **hand to mouth** see ¹HAND — **keep your mouth shut** : to not say anything • When he starts talking about politics, I just keep my mouth shut. • She told me to keep my mouth shut about the news. [=she told me not to tell anyone about the news] —

mouth to feed : a person (such as a child) who needs to be fed ▪ *They can't afford another child. They already have too many (hungry) mouths to feed.* — **put words in/into someone's mouth** see ¹WORD — **put your foot in your mouth** see ¹FOOT — **run your mouth** see ¹RUN — **shoot your mouth off** see ¹SHOOT — **shut your mouth** see ¹SHUT — **take the words right out of someone's mouth** see ¹WORD

²**mouth** /ˈmaʊð/ *vb* [T] **1** : to say or repeat (something) without really meaning it or understanding it ▪ *She was mouthing meaningless slogans.* **2** : to form (words) with your lips without speaking ▪ *silently mouthing the words to a song* — **mouth off** [phrasal vb] *informal* : to talk in a loud, unpleasant, or rude way ▪ *He got in trouble for mouthing off to his teacher.*

-mouthed /ˌmaʊðd/ *adj* : having a mouth of a specified type ▪ *big-mouthed* ▪ *loudmouthed*

mouth·ful /ˈmaʊθˌfʊl/ *n* [C] : as much as a mouth will hold ▪ *a mouthful of food* **2** [*singular*] *informal* **a** : a word, name, or phrase that is very long or difficult to say ▪ *His last name is a real mouthful.* **b** *US* : something said that has a lot of meaning or importance ▪ *You said a mouthful!*

mouth·piece /ˈmaʊθˌpiːs/ *n* [C] **1** : a part of something that is placed between or near your lips ▪ *the mouthpiece of a trumpet/telephone* **2** : someone who speaks for another person or for a group or organization ▪ *The company hired an attorney as a mouthpiece to answer its critics.*

mouth–to–mouth resuscitation *n* [U] : a method of helping a person who is not breathing to start breathing again by blowing air into the person's mouth and lungs — called also **mouth-to-mouth**

mouth·wash /ˈmaʊθˌwɑːʃ/ *n* [C/U] : a liquid that is used to clean your mouth and teeth and to make your breath smell better

mouth–wa·ter·ing /ˈmaʊθˌwɑːtərɪŋ/ *adj* : having a very delicious taste or appealing smell ▪ *mouth-watering aromas/foods*

mov·able *also* **move·able** /ˈmuːvəbəl/ *adj* : able to be moved ▪ *a movable antenna*

¹**move** /ˈmuːv/ *vb* **moved; mov·ing** **1** [T/I] : to go or cause (something or someone) to go from one place or position to another ▪ *The branches moved gently in the breeze.* ▪ *He moved the chair closer to the table.* ▪ *They moved the patient to intensive care.* ▪ *The team moved (up) into second place.* **2 a** [T/I] : to cause (your body or a part of your body) to go from one position to another ▪ *She was unable to move her legs.* ▪ *I moved over so that she could sit next to me.* — *Nobody moved a muscle.* [=nobody moved at all] **b** [I] : to go or walk from one place to another ▪ *We moved into the shade.* **3** [T] **a** : to cause (something) to go to a specified place or to proceed in a specified way ▪ *She moved large amounts of money to a foreign bank account.* **b** : to cause (something) to happen at a different time ▪ *The meeting has been moved to this afternoon.* **4** [T/I] : to change the place where you live, work, etc. ▪ *He moved to the city.* ▪ *The company is moving (its offices) from New York to Chicago.* ▪ *(Brit)* *We've had to move house twice in the past year.* **5** [T] **a** : to affect the feelings of (someone) : to cause (someone) to feel an emotion and especially sadness or sympathy ▪ *The sad story moved us deeply.* ▪ *I was greatly moved by his kindness.* ▪ *He's not easily moved to anger.* [=he does not become angry easily] **b** : to cause (someone) to act or think in a specified way ▪ *His argument moved them to reconsider the plan.* **6** [I] : to take action : ACT ▪ *We need to move quickly to close this deal.* **7** [T/I] : to formally make a suggestion, proposal, or request at a meeting ▪ *She moved to adjourn the meeting.* ▪ *His lawyer moved for a mistrial.* **8** [I] : to make progress ▪ *They're moving closer to making a decision.* **9** [T/I] *informal* : SELL ▪ *a store that moves a lot of merchandise* **10** [I] *informal* : to go fast ▪ *When the police car passed us it was really moving.* **11** [I] : to spend time with a particular group of people or at a particular level of society ▪ *She moves in high circles.* [=she is friendly with wealthy and powerful people] — **move ahead/along 1** : to make progress ▪ *The project is starting to move ahead.* **2** : to go on to something else ▪ *Let's move along to the next item.* — **move heaven and earth** : to work very hard to do something ▪ *He said he'd move heaven and earth to finish the project on schedule.* — **move in** [phrasal vb] **1** : to start living in a house, apartment, etc. ▪ *He moved in with his girlfriend.* **2 move in on** : to move closer or nearer to (someone or something that you are trying to reach, get, etc.) ▪ *The lion moved in on its prey.* — **move in** *US*, *informal* : to start moving or going quickly ▪ *We'd better move it if we don't want to be late.* — **move on** [phrasal vb] : to go on to a different place, subject, activity, etc. ▪ *Let's put that issue aside and move on.* — **move out** [phrasal vb] : to leave your house, apartment, etc., and go to live somewhere else ▪ *He was 20 when he moved out (of his parents' house).*

²**move** *n* [C] **1** : an act of moving your body or a part of your body ▪ *fancy dance moves* ▪ *No one made a move toward the exits.* **2** : an action ▪ *They're watching his every move.* = *They're watching every move he makes.* [=watching everything he does] ▪ **3** : the act of moving to a different place ▪ *He's preparing for his move to California.* **4** : something done to achieve a desired result or goal ▪ *Starting her own business was a risky/bold move.* **5** : an act of moving a piece in a game ▪ *the opening moves in a game of chess* — **get a move on** *informal* : to start moving or going quickly — **on the move 1** : moving or going from place to place ▪ *As a young man, he was always*

on the move. **2** : making progress ▪ *After a slow start, the project is finally on the move.*

move·ment /'muːvmənt/ *n* **1** [C/U] **a** : the act or process of moving people or things from one place or position to another ▪ *a system for the movement of raw materials to the factory* **b** : the act of moving from one place, position, etc., to another ▪ *cell movement* ▪ *the graceful movements of a dancer* **2** [*plural*] : a person's actions or activities ▪ *The police have been watching his movements.* **3** [C] : a series of organized activities in which many people work together to do or achieve something ▪ *the civil rights movement* **4** [C/U] **a** : a noticeable change in the way people behave or think ▪ *There has been a/some movement back to older methods in recent years.* **b** : a noticeable change in a situation ▪ *There hasn't been any movement in the negotiations.* **5** [C] *music* : a main section of a longer piece of music ▪ *the first movement of the symphony* **6** [C] *medical* : an act of passing solid waste from the body — called also *bowel movement*

mov·er /'muːvə/ *n* [C] **1** : someone or something that moves in a certain way ▪ *a slow/fast mover* **2** : a machine that moves people or things from one place to another **3** *US* : a person or company that moves furniture and other possessions from one home or place of business to another — *movers and shakers* : people who are active or powerful in some field ▪ *political movers and shakers*

mov·ie /'muːvi/ *n, chiefly US* **1** [C] : a recording of moving images that tells a story and that people watch on a screen or television ▪ *a Hollywood movie* [=*film*] ▪ *a movie star/producer/director* **2** *the movies* **a** : a showing of a movie in a theater ▪ *We're going to the movies tonight.; also* : a movie theater ▪ *What's (playing/showing) at the movies?* **b** : the business of making movies : the film industry ▪ *a career in the movies*

moving *adj* **1** : changing place or position ▪ *the machine's moving parts* **2** : having a strong emotional effect ▪ *a moving story* — *moving force/spirit* : someone or something that causes something to happen ▪ *He was the moving force/spirit behind the project.* — **mov·ing·ly** *adv*

moving picture *n* [C] *old-fashioned* : MOVIE

moving van *n* [C] *US* : a large vehicle in which furniture and other things are moved from one home or building to another

mow /'moʊ/ *vb* **mowed; mowed** *or* **mown** /'moʊn/; **mow·ing** [T] : to cut (something) with a machine or a blade ▪ *mow the grass/lawn* — *mow down* [*phrasal vb*] *mow (someone) down or mow down (someone) informal* : to kill or knock down (a person or many people) in a sudden and violent way ▪ *The soldiers were mowed down by machine guns.* — **mow·er** /'moʊə/ *n* [C]

moz·za·rel·la /ˌmɑːtsəˈrɛlə/ *n* [U] : a soft Italian cheese that has a mild flavor

MP /'ɛmˈpiː/ *n* [C] **1** : a member of the military police **2** *Brit* : an elected member of Parliament

mpg *abbr* miles per gallon ▪ *a car that gets 30 mpg*

mph *abbr* miles per hour ▪ *a car traveling 60 mph*

MP3 /ˌɛmˌpiːˈθriː/ *n* [C/U] : a computer format for creating sound files (such as songs) or a file created in that format ▪ *an MP3 player* [=a device that stores and plays songs in the MP3 format]

Mr. (*US*) *or Brit* **Mr** /'mɪstə/ *n* **1** — used as a title before the name of a man or his title of office ▪ *Mr. Jones* ▪ *Mr. President* **2** — used as a title when speaking to a man who has an honored position or office ▪ *"It's an honor to meet you, Mr. President/Chairman."*

MRI /ˌɛmˌɑːˈraɪ/ *n, medical* **1** [U] : MAGNETIC RESONANCE IMAGING **2** [C] : a procedure in which magnetic resonance imaging is used ▪ *He had an MRI (done) on his knee.*

Mrs. (*US*) *or Brit* **Mrs** /'mɪsəz/ *n* — used as a title for a married woman ▪ *Mrs. Smith* ▪ *Mrs. Jane Smith* ▪ *Mrs. Robert Smith* [=the wife of Robert Smith]

Ms. (*US*) *or Brit* **Ms** /'mɪz/ *n* — used as a title before a woman's name instead of *Miss* or *Mrs.* ▪ *Ms. Smith*

MS *abbr* **1** Mississippi **2** multiple sclerosis

MT *abbr* Montana

¹much /'mʌtʃ/ *adj* : large in amount or extent ▪ *There isn't much difference between them.* ▪ *Fixing the problem will require much effort.* [=a lot of effort] ▪ *How much time do you have?* ▪ *It doesn't cost much money.* ▪ *The project is taking too much time.* [=is taking more time than it should] — *too much* **1** : too difficult to accept or deal with ▪ *Working two jobs was too much (for him).* **2** *informal* : very unusual in either an enjoyable or annoying way ▪ *I can't believe the way he talks. That guy is too much.*

²much *adv* **1** : to a great degree or extent ▪ *I'm feeling much better.* ▪ *Do you travel much?* [=frequently, often] ▪ *a much-deserved vacation* ▪ *He didn't arrive much before noon.* [=he didn't arrive until almost noon] ▪ *They both talk too much.* **2** : very nearly ▪ *The town looks much the way it did years ago.* — *as much* : the same ▪ *He likes baseball but he likes hockey just as much.* — *much less* see ²LESS — *pretty much* see ²PRETTY — *so much as* see ¹SO — *so much the better* see ³BETTER — *very much* — used for emphasis ▪ *She is very much in control of the situation.*

³much *pron* **1** : a large amount ▪ *Much that was said is false.* ▪ *He gave away much of what he owned.* ▪ *She did much to improve the city.* ▪ *She's trying to do too much.* [=trying to do more than she should] **2** : something that is important or impressive ▪ *The evidence didn't amount to much.* ▪ *The house is not much to look at.* — *as much as* — used to say that an amount is as large as another amount ▪ *She earns as much as he does.* — *make much of* see ¹MAKE — *not*

much of a — used to say that someone or something is not very good • *He's not much of a cook.* — **not much on** : not known for, good at, or interested in (something) • *He's not much on looks.* [=he is not very attractive] — **not think much of** see THINK — **so much** see ¹SO

¹muck /'mʌk/ n [U] *informal* **1** : wet dirt or mud • *Clean that muck off your shoes.* **2** *chiefly Brit* : MANURE — **mucky** /'mʌki/ *adj* **muck·i·er; -est** • *mucky shoes*

²muck vb — **muck about/around** [*phrasal vb*] *Brit, informal* **1** : to spend time doing things that are not useful or serious : to waste time • *We just mucked about all afternoon.* **2 muck (someone) about/around** : to be unfair or dishonest with (someone) • *I want them to stop mucking me around.* — **muck in** [*phrasal vb*] *Brit, informal* : to help out especially by doing work — **muck out** [*phrasal vb*] **muck (something) out** or **muck out (something)** *informal* : to clean (the place where a farm animal lives) • *mucking out the stalls* — **muck up** [*phrasal vb*] **muck (something) up** or **muck up (something)** *chiefly Brit, informal* **1** : to make (something) dirty • *His dirty shoes mucked up the floor.* **2** : to make mistakes in doing or making (something) • *He mucked up the speech.*

muck·rak·er /'mʌkˌreɪkə/ n [C] : someone (such as a reporter) who tries to find embarrassing or shocking information about famous people — **muck·rak·ing** /'mʌkˌreɪkɪŋ/ n [U]

mu·cus /'mju:kəs/ n [U] : a thick liquid that is produced in some parts of the body (such as the nose and throat)

mud /'mʌd/ n [U] : soft, wet dirt • *The car was stuck in the mud.* — **sling/throw mud** *chiefly US* : to publicly say false or bad things about someone • *The candidates started slinging mud (at each other) early in the campaign.* — **your name is mud** *informal* ✧ If *your name is mud*, people do not like or trust you.

¹mud·dle /'mʌdl/ vb **mud·dled; mud·dling** [T] **1** : to cause confusion in (someone or someone's mind) • *a mind muddled by too much advice* : to mix up (something) in a confused way • *I always get their names muddled (up).* — **muddle along** [*phrasal vb*] *informal* : to think, act, or proceed in a confused way or without a plan • *She muddled along for a few years before going to college.* — **muddle through** [*phrasal vb*] *informal* : to do something without doing it very well or easily • *I had a hard time with the class, but somehow I muddled through.*

²muddle n [*singular*] **1** : a state of confusion or disorder • *Her thoughts were in a muddle.* **2** : a confused mess • *a muddle of documents*

¹mud·dy /'mʌdi/ *adj* **mud·di·er; -est 1** : filled or covered with mud • *a muddy pond* **2** : similar to mud • *muddy coffee* **3** : not clear or bright • *a muddy recording* • *muddy thinking*

²muddy vb **-dies; -died; -dy·ing** [T] **1** : to cover (something) with mud • *His shoes were muddied.* **2** : to cause (some-

thing) to become unclear or confused • *muddying the line between fact and fiction* — **muddy the waters** : to make something more complicated or difficult to understand • *The latest study muddies the waters by suggesting an alternate explanation.*

mud flap n [C] : a sheet of thin material that hangs behind a wheel of a vehicle and that stops mud and water from hitting the vehicle or other vehicles

mud·guard /'mʌdˌgɑːd/ n [C] **1** *US* : MUD FLAP **2** *Brit* : FENDER 2

mud·room /'mʌdˌruːm/ n [C] *US* : a room at an entrance to a house where people can leave wet or dirty shoes and clothing

mud·slide /'mʌdˌslaɪd/ n [C] : a large mass of wet earth that suddenly and quickly moves down the side of a mountain or hill

mud·sling·ing /'mʌdˌslɪŋɪŋ/ n [U] : the act or practice of publicly saying false or bad things about someone (such as a political opponent) in order to harm that person's reputation — **mud·sling·er** /'mʌdˌslɪŋə/ n [C]

¹muff /'mʌf/ n [C] : a warm covering for your hands that is shaped like a tube with open ends in which both hands may be placed

²muff vb [T] *informal* : to make a mistake in doing or handling (something) • *The outfielder muffed an easy catch.*

muf·fin /'mʌfən/ n [C] **1** : a small bread or cake that is usually eaten at breakfast • *a blueberry muffin* **2** *Brit* : ENGLISH MUFFIN

muf·fle /'mʌfəl/ vb **muf·fled; muf·fling** [T] **1** : to make (a sound) quieter • *They tried to muffle the noise.* : to decrease the noise made by (something) • *muffle a cough* **2** *chiefly Brit* : to wrap or cover (someone or something) in clothing or cloth for warmth or protection • *She was muffled (up) in a huge overcoat.*

muf·fler /'mʌflə/ n [C] **1** *US* : a device that is attached to the engine of a vehicle to make it quieter — called also (*Brit*) **silencer** **2** : a scarf worn around your neck

¹mug /'mʌg/ n [C] **1** : a large drinking cup with a handle • *a beer/coffee mug* **2** *slang* : the face or mouth of a person • *his ugly mug* **3** *Brit, informal* : a foolish person who is easily tricked

²mug vb **mugged; mug·ging 1** [T] : to attack and rob (someone) • *He was mugged in the park.* **2** [I] *chiefly US* : to act or pose in a silly way or make silly facial expressions especially to attract attention or when being photographed • *She was mugging for the camera/crowd.* — **mug up** [*phrasal vb*] **mug up** or **mug (something) up** or **mug up (something)** or **mug up on (something)** *Brit, informal* : to study or try to learn a lot of information quickly for a test, exam, etc. • *She had better mug up (on his background) before she interviews him.*

mug·ger /'mʌgə/ n [C] : a person who attacks and robs someone

mugging n [C/U] : the act of attacking

and robbing someone ▪ *There have been several muggings in the park recently.*

mug·gy /ˈmʌgi/ *adj* **mug·gi·er; -est** : unpleasantly warm and humid ▪ *a muggy day* ▪ *muggy weather*

mug shot *n* [C] : a photograph taken by the police of someone who has been arrested

mul·ber·ry /ˈmʌlˌberi, *Brit* ˈmʌlbəri/ *n, pl* **-ries** [C] **1** : a type of tree that has purple berries that can be eaten **2** : a berry from a mulberry tree

mulch /ˈmʌltʃ/ *n* [C/U] : a material (such as straw, leaves, or small pieces of wood) that is spread in a garden to protect the plants or help them grow and to stop weeds from growing — **mulch** *vb* [T] ▪ *She mulched* [=spread mulch in] *the flower beds.*

mule /ˈmjuːl/ *n* [C] : an animal that has a horse and a donkey as parents

mull /ˈmʌl/ *vb* [T] : to think about (something) slowly and carefully — usually + *over* ▪ *They're mulling the offer over.*

mul·let /ˈmələt/ *n* **1** *pl* **mullet** or **mullets** [C/U] : a type of fish that lives in the ocean and is often eaten as food **2** *pl* **mullets** [C] : a hairstyle in which the hair is short on the top and sides and long in the back

multi- *combining form* **1 a** : many : much ▪ *multicolored* **b** : more than two ▪ *multinational* **2** : many times over ▪ *multimillionaire*

mul·ti·col·ored (*US*) or *Brit* **mul·ti·col·oured** /ˈmʌltiˌkʌləd/ *adj* : having, made up of, or including many colors ▪ *multicolored balloons*

mul·ti·cul·tur·al /ˌmʌltiˈkʌltʃərəl/ *adj* : relating to or including many different cultures ▪ *a multicultural society* — **mul·ti·cul·tur·al·ism** /ˌmʌltiˈkʌltʃərəlɪzəm/ *n* [U]

mul·ti·eth·nic /ˌmʌltiˈɛθnɪk/ *adj* : relating to or including people from many ethnic groups ▪ *a multiethnic country*

mul·ti·fac·et·ed /ˌmʌltiˈfæsətəd/ *adj* : having many different parts ▪ *a multifaceted approach to health care*

mul·ti·far·i·ous /ˌmʌltəˈferijəs/ *adj, formal* : of many and various kinds ▪ *multifarious activities*

mul·ti·lat·er·al /ˌmʌltiˈlætərəl/ *adj* : involving more than two groups or countries ▪ *a multilateral treaty*

mul·ti·lay·ered /ˌmʌltiˈlejəd/ *adj* : having or involving three or more layers or levels ▪ *a multilayered cake/plot*

mul·ti·lin·gual /ˌmʌltiˈlɪŋgwəl/ *adj* **1** : able to speak and understand several languages ▪ *multilingual students* **2** : using or expressed in several languages ▪ *multilingual countries*

mul·ti·me·dia /ˌmʌltiˈmiːdijə/ *adj, always before a noun* : using or involving several forms of communication or expression ▪ *a multimedia exhibit of photographs, films, and music*

mul·ti·mil·lion·aire /ˌmʌltiˌmɪljəˈneə/ *n* [C] : a person who has property or money worth millions of dollars or pounds

¹**mul·ti·na·tion·al** /ˌmʌltiˈnæʃənəl/ *adj* **1** : of, relating to, or involving more than two nations ▪ *a multinational alliance* **2** : working in several countries ▪ *a multinational corporation*

²**multinational** *n* [C] : a company that works in several countries

¹**mul·ti·ple** /ˈmʌltəpəl/ *adj, always before a noun* **1** : more than one ▪ *He suffered multiple injuries in the accident.* ▪ *a multiple birth* [=the birth of more than one baby at a time] **2** : shared by many people ▪ *multiple ownership*

²**multiple** *n* [C] *mathematics* : a number that can be produced by multiplying a smaller number ▪ *12 is a multiple of 6.*

multiple–choice *adj* **1** : having several answers from which one is to be chosen ▪ *a multiple-choice question* **2** : made up of multiple-choice questions ▪ *a multiple-choice test*

multiple sclerosis *n* [U] : a disease of the nervous system that causes the gradual loss of muscle control

mul·ti·pli·ca·tion /ˌmʌltəpləˈkeɪʃən/ *n* **1** [U] *mathematics* : the process of adding a number to itself a certain number of times ▪ *Students are learning multiplication and division.* **2** [U, *singular*] : an increase in the number or amount of something ▪ *(an) uncontrolled multiplication of cells*

multiplication sign *n* [C] *mathematics* : a symbol (such as "x") that is used to show that two numbers are to be multiplied

mul·ti·plic·i·ty /ˌmʌltəˈplɪsəti/ *n* [*singular*] *formal* : a very large number ▪ *a multiplicity of colors*

mul·ti·ply /ˈmʌltəˌplaɪ/ *vb* **-plies; -plied; -ply·ing** [T/I] **1** : to increase or cause (something) to increase greatly in number or amount ▪ *Her responsibilities (were) multiplied when she was promoted.* **2** *mathematics* : to add a number to itself a certain number of times ▪ *If you multiply 5 by 2 you get 10. = 5 multiplied by 2 equals 10.*

mul·ti·pur·pose /ˌmʌltiˈpəpəs/ *adj* : having more than one use or purpose ▪ *a multipurpose tool*

mul·ti·ra·cial /ˌmʌltiˈreɪʃəl/ *adj* : relating to or including more than one race of people ▪ *a multiracial society*

mul·ti·sto·ry (*US*) or *Brit* **mul·ti·sto·rey** /ˌmʌltiˈstori/ *adj* : having many stories ▪ *a multistory building*

mul·ti·task·ing /ˈmʌltiˌtæskɪŋ, *Brit* ˈmʌltiˌtɑːskɪŋ/ *n* [U] : the act of doing several things at the same time ▪ *The job requires someone who is good at multitasking.*

mul·ti·tude /ˈmʌltəˌtuːd, *Brit* ˈmʌltəˌtjuːd/ *n* [C] : a great number of things or people ▪ *A vast multitude* [=a great crowd of people] *waited to hear the news.* ▪ *a multitude of choices*

mul·ti·vi·ta·min /ˌmʌltiˈvaɪtəmən, *Brit* ˌmʌltiˈvɪtəmən/ *n* [C] : a pill that contains many vitamins

¹**mum** /ˈmʌm/ *adj, informal* : not talking about something ▪ *She told him to keep/stay mum about the party.* [=she told him not to tell anyone about the party] — **mum's the word** *informal* — used to

say that some information is being kept secret or should be kept secret

²**mum** n [C] **1** US : CHRYSANTHEMUM **2** Brit, informal : MOTHER, MOM

mum·ble /ˈmʌmbəl/ vb **mum·bled; mum·bling** [T/I] : to say (something) in a quiet and unclear way • He mumbled "Goodbye" and then left. • I can't understand you when you mumble. — **mumble** n [singular] • She spoke in a mumble. — **mum·bler** /ˈmʌmblə/ n [C]

mum·bo jum·bo /ˌmʌmboʊˈdʒʌmboʊ/ n [U] informal : confusing or meaningless words or activity • His explanation was just a lot of mumbo jumbo.

mum·mi·fy /ˈmʌmɪˌfaɪ/ vb **-fies; -fied; -fy·ing** [T] : to preserve (a dead body) by treating it with oils and wrapping it in strips of cloth • The ancient Egyptians mummified their dead. • a mummified body

mum·my /ˈmʌmi/ n, pl **-mies** [C] **1** : a dead body of a person or animal prepared for burial in the manner of the ancient Egyptians by treating it with oils and wrapping it in strips of cloth **2** Brit, informal : MOTHER, MOMMY

mumps /ˈmʌmps/ n [U] : a disease that causes fever and swelling in the lower part of the cheek

munch /ˈmʌntʃ/ vb [T/I] : to chew or eat (something) especially in a noisy way • cattle munching (on) grass

munch·ies /ˈmʌntʃiz/ n, informal **1** [plural] US : light foods that are eaten as a snack • Munchies are served at the bar. **2** the munchies : a feeling of hunger • I have a serious case of the munchies. [=I'm very hungry]

mun·dane /ˌmʌnˈdeɪn/ adj **1** : dull and ordinary • mundane chores **2** : relating to ordinary life on earth rather than to spiritual things • mundane worries

mu·nic·i·pal /mjʊˈnɪsəpəl/ adj, always before a noun : of or relating to the government of a city or town • a municipal building/library/election

mu·nic·i·pal·i·ty /mjʊˌnɪsəˈpæləti/ n, pl **-ties** [C] : a city or town that has its own government • laws that have been enacted by many states and municipalities

mu·nif·i·cent /mjʊˈnɪfəsənt/ adj, formal : very generous • a munificent gift/donation — **mu·nif·i·cence** /mjʊˈnɪfəsəns/ n [U]

mu·ni·tions /mjʊˈnɪʃənz/ n [plural] : military supplies and especially weapons • rockets and other munitions • a munitions factory

mu·ral /ˈmjʊrəl/ n [C] : a usually large painting that is done directly on the surface of a wall

¹**mur·der** /ˈmʌrdə/ n **1** [C/U] : the crime of deliberately killing a person • He was found guilty of (committing) murder. • a string of unsolved murders • a murder suspect/victim/case **2** [U] informal : something that is very difficult or unpleasant • Traffic is murder this time of day. • Carrying the luggage was murder on my back. [=hurt or strained my back very badly] — **get away with murder 1** : to murder someone without being captured or punished **2** : to do something very bad

or wrong without being criticized or punished • The company had been getting away with murder for years before the scandal broke. — **scream bloody murder** see ¹SCREAM

²**murder** vb [T] **1** : to kill (a person) in a deliberate and unlawful way • He was arrested and accused of murdering his wife. **2** informal : to spoil or ruin (something) • a writer who murders the English language : to perform (something) very badly • The band murdered that song. — **mur·der·er** /ˈmʌrdərə/ n [C]

mur·der·ous /ˈmʌrdərəs/ adj **1** : very violent or deadly • a murderous dictator/attack **2** : very harsh or severe • murderous heat — **mur·der·ous·ly** adv

murk /ˈmʌrk/ n [U] : darkness or fog that is hard to see through • A figure emerged from the murk. [=gloom]

murky /ˈmʌrki/ adj **murk·i·er; -est 1** : very dark, foggy, or cloudy • murky skies/water **2 a** : not clearly expressed or understood • a murky explanation **b** : involving dishonest or illegal activities that are not clearly known • a politician with a murky past — **murk·i·ness** /ˈmʌrkinəs/ n [U]

¹**mur·mur** /ˈmʌrmə/ n [C] **1 a** : a low sound made when many people are speaking • a murmur of voices **b** : a quiet expression of an opinion or feeling • murmurs of agreement/protest • They accepted the decision without a murmur (of protest/complaint). [=they accepted the decision without protesting/complaining at all] **2** medical : an unusual heart sound that may indicate a problem with the heart's function or structure

²**murmur** vb **1** [T] : to say (something) in a quiet voice • He murmured something about having to get home. **2** [I] : to make a low, continuous sound • a murmuring breeze

¹**mus·cle** /ˈmʌsəl/ n **1** [C/U] : a body tissue that can contract and produce movement • the muscles of the arm • stomach muscles • lifting weights to build muscle • Wait here and don't move a muscle. [=don't move at all] **2** [U] **a** : physical strength • To clean that floor you have to put some muscle into it. **b** : power and influence • political muscle

²**muscle** vb **mus·cled; mus·cling 1** [T] : to move (something) by using physical strength and force • They muscled the furniture up the stairs. • (figurative) She was muscled out of office by political opponents. **2** [T/I] : to move forward by using physical force • He muscled (his way) through the crowd. • (figurative) The company muscled in on the market.

mus·cle-bound /ˈmʌsəlˌbaʊnd/ adj : having large muscles that do not move and stretch easily • a muscle-bound athlete

mus·cu·lar /ˈmʌskjələ/ adj **1** : of or relating to muscles • muscular strength **2** : having large and strong muscles • muscular athletes/legs — **mus·cu·lar·i·ty** /ˌmʌskjəˈlerəti/ n [U]

muscular dys·tro·phy /-ˈdɪstrəfi/ n [U] : a serious disease that causes increasing weakness of muscles

mus·cu·la·ture /ˈmʌskjələˌʧʊə/ n [U] formal : the muscles of the body or of one of its parts ▪ an athlete with well-developed musculature

¹**muse** /ˈmjuːz/ vb mused; mus·ing [T/I] : to think about something carefully or thoroughly ▪ She mused about/on/over the possibility of changing jobs. — musing n [C/U] ▪ He recorded his musings [=thoughts] in his diary.

²**muse** n [C] : a person who inspires an artist, writer, etc. ▪ The writer lost his muse when his wife left him.

mu·se·um /mjuˈziːjəm/ n [C] : a building in which interesting and valuable things are displayed ▪ an art museum ▪ a history/science museum

mush /ˈmʌʃ/ n 1 [U, singular] : a soft, wet mass of material ▪ The rotting apples turned into/to mush. ▪ (figurative) I was so tired my brain turned into/to mush. [=I was too tired to think well] 2 [U] US : a soft food made by boiling cornmeal in water or milk ▪ a bowl of mush 3 /ˈmuːʃ/ [U] informal + disapproving : a story or part of a story in a book, movie, etc., that is too romantic or sentimental ▪ a movie full of mush

¹**mush·room** /ˈmʌʃˌruːm/ n [C] : a fungus that is shaped like an umbrella ▪ wild mushrooms ▪ mushroom soup

²**mushroom** vb [I] : to increase or develop very quickly ▪ The population has mushroomed over the past 10 years.

mushroom cloud n [C] : a large cloud that forms after the explosion of a nuclear weapon

mushy /ˈmʌʃi/ adj mush·i·er; -est 1 : soft and wet ▪ The rotting apples turned mushy. 2 informal + disapproving : too romantic or sentimental ▪ a mushy movie

mu·sic /ˈmjuːzɪk/ n [U] 1 : sounds that are sung by voices or played on musical instruments ▪ dancing/listening to the music of a big band ▪ writing/composing/performing music ▪ the music industry ▪ They like to make music [=play or sing music] with friends. 2 : written or printed symbols showing how music should be played or sung ▪ learning to read music 3 : the art or skill of creating or performing music ▪ She studied music in college. 4 : a pleasant sound ▪ Her words were music to my ears. [=I was very happy to hear what she said] — face the music see ²FACE

¹**mu·si·cal** /ˈmjuːzɪkəl/ adj 1 always before a noun : of or relating to music ▪ musical notes/instruments 2 : having the pleasing qualities of music ▪ a musical voice 3 : having a talent for playing music ▪ a musical family 4 always before a noun : having music and songs as a main feature ▪ a musical film/play — mu·si·cal·i·ty /ˌmjuːzɪˈkæləti/ n [U] — mu·si·cal·ly /ˈmjuːzɪkli/ adv

²**musical** n [C] : a movie or play that tells a story with songs and often dancing ▪ a Broadway musical — called also musical comedy

music box n [C] : a box that contains a device which plays a tune when the box is open

mu·si·cian /mjuˈzɪʃən/ n [C] : a person who writes, sings, or plays music — mu·si·cian·ship /mjuˈzɪʃənˌʃɪp/ n [U] ▪ The critics praised her musicianship. [=musical skill]

musk /ˈmʌsk/ n [U] : a strong-smelling substance used in perfume — musky /ˈmʌski/ adj musk·i·er; -est ▪ a musky perfume/odor

mus·ket /ˈmʌskət/ n [C] : a type of long gun that was used by soldiers before the invention of the rifle

mus·ke·teer /ˌmʌskəˈtiə/ n [C] : a soldier who has a musket

musk·rat /ˈmʌskˌræt/ n, pl muskrat or musk·rats [C] : a North American animal that lives in or near water

Mus·lim /ˈmæzləm/ n [C] : a person whose religion is Islam — Muslim adj ▪ the Muslim faith

mus·lin /ˈmæzlən/ n [U] : a thin and loosely woven cotton cloth

muss /ˈmʌs/ vb [T] US, informal : to make (something) messy or untidy — often + up ▪ The wind mussed up my hair.

mus·sel /ˈmʌsəl/ n [C] : a type of shellfish that has a long dark shell

¹**must** /ˈmʌst/ vb [modal vb] 1 somewhat formal in US English — used to say that something is required or necessary ▪ You must stop. [=you have to stop] ▪ I told him what he must do. ▪ One must eat to live. ▪ "Must you go?" [=do you have to go?] "Yes, I'm afraid I really must." ▪ You must not do it. [=I command you not to do it] 2 somewhat formal in US English — used to say that someone should do something ▪ You must come visit us soon. [=we would like to have you come visit us soon] 3 — used to say that something is very likely ▪ It must be almost dinner time. ▪ She must think I'm a fool. ▪ It must have been the coffee that kept me awake. 4 — used in various phrases to emphasize a statement ▪ I must say, I was surprised to hear from him. ▪ She's a talented actress, you must admit. ▪ I must admit, I expected better results. ▪ I must confess, I haven't actually read the book yet. 5 somewhat formal in US English — used in questions that express annoyance or anger ▪ Must you be so unreasonable? ▪ Why must it always rain on the weekend? — if you must — used to say that you will allow someone to do something even though you do not approve of it ▪ You can smoke if you must, but please do it outdoors.

²**must** n [C] : something that is or seems to be required or necessary ▪ If you're going to hike this trail, sturdy shoes are a must.

mus·tache (US) or chiefly Brit mous·tache /ˈmʌˌstæʃ, Brit məˈstɑːʃ/ n [C] : hair growing on a man's upper lip ▪ He decided to grow a mustache. — mus·tached (US) or chiefly Brit mous·tached /ˈmʌˌstæʃt, Brit məˈstɑːʃt/ adj ▪ a mustached man

mus·tang /ˈmʌˌstæŋ/ n [C] : a small and strong wild horse of western North America

mus·tard /ˈmʌstəd/ n [C/U] 1 : a thick and spicy yellow or brownish-yellow sauce ▪ Would you like some mustard on your hot dog? 2 : a plant with yellow flowers, leaves that can be used for food, and seeds that are used in making mustard — **cut the mustard** *informal* : to be good enough to succeed or to do what is needed • *She tried to join the soccer team, but she couldn't cut the mustard.*

mustard gas *n* [*U*] : a poison gas used as a weapon in a war

¹**mus·ter** /ˈmʌstɚ/ *vb* **1** [*T*] : to work hard to find or get (courage, support, etc.) • *He mustered (up) the courage to ask her on a date.* **2** [*T/I*] : to gather together (a group of people, soldiers, etc.) especially for battle or war • *muster (up) the troops*

²**muster** *n* [*C*] : a formal military gathering to examine or test soldiers — **pass muster** : to be judged as acceptable or good enough • *These excuses will not pass muster.*

mustn't /ˈmʌsn̩t/ — used as a contraction of *must not* • *You mustn't say such things.*

must've /ˈmʌstəv/ — used as a contraction of *must have* • *He must've left already.*

musty /ˈmʌsti/ *adj* **must·i·er; -est** : having a bad smell because of wetness, old age, or lack of fresh air • *musty old books*

mu·ta·ble /ˈmjuːtəbəl/ *adj, formal* : able or likely to change often • *mutable opinions*

mu·tant /ˈmjuːtn̩t/ *n* [*C*] *biology* : a plant or animal that is different from other plants or animals of the same kind because of a change in the structure of its genes

mu·tate /ˈmjuːˌteɪt/ *vb* **-tat·ed; -tat·ing** **1** [*T/I*] *biology* : to change and create an unusual characteristic in a plant or animal • *a disease that mutates genes in humans* • *The cells mutated.* **2** [*I*] : to change *into* something very different • *Her feelings mutated from hatred into love.* — **mu·ta·tion** /mjuˈteɪʃən/ *n* [*C/U*] • *The cat's short tail is the result of (a) genetic mutation.*

¹**mute** /ˈmjuːt/ *adj* **1** : not able or willing to speak • *mute witnesses* **2** : felt or expressed without the use of words • *a mute plea for help* — **mute·ly** *adv* • *We stood staring mutely at the sky.*

²**mute** *n* [*C*] **1** *sometimes offensive* : a person who cannot speak **2** : a device on a musical instrument (such as a trumpet) that makes its sound much softer

³**mute** *vb* **mut·ed; mut·ing** [*T*] **1 a** : to make (a sound) softer or quieter • *We muted our voices.* **b** : to make (something, such as a television) silent • *He used the remote control to mute the TV.* **2** : to make (something) softer or less harsh • *He muted his criticism of the president.* [=he expressed his criticism less harshly] • *muted colors/lighting*

mu·ti·late /ˈmjuːtəˌleɪt/ *vb* **-lat·ed; -lat·ing** [*T*] : to cause severe damage to (something) • *Her arm was mutilated in a car accident.* — **mutilated books** — **mu·ti·la·tion** /ˌmjuːtəˈleɪʃən/ *n* [*C/U*]

mu·ti·neer /ˌmjuːtəˈniɚ/ *n* [*C*] : a person who is involved in a mutiny

mu·ti·nous /ˈmjuːtənəs/ *adj* **1** : involved in a mutiny • *mutinous sailors* **2**

: feeling or showing a desire not to do what someone has told or ordered you to do • *Several mutinous party members threatened to defect to the opposition.*

mu·ti·ny /ˈmjuːtəni/ *n, pl* **-nies** [*C*] : a situation in which a group of people refuse to obey orders and try to take control away from the person who commands them • *The sailors staged a mutiny.* — **mutiny** *vb* **-nies; -nied; -ny·ing** [*I*] • *The crew was threatening to mutiny.*

mutt /ˈmʌt/ *n* [*C*] *informal* : a dog with parents of different breeds

mut·ter /ˈmʌtɚ/ *vb* **1** [*T/I*] : to speak quietly so that it is difficult for other people to hear what you say • *He muttered an apology.* **2** [*I*] : to complain in a quiet or indirect way • *Some employees are muttering about the changes in the pension plan.* — **mutter** *n* [*C*] • *She answered with/in a mutter.*

mut·ton /ˈmʌtn̩/ *n* [*U*] : the meat of an adult sheep used as food

mu·tu·al /ˈmjuːtʃəwəl/ *adj* : shared between or by two or more people or groups • *mutual trust* • *Her fans love her, and the feeling is mutual.* [=and she loves her fans] • *They met through a mutual friend.* [=a person who was a friend of both of them] • *a mutual agreement* — **mu·tu·al·i·ty** /ˌmjuːtʃəˈwælət̬i/ *n* [*U*] *formal* — **mu·tu·al·ly** /ˈmjuːtʃəwəli/ *adv*

mutual fund *n* [*C*] *US* : a type of investment in which the money of many people is used to buy stock from many different companies

mutually exclusive *adj* : not able to be true at the same time or to exist together • *War and peace are mutually exclusive.* [=war and peace cannot exist at the same time]

¹**muz·zle** /ˈmʌzəl/ *n* [*C*] **1** : the usually long nose and mouth of a dog, horse, pig, etc. **2** : a covering for the mouth of a dog that stops it from biting people **3** : the hole at the end of a gun where the bullet comes out

²**muzzle** *vb* **muz·zled; muz·zling** [*T*] **1** : to put a muzzle on (a dog) • *a dangerous dog that should be muzzled* **2** : to prevent (a person or group) from speaking or writing in a free or normal way • *attempts by the government to muzzle the press*

my /ˈmaɪ/ *adj, possessive form of* I **1** : always before a noun : relating to or belonging to me • *Welcome to my home.* • *My name is John.* : made or done by me • *I always keep my promises.* **2** *informal* — used by itself and in phrases to express surprise, excitement, or fear • *Oh, my (goodness/Lord/God).* *What happened to you?*

my·o·pia /maɪˈoʊpijə/ *n* [*U*] *medical* : a condition of the eye that makes it difficult to see objects that are far away

my·o·pic /maɪˈɑːpɪk/ *adj* **1** *medical* : not able to clearly see objects that are far away : NEARSIGHTED • *myopic vision* **2** *disapproving* : only thinking or caring about things that are happening now or that relate to a particular group rather than things that are in the future or that relate to many people • *myopic politicians*

¹myr·i·ad /ˈmirijəd/ *n [C] somewhat formal* : a very large number *of* things • *myriads of stars*

²myriad *adj, somewhat formal* : very many • *myriad problems*

my·self /maɪˈsɛlf/ *pron* **1** — used as the object of a verb or preposition to refer to yourself after you have already been mentioned • *I accidentally cut myself while cooking.* • *I bought myself a new suit.* • *I am proud of myself for finishing college.* • *I had the house (all) to myself.* [=I was alone in the house] • *I wanted to see it for myself.* [=to see it rather than have someone tell me about it, describe it to me, etc.] — often used for emphasis • *I told him so myself.* • *I myself have never been to Italy.* **2** : my normal or healthy self • *I'm not (feeling like) myself today.* • *I find it hard to be myself when I'm with people I don't know well.* — **by myself 1** : without any help from other people • *I can't do it (all) by myself.* **2** : with nobody else • ALONE • *I went to the movies by myself.*

mys·te·ri·ous /mɪˈstirijəs/ *adj* : strange, unknown, or difficult to understand • *A mysterious illness has been spreading through the city.* • *Her behavior was very mysterious.* • *the movie's handsome and mysterious main character* — **be mysterious** : to talk or behave in a way that makes other people feel that you must have a secret • *What are you being so mysterious about?* — **mys·te·ri·ous·ly** *adv* • *He died mysteriously at the age of 32.*

mys·tery /ˈmɪstəri/ *n, pl* **-ter·ies 1** [C] : something that is not known or that is difficult to understand or explain • *His name/success/illness is a mystery (to me).* **2** [U] : the quality of being difficult to understand or explain • *The experiment is cloaked/shrouded/veiled in mystery.* • *There's no mystery (to/as to/about) why we're here.* **3** [C] : a book, play, or movie that describes a crime and the process of solving it • *She writes murder mysteries.* • *mystery novels/stories*

¹mys·tic /ˈmɪstɪk/ *n [C]* : a person who tries to gain religious or spiritual knowledge through prayer and deep thought

²mystic *adj* : MYSTICAL • *She had a mystic vision while praying.*

mys·ti·cal /ˈmɪstɪkəl/ *adj* **1** : having a spiritual meaning that is difficult to see or understand • *a symbol that has mystical powers* **2** : resulting from prayer or deep thought • *a mystical journey* — **mys·ti·cal·ly** /ˈmɪstɪkli/ *adv*

mys·ti·cism /ˈmɪstəˌsɪzəm/ *n [U]* : a religious practice based on the belief that knowledge of spiritual truth can be gained by praying or thinking deeply

mys·ti·fy /ˈmɪstəˌfaɪ/ *vb* **-fies; -fied; -fy·ing** [T] : to confuse (someone) completely • *Her strange behavior has mystified her friends and family.* • *a mystifying decision* — **mys·ti·fi·ca·tion** /ˌmɪstəfəˈkeɪʃən/ *n [U]*

mys·tique /mɪˈstiːk/ *n [singular]* : a special quality that makes a person or thing interesting or exciting • *There's a certain mystique to/about people who fight fires.*

myth /ˈmɪθ/ *n* **1** [C/U] : an idea or story that is believed by many people but that is not true • *It's an enduring/persistent myth that money brings happiness.* — *Contrary to popular myth, no monster lives in this lake.* **2 a** [C] : a story that was told in an ancient culture to explain a practice, belief, or natural occurrence • *creation myths* **b** [U] : such stories as a group • *a student of Greek myth* [=*mythology*]

myth·ic /ˈmɪθɪk/ *adj* **1** : of, relating to, or described in a myth • *a mythic story/hero* **2** : very famous or important • *She's one of the mythic figures in ice-skating.* • *His fame has grown to mythic proportions.*

myth·i·cal /ˈmɪθɪkəl/ *adj* **1** : based on or described in a myth • *a mythical hero* • *mythical beasts/creatures* **2** : existing only in the imagination • IMAGINARY • *The benefits of the new policy proved to be mythical.* — **myth·i·cal·ly** /ˈmɪθɪkli/ *adv*

my·thol·o·gy /mɪˈθɑːlədʒi/ *n, pl* **-gies 1** [C/U] : the myths of a particular group or culture • *Greek mythology* **2** [U, singular] : ideas that are believed by many people but that are not true • *Contrary to popular mythology, he did not actually discover the cause of the disease by himself.* — **myth·o·log·i·cal** /ˌmɪθəˈlɑːdʒɪkəl/ *adj* • *a mythological story/hero*

N

¹n *or* **N** /ˈɛn/ *n, pl* **n's** *or* **ns** *or* **N's** *or* **Ns** /ˈɛnz/ [C/U] : the 14th letter of the English alphabet • *a word that starts with (an) n*

²n *abbr* noun

'n *also* **'n** /ən, n̩/ *conj* : AND • *rock 'n' roll*

N *abbr* north, northern

NA 1 North America **2** not applicable — often written as *N/A* **3** not available — often written as *N/A*

NAACP *abbr* National Association for the Advancement of Colored People ✧ The NAACP is an American organization that works to protect the rights of African-Americans.

nab /ˈnæb/ *vb* **nabbed; nab·bing** [T] *informal* **1** : to catch and stop or arrest (someone) • *The police nabbed him.* **2** : to take or get (something) quickly and often in a way that is clever or rude • *We* nabbed seats in the front row of the theater.

na·chos /ˈnɑːˌtʃoʊz/ n [plural] : tortilla chips that are covered with warm melted cheese and often with hot peppers, beans, salsa, etc.

na·dir /ˈneɪˌdiə/ n [singular] formal : the worst or lowest point of something ▪ The relationship between the two countries reached a/its nadir in the 1920s.

¹**nag** /ˈnæg/ vb nagged; nag·ging [T/I]
1 a : to annoy (someone) by often complaining about his or her behavior, appearance, etc. ▪ Mom's always nagging me about my hair. ▪ All you ever do is nag. **b** : to annoy (someone) with repeated questions, requests, or orders ▪ My parents are always nagging me to clean my room. **2** : to cause (someone) to feel annoyed or worried for a long period of time ▪ She's still nagged by the thought that she could have done better. ▪ a nagging fear/suspicion/cough/problem ▪ The problem has been nagging at me for weeks.

²**nag** n [C] **1** informal : a person who nags or complains too often ▪ His wife's an awful nag. **2** : a horse that is old and usually in bad condition

¹**nail** /ˈneɪl/ n [C] **1** : a long, thin piece of metal that is sharp at one end and flat at the other end and that is used chiefly to attach things to wood **2** : a fingernail or toenail ▪ a pair of nail clippers — **a nail in the/someone's coffin** : something that makes it more likely that someone or something will fail, be destroyed, etc. ▪ Every mistake is one more nail in the coffin of his baseball career. — (as) hard/tough as nails of a person : very tough ▪ an athlete who's as tough as nails — hit the nail on the head see ¹HIT — tooth and nail see TOOTH

²**nail** vb [T] **1** : to attach (something) with a nail ▪ Nail the picture to the wall. ▪ nailing boards together **2** informal **a** : to catch (someone) doing something illegal or wrong ▪ He got nailed by his parents while trying to sneak out of the house. **b** : to arrest or punish (someone) for doing something that is illegal or wrong ▪ He got nailed for not paying his taxes. **3** informal : to hit (someone or something) forcefully ▪ Someone nailed him on the head with a rock. **4** US, informal : to make or do (something) in a perfect or impressive way ▪ She nailed a three-point shot. — nail down [phrasal vb] nail (something) down or nail down (something) **1** : to make (something, such as a victory) certain to happen ▪ That goal nailed down the victory. **2** : to find out or identify (something) exactly ▪ They're trying to nail down the cause of the problems. **3** : to make (something) definite or final ▪ nail down a decision

nail file n [C] : a small, flat piece of metal or cardboard that has a rough surface and that is used for shaping your fingernails

nail polish n [U] : a liquid that is used to paint fingernails and toenails

na·ive or **na·ïve** /nɑˈiːv, naɪˈiːv/ adj : having or showing a lack of experience or knowledge ▪ a naive belief/question/person ▪ when I was young and naive — **na·ive·ly** or **na·ïve·ly** adv — **na·ive·té** also **na·ive·te** or **na·ïve·té** /nɑˌiːvˈteɪ, naɪˌiːvˈteɪ/ n [U] — **na·ive·ty** also **na·ïve·ty** /nɑˈiːvəti, naɪˈiːvəti/ n [U] chiefly Brit

na·ked /ˈneɪkəd/ adj **1** : not wearing any clothes ▪ a naked man ▪ He was naked from the waist up. ▪ She was half naked [=partly dressed] when the doorbell rang. ▪ He's stark naked. [=he's completely naked] **2** : not having a usual covering ▪ a naked light bulb **3** : not having any decorations ▪ the room's naked walls **4** always before a noun : stated in a very clear and direct way ▪ the naked facts of the case ▪ the naked truth [=the complete truth] **b** : completely obvious ▪ an act of naked aggression **5** always before a noun : without the use of a telescope, microscope, etc. ▪ distant stars that cannot be seen with the naked eye — naked·ly adv ▪ nakedly ambitious — na·ked·ness n [U]

nam·by–pam·by /ˌnæmbiˈpæmbi/ adj, informal + disapproving : too weak or gentle ▪ namby-pamby politicians

¹**name** /ˈneɪm/ n [C] **1** : a word or phrase that refers to or that can refer to a specific person ▪ "What's his (first) name?" "His name is Jacob." **2** : a word or phrase that refers to a place or thing ▪ We had to memorize the names of all the countries in Africa. **3** : the general opinion that most people have about someone or something ▪ They have given the sport a bad name. [=have made people think badly about the sport] ▪ You ruined our family's good name. [=good reputation] ▪ He's trying to clear his name. [=to prove that he is not guilty of a crime] **4** : a famous person or thing ▪ He's one of the biggest names in music. **5** : a word or phrase that is used to describe and insult someone ▪ "You're such a stupid jerk!" "Hey, stop calling me names!" — by name : by saying the name of someone or something ▪ He never mentioned her by name. [=he never said her name] — in all/everything but name : not in an official way but in every other way ▪ Their marriage was over in all but name five years ago. — in name only — used to describe a person or thing that does not have the qualities that its name suggests ▪ She's my boss in name only. We're really more like partners. — in someone's/something's name or in the name of someone/something **1 a** — used to say that something officially or legally belongs to a specified person ▪ We both own the house, but the car is in my name. **b** — used to say that something has or uses the name of a specified person ▪ Our reservation at the restaurant is in my name. **2** — used to say that something is done with the authority of a specified person or thing ▪ Stop in the name of the law! **3** — used to say that something is given as the official reason for doing something ▪ They're tearing down historic buildings in the name of progress! — know (someone) by name **1** : to

know a person well enough to know the person's name • *The police know him by name.* **2 :** to know a person's name only • *He only knew him by name.* — **make your name** or **make a name for yourself :** to become well-known or famous • *She made her name in politics.* — **put a name to (someone or something) :** to think of and say the name of (someone or something) • *Can you put a name to the face in this photograph?* — **the name of the game** *informal* **:** the basic goal or purpose of an activity • *In business, profit is the name of the game.* — **to your name :** belonging to you • *I haven't a dollar/dime/penny to my name.* [=I have no money] — **under someone's/something's name** or **under the name (of) someone/something 1** — used to say that something officially or legally belongs to a specified person • *We both own the house, but the car is under my name.* **2** — used to say that something has or uses the name of a specified person • *We have dinner reservations under the name of Jones.*

²**name** *vb* **named; nam·ing** [*T*] **1 :** to give a name to (someone or something) • *We named our daughter "Mary."* **2 :** to say the name of (someone or something) • *Can you name the person who attacked you?* **3 :** to choose (someone) to be (something) • *The company president named me (as) his successor.* **4 :** to decide on or choose (something) • *We're getting married, but we haven't named the day (of the wedding) yet.* — **name names :** to say the names of people who were involved in something • *He said he knew who did it, but he wouldn't name names.* — **name your price :** to say how much you want to pay for something or how much you want to sell something for • *Customers can name their price.* — **you name it** *informal* **:** anything you could say or think of • *You name it, we sell it!*

name brand *n* [*C*] **:** a product that is made by a well-known company — **name–brand** *adj, always before a noun* • *name-brand clothing*

name-call·ing /ˈneɪmˌkɑːlɪŋ/ *n* [*U*] **:** the act of using offensive names to insult someone • *They should discuss the issues without resorting to name-calling.*

name-drop·ping /ˈneɪmˌdrɑːpɪŋ/ *n* [*U*] **:** the act of trying to impress someone by saying the names of well-known people that you know or have met — **name–drop·per** /ˈneɪmˌdrɑːpɚ/ *n* [*C*]

name·less /ˈneɪmləs/ *adj* **1 :** having a name that is not known or told • *the nameless author of the editorial* **2 :** not having a name • *a nameless stream/road* **3 :** not marked with a name • *nameless graves* **4 a :** not able to be identified by name • *nameless fears and worries* **b :** too bad to talk about • *nameless horrors*

name·ly /ˈneɪmli/ *adv* — used when giving exact information about something you have already mentioned • *They brought lunch, namely sandwiches, chips, and soda.*

name·plate /ˈneɪmˌpleɪt/ *n* [*C*] **:** a metal

or plastic sign that is attached to a door or wall and that shows the name of the person, group, or company that lives or works there

name·sake /ˈneɪmˌseɪk/ *n* [*C*] **:** someone or something that has the same name as another person or thing

name tag *n* [*C*] **:** a piece of paper, cloth, plastic, or metal that has a person's name written on it and that is attached to the person's clothing

nan·ny /ˈnæni/ *n, pl* **-nies** [*C*] **:** a woman who is paid to care for a young child usually in the child's home

nanny goat *n* [*C*] **:** a female goat

nano·sec·ond /ˈnænoʊˌsɛkənd/ *n* [*C*] **1** *technical* **:** one billionth of a second **2 :** a very short time

nano·tech·nol·o·gy /ˌnænoʊtɛkˈnɑːlə-dʒi/ *n* [*U*] *technical* **:** the science of working with atoms and molecules to build devices (such as robots) that are extremely small

¹**nap** /ˈnæp/ *n* [*C*] **1 :** a short period of sleep especially during the day • *He takes a nap every afternoon.* **2 :** a soft layer of threads on the surface of a piece of cloth, a carpet, etc.

²**nap** *vb* **napped; nap·ping** [*I*] **1 :** to sleep for a short period of time especially during the day • *He's napping on the couch.* **2 :** to be in a state in which you are not prepared to deal with something because you were not paying attention • *When the problem arose, the government was caught napping.*

na·palm /ˈneɪˌpɑːm/ *n* [*U*] **:** a thick substance that contains gasoline and that is used in bombs that cause a destructive fire over a wide area

nape /ˈneɪp/ *n* [*singular*] **:** the back of the neck • *the nape of your neck*

nap·kin /ˈnæpkən/ *n* [*C*] **:** a small piece of cloth or paper used during a meal to clean your lips and fingers and to protect your clothes

nap·py /ˈnæpi/ *n, pl* **-pies** [*C*] *Brit* **:** DIAPER

narc *also* **nark** /ˈnɑɚk/ *n* [*C*] *US, informal* **:** a person (such as a government agent) who tries to catch criminals who buy and sell illegal drugs

nar·cis·sis·tic /ˌnɑɚsəˈsɪstɪk/ *adj, formal + disapproving* **:** loving and admiring yourself and especially your appearance too much • *a narcissistic young actor* — **nar·cis·sism** /ˈnɑɚsəˌsɪzəm/ *n* [*U*]

nar·cot·ic /nɑɚˈkɑːtɪk/ *n* [*C*] **1 :** a drug (such as cocaine, heroin, or marijuana) that affects the brain and that is usually dangerous and illegal • *He was arrested for selling narcotics.* **2** *medical* **:** a drug that is given to people in small amounts to make them sleep or feel less pain — **narcotic** *adj* • *The drug has a mild narcotic effect.* [=makes you feel slightly sleepy]

nar·rate /ˈneɚˌeɪt, *Brit* nəˈreɪt/ *vb* **-rat·ed; -rat·ing** [*T*] **1 :** to tell (a story) • *The author narrates her story in great detail.* **2 :** to say the words that are heard as part of (a movie, television show, etc.) and that describe what is being seen • *Who narrated that film?* — **nar·ra·tor** /ˈneɚ-

,eɪtə, Brit nəˈreɪtə/ n [C]

nar·ra·tion /næˈreɪʃən/ n [C/U] **1** somewhat formal : the act or process of telling a story or describing what happens • the narration of events **2** : words that are heard as part of a movie, television show, etc., and that describe what is being sent • Who did the narration for the documentary?

¹**nar·ra·tive** /ˈnerətɪv/ n [C] formal : a story that is told or written • a detailed narrative

²**narrative** adj, always before a noun **1** : of or relating to the process of telling a story • her narrative style/technique **2** : having the form of a story • a narrative poem

¹**nar·row** /ˈneroʊ/ adj **1** : not wide : small from one side to the other side • a narrow hallway/passageway/street **2** : including or involving a small number of things or people • a narrow range/choice/view/perspective **3** : very close to failure • a narrow escape/victory : almost not enough for success • They won by a narrow margin. — **the straight and narrow** see ³STRAIGHT — **nar·row·ness** n [U]

²**narrow** vb [T/I] **1** : to make (something) less wide or to become less wide • She narrowed her eyes and stared at me. • The vase narrows at its top. **2** : to make (something) smaller in amount or range or to become smaller in amount or range • The field was narrowed (down) from eight to two candidates. • narrowing the range of options • The gap between their salaries began to narrow.

nar·row·ly /ˈneroʊli/ adv **1** : by a very small number, amount, or distance • He narrowly won the election. **2** : in a way that does not include or involve many things or people • They define the term "family" very narrowly.

nar·row-mind·ed /ˈneroʊˈmaɪndəd/ adj : not willing to accept opinions, beliefs, or behaviors that are unusual or different from your own • a narrow-minded view of racial/religious/political issues — **nar·row-mind·ed·ness** n [U]

NASA /ˈnæsə/ abbr National Aeronautics and Space Administration ◇ NASA is a U.S. government organization that is responsible for space travel and research.

na·sal /ˈneɪzəl/ adj **1** always before a noun : of or relating to the nose • nasal congestion/passages **2 a** always before a noun : produced by pushing air out through the nose when you speak • nasal sounds • the nasal consonants /m/ and /n/ **b** : producing nasal sounds • a nasal voice — **na·sal·ly** adv

NASCAR /ˈnæsˌkɑɚ/ abbr, US National Association for Stock Car Auto Racing

na·scent /ˈnæsn̩t/ adj, formal : beginning to exist • a nascent technology

nas·tur·tium /nəˈstɚʃəm/ n [C] : a plant with circular leaves and yellow, orange, or red flowers that are sometimes eaten

nas·ty /ˈnæsti, Brit ˈnɑːsti/ adj **nas·ti·er; -est 1** : very unpleasant to see, smell, taste, etc. • a nasty habit/smell/taste **2** : indecent and offensive • nasty language **3** : unpleasant and unkind • a nasty

person/trick/e-mail **4** : very bad or unpleasant • nasty weather/storms **5** : very serious or severe • a nasty wound — **nas·ti·ly** /ˈnæstəli, Brit ˈnɑːstəli/ adv — **nas·ti·ness** /ˈnæstinəs, Brit ˈnɑːstinəs/ n [U]

na·tion /ˈneɪʃən/ n **1 a** [C] : a large area of land that is controlled by its own government : COUNTRY • the world's richest/poorest nations **b** the nation : the people who live in a nation • The President will speak to the nation tonight. **2** Nation [C] : a tribe of Native Americans or a group of Native American tribes that share the same history, traditions, or language — **na·tion·hood** /ˈneɪʃənˌhʊd/ n [U]

¹**na·tion·al** /ˈnæʃənl̩/ adj **1** : of or relating to an entire nation or country • national governments/politics • national security/defense **2** always before a noun : owned and controlled or operated by a national government • a national bank/forest — **na·tion·al·ly** /ˈnæʃənəli/ adv

²**national** n [C] formal : a person who is a citizen of a country • foreign nationals

national anthem n [C] : a song that praises a particular country and that is officially accepted as the country's song

National Guard n [singular] : a military group that is organized in each U.S. state but given money and supplies by the national government and that can be used by the state or the country

National Health Service n — the National Health Service : the public system of medical care in Britain that is paid for by taxes

na·tion·al·ism /ˈnæʃənəˌlɪzəm/ n [U] **1** : a feeling that people have of being loyal to and proud of their country often with the belief that it is better and more important than other countries **2** : a desire by a large group of people (such as people who share the same culture, history, language, etc.) to form a separate and independent nation of their own

na·tion·al·ist /ˈnæʃənəlɪst/ n [C] **1** : a supporter of or believer in nationalism • German/American/Russian nationalists **2** or **Nationalist** : a member of a political group that wants to form a separate and independent nation • Irish Nationalists — **nationalist** adj • nationalist beliefs/ideologies/sentiments

na·tion·al·is·tic /ˌnæʃənəˈlɪstɪk/ adj : relating to or showing a belief that your country is better and more important than other countries • the political party's nationalistic ideology

na·tion·al·i·ty /ˌnæʃəˈnæləti/ n, pl **-ties 1** [C] : a group of people who share the same history, traditions, and language, and who usually live together in a particular country • people of all races and nationalities **2** [C/U] formal : the fact or status of being a member or citizen of a particular nation • She's American, but her parents are of Japanese nationality.

na·tion·al·ize /ˈnæʃənəˌlaɪz/ also Brit **na·tion·al·ise** vb **-ized; -iz·ing** [T] : to cause (something) to be under the control of a national government • nationalizing the country's oil supply — **na·tion-**

al·i·za·tion also Brit **na·tion·al·i·sa·tion** /ˌnæʃənələˈzeɪʃən, Brit ˌnæʃənəˌlaɪˈzeɪʃən/ n [U]

national monument n [C] : a place (such as an old building or an area of land) that is owned and protected by a national government because of its natural beauty or its importance to history or science

national park n [C] : an area of land that is owned and protected by a national government because of its natural beauty or its importance to history or science

na·tion·wide /ˌneɪʃənˈwaɪd/ adj : including or involving all parts of a nation or country • a nationwide problem/shortage — **nationwide** adv

¹**na·tive** /ˈneɪtɪv/ adj **1** always before a noun **a** : born in a particular place • a native New Yorker **b** — used to refer to the place where a person was born and raised • his native country/land **2 a** always before a noun : belonging to a person since birth or childhood • her native language/tongue **b** : existing naturally as an ability, quality, etc., that someone has • his native wit **3 a** : produced, living, or existing naturally in a particular region • native birds and animals **b** — used to refer to the place or type of place where a plant or animal normally or naturally lives • the plant's native habitat **4** always before a noun : of or relating to a group of people who were living in an area (such as North America or Africa) when a new group of usually European people arrived • native inhabitants/peoples

²**native** n [C] **1** : a person who was born or raised in a particular place • I'm a California native. = I'm a native of California. **2** : a person from a group of people who were living in an area (such as South America or Africa) when Europeans first arrived ✧ This sense of native was commonly used in the past but is now often considered offensive. **3** : a kind of plant or animal that originally grew or lived in a particular place

Native American n [C] : a member of any of the first groups of people living in North America or South America; especially : a member of one of these groups from the U.S.

> **usage** Native American is the term that is now most often used for people whose ancestors lived in North and South America before the arrival of Europeans in 1492. The term American Indian is also often used, but it is offensive to some people. The term Indian by itself is also still used but is now often considered offensive and should usually be avoided.

— **Native American** adj

native speaker n [C] : a person who learned to speak the language of the place where they were born as a child rather than learning it as a foreign language

Na·tiv·i·ty /nəˈtɪvəti/ n — **the Nativity** : the birth of Jesus • a painting of the Nativity

NATO /ˈneɪtoʊ/ abbr North Atlantic Treaty Organization ✧ NATO is an organization of countries that have agreed to provide military support to each other. It includes many European countries as well as the U.S. and Canada.

nat·ter /ˈnætɚ/ vb [I] chiefly Brit : to talk about unimportant things for a long time • She nattered about herself through our entire meal.

nat·ty /ˈnæti/ adj **nat·ti·er; -est** informal : very neat and clean • He's a natty dresser. — **nat·ti·ly** /ˈnætəli/ adv

¹**nat·u·ral** /ˈnætʃərəl/ adj **1 a** : coming from nature • natural silk/light/materials • a country rich in natural resources [=valuable plants, animals, minerals, etc.] • learning more about the natural world [=animals, plants, etc.] **b** : not containing anything artificial • natural soap/yogurt • natural foods like whole grain bread and fresh vegetables • all-natural ingredients **2** : usual or expected • Gray hair is a natural consequence of getting older. • He died of natural causes. [=he died because he was ill or old and not by being killed in an accident, battle, etc.] **3** always before a noun — used to describe a quality, ability, etc., that a person or animal is born with and does not have to learn • a natural ability/curiosity/talent **4** ✧ To be/act/look natural is to be normal and relaxed in the way you behave and look. **5** always before a noun : related by blood • his natural mother [=the woman who gave birth to him] **6** of a choice, decision, etc. : logical and reasonable • He is the natural choice to be company president. **7** music : neither sharp nor flat • B/F natural — **nat·u·ral·ness** /ˈnætʃərəlnəs/ n [U]

²**natural** n [C] **1 a** : someone who is good at doing something from the first time it is done • She's a natural at golf. **b** : someone or something that is suited for a particular job, purpose, etc. • He's a natural for the job. **2** : a musical note that is neither sharp nor flat

natural disaster n [C] : a sudden and terrible event in nature (such as a hurricane, tornado, or flood) that usually results in serious damage and many deaths

natural gas n [U] : gas that is taken from under the ground and used as fuel

natural history n [U] : the study of plants, animals, and sometimes ancient human civilizations • a natural history museum

nat·u·ral·ism /ˈnætʃərəˌlɪzəm/ n [U] : a style of art or literature that shows people and things as they actually are

nat·u·ral·ist /ˈnætʃərəlɪst/ n [C] : a person who studies plants and animals as they live in nature

nat·u·ral·is·tic /ˌnætʃərəˈlɪstɪk/ adj **1** : looking like what appears in nature • a naturalistic setting **2** : showing people or things as they really are • naturalistic writing/paintings

nat·u·ral·ize also Brit **nat·u·ral·ise** /ˈnætʃərəˌlaɪz/ vb **-ized; -iz·ing 1** [T] : to allow (someone who was born in a different country) to become a new citizen • naturalized citizens of the U.S. **2**

[T/I] : to cause (a plant or animal from another place) to begin to grow and live in a new area ▪ *Several Asian fish have become naturalized in these lakes.* — **nat·u·ral·i·za·tion** *also Brit* **nat·u·ral·i·sa·tion** /ˌnætʃərələˈzeɪʃən, *Brit* ˌnætʃərəˌlaɪˈzeɪʃən/ *n* [U]

nat·u·ral·ly /ˈnætʃərəli/ *adv* **1** — used to describe something that happens or exists by itself without being controlled or changed by someone ▪ *naturally curly hair* ▪ *a naturally sweet tea* **2** — used to say that something is expected or normal ▪ *Naturally, some mistakes were made.* **3** : because of a quality or skill that a person or animal is born with ▪ *She's naturally competitive/curious.* **4** : in a way that is relaxed and normal ▪ *acting/speaking naturally* **5** : in a logical and reasonable way ▪ *Her conclusions follow naturally from the theory.* — **come naturally** ✧ If something *comes naturally* to you, you are able to do or learn it easily.

natural selection *n* [U] : the process by which plants and animals that can adapt to changes in their environment are able to survive and reproduce while those that cannot adapt do not survive

natural wastage *n* [U] *Brit* : ATTRITION 1

na·ture /ˈneɪtʃɚ/ *n* **1** *also* **Nature** [U] **a** : the physical world and everything in it (such as plants, animals, mountains, oceans, stars, etc.) that is not made by people ▪ *the beauty of nature* **b** : the natural forces that control what happens in the world ▪ *the forces/laws of nature* **2** [C/U] : the character or personality of a person or animal ▪ *She has a competitive nature.* [=she is competitive] **3** [C/U] : a basic quality that something has ▪ *the nature of democracy/steel* **4** [*singular*] : a particular kind of thing ▪ *What is the nature of your problem?* [=what kind of problem do you have?] ▪ *papers of a confidential nature* [=papers that are confidential] — **get/go back to nature** *also* **return to nature** : to spend time living in a simple way without modern machines, electricity, etc. — **let nature take its course** : to allow something to happen without trying to control it ▪ *The injury should heal within a few weeks if you just let nature take its course.*

na·tur·ism /ˈneɪtʃəˌrɪzəm/ *n* [U] *Brit* : NUDISM — **na·tur·ist** /ˈneɪtʃərɪst/ *n* [C]

naught (*chiefly US*) *or chiefly Brit* **nought** /ˈnɑːt/ *pron, old-fashioned* : ¹NOTHING ▪ *All our efforts came to naught.* = (*US*) *All our efforts came to naught.* [=we did not succeed] ▪ (*chiefly US*) *It was all for naught.* [=it was all for nothing]

naugh·ty /ˈnɑːti/ *adj* **naugh·ti·er; -est** **1** : behaving badly : used especially to describe a child who does not behave properly or obey a parent, teacher, etc. ▪ *a naughty boy/girl* **2** *informal* : relating to or suggesting sex in usually a playful way ▪ *a naughty joke/smile* — **naugh·ti·ly** /ˈnɑːtəli/ *adv* — **naugh·ti·ness** /ˈnɑːtinəs/ *n* [U]

nau·sea /ˈnɑːzijə/ *n* [U] : the feeling you

have in your stomach when you think you are going to vomit

nau·se·ate /ˈnɑːziˌeɪt/ *vb* **-at·ed; -at·ing** [T] **1** : to cause (someone) to feel like vomiting ▪ *The smell of gasoline nauseates me.* ▪ *I felt/was nauseated.* **2** : to cause (someone) to feel disgusted ▪ *It nauseated him to see the way the animals were treated.* — **nauseating** *adj* ▪ *a nauseating smell* — **nau·se·at·ing·ly** *adv*

nau·seous /ˈnɑːʃəs, ˈnɑːzijəs/ *adj* **1** : feeling like you are about to vomit ▪ *The smell made me nauseous.* ▪ *feeling nauseous* **2** : causing you to feel like you are going to vomit ▪ *a nauseous smell*

nau·ti·cal /ˈnɑːtɪkəl/ *adj* : relating to ships and sailing ▪ *nautical charts*

nautical mile *n* [C] : a unit of distance equal to 1,852 meters or 1.15 miles that is used for sea and air travel

na·val /ˈneɪvəl/ *adj* : of or relating to a country's navy ▪ *naval history/officers*

nave /ˈneɪv/ *n* [C] : the long center part of a church where people sit

na·vel /ˈneɪvəl/ *n* [C] : the small, hollow or raised area in the middle of your stomach — called also *belly button*

nav·i·ga·ble /ˈnævɪgəbəl/ *adj* : deep and wide enough for boats and ships to travel on or through ▪ *a navigable river*

nav·i·gate /ˈnævəˌgeɪt/ *vb* **-gat·ed; -gat·ing** **1** [T/I] : to find the way to get to a place when you are traveling in a ship, airplane, car, etc. ▪ *You can drive and I'll navigate.* ▪ *I'd need a map to navigate the city.* ▪ (*figurative*) *We navigated (our way) through all the rules and regulations.* **2** [T/I] **a** : to sail on, over, or through an area of water ▪ *navigating (through) the canal* **b** : to travel on, over, or through (an area or place) ▪ *She has trouble navigating the stairs with her crutches.* **3** [T] : to control the direction of (something, such as a ship or airplane) ▪ *The captain navigated the ship.* ▪ (*figurative*) *She navigated the company through some difficult times.* **4** [T/I] *computers* : to go to different places on the Internet or on a particular Web site in order to find what you want ▪ *navigating (on) the Web/Internet*

nav·i·ga·tion /ˌnævəˈgeɪʃən/ *n* [U] **1** : the act, activity, or process of finding the way to get to a place when you are traveling in a ship, airplane, car, etc. ▪ *navigation by satellite* ▪ *a navigation system* **2** : the act of moving in a boat or ship over an area of water ▪ *navigation of the river/canal* **3** *computers* : the act of going to different places on the Internet or on a particular Web site in order to find what you want ▪ *faster Internet navigation* — **nav·i·ga·tion·al** /ˌnævəˈgeɪʃənl/ *adj*

nav·i·ga·tor /ˈnævəˌgeɪtɚ/ *n* [C] **1** : a person who finds out how to get to a place in a ship, airplane, etc. **2** : a device (such as a computer) that is used to plan or find the route to a place

na·vy /ˈneɪvi/ *n, pl* **-vies** **1** [C] : the part of a country's military forces that fights at sea using ships, submarines, airplanes, etc. ▪ *a career in the navy* ▪ *the U.S. Army,*

Navy, Air Force, and Marines **2** [U] : NAVY BLUE • *a navy sweater*

navy blue *n* [U] : a very dark blue — **navy blue** *adj* • *a navy blue dress*

nay /ˈneɪ/ *n* [C] *formal* : a no vote • *We have 6 nays and 12 yeas, so the measure passes.*

nay·say·er /ˈneɪˌseɪjə/ *n* [C] *formal* : a person who says something will not work or is not possible • *There are always naysayers who say it can't be done.*

Na·zi /ˈnɑːtsi/ *n* [C] : a member of a German political party that controlled Germany from 1933 to 1945 under Adolf Hitler — **Nazi** *adj* — **Na·zism** /ˈnɑːtˌsɪzəm/ *n* [U]

NB *also* **N.B.** *abbr* please note — used in writing to tell the reader that something is important • *NB: applications will not be accepted after May 5.* ✧ *NB* comes from the Latin phrase "nota bene," which means "mark well."

NBA *abbr*, *US* National Basketball Association ✧ *The NBA is the major professional basketball league in the U.S.*

NBC *abbr*, *US* National Broadcasting Company

NC *abbr* North Carolina

NCAA *abbr*, *US* National Collegiate Athletic Association ✧ *The NCAA is an organization that organizes athletic activities for many U.S. colleges and universities.*

NCO /ˌɛnˌsiːˈoʊ/ *n, pl* **NCOs** [C] : NON-COMMISSIONED OFFICER

NC-17 /ˈɛnˌsiːˌsɛvənˈtiːn/ — used as a special mark to indicate that no one who is 17 years old or younger may see a particular movie in a movie theater • *The movie is rated NC-17.*

-nd *symbol* — used in writing after the number 2 for the word *second* • *He's in 2nd grade.*

ND *abbr* North Dakota

NE *abbr* **1** Nebraska **2** New England **3** northeast

Ne·an·der·thal /niˈændərˌtɑːl/ *n* [C] **1** : a type of early human being that existed very long ago in Europe — called also *Neanderthal man* **2** *informal* + *disapproving* **a** : a man who is stupid and rude **b** : a person who has very old-fashioned ideas and who does not like change • *Some Neanderthals continue to resist the education reform bill.*

¹**near** /ˈniə/ *adv* **1** : close to someone or something in distance • *Don't come any nearer (to me).* • *(figurative) We're getting nearer to the truth.* **2** : not far away in time • *The end of winter is near.* • *The day of the wedding drew near.* [=approached; got closer] **3** : almost or nearly • *a near perfect score* • *The job is (damn/damned/darn) near impossible.* — **(as) near as I can tell/figure** *US, informal* : based on what I know • *As near as I can tell, we'll arrive by six o'clock.*

²**near** *prep* : close to (something or someone) • *near the door/house/office* • *near midnight*

³**near** *adj* **1** : located a short distance away • *The nearest grocery store is three blocks away.* • *The airport is quite near.* **2** : not far away in time • *I hope to visit in the near future.* **3** *always before a noun* — used to refer to the side, end, etc., that is closer • *the near side of the lane* **4** *always before a noun* : almost happening • *The ceremony was a near disaster.* [=was nearly a disaster!] **5** *always before a noun* : close to being something • *a near celebrity/certainty/miracle* **6** *always before a noun* : closely related • *near relatives/relations* — **near and dear** : very close in relationship • *my nearest and dearest friend* — **near·ness** *n* [U]

⁴**near** *vb* [T/I] : to come closer in space or time to someone or something • *He always cheers up when baseball season nears.* • *We are nearing a decision.* • *The project is nearing completion.* [=is almost finished]

near·by /niəˈbaɪ/ *adj* : not far away • *a nearby village/river* — **nearby** *adv* • *They live nearby.*

Near East *n* — **the Near East** : MIDDLE EAST

near·ly /ˈniəli/ *adv* : not completely • *I see her nearly every day.* • *We nearly missed our flight.* • *I am nearly finished.* • *Nearly 100 people attended.* — **not nearly** : much less than : not at all • *It's not nearly as late as I thought it was.*

near miss *n* [C] **1** : an attempt that is almost successful • *After years of near misses, the team has finally won a championship.* **2** : an accident that is just barely avoided • *There have been two near misses at that airport recently.* **3** : a bomb that misses its target but still causes damage

near·sight·ed /ˈniəˌsaɪtəd/ *adj, chiefly US* : able to see things that are close more clearly than things that are far away • *He needs glasses because he's nearsighted.* [=(chiefly Brit) shortsighted] — **near·sight·ed·ness** /ˈniəˌsaɪtədnəs/ *n* [U]

neat /ˈniːt/ *adj* **1** : not messy • *His apartment is neat and clean.* • *neat handwriting* **2** : liking to keep things very clean and orderly • *They are both pretty neat people.* **3 a** : simple and clever • *a neat trick* **b** *US, informal* : pleasant, fun, or interesting • *a neat idea* • *She's a neat person who has traveled a lot.* **4** *of alcoholic drinks* : made without ice or water added • *I like my whiskey neat.* [=(US) straight] — **neat·ly** *adv* — **neat·ness** *n* [U]

neb·u·lous /ˈnɛbjələs/ *adj, formal* : difficult to see, understand, describe, etc. • *a nebulous answer/concept*

nec·es·sar·i·ly /ˌnɛsəˈserəli/ *adv, formal* — used to say that something is necessary and cannot be changed or avoided • *This endeavor necessarily involves some risk.* — **not necessarily** : possibly but not certainly — used to say that something is not definitely true • *Seats in the front row are not necessarily the best.*

nec·es·sary /ˈnɛsəˌseri/ *adj* **1** : so important that you must do it or have it : absolutely needed • *Is surgery really/absolutely necessary?* • *Food is necessary for life.* • *necessary ingredients* • *Add more water if/when necessary.* [=if/when it is needed] • *Take as much time as necessary.* [=as much time as you need] **2**

always before a noun, formal : unable to be changed or avoided ▪ *Higher prices are a **necessary** consequence of the new services.* ▪ *a **necessary** evil*

ne·ces·si·tate /nɪˈsɛsəˌteɪt/ *vb* **-tat·ed;** **-tat·ing** [*T*] *formal* : to make (something) necessary ▪ *A tight deadline necessitated working overtime.*

ne·ces·si·ty /nɪˈsɛsəti/ *n, pl* **-ties** **1** [*C*] : something that you must have or do ▪ *food, clothes, and other basic necessities* **2** [*U*] *formal* : the quality of being necessary ▪ *She talked about the necessity of having the right training.* **— by necessity** *or* **out of necessity** : because of conditions that cannot be changed ▪ *He works two jobs out of necessity.* **— necessity is the mother of invention** *see* ¹MOTHER **— of necessity** *formal* — used to say that something must happen or must be the way it is ▪ *Further changes will occur of necessity.*

¹**neck** /ˈnɛk/ *n* [*C*] **1** : the part of the body between the head and the shoulders ▪ *A giraffe is an animal with a very long neck.* **2** : the part of a piece of clothing that fits around your neck ▪ *T-shirts with round necks* **3** : a long and narrow part of something ▪ *the neck of a bottle* ▪ *a neck of land* **— breathe down someone's neck** *see* BREATHE **— neck and neck** : extremely close together in a race or contest ▪ *The two horses were neck and neck at the finish line.* **— neck of the woods** *informal* : the place or area where someone lives ▪ *He's from my neck of the woods.* **— risk your neck** : to do something that puts you in danger of serious injury or death ▪ *I would never risk my neck on a sport like skydiving.* **— save someone's neck** *see* ¹SAVE **— stick your neck out** : to do or say something you think is important even though it may have bad results ▪ *He's not afraid to stick his neck out to help other people.* **— up to your neck in** : deeply involved in or affected by (something) ▪ *She's up to her neck in work.*

²**neck** *vb* [*I*] *old-fashioned + informal* : to kiss for a long time in a sexual way ▪ *They were necking on the couch.*

neck·lace /ˈnɛkləs/ *n* [*C*] : a piece of jewelry that is worn around your neck ▪ *a gold/diamond/pearl necklace*

neck·line /ˈnɛkˌlaɪn/ *n* [*C*] : the shape of the opening of a piece of woman's clothing around the neck ▪ *The dress has a square/round neckline.*

neck·tie /ˈnɛkˌtaɪ/ *n* [*C*] *US* : a long piece of cloth that is worn by men around the neck and under a collar and that is tied in front with a knot at the top — called also *tie*

nec·tar /ˈnɛktɚ/ *n* [*U*] **1** *literary* : the drink that the Greek and Roman gods drank **2** : a thick juice made from a particular fruit ▪ *apricot/mango nectar* **3** : a sweet liquid produced by plants and used by bees in making honey

nec·tar·ine /ˌnɛktəˈriːn, *Brit* ˈnɛktəˌriːn/ *n* [*C*] : a sweet fruit that is like a peach but has smooth skin

née *or* **nee** /ˈneɪ/ *adj* — used after a married woman's name to identify the family name that she had when she was born ▪ *Mrs. Jane Doe, née Smith*

¹**need** /ˈniːd/ *vb* **1** [*T*] : to be in a condition or situation in which you must have (something) : to require (something) ▪ *I need some advice/help.* ▪ *Most babies need about 12 hours of sleep a day.* ▪ *a badly needed vacation = a much-needed vacation* ▪ *This plant needs lots of sunlight.* ▪ *Another delay is the last thing I need!* **2** [*T*] **a** — used to say that some action is necessary ▪ *laundry that needs washing = laundry that needs to be washed* **b** — used to say that it is important and necessary for someone to do something ▪ *We need you to answer a few questions.* **3** [*modal vb*] — used to say that something is necessary ▪ *All you need do is ask.* [=all you need to do is ask] — usually used in negative statements and in questions for which the answer is assumed by the speaker to be "no" ▪ *You need not answer these questions.* [=you don't have to answer these questions] ▪ *Need I point out that your father disagrees?* ✧ The modal verb *need* is used especially in British English. In U.S. English, it is commonly used in phrases like *need not apply* and *need I say more.* ▪ *High school dropouts need not apply.* [=they should not apply because they will not get the job] ▪ *The movie was a complete waste of time. Need I say more?* [=that is all I need to say]

²**need** *n* **1** [*C/U*] : a situation in which someone or something must do or have something ▪ *There is still a need for further discussion.* **2** [*C*] : something that a person must have : something that is needed ▪ *the basic needs of every human being* ▪ *The house is large enough for our needs.* **3** [*C*] : a strong feeling that you must have or do something ▪ *emotional needs* ▪ *a need to be loved* **4** [*U*] : a situation in which people do not have things that they need ▪ *They helped me in my hour of need.* [=when I most needed help] ▪ *He helped us in times of need.* ▪ *people in need* [=who are poor] **— if need be** : if something becomes necessary ▪ *You can call me at home if need be.* **— in need of** — used to say that someone or something needs to have something ▪ *The truck is in need of repair.* **— no need** — used to say that something is not necessary ▪ *There's no need to get angry/excited.* ▪ *"I'll get someone to help you." "No need. I can do it myself."*

need·ful /ˈniːdfəl/ *adj* **1** *formal + somewhat old-fashioned* : needed or necessary ▪ *What's most needful now is patience.* **2** *chiefly US* : in a state of needing something ▪ *needful children*

¹**nee·dle** /ˈniːdl̩/ *n* [*C*] **1 a** : a small, very thin object that is used in sewing and that has a sharp point at one end and a hole for thread **b** : one of the two long, thin sticks that are used in knitting and that are pointed at one end **c** : a very thin, pointed steel tube that is pushed through the skin so that something (such as a drug) can be put into your body or so that blood or other fluids can be taken from it ▪ *a hypodermic needle* **d** : a very thin tube used with a pump to put air

into a ball (such as a basketball or football) **2** : a long, thin object that moves to point to something (such as a measurement or direction) ▪ *a compass needle* **3** : a leaf that is shaped like a very thin stick ▪ *pine needles* **4** : a very small piece of metal that touches a record and produces sound when the record is played — *a needle in a haystack* *informal* : someone or something that is very hard to find ▪ *Searching for my lost earring was like looking for a needle in a haystack.* — see also PINS AND NEEDLES

²**needle** *vb* **nee·dled; nee·dling** [T] *informal* : to criticize and laugh at (someone) in either a friendly or an unkind way : TEASE ▪ *She needled him about his haircut.*

need·less /'ni:dləs/ *adj* : not needed or necessary — used to describe something bad that did not have to happen ▪ *needless suffering/waste* — *needless to say* — used to say that the statement you are making is obvious ▪ *The two candidates were equally popular. Needless to say, the election was very close.* — **need·less·ly** *adv*

nee·dle·work /'ni:dl̩ˌwɚk/ *n* [U] : things that are made by hand with a needle and thread or the activity or art of making such things ▪ *She enjoys doing needlework.*

needn't /'ni:dn̩t/ — used as a contraction of *need not* ▪ *You needn't worry.*

needy /'ni:di/ *adj* **need·i·er; -est** **1** : not having enough money, food, etc., to live properly ▪ *needy families* **2** : needing a lot of attention, affection, or emotional support ▪ *emotionally needy people* — **the needy** : poor people ▪ *collecting food for the needy* — **need·i·ness** *n* [U]

ne·far·i·ous /nɪˈferijəs/ *adj, formal* : evil or immoral ▪ *a nefarious plot/scheme*

ne·gate /nɪˈgeɪt/ *vb* **-gat·ed; -gat·ing** [T] *formal* : to cause (something) to not be effective ▪ *Alcohol negates the effects of the medicine.* [=prevents the medicine from working] ▪ *negate a contract* — **ne·ga·tion** /nɪˈgeɪʃən/ *n* [C/U] *formal* ▪ *The verdict was a negation of justice.* [=was unjust] ▪ *actions done in negation of the rules*

¹**neg·a·tive** /'nɛgətɪv/ *adj* **1** : harmful or bad ▪ *a negative effect/impact/experience* **2** : thinking about the bad qualities of someone or something ▪ *a negative attitude/outlook* **3 a** : expressing dislike or disapproval ▪ *The reviews were mostly negative.* ▪ *negative feedback/feelings* **b** : showing or talking about the bad qualities of someone or something ▪ *a negative political campaign* ▪ *negative advertising* **4** : expressing denial or refusal ▪ *a negative reply/answer* ▪ *negative words like "no" and "not"* **5** *mathematics* : less than zero ▪ *-2 is a negative number.* **6** *technical* **a** : containing or producing electricity that is charged by an electron ▪ *a negative charge/current* **b** : having more electrons than protons ▪ *a negative particle* **7** : not showing the presence of a particular germ, condition, or substance ▪ *a negative HIV/pregnancy test* — **neg·a·tive·ly** *adv*

²**negative** *n* [C] **1** : something that is harmful or bad ▪ *One of the negatives of the house is that it's on a busy street.* **2** : a word or statement that means "no" or that expresses a denial or refusal ▪ *"No" and "not" are negatives.* **3** : an image on film that is used to make a printed photograph and that has light areas where the photograph will be dark and dark areas where the photograph will be light; *also* : the film that has such an image **4** : the result from a test that shows that a particular germ, condition, or substance is not present ▪ *a false negative* [=a test result that incorrectly indicates that something is not present when it really is] — *in the negative formal* : with a reply that means "no" ▪ *She answered (the question) in the negative.* [=she answered "no"]

neg·a·tiv·i·ty /ˌnɛgəˈtɪvəti/ *n* [U] : an attitude in which someone considers only the bad qualities of a person or thing ▪ *Her negativity began to depress me.*

¹**ne·glect** /nɪˈglɛkt/ *vb* [T] **1** : to fail to take care of or to give attention to (someone or something) ▪ *The building was neglected for years.* ▪ *She neglected her child.* **2** : to fail to do (something) ▪ *The officer neglected his duty.* ▪ *He neglected to mention his name.* — **neglect·ed** /nɪˈglɛktəd/ *adj* ▪ *She felt lonely and neglected.*

²**neglect** *n* [U] **1** : lack of attention or care that someone or something needs ▪ *The parents were charged with child neglect.* **2** : the condition of not being taken care of ▪ *The house is in a state of neglect.* — **ne·glect·ful** /nɪˈglɛktfəl/ *adj* ▪ *neglectful parents* ▪ *She is neglectful of her appearance.*

neg·li·gee /ˌnɛgləˈʒeɪ/ *n* [C] : a long piece of clothing made of a thin material (such as silk) that is worn in bed by women

neg·li·gent /'nɛglɪdʒənt/ *adj* : failing to take proper or normal care of something or someone ▪ *negligent parents* ▪ *He was negligent in not reporting the accident to the police.* — **neg·li·gence** /'nɛglɪdʒəns/ *n* [U] — **neg·li·gent·ly** *adv*

neg·li·gi·ble /'nɛglɪdʒəbəl/ *adj* : very small or unimportant ▪ *a negligible amount of damage/money*

ne·go·tia·ble /nɪˈgoʊʃijəbəl/ *adj* **1** : able to be discussed and changed before an agreement or decision is made ▪ *The price was not negotiable.* **2** : able to be successfully traveled over ▪ *a rough but negotiable road* **3** *finance* : able to be passed from one person to another in return for something of equal value ▪ *negotiable bonds/securities*

ne·go·ti·ate /nɪˈgoʊʃiˌeɪt/ *vb* **-at·ed; -at·ing** **1 a** [T/I] : to discuss something formally in order to make an agreement ▪ *She is negotiating a higher salary.* ▪ *The team is negotiating with the player's agent.* **b** [T] : to agree on (something) by formally discussing it ▪ *We negotiated a fair price/contract.* **2** [T] : to get over, through, or around (something) successfully ▪ *The driver carefully negotiated the winding road.*

negotiating table *n* — **the negotiating table** — used to say that people are having formal discussions in order to reach an agreement ▪ *The two sides in this dispute have returned to the negotiating table.*

ne·go·ti·a·tion /nɪˌgouʃiˈeɪʃən/ *n* [*C/U*] : a formal discussion between people who are trying to reach an agreement ▪ *Negotiations with the protesters began today.* ▪ *The contract is under negotiation.* [=the details of the contract are being discussed]

ne·go·ti·a·tor /nɪˈgouʃiˌeɪtɚ/ *n* [*C*] : a person who is involved in formal financial or political discussions in order to try to reach an agreement

Ne·gro /ˈniːˌgrou/ *n, pl* **-groes** [*C*] *old-fashioned + sometimes offensive* : a person who has dark skin and who belongs to a race of people who are originally from Africa — **Negro** *adj, sometimes offensive*

neigh /ˈneɪ/ *vb* [*I*] *of a horse* : to make a loud, long sound — **neigh** *n* [*C*] ▪ *the neigh of a horse*

neigh·bor (*US*) *or Brit* **neigh·bour** /ˈneɪbɚ/ *n* [*C*] **1** : a person who lives next to or near another person ▪ *our next-door neighbors* [=the people who live in the house next to us] **2** : a person or thing that is next to or near another ▪ *Canada is a neighbor of the U.S.*

neigh·bor·hood (*US*) *or Brit* **neigh·bour·hood** /ˈneɪbɚˌhud/ *n* [*C*] **1** : a section of a town or city ▪ *a beautiful/quiet neighborhood* ▪ *the neighborhood school/park/children* **2** [*U*] : the people who live near each other ▪ *The whole neighborhood heard about it.* — **in the neighborhood** : in the area that is close to something ▪ *We'll visit them when we're in the neighborhood.* — **in the neighborhood of 1** : close to (a place) ▪ *somewhere in the neighborhood of southern California* **2** : close to or around (an amount) ▪ *The album sold in the neighborhood of 1,000 copies.*

neigh·bor·ing (*US*) *or Brit* **neigh·bour·ing** /ˈneɪbɚrɪŋ/ *adj, always before a noun* : near or next to something or someone ▪ *neighboring cities/countries*

neigh·bor·ly (*US*) *or Brit* **neigh·bour·ly** /ˈneɪbɚli/ *adj* : helpful and friendly ▪ *neighborly people/relations*

¹**nei·ther** /ˈniːðɚ, ˈnaɪðɚ/ *adj* : not one or the other of two people or things ▪ *Neither answer is correct.* [=both are wrong]

²**neither** *pron* : not the one and not the other of two people or things ▪ *Neither (of the two answers) is correct.*

> **usage** According to the rules of grammar, the pronoun *neither* is singular and requires a singular verb. ▪ *Neither is correct.* However, in informal writing and speech, a plural verb is common when *neither* is followed by *of*. ▪ *Neither of the answers is/are correct.*

³**neither** *conj* **1** — used with *nor* to indicate two or more people, things, actions, etc., about which something is not true ▪

Neither my wife nor I can attend the party. ▪ *I'm neither happy nor sad.* **2** : also not — used after a negative statement ▪ *"I don't believe him." "Neither do I."* [=I also do not believe him] — **neither here nor there** see ¹HERE

nem·e·sis /ˈnɛməsəs/ *n, pl* **-ses** /-ˌsiːz/ [*C*] : an opponent or enemy that is very difficult to defeat

Neo·lith·ic /ˌniːjəˈlɪθɪk/ *adj* : of or relating to the time during the Stone Age when people used stone tools and began to grow crops, raise animals, and live together in large groups but did not read or write ▪ *the Neolithic age/period*

ne·on /ˈniːˌɑːn/ *n* [*U*] : a type of gas that is used in brightly colored electric signs and lights — **neon** *adj* ▪ *neon lights/signs*

neo·na·tal /ˌniːjouˈneɪtl̩/ *adj, medical* : of, relating to, or taking care of babies in the first month after their birth ▪ *a neonatal intensive care unit*

neo·phyte /ˈniːjəˌfaɪt/ *n* [*C*] *formal* : a person who has just started learning or doing something : BEGINNER ▪ *a political neophyte*

neph·ew /ˈnɛfjuː/ *n* [*C*] : a son of your brother or sister

nep·o·tism /ˈnɛpəˌtɪzəm/ *n* [*U*] *disapproving* : the unfair practice by a powerful person of giving jobs and other favors to relatives

Nep·tune /ˈnɛpˌtuːn, *Brit* ˈnɛpˌtjuːn/ *n* [*singular*] : the planet that is eighth in order from the sun

nerd /ˈnɚd/ *n* [*C*] *informal + usually disapproving* **1** : a person who behaves awkwardly around other people and usually has unstylish clothes, hair, etc. **2** : a person who is very interested in technical subjects, computers, etc. ▪ *a computer nerd* — **nerd·i·ness** /ˈnɚdinəs/ *n* [*U*] — **nerdy** /ˈnɚdi/ *adj* **nerd·i·er; -est** ▪ *nerdy clothes* ▪ *a nerdy scientist*

nerve /ˈnɚv/ *n* **1** [*C*] : one of the many thin parts that control movement and feeling by carrying messages between the brain and other parts of the body **2** [*U*] : courage that allows you to do something that is dangerous, difficult, or frightening ▪ *It takes a lot of nerve to start a new career.* **3** [*U, singular*] : the rude attitude of someone who says or does things that make other people angry or upset ▪ *I can't believe she had the nerve to call me a liar.* **4** [*plural*] : feelings of being worried or nervous ▪ *The singer still suffers from nerves before a performance.* ▪ *Her nerves were on edge* [=she was nervous] *before her exam.* — **a bag/bundle of nerves** *informal* : an extremely nervous person — **get on someone's nerves** : to become extremely annoying to someone ▪ *That noise is getting on my nerves.* — **hit/strike/touch a nerve** : to make someone feel angry, upset, embarrassed, etc. ▪ *Something she said to him must have hit/struck/touched a nerve. I've never seen him so angry.* — **nerves of steel** : an impressive ability to remain calm in dangerous or difficult situations ▪ *a dangerous job that requires nerves of steel* — **war of nerves** : a situation in which people do or say things to make other people feel afraid or nervous about what will happen • *The company and the union are engaged in a war of nerves, with each side threatening the other.*

nerve cell *n [C]* : NEURON

nerve center *(US)* or *Brit* **nerve centre** *n [C]* : a place from which the activities of an organization, system, etc., are controlled • *the economic nerve center of a nation*

nerve gas *n [U]* : a poisonous gas that is used as a weapon in war

nerve–rack·ing or **nerve–wrack·ing** /ˈnɚvˌrækɪŋ/ *adj* : causing a person to feel very nervous • *a nerve-racking experience*

ner·vous /ˈnɚvəs/ *adj* **1 a** : having or showing feelings of being worried and afraid about what might happen • *She is/feels nervous about her job interview.* • *a nervous smile* • *He was a nervous wreck.* [=he was extremely nervous] **b** : often or easily becoming worried and afraid about what might happen • *He has a nervous disposition.* **c** : causing someone to feel worried and afraid • *It was a very nervous situation.* **2** *always before a noun* : of or relating to the nerves in your body • *nervous tissue* : caused by or affected by nerves • *a nervous habit/twitch* — **ner·vous·ly** *adv* — **ner·vous·ness** *n [U]*

nervous breakdown *n [C]* : a sudden failure of mental health that makes someone unable to live normally

nervous system *n [C]* : the system of nerves in your body that sends messages for controlling movement and feeling between the brain and the other parts of the body

nervy /ˈnɚvi/ *adj* **nerv·i·er; -est** *informal* **1** *US, approving* : having or showing courage or confidence • *a nervy performance* **2** *US, disapproving* — used to describe someone who says or does rude or shocking things that make other people angry or upset • *She was nervy enough to criticize the food we served her.* **3** *Brit* : unpleasantly nervous or excited • *Too much coffee makes me nervy.*

-ness /nəs/ *n combining form* : state : condition : quality • *goodness* • *friendliness* • *sickness*

¹nest /ˈnɛst/ *n [C]* **1 a** : the place where a bird lays its eggs and takes care of its young **b** : a place where an animal or insect lives and usually lays eggs or takes care of its young **2** : a home where people live • *a cozy little nest in the suburbs* • *when children leave/flee the nest* [=move away from home] **3** : a group of objects that are made in different sizes that fit inside each other • *a nest of boxes/tables* — **feather your (own) nest** see ²FEATHER

²nest *vb [I]* **1** : to build or live in a nest • *Robins nested in the tree.* **2** : to fit inside each other • *The smaller bowl can nest inside the larger one.*

nest egg *n [C]* : an amount of money that is saved over a usually long period of time to pay for something in the future

nes·tle /ˈnɛsəl/ *vb* **nes·tled; nes·tling** **1** *[I]* : to lie comfortably close to or against someone or something • *The puppy nestled (up) against him.* **2** *[T]* : to place (something) close to, next to, or within something • *He nestled his head against her shoulder.* • *The resort is nestled among the hills.* **3** *[I]* : to rest or settle softly into something • *The fly ball nestled into the outfielder's glove.*

nest·ling /ˈnɛstlɪŋ/ *n [C]* : a young bird that is not yet able to fly away from the nest

¹net /ˈnɛt/ *n* **1 a** *[C]* : a device that is used for catching or holding things or for keeping things out of a space and that is made of pieces of string, rope, wire, etc., woven together with spaces in between **b** *[U]* : the material used to make nets • *net curtains* **2** *[C] sports* **a** : a net that is hung across the middle of a playing area in some games (such as tennis, badminton, or volleyball) **b** : a net that is attached to a frame and that is used as the goal in some games (such as soccer, hockey, or basketball) • *He shot the puck into the net.* **3** *the Net* : the Internet — *doing business on the Net* — **slip/fall through the net** : to fail to be noticed or included with others • *talented players who slip through the net and never get to play professionally*

²net *vb* **net·ted; net·ting** *[T]* **1** : to catch (something) in a net • *We netted nine fish during the trip.* **2** *sports* **a** : to hit (a ball) into the net during a game (such as tennis) • *She netted her first two serves.* **b** : to score (a goal or point) by hitting, kicking, or shooting a ball or puck into a net • *She netted 15 points in the first half.* **3** : to gain or receive (an amount) as a profit • *We netted $50 on the sale.* **4** : to produce or get (something) as the result of an effort • *The investigation netted no clues.*

³net *also Brit* **nett** *adj, always before a noun* **1** — used to describe the amount or value of something after all costs and all expenses have been taken away • *the company's net profit/value* • *his net worth* **2** — used to describe the weight of something without its packaging or container • *the net weight of the shipment* **3** : after everything is completed • *The net result/outcome/effect of the new bridge will be fewer traffic jams.*

neth·er·world /ˈnɛðɚˌwɜld/ *n* **1** *the netherworld literary* : HELL **2** *[C]* : a place unknown to most people where secret and often illegal things are done • *a criminal netherworld*

netting *n [U]* : material that is used to make nets • *wire netting*

¹net·tle /ˈnɛtl̩/ *vb* **net·tled; net·tling** *[T]* : to make (someone) angry • *The mayor's recent actions have nettled many people.*

²nettle *n [C]* : a tall plant that has leaves with hairs that sting you if you touch them — **grasp the nettle** *Brit* : to deal with an unpleasant situation without delay

¹net·work /ˈnɛtˌwɚk/ *n [C]* **1 a** : a system of lines, wires, etc., that are connected to each other • *a network of blood ves-*

sels **b** : a system of computers and other devices (such as printers) that are connected to each other **2** : a group of people or organizations that are closely connected and that work with each other ▪ *a network of political allies* **3** : a group of radio or television stations that usually broadcast the same programs ▪ *a network news program*

²**network** *vb* **1** [*T*] : to connect (computers) in a way that allows information and equipment to be shared ▪ *The computers are networked to one main server.* **2** [*I*] : to talk with people whose jobs are similar to yours especially for business opportunities or advice ▪ *She spent the day networking with other executives.* — **net·work·ing** *n* [*U*]

neu·ral /ˈnɜrəl, *Brit* ˈnjʊərəl/ *adj, medical* : of, relating to, or involving a nerve or the nervous system ▪ *neural activity/impulses/pathways*

neu·ral·gia /nʊˈrældʒə, *Brit* njuˈrældʒə/ *n* [*U*] *medical* : a sharp pain that is felt along the length of a nerve — **neu·ral·gic** /nʊˈrældʒɪk, *Brit* njuˈrældʒɪk/ *adj*

neu·rol·o·gy /nʊˈrɑːlədʒi, *Brit* njuˈrɒlədʒi/ *n* [*U*] *medical* : the scientific study of the nervous system and the diseases that affect it — **neu·ro·log·i·cal** /ˌnʊrəˈlɑːdʒɪkəl, *Brit* ˌnjʊərəˈlɒdʒɪkəl/ *or chiefly US* **neu·ro·log·ic** /ˌnʊrəˈlɑːdʒɪk, *Brit* ˌnjʊərəˈlɒdʒɪk/ *adj* — **neu·rol·o·gist** /nʊˈrɑːlədʒɪst, *Brit* njuˈrɒlədʒɪst/ *n* [*C*]

neu·ron /ˈnɜrˌɑːn, ˈnjʊərɒn/ *also Brit* **neu·rone** /ˈnɜrˌoʊn, *Brit* ˈnjʊərəʊn/ *n* [*C*] *medical* : a cell that carries messages between the brain and other parts of the body and that is the basic unit of the nervous system

neu·ro·sci·ence /ˌnɜroʊˈsajəns, *Brit* ˌnjʊərəʊˈsajəns/ *n* [*U*] : the scientific study of nerves and especially of how nerves affect learning and behavior

neu·ro·sis /nʊˈroʊsəs, *Brit* njuˈrəʊsəs/ *n, pl* -**ses** /-ˌsiːz/ [*C/U*] : an emotional illness in which a person experiences strong feelings of fear or worry

neu·rot·ic /nʊˈrɑːtɪk, *Brit* njuˈrɒtɪk/ *adj* **1** *medical* : having or suggesting neurosis ▪ *neurotic patients/symptoms* **2** : often or always fearful or worried about something ▪ *He is neurotic about his job.* — **neurotic** *n* [*C*] — **neu·rot·i·cal·ly** /nʊˈrɑːtɪkli, *Brit* njuˈrɒtɪkli/ *adv*

¹**neu·ter** /ˈnuːtɚ, *Brit* ˈnjuːtə/ *adj, grammar, in some languages* : of or belonging to the class of words (called a gender) that ordinarily includes most of the words referring to things that are neither masculine nor feminine ▪ *The pronoun "it" is neuter.*

²**neuter** *vb* [*T*] **1** : to remove the sex organs from (an animal, especially a male animal) ▪ *She had her dog neutered by the veterinarian.* **2** *disapproving* : to make (something) much less powerful or effective ▪ *The bill was neutered by the changes made by the legislature.*

¹**neu·tral** /ˈnuːtrəl, *Brit* ˈnjuːtrəl/ *adj* **1 a** : not supporting either side of an argument, fight, war, etc. ▪ *neutral countries* **b** : not supporting one political view over another ▪ *a neutral journalist/maga-*

zine **2** : not connected with either side involved in a war, contest, etc. ▪ *neutral territory* **3** : not expressing strong opinions or feelings ▪ *The report was written in neutral language.* ▪ *a neutral tone of voice* **4** : not bright or strong in color : able to go easily with other colors ▪ *neutral tones/colors/fabrics* **5** *technical* : neither an acid nor a base ▪ *a neutral compound* **6** *technical* : not having an electrical charge ▪ *a neutral molecule* — **neu·tral·ly** *adv*

²**neutral** *n* **1** [*C*] : a color that is not bright or strong ▪ *She painted the room in neutrals.* **2** [*U*] : the position of the gears in a car, truck, etc., when they do not touch each other and power from the engine does not move the wheels ▪ *He put/left the car in neutral.* **3** [*C*] : a person, country, etc., that does not support either side of an argument, fight, war, etc.

neu·tral·i·ty /nuːˈtræləti, *Brit* njuːˈtræləti/ *n* [*U*] : the quality or state of not supporting either side in an argument, fight, war, etc. ▪ *political neutrality*

neu·tral·ize *also Brit* **neu·tral·ise** /ˈnuːtrəˌlaɪz, *Brit* ˈnjuːtrəˌlaɪz/ *vb* -**ized**; -**iz·ing** [*T*] **1** : to stop (someone or something) from being effective or harmful ▪ *The soldiers tried to neutralize the attack.* **2** *technical* : to cause (a chemical) to be neither an acid nor a base ▪ *This medicine neutralizes stomach acids.*

neu·tron /ˈnuːˌtrɑːn, *Brit* ˈnjuːˌtrɒn/ *n* [*C*] *physics* : a very small particle of matter that has no electrical charge and is part of the nucleus of all atoms except hydrogen atoms

nev·er /ˈnɛvɚ/ *adv* **1** : not ever : not at any time ▪ *I will never shop there again.* ▪ *We will never forget him.* ▪ *I never meant to hurt you.* **2** *chiefly Brit* — used to express surprise, doubt, or disbelief ▪ *"He's won the lottery." "Never!"* ▪ *"They're getting married." "Well, I never!"* [=I am very surprised or shocked to hear that] — **never ever** *see* EVER — **never fear** — used to tell someone not to worry or be afraid ▪ *Never fear, I think I have a solution.* — **never mind, never you mind** *see* ²MIND — **never so much as** — used to say that someone did not do something that was expected or should have been done ▪ *She never so much as thanked me.*

never–end·ing *adj* : ENDLESS ▪ *a never-ending chore/fight*

nev·er·more /ˌnɛvɚˈmoɚ/ *adv, literary* : never again ▪ *Nevermore shall I call you a friend.* [=I shall never call you a friend again]

nev·er·the·less /ˌnɛvɚðəˈlɛs/ *adv* : in spite of what has just been said ▪ *It was difficult, but they enjoyed it nevertheless.* ▪ *It was a predictable, but nevertheless funny, story.*

¹**new** /ˈnuː, *Brit* ˈnjuː/ *adj* **1 a** : not old : recently born, built, or created ▪ *a new library/store/baby* **b** : not used by anyone else previously ▪ *a new car/watch* **2 a** : recently bought, rented, etc. ▪ *his new apartment/house/dog* **b** : having recently become someone's relative, friend,

employee, etc. ▪ *his new wife/employee* **c** : recently added to an existing group, organization, etc. ▪ *There was a new kid in school today.* ▪ *She is new to the job.* **3** : replacing someone or something that came before ▪ *The team has a new coach.* **4** : recently discovered or learned about ▪ *a new species of fish* ▪ *This kind of work is still new to me.* **5** — used to describe a time, period, etc., that is beginning again and that is different from what came before ▪ *A new semester starts in the fall.* ▪ *He moved to the city to begin a new life.* [=a time in a person's life that is different in some important way from what came before] **6** : healthier or more energetic ▪ *I felt like a new man/woman after my vacation.* — **(as) good as new** or **like new** : in very good condition ▪ *He fixed the bicycle, and now it's as good as new.* — **the new** : new things ▪ *a mixture of the old and the new* — **turn over a new leaf** see ¹LEAF — **what else is new?** see ²ELSE — **what's new?** *US, informal* — used as a friendly greeting ▪ *Hey man, what's new?* — **new·ness** *n* [*U*]

²**new** *adv* : newly or recently — usually used in combination ▪ *new-laid cement*

New Age *n* [*U*] **1** : of or relating to ways of thinking and living that are similar to those of older cultures and that have been accepted in recent times by a group of people in place of the usual beliefs and methods of modern society ▪ *New Age spirituality* **2** — used to describe a type of instrumental music that is usually soft and relaxing ▪ *New Age music* — **New Ager** /-ˈeɪdʒɚ/ *n* [*C*]

new·bie /ˈnuːbi, *Brit* ˈnjuːbi/ *n* [*C*] *chiefly US, informal* : a person who has recently started a particular activity ▪ *a newbie on the Internet = an Internet newbie*

new·born /ˈnuːˌboɚn, *Brit* ˈnjuːˌbɔːn/ *adj, always before a noun* : recently born ▪ *a newborn baby/calf* — **newborn** *n, pl* **newborn** or **new·borns** [*C*] ▪ *a mother goat and all of her newborn*

new·com·er /ˈnuːˌkʌmɚ, *Brit* ˈnjuːˌkʌmə/ *n* [*C*] **1** : a person who has recently arrived somewhere or who has recently started a new activity ▪ *a newcomer to the city* **2** : something new that has recently been added or created ▪ *Our company is a newcomer to this market.*

new·fan·gled /ˈnuːˈfæŋgəld, *Brit* ˈnjuːˈfæŋgəld/ *adj, always before a noun* : recently invented or developed and hard to understand ▪ *newfangled electronics/gadgets*

new·found /ˈnuːˈfaʊnd, *Brit* ˈnjuːˈfaʊnd/ *adj, always before a noun* : recently discovered, acquired, or achieved ▪ *his newfound fame/freedom*

new·ly /ˈnuːli, *Brit* ˈnjuːli/ *adv* : a short time ago : RECENTLY ▪ *a newly married couple* ▪ *The room is newly painted.*

new·ly·wed /ˈnuːliˌwɛd, ˈnjuːliˌwɛd/ *n* [*C*] : a person who has recently married ▪ *the happy newlyweds*

new moon *n* [*C*] : the moon when it is completely dark

news /ˈnuːz, *Brit* ˈnjuːz/ *n* **1** [*U*] : new information or a report about something that has happened recently ▪ *What's the* big/latest news? ▪ *It was late summer when news of his death arrived.* [=when we learned that he had died] ▪ *We tried to* **break the news** [=tell the bad news] *to her gently.* ▪ *"The concert has been canceled." "Well, that is news to me."* [=I didn't know that] ▪ *Lower ticket prices are* **good news for** [=make things easier for] *sports fans.* ▪ *We haven't heard from his teacher lately, but* **no news is good news**. [=if he was doing badly, his teacher would have told us] **2** [*U*] **a** : information that is reported in a newspaper, magazine, television news program, etc. ▪ *local/international news* ▪ *The company has been* **in the news** *recently.* ▪ *TV news reporters* **b** *informal* : someone or something that is exciting and in the news ▪ *She's big news here in the city.* ▪ *That band is* **old news**. *= The band is* **yesterday's news**. [=that band isn't new or exciting anymore] **3** **the news** : a television news program ▪ *We saw it on the evening/nightly news.* — **have news for someone** — used when you are making a definite and forceful statement that someone does not expect, know about, or agree with ▪ *"You think you're going to win? Well, I've got news for you: you're not."*

news agency *n* [*C*] : an organization that collects and gives news to newspapers, magazines, television news programs, and radio stations

news·agent /ˈnuːzˌeɪdʒənt, *Brit* ˈnjuːzˌeɪdʒənt/ *n* [*C*] *chiefly Brit* : a person or shop that sells newspapers, magazines, and often paperback books

news·boy /ˈnuːzˌbɔɪ, *Brit* ˈnjuːzˌbɔɪ/ *n* [*C*] *chiefly US, old-fashioned* : a boy who sells or delivers newspapers

news·cast /ˈnuːzˌkæst, *Brit* ˈnjuːzˌkɑːst/ *n* [*C*] *chiefly US* : a radio or television program that reports the news

news·cast·er /ˈnuːzˌkæstɚ, *Brit* ˈnjuːzˌkɑːstə/ *n* [*C*] *chiefly US* : a person who reports and sometimes discusses the news on a radio or television show

news conference *n* [*C*] : PRESS CONFERENCE

news flash *n* [*C*] : a report on an important piece of news that is given in the middle of another television or radio show

news·group /ˈnuːzˌgruːp, *Brit* ˈnjuːzˌgruːp/ *n* [*C*] : a place on the Internet where people can talk about a particular subject by reading and leaving messages

news·let·ter /ˈnuːzˌlɛtɚ, *Brit* ˈnjuːzˌlɛtə/ *n* [*C*] : a short written report that tells about the recent activities of an organization and that is sent to members of the organization

news·man /ˈnuːzmən, *Brit* ˈnjuːzmən/ *n, pl* **-men** /-mən/ [*C*] : a person (usually a man) who gathers, reports, or comments on the news

news·pa·per /ˈnuːzˌpeɪpɚ, *Brit* ˈnjuːzˌpeɪpə/ *n* **1** [*C*] : a set of large sheets of paper that have news stories, information about local events, advertisements, etc., and that are folded together and sold every day or every week ▪ *a daily/weekly newspaper* ▪ *newspaper headlines/*

articles/reporters **2** [U] : the paper on which a newspaper is printed ▪ *an object wrapped in newspaper* **3** [C] : a company that publishes a newspaper ▪ *She worked for the newspaper for 20 years.*

news·print /'nuːzˌprɪnt, *Brit* 'njuːzˌprɪnt/ *n* [U] : the thin paper that is used for newspapers

news·read·er /'nuːzˌriːdɚ, *Brit* 'njuːzˌriːdə/ *n* [C] *Brit* : NEWSCASTER

news·reel /'nuːzˌriːl, *Brit* 'njuːzˌriːl/ *n* [C] : a short film that reported the news and that was shown in theaters in the past ▪ *old newsreels from World War II*

news·room /'nuːzˌruːm, *Brit* 'njuːzˌruːm/ *n* [C] : an office where the news is prepared for a newspaper or a television or radio program

news·stand /'nuːzˌstænd, *Brit* 'njuːzˌstænd/ *n* [C] : a place (such as a small outdoor store) where newspapers and magazines are sold

news·wom·an /'nuːzˌwʊmən, *Brit* 'njuːzˌwʊmən/ *n, pl* **-wom·en** /-ˌwɪmən/ [C] : a woman who gathers, reports, or comments on the news

news·wor·thy /'nuːzˌwɚði, *Brit* 'njuːzˌwəːði/ *adj* : interesting or important enough to report as news ▪ *a newsworthy story*

newsy /'nuːzi, *Brit* 'njuːzi/ *adj* **news·i·er; -est** *informal* : containing or full of a lot of news ▪ *a newsy letter/magazine*

newt /'nuːt, *Brit* 'njuːt/ *n* [C] : a small animal that lives mostly in water and that has four short legs, a long, low body and tail, and soft, wet skin

New Testament *n* — **the New Testament** : the second part of the Christian Bible that describes the life of Jesus Christ and the lessons that he taught — compare OLD TESTAMENT

new wave *n* **1** [C] : a movement in which a group of people introduce new styles or ideas in art, music, politics, etc. **2** *New Wave* [U] : a style of rock music that was popular especially in the 1970s and 1980s, has a strong beat, and uses many electronic instruments (such as keyboards) **3** [U] : a modern style of art, film, or fashion that tries to be very different or unusual often in a shocking way

New World *n* — **the New World** : North, Central, and South America, especially in the past ▪ *Columbus reached the New World in 1492.*

New Year *n* **1** *or chiefly US* **New Year's** [U] : the first day of the year celebrated as a holiday; *especially* : NEW YEAR'S DAY ▪ *Happy New Year!* ▪ *(chiefly US) a New Year's party* = *(Brit) a New Year party* **2** *or* **new year** [singular] : the year that is about to start or that has just started — usually used with *the* ▪ *It's sure to be the best film of the new year.* ▪ *We stayed up on New Year's Eve to* **see the new year in.** [=to see the beginning of the new year]

New Year's Day *n* [C/U] : January 1 celebrated as a holiday

New Year's Eve *n* [C/U] : December 31; *especially* : the evening of December 31

¹**next** /'nɛkst/ *adj* **1** : coming after this one ▪ *the next day* [=the day that comes

after this day] ▪ *I'll see you next week/ Monday.* ▪ *Next year's party will be even better.* ▪ *For the next two years* [=two years after this point], *she did nothing but eat, sleep, and study.* ▪ *Can I help the next person in line? = Who's next?* ▪ **Next time,** please bring your books to class. ▪ *I slipped, and the* **next thing I knew** [=right after that happened], *I was lying on the ground.* **2** : any other ▪ *I'm as patriotic* **as the next man.** [=as patriotic as anyone else] ▪ *She knew the answer as well* **as the next person.** — **next to** : almost but not quite ▪ *It's next to impossible to drive in this snow.* ▪ *You ate next to nothing at dinner.* ▪ *We were* **next to last** in line. [=there was one person or group behind us]

²**next** *adv* **1** : in the time or place that follows or comes directly after someone or something ▪ *What happens next?* ▪ *Next, I need to ask you a few questions about your family.* **2** : at the first time after this ▪ *when we next see each other* = *when we see each other next* = *(formal) when next we see each other* — **next to 1** : at the side of (someone or something) ▪ *He sat next to his grandmother.* ▪ *The house next to ours is for sale.* **2** : following or coming immediately after (someone or something) ▪ *Next to math, science was my worst subject in school.* **3** : in comparison with (someone or something) ▪ *Next to you, I'm wealthy.*

³**next** *pron* : a person or thing that immediately follows another person or thing ▪ *Her first novel was good, but I hope her next will be even better.* ▪ *We'll meet the week* **after next.** ▪ *She finished one project and began working on the next.* ▪ *Who will be the next to leave the company?* — **next of kin** : the person or people most closely related to you (such as your husband, wife, child, parent, sister, or brother) ▪ *We notified his next of kin of his death.*

next door *adv* **1 a** : in the next house, apartment, room, etc. ▪ *the people (who live) next door* ▪ *We've lived next door to each other for many years.* ▪ *the boy/girl* **next door** [=a wholesome young man/ woman from a middle-class family] **b** : next to your or someone else's house, apartment, room, etc. ▪ *He bought the house next door.* **2** : in a place that is very close to something else ▪ *Canada is right next door to the U.S.* — **next–door** /'nɛkstˈdoɚ/ *adj, always before a noun* ▪ *We've been* **next-door neighbors** *for many years.* ▪ *the next-door house*

NFC *abbr, US* National Football Conference ◆ The NFC and the AFC make up the NFL.

NFL *abbr, US* National Football League ◆ The NFL is the major professional (American) football league in the U.S.

NH *abbr* New Hampshire

NHL *abbr, US* National Hockey League ◆ The NHL is the major professional league for ice hockey in the U.S. and Canada.

ni·a·cin /'najəsən/ *n* [U] *technical* : a type of natural substance (called a vitamin) that is found in certain foods and that helps your body to be healthy

nib /'nɪb/ n [C] : the pointed metal tip of a pen

¹**nib·ble** /'nɪbəl/ vb **nib·bled; nib·bling**
1 [T/I] : to eat slowly or with small bites ▪ *We nibbled (on) cheese and crackers.* **2** [T] : to bite (something) very gently ▪ *He nibbled her ear.* — **nibble (away) at** [phrasal vb] : to make (something) disappear or go away very slowly ▪ *Police have been nibbling (away) at crime in the city for years.*

²**nibble** n **1** [C] : a small bite ▪ *May I have a nibble of your sandwich?* **2** [C] : an expression of interest in something ▪ *We've gotten a couple of nibbles on our house.* [=a couple of people have said that they were thinking about buying our house] **3** [plural] informal : small things to eat before a meal or at a party ▪ *They served some delicious nibbles before dinner.*

nice /'naɪs/ adj **nic·er; -est 1** : good and enjoyable ▪ *I hope you had a nice time.* ▪ *What a nice surprise!* ▪ *It's so nice to see you again.* ▪ **(US)** Thank you. **Have a nice day!** [=goodbye] ▪ "*Hello, my name is Sara.*" "*It's nice to meet you, Sara.*" ▪ *It's nice to see you, Luis. How have you been?* — often used with another adjective for emphasis ▪ *nice green grass* ▪ *The hotel has nice big rooms.* ▪ *The soup is nice and hot.* **2** : attractive or of good quality ▪ *a nice car/house/restaurant* ▪ *She wears the nicest clothes.* ▪ *She looks nice.* [=she is attractive] ▪ *It's a nice idea, but I don't think it'll work.* **3** : kind, polite, and friendly ▪ *He's such a nice young man.* ▪ *He said some very nice things about you.* ▪ *That wasn't a very nice thing to do.* **4** : proper and well-behaved ▪ *They have such nice children.* **5** : done very well ▪ *That was a nice shot!* ▪ *Nice work!* **6** formal : involving a small difference ▪ *There is a nice distinction between those two words.* — **make nice** US, informal : to behave in a polite or friendly way toward other people even though you do not have kind or polite feelings towards them ▪ *It's time to forget about the past and make nice.* — **nice and easy** informal : in a way that is slow, careful, gentle, or easy ▪ *The pilot brought the plane down nice and easy.* — **nice·ness** n [U]

nice–looking adj : ATTRACTIVE ▪ *She's a nice-looking young lady.*

nice·ly /'naɪsli/ adv : in a pleasant or correct way ▪ *a nicely dressed man* ▪ *a very nicely written essay* ▪ *Good work.* **Nicely done.** ▪ *The project seems to be moving along nicely.* "*Thanks. It will do nicely.*" [=it is suitable for what I want to do]

nice·ty /'naɪsəti/ n, pl **-ties** [C] : a small detail and especially one that is a part of polite or proper behavior ▪ *social/legal niceties*

niche /'nɪtʃ, 'ni:ʃ/ n [C] **1** : a job, activity, etc., that is very suitable for someone ▪ *She finally found her niche as a teacher.* **2** : the situation in which a business's products or services can succeed by being sold to a particular kind or group of people ▪ *This product fills a niche in the market.* [=provides something that cer-

tain kinds of people want to buy] ▪ *niche products/publications* [=products/publications that appeal to a particular kind or group of people] **3** technical : an environment that has all the things that a particular plant or animal needs in order to live ▪ *an environmental/ecological niche* **4** : a curved space in a wall that is designed to hold a statue, vase, etc.

¹**nick** /'nɪk/ n **1** [C] **a** : a small broken area that appears on something after something else hits or cuts it ▪ *There is a nick in the cup.* ▪ *a small cut on your skin* ▪ *He had a nick on his chin.* **2 the nick** Brit slang : a prison or police station ▪ *She spent a night in the nick.* **3** [U] Brit, informal : the condition that someone or something is in ▪ *in good/bad nick* [=in good/bad condition] — **in the nick of time** informal : just before the last moment when something can be changed to keep something bad from happening ▪ *Help arrived in the nick of time.*

²**nick** vb [T] **1** : to cut or damage a small part of the surface of (something) ▪ *Something nicked the painting.* : to make a small cut on (someone) ▪ *He nicked himself shaving.* **2** Brit slang **a** : to catch and arrest (someone) ▪ *She was nicked for the theft.* **b** : to steal (something) ▪ *Someone nicked my wallet.*

nick·el /'nɪkəl/ n **1** : a hard silver-white metal **2** [C] : a U.S. or Canadian coin that is worth five cents

nick·name /'nɪkˌneɪm/ n [C] : a name (such as "Moose" or "Lady Bird") that is different from your real name but is what your family, friends, etc., call you when they are talking to you or about you ▪ *His mother gave him the nickname "Winky" when he was a baby.* — **nickname** vb **-named; -nam·ing** [T] ▪ *She nicknamed him "Winky."*

nic·o·tine /'nɪkəˌti:n/ n [U] : a poisonous substance in tobacco that makes it difficult for people to stop smoking cigarettes

niece /'ni:s/ n [C] : a daughter of your brother or sister

nif·ty /'nɪfti/ adj **nif·ti·er; -est** informal : very good, useful, or attractive ▪ *a nifty little machine*

nig·gard·ly /'nɪgədli/ adj, formal + disapproving **1** : hating to spend money ▪ *a niggardly old woman* **2** : very small in amount ▪ *a niggardly allowance*

nig·gling /'nɪgəlɪŋ/ adj, always before a noun : causing you to feel a slight pain or to be worried or annoyed for a long time ▪ *a niggling injury/doubt*

nigh /'naɪ/ adv, old-fashioned + literary **1** : close in time or place : NEAR ▪ *Spring is (drawing) nigh.* **2** : almost or nearly ▪ *a nigh perfect evening* ▪ *We've lived here for nigh on* [=almost] *40 years.*

night /'naɪt/ n **1** [C/U] : the time of darkness between one day and the next ▪ *a cold, rainy night* ▪ *the night of June 20th* ▪ *It's eleven o'clock at night* ▪ *They were up all night (long) talking.* ▪ *Did you have a good night's sleep?* [=did you sleep well during the night?] ▪ *Last night, I had a strange dream.* ▪ *She'll have to spend/stay the night* [=to sleep overnight] *in the* *hospital.* **2** [U] : the darkness that occurs during the nighttime ▪ *Her eyes were as black/dark as (the) night.* **3** [C] : the early part of the night : EVENING ▪ *We went bowling on Tuesday night.* ▪ *a night out* [=an evening that you spend outside of your home doing something fun] **4** [C] **a** : an evening that has a special event ▪ *Friday night is our family night.* [=the night that our family does things together] ▪ *the play's opening night* [=the first time that the play will be performed for an audience] **b** : the part of a special day that occurs during the nighttime ▪ *Christmas night* ▪ *They spent their wedding night in a hotel.* — **day and night** or **night and day** see DAY — **night** *adj, always before a noun* ▪ *the night sky/air* ▪ *a night game* [=a game in the evening] ▪ *a night manager at the supermarket*

night·cap /ˈnaɪtˌkæp/ *n* [C] : a drink with alcohol in it that you have before you go to bed

night·club /ˈnaɪtˌklʌb/ *n* [C] : a place that is open at night, has music, dancing, or a show, and usually serves alcoholic drinks

night·dress /ˈnaɪtˌdrɛs/ *n* [C] *Brit* : NIGHTGOWN

night·fall /ˈnaɪtˌfɑːl/ *n* [U] : the time when the sky gets dark ▪ *We'll be back by nightfall.*

night·gown /ˈnaɪtˌgaʊn/ *n* [C] : a loose dress that is worn in bed

night·ie /ˈnaɪti/ *n* [C] *informal* : an often sexy nightgown

night·in·gale /ˈnaɪtɪnˌgeɪl/ *n* [C] : a small European bird that sings a beautiful song especially at night

night·life /ˈnaɪtˌlaɪf/ *n* [U] : activities and entertainment that are available at night in bars, nightclubs, etc. ▪ *The city is famous for its nightlife.*

night·light /ˈnaɪtˌlaɪt/ *n* [C] : a small light that is on during the night ▪ *a bedroom nightlight*

night·ly /ˈnaɪtli/ *adj* : happening or done every night ▪ *a nightly event* ▪ *the nightly news* ▪ *It happens on a nightly basis.* [=every night] — **nightly** *adv* ▪ *She performs there nightly.*

night·mare /ˈnaɪtˌmeɚ/ *n* [C] **1** : a very bad dream ▪ *I've been having nightmares.* **2** : a very bad or frightening experience or situation ▪ *The party was a complete nightmare.* ▪ *Losing a child is every parent's worst nightmare.* [=the thing every parent fears most] — **night·mar·ish** /ˈnaɪtˌmeriʃ/ *adj* ▪ *a nightmarish event*

night owl *n* [C] *informal* : a person who enjoys staying up late at night

nights /ˈnaɪts/ *adv, chiefly US* : during the nighttime ▪ *He works nights.*

night school *n* [U] : high school or college classes that are taught at night ▪ *She goes to night school.*

night·shirt /ˈnaɪtˌʃɚt/ *n* [C] : a long, loose shirt that you wear in bed

night·spot /ˈnaɪtˌspɑːt/ *n* [C] : NIGHTCLUB

night·stand /ˈnaɪtˌstænd/ *n* [C] *US* : a small table that is next to a bed — called also *night table*

night·stick /ˈnaɪtˌstɪk/ *n* [C] *US* : a heavy stick that is carried by police officers and is used as a weapon

night·time /ˈnaɪtˌtaɪm/ *n* [U] : the time of darkness between one day and the next ▪ *It's almost nighttime.*

ni·hil·ism /ˈnajəˌlɪzəm/ *n* [U] *formal* **1** : the belief that traditional morals, ideas, beliefs, etc., have no value **2** : the belief that a society's political and social institutions are so bad that they should be destroyed — **ni·hil·ist** /ˈnajəlɪst/ *n* [C] — **ni·hil·is·tic** /ˌnajəˈlɪstɪk/ *adj*

nil /ˈnɪl/ *n* [U] **1** : none at all : ZERO ▪ *The chances of that happening are nil.* **2** *Brit* : a score of zero ▪ *They took a 2 to nil lead.*

nim·ble /ˈnɪmbəl/ *adj* **nim·bler; nim·blest** **1** : able to move quickly, easily, and lightly ▪ *the pianist's nimble fingers* **2** : able to learn and understand things quickly and easily ▪ *a nimble mind* — **nim·bly** /ˈnɪmbli/ *adv*

nin·com·poop /ˈnɪŋkəmˌpuːp/ *n* [C] *informal* : a foolish or stupid person

nine /ˈnaɪn/ *n* **1** [C] : the number 9 **2** [C] : the ninth in a set or series ▪ *She wears a size nine.* **3** [U] : nine o'clock ▪ *He woke up at nine.* ▪ *a nine-to-five job* [=a job that you work during regular business hours] **4** : the first or last nine holes of an 18-hole golf course — *usually singular* ▪ *She played well on the front nine* [=holes 1 through 9], *but not on the back nine.* [=holes 10 through 18] — **on cloud nine** see ¹CLOUD — **the whole nine yards** see ¹YARD — **to the nines** : in a very fancy or impressive way ▪ *dressed to the nines* — **nine** *adj* ▪ *nine people* — **nine** *pron* ▪ *I would like nine, please.*

nine·teen /ˌnaɪnˈtiːn/ *n* [C] : the number 19 — **nineteen** *adj* ▪ *nineteen hours* — **nineteen** *pron* — **nine·teenth** /ˌnaɪnˈtiːnθ/ *n* [C] — **nineteenth** *adj* — **nineteenth** *adv*

nine·ty /ˈnaɪnti/ *n, pl* **-ties** **1** [C] : the number 90 **2** [*plural*] **a** : the numbers ranging from 90 to 99 ▪ *temperatures in the nineties* **b** : a set of years ending in digits ranging from 90 to 99 ▪ *I studied there in/during the nineties.* [=between 1990–1999] ▪ *He lived into his nineties.* [=until he was over ninety years old] — **nine·ti·eth** /ˈnaɪntijəθ/ *n* [C] ▪ *one ninetieth of the cost* — **ninetieth** *adj* ▪ *her ninetieth birthday* — **ninety** *adj* ▪ *ninety dollars* — **ninety** *pron* ▪ *We spent ten and had ninety left.*

nin·ny /ˈnɪni/ *n, pl* **-nies** [C] *informal + old-fashioned* : a foolish or stupid person

¹ninth /ˈnaɪnθ/ *n* **1** [*singular*] : the number nine in a series ▪ *We left on the ninth of May.* ▪ *a home run in the ninth* [=the ninth inning of a baseball game] **2** [C] : one of nine equal parts of something ▪ *She owns one ninth of the company.*

²ninth *adj* : occupying the number nine position in a series ▪ *She's in (the) ninth grade.* — **ninth** *adv* ▪ *the ninth largest city*

¹nip /ˈnɪp/ *vb* **nipped; nip·ping** **1** [T/I] : to bite or pinch (someone or something) lightly ▪ *The dog nipped (at) my ankles.* **2** [I] *chiefly Brit, informal* : to go to a place quickly or for a short period of time ▪ *I had to nip back to my place.* **3** [*T/I*] : to harm or hurt (something) with cold ▪ *The wind was nipping (at) my nose.* — **nip off** [*phrasal vb*] **nip off (something)** or **nip (something) off** : to remove (something) by squeezing it tightly between your fingers or the parts of a tool ▪ *He nipped off the bud with his fingers/clippers.* — **nip (something) in the bud** *informal* : to stop (something) so that it does not become a worse problem ▪ *Her bad behavior needs to be nipped in the bud.*

²**nip** *n* **1** [*singular*] : a feeling of cold ▪ *There's a nip in the air.* **2** [*C*] : a light bite or pinch ▪ *The dog gave me a nip on the leg.* **3** [*C*] *informal* : a small amount of liquor ▪ *a nip of whiskey* — **nip and tuck** *US* : so close that the lead changes quickly and often from one person or team to another ▪ *The race was nip and tuck for a while.*

nip·per /ˈnɪpɚ/ *n* **1** [*plural*] : a device or tool that is used for cutting something **2** [*C*] *chiefly Brit, informal* : a small child

nip·ple /ˈnɪpəl/ *n* [*C*] **1** : either one of the two small, round parts on a person's chest **2** *US* : a plastic device with a small opening that is attached to a baby's bottle — called also (*Brit*) **teat**

nip·py /ˈnɪpi/ *adj* **nip·pi·er; -est** *informal* **1** : somewhat cold ▪ *a nippy morning* **2** *Brit* : able to move quickly : FAST ▪ *a nippy car*

nir·va·na /nɪəˈvɑːnə, nəɚˈvɑːnə/ *n* [*U*] : the state of perfect happiness and peace in Buddhism

nit·pick·ing /ˈnɪtˌpɪkɪŋ/ *n* [*U*] *informal* : the act of arguing about small details or criticizing small mistakes that are not important ▪ *She was tired of all the nitpicking.* — **nit·pick·er** /ˈnɪtˌpɪkɚ/ *n* [*C*]

ni·trate /ˈnaɪˌtreɪt/ *n* [*C/U*] : a chemical compound used in fertilizer

ni·tric acid /ˈnaɪtrɪk-/ *n* [*U*] : a strong acid used in fertilizers, explosives, etc.

ni·tro·gen /ˈnaɪtrədʒən/ *n* [*U*] : a chemical that makes up a large part of the atmosphere

ni·tro·glyc·er·in *or* **ni·tro·glyc·er·ine** /ˌnaɪtrəˈɡlɪsərən/ *n* [*U*] : a liquid used in explosives and in medicine

nit·ty-grit·ty /ˈnɪtiˌɡrɪti/ *n* — **the nittygritty** *informal* : the most important and basic facts or details about something ▪ *Let's get down to the nitty-gritty of the problem.*

nit·wit /ˈnɪtˌwɪt/ *n* [*C*] *informal* : a stupid or silly person

nix /ˈnɪks/ *vb* [*T*] *US, informal* : to say no to (a suggestion, plan, etc.) ▪ *We nixed his idea.*

NJ *abbr* New Jersey

NM *abbr* New Mexico

NNE *abbr* north-northeast

NNW *abbr* north-northwest

¹**no** /ˈnoʊ/ *adv* **1 a** — used to give a negative answer or reply to a question, request, or offer ▪ *"Are you going?" "No, I'm not."* ▪ *"Do you need a ride?" "No, thank you."* ▪ *No, you can't have more candy.* ▪ *I said I couldn't come, but he wouldn't take no for an answer.* [=he insisted that I

come] **b** : in a way that shows a negative response ▪ *She shook her head no.* **2** — used to introduce a statement that corrects an earlier statement ▪ *No, that's not what happened.* ▪ *I saw him yesterday—no, the day before.* **3** : not at all — used in comparisons ▪ *He worked no more than 12 hours.* ▪ *Your experience was no different from mine.* **4** — used before an adjective to indicate a meaning that is the opposite of the adjective's meaning ▪ *It is a matter of no small importance.* [=a matter of much importance] **5** — used to show surprise, doubt, or disbelief ▪ *Oh, no. Not again.* ▪ *No, that's impossible.* **6** — used to express agreement with a negative statement ▪ *"She shouldn't do it." "No, she really shouldn't."* **7** — used to tell someone not to do something ▪ *No, don't touch that switch.*

²**no** *adj, always before a noun* **1** : not any ▪ *She had no money.* ▪ *people with little or no experience with computers* ▪ *The sign says "No smoking."* [=smoking is not allowed] ▪ *There's no disputing* [=it is not possible to dispute] *the decision.* **2** — used to say that someone or something is not the kind of person or thing being described ▪ *She's no fool.* ▪ *This is no joke.* [=this is not a joke]

³**no** *n, pl* **noes** *or* **nos** **1** [*C*] : an answer of no — usually singular ▪ *I asked for the day off and received a no in reply.* **2 a** [*C*] : a vote of no ▪ *There were 110 ayes and only 16 noes.* **b** [*plural*] : people who are voting no ▪ *The noes raised their hands.*

No. *or* **no.** *abbr* **1** number ▪ *He lives at No. 35 Main Street.* **2** north, northern

nob·ble /ˈnɑːbəl/ *vb* **nob·bled; nob·bling** [*T*] *Brit, informal* **1** : to give a drug to (a horse) to keep it from winning a race **2** : to cause or force (someone) to do something by offering money, making threats, etc. ▪ *nobble a witness/jury*

No·bel Prize /noʊˈbɛl-/ *n* [*C*] : one of six annual prizes that are awarded to people for work in literature, physics, chemistry, medicine, economics, and world peace

no·bil·i·ty /noʊˈbɪləti/ *n* **1** [*U*] : the quality or state of being noble in character or quality ▪ *the nobility of her character* **2 the nobility** : the group of people who are members of the highest social class in some countries ▪ *a member of the nobility*

¹**no·ble** /ˈnoʊbəl/ *adj* **no·bler; no·blest** **1** : having, showing, or coming from personal qualities that people admire (such as generosity, courage, etc.) ▪ *a man of noble character* ▪ *It was noble of her to accept the blame.* ▪ *a noble ideal/ambition/cause* **2** *always before a noun* : of, relating to, or belonging to the highest social class ▪ *a woman of noble birth/rank* **3** : impressive in size or appearance ▪ *a noble cathedral* — **no·bly** /ˈnoʊbli/ *adv*

²**noble** *n* [*C*] : a member of the nobility

no·ble·man /ˈnoʊbəlmən/ *n, pl* **-men** /-mən/ [*C*] : a man who is a member of the nobility

no·ble·wom·an /ˈnoʊbəlˌwʊmən/ *n, pl*

-wom·en /-ˌwɪmən/ [C] : a woman who is a member of the nobility

¹no·body /'noʊbədi/ *pron* : no person • *There's nobody here.* • **Nobody else will do it.** — **nobody's fool** see ¹FOOL

²nobody *n, pl* **-bod·ies** [C] : someone who is not important or has no influence • *He was a nobody in high school.*

no–brain·er /'noʊˈbreɪnɚ/ *n* [C] *informal* : a decision or choice that is very easy to make • *Choosing the winner was a no-brainer.*

noc·tur·nal /nɑkˈtɚnl/ *adj* **1** : active mainly during the night • *nocturnal animals* **2** *formal* : happening at night • *a nocturnal journey*

noc·turne /'nɑːkˌtɚn/ *n* [C] : a soft piece of music for the piano

¹nod /'nɑːd/ *vb* **nod·ded; nod·ding** **1** [*T/I*] **a** : to move your head up and down as a way of answering "yes" or of showing agreement, understanding, or approval • *He nodded (in) agreement/approval.* • *I asked her if she could hear me, and she nodded her head.* **b** : to move your head up and down as a signal to someone or as a way of saying hello or goodbye to someone • *She nodded hello. The guard nodded to/at us as we walked in.* **2** [*I*] : to slightly move your head in a specified direction • *"She's in there," he said, nodding toward the kitchen.* **3** [*I*] : to move up and down • *The tulips nodded in the breeze.* — **nod off** [*phrasal vb*] *informal* : to fall asleep • *I nodded off during his speech.*

²nod *n* **1** [C] : an up and down movement of the head : an act of nodding your head • *He gave me a nod as he walked by.* **2** [*singular*] : something done to show that someone or something has been chosen, approved, etc. • *She received/got the party's nod* [=the party chose her] *as candidate for governor.* • *We got the nod* [=got approval] *from the city to start the project.*

node /'noʊd/ *n* [C] *technical* **1** : a small lump of tissue in your body; *especially* : LYMPH NODE **2** : the small round part on the stem of a plant where a leaf grows

nod·ule /'nɑːdʒul, *Brit* 'nɒdjul/ *n* [C] *technical* : a small lump on a part of the body or on the root of a plant

noes *plural of* ³NO

no–fault *adj, always before a noun, chiefly US* **1** — used to describe a type of insurance in which someone involved in a car accident is paid a certain amount of money for damages without the need to decide who caused the accident • *a no-fault insurance policy/claim* **2** *law* — used to describe a type of divorce in which no one is blamed for the end of the marriage • *a no-fault divorce*

nog·gin /'nɑːgən/ *n* [C] *informal* : a person's head • *She got a bump on her noggin.*

no–good *adj, always before a noun, informal* : having no worth, use, or chance of success • *her lying no-good brother*

no–hit·ter /ˌnoʊˈhɪtɚ/ *n* [C] *baseball* : a game in which a pitcher does not allow the batters from the other team to get a base hit • *He pitched a no-hitter.*

no–holds–barred /ˌnoʊˌhoʊldzˈbɑɚd/ *adj* : free from the usual limits or rules • *a no-holds-barred interview*

noise /'nɔɪz/ *n* **1 a** [U] : a loud or unpleasant sound • *I can't hear you over all the noise.* **b** [C/U] : a sound that someone or something makes • *The car was making a rattling/banging noise.* **2** [U] *technical* : unwanted electronic signals in a radio or TV broadcast, a digital photograph, etc. — **make noise** : to talk or complain about something • *People have been making (a lot of) noise about the price increases.* — **noise·less** /'nɔɪzləs/ *adj*

noise·mak·er /'nɔɪzˌmeɪkɚ/ *n* [C] *US* : a device used to make noise at parties

noi·some /'nɔɪsəm/ *adj, literary* : unpleasant or disgusting • *a noisome odor*

noisy /'nɔɪzi/ *adj* **nois·i·er; -est** **1** : making a lot of loud or unpleasant noise • *The kids were being noisy.* • *a noisy crowd* **2** : full of loud or unpleasant noise • *a noisy restaurant* — **nois·i·ly** /'nɔɪzəli/ *adv*

no·mad /'noʊˌmæd/ *n* [C] : a member of a group of people who move from place to place instead of living in one place all the time • *a tribe of nomads* — **no·mad·ic** /noʊˈmædɪk/ *adj* • *a nomadic tribe/lifestyle*

no–man's–land /'noʊˌmænzˌlænd/ *n* [*singular*] : an area of land between two countries or armies that is not controlled by anyone • *(figurative) a no-man's-land of abandoned buildings*

no·men·cla·ture /'noʊmənˌkleɪtʃɚ, *Brit* nəʊˈmɛnkləʧə/ *n* [C/U] *formal* : a system of names for things especially in science • *botanical nomenclature*

nom·i·nal /'nɑːmənl/ *adj, formal* **1** : existing as something in name only • *He was the nominal head of the party.* [=he was called the head of the party but he did not actually run the party] **2** : very small in amount • *a nominal price/charge* — **nom·i·nal·ly** *adv*

nom·i·nate /'nɑːməˌneɪt/ *vb* **-nat·ed; -nat·ing** [T] **1 a** : to formally choose (someone) as a candidate for a job, position, office, etc. • *The party nominated him for president.* **b** : to choose (someone) for a job, position, office, etc. • *She was nominated to the Supreme Court.* **2** : to choose (someone or something) as a candidate for receiving an honor or award • *He was nominated for an Academy Award.* — **nom·i·na·tion** /ˌnɑːməˈneɪʃən/ *n* [C/U] • *The Senate approved his nomination.* • *Academy Award nominations*

nom·i·na·tive /'nɑːmənətɪv/ *n* [U] *grammar* : the form of a noun or pronoun when it is the subject of a verb • *"He" in "He sees her" is in the nominative (case).*

nom·i·nee /ˌnɑːməˈniː/ *n* [C] : a person or thing that has been nominated for a job, position, office, honor, award, etc. • *the Democratic nominee* • *the nominee for Attorney General*

non- /nɑn/ *prefix* : not • *nonfiction* • *nonprofit*

non·ag·gres·sion /ˌnɑːnəˈgrɛʃən/ *n* [U] : a situation in which countries promise that they will not attack each other • *a policy of nonaggression*

non·al·co·hol·ic /ˌnɑːnˌælkəˈhɑːlɪk/ *adj* : not containing any alcohol • *nonalcoholic drinks/beer*

non·be·liev·er /ˌnɑːnbəˈliːvə/ *n* [C] : a person who does not believe in a religious belief, a scientific idea, etc. • *trying to convince the nonbelievers*

non·bind·ing /nɑnˈbaɪndɪŋ/ *adj, law* : not able to be enforced by law • *We entered/signed a **nonbinding** agreement to buy our competitor, but we did not make an official promise to buy it*]

non·cha·lant /ˌnɑːnʃəˈlɑːnt/ *adj* : relaxed and calm in a way that shows that you do not care or are not worried about anything • *He was surprisingly nonchalant about winning the award.* — **non·cha·lance** /ˌnɑːnʃəˈlɑːns/ *n* [U] — **non·cha·lant·ly** *adv*

non·com·ba·tant /ˌnɑːnkəmˈbætnt/ *n* [C] **1** : a person (such as a military chaplain or doctor) who is in the army, navy, etc., but does not fight **2** : a person who is not in the army, navy, etc. : CIVILIAN

non·com·mis·sioned officer /ˌnɑːnkəˈmɪʃənd-/ *n* [C] : an officer who has a low rank in the army, air force, or marine corps — called also *NCO*

non·com·mit·tal /ˌnɑːnkəˈmɪtl/ *adj* : not telling or showing what you think about something • *He was noncommittal about how to spend the money.* — **non·com·mit·tal·ly** *adv*

non·con·form·ist /ˌnɑːnkənˈfoɚmɪst/ *n* [C] : a person who does not behave the way most people behave • *a political nonconformist* — **nonconformist** *adj* • *nonconformist behavior/views* — **non·con·for·mi·ty** /ˌnɑːnkənˈfoɚməti/ *n* [U]

non·count noun /ˈnɑːnˈkaʊnt-/ *n, grammar* : a noun (such as "sand" or "butter") that refers to something that cannot be counted ◇ Noncount nouns do not have a plural form and are not used with the indefinite articles *a* and *an.* — compare COUNT NOUN

non·dairy /nɑnˈderi/ *adj* : not containing or made with milk • *nondairy creamer*

non·de·nom·i·na·tion·al /ˌnɑːndiˌnɑːməˈneɪʃənl/ *adj* : not restricted to a single religious group • *a nondenominational church/service*

non·de·script /ˌnɑːndɪˈskrɪpt/ *adj* : having no special or interesting qualities, parts, etc. • *a nondescript office building*

¹**none** /ˈnʌn/ *pron* : not any of a group of people or things : no amount or part of something • *None of the birds was/were singing.* • *"Can I have some soup?" "I'm afraid there's none left."* • *"You have no doubts?" "None whatsoever."* • *This is none of your business.* [=you should not interfere in this situation] — **have none of** : to refuse to accept, allow, or be influenced by (a particular behavior) • *I will have none of that kind of talk in my house.* — **none but** *formal* : no person or kind of person except : ONLY • *a sport for none but the most brave* — **none other than** — used to show that you are

surprised or impressed by the person or thing you are about to mention • *I was sitting next to none other than the founder of the magazine.* — **none the less** : NONETHELESS — **second to none** : better than all others of the same kind • *His cakes are second to none.*

²**none** *adv* — **none the** — used in phrases to say that someone or something is not any worse, better, etc., than before • *We had to change our plans, but we were **none the worse** for it in the end.* • *She's been traveling for five days but seems **none the worse for wear**.* • *They replaced the lobster with crab, and we were **none the wiser**.* [=we did not know that it was not lobster] — **none too** : not at all • *He was none too happy about it.*

non·en·ti·ty /nɑnˈɛntəti/ *n, pl* **-ties** [C] : a person who is not famous or important • *She went from being a nonentity to being extremely famous.*

non·es·sen·tial /ˌnɑːnɪˈsɛnʃəl/ *adj* : not completely necessary • *All nonessential personnel were laid off.* — **nonessential** *n* [C] • *money for nonessentials like haircuts and vacations*

none·the·less /ˌnʌndəˈlɛs/ *adv* : in spite of what has just been said : NEVERTHELESS • *The hike was difficult, but fun nonetheless.* [=the hike was fun even though it was difficult]

non·event /ˈnɑːnɪˌvɛnt/ *n* [C] *informal* : an event that is much less interesting or important than it was expected to be • *Her resignation was a nonevent.*

non·ex·ec·u·tive (*chiefly US*) or *chiefly Brit* **non·ex·ec·u·tive** /ˌnɑːnɪgˈzɛkjətɪv/ *adj, always before a noun, business* : allowed to give advice but not allowed to make important decisions • *a nonexecutive director/chairman*

non·ex·is·tent /ˌnɑːnɪgˈzɪstənt/ *adj* : not present or real • *The disease is nonexistent in most places.* • *nonexistent dangers/threats* — **non·ex·is·tence** /ˌnɑːnɪgˈzɪstəns/ *n* [U]

non·fat /ˈnɑːnˈfæt/ *adj* : with the fat removed • *nonfat milk*

non·fa·tal /ˈnɑːnˈfeɪtl/ *adj* : not causing death • *a nonfatal shooting*

non·fic·tion /ˈnɑːnˈfɪkʃən/ *n* [U] : writing that is about facts or real events • *He reads a lot of nonfiction.* • *nonfiction books*

non·flam·ma·ble /ˈnɑːnˈflæməbəl/ *adj* : not easily set on fire • *nonflammable fabric*

non·gov·ern·men·tal /ˌnɑnˌgʌvənˈmɛntl/ *also* **non·gov·ern·ment** /nɑnˈgʌvənmənt/ *adj* : not belonging to or controlled by a government • *nongovernmental charities/organizations*

non·hu·man /nɑnˈhjuːmən/ *adj* : not a human being • *nonhuman primates*

non·in·ter·ven·tion /ˌnɑːnˌɪntəˈvɛnʃən/ *n* [U] : refusal to become involved in another country's business, problems, etc. • *a policy of nonintervention*

non·in·va·sive /ˌnɑːnɪnˈveɪsɪv/ *adj, medical* : done without cutting the body or putting something into the body • *noninvasive treatments*

non·is·sue /ˈnɑːnˈɪʃu/ *n* [C] : an issue

that is not important • *She's good at her job. Her disability is a nonissue.*

non·mem·ber /ˈnɑːnˈmɛmbɚ/ *n* [C] : someone who is not a member of an organization • *The fee is $10 for nonmembers.*

non·na·tive /nɑnˈneɪtɪv/ *adj* 1 : living or growing in a place that is not the region where it naturally lives and grows • *non-native plants/animals/species* 2 : not born or raised in the place where a particular language is spoken • *nonnative speakers of English* — **nonnative** *n* [C] • *classes for non-natives*

no-no /ˈnoʊˌnoʊ/ *n, pl* **no-no's** *or* **no-nos** [C] *informal* : something that people are not supposed to do because it is not proper, safe, fashionable, etc. • *Sharing your prescription medication is a definite no-no.*

no-nonsense *adj* : very serious about doing things in a direct and efficient way without any foolishness • *a doctor who is very no-nonsense* • *a no-nonsense attitude*

non·par·ti·san /ˈnɑːnˈpɑɚtəzən/ *adj* : not supporting one political party or group over another • *a nonpartisan organization*

non·plussed *also US* **non·plused** /ˌnɑːnˈplʌst/ *adj, not before a noun, formal* : so surprised or confused that you do not know what to say, think, or do • *He was nonplussed by her reaction.*

non·prof·it /ˈnɑːnˈprɑːfət/ *adj* : not existing or done to make a profit • *a nonprofit group/organization that helps the homeless* — **nonprofit** *n* [C] • *She works for a nonprofit.* [=a nonprofit organization]

non–prof·it–making *adj, Brit* : NON-PROFIT

non·pro·lif·er·a·tion /ˌnɑːnprəˌlɪfəˈreɪʃən/ *n* [U] : the act of stopping or limiting the production of nuclear and chemical weapons • *a nonproliferation treaty*

non·re·fund·able /ˌnɑːnrɪˈfʌndəbəl/ *adj* 1 *of something you buy* : not allowed to be returned in exchange for the money you paid • *The tickets are nonrefundable.* 2 *of a payment* : not to be returned • *a nonrefundable deposit*

non·re·new·able /ˌnɑːnrɪˈnuːwəbəl/ *adj* 1 : not able to be replaced by nature • *nonrenewable resources such as oil* 2 : not continued or repeated after a period of time has ended • *a nonrenewable contract/lease*

non·re·stric·tive /ˌnɑːnrɪˈstrɪktɪv/ *adj* 1 : not limiting or controlling something • *nonrestrictive clothing* [=clothes that do not make it difficult to move freely] 2 *grammar* : giving information about a person or thing but not needed to understand which person or thing is meant • *In the sentence "My son, who works at a deli, just got his first car," "who works at a deli" is a nonrestrictive clause.*

non·sense /ˈnɑːnˌsɛns/ *n* [U] 1 : words or ideas that are foolish or untrue • *The story was sheer/utter/complete/absolute nonsense.* [=it was completely false] • *You were attacked by a frog? Nonsense.* [=I do not believe that you were attacked by a frog] • *Don't listen to him. He's talking nonsense.* 2 : behavior that is silly, annoying, or unkind • *She doesn't take any nonsense from anyone.* 3 : language that has no meaning • *Her stories are full of nonsense words.* — **make (a) nonsense of** *Brit* : to take away the value or usefulness of (something) • *The lack of guards makes a nonsense of the security checkpoint.*

non·sen·si·cal /ˌnɑːnˈsɛnsɪkəl/ *adj* : very foolish or silly • *a nonsensical argument*

non se·qui·tur /ˈnɑːnˈsɛkwətɚ/ *n* [C] : a statement that is not connected in a logical or clear way to anything said before it

non·sex·ist /nɑnˈsɛksɪst/ *adj* : treating men and women equally and fairly • *nonsexist language*

non·slip /ˈnɑːnˈslɪp/ *adj* : made to prevent slipping • *a nonslip handle*

non·smok·er /ˌnɑːnˈsmoʊkɚ/ *n* [C] : a person who does not smoke

non·smok·ing /nɑnˈsmoʊkɪŋ/ *adj* — used to describe a place where people are not allowed to smoke • *the restaurant's nonsmoking section*

non·spe·cif·ic /ˌnɑːnspɪˈsɪfɪk/ *adj* 1 *medical* : not clearly having one specific cause • *nonspecific symptoms* 2 : lacking specific details • *a nonspecific threat*

non·stan·dard /ˌnɑːnˈstændɚd/ *adj* 1 : not accepted or used by most of the educated speakers and writers of a language • *a nonstandard word/dialect* 2 : not the usual size or kind • *a nonstandard-sized card*

non·start·er /ˌnɑːnˈstɑɚtɚ/ *n* [C] *informal* : someone or something that will not be effective or successful — usually singular • *As a candidate, he's a nonstarter.* [=he has no chance to succeed] • *The proposal was a political nonstarter.*

non·stick /ˈnɑːnˈstɪk/ *adj* : allowing easy removal of cooked food • *a nonstick pan*

non·stop /ˈnɑːnˈstɑːp/ *adj* 1 : done or made without stopping • *a nonstop flight* 2 : not stopping • *The action in the movie is nonstop.* [=action happens throughout the movie] — **nonstop** *adv* • *The baby cried nonstop for hours.*

non·threat·en·ing /nɑnˈθrɛtnɪŋ/ *adj* : not likely to cause someone to be afraid or worried • *Approach the dog in a calm, nonthreatening way.*

non·union /ˈnɑːnˈjuːnjən/ *adj* 1 : not belonging to a labor union • *nonunion workers* 2 : not having employees who are members of a labor union • *a nonunion construction firm*

non·ver·bal /ˈnɑːnˈvɚbəl/ *adj* 1 : not involving or using words • *nonverbal communication* 2 : not able to speak • *a nonverbal child* — **non·ver·bal·ly** *adv*

non·vi·o·lence /ˈnɑːnˈvajələns/ *n* [U] : the practice of refusing to respond to anything (such as unfair or violent acts by a government) with violence • *The group promotes nonviolence.* — **non·vi·o·lent** /ˈnɑːnˈvajələnt/ *adj* • *a nonviolent protest* — **non·vi·o·lent·ly** *adv*

non·white /ˈnɑːnˈwaɪt/ *n* [C] : a person who does not have the light-colored skin of Europeans — **nonwhite** *adj* • *nonwhite students*

noo·dle /ˈnuːdl̩/ *n* [C] : a thin strip of dough that is cooked in boiling liquid ▪ *chicken noodle soup* [=soup made with chicken and noodles]

nook /ˈnʊk/ *n* [C] **1** : a small space or corner that is inside something ▪ *an old house full of nooks and crannies* ▪ (*figurative*) *We searched every nook and cranny.* [=we searched everywhere] **2** : a part of a room that is used for a specific purpose ▪ *a breakfast nook*

noon /ˈnuːn/ *n* [U] : 12 o'clock in the daytime ▪ *Meet me at/around noon.* — **morning, noon, and night** see MORNING

noon·day /ˈnuːnˌdeɪ/ *n* [U] *literary* : the middle of the day ▪ *the heat of the noonday sun*

no one *pron* : no person : NOBODY ▪ *No one was home.* ▪ *No one knows her better than I do.*

noon·time /ˈnuːnˌtaɪm/ *n* [U] : NOON ▪ *The traffic gets heavy at noontime.*

noose /ˈnuːs/ *n* [C] : a large loop at the end of a rope that gets smaller when you pull the rope and that is used to hang people, to capture animals, etc. ▪ (*figurative*) *The law will tighten the noose on* [=make a situation more difficult for] *drug offenders.*

nope /ˈnoʊp/ *adv, informal* : ¹NO ▪ *"Are you finished?" "Nope."*

nor /ˈnoɚ/ *conj* **1** — used after *neither* to show something is also not true, allowed, etc. ▪ *It's neither good nor bad.* ▪ *I neither know nor care what they think.* **2** — used after a negative statement to introduce a related negative word or statement ▪ *He is not going to the meeting* (*and*) *nor am I.*

Nor·dic /ˈnoɚdɪk/ *adj* : of or relating to Sweden, Norway, Denmark, and sometimes Finland and Iceland, or to the people who live there ▪ *Nordic countries/languages*

norm /ˈnoɚm/ *n* **1** [*plural*] : standards of proper or acceptable behavior ▪ *social/cultural norms* **2 the norm** : an average level of development or achievement ▪ *She scored well above the norm in math.* **3 the norm** : a behavior, way of doing something, etc., that is usual or expected ▪ *Smaller families have become the norm.*

¹**nor·mal** /ˈnoɚməl/ *adj* **1** : usual or ordinary : not strange ▪ *a normal day* ▪ *He had a normal childhood.* ▪ *a normal part of life* **2** : mentally and physically healthy ▪ *a normal, healthy baby* ▪ *It's* (*perfectly*) *normal to feel that way.* — **nor·mal·ly** *adv* ▪ *Normally, I would say no, but I'll make an exception.* ▪ *The dog is not behaving normally.*

²**normal** *n* [U] : the usual or expected state, level, amount, etc. ▪ *Things are back to normal.* ▪ *Oil prices are below normal.*

nor·mal·cy /ˈnoɚməlsi/ *n* [U] *chiefly US* : a normal condition or situation : NORMALITY ▪ *a return to normalcy*

nor·mal·i·ty /noɚˈmæləti/ *n* [U] : a condition or situation in which things happen in the normal or expected way ▪ *I'm trying to maintain a sense of normality.*

nor·mal·ize *also Brit* **nor·mal·ise** /ˈnoɚməˌlaɪz/ *vb* **-ized; -iz·ing** [T/I] *for-*

mal : to bring (someone or something) back to a usual or expected state or condition ▪ *The talks are aimed at normalizing relations between the countries.* ▪ *The situation has not yet normalized.* — **nor·mal·i·za·tion** *also Brit* **nor·mal·i·sa·tion** /ˌnoɚmələˈzeɪʃən, *Brit* ˌnɔːməˌlaɪˈzeɪʃən/ *n* [U]

Norse /ˈnoɚs/ *n* **1 the Norse** : the people of ancient Norway, Sweden, Denmark, or Iceland ▪ *The Norse arrived in the ninth century.* **2** [U] : the language of the Norse — **Norse** *adj, always before a noun* ▪ *Norse mythology*

north /ˈnoɚθ/ *n* **1** [U] : the direction that is to your left when you are facing the rising sun ▪ *The wind is coming from the north.* **2 the north or the North** : regions or countries north of a certain point ▪ *The birds migrate from the North.*; *especially* : the northern part of the U.S. ▪ *The American Civil War was between the North and the South.* — **up north** *informal* : in or to the northern part of a country or region ▪ *We headed up north for the summer.* — **north** *adj* ▪ *North America* ▪ *a north wind* [=a wind that comes from the north] — **north** *adv* ▪ *Turn north onto Elm Street.*

north·bound /ˈnoɚθˌbaʊnd/ *adj* : going or heading north ▪ *a northbound train*

north·east /noɚˈθiːst/ *n* **1** [U] : the direction between north and east **2 the northeast or the Northeast** : the northeastern part of a country or region; *especially* : the northeastern part of the U.S. ▪ *I grew up in the Northeast.* — **northeast** *adj* ▪ *northeast India* ▪ *a northeast wind* [=a wind that comes from the northeast] — **northeast** *adv* ▪ *We headed northeast.* — **north·east·ern** /noɚˈθiːstən/ *adj* ▪ *the northeastern corner of the state*

north·east·er·ly /noɚˈθiːstɚli/ *adj* **1** : located in or moving toward the northeast ▪ *sailing in a northeasterly direction* **2** : blowing from the northeast ▪ *northeasterly winds*

north·er·ly /ˈnoɚðɚli/ *adj* **1** : located in or moving toward the north ▪ *a northerly direction* **2** : blowing from the north ▪ *northerly winds*

north·ern /ˈnoɚðɚn/ *adj* **1** : located in or toward the north ▪ *northern Europe* **2** : of or relating to the north ▪ *northern winters/cities*

north·ern·er *or* **Northerner** /ˈnoɚðɚnɚ/ *n* [C] : a person born, raised, or living in the north

Northern Lights *n* — **the Northern Lights** : large areas of green, red, blue, or yellow light that sometimes appear in the night sky in far northern regions

north·ern·most /ˈnoɚðɚnˌmoʊst/ *adj* : furthest to the north ▪ *the northernmost tip of the island*

North Pole *n* — **the North Pole** : the most northern point of the Earth

North Star *n* — **the North Star** : a bright star that can be seen in northern parts of the world when you look directly toward the north

north·ward /ˈnoɚθwɚd/ *also chiefly Brit* **north·wards** /ˈnoɚθwɚdz/ *adv* : toward the north • *The storm is moving northward.* — **northward** *adj* • *a northward advance*

north·west /noɑθ'wɛst/ *n* **1** [U] : the direction between north and west **2** *the northwest* *or* *the Northwest* : the northwestern part of a country or region; *especially* : the northwestern part of the U.S. • *We traveled throughout the Northwest.* • *the Pacific Northwest* [=the northwestern part of the U.S. near the Pacific coast] — **northwest** *adj* • *northwest China* • *a northwest wind* [=a wind blowing from the northwest] — **northwest** *adv* • *Head northwest on Route 1.* — **northwest·ern** /noɑθ'wɛstɚn/ *adj* • *the northwestern corner of the state*

north·west·er·ly /noɑθ'wɛstɚli/ *adj* **1** : located in or moving toward the northwest • *in a northwesterly direction* **2** : blowing from the northwest • *northwesterly winds*

Nor·we·gian /noɑ'wi:dʒən/ *n* **1** [C] : a person from Norway **2** [U] : the language of Norway — **Norwegian** *adj* • *She's Norwegian.*

nos *plural of* ³NO

nos. *abbr* numbers

¹**nose** /'nouz/ *n* **1** [C] : the part of the face through which a person or animal smells and breathes • *The ball hit me right on/in the nose.* • *You need to wipe/blow your nose.* • *the long nose of the anteater* • *Our horse won the race by a nose!* [=by a very short distance] • *The smell was so bad we had to hold our noses.* [=hold our nostrils together so that we could not smell anything] • *(figurative) She looks down her nose at us.* [=she does not respect us] • *(figurative) You'll do well at school if you just keep your nose to the grindstone.* [=do hard, continuous work] **2** [*singular*] : the ability to smell things • *(figurative) a reporter with a nose for news* [=who is good at finding news] **3** [C/U] : the front end or part of something • *the nose of an airplane* — **as plain as the nose on your face** *informal* : very clear or obvious • *The solution is as plain as the nose on your face.* — **cut off your nose to spite your face** : to do something that is meant to harm someone else but that also harms you — **follow your nose** see FOLLOW — **get up someone's nose** *Brit, informal* : to annoy or irritate (someone) • *He really gets up my nose.* [=(US) gets on my nerves] — **have your nose in** ✧ If you *have your nose in* a book, magazine, newspaper, etc., you are reading it. — **keep your nose clean** : to stay out of trouble by behaving well • *He has kept his nose clean since he got out of prison.* — **keep your nose out of** : to avoid becoming involved in (someone else's situation, problem, etc.) • *It's not your problem, so keep your nose out of it.* — **nose in the air** ✧ If you have your *nose in the air*, you behave in a way that shows you think you are better than other people. — **on the nose** *informal* : very accurate : done very accurately • *You hit it on the nose.* [=you are exactly right] • *Her prediction was right on the nose.* — **pay**

through the nose *informal* : to pay a very high price • *I paid through the nose for this dress.* — **rub someone's nose in** see ¹RUB — **stick/poke your nose in/into** : to get involved in or want information about (something that does not concern you) • *Stop poking your nose into other people's business.* — **thumb your nose at** see ²THUMB — **turn up your nose** *or* **turn your nose up** : to refuse to take or accept something because it is not good enough • *We made them an offer, but they turned up their nose at it.* — **under your nose** — used to describe something that you fail to see or notice even though you should • *They were embezzling funds right under his nose.* • *The answer was right under our noses* [=it was very obvious] *the whole time.* — **nosed** /'nouzd/ *adj* • *a long-nosed animal* [=an animal with a long nose]

²**nose** *vb* **nosed; nos·ing** **1** [T] : to push or move (something) with the nose • *The horse nosed my hand.* **2** [I] : to search for or find something by smelling • *The dogs were nosing around in the garbage.* **3** [T/I] : to move forward slowly or carefully • *The car nosed its way into the street.* — **nose around/about** [*phrasal vb*] : to search for something (such as private information) in usually a quiet or secret way • *She caught him nosing around (in her office).* — **nose out** [*phrasal vb*] **nose (someone or something) out** *or* **nose out (someone or something)** : to defeat (someone or something) by a small amount in a race or other competition • *My horse was/got nosed out at the finish line.*

nose·bleed /'nouz,bli:d/ *n* [C] : a condition in which you are bleeding from your nose • *I had/got a nosebleed.*

nose cone *n* [C] : the pointed front end of an aircraft, missile, etc.

nose·dive /'nouz,daɪv/ *n* [C] **1** : a sudden sharp drop made by an airplane with its front end pointing down • *The plane went into a nosedive.* **2** : a sudden sharp drop in price, value, condition, etc. • *The stock market took a nosedive.* — **nose-dive** /'nouz,daɪv/ *vb* **-dived; -div·ing** [I] • *Prices nosedived.*

nose job *n* [C] *informal* : a medical operation on your nose to improve its appearance • *He got/had a nose job.*

nosey *variant spelling of* NOSY

¹**nosh** /'nɑːʃ/ *vb* [I] *informal* : to eat food • *We noshed on chips.*

²**nosh** *n, informal* **1** [C] *US* : a light meal : SNACK • *Let's have a quick nosh.* **2** [C/U] *Brit* : food or a meal • *have some/a nosh*

no-show /'nou,ʃou/ *n* [C] : someone who is expected to be somewhere but does not arrive or appear • *My sister was a no-show at the party.*

nos·tal·gia /nɑ'stældʒə/ *n* [U] : pleasure and sadness caused by remembering something from the past and wishing that you could experience it again • *He was filled with nostalgia for his college days.* — **nos·tal·gic** /nɑ'stældʒɪk/ *adj* • *I was feeling nostalgic.* — **nos·tal·gi-**

cal·ly /nɑˈstældʒɪkli/ adv • She spoke nostalgically about her childhood.

nos·tril /ˈnɑːstrəl/ n [C] : one of the two openings of the nose

nos·trum /ˈnɑːstrəm/ n [C] formal : a suggested solution for a problem that will probably not succeed • all the usual nostrums about the economy

nosy also **nos·ey** /ˈnouzi/ adj **nos·i·er; -est** informal + disapproving : wanting to know about other people's lives, problems, etc. • nosy neighbors

not /ˈnɑːt/ adv **1 a** — used to form the negative of modal verbs (such as "should" and "could") and auxiliary verbs (such as "do" and "have") • He would/could not stay. • We have not spoken with them. • He did not seem to care. **b** — used before a verb or clause to make it negative or give it an opposite meaning • They gave us the option of not attending. • She told me not to do it. **2 a** — used with a word or phrase to make it negative or give it an opposite meaning • The books are not here. • No, that's not what I said. • She is not (at all/very) happy. • It is not as easy as it seems. • Things are not going well. • "Is there any left?" "Not much." • It is not just [=more than just] a novel; it is a classic. • Not many [=few] people showed up. **b** — used with a negative word to make a positive statement • Their request is not unreasonable. [=it is reasonable] • "What do you think of the food?" "It's not bad." [=it's pretty good] **3** : less or fewer than • Not all of us agree. [=some of us do not agree] **4** — used to refer to a possible situation, condition, etc., that is different from or opposite to another situation, condition, etc. • It works in theory if not in practice. [=even if it doesn't work in practice] • Like it or not [=whether you like it or don't like it], you'll do as she says. **5** — used to give a negative answer to a question • "Do you think they forgot?" "I hope not." • "Do you mind?" "Not at all." — **as like as not** or **like as not** see [5]LIKE — **more often than not** : happening more than half the time • He wins more often than not. — **not a/one** : no thing or person • Not a/one single person showed up. [=no one showed up] — **not that** — used to say that something said before is not important • I saw him with some other woman, not that I care. [=but I don't care]

[1]**no·ta·ble** /ˈnoutəbəl/ adj **1** : unusual and worth noticing : REMARKABLE • a notable example/improvement **2** : very successful or respected • a notable author

[2]**notable** n [C] : a famous or important person • They introduced her to all the town's notables.

no·ta·bly /ˈnoutəbli/ adv **1** : in a way that attracts or deserves attention • She was notably absent from the meeting. **2** : especially or particularly • Some patients, (most) notably the elderly and the very young, have greater risks.

no·ta·rize also Brit **no·ta·rise** /ˈnoutəˌraɪz/ vb **-rized; -riz·ing** [T] law : to sign (a document) as a notary public

no·ta·ry public /ˈnoutəriˈpʌblɪk/ n, pl **no·ta·ries public** or **notary pub·lics**

[C] law : a person who has the authority to act as an official witness when legal documents are signed — called also notary

no·ta·tion /nouˈteɪʃən/ n [C/U] technical : a system of marks, signs, figures, or characters that is used to represent information • (a) musical/scientific notation

[1]**notch** /ˈnɑːtʃ/ n [C] **1** : a small cut that is shaped like a V and that is made on an edge or a surface • He cut a small notch into the wood. • The tool has a notch for prying out nails. **2** US : a narrow passage between mountains **3** : a slightly higher or lower level in a series of levels that measure something • Turn the radio up/down a notch. [=up/down slightly]

[2]**notch** vb [T] **1** : to cut a notch in (something) • Notch the ends so that they fit together. **2** informal : to achieve or get (something) • He notched (up) his fifth victory this year.

[1]**note** /ˈnout/ n **1 a** [C] : a short piece of writing that is used to help someone remember something • I left you a note on the table. • She jotted down a few notes during the interview. **b** [plural] : an informal written record of things that are said and done • The students were taking notes during class. **2** [C] : a short comment or piece of writing that gives you information • Write a brief note about where the picture was taken. • One final note: tickets will be available at the door on the night of the concert. **3** [C] : a short and usually informal letter • I sent a note thanking him for the gift. = I sent him a thank-you note. • If you are out sick, you will need a note from your doctor. • The kidnappers left a **ransom note**. **4** [C] music **a** : a specific musical tone • That note's a B not a C. **b** : a written symbol that is used to show what note should be played and how long it should last **5** [singular] : a characteristic or quality that expresses a mood or feeling • I detected a note of sadness in his voice. • The movie hits/strikes/sounds just the right note with young audiences. — often used after on • If I may end on a personal note, I'd like to wish my dad a happy birthday! • The party ended on a high/sour note. [=it ended well/badly] **6** [C] Brit : BILL • a ten-pound note — **compare notes** see [1]COMPARE — **of note** : important and deserving to be noticed or remembered • American writers of note — **take note** : to notice or give special attention to someone or something • She took note of the time.

[2]**note** vb **not·ed; not·ing** [T] formal **1** : to notice or pay attention to (something) • It's interesting to note the many changes. • Their objections were duly noted. **2** : to say or write (something) • As noted above/earlier, many people survive the disease. • It's worth noting that he gave no reason for his decision. — **note down** [phrasal vb] **note (something) down** or **note down (something)** : to write down (information that you want to remember) • Let me note down your phone number.

note·book /ˈnoutˌbuk/ n [C] **1** : a book

with blank pages that is used for writing notes ▪ *She kept a notebook for her poetry.* **2 :** a small computer that is designed to be easily carried — called also *notebook computer*

not·ed /'noʊtəd/ *adj* : famous or well-known ▪ *a noted scholar* ▪ *a city noted for its nightlife*

note·pad /'noʊt͵pæd/ *n [C]* : sheets of paper that are attached at one end ▪ *I wrote her number on my notepad.*

note·wor·thy /'noʊt͵wɚði/ *adj* : important or interesting enough to be noticed : NOTABLE ▪ *a noteworthy performance/achievement*

not–for–profit *adj, chiefly US* : NONPROFIT ▪ *a not-for-profit organization*

¹noth·ing /'nʌθɪŋ/ *pron* **1 :** not anything : not a thing ▪ *There's nothing in my hands.* ▪ *I know nothing about it.* ▪ *You have nothing to worry about.* ▪ *"What are you doing?" "Nothing (much)."* ▪ *I have nothing against them.* [=I do not dislike or resent them] ▪ *It costs nothing* [=it costs no money] *for the first month.* ▪ *The phone call was nothing more than a sales pitch.* [=it was just a sales pitch and not anything else] ▪ *This has nothing to do with you.* [=it does not involve you in any way] ▪ *There's nothing else to say.* ▪ *If nothing else, you should send him a card.* [=you should at least send him a card] ▪ *I've had next to nothing to eat.* [=I have had very little to eat] ▪ *We discussed our plans, but nothing came of them.* [=we did not do anything about our plans] ▪ *He left nothing to chance.* [=he planned for every possibility] ▪ *The food leaves nothing to be desired.* [=the food is excellent] ▪ *Their children lack/want for nothing.* [=they have everything they need] ▪ *Why should we help? There's nothing in it for us.* [=we will not gain anything for ourselves by helping] ▪ *Those kids are nothing but trouble.* [=they are always causing trouble] ▪ *He is nothing if not persistent.* [=he is extremely persistent] ▪ *"I'm quitting school." "You'll do nothing of the sort!"* [=I will not allow you to do that] ▪ *There's nothing to it* [=it is very easy to do] *once you know how.* ▪ *She'll stop at nothing* [=she will do anything] *to get what she wants.* **2 :** someone or something that has no interest, value, or importance ▪ *That's nothing compared to what I went through.* ▪ *"Thanks for your help." "It was nothing."* [=it was no trouble] — **double or nothing** see ³DOUBLE — **have nothing on** see *have on* at HAVE — **here goes nothing** see ¹HERE — **nothing doing** *informal* — used as a forceful way of saying "no" to a question or suggestion ▪ *He asked her to lend him the money, but she said nothing doing.* [=she said that she would definitely not lend him the money] — **nothing in/to** ◇ If you say that there is *nothing in/to* something, you mean that it is not true at all. ▪ *There is nothing in the rumor.* — **nothing like 1** — used to say that something is very enjoyable or satisfying ▪ *There's nothing like a cool swim on a hot day.* **2** *Brit, infor-*

mal : not nearly ▪ *The report is nothing like thorough enough.* — **to say nothing of** see ¹SAY

²nothing *adv* : not at all : in no way ▪ *She is nothing like her sister.* — **nothing less than 1** — used to give emphasis to a description ▪ *The idea is nothing less than crazy.* [=the idea is crazy] **2** — used to say that something is the least that a situation, person, etc., requires or will accept ▪ *I want nothing less than a full refund!* [=I want a full refund] — **nothing short of** — used to give emphasis to a description ▪ *His recovery was nothing short of miraculous.* [=it was miraculous]

³nothing *n* **1** *[U]* : empty space ▪ *It appeared out of nothing.* **2** *[U]* : the number 0 : ZERO ▪ *The score is two (to) nothing.* **3** *[C/U]* : someone or something that has little or no worth, importance, or influence ▪ *My children are my life—I'm nothing without them.* — **for nothing 1** : for no reason ▪ *We did all that work for nothing.* [=when we did not need to] **2** : at no charge : for free ▪ *He gave it to me for nothing.* — **sweet nothings** : romantic words ▪ *He whispered sweet nothings in her ear.*

noth·ing·ness /'nʌθɪŋnəs/ *n [U]* **1** : empty space ▪ *He was staring into nothingness.* **2** : the state of being no longer seen, heard, or felt ▪ *The sound faded into nothingness.*

¹no·tice /'noʊtəs/ *n* **1** *[U]* **a :** information that tells you or warns you about something that is going to happen ▪ *Please give us enough (advance) notice to prepare for your arrival.* ▪ *Terms of the agreement are subject to change without notice.* [=they may be changed without telling you before they are changed] ▪ *The beach is closed until further notice.* [=until there is an announcement saying that it is open] ▪ *I received written notice* [=I received a letter telling me] *that my account is overdue.* ▪ *The senator served notice* [=made it known] *that he will be opposing the new regulations.* **b :** a statement telling someone that an agreement, job, etc., will end soon ▪ *I gave (my employer) two weeks' notice.* [=I told my employer that I would be quitting my job in two weeks] **2** *[U]* : attention that people give to someone or something ▪ *The error escaped my notice.* [=I did not notice the error] ▪ *Take no notice of them.* [=ignore them] ▪ *People are starting to (sit up and) take notice of* [=starting to notice and give attention to] *the team.* **3** *[C]* : a written or printed statement that gives information ▪ *Notices were sent to parents about the school trip.* — **at/on a moment's/minute's notice** or **at/on short notice** : immediately after you have been told about something ▪ *They can be ready to leave at/on a moment's notice.* — **on notice** *formal* : warned or told about something ▪ *The police are on notice* [=they have been warned] *to have more security at the concert.*

²notice *vb* **-ticed; -tic·ing** *[T]* : to become aware of (something or someone) by seeing, hearing, etc. ▪ *She noticed a smell of gas.* ▪ *I noticed (that there was) a man* standing in the corner. ▪ *I couldn't help noticing the spot on his tie.* = *I couldn't help but notice the spot on his tie.* [=I saw the spot even though I wasn't trying to look for it] — **get noticed** : to get attention that you want from other people ▪ *You'll get noticed in that new sports car.* —

no·tice·a·ble /ˈnoʊtəsəbəl/ *adj* ▪ *a noticeable change in her behavior* — **no·tice·a·bly** /ˈnoʊtəsəbli/ *adv*

no·tice·board /ˈnoʊtəsˌboɚd/ *n* [C] *Brit* : BULLETIN BOARD 1

no·ti·fy /ˈnoʊtəˌfaɪ/ *vb* **-fies; -fied; -fy·ing** [T] : to tell (someone) officially about something ▪ *She notified the police about the accident.* ▪ *I was notified that I did not get the job.* — **no·ti·fi·ca·tion** /ˌnoʊtəfəˈkeɪʃən/ *n* [C/U] ▪ *You will be sent (a) written notification.*

no·tion /ˈnoʊʃən/ *n* **1** [C] : an idea or opinion ▪ *He has some pretty strange notions.* ▪ *I only have a (slight) notion of the poem's meaning.* **2** [C] : a sudden wish or desire ▪ *She had a notion to try skydiving.* **3** [*plural*] *US* : small things (such as pins, thread, and buttons) that are used for sewing ▪ *a shop that sells fabrics and notions*

no·tion·al /ˈnoʊʃənl/ *adj* : existing as an idea rather than as something real ▪ *the company's notional earnings* — **no·tion·al·ly** *adv*

no·to·ri·ous /noʊˈtorijəs/ *adj* : well-known or famous especially for something bad ▪ *The coach is notorious for his violent outbursts.* — **no·to·ri·e·ty** /ˌnoʊtəˈrajəti/ *n* [U, singular] ▪ *She gained notoriety when she appeared nude in a magazine.* — **no·to·ri·ous·ly** *adv*

not·with·stand·ing /ˌnɑːtwɪθˈstændɪŋ/ *prep, formal* : without being prevented by (something) : DESPITE ▪ *Notwithstanding their inexperience, they won the championship.* = *Their inexperience notwithstanding, they won the championship.* — **notwithstanding** *adv* ▪ *Although many oppose the plan, we will go through with it notwithstanding.* [=nevertheless]

¹**nought** /ˈnɑːt/ *n* [C/U] *Brit* : the number 0 : ZERO ▪ *a 1 with six noughts after it*

²**nought** *chiefly Brit* spelling of NAUGHT

noughts and crosses *n* [U] *Brit* : TIC-TAC-TOE

noun /ˈnaʊn/ *n* [C] : a word that is the name of something (such as a person, animal, place, thing, quality, idea, or action)

noun phrase *n* [C] : a group of words that acts like a noun in a sentence ▪ *In the sentence "I found the owner of the dog," "the owner of the dog" is a noun phrase.*

nour·ish /ˈnɚɪʃ/ *vb* [T] **1** : to provide (someone or something) with food and other things that are needed to live, be healthy, etc. ▪ *Plants are nourished by rain and soil.* ▪ *Vitamins in the shampoo nourish the hair.* ▪ *a nourishing meal* **2** : to cause (something) to develop or grow stronger ▪ *a friendship nourished by trust*

nour·ish·ment /ˈnɚɪʃmənt/ *n* [U] : food and other things that are needed for health, growth, etc. ▪ *These children lack*

adequate nourishment. ▪ *(figurative) emotional/spiritual nourishment*

nous /ˈnaʊs/ *n* [U] *Brit, informal* : COMMON SENSE ▪ *She had the nous to save the money.*

nou·veau riche /ˌnuːvoʊˈriːʃ/ *n, pl* **nouveaux riches** /ˌnuːvoʊˈriːʃ/ [C] *disapproving* : a person who has recently become rich and who likes to spend a lot of money — **nouveau riche** *adj* ▪ *a nouveau riche couple*

Nov. *abbr* November

¹**nov·el** /ˈnɑːvəl/ *n* [C] : a long written story usually about imaginary characters and events ▪ *a detective/romance novel*

²**novel** *adj* : new and different ▪ *a novel idea* ▪ *a novel approach to the problem*

nov·el·ist /ˈnɑːvəlɪst/ *n* [C] : a person who writes novels

no·vel·la /noʊˈvɛlə/ *n* [C] : a short novel

nov·el·ty /ˈnɑːvəlti/ *n, pl* **-ties 1** [U] : the quality or state of being new, different, and interesting ▪ *The toy's novelty wore off.* [=the toy became uninteresting] **2** [C] **a** : something that is new or unusual ▪ *Eating shark meat is a novelty to many people.* **b** : something entertaining that is popular for a short time ▪ *novelty songs/acts* **3** [C] : a small and unusual decoration or toy ▪ *a novelty shop/item*

No·vem·ber /noʊˈvɛmbɚ/ *n* [C/U] : the 11th month of the year ▪ *in (early/late) November* ▪ *on November the fourth* = (US) *on November fourth* = *on the fourth of November* ▪ *It happens every November.* — *abbr.* Nov.

nov·ice /ˈnɑːvəs/ *n* [C] **1** : a person who has just started learning or doing something ▪ *I'm a novice at skiing.* ▪ *novice chess players* **2** : a person who is preparing to become a nun or a monk

no·vo·caine /ˈnoʊvəˌkeɪn/ *n* [U] *medical* : a drug that causes part of your body to feel no pain

¹**now** /ˈnaʊ/ *adv* **1** : at the present time ▪ *I'm feeling better now.* ▪ *Now's the time for action.* ▪ *"Can we talk?" "Not now. I'm busy."* ▪ *The room is now used as a home office.* = *They now use the room as a home office.* ▪ *the president's now famous speech* ▪ *This is the only chance you'll ever get. It's now or never.* — often used to show that you are annoyed about something ▪ *"Can I ask another question?" "What now?"* = *"What is it now?" = "Now what?"* **2** : in the next moment ▪ *I have to leave (right) now.* ▪ *They'll be back any minute now!* ▪ *What now? = Now what?* [=what next?] **3** : in the present situation ▪ *He'll never believe me now!* **4** : at the time referred to in the past ▪ *I met her again two years later. She was now 30 years old.* **5** : for an amount of time until the present time ▪ *It's been a year now since I last saw her.* [=I haven't seen her for a year] — often used with *for* ▪ *We've lived here for a while now.* **6** — used to make a command or request or to express disapproval ▪ *Hurry up, now.* ▪ *Now you be sure to write, you hear?* ▪ *Come (on) now. You know that's not true.* ▪ *Now, Billy, that's no way to talk to your mother!* ▪ *Now, you listen to me.* **7** — used to introduce an important idea

or to show a change in subject • *Now that was a great song!* • *Now you've done it!* • *Now who could that be?* • **Now then**, what shall we do next? ✧ The phrase **now for** is often used to introduce a different idea or activity. • *That was an easy question. Now for something a bit more challenging.* — **(every) now and then/again** : not often but sometimes • *We still see each other (every) now and then.* • **Now and again** she would check on me. — **just now** see ²JUST — **now, now** 1 — used to tell someone not to be worried or unhappy • *Now, now, don't cry.* 2 — used to express criticism or disapproval • *Now, now. There's no need to be mean.* — **now you're talking** see ¹TALK — **right now** see ²RIGHT

²**now** *conj* : since something happened or is true • *Now (that) you mention it, I am hungry.* • *Let's start now that everyone's here.*

³**now** *n* [*singular*] : the present time or moment • *A lot can happen between now and then.* • **By now**, you must have heard the news. • *You should be in bed by now.* • *That's enough for now, but we may need more later.* • *We'll be here from now until May.* • **From now on** [=from this moment and forever into the future], *I'll always tell you the truth.* • *Until now, doctors had no idea what caused the disease.* • **Up to now**, they didn't know what caused it. — see also *here and now* at ¹HERE

now·a·days /'nawə,deɪz/ *adv* : at the present time • *People don't wear hats much nowadays.*

¹**no·where** /'noʊ,weə/ *adv* : not in or at any place • *I have nowhere to go/sit/live.* • *The book is nowhere to be found/seen.* = *The book is nowhere in sight.* — **get nowhere** 1 or **go nowhere** : to make no progress • *The research is going nowhere.* 2 **get (someone) nowhere** : to not make a situation any better for (someone) • *Arguing will get us nowhere.* — **nowhere near** *informal* : not at all : not nearly • *That is nowhere near enough water.*

²**nowhere** *n* [*U*] : no place — used figuratively • *They live miles from nowhere.* [=in a place that is very far from other people] • *We got lost in the middle of nowhere.* [=in a place far away from other people, houses, etc.] — **from nowhere** or **out of nowhere** — used to say that someone or something appears, happens, etc., in a sudden and unexpected way • *The car came from nowhere!* • *She rose to fame out of nowhere.* • **From out of nowhere** *he asked her to marry him.*

no–win /'noʊ'wɪn/ *adj*, always before a noun — used to describe (a situation, war, etc.) that cannot have a good result • *We're in a no-win situation.* • *a no-win battle*

nox·ious /'nɑːkʃəs/ *adj* : harmful to living things : TOXIC • *noxious fumes*

noz·zle /'nɑːzəl/ *n* [*C*] : a short tube that is put on the end of a hose or pipe to control the flow of a liquid or gas

NRA *abbr* National Rifle Association ✧ The NRA is an organization that is active in supporting the rights of U.S. citizens to own guns.

NS *abbr* Nova Scotia

NSW *abbr* New South Wales

NT *abbr* 1 New Testament 2 Northern Territory 3 Northwest Territories

nth /'ɛnθ/ *adj* — used to refer to an unknown number in a series • *I told him "no" for the nth time.* [=I told him "no," as I have told him many times before] • *He is brave to the nth degree.* [=he is extremely brave]

nu·ance /'nuː,ɑːns, *Brit* 'njuː,ɑːns/ *n* [*C/U*] : a very small difference in color, tone, meaning, etc. • *nuances of color/ meaning* • *the subtle nuances in the song* — **nu·anced** /'nuː,ɑːnst, *Brit* 'njuː-,ɑːnst/ *adj* • *a complex and nuanced poem*

nub /'nʌb/ *n* [*C*] : a small piece or end • *The dog chewed the bone down to a nub.* — **the nub** : the main part or point of something • *the nub of the story/problem*

nu·cle·ar /'nuːklijə, *Brit* 'njuːklijə/ *adj*, always before a noun 1 **a** : of, relating to, producing, or using energy created when the nuclei of atoms are split apart or joined together • *nuclear weapons/ bombs/fuel* **b** : having or involving nuclear weapons • *a nuclear war/attack* • *nuclear powers* [=countries that have nuclear weapons] 2 : of or relating to the nucleus of an atom • *nuclear physics/fusion*

nuclear energy *n* [*U*] : energy created by splitting apart the nuclei of atoms — called also *atomic energy, nuclear power*

nuclear family *n* [*C*] : the part of a family that includes only the father, mother, and children

nuclear fission *n* [*U*] : FISSION

nuclear fusion *n* [*U*] : FUSION 2

nuclear reaction *n* [*C*] : REACTION 5b

nuclear reactor *n* [*C*] : REACTOR

nu·cle·ic acid /nʊ'kliːjɪk-/ *n* [*C*] *technical* : any of various acids (such as DNA or RNA) that are found in living cells

nu·cle·us /'nuːklijəs/ *n, pl* **nu·clei** /'nuːkli,aɪ/ *also* **nu·cle·us·es** [*C*] 1 *biology* : the central part of most cells that contains genetic material and is enclosed in a membrane 2 *physics* : the central part of an atom that is made up of protons and neutrons 3 : a central or most important part of something • *She is the nucleus of our family.*

¹**nude** /'nuːd, *Brit* 'njuːd/ *adj* 1 : having no clothes on : NAKED • *a nude model* 2 : of or involving people who have no clothes on • *nude photos* — **nude** *adv* • *She posed nude for the magazine.* — **nu·di·ty** /'nuːdəti, *Brit* 'njuːdəti/ *n* [*U*] • *The movie has scenes of nudity.* [=scenes in which people are nude/naked]

²**nude** *n* [*C*] : a painting, sculpture, etc., that shows a nude person • *a famous nude* — **in the nude** : without any clothes on • *He painted her in the nude.*

nudge /'nʌdʒ/ *vb* **nudged**; **nudg·ing** [*T*] **a** : to touch or push (someone or something) gently • *I nudged the plate closer to her.* **b** : to push (someone) gently with your elbow in order to get that person's attention • *He nudged me and pointed to the deer.* 2 [*T*] : to encourage (someone) to do something • *The sales-*

man nudged her into testing out the car.
3 a [T] : to come close to (a particular level or amount) ▪ *Album sales are nudging the one million mark.* **b** [I] : to move slightly to a different level or amount ▪ *The price of gold has nudged a little higher.* — **nudge** n [C] ▪ *He gave me a nudge.*

nud·ism /ˈnuːˌdɪzəm, Brit ˈnjuːˌdɪzəm/ n [U] : the practice of not wearing any clothes especially in private places (such as camps or beaches) that are separated from public areas — called also (Brit) **naturism** — **nud·ist** /ˈnuːdɪst, Brit ˈnjuːdɪst/ n [C] ▪ *a beach for nudists* ▪ *a nudist colony*

nug·get /ˈnʌgət/ n [C] **1** : a solid lump of a valuable metal ▪ *gold nuggets* **2** : a small piece of food ▪ *chicken nuggets* **3** : a piece of valuable information ▪ *nuggets of wisdom*

nui·sance /ˈnuːsns, Brit ˈnjuːsns/ n [C] : a person or thing that is annoying or that causes problems — usually singular ▪ *Filling out the paperwork is a nuisance.* ▪ *I'm sorry to be a nuisance* [=I'm sorry to bother you], *but I need your help again.* ▪ *He made a nuisance of himself.* [=he behaved in an annoying way]

¹**nuke** /ˈnuːk, Brit ˈnjuːk/ n [C] *informal* : a nuclear weapon

²**nuke** vb **nuked; nuk·ing** [T] *informal* **1** : to attack or destroy (something) with a nuclear weapon **2** : to heat or cook (food) in a microwave ▪ *nuke a pizza*

null /ˈnʌl/ adj, law : having no legal power : INVALID ▪ *The contract was declared null and void.*

nul·li·fy /ˈnʌləˌfaɪ/ vb **-fies; -fied; -fy·ing** [T] **1** : to make (something) legally null ▪ *The law was nullified.* **2** : to cause (something) to lose its value or to have no effect ▪ *The penalty nullified the goal.*

num. abbr numeral

¹**numb** /ˈnʌm/ adj **1** : unable to feel anything in a part of your body because of cold, injury, etc. ▪ *The dentist made my mouth numb.* ▪ *My fingers went numb.* **2** : unable to think, feel, or react normally because of something that shocks or upsets you ▪ *He stood there numb with fear/rage.* — **numb·ly** adv — **numb·ness** n [U, singular]

²**numb** vb [T] **1** : to cause (a part of the body) to be unable to feel anything ▪ *The cold wind numbed my face.* **2** : to make (someone) unable to think, feel, or react normally ▪ *She was numbed by the news of her son's death.* — **numb·ing** adj ▪ *the numbing cold* ▪ *a numbing* [=very boring] *lecture* — **numb·ing·ly** adv

¹**num·ber** /ˈnʌmbɚ/ n **1** [C] : a word or symbol (such as "five" or "16") that represents a specific amount or quantity ▪ *the number two* ▪ *a three-digit number like 429* ▪ *2, 4, 6, and 8 are even numbers; 1, 3, 5, and 7 are odd numbers.* **2** [C] **a** : a number or a set of numbers and other symbols used to identify a person or thing ▪ *a student's ID/identification number* ▪ *your credit card number* ▪ *What's the account number on your phone bill?* ▪ *the book's page numbers* ▪ *flight number 101* — abbr. *No.* or *no.* **b** : PHONE NUMBER ▪ *My home/work/daytime/office number is*

(413) 555-2917. ▪ *I'm sorry. You must have the wrong number.* **3 a** [C/U] : the total amount of people or things ▪ *a large/small number of patients* ▪ *a decrease in the number of violent crimes* ▪ *There are a number of* [=several] *options to choose from.* ▪ *A good number of students* [=many students] *have entered the contest.* ▪ *The dish can be made in any number of ways.* [=many different ways] ▪ *New houses are being built in record numbers.* [=more new houses are being built now than ever before] ▪ *They have declined in number.* [=there are not as many of them as there were before] **b** [plural] : a large group of people or things ▪ *There's safety/strength in numbers.* [=people are safer/stronger when they are together in a group] **4** [C] **a** — used to indicate the position of someone or something in a list or series ▪ *You're number 7 on the waiting list.* — abbr. *No.* or *no.* **b** : the version of a magazine, newspaper, etc., that is published at a particular time ▪ *The article is in volume 36, number 2 of this journal.* — abbr. *No.* or *no.* **5** [C] : a song or dance that is usually performed as part of a concert or performance ▪ *The actors broke into a song and dance number.* **6** [C] *informal* : an item of clothing ▪ *a little black number* [=a small black dress] **7** [plural] : numbers that show amounts of money that are spent, earned, or needed ▪ *I don't know if we can afford it. I have to look at the numbers.* ▪ *I ran/crunched the numbers* [=determined the amount of money to be spent, earned, etc.], *and I just don't think we can afford it.* **8** [U] *grammar* : the quality of a word form that shows whether the word is singular or plural ▪ *A verb and its subject must agree in number.* [=if the subject is singular/plural, the verb must be singular/plural] — **bad/good (etc.) with numbers** : bad, good, etc., at adding, subtracting, etc. ▪ *Ask her to do the books, she's good with numbers.* — **by (the) numbers** : in a way that follows the rules or instructions but that is not interesting or original ▪ *painting/dancing by the numbers* — **do a number on** *informal* : to hurt or damage (someone or something) ▪ *This heavy backpack is doing a number on my back.* — **have someone's number** *informal* : to be able to deal with or defeat someone easily especially because you know or understand that person so well ▪ *She thinks she's got my number, but I'm going to prove her wrong.* — **your number is up** ✧ *If your number is up,* you are about to suffer or die.

²**number** vb **1** [T] : to label (people or things in a series) with a number ▪ *She numbers and arranges the photographs according to when they were taken.* ▪ *Each print is signed and numbered by the artist.* ▪ *The players were wearing numbered jerseys.* **2** [I, linking vb] — used to indicate a total amount ▪ *The population now numbers* [=the population is now] *about 400,000.* ▪ *The animal, which once numbered in the millions, is now extinct.* **3**

[T/I] *formal* : to include (someone or something) as part of a larger group • *John Keats is numbered among the greatest English poets.* — **days are numbered** — used to say that someone or something will die, fail, or end soon • *The doctors say that my days are numbered.* [=I will die soon] • *Her days as the team's coach were numbered.*

number cruncher /-'krʌntʃ ə/ *n* [C] : a person who collects and studies information in the form of numbers — **number crunching** *n* [U] • *doing some number crunching*

num·ber·less /'nʌmbələs/ *adj, literary* : too many to count • *the numberless stars in the sky*

¹**number one** *or* **No. 1** *n* [U] **1 a** : the most important person or thing in a group • *Getting the car fixed is number one on my list of priorities.* **b** : the most successful person or thing in a group of people or things • *Her movie is currently number one at the box office.* **2** : your own happiness, health, or success : YOURSELF • *If you don't look out for number one* [=if you don't take care of yourself], *who will?*

²**number one** *or* **No. 1** *adj* : highest in rank or importance • *Heart disease is the number one killer of women.* • *my number one concern*

number plate *n* [C] *chiefly Brit* : LICENSE PLATE

number sign *n* [C] *US* : ¹POUND 4

Number Ten *or* **Number 10** *n* [*singular*] *Brit* **1** : the place in London where the British Prime Minister lives **2** : the British government

numb·skull *also* **num·skull** /'nʌm,skʌl/ *n* [C] *informal* : a stupid or foolish person

nu·mer·al /'nu:mərəl, *Brit* 'nju:mərəl/ *n* [C] : a symbol (such as 1, 2, or 3) that represents a number

nu·mer·a·tor /'nu:mə,reɪtə, *Brit* 'nju:mə,reɪtə/ *n* [C] *mathematics* : the number in a fraction that is above the line and that is divided by the number below the line • *The numerator in the fraction ⅗ is 3.* — compare DENOMINATOR

nu·mer·ic /nu'merɪk, *Brit* nju'merɪk/ *adj* : of or relating to numbers • *a numeric code*

nu·mer·i·cal /nu'merɪkəl, *Brit* nju-'merɪkəl/ *adj* : of or relating to numbers or a system of numbers • *The files are in numerical order.* — **nu·mer·i·cal·ly** /nu'merɪkli, *Brit* nju'merɪkli/ *adv*

nu·mer·ous /'nu:mərəs, *Brit* 'nju:mərəs/ *adj, somewhat formal* : existing in large numbers • *She decided to leave for numerous reasons.*

numskull *variant spelling of* NUMBSKULL

nun /'nʌn/ *n* [C] : a woman who is a member of a religious community and who usually promises to remain poor, unmarried, and separate from the rest of society

nup·tial /'nʌpʃəl/ *adj, always before a noun, formal* : of or relating to marriage or weddings • *nuptial vows*

nup·tials /'nʌpʃəlz/ *n* [*plural*] *formal* : a wedding ceremony • *The nuptials will take place outside.*

¹**nurse** /'nəs/ *n* [C] : a person who is trained to care for sick or injured people • *The nurse will take your blood pressure before the doctor sees you.*

²**nurse** *vb* **nursed; nurs·ing 1** [T] : to take care of or help (someone who is sick or injured) • *She nursed me back to health.* [=she cared for me until I was healthy again] • *He went to nursing school.* [=a school that trains people to be nurses] **2** [T] : to give special care or attention to (something) • *The couple nursed the business through hard times.* • *She is still out nursing an ankle injury.* [=is still caring for her injured ankle] **3 a** [T] : to feed (a baby or young animal) with milk from the mother's body • *She is nursing her baby.* **b** [I] *of a baby or young animal* : to take milk from the mother's body • *The puppies nursed for eight weeks.* **4** [T] : to hold (an idea, a feeling, etc.) in your mind for a long time • *nurse a grievance/grudge* • *She nurses a secret desire to move to the city.* **5** [T] : to drink (something) very slowly over a long period of time • *He nursed his glass of wine.*

nurse·maid /'nəs,meɪd/ *n* [C] *old-fashioned* : a girl or woman whose job is to take care of children

nurse prac·ti·tion·er /nə'spræk,tɪʃənə/ *n* [C] : a nurse who is trained to do some of the things a doctor does

nurs·ery /'nəsəri/ *n, pl* -er·ies [C] **1 a** *US* : the room where a baby sleeps **b** : the room in a hospital where new babies are cared for by nurses **2** : a place where plants are grown and sold • *We get our flowers from a local nursery.* **3** *Brit* : a place where children are cared for during the day while their parents are working • *She dropped her daughter off at the (day) nursery.* [=(US) day care center]

nursery rhyme *n* [C] : a short poem or song for children

nursery school *n* [C/U] : a school for very young children

nurse's aide *n* [C] *US* : a person whose job is to help nurses to take care of patients

nursing home *n* [C] : a place where people who are old can live and be taken care of

¹**nur·ture** /'nətʃə/ *vb* -tured; -tur·ing [T] **1** : to help (something or someone) to grow, develop, or succeed • *Teachers should nurture their students' creativity.* **2** : to take care of (someone or something that is growing or developing) by providing food, protection, a place to live, etc. • *You have to carefully nurture the grape vines.* **3** : to hold (an idea, a feeling, etc.) in your mind for a long time • *She nurtures a secret ambition to be a singer.* — **nur·tur·er** /'nətʃərə/ *n* [C]

²**nurture** *n* [U] *formal* : the way people are treated and taught to behave when they are young • *Is our character affected more by nature or by nurture?*

nut /'nʌt/ *n* **1** [C] : a small dry fruit with a hard shell • *almonds, peanuts, and other* nuts • (figurative) The guy/problem is a **hard/tough nut to crack**. [=he/it is difficult to deal with or understand] **2** [C] : a piece of metal that has a hole through it so that it can be screwed onto a bolt or screw • (figurative) She's still learning the **nuts and bolts** [=the basic parts or details] of the business. **3** [C] informal : a crazy or strange person • That guy's a nut. **b** : a person who is very interested in or enthusiastic about something • She's a real health/movie nut. **4** [plural] informal + impolite : a man's testicles

nut·case /ˈnʌtˌkeɪs/ n [C] informal : a crazy or very strange person • He's a total/complete nutcase.

nut·crack·er /ˈnʌtˌkrækɚ/ n [C] : a tool or device used to open the shells of nuts

nut·house /ˈnʌtˌhaʊs/ n [C] US, informal : a hospital for people who are mentally ill • (figurative) This office is a nuthouse. [=a place where there is a lot of confusion, disorganization, etc.]

nut·meg /ˈnʌtˌmɛg/ n [U] : a spice used in cooking and baking

nu·tri·ent /ˈnuːtrijənt, Brit ˈnjuːtrijənt/ n [C] technical : a substance that plants, animals, and people need to live and grow • Fruits and vegetables have important nutrients. • The disease is caused by nutrient deficiencies.

nu·tri·tion /nuˈtrɪʃən, Brit njuˈtrɪʃən/ n [U] : the process of eating the right kind of food so you can be healthy • exercise and good nutrition — **nu·tri·tion·al** /nuˈtrɪʃənəl, Brit njuˈtrɪʃənəl/ adj • a nutritional supplement [=a vitamin, herb, etc., that you take to be healthy] — **nu·tri·tion·al·ly** adv

nu·tri·tion·ist /nuˈtrɪʃənɪst, Brit njuˈtrɪʃənɪst/ n [C] : a person whose job is to give advice on how food affects your health

nu·tri·tious /nuˈtrɪʃəs, Brit njuˈtrɪʃəs/ adj : having substances that a person or animal needs to be healthy and grow properly • highly nutritious food/vegetables

nu·tri·tive /ˈnuːtrətɪv, Brit ˈnjuːtrətɪv/ adj, always before a noun, technical : of or relating to nutrition • the nutritive value of wheat

¹**nuts** /ˈnʌts/ adj, not before a noun, informal **1** : CRAZY • They thought I was nuts. **2 a** : very enthusiastic about or interested in something • He's nuts about baseball. **b** : feeling affection or love for someone or something • She's nuts for/about him. [=she's deeply in love with him] — **go nuts 1** : to become crazy or insane • She went nuts and thought everyone was trying to kill her. **2** : to act in a way that is wild or out of control because of strong emotion • The crowd went nuts when the team won.

²**nuts** interj, US, informal — used to express anger, disappointment, etc. • Aw nuts! I broke my glasses!

nut·shell /ˈnʌtˌʃɛl/ n [C] : the hard outer shell of a nut — **in a nutshell** : very briefly • And that, in a nutshell, is what happened.

nut·ter /ˈnʌtɚ/ n [C] Brit, informal : a crazy or strange person : NUT

nut·ty /ˈnʌti/ adj **nut·ti·er; -est 1 a** : tasting or smelling like nuts • a nutty coffee **b** : containing nuts • a nutty candy bar **2** informal **a** : silly, strange, or foolish • What a nutty idea. **b** : crazy or mentally ill • She's a little nutty. — **nut·ti·ness** n [U]

nuz·zle /ˈnʌzəl/ vb **nuz·zled; nuz·zling** [T/I] : to gently rub your nose or face against (someone or something) to show affection • She nuzzled (against) his neck.

NV abbr Nevada

NW abbr northwest, northwestern

NWT abbr Northwest Territories

NY abbr New York

NYC abbr New York City

ny·lon /ˈnaɪˌlɑːn/ n **1** [U] : a strong material used for making clothes, ropes, etc. • a nylon jacket/rope/tent **2** [plural] : PANTYHOSE • a pair of nylons

nymph /ˈnɪmf/ n [C] in stories : a spirit in the shape of a young woman who lives in mountains, forests, meadows, and water

nym·pho·ma·ni·ac /ˌnɪmfəˈmeɪniˌæk/ n [C] : a woman who has an unusually strong desire to have sex very often — **nym·pho·ma·ni·a** /ˌnɪmfəˈmeɪnijə/ n [U]

NZ abbr New Zealand

o or **O** /ˈoʊ/ n, pl **o's** or **os** or **O's** or **Os** /ˈoʊz/ **1** [C/U] : the 15th letter of the English alphabet • a word that starts with (an) o **2** [C] : the number zero — used in speech • three o two [=302]

O variant spelling of OH 3

oaf /ˈoʊf/ n [C] : a stupid or awkward person — **oaf·ish** /ˈoʊfɪʃ/ adj • an oafish bore

oak /ˈoʊk/ n, pl **oaks** or **oak 1** [C] : a type of tree that grows in northern parts of the world and that produces acorns — called also oak tree **2** [U] : the wood of an oak tree • The table is solid oak. — **oak·en** /ˈoʊkən/ adj

oar /ˈoɚ/ n [C] : a long pole that is flat and wide at one end and that is used for rowing and steering a boat ◆ Oars are usually used in pairs with one oar on each side of the boat.

oa·sis /oʊˈeɪsəs/ n, pl **oa·ses** /oʊˈeɪˌsiːz/ [C] **1** : an area in a desert where there is water and plants **2** : a pleasant place that is surrounded by something unpleasant • The park is an oasis amid the city's factories.

oat /ˈoʊt/ n **1** [U] : a kind of grain that is

widely grown • *oat bran/flour* **2** [*plural*] : the seeds of the oat plant used as feed for farm animals and in foods for people — **feel your oats** *US, informal* : to feel new confidence and energy • *He's been feeling his oats since he got his promotion.* — **sow your (wild) oats** see ¹SOW

oath /'oʊθ/ *n, pl* **oaths** /'oʊðz/ [*C*] **1** : a formal and serious promise to tell the truth or to do something • *taking/swearing an oath of loyalty* [=formally promising to be loyal] • *an oath of office* [=an official promise by a person who has been elected to a public office to fulfill the duties of the office] **2** : an offensive or rude word • *He uttered an oath and walked away.* — **under oath** also **on oath** *law* : having made a formal promise to tell the truth in a court of law • *testimony given under oath*

oat·meal /'oʊt₁miːl/ *n* [*U*] **1** : oats that have been ground into flour or flattened into flakes • *oatmeal cookies* **2** *US* : a hot breakfast food that is made from oats • *a bowl of oatmeal*

obe·di·ent /oʊ'biːdijənt/ *adj* : willing to do what someone tells you to do or to follow a law, rule, etc. • *an obedient child/dog* — **obe·di·ence** /oʊ'biːdijəns/ *n* [*U*] • *acting in obedience to the rules* [=obeying the rules] — **obe·di·ent·ly** *adv*

obe·lisk /'ɑːbə₁lɪsk/ *n* [*C*] : a tall, four-sided stone column that becomes narrower toward the top and that ends in a point

obese /oʊ'biːs/ *adj* : very fat • *treatment for obese patients* — **obe·si·ty** /oʊ-'biːsəti/ *n* [*U*]

obey /oʊ'beɪ/ *vb* [*T/I*] : to do what someone tells you to do or what a rule, law, etc., says you must do • *obey the law/rules* • *Falling objects obey the laws of physics.* [=move in a way that agrees with the laws of physics] • *a child learning to obey*

OB–GYN *abbr* obstetrics-gynecology

obit /oʊ'bɪt, *Brit* 'ɒbɪt/ *n* [*C*] *informal* : OBITUARY

obit·u·ary /oʊ'bɪtʃə₁weri, *Brit* ə'bɪtʃuəri/ *n, pl* **-ar·ies** [*C*] : an article in a newspaper about the life of someone who has died recently

¹**ob·ject** /'ɑːbdʒɪkt/ *n* **1** [*C*] : a thing that you can see and touch and that is not alive • *an inanimate object* [=a thing that is not alive, such as a rock, a chair, etc.] **2** [*C*] **a** : someone or something that makes you feel a specified emotion • *The book's lead character is both an object of desire and an object of pity.* [=is both desired and pitied by others] **b** : someone or something that your attention or interest is directed toward • *an object of study* **3** [*singular*] : the reason or purpose for an activity • *The object of the game is to score the most points.* **4** [*C*] *grammar* : a noun, noun phrase, or pronoun that receives the action of a verb or completes the meaning of a preposition — compare SUBJECT; see also DIRECT OBJECT, INDIRECT OBJECT — **no object** — used to say that something is not important or worth worrying about • *Money is no object to them.* [=they don't wor-

ry about how much things cost]

²**ob·ject** /əb'dʒɛkt/ *vb* **1** [*I*] : to disagree with something or oppose something • *I object to the proposed changes.* • (*law*) *"Your Honor, I object. That question is misleading."* **2** [*T*] : to say (something that explains why you oppose something or disagree) • *He objected that the chair was too big.* — **ob·jec·tor** /əb'dʒɛktɚ/ *n* [*C*]

ob·jec·ti·fy /əb'dʒɛktə₁faɪ/ *vb* **-fies; -fied; -fy·ing** [*T*] *disapproving* : to treat (someone) as an object rather than as a person • *beauty pageants that objectify women*

ob·jec·tion /əb'dʒɛkʃən/ *n* **1** [*C/U*] : a reason for disagreeing with or opposing something • *She has/makes no objection to going.* • *People raised/voiced a number of objections to the proposed changes.* **2** [*C*] *law* : an act of formally objecting to something during a trial • *The prosecutor's objection was overruled by the judge.*

ob·jec·tion·able /əb'dʒɛkʃənəbəl/ *adj* : not good or right • *an objectionable* [=*unpleasant*] *taste/odor* : causing people to be offended • *objectionable* [=*offensive*] *language* — **ob·jec·tion·ably** /əb-'dʒɛkʃənəbli/ *adv*

¹**ob·jec·tive** /əb'dʒɛktɪv/ *adj* **1** : based on facts rather than feelings or opinions • *an objective analysis* : not influenced by feelings • *It's hard to be objective about my own family.* **2** *philosophy* : existing outside of the mind • *objective reality* **3** *grammar* : relating to nouns, noun phrases, or pronouns that are the objects of verbs or prepositions • *The pronoun "her" is in the objective case in the sentence "I saw her."* — **ob·jec·tive·ly** *adv* • *looking at facts objectively* — **ob·jec·tiv·i·ty** /₁ɑːb₁dʒɛk'tɪvəti/ *n* [*U*] • *She questioned the author's objectivity.*

²**objective** *n* **1** [*C*] : a goal or purpose • *Our main/primary objective is to improve efficiency.* **2** [*U*] *grammar* : ACCUSATIVE

object lesson *n* [*C*] : an example from real life that teaches a lesson or explains something • *His life story is an object lesson in how not to run a business.*

ob·li·gate /'ɑːblə₁geɪt/ *vb* **-gat·ed; -gat·ing** [*T*] : to make (a person or organization) do something because the law requires it or because it is the right thing to do • *I feel obligated to return his call.* • *legally obligated = obligated by law*

ob·li·ga·tion /₁ɑːblə'geɪʃən/ *n* [*C/U*] **1** : something that you must do because of a law, rule, promise, etc. • *legal/financial obligations* • *Try it for free without obligation.* [=without being required to buy it or to do anything else] • *You're under no (legal) obligation to do it.* [=there is no law that requires you to do it] **2** : something that you must do because it is morally right • *moral/family/social obligations* • *We did it out of a sense of obligation.* [=a feeling that it was the right thing to do]

oblig·a·to·ry /ə'blɪgə₁tori, *Brit* ə'blɪgətri/ *adj* **1** *formal* : required by a law or rule • *obligatory military service* **2** *always before a noun, humorous* : always or often included as a familiar and expected part of something ▪ *an action movie with the obligatory chase scenes*

oblige /əˈblaɪdʒ/ *vb* **obliged; oblig·ing** **1** [*T*] : to force or require (someone or something) to do something because of a law or rule or because it is necessary ▪ *The government is obliged by law to release the documents to the public.* **2** [*T/I*] : to do a favor for (someone) ▪ *She's always ready to oblige her friends.*

obliged *adj, not before a noun, old-fashioned* : very grateful ▪ *I'd be much obliged if you'd hold the door for me.*

obliging *adj* : helpful in a friendly way ▪ *An obliging passerby helped her with her packages.* — **oblig·ing·ly** *adv*

oblique /oʊˈbliːk/ *adj* **1** : not stated directly ▪ *an oblique* [=*indirect*] *reference* **2** : having a slanting direction or position ▪ *an oblique line* — **oblique·ly** *adv*

oblit·er·ate /əˈblɪtəˌreɪt/ *vb* **-at·ed; -at·ing** [*T*] : to destroy (something) completely so that nothing is left ▪ *The dock was obliterated by the hurricane.* — **oblit·er·a·tion** /əˌblɪtəˈreɪʃən/ *n* [*U*]

obliv·i·on /əˈblɪvijən/ *n* [*U*] **1** : the state of something that is not remembered, used, or thought about any more ▪ *a technology destined/headed for oblivion* **2** : the state of being unconscious or unaware ▪ *She drank herself into oblivion.* **3** : the state of being destroyed ▪ *a village bulldozed into oblivion*

obliv·i·ous /əˈblɪvijəs/ *adj* : not conscious or aware of someone or something ▪ *She kept dancing, oblivious to everyone around her.* — **obliv·i·ous·ly** *adv* — **obliv·i·ous·ness** *n* [*U*]

ob·long /ˈɑːˌblɑːŋ/ *adj* **1** *US* : longer in one direction than in the other direction ▪ *an oblong loop/leaf* **2** *chiefly Brit* : shaped like a rectangle : RECTANGULAR — **oblong** *n* [*C*]

ob·nox·ious /ɑbˈnɑːkʃəs/ *adj* : unpleasant in a way that makes people feel offended, annoyed, or disgusted ▪ *They were being loud and obnoxious.* ▪ *an obnoxious smell* — **ob·nox·ious·ly** *adv* ▪ *obnoxiously loud*

oboe /ˈoʊboʊ/ *n* [*C*] : a musical instrument that is shaped like a tube and that is played by blowing into a small, thin piece at the top of the tube — **obo·ist** /ˈoʊboʊwɪst/ *n* [*C*]

ob·scene /ɑbˈsiːn/ *adj* **1 a** : relating to sex in an indecent or offensive way ▪ *obscene pictures* **b** : very offensive in usually a shocking way ▪ *an obscene gesture* **2** : so large an amount or size as to be very shocking or unfair ▪ *an obscene amount of money* ▪ *an obscene* [=*disgusting*] *waste of money* — **ob·scene·ly** *adv* ▪ *obscenely wealthy/rich*

ob·scen·i·ty /ɑbˈsɛnəti/ *n, pl* **-ties** **1** [*U*] : the quality or state of being obscene ▪ *He was arrested for obscenity.* **2** [*U*] : obscene words or actions ▪ *The author uses obscenity to make a point about the culture.* **3** [*C*] : an offensive word : SWEARWORD ▪ *shouting obscenities*

¹ob·scure /ɑbˈskjɚ/ *adj* **1** : not known to most people ▪ *obscure books/titles* ▪ *an ob-*

scure corner of the city **2 a** : likely to be understood by only a few people ▪ *obscure references to minor events* **b** : difficult or impossible to know completely and with certainty ▪ *The origins of the language are obscure.* — **ob·scure·ly** *adv*

²obscure *vb* **-scured; -scur·ing** [*T*] : to make (something) difficult to understand or know ▪ *The true history has been obscured by legends about what happened.* **2** : to be in front of (something) so that it cannot be seen ▪ *Clouds obscured the mountains.* = *The mountains were obscured by clouds.*

ob·scu·ri·ty /ɑbˈskjɚəti/ *n, pl* **-ties** **1** [*U*] : the state of being unknown or forgotten ▪ *an old tradition that has emerged from obscurity* ▪ *He was living in relative obscurity in a small town.* **2 a** [*C*] : something that is difficult to understand ▪ *an essay full of obscurities* **b** [*U*] : the quality of being difficult to understand ▪ *Avoid obscurity of language.* [=do not use words people are not likely to understand]

ob·serv·able /əbˈzɚvəbəl/ *adj* : possible to see or notice ▪ *the observable universe*

ob·ser·vance /əbˈzɚvəns/ *n* **1** [*U*] : the practice of following a custom, rule, law, etc. ▪ *The office is closed in observance of the holiday.* ▪ *strict observance of the law* **2** [*C*] : an act that is part of a ceremony or ritual ▪ *religious/ritual observances*

ob·ser·vant /əbˈzɚvənt/ *adj* **1** : good at noticing what is going on around you ▪ *a keenly observant reporter* **2** : careful to follow religious teachings or customs ▪ *an observant Jew/Muslim* = *a Jew/Muslim who is observant of Jewish/Islamic law*

ob·ser·va·tion /ˌɑːbsɚˈveɪʃən/ *n* **1** [*C*] : a statement about something you have noticed ▪ *You like to relax. I'm not criticizing you. I'm just making an observation.* **2 a** [*U*] : the act of careful watching and listening ▪ *close/careful observation of the behavior of wild birds* ▪ *She used her powers of observation* [=ability to notice and pay close attention to things] *to solve the crime.* ▪ *patients under observation* [=being carefully watched by doctors, nurses, etc.] **b** [*C*] : something you notice by watching and listening ▪ *scientific observations* **c** [*C*] : a written or spoken report or description of something that you have noticed or studied ▪ *He recorded his observations in a notebook.* — **ob·ser·va·tion·al** /ˌɑːbsɚˈveɪʃənl/ *adj*

ob·ser·va·to·ry /əbˈzɚvəˌtori, *Brit* əbˈzɚːvətri/ *n, pl* **-ries** [*C*] : a building from which scientists study and watch the sky

ob·serve /əbˈzɚv/ *vb* **-served; -serv·ing** **1** [*T/I*] : to watch and sometimes also listen to (someone or something) carefully ▪ *observing the movements of fish* ▪ *The patient must be observed constantly.* **2** [*T*] : to see and notice (someone or something) ▪ *We observed a flock of birds heading north.* ▪ *diseases that have been observed in humans* **3** [*T*] : to make a comment about something you notice ▪ *"The paint," she observed, "is faded."* **4** [*T*] : to do what a custom, rule, law, etc., says you should do ▪ *Players must observe*

[=*follow*] *the rules of the game.* **5** [*T*] : to celebrate (a holiday) or honor (a person or event) ▪ *observing Veterans Day* ▪ *They observed a moment of silence.*

ob·serv·er /əbˈzɚvɚ/ *n* [*C*] **1** : a person who sees and notices someone or something ▪ *Even a casual observer can tell that the building is in need of repair.* **2** : a person who pays close attention to something and is considered to be an expert on that thing ▪ *industry/military observers* **3** : a person who is present at something in order to watch and listen to what happens ▪ *There was an observer present at the meeting.*

ob·sess /əbˈsɛs/ *vb* **1** [*T*] : to be the only person or thing that someone thinks or talks about ▪ *The war obsesses him.* = *He's obsessed by the war.* ▪ *She's obsessed with him.* [=she thinks about him all the time] **2** [*I*] *informal* : to think and talk about someone or something too much ▪ *He's always obsessing over money.* ▪ *Stop obsessing (about it) and just deal with the problem.*

ob·ses·sion /əbˈsɛʃən/ *n* **1** [*C/U*] : a state in which someone thinks about someone or something constantly or frequently especially in a way that is not normal ▪ *the object of her obsession* [=the thing that she is obsessed about] ▪ *He's concerned about money to the point of obsession.* **2** [*C*] **a** : someone or something that a person thinks about constantly or frequently ▪ *Money is an obsession for him.* **b** : an activity that someone is very interested in or spends a lot of time doing ▪ *Stamp collecting has become an obsession for me.*

ob·ses·sive /əbˈsɛsɪv/ *adj* : thinking about something or someone too much or in a way that is not normal ▪ *dancers who are obsessive about their weight* : showing or relating to an obsession ▪ *obsessive thoughts* ▪ *obsessive attention to detail* — **ob·ses·sive·ly** *adv*

ob·so·lete /ˌɑːbsəˈliːt/ *adj* **1** : no longer used because something newer exists ▪ *obsolete computers* : replaced by something newer ▪ *obsolete mills and factories* **2** : no longer used by anyone ▪ *an obsolete word*

ob·sta·cle /ˈɑːbstɪkəl/ *n* [*C*] **1** : something that makes it difficult to do something ▪ *Lack of experience is a major obstacle for her opponent.* ▪ *an obstacle to learning/progress* **2** : an object that you have to go around or over ▪ *She swerved to avoid an obstacle in the road.*

obstacle course *n* [*C*] **1** : a series of objects that people or animals in a race have to jump or climb over, go around, go under, etc. **2** : a training area for soldiers that is filled with objects that the soldiers have to jump or climb over, go around, go under, etc.

ob·ste·tri·cian /ˌɑːbstəˈtrɪʃən/ *n* [*C*] *medical* : a doctor who specializes in obstetrics

ob·stet·rics /əbˈstɛtrɪks/ *n* [*U*] *medical* : a branch of medicine that deals with the birth of children and with the care of women before, during, and after they give birth to children — **ob·stet·ric**

/əbˈstɛtrɪk/ *or US* **ob·stet·ri·cal** /əbˈstɛtrɪkəl/ *adj*

ob·sti·nate /ˈɑːbstənət/ *adj* : refusing to change your behavior or your ideas : STUBBORN ▪ *obstinate children/behavior* — **ob·sti·na·cy** /ˈɑːbstənəsi/ *n* [*U*] — **ob·sti·nate·ly** *adv*

ob·struct /əbˈstrʌkt/ *vb* [*T*] *somewhat formal* **1** : to block (something, such as a pipe or street) so that things cannot move through easily ▪ *A fallen tree obstructed the road.* **2** : to slow or block the movement, progress, or action of (something or someone) ▪ *She was charged with obstructing justice by lying to investigators.* **3** : to be in front of (something) : to make (something) difficult to see ▪ *a wall that obstructs* [=blocks] *the view of the ocean* — **ob·struc·tive** /əbˈstrʌktɪv/ *adj* ▪ *deliberately obstructive tactics*

ob·struc·tion /əbˈstrʌkʃən/ *n* **1** [*C*] : something that blocks something else and makes it difficult for things to move through ▪ *fallen trees and other obstructions in the road* **2** [*C/U*] : the condition of being blocked so that things cannot move through easily ▪ *an obstruction of the airway* **3** [*U*] : the act of making it difficult for something to happen or move forward ◆ *Obstruction of justice* is the crime of trying to stop police from learning the truth about something.

ob·tain /əbˈteɪn/ *vb* [*T*] *somewhat formal* : to gain or get (something) usually by effort ▪ *The information was difficult to obtain.* ▪ *We obtained a copy of the original letter.* — **ob·tain·able** /əbˈteɪnəbəl/ *adj*

ob·tru·sive /əbˈtruːsɪv/ *adj* **1** : tending to bother people by appearing where you are not welcome or invited ▪ *The waiter was attentive without being obtrusive.* **2** : noticeable in an unpleasant or annoying way ▪ *obtrusive advertising* — **ob·tru·sive·ly** *adv*

ob·tuse /əbˈtuːs, Brit əbˈtjuːs/ *adj* **1** *formal* : stupid or unintelligent ▪ *an incredibly obtuse person* **2** *mathematics* : measuring between 90 degrees and 180 degrees ▪ *an obtuse angle* — **ob·tuse·ness** *n* [*U*]

ob·vi·ous /ˈɑːbvijəs/ *adj* **1** : easy to see or notice ▪ *obvious signs of the disease* ▪ *obvious differences* **2** : easy for the mind to understand or recognize ▪ *It was obvious that the plan wasn't working.* ▪ *The answer seems obvious to me.* ▪ *He's the obvious choice for the job.* — **the obvious** : something that is obvious ▪ *Don't state the obvious. Tell me something I don't already know.* — **ob·vi·ous·ness** *n* [*U*]

ob·vi·ous·ly /ˈɑːbvijəsli/ *adv* **1** : in a way that is easy to see, understand, or recognize ▪ *She obviously enjoys her work.* ▪ *That's obviously not true.* **2** — used to emphasize that you are talking about something that is easy to see, understand, or recognize ▪ *Obviously, something is wrong.*

oc·ca·sion /əˈkeɪʒən/ *n* **1** [*C*] : a special event or time ▪ *birthdays, anniversaries, and other special occasions* ▪ *formal occasions* ▪ *a memorable/historic occasion* ▪ *On the occasion of their 25th wedding*

anniversary, they took a vacation to Paris.
2 [C] *somewhat formal* : a particular time when something happens ▪ *We usually meet at noon, but on this particular occasion, we met at two o'clock.* **3** [U, singular] *somewhat formal* : a situation that allows something to happen ▪ *We had occasion to watch her perform last summer.* ▪ *She never found an occasion to suggest her ideas.* **4** [singular] *somewhat formal* : a reason to do something ▪ *The team's win was an occasion for celebration.* — **on occasion** : sometimes but not often ▪ *On occasion* [=occasionally], we'll eat outside. — **rise to the occasion** see ¹RISE

oc·ca·sion·al /ə'keɪʒənl/ *adj, always before a noun* **1** : happening or done sometimes but not often ▪ *We had occasional rain showers throughout the morning.* ▪ *She makes occasional appearances on television.* = *She appears on the occasional television show.* **2** : sometimes doing a particular job or activity ▪ *occasional smokers* [=people who smoke occasionally]

oc·ca·sion·al·ly /ə'keɪʒənəli/ *adv* : sometimes but not often ▪ *You should stir the soup occasionally as it cooks.* ▪ *Very occasionally* [=rarely], *she will have a glass of wine.*

occult /ə'kʌlt/ *adj, always before a noun* : of or relating to supernatural powers or practices ▪ *the occult sciences/arts* — **the occult** : supernatural powers or practices and the things (such as gods, ghosts, and magic) that are connected with them ▪ *He's a student of the occult.*

oc·cu·pan·cy /'ɑːkjəpənsi/ *n* [U] **1** : the act of living or staying in a particular place ▪ *a building that is unsafe for human occupancy* **2** : the number of people who are in a particular building or room at one time ▪ *The auditorium's maximum occupancy is 500 people.*

oc·cu·pant /'ɑːkjəpənt/ *n* [C] **1** : a person who is using or living in a particular building, apartment, or room ▪ *the building's/apartment's occupants* **2** : a person who is in a room, vehicle, etc., at a particular time ▪ *Both of the car's occupants were injured.*

oc·cu·pa·tion /,ɑːkjə'peɪʃən/ *n* **1** [C] : a person's job or profession ▪ *occupations such as farmer, electrician, or teacher* **2** [C] : an activity that a person spends time doing ▪ *My favorite occupation is playing chess.* **3** [U] : the activity of living in or using a particular place ▪ *The offices are ready for occupation.* **4** [U] : a situation in which the military of a foreign government goes into an area or country and takes control of it ▪ *occupation of a foreign country* ▪ *people living under occupation*

oc·cu·pa·tion·al /,ɑːkjə'peɪʃənl/ *adj, always before a noun* : of or relating to a person's job or occupation ▪ *occupational training* ▪ *an occupational hazard* [=something bad that might happen to you because of the kind of work you do] — **oc·cu·pa·tion·al·ly** *adv*

occupied *adj* **1** *not before a noun, somewhat formal* : busy doing something ▪ *She*

keeps herself occupied with volunteer work.* **2** *somewhat formal* : being used by someone ▪ *This chair is occupied.* **3** : controlled by foreign soldiers or a foreign government ▪ *an occupied territory*

oc·cu·pi·er /'ɑːkjə,pajə/ *n* [C] **1** : a soldier in an army that has taken control of a foreign place ▪ *foreign occupiers* **2** *Brit* : OCCUPANT 1

oc·cu·py /'ɑːkjə,paɪ/ *vb* **-pies**; **-pied**; **-py·ing** [T] **1** *somewhat formal* : to live in (a house, apartment, etc.) ▪ *They occupied the apartment for a year.* **2 a** : to fill or be in (a place or space) ▪ *Their house occupies a beautiful spot next to the ocean.* ▪ (figurative) *That day occupies* [=has] *a special place in my memory.* **b** : to fill or use (an amount of time) ▪ *Studying occupies nearly all of my time.* **3** : to make (someone, someone's mind, etc.) busy ▪ *the questions that occupy her mind/thoughts* ▪ *I occupied myself with reading.* **4** : to take and keep control of (a town, foreign country, etc.) by using military power ▪ *Enemy troops occupied the town.* **5** *somewhat formal* : to have (a job or position) ▪ *occupying a position of power*

oc·cur /ə'kɚ/ *vb* **-curred**; **-cur·ring** [I] **1** *somewhat formal* : to happen ▪ *A similar event may occur in the future.* ▪ *The disease tends to occur in children.* **2** *formal* : to appear or exist ▪ *a naturally occurring compound/chemical/substance* — **occur to** [phrasal vb] : to be thought of by (someone) ▪ *An idea just occurred to me.* [=I just had an idea] ▪ *It suddenly occurred to me that they might be lost.*

oc·cur·rence /ə'kɚrəns/ *n* [C] : something that happens ▪ *Getting headaches is a common/frequent/everyday occurrence for me.* **2** [U] : the fact of happening or occurring ▪ *preventing the occurrence of further problems*

ocean /'oʊʃən/ *n* **1** [U] : the salt water that covers much of the Earth's surface ▪ *crossing miles of ocean* ▪ *We live near the ocean.* [=sea] ▪ *the ocean floor/surface* ▪ *an ocean voyage* **2** *or* **Ocean** [C] : one of the five large areas of salt water that cover much of the Earth's surface ▪ *the Atlantic/Pacific Ocean* **3** [C] *informal* : a very large number or amount of something ▪ *an ocean of sadness* ▪ *oceans of time* [=lots of time]

ocean·go·ing /'oʊʃən,gowɪŋ/ *adj* : made for traveling on or across the ocean ▪ *oceangoing ships*

ocean·og·ra·phy /,oʊʃə'nɑːgrəfi/ *n* [U] : a science that studies the ocean — **ocean·og·ra·pher** /,oʊʃə'nɑːgrəfə/ *n* [C] — **ocean·o·graph·ic** /,oʊʃənə'græfɪk/ *adj*

ochre *or US* **ocher** /'oʊkə/ *n* [U] **1** : a type of red or yellow dirt **2** : the color of ochre and especially of yellow ochre

o'·clock /ə'klɑːk/ *adv* : according to the clock — used when the time is a specific hour ▪ *It's three o'clock in the afternoon.* [=it's three p.m.] ▪ *an 8 o'clock appointment*

Oct. *abbr* October

oc·ta·gon /'ɑːktə,gɑːn/ *n* [C] *mathematics* : a flat shape that has eight sides and eight angles — **oc·tag·o·nal** /ɑk-ˈtæɡənl/ adj

oc·tane /ˈɑːkˌteɪn/ n [U] : a chemical in petroleum that is used to rate the quality of different kinds of gasoline

oc·tave /ˈɑːktɪv/ n [C] music : the difference in sound between the first and eighth note on a musical scale

Oc·to·ber /ɑkˈtoʊbɚ/ n [C/U] : the 10th month of the year • in (early/late) October • on October the third = (US) on October third = on the third of October • It happens every October. — abbr. Oct.

oc·to·pus /ˈɑːktəˌpʊs/ n, pl **-pus·es** or **-pi** /-ˌpaɪ/ [C] : a sea animal that has a soft body and eight long arms

OD /ˌoʊˈdiː/ vb **OD's; OD'd** or **ODed; OD'·ing** [I] informal **1** : to become sick or die from taking too much of a drug : OVERDOSE • She OD'd on heroin. **2** : to have or experience too much of something • OD'ing on video games

odd /ˈɑːd/ adj **1** : strange or unusual • odd behavior/habits • a really odd sense of humor • What an odd-looking animal. • They make an odd couple. [=they are very different from each other] **2** always before a noun : happening in a way that is not planned or regular • at odd moments • He does odd jobs to earn extra money. **3** always before a noun : of different kinds or types • They were selling an odd assortment of candy and jewelry. • a few odd bits of information **4** always before a noun : not matched or paired with another thing or person • an odd shoe/sock **5 a** : not able to be divided into two equal whole numbers • The numbers 1, 3, 5, and 7 are odd, while 2, 4, 6, and 8 are even. **b** : marked by an odd number • even and odd pages **6** informal : a little more than a particular number — used in combination with a number • The book's 100-odd pages long. [=slightly more than 100 pages long] • 30-odd years ago — **the odd man/one out** : the person or thing that is different from the other members of a group • All my friends are married. I'm the odd man out.
— **odd·ness** n [U]

odd·ball /ˈɑːdˌbɑːl/ n [C] informal : a person who behaves in strange or unusual ways — **oddball** adj, always before a noun • oddball characters/behavior

odd·i·ty /ˈɑːdəti/ n, pl **-ties** **1** [C] : a strange or unusual person or thing • Her shyness makes her an oddity in the business world. **2** [U] : the quality or state of being strange or unusual • the oddity of the situation

odd·ly /ˈɑːdli/ adv **1** : in a strange or unusual way • the house's oddly shaped roof • The hotel seemed oddly familiar. **2** — used to say that something is strange, odd, or surprising • It was rainy, but **oddly enough**, everyone seemed to be enjoying themselves.

odds /ˈɑːdz/ n [plural] **1** : the chance that one thing will happen instead of a different thing • What are her odds [=chances] of winning? • I know the odds are against me. [=I know that I am not likely to succeed] • The odds are good that he'll survive. [=he is likely to survive]

• Surgery will increase his odds of survival. • It might rain, but (the) odds are that it'll be sunny tomorrow. [=it is more likely to be sunny than rainy tomorrow] • The team faces long odds. [=the team is not likely to win] **2** : conditions that make it difficult for something to happen • They defied/overcame the odds. • He was able to do it, against all odds. [=even though it was very difficult and unlikely] • Despite/against the odds, she has survived. • I tried to beat the odds. [=to succeed even though I was not likely to succeed] — **at odds** : in a state of disagreement • The groups have long been at odds with each other. • These results are at odds with our previous findings.

odds and ends n [plural] informal : different kinds of things that are usually small and unimportant • A few odds and ends still need to be done. • a box full of odds and ends

odds–on /ˈɑːdzˈɑːn/ adj : believed to be likely to win • They're the odds-on favorite to win. = They are odds-on to win.

ode /ˈoʊd/ n [C] : a poem in which a person expresses a strong feeling of love or respect for someone or something

odi·ous /ˈoʊdijəs/ adj, formal : causing hatred or strong dislike • an odious crime/criminal

odom·e·ter /oʊˈdɑːmətɚ/ n [C] chiefly US : a device in a car, truck, etc., that measures the distance that the vehicle has traveled

odor (US) or Brit **odour** /ˈoʊdɚ/ n [C/U] : a particular smell • a strong/fishy odor — see also BODY ODOR — **odor·less** (US) or Brit **odour·less** /ˈoʊdɚləs/ adj • a colorless and odorless gas

od·ys·sey /ˈɑːdəsi/ n, pl **-seys** [C] **1** literary : a long journey full of adventures **2** : a series of experiences that give knowledge or understanding to someone • a spiritual odyssey

oesophagus, oestrogen Brit spellings of ESOPHAGUS, ESTROGEN

of /ˈʌv, əv, ə, Brit ˈɒv, əv, ə/ prep **1** : belonging to, relating to, or connected with (someone or something) • a friend of mine • that shirt of yours • the plays of Shakespeare • the name of the band • the Queen of England • the results of the experiment • the color of the dress • the fourth of July [=the fourth day in the month of July] • a story of [=about] her travels **2** — used to indicate that someone or something belongs to a group of people or things • He is one of my friends. • This is page one of two (pages). • many/most of the students • members of the team **3** : living or occurring in (a specified country, city, town, etc.) • the people of Guam • a plant of the tropics **4** : showing (someone or something) • a picture/painting of a child **5** — used to indicate the thing that is being referred to • the city of Rome • the month of June • a piece of advice • several kinds of flowers = flowers of several kinds **6** : involving or dealing with (something) • a test of basic skills • the Department of Agriculture **7** — used to indicate what something is made from or includes • a throne of gold = a throne *made (out) of gold* ▪ *a bar of chocolate* ▪ *a group of people* **8** — used to indicate what an amount, number, etc., refers to ▪ *a large amount of rain* ▪ *two acres of land* ▪ *a pair of scissors* ▪ *a hot cup of coffee = a cup of hot coffee* ▪ *He is 40 years of age.* [=40 years old] **9** — used to indicate a quality or characteristic that someone or something has ▪ *He is of Polish descent.* ▪ *a boy of 12 (years of age)* ▪ *a woman of great wealth* ▪ *a matter of no importance* **10** — used to indicate the location of something ▪ *The cabins are north of the lake.* **11 a** — used to indicate the subject of an action ▪ *the arrival of guests* ▪ *the departure of the ship* **b** — used to indicate the object of an action ▪ *the destruction of property* ▪ *an investigation of the crime* ▪ *She asked a favor of me.* **c** — used to indicate the cause of a specified feeling or opinion ▪ *a love of nature* ▪ *I'm so proud of you.* **d** — used to indicate the reason for something ▪ *He died of pneumonia.* **12** — used to indicate what has been taken away, removed, or given away ▪ *She was robbed of her fortune.* ▪ *He gave generously of his time.* [=he gave his time generously] **13** — used to indicate that someone has behaved in a specified way ▪ *It was very kind/nice of you to say that.* **14** *US* — used to indicate that there is a specified amount of time left before the next hour begins ▪ *It's a quarter of ten.* [=9:45] — **as of** see ²AS — **of a** *US, informal* — used to indicate that someone or something is a particular type of person or thing ▪ *It's not much of a problem.* [=it is not a big problem] ▪ *How big of a piece do you want?* — **of course** see ¹COURSE

¹off /ˈɑːf/ *adv* **1 a :** away from a place ▪ *The dog ran off.* ▪ *We get off at the next bus stop.* [=we exit the bus at the next stop] **b :** away from a main road, path, etc. ▪ *The car turned off onto a side street.* **2 :** at a distance in time or space ▪ *Football season is not far off.* [=football season will start soon] **3** — used to describe something that moves or is moved so that it is no longer on something or attached to something ▪ *His hat fell off.* ▪ *She took off her coat.* **4 :** into sleep ▪ *dozing/drifting off (to sleep)* **5 a** — used to describe stopping something ▪ *Shut off the water/engine.* **b** — used to describe getting something into a desired condition especially by removing something ▪ *Dust off the shelves.* ▪ *Wipe the counter off.* **c** — used to describe finishing something ▪ *We paid off our debts.* ▪ *finishing off a pie* **6 :** away from regular work ▪ *I took the day off (from work).* ▪ *I have weekends off.* [=I do not go to work on the weekends] — **off and on** or **on and off :** starting, stopping, and starting again ▪ *It rained off and on all day.* ▪ *They've had an on-and-off relationship.*

²off *prep* **1** — used to indicate separation, distance, or removal from someone or something ▪ *The ball bounced off the wall.* ▪ *She stepped off the train.* ▪ *Keep off the grass.* ▪ *The discussion got/moved off the original subject.* **2 :** on money, food, energy, etc., supplied by (someone or

something) ▪ *She's living off her parents.* ▪ *They live off the land.* ▪ *The machine runs off* [=on] *diesel fuel.* **3** — used to indicate something that someone is no longer doing or using ▪ *He is off his diet.* ▪ *I'm off duty.* ▪ *a day off work* **4** — used to indicate the object of an action ▪ *I borrowed a dollar off* [=from] *him.* **5** — used to indicate the source or cause of something ▪ *money I made off* [=from] *gambling* **6 :** below the usual standard or level of (something) ▪ *(chiefly US) He is off his game.* [=he is not playing as well as he usually does] ▪ *15 percent off the regular price* — **off of** *chiefly US, informal* **:** OFF ▪ *She fell off of the swing.* ▪ *farmers who live off of the land* ▪ *15 percent off of the regular price*

³off *adj* **1** *not before a noun* **:** not attached to or covering something **:** not on ▪ *The lid is off.* **2 a** *not before a noun* **:** not operating, functioning, or flowing ▪ *The radio/electricity/water is off.* **b :** in a position that stops the flow of electricity, water, etc. ▪ *The switch is off.* ▪ *a lever in the off position* **3 :** away from home or work ▪ *She is off on a trip/vacation.* ▪ *He's off today.* ▪ *their off days* [=the days when they are not working] **4** *not before a noun* **:** not happening ▪ *The deal/game is off.* [=has been canceled] **5** *not before a noun, chiefly US* **:** ¹WRONG 1 ▪ *I must be off in my calculations.* ▪ *Your guess is way off!* **6** *always before a noun* **:** very small in degree ▪ *There's an off chance that you'll win.* **7** *always before a noun* **:** not as busy or active as other periods of time ▪ *an off time of year* ▪ *the off season* **8** *not before a noun* **:** not completely sane ▪ *He's a little off (in the head).* **9** *not before a noun* — used to ask about or describe someone's situation or condition ▪ *Are you better/worse off financially now?* ▪ *The other patients are worse off than she is.* ▪ *(chiefly Brit) We're comfortably off.* **10** *not before a noun, chiefly US* **:** below the usual price or value ▪ *Stocks are off* [=down] *today.* **11** *chiefly US* **:** not as good as usual ▪ *My golf game is off today.* ▪ *I am having an off day.* — **be off :** to start going, running, etc. ▪ *I must be off.* [=I must leave now] ▪ *They're off and running!*

off·beat /ˈɑːfˌbiːt/ *adj, informal* **:** different from the ordinary, usual, or expected ▪ *an offbeat sense of humor*

off–center *(US)* or *Brit* **off–centre** *adj* **1** *not before a noun* **:** not exactly in the center of something ▪ *The mirror over the sink is a little bit off-center.* **2 :** different or unusual ▪ *an off-center sense of humor*

off–col·or *(US)* or *Brit* **off–col·our** /ˈɑːfˈkʌlɚ/ *adj, chiefly US* **:** indecent or improper ▪ *an off-color joke/remark*

off–duty *adj* **:** not working at a particular time ▪ *an off-duty cop*

of·fend /əˈfɛnd/ *vb* **1** [*T/I*] **:** to cause (a person or group) to feel hurt, angry, or upset by something said or done ▪ *She spoke carefully so as not to offend anyone.* ▪ *It offends me that you would say that.* ▪ *Some people are offended by the song's lyrics.* ▪ *I'm sorry, I didn't mean to offend (you).* **2** [*T*] **:** to be unpleasant to (someone or something) ▪ *The billboard* **of-fends** *the eye.* [=it is not attractive] **3** [*I*] *formal* : to commit a crime ▪ *Is he likely to offend again after his release from prison?*

of·fend·er /ə'fɛndə/ *n* [*C*] **1** : a person who commits a crime ▪ *a repeat offender* [=someone who has committed a crime more than once] ▪ *a sex/sexual offender* [=someone who commits sex crimes] **2** : someone or something that does something harmful or wrong ▪ *The factory is one of the worst offenders in terms of air pollution.*

of·fense (*US*) or Brit **of·fence** /ə'fɛns/ *n*
1 a [*U*] : something that causes a person to be hurt, angry, or upset ▪ *I don't mean to give/cause offense.* = *I mean no offense.* [=I don't mean/want to offend anyone] ▪ *No offense* [=I do not want to offend you when I say this], *but I think you're wrong.* **b** [*C*] : something that is wrong or improper ▪ *actions that are an offense to/against public morals* **2** [*C*] : a criminal act ▪ *a first offense* ▪ *a capital/federal/criminal offense* **3** /'a:ˌfɛns/ *US, sports* **a** [*C/U*] : the group of players on a team who try to score points or goals against an opponent ▪ *Our team has the best offense in the league.* ▪ *She's on offense.* [=playing on the part of the team that tries to score points or goals] **b** [*U*] : the way that players on a team try to score points or goals against an opponent ▪ *The team plays good offense.* — **take offense** : to become angry or upset by something that another person has said or done ▪ *He took offense when I suggested that he was wrong.* ▪ *She takes offense at any criticism.*

¹of·fen·sive /ə'fɛnsɪv/ *adj* **1** : causing someone to feel hurt, angry, or upset : rude or insulting ▪ *offensive words/terms/remarks* ▪ *behavior that's offensive to many people* **2** : very unpleasant ▪ *an offensive odor* **3** *always before a noun, sports* : of or relating to the way that players try to score against an opponent in a game or contest ▪ *an offensive position/strategy* **4** *always before a noun* : relating to or designed for attacking an enemy ▪ *offensive weapons/maneuvers* — **of·fen·sive·ly** *adv* — **of·fen·sive·ness** *n* [*U*]

²offensive *n* [*C*] : a large military attack ▪ *an air offensive* ▪ (*figurative*) *Union leaders have mounted an offensive against the company's proposal to limit health benefits.* — **on the offensive** : in or into a situation or position in which you attack or fight against someone or something ▪ *soldiers on the offensive* ▪ *She went on the offensive to fight the charges against her.* — **take the offensive** : to begin to attack or fight against someone or something ▪ *Opponents of the project took the offensive and defeated the land sale.*

¹of·fer /'a:fə/ *vb* **1 a** [*T*] : to give someone the opportunity to accept or take (something) ▪ *We'd like to offer the job to you.* = *We'd like to offer you the job.* ▪ *She offered* [=said that she would pay] *$250,000 for the house.* ▪ *I offered my assistance/advice.* **b** [*T/I*] : to say that you

are willing *to do something* ▪ *She offered to help us.* ▪ *We don't need help, but thank you for offering.* **2** [*T*] : to provide or supply (something) ▪ *They offer a wide range of products/services.* ▪ *Living in a large city offers a number of advantages.* ▪ *They serve the best food this town has to offer.* [=the best food in the town] ▪ *She has a great deal to offer.* [=she has many talents, abilities, good qualities, etc.] ▪ *The restaurant offers (up) a new menu every season.* **3** [*T*] : to say or express (something) as an idea to be thought about or considered ▪ *offer (up) an opinion* ▪ *The film offers a unique perspective on the issue.* **4** [*T*] : to say or give (something, such as a prayer or a sacrifice) as a form of religious worship ▪ *offer (up) a prayer of thanks* — **offer resistance** : to try to resist or fight ▪ *They offered no resistance when the enemy entered the town.*

²offer *n* [*C*] **1** : the act of giving someone the opportunity to accept something ▪ *I don't need help, but I appreciate the offer.* [=thanks for offering to help] ▪ *She received several job offers.* ▪ *an offer of marriage* [=a marriage proposal] **2** : an amount of money that someone is willing to pay for something ▪ *I'll pay $500. That's my final/best offer.* [=I won't pay more] ▪ *They made an offer on our house.* [=they said that they would pay a specified amount of money for our house] — **on offer** *chiefly Brit* : available to be bought especially at low prices ▪ *Eggs are on offer this week.*

of·fer·ing /'a:fərɪŋ/ *n* [*C*] **1 a** : something that is given to God or a god as a part of religious worship ▪ *ceremonial/sacrificial offerings* **b** : an act of giving a religious offering ▪ *They made daily offerings to the gods.* **2** : something that is available for sale or use ▪ *the café's tasty dessert offerings*

off·hand /'a:f'hænd/ *also* **off·hand·ed** /'a:f'hændəd/ *adj* **1** : done or made without previous thought or preparation ▪ *an offhand remark* **2** : casual or informal ▪ *She spoke in an offhand manner.* — **offhand** *adv* ▪ *Do you happen to know, offhand, when he'll be back?*

of·fice /'a:fəs/ *n* **1** [*C*] **a** : a building or room in which people work at desks doing business or professional activities ▪ *She works at/in our Chicago office.* ▪ *Are you going to the office today?* ▪ *an office building* [=a building with offices] ▪ *office equipment/supplies/workers* ▪ *office workers/staff* **b** : a room with a desk where a particular person works ▪ *Her office is on the top floor.* **c** *chiefly US* : a building or room where a doctor, lawyer, etc., works and meets with patients or clients ▪ *the doctor's office* **2** [*C/U*] : the job or position of someone who has authority especially in the government ▪ *He's been in office for a year.* ▪ *He was voted out of office.* ▪ *She has held several public offices.* ▪ *He'll take office soon.* ▪ *She's leaving office after two terms.* ▪ *She plans to run for office.* [=campaign to be elected to an office] **3** [*C*] : a department of a company, organization, government, or school ▪ *the unemployment office* ▪ *the U.S. Patent Office*

— **good offices** *formal* : help from someone who has power or authority • *I got the interview through the good offices of a former classmate.*

of·fice·hold·er /ˈɑːfəsˌhouldə/ *n [C]* : a person who has an official job or position especially in the government

office hours *n [plural]* **1** : the time during the day when people work in an office • *Our office hours are 8:30 to 4:00 Monday through Friday.* **2** *US* : a time during the day when people can see a doctor or dentist

of·fi·cer /ˈɑːfəsə/ *n [C]* **1** : POLICE OFFICER • *Officer Ruiz* **2** : a person who has an important position in a company, organization, or government • *the bank's officers [=executives]* **3** : a person who has a position of authority or command in the military • *an officer in the navy* = *a naval officer*

¹**of·fi·cial** /əˈfɪʃəl/ *adj* **1** *always before a noun* : of or relating to the job or work of someone in a position of authority • *official responsibilities/documents* • *an official trip/visit* **2 a** — used to describe something that is said in a public way by someone in a position of authority • *an official announcement* • *It's official. His resignation has been accepted.* **b** — used to describe something that is done in a public and often formal way • *The museum's official opening will be next month.* **3** *always before a noun* : proper for or used by someone who has a position of authority • *the mayor's official residence* **4** *always before a noun* : having authority • *Official sources have confirmed the rumor.* : having authority to perform a service or duty • *the president's official representative* **5** : permitted, accepted, or approved by the government or by a person or organization that has authority • *the country's official language* • *The policy change will soon be official.* — **of·fi·cial·ly** *adv* • *The company's name was officially changed in 1982.*

²**official** *n [C]* **1** : a person who has a position of authority in a company, organization, or government • *a senior official* • *public/government/city/company officials* **2** : a person (such as a referee or umpire) who makes sure that players are following the rules of a game • *a football official*

of·fi·ci·ate /əˈfɪʃiˌeɪt/ *vb* **-at·ed; -at·ing** *[T/I]* **1** *formal* : to perform the official duties of a ceremony • *the priest who officiated at our wedding* **2** *sports* : to be a referee, umpire, or judge at a game, tournament, etc. • *officiating (at) a hockey game*

of·fi·cious /əˈfɪʃəs/ *adj, disapproving* — used to describe an annoying person who tries to tell other people what to do in a way that is not wanted or needed • *the boss's officious assistant* — **of·fi·cious·ly** *adv*

off·ing /ˈɑːfɪŋ/ *n* — **in the offing** : likely to happen soon • *Some big changes are in the offing.*

off–key /ˈɑːfˈkiː/ *adj* : above or below the proper pitch • *off-key notes/singing* — **off–key** *adv* • *He sang off-key.*

off–lim·its /ˈɑːfˈlɪməts/ *adj, not before a noun* **1** — used to say that people are not allowed to enter a place or use something • *This area of the museum is off-limits to visitors.* **2** — used to say that people are not allowed to talk about something • *The subject of sex was off-limits in her family.*

off–line /ˈɑːfˈlaɪn/ *adj* **1** : not connected to a computer, a computer network, or the Internet • *The system/printer is off-line.* **2** : not done on a computer network or the Internet • *off-line storage* — **off–line** *adv* • *working off-line*

off–load /ˌɑːfˈloud/ *vb [T]* **1** : to remove (something) from a truck, ship, etc. • *Workers off-loaded the equipment from the trailer.* **2** : to give away or sell (something unwanted) to someone • *She tried to off-load the stock before prices fell.*

off–peak /ˈɑːfˈpiːk/ *adj* : less busy or active than other times • *telephone rates during off-peak hours*

off–put·ting /ˈɑːfˌpʊtɪŋ/ *adj* : not pleasing or likable • *an off-putting [=unfriendly] manner*

off–ramp /ˈɑːfˌræmp/ *n [C] US* : a short road that is used to gradually slow down after leaving a highway

off–road /ˈɑːfˈroud/ *adj, always before a noun* **1** : designed to be used on trails or dirt roads • *off-road vehicles* **2** : involving or used by off-road vehicles • *off-road trails*

off–screen /ˈɑːfˈskriːn/ *adv* **1** : not happening or present in the scene that is being shown on a television or movie screen • *Strange sounds were heard offscreen.* **2** *of an actor* : in private life • *What's she like offscreen?* — **offscreen** *adj*

off–sea·son /ˈɑːfˌsiːzən/ *n [C]* **1** : a period of time when travel to a particular place is less popular and prices are usually lower • *off-season rates/travel* **2** *sports* : a period of time when official games, tournaments, etc., are not being played — **off–season** *adv* • *traveling off-season*

off·set /ˈɑːfˌsɛt/ *vb* **-set; -set·ting** *[T]* : to cancel or reduce the effect of (something) • *Gains in one area offset losses in another.*

off·shoot /ˈɑːfˌʃuːt/ *n [C]* **1** : something that develops from something larger • *The business is an offshoot of a design company.* **2** : a branch that grows on one of the main stems of a plant

off·shore /ˈɑːfˈʃoə/ *adj* **1** : moving away from the shore toward the water • *an offshore breeze* **2** : located in the ocean away from the shore • *an offshore oil rig* **3** : located in a foreign country • *an offshore bank account* — **offshore** *adv*

off·side /ˈɑːfˈsaɪd/ *adj* **1** *sports* : in a position in a game (such as football or hockey) on the opponent's part of the field where you are not allowed to be • *One of the players was offside.* **2** *Brit* : RIGHT-HAND • *the car's offside mirror/headlight* — **the offside** *Brit* : the right-hand side • *the mirror on the offside* — **offside** *adv*

off·spring /ˈɑːfˌsprɪŋ/ *n, pl* **offspring** *[C]* **1** : a person's child • *parents and their off-*

spring **2** : the young of an animal or plant

off·stage /'ɑ:f'steɪʤ/ *adv* **1** : on the part of the stage that the audience cannot see ▪ *We heard a loud crash offstage.* **2** *of a performer* : in private life ▪ *Offstage, the actress is very down-to-earth.*

off–the–cuff *adj* : done without planning or preparation ▪ *off-the-cuff remarks*

off–the–record *adj* — used to describe statements that are made to a reporter but that are not supposed to be included in a story, newspaper report, etc. ▪ *off-the-record comments*

off–the–wall *adj, informal* : very unusual or strange ▪ *an off-the-wall sense of humor* ▪ *ideas that are off-the-wall*

off–white /'ɑ:f'waɪt/ *n* [U] : a yellowish or grayish white ▪ *They painted the walls in off-white.* — **off–white** *adj*

off year *n* [C] **1** : a year in which activity or production is lower than usual ▪ *an off year for auto sales* **2** *US, politics* : a year in which no major elections are held

oft /'ɑ:ft/ *adv, literary* : OFTEN ▪ *an oft-repeated story*

of·ten /'ɑ:fən/ *adv* : many times : on many occasions ▪ *They visit fairly often.* ▪ *How often do you see her?* ▪ *Often, she works late.* ▪ *She calls every so often.* [=occasionally] ▪ *More often than not* [=typically, usually], *he forgets his hat.* ▪ *She works late, as often as not.* [=very often] ▪ *We see this problem all too often.* [=too commonly]

of·ten·times /'ɑ:fən,taɪmz/ *adv, US* : OFTEN ▪ *Oftentimes, he is the only man in the aerobics class.*

ogle /'ougəl/ *vb* **ogled; ogling** [T] *usually disapproving* : to look at (someone) in a way that shows sexual attraction ▪ *people ogling models*

ogre /'ougɚ/ *n* [C] **1** : an ugly giant in children's stories that eats people **2** : someone or something that is very frightening, cruel, or difficult to deal with ▪ *an ogre of a boss* ▪ *the ogre of inflation*

oh /'ou/ *interj* **1** — used to express surprise, happiness, disappointment, or sadness ▪ *Oh, I'm so sorry to hear that.* ▪ *Oh no! I forgot my purse.* **2** — used in response to a physical sensation (such as pain) ▪ *Oh, that hurt.* **3** *also* **O** — used to address someone directly ▪ *Oh sir, you forgot your change.* ▪ *Bless us, O Lord.* **4** — used for emphasis when responding to a question or statement or when making a statement ▪ *"He's leaving." "Oh? Really?"* ▪ *Oh all right. If you insist.* **5** — used to show that something is understood ▪ *"I'm going now." "Oh, okay. I'll see you later."* **6** — used during a pause in speaking ▪ *Their house is about, oh, a mile from here.*

OH *abbr* Ohio

ohm /'oum/ *n* [C] *technical* : a unit for measuring electrical resistance

¹**oil** /'ojəl/ *n* **1** [U] **a** : a thick, black liquid that comes from the ground and that is used in making various products (such as gasoline) ▪ *drilling for oil* ▪ *oil prices/companies/wells/refineries* ▪ *the oil industry* **b** : a type of oil that is used as a fuel to produce heat or light ▪ *heating oil* **c** : a type of oil that makes the different parts in an engine, machine, etc., run smoothly **2** [C/U] : a liquid substance that comes from a plant or animal, that contains fat, and that is often used in cooking ▪ *Cook the onions in a little oil.* ▪ *salad dressed with oil and vinegar* **3** [C/U] : a smooth substance that is used on the skin, hair, or body to make it soft or healthy ▪ *bath oils* **4 a** [*plural*] : oil paints ▪ *a painter who works in oils* **b** [C] : an oil painting ▪ *an exhibit of oils and watercolors* — **burn the midnight oil** see ¹BURN

²**oil** *vb* [T] : to put oil in or on (something) ▪ *oil the gears*

oiled /'ojəld/ *adj* : treated or covered with oil ▪ *an oiled pan*

oil paint *n* [C/U] : paint that contains oil

oil painting *n* **1** [U] : the art of painting with oil paints ▪ *He studied oil painting in college.* **2** [C] : a picture that is painted with oil paints ▪ *A large oil painting hangs above the mantel.*

oil slick *n* [C] : a thin layer of oil that is floating on the surface of the ocean, a lake, etc.

oil tanker *n* [C] : a large ship that carries oil

oil well *n* [C] : a hole that has been drilled into the ground through which oil can be removed

oily /'ojli/ *adj* **oil·i·er; -est** **1** : having the smooth or greasy quality of oil ▪ *a liquid with an oily feel* **2 a** : covered or soaked with oil ▪ *oily rags* **b** : containing or producing a large amount of oil ▪ *Her skin/hair is oily.* ▪ *an oily fish* — **oil·i·ness** *n* [U]

oink /'oɪŋk/ *n* [C] : the sound made by a hog or pig — **oink** *vb* [I] ▪ *an oinking pig*

oint·ment /'oɪntmənt/ *n* [C/U] : a smooth substance that is rubbed on the skin to help heal a wound or to reduce pain or discomfort — **fly in the ointment** see ³FLY

OJ *abbr, US* orange juice

¹**OK** *or* **okay** /ou'keɪ/ *adv, informal* **1 a** — used to ask for or express agreement, approval, or understanding ▪ *"I'm going, OK?" "Yes, that's fine."* ▪ *"Let's go." "OK."* ▪ *"I'll be there in a minute, okay?"* **b** — used for emphasis at the beginning of a statement ▪ *OK everybody, let's get started.* ▪ *"Hurry up!" "Okay, okay, I'm almost ready."* **2** : well enough ▪ *How did you do at the interview?" "I think I did okay."*

²**OK** *or* **okay** *adj, informal* **1** : not very good or very bad ▪ *I'm an OK golfer.* ▪ *He's okay at math.* ▪ *The movie was just OK.* **2** : acceptable or agreeable ▪ *Is it OK if I take tomorrow off?* ▪ *Is she OK with the change?* **3** *not before a noun* **a** : not ill, hurt, unhappy, etc. ▪ *"Are you feeling OK?" "Yes, I'm fine."* **b** : not marked by problems, danger, etc. ▪ *Don't worry. Everything will be OK.* [=all right] **4** : likable, acceptable, or honest ▪ *He's an okay guy.*

³**OK** *or* **okay** *vb* **OK's** *or* **okays; OK'd** *or* **okayed; OK'·ing** *or* **okay·ing** [T] *informal* : to approve (something) ▪ *The boss needs to OK this before we place the order.*

4OK or **okay** n [singular] informal : approval or permission • We need her OK on this.

5OK abbr Oklahoma

okra /ˈoukrə/ n [U] : a tall plant whose pods are eaten as a vegetable and are used in soups and stews; also : the pods of this plant

1old /ˈould/ adj **1 a** : having lived for many years : not young • an old woman/man **b** — used to talk about or ask about a person's age • She's older than she looks. [=she has a young appearance] • He's dating an older woman. [=a woman who is older than he is] • "How old is your daughter?" "She's six." **c** : having a specified age • He's 30 years old. **2 a** : having existed or been in use for a long time : not new • an old movie • old newspapers/magazines • an old tradition/problem • an old shirt **b** : having existed for a specified amount of time • The house is 50 years old. **3** always before a noun **a** : belonging to, used by, or known by someone in the past • my old house/neighborhood/job • one of my old [=former] teachers **b** — used to say that someone or something has been your friend, enemy, etc., for a long time • an old friend of mine [=a friend I have known for a very long time] **4** informal — used for emphasis after adjectives like big, good, etc. • We had a big old party. • You poor old thing. You must be exhausted! • **Good old Joe.** He's always helping people in need. — **any old** informal — used to describe someone or something that is not special or specific • I don't care where I sleep. Any old couch will do. • Give me beer over champagne any old day. — **chip off the old block** see 1CHIP — **for old times' sake** see 1SAKE — **old boy/chap/man (etc.)** Brit, old-fashioned — used to address a man • Don't worry, old chap, it'll be all right.

2old n **1** [C] : a person who has a specified age — used in combination • six-year-olds [=children who are six years old] **2 old** [plural] : old people • a movie enjoyed by young and old alike • caring for the old [=(more commonly) the elderly] and sick — of old formal + literary : in a time that was long ago • in (the) days of old

old age n [U] : the fact of being old • She died of old age. : the time of life when a person is old • He got sweeter in his old age.

old country n — **the old country** : the country where a person was born or lived before moving to a new country • This music reminds me of the old country.

old·en /ˈouldən/ adj, always before a noun : of or relating to a time in the distant past • life in the olden days

old–fash·ioned /ˈouldˈfæʃənd/ adj **1** : no longer used or accepted • an old-fashioned word • views that are terribly old-fashioned **b** : typical of the past in a pleasing or desirable way • old-fashioned courtesy • She became successful the old-fashioned way. **2** of a person : using or preferring traditions or ideas from the

past • I'm rather old-fashioned when it comes to dating.

Old Glory n [U] : the flag of the United States

old guard n — **the old guard** : the usually older members of an organization (such as a political party) who do not want or like change • She's not popular with the old guard.

old hand n [C] : a person who has a lot of experience doing something • He's an old hand at working on cars.

old hat adj, not before a noun : seen or done many times and no longer interesting • The joke's a bit old hat now.

old·ie /ˈouldi/ n [C] informal : someone or something that is not new • This song is an oldie but a goodie.

old lady n [C] informal : someone's wife, girlfriend, or mother • He introduced me to his old lady.

old maid n [C] old-fashioned + offensive : a woman who has never been married and who is no longer young

old man n [C] informal : someone's husband, boyfriend, or father • I used to work with her old man.

old master or **Old Master** n [C] **1** : a famous and highly skilled artist; especially : a famous painter of the 16th, 17th, or early 18th century **2** : a work of art created by an Old Master • a collection of old masters

old–school adj, informal : typical of an earlier style or form • old-school comedians • old-school [=traditional] values

old school n — **the old school** : the people who support traditional policies and practices • a politician of the old school

old·ster /ˈouldstɚ/ n [C] informal : an old person • active and lively oldsters

Old Testament n — **the Old Testament** : the first part of the Christian Bible that tells about the Jews, their history, and God's words to them in the time before Jesus Christ was born — compare NEW TESTAMENT

old–time /ˈouldˈtaɪm/ adj, always before a noun **1** : of a kind or style that was typical of the past • old-time songs **2** US : having been something specified for a long time : LONGTIME • old-time residents of the neighborhood

old–tim·er /ˈouldˈtaɪmɚ/ n [C] **1** : someone who has been a member of a company or organization for a long time **2** US : an old person • Only a few old-timers still speak the language.

old wives' tale n [C] disapproving : a common belief about something that is not based on facts and that is usually false • an old wives' tale about frogs causing warts

Old World n — **the Old World** : Africa, Asia, and especially Europe • an animal found throughout the Old World

old–world /ˈouldˈwɚld/ adj, always before a noun : old-fashioned or traditional in a way that pleasantly reminds you of the past • the restaurant's old-world elegance

O level n [C] Brit : a basic test in a particular subject taken by students in England, Wales, and Northern Ireland usually at the age of 18

oli·gar·chy /ˈɑːləˌgɑɚki/ n, pl **-chies 1** [C] **a** : a country, business, etc., that is controlled by a small group of people ▪ the people that control a country, business, etc. ▪ *An oligarchy rules their nation.* **2** [U] : government or control by a small group of people ▪ *The corporation is ruled by oligarchy.*

ol·ive /ˈɑːlɪv/ n **1** [C] **a** : a small, eggshaped black or green fruit that is used as food or for making oil ▪ **b** : a tree on which olives grow — called also *olive tree* **2** [U] : a yellowish-green color — called also *olive green* — **olive** *adj*

olive branch n [C] : something that is said or done to make peace or to show that you want peace ▪ *The winner extended/offered an olive branch to his opponent by calling him a great player.*

olive drab n [U] *chiefly US* : a grayishgreen color; *also* : clothing of this color ▪ *The soldiers were dressed in olive drab.*

olive oil n [C/U] : a yellow to yellowishgreen oil that is made from olives and used in cooking

Olym·pi·ad /əˈlɪmpiˌæd/ n [C] : an occasion when the modern Olympics are held ▪ *the games of the 24th Olympiad*

Olym·pi·an /əˈlɪmpijən/ n [C] : an athlete who competes in the Olympics ▪ *modern Olympians*

Olym·pic /əˈlɪmpɪk/ adj, *always before a noun* : of or relating to the Olympics ▪ *an Olympic medal/athlete*

Olym·pics /əˈlɪmpɪks/ n — **the Olympics** : a series of international athletic contests held in a different country once every four years — called also (*formal*) *the Olympic Games*

om·buds·man /ˈɑːmˌbʊdzmən/ n, pl **-men** /-mən/ [C] : a person (such as a government official or an employee) who investigates complaints and tries to deal with problems fairly

om·e·let *or* **om·e·lette** /ˈɑːmlət/ n [C] : a dish made from eggs that are mixed together, cooked without stirring, and served folded in half often with a filling of cheese, vegetables, or meat

omen /ˈoʊmən/ n [C] : something that is believed to be a sign or warning of something that will happen in the future ▪ *They regarded the win as a good omen for the team.*

om·i·nous /ˈɑːmənəs/ adj : suggesting that something bad is going to happen in the future ▪ *ominous clouds* ▪ *speaking in ominous tones* — **om·i·nous·ly** *adv*

omis·sion /oʊˈmɪʃən/ n **1** [C] : something that has not been included or done ▪ *There are a few omissions in the list/book.* **2** [U] **a** : the act of not including or doing something ▪ *the omission of my name from the list* **b** : the state of being not included in something ▪ *her omission from the team*

omit /oʊˈmɪt/ vb **omit·ted; omit·ting** [T] **1** : to not include (someone or something) ▪ *Don't omit any details.* ▪ *My name was omitted from the list.* **2** *formal* : to fail to do (something) ▪ *I omitted [=neglected] to mention it.*

om·nip·o·tent /ɑːmˈnɪpətənt/ adj, *formal* : having complete or unlimited power ▪ *omnipotent gods* — **om·nip·o·tence** /ɑːmˈnɪpətəns/ n [U]

om·ni·pres·ent /ˌɑːmnɪˈprɛznt/ adj, *formal* : present in all places at all times ▪ *an omnipresent threat* — **om·ni·pres·ence** /ˌɑːmnɪˈprɛzns/ n [U]

om·ni·scient /ɑːmˈnɪʃənt/ adj, *formal* : having unlimited understanding or knowledge ▪ *an omniscient deity* — **om·ni·science** /ɑːmˈnɪʃəns/ n [U]

om·ni·vore /ˈɑːmnɪˌvoɚ/ n [C] *technical* : a person or animal that eats both plants and animals

om·niv·o·rous /ɑːmˈnɪvərəs/ adj **1** : eating both plants and animals ▪ *omnivorous animals* **2** : eager to learn about many different things ▪ *an omnivorous reader*

¹**on** /ˈɑːn/ prep **1 a** : touching and being supported by the top surface of (something) ▪ *The book is (lying) on the table.* **b** : to a position that is supported by (something) ▪ *getting on* [=*onto*] *a horse* ▪ *I climbed out on the roof.* **c** — used to indicate the part or object by which someone or something is supported ▪ *He stood on the stool.* **2** — used to say that something is attached to something ▪ *He hung the painting on the wall.* **3** — used to indicate where someone or something is hit or touched ▪ *She kissed him on the cheek.* **4 a** — used to indicate the surface or part where something is seen or located ▪ *I have a cut on my finger.* **b** — used to say that something (such as jewelry) is being worn by someone ▪ *the ring on her finger* **5** : near or close to (something or someone) ▪ *a village on* [=*by*] *the sea* **6** — used to indicate the location or position of something or someone ▪ *the house on the left* ▪ *on page 102 in/of the book* ▪ *Which side is it on?* **7** — used to indicate the time when something happened or will happen ▪ *We met on July 1st.* ▪ *I called on my way home.* [=when I was going home] ▪ *The TV station gives news every hour on the hour.* [=at 6:00, 7:00, 8:00, etc.] ▪ *We finished on schedule/time.* [=when we were supposed to finish] **8** : immediately after (something) ▪ *What was her reaction on hearing the news?* [=when she heard the news] **9** — used to indicate the subject of something ▪ *a book on* [=*about*] *birds* ▪ *a discussion on current events* **10 a** — used to indicate the device or instrument that is used to do something ▪ *He played a song on the piano.* **b** — used to say that someone is using a telephone, computer, etc. ▪ *talking on the phone* ▪ *She's on the phone/computer.* **c** — used to describe the device, system, etc., that is used for seeing something, hearing something, etc. ▪ *the best show on television* ▪ *I heard that song on the radio.* ▪ *I have the movie on DVD.* **11** — used to indicate a source of something (such as money, food, information, or energy) ▪ *She lives on a small salary.* ▪ *The animal feeds on insects.* ▪ *The machine runs on diesel fuel.* ▪ *a story based on fact* **12** — used to indicate the vehicle or animal by which someone or something is moved from

one place to another • *going to work on a bus* [=taking a bus to get to work] **13** — used to say that you have something in your possession at a particular time • *He had a knife on him.* **14** — used to indicate the state of something • *The house is on fire!* • *shoes on sale* **15** — used to indicate an activity that someone did or is now doing • *She did well on the exam/test.* • *The band is on tour.* • *I'm on a diet.* **16** — used to indicate something (such as a medicine or drug) that a person or animal is using • *a person on drugs/antibiotics* • *(informal) What (drugs) is she on?* **17** — used to indicate the person or thing that is responsible for something • *The drinks are on me.* [=I will pay for the drinks] • *They blamed it on me.* **18 a** — used to indicate the person or thing that something is directed toward • *an attack on religion* • *They made a down payment on the house.* • *He pulled a gun on me.* • *a ban on smoking* • *Her eyes are on the road.* [=she is watching the road] **b** — used to say that someone has been affected by something • *Her husband walked out on her.* **19** — used after an adjective to indicate the thing that a statement relates to • *I am short on cash.* [=I don't have much cash] • *Opinions are divided on this issue.* **20** : as stated or shown by (someone or something) • *I have it on good authority* [=a trustworthy person has told me] *that the company will be relocating.* **21** — used to indicate that someone or something is included as part of a team, list, etc. • *She's on the team/jury/committee.* • *His name was on the list.* **22** — used to say that someone or something has an advantage • *She has three inches in height on me.* [=she is three inches taller than I am] **23** *chiefly US* — used to say that someone is playing or performing well • *He is on his game.* [=is playing very well] — **on about** *Brit, informal + disapproving* : talking about • *I don't know what you're on about!* — **on it** : actively dealing with a problem, job, etc. • *"We need to finish." "Don't worry; I'm on it"* [=I am taking care of it]

²on *adv* **1 a** — used to indicate that something is attached to, covering, or supported by something else • *Put the lid on.* • *She put on her glasses.* **b** — used to describe something that is being worn by someone • *He put on his coat.* • *Keep your shoes on.* • *He had on a black shirt and jeans.* **2** — used to indicate movement forward • *The car stopped and then drove on.* • *We traveled on to the next town.* **3 a** — used to indicate that an activity, event, or condition continues • *The argument went on for weeks.* • *The teams played on.* • *She rambled on (and on) about it.* — **From now on** [=from this time forward], *be sure to double-check your answers.* • *From here on (out), things should get easier.* = *From this point on, things should get easier.* **b** : at an advanced state • *We're far/well on with/in our project.* **c** : at a more advanced time : at a later time • *I'll come by later on.* **4** : from one person or thing to another • *Pass the word/note on.* • *Let's move/go on*

to the next point. **5 a** — used to indicate that something is operating, flowing, etc. • *Switch/Turn the light on.* • *The lights came on.* **b** — used to indicate that something is being heated, prepared, etc. • *Put the kettle/tea/coffee on (to boil).* **6** : in or into a train, bus, etc. • *She got on at the last station.* — **on and off** see **¹OFF**

³on *adj* **1** *not before a noun* : attached to or covering something • *The lid is on tight.* **2** *not before a noun* : performing or speaking in public • *The band will be on in 10 minutes.* **3** *not before a noun* : working at a job • *He is on tomorrow from 6 a.m to 6 p.m.* **4 a** *not before a noun* : operating or flowing • *The radio/water is on.* **b** : in a position that starts the flow of electricity, water, etc. • *The switch is on.* • *The lever is in the on position.* **5** *not before a noun* **a** : taking place or happening • *The deal/game is on.* **b** : doing something as planned • *Are we still on for dinner tomorrow?* [=are we still having dinner tomorrow, as we planned to do?] **6** *not before a noun* : being broadcast on television or radio • *The show/game is on at 8 p.m.* **7** *not before a noun, chiefly US* — used to say that you are able to do something well at a particular time • *My golf game was off yesterday, but it/I was on today.* [=I played well today] — **not on** *Brit, informal* **1** : not acceptable or proper • *Cheating old ladies out of their savings just isn't on.* [=is not acceptable] **2** : not possible • *I'm afraid that scheme's just not on.* — **you're on** *informal* — used to say that you accept a bet or challenge • *"I bet I can run faster than you can." "OK, you're on."*

on–again, off–again *adj, chiefly US* : happening or existing at some times and not at other times • *his on-again, off-again girlfriend* [=his girlfriend at certain times but not at other times]

on·board /ˈɑːnˈboɚd/ *adj, always before a noun* : carried or happening on a vehicle • *onboard electronics/systems*

¹once /ˈwʌns/ *adv* **1** : one time only • *We meet once a/every month.* • *I've been here once or twice (before).* **2** : at any one time • *She didn't once thank me.* **3** : at some time in the past • *A river once flowed through this canyon.* • *a once-successful actor* — **(every) once in a while** : sometimes but not often : OCCASIONALLY • *We go out dancing once in a while.* — **once again/more** : one more time • *Once again, you've misunderstood me.* • *Let me explain once again.* — **once and for all** : now and for the last time • *Let's settle this matter once and for all.* — **once upon a time** : at some time in the past • *Once upon a time, there was a beautiful princess.*

²once *n* [U] : one single time • *I've been there more than once.* • *Please be on time just this once.* • *For once she agreed with us.* — **at once** **1** : at the same time • *several people talking (all) at once* **2** : right away : IMMEDIATELY • *We left at once.*

³once *conj* : as soon as • *Things got better once he found a job.*

once·over /ˌwʌnsˈoʊvɚ/ *n* [*singular*] : a

quick look or examination ▪ *He was giving me a/the once-over.* [=he was looking at me]

on·col·o·gy /ɑnˈkɑːlədʒi/ *n* [U] *medical* : the study and treatment of cancer — **on·col·o·gist** /ɑnˈkɑːlədʒɪst/ *n* [C]

on·com·ing /ˈɑːnˌkʌmɪŋ/ *adj, always before a noun* : coming toward you ▪ *oncoming traffic*

¹**one** /ˈwʌn/ *n* **1** [C] : the number 1 ▪ *one, two, three, …* **2** [C] *US* : a one-dollar bill ▪ *a five and two ones* **3** [U] : one o'clock ▪ *I'll be there at one.* **4** [C] : the first in a set or series ▪ *on day one of his diet* — **(all) in one** : combined in a single thing ▪ *a DVD and VCR player all in one* — **as one** *formal* : at the same time ▪ *They rose as one and left.* — **at one with** : in a peaceful state as a part of something else ▪ *I feel at one with nature.* — **for one** : as an example ▪ *I, for one, disagree.* [=I disagree] — **one·ness** /ˈwʌnnəs/ *n* [U, singular] ▪ *I felt a (sense of) oneness with nature.*

²**one** *pron* **1** : that person or thing ▪ *This pen doesn't work, so I'll have to get another one.* ▪ *Have you heard the one about* [=the joke about] *the priest and the rabbi?* — sometimes used in the plural form **ones** ▪ *Those are the ones that I bought.* **2** : someone or something that is a part of a particular group ▪ *I met one of your friends.* ▪ *He'll come back one of these days.* [=someday] ▪ *She's one of us.* [=she is part of our group and can be trusted] **3** *formal* : people in general ▪ *One never knows what the weather will be.* — **one by one** : separately in a series ▪ *They left the room one by one.* — **one in a million** *see* MILLION

³**one** *adj* **1** *always before a noun* : having the value of 1 ▪ *a one-dollar bill* **2** *always before a noun* — used to refer to a single person or thing ▪ *There is one cookie left. There is only/just one more thing to do.* ▪ *Not one person knew* [=no one knew] *the answer.* **3 a** — used before a noun to indicate that someone or something is part of a group of similar people or things ▪ *She is one member of the team.* ▪ *That's one possible solution.* ▪ *I don't like being around him.* **For one thing**, *he smokes.* ▪ *It's one thing to understand the problem, but another thing to actually fix it.* **b** *chiefly US, informal* — used to emphasize a description ▪ *That is one ugly dog.* **4** *always before a noun* : not known exactly : SOME ▪ *He'll come back one day.* **5** — used to indicate that two or more people or things are actually the same person or are the same kind of thing ▪ *The writer and her main character are one.* = *They are one and the same.* — **the one and only** — used before a name to say that there is no one else like that person ▪ *the one and only Elvis Presley*

one another *pron* : EACH OTHER ▪ *We shared our thoughts with one another.*

one–lin·er /ˌwʌnˈlaɪnɚ/ *n* [C] : a very short joke or funny remark

one–night stand *n* [C] : a situation in which you have sex with someone once

and you do not continue in a relationship afterwards

one–on–one /ˌwʌnɑnˈwʌn/ *adj* : involving two people who are dealing with or competing against each other directly ▪ *a one-on-one meeting* — **one–on–one** *adv* ▪ *I'd like to talk with you one-on-one.*

oner·ous /ˈɑːnərəs/ *adj, formal* : difficult and unpleasant to do or deal with ▪ *an onerous chore/duty*

one·self /ˌwʌnˈsɛlf/ *pron, formal* **1** — used as the object of a verb or preposition when *one* is the stated subject or is understood to be the subject ▪ *One can easily teach oneself how to sew.* ▪ *having good feelings about oneself* **2** — used for emphasis to refer again to the subject when *one* is the subject ▪ *If one does not have the information oneself, one can ask others.*

one–shot /ˈwʌnˌʃɑːt/ *adj, always before a noun, chiefly US, informal* : done or happening only once ▪ *a one-shot offer/deal*

one–sid·ed /ˈwʌnˈsaɪdəd/ *adj* **1** *disapproving* : showing only one opinion or point of view ▪ *one-sided interpretations* **2** : led or controlled by one of the two people or groups involved ▪ *a one-sided conversation* — **one–sid·ed·ness** *n* [U]

one·time /ˈwʌnˌtaɪm/ *adj, always before a noun* **1** : FORMER ▪ *a onetime actor* **2** : done or happening only once ▪ *a one-time offer*

one–to–one /ˌwʌntəˈwʌn/ *adj* **1** : involving two people who are dealing with each other directly ▪ *a one-to-one meeting* **2** *formal* : perfectly matching one thing in a group to another thing in another group ▪ *There was a one-to-one correspondence between the number of times the bell rang and the number of times the dog barked.* — **one–to–one** *adv*

one–track *adj, always before a noun* : thinking about only one particular subject ▪ *You've got a one-track mind.*

one up *adj, not before a noun, informal* : having an advantage over someone ▪ *You're one up on me.*

one–up /ˌwʌnˈʌp/ *vb* **-upped; -up·ping** [T] *US, informal* : to get an advantage over (someone) ▪ *They try to one-up each other by buying the latest gadgets.*

one–up·man·ship /ˈwʌnˈʌpmənˌʃɪp/ *n* [U] : behavior in which someone tries to get an advantage by doing, saying, or having better things than someone else ▪ *a round of verbal one-upmanship*

one–way *adj* **1** : moving in or allowing movement in only one direction ▪ *one-way streets/traffic* **2** *US* : allowing travel to a place but not back from the place ▪ *a one-way* [=(Brit) *single*] *ticket*

on·go·ing /ˈɑːnˌgowɪŋ/ *adj* : continuing to exist, happen, or progress ▪ *an ongoing debate/investigation/problem*

on·ion /ˈʌnjən/ *n* [C/U] : a round vegetable that is usually white, yellow, or red and has a strong smell and taste

onion ring *n* [C] : a ring of sliced onion that is covered with batter or bread crumbs and fried

on·line /ˈɑːnˌlaɪn/ *adj* **1** : connected to a computer, a computer network or the Internet ▪ *The library/printer is online.* **2**

: done over the Internet • *online chats/ shopping* — **online** *adv* • *spending time online*

on·look·er /ˈɑːnˌlʊkɚ/ *n* [C] : a person who watches an activity or event without being involved in it • *curious onlookers*

¹**on·ly** /ˈoʊnli/ *adj, always before a noun* : existing with no other or others of the same kind • *You're the only person I trust.* • *He was her only brother.* • (*informal*) *I would come. The only thing* [=the one problem] *is that my car is in the shop.* • *That was one of the only* [=one of very few] *times I ever saw him cry.* — **the only** — used to emphasize that a particular person or thing should be the one chosen; usually + *for* • *She's the only person for the job.*

²**only** *adv* **1 a** : no more than • *There are only two more weeks until vacation.* • *He was only a baby when his father died.* **b** : nothing other than — used to indicate that a single thing was done, is needed, is possible, etc. • *I asked him a question, but he only smiled in response.* • *We can only guess* [=we cannot know] *what they will do next.* **c** — used for emphasis • *I only wish* [=wish very much] *you'd told me sooner.* • *I only hope it won't happen again.* • *It's only natural* [=it's normal] *(that) you would feel that way.* • *Our trip had only just begun.* **2** : excluding all others • *a club for women only* • *Only employees can use that door.* : nobody or nothing except • *I love only you.* **3 a** : in no time, place, or situation except the one specified • *The animal is found only in Australia.* • *I'll go (if and) only if you go with me.* • *We made the change only after careful consideration.* **b** : for no other reason than • *I came only to help.* **4** : nothing more important or serious than • *I'm fine. It's only a scratch.* • *He was only following orders.* **5** — used to emphasize that something happened recently • *I saw her here only a moment ago.* **6 a** — used to say that something has or will have a particular and usually bad result • *Don't eat that. It will only make you sick.* **b** — used to indicate something bad or surprising that happens after something else • *I ran to the station only to find that I had missed the train.* — **for your eyes only** see ¹EYE — **if only** see ¹IF — **in name only** see ¹NAME — **not only** — used to say that both of two related statements are true • *The game is not only fun, it's educational too!* • *I'm concerned not only for myself, but (also) for my children.* — **only too** : very or completely • *They were only too ready to agree.*

³**only** *conj, informal* : BUT, HOWEVER • *We had a radio, only it was broken.*

only child *n* [C] : a person who never had a brother or sister

on–ramp /ˈɑːnˌræmp/ *n* [C] *US* : a short road that is used for driving onto a highway

on·rush /ˈɑːnˌrʌʃ/ *n* [*singular*] **1** : a strong, fast movement forward • *an onrush of water/traffic* **2** : a sudden appearance of something • *an onrush of tears/memories* — **on·rush·ing** /ˈɑːn-

ˌrʌʃɪŋ/ *adj, always before a noun* • *onrushing events*

on–screen /ˈɑːnˈskriːn/ *adv* **1** : in a movie or TV program • *They play newlyweds on-screen.* **2** : on a computer, TV, or movie screen • *The images appear on-screen.* — **on–screen** *adj* • *an on-screen family*

on·set /ˈɑːnˌsɛt/ *n* [*singular*] : the beginning of something • *the onset of a disease*

on·shore /ˈɑːnˌʃoɚ/ *adj* **1** : moving from an ocean, lake, etc., toward land • *onshore winds* **2** : on land • *an onshore oil field*

on–site /ˈɑːnˈsaɪt/ *adv* : at the place where a business or activity happens • *All parts are made on-site.*

on·slaught /ˈɑːnˌslɑːt/ *n* [C] : a violent attack • *an onslaught by the enemy* • (*figurative*) *preparing for an onslaught of tourists* [=preparing to be visited by many tourists]

on–the–job *adj, always before a noun* : received, learned, or done while working at a job • *on-the-job training/injuries*

on·to /ˈɑːntu/ *prep* **1** : to a position that is on (a surface, area, object, etc.) • *We climbed onto the roof.* • *Put the data onto a disk.* • *Turn left onto Third Street.* • (*figurative*) *Don't shift the blame onto me.* [=don't blame me instead of the person who should be blamed] **2** : in a direction that allows you to get to or see (something) • *This room/door opens onto a courtyard.* **3 a** — used to say that someone knows about what someone is doing or has done • *I'm onto you.* [=I know what you did or are doing] **b** — used to say that someone is becoming aware of something • *We are onto something (big).* [=we have discovered something important, special, etc.]

onus /ˈoʊnəs/ *n* [*singular*] *formal* : the responsibility for something • *The onus is on you to prove your point.*

on·ward (*chiefly US*) /ˈɑːnwɚd/ *or chiefly Brit* **on·wards** /ˈɑːnwɚdz/ *adv* : to or toward what is ahead in space or time • *The troops moved onward.* • *Technology is moving onward and upward.* [=toward a better condition or higher level] — **on·ward** *adj, always before a noun* • *the onward march of time*

on·yx /ˈɑːnɪks/ *n* [U] : a kind of stone that is often used in jewelry

oo·dles /ˈuːdlz/ *n* [*plural*] *informal* : a large amount of something • *oodles of money*

¹**ooh** /ˈuː/ *interj* — used to express pleasure or surprise • *Ooh, that's beautiful!*

²**ooh** *vb* [I] *informal* : to express pleasure, surprise, or both pleasure and surprise • *We oohed and aahed at/over the fireworks.* — **ooh** *n* [C] • *oohs and aahs from the crowd*

oomph /ˈʊmf/ *n* [U] *informal* : power, energy, or effectiveness • *His argument lacks oomph.*

oops /ˈʊps/ *interj* — used to express surprise or distress or to say that you have done or said something wrong • *Oops, I spilled my drink.*

¹**ooze** /ˈuːz/ *vb* **oozed; ooz·ing 1 a** [I] : to flow out slowly • *Sap oozed from the*

tree. **b** [*T*] : to have (something) flow out slowly ▪ *The wound was oozing blood.* **2** [*T/I*] : to show (a quality, emotion, etc.) very clearly or strongly ▪ *She oozes (with) confidence.*

²**ooze** *n* [*U*] : soft mud or slime (such as on the bottom of a lake)

op *abbr* **1** operation; operative; operator **2** opportunity **3** opus

opac·i·ty /ouˈpæsəti/ *n* [*U*] : the quality of being opaque ▪ *the opacity of the glass/theory*

opal /ˈoupəl/ *n* [*C/U*] : a kind of white or clear stone that is used in jewelry

opaque /ouˈpeɪk/ *adj* **1** : not letting light through ▪ *opaque glass* **2** : difficult to understand or explain ▪ *opaque writing/theories*

op—ed /ˈɑːpˈɛd/ *n* [*C*] *US* : an essay in a newspaper or magazine that gives the opinion of someone who is not employed by the newspaper or magazine ▪ *an op-ed writer*

¹**open** /ˈoupən/ *adj* **1 a** : not covering an opening ▪ *an open window* ▪ *The door swung/flew (wide) open.* **b** : having an opening that is not covered ▪ *an open box* ▪ *open wounds* [=wounds not covered by skin] ▪ *Her eyes were wide open.* **2** : not sealed or locked ▪ *open bottles of wine* ▪ *The house/door is open.* **3** : allowing movement or travel ▪ *Is that road open?* **4** : able to be entered and used by customers, visitors, etc. ▪ *The store/library is open (from 9 a.m. to 10 p.m.) on Saturdays.* **5** : having parts that are spread apart ▪ *an open umbrella/book/hand* ▪ *His shirt was open* [=was not buttoned] *at the neck/collar.* ▪ *They'll welcome you with* **open arms.** [=in a very kind and friendly way] **6 a** : not containing or surrounded by walls, fences, buildings, etc. ▪ *hanging clothes to dry in the open air* [=outside] ▪ *miles and miles of* **open country** [=land with few buildings] ▪ *the* **wide open** *spaces of the American West* **b** *of a building or room* : having few walls ▪ *a bright, open kitchen* **7 a** : including or allowing a particular group of people ▪ *The beach is* **open** *to the public.* **b** : including or allowing all people ▪ *open debate/registration* **8 a** : available to be used ▪ *It's the only course open to us.* ▪ *We have an* **open invitation** *to visit.* [=we have been invited to visit any time we want] **b** *of a job, position, etc.* : not yet taken or filled ▪ *The job/position is still open.* **9** : happening or done in public so that people can participate in or know what is being said or done ▪ *open sessions/meetings* **10** : not hidden or secret ▪ *open hostility* **11** : expressing thoughts and feelings in a direct and honest way ▪ *open communication/discussion* **12** : willing to listen to or accept different ideas or opinions ▪ *an open society* ▪ *I am* **open to** *suggestions.* ▪ *She listened with an* **open mind/heart.** **13 a** : not yet finished or decided ▪ *The case remains open.* [=it has not been solved] ▪ *an* **open investigation** ▪ *The mayoral race is still* **wide open.** [=any of the candidates could still win] **b** : allowing further comments or discussion ▪ *The question/issue is still open (for*

discussion). **14** : able to be criticized, harmed, doubted, etc. ▪ *He lays/makes himself* **open** *to criticism with such remarks.* **15** *sports* : not blocked or guarded by players from the other team ▪ *I'm open! Pass me the ball!* **16** *computers* — used to describe a file, document, etc., that is being used ▪ *an open program/document*

²**open** *vb* **1 a** [*T*] : to move (a door, window, etc.) so that an opening is no longer covered ▪ *May I open a window?* ▪ *Let me open the door for you.* ▪ *(figurative) Education can* **open** *the* **door/way** *for/to many opportunities.* [=make opportunities easier or more likely to happen] ▪ *(figurative) Her father's fame* **opened doors for** [=gave special opportunities to] *her in Hollywood.* **b** [*I*] : to move and no longer cover an opening ▪ *The car door opened and a woman stepped out.* **2** [*T*] : to cause (something) to no longer be covered, sealed, or blocked ▪ *open a can/present* ▪ *The janitor opened* [=unlocked] *the building.* **3** [*T/I*] : to separate the parts or edges of something ▪ *Open your book/umbrella.* ▪ *She opened her eyes (wide).* ▪ *Her eyes opened.* ▪ *You haven't opened your mouth* [=haven't said anything] *all night.* **4** [*T/I*] : to make a hole or opening in (something) ▪ *The surgeon opened (up) the patient's chest.* ▪ *The heavens opened and the rain poured down.* [=it began to rain hard] **5** [*T/I*] : to allow (a park, road, etc.) to be used ▪ *They've finally opened the bridge (up) to traffic again.* ▪ *The park opens every morning at dawn.* **6** [*T/I*] **a** : to begin the regular services or activities of (a business, school, etc.) ▪ *We'll open (the store) at 9 a.m.* ▪ *What time does the library open (up)?* **b** : to begin the activities or services of (a business, school, etc.) for the first time ▪ *I've always dreamed of opening (up) a café.* ▪ *The film opens* [=begins being shown] *in May.* **7** [*T/I*] : to begin (something) ▪ *The police have opened (up) an inquiry/investigation into the matter.* ▪ *He opened (his speech) with a joke.* **8** [*T*] : to begin keeping money in (a bank account) ▪ *open an account* **9** [*T*] *computers* : to begin to use (a file, document, etc.) on a computer ▪ *Open the program by clicking on the icon.* **10** [*I*] : to allow movement or passage through a doorway or other opening ▪ *The hallway opens (up) into a family room.* **11** [*I*] : to have a specified price or be at a specified level at the beginning of the day ▪ *The stock opened at $19 a share.* — **open fire** : to begin shooting ▪ *The soldiers* **opened fire on** [=began shooting at] *enemy troops.* — **open for** [*phrasal vb*] : to perform before (the main performer at a concert, show, etc.) ▪ *They once opened for the Rolling Stones.* — **open someone's eyes** see ¹EYE — **open to** [*phrasal vb*] **1 open (something) to** : to allow (a particular group of people) to enter, use, or participate in (something) ▪ *They opened the meeting to the public.* **2 open (someone or something) to** : to cause or allow (someone or something) to be affected by (something bad) ▪ *She opened*

herself (up) to political attacks. [=made herself able to be attacked politically] — **open up** [*phrasal vb*] **1** : to become less shy and speak more freely ▪ *He finally began opening up to her.* **2** — used to demand that someone who is inside a room, building, etc., let you in ▪ *This is the police! Open up!* **3 open up** *or* **open up (something)** *or* **open (something) up a** : to become or cause (something) to become available or possible ▪ *Many opportunities opened up for him.* ▪ *She opened up her home to us.* [=she invited us to stay in her home] **b** : to become or cause (something) to become wider or less crowded ▪ *It looks like the road/traffic opens up ahead.* **c** : to develop or cause (something) to develop ▪ *A wide gap in the polls has opened up between the two candidates.* — **open your heart** : to behave in a kind and generous way ▪ *Please, open your hearts to our plight.* — **open your mind** : to become able to understand different ideas or ways of thinking ▪ *The experience opened my mind to new ideas.*

³**open** *n* **1** [*C*] : a tournament that allows both professionals and amateurs to participate ▪ *the French Open* **2 the open a** : an area or place that is not covered or enclosed ▪ *We slept (out) in the open under the stars.* **b** : a situation in which something is no longer hidden or kept secret ▪ *Her true feelings were finally (out) in the open.*

open–air *adj* : located outside rather than inside a building ▪ *an open-air market/restaurant*

open–and–shut *adj* : able to be settled or decided very quickly and easily ▪ *Our lawyer says this is an open-and-shut case.*

open day *n* [*C*] *Brit* : OPEN HOUSE 1

open–door *adj* : allowing all people to enter or participate ▪ *an open-door immigration policy* ▪ *The school has an open-door policy with parents.*

open–end·ed /ˌoʊpənˈɛndəd/ *adj* **1** : able to change ▪ *open-ended plans* : not ending in a certain way or on a certain date ▪ *open-ended military involvement* **2** : allowing people to talk in a way that is not planned or controlled ▪ *an open-ended conversation/question*

open·er /ˈoʊpənɚ/ *n* [*C*] **1** : a tool, device, or machine that is used to open something ▪ *a bottle opener* **2** : the first game, performance, etc., in a series ▪ *Today's game is the season opener.* — **for openers** *informal* : as the first thing to be thought about or said ▪ *She asked what we'd done with her money. And that was just for openers!*

open·hand·ed /ˌoʊpənˈhændəd/ *adj* : having or showing generosity ▪ *open-handed hospitality* **2** : done with the hand held open ▪ *an openhanded slap*

open–heart *adj, always before a noun, medical* : done by stopping the heart, opening it, and repairing damage ▪ *open-heart surgery*

open–hearted *adj* : kind and generous ▪ *an open-hearted woman*

open house *n* [*C*] *US* **1** : an event in which a school, company, etc., invites

the public to visit ▪ *colleges holding open houses for prospective students* **2** : an event in which anyone who is interested in buying a particular house, apartment, etc., is invited to go inside and look at it

¹**open·ing** /ˈoʊpənɪŋ/ *n* **1** [*C*] : a hole or empty space that you can go through ▪ *the opening of a cave* **2** [*C*] : BEGINNING ▪ *We missed the opening of her speech.* ▪ *the opening of the school year* **3** [*C*] : the first time that something happens ▪ *We went to the play's opening.* [=first performance] **4** [*C*] : an event that is held in order to announce that something is ready to accept customers or visitors ▪ *the official opening of the new library* **5** [*C*] : a job or position that is available ▪ *We have an opening for someone with your qualifications.* **6** [*C*] : a chance or opportunity to do or say something ▪ *She waited for an opening to tell her story.* **7** [*U*] : the act of causing something to open or of becoming open ▪ *the opening of a bank account*

²**opening** *adj, always before a noun* **1** : first or beginning ▪ *the opening day of the fishing season* ▪ *the opening lines of a poem* **2** — used to describe the time when something is performed or shown for the first time ▪ *the play's opening night*

open letter *n* [*C*] : a letter that is published in a newspaper but that is addressed to a well-known person or to an organization

open·ly /ˈoʊpənli/ *adv* : in a direct and honest way ▪ *She spoke openly about her divorce.* ▪ *They have been openly critical of the President.*

open market *n* [*singular*] : FREE MARKET ▪ *bought/sold/traded* **on the open market**

open mike *n* [*C*] : an event in which anyone may sing, read poetry, etc., for an audience ▪ *an open mike night at a café*

open–mind·ed /ˌoʊpənˈmaɪndəd/ *adj* : willing to consider different ideas or opinions ▪ *Try to be open-minded about the changes.* — **open–mind·ed·ness** *n* [*U*]

open·ness /ˈoʊpənnəs/ *n* [*U*] **1** : the fact of not hiding your opinions, feelings, etc. ▪ *her lack of openness with the public* **2** : the quality of being willing to consider different ideas or opinions ▪ *an openness to new ideas* **3** : the state of not being surrounded or covered ▪ *the openness of the desert/plains*

open season *n* [*U*] **1** : a time of year when it is legal to kill certain fish or animals ▪ *open season for deer/bear* **2** : a time when someone or something is being attacked or criticized by many people ▪ *It's always open season on politicians!*

open secret *n* [*C*] : something that many people know about but that is supposed to be a secret ▪ *It's an open secret that he's having an affair.*

¹**op·era** /ˈɑːpərə/ *n* [*C/U*] : a show in which actors sing all or most of the words of a play ▪ *I enjoy going to the opera.* ▪ *an opera singer* — **op·er·at·ic** /ˌɑːpəˈrætɪk/ *adj* ▪ *an operatic singer/voice*

²**opera** plural of OPUS

op·er·a·ble /ˈɑːpərəbəl/ adj **1** formal : able to be used • The system is fully operable. [=functional] **2** medical : able to be corrected or removed by surgery • an operable cancer

opera glasses n [plural] : small binoculars for use in a theater

opera house n [C] : a theater where operas are performed

op·er·ate /ˈɑːpəˌreɪt/ vb **-at·ed; -at·ing** **1** [I] : to function or behave in a proper or particular way • The camera also operates underwater. **2** [T] : to use and control (something) • instructions for operating the new oven • a coin-operated washing machine [=a washing machine that you put coins in order to use] **3 a** [T] : to have control of (a business, program, etc.) • They own and operate a café. **b** [I] : to function as a business, group, etc. • It's the only casino operating in the state. **4** [I] medical : to perform surgery • The doctors needed to operate (on the patient) immediately. — **operating** adj, always before a noun • operating conditions/costs

operating room n [C] US : a room in a hospital where operations are done — called also (Brit) operating theatre

operating system n [C] computers : the main program in a computer that controls the way the computer works and makes it possible for other programs to function

operating table n [C] : a special table in an operating room that a person lies on while having an operation

op·er·a·tion /ˌɑːpəˈreɪʃən/ n **1** [C] : a process in which a doctor cuts into someone's body in order to repair or remove a damaged or diseased part • a heart operation [=heart surgery] • a minor/routine operation **2** [C] **a** : a usually small business or organization • They run a small farming operation. **b** : an activity of a business or organization — usually plural • a company's banking operations **3** [U] : the state of functioning or being used • The system is now in operation. • The dam will go into operation next month. **4** [U] : the way something functions or is used • the printer's quiet operation **5** [C] : a set of planned actions for a particular purpose • a rescue/military operation **6** [C] : a single action performed by a computer • performing millions of operations per second **7** [U] : the act of using and controlling something • dangerous operation of a motor vehicle **8** [C] : a mathematical process (such as addition or multiplication) that is used for getting one number or set of numbers from others according to a rule

op·er·a·tion·al /ˌɑːpəˈreɪʃənl/ adj **1** : able to be used • The new airport is now fully operational. **2** always before a noun : of or relating to the operation of a business or machine • operational costs

¹**op·er·a·tive** /ˈɑːpərɑtɪv/ adj **1** : ready to be used • The system is fully operative. **2** : most important • If I go, I will bring a salad. "If," however, is the **operative** word, since I am not sure that I can go.

²**operative** n [C] chiefly US : SPY, SECRET AGENT • CIA/FBI operatives

op·er·a·tor /ˈɑːpəˌreɪtər/ n [C] **1** : a person who uses and controls (a machine, device, business, etc.) • a computer/crane operator **2** : a person whose job is to help to connect telephone calls • Call the operator for the phone number.

op·er·et·ta /ˌɑːpəˈrɛtə/ n [C] : a usually short and funny opera that includes dancing

oph·thal·mol·o·gy /ˌɑːfθəlˈmɑːlədʒi/ n [U] medical : the study of the structure, functions, and diseases of the eye — **oph·thal·mol·o·gist** /ˌɑːfθəlˈmɑːlədʒɪst/ n [C]

opi·ate /ˈoʊpijət/ n [C] **1** : a drug (such as morphine) that is used to reduce pain or cause sleep **2** disapproving : something that causes people to ignore problems and to relax instead of doing things that need to be done • He sees TV as an opiate for/of the masses.

opine /oʊˈpaɪn/ vb **opined; opin·ing** [T/I] formal : to express an opinion about something • You can opine about/on any subject you like.

opin·ion /əˈpɪnjən/ n **1** [C/U] : a belief, judgment, or way of thinking about something • We asked for their opinions about/on the new stadium. • In my opinion, it's the best car on the market. • I have a high/low opinion of them. [=I think that they are good/bad] • It's a matter of opinion. [=people have different opinions about it] • We had a difference of opinion. [=we disagreed] • They are of the opinion [=they think/believe] that his death was not an accident. • swaying/changing public opinion [=changing what most people think] **2** [C] : advice from an expert • seeking medical opinions [=advice from doctors] • You should get a second opinion. [=advice from a second doctor to make sure advice from the first doctor is correct] **3** [C] technical : a formal statement by a judge, court, etc., explaining the reasons a decision was made according to laws or rules • discussing a recent Supreme Court opinion

opin·ion·at·ed /əˈpɪnjəˌneɪtəd/ adj, often disapproving : expressing strong beliefs or judgments about something • an opinionated critic

opi·um /ˈoʊpijəm/ n [U] : a powerful illegal drug that is made from a type of poppy

opos·sum /əˈpɑːsəm/ n, pl **opos·sums** also **opossum** [C] : a somewhat small white or gray animal that is active at night and that lives in North and South America and in Australia — called also possum

opp or **opp.** abbr opposite

op·po·nent /əˈpoʊnənt/ n [C] **1** : a person, team, group, etc., that is competing against another in a contest • a formidable political opponent **2** : a person, group, etc., that is against something (such as an action, law, or system) • opponents of the war • abortion opponents

op·por·tune /ˌɑːpəˈtuːn, Brit ˈɒpətjuːn/ adj : suitable or right for a particular situation • an opportune time to invest

op·por·tun·ist /ˌɑːpəˈtuːnɪst, Brit ˌɒpə-ˈtjuːnɪst/ n [C] disapproving : someone who tries to get an advantage or something valuable from a situation without thinking about what is fair or right ▪ *a political opportunist* — **op·por·tun·ism** /ˌɑːpəˈtuːˌnɪzəm, Brit ˌɒpəˈtjuːˌnɪzəm/ n [U] — **op·por·tu·nis·tic** /ˌɑːpətuˈnɪstɪk, Brit ˌɒpətjuˈnɪstɪk/ adj

op·por·tu·ni·ty /ˌɑːpəˈtuːnəti, Brit ˌɒpə-ˈtjuːnəti/ n, pl **-ties** [C/U] : an amount of time or a situation in which something can be done ▪ *You'll have an/the opportunity to ask questions later.* ▪ *job/employment opportunities* ▪ *Don't miss this golden opportunity.* [=an excellent chance to do or get something] ▪ *I would like to take this opportunity to thank my fans.* ▪ *He was given every opportunity to succeed.* ▪ *We will correct the error at the first opportunity.* [=as soon as we are able to] ▪ *a brief window of opportunity* [=a short period of time when it is possible to do something that you want to do] ▪ *the land of opportunity* [=a place where there are many opportunities] ▪ *Be ready when opportunity knocks.* [=when you get the chance to do something you want to do] — **equal opportunity employer** (US) or Brit **equal opportunities employer** : an employer who does not discriminate against people because of their race, religion, etc.

op·pos·able /əˈpoʊzəbəl/ adj, technical : able to be placed against one or more of the other fingers or toes on the same hand or foot ▪ *Humans have opposable thumbs.*

op·pose /əˈpoʊz/ vb **-pos·es; -posed; -pos·ing** [T] **1** : to disagree with or disapprove of (something or someone) ▪ *She opposes the death penalty.* **2 a** : to compete against (someone) ▪ *the man who opposed him in the last election* **b** : to try to stop or defeat (something) ▪ *senators who oppose the legislation*

opposed /əˈpoʊzd/ adj, not before a noun **1** : not agreeing with or approving of something or someone ▪ *He is opposed to the new law.* [=he opposes the new law] **2** : completely different ▪ *Their political philosophies are diametrically opposed (to each other).* — **as opposed to** — used to refer to something that is different from what has just been mentioned ▪ *The car gets 30 miles per gallon, as opposed to* [=unlike] *last year's model, which got only 25.*

opposing adj, always before a noun **1** : fighting or competing against another person or group ▪ *The crowd booed the opposing team.* **2** : completely different ▪ *opposing viewpoints*

¹**op·po·site** /ˈɑːpəzət/ adj **1** : located at the other end, side, or corner of something ▪ *The two boys lived on opposite sides of the street.* **2** : completely different ▪ *The two scientists reached opposite conclusions.* ▪ *They ran in opposite directions.* — **the opposite side of the coin** see ¹COIN

²**opposite** adv : on the other side of someone or something : across from someone or something ▪ *He sat down opposite to me.*

³**opposite** n [C] **1** : someone or something that is completely different from someone or something else ▪ *We thought the job might be difficult, but it was quite the opposite.* [=it was easy] ▪ *My two sisters are polar/complete/exact opposites (of each other).* **2** : ANTONYM ▪ *"Wet" is the opposite of "dry."* — **opposites attract** — used to say that people who are very different from each other are often attracted to each other

⁴**opposite** prep **1** : across from (something or someone) ▪ *He sat opposite me.* **2** of an actor : in a play, movie, etc., with (another actor) ▪ *She stars/plays opposite Tom Cruise in the movie.*

opposite sex n — **the opposite sex** : the people who are not the same sex as you ▪ *members of the opposite sex*

op·po·si·tion /ˌɑːpəˈzɪʃən/ n **1** [U] : actions or opinions that show that you disagree with or disapprove of someone or something ▪ *The plan has met with opposition from residents.* ▪ *He expressed his opposition to the new law.* **2** [U] : action that is done to stop or defeat someone or something ▪ *the rebels' opposition to advancing troops* **3** **the opposition** **a** : a person or group that you are trying to defeat or succeed against ▪ *She warned her team not to underestimate the opposition.* **b or the Opposition** : a political party that is trying to replace the political party in power ▪ *The opposition is likely to win (in) the upcoming elections.* ▪ *the country's opposition party* **4** [U] formal : the state of being completely different ▪ *the opposition between science and religion* — **in opposition to** **1** : in a way that is against someone or something ▪ *He spoke in opposition to the new law.* **2** : in a way that shows how two things are different ▪ *two words that can be defined in opposition to each other* — **op·po·si·tion·al** /ˌɑːpəˈzɪʃənl/ adj, formal ▪ *oppositional groups*

op·press /əˈprɛs/ vb [T] **1** : to treat (a person, group, etc.) in a cruel or unfair way ▪ *The citizens are being oppressed by a ruthless dictator.* ▪ *freedom for oppressed people = freedom for the oppressed* **2** : to make (someone) feel sad or worried for a long period of time ▪ *She was oppressed by grief.* — **op·pres·sion** /əˈprɛʃən/ n [U] — **op·pres·sor** /əˈprɛsɚ/ n [C]

op·pres·sive /əˈprɛsɪv/ adj **1** : very cruel or unfair ▪ *oppressive laws/regimes* **2** : very unpleasant or uncomfortable ▪ *oppressive heat = an oppressive work environment* — **op·pres·sive·ly** adv

opt /ˈɑːpt/ vb [I] : to choose one thing instead of another ▪ *I opted for coffee instead of tea.* ▪ *She was offered a job but opted to go to college instead.* — **opt in** [phrasal vb] : to choose to do or be involved in something ▪ *When the new pension plan was offered, most employees opted in* — **opt out** [phrasal vb] : to choose not to do or be involved in something ▪ *A few employees opted out of the pension plan.*

op·tic /'ɑ:ptɪk/ adj, always before a noun, technical : of or relating to the eyes • *the optic nerve*

op·ti·cal /'ɑ:ptɪkəl/ adj, technical **1** : used to help a person see • *microscopes and other optical instruments* **2** : relating to or using light • *an optical laser/scanner* — **op·ti·cal·ly** /'ɑ:ptɪkli/ adv

optical disk n [C] : a computer disk on which information is recorded in a way that can be read by a laser

optical illusion n [C] : something that you seem to see but that is not really there

op·ti·cian /ɑp'tɪʃən/ n [C] : a person whose job is to sell eyeglasses and contact lenses

op·ti·mal /'ɑ:ptəməl/ adj, formal : best or most effective • *optimal performance/ health/conditions* — **op·ti·mal·ly** adv

op·ti·mism /'ɑ:ptə‚mɪzəm/ n [U] : a feeling or belief that good things will happen in the future • *He expressed optimism about the future.* • *The early reports are cause for optimism.* — **op·ti·mist** /'ɑ:ptəmɪst/ n [C] • *She's an optimist.* [=a person who usually expects good things to happen] — **op·ti·mis·tic** /‚ɑ:ptə-'mɪstɪk/ adj • *I feel optimistic about our chances of winning.* • *an optimistic attitude* — **op·ti·mis·ti·cal·ly** /‚ɑ:ptə-'mɪstɪkli/ adv

op·ti·mize also Brit **op·ti·mise** /'ɑ:ptə‚maɪz/ vb **-mized**; **-miz·ing** [T] formal : to make (something) as good or as effective as possible • *efforts to optimize service/performance* • *The car is optimized for speed.* [=has been made to go as fast as possible]

op·ti·mum /'ɑ:ptəməm/ adj, formal : OPTIMAL • *optimum conditions/results*

op·tion /'ɑ:pʃən/ n [C] **1** : the opportunity or ability to choose something or to choose between two or more things • *You have the option of staying or leaving.* • *I'm leaving/keeping my options open for now.* [=I'm not making a final decision yet] **2** : a choice or possibility • *I had no option but to start over.* • *For us, quitting is not an option.* [=we cannot quit] **3** : a right to buy or sell something for a specified price during a specified period of time • *Employees will be granted/given options to buy 1,000 shares of company stock.* **4** : an extra feature that you can pay to have in addition to the regular features that come with something you are buying • *A sunroof was one of the car's options.* **5** Brit : ²ELECTIVE

op·tion·al /'ɑ:pʃənl/ adj : available as a choice but not required • *Jackets are required, but ties are optional.*

op·tom·e·try /ɑp'tɑ:mətri/ n [U] : the profession of examining people's eyes to find out if they need eyeglasses or medical treatment — **op·tom·e·trist** /ɑp-'tɑ:mətrɪst/ n [C]

op·u·lent /'ɑ:pjələnt/ adj **1** : very comfortable and expensive • *opulent furnishings/lifestyles* **2** : very wealthy • *an opulent widow* — **op·u·lence** /'ɑ:pjələns/ n [U]

opus /'oupəs/ n, pl **op·era** /'oupərə/ also **opus·es** /'oupəsəz/ [C] formal : an important work done by a writer, painter, etc. • *the author's latest opus*

or /'ɔɚ, ɚ/ conj **1** — used to introduce another choice or possibility • *You can have coffee or tea.* • *I'll call (either) today or tomorrow.* • (informal) *I didn't mean to annoy you or anything.* • (informal) *Can I get you a soda or something?* **2** — used in negative statements to introduce something else that is also true • *They have no food or water.* **3** — used to say what will happen if a specified thing is not done • *Be at the station by 5 o'clock or you will miss the bus.* **4** — used to introduce another number or amount that is possibly the correct one • *It's been two or three years since I've seen her.* • *We waited for an hour or more.* **5** — used to introduce the reason why something said previously is true • *He must be hiding something or he wouldn't be lying.* **6 a** — used to introduce a word or phrase that defines or explains what another word or phrase means • *Botany, or the science of plants, is a fascinating subject.* **b** — used to introduce a word or phrase that corrects or states more precisely something you have just said • *We got here quickly— or at least more quickly than last time.* — **or else** see ¹ELSE — **or so** see ²SO

OR abbr **1** Oregon **2** operating room

or·a·cle /'ɔrəkəl/ n [C] **1** in ancient Greece : a person (such as a priestess) through whom a god was believed to speak • *consulting an oracle* **2** : a person whose opinions and advice about something are highly valued • *an oracle of pop culture* — **orac·u·lar** /oʊ'rækjələ/ adj, formal • *an oracular pronouncement*

¹oral /'ɔrəl/ adj **1** : of or relating to the mouth • *oral hygiene/cancer/surgery* **2** — used to describe a medicine that you eat or swallow • *an oral contraceptive* **3** : spoken rather than written • *an oral exam* — **oral·ly** adv

²oral n [C] : a test in which you answer questions by speaking rather than by writing • *He's preparing for his orals.*

oral sex n [U] : sexual activity that involves stimulating someone's genitals with the tongue or mouth

or·ange /'ɑrɪndʒ, 'ɔrɪndʒ/ n [C/U] **1** : a round citrus fruit that has orange skin • *a slice of orange* • *a glass of orange juice* **2** : a color between red and yellow that is like the color of carrots — **orange** adj — **or·ang·ish** /'ɑrɪndʒɪʃ, 'ɔrɪndʒɪ/ adj

orang·u·tan /ə'ræŋə‚tæn/ n [C] : a large ape that has very long arms and reddish-brown hair

ora·tion /ə'reɪʃən/ n [C] formal : a formal speech • *funeral orations*

or·a·tor /'ɔrətɚ/ n [C] formal : a person who is very good at making speeches

or·a·to·ry /'ɔrə‚tori, Brit 'brətri/ n [U] formal : the art or skill of speaking to groups of people in a way that is effective • *political oratory* — **or·a·tor·i·cal** /‚ɔrə'tɔrɪkəl/ adj • *oratorical skills*

orb /'ɔɚb/ n [C] literary : something that is shaped like a ball • *The moon was a silvery orb.*

¹or·bit /'ɔɚbət/ n [C/U] : the curved path that something (such as a moon) follows as it goes around something else (such as a planet) ▪ *the orbit of the Earth around the Sun* ▪ *The satellite remains in orbit.* — **or·bit·al** /ˈoɚbət̬l/ *adj*

²**orbit** *vb* [T/I] : to travel around (something) in a curved path ▪ *The Moon orbits (around) the Earth.* — **or·bit·er** /ˈoɚbət̬ɚ/ *n* [C] ▪ *a lunar orbiter*

or·chard /ˈoɚtʃɚd/ *n* [C] : a place where people grow fruit trees ▪ *an apple orchard*

or·ches·tra /ˈoɚkəstrə/ *n* 1 [C] : a group of musicians who play usually classical music together and who are led by a conductor 2 **the orchestra** *US* : a group of seats in a theater that are close to the stage ▪ *Our seats were in the orchestra (section).* — **or·ches·tral** /oɚˈkestrəl/ *adj* ▪ *orchestral music*

or·ches·trate /ˈoɚkəˌstreɪt/ *vb* **-trat·ed; -trat·ing** [T] 1 : to write or change (a piece of music) so that it can be played by an orchestra ▪ *He orchestrates musicals.* 2 : to organize or plan (something that is complicated) ▪ *She orchestrated the entire event.* ▪ *a carefully orchestrated campaign/plot* — **or·ches·tra·tion** /ˌoɚkəˈstreɪʃən/ *n* [C/U]

or·chid /ˈoɚkəd/ *n* [C] : a plant with flowers that have unusual shapes

or·dain /oɚˈdeɪn/ *vb* [T] 1 : to officially make (someone) a minister, priest, rabbi, etc. ▪ *He was ordained (as) a priest.* ▪ *an ordained minister* 2 *formal* : to officially establish or order (something) ▪ *a process ordained by law* ▪ *(figurative) trying to avoid what destiny has ordained*

or·deal /oɚˈdiːl/ *n* [C] : an experience that is very unpleasant or difficult ▪ *Being trapped in the elevator was a harrowing ordeal.*

¹**or·der** /ˈoɚdɚ/ *n* 1 [C/U] : an instruction or command that must be obeyed ▪ *The captain was barking out orders.* ▪ *She left the hospital against her doctor's orders.* [=even though her doctor told her not to leave] ▪ *The soldiers were under (strict) orders not to shoot.* ▪ *The city was evacuated by order of the mayor.* 2 a [C/U] : a specific request asking a company to supply products to a customer ▪ *The store received an order for 200 roses.* ▪ *place/ cancel an order* ▪ *The book is on order.* [=it has been ordered but has not yet been delivered] b [C] : a product or a group of products that someone has requested from a company ▪ *We shipped your order today.* 3 [C] a : a request for food or drinks made at a restaurant ▪ *The waiter took our order.* b : the food and drinks that someone has requested at a restaurant ▪ *Your order will be ready soon.* c : an amount of food that is served at a restaurant ▪ *a large order of fries* 4 [U, singular] : the particular way that things or events are arranged in a list or series ▪ *The names were listed in no particular order.* ▪ *a series of jobs listed in order of difficulty/importance/size* ▪ *The books are out of order. They need to be put in order.* 5 [U] a : an organized and proper state or condition ▪ *bringing order out of (the) chaos* ▪ *All her documents were in order.* ▪ *Their finances are in good order.* ▪ *The machine is in (good)*

working order. [=working properly] b : the state in which people behave properly, follow rules or laws, and respect authority ▪ *We must restore order to the city.* ▪ *maintaining order in the classroom* 6 [*singular*] : the way that a society is organized or controlled ▪ *activists who challenge the established social order* ▪ *They accept poverty as part of the **natural order of things.*** 7 [*singular*] : a level of quality or excellence ▪ *a teacher of the first/ highest order* [=an excellent teacher] 8 [C] *chiefly Brit* : a social class ▪ *members of the lower orders* 9 [C] *biology* : a group of related plants or animals that is larger than a family ▪ *humans, apes, and other members of the order Primates* 10 [C] : a large organization of people who have similar jobs or interests and who give help to other members ▪ *the Fraternal Order of Police* 11 [C] : a religious organization whose members usually live together and follow special rules ▪ *joining a religious/monastic order* 12 [C] : a group of people who have been given an honor by a country's ruler ▪ *The Queen made him a Member of the Order of the British Empire.* — **call (something) to order** : to say that (a meeting, court session, etc.) should begin ▪ *She called the meeting to order.* — **house in order** see ¹HOUSE — **in order** : appropriate or desirable ▪ *An apology is in order, I believe.* — **in order for** : to make it possible for someone or something to be or to do something ▪ *We all have to work together in order for us to win.* — **in order that** *formal* — used to say the reason for something ▪ *He gave his life in order that* [=so that] *we might live.* — **in order to** : to make it possible for something to happen ▪ *She works two jobs in order to* [=so that she can] *support her family.* — **in short order** see ¹SHORT — **law and order** see LAW — **on the order of** (*chiefly US*) *or Brit* **in/of the order of** : around or about (a specified number) ▪ *He receives something on the order of 100 e-mails a day.* — **out of order** 1 : not working properly ▪ *The elevator is out of order.* 2 : not following the formal rules of a meeting, court session, etc. ▪ *The mayor ruled her out of order.* 3 *Brit, informal* : beyond what is reasonable or allowable ▪ *Your behavior was out of order.* [=out of line] — **to order** : in response to a specific order or request ▪ *Everything was cooked to order.* — **or·der·less** /ˈoɚdɚləs/ *adj*

²**order** *vb* 1 [T] a : to use your authority to tell someone to do something ▪ *The police officer ordered him to drop his weapon.* ▪ *"Stop! Drop your weapon!" ordered the officer.* b : to say that (something) must be done ▪ *The judge ordered that the charges be dismissed.* 2 [T/I] a : to request (something) from a company ▪ *I ordered the books from the company's Web site.* ▪ *Call this number to order.* b : to request (food or drinks) from a restaurant ▪ *I'd like to order a large cheese pizza.* ▪ *"Are you ready to order?"* 3 [T] : to put things in a particular order or position ▪ *The books are ordered* [=ar-

ranged] *by author.* — **order around** or
chiefly *Brit* **order about** [*phrasal vb*] **order (someone) around/about** 1 : to tell
(someone) what to do ▪ *He was tired of
being ordered around.* — **or·der·er**
/ˈoɚdərɚ/ *n* [C]

or·dered /ˈoɚdəd/ *adj* : carefully organized or controlled ▪ *an ordered sequence
of events* ▪ *an ordered* [=orderly] *life*

order form *n* [C] : a form that customers
can use to order products from a company

¹**or·der·ly** /ˈoɚdəli/ *adj* 1 : arranged or
organized in a logical or regular way ▪ *I
keep my desk neat and orderly.* 2
: peaceful or well-behaved ▪ *an orderly
crowd* ▪ *Please exit the building in an orderly fashion.* — **or·der·li·ness**
/ˈoɚdəlinəs/ *n* [U]

²**orderly** *n, pl* **-lies** [C] 1 : a person who
works in a hospital and does various jobs
(such as moving patients or cleaning) 2
: a soldier who performs various services
(such as carrying messages) for a superi-
or officer

order of business *n* [*singular*] : a job
that must be done or an issue that must
be discussed ▪ *The first order of business is
the budget.*

order of magnitude *n* [C] : a range of
numbers or sizes that goes from a particular number or size to 10 times larger or
10 times smaller ▪ *These molecules are
several orders of magnitude smaller than a
grain of sand.* ▪ (*figurative*) *two problems
of the same order of magnitude* [=that are
equally important]

order of the day *n* — **the order of the
day** : a characteristic or activity that is
common during a particular period of
time or in a particular situation ▪ *Wasteful government spending seems to be the
order of the day.*

or·di·nal number /ˈoɚdənəl-/ *n* [C] : a
number (such as first, fifth, or 22nd) that
is used to show the position of someone
or something in a series

or·di·nance /ˈoɚdənəns/ *n* [C/U] *US* : a
law or regulation made by a city or town
government ▪ *Gambling is prohibited by
(a) local/city ordinance.*

¹**or·di·nary** /ˈoɚdəˌneri, Brit ˈɔːdɪnri/ *adj*
1 *always before a noun* : normal or usual
▪ *an ordinary day at work* ▪ *ordinary people* [=people who are not famous, rich,
etc.] 2 *disapproving* : not very good or
impressive ▪ *The meal was ordinary and
uninspired.* — **or·di·nar·i·ly** /ˌoɚdə-
ˈnerəli, Brit ˈɔːdənrəli/ *adv* ▪ *She doesn't
ordinarily work on Mondays.* — **or·di·
nar·i·ness** /ˈoɚdəˌnerinəs/ *n* [U]

²**ordinary** *n* — **out of the ordinary** : unusual, different, or strange ▪ *Nothing was
out of the ordinary.*

or·di·na·tion /ˌoɚdəˈneɪʃən/ *n* [C/U]
: the official act or process of making
someone a priest, minister, etc. ▪ *ten
years after his ordination*

ord·nance /ˈoɚdnəns/ *n* [U] *technical*
: military supplies

ore /ˈoɚ/ *n* [C/U] : rocks, earth, etc., from
which a valuable metal can be taken ▪ *a
mine that contains iron ore*

oreg·a·no /əˈrɛgənoʊ, Brit ˌɒrɪˈgɑːnəʊ/ *n*

[U] : an herb that has small green leaves
that are used in cooking

or·gan /ˈoɚgən/ *n* [C] 1 : a part of the
body (such as the heart or liver) that has
a particular function ▪ *internal/vital organs* 2 : a musical instrument that has a
keyboard and pipes of different lengths
— called also *pipe organ*

or·gan·ic /oɚˈgænɪk/ *adj* 1 **a** : grown or
made without the use of artificial chemicals ▪ *organic vegetables/cotton* **b** : not
using artificial chemicals ▪ *an organic
farm* 2 : of, relating to, or obtained
from living things ▪ *organic materials/fer-
tilizers* 3 : happening or developing in a
slow and natural way ▪ *a period of steady
organic growth* 4 *formal* : having a curving form similar to the shapes found in
nature ▪ *organic architectural elements* —
or·gan·i·cal·ly /oɚˈgænɪkli/ *adv*

organic chemistry *n* [U] : a branch of
chemistry that is concerned with carbon
compounds which are found in living
things

or·gan·ism /ˈoɚgəˌnɪzəm/ *n* [C] 1 : an
individual living thing ▪ *a microscopic organism* 2 : a system with many parts
that depend on each other and work together ▪ *The city is a complex organism.*

or·gan·ist /ˈoɚgənɪst/ *n* [C] *music* : a person who plays an organ

or·ga·ni·za·tion *also Brit* **or·ga·ni·sa·
tion** /ˌoɚgənəˈzeɪʃən, Brit ˌɔːgənaɪ-
ˈzeɪʃən/ *n* [C] 1 : a company, club, etc.,
that is formed for a particular purpose ▪
a charitable/religious organization 2 [U]
a : the act or process of putting the different parts of something in a certain order ▪ *the organization of notes into an outline* **b** : the act or process of planning
and arranging the different parts of an
event or activity ▪ *the organization of a
party* 3 [U] : the way in which the different parts of something are arranged ▪
*They made changes to the company's or-
ganization.* 4 [U] : the quality of being
arranged in a way that is sensible and
useful ▪ *Your thoughts lack organization.*
— **or·ga·ni·za·tion·al** *also Brit* **or·ga·
ni·sa·tion·al** /ˌoɚgənəˈzeɪʃənļ, Brit
ˌɔːgəˌnaɪˈzeɪʃənļ/ *adj* ▪ *She has strong or-
ganizational skills.* [=she is very skillful at
arranging things in a sensible and useful
way]

or·ga·nize *also Brit* **or·ga·nise** /ˈoɚgə-
ˌnaɪz/ *vb* **-nized; -niz·ing** 1 [T] : to arrange and plan (an event or activity) ▪ *organizing a fund-raiser* 2 [T/I] : to arrange or order things so that they can be
found or used easily and quickly ▪ *I organized my closet last night.* 3 [T/I] **a**
: to gather (people) into a group that will
work on something together ▪ *She organized people to register voters.* **b** : to
form a labor union ▪ *The company prevented the workers from organizing.* —
or·ga·niz·er *also Brit* **or·ga·nis·er**
/ˈoɚgəˌnaɪzɚ/ *n* [C]

organized *also Brit* **organised** *adj* 1 **a**
: arranged into formal groups with lead-
ers and with rules for doing or planning
things ▪ *organized baseball/crime/religion*
b : arranged into or belonging to a labor
union ▪ *organized workers/labor* 2 : ar-

ranged or planned in a particular way ▪ *a well-organized campaign* **3 a** : having things arranged in a neat and effective way ▪ *an organized office* **b** : able to keep things arranged in a neat or effective way ▪ *an organized person*

or·gasm /ˈɔɚˌgæzəm/ *n* [C/U] : the point during sexual activity when sexual pleasure is strongest ▪ *achieve/experience/ reach orgasm* ▪ *have an orgasm* — **or·gas·mic** /ɔɚˈgæzmɪk/ *adj*

or·gy /ˈɔɚdʒi/ *n, pl* **-gies** [C] **1** : a wild party and especially one in which many people have sex together ▪ *a drunken orgy* **2** : something that is done too much and in a wild way ▪ *an orgy of crime*

ori·ent /ˈori,ɛnt/ *vb* [T] **1** : to change or create (something) so that it is suitable for a particular group of people ▪ *The movie was oriented to/toward teenagers.* ▪ *a family-oriented amusement park* **2** : to direct (someone) toward a goal ▪ *The program orients students toward a career in law.* **3** : to place (something) in a particular position or direction ▪ *The house is oriented so that it faces west.* ▪ *(figurative) politically oriented journalists* [=journalists who are interested in politics] **4** : to help (someone) become familiar with a new situation, place, etc. ▪ *The guide helps orient travelers (to their surroundings).*

Ori·ent /ˈorijənt/ *n* — **the Orient** *old-fashioned* : the countries of eastern Asia

ori·en·tal or **Ori·en·tal** /ˌoriˈɛntl̩/ *adj, old-fashioned* : of, relating to, or from Asia and especially eastern Asia ▪ *oriental art/food* ◆ *Oriental* is now often considered offensive when it is used to describe a person. *Asian* should be used instead.

Oriental rug *n* [C] : a rug or carpet that is made in central or southern Asia and that usually has very fancy designs on it

ori·en·tate /ˈorijənˌteɪt/ *vb* **-tat·ed; -tat·ing** [T] *chiefly Brit* : ORIENT

ori·en·ta·tion /ˌorijənˈteɪʃən/ *n* **1** [C/U] **a** : a person's feelings, interests, and beliefs ▪ *his political/religious/spiritual orientation* ▪ SEXUAL ORIENTATION ▪ *people who are bisexual in orientation* **2** [C/U] : a main interest, quality, or goal ▪ *The organization has a conservative orientation.* ▪ *Her later works were more introspective in orientation.* **3** [C/U] : the process of giving people training and information about a new job, situation, etc. ▪ *New students/employees are expected to go through a short orientation.* ▪ *an orientation meeting/session* **4** [C] : the position or direction of something ▪ *The valley has a north-south orientation.*

or·i·fice /ˈorəfəs/ *n* [C] *formal* : a hole or opening and especially one in your body (such as your mouth, ear, etc.)

ori·ga·mi /ˌorəˈgɑːmi/ *n* [U] : the Japanese art of folding paper into shapes that look like birds, animals, etc.

or·i·gin /ˈorədʒən/ *n* [C/U] **1** : the point or place where something begins or is created ▪ *the origin of a custom/word* ▪ *That word is French in origin.* ▪ *a wine named for its place of origin* [=the place where it was made] ▪ *a custom/word of recent/unknown origin* **2** : the place, so-

cial situation, or type of family that a person comes from ▪ *What is her country of origin?* [=what country does she come from?] ▪ *He comes from humble origins.* [=from a family that did not have high social status or much money]

¹**orig·i·nal** /əˈrɪdʒənl̩/ *adj* **1** *always before a noun* : happening or existing first or at the beginning ▪ *Our original idea was to fix the car, but we bought a new one instead.* ▪ *the home's original owners* **2** *always before a noun* : not a copy, translation, etc. ▪ *I gave her a copy and kept the original document myself.* **3 a** : new, different, and appealing ▪ *The concept/design is very original.* **b** : able to think of or make new and creative things ▪ *She's a very original filmmaker.* — **orig·i·nal·i·ty** /əˌrɪdʒəˈnæləti/ *n* [U] ▪ *the design's/artist's originality* — **orig·i·nal·ly** /əˈrɪdʒənli/ *adv* ▪ *We originally planned to fix the car, but we bought a new one instead.*

²**original** *n* **1** [C] : a document, film, painting, etc., which is created by someone and from which a copy or translation is made ▪ *I gave her a copy of the report and kept the original.* **2** [singular] : a person who is different from other people in an appealing or interesting way ▪ *That actress is a true original.*

orig·i·nate /əˈrɪdʒəˌneɪt/ *vb* **-nat·ed; -nat·ing** [T/I] : to begin to exist or to cause (something) to exist ▪ *No one knows when or where the idea (first) originated.* ▪ *I did not originate the idea. = The idea did not originate with me.* [=I was not the first person to have the idea] — **orig·i·na·tor** /əˈrɪdʒəˌneɪtɚ/ *n* [C]

ori·ole /ˈoriˌoul/ *n* [C] : a bird that has an orange or yellow body with black wings

¹**or·na·ment** /ˈɔɚnəmənt/ *n* [C] : a small, fancy object that is put on something else to make it more attractive ▪ *(US)* a **hood ornament** [=a small metal figure on the front edge of a car's hood] ▪ *Christmas ornaments* [=small balls, figures, etc., that are hung on a Christmas tree]

²**ornament** *vb* [T] *formal* : to make (something) more attractive by adding small objects to it : DECORATE ▪ *A dress ornamented with pearls* ▪ *ornamented ceilings*

or·na·men·tal /ˌoɚnəˈmɛntl̩/ *adj* : used for decoration ▪ *ornamental vases/shrubs* — **or·na·men·tal·ly** *adv*

or·na·men·ta·tion /ˌoɚnəmənˈteɪʃən/ *n* [U] *formal* : something that is added to make something else more attractive ▪ *Ribbons were used for ornamentation.*

or·nate /ɔɚˈneɪt/ *adj* **1** : covered with fancy patterns and shapes ▪ *ornate candlesticks/jewelry* **2** : using many fancy words ▪ *an ornate writing style* — **or·nate·ly** *adv* — **or·nate·ness** *n* [U]

or·nery /ˈoɚnəri/ *adj* or·neri·er; -est *US, informal • often humorous* **1** : easily annoyed or angered ▪ *He's getting ornery in his old age.* **2** : difficult to deal with or control ▪ *an ornery mule* — **or·neri·ness** *n* [U]

or·ni·thol·o·gy /ˌoɚnəˈθɑːlədʒi/ *n* [U] : the study of birds — **or·ni·tho·log·i·cal** /ˌoɚnəθəˈlɑːdʒɪkəl/ *adj* — **or·ni·thol·o·gist** /ˌoɚnəˈθɑːlədʒɪst/ *n* [C]

¹**or·phan** /ˈoəfən/ *n* [C] : a child whose parents are dead

²**orphan** *vb* [T] : to cause (a child) to become an orphan • *children who were orphaned by the war*

or·phan·age /ˈoəfənɪdʒ/ *n* [C] : a place where children whose parents have died can live and be cared for

or·tho·don·tia /ˌoəθəˈdɑːnʃijə/ *n* [U] *US, technical* : treatment and devices used on teeth to make them grow straight

or·tho·don·tics /ˌoəθəˈdɑːntɪks/ *n* [U] : a branch of dentistry that deals with helping teeth to grow straight — **or·tho·don·tic** /ˌoəθəˈdɑːntɪk/ *adj* — **or·tho·don·tist** /ˌoəθəˈdɑːntɪst/ *n* [C] • *The orthodontist put braces on my teeth.*

or·tho·dox /ˈoəθəˌdɑːks/ *adj* 1 : accepted as true or correct by most people : CONVENTIONAL • *orthodox thinking* 2 **a** *or* **Orthodox** : accepting and closely following the traditional beliefs and customs of a religion • *Orthodox Jews/Muslims* **b** **Orthodox** : of or relating to a branch of Christianity that has members mainly in the area from eastern Europe to eastern Africa • *She is Russian Orthodox.* • *the Eastern/Greek/Ethiopian Orthodox Church* — **or·tho·doxy** /ˈoəθəˌdɑːksi/ *n, pl* **-dox·ies** [C/U] *formal* • *the orthodoxy of her political views* • *Eastern Orthodoxy*

or·tho·pe·dic (*chiefly US*) *also chiefly Brit* **or·tho·pae·dic** /ˌoəθəˈpiːdɪk/ *adj, medical* 1 : used in the treatment of illnesses and injuries that affect bones and muscles • *orthopedic medicine/surgery/shoes* 2 : affecting bones or muscles • *orthopedic injuries*

or·tho·pe·dics (*chiefly US*) *also chiefly Brit* **or·tho·pae·dics** /ˌoəθəˈpiːdɪks/ *n* [U] *medical* : a branch of medicine that tries to prevent and correct problems that affect bones and muscles — **or·tho·pe·dist** (*chiefly US*) *also chiefly Brit* **or·tho·pae·dist** /ˌoəθəˈpiːdɪst/ *n* [C]

OS *abbr, computers* operating system

os·cil·late /ˈɑːsəˌleɪt/ *vb* **-lat·ed; -lat·ing** [I] 1 : to move in one direction and then back again many times • *an oscillating fan* • *Prices have continued to oscillate.* [=to go up and down] 2 *formal* : to keep changing from one belief, feeling, condition, etc., to an opposite one • *The mood of voters has oscillated between optimism and pessimism.* 3 *technical* : to change in strength or direction regularly • *an oscillating electric current* — **os·cil·la·tion** /ˌɑːsəˈleɪʃən/ *n* [C/U]

os·mo·sis /ɑzˈmoʊsəs/ *n* [U] 1 *biology* : the process that causes a liquid (especially water) to pass through the wall of a living cell • *(figurative) She seems to learn foreign languages by/through osmosis.* [=gradually and without much effort]

os·prey /ˈɑːspri, ˈɑːˌspreɪ/ *n, pl* **-preys** [C] : a large bird that eats fish

os·si·fy /ˈɑːsəˌfaɪ/ *vb* **-fies; -fied; -fy·ing** [T/I] 1 *formal + disapproving* : to become or to cause something to become unable to change • *Her opinions have ossified.* • *ossified ideologies* 2 *technical* : to become or to cause something to become hard like bone • *The cartilage will ossify.* • *a disease that ossifies the joints* — **os·si·fi·ca·tion** /ˌɑːsəfəˈkeɪʃən/ *n* [U]

os·ten·si·ble /ɑˈstɛnsəbəl/ *adj, always before a noun* : seeming or said to be true or real but very possibly not true or real • *The ostensible reason for his visit was to see an old friend.* [=he said the reason was to see an old friend, but the real reason may have been something different] — **os·ten·si·bly** /ɑˈstɛnsəbli/ *adv*

os·ten·ta·tion /ˌɑːstənˈteɪʃən/ *n* [U] *disapproving* : an unnecessary display of wealth, knowledge, etc., that is done to attract attention, admiration, or envy • *She dressed without ostentation.* [=in a simple way] — **os·ten·ta·tious** /ˌɑːstənˈteɪʃəs/ *adj* • *the ostentatious* [=very large and expensive] *homes of the rich* — **os·ten·ta·tious·ly** *adv* • *He dresses ostentatiously.*

os·te·o·po·ro·sis /ˌɑːstijoʊpəˈroʊsəs/ *n* [U] *medical* : a condition in which the bones become weak and break easily

os·tra·cize *also Brit* **os·tra·cise** /ˈɑːstrəˌsaɪz/ *vb* **-cized; -ciz·ing** [T] : to not allow (someone) to be included in a group • *The other girls ostracized her because of the way she dressed.* — **os·tra·cism** /ˈɑːstrəˌsɪzəm/ *n* [U]

os·trich /ˈɑːstrɪtʃ/ *n* [C] : a very large African bird that runs very fast but cannot fly

O.T. *abbr* 1 Old Testament 2 *US* overtime • *He scored a goal in O.T. to win the game.*

¹**oth·er** /ˈʌðə/ *adj, always before a noun* 1 — used to refer to the one person or thing that remains or that has not been mentioned • *What's in your other hand?* • *My other son is a doctor.* 2 — used to refer to all the members of a group except the person or thing that has already been mentioned • *She is taller than the other girls in her class.* 3 : in addition to the person or thing that has already been mentioned • *Does anyone have any other ideas?* 4 : different from the person or thing that has already been mentioned • *Some people believe it while other people don't.* • *Prices are even higher in other parts of the country.* — **every other** — used to indicate how often a repeated activity happens or is done • *I run every other day.* [=I run one day, then the next day I do not run, then the day after that I run, etc.] — **none other than** see ¹NONE — **other than** 1 : not including (something or someone) • *We're open every day other than* [=except] *Sunday.* • *I saw a movie, but other than that, I didn't do much last weekend.* 2 : different from (something) • *any color other than red* 3 : EXCEPT — used to introduce a statement that indicates the only person or thing that is not included in or referred to by a previous statement • *You can't get there other than by boat.* — **the other day/night/evening (etc.)** : on a day/night/evening (etc.) in the recent past • *I talked to him just the other day.* [=a few days ago]

²**other** *pron* 1 **a** : a different or additional person or thing • *This car is like no other!* [=this is a very special car] **b** **others**

: different or additional people or things ▪ *She and two others were injured.* ▪ *Some (people) believe it while others don't.* **2 a the other** : the person or thing that remains or that has not been shown or mentioned yet ▪ *She sat at one end of the table while I sat at the other.* ▪ *You can have (either)* **one or the other**—*but not both.* **b the others** : all the members of a group except the person or thing that has already been mentioned ▪ *He got a drink of water while the others continued playing.* **3** — used in phrases like **something or other** or **somehow or other** when the specific details about something are not important or have been forgotten ▪ *He had to go buy something or other at the grocery store.* ▪ *Somehow or other, we managed to finish on time.*

¹**oth·er·wise** /ˈʌðɚˌwaɪz/ *adv* **1** : in a different way or manner ▪ *The books were burned or otherwise destroyed.* ▪ *All shows begin at 7:00 unless otherwise noted.* ▪ *He claims to be innocent, but the evidence suggests otherwise.* [=the evidence suggests that he's guilty] ▪ *France's King Louis XIV, otherwise known as the Sun King, died in 1715.* **2** : if something did not happen, was not true, etc. ▪ *Something must be wrong; otherwise, he would have called.* ▪ *The test identifies problems that might otherwise go unnoticed.* **3** : in all ways except the one mentioned ▪ *I didn't like the ending, but otherwise it was a very good book.* **4** : if not : or else ▪ *Finish your dinner. Otherwise, you won't get any dessert.*

²**otherwise** *adj* : not the same : DIFFERENT ▪ *If conditions were otherwise, I wouldn't be so worried.*

oth·er·world·ly /ˌʌðɚˈwɚldli/ *adj* : seeming to belong to or come from another world ▪ *otherworldly creatures/beauty*

ot·ter /ˈɑːtɚ/ *n, pl* **otter** or **ot·ters** [C] : an animal that has dark brown fur and webbed feet with claws and that eats fish

ouch /ˈaʊtʃ/ *interj* — used to express sudden pain ▪ *Ouch! That hurt!*

ought /ˈɑːt/ *vb* [*modal vb*] ✧ *Ought* is almost always followed by *to* and the infinitive form of a verb. The phrase **ought to** has the same meaning as *should* and is used in the same ways, but it is less common and somewhat more formal. The negative forms **ought not** and **oughtn't** are often used without a following *to*. **1** — used to indicate what is expected ▪ *They ought to be here by now.* ▪ *She ought to be ashamed of herself.* **2** — used to say or suggest what should be done ▪ *You ought to get some rest.* ▪ *We ought to go now.* ▪ *Children ought not* [=*should not*] *run near the pool.*

oughtn't /ˈɑːtn̩t/ — used as a contraction of *ought not*

ounce /ˈaʊns/ *n* **1** [C] : a unit of weight equal to ¹⁄₁₆ pound (about 28 grams) **2** [C] : FLUID OUNCE **3** [*singular*] *informal* : a very small amount of something ▪ *That story doesn't have an ounce of truth in it.*

our /ˈawɚ, ɑɚ/ *adj, always before a noun, possessive form of* WE : relating to or belonging to us ▪ *our house/rights* : made or done by us ▪ *We were criticized for our actions.*

ours /ˈawɚz, ɑɚz/ *pron* : that which belongs to or is connected with us ▪ *That house is ours.* [=that is our house] ▪ *Ours is the house on the left.* ▪ *He is a friend of ours.* [=he is our friend]

our·selves /ˌawɚˈsɛlvz, ɑɚˈsɛlvz/ *pron* **1** — used as the object of a verb or preposition to refer to a group that includes you after that group has already been mentioned ▪ *We consider ourselves lucky.* ▪ *We kept the money for ourselves.* ▪ *We want to see it for ourselves.* [=to see it rather than have someone tell us about it, describe it to us, etc.] — often used for emphasis ▪ *We did it ourselves.* **2** : our normal or healthy selves ▪ *We are tired and just not ourselves.* — **by ourselves** **1** : without any help from other people ▪ *We did it (all) by ourselves.* **2** : with nobody else except us ▪ *We went to the movies by ourselves.*

oust /ˈaʊst/ *vb* [T] : to cause or force (someone or something) to leave a position of power, a competition, etc. ▪ *The rebels ousted the dictator from power.* ▪ *The team was ousted from the tournament.*

oust·er /ˈaʊstɚ/ *n* [*singular*] *US* : the act of removing someone or something from a position of power or authority ▪ *the dictator's ouster by the rebels*

¹**out** /ˈaʊt/ *adv* **1** : in a direction away from the inside or center of something ▪ *He went out to the garden.* ▪ *She poured the tea out.* ▪ *I heard a noise in the bushes and out jumped a cat!* **2** : in or to a place outside of something (such as a building, room, etc.) ▪ *He waited out in the hall.* ▪ *A car pulled up and two men got out.* ▪ *It is raining out.* **3** : away from home, work, etc. ▪ *We went out for/to lunch.* ▪ *The house is out in the country.* ▪ *The tide is going out.* ▪ *Are you going to ask her out (on a date)?* **4** — used to indicate that something is not in the usual or proper place ▪ *You left out a comma here.* **5** : from among a group of things ▪ *She picked out a shirt to wear.* **6** : in or into the control or possession of another person ▪ *The library book I want is still out.* ▪ *They passed out free samples.* **7 a** : to a state in which something has been used or removed completely ▪ *Their food supply ran out.* ▪ *I couldn't get the stain out.* **b** : to a state in which something is completed ▪ *Please fill out this form.* **8** : in the position of someone who is not involved or participating in something ▪ *Count me out.* [=do not include me in your plans] **9** : in the position of someone who is no longer in a political office or job ▪ *They voted him out (of office).* **10** : to the full or a great extent ▪ *She stretched out on the couch.* **11** : in a way that can be clearly heard, understood, or seen ▪ *She read out the names.* ▪ *He cried out in pain.* ▪ *The sun is out.* **12** *baseball* : no longer batting or on a base because of a play made by the other team ▪ *He threw/tagged the runner out.* ▪ *The runner/batter was (called) out.* **13** : no longer operating, burning, etc. ▪ *The electricity/*

fire is out. **14** : at an end • *before the day is out* [=done] **15** : no longer in fashion • *That style of dress is definitely out.* **16** : available to the public • *The band's new CD is not out yet.* **17** : not possible : not to be considered • *That choice was out as far as we were concerned.* **18** : in or into a state of being asleep or unconscious • *She was out cold.* **19** : known publicly as a homosexual • *He's been out for a long time.* **20** *sports* : not in the area in which a game is played • *Her last serve was out.* [=out of bounds] — **out and about** : going to different places • *She was out and about all day.* — **out back** see ¹BACK — **out front** see ¹FRONT — **out loud** see LOUD — **out of 1** — used to show the direction or movement of a person or thing from the inside to the outside of something • *She walked out of the room.* • *Take your hands out of your pockets.* **2** — used to say that a person or thing is not or no longer in a particular place • *He just got out of the hospital.* • *Move! Get out of the way!* **3** — used to say that a person or thing is not or no longer in a particular state or situation • *trying to stay out of trouble* • *We're not out of danger yet.* • *clothes that are out of fashion/style* • *I think your guitar is out of tune.* **4** — used to say that a person or thing is beyond the range or limits of something • *Try to stay out of the sun.* • *The train was soon out of sight.* **5 a** — used to say what something is made from • *a boat built/made out of wood* **b** — used to say where a person or thing comes from • *I got the idea out of the book.* **6** — used to say where an activity takes place • *He runs his business out of his home.* **7** — used to say what causes something • *We watched the show out of curiosity.* [=because we were curious] **8** — used to say that a person or thing no longer has something • *We're out of milk.* • *I ran out of time.* • *She's been out of* [=without] *a job for two months now.* **9** — used to compare a small number to a larger number in order to say how many people or things are selected, do something, etc. • *The disease occurs in one out of a thousand people.* — **out of it** *informal* : in a state in which you are not thinking clearly • *I had just woken up and was still out of it.* — **out there** see ¹THERE

²**out** *prep, chiefly US* **1** — used to indicate that a person or animal is looking at something that is outside of a building, room, etc. • *She looked out the window.* **2** — used to indicate that a person or animal is moving from the inside of a building, room, etc., to the outside • *He ran out the door.*

³**out** *vb* **1** [T] **a** : to tell people that (someone) is a homosexual • *a gay actor who was outed in a magazine article* **b** : to tell people that (someone) is or does a particular thing • *He outed other players who have used steroids.* **2** [I] : to become publicly known • *The truth will out.*

⁴**out** *n* **1** [C] *baseball* : the act of causing a player to be out or the situation that exists when a player has been put out • *The play resulted in an out.* **2** [singular] : a

way of avoiding an embarrassing or difficult situation • *He changed the wording of the contract to give himself an out.* — **on the outs** *US, informal* : in an unfriendly or bad relationship • *She's on the outs with her husband.* — see also INS AND OUTS

out- /ˌaʊt/ *prefix* : in a manner that is greater, better, or more than something else • *outgrow* • *outrun*

out·age /ˈaʊtɪdʒ/ *n* [C] *US* : a period of time when there is no electricity in a building or area • *a power outage*

out-and-out /ˌaʊtn̩ˈaʊt/ *adj, always before a noun* — used to emphasize a description • *an out-and-out liar/lie*

out·back /ˈaʊtˌbæk/ *n* — **the outback** : the part of Australia that is far from cities and where few people live

out·bid /ˈaʊtˈbɪd/ *vb* **-bid**; **-bid·ding** [T] : to offer to pay a higher price than (someone) • *He outbid me for the painting I wanted.*

out·board /ˈaʊtˌboɚd/ *adj, technical* : located on or toward the outside of an airplane, boat, etc. • *an outboard engine/motor*

out·bound /ˈaʊtˌbaʊnd/ *adj* : traveling away from a place • *outbound flights*

out·box /ˈaʊtˌbɑːks/ *n* [C] **1** *US* : a box or other container on a desk in which letters, notes, etc., that are being sent from the desk are placed **2** *computers* : a computer folder that holds e-mail messages you have not yet sent

out·break /ˈaʊtˌbreɪk/ *n* [C] : a sudden start or increase of fighting or disease • *an outbreak of violence/cholera*

out·build·ing /ˈaʊtˌbɪldɪŋ/ *n* [C] : a small building that is separated from a main building

out·burst /ˈaʊtˌbɚst/ *n* [C] **1** : a sudden expression of strong feeling • *He apologized for his outburst (of anger).* **2** : a sudden increase in activity • *an outburst of violence*

out·cast /ˈaʊtˌkæst, Brit ˈaʊtˌkɑːst/ *n* [C] : someone who is not accepted by other people • *a social outcast*

out·class /ˌaʊtˈklæs, Brit ˌaʊtˈklɑːs/ *vb* [T] : to be or do much better than (someone or something) • *She was outclassed in the tennis tournament.* [=other people played better than she did]

out·come /ˈaʊtˌkʌm/ *n* [C] : a result of an activity or process • *the outcome of the election/game*

out·cry /ˈaʊtˌkraɪ/ *n, pl* **-cries** [C/U] : an expression of strong anger or disapproval by many people • *There was (a) public outcry over his racial comments.*

out·dat·ed /ˌaʊtˈdeɪtəd/ *adj* : no longer useful or acceptable : not modern or current • *outdated computers/technology*

out·dis·tance /ˌaʊtˈdɪstəns/ *vb* **-tanced**; **-tanc·ing** [T] : to go far ahead of or beyond (someone or something) • *She easily outdistanced the other runners.*

out·do /ˌaʊtˈduː/ *vb* **-did** /-ˈdɪd/; **-done** /-ˈdʌn/; **-do·ing** /-ˈduːwɪŋ/ [T] : to be or do better than (someone or something) • *Smaller companies often outdo larger ones in customer service.* • *She really outdid herself this time.* [=she did better than she ever had] ▪ *She scored 20 points in the first game.* **Not to be outdone,** *I scored 30 points in the second game.*

out·door /ˈaʊtˌdoɚ/ *adj, always before a noun* : done, used, or located outside a building ▪ *outdoor sports/clothing/tracks*

out·doors /ˌaʊtˈdoɚz/ *adv* : outside a building ▪ *I went outdoors for some fresh air.* — **the outdoors** : the places outside where you can enjoy nature ▪ *They love the outdoors.*

out·er /ˈaʊtɚ/ *adj, always before a noun* : located on or toward the outside of something ▪ *an outer wall*

out·er·most /ˈaʊtɚˌmoʊst/ *adj, always before a noun* : farthest from the center of something ▪ *the outermost planet in our solar system*

outer space *n* [U] : the region beyond the Earth's atmosphere in which there are stars and planets

out·er·wear /ˈaʊtɚˌweɚ/ *n* [U] : sweaters, coats, etc., that you wear over other clothing

out·field /ˈaʊtˌfiːld/ *n* [C] **1** : the part of a baseball field that includes the area beyond the infield and between the foul lines **2** : the part of a cricket field that is away from the wickets — **out·field·er** /ˈaʊtˌfiːldɚ/ *n* [C] *US* ▪ *a young outfielder* [=a baseball player who plays in the outfield]

¹**out·fit** /ˈaʊtˌfɪt/ *n* [C] **1** : a set of clothes that are worn together ▪ *She bought a new outfit for the party.* **2** : a group of people working together in the same activity ▪ *He works for a publishing outfit.*

²**outfit** *vb* **-fit·ted; -fit·ting** [T] : to provide (someone or something) with equipment, clothes, etc. ▪ *The company outfitted us with food and supplies.* ▪ *The car was outfitted with a new stereo system.* — **out·fit·ter** /ˈaʊtˌfɪtɚ/ *n* [C]

out·flank /ˌaʊtˈflæŋk/ *vb* [T] : to move around the side of (something) to attack from behind ▪ *The army outflanked the enemy.*

out·flow /ˈaʊtˌfloʊ/ *n* [C/U] : an outward flow or movement of something ▪ *(an) outflow of water/money/air*

out·fox /ˌaʊtˈfɑːks/ *vb* [T] : to defeat or trick (someone) by being more intelligent or clever ▪ *He outfoxed the police.*

out·go·ing /ˈaʊtˌgoʊɪŋ/ *adj* **1** — used to describe someone who is friendly and likes being with and talking to other people ▪ *an outgoing personality/person* **2** : leaving a place or position ▪ *outgoing ships/mail* ▪ *the outgoing president*

out·grow /ˌaʊtˈgroʊ/ *vb* **-grew** /-ˈgruː/; **-grown** /-ˈgroʊn/; **-grow·ing** [T] : to grow too large or too old for (someone or something) ▪ *Kids outgrow their clothes quickly.* ▪ *I'm sure he'll outgrow this behavior.* [=will stop this behavior as he becomes older and more mature]

out·growth /ˈaʊtˌgroʊθ/ *n* [C] : something that develops or results from something else — often + *of* ▪ *This project is a natural outgrowth of our research.*

out·gun /ˌaʊtˈgʌn/ *vb* **-gunned; -gun·ning** [T] : to have more military weapons and power than (someone or something) ▪ *We were outgunned (by the enemy).*

out·house /ˈaʊtˌhaʊs/ *n* [C] **1** *US* : a small outdoor building that is used as a toilet **2** *Brit* : a small building that is separated from a main building

out·ing /ˈaʊtɪŋ/ *n* [C] **1** : a brief trip that people take for fun ▪ *an outing to the zoo* **2** : a time when an athlete competes in a game or contest ▪ *The pitcher had a good/bad outing.* [=he pitched well/poorly]

out·land·ish /ˌaʊtˈlændɪʃ/ *adj* : very strange or unusual ▪ *an outlandish story* — **out·land·ish·ly** *adv*

out·last /ˌaʊtˈlæst, Brit ˌaʊtˈlɑːst/ *vb* [T] : to continue to exist, be active, etc., longer than (someone or something) ▪ *He outlasted his opponent.*

¹**out·law** /ˈaʊtˌlɑː/ *n* [C] : a person who has broken the law and who is hiding or running away to avoid punishment ▪ *a gang of outlaws*

²**outlaw** *vb* [T] : to make (something) illegal ▪ *a bill outlawing the hiring of children under the age of 12*

out·lay /ˈaʊtˌleɪ/ *n* [C/U] *formal* : an amount of money that is spent ▪ *an outlay of $2,000* ▪ *large cash outlays*

out·let /ˈaʊtˌlɛt/ *n* [C] **1** : something that people use to express their emotions or talents ▪ *She used poetry as an outlet for her sadness.* **2** : a store that sells products made usually by one company and often at reduced prices ▪ *a discount furniture outlet* ▪ *outlet stores* **3** : a television, radio, or publishing company ▪ *media/news outlets* **4** *US* : a device in a wall into which an electric cord can be plugged in order to provide electricity for a lamp, television, etc. ▪ *electrical outlets* **5** : a place or opening through which something can go out ▪ *the river's outlet to the sea*

¹**out·line** /ˈaʊtˌlaɪn/ *n* **1** [C/U] : a drawing or picture that shows only the shape of an object ▪ *an outline of his face* **2** [C] : a line that is drawn around the edges of something ▪ *The leaves etched into the vase have a gold outline.* **3** [C/U] : a written list or description of only the most important parts of an essay, plan, etc. ▪ *a brief outline of American history*

²**outline** *vb* **-lined; -lin·ing** [T] **1** : to draw a line around the edges of (something) ▪ *The leaves on the vase are outlined in gold.* **2** : to list or describe only the most important parts of (an essay, plan, etc.) ▪ *The President outlined his agenda for the next term.*

out·live /ˌaʊtˈlɪv/ *vb* **-lived; -liv·ing** [T] **1** : to live longer than (someone) ▪ *He outlived his wife by 10 years.* **2** : to continue to exist longer than (something) ▪ *The law has outlived its usefulness.* [=the law still exists, but it is no longer useful]

out·look /ˈaʊtˌlʊk/ *n* **1** [C/U] : the way that a person thinks about things ▪ *The students all seemed to have the same outlook.* ▪ *a positive/optimistic outlook on life* **2** [C] : a set of conditions that will probably exist in the future ▪ *the country's economic outlook* ▪ *The financial outlook for the company is hopeful.* **3** [C] : a place where you can look out over a wide area or the view from such a place • *a beautiful outlook*

out·ly·ing /ˈaʊtˌlajɪŋ/ *adj, always before a noun* : far away from the center of a place • *the country's outlying islands*

out·ma·neu·ver (*US*) *or Brit* **out·ma·noeu·vre** /ˌaʊtməˈnuːvɚ/ *vb* [*T*] : to use cleverness or skill to gain an advantage over (someone) • *She outmaneuvered her political opponents.*

out·mod·ed /ˌaʊtˈmoʊdəd/ *adj* : no longer useful or acceptable : not modern or current • *outmoded technology*

out·num·ber /ˌaʊtˈnʌmbɚ/ *vb* [*T*] : to be more than (someone or something) in number • *Their wins outnumber their losses.* [=they have more wins than losses]

out-of-date /ˌaʊtəvˈdeɪt/ *adj* : no longer useful or acceptable : not modern or current • *an out-of-date history book*

out of doors *adv* : OUTDOORS • *The play was performed out of doors.*

out-of-the-way /ˌaʊtəðəˈweɪ/ *adj* : located far from other places that are well-known • *out-of-the-way restaurants*

out·pace /ˌaʊtˈpeɪs/ *vb* **-paced**; **-pac·ing** [*T*] : to go or grow faster than (something) • *Population growth is outpacing job growth.*

out·pa·tient /ˈaʊtˌpeɪʃənt/ *n* [*C*] : a person who goes to a doctor's office or hospital for treatment but does not spend the night there • *outpatient surgery*

out·per·form /ˌaʊtpɚˈfoɚm/ *vb* [*T*] : to do or perform better than (someone or something) • *He outperformed the competition.*

out·play /ˌaʊtˈpleɪ/ *vb* [*T*] : to play better than (a person or team) • *They outplayed the visiting team.*

out·post /ˈaʊtˌpoʊst/ *n* [*C*] **1** : a large military camp that is in another country or that is far from a country's center of activity • *an American outpost in Africa* **2** : a small town in a place that is far away from other towns or cities

out·pour·ing /ˈaʊtˌpoɚŋ/ *n* [*C*] **1** : an act of expressing an emotion or feeling in a very powerful way • *an outpouring of support/love* **2** : a large amount of something that is given or received in a short period of time • *an outpouring of money*

¹**out·put** /ˈaʊtˌpʊt/ *n* **1** [*C/U*] : the amount of something that is produced by a person or thing • *yearly agricultural output* • *the daily output of each worker* **2** *technical* **a** [*C/U*] : power, energy, information, etc., that is produced by a machine or system • *The computer's output is shown on this screen.* **b** [*C*] : the place at which information, power, etc., comes out of a machine or system • *the television's video and audio outputs*

²**output** *vb* **-put·ted** *or* **-put**; **-put·ting** [*T*] : to produce and send out (something) • *Computers output data very quickly.*

¹**out·rage** /ˈaʊtˌreɪdʒ/ *n* **1** [*U*] : extreme anger because of something bad, hurtful, or morally wrong • *Many people expressed outrage at the court's decision.* • *moral outrage* **2** [*C*] : something that hurts people or is morally wrong • *The rule is an outrage against women.*

²**outrage** *vb* **-raged**; **-rag·ing** [*T*] : to make (someone) very angry • *Parents were outraged by the teacher's actions.*

out·ra·geous /aʊtˈreɪdʒəs/ *adj* **1** : very bad or wrong in a way that causes anger • *outrageous behavior/prices* **2** : very strange or unusual : surprising or shocking • *outrageous costumes/claims* — **out·ra·geous·ly** *adv* — **out·ra·geous·ness** *n* [*U*]

out·rank /ˌaʊtˈræŋk/ *vb* [*T*] : to have a higher rank or position than (someone) • *A general outranks a colonel.*

out·reach /ˈaʊtˌriːtʃ/ *n* [*U*] : the activity or process of bringing information or services to people • *She was hired to do community outreach* [=to do helpful things in the community] *for the company.*

out·right /ˈaʊtˈraɪt/ *adv* **1** : in a full and complete way • *They rejected the idea outright.* • *The painting is now owned outright by the museum.* **2** : quickly and completely • *Several people were killed outright and many were injured.* **3** : in a direct and open way • *Some people laughed outright when he told us his idea.* — **out·right** /ˈaʊtˌraɪt/ *adj, always before a noun* • *That's an outright* [=absolute] *lie!* • *an outright* [=complete, total] *ban on guns*

out·run /ˌaʊtˈrʌn/ *vb* **-ran** /-ˈræn/; **-run**; **-run·ning** [*T*] **1** : to run or move faster than (someone or something) • *The rabbit had no chance of outrunning the dogs.* **2** : to be or become more or greater than (something) • *Demand quickly outran* [=exceeded] *supply.*

out·sell /ˌaʊtˈsɛl/ *vb* **-sold** /-ˈsoʊld/; **-sell·ing** [*T*] **1** : to be sold more than (something) • *Diet sodas are beginning to outsell regular sodas.* **2** : to sell more than (another person, store, etc.) • *We've been outselling our competitors.*

out·set /ˈaʊtˌsɛt/ *n* [*singular*] : the start or beginning of something • *There have been problems with the project from the outset.* • *at the outset of her career*

out·shine /ˌaʊtˈʃaɪn/ *vb* **-shone** /-ˈʃoʊn, Brit -ˈʃɒn/ *or* **-shined**; **-shin·ing** [*T*] : to do better than (someone or something) • *She outshines the other actors in the film.*

¹**out·side** /ˌaʊtˈsaɪd, ˈaʊtˌsaɪd/ *n* **1 the outside** : an area around or near something (such as a building) • *The house looks nice from the outside.* **2** [*C*] : an outer side, edge, or surface of something • *The door can be locked from the inside or outside.* • *the outside of the building* — **at the outside** : not more than a specified amount, level, etc. : at the most • *It took him an hour or less than an hour* [=it took him an hour or less than an hour] — **on the outside 1** : on the outer side, edge, or surface of something • *The car tried to pass the leader on the outside (of the track).* **2** — used to describe someone's appearance • *I might seem calm on the outside, but I'm actually really nervous.*

²**outside** *adj* **1** : located on or near an outer side, edge, or surface of something • *an outside wall/corner/door* • *the outside edge of the foot* • *(baseball) an outside*

pitch **2** *always before a noun* **a** : located in or near the area around a building and not inside it ▪ *She turned on the outside light.* **b** : involving people who are not in the same building, group, etc., as you ▪ *The phone will not let you make outside calls.* ▪ *an outside consultant* **3** *always before a noun* : not involving your regular job or duties ▪ *a businessman with few outside interests besides golf* **4** *always before a noun* : barely possible : very unlikely ▪ *She has an outside chance of winning.*

³**outside** *adv* **1 a** : in or to a place that is near but separate from another place ▪ *He waited outside in the hall.* **b** : OUTDOORS ▪ *It's raining outside.* ▪ *He ran outside to see what the noise was about.* **2** : on the outer side, edge, or surface of something ▪ *The candy was hard outside but chewy inside.*

⁴**outside** *prep* **1** : in a place that is near but separate from (something) ▪ *We waited outside the store.* **2** : beyond the limits or borders of (something) ▪ *activities outside the law* [=unlawful activities] ▪ *traveling outside the U.S.* **3** : not belonging to (a group or organization) ▪ *No one outside the group knew of their plans.* **4** : EXCEPT, BESIDES ▪ *Nobody knew outside a few close friends.* — **outside of** *chiefly US* : OUTSIDE ▪ *We waited outside of the store.* ▪ *I live outside of the city.* ▪ *Nobody knew outside of a few close friends.* — **think outside the box** see ¹BOX

out·sid·er /ˌaʊtˈsaɪdɚ, ˈaʊtˌsaɪdɚ/ *n* [C] : a person who does not belong to or is not accepted as part of a particular group or organization ▪ *She felt like an outsider in her new school.*

out·size /ˈaʊtˌsaɪz/ *also* **out·sized** /ˈaʊtˌsaɪzd/ *adj* : very large in size ▪ *outsize boots* ▪ *outsized trucks*

out·skirts /ˈaʊtˌskɚts/ *n* [*plural*] : the parts of a city or town that are far from the center ▪ *We live on the outskirts of town.*

out·smart /ˌaʊtˈsmɑɚt/ *vb* [*T*] : to defeat or trick (someone) by being more intelligent or clever ▪ *He outsmarted* [=outwitted] *his attackers and escaped unharmed.*

out·source /ˈaʊtˌsoɚs/ *vb* **-sourced;** **-sourc·ing** [*T*] : to send away (some of a company's work) to be done by people outside the company ▪ *The company outsources jobs to other countries.*

out·spo·ken /ˌaʊtˈspoʊkən/ *adj* : talking in a free and honest way about your opinions ▪ *an outspoken supporter/critic of the war* — **out·spo·ken·ly** *adv* — **out·spo·ken·ness** /ˌaʊtˈspoʊkənnəs/ *n* [U]

out·stand·ing /aʊtˈstændɪŋ/ *adj* **1** : extremely good or excellent ▪ *an outstanding student/teacher/performer/job* **2** : not yet paid ▪ *outstanding bills* ▪ *He left 50 dollars outstanding on his account.* **3** : continuing to exist ▪ *There are several outstanding issues between the two countries.* — **out·stand·ing·ly** *adv* ▪ *He played outstandingly.*

out·stay /ˌaʊtˈsteɪ/ *vb* — **outstay your welcome** see ⁴WELCOME

out·stretched /ˌaʊtˈstrɛtʃt/ *adj* : stretched out ▪ *She ran toward him with outstretched arms.*

out·strip /ˌaʊtˈstrɪp/ *vb* **-stripped;** **-strip·ping** [*T*] **1** : to be or become better or more than (someone or something) ▪ *Their achievements (far) outstrip our own.* ▪ *Demand continues to outstrip supply.* **2** : to do better than (someone or something) ▪ *She outstripped her competitor.* **3** : to go faster than (someone or something) ▪ *The fullback outstripped the defenders.*

out·take /ˈaʊtˌteɪk/ *n* [C] **1** : a scene that is not used in the final version of a movie or television show **2** : a song that is not used for a music album

out·vote /ˌaʊtˈvoʊt/ *vb* **-vot·ed;** **-vot·ing** [*T*] : to defeat (a person or idea) by winning a larger number of votes ▪ *I was outvoted by the rest of the group.*

¹**out·ward** /ˈaʊtwɚd/ *adj, always before a noun* **1** : showing on the outside ▪ *Despite her outward calm, she was extremely nervous.* ▪ *the outward symptoms of the disease* ▪ *To/By/From all outward appearances, their marriage was quite normal.* **2** : moving or directed away from something ▪ *an outward movement/flight*

²**outward** (*chiefly US*) *or chiefly Brit* **out·wards** /ˈaʊtwɚdz/ *adv* : toward the outside of something : away from a center ▪ *The window faces outward toward the street.* ▪ *air flowing outward from the lungs* ▪ *They turned their attention outward.* [=away from themselves]

out·ward·ly /ˈaʊtwɚdli/ *adv* : on the outside : in a way that can be seen ▪ *Though extremely nervous, she was able to remain outwardly calm during the interview.* ▪ *Outwardly, their marriage seemed quite normal.*

out·weigh /ˌaʊtˈweɪ/ *vb* [*T*] : to be greater than (someone or something) in weight, value, or importance ▪ *She outweighs her sister by 10 pounds.* ▪ *The advantages far outweigh the disadvantages.*

out·wit /ˌaʊtˈwɪt/ *vb* **-wit·ted;** **-wit·ting** [*T*] : to defeat or trick (someone) by being more intelligent or clever ▪ OUTSMART ▪ *The fox managed to outwit the hunter by hiding in a tree.*

out·worn /ˌaʊtˈwoɚn/ *adj* : no longer useful or acceptable : OUTDATED ▪ *an outworn set of beliefs*

ova *plural of* OVUM

oval /ˈoʊvəl/ *adj* : having the shape of an egg ▪ *an oval mirror* ▪ *an oval racetrack* — **oval** *n* [C] ▪ *The racetrack is an oval.*

Oval Office *n* — **the Oval Office** : the office of the U.S. President in the White House

ova·ry /ˈoʊvəri/ *n, pl* **-ries** [C] **1** : one of usually two organs in women and female animals that produce eggs and female hormones **2** : the part of a flower where seeds are formed — **ovar·i·an** /oʊˈverijən/ *adj* ▪ *ovarian cancer*

ova·tion /oʊˈveɪʃən/ *n* [C] : an occurrence in which a group of people show enthusiastic approval or appreciation by clapping ▪ *They gave her a long ovation.* [=they applauded her for a long time] ▪ *The crowd gave her a standing ovation.* [=they stood and applauded her]

ov·en /'ʌvən/ *n* [C] : a piece of cooking equipment that is used for baking or roasting food — *like an oven informal* : very hot • *Open the window. It's like an oven in here.*

¹over /'oʊvɚ/ *adv* **1** : in an upward and forward direction across something • *We came to a stream and jumped over.* **2 a** : downward from an upright position • *She leaned/bent over and kissed him.* **b** : downward to a flat or horizontal position • *She knocked over the lamp.* • *He tripped and fell over.* **3** : so that the bottom or opposite side is on top • *The baby rolled over.* • *Turn/Flip your cards over.* **4 a** : from one place to another • *The teacher called the girl over.* • *Come over here. I need to talk to you.* • *I'll be right over.* **b** : to your home • *I invited some friends over for dinner.* **c** : in a particular place • *They're building a new library over by the high school.* **5** : from one person or group to another • *They turned over the stolen money to the police.* • *He's gone over to the opposition.* **6** : more than an expected or stated amount or number • *The show ran a minute over.* = *The show ran over by a minute.* • *women 65 and/or over* **7** : remaining and not used • *We ate the turkey that was left over from dinner.* **8** : so as to cover the entire surface of something • *The sky clouded over.* • *He's become famous the world over.* [=throughout the world] **9** : in a complete and thorough way • *She's thinking/reading it over.* **10 a** *chiefly US* : one more time • *You've done it wrong. Do it over.* • *Let's start over (again) from the beginning.* • *I remind him over and over (again) not to leave the door open.* **b** — used to say how many times something is done or repeated • *I had to read the poem twice over* [=two times] *before I understood it.* **11** — used when talking on a radio to show that a message is complete • *"We are ready for takeoff instructions. Over."* — **all over** see ²ALL — **over (and done) with** : finished or completed • *Let's get this over with.* • *The test is over and done with.*

²over *prep* **1** : above in place or position • *He looked over the fence.* • *The meat was cooked over an open fire.* **2** : on top of (something) • *Someone hit him over the head with a rock.* • *His hat was pulled low over his eyes.* **3** : beyond and down from (something) • *He fell over the cliff's edge.* **4 a** : from one side to the other side of (something or someone) • *She walked over* [=across] *the bridge.* • *Excuse me, I need to reach over you to get the salt.* • *I jumped over the stream.* **b** : on the other side of (something) • *Our house is just over that hill.* **5** : in the direction of (something) • *Hey, look over there!* **6** : more than (a specified number or amount) • *I've been waiting for over an hour.* • *The condition is most common in women over 65.* • *They had over 300 people at their wedding.* • *That car costs well over* [=much more than] *$50,000.* **7** — used to say that a person or thing is better than (someone or something else) • *This is a big improvement over our last*

apartment. • *She had a lead over the other runners.* • *When it comes to creative thinking, humans have it over computers.* **8** : in a position of power and authority that allows a person or thing to control (someone or something) • *She should be given more authority over her staff.* • *We have no control over the situation.* **9 a** : so as to cover the surface of (something) • *A strange expression came over his face.* **b** : in every part of (a place) • *These trees once flourished over* [=throughout] *much of North America.* **10** : throughout or during (something) • *I'll think about it over the weekend.* • *I met with my advisers over lunch.* • *Over time, the paper began to turn yellow.* **11** : by using (a radio, television, computer, etc.) • *I heard it over the radio.* • *We spoke over the phone.* **12** : because of (someone or something) • *Don't get angry over something so silly.* **13** : concerning or regarding (something) • *a dispute over the land* **14** : finished with (something) : past or beyond (something) • *I think we're over the worst of it. Things should get better.* • *He's upset now, but he'll get over it.* [=he'll stop being upset about it] **15** : without being stopped or prevented by (something) : DESPITE • *She spoke to the police over the objections of her lawyer.* **16** : without including or considering (someone or something) • *You can skip over that paragraph.* **17** : more loudly and clearly than (another sound) • *talking/shouting over the noise of the engines* — **over and above** : in addition to (something) : along with (something) • *We each received a bonus over and above our regular paychecks.*

³over *adj, not before a noun* : having reached the end : FINISHED • *The storm is over.* • *It's over between them.* [=their relationship has ended] — **over easy** see ¹EASY

over- /,oʊvɚ/ *prefix* **1** : more than usual, normal, or proper • *overconfident* [=too confident] • *overachieve* • *overjoyed* **2** : above • *overhang*

over·achiev·er /,oʊvɚrə'tʃiːvɚ/ *n* [C] : someone who has much more success than is normal or expected • *She is an overachiever who plans to attend a top college.* — **over·achieve** /,oʊvɚrə'tʃiːv/ *vb* **-achieved; -achiev·ing** [I] • *an overachieving student*

over·act /,oʊvɚ'ækt/ *vb* [I] *disapproving* : to show too much emotion when you are acting in a play, movie, etc.

¹over·all /,oʊvɚ'ɑːl/ *adv* : with everyone or everything included • *He scored highest overall.* • *He made a few mistakes but did well overall.* — **overall** *adj, always before a noun* • *What is the overall* [=total] *cost? • Your overall health is sound.*

²over·all /'oʊvɚˌɑːl/ *n* **1** [*plural*] *US* : a pair of pants with an extra piece attached that covers the chest and has straps that go over the shoulders • *wearing (a pair of) overalls* — called also (*Brit*) *dungarees* **2** [C] *Brit* : a loose coat that is worn over clothes so that they do not get dirty : SMOCK **3** [*plural*] *Brit* : COVERALL

over·arm /ˈoʊvəˌɑɚm/ adj, Brit : OVERHAND • He made an overarm throw. — **overarm** adv, Brit

over·bear·ing /ˌoʊvəˈberɪŋ/ adj, disapproving : often trying to control the behavior of other people in an annoying or unwanted way • an overbearing boss/manner

over·blown /ˌoʊvəˈbloun/ adj, disapproving : made to seem very important, intelligent, or great especially in order to impress people • overblown claims/rhetoric • The problem is overblown. [=it is not as bad as people say it is]

over·board /ˈoʊvəˌboəd/ adv : over the side of a ship into the water • The boy fell overboard. — **go overboard** informal : to do too much of something • Don't go overboard on/with the spices. [=don't add too many spices]

over·book /ˌoʊvəˈbʊk/ vb [T/I] : to allow too many people to buy tickets or to reserve seats, tables, rooms, etc. • The airline overbooked the flight.

over·bur·den /ˌoʊvəˈbədən/ vb [T] : to give (someone or something) too much work, worry, etc. • He was overburdened by work.

over·cast /ˈoʊvəˌkæst, Brit ˈoʊvəˌkɑːst/ adj : covered or darkened by clouds • The sky was overcast. • an overcast morning

over·charge /ˌoʊvəˈtʃɑɚdʒ/ vb -charged; -charg·ing 1 [T/I] : to make someone pay too much money for something • The store overcharged me for my skirt. 2 [T] : to give too much of an electric charge to (something) • overcharge a battery

over·coat /ˈoʊvəˌkout/ n [C] : a long coat that is worn to keep a person warm during cold weather

over·come /ˌoʊvəˈkʌm/ vb -came /-ˈkeɪm/; -come; -com·ing [T] 1 : to defeat (someone or something) • They overcame the enemy. 2 : to successfully deal with or gain control of (something difficult) • a story about overcoming adversity 3 : to affect (someone) very strongly or severely • The family was overcome by grief.

over·cook /ˌoʊvəˈkʊk/ vb [T] : to cook (food) for too long • She overcooked the steak.

over·do /ˌoʊvəˈduː/ vb -did /-ˈdɪd/; -done /-ˈdʌn/; -do·ing [T] 1 : to do too much of (something) : to do (something) in an excessive or extreme way • You should exercise every day, but don't overdo it. 2 : to use too much of (something) • Don't overdo the salt in this recipe. 3 : to cook (food) for too long • My steak was slightly overdone.

over·dose /ˈoʊvəˌdous/ n [C] 1 : an amount of a drug or medicine that is too much and usually dangerous • She died from a cocaine overdose. • an overdose of pills 2 : an amount of something that is too much • a sugar overdose — **overdose** /ˈoʊvəˌdous/ vb -dosed; -dos·ing [I] • She overdosed on cocaine.

over·draw /ˌoʊvəˈdrɑː/ vb -drew /-ˈdruː/; -drawn /-ˈdrɑːn/; -draw·ing [T] : to withdraw more money from (an account) than is available • She overdrew her account by $100. — **overdrawn** adj • Your account is overdrawn.

over·dress /ˌoʊvəˈdrɛs/ vb [T/I] : to dress in clothes that are too fancy, formal, or warm for an occasion • He (was) overdressed for the party.

over·drive /ˈoʊvəˌdraɪv/ n [U] 1 : a gear in an automobile that allows it to be driven at higher speeds 2 : a state of great activity especially in order to achieve something • His acting career has gone into overdrive.

over·due /ˌoʊvəˈduː, Brit ˌoʊvəˈdjuː/ adj 1 : not paid at an expected or required time • The rent was overdue. • overdue bills 2 : not appearing or presented by a stated, expected, or required time • an overdue library book 3 — used to say that something should have happened or been done before now • His promotion is long overdue. = He is long overdue for a promotion.

over·eat /ˌoʊvəˈiːt/ vb -ate /-ˈeɪt/; -eat·en /-ˈiːtn̩/; -eat·ing [I] : to eat more than is needed or more than is healthy • When I'm tired or stressed, I tend to overeat.

over·es·ti·mate /ˌoʊvəˈɛstəˌmeɪt/ vb -mat·ed; -mat·ing [T] 1 : to estimate (something) as being greater than the actual size, quantity, or number • We overestimated the value of the coins. 2 : to think of (someone or something) as being greater in ability, influence, or value than that person or thing actually is • She overestimated his ability to do the job. • The importance of a good education cannot be overestimated. [=a good education is very important] — **over·es·ti·mate** /ˌoʊvəˈɛstəmət/ n [C]

over·ex·pose /ˌoʊvərɪkˈspouz/ vb -posed; -pos·ing [T] 1 : to leave (something) without covering or protection for too long • You shouldn't overexpose your skin to the sun's rays. 2 : to let too much light fall on (film in a camera) when you are taking a photograph • an overexposed picture/image 3 : to give too much public attention or notice to (someone or something) • an overexposed celebrity — **over·ex·po·sure** /ˌoʊvərɪkˈspouʒə/ n [U]

over·ex·tend /ˌoʊvərɪkˈstɛnd/ vb [T] : to extend or stretch (something) too far • He overextended a muscle in his arm. — **overextend yourself** 1 : to try to do too much 2 : to spend more money than you can afford to spend • Young people with credit cards often overextend themselves.

¹**over·flow** /ˌoʊvəˈflou/ vb [T/I] 1 : to flow over the edge or top of (something) • The river overflowed its banks. • (figurative) The crowd filled the room and overflowed into the lobby. 2 : to fill or cover (something) completely • Papers overflowed his desk. = His desk was overflowing with papers. • (figurative) Her heart was overflowing with joy. [=was filled with joy] • The hotels are all filled/full to overflowing [=completely filled] with tourists.

²**over·flow** /ˈoʊvəˌflou/ n [C] 1 : an act of flowing over the edge or top of some-

thing • *the overflow of the river* **2 a** : the amount of something that flows over the edge or top of something else • *The overflow from the river flooded the field.* **b** : the number of people or things that goes over a limit • *The police tried to control the overflow of traffic.* **3** : a pipe or container for liquid that overflows from something else

over·ground /'ouvɚˌɡraʊnd/ *adv, Brit* : on or above the ground • *These trains all run overground.* — **overground** *adj*, always before a noun • *an overground train*

over·grow /ˌouvɚˈɡroʊ/ *vb* **-grew** /-ˈɡruː/; **-grown** /-ˈɡroʊn/; **-grow·ing** [T] : to grow in an uncontrolled way and completely cover or fill (something) • *The weeds have overgrown the garden.* — **over·growth** /'ouvɚˌɡroʊθ/ *n* [U]

overgrown *adj* **1** : covered with plants that have grown in an uncontrolled way • *The garden is overgrown with weeds.* • *an overgrown path* **2** : grown to a size that is unusually or too large • *an overgrown plant/child/ego*

over·hand /'ouvɚˌhænd/ *adj, US* : made with the hand brought forward and down from above the shoulder • *an overhand throw* — **overhand** *adv* • *pitching overhand*

¹**over·hang** /ˌouvɚˈhæŋ/ *vb* **-hung** /-ˌhʌŋ/; **-hang·ing** [T/I] : to stick out beyond or hang over (something) • *A cliff overhangs the trail.* • *overhanging branches*

²**overhang** *n* [C] : a part that sticks out or hangs over something • *the overhang of the roof*

over·haul /ˌouvɚˈhɑːl/ *vb* [T] **1** : to look at every part of (something) and repair or replace the parts that do not work • *The mechanic overhauled the car's engine.* **2** : to change (something) completely in order to improve it • *They had to overhaul their original plans.* — **over·haul** /'ouvɚˌhɑːl/ *n* [C] • *The engine underwent a complete overhaul.*

¹**over·head** /ˌouvɚˈhɛd/ *adv* : above someone's head • *Geese were flying overhead.* — **over·head** /'ouvɚˌhɛd/ *adj* • *overhead branches*

²**over·head** /'ouvɚˌhɛd/ *n* [U] *US* : costs for rent, heat, electricity, etc., that a business must pay and that are not related to what the business sells • *Her company has very little overhead.* — called also (*Brit*) **overheads**

over·hear /ˌouvɚˈhiɚ/ *vb* **-heard** /-ˈhɚd/; **-hear·ing** [T/I] : to hear (something that was said to another person) by accident • *I overheard a rumor about you.*

over·heat /ˌouvɚˈhiːt/ *vb* [T/I] : to make (something) too hot or to become too hot • *I overheated the food in the microwave.* • *The car's engine overheated.*

over·joyed /ˌouvɚˈdʒɔɪd/ *adj* : filled with great joy : very happy • *She was overjoyed to see her sister again.*

over·kill /ˌouvɚˈkɪl/ *n* [U] *disapproving* : something that is much larger, greater, etc., than what is needed for a particular purpose • *Yes, we need a new car, but this huge truck seems like overkill.*

over·land /'ouvɚˌlænd/ *adv* : on or across land • *We traveled overland by horse.* — **overland** *adj* • *an overland journey*

over·lap /ˌouvɚˈlæp/ *vb* **-lapped**; **-lap·ping** [T/I] **1** : to lie over the edge of (something) • *The roof shingles overlap (each other).* **2** : to happen at the same time as something else • *Baseball season overlaps (with) football season in September.* **3** : to have parts that are the same as parts of something else • *Some of your duties overlap (with) his.* — **over·lap** /'ouvɚˌlæp/ *n* [C/U] • *There is some overlap between the two courses.* [=the courses cover some of the same material]

¹**over·lay** /ˌouvɚˈleɪ/ *vb* **-laid** /-ˈleɪd/; **-lay·ing** [T] : to cover (something) with a layer of another material • *The tabletop is overlaid with marble.*

²**over·lay** /'ouvɚˌleɪ/ *n* [C/U] : material that covers the complete surface or part of the surface of something • *a silver ring with (a) gold overlay*

over·load /ˌouvɚˈloʊd/ *vb* [T] **1** : to put too great a load on or in (something) • *Don't overload the washing machine.* • *The truck was overloaded with wood.* **2** : to give too much work to (someone) • *My boss is overloading me with extra work.* — **over·load** /'ouvɚˌloʊd/ *n* [C/U] • *The truck had an overload of wood.* • *I'm suffering from advertising overload.* [=I have been seeing too many advertisements]

over·look /ˌouvɚˈlʊk/ *vb* [T] **1 a** : to fail to see or notice (something) • *The detective overlooked an important clue.* **b** : to pay no attention to (something) • *She overlooked her boyfriend's minor faults.* **2** : to not consider (someone) for a job, position, etc. • *I was overlooked for a promotion.* **3** : to rise above (something) • *the mountains that overlook the village*

over·lord /'ouvɚˌloɚd/ *n* [C] : a person who has power over a large number of people • *a colonial overlord*

over·ly /'ouvɚli/ *adv* : to an excessive degree : TOO • *These directions are overly complex.* • *I'm not overly concerned.*

¹**over·night** /ˌouvɚˈnaɪt/ *adv* **1** : for or during the entire night • *He stayed overnight.* **2** : very quickly or suddenly • *The novel made her famous overnight.*

²**overnight** *adj* **1** : happening, traveling, or staying during the night • *an overnight bus trip* • *overnight guests* **2** : happening very quickly or suddenly • *an overnight success*

over·pass /'ouvɚˌpæs, Brit 'ouvɚˌpɑːs/ *n* [C] *US* : a bridge that allows a road or railroad to cross over another • *a highway overpass*

over·pay /ˌouvɚˈpeɪ/ *vb* **-paid** /-ˈpeɪd/; **-pay·ing** **1** [T/I] : to pay too much for something • *He overpaid for his car.* **2** [T] : to pay (someone) more money for a job than is deserved • *She is overpaid for the work she does.*

over·play /ˌouvɚˈpleɪ/ *vb* [T] : to give too much attention to (something) : to make (something) seem more important than it really is • *The media overplayed the story.* — **overplay your hand** *also* **over-**

play your cards : to make a mistake because you believe that your position is stronger or better than it really is • *The labor union overplayed its hand by demanding too much.*

over·pop·u·la·tion /ˌouvɚˌpɑːpjəˈleɪʃən/ *n* [U] : a situation in which too many people or animals live in a certain area • *the problem of world overpopulation* — **over·pop·u·lat·ed** /ˌouvɚˈpɑːpjəˌleɪtəd/ *adj* • *overpopulated cities*

over·pow·er /ˌouvɚˈpawɚ/ *vb* [T] **1** : to defeat or gain control of (someone or something) by using force • *She was able to overpower her attacker.* **2** : to affect (someone) very strongly or severely • *The smell overpowered us.* **3** : to have more strength, force, or effect than (someone or something) • *The taste of the wine was overpowered by the spiciness of the food.*

over·pow·er·ing /ˌouvɚˈpawɚɪŋ/ *adj* : very strong or powerful • *an overpowering smell/urge/personality*

over·price /ˌouvɚˈpraɪs/ *vb* **-priced**; **-pric·ing** [T] : to give a price that is too high to (something) • *overpriced jewelry*

over·rate /ˌouvɚˈreɪt/ *vb* **-rat·ed**; **-rat·ing** [T] : to rate, value, or praise (someone or something) too highly • *The coach tends to overrate the players on his own team.* — **overrated** *adj* • *That movie was highly/very overrated.*

over·re·act /ˌouvɚriˈækt/ *vb* [I] : to respond to something with an emotion that is too strong or an action that is unnecessary • *My mother overreacted when she learned that I had been in an accident.* — **over·re·ac·tion** /ˌouvɚriˈækʃən/ *n* [C/U] • *His angry response was an overreaction.*

over·ride /ˌouvɚˈraɪd/ *vb* **-rode** /-ˈroud/; **-rid·den** /-ˈrɪdn̩/; **-rid·ing** [T] **1** : to make (something) no longer valid • *Congress overrode the President's veto.* **2** : to have more importance or influence than (something) • *Don't let anger override common sense.* • *an overriding concern/ need* **3** : to stop an action that is done automatically by using a special command • *You must enter a code to override the alarm.*

over·rule /ˌouvɚˈruːl/ *vb* [T] : to decide that (something or someone) is wrong • *The judge overruled the objection/attorney.*

¹**over·run** /ˌouvɚˈrʌn/ *vb* **-ran** /-ˈræn/; **-run**; **-run·ning** [T] **1** : to enter and be present in (a place) in large numbers • *The city was overrun by enemy troops.* : to spread over or throughout (something) • *Weeds overran the garden.* = *The garden was overrun with/by weeds.* **2** : to run or go beyond or past (something) • *The plane overran the runway.* • *The stream has overrun* [=*overflowed*] *its banks.* • *His speech overran the time allowed.*

²**over·run** /ˈouvɚˌrʌn/ *n* [C] : an amount of money that is spent and that is more than the expected or planned amount • *cost/budget overruns*

over·seas /ˌouvɚˈsiːz/ *adv* : in or to a foreign country that is across a sea or ocean • *Troops were sent overseas.* — **over-**

seas /ˈouvɚˌsiːz/ *adj* • *overseas flights*

over·see /ˌouvɚˈsiː/ *vb* **-saw** /-ˈsɑː/; **-seen** /-ˈsiːn/; **-see·ing** [T] : to watch and direct (an activity, a group of workers, etc.) in order to be sure that a job is done correctly • *He was hired to oversee construction of the new facility.* — **over·seer** /ˈouvɚˌsiːɚ/ *n* [C] • *government/industry overseers*

over·sell /ˌouvɚˈsɛl/ *vb* **-sold** /-ˈsould/; **-sell·ing** [T] : to accept payment or reservations for more rooms, seats, tickets, etc., than you have available • *The concert was oversold.* [=*more tickets were sold than there were seats*]

over·shad·ow /ˌouvɚˈʃædou/ *vb* [T] **1** : to cause (something or someone) to seem less important or impressive when compared to something or someone else • *She felt overshadowed by the success of her brother.* **2** : to make (something) less enjoyable because of sadness, fear, or worry • *Recent peace efforts have been overshadowed by violence.* **3** : to cast a shadow over (something) • *a house overshadowed by tall trees*

over·shoe /ˈouvɚˌʃuː/ *n* [C] : a rubber shoe worn over another shoe in bad weather

over·shoot /ˌouvɚˈʃuːt/ *vb* **-shot** /-ˈʃɑːt/; **-shoot·ing** [T] : to go over or beyond (something) • *The plane overshot the runway.*

over·sight /ˈouvɚˌsaɪt/ *n* **1** [C] : a mistake made because someone forgets or fails to notice something • *The error was a simple oversight.* **2** [U] : the act or job of directing work that is being done • *He was given oversight of the project.*

over·sim·pli·fy /ˌouvɚˈsɪmpləˌfaɪ/ *vb* **-fies**; **-fied**; **-fy·ing** [T/I] : to describe (something) in a way that does not include all the facts and details and that causes misunderstanding • *The article oversimplifies the problem.* — **over·sim·pli·fi·ca·tion** /ˌouvɚˌsɪmpləfəˈkeɪʃən/ *n* [C/U]

over·size /ˌouvɚˈsaɪz/ *or* **over·sized** /ˌouvɚˈsaɪzd/ *adj* : larger than the normal size • *an oversize package*

over·sleep /ˌouvɚˈsliːp/ *vb* **-slept** /-ˈslɛpt/; **-sleep·ing** [I] : to sleep past the time when you planned to get up • *I overslept this morning and was late for work.*

over·spill /ˈouvɚˌspɪl/ *n* [U, singular] *Brit* : the movement of people from crowded cities to less crowded areas • *a new town built to absorb London's overspill*

over·state /ˌouvɚˈsteɪt/ *vb* **-stat·ed**; **-stat·ing** [T] : to say that (something) is larger or greater than it really is • *The company overstated revenue for the past year.* • *It would be difficult to overstate the damage done by the storm.* [=*the storm did a great amount of damage*] — **over·state·ment** /ˌouvɚˈsteɪtmənt/ *n* [C/U]

over·stay /ˌouvɚˈsteɪ/ *vb* [T] : to stay longer than you are expected or allowed to stay • *Don't overstay your welcome.* [=*don't stay longer than you should*]

over·step /ˌouvɚˈstɛp/ *vb* **-stepped**; **-step·ping** [T] : to go beyond what is proper or allowed by (something) • *They* *overstepped their authority.* • *He overstepped the bounds/limits of good taste.* [=he did something that was not proper]

over·sub·scribed /ˌoʊvəsəbˈskraɪbd/ *adj* — used to describe a situation in which something is wanted by many people but there are not enough copies, rooms, etc., for everyone • *an oversubscribed course/school*

overt /oʊˈvət/ *adj* : easily seen : not secret or hidden • *overt hostility* — **overt·ly** *adv*

over·take /ˌoʊvəˈteɪk/ *vb* -took /-ˈtʊk/; -tak·en /-ˈteɪkən/; -tak·ing 1 [T/I] : to move up to and past (someone or something that is in front of you) • *The car overtook the leader of the race.* • *(figurative)* *The other candidates hope to overtake the front-runner by election day.* 2 [T] : to happen to or affect (someone) in a sudden and unexpected way • *The pain overtook him.* — **overtaken by events** : forced to be changed because of something that has suddenly and unexpectedly happened • *The original date for the meeting was overtaken by events and had to be changed.*

over·tax /ˌoʊvəˈtæks/ *vb* [T] 1 : to make (someone or something) do more than that person or thing is able to do or should do • *We are afraid the trip might overtax his health/strength.* • *The children overtaxed her patience.* • *The hospital's overtaxed emergency room needs more doctors.* 2 : to make (people) pay too much in taxes • *The city is overtaxing its residents.*

over-the-counter *adj, always before a noun* 1 : available for purchase without a prescription from a doctor • *over-the-counter drugs* 2 US, business : not traded on an organized stock exchange • *an over-the-counter stock*

over-the-top *adj, informal* : going beyond what is expected, usual, normal, or appropriate • *an over-the-top performance*

over·throw /ˌoʊvəˈθroʊ/ *vb* -threw /-ˈθruː/; -thrown /-ˈθroʊn/; -throw·ing [T] 1 : to remove (someone or something) from power especially by force • *overthrow a government* 2 US, sports : to throw a ball over or past (someone) • *He overthrew the first baseman.* = *He overthrew first base.* — **over·throw** /ˈoʊvəˌθroʊ/ *n* [C/U]

over·time /ˈoʊvəˌtaɪm/ *n* [U] 1 : time spent working at your job that is in addition to your normal working hours • *I worked two hours of overtime last week.* 2 : extra time added to a game when the score is tied at the end of the normal playing time • *an overtime win/period/game* • *The game went into overtime.* • *They lost the game in overtime.* — **overtime** *adv* • *He has been working overtime.* • *(figurative)* *Her imagination was working overtime.* [=was extremely active]

over·tone /ˈoʊvəˌtoʊn/ *n* [C] : an idea or quality that is suggested without being said directly • *racist/political overtones*

over·ture /ˈoʊvəʧə/ *n* [C] 1 : a piece of music played at the start of an opera, a musical play, etc. 2 : something that is offered or suggested with the hope that it will start a relationship, lead to an agreement, etc. • *He was making (romantic/sexual) overtures to her during dinner.* • *The company's board rejected overtures for a merger.*

over·turn /ˌoʊvəˈtən/ *vb* 1 [T/I] : to turn over • *The truck went off the road and overturned.* • *The dog overturned the bowl.* 2 [T] : to decide that (a ruling, decision, etc.) is wrong and change it • *The court overturned his conviction.*

over·view /ˈoʊvəˌvju/ *n* [C] : a general explanation or description of something • *an overview of American history*

over·ween·ing /ˌoʊvəˈwiːnɪŋ/ *adj, formal + disapproving* 1 : too confident or proud • *overweening politicians* 2 : too great : excessive and unpleasant • *overweening ambition/pride*

over·weight /ˌoʊvəˈweɪt/ *adj* : weighing more than normal or expected • *He's slightly overweight.* • *an overweight package*

over·whelm /ˌoʊvəˈwɛlm/ *vb* [T] 1 : to affect (someone) very strongly • *Grief overwhelmed her.* = *She was overwhelmed by grief.* 2 : to cause (someone) to have too many things to deal with • *They were overwhelmed with work.* 3 : to defeat (someone or something) completely • *The city was overwhelmed by the invading army.*

over·whelm·ing /ˌoʊvəˈwɛlmɪŋ/ *adj* 1 : very great in number, effect, or force • *The response was overwhelming.* • *overwhelming support* 2 : very difficult or confusing • *She found the job overwhelming at first.* — **over·whelm·ing·ly** *adv* • *The town voted overwhelmingly for the new library.* • *an overwhelmingly difficult task*

over·work /ˌoʊvəˈwək/ *vb* 1 [T/I] : to work too hard • *The captain overworked the crew.* 2 [T] : to use (something) too much or too often • *overwork a phrase* • *an overworked expression* 3 [T] : to work on (something) too much • *She overworked the painting.* — **overwork** *n* [U] • *They were exhausted from overwork.*

over·wrought /ˌoʊvəˈrɑːt/ *adj* : very excited or upset • *The witness became overwrought as she described the crime.*

over·zeal·ous /ˌoʊvəˈzɛləs/ *adj* : too eager or enthusiastic • *overzealous fans*

ovu·late /ˈɑːvjəˌleɪt/ *vb* -lat·ed; -lat·ing [I] biology, of a woman or a female animal : to produce eggs within the body — **ovu·la·tion** /ˌɑːvjəˈleɪʃən/ *n* [U]

ovum /ˈoʊvəm/ *n, pl* **ova** /ˈoʊvə/ [C] biology : ¹EGG 3

ow /ˈaʊ/ *interj* — used to express sudden pain • *Ow! That hurts!*

owe /ˈoʊ/ *vb* owed; ow·ing 1 [T/I] : to need to pay or repay money to a person, bank, etc. • *I owe the bank a lot of money.* • *I still owe (money) on the car.* • *He owes me $5.* • *Additional payments are owed on the mortgage.* 2 [T] **a** : to need to do or give something to someone who has done something for you or given something to you • *I owe you a favor.* • *I owe you my thanks.* • *She owes me for all the times I've helped her out.* • *Thanks for* *your help. I* **owe you one**. [=I will give you help when you need it] **b** — used to say that something should be done for or given to someone • *I* **owe you** *an apology.* • *The senator is owed a degree of respect.* • *We* **owe it to** *the veterans to build a memorial.* [=we should build a memorial to honor and thank the veterans] • *You* **owe it to** *yourself to have fun.* [=you deserve to let yourself have fun] **3** [*T*] — used to indicate the person or thing that made something possible • *I* **owe** *my success to my teachers.* • *His success* **owes** *more to luck than skill.* [=is more because of luck than skill]

owing to *prep* : because of (something) • *The ambassador was absent owing to illness.*

owl /ˈawəl/ *n* [*C*] : a bird that usually hunts at night and that has a large head and eyes, a powerful hooked beak, and strong claws — see also NIGHT OWL

¹**own** /ˈoʊn/ *adj, always before a noun* — used to say that something belongs or relates to a particular person or thing and to no other • *We each had our own book.* • *I've got my own problems; I don't have time to listen to yours.* • *They built their own home.* • *I now have my* **very own** *office!*

²**own** *pron* : something or someone that belongs or relates to a particular person or thing and to no other — always used after a possessive (such as "my," "your," or "their") • *The teacher gave out books so that each of us had our own.* • *We've got problems of our own.* • *The band has a style* **all its own**. [=no other band has the same style] • *I don't need much—just a little place to* **call my own**. [=just a little place that belongs only to me] • **Through no fault of their own**, *these children are forced to live in poverty.* • *When you're a little older, you can have a bike of your* **very own**. — **come into your own** see COME — **get your own back** see get back at GET — **hold your own** see ¹HOLD — **on your own 1** : without being helped by anyone or anything • *He's too weak to stand on his own.* • *I found out on my own.* • *I came up with the idea* **all on my own**. **2 a** : without anyone or anything else : ALONE • *She lived on her own for a few years.* **b** : in a state or condition in which there is nobody to help you • *They can't survive on their own in the wilderness.* — **to each his own** or **each to his own** see ²EACH

³**own** *vb* **1** [*T*] : to have (something) as property : to legally possess (something) • *We hope to someday own our own home.* • *The truck was originally owned by her grandfather.* • *He owns the rights to the band's music.* **2** [*T/I*] *old-fashioned* : to admit that something is true • *He owned that he was at fault.* • *She* **owned to** [=admitted] *her mistake.* — **own up** [*phrasal vb*] : to admit that you have done a usu-

ally bad thing : to confess to something • *I know he broke the window, but so far, he hasn't* **owned up**. • *She finally* **owned up** *to her mistake.*

own·er /ˈoʊnɚ/ *n* [*C*] : a person or group that owns something • *the owner of the car* = *the car's owner*

own·er·ship /ˈoʊnɚˌʃɪp/ *n* [*U*] : the state or fact of owning something • *home ownership* • *The café is under new ownership.* [=different people now own the café]

own goal *n* [*C*] *chiefly Brit, sports* : a goal in soccer, hockey, etc., that a player accidentally scores against his or her own team

ox /ˈɑːks/ *n, pl* **ox·en** /ˈɑːksən/ *also* **ox** [*C*] **1** : a bull that has had its sex organs removed **2** : a cow or bull

ox·ford /ˈɑːksfɚd/ *n* **1** [*C*] *chiefly US* : a low shoe usually made of leather and fastened with laces • *a pair of oxfords* **2 a** [*U*] : strong, soft cotton usually used for making shirts **b** [*C*] *US* : a shirt made of oxford • *a blue oxford shirt*

ox·ide /ˈɑːkˌsaɪd/ *n* [*C/U*] *chemistry* : a compound of oxygen and another substance • *iron oxide*

ox·i·dize /ˈɑːksəˌdaɪz/ *also Brit* **ox·i·dise** *vb* **-dized; -diz·ing** [*T/I*] : to become combined or to cause (something) to become combined with oxygen • *The paint oxidizes and discolors rapidly.* — **ox·i·da·tion** /ˌɑːksəˈdeɪʃən/ *n* [*U*]

ox·y·gen /ˈɑːksɪdʒən/ *n* [*U*] : a chemical that is found in the air, that has no color, taste, or smell, and that is necessary for life

ox·y·gen·ate /ˈɑːksɪdʒəˌneɪt/ *vb* **-at·ed; -at·ing** [*T*] *technical* : to add oxygen to (something) • *oxygenate the blood*

oxygen mask *n* [*C*] : a mask worn to breathe oxygen from a storage tank

oxygen tent *n* [*C*] : a piece of medical equipment that surrounds the body or head of a patient and that is filled with flowing oxygen

ox·y·mo·ron /ˌɑːksɪˈmoɚˌɑːn/ *n* [*C*] : a combination of words that have opposite or very different meanings • *The phrase "cruel kindness" is an oxymoron.*

oys·ter /ˈɔɪstɚ/ *n* [*C*] : a type of shellfish that has a rough shell with two parts and that is eaten both cooked and raw — **the world is your oyster** *informal* ✧ If the world is your oyster, your life is good and you have the ability to do whatever you want to do.

oz. *abbr, US* ounce; ounces

ozone /ˈoʊˌzoʊn/ *n* [*U*] : a form of oxygen that is found in a layer high in the Earth's atmosphere • *Scientists are concerned about ozone depletion.*

ozone hole *n* [*C*] : an area of the ozone layer where there is very little ozone

ozone layer *n* [*U*] : a layer of ozone in the upper atmosphere that prevents dangerous radiation from the Sun from reaching the surface of the Earth

P

¹p *or* **P** /ˈpiː/ *n, pl* **p's** *or* **ps** *or* **P's** *or* **Ps** /ˈpiːz/ [C/U] : the 16th letter of the English alphabet ▪ *a word that starts with (a) p* — **mind your p's and q's** *also US* **watch your p's and q's** : to be careful about behaving in a polite or proper way ▪ *We knew to mind our p's and q's around our aunt.*

²p *abbr* **1** *or* **p.** page ▪ *p. 46* ◇ The abbreviation for "pages" is **pp.** ▪ *pp. 46–48* **2** per ▪ *mph* [=miles per hour] **3** *Brit* pence; penny

pa /ˈpɑː/ *n* [C] *informal + old-fashioned* : a person's father ▪ *my ma and pa*

p.a. *abbr, chiefly Brit* per annum

¹PA *abbr* Pennsylvania

²PA /ˌpiːˈeɪ/ *n* [C] **1** : a machine with a microphone and speakers used for making announcements in a public place ▪ *The winner was announced over the PA.* — called also *public address system* **2** *US* : PHYSICIAN'S ASSISTANT

PAC /ˈpæk/ *n* [C] *US* : POLITICAL ACTION COMMITTEE

¹pace /ˈpeɪs/ *n* **1** [*singular*] : the speed at which someone or something moves or something happens ▪ *We walked at a quick/leisurely pace.* ▪ *The pace of the story was slow.* **2** [C] : a single step or the length of a single step ▪ *The tree is about 30 paces from the front door.* — **go through your paces** : to do something in order to show others how well you do it ▪ *The athletes went through their paces as the coaches looked on.* — **keep pace with** : to go or make progress at the same speed as (someone or something else) ▪ *Our production can't keep pace with the orders coming in.* — **off the pace** *US* : behind in a race, competition, etc. ▪ *The runner in second place was three seconds off the pace.* — **put someone or something through his/her/its paces** : to test what someone or something can do ▪ *We put the computer through its paces.* — **set the pace** : to be the one that is at the front in a race and that controls how fast the other racers have to go ▪ *He usually sets the pace for the rest of the team.*

²pace *vb* **paced; pac·ing 1** [T/I] : to walk back and forth across the same space again and again especially because you are nervous ▪ *He paced the floor/room.* ▪ *pacing back and forth* **2** [T] : to control or set the speed of (someone or something) ▪ *She paced the other runners for the first half of the race.* — **pace off** [*phrasal vb*] **pace (something) off** *or* **pace off (something)** : to measure (something) by walking and counting the number of steps you take ▪ *The new garden is 25 feet long. I paced it off.* ▪ *Pace off 20 feet.* — **pace yourself** : to do something at a speed that is steady and that allows you to continue without becoming too tired ▪ *He learned to pace himself so he could get*

all of his work done. — **paced** *adj* ▪ *a moderately paced stroll* ▪ *fast-paced music*

pace·mak·er /ˈpeɪsˌmeɪkɚ/ *n* [C] **1** *medical* : a small electrical machine put inside a person to make the heart beat evenly **2** *Brit* : PACESETTER

pace·set·ter /ˈpeɪsˌsɛtɚ/ *n* [C] *US* : a person who runs ahead of the other runners in a race in order to set a pace ▪ *(figurative) The company has continued to be the industry's pacesetter.*

pac·i·fi·er /ˈpæsəˌfajɚ/ *n* [C] *US* : a rubber object shaped like a nipple for babies to suck or bite on — called also (*Brit*) *dummy*

pac·i·fist /ˈpæsɪfɪst/ *n* [C] : someone who believes that war and violence are wrong and who refuses to participate in or support a war — **pac·i·fism** /ˈpæsəˌfɪzəm/ *n* [U] — **pacifist** *adj, always before a noun* ▪ *pacifist beliefs/ideals*

pac·i·fy /ˈpæsəˌfaɪ/ *vb* **-fies; -fied; -fy·ing** [T] **1** : to cause (someone who is angry or upset) to become calm or quiet ▪ *pacify a crying child* **2** : to cause or force (a country, a violent group of people, etc.) to become peaceful ▪ *trying to pacify the protesters* — **pac·i·fi·ca·tion** /ˌpæsəfəˈkeɪʃən/ *n* [U]

¹pack /ˈpæk/ *n* [C] **1** : a bag or bundle of objects that is carried on a person's or animal's back **2** *chiefly US* **a** : a small paper or cardboard package in which small things are sold ▪ *a pack of gum/cigarettes/needles* **b** : the amount contained in one pack ▪ *He smokes two packs (of cigarettes) a day.* **3** *Brit* : PACKET 2b ▪ *an informational pack* **4** : a complete set of playing cards ▪ DECK **5** : a group of similar people or things ▪ *a pack of teenagers/lawyers/thieves* ▪ *It was all a pack of lies.* [=all lies] ▪ *She's not content to simply follow the pack.* [=to do what everyone else does] **6** : a large number of people who are grouped together during a race or competition ▪ *The company is trying to stay ahead of the pack.* [=ahead of their competitors] **7** : a group of usually wild animals that hunt together ▪ *a wolf pack*

²pack *vb* **1 a** [T] : to put (something) into a bag, suitcase, etc., so that you can take it with you ▪ *I've packed a picnic lunch for us.* ▪ *Pack your things/gear. We're leaving tonight.* **b** [T/I] : to put things into (a bag, box, etc.) ▪ *We packed (our bags) for the trip.* **2** [T] : to put (something) into a box or other container so that it can be moved, stored, or protected ▪ *They packed (up) the dishes in a box.* **3 a** [T] : to fill a place with as many people as possible ▪ *Over 25,000 fans packed the stadium.* ▪ *Concert organizers pack hundreds of people into tiny nightclubs.* **b** [I] : to gather close together as a group ▪ *We all packed into the car.* **4** [T] : to put a large amount of something into (something) ▪ *directors who pack their movies full of violence* ▪ *They pack their magazine with lots of information.* **5** [*T*] : to make (dirt, snow, etc.) more firm or solid by pressing down on it ▪ *Pack the soil firmly around the roots of the plant.* **6** [*T*] *US* : to unfairly control the kinds of people or things that are in (a group, list, etc.) in order to get the result you want ▪ *They packed the meeting with their supporters.* **7** [*T*] *somewhat informal* : to have or be able to produce (something powerful) ▪ *an engine that packs a lot of power* [=a very powerful engine] **8** [*T/I*] *US, informal* : to wear or carry (a weapon) ▪ *They were packing guns.* — **pack a punch/wallop** *informal* : to be very forceful or effective ▪ *These hot peppers really pack a punch.* [=they are very hot and spicy] — **pack away** [*phrasal vb*] **pack (something) away** or **pack away (something)** : to put (something) in a safe place to be used at a later time ▪ *The toys were packed away in the attic.* — **pack in** [*phrasal vb*] **1** *Brit, informal* : to stop or quit ▪ *I have no intention of packing in just yet.* **2 pack in (someone or something)** or **pack (someone or something) in** a : to cause (someone or something) to fit into a small space ▪ *My suitcase was full, but I managed to pack in one more sweater.* **b** : to cause (large groups of people) to come to a show or performance ▪ *His show still packs in (the) crowds/audiences.* ▪ *The movie has been packing them in at theaters across the country.* **3** *informal* **a** *US* : to stop using (something) forever ▪ *She decided to pack in her skis.* [=to give up skiing] **b** *Brit* : to give up doing (something) ▪ *He packed in his job.* **4 pack it in** *informal* : to stop doing a job or an activity : QUIT ▪ *I was ready to pack it in for the day.* — **pack in/into** [*phrasal vb*] **pack (something) in/into** : to put (a large amount of something) into (something) ▪ *She packs a lot of information in her short essays.* — **pack off** [*phrasal vb*] **pack (someone) off** : to send (someone) away to a different place ▪ *His mom packed him off to bed.* — **pack on the pounds** or **pack on five/ten/fifteen (etc.) pounds** *chiefly US, informal* : to gain weight or a certain amount of weight ▪ *Americans are continuing to pack on the pounds.* — **pack up** [*phrasal vb*] **1 pack up** or **pack up (something)** or **pack (something) up** a : to gather things together so that you can take them with you ▪ *He packed up and left town.* ▪ *You should pack up your tools at the end of the day.* **b** *Brit, informal* : to stop or quit ▪ *She packed up her teaching job after five years.* **2** *Brit, informal* : to stop working properly ▪ *The lift has packed up.* — **send (someone or something) packing** see SEND — **pack·er** /ˈpækɚ/ *n* [*C*]

¹**pack·age** /ˈpækɪdʒ/ *n* [*C*] **1** *chiefly US* : a box or large envelope that is sent or delivered usually through the mail or by another delivery service **2** *US* : a wrapper or container that covers or holds something ▪ *All ingredients are listed right on the package.* ▪ *a package* [=(Brit) packet] *of cookies* **3 a** : a group of related things that are sold together for a single price ▪ *a vacation package* ▪ *a software package* **b** : a group of related things that go together ▪ *My new job offers a great benefits package.* [=my new job offers great benefits] ▪ *a student's financial aid package*

²**package** *vb* **-aged; -ag·ing** [*T*] **1** : to put (something) in a package in order to sell it or send it somewhere ▪ *The china needs to be packaged properly.* ▪ *packaged goods/foods* **2** : to show or present (something or someone) in a particular way ▪ *If the issue is not packaged correctly, it will not get voters to come to the polls.*

package deal *n* [*C*] : a group of people or things which must be accepted together ▪ *They presented their proposals to the committee as a package deal.*

package store *n* [*C*] *US* : a store that sells alcoholic beverages

packaging *n* [*U*] **1** : material used to enclose or contain something **2** : the way something or someone is presented in order to be more attractive or appealing ▪ *the packaging of a political candidate*

packed /ˈpækt/ *adj* **1** : pressed together so there is very little space between the parts or pieces ▪ *packed snow/dirt/earth* **2** : filled with a large amount of something ▪ *a room packed with books* ▪ *Oranges are packed full of vitamin C.* **3 a** : full of people ▪ *a packed auditorium* **b** *of a crowd of people* : large enough to fill a space or place ▪ *bands playing to packed audiences/crowds* **4** — used to say that you have finished putting things into bags, boxes, etc. ▪ *We're (all) packed and ready to go.*

packed lunch *n* [*C*] *chiefly Brit* : BAG LUNCH

pack·et /ˈpækət/ *n* **1** [*C*] **a** *US* : a small, thin package ▪ *a packet of sugar* **b** *Brit* : a package in which something is sold and bought ▪ *a packet* [=(US) box] *of crackers* **2** [*C*] *a US* : a group of things that have been gathered together for a particular purpose and usually put into a container (such as a folder or a large envelope) ▪ *an information packet* **b** *chiefly Brit* : a small, thin package sent through the mail or delivered to a person **3** [*singular*] *Brit, informal* : a large amount of money ▪ *We spent a packet on shipping charges.*

pack·ing /ˈpækɪŋ/ *n* [*U*] : material that is used to hold or protect things so that they can be moved or sent somewhere ▪ *I used some old newspapers for packing.*

pack rat *n* [*C*] *US, informal* : a person who collects or keeps things that are not needed

pact /ˈpækt/ *n* [*C*] : a formal agreement between two countries, people, or groups especially to help each other or to stop fighting ▪ *a peace/free-trade/nonaggression pact*

¹**pad** /ˈpæd/ *n* **1 a** : an object that is thin, flat, and usually soft ▪ *a gauze pad* ▪ *a heating pad* [=an electric mat that heats up and is held against the body to reduce pain] ▪ *a mattress pad* [=a cover-

ing that goes under a sheet on a bed to protect the mattress] ▪ *a car's* **brake pads** [=the part of the brakes that are pressed on the wheel when you stop or slow down the car] **b** *sports* : a covering for a specific part of the body that is worn to protect that part from injury ▪ *knee pads* **2** : a set of paper sheets for writing or drawing that are glued or fastened at one edge ▪ *They keep a pad and pencil by the phone.* **3** : the soft part on the bottom of the foot of a dog, cat, etc. **4** *informal + old-fashioned or humorous* : the place where someone lives ▪ *his* **bachelor pad** **5** : a flat area on the ground where helicopters can take off or land ▪ *a landing pad*

²**pad** *vb* **pad·ded; pad·ding** **1** [*T*] : to cover or fill (something) with soft material especially to protect it or make it more comfortable ▪ *He padded the inside of the box with crumpled newspaper.* **2** [*T*] : to make (something) larger, longer, or more attractive by adding things that are unnecessary, unimportant, or false ▪ *He padded his résumé.* **3** [*T*] *US* : to dishonestly add more charges to (a bill) in order to collect more money than is owed ▪ *He padded the bill for his consulting work.* **4** [*I*] : to move with quiet steps ▪ *She padded around/about (the house) in her pajamas.*

padded *adj* : filled or covered with soft material ▪ *a padded envelope/bra/seat*

padding *n* [*U*] **1** : soft material used to cover a hard surface in order to make it more comfortable ▪ *the padding on the seat of the chairs* **2** : unnecessary words used to make a speech or a piece of writing longer ▪ *Her speech contained a lot of padding.*

¹**pad·dle** /ˈpædl/ *n* [*C*] **1** : a long, usually wooden pole that has a wide, flat part at the end and is used to move and steer a small boat (such as a canoe) **2** *US* : an object with a short handle and a wide, flat part that is used to hit the ball in various games (such as table tennis) **3** : any one of various tools or devices that are wide, flat, and thin — **WADE**

²**paddle** *vb* **pad·dled; pad·dling** **1** [*T/I*] : to move a boat forward through water with a paddle ▪ *We paddled (our canoe) across the lake.* **2** [*I*] : to swim by moving your hands and feet in short quick motions ▪ *The dog paddled across the lake.* **3** [*T*] *US* : to beat or hit (someone or something) with a flat piece of wood ▪ *In those days many people believed it was okay to paddle children.* **4** [*I*] *Brit* : to walk or play in shallow water for pleasure ▪ WADE

pad·dock /ˈpædək/ *n* [*C*] **1** : a small field where animals (such as horses) are kept **2** : an enclosed area at a racetrack where horses, dogs, etc., are kept before a race

pad·dy /ˈpædi/ *n, pl* **-dies** [*C*] : a wet field where rice is grown

pad·lock /ˈpædˌlɑːk/ *n* [*C*] : a strong lock with a curved bar that connects to the main part of the lock and holds together two parts of something (such as a chain or a gate) — **padlock** *vb* [*T*] ▪ *The gate was padlocked.*

pa·dre /ˈpɑːdreɪ/ *n* [*C*] *informal* **1** : a Christian priest **2** : a Christian clergyman who works in the military

pae·an /ˈpiːjən/ *n* [*C*] *literary* : a song of joy, praise, or victory

paediatrician, paediatrics *chiefly Brit* spellings of PEDIATRICIAN, PEDIATRICS

paedophile *Brit spelling of* PEDOPHILE

pa·gan *also* **Pagan** /ˈpeɪɡən/ *n* [*C*] **1** : a person who worships many gods or goddesses or the earth or nature **2** *old-fashioned + often offensive* : a person who is not religious or whose religion is not Christianity, Judaism, or Islam — **pagan** *adj* — **pa·gan·ism** /ˈpeɪɡəˌnɪzəm/ *n* [*U*]

¹**page** /ˈpeɪdʒ/ *n* [*C*] **1 a** : one side of a sheet of paper especially in a book, magazine, etc. ▪ *The book is 237 pages long.* **b** : a sheet of paper in a book, magazine, etc. ▪ *He ripped a page out of the phone book.* **2** *literary* : an important event or period in history ▪ *an event that holds a special place in the* **pages of history** **3** *US* : a student who works as an assistant for a member of Congress — **borrow/take a page from someone** *or* **borrow/take a page from someone's book** *US* : to do the same thing that someone else has done ▪ *I borrowed a page from his book and studied harder.* — **jump/leap off the page** *of writing, a picture, etc.* : to be very noticeable, interesting, exciting, etc. ▪ *The characters leap off the page.* — **on the same page** *chiefly US, informal* : agreeing about something (such as how things should be done) ▪ *trying to get everyone on the same page*

²**page** *vb* **paged; pag·ing** [*T*] **1** : to call the name of (someone) in a public place usually over a speaker in order to find that person, deliver a message, etc. ▪ *You can page the manager if you need help.* **2** : to send a message to (someone) by using a special device (called a pager or beeper) ▪ *page a doctor* ▪ *a paging service* — **page through** [*phrasal vb*] : to turn the pages of (a book, magazine, etc.) especially in a quick, steady manner ▪ *He paged through the magazine.*

pag·eant /ˈpædʒənt/ *n* [*C*] **1** *US* : BEAUTY CONTEST **2** : a play or performance made of scenes from a historical event or a legend ▪ *an annual Christmas pageant*

pag·eant·ry /ˈpædʒəntri/ *n* [*U*] : the use of special clothing, traditions, and ceremonies as part of a special event or celebration

pag·er /ˈpeɪdʒə/ *n* [*C*] : a small electronic device that beeps or vibrates and shows a telephone number for the person carrying the device to call

pa·go·da /pəˈɡoʊdə/ *n* [*C*] : a type of tall building in eastern Asia that has many floors with roofs that stick out on each floor and curve up

¹**paid** /ˈpeɪd/ *past tense and past participle of* ¹PAY

²**paid** *adj* **1 a** : receiving money for work ▪ *paid public officials* **b** — used to indicate if someone receives low or high pay for work ▪ *a highly paid consultant* ▪ *low-*

paid workers **2** *chiefly US* : having been paid for ▪ *a paid advertisement* **3** : including payment of normal wages, salary, etc. ▪ *two weeks of paid vacation* — **put paid to** *chiefly Brit, informal* : to end or stop (something) ▪ *The pressure of work put paid to his holiday plans.*

pail /ˈpeɪl/ *n* [C] *chiefly US* **1** : a round container that is open at the top and usually has a handle ▪ *a garbage pail* **2** : the amount held by a pail ▪ *a pail of water*

¹**pain** /ˈpeɪn/ *n* **1** [C/U] : the physical feeling caused by disease, injury, or something that hurts the body ▪ *a dull/sharp pain* ▪ *She was in pain.* [=feeling pain] **2** [C/U] : mental or emotional suffering ▪ *life's joys and pains* ▪ *the pain of a difficult childhood* **3** [*singular*] *informal* : someone or something that causes trouble or makes you feel annoyed or angry ▪ *He can be such a pain.* — often used in phrases like **pain in the neck** — **be at pains** : to try hard *to do* something ▪ *They were at pains to distance themselves from the scandal.* — **go to great pains** *or* **take (great) pains** : to be careful in doing something ▪ *We went to great pains not to offend anyone.* — **on/under pain of** *formal* : at the risk of being given (a particular form of punishment) ▪ *He cannot return to the country on pain of death.* [=he will be killed if he returns to the country]

²**pain** *vb* [T] *formal* : to make (someone) upset, sad, worried, etc. ▪ *It pains me to admit it, but she was right.*

pained /ˈpeɪnd/ *adj* : appearing upset, sad, worried, etc. ▪ *She wore/had a pained expression on her face.*

pain·ful /ˈpeɪnfəl/ *adj* **1** : causing pain to your body ▪ *a painful sunburn/condition* **2** : causing emotional pain ▪ *painful memories*

pain·ful·ly /ˈpeɪnfəli/ *adv* **1** : very or extremely — used especially to describe something that is bad, unpleasant, or upsetting ▪ *It was painfully obvious/clear that we were not welcome.* ▪ *Progress was painfully slow.* ▪ *She is painfully shy.* **2** : in a way that causes pain ▪ *Her jaw was painfully swollen.*

pain·kill·er /ˈpeɪnˌkɪlɚ/ *n* [C] : a drug that decreases or removes pain that you feel in your body — **pain·kill·ing** /ˈpeɪnˌkɪlɪŋ/ *adj* ▪ *painkilling drugs*

pain·less /ˈpeɪnləs/ *adj* **1** : not causing pain to the body ▪ *a painless medical procedure* **2** : not upsetting, disturbing, or difficult ▪ *a painless experience* — **pain·less·ly** *adv*

pains·tak·ing /ˈpeɪnˌsteɪkɪŋ/ *adj* : showing or done with great care and effort ▪ *painstaking work/research* — **pains·tak·ing·ly** *adv*

¹**paint** /ˈpeɪnt/ *n* [C/U] : a liquid that dries to form a thin colored layer when it is spread on a surface ▪ *The old walls are coated with several layers of paint.* ▪ *The house needs a fresh/second coat of paint.*

²**paint** *vb* **1** [T] : to cover (something) with paint ▪ *We painted the room yellow.* **2** [T/I] : to make (a picture or design) by using paints ▪ *He painted a portrait/landscape.* ▪ *She paints well.* **3** [T] : to de-scribe (someone or something) in a particular way ▪ *The study paints a bleak/grim picture of the effects of pollution on animal life.* **4** [T] : to put makeup on (a part of the body) ▪ *She painted her nails with pink nail polish.* — **paint over** [*phrasal vb*] : to cover (something) with a layer of paint ▪ *They painted over the graffiti.* — **paint the town (red)** *informal* : to go out drinking, dancing, etc., to have a good time

paint·ball /ˈpeɪntˌbɑːl/ *n* [U] : a game in which two teams use special guns to shoot balls filled with paint at each other

paint·brush /ˈpeɪntˌbrʌʃ/ *n* [C] : a brush used for putting paint on a surface

paint·er /ˈpeɪntɚ/ *n* [C] **1** : a person whose job it is to paint walls, houses, etc. **2** : an artist who paints pictures ▪ *a famous painter*

paint·ing /ˈpeɪntɪŋ/ *n* **1** [C] : a picture that is painted ▪ *They hung the painting in the living room.* **2** [U] : the art or act of making pictures using paint ▪ *I like painting more than sculpture.* **3** [U] : the activity of painting houses, walls, etc. ▪ *The room is ready for painting.*

¹**pair** /ˈpeɚ/ *n*, *pl* **pairs** *or* **pair** [C] **1** : two things that are the same and are meant to be used together ▪ *a pair of gloves/shoes/socks* **2** : a thing that has two parts which are joined ▪ *a pair of glasses/pants/underwear/scissors* **3** : two people who are related in some way or who do something together ▪ *Those two kids make quite a pair.* **4** : two animals that mate together — **in pairs** : in a group of two people or things ▪ *The students worked in pairs.*

²**pair** *vb* [T] : to put (two people or things) together ▪ *The teacher paired students with partners for the assignment.* — **pair off** [*phrasal vb*] **1** : to join together in a romantic relationship ▪ *His friends were pairing off and having kids.* **2 pair off** *or* **pair (someone or something) off** *or* **pair off (someone or something)** : to join with someone or something else to form a group of two ▪ *People paired off for the next dance.* — **pair up** [*phrasal vb*] **pair up** *or* **pair (someone or something) up** *or* **pair up (someone or something)** : to join together or to cause (two people or things) to join together for a purpose, job, etc. ▪ *They paired me up with a new partner for the last game.*

pais·ley /ˈpeɪzli/ *adj* : covered in a pattern made up of colorful curved shapes ▪ *a paisley print/tie* — **paisley** *n*, *pl* **-leys** [C/U]

pa·ja·mas (*US*) *or Brit* **py·ja·mas** /pəˈdʒɑːməz/ *n* [*plural*] : clothing that people wear in bed or while relaxing at home — **pa·ja·ma** (*US*) *or Brit* **py·ja·ma** /pəˈdʒɑːmə/ *adj, always before a noun* ▪ *a pajama party* [=a party for children who spend the night at the house of a friend]

¹**pal** /ˈpæl/ *n* [C] *informal* : a close friend ▪ *We've been pals since we were kids.* — see also **PEN PAL**

²**pal** *vb* **palled**; **pal·ling** — **pal around with** [*phrasal vb*] *chiefly US, informal* : to spend time with (someone) as a friend ▪

She's been palling around with a girl from her school.

pal·ace /ˈpæləs/ *n [C]* **1** : the official home of a king, queen, president, etc. ▪ *the royal/imperial/presidential palace* ▪ *a palace guard/official* **2** : a very large and impressive house or public building

palaeolithic, palaeontology *Brit spellings of* PALEOLITHIC, PALEONTOLOGY

pal·at·able /ˈpælətəbəl/ *adj, somewhat formal* **1** : having a pleasant or agreeable taste ▪ *palatable food* **2** : pleasant or acceptable to someone ▪ *attempting to make the play more palatable to modern audiences*

pal·ate /ˈpælət/ *n [C]* **1** : the top part of the inside of your mouth **2** : the sense of taste ▪ *The restaurant serves Korean food adapted for the American palate.*

pa·la·tial /pəˈleɪʃəl/ *adj* : very large and impressive like a palace ▪ *a palatial home*

[1]**pale** /ˈpeɪl/ *adj* **pal·er; pal·est 1** : light in color ▪ *the pale wood of the table* ▪ *a pale blue* **2** : having a skin color that is closer to white than is usual or normal ▪ *Are you feeling well? You look pale.* **3** : not bright or intense ▪ *the pale light of dawn* **4** : not as good as something else ▪ *The new version is a pale imitation of the original.* — **pale·ness** /ˈpeɪlnəs/ *n [U]*

[2]**pale** *vb* **paled; pal·ing** /ˈpeɪlɪŋ/ *[I]* **1** : to lose color ▪ *His face paled (in fear) when he saw her.* **2** : to appear less important, good, serious, etc., when compared with something else ▪ *His accomplishments pale beside those of his father.* ▪ *Once you've tasted the local apples, all others pale by/in comparison.*

[3]**pale** *n* — **beyond the pale** : offensive or unacceptable ▪ *conduct that was beyond the pale*

Pa·leo·lith·ic (*chiefly US*) *or Brit* **Pal·aeo·lith·ic** /ˌpeɪlijəˈlɪθɪk, *Brit* ˌpæliə-ˈlɪθɪk/ *adj* : of or relating to the time during the early Stone Age when people made rough tools and weapons out of stone ▪ *Paleolithic artifacts/tools/hunters*

pa·le·on·tol·o·gy (*chiefly US*) *or Brit* **pal·ae·on·tol·o·gy** /ˌpeɪliˌɑːnˈtɑːlədʒi, *Brit* ˌpæliənˈtɒlədʒi/ *n [U]* : the science that deals with the fossils of animals and plants that lived very long ago especially in the time of dinosaurs — **pa·le·on·tol·o·gist** (*chiefly US*) *or Brit* **pal·ae·on·tol·o·gist** /ˌpeɪliˌɑːnˈtɑːlədʒɪst, *Brit* ˌpæli-ˌɒnˈtɒlədʒɪst/ *n [C]*

pal·ette /ˈpælət/ *n [C]* **1** : a thin board that is used by a painter to mix colors while painting **2** : the range of colors used by someone ▪ *a designer with an unusual color palette*

pal·i·mo·ny /ˈpæləˌmouni/ *n [U] chiefly US* : money that a court orders one person to pay to his or her former partner after they have stopped living together

pal·in·drome /ˈpælənˌdroum/ *n [C]* : a word, phrase, or number that reads the same backward or forward ▪ *The word "dad" and the number "1881" are palindromes.*

pal·i·sade /ˌpæləˈseɪd/ *n* **1** [C] : a high fence made of pointed stakes that was used in the past to protect a building or area **2** [*plural*] *US* : a line of steep cliffs

especially along a river or ocean

[1]**pall** /ˈpɑːl/ *n [C] formal* **1** : something (such as a cloud of smoke) that covers a place and makes it dark ▪ *a pall of smoke* ▪ (*figurative*) *a pall of grief/sadness* **2** : a heavy cloth that is used for covering a coffin, hearse, or tomb

[2]**pall** *vb [I] formal* **1** : to stop being enjoyable or interesting ▪ *He found that his retirement hobbies palled after a couple of years.* **2** : to lessen or fade ▪ *Her interest in politics has palled over the years.*

pall·bear·er /ˈpɑːlˌberə/ *n [C]* : a person who helps to carry the coffin at a funeral

pal·let /ˈpælət/ *n [C]* **1** : a wooden or metal platform that is used to support heavy things while they are being stored or moved **2 a** : a cloth bag that is filled with straw and used as a bed **b** : a small, hard bed

pal·lid /ˈpæləd/ *adj, formal* : very pale in a way that suggests poor health ▪ *the patient's pallid face*

pal·lor /ˈpælə/ *n [singular] formal* : paleness especially of the face that is caused by illness ▪ *a sickly pallor*

[1]**palm** /ˈpɑːm/ *n [C]* **1** : the inside part of the hand between the wrist and the fingers ▪ *It was small enough to fit in the palm of my hand.* **2 a** : a kind of tree that grows in tropical regions and has a straight, tall trunk and many large leaves at the top of the trunk — called also *palm tree* **b** : a bush or large plant that is related to the palm and can be grown indoors — **have someone in the palm of your hand** : to be able to control someone easily ▪ *She has her boss in the palm of her hand.*

[2]**palm** *vb [T]* : to hide (something) in the palm of your hand ▪ *To do the card trick, you have to learn to palm one of the cards.* — **palm off** [*phrasal vb*] *informal* **1** **palm (something) off** *or* **palm off (something) a** : to sell (something) for more than it is worth by being dishonest about it ▪ *She tried to palm the painting off as an original.* **b** : to get someone to accept or do (something) ▪ *He tried to palm off science fiction as truth.* **2** **palm yourself off as** : to pretend to be (someone you are not) ▪ *He palmed himself off as a lawyer.*

Palm Sunday *n [U]* : the Christian holiday celebrated on the Sunday before Easter

palm tree *n [C]* : [1]PALM 2a

pal·pa·ble /ˈpælpəbəl/ *adj, formal* : obvious and noticeable ▪ *a palpable sense of relief* — **pal·pa·bly** /ˈpælpəbli/ *adv*

pal·pi·tate /ˈpælpəˌteɪt/ *vb* **-tat·ed; -tat·ing** *[I] of the heart* : to beat quickly and strongly and often in a way that is not regular because of excitement, nervousness, etc. ▪ *My heart was palpitating.* — **pal·pi·ta·tion** /ˌpælpəˈteɪʃən/ *n [C] medical* : *Symptoms include dizziness and (heart) palpitations.*

pal·sy /ˈpɑːlzi/ *n [U] medical* : a condition that causes paralysis in part of your body ▪ *facial palsy* — see also CEREBRAL PALSY — **pal·sied** /ˈpɑːlzid/ *adj*

pal·try /ˈpɑːltri/ *adj* **pal·tri·er; -est** *formal* **1** : very small or too small in amount ▪ *a paltry salary* **2** : having little meaning, importance, or worth • *a paltry excuse*

pam·per /'pæmpə/ *vb* [T] : to treat (someone or something) very well • *They really pamper their guests at that hotel.* • *She pampered herself with a day at the spa.* • *a pampered pet*

pam·phlet /'pæmflət/ *n* [C] : a small, thin book with no cover or only a paper cover that has information about a particular subject

¹**pan** /'pæn/ *n* [C] : a usually shallow and open metal container that has a handle and that is used especially for cooking or baking • *The rice is in a pan on the stove.* • *a cake/loaf/roasting pan* — **flash in the pan** see ²FLASH

²**pan** *vb* **panned; pan·ning** 1 [T/I] : to move (a movie, video, or television camera) across a scene or along with someone or something that is moving • *The camera panned the stadium.* • *The director/camera panned past the child to the school.* 2 [T] *informal* : to criticize (a book, movie, play, etc.) severely • *The book was panned by the critics.* 3 [T/I] : to wash pieces of earth or stones with water in a special kind of pan in order to find pieces of gold or other metals • *They were panning for gold.* — **pan out** [*phrasal vb*] 1 : to develop or happen • *We'll have to see how things pan out.* 2 : to succeed or turn out well • *Her plans never panned out.*

pan- *prefix* : involving all of a specified group • *Pan-American*

pan·a·cea /ˌpænə'si:jə/ *n* [C] *somewhat formal* : something that will make everything about a situation better • *The new law will be helpful, but it is no panacea.*

pa·nache /pə'næʃ/ *n* [U] : lots of energy and style • *She played the role of hostess with great panache.*

pan·a·ma hat *or* **Pan·a·ma hat** /'pænə-ˌmɑ:-/ *n* [C] : a light hat with a broad brim that is made from straw — called also *panama*

Pan-Amer·i·can /ˌpænə'merıkən/ *adj* : of, relating to, or involving the countries of North and South America • *the Pan-American highway*

pan·cake /'pænˌkeık/ *n* [C] : a thin, flat, round cake that is made by cooking batter on both sides in a frying pan or on a hot surface (called a griddle) • *We had blueberry pancakes for breakfast.* — **(as) flat as a pancake** see ¹FLAT

pan·cre·as /'pæŋkrijəs/ *n* [C] : a large gland of the body that is near the stomach and that produces insulin and other substances that help the body digest food — **pan·cre·at·ic** /ˌpæŋkri'ætık/ *adj* • *pancreatic cancer/tissue*

pan·da /'pændə/ *n* [C] : a large animal with black-and-white fur that looks like a bear, lives in China, and eats mostly bamboo shoots — called also *giant panda, panda bear*

pan·dem·ic /pæn'dɛmık/ *n* [C] *medical* : an occurrence in which a disease spreads very quickly and affects a large number of people over a wide area or throughout the world • *a flu pandemic*

pan·de·mo·ni·um /ˌpændə'mounijəm/ *n*

[U] : a situation in which a crowd of people act in a wild, uncontrolled, or violent way because they are afraid, excited, or confused • *Pandemonium erupted in the courtroom when the verdict was announced.*

pan·der /'pændə/ *vb* [I] *disapproving* : to do or provide what someone wants or demands even though it is not proper, good, or reasonable • *politicians pandering to voters*

Pan·do·ra's box /pæn'dorəz-/ *n* [*singular*] : something that will lead to many problems • *Her parents are afraid of opening a Pandora's box* [=causing many worries and problems] *if they buy her a car.*

pane /'peın/ *n* [C] : a sheet of glass in a window or door • *a pane of glass*

¹**pan·el** /'pænl/ *n* [C] 1 a : a group of people who answer questions, give advice or opinions about something, or take part in a discussion for an audience • *The university is hosting a panel on free speech.* • *a panel discussion on education* b : a group of people with special knowledge, skill, or experience who give advice or make decisions • *a panel of judges* 2 a : one of the flat pieces that make up a door, wall, or ceiling b : a piece of cloth that makes up part of something sewn together c : a piece of metal or plastic that forms part of the outside surface of a vehicle • *the side panels of a car* 3 : a flat surface where the controls of a vehicle, machine, etc., are located • *the control panel* • *the phone's display panel* • *an airplane's instrument panel*

²**panel** *vb* **-eled** *or Brit* **-elled;** *US* **-el·ing** *or Brit* **-el·ling** [T] : to cover (a wall, ceiling, etc.) with flat pieces of wood, glass, etc. • *The walls are paneled in oak.* • *a paneled room*

paneling (*US*) *or Brit* **panelling** *n* [U] : square or rectangular pieces of wood that are joined together to cover a wall or ceiling • *The dining room had dark paneling.*

pan·el·ist /'pænlıst/ *n* [C] : a person who is a member of a panel of people who answer questions, give advice or opinions, etc.

panel truck *n* [C] *US* : a small truck or van with a fully enclosed body that is often used to deliver goods

pang /'pæŋ/ *n* [C] : a sudden, strong feeling of physical or emotional pain • *hunger pangs* • *a pang of guilt*

¹**pan·han·dle** /'pænˌhændl/ *n* [C] *US* : a part of a land area (such as a state) that is narrow and sticks out from a larger area • *the panhandle of Florida = the Florida Panhandle*

²**panhandle** *vb* **-han·dled; -han·dling** [I] *chiefly US* : to ask strangers for money in a public place (such as on a sidewalk) • *There is a law against panhandling in the subway.* — **pan·han·dler** /'pænˌhændlə/ *n* [C]

¹**pan·ic** /'pænık/ *n* 1 [U, *singular*] : a state or feeling of extreme fear that makes someone unable to act or think normally. • *He was in a (state of) panic when he realized how late he was.* • *The*

villagers fled in panic from the approaching army. ▪ *She has* **panic attacks** *whenever she has to speak in public.* **2** [C] : a situation that causes many people to become afraid and to rush to do something ▪ *The recent panic over/about unsafe drinking water resulted in a shortage of bottled water in the stores.* — **push/hit/ press the panic button** : to become extremely afraid or nervous when something bad happens or might happen ▪ *Medical officials say there is no need to push the panic button over two isolated cases of the disease.* — **pan·icky** /ˈpænɪki/ *adj*

²**panic** *vb* **-icked; -ick·ing 1** [*I*] : to be affected by extreme fear or panic ▪ *If something goes wrong, don't panic.* **2** [*T*] : to cause (a person or animal) to feel extreme fear ▪ *The deer, panicked by the headlights, ran in front of the car.*

pan·ic–strick·en /ˈpænɪkˌstrɪkən/ *adj* : too frightened to think or act normally ▪ *She looked panic-stricken.*

pan·o·ply /ˈpænəpli/ *n, pl* **-plies** [C] *formal* : a group or collection that is impressive because it is so big or because it includes so many different kinds of people or things ▪ *the full panoply of American literature*

pan·o·rama /ˌpænəˈræmə, Brit ˌpænəˈrɑːmə/ *n* [C] **1** : a full and wide view of something ▪ *a beautiful panorama* **2 a** : a way of showing or telling something that includes a lot of information and covers many topics ▪ *The book presents a panorama of immigration in America.* **b** : a group that includes many different people or things ▪ *a panorama of cultures* — **pan·o·ram·ic** /ˌpænəˈræmɪk/ *adj* ▪ *a panoramic photograph/view*

pan·sy /ˈpænzi/ *n, pl* **-sies** [C] : a small plant that is grown in gardens and has colorful flowers with five petals; *also* : its flower

pant /ˈpænt/ *vb* **1 a** [*I*] : to breathe hard and quickly ▪ *Dogs pant when they are hot.* ▪ *The patient was panting for breath.* [=breathing heavily] **b** [*T*] : to say (something) while you are breathing quickly and heavily ▪ *"I've run far enough," he panted.* **2** [*I*] *informal* : to wish for or want something very eagerly ▪ *The crowd was panting to hear him speak.*

pan·ta·loons /ˌpæntəˈluːnz/ *n* [*plural*] *old-fashioned* : pants with wide legs that become narrow at the bottom

pan·the·on /ˈpænθiˌɑːn/ *n* [C] **1** : the gods of a particular country or group of people ▪ *the Greek and Roman pantheons* **2** *somewhat formal* : a group of people who are famous or important ▪ *He occupies a place in the pantheon of great American writers.*

pan·ther /ˈpænθɚ/ *n, pl* **pan·thers** *also* **panther** [C] **1** : a large, black wildcat **2** *US* : COUGAR

pant·ies /ˈpæntiz/ *n* [*plural*] *chiefly US* : a piece of girl's or woman's underwear that covers the area between the waist and the top of the legs — called also (*Brit*) **knickers**

¹**pan·to·mime** /ˈpæntəˌmaɪm/ *n* **1 a** [U]

: a way of expressing information or telling a story without words by using body movements and facial expressions **b** [*C/U*] : a performance in which a story is told without words by using body movements and facial expressions ▪ *a ballet that is part dance and part pantomime* **2** [C] *Brit* : a play for children performed during the Christmas season that is based on a fairy tale and includes singing and dancing

²**pantomime** *vb* **-mimed; -mim·ing** [*T*] : to make the movements of someone who is doing something without actually doing it : MIME ▪ *He pantomimed someone talking on the phone.*

pan·try /ˈpæntri/ *n, pl* **-tries** [C] : a small room in a house in which food is stored

pants /ˈpænts/ *n* [*plural*] **1** *chiefly US* : a piece of clothing that covers your body from the waist to the ankle and has a separate part for each leg ▪ *a pair of pants* [=*trousers*] ▪ *a pants leg* — sometimes used in the singular form **pant** especially before another noun and in clothing catalogs ▪ *a pant leg* **2** *Brit* : UNDERPANTS **1** — **by the seat of your pants** see ¹SEAT — **keep your pants on** *US, informal* — used to tell someone to be patient ▪ *"Aren't you ready yet?" "Keep your pants on! I'll be ready in a minute."* — **the pants off** *informal* — used for emphasis after words like *charm, scare, frighten, bore,* and *beat* ▪ *He can charm the pants off anybody.* [=he is very charming] — **wear the pants** see ¹WEAR — **with your pants down** *US, informal* : in an embarrassing or unprepared position ▪ *We prepared for the meeting thoroughly because we didn't want to be caught with our pants down.*

pant·suit /ˈpæntˌsuːt/ *n* [C] *US* : a woman's suit consisting of a jacket and pants that are made of the same material

panty·hose /ˈpæntiˌhoʊz/ *n* [*plural*] *US* : clothing for women made of thin material that fits closely over the feet and legs and goes up to the waist ▪ *a pair of pantyhose* — called also **nylons**, (*Brit*) **tights**

pap /ˈpæp/ *n* [U] *informal* : books, television programs, etc., that are worthless or dull ▪ *That show is better than most of the pap on TV.*

pa·pa *also US* **pop·pa** /ˈpɑːpə/ *n* [C] *informal + somewhat old-fashioned* : a person's father

pa·pa·cy /ˈpeɪpəsi/ *n, pl* **-cies 1 the papacy** : the office or position of the pope **2** [C] : the time when a particular pope is in power ▪ *during the papacy of John Paul II*

pa·pal /ˈpeɪpəl/ *adj, always before a noun* : of or relating to the pope or the government of the Roman Catholic Church ▪ *a papal decree/visit* ▪ *papal authority*

pa·pa·raz·zo /ˌpɑːpəˈrɑːtsoʊ, Brit ˌpæpəˈrætsoʊ/ *n, pl* **pa·pa·raz·zi** /ˌpɑːpəˈrɑːtsi, Brit ˌpæpəˈrætsi/ [C] : a photographer who follows famous people in order to take their pictures and then sells the pictures to newspapers or magazines — usually plural ▪ *a movie star surrounded by a swarm of paparazzi*

pa·pa·ya /pə'pajə/ n [C/U] : a yellowish-green fruit with black seeds that grows on a tropical tree

¹pa·per /'peɪpər/ n 1 [U] : the material that is used in the form of thin sheets for writing or printing on, wrapping things, etc. ▪ *a pad/piece/scrap/sheet of paper* ▪ *a paper bag/plate* 2 **a** [C] : a sheet of paper with information written or printed on it — usually plural ▪ *A pile of papers blew off the desk.* **b** [plural] : official documents that give information about something or that are used as proof of something ▪ *The border guards asked to see my papers.* ▪ *divorce/legal papers* 3 [C] **a** : a piece of writing usually on an academic or official subject ▪ *a scientific paper* **b** US : a piece of writing that is done for a course at a school ▪ *The teacher was busy grading papers.* **c** Brit : an exam or test in which students write answers to written questions 4 [C] : NEWSPAPER ▪ *a news story in the local paper* ▪ *the morning paper* ▪ *It was reported in the papers.* — **on paper** 1 : in a written form ▪ *He finally put his ideas on paper.* [=he finally wrote down his ideas] 2 — used to say that something seems to be true or likely when you read or hear what is known about it but that the real situation may be different ▪ *The other team looks good on paper.* — **push paper(s)** informal : to do boring or unimportant work in an office ▪ *She ended up pushing papers in a government job.*

²paper vb [T] : to cover (something, such as a wall) with paper ▪ *We papered the bedroom (walls).* — **paper over** [phrasal vb] **paper (something) over** or **paper over (something)** : to hide (something bad, such as differences or problems) ▪ *They papered over their disagreements.*

pa·per·back /'peɪpər,bæk/ n [C/U] : a book that has a thick paper cover ▪ *a new paperback* ▪ *The book is sold only in paperback.* — **paperback** adj ▪ *a paperback novel/edition*

pa·per·boy /'peɪpər,bɔɪ/ n [C] : a boy who delivers newspapers to people's houses

paper clip n [C] : a piece of wire bent into flat loops that is used to hold sheets of paper together

pa·per·girl /'peɪpər,gəl/ n [C] : a girl who delivers newspapers to people's houses

paper money n [U] : money that is made of paper

pa·per–thin /'peɪpər,θɪn/ adj : very thin ▪ *The walls are paper-thin.*

paper tiger n [C] : someone or something that appears powerful or dangerous but is not

paper towel n [C/U] : a sheet of soft and thick paper that can soak up liquid and that is used for drying your hands, cleaning up spills, etc.

paper trail n [C] chiefly US : documents (such as financial records or memos) that make it possible for someone at a later time to know what was done, discussed, etc. ▪ *They were careful not to leave a paper trail.*

pa·per·weight /'peɪpər,weɪt/ n [C] : a small, heavy object that is used to hold

down loose papers on a surface

pa·per·work /'peɪpər,wək/ n [U] 1 : routine work that involves writing letters, reports, etc. ▪ *He spent most of the morning doing (his) paperwork.* 2 : the official documents that are needed for something to happen or be done ▪ *She failed to file the paperwork on time.*

pa·pery /'peɪpəri/ adj : very thin or dry like paper ▪ *a berry with papery skin*

pa·pier–mâ·ché /ˌpeɪpəmə'ʃeɪ, Brit ˌpæpjeɪ'mæˌʃeɪ/ n [U] : a material that is made of paper mixed with water, glue, and other substances and that hardens as it dries ▪ *a large papier-mâché sculpture*

pa·pri·ka /pə'priːkə/ n [U] : a red powder that is made from sweet peppers and used as a spice for food

Pap smear /'pæp'smɪə/ n [C] US, medical : a test for the early detection of cancer of the uterus and cervix

pa·py·rus /pə'paɪrəs/ n, pl **pa·py·ri** /pə'paɪri/ or **pa·py·rus·es** 1 [U] : a tall plant that is like grass and that grows in marshes especially in Egypt 2 **a** [U] : paper made from papyrus that was used in ancient times ▪ *a roll/scroll of papyrus* **b** [C] : a piece of paper made from papyrus that has writing on it

par /'paə/ n 1 [C/U] : the number of strokes a good golfer is expected to take to finish a golf hole or course ▪ *She made/scored (a) par on the first hole.* ▪ *three strokes under/over par* 2 [U] business : the value of a stock or bond that is printed on the paper of the stock or bond itself or that is decided upon when the stock or bond is issued ▪ *That stock is trading (at) 16 percent above/below par.* — called also *par value* — **above par** : better than normal or expected ▪ *The performance was above par.* — **below par** also **under par** : worse than expected ▪ *I'm feeling a little below par.* — **on (a) par with** : at the same level or standard as (someone or something else) ▪ *His new book is on par with his earlier one.* — **par for the course** disapproving : normal or typical ▪ *His son's bad behavior is just par for the course.* — **up to par** : good enough ▪ *His work is not up to par.*

par·a·ble /'perəbəl/ n [C] : a short story that teaches a moral or spiritual lesson ▪ *the parable of the Good Samaritan*

pa·rab·o·la /pə'ræbələ/ n [C] technical : a curve that is shaped like the path of something that is thrown forward and high in the air and falls back to the ground — **par·a·bol·ic** /ˌperə'bɑːlɪk/ adj ▪ *a parabolic curve*

¹para·chute /'perə,ʃuːt/ n [C] : a piece of equipment usually made of cloth that is fastened to people or things and that allows them to fall slowly and land safely after they have jumped or been dropped from an aircraft

²parachute vb **-chut·ed; -chut·ing** 1 [I] : to jump from an aircraft using a parachute ▪ *The troops parachuted into enemy territory.* 2 [T] : to drop (someone or something) from an aircraft using a parachute ▪ *New troops were parachuted into enemy territory.* — **para·chut·ist** /'perə,ʃuːtɪst/ n [C]

¹pa·rade /pə'reɪd/ n [C] **1** : a public celebration of a special day or event that usually includes many people and groups moving down a street by marching or riding in cars or on special vehicles (called floats) • *the annual Thanksgiving Day parade* • *The city threw/had a parade for the winning team.* **2** : a military ceremony in which soldiers march or stand in lines so that they can be examined by officers or other important people **3** : a long series of people or things that come one after the other • *We had a parade of visitors* [=many visitors] *this morning.* **4** *Brit* : a street with a row of small shops — **on parade 1** : shown or displayed especially in a way that attracts attention or notice • *Her engagement ring was on parade for everyone to see.* **2** : marching or standing in a military parade • *a military honor guard on parade* — **rain on someone's parade** see ²RAIN

²parade vb **-rad·ed; -rad·ing 1** [I] : to walk or march together in public especially as a way of celebrating or protesting something • *Protesters parade in front of City Hall.* **2** [I] : to walk in a way that attracts attention • *She paraded around on the beach in her bikini.* **3** [T] : to force (someone) to walk or march in public • *The victors paraded the prisoners through the streets.* **4** [T/I] *of soldiers* : to march in lines in order to be examined by officers or other important people • *The soldiers (were) paraded past the generals.* **5** [T] : to show or present (someone or something) proudly or in a way that attracts attention • *Her personal problems were paraded in print for everyone to see.* **6** [T/I] *disapproving* : to be falsely presented *as* something good • *The book is just propaganda parading as literature.* • *lies being paraded as the truth*

par·a·digm /'perə,daɪm/ n [C] *formal* **1** : a model or pattern for something that may be copied • *Her recent book provides us with a new paradigm for modern biography.* **2** : a theory or a group of ideas about how something should be done, made, or thought about • *the Freudian paradigm of psychoanalysis* — **par·a·dig·mat·ic** /,perədɪg'mætɪk/ adj

paradigm shift n [C] *formal* : an important change that happens when the usual way of thinking about or doing something is replaced by a new and different way • *Their discovery brought about a paradigm shift in our understanding of evolution.*

par·a·dise /'perə,daɪs/ n **1 a** [C] : a very beautiful, pleasant, or peaceful place that seems to be perfect • *tropical paradises* **b** [*singular*] : a place that is perfect for a particular activity or for a person who enjoys that activity • *a birdwatcher's paradise* **c** [U] : a state of complete happiness • *When I'm with you, I'm in paradise.* [=I'm very happy] **2** *or* **Paradise** [*singular*] **a** : HEAVEN 1 **b** : the place where Adam and Eve first lived according to the Bible

par·a·dox /'perə,dɑːks/ n [C] **1 a** : something (such as a situation) that is

made up of two opposite things and that seems impossible but is actually true or possible • *It is a paradox that computers need maintenance so often since they are meant to save people time.* **b** : someone who does two things that seem to be opposite to each other or who has qualities that are opposite • *As an actor, he's a paradox—he loves being in the public eye but also deeply values his privacy.* **2** : a statement that seems to say two opposite things but that may be true — **par·a·dox·i·cal** /,perə'dɑːksɪkəl/ adj — **par·a·dox·i·cal·ly** /,perə'dɑːksɪkli/ adv

par·af·fin /'perəfən/ n [U] **1** : a soft, waxy substance that is usually made from petroleum or coal and is used in candles and other products — called also *paraffin wax* **2** *Brit* : KEROSENE

par·a·gon /'perə,gɑːn, Brit 'pærəgən/ n [C] *formal* : a person or thing that is perfect or excellent in some way and should be considered a model or example to be copied • *The company is a paragon of modern manufacturing techniques.* • *a paragon of virtue* [=a very virtuous person]

para·graph /'perə,græf, Brit 'pærə,grɑːf/ n [C] : a part of a piece of writing that usually deals with one subject, that begins on a new line, and that is made up of one or more sentences

par·a·keet /'perə,kiːt/ n [C] : a small, brightly colored tropical bird that has a long tail and that is often kept as a pet

para·le·gal /'perə,liːgəl/ n [C] *US* : a person who is trained to help a lawyer by doing research, office work, etc. — **para·le·gal** /,perə'liːgəl/ adj

¹par·al·lel /'perə,lɛl/ adj **1** — used to describe lines, paths, etc., that are the same distance apart along their whole length and do not touch at any point • *parallel lines/tracks* • *The lines are parallel to each other.* **2** : very similar and often happening at the same time • *the parallel careers of the two movie stars* — **parallel** adv

²parallel n **1 a** [C] : a way in which things are similar • *There are many parallels between them.* • *The essay draws parallels between the lives of the two presidents.* [=describes ways in which the lives of the two presidents were similar] **b** [U] : something that is equal or similar — usually used in negative statements • *a masterpiece that has no parallel* = *a masterpiece without parallel* [=better than all others] **2** [C] : any one of the imaginary lines on the surface of the Earth that are parallel to the equator and that are shown as lines on maps — **in parallel (with)** : at the same time and in a way that is related or connected • *Prices are rising in parallel with increasing fuel costs.*

³parallel vb [T] **1** : to be similar or equal to (something) • *Their test results parallel our own.* **2** : to happen at the same time as (something) and in a way that is related or connected • *Rising prices parallel increasing fuel costs.* **3** : to go or extend in the same direction as (something) • *The highway parallels the river.*

parallel bars n [plural] sports : a pair of long bars on posts that are parallel to each other and are used in gymnastics

par·al·lel·o·gram /ˌperəˈlɛləˌgræm/ n [C] geometry : a four-sided shape made up of two pairs of straight parallel lines that are equal in length

pa·ral·y·sis /pəˈræləsəs/ n [U, singular] **1** medical : a condition in which you are unable to move or feel all or part of your body • partial/temporary paralysis • (a) paralysis of the legs **2** formal : a state of being unable to function, act, or move • a state of political paralysis/a paralysis of fear

par·a·lyt·ic /ˌperəˈlɪtɪk/ adj, always before a noun, medical : affected with or causing paralysis • a paralytic patient/drug/stroke/disease — **paralytic** n [C] • treatment for paralytics [=paralyzed people]

par·a·lyze (US) or Brit **par·a·lyse** /ˈperəˌlaɪz/ vb -**lyzed**; -**lyz·ing** [T] **1** : to make (a person or animal) unable to move or feel all or part of the body • The accident paralyzed him from the neck down. **2** : to make (someone or something) unable to function, act, or move • The company was paralyzed by debt. — **paralyzed** adj • The accident left him paralyzed. — **paralyzing** adj • a paralyzing fear

para·med·ic /perəˈmɛdɪk/ n [C] : a person whose job is to provide emergency medical care to sick or injured people who are being taken to a hospital

pa·ram·e·ter /pəˈræmətər/ n [C] : a rule or limit that controls what something is or how something should be done • We need to set/define the parameters of the project.

para·mil·i·tary /ˌperəˈmɪləˌteri, Brit ˌpærəˈmɪlətri/ adj, always before a noun : of or relating to a group that is not an official army but that operates and is organized like an army • paramilitary groups/militias — **paramilitary** n, pl -**tar·ies** [C] • a group of paramilitaries

par·a·mount /ˈperəˌmaʊnt/ adj : of highest rank or importance • Safety is of paramount importance. = Safety is paramount.

para·noia /ˌperəˈnɔjə/ n [U] **1** : a serious mental illness that causes you to falsely believe that other people are trying to harm you **2** : an unreasonable feeling that people are trying to harm you, do not like you, etc. • I had to admit that my fears were just paranoia.

para·noid /ˈperəˌnɔɪd/ adj **1** medical : of, relating to, or suffering from a mental illness that causes you to falsely believe that people are trying to harm you • paranoid behavior/patients **2** : having or showing an unreasonable feeling that people are trying to harm you, do not like you, etc. • I was just being paranoid. She's a little paranoid about her job. — **paranoid** n [C] • a new treatment for paranoids

para·nor·mal /ˌperəˈnɔərməl/ adj : very strange and not able to be explained by what scientists know about nature and the world • paranormal phenomena/powers

par·a·pet /ˈperəpət/ n [C] : a low wall at the edge of a platform, roof, or bridge

par·a·pher·na·lia /ˌperəfəˈneɪljə/ n [U] : objects of a particular kind • Drug paraphernalia was found in his car.

para·phrase /ˈperəˌfreɪz/ vb -**phrased**; -**phras·ing** [T/I] : to say (something that someone else has said or written) using different words • He paraphrased the quote. — **paraphrase** n [C] • This is just a paraphrase of what he said, not an exact quote.

para·ple·gic /ˌperəˈpliːdʒɪk/ n [C] : a person who is permanently unable to move or feel the legs or lower half of the body because of injury or illness — **para·ple·gia** /ˌperəˈpliːdʒijə/ n [U] — **paraplegic** adj, always before a noun • a paraplegic war veteran

para·pro·fes·sion·al /ˌperəprəˈfɛʃənl/ n [C] US : a person whose job is to help a professional person (such as a teacher)

para·psy·chol·o·gy /ˌperəˌsaɪˈkɑːlədʒi/ n [U] : the scientific study of events that cannot be explained by what scientists know about nature and the world

par·a·site /ˈperəˌsaɪt/ n [C] **1** : an animal or plant that lives in or on another animal or plant and gets food or protection from it **2** disapproving : a person or thing that takes something from someone or something else and does not do anything to earn it or deserve it • She's a parasite who only stays with him for the money. — **par·a·sit·ic** /ˌperəˈsɪtɪk/ adj : parasitic plants/insects • a parasitic disease [=a disease caused by a parasite]

para·sol /ˈperəˌsɑːl/ n [C] : a light umbrella that you use to protect yourself from the sun

para·troop·er /ˈperəˌtruːpər/ n [C] : a member of a group of soldiers who are trained to jump out of airplanes using a parachute

para·troops /ˈperəˌtruːps/ n [plural] : soldiers who are trained to jump out of airplanes using a parachute

par·boil /ˈpɑːrˌbɔjəl/ vb [T] : to boil (a piece of food) for a short time often before cooking it fully in another way • Parboil the potatoes before you roast them.

¹**par·cel** /ˈpɑːrsəl/ n [C] **1** : a section or area of land • a parcel of real estate **2** : a box or large envelope that is usually given, sent, or delivered to a person • The parcel [=(chiefly US) package] was shipped today. — **part and parcel** of see ¹PART

²**parcel** vb, US -**celed** or Brit -**celled**; US -**cel·ing** or Brit -**cel·ling** — **parcel off** [phrasal vb] **parcel (something) off** or **parcel off (something)** : to divide (something, such as land) into separate, smaller parts especially in order to sell it • The property was parceled off and sold. — **parcel out** [phrasal vb] **parcel (something) out** or **parcel out (something)** : to divide or share (something) among different people, groups, etc. • The money was parceled out to local charities.

parcel post n [U] : a service that people in the U.S. can use to mail packages

parch /ˈpɑːrtʃ/ vb [T] formal : to make

(something) very dry ▪ *The desert sun parched the land.*

parched /'pɑɚʃt/ *adj* **1** : very dry ▪ *parched land* **2** *somewhat informal* : very thirsty ▪ *I'm parched.*

parch·ment /'pɑɚʃmənt/ *n* **1 a** [U] : paper made from the skin of a sheep or goat **b** [C] : a document written on parchment ▪ *a parchment dating back to ancient times* **2** [U] : strong and thick paper; *especially*, *chiefly US* : strong, tough paper that is used by cooks

¹**par·don** /'pɑɚdn/ *vb* [T] **1** : to officially say that someone who is guilty of a crime will be allowed to go free and will not be punished ▪ *pardon a criminal* **2** : to say that someone should not be blamed for thinking, doing, or saying something ▪ *He can/should/could be pardoned for believing them.* **3** : to officially say that a person, country, etc., does not have to pay (a debt) ▪ *His debt was pardoned.* [=forgiven] **4** — used to be polite in asking questions or saying things that could be considered rude ▪ *Pardon my saying so, but you look tired today.* ▪ *Pardon me for asking, but how old are you?* — **pardon me 1** — used as a polite way of starting to say something when you are interrupting someone, trying to get someone's attention, or disagreeing with someone ▪ *Pardon me, but can I speak to you privately for a moment?* ▪ *Pardon me, (but) you dropped this envelope.* **2** *also* **pardon** — used as a polite apology for a minor fault or offense (such as laughing, coughing, or bumping into someone) ▪ *Oh, pardon me. I didn't see you standing there.* **3** *also* **pardon** — used as a polite way of asking someone to repeat something spoken ▪ *Pardon me? I didn't hear you.*

²**pardon** *n* [C] **1** : an act of officially saying that someone who was judged to be guilty of a crime will be allowed to go free and will not be punished ▪ *The governor granted him a pardon.* **2** *formal* : forgiveness for something ▪ *He asked/ begged my pardon for taking so much of my time.* — see also **beg your pardon** at BEG

par·don·able /'pɑɚdnəbəl/ *adj* : able to be forgiven ▪ *a pardonable mistake/error*

pare /'peɚ/ *vb* **pared; par·ing** [T] **1** : to carefully cut off the outside or the ends of (something) ▪ *pare an apple* **2** : to make (something) smaller ▪ *The company has pared (down) expenses.* ▪ *The budget has been pared to the bone.* [=reduced as much as possible]

par·ent /'perənt/ *n* [C] **1 a** : a person who is a father or mother : a person who has a child ▪ *My parents live in New York.* ▪ *They recently became parents.* **b** : an animal or plant that produces a young animal or plant ▪ *The parent (bird) brings food to the chicks.* **2 a** : something out of which another thing has developed ▪ *a parent language* **b** : a company or organization that owns and controls a smaller company or organization ▪ *the hospital's corporate parent* ▪ *a parent bank* — **pa·ren·tal** /pə'rɛntl/ *adj* ▪ *parental responsibility/guidance*

par·ent·age /'perəntɪʤ/ *n* [U] *formal* : a person's parents — used especially to describe the origins or social status of someone's parents ▪ *a person of noble/ wealthy parentage*

pa·ren·the·sis /pə'rɛnθəsəs/ *n, pl* **-the·ses** /-θəˌsiːz/ [C] : one of a pair of marks ( ) that are used around a word, phrase, sentence, number, etc. — usually plural ▪ *The plant's common name is followed by its Latin name in parentheses.*

par·en·thet·i·cal /ˌperən'θɛtɪkəl/ *adj* : included or added to give information which is not directly related to the main subject that is being discussed ▪ *parenthetical comments/remarks/references* — **par·en·thet·i·cal·ly** /ˌperən'θɛtɪkli/ *adv*

par·ent·hood /'perəntˌhʊd/ *n* [U] : the state of being a mother or a father ▪ *the joys of parenthood*

par·ent·ing /'perəntɪŋ/ *n* [U] : the things that parents do to raise a child ▪ *They share the responsibilities of parenting.* ▪ *parenting skills*

par ex·cel·lence /ˈpɑrˌɛksə'lɑːns, Brit ˌpɑːˈrɛksəˌlɑːns/ *adj, always after a noun, formal* : better than all others ▪ *a chef par excellence*

par·fait /pɑɚ'feɪ/ *n* [C/U] *US* : a cold dessert made usually of layers of ice cream, fruit, and syrup with whipped cream on top

pa·ri·ah /pə'rajə/ *n* [C] : a person who is hated and rejected by other people ▪ *a social pariah*

par·ings /'perɪŋz/ *n* [plural] : thin pieces that have been cut from something ▪ *fingernail/cheese parings*

par·ish /'perɪʃ/ *n* [C] **1 a** : an area that has its own local church and priest or minister **b** : the group of people who go to the church in a particular area **2 a** *US* : an area in Louisiana that is like a county **b** *Brit* : a small area that has its own local government — **parish** *adj, always before a noun* ▪ *a parish priest/minister* ▪ *the parish church*

pa·rish·io·ner /pə'rɪʃənɚ/ *n* [C] : a person who goes to a particular local church ▪ *the parishioners of First Baptist Church*

par·i·ty /'perəti/ *n* [U] *formal* : the state of being equal ▪ *Women have fought for parity with men in the workplace.*

¹**park** /'pɑɚk/ *n* **1** [C] **a** : a piece of public land in or near a city that is kept free of houses and other buildings and can be used for pleasure and exercise ▪ *We went for a walk in the park.* **b** : a large area of public land kept in its natural state to protect plants and animals ▪ *Yellowstone (National) Park* **2** [C] *sports* **a** : a field or stadium where a sport (especially baseball) is played ▪ *a baseball park* **b** *Brit* : a soccer or rugby field **3** [C] : an area that is designed for a specified use ▪ *an office park* [=an area for office buildings] ▪ *a mobile home park* [=an area for people to live in mobile homes] **4** [U] *US* : a condition in which the gears of a vehicle are in a position that prevents the vehicle from moving ▪ *The car is in park.*

²**park** *vb* **1 a** [T/I] : to leave a car, truck, motorcycle, etc., in a particular place ▪ *I*

parked (my car) on the street. ▪ *a parked car* **b** [*I*] *of a car, truck, etc.* : to be left in a particular place by a driver ▪ *The bus parked behind the museum.* **2** [*T*] *informal* **a** : to temporarily leave (something) in a particular place ▪ *Park your bags in the hallway.* **b** : to leave (something) in a particular place for a long time or what seems like a long time ▪ *She parked the money in a savings account.* —
park yourself *informal* : to sit in a particular place especially for a long time ▪ *The kids parked themselves in front of the TV.*

par·ka /ˈpɑɚkə/ *n* [*C*] : a very warm jacket with a hood

park·ing /ˈpɑɚkɪŋ/ *n* [*U*] **1** : the act of leaving a car, truck, motorcycle, etc., in a particular place ▪ *There is no parking in this area.* [=you are not allowed to park in this area] **2** : space in which vehicles can be parked ▪ *They have plenty of free parking.*

parking garage *n* [*C*] *US* : a building in which people usually pay to park their cars, trucks, etc. — called also (*Brit*) **car park**

parking light *n* [*C*] *US* : either one of two small lights that are on the front of a vehicle next to the headlights

parking lot *n* [*C*] *US* : an area outside a building for parking cars, trucks, etc. — called also (*Brit*) **car park**

parking meter *n* [*C*] : a machine near a parking place on the side of a road that you put coins into in order to legally park there

parking ticket *n* [*C*] : a piece of paper that officially tells you that you have parked your car, truck, etc., illegally or for too long and will have to pay a fine

Par·kin·son's disease /ˈpɑɚkənsənz-/ *n* [*U*] : a disease that affects the nervous system and causes people's muscles to become weak and their arms and legs to shake — called also **Parkinson's**

park·land /ˈpɑɚkˌlænd/ *n* [*C/U*] : land with trees, bushes, etc., that is or could be used as a park ▪ *an area of beautiful parkland*

park·way /ˈpɑɚkˌweɪ/ *n* [*C*] *US* : a wide road with trees and grass along the sides and often in the middle

par·lance /ˈpɑɚləns/ *n* [*U*] *formal* : language used by a particular group of people ▪ *military/legal/official parlance*

par·lay /ˈpɑɚˌleɪ, Brit ˈpɑɚli/ *vb* [*T*] *US* : to use or develop (something) to get something else that has greater value — + *into* ▪ *He hopes to parlay his basketball skills into a college scholarship.*

par·lia·ment /ˈpɑɚləmənt/ *n* **1 a** [*C/U*] : the group of people who are responsible for making the laws in some kinds of government **b** *Parliament* [*U*] : a particular parliament; *especially* : the parliament of the United Kingdom that includes the House of Commons and the House of Lords ▪ *a member of Parliament* **2** [*C*] : the period of time during which a parliament is working ▪ *The law was passed in the present parliament.*

par·lia·men·tar·i·an /ˌpɑɚləˌmɛnˈtɛrijən/ *n* [*C*] : a member of a parliament; es-

pecially : a member who knows a lot about the way things are done in a parliament

par·lia·men·ta·ry /ˌpɑɚləˈmɛntri/ *adj* : relating to or including a parliament ▪ *a parliamentary democracy/government/election/candidate*

par·lor (*US*) *or Brit* **par·lour** /ˈpɑɚlɚ/ *n* [*C*] **1** : a store or business that sells a specified kind of food or service ▪ *an ice-cream parlor* ▪ *a pizza parlor* ▪ *a beauty/funeral/tattoo/massage parlor* **2** *old-fashioned* : a room in a house or apartment that is used for conversation or for spending time with guests

parlor game (*US*) *or Brit* **parlour game** *n* [*C*] *somewhat old-fashioned* : a game (such as a board game or card game) that you play inside your home

par·lous /ˈpɑɚləs/ *adj, formal* : full of danger or risk ▪ *a parlous financial situation*

Par·me·san /ˈpɑɚməˌzɑːn, Brit ˌpɑːməˈzæn/ *n* [*U*] : a hard Italian cheese — called also *Parmesan cheese*

pa·ro·chi·al /pəˈroʊkijəl/ *adj* **1** *always before a noun* : of or relating to a church parish and the area around it ▪ *our pastor and other parochial leaders* **2** *formal* + *usually disapproving* : limited to only the things that affect your local area ▪ *his parochial point of view* — **pa·ro·chi·al·ism** /pəˈroʊkijəˌlɪzəm/ *n* [*U*]

parochial school *n* [*C*] *US* : a private school that is run by a church parish

¹**par·o·dy** /ˈpɛrədi/ *n, pl* **-dies** **1** [*C/U*] : a piece of writing, music, etc., that imitates the style of someone or something else in an amusing way ▪ *a political parody* **2** [*C*] *disapproving* : a bad or unfair example of something ▪ *The trial was a parody of justice.* [=was very unfair]

²**parody** *vb* **-dies; -died; -dy·ing** [*T*] : to imitate (someone or something) in an amusing way ▪ *She parodied his poetry.*

pa·role /pəˈroʊl/ *n* [*U*] : permission given to a prisoner to leave prison before the end of a sentence usually as a reward for behaving well ▪ *He was granted/denied parole.* ▪ *She is out on parole.* — **parole** *vb* **-roled; -rol·ing** [*T*] ▪ *He was paroled after three years in prison.*

pa·rol·ee /pəˌroʊˈliː/ *n* [*C*] : a prisoner who is released on parole

par·ox·ysm /ˈpɛrəkˌsɪzəm/ *n* [*C*] **1** : a sudden attack or increase of symptoms of a disease that often occurs again and again ▪ *paroxysms of pain/coughing* **2** *formal* : a sudden strong feeling or expression of emotion that cannot be controlled ▪ *a paroxysm of rage/laughter*

par·quet /ˈpɑɚˌkeɪ/ *n* [*U*] : a surface (such as a floor) made of small pieces of wood that fit together to form a pattern

¹**par·rot** /ˈpɛrət/ *n* [*C*] : a bright-colored tropical bird that has a curved bill and the ability to imitate speech

²**parrot** *vb* [*T*] *disapproving* : to repeat (something, such as words, ideas, etc.) without understanding the meaning ▪ *He was just parroting what the teacher said.*

par·ry /ˈpɛri/ *vb* **-ries; -ried; -ry·ing** **1** [*T/I*] : to defend yourself by turning or pushing aside (a punch, a weapon, etc.) ▪

parry a blow **2** [*T*] : to avoid giving a direct answer to (a question) by being skillful or clever • *She cleverly parried the reporters' questions.* — **parry** *n, pl* **-ries** [*C*]

parse /ˈpɑɚs, *Brit* ˈpɑːz/ *vb* **parsed;** **pars·ing** [*T*] **1** : to divide (a sentence) into grammatical parts and identify the parts and their relations to each other **2** : to study (something) by looking at its parts closely • *Economists parsed the census data.*

par·si·mo·ny /ˈpɑɚsəˌmouni/ *n* [*U*] *formal* : the quality of being very unwilling to spend money • *The charity was surprised by the parsimony* [=stinginess] *of some larger corporations.* — **par·si·mo·ni·ous** /ˌpɑɚsəˈmounijəs/ *adj*

pars·ley /ˈpɑɚsli/ *n* [*U*] : a plant with small green leaves that are used to season or decorate food

pars·nip /ˈpɑɚsnəp/ *n* [*C/U*] : a vegetable that is the long white root of a plant related to the carrot

par·son /ˈpɑɚsn/ *n* [*C*] *old-fashioned* **1** : a minister who is in charge of a parish **2** : a member of the clergy and especially a Protestant pastor

par·son·age /ˈpɑɚsənɪdʒ/ *n* [*C*] : the house in which a parson lives

¹**part** /ˈpɑɚt/ *n* **1** [*C*] **a** : one of the pieces, sections, qualities, etc., that make or form something • *This is the best part of the movie.* • *He's from the western part of the state.* • *Babies spend a good part of* [=a large amount of] *the day sleeping.* **b** : one of the pieces that are put together to form a machine • *The mechanic had to order the part from the manufacturer.* • *an auto parts warehouse* **c** : one of the pieces or areas of the body of a plant or animal • *body parts* **2** [*U*] : some but not all of something — + *of* • *We spent part of the day at the beach.* • *That's only part of the story.* **3** [*C/U*] : a person who is a member of a group or who is included in an activity • *He's an important part of the team.* • *She's like part of the family.* **4** [*C*] : the character played by an actor in a play, movie, etc. • *He got/landed the part of Romeo in his high school play.* **5** [*C*] : an influence in producing a result or causing something • *My father's part in my upbringing was minimal.* • *Did alcohol* **play a part in** *the car accident? =* **Did** *alcohol* **have a part in** *causing the accident?* [=was alcohol involved in the accident?] • *She* **takes an active part in** *running her family's farm.* **6** [*plural*] *somewhat old-fashioned* : a general area with no exact limits or boundaries • *She's not from* **around these parts.** [=not from around here] **7** [*C*] *US* : the line where a person's hair is separated and combed to opposite sides of the head • *a part down the middle of her head* **8** [*C*] : an amount that is equal to another amount • *Mix one part sugar with two parts flour.* — **do your part** : to do what you are responsible for doing or are able to do • *I've done my part, and now it's time for him to do his.* — **for someone's part** : in someone's opinion • *She doesn't trust him, but for my part, I think he's a nice guy.* — **for**

the most part see ¹MOST — **in good/ great/large part** : not entirely but mostly • *The success of our company depends, in good part, on the condition of the economy.* — **in no small part** see SMALL — **in part** : partially or partly • *The project failed in part because of a lack of funds.* — **of parts** : having many talents or skills • *a man/woman of (many) parts* — **on someone's part** *or* **on the part of someone** : by or from someone • *It took a lot of hard work on everyone's part to finish the project on time.* — **part and parcel of** : a basic and necessary part of (something) • *Stress was part and parcel of the job.* — **take part** : to be involved in something • *They refused to take part in the discussion.* • *He swore that he* **took no part** [=was not involved] *in those activities.* — **the best/better/greater part of something** : most of something • *We waited for the better part of an hour.* — **want no part of/in something** : to refuse to be involved in something • *I want no part of this scheme.*

²**part** *vb* **1** [*T/I*] : to separate into two or more parts that move away from each other • *The rain stopped and the clouds parted.* • *Her lips were parted.* **2** [*T*] : to separate (the hair on a person's head) into two parts on each side of a line by using a comb • *She parts her hair on the side.* **3** *formal* **a** [*I*] : to leave each other • *The two lovers parted at dawn.* : to go or move away from someone • *She couldn't bear the thought of parting from her family.* **b** [*T*] : to cause (someone) to be separated from someone • *She couldn't bear to be parted from her family.* **4** [*I*] *somewhat formal* : to end a relationship • *We parted on friendly terms.* — **part company** *formal* **1** : to end a relationship • *The football team and its coach have parted company.* **2** : to leave each other • *Much has happened since we parted company.* **3** : to disagree with someone about something • *The president and I part company on some important issues.* — **part ways** *chiefly US* **1** : to end a relationship • *The band parted ways after releasing their third album.* **2** : to leave each other • *We said our goodbyes and parted ways.* **3** : to disagree with someone about something • *We part ways on that issue.* — **part with** [*phrasal vb*] : to give up possession or control of (something) • *He hated to part with that old car.*

³**part** *adv* : somewhat but not completely • *She's part French and part Italian.* [=some of her relatives or ancestors are from France and some are from Italy]

⁴**part** *adj, always before a noun* : not complete or total • *She's part owner of the restaurant.* [=she and other people own the restaurant as partners]

par·take /pɑɚˈteɪk/ *vb* **-took** /-ˈtʊk/; **-tak·en** /-ˈteɪkən/; **-tak·ing** [*I*] *formal* **1** : to have a share or part of something along with others • *There was food available, but he chose not to partake.* = *He chose not to* **partake of** *the food.* **2** : to join with others in doing something • *Let us all* **partake in** *this celebration.* — **par·tak·er** *n* [*C*]

par·tial /ˈpɑɚʃəl/ adj **1** : not complete or total • *partial shade* • *The play was only a partial success.* • *a partial eclipse* **2** : tending to treat one person, group, or thing better than another • *A referee must not be partial toward either team.* — **partial to** : liking something or someone very much and usually more than other things or people • *I'm not partial to red wine.* — **par·tial·i·ty** /ˌpɑɚʃiˈæləti/ n [U, singular] • *Judges must not show partiality during the competition.* • *He has a partiality to modern art.* [=he likes modern art]

par·tial·ly /ˈpɑɚʃəli/ adv : somewhat but not completely • PARTLY • *I'm partially responsible for what happened.*

par·tic·i·pant /pɑɚˈtɪsəpənt/ n [C] : a person who is involved in an activity or event • *They were active participants in the project.*

par·tic·i·pate /pɑɚˈtɪsəˌpeɪt/ vb **-pat·ed; -pat·ing** [I] : to be involved with others in doing something • *He never participated in sports in high school.* — **par·tic·i·pa·tion** /pɑɚˌtɪsəˈpeɪʃən/ n [U] • *He is known for his active participation in community affairs.* • *the participation of women in politics*

par·tic·i·pa·to·ry /pɑɚˈtɪsəpəˌtori, Brit pɑˌtɪsəˈpeɪtri/ adj, formal : providing the opportunity for people to be involved in deciding how something is done • *participatory democracy/management*

par·ti·ci·ple /ˈpɑɚtəˌsɪpəl/ n [C] grammar : a form of a verb that is used to indicate a past or present action and that can also be used like an adjective • *In the phrases "the finishing touches" and "the finished product," "finishing" and "finished" are participles formed from the verb "finish."* — see also PAST PARTICIPLE, PRESENT PARTICIPLE — **par·ti·cip·i·al** /ˌpɑɚtəˈsɪpijəl/ adj • *a participial phrase*

par·ti·cle /ˈpɑɚtɪkəl/ n [C] **1 a** : a very small piece of something • *food particles* **b** : a very small amount of something • *There is not a particle of truth in what he said.* **2** physics : any one of the very small parts of matter (such as a molecule, atom, or electron) • *subatomic particles* **3** grammar : an adverb or preposition that when combined with a verb creates a phrasal verb • *The phrasal verb "look up" consists of the verb "look" and the adverbial particle "up."*

¹par·tic·u·lar /pɚˈtɪkjələɚ/ adj **1** — used to indicate that one specific person or thing is being referred to and no others • *a/one particular brand/kind/city/car* • *He called for no particular reason.* • *Are you looking for anything particular?* [=(more commonly) in particular] **2** always before a noun : special or more than usual • *Pay particular attention to the poet's choice of words.* **3** : having very definite opinions about what is good or acceptable • *She's very particular about her clothes.*

²particular n [C] : a specific detail or piece of information • *Just give us a brief report; you can tell us about the particulars later.* — **in particular 1** : special or unusual • *"What are you doing?" "Nothing in particular."* • *Are you looking for any-*

thing in particular? [=specific] • *I made the cookies for no one in particular.* [=for no particular person] **2** : PARTICULARLY — used to indicate someone or something that deserves special mention • *The whole family, but Mom in particular, loves to ski.*

par·tic·u·lar·i·ty /pɚˌtɪkjəˈlerəti/ n, pl **-ties** formal **1** [C] : a small detail • *The actors studied all of the particularities of the script.* **2** [C/U] : a quality or feature that makes a person or thing different from others • *the special particularities of the South* • *the particularity of each sculpture* **3** [U] : careful attention to detail • *She described the scene with great particularity.*

par·tic·u·lar·ly /pɚˈtɪkjələli/ adv **1** : VERY, EXTREMELY • *a particularly dry summer* **2** — used to indicate someone or something that deserves special mention • *I liked all the food, particularly the dessert.* — **not particularly** : only a little • *He is not particularly good at math.* • *"Did you like the movie?" "No, not particularly."*

¹part·ing /ˈpɑɚtɪŋ/ n **1** [C/U] : a time or occurrence when people leave each other • *a bitter/sad/tearful parting* **2** [C] Brit : the line where a person's hair is separated : PART — **parting of the ways** : a point at which two people or groups decide to end a relationship • *She and her political party came to a parting of the ways over the war.*

²parting adj, always before a noun : given, taken, or done when leaving someone • *a parting gift/kiss/glance* • *his parting words*

¹par·ti·san /ˈpɑɚtəzən, Brit ˌpɑːtəˈzæn/ n [C] **1** : a person who strongly supports a particular leader, group, or cause • *political partisans* **2** : a member of a military group that fights against soldiers who have taken control of its country — **par·ti·san·ship** /ˈpɑɚtəzənˌʃɪp, Brit ˌpɑːtəˈzænʃɪp/ n [U]

²partisan adj, often disapproving : strongly supporting one leader, group, or cause over another • *partisan interests/loyalties/politics*

¹par·ti·tion /pɑɚˈtɪʃən/ n **1** [C] : a wall or screen that separates one area from another • *a glass partition* **2** [U] : the division of a country into separate political units • *the partition of former Yugoslavia*

²partition vb [T] **1** formal : to divide (something) into parts or shares • *The room is partitioned into four sections.* **2** : to divide (a country) into two or more parts having separate political status • *After the war, the country was partitioned.* — **partition off** [phrasal vb] **partition (something) off** or **partition off (something)** : to separate (an area or part of a room) by using a wall, screen, etc. • *The storage area was partitioned off from the rest of the basement.*

part·ly /ˈpɑɚtli/ adv : somewhat but not completely • *That is only partly true.* • *partly cloudy skies*

¹part·ner /ˈpɑɚtnɚ/ n [C] **1** : someone's husband or wife or the person someone has sexual relations with • *marital/sexual partners* **2** : one of two or more people, businesses, etc., that work together or do business together ▪ *They are partners in the real estate business.* ▪ *law* **partners 3** : someone who participates in an activity or game with another person ▪ *a golf/tennis/dance partner*

²**partner** *vb* [*T/I*] : to be or become a partner : to join *with* someone or something as a partner ▪ *She partnered with her sister, and they opened a candy shop together.* ▪ *I was partnered with her in the tournament.*

part·ner·ship /ˈpɑɚtnɚˌʃɪp/ *n* **1** [*U*] : the state of being partners ▪ *two people joined in* **partnership** ▪ *The companies went/entered into* **partnership** *(with each other).* **2** [*C*] : a relationship between partners ▪ *Their marriage is a partnership.* **3** [*C*] : a business that is owned by partners ▪ *He joined the partnership last year.*

part of speech *n* [*C*] : a class of words (such as adjectives, adverbs, nouns, verbs, etc.) that are identified according to the kinds of ideas they express and the way they work in a sentence

par·tridge /ˈpɑɚtrɪdʒ/ *n, pl* **partridge** or **par·tridg·es** [*C*] : a brown bird with a round body and short tail that is often hunted for food and sport

part–time /ˈpɑɚtˈtaɪm/ *adj* : working or involving fewer hours than is considered normal or standard ▪ *part-time employees/students/jobs* — **part-time** *adv* ▪ *working part-time*

part·way /ˈpɑɚtˈweɪ/ *adv* : at a distance or time that is between two points ▪ *I was partway to school when it started to rain.* ▪ *Partway down the mountain, he sprained his ankle.*

¹**par·ty** /ˈpɑɚti/ *n, pl* **-ties** [*C*] **1** : a social event in which entertainment, food, and drinks are provided ▪ *have/give/throw a party* ▪ *a dinner/birthday party* ▪ *a party hat/dress* **2** : an organization of people who have similar political beliefs and who work to have their members elected to the government ▪ *political parties* ▪ *the Democratic/Republican Party* ▪ *party members/policy* **3** *law* : a person who is involved in a legal case or contract ▪ *the two parties in the lawsuit/contract* ▪ *the guilty party* — see also THIRD PARTY **4** *formal* : someone or something that is involved in an activity ▪ *Interested parties may contact us.* ▪ *He refused to be a party to any gambling.* **5** : a group of people who do something together ▪ *a rescue/search party* ▪ *dinner reservations for a party of four*

²**party** *vb* **-ties; -tied; -ty·ing** [*I*] *informal* : to have a party or be involved in a party ▪ *We partied all night.* — **par·ty·er** /ˈpɑɚtijɚ/ *n* [*C*]

par·ty-go·er /ˈpɑɚtiˌgowɚ/ *n* [*C*] : a person who goes to a party

party line *n* [*C*] : the official policy or opinion of a political party or other organization that members are expected to support

party poop·er /-ˈpuːpɚ/ *n* [*C*] *chiefly US, informal* : a person who spoils the fun for other people ▪ *Don't be such a party pooper!*

¹**pass** /ˈpæs, *Brit* ˈpɑːs/ *vb* **1** [*T/I*] **a** : to

move past someone or something ▪ *boats passing beneath/under the bridge* ▪ *Planes passed overhead.* ▪ *Stand here and don't let anyone pass.* ▪ *We passed each other in the hallway.* ▪ *We pass (by) the library every day.* ▪ *I just happened to be passing by.* ▪ *He passed her (by) without saying hello.* **b** : to move past a person, car, etc., that is moving more slowly in the same direction ▪ (*US*) *Is it safe to pass?* [=(*Brit*) *overtake*] ▪ *She passed two other runners just before the finish line.* **2 a** [*I*] : to move or go into or through a particular place ▪ *The drug passes quickly into the bloodstream.* ▪ *The river passes between/through the mountains.* ▪ *The bullet passed through his leg.* ▪ *We passed through Texas on our way to Mexico.* ▪ *We're not staying here; we're just* **passing through.** **b** [*T*] : to cause (something) to move or go in a specified way ▪ *He passed the rope around the pole.* **3** [*T*] : to give (something) to someone using your hands ▪ *She passed the baby back to his mother.* ▪ *Please pass (me) the salt.* ▪ *They passed around pictures of their trip.* **4** [*T/I*] *sports* : to throw, hit, or kick a ball or puck to a teammate ▪ *Pass me the ball!* = *Pass the ball to me!* ▪ *She passed to her teammate.* **5** [*T*] **a** : to cause someone to have or be affected by (something that you have had or been affected by) ▪ *The disease was passed from mother to child.* = *She passed the disease (on) to her child.* ▪ *Companies are passing the cost (on/along) to their customers.* **b** : to give (information) to another person ▪ *Please pass this information on/along to the staff.* ▪ *Everyone's invited.* **Pass it on!** [=tell more people] **6** [*I*] **a** : to go from one person to another ▪ *The rumor passed* [=*spread*] *from person to person.* **b** : to be given to someone especially according to a law, rule, etc. ▪ *The throne passed to the king's son.* **7** *of time* **a** [*I*] : to go by ▪ *Several months passed.* ▪ *Another day passed without any news.* **b** [*T*] : to let (time) go by especially while you are doing something enjoyable ▪ *They passed the evening playing cards.* ▪ *We played games to* **pass the time.** ▪ *My sister dropped by to* **pass the time of day.** [=to have a friendly conversation] **8** [*I*] **a** : to happen or take place ▪ *The meeting passed without incident.* ▪ *A meaningful glance passed between them.* ▪ *The mistake* **passed unnoticed.** **b** : to end or go away ▪ *waiting until the danger/storm/crisis passed* ▪ *That time/era has passed (into history).* **9** [*I*] : to be done, said, etc., without producing a response ▪ *She let his remark pass (without comment).* **10** [*I*] **a** : to not take, accept, or use something that is offered to you ▪ *Thanks for the offer, but I'll pass.* ▪ *He passed on their offer.* [=he did not accept their offer] **b** : to decide not to do something at a particular point in a game when it is your turn ▪ *"I bid three hearts." "I pass."* **11 a** [*T/I*] : to complete (a test, class, etc.) successfully ▪ *I passed (the class/test).* **b** [*T*] : to decide that (someone) has passed an examination or course of study ▪ *The teacher didn't pass me.* **12 a** [*T*] : to officially approve (a law, bill, etc.) ▪ *Congress passed the law.* = *The law was passed by Congress.* **b** [*T*/*I*] *chiefly US* : to become approved by (a legislature) ▪ *The bill passed (in) both the House and the Senate.* **13** [*T*] *formal* : to say or state (something) especially in an official way ▪ *The judge passed sentence.* [=announced the punishment] ▪ *The court is ready to pass judgment.* ▪ *Don't pass judgment on me.* [=don't criticize me] **14** [*T*] : to go beyond (a number or amount) — usually used with *mark* ▪ *Donations have just passed the $1 million mark.* **15** [*I*] : to change from one state or form to another ▪ *The water passes from a liquid to a gas.* ▪ *passing through the different stages of life* **16** [*T*] : to illegally use (checks, bills, etc., with no real value) as money ▪ *He tried to pass a bad check.* **17** [*T*] : to have (something) come out from your body ▪ *pass a kidney stone* **18** [*I*] : to die ▪ *I'm sorry, but your grandfather has passed.* — **pass as** [*phrasal vb*] **1** : to cause people to believe that you are (someone or something that you are not) ▪ *teens trying to pass as adults* **2** : to be accepted or regarded as (something) ▪ *folk beliefs that once passed as science* — **pass away** [*phrasal vb*] : to die ▪ *Her father passed away.* — **pass by** [*phrasal vb*] **pass (someone) by** : to happen without being noticed or acted upon by (someone) ▪ *Don't let this opportunity pass (you) by!* ▪ *letting life pass me by* — **pass down** [*phrasal vb*] **pass (something) down** *or* **pass down (something)** : to give (something) to a younger person especially within the same family ▪ *The ring was passed down to me by/from my mother.* — **pass for** [*phrasal vb*] : to be accepted or regarded as (something) ▪ *I can't believe the garbage that's passing for art these days.* — **pass in** [*phrasal vb*] **pass (something) in** *or* **pass in (something)** : to give (something) to a person who will review it ▪ *He passed in* [=handed in] *his test.* — **pass off** [*phrasal vb*] **1** **pass (someone or something) off** *or* **pass off (someone or something) as** : to cause people to wrongly believe that someone or something is someone or something else ▪ *amateurs passing themselves off as professionals* ▪ *She passed the poem off as her own.* **2** *Brit* : to happen or take place in a particular way ▪ *The event passed off* [=went off] *without problems.* — **pass on** [*phrasal vb*] : to die ▪ *Her parents have passed on.* — **pass out** [*phrasal vb*] **1** : to fall asleep or become unconscious ▪ *pass out from exhaustion* ▪ *He drank until he passed out.* ▪ *Someone was passed out on the floor.* [=was lying unconscious on the floor] **2** **pass out (something)** *or* **pass (something) out** : to give (something) to several or many people ▪ *passing out flyers* — **pass over** [*phrasal vb*] **pass over (someone or something)** *or* **pass (someone or something) over** **1** : to not choose (someone) for a job, position, etc. ▪ *She was passed over for a promotion.* **2** : to leave out (something) : to not discuss or deal with (something) ▪ *Let's pass over the technical*

details. — **pass the buck** see ¹BUCK — **pass the torch** see ¹TORCH — **pass up** [*phrasal vb*] **pass up (something)** *or* **pass (something) up** : to not take or accept (something that is offered to you) ▪ *Her offer was too good to pass up.*

²pass *n* [*C*] **1** *sports* : an act of throwing, hitting, or kicking a ball or puck to a teammate ▪ *throw/make/complete a pass* ▪ *a forward/touchdown pass* **2** : a card or ticket which shows that you are allowed to enter or leave a place or to ride a vehicle ▪ *a one-day/weekend/season pass to the amusement park* ▪ *a bus pass* **3** : a set of actions that are done together as a stage in a process ▪ *The paint is applied in several passes.* **4** : an act of moving over a place ▪ *The planes made several passes over the area.* **5** *chiefly Brit* : a grade which shows that you have passed a test or class ▪ *I got a pass in my History class.* **6** : a low place in a mountain range where a road or path goes through ▪ *a mountain pass* — **make a pass at** : to do or say something that shows you want to begin a romantic or sexual relationship with (someone) ▪ *He made a pass at me.* — **pass·er** /ˈpæsɚ, *Brit* ˈpɑːsə/ *n* [*C*]

pass·able /ˈpæsəbəl, *Brit* ˈpɑːsəbəl/ *adj* **1** : capable of being passed, crossed, or traveled on ▪ *The river/road is still passable.* **2** : adequate or satisfactory ▪ *He did a passable job.* ▪ *Her Italian is passable.* — **pass·ably** /ˈpæsəbli, *Brit* ˈpɑːsəbli/ *adv* ▪ *She speaks French passably (well).*

pas·sage /ˈpæsɪʤ/ *n* **1** [*C*] : a long, narrow space that connects one place to another ▪ *a secret underground passage* [=passageway] ▪ (*Brit*) *Her office is at the end of the passage.* [=hallway] **2** [*C*] : a narrow space that people or things can move through ▪ *a narrow passage between the rocks* ▪ *the nasal passages* **3** [*U*, *singular*] : an act of moving or passing from one place or state to another ▪ *the passage of goods through the territory* ▪ *He guaranteed us safe passage.* ▪ *the passage of air into the lungs* ▪ *the passage of time* ▪ *a child's passage into adulthood* **4** [*C*] : a usually short section of a book, poem, etc. ▪ *He quoted a passage from the Bible.* **5** [*C/U*] : an act of officially approving a bill, law, etc. ▪ *a bill's passage into law* **6** *old-fashioned* **a** [*C*] : a voyage or journey usually on a boat ▪ *an ocean passage* **b** [*U*] : the right to travel on a boat, airplane, etc. ▪ *They booked passage on a ship/train.*

pas·sage·way /ˈpæsɪʤˌweɪ/ *n* [*C*] : a long, narrow space that connects one place to another ▪ *an underground passageway*

pas·sé /pæˈseɪ, *Brit* ˈpɑːˌseɪ/ *adj* : no longer fashionable or popular ▪ *That style is now considered passé.*

pas·sel /ˈpæsəl/ *n* [*C*] *US, informal* : a large number or group of people or things ▪ *a passel of children*

pas·sen·ger /ˈpæsənʤɚ/ *n* [*C*] : a person who is traveling in a car, bus, airplane, etc., and who is not driving or working on it ▪ *a driver and two passengers* ▪ *a passenger train/ship*

pass·er·by /ˌpæsəˈbaɪ, Brit ˌpɑːsəˈbaɪ/ n, pl **pass·ers·by** /ˌpæsəzˈbaɪ, Brit ˌpɑːsəz-ˈbaɪ/ [C] : a person who walks by something on a street or road • A passerby saw the accident.

¹**pass·ing** /ˈpæsɪŋ, Brit ˈpɑːsɪŋ/ n [U] **1** : the act of moving toward and beyond something — usually + of • I heard the passing of a distant train. **2** — used to talk about the movement of time; usually + of • the passing of the years/seasons **3** formal : a person's death • We all mourned his passing. **4** : the act of officially approving a bill, law, etc. • the passing [=passage] of the bill — **in passing** : in a brief way while discussing something else • She mentioned in passing that she was studying law.

²**passing** adj, always before a noun **1** : moving past someone or something • a passing train **2** — used to talk about time that is going past • I love you more with each passing day. **3** : lasting for only a short time • a passing fad **4** : done or made quickly • He made a few passing remarks about his work. • a passing thought/glance/mention **5** : not very strong or thorough • SLIGHT • a passing knowledge/interest/resemblance **6** : showing that you completed a test or class in an acceptable way • a passing grade/mark

pas·sion /ˈpæʃən/ n **1 a** [C/U] : a strong feeling of enthusiasm or excitement • a controversy that has stirred passions in Congress • She performed/spoke with passion. **b** [U] : a strong feeling (such as anger) that causes you to act in a dangerous way • a crime of passion **c** [singular] informal : a very strong dislike • She hates him/it with a passion. **2** [C/U] : a strong sexual or romantic feeling for someone • his passion for her • sexual passions **3** [C] **a** : something that you enjoy or love doing very much • Music/golf/writing is his passion. **b** : a strong feeling of love for something • a passion for opera — **pas·sion·less** /ˈpæʃənləs/ adj

pas·sion·ate /ˈpæʃənət/ adj **1** : having, showing, or expressing strong emotions or beliefs • a passionate coach/teacher • a passionate plea/performance/interest **2** : expressing or relating to strong sexual or romantic feelings • a passionate kiss/affair — **pas·sion·ate·ly** adv

pas·sive /ˈpæsɪv/ adj **1** — used to describe someone who allows things to happen without trying to change anything • His passive acceptance of the decision surprised us. **2** grammar **a** of a verb or voice : showing that the subject of a sentence is acted on or affected by the verb • "He was hit by the ball" is in the **passive voice**. **b** : containing a passive verb form • a passive sentence — **pas·sive·ly** adv — **pas·siv·i·ty** /pæˈsɪvəti/ n [U]

Pass·over /ˈpæsˌoʊvə, Brit ˈpɑːsˌoʊvə/ n [U] : a Jewish holiday in March or April that celebrates the freeing of the Jews from slavery in Egypt

pass·port /ˈpæsˌpoət, Brit ˈpɑːsˌpɔːt/ n [C] : an official document issued by the government of a country that identifies someone as a citizen of that country

pass·word /ˈpæsˌwəd, Brit ˈpɑːsˌwəːd/ n [C] **1** : a secret word or phrase that you must say to be allowed to enter a place **2** : a secret series of numbers or letters that allows you to use a computer system • Please enter your password.

¹**past** /ˈpæst, Brit ˈpɑːst/ adj **1** always before a noun : from, done, or used in an earlier time • past civilizations • her past **experience** in sales **2** always before a noun — used to refer to a time that has gone by recently • the past few months • this past weekend **3** always before a noun — used to say what someone or something was in the past • a past [=former] president/employee **4** — used to describe something that ended or was completed in the past • The time is past for apologies. • in years past = in past years

²**past** prep **1** : at the farther side of (something) : beyond (a particular place) • The office is two blocks past the intersection. **2** : up to and beyond (a person or place) • I walked/drove past the house. • He looked right past me. **3** : later than (a time) • half past two [=2:30] • It's past his bedtime. **4** : older than (an age) • He is past 60. **5** : beyond or no longer at (a particular point) • The milk is past its expiration date. • She is past (the age for) playing with dolls. • As a singer, he is past his prime. — **I wouldn't put it past (someone)** — used to say that you would not be surprised if someone did something bad • I don't know if she lied, but I wouldn't put it past her.

³**past** n **1** [U] : an earlier time : the time before the present • memories of **the past** • things that happened **in the past** • Let's put the past behind us and start over. • The disease is **a thing of the past**. [=it no longer exists] • Those problems are all **in the past**. [=they are over now] **2** [C] : the events of a person's life, of a place, etc., before the present time • I know nothing about her past. • We learned about the city's past. **3** the past grammar : PAST TENSE

⁴**past** adv : to and beyond a certain point or time • He drove past [=by] slowly. • Several weeks went past.

pas·ta /ˈpɑːstə, Brit ˈpæstə/ n [C/U] : a food made from a mixture of flour, water, and sometimes eggs that is formed into different shapes and usually boiled • pasta with meat sauce

¹**paste** /ˈpeɪst/ n **1** [singular] : a soft, wet mixture of usually a powder and a liquid • a paste of flour and water **2** [U] : a type of glue that is used to make things stick together • wallpaper paste **3** [U] : a soft, smooth food that is made by grinding something into very small pieces • tomato/almond/bean paste **4** [U] : a type of glass that is used to make artificial gems

²**paste** vb past·ed; past·ing [T] **1** : to stick (something) to or onto something by using paste • She pasted the photo into a scrapbook. **2** : to put (something cut or copied from a computer document) into another part of the document or into another document • Cut and paste the picture/text.

pas·tel /pæˈstɛl, *Brit* ˈpæstl/ *n* **1 a** [C/U] : a type of soft chalk that is used for drawing and comes in many colors ▪ *a drawing done in pastel(s)* = *a pastel drawing* **b** [C] : a drawing that is done using pastels ▪ *She has a collection of pastels.* **2** [C] : a pale or light color ▪ *wearing pastels* ▪ *a pastel sweater*

pas·teur·iza·tion *also Brit* **pas·teur·isa·tion** /ˌpæstʃərəˈzeɪʃən, *Brit* ˌpɑːstʃəˌraɪˈzeɪʃən/ *n* [U] : a process in which milk, cream, etc., is heated to a temperature that kills harmful germs and then cooled quickly — **pas·teur·ize** *also Brit* **pas·teur·ise** /ˈpæstʃəˌraɪz, *Brit* ˈpɑːstʃəˌraɪz/ *vb* -**ized**; -**iz·ing** [T] ▪ *pasteurized milk/cream*

pas·tiche /pæˈstiːʃ/ *n* **1** [C/U] : a piece of writing, music, etc., that is made up of selections from different works **2** [C] : a mixture of different things ▪ *a pastiche of styles*

pas·time /ˈpæsˌtaɪm, *Brit* ˈpɑːsˌtaɪm/ *n* [C] : an activity that you enjoy doing during your free time ▪ *Her favorite pastime is gardening.*

pas·tor /ˈpæstər, *Brit* ˈpɑːstə/ *n* [C] : a minister or priest in charge of a church or parish

pas·to·ral /ˈpæstərəl, *Brit* ˈpɑːstərəl/ *adj* **1** : of or relating to the countryside or to the lives of people who live in the country ▪ *pastoral scenes* ▪ *a pastoral poem* **2** : of or relating to the spiritual care or guidance of people who are members of a religious group ▪ *pastoral counseling* **3** : of or relating to the pastor of a church ▪ *pastoral duties/responsibilities*

past participle *n* [C] *grammar* : the form of the verb that is used with "have" in perfect tenses and with "be" in passive constructions ▪ *In "the ball has been thrown" and "many hands were raised," "thrown" and "raised" are past participles.*

past perfect *n* — **the past perfect** *grammar* : the form of the verb that is used in referring to an action that was completed by a particular time in the past ✧ The *past perfect* in English is formed by using *had* and the past participle of a verb, as in "She had visited there once before."

pas·tra·mi /pəˈstrɑːmi/ *n* [U] : highly seasoned smoked beef ▪ *a pastrami sandwich*

past·ry /ˈpeɪstri/ *n, pl* -**ries** **1** [U] : dough that is used to make pies and other baked goods ▪ *pie pastry* **2** [C] : a small, baked food made from pastry ▪ *a pastry shop*

past tense *n* [C] *grammar* : a verb tense that is used to refer to the past

pas·ture /ˈpæstʃər, *Brit* ˈpɑːstʃə/ *n* [C/U] : a large area of land where animals feed on the grass ▪ *horses grazing in the pasture* ▪ *They put/sent/turned the sheep* **out to pasture**. — **greener pastures** *or* **fresh pastures new** : a new and better place or situation ▪ *He left his job for greener pastures.* — **put (someone) out to pasture** : to force (someone) to leave a job because of old age ▪ *I'm not ready to be put out to pasture.*

¹**pasty** /ˈpeɪsti/ *adj* **past·i·er**; -**est 1** : re-

sembling paste ▪ *a pasty consistency* **2** : pale and unhealthy in appearance ▪ *a pasty complexion*

²**pas·ty** /ˈpæsti/ *n, pl* -**ties** [C] *chiefly Brit* : a small pie that usually contains meat

¹**pat** /ˈpæt/ *vb* **pat·ted; pat·ting** [T] : to lightly touch or press (someone or something) with your hand usually several times ▪ *She patted the dog's head.* ▪ *He patted (me on) my knee and reassured me.* ▪ *He patted* [=*smoothed*] *his hair down.* ▪ *Pat the dough into a square.* ▪ *I patted the lettuce dry.* — **pat down** [*phrasal vb*] **pat (someone) down** *or* **pat down (someone)** *US* : to move your hands over (someone) in order to search for weapons, drugs, etc., that may be hidden in clothing ▪ *The police patted him down.* — **pat (someone) on the back** : to praise or give credit to (someone) for doing good work

²**pat** *n* [C] **1** : an act of lightly touching someone or something with your hand ▪ *She gave the dog a pat on the head.* **2** : a small, flat, usually square piece of something ▪ *a pat of butter* — **a pat on the back** *informal* : a show of praise or approval ▪ *She deserves a pat on the back.*

³**pat** *adv* : learned completely or perfectly ▪ (*US*) *She has her lines* **down pat**. ▪ (*Brit*) *He had his story* **off pat**. — **stand pat** *US* : to refuse to change your opinion or decision ▪ *They are standing pat with their decision.*

⁴**pat** *adj, disapproving* : said or done without any real thought or effort to be truthful or original ▪ *a pat response/ending*

¹**patch** /ˈpætʃ/ *n* [C] **1** : a piece of material that is used especially to cover a hole in something ▪ *His pants have patches on the knees.* **2 a** : a piece of material that is worn over your eye especially because of injury **b** : a piece of material that contains a drug and that is worn on your skin to allow the drug to slowly enter your body over a long period of time ▪ *a nicotine patch* **3** : a small spot or area that is different from the surrounding area ▪ *an icy patch* = *a patch of ice* ▪ *a bald patch* **4** : a small area of land where a particular fruit or vegetable grows ▪ *a pumpkin/strawberry patch* **5** : a period of time ▪ *He's going through a bad/difficult/rough patch.* **6** *US* : a piece of cloth with words or pictures that is sewn on clothing : BADGE **7** *computers* : a program that corrects or updates an existing program ▪ *a software patch* — **be not a patch on** *Brit, informal* : to be much less good, appealing, impressive, etc., than (someone or something) ▪ *The new chairman isn't a patch on his predecessor.*

²**patch** *vb* [T] **1** : to cover a hole in (something) with a piece of material ▪ *patch (a hole in) the pants/fence/roof* **2** : to connect (a person, telephone call, etc.) to a communication system ▪ *The operator patched her through.* — **patch together** [*phrasal vb*] **patch (something) together** *or* **patch together (something)** : to put (something) together usually in a quick or careless way ▪ *They patched together a new plan.* — **patch up** [*phrasal vb*] **patch (something or someone) up** *or* **patch up**

(something or someone) **1** : to deal with (a problem, disagreement, etc.) in a relationship ▪ *They patched up [=settled] their differences.* ▪ *tried to patch things up with his girlfriend* **2** : to give quick and usually temporary medical treatment to (someone or something) ▪ *The doctor patched him up.* ▪ *She patched up his arm.*

patch·work /ˈpætʃˌwək/ *n* **1** [*singular*] : something that is made up of different things ▪ *a patchwork (system) of laws* **2** [*U*] : pieces of cloth of different colors and shapes that are sewn together in a pattern ▪ *a patchwork quilt*

patchy /ˈpætʃi/ *adj* **patch·i·er; -est** **1** : having some parts that are good and some that are bad ▪ *a patchy performance* **2** : existing or seen in some areas but not others ▪ *patchy fog* **3** : not thorough or complete enough to be useful ▪ *His knowledge of the language is patchy.*

pate /ˈpeɪt/ *n* [*C*] *somewhat old-fashioned* : the top of a person's head ▪ *his bald pate*

pâ·té *also* **pa·te** /pɑːˈteɪ, *Brit* ˈpæteɪ/ *n* [*C/U*] : liver or meat that has been chopped into very small pieces and that is usually spread on bread or crackers

¹pat·ent /ˈpætnt, *Brit* ˈpeɪtnt/ *n* [*C/U*] : an official document that gives a person or company the right to be the only one that makes or sells a product for a certain period of time ▪ *The company holds a patent for/on the product.* ▪ *apply for a patent* ▪ *They took out a patent on the process.*

²pat·ent *adj, always before a noun* **1** /ˈpætnt, *Brit* ˈpeɪtnt/ : of, relating to, or concerned with patents ▪ *patent rights/laws* ▪ *a patent dispute* **2** /ˈpeɪtnt/ *formal* : obvious or clear ▪ *a patent lie* — **pat·ent·ly** *adv* ▪ *patently obvious*

³pat·ent /ˈpætnt, *Brit* ˈpeɪtnt/ *vb* [*T*] : to get a patent for (something) ▪ *They patented their invention.* ▪ *a patented process/drug*

patent leather /ˈpætnt-, *Brit* ˈpeɪtnt-/ *n* [*U*] : a type of leather that has a hard and shiny surface

pa·ter·nal /pəˈtɚnl/ *adj* **1** : of or relating to a father ▪ *paternal responsibilities/advice* **2** *always before a noun* : related through the father ▪ *his paternal grandparents* [=the parents of his father] — compare MATERNAL — **pa·ter·nal·ly** *adv*

pa·ter·nal·ism /pəˈtɚnəˌlɪzəm/ *n* [*U*] *usually disapproving* : the attitude or actions of a person, organization, etc., that protects people and gives them what they need but does not give them responsibility or freedom — **pa·ter·nal·ist** /pəˈtɚnəlɪst/ *or* **pa·ter·nal·is·tic** /pəˌtɚnəlˈɪstɪk/ *adj*

¹pa·ter·ni·ty /pəˈtɚnəti/ *n* [*U*] *formal* : the state or fact of being the father of a particular child ▪ *He acknowledged paternity of her child.* [=he admitted that he was the father of her child] — compare MATERNITY

²paternity *adj, always before a noun* **1** : relating to the time when a father's child is born ▪ *paternity rights* **2** : done to prove that a man is the father of a particular child ▪ *a paternity test*

path /ˈpæθ, *Brit* ˈpɑːθ/ *n, pl* **paths** /ˈpæðz, *Brit* ˈpɑːðz/ [*C*] **1 a** : a track that is made by people or animals walking over the ground ▪ *a winding path* **b** : a track that is made for people to walk or ride on ▪ *a paved path* **2** : the area in front of someone or something that is moving ▪ *The fire destroyed everything in its path.* ▪ *They tried to block his path.* **3** : a way of living or proceeding that leads to something ▪ *the path to peace/success* ▪ *a career path* — **cross paths** see ²CROSS

pa·thet·ic /pəˈθɛtɪk/ *adj* **1** : causing feelings of sadness and sympathy ▪ *her pathetic cries for help* **2** *informal + disapproving* : very bad, poor, weak, etc. ▪ *a pathetic excuse* — **pa·thet·i·cal·ly** /pəˈθɛtɪkli/ *adv*

path·o·gen /ˈpæθədʒən/ *n* [*C*] *medical* : something (such as a type of bacteria) that causes disease ▪ *a deadly pathogen* — **path·o·gen·ic** /ˌpæθəˈdʒɛnɪk/ *adj*

path·o·log·i·cal /ˌpæθəˈlɑːdʒɪkəl/ *also US* **path·o·log·ic** /ˌpæθəˈlɑːdʒɪk/ *adj* **1** : extreme in a way that is not normal ▪ *a pathological liar/gambler* ▪ *pathological fears* **2** *medical* : relating to or caused by disease ▪ *a pathological condition* **3** *technical* : of or relating to the study of diseases ▪ *pathological research* — **path·o·log·i·cal·ly** /ˌpæθəˈlɑːdʒɪkli/ *adv*

pa·thol·o·gy /pəˈθɑːlədʒi/ *n* [*U*] *technical* **1** : the study of diseases and of the changes that they cause ▪ *a professor of pathology* **2** : changes in a person, an animal, or a plant that are caused by disease ▪ *the pathology of cancer* — **pa·thol·o·gist** /pəˈθɑːlədʒɪst/ *n* [*C*]

pa·thos /ˈpeɪˌθɑːs/ *n* [*U*] *literary* : a quality that causes people to feel sympathy and sadness ▪ *There is an element of pathos in the story.*

path·way /ˈpæθˌweɪ, *Brit* ˈpɑːθˌweɪ/ *n* [*C*] : PATH ▪ *a winding pathway* ▪ *a pathway to success*

pa·tience /ˈpeɪʃəns/ *n* [*U*] **1 a** : the ability to not become annoyed or upset when you have to wait or deal with problems or difficult people ▪ *I don't have the patience to wait much longer.* ▪ *I have little/no patience for his nonsense.* ▪ *I lost patience (with him).* ▪ *I am running out of patience.* ▪ *Her questions were trying my patience.* **b** : the ability to give attention to something for a long time ▪ *I don't have the patience to knit.* **2** *Brit* : SOLITAIRE 1

¹pa·tient /ˈpeɪʃənt/ *adj* **1** : able to remain calm and not become annoyed when waiting or when dealing with problems or difficult people ▪ *I hate waiting. I'm not very patient.* ▪ *Be patient. I'll be done soon.* ▪ *She was very patient with us.* **2** : done in a careful way over a long period of time without hurrying ▪ *Proofreading requires patient attention to detail.* — **pa·tient·ly** *adv* ▪ *waiting patiently*

²patient *n* [*C*] : a person who receives medical care or treatment ▪ *hospital/cancer patients*

pa·ti·na /pəˈtiːnə/ *n* [*C*] **1** : a thin usually green layer that forms naturally on copper and bronze when they are exposed to the air for a long time **2** : a shiny or dark surface that forms naturally on wood, leather, etc., that is used for a long time **3** : a thin layer ▪ *a patina of grease* ▪ (*figurative*) *a patina of respectability*

pa·tio /ˈpæti̱ˌoʊ/ *n, pl* **-ti·os** [C] : a flat area of ground covered in bricks, concrete, etc., that is near a house and that is used for sitting and relaxing

pa·tri·arch /ˈpeɪtriˌɑɚk/ *n* [C] **1** : a man who controls a family, group, or government ▪ *Our grandfather was the family's patriarch.* **2** : an official (called a bishop) of very high rank in the Orthodox Church — **pa·tri·ar·chal** /ˌpeɪtriˈɑɚkəl/ *adj* ▪ *patriarchal cultures/societies* [=cultures/societies that are controlled by men]

pa·tri·ar·chy /ˈpeɪtriˌɑɚki/ *n, pl* **-chies 1** [C] : a family, group, or government controlled by a man or a group of men **2** [U] : a social system in which family members are related to each other through their fathers

pa·tri·cian /pəˈtrɪʃən/ *n* [C] *formal* : ARISTOCRAT — **patrician** *adj* ▪ *patrician families*

pat·ri·cide /ˈpætrəˌsaɪd/ *n* [C] : the act of murdering your own father

pat·ri·mo·ny /ˈpætrəˌmoʊni/ *n* [*singular*] *formal* **1** : property that you receive from your father when he dies : INHERITANCE **2** : things that are from the past : HERITAGE ▪ *our cultural patrimony*

pa·tri·ot /ˈpeɪtrijət, Brit ˈpætrijət/ *n* [C] : a person who loves and strongly supports or fights for his or her country — **pa·tri·ot·ic** /ˌpeɪtriˈɑːtɪk, Brit ˌpætriˈɒtɪk/ *adj* ▪ *patriotic people/songs/speeches* — **pa·tri·ot·i·cal·ly** /ˌpeɪtriˈɑːtɪkli, Brit ˌpætriˈɒtɪkli/ *adv* — **pa·tri·ot·ism** /ˈpeɪtrijəˌtɪzəm, Brit ˈpætrijəˌtɪzəm/ *n* [U, *singular*]

¹pa·trol /pəˈtroʊl/ *n* **1** [C/U] : the act of walking or going around or through an area, building, etc., in order to make sure that it is safe : the act of patrolling an area ▪ *He made a patrol of the building.* ▪ *soldiers on patrol* **2** [C] : a group that patrols an area ▪ *army patrols* ▪ *the highway patrol* ▪ *a foot patrol* [=a group that patrols by walking]

²patrol *vb* **-trolled; -trol·ling** [T/I] : to walk or go around or through (an area, building, etc.) especially in order to make sure that it is safe ▪ *police patrolling the streets*

patrol car *n* [C] : a car that is used by the police to patrol an area

pa·trol·man /pəˈtroʊlmən/ *n, pl* **-men** [C] *US* : a police officer who patrols an area

pa·tron /ˈpeɪtrən/ *n* [C] **1** : a person who gives money and support to an artist, organization, etc. ▪ *a patron of the arts* ▪ *his wealthy patron* **2** *somewhat formal* : a person who buys the goods or uses the services of a business, library, etc. ▪ *restaurant patrons* [=*customers*] ▪ *library patrons*

pa·tron·age /ˈpætrənɪdʒ/ *n* [U] **1** : money and support that is given to an artist, organization, etc. ▪ *The college relies on the patronage of its graduates.* **2** *chiefly*

US, somewhat formal : support that is given to a business, library, etc., by buying its goods or using its services ▪ *promoting patronage of local businesses* **3** *often disapproving* : the power to give jobs or provide other help to people as a reward for their support ▪ *political patronage*

pa·tron·ess /ˈpeɪtrənəs/ *n* [C] : a female patron ▪ *a patroness of the arts*

pa·tron·ize *also Brit* **pa·tron·ise** /ˈpeɪtrəˌnaɪz, Brit ˈpætrəˌnaɪz/ *vb* **-ized; -iz·ing** **1** [T] : to give money or support to (someone or something) ▪ *patronize the arts/symphony* **2** [T/I] *disapproving* : to talk to (someone) in a way that shows that you believe you are more intelligent or better than other people ▪ *Please don't patronize me.* **3** [T] *somewhat formal* : to be a frequent or regular customer or user of (a place) ▪ *people who patronize the store/library* — **pa·tron·iz·ing** *adj, disapproving* ▪ *her patronizing tone/smile* — **pa·tron·iz·ing·ly** *adv*

patron saint *n* [C] : a saint who is believed to protect a particular place or type of person ▪ *St. David is the patron saint of Wales.*

pat·sy /ˈpætsi/ *n, pl* **-sies** [C] *chiefly US, informal* : a foolish person who is easily tricked or cheated

pat·ter /ˈpætɚ/ *n* [*singular*] **1** : fast, continuous talk that is used to sell something or to entertain people ▪ *sales patter* ▪ *kept up a running patter* **2** : a quick series of light sounds or beats ▪ *the patter of little feet* ▪ *the patter of rain* — **patter** *vb* [I] ▪ *rain pattering on the roof*

¹pat·tern /ˈpætɚn/ *n* [C] **1** : a repeated form or design used especially for decoration ▪ *a fabric with a floral/geometric pattern* **2 a** : the regular and repeated way in which something happens or is done ▪ *studying behavior/weather patterns* ▪ *His daily routine followed a* **set pattern.** [=it was always the same] **b** : something that happens in a regular and repeated way ▪ *trying to break the pattern of violence* [=to stop the violence] **3** : a shape or model that is used as a guide for making something ▪ *a dress pattern* — **pat·terned** /ˈpætɚnd/ *adj* ▪ *patterned fabrics/rugs/wallpaper* — **pat·tern·ing** /ˈpætɚnɪŋ/ *n* [U] ▪ *wallpaper with floral patterning*

²pattern *vb* [T] : to make or design (something) so that it is similar to something else of the same type ▪ *Her house is patterned on a Spanish villa.* = (*US*) *Her house is patterned after a Spanish villa.* — **pattern yourself on** *or US* **pattern yourself after** : to try to be like and to behave like (someone you admire) ▪ *He patterned himself after his father.*

pat·ty *also* **pat·tie** /ˈpæti/ *n, pl* **-ties** [C] **1** *chiefly US* : a small, flat cake of chopped food ▪ *hamburger/beef/chicken patties* **2** *US* : a soft, flat candy ▪ *a peppermint patty*

pau·ci·ty /ˈpɑːsəti/ *n* [*singular*] *formal* : an amount that is less than what is needed or wanted — + *of* ▪ *a paucity of evidence*

paunch /ˈpɑːntʃ/ n [C] : a belly that sticks out especially on a man • He has a slight paunch. — **paunchy** /ˈpɑːntʃi/ adj **paunch·i·er; -est** • a paunchy middle-aged man

pau·per /ˈpɑːpɚ/ n [C] old-fashioned : a very poor person who has no money to pay for food, clothing, etc.

¹**pause** /ˈpɑːz/ n 1 [C/U] : a period of time in which something is stopped before it is started again • There was a brief, long pause in the conversation. • He talked for an hour without pause. 2 [U] : a control that you use when you want to stop a recorded song, movie, etc., for a short time • Please hit pause. = Please hit the pause button. — **give (someone) pause** also **give (someone) pause for thought** : to cause (someone) to stop and think about something carefully or to have doubts about something • The look on her face gave me pause.

²**pause** vb paused; paus·ing 1 [I] : to stop doing something for a short time before doing it again • We paused to look at the scenery. 2 [T] : to cause (a recorded song, movie, etc.) to stop for a short time by pushing a button on a device • He paused the movie.

pave /ˈpeɪv/ vb paved; pav·ing [T] : to cover (something) with a hard material to form a level surface for walking, driving, etc. • pave a road • a paved highway • All this land will be paved over. [=covered with parking lots, roads, etc.] — **pave the way for** : to make it easier for something to happen or for someone to do something • The discovery paves the way for new treatments.

pave·ment /ˈpeɪvmənt/ n 1 [U] US : the hard surface of a road, driveway, etc. 2 [C] Brit : SIDEWALK

pa·vil·ion /pəˈvɪljən/ n [C] 1 : a building in a park or garden that usually has open sides and is used for parties, concerts, etc. 2 : a temporary building that is used at public events and exhibitions

paving n [U] : material that is used to form the hard surface of a road, walk, etc. • concrete paving • a paving stone

¹**paw** /ˈpɑː/ n [C] 1 : the foot of an animal that has claws • The dog injured his paw. 2 informal + disapproving : a person's hand • Keep your dirty paws off me!

²**paw** vb 1 [T/I] of an animal : to touch or hit (someone or something) with a paw or foot • The bull was pawing the dirt/ground. • The dog pawed at the door. 2 [T] : to touch (someone or something) in a rough or sexual way • He was pawed by a mob of fans. • He got drunk and tried to paw her. 3 [I] : to search by using your hands in an awkward or careless way • She pawed through her purse.

¹**pawn** /ˈpɑːn/ n [C] 1 : one of the eight small pieces that have the least value in the game of chess 2 : a person or group that is controlled by a more powerful person or group • He became a pawn in the power struggle.

²**pawn** vb [T] : to give (something that you own) to a pawnbroker in exchange for money • She pawned her diamond ring. — **pawn off** [phrasal vb] **pawn (something) off** or **pawn off (something)** US, informal 1 : to sell (something) for more than it is worth by being dishonest about it • I pawned off my old computer on him. 2 : to get someone to accept or do (something) • He tried to pawn off fiction as truth.

pawn·bro·ker /ˈpɑːnˌbroʊkɚ/ n [C] : a person who lends money to people in exchange for personal property that can be sold if the money is not returned within a certain time

pawn·shop /ˈpɑːnˌʃɑːp/ n [C] : a pawnbroker's shop

paw-paw /pɔˈpɑː, ˈpɑːˌpɑː/ n [C/U] chiefly Brit : PAPAYA

¹**pay** /ˈpeɪ/ vb paid /ˈpeɪd/; pay·ing 1 [T/I] **a** : to give money to someone for goods or services • I already paid (you) last week. • I paid $200 to him. = I paid him $200. • We paid him to mow the lawn. • They left without paying. • He paid for our dinner. • She paid a lot for that car. • We get paid on Fridays. • They get paid well. = They are well-paid. • paying customers/passengers **b** — used to say how much someone earns for doing a job • My job doesn't pay very well. [=I don't earn much money from my job] • The job pays $150,000 a year. 2 [T] : to give the money that you owe for (something) • pay the rent/bills • paying taxes/fines/penalties • The bill was paid in full. 3 [T/I] : to be worth the expense or effort to do something • It pays to advertise. • Crime doesn't pay. • Our efforts are paying dividends. [=getting good results] 4 [T] : to give (a percentage of money) as the profit from an investment or business • a savings account paying four percent interest 5 **a** [I] : to deal with the bad result of something that you did : to be punished for doing something • I'll make you pay (for this)! • She paid dearly for her mistakes. **b** [T] : to give, lose, or suffer (something) as a punishment for or result of something else • He commited a crime and he must pay the price. = (Brit) He must pay the penalty. • She paid a (heavy) price for telling the truth. • There is a price to pay for fame. 6 [T] — used in various phrases that describe giving your attention to something • Are you paying attention? • Pay close attention to the instructions. • Don't pay any attention to him. = Pay no attention to him. 7 [T] — used to describe saying or doing something that expresses respect, admiration, etc., for someone • She paid me a compliment. • pay tribute/homage to someone — **hell to pay** or **the devil to pay** — used to say that if a specific thing happens, there will be a very bad result or someone will get very upset • There'll be hell to pay if we don't finish on time. — **pay a call/visit** : to go somewhere to visit someone • She paid me a visit. = She paid a call on me. — **pay back** [phrasal vb] **pay back (something or someone)** or **pay (something or someone) back** 1 : to return (an amount of money) that someone allowed you to borrow • She has to pay back the $100 she borrowed. • paying back a loan

2 a : to give (someone) the amount of money that you borrowed ▪ *I'll pay you back tomorrow.* **b** : to punish or hurt (someone who did something bad to you) ▪ *I'll pay him back for what he did.* **c** : to do something good for (someone who did something good for you) ▪ *How can I pay you back for all your help?* — **pay off** [*phrasal vb*] **1** : to produce a result that you want ▪ *All of our hard work has finally paid off.* **2 pay off (something or someone) or pay (something or someone) off a** : to give all of the money that you owe for (something that you pay for over a period of time) ▪ *paying off debts* ▪ *She finally got her car paid off.* **b** : to give money to (someone) in order to make that person do something illegal or dishonest for you or to convince that person not to talk about something ▪ *She tried to pay off [=bribe] a police officer.* — **pay out** [*phrasal vb*] **pay out (something) or pay (something) out** : to give (an amount of money) to someone usually over a period of time ▪ *The money will be paid out over the course of five years.* — **pay up** [*phrasal vb*] *somewhat informal* **1** : to pay what you owe ▪ *He paid up after they threatened to sue him.* **2** ✧ If you **are paid up**, you have given all of the money that you owe until a specific date. ▪ *You're (all) paid up through June.* — **pay your (own) way** : to use your own money to pay for the things you need or do ▪ *She paid her own way through college.* — **pay your respects** *formal* : to visit or speak with someone in a polite way as a sign of respect ▪ *I stopped by and paid my respects.* ▪ *We paid our last respects at his funeral.* — **put paid to** *Brit, informal* : to stop (something) ▪ *They hope to put paid to the argument.*

²pay *n* [*U*] : money paid to someone for doing work ▪ *The work is hard, but the pay is good.* ▪ *higher/better/lower pay* ▪ *a week's pay* — **pay·er** *also* **pay·or** /ˈpeɪɚ/ *n* [*C*]

pay·able /ˈpeɪəbəl/ *adj, always after a noun* : possible or necessary to pay ▪ *The bill was payable on the first of February.* ✧ If a check is **made payable to** someone, the name of that person or business is written on the check.

pay·back /ˈpeɪˌbæk/ *n* **1** [*U*] : punishment for something that was done in the past ▪ *This is payback for all the pain you've caused me.* **2** [*C*] : an amount of money that you receive after investing in something and that is equal to or greater than the amount of money that you originally invested ▪ *The investment yielded a big payback.*

pay·check (*US*) /ˈpeɪˌtʃɛk/ *or Brit* **pay cheque** *n* [*C*] **1** : a check that is used to pay an employee **2** *chiefly US* : a wage or salary ▪ *Your weekly paycheck will be almost $600.*

pay·day /ˈpeɪˌdeɪ/ *n* [*C/U*] : the day when you are regularly paid your wages ▪ *Next Friday is (a) payday.*

pay dirt *n* — **hit/strike pay dirt** *chiefly US, informal* : to do, find, or get something that results in money or success ▪

The band hit pay dirt with their first single.

pay·ee /peɪˈiː/ *n* [*C*] *technical* : a person or organization that receives a payment ▪ *The payee must endorse the back of the check.*

pay·load /ˈpeɪˌloʊd/ *n* [*C*] **1** : the people or things that are carried by a vehicle ▪ *a truck with a heavy payload* ▪ *a payload of 2,580 pounds* **2** : the power of the explosive material in a bomb or missile

pay·ment /ˈpeɪmənt/ *n* **1** [*U*] **a** : the act of giving money for something : the act of paying ▪ *Payment is due on the first of every month.* ▪ *a payment plan* **b** : something that is given to someone in exchange for something else ▪ *He accepted the tickets as payment (for his services).* ▪ *We fed them dinner in payment for their help.* **2** [*C*] : an amount of money that is paid for something ▪ *He made a payment of $20.* ▪ *mortgage/loan payments* ▪ *a late payment*

pay·off /ˈpeɪˌɑːf/ *n* **1** [*C/U*] : the advantage or benefit that is gained from doing something ▪ *a big/large payoff* ▪ *A lot of work with little payoff* **2** [*C*] : something valuable (such as money) that you give to someone for doing something and especially for doing something illegal or dishonest : BRIBE ▪ *officials accused of receiving payoffs* **3** [*C*] *Brit* : money that a company gives to a worker who is being forced to leave a job

payor *variant spelling of* PAYER

pay·out /ˈpeɪˌaʊt/ *n* [*C*] : a usually large amount of money that is given to someone ▪ *government payouts* ▪ *a large insurance payout*

pay-per-view *n* [*U*] : cable television channels that charge a fee for each show you watch

pay phone *n* [*C*] : a public telephone that you can use if you pay for your call

pay·roll /ˈpeɪˌroʊl/ *n* [*C*] **1** : a list of the people who work for a company and the amount of money that the company has agreed to pay them ▪ *the payroll department* ▪ *They have 30 employees on the payroll.* **2** : the total amount of money that a company pays to all of its employees ▪ *a $50 million payroll*

pay-TV *n* [*U*] : television channels that you must order and pay for ▪ *a movie on pay-TV*

PBS *abbr* Public Broadcasting Service ✧ PBS is an organization that produces educational television programs that are shown without commercials in a network of stations throughout the U.S.

¹PC /ˌpiːˈsiː/ *n, pl* **PCs** *or* **PC's** [*C*] : PERSONAL COMPUTER

²PC *abbr* **1** Peace Corps **2** politically correct; political correctness **3** *Brit* police constable

PCP *abbr, US* primary care physician; primary care provider

pct *abbr* percent; percentage

PD *abbr, US* police department

PDA /ˌpiːˌdiːˈeɪ/ *n* [*C*] : a small electronic device that is used for storing and organizing information (such as phone numbers, addresses, appointments, and notes) ✧ *PDA* is an abbreviation of "personal digital assistant."

PDQ or **pdq** or **p.d.q.** /ˌpiːˌdiːˈkjuː/ adv, informal : as quickly as possible : immediately • We need to hire someone PDQ. ✧ PDQ is an abbreviation of the phrase "pretty damned quick."

P.E. (US) or **PE** abbr physical education

pea /ˈpiː/ n [C] : a small, round, green seed that is eaten as a vegetable and that is formed in a seed case (called a pod) of a climbing plant; also : a plant that produces peas • growing peas in the garden — **two peas in a pod** : two people or things that are very similar to each other • My brother and I are two peas in a pod.

peace /ˈpiːs/ n 1 a [U, singular] : a state in which there is no war or fighting • longing/praying for world peace • an uneasy peace • They lived in peace. • The nation was at peace. [=not fighting a war] • troops sent in to keep (the) peace b [singular] : an agreement to end a war • negotiate a peace • After many years of war, the two countries have finally made peace (with each other). • a peace treaty • peace talks 2 [U] a : a quiet and calm state • a few moments of peace = a little peace and quiet • Leave him in peace. [=stop bothering him] b : a safe and calm state in a public place • Peace and order were restored. • arrested for a breach of the peace • arrested for disturbing the peace [=for behaving in a loud or violent way in a public place] 3 [U, singular] : a state in which a person is not bothered by thoughts or feelings of doubt, guilt, worry, etc. • trying to find/achieve (an) inner peace • Insurance provides peace of mind. • They are at peace with each other. • (of a dead person) May she rest in peace. 4 [U] : a state in which people do not argue or cause trouble • There will be no peace until she gets what she wants. — **make your peace with** : to end an argument or disagreement with (someone) • He finally made his peace with his father.

peace·able /ˈpiːsəbəl/ adj 1 : not liking or wanting to fight or argue • He has a peaceable [=peaceful] nature. 2 : not involving violence or fighting • The crowd dispersed in a peaceable manner. — **peace·ably** /ˈpiːsəbli/ adv

Peace Corps n — **the Peace Corps** : a U.S. organization that trains and sends people who work without pay to help poor people in other countries

peace·ful /ˈpiːsfəl/ adj 1 : quiet and calm • a peaceful countryside 2 : not fighting a war • peaceful nations 3 : not involving violence or force • a peaceful demonstration 4 : not liking or wanting to fight • a peaceful people — **peace·ful·ly** adv — **peace·ful·ness** n [U]

peace·keep·er /ˈpiːsˌkiːpɚ/ n [C] : someone (such as a soldier) who helps to prevent or stop fighting between countries or groups — **peace·keep·ing** /ˈpiːsˌkiːpɪŋ/ adj • a peacekeeping force/mission

peace·mak·er /ˈpiːsˌmeɪkɚ/ n [C] : a person who helps to prevent or stop an argument, a fight, or a war — **peace·mak·ing** /ˈpiːsˌmeɪkɪŋ/ adj • peacemaking efforts — **peacemaking** n [U]

peace officer n [C] US, law : a police officer or similar official

peace·time /ˈpiːsˌtaɪm/ n [U] : a period of time during which a country is not fighting a war • during/in peacetime • the peacetime economy

peach /ˈpiːtʃ/ n 1 [C] : a round, sweet fruit that has white or yellow flesh, soft yellow or pink skin, and a large, hard seed at the center 2 [U] : a yellowish-pink color 3 [singular] informal + old-fashioned : a person or thing that is liked or admired very much • He's a real peach. — **peaches and cream** 1 — used to describe someone who has smooth and pale skin with light pink cheeks • She has a peaches and cream complexion. 2 chiefly US, informal : a situation, process, etc., that has no trouble or problems • Life isn't all peaches and cream.

peachy /ˈpiːtʃi/ adj **peach·i·er**; **-est** 1 : like a peach • a peachy flavor/color 2 chiefly US, informal : very good : fine or excellent • At first, everything was peachy.

pea·cock /ˈpiːˌkɑːk/ n [C] : a large male bird that has a very long bright blue and green tail that it can lift up and spread apart like a fan

¹**peak** /ˈpiːk/ n [C] 1 a : the pointed top of a mountain • rocky peaks b : a tall mountain with a pointed or narrow top c : something that looks like a pointed top of a mountain • the peak of a roof 2 : the highest level or degree of excellence, quantity, activity, etc. • the peak of perfection • a singer at the peak of her career = a singer at her peak • Violence reached a peak last year. • **the peaks and valleys** in electricity usage 3 chiefly Brit : VISOR 2

²**peak** adj, always before a noun 1 : at the highest point or level • He is in peak physical condition. • at peak capacity/performance 2 : filled with the most activity • the peak season for fishing

³**peak** vb [I] : to reach the highest level • His popularity peaked last year.

¹**peaked** /ˈpiːkt/ adj : having a peak • a peaked roof • (chiefly Brit) a peaked cap — compare ²PEAKED

²**peak·ed** /ˈpiːkəd/ adj, US, informal : pale and sick • She looks a bit peaked today. — compare ¹PEAKED

peal /ˈpiːl/ n [C] 1 : a loud ringing • the peal of bells 2 : a loud sound or series of sounds • peals of laughter • a peal of thunder — **peal** vb [I] • Wedding bells pealed.

pea·nut /ˈpiːˌnʌt/ n 1 [C] : a nut with a thin shell that grows under the ground and that can be eaten • roasted peanuts • peanut oil 2 [plural] informal : a very small amount of money • He works for peanuts.

peanut butter n [U] : a creamy food made from peanuts • a jar of peanut butter

pear /ˈpeɚ/ n [C] : a sweet fruit that is narrow near the stem and rounded at the other end and that grows on a tree; also : the tree that this fruit grows on

pearl /ˈpɚl/ n 1 [C] : a hard, shiny, white ball that is formed inside the shell of an oyster and that is often used as jewelry •

a string of pearls = *a pearl necklace* **2** [U] : MOTHER-OF-PEARL **3** [C] : something that is shaped like a pearl ▪ *pearls of dew* ▪ *pearl onions* **4** [C] : someone or something that is very good or admired ▪ *The island is a cultural pearl of the Pacific.* ▪ *He offered some pearls of wisdom* [=good advice] *about raising children.*

pearl·y /ˈpɚli/ *adj* : having the shiny, white color of pearls ▪ *Her teeth were pearly white.*

pear–shaped /ˈpeɚˌʃeɪpt/ *adj* : shaped like a pear ▪ *a pear-shaped fruit* — **go pear-shaped** *Brit, informal* : to go wrong

peas·ant /ˈpɛznt/ *n* [C] **1** : a poor farmer or farm worker who has low social status ▪ *medieval peasants* ▪ *a peasant farm/girl/community* **2** *disapproving* : a person who is not educated and has low social status ▪ *They treated us like a bunch of peasants.*

peas·ant·ry /ˈpɛzntri/ *n* — **the peasantry** : all the peasants in an area or country ▪ *He tried to organize the peasantry for a revolt.*

peat /ˈpiːt/ *n* [U] : a dark material made of decaying plants that is burned for heat or added to garden soil — **peaty** /ˈpiːti/ *adj* **peat·i·er; -est** ▪ *peaty ground*

peat moss *n* [U] *chiefly US* : a type of moss that usually grows on wet land and that is used as a fertilizer, for growing plants in pots, etc.

peb·ble /ˈpɛbəl/ *n* [C] : a small, round stone — **peb·bly** /ˈpɛbəli/ *adj* ▪ *a pebbly beach*

pe·can /pɪˈkɑːn, ˈpiːˌkæn, *Brit* pɪˈkæn, ˈpiːkən/ *n* [C] : a nut that grows on a tall tree in the U.S. and Mexico and that can be eaten ▪ *pecan pie*

pec·ca·dil·lo /ˌpɛkəˈdɪloʊ/ *n, pl* **-loes** *or* **-los** [C] : a small mistake or fault that is not regarded as very bad or serious ▪ *a politician's sexual peccadillos*

¹peck /ˈpɛk/ *vb* **1** [T/I] *of a bird* : to strike sharply at something with the beak ▪ *The hen pecked (at) my finger.* **2** [T] : to kiss (someone) lightly and quickly ▪ *He pecked his wife on the cheek.*

²peck *n* [C] **1 a** : a quick, sharp strike with the beak ▪ *The bird took a peck at the corn.* [=the bird pecked the corn] **b** *informal* : a quick kiss ▪ *She gave him a peck on the cheek.* **2** : a unit for measuring an amount of fruit, vegetables, or grain that is equal to about 8.8 liters in the U.S. and about 9.1 liters in the U.K.

pecking order *n* [C] : the way in which people or things in a group or organization are placed in a series of levels with different importance or status ▪ *He was low in the company's pecking order.*

peck·ish /ˈpɛkɪʃ/ *adj, chiefly Brit, informal* : slightly hungry ▪ *feeling peckish*

pecs /ˈpɛks/ *n* [plural] *informal* : PECTORALS

pec·tin /ˈpɛktən/ *n* [U] : a substance in some fruits that makes fruit jellies thick when they are cooked

pec·to·ral /ˈpɛktərəl/ *adj, technical* : relating to or located on the chest ▪ *pectoral muscles*

pec·to·rals /ˈpɛktərəlz/ *n* [plural] : the muscles of the chest — called also (*informal*) *pecs*

pe·cu·liar /pɪˈkjuːljɚ/ *adj* **1** : not usual or normal : STRANGE ▪ *peculiar behavior* ▪ *a peculiar feeling* **2** *not before a noun, Brit, informal* : somewhat ill ▪ *feeling peculiar* — **peculiar to** : of, relating to, or found in (only one person, thing, or place) ▪ *a custom peculiar to America* — **pe·cu·liar·i·ty** /pɪˌkjuːlˈjerəti/ *n, pl* **-ties** [C/U] ▪ *the peculiarity of his appearance* ▪ *She noted some peculiarities in the test results.* — **pe·cu·liar·ly** *adv*

pe·cu·ni·ary /pɪˈkjuːniˌeri, *Brit* -ˈkjuːnri/ *adj, formal* : relating to or in the form of money ▪ *pecuniary losses*

ped·a·gogue /ˈpɛdəˌgɑːg/ *n* [C] *formal + old-fashioned* : TEACHER

ped·a·go·gy /ˈpɛdəˌgoʊdʒi/ *n* [U] *formal* : the art, science, or profession of teaching — **ped·a·gog·i·cal** /ˌpɛdəˈgɑːdʒɪkəl/ *also* **ped·a·gog·ic** /ˌpɛdəˈgɑːdʒɪk/ *adj* ▪ *pedagogical methods/practices*

¹ped·al /ˈpɛdl/ *n* [C] **1** : a flat part that you push with your foot to make a machine move, work, or stop ▪ *a bike's pedals* ▪ *a car's gas/brake pedal* **2** : a lever on a piano, organ, etc., that you push with your foot to make or change a sound

²pedal *vb, US* **-aled** *or Brit* **-alled**; *US* **-al·ing** *or Brit* **-al·ling** **1** [T/I] : to push the pedals of (something) ▪ *He pedaled (the bike) as fast as he could.* **2** [I] : to ride a bicycle ▪ *He pedaled down to the store.*

ped·ant /ˈpɛdnt/ *n* [C] *disapproving* : a person who annoys other people by correcting small errors and giving too much attention to minor details ▪ *a dull pedant* — **pe·dan·tic** /pɪˈdæntɪk/ *adj* ▪ *a pedantic teacher* — **ped·ant·ry** /ˈpɛdntri/ *n* [U]

ped·dle /ˈpɛdl/ *vb* **ped·dled; ped·dling** [T] **1** : to sell (something) usually in small amounts and often by traveling to different places ▪ *peddling fruits/drugs* ▪ *peddle your wares* [=sell your products] **2** : to try to get people to accept or believe (something) ▪ *peddling gossip*

ped·dler /ˈpɛdlɚ/ *n* [C] **1** *US* : someone who sells things in small amounts : a person who peddles something ▪ *a fruit peddler* **2** : a person who sells illegal drugs ▪ *drug peddlers*

ped·es·tal /ˈpɛdəstl/ *n* [C] : the base of a column or other tall object ▪ *the pedestal of a vase/lamp/statue* — **put/place someone on a pedestal** : to respect or admire someone very much or too much

¹pe·des·tri·an /pəˈdɛstrijən/ *n* [C] : a person who is walking in a city, along a road, etc. ▪ *a group of pedestrians*

²pedestrian *adj* **1** : not interesting or unusual : ORDINARY ▪ *a pedestrian life* ▪ *pedestrian concerns* **2** *always before a noun* : relating to or designed for people who are walking ▪ *pedestrian traffic* ▪ *a pedestrian mall* ▪ (*formal*) *a pedestrian crossing* [=crosswalk]

pe·di·a·tri·cian (*US*) *or Brit* **pae·di·a·tri·cian** /ˌpiːdijəˈtrɪʃən/ *n* [C] : a doctor who treats babies and children

pe·di·at·rics (*US*) *or Brit* **pae·di·at·rics** /ˌpiːdiˈætrɪks/ *n* [U] : a branch of medicine that deals with the development, care, and diseases of babies and children ▪ *a doctor who specializes in pediatrics* — **pe·di·at·ric** /ˌpiːdiˈætrɪk/ *adj* ▪ *a pediatric surgeon*

ped·i·cure /ˈpɛdɪˌkjɚ/ *n* [C] : a treatment to improve the appearance and health of the feet or toenails

ped·i·gree /ˈpɛdəˌgriː/ *n* [C/U] **1** : the history of the family members in a person's or animal's past ▪ *That horse has an impressive pedigree.* ▪ *He has an aristocratic pedigree.* **2** : the origin and history of something especially when it is good or impressive ▪ *a school with an excellent pedigree* — **ped·i·greed** /ˈpɛdəˌgriːd/ *or* **pedigree** *adj* ▪ *a pedigreed horse/school/family*

ped·i·ment /ˈpɛdəmənt/ *n* [C] : a triangular area on the face of a building below the roof, above an entrance, etc.

ped·lar /ˈpɛdlə/ *n* [C] *Brit* : PEDDLER 1

pe·do·phile (*US*) *or Brit* **pae·do·phile** /ˈpɛdəˌfajəl, *Brit* ˈpiːdəˌfajəl/ *n* [C] : a person who has a sexual interest in children — **pe·do·phil·ia** (*US*) *or Brit* **pae·do·phil·ia** /ˌpɛdəˈfɪlijə, *Brit* ˌpiːdəˈfɪlijə/ *n* [U]

pee /ˈpiː/ *n, informal* **1** [U] : URINE **2** [*singular*] : an act of passing urine from the body ▪ *take a pee* = (*Brit*) *have a pee* [=*urinate*] — **pee** *vb* **peed; pee·ing** [I] ▪ *The dog peed* [=*urinated*] *on the floor.*

peek /ˈpiːk/ *vb* [I] **1 a** : to look at someone or something secretly especially from a hidden place ▪ *She peeked through the keyhole.* **b** : to look at something briefly ▪ *She peeked ahead to the next chapter.* **2** : to show slightly : to be slightly visible ▪ *The sun peeked out from behind the clouds.* — **peek** *n* [C] ▪ *He took a peek in the oven.* ▪ *They sneaked a peek behind the curtain.*

peek·a·boo /ˈpiːkəˌbuː/ *n* [U] : a game played with a baby in which you cover and then uncover your face and say "Peekaboo!"

¹peel /ˈpiːl/ *vb* **1** [T] : to remove the skin from (a fruit, vegetable, etc.) ▪ *peel an apple* **2** [T] : to remove (a covering, shell, etc.) from something ▪ *They peeled back the tarp.* ▪ *We peeled the wallpaper off/ from the wall.* ▪ (*informal*) *She peeled off her wet clothes.* **3** [I] : to come off in pieces ▪ *The paint is peeling (off).* ▪ *She got sunburned and her skin is peeling (off).* — **peel off** [*phrasal vb*] *informal* : to turn and go away from something quickly ▪ *The jet peeled off from the formation.* — **peel out** [*phrasal vb*] *US, informal* : to speed away from a place in a car, truck, etc. ▪ *He peeled out into the street.* — **peel·er** *n* [C] ▪ *a potato peeler*

²peel *n* [C] : the skin of a fruit ▪ *a banana peel*

¹peep /ˈpiːp/ *n* **1** [C] : a quick, high sound (such as the sound made by a young bird) **2** [*singular*] *informal* : a word or sound ▪ *I don't want to hear a single peep out of you!*

²peep *vb* [I] **1** : to make a quick, high sound ▪ *I heard a chick peeping.* **2** : to look very quickly at someone or something ▪ *He peeped through the keyhole.* **3**

: to show slightly ▪ *flowers peeping through the snow*

peep·hole /ˈpiːpˌhoʊl/ *n* [C] : a hole that is used to look through something (such as a door)

peeping Tom *n* [C] : a person who secretly looks into other people's windows to see them naked

peeps /ˈpiːps/ *n* [*plural*] *US slang* : people and especially the people who are your friends ▪ *just me and my peeps*

peep show *n* [C] : a show in which someone looks into a box, room, etc., through a small hole or window and sees pictures or a performance usually involving sex

¹peer /ˈpiɚ/ *n* [C] **1** : a person who belongs to the same age group or social group as someone else ▪ *his academic peers* ▪ *She is respected by her peers.* ▪ *a child's peer group* ▪ *teens giving in to peer pressure* [=social pressure] ▪ (*chiefly US, law*) *a jury of your peers* [=a jury whose members are from the same community as you] **2** : a member of the British nobility

²peer *vb* [I] : to look closely or carefully especially because something or someone is difficult to see ▪ *He peered down/ into the well.* ▪ *She peered over the fence.*

peer·age /ˈpiːrɪdʒ/ *n, formal* **1 the peerage** : the people who are members of the British nobility **2** [C] : the rank of a British peer ▪ *He was given the peerage.*

peer·ess /ˈpiːrəs/ *n* [C] **1** : a woman who is a member of the British nobility **2** : the wife or widow of a peer (sense 2)

peer·less /ˈpiːrləs/ *adj* : better than all others ▪ *As an athlete he is peerless.*

peeve /ˈpiːv/ *n* [C] : something that annoys someone ▪ *One of her peeves is people who are always late.* — see also PET PEEVE

peeved /ˈpiːvd/ *adj, informal* : angry or annoyed ▪ *He's peeved at me.* ▪ *I'm feeling pretty peeved.*

pee·vish /ˈpiːvɪʃ/ *adj* : feeling or showing irritation ▪ *a peevish child/frown* — **pee·vish·ly** *adv*

¹peg /ˈpɛg/ *n* [C] **1** : a small piece of wood, metal, or other material that is used to hold or fasten things or to hang things on ▪ *Her coat hung on a peg.* **2** : a piece in a musical instrument (such as a violin) that is turned to tighten or loosen a string ▪ *a tuning peg* **3** *Brit* : CLOTHESPIN — *a square peg in a round hole* : someone who does not fit in a particular place or situation — *off the peg Brit* : in a store where clothes are sold in different sizes that are not made to fit a particular person ▪ *He bought that suit off the peg.* [=(US) off the rack] — *take/knock/bring someone down a peg* : to make (someone) feel less important or proud ▪ *She needs to be taken down a peg.*

²peg *vb* **pegged; peg·ging** [T] **1** : to put a peg into (something) especially to fasten it ▪ *peg down a tent* = *peg a tent to the ground* **2 a** : to keep (a price, wage, etc.) at a particular level or rate ▪ *peg the price of wheat at its current level* **b** : to link (something) to another amount or value • *The foreign currency is pegged to the U.S. dollar.* [=its value changes when the U.S. dollar's value does] **3** *informal* : to think of or identify (someone) as a certain kind of person • *She pegged him for/as a liar.* • *I had him pegged.* [=I understood what kind of person he is] **4** *US, informal* : ¹THROW • *He pegged the ball to first base.*

pe·jo·ra·tive /pɪˈdʒɔrətɪv/ *adj, formal* : insulting to someone or something : expressing criticism • *a pejorative term* — **pejorative** *n* [C] • *a word that is used as a pejorative* — **pe·jo·ra·tive·ly** *adv*

Pe·king·ese *or* **Pe·kin·ese** /ˌpiːkəˈniːz/ *n, pl* **Pekingese** *or* **Pekinese** [C] : a small dog with a flat face and long, soft fur

pel·i·can /ˈpɛlɪkən/ *n* [C] : a large ocean bird that has a large bag that is part of its lower bill for catching and holding fish

pelican crossing *n* [C] *Brit* : a place where a person can stop traffic in order to cross the road by pressing a button that controls the traffic lights

pel·let /ˈpɛlət/ *n* [C] **1** : a small, hard ball of food, medicine, etc. • *a small metal object that is shot from a gun* • *shotgun pellets*

pell–mell /ˌpɛlˈmɛl/ *adv* : in a confused and hurried way • *a car racing pell-mell through the streets*

¹**pelt** /ˈpɛlt/ *vb* **1** [T] : to repeatedly hit (someone or something) with things thrown from a distance • *They pelted him with rocks.* **2** [T] : to hit against (something) repeatedly • *Rain pelted the windowpanes.* **3** [I] : to move very quickly • *They came pelting down the street.*

²**pelt** *n* [C] : the skin of a dead animal especially with its hair, wool, or fur still on it • *a lion's pelt*

pel·vis /ˈpɛlvəs/ *n* [C] : the wide curved bones between the spine and the leg bones — **pel·vic** /ˈpɛlvɪk/ *adj*

¹**pen** /ˈpɛn/ *n* [C] **1** : a writing instrument that uses ink • *write with a pen = write in pen* **2** : a small enclosed area for farm animals • *a sheep pen* — **the pen** *US, informal* : PRISON, PENITENTIARY • *He was sent to the pen.*

²**pen** *vb* **penned; pen·ning** [T] **1** : to write (something) • *pen a letter/novel* • *a poem penned by Shakespeare* **2** : to put or keep (a person or animal) in an enclosed area • *The cows were penned behind the barn.* • *We were penned up inside for days.* • (figurative) *She felt penned in by their relationship.*

pe·nal /ˈpiːnl/ *adj* : relating to or used for punishment • *penal laws* • *the state penal code* • *a penal institution* [=prison] • *a penal colony*

pe·nal·ize *also Brit* **pe·nal·ise** /ˈpiːnəˌlaɪz/ *vb* **-ized; -iz·ing** [T] **1** : to punish (someone or something) for breaking a rule or a law • *The company was penalized for not paying taxes.* **2** : to give (someone) an unfair disadvantage • *a law that unfairly penalizes immigrants*

pen·al·ty /ˈpɛnlti/ *n, pl* **-ties 1** [C/U] : punishment for breaking a rule or law • *He was given/assessed a severe/stiff penalty.* • *They allowed him to pay back the*

money without (a) penalty. **2** [C] : a disadvantage or difficulty you experience • *the penalties you pay for fame* **3** [C] : a punishment or disadvantage given to a team or player for breaking a rule in a game • *He got a penalty for holding.*

pen·ance /ˈpɛnəns/ *n* [C/U] : something that you do or are asked to do in order to show that you are sad or sorry about doing something wrong • *She did/performed (an act of) penance for her sins.*

pence *Brit plural of* PENNY

pen·chant /ˈpɛntʃənt/ *n* [C] : a strong liking or tendency • *He has a penchant for lying.* • *her penchant for mathematics*

¹**pen·cil** /ˈpɛnsəl/ *n* [C/U] : an instrument used for writing and drawing that has a hard outer part and a black or colored center part • *Use a pencil instead of a pen.* • *Write in pencil.*

²**pencil** *vb, US* **-ciled** *or Brit* **-cilled;** *US* **-cil·ing** *or Brit* **-cil·ling** [T] : to draw or write (something) with a pencil • *penciled some notes* — **pencil in** [*phrasal vb*] **pencil (someone or something) in** *or* **pencil in (someone or something)** : to put (someone or something that may be changed later) on a schedule, list, etc. • *Would you like me to pencil you in* [=to schedule you] *for Thursday morning at 11?*

pen·dant /ˈpɛndənt/ *n* [C] : a piece of jewelry that hangs on a chain or a cord which is worn around your neck

¹**pend·ing** /ˈpɛndɪŋ/ *prep, formal* : while waiting for (something) • *He is being held in jail pending trial.*

²**pending** *adj, formal* **1** : not yet decided or acted on • *bills pending in Congress* • *a pending application/lawsuit* **2** : happening or likely to happen soon • *the company's pending move*

pen·du·lous /ˈpɛndʒələs/ *adj, formal + literary* : hanging down and swinging freely • *pendulous earrings*

pen·du·lum /ˈpɛndʒələm/ *n* [C] : a stick with a weight at the bottom that swings back and forth inside a clock • (figurative) *The fashion pendulum swung from silver jewelry to gold and back again.* [=silver jewelry was popular, then gold became popular, and then silver became popular again]

pen·e·trate /ˈpɛnəˌtreɪt/ *vb* **-trat·ed; -trat·ing 1** [T/I] : to go through or into something • *These bullets can penetrate armor.* • *The heat penetrated through the wall.* **2** [T] : to see or show the way through (something) • *Our eyes/lights couldn't penetrate the fog/darkness.* **3** [T] : to succeed in becoming part of (a group, community, etc.) • *a foreign agent who penetrated the CIA* **4** [T] : to succeed in understanding or finding (something) • *trying to penetrate the secrets/mysteries of life* **5** [T/I] : to be understood or noticed by someone • *The truth had not yet penetrated (my consciousness).* [=I had not yet realized the truth] — **pen·e·tra·tion** /ˌpɛnəˈtreɪʃən/ *n* [C/U]

penetrating *adj* **1 a** : able to understand something clearly and fully • *a penetrating mind/thinker* **b** : helping people to understand something clearly and ful-

ly • *her penetrating social commentary* **2**
: spreading out deeply or widely • *penetrating cold* **3** *of sounds* : loud and clear and sometimes unpleasant • *a penetrating voice/cry* **4** ✧ People who have **penetrating eyes** or a **penetrating gaze/look/ stare** look at you in a way that makes you feel that they know what you are thinking. — **pen·e·trat·ing·ly** *adv*

pen friend *n* [C] *Brit* : PEN PAL

pen·guin /ˈpɛŋgwən/ *n* [C] : a black-and-white bird that cannot fly, that uses its wings for swimming, and that lives in or near the Antarctic

pen·i·cil·lin /ˌpɛnəˈsɪlən/ *n* [U] : a medicine that is used to kill harmful bacteria

pe·nile /ˈpiːˌnajəl/ *adj, always before a noun, formal* : of or relating to the penis

pen·in·su·la /pəˈnɪnsələ, *Brit* pəˈnɪnsjələ/ *n* [C] : a piece of land that is almost entirely surrounded by water and is attached to a larger land area • *the Yucatan Peninsula*

pe·nis /ˈpiːnəs/ *n* [C] : the part of the body of men and male animals that is used for sex and through which urine leaves the body

pen·i·tent /ˈpɛnətənt/ *adj, formal* : feeling or showing sorrow and regret because you have done something wrong • *a penitent sinner/gesture* — **pen·i·tence** /ˈpɛnətəns/ *n* [U] — **penitent** *n* [C] • *penitents* [=penitent people] *seeking God's forgiveness* — **pen·i·ten·tial** /ˌpɛnəˈtɛnʃəl/ *adj* • *penitential prayers*

pen·i·ten·tia·ry /ˌpɛnəˈtɛnʃəri/ *n, pl* **-ries** [C] *US* : PRISON — often used in the names of prisons • *Colorado State Penitentiary*

pen·knife /ˈpɛnˌnaɪf/ *n, pl* **-knives** [C] : a small knife with a folding blade : POCKETKNIFE

pen·light /ˈpɛnˌlaɪt/ *n* [C] : a small flashlight that looks like a pen

pen·man·ship /ˈpɛnmənˌʃɪp/ *n* [U] *formal* **1** : the art or practice of writing by hand • *children learning penmanship* **2** : the quality or style of someone's handwriting • *poor penmanship*

pen name *n* [C] : a name used by a writer instead of the writer's real name • *Samuel L. Clemens' pen name was "Mark Twain."*

pen·nant /ˈpɛnənt/ *n* [C] **1** : a long, thin, pointed flag **2** : the prize that is awarded to the champions of the two major professional baseball leagues each year • *Our team won the pennant.*

pen·ni·less /ˈpɛnɪləs/ *adj* : having no money : very poor • *a penniless vagrant*

pen·ny /ˈpɛni/ *n, pl US* **pen·nies** /ˈpɛniz/ *or Brit* **pence** /ˈpɛns/ [C] **1 a** *pl* **pennies** : a coin or a unit of money equal to ¹⁄₁₀₀ of a dollar : CENT **b** *pl* **pence** : a coin or a unit of money equal to ¹⁄₁₀₀ of a British pound — *abbr. p* **c** *pl* **pence** : a British coin used before 1971 that was equal to ¹⁄₁₂ of a shilling — *abbr. p* **2 a** : a small amount of money • *I bought it for just pennies.* • *Every penny helps/ counts.* [=even a small amount of money is important] • *It was expensive, but it was worth every penny.* • *I'll buy/sell it for 100 dollars and not a penny more/less.* **b**

: the least amount of money • *I didn't have a penny (to my name).* [=I did not have any money] — *a penny saved (is a penny earned)* — used to say that it is important to save your money • *You know what they say: a penny saved.* — *a pretty penny* : a large amount of money • *That car must have cost a pretty penny.* — *pinch pennies* see ¹PINCH — *the penny drops Brit, informal* — used to say that someone finally understands something after not understanding for a time • *I had to explain it to him three times, but finally the penny dropped.* [=he understood the explanation]

penny arcade *n* [C] *US* : ARCADE 3

pen·ny-pinch·ing /ˈpɛniˌpɪntʃɪŋ/ *adj* : very careful or too careful about spending money • *a penny-pinching shopper* — **pen·ny-pinch·er** /ˈpɛniˌpɪntʃə/ *n* [C]

pen pal *n* [C] : a person who you exchange letters with even though you have never met

¹**pen·sion** /ˈpɛnʃən/ *n* [C] : an amount of money that a company or the government pays to a person who is old or sick and no longer works • *collect/receive a pension* • *living on/off a pension* • *a company with a good pension plan*

²**pension** *vb* — **pension off** [*phrasal vb*] **pension (someone) off** *or* **pension off (someone)** *chiefly Brit* : to allow or force (an employee) to leave a job and accept a pension • *She was pensioned off after 35 years with the company.*

pen·sion·able /ˈpɛnʃənəbəl/ *adj, chiefly Brit* : allowing someone to receive a pension • *pensionable employment* • *She had reached pensionable age.*

pen·sion·er /ˈpɛnʃənə/ *n* [C] *chiefly Brit* : a person who receives or lives on a pension • *an old-age pensioner*

pen·sive /ˈpɛnsɪv/ *adj* : quietly sad or thoughtful • *He sat alone, looking pensive.* • *a pensive mood* — **pen·sive·ly** *adv* — **pen·sive·ness** *n* [U]

pen·ta·gon /ˈpɛntəˌgɑːn/ *n* [C] *mathematics* : a flat shape that has five sides and five corners **2 the Pentagon a** : the building in Washington, D.C., that is the headquarters of the U.S. Department of Defense • *a meeting at the Pentagon* • *Pentagon officials* **b** : the leaders of the U.S. military — **pen·tag·o·nal** /pɛnˈtægənl/ *adj, mathematics* • *a pentagonal shape*

pen·tam·e·ter /pɛnˈtæmətə/ *n* [U] *technical* : a rhythm in poetry that has five stressed syllables in each line

pen·tath·lon /pɛnˈtæθlən/ *n* [C] : a sports contest for men that consists of five different events • *the Olympic pentathlon* — **pen·tath·lete** /pɛnˈtæθˌliːt/ *n* [C]

Pen·te·cost /ˈpɛntɪˌkɑːst/ *n* [U] : a Christian holiday on the seventh Sunday after Easter that celebrates the appearance of the Holy Spirit to the apostles

Pen·te·cos·tal /ˌpɛntɪˈkɑːstl/ *adj* : of, relating to, or belonging to a Christian group that emphasizes the power of the Holy Spirit and the authority of the Bible • *a Pentecostal church*

pent·house /ˈpɛnt.haʊs/ n [C] : an apartment on the top floor or roof of a building ▪ *She lives in a penthouse (apartment).*

pent–up adj : held or kept inside : not released ▪ *The children were full of pent-up energy.* ▪ *pent-up anger/frustration*

pen·ul·ti·mate /pɪˈnʌltəmət/ adj, always before a noun, formal : occurring immediately before the last one : next to the last ▪ *the book's penultimate chapter*

pe·nu·ri·ous /pəˈnərijəs, Brit pəˈnjʊərijəs/ adj, formal : very poor ▪ *penurious peasants* — **pen·u·ry** /ˈpɛnjəri/ n [U] formal ▪ *living in penury* [=extreme poverty]

pe·on /ˈpiːˌɑːn/ n [C] **1** US : a person who is not very important in a society or organization ▪ *the office peons* [=the lowest paid workers in the office] **2** : a poor farm worker especially in Latin America

pe·o·ny /ˈpiːjəni/ n, pl **-nies** [C] : a type of plant that has large round red, pink, or white flowers; also : the flower

¹peo·ple /ˈpiːpəl/ n **1** [plural] **a** : individual human beings ◆ This sense of *people* is the plural of *person*. ▪ *We met all sorts of people on the trip.* ▪ *rich/poor people* ▪ *the people next door* ▪ *Of all people, she's the one I least/most expected to win.* **b** : human beings as a group : all or most people ▪ *I don't care what people think of me.* ▪ *People think/say he should be fired.* ▪ *She tends to annoy people.* **2** [plural] : a group of people who share a quality, interest, etc. ▪ *a book for young people* ▪ *the American people* — often used in compounds ▪ *businesspeople* ▪ *salespeople* **3** pl **peo·ples** [C] : a group of people who make up a race, tribe, nation, etc. ▪ *the native peoples of Mexico* **4 a the people** : the ordinary people in a country who do not have special power or privileges ▪ *the common people* ▪ *He is a man of the people.* [=he understands or is like ordinary people] **b the People** US, law — used to refer to the government in the name of a legal case ▪ *The People vs. John Doe* — **good people** US, informal + old-fashioned : an honest, helpful, or morally good person ▪ *He's good people.*

²people vb **peo·pled; peo·pling** [T] formal **1** of people : to live or be in (a place) ▪ *The town is peopled* [=inhabited] *by factory workers.* **2** : to put people in (something, such as a story) ▪ *The story is peopled with odd characters.*

¹pep /ˈpɛp/ n [U] : energy or enthusiasm ▪ *He was full of pep.*

²pep vb **pepped; pep·ping — pep up** [phrasal vb] informal **1** : to become more lively or active ▪ *The economy has started to pep up.* **2 pep (someone or something) up or pep up (someone or something)** : to cause (someone or something) to become more lively or active ▪ *an ad campaign to pep up sales* ▪ *The coach tried to pep us up.*

¹pep·per /ˈpɛpɚ/ n **1** [U] : a food seasoning that is made by grinding the dried berries of an Indian plant along with their hard, black covers ▪ *salt and pepper* **2** [C] : a hollow vegetable that is usually red, green, or yellow and that is eaten

raw or cooked ▪ *The steak was served with peppers and onions.* ▪ *hot peppers*

²pepper vb [T] **1** : to add pepper to (food) ▪ *pepper the stew* — **pepper with** [phrasal vb] **pepper (someone or something) with 1** : to hit (someone) repeatedly with your fists or with objects ▪ *He peppered his opponent with punches.* ▪ *(figurative) They peppered her with questions.* **2 a** : to put a small amount of (something) on many different parts of (a surface) ▪ *His face is peppered with freckles.* **b** : to put something in many places in (a story, speech, etc.) ▪ *She peppered the report with statistics.*

pep·per·corn /ˈpɛpɚˌkoɚn/ n [C] : a dried berry from an Indian plant that is ground to make pepper

pep·per·mint /ˈpɛpɚˌmɪnt/ n **1** [U] : a plant that produces an oil that is used especially to flavor candies **2** [C] : a candy flavored with peppermint

pep·per·o·ni /ˌpɛpəˈrouni/ n [U] : a spicy sausage that is usually eaten on pizza

pep·pery /ˈpɛpəri/ adj **1** : containing pepper or having the qualities of pepper ▪ *a peppery soup/flavor* **2** : having a lively, aggressive, or somewhat shocking quality ▪ *peppery language*

pep·py /ˈpɛpi/ adj **pep·pi·er; -est** chiefly US, somewhat old-fashioned **1** : full of energy or enthusiasm ▪ *peppy cheerleaders* ▪ *a peppy little tune* **2** : able to move fast ▪ *a peppy little car*

pep rally n [C] US : an event before a school sports event that is meant to get students and fans excited and to encourage the team to win

pep talk n [C] informal : a short speech that is given to encourage someone to work harder, to feel more confident and enthusiastic, etc. ▪ *The coach gave us a pep talk before the game.*

pep·tic ulcer /ˈpɛptɪk-/ n [C] medical : a painful sore inside the stomach or another part of the digestive system

per /ˈpɚ/ prep **1** : for each ▪ *The pay is $12 per hour.* ▪ *The tickets are $25 per person.* ▪ *The speed limit is 35 miles per hour.* **2** somewhat formal : ACCORDING TO ▪ *Per her advice, I accepted their offer.* ▪ *The work was done as per your instructions.* ▪ *As per usual* [=as usual], *I paid for our meal.*

per an·num /pɚˈænəm/ adv, somewhat formal : in or for each year : per year ▪ *She earns $60,000 per annum.*

per cap·i·ta /pɚˈkæpətə/ adv : by or for each person : per person ▪ *the average income per capita* — **per capita** adj ▪ *the average per capita income*

per·ceive /pɚˈsiːv/ vb **-ceived; -ceiv·ing** [T] **1** formal : to notice or become aware of (something) ▪ *I perceived a change in her attitude.* **2** : to think of (someone or something) as being something stated ▪ *He is perceived as one of the best players in baseball.*

per·cent (US) or Brit **per cent** /pɚˈsɛnt/ n, pl US **percent** or Brit **per cent 1** [C] : an amount that is equal to one one-hundredth of something ▪ *The value has increased half a percent.* ▪ *Thirty percent* [=³⁄₁₀] *of the class failed.* **2** [singular] : a part of a whole : PORTION ▪ *a large percent* [=(*more commonly*) *percentage*] *of their profits* — **percent** (*US*) *or Brit* **per cent** *adv* ▪ *Prices rose 15 percent.* [=15%] ▪ *I'm 99 percent sure.* [=I am almost completely sure] ▪ *I agree 100 percent.* [=*completely*] — **percent** (*US*) *or Brit* **per cent** *adj* ▪ *a five percent* [=5%] *increase*

per·cent·age /pɚˈsɛntɪdʒ/ *n* 1 [*C*] : a number or rate that is expressed as a percent ▪ *The percentage of students who passed was 95 percent.* ▪ *Rates fell two percentage points.* 2 [*singular*] : a part of a whole : PORTION ▪ *A large percentage of students passed the test.* 3 [*C*] : a part or share of the profit earned when something is sold ▪ *He gets a percentage for every car he sells.* — **no percentage** *informal* — used to say that there is no chance that something will produce a good result ▪ *There's no percentage* [=no use] *in arguing with him.*

per·cen·tile /pɚˈsɛnˌtajəl/ *n* [*C*] : one of 100 equal parts that a group of people can be divided into in order to rank them ▪ *She scored in the 95th percentile in math.* [=she scored higher in math than 95 percent of her classmates]

per·cep·ti·ble /pɚˈsɛptəbəl/ *adj* : able to be seen or noticed : able to be perceived ▪ *The sound was barely perceptible.* ▪ *a perceptible difference* — **per·cep·ti·bly** /pɚˈsɛptəbli/ *adv*

per·cep·tion /pɚˈsɛpʃən/ *n* 1 a [*C*] : the way you think about or understand someone or something ▪ *the public/public's perception of nuclear power* b [*U*] *somewhat formal* : the ability to understand or notice something easily ▪ *She shows remarkable perception.* 2 [*U*] *somewhat formal* : the way that you notice or understand something using some of your senses ▪ *visual/spatial perception*

per·cep·tive /pɚˈsɛptɪv/ *adj* : having or showing an ability to understand or notice something easily or quickly ▪ *a perceptive analysis/observation/comment* ▪ *a perceptive young man* — **per·cep·tive·ly** *adv* — **per·cep·tive·ness** *n* [*U*]

¹**perch** /ˈpɚtʃ/ *vb* 1 [*I*] : to sit on or be on something high ▪ *birds perching on a ledge* 2 [*T*] : to put (someone or something) on something high ▪ *Their house is perched on a cliff.* ▪ *We perched ourselves on the railing.*

²**perch** *n* 1 [*C*] : something (such as a tree branch) that a bird sits on 2 [*C*] : a high seat or location ▪ *a lifeguard watching swimmers from her perch* 3 *pl* **perch** *or* **perch·es** [*C/U*] : a fish that lives in rivers and streams and that is eaten as food

per·co·late /ˈpɚkəˌleɪt/ *vb* -**lat·ed**; -**lat·ing** 1 [*I*] : to pass slowly through something that has many small holes in it ▪ *water percolating through sand* 2 [*I*] : to spread slowly ▪ *Rumors percolated through the town.* 3 [*T/I*] : to make (coffee) in a percolator ▪ *Coffee was percolating on the stove.* 4 [*I*] : to develop slowly ▪ *ideas percolating in my mind*

per·co·la·tor /ˈpɚkəˌleɪtɚ/ *n* [*C*] : a covered pot used for making coffee

per·cus·sion /pɚˈkʌʃən/ *n* [*U*] : musical instruments (such as drums or cymbals)

that you play by hitting or shaking

per·cus·sion·ist /pɚˈkʌʃənɪst/ *n* [*C*] : a person who plays a percussion instrument

per di·em /pɚˈdiːjəm/ *adv, formal* : for each day : per day ▪ *You'll get $20 per diem for expenses.* — **per diem** *adj, always before a noun* ▪ *a per diem allowance*

pe·remp·to·ry /pɚˈrɛmptəri/ *adj, formal* 1 : requiring something to be done without any questions or excuses ▪ *a peremptory order/instruction from the court* 2 *disapproving* : having or showing arrogance ▪ *her peremptory* [=*arrogant*] *tone/attitude* — **pe·remp·to·ri·ly** /pɚˈrɛmptərəli/ *adv*

pe·ren·ni·al /pɚˈrɛnijəl/ *adj* 1 *of a plant* : living for several years or many years 2 a : existing or continuing in the same way for a long time ▪ *a perennial favorite* [=something people always like] b : happening again and again ▪ *Flooding is a perennial problem here.* — **perennial** *n* [*C*] ▪ *planting annuals and perennials* [=perennial plants] — **pe·ren·ni·al·ly** *adv* ▪ *perennially popular*

¹**per·fect** /ˈpɚfɪkt/ *adj* 1 a : having no mistakes or flaws ▪ *a perfect diamond/performance* ▪ *a car in perfect condition* ▪ *the* **perfect crime** [=a crime that is done so carefully that the criminal will never be caught] ▪ *It's okay; nobody's perfect.* [=everyone makes mistakes] ▪ *Remember,* **practice makes perfect**. [=you become better at something if you practice it often] b : completely correct or accurate ▪ *She spoke perfect English.* ▪ *a perfect circle/replica* 2 : exactly right for a particular purpose, situation, or person ▪ *a perfect time/place/day for a picnic* ▪ *They're a perfect match for each other.* = *They're* **perfect for** *each other.* ▪ *You have* **perfect timing**. [=you are present, ready, etc., at exactly the right time] 3 *always before a noun* : complete and total — used for emphasis ▪ *a perfect stranger/fool/gentleman*

²**per·fect** /pɚˈfɛkt/ *vb* [*T*] : to make (something good) perfect or better ▪ *perfecting* [=*improving*] *a method*

per·fec·tion /pɚˈfɛkʃən/ *n* 1 [*U, singular*] : the state or condition of being perfect ▪ *The coach expects perfection from his players.* [=expects the players to make no mistakes] ▪ *The meat was cooked to* **perfection**. [=it was perfectly cooked] 2 [*U*] : the act of making something perfect or better ▪ *the* **perfection of** *surgical techniques* 3 [*U*] : something that cannot be improved ▪ *The meal was sheer perfection.*

per·fec·tion·ist /pɚˈfɛkʃənɪst/ *n* [*C*] : a person who wants things to be done perfectly — **per·fec·tion·ism** /pɚˈfɛkʃəˌnɪzəm/ *n* [*U*]

per·fect·ly /ˈpɚfɪkli/ *adv* 1 : in every way : COMPLETELY — used for emphasis ▪ *Don't throw out a perfectly good sofa.* ▪ *a perfectly normal/natural feeling* ▪ *You know perfectly well what I mean.* [=you know exactly what I mean] ▪ *It's perfectly safe.* 2 : without errors, mistakes, or flaws : in a perfect way ▪ *She sang perfectly.* ▪ *a perfectly cooked steak*

perfect tense n [C] grammar : a verb tense that is used to refer to an action or state that is completed at the time of speaking or at a time spoken of

per·fo·rate /ˈpɚfəˌreɪt/ vb -rat·ed; -rat·ing [T] : to make a hole or a series of holes in (something) • a perforated [=punctured] eardrum • a pad with perforated sheets of paper

per·fo·ra·tion /ˌpɚfəˈreɪʃən/ n 1 [C] : a small hole or series of small holes in paper, cardboard, etc. 2 [C/U] medical : a hole in part of the body caused by an accident or disease

per·form /pɚˈfoɚm/ vb 1 [T] : to do an action or activity that usually requires training or skill • We had to perform surgery immediately. • scientists performing an experiment • He was unable to perform his duties. • performing community service • The wedding (ceremony) was performed by a rabbi. • trying to perform miracles [=to do something that is impossible] 2 [T/I] : to entertain an audience by singing, acting, etc. • The band will be performing (songs) on the main stage. • actors performing (in) a play 3 [I] — used to describe how effective or successful someone or something is • The stock market is performing well/badly. • I perform best under pressure.

per·for·mance /pɚˈfoɚməns/ n 1 [C] a : an activity (such as acting in a play) that a person or group does to entertain an audience • orchestra performances • (figurative) That tearful apology was quite a performance! b : the way an actor performs a part in a play, movie, etc. • She gave a brilliant performance. 2 [U, singular] : the act of doing a job, an activity, etc. • the performance of duties 3 [C/U] : how well someone or something functions, works, etc. • employees with strong job performances • the team's poor performance [=the team's poor playing] • a company's stock performance [=the changing value of a company's stock] • improving engine performance • performance-enhancing drugs [=drugs that improve your ability to do something (such as play a sport)] 4 [singular] Brit, informal : PRODUCTION 4

per·form·er /pɚˈfoɚmɚ/ n [C] 1 : a person (such as an actor or a musician) who acts, sings, dances, etc., for an audience 2 : someone or something that works, functions, or behaves in a particular way • The top performers of the sales team will receive a bonus.

performing arts n [plural] : types of art (such as music, dance, or drama) that are performed for an audience • a school for the performing arts

¹**per·fume** /ˈpɚˌfjuːm/ n [C/U] : a liquid that you put on your body in small amounts in order to smell pleasant • Are you wearing perfume?

²**per·fume** /pɚˈfjuːm/ vb -fumed; -fum·ing [T] 1 literary : to fill or cover (something) with a pleasant smell • Roses perfumed the air. 2 : to put perfume in or on (something) • She perfumed her wrists.

per·func·to·ry /pɚˈfʌŋktəri/ adj, formal : done without enthusiasm because of habit or because it is expected • a perfunctory smile/statement — **per·func·to·ri·ly** /pɚˈfʌŋktərəli/ adv

per·haps /pɚˈhæps/ adv, somewhat formal : possibly but not certainly : MAYBE • "Perhaps we'll meet again." "Perhaps, perhaps not." • Perhaps it would be better if you left. • It's not her best book, perhaps, but it's still worth reading.

per·il /ˈperəl/ n, literary 1 [U] : DANGER 1 • the peril miners face each day • Her career is in peril. [=in jeopardy] 2 [C] : DANGER 2 • They faced many perils on their journey. — **at your (own) peril** : with the understanding that what you are doing is dangerous and that you could be injured, punished, etc. • No lifeguard is on duty: swim at your own peril. [=at your own risk] — **per·il·ous** /ˈperələs/ adj • a perilous [=dangerous] journey — **per·il·ous·ly** adv

pe·rim·e·ter /pəˈrɪmətɚ/ n [C] 1 : the outside edge of an area or surface • the perimeter of a camp/yard 2 : the total length of the lines that form a shape • the perimeter of a rectangle

¹**pe·ri·od** /ˈpirijəd/ n [C] 1 : a length of time during which a series of events or an action takes place or is completed • the busy period between Christmas and New Year's • We had two snowstorms in a period of one week. • the period of economic growth • the period of adolescence • a long period of time 2 : a length of time that is very important in the history of the world, a nation, etc. • the country's colonial period 3 a : one of the parts that a school day is divided into b : one of the parts that the playing time of a game (such as hockey) is divided into 4 US a : a point . used to show the end of a sentence or an abbreviation — called also (Brit) full stop b — used in speech to emphasize that a decision, command, or opinion has been made and will not be changed • I won't do it, period. 5 : MENSTRUAL PERIOD

²**period** adj, always before a noun : of, relating to, or typical of a particular time in history • period costumes/furniture

pe·ri·od·ic /ˌpiriˈɑːdɪk/ adj, always before a noun : happening regularly over a period of time • periodic checkups — **pe·ri·od·i·cal·ly** /ˌpiriˈɑːdɪkli/ adv • We get updates periodically.

pe·ri·od·i·cal /ˌpiriˈɑːdɪkəl/ n [C] : a magazine that is published every week, month, etc.

periodic table n [singular] chemistry : a list that shows the chemical elements arranged according to their properties

peri·pa·tet·ic /ˌperəpəˈtetɪk/ adj, formal : going from place to place • a peripatetic journalist/salesman

¹**pe·riph·er·al** /pəˈrɪfərəl/ adj 1 formal : not relating to the main or most important part • focusing on peripheral issues • a character peripheral to the story 2 computers : connected to a computer but not an essential part of it • peripheral devices/equipment such as printers and scanners 3 : of or relating to the area that is

to the side of the area you are looking at • *good **peripheral** vision* — **pe·riph·er·al·ly** *adv*

²**peripheral** *n [C] computers* : a peripheral piece of equipment (such as a printer or speaker)

pe·riph·ery /pə'rɪfəri/ *n, pl* **-er·ies** *[C] formal* : the outside edge of an area • *the periphery of the city* • *(figurative) the periphery of society*

per·ish /'pɛrɪʃ/ *vb [I]* **1** *formal + literary* : to die or be killed • *They perished at sea.* **2** *Brit* : to slowly break apart by a natural process • *The rubber will perish with age.* — **perish the thought** — *used to say that you hope that something does not happen* • *Who would replace him if, perish the thought, he got injured?*

per·ish·able /'pɛrɪʃəbəl/ *adj* : not likely to stay fresh for a long time • *perishable foods* — **per·ish·ables** /'pɛrɪʃəbəlz/ *n [plural]* • *Store perishables [=perishable foods] in the refrigerator.*

per·jure /'pɚdʒɚ/ *vb* **-jured; -jur·ing** — **perjure yourself** *law* : to tell a lie in a court of law • *to commit perjury* • *He perjured himself by giving a false testimony.*

per·ju·ry /'pɚdʒəri/ *n [U] law* : the crime of telling a lie in a court of law after promising to tell the truth • *He was convicted of perjury.*

¹**perk** /'pɚk/ *vb* — **perk up** [*phrasal vb*] *informal* **1 perk up** or **perk (someone) up** or **perk up (someone)** : to become or make (someone) become more lively or cheerful • *We perked up when we heard the good news.* • *The good news perked us up.* **2 perk (something) up** or **perk up (something)** : to make (something) fresher or more appealing • *Fresh paint can perk up any room.* **3** *chiefly US* a **perk (ears) up** or **perk up (ears)** *of an animal* : to lift (the ears) in an alert way • *The dog heard its name and perked up its ears.* **b** *of ears* : to be lifted in an alert way • *The dog's ears perked up.* • *(figurative) My ears perked up* [=I began to listen closely] *when she said my name.*

²**perk** *n [C]* **1** : something extra that someone receives in addition to regular pay for doing a job • *The job's perks include health insurance.* **2** : a good thing that you have or get because of your situation • *the perks of being famous*

perky /'pɚki/ *adj* **perk·i·er; -est** *informal* : lively in manner or appearance • *a perky teenager/car* — **perk·i·ness** *n [U]*

perm /'pɚm/ *n [C]* : a process in which someone's hair is curled and treated with chemicals so that it remains curly for a long time • *She got a perm.* — **perm** *vb [T] permed hair*

per·ma·frost /'pɚmə,frɑːst/ *n [U] technical* : a layer of soil that is always frozen in very cold regions of the world

¹**per·ma·nent** /'pɚmənənt/ *adj* : lasting or continuing for a very long time or forever • *permanent skin damage* • *a permanent record of the proceedings* — **per·ma·nence** /'pɚmənəns/ *n [U]* — **per·ma·nent·ly** *adv*

²**permanent** *n [C] US* : PERM

per·me·able /'pɚmijəbəl/ *adj, technical* : allowing liquids or gases to pass through • *a cell's permeable membrane*

per·me·ate /'pɚmi,eɪt/ *vb [T/I] formal* : to pass or spread through (something) • *The smell of baking bread permeated the kitchen.*

per·mis·si·ble /pɚ'mɪsəbəl/ *adj, formal* : allowed or permitted by laws or rules • *It is not permissible to smoke in restaurants.*

per·mis·sion /pɚ'mɪʃən/ *n [U]* : the right or ability to do something that is given by someone who has the power to decide if it will be allowed • *My boss gave me permission to go home early.*

per·mis·sive /pɚ'mɪsɪv/ *adj, often disapproving* : giving people a lot of freedom to do what they want to do • *permissive parents/laws* — **per·mis·sive·ness** *n [U]*

¹**per·mit** /pɚ'mɪt/ *vb* **-mit·ted; -mit·ting** **1** *[T]* a : to allow (something) to happen • *Smoking is not permitted.* b : to allow (someone) to do or have something • *Her parents would not permit them to marry.* **2** *[T/I]* : to make something possible • *if time permits* [=if there is enough time] • *We will eat outside, **weather permitting.*** [=if the weather is good enough]

²**per·mit** /'pɚ,mɪt/ *n [C]* : an official document that shows that a person is allowed to do or have something • *a fishing/building permit* • *No parking here without a permit.*

per·mu·ta·tion /,pɚmju'teɪʃən/ *n [C] formal* : one of the many different ways or forms in which something exists or can be arranged • *early permutations of the design*

per·ni·cious /pɚ'nɪʃəs/ *adj, formal* : causing great harm or damage often in a way that is not easily seen or noticed • *the pernicious effects of jealousy* — **per·ni·cious·ly** *adv*

per·ox·ide /pɚ'rɑːk,saɪd/ *n [U]* : a chemical that is used chiefly to kill bacteria or to make hair lighter in color

perp /'pɚp/ *n [C] US slang* : a person who commits a crime or does something wrong : PERPETRATOR

per·pen·dic·u·lar /,pɚpən'dɪkjələr/ *adj* : connecting to another line or surface at a 90 degree angle • *a perpendicular line* — **per·pen·dic·u·lar·ly** *adv*

per·pe·trate /'pɚpə,treɪt/ *vb* **-trat·ed; -trat·ing** *[T] formal* : to do (something that is illegal or wrong) • *perpetrate a robbery* — **per·pe·tra·tion** /,pɚpə'treɪʃən/ *n [U]* — **per·pe·tra·tor** /'pɚpə,treɪtɚ/ *n [C]*

per·pet·u·al /pɚ'pɛtʃəwəl/ *adj* **1** : continuing forever or for a very long time without stopping • *a state of perpetual war* **2** : happening all the time or very often • *a perpetual [=constant] problem* — **per·pet·u·al·ly** *adv*

per·pet·u·ate /pɚ'pɛtʃə,weɪt/ *vb* **-at·ed; -at·ing** *[T] formal* : to cause (something that should be stopped, such as a mistaken idea) to continue • *Fears about an epidemic were perpetuated by the media.* • *perpetuating a myth* — **per·pet·u·a·tion** /pɚ,pɛtʃə'weɪʃən/ *n [U]*

per·pe·tu·ity /,pɚpə'tuːwəti, Brit ,pɔː-

'tju:wəti/ *n* [U] *formal* : the state of continuing forever or for a very long time ▪ *Her work will live on in perpetuity.*

per·plex /pə˞'plɛks/ *vb* [T] : to confuse (someone) very much ▪ *Her attitude perplexes me.* = *I'm perplexed* [=confused] *by her attitude.* ▪ *perplexing* [=difficult to understand] *questions*

per·plex·i·ty /pə˞'plɛksəti/ *n, pl* **-ties 1** [U] : the state of being very confused because something is difficult to understand ▪ *He had a look of perplexity on his face.* **2** [C] : something that is confusing and difficult to understand ▪ *the perplexities of life*

per·qui·site /'pə˞kwəzət/ *n* [C] *formal* : ²PERK

per se /pə˞'seɪ/ *adv, formal* : by, of, or in itself — used to indicate that something is being considered by itself and not along with other things ▪ *I don't think gambling is bad per se, but it should be done in moderation.*

per·se·cute /'pə˞sɪˌkjuːt/ *vb* **-cut·ed; -cut·ing** [T] : to treat (someone) cruelly or unfairly especially because of race, religion, or politics ▪ *people persecuted for their beliefs* — **per·se·cu·tion** /ˌpə˞sɪ-'kjuːʃən/ *n* [C/U] ▪ *victims of religious persecution* — **per·se·cu·tor** /'pə˞sɪˌkjuːtə˞/ *n* [C]

per·se·ver·ance /ˌpə˞sə'virəns/ *n* [U] : the quality that allows someone to continue trying to do something even though it is difficult ▪ *hard work and perseverance*

per·se·vere /ˌpə˞sə'viə˞/ *vb* **-vered; -ver·ing** [I] : to continue doing something or trying to do something even though it is difficult ▪ *disabled students who persevere and succeed* ▪ *a very determined and persevering woman*

per·sim·mon /pə˞'sɪmən/ *n* [C] : a small, round, orange fruit

per·sist /pə˞'sɪst/ *vb* [I] **1** : to continue to do something even though it is difficult or other people want you to stop ▪ *The reporter persisted with his questioning.* **2** : to continue to occur or exist beyond the usual, expected, or normal time ▪ *If the pain persists, see a doctor.* ▪ *The rumors persist.* — **per·sis·tence** /pə˞-'sɪstəns/ *n* [U] ▪ *They admired her persistence.* ▪ *the persistence of a rash* — **per·sis·tent** /pə˞'sɪstənt/ *adj* — **per·sis·tent·ly** *adv*

per·snick·e·ty /pə˞'snɪkəti/ *adj, US, disapproving* : giving a lot of attention to details that are minor or not important ▪ *a persnickety teacher*

per·son /'pə˞sn/ *n, pl* **people** *or* **persons** [C] ✧ The plural of *person* is usually *people* except in formal or legal contexts, where the plural is often *persons.* **1 a** : a human being ▪ *a nice/shy/interesting person* ▪ *Most people here are quite friendly.* ▪ *Tickets are $25 per person.* ▪ *I like her as a person, but she's not a good writer.* ▪ *a disease transmitted from person to person* — sometimes used in compounds ▪ *a spokesperson* ▪ *salespeople* **b** : a person who likes or enjoys something specified ▪ *I'm not a city person.* [=I do not like cities] ▪ *She's a cat person.*

[=she likes cats] **2** *pl* **persons** *law* : the body or clothing of a person especially when considered as a place to hide things ▪ *He had illegal drugs on his person.* — **in person** — used to say that a person is actually present at a place ▪ *They met in person after meeting online.*

per·so·na /pə˞'soʊnə/ *n, pl* **per·so·nae** /pə˞'soʊni/ *or* **per·so·nas** [C] : the way you behave, talk, etc., with other people that causes them to see you as a particular kind of person ▪ *Her public persona is very different from how she is in private.*

per·son·able /'pə˞sənəbəl/ *adj* : friendly or pleasant ▪ *a personable young man*

per·son·age /'pə˞sənɪdʒ/ *n* [C] *formal* : an important or famous person ▪ *no less a personage than the president himself*

per·son·al /'pə˞sənəl/ *adj* **1** *always before a noun* **a** : belonging or relating to a particular person ▪ *personal property/belongings* ▪ *my personal opinion/preference* ▪ *I know about it from personal experience.* ▪ *We don't accept personal checks.* **b** : made or designed to be used by one person ▪ *a personal stereo* **c** : working for or helping a particular person ▪ *a personal trainer/assistant* **2 a** : relating to a person's private feelings, thoughts, problems, etc. ▪ *May I ask you a personal question?* ▪ *personal information* **b** : relating to the parts of your life that do not involve your work or job ▪ *my personal life* ▪ *personal matters/problems/issues* ▪ *a personal phone call* **c** — used to describe the feelings of two people who know and deal with each other ▪ *a close personal relationship* ▪ *getting to know your boss on a personal level* **3** : relating to a particular person's character, opinions, etc., in a way that is offensive or hurtful ▪ *a personal insult* ▪ *It's nothing personal* [=I don't mean to offend you], *but I want to be alone.* ▪ *Let's not get personal here.* **4** *always before a noun* : done by a particular person instead of by someone else who is working or acting for that person ▪ *The mayor made a personal appearance at the ceremony.* **5** *always before a noun* : relating to a person's physical body or health ▪ *good personal hygiene*

personal ad *n* [C] : a short message in a newspaper, magazine, etc., that is written by someone who wants to form a relationship with someone else

personal computer *n* [C] : a small computer designed for use by one person — called also *PC*

per·son·al·i·ty /ˌpə˞sə'næləti/ *n, pl* **-ties 1** [C/U] : the set of emotional qualities, ways of behaving, etc., that makes a person different from other people ▪ *a pleasant/strong/unique personality* ▪ *personality disorders/traits* **2** [U] **a** : attractive qualities (such as friendliness and humor) that make a person interesting or pleasant to be with ▪ *He has lots of personality.* **b** : attractive qualities that make something interesting ▪ *a house/city with personality* **3** [C] : a person who is famous ▪ *a sports/radio/TV personality*

per·son·al·ize *also* Brit **per·son·al·ise** /'pə˞sənəˌlaɪz/ *vb* **-ized; -iz·ing** [T] **1** : to mark (something) in a way that shows it belongs to a particular person • *The stationery was personalized with her initials.* • *personalized towels* **2** : to change or design (something) for a particular person • *We can personalize the program to fit your needs.*

per·son·al·ly /'pɜsənəli/ *adv* **1** — used to say that something is done by a particular person and not by someone else • *I'll attend to the matter personally.* **2** : from personal experience and not because of someone else • *I know the president personally.* **3** : in a way that involves a particular person and no one else • *You'll be held personally responsible.* • *I was personally offended by the joke.* **4** : in a way that relates to a particular person and is offensive or hurtful • *Don't take the joke personally.* **5** — used to say what your opinion is • *Personally, I like it.* = *I personally like it.* **6** : in a way that involves someone's personal life rather than someone's work or job • *I know her personally and professionally.*

personal pronoun *n* [C] *grammar* : a pronoun (such as *I, you, they,* or *it*) that is used to refer to a specific person or thing

per·son·als /'pɜsənəlz/ *n* — **the personals** *US* : a special section of a newspaper, magazine, etc., where people can place personal ads

per·son·i·fy /pɚ'sɑːnəˌfaɪ/ *vb* **-fies; -fied; -fy·ing** [T] **1** : to be the perfect example of a person who has (a quality) • *She personifies kindness.* = *She is kindness personified.* [=she is very kind] **2** : to think of or represent (a thing or idea) as a person or as having human qualities or powers • *Justice is personified as a woman with her eyes covered.* — **per·son·i·fi·ca·tion** /pɚˌsɑːnəfə'keɪʃən/ *n* [C/U] • *She's the personification of kindness.* • *a personification of justice*

per·son·nel /ˌpɜsə'nɛl/ *n, pl* **personnel 1** [*plural*] : the people who work for a particular company or organization • *the number of personnel working on the project* • *medical/security/administrative personnel* **2** [U] : HUMAN RESOURCES • *the director of personnel = the personnel director*

person–to–person *adj* : involving two people or going directly from one person to another person • *a person-to-person phone call* — **person–to–person** *adv* • *talking person-to-person*

per·spec·tive /pɚ'spɛktɪv/ *n* **1** [C/U] : a way of thinking about and understanding something • *Try to look at the problem from a new perspective.* • *a story told from the perspective of a child* • *They have different perspectives on the war.* • *a complete change of perspective* **2** [U] **a** : a condition in which a person knows which things are important and does not worry about unimportant things • *Seeing how hard her life is has put my own problems into perspective.* • *I had lost all sense of perspective.* **b** : the ability to understand which things are truly important and which things are not • *keep/maintain your perspective* **3** [C] : the angle or direction that a person uses to look at an

object • *photos from different perspectives* **4** [U] : a way of showing depth or distance in a painting or drawing • *a drawing done in perspective = a perspective drawing*

per·spire /pɚ'spajɚ/ *vb* **-spired; -spir·ing** [I] *somewhat formal* : 'SWEAT **1** — **per·spi·ra·tion** /ˌpɜspə'reɪʃən/ *n* [U] • *runners covered in perspiration* [=sweat] • *fluid lost by perspiration*

per·suade /pɚ'sweɪd/ *vb* **-suad·ed; -suad·ing** [T] **1** : to cause (someone) to do something by asking, arguing, or giving reasons • *She couldn't be persuaded (to go).* **2** : to cause (someone) to believe something • *They persuaded us that we were wrong.* — **per·sua·sive** /pɚ'sweɪsɪv/ *adj* • *a very persuasive* [=convincing] *argument/salesman* — **per·sua·sive·ly** *adv* • *arguing persuasively* — **per·sua·sive·ness** *n* [U]

per·sua·sion /pɚ'sweɪʒən/ *n* **1** [U] : the act of persuading people • *Many voters are still open to persuasion.* [=can still be convinced to change their opinions] **2** [C] *formal* : a particular type of belief or way of thinking • *people of all different (religious/moral) persuasions* • (*humorous*) *artists of the female/feminine persuasion* [=artists who are women]

pert /'pɜt/ *adj* **1** : having or showing confidence and a lack of respect or seriousness especially in an appealing way • *a pert actress/answer* **2** : small and attractive • *a pert nose* — **pert·ly** *adv*

per·tain /pɚ'teɪn/ *vb* [I] *formal* : to have a connection *to* a person or thing • *The law doesn't pertain* [=apply] *to you.* • *questions pertaining to* [=questions about] *law*

per·ti·nent /'pɜtənənt/ *adj, formal* : relating to the thing that is being thought about or discussed : RELEVANT • *His comments/questions weren't pertinent (to the discussion).* — **per·ti·nence** /'pɜtənəns/ *n* [U] — **per·ti·nent·ly** *adv*

per·turb /pɚ'tɝb/ *vb* [T] : to cause (someone) to be worried or upset • *It perturbs me that you're considering quitting.* • *He looked perturbed.*

per·tus·sis /pɚ'tʌsəs/ *n* [U] *medical* : WHOOPING COUGH

pe·ruse /pə'ruːz/ *vb* **-rused; -rus·ing** [T] *formal* **1** : to look at or read (something) in an informal or relaxed way • *perusing a newspaper/menu* **2** : to examine or read (something) in a very careful way • *She perused the lists closely.* — **pe·rus·al** /pə'ruːzəl/ *n* [C/U] • *a quick perusal of the menu*

per·vade /pɚ'veɪd/ *vb* **-vad·ed; -vad·ing** [T] *formal* : to spread through all parts of (something) • *An odor pervaded the room.* : to exist in every part of (something) • *Sadness pervades the film.*

per·va·sive /pɚ'veɪsɪv/ *adj* : existing in every part of something : spreading to all parts of something • *a pervasive odor* • *the pervasive nature of the problem*

per·verse /pɚ'vɝs/ *adj* : wrong or different in a way that others feel is strange or offensive • *a perverse fascination with death* • *He takes perverse pleasure/delight in causing problems.* • *a perverse sense of humor* • *perverse* [=perverted] *sexual de-*

sires — **per·verse·ly** adv • perversely amusing — **per·ver·si·ty** /pəˈvɚsəti/ n, pl -ties [C/U]

per·ver·sion /pəˈvɚʒən/ n 1 [C/U] : sexual behavior that people think is not normal or natural • sexual perversions/ perversion 2 a [C] : something that improperly changes something good • perversions of the truth b [U] : the process of improperly changing something that is good • the perversion of justice/science

¹**per·vert** /pəˈvɚt/ vb [T] 1 : to change (something good) so that it is no longer what it was or should be • perverting the truth 2 : to cause (a person's mind, sexual behavior, etc.) to become immoral or not normal • movies that pervert the minds of young people — **pervert (the course of) justice** Brit : to try to stop the police from learning the facts about a criminal case • convicted of perverting justice [=(US) obstructing justice]

²**per·vert** /ˈpɚvɚt/ n [C] : a person whose sexual behavior is not normal or acceptable

per·vert·ed /pəˈvɚtəd/ adj 1 : having or showing sexual desires that are not normal or acceptable • perverted minds/criminals 2 : not considered normal or acceptable : PERVERSE • He took a perverted pleasure/delight in watching them suffer

pes·ky /ˈpɛski/ adj pes·ki·er; -est US, informal : making someone annoyed or irritated • pesky insects/reporters

pe·so /ˈpeɪsoʊ/ n, pl -sos [C] : the basic unit of money of several Latin-American countries and the Philippines; also : a coin or bill representing one peso

pes·si·mism /ˈpɛsəˌmɪzəm/ n [U] : a feeling or belief that bad things will happen in the future or that what you hope for will not happen • a sense of pessimism about the economy — **pes·si·mist** /ˈpɛsəmɪst/ n [C] • She's a pessimist. [=a person who usually expects bad things to happen] — **pes·si·mis·tic** /ˌpɛsəˈmɪstɪk/ adj • Are they pessimistic or optimistic about the economy? • a pessimistic attitude — **pes·si·mis·ti·cal·ly** /ˌpɛsəˈmɪstɪkli/ adv

pest /ˈpɛst/ n [C] 1 : an animal or insect that causes problems for people especially by damaging crops • mice and other household pests • pest control 2 informal : a person who bothers or annoys other people • Stop being such a pest.

pes·ter /ˈpɛstɚ/ vb [T] : to annoy or bother (someone) in a repeated way • Stop pestering me.

pes·ti·cide /ˈpɛstəˌsaɪd/ n [C/U] : a chemical that is used to kill animals or insects that damage plants or crops

pes·ti·lence /ˈpɛstələns/ n [C/U] literary : a disease that causes many people to die • war and pestilence

pes·tle /ˈpɛsəl/ n [C] : a hard tool used for pounding or crushing seeds, spices, etc., in a heavy bowl (called a mortar)

pes·to /ˈpɛstoʊ/ n [U] : a sauce made especially of fresh basil, garlic, oil, and grated cheese

¹**pet** /ˈpɛt/ n [C] 1 : an animal (such as a dog, cat, bird, or fish) that people keep mainly for pleasure • No pets (are) allowed. • a pet cat/dog • pet food • a family pet [=a pet kept by a family] 2 Brit — used to address someone in a loving or friendly way • What's the matter, pet?

²**pet** adj, always before a noun : very interesting or important to a particular person • the mayor's pet project

³**pet** vb pet·ted; pet·ting 1 [T] : to touch (a cat, dog, child, etc.) with your hand in a loving or friendly way • My dog loves to be petted. 2 [I] informal : to kiss and touch someone in a sexual way • heavy petting

pet·al /ˈpɛtl̩/ n [C] : one of the soft, colorful parts of a flower

pe·ter /ˈpiːtɚ/ vb — **peter out** [phrasal vb] informal : to gradually become smaller, weaker, or less before stopping or ending • Interest in the sport is petering out.

pet hate n [C] Brit : PET PEEVE

pe·tite /pəˈtiːt/ adj : having a small and thin body — usually used to describe a woman or girl • clothes in petite sizes [=sizes that fit petite women]

¹**pe·ti·tion** /pəˈtɪʃən/ n [C] 1 : a written document that people sign to show that they want a person or organization to do or change something • She signed a petition demanding that women be allowed to join the club. 2 a : a formal written request to an official person or organization • They presented a petition to the legislature. b law : a formal written request to have a legal case decided by a court • She filed a petition for divorce. 3 formal : a prayer or request to God or to a very powerful person or group

²**petition** vb [T/I] : to ask (a person, group, or organization) for something in a formal way • The government was petitioned to investigate the issue.

pe·ti·tion·er /pəˈtɪʃənɚ/ n [C] 1 : a person who creates or signs a petition in order to change or ask for something 2 law : a person who asks to have a legal case decided by a court

pet·it larceny /ˈpɛti-/ n [U] US, law : the crime of stealing something that does not have a high value

pet name n [C] : a name that a person uses for someone to show love or affection

pet peeve n [C] US : something that annoys or bothers a person very much • One of my biggest pet peeves is people driving too slowly on the highway.

Pe·tri dish /ˈpiːtri-/ n [C] : a small dish that is used in scientific experiments

pet·ri·fy /ˈpɛtrəˌfaɪ/ vb -fies; -fied; -fy·ing 1 [T] : to make (someone) very afraid • It petrifies me to think of it. • We were petrified (with fear). 2 [T/I] technical : to slowly change (something) into a substance like stone over a very long period of time • petrified wood

pet·rol /ˈpɛtrəl/ n [U] Brit : GASOLINE

petrol bomb n [C] Brit : MOLOTOV COCKTAIL

pe·tro·leum /pəˈtroʊlijəm/ n [U] : a kind of oil that is the source of gasoline and other products

petroleum jelly n [U] : an oily substance

that is used especially in products that are rubbed on the skin

pet·ti·coat /'peti,kout/ n [C] : a skirt worn under a dress or outer skirt

petting zoo n [C] US : a collection of animals that children can touch and feed

pet·ty /'peti/ adj **pet·ti·er; -est 1 a** : not very important or serious • arguing over petty details • petty crimes **b** : relating to things that are not very important or serious • a petty argument **c** : committing crimes that are not very serious • petty thieves/crooks **2** : treating people harshly and unfairly because of things that are not very important • a petty person — **pet·ti·ness** /'petinəs/ n [U]

petty cash n [U] : a small amount of money that is kept in an office to pay for small items

petty larceny n [U] : PETIT LARCENY

petty officer n [C] : an officer with a low rank in the Navy or U.S. Coast Guard

petty theft n [U] : PETIT LARCENY

pet·u·lant /'petʃələnt/ adj, disapproving : having or showing the attitude of people who become angry when they do not get what they want • a petulant child/tone — **pet·u·lance** /'petʃələns/ n [U] — **pet·u·lant·ly** adv

pe·tu·nia /pɪ'tuːnjə/ n [C] : a plant with colorful flowers that are shaped like funnels

pew /'pjuː/ n [C] : one of the benches in a church

pew·ter /'pjuːtə/ n [U] : a dull gray metal • pewter cups

PG /'piː'dʒiː/ — used as a special mark to indicate that parents may want to watch a particular movie with their children

pg. abbr page • pg. 26

PGCE abbr, Brit Postgraduate Certificate of Education

PG–13 /'piː'dʒiː'θəˈtiːn/ — used as a special mark to indicate that parents may want to watch a particular movie with their children especially when their children are younger than 13 years old

pH /'piː'eɪtʃ/ n [singular] technical : a number between 0 and 14 that indicates if a chemical is an acid or a base

pha·lanx /'feɪ,læŋks, Brit 'fæ,læŋks/ n [C] formal : a large group of people or things often placed close together • a phalanx of armed guards

phal·lic /'fælɪk/ adj : of, relating to, or resembling a penis • a phallic symbol representing fertility

phal·lus /'fæləs/ n, pl **phal·li** /'fæ,laɪ/ or **phal·lus·es** /'fæləsəz/ [C] **1** : an image or representation of a penis **2** : PENIS

¹phan·tom /'fæntəm/ n [C] **1** : GHOST 1 • haunted by phantoms **2** : something that is not real and exists only in a person's mind • I think the crisis is a phantom. **3** : something that is hard to see or achieve • the phantoms of fame and fortune

²phantom adj, always before a noun **1** : coming from or associated with the world of ghosts • a phantom ship **2 a** : not real or true or not based on something real or true • phantom fears **b** : not real but felt or experienced as something real • phantom illnesses

pha·raoh or **Pharaoh** /'ferou/ n [C] : a ruler of ancient Egypt

¹phar·ma·ceu·ti·cal /,fɑːməˈsuːtɪkəl/ adj, always before a noun : of or relating to the production and sale of drugs and medicine • a pharmaceutical company

²pharmaceutical n [C] technical : a drug or medicine • The company manufactures pharmaceuticals.

phar·ma·cist /'fɑːməsɪst/ n [C] : a person whose job is to prepare and sell the drugs and medicines that a doctor prescribes for patients

phar·ma·col·o·gy /,fɑːməˈkɑːlədʒi/ n [U] technical **1** : the scientific study of drugs and how they are used in medicine **2** : a drug's qualities and effects • the new drug's pharmacology

phar·ma·cy /'fɑːməsi/ n, pl **-cies 1** [C] **a** : a store or part of a store in which drugs and medicines are prepared and sold **b** : a place in a hospital where drugs and medicines are prepared and given out **2** [U] : the profession of preparing drugs and medicines

¹phase /'feɪz/ n [C] **1** : a part or step in a process • The project was done in three phases. • He's in the final phase of treatment. **2** [C] : a short period of time during which a person behaves in a particular way or likes a particular thing • He has tantrums a lot, but the doctor says it's just a phase. **3** [C] : the shape of the part of the moon that is visible at different times during a month **4** [U] Brit : the state in which things work together with each other • He's out of phase [=(US) out of step] with the rest of the team. • keeping in phase

²phase vb **phased; phas·ing** — **phase in** [phrasal vb] **phase (something) in** or **phase in (something)** : to start to use or do (something) gradually over time • phasing tax cuts in — **phase out** [phrasal vb] **phase (something) out** or **phase out (something)** : to stop using, making, or doing (something) gradually over time • The airplane is being phased out.

phased adj : done gradually in steps and according to a plan • a phased withdrawal of troops

phase-out /'feɪz,aʊt/ n [C] US : the act of stopping something gradually in a planned series of steps • a phaseout of unhealthy menu items

PhD /,piː,eɪtʃ'diː/ n [C] **1** : the highest degree given by a university or college • He got his PhD [=doctorate] from Harvard. **2** : a person who has a PhD • Sheila Jones, PhD

pheas·ant /'fɛznt/ n, pl **pheasant** or **pheas·ants 1** [C] : a large bird that has a long tail and is often hunted for food or sport **2** [U] : the meat of the pheasant eaten as food

phe·nom /'fiː,nɑːm/ n [C] US, informal : a person who is very good at doing something • a baseball phenom [=(more formally) phenomenon]

phenomena plural of PHENOMENON 1

phe·nom·e·nal /fɪ'nɑːmənl/ adj : unusual in a way that is very impressive • a phenomenal [=amazing] performance

phe·nom·e·nal·ly /fɪ'nɑːmənli/ adv **1**

: in a very great or impressive way ▪ *a phenomenally* [=*hugely*] *successful book* **2** : very or extremely ▪ *phenomenally boring*

phe·nom·e·non /fɪˈnɑːmɪˌnɑːn/ *n* [C] **1** *pl* **-e·na** /-ənə/ : something (such as an interesting fact or event) that can be observed and studied and that typically is unusual or difficult to understand or explain fully ▪ *natural phenomena like earthquakes* **2** *pl* **-enons** : someone or something that is very impressive or popular especially because of an unusual ability or quality ▪ *The movie became a cultural phenomenon.*

pher·o·mone /ˈferəˌmoʊn/ *n* [C] *biology* : a chemical substance produced by animals in order to attract mates

phew /fjuː/ *interj* — used to show that you are relieved, tired, hot, or disgusted ▪ *Phew! I thought we were going to miss the bus!*

phi·al /ˈfajəl/ *n* [C] *Brit* : VIAL

phi·lan·der·er /fəˈlændərɚ/ *n* [C] *disapproving* : a man who has sex with many women — **phi·lan·der·ing** /fɪˈlændərɪŋ/ *adj* ▪ *a philandering husband* — **philandering** *n* [U] ▪ *She won't tolerate his philandering.*

phi·lan·thro·py /fəˈlænθrəpi/ *n* [U] : the practice of giving money and time to help make life better for other people — **phil·an·throp·ic** /ˌfɪlənˈθrɑːpɪk/ *adj* ▪ *a philanthropic* [=*charitable*] *foundation* — **phi·lan·thro·pist** /fəˈlænθrəpɪst/ *n* [C] ▪ *wealthy philanthropists*

Phil·har·mon·ic /ˌfɪlhɑːrˈmɑːnɪk/ *n* [C] : SYMPHONY ORCHESTRA — usually used in the names of orchestras

phi·lis·tine *or* **Phi·lis·tine** /ˈfɪləˌstiːn, *Brit* ˈfɪləˌstaɪn/ *n* [C] *formal + disapproving* : a person who does not understand or care about art or culture

phi·los·o·pher /fəˈlɑːsəfɚ/ *n* [C] : a person who studies philosophy ▪ *the Greek philosopher Plato*

phi·los·o·phize *also Brit* **phi·los·o·phise** /fəˈlɑːsəˌfaɪz/ *vb* **-phized; -phiz·ing** [I] : to talk about something in a serious way for a long time ▪ *philosophizing on/about the meaning of life*

phi·los·o·phy /fəˈlɑːsəfi/ *n, pl* **-phies 1 a** [U] : the study of ideas about knowledge, truth, the nature and meaning of life, etc. ▪ *a professor of philosophy* = *a philosophy professor* **b** [C] : a particular set of ideas about knowledge, truth, etc. ▪ *political philosophies* ▪ *the philosophy of Plato* **2** [C] : a set of ideas about how to do something or how to live ▪ *Her cooking philosophy is to use fresh ingredients.* — **philo·soph·i·cal** /ˌfɪləˈsɑːfɪkəl/ *also* **philo·soph·ic** /ˌfɪləˈsɑːfɪk/ *adj* ▪ *a philosophical debate about what it means to be "natural"* ▪ *philosophical texts* — **philo·soph·i·cal·ly** /ˌfɪləˈsɑːfɪkli/ *adv* ▪ *She's philosophically opposed to violence.*

phlegm /ˈflɛm/ *n* [U] : a thick, yellowish liquid that is produced in the nose and throat

phleg·mat·ic /flɛgˈmætɪk/ *adj, literary* : not easily upset, excited, or angered ▪ *our phlegmatic leader*

phlox /ˈflɑːks/ *n, pl* **phlox** *or* **phlox·es**

[C/U] : a plant that has white, pink, or purple flowers

pho·bia /ˈfoʊbijə/ *n* [C] : an extremely strong dislike or fear of someone or something ▪ *a fear of crowds that developed into a phobia*

pho·bic /ˈfoʊbɪk/ *adj* : of, relating to, or having an extremely strong fear or dislike of someone or something ▪ *I'm phobic about heights.* — **phobic** *n* [C]

phoe·nix /ˈfiːnɪks/ *n* [C] : a magical bird in ancient stories that burns itself to death and then is born again from its ashes

¹**phone** /ˈfoʊn/ *n* [C/U] : ¹TELEPHONE ▪ *The phone is ringing.* ▪ *We spoke by phone.* ▪ *a phone bill/conversation* ▪ *I have to make a phone call.* ▪ *ordering over the phone* [=by calling on the telephone] ▪ *I was on the phone* [=using a telephone to talk to] *my sister.*

²**phone** *vb* **phoned; phon·ing** [T/I] : ²TELEPHONE ▪ *She phoned* [=*called*] *them already.* ▪ *He phoned with a question.* ▪ (*Brit*) *I will phone up later.* — **phone in** [*phrasal vb*] **1 a** : to make a telephone call to a place (such as the place where you work) ▪ *I'll phone in tomorrow.* **b** : to make a telephone call to a radio or TV program ▪ *people phoning in* [=*calling in*] *to make a donation* **2 phone (something) in** *or* **phone in (something)** : to deliver (a message, order, etc.) by making a telephone call ▪ *I just phoned in a pizza order.*

phone book *n* [C] : a book that lists the names, addresses, and phone numbers of the people and businesses in a certain area — called also *phone directory*

phone booth *n* [C] *US* : an enclosed structure with a public telephone in it — called also (*Brit*) *phone box*

phone card *n* [C] : CALLING CARD 1

phone-in /ˈfoʊnˌɪn/ *n* [C] *chiefly Brit* : CALL-IN

phone number *n* [C] : a number that you dial on a telephone to reach a particular person, business, etc. ▪ *What's your phone number?*

pho·net·ic /fəˈnɛtɪk/ *adj, linguistics* **1** : of or relating to spoken language, speech sounds, or the science of phonetics ▪ *the phonetic units of a language* **2** : representing each speech sound with a single symbol ▪ *the International Phonetic Alphabet* — **pho·net·i·cal·ly** /fəˈnɛtɪkli/ *adv* ▪ *spelling words phonetically*

pho·net·ics /fəˈnɛtɪks/ *n* [U] *linguistics* : the study of speech sounds

phoney *chiefly Brit spelling of* PHONY

phon·ics /ˈfɑːnɪks/ *n* [U] : a method of teaching people to read and pronounce words by learning the sounds of letters, letter groups, and syllables

pho·no·graph /ˈfoʊnəˌgræf, *Brit* ˈfəʊnəˌgrɑːf/ *n* [C] *old-fashioned* : RECORD PLAYER

¹**pho·ny** (*US*) *or chiefly Brit* **pho·ney** /ˈfoʊni/ *adj* **pho·ni·er; -est** *informal* **1** : not true, real, or genuine ▪ *a phony $100 bill* ▪ *talking in a phony Irish accent* **2** *of a person* : not honest or sincere ▪ *phony politicians* — **pho·ni·ness** *n* [U]

²**pho·ny** (*US*) *or chiefly Brit* **phoney** *n, pl*

US **pho·nies** *or chiefly Brit* **pho·neys** [C] *informal* **1** : a person who is not sincere ▪ *I think a lot of politicians are phonies.* **2** : something that is not real or genuine ▪ *The diamond is a phony.*

phos·phate /'fɑːsˌfeɪt/ *n* [C/U] *chemistry* : a salt or compound that is used especially in fertilizers

phos·pho·rus /'fɑːsfərəs/ *n* [U] *chemistry* : a poisonous chemical element that glows in the dark and burns when it is touched by air

pho·to /'foʊtoʊ/ *n, pl* **-tos** [C] : ¹PHOTOGRAPH ▪ *a photo album* [=a book that holds photographs]

pho·to·copi·er /'foʊtəˌkɑːpijɚ/ *n* [C] : COPIER

pho·to·copy /'foʊtəˌkɑːpi/ *n, pl* **-copies** [C] : a paper copy of a document, picture, etc., that is made with a special machine ▪ *Make a photocopy of the letter.* — **photocopy** *vb* **-copies; -cop·ied; -copy·ing** [T/I] ▪ *Photocopy the letter.*

pho·to·elec·tric /ˌfoʊtowɪ'lɛktrɪk/ *adj, technical* : involving, relating to, or using an electric current that is controlled by light

photo finish *n* [*singular*] : a finish in a race in which the racers are so close that the judges have to look at a photograph of the racers crossing the finish line to see who has won

pho·to·ge·nic /ˌfoʊtə'dʒɛnɪk/ *adj* : tending to look good in photographs ▪ *a photogenic child*

¹**pho·to·graph** /'foʊtəˌgræf, *Brit* 'foʊtəˌgrɑːf/ *n* [C] : a picture made by a camera ▪ *He took a photograph of her.* ▪ *a digital photograph*

²**photograph** *vb* **1** [T] : to take a photograph of (someone or something) ▪ *He photographed her.* **2** [I] : to appear in photographs ▪ *He photographs well.* [=he is photogenic] — **pho·tog·ra·pher** /fə'tɑːgrəfɚ/ *n* [C] ▪ *a fashion photographer*

pho·to·graph·ic /ˌfoʊtə'græfɪk/ *adj* : relating to or used to make photographs ▪ *photographic paper/images* — **pho·to·graph·i·cal·ly** /ˌfoʊtə'græfɪkli/ *adv*

photographic memory *n* [C] : an unusual ability to remember things completely and exactly as they were seen, read, etc.

pho·tog·ra·phy /fə'tɑːgrəfi/ *n* [U] : the art, process, or job of taking pictures with a camera ▪ *fashion photography*

pho·to·jour·nal·ism /ˌfoʊtoʊ'dʒɚnəˌlɪzəm/ *n* [U] : the job or activity of using photographs to report news stories — **pho·to·jour·nal·ist** /ˌfoʊtoʊ'dʒɚnəlɪst/ *n* [C]

pho·ton /'foʊˌtɑːn/ *n* [C] *physics* : a tiny particle of light or electromagnetic radiation

photo opportunity *n* [C] : a situation in which a famous person can be photographed while doing something that is meant to be seen in a favorable way by the public — called also *photo op*

photo shoot *n* [C] : an occasion when a photographer takes pictures of someone famous for use in a magazine or for some other purpose

pho·to·syn·the·sis /ˌfoʊtoʊ'sɪnθəsəs/ *n*

[U] *biology* : the process by which a green plant uses light to turn water and carbon dioxide into food

phras·al verb /'freɪzəl-/ *n* [C] *grammar* : a group of words (such as *take off* and *look down on*) that functions as a verb and is made up of a verb and a preposition, an adverb, or both

¹**phrase** /'freɪz/ *n* [C] **1** : a group of two or more words that express a single idea but do not usually form a complete sentence ▪ *She uses the phrase "I strongly believe" too often.* ▪ *an adverbial/adjectival phrase* **2** : a brief expression that is commonly used ▪ *a famous phrase*

²**phrase** *vb* **phrased; phras·ing** [T] : to say (something) in a particular way ▪ *an awkwardly phrased question*

phrasing *n* [U] **1** : the way something is expressed in words ▪ *The phrasing of the instructions was confusing.* **2** *music* : the act of grouping notes together in a particular way ▪ *a singer's phrasing*

phyl·lo /'fiːloʊ/ *n* [U] : very thin dough that is used in pastries — called also *phyllo dough, phyllo pastry*

phys ed /'fɪz'ɛd/ *n* [U] *chiefly US, informal* : PHYSICAL EDUCATION

¹**phys·i·cal** /'fɪzɪkəl/ *adj* **1** : relating to the body of a person instead of the mind ▪ *physical contact/abuse* ▪ *physical and emotional health* ▪ *I'm in good physical condition.* [=strong and healthy] ▪ *physical fitness* [=good health and strength that you get through exercise] **2** : existing in a form that you can touch or see ▪ *physical evidence of the crime* **3** : involving or related to sex ▪ *physical attraction* ▪ *a purely physical relationship* **4 a** : involving or having a lot of movement or activity ▪ *physical comedy* [=comedy in which people hit each other, fall down, etc.] **b** : involving or having very violent and forceful activity ▪ *Ice hockey is a very physical sport.* **5 a** : of or relating to the laws of nature ▪ *physical phenomena* **b** *always before a noun* : of or relating to the study of physics ▪ *physical forces* — **phys·i·cal·i·ty** /ˌfɪzə'kæləti/ *n* [U] ▪ *a comedian known for his physicality*

²**physical** *n* [C] : a medical examination to see if a person's body is healthy ▪ *an annual physical* — called also *physical examination*

physical education *n* [U] : sports and exercise taught in schools — abbr. *P.E.*

phys·i·cal·ly /'fɪzɪkli/ *adv* **1** : related to or involving the body or physical form ▪ *She's not physically able to climb the stairs.* ▪ *a physically attractive/disabled person* **2** — used to say what can truly happen or be done by physical effort ▪ *It's physically impossible to be in two places at one time.*

physical therapy *n* [U] *US, medical* : the treatment of a disease or an injury of the muscles or joints with massage, exercises, etc. — abbr. *PT* — called also (*Brit*) *physiotherapy* — **physical therapist** *n* [C]

phy·si·cian /fə'zɪʃən/ *n* [C] *chiefly US* : a medical doctor who is not a surgeon

physician's assistant *n* [C] *US* : a person who provides basic medical care and who usually works with a doctor — called also (*US*) **PA**, (*US*) *physician assistant*

phys·i·cist /ˈfɪzəsɪst/ *n* [*C*] : a scientist specializing in physics

phys·ics /ˈfɪzɪks/ *n* [*U*] : a science that deals with matter and energy • *nuclear physics* • *the laws of physics*

phys·i·ol·o·gy /ˌfɪziˈɑːlədʒi/ *n* [*U*] **1** : a science that deals with the ways that living things function • *anatomy and physiology* **2** : the ways that living things or their parts function • *the physiology of diseased organs* — **phys·i·o·log·i·cal** /ˌfɪziːəˈlɑːdʒɪkəl/ *also chiefly US* **phys·i·o·log·ic** /ˌfɪziːəˈlɑːdʒɪk/ *adj* • *physiological changes/processes* — **phys·i·o·log·i·cal·ly** /ˌfɪziəˈlɑːdʒɪkli/ *adv* — **phys·i·ol·o·gist** /ˌfɪziˈɑːlədʒɪst/ *n* [*C*]

phys·io·ther·a·py /ˌfɪzijouˈθerəpi/ *n* [*U*] *Brit* : PHYSICAL THERAPY

phy·sique /fəˈziːk/ *n* [*C*] : the size and shape of a person's body • *a dancer's physique*

pi·a·nist /piˈænɪst, ˈpiːjənɪst/ *n* [*C*] : a person who plays the piano

pi·ano /piˈænou/ *n*, *pl* **-an·os** [*C*] : a large musical instrument with a keyboard that you play by pressing black and white keys and that produces sound when small hammers inside the piano hit steel wires • *I play (the) piano.* • *a concerto that is played on the piano* • *a piano concerto*

pic /ˈpɪk/ *n*, *pl* **pics** *or* **pix** /ˈpɪks/ [*C*] *informal* **1** : ¹PHOTOGRAPH • *vacation pics* **2** : MOVIE • *an exciting action pic*

pic·a·yune /ˌpɪkiˈjuːn/ *adj*, *US*, *informal* : not very valuable or important • *picayune details*

pic·co·lo /ˈpɪkəˌlou/ *n*, *pl* **-los** [*C*] : a musical instrument that looks like a small flute

¹**pick** /ˈpɪk/ *vb* [*T/I*] **1** : to choose or select (someone or something) from a group • *winners picked by lottery* • *She was picked to replace the retiring CEO.* • *He picked the right/wrong answer.* • *With so many candidates, we can afford to pick and choose.* [=to choose only the best candidate] **2** : to remove (a fruit, flower, etc.) from a plant especially by using your hand • *picking flowers* • *freshly picked vegetables* **3 a** : to remove unwanted material from (something) by using your finger, a small tool, etc. • *Don't pick your nose.* **b** : to remove (something) from something by using your fingers • *Pick the meat from/off the bones.* • *The bones were picked clean by the birds.* **4** *chiefly US* : to play (a guitar, banjo, etc.) by pulling the strings — **bone to pick** see ¹BONE — **pick a fight/quarrel** : to deliberately start a fight with someone • *Never pick a fight you can't win.* — **pick a lock** : to open a lock by using something that is not the key • *He used a knife to pick the lock.* — **pick apart** [*phrasal vb*] **pick (someone or something) apart** *or* **pick apart (someone or something)** *chiefly US* : to say all of the things that are bad or wrong about (someone or something) • *Critics picked the film apart.* — **pick at** [*phrasal vb*] **1** **a** : to eat small amounts of (food) very slowly usually because you do not want to eat • *The kids picked at their salads.* **b** : to pull on (something) with your fingertips or your fingernails often because you are nervous • *She was picking at the buttons on her jacket.* **2** : to criticize (someone or something) especially for small mistakes • *They're constantly picking at each other.* — **pick off** [*phrasal vb*] **pick off (someone or something)** *or* **pick (someone or something) off** : to aim at and shoot (someone or something) • *a sniper picking off soldiers from a rooftop* — **pick on** [*phrasal vb*] **1** : to laugh at or make fun of (someone) in an unkind way • *Kids picked on me for wearing worn-out clothes.* • *Stop picking on me.* **2** : to unfairly criticize (one person or group) when others also deserve to be criticized • *They pick on teachers, but the schools are in trouble because of a lack of funding.* — **pick out** [*phrasal vb*] **pick (something or someone) out** *or* **pick out (something or someone)** **1** : to choose or select (the best or most appropriate person or thing) from a group • *picking out a gift for a friend* **2** : to see and identify (something or someone) • *His red hair makes it easy to pick him out of/in a crowd.* — **pick over** [*phrasal vb*] **pick over (something)** *or* **pick (something) over** : to look at (a group of objects or an amount of material) in order to choose the best ones or to remove pieces you do not want • *Pick over the fish to remove any bones.* — **pick pockets** *or* **pick someone's pocket** : to steal money or objects from someone's pockets or purse • *One boy distracted her while the other picked her pocket.* — **pick (someone or something) to pieces/shreds** : to study and criticize all of the parts of (someone or something) • *The media picked his life to pieces.* — **pick someone's brain/brains** see ¹BRAIN — **pick up** [*phrasal vb*] **1** **pick (someone or something) up** *or* **pick up (someone or something)** **a** : to lift (someone or something) from the ground or a low surface • *Pick up the ball!* **b** : to go somewhere in order to get and bring back (someone or something) • *picking up your kids at school* = *picking your kids up from school* • *I have to pick up the car from the repair shop.* **c** : to let or put (people or things) into or onto a car, bus, ship, etc. • *She had a taxi pick her up at the airport.* • *a ship picking up cargo* **2 a** **pick up** *or* **pick (something) up** *chiefly US* : to make an area clean and organized • *Pick up* [=*clean up*] *that mess!* • *We all helped pick up (the kitchen) after dinner.* **b** **pick up after (someone)** : to clean the mess created by (someone) • *Pick up after yourself.* **3** : to answer a telephone • *I called your house, but no one picked up.* **4** : to become busy usually after a period of little activity • *Business picked up last month.* • *The economy is picking up.* **5 a** : to increase in speed or strength • *The wind picked up.* • *The pace of the movie picks up near the end.* **b** **pick up speed/**

momentum (etc.) : to begin to have more speed/momentum (etc.) ▪ *The cyclists picked up speed.* [=began to go faster] ▪ *The idea is **picking up steam**.* [=becoming more popular] **c pick up the pace** : to go faster ▪ *Come on. Let's pick up the pace.* **6 a** : to begin again after a temporary stop ▪ *After being apart for a year, they picked up (right) where they left off.* **b pick (something) up or pick up (something)** : to start (something) again after a temporary stop ▪ *We'll pick up this discussion tomorrow.* **7 pick (something) up or pick up (something) a** : to buy or get (something) ▪ *I just picked up her new CD.* ▪ *I'll stop to pick up some groceries.* **b** : to earn or gain (something) ▪ *She picked up an award for the performance.* **c** : to become aware of (something) and begin to write about it, work on it, etc. ▪ *The press hasn't picked up the story yet.* **d** : to learn (something) usually in an informal way ▪ *I picked up some French on my trip to Paris.* ▪ *picking up bad habits* **e** : to become sick with (an illness) from someone or something ▪ *I picked up* [=caught] *a cold from my kid.* **f** : to be able to see, hear, or smell (something) ▪ *This radio doesn't pick up many stations.* ▪ *The dogs picked up the scent.* : to become aware of (something) ▪ *picking up clues* **8 pick (someone) up or pick up (someone) a** : to meet and begin a usually brief sexual relationship with (someone) ▪ *going to bars to pick up men* **b** *of the police* : to use the power of the law to take and keep (someone) ▪ *The cops picked up the suspect at a local bar.* **c** : to make (someone) feel more energetic and lively ▪ *Some coffee will pick you up.* **d** *sports* : to get (a player) to join your team ▪ *We picked up two new players.* **9 pick (yourself) up a** : to stand up again after falling ▪ *If you fall, pick yourself up and keep going.* **b** : to recover from a difficult situation ▪ *After his divorce, he picked himself up and started dating again.* **10 pick up and leave/go** : to leave suddenly with your possessions ▪ *He picked up and left without saying goodbye.* **11 pick up the tab/bill/check** : to pay the money that is owed for something ▪ *She picked up the check when we went out to dinner.* **12 pick up the pieces** : to try to make a situation better after something bad has happened ▪ *They created the problem, and now we have to pick up the pieces.* — **pick up on** [*phrasal vb*] **1 a** : to notice or become aware of (something) ▪ *She was nervous, but no one picked up on it.* **b** : to take (an idea, trend, etc.) from another person or group and use it ▪ *Other students quickly picked up on the expression.* **c** : to continue talking about (a statement, subject, etc.) ▪ *I'd like to pick up on your last comment.* **2 pick (someone) on or pick (someone) up on** *Brit* : to question (someone) about (something said or done) ▪ *I'd like to pick you up on one of the points you made.* — **pick your way** : to walk very slowly while carefully choosing where to put your feet ▪ *We picked our way down the path.*

²**pick** *n* **1** [*singular*] : the ability to choose the person or thing that you want ▪ *If you get there early, you'll **have your pick** of seats. ▪ They're all good. **Take your pick**.* [=choose any of them] **2** [*C*] : someone or something that is chosen ▪ *She was their **first/top pick**.* [=the person they wanted most] **3** [*C*] : a tool that has a long handle and a heavy, pointed, metal bar that is used for breaking rocks or digging in hard ground **4** [*C*] : a small, thin piece of plastic or metal that is used to play a guitar or similar instrument

pick·ax *(US)* or *chiefly Brit* **pick·axe** /ˈpɪkˌæks/ *n* [*C*] : ²PICK 3

pick·er /ˈpɪkɚ/ *n* [*C*] : a person or machine that picks crops ▪ *fruit pickers*

¹**pick·et** /ˈpɪkət/ *n* [*C*] **1** : a stick or post that is pointed at the end ▪ *a white **picket fence*** **2 a** : a person or group of people who are picketing ▪ *Pickets marched in front of the company headquarters. ▪ The strikers held **picket signs**.* **b** *Brit* : a protest or strike involving pickets ▪ *Students planned a picket.*

²**picket** *vb* [*T/I*] : to stand or march in a public place in order to protest something ▪ *Workers picketed (outside) the factory.* — **pick·et·er** /ˈpɪkətɚ/ *n* [*C*] *US* ▪ *a crowd of picketers*

picket line *n* [*C*] : a line or group of people who are refusing to go to work until their employer agrees to certain demands ▪ *They refused to **cross the picket line.*** [=to work while other workers were picketing]

pick·ing /ˈpɪkɪŋ/ *n* [*U*] : the activity of removing fruits from a plant for use ▪ *We're going apple picking.*

pick·ings /ˈpɪkɪŋz, ˈpɪkənz/ *n* [*plural*] *informal* : opportunities for getting the things you want or need ▪ *It's **slim pickings**.* [=there are few good things to choose from] ▪ *thieves looking for **easy pickings***

¹**pick·le** /ˈpɪkəl/ *n* **1** [*C*] *chiefly US* : a cucumber that is preserved in salt water or vinegar **2** [*U*] *Brit* : a thick, cold sauce made of chopped vegetables in vinegar **3** [*singular*] *informal* : an unpleasant or difficult situation ▪ *I'm **in a pickle**. Can you help me?*

²**pickle** *vb* **pick·led; pick·ling** [*T*] : to preserve (food) with salt water or vinegar ▪ *pickled cabbage/ginger/herring*

pick-me-up /ˈpɪkmiˌʌp/ *n* [*C*] : something (such as a drink) that makes you feel better and more lively ▪ *Coffee is my usual morning pick-me-up.*

pick·pock·et /ˈpɪkˌpɑːkət/ *n* [*C*] : a thief who steals things from people's pockets and purses

¹**pick·up** /ˈpɪkˌʌp/ *n* **1** [*C*] : a small truck that has an open back with low sides — called also *pickup truck* **2** [*C/U*] : the act of going somewhere to get a person or thing that you will then take to another place ▪ *garbage/trash pickup ▪ Is this order for pickup or delivery?* [=do you want to come and get the order yourself, or do you want us to deliver the order to you?] **3** [*C*] : an increase in activity ▪ *a pickup in business/orders* **4** [*U*] *US* : the ability of a vehicle to increase speed quickly

The car has good pickup.

²**pickup** *adj, always before a noun, US* **1** : organized informally with people who are available at the time • *playing pickup basketball* **2** : of or relating to the act of trying to meet strangers in order to have sexual relationships with them • *pickup lines* [=comments used to start a conversation with someone you are attracted to]

picky /ˈpɪki/ *adj* **pick·i·er**; **-est** : too careful about choosing or accepting things • *a picky* [=*fussy*] *eater*

pic·nic /ˈpɪknɪk/ *n* [C] **1 a** : a meal that is eaten outdoors especially away from home • *We had a picnic on the beach.* • *Let's go on a picnic.* **b** : a trip or party that includes a meal eaten outdoors • *a school/company picnic* **2** *informal* : something that is pleasant or easy • *This job is no picnic.* [=it is not easy] — **pic·nic** *vb* **-nicked**; **-nick·ing** [*I*] • *We picnicked* [=had a picnic] *in the park.* — **pic·nick·er** *n* [C]

pic·to·ri·al /pɪkˈtorijəl/ *adj, always before a noun* : of, relating to, or having pictures • *a pictorial record of the trip* — **pic·to·ri·al·ly** *adv*

¹**pic·ture** /ˈpɪktʃɚ/ *n* **1** [C] : a painting, drawing, or photograph of someone or something • *Hang the picture on the wall.* • *The book has many pictures.* • *Draw a picture of a cat.* • *Let me take your picture.* [=*photograph*] • *a picture frame* [=a frame for holding a picture] **2** [C] : an idea of how something or someone looks, of what something is like, etc. • *She gave us a clear picture of what to expect.* • (*informal*) *Okay, I get the picture.* [=I understand] **3** [U] : a general situation • *The overall economic picture is improving.* • *Her boyfriend is back in the picture.* [=she is dating him again] **4** [C] : an image on the screen of a TV set • *a clear picture* **5** [C] : a movie or film • *an award for best picture* **6** [U] **a** : someone or something that looks exactly like someone or something else • *He's the picture of* [=he looks just like] *his father.* **b** : a perfect example of something • *She's the picture of health.* [=she is very healthy] — *a picture is worth a thousand words* see ¹WORTH — *keep/put someone in the picture chiefly Brit* : to give someone the information that is needed to understand something • *I'll put you in the picture when a decision has been made.* — *paint/draw a picture of* : to create an idea or understanding of something or someone through words, facts, etc. • *The author paints a disturbing picture of life in the camp.*

²**picture** *vb* **-tured**; **-tur·ing** [*T*] **1** : to have a thought or idea about (something or someone) : IMAGINE • *I can't picture changing jobs now.* • *Picture him as a teacher.* **2** : to show (someone or something) in a painting, drawing, or photograph • *She's pictured here with her sister.*

picture–perfect *adj, US* : completely perfect • *a picture-perfect day*

pic·tur·esque /ˌpɪktʃəˈrɛsk/ *adj* : very pretty or charming • *a picturesque village/setting*

picture window *n* [C] : a large window made from one piece of glass

pid·dling /ˈpɪdlɪŋ/ *adj, always before a noun, informal + disapproving* : small or unimportant • *piddling details*

pid·dly /ˈpɪdli/ *adj, always before a noun, informal + disapproving* : PIDDLING

pid·gin /ˈpɪdʒən/ *n* [C/U] : a language that is formed from a mixture of several languages when speakers of different languages need to talk to each other

pie /ˈpaɪ/ *n* [C/U] : a pastry crust that is filled with fruit, meat, etc. • *a piece/slice of apple pie* • *I'd love some pie.* — *a piece/slice/share of the pie* : a portion of a particular amount of money • *Schools need a larger piece of the pie.* [=schools need more money from the government] — *eat humble pie* see EAT — *have a finger in a/the pie* see ¹FINGER

¹**piece** /ˈpiːs/ *n* **1** [C] **a** : an amount that is cut or separated from a larger section of something • *Divide the pie into six equal pieces.* • *a piece of wood/plastic/cloth* • *a big piece of steak/fish* • *two pieces* [=*slices*] *of pizza/bread* **b** : an amount of something considered separately from the rest • *a piece of land/property* **2** [C] : a small often broken part of something • *pieces of broken glass* • *The bike lay in pieces.* • *She ripped the letter to/into pieces.* **3** [C] : one of the parts that form a complete thing when they are put together • *a jigsaw puzzle with 500 pieces* • *a three-piece suit* • *a five-piece band* • *building a wall one piece at a time* • *building a wall piece by piece* • (*Brit*) *The rifle comes to pieces* [=separates into parts] *for easy storage.* **4** [*singular*] : a part of someone or something that is shared with other people — + *of* • *a piece of the jackpot* • *Once she became famous, everyone wanted a piece of her.* [=everyone wanted her to do things for them] **5** [C] : one of a particular type of thing — + *of* • *a piece of paper* • *a plum and two other pieces of fruit* • *a piece of candy/chalk* • *pieces of mail/furniture/clothing/jewelry* • *The car is a piece of junk.* [=it is of poor quality] **6** [C] : an example or amount of something — + *of* • *a piece of information/evidence/advice* • *a famous piece of art/literature/music* **7** [C] **a** : a work of art, music, drama, or literature • *a piece painted by Picasso* **b** : a news article or one of the parts of a TV or radio news program • *a piece about/on local charities* • *an opinion piece* [=an article that expresses someone's views] **8** [C] : one of the small movable objects in a game like chess or checkers **9** [C] : a coin • *a 50-cent piece* • *30 gold pieces* **10** [*singular*] *US, informal* : an amount of distance that is not specified • *It's down the road a piece.* — *bits and pieces* see ¹BIT — *fall to pieces* **1** : to break into parts • *The old map fell to pieces in my hands.* **2** : to become ruined or destroyed • *His life fell to pieces after his divorce.* **3** : to become unable to control your emotions • *I fall to pieces when I think about it.* — *give someone a piece of your mind* see ¹MIND — *go to pieces* : to become

unable to behave normally because you are very nervous or upset • *I go (all) to pieces if I have to give a speech.* — **in one piece** : without being hurt or damaged • *We made it home in one piece.* [=safe and sound] — **of a piece 1** : having similar qualities or characteristics • *The two crimes are of a piece.* [=are very similar] **2** : in agreement or harmony with something • *The theory is of a piece* [=consistent] *with her earlier work.* — **pick (someone or something) to pieces** see ¹PICK — **pick up the pieces** see ¹PICK — **say your piece** : to say what you want to say • *You've said your piece, now let me respond.* — **tear (someone or something) to pieces** see ¹TEAR — **to pieces** *informal* : very much • *We're thrilled to pieces!* — see also ¹PIECE 2, 3 (above)

²**piece** *vb* **pieced; piec·ing** — **piece together** [*phrasal vb*] **piece (something) together** *or* **piece together (something)** : to make (something) by bringing together various parts or pieces • *She pieces quilts together from scraps of old cloth.* : to bring together (parts or pieces) to form one complete thing • *piecing together the clues/evidence*

piece·meal /ˈpiːsˌmiːl/ *adj* : done or made in a gradual way in a series of separate steps • *piecemeal repairs/approaches* — **piecemeal** *adv* • *selling land piecemeal* [=piece by piece]

piece of cake *n* [*singular*] *informal* : something that is easy to do • *The test was a piece of cake.*

piece of work *n* [C] *chiefly US, informal + often disapproving* : someone who is difficult to understand • *She's a piece of work, isn't she?* — **a nasty piece of work** *chiefly Brit* : an unkind or unpleasant person

piece·work /ˈpiːsˌwɚk/ *n* [U] : work in which you are paid for each thing you make • *doing piecework in a factory* • *piecework rates/earnings*

pie chart *n* [C] : a chart consisting of a circle that is divided into parts to show the size of the different amounts that are a part of a whole amount

pie in the sky *n* [U] : a very unlikely or unrealistic goal, plan, etc. • *a plan that seems like pie in the sky* — **pie-in-the-sky** *adj* • *pie-in-the-sky plans/promises*

pier /ˈpɪɚ/ *n* [C] : a structure that goes out from a shore into the water • *We walked down the pier and boarded the ship.*

pierce /ˈpɪɚs/ *vb* **pierced; pierc·ing** [T/I] **1** : to make a hole in or through (something) • *The bullet pierced (through) his lung.* • *She got her ears pierced.* [=she had holes made in her ears so that she could wear earrings] • *She has pierced ears.* **2** : to go through or into (something) in a forceful or noticeable way • *The flashlight pierced (through) the darkness.*

piercing *adj* **1** : seeming to have the power to sense a person's thoughts or feelings • *I tried to avoid his piercing eyes/stare.* **2** : very loud and high-pitched • *a piercing scream/voice* **3** : felt in a very noticeable way • *a piercing sadness* **4** : very cold • *a piercing wind* — **pierc·ing·ly** *adv*

pi·e·ty /ˈpajəti/ *n* [U] : devotion to God • *an act of piety*

pif·fling /ˈpɪfəlɪŋ/ *adj, chiefly Brit, informal + disapproving* : small and unimportant : PIDDLING

¹**pig** /ˈpɪg/ *n* [C] **1** : an animal that has a fat body with short legs, a small tail, and a wide nose and that is raised on a farm or lives in the wild **2** *informal + disapproving* **a** : someone who eats too much food • *I made a pig of myself* [=I ate too much] *at dinner.* **b** : a greedy person • *a selfish pig* **c** : someone who is unpleasant or offensive • *Don't be a pig. Say "excuse me" after you burp.* • *They live like pigs.* [=they live in a dirty environment] • *He is a sexist pig.* — **make a pig's ear (out) of** *Brit, informal* : to do or manage something badly — **when pigs fly** *US, informal* — used to say that you think that something will never happen • *They'll win the championship when pigs fly.* [=they'll never win the championship]

²**pig** *vb* **pigged; pig·ging** — **pig out** [*phrasal vb*] *informal* : to eat a lot of food at one time • *pigging out on pizza*

pi·geon /ˈpɪdʒən/ *n* [C] : a gray bird that is common in cities

pi·geon·hole /ˈpɪdʒənˌhoʊl/ *vb* **-holed; -hol·ing** [T] *disapproving* : to unfairly think of or describe (someone or something) as belonging to a particular group, having only one skill, etc. • *She was pigeonholed as a folk musician.* — **pigeonhole** *n* [C] • *She was put in a pigeonhole.* [=she was pigeonholed]

pi·geon–toed /ˈpɪdʒənˌtoʊd/ *adj* : having feet that are turned toward each other • *a pigeon-toed child*

pig·gish /ˈpɪgɪʃ/ *adj, chiefly US, informal + disapproving* : greedy, offensive, or unpleasant • *a piggish attitude toward women* — **pig·gish·ly** *adv*

¹**pig·gy·back** /ˈpɪgiˌbæk/ *n* [C] : the act of carrying someone on your back or shoulders • *Her father gave her a piggyback ride.* [=he carried her on his back] — **piggyback** *adv* • *carrying someone piggyback*

²**piggyback** *vb* [T/I] : to be carried by or connected to something else or to cause (something) to be carried by or connected to something else • *(figurative) The legislation is being piggybacked on another bill.* [=is being added to another bill so that they will both be passed together]

piggy bank *n* [C] : a container that is often shaped like a pig and that is used for saving coins

pig·head·ed /ˈpɪgˌhɛdəd/ *adj, disapproving* : very stubborn • *He's too pigheaded to listen to advice.* — **pig·head·ed·ness** *n* [U]

pig·let /ˈpɪglət/ *n* [C] : a baby pig

pig·ment /ˈpɪgmənt/ *n* **1** : a natural substance that gives color to animals and plants • *skin pigment* **2** : a substance that gives color to something else • *pigments used to give color to paint and ink* — **pig·ment·ed** /ˈpɪgˌmɛntəd/ *adj* • *pigmented paints*

pig·men·ta·tion /ˌpɪgmənˈteɪʃən/ n [U]
: the natural coloring of people, animals,
or plants ▪ *dark skin pigmentation*

pigmy *variant spelling of* PYGMY

pig·pen /ˈpɪgˌpen/ n [C] *US*   **1** : PIGSTY 1
2 : PIGSTY 2

pig·sty /ˈpɪgˌstaɪ/ n, pl **-sties** [C]   **1** : a
place where pigs are kept   **2** *informal* : a
dirty or messy place ▪ *His room was a pigsty.*

pig·tails /ˈpɪgˌteɪlz/ n [plural] : hair tied
in two ponytails or braids with one on
each side of the head ▪ *She wore her hair
in pigtails.* — **pig·tailed** /ˈpɪgˌteɪld/ adj,
always before a noun ▪ *a pigtailed girl*

pike n [C]   **1** pl **pike** or **pikes** : a large,
long fish that lives in rivers and lakes   **2**
US, informal : TURNPIKE — **come
down the pike** *US, informal* : to happen
or appear ▪ *A chance like this doesn't
come down the pike every day.*

pi·laf /ˈpiːˌlɑːf, ˈpɪˌlɑːf, Brit ˈpiːˌlæf/ n
[C/U] : a dish that is made of seasoned
rice and vegetables and often meat ▪ *a
serving of rice pilaf*

Pi·la·tes /pəˈlɑːtiz/ n [U] : a system of exercises

pi·lau /pəˈloʊ, Brit ˈpiːˌlaʊ/ n [C/U] *chiefly
Brit* : PILAF

¹**pile** /ˈpajəl/ n   **1** [C] : a group of things
that are put one on top of another ▪ *Put
the magazines in a pile.* ▪ *raking leaves
into piles* ▪ *a pile of wood/clothes* ▪
(*figurative*) *The team finished the season
at the top/bottom of the pile.* [=in a high/
low position]   **2** [C] *informal* : a very
large amount of something ▪ *piles of
work/money*   **3** [U, singular] : a soft surface of short threads on a rug, carpet,
etc. ▪ *a rug with (a) thick pile*

²**pile** vb **piled; pil·ing**   **1** [T] : to put
(something) in a pile ▪ *Books were piled
(up) high on the table.*   **2** [T] : to put a
large amount of things on or in (something) ▪ *The chair was piled (high) with
clothes.* [=there was a pile of clothes on
the chair]   **3** [T] : to put (things or people) *into* or *onto* something ▪ *He piled potatoes onto his plate.* ▪ *piling clothes into a
suitcase*   **4** [I] of a group of people, animals, etc. : to go into or onto something ▪
The kids piled into the van. ▪ *We piled onto
the couch.* — **pile in** [phrasal vb] of a
group of people, animals, etc. : to move
into a place or vehicle ▪ *She parked the
van and we all piled in.* — **pile on** [phras-
al vb]   **1** : to put a large amount of
(something) on something or someone ▪
He piled on the gravy. ▪ *The teacher piled
on more work.* [=gave the class more
work] ◊ If you **pile on the pounds**, you
gain a lot of weight.   **2** *US, informal* : to
join other people in criticizing something
or someone ▪ *After one negative review, all
the other critics started piling on.* — **pile
out** [phrasal vb] of a group of people, animals, etc. : to move out of a place or a
vehicle ▪ *The crowd piled out of the theater.* — **pile up** [phrasal vb] : to increase
in amount or number to a total that is
difficult to manage ▪ *The bills are piling
up.* ▪ *Traffic piled up because of the accident.*

pile-up /ˈpajəlˌʌp/ n [C]   **1** : an accident

in which several vehicles crash into each
other ▪ *a five-car pileup*   **2** : a large
amount of something that has increased
gradually ▪ *a pileup of debt*

pil·fer /ˈpɪlfə/ vb [T/I] : to steal things
that are not very valuable ▪ *He was
caught pilfering (stamps and paper).*

pil·grim /ˈpɪlgrəm/ n [C]   **1** : someone
who travels to a holy place ▪ *pilgrims
traveling to Mecca*   **2 Pilgrim** : one of the
people who traveled by boat from England and created the first permanent
settlement in New England at Plymouth
in 1620

pil·grim·age /ˈpɪlgrəmɪdʒ/ n [C/U]   **1** : a
journey to a holy place ▪ *He made a pilgrimage to Mecca.*   **2** : a journey to a
special or unusual place ▪ *a pilgrimage to
historical battlefields*

pill /ˈpɪl/ n   **1 a** [C] : a small, rounded object that you swallow and that contains
medicine, vitamins, etc.   **b the pill** : a
pill that a woman takes so that she will
not become pregnant ▪ *She is on the pill.*
[=she is taking birth control pills regular-
ly]   **2** [C] *US, informal* : an annoying
person ▪ *Don't be such a pill.*

pil·lage /ˈpɪlɪdʒ/ vb **-laged; -lag·ing** [T/I]
: to take things from (a place, such as a
city or town) by force especially during a
war : to loot or plunder (a place) ▪ *The
town was pillaged.* — **pillage** n [U]
: *looting and pillaging*

pil·lar /ˈpɪlə/ n [C]   **1** : a large post that
helps to hold up something (such as a
roof)   **2** : someone who is an important
member of a group ▪ *a pillar of society*   **3**
: a basic fact, idea, or principle of something ▪ *The right to vote is a pillar of democracy.*   **4** : something that rises into
the air in a tall, thin shape ▪ *pillars of
smoke* — **pillar of strength** : someone
or something that gives support or help
during difficult times ▪ *He was my/a pillar of strength during my illness.*

pill·box /ˈpɪlˌbɑːks/ n [C]   **1** : a small box
for holding pills   **2** : a small, low shelter
for machine guns and other weapons   **3**
: a small, round hat without a brim

pil·lo·ry /ˈpɪləri/ vb **-ries; -ried; -ry·ing**
[T] : to publicly criticize (someone) in a
very harsh way ▪ *The mayor was pilloried
by the press for his comments.*

pil·low /ˈpɪloʊ/ n [C] : a bag filled with
soft material that is used as a cushion
usually for the head of a person who is
lying down

pil·low·case /ˈpɪloʊˌkeɪs/ n [C] : a removable covering for a pillow

pil·low·slip /ˈpɪloʊˌslɪp/ n [C] : PILLOW-
CASE

pillow talk n [U] *informal* : a conversation between lovers in bed

¹**pi·lot** /ˈpaɪlət/ n [C]   **1** : a person who
flies an airplane, helicopter, etc.   **2** : a
person who steers or guides a ship into
and out of a port or in dangerous waters
3 : a single television show that is made
as a test to see if a television series based
on the show would be popular and successful ▪ PILOT LIGHT

²**pilot** vb [T]   **1** : to fly (an airplane, spacecraft, etc.) ▪ *piloting a helicopter*   **2** : to
steer or guide (a ship) ▪ *He piloted the
ship into port.* ▪ (*figurative*) *The education*

bill was piloted through the House and Senate.

³**pilot** *adj, always before a noun* : done as a test to see if a larger program, study, etc., should be done ▪ *a pilot program/project/study*

pilot light *n [C]* : a small flame that is always burning in a gas stove, burner, etc., and that is used to light a larger flame

pi·men·to /pə'mɛntoʊ/ *n, pl* **pi·men·tos** *or* **pi·men·toes** *[C]* : PIMIENTO

pi·mien·to /pəm'jɛntoʊ/ *n, pl* **-tos** *[C]* : a type of small, mildly sweet pepper

pimp /'pɪmp/ *n [C]* : a man who makes money illegally by getting customers for prostitutes

pim·ple /'pɪmpəl/ *n [C]* : a small, red, swollen spot on the skin — **pim·pled** /'pɪmpəld/ *adj* ▪ *a pimpled face* — **pim·ply** /'pɪmpəli/ *adj* **pim·pli·er; -est** ▪ *pimply skin*

¹**pin** /'pɪn/ *n [C]* **1** : a thin, small, pointed piece of stiff wire with a rounded head at one end that is used especially for fastening pieces of cloth **2 a** : a thin, pointed piece of stiff wire with a decoration at one end **b** *chiefly US* : BROOCH **c** : a small usually circular object that has writing and often a picture on it and that has a pin on the back so that it can be fastened to clothing, bags, etc. ▪ *political campaign pins* **3** : a thin piece of wood, metal, or plastic that is used for holding things together or for hanging one thing from another **4** : a thin piece of metal that is removed to trigger the explosion of a grenade ▪ *pull the pin* **5** *golf* : a long stick with a flag at the top that shows where the hole is on a green **6** *bowling* : one of the usually white standing pieces that are knocked down with the ball — **you could hear a pin drop** — used to say that it was so quiet that the smallest noise could be heard ▪ *After he announced that he was leaving, you could hear a pin drop in the office.*

²**pin** *vb* **pinned; pin·ning** *[T]* **1** : to fasten or attach (something) with a pin ▪ *She pinned a rose to her dress.* ▪ *She pinned up/back her hair.* **2** : to prevent or stop (someone or something) from moving by holding or pressing firmly against something ▪ *He was pinned under the wreckage.* ▪ *The guards pinned his arms to his sides.* ▪ *(figurative) The soldiers were pinned down by enemy fire.* ▪ *They were unable to move because they were being shot at by the enemy)* — **pin down** *[phrasal vb]* **1 pin (someone) down** : to cause or force (someone) to make a definite statement or decision about something ▪ *He talked in a general way, but they couldn't pin him down to specifics.* **2 pin down (something)** *or* **pin (something) down** : to find out (something) with certainty ▪ *I'm trying to pin down the source of the problem.* — **pin on** *[phrasal vb]* **1 pin (something) on** : to say that (something) was done or caused by (someone) ▪ *The police pinned the robbery on him.* **2 pin (all) your hopes on** : to hope very much that (something) will help you or allow you to succeed ▪ *You shouldn't pin all your hopes on getting the job.*

PIN /'pɪn/ *abbr* personal identification number ✧ A personal identification number is a secret number that is used to get money from a bank account through a machine, to get personal information on a Web site, etc.

pi·ña co·la·da /'pi:njəkoʊ'lɑːdə/ *n [C]* : a drink that is made of rum, coconut juice, and pineapple juice mixed with ice

pin·a·fore /'pɪnə,foɚ/ *n [C]* : JUMPER 2

pin·ball /'pɪn,bɑːl/ *n [U]* : a game played on a special machine in which a ball scores points by hitting targets while rolling down a slanting surface and the player tries to control the ball with a set of levers ▪ *playing pinball* ▪ *a pinball machine*

pin·cer /'pɪnsɚ/ *n* **1** *[plural]* : a small tool that is used for holding or gripping small objects **2** *[C]* : a claw of a lobster or crab and some insects

¹**pinch** /'pɪntʃ/ *vb* **1** *[T]* **a** : to squeeze (someone's skin) between your thumb and finger often in a painful way ▪ *He pinched her cheek/arm.* **b** : to squeeze or press (something) together with your thumb and finger ▪ *Pinch together the edges of the dough.* **2** *[T/I]* : to press against or squeeze (a part of the body) in a painful way ▪ *I pinched my fingers in the door.* ▪ *These shoes pinch (my toes).* ▪ *a pinched nerve* [=a nerve pressed against a bone in a painful way] **3** *[I]* : to spend as little money as possible ▪ *By pinching and scraping, she managed to save enough money to buy a new car.* **4** *[T]* *chiefly Brit, informal* : to steal (something) ▪ *Someone pinched her purse.* — **pinch pennies** *informal* : to spend as little money as possible ▪ *He pinched pennies to live on his small paycheck.*

²**pinch** *n [C]* **1** : the act of pinching someone or something ▪ *He gave me a pinch on the cheek.* [=he pinched my cheek] **2** : the amount of something that can be held between your finger and thumb ▪ *a pinch of salt* — **feel the pinch** : to experience the problems caused by not having enough money or by paying higher costs ▪ *We are starting to feel the pinch of high fuel costs.* — **in a pinch** *(US)* or Brit **at a pinch** : in a bad situation when help is needed ▪ *I can help out in a pinch if you need a babysitter.*

³**pinch** *adj, always before a noun, US, baseball* **1** : used as a substitute for another player ▪ *a pinch runner/hitter* **2** : made by a pinch hitter ▪ *a pinch hit*

pinched *adj* : having a thin and unhealthy appearance ▪ *pinched cheeks* — **pinched for** *chiefly US, informal* : not having enough of (something) ▪ *I was pinched for cash/money/time.*

pinch–hit /'pɪntʃ'hɪt/ *vb* **-hit; -hit·ting** *[I]* US **1** *baseball* : to bat in the place of another player ▪ *Who is pinch-hitting for the pitcher?* **2** *informal* : to act or serve in place of another person : SUBSTITUTE ▪ *She wasn't able to attend the ceremony, so he went to pinch-hit for her.* — **pinch hitter** *n [C]*

pin·cush·ion /'pɪn,kʊʃən/ *n [C]* : a small bag filled with a soft material that pins and needles can be pushed into when they are not being used

¹**pine** /ˈpaɪn/ n, pl **pines** or **pine** **1** [C] : a tree that has long, thin needles instead of leaves and that stays green throughout the year — called also *pine tree* **2** [U] : the wood of a pine tree — **pine** adj • *pine bark/needles/forests/floors* — **pin·ey** also **piny** /ˈpaɪni/ adj, chiefly US • *a piney aroma*

²**pine** vb **pined; pin·ing** [I] **1** : to become thin and weak because of sadness or loss • *Since his wife left him, he spends his days alone, pining away.* — **pine after** [phrasal vb] US : to want or desire (someone or something) very much • *teenage girls pining after rock stars* — **pine for** [phrasal vb] : to feel very sad because you want (something) or because you are not with (someone) • *He's pining for his college sweetheart.*

pine·ap·ple /ˈpaɪˌnæpəl/ n [C/U] : a large fruit that grows on a tropical tree and that has thick skin and very sweet, juicy, yellow flesh

pine·cone /ˈpaɪnˌkoʊn/ n [C] : a hard and dry part that is the fruit of a pine tree and contains many seeds

pine nut n [C] : the seed of some pine trees that is used as food

ping /ˈpɪŋ/ vb [I] **1** : to make the high, sharp sound of a small, hard object bouncing off metal or glass • *The engine in my car keeps pinging.* **2** : to bounce off something with a sharp, high sound • *Pebbles pinged off the car.* — **ping** n [C]

Ping–Pong /ˈpɪŋˌpɑːŋ/ trademark — used for table tennis

pin·head /ˈpɪnˌhɛd/ n [C] **1** : the rounded end of a pin **2** US, informal : a stupid or foolish person

pin·hole /ˈpɪnˌhoʊl/ n [C] : a very small hole made by a pin or in some other way

pin·ion /ˈpɪnjən/ vb [T] : to tie up (someone's arms or legs) very tightly • *They pinioned his arms behind his back.*

pink /ˈpɪŋk/ n **1** [C/U] : a pale red color **2** [C] : a plant with narrow leaves and colorful flowers — **pink** adj • *pink roses* — **pink·ness** n [U]

pink·eye /ˈpɪŋkˌaɪ/ n [U] chiefly US, medical : CONJUNCTIVITIS

pin·kie or **pin·ky** /ˈpɪŋki/ n, pl **-kies** [C] chiefly US + Scotland, informal : LITTLE FINGER

pink slip n [C] chiefly US, informal : a notice that is given to a worker by an employer saying that the worker's job is ending • [=were laid off; lost their jobs] — *Many workers were given the pink slip.* = *Many workers got the pink slip.* — **pink–slip** vb **-slipped; -slip·ping** [T] • *Many workers have been/gotten pink-slipped.*

pin·na·cle /ˈpɪnɪkəl/ n [C] **1** : a high mountaintop **2** : the best or most important part of something • *achieving the pinnacle of success* **3** : a tower on the roof of a building that comes to a narrow point at the top

pi·noch·le /ˈpiːˌnʌkəl/ n [U] : a card game played with a special deck of 48 cards

¹**pin·point** /ˈpɪnˌpɔɪnt/ n [C] : a very small point or dot • *a pinpoint of light*

²**pinpoint** adj, always before a noun : very

exact or precise • *pinpoint accuracy/control/precision*

³**pinpoint** vb [T] **1** : to find out (something) with certainty • *Can they pinpoint the cause of the fire?* **2** : to find or locate the exact position of (something) • *He pinpointed the address on the map.*

pin·prick /ˈpɪnˌprɪk/ n [C] **1** : PINHOLE **2** : a very small point or dot • *a pinprick of light* **3** : a slight but sharp pain caused by a pin or needle • *(figurative) I felt a pinprick of jealousy when I saw them together.*

pins and needles n [U] : the unpleasant tingling feeling in a part of your body (such as your arm or leg) as it becomes numb or recovers from being numb — **on pins and needles** US : feeling very nervous and unsure about what will happen • *Everyone was on pins and needles waiting to hear the jury's verdict.*

pin·stripe /ˈpɪnˌstraɪp/ n **1** [C] : a thin vertical stripe on cloth • *a dark suit with white pinstripes* **2** [plural] : a suit with pinstripes • *a man dressed in pinstripes* — **pin–striped** /ˈpɪnˌstraɪpt/ adj • *a pin-striped suit*

pint /ˈpaɪnt/ n [C] **1** US : a unit for measuring liquids that is equal to 0.473 liters **2** Brit : a unit for measuring liquids that is equal to 0.568 liters **3** chiefly Brit : a pint of beer • *I'd like another pint, please.*

pin·to /ˈpɪntoʊ/ n, pl **-tos** [C] US : a horse or pony that has patches of white and another color

pinto bean n [C] : a type of small bean that is grown for food

pint–sized /ˈpaɪntˌsaɪzd/ or **pint–size** /ˈpaɪntˌsaɪz/ adj, informal : very small • *a pint-sized boy*

pin·up /ˈpɪnˌʌp/ n [C] **1** : a photograph of an attractive person (such as an actress or model) that is hung or pinned on a wall **2** : a person who appears in or is attractive enough to appear in a pinup

pin·wheel /ˈpɪnˌwiːl/ n [C] US : a toy that has a set of thin blades that are arranged like a fan on the end of a stick and that spin like a wheel when air is blown on them

¹**pi·o·neer** /ˌpajəˈniɚ/ n [C] **1** : a person who helps create or develop new ideas, methods, etc. • *They were pioneers in the field of American medicine.* **2** : someone who is one of the first people to move to and live in a new area • *the pioneers who settled in the American West in the 19th century*

²**pioneer** vb [T/I] : to help create or develop (new ideas, methods, etc.) • *a painter who pioneered a new art form* • *pioneering a new cancer treatment* — **pi·o·neer·ing** /ˌpajəˈnirɪŋ/ adj • *pioneering studies/experiments*

pi·ous /ˈpajəs/ adj **1** : deeply religious • *pious people* **2** disapproving : falsely appearing to be good or moral • *a politician's pious pronouncements* — **pious hope/wish** : something that is hoped for but will probably not happen • *His speech contained no practical solutions, just the pious hope that the war would end soon.* — **pi·ous·ly** adv

pip /ˈpɪp/ n [C] **1** US **a** : one of the dots on dice or dominoes that show their value **b** : a design on a playing card that shows the suit and value **2** chiefly Brit : a small, hard seed of some fruits ▪ orange/apple pips **3** Brit : a short, high sound ▪ BEEP

¹**pipe** /ˈpaɪp/ n **1** [C] : a long, hollow tube for carrying water, steam, gas, etc. **2** [C] : a tube with a small bowl at one end that is used for smoking tobacco ▪ He smokes a pipe. **3 a** [C] : a musical instrument that is in the shape of a tube, has holes along the top, and is played by blowing **b** [C] : any one of the large tubes of an organ that produce sound when air goes through them **c** [plural] : BAGPIPE **d** [plural] US, informal : a singer's voice ▪ a singer with a fine set of pipes

²**pipe** vb **piped**; **pip·ing 1** [T] : to carry or move (something, such as water or oil) in a pipe ▪ Water is piped into the cabin from an underground stream. **2** [T] : to send (music or recorded sound) from one place to another through an electrical connection ▪ Music is piped into every store in the mall. **3 a** [I] : to play a pipe or the bagpipes ▪ The pipers piped while the drummers drummed. **b** [T] : to play (a tune or song) on a pipe or the bagpipes ▪ piping a tune — **pipe down** [phrasal vb] informal : to stop talking ▪ The teacher told the students to pipe down. — **pipe up** [phrasal vb] informal : to start talking ▪ He suddenly piped up to ask where we were going.

pipe cleaner n [C] : a piece of wire that is covered with soft cloth and used to clean the inside of a tobacco pipe

pipe dream n [C] : a hope, wish, or dream that is impossible to achieve or not practical ▪ His plan for starting his own business was just a pipe dream.

pipe·line /ˈpaɪpˌlaɪn/ n **1** [C] : a line of connected pipes that are used for carrying liquids and gases over a long distance ▪ a natural gas pipeline ▪ (figurative) a weapons/news pipeline **2** the pipeline : the system for developing and producing something ▪ the next wave of products to come down the pipeline [=to be produced] ▪ Newer treatments for the disease are in the pipeline. [=are being developed]

pipe organ n [C] : ORGAN 2

pip·er /ˈpaɪpɚ/ n [C] : a person who plays a pipe or the bagpipes — **pay the piper** informal **1** : to pay the cost of something ▪ They're the ones who are paying the piper. **2** chiefly US : to pay money or suffer in some way because of something you have done ▪ They have mismanaged the company for years, and now they have to pay the piper.

pi·pette /paɪˈpɛt, Brit pɪˈpɛt/ n [C] technical : a narrow glass tube used for measuring liquid or for moving small amounts of liquid from one place to another

¹**pip·ing** /ˈpaɪpɪŋ/ n [U] **1** : pipes that carry water, gas, etc. ▪ kitchen/bathroom piping **2** : a narrow tube of cloth that is used to decorate clothes, furniture, etc. ▪

a sofa trimmed with blue piping

²**piping** adj : having a high-pitched sound or tone ▪ the piping voices of small children

piping hot adj, of food or drink : very hot ▪ piping hot coffee/soup

pip·squeak /ˈpɪpˌskwiːk/ n [C] informal : a person who is very small or unimportant

pi·quant /ˈpiːkənt/ adj, formal **1** : having a pleasant, spicy taste ▪ a piquant sauce **2** : interesting and exciting ▪ a piquant bit of gossip — **pi·quan·cy** /ˈpiːkənsi/ n [U]

¹**pique** /ˈpiːk/ n [U] formal : a sudden feeling of annoyance or anger when someone has offended you ▪ He slammed the door in a fit of pique.

²**pique** vb **piqued**; **piqu·ing** [T] **1** chiefly US : to cause (curiosity or interest) ▪ The package piqued my curiosity. **2** chiefly Brit : to make (someone) annoyed or angry ▪ I was piqued by his rudeness.

pi·ra·cy /ˈpaɪrəsi/ n [U] **1** : the act of attacking and stealing from a ship at sea **2 a** : the act of illegally copying someone's product or invention without permission ▪ software/music/video piracy **b** : the act of illegally making television or radio broadcasts ▪ radio piracy

pi·ra·nha /pəˈrɑːnə/ n [C] : a small South American fish that has sharp teeth and that eats the flesh of animals

¹**pi·rate** /ˈpaɪrət/ n [C] **1** : someone who attacks and steals from a ship at sea **2 a** : someone who illegally copies a product or invention without permission ▪ software pirates ▪ a pirate version of the CD **b** : a person or organization that illegally makes television or radio broadcasts ▪ pirate radio

²**pirate** vb **-rat·ed**; **-rat·ing** [T] : to illegally copy (something) without permission ▪ He was accused of pirating their invention. ▪ pirated videotapes

pir·ou·ette /ˌpɪrəˈwɛt/ n [C] : a full turn on the front of one foot in ballet — **pirouette** vb **-ett·ed**; **-ett·ing** [I] ▪ The dancers pirouetted across the stage.

Pi·sces /ˈpaɪˌsiːz/ n, pl **Pisces 1** [U] : the 12th sign of the zodiac that comes between Aquarius and Aries and is symbolized by a pair of fish **2** [C] : a person born between February 19 and March 20

¹**piss** /ˈpɪs/ vb, informal + impolite **1** [I] : URINATE **2** [T] : to urinate in or on (something) ▪ He pissed the bed. — **piss about/around** [phrasal vb] Brit, informal + impolite : to spend time doing things that are not useful or serious — **piss and moan** US, informal + impolite : to complain in a constant or annoying way ▪ He's always pissing and moaning about something. — **piss away** [phrasal vb] **piss (something) away** or **piss away (something)** US, informal + impolite : to foolishly waste (something, such as money, talent, opportunities, etc.) ▪ He pissed a fortune away on gambling and drinking. — **piss off** [phrasal vb] informal + impolite **1** Brit : to go away ▪ Why don't you piss off? **2 piss (someone) off** or **piss off (someone)** : to make (someone) very angry or annoyed ▪ That really pisses me off.

²**piss** *n, informal + impolite* **1** [U] : URINE **2** [*singular*] : an act of urinating • *He says he has to take a piss.* = (*Brit*) *He says he has to have a piss.* — **piss and vinegar** *US, informal + impolite* : strength and energy • *We were full of piss and vinegar back then.* — **take the piss out of** *Brit, informal + impolite* : to make fun of or laugh at (someone or something)

pissed /ˈpɪst/ *adj* **1** *or* **pissed off** *chiefly US, informal + impolite* : very angry or annoyed at someone **2** *Brit slang* : very drunk or intoxicated

pis·ta·chio /pəˈstæʃijoʊ/ *n, pl* **-chios** [C] : a small green nut

pis·tol /ˈpɪstl̩/ *n* [C] : a small gun made to be aimed and fired with one hand

pis·ton /ˈpɪstən/ *n* [C] : a part of an engine that moves up and down inside a tube and that causes other parts of the engine to move

¹**pit** /ˈpɪt/ *n* **1** [C] : a hole in the ground usually made by digging • *We dug a pit for the fire.* **2** [C] **a** : a large, deep hole in the ground from which stones or minerals are dug out • *a gravel/chalk/tar pit* **b** *chiefly Brit* : a coal mine **3** [C] : something that uses up or holds a very large amount of money, food, information, etc. • *His stomach is a bottomless pit.* [=he eats constantly] **4** [C] : an area separated from and often placed below the areas next to it: such as **a** : an outdoor area where food is cooked • *a barbecue pit* **b** : an area where animals are brought to fight **c** : the space in a theater where an orchestra plays • *the orchestra pit* **d** : an area of dirt or grass used for playing certain games • *a horseshoe pit* **e** : an area beside a racetrack used for servicing cars during a race • *The driver stopped in the pits to refuel.* **5** [C] : a small hole or dent on the surface of something **6** *a* [C] : a very bad or unpleasant place or situation • *The area is a pit of depression/despair/hopelessness.* • **the pits** *informal* : something that is very bad or unpleasant • *Her new movie is the pits!* [=her new movie is terrible] **7** [C] *informal* : ARMPIT **8** [C] *US* : the hard middle part of a fruit • *peach/cherry/olive pits* — **the pit of your/the stomach** : the part of a person's stomach where strong feelings of nervousness, excitement, etc., can be felt • *She felt a flutter in the pit of her stomach.*

²**pit** *vb* **pit·ted; pit·ting 1** [T] : to make small holes or dents in (something) • *A hailstorm badly pitted the car's roof.* **2** [I] *car racing* : to make a pit stop • *The driver had to pit because of engine problems.* **3** [T] *US* : to remove the pit from (a piece of fruit) • *pitting a plum/peach* — **pit against** [*phrasal vb*] **pit (someone or something) against** : to cause (someone or something) to fight or compete against (another person or thing) • *The team will be pitted against* [=will be playing against] *last year's champion in the finals.*

pi·ta (*US*) *or Brit* **pit·ta** /ˈpiːtə, *Brit* ˈpɪtə/ *n* [C/U] : a type of thin, flat bread that can be separated to form a pocket for holding food — called also (*US*) *pita bread*, (*Brit*) *pitta bread*

pit bull *n* [C] : a type of dog that is known for its strength and its ability to fight — called also *pit bull terrier*

¹**pitch** /ˈpɪtʃ/ *n* **1** [C/U] : the highness or lowness of a sound • *Her voice has a high pitch.* • *You were a little off pitch* [=too high or too low] *on that last note.* • *His singing was perfectly on pitch.* **2** [C] *baseball* : an act of throwing a baseball to a batter or the ball that is thrown to a batter • *She fouled off the first pitch.* **3** [C] : things that are said by someone (such as a salesman) in order to make someone want to buy, do, or accept something • *an advertising pitch* — see also SALES PITCH **4** [*singular*] : a state of intense feeling • *Tensions have risen to a high/feverish pitch.* **5** [C] : the amount or degree of slope on a roof or other surface • *a roof with a steep pitch* **6** [U] : up and down movement of a ship or airplane **7** [C] *Brit* : PLAYING FIELD • *a rugby/cricket pitch* **8** [U] **a** : a thick, black, sticky substance that is used on roofs, boats, etc., to keep out water • *ships sealed/coated with pitch* • *The sky was as black/dark as pitch.* [=extremely black/dark] **b** : a sticky substance that is produced by some trees (such as pines) • *pine pitch*

²**pitch** *vb* **1** [T] : to throw or toss (something) • *pitching horseshoes* • *She pitched the empty box into the garbage.* **2** [T/I] *baseball* **a** : to throw a baseball to a batter • *He pitched me a curveball.* • *the team's pitching coach/staff* **b** : to play baseball as a pitcher • *He pitched in the major leagues for several years.* **3** [T] : to talk about or describe (something) in a favorable way so that people will want to buy it, accept it, etc. • *She pitched the story to her editor.* **4** [T] **a** : to cause (a sound, your voice, etc.) to be high or low • *differently pitched sounds* **b** : to cause (a song, an instrument, etc.) to be in a particular musical key • *a tune pitched in the key of C* **5** [T] **a** : to make or design (something) for people at a particular level • *They pitched the test at a fifth-grade reading level.* **b** : to cause (something) to be at a particular level • *Try not to pitch your hopes/ambitions too high.* **6** [I] *of a surface* : to slope downward • *The road pitches steeply down the side of the mountain.* **7** [I] : to fall or move suddenly in a particular direction • *The nose of the airplane suddenly pitched downward.* **8** [T/I] *golf* : to hit a golf ball so that it goes very high in the air and rolls very little after hitting the ground • *She pitched (the ball) onto the green.* **9** [T] : to set up (a tent or camp) • *We pitched our tent next to the river.* — **pitch a fit/tantrum** *US, informal* : to become very upset and angry in a loud and uncontrolled way • *He pitched a fit about the bill.* — **pitch in** [*phrasal vb*] *informal* : to do something or give something (such as money) to help a person, group, or cause • *We all pitched in to help.*

pitch–black /ˈpɪtʃˈblæk/ *adj* : very dark

or black • *a pitch-black night*

pitched /'pɪtʃt/ *adj* : not flat • *a pitched roof*

pitched battle *n [C]* **1** : a major battle that is fought by large groups of soldiers **2** : a long argument or fight between people who have become very angry or emotional

pitch·er /'pɪtʃə/ *n [C]* **1** : the player who throws the ball to the batter in baseball **2 a** *US* : a container with a lip and handle that is used for holding and pouring out liquids **b** : the amount held by a pitcher • *a pitcher of water* **3** *Brit* : JUG 1

pitch·fork /'pɪtʃ,foək/ *n [C]* : a tool that has two or three long, thin metal bars on a long handle and that is used for lifting hay

pitch shot *n [C] golf* : a high shot that is made from an area near the green

pit·e·ous /'pɪtijəs/ *adj, literary* : deserving or causing feelings of sympathy or pity • *a piteous tale/voice* — **pit·e·ous·ly** *adv*

pit·fall /'pɪt,fɑːl/ *n [C]* : a danger or problem that is hidden or not obvious at first • *I warned him about the (hidden) pitfalls of online dating.*

pith /'pɪθ/ *n [U]* : the white covering that is found under the skin of oranges, lemons, etc.

pith helmet *n [C]* : a light, hard hat that is worn for protection from the sun in hot countries

pithy /'pɪθi/ *adj* **pith·i·er; -est** **1** : using few words in a clever and effective way • *pithy sayings* **2** : resembling or having a lot of pith • *a white, pithy substance*

piti·able /'pɪtijəbəl/ *adj, formal* : deserving pity or sympathy : PITIFUL • *a pitiable orphan* — **piti·ably** /'pɪtijəbli/ *adv*

piti·ful /'pɪtɪfəl/ *adj* **1** : deserving or causing feelings of pity or sympathy • *the dog's pitiful cries* **2** : causing feelings of dislike or disgust by not being enough or not being good enough • *a pitiful excuse/performance* — **piti·ful·ly** *adv*

piti·less /'pɪtɪləs/ *adj* **1** : very cruel • *a pitiless ruler/critic* **2** : very harsh or severe • *a pitiless storm* — **piti·less·ly** *adv*

pit stop *n [C]* **1** : a stop for fuel and minor repairs during a car race **2** *US, informal* : a short stop during a journey for rest or food or to use a bathroom

pitta *Brit spelling of* PITA

pit·tance /'pɪtns/ *n [C]* : a very small amount of money • *He bought the car for a pittance.*

pit·ted /'pɪtəd/ *adj* **1** *of a fruit* : with the pit removed • *pitted olives/dates* **2** : having many small holes or dents • *the pitted surface of the bowl*

pi·tu·i·tary /pə'tuːwə,teri, *Brit* pə-'tjuːwətri/ *n, pl* **-tar·ies** *[C] medical* : a small organ in the brain that produces hormones and influences growth and development — called also *pituitary gland*

¹**pity** /'pɪti/ *n* **1** *[U]* : a strong feeling of sadness or sympathy for someone or something • *Those poor people deserve your pity.* **2** *[singular]* : something that causes sadness or disappointment • *It's a pity that you can't go.* • *He didn't live to see his daughter grow up, and that's a pity. —*

more's the pity : UNFORTUNATELY — used to say that something is disappointing • *"Did you see her before she left?" "No, more's the pity." —* **take pity on** : to feel pity for (a person or animal) and do something to help • *I took pity on the stray cat and fed him.*

²**pity** *vb* **pit·ies; pit·ied; pity·ing** *[T]* : to feel pity for (someone or something) • *I pity anyone who has to work at that place.* — **pitying** *adj* • *a pitying look/smile*

¹**piv·ot** /'pɪvət/ *n [C]* **1** : a pin or shaft on which a mechanical part turns **2** : the action of turning around a point • *The quarterback made/did a quick pivot to his left.*

²**pivot** *vb [I]* : to turn on or around a central point • *The door hinge pivots around the pin.* — **pivot on/around** [*phrasal vb*] : to be based on (something) • *The book's plot pivots on the main character's need for revenge.*

piv·ot·al /'pɪvətl/ *adj* : very important • *a pivotal moment/decision*

pix *plural of* PIC

pix·el /'pɪksəl/ *n [C]* : any one of the very small dots that together form the picture on a television screen, computer monitor, etc.

pix·ie *also* **pixy** /'pɪksi/ *n, pl* **pix·ies** *[C]* : an imaginary creature that looks like a small person and has magical powers

piz·za /'piːtsə/ *n [C/U]* : a food made from flat, usually round bread that is topped with usually tomato sauce and cheese and often with meat or vegetables • *We had (a) pizza for supper.*

piz·zazz *or* **pi·zazz** /pə'zæz/ *n [U] informal* : a quality or style that is exciting and interesting • *a performer who has a lot of pizzazz*

piz·ze·ria /ˌpiːtsə'riːjə/ *n [C]* : a restaurant where mainly pizzas are served

pj's /'piːˌdʒeɪz/ *n [plural] informal* : PAJAMAS

pkg. *abbr* package

pkt *abbr* packet

pl. *abbr* **1** place **2** plural

plac·ard /'plækəd/ *n [C]* : a large notice or sign put up in a public place or carried by people

pla·cate /'pleɪˌkeɪt, *Brit* plə'keɪt/ *vb* **-cat·ed; -cat·ing** *[T] formal* : to cause (someone) to feel less angry about something • *The clerk tried to placate the customer.*

¹**place** /'pleɪs/ *n* **1** *[C]* : a specific area or region of the world : a particular city, country, etc. • *This town is a good place to raise children.* • *the hottest place on earth* **2** *[C]* : a building or area that is used for a particular purpose • *a place of learning/business/worship* • *a local gathering/meeting place* **3** *[C]* **a** : a building, part of a building, or area that is used for shelter • *They gave him a place to stay for the night.* **b** : a house, apartment, etc., where a person lives • *our summer place* **4** *[C]* : a particular space or area • *This looks like a good place to stop and rest.* • *My leg was broken in two places.* • *Wires carry the information from place to place.* = *They carry it from one place to another.* **5** *[C]* : a particular point that you reach in a discussion, book, etc. — usually singular

• *a good place to end the discussion* • *She dropped the magazine and lost her place.* **6** [*C*] : an available seat, space, or amount of room • *There's no place to sit down.* • *He was given a place of honor.* [=a seat for someone who is being honored] **7** [*C*] : a particular position in a line especially of people or vehicles • *Would you save/hold our places (in line), please?* **8** [*C*] : a particular position during or at the end of a race or competition • *Their horse finished in second/last place.* **9** [*C*] **a** : a position in a group, course, organization, school, etc. • *There are two places still open in the course/class.* **b** : the proper position of someone in a group or society • *It was not his place to make the decision.* **10 a** [*singular*] : an appropriate situation or setting • *There's a time and a place for everything.* **b** [*C*] : a particular situation or set of conditions • *I love my life and wouldn't change/trade/swap/switch places with anyone!* — **all over the place** *informal* **1** : EVERYWHERE • *New houses are being built all over the place.* **2** : not organized in a logical way • *Your essay lacks organization; your ideas are all over the place.* — **between a rock and a hard place** see ²ROCK — **fall into place** see ¹FALL — **give place to (something)** *formal* : to be replaced by (something) • *Confidence gave place to fear.* — **go places** : to become successful • *The band is clearly going places.* — **keep (someone) in his/her place** : to prevent (someone) from achieving a higher social status • *Such social rules were used to keep women in their place.* — **in place 1** : in the proper position • *Tape held/kept the photo in place.* **2** : in the state of being used or active • *The new computer system is now in place.* **3** *US* : in the same location without moving forward or backward • *running in place* — **in place of someone or something** *or* **in someone's or something's place** : as a substitute or replacement for someone or something • *Use milk in place of [=instead of] water.* • *He went to the meeting in my place.* — **in the first place** — used at the end of a sentence to indicate what was true or what should have been done at the beginning of a situation • *We should never have gone there in the first place.* — **in the first/second place** — used when listing the most important parts of something or the most important reasons for something • *I'm not going to tell you because, in the first place, it's none of your business, and in the second place, you would tell everyone else.* — **into place 1** : into the proper position • *She pushed her glasses into place.* **2** : into the state of being used or active • *The plan was put into place over several months.* — **no place for** — used to say that someone or something does not belong in a particular place, situation, etc. • *This party is no place for children.* — **of all places** — used to say that it is unusual or surprising that something happened in or is true about a particular place • *She met her future husband in a grocery store, of all plac-* es. — **out of place 1** : not in the correct location or position • *Nothing in the room was out of place.* **2** : not in a typical or appropriate situation or setting • *I feel a bit out of place* [=I feel like I don't belong] *with my wife's family.* — **put someone in his/her place** ◇ Someone who *puts you in your place* shows you that you are not better than other people and should not be acting in such a confident and proud way. — **take place** : to happen • *The wedding is set to take place this July.* • *Where does the story take place?* — **take someone's or something's place** *or* **take the place of someone or something** : to replace someone or something • *My secretary took my place at the meeting.* — **take your place** : to go to the location where you are supposed to sit, stand, etc. • *The actors took their places on the stage.*

²**place** *vb* **placed; plac·ing 1** [*T*] : to put (something or someone) in a particular place or position • *Please place the book on my desk.* • *Her name was placed on the list.* • *The husbands and wives were placed in separate groups.* **2** [*T*] : to put (someone or something) in a particular state, condition, or situation • *Working with sick people places him at risk for infection.* • *He placed his future in the hands of the jury.* • *We placed him under arrest.* **3** [*T*] **a** — used to say that something is thought of as important, valuable, etc. • *They place great importance on both work and family.* **b** — used to say who or what you believe should be trusted, blamed, etc. • *We placed our faith in the legal system.* **4** [*T*] : to cause or require someone or something to deal with (a demand, burden, etc.) • *The growing population is placing increasing demands on our schools.* • *restrictions placed upon a person's freedom* **5** [*T*] **a** : to perform the actions that are required for (something) • *He placed a collect (phone) call to his wife.* • *They placed their bets.* **b** : to give (an order) to someone • *"Are you ready to place your order?" asked the waiter.* **c** : to cause (something, such as an advertisement) to appear somewhere • *placing an ad in the newspaper* **6** [*T*] : to find an appropriate place for (someone) to live, work, or learn • *The children were placed with a foster family.* **7** [*T*] : to show or prove the location of (someone or something) at a particular time • *The evidence places you at the scene of the crime.* **8** [*T*] : to remember where you saw (someone or someone's face) in the past • *He looks familiar but I can't quite place him.* **9 a** [*I*] *US* : to end a race or competition in a particular position • *He placed fifth in the race.* **b** [*T*] *Brit* ◇ Someone who **is placed** first, second, etc., in a race or competition has finished in that position. • *He was placed fifth in the race.* **10** [*T*] : to give (someone or something) a particular rank in a series or category • *He is often placed* [=ranked] *among the greatest writers in the world.*

pla·ce·bo /pləˈsiːboʊ/ *n, pl* **-bos** [*C*] *medical* : a pill or substance that is given to a patient like a drug but that has no physical effect on the patient ✧ Patients who have been given a placebo may feel better because they believe that they are getting actual medicine. The improvement that they experience is called the *placebo effect.* Placebos are also used in tests to compare the effect of a real drug with a substance that does not have any physical effect.

place-kick /ˈpleɪsˌkɪk/ n [C] : a kick that is made in sports like American football and rugby when the ball has been put on the ground or is being held on the ground — **place-kick-er** /ˈpleɪsˌkɪkɚ/ n [C]

place mat n [C] : a small mat on which a set of dishes, knives, forks, etc., for one person are placed at a table

place-ment /ˈpleɪsmənt/ n **1** [C/U] : the act of putting something in a particular place ▪ *the placement of microphones around the room* ▪ *camera placements* **2** [U] : the act of finding an appropriate place for someone to live, work, or learn ▪ *the placement of children in foster homes*

place name n [C] : the name of a city, town, lake, country, etc.

pla-cen-ta /pləˈsɛntə/ n [C] : the organ in mammals that forms inside the mother's uterus, nourishes the unborn baby, and is pushed out of the mother after the birth of the baby — **pla-cen-tal** /pləˈsɛntl̩/ adj

place setting n [C] : a set of dishes, knives, forks, etc., that are put on a table for one person

plac-id /ˈplæsəd/ adj **1** : not easily upset or excited ▪ *a placid disposition* **2** : calm and steady ▪ *the placid surface of the lake* — **pla-cid-i-ty** /pləˈsɪdəti/ n [U] — **plac-id-ly** adv

pla-gia-rize also Brit **pla-gia-rise** /ˈpleɪdʒəˌraɪz/ vb **-rized; -riz-ing** [T/I] : to use the words or ideas of another person as if they were your own words or ideas ▪ *He plagiarized (from) a classmate's report.* — **pla-gia-rism** /ˈpleɪdʒəˌrɪzəm/ n [U] ▪ *a writer who has been accused of plagiarism* — **pla-gia-rist** /ˈpleɪdʒərɪst/ n [C]

¹**plague** /ˈpleɪg/ n **1** [C] old-fashioned : a large number of harmful or annoying things ▪ *a plague of natural disasters* **2 a** [C/U] : a disease that causes death and that spreads quickly to a large number of people **b** [U] : BUBONIC PLAGUE — *avoid (someone or something) like the plague* informal : to stay away as much as possible from (someone or something) ▪ *I avoid him like the plague.*

²**plague** vb **plagued; plagu-ing** [T] **1** : to cause constant or repeated trouble, illness, etc., for (someone or something) ▪ *parasites that plague deer* ▪ *Crime plagues the inner city.* ▪ *an athlete plagued by knee injuries* **2** : to cause constant worry or distress to (someone) ▪ *I was plagued with/by doubt.*

plaid /ˈplæd/ n **1** [U] : a pattern on cloth of stripes with different widths that cross each other to form squares ▪ *a plaid pattern/shirt* **2** [plural] US : clothes with plaid patterns ▪ *She likes to wear plaids.*

¹**plain** /ˈpleɪn/ adj **1** : having no pattern

or decoration ▪ *a plain fabric/room/dress* **2** : not having any added or extra things ▪ *a glass of plain water* ▪ *plain yogurt* **3** : easy to see or understand ▪ *It's plain to see that you don't like dogs.* ▪ *What he said is a lie, plain and simple.* ▪ *The evidence makes it plain* [=clearly shows] *that he is guilty.* ▪ *The answer is (as) plain as day.* = *The answer is as plain as the nose on your face.* [=the answer is very obvious] **4** : simple and honest ▪ *plain speaking* ▪ *Let me say it in plain English: you're fired.* **5** : ¹ORDINARY ▪ *plain common sense* ▪ (US) *I'm just a plain old country boy.* **6** : not handsome or beautiful ▪ *She's kind of plain.* ▪ *She describes herself as a plain Jane.* [=a woman who is ordinary looking and not beautiful or glamorous] — *in plain sight/view* chiefly US : in a place that is easily seen ▪ *His gun was in plain sight.* — *plain clothes* : the ordinary clothes of a police officer who is not wearing a uniform ▪ *The officer was wearing plain clothes.* — *plain sailing* see SAILING — **plain-ly** adv ▪ *The star was plainly visible in the sky.* ▪ *The book states the facts plainly.* ▪ *She dresses plainly.* — **plain-ness** n [U]

²**plain** n [C] : a large area of flat land with out trees ▪ *the Great Plains of the United States*

³**plain** adv, informal : truly or completely ▪ *Her answer was misleading, if not plain dishonest.* — used to make a statement or description more forceful ▪ *She plain forgot to call me.* ▪ *You are just plain wrong.*

plain-clothes /ˈpleɪnˈkloʊz/ adj, always before a noun : dressed in ordinary clothes and not a uniform while on duty ▪ *a plainclothes police officer*

plain-spo-ken /ˈpleɪnˈspoʊkən/ adj : expressing opinions, ideas, etc., in a simple and honest way ▪ *a plainspoken man*

plain-tiff /ˈpleɪntəf/ n [C] law : a person who sues another person or accuses another person of a crime in a court of law — compare DEFENDANT

plain-tive /ˈpleɪntɪv/ adj, formal : expressing suffering or sadness ▪ *a plaintive cry/sigh* — **plain-tive-ly** adv

plait /ˈpleɪt, Brit ˈplæt/ n [C] chiefly Brit : an arrangement of hair made by weaving three sections together : BRAID — **plait** vb [T] ▪ *She plaited her hair.*

¹**plan** /ˈplæn/ n **1** [C/U] : a set of actions that have been thought of as a way to do or achieve something ▪ *the President's economic plan* ▪ *We agreed on a plan of action.* ▪ *Everything went according to plan.* [=the way it was supposed to] [C/U] : something that a person intends to do ▪ *Our plan is to leave early.* ▪ *We made plans to go out tonight.* ▪ *There was a change of/in plan.* **3** [C] : a detailed agreement for telephone service, medical care, insurance, etc. ▪ *a health/medical plan* ▪ *a retirement/pension plan* **4** [C] : a drawing that shows the parts or details of something (such as a building, town, machine, etc.) ▪ *a street plan of Washington, D.C.* ▪ *the plans for their new house* ▪ *a seating plan* [=a drawing that shows the

places where particular people will sit at a gathering.

²plan vb **planned; plan·ning 1** [T/I] : to think about and arrange the parts or details of (something) before it happens or is made ▪ *planning a lesson/party/protest/wedding* ▪ *They planned (out) the whole thing.* ▪ *Things don't always* **go as planned.** ▪ *Remember to* **plan ahead. 2 a** [T/I] : to intend or expect to do (something) ▪ *I plan to attend.* = *I plan on attending.* **b** [I] : to expect something to happen ▪ *Plan for a long wait.* ▪ *She didn't plan on such cold weather.*

¹plane /ˈpleɪn/ n **1** [C/U] : AIRPLANE ▪ *a cargo plane* ▪ *traveling by plane* **2** [C] *geometry* : a flat or level surface ▪ *a horizontal plane* **3** [C] : a level of thought, existence, or development ▪ *a higher spiritual plane* **4** [C] : a sharp tool that is pushed along a piece of wood to smooth or shape the surface

²plane vb **planed; plan·ing** [T] : to make (a piece of wood) smooth or level by cutting off thin pieces with a special tool (called a plane) ▪ *I planed the edge of the door.*

plane·load /ˈpleɪnˌloʊd/ n [C] : an amount or number of people or things that will fill an airplane

plan·et /ˈplænət/ n **1** [C] : a large, round object in space (such as the Earth) that travels around a star (such as the sun) **2** **the planet** : the planet Earth ▪ *We must help preserve the planet.* — **plan·e·tary** /ˈplænəˌteri, Brit ˈplænətri/ adj ▪ *planetary motion/orbit/systems*

plan·e·tar·i·um /ˌplænəˈterijəm/ n, pl **-i·ums** or **-ia** /-ijə/ [C] : a building or room in which images of stars, planets, etc., are shown on a high, curved ceiling

plank /ˈplæŋk/ n [C] **1** : a long, thick board that is used especially in building something **2** *formal* : one of the official beliefs and goals of an organization (such as a political party) ▪ *the party's foreign policy and economic planks*

plank·ing /ˈplæŋkɪŋ/ n [U] : heavy boards that are used to build something

plank·ton /ˈplæŋktən/ n [U] : the very small animal and plant life in an ocean, lake, etc.

plan·ner /ˈplænə/ n [C] : a person who plans things; *especially* : a person whose job is to plan things for other people ▪ *a financial/wedding planner*

¹plant /ˈplænt/ n **1** : a living thing that grows in the ground, usually has leaves or flowers, and needs sun and water to survive **2 a** : a building or factory where something is made ▪ *an auto plant* — see also POWER PLANT **b** *US* : the land, buildings, and equipment of an organization ▪ *the college's* **physical plant**

²plant vb [T] **1 a** : to put (something) in the ground to grow ▪ *plant seeds/flowers* **b** : to fill (an area) *with* seeds, flowers, or plants ▪ *I planted the border with roses.* **2 a** : to put or place (something) in the ground ▪ *She planted stakes in the garden to hold the vines.* **b** : to put or place (something or yourself) firmly or forcefully on a surface or in a particular position ▪ *I firmly planted my feet and refused*

to move. ▪ *He planted himself in front of the TV.* ▪ *She planted a big kiss on his cheek.* [=she gave him a big kiss on his cheek] **3 a** : to put (someone or something) in a place secretly ▪ *Terrorists planted a bomb in the bus station.* ▪ *She claims they planted the drugs in her car.* **b** : to cause (a story, rumor, etc.) to be reported or talked about usually for some secret purpose ▪ *planting a rumor/story* **4** : to cause (an idea, feeling, etc.) to be in someone's mind ▪ *She planted the first seeds of doubt in my mind.*

plan·tain /ˈplæntn̩/ n [C/U] **1** : a greenish fruit that comes from a kind of banana plant and is eaten after it has been cooked **2** : a common weed with leaves that grow near the ground and small greenish flowers

plan·ta·tion /plænˈteɪʃən/ n [C] : a large area of land especially in a hot part of the world where crops (such as cotton) are grown ▪ *a southern plantation*

plant·er /ˈplæntə/ n [C] **1** : a container in which plants are grown **2** : a person who owns a plantation ▪ *a wealthy South American planter* **3** : a machine that plants seeds in the ground

plaque /ˈplæk/ n **1** [C] : a flat, thin piece of metal or wood with writing on it that is used especially as a reminder of something (such as a historic event or an achievement) **2** [U] **a** : a thin coating that forms on teeth and contains bacteria **b** *medical* : a harmful material that can form in arteries and be a cause of heart disease

plas·ma /ˈplæzmə/ n **1** [U] *medical* : the watery part of blood that contains blood cells **2** [U] *technical* : a substance that is similar to a gas but that can carry electricity **3 a** [U] : a type of visual display for computers, televisions, etc., that produces pictures that are very clear and bright ▪ *a plasma screen/TV* **b** [C] : a television with a plasma screen ▪ *a 50-inch plasma*

¹plas·ter /ˈplæstə, Brit ˈplɑːstə/ n **1** [U] **a** : a wet substance that hardens when it becomes dry and that is used to make smooth walls and ceilings **b** : PLASTER OF PARIS **2** [C] *Brit* : a piece of material that is put on the skin over a small wound

²plaster vb [T] **1 a** : to cover (a surface) with plaster ▪ *We plastered and sanded the walls.* **b** : to cover (a surface or area) *with* something ▪ *The walls were plastered with posters.* **2** : to put (something, such as a poster or sign) *on* a surface ▪ *He plastered posters on the walls.* ▪ (*figurative*) *He had a silly smile plastered on his face.* [=he was smiling in a silly way] **3** : to make (something) lie flat against or stick to something ▪ *He plastered his hair down/back with gel.* — **plaster over** [*phrasal vb*] **plaster over** (*something*) or **plaster** (*something*) **over** : to cover (something) with plaster ▪ *We plastered over the holes in the wall.*

plas·ter·board /ˈplæstəˌboəd, Brit ˈplɑːstəˌbɔːd/ n [U] : DRYWALL

plas·tered /ˈplæstəd, Brit ˈplɑːstəd/ adj, not before a noun, informal : very drunk ▪

I got/was plastered last night.

plas·ter·er /ˈplæstərɚ, Brit ˈplɑːstərə/ *n* [C] : a person whose job is to put plaster on walls and ceilings

plaster of par·is *or* **plaster of Paris** /-ˈpɛrəs/ *n* [U] : a white powder that is mixed with water to form a paste which hardens quickly

¹**plas·tic** /ˈplæstɪk/ *n* **1** [C/U] : a light, strong substance that can be made into different shapes and that is used for making many common products ▪ *The toy was made of plastic.* ▪ *manufacturing plastics* **2** [U] *informal* : a credit card when used for payment ▪ *She used plastic to pay for her new computer.*

²**plastic** *adj* **1** : made or consisting of plastic ▪ *a plastic dish/toy/bag/bottle* **2** *informal* : not real or sincere ▪ *a plastic smile* **3** *technical* : capable of being made into different shapes ▪ *plastic clay*

plastic explosive *n* [C/U] : an explosive that is made of a soft substance like clay that can be formed into different shapes

plas·tic·i·ty /plæˈstɪsəti/ *n* [U] *technical* : the quality of being able to be made into different shapes ▪ *the plasticity of clay*

plastic surgery *n* [U] : surgery that improves or repairs the form or appearance of body parts — **plastic surgeon** *n* [C]

plastic wrap *n* [U] *US* : thin, clear plastic that is used to wrap food or to cover containers that have food in them

¹**plate** /ˈpleɪt/ *n* **1** [C] : a flat and usually round dish that is used for eating or serving food ▪ *plates, bowls, and cups* ▪ *a paper plate* **b** : the food that is served on a plate ▪ *I ate a salad and a plate of spaghetti.* **2** [C] : a thin, flat piece of metal **3** [C] : LICENSE PLATE — usually plural ▪ *a car with New York plates* **4** [C] : one of the usually flat, hard pieces that cover the body of some animals **5** *the plate baseball* : HOME PLATE **6** [C] *geology* : one of the very large sections of the Earth's surface that are believed to move around and cause earthquakes where they touch each other **7** [U] : metal that is covered with a thin layer of gold or silver ▪ *gold/silver plate* **8** [C] : a special page in a book that has pictures on it ▪ *The book contains over 50 color plates.* **9** [C] : a surface of metal, plastic, or wood that is used in printing words or pictures on paper ▪ *printing plates* **10** [C] : a sheet of glass or plastic that is treated with a special chemical and used in photography ▪ *photographic plates* **11** [C] : the part of a set of false teeth that attaches to the mouth — **on a plate** *informal* : in a way that requires no effort ▪ *He was handed the job on a plate.* — **on your plate** *informal* — used to refer to the things that a person has to do or deal with at one time ▪ *She has a lot on her plate right now.* — **step up to the plate** *baseball* : to move into position next to home plate in order to bat ▪ *(US, figurative) He finally stepped up to the plate* [=he finally took action] *and asked her to marry him.*

²**plate** *vb* **plat·ed; plat·ing** [T] : to add a layer of metal to the outside of (something) ▪ *tin plated with silver*

pla·teau /plæˈtoʊ/ *n, pl* **pla·teaus** *also* **pla·teaux** /plæˈtoʊz/ [C] **1** : a large flat area of land that is higher than other areas of land that surround it **2** : a period when something does not increase or advance any further ▪ *The price of gas seems to have reached a plateau.* — **plateau** *vb* [I] ▪ *The price of gas has plateaued.*

plate·ful /ˈpleɪtˌfʊl/ *n* [C] : the amount of food that fills a plate

plate glass *n* [U] : large sheets of very clear and thick glass ▪ *plate glass windows*

plate·let /ˈpleɪtlət/ *n* [C] : a small, round, thin blood cell that helps blood to stop flowing from a cut by becoming thick and sticky

plate tectonics *n* [U] *geology* : a scientific theory that the Earth's surface is made of very large sections that move very slowly; *also* : the movements of the large sections that form the Earth's surface ▪ *earthquakes caused by plate tectonics*

plat·form /ˈplætˌfoɚm/ *n* [C] **1 a** : a flat surface that is raised higher than the floor or ground and that people stand on when performing or speaking **b** : a flat area next to railroad tracks where people wait for a train or subway **c** : a usually raised structure that has a flat surface where people or machines do work ▪ *a viewing/observation platform* ▪ *oil drilling platforms* **2** : the official beliefs and goals of a political party or candidate ▪ *the Republican/Democratic platform* **3** : something that allows someone to tell a large number of people about an idea, product, etc. ▪ *They used the show as a platform to launch a new product.* **4** : a shoe with a very thick sole — called also **platform shoe** **5** *computers* : OPERATING SYSTEM ▪ *a program that runs on different platforms*

plat·ing /ˈpleɪtɪŋ/ *n* [U] **1** : a thin layer of metal that has been added to the outside of something ▪ *spoons covered in silver plating* **2** : a layer of wide, thin pieces of metal ▪ *armor plating*

plat·i·num /ˈplætnəm/ *n* [U] : a heavy, silver-colored metal that is difficult to melt and that is used especially in expensive jewelry

platinum record *n* [C] : an award that is given to a singer or musical group for selling at least one million copies of a record

plat·i·tude /ˈplætəˌtuːd, Brit ˈplætəˌtjuːd/ *n* [C] *disapproving* : a statement that expresses an idea that is not new ▪ *familiar platitudes about the value of hard work*

pla·ton·ic /pləˈtɑːnɪk/ *adj* : of, relating to, or having a close relationship in which there is no romance or sex ▪ *a platonic relationship*

pla·toon /pləˈtuːn/ *n* [C] : a group of soldiers that includes two or more squads usually led by one lieutenant

plat·ter /ˈplætɚ/ *n* [C] **1** : a large plate that is used for serving food and especially meat **2** : a meal in a restaurant that has a particular type of food ▪ *She ordered the seafood platter.* — **on a (silver) platter** : in a way that requires no effort ▪ *He has had everything handed/given to him on a silver platter.* [=he has not had to work for the things that he has]

platy·pus /ˈplætɪpəs/ *n* [*C*] : a small animal from Australia that has a bill like the bill of a duck, webbed feet, and wide flat tail

plau·dits /ˈplɔːdəts/ *n* [*plural*] *formal* : strong approval • *He has earned/won plaudits for his work abroad.*

plau·si·ble /ˈplɔːzəbəl/ *adj* : possibly true • *a plausible conclusion/excuse/explanation* — **plau·si·bil·i·ty** /ˌplɔːzəˈbɪləti/ *n* [*U*] — **plau·si·bly** /ˈplɔːzəbli/ *adv*

¹**play** /ˈpleɪ/ *vb* **1** [*I*] : to do activities for fun or enjoyment • *The children were playing in the yard.* • *She's playing with her toys/friends.* ◆ If children **play teacher/school (etc.)**, they play by pretending to be adults. **2 a** [*T/I*] : to participate in (a game or sport) • *They play soccer.* • *play (a game of) cards/poker* ◆ If you **play for** a particular team, you are a member of that team. • *He plays for the Giants.* **b** [*T/I*] : to compete against (someone) in a game • *The Yankees play the Red Sox tonight.* **c** [*T*] : to have (a particular position on a sports team) • *She plays third base.* **d** [*T*] : to allow (someone) to play during a game especially in a particular position • *They decided to play him at first base.* **e** [*T*] : to place (a playing card) on the table during your turn in a card game • *I played the ace of hearts.* **b** (*figurative*) *lawyers who play the race card to defend their clients* [=who say that their clients were treated unfairly because of their race] **f** [*T*] : to hit, kick, throw, or catch (a ball, puck, etc.) • *The shortstop played the ball perfectly.* **3** [*T*] **a** : to bet money on (something) • *He plays the races/horses/slots.* • *Do you play the lottery?* **b** : to invest money in (the stock market) in order to try to earn money • *playing the (stock) market* **4 a** [*T/I*] : to perform music on (an instrument) • *She plays (the) piano/guitar/violin.* • *He plays in a band.* **b** [*I*] of an instrument : to produce music • *I could hear a guitar playing.* **c** [*T*] : to perform (a song, a piece of music, etc.) on an instrument • *The band played a waltz.* **d** [*T/I*] : to perform music in (a particular place) • *The band has been playing (in) bars and nightclubs.* **5** [*T/I*] : to cause (a song, a piece of music, a movie, etc.) to be heard or seen • *The radio station plays mostly hip-hop.* • *Our favorite song was playing on the radio.* **6** [*I*] : to be shown or performed usually more than one time • *What's playing at the theater?* **7 a** [*T*] : to act the part of (a particular character) in a film, play, etc. • *She's not a doctor, but she plays one on TV.* • (*figurative*) *We all have a part/role to play in the future of this company.* [=we all are involved in the future of this company] **b** [*I*] : to pretend that you have a particular quality or are in a particular condition • *Don't play innocent with me!* • *She taught her dog to play dead.* [=to lie on its back and pretend to be dead] • *If anyone asks you about it, play dumb.* [=act like you do not know anything about it] **8** [*T/I*] : to act or behave in a particular way • *He*

didn't play fair. = *He didn't play by the rules.* • *She played it cool.* [=acted calm] • *I decided to play it safe* [=to avoid possible problems or danger] *and leave early.* **9** [*I*] : to do or say things in a joking way • *Don't take him seriously. He's just playing (around).* **10** [*T*] : to do (something) to someone in order to amuse yourself or others — usually + *on* • *He played a trick on her.* **11** [*T*] : to base a decision or action on (something) • *play the odds* • *play a hunch* — **play along** [*phrasal vb*] : to agree to do or accept what other people want • *I refused to play along (with their plan).* — **play around** also Brit **play about** [*phrasal vb*] **1** : to have sex with someone who is not your husband, wife, or regular partner • *She's been playing around on her husband.* **2** : to deal with or treat something in a careless way • *You can't play around with diabetes; it's a very serious disease.* **3** : to use or do something in a way that is not very serious • *playing around on the piano/computer/Internet* • *play around with paints* **4 play around with** : to move or change (something) or to think about (something) in different ways often in order to find out what would work best • *We played around with the idea for a while.* — **play at** [*phrasal vb*] **1** : to do (something) in a way that is not serious • *They were only playing at trying to fix the problem.* **2** *chiefly Brit* : to play by pretending to be someone or something • *boys playing at being soldiers* **3** *Brit* — used to say in an annoyed way that you do not know the reason for someone's behavior • *What are you playing at?* — **play back** [*phrasal vb*] **play back (something)** or **play (something) back** : to cause (recorded sounds or pictures) to be heard or seen • *He played the tape back to/for us.* — **play down** [*phrasal vb*] **play down (something)** or **play (something) down** : to make (something) seem smaller or less important • *She played down her role in the research.* — **play fast and loose** : to behave in a clever and dishonest way • *reporters playing fast and loose with the facts/truth* — **play for time** : to try to make something happen later instead of sooner • *They're just playing for time, hoping that the problem will resolve itself.* — **play God** *usually disapproving* : to make decisions that have a very powerful and important effect on other people's lives • *lawyers who play God with people's lives* — **play hard to get** : to pretend that you are not interested in having a romantic or sexual relationship with someone in order to make that person more attracted to you — **play into** [*phrasal vb*] : to help support (something, such as an idea) • *This new evidence plays into their theory nicely.* — **play into someone's hands** or **play into the hands of someone** : to do something that you do not realize will hurt you and help someone else • *You're only playing into their hands by making such ridiculous accusations.* — **play off** [*phrasal vb*] **1** *chiefly Brit* : to participate in a game that decides a winner from people or teams that had the same results in an earlier game ▪ *The two teams played off for third place.* **2** *US* : to combine with (someone or something) in a way that makes each part better ▪ *The two actors play off each other extremely well.* **3** *play (someone or something) off against* : to cause two people or groups to fight or compete with each other in a way that helps you ▪ *He played one side off against the other.* — *play on also play upon* [*phrasal vb*] : to make people do what you want by using (their emotions, fears, concerns, etc.) in an unfair way ▪ *Politicians often win votes by playing on people's emotions.* — *play out* [*phrasal vb*] **1** : to happen or occur in usually a gradual way ▪ *Let's wait and see how things play out.* ▪ *Their personal tragedy was being played out in public.* **2** *play out (something) or play (something) out* **a** : to make (something) happen ▪ *She got to play out her fantasy of being on TV.* ▪ *This scene plays itself out* [=*happens*] *daily in every large city in this country.* ▪ *Her coach let her play out the rest of the season.* — *play the field* : to have romantic or sexual relationships with more than one person at a time — *play up* [*phrasal vb*] **1** *play up (something) or play (something) up* : to emphasize or stress (something) ▪ *During the interview, you should play up your strengths.* **2** *play up or play (someone) up* *Brit* : to cause problems or pain ▪ *The children have been playing up again.* ▪ *My back has been playing me up again.* — *play with* [*phrasal vb*] **1** : to move or handle (something) with your hands or fingers often without thinking ▪ *She played with her hair while she talked.* **2** : to handle, change, or deal with (something) in a careless way ▪ *It's important to teach your children not to play with guns/fire/matches.* **3** : to think about (something) briefly and not very seriously ▪ *I played with the idea of moving to Chicago.* — *play with fire* : to do something that is risky or dangerous ▪ *People who use drugs are playing with fire.*

²**play** *n* **1** [*C*] : a piece of writing that tells a story through the actions and words of characters and that is performed on a stage ▪ *plays by Shakespeare* ▪ *They are putting on a play about her life.* **2** [*U*] : activities that are done especially by children for fun or enjoyment ▪ *imaginative play* ▪ *children at play* **3 a** [*U*] : the action that happens during a game ▪ *Rain held up play for an hour.* **b** [*C/U*] : the time when a person playing a game is supposed to do something ▪ *It's your play.* [=*(more commonly) turn*] **4** [*C*] *US* : a particular action or set of actions that happens during a game ▪ *(American football) a running/passing/defensive/offensive play* ▪ *(baseball) a close play at first base* ▪ *the opening play* [=*move*] *in a game of chess* **5** [*U*] : the state of being active or having an effect ▪ *She promotes the free play of ideas in her classroom.* ▪ *issues that are at play* [=*involved*] ▪ *Their creativity was brought/called/put into play.* [=they had to use their creativity] ▪ *factors that*

came into play [=were involved] **6** [*U*] *US* : attention in newspapers, on television, etc. ▪ *The story hasn't gotten much play in the press.* **7** [*C*] : a humorous or clever way of using a word or phrase so that more than one meaning is suggested ▪ *a clever play on words* **8** [*U*] ▪ **a** : a function of a machine that causes recorded sounds or pictures to be heard or seen ▪ *Press "Play" to start the movie.* **b** : time when a machine is being used to hear or see recorded sounds or pictures ▪ *The CD player's batteries only provided three to four hours of play.* **9** [*singular*] : the irregular or lively movement of something ▪ *a play of shadow and light* **10** [*U*] : loose and free movement of something (such as part of a machine) ▪ *There's too much play in the car's steering wheel.* — *in/into play of a ball* : in or into the area where players must stay in sports ▪ *He put the ball back into play.* — *make a play for* : to try to get (someone or something) ▪ *He made a play for her.* [=he tried to start a romantic or sexual relationship with her] — *out of play of a ball* : outside the area where players must stay in sports ▪ *The ball was kicked out of play.*

play•able /ˈpleɪjəbəl/ *adj* **1** : capable of being played ▪ *The ball was out-of-bounds and no longer playable.* **2** : suitable for being played on ▪ *making the golf course more playable*

play•act•ing /ˈpleɪˌæktɪŋ/ *n* [*U*] : behavior that is not honest or sincere

play•back /ˈpleɪˌbæk/ *n* **1** [*U*] : the act of causing recorded sounds or pictures to be heard or seen again **2** [*C*] : a recording that is heard or seen again ▪ *We listened to a playback of the recording.*

play•book /ˈpleɪˌbʊk/ *n* [*C*] *American football* : a book that contains descriptions of the different offensive and defensive plays that are used by a team ▪ *(figurative) The competition used a play straight from our own playbook.*

play•boy /ˈpleɪˌbɔɪ/ *n* [*C*] : a man who spends most of his time doing things that give him pleasure

play–by–play /ˈpleɪˌbaɪˌpleɪ/ *n* [*C/U*] : a description of a game that is given while the game is being played ▪ *listening to a play-by-play of the game* — **play–by–play** *adj, always before a noun* ▪ *a play-by-play announcer/description*

play•date /ˈpleɪˌdeɪt/ *n* [*C*] *chiefly US* : a time that parents arrange for their young children to play together

play•er /ˈpleɪjə/ *n* [*C*] **1** : a person who plays a sport or game ▪ *a football player* **2** : a person who performs music usually on a particular instrument ▪ *a piano player* **3** : a machine that causes recorded sounds or pictures to be heard or seen ▪ *a record/DVD/CD player* **4** : a person who participates in a usually competitive field or activity ▪ *She's a key/major/top player in the negotiations.*

play•ful /ˈpleɪfəl/ *adj* **1** : happy and full of energy ▪ *playful kittens* **2** : showing that you are having fun and not being serious ▪ *a playful expression/mood* — **play•ful•ly** *adv* — **play•ful•ness** *n* [*U*]

play·ground /'pleɪˌgraʊnd/ *n [C]* **1** : an outdoor area where children can play that usually includes swings, slides, etc. **2** : a place where people go to do enjoyable things ▪ *These mountains are a playground for hikers and skiers.*

play·group /'pleɪˌgruːp/ *n [C]* **1** *US* : an organized group of young children and their parents that meet regularly so the children can play together **2** *Brit* : a school where children younger than five years old go to play and learn

play·house /'pleɪˌhaʊs/ *n [C]* **1** : THEATER — usually used in names ▪ *the Provincetown Playhouse* **2** : a small house for children to play in

playing card *n [C]* : ¹CARD 1a

playing field *n [C]* : an area that is used for playing some sports; *especially* : the part of a field that is officially marked as the place where the action of a game happens — *level the playing field* see ³LEVEL

play·mate /'pleɪˌmeɪt/ *n [C]* : a friend with whom a child plays

play·off /'pleɪˌɑːf/ *n [C]* **1** *US* : a series of games that is played after the end of the regular season in order to decide which player or team is the champion ▪ *The teams faced each other in the playoffs.* **2** : a game or series of games that is played to decide the winner when people or teams are tied ▪ *an 18-hole play-off*

play·pen /'pleɪˌpɛn/ *n [C]* : a structure with high sides that provides an enclosed area in which a baby or young child can play

play·room /'pleɪˌruːm/ *n [C]* : a room for children to play in

play·thing /'pleɪˌθɪŋ/ *n [C]* **1** : a toy ▪ *a child's plaything* **2** : a person or thing that you treat in a careless way and use for your own amusement or advantage ▪ *He used other people as his playthings.*

play·wright /'pleɪˌraɪt/ *n [C]* : a person who writes plays

pla·za /'plɑːzə/ *n [C]* **1** : an open public area that is usually near city buildings and that often has trees and bushes and places to sit, walk, and shop **2** *chiefly US* : SHOPPING CENTER **3** *US* **a** : an area on or next to a highway having restaurants, gas stations, restrooms, etc. ▪ *a rest/information/service plaza* **b** : a place where you stop to pay money before going onto a highway — called also *toll plaza*

plea /'pliː/ *n [C]* **1** : a serious and emotional request for something ▪ *a plea for mercy* **2** *law* **a** : a statement in which a person who has been accused of a crime says in court that he or she is guilty or not guilty of the crime ▪ *a plea of not guilty* ▪ *a guilty plea* **b** : a reason or excuse for committing a crime ▪ *He got off on an insanity plea.* [=the court said that he was not guilty because he was insane] — *cop a plea* see ²COP

plea bargaining *n [U]* : a process in which a person who is accused of a crime is allowed to say that he or she is guilty of a less serious crime in order to be given a less severe punishment — **plea bargain** *n [C]* ▪ *He refused to ac-*cept a plea bargain. — **plea–bargain** *vb [I]* ▪ *He plea-bargained to avoid spending time in jail.*

plead /'pliːd/ *vb* **plead·ed** /'pliːdəd/ or **pled** /'plɛd/; **plead·ing** **1** [*I*] : to ask for something in a serious and emotional way ▪ *pleading for help/mercy* **2** [*T*] : to try to prove (a case) in a court of law ▪ *She hired a lawyer to plead her case.* **3** [*I*] : to say in court that you are either guilty or not guilty of a crime ▪ *"How do you plead?" asked the judge.* ▪ *He pled guilty.* **4** [*T*] : to give (something) as a reason or excuse for something ▪ *He pleaded that he didn't have enough money to pay his bill.* ▪ *On that issue, I have to plead ignorance.* [=to say that I do not know anything about it] **5** [*T/I*] : to argue in support of (a cause) ▪ *pleading my cause*

pleas·ant /'plɛznt/ *adj* **1** : causing a feeling of happiness or pleasure ▪ *a pleasant day/conversation* ▪ *What a pleasant surprise!* **2** : friendly and likable ▪ *a pleasant young man* — **pleas·ant·ly** *adv* — **pleas·ant·ness** *n [U]*

pleas·ant·ry /'plɛzntri/ *n, pl* **-ries** [C] *formal* : something (such as a greeting) that people say in order to be polite ▪ *We exchanged pleasantries.*

¹**please** /'pliːz/ *adv* **1 a** — used to ask for something in a polite way ▪ *Please come in.* ▪ *I'll have a glass of red wine, please.* ▪ *Next, please!* = *Will the next person please come forward?* **b** — used to show that a request is serious or important ▪ *Will everyone please be quiet and listen?* **2** — used as a polite way of saying yes ▪ *"Would you like some tea?" "Please."* ▪ *"How about a piece of cake?" "Yes, please."* **3** *informal* — used to show that you do not agree with or believe something that was said ▪ *Oh, please. You can't be serious!*

²**please** *vb* **pleased; pleas·ing** **1** [*T/I*] : to make (someone) happy or satisfied ▪ *He joined the football team to please his father.* ▪ *We were pleased by her decision.* ▪ *She is hard/easy to please.* ▪ *She's always eager to please.* **2** [*I*] : to make a choice about what to do, have, etc. ▪ *He can come and go as he pleases.* [=whenever he wants to] ▪ *I can do whatever I please.* ▪ *You can do as you please.* [=you can do whatever you want/choose to do] — *as you please Brit, informal* — used to make a statement more forceful especially when describing behavior that is surprising ▪ *She walked right in, bold as you please.* — *if you please old-fashioned + formal* — used to make a polite request ▪ *Follow me, if you please.* — *please yourself* — used to say that you can do what you want to do ▪ *"I'm going to skip the party tonight." "OK, please yourself."*

pleased *adj* : happy or satisfied ▪ *We're pleased that you came.* ▪ *I was pleased to hear that they won.* ▪ *My father was none too pleased* [=not pleased at all; very angry or unhappy] *when he found out that my brother had wrecked the car.* ▪ *"(I'm) Pleased to meet you."* — *(as) pleased as punch informal* : very happy or satisfied • *I was pleased as punch that he decided to visit.*

pleas·ing *adj* : attractive or appealing • *pleasing sounds/sights* — **pleas·ing·ly** *adv*

plea·sur·able /ˈplɛʒərəbəl/ *adj, somewhat formal* : causing a feeling of pleasure or enjoyment • *a pleasurable activity/experience/memory* — **plea·sur·ably** /ˈplɛʒərəbli/ *adv*

plea·sure /ˈplɛʒə/ *n* **1** [U] **a** : a feeling of happiness, enjoyment, or satisfaction : a pleasant or pleasing feeling • *She gets pleasure from helping others.* • *She takes pleasure in* [=enjoys] *her work.* **b** : activity that is done for enjoyment • *Is this trip for business or pleasure?* **2** [C] : something or someone that causes a feeling of happiness, enjoyment, or satisfaction • *It's been a pleasure working with you.* = *You were a pleasure to work with.* [=I enjoyed working with you] • *enjoying life's simple pleasures* • *"Thanks for your help." "(It was) My pleasure."* [=I was happy to help] — **at someone's pleasure** *or* **at the pleasure of someone** — used to say that something is done or can be done because someone wants it to be done • *I serve at the pleasure of the president.* — **with pleasure** — used to say that you are happy to do something for someone • *"Would you deliver a message for me?" "Yes, with pleasure."*

pleat /ˈpliːt/ *n* [C] : a fold in cloth that is made by folding the material onto itself — **pleat·ed** /ˈpliːtəd/ *adj* • *a pleated skirt*

ple·be·ian /plɪˈbiːjən/ *n* [C] **1** : a member of the common people of ancient Rome **2** : a common person — **plebeian** *adj* • *plebeian tastes*

pleb·i·scite /ˈplɛbəˌsaɪt/ *n* [C/U] : a vote by which the people of a country or region express their opinion for or against an important proposal

¹pledge /ˈplɛdʒ/ *n* [C] **1** : a serious promise or agreement • *a pledge to cut taxes* **2** : a promise to give money • *To make a pledge or donation, please call the charity's office.* **3** *US* : a person who has promised to join a college fraternity or sorority but who has not been officially accepted into the group — **the Pledge of Allegiance** *US* : a formal promise of loyalty to the United States that groups of people say together

²pledge *vb* **pledged; pledg·ing 1** [T] : to formally promise to give or do (something) • *She pledged $100,000 toward the new school.* • *We've all pledged (our) loyalty/support/allegiance to the organization.* **2** [T] : to cause (someone) to formally promise something • *She pledged herself to silence.* **3** [T] *US* : to promise to join (a college fraternity or sorority) • *She pledged the sorority as a freshman.*

ple·na·ry /ˈpliːnəri/ *adj, always before a noun, formal* **1** : attended by all the people who have the right to attend • *plenary sessions of the legislature* **2** : complete in every way • *plenary power*

plen·ti·ful /ˈplɛntɪfəl/ *adj* **1** : present in large amounts • *Jobs were plentiful then.* • *plentiful amounts of rain* • *a plentiful re-*

source • *a plentiful supply of food* **2** : containing or giving large amounts of something • *a plentiful source of vitamins* — **plen·ti·ful·ly** *adv*

¹plen·ty /ˈplɛnti/ *pron* : a large number or amount of something • *"Would you like more pie?" "No, thanks. I've had plenty."* • *There's plenty of food for everyone.* • *There's plenty to see and do here.*

²plenty *n* [U] *formal* : the state of having enough of the things that make life good and easy • *They thought of America as the land of plenty.* — **in plenty** — used to say that something is present or exists in large amounts • *She has patience and courage in plenty.*

³plenty *adv, informal* : to a great degree • *We're plenty busy.* • *It's plenty cold/hot outside.* • *There's plenty more where that came from.*

pleth·o·ra /ˈplɛθərə/ *n* [singular] *formal* : a very large amount or number • *a plethora of information*

pleu·ri·sy /ˈplʊrəsi/ *n* [U] : a serious and painful disease of the lungs

Plex·i·glas /ˈplɛksɪˌglæs/ *trademark* — used for sheets of strong, clear plastic

plexus see SOLAR PLEXUS

pli·able /ˈplaɪəbəl/ *adj* **1** : able to bend, fold, or twist easily : FLEXIBLE • *pliable leather* **2** : too easily influenced or controlled by other people • *pliable people/principles* — **pli·abil·i·ty** /ˌplaɪəˈbɪləti/ *n* [U]

pli·ant /ˈplaɪənt/ *adj* **1 a** : able to bend without breaking : FLEXIBLE • *a pliant material* **b** : able to move freely • *the dancer's pliant body* **2** : too easily influenced or controlled by other people • *a pliant wife/husband* — **pli·an·cy** /ˈplaɪənsi/ *n* [U]

pli·ers /ˈplaɪəz/ *n* [plural] : a tool that is used for holding small objects or for bending and cutting wire • *using (a pair of) pliers*

plight /ˈplaɪt/ *n* [C] : a very bad or difficult situation • *the plight of the homeless*

plod /ˈplɑːd/ *vb* **plod·ded; plod·ding 1** [T/I] : to walk slowly and usually heavily : TRUDGE • *I plodded (my way) through the mud.* **2** [T] : to progress or develop slowly • *He plodded through his work.* — **plod** *n* [singular] • *The pace slowed to a plod.* — **plod·der** /ˈplɑːdə/ *n* [C] — **plodding** *adj, always before a noun* • *the movie's plodding pace*

plonk *vb* [T] *Brit, informal* : PLUNK • *He plonked the suitcase onto the bench.* — **plonk down** [phrasal vb] **plonk down** *or* **plonk yourself down** *Brit, informal* : to sit or lie down suddenly in a careless way • *He plonked down* [=(chiefly US) plunked down] *beside me.*

plonk·er /ˈplɑːŋkə/ *n* [C] *Brit, informal* : a stupid person

plop /ˈplɑːp/ *vb* **plopped; plop·ping** *informal* **1** [I] : to fall, drop, or move with a sound like something dropping into liquid • *An ice cube plopped noisily into the glass.* **2** [T] : to drop (something) into a liquid so that it makes a splashing sound • *I plopped an ice cube into my drink.* **3** [T/I] : to sit or lie down in a heavy or careless way • *He plopped (him-*

self) *down in the chair.* **4** [T] : PLUNK ▪ *He plopped the tray down.* — **plop down** [*phrasal vb*] **plop down (money) or plop (money) down** *US, informal* : to pay or spend (money) ▪ *I can't afford to just plop down $30 for a T-shirt.* — **plop** *n* [C] ▪ *The rock landed in the water with a plop.*

¹**plot** /ˈplɑːt/ *n* **1** [C] **a** : an area of land that has been measured and is considered as a unit **b** : a usually small piece of land that is used for a particular purpose ▪ *a garden plot* **2** [C/U] : a series of events that form the story in a novel, movie, etc. ▪ *The movie has a weak/strong plot.* ◇ When **the plot thickens** in a novel, movie, etc., the story becomes more complicated or interesting. **3** [C] : a secret plan to do something that is usually illegal or harmful ▪ *plots against the government* ▪ *They hatched a plot* [=made a plan] *to steal the painting.*

²**plot** *vb* **plot·ted; plot·ting 1 a** [T/I] : to plan secretly to do something usually illegal or harmful ▪ *He plotted his escape/revenge.* ▪ *They were plotting against him.* **b** [T] : to plan (something) ▪ *She carefully plotted her career path.* **2** [T] : to mark (something, such as a location or path) on a map, graph, chart, etc. ▪ *Have you plotted (out) the route for your trip yet?* ▪ *plotting temperatures on a graph* **3** [T] : to create a plot for (a novel, movie, etc.) ▪ *a brilliantly plotted novel* — **plot·ter** /ˈplɑːtɚ/ *n* [C]

plough *Brit spelling of* PLOW

plo·ver /ˈplʌvɚ/ *n, pl* **plover** *or* **plo·vers** [C] : a type of bird that has a short beak and that lives near the sea

¹**plow** (*US*) *or Brit* **plough** /ˈplaʊ/ *n* [C] **1** : a piece of farm equipment that is used to dig into and turn over soil **2** : SNOWPLOW

²**plow** (*US*) *or Brit* **plough** *vb* **1** [T] : to dig into or break up (dirt, soil, land, etc.) with a plow ▪ *plow a field* [T/I] *chiefly US* : to use a snowplow to remove snow from a road, parking lot, etc. ▪ *They didn't plow (the street/snow) until the storm was over.* **3** [T/I] : to move through, over, or across (something) in a forceful and steady way ▪ *They plowed (their way) through the tall grass.* **4** [I] : to do something difficult in a slow or steady way ▪ *She was plowing through the paperwork on her desk.* — **plow into** [*phrasal vb*] **1** : to crash into (someone or something) usually at a high speed ▪ *The car plowed into the guardrail.* **2 plow (money, profits, etc.) into (something)** : to invest (money, profits, etc.) in (something) ▪ *The company plowed millions of dollars into research.*

ploy /ˈplɔɪ/ *n* [C] : a clever trick or plan that is used to get someone to do something or to gain an advantage over someone ▪ *Her sad story is a ploy to get you to give her money.* ▪ *a marketing ploy*

¹**pluck** /ˈplʌk/ *vb* **1** [T] : to pull (something) quickly to remove it ▪ *plucking petals off/from a flower* **2** [T] : to remove some or all of the feathers or hairs from (something) ▪ *pluck a chicken* ▪ *She plucks her eyebrows.* **3** [T] : to select or take (something) usually from a group,

container, or place ▪ *He plucked a stone out of the river.* ▪ (*figurative*) *He'd been plucked from obscurity and thrust into the national spotlight.* **4** [T/I] **a** : to pull and release (a string on a musical instrument) with your fingers in order to make a sound ▪ *pluck (on) a guitar string* **b** : to play (a guitar, banjo, etc.) by pulling and releasing the strings with your fingers ▪ *plucking (on/at) a banjo* — **pluck at** [*phrasal vb*] : to pull part of (something) with your fingers especially more than once ▪ *He nervously plucked at the blanket.* — **pluck up (the) courage** ◇ If you **pluck up (the) courage** to do something, you become brave enough to do it. ▪ *He finally plucked up the courage to ask her on a date.*

²**pluck** *n* [U] *old-fashioned + informal* : courage and determination ▪ *It takes pluck to do what she did.* — **plucky** /ˈplʌki/ *adj* **pluck·i·er; -est** ▪ *a plucky young man*

¹**plug** /ˈplʌg/ *n* [C] **1 a** : a part at the end of an electric cord that has two or three metal pins that connect the cord to a source of electricity ▪ *the lamp's plug* **b** : a part at the end of a wire or cable that is used to connect machines or devices ▪ *a microphone plug* **c** *chiefly Brit* : OUTLET **4 2** : a thing that is used to fill a hole or empty area ▪ *a wooden plug* ▪ *a drain plug* [=a thing used to close a drain so the water does not drain out] **3** : SPARK PLUG **4** : something that is said on the radio, on television, etc., in order to create interest in something (such as a book, movie, or restaurant) ▪ *He gave/made a plug for* [=talked about] *his new film.* — **pull the plug** *informal* **1** : to turn off the machine that is keeping a very sick or injured person alive and allow that person to die **2** : to allow or cause something to end by stopping the money or support that is needed for it ▪ *The network is pulling the plug on the show.*

²**plug** *vb* **plugged; plug·ging** [T] **1** : to fill or cover (a hole, space, etc.) with something ▪ *We were able to plug the hole with cement.* ▪ *The drain was plugged (up).* [=clogged] ▪ (*figurative*) *trying to plug the holes/gaps in the security system* **2** : to advertise (something) by talking about it especially on the radio or television ▪ *plugging the band's new album* — **plug away** [*phrasal vb*] *informal* : to continue doing something even though it is difficult or boring ▪ *She kept plugging away at her homework.* — **plug in** [*phrasal vb*] **plug (something) in** *or* **plug in (something)** **1** : to connect (something) to an electrical source or to another device by using a plug ▪ *The microphone isn't plugged in.* **2** : to put (information, such as a word or number) in something ▪ *Just plug in* [=insert] *your name and address.* — **plug into** [*phrasal vb*] **1 plug in (something)** *or* **plug (something) into** : to become connected or to cause (something) to become connected to an electrical source or another device ▪ *The heater plugs into the dashboard of your car.* ▪ *Plug the scanner into the computer.* **2**

plug (something) into : to put (information, such as a word or number) into something ▪ *plugging numbers into an equation*

plug·hole /ˈplʌɡˌhoʊl/ *n* [C] *Brit* : ²DRAIN 1

plug–in /ˈplʌɡˌɪn/ *n* [C] *computers* : a small piece of software that adds a feature to a larger program or makes a program work better ▪ *a (Web) browser plug-in*

plum /ˈplʌm/ *n* [C] **1** : a round, juicy fruit that has red or purple skin, sweet yellow flesh, and a hard seed at the center **2** : something that many people want or think is very good ▪ *a plum job/role*

plum·age /ˈpluːmɪdʒ/ *n* [U] : the feathers that cover the body of a bird ▪ *a bird with colorful plumage*

¹**plumb** /ˈplʌm/ *adv* **1** *US, informal + old-fashioned* : to a complete degree : COMPLETELY ▪ *I plumb forgot about the party.* **2** *informal* : EXACTLY ▪ *plumb [=right] in the middle of the road*

²**plumb** *vb* [T] **1** *literary* : to examine (something) in a careful and complete way in order to understand it ▪ *The book plumbs the depths of human nature.* **2** : to experience or reach (something) ▪ *The stock plumbed new depths* [=reached its lowest value] *this week.*

plumb·er /ˈplʌmɚ/ *n* [C] : a person whose job is to install or repair sinks, toilets, water pipes, etc.

plumb·ing /ˈplʌmɪŋ/ *n* [U] **1** : a system of pipes that carries water through a building ▪ *The house has old plumbing.* **2** : the job of installing and repairing sinks, toilets, water pipes, etc.

plume /ˈpluːm/ *n* [C] **1** : a feather or group of feathers ▪ *a hat with ostrich plumes* **2** : something (such as smoke, steam, or water) that rises into the air in a tall, thin shape ▪ *a plume of smoke* — **plumed** /ˈpluːmd/ *adj* ▪ *plumed helmets*

plum·met /ˈplʌmət/ *vb* [I] : to fall suddenly straight down especially from a very high place ▪ *The satellite plummeted into/toward the ocean.* ▪ (*figurative*) *Stock prices plummeted 40 percent.*

¹**plump** /ˈplʌmp/ *adj* : having a full, rounded shape ▪ *a plump, juicy peach* : slightly fat ▪ *a plump little boy*

²**plump** *vb* [T] : to shake or hit (something) to make it fuller, softer, or rounder ▪ *She plumped (up) the pillows.* — **plump for** [*phrasal vb*] *informal* **1** *US* : to express support for (someone or something) ▪ *The President plumped for the incumbent candidate in the election.* **2** *Brit* : to choose (someone or something) after thinking carefully ▪ *I finally plumped for the blue dress.*

¹**plun·der** /ˈplʌndɚ/ *vb* [T/I] : to steal things from (a city, town, etc.) especially by force ▪ *Thieves plundered the tomb.* — **plun·der·er** *n* [C]

²**plunder** *n* [U] **1** : the act of stealing things from a place especially by force ▪ *the plunder of the village* **2** : things that are stolen or taken by force especially during a war ▪ *The thieves divided the plunder among themselves.*

¹**plunge** /ˈplʌndʒ/ *vb* **plunged; plung·ing** [I] **1** : to fall or jump suddenly from a high place ▪ *Her car plunged off a bridge.* ▪ *He plunged [=dove] into the pool.* **2** : to fall or drop suddenly in amount, value, etc. ▪ *The stock market plunged yesterday.* **3** : to have a steep slope or drop downward ▪ *The road plunges down the mountain.* — **plunge in/into** [*phrasal vb*] **1 plunge (something) in or plunge (something) into** : to push (something) quickly and forcefully ▪ *He plunged the knife into the cake.* **2** : to start doing (something) with enthusiasm and energy ▪ *We had to plunge in.* ▪ *She plunged (right) into the assignment.* **3** : to suddenly begin to be in or to cause (someone or something) to be in (a particular condition or situation) ▪ *He plunged into a severe depression.* ▪ *The city was plunged into darkness.* [=the city suddenly became dark]

²**plunge** *n* [C] **1** : a sudden fall or jump usually from a high place ▪ *The cat survived its plunge from the roof.* ▪ (*figurative*) *The store experienced a sharp plunge in sales.* [=sales dropped very quickly and sharply] **2** : a sudden quick fall in amount, value, etc. ▪ *a price plunge* **3** : the act of suddenly beginning to be in a particular condition or situation ▪ *his plunge into severe depression* — **take the plunge** *informal* : to do something after thinking about it especially for a long time ▪ *Yesterday we finally took the plunge and bought a new car.*

plung·er /ˈplʌndʒɚ/ *n* [C] **1** : a tool made of a stick with a rubber cup on the end that is used to clear a blocked pipe in a toilet or sink **2** : a part that moves up and down usually inside a tube or cylinder (such as a syringe) to push something out

plunk /ˈplʌŋk/ *vb* [T] *chiefly US, informal* : to drop or place (something or someone) in a forceful and often careless way ▪ *She plunked a mug of coffee on the counter.* ▪ (*figurative*) *He was plunked into the middle of a terrible situation.* — **plunk down** [*phrasal vb*] *informal* **1 plunk down (money) or plunk (money) down** *US* : to pay or spend (money) ▪ *He plunked down $25,000 for a new car.* **2 plunk down or plunk yourself down** *chiefly US* : to sit or lie down suddenly in a careless way ▪ *She plunked herself down on the sofa.*

plu·per·fect /ˌpluːˈpɚfɪkt/ *n* [U] *grammar* : PAST PERFECT

plu·ral /ˈplɚrəl/ *n* [C] : a form of a word that is used to refer to more than one person or thing ▪ *English plurals usually end in an "s."* ▪ *The plural of (the word) "child" is "children."* — abbr. *pl.* — **plural** *adj* ▪ *The plural form of "child" is "children."* ▪ *a plural verb form, like "are"*

plu·ral·i·ty /plʊˈræləti/ *n, pl* **-ties** [C] **1** *formal* : a usually large number of things ▪ *They studied a plurality of approaches.* **2** *chiefly US, technical* : a number of votes that is more than the number of votes for any other candidate or party but that is not more than half of the total number of votes ▪ *He was elected with a* *plurality of the votes, but not with a major-ity.*

¹**plus** /ˈplʌs/ *adj* **1** *always before a noun* : having a value that is above zero ▪ *The temperature was plus 10 degrees.* [=10 degrees above zero] **2** — used after a letter grade to show that the work is slightly better than the letter by itself would indicate ▪ *He got a C plus in history.* **3** — used after a number to indicate a range greater than that number ▪ *This stadium seats 20,000-plus people.* [=more than 20,000 people] — **on the plus side** — used to describe the more appealing or attractive part of something ▪ *On the plus side, the job is close by and the hours are good.*

²**plus** *n* [C] **1** *informal* : something that is useful or helpful ▪ *The job doesn't pay well, but the hours are a definite plus.* **2** *mathematics* : PLUS SIGN

³**plus** *prep* **1** — used to indicate that one number or amount is being added to another ▪ *4 plus 5 equals/is 9* ▪ *The cost is $10 plus $2 for shipping.* **2** : and also ▪ *The hotel has two restaurants, plus a bar and a swimming pool.* — **plus or minus** — used to indicate that a value, number, or amount may be above or below a certain number ▪ *It should take a month, plus or minus a few days.*

⁴**plus** *conj, informal* : AND ▪ *I enjoy gardening, plus it's good exercise.*

plush /ˈplʌʃ/ *adj* **1** : made of a thick, soft fabric ▪ *plush carpeting* **b** : thick and soft ▪ *plush fabric* **2** : very fancy and usually expensive ▪ *a plush apartment/office/suite*

plus sign *n* [C] : the symbol + used to show that a number is being added to another number or that a quantity is greater than zero

Plu·to /ˈpluːtoʊ/ *n* [*singular*] : the object in our solar system that in the past was thought to be the planet farthest from the sun but that is no longer considered to be a planet

plu·to·ni·um /pluˈtoʊnijəm/ *n* [U] : a radioactive element that is used to make nuclear energy and nuclear weapons

¹**ply** /ˈplaɪ/ *vb* **plies; plied; ply·ing** *formal* **1** [T] : to work at (a job, activity, etc.) ▪ *Wood-carvers were plying their trade.* [=doing their work] ▪ *a street where many artists ply their wares* [=sell their goods] **2** [T/I] : to travel on a particular road, way, etc., regularly ▪ *Barges plied back and forth along the canal.* ▪ *ships plying the country's northern coast* — **ply with** [*phrasal vb*] **ply (someone) with** : to offer or give (something) to (someone) repeatedly or constantly ▪ *Waiters plied guests with wine and hors d'oeuvres.*

²**ply** *n, pl* **plies** [C] : one of the layers, folds, or strands that make something (such as yarn or plywood) ▪ *four-ply yarn*

ply·wood /ˈplaɪˌwʊd/ *n* [U] : a strong board that is made by gluing together thin sheets of wood ▪ *a floor made of plywood* ▪ *a plywood floor*

p.m. *or* **PM** *or Brit* **pm** *abbr* in the afternoon or evening — used with numbers to show the time of day ▪ *She went to bed at 10 p.m.* ◆ The abbreviation *p.m.* stands for the Latin phrase *post meridiem,* which means "after noon." — compare A.M.

PM *abbr* prime minister

PMS /ˌpiːˌɛmˈɛs/ *n* [U] *US* : PREMENSTRUAL SYNDROME

PMT /ˌpiːˌɛmˈtiː/ *n* [U] *Brit* : PREMENSTRUAL SYNDROME

pneu·mat·ic /nʊˈmætɪk, Brit njuˈmætɪk/ *adj* **1** : using air pressure to move or work ▪ *a pneumatic hammer* **2** : filled with air ▪ *pneumatic tires*

pneu·mo·nia /nʊˈmoʊnjə, Brit njuˈmoʊnjə/ *n* [U] : a serious disease that affects the lungs and makes it difficult to breathe

P.O. *abbr* **1** post office **2** postal order

poach /ˈpoʊtʃ/ *vb* **1** [T] **a** : to cook (something) in a small amount of liquid that is almost boiling ▪ *The vegetables were poached in chicken broth.* **b** : to cook (an egg without its shell) in boiling water or in a small cup over boiling water ▪ *poach an egg* **2** [T/I] : to catch or kill an animal illegally ▪ *Elephants are often poached for their ivory tusks.* **3** [T] : to take (something or someone) from someone else illegally or unfairly ▪ *She poached the material for her essay from a Web site.* ▪ *poaching clients/employees* — **poached** /ˈpoʊtʃt/ *adj* ▪ *We had poached eggs for breakfast.* — **poach·er** *n* [C]

P.O. Box *n* [C] : a box at a post office where you can have mail delivered ▪ *Write to P.O. Box 100, New York, New York.*

¹**pock·et** /ˈpɑːkət/ *n* [C] **1** : a usually small cloth bag that is sewn into a piece of clothing, a larger bag, etc., and that is open at the top or side so that you can put things into it ▪ *his coat pocket* ▪ *She put her hands in her pockets.* **2** : the amount of money that someone has available to spend ▪ *The governor paid for the event out of his own pocket.* [=with his own money] ▪ *a company with deep pockets* [=with large amounts of money] **3** : a small area or group that is different from the larger area or group it is in or near ▪ *pockets of resistance* **4** : a bag or cup that you hit the ball into at the corner or side of a pool table or billiard table ▪ *the corner/side pocket* — **in someone's pocket** or **in the pocket of someone** *disapproving* : under someone's control or influence ▪ *scientists who are in the pocket of pharmaceutical companies* — **in your pocket** *informal* ◆ If you have something *in your pocket,* you are certain to win or get it. ▪ *She had the game/match in her pocket.* [=she was sure to win the game] — **line your pockets** see ²LINE

²**pocket** *vb* [T] **1** : to put (something) in a pocket ▪ *He pocketed the change.* **2 a** : to take or keep (something that does not belong to you) ▪ *The chairman was fired for pocketing funds.* **b** : to earn or win (something, such as money) ▪ *a professional golfer who pocketed more than four million dollars in winnings*

³**pocket** *adj, always before a noun* **1** : small enough to fit in a pocket ▪ *a pocket calculator/dictionary* **2** : carried in a

pocket • *pocket change*

pock·et·book /ˈpɑːkət,bʊk/ *n* [C] *US* **1** : HANDBAG, PURSE • *a woman's pocketbook* **2** : the amount of money that someone has available to spend • *The restaurant has meals priced for every pocketbook.* [=meals that everyone can afford]

pock·et·ful /ˈpɑːkət,fʊl/ *n, pl* **pock·et·fuls** *or* **pock·ets·ful** /ˈpɑːkəts,fʊl/ [C] : an amount of something that can be carried in a pocket • *a pocketful of money*

pock·et·knife /ˈpɑːkət,naɪf/ *n, pl* **-knives** [C] : a small knife that has one or more blades that fold into the handle

pocket money *n* [U] **1** : a small amount of extra money • *earning a little pocket money* **2** *Brit* : money that is regularly given to children by their parents

pock·et·size /ˈpɑːkət,saɪz/ *also* **pock·et·sized** /ˈpɑːkət,saɪzd/ *adj* : small enough to be carried in a pocket • *a pocket-size dictionary*

pock·mark /ˈpɑːk,mɑːk/ *n* [C] **1** : a mark or scar on the skin that is usually caused by a disease **2** : a hole in or mark on something • *The bullets left pockmarks in the wall.* — **pock·marked** /ˈpɑːk,mɑːkt/ *adj* : pockmarked skin

pod /ˈpɑːd/ *n* [C] : a long, thin part of some plants that has seeds inside • *pea pods* • *a seed pod* — **two peas in a pod** see PEA

podgy /ˈpɑːdʒi/ *adj* **podg·i·er**; **-est** *Brit, informal* : PUDGY

po·di·a·trist /poʊˈdajətrɪst/ *n* [C] *chiefly US* : a doctor who treats injuries and diseases of the foot — **po·di·a·try** /poʊˈdajətri/ *n* [U]

po·di·um /ˈpoʊdijəm/ *n* [C] **1** : a raised platform for a speaker, performer, or the leader of an orchestra **2** *US* : a stand with a slanted surface that holds a book, notes, etc., for someone who is reading, speaking, or teaching

po·em /ˈpoʊəm/ *n* [C] : a piece of writing that usually has figurative language and that is written in separate lines that often have a repeated rhythm and sometimes rhyme

po·et /ˈpoʊət/ *n* [C] : a person who writes poems

po·et·ic /poʊˈɛtɪk/ *adj* **1** : of, relating to, or characteristic of poets or poetry • *poetic words/meter* **2** : having a beautiful or graceful quality • *poetic language* — **po·et·i·cal·ly** /poʊˈɛtɪkli/ *adv*

poetic justice *n* [U] : a result or occurrence that seems proper because someone who has done bad things to other people is being harmed or punished • *After the way he treated his staff, it was poetic justice that he was fired.*

poet laureate *n, pl* **poets laureate** *or* **poet laureates** [C] : a poet who is honored by being chosen for an official position by a ruler or government

po·et·ry /ˈpoʊətri/ *n* [U] **1** : the writings of a poet • *a collection of poetry* [=poems] **2** : something that is very beautiful or graceful • *Her dancing is pure poetry.*

po–faced /ˈpoʊˌfeɪst/ *adj, Brit, informal* : having a serious expression on the face • *a po-faced police officer*

po·grom /pəˈɡrɑːm, Brit ˈpɒɡrəm/ *n* [C] : the organized killing of many helpless people usually because of their race or religion

poi·gnant /ˈpɔɪnjənt/ *adj* : causing a strong feeling of sadness • *a poignant reminder of her childhood* — **poi·gnan·cy** /ˈpɔɪnjənsi/ *n* [U] — **poi·gnant·ly** *adv*

poin·set·tia /pɔɪnˈsɛtijə/ *n* [C] : a plant with large red, pink, or white leaves that look like petals

¹**point** /ˈpɔɪnt/ *n* **1 a** [C] : an idea that you try to make other people accept or understand • *I see your point, but I don't think everyone will agree.* • *He made a very good point.* • *He'll do anything to prove a point.* [=to show that he is right about something] **b** [C] : a particular detail of an idea or argument • *There are two critical/crucial/key points that I would like to discuss.* • *We debated the fine/finer points of the law.* **c** *the point* : the main or most important idea of something that is said or written • *We were waiting for her to come/get to the point.* **2** [U, singular] : a reason for doing something • *Is there a point to/for all of this paperwork?* • *There's no point in getting upset.* [=there is no reason to get upset] • *What's the point of having* [=why have] *a pool if you never use it?* • *There's not much point in going.* **3** [C] : a particular position, location, or place • *the country's northernmost point* • *the old capitol building and other points of interest* **4** [C] : a particular time or a particular stage in the development of something • *At no point (in time) did the defendant ask for a lawyer.* • *The cutoff point of the negotiations* • *At this point in my life, I can't afford to take any risks.* • *Things will be different from this point on.* • *Up to that point it had been a successful meeting.* • *The animals were hunted to the point of extinction.* [=were hunted until they were extinct] **5** [C] **a** : a unit of measurement • *Her blood pressure had risen 16 points since her last checkup.* • *two percentage points* [=two percent] **b** : a unit that is used to score a game or contest • *We won the game by three points.* • *(figurative) He gets points for effort.* [=he should be given credit for the effort he makes] **6** [C] : the usually sharp end of something • *the sharp point of the needle/pencil* **7** [C] **a** : a small dot • *a line drawn between two points* **b** : DECIMAL POINT — used especially in speech • *He had a temperature of one hundred and four point two.* [=104.2] **8** [C] : a piece of land that sticks out into a lake, ocean, etc. • *the lighthouse on the point* **9** [C] *Brit* : OUTLET 4 **10** [C] : a unit that measures the size of letters typed on a computer or printed in a published work • *12-point type* — **beside the point** : not related to the main idea being discussed • *What we had for dinner is beside the point. The point is, we went out on a date.* — **from point A to point B** see ¹A — **make a point** ✧ If you **make a point of** doing something or **make it a point** to do something, you give your attention to it so that you are sure that it happens. • *She makes a point of treating her employees fairly.* — **on point** *US* : re-

lating very well to the subject that is being discussed • *Her message is (right) on point.* — **to the point** : relating to the thing that is being thought about or discussed • *Please keep your questions brief and to the point.* — **up to a point** — used to indicate that a statement is partly but not completely true • *Competition is good but only up to a certain point.*

²**point** *vb* **1** [*T/I*] : to show someone where to look by moving your finger or an object held in your hand in a particular direction • *It's not polite to point (at people).* • *She pointed the stick at the blackboard.* • *He pointed toward the door.* **2** [*T*] : to cause the front or tip of (something) to be turned toward someone or something • *Point the flashlight into the hole.* • *A gun was pointed at his head.* **3** [*I*] : to have the end or tip extended, aimed, or turned in a specified direction • *The ship was pointing into the wind.* **4** [*T/I*] *computers* : to use a mouse or other device to move the pointer on a computer screen to a particular object or place • *Just point (the arrow) and click.* **5** [*T*] : to show (someone) which direction to travel in order to reach a particular place • *Could you point me in the direction of the train station?* — **point out** [*phrasal vb*] **point out (someone or something)** or **point (someone or something) out 1** : to direct someone's attention to (someone or something) by pointing • *He pointed out the houses of famous people as we drove by.* **2** : to talk about or mention (something that you think is important) • *He pointed out the benefits/importance of daily exercise.* — **point the way** : to show the way to go in order to get somewhere • *She pointed the way to the exit.* • *(figurative) Their work pointed the way for future scientific research.* — **point to** [*phrasal vb*] : to mention or refer to (something) as a way of supporting an argument or claim • *They are unable to point to anything that proves their theory.* — **point to/toward** [*phrasal vb*] : to show that something is true or probably true • *All the evidence points to him as the murderer.* [=indicates that he is the murderer] • *Everything points to a bright future.*

point–and–shoot *adj* : having simple controls that do not need to be changed by the user and that make it possible to take pictures easily • *point-and-shoot cameras/camcorders*

point–blank /ˈpɔɪntˈblæŋk/ *adv* **1** : from a very close distance • *The victim was shot point-blank.* **2** : in a direct and open way that does not hide anything • *I asked her point-blank what she wanted.* — **point–blank** *adj* • *The shots were taken at/from point-blank range.*

point·ed /ˈpɔɪntəd/ *adj* **1 a** : ending in a point • *He had a short pointed beard.* **b** : having a particular number of points • *a six-pointed star* **2** : clearly directed toward a particular person or group • *pointed remarks/criticism* • *a pointed reference* **3** : very easy to see or notice • *She reacted to the news with pointed indifference.* — **point·ed·ly** /ˈpɔɪntədli/ *adv* •

He pointedly ignored the question.

point·er /ˈpɔɪntɚ/ *n* [*C*] **1** : a useful suggestion about how to do or understand something better • *She got some pointers about/on the use of commas.* **2** *Brit* : a sign that shows the condition or existence of something • *The latest data gives a pointer to the economy's overall growth.* **3** : a thin stick that a person uses to show people where to look on a screen, map, etc. **4** *computers* : a small object (such as an arrow or cursor) that is moved on a computer screen by a mouse and that is used to make selections or change where work is being done

point·less /ˈpɔɪntləs/ *adj* : having no meaning, purpose, or effect • *pointless remarks/exercises* — **point·less·ly** *adv*

point of no return *n* [*singular*] : the time when it becomes no longer possible for you to make a different decision or to return to an earlier place or state • *If you've signed the contract, you've already reached the point of no return.*

point of reference *n* [*C*] : something that is used to judge or understand something else • *The study was a point of reference for evaluating other theories.*

point of view *n* [*C*] : a way of looking at or thinking about something • *Try to see things from her point of view.*

pointy /ˈpɔɪnti/ *adj* **point·i·er; -est** *informal* : having a somewhat sharp end • *pointy shoes = shoes with pointy toes*

¹**poise** /ˈpɔɪz/ *n* [*U*] : a calm, confident manner • *She kept her poise even when under attack.*

²**poise** *vb* **poised; pois·ing** [*T*] : to hold (something) in a balanced and steady position • *She poised her pencil above the paper.*

poised *adj* **1** *not before a noun* : not moving but ready to move • *The actors were poised on the stage, ready for the curtain to come up.* • *(figurative) The company is poised [=ready] for success.* **2** *not before a noun* : in a state, place, or situation that is between two different or opposite things • *We were poised between hope and fear.* **3** : having or showing a calm, confident manner • *a very poised young woman*

¹**poi·son** /ˈpɔɪzn/ *n* [*C/U*] **1** : a substance that can cause people or animals to die or to become very sick if it gets into their bodies especially by being swallowed • *a jar of rat poison* • *deadly poisons* **2** : something (such as an idea, emotion, or situation) that is very harmful or unpleasant • *Jealousy is (a) poison to a relationship.* [=jealousy can destroy a relationship]

²**poison** *vb* [*T*] **1 a** : to cause (a person or animal) to die or to become very sick with poison • *Hundreds were poisoned from drinking the contaminated water.* **b** : to put a harmful or deadly substance in or on (something) • *The food was poisoned.* **2** : to change (something) in a very harmful or unpleasant way • *He poisoned their minds with hatred for her.* • *The disagreement poisoned their friendship.* — **poi·son·er** /ˈpɔɪznɚ/ *n* [*C*] — **poisoning** *n* [*C/U*] • *alcohol/lead poi-*

soning [=illness caused by having too much alcohol/lead in your body]

poison ivy *n* [*U*] **1** : a common plant in the central and eastern U.S. that has leaves which cause a very itchy and painful rash on your skin if you touch them **2** : the rash that is caused by poison ivy ▪ *I got/have poison ivy on my arm.*

poi·son·ous /ˈpɔɪznnəs/ *adj* **1 a** : causing sickness or death by entering or touching the body ▪ *poisonous mushrooms* ▪ *Chocolate is poisonous to dogs.* **b** : capable of putting poison into another animal's body by biting or stinging it ▪ *poisonous snakes/spiders* **2** : very harmful or unpleasant ▪ *poisonous rumors*

poke /ˈpoʊk/ *vb* **poked; pok·ing** **1 a** [*T/I*] : to push your finger or something thin or pointed into or at someone or something ▪ *He poked (a stick) at the snake.* ▪ *He poked me in the ribs.* **b** [*T*] : to make (a hole) in something by pushing something sharp or pointed through or into it ▪ *She poked a hole in the paper.* **2** [*T/I*] : to stick out so that a part can be seen ▪ *Your toe is poking out/through the hole in your sock.* ▪ *She poked her head out the window.* — **poke along** [*phrasal vb*] *US, informal* : to move along very slowly ▪ *The car poked along down the street.* — **poke around** *or Brit* **poke about** [*phrasal vb*] *informal* : to look around or search through something ▪ *He poked around (in) his closet for something to wear.* ▪ *(figurative) I don't want you poking around in my personal life.* — **poke fun at** see ¹FUN — **poke your nose in/into** see ¹NOSE — **poke** *n* [*C*] ▪ *She gave me a poke to tell me it was my turn.*

po·ker /ˈpoʊkɚ/ *n* **1** [*U*] : a card game in which players bet money on the value of their cards **2** [*C*] : a metal rod for moving coal or wood in a fire

poker face *n* [*C*] : an expression on your face that does not show your thoughts or feelings — **pok·er–faced** /ˈpoʊkɚˌfeɪst/ *adj* ▪ *a poker-faced guard*

poky *or* **pok·ey** /ˈpoʊki/ *adj* **pokier; -est** *informal* **1** *US* : very slow ▪ *a poky car/driver* **2** *Brit,* of a room or building : small and uncomfortable ▪ *a poky little room*

pol /ˈpɑːl/ *n* [*C*] *US, informal* : POLITICIAN ▪ *local pols*

po·lar /ˈpoʊlɚ/ *adj, always before a noun* **1** : of or relating to the North or South Pole or the region around it ▪ *polar ice caps* **2** : completely different or opposite ▪ *She and I are good friends even though we're polar opposites.*

polar bear *n* [*C*] : a large white bear that lives near the North Pole

po·lar·i·ty /poʊˈlerəti/ *n, pl* **-ties** [*C/U*] *formal* : a state in which two ideas, opinions, etc., are completely opposite or very different from each other ▪ *There is (a) considerable polarity of opinion on this issue.* [=there are two sides with completely different opinions]

po·lar·ize *also Brit* **po·lar·ise** /ˈpoʊləˌraɪz/ *vb* **-ized; -iz·ing** [*T/I*] : to cause (people, opinions, etc.) to separate into opposing groups ▪ *The war has polarized*

the nation. — **po·lar·i·za·tion** *also Brit* **po·lar·i·sa·tion** /ˌpoʊlərəˈzeɪʃən, *Brit* ˌpoʊləˌraɪˈzeɪʃən/ *n* [*U*]

Po·lar·oid /ˈpoʊləˌrɔɪd/ *trademark* — used for a camera that produces developed pictures or the pictures this camera produces

pole /ˈpoʊl/ *n* [*C*] **1** : a long, straight piece of wood, metal, etc., that is often placed in the ground so that it stands straight up ▪ *a bird feeder hanging from a pole* ▪ *a fishing pole* [=rod] **2 a** : either end of the imaginary line around which something (such as the earth) turns — see also NORTH POLE, SOUTH POLE **b** : either one of two opposite positions, situations, etc. ▪ *When it comes to politics, we're on opposite poles.* = *When it comes to politics, we're poles apart.*

Pole /ˈpoʊl/ *n* [*C*] : a Polish person

po·lem·ic /pəˈlɛmɪk/ *n, formal* **1** [*C*] : a strong written or spoken attack against someone else's opinions, beliefs, etc. ▪ *Her book is a fierce polemic against inequality.* **2** [*plural*] : the art or practice of using language to defend or harshly criticize something or someone ▪ *They can discuss the issues without resorting to polemics.* — **po·lem·i·cal** /pəˈlɛmɪkəl/ *also* **po·lem·ic** /pəˈlɛmɪk/ *adj* ▪ *polemical writing* — **po·lem·i·cist** /pəˈlɛməsɪst/ *n* [*C*]

pole position *n* [*C/U*] : the front position at the start of a car race

Pole Star *n* — **the Pole Star** : NORTH STAR

pole vault *n* — **the pole vault** : an athletic event in which people compete by using a pole to jump over a bar that is high above the ground — **pole–vault** *vb* [*I*] — **pole–vault·er** *n* [*C*]

¹po·lice /pəˈliːs/ *n* [*plural*] : the people or the department of people who enforce laws, investigate crimes, and make arrests ▪ *(The) Police arrested a man whom they identified as the murderer.* ▪ *a police report/investigation* ▪ *the chief of police* [=the chief of the police department]

²police *vb* **-liced; -lic·ing** [*T*] **1** : to control and keep order in (an area) by the use of police or military forces ▪ *The coast is policed by the military.* **2** : to control (something) by making sure that rules and regulations are being followed ▪ *The international agency polices the development of atomic energy facilities.* — **policing** /pəˈliːsɪŋ/ *n* [*U*] ▪ *The industry is operating without adequate policing.*

police car *n* [*C*] : a car used by police officers

police constable *n* [*C*] *chiefly Brit* : a police officer of the lowest rank — *abbr.* PC

police force *n* [*C*] : the police organization in a particular area ▪ *He joined the local police force.*

po·lice·man /pəˈliːsmən/ *n, pl* **-men** /-mən/ [*C*] : a man who is a police officer

police officer *n* [*C*] : a member of the police

police state *n* [*C*] : a country in which the activities of the people are strictly controlled by the government with the help of a police force

police station n [C] : a place where local police officers work • *They brought him to the police station for questioning.*

po·lice·wom·an /pəˈliːsˌwʊmən/ n, pl **-wom·en** /-ˌwɪmən/ [C] : a woman who is a police officer

pol·i·cy /ˈpɑːləsi/ n, pl **-cies** 1 [C/U] : an officially accepted set of rules or ideas about what should be done • *Each employee is given a handbook on company policy.* • *American foreign policy* 2 [C/U] : an idea or belief that guides the way you live or behave • *I make it a policy not to lend my friends money.* [=I don't lend my friends money] 3 [C] : a document that contains the agreement that an insurance company and a person have made • *an insurance policy*

pol·i·cy·hold·er /ˈpɑːləsiˌhoʊldɚ/ n [C] : a person who owns an insurance policy

po·lio /ˈpoʊlijoʊ/ n [U] : a serious disease that affects the nerves of the spine and often makes a person permanently unable to move particular muscles

po·lio·my·eli·tis /ˌpoʊlijoʊˌmajəˈlaɪtəs/ n [U] : POLIO

¹**pol·ish** /ˈpɑːlɪʃ/ vb [T] 1 : to make (something) smooth and shiny by rubbing it • *She polished the silverware.* 2 : to improve (something) • *He spent the summer polishing (up) his math skills.* — **polish off** [phrasal vb] informal **polish (something) off** or **polish off (something)** : to finish (something) completely • *He polished off the whole pie/book.* — **pol·ish·er** n [C]

²**polish** n 1 [C/U] : a substance that is rubbed on a surface to make it smooth and shiny • *shoe/furniture polish* 2 [U] : good quality or style that comes from practice or effort • *His performance lacked polish.* 3 [singular] : the act of polishing something • *She gave the statue a quick polish.*

Pol·ish /ˈpoʊlɪʃ/ n 1 [U] : the language of Poland • *Do you speak Polish?* 2 **the Polish** : the people of Poland — **Polish** adj • *Polish food/traditions*

pol·ished /ˈpɑːlɪʃt/ adj 1 : made smooth and shiny by polishing • *polished silver/granite* 2 : very impressive or skillful • *a polished actress/performance* 3 somewhat old-fashioned : very polite : having good manners • *a polished gentleman*

po·lite /pəˈlaɪt/ adj **po·lit·er**; **-est** 1 : having or showing good manners or respect for other people • *polite children* • *It isn't polite to interrupt people when they're talking.* 2 always before a noun : socially correct or proper • **polite speech** [=somewhat formal speech that is not offensive and can be used in all situations] • *Certain words should not be used in polite society/company.* [=with people who value good manners] — **po·lite·ly** adv — **po·lite·ness** n [U] • *She only did it out of politeness.* [=to be polite; because she wanted to show good manners]

po·lit·i·cal /pəˈlɪtɪkəl/ adj 1 : of or relating to politics or government • *the American political system* [=the way the American government is officially organized, managed, etc.] • *political parties/issues* • *a*

group of political activists 2 : interested in or active in politics • *She is very political.* 3 : involving, concerned with, or accused of acts against a government • *political prisoners* [=people who are put in prison because of their political beliefs and activities] 4 : relating to the things people do to gain or keep power or an advantage within a group, organization, etc. • *His promotion was political.* [=he was promoted because a powerful person wanted him to be promoted and not because he was qualified] — **po·lit·i·cal·ly** /pəˈlɪtɪkli/ adv • *a politically motivated crime*

political action committee n [C] US : a group that is formed to give money to the political campaigns of people who are likely to make decisions that would benefit the group's interests — called also **PAC**

politically correct adj, sometimes disapproving : agreeing with the idea that people should be careful to not use language or behave in a way that could offend a particular group of people • *politically correct language/terms* — abbr. **PC** — **political correctness** n [U]

politically incorrect adj : not avoiding language or behavior that could offend a particular group of people • *a politically incorrect comment/joke* — **political incorrectness** n [U]

political science n [U] : the study of governments and how they work — **political scientist** n [C]

pol·i·ti·cian /ˌpɑːləˈtɪʃən/ n [C] : someone who is active in government usually as an elected official

po·lit·i·cize also Brit **po·lit·i·cise** /pəˈlɪtəˌsaɪz/ vb **-cized**; **-ciz·ing** [T] 1 disapproving : to relate (an idea, issue, etc.) to politics in a way that makes people less likely to agree • *They have politicized the budget process.* 2 : to cause (someone) to become involved or interested in government or politics • *students politicized by the war*

pol·i·tick·ing /ˈpɑːləˌtɪkɪŋ/ n [U] often disapproving : political activity that is done especially in order to win support or gain an advantage • *a lot of behind-the-scenes politicking*

po·lit·i·co /pəˈlɪtɪˌkoʊ/ n, pl **-cos** [C] somewhat informal + often disapproving : POLITICIAN

pol·i·tics /ˈpɑːləˌtɪks/ n 1 [U] : activities that relate to influencing the actions and policies of a government or getting and keeping power in a government • *The students discussed the latest news in national/local politics.* • *Politics has/have always interested her.* = *She's always been interested in politics.* 2 [U] : the work or job of people who are part of a government • *She plans on going into politics.* [=getting a job that involves politics] 3 [plural] : the opinions that someone has about what should be done by governments • *His politics are very liberal/conservative.* 4 [U] often disapproving : the activities, attitudes, or behaviors that are used to get or keep power or an advantage within a group, organization, etc. • *I* *don't want to get involved in office politics.* **5** [U] *chiefly Brit* : POLITICAL SCIENCE • *a degree in politics* — **play politics** *disapproving* : to say or do things for political reasons instead of doing what is right or what is best for other people • *She's been accused of playing politics with the investigation.*

pol·ka /ˈpoʊlkə, *Brit* ˈpɒlkə/ *n* [C] : a lively dance for couples or the music for this dance • *The band played a polka.*

polka dot *n* [C] : one of a series of dots that make a pattern especially on fabric or clothing • *The dress has polka dots on it.* — **polka-dot** or **pol·ka–dot·ted** /ˈpoʊkəˌdɑːtəd/ *adj* • *a polka-dotted skirt*

¹**poll** /ˈpoʊl/ *n* **1** [C] : an activity in which several or many people are asked a question or a series of questions in order to get information about what most people think about something • *A recent poll shows a decrease in the number of teenagers who smoke.* • *an opinion poll* **2 a** [C] : the record of votes that were made by people in an election • *The polls show that she's ahead.* = *She's ahead in the polls.* **b** [U] *Brit* : the number of votes made in an election • *The candidate won with 55 percent of the poll.* [=(US) vote] **3 the polls** : the places where people vote during an election • *The polls are open until 8:00 tonight.*

²**poll** *vb* [T] **1** : to ask (people) a question or a series of questions in order to get information about what most people think about something • *The magazine polled its readers on their eating habits.* **2** : to receive (a specified number or percentage of votes) in an election • *The conservative candidate polled more than 10,000 votes.*

pol·len /ˈpɑːlən/ *n* [U] : the very fine usually yellow dust that is produced by a plant and that is carried to other plants usually by wind or insects so that the plants can produce seeds

pollen count *n* [C] : a number that indicates the amount of pollen in the air and that is used by people who get sick from breathing in pollen

pol·li·nate /ˈpɑːləˌneɪt/ *vb* **-nat·ed; -nat·ing** [T] : to give (a plant) pollen from another plant of the same kind so that seeds will be produced • *The plants/flowers are pollinated by bees.* — **pol·li·na·tion** /ˌpɑːləˈneɪʃən/ *n* [U]

poll·ing /ˈpoʊlɪŋ/ *n* [U] **1** : the act of asking a person a question as part of a survey or poll • *The polling was done by telephone.* **2** *chiefly Brit* : the act of voting in an election • *Polling starts at 8 a.m.*

polling booth *n* [C] *Brit* : VOTING BOOTH

polling place *n* [C] *US* : a building where people go to vote in an election — called also (*Brit*) **polling station**

poll·ster /ˈpoʊlstɚ/ *n* [C] : someone who makes questions for a poll, asks questions in a poll, or collects and presents results from a poll

poll tax *n* [C] : a tax that each adult has to pay in order to vote in an election ◇ Poll taxes are no longer legal in the U.S.

pol·lut·ant /pəˈluːtn̩t/ *n* [C] : a substance that makes land, water, air, etc., dirty and not safe or suitable to use • *environmental/industrial pollutants*

pol·lute /pəˈluːt/ *vb* **-lut·ed; -lut·ing** [T] : to make (land, water, air, etc.) dirty and not safe or suitable to use • *Miles of beaches were polluted by the oil spill.* • (*figurative*) *Violence on television is polluting the minds of children.* — **polluted** *adj* • *polluted beaches/air* — **pol·lut·er** *n* [C]

pol·lu·tion /pəˈluːʃən/ *n* [U] **1** : the action or process of making water, land, air, etc., dirty and not safe or suitable to use • *industrial practices that have caused pollution of the air and water* **2** : substances that make water, land, air, etc., dirty and not safe or suitable to use • *The fish are dying off from pollution.*

po·lo /ˈpoʊloʊ/ *n* [U] : a game played by two teams of four players who ride horses while using long mallets to hit a wooden ball into a goal

polo neck *n* [C] *Brit* : TURTLENECK

polo shirt *n* [C] : a shirt with a collar and a few buttons at the neck that you put on by pulling over your head

pol·ter·geist /ˈpoʊltɚˌgaɪst/ *n* [C] : a ghost that makes strange noises and causes objects to move

poly·es·ter /ˌpɑːliˈɛstɚ/ *n* [U] : a material that is made from a chemical process and that is used for making many different products including fabrics • *a polyester shirt*

poly·eth·yl·ene /ˌpɑːliˈɛθəˌliːn/ *n* [U] *US* : a light and strong plastic that is used mainly in sheets for packaging

po·lyg·a·my /pəˈlɪgəmi/ *n* [U] : the state or practice of being married to more than one person at the same time • *Some cultures practice polygamy.* — **po·lyg·a·mist** /pəˈlɪgəmɪst/ *n* [C] — **po·lyg·a·mous** /pəˈlɪgəməs/ *adj* • *a polygamous marriage*

poly·gon /ˈpɑːliˌgɑːn/ *n* [C] *mathematics* : a flat shape that has three or more straight lines and angles

poly·graph /ˈpɑːliˌgræf, *Brit* ˈpɒliˌgrɑːf/ *n* [C] **1** : LIE DETECTOR **2** *US* : a test that is done with a lie detector to see if someone is telling the truth • *She took a polygraph.*

poly·mer /ˈpɑːləmɚ/ *n* [C] *chemistry* : a chemical compound that is made of small molecules that are arranged in a simple repeating structure to form a larger molecule

pol·yp /ˈpɑːləp/ *n* [C] **1** *medical* : a small lump that grows inside your body (such as inside your colon or on your vocal cords) **2** : a small sea animal (such as a coral) that has a body shaped like a tube

poly·syl·lab·ic /ˌpɑːlisɪˈlæbɪk/ *adj, technical* : having more than three syllables • *polysyllabic words*

poly·thene /ˈpɑːləˌθiːn/ *n* [U] *Brit* : POLYETHYLENE

poly·un·sat·u·rat·ed /ˌpɑːliˌʌnˈsætʃəˌreɪtəd/ *adj, technical* — used to describe a type of oil or fat that is found especially in nuts and fish and that is better for your health than saturated fats and trans fats ▪ *polyunsaturated fats/oils*

poly·ure·thane /ˌpɑliˈjɚəˌθeɪn/ *n* [U] : a type of plastic that is used to make various products and especially to make a clear liquid that is spread on a surface (such as a wooden floor) and that becomes hard when it dries

pome·gran·ate /ˈpɑːməˌgrænət/ *n* [C] : a round, red fruit that has a thick skin and many large seeds

pomp /ˈpɑːmp/ *n* [U] : the impressive decorations, music, clothing, etc., that are part of some formal events ▪ *the pomp of a ceremony* — **pomp and circumstance** : impressive formal activities or ceremonies ▪ *the pomp and circumstance of a presidential inauguration*

pom–pom /ˈpɑːmˌpɑːm/ *n* [C] **1** : a small, soft ball that is used as a decoration especially on clothing **2** : a large collection of plastic strings attached to a handle that is waved by cheerleaders

pomp·ous /ˈpɑːmpəs/ *adj, disapproving* : having or showing the attitude of people who speak and behave in a very formal and serious way because they believe that they are better, smarter, or more important than other people ▪ *a pompous politician/remark* — **pom·pos·i·ty** /ˌpɑːmˈpɑːsəti/ *n, pl* -**ties** [C/U] ▪ *the pomposities* [=pompous remarks and actions] *of elected officials* — **pomp·ous·ly** *adv*

pon·cho /ˈpɑːntʃoʊ/ *n, pl* -**chos** [C] : a piece of clothing that is used as a coat and that is made of a single piece of cloth or plastic with a hole in the middle for a person's head to go through

pond /ˈpɑːnd/ *n* [C] : an area of water that is surrounded by land and that is smaller than a lake

pon·der /ˈpɑːndɚ/ *vb* [T/I] : to think about or consider (something) carefully ▪ *He pondered the question before he answered.* ▪ *We pondered over/about what to do.*

pon·der·ous /ˈpɑːndərəs/ *adj* **1** : very boring or dull ▪ *a ponderous lecture* **2** : slow or awkward because of weight and size ▪ *the elephant's ponderous movements* — **pon·der·ous·ly** *adv*

pong /ˈpɑːŋ/ *n* [C] *Brit, informal* : an unpleasant smell ▪ *the pong of stale cigarette smoke*

pon·tiff *or* **Pon·tiff** /ˈpɑːntəf/ *n* [C] *formal* : POPE

pon·tif·i·cate /pɑnˈtɪfəˌkeɪt/ *vb* -**cat·ed**; -**cat·ing** [I] *disapproving* : to speak or express your opinion about something in a way that shows that you think you are always right ▪ *We had to listen to her pontificate about/on the best way to raise children.*

pon·toon /pɑnˈtuːn/ *n* [C] : a large hollow container filled with air that is used to make a structure (such as a boat, airplane, or bridge) float on top of water ▪ *a pontoon bridge* [=a bridge that floats on the water and is held up by pontoons]

¹**po·ny** /ˈpoʊni/ *n, pl* -**nies** [C] : a small horse — **dog and pony show** *see* ¹DOG

²**pony** *vb* -**nies**; -**nied**; -**ny·ing** — **pony up** [*phrasal vb*] *US, informal* : to pay

money for something ▪ *We ponied up $160 for the concert tickets.*

po·ny·tail /ˈpoʊniˌteɪl/ *n* [C] : a way of arranging hair by gathering it together at the back of the head and letting it hang down freely ▪ *She wore/had her hair pulled/tied back in a ponytail.*

pooch /ˈpuːtʃ/ *n* [C] *informal* : a dog ▪ *a cute little pooch*

poo·dle /ˈpuːdl̩/ *n* [C] : a type of dog that has thick, curly hair

poof /ˈpuːf/ *interj* — used to say that something has happened suddenly or that someone or something has disappeared ▪ *One minute she was here, then poof, she was gone.*

pooh–pooh /ˈpuːˌpuː/ *vb* [T] *informal* : to think or say that (something) is not very good or not true ▪ *They pooh-poohed my idea/suggestion/warning.*

¹**pool** /ˈpuːl/ *n* **1** [C] : SWIMMING POOL ▪ *She dove into the pool.* **2** [C] **a** : a small area of water ▪ *a garden pool* **b** : a small amount of liquid or light that is on a surface ▪ *a pool of blood/light* **3** [U] : a game played on a long table in which players use a long stick and a white ball to hit 15 colored balls into one of six pockets around the table ▪ *He enjoys playing/shooting pool.* ▪ *a pool table/cue* **4** [C] : an amount of money that has been collected from many people for some purpose ▪ *He put $20 into the pool.* ▪ *an investment pool* **5** [C] : a supply of things or people that are available for use ▪ *a pool of jurors/resources* ▪ *the secretarial pool* [=a group of secretaries]

²**pool** *vb* **1** [I] : to form a pool or puddle ▪ *Water pooled on the floor.* **2** [T] : to combine (something) to form a supply which can be used by a group of people ▪ *We pooled our money together.* ▪ *pooling ideas/resources*

poop /ˈpuːp/ *vb* [I] *US, informal* : to pass solid waste from the body : DEFECATE ▪ *The dog pooped on the lawn.* — **poop out** [*phrasal vb*] *US, informal* **1** : to stop working properly ▪ *The radio finally pooped out.* **2 poop out** *or* **poop (someone) out** : to become very tired or make (someone) very tired ▪ *That hike really pooped me out.* — **poop** *n* [U] *US, informal* ▪ *dog poop* [=feces]

poop deck *n* [C] : the flat surface on the raised structure at the rear of a ship

pooped /ˈpuːpt/ *adj, not before a noun, US, informal* : very tired ▪ *I'm pooped.*

poor /ˈpuɚ/ *adj* **1** : having little money or few possessions ▪ *We were too poor to buy new clothes.* ▪ *a poor country/neighborhood* **2** : having a very small amount of something ▪ *She has a poor vocabulary.* **3** : not good in quality or condition ▪ *a poor effort/performance* ▪ *poor health* ▪ *The joke was in poor taste.* [=the joke was offensive or not polite] **4** : not skilled at something ▪ *a poor golfer* ▪ *She is a poor judge of character.* **5** *always before a noun* — used to refer to someone or something in a way that shows sympathy ▪ *Leave the poor guy alone.* — **the poor** : poor people ▪ *He gave money to the poor.*

poor·house /ˈpuɚˌhaʊs/ *n* [C] *old-*

fashioned : a place for poor people to live that is paid for by the taxes, donations, etc., of other people

¹poor·ly /ˈpʊɚli/ *adv* : in a way that is not good or satisfactory • *a poorly written paper*

²poorly *adj, Brit, informal* : somewhat ill • *feeling poorly*

¹pop /ˈpɑːp/ *vb* **popped; pop·ping** **1 a** [T/I] : to suddenly break open or come off of something often with a short, loud noise • *The balloon popped.* [=burst] • *One of the buttons popped off my sweater.* • *She popped the cork on the champagne.* [=she opened the bottle of champagne by removing the cork] **b** [I] : to make a short, loud noise • *Guns were popping in the distance.* **2** [T/I] : to cook (popcorn) • *We popped some popcorn in the microwave.* **3** [I] *informal* : to move from, into, or out of a place suddenly or briefly • *My neighbor popped in for a visit.* • *I need to pop into the drugstore for some film.* • *She popped out for a minute. She should be back soon.* • *A funny thought just popped into my head.* [=I just thought of something funny] • *The cathedral popped into view.* [=I could see the cathedral] **4** [T] *informal* : to put (something) in, into, or onto a place suddenly or briefly • *She popped a CD in the player.* • *I popped a grape into my mouth.* **5 ◇** When your **ears pop**, you feel a sudden change of pressure in your ears as you are going up or down in an airplane, on a steep road, etc. **6 ◇** If your **eyes pop**, they open very wide because you are surprised, afraid, excited, etc. **7** [T] *US, informal* : to hit (someone) • *I felt like popping him (one).* — **pop open** : to open suddenly and quickly • *The suitcase/lid popped open.* • *She popped the umbrella open.* — **pop pills** *informal* : to take a lot of pills regularly • *He spends his time getting drunk and popping pills.* — **pop the question** *informal* : to ask someone to marry you • *He finally popped the question.* — **pop up** [*phrasal vb*] *informal* **1** : to appear in usually a sudden or unexpected way • *Coffee shops seem to be popping up everywhere.* • *Problems kept popping up.* **2** *baseball* : to hit a high fly ball that does not go very far : to hit a pop fly • *The batter popped up to the second baseman.*

²pop *n* **1** [C] : a short, loud sound • *We heard a loud pop when the lights went out.* **2** [C/U] *informal* : SODA POP • *a bottle of pop* **3** *baseball* : POP FLY **4** [U] **a** : music that is popular • *The radio station plays pop.* **b** *Pops US* : an orchestra that plays popular music — used in names • *the Boston Pops* **5** *US, informal* + *old-fashioned* [C] : a person's father • *Hey Pop, can I borrow one of your ties?* **b** *pops* — used as a form of address for an old man • *Need help with that package, pops?* — **a pop** *US, informal* : for each one : APIECE • *The tickets are selling at $50 a pop.* — **take a pop at** *informal* **1** : to try to hit (someone) • *She took a pop at me.* **2** *chiefly Brit* : to criticize (someone) publicly • *He took a pop at his rival.*

³pop *adj, always before a noun* **1** : of or

relating to things that are popular and often talked about on television, in newspapers, etc. • *pop culture/psychology* **2** : of or relating to popular music • *pop rock* • *a pop singer/star*

pop. *abbr* population

pop art *or* **Pop Art** *n* [U] : art in which common objects are used or shown

pop·corn /ˈpɑːpˌkoɚn/ *n* [U] : corn in the form of hard yellow seeds that burst open and become soft and white when they are heated • *We ate (a bag of) popcorn.*

pope *or* **Pope** /ˈpoʊp/ *n* [C] : the head of the Roman Catholic Church • *Pope Benedict XVI*

pop-eyed /ˈpɑːpˌaɪd/ *adj* : having eyes that stick out or are open very wide • *pop-eyed bullfrogs* • *She stared pop-eyed at the huge buildings.*

pop fly *n* [C] *baseball* : a very high fly ball that does not go very far — called also *pop, pop-up*

pop·lar /ˈpɑːplɚ/ *n* [C] : a tall, thin tree that has rough bark, soft wood, and very small groups of flowers

pop·over /ˈpɑːpˌoʊvɚ/ *n* [C] *US* : a type of bread roll that is very light and that is made from eggs, milk, and flour

poppa *variant spelling of* PAPA

pop·per /ˈpɑːpɚ/ *n* [C] **1** : a pan or electric machine for making popcorn • *a popcorn popper* **2** *Brit* : ˈSNAP 3

pop·py /ˈpɑːpi/ *n, pl* **-pies** [C] : a type of plant that has bright red or orange flowers and that is the source of opium; *also* : its flower

pop quiz *n* [C] *US* : a short test that a teacher gives to students without warning

Pop·si·cle /ˈpɑːpsɪkəl/ *trademark* — used for flavored and colored water frozen on a stick

pop·u·lace /ˈpɑːpjələs/ *n* [*singular*] *formal* : the people who live in a country or area • *The populace has suffered greatly.* • *a diverse/educated populace*

pop·u·lar /ˈpɑːpjələ/ *adj* **1 a** : liked or enjoyed by many people • *a popular performer* • *Spicy foods have become increasingly popular.* • *The bar is popular with/among college students.* **b** : accepted, followed, used, or done by many people • *a popular misconception* • *The word "groovy" was popular in the 1960s.* • *Contrary to popular belief/opinion* [=in spite of what many people believe], *fame has its drawbacks.* **2** *always before a noun* : of, relating to, or coming from most of the people in a country, society, or group • *popular culture* • *the popular vote* **3** *always before a noun, somewhat formal* : capable of being understood by ordinary people • *popular mechanics* • *a popular history of physics*

pop·u·lar·i·ty /ˌpɑːpjəˈlerəti/ *n* [U] : the state of being liked, enjoyed, accepted, or done by a large number of people • *the increasing popularity of cell phones* • *The candidate is winning/losing popularity with/among voters.* [=is becoming more/less popular with/among voters]

popularity contest *n* [C] : a contest or situation in which the person who wins or is most successful is the one who is most popular rather than the one who is most skillful, qualified, etc. — often used to say that someone or something is not popular • *He's not going to win any popularity contests around here.* [=he's not well liked]

pop·u·lar·ize *also Brit* **pop·u·lar·ise** /ˈpɑːpjələˌraɪz/ *vb* **-ized; -iz·ing** [T] : to cause (something) to be liked, enjoyed, accepted, or done by many people • *a phrase that was popularized by a hit TV show* — **pop·u·lar·i·za·tion** *also Brit* **pop·u·lar·i·sa·tion** /ˌpɑːpjələrəˈzeɪʃən, Brit ˌpɒpjələˌraɪˈzeɪʃən/ *n* [U]

pop·u·lar·ly /ˈpɑːpjələli/ *adv* **1** : by many people or most people • *a popularly held belief* **2** : by being chosen or voted for by most of the people • *the country's first popularly elected leader* [=the country's first leader who was chosen in an election rather than in some other way]

pop·u·late /ˈpɑːpjəˌleɪt/ *vb* **-lat·ed; -lat·ing** [T] : to live in (a country, city, area, etc.) • *Strange creatures populate the ocean depths.* • *The country is populated by many ethnic groups.* • *(figurative) His stories are populated with real-life characters.* — **populated** *adj* • *a densely/heavily populated area* [=an area where many people live]

pop·u·la·tion /ˌpɑːpjəˈleɪʃən/ *n* **1** [C/U] : the number of people who live in a place • *the population of New York City* • *an increase in population* • *population growth/control* **2** [C] : a group of people or animals of a particular kind that live in a place • *the rural/urban/educated/adult population*

pop·u·list /ˈpɑːpjəlɪst/ *adj* : of or relating to a political party that claims to represent ordinary people • *populist leaders* — **pop·u·lism** /ˈpɑːpjəˌlɪzəm/ *n* [U] — **populist** *n* [C] • *She is a populist.*

pop·u·lous /ˈpɑːpjələs/ *adj, formal* : having a large population • *the most populous state in the U.S.*

¹**pop-up** /ˈpɑːpˌʌp/ *adj, always before a noun* **1** : having a picture that stands up when a page is opened • *a pop-up book* **2** *computers* : appearing on the screen over another window or document • *pop-up ads*

²**pop-up** *n* [C] **1** *baseball* : POP FLY **2** *computers* : a window that appears on the screen over other windows or documents and that often advertises something • *The Web site is full of pop-ups.*

por·ce·lain /ˈpoɚsələn/ *n* [U] : a hard, white substance that is very delicate and that is made by baking clay • *a porcelain bowl/doll*

porch /ˈpoɚtʃ/ *n* [C] **1** *US* : a structure attached to the entrance of a building that has a roof and that may or may not have walls • *The house has a large front/back porch.* **2** *Brit* : an entrance to a building that has a separate roof

por·cu·pine /ˈpoɚkjəˌpaɪn/ *n, pl* **por·cu·pines** *also* **porcupine** [C] : a small animal that has very stiff, sharp parts (called quills) all over its body

¹**pore** /ˈpoɚ/ *vb* **pored; por·ing** — **pore**

over [*phrasal vb*] : to read or study (something) very carefully • *He pored over the map for hours.*

²**pore** *n* [C] **1** : a very small opening on the surface of your skin that liquid comes out through when you sweat **2** : a small opening on the surface of a plant, a rock, etc.

pork /ˈpoɚk/ *n* [U] **1** : the meat of a pig that is used for food • *roast pork* • *pork chops* **2** *US, informal + disapproving* : government money that is spent on projects done to help the political careers of elected officials • *We need to cut the pork out of the federal budget.*

pork barrel *n* [U] *US, informal + disapproving* : government projects that benefit people in a particular part of the country and that are done in order to help the political careers of elected officials • *pork barrel projects/spending*

pork·er /ˈpoɚkɚ/ *n* [C] *informal* **1** : a very fat pig used for food **2** *impolite* : a fat person

porn /ˈpoɚn/ *also* **por·no** /ˈpoɚnoʊ/ *n* [U] *informal* : PORNOGRAPHY • *making/selling porn* • *the porn industry*

por·no·graph·ic /ˌpoɚnəˈgræfɪk/ *adj* : showing or describing naked people or sex in a very open and direct way in order to cause sexual excitement • *pornographic magazines/movies*

por·nog·ra·phy /poɚˈnɑːgrəfi/ *n* [U] : movies, pictures, magazines, etc., that show or describe naked people or sex in a very open and direct way in order to cause sexual excitement • *a store that sells pornography* — **por·nog·ra·pher** /poɚˈnɑːgrəfɚ/ *n* [C]

po·rous /ˈpoɚəs/ *adj* : having small holes that allow air or liquid to pass through • *a porous membrane/surface* • *(figurative) The country has a porous border.* [=it is very easy to cross or get through the country's border]

por·poise /ˈpoɚpəs/ *n* [C] : a small usually gray and white whale that has a rounded nose

por·ridge /ˈpoɚɪdʒ/ *n* [U] *Brit* : OATMEAL 2

port /ˈpoɚt/ *n* **1** [C/U] **a** : a town or city where ships stop to load and unload cargo • *Boston is a major U.S. port.* • *The ship is now in port but will be leaving port soon.* **b** : a place where ships can find shelter from a storm • *The ship reached the port safely.* **2** [U] : the side of a ship or aircraft that is on the left when you are looking toward the front • *The ship turned to port.* **3** [C/U] : a strong, sweet, usually dark red wine that is made in Portugal **4** [C] : a place where you can connect a printer, mouse, etc., to a computer — **port** *adj* • *the port side of the ship*

portabella *variant spelling of* PORTO-BELLO

por·ta·ble /ˈpoɚtəbəl/ *adj* : easy to carry or move around • *a portable radio/computer* — **portable** *n* [C] • *laptop computers and other portables* — **por·ta·bil·i·ty** /ˌpoɚtəˈbɪləti/ *n* [U]

por·tal /ˈpoɚtl̩/ *n* [C] **1** *formal + literary* : a large door or gate to a building (such as a church) **2** *computers* : a Web site that helps you find other sites ▪ *a Web portal for baseball fans*

por·tend /pɔɚˈtɛnd/ *vb* [T] *formal + literary* : to be a sign or warning that something usually bad or unpleasant is going to happen ▪ *The distant thunder portended a storm.*

por·tent /ˈpɔɚˌtɛnt/ *n* [C] *formal + literary* : a sign or warning that something usually bad or unpleasant is going to happen ▪ *a portent of evil*

por·ten·tous /pɔɚˈtɛntəs/ *adj* **1** *formal + literary* : giving a sign or warning that something usually bad or unpleasant is going to happen ▪ *a portentous dream/event* **2** *formal + disapproving* : trying to seem important, serious, or impressive ▪ *a portentous manner/tone* — **por·ten·tous·ly** *adv*

por·ter /ˈpɔɚtɚ/ *n* [C] **1** : a person whose job is to carry bags or luggage at a hotel, airport, etc. **2** *US* : a person whose job is to help passengers on a train **3** *Brit* : a person whose job is to let people into a hotel, college, hospital, etc. ▪ *the night porter* **4** *Brit* : a person whose job is to move patients from one part of a hospital to another

port·fo·lio /pɔɚtˈfouliˌou/ *n, pl* **-li·os** [C] **1** : a flat case for carrying documents or drawings **2** : a set of drawings, paintings, or photographs that are presented together in a folder **3** *finance* : the investments that are owned by a person or organization ▪ *an investment/retirement portfolio* **4** *Brit* : the responsibilities of a minister of state or member of a cabinet ▪ *That's not part of his portfolio.*

port·hole /ˈpɔɚtˌhoʊl/ *n* [C] : a small round window in the side of a ship or aircraft

por·ti·co /ˈpɔɚtiˌkoʊ/ *n, pl* **-coes** *or* **-cos** [C] *formal* : a row of columns supporting a roof at the entrance of a building

¹**por·tion** /ˈpɔɚʃən/ *n* [C] **1** : a part of a larger amount, area, etc. ▪ *Portions of land were used for farming.* ▪ *A considerable/significant portion of the city was flooded.* **2** : a part of something that is shared with other people ▪ *He did a large portion of the work.* **3** : the amount of food that is served to a person at one time ▪ *The restaurant gives large/generous portions.*

²**portion** *vb* [T] : to divide (something) into parts and give those parts to people ▪ *The supplies were portioned (out) among the troops.*

port·ly /ˈpɔɚtli/ *adj* **port·li·er**; **-est** *somewhat formal* : having a round and somewhat fat body ▪ *a portly gentleman*

por·to·bel·lo /ˌpɔɚtəˈbɛloʊ/ *also* **por·ta·bel·la** /ˌpɔɚtəˈbɛlə/ *n, pl* **-los** *also* **-las** [C] *chiefly US* : a large brown mushroom used in cooking

port of call *n* [C] : a place where a ship stops during a journey ▪ *Our next port of call is Jamaica.*

port of entry *n* [C] : a city, airport, etc., where people or goods enter a country

por·trait /ˈpɔɚtrət/ *n* **1** [C] : a painting, drawing, or photograph of a person that usually only includes the person's head

and shoulders ▪ *The queen posed for her portrait.* **2** [C] : a detailed description of something or someone ▪ *The book/film presents a portrait of life in a small town.* **3** [U] : a way of printing a page so that the shorter sides are on the top and bottom and the longer sides are on the left and right

por·trait·ist /ˈpɔɚtrətɪst/ *n* [C] : a person who paints or draws portraits

por·trai·ture /ˈpɔɚtrətʃɚ/ *n* [U] : the art of making portraits ▪ *a painter who is a master at portraiture*

por·tray /pɔɚˈtreɪ/ *vb* [T] **1** : to describe (someone or something) in a particular way ▪ *He portrayed himself as a victim.* **2** : to show (someone or something) in a painting, book, etc. ▪ *The novel portrays* [=depicts] *life in a small southern town.* **3** : to play (a character) in a film, play, or television show ▪ *Laurence Olivier portrayed Hamlet beautifully.*

por·tray·al /pɔɚˈtreɪjəl/ *n* [C] **1** : the act of showing or describing someone or something especially in a painting, book, etc. ▪ *The book is an accurate portrayal of his life.* **2** : the way in which an actor plays a character ▪ *Laurence Olivier's portrayal of Hamlet was brilliant.*

Por·tu·guese /ˌpɔɚtʃəˈgiːz/ *n* **1** [U] : the language spoken in Portugal and Brazil **2** *the Portuguese* : the people of Portugal ▪ *the customs of the Portuguese* — **Portuguese** *adj* ▪ *Portuguese food/customs*

¹**pose** /ˈpoʊz/ *vb* **posed**; **pos·ing** **1** [T] : to be or create (a possible threat, danger, problem, etc.) ▪ *Smog poses a threat to our health.* [=smog threatens our health] ▪ *Physical sports pose a risk of injury.* ▪ *The weather should not pose a problem for us.* **2** [T] : to ask or suggest (a question) ▪ *These contradictions pose questions about his honesty.* **3** [T/I] : to stand, sit, or lie down in a particular position as a model for a photograph, painting, etc. ▪ *Everyone posed for the group photo.* ▪ *The photographer posed her in a chair.* — **pose as** [*phrasal vb*] : to pretend to be (someone or something) in order to deceive people ▪ *She posed as a student to get free admission to the museum.*

²**pose** *n* [C] **1** : the position in which someone stands, sits, lies down, etc., especially as a model for a photograph, painting, etc. ▪ *Hold that pose for the photographer.* **2** *disapproving* : a kind of behavior that is intended to impress other people and that is not sincere ▪ *His sympathetic manner is just a pose.*

pos·er /ˈpoʊzɚ/ *n* [C] **1** *disapproving* : a person who dresses or behaves in a deceptive way that is meant to impress other people ▪ *He's not really interested in music. He's just a poser.* **2** *informal* : a difficult question or problem ▪ *Her question is quite a poser.*

po·seur /poʊˈzɚ/ *n* [C] *disapproving* : POSER 1

posh /ˈpɑːʃ/ *adj, informal* **1** : very attractive, expensive, and popular ▪ *a posh neighborhood/hotel* **2** *Brit* : typical of people who have high social status ▪ *a posh accent*

pos·it /ˈpɑːzət/ *vb* [T] *formal* : to suggest (an idea, theory, etc.) especially in order to start a discussion ▪ *I would posit* [=*propose*] *that beauty is not subjective.*

¹po·si·tion /pəˈzɪʃən/ *n* **1 a** [C] : the place where someone or something is in relation to other people or things ▪ *the positions of the constellations* **b** [U] : the place where someone or something should be ▪ *The actors were all in position.* ▪ *The defensive players were out of position before the play.* ▪ *He maneuvered the car into position.* **2 a** [C/U] : the way someone stands, sits, or lies down ▪ *She fell asleep in a sitting position.* ▪ *I was uncomfortable, so I shifted position.* **b** [C] : the way something is arranged or placed ▪ *Return your seat to an upright position for landing.* **3** [C] : the situation that someone or something is in ▪ *The company's financial position has worsened over the past year.* ▪ *I'm in no position to lend you any money.* [=I cannot lend you any money.] **4** [C] : an opinion or judgment on a particular subject ▪ *He criticized her for her position on gun control.* **5** [C/U] : the rank or role of someone or something in an organization or society ▪ *a position of leadership and authority* ▪ *Wealth and position are not important to her.* **6** [C] : JOB ▪ *Does your company have any positions available?* ▪ *The position has been filled.* [=someone has been hired for the job] **7** [C/U] : the place of someone or something in a race, contest, competition, etc. ▪ *She finished the race in fourth position.* ▪ *The cars jockeyed for position in the first lap.* [=each car tried to get into a better position] **8** [C] *sports* : the particular place and job of a player on a sports team ▪ *I think goalie is the hardest position to play in hockey.*

²position *vb* [T] : to put (something or someone) in a particular position ▪ *The company is positioning itself to take advantage of a new market.* ▪ *She positioned herself by the door.*

¹pos·i·tive /ˈpɑːzətɪv/ *adj* **1** : good or useful ▪ *a positive effect/experience/influence* **2** : thinking about the good qualities of someone or something ▪ *a positive attitude/outlook* ▪ *You should try to be more positive.* **3** *not before a noun* : completely certain or sure that something is correct or true ▪ *We were positive that we would win the game.* **4** : showing or expressing support, approval, or agreement ▪ *The reviews were mostly positive.* ▪ *positive feedback* **5** : certainly true ▪ *The police have not yet made a positive identification of the victim.* ▪ *That is proof positive that he is not the father.* **6** : showing the presence of a particular germ, condition, or substance ▪ *He tested positive for steroids.* [=the test showed that he had used steroids] **7** *mathematics* : greater than zero ▪ *a positive integer* **8** *technical* : a : containing or producing electricity that is charged by a proton ▪ *a positive charge/current* **b** : having more protons than electrons ▪ *a positive ion/particle* **9** *always before a noun, infor-*

mal : absolute or complete ▪ *The way poor people are ignored is a positive disgrace.*

²positive *n* [C] **1** : something that is good or useful ▪ *The positives of the job outweigh the negatives.* [=there are more good things about the job than bad things] **2** : the result from a test that shows that a particular germ, condition, or substance is present ▪ *The test showed a positive.* ▪ *false positives* [=results that show something is present when it really is not]

positive discrimination *n* [U] *Brit* : AFFIRMATIVE ACTION

pos·i·tive·ly /ˈpɑːzətɪvli/ *adv* **1 a** — used to stress the truth of a statement ▪ *The new building is positively* [=*downright*] *ugly.* **b** — used to stress that you really mean what you are saying ▪ *This is positively* [=*definitely*] *the last time I'm doing this!* **2 a** : in a way that shows that you are hopeful and thinking about the good qualities of a situation ▪ *thinking positively* **b** : in a way that shows that you agree with or approve of someone or something ▪ *Customers responded positively to the new product.* **c** : in a certain or definite way ▪ *The victim has not yet been positively identified.*

pos·se /ˈpɑːsi/ *n* [C] **1** : a group of people who were gathered together by a sheriff in the past to help search for a criminal ▪ *The posse rode out to look for the bandits.* **2 a** *informal* : a group of people who are together for a particular purpose ▪ *a posse of reporters* **b** *informal* : a group of friends ▪ *a movie star and his posse*

pos·sess /pəˈzɛs/ *vb* [T] **1** *formal* : to have or own (something) ▪ *nations that possess nuclear weapons* ▪ *The defendant was charged with possessing cocaine.* **2** : to have or show (a particular quality, ability, skill, etc.) ▪ *He possesses a keen wit.* **3 a** *of spirits* : to enter into and control (someone) ▪ *a movie about a child who is possessed by the devil* **b** *of emotions* : to have a powerful effect on (someone) ▪ *They were possessed by fear.* [=they were very afraid] ▪ *Whatever/What possessed him to say such a stupid thing?* [=why did he say such a stupid thing?] — **be possessed of** *literary* : to have (a particular quality, ability, skill, etc.) ▪ *He is a man who is possessed of great talent.* [=who has great talent] — **pos·ses·sor** /pəˈzɛsɚ/ *n* [C] ▪ *I'm the proud possessor of a new car.*

pos·sessed /pəˈzɛst/ *adj* : controlled by a usually evil spirit ▪ *a horror movie about a possessed child* — **like a man/woman possessed** : with a lot of energy or force ▪ *He pounded on the door like a man possessed, yelling for someone to let him in.*

pos·ses·sion /pəˈzɛʃən/ *n* **1** [U] *formal* : the condition of having or owning something ▪ *I have in my possession* [=I possess] *a letter from Abraham Lincoln.* ▪ *The city can take possession of the abandoned buildings.* **2** [C] : something that is owned or possessed by someone ▪ *The family lost all of its possessions in the fire.* ▪

personal possessions **3** [U] *law* : the crime of having something that is illegal (such as a drug or weapon) ▪ *The defendant was charged with possession of stolen property.* **4** *sports* **a** [U] : control of the ball or puck in a game ▪ *He lost possession of the ball/puck.* **b** [C] *American football* : a time when a team has control of the ball and is trying to score ▪ *They scored a touchdown on each of their first two possessions.* **5** [U] : the state of being controlled by a usually evil spirit ▪ *demonic possession*

¹**pos·ses·sive** /pəˈzɛsɪv/ *adj* **1** : not willing to share things with or lend things to other people ▪ *She is very possessive about/of her toys.* **2** : wanting all of someone's attention and love ▪ *a possessive boyfriend* **3** *grammar* : relating to a word or a form of a word that shows that something or someone belongs to something or someone else ▪ *The possessive form of "dog" is "dog's."* ▪ *"His" and "her" are possessive pronouns.* — **pos·ses·sive·ness** *n* [U]

²**possessive** *n, grammar* **1** [C] : a possessive word or phrase ▪ *"Your" and "yours" are possessives.* **2 the possessive** : the form of a word that shows possession or belonging ▪ *The possessive of "it" is "its."*

pos·si·bil·i·ty /ˌpɑːsəˈbɪləti/ *n, pl* **-ties** **1** [C/U] : a chance that something might exist, happen, or be true ▪ *There is a strong/real/remote/faint possibility that I will get the job.* ▪ *the possibility of success/failure* ▪ *It is not outside the range/realm of possibility that he could win.* [=he might win] **2** [C] : something that might be done or might happen ▪ *Rain is a possibility today.* [=it might rain today] ▪ *We exhausted all the possibilities.* [=we did everything that we could think of doing] **3** [*plural*] : abilities or qualities that could make someone or something better in the future ▪ *The old house might not look like much now, but it has possibilities.*

pos·si·ble /ˈpɑːsəbəl/ *adj* **1** *not usually before a noun* : able to be done ▪ *Would it be possible for me to use your phone?* [=may I use your phone?] ▪ *Advances in medicine have made it possible for people to live longer.* ▪ *We tried to spend as little money as possible.* ▪ *I like to go swimming whenever possible.* [=whenever there is an opportunity to swim] ▪ *Do your best to come home from work early, if (at all) possible.* [=if it can be done] ▪ *Come as soon/quickly as (humanly) possible.* [=as soon as you can] **2** : able to happen or exist ▪ *possible dangers* ▪ *The highest possible score is 100.* ▪ *It is possible that life exists on other planets.* **3** *always before a noun* : able or suited to be or to become something specified ▪ *She suggested a possible solution to the problem.* **4** : perhaps true ▪ *Robbery is one possible motive for the murder.*

pos·si·bly /ˈpɑːsəbli/ *adv* **1** — used to say something might happen, exist, or be true but is not certain ▪ *The fire could possibly have been caused by faulty wiring.* ▪ *It's possibly the worst movie I've ever seen.* **2** — used to show shock or sur-

prise at something ▪ *That cannot possibly be true!* **3** — used to ask for something politely ▪ *Could you possibly get me some milk while you're out?* **4** — used to say that someone will do or has done everything that can be done to achieve something ▪ *I will come as soon as I possibly can.* **5** — used in negative statements to emphasize that something cannot or could not happen or be done ▪ *You couldn't possibly understand what I'm going through.*

pos·sum /ˈpɑːsəm/ *n, pl* **pos·sums** *also* **possum** [C] : OPOSSUM — **play possum** *informal* : to pretend to be asleep or dead ▪ *The wounded soldier played possum, hoping the enemy would pass him by.*

¹**post** /ˈpoʊst/ *n* **1** [C] : a piece of wood or metal that is set in an upright position into or on the ground especially as a support or marker ▪ *fence posts* **2** [C] : a pole that marks the starting or finishing point of a horse race ▪ *a horse's post position* [=the position of a horse in the line of horses at the start of a race] **3 a** [C] : GOALPOST ▪ *The shot hit the post.* **b the post** *basketball* : the position of a player who plays near the basket ▪ *She usually plays the post.* **4** [C] : the place where someone does a job ▪ *The bartender returned to her post behind the counter.* ▪ *The soldiers could not leave their post.* [=could not leave the place they were supposed to be] **5** [C] : a usually important job or position in a large organization ▪ *He resigned from his post as superintendent of schools.* **6** [U] *chiefly Brit* **a** : ¹MAIL 1 ▪ *Contact us by post.* **b** : ¹MAIL 2 ▪ *Has the post come?* **7** [C] : a message on an online message board ▪ *The Internet newsgroup is very active, with over 50 posts per day.* — called also **posting**

²**post** *vb* **1** [T] **a** : to put up (a sign, notice, etc.) so that it can be seen by many people ▪ *The professor posted (up) the grades outside her office.* **b** : to make (something) officially known to many people ▪ *A storm warning was posted* [=announced] *for our area.* **2** [T] : to assign (a person) to stand or stay at a particular place ▪ *The general posted a guard outside his door.* **3** [T] *chiefly Brit* : to send (someone) to a place to work for a long period of time as part of a job ▪ *He was posted to Munich, Germany.* **4** [T/I] : to add (a message) to an online message board ▪ *She posts (messages) regularly to several newsgroups.* **5** [T] *chiefly Brit* : to send (a letter or package) by mail ▪ *I will post the book to you.* — **keep (someone) posted** : to regularly give (someone) the most recent news about something ▪ *Keep me posted on how the project is doing.*

post- /ˌpoʊst/ *prefix* : after or later than ▪ *the postwar period* [=the time after a war] ▪ *post-1990*

post·age /ˈpoʊstɪdʒ/ *n* [U] **1** : the cost of sending a letter or package by mail ▪ *How much is the postage for this package?* **2** : the stamps attached to a letter or package ▪ *I hope I put enough postage on the package.*

postage–paid *adj, always before a noun* : costing nothing to mail because the postage has been paid already ▪ *a postage-paid envelope/postcard*

postage stamp *n [C]* : ¹STAMP 1

post·al /ˈpoʊstl/ *adj, always before a noun* : relating to or involved in the sending, handling, and delivery of mail ▪ *postal workers* [=post office employees] ▪ *Postal rates are going up.* — **go postal** *US, informal* : to suddenly behave in a very violent or angry way ▪ *She suddenly went postal and started yelling at the customers.*

postal order *n [C] Brit* : MONEY ORDER

Postal Service *n* — **the Postal Service** *US* : the U.S. government department in charge of collecting and delivering mail ▪ *the United States Postal Service*

post·box /ˈpoʊstˌbɑːks/ *n [C] Brit* : MAIL-BOX 1

post·card /ˈpoʊstˌkɑɚd/ *n [C]* : a card on which a message may be sent by mail without an envelope and that often has a picture on one side

post·code /ˈpoʊstˌkoʊd/ *n [C] Brit* : a group of numbers and letters that is used especially in the United Kingdom and Australia as part of an address to identify a mail delivery area — compare ZIP CODE

post·date /ˌpoʊstˈdeɪt/ *vb* -**dat·ed**; -**dat·ing** *[T]* : to give (something) a date that is later than the actual or current date ▪ *postdate a check*

post·doc·tor·al /ˌpoʊstˈdɑːktərəl/ *adj, always before a noun* : relating to work that is done after a PhD has been completed ▪ *a postdoctoral fellowship*

post·er /ˈpoʊstɚ/ *n [C]* **1 a** : a usually large printed notice often having a picture on it that is put in a public place to advertise something ▪ *Posters for the concert have been going up all over town.* **b** : a usually large picture that is put on walls as a decoration ▪ *His walls were covered with posters of his favorite bands.* **2** : a person who writes messages on an online message board

poster boy *n [C]* : a male poster child

poster child *n [C] US* : a person who represents or is identified with something (such as a cause or product) ▪ *She became the poster child of the antiwar movement.* ▪ *(humorous) My brother is the poster child for laziness.* [=he is very lazy]

poster girl *n [C]* : a female poster child

¹**pos·te·ri·or** /poʊˈstirijɚ/ *adj, technical* : near or toward the back of something (such as the body) ▪ *the posterior part of the brain*

²**pos·te·ri·or** /pɑˈstirijɚ/ *n [C] humorous* : BUTTOCKS ▪ *I got my large posterior into the chair.*

pos·ter·i·ty /pɑˈsterəti/ *n [U] formal* : people in the future ▪ *A record of the events was preserved for posterity.*

post-game /ˈpoʊstˈgeɪm/ *adj, always before a noun, US* : happening immediately or very soon after the end of a sports game ▪ *a postgame interview/celebration*

¹**post·grad·u·ate** /ˌpoʊstˈgrædʒəwət/ *adj, always before a noun* : of or relating to studies done after earning a bachelor's degree or other degree ▪ *a postgraduate student/course/program*

²**postgraduate** *n [C] chiefly Brit* : a student who has to study for an advanced degree after earning a bachelor's degree or other first degree ▪ *a graduate student*

post·hu·mous /ˈpɑːstʃəməs/ *adj* : happening, done, or published after someone's death ▪ *a posthumous novel/award* — **post·hu·mous·ly** *adv* ▪ *Her last book was published posthumously.* [=after her death]

post·ing /ˈpoʊstɪŋ/ *n [C]* **1** *US* : a public announcement of something ▪ *a job posting* [=an announcement telling people that a position is open] **2** *chiefly Brit* : the act of sending someone to a place to work for a long period of time as part of a job ▪ *a posting in Paris* **3** : ¹POST 7

Post-it /ˈpoʊstˌɪt/ *trademark* — used for a small, colored slip of paper with a sticky edge

post·man /ˈpoʊstmən/ *n, pl* -**men** /-mən/ *[C]* : MAILMAN

post·mark /ˈpoʊstˌmɑɚk/ *n [C]* : a mark placed over the stamp on a piece of mail that shows when the mail was sent and where it was sent from and that makes it impossible to use the stamp again — **postmark** *vb [T]* ▪ *The package was postmarked 13 February.*

post·mas·ter /ˈpoʊstˌmæstɚ, Brit ˈpoʊstˌmɑːstɚ/ *n [C]* : a person who is in charge of a post office

Postmaster General *n, pl* **Postmasters General** *[C]* : the person who is in charge of the U.S. Postal Service

post·mod·ern·ism /ˌpoʊstˈmɑːdɚˌnɪzəm/ *n [U]* : a style of art, architecture, literature, etc., that developed after modernism and that differs from modernism in some important way (such as by combining traditional materials and forms with modern ones or by having an ironic tone or attitude) — **post·mod·ern** /ˌpoʊstˈmɑːdɚn/ *adj* ▪ *postmodern architecture/literature* — **post·mod·ern·ist** /ˌpoʊstˈmɑːdɚnɪst/ *adj* ▪ *a postmodernist author* ▪ *postmodernist art* — **postmodernist** *n [C]*

¹**post·mor·tem** /ˌpoʊstˈmoɚtəm/ *adj, always before a noun, medical* : happening after death ▪ *a postmortem examination*

²**postmortem** *n [C]* **1** *medical* : AUTOPSY ▪ *A postmortem showed he had been poisoned.* **2** : a discussion or analysis of something after it has ended ▪ *conducting a postmortem of the election*

post·na·tal /ˌpoʊstˈneɪtl/ *adj, medical* : relating to the period of time following the birth of a child ▪ *postnatal care/depression*

post office *n* **1** *[C]* : a building where the mail for a local area is sent and received — abbr. *P.O.* **2 the Post Office** : the government department in charge of collecting and delivering mail ▪ *She works for the Post Office.*

post office box *n [C]* : P.O. BOX

post-op /ˈpoʊstˈɑːp/ *adj, always before a noun, medical* : POSTOPERATIVE ▪ *a post-op procedure/patient*

post·op·er·a·tive /ˌpoʊstˈɑːprətɪv/ *adj, always before a noun, medical* **1** : happening after an operation ▪ *postoperative care* **2** : having had an operation recently ▪ *a postoperative patient*

post·par·tum depression /ˌpoust-ˈpɑɚtəm-/ *n* [U] *chiefly US, medical* : a feeling of deep sadness, anxiety, etc., that a woman feels after giving birth to a child

post·pone /ˌpoustˈpoun/ *vb* **-poned; -pon·ing** [T] : to decide that something which had been planned for a particular time will be done at a later time instead ▪ *The game was postponed until/to tomorrow because of rain.* — **post·pone·ment** /ˌpoustˈpounmənt/ *n* [C/U] ▪ *The rain caused (a) postponement of the game.*

post·script /ˈpoustˌskrɪpt/ *n* [C] **1** : a note or series of notes added at the end of a letter, article, or book ▪ *a postscript to her letter* — abbr. *PS* **2** : an additional fact or piece of information about a story that occurs after the main part ▪ *An interesting postscript to the story is that the two people involved later got married.*

post·sea·son /ˈpoustˌsiːzn̩/ *n* [C] *US, sports* : a period of time immediately after the regular season when teams play against each other in a series of games to determine a champion ▪ *The team has never played in the postseason.* ▪ *postseason games*

post–traumatic stress disorder *n* [U] *medical* : a mental condition that can affect a person who has had a very shocking or difficult experience and that is usually characterized by depression, anxiety, etc.

pos·tu·late /ˈpɑːstʃəˌleɪt/ *vb* **-lat·ed; -lat·ing** [T] *formal* : to suggest (an idea, theory, etc.) especially in order to start a discussion ▪ *The theory postulates that carbon dioxide emissions contribute to global warming.*

pos·ture /ˈpɑːstʃɚ/ *n* **1** [C/U] : the way in which your body is positioned when you are sitting or standing ▪ *a rigid/stiff posture* ▪ *He has good/bad/poor posture.* **2** [C] *formal* : the attitude a person or group has toward a subject ▪ *He's taken an aggressive posture on immigration.*

pos·tur·ing /ˈpɑːstʃərɪŋ/ *n* [U] *disapproving* : behavior that is intended to impress other people and that is not sincere ▪ *Don't be fooled by his macho posturing.*

post·war /ˈpoustˌwɔɚ/ *adj, always before a noun* : happening, existing, or made after a war and especially World War II ▪ *the postwar generation* ▪ *postwar Europe*

po·sy /ˈpouzi/ *n, pl* **-sies** [C] *old-fashioned* : a small bunch of flowers ▪ *a posy of violets*

¹pot /ˈpɑːt/ *n* **1** [C] **a** : a deep, round container that is used for cooking ▪ *a soup pot* **b** : a container that is used for storing or holding something ▪ *clay pots* ▪ (*Brit*) *a yogurt/paint pot* **2** [C] : the amount of something held by a pot ▪ *She made a pot of tea.* **3** *the pot chiefly US* : the total amount of money that can be won in a card game ▪ *He took the pot.* [=he won all the money that was bet] **4** [C] *informal* : TOILET **5** [U] *informal* : MARIJUANA ▪ *a pot smoker/plant* — **go to pot** *informal* : to be ruined : to fail ▪

Their business is going to pot.

²pot *vb* **pot·ted; pot·ting** [T] : to plant or place (something) in a pot ▪ *She spent the afternoon potting tulip bulbs.* ▪ *a potted plant*

po·ta·ble /ˈpoutəbəl/ *adj, technical* : safe to drink ▪ *potable water*

pot·ash /ˈpɑːtˌæʃ/ *n* [U] : a form of potassium that is used especially to improve soil or to make soap

po·tas·si·um /pəˈtæsijəm/ *n* [U] : a soft, silver-white metal

po·ta·to /pəˈteɪtou/ *n, pl* **-toes** [C/U] : a round root of a plant that has brown, yellow, or red skin and white or yellow flesh and that is eaten as a vegetable ▪ *baked/mashed/roasted/boiled potatoes* ▪ *potato salad*

potato chip *n* [C] *US* : a thin slice of potato that is fried or sometimes baked and usually salted

pot·bel·ly /ˈpɑːtˌbɛli/ *n, pl* **-lies** [C] : a large, round stomach that sticks out ▪ *a man with a potbelly* — **pot·bel·lied** /ˈpɑːtˌbɛlid/ *adj* ▪ *a potbellied man*

po·tent /ˈpoutn̩t/ *adj* **1** : very effective or strong ▪ *potent medicine/tea* **2** : having a very powerful effect or influence ▪ *Her story serves as a potent reminder of the dangers of drug use.* **3** *of a man* : able to have sex — **po·ten·cy** /ˈpoutn̩si/ *n, pl* **-cies** [C/U] ▪ *the potency of the drug* ▪ *sexual potency* — **po·tent·ly** *adv*

po·ten·tate /ˈpoutn̩ˌteɪt/ *n* [C] *literary* : a powerful ruler

¹po·ten·tial /pəˈtɛnʃəl/ *adj, always before a noun* : capable of becoming real : POSSIBLE ▪ *the school's potential growth* ▪ *He is a potential candidate for president.* ▪ *potential risks/advantages* — **po·ten·tial·ly** *adv*

²potential *n* **1** [C] : a chance or possibility that something will happen or exist in the future — usually + *for* ▪ *Wet roads increase the potential for an accident.* [=make an accident more likely to happen] ▪ *a potential for success* **2 a** [C/U] : a quality that can be developed to make something better ▪ *Scientists are exploring the potentials of the new drug.* **b** [U] : an ability that can be developed to help a person become successful ▪ *He has the potential to be one of the team's best players.* ▪ *The school helps students reach/ realize their full potential.* [=to become the best they can be]

po·ten·ti·al·i·ty /pəˌtɛnʃiˈæləti/ *n, pl* **-ties** *formal* [C/U] : a quality that can be developed to make someone or something better ▪ *The teacher sees potentiality in every student.* **2** [C] : a chance or possibility that something will happen or exist in the future ▪ *the potentiality for good in all people*

pot·head /ˈpɑːtˌhɛd/ *n* [C] *US, informal* : a person who smokes a lot of marijuana

pot·hold·er /ˈpɑːtˌhouldɚ/ *n* [C] *US* : a small, thick cloth pad for holding hot pots, pans, etc.

pot·hole /ˈpɑːtˌhoul/ *n* [C] : a deep hole in a road or some other surface — **pot·holed** /ˈpɑːtˌhould/ *adj* ▪ *the city's potholed streets*

po·tion /ˈpouʃən/ n [C] : a drink that is meant to have a special or magical effect on someone • *a fatal potion* • *sleeping potions*

pot·luck or Brit **pot luck** /ˈpɑːtˈlʌk/ n [C] *US* : a meal to which everyone who is invited brings food to share • *a potluck dinner* **2** [U] *chiefly Brit* : a meal for a guest that is prepared from whatever is available • (*figurative*) *We don't have definite plans. We're just going to take pot luck.* [=we're going to take/accept whatever is available]

pot·pie /ˈpɑːtˈpai/ n [C] *US* : a mixture of meat and vegetables that is covered with a layer of pastry and cooked in a deep dish

pot·pour·ri /ˌpoupuˈriː/ n **1** [C/U] : a mixture of dried flower petals, leaves, and spices that is used to make a room smell pleasant **2** [*singular*] : a collection of different things • *The book is a potpourri of stories about family, religion, and food.*

pot roast n [C/U] : a piece of beef that is cooked slowly in a pot

pot·shot /ˈpɑːtˌʃɑːt/ n [C] : a gunshot that is fired in a careless way or at an easy target • (*figurative*) *She uses her newspaper column to take potshots at anyone who disagrees with her.*

¹**pot·ter** /ˈpɑːtə/ n [C] : a person who makes pottery

²**potter** vb — **potter around/about** [*phrasal verb*] *Brit* : to spend time in a relaxed way doing small jobs and other things that are not very important • **pottering around** [=(*US*) **puttering around**] *the house/garden*

pot·tery /ˈpɑːtəri/ n, pl **-ter·ies** **1** [U] : bowls, plates, etc., that are made out of clay usually by hand and then baked at high temperatures so that they become hard • *a collection of pottery* **2** [U] : the art or activity of making objects out of clay • *a pottery class* **3** [C] : a place where clay bowls, plates, etc., are made

pot·ty /ˈpɑːti/ n, pl **-ties** [C] *informal* : a toilet or bathroom — used by children or when talking to children • *Mommy, I need to use the potty.*

pouch /ˈpautʃ/ n [C] **1 a** : a small bag • *a tobacco pouch* **b** : a bag that is used to carry letters or important papers • *a mail pouch* **2** : a pocket of skin on the stomachs of some female animals (such as kangaroos and koalas) that is used to carry young

poul·tice /ˈpoultəs/ n [C] : a soft, usually heated substance that is spread on cloth and then placed on the skin to heal a sore or reduce pain

poul·try /ˈpoultri/ n [U] **1** : birds (such as chickens and ducks) that are raised on farms for their eggs or meat **2** : meat from a bird • *This wine goes well with poultry.*

pounce /ˈpauns/ vb **pounced; pouncing** [I] : to suddenly jump toward and take hold of someone or something — usually + *on* • *The cat pounced on the ball.* • (*figurative*) *A salesperson pounced on me* [=quickly approached me] *when I walked into the store.* • (*figurative*) *He pounced on the job offer.*

¹**pound** /ˈpaund/ n, pl **pounds** also **pound** [C] **1** : a unit of weight that is equal to 16 ounces or 0.4536 kilograms • *a pound of beef* • *a 50-pound dog* • *a dog that weighs 50 pounds* • *trying to lose a few pounds* • *Pound for pound, it's the most valuable crop being grown in the state.* [=when comparing a pound of this crop with a pound of other crops, a pound of this crop is more valuable] **2 a** : a basic unit of money in the United Kingdom and some other countries • *The bill came to 30 pounds 10 pence.* **b** : a bill or coin that is worth one pound **3 a** : a place where dogs and cats that are found on the streets without an owner are kept until their owners come and get them **b** : a place to which cars that have been parked illegally are towed and kept until their owners pay to get them back **4** *US* : the symbol # — called also (*US*) **pound sign**

²**pound** vb **1** [T/I] : to hit with force again and again • *Heavy waves pounded the shore.* • *She pounded the nails into the wood.* • *The boxers were pounding each other.* • *The wheat is pounded* [=crushed] *into flour.* • *pound on a drum* **2** [I] : to walk or run with heavy, loud steps • *He came pounding down the stairs.* **3** [I] : to work hard at something for a long time • *He pounded away all night at his computer, writing the report.* **4** [I] : to beat loudly and quickly • *His heart was pounding* (*in his ears*). • *a pounding headache* — **pound out** [*phrasal verb*] **pound out (something)** or **pound (something) out** **1** : to make or produce (something) quickly • *Every week he pounds out another column for the newspaper.* **2** : to play (a song, melody, etc.) loudly • *She was pounding out a tune on the piano.* — **pound the streets/pavement** : to walk or run on the streets especially in search of something • *She's out there every day pounding the pavement, looking for work.*

pound cake n [C/U] *US* : a rich cake made with a large amount of butter and eggs

pound·er /ˈpaundə/ n [C] : a person or thing that has a specified weight in pounds • *The fish was a 22-pounder.*

pound·ing /ˈpaundɪŋ/ n **1** [C] : the act of hitting someone or something with force again and again • *the pounding of waves against the shore* • *The boxer took a pounding in the ring.* • (*figurative*) *The company's stocks took a pounding.* **2** [*singular*] : the act of beating loudly and quickly • *I could feel the pounding of my heart in my chest.*

pound sign n [C] **1** : the symbol £ that represents the British pound **2** *US* : ¹POUND 4

pound sterling n, pl **pounds sterling** [C] : a basic unit of money in the United Kingdom

pour /ˈpoɚ/ vb **1** [T] : to cause (something) to flow from or into a container or place • *He poured the water into her glass.* • *The burst pipe poured out water.* • (*figurative*) *She poured scorn on the plan.* [=she talked about the plan in a very critical and scornful way] **2** [T/I] : to fill a cup or glass with a drink for someone ▪ *Will you pour (out) the wine?* [=will you fill everyone's glass with wine?] ▪ *Pour a drink for me, please.* = *Pour me a drink, please.* **3** [I] : to flow or move continuously in a steady stream ▪ *Smoke poured out from the chimney.* ▪ *(figurative) Music poured out of the dance club.* ▪ *(figurative) Thousands of people poured into the stadium for the game.* **4** [I] **a** : to rain heavily ▪ *It poured all day.* **b** *of rain* : to come down heavily ▪ *The rain poured down. We waited in the pouring rain.* — **pour cold water on** *see* ¹WATER — **pour into** [phrasal vb] **pour (something) into** : to spend (a large amount of money, time, etc.) on something ▪ *She poured thousands (of dollars) into the business.* — **pour on** [phrasal vb] **1 pour on (something) or pour (something) on** : to produce a lot of (something) in order to achieve something ▪ *He really poured on the charm to get her to have dinner with him.* **2 pour it on** *informal* **a** : to talk about something in an emotional way that is not sincere in order to get sympathy, attention, etc. ▪ *When he saw that she felt sorry for him, he really poured it on.* **b** *chiefly US* : to do something in a very energetic and effective way ▪ *After they took the lead, they really started to pour it on.* [=they started to score a lot of points very quickly] — **pour out** [phrasal vb] **pour out (something) or pour (something) out** : to talk freely about (something personal) ▪ *I listened while he poured out his anger and frustration.* ▪ *She poured out her heart/soul.* — **when it rains, it pours** *see* ¹RAIN

pout /'paʊt/ *vb* **1** [T/I] : to push out your lips to show that you are angry or annoyed or to look sexually attractive ▪ *She pouted (her lips) and stared at him angrily.* **2** [I] *chiefly US* : to refuse to talk to people because you are angry or annoyed about something ▪ *Quit pouting!* — **pout** *n* [C]

pov·er·ty /'pɑːvəti/ *n* **1** [U] : the state of being poor ▪ *families living in poverty* **2** [singular] *formal* : a lack of something ▪ *a poverty of information*

poverty line *n* — **the poverty line** : the level of income that makes it possible for a person to pay for basic food, clothing, and shelter ▪ *families living below/at the poverty line* — called also *poverty level*

pov·er·ty–strick·en /'pɑːvətiˌstrɪkən/ *adj* : very poor ▪ *poverty-stricken neighborhoods*

POW /ˌpiːˌoʊ'dʌbəlˌjuː/ *n* [C] : PRISONER OF WAR

¹**pow·der** /'paʊdə/ *n* **1** [C/U] : a dry substance made up of very tiny pieces of something ▪ *garlic/cocoa powder* ▪ *She crushed the peppercorns into a fine powder.* **2** [U] : a very fine, dry substance that is put on your body or face especially to make it dry or less shiny **3** [U] : snow that is very light and dry ▪ *powder skiing/snow* **4** [U] : GUNPOWDER

²**powder** *vb* [T] : to put powder on (your face or body) ▪ *She powdered her face and put on lipstick.*

pow·dered *adj, always before a noun* **1** : in the form of a powder ▪ *powdered milk* **2** : covered in powder ▪ *powdered wigs/cheeks*

powdered sugar *n* [U] *US* : sugar that has been ground into a fine powder

powder keg *n* [C] : a place or situation that is likely to become dangerous or violent soon ▪ *Political instability has made the region a powder keg.*

powder room *n* [C] : a public bathroom for women in a restaurant, hotel, etc.

pow·dery /'paʊdəri/ *adj* **1** : like powder ▪ *powdery ashes/snow* **2** : covered with powder ▪ *powdery slopes*

¹**pow·er** /'paʊə/ *n* **1** [U] : the ability or right to control people or things ▪ *a wealthy family with a lot of social power* ▪ *The company abused its power, forcing workers to work overtime without pay.* ▪ *He has no power over me.* **2** [U] : political control of a country or area ▪ *After the emperor died, power passed to his eldest son.* ▪ *The new government has **taken** power.* ▪ *The latest elections put a new (political) party **in** power.* **3** [C] **a** : a person or organization that has a lot of control and influence over others ▪ *Our state is now the region's leading economic power.* **b** : a country that has a lot of influence and military strength ▪ *a foreign power* **4** [U] **a** : physical force or strength ▪ *muscle power* ▪ *the power of hurricane winds* **b** : military force ▪ *threatening to use air/military power* **c** : the energy or force that is used to do work, operate machines, etc. ▪ *electrical/ nuclear/solar/wind/battery power* ▪ *We lost (electrical) power during the storm.* ▪ *The machines are running at full power.* **5** **a** [C/U] : an ability or a right to do something ▪ *You have the power to change your life.* ▪ *The President has the power to veto laws.* ▪ *She lost the power of speech.* [=she was no longer able to speak] ▪ *I'll do everything within/in my power to help.* [=I'll do everything I can to help] **b** [U] : the ability to influence or affect people or things ▪ *It was a speech of great power.* ▪ *the power of art/love* **6** [C] *mathematics* **a** : the number of times that a number is to be multiplied by itself ▪ *5 (raised) to the third power is 125.* [=5 × 5 × 5 = 125] **b** : a number that results from multiplying a number by itself ▪ *8 is a power of 2 because 2 × 2 × 2 is equal to 8.* — **more power to you** (*US*) or *Brit* **more power to your elbow** *informal* — used to say that you approve of what someone is doing and hope it will be successful ▪ *If he wants to write a book, more power to him!* — **the powers that be** : the people who decide what is allowed or acceptable ▪ *The students wanted to have a party, but the powers that be didn't approve.*

²**power** *vb* **1** [T] : to supply (something) with power ▪ *a motor that is powered by a battery* = *a battery-powered motor* **2** [T/I] : to move with great speed or force ▪ *He powered the ball past the goalie.* — **power up** [phrasal vb] **power up (something) or power (something) up** : to make (a machine) ready for use by sup-

plying it with electricity • *I powered up the computer.*

³**power** *adj, always before a noun* **1** : of or relating to electrical power • *a power supply/failure* **2** : operated by using electricity • *power tools*

pow·er·boat /ˈpawəˌbout/ *n [C]* : MOTORBOAT; *especially* : SPEEDBOAT

power cut *n [C] Brit* : OUTAGE

pow·er·ful /ˈpawəfəl/ *adj* : having a lot of power : having great influence, strength, or effect • *rich and powerful people* • *a powerful drug/smell/speech/voice* • *a powerful country* — **pow·er·ful·ly** *adv*

pow·er·house /ˈpawəˌhaus/ *n [C]* **1** : a group of people or an organization that has a lot of power • *The company is a powerhouse in the video game industry.* **2** : a person, team, etc., that has a lot of energy, strength, and skill • *She's a powerhouse on the tennis court.*

pow·er·less /ˈpawələs/ *adj* : having no power : unable to do something or to stop something • *powerless victims* • *We were powerless against them.* • *People are not powerless to prevent heart disease.* — **pow·er·less·ness** *n [U]*

power of attorney *n, law* **1** *[C/U]* : the right to act and make decisions for another person in business and legal matters **2** *[C]* : a document that gives someone the right of power of attorney

power plant *n [C] US* : a building or group of buildings in which electricity for a large area is produced — called also *power station*

power play *n [C] ice hockey* : a situation in which one team has more players on the ice than the other team for a period of time because of a penalty • *They scored on a power play.*

power point *n [C] Brit* : OUTLET 4

power steering *n [U]* : a steering system in cars that uses power from the engine to make it easier to turn the steering wheel

power trip *n [C]* : an activity or way of behaving that makes a person feel powerful : something that a person does for the pleasure of using power to control other people • *She's been on a power trip since she was promoted to manager.*

pow·wow /ˈpauˌwau/ *n [C]* **1** : a social gathering of Native Americans that usually includes dancing **2** *informal* : a meeting for people to discuss something

pox /ˈpɑːks/ *n [U, singular]* : a disease that causes a rash on the skin — see also CHICKEN POX, SMALLPOX

pp. *abbr* pages • *The article is on pp. 22–27.*

¹**PR** /ˈpiːˈɑːr/ *n [U]* : PUBLIC RELATIONS • *a job in PR* • *a PR agency/firm/representative*

²**PR** *abbr* Puerto Rico

prac·ti·ca·ble /ˈpræktɪkəbəl/ *adj* : able to be done or used • *a practicable plan* — **prac·ti·ca·bil·i·ty** /ˌpræktɪkəˈbɪləti/ *n [U]*

prac·ti·cal /ˈpræktɪkəl/ *adj* **1** : relating to what is real rather than to what is possible or imagined • *practical problems/matters* • *She has a lot of practical experi-*

ence in dealing with these kinds of problems. **2 a** : likely to succeed and reasonable to do or use • *practical solutions* : appropriate or suited for actual use • *The shoes are nice but not very practical.* **b** : relating to what can or should be done in an actual situation • *practical advice/help* **3** : tending to make good decisions and to deal with daily life in a sensible way • *She's very practical about money.* — **for (all) practical purposes** — used to say that one thing has the same effect or result as something else • *His effort to hide the document was, for practical purposes, an admission that he had made a mistake.* — **prac·ti·cal·i·ty** /ˌpræktɪˈkæləti/ *n, pl* **-ties** *[C/U]* • *They doubt the practicality of her proposal.* • *His practicality makes him a skilled businessman.* • *learning about the practicalities of teaching* [=the real things that teachers have to do or deal with]

practical joke *n [C]* : a joke involving something that is done rather than said : a trick played on someone • *One of the children filled the sugar bowl with salt as a practical joke.* — **practical joker** *n [C]*

prac·ti·cal·ly /ˈpræktɪkli/ *adv* **1** : almost or nearly • *I talk to him practically every day.* **2** : in a way that is reasonable or logical • *Practically speaking, Alaska is too far to go for just a few days.*

practical nurse *n [C] US* : a nurse who cares for sick people but does not have as much training or experience as a registered nurse

¹**prac·tice** *(US) or Brit* **prac·tise** /ˈpræktəs/ *vb* **-ticed; -tic·ing** **1** *[T/I]* : to do something again and again in order to become better at it • *To be a good musician, you have to practice.* • *Have you been practicing your lines for the play?* **2** *[T]* : to do (something) regularly or constantly as an ordinary part of your life • *He practices yoga daily.* • *You should practice what you preach.* [=you should do the things that you tell other people to do] **3** *[T]* : to live according to the customs and teachings of (a religion) • *He practices Buddhism.* • *a practicing Catholic* **4** *[T/I]* : to have a professional medical or legal business • *practicing medicine/law/dentistry*

²**practice** *n* **1 a** *[U]* : the activity of doing something again and again in order to become better at it • *Being a good musician takes a lot of practice.* • *To be a good musician, you have to stay in practice.* [=you have to practice enough to improve and keep your skills] • *I used to be pretty good at playing the piano, but I'm out of practice now.* [=I haven't practiced so my skills are not as good as they were] • *Remember, practice makes perfect.* [=you become better at something if you practice it often] **b** *[C/U]* : a regular occasion at which you practice something • *I'm late for soccer practice.* **2** *[C/U]* : something that is done often or regularly • *It's his practice* [=habit] *to read the newspaper each morning.* • *Burial practices vary around the world.* **3** *[U]* : the action of doing or using something • *the practice of law/medicine* • *Her advice is*

good, but it's hard to put into practice. [=to use it in actual situations] **4** [C] : a professional medical or legal business ▪ *Her law practice is downtown.* — **in practice** — used to say what is actually done or what the actual effect or result of something is ▪ *In actual practice, people sometimes forget to take their medication.*

practiced /ˈpræktɪst/ *or Brit* **practised** *adj* : good at doing something because of having done it many times ▪ *a practiced chef*

prac·ti·tion·er /prækˈtɪʃənər/ *n* [C] *formal* **1** : a person who works in a professional medical or legal business ▪ *a health/legal practitioner* **2** : a person who regularly does an activity that requires skill or practice ▪ *practitioners of the art of teaching*

prag·mat·ic /prægˈmætɪk/ *adj, formal* : dealing with problems in a reasonable and logical way instead of depending on ideas and theories ▪ *a pragmatic approach to health care* — **prag·mat·i·cal·ly** /prægˈmætɪkli/ *adv*

prag·ma·tism /ˈprægməˌtɪzəm/ *n* [U] *formal* : a reasonable and logical way of doing things or of thinking about problems that is based on dealing with specific situations instead of on ideas and theories — **prag·ma·tist** /ˈprægmətɪst/ *n* [C]

prai·rie /ˈpreri/ *n* [C/U] : a large, mostly flat area of land in North America that has few trees and is covered in grasses

prairie dog *n* [C] : a small animal that lives on the prairies of the central and western U.S.

praise /ˈpreɪz/ *vb* **praised; prais·ing** [T] **1** : to say or write good things about (someone or something) : to express approval of (someone or something) ▪ *He praised her cooking.* ▪ *His poems praise nature.* **2** : to express thanks to or love and respect for (God) ▪ *We praise God for your safe arrival.* — **praise** *n* [U, plural] ▪ *He deserves praise for the way he's handled this crisis.* ▪ *songs of praise* ▪ *The critics heaped praises on her performance.* = *The critics sang the praises of her performance.* = *The critics sang her praises.* [=the critics praised her performance very enthusiastically]

praise·wor·thy /ˈpreɪzˌwəði/ *adj* : deserving or worthy of praise ▪ *praiseworthy efforts*

pra·line /ˈprɑːˌliːn/ *n* [C/U] : a candy made of nuts and boiled sugar

pram /ˈpræm/ *n* [C] *Brit* : BABY CARRIAGE

prance /ˈpræns/ *vb* **pranced; pranc·ing** [I] **1** : to walk or move in a lively and proud way ▪ *The singer pranced around on stage.* **2** *of a horse* : to move by taking high steps

prank /ˈpræŋk/ *n* [C] : a trick that is done to someone usually as a joke ▪ *a childish prank*

prank·ster /ˈpræŋkstər/ *n* [C] : a person who plays pranks on other people

prat /ˈpræt/ *n* [C] *Brit, informal* : a stupid or foolish person

prat·fall /ˈprætˌfɑːl/ *n* [C] **1** : a sudden fall in which you end up sitting on the

ground **2** : an embarrassing mistake or accident ▪ *verbal pratfalls* [=*blunders*]

prat·tle /ˈprætl/ *vb* **prat·tled; prat·tling** [I] : to talk for very long about something that is not important or interesting ▪ *They prattled on for hours.* — **prattle** *n* [U] ▪ *I was tired of listening to their prattle.*

prawn /ˈprɑːn/ *n* [C] **1** *US* : a large shrimp **2** *Brit* : SHRIMP

pray /ˈpreɪ/ *vb* **1** [T/I] **a** : to speak to God especially in order to give thanks or to ask for something ▪ *We prayed (to God) for their safe return.* **b** : to hope or wish very much for something to happen ▪ *She's praying for a chance to play in the game.* **2** — used to introduce a question or request in a polite or deliberately old-fashioned way ▪ *Pray be careful.* ▪ *Why should I trust them, pray tell?* [=tell me why I should trust them]

prayer /ˈpreər/ *n* **1** [C] : words spoken to God especially in order to give thanks or to ask for something ▪ *say a prayer* ▪ *a book of hymns and prayers* **2** [U] : the act of speaking to God : the act of praying ▪ *a moment of silent prayer* **3** [C] : a strong hope or wish ▪ *The house was the answer to all my prayers.* [=was everything that I hoped for] **4** [*singular*] *informal* : a slight chance of doing or getting something ▪ *No one thought the team had a prayer (of winning).*

pre- /priː/ *prefix* **1** : earlier than : before ▪ *prehistoric* ▪ *preseason* **2** : in advance ▪ *prepay*

preach /ˈpriːtʃ/ *vb* **1** [T/I] : to make a speech about religion in a church or other public place ▪ *The minister preached (a sermon) to the congregation.* **2** [T/I] : to say that (something) is good or necessary ▪ *She continues to preach patience.* ▪ *Practice what you preach—don't smoke if you tell your children not to smoke.* **3** [I] : to write or speak in an annoying way about the right way to behave ▪ *It's important to give teenagers helpful advice without preaching (to/at them).* — **preach to the choir** (*chiefly US*) *or* **preach to the converted** : to speak for or against something to people who already agree with your opinions

preach·er /ˈpriːtʃər/ *n* [C] : a person who speaks publicly about religious subjects in a Christian church or other public place

pre·am·ble /ˈpriːˌæmbəl/ *n* [C/U] : a statement that is made at the beginning of something (such as a legal document) and usually gives the reasons for the parts that follow ▪ *the preamble to the U.S. Constitution*

pre·ar·range /ˌpriːjəˈreɪndʒ/ *vb* **-ranged; -rang·ing** [T] : to plan or decide (something) before it happens ▪ *The details of the ceremony were carefully prearranged.* — **prearranged** *adj* ▪ *a prearranged meeting/time*

pre·car·i·ous /prɪˈkerijəs/ *adj* : not safe, strong, or steady ▪ *Her health is precarious.* ▪ *a precarious situation/position* — **pre·car·i·ous·ly** *adv*

pre·cau·tion /prɪˈkɑːʃən/ *n* [C] : something that is done to prevent possible harm or trouble from happening in the future • *safety precautions* • *Every home owner should* **take** *precautions against fire.* — **pre·cau·tion·ary** /prɪˈkɔːʃəˌneri, Brit prɪˈkɔːʃənri/ *adj* • *a precautionary measure*

pre·cede /prɪˈsiːd/ *vb* -ced·ed; -ced·ing [T] *somewhat formal* : to happen, go, or come before (something or someone) • *She preceded him into the room.* • *The meeting was preceded by a brief speech.* • *the preceding year*

pre·ce·dence /ˈprɛsədəns/ *n* [U] *somewhat formal* : the condition of being more important than something or someone else and therefore coming or being dealt with first • *The safety of the children* **has/takes precedence over** [=is more important than] *everything else.* • *The government's policies* **give precedence** *to large corporations.*

prec·e·dent /ˈprɛsədənt/ *n* [C/U] *somewhat formal* **1** : a similar action or event that happened at an earlier time • *There are no precedents for these events.* = *These events are* **without precedent**. [=nothing like these events has ever happened before] **2** : something done or said that can be used as an example or rule to be followed in the future • *The judge's ruling was based on a precedent established by an earlier decision.*

pre·cept /ˈpriːˌsɛpt/ *n* [C/U] *formal* : a rule that says how people should behave • *the basic/moral precepts of a religion*

pre·cinct /ˈpriːˌsɪŋkt/ *n* [C] **1** *US* : any one of the sections that a town or city is divided into for voting or for organizing police forces • *an electoral precinct* • *a police precinct* **2** *Brit* : an area in a town or city where people may walk and vehicles are not allowed **3** : the area that is near or around a place • *within the precincts of the college*

¹**pre·cious** /ˈprɛʃəs/ *adj* **1** : rare and worth a lot of money • *precious jewels/metals* **2** : very valuable or important • *precious resources/time/memories*

²**precious** *adv* : very or extremely • *She had* **precious little** *to say.* • *There are* **precious few** *hours of sunlight left.*

prec·i·pice /ˈprɛsəpəs/ *n* [C] : a very steep side of a mountain or cliff

¹**pre·cip·i·tate** /prɪˈsɪpəˌteɪt/ *vb* -tat·ed; -tat·ing **1** [T] *formal* : to cause (something) to happen quickly or suddenly • *Her death precipitated a family crisis.* **2** [T/I] *technical* : to become or cause (something) to become separated from a liquid especially by a chemical process • *minerals that precipitate from seawater*

²**pre·cip·i·tate** /prɪˈsɪpətət/ *adj, formal* : happening very quickly or too quickly without enough thought or planning • *a precipitate decision* — **pre·cip·i·tate·ly** *adv*

pre·cip·i·ta·tion /prɪˌsɪpəˈteɪʃən/ *n* [U] : water that falls to the ground as rain, snow, etc.

pre·cip·i·tous /prɪˈsɪpətəs/ *adj, formal* **1** : very steep • *a precipitous slope* **2** : happening in a very quick and sudden way • *a precipitous decline in home sales* **3** : done too quickly and without enough thought or planning • *a precipitous action*

— **pre·cip·i·tous·ly** *adv*

pré·cis /preɪˈsiː/ *n, pl* **pré·cis** /preɪˈsiːz/ [C] : a brief summary of the main points and ideas of a piece of writing or speech • *a précis of the book's plot*

pre·cise /prɪˈsaɪs/ *adj* **1** : very accurate and exact • *precise measurements* • *a precise definition* **2** *always before a noun* — used to refer to an exact and particular time, location, etc. • *She quietly closed the door, and at that precise moment the phone rang.* — **to be precise** — used to indicate that a statement is accurate and specific • *one night in early summer— June 22, to be precise* — **pre·cise·ly** *adv* • *It is precisely two o'clock.* • *He knows precisely how much money he has.* • *"Do you mean that the system is outdated?" "Precisely." — "Yes, that's precisely what I mean."* — **pre·cise·ness** *n* [U]

pre·ci·sion /prɪˈsɪʒən/ *n* [U] : the quality of being precise : exactness or accuracy • *The cause of the fire cannot be determined with any (degree of) precision.*

pre·clude /prɪˈkluːd/ *vb* -clud·ed; -clud·ing [T] *formal* : to make something impossible : PREVENT • *Bad weather precluded any further attempts to reach the summit.* • *The injury precluded her from having an athletic career.*

pre·co·cious /prɪˈkouʃəs/ *adj, of a child* : having or showing the qualities or abilities of an adult at an unusually early age • *a precocious child/musician* — **pre·co·cious·ly** *adv* — **pre·co·cious·ness** *n* [U] — **pre·coc·i·ty** /prɪˈkɑːsəti/ *n* [U]

pre·con·ceived /ˌpriːkənˈsiːvd/ *adj* : formed before having actual knowledge about something or before experiencing something • *preconceived ideas about/of what the job would be like*

pre·con·cep·tion /ˌpriːkənˈsɛpʃən/ *n* [C] : an idea or opinion that someone has before learning about or experiencing something directly • *preconceptions about/of modern art*

pre·cur·sor /prɪˈkɚsɚ/ *n* [C] *somewhat formal* : something that comes before something else and that often leads to or influences its development • *Small tremors may be precursors to/of big earthquakes.*

pre·date /ˌpriːˈdeɪt/ *vb* -dat·ed; -dat·ing [T] : to exist or happen at an earlier time than (something or someone) • *modes of transportation that predate the car*

pre·da·tion /prɪˈdeɪʃən/ *n* [U] *technical* : the act of killing and eating other animals • *predation by lions*

pred·a·tor /ˈprɛdətɚ/ *n* [C] **1** : an animal that lives by killing and eating other animals • *predators like bears and wolves* **2** : a person who looks for other people in order to use, control, or harm them in some way • *a sexual predator* [=a person who commits sexual crimes against other people]

pred·a·to·ry /ˈprɛdəˌtori, Brit ˈprɛdətri/ *adj* **1** *technical* : living by killing and eating other animals • *predatory animals* **2** : wrongly harming or using others for pleasure or profit • *predatory business practices*

pre·de·ces·sor /ˈprɛdəˌsɛsɚ, Brit ˈpriːdə-

,sɛsə/ n [C] **1** : a person who had a job or position before someone else ▪ *She changed many of the policies that were introduced by her predecessor.* **2** : something that comes before something else ▪ *Today's computers are much faster than their predecessors were.*

pre·des·ti·na·tion /ˌpriːˌdɛstəˈneɪʃən/ n [U] : the belief that everything that will happen has already been decided by God or fate and cannot be changed

pre·des·tined /ˌpriːˈdɛstənd/ adj : certain to do or be something or certain to happen ▪ *He felt as though he was predestined to marry her when they first met.* ▪ *a predestined outcome*

pre·de·ter·mined /ˌpriːdəˈtəːmənd/ adj, formal : decided or determined at an earlier time ▪ *They met at a predetermined time and place.*

pre·dic·a·ment /prɪˈdɪkəmənt/ n [C] : a difficult or unpleasant situation ▪ *He got himself into quite a predicament.*

¹**pred·i·cate** /ˈprɛdəkət/ n [C] grammar : the part of a sentence that expresses what is said about the subject ▪ *In the sentence "The child threw the ball," the subject is "the child" and the predicate is "threw the ball."*

²**predicate** adj, always before a noun, grammar : used after a linking verb to describe a noun that comes before the verb ▪ *In "The sun is hot," "hot" is a predicate adjective.*

pre·dict /prɪˈdɪkt/ vb [T] : to say that (something) will or might happen in the future ▪ *The local forecasters are predicting rain.* ▪ *She won the election, as I predicted (she would).* ▪ *Sales are predicted to be the same as last year.* — **pre·dic·tive** /prɪˈdɪktɪv/ adj, formal ▪ *The test does not have much predictive value.*

pre·dict·able /prɪˈdɪktəbəl/ adj **1** : capable of being known before happening or being done ▪ *novels with predictable plots* **2** : behaving in a way that is expected ▪ *I knew he would say that. He's so predictable.* — **pre·dict·abil·i·ty** /prɪˌdɪktəˈbɪləti/ n [U] — **pre·dict·ably** /prɪˈdɪktəbli/ adv

pre·dic·tion /prɪˈdɪkʃən/ n **1** [C] : a statement about what will happen or might happen in the future ▪ *Despite predictions that the store would fail, it has done very well.* **2** [U] : the act of saying what will happen in the future ▪ *statistics used for the prediction of future economic trends*

pre·di·lec·tion /ˌprɛdəˈlɛkʃən, Brit ˌpriːdəˈlɛkʃən/ n [C] formal : a natural liking for something : a tendency to do or to be attracted to something ▪ *a predilection for adventure stories*

pre·dis·pose /ˌpriːdɪˈspoʊz/ vb -posed; -pos·ing [T] formal : to cause (someone) to be more likely to behave in a particular way or to be affected by a particular condition ▪ *people who are genetically predisposed to (develop/developing) the disease* ▪ *predisposed to/toward criminal behavior* — **pre·dis·po·si·tion** /ˌpriːˌdɪspəˈzɪʃən/ n [C/U] ▪ *patients with a predisposition toward cancer*

pre·dom·i·nant /prɪˈdɑːmənənt/ adj : more important, powerful, successful, or noticeable than other people or things ▪ *Religion is the predominant theme of the play.* ▪ *Older people are predominant in the neighborhood.* — **pre·dom·i·nance** /prɪˈdɑːmənəns/ n [U, singular] ▪ *The tribe fought to maintain its predominance.* ▪ *There is a predominance of older people in the neighborhood.* [=most of the people in the neighborhood are older] — **pre·dom·i·nant·ly** adv ▪ *The speech was predominantly* [=mainly] *about tax cuts.*

pre·dom·i·nate /prɪˈdɑːməˌneɪt/ vb -nat·ed; -nat·ing [I] : to be greater than others in number, amount, strength, success, or influence ▪ *One ethnic group predominates over others in that country.* ▪ *Cottages predominate along the beach.* [=most of the buildings along the beach are cottages]

pre·em·i·nent /priˈɛmənənt/ adj, formal : more important, skillful, or successful than others ▪ *The poem is a preeminent example of his work.* — **pre·em·i·nence** /priˈɛmənəns/ n [U]

pre·em·i·nent·ly /priˈɛmənəntli/ adv, formal : to a very great degree ▪ *He is preeminently qualified for the position.*

pre·empt /priˈɛmpt/ vb [T] **1** formal : to prevent (something) from happening ▪ *The contract preempts lawsuits by the company's clients.* **2** formal : to take the place of (something) ▪ *The state law was preempted by a federal law.* **3** US : to be shown instead of (another television program) ▪ *The President's speech preempted regular programming.* — **pre·emp·tion** /priˈɛmpʃən/ n [C/U]

pre·emp·tive /priˈɛmptɪv/ adj : done to stop an unwanted act from happening ▪ *a preemptive attack by the army*

preen /ˈpriːn/ vb [T/I] **1** of a bird : to use the beak to clean and arrange feathers **2** : to make (yourself) neat and tidy ▪ *She stood preening (herself) in front of the mirror.*

pre·ex·ist·ing /ˌpriːɪgˈzɪstɪŋ/ adj : existing at an earlier time ▪ *They made changes to the preexisting law.*

pre·fab·ri·cated /ˌpriːˈfæbrɪˌkeɪtəd/ adj : made of parts that are made at a factory and that can be put together later ▪ *prefabricated houses*

¹**pref·ace** /ˈprɛfəs/ n [C] : an introduction to a book or speech

²**preface** vb -aced; -ac·ing [T] : to introduce (a piece of writing, speech, etc.) by writing or saying something ▪ *Each chapter in the book is prefaced by/with a quotation.*

pref·a·to·ry /ˈprɛfəˌtori, Brit ˈprɛfətri/ adj, always before a noun, formal : included at the beginning of a book, speech, etc., as an introduction ▪ *prefatory remarks*

pre·fect /ˈpriːˌfɛkt/ n [C] **1** : a chief officer or government official who is responsible for a particular area in some countries (such as Japan and France) **2** chiefly Brit : an older student who is given the job of helping to watch and control younger students in a school

pre·fec·ture /ˈpriːˌfɛktʃər/ n [C] : any one of the areas into which some countries (such as Japan and France) are divided for local government

pre·fer /prɪˈfɚ/ vb **-ferred; -fer·ring** [T] : to like (someone or something) better than someone or something else ▪ *I prefer this dictionary because of its helpful examples.* ▪ *I would prefer it if you smoked outside.* ▪ *I suggested that we play a game, but they preferred to watch TV.* ▪ *He prefers a good book to/over a movie.*

pref·er·a·ble /ˈprɛfrəbəl/ adj : better or more desirable ▪ *the preferable choice* ▪ *The book is far/much preferable to the movie.* [=is much better than the movie] — **pref·er·a·bly** /ˈprɛfrəbli/ adv ▪ *I'd like to have the work done soon, preferably by the end of the week.*

pref·er·ence /ˈprɛfrəns/ n **1** [C/U] : a feeling of liking or wanting one person or thing more than another person or thing ▪ *Car buyers have shown a growing/strong preference for smaller vehicles.* ▪ *She listed her favorite restaurants in order of preference.* **2** [U] : an advantage that is given to some people or things and not to others ▪ *Their policy is to give preference to minority candidates.* — **in preference to** : instead of (something or someone) ▪ *They chose her in preference to me.*

pref·er·en·tial /ˌprɛfəˈrɛnʃəl/ adj : giving an advantage to a particular person or group ▪ *powerful people who demand preferential treatment from politicians* — **pref·er·en·tial·ly** adv

pre·fer·ment /prɪˈfɚmənt/ n [U] formal : the act of moving someone to a higher or more important position or rank in an organization ▪ *He has hopes for preferment.*

pre·fix /ˈpriːˌfɪks/ n [C] : a letter or group of letters that is added at the beginning of a word to change its meaning ▪ *The prefix "re-" is used in the words "retell" and "recall."*

preg·nant /ˈprɛgnənt/ adj **1** of a woman or female animal : having a baby or babies developing inside the body ▪ *She got/became pregnant.* ▪ *She is pregnant with her first child.* **2** formal : filled with meaning or emotion ▪ *There was a pregnant pause/silence before the winner was announced.* — **preg·nan·cy** /ˈprɛgnənsi/ n, pl **-cies** [C/U]

pre·heat /ˈpriːˈhiːt/ vb [T] : to heat (an oven) to a particular temperature before putting food to be cooked inside ▪ *Preheat the oven to 375 degrees.*

pre·his·tor·ic /ˌpriːhɪˈstorɪk/ also **pre·his·tor·i·cal** /ˌpriːhɪˈstorɪkəl/ adj **1** : of, relating to, or existing in the time before people could write ▪ *prehistoric animals/times* **2** informal + disapproving : very old or outdated ▪ *His attitudes about women are prehistoric.*

pre·judge /ˈpriːˈdʒʌdʒ/ vb **-judged; -judg·ing** [T] : to form an opinion about (someone or something) before you have enough understanding or knowledge ▪ *She was wrong to prejudge him.*

¹prej·u·dice /ˈprɛdʒədəs/ n **1** [C/U] : an unfair feeling of dislike for a person or group because of race, religion, etc. ▪ *religious/racial/sexual prejudice* **2** [C] : a feeling of like or dislike for someone

or something especially when it is not reasonable or logical ▪ *He has a prejudice against fast-food restaurants.*

²prejudice vb **-diced; -dic·ing** [T] **1** : to cause (someone) to have an unfair feeling of dislike for someone or something ▪ *The incident prejudiced many people against the company.* **2** formal : to have a harmful effect on (something) ▪ *The media coverage prejudiced the trial.*

prejudiced adj **1** : having or showing an unfair feeling of dislike for a person or group because of race, sex, religion, etc. ▪ *a prejudiced person/comment* **2** : having a feeling of like or dislike for something or someone ▪ *I was prejudiced against the movie because of its title.*

prej·u·di·cial /ˌprɛdʒəˈdɪʃəl/ adj, formal : causing or likely to cause injury or harm to someone or something ▪ *The court ruled that the testimony was unfairly prejudicial to the defendant.*

prel·ate /ˈprɛlət/ n [C] formal : a high-ranking Christian priest : a bishop, cardinal, etc.

¹pre·lim·i·nary /prɪˈlɪməˌneri, Brit prɪˈlɪmənri/ adj : coming before the main part of something ▪ *Preliminary findings/studies/tests show that the drug could be helpful.* ▪ *a preliminary hearing*

²preliminary n, pl **-nar·ies** [C] : something that comes before and leads to the main part, event, etc. ▪ *There were the usual preliminaries before the ceremony.*

pre·lude /ˈprɛlˌjuːd/ n [C] **1** : something that comes before and leads to something else ▪ *The dark clouds were a prelude to the storm.* **2** : a short piece of music that introduces a longer piece

pre·mar·i·tal /ˌpriːˈmɛrətl/ adj, always before a noun : happening before marriage ▪ *premarital sex*

pre·ma·ture /ˌpriːməˈtuɚ, ˌpriːməˈtʃuɚ, Brit ˈprɛmətʃə/ adj **1** : happening too soon or earlier than usual ▪ *His retirement seems premature.* ▪ *a premature birth/death* **2** : born before the normal time ▪ *premature babies* — **pre·ma·ture·ly** adv

pre·med /ˈpriːˈmɛd/ n [U] US : a course of study at a college or university that prepares students to enter medical school ▪ *premed students/classes*

pre·med·i·tat·ed /ˌpriːˈmɛdəˌteɪtəd/ adj : planned in advance ▪ *premeditated murder*

pre·men·stru·al /ˌpriːˈmɛnstrəwəl/ adj : happening just before a woman's menstrual period ▪ *premenstrual symptoms*

premenstrual syndrome n [U] : a condition experienced by some women before menstruation that may include tiredness, irritability, anxiety, depression, headache, and stomach pain — called also (Brit) **premenstrual tension**

¹pre·mier /prɪˈmiɚ, Brit ˈprɛmiə/ n [C] : PRIME MINISTER ▪ *the Russian premier*

²premier adj, always before a noun : most important or best ▪ *the city's premier restaurant*

pre·miere also **pre·mière** /prɪˈmiɚ, Brit ˈprɛmiˌeə/ n [C] : the first time a film, play, etc., is shown or performed ▪ *the world premiere* [=the first public performance

mance anywhere in the world] *of a new symphony* — **premiere** *also* **première** *vb* -miered *also* -mièred; -mier·ing *also* -mièr·ing [T/I] ▪ *The play premieres next week.* ▪ *The movie was premiered at the film festival.*

prem·ise /ˈprɛməs/ *n* **1** [*plural*] : a building and the area of land that it is on ▪ *The premises were searched by the police.* ▪ *Police escorted her off the premises.* ▪ *The hotel has a restaurant on the premises.* [=inside the hotel] **2** *also Brit* **pre·miss** [C] *formal* : a statement or idea that is accepted as being true and that is used as the basis of an argument ▪ *the basic premises of the argument* — **pre·mised** /ˈprɛməst/ *adj* ▪ *The plan is premised [=based] on the belief that people are willing to pay more to use alternative fuel sources.*

¹**pre·mi·um** /ˈpriːmijəm/ *n* **1** [C] : the amount paid for insurance ▪ *the monthly premium for health insurance* **2** [*singular*] : a price that is higher than the regular price ▪ *paying a premium for hotel rooms that have views of the beach* **3** [*singular*] : a high or extra value ▪ *Publishers put/place a premium on accuracy.* [=value accuracy very highly] — **at a premium** : difficult to get because there is little available ▪ *Space in the apartment is at a premium.*

²**premium** *adj, always before a noun* : of high quality, value, or price ▪ *premium prices/gasoline*

pre·mo·ni·tion /ˌpriːməˈnɪʃən/ *n* [C] : a feeling or belief that something is going to happen ▪ *She had a premonition that he would call.*

pre·na·tal /ˌpriːˈneɪtl̩/ *adj, always before a noun, medical* : relating to pregnant women and their unborn babies ▪ *prenatal care/development*

pre·nup·tial agreement /ˌpriːˈnʌpʃəl-/ *n* [C] *law* : an official agreement that two people make before they marry in which they state how much of each other's property each will receive if they divorce or if one of them dies

pre·oc·cu·pa·tion /ˌpriːˌɑːkjəˈpeɪʃən/ *n* [C] **1** : a state in which you give all your attention to something ▪ *I don't understand her preoccupation with her appearance.* **2** : something that you give all or most of your attention to ▪ *our problems and preoccupations*

pre·oc·cu·pied /ˌpriːˈɑːkjəˌpaɪd/ *adj* : thinking about something a lot or too much ▪ *She is too preoccupied with family problems to focus on her work.*

pre·oc·cu·py /ˌpriːˈɑːkjəˌpaɪ/ *vb* -pies; -pied; -py·ing [T] : to be thought about or worried about by (someone) very often or constantly ▪ *Her family problems continue to preoccupy her.*

pre·or·dained /ˌpriːˌoəˈdeɪnd/ *adj, formal* : decided in advance and certain to happen ▪ *a preordained conclusion*

pre·owned /ˌpriːˈoʊnd/ *adj* : owned by someone else before ▪ *pre-owned cars*

¹**prep** /ˈprɛp/ *vb* prepped; prep·ping [T/I] *US, informal* : PREPARE ▪ *She spent all night prepping (herself) for the test.* ▪ *The patient is being prepped for surgery.*

²**prep** *n* [U] *US, informal* : PREPARATION ▪ *college prep courses* [=classes that students take to prepare for college]

³**prep** *abbr* preposition

pre·pack·age /ˌpriːˈpækədʒ/ *vb* -aged; -ag·ing [T] : to put (a product) in a package before selling it ▪ *The meals are prepackaged and ready to eat.* ▪ *prepackaged software*

prepaid past tense and past participle of PREPAY

prep·a·ra·tion /ˌprɛpəˈreɪʃən/ *n* **1** [U] : the activity or process of making something ready or of becoming ready for something ▪ *The festival involves a lot of preparation.* ▪ *food preparation* ▪ *The boxer exercised daily in preparation for the fight.* **2** [*plural*] : things that are done to make something ready or to become ready for something ▪ *They are busy with preparations for their wedding.* ▪ *The staff is making preparations to move to another building.* **3** [C] : a cream, lotion, etc., that you use as medicine or to improve your appearance ▪ *skin care preparations*

pre·pa·ra·to·ry /prɪˈpɛrəˌtori, Brit prɪˈpærətri/ *adj, always before a noun* : used or done to prepare for something ▪ *preparatory work/training* — **preparatory to** *formal* : as a way of becoming ready for (something) ▪ *Preparatory to the job interview, I researched the company.*

preparatory school *n* [C] : PREP SCHOOL

pre·pare /prɪˈpeə/ *vb* -pared; -par·ing **1 a** [T] : to make (someone or something) ready for something ▪ *The teacher prepared the students for the test.* **b** [T/I] : to make yourself ready for something ▪ *The sailors are preparing (themselves) for a long voyage.* **2** [T] : to make or create (something) so that it is ready for use ▪ *She prepared dinner.* ▪ *He prepared a report for his boss.*

prepared *adj* **1** : made at an earlier time for later use ▪ *The president read a prepared statement.* **2** : ready for something ▪ *The campers were not prepared for the rain.* ▪ *She was well-prepared and scored high on the test.* **3** *not before a noun* : willing to do something ▪ *How much are you prepared to pay?* — **pre·pared·ness** /prɪˈpeədnəs/ *n* [U] *formal*

pre·pay /ˌpriːˈpeɪ/ *vb* -paid /-ˈpeɪd/; -pay·ing [T] **1** : to pay for (something) before you receive or use it ▪ *Special orders must be prepaid.* **2** : to pay (something) before you are required to pay it ▪ *prepay a loan* — **prepaid** *adj* ▪ *a prepaid envelope* [=an envelope for which the postage has already been paid] — **pre·pay·ment** /ˌpriːˈpeɪmənt/ *n* [C/U]

pre·pon·der·ance /prɪˈpɑːndərəns/ *n* [*singular*] *formal* : a greater amount or number of something ▪ *A preponderance of the evidence* [=most of the evidence] *shows that the accused is guilty.*

prep·o·si·tion /ˌprɛpəˈzɪʃən/ *n* [C] *grammar* : a word or group of words that is used with a noun, pronoun, or noun phrase to show direction, location, or time, or to introduce an object ▪ *The preposition "on" in "The keys are on the table" shows location.*

prep·o·si·tion·al phrase /ˌprɛpəˈzɪʃə-nl/ *n* [C] *grammar* : a phrase that begins with a preposition and ends in a noun, pronoun, or noun phrase ▪ *In "He is from Russia," "from Russia" is a prepositional phrase.*

pre·pos·ter·ous /prɪˈpɑːstərəs/ *adj* : very foolish or silly ▪ *a preposterous excuse* — **pre·pos·ter·ous·ly** *adv*

prep·py *or* **prep·pie** /ˈprɛpi/ *n, pl* **-pies** [C] *US, informal* ▪ *often disapproving* : someone who dresses or acts like a student at a prep school (such as by wearing somewhat formal clothing or by using particular words) ▪ *a rich preppy* — **preppy** *or* **preppie** *adj* ▪ *preppy clothes*

prep school *n* [C] **1** *US* : a private school that prepares students for college **2** *Brit* : a private school for children between the ages of 7 and 13

pre·quel /ˈpriːkwəl/ *n* [C] : a movie, book, etc., that tells the part of a story that happened before the story in another movie, book, etc.

pre·re·cord /ˌpriːrɪˈkoəd/ *vb* [T] : to record (something) before showing it to the public, broadcasting it, etc. ▪ *a prerecorded program/interview*

pre·req·ui·site /ˌpriːˈrɛkwəzət/ *n* [C] : something that you officially must have or do before you can have or do something else ▪ *Citizenship is a prerequisite for voting.*

pre·rog·a·tive /prɪˈrɑːgətɪv/ *n* [C] *formal* : a right or privilege ▪ *If you'd rather sell the tickets than use them, that's your prerogative.*

pres. *abbr* **1** present **2** president

pre·sage /ˈprɛsɪdʒ/ *vb* **-saged; -sag·ing** [T] *formal* : to give or be a sign of (something that will happen or develop in the future) ▪ *events that presaged the civil rights movement*

Pres·by·te·ri·an /ˌprɛzbəˈtirijən/ *adj* : of or relating to a Christian church in Scotland, the U.S., and other countries that is officially led by a group of ministers and elders ▪ *a Presbyterian doctrine/church* — **Presbyterian** *n* [C] — **Pres·by·te·ri·an·ism** /ˌprɛzbəˈtirijəˌnɪzəm/ *n* [U]

¹**pre·school** /ˈpriːˌskuːl/ *n* [C/U] *chiefly US* : a school for very young children

²**preschool** *adj, always before a noun* : relating to the time when a child is old enough to talk and walk but is not ready to go to school ▪ *preschool age/children* — **pre·school·er** /ˈpriːˌskuːləʳ/ *n* [C] *US*

pre·scient /ˈprɛʃijənt, Brit ˈprɛsɪənt/ *adj, formal* : having or showing an ability to know what will happen before it does ▪ *a prescient remark/investor* — **pre·science** /ˈprɛʃijəns, Brit ˈprɛsɪəns/ *n* [U]

pre·scribe /prɪˈskraɪb/ *vb* **-scribed; -scrib·ing** [T] **1** : to officially tell someone to use (a medicine, therapy, diet, etc.) as a remedy or treatment ▪ *This drug should not be prescribed to children.* ▪ *The doctor prescribed physical therapy for my leg injury.* **2** : to make (something) an official rule ▪ *The law prescribes a prison sentence of at least five years for the crime.* ▪ *prescribed rules*

pre·scrip·tion /prɪˈskrɪpʃən/ *n* **1 a** [C/U] : a written message from a doctor that officially tells someone to use a medicine, therapy, etc. ▪ *The doctor wrote me a prescription for cough syrup.* ▪ *(US) The drug is only available* **by prescription**. = *(Brit) The drug is only available* **on prescription**. [=you can only get the drug if you have a prescription] **b** [C] : a medicine or drug that a doctor officially tells someone to use ▪ *prescription drugs/medicine/costs* **2** [C] : something that is suggested as a way to do something or to make something happen ▪ *a prescription for economic recovery*

pre·scrip·tive /prɪˈskrɪptɪv/ *adj* : giving exact rules, directions, or instructions about how you should do something ▪ *The new regulations are too prescriptive.*

pres·ence /ˈprɛzns/ *n* **1** [C] : the fact of being in a particular place : the state of being present ▪ *No one was aware of the stranger's presence.* ▪ *the growing presence of women in the construction industry* [=the increasing number of women working in the construction industry] **2** [U] : the area that is close to someone ▪ *Please don't smoke* **in my presence**. [=near me] ▪ *She's shy* **in the presence** [=around] *of strangers.* **3** [C] : someone or something that is seen or noticed in a particular place, area, etc. ▪ *Her mother was a constant presence at the swim meets.* ▪ *There is a heavy military presence in the city.* [=a lot of soldiers, military vehicles, etc., in the city] **4** [singular] : a way of moving, standing, speaking, etc. ▪ *an actor with a commanding* **stage presence** [=an actor with a powerful quality that attracts attention on the stage] — **grace (a person, group, etc.) with your presence** *see* ²**GRACE** — **make your presence felt/heard/known** : to make people aware of you by gaining power or influence over them ▪ *Women are making their presence felt in the industry.*

presence of mind *n* [U] : the ability to think clearly and act quickly especially in an emergency ▪ *The child had the presence of mind to call for an ambulance.*

¹**pres·ent** /ˈprɛznt/ *n* **1** [C] : something that you give to someone especially as a way of showing affection or thanks : GIFT ▪ *a birthday present* **2** [C/U] : the period of time that exists now : the present time ▪ *from 2000 to the present* ▪ *He was trying to escape his present by living in the past.* ▪ **At present** *I am working as a substitute teacher.* [=I am now working as a substitute teacher] **3** *the* **present** *grammar* : PRESENT TENSE ▪ *The verb is in the present.*

²**pre·sent** /prɪˈzɛnt/ *vb* **1** [T] : to give something to someone in a formal way ▪ *He presented the queen with a diamond necklace.* **2** [T/I] : to formally talk about (something) to a group of people ▪ *The scientist presented his results/report to the committee.* **3** [T] : to make (something) available to be seen, used, or considered ▪ *He presented his ID to the security guard.* ▪ *The theater company is presenting Shakespeare's Othello.* ▪ *An offer was presented for our consideration.* ▪ *The opportunity presented itself* [=became available]*, and she took advantage*

of it. **4** [T] : to describe or show (someone or something) in a particular way ▪ *The article presents an accurate picture of the lives of Japanese women.* ▪ *She presents herself as a very ambitious person.* **5** [T] : to create (a problem, challenge, etc.) for someone or something ▪ *The conflicting information presents a dilemma (for us).* ▪ *We have been presented with a difficult task.* **6** [T] : to introduce (someone or something) to a person or group ▪ *I am pleased to present our first comedian of the night.* — **pre·sent·er** n [C] ▪ *the presenter of the award*

³**pres·ent** /ˈprɛznt/ adj **1** : not past or future : existing or happening now ▪ *the present situation* ▪ *No further changes are planned* **at the present time.** [=now] **2 a** : at the particular place or event that is being referred to ▪ *She was present at the meeting.* ▪ *There was a large crowd present in the auditorium.* **b** : existing in something ▪ *There were high levels of lead present in the water.* [=the water contained high levels of lead]

pre·sent·able /prɪˈzɛntəbəl/ adj : in good enough condition to be seen by someone ▪ *I have to make myself presentable before our guests arrive.*

pre·sen·ta·tion /ˌprɛznˈteɪʃən/ n **1** [C] : an activity in which someone shows, describes, or explains something to a group of people ▪ *make/give a presentation* **2** [U] : the way in which something is arranged, designed, etc. ▪ *The presentation of the food made it look very appetizing.* **3** [C/U] : the act of giving something to someone in a formal way or in a ceremony ▪ *The choir sang during the presentation of the gifts.* ▪ *an awards presentation* **4** [U] : the act of showing or presenting something to someone so that it can be seen or considered ▪ *The state has a law that prohibits the presentation of new evidence 30 days after conviction.*

pres·ent·ly /ˈprɛzntli/ adv **1** : at the present time : NOW ▪ *She is presently at work on a new novel.* **2** : after a short time : SOON ▪ *He'll be back presently.*

present participle n [C] grammar : a verb form that ends in "-ing" and that is used with "be" to refer to action that is happening at the time of speaking or a time spoken of ▪ *The verb "crying" in "The baby is crying" is a present participle.*

present perfect n — **the present perfect** grammar : a verb tense that is used to refer to an action that began in the past and is completed at the time of speaking ✧ *The present perfect* in English is formed with "has" and "have" and the past participle of a verb, as in "He has left" and "They have found what they were looking for."

present tense n [C] : a verb tense that is used to refer to the present

pre·ser·va·tive /prɪˈzɚvətɪv/ n [C/U] : a substance that is used to preserve something ▪ *This food does not contain any artificial preservatives.* ▪ *The wood was treated with preservative.*

¹**pre·serve** /prɪˈzɚv/ vb **-served; -serv·ing** [T] **1** : to keep (something) in its original state or in good condition ▪ *pre-*

serving *the city's historical buildings* **2** : to keep (something) safe from harm or loss : PROTECT ▪ *These laws are intended to help preserve our natural resources.* ▪ *a substance that preserves wood* **3** : to prevent (food) from decaying ▪ *Salt can be used to preserve meat.* — **pres·er·va·tion** /ˌprɛzɚˈveɪʃən/ n [U] — **pre·serv·er** n [C]

²**preserve** n **1** [C/U] : a sweet food made of fruit cooked in sugar ▪ *a jar of strawberry preserves* **2** [C] : an area where plants, animals, minerals, etc., are protected ▪ *nature/wildlife preserves* **3** [singular] : an activity, job, interest, etc., that is available to or considered suitable for only a particular group of people ▪ *Raising children used to be the (exclusive) preserve of women.* [=used to be thought of as something done only by women]

pre·side /prɪˈzaɪd/ vb **-sid·ed; -sid·ing** [I] : to be in charge of something ▪ *He has presided over the company for 15 years.* ▪ *The vice president presided at/over the meeting.* ▪ *the presiding judge/officer*

pres·i·den·cy /ˈprɛzədənsi/ n, pl **-cies** [C] : the job of a president or the period of time when a person is president ▪ *the third year of his presidency*

pres·i·dent /ˈprɛzədənt/ n [C] **1** : the head of the government in some countries ▪ *the President of the United States* ▪ *President Abraham Lincoln* **2** : someone who has the highest position in an organization or business ▪ *the president of the club/bank* — **pres·i·den·tial** /ˌprɛzə-ˈdɛnʃəl/ adj ▪ *a presidential candidate/ election*

Presidents' Day n [U] : the third Monday in February celebrated in most states of the U.S. as a holiday in honor of the birthdays of George Washington and Abraham Lincoln

¹**press** /ˈprɛs/ n **1 a** [U] : newspapers, magazines, and radio and television news reports ▪ *Reports in the press suggested there had been many casualties.* ▪ **freedom of the press** [=the right of newspapers, magazines, etc., to report news without being controlled by the government] **b** *the press* : the reporters, photographers, etc., who work for newspapers, magazines, etc. ▪ *She refused to talk to the press.* **c** [U] — used to talk about how often or how well or badly someone or something is described in newspapers, magazines, etc. ▪ *The trial has been getting a lot of press.* ▪ *He has gotten some bad press lately.* **2 a** [C] : PRINTING PRESS ▪ *Stop the presses!* — see also *hot off the press* at HOT **b** [U] : the act or the process of being printed ▪ *The story is going to press.* [=is about to be printed] **c** [C] : a printing or publishing business ▪ *a university press* **3** [C] : a machine that uses pressure to shape, flatten, or squeeze something ▪ *a garlic/trouser press* **4** [C] : the act of pushing or flattening something with your finger or hand or with a device (such as an iron) ▪ *The machine turns on with the press of a button.*

²**press** vb **1** [T/I] **a** : to push (something) with strong or steady force ▪ *She pressed the pieces of clay together.* ▪ *People*

were pressed against each other in the crowd. ▪ *He lightly pressed (down) on the pedal.* **b** : to push (a button, lever, etc.) with your finger or hand ▪ *Don't press that button.* **2** [*T/I*] : to force or try to persuade (someone) to do something especially by repeatedly asking for it to be done ▪ *She pressed him to go with her.* ▪ *The CEO was pressed into resigning.* **3** [*T*] : to repeat (something) often in a way that is annoying to show that it is very important ▪ *press the issue* **4** [*T*] : to flatten or smooth out (something) with your hand, an iron, etc. ▪ *He pressed his shirt and pants.* **5** [*I*] : to continue moving forward ▪ *The troops pressed on/forward in spite of the snow.* ▪ *Now that we have answered that question, let's press on.* **6** [*I*] : to move in a large group toward or near someone or something ▪ *Reporters pressed around the players as they left the field.* — **press charges** : to officially accuse someone of a crime ▪ *He was caught shoplifting, but the store owner didn't press charges.* — **press for** [*phrasal vb*] : to make a demand for (something) ▪ *Laborers are pressing for higher wages.* — **press on** *also* **press upon** [*phrasal vb*] **press (something) on/upon** : to force (someone) to take or accept (something) ▪ *I tried to press money on him for the bill, but he refused to take it.* — **press (someone or something) into service** : to use (someone or something) for a particular job or purpose when a special need occurs ▪ *The backup computer was pressed into service when the main computer failed.* — **press the flesh** *informal* : to greet and shake hands with people especially while campaigning for a political office

press agent *n* [*C*] : a person whose job is to give information about an important or famous person or organization to news reporters

press conference *n* [*C*] : a meeting in which someone gives information to news reporters and answers questions

pressed /ˈprɛst/ *adj, not before a noun* : lacking something that is needed or desired — + *for* ▪ *I am really pressed for time/money right now.*

press·ing /ˈprɛsɪŋ/ *adj* : very important and needing immediate attention ▪ *a pressing problem*

press secretary *n* [*C*] : a person whose job is to give information about an important or famous person or organization to news reporters ▪ *the White House press secretary*

press stud *n* [*C*] *Brit* : ²SNAP 3

press–up /ˈprɛsˌʌp/ *n* [*C*] *Brit* : PUSH-UP

¹**pres·sure** /ˈprɛʃɚ/ *n* **1** [*U, singular*] : the weight or force that is produced when something presses or pushes against something else ▪ *Apply pressure to the wound to stop the bleeding.* ▪ *high/low* **water pressure** [=a force that makes a flow of water strong/weak] ▪ *The contents of the bottle are* **under pressure.** [=the contents are tightly pressed into the bottle] **2** [*U*] : the weight of the air in the Earth's atmosphere ▪ *atmospheric pressure* ▪ *An area of high/low pressure is mov-*

ing over the west coast. **3** [*C/U*] : the force that you feel when people are trying to persuade or force you to do something by using arguments, threats, etc. ▪ *He felt pressure from his father to become a doctor. = His father put pressure on him to become a doctor.* ▪ *The mayor is* **under pressure** *to resign.* ▪ *the social pressures to act and dress like everybody else* **4** [*C/U*] : a feeling of stress or anxiety that you have too much to do or because people are depending on you for something ▪ *the pressures of everyday life* ▪ *He works well* **under pressure.**

²**pressure** *vb* **-sured; -sur·ing** [*T*] *chiefly US* : to use pressure to force or try to force (someone) to do something ▪ *They're pressuring him to make a decision.* ▪ *The defense pressured the quarterback into throwing a bad pass.*

pressure cooker *n* [*C*] : a special pot that is used to cook food quickly by using the pressure of steam

pressure group *n* [*C*] : a group of people who share an interest, concern, or set of opinions and who try to influence politics, business, etc.

pres·sur·ize *also Brit* **pres·sur·ise** /ˈprɛʃəˌraɪz/ *vb* **-ized; -iz·ing** [*T*] *technical* : to cause the air pressure inside (something, such as an airplane) to be the same as or close to the pressure of air on the Earth's surface ▪ *the airplane's pressurized cabin* **2** *Brit* : ²PRESSURE

pres·sur·i·za·tion *also Brit* **pres·sur·i·sa·tion** /ˌprɛʃərəˈzeɪʃən, *Brit* ˌprɛʃəˌraɪˈzeɪʃən/ *n* [*U*]

pres·tige /prɛˈstiːʒ/ *n* [*U*] : the respect and admiration that someone or something gets for being successful or important ▪ *Her career as a diplomat has brought her enormous prestige.* — **pres·ti·gious** /prɛˈstɪdʒəs/ *adj* ▪ *a prestigious college/award*

pre·sum·ably /prɪˈzuːməbli, *Brit* prɪˈzjuːməbli/ *adv* : very likely ▪ *Presumably, he'll come later.* [=it is reasonable to think that he will come later]

pre·sume /prɪˈzuːm, *Brit* prɪˈzjuːm/ *vb* **-sumed; -sum·ing** [*T*] **1 a** : to think that (something) is true without knowing that it is true ▪ *I presume (that) the car was very expensive. = The car was very expensive, I presume.* **b** : to accept legally or officially that something is true until it is proved not true ▪ *A person is presumed (to be) innocent until proven guilty in a court of law.* ▪ *Several people are missing and* **presumed dead.** [=believed to be dead] **2** *formal* : to do (something) that you do not have the right or permission to do ▪ *I'm not going to presume to tell you how to do your job.* **3** : to expect that someone has (a certain level of knowledge, skill, etc.) ▪ *The course presumes familiarity with basic computer programming.* — **presume on/upon** [*phrasal vb*] *formal* : to go beyond the proper limits of (a relationship) ▪ *I don't want to presume on/upon our friendship by asking for too many favors.*

pre·sump·tion /prɪˈzʌmpʃən/ *n* **1** [*C*] : a belief that something is true even though it has not been proved ▪ *The pre-*

sumption is that the thief had a key to the store. • Thousands of people used this drug **on the presumption that** it was safe. **2** [U, singular] law : an act of accepting that something is true until it is proved not true • a defendant's right to a presumption of innocence **3** [U] formal : willingness to do something without the right or permission to do it • I can't believe he has the presumption to tell me what to do!

pre·sump·tu·ous /prɪˈzʌmpʃəwəs/ adj, formal : too confident especially in a way that is rude • It would be presumptuous (of me) to tell her what to do. • a presumptuous question — **pre·sump·tu·ous·ly** adv

pre·sup·pose /ˌpriːsəˈpoʊz/ vb **-posed; -pos·ing** [T] formal **1** : to be based on the idea that something is true or will happen • The plan presupposes (that) the state has enough money to carry it out. **2** : to require or depend on (something) in order to be true or exist • Prayer presupposes a belief in a higher being. — **pre·sup·po·si·tion** /ˌpriːˌsʌpəˈzɪʃən/ n [C/U]

pre·teen /ˈpriːˈtiːn/ n [C] : a boy or girl who is 11 or 12 years old

¹**pre·tend** /prɪˈtɛnd/ vb [T/I] **1** : to act as if something is true when it is not true • She pretended to be angry. = She pretended (that) she was angry. • She looked like she was enjoying the party, but she was just pretending. • It was a mistake, and to **pretend otherwise** would be foolish. **2** : to imagine and act out (a particular role, situation, etc.) • Pretend (that) I'm your boss. What would you say? • The children were pretending to be animals. — **pretend to** [phrasal vb] formal : to claim that you have (something) • I don't pretend to any expertise in these matters.

²**pretend** adj, informal : not real : IMAGINARY • The little girl has a pretend friend.

pre·tend·er /prɪˈtɛndɚ/ n [C] : someone who claims to have the right to a particular title or position (such as king or queen) when others do not agree • a pretender to the throne

pre·tense (US) or Brit **pre·tence** /ˈpriː-ˌtɛns, Brit prɪˈtɛns/ n **1** [C] : a false reason or explanation that is used to hide the real purpose of something • He called her **under/on the pretense of** asking about the homework assignment. • She obtained the documents **under false pretenses. 2** [U, singular] : an act or appearance that looks real but is false • Their indifference is only a pretense. • She couldn't even **make a pretense of** liking him. • He abandoned/dropped all **pretense at** politeness. **3** [C] formal : a claim of having a particular quality, ability, condition, etc. • I make no pretense of being a history expert.

pre·ten·sion /prɪˈtɛnʃən/ n, formal **1** [U] : the unpleasant quality of people who think of themselves as more impressive, successful, or important than they really are • He spoke about his achievements without pretension. **2** [C] : a desire to do something or a claim to be something that is impressive or impor-

tant • The movie has no artistic pretensions. = The movie has no pretensions to/of being great art.

pre·ten·tious /prɪˈtɛnʃəs/ adj, disapproving : having or showing the unpleasant quality of people who want to be regarded as more impressive, successful, or important than they really are • a pretentious snob/movie — **pre·ten·tious·ly** adv — **pre·ten·tious·ness** n [U]

pre·text /ˈpriːˌtɛkst/ n [C] : a reason that you give to hide your real reason for doing something • The leaders used a minor clash at the border as a pretext for war.

¹**pret·ty** /ˈprɪti/ adj **pret·ti·er; -est 1 a** : attractive to look at usually in a simple or delicate way • pretty flowers • She has a pretty face. **b** : pleasant to look at or listen to • a pretty sunset/song **2** always before a noun : large or impressive • She received a pretty sum of money. **3** : pleasant to see or experience • a pretty day • The game wasn't pretty but at least we won. • The kitchen was **not a pretty sight** after we finished making breakfast. — **a pretty penny** see PENNY — **pret·ti·ly** /ˈprɪtəli/ adv — **pret·ti·ness** /ˈprɪtinəs/ n [U]

²**pretty** adv **1** : to some degree or extent but not very or extremely : FAIRLY • It's pretty cold outside. • "Did you put the keys on the table?" "I'm pretty sure I did." • I have to leave pretty soon. • The movie was pretty good but not great. — **pretty much/well** informal : not completely but mostly • It is pretty much the same color. — **sit pretty** see SIT

³**pretty** vb **-ties; -tied; -ty·ing** [T] : to make (something) pretty — usually + up • The curtains prettied up the room.

pret·zel /ˈprɛtsəl/ n [C] : a long, thin piece of bread that is usually salted and shaped like a knot or stick

pre·vail /prɪˈveɪl/ vb [I] formal **1** : to defeat an opponent especially in a long or difficult contest • He prevailed against last year's champion. • (figurative) Truth will prevail over lies. **2** : to be usual, common, or popular • Mutual respect prevails among students and teachers here. • the prevailing opinion **3** : to be or continue to be in use • The law still prevails in some states. — **prevail on/upon** [phrasal vb] : to ask or persuade (someone) to do something • They prevailed on me to play a few tunes on the piano.

prev·a·lent /ˈprɛvələnt/ adj : accepted, done, or happening often or over a large area at a particular time • prevalent beliefs • a fashion that is prevalent among teenagers — **prev·a·lence** /ˈprɛvələns/ n [U]

pre·var·i·cate /prɪˈvɛrəˌkeɪt/ vb **-cat·ed; -cat·ing** [I] formal : to avoid telling the truth by not directly answering a question • Government officials prevaricated about the real costs of the project. — **pre·var·i·ca·tion** /prɪˌvɛrəˈkeɪʃən/ n [C/U]

pre·vent /prɪˈvɛnt/ vb [T] **1** : to stop (something) from happening or existing • Can exercise prevent heart disease? **2** : to stop (someone or something) from doing something • Bad weather prevented us from leaving. — **pre·vent·able** /prɪ-

ˈven·tət/ adj • a preventable disease •
pre·ven·tion /prɪˈvɛnʃən/ n [U] • crime/
fire prevention

pre·ven·ta·tive /prɪˈvɛntətɪv/ adj : PRE-
VENTIVE — **preventative** n [C]

pre·ven·tive /prɪˈvɛntɪv/ adj : used to
stop something bad from happening •
preventive measures/actions • preventive
medicine [=medicine that keeps you
healthy] — **preventive** n [C] • The drug
is a preventive against cancer.

¹**pre·view** /ˈpriːˌvjuː/ n [C] **1** : a special
show that allows some people to see a
movie, play, etc., before it is shown to
the public • a special preview of the movie
2 US : a group of scenes that are shown
to advertise a movie or TV show • They
show previews before the movie starts. **3**
: a description of something that will
happen or be available in the future • a
preview of new fall fashions **4** : an example of what something will look like •
You can see a preview of the page/photo
before you print it.

²**preview** vb [T] : to see or give a preview
of (something) • preview a new movie •
They previewed the upcoming football season. • preview a photo before you print it

pre·vi·ous /ˈpriːvijəs/ adj **1** : existing or
happening before the present time • She
has a child from a previous marriage. • No
previous experience is necessary. **2 a**
: earlier in time or order • the previous
owners of the house **b** : immediately before in time or order • It was Tuesday,
and we'd met the previous day. [=the day
before; Monday] • I was living in Boston
and previous to that, I lived in Miami. —
pre·vi·ous·ly adv • previously published
material

pre·war /ˌpriːˈwoɚ/ adj : happening or
existing before a war and especially before World War II • prewar Europe

¹**prey** /ˈpreɪ/ n [U] **1** : an animal that is
hunted or killed by another animal for
food • a lion stalking its prey — see also
BIRD OF PREY **2** : someone who is easily harmed by someone or something •
Elderly people are often easy prey for
swindlers. — **be/fall prey to 1** : to be
killed by (an animal, disease, etc.) • The
deer fell prey to coyotes. **2** : to be
harmed by (someone or something) • She
fell prey to an online scam.

²**prey** vb — **prey on/upon** [phrasal vb] **1**
: to hunt and kill (something) for food •
Wolves prey on small animals. **2** : to
hurt, cheat, or steal from (someone) •
criminals who prey on tourists **3 prey on/
upon someone's mind** : to make someone worry constantly • Her growing debts
preyed on her mind.

¹**price** /ˈpraɪs/ n [C/U] **1** : the amount of
money that something costs • oil/gas prices • We bought the house at a good/low/
reasonable price. • The price of milk rose/
fell. • Buy two pizzas for the price of one.
[=for the same amount of money it costs
to buy one] • price cuts/increases • Children 12 and over pay full price. [=the
main or highest price] • (figurative) You
can't put a price on love. [=love is more
valuable than any amount of money] **2**
[singular] : the thing that is lost, dam-

aged, or given up in order to get or do
something • She paid a **high price** for her
mistakes. • We won the war, but **at what
price**? [=did we lose too much in order to
win the war?] **3** [U] : the amount of
money needed to persuade someone to
do something • He'll do it once we find his
price. — **a price on someone's head**
: an amount of money that will be given
to anyone who kills or captures someone
• He has a price on his head. — **at any
price 1** : for any amount of money • It's
the best education you can get at any
price. **2** : without caring about what
might be lost or given up • They want
peace at any price. — **at a price 1** : by
losing or giving up something or doing
something unpleasant • Success came at
a price. **2** : for a very large amount of
money • It is available, but at a price.

²**price** vb **priced; pric·ing** [T] **1** : to say
or decide how much something costs •
The car is priced at $19,000. • a reason-
ably priced car **2** : to learn the price of
(something that you are thinking about
buying) • I've been pricing TVs. [=compar-
ing the prices of different TVs]

price·less /ˈpraɪsləs/ adj **1** : extremely
valuable or important • The painting/in-
formation is priceless. **2** informal : very
funny • The look on his face was priceless.

price tag n [C] **1** : a label with a price
written on it that is attached to a product
• The shirt's price tag says it's $19.95. **2**
: the cost or price of something • The car
has a $30,000 price tag.

pricey also **pricy** /ˈpraɪsi/ adj **pric·i·er;
-est** informal : EXPENSIVE • a pricey car/
store

¹**prick** /ˈprɪk/ vb **1** [T] : to make a very
small hole in (something) with a sharp
pointed object • She pricked her finger
with a pin. = The pin pricked her (finger).
2 [T/I] of an animal : to cause (the ears)
to point upward • The dog pricked (up) its
ears. • (figurative) My **ears pricked (up)**
[=I started to listen carefully] when I
heard them say my name.

²**prick** n [C] **1** : an act of pricking something • The nurse gave my finger a prick
and squeezed out some blood. **2 a** : a
pain caused by being touched by something pointed • You'll just feel a little prick.
b : a slight, sharp feeling of sadness, regret, etc. • He felt a **prick of conscience**.
[=a feeling of guilt]

prick·le /ˈprɪkəl/ vb **prick·led; prickling** [T/I] : to cause or experience an unpleasant feeling that is like having many
small, sharp points against your skin •
She felt a prickling sensation in her shoulder.

prick·ly /ˈprɪkli/ adj **prick·li·er; -est 1**
: having many sharp points • a prickly
cactus/leaf **2 a** : caused or seeming to
be caused by something that has many
points • a prickly sensation **b** : causing a
prickly feeling on your skin • a prickly
wool sweater **3** : requiring careful treatment • a prickly issue **4** : easily annoyed
or angered • a prickly old man

prickly pear n [C/U] : a cactus that has
fruits shaped like pears; also : the fruit of
this plant

pricy *variant spelling of* PRICEY

¹**pride** /ˈpraɪd/ *n* **1** [*U*] **a** : a feeling that you respect yourself and deserve to be respected by other people ▪ *Having a job again gave him his pride back.* **b** : a feeling that you are more important or better than other people ▪ *I had to swallow my pride and admit I made a mistake.* **2 a** [*U*, *singular*] : a feeling of happiness that you get when you or someone you know does something good, difficult, etc. ▪ *She spoke with pride* [=she spoke proudly] *about her son.* ▪ *He takes pride in his work.* **b** [*singular*] : a person or thing that makes you feel proud ▪ *She is the pride of her town.* ▪ *The car is his pride and joy.* **3** [*C*] : a group of lions — **pride·ful** /ˈpraɪdfəl/ *adj*, *US* ▪ *He was too prideful to ask for help.*

²**pride** *vb* **prid·ed**; **prid·ing** — **pride yourself** *on* : to be proud because of having (an ability, quality, etc.) ▪ *The restaurant prides itself on* [=is proud of] *its excellent pizza.*

priest /ˈpriːst/ *n* [*C*] : a person who performs ceremonies in some religions ▪ *a Catholic priest* — **priest·hood** /ˈpriːstˌhʊd/ *n* [*C/U*] ▪ *He entered the priesthood.* [=became a priest] — **priest·ly** /ˈpriːstli/ *adj* ▪ *priestly robes/vows*

priest·ess /ˈpriːstəs/ *n* [*C*] : a woman who performs ceremonies in some religions ▪ *a tribal priestess*

prig /ˈprɪg/ *n* [*C*] : someone who annoys people by being very careful about proper behavior and by criticizing the behavior of other people — **prig·gish** /ˈprɪgɪʃ/ *adj* ▪ *She is too priggish.* — **prig·gish·ly** *adv*

prim /ˈprɪm/ *adj* **prim·mer; prim·mest 1 a** : very formal and proper ▪ *a prim manner* **b** : easily upset by rude behavior, comments, etc. ▪ *Her aunts were very prim and proper.* **2** : very neat in appearance ▪ *a prim cottage* — **prim·ly** *adv* ▪ *She was primly dressed.*

pri·ma ballerina /ˈpriːmə-/ *n* [*C*] : the main female dancer in a ballet company

pri·ma·cy /ˈpraɪməsi/ *n* [*U*] *formal* : the state of being most important or strongest ▪ *Civil law took primacy over religious law.*

pri·ma don·na /ˌprɪməˈdɑːnə/, *Brit* /ˌprɪməˈdɒnə/ *n* [*C*] **1** : the main female singer in an opera company : DIVA **2** *disapproving* : a person who thinks she or he is better than everyone else and who does not work well as part of a group

primaeval *Brit spelling of* PRIMEVAL

pri·mal /ˈpraɪməl/ *adj*, *formal* : very basic and powerful — used to describe feelings that are like the feelings of animals ▪ *primal instincts*

pri·mar·i·ly /praɪˈmerəli/, *Brit* /ˈpraɪmərəli/ *adv* — used to indicate the main purpose of something ▪ *The game is designed primarily* [=mainly] *for children.*

¹**pri·ma·ry** /ˈpraɪˌmeri, *Brit* ˈpraɪməri/ *adj*, *always before a noun* **1 a** : most important : MAIN ▪ *our primary objective/goal* **b** : most basic or essential ▪ *primary needs/responsibilities* **2** : happening or coming first ▪ *We just started our primary flight training.* **3** : not coming from or dependent on something else ▪ *The reporter used both primary and secondary sources.* **4** *chiefly Brit* : ELEMENTARY 2 ▪ *primary education/teachers*

²**primary** *n*, *pl* **-ries** [*C*] *US* : an election in which members of the same political party run against each other for the chance to be in a more important election ▪ *a presidential primary*

primary care *n* [*U*] : medical care from a doctor who sees a patient first and provides basic treatment ▪ *(US) a primary care physician*

primary color (*US*) *or Brit* **primary colour** *n* [*C*] : one of the three colors red, yellow, or blue

primary school *n* [*C/U*] : a school for young children ▪ *She goes to (a) primary school.*

pri·mate *n* [*C*] **1** /ˈpraɪˌmeɪt/ : any member of the group of animals that includes humans, apes, and monkeys **2** *or* **Pri·mate** /ˈpraɪmət/ *formal* : the highest ranking person in a country or area in some Christian churches ▪ *the Primate of England and Wales*

¹**prime** /ˈpraɪm/ *adj*, *always before a noun* **1** : most important ▪ *the prime suspect in the case* **2** : of the highest quality or value ▪ *prime beef/farmland* ▪ *The melting of ice caps is a prime example* [=a very good example] *of the effects of global warming.* **3** : very likely to be chosen for something, to experience something, etc. ▪ *a prime target for criticism* ▪ *He was a prime candidate for* [=he was someone who was likely to have] *a heart attack.*

²**prime** *n* [*singular*] : the most active or successful time of a person's life ▪ *She's still in her prime.* ▪ *Their pitcher is past his prime.* [=is not as good as he was in the past]

³**prime** *vb* **primed; prim·ing** [*T*] **1** : to make (someone) ready to do something ▪ *They are primed for battle.* **2** : to make (something) ready for use ▪ *prime a bomb/gun* ▪ *prime a pump* ▪ *prime an engine* **3** : to paint (a surface) with special paint in order to prepare it for the final layer of paint ▪ *We primed and painted the walls.*

prime meridian *n* — **the prime meridian** : an imaginary line that runs from the North Pole to the South Pole through Greenwich, England

prime minister *or* **Prime Minister** *n* [*C*] : the head of the government in some countries ▪ *the Prime Minister of England* — *abbr.* PM

prime number *n* [*C*] *mathematics* : a number (such as 2, 3, or 5) that can only be exactly divided by itself and by 1

¹**prim·er** /ˈprɪmɚ, *Brit* ˈpraɪmə/ *n* [*C*] **1** *chiefly US* : something that gives basic information on a subject ▪ *The article is a good primer on economics.* **2** : a small book that helps teach children how to read — compare ²PRIMER

²**prim·er** /ˈpraɪmɚ/ *n* [*C/U*] : a kind of paint that is used to prepare a surface for a final layer of paint of a different paint — compare ¹PRIMER

prime rate *n* [*C*] : the lowest interest rate

that banks will give to people who borrow money from them

prime time *n* [U] **1 a** : the time when the largest number of people are watching TV • *a prime-time program* **b** : the TV shows that are on during prime time • *He's the best actor in prime time.* **2** *chiefly US, informal* : the highest or most difficult level of use • *This software isn't ready for prime time.* [=it is not yet good enough to be used]

pri·me·val *also Brit* **pri·mae·val** /praɪˈmiːvəl/ *adj* : very old or ancient • *primeval forests*

prim·i·tive /ˈprɪmətɪv/ *adj* : of, belonging to, or seeming to come from the very ancient past • *the time when primitive man first learned to use fire* • *primitive animals/plants* **2** : not having a written language, advanced technology, etc. • *primitive societies* **3** : very simple and basic • *primitive tools/technology* **4** : not based on reason • *primitive instincts/fears*

pri·mor·di·al /prɪˈmoɚdijəl/ *adj, formal* : very ancient : PRIMEVAL • *primordial forests*

primp /ˈprɪmp/ *vb* [T/I] : to make small changes to your clothes, hair, etc., while looking in a mirror • *She was primping (herself) in front of the mirror.*

prim·rose /ˈprɪmˌroʊz/ *n* [C] : a small plant with yellow, white, pink, or purple flowers

prince /ˈprɪns/ *n* [C] **1** : the son or grandson of a king or queen **2** : a male ruler in some countries • *the Prince of Monaco*

prince·ly /ˈprɪnsli/ *adj* **1** : very large or impressive • *a princely gift* • *a princely sum* [=a large amount of money] **2** : of, relating to, or suitable for a prince • *princely duties*

prin·cess /ˈprɪnsəs, *Brit* ˌprɪnˈsɛs/ *n* [C] **1** : a daughter or granddaughter of a king or queen **2** : the wife of a prince • *Princess Diana* **3** *informal + sometimes disapproving* : a girl or woman who is treated with special attention • *a pop music princess*

¹prin·ci·pal /ˈprɪnsəpəl/ *adj, always before a noun* : most important : CHIEF • *the soup's principal ingredients* — **prin·ci·pal·ly** /ˈprɪnsəpəli/ *adv* • *He is principally* [=mainly] *known as a poet.*

²principal *n* [C] **1 a** *US* : the person in charge of a public school • *a high school principal* **b** *Brit* : the person in charge of a university **2** : an amount of money that is put in a bank or lent to someone • *The payment covers the interest on our loan and some of the principal.* **3** : the most important person in a group • *One of the principals in the plot was arrested.* • *the ballet's two principals* [=lead dancers]

prin·ci·pal·i·ty /ˌprɪnsəˈpæləti/ *n, pl* **-ties** [C] *formal* : a small area or country that is ruled by a prince

principal parts *n* [plural] *grammar* : the main forms of a verb • *The principal parts of the verb "write" include the infinitive "write," the past tense "wrote," the past participle "written," and the present participle "writing."*

prin·ci·ple /ˈprɪnsəpəl/ *n* **1** [C/U] : a

moral rule or belief that influences your actions • *It's against my principles to cheat.* [=I believe that cheating is wrong] • *She refused to steal as a matter of principle.* [=because of her beliefs] **2** [C] : an idea that forms the basis of something • *economic principles* **3** [C] : a law or fact of nature that explains how or why something happens • *the basic principles of magnetism* — **in principle 1** — used to say that something should be possible according to what is known • *In principle, it should work perfectly.* **2** : in a general way and without giving attention to details • *They accepted the offer in principle.*

prin·ci·pled /ˈprɪnsəpəld/ *adj* : having, based on, or relating to strong beliefs about what is right and wrong • *a principled person* [=a person who tries to do what is morally right]

¹print /ˈprɪnt/ *vb* **1** [T/I] : to use a printer to cause (words, images, etc.) to appear on paper • *We printed 50 invitations/photos.* • *Your receipt is printing now.* • *printed documents* **2** [T] : to use a printing press to produce (books, newspapers, etc.) • *They printed 10,000 copies of the book.* **3** [T] : to include (something) in a book, newspaper, etc. • *Her picture was printed in a magazine.* **4** [T/I] : to write (something) using separate letters that do not join together • *Print your name below your signature.* — **print out** *also* **print off** [phrasal vb] **print (something) out/off** *or* **print out/off (something)** : to produce a paper copy of (a document that is on a computer) • *He printed out 200 copies.*

²print *n* **1** [U] : the process of making a book, magazine, etc. • *Her first novel is still in print.* [=being printed for sale] • *His book is out of print.* [=no longer being printed] **2** [U] : the letters, numbers, or symbols used in printing something • *books with large print* **3** [C] : a photograph that is printed on paper • *black-and-white prints* **4** [C] **a** : FINGERPRINT • *Police dusted the house for prints.* **b** : FOOTPRINT • *a muddy print* **5** [C] : cloth that has a pattern printed on it • *a floral print dress*

³print *adj, always before a noun* : of, relating to, or writing for books, magazines, newspapers, etc. • *print ads/journalism*

print·able /ˈprɪntəbəl/ *adj* **1** : suitable to be printed or published • *His exact words are not printable.* [=they are too offensive to be printed] **2** : able to be printed by using a computer's printer • *a Web site with printable maps*

print·er /ˈprɪntɚ/ *n* [C] **1** : a machine used for printing documents, photographs, etc. **2** : a person or company that prints books, magazines, etc.

print·ing /ˈprɪntɪŋ/ *n* **1** [U] : the process of producing books, magazines, etc. • *a printing error* **2** [C] : the act or process of printing a set number of copies of a book at one time • *The book is in its second printing.*

printing press *n* [C] : a machine that prints books, magazines, etc.

print·out /ˈprɪntˌaʊt/ *n* [C] : a copy of a

document produced by a printer ▪ *a computer printout*

¹pri·or /ˈprajɚ/ *adj, always before a noun* : existing earlier in time : PREVIOUS ▪ *The job requires prior experience in sales.* ▪ *We have a prior commitment that night.* — **prior to** : before (a time, event, etc.) ▪ *They were married just prior to the war.*

²prior *n* [C] 1 : a monk who is the head of a religious house or order 2 *US, informal* : a previous time of being arrested for or found guilty of a crime ▪ *He has two priors* [=has been arrested/convicted twice before] *for robbery.*

pri·or·ess /ˈprajɚrəs/ *n* [C] : a nun who is head of a religious house or order

pri·or·i·tize *also Brit* **pri·or·i·tise** /praɪˈorəˌtaɪz/ *vb* **-tized**; **-tiz·ing** [T/I] : to organize (things) so that the most important thing is dealt with first ▪ *It's difficult to prioritize work, school, and family.*

pri·or·i·ty /praɪˈorəti/ *n, pl* **-ties** 1 [C] : something that is more important than other things and that needs to be done or dealt with first ▪ *a top priority* ▪ *Exercising is not high on her list of priorities.* [=it's not important to her] ▪ *You need to get your priorities straight and go back to school.* [=you need to realize that going back to school is important] 2 [U] : the condition of being the most important thing and therefore coming or being dealt with first ▪ *These problems should be given priority (over others).* [=they should be dealt with first] ▪ *Saving for college has to take priority.*

pri·o·ry /ˈprajɚri/ *n, pl* **-ries** [C] : a place where a group of monks or nuns live

prism /ˈprɪzəm/ *n* [C] : a clear object with three sides that separates the light that passes through it into different colors — often used figuratively to describe a way of looking at or thinking about something that causes you to see or understand it in a different way ▪ *The novel is a history of early 19th-century America told through the prism of one life.*

pris·on /ˈprɪzn/ *n* [C/U] : a building where people are kept usually as punishment for a crime ▪ *a state/federal prison* ▪ *a prison cell/guard* ▪ *a ten-year prison sentence* ▪ *She was sent/sentenced to prison for robbery.* ▪ *He was released from prison.* 2 [C] : a place or situation from which you cannot escape ▪ *Her house became a prison.*

prison camp *n* [C] : a camp where prisoners are kept especially during a war

pris·on·er /ˈprɪznɚ/ *n* [C] 1 : a person who is kept in a prison ▪ *a political prisoner* [=a person in prison because of his or her political beliefs] 2 : a person who has been captured and is being kept somewhere ▪ *They took him prisoner.* = *He was taken prisoner.* [=they captured him and made him their prisoner] ▪ *(figurative) She's a prisoner of* [=she is controlled by] *her fears.* — **take no prisoners** : to deal with your competitors in a very harsh way ▪ *a business man who takes no prisoners*

prisoner of war *n* [C] : a soldier who has been captured during a war by the enemy — called also *POW*

pris·sy /ˈprɪsi/ *adj* **pris·si·er**; **-est** *informal + disapproving* : caring too much about dressing and behaving properly ▪ *She's too prissy to wear jeans.* — **pris·si·ness** /ˈprɪsinəs/ *n* [U]

pris·tine /ˈprɪˌstiːn/ *adj* 1 : in perfect condition : completely clean, fresh, neat, etc. ▪ *Her office is always pristine.* ▪ *The car is in pristine condition.* [=it looks the way it did when it was new] 2 : not changed by people ▪ *a pristine forest*

pri·va·cy /ˈpraɪvəsi, *Brit* ˈprɪvəsi/ *n* [U] : the state of being alone ▪ *She went upstairs for some privacy.* 2 : the state of being away from public attention ▪ *The search was an invasion of (her) privacy.* [=it did not respect her privacy]

¹pri·vate /ˈpraɪvət/ *adj* 1 : belonging to one person or group : not public ▪ *a private beach/club/jet* 2 : not relating to a person's official position or job ▪ *He kept his public and private life separate.* 3 a : not known by the public or by other people : SECRET ▪ *private dealings/meetings* b : not telling others about yourself ▪ *He's a very private person.* 4 : away from other people ▪ *Let's go somewhere private.* 5 : always before a noun : not holding a public or elected office ▪ *private individuals/citizens* 6 a : not paid for or controlled by the government ▪ *a private hospital/college* b : not having stocks traded on the open market ▪ *a private company* 7 : involving or done with a single person rather than a group ▪ *private piano lessons* — **pri·vate·ly** *adv*

²private *n* 1 [C] : a person of the lowest rank in the U.S. or British Army or the U.S. Marines 2 [*plural*] *informal* : PRIVATE PARTS — **in private** : in a private place ▪ *They spoke in private.* [=privately] ▪ *The group meets in private.*

private enterprise *n* [U] : FREE ENTERPRISE

private investigator *n* [C] : someone who works as a detective and who is not a member of a police force — called also *private detective, (informal) private eye*

private parts *n* [*plural*] *informal* : a person's external sexual organs ▪ *A cloth covered his private parts.*

private practice *n* [C/U] : a business of a lawyer, doctor, etc., that is not controlled by the government or a larger company ▪ *She left the hospital clinic and now has a private practice.* ▪ *a lawyer in private practice*

private school *n* [C] : a school that does not get money from the government

private sector *n* [*singular*] : the part of an economy which is not controlled or owned by the government ▪ *businesses in the private sector*

pri·va·tion /praɪˈveɪʃən/ *n* [C/U] *formal* : a lack or loss of the basic things that people need to live properly ▪ *economic privation*

pri·vat·ize *also Brit* **pri·vat·ise** /ˈpraɪvəˌtaɪz/ *vb* **-ized**; **-iz·ing** [T] : to remove (something) from government control and place it in private control or ownership ▪ *privatizing the health-care system* — **pri·vat·i·za·tion** *also Brit* **pri·vat·i·sa-**

tion /ˌpraɪvəˈzeɪʃən, Brit ˌpraɪvəˌtaɪˈzeɪʃən/ n [U]

priv·et /ˈprɪvət/ n [U] : a bush that is often used for hedges

¹**priv·i·lege** /ˈprɪvlɪdʒ/ n **1** [C] : a right or benefit that is given to some people and not to others ▪ Health care should be a right and not a privilege. **2** [singular] : an opportunity to do something that makes you proud ▪ I had the privilege of knowing your father. **3** [U] : the advantage that wealthy and powerful people have in a society ▪ sons of privilege [=sons from wealthy families] **4** [U] : the right to keep important information private ▪ attorney-client privilege [=the right an attorney has to keep information shared by a client secret] **5** [U] Brit : the right to say or do something without being punished for it ▪ parliamentary privilege

²**privilege** vb **-leged; -leg·ing** [T] formal : to give an advantage that others do not have to (someone or something) ▪ The tax laws unfairly privilege the rich.

privileged adj **1** : having special rights or advantages that most people do not have ▪ wealthy, privileged people ▪ Only the privileged few can become members of the club. ▪ I was privileged to be [=I had the good fortune of being] part of the winning team. **2** law : known only by the people who need to know ▪ privileged information

privy /ˈprɪvi/ adj — **privy to** : allowed to know about (something secret) ▪ I wasn't privy to [=I didn't know about] their plans.

Privy Council n — **the Privy Council** : the group of people chosen by the British king or queen to serve as advisers

¹**prize** /ˈpraɪz/ n [C] **1** : something that is won in a contest or given as an award ▪ He won first/second/third prize. ▪ The grand prize [=the best prize] was $5000. **2** : something that is very valuable or desirable ▪ the prize of the museum's collection

²**prize** adj, always before a noun **1 a** : given as an award or prize ▪ prize money **b** : winning a prize ▪ the prize pig .**2** : very impressive : deserving a prize ▪ a prize student

³**prize** vb **prized; priz·ing** [T] **1** : to value (someone or something) very highly ▪ I prize our friendship. ▪ prized possessions **2** also Brit **prise** : to open or move (something) with a tool ▪ prize [=(US) pry] the lid off a jar

prize·fight /ˈpraɪzˌfaɪt/ n [C] : a fight between two professional boxers for money — **prize·fight·er** /ˈpraɪzˌfaɪtɚ/ n [C] — **prize·fight·ing** /ˈpraɪzˌfaɪtɪŋ/ n [U]

prize·win·ner /ˈpraɪzˌwɪnɚ/ n [C] : someone or something that wins a prize — **prize·win·ning** /ˈpraɪzˌwɪnɪŋ/ adj ▪ a prizewinning recipe

¹**pro** /ˈproʊ/ n, pl **pros** [C] **1** : a reason to do something — usually plural ▪ The pros outweigh the cons. [=there are more advantages than disadvantages] **2** : ²PROFESSIONAL **2** ▪ tennis/golf pros ▪ He turned pro. [=he became a professional] **3** : ²PROFESSIONAL **3** ▪ She handled the crisis like an old pro. — **the pros** US, in-

formal : the professional level of competition in a sport ▪ He is playing in the pros now.

²**pro** adv : in favor of something ▪ Much was written pro and con about the law. [=both for and against the law]

³**pro** adj, always before a noun : ¹PROFESSIONAL **2** ▪ a pro athlete ▪ pro basketball

pro- prefix : in favor of : supporting ▪ pro-Democracy

pro·ac·tive /proʊˈæktɪv/ adj : controlling a situation by making things happen or by preparing for possible future problems ▪ The city is taking a proactive approach to fighting crime by hiring more police officers. — **pro·ac·tive·ly** adv

pro-am /ˈproʊˈæm/ n [C] : an event or tournament in which both professionals and amateurs compete

prob·a·bil·i·ty /ˌprɑːbəˈbɪləti/ n, pl **-ties 1** [C/U] : the chance that something will happen ▪ The probability of an earthquake is low/high. ▪ There is a low/high probability that you will be chosen. **2** [singular] : something that has a good chance of happening ▪ Rain today is a real probability. **3** [C/U] : a measure of how often an event will happen if something is done repeatedly ▪ the laws of probability — **in all probability** — used to say that something is very likely to happen or be done ▪ In all probability, he will go home today.

prob·a·ble /ˈprɑːbəbəl/ adj : likely to happen or to be true but not certain ▪ a probable result/explanation

probable cause n [U] chiefly US, law : evidence that gives someone a reason to think that a crime was or is being committed ▪ The police had probable cause to arrest him.

prob·a·bly /ˈprɑːbəbli/ adv : very likely ▪ It will probably rain today. ▪ You are probably right. ▪ "Are you going to the picnic?" "Probably (not)."

pro·bate /ˈproʊˌbeɪt/ n [U] law : the process of proving in court that a person's will is valid ▪ Her will was offered for probate.

probate court n [C/U] US, law : a court that proves wills are valid

pro·ba·tion /proʊˈbeɪʃən/ n **1** [U, singular] : a period of time in which a new employee is tested to see if he or she is able to do the job ▪ a three-month probation (period) ▪ I was on probation for three months. **2** [U] law : a period of time in which a criminal is allowed to stay out of prison if he or she behaves well, does not commit another crime, etc. ▪ She was sentenced to one year's probation. ▪ He violated his probation. **3** [U] US : a situation in which a person who has done something bad must behave well in order not to be seriously punished ▪ The student was put/placed on probation.

probation officer n [C] law : a person who watches, works with, and helps criminals who are on probation

¹**probe** /ˈproʊb/ vb **probed; prob·ing 1** [T/I] : to ask a lot of questions in order to find secret or hidden information about someone or something ▪ probing for information **2** [T] **a** : to touch or

reach into (something) with your finger, a tool, etc., to see or find something ▪ *Searchers probed the mud with poles.* **b** : to examine (something) carefully ▪ *She probed the files for evidence.* — **probing** *adj* ▪ *Reporters asked a lot of probing questions.*

²**probe** *n* [C] **1** : a careful examination or investigation of something ▪ *The FBI probe produced new evidence.* **2** : a thin, long instrument used for examining the body **3** : SPACE PROBE

¹**prob·lem** /ˈprɑːbləm/ *n* **1** [C] : something that is difficult to deal with : something that is a source of trouble, worry, etc. ▪ *financial/medical/personal problems* ▪ *She has a weight problem.* [=her weight is not healthy] ▪ *There is one problem with your argument.* ▪ *The problem with you is that you're stubborn.* ▪ *It's not my problem.* [=I am not responsible for dealing with the problem] **2** [*singular*] : a feeling of not liking or wanting to do something ▪ *I don't have a problem with it.* [=it doesn't bother me] ▪ *"He says he won't go." "What's his problem?"* [=why is he being so unreasonable?] **3** [C] : a mathematical question to be solved ▪ *solving a math problem* — **no problem** *also* **not a problem** *informal* — used to say that you are happy to do something or that you are not bothered by something ▪ *"Thanks for your help." "No problem."* ▪ *"I'm sorry to interrupt you." "No problem."*

²**problem** *adj, always before a noun* : difficult to deal with ▪ *a problem child*

prob·lem·at·ic /ˌprɑːbləˈmætɪk/ *also* **prob·lem·at·i·cal** /ˌprɑːbləˈmætɪkəl/ *adj* : difficult to understand, solve, or fix ▪ *a problematic situation*

pro·ce·dure /prəˈsiːdʒɚ/ *n* **1** [C/U] : a series of actions that are done in a certain way or order ▪ *Installing a car battery is a simple procedure.* ▪ *safety procedures* ▪ *court/legal/parliamentary procedure* **2** [C] : a medical treatment or operation ▪ *surgical procedures* — **pro·ce·dur·al** /prəˈsiːdʒərəl/ *adj, formal* ▪ *a procedural matter*

pro·ceed /prouˈsiːd/ *vb* **1** [I] **a** : to continue to do something ▪ *We will proceed according to plan.* ▪ *How should we proceed?* ▪ *Proceed to the next step.* **b** : to continue being done ▪ *The work is proceeding well.* **2** [T] : to do something after you have done something else — often used to describe behavior that is surprising, annoying, etc. ▪ *He said he was in a rush and then proceeded to talk about his vacation.* **3** [I] *formal* : to go or move in a particular direction ▪ *The crowd proceeded toward the exits.*

pro·ceed·ing /prouˈsiːdɪŋ/ *n* **1** [C] *law* : the process of appearing before a court of law so a legal decision can be made ▪ *bankruptcy/divorce/criminal proceedings* **2** [*plural*] **a** : things that are said or done at a meeting, conference, etc. ▪ *She started the proceedings with a brief speech.* **b** *formal* : an official record of the things said or done at a meeting, conference, etc. ▪ *the conference's published proceedings*

pro·ceeds /ˈprouˌsiːdz/ *n* [*plural*] : the total amount of money or profit that is made ▪ *The proceeds from/of the concert went to charity.*

¹**pro·cess** /ˈprɑːˌsɛs, *Brit* ˈprəʊˌsɛs/ *n* [C] **1** : a series of actions that lead to a particular result ▪ *How does the election process work?* ▪ *Learning a language can be a slow process.* **2** : a series of changes that happen naturally ▪ *the aging process* **3** *medical* : something that sticks out of something else ▪ *a bony process on the foot* — **in the process 1** : while doing something ▪ *He scored the goal but was injured in the process.* **2** ◇ If you are **in the process** of doing something, you are doing something that takes a certain amount of time to do. ▪ *I am in the process of buying a house.*

²**process** *vb* [T] **1 a** : to change (something) by preparing, handling, or treating it in a special way ▪ *The food is processed, packaged, and sold.* **b** : to deal with (something) by using a particular method or system ▪ *processing insurance claims* **2** : to take in and use (information) ▪ *Computers process data.* ▪ *I couldn't process* [=*understand*] *what he was saying.*

pro·ces·sion /prəˈsɛʃən/ *n* **1** [C/U] : an organized group or line of people or vehicles that move together slowly as part of a ceremony ▪ *a funeral/wedding procession* **2** [C] : a number of people or things that come or happen one after another : SERIES ▪ *We had a procession of visitors today.*

pro·ces·sion·al /prəˈsɛʃənl̩/ *n* [C] **1** : a piece of music that is played during a procession ▪ *a wedding processional* **2** : PROCESSION 1

pro·ces·sor /ˈprɑːˌsɛsɚ/ *n* [C] **1** : a machine, company, etc., that treats, prepares, or handles something ▪ *a film processor* — see also FOOD PROCESSOR **2** : CPU

pro·choice /prouˈtʃois/ *adj* : believing that women should be able to have abortions ▪ *pro-choice supporters* ▪ *The governor is pro-choice.*

pro·claim /prouˈkleɪm/ *vb* [T] : to declare or announce (something) ▪ *The President proclaimed a national day of mourning.* ▪ *He proclaimed himself emperor.* ▪ *She proclaimed her love for him in a poem.*

proc·la·ma·tion /ˌprɑːkləˈmeɪʃən/ *n* **1** [C/U] : the act of proclaiming something ▪ *the proclamation of martial law* **2** [C] : an official announcement made by a person in power or by a government ▪ *The President issued a proclamation which freed the slaves.*

pro·cliv·i·ty /prouˈklɪvəti/ *n, pl* **-ties** [C] *formal* : a tendency to do something that is usually bad ▪ *She has a proclivity to assume the worst.* ▪ *a proclivity for violence*

pro·cras·ti·nate /prəˈkræstəˌneɪt/ *vb* **-nat·ed; -nat·ing** [I] : to delay doing something until a later time because you do not want to do it, because you are lazy, etc. ▪ *She procrastinated and missed the deadline.* — **pro·cras·ti·na·tion** /prəˌkræstəˈneɪʃən/ *n* [U] — **pro·cras-**

ti·na·tor /prəˈkræstəneɪtə/ n [C]

pro·cre·ate /ˈproʊkriˌeɪt/ vb -at·ed; -at·ing [I] formal : to produce children or offspring • a natural instinct to procreate — **pro·cre·ation** /ˌproʊkriˈeɪʃən/ n [U]

pro·cure /prəˈkjɚ/ vb -cured; -cur·ing [T] formal 1 : to get or obtain (something) • The group is procuring weapons. 2 : to find or provide (a prostitute) for someone • illegally procuring women for wealthy clients — **pro·cure·ment** /prəˈkjɚmənt/ n [U] • the procurement of a license

¹**prod** /ˈprɑːd/ vb prod·ded; prod·ding 1 [T/I] : to push someone or something with your finger or a pointed object : POKE • He prodded (at) the snake with a stick. 2 [T] : to persuade or try to persuade (someone) to do something • She was prodded into staying. — **prodding** n [U]

²**prod** n [C] 1 a : the act of pushing someone or something with your finger or a pointed object : POKE • She gave him a prod in the back. b : something (such as a stick) that is used to prod an animal — see also CATTLE PROD 2 : something said or done to encourage or remind someone to do something • He needed a few prods to remember his lines.

prod·i·gal /ˈprɑːdɪgəl/ adj, always before a noun, formal : carelessly and foolishly spending money, time, etc. • a prodigal spender • the return of a **prodigal son/daughter** [=a son/daughter who leaves to do things that his or her parents do not approve of but then feels sorry and returns home]

pro·di·gious /prəˈdɪdʒəs/ adj, formal 1 : very impressive • a prodigious achievement 2 : very big • a prodigious amount — **pro·di·gious·ly** adv, formal

prod·i·gy /ˈprɑːdədʒi/ n, pl -gies [C] : a young person who is unusually talented in some way • a tennis/math prodigy

¹**pro·duce** /prəˈduːs, Brit prəˈdjuːs/ vb -duced; -duc·ing 1 [T] a : to make (something) especially by using machines • The factory produces [=manufactures] steel. b : to make or create (something) by a natural process • The tree produces small apples. 2 [T] : to cause (a particular result or effect) • The insect bite produced a rash. 3 [T] : to be the place where (something or someone) comes from • The college produced some well-known scientists. 4 [T/I] : to be in charge of making and providing money for (a movie, record, etc.) • She produces and directs (plays). 5 [T] a : to cause (something) to be seen • He produced his ID for the guard. b : to provide (something that is wanted or needed) • They produced evidence that proved she was guilty.

²**pro·duce** /ˈproʊˌduːs, Brit ˈprɒˌdjuːs/ n [U] : fresh fruits and vegetables • local produce

pro·duc·er /prəˈduːsɚ, Brit prəˈdjuːsə/ n [C] 1 : someone who produces a movie, record, etc. • a record producer 2 : someone or something that makes particular goods or products • wine/oil producers

prod·uct /ˈprɑːˌdʌkt/ n 1 [C/U] : something that is made or grown to be sold or used • dairy/software products • (technical) We need to sell more product. 2 [C] : something that is the result of a process • This book is the product of many years of hard work. • The finished/end product was a beautiful vase. 3 [C] : someone or something that is produced or influenced by a particular environment or experience • She is a product of good parenting. 4 [C] mathematics : the number that is the result of multiplying two or more numbers • 15 is the product of 3 and 5.

pro·duc·tion /prəˈdʌkʃən/ n 1 [U] a : the process of making or growing something for sale or use • steel production • The car is in production. = The car has gone into production. [=the car is being made] b : the process of making something naturally • the body's production of insulin c : the process of making a movie, record, etc. • a job in TV production 2 [C] : a play, movie, etc., that is presented to the public • the director's next production 3 [U] : the amount of something that is made or grown for sale or use • a rise in oil production 4 [singular] informal : something that is very difficult or complicated • It's a major production to get the kids ready for school in the morning.

production line n [C] : a line of machines, workers, etc., in a factory that builds a product by passing work from one station to the next

pro·duc·tive /prəˈdʌktɪv/ adj 1 : doing or achieving a lot • a productive day/meeting/worker 2 : producing or able to produce a lot of something • productive farmland — **pro·duc·tive·ly** adv

pro·duc·tiv·i·ty /ˌproʊdəkˈtɪvəti/ n [U] : the rate at which goods are produced or work is completed • trying to improve worker productivity

Prof. abbr professor • Prof. Smith

pro·fane /proʊˈfeɪn/ adj, formal 1 : having or showing disrespect for religious things • profane language 2 : not religious or spiritual • sacred and profane customs

pro·fan·i·ty /proʊˈfænəti/ n, pl -ties 1 [U] : offensive language • He doesn't tolerate profanity. 2 [C] : an offensive word • a song filled with profanities

pro·fess /prəˈfɛs/ vb [T] formal 1 : to say or declare (something) openly • They profess loyalty to the king. • He is a professed enemy of the state. [=he has openly said that he is an enemy of the state] 2 : to say that you are, do, or feel something when other people doubt what you say • She professes to be our friend.

pro·fes·sion /prəˈfɛʃən/ n 1 [C] : a type of job that requires special education or skill • the legal profession • His profession is carpentry. 2 [singular] : the people who work in a particular profession • a member of the medical/teaching profession 3 [C] formal : the act of declaring or saying something openly • a profession of religious faith

¹**pro·fes·sion·al** /prəˈfɛʃənl/ adj 1 al-

ways before a noun **a** : relating to a job that requires special education, training, or skill ▪ *Do you have any professional experience?* ▪ *professional photographers* **b** : done or given by a person who has a particular profession ▪ *You need professional help/advice.* **2** *always before a noun* **a** : paid to participate in a sport or activity ▪ *professional athletes* ▪ *a golfer who has turned professional* **b** : done by people who are paid to play or compete ▪ *professional sports* **3** : having or showing skill, good judgment, and polite behavior ▪ *He deals with customers in a very professional way.* ▪ *The presentation was very professional.* — **pro·fes·sion·al·ism** /prəˈfɛʃənəˌlɪzəm/ *n* [*U*] ▪ *I admire her professionalism.* [=her professional skill, good judgment, etc.] — **pro·fes·sion·al·ly** /prəˈfɛʃənəli/ *adv* ▪ *a professionally trained staff* ▪ *He plays soccer professionally.* ▪ *The problem was dealt with very professionally.*

²**professional** *n* [*C*] **1** : someone who does a job that requires special training, education, or skill ▪ *She is a medical/legal professional.* **2** : someone who is paid to participate in a sport or activity ▪ *amateurs and professionals* **3** : someone who has a lot of experience or skill in a particular job or activity ▪ *She handles stress like a professional.*

pro·fes·sor /prəˈfɛsɚ/ *n* [*C*] : a teacher especially of the highest rank at a college or university ▪ *a chemistry/history professor* ▪ *Professor Jones teaches the class.* — **pro·fes·so·ri·al** /ˌproʊfəˈsorijəl/ *adj*

pro·fes·sor·ship /prəˈfɛsɚˌʃɪp/ *n* [*C*] : the job or duties of a professor ▪ *She accepted a professorship at the college.*

prof·fer /ˈprɑːfɚ/ *vb* [*T*] *formal* : to offer or give (something) to someone ▪ *He proffered advice on how to proceed.*

pro·fi·cient /prəˈfɪʃənt/ *adj* : good at doing something ▪ *a proficient reader* ▪ *She is proficient in two languages.* — **pro·fi·cien·cy** /prəˈfɪʃənsi/ *n* [*U*] ▪ *a reading proficiency test* [=a test to see how well you can read]

¹**pro·file** /ˈproʊˌfajəl/ *n* **1 a** [*C/U*] : the shape of a head or face that is seen or drawn from the side ▪ *The President's profile appears on the coin.* **b** [*C*] : the shape of something that is seen against a background ▪ *the profile of a boat against a sunset* **2** [*C*] : a brief written description that gives information about someone or something ▪ *I read a profile of her in a magazine.* ▪ *a company profile* ▪ **high/low profile** — used to describe the amount of attention that someone or something is given ▪ *I try to keep a low profile.* [=I try to avoid doing things that will cause people to notice me] ▪ *a job with a high profile*

²**profile** *vb* **-filed; -fil·ing** [*T*] : to write a profile about (someone or something) ▪ *The company was profiled in the magazine.*

profiling *n* [*U*] : the act or practice of regarding people as more likely to commit crimes because of their appearance, race, etc. ▪ *racial profiling*

¹**prof·it** /ˈprɑːfət/ *n* [*C/U*] : money that is

made after all costs and expenses are paid ▪ *The company made/turned a profit this year.* ▪ *a rise/fall/increase/decrease in profits* ▪ *We sold the house at a profit.* [=we made a profit when we sold our house] — **prof·it·less** /ˈprɑːfətləs/ *adj* ▪ *a profitless company*

²**profit** *vb* **1 a** [*I*] : to get an advantage or benefit from something ▪ *Everyone can profit by/from reading this book.* **b** [*T*] : to be an advantage to (someone) ▪ *It would profit him to take some classes.* **2** [*I*] : to earn or get money by or from something ▪ *The company has profited by/from selling its products online.* — **prof·it·abil·i·ty** /ˌprɑːfətəˈbɪləti/ *n* [*U*] — **prof·it·able** /ˈprɑːfətəbəl/ *adj* ▪ *a profitable business* — **prof·it·ably** /ˈprɑːfətəbli/ *adv*

prof·i·teer·ing /ˌprɑːfəˈtirɪŋ/ *n* [*U*] *disapproving* : the act of selling things at very high prices at a time when they are hard to get ▪ *The company was accused of profiteering during the war.* — **prof·i·teer** /ˌprɑːfəˈtiɚ/ *n* [*C*]

profit margin *n* [*C*] : the difference between the cost of buying or making something and the price at which it is sold

profit sharing *n* [*U*] : a system in which employees receive a part of the company's profits

prof·li·gate /ˈprɑːflɪgət/ *adj, formal* : very wasteful ▪ *She is profligate in her spending.* — **prof·li·ga·cy** /ˈprɑːflɪgəsi/ *n* [*U*] — **profligate** *n* [*C*]

pro for·ma /proʊˈfoɚmə/ *adj* : usual or required but having little true meaning ▪ *The meeting was pro forma, since the decision had already been made.*

pro·found /prəˈfaʊnd/ *adj* **1 a** : having or showing great knowledge or understanding ▪ *a profound thinker/insight* **b** : requiring deep thought or wisdom ▪ *profound questions* **2 a** : very strongly felt ▪ *a profound sense of loss* **b** : major or significant ▪ *Computers have made profound changes in our lives.* **3** : absolute or complete ▪ *a profound silence* — **pro·found·ly** *adv* ▪ *profoundly different/important* — **pro·fun·di·ty** /prəˈfʌndəti/ *n, pl* **-ties** [*C/U*] *formal* ▪ *the profundity of his thoughts/sadness*

pro·fuse /prəˈfjuːs/ *adj* : given, produced, or existing in large amounts ▪ *He offered profuse apologies for being late.* ▪ *profuse sweating* — **pro·fuse·ly** *adv* ▪ *He apologized profusely.* — **pro·fu·sion** /prəˈfjuːʒən/ *n* [*U, singular*] *formal* ▪ *a profusion* [=large amount] *of flowers* ▪ *The flowers grow in profusion.*

pro·gen·i·tor /proʊˈdʒɛnətɚ/ *n* [*C*] **1** *formal* : a person who begins something ▪ *the progenitors of modern art* **b** : something that is a model for something else ▪ *a mechanical progenitor of the modern computer* **2** *biology* : ANCESTOR ▪ *wild cats that were the progenitors of the house cat*

prog·e·ny /ˈprɑːdʒəni/ *n, pl* **progeny** [*C*] **1** : the child or descendant of someone ▪ *Many Americans are the progeny of immigrants.* **2** : the young of an animal or plant ▪ *the progeny of an oak tree*

pro·ges·ter·one /prou'dʒɛstə,roun/ n [U] medical : a hormone that occurs in women and female animals

prog·no·sis /prɑg'nousəs/ n, pl **-no·ses** /-'nou,si:z/ [C] **1** : a doctor's opinion about how someone will recover from an illness or injury ▪ Doctors say his prognosis is/isn't good. **2** : a judgment about what is going to happen in the future ▪ a hopeful prognosis about the company's future

prog·nos·ti·ca·tion /prɑg,nɑ:stə'keɪʃən/ n [C] formal : PREDICTION ▪ His prognostications are usually right. — **prog·nos·ti·ca·tor** /prɑg'nɑ:stə,keɪtə/ n [C]

¹**pro·gram** (US) or Brit **pro·gramme** /'prou,græm/ n [C] **1** : a plan of things that are done in order to achieve a specific result ▪ government programs **2** : a set of instructions that tell a computer what to do ▪ He writes computer programs. ✧ In this sense, the spelling program is used in both U.S. and British English. **3** : a thin book or a piece of paper that gives information about a concert, play, etc. **4** : something that is broadcast on TV or radio ▪ a news program **5** US : a course of study ▪ the university's graduate program — **get with the program** informal : to start doing what others need or want you to do ▪ You'd better get with the program if you want to keep your job. — **pro·gram·mat·ic** /,prougrə'mætɪk/ adj, formal ▪ programmatic reforms

²**program** (US) or Brit **programme** vb **-grammed** or **-gramed**; **-gram·ming** or **-gram·ing** **1** [T/I] : to create a program for (a computer) ▪ She programmed the computer to calculate her monthly expenses. ✧ In this sense, the spelling program is used in both U.S. and British English. **b** [T] : to give (a machine) a set of instructions to perform a particular action ▪ program a VCR **2** [T] : to make (a person or animal) behave or think in a particular way ▪ instinctive behaviors that are genetically programmed in animals — **pro·gram·ma·ble** /'prou,græməbəl/ adj

pro·gram·mer /'prou,græmə/ n [C] : a person who creates computer programs

pro·gram·ming /'prou,græmɪŋ/ n [U] **1** : the act or job of creating computer programs **2** : a schedule of TV or radio broadcasts ▪ regular television programming

¹**prog·ress** /'prɑ:grəs, Brit 'prəu,grɛs/ n [U] **1** : movement forward or toward a place ▪ We made slow progress up the mountain. **2** : the process of improving or developing something over a period of time ▪ The project showed slow but steady progress. ▪ We're **making progress.** [=we are moving forward in our work] ▪ Filming is already **in progress.** [=happening or being done]

²**pro·gress** /prə'grɛs/ vb [I] **1** : to move forward in time ▪ It got colder as the day progressed. **2** : to improve or develop over a period of time ▪ The project is progressing slowly. **3** formal : to move forward or toward a place ▪ The caravan progressed slowly across the desert.

pro·gres·sion /prə'grɛʃən/ n [C] **1** : the process of developing over a period of time ▪ the rapid progression of the disease **2** : a sequence or series of actions, events, etc. ▪ a progression of activities

¹**pro·gres·sive** /prə'grɛsɪv/ adj **1** : moving forward ▪ progressive movements **2** : happening or developing gradually ▪ a progressive disease **3** : using or favoring modern ideas especially in politics and education ▪ a progressive candidate/ school **4** grammar : of or relating to the progressive tense of a verb ▪ a progressive verb form — **pro·gres·sive·ly** adv

²**progressive** n **1** [C] : a person who favors modern ideas ▪ social progressives **2** the progressive grammar : PROGRESSIVE TENSE ▪ "Believe" is never used in the progressive.

progressive tense n [C] grammar : a verb tense that is used to refer to an action or a state that is continuing to happen ✧ A progressive verb form in English consists of a form of "be" and the main verb's present participle.

pro·hib·it /prou'hɪbət/ vb [T] **1 a** : to order (someone) not to use or do something — + from ▪ The town prohibits people from smoking in bars. **b** : to say that (something) is not allowed ▪ Alcohol is prohibited in the park. **2** : to make (something) impossible to do ▪ The prison's fence prohibits escape.

pro·hi·bi·tion /,prouə'bɪʃən/ n **1** [U] : the act of not allowing something to be used or done ▪ the prohibition of smoking in bars **2** [C] : a law or order that stops something from being used or done ▪ a prohibition against hitchhiking **3 Prohibition** [U] : the period of time from 1920 to 1933 in the U.S. when it was illegal to make or sell alcohol

pro·hi·bi·tion·ist /,prouə'bɪʃənɪst/ n [C] : someone who supported the laws of Prohibition in the U.S.

pro·hib·i·tive /prou'hɪbətɪv/ adj **1** : so high that people cannot use or buy something ▪ the prohibitive cost of rent **2** US : almost certain to perform, win, etc., in the expected way ▪ She is the prohibitive favorite to win. [=she is almost certain to win] **3** formal : stopping people from using or doing something ▪ prohibitive legislation — **pro·hib·i·tive·ly** adv

¹**proj·ect** /'prɑ:,dʒɛkt/ n [C] **1** : a planned piece of work that has a specific purpose and that requires a lot of time ▪ a research/construction project **2** : a task in school that requires work over a long period of time ▪ a science project **3** US : HOUSING PROJECT ▪ He grew up in the projects.

²**pro·ject** /prə'dʒɛkt/ vb **1** [T] : to plan, calculate, or estimate (something) for a time in the future ▪ The bridge is projected to be finished in the fall. ▪ the projected cost of the project **2** [T] : to cause (light, a picture, a movie, etc.) to appear on a surface ▪ projecting images on/onto a screen **3** [T] : to have or show (a particular quality, image, etc., that can be seen by other people) ▪ He projects strength. **4** [I] : to stick out beyond an edge or sur-

face • *A balcony projects out over the seats below.* **5** [*T*] : to send or throw (something) forward, upward, or outward • *Actors need to project their voices.* [=to speak loudly and clearly] — **project onto** [*phrasal vb*] **project (something) onto** : to imagine that (your ideas, feelings, etc.) are shared by (another person) • *She projected her fears onto him.* [=she thought he had the same fears she had]

pro·jec·tile /prə'dʒɛktajəl/ *n* [*C*] *formal* **1** : something (such as a bullet or rocket) that is shot from a weapon **2** : something (such as a rock) that is thrown as a weapon

pro·jec·tion /prə'dʒɛkʃən/ *n* **1** [*C*] : an estimate of what might happen in the future • *a projection of future expenses* **2** [*C*] : something that sticks out from a surface • *projections on a rock wall* **3** [*U*] : the act or process of projecting something • *the projection of future costs* • *movie projection* • *his projection of strength* • *the projection of your fears onto others*

pro·jec·tion·ist /prə'dʒɛkʃənɪst/ *n* [*C*] : a person who operates a projector in a theater • *a movie projectionist*

pro·jec·tor /prə'dʒɛktɚ/ *n* [*C*] : a machine that projects a movie or picture onto a screen • *a movie/slide projector*

pro·le·tar·i·an /ˌproʊlə'terijən/ *n* [*C*] : a member of the working class — **proletarian** *adj*

pro·le·tar·i·at /ˌproʊlə'terijət/ *n* — **the proletariat** : the working class • *a member of the proletariat*

pro—life /proʊ'laɪf/ *adj* : opposed to abortion • *the pro-life movement* • *She is pro-life.* — **pro—lifer** *n* [*C*]

pro·lif·er·ate /prə'lɪfəˌreɪt/ *vb* **-at·ed; -at·ing** [*I*] : to increase in number or amount quickly • *Problems have proliferated recently.* — **pro·lif·er·a·tion** /prəˌlɪfə'reɪʃən/ *n* [*U, singular*] • *the/a proliferation of nuclear weapons*

pro·lif·ic /prə'lɪfɪk/ *adj* : producing a large amount of something • *a prolific author* [=an author who writes many books] — **pro·lif·i·cal·ly** /prə'lɪfɪkli/ *adv*

pro·lix /proʊ'lɪks/ *adj, formal* : using too many words • *a prolix speech/writer*

pro·logue /'proʊˌlɑːg/ *n* [*C*] : an introduction to a book, play, etc. • *the novel's prologue* • *(figurative) events that were a prologue to war* [=that led to war]

pro·long /prə'lɑːŋ/ *vb* [*T*] : to make (something) continue for a longer time • *Chemotherapy prolonged her life.* — **pro·lon·ga·tion** /proʊˌlɑːŋ'geɪʃən/ *n* [*C/U*] — **prolonged** *adj* • *a prolonged illness* [=an illness that lasts a long time]

prom /'prɑːm/ *n* [*C*] *US* : a formal dance for high school students • *the junior/senior prom* • *the prom queen*

prom·e·nade /ˌprɑːmə'neɪd, ˌprɑːmə'nɑːd/ *n* [*C*] **1** *Brit* : a public place for walking especially along a beach **2** *old-fashioned* : a walk taken in a public place for pleasure • *They went for a promenade around town.* — **promenade** *vb* **-nad·ed; -nad·ing** [*I*] • *promenading along the beach*

prom·i·nent /'prɑːmənənt/ *adj* **1** : important and well-known • *politically prominent families* **2 a** : easily noticed or seen • *He put the award in a prominent place on his desk.* **b** : sticking out in a way that is easily noticed • *a prominent nose/chin* — **prom·i·nence** /'prɑːmənəns/ *n* [*U, singular*] • *She gained prominence* [=became well-known] *in medical circles.* — **prom·i·nent·ly** *adv*

pro·mis·cu·ous /prə'mɪskjəwəs/ *adj, disapproving* **1** : having or involving many sexual partners • *promiscuous sex/behavior/men.* **2** *formal* : not limited in a careful or proper way • *a promiscuous selection of poems* — **pro·mis·cu·i·ty** /ˌprɑːmə'skjuːwəti/ *n* [*U*] • *sexual promiscuity*

¹**prom·ise** /'prɑːməs/ *n* **1** [*C*] : a statement telling someone that you will definitely do something or that something will definitely happen • *I'll be there, and that's a promise.* • *He made a promise to help her.* • *He kept/fulfilled his promise.* [=he did what he said he would do] • *He broke his promise.* = *He went back on his promise.* [=he didn't do what he said he would do] **2** [*U*] : an indication of future success or improvement • *a young artist who shows/holds/has (a lot of) promise* [=who seems talented and likely to do good work in the future] • *Her early novels were full of promise.* [=very promising] **3** [*U, singular*] : a reason to expect that something will happen in the future • *There is (a) promise of better days ahead.*

²**promise** *vb* **-ised; -is·ing 1** [*T/I*] : to make a promise to someone • *He promised (to buy) his son a new bicycle.* • *I promise to be careful.* • *The country has promised further aid.* • *"I won't tell anyone." "Promise?" "Yes, I promise."* **2** [*T*] : to make (something) seem likely • *It promises to be* [=it is expected to be] *a good game.* — **I (can) promise you** — used to emphasize a statement • *He only cares about himself, I promise you.*

promising *adj* : likely to succeed or to be good • *a promising student/debut* — **prom·is·ing·ly** *adv*

prom·is·so·ry note /'prɑːməˌsori-, *Brit* 'prɒməsri-/ *n* [*C*] *business* : a written promise to pay an amount of money before a particular date

pro·mo /'proʊmoʊ/ *n, pl* **-mos** [*C*] *informal* : something (such as a brief film or an appearance) that is used to promote a new product, movie, etc. • *radio promos* • *a promo shoot*

prom·on·to·ry /'prɑːmənˌtori, *Brit* 'prɒməntri/ *n, pl* **-ries** [*C*] : a high area of land or rock that sticks out into the sea

pro·mote /prə'moʊt/ *vb* **-mot·ed; -mot·ing** [*T*] **1 a** : to give (someone) a higher or more important rank or position • *She was promoted to senior editor.* **b** *Brit* : to move (a sports team) to a higher position in a league • *a team promoted to the First Division* **2** : to help (something) happen, develop, or increase • *Good soil promotes plant growth.* • *pamphlets promoting dental hygiene* **3** : to make (something) more popular, well-known, etc. ▪ *promoting a new clothing line —*

pro·mo·tion /prə'mouʃən/ *n* [C/U] ▪ *She was given a promotion.* ▪ *a special promotion to increase car sales* ▪ *the promotion of alternative fuels*

pro·mot·er /prə'mouṭɚ/ *n* [C] **1** : a person or organization that organizes or provides money for a sports event, a concert, etc. ▪ *concert promoters* **2** : a person or organization that helps something to happen, develop, or increase ▪ *a promoter of alternative fuels*

pro·mo·tion·al /prə'mouʃənl/ *adj* : done or used to make people aware of (a new product, book, etc.) and increase its sales or popularity ▪ *promotional displays*

¹**prompt** /'prɑːmpt/ *vb* [T] **1 a** : to cause (someone) to do something ▪ *What prompted you to ask the question?* **b** : to be the cause of (something) ▪ *The evidence prompted an investigation.* **2 a** : to say (something that encourages a person to talk) ▪ *"Tell me more," he prompted.* **b** : to say the lines of a play to (an actor who has forgotten them) ▪ *She was prompted by someone offstage.* **3** *computers* : to show a message that tells (a user) to do something ▪ *The computer/program prompted me to type in a number.* — **prompt·er** *n* [C]

²**prompt** *adj* **1** : done or given without delay ▪ *We got prompt service at the diner.* ▪ *a prompt response* **2** : arriving or doing something without delay ▪ *They were prompt about responding to my request.* — **prompt·ly** /'prɑːmptli/ *adv* ▪ *My request was handled promptly.* ▪ *She arrived promptly at 7:00 p.m.* [=exactly at 7:00 p.m.] — **prompt·ness** *n* [U]

³**prompt** *n* [C] **1** : the lines of a play that are said to an actor who has forgotten them ▪ *She got a prompt from someone offstage.* **2** *computers* : a message that appears on a computer screen asking the user to do something

pro·mul·gate /'prɑːməlˌgeɪt/ *vb* -gat·ed; -gat·ing [T] **1** *formal* : to make (an idea, belief, etc.) known to many people ▪ *The theory was promulgated on the Internet.* **2** *technical* : to make (a new law) known officially and publicly ▪ *The law was promulgated in 1988.* — **pro·mul·ga·tion** /ˌprɑːməlˈgeɪʃən/ *n* [U]

prone /'proun/ *adj* **1** : likely to do, have, or suffer from something ▪ *They are prone to (making) mistakes.* ▪ *She is accident-prone.* [=she has many accidents] **2** : lying with the front of your body facing downward ▪ *lying in a prone position* — **prone·ness** /'prounnəs/ *n* [U] ▪ *proneness to accidents*

prong /'prɑːŋ/ *n* [C] **1** : one of the long points of a fork or similar object **2** : one of the small metal parts of an electrical plug that fit into an outlet

pronged /'prɑːŋd/ *adj* **1** : having a specified number of prongs ▪ *a three-pronged fork/outlet* **2** : having a specified number of parts ▪ *a two-pronged strategy*

pro·noun /'prouˌnaun/ *n* [C] *grammar* : a word (such as *I, he, she, you, it, we,* or *they*) that is used instead of a noun or noun phrase

pro·nounce /prə'nauns/ *vb* -nounced; -nounc·ing **1** [T] **a** : to make the sound of (a word or letter) with your voice ▪ *The "k" in "know" is not pronounced.* [=it is silent] **b** : to say or speak (a word) correctly ▪ *I can't pronounce her name.* **2** [T] *formal* **a** : to say or announce (something) in an official or formal way ▪ *The judge pronounced sentence.* [=stated the punishment for a criminal] **b** : to say or state that (someone or something) is something in an official or definite way ▪ *I now pronounce you husband and wife.* [=I now declare that you are married] ▪ *She pronounced the party a success.* [=she said that the party was a success] ▪ *He was pronounced dead upon arrival at the hospital.* **3** [I] *formal* **a** : to state an opinion on something ▪ *a grammarian who pronounces on/upon questions of proper English* **b** : to give a judgment for or against someone or something ▪ *The judge pronounced for the defendant.* — **pro·nounce·able** /prə'naunsəbəl/ *adj* ▪ *an easily pronounceable name*

pro·nounced /prə'naunst/ *adj* : very noticeable ▪ *a pronounced limp* ▪ *The symptoms of her disease are pronounced.*

pro·nounce·ment /prə'naunsmənt/ *n* [C] *formal* : an official public statement ▪ *pronouncements on government policy*

pron·to /'prɑːnˌtou/ *adv, informal* : without delay : right away ▪ *I need you there pronto.*

pro·nun·ci·a·tion /prəˌnʌnsiˈeɪʃən/ *n* **1** [C/U] : the way in which a word or name is pronounced ▪ *What is the correct pronunciation of her name?* **2** [singular] : a particular person's way of pronouncing a word or the words of a language ▪ *He has flawless pronunciation.* [=he pronounces words flawlessly]

¹**proof** /'pruːf/ *n* **1** [U] : something which shows that something else is true or correct ▪ *He claims he is innocent, but he has no proof.* ▪ *The photo is proof positive* [=definite proof] *that she was there.* ▪ *I'm living proof that success is possible.* [=my success shows that other people can succeed too] ▪ *Keep the receipt as proof of purchase.* [=evidence showing that you bought something] **2** [C] **a** : an act or process of showing that something is true ▪ *The burden of proof* [=the need to show that something is true] *is on the case's prosecutors.* **b** *mathematics* : a test which shows that a calculation is correct **3** [C] *technical* : a copy of something that is going to be printed which is examined and used to make corrections before the final printing is done ▪ *He edited the proofs of the manuscript.* **4.** [U] : a measurement of how much alcohol is in an alcoholic drink ▪ *The whiskey is 80 proof.* — **the proof is in the pudding** see PUDDING

²**proof** *adj, formal* : designed or made to prevent or protect *against* something harmful ▪ *waterproof* ▪ *bulletproof*

proof·read /'pruːfˌriːd/ *vb* -read /-ˌrɛd/; -read·ing [T] : to read and correct mistakes in (a piece of writing) ▪ *Proofread* the essay carefully. — **proof·read·er** *n* [C]

¹**prop** /'prɑːp/ *vb* **propped; prop·ping** [T] : to support (something) by placing it against something else or by placing something under it ▪ *The window was propped open.* — **prop up** [*phrasal vb*] **prop up (something or someone)** *or* **prop (something or someone) up** 1 : to stop (something) from falling or slipping by placing something under or against it ▪ *We propped up the fence with rocks.* 2 : to help or support (someone) ▪ *His faith props him up in times of crisis.*

²**prop** *n* [C] 1 a : something that is used to support something and keep it in position ▪ *We used rocks as props to keep up the fence.* b : someone or something that helps or supports someone or something else ▪ *His faith is his prop during a crisis.* 2 : an object that is used by actors or as part of a scene in a play, movie, etc. ▪ *They use props in their comedy routine.* 3 *informal* : PROPELLER

pro·pa·gan·da /ˌprɑːpə'gændə/ *n* [U] : ideas that are often false or exaggerated and that are spread to help a cause, a government, etc. ▪ *The report was nothing but propaganda.* — **pro·pa·gan·dist** /ˌprɑːpə'gændɪst/ *n* [C] — **pro·pa·gan·dis·tic** /ˌprɑːpəˌgæn'dɪstɪk/ *adj*

pro·pa·gan·dize *also Brit* **pro·pa·gan·dise** /ˌprɑːpə'gænˌdaɪz/ *vb* **-dized; -diz·ing** [T/I] *formal* : to spread propaganda ▪ *movies that propagandize for the state*

prop·a·gate /'prɑːpəˌgeɪt/ *vb* **-gat·ed; -gat·ing** 1 [T] *formal* : to make (an idea, belief, etc.) known to many people ▪ *The group propagates its doctrine on the Web.* 2 [T/I] *technical* : to produce (a new plant) ▪ *ways to propagate plants without seeds* — **prop·a·ga·tion** /ˌprɑːpə'geɪʃən/ *n* [U] — **prop·a·ga·tor** /'prɑːpəˌgeɪtə/ *n* [C] ▪ *a propagator of new ideas*

pro·pane /'proʊˌpeɪn/ *n* [U] : a gas used for cooking and heating

pro·pel /prə'pɛl/ *vb* **-pelled; -pel·ling** [T] : to push or drive (someone or something) in a particular direction ▪ *The train is propelled by steam.* ▪ *(figurative) The song propelled the band to fame.*

pro·pel·lant *also* **pro·pel·lent** /prə-'pɛlənt/ *n* [C/U] *technical* 1 : a gas under pressure in a can that is used to spray out the can's contents 2 : a fuel used to make something go forward ▪ *rocket propellant*

pro·pel·ler /prə'pɛlə/ *n* [C] : a device with two or more blades that turn quickly and cause a ship or aircraft to move

pro·pen·si·ty /prə'pɛnsəti/ *n, pl* **-ties** [C] *formal* : a strong natural tendency to do something ▪ *They have a propensity for/to-ward violence.* [=*they are violent*] ▪ *a propensity to complain*

prop·er /'prɑːpə/ *adj* 1 a : correct according to social or moral rules ▪ *proper behavior* ▪ *It is not proper to speak/behave that way.* b : behaving in a socially correct way ▪ *She is a very proper young lady.* 2 *always before a noun* : exactly correct ▪ *proper punctuation* 3 *always before a noun* : right or suitable for some purpose

or situation ▪ *You need to eat a proper meal instead of junk food.* ▪ *Each step must be done in the proper order.* 4 *always after a noun* — used to emphasize that you are referring to the specific thing that is being named ▪ *We live outside the city proper.* [=*close to the city but not in the city*] 5 *always before a noun, Brit* : complete or absolute ▪ *I felt a proper fool.*

prop·er·ly /'prɑːpəli/ *adv* 1 : in an acceptable or suitable way ▪ *The children usually behave properly.* ▪ *The oven is not working properly.* 2 : in an accurate or correct way ▪ *The boxes were not properly labeled.*

proper noun *n* [C] : a word or group of words that is the name of a particular person, place, or thing and that usually begins with a capital letter — called also *proper name*

prop·er·tied /'prɑːpətid/ *adj, formal* : owning a lot of property or land ▪ *a propertied family*

prop·er·ty /'prɑːpəti/ *n, pl* **-ties** 1 [U] : something that is owned by a person, business, etc. ▪ *That book is my property.* [=*I own that book*] ▪ *the loss of personal property* ▪ *The library is public property.* [=*the library is owned by the city, town, or state*] 2 [C/U] : a piece of land often with buildings on it that is owned by a person, business, etc. ▪ *trespassing on private property* ▪ *commercial/residential properties* ▪ *property values/taxes* 3 [C] : a special characteristic of something ▪ *The herb has medicinal properties.* ▪ *the chemical properties of water*

proph·e·cy /'prɑːfəsi/ *n, pl* **-cies** 1 [C] : a statement that something will happen in the future : PREDICTION ▪ *His prophecies have all come true.* 2 [U] : the power or ability to know what will happen in the future ▪ *She has the gift of prophecy.*

proph·e·sy /'prɑːfəˌsaɪ/ *vb* **-sies; -sied; -sy·ing** [T] : to state that something will happen in the future : PREDICT ▪ *The book claims that modern events were prophesied in ancient times.*

proph·et /'prɑːfət/ *n* [C] 1 : a person who delivers messages that are believed to have come from God ▪ *the Prophet Isaiah/Muhammad* 2 : a person who states that something will happen in the future ▪ *a prophet of doom* [=*someone who says that bad things will happen*]

pro·phet·ic /prə'fɛtɪk/ *adj* 1 : correctly stating what will happen in the future ▪ *Her warning was prophetic.* [=*the thing that she warned could happen did happen*] 2 : of or relating to a prophet or to prophecy ▪ *the prophetic books of the Bible* — **pro·phet·i·cal·ly** /prə'fɛtɪkli/ *adv*

¹**pro·phy·lac·tic** /ˌproʊfə'læktɪk, *Brit* ˌprɒfə'læktɪk/ *adj, medical* : designed to prevent disease ▪ *a prophylactic treatment*

²**prophylactic** *n* [C] 1 *medical* : something designed to prevent the spread of disease 2 *US* : CONDOM

pro·pi·ti·ate /proʊ'pɪʃiˌeɪt/ *vb* **-at·ed; -at·ing** [T] *formal* : to make (someone) pleased or less angry by giving or saying something desired : APPEASE ▪ *He made*

an offering to propitiate the angry gods. —
pro·pi·ti·a·tion /prouˌpɪʃiˈeɪʃən/ *n* [U]

pro·pi·tious /prəˈpɪʃəs/ *adj, formal*
: likely to have or produce good results ▪
Now is a propitious time to start a business.

pro·po·nent /prəˈpoʊnənt/ *n* [C] : a person who argues for or supports something ▪ *a proponent of gun control*

pro·por·tion /prəˈpoəʃən/ *n* **1** [C] : an amount that is a part of a whole ▪ *A large proportion of the proceeds are donated to charity.* **2** [C/U] : the relationship that exists between the size, number, or amount of two things ▪ *The proportion of boys to girls in our class is two to one.* [=there are two boys for each girl in our class] **3** [C/U] : the correct or appropriate relationship between the size, shape, and position of the different parts of something ▪ *The garage is not in proportion to the house.* [=the garage is too small/big for the house] ▪ *His ears were drawn out of proportion with his head.* **4** [*plural*] : the size, shape, or extent of something ▪ *the proportions of the room* ▪ *a disaster of biblical/epic proportions* [=a terrible disaster that affected many people] **5** [U] : the importance of something when it is compared to other things ▪ *Let's keep things in proportion.* [=let's not become upset by small things that are not important] ▪ *The story was blown out of proportion.* [=it was treated as something worse or more important than it really was]

pro·por·tion·al /prəˈpoəʃənl/ *adj* **1** : having a size, number, or amount that is directly related to or appropriate for something ▪ *Your share of the profits will be proportional to the amount of work you did.* **2** : having parts that are the appropriate size in relation to each other ▪ *The head was not proportional (to the body).* [=the head was too large/small (for the body)] — **pro·por·tion·al·ly** /prəˈpoəʃənli/ *adv*

pro·por·tion·ate /prəˈpoəʃənət/ *adj* : PROPORTIONAL **1** ▪ *The property tax is proportionate to the size of the house.* — **pro·por·tion·ate·ly** *adv*

pro·por·tioned /prəˈpoəʃənd/ *adj* : having parts that relate in size to the other parts in a particular way ▪ *a well-proportioned body*

pro·pos·al /prəˈpoʊzəl/ *n* **1** [C] : something (such as a plan or suggestion) that is presented to a person or group of people to consider ▪ *They rejected/accepted/considered/approved my proposal.* **2** [U] : the act of presenting a plan, suggestion, etc., to a person or group of people ▪ *the proposal of a new law* **3** [C] : the act of asking someone to marry you ▪ *She accepted his proposal (of marriage).* ▪ *a marriage proposal*

pro·pose /prəˈpoʊz/ *vb* **-posed; -pos·ing** **1** [T] : to suggest (a plan, theory, etc.) to a person or group of people to consider ▪ *The mayor proposed a plan for a new bridge.* ▪ *The senator proposes raising the tax.* ▪ *a proposed tax increase* **2** [T] : to plan or intend to do (something) ▪ *How do you propose to solve this prob-*

lem? **3** [T/I] : to ask someone to marry you ▪ *He proposed (marriage) to his girlfriend.*

¹prop·o·si·tion /ˌprɑːpəˈzɪʃən/ *n* [C] **1** : a plan, offer, etc., that is presented to a person or group of people to consider ▪ *a business proposition* [=proposal] **2** : a statement to be proved, explained, or discussed ▪ *They reject the proposition that humans evolved from apes.* **3** : something that someone intends to do or deal with ▪ *Fixing the car will not be an easy/simple proposition.* [=matter] **4** US : a suggestion for a change in the law on which people must vote ▪ *Proposition 12 passed by a wide margin.*

²proposition *vb* [T] : to offer to have sex with (someone) in a direct way ▪ *He was propositioned by a prostitute.*

pro·pound /prəˈpaʊnd/ *vb* [T] *formal* : to suggest (an idea, theory, etc.) to a person or group of people to consider ▪ *propound a theory*

pro·pri·e·tary /prəˈprajəˌteri, Brit prəˈprajətri/ *adj, formal* **1** : of or like that of an owner ▪ *Investors have a proprietary interest in the land.* **2** : used, made, or sold only by the particular person or company that has the legal right to do so ▪ *a proprietary drug* **3** : kept private by an owner ▪ *the company's proprietary information*

pro·pri·e·tor /prəˈprajətəʳ/ *n* [C] *formal* : a person who owns a business or property ▪ *She is the store's proprietor.*

pro·pri·e·ty /prəˈprajəti/ *n, pl* **-ties** *formal* **1** [U] : behavior that is socially or morally correct and proper ▪ *acting with propriety* **2** [*plural*] : rules of correct social behavior ▪ *When attending a wedding, there are certain proprieties that must be observed.*

props /ˈprɑːps/ *n* [*plural*] US *slang* **1** : something that is said to publicly thank and give special attention to someone ▪ *He gave her props for her help with the project.* **2** : RESPECT ▪ *She earned our props.*

pro·pul·sion /prəˈpʌlʃən/ *n* [U] *technical* : the force that propels something forward ▪ *rocket propulsion* — **pro·pul·sive** /prəˈpʌlsɪv/ *adj*

pro ra·ta /prouˈreɪtə/ *adj, formal* : calculated according to the specific amount that someone has done, used, etc. ▪ *Each investor will receive a pro rata share of the profits.* — **pro rata** *adv* ▪ *They were paid pro rata.*

pro·rate /prouˈreɪt/ *vb* **-rat·ed; -rat·ing** [T] US : to calculate (something) according to the specific amount that someone has done, used, etc. ▪ *We will prorate your monthly rent for the remaining 10 days on your lease.* [=you will pay 10 days' worth of a month's rent]

pro·sa·ic /prouˈzejɪk/ *adj, formal* : dull or ordinary ▪ *a prosaic writing style* — **pro·sa·i·cal·ly** /prouˈzejəkli/ *adv*

pro·scribe /prouˈskraɪb/ *vb* **-scribed; -scrib·ing** [T] *formal* : to not allow (something) ▪ *Hats are proscribed* [=banned] *in school.* — **pro·scrip·tion** /prouˈskrɪpʃən/ *n* [C/U]

prose /ˈprouz/ *n* [U] : writing that is not

poetry • *She writes in clear prose.*

pros·e·cute /ˈprɑːsɪˌkjuːt/ *vb* **-cut·ed; -cut·ing 1** [*T/I*] *law* : to hold a trial against a person who is accused of a crime • *Shoplifters will be prosecuted.* **2** [*T/I*] : to work as a lawyer to try to prove a case against someone accused of a crime • *The case is being prosecuted by the assistant district attorney.* **3** [*T*] *formal* : to continue to do (something) • *the way governments prosecute wars* — **pros·e·cut·able** /ˌprɑːsəˈkjuːtəbəl/ *adj* • *a prosecutable offense* — **pros·e·cu·tion** /ˌprɑːsɪˈkjuːʃən/ *n* [*C/U*] • *The defendant is awaiting prosecution.* • *The* **prosecution** [=the lawyer or lawyers who prosecute in a court case] *called their first witness.* — **pros·e·cu·tor** /ˈprɑːsɪˌkjuːtə/ *n* [*C*] • *a federal prosecutor*

pros·e·ly·tize *also Brit* **pros·e·ly·tise** /ˈprɑːsələˌtaɪz/ *vb* **-tized; -tiz·ing** [*T/I*] *formal + often disapproving* : to try to persuade people to join a religion, cause, or group • *They are encouraged to proselytize (their faith).*

¹pros·pect /ˈprɑːˌspɛkt/ *n* **1** [*U, singular*] : the possibility that something will happen in the future • *There's no/little prospect that they will reach an agreement soon.* **2** [*C*] : an opportunity for something to happen • *employment prospects* **3** [*C*] : someone or something that is likely to succeed or to be chosen • *We went car shopping and found a few prospects.*

²pros·pect /ˈprɑːˌspɛkt, Brit prəˈspɛkt/ *vb* [*I*] : to search an area for gold, minerals, oil, etc. • *Men were prospecting for gold along the river.* — **pros·pec·tor** /ˈprɑːˌspɛktə/ *n* [*C*]

pro·spec·tive /prəˈspɛktɪv/ *adj, always before a noun* **1** : likely to be something specified in the future • *prospective students/employers* **2** *formal* : likely to happen • *The new law has many prospective benefits.*

pro·spec·tus /prəˈspɛktəs/ *n* [*C*] **1** : a printed statement that describes a new business, investment, etc., and that is sent to people who may want to be involved in it or invest in it **2** *chiefly Brit* : a book or document that provides information about a school, business, etc. : BROCHURE

pros·per /ˈprɑːspə/ *vb* [*I*] **1** : to become very successful usually by making a lot of money • *Her business prospered.* **2** : to become very active, healthy, or strong • *The city is prospering.*

pros·per·i·ty /prɑːˈspɛrəti/ *n* [*U*] : the state of being successful usually by making a lot of money • *economic prosperity*

pros·per·ous /ˈprɑːspərəs/ *adj* : having success usually by making a lot of money • *a prosperous town*

pros·tate /ˈprɑːˌsteɪt/ *n* [*C*] : an organ found in men and male animals that produces the liquid in which sperm is carried — called also **prostate gland**

pros·the·sis /prɑːsˈθiːsəs/ *n, pl* **-the·ses** /-ˌsiːz/ [*C*] *medical* : an artificial device that replaces a missing part of the body (such as an arm or leg) — **pros·thet·ic**

/prɑːsˈθɛtɪk/ *adj* • *a prosthetic leg*

¹pros·ti·tute /ˈprɑːstəˌtuːt, Brit ˈprɒstəˌtjuːt/ *n* [*C*] : a person who has sex in exchange for money

²prostitute *vb* **-tut·ed; -tut·ing** [*T*] **1** : to work as a prostitute • *She prostituted herself for drug money.* **2** : to use (something valuable) in a way that is not respectable • *a writer who prostituted his talents by writing commercials* — **pros·ti·tu·tion** /ˌprɑːstəˈtuːʃən, Brit ˌprɒstəˈtjuːʃən/ *n* [*C*]

¹pros·trate /ˈprɑːˌstreɪt/ *adj* **1** : lying with the front of your body turned toward the ground • *She was lying prostrate on the bed.* **2** : so tired, upset, etc., that you are unable to do anything • *He was prostrate with grief.*

²pros·trate /ˈprɑːˌstreɪt, Brit prəˈstreɪt/ *vb* **-trat·ed; -trat·ing** [*T*] **1** : to make (someone) weak or powerless • *He was prostrated* [=overcome] *with/by grief.* — **prostrate yourself** : to lie down with your face turned toward the ground • *They prostrated themselves before the shrine.* — **pros·tra·tion** /prɑːˈstreɪʃən/ *n* [*C/U*]

pro·tag·o·nist /proʊˈtægənɪst/ *n* [*C*] : the main character in a novel, play, movie, etc.

pro·tect /prəˈtɛkt/ *vb* **1** [*T/I*] : to keep (someone or something) from being harmed, lost, etc. • *The jewelry was protected in a safe.* • *The forest is protected by/under federal law.* • *a protected species* • *Sunscreen protects against sunburn.* **2** [*T/I*] : to save (someone) from financial loss caused by fire, injury, damage, etc. • *The insurance protects you against flooding.* **3** [*T*] *sports* : to try to stop opponents from scoring at (your goal) • *She helped protect the goal.*

pro·tec·tion /prəˈtɛkʃən/ *n* **1** [*U*] : the state of being kept from harm, loss, etc. • *the protection of the environment* • *protection from/against disease* • *The witness was placed under police protection.* **2** [*C/U*] : something that keeps a person or thing from being harmed, lost, etc. • *He keeps a gun for protection.* • *legal protections against/from harrassment* **3** [*U*] : a device (such as a condom) that is used during sex to prevent pregnancy or the spread of diseases • *Do you have protection?* **4** [*U*] : insurance against financial loss caused by fire, injury, damage, etc. • *The policy offers fire and theft protection.* — **pro·tec·tive** /prəˈtɛktɪv/ *adj* • *protective clothing/gear* • *She is very protective of her children.* [=she has a strong desire to protect her children] • *The police kept him in protective custody.* [=in jail and away from others so that he would not be harmed] — **pro·tec·tive·ly** *adv* — **pro·tec·tor** /prəˈtɛktə/ *n* [*C*]

pro·tec·tion·ism /prəˈtɛkʃəˌnɪzəm/ *n* [*U*] : the practice of helping businesses in your own country by making laws that limit and tax imports — **pro·tec·tion·ist** /prəˈtɛkʃənɪst/ *n* [*C*] — **protection·ist** *adj*

pro·tec·tor·ate /prəˈtɛktərət/ *n* [*C*] : a small country that is controlled and protected by a larger one

pro·té·gé /ˈproʊtəˌʒeɪ/ *n* [*C*] : a young

person who is taught and helped by someone who has a lot of knowledge and experience • *protégés of great writers*

pro·té·gée /ˈprouṭəˌʒeɪ/ *n* [C] : a woman who is a protégé

pro·tein /ˈprouˌtiːn/ *n* [C/U] : a substance found in foods (such as meat, milk, eggs, and beans) that is an important part of the human diet • *You need more protein in your diet.*

pro tem /ˌprouˈtɛm/ *adv, formal* : for the present time but not permanently • *He is serving as the chairman pro tem.* — **pro tem** *adj* • *the Senate president pro tem*

pro tem·po·re /prouˈtɛmpəri/ *adv, formal* : PRO TEM — **pro tempore** *adj*

¹**pro·test** /prəˈtɛst/ *vb* **1** [T/I] **a** : to show or express strong disagreement or disapproval • *The victim's family protested (at/against) the judge's sentence.* **b** /ˈprouˌtɛst/ : to show or express strong disapproval of something at a public event with other people • *gathering to protest against the war* • *(US) They protested the war.* **2** [T] : to say (something that other people do not agree with) in a forceful way • *"But I'm innocent!" he protested.* — **pro·tes·ta·tion** /ˌprɑːtəˈsteɪʃən/ *n* [C] *formal* • *He was arrested despite his protestations.* — **pro·test·er** *or* **pro·tes·tor** /prəˈtɛstə, ˈprouˌtɛstə/ *n* [C]

²**pro·test** /ˈprouˌtɛst/ *n* **1** [C/U] : something said or done that shows disagreement with or disapproval of something • *He heard protests from the crowd.* • *She was so upset by their decision that she resigned in protest.* **2** [C] : an event at which people gather together to show strong disapproval about something • *holding/staging a protest*

Prot·es·tant /ˈprɑːtəstənt/ *n* [C] : a member of one of the Christian churches that separated from the Roman Catholic Church in the 16th century — **Protestant** *adj* — **Prot·es·tant·ism** /ˈprɑːtəstənˌtɪzəm/ *n* [U]

pro·to·col /ˈprouṭəˌkɑːl/ *n* **1** [C/U] : a system of rules that explain the correct conduct and procedures to be followed in formal situations • *diplomatic protocols* • *a breach of protocol* **2** [C] : a plan for a scientific experiment or for medical treatment • *a treatment protocol* **3** [C] *formal* : a document that describes the details of a treaty • *the Geneva Protocol* **4** [C] *computers* : a set of rules used in programming computers so that they can communicate with each other • *an Internet protocol*

pro·ton /ˈprouˌtɑːn/ *n* [C] *physics* : a part of the nucleus of an atom that has a positive electrical charge

pro·to·type /ˈprouṭəˌtaɪp/ *n* [C] **1** : an original model of something from which other forms are copied or developed • *testing the prototype of the car* **2** : a first or early example that is used as a model for what comes later • *the prototypes of the modern novel*

pro·to·typ·i·cal /ˌprouṭəˈtɪpɪkəl/ *adj* : having the typical qualities of a particular group or kind of person or thing : very typical • *a prototypical gangster*

pro·tract·ed /prouˈtræktəd/ *adj* : continuing a long time • *a protracted battle/war*

pro·trac·tor /prouˈtræktə/ *n* [C] : a device that has the form of a half circle and that is used for drawing and measuring angles

pro·trude /prouˈtruːd/ *vb* **-trud·ed; -trud·ing** [I] : to extend outward beyond an edge or surface • *His jaw protrudes slightly.* — **protruding** *adj* — **pro·tru·sion** /prouˈtruːʒən/ *n* [C/U] • *bony protrusions* • *the protrusion of a disc*

pro·tu·ber·ance /prouˈtuːbərəns, *Brit* prəˈtjuːbərəns/ *n* [C] : a usually rounded part that sticks out from a surface • *a protuberance on the skull*

proud /ˈpraʊd/ *adj* **1 a** : very happy and pleased because of something you have done, someone you know, etc. • *the proud parents of a hero* • *We're so proud of you!* • *I'm proud to say that we won.* • *It did me proud* [=made me feel proud] *to see her graduate.* • *She did herself proud.* [=she did something that she can be proud of] **b** : causing a feeling of pride • *her proudest accomplishment* **2** *disapproving* : having or showing too much pride • *an arrogant and proud person/manner* **3** : not willing to accept help from other people • *She's too proud to accept their charity.* **4** : excellent or impressive • *They have a proud record of public service.* — **proud·ly** *adv* • *He spoke proudly of his son.*

prove /ˈpruːv/ *vb* **proved; proved** *or chiefly US* **prov·en** /ˈpruːvən/; **prov·ing** **1** [T] : to show the existence, truth, or correctness of (something) by using evidence, logic, etc. • *The lawyers failed to prove their case.* • *Suspects are considered innocent until proved/proven guilty.* • *What are you trying to prove by behaving so recklessly?* [=why are you behaving so recklessly?] • *He'll do anything to prove a/his point.* [=to show that he is right] **2** [T] : to show that (someone or something) has a particular quality, ability, etc. • *The evidence proved him (to be) guilty.* **3** [linking vb] : to turn out to be — used to say that something or someone is eventually found to have a particular quality, ability, etc. • *The vaccine has proven (to be) effective.* — **prove yourself** : to show that you are able to do something or to succeed • *She was eager to prove herself in her new job.* — **prov·able** /ˈpruːvəbəl/ *adj*

prov·e·nance /ˈprɑːvənəns/ *n* [C/U] *formal* : the origin or source of something • *an artifact of unknown provenance*

prov·erb /ˈprɑːˌvəb/ *n* [C] : a brief popular saying (such as "Too many cooks spoil the broth") that gives advice or that expresses a popular belief

pro·ver·bi·al /prəˈvəbijəl/ *adj* **1** : of, relating to, or resembling a proverb • *proverbial wisdom* **2** : widely known • *the proverbial beginner's luck* — **pro·ver·bi·al·ly** *adv*

pro·vide /prəˈvaɪd/ *vb* **-vid·ed; -vid·ing** [T] **1 a** : to supply (something that is wanted or needed) • *The school provided uniforms for the band.* • *providing infor-*

mation/services/privacy **b** : to supply (someone or something) *with* something ▪ *The school provided the band with uniforms.* **2** *formal* : to say that something will or should happen ▪ *The contract provides that certain deadlines will be met.* — **provide against** [*phrasal vb*] : to do what is needed to prepare for (something bad that might happen) ▪ *We have extra supplies to provide against a possible scarcity.* — **provide for** [*phrasal vb*] **1** : to cause (something) to be available or to happen in the future ▪ *The grant provides for more research.* **2** : to supply what is needed for (something or someone) ▪ *She works two jobs to provide for her family.*

provided *conj* : IF — used to say that one thing must happen or be true in order for another thing to happen ▪ *You can still get health care, provided (that) you pay the cost yourself.*

Prov·i·dence /'prɑːvədəns/ *n* [*U*] : God or fate thought of as the guide and protector of all people ▪ *putting faith in Providence*

prov·i·den·tial /ˌprɑːvəˈdɛnʃəl/ *adj*, *formal* : LUCKY 2 ▪ *a providential escape* — **prov·i·den·tial·ly** *adv*

pro·vid·er /prəˈvaɪdɚ/ *n* [*C*] **1** : a group or company that provides a specified service ▪ *health-care providers* **2** : a person (such as a mother or father) who earns the money that is needed to support a family ▪ *a good provider*

providing *conj* : IF, PROVIDED ▪ *We'll go tomorrow, providing it doesn't rain.*

prov·ince /'prɑːvəns/ *n* **1** [*C*] : any one of the large parts that some countries are divided into **2** [*C*] : a subject or area of interest that a person knows about or is involved in ▪ *a subject that is/falls outside my province* [=that I do not know about] **3** [*plural*] : the parts of a country that are away from large cities ▪ *life in the provinces*

pro·vin·cial /prəˈvɪnʃəl/ *adj* **1** : of, relating to, or coming from a province ▪ *a provincial accent/official* **2** *disapproving* : not knowing or caring about people and events in other places ▪ *a provincial person/attitude* — **pro·vin·cial·ism** /prəˈvɪnʃəˌlɪzəm/ *n* [*C/U*] *disapproving*

proving ground *n* [*C*] : a place where things or people are tested for the first time ▪ *a proving ground for young actors*

¹**pro·vi·sion** /prəˈvɪʒən/ *n* **1** [*U*] : the act or process of providing something **2** [*C/U*] : something that is done in advance to prepare for something else ▪ **making provision/provisions** for emergencies **3** [*plural*] : a supply of food and other things that are needed ▪ *We brought enough provisions to last a week.* **4** [*C*] : a condition that is included as part of an agreement or law ▪ *Under the provisions of the contract, the work must be completed in two months.*

²**provision** *vb* [*T*] : to supply (someone or something) with food or other provisions ▪ *provisioning a ship*

pro·vi·sion·al /prəˈvɪʒənl/ *adj* : TEMPORARY ▪ *provisional arrangements* — **pro·vi·sion·al·ly** *adv*

pro·vi·so /prəˈvaɪzoʊ/ *n*, *pl* **-sos** [*C*] : a

condition that must be accepted in order for someone to agree to do something ▪ *I'll do it with one proviso: I must work alone.*

prov·o·ca·tion /ˌprɑːvəˈkeɪʃən/ *n* [*C/U*] : an action or occurrence that causes someone to become angry or to begin to do something ▪ *He turns violent at the smallest provocation.*

pro·voc·a·tive /prəˈvɑːkətɪv/ *adj* **1** : causing discussion, thought, argument, etc. ▪ *a provocative book/idea/comment/style* **2** : SEXY ▪ *provocative clothing* — **pro·voc·a·tive·ly** *adv*

pro·voke /prəˈvoʊk/ *vb* **-voked**; **-voking** [*T*] **1** : to make (something) happen ▪ *His remarks provoked both tears and laughter.* **2** : to cause (a person or animal) to become angry, violent, etc. ▪ *The animal will attack if it is provoked.*

pro·vost /'proʊˌvoʊst, *Brit* 'prɒvəst/ *n* [*C*] **1** *US* : an official of high rank at a university **2** *Brit* : the head of a college at a university **3** : the head of a Scottish town

prow /'praʊ/ *n* [*C*] : the front of a ship

prow·ess /'praʊəs/ *n* [*U*] : great ability or skill ▪ *athletic/physical/technical prowess*

¹**prowl** /'praʊl/ *vb* [*T/I*] **1** *of an animal* : to move quietly through an area while hunting ▪ *a tiger prowling (in) the jungle* **2** : to move through a place especially while searching for something often in a quiet or secret way ▪ *I prowled (through) the store looking for sales.*

²**prowl** *n* [*singular*] : an act of moving through a place while searching for something ▪ *reporters* **on the prowl** *for a good story*

prowl·er /'praʊlɚ/ *n* [*C*] : a person who moves through an area in a quiet way in order to commit a crime ▪ *There were reports of a prowler in the neighborhood.*

prox·i·mate /'prɑːksəmət/ *adj*, *always before a noun*, *formal* : related or connected to something in a direct way ▪ *the proximate cause of the fire*

prox·im·i·ty /prɑːkˈsɪmət/ *n* [*U*] : the state of being near ▪ *the proximity of the beach to our hotel* ▪ *The bus stop is located* **in close proximity** *to my home.*

proxy /'prɑːksi/ *n*, *pl* **prox·ies** **1** [*C*] : a person who is given the authority to do something (such as to vote) for someone else ▪ *He served as a proxy for his uncle.* **2** [*U*] : authority that is given to allow a person to act for someone else ▪ *I voted* **by proxy**. [=by giving another person the authority to vote for me]

prude /'pruːd/ *n* [*C*] *disapproving* : a person who is easily shocked or offended ▪ *Don't be such a prude.* — **prud·ery** /'pruːdəri/ *n* [*U*] — **prud·ish** /'pruːdɪʃ/ *adj*

pru·dent /'pruːdnt/ *adj* : having or showing careful good judgment that allows someone to avoid danger or risks ▪ *a prudent person/choice/decision* — **pru·dence** /'pruːdəns/ *n* [*U*] — **pru·dent·ly** *adv* ▪ *investing prudently*

¹**prune** /'pruːn/ *n* [*C*] : a dried plum

²**prune** *vb* **pruned**; **prun·ing** [*T*] **1** : to cut off some of the branches of (a tree or

bush) • *pruning (back) a hedge* **2** : to reduce (something) by removing parts that are not necessary or wanted • *pruning the budget*

pruning shears *n [plural] US* : a garden tool that is used for cutting off branches • *a pair of pruning shears* — called also *(Brit)* secateurs

pru·ri·ent /'prərijənt/ *adj, formal + usually disapproving* : having or showing too much interest in sex • *He took a prurient interest in her personal life.* — **pru·ri·ence** /'prərijəns/ *n [U]*

pry /'praɪ/ *vb* **pries; pried; pry·ing** **1** [*I*] : to try to find out about other people's private lives • *They tried to pry into my past.* **2** [*T*] : to raise, move, or open (something) with a tool • *prying open a door with a crowbar* • *(figurative) I pried the secret out of her.* [=I got her to reveal the secret] — **prying** *adj* • *prying questions*

PS *abbr* **1** postscript — used to introduce an added comment that comes after your name at the end of a letter **2** *US* public school

psalm /'saːm/ *n [C]* : a song or poem used in worship and especially one from the Bible

pseu·do /'suːdoʊ/ *adj, always before a noun, chiefly US* : ¹FAKE • *a pseudo event*

pseu·do·nym /'suːdəˌnɪm/ *n [C]* : a name that someone uses instead of his or her real name • *Mark Twain is the pseudonym of the writer Samuel L. Clemens.* • *She writes under a pseudonym.* [=using a false name] — **pseu·don·y·mous** /suː'dɑːnəməs/ *adj*

psi *abbr* pounds per square inch

pso·ri·a·sis /sə'rajəsəs/ *n [U] medical* : a type of skin disease

psst /'pst/ *interj* — used to get someone's attention • *Psst! I'm over here.*

¹psych /'saɪk/ *vb* [*T*] *informal* : to make (yourself or another person) mentally ready to perform or compete • *He psyched himself (up) for the race.* — **psych out** [*phrasal vb*] **psych (some-one) out** or **psych out (someone)** *informal* : to say or do something to make (someone) feel less confident • *psyching out her competition*

²psych *abbr* psychology

psy·che /'saɪki/ *n [C] formal* : the soul, mind, or personality of a person or group • *the nation's psyche*

psyched /'saɪkt/ *adj, informal* : very eager, ready, or excited about something • *Are you psyched for this party?*

psy·che·del·ic /ˌsaɪkə'dɛlɪk/ *adj* **1 a** — used to describe a drug (such as LSD) that causes you to see things that are not real • *psychedelic drugs* **b** : caused by the use of psychedelic drugs • *psychedelic experiences* **2** : having bright colors, strange sounds, etc. • *psychedelic music/clothing* — **psy·che·del·i·cal·ly** /ˌsaɪkə'dɛlɪkli/ *adv*

psy·chi·a·try /saɪ'kajətri/ *n [U]* : a branch of medicine that deals with mental or emotional disorders — **psy·chi·at·ric** /ˌsaɪki'ætrɪk/ *adj* — **psy·chi·a·trist** /saɪ'kajətrɪst/ *n [C]* • *a drug prescribed by his psychiatrist*

psy·chic /'saɪkɪk/ *adj* **1 a** — used to describe strange mental powers and abilities (such as the ability to predict the future) • *psychic powers/phenomena* **b** : having strange and unnatural mental abilities • *She claims to be psychic.* **2** : of or relating to the mind • *psychic disorders/disturbances* — **psychic** *n [C]* • *She claims to be a psychic.* — **psy·chi·cal·ly** /'saɪkɪkli/ *adv*

psy·cho /'saɪkoʊ/ *n, pl* **-chos** [*C*] *informal* : PSYCHOPATH — **psycho** *adj* • *psycho creeps/killers*

psy·cho·anal·y·sis /ˌsaɪkowə'næləsəs/ *n [U]* : a method of treating mental and emotional problems by having the patient talk about feelings, memories, etc. — **psy·cho·an·a·lyt·ic** /ˌsaɪkouˌænə'lɪtɪk/ *also* **psy·cho·an·a·lyt·i·cal** /ˌsaɪkouˌænə'lɪtɪkəl/ *adj* — **psy·cho·an·a·lyt·i·cal·ly** /ˌsaɪkouˌænə'lɪtɪkli/ *adv*

psy·cho·an·a·lyst /ˌsaɪkou'ænəlɪst/ *n [C]* : a doctor who helps people with mental and emotional problems by talking to them about their dreams, memories, etc.

psy·cho·an·a·lyze *also Brit* **psy·cho·an·a·lyse** /ˌsaɪkou'ænəˌlaɪz/ *vb* **-lyzed; -lyz·ing** [*T*] : to treat (someone) by using psychoanalysis

psy·cho·bab·ble /'saɪkouˌbæbəl/ *n [U] informal* : language that is used by people who talk about mental and emotional problems and that is seen as silly or meaningless

psy·cho·log·i·cal /ˌsaɪkə'lɑːdʒɪkəl/ *also US* **psy·cho·log·ic** /ˌsaɪkə'lɑːdʒɪk/ *adj* **1** : of or relating to the mind : MENTAL • *a psychological condition/disorder* **2** : of or relating to the study of the mind • *psychological analysis/research* — **psy·cho·log·i·cal·ly** /ˌsaɪkə'lɑːdʒɪkli/ *adv*

psy·chol·o·gy /saɪ'kɑːlədʒi/ *n, pl* **-gies** **1** [*U*] : the science or study of the mind and behavior • *She studied psychology in college.* **2** [*C/U*] : the way a person or group thinks • *the psychology of an athlete* — **psy·chol·o·gist** /saɪ'kɑːlədʒɪst/ *n [C]*

psy·cho·path /'saɪkəˌpæθ/ *n [C]* : a person who is mentally ill, who does not care about other people, and who is usually violent • *a murderous psychopath* — **psy·cho·path·ic** /ˌsaɪkə'pæθɪk/ *adj* • *a psychopathic murderer*

psy·cho·sis /saɪ'koʊsəs/ *n, pl* **-cho·ses** /-'koʊˌsiːz/ *[C/U]* : a serious mental illness that makes you behave strangely or believe things that are not true

psy·cho·so·mat·ic /ˌsaɪkousə'mætɪk/ *adj* : caused by mental or emotional problems rather than by physical illness • *psychosomatic symptoms*

psy·cho·ther·a·py /ˌsaɪkou'θerəpi/ *n, pl* **-pies** *[C/U]* : treatment of mental or emotional illness by talking about problems — **psy·cho·ther·a·pist** /ˌsaɪkou'θerəpɪst/ *n [C]*

psy·chot·ic /saɪ'kɑːtɪk/ *adj* : having or relating to a very serious mental illness that makes you act strangely or believe things that are not true • *psychotic behavior/patients* — **psychotic** *n [C]* • *He's a* *psychotic.* — **psy·chot·i·cal·ly** /saɪˈkɑːtɪkli/ *adv*

pt *or* **Pt** *abbr* **1** part **2** pint **3** *pt. or Pt.* point **4** *Pt.* pot

PT *abbr* **1** part-time **2** *US* physical therapist; physical therapy **3** *Brit* physical training

PTA *abbr* Parent-Teacher Association ▪ *a PTA meeting*

Pte *abbr, Brit* private ▪ *Pte Daniel Kyle*

ptero·dac·tyl /ˈterəˈdæktl/ *n* [C] : a large flying dinosaur

PTO *abbr* **1** *US* Parent-Teacher Organization **2** *chiefly Brit* please turn over ✧ *PTO* tells a reader to continue reading on the back of a page.

PTSD *abbr* post-traumatic stress disorder

Pty *abbr, Brit* proprietary ✧ *Pty* is used after the names of companies in Australia, New Zealand, and South Africa. ▪ *Laura Russ Yachts, Pty Ltd*

pub /ˈpʌb/ *n* [C] : a building where alcoholic drinks and often food are served ▪ *an Irish pub*

pub. *abbr* published; publisher; publishing

pub crawl *n* [C] *informal* : a visit to several or many pubs or bars in one night

pu·ber·ty /ˈpjuːbəti/ *n* [U] : the period of life when a person's sexual organs mature ▪ *reaching/entering puberty*

pu·bes·cent /pjuˈbɛsn̩t/ *adj* : beginning to physically develop into an adult ▪ *pubescent boys/girls*

pu·bic /ˈpjuːbɪk/ *adj, always before a noun* : of, relating to, or near the sexual organs ▪ *pubic hair*

¹pub·lic /ˈpʌblɪk/ *adj* **1** *always before a noun* : of, relating to, or affecting all or most of the people of a country, state, etc. ▪ *public opinion/outrage* ▪ *public policy* [=government policies that affect the whole population] ▪ *the director of public affairs* [=work involving activities that a company does for the public] **2** *always before a noun* **a** : of, relating to, paid for by, or working for a government ▪ *She was elected to a public office.* ▪ *public education/housing* **b** : supported by money from people and the government rather than by commercials ▪ *public television/radio* **3 a** : able to be used by anyone ▪ *a public library/restroom/beach* ▪ *public property* ▪ *a public meeting* **b** : able to be seen or heard by many people ▪ *a public apology/performance* **4** : known to many people ▪ *her private life and public life* ▪ *The scandal ruined his public image.* [=caused many people to have a bad opinion of him] ▪ *a public figure* [=a well-known person] ▪ *The results of the study were made public.* [=were announced, published, etc.] ▪ *He went public with* [=he announced, published, etc.] *his research.* **5** : offering shares or stock that can be traded on the open market ▪ *a public corporation* ▪ *The company went public.* [=became a public company] — **in the public eye** see ¹EYE — **pub·lic·ly** /ˈpʌblɪkli/ *adv* ▪ *publicly approved policies* ▪ *publicly owned land* ▪ *He publicly announced his resignation.* ▪ *publicly traded stock*

²public *n* **1** *the public* : the people of a country, state, etc. ▪ *The beach is open to the public.* ▪ (*US*) *The public is angry.* = (*Brit*) *The public are angry.* **2** [*singular*] : a group of people who have a shared interest, quality, etc. ▪ *the reading public* [=people who read a lot] — **in public** : in a public place ▪ *She is rarely seen in public.*

public address system *n* [C] : ²PA 1

public assistance *n* [U] *US* : money that the government gives to people who are poor, old, or disabled ▪ *She went on public assistance* [=received money from the government] *when she lost her job.*

pub·li·ca·tion /ˌpʌbləˈkeɪʃən/ *n* **1** [U] : the act or process of producing a book, magazine, etc., and making it available to the public ▪ *the publication of a novel* **2** [C] : a book, magazine, etc., that has been printed and made available to the public ▪ *scholarly/scientific publications* **3** [U] : the act of printing something in a magazine, newspaper, etc. ▪ *the publication of a photo*

public defender *n* [C] *US* : a lawyer who is paid by the government to defend people who are accused of a crime and are unable to pay for a private lawyer

public domain *n* — **the public domain** **1** : the state of something that is not owned by a particular person or company and is available for anyone to use ▪ *software in the public domain* **2** *US* : land that is owned by the government

public health *n* [U] **1** : the health of people in general ▪ *a threat to public health* **2** *US* : the science of caring for a community by giving people basic health care, improving living conditions, etc. ▪ *Public health officials warned of an influenza outbreak.*

public house *n* [C] *Brit, formal* : PUB

pub·li·cist /ˈpʌbləsɪst/ *n* [C] : a person whose job is to give information about a person or organization to news reporters ▪ *The actor's publicist declined to comment.*

pub·lic·i·ty /pəˈblɪsəti/ *n* [U] **1** : attention that is given to someone or something by TV, newspapers, etc. ▪ *The film got some good/bad publicity.* **2** : the activity of getting people to give attention to someone or something ▪ *The studio spent a lot of money on publicity for the movie.*

pub·li·cize *also Brit* **pub·li·cise** /ˈpʌbləˌsaɪz/ *vb* **-cized; -ciz·ing** [T] : to cause (something) to be publicly known ▪ *a highly publicized murder trial*

public relations *n* **1** [U] : the activity of providing favorable information about a person or organization to the public ▪ *a public relations firm* — called also *PR* **2** [*plural*] : the relationship between an organization and the public ▪ *It's good for public relations.* — called also *PR*

public school *n* [C/U] **1** *US* : a school that gets money from and is controlled by a local government ▪ *He attends (a) public school.* **2** *Brit* : a private school that prepares students for college or for public service

public sector *n* [*singular*] : the part of an economy which is controlled or owned by the government ▪ *She has a job in the public sector.*

public servant *n* [C] : a government official or employee

public service *n* **1** [C/U] : the business or activity of supplying electricity, transportation, etc., to the members of a community **2** [C/U] : something that is done to help people rather than to make a profit ▪ *The station is running antismoking commercials as a public service.* ▪ *doing a public service* **3** [U] : work that someone does as part of a government ▪ *She devoted her life to public service.*

public speaking *n* [U] : the act or skill of speaking to a usually large group of people ▪ *He has a fear of public speaking.* — **public speaker** *n* [C]

public transit *n* [U] *US* : MASS TRANSIT

public utility *n* [C] : a company (such as an electric company) that provides a public service

public works *n* [*plural*] : buildings and structures (such as schools and highways) that are built by a government

pub·lish /ˈpʌblɪʃ/ *vb* **1** [T] : to prepare and produce (a book, magazine, etc.) for sale ▪ *The newspaper is published daily.* **2** [T/I] : to have something you wrote included in a book, magazine, newspaper, etc. ▪ *professors who publish regularly* **3** [T] : to include (an article, photograph, etc.) in a magazine or newspaper ▪ *The magazine published my poem.* **4** [T] *formal* : to make (something) known to many people ▪ *She published her findings.* — **pub·lish·er** /ˈpʌblɪʃɚ/ *n* [C] ▪ *a publisher of novels* — **pub·lish·ing** /ˈpʌblɪʃɪŋ/ *n* [U] ▪ *She got a job in publishing.*

puck /ˈpʌk/ *n* [C] : the small, hard, rubber object that is used in ice hockey

puck·er /ˈpʌkɚ/ *vb* [T/I] : to pull the sides of (something) together so that folds or wrinkles are formed ▪ *He puckered his lips* [=he squeezed his lips together] *and kissed her.* = ▪ *He puckered up and kissed her.*

puck·ish /ˈpʌkɪʃ/ *adj, literary* : MISCHIEVOUS 2 ▪ *a puckish smile/look*

pud·ding /ˈpʊdɪŋ/ *n* [C/U] **1** *US* : a thick, sweet, soft, and creamy dessert ▪ *chocolate/vanilla/butterscotch pudding* **2** : a sweet, soft food made of rice, bread, etc. **3** *Brit* : DESSERT ▪ *What's for pudding?* **4** *Brit* : a hot dish like a pie that has meat or vegetables inside it — **the proof is in the pudding** — used to say that you can only know if something is good or bad by trying it

pud·dle /ˈpʌdl/ *n* [C] : a small amount of water, mud, etc., on the ground ▪ *I stepped in a puddle.*

pudgy /ˈpʌdʒi/ *adj* **pudg·i·er**; **-est** *informal* : somewhat fat ▪ *the baby's pudgy cheeks*

pu·er·ile /ˈpjɚrəl/ *adj, formal + disapproving* : silly or childish ▪ *puerile behavior*

¹**puff** /ˈpʌf/ *vb* **1** [T/I] : to breathe smoke from a cigarette, pipe, etc., in and out of the lungs ▪ *puffing (on) a cigar* **2** [T/I] : to produce or send out small clouds of smoke or steam ▪ *Steam puffed (out) from the pot.* **3** [I] *informal* : to breathe loudly especially because of hard physical activity ▪ *He was puffing and panting from running.* **4** [T/I] : to become or make (something) become larger and rounder than normal ▪ *He puffed his chest.* ▪ *Her face puffed up from an allergic reaction.* — **huff and puff** see ¹HUFF — **puff out** [*phrasal vb*] **puff (something) out** or **puff out (something)** : to make (something) larger and rounder by filling it with air ▪ *She puffed out her cheeks and blew out the candles.*

²**puff** *n* [C] **1** : an act of breathing something into your lungs ▪ *He took a puff off his pipe.* **2** : a movement of gas, smoke, or air that can be seen or felt ▪ *a puff of smoke* **3** : a light, round pastry that contains a sweet filling ▪ *a cream puff*

puf·fin /ˈpʌfən/ *n* [C] : a black-and-white seabird that has a colorful bill

puff pastry *n* [U] : dough that is made of thin layers

puff piece *n* [C] *chiefly US, informal + disapproving* : a story, news report, etc., that praises someone or something too much

puffy /ˈpʌfi/ *adj* **puff·i·er**; **-est 1** : larger than normal : SWOLLEN ▪ *puffy eyes* **2** : soft and light ▪ *puffy clouds*

pug /ˈpʌg/ *n* [C] : a small dog that has a wide wrinkled face

pug·na·cious /ˌpʌgˈneɪʃəs/ *adj, formal* : showing a readiness or desire to fight or argue ▪ *a pugnacious student* — **pug·na·cious·ly** *adv* — **pug·nac·i·ty** /ˌpʌgˈnæsəti/ *n* [U]

puke /ˈpjuːk/ *vb* **puked**; **puk·ing** [T/I] *informal* : ¹VOMIT ▪ *I almost puked.* — **puke** *n* [U]

¹**pull** /ˈpʊl/ *vb* **1** [T/I] : to hold onto and move (someone or something) in a particular direction and especially toward yourself ▪ *He pulled the door open.* ▪ *Don't pull the cat's tail.* ▪ *She pulled the blanket over her head.* ▪ *Grab the rope and pull.* **2** [T] : to remove (something) by holding it and using force ▪ *We were pulling weeds in the garden.* ▪ *I had two teeth pulled (out).* **3** [T] **a** : to cause (something) to move with you as you go in a particular direction ▪ *She pulled a wagon behind her.* **b** : to cause (something) to move or be directed toward something ▪ *The colors pull the eye toward the top of the painting.* **4 a** [I] *of a car, train, etc.* : to move from or to a particular place ▪ *The train pulled into the station.* **b** [T/I] : to move a vehicle from or to a particular place ▪ *He pulled (the car) into the parking space.* ▪ *pulling off the highway* **5** [I] *of a car, wheel, etc.* : to move toward the left or right instead of straight ahead ▪ *The car pulls to the right/left.* **6** [T/I] : to move (your body or a part of your body) in a particular direction ▪ *Her hair was pulled back in a ponytail.* ▪ *When I tried to kiss her, she pulled away.* **7** [T] : to move (something) in order to operate a device or machine ▪ *pulling the trigger of a gun* **8** [T/I] : to move a boat through water using oars : ROW ▪ *The crew pulled (the boat) toward shore.* **9** [T] : to remove (someone or something) from a

place or situation • *The pitcher was pulled (from the game).* **b** : to take (something) away • *The company pulled its sponsorship of the project.* **10** [*T*] : to take (a weapon) out of a pocket or other hidden place • *Someone pulled a knife/gun on him.* **11** [*T*] : to do (something) • *Don't you ever pull a crazy stunt like that again!* • *I pulled an all-nighter.* [=worked all night] **12** [*T*] : to hurt (a muscle, tendon, or ligament) by stretching it too much • *She pulled a muscle in her back.* **13** [*T*] *sports* : to hit (a ball) toward the left from a right-handed swing or toward the right from a left-handed swing • *(baseball) He pulled the ball down the left-field line.*

> In addition to the phrases shown below, *pull* occurs in many idioms that are shown at appropriate entries throughout the dictionary. For example, *pull someone's leg* can be found at ¹LEG, and *pull the wool over someone's eyes* can be found at WOOL.

— **pull a fast one** *informal* : to deceive or trick someone • *He tried to pull a fast one on you.* — **pull ahead** [*phrasal vb*] : to take the lead in a race, contest, etc. • *She pulled ahead in the race.* — **pull apart** [*phrasal vb*] **pull apart** or **pull (something) apart** or **pull apart (something)** : to separate (something) or be separated into parts or pieces by pulling • *She pulled the rolls apart.* — **pull aside** [*phrasal vb*] **pull (someone) aside** : to take (someone) away from other people for a private conversation • *She pulled me aside and asked for a favor.* — **pull away** [*phrasal vb*] : to begin to move farther ahead in a race, contest, etc. • *They pulled away in the second half and won the game easily.* — **pull back** [*phrasal vb*] **pull back** or **pull back (someone or something)** or **pull (someone or something) back** : to move back or to cause (someone or something) to move back from a place or position • *The soldiers had to pull back.* — **pull down** [*phrasal vb*] **1 pull down (something)** or **pull (something) down** **a** : to move (something) down • *I pulled down the shade.* **b** : to make (something) smaller in amount or number • *The rumors pulled the company's stock prices down.* **2 pull down (someone)** or **pull (someone) down** *US, informal* : to cause (someone) to become sad or depressed • *The loss really pulled the team down.* **3** *informal* **a** : to earn (a usually large amount of money) • *He pulls down a million dollars a year.* **b** : to get (something) • *The show pulls down high ratings.* — **pull for** [*phrasal vb*] *US, informal* : to say or show that you hope (someone or something) will succeed, get well, etc. • *We're all pulling for you (to win).* — **pull in** [*phrasal vb*] **1** : to arrive at a place and come to a stop • *The train pulled in on time.* **2 pull in (someone or something)** or **pull (someone or something) in** **a** : to attract (someone or something) • *pulling customers in* **b** *informal* : to earn (a usually large amount of money) • *She pulls in*

$100,000 a year. **c** : to bring (someone) to a police station • *The police pulled him in for questioning.* — **pull off** [*phrasal vb*] **pull off (something)** or **pull (something) off** **1** : to remove (something) from something • *She pulled her boots off.* **2** *informal* : to do (something difficult) successfully • *The team pulled off a win/upset.* • *I hope we can pull it off.* — **pull on** [*phrasal vb*] **1** : to hold onto and pull (something) repeatedly • *When she's nervous, she pulls on her ear.* **2** : to breathe in the smoke from (a cigarette, pipe, etc.) • *He pulled on his pipe.* **3 pull on (something)** or **pull (something) on** : to dress yourself in (clothing) • *She pulled on her sweater.* — **pull out** [*phrasal vb*] **1** : to decide not to do something that you had intended to do or started to do • *The buyers of the house pulled out at the last minute.* **2 pull out** or **pull out (someone or something)** or **pull (someone or something) out** : to leave a place or position or to cause (someone or something) to leave a place or position • *Military leaders pulled the troops out of the war zone.* • *Companies are pulling out of the state.* — **pull over** [*phrasal vb*] **pull over** or **pull over (something)** or **pull (something) over** : to move a vehicle to the side of the road and stop • *Let's pull over and look at the map.* **2 pull over (someone or something)** or **pull (someone or something) over** : to force (a driver or vehicle) to move to the side of the road and stop • *He was pulled over (by the police) for speeding.* — **pull through** [*phrasal vb*] **1** : to survive a serious illness, injury, operation, etc. • *We prayed that he would pull through.* **2 a** : to get through a difficult situation • *It was a bad time for us, but we pulled through (it).* **b pull (someone or something) through** : to help (someone or something) to continue to live or succeed in a difficult situation • *His determination pulled him through.* — **pull together** [*phrasal vb*] **1** : to work together as a group in order to get something done • *We all pulled together to finish the project.* **2 pull together (someone or something)** or **pull (someone or something) together** **a** : to bring (people or things) together and organize them in order to make or do something • *She pulled a team of researchers together.* **b** : to make (something) by bringing together different things • *pulling together a report* **3 pull (yourself) together** : to become calm again • *You need to pull yourself together.* — **pull up** [*phrasal vb*] **1 pull up (something)** or **pull (something) up** **a** : to move (something) up • *I pulled up the shade.* **b** : to move (something) forward or into a position where it can be seen, used, etc. • *Pull up a chair and join us.* **2 pull up** or **pull (something) up** or **pull up (something)** : to stop a vehicle at a particular place • *We pulled up in front of the house.*

²**pull** *n* **1** [*C*] : the act of pulling something • *Give the rope a pull.* **2** [*U*] : special influence and power over other people • *He has a lot of pull in local political*

circles. **3** [C] : the power to make someone want to go somewhere, do something, etc. — usually singular • *the pull of big cities* **4** [*singular*] : a natural force that causes one thing (such as a planet) to be pulled toward another • *the moon's gravitational pull* **5** [C] : an injury that is caused by stretching a muscle, tendon, or ligament too much • *a muscle/groin pull* **6** [C] **a** : the act of breathing in smoke from a cigarette, cigar, pipe, etc. • *He took a pull on/off/at his cigar.* **b** : the act of taking a long drink of something • *He took a long pull on his beer.*

pul·ley /'pʊli/ *n, pl* **-leys** [C] : a wheel or set of wheels that is used with a rope, chain, etc., to lift or lower heavy objects

pull-out /'pʊl,aʊt/ *n* [C] **1** : an act of removing military troops from a position or an area • *a pullout of troops from the region* **2** : a section of a newspaper, magazine, etc., that is meant to be removed and looked at separately • *a ten-page pullout*

pull-over /'pʊl,oʊvə/ *n* [C] : a piece of clothing (such as a sweater) that is put on by pulling it over your head

pull-up /'pʊl,ʌp/ *n* [C] : an exercise in which you hold onto a bar above your head and then pull your body up until your chin is above the bar — called also *(US) chin-up*

pul·mo·nary /'pʊlmə,neri, Brit 'pʊlmənri/ *adj, always before a noun, medical* : relating to the lungs • *the pulmonary arteries/veins*

pulp /'pʌlp/ *n* **1 a** [U] : the inner, juicy part of a fruit or vegetable **b** [U] : the substance that is left after the liquid has been squeezed from a fruit or vegetable • *orange juice that has pulp in it* **c** [U, *singular*] : a soft, wet substance that is made by crushing something • *The grain was mashed to (a) pulp.* • *(figurative) He threatened to beat them to a pulp.* [=to hurt them very badly] **2** [U] : a soft material that is made mostly from wood and is used in making paper **3** [C] *US* : a magazine, book, etc., that is cheaply made and that deals with sex, violence, etc., in a shocking way • *a pulp magazine* **4** [C/U] *technical* : the soft tissue that is inside a tooth — **pulpy** /'pʌlpi/ *adj* **pulp·i·er; -est**

pul·pit /'pʊl,pɪt/ *n* [C] : a raised platform where a priest or minister stands when leading a worship service • *(figurative) Their crimes were denounced from the pulpit.* [=by church leaders]

pul·sate /'pʌl,seɪt, Brit ,pʌl'seɪt/ *vb* **-sated; -sat·ing** [I] **1** : to make strong and regular beats, sounds, flashes, etc. • *pulsating lights/music* **2** : to be filled with activity or a feeling • *a movie pulsating with suspense* — **pul·sa·tion** /,pʌl'seɪʃən/ *n* [C/U]

¹**pulse** /'pʌls/ *n* [C] **1** : the regular movement of blood through your body that is caused by the beating of your heart and that can be felt by touching certain parts of your body • *The nurse checked/took my pulse.* [=measured how fast my heart was beating] **2** : a brief increase in an amount of electricity, light, or sound •

pulses of light **3** : the ideas, feelings, or opinions that are shared by a group of people • *the political pulse of the nation* • **finger on the pulse** see ¹**FINGER**

²**pulse** *vb* **pulsed; puls·ing** [I] **1 a** : to move with strong, regular beats • *He could feel the blood pulsing through his veins.* **b** : to produce a strong, regular beat • *Music pulsed from the speakers.* **2** : to be filled with activity or a feeling • *The city pulses with life.*

pul·ver·ize also Brit **pul·ver·ise** /'pʌlvə,raɪz/ *vb* **-ized; -iz·ing** [T] **1** *technical* : to crush, beat, or grind (something) into powder or dust • *pulverized rock* **2** *informal* : to destroy or defeat (someone or something) • *They pulverized the opposition.*

pu·ma /'pu:mə, Brit 'pju:mə/ *n, pl* **pumas** also **puma** [C] : COUGAR

pum·ice /'pʌmɪs/ *n* [U] : a gray stone that is full of small holes — called also **pumice stone**

pum·mel /'pʌməl/ *vb, US* **-meled** or Brit **-melled;** *US* **-mel·ing** or Brit **-mel·ling** [T] : to repeatedly hit or punch (someone or something) very hard • *He pummeled the intruder.* • *(figurative) The movie was pummeled by critics.*

¹**pump** /'pʌmp/ *n* [C] **1** : a device that forces liquid, air, or gas into or out of something • *an air/water pump* • *(US) a gas pump* = *(Brit) a petrol pump* • *(US, figurative) higher prices at the pump* [=at places where people buy gasoline] **2** : the act of pumping something • *two pumps of the handle* **3 a** *US* : a woman's dress shoe with a high heel **b** *Brit* : a soft shoe that is worn for dancing or exercise

²**pump** *vb* **1 a** [T/I] : to move something (such as water, air, or gas) to or from a particular place with a pump • *pumping water* • *balloons pumped full of helium* • *(figurative) She pumped all of her resources into her business.* • *(figurative) She pumped herself full of caffeine.* **b** [T] : to remove water, air, etc., from (something) with a pump • *We had to pump the basement out.* **c** [T] : to remove the contents of (someone's stomach) • *Doctors pumped (out) her stomach.* **2** [T/I] *of the heart* : to move blood through your body by beating • *My heart was pumping fast.* **3** [I] *of a liquid* : to flow by the action of a pump, by the beating of your heart, etc. • *the blood that pumps through my veins* **4** [T/I] : to move (something) up and down or in and out quickly and repeatedly • *He pumped his arms as he ran.* **5** [T] *informal* : to question (someone) repeatedly • *He pumped them for information.* — **pump iron** *informal* : to lift weights to make your muscles stronger — **pump out** [*phrasal vb*] **pump out (something)** or **pump (something) out** *informal* : to produce (something) quickly and frequently • *The author pumps out a book every year.* — **pump up** [*phrasal vb*] **1 pump (something) up** or **pump up (something) a** : to fill (something, such as a tire) with air by using a pump • *pumping up the bike's tires* **b** *informal* : to increase the amount, size, or value of

(something) ▪ *pumping up sales/egos* **2 pump (someone) up or pump up (someone)** : to fill (someone) with excitement or enthusiasm ▪ *They were (all) pumped up for the game.*

pumped /ˈpʌmpt/ *adj, US, informal* : excited and enthusiastic about something ▪ *I'm pumped for the game.*

pum·per·nick·el /ˈpʌmpɚˌnɪkəl/ *n [U]* : a dark bread made from rye

pump·kin /ˈpʌmpkən/ *n [C/U]* : a large, round, orange vegetable used as food and sometimes as a decoration

pun /ˈpʌn/ *n [C]* : a humorous way of using a word or phrase so that more than one meaning is suggested ▪ *She made a pun.* ▪ *a pilot whose career has—no pun intended—taken off* — **pun** *vb* **punned; pun·ning** *[T/I]* ▪ *"Firefighting sparks my interest," he punned.*

¹**punch** /ˈpʌntʃ/ *vb [T]* **1** : to hit (someone or something) hard with your fist ▪ *She punched him in the face.* **2** : to make (a hole, dent, etc.) by pressing or cutting *in, into,* or *through* something ▪ *The tool punches holes in paper.* **3** : to make a hole in (something) with a special tool ▪ *The conductor punched my ticket.* ▪ *(figurative)* He tried to *punch holes* in my theory. [=to weaken or destroy my theory by proving that parts of it are wrong] — **punch in** *[phrasal vb] US* **1** : to place a card in a time clock at the beginning of a workday ▪ *I punched in at 8:00.* **2 punch (something) in or punch in (something)** : to enter (information) into a computer by pressing buttons or keys ▪ *She punched in her secret code.* — **punch out** *[phrasal vb] US* **1** : to place a card in a time clock at the end of a workday ▪ *It's time to punch out.* **2 punch (someone) out or punch out (someone)** *informal* : to hit (someone) repeatedly ▪ *He threatened to punch me out.* — **punch someone's lights out** *informal* : to hit someone's face hard with your fist ▪ *I'd like to punch his lights out.* — **punch up** *[phrasal vb]* **punch (something) up or punch up (something)** *US, informal* : to make (something) more exciting, attractive, etc. ▪ *The steak was punched up with a pepper sauce.* — **punch·er** *n [C]*

²**punch** *n* **1** *[C]* : a quick hit with your fist **2** *[U]* : energy or forcefulness ▪ *The story lacks punch.* **3** *[C/U]* : a drink made usually by mixing fruit juices and often alcohol ▪ *a bowl/glass of punch* **4** *[C]* : a tool or machine for cutting holes in paper, leather, etc. ▪ *a paper punch* **5** *[C]* : a hole made by a cutting tool or machine — **(as) pleased as punch** see PLEASED — **beat (someone) to the punch** : to do or achieve something before someone else is able to ▪ *I was going to tell them but he beat me to the punch.* — **pack a punch** see ²PACK — **pull punches** : to express criticism in a mild or kind way ▪ *The report pulls no punches in blaming him.* — **roll with the punches** see ¹ROLL

punch–drunk /ˈpʌntʃˌdrʌŋk/ *adj* **1** : confused and unable to act normally because of being punched many times in

the head ▪ *punch-drunk fighters* **2** *informal* : unable to think or act normally because you are very tired, excited, etc. ▪ *I was punch-drunk with fatigue.*

punching bag *n [C] US* : a very heavy bag that is punched for exercise or training ▪ *(figurative)* I'm tired of being your *punching bag.* [=I'm tired of being criticized/hit/defeated by you] — called also *(Brit)* **punch bag**

punch line *n [C]* : the words at the end of a joke or story that make it funny, surprising, etc.

punchy /ˈpʌntʃi/ *adj* **punch·i·er; -est** *informal* : very exciting or lively ▪ *a punchy color/sauce/tune*

punc·til·i·ous /ˌpʌŋkˈtɪliəs/ *adj, formal* : very careful about behaving properly and doing things in a correct way ▪ *She's punctilious about grammar.*

punc·tu·al /ˈpʌŋktʃəwəl/ *adj* : arriving or doing something at the expected or planned time ▪ *a punctual employee/train* — **punc·tu·al·i·ty** /ˌpʌŋktʃəˈwæləti/ *n [U]* — **punc·tu·al·ly** *adv* ▪ *She arrived punctually at 7:00.*

punc·tu·ate /ˈpʌŋktʃəˌweɪt/ *vb* **-at·ed; -at·ing** *[T]* **1** : to use punctuation marks in (a piece of writing) ▪ *a properly punctuated sentence* **2** : to occur in (something) repeatedly ▪ *Her speech was punctuated by applause.*

punc·tu·a·tion /ˌpʌŋktʃəˈweɪʃən/ *n [U]* : the marks (such as periods and commas) in a piece of writing ▪ *good punctuation and spelling*

punctuation mark *n [C]* : a mark (such as a period or comma) used to divide writing into sentences, clauses, etc.

¹**punc·ture** /ˈpʌŋktʃɚ/ *n [C]* : a hole or wound made by a sharp point

²**puncture** *vb* **-tured; -tur·ing** **1** *[T/I]* : to make a hole in (something) with a sharp point ▪ *A nail punctured the tire.* ▪ *a punctured tire* **2** *[T]* of a sound : to interrupt (silence) in a sudden and unexpected way ▪ *The silence was punctured by her cry.*

pun·dit /ˈpʌndət/ *n [C]* : a person who expresses opinions about a particular subject publicly ▪ *political pundits*

pun·gent /ˈpʌndʒənt/ *adj* : having a strong, sharp taste or smell ▪ *a pungent aroma/sauce* — **pun·gen·cy** /ˈpʌndʒənsi/ *n [U]* — **pun·gent·ly** *adv*

pun·ish /ˈpʌnɪʃ/ *vb [T]* **1 a** : to make (someone) suffer for a crime or for bad behavior ▪ *He was punished by/with a year in prison.* **b** : to make someone suffer for (a crime or bad behavior) ▪ *State law punishes fraud with fines.* **2** : to treat (someone or something) severely or roughly ▪ *These shoes punish my feet.* ▪ *a punishing schedule* — **pun·ish·able** /ˈpʌnɪʃəbəl/ *adj* ▪ *a punishable crime/offense*

pun·ish·ment /ˈpʌnɪʃmənt/ *n* **1** *[C/U]* : the act of punishing someone or a way of punishing someone ▪ *I took away her toy as (a) punishment for her bad behavior.* ▪ *cruel and unusual punishment* [=punishment that is very painful or too severe] **2** *[U]* : rough physical treatment ▪ *These boots can take a lot of punishment.*

pu·ni·tive /'pjuːnətɪv/ adj **1** : intended to punish someone or something • *taking punitive measures/action* **2** : extremely or unfairly severe or high • *imposing punitive taxes* — **pu·ni·tive·ly** adv

punk /'pʌŋk/ n **1** [C] US, informal + disapproving : a rude and violent young man **2 a** [U] : a kind of loud and intense rock music — called also *punk rock* **b** [C] : a person who is a fan of punk — called also *punk rocker*

¹**punt** /'pʌnt/ vb **1** [T/I] sports : to drop a ball and kick it before it touches the ground in sports like American football and rugby • *The team's kicker punted (the ball) from midfield.* **2** [T/I] US, informal : to avoid dealing with a problem or answering a question • *The legislature punted on the issue.* **3** [I] Brit : to go on a river, canal, etc., in a long, thin boat (called a punt) • *We went punting.*

²**punt** n [C] **1** sports : a kick made by dropping a ball and kicking it before it touches the ground : the act of punting a ball • *a 40-yard punt* **2** : a long, thin boat with square ends that is moved by pushing a pole against the bottom of a river, canal, etc. **3** : the basic unit of money used in Ireland before the euro

punt·er /'pʌntər/ n [C] **1** American football : a player whose job is to punt the ball **2** chiefly Brit : a person who goes on a river, canal, etc., in a long, thin boat (called a punt)

pu·ny /'pjuːni/ adj **pu·ni·er**; **-est** informal **1** : small and weak • *a puny little guy* **2** : not very large, impressive, or effective • *a puny car/house*

pup /'pʌp/ n [C] : a young dog; also : one of the young of various animals other than dogs • *seal pups*

pu·pa /'pjuːpə/ n, pl **pu·pae** /'pjuːˌpiː/ [C] biology : an insect in the stage of development between larva and adult — **pu·pal** /'pjuːpəl/ adj • *the pupal stage*

pu·pil /'pjuːpəl/ n [C] **1** : a young student **2** : the small, black, round area at the center of the eye

pup·pet /'pʌpət/ n [C] **1** : a doll that is moved by putting your hand inside it or by pulling strings or wires that are attached to it **2** : a person or an organization that is controlled by another person or organization • *a puppet regime* [=a government controlled by another country]

pup·pet·ry /'pʌpətri/ n [U] : the activity of using puppets to entertain people — **pup·pe·teer** /ˌpʌpə'tiər/ n [C]

pup·py /'pʌpi/ n, pl **-pies** [C] **1** : a young dog **2** US, informal — used in a playful way to refer to a person or thing • *Why isn't the grill on? This thing turned up!* [=turn on the grill] • *He's one sick puppy.* [=he is crazy, cruel, or disgusting]

puppy fat n [U] Brit : BABY FAT

puppy love n [U] : romantic love that is felt by a child or teenager

pup tent n [C] US : a small tent

¹**pur·chase** /'pɜːtʃəs/ vb **-chased**; **-chasing** [T] formal : to buy (property, goods, etc.) • *purchase a house/suit/gift* — **pur·chas·er** n [C]

²**purchase** n **1** [C/U] : an act of buying something • *credit card purchases* **2** [C] : something that is bought • *an expensive purchase* **3** [U, singular] : a firm hold or grip that makes movement possible • *The ice made it impossible for the car's wheels to gain/get a purchase on the road.*

purchase price n [C] : the amount of money someone pays for something

pure /'pjʊr/ adj **pur·er**; **-est** **1** : not mixed with anything else • *pure gold/silk/honey* • *pure intuition/instinct* **2** : clean and not harmful in any way • *pure air/water* **3** : having a smooth and clear sound • *the pure notes of the flute* **4** always before a noun : COMPLETE, TOTAL — used for emphasis • *pure nonsense/fiction/fantasy/joy/evil* **5** : morally good • *a pure heart/thought* — **pure and simple** : with nothing other than what has been mentioned — used to add emphasis • *I was wrong, pure and simple.* — **pure·ly** /'pjʊrli/ adv • *He reads purely* [=completely, only] *for enjoyment.* — **pure·ness** n [U]

pure·bred /'pjʊrˌbrɛd/ adj, of animals : having parents that are of the same breed • *a purebred dog/horse* — **pure·bred** n [C]

¹**pu·ree** or **pu·rée** /pjʊ'reɪ, Brit 'pjʊəreɪ/ n [C/U] : a thick liquid made by crushing usually cooked fruits, vegetables, etc. • *a spoonful of apple puree* • *vegetable/fruit purees*

²**puree** or **purée** vb **-reed**; **-ree·ing** [T] : to crush (food) until it is a thick liquid • *She pureed the fruit.* • *pureed carrots*

pur·ga·to·ry /'pɜːgəˌtori, Brit 'pɜːgətri/ n, pl **-ries** **1** Purgatory [singular] : a state according to Roman Catholic belief in which the souls of dead people are made pure before going to heaven **2** [C/U] : a place or state of suffering • *a/the purgatory of drug abuse*

¹**purge** /'pɜːdʒ/ vb **purged**; **purg·ing** [T] **1** : to remove people from an area, organization, etc., often in a violent and sudden way • *Many officials were purged from the company.* **2** : to cause something to leave the body • *medicines that purge toxins from the body* • (figurative) *He purged himself* [=freed himself] *of old fears.* — **binge and purge** see ²BINGE

²**purge** n [C] : the removal of people from an area, organization, etc. • *a corporate/postwar purge*

pu·ri·fi·er /'pjʊrəˌfajər/ n [C] : a device that removes dirty or harmful substances • *a water/air purifier*

pu·ri·fy /'pjʊrəˌfaɪ/ vb **-fies**; **-fied**; **-fy·ing** [T] : to make (something or someone) pure • *purifying the air/water/mind/soul* — **pu·ri·fi·ca·tion** /ˌpjʊrəfə'keɪʃən/ n [U]

pur·ist /'pjʊrɪst/ n [C] : a person who has very strong ideas about what is correct or acceptable • *jazz/music purists* • *a grammatical purist* — **pur·ism** /'pjʊrˌɪzəm/ n [U]

pu·ri·tan /'pjʊrətən/ n [C] **1** Puritan : a member of a Protestant group in England and New England in the 16th and 17th centuries **2** : a person who follows strict moral rules and who believes that pleasure is wrong • *She's a puritan about* *sex.* — **Puritan** /ˈpjʊrətn̩/ *— pu·ri·tan·i·cal* /ˌpjʊrəˈtænɪkəl/ *adj, disapproving ▪ puritanical attitudes/rules —* **pu·ri·tan·ism** /ˈpjʊrətənˌɪzəm/ *n [U]*

pu·ri·ty /ˈpjʊrəti/ *n [U]* : the quality or state of being pure ▪ *water/moral purity*

pur·loin /pɚˈlɔɪn/ *vb [T] formal + humorous* : STEAL 1 ▪ *He purloined a bottle of whiskey.*

pur·ple /ˈpɚpəl/ *n [C/U]* : a color that is between red and blue — **purple** *adj* — **pur·pler** ; **pur·plest** — **pur·plish** /ˈpɚplɪʃ/ *adj ▪ a purplish blue*

Purple Heart *n [C]* : a U.S. military award that is given to a soldier who is wounded or killed in battle

¹**pur·port** /ˈpɚˌpoɚt/ *n [U] formal* : the main or general meaning of something ▪ *the purport of the letter/visit*

²**pur·port** /pɚˈpoɚt/ *vb [T]* : to claim to be or do a particular thing when this claim may not be true ▪ *The report purports to be objective.* ▪ *the purported* [=*alleged*] *crime* — **pur·port·ed·ly** *adv ▪ diaries purportedly* [=*supposedly*] *written by a famous author*

pur·pose /ˈpɚpəs/ *n* **1** [C] : the reason why something is done or used ▪ *What is the purpose of your visit?* ▪ *a tool's purpose* ▪ *keeping receipts for tax purposes* ▪ *Everything on the boat* **serves a purpose**. [=has a particular use] ▪ *The money was used* **for a good purpose**. [=for something useful, important, etc.] ▪ *For the purpose(s) of this discussion, let's assume that sales will increase next year.* **2** [U] : the feeling of being determined to do or achieve something ▪ *My life lacked purpose and meaning.* ▪ *We started again with a new* **sense of purpose**. **3** [C] : the aim or goal of a person ▪ *Her sole purpose (in life) was to be a writer.* ▪ *We shared a* **common purpose**. [=we had the same goals] ▪ *searching for a* **higher purpose** [=a more meaningful reason to live, work, etc.] ▪ **on purpose** : in a way that is planned or intended ▪ *I didn't do it on purpose.* [=*purposely*] — **to/for all intents and purposes** see ¹INTENT

pur·pose·ful /ˈpɚpəsfəl/ *adj* : having a clear aim or purpose ▪ *a purposeful glance* — **pur·pose·ful·ly** *adv*

pur·pose·less /ˈpɚpəsləs/ *adj* : having or seeming to have no purpose or reason ▪ *a purposeless meeting*

pur·pose·ly /ˈpɚpəsli/ *adv* : in a way that is planned or intended ▪ *She purposely raised her voice.*

¹**purr** /ˈpɚ/ *n [C]* **1** : the soft sound that a cat makes when it is happy **2** : a sound that is like the purr of a cat ▪ *the soft purr of a car engine*

²**purr** *vb [I]* : to make a purr or a sound like a purr ▪ *a purring cat* ▪ *The car/engine purred smoothly.*

¹**purse** /ˈpɚs/ *n [C]* **a** *US* : HANDBAG **b** *chiefly Brit* : CHANGE PURSE **2** [*singular*] : an amount of money that a person or organization has available to use ▪ *The government* **holds/controls the purse strings**. [=makes the decisions about how money is spent] ▪ *They* **loosened/tightened the purse strings**. [=made more/less money available for spending]

3 [C] : an amount of money that is offered as a prize in a competition ▪ *a golf tournament with a million dollar purse*

²**purse** *vb* **pursed; purs·ing** [T] : to form (your lips) into a tight circle or line ▪ *She pursed her lips in concentration.*

purs·er /ˈpɚsɚ/ *n [C]* : an officer on a ship whose job is to handle matters relating to money and to make sure passengers are comfortable and have what they need

pur·su·ance /pɚˈsuːwəns, *Brit* pəˈsjuːəns/ *n* — **in pursuance of** *formal* : in order to do (something) or to do what is required by (something) ▪ *making changes in pursuance of the contract*

pur·su·ant to /pɚˈsuːwənt-, *Brit* pəˈsjuːənt-/ *prep, formal* : in a way that agrees with or follows (something) ▪ *Pursuant to the terms of the sale, the owner shall be responsible for damages.*

pur·sue /pɚˈsuː, *Brit* pəˈsjuː/ *vb* **-sued; -su·ing** [T] **1** : to follow and try to catch (someone or something) for usually a long distance or time ▪ *He was pursued by police.* **2** : to try to get or do (something) over a period of time ▪ *pursuing a teaching career/degree* **3** : to be involved in (an activity) ▪ *pursue a hobby* **4** : to move along (a course) ▪ *The ship pursued a northerly course.* **5** : to make an effort to find out more about (something) ▪ *I'd like to pursue the matter further.* — **pur·su·er** *n [C]*

pur·suit /pɚˈsuːt, *Brit* pəˈsjuːt/ *n* **1** [U] : the act of pursuing someone or something ▪ *police* **in pursuit of** *a fugitive* ▪ *the* **pursuit of** *excellence/knowledge* **2** [C] : an activity that is done for pleasure ▪ *She enjoys reading, knitting, and other quiet pursuits.*

pur·vey /pɚˈveɪ/ *vb [T] formal* : to make (something, such as a product) available ▪ *a shop purveying handmade merchandise* — **pur·vey·or** /pɚˈveɪjɚ/ *n [C]* ▪ *a purveyor of kitchen supplies*

pur·view /ˈpɚˌvjuː/ *n [U] formal* : an area within which someone or something has authority or knowledge ▪ *That question is outside/beyond my purview.*

pus /ˈpʌs/ *n [U] medical* : a thick, yellowish substance that is produced when a part of the body or a wound becomes infected

¹**push** /ˈpʊʃ/ *vb* **1** [T/I] : to use force to move (someone or something) forward or away from you ▪ *Push the button to turn on the computer.* ▪ *Stop pushing me.* ▪ *He pushed me out of the way.* ▪ *pushing a shopping cart* ▪ *Push the door open.* ▪ *She pushed against/on the door.* ▪ (*figurative*) *Poverty pushed them to the breaking point.* ▪ (*figurative*) *He* **pushed aside** [=*put aside*] *his fears.* **2** [T/I] : to go forward while using your hands, arms, etc., to forcefully move people or things that are blocking you ▪ *I pushed (my way) through the crowd.* **3** [T] : **a** : to force or try to force or persuade (someone) to do something ▪ *We pushed him to play football.* ▪ *He pushed them into accepting his plan.* **b** : to force (someone) to work hard at something ▪ *The coach pushes his players too hard.* ▪ *She pushed herself to keep*

working. **c** : to do or say things that cause trouble for (someone) ▪ *If you push her too far, you'll regret it.* **4** [*I*] **a** : to continue moving forward in a forceful or steady way ▪ *They pushed ahead/forward/ on in spite of the snow.* **b** : to continue to do something especially in a determined way ▪ *They pushed ahead/forward/on with their plans.* **5** [*T*] : to force (someone or something) to move away from a place ▪ *Settlers pushed the native people off their land.* **6** [*T*] : to cause (something) to be accepted, completed, etc., by making a special effort ▪ *The senators pushed the bill through Congress.* **7** [*I*] : to make a strong, continuous effort to get or do something ▪ *Workers are pushing hard for raises.* **8** [*T*] **a** : to make a strong effort to sell (something) ▪ *pushing last year's models* **b** : to try to make (something) more popular, well-known, etc., by talking about it ▪ *He's pushing his new film.* **c** : to repeat (something) in order to show that it is important ▪ *She kept pushing the issue/point.* **9** [*T*] *informal* : to sell (illegal drugs) ▪ *pushing drugs* **10** [*T*] **a** : to go up to and often beyond (a limit) ▪ *His humor pushes the limits of bad taste.* **b** *informal* : to get close to (an age or number) ▪ *She is pushing 80.* [=she is almost 80 years old] **11** [*T*] : to cause or force (something) to change in a specified way ▪ *The cost of oil has pushed gas prices higher/up.* [=has raised gas prices] **12** [*T*] *sports* : to hit (a ball) toward the right from a right-handed swing or toward the left from a left-handed swing ▪ *(golf) She pushed her drive into the rough.* — **push around** *also Brit* **push about** [*phrasal vb*] **push (someone) around/ about** : to try to force (someone) to do what you want by making threats, using force, etc. ▪ *Don't let him push you around!* — **push back** [*phrasal vb*] **push back (something) or push (something) back** : to change (a planned event) to start at a later date or time ▪ *The meeting has been pushed back to Thursday.* — **push in** [*phrasal vb*] *Brit* : to move in front of other people who are waiting in a line ▪ *She pushed in at the head of the queue.* — **push it/things** *informal* : to continue to do or to try to do something when you should stop ▪ *I already said "no" twice, so don't push it.* [=don't keep asking me] — **push off** [*phrasal vb*] **1** : to move from a place or position by pushing against a surface with something ▪ *She pushed off (from shore) with her oar.* — **push on** [*phrasal vb*] **push (something) on** : to force (someone) to accept (something) ▪ *He tried to push his beliefs on me.* — **push over** [*phrasal vb*] **1 push (someone or something) or push (someone or something) over** : to make (someone or something) fall to the ground by pushing ▪ *He pushed me over.* **2** *US, informal* : to move so that there is room for someone else to sit next to you ▪ *Push over so I can sit down.* — **push pa-per(s)** see ¹PAPER — **push the enve-lope** see ENVELOPE — **push your luck** see ¹LUCK

²**push** *n* [*C*] **1** : an act of pushing some-

thing or someone ▪ *He gave me a push.* [=he pushed me] ▪ *The car starts with the push of a button.* **2** : a large, organized military attack ▪ *making a final push* **3** : a strong, continuous effort to get or achieve something ▪ *Workers are making a push for higher wages.* — **push comes to shove** *informal* — used to describe what happens when a situation becomes very serious or difficult and action needs to be taken ▪ *He backed down when push came to shove.*

push button *n* [*C*] : a small button or knob that is pushed to operate a machine — **push–button** *adj, always before a noun* ▪ *a push-button phone*

push·chair /ˈpʊʃˌtʃeɚ/ *n* [*C*] *Brit* : STROLLER 1

pushed /ˈpʊʃt/ *adj, not before a noun, Brit, informal* **1** : HARD-PRESSED ▪ *You'd be (hard) pushed to find a better offer.* **2** : lacking something that is needed or desired : PRESSED ▪ *I'm pushed for time/money.* **3** : busy or active ▪ *We've been a bit pushed lately.*

push·er /ˈpʊʃɚ/ *n* [*C*] : someone who sells illegal drugs ▪ *drug pushers*

push·over /ˈpʊʃˌouvɚ/ *n* [*C*] *informal* **1** : an opponent that is easy to defeat **2** : someone who is easy to persuade or influence ▪ *Dad's a pushover. He'll let me do anything I want.*

push–up /ˈpʊʃˌʌp/ *n* [*C*] *chiefly US* : an exercise in which you lie on your stomach and raise and lower your body by bending your arms — called also *(Brit)* press-up

pushy /ˈpʊʃi/ *adj* **push·i·er; -est** : aggressive and rude ▪ *a pushy salesperson* — **push·i·ness** /ˈpʊʃinəs/ *n* [*U*]

puss /ˈpʊs/ *n, informal* [*C*] : ¹FACE 1 **2** [*singular*] *Brit* : a cat or kitten

pussy /ˈpʊsi/ *n, pl* **puss·ies** [*C*] *informal* : a cat or kitten

pussy·cat /ˈpʊsiˌkæt/ *n* [*C*] *informal* **1** : a cat or kitten **2** : a kind and gentle person ▪ *He looks tough, but he's really a pussycat.*

pussy·foot /ˈpʊsiˌfʊt/ *vb* [*I*] *informal + disapproving* : to avoid making a decision or statement because of fear, doubt, etc. ▪ *Stop pussyfooting (around) and tell us what happened.*

pussy willow *n* [*C*] : a small tree with large, soft flowers

¹**put** /ˈpʊt/ *vb* **put; put·ting** [*T*] **1 a** : to cause (someone or something) to be in a particular place or position ▪ *I put the keys on the table.* ▪ *He put his arms around her.* **b** : to send (someone) to a particular place ▪ *The illness put her in the hospital.* ▪ *They put her in a special school.* **2** : to write (something) in or on something ▪ *Put your name on your homework.* ▪ *Put a circle around the correct answer.* **3** : to cause (someone or something) to be in a particular state or condition ▪ *Who put you in charge?* ▪ *The music put her in/into a good mood.* ▪ *Their actions have put them in danger.* ▪ *She put us at ease.* [=made us feel calm and relaxed] ▪ *Put it out of your mind.* [=stop thinking about it] ▪ *We put our competitors out of business.* ▪ *He put the children to bed.*

[=helped them get into their beds] **4 a** : to cause (someone or something) to do work or perform a task ▪ *She put me to work in the yard.* **b** : to use (something) ▪ *They put the plan in action/motion.* ▪ *The donations will be put to good use.* **5** : to cause (something) to have an effect on someone or something ▪ *She put pressure on us to finish the job early.* ▪ *a tax put on luxury items* ▪ *putting a limit on government spending* **6** : to say or express (something) ▪ *As she put it, "You can't please everyone."* ▪ *It was difficult, to put it mildly.* [=it was very difficult] **7 a** : to ask (a question) or make (a suggestion) to someone ▪ *I put my plan before them for consideration.* **b** : to ask a group of people to formally vote on (something) ▪ *They will put the resolution to a vote to-day.* **8** : to add music to (words) ▪ *She put the lyrics to music.* — **put about** [*phrasal vb*] **1 put (something) about or put about (something)** *Brit* : to tell many people about (something) ▪ *They put about the news that he was resigning.* **2 put about or put (something) about of** a boat or ship : to change direction ▪ *The ship put about.* ▪ *They put the ship about.* — **put across** [*phrasal vb*] **1 put (something) across or put across (something)** : to cause (something) to be understood ▪ *putting the message across to voters* **2 put (yourself) across as** : to cause (yourself) to appear to be (a particular type of person) ▪ *He puts himself across as a nice guy.* — **put aside** [*phrasal vb*] **put (something) aside or put aside (something) 1** : to save or keep (something) to be used at a later time ▪ *putting aside money for a vacation* **2** : to stop worrying or thinking about (something) ▪ *Let's put aside our differences.* — **put at** [*phrasal vb*] **put (something) at** : to guess (something) to be (something) ▪ *Estimates put the number of cases at 2,000 each year.* — **put away** [*phrasal vb*] **1 put (something) away or put away (something) a** : to return (something) to the place where it belongs ▪ *He put away the dishes.* **b** : to save or keep (something) to be used at a later time ▪ *putting away money for college* **c** *informal* : to eat (a large amount of food) ▪ *He can really put it away!* **2 put (someone) away or put away (someone)** *informal* : to cause (someone) to be kept in a prison or mental hospital ▪ *They put him away for the rest of his life.* — **put back** [*phrasal vb*] **put (something) back or put back (something) 1** : to return (something) to the place where it belongs ▪ *Put the books back on the shelf.* **2** *Brit* : POSTPONE ▪ *They put back the game until next week.* — **put before** [*phrasal vb*] **put (something) before** : to ask (a person or group) to make a decision about (something) ▪ *We'll put the question before the voters.* — **put behind** [*phrasal vb*] **put (something) behind you** : to stop worrying about or being upset by (something in the past) ▪ *Let's put our loss behind us and focus on the next game.* — **put by** [*phrasal vb*] **put (something) by or put by (something)** *chiefly Brit* : to save (money)

for a later time ▪ *putting money by* — **put down** [*phrasal vb*] **1 put (someone or something) down also put down (someone or something) a** : to place (someone or something that you have been holding or carrying) on a table, on the floor, etc. ▪ *Put down the gun.* **b** : to add (someone or something) to a list ▪ *Put down milk on the shopping list.* **c** *informal* : to say critical things about (someone or something) ▪ *He often puts down her work.* ▪ *Stop putting her down.* **2 put (something) down or put down (something) a** : to write (something) ▪ *putting my thoughts down on paper* **b** : to give (an amount of money) as a first payment ▪ *We put 10 percent down on the house/car.* **c** : to put (something) in place on the floor or ground ▪ *putting down carpet/tile/mulch* **d** : to stop (a violent activity) by using force ▪ *put down a rebellion* **e** : to kill (an animal) in a way that causes it little pain ▪ *The sick/injured horse had to be put down.* **f** *Brit* : to end a telephone connection ▪ *She put down the phone.* [=hung up the phone] **g** *Brit* : to propose or introduce (something) ▪ *putting down an amendment* **3 put down or put (something) down or put down (something)** *chiefly Brit* : to land or to cause (an airplane) to land ▪ *Our plane put down at 2 p.m.* **4 put (someone) down or put down (someone)** : to place (a baby or child) in a bed to sleep ▪ *He put the baby down for a nap.* **5 put (someone) down as** : to think of (someone) as (a specified kind of person) ▪ *Most people put him down as a fanatic.* **6 put (someone) down for** : to write the name of (someone) on a list of people who will do or give (something) ▪ *Can I put you down for a donation?* ▪ *Sure, put me down for $20.* **7 put (something) down to** : to say or think that (something) happened because of (something) ▪ *We put the mistake down to inexperience.* — **put forth** [*phrasal vb*] **put forth (something) or put (something) forth** *somewhat formal* **1** : PROPOSE 1 ▪ *putting forth a plan/theory* **2** : to use (something, such as energy) for a particular purpose ▪ *They put forth a good effort.* — **put forward** [*phrasal vb*] **put (something) forward or put (something) forward (something)** *somewhat formal* : PROPOSE 1 ▪ *putting forward a theory* — **put in** [*phrasal vb*] **1 put (something) in or put in (something) a** : INSTALL 1 ▪ *We put in new cabinets.* **b** : to add (a comment) to a conversation or argument ▪ *Would you put in a good word for me?* [=would you say something good about me?] ▪ *Can I put in my two cents?* [=express my opinion] **c** : to make an official statement, offer, or request ▪ *I put in a report about this.* ▪ *We put in a bid for the job.* **d** : to perform (a particular action) ▪ *They put in a fine performance.* ▪ *He put in a call to his boss.* **e** : to work or do something for (an amount of time) ▪ *She put in a long day at work.* **2 put in (something) or put (something) in** : to use (an amount of energy or effort) when doing something ▪ *He puts a lot of energy in his work.*

3 put (something) in　a : to invest (money) into (something) ▪ *She put her money in stocks.*　**b** — used to say what causes you to have faith, confidence, etc. ▪ *putting her faith in God/science*　**4 put in for** : to ask for (something) in an official way ▪ *putting in for a promotion*　**5** *of a boat or ship* : to enter a harbor or port ▪ *The ship put in at Sydney.* — **put into** [*phrasal vb*] **put (something) into　1** : to use (an amount of energy or effort) when doing (something) ▪ *She put her heart into* [=she expressed her true feelings in] *the letter.*　**2** : to invest (time, money, etc.) in (something) ▪ *We put a lot of money into (fixing up) that house.* — **put it/her there** *informal* — used to invite someone to shake hands with you ▪ *Put her there, pal!* — **put off** [*phrasal vb*] **1 put (something) off** *or* **put off (something)** : to decide that (something) will happen at a later time : POSTPONE ▪ *The meeting was put off until next week.* ▪ *I've been putting off calling him.*　**2 put (someone) off** *or* **put off (someone)　a** : to cause (someone) to wait ▪ *putting off a bill collector*　**b** : to cause (someone) to dislike someone or something ▪ *I was put off by his rudeness.* = (*chiefly Brit*) *His rudeness put me off him.*　**c** *Brit* : to allow (someone) to get off a bus or other vehicle ▪ *Put me off (the bus) at the next stop, please.* — **put on** [*phrasal vb*] **1 put (something) on** *or* **put on (something)　a** : to dress yourself in (clothing) ▪ *She put on her hat.*　**b** : to apply (something) to your face or body ▪ *putting on lipstick/lotion* ▪ *She put on a happy/brave face.* [=tried to appear happy/brave]　**c** : to add to or increase the amount of (something) ▪ *He's put on some weight.*　**d** : to cause (a machine, a light, etc.) to begin to work ▪ *Put on the lights.*　**e** : to cause (something) to begin to be heard, produced, etc. ▪ *putting on some music/CDs/heat*　**f** : to start cooking or making (something) ▪ *He put on a pot of coffee.*　**g** : to produce (something that entertains people) ▪ *put on a concert/party/play/show*　**2 put (something) on　a** : to say that (someone or something) is responsible for or guilty of (something) ▪ *Don't put the blame on her.*　**b** : to bet (an amount of money) on (someone or something) ▪ *putting money on horse races*　**3 put (someone or something) on** : to add (someone or something) to (a list or group) ▪ *We put a new dish on the menu.*　**4 put (someone) on** *or* **put on (someone)** *chiefly US, informal* : to trick or fool (someone) for amusement ▪ *Are you putting me on?*　**5 put (someone) on** — used to say that you would like to speak to someone on the phone ▪ *Put Dave on (the phone), please.*　**6 put (someone) on** : to tell (someone) to use or do (something) ▪ *He put himself on a diet.* [=went on a diet]　**7 put (someone) on to** : to give (someone) information about (something) ▪ *He put me on to this book.* — **put out** [*phrasal vb*] **1 put (something) out** *or* **put out (something)　a** : to cause (something) to stop burning : EXTINGUISH ▪ *Put the fire out.*　**b** : to

stop (something) from working ▪ *Who put out the lights?*　**c** : to take (something) outside and leave it there ▪ *I put the dog out.* ▪ *putting out the trash/garbage/rubbish*　**d** : to extend (something) outward ▪ *I put out my hand and he shook it.*　**e** : to place (something) where people may use it ▪ *He put out a bowl of apples.*　**f** : to produce (something) ▪ *putting out effort/heat*　**g** : to make (something) available to be bought, used, etc. ▪ *putting out a new album/CD* ▪ *She put the word out* [=started telling people] *about the sale.*　**2 put (someone) out** *or* **put out (someone)　a** : to annoy or bother (someone) ▪ *I'm a little put out that he never called.*　**b** : to cause (someone) to do extra work ▪ *I hope we're not putting you out.*　**c** *sports* : to cause (someone) to be out in baseball or cricket ▪ *She was put out at second base.*　**3** : to leave a harbor or port ▪ *The ship put out to sea.* — **put over** [*phrasal vb*] **put (something) over on** : to trick or deceive someone ▪ *He tried to put something over on us.* — **put paid to** see ²PAID — **put (someone) in mind of** see ¹MIND — **put through** [*phrasal vb*] **1 put (something) through** *or* **put through (something)** : to cause (something) to be accepted or done successfully ▪ *putting through tax cuts*　**2 put (someone) through** : to pay for (someone) to attend (school) ▪ *She put herself through college.*　**3 put (someone or something) through** : to cause (someone or something) to experience (something) ▪ *They put the car through a series of tests.* ▪ *I've been put through hell!*　**4 put (someone or something) through　a** : to send a phone call from (someone) to another person's phone ▪ *Please hold while I put you through (to the manager).*　**b** : to send (a phone call) to another person's phone ▪ *I'll put your call through.* — **put together** [*phrasal vb*] **1 put (something) together** *or* **put together (something)　a** : to create (something) by joining or gathering parts together ▪ *putting a toy/proposal/outfit together*　**b** — used to say that someone or something is greater than the total of all the other people or things mentioned ▪ *You're smarter than all of them put together.*　**2 put (something) together with** : to add or combine (something) with (something) ▪ *The lack of rain put together with the heat ruined our crops.* — **put up** [*phrasal vb*] **1 put (something) up** *or* **put up (something)　a** : to place (something) in a higher position ▪ *They put up the flag.* ▪ *Put your feet up and relax.* ▪ *She put her hair up (in a bun/ponytail).*　**b** : to hang (something) on a wall, from a ceiling, etc. ▪ *put up curtains*　**c** : to set (something) so that it stands up ▪ *putting up a tent/sign*　**d** : to build (something) ▪ *They put up a fence/building.*　**e** : to make (something) available for people to buy or have ▪ *They put the house up for sale.*　**f** : to provide (money, property, etc.) to pay for something ▪ *Who put up the money for her bail?*　**g** *chiefly Brit* : to increase (something) ▪ *put up interest rates*　**2 a** : to do (something) as a way of resisting or struggling ▪

putting up a fight/fuss/argument **b** : to
score (points) ▪ *They put up 20 points in
the first half.* **3 a** *put (someone) up* : to
give food and shelter to (someone) ▪
They put him up at a hotel. **b** *chiefly Brit*
: to stay in someone's home, a hotel, etc.,
for the night ▪ *He put up with a friend.* **4**
put (someone) up to : to convince
(someone) to do (something stupid or
foolish) ▪ *Who put you up to this?* **5** *put
up with* : to allow (someone or something unpleasant or annoying) to exist or
happen : TOLERATE ▪ *I can't put up with
his behavior.*

²**put** *adj* — *stay put* : to not move or go
anywhere ▪ *Stay put until I get back.*

pu·ta·tive /'pjuːtətɪv/ *adj, always before a
noun, formal* : generally believed to be
something ▪ *a putative expert*

put-down /'pʊt،daʊn/ *n [C]* : a critical or
insulting statement ▪ *humiliating put-
downs*

put-on /'pʊt،ɑːn/ *n [C] chiefly US* : the
act of saying things that are not true in a
joking way ▪ *Are you serious, or was that a
put-on?*

put·out /'pʊt،aʊt/ *n [C] baseball* : an action that causes a batter or runner on the
opposite team to be out

pu·tre·fy /'pjuːtrə،faɪ/ *vb* **-fies; -fied; -fy-
ing** *[I] formal* : to rot and become putrid
▪ *putrefying meat/flesh*

pu·trid /'pjuːtrəd/ *adj* **1** : decayed with
usually a very bad smell ▪ *putrid meat/
odors* **2** *informal* : very ugly, bad, or unpleasant ▪ *a putrid color*

putt /'pʌt/ *vb [I]* : to hit a golf ball when it
is close to the hole with a special club
(called a putter) — **putt** *n [C]* ▪ *She
missed/made the putt.*

¹**putt·er** /'pʌtɚ/ *n [C]* **1** : a golf club that
is used to putt the ball **2** : a person who
putts golf balls ▪ *I'm a good/bad putter.*

²**put·ter** /'pʌtɚ/ *vb [I] Brit* : to make small
popping sounds while moving slowly ▪
The motorboat puttered across the lake.
— **putter around** [*phrasal vb*] *US* : to
spend time in a relaxed way doing small
jobs ▪ *I was just puttering around the
house/garden.*

¹**put·ting** *present participle of* ¹PUT

²**putt·ing** *present participle of* PUTT

putt·ing green /'pʌtɪŋ-/ *n [C] golf* : an
area covered with very short grass
around the hole into which the ball must
be played : GREEN; *also* : a similar area
that has many holes and that is used for
practice

put·ty /'pʌti/ *n [U]* : a soft, sticky substance that becomes hard when it dries
and that is used in construction ▪
(*figurative*) *He's putty in her hands.* [=she
is able to control him easily] — **putty** *vb*
put·ties; put·tied; put·ty·ing *[T]* ▪ *She
puttied the holes in the wood.*

put–up·on /'pʊtə،pɑːn/ *adj* : feeling that

someone is taking advantage of you ▪ *I
felt put-upon by her request.*

putz /'pʌts/ *n [C] US, informal* : a stupid
or foolish person who is not well liked

¹**puz·zle** /'pʌzəl/ *n [C]* **1** : a question or
problem that requires skill or cleverness
to be answered or solved **2** : JIGSAW
PUZZLE ▪ (*figurative*) *Researchers have
found the final piece of the puzzle.* **3**
: something or someone that is difficult
to understand ▪ *His strange behavior is a
puzzle to his friends.*

²**puz·zle** *vb* **puz·zled; puz·zling** *[T]* : to
confuse (someone) ▪ *The question puzzled
me.* ▪ *I was puzzled by his behavior.* ▪ *He
had a puzzled* [=*confused*] *look on his
face.* ▪ *a puzzling* [=*confusing*] *question* —
puzzle over [*phrasal vb*] : to think or
worry for a long time about (something)
▪ *We puzzled over how to arrange the furniture.* — **puz·zler** /'pʌzlɚ/ *n [C] formal*
▪ *The question is a real puzzler.*

puz·zle·ment /'pʌzəlmənt/ *n, formal* **1**
[*U*] : a feeling of being confused because
something is difficult to understand ▪
*The explanation only increased their puz-
zlement.* **2** [*singular*] *chiefly US* : something that is difficult to understand ▪ *The
cause of the accident is a puzzlement.*

PVC /،piːˌviːˈsiː/ *n [U]* : a type of plastic
used especially for pipes

Pvt. *abbr, US private* ▪ *Pvt. David Logan*

Pyg·my /'pɪgmi/ *n, pl* **-mies** *[C]* : a member of a group of very small people who
live in Africa

pygmy *also* **pigmy** *adj, always before a
noun, biology* — used to describe a type
of plant or animal that is smaller than
the usual size ▪ *a pygmy elephant*

pyjamas *Brit spelling of* PAJAMAS

py·lon /'paɪˌlɑːn/ *n [C]* : a tall tower or
similar structure

pyr·a·mid /'pɪrəˌmɪd/ *n [C]* **1** : a very
large structure that has a square base
and four triangular sides which form a
point at the top ▪ *the ancient pyramids of
Egypt* **2** : something that resembles a
pyramid ▪ *a pyramid of boxes* ▪ (*US*) *the
food pyramid* [=a drawing that is shaped
like a pyramid and that shows the type of
food you should eat for a healthy diet]

pyre /'pajɚ/ *n [C]* : a pile of wood for
burning a dead body ▪ *a funeral pyre*

py·ro·ma·nia /،paɪrouˈmeɪnijə/ *n [U]* : a
strong desire to set fires — **py·ro·ma·
ni·ac** /،paɪrouˈmeɪniˌæk/ *n [C]*

py·ro·tech·nics /،paɪrəˈtɛknɪks/ *n* [*plural*] **1** : a display of fireworks **2** : a
very impressive show or display that requires great skill ▪ *verbal/musical pyro-
technics*

Pyr·rhic victory /'pɪrɪk-/ *n [C]* : a victory that is not worth winning because so
much is lost to achieve it

py·thon /'paɪˌθɑːn/ *n [C]* : a type of very
large snake

Q

q *or* **Q** /ˈkjuː/ *n, pl* **q's** *or* **qs** *or* **Q's** *or* **Qs** [C/U] : the 17th letter of the English alphabet ▪ *The word "quart" begins with (a) q.* — **mind your p's and q's** see ¹P

Q and A *or* **Q & A** *n* [C] : a period of time or an occasion when someone answers questions from a reporter, people in an audience, etc. ▪ *a brief Q and A (session)*

qt. *abbr* quart

q.t. /ˌkjuːˈtiː/ — **on the q.t.** *or* **on the Q.T.** *informal* : in a secret or quiet way ▪ *Keep this on the q.t.* [=don't tell anyone about this]

Q–tips /ˈkjuːˌtɪps/ *trademark* — used for short sticks that have pieces of soft cotton at both ends

qtr. *abbr* quarter

qty. *abbr* quantity

quack /ˈkwæk/ *n* [C] **1** : the loud sound that is made by a duck **2** *informal* : an unskillful doctor or a person who falsely claims to have medical skills — **quack** *vb* [I] ▪ *We could hear the ducks quacking.*

quack·ery /ˈkwækəri/ *n* [U] *disapproving* : the methods and treatments used by unskillful doctors or by people who pretend to be doctors

quad /ˈkwɑːd/ *n* [C] *informal* : QUADRANGLE 2

quad·ran·gle /ˈkwɑːˌdræŋgəl/ *n* [C] **1** *geometry* : a flat shape that has four sides and four angles : QUADRILATERAL **2** : an open square or rectangular area at a college, school, etc., that is surrounded by buildings on all four sides

quad·rant /ˈkwɑːdrənt/ *n* [C] : one part of something that is evenly divided into four parts ▪ *the northwest quadrant of the state*; *especially, geometry* : one part of a circle that is evenly divided into four parts

quad·ri·ceps /ˈkwɑːdrəˌsɛps/ *n, pl* **quadriceps** [C] : a large muscle at the front of your upper leg

quad·ri·lat·er·al /ˌkwɑːdrəˈlætərəl/ *n* [C] *geometry* : a flat shape that has four sides and four angles

quad·ri·ple·gic /ˌkwɑːdrəˈpliːdʒɪk/ *n* [C] *medical* : a person who is permanently unable to move or feel both arms and both legs because of injury or illness — **quadriplegic** *adj*

¹**qua·dru·ple** /kwɑːˈdruːpəl/ *vb* **-dru·pled; -dru·pling** [T/I] : to become or to cause (something) to become four times bigger in value or number ▪ *The value of the stock has quadrupled in the past year.* ▪ *quadrupling your winnings*

²**quadruple** *adj* **1** : four times bigger in size or amount ▪ *a quadruple dose* **2** *always before a noun* : having four parts or including four people or things ▪ *a quadruple murder*

qua·dru·plet /kwɑːˈdruːplət/ *n* [C] : one of four babies that are born at the same time to the same mother

quag·mire /ˈkwæɡˌmajɚ/ *n* [C] **1** : an

area of soft, wet ground **2** : a situation that is hard to deal with or get out of ▪ *a legal quagmire*

quail /ˈkweɪl/ *n, pl* **quail** *or* **quails** **1** [C] : a kind of small wild bird that is often hunted **2** [U] : the meat of quail eaten as food

quaint /ˈkweɪnt/ *adj* : having an old-fashioned or unusual quality or appearance that is usually attractive or appealing ▪ *a quaint village* ▪ *quaint* [=*outdated*] *notions* — **quaint·ly** *adv*

¹**quake** /ˈkweɪk/ *vb* **quaked; quak·ing** [I] **1** : to shake because of fear, anger, etc. ▪ *She was quaking with rage/fear.* **2** : to shake violently ▪ *The house quaked.*

²**quake** *n* [C] *informal* : EARTHQUAKE

Quak·er /ˈkweɪkɚ/ *n* [C] : a member of a Christian religious group whose members dress simply, are against violence, and have meetings without any special ceremony or priests — **Quaker** *adj*

qual·i·fi·ca·tion /ˌkwɑːləfəˈkeɪʃən/ *n* **1** [C] **a** : a special skill or type of experience or knowledge that makes someone suitable to do a particular job or activity ▪ *He has the proper qualifications for the job.* ▪ *technical qualifications* **b** : something that is necessary in order for you to do, have, or be a part of something ▪ *the qualifications for getting a permit* **2** [C/U] *formal* : something that is added to a statement to limit or change its effect or meaning ▪ *I agree without qualification.* [=I agree completely] **3** [C] *Brit* : an official record or document (such as a degree, certificate, or diploma) which shows that you have completed a course of study or training and are qualified to do something ▪ *a teaching qualification*

qual·i·fied /ˈkwɑːləˌfaɪd/ *adj* **1** : having the necessary skill, experience, or knowledge to do a particular job or activity ▪ *She's highly qualified for the job.* ▪ *fully qualified teachers/nurses* **2** *formal* : not complete : limited in some way ▪ *The plan was given qualified approval.*

qual·i·fi·er /ˈkwɑːləˌfajɚ/ *n* [C] **1** : a person or team that has defeated others to enter a competition **2** : a game or contest that a person or team must win in order to enter a particular competition ▪ *She won the qualifier.* **3** *grammar* : MODIFIER

qual·i·fy /ˈkwɑːləˌfaɪ/ *vb* **-fies; -fied; -fy·ing** **1 a** [T] : to give (someone) the necessary skill or knowledge to do a particular job or activity ▪ *experience/training that qualifies you for the job* **b** [I] : to have the necessary skill or knowledge to do a particular job or activity ▪ *She qualifies for the job.* **2** [I] : to pass an exam or complete a course of study that is required in order to do something ▪ *studying to qualify as a pilot* **3 a** [I] : to have the right to do, have, or be a part of something ▪ *students who qualify for fi-*

nancial aid **b** [T] : to give (someone) the right to do, have, or be a part of something • *training that qualifies employees for pay increases* **4** [I] : to have the skills that are required or do the things that are required to become a member of a team or to be allowed in a competition • *athletes who qualify for the Olympics* **5 a** [I] : to have all the necessary qualities to be thought of or described in a particular way — + *as* • *clothes that qualify as business attire* • *The book is too short to qualify as a novel.* **b** [T] : to give (someone or something) the right to be thought of or described in a particular way — + *as* • *experience that qualifies someone as an expert* **6** [T] *formal* : to make (a statement) more specific or limited in meaning or effect • *I need to qualify* [=*modify*] *what I said earlier.*

qual·i·ta·tive /ˈkwɑːləˌteɪtɪv/ *adj* : of or relating to how good something is • *qualitative analysis of a product* — **qual·i·ta·tive·ly** *adv*

¹**qual·i·ty** /ˈkwɑːləti/ *n, pl* **-ties** **1** [U] : how good or bad something is • *air/water quality* • *the quality of products/services* • *your quality of life* [=how pleasant and enjoyable your life is] **2** [C] : a characteristic or feature that someone or something has • *the qualities of a good leader* • *a house/person with many fine qualities* **3** [U] : a high level of value or excellence • *Their store offers quality at reasonable prices.*

²**quality** *adj, always before a noun* : very good or excellent • *quality service/products*

quality time *n* [U] : time that you spend giving all of your attention to someone who is close to you (such as your child) • *Dad and I spent some quality time together.*

qualm /ˈkwɑːm/ *n* [C] : a feeling of doubt or uncertainty about whether you are doing the right thing • *I had/felt some qualms about leaving.*

quan·da·ry /ˈkwɑːndri/ *n, pl* **-ries** [C] *formal* : a situation in which you are confused about what to do • *I'm in a quandary* [=*unsure, confused*] *about which one to choose.*

quan·ti·fi·er /ˈkwɑːntəˌfajɚ/ *n* [C] *grammar* : a word or number (such as "many," "few," "some," "two," or "2") that is used with a noun to show the amount of something

quan·ti·fy /ˈkwɑːntəˌfaɪ/ *vb* **-fies; -fied; -fy·ing** [T] *formal* : to find or calculate the quantity or amount of (something) • *quantifying risks* — **quan·ti·fi·able** /ˌkwɑːntəˈfajəbəl/ *adj*

quan·ti·ta·tive /ˈkwɑːntəˌteɪtɪv/ *adj* : of or relating to how much there is of something • *a quantitative analysis/measurement* — **quan·ti·ta·tive·ly** *adv*

quan·ti·ty /ˈkwɑːntəti/ *n, pl* **-ties** [C/U] **1** : an amount or number of something • *small/large quantities of food* • *an increase in quantity* — abbr. *qty.* **2** : a large amount or number of something • *shipping quantities of books* • *buying supplies in quantity* [=in large amounts] — **known quantity** : someone or some-

thing whose abilities or characteristics are well known — **unknown quantity** : someone or something whose abilities or characteristics are not yet known • *She has very little experience as an actress so she's an unknown quantity.*

quan·tum leap /ˈkwɑːntəm-/ *n* [C] : a sudden large change, development, or improvement • *The new drug is a quantum leap in the fight against cancer.* — called also **quantum jump**

quantum mechanics *n* [U] *physics* : a branch of physics that deals with the structure and behavior of very small pieces of matter

quantum theory *n* [U] *physics* : a theory in physics that is based on the idea that energy (such as light) is made of small separate units of energy

quar·an·tine /ˈkwɔrənˌtiːn/ *n* **1** [C] : the period of time during which a person or animal that has a disease or that might have a disease is kept away from others to prevent the disease from spreading • *a six-month quarantine* **2** [U] : the situation of being kept away from others to prevent a disease from spreading • *cows being kept/held in quarantine* • *The dog was put/placed under quarantine.* — **quarantine** *vb* **-tined; -tin·ing** [T] • *The dog was quarantined.*

quark /ˈkwɑrk/ *n* [C] *physics* : any one of several types of very small particles that make up matter

¹**quar·rel** /ˈkwɔrəl/ *n* [C] **1** : an angry argument or disagreement • *a lover's quarrel* = *a quarrel between lovers* • *a quarrel about/over money* **2** : a reason to disagree with or argue about something • *I have no quarrel with your plan.*

²**quarrel** *vb, US* **-reled** *or Brit* **-relled; US -rel·ing** *or Brit* **-rel·ling** [I] : to argue about or disagree with something • *They were quarreling about/over money.*

quar·rel·some /ˈkwɔrəlsəm/ *adj* : ready or likely to argue or disagree • *a quarrelsome person*

¹**quar·ry** /ˈkwɔri/ *n, pl* **-ries** **1** [*singular*] : an animal or person that is being hunted or chased • *dogs chasing their quarry* **2** [C] : a place where large amounts of stone are dug out of the ground • *a limestone quarry*

²**quarry** *vb* **-ries; -ried; -ry·ing** **1** [T/I] : to dig or take (stone or other materials) from a quarry • *quarrying (for) limestone* **2** [T] : to make a quarry in (a place) • *an area quarried for limestone*

quart /ˈkwoɚt/ *n* [C] **1** *US* : a unit of liquid measurement equal to two U.S. pints or 0.946 liters — abbr. *qt.* **2** *Brit* : a unit of liquid measurement equal to two British pints or 1.14 liters — abbr. *qt.*

¹**quar·ter** /ˈkwoɚtɚ/ *n* **1** [C] : one of four equal parts of something • *Cut the pie into quarters.* • *a quarter* [=*fourth*] *of the class* **2** [C] : a unit of something (such as weight or length) that equals one fourth of some larger unit • *three quarters of a century* [=75 years] **3** [C] : one of four divisions of an hour : a period of 15 minutes • *It's (a) quarter of four.* [=15 minutes before four o'clock] • *It's (a) quarter past/after six.* [=15 minutes after

six o'clock) **4** [C] : one of four divisions of a year : a period of three months • *Profits rose in the second quarter.* **5** [C] : one of four divisions of a school term usually lasting about 12 weeks **6** [C] : one of the four equal parts of the playing time of a game (such as basketball or American football) • *There are two minutes left in the third quarter.* **7** [C] : a coin of the United States and Canada that is worth 25 cents **8** [C] : a person or group of people or an area in which people live • *complaints* **from** *all quarters* [=from many people or places] **9** [C] : a part or area of a city • *the historic quarter* [=*district*] **10** [*plural*] : the place where someone lives • *our living quarters* — **at/in close quarters** : close together usually in a very small space • *The sailors were living in close quarters.*

²**quarter** *vb* [T] **1** : to divide or separate (something) into four parts • *quartering potatoes* **2** : to provide (someone) with a place to stay for a usually short period of time • *We were quartered in log cabins at the camp.*

³**quarter** *adj, always before a noun* : equal or about nearly equal in size, value, amount, etc., to one fourth of something • *a quarter acre/mile* • *a quarter hour* [=15 minutes]

quar·ter·back /ˈkwoɚtɚˌbæk/ *n* [C] *American football* : a player who leads a team's attempts to score usually by passing the ball to other players

quar·ter·fi·nal (*US*) *or Brit* **quar·ter-final** /ˌkwoɚtɚˈfaɪnl/ *n* [C] : one of four matches, games, or contests that will decide the four people or teams that will continue playing in a competition (such as a tennis tournament)

¹**quar·ter·ly** /ˈkwoɚtɚli/ *adj* : happening, done, or produced four times a year • *a quarterly report/meeting* — **quarterly** *adv* • *payments made quarterly*

²**quarterly** *n, pl* **-lies** [C] : a magazine that is published four times a year

quarter note *n* [C] *US* : a musical note equal in time to ¼ of a whole note

quar·tet /kwoɚˈtɛt/ *n* [C] **1** : a group of four singers or musicians who perform together • *a jazz quartet* **2** : a group or set of four people or things • *a quartet of novels*

quartz /ˈkwoɚts/ *n* [U] : a mineral that is often found in the form of a hard crystal and that is used especially to make clocks and watches

quash /ˈkwɑːʃ/ *vb* [T] : to stop (something) from continuing by doing or saying something • *The riot was quashed by police.* • *quashing rumors*

qua·si- /ˈkweɪˌzaɪ, ˈkwɑːˌzi/ *combining form* : in some way or sense but not in a true, direct, or complete way • *a quasi-historical novel* • *a quasi-official organization*

qua·ver /ˈkweɪvɚ/ *vb* [I] *of your voice* : to produce sound in an unsteady way especially because you are afraid or nervous • *My voice quavered.* — **quaver** *n* [C] • *a quaver in my voice*

quay /ˈkiː/ *n* [C] : a structure built next to water for boats to stop for loading and unloading freight and passengers

quea·sy /ˈkwiːzi/ *adj* **quea·si·er; -est** : having a sick feeling in the stomach • *I feel a little queasy.* — **quea·si·ness** *n* [U]

queen /ˈkwiːn/ *n* [C] **1 a** : a woman who rules a country and who usually inherits her position and rules for life **b** : the wife of a king • *the king and his queen* **2 a** : a girl or woman who is highly respected and very successful or popular • *the queen of the blues* **b** : a girl or woman who is awarded the highest honor for an event or contest • *a homecoming queen* **c** : something that is thought of as female and that is considered better than all others • *This ship is the queen of ocean liners.* **3** : the most powerful piece in the game of chess that can move any number of free squares in any direction **4** : a playing card that has a picture of a queen • *the queen of hearts/spades* **5** : a female insect (such as a bee or ant) that lays eggs • *a queen bee*

queen-size /ˈkwiːnˌsaɪz/ *or* **queen-sized** /ˈkwiːnˌsaɪzd/ *adj, US, of a bed* : having a size of about 60 inches by 80 inches (about 1.5 by 1.9 meters)

¹**queer** /ˈkwiɚ/ *adj* **1** *old-fashioned* : odd or unusual • *a queer feeling* **2** *informal + usually offensive* : HOMOSEXUAL ✧ *Queer* in this sense is offensive in most of its uses, but it is also now sometimes used in a neutral or positive way especially by some homosexual and bisexual people. — **queer·ness** *n* [U]

²**queer** *n* [C] *informal + usually offensive* : a homosexual person

quell /ˈkwɛl/ *vb* [T] **1** : to end or stop (something) usually by using force • *Police quelled the riot.* **2** : to calm or reduce (something, such as fear or worry) • *words that quelled* [=*eased*] *our fears*

quench /ˈkwɛntʃ/ *vb* [T] *formal* : to stop (a fire) from burning • *Firefighters quenched the flames.* — **quench your thirst** : to cause you to stop feeling thirsty • *a drink to quench your thirst*

¹**que·ry** /ˈkwiri/ *n, pl* **-ries** [C] : a question or a request for information about something • *I have a query about my order.* • *an Internet query*

²**query** *vb* **-ries; -ried; -ry·ing** [T] **1** *chiefly US* : to ask (someone) a question • *a survey in which people were queried about their diets* **2** : to ask questions or express doubt about (something) • *She queried* [=*questioned*] *their decision.* **3** : to ask (a question) • *"What's that?" he queried.*

quest /ˈkwɛst/ *n* [C] *formal + literary* **1** : a journey made in search of something • *a quest for gold* **2** : a long and difficult effort to find or do something • *a quest for answers* — **in quest of** : searching for (something) • *in quest of the perfect wine* — **quest** *vb* [I] • *They were questing for gold.*

¹**ques·tion** /ˈkwɛstʃən/ *n* **1** [C] : a sentence, phrase, or word that asks for information or is used to test someone's knowledge • *Can I ask you a question?* • *Please answer my question.* • *The exam included several questions on/about cur-*

rent events. ▪ *Whether voters will approve it is an* **open question**. [=no one knows yet whether voters will approve it] ▪ *"Will the plan work?" "(That's a)* **good question**." [=I don't know] ▪ *The* **big question** [=the thing everyone would like to know] *is, will the plan work?* ▪ *a* **question and answer session** [=a period of time when people can have their questions answered] **2** [C] : a subject or topic ▪ *Her paper raises several questions* [=issues] *that need to be addressed.* **3** [U] ▪ : doubt or uncertainty about something ▪ *There's no question of/about their loyalty.* ▪ *Without question, the party was a success.* **b** : a state of doubt or uncertainty ▪ *The results have* **come into question.** = *The results have been* **called into question.** [=people are expressing doubts about the results] **4** [U] : the possibility or chance *of* something happening or *of* someone doing something ▪ *There was* **no question** *of escape.* [=escape was not possible] — *a* **question of** — used to say that one thing results from or requires another ▪ *It's only a* **question of time** [=a matter of time] *before/until they win.* — **beg the question** see BEG — **beyond question 1** : completely certain or definite ▪ *His genius is beyond question.* **2** : in a way that is completely certain ▪ *evidence that establishes his innocence beyond (all) question* — **in question 1** — used to indicate the specific thing that is being discussed or referred to ▪ *The painting in question is by Rembrandt.* **2** : in a state of doubt or uncertainty ▪ *The results are in question.* — **open to question** : not known for sure ▪ *The exact meaning is open to question.* — **out of the question** : not possible or allowed ▪ *Leaving was completely out of the question.* — **pop the question** see ¹POP

²**question** *vb* [T] **1** : to ask (someone) questions about something ▪ *I questioned her at length about it.* ▪ *police questioning a suspect* **2** : to have or express doubt about (something) ▪ *She questioned my decision/ability.* ▪ *They questioned the truth of her statement.* ▪ *questioning whether it's true* — **ques·tion·er** *n* [C]

ques·tion·able /ˈkwɛstʃənəbəl/ *adj* **1** : not likely to be true or correct ▪ *a highly questionable decision/conclusion* **2** : not worthy of trust ▪ *water of questionable quality* ▪ *acquiring money by questionable means* **3** : unknown or undecided ▪ *facing a questionable future*

¹**ques·tion·ing** /ˈkwɛstʃənɪŋ/ *adj* : showing a feeling of doubt or a desire to ask a question in order to get information ▪ *She gave him a questioning look.* — **ques·tion·ing·ly** *adv*

²**questioning** *n* [U] : the activity or process of asking questions ▪ *The police took him in for questioning.*

question mark *n* [C] **1** : the punctuation mark ? that is used after a direct question or to indicate that something (such as a birth date) is uncertain **2** *chiefly US* : someone or something that causes feelings of doubt or uncertainty ▪

The company's future remains a question mark.

ques·tion·naire /ˌkwɛstʃəˈneər/ *n* [C] : a written set of questions that are given to people in order to collect facts or opinions about something

queue /ˈkjuː/ *n* [C] **1** *chiefly Brit* : a line of people who are waiting for something ▪ *standing/waiting in a queue* [=(US) line] ▪ *a bus/taxi queue* **2** *computers* : a series of instructions that are stored in a computer so that they can be processed later ▪ *the printer queue* — **jump the queue** *Brit* : to go ahead of the other people in a queue — **queue** *vb* **queued; queu·ing** *or* **queue·ing** [I] *chiefly Brit* ▪ *People were queuing (up)* [=(US) lining up] *at the ticket window.*

¹**quib·ble** /ˈkwɪbəl/ *vb* **quib·bled; quib·bling** [I] : to argue or complain about small, unimportant things ▪ *Why are you quibbling about/over such a small amount of money?*

²**quibble** *n* [C] : a small complaint or criticism usually about something unimportant ▪ *Our only quibble about the trip was that it rained a lot.*

quiche /ˈkiːʃ/ *n* [C/U] : a pie made with eggs, milk, cheese, and vegetables or meat

quick /ˈkwɪk/ *adj* **1** : done or happening in a short amount of time ▪ *a quick look/shower* ▪ *You're back already? That was quick!* ▪ *a quick decision/reply* **2** : fast in thinking, learning, or understanding ▪ *a quick mind/learner* ▪ *quick students* ▪ *his quick wit* **3 a** : fast in moving or reacting ▪ *walking with quick steps* ▪ *Please be quick. We can't wait much longer.* ▪ *He has a* **quick temper.** [=he gets angry very quickly and easily] **b** : tending to do something very quickly or too quickly — followed by *to* + *verb* ▪ *She's quick to criticize/praise other people.* **4** : able to be done, obtained, or achieved easily and in a short amount of time ▪ *a quick and easy recipe* ▪ *a quick profit/buck* ▪ *a* **quick fix** *for the problem* [=a fast and easy solution for the problems] — **quick·ness** *n* [U]

²**quick** *adv, informal* : in a fast or quick manner : QUICKLY ▪ *a scheme to get rich quick* ▪ *Come quick!* ▪ *quick-growing trees* ▪ *Quick!* [=come/move quickly] *The train is leaving.* ▪ *They came* **quick as a flash.** [=very quickly]

³**quick** *n* — **cut (someone) to the quick** : to make (someone) very upset ▪ *Her harsh words cut him to the quick.*

quick·en /ˈkwɪkən/ *vb* [T/I] : to become faster or to cause (something) to become faster ▪ *a quickening tempo* ▪ *She quickened her steps.* ▪ *stimulants that quicken the heart rate*

quick·ie /ˈkwɪki/ *n* [C] *informal* : something that is done very quickly ▪ *a quickie divorce*

quick·ly /ˈkwɪkli/ *adv* : in a fast or quick manner ▪ *eat/act quickly* ▪ *Get here as quickly as possible.*

quick·sand /ˈkwɪkˌsænd/ *n* **1** [U] : deep, wet sand into which heavy objects sink easily **2** [U, *singular*] : a situation that is dangerous and difficult to escape from • *the quicksand of depression*

quick-tem-pered /'kwɪk'tɛmpəd/ *adj*
: becoming angry quickly and easily • *a quick-tempered coach*

quick-wit-ted /'kwɪk'wɪtəd/ *adj* : having or showing the ability to think and understand things quickly • *a quick-witted speaker/reply*

quid /'kwɪd/ *n, pl* **quid** *also* **quids** [C] *Brit, informal* : one pound in money • *The ticket costs five quid.*

quid pro quo /ˌkwɪdˌprouˈkwou/ *n* [C] : something that is given to you or done for you in return for something else • *If he helps us, he'll expect a quid pro quo.* [=he'll expect us to do something for him]

¹**qui-et** /'kwajət/ *adj* **1** : making very little noise • *a quiet engine/voice* • *She was as quiet as a mouse.* [=very quiet] **2 a** : not talking • *The class/crowd was quiet.* • *Be quiet!* **b** : tending not to talk very much • *He's a very quiet person.* • *a quiet temperament* **3** : not having much activity or movement • *Business was quiet.* • *a quiet town/village/neighborhood* • *a quiet life* **4** : not disturbed by noise or people • *We enjoyed a quiet dinner.* **5** : not shown or done in an obvious way • *quiet determination/confidence/rage* — **keep quiet 1** : to not say anything or make any noise • *Please keep quiet during the movie.* • *witnesses to the crime who decided to keep quiet* [=to not say anything] **2** **keep quiet about (something) or keep (something) quiet** : to not say anything about (something) • *She kept quiet about her plans.* = *She kept her plans quiet.* **3 keep (someone or something) quiet a** : to prevent (someone or something) from speaking or making noise • *Give the dog a bone to keep him quiet.* **b** : to prevent (someone) from revealing information • *What'll it take to keep you quiet?* — **qui-et-ly** *adv* • *speaking/moving quietly* — **qui-et-ness** *n* [U] • *the quietness of the forest/neighborhood*

²**quiet** *vb* [T] *chiefly US* : to make (someone or something) quieter, calmer, or less intense • *trying to quiet* [=(Brit) *quieten*] (*down*) *the crowd* • *quiet a crying baby* • *His efforts did little to quiet our doubts.* — **quiet down** [*phrasal vb*] *chiefly US* : to become quiet or quieter • *Quiet down* [=(Brit) *quieten down*], *please.* • *Things quieted down in town.* [=the town became less busy]

³**quiet** *n* [U] : the quality or state of being quiet or calm • *the quiet of a wooded trail* • *I need some* **peace and quiet.** — **on the quiet** : in a secret or quiet way • *a deal made on the quiet*

qui-et-en /'kwajətən/ *vb* [T] *Brit* : ²QUIET • *trying to quieten (down) the crowd* — **quieten down** [*phrasal vb*] *Brit* : to become quiet or quieter • *They've quietened down some.*

qui-etude /'kwajə,tu:d, Brit 'kwajə,tju:d/ *n* [U] *literary* : the state of being quiet or calm : QUIETNESS

quill /'kwɪl/ *n* [C] **1** : a large, stiff feather from the wing or tail of a bird **2** : a pen that is made from a feather — called also

quill pen **3** : one of the hollow, sharp parts on the back of a porcupine

quilt /'kwɪlt/ *n* [C] : a bed cover with stitched designs that is made of two layers of cloth filled with wool, cotton, or soft feathers

quilt-ed /'kwɪltəd/ *adj* : having two layers of stitched cloth filled with wool, cotton, or soft feathers • *a quilted coat*

quilt-ing /'kwɪltɪŋ/ *n* [U] : the activity or process of making a quilt

quince /'kwɪns/ *n* **1** [C/U] : the yellow fruit of an Asian tree that is used for making jam, jelly, etc. **2** [C] : the tree that produces quince

qui-nine /'kwaɪ,naɪn, Brit 'kwɪ,ni:n/ *n* [U] : a drug that is made from the bark of a tree and used especially to treat malaria

quint-es-sen-tial /ˌkwɪntəˈsɛnʃəl/ *adj* : perfect as an example of a specified thing • *He was the quintessential cowboy.* [=he was the perfect example of a cowboy] • *She's the quintessential New Yorker.* — **quint-es-sen-tial-ly** *adv* • *the movie's quintessentially British humor*

quin-tet /kwɪn'tɛt/ *n* [C] : a group of five singers or musicians who perform together • *a brass/jazz quintet*

¹**quin-tu-ple** /kwɪn'tʌpəl, Brit 'kwɪntjʊpl/ *vb* -**tu-pled**; -**tu-pling** [T/I] : to become or to cause (something) to become five times bigger in value or number • *The town's population has quintupled in the past 50 years.* • *We quintupled our earnings.*

²**quintuple** *adj* **1** : five times bigger in size or amount • *prices that are quintuple what they were* **2** *always before a noun* : having five parts or including five people or things • *quintuple bypass surgery*

quin-tu-plet /kwɪn'tʌplət, Brit 'kwɪntjʊplət/ *n* [C] : one of five babies that are born at the same time to the same mother

quip /'kwɪp/ *n* [C] : a clever remark • *witty/amusing quips* — **quip** *vb* **quipped**; **quip-ping** [T]

quirk /'kwɚk/ *n* [C] **1** : an unusual habit or way of behaving • *We all have our quirks.* **2** : something strange that happens by chance • *Our meeting was a (strange) quirk of fate/nature.*

quirky /'kwɚki/ *adj* **quirk-i-er**; -**est** : unusual especially in an interesting or appealing way • *a quirky sense of humor*

quit /'kwɪt/ *vb* **quit** *also* **quit-ted**; **quit-ting 1** [T/I] *informal* : to leave (a job, school, career, etc.) • *He quit his job.* • *quitting college/teaching* • *She hates her job and is thinking about quitting.* • *I quit!* **2** [T/I] *chiefly US, informal* : to stop doing (an action or activity) • *She quit smoking.* • *Quit bothering her.* • *Quit it.* [=stop doing what you are doing] • *workers ready to quit for the day* **3** [I] *informal* : to stop working • *The engine suddenly quit.* **4** [T/I] *formal* : to leave (the place where you live) • *The landlord gave the tenants notice to quit (the premises).* [=the landlord formally told them that they had to leave]

quite /'kwaɪt/ *adv* **1 a** : VERY ✧ *Quite* is a more forceful word than *fairly* but it is a less forceful word than *extremely*. It is used more often in British English than in U.S. English, but it is not an unusual or rare word in U.S. English. ▪ *She did quite well.* ▪ *He's quite ill/rich/busy.* ▪ *It's quite large/small/near/far.* ▪ *We see them quite frequently.* ▪ *Quite simply, I can't afford it.* ▪ *She sings quite wonderfully.* **b** — used to make a statement more forceful ▪ *"We're sorry for the trouble." "That's* **quite all right."** ▪ *I haven't seen her for* **quite some time.** [=a long period of time] ▪ *I've heard* **quite enough.** ▪ *It was* **quite something** [=a major event] *when our team won.* — often used with *a, an,* or *the* before a noun ▪ *She's quite a beauty.* [=she's very beautiful] ▪ *It was quite a surprise/shock.* [=it was very surprising/shocking] ▪ *quite a lot of food* ▪ *It was quite an eventful week.* ▪ *waiting for quite a while* ▪ *The award is quite an honor.* [=is a very impressive honor] **2** : completely or entirely ▪ *I'm not quite ready.* ▪ *I'm quite capable of doing it myself.* ▪ *You're quite mistaken.* ▪ *Something wasn't quite right.* ▪ *We hadn't quite finished.* **3** : exactly or precisely ▪ *No one realized quite what was happening.* ▪ *That's not quite what I said.* **4** *Brit* — used to express agreement ▪ *"They have no one but themselves to blame." "Quite right/so."* — **quite a bit** see ¹BIT — **quite a few** see ¹FEW — **quite the contrary** see ¹CONTRARY

quits /ˈkwɪts/ *adj* — **call it quits** *informal* : to quit or end something (such as a job, relationship, or activity) ▪ *After eight years of marriage, she and her husband are calling it quits.* — **double or quits** see ³DOUBLE

quit·ter /ˈkwɪtɚ/ *n* [C] *informal + disapproving* : a person who easily gives up or stops doing something ▪ *Don't be a quitter.*

¹**quiv·er** /ˈkwɪvɚ/ *vb* [I] : to shake because of fear, cold, nervousness, etc. ▪ *He was quivering with excitement/rage.*

²**quiver** *n* [C] **1** : a shaking sound, movement, or feeling that is caused by fear or other strong emotions ▪ *a quiver of excitement* **2** : a case used for carrying arrows

quix·ot·ic /kwɪkˈsɑːtɪk/ *adj, formal* : hopeful or romantic in a way that is not practical ▪ *a quixotic solution/dream*

¹**quiz** /ˈkwɪz/ *n, pl* **quiz·zes** [C] **1** *US* : a short spoken or written test that is often taken without preparation **2** : a set of questions about a particular subject that people try to answer as a game or competition ▪ *a trivia/health quiz*

²**quiz** *vb* **quizzes; quizzed; quiz·zing** [T] **1** : to ask (someone) questions about something ▪ *They quizzed him on his knowledge of jazz.* **2** *US* : to give (someone) a quiz ▪ *The teacher quizzed us on the new material.*

quiz show *n* [C] : a radio or television program during which people compete with each other by trying to answer questions

quiz·zi·cal /ˈkwɪzɪkəl/ *adj* : showing that you do not understand something or that you find something strange or amusing ▪ *a quizzical look/expression* — **quiz·zi·cal·ly** /ˈkwɪzɪkli/ *adv*

quo·rum /ˈkwoʊrəm/ *n* [*singular*] : the smallest number of people who must be present at a meeting in order for decisions to be made

quo·ta /ˈkwoʊtə/ *n* [C] **1** : an official limit on the number or amount of people or things that are allowed ▪ *import/export quotas* ▪ *fishing/hunting quotas* **2** : a specific amount or number that is expected to be achieved ▪ *a sales quota*

quot·able /ˈkwoʊtəbəl/ *adj* : interesting or clever enough to be quoted ▪ *a quotable phrase/author*

quo·ta·tion /kwoʊˈteɪʃən/ *n* [C] **1** : something that a person says or writes that is repeated or used by someone else in another piece of writing or a speech ▪ *literary quotations* [=*quotes*] **2** : a written statement of how much money a particular job will cost to do ▪ *We should get price quotations* [=*quotes*] *from several builders.*

quotation mark *n* [C] : one of a pair of punctuation marks " " or ' ' that are used to show the beginning and the end of a quotation, to show that something is a title, to show that a word or phrase is being used in a special way, etc. ▪ *There were quotation marks around the phrase.* = *The phrase was in quotation marks.* — called also (*Brit*) **inverted comma**

¹**quote** /ˈkwoʊt/ *vb* **quot·ed; quot·ing** **1 a** [T] : to repeat (something written or said by another person) exactly ▪ *She quoted a passage from the book in her article.* **b** [T] : to write or say the exact words of (someone) ▪ *He began his speech by quoting Shakespeare.* ▪ *Can I quote you on that?* [=can I tell other people that you said that?] **c** [T/I] : to write or say a line or short section from (a piece of writing or a speech) ▪ *quoting (from) the Bible* **d** [T] — used in speech to show that you are actually repeating someone else's words ▪ *I asked him if he was leaving, and he said, quote, "Not if I can help it."* ▪ *He said, quote, "Not if I can help it."* — often followed by *unquote* ▪ *She said it was quote, "time for a change,"* *unquote.* ▪ *He said he's been living under,* **quote, unquote,** *"intense pressure."* **2** [T] : to tell someone the price at which something can be bought or done ▪ *One builder quoted (us) a much lower price for the job.*

²**quote** *n* [C] **1** : QUOTATION 1 ▪ *She included quotes from the poem in her essay.* ▪ *price quotes* **2** : QUOTATION MARK ▪ *a phrase in quotes* [=with quotation marks around it]

quo·tient /ˈkwoʊʃənt/ *n* [C] **1** *mathematics* : the number that results when one number is divided by another **2** : the degree to which a specific quality or characteristic exists ▪ *an actress with a high likability quotient* [=an actress who is very likable]

Quran *or* **Qur'an** *variant spellings of* KORAN

QWER·TY /ˈkwɚti/ *adj, of a keyboard* : having the letters q, w, e, r, t, and y arranged in a row in the top row of letter keys

R

¹**r** or **R** /ˈɑɚ/ n, pl **r's** or **rs** or **R's** or **Rs** [C/U] : the 18th letter of the English alphabet • *words that begin with (an) r*

²**r** abbr **1** radius **2** or **R** right

¹**R** — used as a special mark to indicate that people over the age of 17 or 18 may see a particular movie but that younger people may only see the movie in a movie theater with a parent or guardian • *The movie is rated R.*

²**R** abbr **1** registered trademark **2** Republican

rab·bi /ˈræˌbaɪ/ n [C] : a person who is trained to make decisions about what is lawful in Judaism, to perform Jewish ceremonies, or to lead a Jewish congregation

rab·bin·ic /rəˈbɪnɪk/ or **rab·bin·i·cal** /rəˈbɪnɪkəl/ adj, always before a noun : of or relating to rabbis, their writings, or their teachings • *rabbinic traditions*

rab·bit /ˈræbət/ n, pl **rab·bits** or **rabbit** **1** [C] : a small animal that usually lives in holes in the ground and has long ears, soft fur, and back legs that are longer than its front legs **2** [U] : the fur or meat of a rabbit • *a rabbit coat/stew*

rab·ble /ˈræbəl/ n, disapproving **1** [singular] : a large group of loud people who could become violent : MOB • *an angry/unruly rabble* **2 the rabble** : ordinary or common people who do not have a lot of money, power, or social status • *celebrities who live in beautiful homes far away from the rabble*

rab·ble–rous·er /ˈræbəlˌrauzɚ/ n [C] disapproving : a person who makes a group of people angry, excited, or violent (such as by giving speeches) — **rab·ble–rous·ing** /ˈræbəlˌrauzɪŋ/ adj • *a rabble-rousing speech/politician* — **rabble–rousing** n [U]

ra·bid /ˈræbəd/ adj **1** : affected with rabies • *rabid dogs* **2** : having or expressing a very extreme opinion about or interest in something • *rabid baseball fans* — **ra·bid·ly** adv

ra·bies /ˈreɪbiz/ n [U] : a very serious and often fatal disease that affects animals (such as dogs) and that can be passed on to people if an infected animal bites them

rac·coon /ræˈkuːn/ n, pl **raccoon** or **rac·coons** [C] : a small North American animal with grayish-brown fur that has black fur around its eyes and black rings around its tail

¹**race** /ˈreɪs/ n **1** [C] **a** : a competition between people, animals, vehicles, etc., to see which one is fastest • *a bicycle/boat/car/yacht race* **b** : a contest or competition in which different people or teams try to win something or to do something first • *the race for governor* • *the race to find a cure for the disease* **c** [singular] : a situation in which someone has to do something very quickly because there is not much time • *It was a race against time to disarm the bomb.* **2 a** [C/U] : one of the groups that people can be divided into based on certain physical qualities (such as skin color) **b** [C] : a group of people who share the same history, language, culture, etc. • *the English race*

²**race** vb **raced**; **rac·ing** **1** [T/I] : to compete in a race against another person, animal, vehicle, etc. • *She's going to race (against) the champion.* **2** [T] : to drive or ride (a car, horse, etc.) in a race • *He races cars for a living.* **3** [T/I] : to go, move, or function at a very fast speed • *The dog raced ahead of me.* • *His heart was racing.* [=was beating very fast] • *Her mind was racing.* [=she had many thoughts going quickly through her mind] • *The truck's engine was racing.* • *Researchers are racing (against time) to find a cure.* — **rac·er** /ˈreɪsɚ/ n [C]

race course (US) or Brit **race·course** /ˈreɪsˌkoɚs/ n [C] : a course or track that is used for racing

race-go·er /ˈreɪsˌgowɚ/ n [C] chiefly Brit : a person who goes to a race

race·horse /ˈreɪsˌhoɚs/ n [C] : a horse that is bred and trained for racing

race·track /ˈreɪsˌtræk/ n [C] : a track or course that is used for racing

ra·cial /ˈreɪʃəl/ adj : relating to or based on race • *racial prejudices/segregation* — **ra·cial·ly** adv

ra·cial·ism /ˈreɪʃəˌlɪzəm/ n [U] chiefly Brit, old-fashioned : RACISM — **ra·cial·ist** /ˈreɪʃəlɪst/ n [C] — **racialist** adj

racing n [U] : the sport or profession of racing horses, cars, etc.

rac·ism /ˈreɪˌsɪzəm/ n [U] disapproving **1** : poor treatment of or violence against people because of their race • *Have you experienced racism?* **2** : the belief that some races of people are better than others • *discrimination based on racism* — **rac·ist** /ˈreɪsɪst/ n [C] — **racist** adj • *racist remarks/attitudes*

¹**rack** /ˈræk/ n **1** [C] : a frame or stand that has shelves, hooks, slots, etc., in which or on which you place things • *a bike/hat/magazine/wine/dish rack* • *Clothes were flying off the rack.* [=people were buying the clothes very quickly] **2** [C/U] : a cut of meat from a lamb or pig that includes some of the ribs • *(a) rack of lamb* **3** [U] : the state of being destroyed or ruined • *The old house has gone to rack and ruin.* [=has become ruined] — **off the rack** US : in a store where clothes are sold in different sizes that are not made to fit a particular person • *He bought that suit off the rack.* [=(Brit) off the peg]

²**rack** vb [T] : to cause (someone or something) to suffer pain or damage • *He was racked with/by jealousy.* — **rack up** [phrasal vb] informal : to achieve or get

(something) as time passes • *The company has racked up huge losses/sales.* — **rack your brain/brains** : to think very hard to try to remember something, solve a problem, etc. • *I've been racking my brain, but I can't remember his name.*

rack·et *or* **rac·quet** /ˈrækət/ *n* **1** [C] : a piece of sports equipment that is used to hit a ball or other object in games like tennis, badminton, squash, etc. • *a tennis racket* **2** [*singular*] : a loud, unpleasant noise • *The kids were making a terrible racket.* **3** [C] : a business that makes money through illegal activities • *a criminal racket*

rack·e·teer /ˌrækəˈtiɚ/ *n* [C] : a person who makes money through illegal activities — **rack·e·teer·ing** /ˌrækəˈtirɪŋ/ *n* [U] • *He was arrested and charged with racketeering.*

rac·quet·ball /ˈrækətˌbɑːl/ *n* **1** [U] : a game played on a court with four walls by two or four players who use rackets to hit a soft ball against the walls **2** [C] : the ball that is used in racquetball

racy /ˈreɪsi/ *adj* **rac·i·er; -est** : exciting, lively, or amusing often in a way that is slightly shocking • *a racy novel*

ra·dar /ˈreɪˌdɑɚ/ *n* [C/U] : a device that sends out radio waves for finding out the position and speed of a moving object (such as an airplane) • *The approaching planes were detected by radar.*

radar gun *n* [C] : a small device that uses radar to measure the speed of a moving object (such as a car or a ball)

¹ra·di·al /ˈreɪdijəl/ *adj* : arranged or having parts arranged in straight lines coming out from the center of a circle • *a radial pattern* — **ra·di·al·ly** *adv*

²radial *n* [C] : a type of strong tire in which cords underneath the rubber run across the tire's surface — called also *radial tire*

ra·di·ant /ˈreɪdijənt/ *adj* **1** : having or showing an attractive quality of happiness, love, health, etc. • *a radiant smile* **2** : bright and shining • *the radiant sun* **3** *always before a noun, technical* : sent out from something in rays or waves that you cannot see • *radiant heat/energy* — **ra·di·ance** /ˈreɪdijəns/ *n* [U, *singular*] • *the youthful radiance of her face/smile* • *the sun's radiance* — **ra·di·ant·ly** *adv* • *She smiled radiantly.*

ra·di·ate /ˈreɪdiˌeɪt/ *vb* **-at·ed; -at·ing 1** [I] : to go out in a direct line from a central point or area • *Spokes radiate (out/outward) from the center of the wheel.* **2** [I] : to move in a specified direction from a source • *The pain radiated down my arm.* **3 a** [T] : to send out (heat, energy, etc.) in rays • *The sun radiates heat and light.* **b** [I] : to come or go out in the form of rays • *Heat radiates from the sun.* **4** [T] : to show (a feeling or quality) very clearly • *a smile that radiates warmth*

ra·di·a·tion /ˌreɪdiˈeɪʃən/ *n* [U] **1** : a type of dangerous and powerful energy that is produced by radioactive substances and nuclear reactions **2 a** : energy that comes from a source in the form of waves or rays you cannot see • *ultraviolet*

radiation **b** *technical* : the process of giving off energy in the form of waves or rays you cannot see • *the sun's radiation of heat*

ra·di·a·tor /ˈreɪdiˌeɪtɚ/ *n* [C] **1** : a large, metal device that provides heat for a room when hot water passes through it **2** : a device that is used to keep the engine of a vehicle from getting too hot

¹rad·i·cal /ˈrædɪkəl/ *adj* **1 a** : very new and different from what is traditional or ordinary • *radical ideas about education* **b** : very basic and important • *radical reforms/differences* **2** : having extreme political or social views that are not shared by most people • *radical liberals/conservatives* — **rad·i·cal·ism** /ˈrædɪkəˌlɪzəm/ *n* [U] • *political radicalism* — **rad·i·cal·ly** /ˈrædɪkli/ *adv* • *a radically different approach to the problem*

²radical *n* [C] : a person who favors extreme changes in government : a person who has radical political opinions

radii *plural of* RADIUS

¹ra·dio /ˈreɪdiˌoʊ/ *n, pl* **-di·os 1** [U] : the system or process that is used for sending and receiving signals through the air without using wires • *The news was sent/received by/over radio.* • *radio signals* **2** [U] : programs that are broadcast by radio • *I heard the song on the radio.* **3** [C] **a** : a device that is used to receive the signals that are broadcast by radio • *There's a problem with the car's radio.* **b** : a device that is used to send and receive messages by radio • *The pilot's radio wasn't working.* **4** [U] : the business that makes and broadcasts radio programs • *She has a job in radio.*

²radio *vb* **-dios; -di·oed; -di·o·ing** [T/I] : to send a message to someone by radio • *The police radioed for help.* • *They radioed a report back to the station.*

ra·dio·ac·tive /ˌreɪdijoʊˈæktɪv/ *adj* : having or producing a powerful and dangerous form of energy (called radiation) • *radioactive waste* — **ra·dio·ac·tive·ly** *adv* — **ra·dio·ac·tiv·i·ty** /ˌreɪdijoʊˌækˈtɪvəti/ *n* [U]

ra·di·og·ra·phy /ˌreɪdiˈɑːgrəfi/ *n* [U] *medical* : the process of taking a photograph of the inside of a person's body by using X-rays — **ra·di·og·ra·pher** /ˌreɪdiˈɑːgrəfɚ/ *n* [C] *medical*

ra·di·ol·o·gy /ˌreɪdiˈɑːlədʒi/ *n* [U] *medical* : a branch of medicine that uses some forms of radiation (such as X-rays) to diagnose and treat diseases — **ra·di·ol·o·gist** /ˌreɪdiˈɑːlədʒɪst/ *n* [C]

ra·dio·ther·a·py /ˌreɪdioʊˈθerəpi/ *n* [U] *medical* : the use of controlled amounts of radiation for the treatment of diseases (such as cancer) — **ra·dio·ther·a·pist** /ˌreɪdioʊˈθerəpɪst/ *n* [C]

radio wave *n* [C] : an electromagnetic wave that is used for sending signals through the air without using wires

rad·ish /ˈrædɪʃ/ *n* [C] : a small, round vegetable that is red or white, is eaten raw in salads, and has a sharp, spicy taste; *also* : the plant that produces this vegetable

ra·di·um /ˈreɪdijəm/ *n* [U] : a radioactive

ra·di·us /ˈreɪdiəs/ n, pl **ra·dii** /ˈreɪdiˌaɪ/ [C] **1** technical : a straight line from the center of a circle or sphere to any point on the outer edge; also : the length of this line • a circle with a radius of 10 inches **2** : an area that goes outward in all directions from a particular place • There are three restaurants within a one-block radius of our apartment. **3** medical : the bone in the lower part of your arm on the same side as your thumb

ra·don /ˈreɪˌdɑːn/ n [U] : a radioactive element which is a gas that is used medically in cancer treatments

RAF abbr Royal Air Force

raff·ish /ˈræfɪʃ/ adj : not completely acceptable or respectable but interesting and attractive • raffish charm

¹**raf·fle** /ˈræfəl/ n [C] : a contest that a group or organization uses to earn money and that involves people buying numbered tickets in exchange for a chance to win a prize

²**raffle** vb **raf·fled**; **raf·fling** [T] : to give (something) as a prize in a raffle — usually + off • Our church is raffling off turkeys.

raft /ˈræft, Brit ˈrɑːft/ n [C] **1 a** : a flat structure that is used for floating or sailing on water **b** : a plastic or rubber boat that you have to fill with air in order to use **2** : a large amount or number of people or things • a raft of supporters

raf·ter /ˈræftɚ, Brit ˈrɑːftə/ n [C] **1** : one of the large, long pieces of wood that support a roof **2** : a person who makes or travels in a raft

raft·ing /ˈræftɪŋ, Brit ˈrɑːftɪŋ/ n [U] : the activity of traveling down a river on a raft • a rafting trip • We went rafting last weekend.

¹**rag** /ˈræg/ n **1** [C] : a piece of cloth that is old and no longer in good condition • She used a rag to wipe up the spill. **2** [plural] : clothing that is in poor condition • a homeless person (dressed) in rags **3** [C] informal : a newspaper of poor quality • He's a writer for our local rag. — **chew the rag** see CHEW — **from rags to riches** : from being poor to being wealthy • She went from rags to riches overnight.

²**rag** vb **rag·ged**; **rag·ging** [T/I] informal : to laugh at and make jokes about (someone) • The other kids ragged him for having a crush on the teacher. • (US) The other kids were ragging on me.

rag·a·muf·fin /ˈrægəˌmʌfən/ n [C] somewhat old-fashioned : a child who is dressed in rags and is usually dirty and poor

rag·bag /ˈrægˌbæg/ n [C] chiefly Brit : a collection of very different things • a ragbag of ideas

rag doll n [C] : a soft doll made of cloth

¹**rage** /ˈreɪdʒ/ n **1 a** [U] : a strong feeling of anger that is difficult to control • He was shaking with rage. **b** : a sudden expression of violent anger • He flew into a rage. [=he suddenly became extremely angry] **2** [singular] **a** : something that is suddenly very popular • Karaoke is (all)

the rage these days. **b** : a strong desire by many people to have or do something • the current rage for flavored coffee

²**rage** vb **raged**; **rag·ing** [I] **1** : to talk in an extremely angry way • Activists have raged against the company for years. **2** : to happen or continue in a destructive, violent, or intense way • The fire/debate raged (on) for hours.

rag·ged /ˈrægəd/ adj **1** : having an edge or surface that is not straight or even • a ragged outline **2 a** : in bad condition especially because of being torn • ragged clothes **b** : wearing clothes that are torn and in poor condition • a ragged orphan **3** : tired from effort or stress • You look a little ragged. **4** : having good parts and bad parts • a ragged performance **5** : not smooth or even • The patient's breathing is ragged. • a ragged cough — **run (someone) ragged** informal : to make (someone) very tired • All this travel is running me ragged! — **rag·ged·ly** adv

rag·gedy /ˈrægədi/ adj, informal : not in good condition • raggedy clothes

raging adj, always before a noun **1** : very wild and violent • a raging storm **2** : very great, strong, or impressive • The book was a raging success. **3** : causing a lot of pain or distress • a raging headache

rag·tag /ˈrægˌtæg/ adj, always before a noun, informal : not organized or put together well • a ragtag group of musicians

rag·time /ˈrægˌtaɪm/ n [U] : a type of lively music that is often played on the piano and that was popular in the U.S. in the early 20th century

rag·weed /ˈrægˌwiːd/ n [U] : any one of a group of North American plants that release a lot of pollen into the air

¹**raid** /ˈreɪd/ n [C] **1** : a sudden and unexpected attack or invasion • a bombing raid • a drug raid [=an invasion by police to find illegal drugs] **2** chiefly Brit : an act of going into a place to steal something : HEIST • a bank raid

²**raid** vb [T] **1** : to attack (a place or group) in a sudden and unexpected way • The village was raided by a neighboring tribe. **2** : to enter (a place) suddenly and forcefully to look for someone or something or to steal or take something • Police raided the house and found drugs. • Armed men raided the bank. • She raided her sister's closet to find something to wear to the party. — **raid·er** /ˈreɪdɚ/ n [C]

¹**rail** /ˈreɪl/ n **1** [C] **a** : a bar that goes from one post or support to another and that is used to form a barrier • She leaned over the rail of the ship. • a fence rail **b** : a bar used to hang something from • He hung the curtains on the rail. **2 a** [C] : one of the bars of steel that form a train's track • The train went off the rails. **b** [U] : ¹RAILROAD • transportation by rail • rail travel

²**rail** vb **1** [T] : to use rails to create a barrier around or at the edge of (something) • They railed off the garden. — usually + off **2** [I] formal : to complain angrily about something • old men railing at/against the government

rail·ing /ˈreɪlɪŋ/ n [C] : a barrier that is made of rails supported by posts • He *leaned on the deck's railing.*

¹rail·road /ˈreɪlˌroʊd/ *n* [C] *US* **1** : a system of tracks on which trains travel ▪ *railroad stations/cars* **2** : a company that owns and operates trains ▪ *working for the railroad*

²railroad *vb* [T] **1** : to force (something) to be officially approved or accepted without much discussion or thought ▪ *The law was railroaded through Congress.* ▪ *The bill was railroaded into law.* **2** *US* : to convict (someone) of a crime unfairly ▪ *They claim he was railroaded.* **3** : to force (someone) into doing something quickly or without enough information ▪ *He railroaded her into signing the contract.*

rail·road·er /ˈreɪlˌroʊdɚ/ *n* [C] *US* : a person who works for a railroad company

rail·road·ing /ˈreɪlˌroʊdɪŋ/ *n* [U] : the building or operation of a railroad

rail·way /ˈreɪlˌweɪ/ *n* [C] *chiefly Brit* : ¹RAILROAD

¹rain /ˈreɪn/ *n* **1** [C/U] : water that falls in drops from clouds in the sky ▪ *We could hear the sound of (the) rain on the roof.* ▪ *A light/heavy rain began to fall.* **2** [*singular*] : a large amount of something falling from above ▪ *a rain of ash* — **(as) right as rain** see ¹RIGHT — **rain or shine** *or* **come rain, come shine** *or* **come rain or come shine** *or* **come shine** — used to say that something will happen even if it rains ▪ *The party will be on Tuesday, rain or shine.*

²rain *vb* **1** [*I*] — used with *it* to say that rain is falling ▪ *It rained all day.* **2** [*I*] : to fall from above in large amounts ▪ *Sparks from the fireworks rained (down) on the field.* **3** [*T*] : to cause (something) to fall in large amounts ▪ *The volcano rained ashes on the city.* ▪ *The boxers rained blows/punches on each other.* [=hit each other many times] — **be rained out** (*US*) *or Brit* **be rained off** : to be canceled because of rain ▪ *The game was rained out.* — **rain cats and dogs** *informal* : to rain very hard — **rain on someone's parade** *US, informal* : to spoil someone's pleasure — **when it rains, it pours** (*US*) *or chiefly Brit* **it never rains but it pours** *informal* — used to say that when something bad happens other bad things usually happen at the same time

¹rain·bow /ˈreɪnˌboʊ/ *n* [C] : a curved line of different colors that sometimes appears in the sky when the sun shines through rain

²rainbow *adj, always before a noun* : of, relating to, or including people of different races, cultures, etc. ▪ *a rainbow coalition*

rain check *n* [C] *US* **1** : a ticket given to people so that they can go to another event (such as a baseball game) if the one they were watching or planning to go to is canceled or stopped because of rain **2** : a promise to allow someone to buy or do something in the future because it is not possible to buy or do it now ▪ *The store offered rain checks when the sale items had all sold.* ▪ *She asked if she could*

have/take a rain check on the invitation for dinner.

rain·coat /ˈreɪnˌkoʊt/ *n* [C] : a coat that you wear when it rains in order to stay dry

rain date *n* [C] *US* : a date for something to happen if it cannot happen on its original date because of rain

rain·drop /ˈreɪnˌdrɑːp/ *n* [C] : a single drop of rain

rain·fall /ˈreɪnˌfɑːl/ *n* [C/U] : the amount of rain that falls on a particular area ▪ *This area has an average annual rainfall of 12 inches.*

rain forest *n* [C/U] : a tropical forest that receives a lot of rain and that has very tall trees

rain·proof /ˈreɪnˌpruːf/ *adj* : able to keep rain out ▪ *a rainproof jacket/tent*

rain·storm /ˈreɪnˌstoɚm/ *n* [C] : a storm that produces rain

rain·wa·ter /ˈreɪnˌwɑːtɚ/ *n* [U] : water that falls from the sky as rain

rainy /ˈreɪni/ *adj* **rain·i·er; -est** : having a lot of rain ▪ *rainy weather* — **for a rainy day** *informal* : for a time in the future when something will be needed ▪ *He saved some money for a rainy day.*

raise /ˈreɪz/ *vb* **raised; rais·ing** [T] **1** : to lift or move (something or someone) to a higher position or to a standing or more upright position ▪ *Raise your arms above your head.* ▪ *We raised the flag to the top of the pole.* ▪ *I raised her to a sitting position.* ▪ *The men raised (up) the barn's walls with pulleys.* **2** : to increase the amount or level of (something) ▪ *The store is raising its prices.* ▪ *The college is raising its standards for admission.* ▪ *Exposure to secondhand smoke raises the risk of lung cancer.* **3** : to collect (money) from people for a particular cause ▪ *The students are raising money for their school.* **4 a** : to mention (something) for people to think or talk about ▪ *The issue of money was never raised.* **b** : to cause people to think about or be aware of (something) ▪ *The discovery raises the possibility of a cure for the disease.* **5** : to cause (something) to happen or exist ▪ *The news raised hopes for peace.* ▪ *Her comment raised a few smiles/laughs.* **6** *chiefly US* : to take care of and teach (a child) : to bring up or rear (a child) ▪ *She was raised by her grandparents.* ▪ *This is a wonderful place to raise a family.* **7** : to keep and take care of (animals or crops) ▪ *raising chicken/corn* **8** *formal* : to stop or remove (something that is preventing or blocking an activity) often for only a short period of time ▪ *They raised the siege/embargo/blockade.* **9** : to build (a monument, statue, etc.) : ERECT ▪ *The city raised a monument in his honor.* — **raise Cain** *US, old-fashioned* **1** : to behave wildly and make a lot of noise ▪ *They were always getting drunk and raising Cain.* [=raising hell] **2** : to complain in a loud or angry way — **raise hell** see HELL — **raise its ugly head** see ¹HEAD — **raise the roof** see ¹ROOF — **raise your voice** : to speak loudly especially because you are angry ▪ *The baby is sleeping, so try not to raise your voice.*

²**raise** n [C] US : an increase in the amount of your pay • *I asked my boss for a raise.* [=(Brit) *rise*]

raised adj : higher than the surrounding area or surface • *a raised platform*

raised ranch n [C] US : a house that has two floors with its front entryway located between the floors

rai·sin /ˈreɪzn̩/ n [C] : a dried grape used for food

rai·son d'être /ˌreɪˌzoʊnˈdɛtrə/ n, pl **raisons d'être** /ˌreɪˌzoʊnˈdɛtrə/ [C] *formal* : the reason for which a person or organization exists • *Art is his raison d'être.*

ra·ja or **ra·jah** /ˈrɑːdʒə/ n [C] : a king or prince in India

¹**rake** /ˈreɪk/ n [C] : a tool that has a series of metal, wooden, or plastic pieces at the end of a long handle and that is used to gather leaves, break apart soil, make ground smooth, etc.

²**rake** vb **raked; rak·ing** **1** [T/I] : to use a rake to gather leaves, break apart soil, make ground smooth, etc. • *rake (up) leaves* • *rake the lawn* [=use a rake to remove leaves, sticks, etc., from the lawn] **2** [T] : to move (your fingers or something similar) through or along something • *The cat raked its claws down the post.* **3** [T] : to shoot many bullets along (something) • *Two men raked the car with gunfire.* — **rake in** [phrasal vb] **rake (something) in** or **rake in (something)** *informal* : to earn or receive (a large amount of money) • *The movie raked in over $300 million.* • *He's really raking it in.* [=making a lot of money] — **rake over** [phrasal vb] chiefly Brit, informal : to continue to think or talk about (something that happened in the past) • *Don't spend so much time raking over the past.* — **rake (someone) over the coals** see COAL — **rake up** [phrasal vb] **rake (something) up** or **rake up (something)** informal : to talk about (something unpleasant that happened in the past) • *raking up bad memories*

rak·ish /ˈreɪkɪʃ/ adj, somewhat old-fashioned : having an unusual quality that is attractive and stylish • *a rakish smile* • *He wore his hat at a rakish angle.* — **rak·ish·ly** adv

¹**ral·ly** /ˈræli/ n, pl **-lies** [C] **1** : a public meeting to support or oppose someone or something • *a political rally* **2** finance : an increase in price or value after a decrease in price or value • *a stock market rally* **3** sports : an occurrence in which a team or player that has been playing badly begins to play well • *Our team staged a rally in the second half.* **4** sports : a continuous series of hits back and forth between players in tennis or a similar game **5** : a car race that is usually held on public roads • *a road rally*

²**rally** vb **-lies; -lied; -ly·ing** **1 a** [T] : to meet publicly to support or oppose something • *His supporters rallied outside the court.* **b** [T] : to cause (people) to join together to publicly support or oppose something • *The group is trying to rally voters for the election.* **2** [I] : to publicly support or oppose something or

someone as a group • *Parents rallied (together) behind the new dress code.*; also : to join together to do something • *People around the country have rallied (together) to help raise money for the victims.* **3** [T] : to cause (a group of people) to have new energy and enthusiasm in a difficult time or situation • *The coach rallied his players.* **4** [I] : to improve suddenly after a period of weakness, failure, etc. • *We rallied in the fourth quarter and won the game.* • *Stocks rallied at the close of trading.* — **rally around** or chiefly Brit **rally round** [phrasal vb] : to join together to support (someone or something) in a difficult time or situation • *We rallied around our neighbors when their house burned down.*

rallying cry n [C] : a word or phrase that is used to make people join together to support an idea, cause, etc. • *"We believe!" became the rallying cry of the fans.*

rallying point n [C] : someone or something that makes people join together to support a person, cause, etc. • *His promise to improve education has become a rallying point for his supporters.*

¹**ram** /ˈræm/ n [C] **1** : an adult male sheep **2 a** : a piece of machinery that is used to hit or lift something else **b** : BATTERING RAM

²**ram** vb **rammed; ram·ming** **1** [T/I] : to forcefully hit something • *His car rammed (into) mine.* • *He rammed his car into mine.* **2** [T] : to push (something) into a position or place with force • *He rammed the clothes down the chute.* — **ram (something) down someone's throat** see THROAT — **ram (something) home** : to make (something) very clear and obvious in a forceful way • *He tried to ram home the importance of meeting the deadline.*

RAM /ˈræm/ n [U] computers : the part of a computer in which information is stored temporarily when a program is being used • *My computer needs more RAM.* — called also *random-access memory*

Ram·a·dan /ˈrɑːməˌdɑːn, Brit ˈræmə-ˌdæn/ n [C/U] : the ninth month of the Islamic year when Muslims do not eat or drink anything between sunrise and sunset

¹**ram·ble** /ˈræmbəl/ vb **ram·bled; ram·bling** [I] **1** : to walk or go from one place to another place without a specific goal, purpose, or direction • *He rambled around/about the countryside.* **2** : to go from one subject to another without any clear purpose or direction • *She rambled (on) for several minutes before introducing the main speaker.*

²**ramble** n [C] **1** chiefly Brit : a long walk for pleasure • *a solitary ramble* **2** : a long speech or piece of writing that goes from one subject to another without any clear purpose or direction • *a long ramble about politics*

ram·bler /ˈræmblə/ n [C] **1** chiefly Brit : a person who goes on long walks for pleasure **2** : a plant that grows up and over fences, walls, etc.

ram·bling /ˈræmbəlɪŋ/ adj **1** of a build-

ing : big and having many rooms that are arranged in an irregular shape • *a rambling old farmhouse* **2** : not having a specific goal, purpose, or direction • *a rambling lecture*

ram·blings /ˈræmblɪŋz/ *n* [*plural*] : spoken or written words that go from one subject to another without any clear purpose or direction • *drunken ramblings*

ram·bunc·tious /ræmˈbʌŋkʃəs/ *adj, US* : uncontrolled in a way that is playful or full of energy • *a rambunctious crowd*

ram·i·fi·ca·tion /ˌræməfəˈkeɪʃən/ *n* [C] *formal* : something that is the result of an action, decision, etc. • *They discussed the possible ramifications of the new treaty.*

¹ramp /ˈræmp/ *n* [C] **1** *US* : a usually sloping road that connects a road to a highway • *an exit/entrance ramp* **2** : a piece of equipment with a slope that is used to join two surfaces that are at different levels or heights

²ramp *vb* — **ramp up** [*phrasal vb*] **ramp up** or **ramp up (something)** or **ramp (something) up** : to increase or to cause (something) to increase in speed, size, etc. • *The company has been ramping up production.*

ram·page /ˈræmˌpeɪdʒ/ *n* [C] : an occurrence of wild and usually destructive behavior • *a murderous rampage* • *Rioters were/went on a rampage.* — **rampage** *vb* **-paged; -pag·ing** [I] • *Rioters rampaged through the streets.*

ram·pant /ˈræmpənt/ *adj* : spreading or growing very quickly and in a way that is difficult to control • *Rumors of her engagement were rampant.* • *a weed that's rampant in this area* — **ram·pant·ly** *adv*

ram·part /ˈræmˌpɑɚt/ *n* [C] : a tall, thick stone or dirt wall that is built around a castle, town, etc., to protect it from attacks

ram·rod /ˈræmˌrɑːd/ *n* [C] : a metal bar that is used to push explosive material down into the barrel of some old-fashioned guns — **straight as a ramrod** or **ramrod straight** : in a very straight and stiff way • *The guard stood straight as a ramrod.*

ram·shack·le /ˈræmˌʃækəl/ *adj* : in a very bad condition and needing to be repaired • *a ramshackle old house*

ran *past tense of* **¹RUN**

¹ranch /ˈræntʃ/, *Brit* /ˈrɑːntʃ/ *n* [C] **1** : a large farm especially in the U.S. where cattle, horses, sheep, etc., are raised **2** *US* : RANCH HOUSE 2 — see also RAISED RANCH

²ranch *vb* [T/I] : to live or work on a ranch • *They've been ranching (cattle) here for many years.* — **ranch·er** /ˈræntʃɚ/, *Brit* /ˈrɑːntʃə/ *n* [C]

ranch dressing *n* [C/U] *US* : a creamy salad dressing

ranch house *n* [C] **1** : the main house on a ranch **2** *US* : a house that has a single story and a roof that is not very steep

ran·cid /ˈrænsəd/ *adj* **1** *of food* : having a strong and unpleasant smell or taste from no longer being fresh • *rancid butter* **2** *chiefly US* : full of anger and bitterness • *The argument turned rancid.*

ran·cor (*US*) *or Brit* **ran·cour** /ˈræŋkɚ/ *n* [U] *formal* : an angry feeling of hatred or dislike for someone who has treated you unfairly • *She answered her accusers calmly and without rancor.* — **ran·cor·ous** (*US*) *or Brit* **ran·cour·ous** /ˈræŋkərəs/ *adj* • *a rancorous debate*

rand /ˈrænd/ *n, pl* **rand** [C] : the basic unit of money in the Republic of South Africa

R & B *abbr* rhythm and blues

R & D *abbr* research and development • *She works for a computer firm doing R & D.*

ran·dom /ˈrændəm/ *adj* : chosen, done, etc., without a particular plan or pattern • *a random sample/selection of doctors from around the country* • *random drug testing* • *random numbers* — **at random** : in a way that does not follow a particular plan or pattern • *Our names were chosen/selected at random from the list.* — **ran·dom·ly** *adv* — **ran·dom·ness** *n* [U]

random–access memory *n* [U] : RAM

R & R *abbr* rest and recreation; rest and recuperation; rest and relaxation • *We rented a cottage in the country to get a little R & R.*

randy /ˈrændi/ *adj* **rand·i·er; -est** *chiefly Brit, informal* : sexually excited • *a randy bachelor*

rang *past tense of* **³RING**

¹range /ˈreɪndʒ/ *n* **1** [C] : a group or collection of things or people that are usually similar in some way • *a wide range of topics/colors* **2** [C] : a series of numbers that includes the highest and lowest possible amounts • *What's the salary range for the job?* [=what are the highest and lowest salaries that people are paid for the job?] • *The car is out of our price range.* [=it is too expensive] • *children in the 7 to 13 age range* **3** [C] : the total amount of ability, knowledge, experience, etc., that a person has • *The technical vocabulary is outside my range (of expertise).* **4** [C] : all of the notes that a particular person can sing or that a particular musical instrument can make • *The song is out of my vocal range.* **5** [C/U] : the distance over which someone or something can see, hear, or reach someone or something else • *I can't get the radio station west of the mountains because I'm out of range there.* • *The troops were within range of the enemy's artillery.* • *a missile with a 400-mile range* • *The photograph was taken at close/short range.* [=taken from a close distance] **6** [C] : a series of mountains or hills in a line • *a mountain range* **7** [C/U] *US* : open land that cows, sheep, etc., use for grazing and roaming • *areas of open range* **8** [U] : the ability to move around • *free range of motion* **9** [C] **a** : a place where people can practice shooting guns • *a rifle range* **b** : a place where weapons are tested • *a missile range* **c** : a place where people can practice hitting golf balls **10** [C] *US* : a large piece of kitchen equipment that consists of an oven and a stove • *a gas/electric range*

²range *vb* **ranged; rang·ing** **1** [I] : to include everything between specified limits • *The selection of food ranged from mild to very spicy.* • *children whose ages range between 7 and 13* • *The rugs range in size/price/color.* **2** [*I*] : to move around an area • *The farmers let the horses range freely.* **3** [*T*] *formal* : to arrange (people or things) in a particular place or position • *Soldiers were ranged along the palace walls.* • *(figurative) They have ranged themselves in opposition to the proposed new law.*

rang·er /ˈreɪndʒɚ/ *n* [*C*] **1** : a person in charge of managing and protecting part of a public forest or national park **2** : a soldier in the U.S. Army who has special training especially in fighting at close range

rangy /ˈreɪndʒi/ *adj* **rang·i·er; -est 1** *of a person* : tall and thin • *a rangy teenager* **2** *of an animal* : having a long body and long legs • *rangy cattle*

¹**rank** /ˈræŋk/ *n* **1** [*C/U*] : a position in a society, organization, etc. • *people/officers of high rank* • *the upper social ranks* • *He moved up through the ranks to become vice president.* • *a writer of the first rank* [=an excellent writer] **2** [*plural*] **a** : the people or things that belong to a particular organization or group • *The organization's ranks have doubled.* • *More older adults are choosing to join the ranks of college students.* **b** : the people in the army, navy, air force, etc., who are not officers • *Several men were selected from the ranks.* **3** [*C*] : a row of people or things • *The troops stood in ranks.* **4** [*C*] *Brit* : TAXI STAND — **break ranks** also **break rank 1** : to step out of a line • *The soldier was disciplined for breaking ranks.* **2** : to no longer agree with or support a person or group • *One scientist has broken ranks with her colleagues and questioned the research.* — **close ranks** : to join together to support or protect someone or something that is in trouble • *The police officers closed ranks when their captain was being investigated for misconduct.* — **pull rank** : to use your high position in a society, organization, etc., to order someone to do something or to get special treatment or privileges • *He's their boss, but he doesn't like to pull rank (on them) if he can avoid it.*

²**rank** *vb* [*T/I*] : to place (someone or something) in or to be in a particular position among a group of people or things that are being judged according to quality, ability, size, etc. • *The museum is ranked among the best in the U.S.* • *The gymnast is ranked fifth in the world.* • *The city currently ranks as the world's largest.* • *students who rank in the top third of their class* • *Our professor ranks with/among the best in her field.* [=is one of the best in her field]

³**rank** *adj* **1** : having a strong, unpleasant smell • *a rank odor* **2 a** : very bad and obvious • *rank dishonesty* **b** *always before a noun* : complete or total • *a rank beginner* **3** *of plants* : growing too quickly and over too much land • *rank weeds*

rank and file *n* — **the rank and file 1**

: the people in the army, navy, air force, etc., who are not officers **2** : the members of a group or organization who are not leaders • *The rank and file is/are unhappy with the chairman's decision.*

¹**rank·ing** /ˈræŋkɪŋ/ *adj, always before a noun, chiefly US* : having a high position or the highest position in a group or organization • *Who is the ranking officer here?*

²**ranking** *n* **1** [*plural*] : a list of people or things that are ordered according to their quality, ability, size, etc. • *He is number two in the class rankings.* **2** [*C*] : the position of a person or thing in the rankings • *The new coach led the team to a No. 1 ranking.*

ran·kle /ˈræŋkəl/ *vb* **ran·kled; ran·kling** [*T/I*] : to cause (someone) to feel angry or irritated especially for a long time • *The joke about her family rankled him.*

ran·sack /ˈrænˌsæk/ *vb* [*T*] : to search (a place) for something in a way that causes disorder or damage • *Robbers ransacked the apartment.*

¹**ran·som** /ˈrænsəm/ *n* [*C/U*] : money that is paid in order to free someone who has been captured or kidnapped • *The kidnappers demanded a ransom of one million dollars.* • *A group of men is holding the ship's crew for ransom.* — see also **KING'S RANSOM**

²**ransom** *vb* [*T*] : to pay money in order to free (a person who has been captured or kidnapped) • *He was held captive for a week before he was ransomed and returned to his family.*

rant /ˈrænt/ *vb* [*T/I*] : to talk loudly and in a way that shows anger • *He was **ranting and raving** about how badly he'd been treated.* — **rant** *n* [*C*]

¹**rap** /ˈræp/ *n* **1** [*C*] : a quick hit or knock • *a sharp rap on/at the window/door* **2** [*C*] *US, informal* : a statement by police or the government saying that someone has committed a crime • *She faces a murder rap.* [=charge] **3** *the rap informal* : the blame or punishment for something • *He took the rap for his brother.* **4** [*C*] *US, informal* : a complaint or criticism about someone or something • *The main rap against him is that he isn't totally honest.* • *The boys say they've all **gotten a bum rap** because one person damaged some property.* **5 a** [*U*] : a type of music that has words that are spoken with the rhythm instead of being sung • *She listens mostly to rap.* **b** [*C*] : a rap song • *He performed a rap.* — **a rap on/over/ across the knuckles** *informal* : criticism or punishment that is given in a gentle way • *I received a rap on the knuckles for missing the meeting.* — **beat the rap** *US, informal* : to avoid being sent to jail for a crime • *He was arrested for assault, but he beat the rap.*

²**rap** *vb* **rapped; rap·ping 1** [*T/I*] : to quickly hit or knock (something) many times • *The teacher rapped the desk with her knuckles.* • *Someone was rapping on the door.* **2** [*I*] : to perform rap music or a rap song **3** [*I*] *informal* : to talk in a free and informal way • *I enjoyed rapping with him about sports.* **4** [*T*] : to criticize

(someone or something) publicly ▪ *The report raps the organization for failing to develop a plan.* — **rap someone on/over/across the knuckles** or **rap someone's knuckles** : to criticize or punish someone in a gentle way ▪ *The boss rapped me on the knuckles for missing the meeting.*

ra·pa·cious /rə'peɪʃəs/ *adj, formal* : always wanting more money, possessions, etc. ▪ *a rapacious [=greedy] businessman*

¹rape /'reɪp/ *vb* **raped; rap·ing** [T] : to force (someone) to have sex with you by using violence or the threat of violence

²rape *n* **1** [C/U] : the crime of forcing someone to have sex with you by using violence or the threat of violence ▪ *a victim of rape* **2** [U] *literary* : the act of ruining or destroying something ▪ *the rape of the land* **3** [U] : a plant that is grown as food for farm animals and as a source of oil

rape·seed /'reɪp,si:d/ *n* **1** [U] : ²RAPE 3 **2** [C] : the seed of the rape plant

rap·id /'ræpəd/ *adj* : very fast or quick ▪ *rapid growth* ▪ *a rapid heartbeat* — **ra·pid·i·ty** /rə'pɪdəti/ *n* [U] — **rap·id·ly** *adv* ▪ *He was breathing rapidly.*

rap·id-fire /,ræpəd'fajɚ/ *adj, always before a noun* **1** : coming quickly one after another ▪ *rapid-fire changes/jokes* **2** *of a weapon* : able to quickly shoot bullets one after another ▪ *a rapid-fire rifle*

rap·ids /'ræpədz/ *n* [*plural*] : a part of a river where the water flows very fast usually over rocks

rapid transit *n* [U] *chiefly US* : the system that is used in cities for quickly bringing people to and from places on trains, buses, etc.

¹ra·pi·er /'reɪpijɚ/ *n* [C] : a straight sword that has a narrow blade with sharp edges

²rapier *adj, always before a noun* : extremely sharp ▪ *his rapier wit*

rap·ist /'reɪpɪst/ *n* [C] : a person who rapes someone

rap·per /'ræpɚ/ *n* [C] : a person who performs rap music or speaks the words of a rap song

rap·port /ræ'poɚ/ *n* [U, singular] *formal* : a friendly relationship ▪ *She works hard to build (a) rapport with her patients.*

rap·proche·ment /,ræ,prouʃ'mɑːnt, Brit ræ'prɒʃmɒŋ/ *n* [U, singular] *formal* : the development of friendlier relations between countries or groups of people who have been enemies ▪ *Officials hope that these talks will lead to a rapprochement with the rebels.*

rap session *n* [C] *US, informal* : a meeting at which a group of people talk informally about a particular subject ▪ *a rap session for teenagers about/on drunk driving*

rap sheet *n* [C] *US, informal* : a list kept by the police of all the times a person has been arrested ▪ *He has a long rap sheet.* [=he has been arrested many times]

rapt /'ræpt/ *adj, literary + formal* : showing complete interest in something ▪ *The students listened with rapt attention.* — **rapt·ly** *adv*

rap·tor /'ræptɚ/ *n* [C] : a bird (such as an

eagle or hawk) that kills and eats other animals for food

rap·ture /'ræptʃɚ/ *n* [C/U] *literary + formal* : a state or feeling of great happiness, pleasure, or love ▪ *a smile of rapture* ▪ *The music sent the crowd into raptures.* — **rap·tur·ous** /'ræptʃərəs/ *adj* ▪ *rapturous applause* — **rap·tur·ous·ly** *adv*

rare /'reɚ/ *adj* **rar·er; -est** **1** : not often done, seen, or happening ▪ *a rare disease/opportunity* **2** : having only a few of its kind in existence ▪ *rare books/species* **3** *of meat* : cooked for only a short time so that the inside is still red ▪ *a rare steak* — **rare** *adv* ▪ *I like my steak cooked rare.* — **rare·ly** /'reɚli/ *adv* ▪ *She rarely talks about her past.* ▪ *Rarely do we see this kind of weather.* ▪ *Only rarely is surgery necessary.* — **rare·ness** *n* [U]

rar·e·fied /'rerə,faɪd/ *adj* **1** *often disapproving* : understood by only a small group of people ▪ *the rarefied world of art dealers* **2** *technical, of air* : not having much oxygen because of being high up in the atmosphere ▪ *the rarefied air near the mountain's peak*

rar·ing /'rerən/ *adj, informal* : ready and excited to start to do something ▪ *She's been raring to go since dawn.*

rar·i·ty /'rerəti/ *n, pl* **-ties** **1** [C] : a rare person or thing ▪ *In most sports, athletes over the age of 50 are rarities.* ▪ *Snow is a rarity in this area.* **2** [U] : the quality of being rare ▪ *The rarity of the disease makes it difficult to diagnose.*

ras·cal /'ræskəl, Brit 'rɑːskəl/ *n* [C] **1** *informal + humorous* : a person who causes trouble or does things that annoy people ▪ *Which one of you rascals woke me up?* **2** *old-fashioned* : a cruel or dishonest man ▪ *a lying rascal* — **ras·cal·ly** *adj, old-fashioned* ▪ *rascally kids*

¹rash /'ræʃ/ *n* **1** [C/U] : a group of red spots on the skin that is caused by an illness or a reaction to something **2** [*singular*] : a series of usually unpleasant things or events that happen in a short period of time ▪ *a rash of fires*

²rash *adj* : acting quickly or done without thought about what will happen as a result ▪ *Don't be rash about this decision.* ▪ *a rash statement* ▪ *Please don't do anything rash.* — **rash·ly** *adv* — **rash·ness** *n* [U]

rash·er /'ræʃɚ/ *n* [C] *chiefly Brit* : a thin piece of bacon or ham

¹rasp /'ræsp, Brit 'rɑːsp/ *vb* **1** [T] : to speak in a way that sounds rough or harsh ▪ *"Let go of my arm," she rasped.* ▪ *a rasping voice* **2** [I] : to make a rough, harsh sound ▪ *The metal boxes rasped as they were dragged across the floor.*

²rasp *n* **1** [C] : a metal tool that has sharp points and that is used to make rough surfaces smooth **2** [*singular*] : a rough, harsh sound ▪ *speaking in a harsh rasp*

rasp·ber·ry /'ræz,beri, Brit 'rɑːzbri/ *n, pl* **-ries** [C] **1** : a soft, red berry that is sweet and juicy **2** *informal* : a rude sound made by pushing your tongue outside your lips and blowing air out of your mouth ▪ *He made/blew a raspberry at me.*

raspy /'ræspi, Brit 'rɑːspi/ *adj* **rasp·i·er;**

-est : having a rough, harsh sound • *a raspy voice*

Ras·ta·far·i·an /ˌrɑːstəˈfɑːrijən, *Brit* ˌræstəˈfeəriən/ *n* [C] : a member of a religious movement among black Jamaicans which teaches that black people will eventually return to Africa and which worships Haile Selassie, the former Emperor of Ethiopia

¹rat /ˈræt/ *n* [C] **1** : a small animal that has a pointed nose and a long, thin tail **2** *informal* : a person who is not loyal or who cannot be trusted • *He's a dirty rat.* **3** *US, informal* : a person who spends a lot of time in a specified place • *a mall/gym rat* — **smell a rat** *informal* : to think or suspect that something is wrong about a situation • *She smelled a rat when her husband came home with lipstick on his collar.*

²rat *vb* **rat·ted; rat·ting** [T/I] *informal* : to tell someone in authority (such as the police) about something wrong that someone has done • *Somebody ratted on me.* = *Somebody ratted me out.*

¹ratch·et /ˈrætʃət/ *n* [C] : a device made up of a wheel or bar with many teeth along its edge in between which a piece fits so that the wheel or bar can move only in one direction

²ratchet *vb* [T] : to increase or decrease (something) especially by a series of small steps or amounts — usually + *up* or *down* • *Banks are ratcheting up interest rates.*

¹rate /ˈreɪt/ *n* [C] **1** : the speed at which something happens over a particular period of time • *Gun violence is increasing at an alarming rate.* • *Snow was falling at a rate of three inches per hour.* **2** : the number of times something happens or is done during a particular period of time • *There is a high success rate for this surgery.* [=this surgery is often/usually successful] • *the unemployment rate* [=the number of people who are unemployed] • *your heart/pulse rate* [=the number of times your heart beats in a minute] **3** : a price or amount to be paid that is set according to a scale or standard • *The hotel's rates start at $65/night.* • *interest rates* • *What's the going rate for a new computer?* — **at any rate** — used to indicate that something is true or certain regardless of what else has happened or been said • *This restaurant has the best food—or at any rate, the best pasta dishes—in the city.* • *It is possible that she was nervous. At any rate, her singing was still good.* — **at this/that rate** : if things continue to happen in the same way they have been happening • *At this rate, the town's farmland will be gone within 20 years.*

²rate *vb* **rat·ed; rat·ing 1 a** [T] : to make a judgment about the quality, ability, or value of (someone or something) • *On a scale of 1 to 5, I'd rate the book at/a 4.* • *The school is rated above average.* • *the highest rated radio show* **b** [I] : to be judged as having a particular level of quality, ability, or value • *The car rates as one of the best.* • *The shoes rate high as far as comfort goes.* **2** [T] : to consider someone or something to be (something)

• *The boat is large enough to be rated a ship.* **3** [T] : to officially state that a movie, video game, etc., is appropriate for a specific audience • *The movie is rated G.* **4** [T] : to deserve (something) • *The new museum rates a visit.* **5** [I] *US, informal* : to be liked by someone • *He really rates with the boss.* [=the boss really likes him] **6** [T] *Brit, informal* : to think of (someone or something) as being good or of a high quality • *They don't rate him as a player.*

rate of exchange *n, pl* **rates of exchange** [C] : EXCHANGE RATE

rath·er /ˈræðɚ, *Brit* ˈrɑːðə/ *adv* **1** : to some degree or extent • *a rather hot day* • *It rather annoyed me that he was late.* • *He was driving rather fast.* **2 a** — used to introduce a statement that indicates what is true after you have said what is not true • *I don't like chocolate—rather, I love chocolate.* • *It wasn't red but rather bright orange.* **b** — used to introduce a statement that corrects what you have just said • *My father, or rather, my stepfather, will be visiting.* — **rather than 1** : instead of (something or someone) • *Rather than using dried herbs, he picked fresh ones from the garden.* : and not • *He was happy rather than sad.* **2** — used to say what is not chosen or done because something else is chosen or done instead • *Rather than continue the argument, she walked away.* — **would rather** — used to indicate what you want or prefer to do, have, etc. • *She would rather drive than take the train.* • *I would rather you didn't tell them.*

rat·i·fy /ˈrætəˌfaɪ/ *vb* **-fies; -fied; -fy·ing** [T] : to make (a treaty, agreement, etc.) official by signing it or voting for it • *Several countries have refused to ratify the treaty.* — **rat·i·fi·ca·tion** /ˌrætəfəˈkeɪʃən/ *n* [U]

rating *n* **1** [C] : a measurement of how good, difficult, efficient, etc., something or someone is • *The President's approval rating is low.* • *The school has an above-average academic rating.* **2 the ratings** : numbers that show how many people watch or listen to a particular television or radio program • *a show that is doing well/badly in the ratings* **3** [C] : a symbol that is officially given to a movie, video game, etc., to tell people what audience it is appropriate for • *Both movies received G ratings.* **4** [C] *Brit* : someone in the navy who is not an officer

ra·tio /ˈreɪʃiˌou/ *n, pl* **-tios** [C] : the relationship that exists between the size, number, or amount of two things and that is often represented by two numbers • *The college has a 12:1 ratio between students and teachers.* [=for every 12 students, there is one teacher] • *Women outnumbered men by a ratio of three to two.*

ra·tion /ˈræʃən/ *n* **1 a** [C] : a particular amount of food that is given to one person or animal for one day **b** [*plural*] : food or supplies • *The campers were getting low on rations.* **2** [C] : a particular amount of something that the government allows you to have when there is not enough of it • *a gas ration*

²**ration** vb [T] : to control the amount of (something) that people are allowed to have especially when there is not enough of it ▪ *Gasoline was rationed during the war.*

ra·tio·nal /'ræʃənl/ adj **1** : based on facts or reason and not on emotions or feelings ▪ *a rational decision* **2** : having the ability to reason or think about things clearly ▪ *a rational person* ▪ *Humans are rational beings.* — **ra·tio·nal·i·ty** /ˌræʃə'næləti/ n [U] *formal* — **ra·tio·nal·ly** adv

ra·tio·nale /ˌræʃə'næl/ n [C] *somewhat formal* : the reason or explanation for something ▪ *What was her rationale for quitting?* ▪ *I don't understand the rationale behind/of his decision.*

ra·tio·nal·ize also Brit **ra·tio·nal·ise** /'ræʃənəˌlaɪz/ vb -**ized**; -**iz·ing** **1** [T/I] : to think about or describe something in a way that explains it and makes it seem proper, more attractive, etc. ▪ *He couldn't rationalize buying such an expensive car.* **2** [T] *chiefly Brit* : to find ways to make (an industry, a company, etc.) waste less time, effort, and money ▪ *trying to rationalize a production system* — **ra·tio·nal·i·za·tion** also Brit **ra·tio·nal·i·sa·tion** /ˌræʃənələ'zeɪʃən, Brit ˌræʃənəˌlaɪ'zeɪʃən/ n [C/U]

rat race n — **the rat race** : the unpleasant life of people who have jobs that require them to work very hard in order to compete with others for money, power, status, etc. ▪ *I'd like to get out of the rat race.*

rat·tan /ræ'tæn/ n [U] : a plant with very long, strong stems that are woven together to make baskets, furniture, etc. ▪ *a rattan chair*

¹**rat·tle** /'rætl/ vb **rat·tled**; **rat·tling 1 a** [I] : to hit against something repeatedly and make short, loud sounds ▪ *The coins rattled in the box.* **b** [T] : to cause (something) to move or shake and make short, loud sounds ▪ *She rattled the jar with the coins in it.* = *She rattled the coins in the jar.* **2** [I] : to make short, loud sounds while moving ▪ *The train rattled by.* **3** [T] : to upset or disturb (someone) ▪ *The speaker was rattled by the question.* — **rattle off** [phrasal vb] **rattle (something) off** or **rattle off (something)** *informal* : to say (something) quickly or easily from memory ▪ *She rattled off the names of all 50 states.* — **rattle on** [phrasal vb] *informal* : to talk for a long time about things that are not interesting or important ▪ *She rattled on (and on) about the party.* — **rattle someone's cage** see CAGE

²**rattle** n [C] **1** : a series of short, loud sounds ▪ *the rattle of machine guns* **2** : a baby's toy that makes a series of short sounds when it is shaken **3** : the group of hard, loose scales that cover the end of a rattlesnake's tail

rat·tler /'rætlə/ n [C] *informal* : RATTLE-SNAKE

rat·tle·snake /'rætlˌsneɪk/ n [C] : a poisonous American snake with a tail that it shakes to make a rattling noise

rat·ty /'ræti/ adj **rat·ti·er**; -**est** *informal* **1** *US* : in very bad condition ▪ *ratty hair/clothes* **2** *Brit* : easily angered or annoyed ▪ *feeling tired and ratty* [=(chiefly US) cranky]

rau·cous /'rɑːkəs/ adj **1** : loud and unpleasant to listen to ▪ *raucous shouts* **2** : behaving in a very rough and noisy way ▪ *a raucous crowd* — **rau·cous·ly** adv — **rau·cous·ness** n [U]

raun·chy /'rɑːntʃi/ adj **raun·chi·er**; -**est** *informal* **1** : dealing with or suggesting sex in a way that is somewhat shocking ▪ *a raunchy movie* **2** *US, disapproving* : very dirty, smelly, etc. ▪ *raunchy old sneakers* — **raun·chi·ness** /'rɑːntʃinəs/ n [U]

rav·age /'rævɪdʒ/ vb **rav·aged**; **rav·ag·ing** [T] *formal* : to damage or harm (something) very badly ▪ *The forest was ravaged by fire.*

rav·ages /'rævɪdʒəz/ n [plural] *literary* : destruction or damage — usually + *of* ▪ *the ravages of war/disease*

¹**rave** /'reɪv/ vb **raved**; **rav·ing 1** [T/I] : to talk or write about someone or something in an excited or enthusiastic way ▪ *Critics raved about/over the new play.* **2** [I] : to talk loudly in an angry or wild way ▪ *The coach ranted and raved at the referee.*

²**rave** n [C] **1** : a statement of enthusiastic praise or approval ▪ *The movie got raves from the critics.* = *The movie got rave reviews from the critics.* **2** : a large party that lasts all night in which people dance to electronic dance music

¹**ra·ven** /'reɪvən/ n [C] : a bird that has shiny black feathers and looks like a crow but is larger

²**raven** adj, always before a noun, *literary* : shiny and black ▪ *raven hair*

rav·en·ous /'rævənəs/ adj : very hungry ▪ *a ravenous wolf* ▪ *I had a ravenous appetite.* [=I was extremely hungry] — **rav·en·ous·ly** adv

ra·vine /rə'viːn/ n [C] : a small, deep, narrow valley

¹**rav·ing** adj, always before a noun, *informal* **1** : talking or acting in a crazy way ▪ *a raving lunatic* **2** : very great ▪ *a raving success/beauty*

²**raving** adv, *informal* : completely or fully ▪ *That guy is (stark) raving mad.* [=completely insane]

rav·ings /'reɪvɪŋz/ n [plural] : statements that have no meaning or that sound crazy ▪ *the ravings of a madman*

rav·i·o·li /ˌrævi'ouli/ n, pl **ravioli** also **rav·i·o·lis** [C/U] : pasta that is shaped like a square and is filled with meat, cheese, or vegetables

rav·ish /'rævɪʃ/ vb [T] *literary* **1** : to fill (someone) with pleasure, joy, or happiness ▪ *He was ravished by her charm.* **2** : ¹RAPE

rav·ish·ing /'rævɪʃɪŋ/ adj : very beautiful ▪ *a ravishing view of the ocean* — **rav·ish·ing·ly** adv

¹**raw** /'rɑː/ adj **1** : not cooked ▪ *raw meat/vegetables* **2 a** : not treated or prepared ▪ *raw sewage* **b** : not yet organized or changed in any way ▪ *raw data* **3** : damaged and painful from harsh conditions,

rubbing, etc. ▪ *The shoes rubbed my heels raw.* ▪ *(figurative) The article touched a* **raw nerve.** [=it hurt or upset the people who read it] **4** : powerful and not controlled ▪ *raw emotion/anger* **5** : having no experience or training ▪ *raw recruits* **6** : wet and cold ▪ *a raw winter day* — **raw·ness** *n* [*U*]

²**raw** *n* — **in the raw** **1** : in a natural or unfinished state ▪ *The sculpture is still in the raw.* **2** : NAKED 1 ▪ *He sleeps in the raw.*

raw deal *n* [*C*] : an unfair way of treating someone ▪ *I got a raw deal.* [=I was treated unfairly]

raw·hide /ˈrɑːˌhaɪd/ *n* [*U*] : the skin of a cow before it has been prepared or made into leather

raw material *n* [*C/U*] : the basic material that can be used to make or create something ▪ *Wheat and rye are the raw materials for a flour mill.*

ray /ˈreɪ/ *n* [*C*] **1 a** : a line of light that you can see coming from an object ▪ *a ray of sunlight* ◇ In informal English, if you **catch some rays, soak up a few rays,** etc., you sit or lie in the sun. **b** *technical* : a thin beam of energy (such as heat or light) that moves in the form of waves ▪ *ultraviolet rays* **2** : a very small amount of something ▪ *a ray of hope* **3** : a fish with a flat body and a long, narrow tail

ray·on /ˈreɪˌɑːn/ *n* [*U*] : a smooth fiber that is used in making clothing

raze /ˈreɪz/ *vb* **razed; raz·ing** [*T*] : to destroy (something, such as a building) completely ▪ *The old factory was razed.* [=demolished]

ra·zor /ˈreɪzɚ/ *n* [*C*] : a tool or device with a sharp edge that is used to shave or cut hair

razor blade *n* [*C*] : a small, thin, sharp piece of metal that is used in a razor

razor–sharp *adj* **1** : very sharp ▪ *razor-sharp teeth* **2** : showing a lot of intelligence or the ability to think quickly ▪ *a razor-sharp wit/mind*

razor–thin *adj, always before a noun, chiefly US* : very small or thin ▪ *He won by a razor-thin margin.*

razor wire *n* [*U*] : strong wire that has many sharp metal pieces on it and is put around an area to keep people out or in

razz /ˈræz/ *vb* [*T*] *US, informal* : to make playful or unkind comments about (someone) : TEASE ▪ *Quit razzing me!*

razz·ma·tazz /ˌræzməˈtæz/ *also chiefly Brit* **razz·a·ma·tazz** /ˌræzəməˈtæz/ *n* [*U*] : noisy and exciting activity meant to attract attention ▪ *show-business razzmatazz*

RBI /ˌɑːbiːˈaɪ/ *n, pl* **RBIs** *or* **RBI** [*C*] *baseball* : a run that is scored as a result of a specific batter's hit, walk, etc. ◇ *RBI* is an abbreviation for "run batted in."

RC *abbr* Roman Catholic

Rd *or* **Rd.** *abbr* road

-rd *symbol* — used in writing after the number 3 for the word *third* ▪ *my 3rd* [=third] *try*

¹**re** /ˈreɪ/ *n* [*U*] *music* : the second note of a musical scale ▪ *do, re, mi, fa, sol, la, ti*

²**re** /ˈreɪ, ˈriː/ *prep, formal* : on the subject of : regarding or concerning — used in business and legal writing and e-mail before a word or phrase that states the subject you will be discussing ▪ *re your letter of last month*

re- /ri/ *prefix* **1** : again ▪ *refill* [=fill again] **2** : back to an original place, condition, etc. ▪ *recall* [=call something back]

¹**reach** /ˈriːtʃ/ *vb* **1 a** [*T*] : to be able to touch, pick up, or grab (something) by moving or stretching ▪ *She couldn't reach the apple.* **b** [*T/I*] : to move or stretch (your hand, arm, etc.) when you are trying to touch or grab something ▪ *She reached for the salt.* ▪ *I reached my hand out (to her).* ▪ *He reached into his pocket for a dime.* ▪ *(figurative) reaching for success* **2** [*T*] : to arrive at (a place) ▪ *We reached California after driving for two days.* ▪ *(figurative) The team reached the play-offs.* **3** [*T/I*] — used to say that something is big or long enough to touch a certain place or point ▪ *Their land reaches (to) the river.* ▪ *The phone cord isn't long enough to reach the table.* ▪ *Skirts must reach (down) below the knees.* **4** [*T*] **a** : to grow, develop, or increase to (a particular amount, size, etc.) ▪ *You are an adult when you reach 18 years of age.* ▪ *The lottery is expected to reach $50 million.* ▪ *These plants can reach (up to) 6 feet tall.* **b** : to come to (a particular situation or condition) ▪ *The situation has reached a critical point.* **c** : to succeed in achieving (something) after making an effort over a period of time ▪ *We've reached our goal.* ▪ *trying to reach an agreement* ▪ *reach a decision/verdict* **5** [*T*] **a** : to be seen or heard by (someone) ▪ *The news just reached us.* **b** : to call or write to (someone) : to communicate with (someone) ▪ *You can reach me by e-mail/phone.* **6** [*T*] *informal* : to make (someone) understand or accept something ▪ *I don't think I'm reaching my son.* — **reach out** [*phrasal vb*] : to make an effort to do something for other people ▪ *The church is reaching out to help the poor.* ▪ *The students are reaching out to the homeless.* — **reach·able** /ˈriːtʃəbəl/ *adj*

²**reach** *n* **1** [*U, singular*] : the distance that you can stretch your arm to touch, pick up, or grab something ▪ *The toy was within/in (her) reach.* [=she was able to touch/reach the toy] ▪ *Keep chemicals out of the reach of children.* **2** [*U, singular*] : the ability or power to do, achieve, or control something ▪ *Victory was within (their) reach.* [=they were close to victory] ▪ *Buying a new car is beyond our reach right now.* **3** [*plural*] **a** : the parts of an area that are a long way from the center ▪ *the outer reaches of the universe* **b** : levels of an organization ▪ *the upper/lower reaches of the business* **c** : a straight part of a stream or river ▪ *the upper/lower reaches of the river* — **within (easy) reach of** : close to (something) ▪ *Our house is within easy reach of the highway.*

re·act /riˈækt/ *vb* [*I*] **1** : to behave or change in a particular way when something happens, is said, etc. ▪ *The firefighters reacted quickly when they* *heard the alarm.* — often + *to* ▪ *She reacted to the news by getting angry.* **2** *of a chemical substance* : to change after coming into contact with another substance ▪ *The chemicals react (with each other) to form a gas.* — **react against** [*phrasal vb*] : to do things that are opposed to (something or someone that you disagree with) ▪ *artists who reacted against convention by doing things in a completely new way*

re·ac·tant /ri'æktənt/ *n* [*C*] *chemistry* : a substance that changes when it is combined with another substance in a chemical reaction

re·ac·tion /ri'ækʃən/ *n* **1** [*C/U*] : the way someone acts or feels in response to something that happens, is said, etc. ▪ *I was surprised by his angry reaction to the news.* ▪ *She wrote an angry letter in reaction to the story.* **2** [*C/U*] : an action or attitude that shows disagreement with or disapproval of someone or something ▪ *His behavior is a reaction against traditional conventions.* **3** [*plural*] : the ability to act and move quickly in order to avoid sudden danger ▪ *A good driver has quick reactions.* **4** [*C/U*] *medical* : an occurrence in which your body is affected by a drug, food, etc., in usually a bad way ▪ *I had/suffered a (bad) reaction to the medicine.* ▪ *an allergic reaction* **5** [*C/U*] **a** *chemistry* : a chemical change that occurs when two or more substances combine to form a new substance ▪ *chemical reactions* **b** *physics* : a process in which the nucleus of an atom is changed by being split apart or joined with the nucleus of another atom — called also *nuclear reaction*

re·ac·tion·ary /ri'ækʃəˌneri, *Brit* ri-'ækʃənri/ *n, pl* **-ar·ies** [*C*] *disapproving* : a person who is strongly opposed to new political or social ideas — **reactionary** *adj* ▪ *reactionary ideas*

re·ac·tive /ri'æktɪv/ *adj* **1** : reacting to problems when they occur instead of doing something to prevent them ▪ *Their response to the problem was reactive rather than proactive.* **2** *chemistry* : tending to change into something else when mixed with another substance ▪ *a reactive chemical*

re·ac·tor /ri'æktɚ/ *n* [*C*] : a large device that produces nuclear energy — called also *nuclear reactor*

¹**read** /'ri:d/ *vb* **read** /'rɛd/; **read·ing** /'ri:dɪŋ/ **1** [*T/I*] **a** : to look at and understand the meaning of letters, words, symbols, etc. ▪ *She learned to read at an early age.* ▪ *Can you read decimals/music/ Braille?* **b** : to read the words of (a book, magazine, etc.) ▪ *She reads mystery novels.* ▪ *He read through/over the directions.* **c** : to speak aloud the words of (something written) ▪ *He read the poem aloud.* ▪ *The teacher read (a story) to us.* = *The teacher read us a story.* ▪ *I read out the names on the list.* **2** [*T/I*] : to learn information about something from a book, newspaper, etc. ▪ *I read about/of the fire in the newspaper.* ▪ *I read that they got married.* **3** [*T*] : to learn information about (someone or something) by look-

ing at particular characteristics ▪ *I can't read her—I'm not sure if she likes me or not.* ▪ *A good canoeist can read the rapids.* **4** [*T*] : to understand (something) in a particular way ▪ *I read his actions as a cry for help.* **5** [*T*] : to show (words, a number, etc.) ▪ *The sign reads "No Trespassing."* ▪ *The thermometer reads 90 degrees.* ▪ *The clock read 4:30.* **6** [*I*] : to be written in a particular way ▪ *The speech reads well.* **7** [*T*] : to get information from (something) ▪ *The computer can't read that disk.* **8** [*T*] : to hear and understand (someone) over a radio ▪ *I read you loud and clear.* **9** [*T/I*] *Brit* : to study (a subject) especially at a university ▪ *He read history at Oxford.* — **read between the lines** : to look for or find a hidden meaning in something that someone writes or says ▪ *Her letter seems cheerful, but if you read between the lines, you can tell that she's not happy.* — **read into** [*phrasal vb*] : to think of (a comment, situation, etc.) as having a meaning or importance that does not seem likely or reasonable ▪ *You're reading too much into her remarks.* — **read lips** : to understand what people are saying by watching the movement of their lips ▪ *deaf people who know how to read lips* — **read (someone) like a book** : to easily understand the true thoughts and feelings of (someone) by looking at how that person acts or behaves — **read someone's thoughts** or **read someone's mind** : to know or guess what someone is thinking ▪ *She looked deep into his eyes, trying to read his thoughts.* — **read up on** [*phrasal vb*] : to read a lot about (something) in order to learn about it ▪ *I read up on the history of the war.*

²**read** /'ri:d/ *n* [*C*] *informal* **1** : something (such as a book) that is read ▪ *The book is a good/quick read.* **2** : an act of reading a book, article, etc. ▪ *Give this article a read and tell me what you think of it.*

³**read** /'rɛd/ *adj* : having knowledge that has been gained from reading books, articles, etc. — used after an adverb ▪ *She is widely read in* [=has read a lot of] *American literature.*

read·able /'ri:dəbəl/ *adj* **1** : easy and enjoyable to read ▪ *a highly readable book* **2** : clear and easy to read ▪ *His handwriting is not readable.* — **read·abil·i·ty** /ˌri:də'bɪləti/ *n* [*U*]

read·er /'ri:dɚ/ *n* [*C*] **1** : a person who reads a book, magazine, newspaper, etc. ▪ *She's a fast/slow reader.* ▪ *the readers of a newspaper* **2** : a machine that is used for reading text or information that is stored on film, tape, etc. ▪ *a microfilm reader* **3** : a book that is used to learn how to read or to practice reading **4** or **Reader** *Brit* : a teacher at a university who ranks just below a professor

read·er·ship /'ri:dɚˌʃɪp/ *n* [*C*] **1** : the number or group of people who read a particular newspaper or magazine ▪ *The newspaper has a readership of around 5,000.* **2** or **Readership** *Brit* : the position of a reader at a university

read·i·ly /'rɛdəli/ *adv* **1** : quickly and easily ▪ *readily understandable/available*

2 : without hesitating or complaining ▪ *He readily agreed to help us.*

read·i·ness /ˈrɛdinəs/ *n* **1** [*U*] : the state of being ready or prepared for something ▪ *I'm unsure of my son's readiness for school.* ▪ *The soldier lay in readiness.* **2** [*U, singular*] : the state of being willing to do something ▪ *He showed a readiness to help us.*

read·ing /ˈriːdɪŋ/ *n* **1** [*C/U*] : the act or activity of reading something ▪ *The family attended the reading of her will.* ▪ *After several readings, I finally understood the meaning of the poem.* ▪ *The book makes for interesting reading.* **2** [*C/U*] : a book, article, etc., that is being read or that is intended to be read ▪ *The teacher assigned several readings to the class.* **3** [*C*] : a particular opinion or understanding of something ▪ *a strict reading of the law* **4** [*C*] : an event at which something is read aloud to an audience ▪ *a poetry reading* **5** [*C*] : the temperature, weight, etc., that is shown on a measuring instrument ▪ *The thermometer reading was 20 degrees.*

re·ad·just /ˌriːjəˈdʒʌst/ *vb* **1** [*I*] : to change in order to work or do better in a new situation ▪ *The children need time to readjust to the new school.* **2** [*T*] : to change or move the position of (something) slightly ▪ *He readjusted the picture on the wall.* — **re·ad·just·ment** /ˌriːjəˈdʒʌstmənt/ *n* [*C/U*]

read–only *adj, computers* : capable of being viewed but not of being changed or deleted ▪ *a read-only file*

read–only memory *n* [*U*] *computers* : ROM

read·out /ˈriːdˌaʊt/ *n* [*C*] *computers* : a small screen that shows information ▪ *The calculator has a digital readout.*; *also* : the information shown on such a screen

¹**ready** /ˈrɛdi/ *adj* **read·i·er; -est** **1** *not before a noun* : prepared to do something ▪ *I'll be ready to leave in 10 minutes.* ▪ *We didn't have much time to get ready for their visit.* **2** *not before a noun* : properly prepared or finished and available for use ▪ *Dinner is ready.* **3** *not before a noun* : almost about to do something ▪ *He looked like he was ready to cry.* **4** *not before a noun* **a** : willing and eager to do something ▪ *He is always ready to help his friends.* **b** : needing or wanting something as soon as possible ▪ *I'm tired and ready for bed.* [=I want to go to bed] **5** *always before a noun* : quick and clever ▪ *her ready wit* **6** *always before a noun* : available for immediate use ▪ *ready cash* ▪ *She has ready access to the files.* [=she can get and use the files very quickly and easily] — **(get) ready, (get) set, go** *also Brit* **ready, steady, go** — used as a command to start a race

²**ready** *vb* **read·ies; read·ied; ready·ing** [*T*] *formal* : to prepare (someone or something) ▪ *They readied the room for guests.* ▪ *She readied herself to speak.*

³**ready** *n* — **at the ready** : available for immediate use ▪ *The tourists kept their cameras at the ready.*

ready–made /ˌrɛdiˈmeɪd/ *adj* **1** : pre-pared in advance for immediate use ▪ *ready-made meals* **2** *always before a noun* : already created or provided ▪ *a ready-made excuse/solution*

re·af·firm /ˌriːjəˈfɚm/ *vb* [*T*] : to formally state (something) again in order to emphasize that it is true ▪ *She reaffirmed her stance on the issue.*

re·agent /riˈeɪdʒənt/ *n* [*C*] *chemistry* : a substance that is used to test for the presence of another substance by causing a chemical reaction with it

¹**re·al** /ˈriːjəl/ *adj* **1** : actually existing or happening : not imaginary ▪ *The movie is based on real events.* ▪ *a real person/place* ▪ *The team has a real chance at winning.* ▪ *He looks taller on TV than he does in real life.* ▪ *Their son finally went out into the real world* [=the world where people have to work, deal with daily problems, etc.] *and got a job.* **2** : not fake, false, or artificial ▪ *real leather* ▪ *What is his real name?* ▪ *Tell me the real reason you need the money.* **3** : important and deserving to be regarded or treated in a serious way ▪ *This is a very real problem/danger/concern.* **4** *always before a noun* — used for emphasis ▪ *Receiving this award is a real thrill.* ▪ *He's being a real jerk.* **5** : strong and sincere ▪ *I have no real interest in sports.* [=I'm not very interested in sports] — **for real** *informal* **1** : true and genuine ▪ *The information is for real.* **2** *US* **a** : honest and serious ▪ *Is that guy for real?* **b** : genuinely good, skillful, etc. ▪ *The team has proven that it's for real this year.* **3** : seriously or truly ▪ *They're arguing for real.* — **get real** *informal* : to stop having foolish ideas, hopes, etc. ▪ *You think you can get into Harvard with those grades? Get real.* — **keep it real** *informal* : to talk and behave in an honest and serious way that shows who you really are ▪ *He says he's just trying to keep it real.* — **the real deal** see ²**DEAL** — **the real McCoy** see **MCCOY** — **the real thing** see **THING** — **re·al·ness** *n* [*U*]

²**real** *adv, chiefly US, informal* : very or really ▪ *We had a real good time.* ▪ *a real old car*

real estate *n* [*U*] *chiefly US* **1** : property consisting of buildings and land ▪ *He sells real estate.* **2** : the business of selling land and buildings ▪ *She works in real estate.*

real estate agent *n* [*C*] *chiefly US* : a person in the business of selling land and buildings — called also (*Brit*) **estate agent**

re·align /ˌriːjəˈlaɪn/ *vb* [*T*] **1** : to change the position or direction of (something) slightly ▪ *She realigned the mirror.* **2** : to organize (something) in a different way ▪ *The company has realigned several departments.* — **re·align·ment** /ˌriːjəˈlaɪnmənt/ *n* [*C/U*]

re·al·ism /ˈriːjəˌlɪzəm/ *n* [*U*] **1** : the quality of a person who understands what is real and possible in a particular situation and is able to deal with problems in an effective and practical way **2** : the quality of being like real life ▪ *The realism of her dream was alarming.* **3** : a style of art or literature that shows or describes people and things as they are in real life • *the realism of the painting* — **re·al·ist** /ˈriːjəlɪst/ *n* [C] • *I'm a realist when it comes to politics.* — **realist** *adj*

re·al·is·tic /ˌriːjəˈlɪstɪk/ *adj* **1** : able to see things as they really are and to deal with them in a practical way • *He was realistic about the situation.* **2** : based on what is real rather than on what is wanted or hoped for • *a realistic approach/goal* **3** : showing people and things as they are in real life • *a realistic painting/novel* — **re·al·is·ti·cal·ly** /ˌriːjəˈlɪstɪkli/ *adv*

¹**re·al·i·ty** /riˈæləti/ *n, pl* **-ties** **1** [U] : the true situation that exists : the real situation • *He refused to face/accept reality.* • *The reality is that we can't afford to buy a house.* **2** [C] : something that actually exists or happens : a real event, occurrence, etc. • *the realities of war* • *Her dream of competing in the Olympics became a reality.* — **in reality** : in truth — used to stress that something is true or real especially when it is different from what was believed or expected • *In reality, she was 15 years younger than she looked.*

²**reality** *adj, always before a noun* — used to describe television shows in which people who are not actors are shown living with, dealing with, and often competing against each other in real-life situations • *reality television/TV/shows*

reality check *n* [C] *informal* : something which shows you that the real situation is different from what you believed or hoped • *Her friends gave her a reality check about her boyfriend.* [=told her the truth about her boyfriend]

re·al·ize *also Brit* **re·al·ise** /ˈriːjəˌlaɪz/ *vb* **-ized; -iz·ing** [T] **1** : to understand or become aware of (something) • *They did not realize the risk/danger that was involved.* • *I realize (that) this is an unusual situation.* **2** : to cause (something) to become real • *Our worst fears have been realized.* • *He realized a lifelong dream by winning an Olympic medal.* • *She hasn't yet realized* [=achieved] *her full potential as a golfer.* **3** *formal* : to earn or get (money) by sale or effort • *We can realize a profit by selling the stock.* — **re·al·iz·able** *also Brit* **re·al·is·able** /ˌriːjəˈlaɪzəbəl/ *adj* • *a realizable goal* • *realizable assets* — **re·al·i·za·tion** *also Brit* **re·al·i·sa·tion** /ˌriːjələˈzeɪʃən, *Brit* ˌriːəˌlaɪˈzeɪʃən/ *n* [C/U] • *She had a/the sudden realization* [=she suddenly realized] *that things had changed between them.* • *the realization of his lifelong dream* • *the realization of assets* • *He came to the realization* [=he realized] *that he was adding up the wrong numbers.*

real–life *adj, always before a noun* : happening in the real world rather than in a story • *real-life problems/events*

re·al·ly /ˈriːjəli/ *adv* **1** — used to refer to what is true or real • *They really are twins.* • *What really happened?* • *Did you really think that?* **2** : without question or doubt • *You should really see a doctor.* • *She really is a nice person.* • *He really likes her.* **3** : to a great degree : VERY • *The dog runs really fast.* • *I had a really good*

time at the party. **4** — used to reduce the force of a negative statement • *I don't really agree with you.* **5** — used in speech to show surprise, doubt, or interest • *"They're getting divorced." "Really?"* [=I am surprised to hear that and would like to hear more] **6** *US* — used in speech to express agreement with what someone has just said • *"He shouldn't be allowed to do that." "Yeah, really. Who does he think he is?"* **7** — used in speech to show that you are annoyed • *Really, you're being ridiculous.* — **not really** — used to say "no" in a way that is not very forceful or definite • *"Was the movie good?" "Not really."* [=the movie wasn't very good]

realm /ˈrɛlm/ *n* [C] **1** : an area of activity, interest, or knowledge • *new discoveries in the realm of medicine* • *in the political realm* • *A victory seems within/beyond the realm of possibility.* [=seems possible/impossible] **2** : a country that is ruled by a king or queen • *a peaceful realm*

real–time *adj, always before a noun* : happening or shown at the speed at which a computer receives and processes information • *real-time data/video* — **real time** *n* [U] • *We chatted online in real time.*

Re·al·tor /ˈriːjəltɚ/ *service mark* — used for a real estate agent who is a member of a national licensing association

re·al·ty /ˈriːjəlti/ *n* [U] *US* : REAL ESTATE

ream /ˈriːm/ *n* **1** [C] : an amount of paper that equals 480, 500, or 516 sheets **2** [*plural*] *informal* : a large amount of writing • *She took reams of notes.*

reap /ˈriːp/ *vb* **1** [T] : to get (something) as a result of something that you have done • *She is now reaping the benefits/rewards of her hard work.* **2** [T/I] : to cut and collect (a plant, crop, etc.) from a field • *reaping the crops* — **reap what you sow** : to experience the same kind of things that you have caused other people to experience • *If you're rude to everyone, you'll reap what you sow.* [=people will be rude to you] — **reap·er** /ˈriːpɚ/ *n* [C]

re·ap·pear /ˌriːjəˈpiɚ/ *vb* [I] : to appear again after not being seen, felt, etc., for a period of time • *Call the doctor if the symptoms reappear.* [=come back] — **re·ap·pear·ance** /ˌriːjəˈpirəns/ *n* [C/U]

re·ap·praise /ˌriːjəˈpreɪz/ *vb* **-praised; -prais·ing** [T] *formal* **1** : to make a new judgment about the value of (something) • *Our house is being reappraised.* **2** : to think about (something) again in order to decide whether you should change your opinion about it • *I'm reappraising my plans.* — **re·ap·prais·al** /ˌriːjəˈpreɪzəl/ *n* [C/U]

¹**rear** /ˈriɚ/ *n* **1** [U] : the back part of something • *the rear of the building/train* **2** [C] *informal* : BUTTOCKS — **bring up the rear** : to be in the last position in a group, line, etc. • *They entered the room first and I brought up the rear.*

²**rear** *adj, always before a noun* : at or near the back of something • *the hotel's rear entrance*

³**rear** vb 1 [T] : to take care of (a young person or animal) ▪ *His family rears* [=raises] *cattle.* ▪ *books on child-rearing* ▪ *He was reared on comic books.* [=he read a lot of comic books when he was young] 2 [I] *of an animal* : to rise up on the back legs ▪ *The horse reared (up) in fright.* 3 [I] : to rise high in the air ▪ *The cliff wall reared (up) above us.* — **rear its ugly head** see ¹HEAD

rear admiral n [C] : an officer of high rank in the navy

rear end n [C] 1 : BUTTOCKS ▪ *I slipped and fell on my rear end.* 2 : the back part of something (such as a vehicle) ▪ *the car's rear end*

rear–end /ˈrɪəˌɛnd/ vb [T] *chiefly US, informal* : to drive into the back of (a vehicle) ▪ *My car got rear-ended.*

rear·most /ˈrɪəˌmoʊst/ adj, always before a noun : farthest back from the front ▪ *the rearmost seats*

re·ar·range /ˌriːjəˈreɪndʒ/ vb -ranged; -rang·ing [T] 1 a : to change the position or order of (things) ▪ *He rearranged the furniture.* b : to change the position or order of the things in (something) ▪ *rearrange the living room* 2 : to change the time or location of (something) ▪ *rearrange an appointment* — **re·ar·range·ment** /ˌriːjəˈreɪndʒmənt/ n [C/U]

rear·view mirror /ˈrɪəˌvjuː-/ n [C] : a mirror in a vehicle that allows the driver to see what is behind the vehicle

rear·ward /ˈrɪəwəd/ adj, somewhat formal 1 : located at, near, or toward the back of something ▪ *the rearward section of the store* 2 : BACKWARD ▪ *a rearward glance* — **rear·ward** adv ▪ *He glanced rearward.*

¹**rea·son** /ˈriːzn̩/ n 1 [C] : a statement or fact that explains why something is the way it is or why someone does, thinks, or says something ▪ *I gave a reason for my absence.* ▪ *There is a reason why they don't want to come.* ▪ *He wanted to know the reason for their decision.* ▪ *He tends to get upset for no (good) reason.* 2 [U] : a fact, condition, or situation that makes something proper or appropriate ▪ *There's no reason for you to feel that way.* ▪ *He was found not guilty by reason of insanity.* ▪ *We have (every) reason to believe he is lying.* ▪ *The company fired him with/without reason.* ▪ *Poor work conditions are all the more reason to find another job.* 3 [U] : the power of the mind to think and understand in a logical way ▪ *Human beings possess the power of reason.* 4 [U] : ideas and opinions that are fair, sensible, and appropriate ▪ *I can't get him to listen to (the voice of) reason. = I can't get him to see reason.* ▪ *He is not open to reason.* — **rhyme or reason** see ¹RHYME — **stand to reason** : to be sensible or understandable ▪ *If her friends don't want to go, it stands to reason that she won't want to go either.* — **within reason** : within reasonable or sensible limits ▪ *You can do anything you want, within reason.*

²**reason** vb 1 [I] : to think in a logical way ▪ *He lost the ability to reason.* 2 [T] : to form (a conclusion or judgment) by thinking logically ▪ *She reasoned that something must be wrong.* — **reason out** [phrasal vb] **reason (something) out** or **reason out (something)** : to find an explanation or solution to (a problem, question, etc.) by thinking about the possibilities ▪ *He reasoned out the problem by himself.* — **reason with** [phrasal vb] : to talk with (someone) in a sensible way in order to try to change that person's thoughts or behavior ▪ *They tried to reason with him, but he wouldn't listen.*

rea·son·able /ˈriːznəbəl/ adj 1 : fair and sensible ▪ *a reasonable boss/request* ▪ *We finished within a reasonable amount of time.* 2 : fairly or moderately good ▪ *We have a reasonable chance of winning.* 3 : not too expensive ▪ *a reasonable price* — **rea·son·able·ness** /ˈriːznəbəlnəs/ n [U] — **rea·son·ably** /ˈriːznəbli/ adv ▪ *The food was reasonably* [=fairly] *good/inexpensive.* ▪ *a reasonably priced car* ▪ *We need to discuss this problem reasonably.*

rea·soned /ˈriːznd/ adj, always before a noun : based on sensible and logical thinking ▪ *a reasoned argument/conclusion*

rea·son·ing /ˈriːzn̩ɪŋ/ n [U] : the process of thinking about something in a logical way in order to form a conclusion or judgment ▪ *Could you explain your reasoning?* ▪ *scientific/logical/legal reasoning* ▪ *following a particular line of reasoning* [=using a specific set of reasons in order to reach a conclusion]

re·as·sem·ble /ˌriːjəˈsɛmbəl/ vb -sem·bled; -sem·bling 1 [T] : to put the parts of (something) back together ▪ *reassembled a puzzle* 2 [I] : to meet as a group again ▪ *We will reassemble after lunch.*

re·as·sert /ˌriːjəˈsɚt/ vb [T] 1 : to make other people accept or respect (something that has been in doubt) ▪ *He reasserted his authority.* 2 : to state or declare (something) more strongly or clearly ▪ *She reasserted her innocence.* — **reassert itself** : to start to have an effect again ▪ *Traditional values have reasserted themselves.* — **re·as·ser·tion** /ˌriːjəˈsɚʃən/ n [C/U]

re·as·sess /ˌriːjəˈsɛs/ vb [T] : to think about (something) in order to decide whether to change your opinion of it ▪ *The doctor reassessed the injury.* — **re·as·sess·ment** /ˌriːjəˈsɛsmənt/ n [C/U]

re·as·sure /ˌriːjəˈʃɚ/ vb -sured; -sur·ing [T] : to make (someone) feel less afraid, upset, or doubtful ▪ *She reassured me that they were safe.* — **re·as·sur·ance** /ˌriːjəˈʃɚəns/ n [C/U] — **reassuring** adj ▪ *a reassuring smile*

re·bate /ˈriːˌbeɪt/ n [C] 1 : ²REFUND ▪ *a tax rebate* 2 : an amount of money that a company pays back to you because you have bought something ▪ *a mail-in rebate*

¹**reb·el** /ˈrɛbəl/ n [C] 1 : a person who opposes or fights against a government ▪ *armed rebels* ▪ *a rebel leader* 2 : a person who does not obey rules or accept normal standards of behavior, dress, etc. ▪ *a fashion rebel*

²**re·bel** /rɪˈbɛl/ vb **-belled; -bel·ling** [I] **1**
: to oppose or fight against a government
▪ *When the government imposed more taxes, the people rebelled.* **2** : to oppose a
person or group in authority ▪ *She rebelled against her parents.* : to refuse to
obey rules or accept normal standards of
behavior, dress, etc. ▪ *rebelling against social conventions*

re·bel·lion /rɪˈbɛljən/ n **1** [C/U] : an effort by many people to change the government or leader of a country by the
use of protest or violence ▪ *A rebellion
broke out.* **2** [C/U] : open opposition toward a person or group in authority ▪ *a
rebellion against the leaders of the party*
3 [U] : refusal to obey rules or accept
normal standards of behavior, dress, etc.
▪ *teenage rebellion*

re·bel·lious /rɪˈbɛljəs/ adj **1** : fighting
against a government ▪ *a rebellious army*
2 : refusing to obey rules or authority or
to accept normal standards of behavior,
dress, etc. ▪ *a rebellious child* ▪ *He has a
rebellious streak.* — **re·bel·lious·ly**
adv — **re·bel·lious·ness** n [U]

re·birth /riˈbɚθ/ n [C] **1** : a period in
which something becomes popular again
after a long period of time when it was
not popular ▪ *the rebirth of swing music*
2 : a period of new life, growth, or activity ▪ *the cycle of death and rebirth in
plants*

re·boot /riˈbuːt/ vb [T/I] computers : to
turn off a computer and then immediately turn it on ▪ *I had to reboot the computer).*

re·born /riˈbɔɚn/ adj — **be reborn** : to
become alive again after death ▪
(figurative) *The city has been reborn as a
tourist destination.*

¹**re·bound** /ˈriːˌbaʊnd/ n [C] **1** : the act
of bouncing back after hitting something
▪ *I caught the ball on the rebound.*
[=when it bounced back] **2** : a ball,
puck, etc., that bounces back after hitting something ▪ *He caught the rebound.*
3 basketball : the act of catching the ball
after a missed shot ▪ *He leads the league
in rebounds.* **4** : an increase or improvement after a decrease or decline ▪ *a rebound in prices* — **on the rebound 1**
: sad and confused because a romantic
relationship has recently ended ▪ *She refuses to date men who are on the rebound.*
2 chiefly US : getting better ▪ *His health is
on the rebound.*

²**rebound** vb **1** [I] : to bounce back off
something after hitting it ▪ *The ball re-
bounded off the wall.* **2** [I] : to increase
or improve after a recent decrease or decline ▪ *Prices are rebounding.* **3** [T/I]
basketball : to catch the ball after a shot
has missed going in the basket ▪ *She is
good at rebounding (the ball).*

re·buff /rɪˈbʌf/ vb [T] formal : to refuse
(something) in a rude way ▪ *Our suggestion was rebuffed.* — **rebuff** n [C]

re·build /riˈbɪld/ vb **-built** /-ˈbɪlt/; **-build-
ing** [T/I] **1** : to build (something) again
after it has been destroyed ▪ *He rebuilt
(his house) after the fire.* **2** : to make important improvements in (something) ▪
rebuilding [=renovating] *an old house* ▪

*The team is rebuilding after losing most of
its top players.*

re·buke /rɪˈbjuːk/ vb **-buked; -buk·ing**
[T] formal : to speak in an angry and
critical way to (someone) ▪ *He rebuked us
for being late.* — **rebuke** n [C] ▪ *a harsh
rebuke*

re·but /rɪˈbʌt/ vb **-but·ted; -but·ting** [T]
formal : to prove (something) is false by
using arguments or evidence ▪ *rebut a
witness's testimony* — **re·but·tal** /rɪˈbʌtl/
n [C/U] formal ▪ *Her report is a rebuttal of
some common misconceptions.*

re·cal·ci·trant /rɪˈkælsətrənt/ adj, formal
: stubbornly refusing to obey rules or orders ▪ *a recalcitrant prisoner* — **re·cal-
ci·trance** /rɪˈkælsətrəns/ n [U]

¹**re·call** /rɪˈkɑːl/ vb **1** [T/I] : to remember
(something) from the past ▪ *I don't recall
what she said.* **2** [T] **a** : to ask or order
(someone) to return ▪ *The ambassador
was recalled from abroad.* **b** : to ask
people to return (a defective product) ▪
The factory is recalling thousands of toys.
3 [T] : to bring (an image, idea, etc.) into
your mind ▪ *Seeing her again recalled
memories of my childhood.*

²**re·call** /ˈriːˌkɑːl/ n **1** [singular] : an official order for someone or something to
return ▪ *a recall of workers after a layoff*
2 [C] : a request by a company for people to return a defective product ▪ *a
product recall* **3** [U] : the ability to remember what has been learned or experienced in the past ▪ *He has total recall.*
[=he remembers everything that hap-
pened] **4** [singular] US : a way in which
a public official may be removed from
office by a special vote of the people ▪
The mayor is facing a recall. ▪ *a recall
election* — **beyond recall** : not able to
be brought back or remembered ▪ *events
that are beyond recall*

re·cant /rɪˈkænt/ vb [T/I] formal : to publicly say that you no longer have an opinion or belief that you once had ▪ *The witness threatened to recant (her testimony).*
— **re·can·ta·tion** /ˌriːˌkænˈteɪʃən/ n
[C/U]

re·cap /ˈriːˌkæp/ vb **-capped; -cap·ping**
[T/I] : to give a brief summary of what
has been done or said before ▪ *Before we
continue, let's recap (what we have done so
far).* — **recap** n [C] ▪ *a brief recap of the
news*

re·ca·pit·u·late /ˌriːkəˈpɪtʃəˌleɪt/ vb **-lat-
ed; -lat·ing** [T/I] formal : RECAP ▪ *He re-
capitulated (what was said earlier).* — **re-
ca·pit·u·la·tion** /ˌriːkəˌpɪtʃəˈleɪʃən/ n
[C/U]

re·cap·ture /riˈkæptʃɚ/ vb **-tured; -tur-
ing** [T] **1** : to catch (someone or something that has escaped) ▪ *recapture a prisoner* **2** : to gain control of (a place or
position) again after losing it ▪ *The soldiers recaptured the hill.* **3** : to experience or bring back (a feeling, quality, or
situation) again ▪ *They are trying to recapture their youth.* — **recapture** n [U]

re·cast /riˈkæst, Brit riˈkɑːst/ vb **-cast;
-cast·ing** [T] **1 a** : to change the actors
in (a play, movie, etc.) ▪ *The director recast the movie.* **b** : to give a new role to
(an actor) ▪ *I was recast in the leading*

role. **2** : to present (something) in a different way ▪ *He recast his political image.*

rec'd *abbr* received

re·cede /rɪˈsiːd/ *vb* **-ced·ed; -ced·ing** [*I*] **1** : to move away gradually ▪ *The floodwaters receded.* ▪ *The ship receded from view.* **2** : to become smaller or weaker ▪ *The sound/pain receded.* **3** ◆ If your hair is *receding,* you are gradually losing the hair that is at the front of your head. ▪ *He has a receding hairline.*

re·ceipt /rɪˈsiːt/ *n* **1** [*C*] : a piece of paper on which the things that you buy or the services that you pay for are listed with the amounts paid **2** [*U*] *formal* : the act of receiving something ▪ *Open immediately upon/on receipt of the package.* **3** [*plural*] : money that a business, bank, or government receives ▪ *depositing cash receipts*

re·ceiv·able /rɪˈsiːvəbəl/ *adj, always after a noun, business* : not yet paid ▪ *accounts receivable* [=the amounts of money owed to a business]

re·ceive /rɪˈsiːv/ *vb* **-ceived; -ceiv·ing** [*T*] **1** : to get or be given (something) ▪ *We received your letter/payment.* **2** : to react to (something) in a specified way ▪ *Her book was well received.* [=people liked it] **3** *formal* : to welcome (someone) in usually a formal way ▪ *The ambassador received his guests.* **4 a** : to suffer (an injury) ▪ *receive a broken nose* ▪ : to be given (a punishment) ▪ *receive a heavy sentence* **5** : to experience or take (a medical treatment) ▪ *receive an injection* **6 a** : to get (signals that are sent to a TV, radio, etc.) ▪ *We were unable to receive the broadcast.* **b** : to be able to hear (someone who is talking to you on a radio) ▪ *I'm receiving you loud and clear.* **— on/at the receiving end** ◆ If you are *on/at the receiving end* of something bad or unpleasant, you are the person it is directed at. ▪ *I was on the receiving end of his insults.*

received *adj, always before a noun, formal* : widely accepted ▪ *The theory has become received wisdom.*

re·ceiv·er /rɪˈsiːvɚ/ *n* [*C*] **1** : the part of a telephone that you pick up and hold near your face **2** : radio or television equipment that changes signals into sound and pictures ▪ *a satellite receiver* **3** *American football* : a player who catches passes thrown by the quarterback **4** *law* : a person who is chosen to take control of a bankrupt business or its property

re·ceiv·er·ship /rɪˈsiːvɚˌʃɪp/ *n* [*U*] *law* : the state of a business that has been placed under the control of a receiver because it is bankrupt ▪ *The company is in receivership.*

re·cent /ˈriːsn̩t/ *adj* : happening or beginning not long ago ▪ *recent decades/events* ▪ *the biggest earthquake in recent history/memory* **— re·cent·ly** /ˈriːsn̩tli/ *adv* ▪ *She recently graduated from college.*

re·cep·ta·cle /rɪˈsɛptɪkəl/ *n* [*C*] *formal* : CONTAINER ▪ *a trash receptacle*

re·cep·tion /rɪˈsɛpʃən/ *n* **1** [*C*] : the kind of welcome that someone or something is given ▪ *We got a warm/cool recep-* *tion.* **2** [*C*] : a social gathering to celebrate something or to welcome someone ▪ *a wedding reception* **3** [*U*] : the act or process of receiving, welcoming, or accepting something or someone ▪ *the reception of donations* **4** [*U*] — used to describe how well or badly a radio, television, etc., is able to receive signals ▪ *terrible cell phone reception* **5** [*U*] : a desk or area in a hotel, office building, etc., where visitors first go after entering ▪ *Check in at the reception desk.* ▪ *the reception area* [=*lobby*]

re·cep·tion·ist /rɪˈsɛpʃənɪst/ *n* [*C*] : a person whose job is to deal with the people who call or enter a business

re·cep·tive /rɪˈsɛptɪv/ *adj* : willing to listen to or accept ideas, suggestions, etc. ▪ *a receptive audience* **— re·cep·tive·ness** *n* [*U*] **— re·cep·tiv·i·ty** /ˌriːˌsɛpˈtɪvəti/ *n* [*U*]

re·cep·tor /rɪˈsɛptɚ/ *n* [*C*] *biology* : a nerve ending that senses changes in light, temperature, pressure, etc., and causes the body to react in a particular way

¹**re·cess** /ˈriːˌsɛs/ *n* **1** [*U*] *US* : a short period of time during the school day when children can play ▪ *They played outside at/during recess.* **2** [*C/U*] : a usually brief period of time during which regular activity in a court of law or in a government stops ▪ *The Senate wanted to vote on the bill before the(the) recess.* **3** [*C*] : a dark, hidden place or part ▪ *the dark recesses of the forest* ▪ *the recesses of my mind*

²**recess** *vb* [*T/I*] *US* : to stop regular activity in a court of law or in a government for a usually short period of time ▪ *The trial recessed.* ▪ *The judge recessed the trial.*

re·cessed /ˈriːˌsɛst/ *adj* : set back into a wall or ceiling ▪ *recessed lighting/shelves*

re·ces·sion /rɪˈsɛʃən/ *n* **1** [*C/U*] : a period of time in which there is a decrease in economic activity and many people do not have jobs ▪ *The economy is in (a) deep recession.* **2** [*U*] *formal* : the act of moving back or away slowly ▪ *the recession of the floodwaters*

re·ces·sive /rɪˈsɛsɪv/ *adj, biology* : causing or relating to a characteristic or condition that a child will have only if both of the child's parents have it ▪ *recessive genes/traits*

re·charge /ˈriːˈtʃɑɚdʒ/ *vb* **-charged; -charg·ing** [*T/I*] : to refill (a battery) with electricity ▪ *(figurative) Take a break to give yourself time to recharge (your batteries).* [=to regain your energy and strength] **— re·charge·able** *adj*

rec·i·pe /ˈrɛsəpi/ *n* [*C*] **1** : a set of instructions for making food ▪ *a recipe for beef stew* **2** : a way of doing something that will produce a particular result ▪ *a recipe for success/disaster*

re·cip·i·ent /rɪˈsɪpijənt/ *n* [*C*] *formal* : a person who receives something ▪ *welfare recipients* ▪ *a recipient of many honors*

re·cip·ro·cal /rɪˈsɪprəkəl/ *adj* — used to describe a relationship in which two people or groups agree to do something similar for each other, to allow each other to have the same rights, etc. ▪ *a reciprocal exchange of information* **— re·cip·ro-**

cal·ly /rɪˈsɪprəkli/ *adv*

re·cip·ro·cate /rɪˈsɪprəˌkeɪt/ *vb* **-cat·ed;** **-cat·ing** **1** [*T/I*] : to do (something) for or to someone who has done something similar for or to you ▪ *They appreciated her kindness but were not ready to reciprocate (the gesture).* **2** [*T*] : to have (a feeling) for someone who has the same feeling for you ▪ *His love was not reciprocated.* [=the person he loved did not love him] — **re·cip·ro·ca·tion** /rɪˌsɪprəˈkeɪʃən/ *n* [*U*]

rec·i·proc·i·ty /ˌrɛsəˈprɑːsəti/ *n* [*U*] *formal* : a situation or relationship in which two people or groups agree to do something similar for each other, to allow each other to have the same rights, etc. ▪ *reciprocity in trade relations*

re·cit·al /rɪˈsaɪtl̟/ *n* [*C*] **1** : a dance or musical performance ▪ *a dance/piano recital* **2** : the act of reading something out loud or saying something from memory usually for an audience ▪ *a recital of poems*

rec·i·ta·tion /ˌrɛsəˈteɪʃən/ *n* **1** [*C/U*] : the act of saying or repeating something out loud for an audience ▪ *a/the recitation of poetry/prayers* **2** [*C*] : the act of describing or listing many things in a series ▪ *dry recitations of statistics*

re·cite /rɪˈsaɪt/ *vb* **-cit·ed;** **-cit·ing** **1** [*T/I*] : to read (something) out loud or say (something) from memory ▪ *recite a poem* **2** [*T*] : to say or describe (a series or list of things) ▪ *He can recite the facts about any player on the team.*

reck·less /ˈrɛkləs/ *adj* : not showing proper concern about the possible bad results of your actions ▪ *a reckless young man* ▪ **reckless driving** [=driving in a dangerous manner] ▪ *a reckless disregard for safety* ▪ *spending money with reckless abandon* — **reck·less·ly** *adv* — **reck·less·ness** *n* [*U*]

reck·on /ˈrɛkən/ *vb* [*T*] **1** *informal* : to think or suppose (something) ▪ *I reckon (that) it will rain.* ▪ *"Do you think it will rain?" "(I) Reckon so."* **2** : to calculate or guess (something) ▪ *They reckoned that they would arrive by noon.* ▪ *Losses were reckoned to be over a million dollars.* **3** : to think of (someone or something) as being something specified ▪ *She was reckoned to be among the leaders.* = *She was reckoned as one of the leaders.* — **reckon on** [*phrasal vb*] : to expect (something) ▪ *We hadn't reckoned on the train arriving late.* — **reckon with** [*phrasal vb*] **1** : to consider or think about (something) when you are making plans ▪ *They hadn't reckoned with the extra paperwork.* **2** : to deal with (someone or something that can cause problems) ▪ *Anyone who tries to harm you will have me to reckon with.* [=I will oppose/ fight anyone who tries to harm you] ✦ If you are a *person/force to be reckoned with* or a *person/force to reckon with*, you are someone who is strong and cannot be ignored.

reck·on·ing /ˈrɛkənɪŋ/ *n* **1** [*U*] : the act of calculating the amount of something ▪ *By my reckoning* [=by my calculations], *we are short $10.* **2 a** [*U*] : the time

when your actions are judged as good or bad and you are rewarded or punished ▪ *When the day of reckoning comes, we will have to face some unpleasant truths.* **b** [*C*] : the act of judging something ▪ *In the final reckoning, her earliest books are the best.*

re·claim /rɪˈkleɪm/ *vb* [*T*] **1** : to get back (something that was lost or taken away) ▪ *She reclaimed the title of world champion.* **2** : to make (land) available for use by changing its condition ▪ *an area of reclaimed swampland* **3** : to get (a usable material) from materials that have been used before ▪ *The factory reclaims fibers from textile wastes.* — **rec·la·ma·tion** /ˌrɛkləˈmeɪʃən/ *n* [*U*]

re·cline /rɪˈklaɪn/ *vb* **-clined;** **-clin·ing** **1** [*I*] *formal* : to sit back or lie down in a relaxed manner ▪ *She was reclining on the sofa.* **2** [*T/I*] : to lean backward ▪ *He reclined his seat.* ▪ *a reclining seat*

re·clin·er /rɪˈklaɪnɚ/ *n* [*C*] : a comfortable chair which has a back that can lean back at an angle

re·cluse /ˈrɛˌkluːs, *Brit* rɪˈkluːs/ *n* [*C*] : a person who lives alone and avoids other people — **re·clu·sive** /rɪˈkluːsɪv/ *adj* ▪ *my reclusive neighbor*

rec·og·ni·tion /ˌrɛkɪgˈnɪʃən/ *n* **1** [*U*] : the act of knowing who or what someone or something is because of previous knowledge or experience ▪ *She escaped recognition.* [=she was not recognized] ▪ *The house has changed beyond (all) recognition.* [=so much that it looks completely different] **2 a** [*U, singular*] : the act of accepting that something is true or important or that it exists ▪ *The Olympic Committee gave official recognition to the sport.* **b** [*U*] : the act of accepting someone or something as having legal or official authority ▪ *the recognition of the territory as a state* **3** [*U*] : special attention or notice especially by the public for someone's work or actions ▪ *She received recognition from her fellow artists.* ▪ *They were awarded medals in recognition of their bravery.*

re·cog·ni·zance /rɪˈkɑːgnəzəns/ *n* [*U*] *US, law* : a legal promise made by someone before a court of law that must be kept to avoid being punished ▪ *He was released on his own recognizance.* [=after promising to do what the court wanted him to do]

rec·og·nize *also Brit* **rec·og·nise** /ˈrɛkɪgˌnaɪz/ *vb* **-nized;** **-niz·ing** [*T*] **1** : to know and remember (someone or something) because of previous knowledge or experience ▪ *I almost didn't recognize you with your new haircut.* **2** : to accept or be aware that (something) is true or exists ▪ *They soon recognized how much they had in common.* **3** : to accept and approve of (something) as having legal or official authority ▪ *They refused to recognize the treaty.* **4** : to think of (someone or something) as being something specified ▪ *He is recognized as one of America's great poets.* **5** : to publicly give special attention or notice to (someone or something) ▪ *They recognized her years of service with a special award.* —

rec·og·niz·able also Brit **rec·og·nis·able** /ˈrɛkɪgˌnaɪzəbəl/ adj — **rec·og·niz·ably** also Brit **rec·og·nis·ably** /ˈrɛkɪgˌnaɪzəbli/ adv

¹**re·coil** /rɪˈkojəl/ vb [I] **1** : to quickly move away from something that is shocking, frightening, or disgusting ▪ We recoiled in horror at the sight of his wounded arm. ▪ (figurative) We recoiled at the idea of paying such high prices. **2** of a gun : to move back suddenly when fired ▪ The rifle recoiled.

²**re·coil** /ˈriːˌkojəl/ n [singular] : the sudden backward movement of a gun that happens when the gun is fired ▪ a gun with a sharp recoil

rec·ol·lect /ˌrɛkəˈlɛkt/ vb [T] : to remember (something) ▪ I've been trying to recollect what happened.

rec·ol·lec·tion /ˌrɛkəˈlɛkʃən/ n **1** [U] : the act of remembering something or the ability to remember something ▪ Her recollection of the event is different from mine. ▪ To the best of my recollection [=from what I can remember], I never met them. **2** [C] : something from the past that is remembered ▪ recollections of childhood ▪ He has no recollection of what happened. [=he doesn't remember what happened]

re·com·mence /ˌriːkəˈmɛns/ vb **-menced; -menc·ing** [T/I] formal : to begin (something) again after stopping ▪ recommencing peace talks

rec·om·mend /ˌrɛkəˈmɛnd/ vb [T] **1** : to say that (someone or something) is good and deserves to be chosen ▪ A friend recommended this restaurant. **2** : to suggest that someone do (something) ▪ I recommend getting to the theater early. **3** : to make (something or someone) seem attractive or good ▪ The area has much to recommend it. [=the area is appealing] ▪ He has little/nothing to recommend him as a political candidate. — **rec·om·men·da·tion** /ˌrɛkəmənˈdeɪʃən/ n [C/U] ▪ He rejected his doctors' recommendations. [=advice] ▪ a letter of recommendation = (chiefly US) a written recommendation [=a letter recommending that someone be chosen for something, such as a job] ▪ We picked this restaurant on his recommendation. [=because he recommended it]

rec·om·pense /ˈrɛkəmˌpɛns/ n [U, singular] formal : something that is given to or done to thank or reward someone or to pay someone for loss or suffering ▪ a fair recompense — **recompense** /ˈrɛkəmˌpɛns/ vb [T] ▪ She was recompensed for her injuries.

rec·on·cile /ˈrɛkənˌsajəl/ vb **-ciled; -cil·ing** formal **1** [T] : to find a way of making (two different ideas, facts, etc.) exist or be true at the same time ▪ It can be difficult to reconcile your ideals with reality. **2** [T/I] : to cause people or groups to become friendly again after a disagreement ▪ They (are) finally reconciled (with each other). [=they are finally friendly again] — **reconcile to** [phrasal vb] **reconcile (someone) to** : to cause (someone) to accept (something unpleasant) ▪ I reconciled myself to the loss.

rec·on·cil·i·a·tion /ˌrɛkənˌsɪliˈeɪʃən/ n [C/U] formal **1** : the act of causing two people or groups to become friendly again after a disagreement ▪ He contacted us in hopes of a reconciliation. **2** : the process of finding a way to make two different ideas, facts, etc., exist or be true at the same time ▪ a reconciliation of opposing views

re·con·di·tion /ˌriːkənˈdɪʃən/ vb [T] : to return (something) to good condition by repairing it, cleaning it, or replacing parts ▪ a reconditioned engine

re·con·fig·ure /ˌriːkənˈfɪgjɚ, Brit ˌriːkənˈfɪgə/ vb **-ured; -ur·ing** [T] : to change the way (something) is arranged or prepared for a particular purpose ▪ We reconfigured the space to make it easier to work in.

re·con·nais·sance /rɪˈkɑːnəzəns/ n [C/U] : military activity in which soldiers, airplanes, etc., are sent to find out information about an enemy ▪ a reconnaissance of the enemy's position

re·con·noi·ter (US) or Brit **re·con·noi·tre** /ˌriːkəˈnoɪtɚ/ vb [T/I] : to go to (a place or area) in order to find out information about a military enemy ▪ They went ahead to reconnoiter (the coast).

re·con·sid·er /ˌriːkənˈsɪdɚ/ vb [T/I] : to think carefully about (someone or something) again especially in order to change a choice or decision you have already made ▪ She refused to reconsider (her decision). — **re·con·sid·er·a·tion** /ˌriːkənˌsɪdəˈreɪʃən/ n [C/U]

re·con·sti·tute /riˈkɑːnstəˌtuːt, Brit riˈkɒnstəˌtjuːt/ vb **-tut·ed; -tut·ing** [T] **1** formal : to form (an organization or group) again in a different way ▪ a newly reconstituted committee **2** : to return (dried food) to a former state by adding water ▪ reconstituted potatoes — **re·con·sti·tu·tion** /ˌriˌkɑːnstəˈtuːʃən, Brit ˌriˌkɒnstəˈtjuːʃən/ n [U]

re·con·struct /ˌriːkənˈstrʌkt/ vb [T] **1** : to build (something damaged or destroyed) again ▪ The bridge was reconstructed. **2** : to find out and describe or show the way an event or series of events happened ▪ Police reconstructed the crime.

re·con·struc·tion /ˌriːkənˈstrʌkʃən/ n **1** [U] : the act or process of building something that was damaged or destroyed again ▪ the reconstruction of the dam **2** [U] : the process of putting something (such as a country) back into a good condition ▪ the reconstruction of postwar Europe **3** [C/U] : a process in which an event or series of events is carefully examined in order to find out or show exactly what happened ▪ (a) reconstruction of the crime/accident **4** or **Re·construction** [U] US : the period from 1867 to 1877 when the southern states joined the northern states again after the American Civil War

re·con·struc·tive /ˌriːkənˈstrʌktɪv/ adj, medical : done on a body part to return it to a former shape or to change the way that it looks ▪ reconstructive surgery

re·con·vene /ˌriːkənˈviːn/ vb **-vened; -ven·ing 1** [I] : to meet again after a break • *Congress will reconvene next week.* 2 [T] : to cause (a group of people) to meet again after a break • *reconvene a conference*

¹rec·ord /ˈrɛkəd/ n [C] 1 : an official written document that gives proof of something or tells about past events • *medical/financial/court records* 2 — used to talk about the things that someone or something has done in the past • *She has a perfect driving record.* [=she has not had any car accidents, traffic tickets, etc.] • *The defendant does not have a (criminal) record.* [=has not been arrested in the past for a crime] • *The team has a losing/winning record.* [=the team has lost/won most of its games] 3 : a performance or achievement that is the best of its kind • *He broke the record for the high jump.* [=he jumped higher than anyone else had ever jumped] • *She set a record for the most sales.* [=she made more sales than anyone else ever had] • *He holds the school/world/Olympic record for the shot put.* 4 a : a flat, round disc on which sound or music is recorded • *a collection of old records* • (figurative) *He sounds like a broken record.* [=he keeps saying the same thing over and over again] b : a musical recording on a record, CD, etc. • *Have you heard the band's latest record?* • *a record label/company* • *a hit record* [=a record or CD that sells many copies] — **for the record** 1 — used to indicate that a statement will be written down in an official record • *Please state your name for the record.* 2 — used to indicate that you are making a statement which is important and should be remembered • *For the record, I think this is a bad idea.* — **off the record** — used to describe a statement that is not official and should not be repeated or made public by being used in a newspaper, magazine, etc. • *Her remarks were off the record.* — **on record** 1 — used to indicate that someone is making or has made an official or public statement • *The judge's opinion is on record.* 2 : included or described in official records • *It was one of the worst years on record for winter storms.* — **on the record** — used to describe a statement that is official and can be repeated or made public by being used in a newspaper, magazine, etc. • *The interview was on the record.* — **set/put the record straight** : to provide the facts about something that people have a false understanding or idea about

²re·cord /rɪˈkoəd/ vb 1 [T] : to write (something) down so that it can be used or seen again in the future • *He recorded the incident in his journal.* • *There are similar events throughout recorded history.* 2 [T] : to show a measurement of (something) • *The thermometer recorded 40 degrees.* 3 [T/I] : to store (sounds, music, images, etc.) on tape or on a disk so that it can be heard or seen later • *The band spent all night recording (songs).*

³rec·ord /ˈrɛkəd/ adj, always before a noun : best or most remarkable among other similar things • *Prices are at a record high.* [=higher than ever before]

re·cord·er /rɪˈkoədə/ n [C] 1 : a device that records sounds or images or both so that they can be heard or seen again 2 : a musical instrument that is shaped like a tube with holes and that is played by blowing into the top of the tube 3 : a person whose job is to record official information

re·cord·ing /rɪˈkoədɪŋ/ n 1 [C] : music, sounds, or images that have been stored on a record, CD, computer, etc., so that they can be heard or seen again • *a digital recording* 2 [U] : the act or process of storing sounds or images on tape or a disk • *a recording studio/session*

record player n [C] : a device used for playing musical records

¹re·count /rɪˈkaʊnt/ vb [T] : to count (something) again • *They recounted the votes/money.* — compare ³RECOUNT

²re·count /ˈriːˌkaʊnt/ n [C] : a second count of the votes in a very close election • *The losing candidate demanded a recount.*

³re·count /rɪˈkaʊnt/ vb [T] formal : to tell someone about (something that happened) • *He recounted the conversation he'd had earlier.* — compare ¹RECOUNT

re·coup /rɪˈkuːp/ vb [T] : to get back (money that has been spent, invested, etc.) • *It will be hard for us to recoup the loss.*

re·course /ˈriːˌkoəs, Brit rɪˈkɔːs/ n [U] : an opportunity or choice to use or do something in order to deal with a problem or situation • *His only recourse* [=the only thing he can do] *is to file a complaint.*

re·cov·er /rɪˈkʌvə/ vb 1 [I] a : to become healthy after an illness or injury • *She had a heart attack but is recovering well.* • *He's recovering from the flu.* b : to return to a normal state after a period of difficulty • *The team never recovered from the devastating loss.* 2 [T] a : to get (an ability, feeling, etc.) again • *I recovered my balance/confidence.* b : to get back (something stolen or lost) • *The police recovered his wallet.* • *A recovered computer file* c : to get back (money that has been spent, invested, etc.) • *We haven't yet recovered our expenses.* — **re·cov·er·able** /rɪˈkʌvərəbəl/ adj

re·cov·er·ing /rɪˈkʌvərɪŋ/ adj, always before a noun : in a state in which you have stopped or are trying to stop a behavior (such as drug use) • *a recovering alcoholic/addict*

re·cov·ery /rɪˈkʌvəri/ n, pl -er·ies 1 [C] : the act or process of becoming healthy after an illness or injury • *The patient made a miraculous recovery.* 2 [C/U] : the act or process of returning to a normal state after a period of difficulty • *(a) gradual economic recovery* 3 [U] : the return of something that has been lost, stolen, etc. • *the recovery of stolen paintings* 4 [U] : the act or process of stopping the use of drugs, alcohol, etc. • *She used to drink too much, but she's in recovery now.*

re–cre·ate /ˌriːkriˈeɪt/ vb -at·ed; -at·ing [T] : to make (something from the past) exist or seem to exist again • *The movie set re-creates a desert oasis.* — **re·cre·a·tion** /ˌriːkriˈeɪʃən/ *n* [C/U] ▪ *a perfect re-creation of a colonial village*

rec·re·a·tion /ˌrɛkriˈeɪʃən/ *n* [C/U] : something people do to relax or have fun ▪ *Hiking is my favorite (form of) recreation.* ▪ *a recreation center/area* — **rec·re·a·tion·al** /ˌrɛkriˈeɪʃənl/ *adj* ▪ *recreational activities*

recreational vehicle *n* [C] *US* : MOTOR HOME

re·crim·i·na·tion /rɪˌkrɪməˈneɪʃən/ *n* [C/U] : an angry statement in which you accuse or criticize a person who has accused or criticized you ▪ *Recriminations were flying back and forth.* ▪ *words of recrimination*

¹**re·cruit** /rɪˈkruːt/ *vb* **1 a** [T/I] : to find suitable people and get them to join a company, an organization, etc. ▪ *He was recruited by the army.* **b** [T] : to form or build (a team, army, etc.) by getting people to join ▪ *recruit an army* **2** [T] : to persuade (someone) to join you in some activity or to help you ▪ *I recruited him to help us paint.* — **re·cruit·er** *n* [C] — **re·cruit·ment** /rɪˈkruːtmənt/ *n* [U]

²**recruit** *n* [C] : a person who has recently joined the armed forces or some other group ▪ *army recruits* ▪ *the newest recruit on the team*

rec·tal /ˈrɛktl̩/ *adj, medical* : relating to, affecting, or located near the rectum ▪ *rectal cancer*

rect·an·gle /ˈrɛkˌtæŋɡəl/ *n* [C] *geometry* : a four-sided shape that is made up of two pairs of parallel lines and that has four right angles; *especially* : a shape in which one pair of lines is longer than the other pair ▪ *squares and rectangles* — **rect·an·gu·lar** /rɛkˈtæŋɡjələ/ *adj*

rec·ti·fy /ˈrɛktəˌfaɪ/ *vb* **-fies; -fied; -fy·ing** [T] *formal* : to correct (something that is wrong) ▪ *The manager promised to rectify the problem/situation.*

rec·ti·tude /ˈrɛktəˌtuːd, *Brit* ˈrɛktəˌtjuːd/ *n* [U] *formal* : the quality of being honest and morally correct ▪ *moral rectitude*

rec·tor /ˈrɛktə/ *n* [C] **1** : a priest or minister who is in charge of a church or parish **2** *chiefly Brit* : a person who is in charge of a university or school

rec·to·ry /ˈrɛktəri/ *n, pl* **-ries** [C] : the house where the rector of a Christian church lives

rec·tum /ˈrɛktəm/ *n* [C] *medical* : the end of the tube in your body that helps digest food

re·cum·bent /rɪˈkʌmbənt/ *adj, formal* : lying down ▪ *a recumbent position*

re·cu·per·ate /rɪˈkuːpəˌreɪt, *Brit* rɪˈkjuːpəˌreɪt/ *vb* **-at·ed; -at·ing 1** [I] : to return to normal health or strength after being sick, injured, etc. ▪ *He is still recuperating (from surgery).* **2** [T] *Brit* : to get back (money that has been spent, invested, etc.) ▪ *The company hopes to recuperate its losses.* — **re·cu·per·a·tion** /rɪˌkuːpəˈreɪʃən, *Brit* rɪˌkjuːpəˈreɪʃən/ *n* [U] — **re·cu·per·a·tive** /rɪˈkuːpəˌreɪtɪv, *Brit* rɪˈkjuːpərətɪv/ *adj*

re·cur /rɪˈkə/ *vb* **-curred; -cur·ring** [I] : to happen or appear again ▪ *The disease/problem might recur.* ▪ *a recurring in-jury/nightmare* — **re·cur·rence** /rɪˈkərəns/ *n* [C/U] ▪ *preventing (a) recurrence of the disease* — **re·cur·rent** /rɪˈkərənt/ *adj*

re·cy·cle /riˈsaɪkəl/ *vb* **-cy·cled; -cy·cling 1 a** [T] : to make something new from (something that has been used before) ▪ *The company recycles plastic.* **b** [T/I] : to send (used newspapers, bottles, etc.) to a place where they are made into something new ▪ *We recycle (our cans and bottles).* **2** [T] : to use (something) again ▪ *The author recycled a familiar story.* — **re·cy·cla·ble** /riˈsaɪkləbəl/ *adj* — **recy·clable** *n* [C] ▪ *Put all recyclables* [=recyclable materials] *in the green bin.* — **re·cycling** *n* [U] ▪ *(US) Put the recycling* [=recyclable materials] *out by the curb.* ▪ *a recycling program*

¹**red** /ˈrɛd/ *adj* **red·der; red·dest 1** : having the color of blood ▪ *a red fire truck* ▪ *red apples* **2** : reddish brown or reddish orange in color ▪ *red hair* ▪ *a red fox* **3** *of a person's face* : pink because of embarrassment, anger, etc. ▪ *His face turned red.* **4** *of eyes* : BLOODSHOT ▪ *Her eyes were red from crying.* **5** *somewhat old-fashioned, informal + disapproving* : supporting Communism : COMMUNIST — **red·ness** /ˈrɛdnəs/ *n* [U]

²**red** *n* **1** [C/U] : the color of blood **2** **Red** [C] *somewhat old-fashioned, informal + disapproving* : COMMUNIST — **in the red** : spending and owing more money than is being earned ▪ *The company is in the red.* — compare *in the black* at ²BLACK — **see red** *informal* : to become very angry ▪ *The construction delays have many commuters seeing red.*

red blood cell *n* [C] : a red-colored blood cell that carries oxygen from the lungs to other parts of the body

red-blood·ed /ˈrɛdˈblʌdəd/ *adj, informal* : full of energy, strength, and strong emotion ▪ *a red-blooded woman/man*

red carpet *n* — **roll out the red carpet** : to formally greet or welcome an important guest ▪ *The governor rolled out the red carpet for his guests.* — **red-carpet** *adj, always before a noun* ▪ *a red-carpet welcome*

red·coat /ˈrɛdˌkoʊt/ *n* [C] : a British soldier of the 18th and early 19th centuries and especially during the American Revolution

red·den /ˈrɛdn/ *vb* [T/I] : to make something red or to become red ▪ *Her face reddened when her name was announced.*

red·dish /ˈrɛdɪʃ/ *adj* : somewhat red ▪ *reddish-brown hair*

re·dec·o·rate /riˈdɛkəˌreɪt/ *vb* **-rat·ed; -rat·ing** [T/I] : to change the appearance of the inside of a house, building, or room by painting the walls, changing the furniture, etc. ▪ *They redecorated their living room.* — **re·dec·o·ra·tion** /riˌdɛkəˈreɪʃən/ *n* [U]

re·deem /rɪˈdiːm/ *vb* [T] **1** : to make something (that is bad, unpleasant, etc.) better ▪ *The exciting ending partially redeems an otherwise dull movie.* ▪ *He wants to redeem his reputation.* **2** : to exchange (a coupon, lottery ticket, etc.) for money, an award, etc. ▪ *You can redeem* *this coupon at any store.* **3** : to buy back (a stock, bond, etc.) • *The company redeemed some of its stock.* **4** : to pay back (money that is owed) • *redeem a debt* **5** *formal* : FULFILL 1 • *redeem a promise/pledge* **6** *Christianity* : to save (people) from sin and evil • *They believe that Jesus Christ was sent here to redeem us from sin.* — **redeem yourself** : to succeed or do something good after you have failed or done something bad • *They can redeem themselves by winning today's game.* — **re·deem·able** /rɪˈdiːməbəl/ *adj* • *The gift certificate is redeemable at any store location.* • *(US) The movie had no redeemable qualities.* [=nothing about the movie was good, enjoyable, etc.] — **re·deem·er** /rɪˈdiːmɚ/ *n* [C] — **re·deem·ing** /rɪˈdiːmɪŋ/ *adj* • *The movie had no redeeming qualities.*

re·demp·tion /rɪˈdɛmpʃən/ *n* **1** [U] : the act of making something better or more acceptable • *The situation is beyond/past redemption.* [=too bad to be fixed] **2** [C/U] : the act of exchanging something for money, an award, etc. • *stock redemptions* • *the redemption of coupons* **3** [U] *Christianity* : the act of saving people from sin and evil • *the redemption of sinners* : the fact of being saved from sin or evil • *a sinner's search for redemption* • *people who are beyond/past redemption* [=who cannot be saved] — **re·demp·tive** /rɪˈdɛmptɪv/ *adj*

re·de·sign /ˌriːdɪˈzaɪn/ *vb* [T] : to change the design of (something) • *We're redesigning our kitchen.* — **redesign** [C/U]

re·de·vel·op /ˌriːdɪˈvɛləp/ *vb* **1** [T/I] : to change the appearance of an area especially by repairing and adding new buildings, roads, etc. • *The city has plans to redevelop (the neighborhood).* **2** [I] : to happen or develop again • *We need to prevent these problems from redeveloping.* — **re·de·vel·op·ment** /ˌriːdɪˈvɛləpmənt/ *n* [C/U]

red–eye /ˈrɛdˌaɪ/ *n* [C] *US, informal* : a flight in a passenger airplane that happens late at night or that continues through the night • *He caught/took the red-eye.* • *a red-eye flight*

red–faced *adj* : having or showing a red face especially because you are embarrassed, angry, or ashamed • *He was red-faced with rage/shame.*

red–hand·ed /ˈrɛdˈhændəd/ *adv* : while doing something wrong or illegal • *The robbers were caught red-handed.*

red·head /ˈrɛdˌhɛd/ *n* [C] : a person who has red hair — **red·head·ed** /ˈrɛdˌhɛdəd/ *adj*

red herring *n* [C] : something unimportant that is used to stop people from noticing or thinking about something important • *The mystery's plot was full of red herrings.*

red–hot /ˈrɛdˈhɑːt/ *adj* **1 a** : glowing red because of being very hot • *red-hot coals* **b** : extremely hot • *red-hot irons/chili* **2** *informal* **a** : very active or successful • *The economy is red-hot.* **b** : extremely popular • *a red-hot vacation destination* **c** : new and exciting • *red-hot news*

redid *past tense of* REDO

re·di·rect /ˌriːdəˈrɛkt/ *vb* [T] **1** : to change the path or direction of (something) • *Traffic was redirected.* **2** : to use (something) for a different purpose • *redirect tax dollars* — **re·di·rec·tion** /ˌriːdəˈrɛkʃən/ *n* [U]

re·dis·cov·er /ˌriːdɪˈskʌvɚ/ *vb* [T] : to find (something lost or forgotten) again • *She rediscovered her love of ballet.*

re·dis·trib·ute /ˌriːdɪˈstrɪˌbjuːt/ *vb* **-ut·ed; -ut·ing** [T] : to divide (something) among a group in a different way • *Unused funds will be redistributed.* — **re·dis·tri·bu·tion** /ˌriːˌdɪstrəˈbjuːʃən/ *n* [U]

re·dis·trict /riːˈdɪstrɪkt/ *vb* *US* : to divide (a town, state, etc.) into new political or school districts

red–letter day *n* [C] *informal* : a very happy and important day

red–light *adj, always before a noun* : having many prostitutes • *a red-light district*

red meat *n* [U] : meat (such as beef) that is red when it is raw

red·neck /ˈrɛdˌnɛk/ *n* [C] *US, informal + usually disapproving* : a white person who lives in a small town or in the country especially in the southern U.S. and who is seen by others as being uneducated and having offensive opinions and attitudes

re·do /riːˈduː/ *vb* **-does** /-ˈdʌz/; **-did** /-ˈdɪd/; **-done** /-ˈdʌn/; **-do·ing** /-ˈduːwɪŋ/ [T] **1** : to do (something) again especially in order to do it better • *We had to redo our paperwork.* **2** : to change (something) so that it looks new or different • *I want to redo the kitchen and put in new cabinets.*

red·o·lent /ˈrɛdələnt/ *adj, literary + formal* **1** : having a strong smell • *a room redolent of spices* • *The sauce was redolent with the smell of basil.* **2** : causing thoughts or memories of something • *a room redolent of the 1940s*

re·dou·ble /riːˈdʌbəl/ *vb* **-dou·bled; -dou·bling** [T/I] : to greatly increase the size or amount of (something) • *We redoubled our efforts.*

red pepper *n* **1** [C] : a pepper that is red and that can be eaten raw or cooked **2** [C] : a hot pepper that is red and that is added to food to make it spicy; *also* [U] : CAYENNE PEPPER

¹**re·dress** /rɪˈdrɛs/ *vb* [T] *formal* : to correct (something that is unfair or wrong) • *redress injustices*

²**redress** *n* [U] *formal* : something (such as money) that is given to someone to make up for damage, trouble, etc. • *They are seeking redress through the courts.*

red tape *n* [U] *disapproving* : a series of actions or complicated tasks that seem unnecessary but that a government or organization requires you to do • *bureaucratic red tape*

re·duce /rɪˈduːs, Brit rɪˈdjuːs/ *vb* **-duced; -duc·ing** **1** [T] : to make (something) smaller in size, amount, number, etc. : DECREASE • *The medicine reduces the risk of infection.* • *a reduced price* **2** [T] **a** : to cause (someone) to be in a specified state or condition • *The story's ending reduced me to tears.* [=made me cry] • *The crowd was reduced to silence.* **b**

: to cause (something) to be in a specified form by breaking it, burning it, etc. ▪ *Their house was **reduced to ashes**.* [=it burned down] ▪ *The city was **reduced to rubble/ruins**.* **c** : to force (someone) to do something that causes shame, embarrassment, etc. ▪ *He was **reduced to begging**.* **3** [T] : to describe (something) in a way that includes only some of the facts and details ▪ *Her argument can be reduced to a few essential points.* **4** [T/I] : to boil (a liquid) so that there is less of it ▪ *Reduce the broth to 2 cups.* = *Boil the broth until it reduces to 2 cups.* **5** [T] : to change (someone's rank) to a lower or less important one ▪ *The sergeant's rank was reduced to private.* **6** [I] *US, informal* : to gradually decrease your weight by eating less ▪ *He's on a (weight) reducing diet.* **7** [T] *mathematics* : to change (a fraction) so that it is written with the lowest possible numbers ▪ *You can reduce ¾ to ½.* — **reduced circumstances** *formal* : a situation in which you have less money than you used to have ▪ *people living in reduced circumstances* — **re·duc·er** *n* [C] — **re·duc·ible** /rɪˈduːsəbəl, Brit rɪˈdjuːsəbəl/ *adj*

re·duc·tion /rɪˈdʌkʃən/ *n* **1** [C/U] : the act of making something smaller in size, amount, number, etc. ▪ *price/troop reductions* **2** [C] : an amount by which something is reduced ▪ *a 20 percent reduction*

re·dun·dant /rɪˈdʌndənt/ *adj* **1** : repeating something else and therefore unnecessary ▪ *Avoid redundant expressions in your writing.* **2** *technical* — used to describe part of a machine, system, etc., that has the same function as another part and that exists so that the entire machine, system, etc., will not fail if the main part fails ▪ *The design incorporates several redundant features.* **3** *Brit* : dismissed from a job because you are no longer needed ▪ *More than 200 of the company's employees have already been **made redundant**.* [=laid off] — **re·dun·dan·cy** /rɪˈdʌndənsi/ *n, pl* -**cies** [C/U] ▪ *Avoid redundancy/redundancies in your writing.* ▪ *The design incorporates several redundancies.* ▪ *(Brit) The workers are now facing redundancy.* — **re·dun·dant·ly** *adv*

red·wood /ˈrɛdˌwʊd/ *n* **1** [C] : a very tall evergreen tree **2** [U] : the wood of a redwood

reed /ˈriːd/ *n* [C] **1** : a tall, thin grass that grows in wet areas **2 a** : a thin strip of wood, metal, or plastic inside some musical instruments (such as clarinets) that makes a sound when you blow over it **b** : a musical instrument that has a reed ▪ *the orchestra's reeds*

re·ed·u·cate /ˌriːˈɛdʒəˌkeɪt/ *vb* -**cat·ed**; -**cat·ing** [T] **1** : to teach (someone) to do or understand something in a new way ▪ *The program reeducates people about how to eat in a more healthful way.* ▪ *(disapproving) camps that were used to "reeducate" political prisoners* [=to force political prisoners to accept the official beliefs of the government] **2** : to train (someone) for a different job ▪ *reeducating workers who have lost their jobs* — **re-**

ed·u·ca·tion /ˌriːˌɛdʒəˈkeɪʃən/ *n* [U]

reedy /ˈriːdi/ *adj* **reed·i·er**; -**est 1** : full of or covered with reeds ▪ *a reedy marsh* **2** : having a weak, high-pitched sound ▪ *reedy music/voices*

reef /ˈriːf/ *n* [C] : a long line of rocks or coral or a high area of sand near the surface of the water in the ocean

ree·fer /ˈriːfɚ/ *n* [C] *informal* + *old-fashioned* : a marijuana cigarette

reek /ˈriːk/ *vb* [I] **1** : to have a very strong and unpleasant smell ▪ *The room reeked of garbage/smoke.* **2** *usually disapproving* — used to say that it is very obvious that someone or something has a lot of a specified thing ▪ *She reeks of money.*

¹**reel** /ˈriːl/ *n* [C] **1 a** : a device shaped like a cylinder that a string, cord, etc., is wrapped around ▪ *a garden hose reel* **b** : a device that is attached to the handle of a fishing pole and used to wrap and release the line ▪ *a new rod and (fishing) reel* **c** : an object that is used to hold and release film or tape ▪ *a reel of film* **2** : a part of a movie that is on a reel of film ▪ *the chase scene in the movie's second reel* **3** : a lively dance originally from Scotland and Ireland; *also* : the music for this dance

²**reel** *vb* [I] **1** : to be very shocked, confused, and upset ▪ *She is still reeling from the shock.* **2** : to move or fall back suddenly ▪ *The surprise attack sent the enemy reeling.* **3** : to move or walk in an unsteady way ▪ *He was reeling drunkenly down the street.* ▪ *When she opened her eyes, the room was reeling.* [=it seemed to be moving in an unsteady way] — **reel in** [*phrasal vb*] **reel (something) in** or **reel in (something)** : to pull in (a fish) by turning the reel of a fishing rod — **reel off** [*phrasal vb*] **reel (something) off** or **reel off (something)** : to say (something) easily and quickly ▪ *She reeled off the right answers.*

re·elect /ˌriːəˈlɛkt/ *vb* [T] : to elect (someone) again ▪ *He was reelected to the school committee.* — **re·elec·tion** /ˌriːəˈlɛkʃən/ *n* [C/U]

re·emerge /ˌriːɪˈmɚdʒ/ *vb* -**emerged**; -**emerg·ing** [I] **1** : to come out of something you have entered ▪ *The rescuers reemerged from the cave.* **2** : to be seen or known again ▪ *a style that has reemerged* [=become popular again]

re·en·act /ˌriːəˈnækt/ *vb* [T] : to repeat the actions of (an event) ▪ *reenacting a famous battle* — **re·en·act·ment** /ˌriːəˈnæktmənt/ *n* [C/U]

re·en·ter /riˈɛntɚ/ *vb* [T/I] : to enter again ▪ *They reentered the country.* ▪ *I left the theater and wasn't allowed to reenter.* ▪ *We had to reenter the data.* — **re·en·try** /riˈɛntri/ *n, pl* -**tries** [C/U]

re·es·tab·lish /ˌriːɪˈstæblɪʃ/ *vb* [T] **1** : to cause (someone or something) to be widely known and accepted again ▪ *The city is trying to reestablish itself as a tourist destination.* **2** : to make (something) exist again ▪ *We reestablished communication with the ship.* — **re·es·tab·lish·ment** /ˌriːɪˈstæblɪʃmənt/ *n* [U]

re·eval·u·ate /ˌriːɪˈvæljəˌweɪt/ *vb* -**at·ed**;

-at·ing [T] : to judge the value or condition of (someone or something) again • *We will reevaluate your progress after six months.* — **re·e·val·u·a·tion** /ˌriːɪˌvæljəˈweɪʃən/ n [C/U]

re·ex·am·ine /ˌriːɪgˈzæmən/ vb **-ined; -in·ing** [T] : to examine (someone or something) again usually in a new or different way • *The book reexamines traditional family roles.* — **re·ex·am·i·na·tion** /ˌriːɪgˌzæməˈneɪʃən/ n [C/U]

ref abbr reference

ref /ˈrɛf/ n [C] informal : a referee in a game or sport

ref. abbr reference

re·fer /rɪˈfɚ/ vb **-ferred; -fer·ring** [T] : to send (someone or something) to a particular person or place for treatment, help, advice, etc. • *The patient was referred (to a specialist) by her regular doctor.* • *She referred me to his Web site.* — **refer to** [phrasal vb] **1** : to look at or in (something) for information • *Please refer to our Web site for more information.* **2** : to have a direct connection or relationship to (something) • *The word "finch" refers to a kind of bird.* **3 a** : to talk about or write about (someone or something) especially briefly • *No one referred to the incident.* **b refer to (something or someone) as** : to call (something or someone) by (a specified name or title) • *The victim was referred to as "John Doe."*

ref·er·ee /ˌrɛfəˈriː/ n [C] **1** : a person who makes sure that players act according to the rules of a game or sport • *a football/soccer referee* **2** Brit : REFERENCE 3a — **referee** vb **-eed; -ee·ing** [T/I] • *She refereed (the game) last night.*

ref·er·ence /ˈrɛfrəns/ n **1** [C/U] : the act of referring to something or someone • *a reference to an earlier event* • *She made reference to* [=mentioned] *our agreement.* **2** [U] : the act of looking at or in something for information • *File this for future reference.* [=in case we need to look at it later] **3 a** [C] : a person who can be asked for information about another person's character, abilities, etc. • *She listed me as a reference when she applied for the job.* **b** [C/U] : a statement about someone's character, abilities, etc. • *I gave her a (letter of) reference when she applied for the job.* **4** [C] : something (such as a dictionary, encyclopedia, etc.) that people can look at or in to find information about something • *How many references do you use for your essay?* • *a reference book* • *a list of reference materials* — **in reference to** or **with reference to** formal : about or concerning (something or someone) • *I am writing in reference to your ad.*

ref·er·en·dum /ˌrɛfəˈrɛndəm/ n, pl **-da** /-də/ or **-dums** [C/U] : a public vote on a particular issue • *They are having/holding a referendum.* • *The issue was decided by referendum.*

re·fer·ral /rɪˈfɚəl/ n [C] : the act of sending someone to another person or place for treatment, help, advice, etc. • *Her doctor gave her a referral (to a specialist).*

¹**re·fill** /ˌriːˈfɪl/ vb **1** [T] : to fill (something) again • *refill a glass/prescription* **2** [I] : to be filled again • *The reservoir will refill*

once it begins raining. — **re·fill·able** /riˈfɪləbəl/ adj

²**re·fill** /ˈriːˌfɪl/ n [C] : a new supply of something • *This restaurant gives free refills (of soda).*

re·fi·nance /ˌriːfəˈnæns, riˈfaɪˌnæns/ vb **-nanced; -nanc·ing** [T] : to get a new loan to pay (an older debt) • *refinance a mortgage/house*

re·fine /rɪˈfaɪn/ vb **-fined; -fin·ing** [T] **1** : to remove the unwanted substances in (something) • *refine oil/sugar* **2** : to improve (something) by making small changes • *The class helped her refine her writing style.* — **re·fin·er** n [C] • *oil/sugar refiners* [=companies that refine oil/sugar]

refined adj **1** : free of unwanted substances • *refined flour/metals/oil* **2** : improved to be more precise or exact • *refined testing methods* **3** : having or showing the good education, polite manners, etc., that are expected in people who belong to a high social class • *refined people/manners*

re·fine·ment /rɪˈfaɪnmənt/ n **1** [U] : the act or process of removing unwanted substances from something • *oil refinement* **2** [U] : the act or process of improving something • *the refinement of testing methods* **3** [C] : an improved version of something • *The new game is a refinement of last year's version.* **4** [C] : a small change that improves something • *Engine refinements have increased efficiency.* **5** [U] : the quality of a person who has the good education, polite manners, etc., that are expected in people who belong to a high social class • *a person of great refinement*

re·fin·ery /rɪˈfaɪnəri/ n, pl **-er·ies** [C] : a place where the unwanted substances in something are removed • *oil/sugar refineries*

re·fin·ish /riˈfɪnɪʃ/ vb [T] US : to remove the coating on the surface of (furniture, a floor, etc.) and put on a new coating • *We refinished the wood floors.*

re·fit /riˈfɪt/ vb **-fit·ted; -fit·ting** [T] : to make (something) ready for use again especially by adding new parts • *refit a ship for service* — **refit** /ˈriːˌfɪt/ n [C]

re·flect /rɪˈflɛkt/ vb **1 a** [I] of light, sound, etc. : to move in one direction, hit a surface, and then quickly move in a different and usually opposite direction • *The light reflected off the mirror.* **b** [T] ◇ When a surface reflects light, sound, or heat, it causes the light, sound, or heat that hits it to move or bounce away in a different direction. • *A polished surface reflects light.* **2** [T] : to show the image of (something) on a surface • *The old church is reflected in/on the glass exterior of the skyscraper.* **3** [T] : to make (something) known • *Her book clearly reflects her beliefs.* **4** [I] **a** : to cause people to think of someone or something in a specified way — + on or upon • *Her story reflects badly/poorly on him.* [=makes him look bad] **b** : to cause people to disapprove of someone or something — + on or upon • *His bad behavior reflects on all of us.* **5 a** [I] : to think carefully about something • *I need some time to reflect before I make a decision.* • *I've been reflecting on my experiences.* **b** [*T*] : to think or say (something) after careful thought • *She reflected that the situation could have been worse.* — **re·flec·tion** /rɪˈflɛkʃən/ *n* [*C/U*] • *a reflection in a mirror* • *(figurative) The movie is a reflection of life in a small town.* [=shows what life is like in a small town] • *His bad behavior is a reflection on all of us.* • *a moment of reflection* [=careful thought] • *The book features the writer's reflections* [=thoughts] *on democracy.*

re·flec·tive /rɪˈflɛktɪv/ *adj* **1** : causing light, sound, or heat to move away • *a reflective surface* **2** : thinking carefully about something : THOUGHTFUL • *She was in a very reflective mood.* **3** — used to say that one thing shows what something else is like • *The school is reflective of society: the same problems that exist in society exist at the school.* — **re·flec·tive·ly** *adv*

re·flec·tor /rɪˈflɛktɚ/ *n* [*C*] : an object that is used to reflect light • *safety devices such as bicycle reflectors*

re·flex /ˈriːˌflɛks/ *n* **1** [*C*] : an action or movement of the body that happens automatically as a reaction to something • *a reflex action/response* **2** [*C*] : something that you do without thinking as a reaction to something • *Disagreeing has become almost a reflex for him.* **3** [*plural*] : the natural ability to react quickly • *an athlete with quick reflexes*

re·flex·ive /rɪˈflɛksɪv/ *adj* **1** *grammar* : showing that the action in a sentence or clause happens to the person or thing that does the action • *In "I hurt myself," the verb "hurt" is reflexive.* **2** : happening or done without thinking as a reaction to something • *music that triggers reflexive toe tapping* — **re·flex·ive·ly** *adv*

re·flux /ˈriːˌflʌks/ *n* [*U*] *medical* : a backward flow of the contents of the stomach into the esophagus that causes heartburn • *acid reflux*

re·fo·cus /riˈfoʊkəs/ *vb* **-cused; -cus·ing** [*T/I*] : to focus again • *She refocused the camera.* • *She refocused her energies.* • *I've been distracted lately, but I'm ready to refocus and improve my grades.*

re·for·es·ta·tion /riˌfɔrəˈsteɪʃən/ *n* [*U*] : the act of planting tree seeds or young trees in an area where there used to be a forest — **re·for·est** /riˈfɔrəst/ *vb* [*T*] • *They are reforesting the burned areas of land.*

¹**re·form** /rɪˈfoɚm/ *vb* **1** [*T*] : to improve (someone or something) by removing or correcting faults, problems, etc. • *The program is designed to reform prisoners.* • *The laws need to be reformed.* **2** [*I*] : to improve your own behavior or habits • *former gang members who are trying to reform* — **re·formed** /rɪˈfoɚmd/ *adj, always before a noun* • *reformed criminals/laws*

²**reform** *n* **1** [*U*] : the improvement of something by removing or correcting faults, problems, etc. • *economic/educational/political/tax reform* • *a reform movement* **2** [*C*] : an action, plan, rule,

etc., that is meant to improve something • *a list of proposed political reforms*

re–form /riˈfoɚm/ *vb* [*T/I*] : to form (something) again • *They decided to re-form the band.* • *Ice re-formed on the lake.*

ref·or·ma·tion /ˌrɛfɚˈmeɪʃən/ *n* **1** [*C/U*] *formal* : the act or process of improving something or someone by removing or correcting faults, problems, etc. • *a/the reformation of our justice system* **2** *the Reformation* : the 16th-century religious movement that led to the establishment of the Protestant churches

re·form·er /rɪˈfoɚmɚ/ *n* [*C*] : a person who works to change and improve a society, government, etc.

re·form·ist /rɪˈfoɚmɪst/ *adj* **1** : wanting to change and improve a society, government, etc. • *a reformist group/movement* **2** : of or relating to the work of a reformer • *reformist efforts/views*

reform school *n* [*C*] *US, old-fashioned* : a place where young people who have committed crimes are sent to live and be taught to behave in ways that are socially acceptable

re·fract /rɪˈfrækt/ *vb* [*T*] *technical, of an object or substance* : to make (light) change direction when it goes through at an angle • *Prisms refract light.* — **re·frac·tion** /rɪˈfrækʃən/ *n* [*C/U*] — **re·frac·tive** /rɪˈfræktɪv/ *adj*

¹**re·frain** /rɪˈfreɪn/ *vb* [*I*] *formal* : to stop yourself from doing something that you want to do • *Please refrain from smoking.*

²**refrain** *n* [*C*] **1** : a phrase or verse that is repeated regularly in a poem or song **2** : a comment or statement that is often repeated • *A common refrain among teachers is that the schools need more funding.*

re·fresh /rɪˈfrɛʃ/ *vb* [*T*] **1** : to make (someone) have more energy and feel less tired or less hot • *A cold shower will refresh you.* **2** : to fill (someone's glass, cup, etc.) again • *Can I refresh your drink?* **3** *computers* : to cause an updated version of (something, such as an Internet page) to appear on a computer screen • *Refresh* [=reload] *the home page.* — **refresh someone's memory** : to remind someone about something • *I'm not sure of the address. Can you refresh my memory?* — **re·freshed** /rɪˈfrɛʃt/ *adj* • *I felt refreshed after taking a nap.*

re·fresh·er /rɪˈfrɛʃɚ/ *n* [*C*] *chiefly US* : a reminder about something • *I need a refresher on the rules of the game.* [=I need to be reminded about the rules]

refresher course *n* [*C*] : a training class which helps people review information or learn new skills needed for their jobs

re·fresh·ing /rɪˈfrɛʃɪŋ/ *adj* **1** : pleasantly new, different, or interesting • *It is refreshing to hear some good news.* • *a refreshing change* **2** : making you feel more rested, energetic, cool, etc. • *My swim was very refreshing.* — **re·fresh·ing·ly** *adv*

re·fresh·ment /rɪˈfrɛʃmənt/ *n* **1** [*plural*] : drinks and small amounts of food • *Light refreshments will be served.* **2** [*U*] : food and drink • *The workers were in need of refreshment.* **3** [*U*] : the process of becoming rested and regaining strength or energy ▪ *relaxation and refreshment*

re·fried beans /ˌriːˌfraɪd-/ *n* [*plural*] : a Mexican food that consists of beans that are cooked with seasonings, fried, then mashed and fried again

re·frig·er·ate /rɪˈfrɪdʒəˌreɪt/ *vb* **-at·ed;** **-at·ing** [*T*] : to put or keep (something) in a refrigerator in order to make it cold or keep it fresh ▪ *The potato salad needs to be (kept) refrigerated.* — **re·frig·er·a·tion** /rɪˌfrɪdʒəˈreɪʃən/ *n* [*U*] ▪ *The salad needs refrigeration.*

re·frig·er·a·tor /rɪˈfrɪdʒəˌreɪtɚ/ *n* [*C*] : a device or room that is used to keep things (such as food and drinks) cold — called also *fridge*

re·fu·el /riˈfjuːl/ *vb,* US **-eled** or Brit **-elled;** US **-el·ing** or Brit **-el·ling** [*T/I*] : to add fuel to (an airplane, a truck, etc.) ▪ *The crew refueled the airplane.* ▪ *The airplane landed to refuel.*

ref·uge /ˈrɛfjuːdʒ/ *n* **1** [*U*] : shelter or protection from danger or trouble ▪ *They were seeking (a place of) refuge.* [=seeking a safe place] ▪ *We took refuge in* [=we went into] *a barn during the storm.* = *We found refuge from the storm in a barn.* ▪ *They sought refuge in another country.* ▪ *(figurative) During hard times, she took/sought/found refuge in her music.* **2** [*C*] : a place that provides shelter or protection ▪ *a refuge for wildlife*

ref·u·gee /ˌrɛfjʊˈdʒiː/ *n* [*C*] : someone who has been forced to leave a country because of war or for religious or political reasons ▪ *Thousands of refugees have fled the area.* ▪ *refugee camps*

¹**re·fund** /rɪˈfʌnd/ *vb* [*T*] : to give back money that someone paid for something ▪ *If you are not completely satisfied, we will refund your money.* ▪ *They refunded my ticket.* [=gave back the money that I paid for the ticket] — **re·fund·able** /rɪˈfʌndəbəl/ *adj*

²**re·fund** /ˈriːˌfʌnd/ *n* [*C*] : an amount of money that is given back to someone who has returned a product, paid too much, etc. ▪ *No refunds or exchanges are allowed.* ▪ *We received a tax refund.* [=we paid too much income tax so we got some money back]

re·fur·bish /riˈfɚbɪʃ/ *vb* [*T*] : to repair and make improvements to (something) ▪ *They are refurbishing* [=renovating] *the old house.* ▪ *refurbished computers* [=old computers that have been repaired so that they are in good condition] — **re·fur·bish·ment** /riˈfɚbɪʃmənt/ *n* [*C/U*]

re·fus·al /rɪˈfjuːzəl/ *n* [*C*] : an act of saying or showing that you will not do, give, or accept something ▪ *My request was met with a flat/firm refusal.* ▪ *Her refusal of our offer surprised us.* [=we were surprised when she refused our offer] ▪ *his refusal to cooperate* — **(the right of) first refusal** : the right to accept or refuse something before it is offered to anyone else ▪ *If we decide to sell the house, we'll give our tenants first refusal.*

¹**re·fuse** /rɪˈfjuːz/ *vb* **-fused; -fus·ing** **1** [*T/I*] : to say that you will not accept (a gift, offer, etc.) ▪ *He refused* [=did not ac-

cept] *the job.* ▪ *I could hardly refuse* [=could not refuse] *the money.* ▪ *The offer was too good to refuse.* **2** [*T/I*] : to say or show that you are not willing to do something that someone wants you to do ▪ *He refused to answer the question.* ▪ *They asked her to help but she refused.* **3** [*T*] : to not allow someone to have (something) ▪ *They were refused admittance.* ▪ *They refused him a visa.* [=they did not give him a visa]

²**ref·use** /ˈrɛfjuːs/ *n* [*U*] *formal* : trash or garbage ▪ *a pile of refuse* [=*rubbish*]

re·fute /rɪˈfjuːt/ *vb* **-fut·ed; -fut·ing** [*T*] *formal* **1** : to prove that (something) is not true ▪ *The lawyer refuted the testimony.* ▪ *refute an argument/claim* **2** : to say that (something) is not true ▪ *He refuted the rumor.* [=*denied* it] — **ref·u·ta·tion** /ˌrɛfjʊˈteɪʃən/ *n* [*C/U*]

¹**reg** /ˈrɛg/ *n* [*C*] *US, informal* : REGULATION ▪ *a list of proposed regs*

²**reg** *abbr* **1** register; registered; registration **2** regular

re·gain /riˈgeɪn/ *vb* [*T*] **1** : to get back (something that you lost) ▪ *I regained my health/strength.* ▪ *The pilot regained control of the plane.* **2** *literary* : to reach (a place) again ▪ *They finally regained the shore.*

re·gal /ˈriːgəl/ *adj* : of, relating to, or suitable for a king or queen ▪ *He has a regal bearing.* [=he is very dignified, authoritative, etc.] ▪ *regal splendor* — **re·gal·ly** /ˈriːgəli/ *adv*

re·gale /rɪˈgeɪl/ *vb* **-galed; -gal·ing** — **regale with** [*phrasal vb*] **regale (someone) with** *somewhat formal* : to entertain or amuse (someone) by telling stories, describing experiences, etc. ▪ *He regaled us with stories of his adventures.*

re·ga·lia /rɪˈgeɪljə/ *n* [*U*] **1** : special clothes and decorations (such as a crown or scepter) for official ceremonies ▪ *royal/ceremonial regalia* ▪ *The queen was in full regalia.* **2** : special clothing of a particular kind ▪ *cowboy/war regalia*

¹**re·gard** /rɪˈgɑɚd/ *n* **1** [*U*] : care or concern for someone or something ▪ *He has no regard for my feelings.* ▪ *The company acted without regard for the safety of its workers.* ▪ *She was hired without regard to race, age, or gender.* [=race, age, and gender did not influence the decision to hire her] **2** [*U, singular*] : a feeling of respect and admiration for someone or something ▪ *I have a great regard for your ability.* ▪ *I have the highest regard for her.* ▪ *His work is held in high regard.* [=is greatly respected] **3** [*plural*] : friendly greetings ▪ *Give/Send them my (warm/kind) regards.* [=tell them I am thinking of them] — sometimes used to end a letter ▪ *I look forward to seeing you soon. Regards, John* — **in that/this regard** *formal* — used to refer to something just mentioned ▪ *We will supply the food, so you have nothing to worry about in that regard.* — **in/with regard to** *formal* : relating to (something) ▪ *I have a question with regard to your last statement.*

²**regard** *vb* [*T*] **1** : to think of (someone or something) in a particular way ▪ *She regards him as a friend.* ▪ *He is highly re-*

garded by his coworkers. [=his coworkers admire and respect him] **2** *formal* : to look at (someone or something) • *The police officer regarded us with suspicion.* — **as regards** *formal* : relating to (something) • *As regards* [=*regarding*] *your first question, we cannot assist you.*

re·gard·ing /rɪˈgaɚdɪŋ/ *prep, somewhat formal* : relating to (something) : ABOUT • *I have a question regarding your earlier comments.*

re·gard·less /rɪˈgaɚdləs/ *adv* : in spite of difficulty, trouble, etc. • *It may rain, but I will go regardless.* — **regardless of** : without being stopped or affected by (something) • *He runs every day regardless of the weather.* [=no matter what the weather is like]

re·gat·ta /rɪˈgaːtə, Brit rɪˈgætə/ *n* [C] : a race or a series of races between boats (such as sailboats)

re·gen·er·ate /rɪˈdʒɛnəˌreɪt/ *vb* -at·ed; -at·ing **1** [T/I] *biology* : to grow again after being lost, damaged, etc. • *The tissue cells regenerated.* • *The lizard is able to regenerate its tail.* **2** [T] *formal* : to give new life to (something) • *trying to regenerate* [=*revive*] *the economy* — **re·gen·er·a·tion** /rɪˌdʒɛnəˈreɪʃən/ *n* [U] — **re·gen·er·a·tive** /rɪˈdʒɛnəˌreɪtɪv, Brit rɪˈdʒɛnərətɪv/ *adj*

re·gent /ˈriːdʒənt/ *n* [C] : a person who rules a kingdom when the king or queen is not able to rule because he or she is sick, too young, etc. — **re·gen·cy** /ˈriːdʒənsi/ *n, pl* -cies [C] — **Regent** *adj, always after a noun* • *the Prince Regent*

reg·gae /ˈrɛgeɪ/ *n* [U] : popular music that is originally from Jamaica and that combines native styles with elements of rock and soul music

re·gime /reɪˈʒiːm/ *n* [C] **1** : a form of government • *a socialist/Communist/military regime* : a particular government • *a new regime* **2** : REGIMEN • *a strict exercise regime*

reg·i·men /ˈrɛdʒəmən/ *n* [C] : a plan or set of rules about food, exercise, etc., to make someone become or stay healthy • *a regimen of daily exercise* • *a strict treatment/drug regimen*

¹**reg·i·ment** /ˈrɛdʒəmənt/ *n* [C] : a military unit that is usually made of several large groups of soldiers (called battalions) • *infantry/cavalry regiments* — **reg·i·men·tal** /ˌrɛdʒəˈmɛntl̩/ *adj*

²**reg·i·ment** /ˈrɛdʒəˌmɛnt/ *vb* [T] **1** : to organize and control (something) strictly • *They carefully regiment their son's diet/schedule/life.* **2** : to control the behavior of (people) strictly • *She criticized the way the school regiments its students.* — **reg·i·men·ta·tion** /ˌrɛdʒəmənˈteɪʃən/ *n* [U] — **regimented** *adj* • *a regimented diet/schedule*

re·gion /ˈriːdʒən/ *n* [C] **1** : a part of a country, of the world, etc., that is different or separate from other parts in some way • *the agricultural regions of France* • *tropical regions* **2** : a place on your body • *She has a pain in the lower back region.* — **(somewhere) in the region of** : close to (an amount) • *He makes some-*

where in the region of [=*approximately*] $100,000 a year. — **re·gion·al** /ˈriːdʒənl̩/ *adj* • *a regional accent/newspaper/school* — **re·gion·al·ly** *adv*

re·gion·al·ism /ˈriːdʒənl̩ˌɪzəm/ *n* **1** [U] : interest in or loyalty to a particular region • *The residents have a strong sense of regionalism.* **2** [C] : a word that is used in a particular region • *The word "pop" for "soda" is a Midwest regionalism.*

¹**reg·is·ter** /ˈrɛdʒəstɚ/ *n* [C] **1** : an official list, book, or system for keeping records of something • *The church keeps a register of births, marriages, and deaths.* **2** *formal* : a part of the range of musical notes that a person's voice or an instrument can reach • *a singer's upper register* **3** : CASH REGISTER **4** *US* : a cover on an opening (such as a heating vent) that has parts which can be opened or closed to control the flow of air

²**register** *vb* **1 a** [T] : to record information about (something) in a book or system of public records • *The car was registered under my name.* **b** [T/I] : to put your name on an official list • *Did you register to vote?* • *Patients must register at the front desk.* • *The students registered for classes.* • *She is busy registering the students/voters/guests.* ◇ If you **register as something** or if you **are registered as something**, you enter or have entered your name on an official list which indicates what group you belong to. • *He registered as a Republican.* **2** [T] : to show or record (an amount, value, etc.) • *an earthquake that registered 6.3 on the Richter scale* **3** [T] : to get or reach (something) : ACHIEVE • *The company registered over one billion dollars in sales.* **4 a** [I] : to be recognized or remembered • *It took a moment for what she was saying to register.* [=it took a moment before I understood what she was saying] • *The name didn't register with me.* [=I didn't recognize the name] **b** [T] : to notice or realize (something) • *She didn't immediately register my presence.* **5** [T/I] *formal* : to show (a feeling or emotion) • *Her face registered anger/surprise.* • *Fear (was) registered on her face.* **6** [T] *formal* : to make (something) known officially and publicly • *I registered a protest over their decision.* — **re·gis·tered** /ˈrɛdʒəstɚd/ *adj* • *a registered trademark/voter/letter*

registered nurse *n* [C] : a nurse who has had extensive training and has passed a special exam — called also *RN*

reg·is·trar /ˈrɛdʒəˌstraɚ/ *n* [C] **1** : someone who is in charge of keeping records especially of births, marriages, and deaths **2** : an officer of a college or university who is in charge of registering students and keeping academic records

reg·is·tra·tion /ˌrɛdʒəˈstreɪʃən/ *n* **1** [C/U] **a** : the act or process of entering information about something in a book or system of public records • *the registration of motor vehicles* • *trademark registrations* **b** : the act or process of entering names on an official list • *Voter registration begins today.* • *Registrations are low this year.* [=few people have registered this year] • *a registration fee* **2** [C]

US : a document showing that something (such as a vehicle) has been officially registered ▪ *He asked to see my driver's license and registration.*

registration number *n* [C] *Brit* : LICENSE NUMBER

reg·is·try /ˈrɛdʒəstri/ *n, pl* **-tries** [C] **1** : a place where official records are kept ▪ *the Registry of Motor Vehicles* **2** *US* : a book or system for keeping an official list or record of items ▪ *a voter registry* ▪ *a* **gift registry** [=a list kept by a store of the things that someone wants as gifts]

re·gress /rɪˈgrɛs/ *vb* [I] *technical* : to return to an earlier and usually worse or less developed condition or state ▪ *The patient is regressing to a childlike state.* — **re·gres·sion** /rɪˈgrɛʃən/ *n* [C/U]

¹re·gret /rɪˈgrɛt/ *vb* **-gret·ted; -gret·ting** [T] **1** : to feel sad or sorry about (something that you did or did not do) ▪ *I deeply regret what I said.* ▪ *She does not regret leaving him.* ▪ *If you don't go, you might* **live to regret it.** [=you might feel sorry or disappointed later] **2** *formal* — used to express sad feelings about something that is disappointing or unpleasant ▪ *We regret to inform you* [=we are sorry to tell you] *that we have offered the job to someone else.* ▪ *We regret any inconvenience these delays may cause.*

²regret *n* **1** [C/U] : a feeling of sadness or disappointment about something that you did or did not do ▪ *She has no regrets about leaving him.* ▪ *She expressed (her) regret for calling me a liar.* ▪ **To my regret**, *I never visited Europe.* ▪ *I didn't go to college, much to my parents' regret.* ▪ *It is with deep regret that he is announcing his resignation.* **2** [*plural*] : a statement saying politely that you will not be able to go to a meeting, party, etc. ▪ *She gives/sends her regrets for being unable to attend.* — **re·gret·ful** /rɪˈgrɛtfəl/ *adj* ▪ *feeling regretful* — **re·gret·ful·ly** /rɪˈgrɛtfəli/ *adv* ▪ *"I must leave now," he said regretfully.* ▪ *Regretfully* [=unfortunately], *we can't go.* — **re·gret·ta·ble** /rɪˈgrɛtəbəl/ *adj* ▪ *a regrettable mistake* — **re·gret·ta·bly** /rɪˈgrɛtəbli/ *adv* ▪ *Progress was regrettably slow.* ▪ *Regrettably* [=unfortunately], *we lost.*

re·group /riˈgruːp/ *vb* **1** [T/I] : to form into a group again ▪ *Members of the search party will regroup in the morning.* **2** [I] : to stop for a short time and prepare yourself before you continue doing something that is difficult ▪ *Wait a minute. I need to regroup.*

¹reg·u·lar /ˈrɛgjələ/ *adj* **1 a** : happening over and over again at the same time or in the same way ▪ *He works regular hours.* [=he works at the same time every work day] ▪ *a regular routine/schedule* **b** : happening at times that are equally separated ▪ *The town holds regular meetings.* ▪ *They meet on a regular basis.* [=regularly] ▪ *The buses run at regular intervals.* [=there is the same amount of time between buses] **2** *always before a noun* : happening or done very often ▪ *Getting regular exercise is important.* ▪ *a regular* [=common] *occurrence* **b** : doing the same thing or going to the same place

very often ▪ *a regular contributor/customer/guest* **3** : spaced an equal distance apart ▪ *a regular pattern of stripes* ▪ *The boards are placed at regular intervals.* [=the space between each board is the same] **4** *always before a noun* : normal or usual ▪ *Our regular hours are from 9 a.m. to 5 p.m.* ▪ *He is substituting for the regular quarterback.* **b** *chiefly US* : not special or unusual ▪ *Do you use regular or premium gas in your car?* ▪ *a regular* [=normal size] *soda* ▪ *She's a regular* [=average, ordinary] *guy.* ▪ *It's nothing special, just a regular old stereo.* ▪ **regular coffee** [=coffee that has caffeine] **5 a** : having a shape that is smooth or even ▪ *a regular surface/outline* **b** : having parts that are arranged in an even or balanced way ▪ *He has very regular features.* **6** *grammar* : following the normal patterns by which word forms (such as the past tenses of verbs) are usually created ▪ *"Talk" is a regular verb because its past tense is "talked."* **7** *always before a noun, informal* — used for emphasis ▪ *She's become a regular expert on fitness.* **8** *always before a noun* : belonging to a country's official army ▪ *the regular army/troops/soldiers* — **reg·u·lar·i·ty** /ˌrɛgjəˈlɛrəti/ *n, pl* **-ties** [C/U] ▪ *the regularity of the seasons* ▪ *It happens with some regularity.* [=happens frequently] — **reg·u·lar·ly** /ˈrɛgjələli/ *adv* ▪ *We go to church regularly.* [=on a regular basis] ▪ *regularly* [=evenly] *spaced lines*

²regular *n* **1** [C] : someone who goes somewhere very often ▪ *They are regulars at the bar/restaurant.* **2** [C] : someone who often or usually performs, plays, etc. ▪ *He is a regular on the show.* **3** [C/U] *US* : something that is average or usual in quality or size ▪ *Do you drink decaf or regular?* [=regular coffee] ▪ *10 gallons of regular* [=regular gas] ▪ *We'll have one large soda and two regulars.* **4** [C] : a soldier who belongs to a country's permanent army ▪ *The regulars were called to battle.*

reg·u·lar·ize *also Brit* **reg·u·lar·ise** /ˈrɛgjələˌraɪz/ *vb* **-ized; -iz·ing** [T] : to make (something) regular, legal, or officially accepted ▪ *regularize a process*

reg·u·late /ˈrɛgjəˌleɪt/ *vb* **-lat·ed; -lat·ing** [T] **1** : to set or adjust the amount, degree, or rate of (something) ▪ *The dam regulates the flow of water.* ▪ *The room's temperature is regulated by the thermostat.* **2 a** : to bring (something) under the control of authority ▪ *laws that regulate the content of the Internet* **b** : to make rules or laws that control (something) ▪ *The department regulates foreign trade.* — **reg·u·la·tor** /ˈrɛgjəˌleɪtə/ *n* [C] — **reg·u·la·to·ry** /ˈrɛgjələˌtori, *Brit* ˌrɛgjəˈleɪtri/ *adj*

reg·u·la·tion /ˌrɛgjəˈleɪʃən/ *n* **1** [C] : an official rule or law that says how something should be done ▪ *safety/government regulations* **2** [U] : the act of regulating something ▪ *the regulation of gun sales*

re·gur·gi·tate /rɪˈgɚdʒəˌteɪt/ *vb* **-tat·ed; -tat·ing** **1** [T/I] : to bring food that has been swallowed back to and out of the mouth • *The bird regurgitates (food) to feed its young.* **2** [*T*] *disapproving* : to repeat (a fact, idea, etc.) without understanding it • *students who regurgitate information on exams* — **re·gur·gi·ta·tion** /rɪˌgɚdʒəˈteɪʃən/ *n* [*U*]

¹**re·hab** /ˈriːˌhæb/ *n* [*U*] *informal* **1** : a program for helping people who have problems with drugs, alcohol, etc. • *He is in rehab.* • *She checked herself into rehab.* **2** : the process of helping someone to become healthy or sober again • *The rehab for his injury is going well.* • *a rehab program*

²**rehab** *vb* **-habbed; -hab·bing** [*T/I*] *US, informal* : REHABILITATE • *It could take him several months to rehab his knee.* • *He's still rehabbing from the injury.*

re·ha·bil·i·tate /ˌriːəˈbɪləˌteɪt/ *vb* **-tated; -tat·ing** **1** [*T/I*] : to bring (someone or something) back to a normal, healthy condition after an illness, injury, drug problem, etc. • *The clinic rehabilitates drug addicts.* • *He's rehabilitating his knee.* • *She's rehabilitating from an injury.* **2** [*T*] : to teach (a criminal in prison) to live a normal and productive life • *The program is intended to rehabilitate criminals.* **3** [*T*] : to bring (someone or something) back to a good condition • *The city plans to rehabilitate its slum areas.* — **re·ha·bil·i·ta·tion** /ˌriːjəˌbɪləˈteɪʃən/ *n* [*U*]

re·hash /riˈhæʃ/ *vb* [*T*] *disapproving* **1** : to present (something) again in a slightly different form • *You're just rehashing old ideas.* **2** : to talk about or discuss (something) again • *rehashing old memories* — **re·hash** /ˈriːˌhæʃ/ *n* [*C*] • *The book is a rehash of her earlier work.*

re·hears·al /rɪˈhɚsəl/ *n* [*C/U*] : an event at which a person or group practices singing, dancing, etc., in order to prepare for a public performance • *There are only three more rehearsals before the concert.* • *The play has been in rehearsal* [=the actors have been practicing their parts together] *for nearly a month.*

re·hearse /rɪˈhɚs/ *vb* **-hearsed; -hearsing** **1** [*T/I*] : to prepare for a public performance of a play, a piece of music, etc., by practicing the performance • *rehearse a play/scene/dance* • *The band is rehearsing for the show.* **2** [*T*] : to say or do (something) several times in order to practice • *He rehearsed his dance moves.* — **rehearsed** *adj* • *Her story sounded rehearsed.* [=it did not sound natural or true]

re·heat /riˈhiːt/ *vb* [*T*] : to make (cooked food that has become cool) hot again • *reheating leftovers*

re·hire /riˈhajɚ/ *vb* **-hired; -hir·ing** [*T*] : to hire (someone) back into the same company or job • *The company decided to rehire him for another project.*

re·house /riˈhaʊz/ *vb* **-housed; -hous·ing** [*T*] *Brit* : to give (a person or animal) a different and usually better place to live • *rehousing families who were displaced in the fire*

¹**reign** /ˈreɪn/ *n* [*C*] **1** : the period of time during which a king, queen, emperor, etc., is ruler of a country • *the reign of Queen Elizabeth* **2** : the period of time

during which someone is in charge of a group or organization • *her reign as club president* **3** : the period of time during which someone or something is the best or the most important, powerful, etc. • *his reign as champion* • *the reign of digital technology*

²**reign** *vb* [*I*] **1** : to rule as a king, queen, emperor, etc. • *The king reigned (over the land) in a time of peace and prosperity.* **2** : to be the best or the most powerful or important person or thing • *The lion reigns as king of the jungle.* • *As a director, he still reigns supreme.* [=he is still the best] **3** — used to say that a quality exists to such a degree in a place or situation that it affects everything about that place or situation • *Chaos reigned in the city.* [=chaos was everywhere in the city] — **reign·ing** /ˈreɪnɪŋ/ *adj* • *the reigning king/queen/champion*

re·ig·nite /ˌriːɪɡˈnaɪt/ *vb* **nit·ed; nit·ing** **1** [*T/I*] : to begin to burn again or to cause (something) to begin to burn again • *reignite a fire* **2** [*T*] **a** : to give new life or energy to (someone or something) • *The incident reignited racial tensions.* **b** : to cause (something) to suddenly occur again • *The study has reignited debate on the issue.*

re·im·burse /ˌriːəmˈbɚs/ *vb* **-bursed; -burs·ing** [*T*] : to pay someone an amount of money equal to an amount that person has spent • *We will reimburse (you for) your travel expenses.* — **re·im·burse·ment** /ˌriːəmˈbɚsmənt/ *n* [*C/U*]

¹**rein** /ˈreɪn/ *n* [*C*] **1** : a strap that is fastened to a bridle and that is used to guide and control an animal • *The rider pulled on the reins.* **2 a** : the ability to limit or control something • *We need to keep a rein on* [=limit, control] *our spending.* **b** : the power to guide or control someone or something • *They held the reins of government.* [=they controlled the government] • *She handed (over) the reins of the company.* • *The new CEO officially took the reins in January.* — **free/full rein** : the opportunity to act freely • *The director had free rein* [=complete control] *over the movie.*

²**rein** *vb* — **rein in** [*phrasal vb*] **rein (someone or something) in** or **rein in (someone or something)** **1** : to limit or control (someone or something) • *Congress must rein in spending.* **2** : to make (an animal) stop by using reins • *The rider reined in his horse.*

re·in·car·nate /ˌriːɪnˈkɑɚˌneɪt/ *vb* — **be reincarnated** : to be born again with a different body after death • *Some religions teach that we are reincarnated many times.* — **reincarnated** *adj*

re·in·car·na·tion /ˌriːɪnˌkɑɚˈneɪʃən/ *n* **1** [*U*] : the idea or belief that people are born again with a different body after death • *Do you believe in reincarnation?* **2** [*C*] : someone who has been born again with a different body after death • *They believe that he is the reincarnation of their leader.*

rein·deer /ˈreɪnˌdiɚ/ *n, pl* **reindeer** [*C*] : a large type of deer that lives in northern parts of the world

re·in·force /ˌriːjənˈfoɚs/ vb **-forced;**
-forc·ing [T] **1** : to strengthen (a group
of people) with new supplies or more
people ▪ *reinforce the troops* **2** : to
strengthen (clothing, a building, etc.) by
adding more material for support ▪ *The
levees need to be reinforced.* **3** : to encourage or give support to (an idea, behavior, feeling, etc.) ▪ *The movie reinforc-
es negative stereotypes.* — **re·in·force·
ment** /ˌriːjənˈfoɚsmənt/ n [C/U] ▪ *"We're
outnumbered! Call for reinforcements!"* ▪
The bridge needs reinforcement.

re·in·state /ˌriːjənˈsteɪt/ vb **-stat·ed;**
-stat·ing [T] **1** : to put (someone) back
in a job or position that had been taken
away ▪ *He was reinstated as chairperson.*
2 : to begin using or dealing with (a law,
policy, system, etc.) again ▪ *The board
voted to reinstate the policy.* — **re·in·
state·ment** /ˈriːjənˈsteɪtmənt/ n [U]

re·in·ter·pret /ˌriːjənˈtəprət/ vb [T] : to
understand and explain or show (something) in a new or different way ▪ *reinter-
preting evidence* — **re·in·ter·pre·ta·
tion** /ˌriːjənˌtəprəˈteɪʃən/ n [C/U]

re·in·tro·duce /ˌriːjɪmtrəˈduːs, Brit
ˌriːjɪntrəˈdjuːs/ vb **-duced; -duc·ing** [T]
1 : to begin using (something) again ▪ *re-
introduce an old policy* **2** : to return (an
animal or plant) to the area where it used
to live ▪ *Several species are being reintro-
duced into the river.* — **re·in·tro·duc·
tion** /ˌriːjɪntrəˈdʌkʃən/ n [C/U]

re·in·vent /ˌriːjənˈvɛnt/ vb [T] : to make
major changes or improvements to
(something) ▪ *trying to reinvent government programs* — **reinvent the wheel**
informal : to waste time trying to do
something that has already been done
successfully by someone else ▪ *When designing new software, there's no need to reinvent the wheel.* — **reinvent yourself**
: to become a different kind of person,
performer, etc. ▪ *a classical singer who
has reinvented herself as a pop artist* —
re·in·ven·tion /ˌriːjənˈvɛnʃən/ n [C/U]

re·is·sue /ˈriːˌɪʃuː/ vb **-sued; -su·ing** [T]
: to publish or produce (a book, recording, etc.) again ▪ *The album is being reis-
sued on CD.* — **reissue** n [C]

re·it·er·ate /ˈriːˈɪtəˌreɪt/ vb **-at·ed; -at·ing**
[T] *somewhat formal* : to repeat some-
thing you have already said in order to
emphasize it ▪ *reiterate a claim/view/point*
— **re·it·er·a·tion** /riˌɪtəˈreɪʃən/ n [C/U]

¹**re·ject** /rɪˈdʒɛkt/ vb [T] **1** : to refuse to
believe, accept, or consider (something) ▪
The committee rejected my proposal. **2**
: to decide not to publish (something) or
make (something) available to the public
because it is not good enough ▪ *My arti-
cle/book/paper was rejected.* **3 a** : to
refuse to allow (someone) to join a club,
to attend a school, etc. ▪ *The college rejects hundreds of applicants each year.* **b**
: to decide not to offer (someone) a job
or position ▪ *We rejected 5 of the 10 job
applicants right away.* **4** : to refuse to
love, care for, or give attention to (someone) ▪ *He wanted to ask her on a date, but
he was afraid of being rejected.* ▪ *kids who
have been rejected by society* **5** *medical,
of a person's body* : to produce substanc-

es that try to harm or destroy (a transplanted organ, a skin graft, etc.) ▪ *The patient's immune system rejected the
transplanted heart.* — **re·jec·tion** /rɪ-
ˈdʒɛkʃən/ n [C/U]

²**re·ject** /ˈriːˌdʒɛkt/ n [C] **1** : something
that is not good enough for some purpose ▪ *Put the promising applications here,
and put the rejects over there.* **2** : a person who is not accepted or liked by other
people ▪ *the rejects of society* ▪ (*informal*)
Ignore him, he's a (total/complete) reject.

re·joice /rɪˈdʒoɪs/ vb **-joiced; -joic·ing**
[I] : to feel or show that you are very
happy about something ▪ *We rejoiced
over/about/in/at our friend's good luck.* —
rejoicing n [U] ▪ *There was much rejoicing when the soldiers returned home.*

re·join vb **1** [T/I] /ˌriːˈdʒoɪn/ : to become
a member of (a group or organization)
again ▪ *He left the band in 2000 but rejoined (the group) two years later.* **2** [T/I]
/rɪˈdʒoɪn/ : to come together with (something) again ▪ *This trail eventually rejoins
the main trail.* ▪ *The two streams rejoin
downstream.* **3** /ˌrɪˈdʒoɪn/ [T] *formal*
: to reply to something especially in a
rude or angry way ▪ *"You're a fine one to
talk," she rejoined.*

re·join·der /rɪˈdʒoɪndɚ/ n [C] *formal* : a
usually rude or angry reply to something
written or said ▪ *a witty rejoinder*

re·ju·ve·nate /rɪˈdʒuːvəˌneɪt/ vb **-nat·ed;**
-nat·ing [T] **1** : to make (someone) feel
or look young, healthy, or energetic
again ▪ *The spa treatment rejuvenated me.*
2 : to give new strength or energy to
(something) ▪ *I'm trying to rejuvenate my
career.* — **rejuvenating** adj ▪ *The swim
was very rejuvenating.* — **re·ju·ve·na·
tion** /rɪˌdʒuːvəˈneɪʃən/ n [U, singular] ▪
(a) *physical/economic rejuvenation*

re·kin·dle /ˈriːˈkɪndl/ vb **-kin·dled; -kin·
dling** [T] : to cause (something) to be
strong or active again ▪ *The movie rekin-
dled my interest in the trial.* ▪ *rekindle an
old romance*

re·lapse /ˈriːˌlæps/ n [C/U] **1** : the return of an illness after a period of improvement ▪ *A sudden relapse sent her
back to the hospital.* ▪ *a high risk of relapse*
2 : a return to bad behavior that you had
stopped doing ▪ *An addict who has had a
relapse* — **re·lapse** /rɪˈlæps/ vb
-lapsed; -laps·ing [I] ▪ *Without treatment, you could relapse.* [=become ill
again] ▪ *Many former smokers relapse*
[=begin smoking again] *in times of stress.*

re·late /rɪˈleɪt/ vb **-lat·ed; -lat·ing** [T] **1**
: to show or make a connection between
(two or more things) ▪ *I didn't immediately relate my symptoms to the food I'd
eaten.* **2** [I] : to understand and like or
have sympathy for someone or some-
thing ▪ *I just can't relate to him.* ▪ *I had a
similar experience, so I can relate (to what
you are saying).* **3** [T] *formal* : to tell
(something) ▪ *We listened as she related
her story.* **4** [I] — used to describe how
people talk to, behave toward, and deal
with each other ▪ *the way the child relates
to her parents* ▪ *They relate with each other
in a very formal way.* — **relate to** [*phrasal vb*] : to be connected with (someone

or something) • *The readings relate to the class discussions.* • *Success is closely related to hard work.* — **re·lat·able** /rɪˈleɪtəbəl/ *adj*

related *adj* **1** : connected in some way • *ancient history and other related subjects* • *drug-related crimes* **2** *not before a noun* : in the same family • *I call her "auntie," but we're not actually related.* • *My stepmother and I are not **related by blood**.* [=we do not share biological ancestors] • *My sister-in-law and I are **related by marriage**.* **3** : belonging to the same group because of shared characteristics, qualities, etc. • *Horses and donkeys are related.* • *related words*

re·la·tion /rɪˈleɪʃən/ *n* **1** [*plural*] **a** : the way in which two or more people, groups, countries, etc., behave toward each other • *international relations* **b** *formal* : SEXUAL INTERCOURSE • *sexual relations* **2** [C/U] : the way in which two or more people or things are connected • *This movie bears no relation to the book by the same title.* **3** [C/U] : a person who is a member of your family • *friends and relations* [=relatives] • *Is he a relation of yours?* • *I'm Jill Jones, and this is Mike Jones—no relation.* [=we have the same last name, but we are not related] — **in relation to** *formal* **1** — used to talk about what something is like by comparing it to something else or by seeing how it is related to something else • *The monkey's eyes are large in relation to its head.* **2** : about (something or someone) • *I have several comments to make in relation to that topic.*

re·la·tion·ship /rɪˈleɪʃənˌʃɪp/ *n* **1** [C] : the way in which two or more people, groups, countries, etc., behave toward each other • *She has a close relationship with her sister.* • *We have a good **working relationship**.* [=we work well together] • *We have a **love-hate relationship**.* [=we have feelings of both love and hatred for each other] **2** [C] : a romantic or sexual friendship between two people • *Are you in a relationship?* **3** [C/U] : the way in which two or more people or things are connected • *the relationship between mental and physical health* • *"What is your relationship to him?" "He is my boss."* • *Her earlier paintings bear little relationship to* [=are very different from] *her later work.*

¹**rel·a·tive** /ˈrɛlətɪv/ *n* [C] **1** : a member of your family • *At the family reunion, I saw relatives I haven't seen in years.* **2** : something that belongs to the same group as something else because of shared characteristics, qualities, etc. • *The donkey is a relative of the horse.*

²**relative** *adj* **1 a** : compared to someone or something else or to each other • *the relative value of two houses* • *We discussed the **relative merits** of each school.* • *The car might seem expensive, but it's all relative.* [=the car is expensive compared to some cars but not to other cars] **b** : seeming to be something when compared with others • *I'm a relative newcomer to the area.* [=I am more of a newcomer than many people] **2** *grammar*

: referring to a noun, a part of a sentence, or a sentence that was used earlier • *"Who," "whom," "whose," "which," and "that" are all **relative pronouns**.* • *The phrase "that won" in "the book that won" is a **relative clause**.* — **relative to** *formal* **1** — used to describe what someone or something is like when compared with or measured against someone or something else • *Dolphins have large brains relative to their body size.* **2** : concerning or about (something) • *We will discuss matters relative to peace and security.*

rel·a·tive·ly /ˈrɛlətɪvli/ *adv* : when compared to others • *The car's price is relatively low.* • *a relatively warm day* — **relatively speaking** : when compared to others that are similar • *The procedure was quick, relatively speaking.*

rel·a·tiv·ism /ˈrɛlətɪˌvɪzəm/ *n* [U] : the belief that different things are true, right, etc., for different people or at different times • *moral/cultural relativism* — **rel·a·tiv·ist** /ˈrɛlətɪvɪst/ *n* [C] — **relativist** *also* **rel·a·tiv·is·tic** /ˌrɛlətɪˈvɪstɪk/ *adj*

rel·a·tiv·i·ty /ˌrɛləˈtɪvəti/ *n* [U] *physics* : a theory developed by Albert Einstein which says that the way that anything except light moves through time and space depends on the position and movement of someone who is watching

re·launch /ˈriˈlɑːntʃ/ *vb* [T] : to launch (something) again • *relaunch a rocket/product* — **re·launch** /ˈriːˌlɑːntʃ/ *n* [C]

re·lax /rɪˈlæks/ *vb* **1** [T/I] : to become or to cause (something) to become less tense, tight, or stiff • *Her grip relaxed.* = *She relaxed her grip.* • *A massage relaxes the muscles.* **2** [I] : to stop feeling nervous or worried • *Try to relax and enjoy the ride.* **3** [I] : to spend time resting or doing something enjoyable • *relaxing in front of the television* **4** [T/I] : to become or to cause (a rule, law, etc.) to become less severe or strict • *They voted to relax the regulations.* • *Fashion rules have relaxed in recent years.* **5** [T] *formal* : to allow (your attention, concentration, etc.) to become weaker • *We mustn't relax our vigilance!* **6** [T] *chiefly US* : to use a chemical treatment on (hair) in order to make it straighter — **re·lax·er** /rɪˈlæksə/ *n* [C/U] *chiefly US* • *a chemical hair relaxer* — **re·lax·ing** /rɪˈlæksɪŋ/ *adj* • *relaxing music* • *a relaxing weekend*

re·lax·ant /rɪˈlæksənt/ *n* [C] : a substance (such as a drug) that relaxes you, your muscles, etc. • *a muscle relaxant*

re·lax·a·tion /ˌriːˌlækˈseɪʃən/ *n* **1** [U] **a** : a way to rest and enjoy yourself • *I play the guitar for relaxation.* **b** : time that you spend resting and enjoying yourself • *I need some rest and relaxation.* **2** [C/U] : something that you do to stop feeling nervous, worried, etc. • *relaxation techniques* • *(Brit) Her favourite relaxation is listening to music.* **3** [U] : the act of making something less tense, tight, or stiff • *muscle relaxation* **4** [C/U] : the act of becoming or causing something to become less severe or strict • *the relaxation of the dress code*

re·laxed /rɪˈlækst/ *adj* **1** : calm and free from stress, worry, or anxiety • *feeling re-*

laxed ▪ *He's a very relaxed guy.* **2** : informal and comfortable : CASUAL ▪ *a relaxed atmosphere* ▪ *The meeting was very relaxed.* **3** : not strict or carefully controlled ▪ *a relaxed attitude* **4** *of clothing* : not tight ▪ *relaxed jeans*

¹**re·lay** /ˈriːˌleɪ/ *n* [C] **1** : a race between teams in which each team member runs, swims, etc., a different part of the race **2** : the act of passing something from one person or device to another ▪ *a satellite relay of a television signal; also* : a system for doing this ▪ *We set up a relay to move the boxes.* **3** : a group of people, horses, etc., that takes the place of others so that something is done continuously ▪ *They worked in relays.* **4** *technical* : a device that causes a switch to open or close automatically when there is a change in the current that is flowing through a circuit

²**re·lay** /rɪˈleɪ/ *vb* [T] : to pass (information) from one person or device to another ▪ *She relayed the news/message to the rest of the team.* ▪ *The data is relayed by/from/to the aircraft.*

¹**re·lease** /rɪˈliːs/ *vb* **-leased; -leas·ing** [T] **1 a** : to allow (a person or animal) to leave a jail, cage, prison, etc. : to set (someone or something) free ▪ *release a prisoner/hostage* ▪ *The lion was released from its cage.* ▪ *wolves released into the wild* **b** : to stop holding (someone or something) ▪ *I released his hand.* **c** : to allow (something) to enter the air, water, soil, etc. ▪ *release heat/chemicals* ▪ *The drug is released into the blood.* **d** : to cause (an emotion, a feeling, etc.) to go away by expressing it or dealing with it in some way ▪ *exercising to release stress/tension* **2** : to free (someone) from a duty, responsibility, etc. ▪ *I released him from his obligation/promise.* **3** : to give up control or possession of (something) ▪ *The police released the evidence to the FBI.* **4** : to make (something) available to the public ▪ *The band released their new album.* ▪ *The police have not released any details.* ▪ *release a statement* **5** : to allow (part of a machine, device, etc.) to go back to its normal position ▪ *release the button/brake/lever*

²**release** *n* **1** [C/U] : the act of releasing someone or something ▪ *The prisoner was given an early release.* ▪ *the release of heat/chemicals into the atmosphere* ▪ *a request for release from the contract* ▪ *the release of a new book/movie* **2** [U, *singular*] **a** : a way of dealing with and getting rid of unpleasant emotions, feelings, etc. ▪ *activities that offer a release from stress* **b** *formal* : an end to pain, distress, etc. ▪ *Her death brought her (a) release from pain.* **3** [C] : something (such as a product or statement) that is made available to the public ▪ *new movie/CD releases* ▪ *The company office has issued a release about the new software.* **4** [C] : an official document which states that a company, person, etc., is not responsible if you are hurt while doing something ▪ *sign a release (form)* **5** [C] : a device that allows a part of a machine to move freely ▪ *the shutter release on a camera* **6** [C]

US, sports : the action or manner of throwing a ball ▪ *The quarterback has a quick release.*

rel·e·gate /ˈrɛləˌɡeɪt/ *vb* **-gat·ed; -gat·ing** [T] **1** *formal* : to put (someone or something) in a lower or less important position, rank, etc. ▪ *He was relegated to a backup role.* ▪ *old books relegated to the attic* **2** *formal* : to give (a job, responsibility, etc.) *to* another person or group ▪ *The bill has been relegated to committee.* **3** *Brit* : to move (a sports team) to a lower position in a league ▪ *The team have been relegated to the Second Division.* — **rel·e·ga·tion** /ˌrɛləˈɡeɪʃən/ *n* [U]

re·lent /rɪˈlɛnt/ *vb* [I] *somewhat formal* **1** : to agree to do or accept something that you have been resisting or opposing ▪ *She had refused our help, but finally relented.* **2** : to become less severe, harsh, strong, determined, etc. ▪ *He will not relent in his efforts.*

re·lent·less /rɪˈlɛntləs/ *adj* **1** : continuing without becoming weaker, less severe, etc. ▪ *relentless optimism/winds* **2** : remaining strict or determined ▪ *a relentless opponent* — **re·lent·less·ly** *adv*

rel·e·vant /ˈrɛləvənt/ *adj* : relating to a subject in an appropriate way ▪ *a relevant question/comment* ▪ *experience that is relevant to the job* — **rel·e·vance** /ˈrɛləvəns/ *or* **rel·e·van·cy** /ˈrɛləvənsi/ *n* [U] ▪ *The question lacks relevance.* — **rel·e·vant·ly** *adv*

re·li·able /rɪˈlajəbəl/ *adj* **1** : able to be trusted to do or provide what is needed ▪ *a reliable car/income* ▪ *He's not very reliable.* **2** : able to be believed : likely to be true or correct ▪ *a reliable witness/source* ▪ *reliable data/information* — **re·li·abil·i·ty** /rɪˌlajəˈbɪləti/ *n* [U] — **re·li·ably** /rɪˈlajəbli/ *adv* ▪ *a car that works reliably*

re·li·ance /rɪˈlajəns/ *n* [*singular*] : the state of needing someone or something for help, support, etc. ▪ *We should reduce our reliance on gasoline.*

re·li·ant /rɪˈlajənt/ *adj* : needing someone or something for help, support, etc. : DEPENDENT ▪ *He's reliant on his parents' support.* ▪ *Students are too reliant on/upon calculators.*

rel·ic /ˈrɛlɪk/ *n* [C] **1** : something that is from a past time, place, culture, etc. ▪ *relics of ancient China* ▪ *relics from the war* ▪ *a relic of a bygone era = a relic of the past* **2** : an object (such as the bone of a saint) that is considered holy ▪ *holy/sacred relics*

re·lief /rɪˈliːf/ *n* **1** [U, *singular*] : a pleasant and relaxed feeling that someone has when something unpleasant stops or does not happen ▪ *What a relief it is to be home.* ▪ *Much to our relief, there were no problems.* **2** [U] : the removal or reducing of something that is painful or unpleasant ▪ *relief from headaches* ▪ *pain/stress relief* **3** [U] : things (such as food or medicine) that are given to help people who are victims of a war, earthquake, etc. ▪ *sending relief to the flood victims* ▪ *Relief workers delivered supplies.* **4** [U] : a person or group that replaces another person or group that needs rest or has finished a period of work ▪ *a relief* *driver/crew* **5** [*U, singular*] : something that is enjoyable and that replaces for a short time something that is unpleasant ▪ *A sunny day would be a welcome relief from the rain.* ▪ *a little comic relief in a serious movie* **6** [*U*] : a way of decorating wood, stone, metal, etc., with designs that stick out above the surface ▪ *a coin depicting the queen's head in relief; also* [*C*] : a work of art with such designs ▪ *marble reliefs*

relief map *n* [*C*] : a map that uses different colors or textures to show the height or depth of mountains, valleys, etc.

relief pitcher *n* [*C*] *baseball* : a pitcher who comes into a game when another pitcher is removed from the game

re·lieve /rɪˈliːv/ *vb* **-lieved; -liev·ing** [*T*] **1** : to reduce or remove (pain, tension, etc.) ▪ *I took a pill to relieve my headache.* ▪ *relieving stress* **2** : to make (a problem) less serious ▪ *relieve poverty* **3** : to take the place of (someone who has been working, fighting, etc.) ▪ *I've come to relieve the guard on duty.* **4** : to make (something) less boring, dull, etc., by including a part that is different ▪ *a serious novel relieved by the occasional joke* — **relieve of** [*phrasal vb*] **relieve (someone) of 1** *formal* : to take (something difficult or unpleasant) from (someone) ▪ *The contract relieved him of all responsibility/liability.* **2** *informal + humorous* : to steal (something) from (someone) ▪ *Someone relieved him of his wallet.* **3** : to remove (someone who has done something wrong) from (a post, duty, job, etc.) ▪ *The general was relieved of his command.* — **relieve yourself** : to pass waste from your body : URINATE — **re·liev·er** /rɪˈliːvɚ/ *n* [*C*] ▪ *pain relievers like aspirin and ibuprofen*

relieved *adj* : feeling relaxed and happy because something difficult or unpleasant has been stopped, avoided, or made easier ▪ *I was relieved to hear that you're feeling better.*

re·li·gion /rɪˈlɪdʒən/ *n* **1** [*U*] : the belief in a god or in a group of gods **2** [*C/U*] : an organized system of beliefs, ceremonies, and rules used to worship a god or a group of gods ▪ *learning about different religions* **3** [*C/U*] *informal* : an interest, a belief, or an activity that is very important to a person or group ▪ *Where I live, football is (a) religion.* — **find/get religion** *informal + sometimes disapproving* : to become religious ▪ *prisoners who get religion*

re·li·gi·os·i·ty /rɪˌlɪdʒiˈɑːsəti/ *n* [*U*] *sometimes disapproving* : the state of being religious ▪ *a man of deep religiosity*

re·li·gious /rɪˈlɪdʒəs/ *adj* **1** : of or relating to religion ▪ *religious beliefs/groups/leaders* **2** : believing in a god or a group of gods and following the rules of a religion ▪ *She is very religious.* ▪ *a deeply religious man*

re·li·gious·ly /rɪˈlɪdʒəsli/ *adv* **1** : concerned or connected with religion ▪ *He is religiously observant.* **2** : very regularly or carefully ▪ *She exercises religiously.* ▪ *This recipe must be followed religiously.*

re·lin·quish /rɪˈlɪŋkwɪʃ/ *vb* [*T*] *formal*

: to give up (something) ▪ *relinquish rights/control/custody* — **re·lin·quish·ment** /rɪˈlɪŋkwɪʃmənt/ *n* [*U*]

¹**rel·ish** /ˈrɛlɪʃ/ *n* **1** [*C/U*] : a seasoned sauce that is made of chopped fruit or vegetables ▪ *hot dogs with (pickle) relish* **2** [*U*] : enjoyment of or delight in something ▪ *She sang with (great) relish.* ▪ *He took relish in pointing out my error.*

²**relish** *vb* [*T*] : to enjoy or take pleasure in (something) ▪ *I don't relish the idea/prospect/thought of working late.*

re·live /riˈlɪv/ *vb* **-lived; -liv·ing** [*T*] : to experience (something) again in your imagination ▪ *an athlete trying to relive his glory days*

re·load /riˈloʊd/ *vb* [*T/I*] **1** : to put bullets, film, etc., into (a gun, camera, etc.) again ▪ *The soldiers reloaded (their rifles).* **2** : to put data into a computer's memory again ▪ *Try reloading the Web page.*

re·lo·cate /riˈloʊˌkeɪt/ *vb* **-cat·ed; -cat·ing** [*T/I*] : to move to a new place ▪ *He relocated to Los Angeles.* ▪ *They relocated their headquarters.* — **re·lo·ca·tion** /ˌriloʊˈkeɪʃən/ *n* [*C/U*]

re·luc·tant /rɪˈlʌktənt/ *adj* : feeling or showing doubt about doing something ▪ *We were reluctant to get involved.* ▪ *a reluctant participant* — **re·luc·tance** /rɪˈlʌktəns/ *n* [*U, singular*] ▪ *a reluctance to take risks* ▪ *He agreed with reluctance.* — **re·luc·tant·ly** *adv*

re·ly /rɪˈlaɪ/ *vb* **-lies; -lied; -ly·ing** — **rely on/upon** [*phrasal vb*] **1 a** : to need (someone or something) for support, help, etc. ▪ *They rely on a well for water.* ▪ *He relies upon her for money.* ▪ *I'm relying on you to help.* **b** : to trust or believe (someone or something) ▪ *You can rely on him to do it right.* **2** : to be certain that (something) will happen or exist ▪ *The economy may improve, but you can't rely on that.*

re·main /rɪˈmeɪn/ *vb* **1** [*I*] : to be left when the other parts are gone or have been used ▪ *Little remained after the fire.* ▪ *Only two minutes remain in the game.* **2** [*I*] : to be something that still needs to be done, dealt with, etc. ▪ *The question remains: who fired the shot?* ▪ *Much work remains to be done.* ▪ *That remains to be seen.* [=that is uncertain] **3** [*I*] *somewhat formal* : to stay after others have gone ▪ *I remained behind after class.* ▪ *He remained with the team.* **4** [*linking vb*] : to continue in a specified state, condition, or position ▪ *She remained* [=*kept, stayed*] *calm.* ▪ *Please remain standing/seated.* : to continue to be something specified ▪ *The weather remained cold.* ▪ *They have remained friends.* — **re·main·ing** /rɪˈmeɪnɪŋ/ *adj* ▪ *Add the remaining ingredients.* ▪ *a few remaining guests*

re·main·der /rɪˈmeɪndɚ/ *n* **1** *the remainder* : the part that is left when the other people or things are gone, used, etc. ▪ *the remainder of the money/year/students* **2** [*C*] *mathematics* **a** : the number that is left when one number is subtracted from another number ▪ *2 subtracted from 5 gives a remainder of 3.* **b** : the number that is left over when one number does not divide evenly into another number • *5 goes into 29 five times with a remainder of 4.*

re·mains /rɪˈmeɪnz/ *n* [*plural*] **1** : the dead body of a person or animal • *fossil remains* • *human remains* **2** : the parts of something that are left when the other parts are gone or used • *the remains of a castle*

¹**re·make** /riˈmeɪk/ *vb* **-made** /-ˈmeɪd/; **-mak·ing** [*T*] **1** : to make a new or different version of (a movie, song, etc.) • *remake an old film* **2** : to make (something) into something else • *The city remade itself into a center for tourism.*

²**re·make** /ˈriːˌmeɪk/ *n* [*C*] : a new or different version of a movie, song, etc. • *a remake of King Kong*

re·mand /rɪˈmænd, *Brit* rɪˈmɑːnd/ *vb* [*T*] *law* **1** *US* : to send (a case) back to another court of law to be tried or dealt with again **2** : to order (someone) to go somewhere • *He was remanded into custody.*

¹**re·mark** /rɪˈmɑɚk/ *n* **1** [*C*] : something that someone says or writes : COMMENT • *I was offended by his remark.* • *making witty/clever remarks* **2** [*U*] *formal* : the act of noticing or making a comment about something • *The incident passed without remark.*

²**remark** *vb* [*T/I*] : to make a statement about someone or something • *He remarked that the movie was long.* • *She remarked on/upon the weather.*

re·mark·able /rɪˈmɑɚkəbəl/ *adj* : unusual or surprising : likely to be noticed • *a remarkable achievement* — **re·mark·ably** /rɪˈmɑɚkəbli/ *adv* • *Remarkably (enough), no one was hurt.*

re·mar·ry /rɪˈmeri/ *vb* **-ries; -ried; -ry·ing** [*T/I*] : to marry again • *a widow who never remarried* • *He remarried his ex-wife.* — **re·mar·riage** /rɪˈmeridʒ/ *n* [*C/U*]

re·match /ˈriːˌmætʃ/ *n* [*C*] : a second match or game that is played by the same people or teams • *She demanded a rematch.*

re·me·di·al /rɪˈmiːdijəl/ *adj* **1 a** : done to make something better • *remedial action/measures* **b** : done to cure or treat someone • *remedial therapy* **2** : involving students who need special help to improve in a particular subject • *remedial classes/courses* • *(US) a remedial student*

¹**rem·e·dy** /ˈrɛmədi/ *n, pl* **-dies** **1** [*C*] : a medicine or treatment that relieves pain or cures a usually minor illness • *a remedy for fever* **2** [*C/U*] : a way of solving or correcting a problem • *a remedy for traffic congestion* • *a legal remedy* • *The problem was beyond remedy.*

²**remedy** *vb* **-dies; -died; -dy·ing** [*T*] : to solve, correct, or improve (something) • *finding a way to remedy the problem*

re·mem·ber /rɪˈmɛmbɚ/ *vb* **1** [*T/I*] : to think of (something or someone from the past) again • *I remember my first day of school.* • *Do you remember me?* • *Remember when we went hiking?* • *I remember what that felt like.* • *a day to remember* [=a special day] **2** [*T/I*] : to cause (something) to come back into your mind • *I can't remember how to do it.* • *I*

don't remember his name. **3** [*T/I*] : to keep (information) in your mind : to not forget (something) • *She always remembers my birthday.* • *Remember, the test is tomorrow.* **4** [*T*] : to think about (someone who has died) in a respectful way • *She is remembered for her contributions to physics.* — **remember me to** old-fashioned — used to ask someone to give your greetings to another person • *Please remember me to your aunt.*

re·mem·brance /rɪˈmɛmbrəns/ *n, literary* **1** [*U*] : the act of remembering a person, thing, or event • *a time for remembrance* **2** [*U*] : something that is done or made to honor the memory of a person, thing, or event • *a dinner held in remembrance of my mother* **3** [*C*] : a memory of a person, thing, or event • *fond remembrances of my youth*

re·mind /rɪˈmaɪnd/ *vb* [*T*] : to cause (someone) to remember something • *Remind me to call her.* • *I had to remind him that she was coming.* — **remind of** [*phrasal vb*] **remind (someone) of 1** : to cause (someone) to remember (something) • *I reminded him of his promise.* • *This song reminds me of our wedding.* **2** : to cause (someone) to think of (a similar person or thing) • *He reminds me of my uncle.* [=he looks/acts like my uncle]

re·mind·er /rɪˈmaɪndɚ/ *n* [*C*] : something that causes you to remember or to think about something • *a constant reminder of his past* • *I sent/wrote a reminder about the meeting.*

rem·i·nisce /ˌrɛməˈnɪs/ *vb* **-nisced; -nisc·ing** [*I*] : to talk, think, or write about things that happened in the past • *reminiscing about high school*

rem·i·nis·cence /ˌrɛməˈnɪsn̩s/ *n, formal* **1** [*C*] : a story that someone tells about something that happened in the past • *her reminiscences of her childhood* **2** [*U*] : the act of remembering or telling about past experiences • *a time for reminiscence*

rem·i·nis·cent /ˌrɛməˈnɪsn̩t/ *adj* : reminding you of someone or something else • *a song that is reminiscent of early jazz*

re·miss /rɪˈmɪs/ *adj, formal* : not showing enough care and attention • *I was remiss in paying my bills.* [=I neglected to pay my bills]

re·mis·sion /rɪˈmɪʃən/ *n* **1** [*C/U*] : a period of time during a serious illness when the patient's health improves • *Her cancer has gone into remission.* = *Her cancer is in remission.* = *She is in remission.* **2** [*C/U*] *formal* : the act of reducing or canceling the amount of money that you owe • *tax/fee remissions* **3** [*U*] *Brit* : the reduction of a prison sentence • *He was given remission for good behavior.*

¹**re·mit** /rɪˈmɪt/ *vb* **-mit·ted; -mit·ting** [*T*] *formal* **1** : to send (money) as a payment • *Please remit $1,000.* • *remit payment* **2** : to cancel or free someone from (a punishment, debt, etc.) • *remit a prison sentence* — **remit to** [*phrasal vb*] **remit (something)** : to send (a dispute, a court case, etc.) to an authority that can make a decision about it • *The case was remitted to the state court.*

²**remit** *n* [C] *Brit, formal* : an area of responsibility and authority ▪ *The problem was outside/beyond our remit.*

re·mit·tance /rɪˈmɪtn̩s/ *n, formal* 1 [C] : an amount of money that is sent as a payment for something ▪ *Please return the form with your remittance.* 2 [U] : the act of sending money as a payment ▪ *Remittance can be made by check.*

re·mix /ˈriːˌmɪks/ *n* [C] : a new or different version of a recorded song that is made by changing or adding to the original recording — **re·mix** /riːˈmɪks/ *vb* [T] ▪ *He remixed the song for the new album.*

rem·nant /ˈrɛmnənt/ *n* [C] : the part of something that is left when the other parts are gone ▪ *the last surviving remnants of a great civilization*

re·mod·el /riːˈmɑːdl̩/ *vb, US* **-eled** *or Brit* **-elled**; *US* **-el·ing** *or Brit* **-el·ling** [T] : to change the structure, shape, or appearance of (something) ▪ *We remodeled the kitchen.* ▪ *newly remodeled bathrooms*

re·mon·strate /ˈrɛmənˌstreɪt, rɪˈmɑːnˌstreɪt/ *vb* **-strat·ed**; **-strat·ing** [I] *formal* : to disagree and argue or complain about something ▪ *I remonstrated with him about littering.* — **re·mon·stra·tion** /ˌrɛmənˈstreɪʃən, rəˌmɑːnˈstreɪʃən/ *n* [C/U]

re·morse /rɪˈmoɚs/ *n* [U] : a feeling of being sorry for doing something bad or wrong in the past ▪ *He showed (some/no) remorse for his crimes.* — **re·morse·ful** /rɪˈmoɚsfəl/ *adj* ▪ *She was remorseful for what she had done.* — **re·morse·ful·ly** /rɪˈmoɚsfəli/ *adv* — **re·morse·less** /rɪˈmoɚsləs/ *adj* ▪ *a remorseless* [=*merciless*] *murderer* ▪ *his remorseless* [=*relentless*] *pursuit of justice*

¹**re·mote** /rɪˈmoʊt/ *adj* **re·mot·er; -est** 1 **a** : far away : DISTANT ▪ *remote lands/galaxies* **b** : far away from other people, houses, cities, etc. ▪ *a remote island/village* 2 *always before a noun* : far away in time ▪ *imagining life in the remote future/past* 3 : very small : SLIGHT ▪ *a remote chance/possibility* 4 *always before a noun* : not closely related ▪ *remote ancestors* 5 : very different *from* something ▪ *traditions remote from our own* 6 : not friendly or involved with other people ▪ *She became more remote in her old age.* 7 *always before a noun* **a** computer : connected to a computer system from another place ▪ *a remote computer/terminal* ▪ *remote users* ▪ *remote access to the system* **b** : capable of being controlled from a distance ▪ *a remote camera/sensor* — **re·mote·ness** *n* [U]

²**remote** *n* [C] *informal* : REMOTE CONTROL

remote control *n* 1 [C] : a device that is used to operate electronic equipment (such as a television) from a distance 2 [U] : a process or system that makes it possible to control something from a distance ▪ *a device operated by remote control* ▪ *a remote control camera* — **remote–controlled** *adj* ▪ *a remote-controlled toy car*

re·mote·ly /rɪˈmoʊtli/ *adv* 1 : to a very small degree ▪ *It's remotely possible.* ▪ *I've never seen anything remotely like it.* ▪

That's not even remotely true. 2 *technical* : from a distance ▪ *users who log in remotely* ▪ *a remotely operated submarine*

re·mount /riːˈmaʊnt/ *vb* 1 [T] : to attach (something) to a support again ▪ *remount a diamond/tire/door* 2 [T/I] : to get on a horse, bicycle, motorcycle, etc., again after getting off or falling off ▪ *She quickly remounted (her horse).*

re·move /rɪˈmuːv/ *vb* **-moved; -mov·ing** [T] 1 : to move or take (something) away from a place ▪ *Remove the trash from the front yard.* 2 : to cause (something) to no longer exist ▪ *evidence that will remove any doubt* ▪ *remove a stain/obstacle* 3 : to dismiss (someone) from a job ▪ *He was removed from office.* 4 *somewhat formal* : to take off (something you are wearing) ▪ *Please remove your shoes/hat.* — **re·mov·able** /rɪˈmuːvəbəl/ *adj* — **re·mov·al** /rɪˈmuːvəl/ *n* [U] ▪ *trash/waste/snow removal* ▪ *the removal of doubt* ▪ *his removal from office* — **re·mov·er** /rɪˈmuːvɚ/ *n* [C] ▪ *a paint/stain remover*

re·mu·ner·ate /rɪˈmjuːnəˌreɪt/ *vb* **-at·ed; -at·ing** [T] *formal* : to pay someone for work that has been done ▪ *They were remunerated for their services.* = *Their services were remunerated.* — **re·mu·ner·a·tion** /rɪˌmjuːnəˈreɪʃən/ *n* [C/U]

re·nais·sance /ˈrɛnəˌsɑːns, *Brit* rɪˈneɪsn̩s/ *n* 1 **Renaissance** : the period of European history between the 14th and 17th centuries when there was a new interest in science and in ancient art and literature especially in Italy ▪ *a Renaissance painter* ▪ *a book on the Renaissance* 2 [*singular*] : REBIRTH, REVIVAL ▪ *the city's economic renaissance*

re·nal /ˈriːnl̩/ *adj, always before a noun, medical* : relating to or involving the kidneys ▪ *renal disease/failure*

re·name /riːˈneɪm/ *vb* **-named; -nam·ing** [T] : to give a new name to (someone or something) ▪ *The bridge was renamed in her honor.*

rend /ˈrɛnd/ *vb* **rent** /ˈrɛnt/ *also US* **rend·ed; rend·ing** [T] *literary* : to tear (something) into pieces with force or violence ▪ *They rent the cloth to shreds.*

ren·der /ˈrɛndɚ/ *vb* [T] 1 *formal* : to cause (someone or something) to be in a specified condition ▪ *She was rendered helpless/unconscious.* 2 *formal* : to give (something) to someone ▪ *render aid/assistance* ▪ *a fee/payment for services rendered* 3 *law* : to officially report or declare (a legal judgment) ▪ *The jury rendered a verdict of not guilty.* 4 *formal* : to present or perform (something) ▪ *The novel renders a portrait of rural life.* ▪ *perfectly rendered songs* 5 *formal* : TRANSLATE ▪ *render Latin into English* — **ren·der·ing** /ˈrɛndərɪŋ/ *n* [C] ▪ *an emotional rendering* [=*performance*] *of the national anthem* ▪ *The book is a faithful rendering* [=*depiction*] *of rural life.*

ren·dez·vous /ˈrɑːndɪˌvuː/ *n, pl* **ren·dez·vous** /ˈrɑːndɪˌvuːz/ [C] 1 : a meeting with someone at a particular time and place ▪ *a secret rendezvous* 2 **a** : a place where people agree to meet at a particular time ▪ *The restaurant will be* *our rendezvous.* **b** : a place where many people go to spend time ▪ *a popular/favorite rendezvous* — **ren·dez·vous** /ˈrɑːndɪˌvuː/ *vb* **-vouses** /-ˌvuːz/; **-voused** /-ˌvuːd/; **-vous·ing** /-ˌvuːwɪŋ/ [*I*] ▪ *We'll rendezvous at the station.*

ren·di·tion /rɛnˈdɪʃən/ *n* [*C*] : a performance of something ▪ *a moving rendition of an old song*

ren·e·gade /ˈrɛnɪˌgeɪd/ *n* [*C*] **1** : a person who leaves one group, religion, etc., and joins another that opposes it ▪ *a renegade Republican/Democrat* **2** : someone or something that causes trouble and cannot be controlled ▪ *drugs that attack renegade cells in cancer patients*

re·nege /rɪˈnɛg, *Brit* rɪˈniːg/ *vb* **-neged**; **-neg·ing** [*I*] : to refuse to do something that you promised or agreed to do ▪ *They reneged (on their promise).*

re·new /rɪˈnuː, *Brit* rɪˈnjuː/ *vb* [*T*] **1** : to make (something) new, fresh, or strong again ▪ *The body needs rest to renew itself.* ▪ *renew a hope/commitment* **2** : to make (a promise, vow, etc.) again ▪ *They renewed their wedding vows.* **3** : to begin (something) again especially with more force or enthusiasm ▪ *They renewed their efforts.* ▪ *renewing hostilities* ▪ *They recently renewed their acquaintance/friendship.* **4** : to cause (something) to continue to be effective or valid for an additional period of time ▪ *renew a lease/subscription/passport* — **re·new·able** /rɪˈnuːwəbəl, *Brit* rɪˈnjuːwəbəl/ *adj* ▪ *a renewable lease* ▪ *renewable fuel sources* [=fuel sources that can be replaced by natural processes] — **re·newed** /rɪˈnuːd, *Brit* rɪˈnjuːd/ *adj* ▪ *worked with renewed enthusiasm* ▪ *I felt renewed after my nap.* ▪ *their renewed efforts to make peace*

re·new·al /rɪˈnuːwəl, *Brit* rɪˈnjuːwəl/ *n* **1** [*C/U*] : the act of extending the period of time when something is effective or valid ▪ *license/subscription/lease renewals* ▪ *This contract is up for renewal.* [=it is time to consider renewing his contract] **2** [*U, singular*] : the state of being made new, fresh, or strong again ▪ *a renewal of interest* ▪ *a symbol of rebirth and renewal*

re·nounce /rɪˈnaʊns/ *vb* **-nounced**; **-nounc·ing** [*T*] **1** : to say especially in a formal or official way that you will no longer have or accept (something) ▪ *The king renounced the throne.* ▪ *renounce (the use of) violence* **2** : to say in a formal or definite way that you refuse to follow, obey, or support (someone or something) any longer ▪ *His former supporters have renounced him.* ▪ *She renounced her old way of life.*

ren·o·vate /ˈrɛnəˌveɪt/ *vb* **-vat·ed**; **-vat·ing** [*T*] : to make changes and repairs to (an old building, room, etc.) so that it is back in good condition ▪ *renovate a house/bathroom/kitchen* — **ren·o·va·tion** /ˌrɛnəˈveɪʃən/ *n* [*C/U*] — **ren·o·va·tor** /ˈrɛnəˌveɪtɚ/ *n* [*C*]

re·nown /rɪˈnaʊn/ *n* [*U*] *somewhat formal* : great fame and respect ▪ *He achieved/gained/won renown for his discoveries.* ▪ *writers of renown* — **re·nowned** /rɪ-*

ˈnaʊnd/ *adj* ▪ *a renowned scientist/restaurant*

¹rent /ˈrɛnt/ *n* [*C/U*] : money that you pay in return for being able to use an apartment, house, etc., that belongs to someone else ▪ *(The) rent is due next week.* ▪ *Our landlord raised the rent.* — **for rent** *chiefly US* : available to be rented ▪ *houses/rooms for rent* [=to let]

²rent *vb* **1** [*T/I*] : to pay money in return for being able to use (something that belongs to someone else) ▪ *rent a cottage* ▪ *(US) We rented* [=(*Brit*) *hired*] *a car.* ▪ *(US) rent a movie/DVD/video* **2** [*T*] : to allow someone to use (something) in return for payment ▪ *They rented their cottage.* **3** [*I*] : to be available for use in return for payment ▪ *The cottage rents for $400 a week.* — **rent·er** *n* [*C*]

³rent *past tense and past participle of* REND

rent·al /ˈrɛntl̩/ *n* **1** [*C/U*] : the amount of money paid or collected as rent ▪ *The rental (fee) is $400.* **2** [*C/U*] : the act of renting something ▪ *The house is available for rental.* ▪ *a rental agreement* **3** [*C*] *chiefly US* : something that can be rented ▪ *a two-bedroom rental* ▪ *driving a rental (car)*

re·nun·ci·a·tion /rɪˌnʌnsiˈeɪʃən/ *n* [*C/U*] : the act of renouncing something or someone ▪ *the king's renunciation of the throne* ▪ *renunciation of violence*

re·open /riˈoʊpən/ *vb* **1** [*T/I*] : to open again after being closed ▪ *We reopen (the store) at nine a.m.* ▪ *The cut on his knee reopened.* **2 a** [*T/I*] : to start (something) again after a period without activity ▪ *reopen negotiations* **b** [*T*] *US* : to discuss and make changes to (something) again ▪ *reopen a contract* — **re·open·ing** /riˈoʊpənɪŋ/ *n* [*U, singular*]

re·or·der /riˈoɚdɚ/ *vb* **1** [*T/I*] : to order (something) again ▪ *reorder supplies* **2** [*T*] : to arrange (something) in a different order ▪ *reorder a list*

re·or·ga·nize *also Brit* **re·or·ga·nise** /riˈoɚgəˌnaɪz/ *vb* **-nized**; **-niz·ing** [*T/I*] : to organize (something) again or in a different way ▪ *reorganize files* ▪ *The company (was) reorganized.* — **re·or·ga·ni·za·tion** *also Brit* **re·or·ga·ni·sa·tion** /riˌoɚgənəˈzeɪʃən, *Brit* riˌoːgəˌnaɪˈzeɪʃən/ *n* [*U*]

rep /ˈrɛp/ *n* [*C*] **1** *informal* : REPRESENTATIVE ▪ *sales reps* **2** *informal* : a motion or exercise that is repeated ▪ *3 sets of 12 reps* [=repetitions] **3** *US slang* : REPUTATION ▪ *protecting his rep*

Rep. *abbr* **1** Republican **2** representative ▪ *Rep. Richard Jones*

¹re·pair /rɪˈpeɚ/ *vb* [*T*] **1** : to put (something that is broken or damaged) back into good condition ▪ FIX ▪ *He repairs clocks.* ▪ *surgery to repair a torn ligament* ▪ *repairing the damage* **2** : to correct or improve (something) ▪ *trying to repair her damaged reputation* ▪ *Can their marriage be repaired?* — **repair to** [*phrasal vb*] *old-fashioned + formal* : to go to (a place) ▪ *After dinner, we repaired to the drawing room.* — **re·pair·er** /rɪˈpeɚɚ/ *n* [*C*]

²repair *n* **1** [*C/U*] : the act or process of repairing something ▪ *The roof is in need of repair.* ▪ *a shoe/car repair shop* ▪ *The* *car was damaged* **beyond repair.** ▪ *We* **made repairs** *to the roof.* **2** [*U*] : a specified physical condition ▪ *The roof is in good/poor repair.*

re·pair·man /rɪˈpeɚˌmæn/ *n, pl* **-men** /-mən/ [*C*] : a person (especially a man) whose job is to repair things ▪ *a TV repairman*

rep·a·ra·tion /ˌrɛpəˈreɪʃən/ *n* **1** [*plural*] : money that a country or group that loses a war pays because of the damage, deaths, etc., it has caused **2** [*U, plural*] *formal* : something that is done or given as a way of correcting a mistake that you have made or a bad situation that you have caused ▪ *She wants to* **make reparation(s).**

rep·ar·tee /ˌrɛpɚˈtiː, Brit ˌrɛpɑːˈtiː/ *n* [*U*] : conversation in which clever statements and replies are made quickly ▪ *witty repartee*

re·past /rɪˈpæst, Brit rɪˈpɑːst/ *n* [*C*] *literary* : MEAL ▪ *a light repast*

re·pa·tri·ate /riːˈpeɪtriˌeɪt, Brit riˈpætriˌeɪt/ *vb* **-at·ed; -at·ing** [*T*] : to return (someone) to his or her own country ▪ *repatriated refugees* — **re·pa·tri·a·tion** /ˌriːˌpeɪtriˈeɪʃən, Brit riˌpætriˈeɪʃən/ *n* [*C/U*]

re·pay /riˈpeɪ/ *vb* **-paid** /-ˈpeɪd/; **-pay·ing** [*T*] **1 a** : to pay back (money) ▪ *repay a loan/debt* **b** : to make a payment to (a person or organization that has loaned you money) ▪ *repay the bank* **2 a** : to do or give something in return for (something) ▪ *How can I ever repay your kindness?* : to provide something in return for (work, effort, etc.) ▪ *Her efforts were repaid with praise.* **b** : to do something for (someone) in return for something ▪ *How can I ever repay you for your kindness?* — **re·pay·ment** /riˈpeɪmənt/ *n* [*C/U*]

re·peal /rɪˈpiːl/ *vb* [*T*] : to officially make (a law) no longer valid ▪ *The legislature repealed the tax (law).* — **repeal** *n* [*C/U*] ▪ *the repeal of the law*

¹**re·peat** /rɪˈpiːt/ *vb* **1** [*T*] **a** : to say (something) again ▪ *Will you repeat the question?* ▪ *He kept repeating the same thing.* **b** : to say (something) after someone else has said it ▪ *Repeat after me: "I solemnly swear ..."* ▪ *You're just repeating what I already said.* **2** [*T*] : to tell (something that you have heard) to someone else ▪ *Please don't repeat this (to anyone).* **3** [*T*] **a** : to make, do, or achieve (something) again ▪ *We need to avoid repeating the mistakes of the past.* ▪ *repeat a process/procedure* ▪ *repeat a year/grade (in school)* ▪ *Will history repeat itself?* [=will the same thing happen again?] **b** : to present (something) again ▪ *repeat a broadcast* **4** [*I*] : to happen again ▪ *The cycle repeats every 24 hours.* — **repeat yourself** : to say again what you have already said ▪ *I'm not going to repeat myself.* — **re·peat·able** /rɪˈpiːtəbəl/ *adj* ▪ *repeatable test results* ▪ *He said things that aren't repeatable.* [=things that are too impolite, offensive, etc., to say again] — **re·peat·ed** /rɪˈpiːtəd/ *adj, always before a noun* ▪ *his repeated requests/attempts/failures* — **re·peat·ed·ly** *adv* ▪ *I told her repeatedly* [=many times] *not to do it.*

²**re·peat** /rɪˈpiːt, ˈriːˌpiːt/ *n* [*C*] **1 a** : an occurrence in which something happens or is done again ▪ *avoiding a repeat of that incident* **b** : something that happens or is done again ▪ *a repeat win* ▪ *repeat business* [=new business from past customers] **c** : someone who does something again ▪ *repeat customers* ▪ *repeat offenders* [=people who have committed a crime more than once] **2** : a radio or television show that is broadcast again ▪ *That show is a repeat.*

re·pel /rɪˈpɛl/ *vb* **-pelled; -pel·ling** [*T*] **1** : to keep (something) out or away ▪ *a fabric that repels water* **2** : to force (an enemy, attacker, etc.) to stop an attack and turn away ▪ *They repelled the invasion.* **3** *physics* : to force (something) to move away or apart ▪ *Magnets can both repel and attract one another.* **4** : to cause (someone) to feel disgust ▪ *I was repelled by what I saw.*

¹**re·pel·lent** *also* **re·pel·lant** /rɪˈpɛlənt/ *adj* **1** : keeping something out or away ▪ *a water-repellent fabric* [=a fabric that repels water] **2** *formal* : causing someone to feel disgust ▪ *ideas that are repellent to me*

²**repellent** *also* **repellant** *n* [*C/U*] : a substance that is used to keep something out or away ▪ *(an) insect repellent*

re·pent /rɪˈpɛnt/ *vb* [*T/I*] *formal* : to feel or show that you are sorry for something bad or wrong that you did ▪ *repent your sins* ▪ *He has repented (for) his crimes.* — **re·pen·tance** /rɪˈpɛntn̩s/ *n* [*U*] — **re·pen·tant** /rɪˈpɛntn̩t/ *adj* ▪ *repentant sinners*

re·per·cus·sion /ˌriːpɚˈkʌʃən/ *n* [*C*] : a bad or unpleasant result that usually affects people for a long time — usually *plural* ▪ *Their decision had serious repercussions.*

rep·er·toire /ˈrɛpɚˌtwɑɚ/ *n* [*C*] **1** : all the plays, songs, dances, etc., that a performer or group of performers knows and can perform ▪ *the band's repertoire* **2** : all the things that a person is able to do ▪ *a repertoire of techniques/options*

rep·er·to·ry /ˈrɛpɚˌtori, Brit ˈrɛpətri/ *n, pl* **-ries** [*C/U*] : a group of actors who perform many plays with each play being performed for only a short time ▪ *She acted in repertory.* ▪ *a repertory (company)*

rep·e·ti·tion /ˌrɛpəˈtɪʃən/ *n* **1** [*U*] : the act of repeating words, actions, etc. ▪ *Avoid repetition in your writing.* ▪ *mindless repetition* **2** [*C*] : something that is done or said again ▪ *We want to avoid a repetition (of the problem).* — **rep·e·ti·tious** /ˌrɛpəˈtɪʃəs/ *adj* ▪ *repetitious work/lyrics*

re·pet·i·tive /rɪˈpɛtətɪv/ *adj* **1** : repeated many times ▪ *repetitive movements* ▪ *a repetitive pattern* **2** : having parts, actions, etc., that are repeated many times ▪ *dull, repetitive work*

re·phrase /riːˈfreɪz/ *vb* **-phrased; -phras·ing** [*T*] : to say or write (something) again using different words ▪ *Let me rephrase the question.*

re·place /rɪˈpleɪs/ *vb* **-placed; -plac·ing** [*T*] **1 a** : to be used instead of (something) ▪ *Will computers ever replace books?* **b** : to do the job or duty of (someone) • *She was hired to replace the manager.* **2** : to put someone or something new in the place or position of (someone or something) • *I replaced the old rug (with a new one).* • *The manager was replaced.* **3** : to put (something) where it was before • *He replaced the vase on the shelf.* — **re·place·able** /rɪ-ˈpleɪsəbəl/ *adj* • *The broken vase is easily replaceable.*

re·place·ment /rɪˈpleɪsmənt/ *n* **1** [*U*] : the act of replacing something • *The stove is in need of replacement.* • *a hip replacement = hip replacement surgery* **2** [*C*] : a person or thing that replaces someone or something else • *I'm training my replacement.* • *We need a replacement for our old stove.*

¹**re·play** /ˈriːˌpleɪ/ *n* [*C*] **1** : a game that is played again because there was no winner in a previous game **2** : a recording of something that is being shown again • *They showed a replay of the touchdown.* **3** : ¹REPEAT 1a • *We don't want a replay of that incident.*

²**re·play** /riˈpleɪ/ *vb* [*T*] **1** : to play (something) again especially because of a problem that occurred when it was played originally • *replay a baseball game* **2** : to play (recorded images, sounds, etc.) • *The touchdown was replayed several times.* • *(figurative) I replayed the conversation in my mind.*

re·plen·ish /rɪˈplɛnɪʃ/ *vb* [*T*] *somewhat formal* : to fill or build up (something) again • *replenish a supply of food* — **re·plen·ish·ment** /rɪˈplɛnɪʃmənt/ *n* [*U*]

re·plete /rɪˈpliːt/ *adj, not before a noun, formal* **1** : filled with something • *The book is replete with photographs.* **2** : having had plenty to eat • *feeling replete*

rep·li·ca /ˈrɛplɪkə/ *n* [*C*] : an exact or very close copy of something • *an exact replica of an ancient urn*

rep·li·cate /ˈrɛpləˌkeɪt/ *vb* **-cat·ed; -cat·ing** [*T/I*] *formal* : to repeat or copy (something) exactly • *trying to replicate the results of an experiment* • *computers that replicate human speech* — **rep·li·ca·tion** /ˌrɛpləˈkeɪʃən/ *n* [*C/U*]

¹**re·ply** /rɪˈplaɪ/ *vb* **-plies; -plied; -ply·ing** [*T/I*] : to say, write, or do something as an answer or response • *He never replied (to my letter/invitation).* • *I said hello, but no one replied.* • *"How do you feel?" she asked. "Better," he replied.*

²**reply** *n, pl* **-plies** [*C/U*] : something said, written, or done as an answer or response • *a rude reply* • *I never received a reply (to my letter).* • *In reply, she just shrugged.* • *He wrote a note in reply to her letter.*

¹**re·port** /rɪˈpoət/ *n* [*C*] **1** : a story in a newspaper or on radio or television that is about something that happened or that gives information • *a news/weather/financial report* **2 a** : a written or spoken description of a situation, event, etc. • *write/make/give a report* • *a medical/book/police report* • *a progress report* **b** : an official document that gives information about a particular subject • *the company's annual (business) report* **3** : a written or spoken statement about some-

thing • *an eyewitness report* • *By/from all reports, you're a hard worker.* [=everyone says that you are a hard worker] **4** *formal* : a loud noise made by a gun or an explosion • *the report of a rifle* **5** *Brit* : REPORT CARD

²**report** *vb* **1** [*T/I*] : to give information about (something) in a newspaper or on television or radio • *The murder was reported in/on the news.* • *reporting (on) the news* • *It was reported that two people died. = Two people were reported to have died.* **2** [*T/I*] : to make a report about (something) • *report the details of a meeting = report on a meeting* **3** [*T*] **a** : to describe (a feeling, condition, etc.) • *He reported feeling depressed.* • *The doctor reported some improvement in her condition.* **b** : to say or claim (something) • *The herb is reported to reduce anxiety.* **4** [*T*] : to tell the police, fire department, etc., about (a crime, accident, etc.) • *report a fire/burglary* • *They reported him missing.* [=they told the police that he was missing] **5** [*T*] : to tell someone with authority about (someone who has done something wrong) • *She reported him to the police/principal.* **6** [*I*] : to go somewhere and tell someone that you have arrived • *report to the office* • *report for work/duty* — **report back** [*phrasal vb*] **1** : to return to a place in order to report information, do more work, etc. • *Report back (to me) in two hours.* **2** **report back** *or* **report back (something)** *or* **report (something) back** : to give (information) to someone • *They reported their findings back (to us).* — **report sick** : to tell your boss, employer, etc., that you are sick and cannot work — **report to** [*phrasal vb*] : to have (someone) as your boss, supervisor, etc. • *She reports (directly) to the president.* — **re·port·ed** *adj, always before a noun* • *the reported findings/facts* • *a reported crime*

re·port·able /rɪˈpoətəbəl/ *adj, US* : required by law to be publicly reported to the government • *reportable income*

re·port·age /rɪˈpoətɪdʒ/ *n* [*U*] *formal* : REPORTING • *reportage of the news*

report card *n* [*C*] *US* : a written statement of a student's grades that is given to the student's parents

re·port·ed·ly /rɪˈpoətədli/ *adv* : according to what has been said • *They reportedly stole one million dollars.*

re·port·er /rɪˈpoətɚ/ *n* [*C*] : a person who writes news stories for a newspaper, magazine, etc., or who tells people the news on radio or television • *a news/television reporter*

re·port·ing /rɪˈpoətɪŋ/ *n* [*U*] : the act or activity of telling people the news in a newspaper or on television or radio • *firsthand reporting*

¹**re·pose** /rɪˈpoʊz/ *n* [*U*] *formal + literary* : a state of resting or not being active • *drawings of models in repose*

²**repose** *vb* **-posed; -pos·ing** *formal + literary* **1** [*T/I*] : to rest or lay (something) somewhere • *She reposed her head on a cushion.* • *reposing on the couch* **2** [*T*] : to place (trust, hope, etc.) in someone

or something • *They reposed confidence in their leader.*

re·pos·i·to·ry /rɪˈpɑːzəˌtori, *Brit* rɪˈpɒzətri/ *n, pl* **-ries** [C] *formal* **1** : a place where a large amount of something is stored • *huge repositories of data* **2** : a person who possesses a lot of information, wisdom, etc. • *She is the repository of her family's history.*

re·pos·sess /ˌriːpəˈzɛs/ *vb* [T] : to take (something) back from a buyer because payments are not being made • *The bank repossessed her truck.* — **re·pos·ses·sion** /ˌriːpəˈzɛʃən/ *n* [C/U]

rep·re·hen·si·ble /ˌrɛprɪˈhɛnsəbəl/ *adj, formal* : very bad : deserving very strong criticism • *reprehensible acts* — **rep·re·hen·si·bly** /ˌrɛprɪˈhɛnsəbli/ *adv*

rep·re·sent /ˌrɛprɪˈzɛnt/ *vb* **1** [T] **a** : to act or speak officially for (someone or something) • *He represented us at the meeting.* **b** : to have a government position in which you speak or act for (a particular group, state, etc.) • *Senator Smith represents Connecticut.* **c** : to speak or act for (someone or something) in a court of law • *He represented himself at the trial.* **2** [T] **a** : to be part of a competition for (a particular country, city, school, etc.) • *representing China at the Olympics* **b** **be represented** — used to say that people from a particular place or group are present at an event, meeting, etc. • *The town was well represented at the meeting.* **3** [*linking vb*] : to form or be something • *The court's decision represents a victory for small businesses.* **4** [T] : to be an example of (someone or something) • *He represents everything I dislike about politics.* **5** [T] : to be a sign or symbol of (someone or something) • *The flag represents our country.* • *Letters represent sounds.* **6** [T] : to show (someone or something) in a picture • *This painting represents Queen Elizabeth.* **7** [T] : to describe (someone or something) in a particular way • *He falsely represented himself as poor.*

rep·re·sen·ta·tion /ˌrɛprɪˌzɛnˈteɪʃən/ *n* **1** [U] : a person or group that speaks or acts for another person or group • *He had no legal representation.* [=he did not have a lawyer] • *Each state has equal representation in the Senate.* **2** [C] : something that stands for something else • *The letters of the alphabet are representations of sounds.* **3** [C] : a painting, sculpture, etc., that is created to look like a particular thing or person • *carved representations of flowers* **4** [U] : the act of presenting or describing a person or thing in a particular way • *the representation of women in her novels* **5** [C] *formal* **a** : a statement made to influence others • *He was accused of making false representations.* **b** *chiefly Brit* : a formal and official complaint • *They made representations to the government.*

¹**rep·re·sen·ta·tive** /ˌrɛprɪˈzɛntətɪv/ *adj* **1** : typical of a particular group of people or of a particular thing • *a representative example* • *paintings that are representative of the period* **2** : including examples of the different types of people

or things in a group • *a representative sample/sampling* **3** : having people who are chosen in elections to act or speak for the people who voted for them • *representative government/democracy*

²**representative** *n* [C] **1 a** : someone who acts or speaks for another person or group • *a sales/company representative* **b** : a member of the House of Representatives of the U.S. Congress or of a state government • *state representatives* • *Representative Smith* **2** : a person or thing that is typical of a group • *a representative of her age group*

re·press /rɪˈprɛs/ *vb* [T] **1** : to not allow yourself to do or express (something) • *She repressed a laugh.* • *He repressed his anger.* **2** : to not allow yourself to remember (something unpleasant) • *repress a painful memory* **3** : to control (someone or something) by force • *The dictator repressed all political dissent.* • *a repressed minority* — **re·pres·sion** /rɪˈprɛʃən/ *n* [U] • *the state's repression of its citizens* • *sexual repression* — **re·pres·sive** /rɪˈprɛsɪv/ *adj* • *a repressive government/culture*

¹**re·prieve** /rɪˈpriːv/ *n* [C] **1** : an official order that delays the punishment of a prisoner who is sentenced to death • *He won/got a (temporary) reprieve.* **2 a** : a delay that keeps something bad from happening • *The library was going to close but got a reprieve.* **b** : a period of relief from pain, trouble, etc. • *a reprieve from the winter cold*

²**reprieve** *vb* **-prieved; -priev·ing** [T] **1** : to delay the punishment of (someone) • *He was sentenced to death but then reprieved.* **2** : to prevent (something) from being closed, etc., for a period of time • *The old building has been reprieved.*

rep·ri·mand /ˈrɛprəˌmænd, *Brit* ˈrɛprəˌmɑːnd/ *vb* [T] : to speak in an angry and critical way to (someone who has done something wrong) • *Her boss reprimanded her for being late.* — **reprimand** *n* [C/U] • *a severe/mild reprimand* • *a letter of reprimand*

¹**re·print** /riˈprɪnt/ *vb* [T] : to print (something) again • *reprint a book*

²**re·print** /ˈriːˌprɪnt/ *n* [C] **1** : the act of printing more copies of a book • *The novel is on its fifth reprint.* **2** : a book, story, etc., that is printed again • *a reprint of an article*

re·pri·sal /rɪˈpraɪzəl/ *n* [C/U] : something that is done to hurt or punish someone who has done something bad to you • *Enemy officers suffered harsh reprisals.* • *They kept silent for fear of reprisal.*

re·prise /rɪˈpriːz/ *n* [C] : something (such as a piece of music) that is repeated • *a reprise of the opening number* — **reprise** *vb* **-prised; -pris·ing** [T] • *reprise a song/play/film* • *He will reprise his role in the play.*

¹**re·proach** /rɪˈproʊtʃ/ *n, formal* **1** [C/U] : an expression of disapproval or disappointment • *She looked at him with reproach.* • *His actions were above/beyond reproach.* [=not able to be criticized] **2** [U] : loss of reputation : DISGRACE • *He*

brought *reproach to his family.* **3** [C] : something that causes shame or disgrace ▪ *This scandal is a reproach to all of us.* — **re·proach·ful** /rɪˈprouʧfəl/ *adj* ▪ *a reproachful look* — **re·proach·ful·ly** /rɪˈprouʧfəli/ *adv*

²**reproach** *vb* [T] *formal* : to speak in an angry and critical way to (someone) ▪ *She reproached her daughter.* ▪ *He reproached himself* [=felt sorry or ashamed] *for lying.*

rep·ro·bate /ˈrɛprəˌbeɪt/ *n* [C] *formal* : a person who behaves in a morally wrong way ▪ *drunken reprobates*

re·pro·duce /ˌriːprəˈduːs, *Brit* ˌriːprəˈdjuːs/ *vb* **-duced; -duc·ing** **1** [T] **a** : to make a copy of (something) ▪ *reproduce a photograph* **b** : to produce something that is the same as or very similar to (something else) ▪ *reproduce the sound of thunder* **2** [T] : to cause (something) to happen again in the same way ▪ *reproduce the results of an experiment* **3** [T/I] : to produce babies, young animals, new plants, etc. ▪ *studying the ways in which animals reproduce* ▪ *The virus reproduces itself rapidly.* — **re·pro·duc·ible** /ˌriːprəˈduːsəbəl, *Brit* ˌriːprəˈdjuːsəbəl/ *adj* ▪ *The results were not reproducible.*

re·pro·duc·tion /ˌriːprəˈdʌkʃən/ *n* **1** [U] : the process that produces babies, young animals, or new plants ▪ *sexual/asexual reproduction* **2** [U] : the act of copying something (such as a document, book, or sound) ▪ *methods of sound reproduction* **3** [C] : something that is made to look exactly like an original : COPY ▪ *a reproduction of the painting*

re·pro·duc·tive /ˌriːprəˈdʌktɪv/ *adj, always before a noun* : relating to or involved in the production of babies, young animals, or new plants ▪ *the reproductive organs/system*

re·proof /rɪˈpruːf/ *n* [C/U] *formal* : CRITICISM ▪ *fear of reproof* ▪ *hurt by their reproofs*

re·prove /rɪˈpruːv/ *vb* **-proved; -prov·ing** [T] *formal* : to criticize or correct (someone) usually in a gentle way ▪ *The teacher reproved her for being late.*

rep·tile /ˈrɛpˌtajəl/ *n* [C] : an animal (such as a snake or turtle) that has cold blood, that lays eggs, and that has a body covered with scales or hard parts — **rep·til·ian** /rɛpˈtɪlijən/ *adj* ▪ *a reptilian brain/appearance*

re·pub·lic /rɪˈpʌblɪk/ *n* [C] : a country that is governed by elected representatives and by an elected leader (such as a president) rather than by a king or queen ▪ *an independent republic*

¹**re·pub·li·can** /rɪˈpʌblɪkən/ *n* [C] **1** *Republican* : a member of the Republican party of the U.S. **2** : a person who believes in or supports a republican form of government

²**republican** *adj* **1** *Republican US* : of or relating to one of the two major political parties in the U.S. ▪ *Republican candidates/voters* ▪ *the Republican Party* — compare DEMOCRATIC 2 **2** : relating to or based on a form of government in which representatives are elected and there is no king or queen ▪ *a republican government* — **re·pub·li·can·ism** *or* **Republicanism** /rɪˈpʌblɪkəˌnɪzəm/ *n* [U]

re·pu·di·ate /rɪˈpjuːdiˌeɪt/ *vb* **-at·ed; -at·ing** [T] *formal* **1** : to reject (something or someone) ▪ *He repudiated the government's policies.* **2** : to say or show that (something) is not true ▪ *evidence which repudiates the allegations* — **re·pu·di·a·tion** /rɪˌpjuːdiˈeɪʃən/ *n* [C/U]

re·pug·nant /rɪˈpʌgnənt/ *adj, formal* : causing a strong feeling of dislike or disgust ▪ *a morally repugnant act* ▪ *The idea was repugnant to us.* — **re·pug·nance** /rɪˈpʌgnəns/ *n* [U] ▪ *feelings of repugnance* [=disgust]

re·pulse /rɪˈpʌls/ *vb* **-pulsed; -puls·ing** [T] *formal* **1** : to force (someone) to stop attacking you ▪ *The troops repulsed the attack/invaders.* **2** : to cause dislike or disgust in (someone) ▪ *I was repulsed by the movie's violence.* **3** : to reject (someone or something) in a rude or unfriendly way ▪ *He repulsed all attempts to help him.*

re·pul·sion /rɪˈpʌlʃən/ *n* **1** [U, singular] : a feeling of strong dislike or disgust ▪ *reacting with shock and repulsion* **2** [C/U] *physics* : a force that pushes something away from something else ▪ *magnetic repulsion* **3** [U] : the act of repulsing something or someone ▪ *their repulsion of the attack/attackers*

re·pul·sive /rɪˈpʌlsɪv/ *adj* **1** : causing strong dislike or disgust ▪ *a repulsive person/act* **2** *physics* : of or relating to the force that pushes something away from something else ▪ *a repulsive effect/force* — **re·pul·sive·ly** *adv* — **re·pul·sive·ness** *n* [U]

rep·u·ta·ble /ˈrɛpjətəbəl/ *adj* : respected and trusted by most people ▪ *a reputable person/source/company*

rep·u·ta·tion /ˌrɛpjəˈteɪʃən/ *n* [C/U] : the common opinion that people have about a person, business, etc. ▪ *He has a good/bad reputation.* ▪ *The scandal damaged her reputation.* ▪ *They have a reputation for excellence.*

re·pute /rɪˈpjuːt/ *n* [U] *formal* **1** : REPUTATION ▪ *They are held in high/good/bad/low repute.* [=they have a good/bad reputation] **2** : good reputation ▪ *a scientist of repute* — **ill repute** : bad reputation ▪ *a woman of ill repute* [=prostitute] ▪ *a house of ill repute* [=brothel]

re·put·ed /rɪˈpjuːtəd/ *adj* : said to be true, to exist, to have a specified identity, etc. ▪ *He is reputed to be a millionaire.* ▪ *a reputed gang member* — **re·put·ed·ly** *adv*

¹**re·quest** /rɪˈkwɛst/ *n* [C/U] : an act of politely or formally asking for something ▪ *make/file/send/submit a request* ▪ *deny/refuse/reject a request* ▪ *fulfill/grant a request* ▪ *At your request, I am enclosing a refund.* ▪ *Catalogs are available by/on/upon request.* **2** [C] : something (such as a song) that a person asks for ▪ *The DJ plays requests.*

²**request** *vb* [T] **1** : to ask for (something) in a polite or formal way ▪ *He requested a table for two.* ▪ *request an appointment* **2** : to ask (someone) to do

something in a polite or formal way ▪ *Gentlemen are requested to wear a tie.*

re·qui·em *or* **Requiem** /ˈrɛkwijəm/ *n* [C] **1** : a Christian religious ceremony for a dead person **2** : a piece of music for a requiem

re·quire /rɪˈkwajɚ/ *vb* **-quired; -quir·ing** [T] *formal* **1** : to need (something) ▪ *We require your assistance.* ▪ *The game requires skill.* ▪ *Experience is required for this job.* ▪ *a required course/class* [=a course/class that must be taken] **2** : to make it necessary for someone to do something ▪ *The law requires us to pay taxes.* = *The law requires that we pay taxes.* ▪ *the duties that are required of a soldier* ▪ *paid his taxes,* **as required by** *law*

re·quire·ment /rɪˈkwajɚmənt/ *n* [C] **1** : something that is needed or that must be done ▪ *nutritional requirements* ▪ *a legal requirement* **2** : something that is necessary for something else to happen or be done ▪ *He met the minimum requirements for graduation.*

req·ui·site /ˈrɛkwəzət/ *adj, formal* : needed for a particular purpose ▪ *She has the requisite skills/experience for the job.* — **requisite** *n* [C] ▪ *Previous experience is a requisite for this job.*

req·ui·si·tion /ˌrɛkwəˈzɪʃən/ *vb* [T] *formal* : to ask for or demand and take (something) for your use ▪ *The car was requisitioned by the police.* — **requisition** *n* [C]

re·route /riˈruːt/ *vb* **-rout·ed; -rout·ing** [T] : to change the normal route of (something) ▪ *The airplane was rerouted.*

re·run /riˈrʌn/ *vb* **-ran** /-ˈræn/; **-run; -run·ning** [T] **1** : to show (a television program or movie) again ▪ *The show is being rerun tomorrow.* **2** : to do or run (something) again ▪ *They reran the race to break the tie.* ▪ *They reran the lab tests.* — **re·run** /ˈriːˌrʌn/ *n* [C] ▪ *watching summer reruns*

re·sale /ˈriːˌseɪl/ *n* [C/U] : the act of selling something that you have bought ▪ *The resale price/value of the car is $8,000.*

re·sched·ule /riˈskɛˌdʒuːl, *Brit* riˈʃɛˌdjuːl/ *vb* **-uled; -ul·ing** [T] : to schedule (something) for a different time or date ▪ *reschedule an appointment*

re·scind /rɪˈsɪnd/ *vb* [T] *formal* : to say officially that (something) is no longer valid ▪ *rescind a ban* ▪ *The company later rescinded its offer/decision.*

¹**res·cue** /ˈrɛskju/ *vb* **-cued; -cu·ing** [T] : to save (someone or something) from danger or harm ▪ *He rescued them from the fire.* — **res·cu·er** *n* [C] ▪ *Rescuers freed him from the car wreck.*

²**rescue** *n* [C] : an act of saving someone or something from danger, harm, or trouble ▪ *a heroic rescue* ▪ *a rescue team/mission* ▪ *A policeman* **came to our/the** *rescue.*

¹**re·search** /ˈriːˌsɚtʃ/ *n* [U] **1** : careful study that is done to find and report new knowledge about something ▪ *cancer/AIDS/drug research* ▪ *medical/scientific/scholarly research* ▪ *conducting research into/on a disease* ▪ *research findings* ▪ *a research scientist/project/laboratory/paper* ▪ *The company spends a lot of money on re-*

search and development. **2** : the activity of getting information about a subject ▪ *He did a lot of research before buying his car.* — **re·search·er** *n* [C] ▪ *medical researchers*

²**re·search** /rɪˈsɚtʃ/ *vb* [T] **1** : to study (something) carefully ▪ *researching the causes of the disease* **2** : to collect information about or for (something) ▪ *She spent a lot of time researching the story.*

re·sem·blance /rɪˈzɛmbləns/ *n* **1** [U, singular] : the state of looking or being like someone or something else ▪ *There is some/no resemblance between them.* ▪ *He bears/has a close/striking/strong resemblance to his father.* **2** [C] : something that makes one person or thing like another : SIMILARITY ▪ *I noticed some resemblances between them.*

re·sem·ble /rɪˈzɛmbəl/ *vb* **-sem·bled; -sem·bling** [T] : to look or be like (someone or something) ▪ *He strongly resembles his father.*

re·sent /rɪˈzɛnt/ *vb* [T] : to be angry or upset about (someone or something that you think is unfair) ▪ *I resent that remark.* ▪ *She resented being told what to do.* ▪ *He resented his boss.* — **re·sent·ful** /rɪˈzɛntfəl/ *adj* ▪ *feeling resentful toward someone* ▪ *a resentful child/glare* — **re·sent·ful·ly** *adv* — **re·sent·ment** /rɪˈzɛntmənt/ *n* [U] ▪ *feelings of resentment*

res·er·va·tion /ˌrɛzɚˈveɪʃən/ *n* **1** [C] : an arrangement to have a table, seat, room, etc., held for your use at a later time ▪ *making dinner/hotel reservations* **2** [C/U] : a feeling of doubt or uncertainty about something ▪ *She had reservations about leaving.* ▪ *My only reservation is the price.* ▪ *He supported her* **without reservation.** **3** [C] : an area of land in the U.S. that is kept separate as a place for Native Americans to live **4** [C] *US* : an area of land on which hunting animals is not allowed ▪ *a wildlife reservation*

¹**re·serve** /rɪˈzɚv/ *vb* **-served; -serv·ing** [T] **1** : to make arrangements to use or have a table, seat, room, etc., at a later time ▪ *We reserved a hotel room.* ▪ *A table is reserved for you.* **2** : to keep (something) for a special or future use ▪ *reserve a wine for a special occasion* ▪ *a tone of voice that she reserved for her students* [=that she only used for her students] ▪ *I will* **reserve judgment** [=will not make a judgment/decision] *until I know the full story.* **3** : to have or keep (something, such as a right) for possible future use ▪ *We reserve the right to edit submissions.*

²**reserve** *n* **1** [C] : a supply of something that is stored so that it can be used at a later time ▪ *oil reserves* ▪ *inner reserves of strength* **2** [C] : a military force that is additional to the regular forces and that is available if it is needed ▪ *the army reserve* ▪ *a member of the reserves* **3** [C] : RESERVATION **4** ▪ *a forest/wildlife/nature reserve* **4** [U] : the quality of a person who does not express feelings, opinions, etc., in an easy and open way ▪ *his natural reserve* **5** [C] : a player on a team who takes the place of a regular player who is injured or cannot play — **in reserve** : kept for future or special

use • *money kept in reserve — **without reserve*** : in a free and complete way • *They trusted him without reserve.*

re·served /rɪˈzɚvd/ *adj* **1** : not openly expressing feelings or opinions • *a very reserved young woman* **2** : kept for use only by a particular person or group • *a reserved parking space*

re·serv·ist /rɪˈzɚvɪst/ *n* [*C*] : a member of a military reserve • *an army reservist*

res·er·voir /ˈrɛzəˌvwɑɚ/ *n* [*C*] **1** : a usually artificial lake that is used to store a large supply of water **2** : a place (such as a part of a machine) where a liquid is stored • *the engine's oil reservoir* **3** : an extra supply of something • *She has endless reservoirs of energy.*

re·set /rɪˈsɛt/ *vb* **-set; -set·ting** [*T*] **1** : to set (something) again: such as **a** : to move (something) back to an original place or position • *The machine reset the bowling pins.* **b** : to put (a broken bone) back in the correct position for healing • *reset a broken leg* **c** : to put (a gem) into a new piece of jewelry • *reset a diamond* **d** : to change (something) so that it shows a different time or can be used again • *reset a watch/trap*

re·set·tle /rɪˈsɛtl̩/ *vb* **-set·tled; -set·tling** **1** [*T/I*] : to begin to live in a new area after leaving an old one • *He resettled (his family) out west.* **2** [*T*] : to begin to use (an area) again as a place to live • *The area was resettled in the 1800s.* — **re·set·tle·ment** /rɪˈsɛtl̩mənt/ *n* [*U*]

re·shape /rɪˈʃeɪp/ *vb* **-shaped; -shap·ing** [*T*] : to give a new form or shape to (something) • *These changes will reshape the future.*

re·shuf·fle /rɪˈʃʌfəl/ *vb* **-shuf·fled; -shuf·fling** [*T*] **1** : to shuffle (cards) again • *The dealer reshuffled the cards.* **2** : to change the way the parts of (something) are arranged or organized • *The President reshuffled his Cabinet/schedule.* — **reshuffle** *n* [*C*]

re·side /rɪˈzaɪd/ *vb* **-sid·ed; -sid·ing** [*I*] *formal* **1** : to live in a particular place • *He resides in St. Louis.* **2** : to exist or be present • *The power of veto resides with the President.* [=the President has the power of veto]

res·i·dence /ˈrɛzədəns/ *n, formal* **1** [*U*] : the state of living in a particular place • *He ended his residence here.* • *Birds have* **taken up residence** [=made a home] *in the barn.* • (*US*) *a* **residence hall** = (*Brit*) *a* **hall of residence** [=a place where students live at a college or university] **2** [*C*] : the place where someone lives • *a two-story residence* • *the prime minister's residence* **3** [*U*] : legal permission to live in a country • *They were granted/denied residence.* — **in residence** **1** : living in a particular place at a particular time • *The Queen is not in residence.* **2** : having an official position as a writer, artist, etc., who has been chosen to live and work at a college or other institution for a period of time • *the artist in residence*

res·i·den·cy /ˈrɛzədənsi/ *n, pl* **-cies** *formal* **1 a** [*U*] : the state or fact of living in a place • *proof of residency* [=residence] **b** [*singular*] : a period of time when

someone lives in a place • *a four-year residency* **2** [*C*] : legal permission to live in a place • *He was granted/denied residency.* **3** [*C/U*] *chiefly US* : a period when a doctor receives advanced training at a hospital in order to become a specialist in a particular field of medicine • *She completed her residency in pediatrics.*

¹**res·i·dent** /ˈrɛzədənt/ *n* [*C*] **1** : someone who lives in a particular place • *She is a resident of New York.* • *apartment residents* **2** *US* : a doctor who is training at a hospital to become a specialist in a particular field of medicine • *a first-year resident*

²**resident** *adj* **1** : living in a particular place usually for a long period of time • *the city's resident voters* **2** *always before a noun* : working regularly at a particular place • *the magazine's resident critic*

res·i·den·tial /ˌrɛzəˈdɛnʃəl/ *adj* **1** : containing mostly homes • *a residential area/street/neighborhood* **2** : used as a place to live • *residential property* **3** : of or relating to the places where people live • *residential insurance policies* **4** : providing students a place to live • *residential colleges* **5** : relating to a medical facility that requires patients to stay while they receive medical care • *residential drug treatment* • *a residential treatment center*

re·sid·u·al /rɪˈzɪdʒəwəl/ *adj, formal* : remaining after a process has been completed or something has been removed • *residual effects*

res·i·due /ˈrɛzəˌduː, *Brit* ˈrɛzəˌdjuː/ *n* [*C/U*] : a usually small amount of something that remains after a process has been completed or a thing has been removed • *The grill was covered in a greasy residue.*

re·sign /rɪˈzaɪn/ *vb* [*T/I*] : to give up (a job or position) in a formal or official way • *He was forced to resign (his position).* • *She resigned from her job.* — **resign yourself** : to make yourself accept something that is bad or that cannot be changed • *We resigned ourselves to our fate.*

res·ig·na·tion /ˌrɛzɪgˈneɪʃən/ *n* **1** [*C/U*] : an act of giving up a job or position in a formal or official way • *They accepted her resignation.* • *a letter of resignation* **2** [*U*] : the feeling that something unpleasant is going to happen and cannot be changed • *We accepted the news with resignation.* • *a sigh of resignation*

re·signed /rɪˈzaɪnd/ *adj, always before a noun* : feeling or showing acceptance that something unpleasant will happen or will not change • *a resigned sigh* • *She was resigned to her fate.* • *I'm resigned to having to work.* • *He was* **resigned to the fact** *that she wasn't coming.* — **re·sign·ed·ly** /rɪˈzaɪnədli/ *adv* • *She sighed resignedly.*

re·sil·ience /rɪˈzɪljəns/ *n* [*U*] **1** : the ability to become strong, healthy, or successful again after something bad happens • *They showed great courage and resilience.* **2** : the ability of something to return to its original shape after it has been pulled, stretched, etc. • *the resilience of rubber* — **re·sil·ient** /rɪˈzɪljənt/

adj ▪ *resilient young people* ▪ *a resilient material*

re·sil·ien·cy /rɪˈzɪljənsi/ *n* [U] : RESIL·IENCE

res·in /ˈrɛzn/ *n* [C/U] : a yellow or brown sticky substance that comes from some trees and that is used to make various products; *also* : a similar artificial substance that is used to make plastics —
res·in·ous /ˈrɛznəs/ *adj* ▪ *a resinous substance*

re·sist /rɪˈzɪst/ *vb* 1 [T] : to fight to stop or prevent (something) ▪ *He resisted arrest.* ▪ *They resisted the tax increase.* 2 [T] : to remain strong against the force or effect of (something) ▪ *These windows can resist high winds.* ▪ *resist infection* 3 [T/I] : to prevent yourself from doing something that you want to do ▪ *I couldn't resist the urge/temptation.* ▪ *The offer was hard to resist.* — **re·sist·er** /rɪˈzɪstɚ/ *n* [C] ▪ *military draft resisters*

re·sis·tance /rɪˈzɪstəns/ *n* 1 [U, singular] : refusal to accept something new or different ▪ *There was a lot of resistance to the plan.* ▪ *She has shown a stubborn resistance to change.* 2 [U] : effort made to stop or to fight against someone or something ▪ *He offered no resistance when he was arrested.* ▪ *The troops met heavy/stiff resistance.* 3 [U, singular] : the ability to prevent something from having an effect ▪ *resistance to disease* ▪ *The patient could develop a resistance to the drug.* 4 [U] : a force that slows down a moving object (such as an airplane) by going against the direction in which the object is moving ▪ *reducing wind resistance* 5 *or* **Resistance** [singular] : a secret organization that fights against enemy forces who have gained control of a region, country, etc. ▪ *the French Resistance* 6 [U] technical : the ability of a substance to prevent electricity from passing through it — **take/follow the path/line of least resistance** : to choose the easiest way to do something instead of trying to choose the best way

re·sis·tant /rɪˈzɪstənt/ *adj* 1 : opposed to something : wanting to prevent something from happening ▪ *People are often resistant to change.* 2 : not affected or harmed by something ▪ *These plants are resistant to cold temperatures.* ▪ *a water-resistant watch*

re·sis·tor /rɪˈzɪstɚ/ *n* [C] technical : a device that is used to control the flow of electricity in an electric circuit

re·sit /ˈriːsɪt/ *vb* **re·sat** /ˈriːsæt/; **re·sit·ting** [T] *Brit* : to take (an examination) again — **re·sit** /ˈriːˌsɪt/ *n* [C]

res·o·lute /ˈrɛzəˌluːt/ *adj* : very determined ▪ *a resolute competitor/manner* —
res·o·lute·ly *adv* ▪ *He is resolutely opposed to the bill.*

res·o·lu·tion /ˌrɛzəˈluːʃən/ *n* 1 a [U] : the act of finding an answer or solution to a conflict, problem, etc. ▪ *conflict resolution* b [C] : an answer or solution to something ▪ *We found a resolution to the dispute.* 2 [C/U] : the ability of a device to show an image clearly ▪ *computer screens with high resolution(s)* 3 [C] : a promise to yourself that you will do

something that you should do ▪ *I made a resolution to lose weight.* ▪ *a New Year's resolution* 4 [U] : the quality of being very determined to do something : DETERMINATION ▪ *his courage and resolution* 5 [C] : a formal statement that expresses the feelings, wishes, or decision of a group ▪ *The assembly passed a resolution.* 6 [U] : the point in a story at which the main conflict is solved or ended ▪ *the resolution of the plot*

¹**re·solve** /rɪˈzɑːlv/ *vb* **-solved**; **-solv·ing** 1 [T] : to settle or solve (something) ▪ *resolve a conflict* ▪ *The issue was never resolved.* 2 [T] : to make a definite and serious decision to do something ▪ *She resolved to quit smoking.* 3 [T] : to make a formal decision about something usually by a vote ▪ *The committee resolved to override the veto.* 4 [T/I] formal : to gradually change *into* separate parts or a different form ▪ *The mixture was resolved into two parts.* ▪ *The image resolved into a person's face.*

²**resolve** *n* [U] : a strong determination to do something ▪ *Nothing can weaken my resolve.*

resolved *adj* : feeling strong determination to do something ▪ *I was resolved to find out the truth.*

res·o·nant /ˈrɛzənənt/ *adj* 1 : producing a loud, clear, deep sound ▪ *a resonant voice* 2 : strongly affecting someone especially with a particular quality ▪ *His words were resonant with meaning.* —
res·o·nance /ˈrɛzənəns/ *n* [U] — **res·o·nant·ly** *adv*

res·o·nate /ˈrɛzəˌneɪt/ *vb* **-nat·ed**; **-nat·ing** [I] 1 : to continue to produce a loud, clear, deep sound for a long time ▪ *The siren resonated throughout the city.* 2 : to affect or appeal to someone in a personal or emotional way ▪ *Her speech resonated with voters.*

¹**re·sort** /rɪˈzoɚt/ *n* 1 [C] : a place where people go for vacations ▪ *a ski/beach/golf resort* ▪ *a resort hotel* 2 [C] : something that you choose for help ▪ *We'll do that only* **as a last/final resort**. = (Brit) *We'll do that only* **in the last resort.** [=if nothing else works] 3 [U] : the act of doing or using something especially because no other choices are possible ▪ *resolving conflicts* **without resort to force**

²**resort** *vb* — **resort to** [phrasal vb] : to do or use (something) especially because no other choices are possible ▪ *They resolved the crisis without resorting to violence.* ▪ *He had to resort to borrowing money.*

re·sound /rɪˈzaʊnd/ *vb* [I] 1 : to become filled with sound ▪ *The hall resounded with cheers.* 2 : to make a loud, deep sound ▪ *The organ resounded throughout the church.*

re·sound·ing /rɪˈzaʊndɪŋ/ *adj* 1 : producing a loud, deep sound that lasts for a long time ▪ *a resounding crash* 2 : leaving no doubt : very definite ▪ *a resounding success/victory* ▪ *She answered with a resounding no.* — **re·sound·ing·ly** *adv*

re·source /ˈriːˌsoɚs, Brit rɪˈzɔːs/ *n* 1 [C] : something that a country has and can use to increase its wealth ▪ *coal, oil, and other* **natural resources** 2 [plural] : a supply of something (such as money) that someone has and can use when it is needed • *their financial resources* **3** [C] : a place or thing that provides something useful • *The library/Internet is a useful resource.* **4 a** [C] : an ability or quality that allows you to do the things that are necessary • *mental/physical resources* • *She has the inner resources to cope.* **b** [U] *formal* : an ability to deal with and find solutions for problems • *a worker of tremendous resource*

re·source·ful /rɪˈsoɚsfəl, Brit rɪˈzɔːsfəl/ *adj* : able to deal well with new or difficult situations and to find solutions to problems • *a resourceful leader* — **re·source·ful·ly** *adv* — **re·source·ful·ness** *n* [U]

¹**re·spect** /rɪˈspɛkt/ *n* **1** [U, *singular*] : a feeling of admiring someone or something that is good, important, etc. • *He earned/gained/won their respect.* • *I have a lot of respect for him.* • **With all (due) respect**, *I must disagree.* [=I respect your opinion but I disagree with it] **2** [C/U] : a feeling or understanding that someone or something is important, serious, etc., and should be treated appropriately • *We were treated with respect.* • *She showed no respect for my feelings.* • *He has a healthy respect for power tools.* [=he uses the tools carefully] **3** [C] : a particular way of thinking about or looking at something • *The show was perfect in all respects.* • *Your theory makes sense in one respect.* **4** [*plural*] : a polite greeting or expression of kind feelings • *Please give/send my respects to your parents.* • *I paid my respects* [=offered my condolences] *to his family.* • *We went to his funeral to pay our last/final respects.* — **with respect to** *also* **in respect to** *or chiefly Brit* **in respect of** *formal* : about or concerning (something or someone) • *There is a question with respect to your earlier comments.*

²**respect** *vb* [T] **1** : to regard (someone or something) as being worthy of admiration because of good qualities • *We respect him for his honesty.* • *I respect what she has accomplished.* **2** : to act in a way which shows that you are aware of (someone's rights, wishes, etc.) • *respect someone's feelings/property* • *Please respect my privacy.* **3 a** : to treat or deal with (something good or valuable) in a proper way • *respect the environment* **b** : do what is required by (a law, rule, etc.) • *respect the speed limit* — **re·spect·er** /rɪˈspɛktɚ/ *n* [C]

re·spect·able /rɪˈspɛktəbəl/ *adj* **1** : decent or correct in character, behavior, or appearance • *respectable people* • *wearing respectable clothes* **2** : fairly good • *a respectable salary* — **re·spect·abil·i·ty** /rɪˌspɛktəˈbɪləti/ *n* [U] — **re·spect·ably** /rɪˈspɛktəbli/ *adv*

re·spect·ed /rɪˈspɛktəd/ *adj* : admired by many people • *She is a highly respected professor.*

re·spect·ful /rɪˈspɛktfəl/ *adj* : showing or having respect • *a respectful manner* • *Be respectful of your elders.* — **re·spect·ful·ly** /rɪˈspɛktfəli/ *adv*

re·spect·ing /rɪˈspɛktɪŋ/ *prep, formal* : about or relating to (something) • *We have no information respecting his whereabouts.*

re·spec·tive /rɪˈspɛktɪv/ *adj* : belonging or relating to each one of the people or things that have been mentioned • *They are all successful in their respective fields.* — **re·spec·tive·ly** /rɪˈspɛktɪvli/ *adv* • *The boy and girl are 12 and 13 years old, respectively.* [=the boy is 12 and the girl is 13]

res·pi·ra·tion /ˌrɛspəˈreɪʃən/ *n* [U] *medical* : the act or process of breathing • *The doctor checked his heartbeat and respiration.* — see also ARTIFICIAL RESPIRATION

res·pi·ra·tor /ˈrɛspəˌreɪtɚ/ *n* [C] **1** : a device that you wear over your mouth and nose so that you can breathe when there is a lot of dust, smoke, etc., in the air **2** *medical* : a device that helps people to breathe when they are not able to breathe naturally

re·spi·ra·to·ry /ˈrɛspərəˌtori, Brit rɪˈspɪrətri/ *adj, medical* : of or relating to breathing or the organs of the body that are used in breathing • *respiratory diseases/infections* • *the respiratory system*

re·spite /ˈrɛspət, Brit ˈrɛˌspaɪt/ *n* [C/U] : a short period of time when you are able to stop doing something that is unpleasant or when something unpleasant stops or is delayed • *a temporary respite.* • *The bad weather continued without respite.*

re·splen·dent /rɪˈsplɛndənt/ *adj, literary* : very bright and attractive • *resplendent beauty/colors* • *She was resplendent in green satin.*

re·spond /rɪˈspɑːnd/ *vb* **1** [T/I] : to say or write something as an answer to a question or request : REPLY • *He didn't respond to my question/letter/request.* • *She responded that she wasn't ready.* **2** [I] : to do something as a reaction to something • *respond to a call for help* • *She responded to their decision by threatening to quit.* • *He doesn't respond well to criticism.* **3** [I] : to have a good or desired reaction to something • *The patient is responding to the treatment.*

re·spon·dent /rɪˈspɑːndənt/ *n* [C] : a person who gives a response or answer to a question that is asked especially as part of a survey • *A majority of respondents said they disagreed with the plan.*

re·sponse /rɪˈspɑːns/ *n* [C/U] **1** : something that is said or written as a reply to something • *He got a response to his letter.* • *I am writing in response to your letter.* **2** : something that is done as a reaction to something else • *Her response to their decision was to quit her job.* • *The patient suffered an adverse response to the drug.*

re·spon·si·bil·i·ty /rɪˌspɑːnsəˈbɪləti/ *n, pl* **-ties** **1** [U] : the state of being the person who caused something to happen • *She accepted/denied responsibility for the accident.* **2 a** [C/U] : a duty or task that you are required or expected to do • *Mowing the lawn is your responsibility.* • *her family/work responsibilities* • *a new job with more responsibility* **b** [C] : something that you should do because it is morally right, legally required, etc. ▪ *We have a responsibility to protect the environment.* **3** [U] : the state of having the job or duty of dealing with and taking care of something or someone ▪ *The principal has responsibility for 450 students.* **4** [U] : the quality of a person who can be trusted to do what is expected, required, etc. ▪ *She lacks responsibility.* ▪ *developing a **sense of responsibility**

re·spon·si·ble /rɪ'spɑːnsəbəl/ *adj* **1** — used to describe the person or thing that causes something to happen ▪ *the person responsible for the vandalism/accident* ▪ *She's responsible for the improvements.* ▪ *He holds me responsible* [=blames me] *for the error.* **2** : having the job or duty of dealing with or taking care of something or someone ▪ *You are responsible for mowing the lawn.* ▪ *Parents are responsible for their own children.* **3** : able to be trusted to do what is right or to do the things that are expected or required ▪ *She is a very responsible worker.* **4** : involving important duties, decisions, etc., that you are trusted to do ▪ *She got a more responsible position.* **5** : working under the direction and authority of a particular person ▪ *She is directly responsible to the company president.* — **re·spon·si·bly** /rɪ'spɑːnsəbli/ *adv* ▪ *acting responsibly*

re·spon·sive /rɪ'spɑːnsɪv/ *adj* **1** : reacting in a desired or positive way ▪ *The patient was not responsive to the treatment.* ▪ *They weren't very responsive to my suggestion.* **2** : quick to react or respond ▪ *a car with responsive steering* — **re·spon·sive·ness** *n* [U]

¹rest /'rɛst/ *n* **1** [C/U] : a period of time in which you relax, sleep, or do nothing after you have been active or doing work ▪ *a day of rest* ▪ *get some rest* ▪ *I need a rest.* ▪ *a 10-minute rest period* **2** [U] : a state in which there is no motion ▪ *an object in a state of rest* **3** [C] : an object that is designed to support or hold something ▪ *a knife/spoon rest* **4** [C] : a period of silence between musical notes; *also* : a symbol in music that shows this — **at rest 1** : not moving ▪ *The object is at rest.* [=motionless] **2** : no longer living : DEAD ▪ *She is at rest now.* **3** : in a relaxed and comfortable state ▪ *You can set/put your mind at rest.* [=stop worrying] — **come to rest** : to stop moving ▪ *The ball came to rest against the curb.* ▪ *Her eyes came to rest on the letter.* — **give it a rest** *informal* — used to tell someone to stop talking about something ▪ *Oh, give it a rest!* — **lay (someone) to rest** : to bury (someone who has died) ▪ *She was laid to rest in the church's graveyard.* — **lay/put to rest (something) or lay/put (something) to rest** : to make someone stop thinking about or believing (something) by showing it is not true ▪ *I want to lay/put any doubts to rest.* — **the rest** : the part that is left when other people or things are gone, used, etc. ▪ *You bring these in, and I'll bring the rest.* ▪ *Thanks for your help. I can handle the rest.* ▪ *Linda, Joan, Donna, and the rest* ▪

the rest of his life/money ▪ *We finished the rest of the cake.*

²rest *vb* **1** [I] : to stop doing work or an activity ▪ *We will not rest until we discover the truth.* : to spend time relaxing, sleeping, etc., after you have been active or doing work ▪ *The workers were resting in the shade.* ▪ *The patient is resting comfortably.* **2** [T] **a** : to give rest to (someone) ▪ *May God rest his soul.* [=may God give her soul peace now that she has died] **b** : to stop using (something) so that it can become strong again ▪ *He rested his horse.* ▪ *rest your eyes* **3 a** [I] : to sit or lie on something ▪ *The spoon was resting in the cup.* ▪ *The house rests on its foundation.* ▪ (*figurative*) *The authority/blame rests with him.* **b** [T] : to place (something) on or against something else ▪ *She rested her bike against a tree.* ▪ *He rested his chin in his hands.* **4** [I] : to lie in a grave after death ▪ *May she rest in peace.* [=may she have peace in her death] **5** [T/I] : to stop presenting evidence in a legal case ▪ *The defense rests (its case), Your Honor.* — **let (something) rest** : to stop mentioning or talking about (something) ▪ *You just won't let this rest, will you?* — **rest easy** : to not worry about something ▪ *I can rest easy knowing that he is in charge.* — **rest on/upon** [*phrasal vb*] **1 a** : to depend on or rely on (someone or something) ▪ *All our hopes rested on one man.* **b** : to stop moving and look at (someone or something) ▪ *His eyes/gaze rested on the letter.* **2** : to be based on (something) ▪ *His theory rested upon two pieces of evidence.* — **rest with** [*phrasal vb*] : to be the responsibility of (someone or something) ▪ *The final decision rests with you.*

rest area *n* [C] *US* : an area next to a highway where people can stop to rest, use the bathroom, get food, etc.

re·start /ri'stɑːrt/ *vb* **1** [T/I] : to make (something) start again after it has stopped ▪ *Install the update, then restart (your computer).* **2** [I] : to start again after stopping ▪ *The tractor won't restart.* — **restart** *n* [C] ▪ *a computer restart*

re·state /ri'steɪt/ *vb* **-stat·ed; -stat·ing** [T] : to say (something) again or in a different way ▪ *restate an argument* — **re·state·ment** /ri'steɪtmənt/ *n* [C/U]

res·tau·rant /'rɛstərɑːnt/ *n* [C] : a place where you can buy and eat a meal ▪ *a Mexican/Italian/Chinese restaurant*

res·tau·ra·teur /ˌrɛstərə'tɚ/ *also* **res·tau·ran·teur** /ˌrɛstərɑːn'tɚ/ *n* [C] : a person who owns or manages a restaurant

rest·ed /'rɛstəd/ *adj* : having had enough rest or sleep ▪ *They were (well) rested after a long vacation.*

rest·ful /'rɛstfəl/ *adj* : peaceful and quiet in a way that makes you relax ▪ *It's restful here.* ▪ *a restful weekend* — **rest·ful·ly** *adv*

rest home *n* [C] : NURSING HOME

resting place *n* [C] **1** : a place where you can stop and rest **2** : a place where someone is buried ▪ *This is her final/last resting place.*

res·ti·tu·tion /ˌrɛstə'tuːʃən, *Brit* ˌrɛstə-

'tju:ʃən/ n [U] formal 1 : the act of returning something that was lost or stolen to its owner • *the restitution of her stolen property* 2 : payment that is made to someone for damage, trouble, etc. • *He was ordered to make restitution.*

res·tive /'rɛstɪv/ adj, formal : feeling bored or impatient while waiting for something to happen or change • *a restive audience*

rest·less /'rɛstləs/ adj 1 : feeling nervous or bored and tending to move a lot • *restless children* • *The audience was becoming restless.* 2 : unhappy about a situation and wanting change • *He started to feel restless in his job.* 3 : having little or no rest or sleep • *a restless night* — **rest·less·ly** adv — **rest·less·ness** n [U]

re·stock /ri'stɑːk/ vb [T] : to provide a new supply of something to replace what has been used, sold, taken, etc. • *We restocked the shelves/merchandise.*

res·to·ra·tion /ˌrɛstə'reɪʃən/ n 1 [C/U] : the act or process of returning something to its original condition • *The building is undergoing restoration.* • *a careful restoration* 2 [C/U] somewhat formal : the act of bringing back something that existed before • *the restoration of peace* 3 [C/U] somewhat formal : the act of returning something that was stolen or taken • *a restoration of stolen property* 4 **Restoration** : the period in 17th-century English history when Charles II was king after a long period of no king or queen on the throne • *a Restoration play* • *during the Restoration*

re·stor·a·tive /rɪ'storətɪv/ adj, formal : having the ability to make a person feel strong or healthy again • *the restorative powers of rest* — **restorative** n [C] • *Sleep is a powerful restorative.*

re·store /rɪ'stoɚ/ vb -**stored**; -**stor·ing** [T] 1 : to give back (someone or something that was lost or taken) • *The police restored the purse to its owner.* 2 : to put or bring (something) back into existence or use • *Surgery will restore his hearing.* • *The police restored law and order.* • *trying to restore confidence in the economy* 3 : to return (something) to an earlier or original condition by repairing it, cleaning it, etc. • *restore an old house/car* • *He restores old paintings.* 4 a : to bring (someone) back to an earlier and better condition • *Her care restored him to health.* b : to put (someone) back in a position • *They restored the king to the throne.* — **re·stor·er** n [C] • *a restorer of antiques*

re·strain /rɪ'streɪn/ vb [T] 1 : to prevent (a person or animal) from doing something • *I restrained myself from having more cake.* 2 : to prevent (a person or animal) from moving by using physical force • *He was restrained by police.* 3 : to keep (something) under control • *He could barely restrain his anger.* • *restrain costs*

re·strained /rɪ'streɪnd/ adj 1 : showing careful self-control • *her restrained behavior* • *a restrained smile* 2 : not too colorful or fancy • *restrained colors*

restraining order n [C] US, law : a legal order saying that someone is not allowed to go near a particular person

re·straint /rɪ'streɪnt/ n 1 [C] somewhat formal : a way of limiting, controlling, or stopping something • *The government placed/put/imposed restraints on imports.* 2 [C] formal : a device that limits a person's movement • *a child safety restraint* • *The prisoner was placed in restraints.* 3 [U] : control over your emotions or behavior • *his lack of restraint* • *You should exercise restraint.* 4 [U] formal : physical force that prevents someone from moving • *He was placed under restraint.*

re·strict /rɪ'strɪkt/ vb [T] 1 : to limit the amount or range of (something) • *Her eye problem restricts her reading.* • *The law restricts smoking in public.* • *Visits are restricted to 30 minutes.* • *The damage was restricted to one small area.* 2 : to prevent (someone) from doing something • *They tried to restrict her from speaking out.* 3 : to allow (someone) to only have or do a particular thing • *The doctor restricted her to a low-fat diet.* • *He restricts himself to one cup of coffee a day.*

re·strict·ed /rɪ'strɪktəd/ adj 1 : having a set limit • *a restricted number of participants* 2 : having definite rules about what or who is allowed and not allowed • *a very restricted diet* 3 : allowing use or entry by only certain people • *a restricted area* 4 : kept secret from all but a few people : CLASSIFIED • *a restricted document*

re·stric·tion /rɪ'strɪkʃən/ n 1 [C] : a law or rule that limits or controls something • *building/travel restrictions* • *They placed/imposed restrictions on smoking.* 2 [U] : the act of limiting or controlling something • *illegal restriction of free speech*

re·stric·tive /rɪ'strɪktɪv/ adj 1 : limiting or controlling someone or something • *restrictive laws/regulations* • *a very restrictive diet* 2 grammar : giving information about a person or thing that is needed to understand which person or thing is meant • *In the sentence "The book that you ordered is out of print," "that you ordered" is a restrictive clause.*

rest·room /'rɛst,ru:m/ n [C] US : a room in a public place with a sink and toilet : BATHROOM • *a public restroom*

re·struc·ture /ri'strʌktʃɚ/ vb -**tured**; -**tur·ing** [T] : to change the basic organization or structure of (something) • *restructure a sentence* • *The college is restructuring its Humanities Department.* — **restructuring** n [C/U]

rest stop n [C] US : REST AREA

¹re·sult /rɪ'zʌlt/ n 1 [C/U] : something that is caused by something else that happened or was done before • *The book is the result of years of hard work.* • *the end/final result of his work* • *He died as a result of his injuries.* • *The market crashed with the result that many investors lost millions.* 2 [C] : the final score or a description of who won and lost in a game, election, etc. • *waiting for election results* 3 [C] Brit : the grade received on a test or examination — usually plural • *I got my* *exam results.* **4** [*C*] : information that you get from a scientific or medical test • *my blood test result* **5** [*plural*] : something you want that is achieved successfully • *This method gets results.* [=is effective and successful]

²**result** *vb* [*I*] : to be caused by something else • *The fire resulted from an explosion.* — **result in** [*phrasal vb*] : to cause (something) to happen • *The disease resulted in his death.* : to produce (something) as a result • *The trial resulted in an acquittal.* — **re·sul·tant** /rɪˈzʌltn̩t/ *adj, always before a noun, formal* • *the increase in sales and the resultant increase in profit* — **re·sult·ing** *adj, always before a noun* • *the accident and his resulting death*

re·sume /rɪˈzuːm, Brit rɪˈzjuːm/ *vb* **-sumed; -sum·ing** *formal* **1** [*T/I*] : to begin again after stopping • *The game resumed after the rain stopped.* • *resume work/negotiations* **2** [*T*] : to go back to (something) • *She resumed her position at the company.* — **re·sump·tion** /rɪˈzʌmpʃən/ *n* [*U, singular*] *formal* • *waiting for the resumption of the game*

ré·su·mé or **re·su·me** *also* **re·su·mé** /ˈrɛzəˌmeɪ, Brit ˈrɛzjuˌmeɪ/ *n* [*C*] **1** *US* **a** : a short document describing your education, work history, etc., that you give an employer when you are applying for a job • *Please submit your résumé.* **b** : a list of achievements • *His musical résumé includes several performances at Carnegie Hall.* **2** *formal* : SUMMARY

re·sur·face /riˈsɚfəs/ *vb* **-faced; -fac·ing** **1** [*I*] : to rise to the surface again after being underwater or underground • *The submarine resurfaced.* **2** [*I*] : to suddenly be found or appear again • *The stolen paintings have resurfaced.* **3** [*T*] : to put a new surface on (something) • *resurface a table/road*

re·sur·gence /rɪˈsɚdʒəns/ *n* [*U, singular*] : a growth or increase that occurs after a period without growth or increase • *a resurgence of interest/popularity* — **re·sur·gent** /rɪˈsɚdʒənt/ *adj, formal* • *a resurgent market/politician*

res·ur·rect /ˌrɛzəˈrɛkt/ *vb* [*T*] **1** : to bring (a dead person) back to life • *resurrect the dead* **2** : to cause (something) to exist again, to be used again, etc. • *He is trying to resurrect his career.* • *an old theory that has been resurrected*

res·ur·rec·tion /ˌrɛzəˈrɛkʃən/ *n* **1** in Christianity **a the Resurrection** : the event told about in the Bible in which Jesus Christ returned to life after his death **b the resurrection** or **the Resurrection** : the event told about in the Bible in which dead people will be brought back to life before the day of final judgment **2** [*singular*] : the act of causing something to exist again, to be used again, etc. • *the resurrection of his career* • *a resurrection of an old theory*

re·sus·ci·tate /rɪˈsʌsəˌteɪt/ *vb* **-tat·ed; -tat·ing** [*T*] : to bring (someone) back to a conscious or active state again • *He stopped breathing but doctors were able to resuscitate him.* • *(figurative) He is trying to resuscitate his career.* — **re·sus·ci·ta-**

tion /rɪˌsʌsəˈteɪʃən/ *n* [*C/U*]

ret. or **Ret.** *abbr* retired • *General Smith, U.S. Army (Ret.)*

¹**retail** /ˈriːˌteɪl/ *n* [*U*] : the business of selling things directly to customers for their own use • *She has a job in retail.* — **retail** *adj* • *a retail establishment/shop/store* • *Is that price retail or wholesale?* — **retail** *adv* • *The product sells retail for about $100.*

²**re·tail** *vb* **1** [*T*] : to sell (something) to customers for their own use • *a store that retails clothing* **2** [*I*] : to be sold to the final customer for a specified price • *The item retails at $59.* **3** [*T*] *formal* : to tell (something) to one person after another • *retailing gossip* — **re·tail·er** /ˈriːˌteɪlɚ/ *n* [*C*] • *a leading retailer of women's clothing* — **re·tail·ing** /ˈriːˌteɪlɪŋ/ *n* [*U*] • *She works in retailing.*

re·tain /rɪˈteɪn/ *vb* [*T*] *formal* **1** : to continue to have or use (something) : KEEP • *retaining old customs* • *You will retain your rights as a citizen.* • *The TV show has retained its popularity.* **2** : to keep (someone) in a position, job, etc. • *Our goal is to retain good employees.* **3** : to pay for the work of (a person or business) • *retain an attorney* **4** : to keep (something) in your memory especially for a long period of time • *I didn't retain much of what I learned.* **5** : to continue to hold (heat, moisture, etc.) as time passes • *Mulch helps the soil to retain moisture.*

re·tain·er /rɪˈteɪnɚ/ *n* **1** [*C/U*] : an amount of money that you pay to someone (such as a lawyer) to make sure that you will have that person's services when you need them • *They have her on (a) retainer.* **2** [*C*] *US* : a device that you put in your mouth to keep your teeth in the correct position especially after you have had braces **3** [*C*] *old-fashioned* : a servant in a wealthy home • *a faithful old retainer*

re·take /riˈteɪk/ *vb* **-took** /-ˈtʊk/; **-tak·en** /-ˈteɪkən/; **-tak·ing** [*T*] : to take (something) again • *He retook the lead.* • *retake a test/photograph* — **re·take** /ˈriːˌteɪk/ *n* [*C*] • *The director called for a retake.*

re·tal·i·ate /rɪˈtæliˌeɪt/ *vb* **-at·ed; -at·ing** [*I*] : to do something bad to someone who has hurt you or treated you badly • *After the layoffs, the union threatened to retaliate by calling for a strike.* — **re·tal·i·a·tion** /rɪˌtæliˈeɪʃən/ *n* [*C/U*] • *the threat of retaliation* • *a quick retaliation* • *threatened a strike in retaliation for the layoffs* — **re·tal·i·a·to·ry** /rɪˈtæliˌtori/ *adj* • *retaliatory attacks*

re·tard /rɪˈtɑɚd/ *vb* [*T*] *formal* : to slow down the development or progress of (something) • *a chemical that retards the spread of fire*

re·tar·dant /rɪˈtɑɚdn̩t/ *adj, always before a noun, technical* : able to slow down the progress or development of something • *flame-retardant fabrics* [=fabrics that do not catch fire easily] — **retardant** *n* [*C*] • *a fire retardant*

re·tar·da·tion /ˌriːˌtɑɚˈdeɪʃən/ *n* [*U*] **1** *old-fashioned + sometimes offensive* : an unusual slowness of mental development

• *mental retardation* **2** *formal* : an act of slowing down the development or progress of something • *retardation of cell growth*

re·tard·ed /rɪˈtɑɚdəd/ *adj, old-fashioned + often offensive* : slow or limited in mental development

retch /ˈrɛtʃ/ *vb* [*I*] : to vomit or feel as if you are about to vomit • *The smell made him retch.*

re·tell /riˈtɛl/ *vb* -**told** /-ˈtoʊld/; -**tell·ing** [*T*] : to tell (a story) again especially in a different way • *a movie that retells the story of Ulysses* — **retelling** *n* [*C*] • *The story is a retelling of a Greek legend.*

re·ten·tion /rɪˈtɛnʃən/ *n* [*U*] *formal* : the act of keeping or retaining something or someone • *retention of profits* • *water retention* • *The fabric has good color retention.* [=its colors do not fade]

re·ten·tive /rɪˈtɛntɪv/ *adj, formal* : having the ability to remember things easily or for a long time • *a retentive mind/memory*

re·think /riˈθɪŋk/ *vb* -**thought** /-ˈθɑːt/; -**think·ing** [*T/I*] : to think carefully about (someone or something) again especially in order to change a choice or decision • *rethink a decision/policy*

ret·i·cent /ˈrɛtəsənt/ *adj* : not willing to tell people about things • *a quiet, reticent person* • *He's reticent about discussing it.* — **ret·i·cence** /ˈrɛtəsəns/ *n* [*U*]

ret·i·na /ˈrɛtənə/ *n* [*C*] : the tissue at the back of the eye that receives images and sends signals to the brain about what is seen — **ret·i·nal** /ˈrɛtənəl/ *adj*

ret·i·nue /ˈrɛtəˌnuː, *Brit* ˈrɛtəˌnjuː/ *n* [*C*] : a group of helpers, supporters, or followers • *the king and his retinue*

re·tire /rɪˈtajɚ/ *vb* -**tired**; -**tir·ing** **1 a** [*I*] : to stop a job or career because you have reached the age when you are not allowed to work anymore or do not need or want to work anymore • *She'll retire (from her job) next year.* **b** [*T*] : to cause (someone, such as a military officer) to end a job or career • *The general was retired with honors.* **2** [*I*] : to stop playing in a game, competition, etc., especially because of injury **3** [*T*] : to take (something) out of use, service, or production • *retiring an old battleship* **4** [*I*] *formal* : to move to a different place • *They retired to the parlor.* **5** [*I*] *literary* : to go to bed • *She retired for the night.* **6** [*T*] *baseball* : to cause (a batter) to be out • *The pitcher retired seven batters in a row.*

retired *adj* : having ended your working or professional career • *a retired teacher*

re·tir·ee /ˌrɪˌtajˈriː/ *n* [*C*] *US* : a person who has retired

re·tire·ment /rɪˈtajɚmənt/ *n* **1 a** [*C*] : the act of ending your working or professional career • *She took an early retirement.* **b** [*U*] : the state of being retired • *He came out of retirement to play baseball again.* • *a retirement community* [=a place for people who are retired] **2** [*U, singular*] : the period after you have permanently stopped your job or profession • *a long and happy retirement*

retiring *adj* **1** : quiet and shy • *a shy, retiring young woman* **2** — used to describe a person who will be retiring from

a job or profession soon • *a retiring senator*

re·tool /riˈtuːl/ *vb* **1** [*T*] : to change or replace the tools or machines in (a factory, workshop, etc.) • *The factory has been retooled.* **2** [*T/I*] *US* : to make changes to (something) in order to improve it • *The company is retooling its sales strategies.*

re·tort /rɪˈtoɚt/ *n* [*C*] : a quick and often angry reply • *a clever retort* — **retort** *vb* [*T*] • *"You have no proof," she retorted.*

re·touch /riˈtʌtʃ/ *vb* [*T*] : to make small changes to (something, such as a photograph) in order to improve the way it looks • *a retouched photograph*

re·trace /riˈtreɪs/ *vb* -**traced**; -**trac·ing** [*T*] : to go back along the same course, path, etc., that you or someone else has taken earlier • *retrace a path/route* • *carefully retracing our steps/footsteps*

re·tract /rɪˈtrækt/ *vb* **1** [*T/I*] : to pull (something) back into something larger that usually covers it • *A cat can retract its claws.* • *The plane's landing gear failed to retract.* **2** [*T*] : to say that something you said or wrote is not true or correct • *retract* [=*take back*] *a statement/story* **3** [*T*] *formal* : to take back (something, such as an offer or promise) • *retract a job offer* — **re·tract·able** /rɪˈtræktəbəl/ *adj* — **re·trac·tion** /rɪˈtrækʃən/ *n* [*C/U*]

re·train /riˈtreɪn/ *vb* **1** [*T*] : to teach (someone) new skills • *retraining (those who have lost their jobs)* **2** [*I*] : to learn new skills especially for a different job • *I'm retraining for a new job.*

re·tread /ˈriːˌtrɛd/ *n* [*C*] : an old tire whose surface has been given a new layer of rubber

¹**re·treat** /rɪˈtriːt/ *n* **1** [*C/U*] : movement by soldiers away from an enemy because the enemy is winning or has won a battle • *The forces are in (full) retreat.* • *an army's retreat (from the battlefield)* **2** [*C/U*] : movement away from a place or situation especially because it is dangerous, unpleasant, etc. • *her retreat from public life* • *He made/beat a hasty retreat.* [=he left quickly] **3** [*C*] : the act of changing your opinion or position on something because it is unpopular • *She was forced to make a retreat from her earlier position.* **4** [*C/U*] : the act or process of moving away • *the retreat of floodwaters* • *glaciers in retreat* **5 a** [*C*] : a place that is quiet and private • *a mountain retreat* **b** [*C/U*] : a trip to a place where you can quietly pray, think, study, etc. • *a corporate/spiritual retreat* • *going on retreat*

²**retreat** *vb* [*I*] **1** : to move back to get away from danger, attack, etc. • *The troops were forced to retreat.* **2** : to move or go away from a place or situation especially because it is dangerous, unpleasant, etc. • *He quickly retreated from the room.* **3** : to change your opinion or statement about something because it is unpopular • *She has retreated from her original position.* **4** : to move backward • *floodwaters retreating* **5** : to go to a place that is quiet and private • *retreat into the study*

re·tri·al /riˈtrajəl/ *n* [*C/U*] : a second trial

in a court of law in order to make a new judgment on a case that has been judged before

ret·ri·bu·tion /ˌrɛtrəˈbjuːʃən/ n [U] formal : punishment for doing something wrong • *divine retribution* [=punishment by God]

re·triev·al /rɪˈtriːvəl/ n [U] : the act or process of getting and bringing back something • *the retrieval of stolen goods* • *the storage and retrieval of data* — **beyond retrieval 1** : not able to be brought back • *The old data is now beyond retrieval.* **2** : not able to be corrected, cured, etc. • *The situation is beyond retrieval.*

re·trieve /rɪˈtriːv/ vb -**trieved**; -**triev·ing** [T] **1** : to get and bring (something) back from a place • *Police retrieved the stolen goods.* **2** : to find and get (information) from a computer or disk • *retrieving data/information* — **re·triev·able** /rɪˈtriːvəbəl/ adj

re·triev·er /rɪˈtriːvɚ/ n [C] : a dog that is used for retrieving birds or animals that have been shot by a hunter

ret·ro /ˈrɛtroʊ/ adj : looking like or relating to styles or fashions from the past • *retro styles/music*

ret·ro·ac·tive /ˌrɛtroʊˈæktɪv/ adj, formal : effective from a particular date in the past • *a retroactive pay raise* — **ret·ro·ac·tive·ly** adv • *The law was applied retroactively.*

ret·ro·spect /ˈrɛtrəˌspɛkt/ n — **in retrospect** : when thinking about the past or something that happened in the past • *In retrospect, I made the right decision.*

¹**ret·ro·spec·tive** /ˌrɛtrəˈspɛktɪv/ adj : of or relating to the past or something that happened in the past • *a retrospective analysis* • *a retrospective exhibit of Picasso's early works* — **ret·ro·spec·tive·ly** adv

²**retrospective** n [C] : an exhibition of work that an artist has done in the past

¹**re·turn** /rɪˈtɚn/ vb **1** [I] : to come or go to a place again : to come back or go back again • *We waited for you to return.* • *return from a trip* • *return to Paris* **2** [T] **a** : to bring, give, send, or take (something) to the place that it came from or the place where it should go • *return a book to the library* • *Fill out the application and return* [=send] *it to the address below.* **b** : to bring or send (something that you bought) to the place that it came from because it does not work or fit properly, because it is damaged, etc. • *I had to return the shirt and get a bigger size.* **3** [I] : to happen or exist again • *The pain returned.* • *Hope has returned.* [=people are hopeful again] **4** [T] : to respond to (something) in the same way • *He smiled at her, and she returned the smile.* • *return someone's phone calls* • *Thanks for the help. I'll be sure to return the favor.* [=I will help you when you need help] **5** [T] formal : to make an official report of (a decision or order) • *The jury returned a verdict of guilty.* **6** [T] tennis : to hit back (a ball that was hit to you) • *He returned her serve.* **7** [T] finance : to produce or earn (something,

such as a profit or loss) • *investments that return big profits* — **return to** [phrasal vb] **1** : to go to (a place where you work, study, etc.) again after being away for a time • *students returning to college* **2** : to start doing or using (something) again especially after a long time • *returning to work* [=starting to work again] **3** : to start an activity again that relates to (something) • *He returned to his book.* [=started reading his book again] **4** : to change back to (an earlier or original condition or state) • *His breathing returned to normal.* [=became normal again] — **re·turn·able** /rɪˈtɚnəbəl/ adj — **re·turn·er** /rɪˈtɚnɚ/ n [C]

²**return** n **1** [singular] : the act of coming or going back to the place you started from or to a place where you were before • *I'm looking forward to your return.* • *our return to/from Europe* • *Upon/on his return* [=less formally] *when he returned; when he came back], he found a note taped to the door.* **2** [singular] : the act of going back to an activity, job, situation, etc. • *a return to the old ways of farming* **3** [singular] **a** : the fact that something (such as a condition, feeling, or situation) happens again • *the return of peace/spring* **b** : the fact that someone or something changes to a condition or state that existed before • *a return to normal* • *a leader's return to power* **4** [singular] : the act of taking someone or something back to the proper place • *the return of stolen goods* **5** [C] : something that is brought or sent back to a store or business because it does not work or fit properly, is damaged, is not needed, etc. • *The store accepts returns with a receipt.* **6** [C/U] finance : the profit from an investment or business • *a stock with a high rate of return* • *He received a large return on his investment.* **7** [plural] : a report of the results of voting • *election returns* **8** [C] : a report that you send to the government about the money that you have earned and the taxes that you have paid in one year • *filing my (income) tax return* [=sending my tax return to the government] **9** [C] Brit : a ticket for a trip that takes you to a place and back to the place you started from : a round-trip ticket — **happy returns** old-fashioned • *They wished me (many) happy returns.* — **in return** : in payment or exchange • *She helped me and asked nothing in return.* • *lending money in return for a favor*

³**return** adj, always before a noun **1** : used in or taken for returning to a place • *a return flight/trip* **2** : happening or done for the second time • *a return visit*

re·turn·ee /rɪˌtɚˈniː/ n [C] : someone who returns to a country after being in another country in prison, in military service, etc.

re·uni·fy /riˈjuːnəˌfaɪ/ vb -**fies**; -**fied**; -**fy·ing** [T/I] : to make (something, such as a divided country) whole again • *Germany (was) reunified in 1990.* — **re·uni·fi·ca·tion** /riˌjuːnəfəˈkeɪʃən/ n [U]

re·union /riˈjuːnjən/ n [C] **1** : an act of

getting people together again after they have been apart ▪ *an emotional reunion between mother and son* 2 : an organized gathering of people who have not been together for a long time ▪ *a family reunion* [=a usually large gathering for family members] ▪ *(US) a high school reunion*

re·unite /ˌriːjuːˈnaɪt/ *vb* -unit·ed; -unit·ing 1 [*T*] : to bring (people or things) together again especially after they have been apart for a long time ▪ *The police reunited the woman with/and her son.* 2 [*I*] : to be together again after being apart for a long time ▪ *The band reunited for a special concert.*

re-up /riˈʌp/ *vb* -upped; -up·ping [*I*] *US, informal* : to officially agree to stay in the military, on a team, with a company, etc., for an additional period of time ▪ *He re-upped in the navy last year.*

re·use /riˈjuːz/ *vb* -used; -us·ing [*T*] : to use (something) again ▪ *reuse a bag/container* — re·us·able /riˈjuːzəbəl/ *adj* ▪ *reusable containers* — re·use /riˈjuːs/ *n* [*U*]

rev /ˈrɛv/ *vb* revved; rev·ving [*T*] : to cause (an engine) to run more quickly ▪ *revving (up) a car's engine* [=pressing the car's accelerator when the engine is on but the car is not in gear] — **rev up** [*phrasal vb*] *informal* 1 : to become more active ▪ *The campaign is revving up.* 2 **rev (someone or something) up** or **rev up (someone or something)** : to make (someone or something) more active or effective ▪ *trying to rev up the economy*

Rev. *(US)* or *Brit* Rev or *Brit* Revd *abbr* reverend

re·val·ue /riˈvælju/ *vb* -ued; -u·ing 1 [*T/I*] *finance* : to change the value of a country's money so that it is worth less or more when it is traded for another country's money 2 [*T*] : to make a new judgment about the value of (something, such as a house or an investment) ▪ *revalue residential properties* — re·val·u·a·tion /ˌriˌvæljəˈweɪʃən/ *n* [*C/U*]

re·vamp /riˈvæmp/ *vb* [*T*] : to make (something) better or like new again ▪ *revamping the design of a car* — **revamp** or **re·vamp·ing** /riˈvæmpɪŋ/ *n* [*C*] ▪ *a revamp of a car's design*

re·veal /riˈviːl/ *vb* [*T*] 1 a : to make (something) known ▪ *reveal a secret* ▪ *They revealed plans for a new building.* b : to show or prove that (someone or something) is a particular type of person or thing ▪ *Analysis reveals the substance to be mostly carbon.* 2 : to make (something that was hidden) able to be seen ▪ *A curtain was lifted to reveal the prize.*

re·veal·ing /riˈviːlɪŋ/ *adj* 1 : giving information about something that was not known before ▪ *Her comments about family are revealing.* 2 : showing parts of the body that are usually hidden from view ▪ *a revealing shirt* — re·veal·ing·ly *adv*

¹rev·el /ˈrɛvəl/ *vb*, *US* rev·eled or *Brit* rev·elled; *US* rev·el·ing or *Brit* rev·el·ling — **revel in** [*phrasal vb*] : to enjoy (something) very much ▪ *She reveled in her success.*

²revel *n* [*C*] *literary* : a noisy and wild celebration ▪ *holiday revels*

rev·e·la·tion /ˌrɛvəˈleɪʃən/ *n* 1 [*C*] : a usually secret or surprising fact that is made known ▪ *personal revelations* 2 [*C*] : an act of making something known ▪ *the revelation of her gambling problem* 3 [*singular*] : something that surprises you ▪ *Her talent was a revelation.* [=was completely unexpected] 4 [*C/U*] : a sign or message from God ▪ *laws made known by (a) divine revelation*

rev·el·er *(US)* or *Brit* rev·el·ler /ˈrɛvələ/ *n* [*C*] : a person who is celebrating with other people in usually a wild and noisy way

rev·el·ry /ˈrɛvəlri/ *n*, *pl* -ries [*C/U*] : a wild and noisy celebration ▪ *drunken revelry*

¹re·venge /rɪˈvɛndʒ/ *n* [*U*] : the act of doing something to hurt someone because that person did something that hurt you ▪ *seeking/wanting revenge against her enemies* ▪ *He got his revenge.* ▪ *He took (his) revenge on his enemies.* ▪ *attacks in revenge for the assassination of the king*

²revenge *vb* -venged; -veng·ing — **revenge yourself** *on formal* : to do something to hurt (someone who has hurt you) ▪ *She vowed to revenge herself on her father's killer.*

rev·e·nue /ˈrɛvəˌnuː, *Brit* ˈrɛvəˌnjuː/ *n* [*U*, *plural*] *finance* 1 : money that is made by or paid to a business or an organization ▪ *sources of revenue* ▪ *advertising and sales revenues* 2 : money that is collected for public use by a government through taxes ▪ *state and federal tax revenues*

re·ver·ber·ate /rɪˈvɚbəˌreɪt/ *vb* -at·ed; -at·ing [*I*] *somewhat formal* 1 : to continue in a series of quickly repeated sounds that bounce off a surface (such as a wall) ▪ *voices reverberating* [=echoing] *in the hall* 2 : to become filled with a sound ▪ *The room reverberated with laughter.*

re·ver·ber·a·tion /rɪˌvɚbəˈreɪʃən/ *n* 1 [*C/U*] *somewhat formal* : a sound that echoes ▪ *the reverberations of her voice* 2 [*C*] : an effect or result that is not wanted ▪ *economic/political reverberations*

re·vere /rɪˈviɚ/ *vb* -vered; -ver·ing [*T*] *formal* : to have great respect for (someone or something) ▪ *He was revered as a hero.* ▪ *Her poems are revered by other poets.*

rev·er·ence /ˈrɛvərəns/ *n* [*U*, *singular*] *formal* : honor or respect that is felt for or shown to (someone or something) ▪ *a (feeling of) reverence for tradition* — rev·er·ent /ˈrɛvərənt/ *adj* ▪ *reverent* [=deeply respectful] *worshippers* — rev·er·en·tial /ˌrɛvəˈrɛnʃəl/ *adj* ▪ *a reverential* [=*reverent*] *attitude* — rev·er·ent·ly *adv*

rev·er·end /ˈrɛvərənd/ *n* [*C*] : a priest or minister in the Christian church — often used as a title ▪ *(the) Reverend John Smith*

re·ver·sal /rɪˈvɚsəl/ *n* [*C/U*] : a change to an opposite state, condition, etc. ▪ *the reversal of a decision/position/policy* ◇ *Reversal often means a change to a worse state or condition.* ▪ *He suffered a financial reversal.* ▪ *a reversal of fortune*

¹re·verse /rɪˈvəs/ vb **-versed; -vers·ing**
1 [T] : to change (something) to an opposite state or condition • *The runners reversed direction.* • *efforts to reverse the decline in enrollment* **2** [T] : to cause (something, such as a process) to stop or return to an earlier state • *a medicine that may reverse the course of the disease* **3** [T] **a** : to change the order or position of (two things or a series) • *reversing roles* • *Let's reverse our usual order and start with Z.* **b** : to switch the positions of the top and bottom or the front and back of (something) • *reverse a piece of paper* **4** [T/I] *chiefly Brit* : to drive (a vehicle) backward • *Reverse* [=(US) back, back up] *(the car) into/out of the parking space.* — **reverse the charges** *or* **reverse the charge** *Brit* : to arrange to have the cost of a phone call paid by the person who is called — **re·vers·ible** /rɪˈvəsəbəl/ *adj*

²reverse *n* **1 the reverse** : something that is opposite to something else • *The river flows south to north, rather than the reverse.* [=north to south] • *You don't owe me any money. If anything, the reverse is true.* [=I owe you money] **2 the reverse** : the back side of a coin, document, etc. • *Please sign your name on the reverse.* **3** [U] : REVERSE GEAR • *Put the car* **in/into reverse.** • *(figurative) an economy stuck in reverse* [=continuing to get worse] **4** [C] *formal* : a change that makes something worse • *financial reverses* [=setbacks] — **in reverse 1 a** : in an order in which the last part is first and the first part is last • *a story told in reverse, from the main character's death to her birth* **b** : in a way that is opposite to what is normal or to what happened earlier • *American tourists are flocking to Europe in reverse of the situation ten years ago.* **2** : toward an opposite or worse state or condition • *Negotiations seem to be moving in reverse.* — **into reverse** : into an opposite state or condition • *The economy has gone into reverse.* [=has gotten worse]

³reverse *adj, always before a noun* **1** : opposite to what is usual or stated • *saying the alphabet in reverse order* **2** : opposite to the front • *the reverse* [=back] *side of the application*

reverse discrimination *n* [U] : the practice of making it more difficult for a certain type of person (such as a white man) to get a job, to go to a school, etc., because other people who were treated unfairly in the past are now being given an advantage

reverse gear *n* [C/U] : a gear that makes a motor move a vehicle in a backward direction • *Put the car* **in/into reverse gear.**

re·vert /rɪˈvət/ vb — **revert to** [*phrasal vb*] : to go back or return to (an earlier state, condition, situation, etc.) • *reverting (back) to old habits* — **re·ver·sion** /rɪˈvəʒən, *Brit* rɪˈvəːʃən/ *n* [C/U] • *(a) reversion to old habits*

¹re·view /rɪˈvjuː/ *n* **1** [C/U] : an act of carefully looking at or examining the quality or condition of something or someone • *a review of the evidence* • *The medical records were sent to the doctor for review.* • *The policy is* **under review.** [=is being reviewed] **2** [C/U] : a report that gives someone's opinion about the quality of a book, performance, product, etc. • *The movie got mixed reviews.* [=some critics liked it, while other critics did not] • **rave reviews** [=reviews that say something is excellent] **3** [C] : a class, a book, an article, etc., that studies or describes something (such as events from a particular time) • *a review of 19th-century American art* **4** [C/U] *US* : the act of studying information that was studied before • *I did a quick review of my notes before the test.*

²review *vb* **1 a** [T] : to look at or examine (something) carefully especially before making a decision or judgment • *reviewing results/applications* • *I need time to review the situation.* **b** [T/I] *US* : to study or look at (something) again • *She reviewed her notes for the speech.* • *Review your answers before handing in your test.* **c** [T] : to describe or show (a series of things or events from the past) • *The book reviewed her accomplishments.* **2** [T] : to report on or judge the quality of a book, show, product, etc. • *review a movie/book/play* — **re·view·er** /rɪˈvjuːwə/ *n* [C] • *a movie/book reviewer*

re·vile /rɪˈvajəl/ vb **-viled; -vil·ing** [T] *formal* : to speak about (someone or something) in a very critical or insulting way • *a policy reviled as racist*

re·vise /rɪˈvaɪz/ vb **-vised; -vis·ing** [T] : to make changes especially to correct or improve (something) • *revise an essay/estimate* • *We had to revise our plans.* **2** [T/I] *Brit* : to study (something) again • *revising* [=(US) reviewing] *for the exam*

re·vi·sion /rɪˈvɪʒən/ *n* **1** [C/U] : a change or a set of changes that corrects or improves something • *making revisions to a book* • *The essay needs revision.* **2** [C] : something (such as a piece of writing or a song) that has been corrected or changed • *Here is my revision of the essay.* **3** [U] *Brit* : study of information that was studied before

re·vis·it /riˈvɪzət/ vb [T] **1** : to go to (a place) again especially after a long period of time • *I revisited my old house.* **2** : to think about or look at (something) again • *an idea worth revisiting*

re·vi·tal·ize *also Brit* **re·vi·tal·ise** /riˈvaɪtəˌlaɪz/ vb **-ized; -iz·ing** [T] : to make (someone or something) active, healthy, or energetic again • *trying to revitalize a city* — **re·vi·tal·i·za·tion** *also Brit* **re·vi·tal·i·sa·tion** /riˌvaɪtələˈzeɪʃən, *Brit* riˌvaɪtəˌlaɪˈzeɪʃən/ *n* [U, singular]

re·viv·al /rɪˈvaɪvəl/ *n* **1** [C] : a period in which something becomes popular again after a long period of time • *Fashions from the 1970s are* **enjoying a revival.** **2** [C/U] : the growth of something or an increase in the activity of something after a long period of no growth or activity • *The city is showing signs of revival.* • *the recent* **revival of interest** *in mythology* **3** [C] : the showing of a play, a movie, etc., to the public usually many years after it was last shown • *staging a musical revival*

re·vive /rɪˈvaɪv/ vb -**vived**; -**viv·ing** **1 a** [T] : to make (someone or something) strong, healthy, or active again ▪ doctors trying to revive a patient [=to make an unconscious patient conscious again] ▪ revive someone's career ▪ revive the economy **b** [I] : to become strong, healthy, or active again ▪ Business is reviving. **2** [T] : to bring (something) back into use or popularity ▪ trying to revive an old custom **3** [T] : to arrange to have (an old play, opera, etc.) performed in front of an audience

re·voke /rɪˈvoʊk/ vb -**voked**; -**vok·ing** [T] formal : to officially cancel the power or effect of (something, such as a law, license, agreement, etc.) ▪ Their work permits were revoked. — **re·vo·ca·tion** /ˌrɛvəˈkeɪʃən/ n [C/U]

¹re·volt /rɪˈvoʊlt/ vb **1** [I] : to fight in a violent way against the rule of a leader or government ▪ They threatened to revolt (against the king). **2** [I] : to act in a way that shows that you do not accept the control or influence of someone or something ▪ teenagers revolting [=rebelling] against their parents **3** [T] : to cause (someone) to feel disgust or shock ▪ I was revolted by the smell/violence.

²revolt n [C/U] **1** : violent action against a ruler or government ▪ The people staged a revolt. = The people rose (up) in revolt. ▪ a revolt against the government **2** : something which shows that you will not accept something or will not agree to be controlled or influenced by someone or something ▪ a revolt by consumers over high prices ▪ His book is a revolt against conservative thinking.

re·volt·ing /rɪˈvoʊltɪŋ/ adj : extremely unpleasant or offensive ▪ a revolting [=disgusting] smell

rev·o·lu·tion /ˌrɛvəˈluːʃən/ n **1 a** [C/U] : the usually violent attempt by many people to end the rule of one government and start a new one ▪ the American/French Revolution **b** [C] : a sudden, extreme, or complete change in the way people live, work, etc. ▪ the computer revolution [=the changes created by the widespread use of computers] **2** technical **a** [C/U] : the action of moving around something in a path that is similar to a circle : ROTATION ▪ the revolution of the Earth around the Sun **b** [C] : a complete turn that is made by something around its center point or line ▪ This motor operates at a speed of 5,000 revolutions per minute.

¹rev·o·lu·tion·ary /ˌrɛvəˈluːʃəˌneri, Brit ˌrɛvəˈluːʃənri/ adj **1** always before a noun : relating to, involving, or supporting a political revolution ▪ a revolutionary war **2** : causing or relating to a great or complete change ▪ The invention was revolutionary.

²revolutionary n, pl -**aries** [C] : someone who leads, joins, or wants a revolution

rev·o·lu·tion·ize also Brit **rev·o·lu·tion·ise** /ˌrɛvəˈluːʃəˌnaɪz/ vb -**ized**; -**iz·ing** [T] : to change (something) very much or completely ▪ The invention of the airplane revolutionized travel.

re·volve /rɪˈvɑːlv/ vb -**volved**; -**volv·ing** [T/I] : to turn around a center point or line ▪ The Earth revolves on its axis. — **re·volve around** [phrasal vb] **1** : to move around (something) in a path that is similar to a circle ▪ The planets revolve around the sun. **2** : to have (someone or something) as a main subject or interest ▪ The discussion revolved around politics. ▪ Her world revolves around her work/son.

re·volv·er /rɪˈvɑːlvɚ/ n [C] : a small gun with a container for bullets that turns after the gun is fired and puts another bullet into position to be fired next

revolving door n [C] : a type of door that turns in its frame when it is used and allows people to go both in and out of a large building at the same time

re·vue /rɪˈvjuː/ n [C] : a show in a theater that includes funny songs, dances, short plays, etc., usually about recent events

re·vul·sion /rɪˈvʌlʃən/ n [U, singular] somewhat formal : a very strong feeling of dislike or disgust ▪ I felt revulsion at the thought. [=I was revolted by the thought]

revved up adj, informal : very excited ▪ a rousing song that got the crowd all revved up

¹re·ward /rɪˈwoɚd/ n [C/U] : money or another kind of payment that is given or received for something that has been done or that is offered for something that might be done ▪ A (cash) reward is being offered for the return of the lost dog. ▪ reaping the rewards of success [=getting all the good things that come with success] ▪ She got a puppy as a reward for doing well in school. = She got a puppy in reward for doing well in school.

²reward vb [T] : to give money or another kind of payment to (someone or something) for something good that has been done ▪ I rewarded myself with ice cream. ▪ employees rewarded for their work with cash bonuses

re·ward·ing /rɪˈwoɚdɪŋ/ adj **1** : giving you a good feeling that you have done something valuable, important, etc. ▪ a rewarding experience/career **2** : giving you money or profit ▪ financially rewarding work

re·wind /ˈriːˌwaɪnd/ n [U] : a function that causes a recording (such as an audiotape or a videotape) to go backwards ▪ Hit the rewind button. — **re·wind** /riˈwaɪnd/ vb -**wound** /-ˈwaʊnd/; -**wind·ing** [T] ▪ rewind a tape

re·wire /riˈwajɚ/ vb -**wired**; -**wir·ing** [T] : to put new electrical wires in (a building, machine, etc.) ▪ He rewired the entire house.

re·word /riˈwɚd/ vb [T] : to state (something) again using different and often simpler words ▪ reword a question

re·work /riˈwɚk/ vb [T] : to make changes to (something, such as a piece of writing or music) in order to improve it ▪ The design has been reworked.

re·write /riˈraɪt/ vb -**wrote** /-ˈroʊt/; -**writ·ten** /-ˈrɪtn̩/; -**writ·ing** [T] : to write (something) again especially in a different way in order to improve it or to include new information ▪ rewrite an essay ▪ (figurative) You can't rewrite history. [=you can't change the past] — **re·write**

/ˈriːˌraɪt/ *n* [*C*] • *a rewrite of the script*

rhap·so·dize *also Brit* **rhap·so·dise**
/ˈræpsəˌdaɪz/ *vb* -**dized; -diz·ing** [*I*] *for-mal* : to praise or describe something or someone with a lot of enthusiasm and emotion • *He rhapsodized about/over his favorite musician.*

rhap·so·dy /ˈræpsədi/ *n, pl* -**dies** [*C*] : a piece of music that is meant to express a lot of emotion and does not have a regu-lar form

rhet·o·ric /ˈrɛtərɪk/ *n* [*U*] *formal* **1** *often disapproving* : language that is intended to influence people and that may not be honest or reasonable • *a speech free of (empty) rhetoric* **2** : the art or skill of speaking or writing formally and effec-tively especially as a way to persuade or influence people • *a college course in rhet-oric*

rhe·tor·i·cal /rɪˈtɔrɪkəl/ *adj* **1** : of, relat-ing to, or concerned with the art of speaking or writing formally and effec-tively • *a rhetorical device/style* **2** *of a question* : asked in order to make a state-ment rather than to get an answer • *"Should we be leaving soon?" "Is that a rhetorical question?"* [=is that a question you're asking as a way to say that we should be leaving soon?] — **rhe·tor·i·cal·ly** /rɪˈtɔrɪkli/ *adv*

rheu·ma·tism /ˈruːməˌtɪzəm/ *n* [*U*] : a disease that causes stiffness and pain in the muscles and swelling and pain in the joints — **rheu·mat·ic** /ruˈmætɪk/ *adj*

rhine·stone /ˈraɪnˌstoʊn/ *n* [*C*] : a small stone that is made to look like a diamond and that is used in jewelry or for decora-tion

rhi·no /ˈraɪnoʊ/ *n, pl* **rhi·nos** *also* **rhino** [*C*] *somewhat informal* : RHINOCEROS

rhi·noc·er·os /raɪˈnɑːsərəs/ *n, pl* **rhi·noc·er·os·es** *also* **rhinoceros** [*C*] : a large, heavy animal of Africa and Asia that has thick skin and either one or two large horns on its nose

rho·do·den·dron /ˌroʊdəˈdɛndrən/ *n* [*C*] : an evergreen bush that has large, bright flowers

rhom·bus /ˈrɑːmbəs/ *n* [*C*] *geometry* : a shape with four sides that are equal in length and with four angles that are not always right angles

rhu·barb /ˈruːˌbɑːb/ *n* [*U*] : a plant with large green leaves and with thick pink or red stems that are cooked and used in pies, jams, etc. • *rhubarb pie*

rhumba *variant spelling of* RUMBA

¹**rhyme** /ˈraɪm/ *n* **1** [*C*] : one of two or more words or phrases that end in the same sounds • *using "moon" as a rhyme for "June"* **2** [*C*] : a poem or song whose lines end in rhymes • *children's rhymes* **3** [*U*] : the use of rhymes in a poem or song • *learning about meter and rhyme* — **rhyme or reason** : a good reason or ex-planation for something — used in nega-tive statements • *There seems to be no rhyme or reason to/for it.*

²**rhyme** *vb* **rhymed; rhym·ing** **1** [*I*] : to have or end with the same sounds • *"Bug" and "rug" rhyme.* = *"Bug" rhymes with "rug."* **2** [*I*] : to have lines that end with the same sounds • *poems that rhyme* **3**

[*T*] : to use (a rhyme) in a poem, song, etc. • *rhyming "moon" with "June"*

rhythm /ˈrɪðəm/ *n* **1** [*C/U*] : a regular, repeated pattern of sounds or move-ments • *the music's fast/slow/steady rhythm* [=beat] • *the rhythm of her breath-ing* **2** [*C*] : a regular, repeated pattern of events, changes, activities, etc. • *the rhythms of country life*

rhythm and blues *n* [*U*] : a type of pop-ular music usually performed by African-Americans that was developed originally by combining elements of blues and jazz — *abbr. R & B*

rhyth·mic /ˈrɪðmɪk/ *or* **rhyth·mi·cal** /ˈrɪðmɪkəl/ *adj* : having a regular repeat-ed pattern of sounds or movements • *rhythmic drumming/chanting* — **rhyth·mi·cal·ly** /ˈrɪðmɪkli/ *adv*

RI *abbr* Rhode Island

¹**rib** /ˈrɪb/ *n* [*C*] **1** : any one of the curved bones of the chest that connect to the spine **2** : a piece of meat from an ani-mal that includes a rib and that is used as food **3** : a long curved piece of metal, wood, etc., that forms the frame of a boat, roof, etc. • *the ribs of an umbrella*

²**rib** *vb* **ribbed; rib·bing** [*T*] *informal* : to make jokes about (someone) in a friend-ly way • *They ribbed* [=kidded] *me about/ over my silly outfit.* — **ribbing** *n* [*U*] • *a little good-natured ribbing between friends*

rib·ald /ˈrɪbəld/ *adj, formal* : referring to sex in a rude but amusing way • *ribald jokes/comments*

ribbed *adj* : having raised lines • *a ribbed sweater*

rib·bon /ˈrɪbən/ *n* **1** [*C/U*] : a narrow piece of cloth (such as silk) that is used to tie things or for decoration • *She tied a ribbon around the box.* • *a length/piece of ribbon* **2** [*C*] : a short piece of cloth that is given as a military award **3** [*C*] *chiefly US* : a piece of colored cloth that is given as an award in a competition — see also BLUE RIBBON **4** [*C*] : something that is long and narrow like a strip of cloth • *a ribbon of road* **5** [*plural*] : narrow piec-es of something that has been cut or torn apart • *a banner torn/cut to ribbons* [=to pieces]

rib cage *n* [*C*] *medical* : the curved wall of ribs that surrounds and protects the chest

rice /ˈraɪs/ *n* [*U*] **1** : small white or brown grains that come from a southeast Asian plant and that are used for food • *a bowl/grain of brown/white rice* **2** : the plant that produces rice • *a field of rice* = *a rice field/paddy*

rich /ˈrɪtʃ/ *adj* **1** : having a lot of money and possessions • *a rich person/country/ neighborhood* • *(informal + often disap-proving)* She's *filthy/stinking rich.* [=ex-tremely rich] **2** : very expensive and beautiful, impressive, etc. • *rich* [=luxuri-ous] *robes* **3 a** : having or supplying a large amount of something that is want-ed or needed • *a rich source of informa-tion* • *rich* [=fertile] *soils* • *protein-rich foods = foods rich in protein* [=foods that contain a lot of protein] **b** : having a lot of flavor and making your stomach feel full • *rich foods* **c** : very interesting and full of many different things • *a rich cultural heritage* **4** : having a pleasingly strong quality • *a full, rich voice* **5** *informal* — used to say that a person's comment or criticism is surprising or amusing because the same comment or criticism could be made about that person • *"She says we're working too slowly." "Oh, that's rich. She's the one who keeps delaying things with all her meetings."* — **strike it rich** see ¹STRIKE — **the rich** : people who are rich • *the rich and famous* — **rich·ness** /ˈrɪtʃnəs/ *n* [*U*] • *the richness of the soil/food/colors*

rich·es /ˈrɪtʃəz/ *n* [*plural*] **1** : large amounts of money and possessions • *acquiring riches* [=*wealth*] *and fame* **2** : good things that are available to use or choose • *With so many restaurants in the city, diners are faced with an embarrassment of riches.* [=there are so many restaurants that it is difficult to choose one] — **from rags to riches** see ¹RAG

rich·ly /ˈrɪtʃli/ *adv* **1** : in a beautiful and expensive way • *richly dressed* **2** : in a pleasingly strong way • *a richly rewarding* [=very satisfying] *experience* **3** : in a generous way • *They were richly rewarded.* **4** : completely or fully • *a reward that was richly deserved* **5** : having a large amount of something • *a richly illustrated book* [=a book with many illustrations]

Rich·ter scale /ˈrɪktə-/ *n* — **the Richter scale** *technical* : a system of measurement used for showing the strength of an earthquake

rick·ets /ˈrɪkəts/ *n* [*U*] *medical* : a disease in children that is caused by a lack of vitamin D and that causes bones to become soft and to bend

rick·et·y /ˈrɪkəti/ *adj* : not strong or stable and likely to break • *rickety stairs*

rick·shaw /ˈrɪkˌʃɑː/ *n* [*C*] : a small, light vehicle with two wheels that is pulled by one person and that is used in some Asian countries

ric·o·chet /ˈrɪkəˌʃeɪ/ *vb* **-cheted** /-ˌʃeɪd/; **-chet·ing** /-ˌʃeɪɪŋ/ [*I*] : to bounce off a surface and continue moving in a different direction • *The bullet ricocheted off the wall.* — **ricochet** *n* [*C/U*] • *He was hit by a ricochet.* [=by a bullet, stone, etc., that ricocheted off a surface]

ri·cot·ta /rɪˈkɑːtə/ *n* [*U*] : a soft, white Italian cheese — called also *ricotta cheese*

rid /ˈrɪd/ *vb* **rid** *also* **rid·ded**; **rid·ding** — **be rid of** : to no longer have or be affected or bothered by (someone or something that is unwanted or annoying) • *wanting to be rid of a cold* — **get rid of** : to do something so that you no longer have or are affected or bothered by (something or someone that is unwanted) • *I got rid of some old furniture by selling/giving it to my nephew.* — **rid of** [*phrasal vb*] **rid (someone or something) of** : to cause (someone or something) to no longer have or be affected by (someone or something unwanted) • *rid the garden of pests* • *wanting to rid herself of all her worries*

rid·dance /ˈrɪdns/ *n* — **good riddance**

— used to say that you are glad that someone is leaving or that something has gone • *Winter is finally over, and I say good riddance!*

¹**rid·den** /ˈrɪdn/ *adj* : filled with or containing something unpleasant or unwanted • *ridden with guilt* = *guilt-ridden*

²**ridden** *past participle of* ¹RIDE

¹**rid·dle** /ˈrɪdl/ *n* [*C*] **1** : a difficult question that is asked as a game and that has a surprising or funny answer • *trying to solve a riddle* • *(figurative) speaking in riddles* [=speaking in a confusing way] **2** : someone or something that is difficult to understand or solve • *She's a bit of a riddle to me.*

²**riddle** *vb* **rid·dled; rid·dling** [*T*] **1** : to make many holes in (something or someone) *with* something • *a car riddled with bullets* **2** : to fill (something) with something that is bad or unpleasant • *a theory riddled with contradictions*

¹**ride** /ˈraɪd/ *vb* **rode** /ˈroʊd/; **rid·den** /ˈrɪdn/; **rid·ing** **1** [*T/I*] : to sit on and control the movements of (a horse, motorcycle, bicycle, etc.) • *riding (on) a horse/motorcycle* • *She got on her bicycle and rode away.* **2** [*T/I*] **a** : to travel to a place as a passenger on or in (something that is moving) • *(chiefly US) riding a bus/train* • *They rode the elevator/escalator to the top floor.* • *a dog riding in the back of a truck* **b** : to go on a mechanical ride at an amusement park or similar place • *riding (on) the Ferris wheel* **3** [*T*] *chiefly US* : to travel over or on (a road, railway, trail, etc.) in a car, on a train, on a bicycle, etc. • *riding the rails* **4** [*I*] *of a vehicle* : to move over the surface of a road in a specified way • *The car rides smoothly/well.* **5** [*T*] *US, informal* : to criticize or make jokes about (someone) constantly or frequently in usually a harsh or annoying way • *They've been riding him pretty hard.* — **be riding for a fall** *informal* : to be doing something that is likely to lead to failure or disaster — **be riding high** *informal* **1** : to be very happy and excited • *She's riding high after her recent win.* **2** : to be very successful • *The company's stock is riding high.* — **let (something) ride** *informal* : to ignore (something) • *let a comment ride* — **ride herd on** *US, informal* : to keep (someone or something) under close watch or control — **ride on** [*phrasal vb*] **1** : to depend on (something or someone) • *Our hopes are riding on you.* **2** ✧ If you have money *riding* on something or someone, you have bet money on that thing or person. — **ride out** [*phrasal vb*] **ride (something) out** *or* **ride out (something)** : to succeed in surviving or getting through (something dangerous or harmful that cannot be stopped or avoided) • *ride out a storm* — **ride shotgun** *informal* : to ride in the front passenger seat of a vehicle

²**ride** *n* [*C*] **1 a** : a usually short journey in or on a vehicle • *a two-hour car ride* • *He took me for a ride on his motorcycle.* = *He gave me a ride on his motorcycle.* • *I went for a ride on my bike.* • *Can you give me a ride* [=*lift*] *to town?* **b** : a usually short journey on a horse or other animal

• *a pony ride* **2** — used to describe what the experience of riding in a car or other vehicle is like • *The car has/offers a smooth/comfortable ride.* • (figurative) *investors preparing for a bumpy/rough ride* [=a difficult time] *in the stock market* **3 a : a** large machine at an amusement park, fair, etc., that people ride on for enjoyment **b :** the act of riding on such a machine • *a ride on a roller coaster* — **along for the ride** *informal* : doing something with other people without being seriously involved in it or having a serious interest in it • *I'm not interested in buying anything. I just came/went along for the ride.* — **take (someone) for a ride** *informal* : to trick or fool (someone) especially in order to get money

rid·er /'raɪdɚ/ *n* [C] **1 :** a person who rides something • *bike riders* **2 a :** an official document that is attached to another document and that adds to or changes information in the original document **b :** an additional part added to a legislative bill

ridge /'rɪdʒ/ *n* [C] **1 :** a long area of land that is on top of a mountain or hill • *hiking along the ridge* **2 :** a raised part or area on the surface of something • *the ridges on the sole of a boot* **3 :** the place where two sloping surfaces meet • *a roof ridge*

¹**rid·i·cule** /'rɪdə,kjuːl/ *n* [U] : harsh comments made by people who are laughing at someone or something • *He's a subject/object of ridicule to his coworkers.* [=he is ridiculed by his coworkers] • *They held her up to (public) ridicule.* [=they made fun of her publicly]

²**ridicule** *vb* -**culed**; -**cul·ing** [T] **:** to laugh at and make jokes about (someone or something) in a cruel or harsh way • *They ridiculed her suggestions.*

ri·dic·u·lous /rə'dɪkjələs/ *adj* **:** extremely silly or unreasonable • *I look ridiculous in this hat.* • *Don't be ridiculous!* • *a ridiculous suggestion/price* — **ri·dic·u·lous·ly** *adv*

¹**rid·ing** /'raɪdɪŋ/ *n* [U] **:** the sport or activity of riding a horse, bicycle, motorcycle, etc. • *We'll go riding after the rain stops.*

²**riding** *adj, always before a noun* **1 :** related to or used for riding and especially for riding a horse • *riding lessons/gear/boots* **2** *US* **:** controlled by a person who sits on it • *a riding lawn mower* [=a lawn mower that you ride on]

rife /'raɪf/ *adj, not before a noun* **1 :** very common and often bad or unpleasant • *an area where malaria is rife* [=widespread] — **rife with :** having a large amount of (something bad or unpleasant) • *a history rife with scandal*

riff /'rɪf/ *n* [C] **1** *music* **:** a short and usually repeated pattern of notes in a song • *a guitar riff* **2** *US, informal* **:** a short set of comments on a particular subject • *a comedian's riff on modern love*

riff-raff /'rɪf,ræf/ *n* [U] *disapproving* **:** people who are not respectable — often used in a humorous or exaggerated way to suggest the attitudes of wealthy and powerful people • *keeping the riffraff out*

¹**ri·fle** /'raɪfəl/ *n* [C] **:** a gun that has a long

barrel and that is held against your shoulder when you shoot it

²**rifle** *vb* **ri·fled; ri·fling** [T/I] **:** to search through something quickly and carelessly often in order to take or steal something • *He rifled (through) the papers on his desk.* • *rifle a wallet*

rift /'rɪft/ *n* [C] **1 :** a situation in which two people, groups, etc., no longer have a friendly relationship • *a conflict that widened the rift between them* **2 :** a deep crack or opening in the ground, a rock, etc.

¹**rig** /'rɪg/ *vb* **rigged; rig·ging** [T] **1 :** to control or affect (something, such as a game or election) in a dishonest way in order to get a desired result • *rig an election* **2 a :** to build or set up (something) usually quickly and for temporary use • *We rigged (up) a shelter.* **b :** to place (something) in the proper position for use • *rigging (up) lights* **3 :** to provide (a boat or ship) with ropes, sails, etc. **4 a :** to provide (someone or something) with particular clothing or equipment • *firefighters rigged out in protective suits* **b :** to put something secretly in (a place) • *They rigged the enemy base with explosives.* — **rigged** *adj* • *a rigged election* • *a fully-rigged ship*

²**rig** *n* [C] **1 :** equipment or machinery that is used for a particular purpose • *an oil-drilling rig* = *an oil rig* **2** *US* **:** a large truck that is attached to a trailer • *a big rig*

rigamarole *variant spelling of* RIGMA-ROLE

rig·ging /'rɪgɪŋ/ *n* [U] **1 :** the ropes and chains that are used on a ship to help support the masts and sails **2 :** equipment that is used for supporting and using lights, curtains, etc., in a theater

¹**right** /'raɪt/ *adj* **1 :** morally or socially correct or acceptable • *Stealing is not right.* • *You can't treat me like this! It's not right!* • *You were right to tell the police. It was the right thing to do.* **2 a :** accurate or correct • *the right answer* • *Something's not quite right about his story.* • *Let me get this right—you want me to lend you $1,000?!* **b** *not before a noun* **:** speaking, acting, or judging in a way that agrees with the facts or truth • *You're right; the answer is six.* • *You're right about that.* • *You're right to be concerned.* • *Let me put/set you right about one thing: I didn't start this argument!* **c** — used in speech to ask if a statement is correct or to say that a statement is correct • *"You paid our tab, right?" "Yes, I did."* **d** — used in speech to say you understand and accept what someone has said • *"It's late." "Oh, right. We should go."* **e** — used for emphasis at the beginning of a statement • *Right. Let's get this over with.* **f** — used in speech to express disbelief • *"I'm actually quite famous." "Right. And I'm the Pope." "No, it's true." "Yeah, right. I don't believe you."* **3 :** suitable or appropriate for a particular purpose, situation, or person • *the right person/tools for the job* • *They're not right for each other.* • *the right decision* • *Practice until you get it right.* • *I'll buy it if the price is right.* • *Success is of-*

*ten a matter of being in **the right place at the right time.** **4 a** : in a normal or healthy state or condition ▪ *I don't feel quite right.* [=I feel somewhat ill] ▪ *The fish doesn't smell right.* [=it doesn't smell the way it should] ▪ *She's not in her right mind.* [=she is mentally ill] **b** *not before a noun* : in a proper state or condition ▪ *Things are not right between them.* [=they do not have a good/happy relationship] ▪ *He apologized and tried to **put/set things right** (with her).* **5** *always before a noun* **a** : located on the side of your body that is away from your heart ▪ *her right hand/leg/side* **b** : done with your right hand ▪ *a right hook to the jaw* **c** : located nearer to the right side of your body than to the left ▪ *on the right side of the street* ▪ *taking a right turn* **6** *US* — used to refer to the side of something that is meant to be on top, in front, or on the outside ▪ *turn a shirt **right side out*** **7** *always before a noun, Brit, informal* : complete or total — used for emphasis ▪ *We were in a right mess!* — **(as) right as rain** *informal* : in excellent health or condition ▪ *After a few days of rest, you'll be right as rain again.* — **give your right arm** see ¹GIVE — **right·ness** *n* [U] ▪ *questioning the rightness of a decision*

²**right** *adv* **1** : in the exact location, position, or moment that is mentioned ▪ *It's right where I said it was.* ▪ *"Where is it?" "It's right here/there."* ▪ *The bank is right next to the pharmacy.* ▪ *We arrived right at noon.* ▪ *I'm right behind you.* ▪ *You are **right on time.*** **2** : in a direct course or manner ▪ *We went right* [=straight, directly] *home.* ▪ *He walked right past me.* ▪ *Come right this way, please.* ▪ *She came right out and said it.* [=she said it without hesitating] **3** : in a way that agrees with the facts or truth ▪ *You guessed/heard right.* **4** : in a suitable, proper, or desired way ▪ *eating right and exercising* ▪ *You're doing it right.* ▪ *Nothing is going right for me today.* **5** : all the way ▪ *The baby slept right through the night.* **6** : very soon or immediately ▪ *I'll be right back.* **7** : toward the right ▪ *She turned/looked right.* **8** : towards the political right ▪ *a political party that has shifted right* **c** *US* : using the right hand ▪ *He bats/throws right.* [=right-handed] ▪ : in a complete manner ▪ *I feel right at home here.* — **play your cards right** see ¹CARD — **right away** *also* **right off** : without delay or hesitation ▪ *I'll be right off.* ▪ *I knew right off.* — **right now 1** : in the next moment ▪ *Clean this up right now.* **2** : at the present time ▪ *He's not here right now.*

³**right** *n* **1** [C/U] : behavior that is morally good or correct ▪ *I know the difference between right and wrong.* = *right from wrong.* ▪ *You did right* [=you did the right thing] *to tell the teacher.* ▪ *the **rights and wrongs** of genetic cloning* **2** [C] : something that a person is or should be morally or legally allowed to have, get, or do ▪ *women fighting for equal rights* ▪ *The government must protect the rights of its citizens.* ▪ *the constitutional right of/to privacy* ▪ *She has a right to know the truth.*

▪ *He has every right to be angry.* ▪ *You are **within your rights** to demand a refund.* [=you have the right to demand a refund] **3** [plural] : the legal authority to reproduce, publish, broadcast, or sell something ▪ *the movie rights to a book* **4 a** [U] : a location closer to the right side of your body than to the left : the right side ▪ *Swing it from right to left.* ▪ *My house is up that road on your/the right.* ▪ *Move it to the right.* **b** [C] : a turn or movement toward the right ▪ *Take a right at the next intersection.* **5** [C] : a punch made with the right hand ▪ *a right to the jaw* **6 a the Right** : political groups who favor traditional attitudes and practices and conservative policies ▪ *a law opposed by (members of) the country's Right* **b the right** : the position of people who support the beliefs and policies of the political Right ▪ *The party has shifted to the right.* — **by right** : according to what is legally or morally correct ▪ *It's mine by right.* — **by rights** *also* **by all rights** : according to what is proper and reasonable ▪ *By rights, you should have won.* — **dead to rights** *US or Brit* **bang to rights** : with proof that you are guilty ▪ *She was caught dead to rights on a bribery charge.* — **in its own right** : because of its own special qualities and not because of a connection with something else ▪ *It's based on a popular novel, but the movie is great in its own right.* — **in the right** : in the position or situation of being right ▪ *The judge agreed that I was in the right.* — **in your own right** : because of your own efforts, talent, etc., and not because of your connection with someone else ▪ *Her husband is a famous novelist, but she is a successful writer in her own right.* — **might makes right** see ²MIGHT — **two wrongs don't make a right** see ³WRONG

⁴**right** *vb* [T] **1** : to correct (something wrong or unjust) ▪ *righting an old wrong* **2** : to return (something) to a proper state or condition ▪ *trying to right the economy* **3** : to put (something or someone) back in an upright position ▪ *righting a capsized boat*

right angle *n* [C] : an angle that measures 90° ▪ *A square has four right angles.*

righ·teous /ˈraɪtʃəs/ *adj, formal* **1** : following religious or moral laws ▪ *a righteous person/life* **2** *always before a noun* : caused by something that you believe is not morally right or fair ▪ *righteous anger/indignation* — **righ·teous·ly** *adv* — **righ·teous·ness** *n* [U]

right field *n* [U] : the part of a baseball outfield that is to the right when you are looking out from home plate; *also* : the position of the player defending right field ▪ *He plays right field.* — **right fielder** *n* [C]

right·ful /ˈraɪtfəl/ *adj, always before a noun, formal* **1** : according to the law ▪ *the property's rightful owner* **2** : proper or appropriate ▪ *the leader's rightful place in history books* — **right·ful·ly** *adv* ▪ *It's rightfully mine.* ▪ *She was rightfully praised.*

right–hand /ˈraɪtˌhænd/ *adj, always be-*

fore a noun : located closer to your right hand : located on the right side ▪ *Our building is on the right-hand side.* ▪ *the bottom right-hand corner of the page* ▪ *a right-hand turn*

right–hand·ed /ˈraɪtˈhændəd/ *adj* **1** : using the right hand more easily than the left hand ▪ *a right-handed person/pitcher* **2 a** : made for the right hand ▪ *a right-handed glove* **b** : using or done with the right hand ▪ *a right-handed pitch/punch* **3** : swinging from the right side of the body to the left side in sports like baseball and golf ▪ *a right-handed batter/hitter* — **right–handed** *adv* ▪ *She bats right-handed.*

right–hand·er /ˈraɪtˈhændər/ *n* [C] : a right-handed person; *especially* : a right-handed pitcher in baseball

right–hand man *n* [*singular*] : a very important assistant who helps someone do a job ▪ *He/She is the CEO's right-hand man.*

right·ist *or* **Right·ist** /ˈraɪtɪst/ *n* [C] : a person who belongs to or supports the political Right — **rightist** *or* **Rightist** *adj* ▪ *a rightist government*

right·ly /ˈraɪtli/ *adv* **1** : in a way that is correct ▪ *She rightly anticipated a decline in the value of the stock.* ▪ *He points out, quite rightly, that there are flaws in the theory.* **2** : for a good reason ▪ *People are rightly upset about the city's crime rate.* ▪ *She is proud of them, and rightly so.* **3** *informal* : with certainty — usually used in negative statements ▪ *I don't rightly know where she went.* [=I don't know where she went] ▪ *I can't rightly say what happened.*

right–mind·ed /ˈraɪtˈmaɪndəd/ *adj* : having beliefs, opinions, etc., that most people think are morally or socially right ▪ *right-minded citizens*

right–of–way /ˌraɪtəvˈweɪ/ *n, pl* **rights–of–way 1** [U] : the right to move onto or across a road before other people or vehicles ▪ *The other car has the right-of-way.* **2** [C] **a** : a legal right to go across another person's land **b** : a path on a person's land which other people have a legal right to use

right on *adj, US* **1** : exactly correct ▪ *Her assessment was right on.* **2** *informal + somewhat old-fashioned* — used to say that you agree completely with what someone has said ▪ *"Make love, not war!" "Right on, man!"*

right·ward (*chiefly US*) /ˈraɪtwəd/ *or chiefly Brit* **right·wards** /ˈraɪtwədz/ *adv* : toward the right ▪ *moving rightward* — **rightward** *adj* ▪ *a rightward turn*

right wing *n* [*singular*] : the part of a political group that consists of people who support conservative or traditional ideas and policies — **right–wing** /ˈraɪtˈwɪŋ/ *adj* ▪ *right-wing politics/politicians* — **right–wing·er** /ˈraɪtˈwɪŋə/ *n* [C]

right·y /ˈraɪti/ *n, pl* **right·ies** [C] *chiefly US, informal* : RIGHT-HANDER

rig·id /ˈrɪdʒəd/ *adj* **1** : not able to be bent easily ▪ *The patient's legs were rigid.* **2** : not easily changed ▪ *rigid rules/guidelines* ▪ *a rigid adherence to the rules* **3** : not willing to change opinions or be-

havior ▪ *a rigid disciplinarian* — **ri·gid·i·ty** /rəˈdʒɪdəti/ *n* [U] — **rig·id·ly** *adv*

rig·ma·role *or US* **rig·a·ma·role** /ˈrɪgməˌroʊl, ˈrɪgməˌroʊl, Brit* ˈrɪgməˌrəʊl/ *n* [U, *singular*] : a long, complicated, and annoying process, description, etc. ▪ *He just told us what to do without all the usual rigmarole.*

rig·or (*US*) *or Brit* **rig·our** /ˈrɪgə/ *n* **1** [*plural*] : the difficult and unpleasant conditions or experiences that are associated with something ▪ *the rigors of life in the wilderness* **2** [U] : the quality or state of being very exact, careful, or strict ▪ *scientific/intellectual rigor*

rig·or mor·tis /ˌrɪgəˈmoətəs/ *n* [U] : a temporary stiffness of the body that happens soon after death

rig·or·ous /ˈrɪgərəs/ *adj* **1** : very strict and demanding ▪ *rigorous training* ▪ *a rigorous course of study* **2** : done carefully and with a lot of attention to detail ▪ *a rigorous investigation/analysis* — **rig·or·ous·ly** *adv*

rile /ˈrajəl/ *vb* **riled; ril·ing** [T] **1** : to make (someone) angry : to irritate or annoy (someone) ▪ *Her comments riled the professor.* ▪ *Don't get all riled up.* [=angry] **2** *US, informal* : to make (someone) very excited ▪ *getting the kids all riled up*

¹**rim** /ˈrɪm/ *n* [C] **1** : the outer edge of a usually round object ▪ *the bowl's rim* **2** : the part of a wheel that the tire is put on

²**rim** *vb* **rimmed; rim·ming** [T] : to form or put a rim around (something) ▪ *a bowl rimmed with gold*

rimmed /ˈrɪmd/ *adj* : having a particular type of rim — used in combination ▪ *horn-rimmed glasses*

rind /ˈraɪnd/ *n* [C/U] **1** : the tough, outer skin of some fruits that is usually removed before the fruit is eaten ▪ *the rind of a lemon/watermelon* **2** : a tough, outer surface of some foods (such as certain cheeses)

¹**ring** /ˈrɪŋ/ *n* [C] **1 a** : a piece of jewelry that is worn usually on a finger ▪ *an engagement ring* **b** : a piece of jewelry that is shaped like a circle and worn in a special hole made in the skin ▪ *a nose ring* **2 a** : something that is shaped like a circle ▪ *smoke rings* ▪ *a key ring* [=a metal circle to which keys are attached] **b** : something that forms a circle around something else ▪ *a ring of stones around a fire pit* **c** : a circular or curved mark or shape ▪ *a ring of dirt in the bathtub* **3** : an area that is used for shows and contests and is usually surrounded by ropes or a fence ▪ *a boxing/wrestling ring* **4** : a group of people who are involved in some illegal or dishonest activity ▪ *a smuggling ring* **5** *Brit* : the part on the top of a stove where the heat or flame is produced — **rings around** — used in phrases like **run rings around** to say that one person or thing is much better than others ▪ *an architect who runs rings around* [=does much better work than] *her peers* — compare ⁴RING

²**ring** *vb* **ringed; ring·ing** [T] : to form a circle around (something or someone) ▪

Cottages *ring the lake.* — compare
³RING

³**ring** *vb* **rang** /ˈræŋ/; **rung** /ˈrʌŋ/; **ringing**
1 a [*T*] : to cause (an object or device,
such as a bell) to make a sound • *ring a
bell/doorbell* **b** [*I*] *of an object or device*
: to make a sound especially as a signal
of something • *The church bells were ringing.* • *My phone is ringing.* **c** [*I*] : to call
someone or something by ringing a bell •
She rang for a nurse/servant. **2** [*I*] **a** : to
fill a place or area with sound • *Cheers
rang through the hall.* • *Gunshots rang in
the air.* • *(figurative) Her words were still
ringing in my ears/head.* [=I was still
thinking about or remembering what she
had said] **b** : to be filled *with* the sound
of something • *The hall rang with cheers.*
c *of the ears* : to be filled with a sound
that other people cannot hear • *His ears
were ringing after the concert.* **3** [*I*] : to
seem to have a specified quality or character • *Her explanation didn't ring true.*
[=it seemed false] **4** [*T/I*] *chiefly Brit* : to
make a telephone call to someone or
something : CALL • *I'll ring you (up) tomorrow.* • *He's not here. Can you ring
back later?* — **ring a bell** *informal* : to be
familiar • *That name rings a bell.* — **ring
in** [*phrasal vb*] **1** *ring in (something)
also ring (something) in* : to celebrate
the beginning of (something, such as a
new year) • *a party to ring in the New
Year* **2** *chiefly Brit* : to make a telephone
call to a place (such as the place where
you work) • *She rang in sick* [=(*US*)
called in sick] *yesterday.* — **ring off**
[*phrasal vb*] *Brit* : to end a telephone call
— **ring off the hook** *US, of a telephone*
: to ring constantly or frequently • *The
phone was ringing off the hook all morning.* [=many people called during the
morning] — **ring out** [*phrasal vb*] : to be
heard loudly and clearly • *A shot rang
out.* [=a loud shot was heard] — **ring up**
[*phrasal vb*] *ring (something) up or ring
up (something)* **1** : to use a special machine (called a cash register) to calculate
the cost of (something, such as goods or
services) • *The cashier rang up our purchases.* **2** : to achieve (something) • *The
company rang up huge profits.*
— compare ²RING

⁴**ring** *n* **1** [*C*] **a** : the sound that a bell
makes • *the ring of the doorbell* **b** : the
act of making a bell ring • *Give the doorbell a ring.* [=ring the doorbell] **2** [*C*] **a**
: the sound that a telephone makes when
someone is calling • *a phone with a loud
ring* **b** : one of the sounds in the series
of sounds that a telephone makes when
someone is calling • *She waited until the
third ring to answer the phone.* **3** [*singular*] : a specified quality • *The name has a
familiar ring to it.* [=the name is familiar]
— **give (someone) a ring** *chiefly Brit*
: to make a telephone call to (someone) •
I'll give you a ring tomorrow. — compare
¹RING

ring•er /ˈrɪŋɚ/ *n* [*C*] **1** : someone who
rings a bell **2** : the part of a telephone
that rings to signal that someone is calling **3** *informal* : a person or animal that
enters a contest illegally by using a false

name, pretending not to have much skill,
etc. • *One of the players on the winning
team was a ringer.* **4** *informal* : someone
who looks very much like another person • *She's a dead ringer for my cousin.*
[=she looks exactly like my cousin]

ring finger *n* [*C*] : the third finger especially of your left hand when you count
the index finger as the first finger

ring•ing /ˈrɪŋɪŋ/ *adj, always before a noun*
1 a : very loud and clear • *a ringing voice*
b : like the sound a bell or alarm makes •
a ringing sound **2** : made forcefully or
with confidence • *a ringing endorsement/
condemnation*

ring•lead•er /ˈrɪŋˌliːdɚ/ *n* [*C*] : the leader
of a group that causes trouble or is involved in an illegal activity

ring•let /ˈrɪŋlət/ *n* [*C*] : a long curl of hair

ring•mas•ter /ˈrɪŋˌmæstɚ, *Brit* ˈrɪŋ-
ˌmɑːstə/ *n* [*C*] : a person whose job is to
introduce the performers in a circus

ring•side /ˈrɪŋˌsaɪd/ *n* [*U*] : the area that
is closest to the space used for circus
acts, boxing matches, etc. • *We were seated at ringside.* — **ringside** *adj* • *ringside
seats*

ring•tone /ˈrɪŋˌtoʊn/ *n* [*C*] : the sound
that a cell phone makes when someone is
calling

ring•worm /ˈrɪŋˌwɚm/ *n* [*U*] : a disease
that causes ring-shaped marks to appear
on the skin

rink /ˈrɪŋk/ *n* [*C*] : an often enclosed area
that has a special surface of ice, smooth
pavement, etc., and that is used for skating • *an ice-skating/roller-skating rink*

rinky–dink /ˈrɪŋkiˌdɪŋk/ *adj, US, informal + disapproving* : not very large or important • *a rinky-dink operation/business*

¹**rinse** /ˈrɪns/ *vb* **rinsed; rins•ing** [*T*] **1 a**
: to wash (something) with clean water
and without soap • *I rinsed my face.* •
Rinse (off) the apple before you eat it. •
rinse (out) a cup **b** : to wash (something) with a liquid other than clean water • *tools rinsed in alcohol* **2** : to remove
(something) from an object by washing
the object with clean water • *Rinse the
dirt off the lettuce.*

²**rinse** *n* **1** [*C*] : an act of washing something with a liquid and especially with
clean water • *Give the apple a rinse.*
[=rinse the apple] **2** [*C/U*] : liquid that is
used for rinsing something • *a mouth
rinse* **3** [*C/U*] : a dye that you put on
your hair to change its color for a short
time • *a bottle of hair rinse*

¹**ri•ot** /ˈrajət/ *n* **1** [*C*] : a situation in
which a large group of people behave in
a violent and uncontrolled way • *a prison
riot* **2** [*singular*] : a place that is filled
with something • *The woods are a riot of
color in the autumn.* **3** [*singular*] *informal* : someone or something that is very
funny • *She's a riot.* — **read (someone)
the riot act** : to speak in an angry and
critical way to (someone who has done
something wrong) • *His boss read him the
riot act for making careless mistakes.* —
run riot : to behave in a violent and uncontrolled way • *People were running riot
in the streets.*

²**riot** *vb* [*I*] *of a group of people* : to behave

in a violent and uncontrolled way • *People were rioting in the streets.* — **ri·ot·er** *n* [C] — **ri·ot·ing** /ˈrajətɪŋ/ *n* [U] • *Police stopped the rioting.*

ri·ot·ous /ˈrajətəs/ *adj, formal* **1** : behaving in a violent and uncontrolled way • *a riotous crowd* **2** : very exciting, fun, or full of energy • *a riotous party/celebration* — **ri·ot·ous·ly** *adv* • *a riotously funny performance*

¹**rip** /ˈrɪp/ *vb* **ripped; rip·ping 1 a** [T] : to tear, split, or open (something) quickly or violently • *She ripped the paper in half.* • *rip open a package* **b** [I] : to become torn or split • *Her coat ripped.* **2** [T] : to remove (something) quickly or violently • *rip a poster off a wall* • *rip a page out of a book* **3** [I] : to go or move very quickly *through* or *into* something • *The fire ripped through the forest.* **4** [T] : to criticize (someone or something) in a very harsh or angry way • *(US) The coach ripped the team for their sloppy play.* —

let rip *informal* **1** : to do something in a way that is full of anger or energy • *For the concert finale, the band let rip with a fantastic version of the song that made them famous.* **2 let (something) rip** : to make (a car, boat, machine, etc.) go very fast — usually used in phrases like *let it rip* and *let her/'er rip* • *We got in the boat and let 'er rip.* — **rip apart** [*phrasal vb*] **rip (something or someone) apart** *or* **rip apart (something or someone) 1** : to completely destroy (something) by tearing it into pieces • *Strong winds ripped apart the little beach shack.* • (*figurative*) *a tragedy/scandal that almost ripped the family apart* **2** : to criticize (someone or something) in a very harsh or angry way especially by describing weaknesses, flaws, etc. • *an article that rips apart the mayor's plan* — **rip into** [*phrasal vb*] : to criticize (someone or something) in a very harsh or angry way • *She ripped into their performance.* — **rip off** [*phrasal vb*] **rip (someone or something) off** *or* **rip off (someone or something)** *informal* **1** : to steal from or cheat (someone) • *I'm not trying to rip you off. It's a fair price.* **2** : to steal (something) • *Somebody ripped off our equipment.* = *Our equipment got ripped off.* — **rip up** [*phrasal vb*] **rip (something) up** *or* **rip up (something)** : to completely destroy (something) by tearing it into pieces • *rip up a letter*

²**rip** *n* [C] : a long tear in something • *I have a rip in my coat.*

R.I.P. *or chiefly Brit* **RIP** /ˌɑəˌaɪˈpiː/ *abbr* rest in peace ✧ *R.I.P.* is often written on a gravestone as a wish that the person buried there will have peace in death.

rip cord *n* [C] : a cord or wire that is pulled to open a parachute

ripe /ˈraɪp/ *adj* **rip·er; rip·est 1** : fully grown and developed and ready to be eaten • *a ripe tomato/apple* • (*figurative*) *a story ripe with details* [=a story that includes many details] **2** *not before a noun* : ready or suitable for something • *a system that is ripe for abuse* [=a system that is in such bad condition that it can easily be used wrongly] • *The time was ripe for proposing the plan.* — **ripe old age**

: a very old age • *They lived to a ripe old age.* — **ripe·ness** *n* [U]

rip·en /ˈraɪpən/ *vb* **1** [I] : to become ripe and ready to eat • *tomatoes ripening on the vine* **2** [T] : to make (something) ripe • *Ripen the fruit by placing it on the windowsill.*

rip-off /ˈrɪpˌɑːf/ *n* [C] *informal + disapproving* **1** : something that is not worth its price • *The bike was a real rip-off.* **2** : something that is too much like something made by someone else • *The song is an obvious rip-off.*

ri·poste /rɪˈpoʊst/ *n* [C] *formal* : a quick and clever reply • *a witty riposte*

¹**rip·ple** /ˈrɪpəl/ *vb* **rip·pled; rip·pling 1** [T/I] : to move in small waves • *A breeze rippled the water.* **2** [I] : to pass or spread through or over (someone or something) • *Fear/excitement rippled through the room.* [=people in the room suddenly felt fear/excitement]

²**ripple** *n* [C] **1 a** : a small wave on the surface of a liquid • *ripples on a pond* **b** : a shape or pattern having small waves • *ripples of sand* **2** : a sound that gradually becomes louder and then quieter • *ripples of laughter* **3** : something that passes or spreads through or over someone or something • *A ripple of excitement spread through the room.*

ripple effect *n* [C] : a situation in which one event causes a series of other events to happen • *crimes that create a ripple effect* [=that cause more crimes, problems, etc.]

rip-roar·ing /ˈrɪpˈrorɪŋ/ *adj, informal* : very loud, lively, and exciting • *a rip-roaring party* — **rip-roaring** *adv* • *rip-roaring drunk* [=very drunk in a lively and noisy way]

¹**rise** /ˈraɪz/ *vb* **rose** /ˈroʊz/; **ris·en** /ˈrɪzn̩/; **ris·ing** /ˈraɪzɪŋ/ [I] **1 a** : to move upward • *Smoke rose (up) into the air.* • *The airplane rose (up) into the sky.* • (*figurative*) *My spirits rose.* [=I began to feel happier] **b** : to become higher • *The tide/river is rising.* **c** : to slope or extend upward • *The road rose gently/steeply.* **2** : to become more popular, successful, etc. • *a politician who rose to fame/power/prominence very quickly* • *Empires rise and fall.* • *She rose through the ranks of the company to become president.* **3 a** : to increase in amount, number, level, etc. • *Sales have risen in recent months.* • *rising prices* **b** : to become stronger • *The wind rose in the afternoon.* **c** : to become louder • *The music rose and fell.* **4 a** : to stand up • *He rose slowly (to his feet).* • *She quickly rose from her chair.* **b** : to get up from sleeping in a bed • *Rise and shine!* [=wake up and get out of bed] **5** *of the sun or moon* : to appear above the horizon • *The sun rises in the east and sets in the west.* **6** *of bread, cake, etc.* : to become bigger because of being filled with air bubbles made through a chemical process • *Yeast makes the dough rise.* **7** : to begin to fight in order to remove a ruler or government • *The people rose (up) in rebellion/revolt.* **8** : to live again after dying • *a belief that the dead will rise again* [=will live again] — **rise above**

[*phrasal vb*] : to not allow yourself to be hurt or controlled by (something bad or harmful) ▪ *We need to rise above our anger/frustration and find a way to get along.* — **rise to the occasion/challenge** : to make the special effort that is required to successfully deal with a difficult situation ▪ *When things looked desperate, they rose to the challenge and found a way to win.*

²**rise** *n* **1** [*C*] : an increase in amount, number, level, etc. ▪ *a sharp/dramatic rise in property values* ▪ *a rise in prices/taxes* = (chiefly *Brit*) *a price/tax rise* **2** [*singular*] : an upward movement ▪ *the rise and fall of waves* **3** [*singular*] : the process by which something or someone becomes established, popular, successful, etc. ▪ *the empire's rise and fall* ▪ *a politician's rise to fame/power/prominence* **4** [*C*] **a** : an upward slope ▪ *a gentle/steep rise in the road* **b** : a small hill ▪ *coming over the rise* **5** [*C*] *Brit* : an increase in the amount of money paid to a worker : RAISE ▪ *a pay rise* — **get a rise out of** *informal* : to cause (someone) to react in an angry way ▪ *She's trying to get a rise out of you.* — **give rise to** : to cause or produce (something) ▪ *The increase in prices has given rise to concerns about inflation.* — **on the rise** **1** : increasing in amount, number, level, etc. ▪ *Prices are on the rise.* **2** : becoming more successful, popular, etc. ▪ *an actress whose career is on the rise*

ris·er /ˈraɪzɚ/ *n* **1** [*C*] : a person who gets out of bed after sleeping ▪ *I'm an early/late riser.* [=I get out of bed early/late in the morning] **2** [*C*] *technical* : the upright board between two stairs **3** [*plural*] *US* : a set of tall and wide steps for standing or sitting on

rising *n* [*C*] *chiefly Brit* : UPRISING ▪ *an armed rising against the government*

rising star *n* [*C*] : a person who is quickly becoming popular, successful, etc. ▪ *a rising star in the Republican/Democratic Party*

¹**risk** /ˈrɪsk/ *n* **1** [*C/U*] : the possibility that something bad or unpleasant (such as an injury or a loss) will happen ▪ *I'm aware of the risks associated with the treatment.* ▪ *reducing the risk of injury or death in a car accident* ▪ *a product that presents a significant risk to public health* ▪ *To me, skydiving is not worth the risk.* **2** [*C*] : someone or something that may cause something bad or unpleasant to happen ▪ *They don't understand the risks involved in the sport.* ▪ *a risk to national security* **3** [*C*] : a person or thing that someone judges to be a good or bad choice for insurance, a loan, etc. ▪ *a borrower who is a good/bad credit risk* [=who is likely/unlikely to pay back borrowed money] — **at risk** : in a dangerous situation ▪ *a policy that puts the country at risk* ▪ *people who are at risk of developing heart disease* [=who might develop heart disease] ▪ *He placed his life at risk to save them.* [=he risked his life to save them] — **at the risk of (doing something)** : despite the possibility of (doing something that could be considered improper,

wrong, etc.) ▪ *At the risk of sounding repetitive, I want to say again that we need more time.* — **at your own risk** : with full understanding that what you are doing is dangerous and that you are responsible for your own safety ▪ *swim at your own risk* — **run a risk** : to do something that may result in loss, failure, etc. ▪ *He is not afraid of running risks.* [=(more commonly) taking risks] — **run the risk of** : to do something that may result in (something bad or unpleasant happening) ▪ *You run the risk of being misunderstood if you don't explain your purpose carefully.* — **take a risk** : to do something that may result in loss, failure, etc. ▪ *Every time you invest money, you're taking a risk.*

²**risk** *vb* [*T*] **1** : to put (something) in a situation in which it could be lost, damaged, etc. ▪ *She risked her life to save them.* ▪ *risking money to start a business* **2** : to do something that could result in (something bad or unpleasant) ▪ *I'm not willing to risk getting lost. I'm going to buy a map.* **3** : to do (something that may have harmful or bad results) ▪ *We probably have enough gas, but I don't want to risk it.* [=I don't want to possibly not have enough gas]

risk factor *n* [*C*] : something that increases risk; *especially* : something that makes a person more likely to get a particular disease or condition ▪ *Age is one of the risk factors for this disease.*

risk–taking *n* [*U*] : the act or fact of doing something that involves danger or risk in order to achieve a goal ▪ *Starting a business always involves risk-taking.* — **risk–taker** *n* [*C*]

risky /ˈrɪski/ *adj* **risk·i·er**; **-est** : involving the possibility of something bad or unpleasant happening ▪ *This plan/proposal seems risky.* ▪ *Love is a risky business.* [=love involves the possibility of being hurt] ▪ *a risky move* [=an action that may result in something bad or unpleasant happening] — **risk·i·ness** *n* [*U*]

ri·sot·to /rɪˈsɑːtoʊ/ *n, pl* **-tos** [*C/U*] : an Italian dish made with rice and often vegetables or meat

ris·qué /rɪˈskeɪ/ *adj* : referring to sex in a rude and slightly shocking way ▪ *a risqué joke*

rite /ˈraɪt/ *n* [*C*] : an act that is part of a usually religious ceremony ▪ *funeral/purification rites*

rite of passage *n* [*C*] : an act that is a symbol of an important change in someone's life ▪ *For many, going to college is a rite of passage.*

¹**rit·u·al** /ˈrɪtʃəwəl/ *n* [*C/U*] **1** : a formal ceremony or series of acts that is always performed in the same way ▪ *a religious ritual* ▪ *buried without ceremony or ritual* **2** : an act or series of acts done in a particular situation and in the same way each time ▪ *the daily ritual of preparing breakfast* ▪ *bird mating rituals*

²**ritual** *adj, always before a noun* **1** : done as part of a ceremony or ritual ▪ *a ritual dance* **2** : always done in a particular situation and in the same way each time ▪ *a ritual greeting/gesture* — **rit·u·al·ly** *adv*

rit·u·al·is·tic /ˌrɪtʃəwəˈlɪstɪk/ *adj, formal*
: relating to or done as part of a rite or
ritual • *ritualistic acts* — **rit·u·al·is·ti-
cal·ly** /ˌrɪtʃəwəˈlɪstɪkli/ *adv*

ritzy /ˈrɪtsi/ *adj* **ritz·i·er; -est** *informal*
: very fashionable and expensive often in
a showy way • *a ritzy resort/club/wedding*

¹**ri·val** /ˈraɪvəl/ *n* [C] **1** : a person or thing
that tries to defeat or be more successful
than another • *The men are romantic rivals for her affection.* • *a rival team/gang/
candidate* • *the company's chief/main rival* **2** : something or someone that is as
good or almost as good as another person or thing • *The wine is the rival of any
in the world.* [=it is as good as any wine in
the world]

²**rival** *vb, US* **ri·valed** *or Brit* **ri·valled;** *US*
ri·val·ing *or Brit* **ri·val·ling** [T] : to be
as good or almost as good as (someone
or something) • *wine that rivals the
world's best*

ri·val·ry /ˈraɪvəlri/ *n, pl* **-ries** [C/U] : a
state or situation in which people or
groups are competing with each other •
*There is a bitter/friendly rivalry between
them.* • *sibling rivalry* [=competition or
jealousy between sisters and brothers]

riv·er /ˈrɪvɚ/ *n* [C] **1** : a large natural
flow of water that crosses an area of land
and goes into an ocean, a lake, etc. • *the
Mississippi River* • *a house on the river*
[=on land next to the river] • *Large boats
came up/down the river.* [=in the oppo-
site/same direction that the river is flow-
ing] **2** : a large flow of something • *crying a river of tears* [=crying a lot] — **sell
(someone) down the river** see SELL

riv·er·bank /ˈrɪvɚˌbæŋk/ *n* [C] : the
ground at the edge of a river

riv·er·bed /ˈrɪvɚˌbɛd/ *n* [C] : the ground
at the bottom of a river

riv·er·front /ˈrɪvɚˌfrʌnt/ *n* [C] *chiefly US*
: the land that is next to a river • *walking
along the riverfront*

riv·er·side /ˈrɪvɚˌsaɪd/ *n* [C] : the land
that is next to a river • *walking along the
riverside*

¹**riv·et** /ˈrɪvət/ *n* [C] : a special kind of metal bolt or pin that is used to hold pieces
of metal together

²**rivet** *vb* [T] **1** : to attract and hold all of
someone's attention • *I was riveted by her
story.* • *Their performance kept the audience riveted.* **2** : to make (someone) unable to move because of fear, shock, etc.
• *She stood riveted in place, staring
straight ahead.* **3** : to fasten (something)
with rivets • *The iron plates are riveted
rather than welded.* — **riv·et·er** *n* [C] •
working as a riveter in a factory

riv·et·ing /ˈrɪvətɪŋ/ *adj* : very exciting or
interesting • *a riveting story*

riv·u·let /ˈrɪvjələt/ *n* [C] : a small stream
of water or liquid

RN /ˌɑɚˈɛn/ *n* [C] : REGISTERED NURSE

RNA /ˌɑɚˌɛnˈeɪ/ *n* [U] *technical* : a substance in the cells of plants and animals
that helps make proteins

roach /ˈroʊtʃ/ *n* [C] **1** *US* : COCKROACH
2 *informal* : the part of a marijuana cigarette that is left after it has been smoked

road /ˈroʊd/ *n* **1** [C/U] : a hard flat surface for vehicles, people, and animals to

travel on • *a paved/gravel/dirt road* • *a
desolate stretch of road* • *country/moun-
tain roads* • *The library is on River Road.* •
The post office is up/down this road a bit.
[=a short distance further on this road] •
The cabin is accessible by road. • *traveling
on the open road* [=on roads that are
away from cities and towns] **2** [C] : a
process or a course of action that leads
to a certain result • *the road to riches/suc-
cess/victory* • *I'm on the road to recovery.*
[=in the process of becoming healthy
again] • *I've been/gone down this road before.* [=I've had this kind of experience
before] — **down the road** : in or into
the future • *a month/year down the road*
— **for the road** — used to refer to an alcoholic drink that you have quickly before leaving a place • *I'll have one (more)
for the road.* — **get the/this show on
the road** see ²SHOW — **hit the road** *informal* : to begin a journey • *We hit the
road around 7:00.* : to go away : LEAVE •
It's time to hit the road. — **on the road**
1 : traveling especially in a car, truck,
bus, etc. • *We've been on the road since
Tuesday.* **2** *of a vehicle* : being used •
*There aren't many of those cars on the
road anymore.*

road·block /ˈroʊdˌblɑːk/ *n* [C] **1** : a
place where police or military officers
stop drivers especially in order to examine vehicles **2** *US* : something that stops
progress • *roadblocks on the path to success*

road·kill /ˈroʊdˌkɪl/ *n* [U] : animals that
have been killed by being hit by cars and
other vehicles

road map *n* [C] **1** : a map that shows
the roads in a particular area **2** *chiefly
US* : a plan for achieving a goal • *a road
map to/for peace*

road rage *n* [U] : anger and aggressive
behavior by a driver who is upset by how
another person is driving

road·run·ner /ˈroʊdˌrʌnɚ/ *n* [C] : a
North American bird that lives in the
desert and runs very fast

road·side /ˈroʊdˌsaɪd/ *n* [U] : the land
that is along a road • *a roadside restaurant*

road sign *n* [C] : a sign near a road that
has information for drivers

road test *n* [C] **1** : a test to see how well
a vehicle works when it is driven on
roads **2** *US* : a test to see how well
someone is able to drive a car or other
vehicle — **road test** *vb* [T] • *The car has
not yet been road tested.*

road trip *n* [C] *US* **1** : a long trip in a
car, truck, etc. • *a cross-country road trip*
2 : a trip that is taken by a sports team in
order to play one or more games

road·way /ˈroʊdˌweɪ/ *n* [C] : the part of a
road that is used by vehicles

road·work /ˈroʊdˌwɚk/ *n* [U] *US* : work
that is done to build or repair roads —
called also (*Brit*) *roadworks*

road·wor·thy /ˈroʊdˌwɚði/ *adj* : safe and
suitable for using on a road • *a
roadworthy vehicle* — **road·wor·thi-
ness** *n* [U]

roam /ˈroʊm/ *vb* [T/I] : to go to different
places without having a particular pur-

pose or plan • *goats roaming (on) the mountain* • *Tourists roamed (through) the streets.* • *His eyes roamed* [=he looked carefully around] *the room.*

¹**roar** /ˈroɚ/ *vb* **1** [*I*] **a** : to make the loud sound of a wild animal (such as a lion) • *lions roaring* **b** : to make a long, loud sound • *The guns/siren roared.* • *The engine roared (back) to life.* [=it made the loud sound of an engine and began running well] • *(figurative) His career suddenly roared back to life.* **2** [*I*] : to laugh loudly • *The audience roared with laughter.* **3** [*T/I*] : to shout (something) very loudly • *The crowd roared its approval.* **4** [*I*] : to move noisily and quickly • *The truck roared away/off.* • *The wind roared through the open barn.* • *(figurative) The team came roaring back to win the game.*

²**roar** *n* [*C*] **1** : the loud sound of a wild animal (such as a lion) **2** : a loud, long sound that continues for a long time • *the roar of the river/crowd/engine* • *roars of laughter/approval*

¹**roar·ing** /ˈrorɪŋ/ *adj, always before a noun* : very loud, active, or strong • *a roaring fire/river* • *a roaring success* [=a very great success] • *life during the roaring twenties* [=the 1920s, when many people lived in a wild and lively way]

²**roaring** *adv, informal* : extremely or very • *a roaring good time* • *He was roaring drunk.*

¹**roast** /ˈroʊst/ *vb* **1** [*T/I*] **a** : to cook (food such as chicken, potatoes, or beef) with dry heat in an oven or over a fire • *roast a chicken* • *The chicken is roasting in the oven.* **b** : to dry (something, such as a bean or nut) with heat • *We roasted the peanuts over the fire.* **2** [*I*] *informal* : to be very hot • *I'm roasting in this sweater.* **3** [*T*] *informal* : to criticize (someone or something) severely • *The movie was roasted by critics.* **4** [*T*] *US, informal* : to criticize (someone who is being honored at a special event) in a friendly or joking way • *Friends and family roasted him at his 40th birthday party.* — **roast·ed** /ˈroʊstəd/ *adj* • *roasted potatoes/garlic/tomatoes*

²**roast** *n* **1** [*C/U*] : a piece of meat that is roasted • *We're having (a) pork roast for dinner.* **2** [*C*] *US* : an outdoor party at which food is cooked over an open fire • *a pig roast* **3** [*C*] *US* : an event at which someone is honored and people tell jokes or funny stories about that person in a friendly way • *a celebrity roast*

³**roast** *adj, always before a noun* : cooked by roasting • *roast* [=roasted] *chicken/pork/potatoes*

rob /ˈrɑːb/ *vb* **robbed; rob·bing** [*T*] **1** : to take money or property from (a person or a place) illegally and sometimes by using force, violence, or threats • *rob a bank/person* • *They robbed her of her life savings.* **2** : to keep (someone) from getting something expected or wanted • *Her illness robbed her of a normal childhood.* — **rob Peter to pay Paul** : to take money that was meant for one person or thing and use it to pay someone else or to pay for something else — **rob (someone) blind** : to steal a lot of things or

money from someone — **rob the cradle** see ¹CRADLE

rob·ber /ˈrɑːbɚ/ *n* [*C*] : a criminal who steals money or property • *a bank robber*

rob·bery /ˈrɑːbəri/ *n, pl* **-ber·ies** [*C/U*] : the crime of stealing money or property • *a bank robbery* • *She was arrested for robbery.*

robe /ˈroʊb/ *n* [*C*] **1** : a long, loose piece of clothing that is worn on top of other clothes to show that someone has a high rank or an important job • *a judge's robes* **2** *chiefly US* : a loose piece of clothing that wraps around your body and that you wear before or after bathing, swimming, etc., or while resting at home — called also *dressing gown*

robed /ˈroʊbd/ *adj* : dressed in robes • *priests robed in black*

rob·in /ˈrɑːbən/ *n* [*C*] **1** : a North American bird with a grayish back and reddish breast **2** : a small European bird with a brownish back and orange face and breast

ro·bot /ˈroʊˌbɑːt/ *n* [*C*] **1** : a real or imaginary machine that is controlled by a computer and is often made to look like a human or animal • *a toy robot* **2** : a machine that can do the work of a person and that works automatically or is controlled by a computer • *The cars are assembled by robots.* — **ro·bot·ic** /roʊˈbɑːtɪk/ *adj* • *a robotic arm* — **ro·bot·i·cal·ly** /roʊˈbɑːtɪkli/ *adv*

ro·bot·ics /roʊˈbɑːtɪks/ *n* [*U*] : technology that is used to design, build, and operate robots

ro·bust /roʊˈbʌst/ *adj* **1** : strong and healthy • *robust young men and women* **2 a** : successful or impressive and not likely to fail or weaken • *a robust company/economy* **b** : impressively large • *robust profits* **3** : having a rich, strong flavor • *a robust wine* • *sauce with a robust flavor* — **ro·bust·ly** *adv* — **ro·bust·ness** /roʊˈbʌstnəs/ *n* [*C/U*]

¹**rock** /ˈrɑːk/ *vb* **1** [*T/I*] : to move (someone or something) back and forth or from side to side • *She gently rocked the baby to sleep.* • *The boat rocked back and forth.* **2** [*T*] : to cause (something) to shake violently • *The building was rocked by an explosion.* **3** [*T*] *informal* **a** : to cause (someone or something) to be upset or shocked • *News of the murders rocked the town.* **b** : to affect or influence (someone or something) very powerfully • *Their invention rocked the computer industry.* **c** : to entertain (someone) in a very powerful and effective way • *a performance that rocked the house* [=that the audience loved] • *The game will rock your world.* [=you will really like it] **4** [*I*] *informal* : to sing, dance to, or play rock music • *We were rocking all night long.* **5** [*I*] *slang* : to be very enjoyable, pleasing, or effective • *That car rocks.* — **rock the boat** see BOAT

²**rock** *n* **1 a** [*U*] : the hard, solid material that the surface of the Earth is made of • *layers of solid rock* • *rock formations* **b** [*C*] : a piece of rock • *a flat rock* • *(US) throwing rocks* [=stones] *into the water* **c**

[C] : a large piece of rock that sticks up from the surface of the Earth ▪ *The ship crashed into the rocks.* **2** — used in phrases to say that something is very hard, steady, etc. ▪ *The bread is (as) hard as a rock.* = *The bread is rock-hard.* [=the bread is very hard] ▪ *The beat of the drum was rock-steady.* **3** [*singular*] *informal* : a strong person who can be relied on ▪ *He's our rock.* **4** [C] *informal* : a diamond or other jewel ▪ *the rock on her finger* **5** [C] *informal* : a small hard piece of a drug ▪ *a rock of crack cocaine* **6** [U] : a kind of popular music with a strong beat that is played on instruments that are made louder electronically — *listening to jazz and rock (music)* — **between a rock and a hard place** *informal* : in a very difficult or bad position or situation with no good way of getting out of it ▪ *caught/stuck between a rock and a hard place* — **on the rocks** **1** : having a lot of problems and likely to fail ▪ *Their marriage is on the rocks.* [=in trouble] **2** *of an alcoholic drink* : with ice cubes ▪ *a whiskey on the rocks*

rock and roll *or* **rock 'n' roll** /ˌrɑːkənˈroʊl/ *n* [U] : rock music — **rock and roll·er** *or* **rock 'n' roll·er** /ˌrɑːkənˈroʊlɚ/ *n* [C]

rock bottom *n* [U] : the lowest possible level or point ▪ *Prices have hit/reached rock bottom.*

rock–bottom *adj, always before a noun, of a price* : very low ▪ *rock-bottom prices*

rock climbing *n* [U] : the sport or activity of climbing the steep sides of a mountain or cliff ▪ *We're going rock climbing.* — **rock climber** *n* [C] ▪ *She's a skillful rock climber.*

rock·er /ˈrɑːkɚ/ *n* [C] **1** : a curved piece of wood or metal on which an object (such as a cradle or chair) moves back and forth or from side to side **2** *chiefly US* : ROCKING CHAIR **3** : someone who plays or performs rock music — **off your rocker** *informal* : CRAZY ▪ *You must be off your rocker if you think I'm going to do that!*

¹**rock·et** /ˈrɑːkət/ *n* [C] **1** : a type of very powerful engine that is powered by gases that are released from burning fuel **2** : a spacecraft or missile that is powered by a rocket engine ▪ *a rocket launcher* **3** : a firework that goes high in the air before exploding

²**rocket** *vb* **1** [*I*] : to increase quickly and suddenly ▪ *Sales rocketed (up) from 1,000 units to 5,000 units.* **2** [*T/I*] : to move or rise quickly ▪ *The train rocketed through the tunnel.* ▪ *The album rocketed up the charts.* ▪ *The movie rocketed her to fame.*

rocket science *n* [U] **1** : the science of designing or building rockets **2** : something that is very difficult to learn or understand ▪ *The job is challenging, but it's not exactly rocket science.* — **rocket scientist** *n* [C]

rocket ship *n* [C] : a spaceship that is powered by rockets

rocking chair *n* [C] : a chair that moves back and forth on rockers that are attached to its legs

rocking horse *n* [C] : a toy horse that is

attached to rockers and that moves back and forth while a child sits on it

rock 'n' roll *variant spelling of* ROCK AND ROLL

rock salt *n* [U] : salt that is in the form of large pieces or crystals

rock·slide /ˈrɑːkˌslaɪd/ *n* [C] : a large mass of rocks that suddenly and quickly moves down the side of a mountain or hill

rocky /ˈrɑːki/ *adj* **rock·i·er; -est** **1** : full of rocks ▪ *The soil/coastline is rocky.* **2** : full of problems or difficulties ▪ *a rocky relationship* ▪ *You have a long rocky road ahead of you if you want to become a doctor.* [=becoming a doctor will be very difficult]

rod /ˈrɑːd/ *n* [C] **1** : a straight, thin stick or bar ▪ *a curtain rod* **2** : a pole with a line and usually a reel that is used in fishing — **rule with a rod of iron** *see* ²RULE

²**rode** *past tense of* ¹RIDE

ro·dent /ˈroʊdn̩t/ *n* [C] : a small animal (such as a mouse or squirrel) that has sharp front teeth

ro·deo /ˈroʊdiˌoʊ, roʊˈdeɪoʊ/ *n* [C] : an event in which people compete at riding horses and bulls, catching animals with ropes, etc.

roe /ˈroʊ/ *n* [C/U] : the eggs of a fish or sea animal

¹**rogue** /ˈroʊg/ *n* [C] **1** *old-fashioned* : a dishonest or immoral man **2** : a man who causes trouble in a playful way ▪ *a lovable old rogue*

²**rogue** *adj, always before a noun* : different in a dangerous, harmful, or dishonest way ▪ *A rogue wave flipped the boat over.* ▪ *rogue states* [=dangerous states that do not obey international laws]

rogues' gallery *n* [*singular*] **1** : a collection of pictures of criminals **2** : a collection or list of bad or dangerous people or things ▪ *a rogues' gallery of deadly viruses*

rogu·ish /ˈroʊgɪʃ/ *adj* : showing in a playful way that you have done something wrong ▪ *a roguish smile* — **rogu·ish·ly** *adv*

roil /ˈrɔɪəl/ *vb, chiefly US* **1** [*T*] : to upset or disturb (someone or something) ▪ *Financial markets were roiled by the crisis.* **2** [*I*] : to move in a violent and confused way ▪ *roiling river rapids* ▪ *(figurative) Emotions were roiling (around) inside her.*

role /ˈroʊl/ *n* [C] **1** : the character played by an actor ▪ *I had a minor/major/leading role in the play.* ▪ *playing the role of the villain* **2 a** : a part that someone or something has in a particular activity or situation ▪ *He had a key role in winning the game.* ▪ *Religion plays an important role in his life.* **b** : the part that someone has in a family, society, or other group ▪ *the traditional roles of women*

role model *n* [C] : someone who another person admires and tries to be like ▪ *He's a good role model (for his son).*

¹**roll** /ˈroʊl/ *vb* [*T/I*] : to move or cause (something) to move by turning over one or more times ▪ *Roll the ball to me.* = *Roll me the ball.* ▪ *pigs rolling (around) in the mud* ▪ *The car rolled into the ditch.* ▪ *He*

rolled (over) onto his back. ▪ *(figurative) She rolled out of bed* [=rose after sleeping in a bed] *at noon.* **2** [T/I] : to move smoothly on wheels ▪ *The car rolled slowly to a stop.* **3** [I] : to move in a smooth, continuous way ▪ *The clouds rolled past.* ▪ *(figurative) The days rolled by.* **4** [T] : to form (something) into the shape of a ball or tube ▪ *She rolled the dough into a ball.* *He rolls his own cigarettes.* ▪ *She rolled up the meat in a tortilla.* **5** [T] : to make (something) smooth, even, or flat especially with a roller or rolling pin ▪ *She rolled (out) the dough.* ▪ *rolled oats* **b** : to spread (something) *on* a surface with a roller ▪ *She rolled the paint on (the wall).* **6** [I] : to move or lean from side to side ▪ *The ship heaved and rolled in the storm.* **7** [I] **a** : to make a deep, continuous sound ▪ *rolling thunder* **b** : to make a continuous, quick, beating sound ▪ *The drums rolled.* **8** [T/I] : to operate (something, such as a movie camera) ▪ *Roll the cameras when I say "action."* **9** [T/I] : to cause (your eyes) to look upward in an expression which shows that you think someone or something is foolish or annoying ▪ *He rolled his eyes at her suggestion.* **10** [I] *informal* : to start leaving a place or to start doing something ▪ *We ought to get rolling.* ▪ *(chiefly US) "Let's roll," the sergeant shouted to his men.* ▪ *After we got the loan approved, we were ready to roll.* — **get/set/start/keep the ball rolling** see ¹BALL — **heads roll** see ¹HEAD — **roll around** also Brit **roll about** [phrasal vb] informal : to arrive or happen again ▪ *By the time Friday rolls around, I'm ready for the weekend.* — **roll back** [phrasal vb] **roll back (something) or roll (something) back** chiefly US **1** : to reduce (something) ▪ *rolling back prices* **2** : to change (something) back to the way it was at an earlier time ▪ *They rolled back the clock on civil rights.* — **roll down** [phrasal vb] **roll down (something) or roll (something) down** **1** : to move (something) down especially by turning a handle ▪ *She rolled down the car window.* **2** : to unfold the edge of (something) ▪ *He rolled down his sleeves.* — **rolled into one** : combined together into one thing or person ▪ *It's an amusement park and nightclub (all) rolled into one.* — **roll in** [phrasal vb] informal **1 be rolling in (something)** : to have a large amount of (something) ▪ *They were rolling in money/dough.* **2** : to appear or arrive in large numbers or amounts ▪ *The money has been rolling in.* **3** : to arrive at a place especially later than usual or expected ▪ *He finally rolled in at 3:30.* — **roll off the tongue** see TONGUE — **roll out** [phrasal vb] **roll out (something) or roll (something) out** : to offer or sell (something) for the first time ▪ *The company is rolling out a new product.* — **roll out the red carpet** see RED CARPET — **roll over** [phrasal vb] **1** informal : to allow yourself to be easily defeated or controlled ▪ *He just rolls over and lets them do what they want.* **2 roll over (something) or roll (something) over** **a** : to delay the repayment of (something) ▪ *rolling over the*

repayment of a loan **b** : to place (invested money) in a new investment of the same kind ▪ *She rolled over her investments to another fund.* — **roll the dice** see ¹DICE — **roll up** [phrasal vb] **1 roll up (something) or roll (something) up a** : to move (something) up especially by turning a handle ▪ *She rolled up the car window.* **b** : to fold up the ends of (something) ▪ *She rolled up her jeans.* **2** informal : to arrive at a place in a vehicle ▪ *They rolled up in a limousine.* — **roll with the punches** informal : to not allow yourself to become upset by things that happen ▪ *You've got to roll with the punches!* — **roll your r's** : to pronounce the sound /r/ with a trill

²**roll** *n* [C] **1** : a long piece of cloth, paper, film, tape, etc., that is rolled to form the shape of a tube or ring **2 a** : a small loaf of bread for one person to eat **b** : a usually round sweet cake ▪ *cinnamon/sweet rolls* **3** : a food that is rolled up for cooking or serving ▪ *sushi rolls* **4** : a thick fold of fat, skin, etc. **5** : an official list of names ▪ *the voter rolls* **6 a** : an act of rolling something ▪ *a roll of the dice* **b** : a movement in which something rolls ▪ *the roll of the waves* **7 a** : a series of quick hits on a drum **b** : a deep, continuous sound ▪ *We heard the roll of thunder.* — **on a roll** informal : experiencing a series of successes ▪ *The team has been on a roll.*

roll·back /ˈroʊlˌbæk/ *n* [C] *chiefly US* : the act of rolling back something ▪ *rollbacks in prices*

roll call *n* [C/U] : the act of saying each of the names on a list to find out who is present ▪ *She missed roll call.*

roll·er /ˈroʊlɚ/ *n* [C] **1** : a part that rolls and is used to move, press, shape, spread, or smooth something ▪ *They moved the monument on rollers.* ▪ *a paint roller* **2** : a plastic or metal tube around which hair is wrapped to make it curl ▪ *Her hair was in rollers.* — see also HIGH ROLLER

Roll·er·blade /ˈroʊlɚˌbleɪd/ *trademark* — used for a skate that has wheels set in a straight line on the bottom

roll·er coast·er /ˈroʊlɚˌkoʊstɚ/ *n* [C] **1** : a ride at an amusement park which is like a small, open train with tracks that are high off the ground and that have sharp curves and steep hills **2** : a situation or experience that involves sudden and extreme changes ▪ *Their divorce was an emotional roller coaster.*

roller skate *n* [C] : a shoe that has wheels on the bottom for skating on a flat surface — **roller–skate** *vb* **-skated; -skat·ing** [I] ▪ *Let's go roller-skating.* — **roller skater** *n* [C]

rol·lick·ing /ˈrɑːlɪkɪŋ/ *adj, always before a noun, informal* : enjoyable in a lively or noisy way ▪ *We had a rollicking good time.*

roll·ing /ˈroʊlɪŋ/ *adj, always before a noun* : having gentle slopes ▪ *rolling hills*

rolling pin *n* [C] : a cylinder that is used for making dough flat and smooth

roll of honour *n* [C] *Brit* : HONOR ROLL

roll-on /ˈroʊlˌɑːn/ *adj, always before a noun* : rubbed or spread on the body with a bottle that has a rolling ball set into its top • *a roll-on deodorant* — **roll-on** *n* [C]

roll·out /ˈroʊlˌaʊt/ *n* [C/U] : an occasion when a new product or service is first offered for sale or use • *the rollout of a new car*

roll·over /ˈroʊlˌoʊvər/ *n* [C/U] **1 a** : the act of delaying the payment of a debt **b** : the act of placing invested money in a new investment of the same kind **2** *chiefly US* : an accident in which a car, truck, etc., turns over • *He was injured in a rollover.*

ro·ly-po·ly /ˌroʊliˈpoʊli/ *adj, informal* : short and fat • *a roly-poly man*

ROM /ˈrɑːm/ *n* [U] : the part of a computer in which information that cannot be changed is stored — called also *read-only memory*

ro·maine /roʊˈmeɪn/ *n* [U] *US* : a type of lettuce that has long, crisp leaves

¹Ro·man /ˈroʊmən/ *n* **1** [C] : a person who is from Rome or the ancient Roman Empire **2** *roman* [U] : roman type • *Should the word be italicized or set in roman?*

²Roman *adj* **1 a** : of or relating to Rome or the people of Rome • *the Roman population* **b** : of or relating to the ancient Roman Empire • *Roman law* **2** *roman* : having letters, numbers, etc., that stand upright instead of slanting • *roman type*

Roman Catholic *adj* : belonging or relating to the Christian church that is led by the pope • *a Roman Catholic priest* — **Roman Catholic** *n* [C] — **Roman Catholicism** *n* [U]

¹ro·mance /roʊˈmæns/ *n* **1** [C/U] : an exciting and usually short relationship between lovers • *a summer romance* • *a tale of love and romance* **2** [C] **a** : an exciting story often set in the past • *a medieval romance* **b** : a love story • *a romance novel* **3** [U] : the quality of something that makes it exciting and attractive • *the romance of the old West*

²romance *vb* **-manced; -manc·ing** **1** [T] : to have or try to have a romantic relationship with (someone) • *She was romanced by several young men.* **2** [I] : to talk about something in a way that makes it seem better than it really is • *romancing about the past*

Ro·mance language /roʊˈmæns-/ *n* [C] : a language (such as French or Italian) that developed from Latin

Roman numeral *n* [C] : one of the letters that were used by the ancient Romans to represent numbers and that are still used today • *In Roman numerals "X" is equal to the number 10.*

¹ro·man·tic /roʊˈmæntɪk/ *adj* **1 a** : of, relating to, or involving love between two people • *a romantic relationship/movie* **b** : making someone think of love • *a romantic dinner* **c** : showing that you love someone • *Why can't you be more romantic?* **2** : not realistic or practical • *romantic dreams of becoming an actress* **3** *Romantic* : of or relating to Romanticism • *the Romantic poets/movement* — **ro·man·ti·cal·ly** /roʊˈmæntɪkli/ *adv*

²romantic *n* [C] **1** : a person who shows feelings of love for someone **2** : someone who is not realistic or practical • *She's a hopeless romantic.* **3** *Romantic* : a writer, musician, or artist of Romanticism

ro·man·ti·cism /roʊˈmæntəˌsɪzəm/ *n* [U] **1** *Romanticism* : a style of art, literature, etc., during the 18th and 19th centuries that emphasized the imagination and emotions **2** : the quality or state of being impractical or unrealistic • *the romanticism of college students*

ro·man·ti·cize *also Brit* **ro·man·ti·cise** /roʊˈmæntəˌsaɪz/ *vb* **-cized; -ciz·ing** [T/I] : to think about or describe something as being more attractive or interesting than it really is • *romanticized notions of army life*

romp /ˈrɑːmp/ *vb* [I] : to move in a playful and noisy way • *The kids were romping in the yard.* — **romp** *n* [C] • *The dogs love a good romp through the woods.*

¹roof /ˈruːf/ *n* [C] **1** : the cover or top of a building, vehicle, etc. • *We were happy to* **have a roof over our heads.** [=to have somewhere to live] • *They all live* **under the same roof.** [=in the same house] **2** : the top of the inside of your mouth • **go through the roof** *informal* **1** : to become very angry or upset • *His parents went through the roof.* **2** : to rise to a very high level • *Sales have gone through the roof.* — **hit the roof** *see* ¹HIT — **raise the roof** *informal* : to make a lot of noise by playing music, celebrating, shouting, etc. • *We raised the roof when our team won.* — **through the roof** *chiefly US, informal* : at a very high level • *Prices are through the roof.* — **roof·less** /ˈruːfləs/ *adj* • *a roofless stadium*

²roof *vb* [T] : to cover (something) with a roof • *Our house is roofed with asphalt shingles.* • *thatch-roofed houses*

roof·er /ˈruːfər/ *n* [C] : a person whose job is to build or repair roofs

roof·ing /ˈruːfɪŋ/ *n* [U] **1** : material that is used for a roof **2** : the work of building or repairing roofs

roof·top /ˈruːfˌtɑːp/ *n* [C] : the upper surface of a roof • *a rooftop garden*

rook /ˈrʊk/ *n* [C] **1** : a large, black European bird **2** : CASTLE 2

rook·ie /ˈrʊki/ *n* [C] *chiefly US* **1** : a first-year player in a professional sport • *a rookie quarterback* **2** : a person who has just started a job or activity and has little experience • *a rookie cop*

¹room /ˈruːm/ *n* **1** [C] **a** : a part of the inside of a building that is divided from other areas by walls • *Smoke filled the room.* **b** : a room in a house, hotel, etc., where someone sleeps • *She's studying in her room.* **2** [U] : space that is used for something • *The sofa takes up too much room.* • *Is there enough room to turn the car around?* • *Can we* **make/find room** *in the garage for the bicycles?* **3** [singular] : the people in a room • *The whole room cheered.* **4** [U] : the possibility for something to happen or exist • *There is room for improvement.* — **room·ful** /ˈruːmˌfʊl/ *n* [C] • *a roomful of strangers*

²room *vb* [I] *US* : to live in a room, apartment, or house with another person • *He* *roomed with his brother.* ▪ *We roomed together in college.*

room and board *n* [U] *chiefly US* : a place to stay with meals provided and included in the price ▪ *We paid $50 (for) room and board.*

room·ie /ˈruːmi/ *n* [C] *US, informal* : ROOMMATE

rooming house *n* [C] *US* : a house where rooms with furniture are rented to people to live in

room·mate /ˈruːmˌmeɪt/ *n* [C] : a person who shares a room, apartment, or house with someone else

room service *n* [U] : the service that is provided to hotel guests so that they can have food, drinks, etc., brought to their rooms ▪ *He ordered a meal from room service.*

roomy /ˈruːmi/ *adj* **room·i·er**; **-est** : having plenty of space or room ▪ *The car is roomy inside.* — **room·i·ness** *n* [U]

¹**roost** /ˈruːst/ *n* [C] : a place where birds rest or sleep ▪ *(figurative, informal) At home, he ruled the roost.* [=had the most authority in a group]

²**roost** *vb* [I] *of a bird* : to rest or sleep somewhere ▪ *(figurative) Her bad decisions are coming home to roost. = After her bad decisions, her/the chickens are coming home to roost.* [=she is experiencing problems that she deserves because she made bad decisions]

roost·er /ˈruːstɚ/ *n* [C] *chiefly US* : an adult male chicken

¹**root** /ˈruːt/ *n* **1** [C] : the part of a plant that grows underground **2** [C] : the part of a tooth, hair, etc., that is attached to the body **3** [C] : the cause or source of something ▪ *We need to get to the root (cause) of the problem.* ▪ *Rock-and-roll has its roots* [=origins] *in blues music.* **4** [plural] **a** : the family history of a person or a group of people ▪ *She traced her roots back to Africa.* **b** : a special connection to something ▪ *a teacher with roots in the community* **5** [C] : a word from which other words are formed ▪ *"Hold" is the root of "holder."* — **put down roots** : to settle and live in one place ▪ *He put down roots in Canada.* — **take root 1** *of a plant* : to grow and develop roots ▪ *The grass took root before winter.* **2** : to begin to develop ▪ *Democracy is taking root in the country.* — **root·less** /ˈruːtləs/ *adj*

²**root** *vb* **1** [T/I] : to develop or make (a plant) develop roots ▪ *Moss was rooted to the rock.* **2** [T] : to make (someone) unable to move ▪ *I was rooted to my chair by/with fear.* **3** [I] : to search for something by moving things around ▪ *She rooted around in her purse to find her keys.* ▪ *pigs rooting for food* — **root for** [phrasal vb] : to express or show support for (a person, team, etc.) ▪ *Who are you rooting for?* — **root in** [phrasal vb] **root (something) in** : to form, make, or develop (something) by using (something) as a basis ▪ *His art is rooted in reality.* — **root on** [phrasal vb] **root (someone or something) on** *US* : to help (someone or something) to win or succeed by showing strong support ▪ *Her friends came to root*

her on. — **root out** [phrasal vb] **root (something or someone) out** or **root out (something or someone)** : to find or to find and remove (something or someone) ▪ *rooting out the cause of a problem* ▪ *The mayor promised to root out corruption.* — **root·er** /ˈruːtɚ/ ▪ *rooters for the home team*

root beer *n* [C/U] : a sweet, brown drink that is flavored with roots and herbs and that contains bubbles

root canal *n* [C] : a dental procedure to save a tooth by removing the injured tissue in its root

root vegetable *n* [C] : a vegetable (such as a carrot or potato) that grows under the ground

¹**rope** /ˈroʊp/ *n* **1** [C/U] : a strong, thick string made by twisting many threads together **2** [plural] : the special way things are done in a particular place or activity ▪ *I'm still learning the ropes at my new job.* ▪ *He's a director who really knows his/the ropes.* — **jump/skip rope** *US* : to jump over a rope that is being swung near the ground for exercise or as a game

²**rope** *vb* **roped; rop·ing** [T] **1** : to bind, fasten, or tie (something or someone) with a rope ▪ *The boats were roped together at the dock.* **2** *chiefly US* : to catch (an animal) by throwing a circle of rope around it ▪ *roping a calf* **3** *informal* : to use clever or tricky methods to get (someone) to do something ▪ *I was roped into going to the party.* — **rope off** [phrasal vb] **rope off (something)** or **rope (something) off** : to separate (an area) from another area with rope ▪ *Part of the exhibit had been roped off.*

ro·sa·ry /ˈroʊzəri/ *n, pl* **-ries 1** [C] : a string of beads that are used by Roman Catholics for counting prayers **2** *the Rosary* : a set of Roman Catholic prayers that are repeated in a specific order ▪ *say the Rosary*

¹**rose** *past tense of* ¹RISE

²**rose** /ˈroʊz/ *n* **1** [C] : a flower with a sweet smell that grows on a bush which has thorns on the stems ▪ *(figurative, informal) Take some time to (stop and) smell the roses.* [=stop being busy and enjoy the pleasant things in life] ▪ *(figurative, informal) After the scandal, she came out smelling like a rose.* [=her reputation was not harmed at all by the scandal] **2** [U] : a slightly purplish-pink color

rose·bud /ˈroʊzˌbʌd/ *n* [C] : the bud of a rose

rose·bush /ˈroʊzˌbʊʃ/ *n* [C] : a bush that produces roses

rose–col·ored (*US*) *or Brit* **rose–col·oured** /ˈroʊzˌkʌlɚd/ *adj* : tending to think of things as being better than they really are ▪ *taking a rose-colored view of the problem* ▪ *looking at the world through rose-colored glasses/spectacles* [=looking at the world in a too optimistic way]

rose·mary /ˈroʊzˌmeri/ *n* [U] : a sweet herb used in cooking

ro·sette /roʊˈzɛt/ *n* [C] **1** : a ribbon that is folded in the shape of a rose **2** : a design shaped like a rose • *a rosette of frost-ing*

rose water *n* [U] : liquid made from roses that is used as a perfume or flavoring

rose·wood /ˈrouzˌwʊd/ *n* [U] : the hard, dark, red wood of some tropical trees

Rosh Ha·sha·nah /ˌrɑːˈʃɑːˈʃɑːnə/ *n* [U] : the Jewish New Year observed as a religious holiday

ros·in /ˈrɑːzn/ *n* [U] : a hard and slightly sticky substance that has various uses • *She rubbed her violin's bow with rosin.*

ros·ter /ˈrɑːstə/ *n* [C] **1 a** : a list of the people or things that belong to a particular group, team, etc. • *He was added to the team roster.* **b** *US* : the people or things listed on a roster • *a roster of 40 players* **2** : a list that shows the order in which a job or duty is to be done • *a duty roster*

ros·trum /ˈrɑːstrəm/ *n, pl* **ros·trums** or **ros·tra** /ˈrɑːstrə/ [C] *formal* : a small raised platform on a stage

rosy /ˈrouzi/ *adj* **ros·i·er; -est 1** : having a pink color • *rosy cheeks* **2** : having or producing hope for success or happiness in the future • *a rosy outlook* • *He painted a rosy picture of our future.* [=he made our future sound very good]

¹rot /ˈrɑːt/ *vb* **rot·ted; rot·ting** [T/I] : to slowly decay or cause (something) to decay • *The wood rotted away.* • *rotting apples* • *(figurative) He was left to rot in jail.*

²rot *n* [U] **1** : the process of rotting or the condition that results when something rots • *They found rot in the house's roof.* **2** *informal* + *old-fashioned* : NONSENSE 1 • *That's a lot of rot!*

¹ro·ta·ry /ˈroutəri/ *adj, always before a noun* **1** : turning around a central point like a wheel • *a rotary blade* **2** : having a part that turns around a central point • *an old-fashioned rotary phone*

²rotary *n, pl* **-ries** [C] *US* : TRAFFIC CIRCLE

ro·tate /ˈrouˌteɪt, Brit rəʊˈteɪt/ *vb* **-tat·ed; -tat·ing** [T/I] **1** : to move or turn in a circle • *The planets rotate around the sun.* • *a rotating propeller* **2** : to regularly change the person who does something so that all the members of a group do it at different times • *The staff rotates the weekend shift.* **3** : to regularly change the place or position of things or people so that each takes the place of another • *You should rotate your car's tires once a year.* — **ro·ta·tion** /rouˈteɪʃən/ *n* [C/U] • *the rotation of the Moon around the Earth* • *The Earth makes one rotation every day.* • *Alfalfa and corn are planted in rotation.*

ROTC /ˌɑːˌoʊˌtiːˈsiː, ˈrɑːtsi/ *n* [U] *US* : a military program that provides training and financial assistance for college students who become officers in the military at the end of the program • *He joined (the) ROTC.* ✧ *ROTC* is an abbreviation of "Reserve Officers' Training Corps."

rote /ˈrout/ *n* [U] : the process of learning something by repeating it many times • *rote memorization*

ro·tis·ser·ie /rouˈtɪsəri/ *n* [C] : a machine that turns meat over a source of heat

ro·tor /ˈroutə/ *n* [C] *technical* : a part of a machine that turns around a central point • *the rotor (blade) of a helicopter*

¹rot·ten /ˈrɑːtn/ *adj* **1** : having rotted or decayed • *rotten wood/teeth* • *The banana went rotten.* **2** *informal* **a** : very bad or unpleasant • *What rotten luck!* • *I feel rotten about lying.* **b** *not before a noun* : not well or healthy • *I feel rotten today.* — **rot·ten·ness** /ˈrɑːtnnəs/ *n* [U]

²rotten *adv, informal* **1** : very badly or poorly • *He treats her rotten.* **2** : very much • *Those kids are spoiled rotten.*

Rott·wei·ler /ˈrɑːtˌwaɪlə/ *n* [C] : a type of large, black and tan dog

ro·tund /rouˈtʌnd/ *adj, literary + humorous* : fat and round • *a rotund face/man*

ro·tun·da /rouˈtʌndə/ *n* [C] : a large, round room and especially one covered by a dome

rouble *chiefly Brit* spelling of RUBLE

rouge /ˈruːʒ/ *n* [U] *old-fashioned* : a red powder or cream that is used to make your cheeks pinker

¹rough /ˈrʌf/ *adj* **1** : having a surface that is not even or smooth • *rough tree bark* • *rough roads/terrain* **2** : having or causing sudden, violent movements • *The plane made a rough landing.* • *rough waters* **3** *somewhat informal* : difficult or unpleasant to deal with • *Despite a rough start, the team won the game.* • *She had a rough life/time.* = *She had it rough.* **4** : not gentle or careful; causing or likely to cause harm or injury • *rough handling/sports* • *Don't be so rough on them.* [=don't punish or criticize them so harshly] **5** : having a lot of crime or danger • *a rough neighborhood* **6** : made or done in a way that is simple or that needs further changes • *He made a rough sketch of the house.* • *a rough draft of the speech* **7** *always before a noun* : not precise or exact • *a rough guess/estimate* • *She gave us a rough idea of what the house looks like.* **8** : having a harsh sound • *a rough voice* — **rough·ness** *n* [U]

²rough *adv* : in a rough way • *He plays rough with the dog.* • *(Brit) people living/sleeping rough on the streets*

³rough *n* [U] : an area on a golf course covered with tall grass that makes it difficult to hit the ball • *an area of rough* • *He hit his drive into the rough.* — **take the rough with the smooth** *chiefly Brit* : to accept and deal with bad or unpleasant things in addition to good or pleasant things

⁴rough *vb* [T] *American football* + *ice hockey* : to hit (a player) very hard in a way that is not allowed by the rules • *He was called for roughing the kicker.* — **rough it** *informal* : to live without the normal things that make life comfortable • *She was roughing it in the wilderness.* — **rough out** [*phrasal vb*] **rough (something) out** or **rough out (something)** : to make (something) quickly and without including all the details • *roughing out a general plan* — **rough up** [*phrasal vb*] **rough (someone) up** or **rough up (someone)** *informal* : to hit and hurt (someone)

• *He was roughed up by a mugger.*

rough·age /ˈrʌfɪʤ/ n [U] : FIBER 1

rough–and–ready /ˌrʌfənˈrɛdi/ adj 1 : not complete but good enough to be used • *a rough-and-ready solution* 2 : not having polite manners or fancy skills but ready to do what needs to be done • *rough-and-ready soldiers*

rough–and–tum·ble /ˌrʌfənˈtʌmbəl/ adj, always before a noun 1 : disorderly, loud, and rough • *a rough-and-tumble game/crowd* 2 : very competitive and aggressive • *the rough-and-tumble world of politics* — **rough–and–tumble** n [U] • *the rough-and-tumble of politics*

rough diamond n [C] Brit : DIAMOND IN THE ROUGH 1

rough·en /ˈrʌfən/ vb [T/I] : to become rough or cause (something) to become rough • *Roughen the surface with a file.*

rough–hewn /ˈrʌfˈhjuːn/ adj 1 : having a rough and uneven surface • *rough-hewn ceiling beams* 2 : not polite or educated • *a rough-hewn peasant*

rough·house /ˈrʌfˌhaʊs/ vb -housed; -hous·ing [I] US, informal : to play in a rough and noisy way • *The boys were roughhousing in their room.*

rough·ly /ˈrʌfli/ adv 1 : not exactly but close in number, quality, meaning, etc. • *The car is modeled roughly on an earlier design.* • *Roughly 20 percent of our land is farmland.* 2 a : in a way that is not gentle or careful • *The guard spoke to us roughly.* b : in a very simple or basic way • *roughly sketched drawings* c : in a way that produces a rough surface • *roughly cut timber*

rough·neck /ˈrʌfˌnɛk/ n [C] chiefly US, informal : someone who behaves in a rough or rude way 2 : someone who works on an oil rig or at an oil well

rough·shod /ˈrʌfˌʃɑːd/ adv : without thinking or caring about the opinions, rights, or feelings of others • *riding/running roughshod over* [=completely ignoring] *the law*

rou·lette /ruˈlɛt/ n [U] : a game in which players bet on a small ball that is dropped onto a spinning, numbered wheel

¹**round** /ˈraʊnd/ adj 1 : shaped like a circle or ball • *The Earth is round.* • *a round table/face* 2 : shaped like a cylinder • *a round peg* 3 : having curves rather than angles • *round shoulders/corners/leaves* 4 : slightly fat • *a large, round man/belly* 5 always before a noun ◇ A round number is a whole number that is used instead of a more exact number. • *They charge $49.99 rather than the nice round number of $50.00.* — **round·ness** /ˈraʊndnəs/ n [U]

²**round** adv 1 chiefly Brit : AROUND 2 : from beginning to end • *The bush stays green all year round.*

³**round** n 1 [C] : a series of similar actions, events, or things • *a second round of chemotherapy* • *an endless round of business meetings* 2 [plural] : a series of regular visits or stops • (US) *The doctor is making/doing her rounds at the hospital.* • (US, figurative) *Rumors were making the rounds.* [=were spreading] 3 [C, plural]

: a route that is regularly covered as part of a job • (chiefly US) *The mailman was on his rounds.* = (Brit) *The postman was on his round.* 4 [C] a : a stage of a sports competition in which each player or team plays against an opponent and the winner is allowed to continue to the next stage b : one of the three-minute periods into which a boxing match is divided • *The match lasted five rounds.* c : a complete set of 18 holes played in golf • *a round of golf* 5 [C] : a number of drinks that are served at the same time to each person in a group • *I'll buy the next round (of drinks).* 6 [singular] : a usually short period of applause, cheering, etc. • *The winner got a huge round of applause.* 7 [C] : a bullet for one shot • *There was only one round left in the gun.* 8 [C] : a round shape • *Cut the carrots into rounds.*

⁴**round** vb [T] 1 : to go or pass around (something) • *When we rounded the bend, we saw two deer in a field.* 2 : to finish or complete (something) in a good or suitable way • *They rounded off the meal with dessert.* • *Two scientists round out the staff.* 3 : to cause (something) to have a round shape • *He rounded (off) the table's corners.* 4 mathematics : to increase or decrease (a number) to the nearest whole or round number • *She rounded 10.6 (up) to 11.* • *Round off the amounts to the nearest dollar.* — **round up** [phrasal vb] **round up (someone or something)** or **round (someone or something) up** : to find and gather together (people, animals, or things) • *They rounded up all the suspects/cattle.*

⁵**round** prep, chiefly Brit : AROUND 2 : all during : THROUGHOUT • *The bush stays green (all) round the year.*

¹**round·about** /ˈraʊndəˌbaʊt/ adj : not direct • *a roundabout route to town* • *In a roundabout way, he told me that he needed help.*

²**roundabout** n [C] Brit 1 : TRAFFIC CIRCLE 2 : MERRY-GO-ROUND

round·ly /ˈraʊndli/ adv 1 a : thoroughly or completely • *He was roundly defeated.* b : by nearly everyone : WIDELY • *roundly praised* 2 : using plain or strong language • *She roundly criticized the plan.*

round·ta·ble /ˈraʊndˌteɪbəl/ n [C] : a meeting at which people discuss something and everyone has an equal chance to express an opinion • *a roundtable discussion*

round–the–clock adj, always before a noun : AROUND-THE-CLOCK

round trip n [C] : a trip to a place and back usually over the same route — **round trip** adv, US • *The drive is 50 miles round trip.* — **round–trip** /ˈraʊndˌtrɪp/ adj, always before a noun, US • *a round-trip ticket*

round·up /ˈraʊndˌʌp/ n [C] 1 : the act or process of finding and gathering together people or things of the same kind • *a roundup of all the suspects/cattle* 2 : SUMMARY • *a roundup of today's news*

rouse /ˈraʊz/ vb **roused; rous·ing** [T] somewhat formal 1 : to wake (someone) from sleep • *I've been unable to rouse her.*

2 : to cause (an emotional response) in someone ▪ *His performance roused the audience.* ▪ *a rousing speech/victory* ▪ *She was roused to anger by their indifference.* **3** : to cause (something) to happen ▪ *The report roused roused speculation.*

¹rout /ˈraʊt/ *n* **1** [C] : a game or contest in which the winner easily defeats the loser **2** [C/U] : a confused and disorderly retreat

²rout *vb* [T] **1** : to defeat (someone) easily in a game or contest ▪ *He was routed in the election.* **2** : to force (someone or something) to move from a place ▪ *People were routed out of their homes by soldiers.*

¹route /ˈruːt, ˈraʊt/ *n* [C] **1** : a way to get from one place to another ▪ *a parade/escape route* ▪ *We took the scenic route.* [=a way that is not the fastest way but that has beautiful scenery] **2** : a way of achieving or doing something ▪ *I decided to go/take the traditional route* [=do the traditional thing] *and have a big wedding.* **3** *US* : a usually minor highway

²route *vb* **rout·ed; rout·ing** [T] : to send (someone or something) along a particular route ▪ *Traffic was routed around the accident.*

rout·er *n* [C] **1** /ˈraʊtə/ : a machine used for cutting a groove into wood or metal **2** /ˈruːtə, ˈraʊtə/ *technical* : a device that sends data to another place within a computer network or between computer networks

¹rou·tine /ruˈtiːn/ *n* **1** [C/U] : a regular way of doing things in a particular order ▪ *A walk is part of her morning routine.* ▪ *The job was easier once I settled into a routine.* **2** [C] **a** : a series of movements, jokes, etc., that are repeated as part of a performance ▪ *a comedy/dance routine* **b** *informal* : something that is said or done the same way very often ▪ *He gave me the old "I'm too busy" routine.* [=he said "I'm too busy"]

²routine *adj* **1** : done very often ▪ *routine surgery* **2** : done or happening as a normal part of a job, situation, or process ▪ *routine business practices* — **rou·tine·ly** *adv*

rove /ˈroʊv/ *vb* **roved; rov·ing** [T/I] *literary* : to go to different places without having a particular purpose or plan ▪ *a roving reporter*

rov·er /ˈroʊvə/ *n* [C] **1** *literary* : a person who wanders to different places **2** : a machine used for exploring the surface of a moon, planet, etc.

¹row /ˈroʊ/ *n* [C] **1** : a straight line of people or things that are next to each other ▪ *an empty row of seats* **2** : a street or road — used in names ▪ *a house on Church Row* — **in a row** : following one after another ▪ *five trees in a row* ▪ *We ate pizza three nights in a row.* — compare ³ROW

²row /ˈroʊ/ *vb* **1** [T/I] : to move a boat through water using oars ▪ *rowing (a boat) across the lake* **2** [T] : to carry (someone or something) in a boat that you row ▪ *I rowed them out to the island.* — compare ⁴ROW — **row·er** /ˈroʊwə/ *n* [C] ▪ *Olympic rowers*

³row /ˈraʊ/ *n* [C] *chiefly Brit, informal* : a noisy argument, disturbance, etc. ▪ *They got into a row.* ▪ *The proposal caused a huge row.* [=*uproar*] — compare ¹ROW

⁴row /ˈraʊ/ *vb* [I] *Brit* : to have a noisy argument with someone ▪ *He's always rowing with his wife.* — compare ²ROW

row·boat /ˈroʊˌboʊt/ *n* [C] *US* : a small boat that is moved through water using oars — called also (*Brit*) **rowing boat**

row·dy /ˈraʊdi/ *adj* **row·di·er; -est** : rough or noisy ▪ *a rowdy crowd/game* — **row·di·ness** /ˈraʊdinəs/ *n* [U]

roy·al /ˈrojəl/ *adj, always before a noun* **1** : of or relating to a king or queen ▪ *the royal family/palace* **2** : suitable for a king or queen ▪ *The hotel gave us the royal treatment.* — **royal** *n* [C] ▪ *a young royal* [=member of a royal family] — **roy·al·ly** /ˈrojəli/ *adv* ▪ *We were treated royally.* ▪ (*US, informal*) *I messed up royally.* [=very badly]

royal flush *n* [C] : a set of cards that a player has in a card game (such as poker) that are all of the same suit and are the most valuable cards in that suit

roy·al·ist /ˈrojəlɪst/ *n* [C] : a person who believes that a country should have a king or queen or who supports a particular king or queen

roy·al·ty /ˈrojəlti/ *n, pl* **-ties** **1** [U] : members of a royal family ▪ *We were treated like royalty.* **2** [C] **a** : money that is paid to the original creator of a song, book, etc., based on how many copies have been sold ▪ *The book has earned $40,000 in royalties.* **b** : money that is paid by a mining or oil company to the owner of the land the company is using

rpm *abbr* revolutions per minute

RR *abbr* **1** railroad ▪ *RR crossings* **2** *or* **R.R.** *US* rural route

¹RSVP *abbr* — used on invitations to ask invited guests to indicate whether they will be able to attend ◇ *RSVP* comes from the French phrase "répondez s'il vous plaît."

²RSVP /ˌɑːˌɛsˌviˈpiː/ *vb* **RSVP's** *or* **RSVPs; RSVP'd** *or* **RSVPed; RSVP'·ing** *or* **RSVP·ing** [I] *chiefly US* : to respond to an invitation ▪ *Have you RSVP'd?*

Rt *or* **Rt.** *abbr, US* route ▪ *Rt 70*

Rte. *or* **Rte** *abbr, US* route

¹rub /ˈrʌb/ *vb* **rubbed; rub·bing** **1** [T/I] : to move your hand, an object, etc., back and forth along the surface of (something) while pressing ▪ *He rubbed his eyes.* ▪ *The cat rubbed against my leg.* **2** [T/I] : to move (two things) back and forth against each other ▪ *I rubbed my hands (together) to warm them up.* **3** [T/I] : to move back and forth many times against something in a way that causes pain or damage ▪ *There are marks where the chair has been rubbing (against) the wall.* **4** [T] : to spread (something) on a surface by pressing firmly with your hands ▪ *Rub the steaks with spices.* = *Rub spices on/onto the steaks.* ▪ (*figurative*) *She beat me and then rubbed salt in the wound* [=made a difficult situation even worse for me] *by telling everyone.* — **rub**

elbows with (US) or *rub shoulders with* *informal* : to meet and talk with (someone) in a friendly way ▪ *I got to rub elbows with some local politicians.* — *rub in* [*phrasal vb*] *rub (something) in* or *rub in (something)* *informal* : to remind someone of (something that person would like to forget) ▪ *She keeps rubbing in the fact that she makes more money than I do.* — *rub off* [*phrasal vb*] **1** : to be removed from a surface and often stick to another surface when the surfaces touch each other ▪ *The ink may rub off (on your fingers).* ▪ (*figurative*) *I wish some of your good luck would rub off on me.* **2** *rub (something) off* or *rub off (something)* : to remove (something) from a surface by rubbing ▪ *I rubbed the dirt off (of) my knees.* — *rub out* [*phrasal vb*] *rub (something) out* or *rub out (something)* *chiefly Brit* : to remove (something) especially with an eraser ▪ *rubbing out the answer on a test* — *rub someone's nose in* *informal* : to remind someone of (a mistake, failure, etc.) in a mean way ▪ *He beat us and then rubbed our noses in it.* — *rub (someone) the wrong way* (US) or *Brit* *rub (someone) up the wrong way* *informal* : to cause (someone) to be angry or annoyed ▪ *Her suggestion really rubbed me the wrong way.*

²**rub** *n* **1** [*C*] : an act of rubbing a surface with your hands or an object ▪ *He gave the windshield a quick rub with a dry cloth.* ▪ *Let me give you a back rub.* [=let me rub/massage your back] **2** *the rub* *formal* : something that causes a difficulty or problem ▪ *Therein/There lies the rub.* [=that's the problem] **3** [*C*] US : a mixture of spices that is rubbed onto meat before the meat is cooked

rub·ber /ˈrʌbɚ/ *n* **1** [*U*] : a strong substance that stretches ▪ *tires made of rubber* ▪ *a rubber ball* **2** [*C*] Brit : ERASER **3** [*plural*] US, *old-fashioned* : rubber shoes or boots that fit over your regular shoes to keep them dry **4** [*C*] US, *informal* : CONDOM — *burn rubber* *informal* : to drive very fast

rubber band *n* [*C*] : a thin, flexible loop that is made of rubber and used to hold things together

rub·ber·neck /ˈrʌbɚˌnɛk/ *vb* [*I*] *chiefly US, informal* : to stare with great curiosity ▪ *Drivers were rubbernecking as they passed the accident.* — **rub·ber·neck·er** /ˈrʌbɚˌnɛkɚ/ *n* [*C*]

rubber stamp *n* [*C*] **1** : a small tool with a piece of carved rubber on it that is dipped in ink and then pressed on paper to print a date, name, symbol, etc. **2** *disapproving* : a person or group that automatically approves everything that someone does or decides ▪ *The legislature was just a rubber stamp for the President.* — **rubber-stamp** *vb* [*T*] ▪ *They rubber-stamp his proposals.*

rub·bery /ˈrʌbɚi/ *adj* **1** : similar to rubber ▪ *rubbery eggs* **2** *of legs or knees* : weak, shaky, and unstable ▪ *Her legs were/felt rubbery when she stepped off the roller coaster.*

rubbing alcohol *n* [*U*] *US* : a liquid that contains alcohol and water and that is used to clean wounds or skin

rub·bish /ˈrʌbɪʃ/ *n* [*U*] **1** : ¹TRASH **1** ▪ *picking rubbish up off the ground* ▪ (*chiefly Brit*) *Put the potato peels in the rubbish bin.* [=(US) garbage can, (chiefly US) trash can] **2** *chiefly Brit, informal* : NONSENSE **1** ▪ *That's (a load of) rubbish! I didn't do it.* **3** *informal* : something that is worthless, unimportant, or of poor quality ▪ *Why are you reading that rubbish?*

rub·ble /ˈrʌbəl/ *n* [*U*] : broken pieces of stone, brick, etc., from walls or buildings that have fallen ▪ *pulling injured people out of the rubble*

rub·down /ˈrʌbˌdaʊn/ *n* [*C*] *chiefly US* : an act of rubbing someone's body to relax the muscles

ru·bel·la /ruˈbɛlə/ *n* [*U*] *medical* : GERMAN MEASLES

ru·ble (*chiefly US*) or *chiefly Brit* **rou·ble** /ˈruːbəl/ *n* [*C*] **1** : the basic unit of money of Russia ▪ *It costs 40 rubles.* **2** : a coin representing one ruble

ru·bric /ˈruːbrɪk/ *n* [*C*] *formal* **1** : a name or heading under which something is classified ▪ *Their songs fall under the rubric of "world music."* **2** : an explanation or a set of instructions at the beginning of a book, a test, etc.

ru·by /ˈruːbi/ *n, pl* **-bies** **1** [*C*] : a deep red stone that is used in jewelry **2** [*C/U*] : a dark red color ▪ *ruby (red) lips*

ruck·sack /ˈrʌkˌsæk/ *n* [*C*] *chiefly Brit* : BACKPACK

ruck·us /ˈrʌkəs/ *n* [*singular*] *chiefly US, informal* : a noisy argument, fight, etc. ▪ *He raised a ruckus* [=got upset and complained very loudly] *over the cost of the repairs.*

ruc·tions /ˈrʌkʃənz/ *n* [*plural*] *chiefly Brit* : angry arguments or complaints

rud·der /ˈrʌdɚ/ *n* [*C*] : a flat, movable piece that is attached to a ship, airplane, etc., and is used in steering

rud·dy /ˈrʌdi/ *adj* **1** : having a healthy reddish color ▪ *ruddy cheeks* **2** *literary* : RED ▪ *the ruddy surface of Mars*

rude /ˈruːd/ *adj* **rud·er; rud·est** **1** : not having or showing concern or respect for the rights and feelings of other people : not polite ▪ *rude remarks/behavior* ▪ *It is rude (of/for you) to keep us waiting.* **2** : relating to sex or other body functions in a way that offends others ▪ *a rude joke/noise* **3** *always before a noun* : happening suddenly in usually an unpleasant or shocking way ▪ *If you think this job is going to be easy, you're in for a rude awakening.* [=you will be unpleasantly surprised when you realize that this job is not easy] **4** *literary* : made or done in a simple or rough way : CRUDE ▪ *a rude stone farmhouse* — **rude·ly** *adv* ▪ *He rudely interrupted me.* — **rude·ness** *n* [*U*]

ru·di·men·ta·ry /ˌruːdəˈmɛntəri/ *adj, formal* **1** : basic or simple ▪ *a rudimentary knowledge of human anatomy* ▪ *He speaks rudimentary English.* **2** : not very developed or advanced ▪ *rudimentary technology*

ru·di·ments /ˈruːdəmənts/ *n* [*plural*] *for-*

mal : basic facts or skills ▪ *the rudiments of grammar*

rue /'ruː/ *vb* **rued; ru·ing** [T] *formal* : to feel sorrow or regret for (something) ▪ *I rue the day (that) I signed that contract.*

rue·ful /'ruːfəl/ *adj* : showing or feeling regret for something done ▪ *a rueful smile* — **rue·ful·ly** *adv*

ruf·fi·an /'rʌfijən/ *n* [C] *old-fashioned* : a cruel, violent person ▪ *a gang of ruffians*

¹**ruf·fle** /'rʌfəl/ *vb* **ruf·fled; ruf·fling** [T] **1** : to move or lift (something) so that it is no longer smooth ▪ *The bird ruffled (up) its feathers.* ▪ *(figurative, informal) His remarks ruffled (a few) feathers.* [=upset or offended people] **2** : to make (someone) irritated, annoyed, worried, etc. ▪ *She was ruffled by the reporter's question.*

²**ruffle** *n* [C] : a piece of cloth that is gathered together along one edge ▪ *The dress has a ruffle around the collar.* — **ruffled** *adj* ▪ *a ruffled collar*

rug /'rʌg/ *n* [C] **1** : a piece of thick, heavy material that is used to cover a section of a floor **2** *chiefly US, informal* : TOUPEE **3** *Brit* : a blanket that you put over your legs to keep them warm — **pull the rug (out) from under** *informal* : to very suddenly take something needed or expected from (someone or something) ▪ *The mayor pulled the rug out from under us and cut our funding.* — **sweep (something) under the rug** *see* ¹SWEEP

rug·by *also* **Rugby** /'rʌgbi/ *n* [U] : a game played by two teams in which each team tries to carry or kick a ball over the other team's goal line — called also *(chiefly Brit) rugby football*

rug·ged /'rʌgəd/ *adj* **1** : having a rough, uneven surface ▪ *the rugged surface of the moon* **2** *of a man's face* : having rough but attractive features ▪ *People are attracted to his rugged good looks.* **3** : strong and tough ▪ *rugged plastic/pioneers* **4** : involving great difficulties or challenges ▪ *the rugged life of a sailor* — **rug·ged·ly** *adv* — **rug·ged·ness** *n* [U]

¹**ru·in** /'ruːwən/ *vb* [T] **1** : to damage (something) so badly that it is no longer useful, valuable, enjoyable, etc. ▪ *Moths ruined the sweater.* ▪ *The bad weather ruined* [=spoiled] *the party.* ▪ *His low test scores ruined his chances of getting into a good school.* **2** : to cause (someone) to lose money, social status, etc. ▪ *She was ruined by debt.*

²**ruin** *n* **1** [U] : a state of complete destruction : a state of being ruined ▪ *The town fell into ruin.* **2** [C] : the remaining pieces of something that was destroyed ▪ *the ruins of the ancient city* ▪ *The building was/lay in ruins.* ▪ *(figurative) After her death, the family was in ruins.* **3** [U] : the state of having lost money, social status, etc. ▪ *The drought brought financial ruin to farmers.* **4** [*singular*] : something that badly damages someone physically, economically, etc. ▪ *Her drug addiction was her ruin.*

ru·in·a·tion /,ruːwə'neɪʃən/ *n* [U] *formal* : the act or process of destroying something ▪ *Water pollution is causing the ruination of the fishing industry.*

ru·in·ous /'ruːwənəs/ *adj, formal* **1** : causing or likely to cause damage or destruction ▪ *the ruinous effects of smoking* **2** : costing far too much money ▪ *ruinous price increases* — **ru·in·ous·ly** *adv* ▪ *ruinously expensive*

¹**rule** /'ruːl/ *n* **1** [C] : a statement that tells you what is or is not allowed in a particular game, situation, etc. ▪ *the rules of chess/grammar* ▪ *follow/obey/break the rules* ▪ *The new rule allows/permits employees to dress casually on Fridays.* ▪ *It's against the rules to eat during class.* ▪ *(figurative) She has played by the rules throughout her career.* **2** [C] : a piece of advice about the best way to do something ▪ *The first rule of driving is to pay attention.* **3** [*singular*] : the way something usually is done or happens ▪ *As a (general) rule, I don't drive in the snow.* [=I don't usually drive in the snow] **4** [U] : control and power over a country or area ▪ *the country's independence from colonial rule* ▪ *Under her rule, the country prospered.* — **rule of thumb 1** : a method of doing something that is based on experience and common sense ▪ *A good rule of thumb is to get rid of any clothes you haven't worn in the past year.* **2** : a principle that is based on the way something usually happens or is done ▪ *As a rule of thumb, stocks having greater risk also have the potential of earning more money.*

²**rule** *vb* **ruled; rul·ing 1** [T/I] : to have control and power over a country, area, etc. ▪ *The queen ruled (the country) for 25 years.* ▪ *a member of the ruling class/party* ▪ *(figurative) After the overthrow of the government, chaos ruled.* [=there was a lot of chaos] **2** [T] : to have great influence over (someone) ▪ *Football rules their lives.* **3** [T/I] : to make a legal decision about something ▪ *The Supreme Court ruled the law unconstitutional.* ▪ *The court ruled in favor of the defendant.* ▪ *The jury ruled against the tobacco companies.* ▪ *How will the court rule on the motion?* **4** [I] *slang* : to be very good or popular ▪ *That movie rules!* — **rule out** [*phrasal vb*] **rule (someone or something) out** *or* **rule out (someone or something) 1** : to no longer consider (someone or something) as a possibility ▪ *The police ruled them out as suspects.* **2** : to prevent (something) from happening ▪ *The bad weather ruled out a picnic.* — **rule with an iron fist/hand** *(chiefly US) or Brit* **rule with a rod of iron** : to rule a country, area, etc., in a very strict and often cruel way ▪ *The dictator ruled (the country) with an iron fist.*

ruled *adj* : printed with lines on which to write ▪ *wide-ruled notebook paper*

rul·er /'ruːlɚ/ *n* [C] **1** : a king, queen, etc., who rules a country, area, etc. **2** : a straight piece of plastic, wood, or metal that has marks on it and that is used to measure things

rul·ing *n* [C] : an official decision made by a judge, referee, etc. ▪ *the court's ruling on the case*

rum /'rʌm/ *n* [C/U] : an alcoholic drink that is made from sugar

rum·ba *also* **rhum·ba** /'rʌmbə/ *n* **1** [C]

: a type of dance from Cuba in which dancers move their hips a lot   **2** [C/U] : the music for a rumba • *playing (a) rumba*

rum·ble /ˈrʌmbəl/ *vb* **rum·bled; rum·bling** [I] : to make or move with a low, heavy, continuous sound • *Thunder rumbled in the distance.* • *I got hungry and my stomach started rumbling.* • *The train rumbled through town.* — **rumble** *n* [C] • *I heard a rumble of thunder.*

rum·bus·tious /ˌrʌmˈbʌstʃəs/ *adj, Brit* : RAMBUNCTIOUS

ru·mi·nant /ˈruːmənənt/ *n* [C] *technical* : an animal (such as a cow or sheep) that ruminates

ru·mi·nate /ˈruːməˌneɪt/ *vb* **-nat·ed; -nat·ing** [I]   **1** *formal* : to think carefully and deeply about something • *He ruminated over/about the meaning of life.*   **2** *technical, of an animal* : to swallow food and then bring it back up again to continue chewing it • *a ruminating cow* — **ru·mi·na·tion** /ˌruːməˈneɪʃən/ *n* [C/U]

ru·mi·na·tive /ˈruːməˌneɪtɪv/ *adj, formal* : showing careful thought about something • *a ruminative mood*

rum·mage /ˈrʌmɪdʒ/ *vb* **-maged; -mag·ing** [I] : to search for something by looking through the contents of a place • *He rummaged through the attic for his stamp collection.* — **rummage** *n* [singular] *chiefly Brit* • *having a rummage through the fridge*

rummage sale *n* [C] *US* : a sale of old clothes, toys, etc.

rum·my /ˈrʌmi/ *n* [U] : a card game in which each player tries to collect groups of three or more cards

ru·mor (*US*) *or Brit* **ru·mour** /ˈruːmə/ *n* [C/U] : information or a story that is passed from person to person but has not been proven to be true • *starting/spreading rumors about someone* • *Rumor has it that they broke up.*

ru·mored (*US*) *or Brit* **ru·moured** /ˈruːməd/ *adj* — used to describe what is being said in rumors • *The estate sold for a rumored $12 million.* • *The new boss is rumored to be a bit of a tyrant.*

rump /ˈrʌmp/ *n* [C]   **1** : the back part of an animal's body where the thighs join the hips   **2** *humorous* : the part of the body you sit on • *I fell on my rump.*

rum·ple /ˈrʌmpəl/ *vb* **rum·pled; rum·pling** [T] : to make (something) messy or wrinkled • *He rumpled her hair affectionately.* • *a rumpled shirt*

rum·pus /ˈrʌmpəs/ *n* [singular] *chiefly Brit, informal* : RUCKUS

¹**run** /ˈrʌn/ *vb* **ran** /ˈræn/; **run; run·ning**   **1** [I]   **a** : to move with your legs at a speed that is faster than walking • *She ran up the stairs.* • *The dog ran after [=chased] the squirrel.*   **b** : to leave a place quickly by running • *When the alarm sounded, the robbers ran (off/ away).*   **2** [T/I]   **a** : to run as part of a sport or for exercise • *She ran on the track team in college.* • *I run six miles every day.*   **b** *American football* : to carry and run with (the ball) • *He ran (the ball) for a 20-yard gain.*   **c** *baseball* : to

run from base to base • *He runs the bases well.*   **3** [T] : to cause (an animal) to run • *She ran the horse through the fields.*   **4** [I] *chiefly US* : to be a candidate in an election for a particular office • *She is running for mayor.* • *He is running against her in the election.*   **5** [T]   **a** : to direct the business or activities of (something) • *She runs [=manages] the store.* • *The company is badly/privately run.* • *state/family-run companies* • *I can run my own life!*   **b** : to do (a test or check) on someone or something • *The doctors ran tests on the blood samples.*   **6** **a** [T] : to use and control (something) • *run [=operate] a forklift*   **b** [I] : to function or operate • *The car's engine was running.* • *I'll have the computer up and running in no time.* • *The car runs on diesel.*   **7** [I] : to go on a particular route or at particular times • *The bus/ferry runs every hour.*   **8** **a** [T/I] : to make a quick trip to a place or event • *She ran to the store for milk.* • *I have to run the kids to soccer practice.* • *running around* [=going from place to place] *doing errands*   **b** : to do (something that involves making a quick trip) • *I have a few errands to run after work.*   **9** [T/I] : to move or cause (something) to move • *He ran (his car) into a tree.* • *That car tried to run me off the road!*   **10** [T/I] : to pass or cause (something) to pass through, over, along, or into something else • *I ran a comb through my hair.* • *A chill ran up/down my spine.*   **11** [T/I] : to go or extend or cause (something) to extend in a particular direction • *The highway runs from Boston to New York.* • *A path runs along the ridge.* • *He ran the wires up from the basement.* • *(figurative) Lying would run against his moral principles.*   **12** [T] : SMUGGLE • *They've been running drugs into the country.*   **13** **a** [T/I] : to flow or cause (something) to flow • *He left the water running.* • *Sand ran out of the bag.* • *Run the water until it gets hot.*   **b** [T] : to prepare (a bath) by running a faucet • *She ran a bath for her son.*   **14** [I] : to produce a flow of liquid • *My nose/eyes started to run.*   **b** : to spread or flow into another area • *Your mascara is running.*   **15** [I] : to continue or remain effective for a particular period of time • *His contract runs until next season.* • *The play has run for six months.*   **16** [I] : to be or to begin to be something specified • *The well has run dry.* • *Supplies were running low/short.* • *I have to hurry. I'm running late.*   **17** [I] : to include everything between specified limits • *Ticket prices run from $10 to $50.*   **18** [T/I] : to have or reach a particular length, size, price, or amount • *The rooms run $100 a night.* • *The book runs (to) nearly 500 pages.*   **19 a** [T] : to print or broadcast (something) • *The ad/story was run in today's newspaper.*   **b** [I] : to appear in print or on TV • *The show ran for five seasons.*   **20** [T/I] : to have (particular words) in writing or print • *"War Is Over" ran the headline.* • *The definition runs as follows.*   **21** [T] : to drive past or through (a stop sign or red traffic light) illegally without stopping ▪ *She ran the stop sign.*

In addition to the phrases shown below, *run* occurs in many idioms that are shown at appropriate entries throughout the dictionary. For example, *cut* and *run* can be found at ¹CUT and *run a tight ship* can be found at ¹SHIP.

— **run across** [*phrasal vb*] : to meet (someone) or find (something) by chance ▪ *I ran across an old roommate/ photo.* — **run a fever/temperature** : to have a body temperature that is higher than 98.6 degrees Fahrenheit ▪ *You can't keep running away from your problems.* **3 a** *disapproving* : to leave a person or place in order to live with and have a sexual relationship with (someone) ▪ *He left his wife and ran away with his secretary.* **b** : to leave a place with (something that does not belong to you) ▪ *The butler ran away with the family silver.* — **run by/past** [*phrasal vb*] **run (something) by/past** : to tell (something) to (someone) so that it can be considered, approved, etc. ▪ *You'd better run this by the boss.* — **run down** [*phrasal vb*] **1 run (someone or something) down** or **run down (someone or something) a** : to hit and knock down (a person or animal) with a vehicle ▪ *She tried to run him down.* **b** : to chase after and catch (a person or animal) ▪ *The cops ran the robber down.* **c** : to find (someone or something) after searching ▪ *He wasn't in his office, but I finally ran him down in the lounge.* **2 run down** or **run down (something)** or **run (something) down** : to use up or cause (something) to use up all of its power ▪ *Turn off the radio so you don't run down the batteries.* **3** : to say or repeat (a list of people or things) ▪ *Let me run down all the things we need to do.* — **run for it** *informal* : to run to avoid being caught ▪ *It's the cops! Run for it!* — **run high** : to be or become very strong or intense ▪ *Emotions are running high.* — **run into** [*phrasal vb*] **1** : to move into (someone or something) in a sudden or forceful way ▪ *She ran into the table.* **2** : to meet (someone) by chance ▪ *I ran into an old classmate today.* **3** : to experience (problems, difficulties, etc.) ▪ *We ran into some bad weather on our way home.* — **run its course** ✧ When something *runs its course*, it begins, continues for a time, and then ends. ▪ *The disease will run its course in a few days.* — **run off** [*phrasal vb*] **1** : to leave or abandon a person or place ▪ *Her husband ran off and left her.* ▪ *She ran off with all the money.* **2 run off (something)** or **run (something) off** : to repeat or produce (something) quickly ▪ *I ran off five copies of the letter.* — **run on** [*phrasal vb*] : to keep going

without being stopped or interrupted for a long period of time ▪ *The meeting ran on for hours.* — **run out** [*phrasal vb*] **1 a** : to come to an end ▪ *My contract runs out soon.* **b** : to become used up ▪ *The money ran out.* **2 run out** or **run out of** : to use up the available supply of (something) ▪ *We're low on gas. We'd better stop before we run out.* ▪ *We're running out of time.* **3** *informal* : to leave (someone you should stay with) ▪ *She ran out on her husband and children.* — **run over** [*phrasal vb*] **1** : to go beyond a limit ▪ *The meeting ran over.* [=the meeting was longer than it was expected or planned to be] **2** : to flow over the top or edge of something ▪ *The water was running over onto the floor.* **3 run over (someone or something)** or **run (someone or something) over a** : to knock down and drive over or go over (someone or something) ▪ *The dog was run over by a car.* **b** : to read, repeat, or practice (something) quickly ▪ *Let's run the lines over one more time.* — **run past** see RUN BY (above) — **run through** [*phrasal vb*] **1 a** : to spend or use up (something) quickly ▪ *He ran through his winnings in a short time.* **b** : to read, repeat, or practice (something) quickly ▪ *He quickly ran through the dance routine.* **c** : to occur repeatedly in or throughout (something) ▪ *The song has been running through my head all day.* **2 run (something) through** : to enter (information) into (a computer) for processing ▪ *She ran his name through the police computer.* — **run up** [*phrasal vb*] **1 run up (something)** or **run (something) up** : to raise (a flag) to the top of a flagpole ▪ *We ran up the flag.* **b** : to cause (a large score, debt, etc.) to happen or exist ▪ *She ran up a large phone bill.* ▪ : to increase the amount of (something) ▪ *running up the bill* **2** : to experience (something difficult) ▪ *She has run up against a lot of opposition.* — **run with** [*phrasal vb*] *informal* : to use (something) in a very enthusiastic and effective way ▪ *He took the idea and ran with it.* — **run your mouth** *informal* : to talk too much and in a foolish way ▪ *He's always running his mouth about how smart he is.*

²**run** *n* **1** [*C*] : an act of running ▪ *He goes for a six-mile run every day.* ▪ *She took the dogs out on a run.* ▪ *The robbers heard the police sirens and made a run for it.* [=ran away] **2** [*C*] **a** : a continuous series of similar things ▪ *a run of bad luck* ▪ *a long run of wins* **b** : a continuous series of performances or showings ▪ *The play had a six-month run on Broadway.* **3** [*C*] *US* : an attempt to win or do something ▪ *She made a run for* [=she tried to be elected to] *a seat in the Senate.* **4** [*C*] **a** : a score made in baseball when a player reaches home plate after going around the bases **b** : a score made in cricket **5** [*C*] *American football* : a play in which a player tries to move the ball forward by running with it ▪ *a 25-yard run* **6 a** [*C*] : a regular journey that is made by a bus, train, etc. ▪ *The bus makes four runs daily.* ▪ *a delivery run* **b** [*singular*] : a short trip in a vehicle ▪ *I made a quick run to the*

store. **7** [C] : a track that slopes down and that is used for skiing, sledding, etc. **8** [C] : an enclosed area for animals where they feed and exercise • *a chicken run* **9** [C] *US* : a long hole in a stocking **10** [C] : a situation in which many people want to have, get, or do something at the same time • *There is usually a run on bread and milk before a big storm.* • *There was a run on the bank* [=a lot of people were taking their money out of the bank] **11 the runs** *informal* : DIARRHEA • *He had the runs.* — *a run for your money* ✧ *Someone who gives us a (good) run for your money* tries hard and plays or performs well in a game or contest and makes it difficult for you to win. • *We beat them, but they gave us a run for our money.* — *on the run* **1 a** : running away from someone in order to avoid being captured • *an escaped convict on the run* **b** : running away because you are about to be defeated • *The enemy was on the run.* **2** : while going somewhere • *We ate lunch on the run.* — *the run of* : the freedom to go anywhere or do anything you want in (a place) • *With his parents gone, he had the run of the house.*

run·around /'rʌnəˌraʊnd/ *n* — **the runaround** *informal* : a situation in which you are not given the information or help that you need because someone will not answer your questions or deal with your problem directly • *I got the runaround from them.* = *They gave me the runaround.*

¹**run·away** /'rʌnəˌweɪ/ *n* [C] : someone (such as a child) who leaves home without permission • *teenage runaways*

²**runaway** *adj, always before a noun* **1** — used to describe a person who has left home without permission or who has escaped from some place • *a runaway teenager/slave* **2** : running, increasing, etc., in a fast and dangerous way that cannot be controlled • *a runaway horse/train* • *runaway inflation* **3** : extremely successful • *a runaway best seller* **4** : won or winning very easily by a large amount • *a runaway victory* • *the runaway winner*

run–down /'rʌnˈdaʊn/ *adj* **1** : in very bad condition • *a run-down old building* **2** *not before a noun* : in poor health : worn-out or exhausted • *You look rundown.*

run–down /'rʌnˈdaʊn/ *n* [C] : a quick report about the main parts of something • *a rundown on/of the news*

¹**rung** *past participle of* ³RING

²**rung** /'rʌŋ/ *n* [C] **1** : a piece of wood or metal that is between the legs of a chair **2** : a step on a ladder • *(figurative) people on the bottom rung* [=at the bottom position or level] *of society*

run–in /'rʌnˌɪn/ *n* [C] *informal* : an angry argument • *He had a run-in with the cops.*

run·ner /'rʌnɚ/ *n* [C] **1 a** : a person who runs as part of a sport or for exercise • *a fast/marathon runner* **b** : a horse, dog, etc., that runs in a race **2 a** : a person who delivers messages, reports, materials, or products **b** : a person who brings drugs, guns, etc., to a place illegally and secretly • *a drug runner* **3** *baseball*

: BASE RUNNER **4** : a long, thin part on which a skate, drawer, etc., slides **5** : a stem of a plant that grows along the ground and that forms new plants **6 a** : a long, narrow carpet for a hall or staircase **b** : a narrow cloth cover for a table, dresser, etc. — *do a runner* *Brit, informal* : to leave a place quickly by running especially to avoid paying a bill or to escape punishment

run·ner–up /'rʌnɚˈʌp/ *n, pl* **run·ners–up** /'rʌnɚzˈʌp/ [C] : a person or team that does not win first place in a contest but that does well enough to get a prize; *especially* : a person or team that finishes in second place

¹**run·ning** /'rʌnɪŋ/ *n* [U] **1** : the activity or sport of running • *long-distance running* • *They go running every day.* **2** : the activity of managing or operating something • *the day-to-day running of the business* **3** : the activity of bringing drugs, guns, etc., to a place illegally and secretly • *drug running* — *in the running* **1** : competing in a contest • *He's in the running for mayor.* **2** : having a chance to win a contest • *She's in the running for first place.* — *out of the running* **1** : not competing in a contest • *He's officially out of the running for mayor.* **2** : having no chance to win a contest • *She's out of the running for first place.*

²**running** *adj, always before a noun* **1** : operating or flowing • *a running engine/faucet* **2** : going on steadily or repeatedly for a long period of time • *The farmer had a running battle with pests.* • *a running joke between friends* **3** : made during the course of a process or activity • *They provided running commentary on the election results.* • *She kept a running total of her expenses.* **4** : done while running or immediately after running • *a running catch/jump* **5** *American football* — used to describe play in which the ball is moved forward by running rather than by passing • *The team has a strong running game.* **6** : designed for use by runners • *running shoes*

³**running** *adv, always after a noun* : following or happening one after the other • *It has rained (for) three days running.* [=for three days in a row]

running back *n* [C] *American football* : a player who carries the football on running plays

running mate *n* [C] *chiefly US* : the person who runs with someone in an election and who is given the less important position if they are elected • *the presidential candidate and his running mate*

running start *n* [singular] *chiefly US* — used to say that a person or animal is running at the start of a race, jump, etc. • *She took a running start and jumped over the stream.* • *(figurative) He's off to a running start.* [=he has been successful very quickly]

running time *n* [C/U] : the amount of time that a movie, song, etc., lasts from beginning to end

running water *n* [U] : water that comes into a building through pipes • *a cabin with running water*

run·ny /ˈrʌni/ adj **run·ni·er; -est** **1** of a food : soft and with a lot of liquid ▪ The fried eggs are runny. **2** : having a thin flow of liquid flowing out ▪ runny noses/eyes

run-off /ˈrʌnˌɑːf/ n **1** [C] : an additional race, contest, or election that is held because an earlier one has not resulted in a winner **2** [U] : water that flows over the surface of the ground into streams

run-of-the-mill /ˌrʌnəvðəˈmɪl/ adj, often disapproving : average or ordinary ▪ a run-of-the-mill performance

runt /ˈrʌnt/ n [C] : an unusually small animal or person ▪ the runt of the litter ▪ (informal + disapproving) The boy is a skinny, little runt.

run-through /ˈrʌnˌθruː/ n [C] : an activity in which you quickly practice all the different parts of a performance, speech, etc. ▪ She gave her lines a quick run-through.

run-up /ˈrʌnˌʌp/ n [C] **1** : a usually sudden increase in price ▪ a run-up in stock prices **2** : the period immediately before an action or event ▪ during the run-up to the war

run·way /ˈrʌnˌweɪ/ n [C] **1** : a long strip of ground where airplanes take off and land **2** US : CATWALK 2

ru·pee /ˈruːˈpiː/ n [C] : the basic unit of money in some Asian countries

1rup·ture /ˈrʌptʃɚ/ n **1** [C/U] : a crack or break in something (such as a pipe) **2** medical **a** [C/U] : a break or tear in a part of the body ▪ a/the rupture of an artery **b** [C] : HERNIA **3** [C] : a break in good relations between people or countries ▪ a rupture in their marriage

2rupture vb **-tured; -tur·ing** **1 a** [T/I] : to break or burst ▪ ruptured pipes **b** [T] medical : to break or tear (a part of the body) ▪ The impact ruptured his liver. **2** [T] : to damage or destroy (a relationship, situation, etc.) ▪ His lies ruptured their marriage.

ru·ral /ˈrɚrəl/ adj : of or relating to the country and the people who live there instead of the city ▪ rural areas/voters

ruse /ˈruːs, Brit ˈruːz/ n [C] : a trick or act that is used to fool someone ▪ a clever ruse

1rush /ˈrʌʃ/ vb **1** [T/I] : to move or do something very quickly or in a way that shows you are in a hurry ▪ Firefighters rushed to the accident scene. ▪ I rushed home. ▪ She rushed through dinner. ▪ He asked the clerk to rush [=to quickly prepare] his order. **2 a** [T] : to cause or force (someone) to do something too quickly ▪ He got nervous because they rushed him. — often + into ▪ They rushed her into making a decision. **b** [I] : to do something too quickly and often with little thought, attention, or care ▪ He rushed through his work and made a lot of mistakes. — often + into ▪ He rushed into marriage. **3** [I] : to flow or move very quickly in a particular direction ▪ Water rushed through the pipes. ▪ (figurative) When he saw her photo, memories came rushing back. **4** [T] : to bring or send (someone or something) very quickly to a particular place ▪ She rushed

him to the hospital. ▪ (figurative) They rushed the bill through Congress. **5** [T] : to run toward (someone or something) very quickly ▪ The crowd rushed the stage at the concert. **6** [T/I] American football : to move a football down the field by running with it instead of throwing it ▪ He rushed [=ran] (the ball) for 100 yards.

2rush n **1** [singular] : a quick, strong movement ▪ a rush of hot air **2** [singular] : a situation in which someone is doing something very quickly or is hurrying ▪ We are in no rush to finish. **3** [C] : a situation in which a large number of people move to or toward one place at the same time ▪ avoiding the holiday rush [=the time when everyone else is shopping for the holidays] ▪ a gold rush **4** [plural] : the first prints of scenes of a film or movie that have not been edited **5** [C] : a strong feeling or emotion caused by something exciting ▪ The roller-coaster ride gave me a rush. ▪ an adrenaline rush

rush·er /ˈrʌʃɚ/ n [C] American football : a player who carries the ball during running plays ▪ He was the team's leading rusher last year.

rush hour n [C/U] : a time during the day when many people are traveling on roads to go to work or to go home from work ▪ rush hour traffic

Rus·sian /ˈrʌʃən/ n **1** [C] : a person from Russia **2** [U] : the language of the Russian people — **Russian** adj ▪ Russian food/literature

rust /ˈrʌst/ n [U] : a reddish-brown substance that forms on metal — rust vb [T/I] ▪ The chain started to rust. ▪ a rusted iron fence

1rus·tic /ˈrʌstɪk/ adj **1** : of, relating to, or suitable for the country or people who live in the country ▪ a rustic village/cabin **2** : made of rough wood ▪ rustic furniture

2rustic n [C] : a person who lives in the country

1rus·tle /ˈrʌsəl/ vb **rus·tled; rus·tling** **1** [T/I] : to make or cause (something) to make a quick series of soft, light sounds ▪ Her skirt rustled as she walked. ▪ He rustled the papers on his desk. **2** [T] : to steal (sheep, cattle, etc.) from a farm or ranch — **rustle up** [phrasal vb] **rustle (something) up** or **rustle up (something)** informal **1** : to prepare (food, a meal, etc.) quickly ▪ He rustled up some grub. **2** : to find or get (something) ▪ rustle up firewood — **rus·tler** /ˈrʌslɚ/ n [C] ▪ a cattle rustler — **rustling** n [U, singular] ▪ I heard a rustling in the bushes.

2rustle n [singular] : a quick series of soft, light sounds ▪ a rustle of leaves

rust·proof /ˈrʌstˌpruːf/ adj : protected against rusting ▪ a rustproof pipe

rust·y /ˈrʌsti/ adj **rust·i·er; -est** **1** : covered with rust ▪ rusty nails **2** : not as good as usual or as in the past because you have not done or practiced something for a long time ▪ My tennis skills are a little rusty. **3** : reddish brown ▪ rusty hair — **rust·i·ness** /ˈrʌstinəs/ n [U]

1rut /ˈrʌt/ n [C] : a long, narrow mark made by the wheels of a vehicle passing over an area ▪ The truck left deep ruts in *the muddy ground.* **2** [*singular*] : a situation or way of behaving that does not change ▪ *She was **stuck in a rut** at her old job.* — compare ²RUT — **rut·ted** /ˈrʌtəd/ *adj* ▪ *a rutted dirt road*

²**rut** *n* [U] : the time when male animals become sexually active ▪ *a deer in rut* — compare ¹RUT — **rut·ting** /ˈrʌtɪŋ/ *adj* ▪ *a rutting elk*

ru·ta·ba·ga /ˌruːtəˈbeɪgə/ *n* [C/U] *US* : a large, yellowish type of turnip — called also (*Brit*) **swede**

ruth·less /ˈruːθləs/ *adj* : cruel or merciless ▪ *a ruthless killer* — **ruth·less·ly** *adv* ▪ *She was criticized ruthlessly by her peers.* — **ruth·less·ness** *n* [U]

RV /ˌɑɚˈviː/ *n* [C] : RECREATIONAL VEHICLE

rye /ˈraɪ/ *n* **1** [U] : a type of grass that is grown as a grain **2** [C/U] *US* : bread that is made from rye flour ▪ *a ham sandwich on rye (bread)* **3** [C/U] : whiskey that is made from rye ▪ *a bottle of rye*

S

¹**s** *or* **S** /ˈɛs/ *n*, *pl* **s's** *or* **S's** [C/U] : the 19th letter of the English alphabet ▪ *a word that starts with (an) s*

²**s** *or* **S** *abbr* **1** small ▪ *The shirt comes in S, M, L, or XL.* **2 S** south, southern

's /s *after* p, t, k, f, *or* θ; əz *after* s, z, ʃ, ʒ, tʃ, *or* dʒ; z *elsewhere*/ — used as a contraction of *is*, *was*, *has*, and *does* ▪ *She's here.* [=she is here] ▪ *When's* [=when was] *the last time you ate?* ▪ *He's* [=he has] *seen them already.* ▪ *What's he want?* [=what does he want?]

-'s /s *after* p, t, k, f, *or* θ; əz *after* s, z, ʃ, ʒ, tʃ, *or* dʒ; z *elsewhere*/ *n suffix or pron suffix* — used to form the possessive of singular nouns, of plural nouns not ending in *s*, of some pronouns, and of word groups that function as nouns ▪ *boy's books* ▪ *men's shoes* ❖ The possessive of a plural noun that ends in *s* is formed by adding an apostrophe alone instead of *'s.* ▪ *The boys' books were missing.* The possessive of singular nouns and names that end in *s* can usually be formed by adding *'s.* If adding *'s* would make the word difficult to say, an apostrophe alone may be used instead. ▪ *Moses' mother*

Sa. *abbr* Saturday

Sab·bath /ˈsæbəθ/ *n* — **the Sabbath** : a weekly day of rest and worship that is observed on Sunday by most Christians and on Saturday (from Friday evening to Saturday evening) by Jews and some Christians

sab·bat·i·cal /səˈbætɪkəl/ *n* [C/U] : a period of time during which someone does not work at his or her regular job and is able to rest, travel, do research, etc. ▪ *a paid sabbatical* ▪ *Several professors will be **on sabbatical** this year.*

sa·ber (*US*) *or Brit* **sa·bre** /ˈseɪbɚ/ *n* [C] **1** : a long, heavy sword with a curved blade **2** : a lightweight sword that is used in fencing

sa·ble /ˈseɪbəl/ *n*, *pl* **sa·bles** *or* **sable** **1** [C] : a small animal that lives in northern Asia and has soft, brown fur **2** [U] : the fur of the sable ▪ *a brush/coat made of sable*

¹**sab·o·tage** /ˈsæbəˌtɑːʒ/ *n* [U] : the act of destroying or damaging something deliberately ▪ *industrial sabotage*

²**sabotage** *vb* **-taged; -tag·ing** [T] **1** : to destroy or damage (something) deliberately ▪ *They sabotaged the airplane.* **2** : to cause the failure of (something) deliberately ▪ *The lawyer is trying to sabotage the case.*

sab·o·teur /ˌsæbəˈtɚ/ *n* [C] : a person who destroys or damages something deliberately

sac /ˈsæk/ *n* [C] : a part inside the body of an animal or plant that is shaped like a bag and that usually contains liquid or air

sac·cha·rin /ˈsækərən/ *n* [U] : a very sweet, white substance that does not have any calories and that is used instead of sugar to sweeten food

sac·cha·rine /ˈsækərən, *Brit* ˈsækəˌriːn/ *adj*, *formal* : too sweet or sentimental ▪ *a saccharine smile*

sa·chet /sæˈʃeɪ, *Brit* ˈsæʃeɪ/ *n* [C] **1** : small bag filled with something that smells good that is used to give a pleasant smell to clothes, sheets, etc. **2** *Brit* : small, thin package : PACKET

¹**sack** /ˈsæk/ *n* **1** [C] : a bag that is made of strong paper, cloth, or plastic ▪ *a sack of groceries/cement/potatoes* **2** [*singular*] : the act of destroying and taking things from a city, town, etc. ▪ *the sack of Rome* **3 the sack** *chiefly US, informal* : BED ▪ *It's time to **hit the sack**.* [=go to bed] **4 the sack** *informal* : a sudden dismissal from a job ▪ *She **got the sack**.* [=she was fired] **5** [C] *American football* : the act of tackling the quarterback behind the line of scrimmage

²**sack** *vb* [T] **1** : to destroy and take things from a city, town, etc. ▪ *The army sacked the city.* **2** *informal* : to dismiss (someone) from a job ▪ *They sacked her for always being late.* **3** *American football* : to tackle (the quarterback) behind the line of scrimmage **4** *US, informal* : to put (something) in a sack ▪ *sacking groceries* — **sack out** [*phrasal vb*] *US, informal* : to lie down for sleep ▪ *He sacked out on the couch.*

sac·ra·ment /ˈsækrəmənt/ *n* [C] : an important Christian ceremony (such as baptism or marriage) **2** *the Sacrament* : the bread and wine that are eaten and drunk during the Christian ceremony of Communion — **sac·ra·men·tal** /ˌsækrəˈmɛntl̩/ *adj*

sa·cred /ˈseɪkrəd/ *adj* **1** : very holy ▪ *a sacred shrine/image* **2** : relating to religion ▪ *sacred scriptures/songs/texts* **3** : highly valued and important ▪ *a sacred duty/right* — **sa·cred·ness** *n* [U]

sacred cow *n* [C] *disapproving* : someone or something that has been accepted or respected for a long time and that people are afraid or unwilling to criticize or question

¹sac·ri·fice /ˈsækrəˌfaɪs/ *n* [C/U] **1** : the act of giving up something that you want to keep especially in order to get or do something else or to help someone ▪ *The war required everyone to make sacrifices.* **2** : an act of killing a person or animal in a religious ceremony ▪ *a place where priests performed human/animal sacrifices in ancient rituals* — **sac·ri·fi·cial** /ˌsækrəˈfɪʃəl/ *adj* ▪ *sacrificial rites*

²sacrifice *vb* -ficed; -fic·ing **1** [T/I] : to give up (something that you want to keep) especially in order to get or do something else or to help someone ▪ *He sacrificed a lot for his career.* ▪ *He sacrificed his life* [=died] *for his country.* **2** [T] : to kill (a person or animal) in a religious ceremony ▪ *a place where people/animals were sacrificed in ancient rituals*

sacrifice bunt *n* [C] *baseball* : a bunt that allows a runner to go to the next base while the batter is put out

sacrifice fly *n* [C] *baseball* : a fly ball that is caught by a fielder but allows a runner to score

sac·ri·lege /ˈsækrəlɪʤ/ *n* [U, singular] : an act of treating a holy place or object in a way that does not show proper respect ▪ *They accused him of sacrilege.* — **sac·ri·le·gious** /ˌsækrəˈlɪʤəs/ *adj*

sac·ro·sanct /ˈsækroʊˌsæŋkt/ *adj, formal* : too important and respected to be changed, criticized, etc. ▪ *sacrosanct institutions/traditions*

sad /ˈsæd/ *adj* **sad·der; -dest** **1** : not happy ▪ *feeling sad* ▪ *sad eyes* **2** : causing a feeling of unhappiness ▪ *sad news* ▪ *a sad song/poem/movie* **3** : causing feelings of disappointment or pity ▪ *The sad fact/truth of the matter is that they are right.* ▪ *The city is in sad shape.* — **sad·ness** *n* [C/U]

sad·den /ˈsædn̩/ *vb* [T] : to cause (someone) to be sad ▪ *We were saddened by the news.*

¹sad·dle /ˈsædl̩/ *n* [C] **1** : a leather-covered seat that is put on the back of a horse ▪ *a cowboy in the saddle* [=riding on a horse] **2** : a seat on a bicycle or motorcycle

²saddle *vb* **sad·dled; sad·dling** [T] : to put a saddle on (a horse) ▪ *He saddled (up) his horse.* — **saddle up** [*phrasal vb*] : to get on a horse ▪ *He saddled up and rode away.* — **saddle with** [*phrasal vb*] **saddle (someone or something) with** : to cause (someone or something) to have (a problem, burden, responsibility, etc.) ▪ *My boss saddled me with the project.*

sad·dle·bag /ˈsædl̩ˌbæg/ *n* [C] : one of a pair of bags that are laid across the back of a horse behind the saddle or that hang over the rear wheel of a bicycle or motorcycle

sad·dler /ˈsædlə/ *n* [C] : a person who makes, repairs, or sells saddles and other equipment for horses

sa·dism /ˈseɪˌdɪzəm/ *n* [U] : enjoyment from hurting or punishing someone — **sa·dist** /ˈseɪdɪst/ *n* [C] — **sa·dis·tic** /səˈdɪstɪk/ *adj* ▪ *sadistic behavior/criminals* — **sa·dis·ti·cal·ly** /səˈdɪstɪkli/ *adv*

sad·ly /ˈsædli/ *adv* **1** : in a way that shows sadness or unhappiness ▪ *She shook her head sadly.* **2** : in a way that causes feeling of sadness, disappointment, regret, etc. ▪ *Her work had been sadly neglected.* — sometimes used for emphasis ▪ *If you think I'll forget, you are sadly mistaken.* **3** : UNFORTUNATELY — used to say that something is disappointing, sad, etc. ▪ *Sadly, nothing could be done.*

sa·do·mas·och·ism /ˌseɪdoʊˈmæsəˌkɪzəm/ *n* [U] : sexual behavior that involves getting pleasure from causing or feeling pain — **sa·do·mas·och·ist** /ˌseɪdoʊˈmæsəkɪst/ *n* [C] — **sa·do·mas·och·is·tic** /ˌseɪdoʊˌmæsəˈkɪstɪk/ *adj*

SAE *abbr* **1** self-addressed envelope **2** stamped addressed envelope

sa·fa·ri /səˈfɑri/ *n* [C/U] : a journey to see or hunt animals especially in Africa ▪ *a group of hunters on (a) safari*

¹safe /ˈseɪf/ *adj* **saf·er; -est** **1** not before a noun **a** : not able or likely to be hurt or harmed in any way ▪ *I feel safe in this area.* ▪ *We are all safe and sound.* **b** : not able or likely to be lost, taken away, or given away ▪ *"Is the money safe in the bank?"* ▪ *Your secret is safe with me.* ▪ [=I will not tell anyone your secret] **2 a** : not involving or likely to involve danger, harm, or loss ▪ *Have a safe trip.* **b** : providing protection from danger, harm, or loss ▪ *a safe distance/neighborhood/place* **3** : not dangerous ▪ *safe drinking water* **4 a** : not likely to cause a bad result ▪ *a safe investment/bet* **b** : cautious or careful ▪ *a very safe driver* ▪ (*It's*) *Better (to be) safe than sorry.* [=it is better to be careful now so that problems do not occur later on] ▪ *I decided to play it safe.* [=to be careful and avoid risk or danger] **5** : not likely to cause disagreement or argument ▪ *a safe assumption* ▪ *I think it's safe to say that he won't be back.* **6** *baseball* : successful at getting to a base without being put out ▪ *The runner was safe at first base.* — **safe·ly** *adv*

²safe *adv, chiefly US, informal* : in a safe way ▪ *Drive safe.* [=safely]

³safe *n* [C] : a strong metal box with a lock that is used to store money or valuable things

safe-crack·er /ˈseɪfˌkrækə/ *n* [C] *chiefly US* : a person who steals things by opening safes

safe–deposit box *n* [C] : a strong metal box in a bank that has a lock and that is used to store money or other valuable things — called also *safety-deposit box*

safe·guard /'seɪfˌgɑɑd/ n [C] *formal* : something that provides protection against possible loss, damage, etc. • *The new law has safeguards to protect the rights of citizens.* — **safeguard** vb [T/I] • *laws that safeguard [=protect] the rights of citizens*

safe house n [C] : a place where a person hides from the police, stays to be protected by the police, or is involved in secret activities

safe·keep·ing /seɪfˈkiːpɪŋ/ n [U] : the act of keeping something safe or the state of being kept safe • *I gave her my jewelry for safekeeping while I was away.* • *The property is in safekeeping with his lawyer.*

safe·ty /'seɪfti/ n, pl **-ties** 1 [U] : freedom from harm or danger : the state of being safe • *The changes were made in the interest of public safety.* • *improving airline safety* • *She fears for her own safety.* [=she is afraid because she thinks she is in danger] 2 [U] : the state of not being dangerous or harmful • *The car was redesigned for added safety.* 3 [U] : a place that is free from harm or danger • *They were led to safety by the rescuers.* 4 [C] *US* : a device that prevents a gun from being fired accidentally — called also *safety catch* 5 [C] *American football* **a** : a defensive player whose position is far back from the line of scrimmage **b** : a score of two points for the defensive team when an offensive player who has the ball is tackled behind his own team's goal line

safety belt n [C] 1 : a belt that is used to prevent someone from falling or getting injured by holding that person in place 2 : SEAT BELT

safety–deposit box n [C] : SAFE-DEPOSIT BOX

safety net n [C] 1 : a net that is placed below acrobats to catch them if they fall 2 : something that helps someone who is in a difficult situation • *a financial safety net*

safety pin n [C] : a metal pin that is used for attaching things and that has a point at one end and a cover at the other into which the pointed end fits

safety razor n [C] : a razor with a cover for part of the blade to prevent deep cuts in the skin

safety valve n [C] 1 : a part in a machine that opens automatically to release steam, water, gas, etc., when pressure becomes too great 2 : something that allows someone to release mental stress and tension in a harmless way • *His hobbies act as a safety valve, relieving some of the pressure he feels from his job.*

saf·fron /'sæˌfrɑːn, Brit 'sæfrən/ n [U] : an orange powder that is made from a type of flower and that is used to color and flavor food

sag /'sæg/ vb **sagged**; **sag·ging** [I] 1 : to bend or hang down in the middle especially because of weight or weakness • *a sagging mattress* 2 : to become weaker or fewer • *The economy began to sag.* •

sagging sales — **sag** n [C]

sa·ga /'sɑːgə/ n [C] : a long and complicated story • *the saga of a shipwrecked crew*

sa·ga·cious /səˈgeɪʃəs/ adj, *formal* : having or showing wisdom or good judgment : WISE • *sagacious advice/counsel* — **sa·ga·cious·ly** adv — **sa·gac·i·ty** /səˈgæsəti/ n [U]

[superscript]1[/superscript]**sage** /'seɪdʒ/ n 1 [C] *formal* : a person who is very wise 2 [U] : an herb that has grayish-green leaves which are used in cooking

[superscript]2[/superscript]**sage** adj, *always before a noun* **sag·er**; **sag·est** *formal* : very wise • *sage advice* — **sage·ly** adv

sag·gy /'sægi/ adj **sag·gi·er**; **-est** *informal* : bending or hanging down too much : not firm • *a saggy mattress*

Sag·it·tar·i·us /ˌsædʒəˈteriəs/ n 1 [U] : the sign of the zodiac that comes between Scorpio and Capricorn and that has a centaur shooting a bow and arrow as its symbol 2 [C] : a person born between November 22 and December 21

[superscript]1[/superscript]**said** past tense and past participle of [superscript]1[/superscript]SAY

[superscript]2[/superscript]**said** /'sɛd/ adj, *always before a noun, formal + law* : mentioned or referred to before • *by order of the judge of said court*

[superscript]1[/superscript]**sail** /'seɪl/ vb 1 [T/I] **a** : to travel on water in a ship or boat • *sail across/on/over the sea/ocean* • *sail the Atlantic* **b** : to control a ship or boat (especially one that has sails) while traveling on water • *The ship was sailed by a crew of 8.* • *learning to sail* **c** : of a ship or boat : to travel on water • *a ship that has sailed the seven seas* 2 [I] : to begin a journey on water in a ship or boat • *We sail at 9 a.m. tomorrow.* 3 [I] : to move or proceed in an easy, quick, and smooth way • *He sailed into the room.* • *The ball sailed over my head.* • *She sailed through the exam/course.* [=she easily passed the exam/course]

[superscript]2[/superscript]**sail** n [C] : a large piece of strong cloth that is connected to a ship or boat and that is used to catch the wind that moves the ship or boat through the water — **in full sail** also **at full sail** *of a ship or boat* : moving through the water by using all of its sails • *a yacht in full sail* — **set sail** : to begin a journey on water in a ship or boat • *They set sail for/from Boston.* — **take the wind out of someone's sails** see [superscript]1[/superscript]WIND — **under sail** *of a ship or boat* : moving through the water by using sails • *a ship under sail*

sail·boat /'seɪlˌboʊt/ n [C] *US* : a boat that has a sail — called also *(Brit) sailing boat*

sail·ing /'seɪlɪŋ/ n [U] : the sport or activity of traveling on water in a sailboat • *They went sailing.* — **clear sailing** *(US)* or *chiefly US* **smooth sailing** or *chiefly Brit* **plain sailing** : easy progress • *Her time at college wasn't all smooth sailing.* [=she had some problems/difficulties during her time at college]

sailing ship n [C] : a ship that has sails

sail·or /'seɪlə/ n [C] 1 : a person who works on a boat or ship as part of the crew 2 : someone who controls a boat or ship that has sails ▪ *She's a skillful sailor.*

saint /ˈseɪnt/ *n* [C] **1** : a person who is officially recognized by the Christian church as being very holy because of the way he or she lived — *abbr.* **St.** **2** : a person who is very good, kind, or patient ▪ *The salesperson was a saint for putting up with them.* — **saint·hood** /ˈseɪnt‚hʊd/ *n* [U]

Saint Ber·nard /ˈseɪntbɚˈnɑɚd/ *n* [C] : a very large, strong dog

saint·ly /ˈseɪntli/ *adj* **saint·li·er; -est** : very good and kind ▪ *a saintly man/smile* — **saint·li·ness** *n* [U]

Saint Pat·rick's Day /ˌseɪntˈpætrɪks-/ *n* [U] : March 17 celebrated in honor of Saint Patrick

Saint Valentine's Day *n* [U] : VALENTINE'S DAY

¹sake /ˈseɪk/ *n* [C] **1** : the benefit of someone or something — used in phrases with *for* to say that something is done to help a particular person or thing ▪ *Please do it for her sake.* [=do it to help her] ▪ *He sacrificed his life for all our sakes.* [=to help all of us] — used in phrases with *for* to say that something is done for a particular purpose or to achieve a particular goal or result ▪ *For the sake of clarity* [=in order to be clear]*, I've listed each item separately.* **2** *informal* — used in phrases with *for* to express anger, annoyance, surprise, etc. ▪ *For heaven's/Pete's/goodness' sake, could you hurry up?* — **for old times' sake** ◇ If you do something for *old times' sake*, you do it because you did it in the past and you want to experience it again. ▪ *We went back to the bar for old times' sake.* — compare ²SAKE

²sa·ke *or* **sa·ki** /ˈsɑːki/ *n, pl* **-kes** *or* **-kis** [C/U] : a Japanese alcoholic drink that is made from rice — compare ¹SAKE

sal·able *or* **sale·able** /ˈseɪləbəl/ *adj* : good enough to be sold ▪ *a salable commodity/product*

sa·la·cious /səˈleɪʃəs/ *adj, formal + disapproving* : relating to sex in a way that is excessive or offensive ▪ *salacious pictures/messages*

sal·ad /ˈsæləd/ *n* [C/U] **1** : a mixture of raw green vegetables (such as different types of lettuce) usually combined with other raw vegetables ▪ *a spinach salad* ▪ *a bowl of salad* **2** : a mixture of small pieces of raw or cooked food (such as pasta, meat, fruit, eggs, or vegetables) combined usually with a dressing and served cold ▪ *chicken/tuna/fruit salad*

salad bar *n* [C] : a place in a restaurant where there are foods that customers can use to make their own salads

salad dressing *n* [C/U] : DRESSING 1

sal·a·man·der /ˈsæləˌmændɚ/ *n* [C] : a small animal that looks like a lizard with smooth skin and that lives both on land and in water

sa·la·mi /səˈlɑːmi/ *n* [C/U] : a large, spicy, and dry sausage that is usually eaten cold

sal·a·ried /ˈsælərid/ *adj* **1** : receiving a salary ▪ *salaried workers* **2** : giving payment in the form of a salary ▪ *a salaried job*

sal·a·ry /ˈsæləri/ *n, pl* **-ries** [C/U] : an amount of money that an employee is paid each year ▪ *She was offered a salary of $50,000 a year.*

sale /ˈseɪl/ *n* **1** *a* [C] : the act of selling something ▪ *the sale of their house* ▪ *online/Internet sales* ▪ *trying to make a sale* [=sell something] *b* [*plural*] : the total amount of money that a business receives from selling goods or services ▪ *the company's annual sales* **2** [C] : an event or occasion during which a business sells goods or services at prices that are lower than usual ▪ *The store is having/holding a sale.* **3** [*plural*] : the business or activity of selling goods or services ▪ *He has a job in sales.* ▪ *the sales department/manager* **4** [C] : a public event at which things are sold ▪ *They're having/holding a sale of fine antiques next week.* — **for sale** : available to be bought ▪ *That house is (up) for sale.* — **on sale 1** : available to be bought ▪ *These shoes are on sale at most department stores.* ▪ *Tickets go on sale* [=become available to be bought] *next week.* **2** *chiefly US* : selling at a price that is lower than usual ▪ *I bought a shirt on sale for $5.* ▪ *I bought the shirt when it was on sale.*

saleable *variant spelling of* SALABLE

sales·clerk /ˈseɪlzˌklɚk, *Brit* ˈseɪlzˌklɑːk/ *n* [C] *US* : a person whose job is to sell things in a store

sales·man /ˈseɪlzmən/ *n, pl* **-men** /-mən/ [C] : a person (especially a man) whose job is to sell things ▪ *a car salesman*

sales·man·ship /ˈseɪlzmənˌʃɪp/ *n* [U] : the skill of persuading people to buy things or to accept or agree to something ▪ *good/poor salesmanship*

sales·per·son /ˈseɪlzˌpɚsn/ *n, pl* **salespeo·ple** /ˈseɪlzˌpiːpəl/ *also* **sales·persons** [C] : a person whose job is to sell things

sales pitch *n* [C] : a speech that you give in order to persuade someone to buy something

sales slip *n* [C] *US* : a piece of paper on which the things that you have bought are listed : RECEIPT

sales tax *n* [C/U] : a tax that is added to the price of goods and services

sales·wom·an /ˈseɪlzˌwʊmən/ *n, pl* **-wom·en** /-ˌwɪmən/ [C] : a woman whose job is to sell things

sa·lient /ˈseɪljənt/ *adj, formal* : very important or noticeable ▪ *a salient feature/fact* — **sa·lience** /ˈseɪljəns/ *n* [U]

¹sa·line /ˈseɪˌliːn, *Brit* ˈseɪˌlaɪn/ *adj, technical* : containing salt ▪ *a saline solution* — **sa·lin·i·ty** /seɪˈlɪnəti/ *n* [U]

²saline *n* [U] *technical* : a mixture of salt and water

sa·li·va /səˈlaɪvə/ *n* [U] : the liquid produced in your mouth that keeps your mouth moist and makes it easier to swallow food — **sal·i·vary** /ˈsæləˌveri/ *adj*

salivary gland *n* [C] *medical* : a small organ that produces saliva in your mouth

sal·i·vate /ˈsæləˌveɪt/ *vb* **-vat·ed; -vat·ing** [I] **1** : to have a lot of saliva produced in your mouth because you see or smell food that you want to eat • *The smell made me salivate.* **2** : to have great interest in or desire for something • *She was salivating at the prospect of going to Europe.*

sal·low /ˈsæloʊ/ *adj* : slightly yellow in a way that does not look healthy • *a sallow complexion/face*

salm·on /ˈsæmən/ *n, pl* **salmon** **1** [C/U] : a large fish that is born in streams but that lives most of its life in the ocean and that is commonly used for food **2** [U] : SALMON PINK

sal·mo·nel·la /ˌsælməˈnɛlə/ *n* [U] : a kind of bacteria that is sometimes in food and that makes people sick

salmon pink *n* [U] : an orange-pink color

sa·lon /səˈlɑːn, *Brit* ˈsæˌlɒn/ *n* [C] **1** : a business that gives customers beauty treatments (such as haircuts) **2** *old-fashioned* : a large room in a fashionable house that is used for entertaining guests

sa·loon /səˈluːn/ *n* [C] **1** : a place where alcoholic drinks are served; *especially* : such a place in the western U.S. during the 19th century **2** *Brit* : SEDAN — called also (*Brit*) **saloon car**

sal·sa /ˈsɑːlsə/ *n* [C/U] **1** : a spicy sauce made with tomatoes, onions, and hot peppers that is commonly served with Mexican food **2 a** : a type of popular Latin-American music • *a salsa band* **b** : dancing that is done to salsa music

¹**salt** /ˈsɑːlt/ *n* **1** [U] : a natural white substance that is used especially to flavor or preserve food **2** [C] *technical* : a chemical compound formed when part of an acid is replaced by a metal or something like a metal • *mineral salts* — **take (something) with a grain/pinch of salt** *informal* : to not completely believe (something) • *You should take what he says with a grain of salt.* — **the salt of the earth** : a very good and honest person or group of people — **worth your salt** : worthy of ordinary respect • *A detective writer worth his salt* [=a good detective writer] *keeps his readers from solving the mystery.*

²**salt** *vb* [T] **1** : to flavor or preserve (food) with salt • *He salted his food.* **2** : to put salt on (a surface) especially in order to melt ice • *The city salted the roads after the snowstorm.* — **salt away** [*phrasal vb*] **salt (something) away** *or* **salt away (something)** *informal* **1** : to put (money) in a safe place especially secretly or dishonestly • *He salted millions away in a foreign bank account.* **2** *US* : to make your victory in (a game, contest, etc.) certain • *They salted away the game by scoring 21 points in the last quarter.* — **salt with** [*phrasal vb*] **salt (something) with** : to put something in many places in (a story, speech, etc.) • *The book is salted with witty anecdotes.* [=the book has many witty anecdotes throughout it]

³**salt** *adj, always before a noun* **1** : containing salt • *salt water* **2** : preserved or seasoned with salt • *salt pork*

salt–and–pepper *adj* : having many

small spots of black and white • *a salt-and-pepper beard*

salt·ed /ˈsɑːltəd/ *adj* **1** : having salt added • *salted butter/peanuts* **2** : preserved with salt • *salted fish/meat/pork*

sal·tine /sɑlˈtiːn/ *n* [C] *US* : a thin, salty cracker

salt·pe·ter (*US*) *or Brit* **salt·pe·tre** /ˈsɑːltˈpiːtə/ *n* [U] : a white powder that exists naturally in some soils and that is used especially as a fertilizer, in medicine, and to make gunpowder

salt·wa·ter /ˈsɑːltˌwɑːtə/ *adj, always before a noun* : of, relating to, or living in salt water • *saltwater fish*

salty /ˈsɑːlti/ *adj* **salt·i·er; -est** **1** : containing salt or too much salt • *salty foods* **2** *US, old-fashioned* : somewhat rude or shocking • *salty language/talk* — **salt·i·ness** /ˈsɑːltinəs/ *n* [U]

sa·lu·bri·ous /səˈluːbrijəs/ *adj, formal* : making good health possible or likely • *salubrious weather*

sal·u·tary /ˈsæljəˌteri, *Brit* ˈsæljətri/ *adj, formal* : having a good or helpful result especially after something unpleasant has happened • *a salutary effect*

sal·u·ta·tion /ˌsæljəˈteɪʃən/ *n* **1** [C] : a word or phrase (such as "Dear Sir") that is used to begin a letter **2** [C/U] *formal* : the act of greeting someone • *Shaking hands is a form of salutation.*

¹**sa·lute** /səˈluːt/ *vb* **-lut·ed; -lut·ing** **1** [T/I] : to give a sign of respect to (a military officer, flag, etc.) by moving your right hand to your forehead : to give a salute to (someone or something) • *He saluted (the officer).* **2** [T] : to publicly praise (someone or something) • *The president saluted his bravery.*

²**salute** *n* [C/U] **1** : the act of moving your right hand to your forehead as a sign of respect to a military officer, flag, etc. • *The officers gave the general a salute.* **2** : an act or ceremony that shows respect for someone • *a 21-gun salute* [=a military ceremony when 21 guns are fired in the air to honor someone] • *We raise our glasses in salute to the newlyweds.*

¹**sal·vage** /ˈsælvɪʤ/ *n* [U] **1** : the act of saving something (such as a building, a ship, or cargo) that is in danger of being completely destroyed • *salvage attempts/efforts/operations* **2** : something (such as cargo) that is saved from a wreck, fire, etc. • *the salvage from the wrecked ship*

²**salvage** *vb* **-vaged; -vag·ing** [T] **1** : to remove (something) from a place so that it will not be damaged, destroyed, or lost • *Divers salvaged some of the sunken ship's cargo.* **2** : to save (something valuable or important) • *trying to salvage his marriage/reputation* — **sal·vage·able** /ˈsælvɪʤəbəl/ *adj*

sal·va·tion /sælˈveɪʃən/ *n* [U] **1** *in Christianity* : the act of saving someone from sin or evil • *praying for salvation* **2** : something that saves someone or something from danger or a difficult situation • *The new medication has been her salvation.* [=has saved her]

¹**salve** /ˈsæv, *Brit* ˈsælv/ *n* [C/U] : a creamy substance that you put on a wound to

heal it or to make it less painful

[2]**salve** *vb* **salved; salv·ing** [*T*] : to make (something) less painful • *salve the pain* • *salving his guilty conscience*

sal·vo /ˈsælvoʊ/ *n, pl* **-vos** *or* **-voes** [*C*] **1** : the act of firing several guns or bombs at the same time • *a salvo of cannon fire* **2** : a sudden occurrence of applause, laughter, etc., from many people • *a salvo of cheers* **3** : a strong or sudden attack • *He fired the opening salvo of the debate.*

Sa·mar·i·tan /səˈmerətən/ *n* [*C*] : GOOD SAMARITAN

sam·ba /ˈsæmbə/ *n* [*singular*] : a lively Brazilian dance; *also* : the music for this dance

[1]**same** /ˈseɪm/ *adj, always before a noun* **1** : not different — used when referring to a particular person or thing that is connected to more than one person, time, place, etc. • *He lived in the same city/town/place all his life.* • *We go to the same school.* • *I'd met him earlier that exact same day.* = (US) *I'd met him earlier that same exact day.* • *I was thinking the very same thing.* • *The restaurant's owner and chef are one and the same person.* [=the owner is also the chef] **2 a** : exactly like someone or something else • *The words "their" and "there" are pronounced in exactly the same way.* **b** : not changed • *She gave the same answer as before.* **3** — used to describe a quality or characteristic that is shared by more than one person or thing • *The buildings are the same age/style.* — *the same old story informal + usually disapproving* — used to refer to something that has not changed • *He told the same old story again!*

[2]**same** *pron* **1 the same a** : someone or something that is exactly like another person or thing being discussed or referred to • *He ordered coffee, and I had the same.* [=I also had coffee] • *Your idea is the same as his.* • *Everyone else is studying, and I suggest you do the same.* • *He should help us—and the same goes for you!* [=and you should help us too] **b** ✧ Two or more things that are *the same* are exactly like each other or very similar to each other. • *No two fingerprints are ever the same.* **2 the same** : someone or something that has not changed • *After that, he was never quite the same.* — *all/ just the same* : despite what has just been said : NEVERTHELESS • *It won't be easy. But you should try all the same.* — *all the same to* — used to say that someone does not care about what is chosen or done in a particular situation • *We can go either today or tomorrow—it's all the same to me.* — *one and the same* : one person or thing and not two • *The restaurant's owner and chef are one and the same.* [=the owner is also the chef] — *same here informal* — used to say that you think, feel, or want the same thing as someone else • *"I'm tired." "Same here."* [=I'm tired too] — *the same to you* — used to return a greeting or insult • *"Merry Christmas!" "(And) the same to you!"* [=Merry Christmas to you too]

[3]**same** *adv* : in a way that is alike or very

similar — usually used after *the* • *two words that are pronounced the same* • *I feel exactly the same as I did yesterday.* • *He ate a sandwich for lunch, same as usual.* [=as he usually does]

same·ness /ˈseɪmnəs/ *n* [*singular*] : the quality or state of being alike or of not changing • *There is a sameness to his stories that makes them too predictable.*

[1]**sam·ple** /ˈsæmpəl, *Brit* ˈsɑːmpəl/ *n* [*C*] **1** : a small amount of something that gives you information about the thing it was taken from • *a blood/water/soil sample* **2** : a small amount of something that people can try • *Free samples were handed out at the store.* **3** : a group of people or things that are taken from a larger group and studied, tested, or questioned to get information • *a sample group* • *A random sample of people filled out the survey.* **4** : a small part of a recording (such as a song) that is used in another performer's recording

[2]**sample** *vb* **sam·pled; sam·pling** [*T*] **1** : to taste or smell a small amount of (something) • *sample the wine/food* **2** : to try or experience (something) • *She sampled everything the resort had to offer.* **3** : to use a small part of (a recording, such as a song) in another recording • *The rap group sampled the song.*

sam·pler /ˈsæmplɚ, *Brit* ˈsɑːmplə/ *n* [*C*] **1** : a piece of cloth with letters and words sewn in different kinds of stitches and made as an example of a person's sewing skill **2** : a collection that includes different examples of a particular type of thing • *a chocolate sampler*

sam·u·rai /ˈsæməˌraɪ/ *n, pl* **samurai** [*C*] : a member of a Japanese military class in the past

san·a·to·ri·um /ˌsænəˈtoriəm/ *n, pl* **-to·ri·ums** *or* **-to·ria** /-ˈtoriə/ [*C*] *old-fashioned* : a place for the care and treatment of people who are recovering from illness or who have a disease that will last a long time

sanc·ti·fy /ˈsæŋktəˌfaɪ/ *vb* **-fies; -fied; -fy·ing** [*T*] *formal* **1** : to make (something) holy • *sanctify a marriage* **2** : to give official acceptance or approval to (something) • *The constitution sanctified the rights of the people.* — **sanc·ti·fi·ca·tion** /ˌsæŋktəfəˈkeɪʃən/ *n* [*U*]

sanc·ti·mo·nious /ˌsæŋktəˈmoʊnijəs/ *adj, formal + disapproving* : pretending to be morally better than other people • *a sanctimonious speech/politician*

[1]**sanc·tion** /ˈsæŋkʃən/ *n, formal* **1** [*C*] : an action that is taken or an order that is given to force a country to obey international laws by limiting or stopping trade with that country, by not allowing economic aid for that country, etc. • *imposing trade/economic sanctions* **2** [*U*] : official permission or approval • *Their policy has/lacks legal sanction.*

[2]**sanction** *vb* [*T*] *formal* : to officially accept or allow (something) • *The government sanctioned the use of force.*

sanc·ti·ty /ˈsæŋktəti/ *n* [*U*] : the quality or state of being holy, very important, or valuable • *the sanctity of marriage/life/tradition*

sanc·tu·ary /'sæŋkt∫ə,weri, *Brit* 'sæŋkt∫uəri/ *n, pl* **-ar·ies** **1** [C] : a place where someone or something is protected or given shelter ▪ *a bird sanctuary* ▪ *The house was a sanctuary for runaway teens.* **2** [U] : the protection that is provided by a safe place ▪ *The refugees found/sought sanctuary when they crossed the border.* **3** [C] **a** *US* : the room inside a church, synagogue, etc., where religious services are held **b** : the most sacred or holy part of a religious building

sanc·tum /'sæŋktəm/ *n* [C] *somewhat formal* **1** : a place where you are not bothered by other people ▪ *Her office was her sanctum.* — see also INNER SANCTUM **2** : a holy or sacred place

¹**sand** /'sænd/ *n* **1** [U] : the very tiny, loose pieces of rock that cover beaches, deserts, etc. ▪ *a grain of sand* **2 a** [U] : an area of sand ▪ *children playing in the sand* **b** [*plural*] *literary* : the beach or desert ▪ *journeying across the (desert) sands*

²**sand** *vb* **1** [T/I] : to make the surface of something smooth by rubbing it with sandpaper ▪ *sand (down) the shelf/wood/table* **2** [T] *US* : to spread sand over (an icy street, sidewalk, etc.) ▪ *The streets haven't been sanded yet.* — **sand·er** /'sændə/ *n* [C]

san·dal /'sændl/ *n* [C] : a shoe with a bottom part that is held in place with straps around the foot and sometimes the ankle

¹**sand·bag** /'sænd,bæg/ *n* [C] : a bag filled with sand and used as a weight or to build temporary walls, dams, etc.

²**sandbag** *vb* **-bagged; -bag·ging** [T] **1** : to put sandbags around, on, or in (something) ▪ *They sandbagged (the area around) the house to protect it from the flood.* **2** *chiefly US, informal* : to hit (someone) with a sandbag ▪ *(figurative) He got sandbagged by the media.* [=he was treated or criticized unfairly by the media]

sand·bank /'sænd,bæŋk/ *n* [C] : a raised area of sand in a river, ocean, etc.

sand·bar /'sænd,baə/ *n* [C] : a raised area of sand with a top that is near or just above the surface of the water in an ocean, lake, or river

sand·blast /'sænd,blæst, *Brit* 'sænd,blɑːst/ *vb* [T] : to clean, polish, or decorate the surface of (something) by spraying sand on it with a powerful machine ▪ *sandblast a building* — **sand·blast·er** *n* [C]

sand·box /'sænd,bɑːks/ *n* [C] *US* : a low box filled with sand that children can play in — called also *(Brit)* **sandpit**

sand castle *n* [C] : a small model of a castle or other building that is made with wet sand on a beach

sand dune *n* [C] : DUNE

S&L *n* [C] *US* : SAVINGS AND LOAN ASSOCIATION

sand·lot /'sænd,lɑːt/ *n* [C] *US* : an empty area of land in a city where children play games or sports

S and M *or* **S&M** *n* [U] : SADOMASOCHISM

sand·man /'sænd,mæn/ *n* — **the sandman** — used to refer to sleep as an imaginary man who makes people sleepy by sprinkling sand in their eyes ▪ *fighting off the sandman* [=trying not to fall asleep]

sand·pa·per /'sænd,peɪpə/ *n* [U] : stiff paper that has a rough surface on one side and that is rubbed against something (such as a piece of wood) to make it smooth — **sandpaper** *vb* [T] ▪ *sandpapering* [=sanding] *a room*

sand·pip·er /'sænd,paɪpə/ *n* [C] : a type of bird that has long legs and a long bill and that lives near the sea

sand·pit /'sænd,pɪt/ *n* [C] *Brit* : SANDBOX

sand·stone /'sænd,stoʊn/ *n* [C/U] : a type of soft stone that is made from grains of sand stuck together

sand·storm /'sænd,stoəm/ *n* [C] : a storm in the desert with strong winds that blow sand around forcefully

sand trap *n* [C] *US, golf* : an area on a golf course that is filled with sand — called also **bunker**

¹**sand·wich** /'sænd,wɪt∫, *Brit* 'sæn,wɪdʒ/ *n* [C] : two pieces of bread with something (such as meat, peanut butter, etc.) between them ▪ *a ham sandwich*

²**sandwich** *vb* [T] : to put (someone or something) in the space between two other things or people ▪ *The boy was sandwiched between his brother and sister in the back seat.*

sandy /'sændi/ *adj* **sand·i·er; -est** **1** : full of or covered with sand ▪ *sandy soil/beaches* **2** : having a yellowish-gray or yellowish-brown color ▪ *sandy hair*

sane /'seɪn/ *adj* **san·er; san·est** **1** : having a healthy mind ▪ *He is perfectly sane.* [=he is not mentally ill] **2** : based on reason or good judgment ▪ *a sane policy/decision* — **sane·ly** *adv*

sang *past tense of* SING

san·guine /'sæŋgwən/ *adj, formal* : confident and hopeful ▪ *a sanguine disposition/outlook*

san·i·tar·i·um /,sænə'terijəm/ *n, pl* **-i·ums** *or* **-ia** /-ijə/ [C] *US, old-fashioned* : SANATORIUM

san·i·tary /'sænə,teri, *Brit* 'sænətri/ *adj* **1** *always before a noun* : of or relating to good health or protection from dirt, infection, disease, etc. ▪ *poor sanitary conditions* [=conditions that are likely to give people diseases or infection] **2** : free from dirt, infection, disease, etc. ▪ *The public bathrooms were not very sanitary.*

sanitary napkin *n* [C] *US* : a thick piece of soft material that is used to absorb blood during menstruation — called also *sanitary pad*, *(Brit)* *sanitary towel*

san·i·ta·tion /,sænə'teɪ∫ən/ *n* [U] : the process of keeping places free from dirt, infection, disease, etc., by removing waste, trash, and garbage, by cleaning streets, etc. ▪ *Diseases can spread from poor sanitation.*

san·i·tize *also Brit* **san·i·tise** /'sænə,taɪz/ *vb* **-tized; -tiz·ing** [T] **1** : to make (something) free from dirt, infection, disease, etc., by cleaning it ▪ *sanitize a bathroom* **2** *often disapproving* : to make (something) more pleasant and acceptable by taking things that are unpleasant

or offensive out of it ▪ *sanitizing the news*
▪ *a sanitized version of the joke*

san·i·to·ri·um /ˌsænəˈtorijəm/ *n, pl* **-to·ri·ums** *or* **-to·ria** /-ˈtorijə/ *[C] US, old-fashioned* : SANATORIUM

san·i·ty /ˈsænəti/ *n [U]* : the condition of being sane ▪ *People have begun to doubt his sanity.*

sank *past tense of* ¹SINK

San·skrit /ˈsænˌskrɪt/ *n [U]* : a language that was spoken many years ago in India and is still used in the practice of Hinduism — **Sanskrit** *adj*

San·ta Claus /ˈsæntəˌklɑːz/ *n [singular]* : an imaginary fat man with a white beard and a red suit who gives toys to children at Christmas — called also *Santa,* (*Brit*) *Father Christmas*

¹**sap** /ˈsæp/ *n* **1** *[U]* : a watery juice inside a plant that carries the plant's food **2** *[C] chiefly US, informal* : a person who is easily tricked or cheated

²**sap** *vb* **sapped; sap·ping** *[T]* **1** : to use up the supply of (something, such as a person's courage, energy, strength, etc.) ▪ *Moving the furniture sapped her strength.* ▪ *Losing his job sapped his confidence.* **2** : to cause (someone) to lose courage, energy, strength, etc. ▪ *The illness sapped him of his strength.*

sap·ling /ˈsæplɪŋ/ *n [C]* : a young tree

sap·per /ˈsæpə/ *n [C] Brit* : a member of a military unit that builds structures to defend and protect a position

sap·phire /ˈsæˌfajə/ *n* **1** *[C/U]* : a clear, usually deep blue jewel **2** *[U]* : a deep blue color

sap·py /ˈsæpi/ *adj* **sap·pi·er; -est** **1** *US, informal* **a** : sad or romantic in a foolish or exaggerated way ▪ *a sarcastic person/remark/reply* — **sar·cas·ti·cal·ly** /sɑˈkæstɪkli/ *adv*

Sa·ran Wrap /səˈræn-/ *trademark, US* — used for a thin sheet of clear plastic that is used to wrap food

sar·casm /ˈsɑəˌkæzəm/ *n [U]* : the use of words that mean the opposite of what you really want to say especially in order to insult someone, to show irritation, or to be funny ▪ *a voice full of sarcasm*

sar·cas·tic /sɑəˈkæstɪk/ *adj* : using or showing sarcasm ▪ *a sarcastic person/remark/reply* — **sar·cas·ti·cal·ly** /sɑəˈkæstɪkli/ *adv*

sar·dine /sɑəˈdiːn/ *n [C]* : a very small fish that is used for food and is usually packed in a can — **like sardines** : without enough room to move around ▪ *We were crammed/packed like sardines into a small room.*

sar·don·ic /sɑəˈdɑːnɪk/ *adj, formal* : showing that you disapprove of or do not like someone or something ▪ *sardonic humor/comments* — **sar·don·i·cal·ly** /sɑəˈdɑːnɪkli/ *adv*

sarge /ˈsɑədʒ/ *n [singular] informal* : SERGEANT ▪ *What should I do, Sarge?*

sa·ri /ˈsɑri/ *n [C]* : a long piece of cloth that is wrapped around the body and head or shoulder and worn by women in southern Asia

sa·rong /səˈrɑːŋ/ *n [C]* : a long strip of cloth that is wrapped loosely around the body and worn by men and women of Malaysia and many Pacific islands

sar·to·ri·al /sɑəˈtorijəl/ *adj, always before a noun, formal* : of or relating to clothes ▪ *sartorial splendor/taste* — **sar·to·ri·al·ly** *adv*

SASE *abbr, US* self-addressed stamped envelope

sash /ˈsæʃ/ *n [C]* **1** : a long piece of cloth that you wear around your waist or over one shoulder **2** : the frame that holds glass in a window

sa·shay /sæˈʃeɪ/ *vb [I]* : to walk in a slow and confident way that makes people notice you ▪ *She sashayed into the room.*

sass /ˈsæs/ *vb [T] chiefly US, informal* : to talk to (someone) in a rude way that does not show proper respect ▪ *He sassed a cop.* — **sass** *n [U]*

sas·sa·fras /ˈsæsəˌfræs/ *n, pl* **sassafras** **1** *[C/U]* : a tall tree of eastern North America **2** *[U]* : the dried bark from the root of the sassafras that is used in medicine and as a flavoring

sassy /ˈsæsi/ *adj* **sass·i·er; -est** *chiefly US, informal* **1** : having or showing a rude lack of respect ▪ *a sassy answer/child* **2** : very stylish ▪ *her sassy new hairdo* **3** : confident and energetic ▪ *her sassy charm*

sat *past tense and past participle of* SIT

Sat. *abbr* Saturday

SAT *abbr* Scholastic Assessment Test

Sa·tan /ˈseɪtn/ *n [U]* : DEVIL **1a** ▪ *He went to the Halloween party dressed up as Satan.* [=*the Devil*]

sa·tan·ic /seɪˈtænɪk/ *adj* **1** : of, relating to, or worshipping the Devil ▪ *a satanic cult/rite* **2** : very cruel or evil ▪ *a satanic serial killer*

sa·tan·ism /ˈseɪtəˌnɪzəm/ *n [U]* : worship of the Devil — **sa·tan·ist** /ˈseɪtənɪst/ *n [C]*

satch·el /ˈsætʃəl/ *n [C]* : a small bag that is carried over your shoulder and that is used for carrying clothes, books, etc. ▪

sate /ˈseɪt/ *vb* **sat·ed; sat·ing** *[T] formal* **1** : to fill (someone) with food so that no more is wanted ▪ *He was completely sated.* **2** : to end (something, such as hunger or curiosity) by providing everything that is required or wanted ▪ *The information sated their curiosity.*

sat·el·lite /ˈsætəˌlaɪt/ *n* **1 a** *[C]* : an object (such as a moon) that moves around a much larger planet **b** *[C/U]* : a machine that is sent into space and that moves around the earth, moon, sun, or a planet ▪ *Images of the planet are sent by satellite.* ▪ *satellite broadcasting/channels/images/radio/TV* **2** *[C]* : a country, organization, etc., that is controlled by a larger and more powerful country, organization, etc.

satellite dish *n [C]* : a device that is shaped like a large dish and that receives television signals from a satellite high above the earth

sa·ti·ate /ˈseɪʃiˌeɪt/ *vb* **-at·ed; -at·ing** *[T] formal* : to satisfy (a need, desire, etc.) fully ▪ *Her curiosity was satiated.* — **sa·ti·a·tion** /ˌseɪʃiˈeɪʃən/ *n [U]*

sa·ti·ety /səˈtajəti/ *n [U] technical* : a feeling or condition of being full after eating food ▪ *eating beyond the point of satiety*

sat·in /ˈsætn/ n [U] : cloth that has a smooth, shiny surface — **satin** adj • satin sheets — **sat·iny** /ˈsætni/ adj

sat·ire /ˈsæˌtajɚ/ n 1 [U] : a way of using humor to show that someone or something is foolish, weak, bad, etc. 2 [C] : a book, movie, etc., that uses satire • The movie is a political/social satire. — **sa·tir·ic** /səˈtɪrɪk/ or **sa·tir·i·cal** /səˈtɪrɪkəl/ adj : a satiric/satirical novel — **sa·tir·i·cal·ly** /səˈtɪrɪkli/ adv

sat·i·rist /ˈsætərɪst/ n [C] : a person who uses satire in books, movies, etc.

sat·i·rize also Brit **sat·i·rise** /ˈsætəˌraɪz/ vb **-rized; -riz·ing** [T] : to show that (someone or something) is foolish, weak, bad, etc., by using satire • The book satirizes contemporary life.

sat·is·fac·tion /ˌsætəsˈfækʃən/ n 1 [U, singular] : a happy or pleased feeling because of something that you did or something that happened to you • He gets/derives great satisfaction from volunteering. 2 [U] : the act of providing what is needed or desired • the satisfaction of his deep craving for love 3 [C] US : something that makes you happy, pleased, or satisfied • Helping others is one of the greatest satisfactions of my life. — **to someone's satisfaction** : so that someone is happy, pleased, or satisfied • The work was not done to my satisfaction.

sat·is·fac·to·ry /ˌsætəsˈfæktəri/ adj : good enough for a particular purpose : ACCEPTABLE • satisfactory work • a satisfactory account/explanation/conclusion — **sat·is·fac·to·ri·ly** /ˌsætəsˈfæktərəli/ adv

sat·is·fy /ˈsætəsˌfaɪ/ vb **-fies; -fied; -fy·ing** [T] 1 : to cause (someone) to be happy or pleased • His job satisfies him. • I was not satisfied with the movie's ending. • a satisfying experience 2 : to provide, do, or have what is required by (someone or something) • His curiosity was satisfied by their explanation. 3 formal : to cause (someone) to believe that something is true • He has satisfied himself that the story is true. — **sat·is·fy·ing·ly** adv

sat·u·rate /ˈsætʃəˌreɪt/ vb **-rat·ed; -rat·ing** [T] 1 : to make (something) very wet • Saturate the sponge with water. • His shirt was saturated with sweat. 2 : to fill (something) completely with something • Images of the war saturated the news. — **sat·u·ra·tion** /ˌsætʃəˈreɪʃən/ n [U]

sat·u·rat·ed /ˈsætʃəˌreɪtəd/ adj, technical — used to describe a type of oil or fat that is found in foods such as meat and butter and that is bad for your health • saturated fats

Sat·ur·day /ˈsætɚˌdeɪ/ n [C/U] : the day of the week between Friday and Sunday • I'll arrive on Saturday. = (Brit) I will arrive on the Saturday. • next/last Saturday — abbr. **Sat.** — **Sat·ur·days** /ˈsætɚˌdeɪz/ adv • He visits his parents Saturdays. [=every Saturday]

Sat·urn /ˈsætɚn/ n [singular] : the planet that is sixth in order from the sun and that is surrounded by large rings

sauce /ˈsɑːs/ n 1 [C/U] : a thick liquid that is eaten with or on food to add flavor to it • a delicious spaghetti/meat sauce • ice cream with chocolate sauce 2 [C] : boiled or canned fruit • cranberry sauce

sauce·pan /ˈsɑːsˌpæn, Brit ˈsɔːspən/ n [C] : a deep, round cooking pan with a handle

sau·cer /ˈsɑːsɚ/ n [C] : a small, round dish that you put a cup on

saucy /ˈsɑːsi/ adj **sauc·i·er; -est** somewhat old-fashioned : rude usually in a lively and playful way • saucy language

sau·er·kraut /ˈsawɚˌkraʊt/ n [U] : a German food made of a vegetable (called a cabbage) that is cut into small pieces and soaked in a salty and sour liquid

sau·na /ˈsɑːnə/ n [C] 1 : a special heated room in which people get hot and sweat 2 : a health treatment in which people sit or lie down in a sauna • the benefits of taking/having a sauna regularly

saun·ter /ˈsɑːntɚ/ vb [I] : to walk along in a slow and relaxed manner • He sauntered by.

sau·sage /ˈsɑːsɪdʒ/ n [C/U] : spicy ground meat (such as pork) that is usually stuffed into a narrow tube of skin or made into a small flat cake • a spicy sausage

¹**sau·té** /saˈteɪ, Brit ˈsoʊˌteɪ/ n **-tés** also **-tes; -téed** also **-teed; -té·ing** also **-te·ing** [T] : to fry (food) in a small amount of fat • Sauté the onion and garlic.

²**sauté** n [C] : a food that is fried in a small amount of fat • a shrimp sauté = (US) a sauté of shrimp

¹**sav·age** /ˈsævɪdʒ/ adj 1 of an animal : WILD • savage beasts 2 : very cruel or violent • a savage criminal/attack/battle 3 : very critical or harsh • savage criticism 4 old-fashioned + offensive : uncivilized or primitive • a savage tribe — **sav·age·ly** adv

²**savage** n [C] old-fashioned + offensive 1 : a person who has a way of life that is simple and not highly advanced 2 : a person who is very violent or cruel • What kind of savage could have committed such a terrible crime?

³**savage** vb **-aged; -ag·ing** [T] : to attack or treat (someone or something) in a very cruel, violent, or harsh way • He looked like he'd been savaged by a wild animal. • The newspapers savaged her reputation.

sav·age·ry /ˈsævɪdʒri/ n, pl **-ries** 1 [U] : a cruel or violent quality • an act of pure savagery 2 [C] : a cruel or violent act or action • the savageries of war

sa·van·na also **sa·van·nah** /səˈvænə/ n [C] : a large flat area of land with grass and very few trees especially in Africa and South America

¹**save** /ˈseɪv/ vb **saved; sav·ing** 1 [T] a : to keep (someone or something) safe : to stop (someone or something) from dying or being hurt, damaged, or lost • He saved me (from drowning). • saving endangered animals b : to stop (something) from ending or failing • trying to save their marriage 2 [T/I] : to keep (something) from being lost or wasted • This new plan will help us save (on) energy/time. 3 [T/I] a : to keep money instead of spending it • She saves part of her pay every week. • I'm saving (up) for a new

car. **b** : to spend less money ▪ *Buy now and save!* ▪ *She saved $15 (on groceries) by using coupons.* **4** [T] **a** : to keep (something) available for use in the future ▪ *Save some cookies for me.* **b** : to keep (something) for someone to use or have ▪ *She saved a seat for me.* **5** [T] : to make (something) unnecessary ▪ *The shortcut saves an hour's driving.* **6** [T] : to keep (someone) from doing something ▪ *Thanks for sending out that package. It saved me a trip to the post office.* **7** [T] : to collect or keep (something) ▪ *She saved all his letters.* **8** [T/I] : to store (data) in a computer or on a storage device ▪ *Save (your document/work) before you close the file.* **9** [T] *sports* **a** : to stop (an opponent's shot) from scoring a goal ▪ *The goalie saved the kick/shot.* **b** : to keep (a game) from being lost to an opponent ▪ *The relief pitcher saved the game.* **10** [T/I] *in Christianity* : to protect or free (someone) from sin or evil ▪ *He believes that Jesus Christ will save him.* ▪ *Jesus saves.* — **save face** *see* ¹FACE — **save someone's bacon/hide/neck/skin** *informal* : to save or protect someone ▪ *All he's worried about is saving his own skin/neck.* — **save someone's life** : to stop (someone) from dying or being killed ▪ *He saved my life.* ▪ *The use of seat belts can save lives.* — **save the day** : to make a bad situation end successfully ▪ *Just when things looked hopeless, my brother came along and saved the day.*

²**save** *n* [C] **1** : a play that stops an opponent from scoring a goal ▪ *The goalie made a spectacular save.* **2** *baseball, of a relief pitcher* : the act of keeping a team's lead when replacing another pitcher at the end of a game

³**save** *prep, formal* : other than ▪ *We had no hope save* [=except] *one.* ▪ *The park was deserted save for* [=except for] *a few joggers.*

sav·er /ˈseɪvə/ *n* [C] **1** : someone who saves money for future use **2** : something that prevents unnecessary waste or loss — used in combination ▪ *This recipe is a real time-saver.*

saving *n* **1** [C] : an amount of something that is not spent or used ▪ *a saving on fuel* — often plural ▪ *a savings of 50 percent* ▪ *tax savings* **2** [plural] : the amount of money that you have saved especially in a bank over a period of time ▪ *They were able to retire on their savings.* ▪ *She lost her life savings* [=all the money she had] *when the stock market crashed.*

saving grace *n* [C] : a good quality that makes a bad or unpleasant person or thing better or more acceptable ▪ *The machine's saving grace is its ease of operation.*

savings account *n* [C] : a bank account in which people keep money that they want to save

savings and loan association *n* [C] *US* : a business that is like a bank and that holds and invests the money saved by its members and makes loans to home buyers — called also *savings and loan, S&L*

savings bank *n* [C] : a business where

people keep money that they are saving in order to earn interest on it and where they can borrow money to buy homes, cars, etc.

savings bond *n* [C] *finance* : a bond sold by the U.S. government that comes in values of $50 to $10,000

sav·ior (*US*) *or Brit* **sav·iour** /ˈseɪvjə/ *n* **1** [C] : someone who saves something or someone from danger, harm, failure, etc. ▪ *We all felt that she was our savior.* **2** *Savior* (*US*) *or Brit* **Saviour** — used by Christians to refer to Jesus Christ

sa·vor (*US*) *or Brit* **sa·vour** /ˈseɪvə/ *vb* [T] *formal* **1** : to enjoy the taste or smell of (something) for as long as possible ▪ *savoring an aroma* **2** : to enjoy (something) for a long time ▪ *She savored the moment.*

¹**sa·vory** (*US*) *or Brit* **sa·voury** /ˈseɪvəri/ *adj, formal* **1** : having a pleasant taste or smell ▪ *a savory aroma* **2** : having a spicy or salty quality without being sweet ▪ *savory foods*

²**savory** (*US*) *or Brit* **savoury** *n, pl* **-vories** [C] *formal* : a small serving of food that is spicy or salty but not sweet

¹**sav·vy** /ˈsævi/ *n* [U] : practical understanding or knowledge of something ▪ *He is admired for his business savvy.*

²**savvy** *adj* **sav·vi·er; -est** /ˈsævi/ : having practical understanding or knowledge of something ▪ *savvy investors*

¹**saw** *past tense of* SEE

²**saw** /ˈsɑː/ *n* [C] : a tool that has a blade with sharp teeth and that is used to cut through wood, metal, etc.

³**saw** *vb* **sawed** /ˈsɑːd/; **sawed** *or Brit* **sawn** /ˈsɑːn/; **saw·ing** /ˈsɑːɪŋ/ [T/I] : to cut or shape (wood, metal, etc.) with a saw ▪ *He sawed the boards in half.* — **saw at** [*phrasal vb*] : to try to cut (something) by moving a saw, knife, etc., backwards and forwards ▪ *She was sawing (away) at the turkey with a dull knife.* — **saw down** [*phrasal vb*] **saw down (something)** *or* **saw (something) down** : to cut (something) with a saw and bring it to the ground ▪ *The tree was sawed down.* — **saw off** [*phrasal vb*] **saw off (something)** *or* **saw (something) off** : to remove (something) by cutting it with a saw ▪ *She sawed off the branch.* — **saw up** [*phrasal vb*] **saw up (something)** *or* **saw (something) up** : to cut (something) into pieces with a saw ▪ *He sawed up the boards.*

saw·dust /ˈsɑːˌdʌst/ *n* [U] : tiny particles of wood that are formed from sawing or sanding wood

saw·horse /ˈsɑːˌhoəs/ *n* [C] : a frame on which wood is placed when it is being cut with a saw

saw·mill /ˈsɑːˌmɪl/ *n* [C] : a mill or factory where logs are sawed to make boards

sax /ˈsæks/ *n* [C] *informal* : SAXOPHONE

Sax·on /ˈsæksən/ *n* [C] : a member of the Germanic people who entered and conquered England in the fifth century A.D. — **Saxon** *adj*

sax·o·phone /ˈsæksəˌfoʊn/ *n* [C] : a musical instrument that has a curved metal tube and that is played by blowing into a mouthpiece and pressing keys — **sax·o·**

phon·ist /'sæksə₁fʊunɪst, *Brit* sæk-'sɒfənɪst/ *n* [C]

¹**say** /'seɪ/ *vb* **says** /'sɛz/; **said** /'sɛd/; **say·ing** /'seɪɪŋ/ **1** [T/I] : to use your voice to express (something) with words ▪ *"Is anybody there?" he said.* ▪ *"Good morning," said the woman behind the counter.* ▪ *I stopped by to say hello.* ▪ *Don't believe a word he says.* ▪ *What did you say?* ▪ *Did she say how to get there?* ▪ *He said (that) he was a doctor.* ▪ *"What happened next?" "I'd rather not say."* ▪ *Her eyes are hazel,* **which is to say** [=which means that] *they are greenish brown.* **2** [T] : to express (an opinion) ▪ *I say they're wrong.* [=my opinion is that they're wrong] ▪ *"Is the island nice?" "So they/people say."* ▪ *I must* **say** *that was quite a surprise.* = *I* **have to say** *that was quite a surprise.* ▪ *The dress seems too fancy,* **wouldn't you say?** [=don't you agree?] ▪ *I'll* **say** *this for him—he's very generous with his money.* **3** [T/I] : to express (a fact) with certainty ▪ *No one can say for sure what will happen.* ▪ *It is hard to say what caused the injury.* ▪ **There's no saying** [=it is impossible to know] *how many people died in the earthquake.* ▪ *"When will you be done?" "I* **couldn't/can't say."** [=I don't know] **4** [T/I] : to tell someone to do (something) ▪ *Mom said to wait here.* ▪ **What she says goes!** [=you have to do what she tells you to do] ▪ *"Let's try installing the program one more time." "Whatever you* **say**—*you're the expert."* **5** [T] : to pronounce (a word) ▪ *How do you say my name?* **6** [T] : to repeat or recite (something) ▪ *saying our prayers* **7** [T] : to use written words to give (information) ▪ *The instructions say to add two eggs.* **8** [T] : to show or indicate (something) by using numbers, pictures, etc. ▪ *The clock says five minutes after ten.* **9** [T] : to express (a meaning, emotion, etc.) without using words ▪ *I like art that really says something.* ▪ *His face* **said it all.** = *His face* **said everything.** [=his face showed how he felt] **10 a** — used to suggest an example or possibility ▪ *Say you do get accepted to the college. Will you go?* ▪ *Let's* **say** *you're right, for argument's sake.* **b** — used to suggest a possible or approximate amount, value, etc. ▪ *The property is worth,* **say,** *four million dollars.* [=the property is worth about four million dollars] — **go without saying** : to be obvious and true ▪ *It goes without saying that I'll do whatever I can to help you.* — **have something/nothing/much (etc.) to say for yourself** : to be able or unable to say something that explains what you are doing, have done, etc. ▪ *I asked him about school, but he didn't have much to say for himself.* ▪ *What do you have to say for yourself?* — **having said that** or **that said** : despite what I just said ▪ *His work has been fairly good. Having said that, I think he can do better.* — **if I may say so** also **if I might say so** — used to express criticism or disagreement in a polite way ▪ *The meeting—if I may say so—was a waste of time.* — **if I say so myself** — used when you are saying something that praises your own work, skill, etc. ▪ *I'm a*

pretty good golfer, if I say so myself. — *I'll* **say** *informal* — used to indicate that you completely agree with something just said ▪ *"Isn't it hot today!" "I'll say (it is)."* — **not to say** — used to introduce a more forceful or critical way of describing someone or something ▪ *His manner was discourteous, not to say offensive.* — **say no** : to say that you will not accept or agree to something ▪ *We requested more time, but she said no.* ▪ *I never say no to dessert.* — **say something/little/a lot (etc.) for** : to show that (someone or something) does or does not deserve to be praised, admired, etc. ▪ *The students' low test scores don't say much for the education they're receiving.* — **say what** *US, informal* — used to express surprise at what someone has just said ▪ *"I'm moving out." "Say what?"* — **say yes** : to say that you accept or agree to something ▪ *They said yes to our plan.* — **that's not saying much** — used to indicate that a fact, achievement, etc., is not unusual or impressive ▪ *He is a better golfer than me, but that's not saying much (because I'm not a good golfer).* — **there is something/a lot/much (etc.) to be said for** — used to indicate that something has advantages which deserve to be considered when you are thinking about what to do ▪ *There is something to be said for small weddings.* — **to say nothing of** — used when referring to another thing that relates to what you have just said ▪ *We need more time, to say nothing of money.* [=we also need more money] — **to say the least** *see* ²LEAST — **you can say that again** *informal* — used to indicate that you completely agree with something just said ▪ *"She's in a bad mood." "You can say that again."* — **you don't say** — used to express surprise ▪ *"She met him here." "You don't say!"* — **you might say** — used to suggest a possible way of describing or thinking about something ▪ *The experience was, you might say, a glimpse into the future.* — **you said it** *informal* — used to indicate that you completely agree with something just said ▪ *"That was pretty rude of him." "You said it."*

²**say** *n* **1** [*singular*] : an opportunity to express your opinion ▪ *Everybody had a/their* **say** *at the meeting.* **2** [U, *singular*] : the power to decide or help decide something — usually + *in* ▪ *Do I have a say in this?* ▪ *He had no/some/little say in the matter.*

³**say** *interj, chiefly US, informal* **1** — used to express surprise, shock, etc. ▪ *Say, that's a great idea.* **2** — used to attract the attention of someone ▪ *Say there. Can you help me?*

say·ing /'seɪɪŋ/ *n* [C] : an old and well-known phrase that expresses an idea that most people believe is true ▪ *"Two minds are better than one," as the (old) saying goes.*

say-so /'seɪ₁soʊ/ *n* [U] *informal* **1** : a statement that is not supported by any proof ▪ *We have only his say-so that he did the work.* **2** : permission that is given by a person who has authority ▪ *Nothing was* done without his say-so. **3** : the power to decide something • *She has the ultimate say-so on/over what will be taught.*

SC *abbr* **1** South Carolina **2** supreme court

scab /'skæb/ *n* [C] **1** : a hard covering of dried blood that forms over a wound to cover and protect it as it heals **2** *informal + disapproving* : a worker who does not join a strike or who takes the place of another worker who is on strike

scads /'skædz/ *n* [*plural*] *informal* : a large amount of something • *scads of money/time*

scaf·fold /'skæfəld/ *n* [C] **1** : a temporary or movable platform or structure on which a person stands or sits while working high above the floor or ground **2** : a platform or structure on which criminals are killed by being hanged or beheaded

scaf·fold·ing /'skæfəldɪŋ/ *n* [U] : the metal poles and wooden boards that are used to build or support a scaffold (sense 1)

¹**scald** /'skɑːld/ *vb* [T] **1** : to burn (someone or something) with hot liquid or steam • *The steam scalded his skin.* **2 a** : to put (something) in hot liquid or steam for a brief time • *Scald the tomatoes in boiling water.* **b** : to heat (a liquid) until it is very hot but not boiling • *scald milk*

²**scald** *n* [C] : a burn left on the skin that is caused by hot liquid or steam

scald·ing /'skɑːldɪŋ/ *adj* **1** : very hot • *a scalding bowl of soup* • *scalding hot water* **2** : very harsh or critical • *a scalding review of the book*

¹**scale** /'skeɪl/ *n* **1** [C] : a device that is used for weighing people or things • *(US) a bathroom scale = (Brit) the bathroom scales* **2** [C] : a series of musical notes that go up or down in pitch • *the C-minor scale* • *a major scale* **3** [C] : a line on a map or chart that shows a specific unit of measure (such as an inch) used to represent a larger unit (such as a mile) • *The map uses a scale of one centimeter for every 10 kilometers.* **4** [C] : a range of numbers that is used to show the size, strength, or quality of something — usually singular • *On a scale of 1 to 10, I give the movie a 9.* [=the movie was extremely good] **5** [C] : a range of levels of something from lowest to highest • *He is at the top of the pay scale for his position.* **6** [U] — used to describe a model, drawing, etc., in which all of the parts of something relate to each other in the same way that they do in the larger form • *The model of the building is to scale.* [=the model shows exactly how the parts will relate to each other when it is built] • *a scale model of a car* **7** [*singular*] : the size or level of something especially in comparison to something else • *The company does things on a larger scale than most others.* • *They exposed fraud on a grand scale.* **8** [C] : one of many small thin plates that cover the bodies of some animals (such as fish or snakes) **9** [U] *technical* : a hard substance that is formed in pipes or containers holding

water **10** [U] *Brit* : TARTAR

²**scale** *vb* **scaled; scal·ing** [T] **1** : to climb to the top of (something) • *Hikers scaled the mountain.* • *(figurative) She scaled the heights of the publishing industry.* [=she rose to a very high position in the publishing industry] **2** : to remove the scales from (a fish) • *He cleaned and scaled the fish.* — **scale back/down** [*phrasal vb*] **scale back/down (something)** or **scale (something) back/down** : to decrease the size, amount, or extent of (something) • *We scaled back our plans.* — **scale up** [*phrasal vb*] **scale up (something)** or **scale (something) up** : to increase the size, amount, or extent of (something) • *The company hopes to scale up production soon.*

scal·lion /'skæljən/ *n* [C] *US* : GREEN ONION

scal·lop /'skɑːləp, 'skæləp/ *n* [C] **1** : a type of shellfish that has a flat, round shell with two parts and that is often eaten as food **2** : one of a series of similar curves that form a decorative edge on something

scal·loped /'skɑːləpt, 'skæləpt/ *adj* **1** : baked in a sauce usually with bread crumbs on top • *scalloped potatoes* **2** : having a series of similar, decorative curves along the edge • *a scalloped collar/hem*

¹**scalp** /'skælp/ *n* [C] **1** : the skin on the top of your head where hair grows **2** : hair and skin that is cut or torn from the head of an enemy as a sign of victory • *(figurative) His boss wants his scalp.* [=wants to fire him]

²**scalp** *vb* [T] **1** : to remove the hair and skin from the head of (an enemy) as a sign of victory • *Settlers were scalped by the attacking warriors.* **2** *US* : to buy tickets for an event and sell them again at a much higher price • *People were scalping tickets outside the stadium.* — **scalp·er** *n* [C] *US* • *ticket scalpers*

scal·pel /'skælpəl/ *n* [C] : a small knife with a thin, sharp blade that is used in surgery

scaly /'skeɪli/ *adj* **scal·i·er; -i·est** : covered with scales or flakes • *scaly skin*

¹**scam** /'skæm/ *n* [C] : a dishonest way to make money by deceiving people • *She was the victim of an insurance scam.*

²**scam** *vb* **scammed; scam·ming** [T] **1** : to deceive and take money from (someone) • *The company scammed hundreds of people.* **2** : to get (something, such as money) by deceiving someone • *He scammed a lot of money from unwary customers.* — **scam·mer** *n* [C]

scam·per /'skæmpər/ *vb* [I] : to run or move quickly and often playfully • *Mice scampered across the floor.*

¹**scan** /'skæn/ *vb* **scanned; scan·ning 1** [T] : to look at (something) carefully usually in order to find someone or something • *He scanned the field with binoculars.* • *The program scans the computer's files.* **2** [T/I] : to look over or read (something) quickly • *She quickly scanned (through) the list.* **3** [T] : to look at the inside of (something) by using a

special machine • *Our bags were scanned at the airport.* **4** [T/I] : to use a special machine to read or copy (something, such as a photograph or a page of text) into a computer • *She scanned the pictures into her computer.* • *The bar code won't scan.* [=the machine is unable to read the bar code]

²**scan** *n* [C] **1** : the act or process of scanning something • *a careful scan of the area* • *She gave the list a quick scan.* • *The patient underwent a brain scan.* **2** : a picture of the inside of something that is made by a special machine • *The doctor examined the bone scans.* — see also CAT SCAN

scan·dal /'skændl/ *n* **1** [C/U] : an occurrence in which people are shocked and upset because of behavior that is morally or legally wrong • *There was a major scandal involving the mayor's ties with the Mob.* • *a drug/sex scandal* • *His actions brought scandal on the team.* [=his actions disgraced the team] **2** [U] : talk about the shocking or immoral things that people have done or are believed to have done • *a magazine filled with rumors and scandal* **3** [*singular*] : something that is shocking, upsetting, or unacceptable • *The high price of gas these days is a scandal.*

scan·dal·ize *also Brit* **scan·dal·ise** /'skændə,laɪz/ *vb* -**ized**; -**iz·ing** [T] : to shock or offend (someone) by doing something immoral or illegal • *She was scandalized by her son's behavior.*

scan·dal·ous /'skændələs/ *adj* **1** : shocking or offensive • *scandalous behavior/pictures* **2** : involving immoral or shocking things that a person has done or is believed to have done • *scandalous allegations/rumors* — **scan·dal·ous·ly** *adv*

scan·ner /'skænɚ/ *n* [C] **1** : a device that scans things • *a photo/price/luggage scanner* **2** : a radio receiver that searches for a signal • *a police scanner* [=a device that is used for listening to the police as they talk to each other over the radio]

scant /'skænt/ *adj* : very small in size or amount • *She paid scant attention to the facts.* • *scant evidence*

scanty /'skænti/ *adj* **scant·i·er**; -**est** : very small in size or amount • *The cheerleaders wore scanty outfits.* — **scant·i·ly** /'skæntəli/ *adv*

scape·goat /'skeɪp,goʊt/ *n* [C] : a person who is unfairly blamed for something that others have done • *The CEO was made the scapegoat for the company's failures.* — **scapegoat** *vb* [T] • *He was scapegoated for the company's failures.*

¹**scar** /'skɑɚ/ *n* [C] **1** : a mark that is left on your skin after a wound heals • *the soldier's battle scars* • *scar tissue* **2** : a mark on something showing where it has been damaged • *the scars on an old table* **3** : a feeling of great emotional pain or sadness that is caused by a bad experience and that lasts for a long time • *The divorce left her with deep emotional scars.*

²**scar** *vb* **scarred**; **scar·ring** [T] **1** : to mark (something) with a scar • *His arm*

was badly scarred. **2** : to cause (someone) to feel great emotional pain or sadness because of a bad experience • *Divorce can scar a person for life.* **3** : to make marks on (something) that show damage or wear • *The fence was scarred by rust.*

scarce /'skeɚs/ *adj* **scarc·er**; **scarc·est** : very small in amount or number • *Food was getting scarce.* • *scarce resources* — **make yourself scarce** *informal* : to leave so that you will not be seen in a certain place • *You'd better make yourself scarce before my parents get home.* — **scarce·ness** *n* [U]

scarce·ly /'skeɚsli/ *adv* **1** : almost not at all : HARDLY • *He could scarcely control his joy.* **2** : by only a small amount of time, space, etc. : BARELY • *He had scarcely enough money.* **3** : certainly not • *This is scarcely a time to laugh.* — **scarcely ever** see EVER

scar·ci·ty /'skeɚsəti/ *n*, *pl* -**ties** [C/U] : a very small supply • *There was a scarcity of food.* [=there was very little food; there was not enough food]

¹**scare** /'skeɚ/ *vb* **scared**; **scar·ing** **1** [T] : to cause (someone) to become afraid : FRIGHTEN • *Stop scaring the children.* • *You nearly scared me to death.* [=you scared me very much] **2** [I] : to become afraid • *I don't scare easily.* — **scare away/off** [*phrasal vb*] **scare (someone or something) away/off** *or* **scare away/off (someone or something)** : to cause (someone or something) to go away and stay away because of fear or because of possible trouble, difficulty, etc. • *The noise scared off the birds.* — **scare into** [*phrasal vb*] **scare (someone) into** : to cause (someone) to do (something) because of fear • *They tried to scare us into buying more insurance.* — **scare up** [*phrasal vb*] **scare (someone or something) up** *or* **scare up (someone or something)** *US*, *informal* : to find or get (someone or something) with some difficulty • *We scared up the money.*

²**scare** *n* [C] **1** : a sudden feeling of fear • *You gave me (quite) a scare.* [=you scared me] **2** : a situation in which a lot of people become afraid because of some threat, danger, etc. • *a bomb scare* [=a situation in which people are afraid because someone says that a bomb is going to explode] — **scare** *adj*, *always before a noun* • *using scare tactics*

scare·crow /'skeɚ,kroʊ/ *n* [C] : an object that looks like a person and that is placed in a field to scare birds away from crops

scared *adj* : afraid of something • *You look scared.* • *He's scared of snakes.* • *She's scared to walk alone at night.* • *She's scared to death of flying.* = *She's scared stiff of flying.* [=she's very scared of flying]

¹**scarf** /'skɑɚf/ *n*, *pl* **scarves** /'skɑɚvz/ *or* **scarfs** [C] : a long piece of cloth that is worn on your shoulders, around your neck, or over your head

²**scarf** *vb* [T] *US*, *informal* : to eat (something) quickly • *I scarfed (down) my breakfast.* — **scarf up** [*phrasal vb*] **scarf**

(something) up or *scarf up (something)*
US, *informal* : to take (something) in a
quick and eager way ▪ *They scarfed up
the free gifts.*

scar·let /ˈskɑɚlət/ *n* [C/U] : a bright red
color — **scarlet** *adj*

scarlet fever *n* [U] : a very serious disease that causes a fever, sore throat, and
a red rash

scary /ˈskeri/ *adj* **scar·i·er; -est** : causing fear ▪ *a scary movie* ▪ *He is scary looking.* = *He looks scary.* — **scar·i·ly**
/ˈskerəli/ *adv* — **scar·i·ness** *n* [U]

scat /ˈskæt/ *interj* — used to scare away
an animal

scath·ing /ˈskeɪðɪŋ/ *adj, somewhat formal* : very harsh or severe ▪ *a scathing re-
view/look/comment* — **scath·ing·ly** *adv*

scat·o·log·i·cal /ˌskætəˈlɑːdʒɪkəl/ *adj,
formal* : relating to things that are disgusting or offensive ▪ *scatological humor*

scat·ter /ˈskæt̬ɚ/ *vb* **1 a** [T] : to cause
(things or people) to separate and go in
different directions ▪ *The wind scattered
the leaves.* **b** [I] : to separate and go in
different directions ▪ *The kids scattered
when the police arrived.* **2** [T] : to place
or leave (things) in different places ▪ *scatter seeds* ▪ *She scattered the books on the
table.*

scat·ter·brain /ˈskæt̬ɚˌbreɪn/ *n* [C] *informal* : a person who is unable to concentrate or think clearly — **scat·ter-
brained** /ˈskæt̬ɚˌbreɪnd/ *adj* ▪ *scatter-
brained people/ideas*

scat·tered /ˈskæt̬ɚd/ *adj* : placed or
found far apart ▪ *Clothes were scattered
about the room.* ▪ *The weather forecast
calls for scattered* [=occasional] *showers.*

scat·ter·ing /ˈskæt̬ɚɪŋ/ *n* [C] : a small
number or group of things or people that
are seen or found at different places or
times ▪ *The museum had a scattering of
visitors last week.*

scav·enge /ˈskævəndʒ/ *vb* **-enged;
-eng·ing** [T/I] **1** of an animal : to
search for food ▪ *The bears scavenged for
food in the woods.* **2** : to search through
waste, junk, etc., for something that can
be saved or used ▪ *scavenging (the town
dump) for car parts* — **scav·en·ger**
/ˈskævəndʒɚ/ *n* [C]

scavenger hunt *n* [C] : a game in which
players try to find specified items within
a particular period of time

sce·nar·io /səˈnerijoʊ, *Brit* səˈnɑːriəʊ/ *n,
pl* **-i·os** [C] **1** : a description of what
could happen ▪ *A possible scenario would
be that we move to the city.* ▪ *What's the
best-case/worst-case scenario?* [=what's
the best/worst thing that could happen?]
2 *formal* : a written description of a play,
movie, opera, etc.

scene /ˈsiːn/ *n* [C] **1 a** : a part of an act
in a play during which the action hap-
pens in a single place without a break in
time ▪ *The play's opening scene takes
place in the courtyard.* ▪ *Act I, Scene 3* **b**
: a part of a play, movie, story, etc., in
which a particular action or activity occurs ▪ *a famous love/fight/chase scene* **2**
[C] : a view or sight that looks like a picture ▪ *a winter scene* **3** [C] : the place of
an event or action ▪ *a crime scene* ▪ *the*
scene of the accident ▪ *Police are now at/
on the scene.* **4** [C] : an occurrence in
which someone becomes angry and loud
in a noticeable way in a public place ▪ *an
ugly/angry scene* ▪ *The child made a
scene.* **5** [U] **a** : a particular area of
activity that involves many people ▪ *the
music/political scene* ▪ (*informal*) *Nightclubs are not my scene.* [=I do not like to
go to nightclubs] **b** : someone's usual
area of activity or surroundings ▪ *I need a
change of scene.* [=I need to go somewhere else] **6** [C] : an event or occurrence ▪ *a scene of celebration* — *behind
the scenes* : in or into a private or secret place where things are done without
being seen or known by the public ▪ *The
workers behind the scenes made the event
a success.* — *set the scene* **1** : to give
someone information that is needed to
understand something ▪ *First, let me set
the scene (for you).* **2** : to create the conditions in which something can happen ▪
*His comments set the scene for an argu-
ment.*

scen·ery /ˈsiːnəri/ *n* [U] **1** : the walls,
furniture, trees, etc., that are used on a
stage during a play or other performance
to show where the action is taking place
2 : a pleasing view of natural features
(such as mountains, hills, valleys, etc.) ▪
beautiful mountain scenery ▪ *We went for
a drive to enjoy the scenery.* **3** : the
things that can be seen where a person
lives, works, etc. ▪ *I could use a change of
scenery.* [=I need to be in a different
place]

sce·nic /ˈsiːnɪk/ *adj* : having, providing,
or relating to a pleasing or beautiful view
of natural scenery (such as mountains,
hills, valleys, etc.) ▪ *a scenic route/drive/
view*

1scent /ˈsɛnt/ *n* **1** [C] **a** : a pleasant
smell that is produced by something ▪ *the
scent of flowers/perfume* ▪ (*figurative*) *Her
story has a/the scent of truth.* [=her story
seems to be true] **b** : a smell that is left
by an animal or person and that can be
sensed and followed by some animals
(such as dogs) ▪ *The dogs followed the
fox's scent.* ▪ (*figurative*) *The reporter was
on the scent of a big story.* [=was follow-
ing/investigating a big story] **2** [C/U]
: ¹PERFUME ▪ *a bottle of scent*

2scent *vb* [T] **1** : to become aware of
(something) by smell ▪ *The dog scented a
rabbit.* ▪ (*figurative*) *The reporter scented a
big story.* **2** : to give (something) a pleasing smell ▪ *Roses scented the air.* = *The air
was scented by roses.* — **scent·ed**
/ˈsɛntəd/ *adj* ▪ *The soap is scented.*

scep·ter (*US*) or *Brit* **scep·tre** /ˈsɛptɚ/ *n*
[C] : a long decorated stick that is carried by a king or queen

scep·tic, sceptical, scepticism *Brit
spellings of* SKEPTIC, SKEPTICAL, SKEPTI-
CISM

1sched·ule /ˈskɛdʒuːl, *Brit* ˈʃɛˌdjuːl/ *n* **1**
[C/U] : a plan of things that will be done
and the times when they will be done ▪ *I
have a hectic/busy/full schedule this week.*
▪ *The bus arrived on schedule.* [=arrived
at the time it was expected] ▪ *We are
ahead of schedule.* [=we are completing

work earlier than planned] • *We are be-hind/off schedule.* [=we are doing things later than planned] **2** [C] **a** : a written or printed list of things and the times when they will be done • *a class/course schedule* **b** *US* : a list of the times when buses, trains, airplanes, etc., leave or ar-rive • *a bus/train/airplane/flight schedule* [=(*chiefly Brit*) *timetable*] **c** : a list of the television or radio programs that are on a particular channel and the times that they begin • *a programming schedule* **d** : a list of prices or rates • *a tax schedule*

²**schedule** *vb* **-uled; -ul·ing** [T] : to plan (something) at a certain time • *We sched-uled a meeting for next week.* • *He's sched-uled to arrive at noon.* • *a list of scheduled events* • *The train left as scheduled.* [=*on time*]

sche·mat·ic /skɪˈmætɪk/ *adj, technical* : showing the main parts of something usually in the form of a simple drawing or diagram • *a schematic diagram*

¹**scheme** /ˈskiːm/ *n* [C] **1** : a clever and often dishonest plan • *a scheme to cheat people out of their money* **2** *chiefly Brit* : an official plan or program of action • *a training/pension/marketing scheme* **3** : the way that something is arranged or organized • *the color/decorative scheme of a room* — **the scheme of things** : the general way that things are organized and relate to each other • *Our problems aren't really that important in the grand scheme of things.* [=aren't really that im-portant when you think about the larger situation]

²**scheme** *vb* **schemed; schem·ing** [I] : to make plans to do or get something in a secret and often dishonest way • *They were scheming against him.* • *She schemed to take control of the company.* — **schem·er** *n* [C]

schism /ˈsɪzəm, ˈskɪzəm/ *n* [C/U] *formal* : a division among the members of a group that occurs because they disagree on something • *The controversy created a schism in the group.*

schiz·oid /ˈskɪtˌsɔɪd/ *adj* **1** *technical* : relating to or having schizophrenia • *schizoid symptoms/patients* **2** : changing frequently between opposite states • *a schizoid career*

schizo·phre·nia /ˌskɪtsəˈfriːnijə/ *n* [U] *technical* : a very serious mental illness in which someone cannot think or behave normally and often experiences delu-sions

schizo·phren·ic /ˌskɪtsəˈfrɛnɪk/ *adj* **1** *technical* : relating to or having schizo-phrenia • *schizophrenic symptoms/pa-tients* **2** : changing frequently between opposite states • *the government's schizo-phrenic foreign policy* — **schizophren-ic** *n* [C]

schlep *or* **schlepp** /ˈʃlɛp/ *vb* **schlepped; schlep·ping** [T] *US, infor-mal* : to carry or pull (something) with difficulty • *We schlepped our luggage through the airport.*

schlock /ˈʃlɑːk/ *n* [U] *US, informal + usu-ally disapproving* : things that are of low quality or value • *a film director who's known as a master of schlock* —

schlocky /ˈʃlɑːki/ *adj* **schlock·i·er; -est**

schmaltz *also* **schmalz** /ˈʃmɑːlts/ *n* [U] *informal + disapproving* : music, art, etc., that is very sad or romantic in usually a foolish or exaggerated way • *The movie has too much schmaltz for me.* — **schmaltzy** /ˈʃmɑːltsi/ *adj* **schmaltz·i·er; -est**

schmooze *or* **shmooze** /ˈʃmuːz/ *vb* **schmoozed** *or* **shmoozed; schmooz-ing** *or* **shmooz·ing** [T/I] *informal* : to talk with someone in a friendly way of-ten in order to get some advantage for yourself • *She schmoozed (with) the re-porters/boss.* — **schmooz·er** /ˈʃmuːzɚ/ *n* [C]

schmuck /ˈʃmʌk/ *n* [C] *US slang* : a stu-pid or foolish person : JERK

schnapps /ˈʃnæps/ *n, pl* **schnapps** [C/U] : a type of strong liquor

schol·ar /ˈskɑːlɚ/ *n* [C] **1** : an intelligent and well-educated person who knows a particular subject very well • *a biblical/classical scholar* **2** : someone who has been given a scholarship • *a Rhodes scholar*

schol·ar·ly /ˈskɑːlɚli/ *adj* **1** : concerned with or relating to formal study or re-search • *scholarly journals/work/writings* **2** : having the characteristics of a scholar • *a scholarly man* [=a man who studies something seriously]

schol·ar·ship /ˈskɑːlɚˌʃɪp/ *n* **1** [C] : an amount of money that is given by a school, an organization, etc., to a student to help pay for the student's education • *She got/received/won a scholarship to Yale University.* **2** [U] : serious formal study or research of a subject • *The essay is a work of serious scholarship.* • *academic/biblical/literary scholarship*

scho·las·tic /skəˈlæstɪk/ *adj, always be-fore a noun* : of or relating to education • *scholastic achievement/aptitude*

¹**school** /ˈskuːl/ *n* **1 a** [C/U] : a place where children go to learn • *a new school* • *Where do you go to school?* • *He learned to play the flute at/in school.* • *He left/quit school* [=he stopped going to school] *when he was 16.* **b** [C/U] *US* : a college or university • *He is attending (a) law/business/medical school.* **c** [C] : a divi-sion within a university or college for study and research in a particular area of knowledge • *the school of art/engineering* **d** [C] : a place where people go to learn a particular skill • *a driving school* **2** [U] **a** : the activity or process of learning or teaching in a school • (*US*) *She teaches school.* • *I had a job while I was in/at school.* = [=while I was a student in a school] **b** : the period of time during which students are in school • *School starts at 8:00 a.m.* **3** [C] : the students or students and teachers of a school • *The whole school was at the assembly.* **4** [C] : a group of people who share the same opinions, beliefs, or methods • *artists from the Impressionist/Romantic school* • *There are two main schools of thought* [=ways of thinking] *on that topic.* **5** [C] : a large group of fish or other ocean an-imals that are swimming together

²**school** vb [T] somewhat old-fashioned : to teach or train (someone or something) to do something • They schooled the child at home. • She schooled herself in patience. • He is schooled in five different languages.

school age n [U] : the age when a child is allowed to go to a school — **school-age** adj, always before a noun • school-age children

school·bag /ˈskuːlˌbæg/ n [C] : a bag for carrying books and supplies for school

school board n [C] US : a group of people who are in charge of local schools — called also (US) school committee

school·boy /ˈskuːlˌbɔɪ/ n [C] : a boy who goes to a school

school bus n [C] : a bus for carrying children to and from a school

school·child /ˈskuːlˌtʃaɪld/ n, pl -chil·dren [C] : a child who goes to a school

school·girl /ˈskuːlˌgɚl/ n [C] : a girl who goes to a school

school·house /ˈskuːlˌhaʊs/ n [C] : a building that is used as a school

school·ing /ˈskuːlɪŋ/ n [U] : teaching that is done in a school : EDUCATION • He has had little schooling.

school·mas·ter /ˈskuːlˌmæstɚ, Brit ˈskuːlˌmɑːstə/ n [C] old-fashioned : a man who teaches in a school

school·room /ˈskuːlˌruːm/ n [C] : a room where classes meet in a school : CLASSROOM

school·teach·er /ˈskuːlˌtiːtʃɚ/ n [C] : someone who teaches in a school

school·work /ˈskuːlˌwɚk/ n [U] : work that is done in classes in a school or given to students to be done at home

school·yard /ˈskuːlˌjɑɚd/ n [C] : the area next to or surrounding a school where children play

schoo·ner /ˈskuːnɚ/ n [C] : a ship that has usually two masts with the larger mast located toward the center and the shorter mast toward the front

schtick variant spelling of SHTICK

schwa /ˈʃwɑː/ n [C] technical : a vowel that has the sound of the first and last vowels of the English word America ə : the symbol ə that is used for the schwa sound

sci·at·i·ca /saɪˈætɪkə/ n [U] medical : pain in the lower back, hip, and especially the back of the thigh that is caused by pressure on a nerve

sci·ence /ˈsaɪəns/ n **1** [U] : knowledge about or study of the natural world based on facts learned through experiments and observation • a new branch/field of science • science teachers/students/classes **2** [C] : a particular area of scientific study (such as biology, physics, or chemistry) • students majoring in a science **3** [C] : a subject that is formally studied in a college, university, etc. • the science of linguistics — see also POLITICAL SCIENCE, SOCIAL SCIENCE **4** [singular] : an activity that is done by using methods that are known to produce particular results • Cooking is both a science and an art. • He has packing down to a science. [=he can pack quickly and efficiently]

science fiction n [U] : stories about how people and societies are affected by imaginary scientific developments in the future

sci·en·tif·ic /ˌsaɪənˈtɪfɪk/ adj **1** : of or relating to science • scientific techniques/knowledge/research **2** : done in an organized way that agrees with the methods and principles of science • a scientific approach — **sci·en·tif·i·cal·ly** /ˌsaɪənˈtɪfɪkli/ adv

sci·en·tist /ˈsaɪəntɪst/ n [C] : a person who is trained in a science and whose job involves doing scientific research or solving scientific problems

sci-fi /ˈsaɪˈfaɪ/ n [U] informal : SCIENCE FICTION

scin·til·la /sɪnˈtɪlə/ n [singular] : a very small amount of something — usually used in negative statements • There's not even a scintilla of evidence.

scin·til·lat·ing /ˈsɪntəˌleɪtɪŋ/ adj : very clever, amusing, and interesting • a scintillating discussion

sci·on /ˈsaɪən/ n [C] formal : a person who was born into a rich, famous, or important family • He's a scion of a powerful family.

scis·sors /ˈsɪzɚz/ n [plural] : a tool used for cutting paper, cloth, etc., that has two blades joined together in the middle so that the sharp edges slide against each other • He handed her the scissors. = He handed her a pair of scissors.

scoff /ˈskɑːf/ vb **1** [T/I] : to laugh at and talk about someone or something in a way that shows disapproval and a lack of respect • He scoffed at the idea of her becoming an actress. **2** [T] chiefly Brit : to eat (something) quickly • She scoffed her breakfast.

¹**scold** /ˈskoʊld/ vb [T] : to speak in an angry or critical way to (someone who has done something wrong) • He scolded the children for making a mess. — **scold·ing** /ˈskoʊldɪŋ/ n [C/U] • The children got a scolding.

²**scold** n [C] : a person who often criticizes other people in an angry way

sconce /ˈskɑːns/ n [C] : an object that is attached to a wall and that holds a candle or an electric light

scone /ˈskoʊn, ˈskɑːn/ n [C] : a small, often sweet bread that sometimes has pieces of dried fruit in it

¹**scoop** /ˈskuːp/ n **1** [C] **a** : a kitchen tool like a spoon that has a usually thick handle and a deep bowl for taking something from a container • an ice-cream scoop **b** : something that is shaped like a bowl or bucket and used to pick up and move things • a backhoe with a large scoop **c** : the amount of something that is held in a scoop • a scoop of ice cream **2** [C] : a news story that is reported before other news reporters know about it • The story was the political scoop of the year. **3** the scoop US, informal : information about something that is currently important or happening • Did you talk to him? What's the scoop? [=what did he say?] • I've got the inside scoop. [=information known only by a particular group of people] **4** [C] : the act of pick-

1046

ing up something with a quick, continuous motion ▪ *With one scoop, he gathered up all the clothes on the floor.*

²**scoop** *vb* [*T*] **1 a :** to pick up and move (something) with a scoop, a spoon, etc. ▪ *scoop ice cream from a bucket* ▪ *Scoop out the seeds of the melon.* **b :** to pick up (something or someone) in one quick, continuous motion ▪ *He scooped the dice off the table.* ▪ *She scooped up her child.* **2 :** to make (a hole, hollow, etc.) by using a scoop, spoon, etc. ▪ *Scoop (out) a hole in the dough for the filling.* **3 :** to report a news story before (any other newspaper, news program, etc.) ▪ *The leading newspaper got scooped by a smaller competitor.* — **scoop up** [*phrasal vb*] **scoop up (something)** *or* **scoop (something) up** *informal* **:** to take or buy (something) in a quick and eager way ▪ *Customers scooped up the free samples.* — **scoop·er** *n* [*C*]

scoot /ˈskuːt/ *vb, informal* **1** [*I*] **:** to go or leave suddenly and quickly ▪ *I'm late, so I have to scoot.* **2** [*I*] *chiefly US* **:** to move (yourself, your chair, etc.) a short distance in a particular direction ▪ *She scooted her chair back.* ▪ *Can you scoot over a little?*

scoot·er /ˈskuːtə/ *n* [*C*] **1 :** a child's vehicle that is made of a narrow board with two small wheels attached underneath and an upright handle attached on top and that is moved by pushing with one foot while holding onto the handle **2 :** MOTOR SCOOTER

¹**scope** /ˈskoʊp/ *n* **1 a** [*U, singular*] **:** the area that is included in or dealt with by something ▪ *the scope of the book/discussion/law/study* **b** [*U*] **:** space or opportunity for action, thought, etc. ▪ *A bigger budget will allow more scope for innovation.* **2** [*C*] *chiefly US* **:** an instrument (such as a telescope or microscope) that is used to look at things ▪ *the scope of a rifle*

²**scope** *vb* **scoped; scop·ing** — **scope out** [*phrasal vb*] **scope (someone or something) out** *or* **scope out (someone or something)** *US, informal* **:** to look at (someone or something) especially in order to get information ▪ *We scoped out the area/competition.*

scorch /ˈskoːtʃ/ *vb* **1 a** [*T*] **:** to burn the surface of (something) ▪ *The hot pan scorched the table.* **b** [*I*] **:** to be burned on the surface ▪ *The fabric scorches at high temperatures.* **2** [*T*] **:** to damage (something) by making it extremely dry ▪ *The land was scorched by drought.* — **scorch·ing** /ˈskoːtʃɪŋ/ *adj* ▪ *a scorching* [=very hot] *summer day* — **scorching** *adv* ▪ *scorching hot* [=very hot] *weather*

scorch·er /ˈskoːtʃə/ *n* [*C*] *informal* **:** a very hot day ▪ *Today was a real scorcher.*

¹**score** /ˈskoː/ *n* **1** [*C*] **a :** the number of points, goals, runs, etc., that each player or team has in a game or contest ▪ *The score was tied at 1–1.* [=each team had scored once] **b** *chiefly US* **:** the number of points that someone gets for correct answers on a test, exam, etc. ▪ *a low/high score* ▪ *She got a perfect score on the test.* [=she answered all the ques-

tions correctly] **2** [*C*] **a :** a document showing all the notes of a piece of music ▪ *an orchestral score* **b :** the music that is written for a movie or play ▪ *The film's score is by a famous composer.* **3** [*C*] **:** a mark or cut that is made in a surface with a sharp object **4** *pl* **score** [*C*] *formal + literary* **a :** the number 20 ▪ *a score of books* [=20 books] **b :** a group of 20 people or things ▪ *three score years* [=60 years] **5** [*plural*] *formal* **:** a large number or amount of people or things ▪ *scores of suggestions* — **by the score :** in large numbers or amounts ▪ *Factories are closing by the score.* — **even the score 1 :** to tie the score in a game ▪ *They evened the score at 5–5.* **2 :** to harm or punish someone who has harmed you ▪ *They cheated her, and she was determined to even the score.* — **keep score :** to officially record the number of points, goals, runs, etc., that each player or team gets in a game or contest — **know the score** *informal* **:** to have a good understanding of a situation ▪ *Now that she knows the score, she won't be fooled again.* — **on that/this score :** with regard to the thing that is being discussed ▪ *The work will be done on time. You have nothing to worry about on that score.* — **settle a/the score :** to harm or punish someone who has harmed you ▪ *seeking out an old enemy to settle a score* ▪ *He has a few (old) scores to settle.* — **score·less** /ˈskoːləs/ *adj*

²**score** *vb* **scored; scor·ing** **1 a** [*T/I*] **:** to get points, goals, runs, etc., in a game or contest ▪ *He scored (a run/goal/touchdown)!* **b** [*T*] **:** to be worth (a particular number of points) in a game or contest ▪ *Each correct answer scores two points.* **2** [*T/I*] **:** to officially record the number of points, goals, runs, etc., that each player or team gets in a game or contest ▪ *Who's going to score (the game)?* **3** [*T/I*] **:** to give (someone or something) a grade or a particular number of points based on the number of correct answers on a test, the quality of a performance, etc. ▪ *Judges will score (the performances) based on artistic and technical merit.* **4** [*T*] **:** to write the music for (something) ▪ *score a movie* **5** [*T*] **:** to mark or cut the surface of (something) with a sharp object ▪ *score glass* **6** [*T*] **:** to achieve or earn (something) ▪ *He scored a hit in his first movie.* **7** [*I*] **:** to have success ▪ *He has scored again with his latest thriller.* **8 a** [*T/I*] *slang* **:** to buy or get (illegal drugs) ▪ *druggies looking to score (some drugs)* **b** [*T*] *US, informal* **:** to get (something) ▪ *I scored a couple of tickets to the game.* **9** [*I*] *slang* **:** to have sex with someone and especially with someone you do not know well ▪ *Did you score (with her) last night?*

score·board /ˈskoːˌboːd/ *n* [*C*] **:** a large board on which the score of a game or contest is shown

score·card /ˈskoːˌkaːd/ *n* [*C*] **:** a card on which the score of a game or contest is recorded ▪ *a golfer's scorecard*

score·keep·er /ˈskoːˌkiːpə/ *n* [*C*] *chiefly US* **:** a person who records the official score in a game or contest

scor·er /ˈskoɚɚ/ *n* [*C*] **1** : a person who scores points, goals, runs, etc., in a game or contest **2** : SCOREKEEPER

¹**scorn** /ˈskoɚn/ *n* [*U*] **1** : a feeling that someone or something is not worthy of any respect or approval ▪ *They treated him with scorn.* **2** : harsh criticism that shows a lack of respect or approval for someone or something ▪ *Her rivals have poured/heaped scorn on her ideas.* — **scorn·ful** /ˈskoɚnfəl/ *adj* — **scorn·ful·ly** *adv*

²**scorn** *vb* [*T*] **1** : to show that you think (someone or something) is not worthy of respect or approval ▪ *Her actions were scorned by many people.* **2** *formal* : to refuse or reject (someone or something that you do not think is worthy of respect or approval) ▪ *She scorned his invitation.*

Scor·pio /ˈskoɚpiˌoʊ/ *n, pl* **-pios 1** [*U*] : the eighth sign of the zodiac that comes between Libra and Sagittarius and that has a scorpion as its symbol **2** [*C*] : a person born between October 24 and November 21

scor·pi·on /ˈskoɚpijən/ *n* [*C*] : a small animal related to spiders that has two front claws and a curved tail with a poisonous stinger at the end

Scot /ˈskɑːt/ *n* [*C*] : a person born, raised, or living in Scotland

scotch /ˈskɑːtʃ/ *vb* [*T*] : to stop (something) from continuing or spreading ▪ *scotch a rumor*

¹**Scotch** *or* **scotch** /ˈskɑːtʃ/ *n* [*C/U*] : a kind of whiskey that is made in Scotland

²**Scotch** *adj, old-fashioned* : SCOTTISH

³**Scotch** *trademark* — used for a type of adhesive tape

scot-free /ˈskɑːtˈfriː/ *adj, informal* : without the punishment that is deserved ▪ *They got off scot-free.* [=they were not punished at all]

Scots /ˈskɑːts/ *n* [*U*] : the English language of Scotland

Scot·tish /ˈskɑːtɪʃ/ *adj* : of or relating to Scotland or its people ▪ *a Scottish writer/accent*

scoun·drel /ˈskaʊndrəl/ *n* [*C*] *old-fashioned* : a person (especially a man) who is cruel or dishonest ▪ *a rotten scoundrel*

scour /ˈskawɚ/ *vb* [*T*] **1** : to search (something) carefully and thoroughly ▪ *We scoured the woods for the missing child.* **2 a** : to clean (something) by rubbing it hard with a rough object ▪ *scour a pan with steel wool* **b** : to cause parts of (something) to be carried away by the movement of water, ice, etc. ▪ *Rain scoured the hillside.*

scourge /ˈskɚdʒ/ *n* [*C*] **1** *formal + literary* : someone or something that causes a great amount of trouble or suffering ▪ *the scourge of unemployment/poverty* **2** : a whip that was used to punish people in the past — **scourge** *vb* **scourged**; **scourg·ing** [*T*] ▪ *a neighborhood scourged by crime*

¹**scout** /ˈskaʊt/ *n* [*C*] **1** *or* **Scout a** : BOY SCOUT **b** : GIRL SCOUT **2** : a soldier, airplane, etc., that is sent to get informa-

tion about the size, location, etc., of an enemy **3** : a person whose job is to search for talented performers, athletes, etc. ▪ *a baseball scout* ▪ *a talent scout*

²**scout** *vb* **1 a** [*I*] : to search an area or place for something or someone ▪ *I scouted (around) for firewood.* **b** [*T*] : to explore (an area) in order to find information about it ▪ *We went ahead to scout (out) the area.* **2** [*T/I*] : to watch or look at (someone or something) in order to decide if that person or thing is suited for a particular job or purpose ▪ *The pitcher is being scouted by several major-league teams.*

scout·ing *or* **Scouting** /ˈskaʊtɪŋ/ *n* [*U*] : the activities of Boy Scout and Girl Scout groups

scowl /ˈskaʊl/ *vb* [*I*] : to look at someone or something in a way that shows anger or disapproval ▪ *She scowled (at him) in response to his question.* — **scowl** *n* [*C*] ▪ *She responded to his question with a scowl.*

scrag·gly /ˈskrægəli/ *adj* **scrag·gli·er**; **-est** *chiefly US, informal* : growing in a way that is not neat and even ▪ *a scraggly beard*

scram /ˈskræm/ *vb* **scrammed**; **scram·ming** [*I*] *informal* : to leave immediately ▪ *Scram! You're not wanted here!*

scram·ble /ˈskræmbəl/ *vb* **scram·bled**; **scram·bling 1** [*I*] **a** : to move or climb over something quickly especially while also using your hands ▪ *scrambling over boulders* **b** : to move or act quickly to do, find, or get something often before someone else does ▪ *reporters scrambling to meet deadlines* **2** [*T*] : to prepare (eggs) by mixing the clear and yellow parts together and then stirring the mixture in a hot pan ▪ *I had scrambled eggs for breakfast.* **3** [*T*] : to put (parts of something) in the wrong order ▪ *The letters of the words are scrambled.* **4** [*T*] : to change (a radio or electronic signal) so that whoever receives it will not be able to understand it ▪ *We scrambled our radio communications.* — **scramble** *n* [*singular*] ▪ *a quick scramble over boulders* ▪ *a scramble for power* — **scram·bler** /ˈskræmbəlɚ/ *n* [*C*] ▪ *We used a scrambler* [=a device that scrambles radio or electronic signals] *to encode our messages.*

¹**scrap** /ˈskræp/ *n* **1 a** [*singular*] : a very small amount ▪ *There is not a scrap of evidence to support their theory.* **b** [*plural*] : pieces of food that are not eaten and could be thrown away ▪ *dogs begging for scraps* **c** [*C*] : a small piece of something that is left after you have used the main part ▪ *fabric/paper scraps* **d** [*U*] : things from an unwanted or broken object (such as a car) that are useful only in making or fixing something else ▪ *scrap metal* ▪ *He sold the car for scrap.* [=he sold it to someone who wanted the parts of the car] **2** [*C*] *informal* : a physical fight ▪ *He got into a scrap.*

²**scrap** *vb* **scrapped**; **scrap·ping** [*T*] : to get rid of (something) because it is damaged, no longer useful, etc. ▪ *scrap a car/idea*

scrap·book /'skræp,bʊk/ n [C] : a book with blank pages to which you attach photographs, letters, newspaper stories, etc., that help you remember a person or time

¹**scrape** /'skreɪp/ vb scraped; scrap·ing 1 [T] : to damage (the surface of something) or hurt (a part of your body) by rubbing something rough or sharp against it or by making it rub against something rough or sharp ▪ I fell and scraped my knee. 2 [T/I] : to rub or cause (something) to rub against a hard surface and make a harsh and usually unpleasant sound ▪ fingernails scraping against a blackboard 3 [T] : to remove (something) from a surface by rubbing an object or tool against it ▪ We scraped the paint off the wall. 4 [T] : to barely succeed in collecting or gathering (something needed or wanted) by making an effort — + together or up ▪ He managed to scrape together/up enough money for lunch. — bow and scrape see ¹BOW — **scrape by** also **scrape along** [phrasal vb] 1 : to live or function with barely enough money ▪ Money was tight, but we managed to scrape by. 2 or **scrape through** : to succeed at doing something but just barely ▪ He didn't study for the exam and just barely scraped by. — **scrap·er** /'skreɪpɚ/ n [C] ▪ a paint scraper

²**scrape** n [C] 1 : a mark or injury that is caused by something rubbing against something else ▪ I fell and got a scrape on my knee. ▪ There's a scrape on the car door. 2 informal : a bad, dangerous, or unpleasant situation ▪ a scrape with the police/law 3 : a harsh and usually unpleasant sound that is made when something rubs against a hard surface ▪ the scrape of fingernails on a blackboard

scrap heap n [C] : a place where broken or useless things are taken and left ▪ (figurative) a minor event consigned to the scrap heap of history

scrap·py /'skræpi/ adj scrap·pi·er; -est informal 1 US : ready or eager to fight ▪ a scrappy little guy 2 US : willing to work hard in order to succeed ▪ a scrappy athlete/journalist 3 chiefly Brit : not organized or done well ▪ a scrappy essay that should be rewritten

¹**scratch** /'skrætʃ/ vb 1 a [T/I] : to rub skin with something sharp (such as your fingernails) especially in order to stop an itch ▪ The dog scratched its ear. ▪ Don't scratch. It just makes the itch worse. ▪ (figurative) You scratch my back, and I'll scratch yours. [=if you do something to help me, I'll do something to help you] ▪ (figurative) His odd behavior left us scratching our heads. [=we could not understand his odd behavior] b [T/I] : to make a shallow and narrow cut in (your skin) with fingernails, claws, etc. ▪ The cat scratched me. c [I] : to rub a surface or object with something sharp or rough in a way that produces a harsh sound ▪ The dog was scratching at the door. 2 [T] a : to make a line or mark in the surface of (something) by rubbing or cutting it with something rough or

sharp ▪ Someone scratched the paint on my car. ▪ (figurative) I've only scratched **the surface** of this subject. [=only learned a small part of what there is to learn] b : to make (lines, letters, etc.) in the surface of something by using a stick, a sharp tool, etc. ▪ They scratched their initials in the tree. 3 [T] informal a : to decide not to do or continue with (something) ▪ We had to scratch our plans. b : to remove (someone) from the list of players who will be playing in a game ▪ She was scratched from the starting lineup. — **scratch off** [phrasal vb] scratch (something) off or scratch off (something) 1 : to remove (something) from an object or surface by rubbing with a sharp edge or tool ▪ Scratch off the gray box on the ticket to see if you've won! 2 : to draw a line through (something that is written down) ▪ Scratch his name off the list. — **scratch out** [phrasal vb] scratch (something) out or scratch out (something) : to draw a line through (something that is written down) ▪ I scratched out the mistake. — **scratch·er** n [C] ▪ a back scratcher [=a device you can use to scratch your back]

²**scratch** n [C] 1 a : a line or mark in the surface of something that is caused by something rough or sharp rubbing against it ▪ My car has some dents and scratches. b : a shallow and narrow cut in the skin that is caused by something sharp ▪ He escaped without a scratch. [=without getting hurt] 2 : the sound made when something sharp rubs against a surface or object ▪ the scratch of pencils on paper — **from scratch** 1 : with ingredients you have prepared yourself rather than with a prepared mixture of ingredients bought from a store ▪ cookies made from scratch 2 : from a point at which nothing has been done yet ▪ He built the company from scratch. — **up to scratch** chiefly Brit, informal : as good as expected or wanted ▪ Her performance wasn't up to scratch.

scratchy /'skrætʃi/ adj scratch·i·er; -est 1 : having a rough sound ▪ scratchy old records 2 informal : likely to make you itch ▪ scratchy wool 3 : swollen and sore ▪ a scratchy throat

scrawl /'skrɑːl/ vb [T] : to write or draw (something) very quickly or carelessly ▪ She scrawled her signature. — **scrawl** n [C] ▪ Her signature was a scrawl.

scraw·ny /'skrɑːni/ adj scraw·ni·er; -est : very thin in a way that is not attractive or healthy ▪ a scrawny kid

¹**scream** /'skriːm/ vb 1 a [I] : to suddenly cry out in a loud and high voice of pain, surprise, etc. ▪ The crowd screamed with excitement. b [T/I] : to say (something) in a loud and high voice because you are angry, afraid, etc. ▪ He screamed at me. ▪ She screamed (out) my name. ▪ (figurative) Headlines screamed about the spike in crime. ▪ (figurative) Her tax records practically screamed "fraud." [=very strongly suggested that she had committed fraud] ▪ (figurative) These policies just scream (out) for reform. [=they very badly need to be reformed] c [I]

: to make a very loud, high sound ▪ *Sirens were screaming in the distance.* **2** [I] : to move very quickly through a place while making a lot of noise ▪ *Police cars screamed down the street.* — **scream bloody murder** (*US*) *or Brit* **scream blue murder** *informal* : to scream, yell, or complain in a very loud or angry way

²scream *n* **1** [C] : a loud and high cry or sound ▪ *a piercing scream* ▪ *screams of terror* **2** [singular] *informal* + *old-fashioned* : a person or thing that is very funny ▪ *She's an absolute scream.*

¹screech /ˈskriːtʃ/ *n* [C] **1** : a loud and very high cry that usually expresses extreme pain, anger, or fear ▪ *The animal emitted a loud screech.* **2** : a loud and very high sound ▪ *the screech of brakes*

²screech *vb* **1** [T/I] : to cry out or shout in a loud and very high voice because of extreme pain, anger, fear, etc. ▪ *"You can't do this to me!" she screeched.* **2** [I] : to make a loud and very high sound ▪ *The car screeched to a halt/stop.* = *The car came to a screeching halt.* [=made a loud, high sound as it stopped quickly] ▪ (*figurative*) *Her promising career screeched to a halt.* [=suddenly ended]

¹screen /ˈskriːn/ *n* **1** [C] **a** : the part of a television or computer that you look at when you are using it ▪ *a computer/television screen* **b** : a large, flat, white surface on which images or movies are shown **2** [U] : the art or profession of acting in movies ▪ *a star of stage and screen* ▪ *The two actors perform well together on screen.* [=in movies or on TV] ▪ *a screen actor* **3** [C] *chiefly US* : a sheet that is made of very small wire or plastic strings which are woven together and that is set in a frame in a window, door, etc., to let air in but keep insects out ▪ *a window screen* ▪ *a screen door* [=a door that has a screen built into it] **4** [C] : something that is used to hide, protect, cover, or block a person or thing ▪ *You can change your clothes behind the screen.* ▪ *a screen of shrubs* ▪ *His activities were a screen for his real plans.*

²screen *vb* [T] **1** : to examine (people or things) in order to decide if they are suitable for a particular purpose ▪ *screening candidates for a job* ▪ *He usually* **screens his (telephone/phone) calls.** [=lets his answering machine answer his phone so that he can hear who is calling before he decides to talk to whoever it is] **2 a** : to do a test on (someone) to find out if that person has or is likely to develop a disease ▪ *All blood donors are screened for AIDS.* **b** : to do a test on (a person's blood, urine, etc.) to find out if the person has been using an illegal substance ▪ *The players were screened for performance-enhancing drugs.* **3** : to show (a movie, television show, etc.) to the public on a screen ▪ *We'll be screening his latest film in two weeks.* **4** : to hide, protect, cover, or block (someone or something) with a screen ▪ *A row of shrubs screens our backyard.* ▪ *a screened porch* [=a porch that has walls made of screens] — **screen out** [phrasal vb] **screen (someone or something) out** or

screen out (someone or something) 1 : to remove (someone or something that is not suitable for a particular purpose) from a group that is being examined ▪ *Students receiving a D or lower will be screened out.* **2** : to prevent (something harmful) from passing through ▪ *The lotion screens out* [=blocks] *the sun's harmful rays.*

screen pass *n* [C] *American football* : a pass to a receiver who is behind the line of scrimmage and is protected by a line of blockers

screen-play /ˈskriːnˌpleɪ/ *n* [C] : the written form of a movie that also includes instructions on how it is to be acted and filmed

screen saver *n* [C] : a computer program that shows a moving image or set of images on a computer screen when the computer is on but is not being used

screen-writ-er /ˈskriːnˌraɪtɚ/ *n* [C] : a person who writes screenplays

¹screw /ˈskruː/ *n* [C] **1** : a narrow, pointed metal cylinder that has a wide flat or rounded top and a ridge (called a thread) that goes around it in a spiral ✧ A screw is used to hold things together or to attach things. It is inserted into wood, metal, etc., by being turned. ▪ *Tighten the screws.* **2** : an object that has a thread like a screw which is used to attach or connect it to something ▪ *The bottle has a* **screw cap/top.** [=a cap/top that is attached and removed by turning it] — **have a screw loose** or **have a loose screw** *informal* : to be crazy ▪ *He acts like he has a screw loose.*

²screw *vb* **1** [T] : to attach (something) with a screw ▪ *I screwed the boards together.* **2 a** [T] : to turn (something) so that it attaches or connects to something ▪ *Screw the cap on tight.* **b** [I] : to fit onto or into something by being turned ▪ *The lid screws onto the jar.* **3** [T] *informal* **a** : to take something from (someone) by lying or breaking a rule ▪ *They screwed me out of thousands of dollars.* **b** : to prevent (someone) from having or getting something that is deserved or expected ▪ *She was screwed out of the job.* [=she should have gotten the job but she didn't get it] **4** [T] *informal* + *impolite* — used to express anger, disgust, etc. ▪ *They don't like it? Well, screw them.* — **screw around** [phrasal vb] *chiefly US, informal* : to do things that are not useful or serious ▪ *Quit screwing around and get back to work.* — **screw up** [phrasal vb] *informal* **1** : to make a mistake ▪ *Sorry about that. I screwed up.* **2 screw (something or someone) up** or **screw up (something or someone) a** : to make a mistake in (something) ▪ *The waiter screwed up our order.* **b** : to damage or ruin (something) ▪ *Drugs screwed up her life.* **c** : to make (someone) very upset and unhappy for a long time ▪ *The divorce really screwed him up.* **d** : to tighten the muscles of (your face or eyes) ▪ *She screwed up her eyes.* [=she squinted] **3 screw up the/your courage** : to make yourself brave enough to do something difficult • *I finally screwed up the courage to quit.*

screw·ball /'skruː,bɑːl/ *n* [*C*] **1** *baseball* : a pitch that is thrown with spin so that the ball curves in a direction that is opposite to the direction of a curveball **2** *chiefly US, informal* : a crazy person — **screwball** *adj, always before a noun* • *a screwball comedy* [=a very silly comedy]

screw·driv·er /'skruː,draɪvɚ/ *n* [*C*] : a tool that is used for turning screws

screwed–up *adj, informal* : not acting or functioning the way a person or thing should • *a screwed-up kid*

screw·up /'skruː,ʌp/ *n* [*C*] *informal + disapproving* **1** : a mistake or error • *That was a major screwup.* **2** : a person who often makes mistakes • *She's such a screwup!*

screwy /'skruːwi/ *adj* **screw·i·er; -est** *informal* : strange or unusual : not sensible or reasonable • *a screwy idea/policy*

scrib·ble /'skrɪbəl/ *vb* **scrib·bled; scrib·bling** **1** [*T/I*] : to write (something) quickly and in a way that makes it difficult to read • *She scribbled a note.* **2** [*I*] : to draw lines, shapes, etc., that have no particular meaning in a quick and careless way • *The child scribbled all over the paper.* — **scribble** *n* [*C/U*] • *children's scribbles* • *I can't read his scribble.* [=his quick and careless handwriting] — **scrib·bler** *n* [*C*]

scribe /'skraɪb/ *n* [*C*] **1** : a person in the past whose job was to copy manuscripts and books • *medieval scribes* **2** *chiefly US, informal* : a journalist or writer • *a local newspaper scribe*

scrim·mage /'skrɪmɪdʒ/ *n, American football* **1** [*U*] : the point in a game at which the center passes or throws the ball to the quarterback • *They scored on the first play from scrimmage.* — see also LINE OF SCRIMMAGE **2** [*C*] : an informal game that is played for practice — **scrimmage** *vb* **-maged; -mag·ing** [*I*] • *We scrimmage every Saturday.*

scrimp /'skrɪmp/ *vb* [*I*] : to spend as little money as you can • *They scrimped and saved for their big vacation.*

¹**script** /'skrɪpt/ *n* **1** [*C*] : the written form of a play, movie, television show, etc. **2 a** [*U*] : a type of handwriting in which all the letters in a word are connected to each other • *She wrote in script.* **b** [*C/U*] : a particular style of writing or printing • *roman and italic scripts* **c** [*C/U*] : ALPHABET • *the Cyrillic script*

²**script** *vb* [*T*] **1** : to write the script for (a play, movie, etc.) • *The dialogue was carefully scripted.* **2** : to plan how (something) will happen, be done, etc. • *The trip didn't go as scripted.* • *a carefully scripted campaign*

scrip·ture /'skrɪptʃɚ/ *n* **1** *Scripture or the Scriptures* : the Bible • *quoting Scripture* • *the Hebrew Scriptures* **2** [*plural*] : the sacred writings of a religion • *holy scriptures* — **scrip·tur·al** /'skrɪptʃərəl/ *adj*

script·writ·er /'skrɪpt,raɪtɚ/ *n* [*C*] : a person who writes scripts for movies, plays, etc. • *Hollywood scriptwriters*

¹**scroll** /'skroʊl/ *n* [*C*] **1** : a long piece of paper that rolls around one or two cylinders and that usually has something written or drawn on it **2** : a decoration that looks like the curled ends of a scroll

²**scroll** *vb* [*T/I*] *computers* : to move text or images of a Web page, document, etc., up, down, or to the side on a computer screen so that you can see all of it • *She scrolled (down) to the bottom of the screen.*

Scrooge *or* **scrooge** /'skruːdʒ/ *n* [*C*] *informal* : a selfish and unfriendly person who is not willing to spend or give away money

scro·tum /'skroʊtəm/ *n, pl* **scro·tums** *or* **scro·ta** /'skroʊtə/ [*C*] : the sack of skin that contains the testicles of men and male animals

scrounge /'skraʊndʒ/ *vb* **scrounged; scroung·ing** [*T/I*] : to get or find something by looking in different places, asking different people, etc. • *She scrounged some money off/from her friends.* • *We scrounged around for firewood.* • *I managed to scrounge (up) some tickets to the show.* — **scroung·er** *n* [*C*]

¹**scrub** /'skrʌb/ *n* **1** [*U*] **a** : small bushes and trees • *A chipmunk hid in the scrub.* **b** : land that is covered with small bushes and trees • *the desert scrub* **2** [*C*] **a** : the act of scrubbing something • *Give the pan a good scrub.* [=scrub the pan] **b** : a powerful cleanser that is used on the skin • *a face scrub* **3** [*plural*] *US* : special loose clothing that is worn by people who work in hospitals — **scrub·by** /'skrʌbi/ *adj* **scrub·bi·er; -est** • *scrubby land/bushes*

²**scrub** *vb* **scrubbed; scrub·bing** **1** [*T/I*] : to rub (something) hard with a rough object or substance and often with soap in order to clean it • *scrubbing the floor* **2** [*T*] *informal* : to cancel (something) • *They scrubbed the game because of the bad weather.* — **scrub off** [*phrasal vb*] **scrub off (something)** *or* **scrub (something) off** : to remove (something) from a surface by scrubbing • *I scrubbed off the my makeup.* — **scrub out** [*phrasal vb*] **scrub out (something)** *or* **scrub (something) out** **1** : to remove (something) from an object by scrubbing • *a stain that was impossible to scrub out* **2** : to scrub the inside of (something) • *She scrubbed out the pots.* — **scrub·ber** /'skrʌbɚ/ *n* [*C*]

scruff /'skrʌf/ *n* [*singular*] : the skin on the back of the neck • *She held the kitten by the scruff of the neck.*

scruffy /'skrʌfi/ *adj* **scruff·i·er; -est** *informal* : not neat, clean, or orderly • *a scruffy beard*

scrum /'skrʌm/ *n* [*C*] **1** *rugby* **a** : a way of starting play again in which players from each team come together and try to get control of the ball by pushing against each other and using their feet when the ball is thrown in between them **b** : the group of players who are involved in a scrum **2** : a large group of people who are close together in one place • *a media scrum* [=a crowd of reporters, photographers, etc.]

scrump·tious /'skrʌmpʃəs/ *adj, infor-*

mal : very pleasant to taste : DELICIOUS ▪ *a scrumptious cake*

scrunch /ˈskrʌntʃ/ *vb* **1** [*I*] : to make your body lower or shorter by bending your legs, making your back bend forward, lowering your head, etc. ▪ *I scrunched down in the chair.* **2** [*T*] : to tighten the muscles of (your face or nose) ▪ *She scrunched (up) her face.* **3** [*T*] **a** : to put (several or many people or things) in a space that is too small ▪ *The tables were all scrunched together.* **b** : to press or squeeze (something) so that it is no longer flat or smooth ▪ *I scrunched (up) the note and threw it away.*

scru·ple /ˈskruːpəl/ *n* [*C/U*] : a feeling that prevents you from doing something that you think is wrong ▪ *moral/religious scruples*

scru·pu·lous /ˈskruːpjələs/ *adj* **1** : very careful about doing something correctly ▪ *She is scrupulous about her work.* **2** : careful about doing what is honest and morally right ▪ *Less scrupulous companies find ways to evade the law.* — **scru·pu·lous·ly** *adv*

scru·ti·nize *or Brit* **scru·ti·nise** /ˈskruːtəˌnaɪz/ *vb* **-nized** ; **-niz·ing** [*T*] : to examine (something) carefully especially in a critical way ▪ *I scrutinized my opponent's every move.*

scru·ti·ny /ˈskruːtəni/ *n* [*U, singular*] *formal* : the act of carefully examining something especially in a critical way ▪ *(a) careful scrutiny of data* ▪ *public scrutiny* ▪ *Their behavior is under scrutiny.* [=people are examining their behavior in a critical way]

scu·ba /ˈskuːbə/ *adj, always before a noun* : used in scuba diving ▪ *scuba gear/tanks*

scuba diving *n* [*U*] : a sport or activity in which you swim underwater using an air tank and a special breathing machine that you strap on your body ▪ *We went scuba diving yesterday.* — **scuba dive** *vb* ~ **dived**; ~ **div·ing** [*I*] ▪ *He plans to scuba dive while on vacation.* — **scuba diver** *n* [*C*]

scuff /ˈskʌf/ *vb* **1** [*T*] : to make a mark or scratch in the surface of (something) by scraping it ▪ *I scuffed (up) my new shoes.* **2** [*I*] : to drag your feet while you walk ▪ *She scuffed down the hall.*

scuf·fle /ˈskʌfəl/ *vb* **scuf·fled**; **scuf·fling** [*I*] **1** : to fight briefly and usually not very seriously ▪ *Protesters and police scuffled.* **2** : to move quickly and with short steps ▪ *Small creatures scuffled in the underbrush.* — **scuffle** *n* [*C*] ▪ *They got in/into a scuffle.*

scull /ˈskʌl/ *n* [*C*] : a long and very narrow boat that is usually rowed by one or two people — **scull** *vb* [*I*] ▪ *She sculled along the river.*

sculpt /ˈskʌlpt/ *vb* [*T/I*] : to make (something) by carving or molding clay, stone, etc. ▪ *The figures were sculpted from wood.* ▪ *(figurative) She carefully sculpted the plot of the story.* ▪ *(figurative) an athlete with a lean, sculpted* [=muscular and attractive] *body*

sculp·tor /ˈskʌlptɚ/ *n* [*C*] : a person who makes sculptures

sculp·ture /ˈskʌlptʃɚ/ *n* **1** [*C/U*] : a piece of art that is made by carving or molding clay, stone, metal, etc. ▪ *a sculpture of an elephant* ▪ *I like abstract sculpture.* **2** [*U*] : the process or art of carving or molding clay, stone, metal, etc., into a sculpture ▪ *She's studying sculpture.* — **sculp·tur·al** /ˈskʌlptʃ(ə)rəl/ *adj*

scum /ˈskʌm/ *n* **1** [*U*] : a layer of something unpleasant or unwanted that forms on top of a liquid ▪ *pond scum* [=a layer of algae on top of a pond] **2** [*C/U*] *informal* : a dishonest, unkind, or unpleasant person ▪ *Ignore him; he's a (complete) scum.* ▪ *They are the scum of the earth.* [=the worst people on the earth] — **scum·my** /ˈskʌmi/ *adj* **scum·mi·er; -est**

scum·bag /ˈskʌmˌbæg/ *n* [*C*] *slang* : a dishonest, unkind, or unpleasant person

scup·per /ˈskʌpɚ/ *vb* [*T*] *Brit* : to cause (something) to stop or fail ▪ *The latest information could scupper the peace talks.*

scur·ri·lous /ˈskɚrələs/ *adj, formal* : said or done unfairly to make people have a bad opinion of someone ▪ *scurrilous attacks/rumors*

scur·ry /ˈskɚri/ *vb* **-ries; -ried; -ry·ing** [*I*] : to move quickly and with short steps ▪ *Mice scurried around the house.*

scur·vy /ˈskɚvi/ *n* [*U*] : a disease that is caused by not eating enough fruits or vegetables that contain vitamin C

scut·tle /ˈskʌtl/ *vb* **scut·tled; scut·tling** [*T*] **1** *US* : to cause (something) to end or fail ▪ *He tried to scuttle the conference/sale.* **2** : to sink (a ship) by putting holes in the bottom or sides **3** : to move quickly and with short steps ▪ *Crabs scuttled along the ocean floor.*

scythe /ˈsaɪð/ *n* [*C*] : a farming tool with a curved blade and long handle that is used for cutting grass, grain, etc. — **scythe** *vb* **scythed; scyth·ing** [*T/I*] ▪ *scything the wheat* [=cutting the wheat with a scythe] ▪ *(figurative) Her hands scythed* [=cut] *through the air.*

SD *abbr* South Dakota

SE *abbr* southeast; southeastern

sea /ˈsiː/ *n* **1 a** [*U, plural*] : the salt water that covers much of the Earth's surface ▪ *the bottom of the sea* [=the ocean] ▪ *(literary) the uncharted seas* ▪ *a sea creature/voyage* ▪ *We traveled by sea.* [=on a ship] ▪ *sailing the open sea* [=sailing far away from land] ▪ *The boat headed out to sea.* [=away from land] ▪ *The ship put (out) to sea.* [=left the port] ▪ *He went to sea.* [=became a sailor] ▪ *The crew was lost at sea.* [=the crew disappeared while traveling on the sea] ▪ *(figurative) She felt completely at sea.* [=confused and not confident] **b** *or Sea* [*C*] : a large body of water that is part of the sea or that has land around part or all of it ▪ *the Mediterranean Sea* **2** [*C*] : an area of the sea — used to describe the movement of the water in the sea ▪ *a calm/rough sea* ▪ *We sailed in heavy seas.* [=in very large waves] **3** [*C*] : a large amount or number *of* people or things spread over a large area ▪ *a sea of screaming fans*

sea·bed /ˈsiːˌbɛd/ *n* — **the seabed** : the ground that is at the bottom of the sea

sea-bird /'si:,bɚd/ n [C] : a bird that lives on or near the sea and finds food in it • *gulls and other seabirds*

sea-board /'si:,boɚd/ n [C] : the part of a country that is along or near the sea • *the eastern seaboard*

sea-borne /'si:,boɚn/ adj, always before a noun **1** : carried in a ship sailing across the sea • *seaborne cargo* **2** : involving or using ships that sail across the sea • *seaborne trade*

sea change n [C] : a big and sudden change • *a sea change in public opinion*

sea-coast /'si:,koʊst/ n [C/U] : the land along the edge of a sea

sea-far-er /'si:,fɛrɚ/ n [C] *old-fashioned* : SAILOR

sea-far-ing /'si:,fɛrɪŋ/ n [U] : the activity of traveling on the sea especially while working on a boat or a ship • *a life of seafaring* — **seafaring** adj, always before a noun • *a seafaring people*

sea-food /'si:,fu:d/ n [U] : fish and shellfish that live in the ocean and are used for food • *I'm allergic to seafood.* • *a seafood dish/restaurant*

sea-go-ing /'si:,goʊɪŋ/ adj, always before a noun : made or used for traveling on the sea • *a seagoing ship/craft/vessel*

sea-gull /'si:,gʌl/ n [C] : a large, common, usually gray and white bird that lives near the ocean : GULL

sea horse n [C] : a small fish that has a head that looks like a horse's head and that swims with its head above its body and tail

¹**seal** /'si:l/ vb **1 a** [T] : to close (something) tightly so that air, liquid, etc., cannot get in or out • *He sealed the jar.* • *We sealed (up) the cracks in the wall.* **b** [T] : to close (an envelope, bag, etc.) by sticking or pressing two of its parts together • *seal an envelope* **c** [I] : to become closed tightly • *Make sure the bag seals properly.* **2** [T] : to cover the surface of (something) with a substance that will protect it • *We sealed the wood to make it waterproof.* **3** [T] : to make (something) definite and final • *His home run sealed the victory.* [=made it certain that his team would win] • *(informal) They finally sealed the deal.* [=reached an agreement and made a deal] • *Their decision sealed her fate.* [=made it certain that something bad would happen to her] **4** [T] : to prevent someone from going into or through (an area or place) • *Troops have sealed the border.* — **my lips are sealed** see LIP — **seal in** [phrasal vb] **seal (something) in** or **seal in (something)** : to prevent (something that is in something else) from getting out or escaping • *He seared the steak to seal in the juices.* — **seal off** [phrasal vb] **seal off (something)** or **seal (something) off** : to prevent people from entering or leaving (an area or place) • *Police sealed off the crime scene.*

²**seal** n [C] **1 a** : an official mark that is stamped on paper or on a small piece of wax to show that something (such as a document) is genuine and has been officially approved • *a notary's seal* **b** : a small piece of stamped wax or a small sticker that is put on a letter or envelope to keep it closed or to show that it has not been opened **2** : a device with a raised design that can be pressed into paper, wax, etc., to make a seal **3 a** : a piece of material that is used on the lid of a container to keep air, water, etc., out of the container or to show the container has not been opened • *a rubber/plastic seal* **b** : the state of being closed tightly so that no air, water, etc., can pass through • *The caulk gives the window an airtight seal.* **4** : a large animal that lives in the sea near coasts, has flippers, and eats fish — **seal of approval** : an action or statement that shows approval or official acceptance • *The bill has the President's seal of approval.* — **under seal** law, formal : having an official seal that prevents the public from seeing or reading it • *a document under seal*

seal-ant /'si:lənt/ n [C] : a substance that is put on a surface in order to protect it from air, water, etc.

seal-er /'si:lɚ/ n [C] : SEALANT

sea level n [U] : the average height of the sea's surface ✧ Sea level is a standard level that is used when measuring the height or depth of a place on land • *The city is a mile above sea level.*

sea lion n [C] : a large seal that lives near coasts in the Pacific Ocean

seam /'si:m/ n [C] **1** : a line where two pieces of cloth, wood, metal, dough, etc., are joined together • *the seams of a dress/boat* **2** technical : a layer of coal, rock, etc., that is between two other layers of rock underground • *coal seams* • *(figurative) a rich seam [=source] of information* — **be bursting at the seams** see ¹BURST — **come/fall apart at the seams** informal : to break into parts or pieces • *(figurative) The plan is falling apart at the seams.*

sea-man /'si:mən/ n, pl **-men** [C] **1** : an experienced sailor **2** : a sailor in the U.S. or British Navy or the U.S. Coast Guard who is not an officer

sea-man-ship /'si:mən,ʃɪp/ n [U] : skill in sailing or operating a ship • *The captain shows great seamanship.*

seam-less /'si:mləs/ adj **1** : having no seams • *a seamless rug/boat* **2** : moving from one thing to another easily and without any interruptions or problems • *a seamless transition* **3** : perfect and having no flaws or errors • *a seamless performance* — **seam-less-ly** adv

seam-stress /'si:mstrəs/ n [C] : a woman who sews clothes, curtains, etc., as a job

seamy /'si:mi/ adj **seam-i-er; -est** : of or relating to unpleasant and usually illegal things (such as crime, drugs, etc.) • *the seamy side of the city*

sé-ance /'seɪ,ɑːns/ also **se-ance** n [C] : a meeting where people try to communicate with the spirits of dead people • *They're having/holding a séance.*

sea-plane /'si:,pleɪn/ n [C] : an airplane that can take off from and land on water

sea-port /'si:,poɚt/ n [C] : a town or city with a harbor where ships stop to load and unload cargo : PORT ▪ *Boston is a major seaport.*

sear /'siɚ/ *vb* [T] **1** : to burn and damage the surface of (something) with strong and sudden heat ▪ *The tree was seared by lightning.* ▪ *(figurative) The image is seared into my memory.* [=I cannot forget it] **2** *US* : to cook the surface of (something) quickly with intense heat ▪ *sear a steak*

¹search /'sɚtʃ/ *n* **1** [C/U] : the act or process of looking for someone or something ▪ *The search for the crew was called off.* ▪ *We have begun our search for a new manager.* ▪ *We are in search of the answer.* [=we are searching for the answer] **2** [C] : an attempt to find information in a database, network, Web site, etc., by using a computer program ▪ *I did a Web search for restaurants in that area.*

²search *vb* **1 a** [I] : to carefully look for someone or something ▪ *They searched among/through the wreckage (for survivors).* ▪ *They're still searching for the lost child.* ▪ *(figurative) She searched for an answer to his question.* **b** [T] : to carefully look for someone or something in (something) ▪ *Police searched the vehicle.* **c** [T] : to carefully look through the clothing of (someone) for something that may be hidden ▪ *The police searched her for concealed weapons.* **2** [T/I] : to use a computer to find information in (a database, Web site, etc.) ▪ *She searched the Web for information.* = *She searched for information on the Web.* **3** [T] : to look carefully at (something) in order to get information about it ▪ *He searched her face for clues about her mood.* — **search me** *informal* — used in speech to say that you do not know the answer to a question ▪ *"Why did they do that?" "Search me."* — **search out** [*phrasal vb*] **search (someone or something) out** *or* **search out (someone or something)** : to find (someone or something) by carefully looking ▪ *She searched out the information.* — **search·er** *n* [C]

search engine *n* [C] : a computer program that is used to look for information on the Internet

search·ing /'sɚtʃɪŋ/ *adj, always before a noun* : carefully made, done, asked, etc., in order to find out more information about someone or something ▪ *a searching question/look* — **search·ing·ly** *adv*

search·light /'sɚtʃ,laɪt/ *n* [C] : a very bright light that can be aimed in different directions and that is used to find people or things in the dark

search party *n* [C] : an organized group of people who are looking for someone or something that is missing ▪ *A search party was sent out to look for the hikers.*

search warrant *n* [C] : a legal document that gives the police permission to search a place for evidence

sear·ing /'sɪrɪŋ/ *adj* **1** : very hot ▪ *the searing heat of the fire* **2** : extremely intense, severe, etc. ▪ *a searing pain* **3** *of writing or speech* : very strong and critical ▪ *a searing review* — **sear·ing·ly** *adv*

sea·scape /'si:,skeɪp/ *n* [C] : a picture or painting of the sea

sea·shell /'si:,ʃɛl/ *n* [C] : the hard, empty shell of a small sea creature (such as a clam) ▪ *She collects seashells.*

sea·shore /'si:,ʃoɚ/ *n* — **the seashore** : the land along the edge of the sea that is usually covered with sand or rocks ▪ *They built a house near the seashore.*

sea·sick /'si:,sɪk/ *adj* : feeling sick because of the movement of a boat or ship that you are traveling on ▪ *The waves made her seasick.* — **sea·sick·ness** *n* [U]

¹sea·side /'si:,saɪd/ *adj, always before a noun* : located in the area near the sea ▪ *a seaside hotel/town*

²seaside *n* — **the seaside** *chiefly Brit* : the areas or towns along or near the sea ▪ *a trip to the seaside*

¹sea·son /'si:zn/ *n* **1** [C] : one of the four periods (spring, summer, autumn, and winter) into which the year is commonly divided **2 a** [C] : a period of time when a particular sport is being played ▪ *baseball season* ▪ *The team had a good season last year.* [=the team played well last year] **b** [C/U] : a period of time when a particular event, process, activity, etc., occurs ▪ *These plants have a short growing season.* ▪ *the Christmas season* ▪ *flu season* **c** [C/U] : a period of time when people are legally allowed to hunt, fish, etc. ▪ *deer season* ▪ *fishing season* **d** [C/U] : the time of the year during which something grows and can be harvested ▪ *blueberry season* **e** [C/U] : a time of the year during which a particular type of weather usually happens ▪ *the rainy season* **f** [*singular*] : a time of the year when a new fashion, color, hairstyle, etc., is popular ▪ *Pink is in style this season.* **g** [U] : a period of time when a series of new television shows, plays, etc., are being shown or performed ▪ *I can't wait until the new (television) season starts.* — **in season/out of season** **1** ◆ When fruits and vegetables are *in season*, it is the time of year when they are being harvested and are easily available. When they are *out of season*, they are not being harvested in a place near you and are more difficult or expensive to get. **2** ◆ When animals, fish, etc., are *in season*, it is the time of year when they can be legally hunted, caught, etc. When they are *out of season*, they cannot be legally hunted, caught, etc. — **Season's Greetings** — used in writing as a greeting in the time of year when Christmas and several other holidays happen near each other

²season *vb* **1** [T/I] : to add salt, pepper, spices, etc., to (something) to give it more flavor ▪ *He seasoned the stew.* **2** [T] : to make (wood) ready for use by slowly drying it ▪ *season the firewood*

sea·son·able /'si:znəbəl/ *adj, of weather* : normal for a certain time of year ▪ *seasonable weather/temperatures* — **sea·son·ably** /'si:znəbli/ *adv*

sea·son·al /'si:znəl/ *adj* **1** : happening or needed during a particular time of the year ▪ *seasonal workers* **2** : normal for a certain time of year ▪ *seasonal allergies* — **sea·son·al·ly** *adv*

sea·soned /ˈsiːznd/ adj **1** of food : having a lot of spices, herbs, salt, pepper, etc., added ▪ a highly seasoned stew **2** always before a noun : having a lot of experience doing something ▪ a seasoned actor/traveler **3** of wood : dry and ready for use ▪ seasoned lumber

sea·son·ing /ˈsiːznɪŋ/ n [C/U] : a substance (such as salt, pepper, a spice, or an herb) that is used to add flavor to food ▪ The soup needs more seasoning. ▪ Oregano is my favorite seasoning.

season ticket n [C] : a ticket for a certain place, activity, or series of events (such as sports contests) that you can use many times during a particular period of time

¹**seat** /ˈsiːt/ n **1** [C] : something (such as a chair) that you sit on ▪ a car with leather seats ▪ After intermission, he returned to his seat. ▪ She booked a seat on the next flight. ▪ Please have/take a seat. [=sit down] **2 a** [C] : the part of a chair or other piece of furniture that a person sits on ▪ The chairs have woven seats. **b** [singular] : the part of a piece of clothing that you sit on ▪ You have a tear in the seat of your pants. **3** [C] : an official position within an organization and the right to be present when that organization meets ▪ a Senate seat ▪ a seat on the board **4** [singular] **a** : a place or area where a particular activity, function, etc., occurs ▪ The university has been a seat of learning since the Middle Ages. **b** : a place (such as a city) where the people who run a government, religion, etc., are based ▪ the seat of government/power — **by the seat of your pants** : by using your own judgment and feelings to deal with each new problem or task without planning, preparation, or help from others ▪ He was running the company by the seat of his pants. ▪ We were flying by the seat of our pants when we started our business. — **in the driver's seat** see DRIVER — **on the edge of your seat** see ¹EDGE

²**seat** vb [T] **1** : to give (a person) a place to sit ▪ She was seated in the front row. ▪ Please be seated. [=sit down] **2** : to have enough seats for (a certain number of people) ▪ The restaurant seats 120 (people).

seat belt n [C] : a strap on a vehicle's seat that holds a person in the seat if there is an accident ▪ Fasten your seat belt.

seat·ing /ˈsiːtɪŋ/ n **1** [U] : seats or places to sit ▪ The auditorium has seating for 400. ▪ a seating arrangement/plan [=a plan that shows where people should sit] **2** [C] : a scheduled time when people are allowed into a performance, a meal, etc. ▪ There are two seatings for tea.

seat–of–the–pants adj, always before a noun, chiefly US : done or made by using your own judgment and feelings without planning, preparation, or help from others ▪ a seat-of-the-pants decision

sea turtle n [C] : a type of large turtle that lives in the sea

sea urchin n [C] : a small sea animal that lives on the ocean floor and is covered in sharp spines

sea·wall /ˈsiːˌwɑːl/ n [C] : a wall built to keep sea waves from coming up onto land

sea·ward /ˈsiːwəd/ also **sea·wards** /ˈsiːwədz/ adv : toward the sea ▪ She gazed seaward. — **seaward** adj

sea·wa·ter /ˈsiːˌwɑːtə/ n [U] : water in or from the sea

sea·weed /ˈsiːˌwiːd/ n [C/U] : a type of plant that grows in the sea

sea·wor·thy /ˈsiːˌwəði/ adj : fit or safe to travel on the sea ▪ a seaworthy ship — **sea·wor·thi·ness** /ˈsiːˌwəðinəs/ n [U]

¹**sec** abbr **1** section **2 Sec.** secretary ▪ Sec. of Internal Affairs

²**sec** /ˈsɛk/ n [singular] informal : a very brief time : SECOND ▪ Wait just a sec.

SEC abbr, US Securities and Exchange Commission ✧ The Securities and Exchange Commission is a part of the U.S. federal government that enforces laws about securities like stocks.

sec·a·teurs /ˌsɛkəˈtəz/ n [plural] Brit : PRUNING SHEARS

se·cede /sɪˈsiːd/ vb **-ced·ed; -ced·ing** [I] : to separate from a nation or state and become independent ▪ South Carolina seceded from the Union in 1860.

se·ces·sion /sɪˈsɛʃən/ n [C] : the act of separating from a nation or state and becoming independent ▪ the secession of the Southern states — **se·ces·sion·ist** /sɪˈsɛʃənɪst/ n [C]

se·clude /sɪˈkluːd/ vb **-clud·ed; -clud·ing** [T] : to keep (someone) away from other people ▪ He secluded himself in his room.

secluded adj **1** : private and not used or seen by many people ▪ a secluded beach **2** : placed apart from other people ▪ She led a secluded [=solitary] life.

se·clu·sion /sɪˈkluːʒən/ n [U] **1** : the act of placing or keeping someone away from other people ▪ the seclusion of women that occurs in some countries **2** : the state of being away from other people ▪ He lived in seclusion. [=he lived by himself and kept away from other people]

¹**sec·ond** /ˈsɛkənd/ adj, always before a noun **1 a** : occupying the number two position in a series ▪ B is the second letter in the alphabet. **b** : next to the first in importance or rank ▪ I won second prize. **c** : another of the same kind ▪ The chair needs a second coat of paint. ▪ English as a second language [=a language that you learn in addition to the language you first learned when you were a young child] ▪ I gave him a second chance. [=a chance to try again] ▪ a second opinion [=advice from a second person to make sure the first advice is right] **2** : having or playing the part in a group of instruments that is one level lower than the first ▪ She plays second violin in the city orchestra. — see also play second fiddle at ¹FIDDLE — **every second** — used to indicate how often a repeated activity happens or is done ▪ We elect a mayor every second year. [=every other year] — **second only to** : only less important than (something or someone) ▪ Rice is second only to corn as the state's major crop. — **second to none** see ¹NONE

²**second** adv **1** : in a position that only comes after one other in time, order, or importance • *Milan is Italy's second largest city.* • *I placed/finished second in the race.* **2** — used to introduce a statement that is the second in a series of statements • *It's pointless to plan a trip—first, we can't afford one, and second, we don't have time to take one.*

³**second** n **1** [*singular*] : something that is second • *His birthday is on the second of June.* [=on June 2] **2** [*plural*] : another serving of food taken after you are finished with the first serving • *Who wants seconds?* **3** [*singular*] : a statement made to support or approve a motion in a meeting • *There's been a motion to vote on the proposal. Do I hear a second?* **4** [*C*] : a product that is cheaper than normal because it is damaged or imperfect — usually plural • *These curtains are (factory) seconds.* **5** [*U*] baseball : SECOND BASE • *He stole second.* **6** [*C*] **a** : a unit of time that is equal to ¹⁄₆₀ of a minute • *a delay of several seconds* • *a 30-second commercial* **b** *informal* : a very brief period of time • *For a second (there) I thought you were kidding.* • *This will only take a second.* • *I expect her back **any second** now.* [=very soon] **7** [*C*] technical : one of 60 equal parts into which a minute can be divided for measuring angles • *40 degrees, 27 minutes, and 45 seconds*

⁴**second** vb [*T*] **1 a** : to approve (something) during a meeting so that discussion or voting can begin • *I second the motion.* **b** *informal* : to agree with (a suggestion or statement) • *"Let's call it a day." "I'll second that."* **2** /sɪˈkɑːnd/ Brit : to move (someone) from a regular job to a different place, department, etc., for a short period of time • *She was seconded to the Birmingham office for six months.* — **sec·ond·er** n [*C*]

¹**sec·ond·ary** /ˈsɛkənˌderi, Brit ˈsɛkəndri/ adj **1** : not as important or valuable as something else • *Winning is secondary—we mostly play for fun.* • *The book's text is secondary to its illustrations.* • *secondary issues/goals* **2** : of or relating to education of students who have completed primary school • *a secondary* [=high school] *education* **3** : caused by or coming from something else • *a secondary infection* — **sec·ond·ari·ly** /ˌsɛkənˈderəli/ adv

²**secondary** n, pl **-aries** *American football* : the players on the defense who are positioned away from the line of scrimmage and who mainly try to stop passes by the offense • *The team has a strong secondary.*

secondary school n [*C*] **1** *US* : HIGH SCHOOL 1 • *a job that requires at least a secondary school education* **2** Brit : a school for children between the ages of 11 and 16 or 18

second base n [*singular*] *baseball* : the base that must be touched second by a base runner • *He slid into second base.* — **second base·man** /-ˈbeɪsmən/ n [*C*]

second best n [*U*] : something that is good but not the best • *He won't settle for*

second best. — **sec·ond–best** /ˌsɛkənd-ˈbɛst/ adj, always before a noun • *our second-best pitcher*

second class n [*U*] **1** : a level of service on a train, ship, etc., that is just below first class • *The airline offers special services for travelers in first and second class.* **2 a** : a class of mail in the U.S. that includes newspapers, magazines, etc. **b** : a class of mail in the UK that costs less and takes longer to arrive than first class

second–class adj **1** : of or relating to second class • *a second-class seat* **2** : not given the same rights or treatment as the rest of the people in a society • *They treated us like **second-class citizens**.* [=like people who are less important and deserving of respect than other people] — **second–class** adv

Second Coming n — **the Second Coming** : the time when Christians believe that Jesus Christ will return to judge humanity at the end of the world

second cousin n [*C*] : a child of your parent's cousin • *Susan is my second cousin.* — compare FIRST COUSIN

second–degree adj, always before a noun **1** *US, of a crime* : deserving punishment but not the most severe punishment • *second-degree assault/murder* **2** : causing a moderate level of injury • *second-degree burns*

sec·ond–guess /ˌsɛkəndˈgɛs/ vb [*T*] **1** *US* : to criticize or question the actions or decisions of someone • *Don't second-guess the umpire.* = *Don't second-guess the umpire's decision.* **2** : to try to guess or predict what (someone or something) will do • *second-guessing the stock market* — **sec·ond–guess·er** n [*C*]

sec·ond·hand /ˈsɛkəndˈhænd/ adj **1 a** : having had a previous owner : USED • *secondhand furniture* **b** : buying or selling things that have already been owned or used • *a secondhand bookstore* **2** : taken from someone who was not directly involved • *secondhand information* — **secondhand** adv • *She buys all her clothes secondhand.*

secondhand smoke n [*U*] : smoke from a cigarette, cigar, pipe, etc., that can be inhaled by people who are near the person who is smoking

second lieutenant n [*C*] : an officer in the U.S. Army, Air Force, or Marine Corps who ranks below a first lieutenant

sec·ond·ly /ˈsɛkəndli/ adv — used to introduce a statement that is the second statement in a series • *I'm moving because, for one thing, my apartment is too small, and, secondly, I found one closer to my job.*

se·cond·ment /sɪˈkɑːndmənt/ n [*U*] Brit : a period of time when you are away from your regular job while you do another job • *She returned to London after her secondment in/to Birmingham.*

second nature n [*U*] : something you can do easily or without much thought because you have done it many times before • *After a while, using the gearshift becomes second nature.*

second person n [*U*] **1** *grammar* : a

set of words or forms (such as pronouns or verb forms) that refer to the person that the speaker or writer is addressing ▪ *"You" is the second person singular and plural pronoun in English.* **2** : a writing style that uses second person pronouns and verbs ▪ *The author begins the story in the second person with the sentence "You open the door and step into the room."*

sec·ond–rate /ˌsɛkənd'reɪt/ *adj* : not very good ▪ *a second-rate meal/education*

sec·ond–string /ˌsɛkənd'strɪŋ/ *adj*, always before a noun, chiefly *US*, *sports* : not used as one of the regular players on a team ▪ *a second-string quarterback*

second thought *n* [*C*] : a feeling of guilt, doubt, worry, etc., that you have after you have decided to do something or after something has happened ▪ *She was having second thoughts about getting married.* ▪ *Don't give a second thought to* [=don't worry about] *that broken vase.* — **on second thought** (*US*) *or Brit* **on second thoughts** : after thinking about something again ▪ *On second thought, I think I will go.*

second wind *n* [*singular*] : a feeling of new energy that allows you to continue to do something after you had begun to feel tired ▪ *The sight of the finish line gave me a second wind.*

se·cre·cy /'si:krəsi/ *n* [*U*] **1** : the act of keeping information secret ▪ *She swore him to secrecy.* [=made him promise to keep a secret] **2** : the quality or state of being hidden or secret ▪ *The project was cloaked in secrecy.* [=the true nature of the project was kept secret]

¹**se·cret** /'si:krət/ *adj* : kept hidden from others ▪ *a secret hideout/passage/mission/password* ▪ *She has a secret admirer.* [=someone admires her but she does not know who it is] ▪ *He was accused of being a secret agent.* [=a person who tries to get secret information about another country, government, etc., for a foreign government] — **se·cret·ly** *adv*

²**secret** *n* [*C*] **1** : a fact or piece of information that is kept hidden from other people ▪ *Don't tell him about the party—it's a secret.* ▪ *He knows how to keep a secret.* [=if you tell him a secret he won't tell it to anyone else] ▪ *It's no secret* [=many people know] *that he has connections to the Mafia.* **2** : a special or unusual way of doing something to achieve a good result ▪ *You always look great. What's your secret? What is the secret to your success?* [=why are you so successful?] **3** : something that cannot be explained ▪ *the secrets of the universe* — **in secret** : in a private place or manner ▪ *They met in secret.* [=secretly] — **make no secret of** : to show or express (something) openly ▪ *She made no secret of her dislike for him.*

secret agent *n* [*C*] : a person who tries to get secret information about another country, government, etc.

sec·re·tar·i·at /ˌsɛkrə'tɛriət/ *n* [*C*] : a department in a governmental organization that is headed by a secretary or a secretary-general ▪ *the United Nations secretariat*

sec·re·tary /'sɛkrəˌteri, *Brit* 'sɛkrətri/ *n*, *pl* **-tar·ies** [*C*] **1** : a person whose job is to handle records, letters, etc., for another person in an office ▪ *You can set up an appointment with my secretary.* **2** : a person in a club or other organization who is in charge of keeping letters and records **3 a** *US* : an official who is selected by the President and is in charge of a particular department of the government ▪ *the Treasury Secretary* **b** *Brit* : a government official who helps a minister, an ambassador, etc. ▪ *a junior secretary at the embassy* **c** *Brit* : SECRETARY OF STATE **2** — **sec·re·tar·i·al** /ˌsɛkrə'tɛriəl/ *adj* ▪ *secretarial duties*

Secretary–General *n*, *pl* **Secretaries–General** [*C*] : an official who is in charge of an organization ▪ *the Secretary-General of the United Nations*

Secretary of State *n* [*C*] **1** : the head of the U.S. government department that is in charge of how the country relates to and deals with foreign countries **2** : the head of one of several important departments of the British government ▪ *the Secretary of State for Home Affairs*

se·crete /sɪ'kri:t/ *vb* **-cret·ed; -cret·ing** [*T*] **1** *biology* : to produce and give off (a liquid) ▪ *glands that secrete saliva* **2** *somewhat formal* : to put (something) in a hidden place ▪ *He secreted the money under the mattress.*

se·cre·tion /sɪ'kri:ʃən/ *n*, *biology* **1** [*U*] : the production of a liquid by part of a plant or animal ▪ *the secretion of stomach acids* **2** [*C*] : a substance produced and given off by a plant or animal part ▪ *gastric secretions*

se·cre·tive /'si:krətɪv/ *adj* : not letting people see or know what you are doing or thinking : tending to act in secret ▪ *a secretive person/organization* — **se·cre·tive·ness** *n* [*U*]

secret police *n* — **the secret police** : a police organization that is run by a government and that operates in a secret way to control the actions of people who oppose the government

secret service *n* **1 the Secret Service** : a U.S. government department that is in charge of protecting elected leaders of the U.S. and visiting leaders **2** [*singular*] : a government department that protects a country's secrets and obtains secret information about other countries ▪ *the British secret service*

sect /'sɛkt/ *n* [*C*] **1** : a religious group that is a smaller part of a larger group and whose members all share similar beliefs ▪ *Buddhist sects* **2** : a religious or political group that is connected to a larger group but that has beliefs that differ greatly from those of the main group ▪ *a fundamentalist Christian sect*

sec·tar·i·an /sɛk'tɛrijən/ *adj* : relating to religious or political sects and the differences between them ▪ *sectarian violence* — **sec·tar·i·an·ism** /sɛk'tɛrijəˌnɪzəm/ *n* [*U*]

¹**sec·tion** /'sɛkʃən/ *n* [*C*] **1 a** : one of the parts that form something ▪ *the upper section of the bridge* **b** : a particular area that is part of a larger place ▪ *the library's*

reference section **c** : a part of a newspaper, play, book, etc. ▪ *the sports section (of the newspaper)* **d** : a part of a group of people ▪ *ads that target one section of the population* **2** : one of several parts made so that something can be put together easily ▪ *The siding comes in five-foot sections.* **3** : a part of a band or orchestra that has instruments of a particular kind ▪ *the brass section*

²**section** *vb* [T] : to divide (something) into parts ▪ *Peel and section the orange.* — **section off** [*phrasal vb*] **section (something) off** *or* **section off (something)** : to separate (an area) from a larger area ▪ *Part of the field was sectioned off for parking.*

¹**sec·tion·al** /ˈsɛkʃənl/ *adj* **1** : showing how something would look if it were cut from the top to the bottom ▪ *a sectional drawing of a ship* **2** : concerned only with one part of a group or community ▪ *sectional interests/conflicts* **3** : made up of sections that can be put together or taken apart easily ▪ *a sectional couch*

²**sectional** *n* [C] *US* : a sofa that has three or more separate sections ▪ *a leather sectional* — called also *sectional sofa*

sec·tor /ˈsɛktə/ *n* [C] **1** : a part of an economy that includes certain kinds of jobs ▪ *the industrial/agricultural/service sector* — see also PRIVATE SECTOR, PUBLIC SECTOR **2** : an area for which someone (such as a military commander) is responsible ▪ *the northern sector* **3** *geometry* : an area in a circle that lies between two straight lines drawn from the center of the circle to the edge of the circle ▪ *a 90-degree sector*

sec·u·lar /ˈsɛkjələ/ *adj* **1 a** : of or relating to the physical world and not the spiritual world ▪ *secular concerns* **b** : not religious ▪ *secular music/institutions* **c** : of, relating to, or controlled by the government rather than by the church ▪ *secular courts* **2** — used to describe a member of the clergy who does not live in a monastery ▪ *a secular priest*

sec·u·lar·ism /ˈsɛkjələˌrɪzəm/ *n* [U] : the belief that religion should not play a role in government, education, or other public parts of society — **sec·u·lar·ist** /ˈsɛkjələrɪst/ *n* [C] — **secularist** *or* **sec·u·lar·is·tic** /ˌsɛkjələˈrɪstɪk/ *adj*

¹**se·cure** /sɪˈkjʊ/ *adj* **se·cur·er; -est** **1 a** : protected from danger or harm ▪ *The children are safe and secure.* **b** : providing protection from danger or harm ▪ *Store your valuables in a secure place.* **c** : guarded so that no one can enter or leave without approval ▪ *You are now entering a secure area.* **2** : feeling safe and free from worries or doubt ▪ *I feel secure about my place in the company.* ▪ *They are financially secure.* **3 a** : firmly attached ▪ *Is that shelf secure?* **b** : in a firm position that prevents unwanted movement ▪ *a secure grip* **c** : not in danger of being lost or taken away ▪ *He believes his job is secure.* ▪ *a secure investment* **4** : known only to certain people ▪ *a secure password*

²**secure** *vb* **-cured; -cur·ing** [T] *somewhat formal* **1 a** : to make (something) safe by guarding or protecting it ▪ *Police secured the building.* **b** : to put (something) in a place or position so that it will not move ▪ *Secure your belongings under the seat.* ▪ *secure a child safety seat* **2** : to make (something) certain ▪ *She scored a goal to secure the team's victory.* **3** : to guarantee that (an amount owed) will be paid usually by offering your property if you cannot pay ▪ *He secured the loan using his house as collateral.* **4** : to get (something) by using effort : OBTAIN ▪ *He secured her release.* — **se·cure·ly** /sɪˈkjɚli/ *adv*

se·cu·ri·ty /sɪˈkjɚəti/ *n, pl* **-ties** **1** [U] **a** : the state of being protected or safe from harm ▪ *We must insure our national security.* **b** : things done to make people or places safe ▪ *increased security at airports* **c** : the area in a place (such as an airport) where people are checked to make sure they are not carrying weapons or other illegal materials ▪ *We have to go through security at the airport.* **d** : the part of a company or other organization that provides protection for workers, equipment, etc. ▪ *We called security when we found the door open.* **2** [U] : the state of being closely watched or guarded ▪ *The meeting was held under tight security.* **3** [U] : the state of being free from anxiety or worry ▪ *financial/job security* **4** [C] **a** : something given as proof of a promise to make a payment later ▪ *security for a loan* **b** : a document showing that someone owns or has invested in a company, organization, etc. ▪ *government securities*

security deposit *n* [C] : an amount of money that you pay when you begin to rent property (such as an apartment) and that can be used to pay for any damage that you cause to the property

security guard *n* [C] : a person whose job is to guard a place (such as a store or museum) and make sure the people and things in it are not harmed

se·dan /sɪˈdæn/ *n* [C] *US* : a car that has four doors and that has room for four or more people

¹**se·date** /sɪˈdeɪt/ *adj* **1** : slow and relaxed ▪ *a sedate pace* **2** : quiet and peaceful ▪ *a sedate neighborhood*

²**sedate** *vb* **-dat·ed; -dat·ing** [T] : to give (a person or animal) drugs that cause relaxation or sleep ▪ *The doctor sedated the patient heavily.* ▪ *The animal had to be sedated.*

se·da·tion /sɪˈdeɪʃən/ *n* [U] **1** : a relaxed, calm, or sleepy condition that results from taking a drug (called a sedative) ▪ *The patient was under (heavy) sedation.* **2** : the act of giving a person or animal a drug that causes calmness or relaxation ▪ *For some patients, sedation may be necessary.*

sed·a·tive /ˈsɛdətɪv/ *n* [C] : a drug that calms or relaxes someone ▪ *The patient was given a sedative.* ▪ *sedative drugs/medicine*

sed·en·tary /ˈsɛdn̩ˌteri, *Brit* ˈsɛdntri/ *adj* : doing or involving a lot of sitting ▪ *a sedentary job*

sedge /ˈsɛdʒ/ *n* [C/U] : a plant like grass

that grows in wet ground or near water

sed·i·ment /ˈsɛdəmənt/ n [C/U] **1** : material that sinks to the bottom of a liquid ▪ *There was a layer of sediment in the bottom of the tank.* **2** : material (such as stones and sand) that is carried into water by water, wind, etc. — **sed·i·men·ta·ry** /ˌsɛdəˈmɛntəri/ adj, technical ▪ *sedimentary rock* [=a type of rock formed when sediments that were deposited in ancient times were pressed together and became hard] — **sed·i·men·ta·tion** /ˌsɛdəmənˈteɪʃən/ n [U] technical ▪ *rock formed by sedimentation*

se·di·tion /sɪˈdɪʃən/ n [U] formal : the crime of saying, writing, or doing something that encourages people to disobey their government — **se·di·tious** /sɪˈdɪʃəs/ adj ▪ *seditious statements*

se·duce /sɪˈduːs, Brit sɪˈdjuːs/ vb **-duced; -duc·ing** [T] **1** : to persuade (someone) to have sex with you ▪ *He tried to seduce her.* **2** : to persuade (someone) to do something ▪ *He was seduced into a life of crime.* — **se·duc·er** /sɪˈduːsɚ, Brit sɪˈdjuːsə/ n [C] — **se·duc·tion** /sɪˈdʌkʃən/ n [C/U] — **se·duc·tive** /sɪˈdʌktɪv/ adj ▪ a seductive woman/voice/smile ▪ *the seductive* [=very attractive] *power of advertising* — **se·duc·tive·ly** adv — **se·duc·tive·ness** n [U]

see /ˈsiː/ vb **saw** /ˈsɑː/; **seen** /ˈsiːn/; **see·ing** /ˈsiːjɪŋ/ **1 a** [T/I] : to notice or become aware of (someone or something) by using your eyes ▪ *I can't see a thing without my glasses.* ▪ *I saw her take the money.* ▪ *I see (that) you bought a new car.* ▪ *I couldn't see through/out the foggy window.* ▪ *I want to have the ability to see* ▪ *She cannot see.* [=she is blind] **2** [T/I] : to be or become aware of (something) ▪ *He only sees* [=notices] *my faults.* ▪ *It was easy to see that she was lying.* ▪ **As you can see**, *profits have declined.* **3** [T/I] : to learn or find out (something) especially by looking or waiting ▪ *Please see who's at the door.* ▪ *Try on the dress to see if it fits.* ▪ *It remains to be seen* [=it is uncertain] *whether or not she was lying.* ▪ "*Can I go to the party?*" "**We'll see.**" [=maybe, perhaps] **4** [T] **a** : to read (something written or printed) ▪ *Have you seen today's newspaper?* **b** — used to tell someone where to look for information ▪ *For further information, see Appendix A.* **5** [T] **a** : to watch (a television program, movie, etc.) ▪ *I saw that movie last week.* **b** : to go to and watch (a performance, play, event, etc.) ▪ *We saw the parade.* **6** [I] — used in speech to direct someone's attention to something or someone ▪ *See, I told you it would rain.* **7** [T] **a** : to think of (someone or something) in a certain way ▪ *I see things differently now.* ▪ *She sees herself as an independent woman.* **b** — used to say what your opinion is about something ▪ "*Can we do it?*" "*I don't see why not.*" [=yes, I believe that we can do it] ▪ *As I see it*, *you have only two choices.* ▪ *The way he sees it*, *we should be done by Friday.* [=he thinks we should be done by Friday] **8** [T] **a** : to imagine (someone) as being or doing something speci-

fied ▪ *I can see her becoming a doctor.* ▪ *I just can't see him as a banker.* **b** : to form a mental picture of (something) ▪ *He saw a great future for himself in baseball.* **9** [T/I] : to understand (something) ▪ *I don't see the point of your story.* ▪ "*You should hold the club like this.*" "*Oh, I see (what you mean).*" **10** [T] **a** : to meet with (someone) ▪ *Can I see you later this afternoon?* ▪ *You should see a doctor.* **b** : to visit (someone) ▪ *I saw him at the hospital.* **c** : to allow yourself to be visited by (someone) ▪ *He's not seeing anyone today.* **d** : to be with and talk to (someone) ▪ *We'll see you again soon.* **e** — used in phrases like **see more/less of** and **see a lot of** to describe how much time people spend with each other ▪ *I'd like to see more of you.* [=to spend more time with you] ▪ *They've been seeing a lot of each other.* [=been spending a lot of time together] **11** [T] : to spend time with (someone) as part of a romantic relationship ▪ *They've been seeing each other for months.* **12** [T] : to make sure (something) is done ▪ *Please see (that) the work gets finished on time.* **13** [T] : to experience (something) ▪ *He saw a lot of action during the war.* **14** [T] : to be the place or time in which (something) happens ▪ *The city has seen a lot of growth in recent years.* ▪ *This year has seen a drop in profits.* **15** [T] : to go somewhere with (someone) ▪ *I'll see you home.* ▪ *I can see myself out*, *thank you.* [=I can leave without having anyone show me where to go] **16** [T] : to help or support (someone or something) for a particular period of time ▪ *The support of his friends saw him through his depression.* [=helped him to get through his depression] **17** [T] : to make a bet that is equal to (another player's bet) in poker ▪ *I'll see your 10 and raise you 10.* — **I'll be seeing you** *informal* — used to say goodbye — **let me see**, **let's see** see ¹LONG — **long time no see** see ¹LONG — **see about** [phrasal vb] **1** : to do what is required for (something) ▪ *I'll see about getting concert tickets.* **2 we'll (soon) see about that** — used in speech to say that you are not going to allow someone to do something or to behave in a certain way ▪ "*He says that he's not going.*" "*Well, we'll (soon) see about that.*" — **see double** see ⁴DOUBLE — **see eye to eye** : to have the same opinion — usually used in negative statements ▪ *They don't see eye to eye on this issue.* — **see fit** see ¹FIT — **see here** — used to introduce a statement when you want someone to notice what you are saying ▪ *See here*, *you need to start behaving more responsibly.* — **see if I care** see ²CARE — **see in** [phrasal vb] **see (something) in (someone or something)** : to notice or perceive (something good or attractive) in (someone or something) ▪ *I don't know/understand what she sees in him.* [=I don't know why she likes/admires him] — **see off** [phrasal vb] **see (someone) off** or **see off (someone) 1** : to go to an airport, train station, etc., with (someone who is leaving) in order to say goodbye ▪ *She saw him off at the* *train station.* **2** *Brit* **a** : to chase or force (someone) away from a place ▪ *The police finally saw them off.* **b** : to defeat or stop (an enemy, opponent, etc.) ▪ *They saw off the opposition.* — **see out** [*phrasal vb*] **see (something) out** : to continue to work at (something) until it is completed ▪ *He saw the project out to its very end.* — **see red** see ²RED — **see stars** see ¹STAR — **see the back of** see ¹BACK — **see the light** see ¹LIGHT — **see things** : to see things that do not really exist —*you must be seeing things.* — **see through** [*phrasal vb*] **1** : to realize the true nature of (someone or something) ▪ *She saw through his lies.* [=she knew he was lying] ▪ *I can't lie to her—she'd see right through me.* **2** **see (something) through** : to continue to work at (something) until it is completed ▪ *He saw the project through to the end.* — **see to** [*phrasal vb*] **1** : to do or provide what is needed for (something) ▪ *The hotel staff saw to my every need.* : to deal with (something) ▪ *I'll see to your order at once.* **2** **see to it** : to make sure that something is done ▪ *Can you see to it that everyone gets the memo?* — **see you** or **see you around** or **see you later** *informal* — used to say goodbye — **see your way (clear) to** see ¹WAY

¹**seed** /ˈsiːd/ *n* **1** [*C/U*] : a small object produced by a plant from which a new plant can grow ▪ *a packet of sunflower seeds* ▪ *She grows her plants from seed.* [=by planting seeds] **2** [*C*] : the beginning of something which continues to develop or grow ▪ *Her comment planted/sowed a seed of doubt in his mind.* [=caused him to begin to have doubts] **3** [*C*] : a player or team that is ranked as one of the best in a competition in order to be sure that the best players or teams do not play against each other in the early part of the competition ▪ *The top seed won the tennis tournament.* — **go to seed** or **run to seed** **1** : to produce seeds ▪ *The flowers will go to seed and spread.* **2** : to become less attractive, effective, etc., because of age or lack of care ▪ *He let himself go to seed after he lost his job.* — **seed·less** /ˈsiːdləs/ *adj*

²**seed** *vb* **1** [*T*] : to plant (an area of ground) with seeds ▪ *We seeded the field with corn.* ▪ *a newly seeded lawn* **2** [*I*] : to produce seeds ▪ *These plants will seed late in the fall.* **3** [*T*] : to remove (seeds) from a fruit or vegetable ▪ *wash and seed the peppers* **4** [*T*] : to give (a player or team) a particular rank which shows how likely that person or team is to win a competition ▪ *She is seeded first in tomorrow's tennis tournament.* ▪ *the top-seeded player* — **seed itself** *of a plant* : to produce new plants from its own seeds ▪ *This plant spreads quickly because it seeds itself.*

seed·bed /ˈsiːdˌbɛd/ *n* [*C*] : an area of soil prepared for planting seeds

seed·ling /ˈsiːdlɪŋ/ *n* [*C*] : a young plant that is grown from seed

seed money *n* [*U*] : money that is used for starting a new business, program,

project, etc. ▪ *He provided seed money for the campaign.*

seedy /ˈsiːdi/ *adj* **seed·i·er; -est** **1** : dirty or in bad condition ▪ *a seedy motel* **2** : not respectable or decent ▪ *a seedy area of the city* **3** : DISHONEST ▪ *a seedy lawyer* **4** : having a lot of seeds ▪ *seedy fruit*

see·ing /ˈsiːɪŋ/ *conj* — used to explain the reason for a statement ▪ *There's not much we can do, seeing that they've already left.* ▪ *Seeing as you've met my family, I'd like to meet yours.* ▪ *Seeing as how* [=since] *I'm not busy right now, I can help you.*

Seeing Eye *trademark, US* — used for a dog that is trained to guide a blind person

seek /ˈsiːk/ *vb* **sought** /ˈsɑːt/; **seek·ing** [*T*] *somewhat formal* **1** : to try to find (someone or something) ▪ *He is seeking employment.* ▪ *The prince is seeking a wife.* **2** : to ask for (help, advice, etc.) ▪ *The church is seeking donations.* **3 a** : to try to get or achieve (something) ▪ *The mayor is seeking reelection.* ▪ *They came to the city to seek their fortune.* [=to try to become rich] ▪ *They are seeking compensation/damages* [=they are trying to get money] *for their loss.* **b** : to make an attempt *to do* something ▪ *The builders sought to make the bridge stronger.* — **seek out** [*phrasal vb*] **seek (someone or something) out** or **seek out (someone or something)** : to search for and find (someone or something) ▪ *His parents sought out the best doctors in the field.* — **seek·er** *n* [*C*]

seem /ˈsiːm/ *vb* [*linking vb*] **1** : to appear to be something or to do something ▪ *She seemed (to be) happy.* ▪ *Their request seems reasonable.* ▪ *She seems to know our secret.* ▪ *He seems like a nice man.* = *He seems (to be) a nice man.* ▪ *It seemed as if/though the work would never end.* **2** — used with *it* to make a statement about what appears to be true based on what is known ▪ *It seems (that) they forgot about the meeting.* ▪ *They are very rude, or so it seems (to me).* **3** — used to make a statement less definite or more polite ▪ *I seem to remember that you said you'd help me.* ▪ *What seems to be the problem?*

seem·ing /ˈsiːmɪŋ/ *adj, always before a noun, somewhat formal* : appearing to be true but not being true or certain ▪ *I was fooled by the seeming simplicity of the instructions.* — **seem·ing·ly** *adv* ▪ *a seemingly impossible stunt*

seem·ly /ˈsiːmli/ *adj, formal + old-fashioned* : proper or appropriate ▪ *seemly behavior* ▪ *a seemly reply*

seen *past participle of* SEE

seep /ˈsiːp/ *vb* [*I*] : to flow or pass slowly through small openings ▪ *Blood was seeping through the bandage.*

seep·age /ˈsiːpɪdʒ/ *n* [*C/U*] *formal* : an occurrence in which a liquid or gas flows or passes slowly through small openings ▪ *gas/oil seepages*

seer /ˈsiɚ/ *n* [*C*] : someone who predicts things that will happen in the future

seer·suck·er /ˈsiɚˌsʌkɚ/ *n* [*U*] : a light type of cloth that has an uneven surface and a pattern of lines ▪ *a seersucker dress*

see·saw /'si:ˌsɑ:/ *n* [C] **1** : a long, flat board that is balanced in the middle so that when one end goes up the other end goes down ▪ *Let's play/ride on the seesaw.* **2** [*singular*] : a situation in which something keeps changing from one state to another and back again ▪ *Their relationship was an emotional seesaw.* ▪ *a seesaw economy* — **seesaw** *vb* [*I*] ▪ *Stock prices continue to seesaw.* [=to go up and down]

seethe /'si:ð/ *vb* **seethed; seeth·ing** [*I*] **1** : to feel or show strong emotion even though you try to control it ▪ *a seething letter* ▪ *He seethed with anger/jealousy.* **2** : to be in a state of constant activity ▪ *The island is seething with tourists.* [=there are very many tourists moving around on the island] ▪ *His brain was seething with ideas.*

see-through /'si:ˌθru:/ *adj* : thin enough to be seen through ▪ *a see-through blouse*

¹**seg·ment** /'sɛgmənt/ *n* [C] : one of the parts into which something can be divided : SECTION ▪ *a large segment of the population* ▪ *the segments of an orange*

²**seg·ment** /'sɛgˌmɛnt, *Brit* sɛg'mɛnt/ *vb* [*T*] : to divide (something) into parts ▪ *Researchers segmented the population into different age groups.* — **seg·men·ta·tion** /ˌsɛgmən'teɪʃən/ *n* [U]

seg·re·gate /'sɛgrɪˌgeɪt/ *vb* **-gat·ed; -gat·ing** [*T*] **1** : to separate groups of people because of their particular race, religion, etc. ▪ *practices that segregated blacks and whites* ▪ *Women are segregated from men during religious services.* **2** : to not allow people of different races to be together in (a place, such as a school) ▪ *racially segregated schools* — **seg·re·ga·tion** /ˌsɛgrɪ'geɪʃən/ *n* [U] ▪ *racial/religious segregation*

seg·re·ga·tion·ist /ˌsɛgrɪ'geɪʃənɪst/ *n* [C] : a person who supports racial segregation

se·gue /'sɛgˌweɪ/ *vb* **se·gued; se·gue·ing** [*I*] : to move without stopping from one topic, song, etc., to another ▪ *She quickly segued to the next topic.* — **segue** *n* [C] ▪ *She used the question as a segue to her next topic.*

seis·mic /'saɪzmɪk/ *adj, always before a noun* **1** *technical* : of, relating to, or caused by an earthquake ▪ *seismic activity/waves* **2** : very great or important ▪ *a seismic shift/change in public opinion* — **seis·mi·cal·ly** /'saɪzmɪkli/ *adv*

seis·mo·graph /'saɪzməˌgræf, *Brit* 'saɪzməˌgrɑ:f/ *n* [C] : a device that measures the force of an earthquake

seis·mol·o·gy /saɪz'mɑ:lədʒi/ *n* [U] : the scientific study of earthquakes — **seis·mo·log·i·cal** /ˌsaɪzmə'lɑ:dʒɪkəl/ *adj* — **seis·mol·o·gist** /saɪz'mɑ:lədʒɪst/ *n* [C]

seize /'si:z/ *vb* **seized; seiz·ing** [*T*] **1** : to use legal or official power to take (something) ▪ *Police seized weapons and drugs.* ▪ *The bank seized their property.* **2** : to get or take control of (something or someone) in a forceful or sudden way ▪ *A rebel group seized power.* ▪ *She seized the lead in the race.* ▪ *He seized (hold of) the gun.* ▪ *(figurative) Panic seized me.* **3** : to take or use (a chance, moment, etc.) in a

quick and eager way ▪ *He seized the opportunity to talk to his boss.* — **seize on/upon** [*phrasal vb*] : to take or use (something, such as a chance or opportunity) in a quick and eager way ▪ *His critics have seized on the scandal to call for his resignation.* ▪ *She seized on the opportunity to tell her side of the story.* — **seize up** [*phrasal vb*] : to stop working because the moving parts can no longer move ▪ *The engine/brakes seized up.*

sei·zure /'si:ʒɚ/ *n* **1** [U] : the act of taking control of something especially by force ▪ *the seizure of power by the rebels* **2** [C/U] *law* : the act of taking something by legal authority ▪ *the seizure of evidence by the police* **3** [C] *medical* : an abnormal state in which you become unconscious and your body moves in an uncontrolled and violent way ▪ *an epileptic seizure*

sel·dom /'sɛldəm/ *adv* : not often : almost never ▪ *We seldom go to the movies.* ▪ *Seldom do we agree.* — **seldom ever** see EVER — **seldom if ever** see EVER

¹**se·lect** /sə'lɛkt/ *vb* [*T/I*] : to choose (someone or something) from a group ▪ *Please select one item from the list.* ▪ *People were selected at random to take the survey.* ▪ *a book of selected essays* — **se·lec·tor** /sə'lɛktɚ/ *n* [C]

²**select** *adj* **1** : chosen from a group to include the best people or things ▪ *A select number of people are invited.* ▪ *Only a select few will be accepted into the program.* **2** *always before a noun* : of the highest quality ▪ *select wines/hotels*

se·lec·tion /sə'lɛkʃən/ *n* **1** [U] : the act of choosing something or someone from a group ▪ *The selection of the best poem was difficult.* ▪ *the selection process* ▪ *It was not easy to make my selection.* **2** [C] **a** : someone or something that is chosen from a group ▪ *Who is your selection for president?* ▪ *She sang selections from her new album.* **b** : a collection of things chosen from a group of similar things ▪ *The pub has a wide selection of beers.* [=has many different beers]

se·lec·tive /sə'lɛktɪv/ *adj* **1** : careful to choose only the best people or things ▪ *She is very selective about which men she dates.* ▪ *the college's highly selective admissions process* **2** : involving the selection of people or things from a group ▪ *selective breeding* ▪ *She has a selective memory.* [=she remembers only what she wants to remember] — **se·lec·tive·ly** *adv* — **se·lec·tiv·i·ty** /sə,lɛk'tɪvəti/ *n* [U]

self /'sɛlf/ *n, pl* **selves** /'sɛlvz/ **1** [C/U] : the person that someone normally or truly is ▪ *He's not his usual/normal self today.* ▪ *After some sleep, she was her old self again.* [=she returned to behaving/feeling as she normally did] ▪ *She stopped pretending and showed her true/real self.* **2** [C] : a particular part of your personality or character that is shown in a particular situation ▪ *Her public self is very different from her private self.* **3** [C] — used to refer to a person ▪ *a photo of her younger self* ▪ *He puts his whole self into* ▪ *every game.*

self- /ˌsɛlf/ *combining form* **1 a** : yourself or itself • *self-pitying* **b** : of yourself or itself • *self-destructive* **2** : by, of, to, with, for, or toward yourself or itself • *self-made* • *self-addressed* • *self-respect*

self–ab·sorbed /ˌsɛlfəbˈsoɚbd/ *adj, disapproving* : only caring about and interested in yourself • *self-absorbed people* — **self–ab·sorp·tion** /ˌsɛlfəbˈsoɚpʃən/ *n* [U]

self–ad·dressed /ˌsɛlfəˈdrɛst/ *adj* : having the sender's address on it so that it can be sent back to that person • *a self-addressed envelope*

self–ap·point·ed /ˌsɛlfəˈpɔıntəd/ *adj, disapproving* : thinking of yourself as having a particular job, responsibility, etc., without considering the opinions or wishes of other people • *a self-appointed leader*

self–as·sured /ˌsɛlfəˈʃəd/ *adj* : SELF-CONFIDENT • *a self-assured man/manner* — **self–as·sur·ance** /ˌsɛlfəˈʃərəns/ *n* [U]

self–aware·ness /ˌsɛlfəˈwɛənəs/ *n* [U] : knowledge and awareness of your own personality or character — **self–aware** /ˌsɛlfəˈwɛə/ *adj* • *a remarkably self-aware child*

self–ca·ter·ing /ˌsɛlfˈkeıtərıŋ/ *adj, Brit* : provided with equipment that allows you to cook your own food while you are on holiday • *a self-catering cottage/holiday* — **self–catering** *n* [U] *Brit*

self–cen·tered (*US*) or *Brit* **self–cen·tred** /ˌsɛlfˈsɛntəd/ *adj, disapproving* : SELFISH • *He's a self-centered jerk.* — **self–cen·tered·ness** (*US*) or *Brit* **self–cen·tred·ness** *n* [U]

self–con·fessed /ˌsɛlfkənˈfɛst/ *adj, always before a noun* : freely and openly admitting that you are a particular type of person • *a self-confessed TV addict*

self–con·fi·dent /ˌsɛlfˈkɑːnfədənt/ *adj* : having or showing confidence in yourself and your abilities • *a self-confident woman* — **self–con·fi·dence** /ˌsɛlfˈkɑːnfədəns/ *n* [U] — **self–con·fi·dent·ly** *adv*

self–con·grat·u·la·tion /ˌsɛlfkənˌgrætʃəˈleıʃən, ˌsɛlfkənˌgrædʒəˈleıʃən/ *n* [U] *usually disapproving* : a way of behaving or speaking which shows that you are very proud of something you have done — **self–con·grat·u·la·to·ry** /ˌsɛlfkənˈgrætʃələˌtori, ˌsɛlfkənˈgrædʒələˌtori, *Brit* ˌsɛlfkənˌgrætʃəˈleıtri/ *adj* • *a self-congratulatory speech/tone*

self–con·scious /ˌsɛlfˈkɑːnʃəs/ *adj* **1** : uncomfortably nervous about or embarrassed by what other people think about you • *He's very self-conscious about his appearance.* **2** *usually disapproving* : done in a way that shows an awareness of the effect that is produced • *a self-conscious attempt to win people's sympathy* — **self–con·scious·ly** *adv* — **self–con·scious·ness** *n* [U]

self–con·tained /ˌsɛlfkənˈteınd/ *adj* **1** : not requiring help or support from anyone or anything else • *a self-contained community/system* **2** : tending to keep thoughts and feelings private • *a self-contained young man* **3** *Brit* : having a

kitchen and bathroom • *a self-contained flat*

self–con·trol /ˌsɛlfkənˈtroul/ *n* [U] : control over your feelings or actions • *a lack of self-control* — **self–con·trolled** /ˌsɛlfkənˈtrould/ *adj*

self–de·feat·ing /ˌsɛlfdıˈfiːtıŋ/ *adj* **1** : causing more problems than it solves • *Violence is a more self-defeating solution.* **2** : preventing you from doing or achieving something • *Don't assume you'll fail! That's a self-defeating attitude.*

self–de·fense (*US*) or *Brit* **self–de·fence** /ˌsɛlfdıˈfɛns/ *n* [U] **1** : the act of defending yourself, your property, etc. • *She hit back in self-defense.* **2** : skills that make you capable of protecting yourself during an attack • *a self-defense class*

self–dep·re·cat·ing /ˌsɛlfˈdɛprıˌkeıtıŋ/ *adj, formal* : meant to make yourself or the things you do seem unimportant • *self-deprecating humor*

self–de·struct /ˌsɛlfdıˈstrʌkt/ *vb* [I] : to destroy itself • *The missile self-destructs if it goes off course.* • *(figurative) The team self-destructed in the ninth inning and lost.* — **self–destruct** *adj, always before a noun* • *a self-destruct mechanism*

self–de·struc·tion /ˌsɛlfdıˈstrʌkʃən/ *n* [U] : the act of hurting or killing yourself — **self–de·struc·tive** /ˌsɛlfdıˈstrʌktıv/ *adj* • *self-destructive behavior*

self–dis·ci·pline /ˌsɛlfˈdısəplən/ *n* [U] : the ability to make yourself do things that should be done • *You need a lot of self-discipline to exercise every day.* — **self–dis·ci·plined** /ˌsɛlfˈdısəplənd/ *adj* • *self-disciplined students*

self–doubt /ˈsɛlfˈdaut/ *n* [C/U] : a feeling of doubt about your own abilities or actions • *a moment of self-doubt*

self–drive /ˈsɛlfˈdraıv/ *adj, always before a noun, Brit* **1** *of a car* : rented from a company • *a self-drive car* **2** : done by driving yourself • *a self-drive tour*

self–ef·fac·ing /ˌsɛlfıˈfeısıŋ/ *adj, formal* : not trying to get attention or praise for yourself • *a self-effacing manner/scholar* — **self–ef·face·ment** /ˌsɛlfıˈfeısmənt/ *n* [U]

self–em·ployed /ˌsɛlfımˈplɔıd/ *adj* : earning income from your own business or profession rather than by working for someone else • *a self-employed businessman*

self–es·teem /ˌsɛlfəˈstiːm/ *n* [U] : a feeling of having respect for yourself and your abilities • *low/high self-esteem*

self–ev·i·dent /ˌsɛlfˈɛvədənt/ *adj, formal* : clearly true and requiring no proof or explanation • *self-evident truths* — **self–ev·i·dent·ly** *adv*

self–ex·plan·a·to·ry /ˌsɛlfık'splænəˌtori, *Brit* ˌsɛlfık'splænətri/ *adj* : easy to understand without explanation • *a self-explanatory phrase*

self–ex·pres·sion /ˌsɛlfık'sprɛʃən/ *n* [U] : the expression of your thoughts or feelings especially through painting, writing, dancing, etc. • *a form/means of self-expression*

self–ful·fill·ing /ˌsɛlfful'fılıŋ/ *adj* **1** : becoming real or true because it was predicted or expected • *The prediction of a rise in the stock market became a self-fulfilling prophecy when investors heard the report and began buying stock.* **2** : providing happiness and satisfaction • *She finds running her own business very self-fulfilling.* — **self-ful-fill-ment** (*US*) *or Brit* **self-ful-fil-ment** /ˌsɛlfʊl-ˈfɪlmənt/ *n* [*U*] • *She found self-fulfillment by starting her own business.*

self-gov-ern-ment /ˌsɛlfˈgʌvənmənt/ *n* [*U*] : government or control of a country, group, etc., by its own members — **self-gov-ern-ing** /ˌsɛlfˈgʌvənɪŋ/ *adj* • *a self-governing territory/body*

self-help /ˈsɛlfˈhɛlp/ *n* [*U*] : the action or process of improving yourself or solving your problems without the help of others — **self-help** *adj, always before a noun* • *self-help books*

self-im-age /ˈsɛlfˈɪmɪdʒ/ *n* [*U*] : the way you think about yourself and your abilities or appearance • *She has a positive/poor self-image.*

self-im-por-tant /ˌsɛlfɪmˈpoətənt/ *adj, disapproving* : having too high an opinion of your own importance • *a self-important businessman* — **self-im-por-tance** /ˌsɛlfɪmˈpoətns/ *n* [*U*]

self-im-posed /ˌsɛlfɪmˈpouzd/ *adj* : required by you of yourself • *a self-imposed deadline/punishment*

self-in-dul-gent /ˌsɛlfɪnˈdʌldʒənt/ *adj, disapproving* : allowing yourself to have or do whatever you want in a way that is excessive or wasteful • *a self-indulgent lifestyle/millionaire* — **self-in-dul-gence** /ˌsɛlfɪnˈdʌldʒəns/ *n* [*C/U*]

self-in-flict-ed /ˌsɛlfɪnˈflɪktəd/ *adj* : caused by your own actions • *a self-inflicted wound*

self-in-ter-est /ˌsɛlfˈɪntrəst/ *n* [*U*] **1** *disapproving* : concern only for getting what you want or need • *They acted out of self-interest.* **2** : your own interest or advantage • *Our self-interest demands that we help them.* [=it benefits us to help them] — **self-in-ter-est-ed** /ˌsɛlfˈɪntrəstəd/ *adj* • *self-interested behavior/politicians*

self-ish /ˈsɛlfɪʃ/ *adj, disapproving* : having or showing concern only for yourself and not for the needs or feelings of other people • *selfish behavior/children* — **self-ish-ly** *adv* • *I acted selfishly.* — **self-ish-ness** *n* [*U*]

self-less /ˈsɛlfləs/ *adj* : having or showing great concern for other people and little or no concern for yourself • *selfless love/acts* — **self-less-ly** *adv*

self-made /ˈsɛlfˈmeɪd/ *adj* : made rich and successful by your own efforts • *a self-made man*

self-pity /ˈsɛlfˈpɪti/ *n* [*U*] *disapproving* : a state of feeling sad for yourself because you believe you have suffered too much • *He was wallowing in self-pity.* — **self-pity-ing** /ˈsɛlfˈpɪtiɪŋ/ *adj* • *a self-pitying complainer*

self-por-trait /ˈsɛlfˈpoətrət/ *n* [*C*] : a painting or drawing of yourself that is done by yourself

self-pos-sessed /ˌsɛlfpəˈzɛst/ *adj* : having or showing control of your feelings or actions especially in a difficult situation • *a self-possessed young woman* — **self-pos-ses-sion** /ˌsɛlfpəˈzɛʃən/ *n* [*U*]

self-pres-er-va-tion /ˌsɛlfˌprɛzəˈveɪʃən/ *n* [*U*] : protection of yourself from harm or death • *We all have an instinct for self-preservation.*

self-pro-claimed /ˌsɛlfprouˈkleɪmd/ *adj, always before a noun, usually disapproving* : giving yourself a particular name, title, etc. • *the self-proclaimed king of pop* • *a self-proclaimed expert*

self-pro-fessed /ˌsɛlfprəˈfɛst/ *adj, always before a noun, usually disapproving* **1** : SELF-PROCLAIMED **2** : SELF-CONFESSED

self-pro-pelled /ˌsɛlfprəˈpɛld/ *adj* : able to move itself by means of a motor • *a self-propelled lawn mower*

self-rais-ing flour /ˈsɛlfˈreɪzɪŋ-/ *n* [*U*] *Brit* : SELF-RISING FLOUR

self-re-li-ant /ˌsɛlfrɪˈlajənt/ *adj* : not needing help from other people • *a self-reliant adult* — **self-re-li-ance** /ˌsɛlfrɪˈlajəns/ *n* [*U*]

self-re-spect /ˌsɛlfrɪˈspɛkt/ *n* [*U*] : proper respect for yourself as a human being • *I lost my job, but not my self-respect.* — **self-re-spect-ing** /ˌsɛlfrɪˈspɛktɪŋ/ *adj, always before a noun* • *No self-respecting person would say that.*

self-re-straint /ˌsɛlfrɪˈstreɪnt/ *n* [*U*] : control over your own actions or feelings that keeps you from doing things you want to do but should not do • *I know you like to shop, but you need to exercise/show some self-restraint.*

self-righ-teous /ˌsɛlfˈraɪtʃəs/ *adj, disapproving* : having or showing a strong belief that your own actions, opinions, etc., are right and other people's are wrong • *a self-righteous person/tone* — **self-righ-teous-ly** *adv* — **self-righ-teous-ness** *n* [*U*]

self-ris-ing flour /ˈsɛlfˈraɪzɪŋ-/ *n* [*U*] *US* : a mixture of flour, salt, and baking powder

self-rule /ˈsɛlfˈruːl/ *n* [*U*] : SELF-GOVERNMENT

self-sac-ri-fice /ˈsɛlfˈsækrəˌfaɪs/ *n* [*U*] : the act of giving up something in order to help someone else • *the courage and self-sacrifice of soldiers* — **self-sac-ri-fic-ing** /ˈsɛlfˈsækrəˌfaɪsɪŋ/ *adj* • *self-sacrificing parents*

self-sat-is-fac-tion /ˌsɛlfˌsætəsˈfækʃən/ *n* [*U*] *usually disapproving* : a feeling of being very pleased or satisfied with yourself — **self-sat-is-fied** /ˌsɛlfˈsætəsˌfaɪd/ *adj* • *a self-satisfied smirk*

self-ser-vice /ˌsɛlfˈsəvəs/ *adj* : allowing or requiring customers to serve themselves without help from workers • *a self-service gas station* — **self-service** *n* [*U*]

self-serv-ing /ˌsɛlfˈsəvɪŋ/ *adj, disapproving* : having or showing concern only about your own needs and interests • *self-serving motives/politicians*

self-start-er /ˌsɛlfˈstaətə/ *n* [*C*] : a person who is able to work without needing a lot of instruction or help

self-styled /ˌsɛlfˈstajəld/ *adj, always be-*

fore a noun : SELF-PROCLAIMED ▪ *self-styled experts*

self–suf·fi·cient /ˌsɛlfsə'fɪʃənt/ *adj* : able to live or function without help or support from others ▪ *self-sufficient farmers/farms* — **self–suf·fi·cien·cy** /ˌsɛlfsə'fɪʃənsi/ *n* [U]

self–sup·port·ing /ˌsɛlfsə'poɚtɪŋ/ *adj* : earning enough money to live without getting help from other people ▪ *self-supporting college students*

self–taught /'sɛlf'tɑːt/ *adj* **1** : educated by your own efforts (such as by reading books) rather than by a teacher ▪ *a self-taught musician* **2** : learned by your own efforts ▪ *self-taught knowledge*

self–worth /'sɛlf'wɚθ/ *n* [U] : SELF-ESTEEM

sell /'sɛl/ *vb* **sold** /'sould/; **sell·ing 1** [T/I] : to exchange (something) for money ▪ *She sold him a watch (for $20). = She sold a watch to him (for $20).* ▪ *Now is a good time to sell (your stocks).* **2** [T] : to make (something) available to be bought ▪ *Only a few stores sell that brand of paint.* ▪ *She sells insurance.* = *She has a job selling insurance.* ▪ *He is selling his car for $1,000.* **3** [I] : to be able to be bought for a particular price ▪ *Those cookies sell for a dollar apiece.* ▪ *items selling at half price* **4** a [I] : to be bought by someone or by many people ▪ *That house still hasn't sold.* [=no one has bought that house] ▪ *The dictionary is selling well.* [=many people are buying the dictionary] **b** [T] — used to say how many copies of something have been sold ▪ *The album sold more than a million copies.* **5** [T/I] : to cause people to want to buy (something) ▪ *His name on the cover sells the book.* **6** [T] : to persuade someone to accept or approve of (something or someone) ▪ *He had difficulty selling his theory to other scientists.* ▪ *You will really have to sell yourself at the job interview.* — **sell off** [*phrasal vb*] **sell (something) off** or **sell off (something)** : to sell (something) especially in order to get rid of it quickly or to get money that you need ▪ *They sold off some of their property.* — **sell on** [*phrasal vb*] **sell (someone) on** : to persuade (someone) to be interested in and excited about (something) ▪ *He tried to sell them on the idea.* ▪ *She wasn't sold on the idea.* — **sell out** [*phrasal vb*] **1** a : to be bought until no more are available ▪ *Tickets to the concert (were) sold out quickly.* **b** : to sell the entire amount of something ▪ *The concert/store sold out quickly.* ▪ *"Are there any more tickets?" "No, we are (all) sold out."* [=we have sold all the tickets] **2** *disapproving* : to do something that does not agree with your beliefs, values, etc., especially in order to make money ▪ *Fans accused the band of selling out when they appeared in a TV commercial.* ▪ *The union sees the deal as selling out to management.* **3** **sell (someone) out** or **sell out (someone)** *informal* : to betray (someone) ▪ *She sold out her accomplices* [=she told police who her accomplices were] *in exchange for a lower prison sentence.* — **sell (someone) down the river** *informal* : to betray

(someone) ▪ *I can't believe my friend would sell me down the river.* — **sell (someone or something) short** : to put too low a value on the ability, importance, or quality of (someone or something) ▪ *Don't sell yourself short. You have some great skills.* — **sell up** [*phrasal vb*] *Brit* : to sell your possessions, business, etc., especially so that you can move away ▪ *They were forced to sell up and go out of business.* — **sell your soul (to the devil)** : to gain wealth, success, power, etc., by doing something bad or dishonest ▪ *He has sold his soul for fame.* — **sell** *n* [C] *chiefly US* ▪ *We need to raise taxes, but that will be a tough sell.* [=it will be difficult to get people to accept that]

sell·er /'sɛlɚ/ *n* [C] **1** : a person or business that sells something ▪ *a ticket seller* ▪ *the seller of the car* **2** : a product that sells in a particular way or amount ▪ *Her new CD is a hot/big seller.* [=many people are buying her new CD]

selling point *n* [C] : a quality or feature that makes people want to buy something ▪ *The house's main selling point is its location.*

sell·out /'sɛlˌaʊt/ *n* [C] **1** : a game, concert, etc., for which all seats are sold ▪ *The concert was a sellout.* **2** a : an occurrence in which you do something that does not agree with your beliefs, values, etc., especially in order to make money ▪ *The union sees the deal as a sellout.* **b** : someone who does something that does not agree with that person's beliefs or values especially in order to make money ▪ *Angry fans called him a sellout.*

selt·zer /'sɛltsɚ/ *n* [U] : water that has bubbles added to it

selves *plural of* SELF

se·man·tic /sɪ'mæntɪk/ *adj* : of or relating to the meanings of words and phrases ▪ *semantic confusion* — **se·man·ti·cal·ly** /sɪ'mæntɪkli/ *adv* ▪ *semantically related words*

se·man·tics /sɪ'mæntɪks/ *n* [U] *linguistics* : the meanings of words and phrases in a particular context ▪ *The controversy is a matter of semantics.* [=it was caused by people understanding the same words in different ways]

sem·blance /'sɛmbləns/ *n* [*singular*] : the state of being like something but not truly or fully the same thing ▪ *Her life finally returned to some semblance of order/normality.*

se·men /'siːmən/ *n* [U] : the liquid containing sperm that is produced by a male's sex organs

se·mes·ter /sə'mɛstɚ/ *n* [C] *US* : one of two periods that make up the time during a year when a school has classes

semi /'sɛˌmaɪ/ *n, pl* **sem·is** [C] *informal* **1** : SEMIFINAL — usually plural ▪ *The team made it to the semis.* **2** *US* : SEMITRAILER **2** /'sɛmi/ *Brit* : a house that is attached to another house : a semidetached house

semi- *prefix* **1** : half ▪ *a semicircle* **2** : happening twice during a period of time ▪ *semimonthly* **3** : partly : not completely ▪ *semiformal* **4** : partial : not complete ▪ *semiconsciousness*

semi·an·nu·al /ˌsɛmiˈænjəwəl/ adj, chiefly US : happening or produced twice in each year • a semiannual sale/visit — **semi·an·nu·al·ly** adv

semi·au·to·mat·ic /ˌsɛmiˌɑːtoˈmætɪk/ adj, of a gun : able to fire bullets one after the other quickly but not automatically • a semiautomatic rifle — **semiau·to·mat·ic** n [C]

semi·cir·cle /ˈsɛmiˌsɚkəl/ n [C] : half of a circle • The children sat in a semicircle. — **semi·cir·cu·lar** /ˌsɛmiˈsɚkjələ/ adj

semi·co·lon /ˈsɛmiˌkoʊlən/ n [C] : the punctuation mark ; that is used to separate major parts in a sentence

semi·con·duc·tor /ˌsɛmikənˈdʌktɚ/ n [C] : a material or object that allows some electricity or heat to move through it and that is used in electronic devices

semi·con·scious /ˌsɛmiˈkɑːnʃəs/ adj : partially awake and able to understand what is happening around you • a semiconscious patient

semi·de·tached /ˌsɛmɪdɪˈtætʃt/ adj, Brit : attached to another house by a shared wall on one side • a semidetached house

semi·fi·nal /ˈsɛmiˌfaɪnl/ n [C] : either one of two matches, games, or contests to decide which people or teams will be in the final part of a competition • She lost in the semifinals. • She won in the quarterfinals but lost in the semifinals. • the semifinal round — **semi·fi·nal·ist** /ˌsɛmiˈfaɪnlɪst/ n [C]

semi·for·mal /ˌsɛmiˈfoɚməl/ adj US : somewhat formal • a semiformal dress/dinner

semi·month·ly /ˌsɛmiˈmʌnθli/ adj : happening or produced two times in each month • a semimonthly meeting/newsletter

sem·i·nal /ˈsɛmənl/ adj 1 formal : having a strong influence on ideas, events, etc., that come later • a seminal book/writer 2 always before a noun, medical : of or containing semen • seminal fluid

sem·i·nar /ˈsɛməˌnɑɚ/ n [C] 1 : a meeting in which you receive information on and training in a particular subject • a writing/investment seminar 2 : a class offered to a small group of students at a college or university • a graduate seminar

sem·i·nary /ˈsɛməˌneri, Brit ˈsɛmənəri/ n, pl **-nar·ies** [C] : a school for training priests, rabbis, etc. — **sem·i·nar·i·an** /ˌsɛməˈnerijən/ n [C] • his fellow seminarians

Sem·ite /ˈsɛˌmaɪt, Brit ˈsiːˌmaɪt/ n [C] : a member of a group of people that includes Jews and Arabs — **Se·mit·ic** /səˈmɪtɪk/ adj

semi·tone /ˈsɛmiˌtoʊn/ n [C] music : a difference in sound that is equal to ¹⁄₁₂ of an octave

semi·trail·er /ˈsɛˌmaɪˌtreɪlɚ/ n [C] US 1 : a long trailer that has wheels at the rear and is attached at its forward end to a large truck 2 : a large truck with a long trailer attached to the back of it

semi·week·ly /ˌsɛmiˈwiːkli/ adj : happening twice a week • semiweekly classes

sem·o·li·na /ˌsɛməˈliːnə/ n [U] 1 : a type of wheat flour 2 Brit : a sweet dessert made from semolina and milk

sen. abbr 1 Senate; senator 2 senior

Sen·ate /ˈsɛnət/ n — **the Senate** 1 : the smaller group of the two groups of people who meet to discuss and make the laws of a country, state, etc. • the U.S. Senate • The Senate approved the bill. • the New York State Senate 2 : the group of officials who led the ancient Roman government

sen·a·tor /ˈsɛnətɚ/ n [C] : a member of the Senate • a former senator • Senator Smith — **sen·a·to·ri·al** /ˌsɛnəˈtorijəl/ adj • senatorial offices/candidates

send /ˈsɛnd/ vb **sent** /ˈsɛnt/; **send·ing** [T] 1 : to cause (a letter, package, signal, etc.) to go from one place or person to another • He sent me an e-mail. = He sent an e-mail to me. • I sent (off) the package yesterday. • Satellites receive signals in space and send them back to Earth. • Please **send** in your poems [=mail your poems to us] by May 1. 2 : to give (a message) to someone • Please send my compliments to the chef. [=tell the chef that I enjoyed the food] • Tell her that I send my love. 3 : to tell or cause (someone or something) to go to a place • She became ill and was sent home from school. • He was sent to prison. • He asked us to send a taxi for him. • Police were **sent** in to restore order. 4 : to make arrangements that allow (someone) to attend a school, camp, etc. • They send their children to private school. • They sent their daughter to soccer camp. 5 : to tell (someone or something) to go to a particular person or place for treatment, help, etc. • She sent him to the information desk. • My doctor sent me to a specialist. 6 : to cause (someone or something) to move in a particular direction or manner • The surprise attack sent the enemy running. • The punch sent him to the floor. • Her performance **sent** a chill/shiver up/down my spine. [=made me feel very excited and emotional] 7 : to put (someone) into a particular state or condition • Their decision **sent** him into a rage. — **send away** for [phrasal vb] **send away for** or **send away to** (someone) **for** : to ask to receive (something) by sending a letter, coupon, etc., to someone by mail • I sent away for a free sample. • Send away to the manufacturer for a refund. — **send down** [phrasal vb] **send down (someone)** or **send (someone) down** Brit, informal : to send (someone) to prison • He was sent down for six years for the robbery. — **send for** [phrasal vb] 1 : to ask (someone) to come to a place • Someone should send for a doctor. 2 : to ask someone to bring or send (something) to you • Send for our free catalog. • She sent for help. — **send forth** [phrasal vb] formal : to cause (light, heat, sound, etc.) to move outward from a source • The flowers sent forth a sweet fragrance. — **send off** [phrasal vb] : to ask to receive (something) by sending a letter, coupon, etc., to someone by mail • I sent off for a sample. — **send out** [phrasal vb] 1 **send out (something)** or **send (something) out a** : to mail (something) to many different people or places • Have *you sent out the invitations yet?* **b** : to cause (a signal) to go out • *The pilot sent out a distress signal.* **c** : to cause (light, heat, sound, etc.) to move outward from a source • *The coals sent out a reddish glow.* **d** : to produce (something) in the process of growing or developing • *plants sending out new shoots* **2 send out for** : to ask a restaurant to deliver (food) to you • *We sent out for pizza.* — **send (someone or something) packing** *informal* : to force (someone or something) to leave a place or situation • *We were sent packing after the first day of try-outs.* — **send up** [*phrasal vb*] **1 send up (something) or send up (something)** **a** : to cause (something) to move upward • *The fire sent up sparks.* **b** : to produce (something) in the process of growing or developing • *plants sending up new shoots* **c** : to suggest or propose (something) to a more powerful person or group • *The bill has been sent up to the Senate for a vote.* **2 send up (someone or something) or send (someone or something) up** *chiefly Brit, informal* : to imitate (someone or something) in an amusing way : PARODY • *The show sends up soap operas.* — **send·er** /ˈsɛndɚ/ *n* [C]

send-off /ˈsɛnd͵ɑːf/ *n* [C] : an occasion when people gather together to say goodbye to someone who is leaving • *A crowd of friends gave them a fine send-off.*

se·nile /ˈsiːˌnajəl/ *adj* : showing a loss of mental ability (such as memory) in old age • *a senile man* • *She is becoming/going senile.* — **se·nil·i·ty** /sɪˈnɪləti/ *n* [U]

¹se·nior /ˈsiːnjɚ/ *adj* **1** *not before a noun, US* **a** : older in age • *She is five years senior to me.* [=she is five years older than I am] **b** — used chiefly in its abbreviated form *Sr.* to identify a father who has the same name as his son • *John Smith, Jr. and John Smith, Sr.* **2** : higher in standing or rank • *a senior officer/manager* • *He is senior to me.* **3** *always before a noun* : of, relating to, designed for, or done by older people • *senior centers/housing/golf*

²senior *n* [C] **1** : a person who is older than another person • *She is five years my senior.* = *She is my senior by five years.* **2** : a person who is of a higher rank than another person • *She was his senior in rank.* **3** *US* : a student in the final year of high school or college • *the senior class/prom* • *She's in her senior year in college.* **4** *chiefly US* : SENIOR CITIZEN

senior citizen *n* [C] *chiefly US* : an old person • *programs/activities for senior citizens*

senior high school *n* [C] *US* : HIGH SCHOOL 1

se·nior·i·ty /sinˈjɔrəti/ *n* [U] **1** : the amount of time you have worked at a job or for a company compared to other employees • *Promotions are based on merit and seniority.* • *He has worked here longer than I have, so he has seniority over me.* **2** : the state of having a higher rank than another person • *a position of seniority*

sen·sa·tion /sɛnˈseɪʃən/ *n* **1** [C] : a particular feeling or effect that your body

experiences • *a tingling sensation in the arm* • *a sensation of hunger* **2** [C] : a particular feeling or experience that may not have a real cause • *She had the strange sensation that someone was watching her.* **3** [U] : the ability to feel things through your physical senses • *Her injury left her with no sensation in her legs.* **4** [C] **a** : a lot of excitement and interest • *The news created (quite) a sensation.* **b** : someone or something that causes a lot of excitement and interest • *a music/pop sensation*

sen·sa·tion·al /sɛnˈseɪʃənl/ *adj* **1** : causing great interest with shocking details • *sensational news stories* **2** : excellent or great • *a sensational performance/idea* **3** *informal* : very attractive • *You look sensational tonight.* — **sen·sa·tion·al·ly** *adv*

sen·sa·tion·al·ism /sɛnˈseɪʃənəˌlɪzəm/ *n* [U] *disapproving* : the use of shocking details to cause a lot of interest • *The network was accused of sensationalism in its reporting.* — **sen·sa·tion·al·ist** /sɛnˈseɪʃənəlɪst/ *also chiefly US* **sen·sa·tion·al·is·tic** /sɛnˌseɪʃənəˈlɪstɪk/ *adj* • *sensationalist reporting*

sen·sa·tion·al·ize *also Brit* **sen·sa·tion·al·ise** /sɛnˈseɪʃənəˌlaɪz/ *vb* **-ized; -iz·ing** [T] *disapproving* : to describe or show (something) in a way that makes it seem more shocking than it really is • *The reporter sensationalized the story.*

¹sense /ˈsɛns/ *n* **1** [C] : one of the five natural powers (touch, taste, smell, sight, and hearing) through which you receive information about the world around you • *The dog lost his sense of smell.* **2 a** [*singular*] : a particular feeling • *We had a sense that something wasn't right.* • *a sense of fatigue/relief/accomplishment* **b** [C] : a personal quality • *Where's your sense of adventure?* • *She has a great sense of humor.* [=she says funny things and can see the funny side of things] • *his excellent sense of direction* [=his ability to find his way around easily in a new place] **3** [*plural*] : the ability to think clearly or in a reasonable way • *He came to his senses and decided not to quit his job.* • *We hoped she could bring him to his senses.* [=make him act sensibly] • *(chiefly Brit) Are you out of your senses?* [=out of your mind] **4** [U] : an awareness of what is appropriate and what should be done • *She had the (good) sense to stop before she said too much.* • *(informal) I tried to knock some sense into her.* = *I tried to talk sense to her.* [=to cause her to stop thinking or behaving foolishly] **5** [U] : a reason for something • *There's no sense in waiting.* • *I fail to see the sense of/in that decision.* **6** [C] : a way of understanding something • *In a/one sense* [=from one point of view], *you're correct.* • *In some senses* [=in some ways], *it was a wasted effort.* • *The book is in no sense* [=the book is definitely not] *intended for beginners.* **7** [C] : the meaning of a word, phrase, etc. • *Many words have more than one sense.* • *The book is a classic in every sense of the word.* [=in every possible way] — **make (any) sense of**

: to understand (something) • *We couldn't make (any) sense of the instructions.* — **make sense 1** : to have a clear meaning : to be easy to understand • *The instructions don't make any sense.* = *The instructions make no sense.* • *You're not making much sense (to me).* [=I can't understand what you're saying] **2** : to be reasonable • *It makes sense to leave early to avoid traffic.* • *It makes little/no sense* [=it is not reasonable] *to continue.* — **take leave of your senses** see ²LEAVE

²**sense** *vb* **sensed; sens·ing** [T] **1** : to understand or be aware of (something) without being told about it or having evidence that it is true • *We sensed danger.* • *She sensed what was going on.* • *I sense that you're worried.* **2** *of a machine* : to detect the presence or occurrence of (something) • *A motion detector senses movement.*

sense·less /ˈsɛnsləs/ *adj* **1** : done or happening for no reason • *a senseless crime/death* **2** : badly hurt and no longer conscious • *I was knocked senseless by the fall.* [=I fell and hit my head and lost consciousness] • *He was beaten senseless.* [=he was beaten until he was unconscious] **3** : stupid or foolish • *a senseless fool/joke* — **sense·less·ly** *adv*

sense organ *n* [C] : a part of your body (such as your eyes, ears, nose, or tongue) that you use to see, hear, smell, taste, or feel things

sen·si·bil·i·ty /ˌsɛnsəˈbɪləti/ *n, pl* **-ties** *formal* **1** [C] : the kinds of feelings that you have when you hear, see, read, or think about something • *offending the audience's sensibilities* [=upsetting the audience] **2** [C] : the kinds of feelings that a certain type of person tends to have • *The show seems out of line with modern sensibilities.* [=seems strange or offensive to modern people] **3** [C/U] : the ability to feel and understand emotions • *She's a woman of artistic sensibility.*

sen·si·ble /ˈsɛnsəbəl/ *adj* **1** : having or showing good sense or judgment : REASONABLE • *sensible prices/advice/diets* • *She was sensible enough to stop driving when she got too tired.* **2** : designed to be comfortable, useful, etc., rather than stylish • *sensible shoes* — **sen·si·bly** /ˈsɛnsəbli/ *adv*

sen·si·tive /ˈsɛnsətɪv/ *adj* **1 a** : easily upset by the things that people think or say about you • *a sensitive child* • *He is sensitive about his weight.* **b** : likely to cause people to become upset • *sensitive issues* **2** : aware of and understanding the feelings of other people • *a sensitive, caring person* • *She is sensitive to the fears of her patients.* **3** : easily affected by something in a way that is not pleasant or good • *sensitive skin/teeth* **4** *technical* **a** : able to sense very small changes in something • *a highly sensitive instrument* **b** : changing in response to something • *light-sensitive film = film that is sensitive to light* **5** : needing to be handled in a careful or secret way in order to protect someone or something • *highly sensitive information* — **sen·si·tive·ly**

adv — **sen·si·tiv·i·ty** /ˌsɛnsəˈtɪvəti/ *n, pl* **-ties** [C/U] • *his sensitivity about his weight* • *a sensitivity to light* • *the sensitivity of the instrument/document*

sen·si·tize *also Brit* **sen·si·tise** /ˈsɛnsəˌtaɪz/ *vb* **-tized; -tiz·ing** [T] : to make (someone or something) sensitive or more sensitive • *The program is intended to sensitize students to the dangers of drug use.* • *sensitized skin*

sen·sor /ˈsɛnˌsoɚ, ˈsɛnsɚ/ *n* [C] : a device that detects or senses heat, light, sound, etc. • *a motion sensor*

sen·so·ry /ˈsɛnsɚi/ *adj* : of or relating to your physical senses • *sensory stimulation/perception*

sen·su·al /ˈsɛnʃəwəl/ *adj* : relating to, devoted to, or producing physical or sexual pleasure • *sensual desires* • *a very sensual person* — **sen·su·al·i·ty** /ˌsɛnʃəˈwæləti/ *n* [U] — **sen·su·al·ly** /ˈsɛnʃəwəli/ *adv*

sen·su·ous /ˈsɛnʃəwəs/ *adj* : affecting the senses in a pleasing way • *sensuous music* • *a gentle, sensuous breeze* — **sen·su·ous·ly** *adv* — **sen·su·ous·ness** *n* [U]

sent *past tense and past participle of* SEND

¹**sen·tence** /ˈsɛntn̩s/ *n* **1** [C] : a group of words that expresses a statement, question, command, or wish, and that usually contains a subject and a verb ✧ In written English, the first word of a sentence is capitalized and the sentence ends with a period, question mark, or exclamation point. **2** [C/U] *law* : the punishment given by a court of law • *He is serving a 10-year prison sentence for armed robbery.*

²**sentence** *vb* **-tenced; -tenc·ing** [T] *law* : to officially state the punishment given to (someone) by a court of law • *The judge sentenced him to prison.* • *They will return to court for sentencing.* [=to hear what her punishment will be]

sentence fragment *n* [C] *grammar* : a group of words that is written out as a sentence but that lacks a subject or verb

sen·tient /ˈsɛnʃijənt/ *adj, technical + formal* : able to feel, see, hear, smell, or taste • *sentient beings*

sen·ti·ment /ˈsɛntəmənt/ *n* **1** [C/U] : an attitude or opinion • *antiwar sentiments* • *"The lecture was much too long." "My sentiments exactly!"* [=I agree with you completely] **2** [U] : feelings of love, sympathy, kindness, etc. • *There's no room for sentiment in the business world.*

sen·ti·men·tal /ˌsɛntəˈmɛntl̩/ *adj* **1** : based on, showing, or resulting from feelings or emotions • *He has a sentimental attachment to that old shirt.* • *The picture has sentimental value for me.* [=is important to me because of its connection with a happy time of life, a special person, etc.] **2 a** : appealing to the emotions especially in an excessive way • *a sentimental melodrama* **b** : having or expressing strong feelings of love, sadness, etc. • *a sentimental person* • *I get sentimental when I think about my childhood.* — **sen·ti·men·tal·i·ty** /ˌsɛntəˌmɛnˈtæləti/ *n* [U] • *the sentimentality of Romantic poetry* — **sen·ti·men·tal·ly** *adv*

sen·ti·nel /'sɛntənəl/ n [C] : SENTRY • armed sentinels

sen·try /'sɛntri/ n, pl **-tries** [C] : a soldier who guards a door, gate, etc. • A policeman stood sentry [=acted as a guard] by the door.

Sep. abbr September

¹**sep·a·rate** /'sɛpərət/ adj **1** : not joined, connected, or combined : placed or kept apart • two separate buildings • There are separate restrooms for men and women. • They have separate bank accounts. • She keeps her private life and public life separate (from each other). **2** : not related • That's an entirely separate issue. : different from something else • I met him on four separate occasions. • After dinner we will go our separate ways. [=we will go in different directions] • (figurative) After 20 years of marriage, they went their separate ways. [=they ended their marriage]

²**sep·a·rate** /'sɛpəˌreɪt/ vb **-rat·ed; -rat·ing 1** [T/I] : to stop or to cause (people or things) to stop being together, joined, or connected : to make (people or things) separate or to become separate • He separated the fighters (from each other). • A river separates the two towns. = The two towns are separated by a river. • The class separated into small groups. • The oil separated from the water. • My sister and her husband are separated. [=they are no longer living with each other as a couple] • This is the point in the competition where we **separate the men from the boys**. [=show which people are really strong, brave, etc., and which are not] **2** [T] : to see or describe the differences between (two things) • separating fact and/from fiction **3** [T] : to make (people or things) different in some way • Our ability to reason is what separates us from animals. **4** [T] — used to describe the difference in the scores or positions of people or teams in a race, game, etc. • One goal separated the teams at the end of the period. — **separate off** [phrasal vb] **separate (someone or something) off** or **separate off (someone or something)** : to cause (someone or something) to be separate from other people or things • He separated himself off from the crowd. — **sep·a·ra·tor** /'sɛpəˌreɪtə/ n [C]

sep·a·rate·ly /'sɛpərətli/ adv : not together with someone or something else • The software is sold separately from the hardware. • The professor met with each student separately.

sep·a·ra·tion /ˌsɛpəˈreɪʃən/ n **1** [C/U] : the act of separating people or things or the state of being separated • a separation of 30 years from her family • The U.S. Constitution calls for the **separation of church and state**. [=calls for government and religion to be kept separate from each other] **2** [C] : a situation in which a husband and wife live apart from each other • She wanted a separation from her husband.

Sept. abbr September

Sep·tem·ber /sɛpˈtɛmbə/ n [C/U] : the ninth month of the year • in (early/late) September • on September the fifth = (US) on September fifth = on the fifth of Sep-

tember • They moved last September. — abbr. Sep. or Sept.

sep·tic /'sɛptɪk/ adj, chiefly Brit, medical : infected with bacteria • a septic leg

septic tank n [C] : a tank under the ground that holds human waste from toilets

se·pul·chral /səˈpʌlkrəl/ adj **1** literary : very sad and serious • sepulchral silence **2** always before a noun : of or relating to a sepulchre • a sepulchral inscription

sep·ul·chre or US **sep·ul·cher** /'sɛpəlkə/ n [C] old-fashioned : TOMB

se·quel /'siːkwəl/ n [C] **1** : a book, movie, etc., that continues a story begun in another book, movie, etc. **2** : something that happens after something else • There is an interesting sequel to my date with her.

se·quence /'siːkwəns/ n **1** [C/U] : the order in which things happen or should happen • a sequence of events • The pages were out of sequence. [=not in order] **2** [C] : SERIES 1 • a sequence of numbers **3** [C] : a part of a movie, television show, etc., that deals with one subject, action, or idea • a chase sequence in a spy movie • I enjoyed the movie's opening sequence.

se·quen·tial /sɪˈkwɛnʃəl/ adj, formal **1** : of, relating to, or arranged in a particular order or sequence • Put the cards in sequential order. **2** : happening in a series • sequential events — **se·quen·tial·ly** adv

se·ques·ter /sɪˈkwɛstə/ vb [T] : to keep (a person or group) apart from other people • The jury was sequestered until a verdict was reached. • She was sequestered in her room. — **se·ques·tra·tion** /ˌsiːkwəˈstreɪʃən/ n [U]

se·quin /'siːkwən/ n [C] : a small piece of shiny metal or plastic that is sewn onto clothes as a decoration — **se·quined** or **se·quinned** /'siːkwənd/ adj • a sequined dress

se·quoia /sɪˈkwojə/ n [C] : a very tall evergreen tree that grows in California

sera plural of SERUM

ser·e·nade /ˌsɛrəˈneɪd/ n [C] : a love song that is sung or played outdoors at night for someone — **serenade** vb **-nad·ed; -nad·ing** [T] • He serenaded her. [=he sang/played a serenade for her]

ser·en·dip·i·ty /ˌsɛrənˈdɪpəti/ n [U] literary : luck that takes the form of finding valuable or pleasant things that are not looked for • They found each other by pure serendipity. — **ser·en·dip·i·tous** /ˌsɛrənˈdɪpətəs/ adj • a serendipitous discovery

se·rene /səˈriːn/ adj : calm and peaceful • serene faces/music — **se·rene·ly** adv — **se·ren·i·ty** /səˈrɛnəti/ n [U] • a feeling of peace and serenity

serf /'sɚf/ n [C] : a person in the past who lived and worked on land owned by another person • medieval serfs — **serf·dom** /'sɚfdəm/ n [U]

ser·geant /'sɑɚdʒənt/ n [C] **1** : an officer of low rank in the army or marines **2** : an officer in a police force with a rank below captain or lieutenant

¹**se·ri·al** /'sirijəl/ adj, always before a noun **1** : arranged or happening in a series •

Scientists made serial observations over a period of two weeks. **2 a** *of a crime* : committed many times usually in the same way ▪ *serial murders* **b** *of a criminal* : committing a series of crimes ▪ *a serial killer* **3** : broadcast or published in separate parts over a period of time ▪ *a serial novel/publication* — **se·ri·al·ly** *adv*

²**serial** *n* [C] : a story that is broadcast on TV or radio or that is published in a magazine in separate parts over a period of time ▪ *a daytime television serial*

serial number *n* [C] : a number that is put on a product and that is used to identify it ▪ *a computer's serial number*

se·ries /ˈsiriːz/ *n, pl* **series** [C] **1** : a number of things or events that are arranged or happen one after the other ▪ *the summer concert series* ▪ *a series of tests/problems* **2** : a set of TV shows, books, etc., that involve the same group of characters or the same subject ▪ *a TV series on the history of baseball* ▪ *a comic book series* **3** *sports* : a set of games that are played between two teams one after the other on different days ▪ *a three-game series*

se·ri·ous /ˈsirijəs/ *adj* **1** : having an important or dangerous possible result ▪ *a serious injury/mistake* **2** : involving or deserving a lot of thought, attention, or work ▪ *serious questions/conversations* ▪ *a serious contender for the championship* **3** : giving a lot of attention or energy to something ▪ *serious musicians/journalists* ▪ *He's very serious about fishing.* **4** : not joking or funny ▪ *a serious story* ▪ *She is serious about moving.* [=she truly intends to move] ▪ *"I'm joining the army." "You can't be serious."* [=I can't believe that] **5** *always before a noun, informal* : large or impressive in quality or amount ▪ *He makes serious money.* [=he makes a lot of money] **6** : having or involving strong romantic feelings ▪ *Their relationship is getting serious.* **7** : thoughtful or quiet ▪ *a serious person/expression* — **se·ri·ous·ly** /ˈsirijəsli/ *adv* ▪ *seriously injured/mistaken* ▪ *You should seriously consider buying a new car.* ▪ *You should be a lawyer. Seriously, you would be good at it.* ▪ *Police are taking the matter very seriously.* — **se·ri·ous·ness** /ˈsirijəsnəs/ *n* [U] ▪ *the seriousness of her illness* ▪ *The child's seriousness was surprising.* ▪ *In all seriousness* [=in a serious way]*, if he does propose, what will you say?*

ser·mon /ˈsɚmən/ *n* [C] **1** : a speech about a moral or religious subject ▪ *The priest delivered/gave a sermon on the power of prayer.* **2** *informal + usually disapproving* : a serious talk about how someone should behave ▪ *Dad gave me a sermon about doing my homework.*

ser·mon·ize *also Brit* **ser·mon·ise** /ˈsɚməˌnaɪz/ *vb* **-ized; -iz·ing** [I] : to give a sermon to someone ▪ *talking to students without sermonizing*

ser·pent /ˈsɚpənt/ *n* [C] *literary* : SNAKE

ser·pen·tine /ˈsɚpənˌtiːn, *Brit* ˈsɚːpənˌtaɪn/ *adj* : having many bends and turns ▪ *a serpentine path*

ser·rat·ed /ˈseɚˌeɪtəd, səˈreɪtəd/ *adj*

: having a row of small points or teeth along the side like a saw ▪ *a serrated blade/edge*

se·rum /ˈsirəm/ *n, pl* **se·rums** *or* **se·ra** /ˈsirə/ [U] *medical* : the part of blood that is like water and that contains antibodies ▪ *blood serum*

ser·vant /ˈsɚvənt/ *n* [C] : a person who is hired to do household or personal duties (such as cleaning and cooking) ▪ *domestic/household servants* — see also CIVIL SERVANT, PUBLIC SERVANT

¹**serve** /ˈsɚv/ *vb* **served; serv·ing** **1** [T/I] : to give food or drink to someone at a meal, in a restaurant, etc. ▪ *Soup was served first.* ▪ *The waiter served (us) our meals quickly.* ▪ *a restaurant that serves Italian food* ▪ *Dinner is served.* [=dinner is on the table and ready to be eaten] ▪ *You carve the turkey, and I'll serve.* **2** [T] : to be enough food for (a particular number of people) ▪ *The roast should serve six.* **3** [T] : to provide service to (a customer) ▪ *How can we serve our customers better?* **4** [I] **a** : to be used or seen in a particular way ▪ *The accident serves as a reminder of the dangers of drunk driving.* **b** : to have a particular result or effect ▪ *Her efforts only served to bring attention to her lack of experience.* **5 a** [T] : to be useful or helpful to (someone) ▪ *Her quick wit served her well.* **b** [T/I] : to provide what is needed by or for (someone or something) ▪ *The library serves (the needs of) the community.* ▪ *Arguing with him serves no purpose.* [=is not useful or helpful in any way] ▪ *If (my) memory serves me (right/correctly)* [=if I remember correctly]*, she is from Miami.* ▪ *I do not believe that justice has been served.* [=that proper punishment or fair treatment has been given] **6** [T/I] : to hold a particular office, position, etc. : to perform a duty or job ▪ *They served on the jury.* ▪ *He served as the club's adviser.* ▪ *She is serving in the army.* ▪ *those who serve our country* **7** [T] : to be in prison for or during (a period of time) ▪ *serving a life/10-year sentence* ▪ *He served time (in prison) for drug possession.* **8** [T] *law* : to send or give (someone) official legal papers ▪ *He served her with divorce papers.* **9** [T/I] *sports* : to throw a ball into the air and hit it over a net to start play in tennis, volleyball, etc. ▪ *It's your turn to serve (the ball).* — **first come, first served** *see* ¹FIRST — **serve out** [*phrasal vb*] **serve (something) out** *or* **serve out (something)** : to complete (a term in office, a prison sentence, etc.) ▪ *She has served out her prison sentence.* — **serve (someone) right** — used to say that someone deserves a particular punishment, problem, etc. ▪ *"He won't talk to me." "(It) Serves you right for lying to him."* — **serve up** [*phrasal vb*] **serve up (something)** *or* **serve (something) up** : to give (food) to someone at a meal, in a restaurant, etc. ▪ *The café serves up soup and sandwiches.* ▪ *(figurative) The movie serves up a ton of laughs.* [=the movie is very funny]

²**serve** *n* [C] *sports* : the act or action of

serving a tennis ball, volleyball, etc. ▪ *She has a powerful serve.*

serv·er /ˈsɚvɚ/ *n [C]* **1** *US* : a waiter or waitress ▪ *She asked our server for another glass of wine.* **2** : the main computer in a network which provides files and services that are used by the other computers ▪ *the file/mail/Web server* **3** : the player who begins play in tennis, volleyball, etc., by serving the ball **4** : a tray, spoon, etc., that is used to serve food

¹**ser·vice** /ˈsɚvəs/ *n* **1** *[C]* : an organization, company, or system that provides something to the public ▪ *the National Park Service* ▪ *landscaping/government/ health services* **2** *[C/U]* : work done by an organization or person that does not involve producing goods ▪ *a free delivery service* ▪ *bus/Internet service* ▪ *The lawyer offered his services for free.* **3** *[U]* : work done for a business, organization, country, etc. ▪ *She retired from the company after 34 years of service.* ▪ *military service* **4** *[U]* : the act of helping or serving customers at a restaurant, hotel, store, etc. ▪ *The food was good but the service was slow.* ▪ *excellent customer service* **5** *[U]* : the state of being available for use ▪ *The copier is currently* **out of service.** [=out of order] ▪ *The new planes will be* **put into service** *next year.* **6** *[C/U]* : work that is done to repair something or to keep it in good condition ▪ *He brought his car in for service.* = (*Brit*) *He brought his car in for a service.* **7** *[C]* : a religious ceremony ▪ *a funeral service* **8** *US* **the service** or *Brit* **the services** : a country's army, navy, air force, etc. ▪ *He entered/joined the service when he was 19.* **9** *[C]* : a set of dishes, cups, etc., that match each other ▪ *a tea/china/dinner service* **10** *[C]* *sports* : ²SERVE ▪ *a first/second service* **11** *[U]* *law* : the act of giving legal papers to someone ▪ *the service of a subpoena* — **at someone's service** : ready or available for someone's use ▪ *I am at your service.* — **be of service** : to be helpful or useful to someone ▪ *I am glad to be of service (to you).* — **do (someone) a service** : to do something that helps (someone) ▪ *The journalists did the public a service by exposing the corruption.*

²**service** *vb* **-viced; -vic·ing** *[T]* **1** : to do the work that is needed to keep (a machine or vehicle) in good condition ▪ *I need to get my car serviced.* **2** *technical* : to pay interest on (a loan or debt) ▪ *The company was unable to service the loan.* **3** : to provide (someone) with something that is needed or wanted ▪ *The bookstore primarily services people looking for out-of-print books.*

ser·vice·able /ˈsɚvəsəbəl/ *adj* : ready to use or able to be used ▪ *an old but still serviceable bicycle*

service area *n [C]* *chiefly Brit* : REST AREA

service charge *n [C]* **1** : an amount of money that is charged for a particular service in addition to a basic fee ▪ *Tickets are $25 each plus a $3 service charge per ticket.* **2** *Brit* : a charge added to a bill in a restaurant to pay for the work of the waitress or waiter

ser·vice·man /ˈsɚvəsˌmæn/ *n, pl* **-men** /-ˌmɛn/ *[C]* : a man who is a member of the military

service mark *n [C]* : a name, symbol, etc., that an organization uses to identify its services

service station *n [C]* : GAS STATION

ser·vice·wom·an /ˈsɚvəsˌwʊmən/ *n, pl* **-wom·en** /-ˌwɪmən/ *[C]* : a woman who is a member of the military

ser·vi·ette /ˌsɚviˈɛt/ *n [C]* *Brit* : NAPKIN

ser·vile /ˈsɚvəl, *Brit* ˈsɚˌvaɪl/ *adj, formal + disapproving* : very obedient and trying too hard to please someone ▪ *a servile assistant/attitude* — **ser·vil·i·ty** /sɚˈvɪləti/ *n [U]*

¹**serving** *n [C]* : an amount of food or drink that is enough for one person ▪ *The recipe makes four servings.*

²**serving** *adj, always before a noun* : used to serve food ▪ *a serving bowl/spoon*

ser·vi·tude /ˈsɚvəˌtuːd, *Brit* ˈsɚːvəˌtjuːd/ *n [U]* *formal* : the condition of being a slave or of having to obey another person ▪ *involuntary servitude*

ses·a·me /ˈsɛsəmi/ *n [U]* : a plant that produces small, flat seeds that are used in cooking and as a source of oil ▪ *sesame seeds/oil*

ses·sion /ˈsɛʃən/ *n [C/U]* **1** : a period of time that is used to do a particular activity ▪ *a recording/photo/therapy session* ▪ (*US*) *School will be back* **in session** [=school will start again] *in September.* **2** : a formal meeting or series of meetings ▪ *the U.N. Special Session on Disarmament* ▪ *The board met in* **closed session.** [=with no one else present]

¹**set** /ˈsɛt/ *vb* **set; set·ting** **1** *[T]* : to put (something) in a place or position ▪ *Set your books (down) on the table.* ▪ *He set the ladder against the wall.* ▪ *The tiles are set into the wall.* ▪ *a diamond set in a gold band* **2** *[T]* : to cause the action of (a film, story, etc.) to happen in a certain place or during a certain time ▪ *The novel is set in Italy in 1943.* **3** *[T]* **a** : to put (something) in a position to be used ▪ *set the trap/brake* : to put the controls of (a clock or other device) in a particular position ▪ *setting an alarm/timer* ▪ *Set the oven to 350 degrees.* **b** : to put plates, forks, spoons, knives, etc., on a table before serving a meal ▪ *Would you please set the table?* ▪ *We set an extra place at the table for our guest.* **4** *[T]* : to decide on or choose (something) ▪ *setting limits/rules/ goals/priorities* ▪ *NASA has set the date for the shuttle launch.* ▪ *He has* **set his sights on** *becoming* [=he has decided to try to become] *the next president.* **5** *[T]* : to give (a particular price or value) to something ▪ *He set the price too high.* ▪ *Her bail was set at $10,000.* = *The judge set (her) bail at $10,000.* ▪ *They set a high value on their privacy.* **6** *[T]* : to cause (something) to be accepted as an example, rule, etc. ▪ *They are improving the safety of their vehicles and setting a higher standard for other companies (to follow).* ▪ *Try to set a good example for the rest of the children.* ▪ *He set the world record for/ in the 100-meter dash.* **7** *[T/I]* : to cause (someone or something) to be in a speci-

fied condition or to start doing something • *The slaves were set free.* • *They set the house on fire.* • *The plan has been set in motion.* • *She immediately set to work* [=began working] *on the project.* **8** [*T*] *Brit* : to require someone to do (a job or task) • *She set her students an easy assignment.* **9** [*I*] *of the sun or moon* : to move down in the sky and go below the horizon • *We watched the sun set.* **10 a** [*I*] *of a liquid* : to become thick or hard • *The cement/gelatin needs a few hours to set.* **b** [*T/I*] : to become permanent • *The stain has already set.* **11** [*T/I*] : to put (a broken bone) into its normal position so it can heal • *Doctors set her broken leg.* **12** [*T*] : to type or print (a word, sentence, etc.) in a particular form or style • *a word set in italics* **13** [*T*] : to add music to (words) • *The lyrics were set to music.* — **set about** [*phrasal vb*] : to begin to do (something) • *They set about the task of) creating a new Web site.* — **set against** [*phrasal vb*] **1 set (something) against** : to compare (something) to (something else) • *Let's set the advantages against the disadvantages.* • *The fines are small when set against the company's huge profits.* **2 set (yourself) against** : to be or become opposed to (something or someone) • *He has set himself against (joining) them.* **3 set (someone) against** : to cause (someone) to disagree with or oppose (someone) • *The incident set brother against sister.* — **set apart** [*phrasal vb*] **set (someone or something) apart** : to be a quality that makes (someone or something) better than or different from other people or things • *What sets her apart (from the other teachers) is her enthusiasm.* — **set aside** [*phrasal vb*] **set (something) aside** or **set aside (something)** **1** : to move (something) to the side because you are not working on it, dealing with it, etc. • *Mix the ingredients in a bowl and set the mixture aside.* : to wait until later to use or deal with (something) • *Let's set aside this discussion until our next meeting.* **2** : to keep or save (something) for a particular purpose • *We set some money aside for our vacation.* **3** : to stop thinking about, talking about, or being affected by (something) • *They decided to set aside their differences and work together.* — **set back** [*phrasal vb*] **1 set (something or someone) back** or **set back (something or someone)** : to make the progress of (something or someone) slower or more difficult : to cause (something or someone) to go back to an earlier or worse condition • *setting back progress* • *If the law is reversed, it will set us back 20 years.* **2 set (someone) back** *informal* : ²COST • *A new suit will set you back at least $200.* — **set down** [*phrasal vb*] **1** : to create or establish (a rule, requirement, etc.) • *following the guidelines set down by the organization* **2 set (something) down** or **set down (something)** **a** : to record (something) by writing it down • *She set down her thoughts on paper.* • *setting an agreement down in writing* **b** : to land (an airplane) • *We had to set the plane*

down in a field. — **set forth** [*phrasal vb*] **1** *literary* : to begin a journey • *We will set forth at dawn.* **2 set forth (something)** or **set (something) forth** *formal* : to explain or describe (something) • *The author sets forth the book's premise in its first two pages.* — **set forward** [*phrasal vb*] **set (something) forward** or **set forward (something)** : to explain or describe (something) • *She has set forward a plan to fix the health-care system.* — **set in** [*phrasal vb*] : to begin to be present, seen, etc. • *An infection set in after the surgery.* • *Reality was starting to set in. We were not going to win.* — **set in stone** see ¹STONE — **set off** [*phrasal vb*] **1** : to begin traveling in a particular direction • *We set off for home.* **2 set off (something)** also **set (something) off** : to cause (something) to start or happen • *set off an explosion* • *The incident set off a public debate.* **3 set off (something)** or **set (something) off** **a** : to cause (something) to begin making noise • *The smoke set off the fire alarm.* **b** : to cause (fireworks, a bomb, etc.) to explode • *A bomb was set off.* **c** : to make (something) easy to see or notice • *Yellow police tape set off the crime scene.* • *a quote set off by quotation marks* **4 set (someone) off** : to cause (someone) to suddenly start yelling, crying, laughing, etc. • *I wonder what set her off.* — **set on** [*phrasal vb*] **set (someone or something) on** : to make (a person or animal) suddenly attack (someone) • *Police dogs were set on the protesters.* — **set out** [*phrasal vb*] **1 a** : to begin traveling in a particular direction • *They set out toward the east.* **b** : to start doing something • *She set out with the goal of going to the Olympics.* • *I never set out to hurt you.* **2 set (something) out** or **set out (something)** : to place (a group of things) so that they can be seen or used • *We set extra chairs out for our guests.* — **set sail** see ²SAIL — **set (someone or something) loose** see *let loose* at ¹LOOSE — **set the record straight** see ¹RECORD — **set the scene** see SCENE — **set the stage** see ¹STAGE — **set up** [*phrasal vb*] **1** : to prepare for something by putting things where they need to be • *We started setting up for the party.* **2 set up (something)** or **set (something) up** **a** : to create or establish (something) for a particular purpose • *She set up a private practice of her own.* • *A foundation was set up for people with the disease.* **b** : to arrange and plan (something) • *My secretary will set up a meeting.* • *Let's set up a time to get together.* **c** : to put (something) in an upright position • *Help me set the tent up.* **d** : to make (a machine, system, etc.) ready to be used • *She set up my computer for me.* **3 set (someone) up** or **set up (someone)** **a** : to cause (someone) to be in a bad situation or to appear guilty • *He claimed he was set up by the police.* **b** : to give (someone) a job, a place to live, etc. • *She set me up in an apartment.* • *He set his son up with a job at his company.* **c** : to do something that makes it likely or possible for (someone) to do, get, or experience something ▪ *You're setting yourself up to be disappointed.* [=you're expecting something that won't happen] **d** : to cause (someone) to meet someone in order to start a romantic relationship ▪ *"How did you first meet your husband?" "My best friend set us up."* ▪ *I set him up with my sister.* — **set upon** [*phrasal vb*] **set (someone or something) upon** : to attack (someone or something) ▪ *The protesters were set upon by police dogs.* — **set up shop** see ¹SHOP — **set your heart on** see HEART — **set your mind to** see ¹MIND

²**set** *n* [*C*] **1** : a group of similar things that belong together ▪ *a set of keys/dishes/footprints/instructions* ▪ *a complete set of Shakespeare's plays* ▪ *a chess set* ▪ *a dining (room) set* [=a group of furniture for a dining room] **2** : a piece of electronic equipment ▪ *a radio/stereo set* ▪ *a television/TV set* **3** : a place where a movie or TV program is filmed or a play is performed ▪ *Quiet on the set!* **4** : one of the parts into which a tennis or volleyball match is divided ▪ *a five-set match* **5** : a group of songs or pieces that a musician or band performs at a concert ▪ *Her band opened the show with a 30-minute set.*

³**set** *adj* **1** : having a particular position or location ▪ *Their house is set back from the road.* ▪ *deep-set eyes* **2** : particular and not changing ▪ *set prices* ▪ *a set number of days* **3** : not likely to change ▪ *She has very set ideas about how children should behave.* ▪ *We're both set in our ways.* [=unwilling to change the way we do or think about things] **4** *not before a noun, informal* : ready or prepared for something ▪ *Is everyone (all) set to go?* ▪ *If we win the lottery, we'll be set for life.* [=we will have everything we need for the rest of our lives] **5** *not before a noun* : scheduled or supposed to happen at a certain time ▪ *The game is set to begin at 6:00.* ▪ *Her trial is set for May.* — **be set against** : to feel strongly that you do not want (something) or will not do (something) ▪ *Everyone was set against going.* ▪ *He was dead set against the deal.* — **be set on** : to feel strongly that you want (something) or will do (something) ▪ *She has been set on becoming a doctor since she was a child.* — **(get) ready, (get) set, go** see ¹READY — **have your heart set on** see HEART

set·back /ˈsɛtˌbæk/ *n* [*C*] : a problem that makes progress more difficult or success less likely ▪ *Despite some early setbacks, they eventually became successful.*

set·tee /sɛˈtiː/ *n* [*C*] **1** : a long seat that has a back and arms **2** *Brit* : SOFA

set·ter /ˈsɛtɚ/ *n* [*C*] **1** : a person or thing that determines or establishes something ▪ *world record setters* **2** : a large dog that has long ears and long, smooth hair

set·ting /ˈsɛtɪŋ/ *n* [*C*] **1** : the place and conditions in which something happens or exists ▪ *a perfect setting for a picnic* ▪ *animals in their natural setting* ▪ *dining in a casual/formal setting* **2** : the time, place, and conditions in which the action of a book, movie, etc., takes place ▪

Modern-day China is the setting for the book. **3** : a particular way of positioning the controls of a machine, system, etc., in order to produce a desired result ▪ *She changed the settings on her camera.* **4** : the metal that attaches a stone or jewel to a piece of jewelry **5** : PLACE SETTING

set·tle /ˈsɛtl/ *vb* **set·tled; set·tling 1** [*T/I*] : to end (something, such as an argument) by reaching an agreement ▪ *He agreed to settle (the lawsuit) out of court.* ▪ *We need to settle this question once and for all.* ▪ *It's settled* [=decided] *then: you pay for dinner and I'll pay for the movie.* ▪ *The two sides have settled their differences.* **2** [*T/I*] : to move to a place and make it your home ▪ *Many German immigrants settled in Pennsylvania.* ▪ *The region was settled by German immigrants.* **3 a** [*T/I*] : to put or place (someone) in a comfortable position ▪ *He settled back into his chair.* **b** [*I*] : to begin to feel comfortable in a new place, job, etc. ▪ *I'm finally settling in at my new job.* ▪ *The children are settling into their new school just fine.* **4** [*T*] : to make (someone or something) quiet or calm ▪ *She had a drink to settle her nerves.* **5** [*T*] : to relieve pain and discomfort in (the stomach) ▪ *Some tea may settle your stomach.* **6** [*I*] **a** : to move slowly downward ▪ *The foundation of the house has settled.* **b** : to stop flying, moving, etc., and rest on something ▪ *Dust settled on the shelves.* ▪ *The birds settled on a branch.* ▪ *His eyes settled on her necklace.* **7** [*T/I*] : to pay money that is owed ▪ *We settled the bill.* **8** [*T*] **a** : to arrange who will be given (a property, business, etc.) ▪ *She had to settle her uncle's estate after his death.* **b** : to put (something) in order so that nothing else needs to be done ▪ *He settled his affairs before entering the army.* — **settle a/the score** see ¹SCORE — **settle down** [*phrasal vb*] **1 settle down or settle (someone or something) down or settle down (someone or something)** : to become or make (someone or something) become quiet, calm, or orderly ▪ *When things settle down here, I'll come for a visit.* ▪ *settle the dog down* **2** : to begin to live a quiet and steady life ▪ *They settled down and got married.* **3** : to put yourself into a comfortable position ▪ *She settled down for the night.* **4** : to become quiet and begin giving your attention to something ▪ *They settled down to their work.* — **settle for** [*phrasal vb*] : to be happy or satisfied with (something) ▪ *He asked his parents for $20 but settled for $10.* ▪ *I'm determined to win and won't settle for less.* — **settle on/upon** [*phrasal vb*] : to choose (something or someone) after thinking about other possible choices ▪ *We settled on a soft yellow color to paint the kitchen.* ▪ *settling on a plan*

set·tle·ment /ˈsɛtlmənt/ *n* **1 a** [*C*] : a formal agreement or decision that ends an argument or dispute ▪ *I got the house in the divorce settlement.; also* : an amount of money that someone receives as part of such an agreement ▪ *a settlement of two million dollars* **b** [*singular*]

: the act or process of settling an argument or disagreement • *a quick settlement of the dispute* **2** [U] : the act of paying back money that is owed • *the settlement of a debt* **3 a** [C] : a place where people have come to live and where few or no people lived before • *English settlements in North America* **b** [U] : the act or process of settling an area • *the settlement of North America* **c** [C] : a small village

set·tler /'sɛtlər/ n [C] : a person who settles an area • *The town was established by British settlers.*

set·up /'sɛt,ʌp/ n **1** [C/U] : the process of making something ready to be used • *an online account setup* • *The tent is designed for quick and easy setup.* **2** [C] : the way that something is done or organized • *It took me a while to learn the setup of the office's filing system.* **3** [C] *informal* : a situation in which someone is deliberately put in a bad position or made to look guilty • *Those aren't my drugs. This is a setup!*

sev·en /'sɛvən/ n **1** [C] : the number 7 **2** [C] : the seventh in a set or series • *the seven of hearts* **3** [U] : seven o'clock • *Dinner is at seven.* — **at sixes and sevens** see SIX — **seven** *adj* • *seven cars* — **seven** *pron* • *Seven (of them) passed the test.*

seven seas n [plural] : all the oceans of the world • *He sailed the seven seas.*

sev·en·teen /,sɛvən'ti:n/ n [C] : the number 17 — **seventeen** *adj* • *seventeen years* — **seventeen** *pron* — **sev·en·teenth** /,sɛvən'ti:nθ/ n [C] — **seventeenth** *adj*

[1] **sev·enth** /'sɛvənθ/ n **1** [singular] : number seven in a series • *the seventh of June* **2** [C] : one of seven equal parts of something • *Only a seventh of the town voted for her.*

[2] **seventh** *adj* : occupying the number seven position in a series • *the seventh car in line* — **seventh** *adv* • *She finished seventh in the race.*

seventh heaven n [singular] *informal* : a state of extreme happiness and joy • *The winner was in seventh heaven.*

sev·en·ty /'sɛvənti/ n, pl **-ties** **1** [C] : the number 70 **2** [plural] **a** : the numbers ranging from 70 to 79 • *temperatures in the high seventies* **b** : a set of years ending in digits ranging from 70 to 79 • *She grew up in the seventies.* [=1970–1979] *This is in her seventies.* — **sev·en·ti·eth** /'sɛvəntijəθ/ n [C] • *one seventieth of the total* — **seventieth** *adj* • *the seventieth day* — **seventy** *adj* • *seventy days* — **seventy** *pron* • *Seventy (of them) came to the show.*

sev·er /'sɛvər/ vb [T] **1** : to remove (something) by cutting • *He severed the lowest tree limbs.* • *A severed hand/finger* **2** : to end (a relationship, connection, etc.) completely • *She severed her ties to the group.*

[1] **sev·er·al** /'sɛvərəl/ adj, always before a noun : more than two but not very many • *He arrived several hours/days ago.* • *The meat can be cooked several ways.*

[2] **several** *pron* : more than two but not

very many • *Several of the guests left early.*

sev·er·ance /'sɛvərəns/ n [singular] *formal* **1** : the act of ending someone's employment • *a severance of employment* • **severance pay** [=money given to someone who has been fired or laid off from a job] **2** : the act of ending a relationship, connection, etc. • *a severance of diplomatic relations*

se·vere /sə'viər/ adj **se·ver·er; -est** **1** : very bad, serious, or unpleasant • *severe weather/damage/injuries/pain* **2** : very harsh • *severe punishment/criticism* **3** : requiring great effort • *a severe challenge* **4** : very formal, strict, and serious • *a severe woman* **5** : very plain • *severe architecture* • *Her short, straight haircut looks too severe on her.* — **se·vere·ly** *adv* — **se·ver·i·ty** /sə'vɛrəti/ n [U] • *the severity of the situation*

sew /'soʊ/ vb **sewed; sewn** /'soʊn/ or **sewed; sew·ing** [T/I] : to make or repair something by using a needle and thread • *She sews dresses by hand.* • *sewing a button on a shirt* • *The surgeon sewed the wound shut.* — **sew up** [phrasal vb] **sew (something) up** or **sew up (something)** **1** : to close or repair (something) by sewing • *He sewed up the tear in his shirt.* **2** *informal* : to make (something) certain • *sewing up a deal* • *They felt they had the win/game sewn up.*

sew·age /'su:wɪdʒ/ n [U] : waste material (such as human urine and feces) that is carried away from buildings in a system of pipes

[1] **sew·er** /'su:wər, Brit 'sju:ə/ n [C] : a pipe that is usually underground and that is used to carry off water and sewage • *a sewer pipe* • *The water ran into the sewer.* — compare [2]SEWER

[2] **sew·er** /'soʊə/ n [C] : someone who sews things • *I'm a good sewer.* — compare [1]SEWER

sew·er·age /'su:wərɪdʒ, Brit 'sju:ərɪdʒ/ n [U] **1** : a system or process used for carrying away water and sewage **2** : SEWAGE • *raw sewerage*

sewing n [U] **1** : the act or process of sewing something (such as a piece of clothing) • *She enjoys sewing.* **2** : things that are used for sewing or that are being sewn • *She left her sewing in the living room.*

sewing machine n [C] : a machine that is used for sewing things

sewn past participle of SEW

sex /'sɛks/ n **1** [U] : the state of being male or female : GENDER • *The form asks for your name, age, and sex.* **2** [C] : men or male animals as a group or women or female animals as a group • *a movie that appeals to both sexes* [=to both men and women] • *Some feel men are the more aggressive sex.* • *a single-sex dormitory* [=a dormitory for only women or men] **3** [U] : physical activity that is related to and often includes sexual intercourse • *All he ever thinks about is sex.* • *premarital sex*

sex act n [C] : an action performed with another person for sexual pleasure

sex appeal n [U] : the quality of being

sexually attractive ▪ *an actor with sex appeal*

sex·ism /ˈsɛkˌsɪzəm/ *n* [U] : unfair treatment of people and especially of women because of their sex — **sex·ist** /ˈsɛksɪst/ *adj* ▪ *a sexist remark*/*jerk* — **sexist** *n* [C] ▪ *He was accused of being a sexist.*

sex·less /ˈsɛksləs/ *adj* **1** : not having sexual activity ▪ *a sexless marriage* **2** : not looking like either a male or female ▪ *sexless dolls* — **sex·less·ness** *n* [U]

sex object *n* [C] : someone who is thought of only as being sexually attractive or desirable ▪ *He treats women as sex objects.*

sex offender *n* [C] : a person who is guilty of a crime involving sex (such as rape)

sex symbol *n* [C] : a usually famous person who is very sexually attractive

sex·tu·plet /sɛkˈstʌplət, Brit ˈsɛkstjʊplət/ *n* [C] : one of six babies born at the same time to the same mother

sex·u·al /ˈsɛkʃəwəl/ *adj* **1** : of, relating to, or involving sex ▪ *sexual reproduction/relationships/abuse/desire* **2** : of or relating to males and females ▪ *sexual differences* — **sex·u·al·ly** /ˈsɛkʃəwəli/ *adv* ▪ *sexually active teenagers*

sexual intercourse *n* [U] : sexual activity between two people; *especially* : sexual activity in which a man puts his penis into the vagina of a woman

sex·u·al·i·ty /ˌsɛkʃəˈwæləti/ *n* [U] : the sexual habits and desires of a person ▪ *She is comfortable with her sexuality.*

sexually transmitted disease *n* [C] *medical* : STD

sexual orientation *n* [C] : a person's sexual preference or identity as bisexual, heterosexual, or homosexual

sexy /ˈsɛksi/ *adj* **sex·i·er; -est** : sexually appealing, attractive, or exciting ▪ *a sexy skirt/woman/hairstyle* — **sex·i·ly** /ˈsɛksəli/ *adv* — **sex·i·ness** /ˈsɛksinəs/ *n* [U]

Sgt. *abbr* sergeant

sh *or* **shh** *or* **shhh** /ˈʃ/ *often prolonged*/ *interj* — used to tell someone to be quiet ▪ *Shh! The baby is sleeping.*

shab·by /ˈʃæbi/ *adj* **shab·bi·er; -est** **1** : in poor condition especially because of age or use ▪ *a shabby coat* **2** : dressed in clothes that are old and worn ▪ *shabby workmen* **3** *informal* : not fair, generous, or reasonable ▪ *the hotel's shabby treatment of guests* — **not (too) shabby** *informal* : fairly good or quite good ▪ *Placing fifth in a race is not too shabby.* — **shab·bi·ness** /ˈʃæbinəs/ *n* [U]

¹**shack** /ˈʃæk/ *n* [C] : a small house or building that is not put together well

²**shack** *vb* — **shack up** [*phrasal vb*] *informal* : to live with a sexual partner without being married to that person ▪ *She shacked up with her boyfriend.*

shack·le /ˈʃækəl/ *n* [C] : one of two rings or bands that are placed around a person's wrists or ankles and that are connected by a chain ▪ *a prisoner in shackles* ▪ *(figurative) the shackles of tyranny* — **shackle** *vb* **shack·led; shack·ling** [T] ▪ *The guard shackled* [=put shackles on]

the prisoner. ▪ *(figurative) people shackled by poverty*

¹**shade** /ˈʃeɪd/ *n* **1** [U] : an area of slight darkness that is produced when something blocks the light of the sun ▪ *These plants grow well in (the) shade.* ▪ *We sat in the shade of a tree.* **2** [C] **a** : something that is used to block strong light ▪ *an eye shade* **b** : LAMPSHADE **c** *US* : WINDOW SHADE ▪ *She pulled down the shades.* **3** [*plural*] *informal* : SUNGLASSES **4** [C] : a particular type of color that is lighter, darker, etc., than other types ▪ *shades of blue* **5** [C] : a particular form of something that is usually slightly different from other forms ▪ *The word has many shades of meaning.* **6** [C] : a very small amount ▪ *He's just a shade* [=*a bit*] *taller than me.* — **have it made in the shade** *US, informal* : to have a very easy life or to be in a very good situation — **put (someone or something) in the shade** *chiefly Brit, informal* : to be much better than (someone or something) ▪ *Their performance really put ours in the shade.*

²**shade** *vb* **shad·ed; shad·ing** [T] **1** : to shelter (something) from strong light and especially from sunlight ▪ *I shaded my eyes (with my hand).* ▪ *Several large trees shade the house.* **2** : to make an area in a drawing, on a graph, etc., darker than other areas ▪ *shade (in) a circle* **3** *US* : to change (something, such as the truth) slightly in order to deceive people ▪ *shading the truth* — **shade into** [*phrasal vb*] : to slowly or gradually change into (something) or become the same as (something) ▪ *as day shades into night*

shading *n* **1** [U] : the use of dark areas in a drawing, on a graph, etc. **2** [*plural*] : small differences ▪ *shadings of meaning*

¹**shad·ow** /ˈʃædoʊ/ *n* **1** [C] : a dark shape that appears on a surface when someone or something moves between the surface and a source of light ▪ *trees casting/throwing long shadows* ▪ *(figurative) She grew up in the shadow of her famous sister.* **2** [U, *plural*] : an area of darkness created when a source of light is blocked ▪ *Part of the valley was in shadow.* ▪ *hiding in the shadows* **3** [*singular*] : a very small amount of something ▪ *There's not a shadow of (a) doubt.* [=there's no doubt] **4** [C] : a dark area of skin under a person's eyes ▪ *He had dark shadows under his eyes.* **5** [C] : someone or something that is now much weaker, less impressive, etc., than in the past ▪ *He's just a shadow of his former self.*

²**shadow** *vb* [T] **1** : to cover (something) with a shadow ▪ *a yard shadowed* [=shaded] *by trees* **2** : to follow and watch (someone) especially in a secret way ▪ *Police shadowed the suspect for several days.*

shad·owy /ˈʃædowi/ *adj* **1** : full of shade or shadows ▪ *a shadowy lane* **2** : dark and mysterious ▪ *a shadowy figure* **3** : not clearly seen or understood ▪ *He had only a shadowy idea of what to do.*

shady /ˈʃeɪdi/ *adj* **shad·i·er, -est** **1 a** : giving or providing shade ▪ *a shady tree*

b : sheltered from the sun's light ▪ *a shady yard/area* **2** *informal* : seeming to be dishonest ▪ *a shady business deal*

¹**shaft** /ˈʃæft, *Brit* ˈʃɑːft/ *n* **1** [C] : the long, narrow part of a weapon, tool, instrument, etc. **2** [C] : a bar in a machine which holds or turns other parts that move or spin ▪ *a propeller shaft* **3** [C] **a** : an opening or passage straight down through the floors of a building ▪ *an air/elevator shaft* **b** : an opening or passage in a mine ▪ *a mine shaft* **4** [C] *formal + literary* : a narrow beam of light ▪ *a shaft of sunlight* **5** **the shaft** *US, informal* : harsh or unfair treatment ▪ *You got the shaft in that deal.*

²**shaft** *vb* [T] *chiefly US, informal* : to treat (someone) unfairly or harshly ▪ *You got shafted in that deal.*

shag /ˈʃæg/ *n* [U] : long pieces of material (such as wool) that are twisted together to make a rug or carpet ▪ *shag carpeting*

shag·gy /ˈʃægi/ *adj* **shag·gi·er**; **-est** **1** : long and tangled ▪ *shaggy hair* **2** : covered with hair or fur that is long and tangled ▪ *a shaggy dog*

¹**shake** /ˈʃeɪk/ *vb* **shook** /ˈʃʊk/; **shak·en** /ˈʃeɪkən/; **shak·ing** **1 a** [T/I] : to move sometimes violently back and forth or up and down with short, quick movements ▪ *The house shook as the train passed.* = *The passing train shook the house.* ▪ *He shook his fist (in the air) and yelled at us.* **b** [I] : to move or have parts of your body move in short, quick movements and in a way that you are not able to control ▪ *His hand shook.* ▪ *She was shaking with cold/laughter/anger.* ▪ *nervous and shaking like a leaf* **2** [T] : to get away from or get rid of (someone or something) ▪ *He couldn't shake the police.* ▪ *shake (off) a cold* **3** [T] : to cause (a belief, feeling, etc.) to become weaker ▪ *Her confidence was shaken by the accident.* **4** [T] : to cause (someone) to feel fear, anxiety, shock, etc. ▪ *The whole town was shaken by the news.* **5** [T/I] : to grasp (someone's hand) with your hand and move it up and down when you are meeting or saying goodbye to each other or as a sign of friendship or agreement ▪ *I shook his hand.* = *I shook hands with him.* ▪ **shake on a deal** = **shake on it** [=shake hands to show that you both/all agree] **6** [I] *of your voice* : to produce sound in an unsteady way because your are nervous, angry, sad, etc. ▪ *Her voice shook with rage.* — **shake a leg** *informal* : to move or go quickly ▪ *"Shake a leg! We're late."* — **shake down** [*phrasal vb*] *US, informal* **shake (someone) down** or **shake down (someone)** : to get money from (someone) by using deception or threats ▪ *mobsters shaking down store owners* — **shake out** [*phrasal vb*] **1** *informal* : to happen or end in a particular way ▪ *We're waiting to see how things shake out.* [=turn out] **2** **shake (something) out** or **shake out (something)** : to shake (something) back and forth or up and down in order to remove dirt, wrinkles, etc., from it ▪ *shake a rug out* — **shake up** [*phrasal vb*] **shake (someone**

or something) **up** or **shake up (someone or something) 1** : to shock or frighten (someone) ▪ *She was shaken up by the news.* **2** : to make many changes in (something; such as a company or organization) ▪ *The coach shook things up by hiring new assistants.* — **shake your head** : to turn your head from side to side as a way of answering "no" or of showing disagreement or refusal ▪ *When I asked her if she wanted help, she just shook her head.*

²**shake** *n* **1** [C] : a short, quick movement back and forth or up and down ▪ *Give the dice a shake.* **2 the shakes** *informal* : a condition in which parts of your body move in a way that you are not able to control ▪ *Coffee gives me the shakes.* **3** [C] : MILKSHAKE ▪ *a chocolate shake* — **a fair shake** *informal* : fair treatment ▪ *She'll get a fair shake from her boss.* — **no great shakes** *informal* : not very good or skillful at something ▪ *I'm no great shakes at golf.*

shake·down /ˈʃeɪkˌdaʊn/ *n* [C] *informal* **1** *US* : the act of taking something (such as money) from someone by using threats or deception ▪ *a shakedown by mobsters* **2** *US* : a thorough search of something ▪ *The guards conducted a shakedown of the prisoners' cells.* **3** : a thorough test of a new ship, airplane, etc., in order to make sure there are no problems or defects ▪ *a shakedown cruise/flight*

shak·er /ˈʃeɪkɚ/ *n* [C] : a container that is shaken to mix something or to make something come out ▪ *a salt/pepper shaker* — **movers and shakers** see MOVER

shake-up /ˈʃeɪkˌʌp/ *n* [C] : an important change or series of changes in the way a company or other organization is organized or run ▪ *a management shake-up*

shaky /ˈʃeɪki/ *adj* **shak·i·er**; **-est** **1** : tending to shake because of weakness, strong emotion, etc. ▪ *shaky hands* ▪ *taking a few shaky steps* **2** : weak and likely to break down, collapse, or fail ▪ *The company's future looks shaky.* ▪ *Their marriage is on shaky ground.* **3** : not impressive or effective ▪ *a shaky start/performance*

shale /ˈʃeɪl/ *n* [U] : a soft kind of rock that splits easily into flat pieces

shall /ˈʃæl, ʃəl/ *vb, past tense* **should** /ˈʃʊd, ʃəd/ *present tense for both singular and plural* **shall**; *negative* **shall not** or **shan't** /ˈʃænt, *Brit* ˈʃɑːnt/ [*modal vb*] *formal* **1** — used to say that something is expected to happen in the future ▪ *Perhaps it will happen. We shall* [=will] *see.* **2** — used to ask for someone's opinion ▪ *Shall we dance?* [=would you like to dance?] **3** — used to give a command or to say that you will or will not allow something to happen ▪ *They shall not pass.* **4** — used in laws or rules to say that something is required ▪ *The jury alone shall decide the verdict.*

shal·lot /ʃəˈlɑːt, ˈʃælət/ *n* [C/U] : a small type of onion that is used in cooking

shal·low /ˈʃæloʊ/ *adj* **1 a** : having a small distance to the bottom from the surface or highest point ▪ *a shallow dish/*

pond/grave **b** : not going far inward from the outside or the front edge of something ▪ *a shallow closet* **2** *disapproving* : not caring about or involving serious or important things ▪ *a shallow person* **3** : taking in a small amount of air ▪ *shallow breaths/breathing* — **shal·low·ly** *adv* ▪ *breathing shallowly* — **shal·low·ness** *n* [*U*] ▪ *the shallowness of the water*

sham /ˈʃæm/ *n* [*C*] : something that is not what it appears to be and that is meant to trick or deceive people ▪ *The trial/marriage was a sham.* — **sham** *adj, always before a noun* ▪ *sham [=fake] pearls*

sha·man /ˈʃɑːmən, ˈʃeɪmən/ *n* [*C*] : someone who is believed in some cultures to be able to use magic to cure people who are sick, to control future events, etc.

sham·bles /ˈʃæmbəlz/ *n* [*U, singular*] : a place or state in which there is great confusion, disorder, or destruction ▪ *His life was a shambles after the divorce.* ▪ *The room/city was in shambles.*

sham·bol·ic /ʃæmˈbɑːlɪk/ *adj, chiefly Brit* : very messy or disorganized ▪ *a shambolic system of public transportation*

¹**shame** /ˈʃeɪm/ *n* **1** [*U*] : a feeling of guilt, regret, or sadness that you have because you know you have done something wrong ▪ *He felt shame for his lies.* ▪ *Shame on you.* [=you should feel shame] **2** [*U*] : ability to feel guilt, regret, or embarrassment ▪ *How could you be so rude? Have you no shame?* **3** [*U*] : dishonor or disgrace ▪ *Her crimes brought shame upon her family.* **4** [*singular*] : something that is regretted ▪ *It would be a shame to give up now.* — **put (someone or something) to shame** : to be much better than (someone or something) ▪ *Her project put mine to shame.*

²**shame** *vb* **shamed; sham·ing** [*T*] **1** : to cause (someone) to feel ashamed ▪ *Her crimes shamed her family.* **2** : to force (someone) to act in a specified way by causing feelings of shame or guilt ▪ *They were shamed into confessing.*

shame·faced /ˈʃeɪmˌfeɪst/ *adj* : feeling or showing shame ▪ *a shamefaced apology/grin*

shame·ful /ˈʃeɪmfəl/ *adj* : bad enough to make someone ashamed ▪ *shameful behavior* — **shame·ful·ly** /ˈʃeɪmfəli/ *adv*

shame·less /ˈʃeɪmləs/ *adj* : having or showing no shame ▪ *shameless acts/people* — **shame·less·ly** *adv*

sham·poo /ʃæmˈpuː/ *n, pl* -**poos** **1** [*C/U*] **a** : a special liquid that is used for cleaning your hair **b** : a special liquid used for cleaning rugs, carpets, etc. **2** [*C*] : an act of cleaning hair, a carpet, etc., with shampoo ▪ *She got a shampoo and a haircut.* — **shampoo** *vb* [*T*] ▪ *She shampoos her hair* [=cleans her hair with shampoo] *every morning.*

sham·rock /ˈʃæmˌrɑːk/ *n* [*C*] : a small plant with three leaves on each stem that is the national symbol of Ireland

shank /ˈʃæŋk/ *n* [*C*] **1** : the straight, narrow part of a tool that connects the part that does the work with the part

that you hold ▪ *the shank of a drill bit* **2** : a piece of meat cut from the upper part of the leg ▪ *a lamb/beef shank*

shan't /ˈʃænt, Brit ˈʃɑːnt/ : shall not

shan·ty /ˈʃænti/ *n, pl* -**ties** [*C*] : a small, simple building that is roughly made from sheets of wood, plastic, etc., and that is used as a house by poor people

shan·ty·town /ˈʃæntiˌtaʊn/ *n* [*C*] : a town or a part of a town where the people are poor and live in shanties

¹**shape** /ˈʃeɪp/ *n* **1** [*C/U*] : the form or outline of an object ▪ *circles, squares, triangles, and other geometric shapes* ▪ *pieces sorted by size and shape* ▪ *clouds changing shape* ▪ *a cake with a rectangular/circular shape* ▪ *a cake that is rectangular/circular in shape* ▪ *a cookie in the shape of a heart* ▪ *a pipe that's bent out of shape* [=bent to no longer have its usual shape] **2** [*U*] **a** : the condition of something or someone ▪ *a car in good/bad/poor shape* ▪ *athletes in top/exellent shape* **b** : a physically strong and healthy condition ▪ *I'm out of shape.* ▪ *She stays/keeps in shape by exercising.* ▪ *(figurative) get the company back in shape* [=into good condition again] **3** [*U*] : the way something is done ▪ *Computers have changed the shape of communication.* ▪ *They offered help in the shape of a loan.* [=the help they offered was a loan] ▪ *not acceptable in any way, shape, or form* [=not at all acceptable] **4** [*U*] : a definite form or arrangement of something ▪ *A plan is taking shape.* **5** [*C*] : a person or thing that cannot be seen clearly ▪ *dark shapes moving in the shadows*

²**shape** *vb* **shaped; shap·ing** [*T*] **1** : to work with (a material) in order to make something from it ▪ *shaping stone with a hammer and chisel* ▪ *shaping dough into loaves* **2** : to influence the development of (something) ▪ *Ads shape public opinion.* **3** : to make (something, such as a plan) by a process of careful thought ▪ *shaping a strategy* — **shape up** [*phrasal vb*] *informal* **1** : to happen or develop in a particular way ▪ *Our plans are shaping up nicely.* **2** : to start behaving in a better or more acceptable way ▪ *If he doesn't shape up, he's going to be fired.* **3** : to make your body stronger and healthier by exercising ▪ *shaping up at the gym* — **shap·er** *n* [*C*]

shaped /ˈʃeɪpt/ *adj* : having a particular shape or form ▪ *a cookie shaped like a heart* = *a heart-shaped cookie*

shape·less /ˈʃeɪpləs/ *adj* **1** : not having a particular or definite shape ▪ *a shapeless blob* **2** : not organized or arranged in a way that is clear and understandable ▪ *a shapeless essay/argument*

shape·ly /ˈʃeɪpli/ *adj* **shape·li·er; -est** : having an attractive shape or form ▪ *a shapely figure*

shard /ˈʃɑːd/ *also* **sherd** /ˈʃɚd/ *n* [*C*] : a sharp piece of something ▪ *shards of glass*

¹**share** /ˈʃeɚ/ *vb* **shared; shar·ing** **1** [*T*] : to have or use (something) with others ▪ *We share a car (together).* ▪ *I share an office with other people.* **2** [*T*] *of two or more people* : to divide (something) into parts and each take or use a part ▪ *We*

shared the money equally. **3** [T/I] : to let someone else have or use a part of (something that belongs to you) ▪ *children learning to share (toys/games)* **4** [T/I] : to have (something that someone or something else also has) ▪ *We share an interest in baseball.* ▪ *countries that share a border* **5** [T/I] : to tell someone about (your feelings, opinions, thoughts, etc.) ▪ *share your feelings/ideas* ▪ *Thanks for sharing your concerns (with me).* **6** [T/I] : to have equal responsibility for or involvement in (something) ▪ *I share (in) the blame for what happened.* — **share out** [*phrasal vb*] **share out (something)** or **share (something) out** *chiefly Brit* : to divide (something) into parts and give the parts to different people ▪ *She shared out her property to her nephews and nieces.*

²**share** *n* **1** [*singular*] : a part of something that has been divided into parts and given to different people ▪ *a share of the business/profits* **2** [C] : any of the equal parts into which the ownership of a property or business is divided ▪ *100 shares of stock* **3** [*singular*] : the amount of something that someone owes or deserves or is responsible for ▪ *your share of the bill* ▪ *I did my (fair) share of the work.*

share·crop·per /ˈʃeɚˌkrɑːpɚ/ *n* [C] : a farmer especially in the southern U.S. who raises crops for the owner of a piece of land and is paid a portion of the money from the sale of the crops

share·hold·er /ˈʃeɚˌhoʊldɚ/ *n* [C] : someone who owns shares in a company or business : STOCKHOLDER

share—out *n* [C] *Brit* : an act of dividing something into parts and giving them to two or more people ▪ *an equal share-out of the money*

share·ware /ˈʃeɚˌweɚ/ *n* [U] : computer software that you can try for free for a certain period of time before choosing whether or not to buy it

shark /ˈʃɑɚk/ *n* [C] **1** : a large and often dangerous sea fish with very sharp teeth **2** *informal* : a person who wins money in a game by playing well and by being dishonest ▪ *a pool/card shark*

¹**sharp** /ˈʃɑɚp/ *adj* **1** : having a thin edge that is able to cut things or a fine point that is able to make a hole in things ▪ *a sharp knife/pencil* ▪ *sharp teeth/claws* **2 a** : sudden and quick ▪ *a sharp drop/rise in temperature* **b** : involving a sudden change in direction ▪ *a sharp (left) turn* **3 a** : clear and easy to see ▪ *a sharp image/ picture* **b** : very noticeable ▪ *a sharp difference* **4** : having or showing a quick ability to notice and understand things ▪ *a sharp student* **5** : very sudden and severe ▪ *a sharp pain/disappointment* **6** : critical or harsh ▪ *a sharp reply* ▪ *She has a **sharp tongue**.* [=she says very critical things to people] **7** : loud, short, and sudden ▪ *a sharp noise* **8** *of cheese* : having a strong odor and flavor **9** : very strong and cold ▪ *a sharp wind* **10** *disapproving* : clever in a bad or dishonest way ▪ *sharp business practices.* **11** : ending in a point or edge ▪ *a sharp nose* **12** *informal* : stylish or fashionable ▪ *a sharp*

dresser **13** *music* **a** : higher than the true pitch ▪ *Her singing was slightly sharp.* **b** : higher than a specified note by a semitone ▪ *F sharp* — **keep a sharp eye on** : to watch (someone or something) carefully — **sharp·ly** /ˈʃɑɚpli/ *adv* ▪ *a sharply pointed knife* ▪ *The temperature dropped/rose sharply.* ▪ *a sharply defined image* — **sharp·ness** *n* [U]

²**sharp** *adv* **1** : EXACTLY — used to refer to an exact time ▪ *four o'clock sharp* **2** : above the correct musical pitch ▪ *He sang slightly sharp.*

³**sharp** *n* [C] : a musical note that is one semitone higher than a specified note ▪ *C sharp*; *also* : a written symbol # that is placed before a note to show that it should be played a semitone higher

sharp·en /ˈʃɑɚpən/ *vb* **1** [T] : to make (something) sharp or sharper ▪ *sharpen a knife/pencil* **2** [T/I] : to become or to make (something) become clearer or more distinct ▪ *sharpen an image* **3** [T] : to improve (something) ▪ *sharpen (up) skills* **4** [I] : to become more severe ▪ *The pain suddenly sharpened.* — **sharpen up** [*phrasal vb*] : to become better, smarter, more skillful, etc. ▪ *You'd better sharpen up if you want to keep your job.*

sharp·en·er /ˈʃɑɚpənɚ/ *n* [C] : a tool or machine that makes something sharp ▪ *a pencil/knife sharpener*

sharp—eyed /ˈʃɑɚpˈaɪd/ *adj* **1** : having very good eyesight ▪ *a sharp-eyed bird* **2** : having a strong ability to notice things ▪ *a sharp-eyed reader*

sharp—shoot·er /ˈʃɑɚpˌʃuːtɚ/ *n* [C] : someone who is skilled at shooting a target with a gun

shat·ter /ˈʃætɚ/ *vb* **1** [T/I] : to break suddenly into many small pieces ▪ *The window shattered.* ▪ *The rock shattered the window.* **2** [T] : to damage (something) very badly ▪ *His dreams were shattered.* ▪ *an emotionally shattering experience*

¹**shave** /ˈʃeɪv/ *vb* **shaved; shaved** or **shav·en** /ˈʃeɪvən/; **shav·ing** **1** [T/I] : to cut the hair, wool, etc., off someone or something very close to the skin ▪ *He shaves (himself)* [=cuts off the hair that grows on his face] *every morning.* ▪ *shave (off) a beard* ▪ *shaved/shaven heads/legs* **2** [T] : to remove a thin layer of (something) from something ▪ *shave the bark off a tree* **3** [T] : to reduce something by taking away (a small amount) ▪ *They shaved a little off the price.*

²**shave** *n* [C] : an act of shaving ▪ *give yourself a shave* [=shave yourself] — see also CLOSE SHAVE

shav·er /ˈʃeɪvɚ/ *n* [C] **1** : a tool or device that is used to shave hair from your face, body, or head ▪ *an electric shaver* [=razor] **2** : a person who shaves ▪ *a careful shaver*

shaving *n* [C] : a very thin piece removed from something with a sharp tool ▪ *wood shavings*

shaving cream *n* [U] : a special cream or foam that is spread over your face or another part of your body before shaving

shawl /ˈʃɑːl/ *n* [C] : a piece of cloth that is used especially by women as a covering for the head or shoulders

¹she /ˈʃiː/ *pron* **1** : that female ▪ *She is my mother.* **2** *somewhat old-fashioned* — used to refer to something (such as a ship) that is thought of as having female qualities

²she *n* [*singular*] : a girl, woman, or female animal ▪ "*Somebody called for you.*" "*Was it a he or a she?*"

sheaf /ˈʃiːf/ *n, pl* **sheaves** /ˈʃiːvz/ [*C*] **1** : a bunch of stalks and ears of grain that are tied together after being cut **2** : a group of things fastened together ▪ *a sheaf of arrows/papers*

shear /ˈʃiɚ/ *vb* **sheared; sheared** *or* **shorn** /ˈʃoɚn/; **shear·ing** [*T*] : to cut the hair, wool, etc., off an animal ▪ *shearing sheep = shearing (off) wool from sheep* — **shear off** [*phrasal vb*] **1** : to become separated suddenly because of great force ▪ *The bolt sheared off.* **2** *shear (something) off* or *shear off (something)* : to remove (something) with great force ▪ *The impact sheared off the airplane's wing.* — **shear·er** *n* [*C*]

shears /ˈʃiɚz/ *n* [*plural*] : a large, heavy pair of scissors

sheath /ˈʃiːθ/ *n* [*C*] **1** : a cover for the blade of a knife, sword, etc. **2** : a protective covering ▪ *a piece of wire covered with a plastic sheath* **3** *Brit* : CONDOM

sheathe /ˈʃiːð/ *vb* **sheathed; sheath·ing** [*T*] **1** : to put (something) into a sheath ▪ *He sheathed his sword.* **2** : to cover (something) with something that protects it ▪ *The ship's bottom is sheathed with/in copper.*

she-bang /ʃɪˈbæŋ/ *n* — **the whole she-bang** *informal* : everything that is included in something ▪ *You can buy the whole shebang for $50.*

¹shed /ˈʃɛd/ *vb* **shed; shed·ding** **1** [*T*] : to get rid of (something) ▪ *shed extra pounds* ▪ *trying to shed her bad image* **2** [*T/I*] : to lose (leaves, skin, fur, etc.) naturally ▪ *The dog is shedding (its fur).* **3** [*T*] **a** : to take off (something you are wearing) ▪ *He quickly shed his hat and coat.* **b** *Brit* : to lose or drop (a load, cargo, etc.) ▪ *The lorry shed its load.* **4** [*T*] : to cause (water) to flow off instead of soaking into something ▪ *Raincoats shed water.* — **shed blood** see BLOOD — **shed light on** see ¹LIGHT — **shed tears** see ³TEAR

²shed *n* [*C*] **1** : a small, simple building that is used especially for storing things **2** *Brit* : a large industrial building

she'd /ˈʃiːd, ʃɪd/ — used as a contraction of *she had* or *she would* ▪ *She'd* [=*she had*] *left already.* ▪ *She'd* [=*she would*] *prefer to wait.*

sheen /ˈʃiːn/ *n* [*singular*] : a soft, smooth, shiny quality ▪ *the sheen of satin*

sheep /ˈʃiːp/ *n, pl* **sheep** [*C*] **1** : an animal with a thick woolly coat that is often raised for meat or for its wool and skin **2** : a person who does what other people say to do ▪ *following fads like (a flock of) sheep* — **a wolf in sheep's clothing** see ¹WOLF

sheep·dog /ˈʃiːpˌdɑːg/ *n* [*C*] : a dog that is trained to control sheep

sheep·ish /ˈʃiːpɪʃ/ *adj* : showing or feeling embarrassment especially because you have done something foolish or wrong ▪ *a sheepish look/grin/smile* — **sheep·ish·ly** *adv*

sheer /ˈʃiɚ/ *adj* **1** *always before a noun* — used to emphasize the large amount, size, or degree of something ▪ *The sheer amount of work was overwhelming.* **2** *always before a noun* : complete and total ▪ *sheer nonsense* **3** : very steep ▪ *sheer cliffs* **4** : very thin ▪ *sheer curtains*

sheet /ˈʃiːt/ *n* [*C*] **1 a** : a large piece of cloth that is used to cover something **b** : a large piece of thin cloth used on a bed **2** : a usually rectangular piece of paper **3** : a thin, flat, rectangular or square piece of something ▪ *a sheet of iron/glass* **4** : a wide, flat surface or area of something ▪ *a sheet of ice* **5** : a large moving area of something (such as fire or water) ▪ *sheets of rain*

sheet·ing /ˈʃiːtɪŋ/ *n* [*U*] : material (such as plastic) in the form of thin layers used to cover or protect something ▪ *clear plastic sheeting*

sheet music *n* [*U*] : music printed on sheets of paper that are not bound together

sheikh *or* **sheik** /ˈʃiːk/ *n* [*C*] **1** : an Arab chief, ruler, or prince **2** : a leader of a Muslim organization or group

shelf /ˈʃɛlf/ *n, pl* **shelves** /ˈʃɛlvz/ [*C*] **1** : a flat board which is attached to a wall, frame, etc., and on which objects can be placed **2** *geology* : a flat area of rock, sand, etc., especially underwater — **off the shelf** : directly from a store without having to be specially made or ordered ▪ *equipment bought off the shelf* — **on the shelf** : not active or being used ▪ *Our plans to remodel are on the shelf for now.*

shelf life *n* [*C*] : the length of time that food may be stored and still be good to eat ▪ *Rice has a long shelf life.*

¹shell /ˈʃɛl/ *n* [*C/U*] **a** : the hard outer covering of an animal, insect, etc., that protects it ▪ *a turtle's shell* **b** : the hard outer covering of an egg : EGGSHELL **c** : the hard outer covering of a nut, fruit, or seed ▪ *a coconut shell* **2** [*C*] *US* : something (such as pasta) that is shaped like a shell **3** [*C*] : the hard outer structure of a building, car, airplane, etc. ▪ *the shell of an unfinished house* **4** [*C*] *chiefly US* : a hard or crisp piece of bread, dough, etc., that is used to hold a filling ▪ *a pie shell* **5** [*C*] **a** : a metal case that is filled with an explosive and that is shot from a cannon ▪ *mortar shells* **b** *chiefly US* : CARTRIDGE 1 — **shelled** /ˈʃɛld/ *adj* ▪ *a hard-shelled egg* [=an egg with a hard shell]

²shell *vb* [*T*] **1** : to remove the shell or outer covering of (something) ▪ *shell peas* **2** : to shoot shells at (someone or something) using large guns ▪ *shelling enemy troops* — **shell out** [*phrasal vb*] *informal* : to pay a large amount of money for something ▪ *shelling out $400 for tickets*

she'll /ˈʃiːl, ʃɪl/ — used as a contraction of *she will* ▪ *She'll call you.*

shel·lac /ʃəˈlæk/ *n* [*U*] : a clear liquid that dries into a hard coating and that is put on a surface to protect it

shell·fish /ˈʃɛlˌfɪʃ/ *n, pl* **shellfish** [C/U] : an animal (such as a crab or an oyster) that has a hard outer shell and that lives in water

shell shock *n* [U] *old-fashioned* : BATTLE FATIGUE — **shell–shocked** *adj* • *shell-shocked veterans* • *(figurative) She was shell-shocked* [=*very shocked, upset, etc.*] *when she heard the news.*

¹**shel·ter** /ˈʃɛltɚ/ *n* **1 a** [C] : a structure that covers or protects people or things • *a bomb shelter* **b** [C] : a place that provides food and protection for people or animals that need assistance • *homeless shelters* **c** [U] : a place to live • *people in need of food and shelter* **2** [U] : the state of being covered and protected from danger, bad weather, etc. • *We found/took shelter in a cave during the storm.*

²**shelter** *vb* **1** [T] : to protect (someone) from danger, bad weather, etc. • *A cave sheltered the climbers during the storm.* • *sheltering a criminal* [=*giving a criminal a place to hide*] • *(figurative) wanting to shelter children from pain* [=*to prevent children from experiencing pain*] **2** [I] : to be in a place that provides protection from danger, bad weather, etc. • *They sheltered in a cave during the storm.*

shel·tered /ˈʃɛltɚd/ *adj* **1** : providing protection from bad weather • *sheltered bays/harbors* **2** *sometimes disapproving* : protected from dangerous or unpleasant experiences in the world • *a sheltered life* **3** *always before a noun, Brit* : providing care for people (such as old or disabled people) who need help with daily activities • *sheltered accommodation/housing*

shelve /ˈʃɛlv/ *vb* **shelved; shelv·ing** [T] **1** : to put (something) on a shelf • *shelving books/products* **2** : to stop doing or thinking about (something) for a period of time • *The project was shelved.*

shelves *plural of* SHELF

she·nan·i·gans /ʃəˈnænɪgənz/ *n* [*plural*] *informal* : activity or behavior that is not honest or proper • *political/financial shenanigans*

¹**shep·herd** /ˈʃɛpɚd/ *n* [C] : a person whose job is to take care of sheep

²**shepherd** *vb* [T] : to guide (someone or something) • *They shepherded the bill through Congress.*

sher·bet /ˈʃɚbət/ *also US* **sher·bert** /ˈʃɚbɚt/ *n* [C/U] *US* : a frozen sweet dessert made from fruit or fruit juices

sherd *variant spelling of* SHARD

sher·iff /ˈʃerəf/ *n* [C] **1** : an elected official who is in charge of enforcing the law in a county or town of the U.S. **2** *Brit* : the highest official in a county or shire in England or Wales — called also *High Sheriff*

sher·ry /ˈʃeri/ *n, pl* **-ries** [C/U] : a type of strong wine that is made especially in Spain

she's /ˈʃiːz, ʃɪz/ — used as a contraction of *she is* or *she has* • *She's* [=*she is*] *right.* • *She's* [=*she has*] *been here before.*

shied *past tense and past participle of* SHY

¹**shield** /ˈʃiːld/ *n* [C] **1** : a large piece of metal, wood, etc., carried by someone (such as a soldier or police officer) for protection **2** : something that defends or protects someone or something • *Good nutrition is a shield against disease.* **3** *US* : a police officer's badge

²**shield** *vb* [T] **1** : to cover and protect (someone or something) • *She shielded her eyes (from the glare).* • *(figurative) shielding a child from the real world* **2** : to prevent (someone or something) from being seen • *Trees shield the house from view.*

¹**shift** /ˈʃɪft/ *vb* [T/I] **1** : to move or to cause (something or someone) to move to a different place, position, etc. • *I shifted the bag to my other shoulder.* • *The wind shifted.* • *The population is shifting away from the city.* **2** : to change or to cause (something) to change to a different opinion, belief, etc. • *Public opinion has shifted.* • *She won't shift her ground.* [=*change her position*] **3** : to go or to cause (something) to go from one person or thing to another • *He tried to shift the blame onto/to us.* • *shift resources to a project* **4** *US* : to change the gear you are using in a vehicle • *shifting (the car) into first gear* — **shift for yourself** : to do things without help from others — **shift·er** /ˈʃɪftɚ/ *n* [C]

²**shift** *n* [C] **1 a** : a change in position or direction • *a shift of responsibility* • *shifts in weather* **b** : a change in how something is done or how people think about something • *a shift in voter opinion* **2 a** : a group of people who work together during a scheduled period of time • *The day/night shift worked overtime.* **b** : the scheduled period of time during which a person works • *working long shifts* **3** : SHIFT KEY

shift key *n* [C] : a key on a computer keyboard or a typewriter that you press to type capital letters

shift·less /ˈʃɪftləs/ *adj, disapproving* : lacking ambition and energy • *a lazy, shiftless person*

shift·y /ˈʃɪfti/ *adj* **shift·i·er; -est** *informal* : having an appearance or way of behaving that seems dishonest • *shifty eyes*

shill /ˈʃɪl/ *vb* [I] *US, informal + disapproving* : to talk about or describe someone or something in a favorable way because you are being paid to do it • *celebrities shilling for politicians* — **shill** *n* [C] • *a political shill*

shil·ling /ˈʃɪlɪŋ/ *n* [C] : a British coin used before 1971 that was equal to ¹/₂₀ of a British pound

shim·mer /ˈʃɪmɚ/ *vb* [I] : to shine with a light that seems to move slightly • *shimmering colors/light* — **shimmer** *n* [*singular*] • *the shimmer of jewels*

shim·my /ˈʃɪmi/ *vb* **-mies; -mied; -my·ing** [T/I] : to move or shake your body from side to side • *They were shimmying (their hips) on the dance floor.*

shin /ˈʃɪn/ *n* [C] : the front part of the leg below the knee • *She kicked him in the shin.*

shin·dig /ˈʃɪnˌdɪg/ *n* [C] *informal* : a big party

¹**shine** /ˈʃaɪn/ *vb* **shone** /ˈʃoʊn, *Brit* ˈʃɒn/ *or chiefly US* **shined; shin·ing** **1** [I] : to give off light • *The sun was shining*

through the clouds. ▪ (*figurative*) *Her talent began to shine through.* [=to be clearly shown] **2** [*I*] : to have a smooth surface that reflects light ▪ *silver that shines* **3** [*I*] : to be very good or successful at an activity ▪ *a sport where she really shines* **4** [*I*] : to have a bright, glowing appearance ▪ *Her face was shining with joy.* **5** [*T*] : to point (something that produces light) in a particular direction ▪ *Shine the flashlight over here.* **6** *past tense and past participle* **shined** [*T*] : to make (something) bright and shiny by polishing ▪ *shine shoes* — **rise and shine** *informal* — used to tell someone to wake up and get out of bed

²**shine** *n* [*singular*] **1** : the brightness that results when light is reflected from a surface ▪ *the shine of polished silver* **2** : the act of polishing a pair of shoes ▪ *Would you like a shine?* — **rain or shine** see ¹RAIN — **take a shine to** *informal* : to begin to like (someone or something) ▪ *She really took a shine to her new neighbor.*

shin·gle /ˈʃɪŋɡəl/ *n* [*C*] : a small, thin piece of building material that is used to cover the roof or sides of a building — **shingle** *vb* **shin·gled; shin·gling** [*T*] ▪ *shingle a house* [=put shingles on a house]

shin·gles /ˈʃɪŋɡəlz/ *n* [*U*] : a disease that causes pain and red marks on your skin

shin·ny /ˈʃɪni/ *vb* **-nies; -nied; -ny·ing** [*I*] *US* : to climb *up* or *down* something (such as a pole) by grasping it with your arms and legs — + *up* or *down* ▪ *She shinnied down the drainpipe.*

shiny /ˈʃaɪni/ *adj* **shin·i·er; -est** : having a smooth, shining, bright appearance ▪ *a shiny new car*

¹**ship** /ˈʃɪp/ *n* **1** [*C/U*] : a large boat used for traveling long distances over the sea ▪ *a cruise/merchant ship* **2** [*C*] : a large airplane or spacecraft — **jump ship 1** : to leave a ship without the captain's permission **2** : to suddenly or unexpectedly leave a group, team, etc. ▪ *She jumped ship when the competition offered her a better job.* — **run a tight ship** : to manage or handle a group of people in a strict and effective way — **ship comes in** ✧ When **your ship comes in**, you become very successful or wealthy.

²**ship** *vb* **shipped; ship·ping 1** [*T/I*] : to send (something) to a customer, store, etc. ▪ *The goods were shipped from a foreign port.* ▪ *Your order will ship soon.* **2** [*T*] : to send (someone) to a place that is usually far away ▪ *The soldiers were shipped overseas.* — **ship out** [*phrasal vb*] : to leave one place and go to another for military duties ▪ *The troops will be shipping out next month.* — **ship·per** /ˈʃɪpɚ/ *n* [*C*]

-ship /ˌʃɪp/ *n suffix* **1** : the state or condition of being something ▪ *friendship* **2** : the position, status, or duties of something ▪ *professorship* **3** : skill or ability as someone or something ▪ *penmanship*

ship·board /ˈʃɪpˌboɚd/ *adj, always before a noun* : happening or existing on a ship ▪ *shipboard entertainment*

ship·load /ˈʃɪpˌloʊd/ *n* [*C*] : an amount or number that will fill a ship ▪ *a shipload of corn*

ship·ment /ˈʃɪpmənt/ *n* **1** [*C*] : a load of goods that are being sent to a customer, store, etc. ▪ *a shipment of books* **2** [*U*] : the act of sending something to a customer, store, etc. ▪ *This box is ready for shipment.*

ship·ping /ˈʃɪpɪŋ/ *n* [*U*] **1** : the act or business of sending goods to people, stores, etc. ▪ *The fruit was ready for shipping.* ▪ *What do you charge for* **shipping and handling**? [=for packaging and sending something to a customer] **2** *formal* : a group of ships ▪ *international shipping lanes* [=paths through the sea that commercial ships can take]

ship·shape /ˌʃɪpˈʃeɪp/ *adj, not before a noun* : clean, neat, and tidy ▪ *I like to keep everything shipshape.*

ship·wreck /ˈʃɪpˌrɛk/ *n* **1** [*C/U*] : the destruction or sinking of a ship at sea ▪ *Only a few sailors survived the shipwreck.* **2** [*C*] : a ruined or destroyed ship ▪ *a sunken shipwreck* — **shipwreck** *vb* [*T*] ▪ *shipwrecked sailors/boats*

ship·yard /ˈʃɪpˌjɑɚd/ *n* [*C*] : a place where ships are built or repaired

shire /ˈʃajɚ/ *n* [*C*] *Brit* : a county in England

shirk /ˈʃɚk/ *vb* [*T/I*] : to avoid doing something that you are supposed to do ▪ *He never shirks (from doing) his duty.*

shirt /ˈʃɚt/ *n* [*C*] : a piece of clothing for the upper body that usually has sleeves and often a collar and buttons down the front — **keep your shirt on** *informal* — used to tell someone to calm down or be more patient ▪ *"Let's go!" "Keep your shirt on! I'll be ready soon."* — **lose your shirt** *chiefly US, informal* : to lose a lot of money because of a bad bet or investment ▪ *She lost her shirt in the stock market.* — **the shirt off your back** *informal* ✧ People who would **give you the shirt off their back** would do anything to help you.

shirt·sleeve /ˈʃɚtˌsliːv/ *n* [*C*] : the sleeve of a shirt — **in (your) shirtsleeves** : wearing a shirt but no coat or jacket

shirty /ˈʃɚti/ *adj* **shirt·i·er; -est** *Brit, informal* : angry or irritated ▪ *He was/got shirty with me.*

shish ke·bab /ˈʃɪʃkəˌbɑːb, *Brit* ˈʃɪʃkəˌbæb/ *n* [*C*]: KEBAB

¹**shiv·er** /ˈʃɪvɚ/ *vb* [*I*] : to shake slightly because you are cold, afraid, etc. ▪ *It was so cold that I was shivering.*

²**shiver** *n* [*C*] : a small shaking movement caused by cold or strong emotion ▪ *a shiver of delight/pleasure* — **shiv·ery** /ˈʃɪvɚi/ *adj* ▪ *I felt shivery.*

shmooze *variant spelling of* SCHMOOZE

shoal /ˈʃoʊl/ *n* [*C*] **1** : an area where the water in a sea, lake, or river is not deep **2** : a small, raised area of sand just below the surface of the water

¹**shock** /ˈʃɑːk/ *n* **1 a** [*C*] : a sudden usually unpleasant or upsetting feeling caused by something unexpected ▪ *the shock of discovering a terrible secret* ▪ *I got the* **shock of my life**. [=I was very unpleasantly surprised] ▪ *You're in for a big/rude shock if you think it will be easy.* **b**

[C] : something unexpected that causes a sudden usually unpleasant or upsetting feeling ▪ *Seeing them together was a shock.* ▪ *Her death came as (quite) a shock.* [=was very shocking] **c** [U] : a state in which you are experiencing a sudden usually unpleasant or upsetting feeling because of something unexpected ▪ *I was in (a state of) shock after hearing the news.* **2** [U] *medical* : a serious condition in which the body is not able to get enough blood to all the parts of the body ✧ Shock is caused by a severe injury, a large loss of blood, etc. ▪ *She was treated for shock after the accident.* **3** [C] : the effect of a strong charge of electricity passing through the body of a person or animal ▪ *an electric shock* **4** [C] : SHOCK ABSORBER **5** [C/U] : a violent shake ▪ *the shock of the explosion* **6** [C] : a thick and full mass of hair ▪ *a shock of hair*

²**shock** *vb* **1** [T] : to surprise and usually upset (someone) ▪ *The attack shocked the world.* ▪ *I'm shocked at/by how easy it was.* ▪ *shocked into taking action* **2** [T/I] : to cause (someone) to feel horror or disgust ▪ *He enjoys shocking his readers.*

shock absorber *n* [C] : a device that is connected to the wheel of a vehicle in order to reduce the effects of traveling on a rough surface

shock·er /ˈʃɑːkɚ/ *n* [C] *informal* : something that shocks people ▪ *Their divorce was a shocker.*

shock·ing /ˈʃɑːkɪŋ/ *adj* : very surprising and upsetting or causing a sudden feeling of horror or disgust ▪ *a shocking crime/discovery* — **shock·ing·ly** *adv*

shocking pink *n* [U] : a very bright pink color

shock·proof /ˈʃɑːkˌpruːf/ *adj* : not damaged if dropped, hit, etc. ▪ *a waterproof and shockproof watch*

shock wave *n* [C] **1** : a movement of extremely high air pressure that is caused by an explosion, an earthquake, etc. **2** : a usually negative response or reaction that many people have to a particular thing ▪ *The court's ruling sent shock waves throughout the nation.*

shod /ˈʃɑːd/ *adj, literary* : wearing shoes ▪ *His feet were shod in slippers.* [=he was wearing slippers]

shod·dy /ˈʃɑːdi/ *adj* **shod·di·er**; **-est** : poorly done or made ▪ *shoddy work/furniture* — **shod·di·ly** /ˈʃɑːdəli/ *adv*

¹**shoe** /ˈʃuː/ *n* **1** [C] : an outer covering for your foot that usually has a stiff bottom part called a sole with a thicker part called a heel attached to it and an upper part that covers part or all of the top of your foot ▪ *a pair of shoes* ▪ *athletic/running shoes* **2** [*plural*] : another person's situation or position ▪ *I wouldn't want to be in his shoes right now.* ▪ *Put yourself in her shoes.* [=imagine yourself in her situation] ▪ *trying to fill her shoes* [=do what she does as well as she does it] **3** [C] : HORSESHOE 1 **4** [C] : the part of a brake that presses on the wheel of a vehicle ▪ *brake shoes* — **if the shoe fits** or **if the shoe fits, wear it** *US* — used to say that something said or suggested about a

person is true and that the person should accept it as true ▪ *"Are you calling me a liar?" "Well, if the shoe fits, wear it."*

²**shoe** *vb* **shod** /ˈʃɑːd/ *also chiefly US* **shoed** /ˈʃuːd/; **shoe·ing** /ˈʃuːwɪŋ/ [T] : to put a horseshoe on (a horse)

¹**shoe·horn** /ˈʃuːˌhoɚn/ *n* [C] : a curved device that you use to slide the heel of your foot into a shoe

²**shoehorn** *vb* [T] : to force (something or someone) into a small space, a short period of time, etc. ▪ *She's trying to shoehorn a year's worth of classes into a single semester.* ▪ *They somehow shoehorned all of us into a tiny room.*

shoe·lace /ˈʃuːˌleɪs/ *n* [C] : a long, thin material like a string that is used for fastening a shoe ▪ *Tie your shoelaces.*

shoe·mak·er /ˈʃuːˌmeɪkɚ/ *n* [C] : someone who makes or repairs shoes

shoe·shine /ˈʃuːˌʃaɪn/ *n* [C] : the act of polishing someone's shoes in exchange for money ▪ *a shoeshine boy/man* [=a boy/man who earns money by polishing/shining shoes]

shoe·string /ˈʃuːˌstrɪŋ/ *n* **1** [C] *US* : SHOELACE **2** [*singular*] *informal* : a small amount of money ▪ *The newspaper operates/runs on a shoestring (budget).*

shone *past tense and past participle of* ¹SHINE

shoo /ˈʃuː/ *interj* — used when repeatedly moving your hand away from you in a short motion with your fingers down to tell an animal or person to leave ▪ *Shoo! Get out of here!* — **shoo** *vb* [T] ▪ *He shooed the cat out of the house.*

shoo-in /ˈʃuːˌɪn/ *n* [C] *chiefly US, informal* : someone or something that will win easily or is certain to win ▪ *She's a shoo-in for the job/award.*

shook *past tense of* ¹SHAKE

¹**shoot** /ˈʃuːt/ *vb* **shot** /ˈʃɑːt/; **shoot·ing** **1 a** [T/I] : to cause a bullet, arrow, etc., to move forward with great force from a weapon ▪ *a gun that shoots accurately* ▪ *Don't shoot. I surrender.* ▪ *He shot (an arrow) at the deer.* ▪ *shoot a gun/rifle* **b** [T] : to wound or kill (a person or animal) with a bullet, arrow, etc., that is shot from a weapon ▪ *Police shot the suspect in the leg.* ▪ *Two people were shot dead.* [=killed with bullets] **c** [T] : to remove or destroy (something) with a bullet, rocket, etc., that is shot from a weapon ▪ *shoot the lock off a door* ▪ *shoot out the lights* **2** [T/I] : to go, move, or pass quickly and suddenly in a particular direction or to a particular place ▪ *They shot past us on skis.* ▪ *A pain shot through her arm.* ▪ *I've been having shooting pains in my leg.* ▪ *The album shot (the band) straight to the top of the charts.* **3 a** [T/I] *sports* : to kick, hit, or throw (something) toward or into a goal ▪ *shoot a basketball* ▪ *He shot the puck/ball into the goal.* ▪ *She was outside shooting baskets.* [=practicing basketball by making shots] **b** [T] *golf* : to achieve (a particular score) ▪ *He shot a hole in one.* **c** [T] : to play (a sport or game) ✧ This sense is usually used with sports or games that involve shooting a ball. ▪ *Let's shoot some pool.* **4** [T/I] : to film or photograph (some-

thing) ▪ *The movie was shot* [=*filmed*] *in Australia.* ▪ *shoot* [=*take*] *a photo* **5** [*T*] : to direct (a look, comment, etc.) at (someone) ▪ *She shot me an angry look.* = *She shot an angry look at me.* **6** [*I*] *US, informal* — used to tell someone to begin to speak ▪ *You wanted to say something? OK, shoot.* **7** [*T*] *informal* : to inject (an illegal drug) into a vein ▪ *shoot heroin* — **shoot down** [*phrasal vb*] **shoot down (something or someone)** *or* **shoot (something or someone) down 1 a** : to cause (something) to fall to the ground by hitting it with a bullet, rocket, etc., that is shot from a weapon ▪ *shoot down a helicopter* **b** : to end or defeat (something) ▪ *The bill was shot down in the Senate.* **c** : to reject (something) completely ▪ *shoot down an idea* **2 a** : to kill (someone) with a bullet shot from a gun ▪ *Someone shot him down.* **b** *informal* : to refuse to accept the offer made by (someone) ▪ *I asked her out, but she shot me down.* [=she said no to me] — **shoot for** [*phrasal vb*] *chiefly US, informal* : to have (something) as a goal ▪ *"When should we do it?" "Let's shoot for* [=*aim for*] *Friday."* — **shoot from the hip** : to act or speak quickly without thinking about the possible results — **shoot it out** : to shoot guns at someone during a fight until one side is killed or defeated ▪ *The two gangs shot it out in the street.* — **shoot the breeze** *also* **shoot the bull** *US, informal* : to talk informally about unimportant things ▪ *I enjoy shooting the breeze with my neighbors.* — **shoot up** [*phrasal vb*] **1** : to grow or increase quickly and suddenly ▪ *Sales have shot up.* **2** *informal* : to inject an illegal drug into a vein ▪ *shooting up heroin* **3 shoot up (something)** *or* **shoot (something) up** : to shoot many bullets at or inside (something) ▪ *He shot the place up.* — **shoot your mouth off** *also* **shoot off at the mouth** *informal* : to talk foolishly, carelessly, or too much about something — **shoot yourself in the foot** *informal* : to do or say something that causes trouble for yourself — **shoot-er** /ˈʃuːtɚ/ *n* [*C*]

²**shoot** *n* [*C*] **1 a** : the part of a new plant that is just beginning to grow above the ground **b** : a new branch and its leaves on an established plant **2 a** : an occasion when a movie, television show, etc., is being filmed ▪ *She is currently on a movie shoot in London.* **b** : PHOTO SHOOT

³**shoot** *interj, US* — used to show that you are annoyed or surprised ▪ *"We've missed the train!" "Oh, shoot!"*

shooting *n* **1** [*C*] : an occurrence in which a person is shot with a gun ▪ *There was a shooting last night.* **2** [*U*] : the activity or sport of killing wild animals with a gun ▪ *They are going shooting* [=*going hunting*] *this weekend.* **3** [*U*] : the action of photographing or filming someone or something ▪ *Shooting of the movie begins next week.*

shooting star *n* [*C*] : a streak of light in the night sky that looks like a star falling but that is actually a piece of rock or

metal (called a meteor) falling from outer space into the Earth's atmosphere

shoot–out /ˈʃuːtˌaʊt/ *n* [*C*] : a fight in which people shoot guns at each other until one side is killed or defeated

¹**shop** /ˈʃɑːp/ *n* **1** [*C*] **a** : a building or room where goods and services are sold

> **usage** In U.S. English, *store* is more common than *shop*. When *shop* is used, it is usually for particular types of small businesses that sell one kind of product or service. *Store* is used for both small and large businesses, especially ones that sell many kinds of goods and services. In British English *store* is only used for large businesses that sell many kinds of goods and services and for a few types of smaller businesses that sell equipment. ▪ (*US + Brit*) *a gift/sandwich/doughnut/flower shop* ▪ (*US + Brit*) *an antique shop* [=(*US*) *store*] ▪ (*Brit*) *a hardware shop* [=(*US + Brit*) *store*] ▪ (*Brit*) *The shops* [=(*US*) *stores*] *are crowded.*

b : the place where a specified kind of worker works ▪ (*US*) *the butcher shop* = (*Brit*) *the butcher's shop* **2** [*C*] : a place for making or repairing goods, machinery, vehicles, etc. ▪ *a repair shop* **3** [*C*] *US* : a class in school in which students are taught to work with tools and machinery ▪ *I am taking shop this semester.* **4** [*U*] *informal* : talk that is related to or about your work or special interests ▪ *They are always talking shop.* — **all over the shop** *Brit* : all over the place : EVERYWHERE — **close up shop** see ¹CLOSE — **mind the shop** see ²MIND — **set up shop** : to start a business or activity in a particular place ▪ *The restaurant set up shop three blocks from here.*

²**shop** *vb* **shopped; shop-ping 1** [*I*] : to visit places where goods are sold in order to look at and buy things ▪ *I shopped all day.* = *I spent the day shopping.* ▪ *She is (out) shopping for a new car.* ▪ *shopping online* **2** [*T*] *US* : to try to get a company to publish or produce (something) ▪ *She's shopping her idea for a film.* ▪ *shop a manuscript around* **3** [*T*] *Brit, informal* : to give information about the secret or criminal activity of (someone) to an authority (such as the police) ▪ *His own mother shopped him to the police.* — **shop around** [*phrasal vb*] : to visit several different places where a thing is sold in order to find the most suitable item or service for the lowest price ▪ *We're shopping around for a bank with low fees.* — **shop-per** /ˈʃɑːpɚ/ *n* [*C*]

shop-a-hol-ic /ˌʃɑːpəˈhɑːlɪk/ *n* [*C*] *informal* : a person who likes to shop very much

shop-keep-er /ˈʃɑːpˌkiːpɚ/ *n* [*C*] : STOREKEEPER

shop-lift /ˈʃɑːpˌlɪft/ *vb* [*T/I*] : to steal things from a shop or store ▪ *He was caught shoplifting (books).* — **shop-lift-er** /ˈʃɑːpˌlɪftɚ/ *n* [*C*] — **shop-lift-ing** /ˈʃɑːpˌlɪftɪŋ/ *n* [*U*] ▪ *She was arrested for shoplifting.*

shopping *n* [*U*] : the activity of visiting places where goods are sold in order to look at and buy things (such as food, clothing, etc.) ▪ *We do our/the grocery* ***shopping*** *once a week.* = *We* ***go grocery shopping*** *once a week.* [=we shop for groceries once a week] ▪ *I'm going shopping.* ▪ *a* ***shopping cart*** = *a* ***shopping bag*** [= a bag that a store gives you to carry any items you have bought there]

shopping cart *n* [C] : ¹CART 2

shopping center (*US*) *or Brit* **shopping centre** *n* [C] : a group of shops or stores in one area — called also *shopping plaza*

shopping list *n* [C] : a list of things to be bought at a shop or store

shopping mall *n* [C] *chiefly US* : a large building or group of buildings containing many different stores

shop steward *n* [C] : a member of a labor union in a factory or company who is elected by the other members to meet with the managers

shop·talk /ˈʃɑːpˌtɑːk/ *n* [U] *chiefly US* : talk that is related to your work or special interests

shop·worn /ˈʃɑːpˌwoɚn/ *adj*, *US* **1** : faded or damaged from being in a shop or store for too long ▪ *shopworn books* **2** : not interesting because of being used too often ▪ *shopworn clichés*

¹**shore** /ˈʃoɚ/ *n* **1** [C/U] : the land along the edge of an area of water (such as an ocean, lake, etc.) ▪ *a rocky/sandy shore* [=*coast*] ▪ *Houses were built on the shores of the lake.* ▪ *swim/head to shore* ▪ *a mile from shore* **2** [*plural*] *literary* : a country that touches a sea or ocean ▪ *when my family came to these shores* [=came to this country]

²**shore** *vb* **shored**; **shor·ing** — **shore up** [*phrasal vb*] **shore (something) up** *or* **shore up (something) 1** : to support (something) or keep (something) from falling by placing something under or against it ▪ *shore up* [=*prop up*] *a roof/wall* **2** : to support or help (something) ▪ *The tax cuts are supposed to shore up the economy.*

shore·line /ˈʃoɚˌlaɪn/ *n* [C/U] : the land along the edge of an area of water (such as an ocean, lake, etc.) : a coast or shore ▪ *miles of shoreline*

shorn *past participle of* SHEAR

¹**short** /ˈʃoɚt/ *adj* **1 a** : extending a small distance from one end to the other end : not long ▪ *Her hair is short.* = *She has short hair.* ▪ *a short distance* **b** : not great in distance ▪ *a short drive/trip* ▪ *This way is shorter.* **c** : having little height : not tall ▪ *a short girl* **2** : lasting or continuing for a small amount of time ▪ *a short* [=*brief*] *delay/vacation/speech* ▪ *It's a short walk from here.* [=you can walk there from here in a few minutes] ▪ *She has a short memory.* [=she forgets about events, conversations, etc., soon after they happen] **3** : having few pages, items, etc. ▪ *a short book/poem/list* **4** *of clothing* : covering only part of the arms or legs ▪ *boys in short pants* ▪ *a shirt with short sleeves* [=sleeves that end at or above the elbows] ▪ *a short skirt* [=a skirt that ends above the knees and especially several inches above the knees] **5 a** : existing in less than the usual or needed

amount ▪ *Money is short these days.* [=I don't have enough money lately] ▪ *Gasoline is in short supply.* [=little gasoline is available] ▪ (*US*) *We can be ready on* ***short notice.*** = (*Brit*) *We can be ready at* ***short notice.*** [=very quickly] **b** *not before a noun* : having less than what is needed ▪ *We're short on time/money* [=we don't have enough time/money] ▪ *The team was short (by) two players.* = *The team was two players short.* ▪ **short on patience** [=feeling impatient] **c** : less than — used in the phrase ***nothing short of*** to give emphasis to a statement or description ▪ *It's nothing short of a miracle.* = *It's nothing short of miraculous.* [=it's a miracle] **d** : not reaching far enough ▪ *a short throw* **6** : made smaller by having part removed ▪ *a short tax form* ▪ *"Doc" is* ***short for*** *"doctor."* **7** *not before a noun* : talking to someone in a very brief and unfriendly way ▪ *I'm sorry I was short with you.* **8** *linguistics* *of a vowel* — used to identify certain vowel sounds in English (such as the "a" in "bad," the "e" in "bet," the "i" in "sit," the "o" in "hot," and the "u" in "but") ▪ *long and short vowels* — compare ¹LONG 6 — **fall short** see ¹FALL — **in short order** : quickly and without delay ▪ *The work was finished in short order.* — **make short work of** see ²WORK — **short and sweet** : pleasantly brief ▪ *I like meetings that are short and sweet.* — **short of breath** ✧ *If you are short of breath, it is difficult for you to breathe.* ▪ *She was short of breath and unable to talk after her run.* — **short·ness** /ˈʃoɚtnəs/ *n* [U]

²**short** *adv* **1** : to or at a point that is not as far as expected or desired ▪ *The ball fell short.* ▪ *throw a ball short* ▪ *a month short of graduation* [=a month before graduation] ▪ *We made dozens of cookies, but we still* ***came up short.*** [=we had fewer than we needed] ▪ *Sales for the month* ***came short of*** *our estimates.* [=we sold less than we had predicted we would sell] ▪ *She's* ***just short of*** *six feet tall.* [=she is almost six feet tall] ▪ *He* ***stopped short of*** *the line.* [=stopped before reaching the line] ▪ *She said she was unhappy with some employees, but she* ***stopped short of*** *naming which ones.* [=she did not say which ones she was unhappy with] ▪ *Time is* ***running short.*** [=there is little time left] **2** : in a sudden manner ▪ *She stopped* ***short*** [=*suddenly*] *when she saw him.* ▪ *I was* ***brought up short*** *by what I saw.* [=I stopped suddenly because of what I saw] **3** : in a way that makes something short ▪ *Her hair was cut/cropped* ***short.*** [=she had short hair] — **cut short** : to end (something) earlier than expected ▪ *cut a vacation/speech* ***short*** — **fall short** see ¹FALL — **sell (someone or something) short** see SELL — **short of** : except for (something) : other than (something) ▪ *Short of replacing the motor, I've tried everything to fix the car.*

³**short** *n* **1** [*plural*] **a** : pants that end at or above the knees ▪ *a pair of shorts* **b** : BOXER SHORTS **2** [C] : a short movie ▪ *an animated short* **3** [C] : SHORT CIR-

CUIT **4** [C] *Brit* : a small amount of liquor that you drink quickly : SHOT ▪ *a short of vodka* — **for short** : in a shorter form ▪ *My name is Susan, or Sue for short.* — **in short** : in a few words — used to indicate that you are saying something in as few words as possible ▪ *The trip was, in short, a disaster.* — **the long and (the) short of it** see ³LONG

⁴**short** *vb* **1** [T] : to cause (something) to have a short circuit : SHORT-CIRCUIT ▪ *Lightning shorted (out) the TV.* **2** [I] : to stop working because of a short circuit : SHORT-CIRCUIT ▪ *The lamp shorted (out).*

short·age /ˈʃoɚtɪdʒ/ *n* [C/U] : a state in which there is not enough of something that is needed ▪ *a gasoline/water shortage* = *a shortage of gasoline/water* ▪ **There is no shortage of restaurants** [=there are many restaurants] *in the city.*

short·bread /ˈʃoɚtˌbrɛd/ *n* [U] : a thick cookie made of flour, sugar, and a lot of butter or other shortening

short·cake /ˈʃoɚtˌkeɪk/ *n* [U] *chiefly US* : a dessert made with a rich cake that is served with sweetened fruit on top ▪ *strawberry shortcake*

short·change /ˈʃoɚtˈtʃeɪndʒ/ *vb* **-changed; -chang·ing** [T] **1** : to give (someone) less than the correct amount of change ▪ *The cashier shortchanged me.* **2** : to give (someone) less than what is expected or deserved ▪ *I feel that I'm being shortchanged by the policy.*

short circuit *n* [C] : the failure of electricity to flow properly in a circuit because the wires or connections in the circuit are damaged or not connected properly

short–circuit *vb* **1 a** [T] : to cause (something) to have a short circuit ▪ *Lightning short-circuited the TV.* **b** [I] : to stop working because of a short circuit ▪ *The lamp short-circuited.* **2** [T] : to avoid doing (something) ▪ *The owners short-circuited a required inspection.* **3** [T] : to stop (efforts, plans, etc.) from succeeding ▪ *The lawyers short-circuited any attempt to sue the company.*

short·com·ing /ˈʃoɚtˌkʌmɪŋ/ *n* [C] **1** : a weakness in someone's character ▪ *my strengths and shortcomings* **2** : a bad feature ▪ *One shortcoming of this camera is its short battery life.*

short·cut /ˈʃoɚtˌkʌt/ *n* [C] **1** : a shorter, quicker, or easier way to get to a place ▪ *I know a shortcut. Turn left here.* ▪ *We took a shortcut home.* **2** : a quicker or easier way to do something ▪ *There are no shortcuts to/for learning another language.*

short·en /ˈʃoɚtn̩/ *vb* **1** [I] : to become shorter ▪ *The days are shortening.* [=lasting for less time] **2** [T] : to make (something) shorter ▪ *shorten a coat/speech/name* ▪ *a problem that shortened the life of the engine* [=caused the engine to fail sooner]

short·en·ing /ˈʃoɚtnɪŋ/ *n* [U] : a fat (such as butter) that is used in cooking or baking

short·fall /ˈʃoɚtˌfɑːl/ *n* [C] *formal* : a failure to get what is expected or needed ▪ *We had a budget shortfall.* [=our costs

were higher than the available amount of money]; *also* : the amount of such a failure ▪ *a $2 million shortfall = a shortfall of $2 million* [=$2 million less than is needed]

short–haired *adj* : having short fur or hair ▪ *a short-haired cat/student*

short·hand /ˈʃoɚtˌhænd/ *n* [U] **1** : a method of writing quickly by using symbols or abbreviations for sounds, words, or phrases ▪ *The notes were written in shorthand.* [=using special symbols] ▪ *The secretary takes shorthand.* [=writes in shorthand] **2** : a short or quick way of showing or saying something ▪ *"ASAP" is shorthand for "as soon as possible."*

short·hand·ed /ˌʃoɚtˈhændəd/ *adj* : having fewer than the usual number of people available ▪ *We're shorthanded this week.*

short–lived /ˈʃoɚtˈlɪvd/ *adj* **short·er–lived; short·est–lived** : living or lasting for a short time ▪ *Her happiness was short-lived.*

short·ly /ˈʃoɚtli/ *adv* **1** : in or within a short time : SOON ▪ *I'll be ready shortly.* ▪ *I left shortly after/before noon.* ▪ **Shortly after** [=soon after] *she hung up, the phone rang again.* **2** : in a very brief and unfriendly way ▪ *"I can't help you,"* he said *shortly.*

short–or·der /ˈʃoɚtˌoɚdɚ/ *adj, always before a noun* : making or serving food that can be cooked quickly when a customer orders it ▪ *a short-order cook*

short–range /ˈʃoɚtˈreɪndʒ/ *adj, always before a noun* **short·er–range; short·est–range** **1** : able to travel or be used over short distances ▪ *short-range missiles/weapons* **2** : involving a short period of time ▪ *short-range* [=short-term] *goals*

short run *n* — **the short run** : a short period of time at the beginning of something ▪ *seeing results in the short run* [=when a small amount of time has passed]

short shrift *n* [U] : little or no attention or thought ▪ **giving short shrift to the theory** ▪ *They have gotten/received short shrift from the city government.* [=the city government has ignored their problems]

short–sight·ed /ˈʃoɚtˌsaɪtəd/ *adj* **1 a** : not considering what will or might happen in the future ▪ *shortsighted politicians who only care about getting reelected* **b** : made or done without thinking about what will happen in the future ▪ *shortsighted policies/investments* **2** *Brit* : NEARSIGHTED — **short·sight·ed·ness** *n* [U]

short·stop /ˈʃoɚtˌstɑːp/ *n* [C] *baseball* : the player who defends the area between second and third base

short story *n* [C] : a short written story usually dealing with few characters : a short work of fiction

short temper *n* [C] : a tendency to become angry easily ▪ *She has a short temper.* — **short–tem·pered** /ˈʃoɚtˈtɛmpəd/ *adj* ▪ *short-tempered children*

short term *n* — **the short term** : a short period of time at the beginning of something ▪ *It'll work, at least for the short term.*

▪ *It won't make any difference* **in the short term.** [=when a small amount of time has passed]

short—term /ˈʃɔɚtˌtɚm/ *adj* : lasting for, relating to, or involving a short period of time ▪ *the short-term effects of the plan* ▪ *a short-term plan/strategy* ▪ *her short-term memory* [=her ability to remember things that happened recently]

short—wave /ˈʃɔɚtˌweɪv/ *n* [C] **1** : a radio wave with a wavelength between 10 and 100 meters **2** : a radio or receiver that uses shortwaves — **shortwave** *adj, always before a noun* ▪ *a shortwave radio/receiver*

¹**shot** /ˈʃɑːt/ *n* **1** [C] : an act of shooting a gun ▪ *Two shots were heard.* = *Two shots rang out.* ▪ *She fired a warning shot into the air.* [=fired/shot a gun into the air as a warning] ▪ *Someone took a shot at him.* [=tried to shoot him] **2** [U] **a** : BUCKSHOT **b** : the objects (called ammunition) that are shot from cannons and other old-fashioned weapons ▪ *musket/cannon shot* **3** [C] : a person who shoots a gun ▪ *She's a good shot.* [=she is skilled in shooting a gun] — see also BIG SHOT **4** [C] : a critical or hurtful remark ▪ *They* **took shots** *at each other throughout the debate.* ▪ *a* **parting shot** : [=a final critical comment] **5** [C] : the act of hitting someone or something with your hand or an object ▪ *Her shot got in a few good shots on his opponent.* **6** [C] **a** : an act of kicking, hitting, or throwing a ball or puck toward or into a goal ▪ *He* **made the shot.** [=got the ball or puck in the goal] ▪ *She* **took a shot** *but missed.* **b** : a ball or puck that is kicked, hit, or thrown toward or into a goal ▪ *Her shot landed on the putting green.* **7** [C] **a** : an attempt to do something successfully — usually singular ▪ **Give it a shot.** = **Take a shot** *at it.* [=try to do it] ▪ *I gave it my best shot.* [=try, effort] ▪ *I took/had a shot at (guessing) the answer.* **b** : a chance that something will happen or be achieved ▪ *We have a good shot at winning.* **8** [C] *informal* : PHOTOGRAPH ▪ *I got/took some good shots* [=pictures] *of the kids.* **9** [C] : a part of a movie or a television show that is filmed by one camera without stopping ▪ *the movie's opening shot* **10** [C] *chiefly US* : an act of putting something (such as medicine or vaccine) into the body with a needle : INJECTION ▪ *a flu shot* ▪ *a shot of morphine* **11** [C] **a** : a small amount of a drink and especially a strong alcoholic drink ▪ *tequila shots* = *shots of tequila* **b** : a small amount of something ▪ *a shot of humor* **c** : a heavy metal ball that people throw as far as they can in the athletic event called the shot put — **a shot** *US, informal* : for each one : APIECE ▪ *They cost $5 a shot.* — **a shot in the arm** : something that makes someone or something stronger or more active, confident, etc. ▪ *The award has given the school a much needed shot in the arm.* — **a shot in the dark** : a guess that is based on very little or no information or evidence ▪ *Estimating the cost of a project like this is often a shot in the dark.* — **call the shots** *informal* : to

be in charge or control of something ▪ *Who calls the shots here?* — **like a shot** : immediately and very quickly ▪ *The car took off like a shot.*

²**shot** *past tense and past participle of* ¹SHOOT

³**shot** *adj, not before a noun* **1** *informal* : in a very bad condition ▪ *The tires are shot.* ▪ *My nerves are* **shot (to pieces).** **2** : having a particular color, quality, feature, etc., throughout ▪ *black hair shot* **through with** *gray*

shot·gun /ˈʃɑːtˌgʌn/ *n* [C] : a gun with a long barrel that shoots a large number of small metal balls (called buckshot) — **ride shotgun** *see* ¹RIDE

shotgun wedding *n* [C] : a wedding that happens because the bride is pregnant — called also **shotgun marriage**

shot put *n* — **the shot put** : an athletic event in which people compete by trying to throw a heavy metal ball (called a shot) as far as possible — **shot—put·ter** /ˈʃɑːtˌpʊtɚ/ *n* [C]

should /ˈʃʊd, ˈʃəd/ *vb, past tense of* SHALL [*modal vb*] **1 a** — used to say or suggest that something is the proper, reasonable, or best thing to do ▪ *You should* [=ought to] *sleep.* ▪ *They should be punished.* ▪ *My friends say that I should quit the team.* **b** — used with *have* to say that something was the proper, reasonable, or best thing to do but was not done ▪ *You should have told me.* ▪ *What should I have done?* ▪ *I should have known that he'd be late.* [=it would have been reasonable for me to expect him to be late because he is often late] **c** — used with *have* to say that you wish someone had seen, heard, or experienced something ▪ *You should have seen her face.* [=I wish that you had seen her face] ▪ *It was so funny. You should have been there.* **2** — used to ask for someone's opinion ▪ *Should I turn the music down?* ▪ *What should we have for lunch?* **3** — used to say that something is expected or correct ▪ *There should be four bowls, not six.* ▪ *"He feels very sorry." "Well, he should!"* ▪ *They should be here by now.* = *They should have arrived by now.* [=I expected them to be here by now] **4 a** — used when saying that you feel a specified way about someone's words or behavior ▪ *It's strange (that) you should say that.* **b** — used to emphasize what you believe, think, hope, etc. ▪ *I should imagine it'll take no more than an hour.* [=I am fairly certain that it won't take more than an hour] ▪ *I should think not.* [=I really don't think so] **5** — used with *have* in negative statements as a polite way of thanking someone for doing something ▪ *Flowers for me? You shouldn't have.* **6** *somewhat formal* — used to talk about the result or effect of something that may happen or be true ▪ *Should* [=if] *you change your mind, please let us know.* ▪ *I will feel guilty if anything should go wrong.* = *I will feel guilty should anything go wrong.* [=if anything goes wrong] **7** *Brit* — used to say that you would do or feel something if something specified happened; only used after *I* or *we* ▪ *If my husband treated me like that, I should*

[=would] *divorce him.* ▪ *I shouldn't [=wouldn't] be surprised at all.* **8** *Brit* — used when giving someone advice; only used after *I* or *we* ▪ *I should [=would] see a doctor if I were you.* **9** *Brit* — used to say that you want to do or want to have something; only used after *I* or *we* ▪ *I should like to call my lawyer.* — **how/why should I/we know** — used to say that you do not know the answer to a question and are surprised that you were asked it ▪ *"Where did they go?" "How should I know?"* — **what/who should you see but** — used to say that you are surprised to see something or someone ▪ *I looked up and what should I see but a hummingbird hovering over my head.*

¹**shoul·der** /ˈʃoʊldɚ/ *n* **1** [C] : the part of your body where your arm is connected ▪ *carrying a backpack on one shoulder* ▪ *He has broad shoulders.* ▪ (*figurative*) *The responsibility falls squarely on her shoulders.* [=she is completely responsible] **2 a** [C] : the part of an animal's body where a front leg is connected **b** [C/U] : a cut of meat from the shoulder of an animal ▪ *pork shoulder* **3** [C] : the part of a piece of clothing that covers your shoulders ▪ *The jacket is tight in the shoulders.* **4** [C] : a part of something that is near the top and that resembles a person's shoulder in shape ▪ *the shoulder of the hill/bottle* **5** [*singular*] *US* : the outside edge of a road that is not used for travel — **a good head on your shoulders** see ¹HEAD — **a shoulder to cry on 1** : a person who gives you sympathy and support **2** : sympathy and support ▪ *He offered me a shoulder to cry on when my husband left me.* — **have a chip on your shoulder** see ¹CHIP — **head and shoulders above** see ¹HEAD — **look over your shoulder** : to worry or think about the possibility that something bad might happen, that someone will try to harm you, etc. ▪ *She's always looking over her shoulder.* — **shoulder to shoulder 1** : physically close together ▪ *They were standing shoulder to shoulder.* **2** : united together to achieve a shared goal ▪ *I stand shoulder to shoulder with the other legislators in this effort.*

²**shoulder** *vb* **1** [T] : to deal with or accept (something) as your responsibility or duty ▪ *shoulder the blame/costs* **2 a** [T] : to push (something) with your shoulder ▪ *He shouldered the door open.* **b** [T/I] : to move forward by pushing through something with the shoulders ▪ *She shouldered (her way) through the crowd.* **3** [T] : to place or carry (something) on your shoulder ▪ *shoulder a rifle*

shoulder blade *n* [C] : one of the two flat, triangular bones of the shoulder that are located in the upper back

-**shoul·dered** /ˈʃoʊldɚd/ *adj* : having shoulders of a specified kind ▪ *broad-shouldered*

shoulder–length *adj*, *of a person's hair* : reaching your shoulders ▪ *shoulder-length hair*

shoulder strap *n* [C] : a strap that is

used to carry or hold something on your shoulder or to hold up a piece of clothing

shouldn't /ˈʃʊdnt/ — used as a contraction of *should not* ▪ *You shouldn't do that.*

should've /ˈʃʊdəv/ — used as a contraction of *should have* ▪ *I should've known that.*

¹**shout** /ˈʃaʊt/ *vb* **1** [T/I] : to say (something) very loudly ▪ *shouting (out) insults/orders* ▪ *Don't shout (at me).* **2** [I] : to make a sudden, loud cry ▪ *They shouted with delight.* ▪ **shout out** *in pain* — **shout down** [*phrasal vb*] **shout (someone) down** : to shout so that (someone who is speaking) cannot be heard ▪ *The crowd shouted him down when he tried to speak.* [=the crowd stopped him from speaking by shouting]

²**shout** *n* [C] : a sudden, loud cry ▪ *a shout of surprise* — **give (someone) a shout** *informal* : to tell (someone) about something when it happens or is ready to be done ▪ *I'll give you a shout when it's time to leave.*

shouting distance *n* [U] *informal* : a short distance ▪ *We live within shouting distance of them.*

shouting match *n* [C] : a loud, angry argument in which people shout at each other ▪ *He got into a shouting match with his neighbor.*

shout–out /ˈʃaʊtˌaʊt/ *n* [C] *US, informal* : an expression of greeting or praise that is given to someone in the presence of many people ▪ *I'd like to give a shout-out to my parents.*

¹**shove** /ˈʃʌv/ *vb* **shoved**; **shov·ing 1** [T] : to push (something) with force ▪ *shove a door* **2** [T/I] : to push (someone or something) along or away in a rough or careless way ▪ *He shoved me out of the way.* ▪ *She shoved her plate aside.* ▪ *The children were pushing and shoving to see the clowns.* — **shove it** *US, informal + impolite* — used to say that you will not accept or do something ▪ *They can take their suggestion and shove it.* — **shove off** [*phrasal vb*] *informal* : to leave a place ▪ *It's late. I should shove off.* — **shove over** or *chiefly Brit* **shove up** [*phrasal vb*] *informal* : to move over to make room for someone else ▪ *Shove over so that I can sit down, too.* — **shove (something) down someone's throat** see THROAT

²**shove** *n* [C] : a strong, forceful push ▪ *He gave the door a shove.* — **push comes to shove** see ²PUSH

¹**shov·el** /ˈʃʌvəl/ *n* [C] **1** : a tool with a long handle that is used for lifting and throwing dirt, sand, snow, etc. **2** : the part of a machine (such as a backhoe) that picks up and moves dirt, sand, snow, etc.

²**shovel** *vb*, *US* -**eled** or *Brit* -**elled**; *US* -**el·ing** or *Brit* -**el·ling 1** [T] : to lift and throw (dirt, sand, snow, etc.) with a shovel ▪ *shoveling snow* **2** *US* **a** [T/I] : to remove snow from (a sidewalk, driveway, etc.) with a shovel ▪ *I have to shovel the driveway.* **b** [T] : to create (a path) by removing snow with a shovel ▪ *He shoveled a path to the door.* **3** [T] *in-*

formal : to put large amounts of (something, such as food) into something in a quick way ▪ *Stop shoveling food into your mouth.*

¹**show** /'ʃoʊ/ *vb* **showed** /'ʃoʊd/; **shown** /'ʃoʊn/ *or* **showed; show·ing** **1** [*T*] : to cause or allow (something) to be seen ▪ *He showed her a picture.* = *He showed a picture to her.* ▪ *Let them show (you) what they can do.* **2** [*T*] : to give information that proves (something) ▪ *The study/research shows (that there is) a link between cigarettes and lung cancer.* ▪ *They showed the theory to be faulty.* ▪ *He seemed fine before his heart attack. That just* **goes to show** [=*shows, proves*] *that appearances can be deceptive.* **3** [*T*] : to teach (someone) how to do or use something especially by letting that person see you do or use it ▪ *Show me how to play the game.* **4** [*T*] : to tell (someone) what or where something is by touching or pointing to it ▪ *She showed me where it is on the map.* ▪ *Show me where it hurts.* ▪ *The guide showed us the church.* [=pointed to the different parts of the church and told us about them] **5** [*T*] : to lead (someone) to a place ▪ *He showed us to our seats.* ▪ *Please show him in/out.* [=lead him to the entrance/exit] **6** [*T*] — used to describe what can be seen or noticed when you look at or examine something ▪ *Her grades have shown some improvement.* [=her grades have improved] ▪ *His health is* **showing signs** *of improvement.* **7** [*T*] : to have an image or picture of (someone or something) ▪ *The photograph shows her as a young woman.* **8** [*T/I*] : to give (information) in the form of numbers, pictures, etc. ▪ *The chart shows that 9 percent of the money is spent on supplies.* **9 a** [*I*] : to be able to be seen or noticed ▪ *The scar hardly shows.* ▪ *He's been working out, and it shows.* **b** [*T*] : to cause or allow (something) to be easily seen or noticed ▪ *Light-colored carpets show dirt.* **10 a** [*T*] : to cause or allow (a feeling, quality, or condition) to be seen or known ▪ *The expression on his face shows he's disappointed.* ▪ *Show your support by wearing this pin.* **b** [*I*] *of a feeling, quality, or condition* : to be able to be seen ▪ *His disappointment showed in his face.* **11** [*T*] : to give (mercy, respect, etc.) to someone ▪ *The judge showed no mercy.* ▪ *Students must show respect for their teachers.* = *Students must show their teachers respect.* **12** [*T*] : to cause (someone) to see your true ability, power, etc. ▪ *They think I can't win, but* **I'll show them!** [=I'll prove that I can win] **13** [*T/I*] : to make (a movie, television show, piece of art, etc.) available for the public to see ▪ *news programs that showed the video* ▪ *She is showing her paintings at a gallery.* ▪ *a movie now showing* [=*playing*] *in theaters* **14** [*I*] *chiefly US, informal* : to arrive or appear at a place ▪ *Many passengers failed to show.* ▪ *Everyone* **showed up** *on time.* **15** — used in phrases like **have something/nothing to show for** to say what someone has achieved or produced by doing something ▪ *We worked all day but had* **nothing to show for** *it.* [=we

worked all day but did not achieve/accomplish anything] — **show around** *also Brit* **show round** [*phrasal vb*] **show (someone) around/round** : to lead (someone) around a place and point to and talk about the interesting or important things you see ▪ *She showed us around (the city).* — **show off** [*phrasal vb*] *informal* **1** *disapproving* : to try to impress someone with your abilities or possessions ▪ *Stop showing off.* **2 show off (someone or something)** *or* **show (someone or something) off a** : to cause (someone or something that you are proud of) to be seen or noticed by a lot of people ▪ *show off a new car* **b** : to make (something) very noticeable ▪ *She wears tight clothes that show off her figure.* — **show (someone) the door, show (someone) to the door** *see* DOOR — **show up** [*phrasal vb*] **show up (someone)** *or* **show (someone) up** *informal* **1** : to do something that makes (someone) look foolish, weak, etc. ▪ *He was trying to show up the boss.* — **show your face** : to appear in public and allow people to see you ▪ *How can you show your face here after what happened?* — **show your hand** *also* **show your cards 1** : to put down your playing cards on a table so that their values can be seen **2** : to tell other people what you are planning to do, want to do, or are able to do ▪ *The company wants to avoid showing its hand about its decision until next month.* — **show yourself 1** : to move out from a hidden place so that you can be seen **2** : to show that you are a particular kind of person, that you have a particular skill, etc. ▪ *They showed themselves to be cowards.* [=behaved in a cowardly way] ▪ *She's shown herself to be capable of running the company.* [=she has shown that she is capable of running the company] — **show your true colors** *see* ¹COLOR

²**show** *n* **1** [*C*] **a** : a performance in a theater that usually includes singing and dancing ▪ *a Broadway/musical show* ▪ *She was the* **star of the show. b** : a public performance that is intended to entertain people ▪ *a puppet/comedy show* ▪ *The band* **puts on a good show. 2** [*C*] : a television or radio program ▪ *my favorite (TV) show* **3** [*C*] : an event at which things of the same kind are put on display for people to look at or buy ▪ *fashion/auto/boat shows* **4** [*singular*] **a** : an action, performance, etc., which clearly shows an ability, feeling, quality, etc. ▪ *a show of strength/generosity* **b** : an event at which something is done or shown to impress or entertain people ▪ *a spectacular show of fireworks* **5** [*C/U*] *disapproving* : an act of pretending to feel a particular way ▪ *She put on a show of sympathy/friendship, but she didn't really care about my problems.* ▪ *Her friendliness is* **all show.** [=she does not truly have friendly feelings toward people] **6** [*singular*] : an event, business, etc., and all of the activities that are involved in its success ▪ *Who's* **running the show?. 7** [*C*] : a competition at which animals of the same kind are judged against one anoth-

er • *a dog show* — **a show of hands** : an occurrence in which people put a hand in the air to indicate that they want something, agree with something, etc. • *Let's see a show of hands: how many people want cake?* — **for show 1** : intended to be seen but not used or bought • *Don't eat the fruit. It's just for show.* [=it's just being used as decoration] **2** *disapproving* : done in order to make others like or approve of you • *His concern was just for show.* — **get the/this show on the road** *informal* : to begin an activity or journey • *Let's get this show on the road!* — **on show** : put somewhere for people to see • *Her paintings are on show at the art gallery.* — **the show must go on** *informal* — used to say that a performance, event, etc., must continue even though there are problems

show–and–tell /ˈʃoʊənˈtɛl/ *n* [U] : a school activity in which children show an item to the class and talk about it

show·biz /ˈʃoʊˌbɪz/ *n* [U] *informal* : SHOW BUSINESS

show·boat /ˈʃoʊˌboʊt/ *n* [C] **1** : a large boat that has a theater and a group of performers and that gives plays at towns and cities along a river **2** *chiefly US, informal + usually disapproving* : a person (such as an athlete) who behaves or performs in a way that is meant to attract the attention of a lot of people — **showboat** *vb* [I] *chiefly US, informal + usually disapproving* • *an athlete who showboats for the fans*

show business *n* [U] : the entertainment industry involved in making movies, television shows, plays, etc. • *She has been in show business for over 30 years.*

¹**show·case** /ˈʃoʊˌkeɪs/ *n* [C] **1** : a box that has a glass top or sides and that is used for displaying objects in a store, museum, etc. **2** : an event, occasion, etc., that shows the abilities or good qualities of someone or something in an attractive or favorable way • *The program is a showcase for local musicians.*

²**showcase** *vb* **-cased; -cas·ing** [T] : to show (something or someone) in an attractive or favorable way • *The program showcases local musicians.*

show·down /ˈʃoʊˌdaʊn/ *n* [C] **1** : a meeting, argument, fight, etc., that will finally settle a disagreement between people or groups • *a showdown with the opposition* **2** : an important game or competition • *The team is getting ready for tonight's showdown with last year's champions.*

¹**show·er** /ˈʃawɚ/ *n* [C] **1 a** : a device that produces a spray of water for you to stand under and wash your body **b** : a room or an enclosed area in a room that contains a shower • *a shower curtain/stall* • *He's in the shower.* **c** : the act of washing your body with a shower • *She took a shower after her run.* = (Brit) *She had a shower after her run.* **2 a** : a brief fall of rain or sometimes snow over a small area • *light/heavy showers* • *rain/snow showers* **b** : a large number of small things that fall or happen at the same time • *a shower of sparks/tears/kisses* **3** *US* : a party

where gifts are given to a woman who is going to be married or have a baby • *a bridal/baby shower*

²**shower** *vb* **1** [I] : to wash yourself by using a shower • *I showered after I went swimming.* **2** [T/I] : to fall on someone or something in the way that rain falls from the sky • *Sparks from the machine showered onto the floor.* = *The machine showered sparks onto the floor.* **3** [T] : to provide (someone) with something in large amounts • *He showered her with gifts/kisses.* = *He showered gifts/kisses on her.* [=he gave her many gifts/kisses]

show·ery /ˈʃawəri/ *adj* : having a lot of rain showers • *showery weather*

show·girl /ˈʃoʊˌgɚl/ *n* [C] : a woman who sings or dances in a musical show

showing *n* [C] **1** : the act of making a movie, television show, piece of art, etc., available for the public to see • *The movie's last showing tonight is at 10:30.* **2** : a performance or appearance of a particular kind • *Both candidates are expected to make a good/strong showing* [=to get many votes] *in the election.*

show·man /ˈʃoʊmən/ *n, pl* **-men** /-mən/ [C] : a person who is good at entertaining people

show·man·ship /ˈʃoʊmənˌʃɪp/ *n* [U] : the ability to attract attention and entertain people • *political showmanship*

shown *past participle of* ¹SHOW

show–off /ˈʃoʊˌɑːf/ *n* [C] *informal + disapproving* : a person who tries to impress other people with his or her abilities or possessions

show·piece /ˈʃoʊˌpiːs/ *n* [C] **1** : something that is the best or most attractive thing being shown • *The museum's showpiece is a painting by Picasso.* **2** : something that is seen as an excellent or outstanding example of something • *The house is an architectural showpiece.*

show·place /ˈʃoʊˌpleɪs/ *n* [C] : a beautiful or important place that people enjoy seeing • *They transformed their home into a showplace.*

show·room /ˈʃoʊˌruːm/ *n* [C] : a large room where things that are for sale are displayed • *a car showroom*

show·time /ˈʃoʊˌtaɪm/ *n* [U] : the time when a play, movie, etc., begins • *Showtime is in five minutes.* • *(figurative) After months of planning, it's finally showtime.*

showy /ˈʃowi/ *adj* **show·i·er; -est** : having an appearance that attracts attention • *showy blossoms* • *(disapproving) showy jewelry*

shrank *past tense of* ¹SHRINK

shrap·nel /ˈʃræpnəl/ *n* [U] : small metal pieces that scatter outwards from an exploding bomb, shell, or mine

¹**shred** /ˈʃrɛd/ *n* **1** [C] : a long, thin piece cut or torn off of something • *shreds of paper/cloth* **2** [*plural*] : a completely ruined condition • *His reputation was in shreds.* • *Critics picked/pulled/tore/ripped the movie to shreds.* [=criticized the movie very severely] **3** [*singular*] : a very small amount of something • *There's not a shred of proof/evidence he did it.*

²**shred** *vb* **shred·ded; shred·ding** [T] : to

cut or tear (something) into long, thin pieces ▪ *He shredded the documents.*

shred·der /ˈʃrɛdɚ/ *n* [C] : a machine used for cutting something into long, thin pieces ▪ *a paper shredder*

shrewd /ˈʃruːd/ *adj* : having or showing an ability to understand things and to make good judgments ▪ *a shrewd observer/observation* — **shrewd·ly** *adv*

shriek /ˈʃriːk/ *vb* [T/I] : to make a loud, high-pitched cry ▪ *The baby shrieked with delight.* ▪ *"Mommy!" she shrieked.* — **shriek** *n* [C] ▪ *a shriek of delight*

shrift /ˈʃrɪft/ *see* SHORT SHRIFT

shrill /ˈʃrɪl/ *adj* **1** : having a very loud, high-pitched sound ▪ *a shrill whistle/scream* **2** : difficult to ignore but often unreasonable ▪ *shrill protests/accusations*

shrimp /ˈʃrɪmp/ *n*, *pl* **shrimp** *or* **shrimps** [C] **1** : a small shellfish that has a long body and legs and that is eaten as food **2** *informal* : a very small or unimportant person

shrine /ˈʃraɪn/ *n* [C] **1** : a place connected with a holy person or event where people go to worship ▪ *a Buddhist shrine* **2** : a place that people visit because it is connected with someone or something that is important to them ▪ *The writer's house has become a shrine to/for his fans.*

¹shrink /ˈʃrɪŋk/ *vb* **shrank** /ˈʃræŋk/ *or* **shrunk** /ˈʃrʌŋk/; **shrunk** *or* **shrunk·en** /ˈʃrʌŋkən/; **shrink·ing** **1** [T/I] : to become smaller or to make (something) smaller in amount, size, or value ▪ *The sweater shrank when it was washed.* ▪ *The treatment should shrink the tumor.* **2** [I] : to quickly move away from something shocking, frightening, or disgusting ▪ *He shrank (back) in horror.* — **shrink from** [*phrasal vb*] : to try to avoid (something difficult or unpleasant) ▪ *She won't shrink from the task.*

²shrink *n* [C] *informal* : a psychiatrist or psychologist ▪ *He's seeing a shrink.*

shrink·age /ˈʃrɪŋkɪdʒ/ *n* [U] **1** : the amount by which something becomes smaller or less ▪ *a shrinkage of 10 percent* **2** : the act or process of becoming smaller in amount, size, or value ▪ *the shrinkage of the polar ice caps*

shrinking violet *n* [C] *informal* : a person who is very shy ▪ *He's no shrinking violet.*

shrink–wrap /ˈʃrɪŋkˌræp/ *n* [U] : tough, clear, thin plastic that is placed around a product and shrunk in order to wrap it tightly — **shrink–wrapped** /ˈʃrɪŋkˌræpt/ *adj* ▪ *a shrink-wrapped book*

shriv·el /ˈʃrɪvəl/ *vb*, *US* **-eled** *or Brit* **-elled**; *US* **-el·ing** *or Brit* **-el·ling** [T/I] : to become dry and wrinkled or to make (something) dry and wrinkled from heat, cold, old age, etc. ▪ *The plants shriveled (up) in the hot sun.* ▪ *The heat shriveled (up) the plant's leaves.* — **shriveled** *adj* ▪ *a shriveled grape*

¹shroud /ˈʃraʊd/ *n* [C] **1** : a cloth that is used to wrap a dead body **2** *literary* : something that covers or hides something ▪ *a shroud of secrecy/fog*

²shroud *vb* [T] *literary* : to cover or hide (something) ▪ *a place shrouded in fog/secrecy*

shrub /ˈʃrʌb/ *n* [C] : a plant that has stems of wood and is smaller than a tree : BUSH

shrub·bery /ˈʃrʌbəri/ *n*, *pl* **-ber·ies** [C/U] : a group of shrubs planted together ▪ *a patch of tangled shrubbery* ▪ *a large shrubbery*

shrug /ˈʃrʌg/ *vb* **shrugged**; **shrug·ging** [T/I] : to raise and lower your shoulders usually to show that you do not know or care about something ▪ *When I asked him what he thought, he just shrugged (his shoulders).* — **shrug off** [*phrasal vb*] **shrug off (something)** *or* **shrug (something) off** : to think of or treat (something) as not important ▪ *She shrugged off their concerns.* — **shrug** *n* [C] ▪ *He answered my question with a shrug (of his shoulders).*

shrunk *past tense and past participle of* ¹SHRINK

shrunk·en /ˈʃrʌŋkən/ *adj* : made smaller or shorter ▪ *a shrunken old man* [=a man who has gotten smaller/shorter in old age]

shtick *also* **schtick** /ˈʃtɪk/ *n* [C] *US, informal* : a usual way of performing, behaving, speaking, etc. ▪ *That joke is part of his shtick.*

shuck *vb* [T] *US* : to remove the outer covering of (a plant) or the shell of (an oyster or clam) ▪ *shuck the corn/oysters*

shucks /ˈʃʌks/ *interj*, *US, old-fashioned* — used to show that you are disappointed or embarrassed ▪ *Oh, shucks, I forgot.*

shud·der /ˈʃʌdɚ/ *vb* [I] **1** *of a person* : to shake because of fear, cold, etc. ▪ *He shuddered with fear.* ▪ *(figurative)* **I shudder to think** (*of*) *what might happen.* [=I am very worried/fearful about what might happen] **2** *of a thing* : to shake violently ▪ *The old car shuddered to a halt.* — **shudder** *n* [C] ▪ *a shudder of fear*

¹shuf·fle /ˈʃʌfəl/ *vb* **shuf·fled**; **shuf·fling** **1** [T/I] : to slide your feet along the ground or back and forth without lifting them completely ▪ *He shuffled across the room.* ▪ *She shuffled her feet.* **2 a** [T] : to move things or people into a different order or into different positions ▪ *She shuffled the papers on her desk.* **b** [T/I] : to mix (playing cards) before playing a game so that no one knows what order they are in ▪ *Whose turn is it to shuffle (the cards/deck)?*

²shuffle *n* **1** [*singular*] : the act of moving by sliding your feet without lifting them off the ground ▪ *We heard the shuffle of feet outside the door.* **2** [C] : the act of mixing the order of playing cards ▪ *He gave the cards a shuffle.* [=he shuffled the cards] — **lost in the shuffle** *US* : not noticed or given attention because there are many other people or things to consider or deal with ▪ *Her letter got lost in the shuffle.*

shuf·fle·board /ˈʃʌfəlˌboɚd/ *n* [U] : a game in which players use a long stick with a curved piece at one end to slide discs into scoring areas that are marked on the ground

shun /ˈʃʌn/ *vb* **shunned**; **shun·ning** [T]

: to avoid (someone or something) • *She was shunned by many of her former friends.*

shunt /'ʃʌnt/ *vb* [T] : to move (someone or something) to a different and usually less important or noticeable place or position • *The company shunted him (off) to the mail room.* • (*figurative*) *Her suggestions were shunted aside.* [=*ignored*]

¹**shush** /'ʃʌʃ, 'ʃʊʃ/ *vb* [T] : to tell (someone) to be quiet • *The librarian shushed us.*

²**shush** *interj* — used to tell someone to be quiet • *Shush! I can't hear the movie.*

¹**shut** /'ʃʌt/ *vb* **shut; shut·ting** [T/I] **1** : to close (something) or to become closed • *Please shut the door/window/lid/drawer.* • *He shut his eyes.* • *The door shut slowly behind me.* **2** : to stop the services or activities of (a business, school, etc.) for a period of time or forever • *They plan to shut the factory.* — **shut away** [*phrasal vb*] **shut (someone or something) away** : to put (someone or something) in a place that is separate from others • *She was shut away in prison for three years.* — **shut down** [*phrasal vb*] **shut down** *or* **shut down (something)** *or* **shut (something) down 1** : to close or to cause (a business, factory, etc.) to close • *The factory shut down.* **2** : to stop operating or to cause (a machine) to stop operating • *She shut down her computer and went home.* — **shut in** [*phrasal vb*] **shut (someone or something) in** : to put (someone or something) in a room and close or lock the door • *He shut himself in his room to study.* — **shut off** [*phrasal vb*] **1 shut off** *or* **shut off (something)** *or* **shut (something) off a** : to stop operating or to cause (a machine, light, etc.) to stop operating • *It shuts off* [=*turns off*] *automatically.* • *Who shut off the lights?* **b** : to stop the flow or supply of (something) • *Make sure to shut off the water/gas/electricity.* **2 shut (yourself) off** : to keep (yourself) in a place that is away from other people • *He shut himself off from his family.* **3 shut (someone or something) off from** : to separate (someone or something) from (something) • *He is shut off from (contact with) the outside world.* — **shut out** [*phrasal vb*] **shut out (someone or something)** *or* **shut (someone or something) out 1** : to stop (someone or something) from entering a place • *He closed the curtain to shut out the sunlight.* • (*figurative*) *He tried to shut out the memory.* **2** : to not allow (someone) to be involved in your life, to know your personal thoughts and feelings, etc. • *She shut him out of her life.* **3** *chiefly US* : to keep (a player or team) from scoring in a game or contest • *The team was shut out* [=the team did not score any points] *in the first half.* — **shut up** [*phrasal vb*] **1** *informal* **a** : to stop talking, laughing, etc. — often used as a rude way to tell someone to stop talking • *Shut up and listen!* **b shut (someone) up** *informal* : to cause (someone) to stop talking, laughing, etc. • *Nothing shuts her up.* **2 shut up (something or someone)** *or* **shut (something or someone) up a**

: to close and lock all the doors of (a house, store, etc.) • *They shut up the house.* **b** : to put (someone or something) in a place that is away from other people • *He shut himself up in his room.* — **shut your mouth/face/yap/trap (etc.)** *informal* — used to tell someone in a rude way to stop talking • *She angrily told him to shut his mouth.*

²**shut** *adj* **1** : not open • *The door slammed shut.* • *Make sure that all the windows are shut.* **2** *Brit* : not operating or open to the public • *The store is shut* [=*closed*] *for remodeling.*

shut·down /'ʃʌt,daʊn/ *n* [C] : the act of stopping the operation or activity of a business, machine, etc. • *the shutdown of the factory*

shut·eye /'ʃʌt,aɪ/ *n* [U] *informal* : SLEEP • *You'd better get some shut-eye.*

shut-in /'ʃʌt,ɪn/ *n* [C] : a sick or disabled person who rarely or never leaves home • *visits to shut-ins*

shut·out /'ʃʌt,aʊt/ *n* [C] *US* : a game or contest in which one side does not score • *He pitched a shutout.*

shut·ter /'ʃʌtɚ/ *n* [C] **1** : one of a pair of outside covers for a window that open and close like a door • *She opened/closed the shutters.* **2** : the part of a camera that opens to allow light in when a picture is taken — **shutter** *vb* [T] *US* • *shutter the windows* [=close the shutters to cover the windows]

¹**shut·tle** /'ʃʌtl/ *n* [C] **1** : a vehicle that travels back and forth between places • *an airport shuttle* [=a vehicle that takes people to the airport] **2** : SPACE SHUTTLE

²**shuttle** *vb* **shut·tled; shut·tling** [T/I] : to move back and forth between places • *We shuttled between the city and the country.* • *A bus shuttled people from the parking lot to the dock.*

shut·tle·cock /'ʃʌtl,kɑːk/ *n* [C] : a light object shaped like a cone that is hit over the net in the game of badminton

¹**shy** /'ʃaɪ/ *adj* **shi·er** *or* **shy·er** /'ʃajɚ/; **shi·est** *or* **shy·est** /'ʃajəst/ **1 a** : feeling nervous and uncomfortable about meeting and talking to people • *a shy, quiet girl* **b** : showing that you are nervous and uncomfortable about meeting and talking to people • *He gave her a shy smile.* **2** : tending to avoid something because of nervousness, fear, dislike, etc. • *publicity/camera shy* **3** : hesitant about taking what you want or need • *Help yourself if you want more. Don't be shy.* **4** *chiefly US* : not quite reaching a particular place, number, etc. • *The ball stopped just shy* [=*short*] *of the hole.* • *He was two weeks shy of his 19th birthday.* — **fight shy of** *Brit* : to try to avoid something • *She has always fought shy of publicity.* — **once bitten, twice shy** see ¹BITE — **shy·ly** *adv* — **shy·ness** *n* [U]

²**shy** *vb* **shies; shied; shy·ing** [I] : to move away from something because of fear • *The horse shied when the gun went off.* — **shy (away) from** [*phrasal vb*] : to try to avoid (something) because of nervousness, fear, dislike, etc. • *He shied away from discussing his divorce.*

shy·ster /ˈʃaɪstɚ/ n [C] chiefly US, informal : a dishonest person; especially : a dishonest lawyer or politician

Si·a·mese cat /ˈsajəˌmiːz-/ n [C] : a type of cat that has blue eyes and short light-colored hair on the body with darker-colored ears, paws, tail, and face

sib·i·lant /ˈsɪbələnt/ adj, formal : making or having a sound like /s/ or /z/ ▪ sibilant consonants/whispers — **sibilant** n [C] ▪ the /s/ sound and other sibilants

sib·ling /ˈsɪblɪŋ/ n [C] somewhat formal : a brother or sister ▪ younger/older siblings ▪ **sibling rivalry** [=competition between brothers and sisters]

¹sic /ˈsɪk/ vb **sicced** /ˈsɪkt/; **sic·cing** [T] US, informal : to attack (someone or something) — usually used as a command to a dog ▪ Sic 'em, boy. — **sic (something) on** : to order (an animal) to attack (someone or something) ▪ He sicced his dog on me.

²sic — used in writing after an error in a quotation to show that the error was made by the speaker or writer who is being quoted and not by you ▪ His letter said the people were "very freindly [sic] to me."

¹sick /ˈsɪk/ adj **1** : affected with a disease or illness : ILL ▪ She is sick with the flu. ▪ (figurative) a sick economy ▪ I hardly ever **get sick** ▪ (informal) He was (as) **sick as a dog.** [=he was very sick] **2 a** not before a noun, informal : very annoyed or bored by something because you have had too much of it — + of ▪ He was sick of her lies. ▪ I'm getting sick of this cold weather. ▪ I'm sick and tired of hearing you two argue. = I'm **sick to death** of hearing you two argue. **b** : very disgusted or angry ▪ The way they treat people **makes me sick. 3** : not mentally normal or healthy ▪ He has a sick mind. **4** : relating to very unpleasant or offensive things ▪ sick jokes/humor **5** : powerfully affected by a strong and unpleasant emotion ▪ We have been sick with worry about her. = We've been **worried sick** [=worried] about her. — **be sick** : to vomit ▪ Stop the car—I'm **going to be sick.** [=I'm going to throw up] — **feel sick 1** US : to feel ill ▪ I was feeling sick, so I went home early. **2** : to feel like you will vomit ▪ After eating a whole plate of cookies, I felt sick. **3** US : to feel very upset ▪ I feel sick about what happened. — **sick to your stomach 1** US : feeling like you are going to vomit ▪ Just the thought of it makes me sick to my stomach. [=nauseous] **2** : feeling very disgusted or angry ▪ Her behavior **makes me sick to my stomach.** — **the sick** : sick people ▪ the sick and dying

²sick n [U] Brit, informal : VOMIT

sick·bed /ˈsɪkˌbɛd/ n [C] : the bed on which a sick person lies ▪ He called the nurse from his sickbed.

sick day n [C] : a paid day in which an employee does not work because he or she is sick

sick·en /ˈsɪkən/ vb **1** [T/I] somewhat formal : to become sick or to cause (someone) to become sick ▪ Many people sickened and died on the long voyage. ▪ The drinking water sickened the whole village. **2** [T] : to cause (someone) to feel disgusted or angry ▪ We were sickened by the reports of violence.

sick·en·ing /ˈsɪkənɪŋ/ adj **1** : causing you to feel sick ▪ a sickening odor **2** : causing a strong feeling of disgust ▪ a sickening display of selfishness — **sick·en·ing·ly** adv

sick·le /ˈsɪkəl/ n [C] : a tool with a curved metal blade attached to a short handle that is used for cutting grass, grain, etc.

sickle–cell anemia (US) or Brit **sickle–cell anaemia** n [C] : a serious disease that affects the red blood cells

sick·ly /ˈsɪkli/ adj **sick·li·er; -est 1** : not healthy and strong ▪ a sickly child/plant **2 a** : causing a person to feel sick ▪ a sickly odor **b** : causing feelings of dislike or disgust ▪ The walls were a sickly yellow. — **sickly** adv ▪ a sickly sweet taste

sick·ness /ˈsɪknəs/ n **1** [U] : the state of being sick ▪ She missed work due to sickness. **2** [C] : a specific type of disease or illness ▪ an unknown sickness **3** [U] : NAUSEA

sick pay n [U] : money that is paid by an employer to a person who misses work because of sickness

¹side /ˈsaɪd/ n [C] **1** : a place, space, or direction that is away from or beyond the center of something ▪ the right-hand/opposite side of the street ▪ the side of your face ▪ Guards stood on either side of the gate. ▪ She tilted her head to one side. **2 a** : an outer surface or part of something ▪ The box says, "THIS SIDE UP."; especially : one of the surfaces of an object that is not the front, back, top, or bottom ▪ The side of the car was dented. **b** : one of the two surfaces of a thin object ▪ She wrote on both sides of the paper. **3** : a line that forms part of a geometric shape ▪ A square has four sides. : a surface that forms part of a geometric object ▪ A cube has six sides. **4** : one of the slopes of a hill or mountain ▪ the side of the mountain **5 a** : the right or left part of your body ▪ She likes to sleep on her right side. **b** : the place directly to the right or left of someone ▪ I stood at/by her side. ▪ She set/put the book to the/one side. ▪ (figurative) His wife **stood at/by his side** [=remained loyal to him] throughout the scandal. **6** : one of two or more opinions, positions, etc., that disagree with each other ▪ He listened to both sides of the argument. **7** : one of the two or more people or groups that are involved in an argument, war, game, etc. ▪ Each side accused the other of delaying progress. ▪ Our side [=team] won the game. ▪ I don't want to choose/pick/take sides. [=support one person and not the other] ▪ Whose side are you on, anyway? **8 a** : a particular part or feature of something that is opposite to or different from another part or feature ▪ There are good/positive and bad/negative sides to owning your own business. ▪ She kept her side of the bargain/deal. [=she did what she agreed to do] **b** — used in phrases like on the large side, on the heavy side, etc., to describe someone or something as somewhat heavy, large, etc. ▪ *These pants are on the tight side.* [=are a little tight] **9 a** : a part of someone's personality that is opposite or different from another part ▪ *I've never seen this side of you before.* **b** — used in phrases like *be/get on someone's good/bad side* and *be/get on the right/wrong side of someone* to talk about doing things that cause someone to like you or dislike you ▪ *She tries to keep/stay on her boss's good side.* **10** : the ancestors or relatives of your mother or your father ▪ *Both sides of his family are Irish.* **11** *US* : a small amount of food that is ordered in addition to the main meal ▪ *a side of fries* — **(from) side to side** : moving to the left and then to the right ▪ *She shook her head from side to side.* — **let the side down** *Brit* : to disappoint your family, friends, etc., by failing to do what is needed or expected — **on the right/wrong side of 30, 40, 50 (etc.)** *informal* : younger/older than 30, 40, 50 (etc.) ▪ *She's still on the right side of 40.* [=younger than 40] — **on the side 1 a** : in addition to the main item in a meal ▪ *salmon with grilled vegetables on the side* **b** : served next to something rather than on top of it ▪ *For my salad, I'd like Italian dressing on the side.* **2** : in addition to your main job ▪ *She sells insurance on the side.* **3** : as part of a secret romantic relationship that is outside of your marriage or main romantic relationship ▪ *a married man with a girlfriend on the side* — **on your side** : as an advantage ▪ *Time is on our side.* [=we have a lot of time to do what we need to do] — **side by side 1** : next to each other and facing in the same direction ▪ *They stood side by side.* **2** : together or very close to each other ▪ *The tribes have lived peacefully side by side for many years.* — **this side of 1 a** : very nearly (something) ▪ *Their actions were just this side of illegal.* [=were almost but not quite illegal] **b** : that is not (something) ▪ *the worst punishment this side of death* **2** *Brit* : BEFORE ▪ *She's not likely to be back this side of Monday week.* — **to the/one side** : to a place that is on one side ▪ ASIDE ▪ *Please move/step to the side.*

²side *adj, always before a noun* **1** : of or located on the side of something ▪ *the side door/entrance* **2** : happening or done in addition to the main or most important thing ▪ *a side project/job/issue* **3** : in addition to the main meal ▪ *a burger with a side order of fries* ▪ *a side dish*

³side *vb* **sid·ed; sid·ing** [T] *US* : to cover the outside walls of (a building) with long pieces of material (called siding) ▪ *They sided their house.* — **side against** [*phrasal vb*] : to not agree with or support the opinions or actions of (someone) ▪ *They both sided against me.* — **side with** [*phrasal vb*] : to agree with or support the opinions or actions of (someone) ▪ *She sided with her friend.*

side·arm /ˈsaɪdˌɑɚm/ *adj, chiefly US* : done with your arm moving out to the side ▪ *a sidearm pass* — **sidearm** *adv* ▪ *He throws sidearm.*

side·board /ˈsaɪdˌboɚd/ *n* [C] : a piece of

furniture that has drawers and shelves for holding dishes, silverware, etc.

side·burns /ˈsaɪdˌbɚnz/ *n* [*plural*] : hair that grows on the side of a man's face in front of his ears

side·car /ˈsaɪdˌkɑɚ/ *n* [C] : a small vehicle that is attached to the side of a motorcycle for a passenger to ride in

side effect *n* [C] **1** : an often harmful and unwanted effect of a drug or chemical that occurs along with the desired effect **2** : a result of an action that is not expected or intended ▪ *The merger created positive side effects for both companies.*

side·kick /ˈsaɪdˌkɪk/ *n* [C] *informal* : a person who helps and spends a lot of time with someone who is usually more important, powerful, etc. ▪ *the hero and his sidekick*

side·light /ˈsaɪdˌlaɪt/ *n* [C] **1** : a piece of information that is in addition to the main information ▪ *The book includes some amusing sidelights about his childhood.* **2** *Brit* : PARKING LIGHT

¹side·line /ˈsaɪdˌlaɪn/ *n* [C] **1** : a line that marks the outside edge of a sports field or court **2** : the space outside the area where a game is played on a field or court ▪ *We stood on the sidelines to watch the game.* ▪ (*figurative*) *His injury has kept him on the sidelines* [=has kept him from playing] *this season.*

²sideline *vb* **-lined; -lin·ing** [T] : to prevent (a player) from playing in a game especially because of injury, illness, etc. ▪ *He was sidelined with a knee injury.*

side·long /ˈsaɪdˌlɑːŋ/ *adj, always before a noun* : made to the left or right or out of the corner of your eye ▪ *a sidelong look/glance* — **sidelong** *adv*

side·show /ˈsaɪdˌʃoʊ/ *n* [C] : a smaller show that is performed in addition to a main show ▪ *a circus sideshow* ▪ (*figurative*) *The disagreement is just a political sideshow when compared to the real issues at hand.*

side·step /ˈsaɪdˌstɛp/ *vb* **-stepped; -step·ping 1** [T/I] : to avoid walking into or being hit by (someone or something) by stepping to the right or left ▪ *She sidestepped the puddle.* **2** [T] : to avoid answering or dealing with (something) directly ▪ *She sidestepped the question/issue.*

¹side·swipe /ˈsaɪdˌswaɪp/ *vb* **-swiped; -swip·ing** [T] *US* : to hit the side of a vehicle with the side of another vehicle ▪ *The taxi sideswiped a parked car.*

²sideswipe *n* [C] : a critical remark about someone or something that is made while talking about someone or something else ▪ *She took a sideswipe at the senator's voting record.*

side table *n* [C] : a table that is designed to be placed against a wall

side·track /ˈsaɪdˌtræk/ *vb* [T] **1** : to cause (someone) to talk about or do something different and less important ▪ *I got/was sidetracked by a phone call.* **2** *US* **a** : to change the direction or use of (something) ▪ *The money was sidetracked to fund other projects.* **b** : to prevent (something) from being dealt with ▪ *The issue has been sidetracked.*

side·walk /'saɪd,wɑːk/ n [C] US : a usually concrete path along the side of a street for people to walk on — called also (Brit) pavement

side·ways /'saɪd,weɪz/ adv 1 : with one side facing forward • We had to turn sideways to get through the hallway. 2 : to or toward the right or left side • I looked sideways at him. — **sideways** adj • a sideways movement/glance

sid·ing /'saɪdɪŋ/ n [U] US : long pieces of material that are used to cover the outside walls of a building • vinyl siding

si·dle /'saɪdl/ vb **si·dled**; **si·dling** [I] : to move close to someone in a quiet or secret way • He sidled up/over to me.

siege /'siːdʒ/ n [C/U] : a situation in which soldiers or police officers surround a city, building, etc., in order to try to take control of it • the siege of Paris • (figurative) He's recovering from a siege of depression. • The army laid siege to the city. • The city was under siege. 2 [=surrounded by enemy soldiers] • (figurative) The reporter has been under siege [=has been angrily attacked/criticized by many people] for lying.

si·es·ta /si'ɛstə/ n 1 [C/U] : a regular period of sleep or rest in the afternoon in some hot countries • The shops are closed during the (afternoon) siesta. 2 [C] : a brief sleep : NAP • He's taking a little siesta.

sieve /'sɪv/ n [C] : a kitchen tool that has many small holes and that is used to separate smaller particles from larger ones or solids from liquids — **have a memory/mind like a sieve** informal : to be unable to remember things • I've already forgotten her name. I have a mind like a sieve.

sift /'sɪft/ vb 1 [T] **a** : to put (flour, sugar, etc.) through a sifter or sieve • Sift the flour into a mixing bowl. **b** : to separate or remove (something) by using a sifter or sieve • Sift (out) the rocks from the sand. • (figurative) The lawyer sifted out the relevant facts of the case. 2 [T/I] : to go through (something) very carefully in order to find something useful or valuable • The police sifted (the evidence) for clues. • The lawyer sifted through hundreds of pages of testimony. — **sift·er** /'sɪftər/ n [C]

sigh /'saɪ/ vb 1 [I] : to take in and let out a long, loud breath in a way that shows you are bored, disappointed, relieved, etc. • He sighed with/in relief. • (figurative) The wind sighed through the trees. 2 [T] : to say (something) with a sigh • "I may never see her again," she sighed. — **sigh** n [C] • She gave a long, weary sigh. • I can breathe a sigh of relief. [=stop worrying]

¹sight /'saɪt/ n 1 [U] : the ability to see • Your sight weakens as you get older. • He lost his sight. [=he became blind] 2 [U] : the act of seeing someone or something • We lost sight of the plane. [=we could no longer see the plane] • He faints at the sight of [=when he sees] blood. • She caught sight of an eagle. • The officers were ordered to shoot on sight. [=shoot as soon as they saw the enemy] 3 [U] : a position in which someone or something

can be seen • There was no one in sight. [=no one could be seen] • Keep out of sight. • Get out of my sight! [=go away from me; I don't want to see you] • She left her purse out in plain sight. = Her purse was in plain sight of anyone passing by. • A large pole was directly in my line of sight. [=a large pole was blocking my view] • (figurative) The end of the project is finally in/within sight. [=is finally near] ◇ The phrase **out of sight, out of mind** means that you stop thinking about something or someone if you do not see that thing or person for a period of time. 4 [C] **a** : someone or something that is seen • The old dog was a pathetic/sorry sight. • I've seen the damage done, and it's not a pretty sight. • It was a sight to see/behold. [=was an amazing or wonderful thing to see] **b** : a famous or interesting place in an area • We saw all the sights (off in the city). 5 [C] : a device that is used to aim a gun — usually plural • The deer was in her sights. [=she was aiming her gun at the deer] • (figurative) He had a law career in his sights. [=his goal was to have a law career] • (figurative) She has set her sights on becoming a doctor. [=she wants to become a doctor] — **a sight for sore eyes** : a person or thing that you are very glad to see — **at first sight** see ¹FIRST — **sight unseen** : without seeing or examining something • They bought the house sight unseen. [=without first looking at it]

²sight vb [T] : to see (something or someone that is rarely seen or difficult to see) • Several bears have been sighted in the area.

sight·ed /'saɪtəd/ adj : able to see • blind and sighted people

sight·ing /'saɪtɪŋ/ n [C] : an act of seeing something or someone that is rarely seen or difficult to see • a whale sighting

sight·less /'saɪtləs/ adj, literary : BLIND • sightless eyes

sight·see·ing /'saɪt,siːɪŋ/ n [U] : the activity of visiting the famous or interesting places of an area • We did a lot of sightseeing on our vacation. — **sight·seer** /'saɪt,siːjər/ n [C] • The church attracts a lot of sightseers.

¹sign /'saɪn/ n [C] 1 : a piece of paper, wood, etc., with words or pictures on it that gives information about something • road/street/traffic signs • There was a "For Sale" sign on the car. 2 : an action, event, etc., which shows that something else exists, is true, or will happen • We remained alert for any signs of danger. • "The company called me in for a second interview." "That's a good sign." • The planet showed no signs of life. [=there was no evidence of living things on the planet] • We called the police at the first sign of trouble. [=as soon as there was trouble] 3 : a motion, action, or movement that you use to express a thought, command, or wish • They bowed as a sign of respect. 4 : a symbol that is used to represent something • a sign of the zodiac — see also DIVISION SIGN, DOLLAR SIGN, EQUAL SIGN, MINUS SIGN, MULTI-PLICATION SIGN, PLUS SIGN — **a sign**

of the times : something that shows the kinds of things that are happening, popular, important, etc., in a culture at a particular period in history ▪ *Having metal detectors in schools is a sign of the times.*

²**sign** *vb* **1 a** [*T/I*] : to write (your name) on something ▪ *Sign (your name) on the bottom line.* ▪ *She met with fans and signed autographs.* **b** [*T*] : to write your name on (something) especially to show that you accept, agree with, or will be responsible for something ▪ *sign a document/letter/check* ▪ *The contract should be signed, sealed, and delivered by tomorrow.* **2 a** [*T*] : to hire (someone) to do something especially by having that person sign a contract ▪ *The team signed the pitcher to a three-year contract.* **b** [*I*] : to agree to work for or to produce something for an organization, business, etc., especially by signing a contract ▪ *She signed with the studio to direct two movies.* **3** [*T/I*] : to communicate by using sign language ▪ *I'm learning how to sign.* — **sign away** [*phrasal vb*] **sign (something) away** *or* **sign away (something)** : to give (rights, property, etc.) to someone by signing a document ▪ *He signed away his share of the property.* — **sign for** [*phrasal vb*] : to sign a document to show that you have received (something) ▪ *I signed for the package.* — **sign in** [*phrasal vb*] **sign in** *or* **sign (someone or something) in** *or* **sign in (someone or something)** **1** : to sign your name or write (someone else's) name on a list, in a book, etc., when arriving at a place ▪ *All visitors must sign in upon arrival.* ▪ *The receptionist signed the guests in.* **2** : to sign your name on a list, in a book, etc., to show that you have returned (something that you borrowed) ▪ *He signed the video equipment (back) in.* — **sign off** [*phrasal vb*] **1** : to end a letter or broadcast by signing or saying your name ▪ *She signed off with "Yours Truly, Maria."* **2** : to approve something officially by signing your name ▪ *(US) He signed off on the memo.* [=he approved the memo by signing it] — **sign on** [*phrasal vb*] **sign on** *or* **sign (someone) on** *or* **sign on (someone)** : to agree to do or hire (someone) to do a job, project, etc., especially by signing a contract ▪ *He signed on as a member of the crew.* ▪ *She's signed on for another movie.* — **sign out** [*phrasal vb*] **sign out** *or* **sign (someone or something) out** *or* **sign out (someone or something)** **1** : to sign your name or write someone else's name on a list, in a book, etc., in order to leave a place ▪ *Did the visitors sign out?* ▪ *The receptionist signed the guests out.* **2** : to sign your name on a list, in a book, etc., to show that you have borrowed (something) ▪ *The library book is signed out.* — **sign over** [*phrasal vb*] **sign (something) over** *or* **sign over (something)** : to give (something that you own) to someone by signing a document ▪ *He signed over the property to his brother.* — **sign up** [*phrasal vb*] **1** : to sign your name on a document or list in order to get, do, or take something ▪ *She signed up for health insurance.* ▪ *He signed up as*

[=agreed to do the job of] *an Army reservist.* **2** **sign (someone) up** *or* **sign up (someone)** **a** : to add the name of (someone) to an official list in order for that person to get, do, or take something ▪ *We have signed up enough volunteers for the festival.* **b** : to hire (someone) to do something especially by having that person sign a contract ▪ *The record label signed the band up.* — **sign·er** /ˈsaɪnɚ/ *n* [*C*]

sign·age /ˈsaɪnɪʤ/ *n* [*U*] : signs or a system of signs used to show information about something ▪ *There is new lighting and better signage at the airport.*

¹**sig·nal** /ˈsɪgnl̩/ *n* [*C*] **1** : an event, act, motion, sound, etc., which shows that something exists or that gives information about something ▪ *Her strange behavior is a signal that there is a problem.* ▪ *Don't start until I give the signal.* [=until I do something that tells you to start] ▪ *The pilot sent out a distress signal.* [=a message that the airplane was in danger] **2** : a piece of equipment with colored lights that is used on railways and roads to tell people when to go, to slow down, or to stop ▪ *The traffic signal* [=*traffic light*] *was not working.* **3** *technical* : a message, sound, or image that is carried by waves of light or sound ▪ *The video/TV signal is scrambled.*

²**signal** *vb*, *US* -**naled** *or Brit* -**nalled**; *US* -**nal·ing** *or Brit* -**nal·ling** **1** [*T*] : to show the existence of (something) ▪ *The election results signal the start of a new era.* **2** [*T/I*] : to make a sound or motion that tells someone something ▪ *Did he signal before he made the left turn?* ▪ *The umpire signaled a strike.*

sig·na·to·ry /ˈsɪgnəˌtori, *Brit* ˈsɪgnətri/ *n*, *pl* -**ries** [*C*] *formal* : a person, country, or organization that has signed an official document ▪ *the signatories to/of the treaty/ petition*

¹**sig·na·ture** /ˈsɪgnəʧɚ/ *n* [*C*] **1** : a person's name written in that person's handwriting ▪ *This is not my signature.* ▪ *We presented the document to her for her signature.* **2** : something (such as a quality or feature) that is closely associated with someone or something ▪ *That motif has become the artist's signature.*

²**signature** *adj*, *always before a noun* : closely associated with someone or something ▪ *the chef's signature dish* [=the dish that the chef is known for making]

sig·nif·i·cance /sɪgˈnɪfɪkəns/ *n* [*U*, *singular*] **1** : the quality of being important ▪ *The discovery has great/little significance to researchers.* **2** : the meaning of something ▪ *I failed to understand/grasp/appreciate the significance of her remarks.*

sig·nif·i·cant /sɪgˈnɪfɪkənt/ *adj* **1** : large enough to be noticed or have an effect ▪ *A significant number of customers complained.* ▪ *a significant difference* **2** : very important ▪ *a significant event* — **sig·nif·i·cant·ly** *adv* ▪ *a significantly lower price* ▪ *Her health has improved significantly.*

significant other *n* [*C*] : your husband, wife, boyfriend, or girlfriend

sig·ni·fy /ˈsɪgnəˌfaɪ/ *vb* -**fies**; -**fied**; -**fy-**

ing [T] **1** : to be a sign of (something) • *A check mark next to your name signifies that you have met all the requirements.* **2** : to show (your feelings, intentions, opinions, etc.) by doing something • *He nodded to signify that he approved.*

sign language *n* [C/U] : a system of hand movements used for communication especially by people who are deaf

sign·post /ˈsaɪnˌpoʊst/ *n* [C] : a sign beside a road showing the direction and distance to a place • *(figurative) There are no signposts pointing to a solution.*

Sikh /ˈsiːk/ *n* [C] : a follower of Sikhism — **Sikh** *adj*

Sikh·ism /ˈsiːˌkɪzəm/ *n* [U] : a religion founded in India around 1500 that is based on the belief that there is one God

¹**si·lence** /ˈsaɪləns/ *n* **1** [U] : a lack of sound or noise • *The silence was broken by the sound of footsteps.* **2** [C/U] : a situation, state, or period of time in which people do not talk • *We sat there in dead/total/complete silence.* • *an awkward silence* **3** [C/U] : a situation or state in which someone does not talk about or answer questions about something • *She finally ended her silence and spoke about what happened.* — **silence is golden** — used to say that it is often better to remain silent than to speak

²**silence** *vb* **-lenced; -lenc·ing** [T] **1** : to cause (someone or something) to stop speaking or making noise • *Disconnecting the battery will silence the alarm.* **2** : to stop (someone) from expressing opinions that are opposed to your own or from telling people about bad things that you have done • *The mayor tried to silence his critics.*

si·lenc·er /ˈsaɪlənsər/ *n* [C] **1** *US* : a device that is attached to a handgun to reduce the noise that the gun makes when it is fired **2** *Brit* : MUFFLER 1

si·lent /ˈsaɪlənt/ *adj* **1** : not speaking or making noise : QUIET • *Please be silent.* • *The crowd fell silent as the horrible news was read aloud.* **2** *always before a noun* : tending not to talk much • *My father was a very silent man.* **3** *always before a noun* : done, felt, or expressed without speaking • *a silent prayer* • *He turned his back on the president in silent protest.* **4** : giving no information about something or refusing to discuss something • *History books are silent on this topic.* • *You have the right to remain silent.* [=the legal right not to say anything when you are arrested] **5** *grammar* : written in the spelling of a word but not pronounced • *There is a silent "e" in "cane."* **6** *always before a noun* : not having spoken dialogue • *silent movies/films* — **si·lent·ly** *adv*

silent partner *n* [C] *chiefly US* : a partner who invests money in a business but is not involved in running the business

¹**sil·hou·ette** /ˌsɪləˈwɛt/ *n* **1** [C/U] **a** : a dark shape in front of a light background • *the silhouettes of buildings against the sky* • *The buildings appeared in silhouette against the sky.* **b** : a picture of something (such as a person's face) showing it as a dark shape on a

light background • *a framed silhouette* **2** [C] : the shape or outline of something • *He admired the car's sleek silhouette.*

²**silhouette** *vb* **-ett·ed; -ett·ing** [T] : to make (someone or something) appear as a dark shape in front of a light background • *The house was silhouetted against the sky.*

sil·i·con /ˈsɪlɪkən, ˈsɪləˌkɑːn/ *n* [U] : a chemical element that is found in the Earth's crust and is used especially in computers and electronics

sil·i·cone /ˈsɪləˌkoʊn/ *n* [U] : a chemical that does not let water or heat pass through and that is used to make rubber and grease and in plastic surgery • *silicone breast implants*

silk /ˈsɪlk/ *n* [C/U] : a smooth, soft, and shiny cloth that is made from thread produced by silkworms; *also* : the thread that is used to make silk • *a dress made of blue silk* • *silk threads/dresses/blouses* • *Her hair is as smooth as silk.* [=very smooth]

silk·en /ˈsɪlkən/ *adj* **1** : made of silk or a cloth that is like silk • *silken* [=silk] *robes* **2** : smooth and soft • *her silken black hair*

silk·worm /ˈsɪlkˌwɚm/ *n* [C] : a caterpillar that produces silk which is used to make thread or cloth

silky /ˈsɪlki/ *adj* **silk·i·er; -est 1** : made of silk or of material that is soft, smooth, and shiny like silk • *a silky nightgown* **2** : smooth and soft like silk • *her silky brown hair* **3** *of food* : smooth, soft, and rich • *silky chocolate mousse* **4** *of a sound* : smooth and pleasant to hear • *a silky voice*

sill /ˈsɪl/ *n* [C] **1** : the shelf at the bottom of a window frame : WINDOWSILL **2** : a piece of wood, metal, or stone at the bottom of a door frame

sil·ly /ˈsɪli/ *adj* **sil·li·er; -est 1** : having or showing a lack of thought, understanding, or good judgment • *a silly idea* • *He looks silly in that hat.* **2 a** : not serious, meaningful, or important • *I'm tired of watching silly movies.* **b** : playful and funny • *He made a silly face.* • *a silly sense of humor* **3** *not before a noun* : in a condition in which you are unable to think clearly • *The ball knocked him silly.* • *They drank themselves silly.* [=they got extremely drunk] — **sil·li·ness** /ˈsɪlinəs/ *n* [U]

si·lo /ˈsaɪloʊ/ *n, pl* **-los** [C] **1** : a tower that is used to store food for farm animals **2** : an underground structure that is used for storing and firing a missile

silt /ˈsɪlt/ *n* [U] : sand, soil, mud, etc., that is carried by flowing water and that sinks to the bottom of a river, pond, etc.

sil·ver /ˈsɪlvɚ/ *n* **1** [U] : a soft grayish-white metal that is very valuable and is used to make jewelry, coins, knives, forks, etc. **2** [U] : objects that are made of or covered with silver • *We need to polish the silver.* **3** [C/U] : a shiny light gray color **4** [C] : SILVER MEDAL — **silver** *adj* • *silver jewelry/coins* • *silver hair*

silver dollar *n* [C] *US* : a large silver coin worth one dollar that was used in the past

silver lining *n* [C] : something good that

can be found in a bad situation ▪ *If there's a silver lining to losing my job, it's that now I can go back to school full-time.* ▪ *Remember that every cloud has a silver lining.* [=every bad situation holds the possibility of something good]

silver medal *n* [C] : a medal made of silver that is given as a prize to someone who wins second place in a contest

silver–plated *adj* : covered with a thin layer of silver ▪ *a silver-plated tray*

silver screen *n* — **the silver screen** *old-fashioned* **1** : a screen in a movie theater ▪ *one of the greatest films ever to hit the silver screen* [=one of the greatest films ever shown in movie theaters] **2** : movies in general ▪ *stars of the silver screen* [=movie stars]

sil·ver·smith /ˈsɪlvɚˌsmɪθ/ *n* [C] : a person who makes things out of silver

sil·ver·ware /ˈsɪlvɚˌweɚ/ *n* [U] **1** : objects (such as forks, knives, spoons, etc.) for serving food and drink that are made of or covered with silver **2** *US* : forks, knives, and spoons that are made of stainless steel, plastic, etc. — called also *flatware*

sil·very /ˈsɪlvəri/ *adj, literary* **1** : shiny and white or light gray in color like silver ▪ *Silvery light reflected off the water.* **2** *of sound* : high, clear, soft, and pleasant ▪ *a singer with a beautiful silvery voice*

sim·i·an /ˈsɪmijən/ *n* [C] *technical* : a monkey or ape — **simian** *adj*

sim·i·lar /ˈsɪmələ/ *adj* : almost the same as someone or something else ▪ *Our cats are similar in size/color/appearance.* ▪ *You two look very/quite similar to each other.* ▪ *similar experiences* — **sim·i·lar·ly** /ˈsɪməˌləli/ *adv* ▪ *The houses are decorated similarly.*

sim·i·lar·i·ty /ˌsɪməˈlerəti/ *n, pl* **-ties** [C/U] : a quality that makes one person or thing like another ▪ *I see a lot of similarities in/between them.* ▪ *I see very little similarity between your situation and his.*

sim·i·le /ˈsɪməli/ *n* [C/U] *grammar* : a phrase that uses the words *like* or *as* to describe someone or something by comparing it with someone or something else that is similar ▪ *"She's as fierce as a tiger" is a simile.*

¹**sim·mer** /ˈsɪmɚ/ *vb* **1** [T/I] : to cook (something) so that it is almost boiling for a certain period of time ▪ *Simmer the stew for 40 minutes.* ▪ *Let the stew simmer for 40 minutes.* **2** [I] **a** : to be filled with a strong feeling that is difficult to control or hide ▪ *He was simmering with anger/resentment.* **b** : to be felt strongly by someone without being directly shown or expressed ▪ *Anger simmered inside him.* **3** [I] : to continue for a long time without producing a definite result ▪ *simmering conflicts/controversies* ▪ *The idea simmered in my mind for quite some time.* — **simmer down** [*phrasal vb*] : to become calm after being very angry or excited ▪ *"Simmer down! I was just joking."*

²**simmer** *n* [*singular*] : a way of cooking that is close to boiling : a state of simmering ▪ *Bring the mixture to a simmer.*

sim·per /ˈsɪmpɚ/ *vb* [I] : to smile in a way that is not sincere or natural ▪ *He simpered and smirked while he talked to the boss.* — **simper** *n* [*singular*] ▪ *an annoying simper*

sim·ple /ˈsɪmpəl/ *adj* **sim·pler; -plest** **1** : not hard to understand or do ▪ *a simple task/answer/explanation* ▪ *a simple recipe* **2** : having few parts : not complex or fancy ▪ *a simple machine/tune* **3** *always before a noun* : not special or unusual ▪ *I'm a simple man just trying to make a living.* ▪ *Watching the sunset is one of life's* **simple pleasures.** **4** *always before a noun* : complete and total — used for emphasis ▪ *The simple fact/truth is that he made a mistake.* ▪ *I don't want to go* **for the simple reason** *that I'm very tired.* **5** *grammar, of a sentence* : having only one main clause and no additional clauses ▪ *"Last summer was unusually hot" is a simple sentence.* **6** *old-fashioned* : not very intelligent ▪ *She looked at me as if I were simple.* — **pure and simple** *see* PURE — **the simple life** ◇ If you live *the simple life,* you do not own many things or use many modern machines and you usually live in the countryside.

simple interest *n* [U] *finance* : interest paid only on the original amount of money and not on the interest it has already earned

sim·ple–mind·ed /ˌsɪmpəlˈmaɪndəd/ *adj* : not very intelligent : having or showing a lack of good sense or judgment ▪ *a simpleminded approach/person*

sim·ple·ton /ˈsɪmpəltən/ *n* [C] *old-fashioned* : someone who is not very intelligent or who does not have or show good sense or judgment

sim·plic·i·ty /sɪmˈplɪsəti/ *n* [U] **1** : the quality of being easy to understand or use ▪ *People like the simplicity of the instructions/camera.* ▪ *We have rounded off the numbers* **for the sake of simplicity.** [=to make it simpler] **2** : the state or quality of being plain or not fancy or complicated ▪ *the simplicity of the music/writing/design* **3** : something that is easy to do ▪ *Making the dish is simplicity itself.* [=is very easy]

sim·pli·fy /ˈsɪmpləˌfaɪ/ *vb* **-fies; -fied; -fy·ing** [T] : to make (something) easier to do or understand ▪ *The new software should simplify the process.* ▪ *The forms have been simplified.* ▪ *a simplified version of the instructions* — **sim·pli·fi·ca·tion** /ˌsɪmpləfəˈkeɪʃən/ *n* [C/U]

sim·plis·tic /sɪmˈplɪstɪk/ *adj, disapproving* : too simple : not treating or considering all possibilities or parts ▪ *a simplistic approach to a complicated problem* ▪ *simplistic thinking* — **sim·plis·ti·cal·ly** /sɪmˈplɪstɪkli/ *adv*

sim·ply /ˈsɪmpli/ *adv* **1 a** : only, merely, or just ▪ *Simply add water and stir.* ▪ *You can order new checks simply by calling or going online.* **b** — used to stress the truth of a description or statement ▪ *That is simply* [=just] *not true.* ▪ *We want to buy the car, but we simply can't afford it.* ▪ *He is,* **quite simply,** *one of the best players ever to play the game.* **2 a** : in way that is clear and understandable ▪ *The instructions are simply written.* **b** : in a way that is plain or not fancy or complicated • *She dresses/lives simply.* **c** : in a way that is direct and uses few words • *"Sorry, I can't help you," he said simply.* • **Simply put/ speaking**, *the movie was horrible.*

sim·u·late /ˈsɪmjəˌleɪt/ *vb* **-lat·ed; -lat·ing** [*T*] : to look, feel, or behave like (something) • *The model will be used to simulate the effects of an earthquake.* • *The material simulates the look and feel of real fur.*

simulated *adj* : not real • *simulated leather* • *They are trained in simulated combat.*

sim·u·la·tion /ˌsɪmjəˈleɪʃən/ *n* [*C/U*] : something that is made to look, feel, or behave like something else especially so that it can be studied or used to train people • *a simulation of the planet's surface* • *They use computer simulation to predict weather conditions.*

sim·u·la·tor /ˈsɪmjəˌleɪtɚ/ *n* [*C*] : a machine that is used to show what something looks or feels like and is usually used to study something or to train people • *a flight simulator used by pilots*

si·mul·ta·neous /ˌsaɪməlˈteɪnijəs, *Brit* ˌsɪməlˈteɪnɪəs/ *adj* : happening at the same time • *simultaneous events* — **si·mul·ta·neous·ly** *adv* • *The speech was broadcast simultaneously on radio and TV.*

¹**sin** /ˈsɪn/ *n* **1** [*C/U*] : an action that is considered to be wrong according to religious or moral law • *Murder is a sin.* • *She committed a sin.* • *a world of sin* **2** [*C*] : an action that is considered to be bad • *It's a sin to waste food.* — **(as) guilty/ miserable/ugly as sin** *informal* : very guilty/miserable/ugly • *That house is as ugly as sin.* — **live in sin** see ¹**LIVE**

²**sin** *vb* **sinned; sin·ning** [*I*] : to do something that is considered wrong according to religious or moral law : to commit a sin • *Forgive me, for I have sinned.*

¹**since** /ˈsɪns/ *prep* : from (a point in the past) until the present time • *I haven't seen him since yesterday.* • *Since the party, she has not spoken to him at all.* • *The company started 10 years ago and has grown a lot since then.* [=within that time] — **since when?** — used to show that you are surprised and often angry, annoyed, or doubtful about what someone has said or done • *"I'm a vegetarian." "Since when?"* • *Since when is it okay to cheat?*

²**since** *conj* **1** : in the period after the time when • *He has had two jobs since he graduated.* **2** : from the time in the past when • *I have wanted to be a pilot since* [=*ever since*] *I was a child.* **3** — used to introduce a statement that explains the reason for another statement • *Since you've finished all your chores, you may go out and play.*

³**since** *adv* **1** : from a past time until now • *He moved to New York ten years ago and has lived there since.* [=(*more commonly*) *ever since*] **2** : after a time in the past • *He left home two years ago and has since become a soldier.*

sin·cere /sɪnˈsiɚ/ *adj* **sin·cer·er; -est 1** : having or showing true feelings that are expressed in an honest way • *He sounded sincere in his promises.* **2** : not false, fake, or pretended • *Her apology was sincere.* • *a sincere attempt/effort to quit smoking* — **sin·cer·i·ty** /sɪnˈserəti/ *n* [*U*] • *Some people question her sincerity.* • *In all sincerity, we could not have done this project without your help.*

sin·cere·ly /sɪnˈsiɚli/ *adv* **1** : in a sincere or truthful way • *He sincerely apologized for breaking the vase.* • *I am sincerely sorry for your loss.* **2** ✧ **Sincerely, yours sincerely,** and (*chiefly US*) **sincerely yours** are often used at the end of a formal letter before the sender's signature.

sin·ew /ˈsɪnˌju:/ *n* [*C/U*] : strong tissue that connects muscles to bones • *cutting through bone and sinew*

sin·ewy /ˈsɪnjəwi/ *adj* **1** : having strong and lean muscles • *sinewy arms* **2** : tough and difficult to cut or chew • *a sinewy piece of meat*

sin·ful /ˈsɪnfəl/ *adj* **1** : wrong according to religious or moral law • *It is sinful to steal.* **2** : very bad or wicked • *sinful people* **3** *informal* : extremely enjoyable in a way that makes you feel guilty • *a sinful chocolate cake* — **sin·ful·ly** *adv*

sing /ˈsɪŋ/ *vb* **sang** /ˈsæŋ/ *or* **sung** /ˈsʌŋ/; **sung; sing·ing 1** [*T/I*] : to use your voice to make musical sounds in the form of a song or tune • *sing a song* • *She sings beautifully.* **2** [*I*] : to make pleasant sounds that sound like music • *The birds are singing.* — **sing along** [*phrasal vb*] : to sing a song together with someone who is already singing or with a recording of the song • *He loves to sing along with the radio.* — **sing out** [*phrasal vb*] **sing out** *or* **sing out (something)** *or* **sing (something) out** : to say or shout something loudly • *If you need any help, just sing out.* • *The children sang out "good morning" to the teacher.* — **sing someone's/something's praises** *or* **sing the praises of (someone/something)** : to say good things about someone or something • *His patients all sing his praises.* — **singing** *n* [*U*] • *folk singing* • *There was singing and dancing all night long.*

sing. *abbr* singular

sing-along /ˈsɪŋəˌlɑ:ŋ/ *n* [*C*] : an informal occasion or event at which people sing songs together • *a Christmas sing-along*

singe /ˈsɪndʒ/ *vb* **singed; singe·ing** [*T*] : to burn (something) slightly • *The flame singed his hair.*

sing·er /ˈsɪŋɚ/ *n* [*C*] : someone who sings • *My sister is a pretty good singer.*; *especially* : a performer who sings • *He is the lead singer in the band.*

¹**sin·gle** /ˈsɪŋɡəl/ *adj* **1** *always before a noun* : not having or including another : only one • *They lost by a single point.* [=they lost by one point] — sometimes used to emphasize the largeness or importance of something • *It was the single most important piece of evidence.* — sometimes used in negative statements to emphasize that there is a complete lack of something • *I could not hear a single word.* **2** : not married or not having a serious romantic relationship with some-

one ▪ *Are you single?* ▪ *a single parent/ mother/father* [=a parent/mother/father who takes care of a child alone] **3** — used for emphasis after words like *any, each, every,* etc. ▪ *I drink milk every single day.* **4** *always before a noun* : made for one person to use ▪ *I stayed in a single room.* ▪ *I slept in a single bed.* **5** *Brit* : ONE-WAY ▪ *a single ticket*

²**single** *n* **1** [C] : an unmarried person and especially one who is young and socially active — usually plural ▪ *a singles bar/club* **2** [C] *baseball* : a hit that allows the batter to reach first base **3** [*plural*] : a game of tennis or a similar sport that is played between two players ▪ *Do you want to play singles or doubles?* **4** [C] : one song from a recording that includes many songs ▪ *Have you heard the latest single from the album?* **5** [C] : a room in a hotel, inn, etc., for one person ▪ *The hotel has only singles available.* **6** [C] *US* : a one-dollar bill ▪ *Do you have five singles for this five?* **7** [C] *Brit* : a one-way ticket ▪ *A single to Bath, please.*

³**single** *vb* **sin·gled; sin·gling** [I] : to hit a single in baseball ▪ *He singled to right field.* — **single out** [*phrasal vb*] **single out (someone or something) or single (someone or something) out** : to treat or to speak about (someone or something in a group) in a way that is different from the way you treat or speak about others ▪ *The teacher singled him out as the only student to get an A on the test.*

sin·gle–breast·ed /ˈsɪŋɡəlˈbrɛstəd/ *adj,* of a coat, jacket, or suit : having one row of buttons ▪ *He wore a single-breasted blazer.*

single file *n* [U] : a line of people, animals, or things arranged one behind another ▪ *They stood/walked in single file.* — **single file** *adv* ▪ *They lined up single file.*

sin·gle–hand·ed /ˌsɪŋɡəlˈhændəd/ *adj, always before a noun* : working or done alone ▪ *a single-handed sailor* ▪ *single-handed sailing* — **single–handed** *adv* ▪ *He did the work single-handed.* — **sin·gle–hand·ed·ly** *adv* ▪ *She raised the children single-handedly.* [=by herself]

sin·gle–mind·ed /ˌsɪŋɡəlˈmaɪndəd/ *adj* : having only one purpose, goal, or interest ▪ *He worked with single-minded dedication/determination/devotion to help the poor.* ▪ *She is very single-minded and determined to succeed.*

sin·glet /ˈsɪŋɡlət/ *n* [C] *chiefly Brit* : a shirt that has no sleeves or collar and that is worn for playing sports

sin·gly /ˈsɪŋɡəli/ *adv, formal* : without another ▪ *The books in the set cannot be sold singly.* [=individually]

sing·song /ˈsɪŋˌsɑːŋ/ *n* **1** [*singular*] : a way of speaking in which the sound of your voice rises and falls in a pattern ▪ *a singsong voice* **2** [C] *Brit* : SING-ALONG

¹**sin·gu·lar** /ˈsɪŋɡjələ/ *adj* **1** *grammar* : showing or indicating no more than one thing ▪ *"Walks" in "she walks everyday" is a singular verb.* — *abbr. sing.* **2 a** *formal* : better or greater than what is usual or normal ▪ *her singular talent for music* ▪ *He showed a singular* [=notice-

able, obvious] *lack of interest.* **b** *literary* : strange or odd ▪ *He is a singular man.* — **sin·gu·lar·ly** *adv* ▪ *a singularly important discovery*

²**singular** *n* — **the singular** : a form of a word that is used to refer to one person or thing ▪ *"Mouse" is the singular of "mice."* ▪ *The verb should be in the singular.*

sin·is·ter /ˈsɪnəstə/ *adj* : having an evil appearance : looking likely to cause something bad, harmful, or dangerous to happen ▪ *He looked sinister.* ▪ *sinister black clouds*

¹**sink** /ˈsɪŋk/ *vb* **sank** /ˈsæŋk/ *or* **sunk** /ˈsʌŋk/; **sunk; sink·ing** **1** [T/I] : to go down or to cause (something) to go down below the surface of water, mud, etc. ▪ *a sinking ship* ▪ *The torpedo sank the ship.* ▪ *She sank up to her knees in the snow.* ▪ *The ship sank like a stone.* [=sank very quickly] **2** [I] : to move down to a lower position ▪ *The sun sank behind the hills.* ▪ *He sank to his knees.* [=he knelt down] ▪ *She sank back into the chair.* **3** [I] : to become lower in amount, value, etc. ▪ *The currency's value is sinking.* **4** [T] : to use force to cause (something) to go into the ground or another surface ▪ *He sank the fence posts into the ground.* ▪ *The cat sank its claws into my arm.* **5** [I] **a** : to do something that is morally wrong ▪ *I never thought he could sink so low.* [=do something so wrong] **b** : to begin to feel sad, depressed, etc. ▪ *Her heart sank* [=she became very sad] ▪ *She got a sinking feeling* [=a feeling of dread or discouragement] *as she picked up the phone.* **c** : to go or change to a worse or less active state ▪ *The patient sank into a coma.* **6** [I] *of a person's voice* : to become quieter ▪ *Her voice sank to a whisper.* [=she began to whisper] **7** [T] : to cause (someone or something) to fail ▪ *Bad weather sank their plans for a picnic.* ▪ *If we don't get that money soon, we'll be sunk.* **8** [T] : to spend (a lot of money, work, time, etc.) on something — + *in or into* ▪ *He keeps sinking money into that old car.* **9** [T] : to throw, hit, or roll (a ball) into a hole or basket ▪ *She sank the shot/putt.* — **sink in** [*phrasal vb*] : to become completely known, felt, or understood ▪ *The fact that she's left me still hasn't really sunk in.* — **sink or swim** ◆ A situation in which you either *sink or swim* is one in which you must succeed by your own efforts or fail completely. ▪ *In this job, it's sink or swim.* — **sink your teeth into** see TOOTH

²**sink** *n* [C] : a wide bowl that has a faucet for water and a drain at the bottom and is usually positioned in a counter or on a pedestal ▪ *a kitchen sink* ▪ (*chiefly US*) *a bathroom sink* [=(*chiefly Brit*) *washbasin*]

sink·er /ˈsɪŋkə/ *n* [C] : a weight used for holding a fishing line or net underwater — **hook, line and sinker** see ¹HOOK

sin·ner /ˈsɪnə/ *n* [C] : someone who has done something wrong according to religious or moral law : someone who has sinned

sin·u·ous /ˈsɪnjəwəs/ *adj, formal + literary* **1** : having many twists and turns ▪ *a* *sinuous* [=*winding*] *road* **2** : moving and bending in a smooth and attractive way ▪ *She moved with sinuous grace.* — **sin·u·ous·ly** *adv*

si·nus /'saɪnəs/ *n* [*C*] : any one of several spaces in the skull that connect with the nostrils ▪ *My sinuses are blocked.* [=they are filled with mucus and will not drain properly] ▪ *a sinus infection/problem*

sip /'sɪp/ *vb* **sipped; sip·ping** [*T/I*] : to drink (a liquid) slowly by taking only small amounts into your mouth ▪ *She sipped her coffee.* ▪ *He sipped on the bottle of water.* — **sip** *n* [*C*] ▪ *Have/take a sip of water.*

¹si·phon *also* **sy·phon** /'saɪfən/ *n* [*C*] : a bent tube used to move a liquid from one container to another container by means of air pressure

²siphon *also* **syphon** *vb* [*T*] **1** : to move (a liquid) from one container to another by using a siphon ▪ *He siphoned (off) gas from the car's tank.* **2** : to take and use (something, such as money) for your own purpose ▪ *Funds were siphoned (off) from the schools to build a new stadium.*

sir /'sɚ/ *n* **1** [*U*] **a** — used without a name as a form of polite address to a man you do not know ▪ *May I help you, sir?* **b** — used without a name as a form of polite address to a man of high rank or authority (such as a military or police officer, teacher, or master) ▪ *"At ease, lieutenant." "Yes sir, captain."* **2** *Sir* [*C*] — used without a name as a form of address at the beginning of a formal letter ▪ *Dear Sir or Madam* **3** *Sir* [*U*] — used as a title before the name of a knight ▪ *Sir Lancelot* **4** [*U*] *US, informal* — used in the phrases *no sir* and *yes sir* for emphasis, to show surprise, etc. ▪ *I will not have that man in my home, no sir.* ▪ *"She couldn't have said that." "Yes sir, she sure did."*

sire /'sajɚ/ *n* **1** [*U*] — used formerly to address a man of high rank or authority (such as a king or lord) ▪ *Your horses are ready, sire.* **2** [*C*] *technical* : a male parent of some animals (such as dogs and horses) ▪ *the foal's sire* — **sire** *vb* **sired; sir·ing** [*T*] ▪ *The horse sired several champion racers.*

si·ren /'saɪrən/ *n* [*C*] **1** : a piece of equipment that produces a loud, high-pitched warning sound ▪ *an ambulance siren* **2** : a woman who is very attractive but also dangerous ▪ *a Hollywood siren*

siren song *n* [*C*] : something that is very appealing and makes you want to go somewhere or do something but that may have bad results ▪ *the siren song of fame and money* — called also *siren call*

sir·loin /'sɚˌlɔɪn/ *n* [*C/U*] : a piece of beef from the lower back area of a cow ▪ *a sirloin steak*

sis·sy *also Brit* **cis·sy** /'sɪsi/ *n, pl* **-sies** [*C*] *informal + disapproving* **1** : a boy who is weak or who likes things that girls usually like ▪ *They called him a sissy because he didn't like sports.* **2** : a person who is weak and fearful ▪ *Don't be such a sissy.* — **sissy** *adj* ▪ *a sissy sport*

¹sis·ter /'sɪstɚ/ *n* [*C*] **1** : a girl or woman who has one or both of the same parents as you ▪ *my little/younger sister* ▪ *He has two sisters.* **2** *or Sister* : a member of a religious community of women : NUN ▪ *Sister Mary* — abbr. *Sr.* **3** : a woman who is from the same group or country as you ▪ *her college sorority sisters*

²sister *adj, always before a noun* : belonging to the same kind or group ▪ *sister companies/schools*

sis·ter·hood /'sɪstɚˌhʊd/ *n* **1** [*U*] : the close relationship among women based on shared experiences, concerns, etc. ▪ *the bonds of sisterhood* **2** [*C*] : a community or society of women and especially nuns ▪ *Sister Katherine joined the sisterhood 10 years ago.*

sis·ter–in–law /'sɪstərənˌlɑ:/ *n, pl* **sis·ters–in–law** /'sɪstərzənˌlɑ/ [*C*] **1** : the sister of your husband or wife **2** : the wife of your brother

sis·ter·ly /'sɪstɚli/ *adj* : showing or suggesting the closeness of a sister ▪ *She gave me a sisterly kiss on the cheek.* ▪ *a sisterly friendship*

sit /'sɪt/ *vb* **sat** /'sæt/; **sit·ting 1 a** [*I*] : to be in a position in which your bottom is resting on a chair, the ground, etc., especially with your back upright ▪ *He was sitting in a chair.* ▪ *She sat across from me during dinner.* ▪ *You can't expect young children to sit still.* [=sit without moving around] *for that long.* **b** [*I*] : to put yourself in a sitting position ▪ *He went over and sat in a chair next to the window.* **c** [*T*] : to cause (someone) to be seated ▪ *She sat the toddler in the chair.* **2** [*I*] **a** *of an animal* : to rest with the tail end of the body on the floor and the front legs straight ▪ *He taught the dog to sit (on command).* **b** *of a bird* : to rest on the top or the edge of something ▪ *The bird sat on the ledge.* **3** [*I*] : to be or stay in a particular place, position, or condition ▪ *A vase sat on the table.* **4** [*I*] : to be a member of an official group that has meetings ▪ *She sits on the board of directors.* **5** [*I*] : to meet in order to carry on official business ▪ *The court is now sitting.* **6** [*I*] **a** : BABYSIT ▪ *She sits for the neighbors' kids.* **b** : to take care of something while the owner is away ▪ *Can you dog-sit* [=take care of my dog] *for me this weekend?* **7** [*T*] *US* : to have enough seats for (a certain number of people) ▪ *The car sits* [=seats] *five (people).* **8** [*I*] : to pose for a portrait, photograph, etc. ▪ *She agreed to sit for the painting/painter.* **9** [*T/I*] *Brit* : to take (an examination) ▪ *Students will sit (for) the exam next week.* — **sit around** *also chiefly Brit* **sit about** [*phrasal vb*] : to spend time doing nothing useful ▪ *She just sits around watching television all day.* — **sit back** [*phrasal vb*] **1** : to get into a comfortable and relaxed position in a chair, seat, etc. ▪ *Sit back and enjoy the ride.* **2** : to make no effort to do something ▪ *He sat back and watched us do all the work.* — **sit by** [*phrasal vb*] : to make no effort to stop something bad or unpleasant from happening ▪ *We can't just sit by and watch him ruin his life.* — **sit down** [*phrasal vb*] **1** : to put yourself into a sitting position ▪ *She called just as we were sitting down to* *eat.* **2 be sitting down** : to be in a sitting position ▪ *She made sure everyone was sitting down before she began.* **3 sit (someone) down** : to put or get (someone) in a sitting position ▪ *You need to sit him down and have a talk with him.* — **sit in** [*phrasal vb*] **1** : to take the place of someone who is not present ▪ *He could not attend, so his assistant is sitting in (for him).* **2 sit in on (something)** : to attend (something, such as a class or meeting) without officially participating ▪ *I would like to sit in on one of your classes.* — **sit on** [*phrasal vb*] *informal* : to delay dealing with or talking about (something) ▪ *They have been sitting on my insurance claim for months!* — **sit out** [*phrasal vb*] **sit out (something)** *or* **sit (something) out 1** : to stay in a place and wait for (something) to end ▪ *The movie was boring, but we sat it out to see how it ended.* **2** : to not take part in (something) ▪ *You can start the game without me. I'm going to sit this one out.* — **sit pretty** *informal* : to be in a very good or favorable situation ▪ *He bought stock in the company early on, and now he is sitting pretty.* — **sit through** [*phrasal vb*] : to go to (something) and stay until the end ▪ *We had to sit through another boring meeting.* — **sit tight** : to not change your position or situation ▪ *Sit tight, I'll go get help.* ▪ *This isn't a good time to sell a house. Let's just sit tight and see if the market improves.* — **sit up** [*phrasal vb*] **1** : to stay awake until late at night ▪ *They sat up talking until almost dawn.* **2** : to sit with your back very straight ▪ *Quit slouching and sit up (straight).* **3 sit up** *or* **sit (someone) up** : to move or help (someone) to move into a sitting position ▪ *He sat up in bed.* ▪ *She sat the child up.* — **sit up and take notice** : to suddenly pay attention to (someone or something) ▪ *The news made them sit up and take notice.* — **sit well/comfortably (etc.)** ◊ If something **does not sit well/comfortably (etc.) with you**, you do not like it. ▪ *The decision didn't sit well with him.*

si·tar /sɪˈtɑːʳ/ *n* [*C*] : a musical instrument from India that is like a guitar and that has a long neck and a round body

sit·com /ˈsɪtˌkɑːm/ *n* [*C/U*] : a show that is on television regularly and that is about a group of characters who are involved in different funny situations — called also *situation comedy*

¹**sit-down** /ˈsɪtˈdaʊn/ *adj, always before a noun* **1** : done or used while sitting down ▪ *a sit-down job/interview* ▪ *a sit-down lawn mower* **2 a** : served to people who are sitting down at a table ▪ *a sit-down dinner* **b** : serving sit-down meals ▪ *a sit-down restaurant*

²**sit-down** /ˈsɪtˌdaʊn/ *n* [*C*] **1** : a strike or protest in which a group of people sit down to block a road, entrance, etc., and refuse to leave until they are given what they demand ▪ *a sit-down strike/protest* **2** *chiefly US* : a meeting held to talk about a problem or disagreement ▪ *The group arranged a sit-down with city officials.*

site /ˈsaɪt/ *n* [*C*] **1** : the place where something (such as a building) is, was, or

will be located ▪ *The company has chosen a new site for its office building.* **2** : a place where something important has happened ▪ *the site of the battle* **3** : a place that is used for a particular activity ▪ *a nuclear test site* **4** : WEB SITE

sit-in /ˈsɪtˌɪn/ *n* [*C*] : a strike or protest in which people sit or stay in a place and refuse to leave until they are given what they demand

sit·ter /ˈsɪtəʳ/ *n* [*C*] *chiefly US* : a person who takes care of a child while the child's parents are away : BABYSITTER ▪ *They hired a sitter so they could go out.*

¹**sit·ting** /ˈsɪtɪŋ/ *n* [*C*] **1** : a period of time during which someone sits and does a particular activity ▪ *I got through the book in one sitting.* ▪ *He finished the portrait in one sitting.* **2** : a time when a meal is served to a number of people at the same time ▪ *We have reservations for the 5:30 sitting.* **3** : a formal meeting of a court of law, a legislature, etc. ▪ *a sitting of the legislature*

²**sitting** *adj, always before a noun* : currently holding an office ▪ *a sitting President*

sitting duck *n* [*C*] : a person or thing that is easy to hit, attack, trick, etc. ▪ *The tourists were sitting ducks for local thieves.*

sitting room *n* [*C*] : LIVING ROOM

sit·u·ate /ˈsɪtʃəˌweɪt/ *vb* **-at·ed; -at·ing** [*T*] *formal* : to place (someone or something) in a particular location ▪ *They decided to situate the new hotel near the airport.* ▪ *We situated ourselves in the seats nearest the exit.*

situated *adj, formal* : located in a particular place ▪ *The building is situated in the nice part of town.*

sit·u·a·tion /ˌsɪtʃəˈweɪʃən/ *n* [*C*] **1** : all of the facts, conditions, and events that affect someone or something at a particular time and in a particular place ▪ *He's in a bad/difficult/dangerous situation.* ▪ *I've been in your situation before.* **2** *somewhat formal* + *old-fashioned* : a place or location ▪ *The house is in a wonderful situation overlooking the valley.*

situation comedy *n* [*C*] : SITCOM

sit-up /ˈsɪtˌʌp/ *n* [*C*] : an exercise in which you lie on your back and use your stomach muscles to raise the top part of your body to a sitting position ▪ *She does 50 sit-ups every morning.*

six /ˈsɪks/ *n* **1** [*C*] : the number 6 **2** [*C*] : the sixth in a set or series ▪ *the six of hearts* **3** [*U*] : six o'clock ▪ *I leave each day at six.* — **at sixes and sevens** *chiefly Brit, informal* : disorganized and confused ▪ *The change left everyone at sixes and sevens.* — **hit/knock (someone) for six** *Brit, informal* : to have an unpleasant and shocking effect on (someone) ▪ *The news of the accident really hit me for six.* — **six** *adj* ▪ *six possibilities/hours* — **six** *pron* ▪ *Six (of them) will be coming tonight.*

six-pack /ˈsɪksˌpæk/ *n* [*C*] : a group of six cans or bottles sold together ▪ *a six-pack of soda/beer*

six·teen /ˌsɪkˈstiːn/ *n* [*C*] : the number 16 — **sixteen** *adj* ▪ *sixteen years* — **sixteen** *pron* ▪ *Sixteen (of them) will be com-*

ing tonight. — **six·teenth** /ˌsɪkˈstiːnθ/ *n* [C] • *I'll see you on the sixteenth (of April).* • *one sixteenth of the total* — **sixteenth** *adj* • *the sixteenth century* — **sixteenth** *adv* • *the nation's sixteenth largest city*

¹**sixth** /ˈsɪksθ/ *n* **1** [*singular*] : the number six in a series • *I'll be flying in on the sixth.* [=the sixth day of the month] **2** [C] : one of six equal parts of something • *a sixth of the total*

²**sixth** *adj* : occupying the number six position in a series • *on the sixth day* — **sixth** *adv* • *She finished sixth in the race.*

sixth form *n* [*singular*] *Brit* : the two final years of secondary school in Britain for students aged 16 to 18 — **sixth-former** *n* [C]

sixth sense *n* [*singular*] : a special ability to know something that cannot be learned by using sight, hearing, etc. • *I have a sixth sense for knowing when someone is going to call.*

six·ty /ˈsɪksti/ *n, pl* **-ties** **1** [C] : the number 60 **2** [*plural*] **a** : the numbers ranging from 60 to 69 **b** : a set of years ending in digits ranging from 60 to 69 • *She likes music from the sixties.* [=from 1960 to 1969] • *He is in his sixties.* — **six·ti·eth** /ˈsɪkstijəθ/ *n* [C] — **sixtieth** *adj* • *his sixtieth birthday* — **sixty** *adj* • *sixty books* — **sixty** *pron*

siz·able *or* **size·able** /ˈsaɪzəbəl/ *adj* : fairly large • *a sizable contribution/donation* • *a sizable portion/percentage/proportion of the population*

¹**size** /ˈsaɪz/ *n* **1 a** [C/U] : how large or small someone or something is • *The bug was about the size of a dime.* • *The tomatoes haven't quite reached their full size.* • *The cars are similar in size.* **b** [C/U] : the total number of people or things in a group • *the size of the audience/population* **c** [U] : the very large size of something • *You should have seen the size of the shark!* **2** [U] : a specific size • *The lumber can be cut to size.* [=cut to the specific size you need] **3** [C/U] : one of a series of standard measurements in which clothing, shoes, etc., are made • *The dress is a size 12.* • *She's a size six.* [=the clothes that fit her are size six] • *Try this shoe on for size.* [=try this shoe on to see if it is the correct size] — **down to size** ◆ If people *cut/bring (etc.) you down to size,* they make you realize that you are not as powerful and important as you thought you were. — **that's about the size of it** *informal* — used to say that what has been stated about a situation is correct • *"So there's no chance of getting finished on time?" "That's about the size of it."*

²**size** *vb* **sized; siz·ing** [T] : to make (something) a particular size • *The jeweler sized the ring (up/down) to fit her finger.* — **size up** [*phrasal vb*] **size (something or someone) up** *or* **size up (something or someone)** *informal* : to consider (something or someone) in order to form an opinion or conclusion • *She quickly sized up the situation.*

siz·zle /ˈsɪzəl/ *vb* **siz·zled; siz·zling** [I] **1** : to make a hissing sound like the sound water makes when it hits hot metal • *bacon sizzling in the pan* **2** *chiefly US, informal* : to be very exciting, romantic, etc. • *The book sizzles with excitement.* — **sizzle** *n* [*singular*] • *the sizzle of frying bacon*

sizzling *adj, chiefly US, informal* **1** : very hot • *a sizzling summer* **2** : very exciting, romantic, etc. • *a sizzling love affair*

¹**skate** /ˈskeɪt/ *n* [C] **1** : ICE SKATE **2** : ROLLER SKATE

²**skate** *vb* **skat·ed; skat·ing** [I] **1** : to move or glide over a surface on skates • *We skated around the rink.* **2** : to ride or perform tricks on a skateboard • *We skate at the park.* **3** : to move or glide quickly along a surface • *The bugs skated along the surface of the water.* — **skate over/around** [*phrasal vb*] : to avoid talking about (something) especially because it is difficult to talk about or embarrassing • *He skated over the issue/question.* — **skat·er** /ˈskeɪtɚ/ *n* [C] • *Olympic ice skaters* — **skating** [U] • *I like skating. Let's go skating.*

skate·board /ˈskeɪtˌboɚd/ *n* [C] : a short board that is on wheels and that a person stands on to move along a surface or to perform tricks — **skateboard** *vb* [I] • *He skateboards* [=rides a skateboard] *to school every day.* — **skate·board·er** /ˈskeɪtˌboɚdɚ/ *n* [C] — **skate·board·ing** /ˈskeɪtˌboɚdɪŋ/ *n* [U] • *Skateboarding is not allowed in the parking lot.*

skating rink *n* [C] : an area or place that is used for skating

skein /ˈskeɪn/ *n* [C] : a long piece of yarn or thread that is loosely wound

skel·e·tal /ˈskɛlətl/ *adj* **1** *technical* : of or relating to a skeleton • *skeletal muscles* • *skeletal remains* **2** : very thin • *She was skeletal after her illness.*

¹**skel·e·ton** /ˈskɛlətən/ *n* [C] **1 a** : the structure of bones that supports the body of a person or animal **b** : a set or model of all the bones in the body of a person • *He hung a plastic skeleton on the door for Halloween.* **2 a** : the frame of a building • *Only the charred skeleton of the house remained after the fire.* **b** : a basic outline of a plan, piece of writing, etc. • *We saw a skeleton of the report before it was published.* — **skeletons in the/your closet** *or Brit* **skeletons in the/your cupboard** *informal* : something bad or embarrassing that happened in your past and that is kept secret • *Do you have any skeletons in your closet?*

²**skeleton** *adj, always before a noun* : having the smallest possible number of people who can get a job done • *a skeleton crew/staff*

skep·tic *(US) or Brit* **scep·tic** /ˈskɛptɪk/ *n* [C] : a person who questions or doubts something (such as a claim or statement) • *Skeptics have pointed out flaws in the researchers' methods.*

skep·ti·cal *(US) or Brit* **scep·ti·cal** /ˈskɛptɪkəl/ *adj* : having or expressing doubt about something (such as a claim or statement) • *She's highly skeptical of/about the researchers' claims.* • *He says he* *can win, but I'm skeptical.* — **skep·ti·cal·ly** *(US) or Brit* **scep·ti·cal·ly** /ˈskɛptɪkli/ *adv*

skep·ti·cism *(US) or Brit* **scep·ti·cism** /ˈskɛptəˌsɪzəm/ *n* [U, singular] : an attitude of doubting the truth of something (such as a claim or statement) ▪ *She regarded their claims with skepticism.* ▪ *He maintains a healthy skepticism about fad diets.*

¹**sketch** /ˈskɛtʃ/ *n* [C] **1** : a quick, rough drawing that shows the main features of an object or scene ▪ *I drew a sketch of the house.* **2** : a short description of something ▪ *a biographical sketch of the author* ▪ *She gave us a thumbnail sketch* [=short description] *of the movie's plot.* **3** : a short, funny performance ▪ *a comedy sketch*

²**sketch** *vb* **1** [T/I] : to make a quick, rough drawing of (something) ▪ *He sketched the trees.* ▪ *He likes to sit outside and sketch.* **2** [T] : to describe (something) briefly ▪ *She sketched (out) the plan for us.* — **sketch in** [*phrasal vb*] **sketch in (something) or sketch (something) in** : to add (something, such as details) to a drawing, description, etc. ▪ *The author decided to sketch in some minor characters.*

sketch·book /ˈskɛtʃˌbʊk/ *n* [C] : a book filled with paper that is used for drawing

sketch·pad /ˈskɛtʃˌpæd/ *n* [C] : SKETCHBOOK

sketchy /ˈskɛtʃi/ *adj* **sketch·i·er; -est** **1** : not complete or clear ▪ *The details are still a little sketchy.* ▪ *sketchy information/ reports* **2** : done quickly without many details ▪ *a sketchy drawing* **3** *US, informal* : likely to be bad or dangerous ▪ *a sketchy neighborhood* — **sketch·i·ness** /ˈskɛtʃinəs/ *n* [U]

skew /ˈskju:/ *vb* [T] **1** : to change (something) so that it is not true or accurate ▪ *They skewed the facts to fit their theory.* **2** : to make (something) favor a particular group of people in a way that is unfair ▪ *The tax cuts are skewed toward the wealthy.*

skewed /ˈskju:d/ *adj* **1** : not true or accurate ▪ *skewed facts* **2** : not straight ▪ *The line is skewed.*

¹**skew·er** /ˈskju:wɚ/ *n* [C] : a long pointed piece of metal or wood that is pushed through pieces of food to keep them together or hold them in place for cooking

²**skewer** *vb* [T] **1** : to push a skewer through (food) ▪ *skewer a marshmallow* **2** *chiefly US, informal* : to criticize (someone or something) very harshly ▪ *Critics skewered the movie.*

¹**ski** /ˈski:/ *n* [C] : one of a pair of long narrow pieces of wood, metal, or plastic that curve upward slightly in front, are attached to shoes, and are used for gliding over snow

²**ski** *vb* [T/I] : to move or glide on skis over snow ▪ *He loves to ski.* ▪ *I have skied that mountain.* — **ski·er** *n* [C] — **ski·ing** /ˈski:jɪŋ/ *n* [U] ▪ *We are going skiing tomorrow.*

³**ski** *adj, always before a noun* : of, relating to, or used in skiing ▪ *ski slopes/goggles/ resorts*

¹**skid** /ˈskɪd/ *vb* **skid·ded; skid·ding** [I] : to slide along a road or other surface in an uncontrolled way ▪ *The truck skidded across the icy road.*

²**skid** *n* [C] **1** : a sudden, uncontrolled sliding movement ▪ *The car hit a patch of ice and went into a skid.* **2** : one of a pair of long narrow parts on which a helicopter or airplane rests **3** : PALLET 1 — **hit the skids** *informal* : to begin to fail or get worse very suddenly and quickly ▪ *The stock market has hit the skids.* — **on the skids** *informal* : failing or getting worse ▪ *The company is on the skids.*

skid row *n* [U] *chiefly US, informal* : a poor part of a town or city where people who are homeless or who drink too much often go ▪ *You'll end up on skid row if you don't stop drinking so much.*

skilful *Brit spelling of* SKILLFUL

ski lift *n* [C] : a series of seats or handles that are attached to a moving cable and that are used to carry skiers up a mountain

skill /ˈskɪl/ *n* [C/U] : the ability to do something that comes from training, experience, or practice ▪ *I was impressed by her skill at writing.* ▪ *Cooking is a useful skill.*

skilled /ˈskɪld/ *adj* **1** : having the training, knowledge, and experience that is needed to do something : having a lot of skill ▪ *skilled workers* **2** *always before a noun* : requiring training ▪ *Carpentry is a skilled trade.*

skil·let /ˈskɪlət/ *n* [C] *chiefly US* : FRYING PAN

skill·ful *(US) or Brit* **skil·ful** /ˈskɪlfəl/ *adj* **1** : having the training, knowledge, and experience that is needed to do something well : having a lot of skill ▪ *a skillful artist* **2** : showing or requiring skill ▪ *a skillful performance* — **skill·ful·ly** *(US) or Brit* **skil·ful·ly** *adv* — **skill·ful·ness** *(US) or Brit* **skil·ful·ness** *n* [U]

skim /ˈskɪm/ *vb* **skimmed; skim·ming** **1** [T] : to remove a layer of something from the surface of a liquid ▪ *I skimmed the fat from the broth.* = *I skimmed the broth to remove the fat.* **2** [T/I] : to look over or read (something) quickly especially to find the main ideas ▪ *She skimmed (through/over) the reading assignment.* **3** [T/I] : to move quickly or lightly along, above, or near the surface of something ▪ *The ducks skimmed (across/over) the water before landing.* — **skim off** [*phrasal vb*] **skim off (something) or skim (something) off** : to take (something valuable) for yourself out of something else ▪ *He skimmed off some of the profits.* — **skim·mer** /ˈskɪmɚ/ *n* [C]

skim milk *n* [U] *chiefly US* : milk from which all the cream and fat has been removed — *called also* (*chiefly Brit*) **skimmed milk**

skimp /ˈskɪmp/ *vb* **skimped; skimp·ing** [I] : to spend less time, money, etc., on something than is needed ▪ *The book doesn't skimp on details.* [=it provides plenty of details]

skimpy /ˈskɪmpi/ *adj* **skimp·i·er; -est**

: very small in size or amount ▪ *skimpy evidence/portions* ▪ *a skimpy dress*

¹skin /ˈskɪn/ *n* [C/U] **1** : the natural outer layer of tissue that covers the body of a person or animal ▪ *She has pale/dark skin.* ▪ *The snake sheds its skin once a year.* ▪ *The horrible things I saw* **made my skin crawl/creep.** [=made me feel disgusted, afraid, etc.] **2** : the skin of an animal that has been removed from the body often with its hair or feathers still attached and that is used to make things (such as clothes) ▪ *His boots are made of alligator skin.* **3** : the outer covering of a fruit, vegetable, etc. ▪ *apple skins* — **(a) thick/thin skin** ✧ If you have *(a) thin skin,* you are easily upset or offended by the things other people say or do. If you have *(a) thick skin,* you are not easily upset or offended by the things other people say and do. — **by the skin of your teeth** *informal* : only by a small difference in time, space, or amount ▪ *He escaped by the skin of his teeth.* [=he just barely escaped] — **get under your skin** *informal* **1** : to irritate or upset you ▪ *She really gets under my skin.* **2** : to affect you emotionally even though you do not want or expect to be affected ▪ *I used to hate the city, but after a while it kind of got under my skin.* [=I grew to like it] — **save someone's skin** see ¹SAVE — **skin and bones** *or* **skin and bone** *informal* : very thin in a way that is unattractive and unhealthy ▪ *After the illness, he was skin and bones.* — **skin·less** /ˈskɪnləs/ *adj* ▪ *skinless chicken breast*

²skin *vb* **skinned; skin·ning** [T] **1** : to remove the skin of (a dead animal, a fruit, etc.) ▪ *The hunter skinned the rabbit.* **2** : to scrape or rub off some of the skin from (a body part) ▪ *I skinned my knee when I fell.*

skin–deep /ˈskɪnˈdiːp/ *adj* : not very deep at all : relating to, affecting, or involving only the surface ▪ *Beauty is only skin-deep.*

skin diving *n* [U] : the sport of swimming underwater with special equipment (such as a face mask, snorkel, and flippers) but without a diving suit or air tank — **skin diver** *n* [C]

skin·flint /ˈskɪnˌflɪnt/ *n* [C] *informal + disapproving* : a person who hates to spend money

skin·head /ˈskɪnˌhɛd/ *n* [C] : a person with a shaved head; *especially* : a young white person who belongs to a gang whose members shave their heads and have racist beliefs

skinned /ˈskɪnd/ *adj* : having skin of a specified kind ▪ *dark-skinned* ▪ *smooth-skinned*

skin·ny /ˈskɪni/ *adj* **skin·ni·er, -est** *informal* : very thin or too thin ▪ *a skinny actress* ▪ *skinny legs*

skin·ny–dip /ˈskɪniˌdɪp/ *vb* **-dipped; -dip·ping** [I] *informal* : to swim without wearing any clothes — **skin·ny–dip·per** /ˈskɪniˌdɪpɚ/ *n* [C] — **skinny–dipping** *n* [U]

skin·tight /ˈskɪnˈtaɪt/ *adj* : very closely fitted to the body ▪ *a skintight dress*

¹skip /ˈskɪp/ *vb* **skipped; skip·ping** **1** [T] : to not do (something that is usual or expected) ▪ *He skipped the meeting.* [=he didn't go to the meeting] ▪ *(chiefly US) They got in trouble for* **skipping school/class.** **2** [T/I] : to not do or deal with (something) and go instead to the next thing ▪ *I skipped two questions on the test.* ▪ *I don't like this song. Let's skip to the next one.* ▪ *You can* **skip over** *the introduction if you want.* **3** [I] **a** : to change quickly from one subject, place, etc., to another ▪ *The movie skips around in time.* **b** ✧ If a CD, DVD, record, etc., **skips,** it fails to play part of a song or movie properly because it is damaged. **4** [I] : to move forward in a light or playful way by taking short, quick steps and jumps ▪ *The kids skipped down the street.* **5** [T] *informal* : to leave (a place) in a sudden and unexpected way ▪ *Police are afraid he might try to skip the country.* **6** [T/I] *US* : to throw (a flat stone) along the surface of water so that it bounces ▪ *She's good at* **skipping stones.** **7** [I] *Brit* : to jump over a rope that is being swung near the ground for exercise or as a game — **skip out** *(US)* or *Brit* **skip off** [phrasal vb] *informal* : to leave a place quickly in a secret and improper way ▪ *She skipped out with all the money.* ▪ *(US) She* **skipped out** *on me.* — **skip rope** see ¹ROPE

²skip *n* [C] **1** : a short, quick step and jump forward **2** *Brit* : a large metal container for putting trash in — **a hop, skip, and (a) jump** see ²HOP

skip·per /ˈskɪpɚ/ *n* [C] *informal* **1** : the captain of a ship or boat **2** *informal* : the manager of a baseball team — **skipper** *vb* [T] ▪ *skipper a boat/team*

skir·mish /ˈskɚmɪʃ/ *n* [C] **1** : a brief and usually unplanned fight during a war **2** : a minor or brief argument or disagreement ▪ *a political skirmish* — **skirmish** *vb* [I] ▪ *Rebel groups are skirmishing with military forces.*

¹skirt /ˈskɚt/ *n* [C] **1 a** : a piece of clothing worn by women and girls that hangs from the waist down **b** : the part of a dress, coat, etc., that hangs from the waist down **2** : an outer covering that hangs down to protect something ▪ *a protective skirt*

²skirt *vb* [T/I] **1** : to avoid (something) especially because it is difficult or will cause problems ▪ *He tried to skirt (around) the question/issue.* **2** : to lie or go along the edge of (something) ▪ *The road skirts (around) the lake.*

skirting board *n* [C/U] *Brit* : BASEBOARD — called also *(Brit)* **skirting**

skit /ˈskɪt/ *n* [C] : a short, funny story or performance

skit·ter /ˈskɪtɚ/ *vb* [I] : to move quickly and lightly along a surface ▪ *Mice skittered across the floor.*

skit·tish /ˈskɪtɪʃ/ *adj* **1** *of an animal* : easily frightened or excited ▪ *a skittish horse* **2** : nervous or fearful about doing something ▪ *skittish investors*

skit·tle /ˈskɪtl̩/ *n* **1** **skit·tles** [U] : a British game played by rolling a wooden ball toward a set of objects in order to knock over as many as possible **2** [C] : one of the objects that a player tries to knock over in a game of skittles

skive /'skaɪv/ *vb* **skived; skiv·ing** [*T/I*] *Brit, informal* : to avoid school or work by staying away or by leaving without permission — often + *off* ▪ *He skives off (work) whenever he can.*

skul·dug·gery *or* **skull·dug·gery** /ˌskʌl'dʌgəri/ *n* [*U*] *old-fashioned* : secret or dishonest behavior or activity

skulk /'skʌlk/ *vb* [*I*] : to move or hide in a secret way especially because you are planning to do something bad ▪ *A man was skulking around outside.*

skull /'skʌl/ *n* [*C*] : the structure of bones that form the head and face of a person or animal

skull and cross·bones /ˌskʌlən'krɑːsˌboʊnz/ *n* [*singular*] : a picture of a human skull above two crossed bones that was used on the flags of pirate ships in the past and is now used as a warning label on containers of poisonous or dangerous substances

skull·cap /'skʌlˌkæp/ *n* [*C*] : a small, round cap that fits on top of the head

skunk /'skʌŋk/ *n* [*C*] **1** : a small black-and-white North American animal that produces a very strong and unpleasant smell when it is frightened or in danger **2** *US, informal* : a very bad or unpleasant person

sky /'skaɪ/ *n, pl* **skies** [*C/U*] : the space over the Earth where the sun, moon, stars, and clouds appear ▪ *a starry sky* ▪ *There wasn't a cloud in the sky.* ▪ *sunny/ overcast skies* — **take to the sky/skies** *chiefly US* : to begin flying ▪ *The new airliner will take to the skies next year.* — **the sky's the limit** see [1]**LIMIT**

sky–div·ing /'skaɪˌdaɪvɪŋ/ *n* [*U*] : the sport of jumping from an airplane and falling through the sky before opening a parachute — **sky–dive** /'skaɪˌdaɪv/ *vb* **-dived; -div·ing** [*I*] ▪ *Have you ever skydived?* — **sky–div·er** *n* [*C*]

sky–high /'skaɪˌhaɪ/ *adj* : extremely high ▪ *sky–high prices* — **sky–high** *adv* ▪ *Stock prices rose sky-high.*

sky·lark /'skaɪˌlɑɚk/ *n* [*C*] : a small bird of Europe, Asia, and northern Africa that sings while it flies

sky·light /'skaɪˌlaɪt/ *n* [*C*] : a window in the roof of a house or on a ship's deck

sky·line /'skaɪˌlaɪn/ *n* [*C*] : the outline of buildings, mountains, etc., against the background of the sky ▪ *the New York City skyline*

sky·rock·et /'skaɪˌrɑːkət/ *vb* [*I*] : to increase quickly to a very high level or amount ▪ *Sales have skyrocketed.* — **sky-rocketing** *prices*

sky·scrap·er /'skaɪˌskreɪpɚ/ *n* [*C*] : a very tall building in a city

sky·ward /'skaɪwɚd/ *also chiefly Brit* **sky·wards** /'skaɪwɚdz/ *adv* : toward the sky : up into the sky ▪ *look/soar skyward*

slab /'slæb/ *n* [*C*] **1** : a thick, flat piece of a hard material ▪ *concrete slabs* **2** : a thick, flat piece of food ▪ *a slab of bacon*

[1]**slack** /'slæk/ *adj* **1** : not stretched or held in a tight position : LOOSE ▪ *slack rope* ▪ *Her jaw went slack* [=fell open] *in amazement.* **2** : not busy or active ▪ *a*

slack market/season **3 a** : doing something poorly because you are not putting enough care or effort into it ▪ *I've been a little slack about taking my medication.* **b** : done poorly and carelessly ▪ *slack supervision* — **slack·ly** *adv* — **slack·ness** *n* [*U*]

[2]**slack** *n* **1** [*U*] : the part of a rope, chain, etc., that hangs loosely ▪ *Take in/up the slack of the rope.* **2** [*plural*] *chiefly US* : pants or trousers ▪ *(a pair of) cotton slacks* — **give/cut (someone) some slack** *informal* : to treat (someone) in a less harsh or critical way ▪ *Would you give/cut me some slack? I'm doing the best I can.* — **pick/take up the slack** : to provide or do something that is missing or not getting done ▪ *The manager has to take up the slack when employees don't do their jobs correctly.*

[3]**slack** *vb* — **slack off** [*phrasal vb*] : to become less active, forceful, energetic, etc. ▪ *I was exercising regularly last summer, but I've been slacking off recently.* ▪ *Business has been slacking off.*

slack·en /'slækən/ *vb* [*T/I*] **1** : to become slower or less active or to make (something) slower or less active ▪ *Sales show no sign of slackening (off).* ▪ *She slackened her speed.* [=she slowed down] **2** : to become less tight or to make (something) less tight : LOOSEN ▪ *His grip slackened.* ▪ *He slackened his grip.*

slack·er /'slækɚ/ *n* [*C*] *informal* : a person who avoids work and responsibilities

slag /'slæg/ *n* [*U*] : the material that is left when rocks that contain metal are heated to get the metal out ▪ *a slag heap* [=a large pile of slag]

slain *past participle of* SLAY

slake /'sleɪk/ *vb* **slaked; slak·ing** [*T*] *literary* : to provide, do, or have what is required by (something) : SATISFY ▪ *trying to slake his thirst/curiosity*

sla·lom /'slɑːləm/ *n* [*C/U*] : a race especially on skis over a winding course that is marked by flags

slam /'slæm/ *vb* **slammed; slam·ming** **1** [*T/I*] : to close (something) in a forceful and loud way ▪ *He slammed the door.* ▪ *The window slammed shut.* **2** [*T*] : to set or throw (something) in a forceful and loud way ▪ *She slammed down the phone.* **3** [*T/I*] : to hit something with a lot of force ▪ *The car slid on the ice and slammed into a tree.* ▪ *He slammed on the brakes.* [=pressed down hard on the brakes] **4** [*T*] *informal* : to criticize (someone or something) harshly ▪ *He slammed the company for not paying its workers decent wages.* — **slam** *n* [*C*] ▪ *I heard the slam of a car door.*

slam dunk *n* [*C*] **1** *basketball* : [2]DUNK **2** *US, informal* : something that is sure to happen or be successful ▪ *There's no doubt that he's guilty. The case is a slam dunk.* — **slam–dunk** *vb* [*T/I*] *basketball* ▪ *He slam-dunked the ball.*

slam·mer /'slæmɚ/ *n* — **the slammer** *informal* : a prison or jail ▪ *He got 10 years in the slammer.*

slan·der /'slændɚ/ *n* **1** [*U*] : the act of making a false spoken statement that causes people to have a bad opinion of

someone ▪ *She is being sued for slander.*
2 [C] : a false spoken statement that is made to cause people to have a bad opinion of someone ▪ *We've heard countless slanders about her.* — **slander** *vb* [T] ▪ *She slandered her former boss.* — **slan·der·ous** /ˈslændərəs/ *adj* ▪ *slanderous attacks*

slang /ˈslæŋ/ *n* [U] : words that are not considered part of the standard vocabulary of a language and that are used very informally in speech ▪ *American/military slang* ▪ *slang words* — **slangy** /ˈslæŋi/ *adj* ▪ *slangy expressions*

¹**slant** /ˈslænt/ *vb* **1** [T/I] : to not be level or straight up and down ▪ *The floor slants down slightly.* ▪ *His handwriting slants to the left.* ▪ *She slanted her hat to the right.* ▪ *a slanting table* ▪ *a slanted floor* **2** [T] : to present (something) in a way that favors a particular group, opinion, etc. ▪ *They slanted the story to make themselves look good.* ▪ *The media coverage of the strike was slanted against the union.*

²**slant** *n* **1** [*singular*] : a direction, line, or surface that is not level or straight up and down ▪ *The computer keyboard is positioned at a slant.* ▪ *He sliced the carrots on a/the slant.* **2** [C] : a way of thinking about, describing, or discussing something ▪ *The new evidence puts an entirely different slant on the case.* ▪ *His writings have a religious slant.*

¹**slap** /ˈslæp/ *vb* **slapped; slap·ping 1 a** [T] : to hit (someone or something) with the front or back of your open hand ▪ *She slapped him across/in the face.* ▪ *She slapped his face.* **b** [T/I] : to hit something with a sound like the sound made when your hand slaps something ▪ *Gentle waves slapped (against) the side of the raft.* **2** [T] : to put (something) on a surface quickly or forcefully ▪ *He slapped the book down on the desk.* ▪ *She slapped a coat of paint on the wall.* — **slap around** [*phrasal vb*] **slap (someone) around** *also* **slap around (someone)** *informal* : to hit or slap (someone) many times ▪ *He was slapping her around.* [=beating her up] — **slap on** [*phrasal vb*] **slap (something) on** *or* **slap on (something)** *informal* : to add (something) to an amount ▪ *The judge slapped on an additional fine.* — **slap together** [*phrasal vb*] **slap together (something)** *or* **slap (something) together** *informal* : to create (something) in a quick or careless way ▪ *I slapped a sandwich together as I was running out the door.* — **slap with** [*phrasal vb*] **slap (someone) with** US, *informal* : to punish (someone) with (something) ▪ *They were slapped with a fine.*

²**slap** *n* [C] **1** : a hit with the front or back of your open hand ▪ *She gave him a slap.* ▪ *a friendly slap on the back* **2** : a loud sound made when something hits a flat surface ▪ *the slap of the waves against the side of the boat* — **a slap in the face** : a surprising act that offends or insults someone ▪ *Her decision to leave the company to work for our competitor was a slap*

in the face. — **a slap on the wrist** : a mild punishment ▪ *The fine was just a slap on the wrist.*

slap·dash /ˈslæpˌdæʃ/ *adj* : quick and careless ▪ *slapdash repairs*

slap shot *n* [C] *ice hockey* : a shot that is made by swinging your stick with a lot of force

slap·stick /ˈslæpˌstɪk/ *n* [U] : comedy that involves physical action (such as falling down or hitting people)

¹**slash** /ˈslæʃ/ *vb* [T] **1** : to make a long cut in (something) with a knife or other sharp weapon ▪ *Someone slashed his car's tires.* ▪ *He threatened to slash the man's throat.* **2** : to reduce (something) by a large amount ▪ *The company has slashed prices.* — **slash at** [*phrasal vb*] : to attack (someone or something) violently with a knife or other sharp weapon ▪ *He slashed at me with a knife.* — **slash·er** /ˈslæʃɚ/ *n* [C]

²**slash** *n* [C] **1** : a thin and usually long cut made with a knife or other sharp object **2** : a quick movement with a sharp knife or weapon to cut someone or something ▪ *He cut my cheek with a quick slash of the knife.* **3** : the mark / that is used to mean "or" (as in *and/or*), "and or" (as in *bottles/cans*), or "per" (as in *kilometers/hour*) or as a division sign in fractions (as in ¾)

slat /ˈslæt/ *n* [C] : a thin, narrow strip of wood, plastic, or metal ▪ *the slats of a venetian blind* — **slat·ted** /ˈslætəd/ *adj* ▪ *slatted blinds*

¹**slate** /ˈsleɪt/ *n* **1** [U] : a type of hard rock that splits easily into thin layers **2** [C] : a sheet of slate in a wooden frame that was used for writing on with chalk **3** [C] : a piece of slate that is used with others to cover a roof or wall **4** [C] US : a list of people who are trying to win an election ▪ *an impressive slate of candidates* — **clean slate** see ¹CLEAN — **wipe the slate clean** see ¹WIPE

²**slate** *vb* **slat·ed; slat·ing** [T] **1** *chiefly US* : to arrange or plan for something to happen ▪ *The new museum is slated to open next spring.* ▪ *Her latest album is slated for release in July.* **2** *Brit, informal* : to criticize (someone or something) very harshly ▪ *The film/book was slated by most critics.*

slath·er /ˈslæðɚ/ *vb* [T] : to cover (something) with a thick layer of a liquid, cream, etc. ▪ *She slathered her skin with sunscreen.* = *She slathered sunscreen on her skin.*

¹**slaugh·ter** /ˈslɑːtɚ/ *vb* [T] **1** : to kill (an animal) for food ▪ *slaughter cattle* **2** : to kill (many people) in a very violent way ▪ *Hundreds of people were slaughtered by the invaders.* **3** *informal* : to defeat (someone or something) easily or completely ▪ *Our team got slaughtered.*

²**slaughter** *n* [U] **1** : the act of killing animals for their meat ▪ *Thousands of cows are sent to (the) slaughter every day.* **2** : the violent killing of a large number of people ▪ *the slaughter of innocent people*

slaugh·ter·house /ˈslɑːtɚˌhaʊs/ *n* [C] : a building where animals are killed for their meat

¹**slave** /'sleɪv/ n [C] **1** : someone who is legally owned by another person and is forced to work for that person without pay ▪ *Do it yourself! I'm not your slave!* **2** *disapproving* : a person who is strongly influenced and controlled by something — + *to* or *of* ▪ *She's a slave to fashion.* ▪ *a slave of desire*

²**slave** vb **slaved; slav·ing** [I] : to work very hard ▪ *I slaved all morning to get the work done on time.* ▪ *She's been slaving away at her homework.*

slave driver n [C] **1** : someone who is in charge of slaves and makes them work **2** *disapproving* : someone who makes people work very hard

slave labor (US) or Brit **slave labour** n [U] **1** : work that is done by slaves or by people who are treated like slaves ▪ *prisoners being forced to do slave labor* **2** : slaves doing work ▪ *The pyramids were built by slave labor.*

slav·ery /'sleɪvəri/ n [U] **1** : the state of being a slave ▪ *She was sold into slavery.* **2** : the practice of owning slaves ▪ *the abolition of slavery*

Slav·ic /'slɑːvɪk/ n [U] : a group of related languages that includes Russian, Czech, Polish, etc. — **Slavic** adj ▪ *Slavic languages/lands/people*

slav·ish /'sleɪvɪʃ/ adj, disapproving : copying or following someone or something completely ▪ *a politician and his slavish followers* ▪ *slavish obedience/imitation* — **slav·ish·ly** adv

slay /'sleɪ/ vb **slew** /'sluː/ also **slayed; slain** /'sleɪn/, **slay·ing** [T] : to kill (someone or something) ▪ *The knight slew the dragon.* ▪ *The victims were slain in their homes.* — **slay·er** n [C] — **slay·ing** n [C] chiefly US ▪ *Police have arrested a man in connection with three recent slayings.*

sleaze /'sliːz/ n **1** [U] somewhat informal : behavior that is dishonest or immoral ▪ *political sleaze and corruption* **2** [C] US, informal : a dishonest or immoral person ▪ *He's a real sleaze.*

slea·zy /'sliːzi/ adj **slea·zi·er; -est** informal **1** : dishonest or immoral ▪ *a sleazy lawyer/trick* **2** : dirty and in bad condition ▪ *a sleazy neighborhood* **3** : not decent or socially respectable ▪ *sleazy nightclubs* — **slea·zi·ness** /'sliːzinəs/ n [U]

¹**sled** /'slɛd/ n [C] chiefly US : a small vehicle that has a flat bottom or long, narrow strips of metal or wood on the bottom and that is used for moving over snow or ice

²**sled** vb **sled·ded; sled·ding** [I] chiefly US : to ride on a sled especially down a hill ▪ *We went sledding on the hill.* — **sled·der** n [C]

sledge /'slɛdʒ/ n [C] Brit : ¹SLED — **sledge** vb **sledged; sledg·ing** [I]

sledge·ham·mer /'slɛdʒˌhæmɚ/ n [C] : a large, heavy hammer with a long handle

sleek /'sliːk/ adj **1** : straight and smooth in design or shape ▪ *the sleek lines of a sports car* **2** : smooth and shiny ▪ *sleek, dark hair* **3** : stylish and attractive ▪ *a sleek young executive* — **sleek·ly** adv ▪ *a sleekly modern building* — **sleek·ness** n [U]

¹**sleep** /'sliːp/ vb **slept** /'slɛpt/; **sleep·ing** **1** [I] : to rest your mind and body by closing your eyes and becoming unconscious ▪ *I couldn't sleep last night. I was awake all night long.* ▪ *Did you sleep soundly/well?* ▪ (figurative) *New York is the city that never sleeps.* [=a city that is full of activity all night] **2** [T] : to have enough space for (a specified number of people) to sleep in it ▪ *The tent sleeps five adults.* — **let sleeping dogs lie** see ¹DOG — **sleep around** [phrasal vb] informal + disapproving : to have sex with many different people — **sleep a wink** informal : to sleep for even a very brief time — used in negative statements ▪ *I didn't/couldn't sleep a wink last night.* — **sleep in** [phrasal vb] informal : to get up past the time when you usually get up ▪ *On Sundays, we always sleep in.* — **sleep like a baby/log** informal : to sleep very well ▪ *I slept like a log last night.* — **sleep off** [phrasal vb] **sleep (something) off** or **sleep off (something)** informal : to sleep until the effects of alcohol, medication, etc., are no longer felt ▪ *He had too much to drink, and I'm letting him sleep it off.* — **sleep on it** informal : to think more about something overnight and make a decision about it later ▪ *You've heard my offer. Why don't you sleep on it and let me know what you decide.* — **sleep over** [phrasal vb] : to stay overnight at another person's house ▪ *My mother said that you could sleep over.* — **sleep tight** : to sleep deeply and well ▪ *Good night. Sleep tight.* — **sleep together** [phrasal vb] informal : to have sex with each other — **sleep with** [phrasal vb] informal : to have sex with (someone) ▪ *She found out that her husband was sleeping with his secretary.*

²**sleep** n [U, singular] : the natural state of rest during which your eyes are closed and you become unconscious ▪ *How much sleep did you get last night?* ▪ *The noise woke her from a deep/light sleep.* ▪ *Her roommate talks/walks in her sleep.* ▪ *She sang the baby to sleep.* [=she sang to the baby until it fell asleep] — **get to sleep** : to succeed in beginning to sleep : to fall asleep ▪ *It took me almost an hour to get to sleep last night.* — **go to sleep** **1** : to begin sleeping ▪ *Tell the kids it's time to go to sleep.* **2** ✧ If a part of your body (such as a foot or leg) *goes to sleep*, it is not able to feel anything for a brief time, usually because you have kept it in an awkward position for too long. — **in your sleep** ✧ If you can do something *in your sleep*, you can do it very easily because you have done it many times before. ▪ *She could bake those cookies in her sleep.* — **lose sleep over** : to worry about (something) so much that you cannot sleep ▪ *I'm disappointed about their decision, but I'm not losing (any) sleep over it.* — **put to sleep 1** *put (an animal) to sleep* : to give (a sick or injured animal) drugs that will make it die without pain **2** *put (someone) to sleep* a informal : to use a drug to make (someone) unconscious before a medical operation ▪ *The doctor put the patient to*

sleep. **b** : to get (someone) ready to sleep for the night ▪ *Did you put the kids to sleep?* **c** : to make (someone) fall asleep from boredom ▪ *Her lectures used to put him to sleep.*

sleep·er /ˈsliːpɚ/ *n* [C] **1 a** : a person who sleeps in a particular way ▪ *a light sleeper* [=someone who does not sleep well and wakes up easily] ▪ *a heavy sleeper* [=someone who sleeps well and does not wake up easily] **b** : someone who is asleep ▪ *Sleepers were awakened by the sound of a loud crash.* **2 a** : a place or piece of furniture that can be used for sleeping ▪ *the sleeper cab of a truck* ▪ *a sleeper sofa* [=a sofa that folds out to form a bed] ▪ SLEEPING CAR **3** *chiefly US, informal* : someone or something that suddenly becomes successful in a way that was not expected ▪ *The movie was the summer's sleeper (hit).* **4** *Brit* : one of the heavy beams to which the rails of a railway are attached ▪ TIE

sleeping bag *n* [C] : a warm, long bag that is used for sleeping outdoors or in a tent

sleeping car *n* [C] : a railroad car with beds for people to sleep in — called also *sleeper*

sleeping pill *n* [C] : a pill that contains a drug which helps a person sleep

sleep·less /ˈsliːpləs/ *adj* **1** *always before a noun* : without sleep ▪ *a sleepless night* **2** *not before a noun* : not able to sleep ▪ *He lay sleepless in bed.* — **sleep·less·ly** *adv* — **sleep·less·ness** *n* [U]

sleep·over /ˈsliːpˌoʊvɚ/ *n* [C] : a party where one or more people (especially children) stay overnight at one person's house

sleep·walk /ˈsliːpˌwɑːk/ *vb* [I] : to walk around while you are asleep — **sleep·walk·er** /ˈsliːpˌwɑːkɚ/ *n* [C] — **sleep·walk·ing** /ˈsliːpˌwɑːkɪŋ/ *n* [U]

sleepy /ˈsliːpi/ *adj* **sleep·i·er; -est 1** : tired and ready to fall asleep ▪ *She felt sleepy.* **2** : quiet and not active or busy ▪ *a sleepy town* — **sleep·i·ly** /ˈsliːpəli/ *adv* — **sleep·i·ness** /ˈsliːpinəs/ *n* [U]

sleet /ˈsliːt/ *n* [U] : frozen or partly frozen rain — **sleet** *vb* [I] ▪ *It's sleeting outside.* [=sleet is falling]

sleeve /ˈsliːv/ *n* [C] **1** : the part of a shirt, jacket, etc., that covers all or part of your arm ▪ *a shirt with long/short sleeves* **2** : a part that fits over or around something to protect it or to hold its parts together ▪ *a plastic document sleeve* — **have/keep (something) up your sleeve** *informal* : to have/keep a secret method, trick, etc., that you can use when it is needed ▪ *The coach always keeps a few tricks up his sleeve.* — **on your sleeve** *informal* : in a way that can be clearly seen ▪ *He wears his emotions/heart on his sleeve.* [=his emotions are easy to see] — **sleeved** /ˈsliːvd/ *adj* ▪ *a long-sleeved shirt* — **sleeve·less** /ˈsliːvləs/ *adj* ▪ *a sleeveless dress*

sleigh /ˈsleɪ/ *n* [C] : a large, open vehicle that is usually pulled by a horse over snow or ice

sleight of hand /ˈslaɪt-/ *n* [U] **1** : quick or deceptive hand movements that are used especially to perform magic tricks ▪ *He performs sleight of hand with cards.* **2** : the act of tricking or deceiving someone in a clever way ▪ *financial sleight of hand*

slen·der /ˈslɛndɚ/ *adj* **1 a** : thin especially in an attractive or graceful way ▪ *She has a slender figure.* **b** : very narrow : not wide ▪ *a flower with a slender stem* **2** : small or limited in amount or size ▪ *slender resources* — **slen·der·ness** *n* [U]

slept *past tense and past participle of* ¹SLEEP

sleuth /ˈsluːθ/ *n* [C] *old-fashioned* : DETECTIVE ▪ *a clever sleuth* — **sleuth·ing** /ˈsluːθɪŋ/ *n* [U] ▪ *He did some sleuthing to see if he could turn up any clues.*

S level *n* [C] *Brit* : the highest of three tests in a particular subject that students in England, Wales, and Northern Ireland take usually at the age of 18

¹**slew** *past tense of* SLAY

²**slew** /ˈsluː/ *n* [*singular*] *informal* : a large number of people or things ▪ *He has written a slew of books.*

³**slew** *vb* [T/I] : to turn or slide in another direction very quickly ▪ *His car slewed sideways off the road.*

¹**slice** /ˈslaɪs/ *n* [C] **1 a** : a thin piece of food that is cut from something larger ▪ *a slice of bread/ham* **b** : a piece that is cut from a pie, cake, etc. ▪ *a slice of pie* **2 a** : a shot in golf and other games that curves to the side instead of going straight ▪ *He hit a slice into the right rough.* — **a slice of life** : something (such as a story or movie) that shows what ordinary life is like ▪ *The story is/shows/presents a slice of life in a small Midwestern town.* — **a slice of the pie** see PIE

²**slice** *vb* **sliced; slic·ing** [T/I] **1** : to cut something with a sharp object (such as a knife) ▪ *He sliced the board in two.* ▪ *He accidentally sliced open his finger.* ▪ *The knife sliced through the cake easily.* ▪ *He sliced the banana into pieces.* = *He sliced up the banana.* **2** *sports* : to hit or kick (a ball or shot) in a way that causes it to curve : to hit a slice ▪ *(golf) She sliced her drive into the rough.* **3** : to move quickly and easily through something (such as air or water) ▪ *The ship's hull sliced through the waves.* — **any way you slice it or no matter how you slice it** *US, informal* — used to say that the truth of a statement is not changed or affected by the way you describe or think about a situation ▪ *Losing is disappointing no matter how you slice it.* [=losing is always disappointing] — **slic·er** *n* [C]

¹**slick** /ˈslɪk/ *adj* **1** : very smooth and slippery ▪ *The roads are wet and slick.* **2** : clever in usually a dishonest or deceptive way ▪ *a slick salesman/lawyer* **3 a** : skillful and clever ▪ *The new kid had some slick moves on the basketball court.* **b** : very good : of the highest quality ▪ *The video game has slick graphics.* — **slick·ly** *adv* — **slick·ness** *n* [U]

²**slick** *vb* [T] : to make (something) smooth and slippery ▪ *The rain slicked the roads.* — **slick back/down** [*phrasal vb*] **slick back/down (hair) or slick (hair) back/**

down : to pull (hair) back and make it look smooth or shiny by using water or some wet substance (such as hair gel) • *He climbed out of the pool and slicked back his hair.*

slick·er /ˈslɪkə/ *n* [C] *US* : a long, loose raincoat — see also CITY SLICKER

¹**slide** /ˈslaɪd/ *vb* **slid** /ˈslɪd/; **slid·ing** **1** [T/I] : to move smoothly along a surface • *The door slides open easily.* • *She slid the paper under the door.* **2** [I] : to slip and fall • *Her purse slid out of her hands.* **3** [T/I] : to move or pass smoothly and easily into or out of something • *She slid into the booth beside us.* • *He slid the key into his pocket.* • *He slid in a reference to his new book.* **4** [I] : to become gradually worse over time • *Their son's grades have started to slide.* **5** [I] *baseball* : to dive toward a base to avoid being tagged out • *He slid into second base.* — **let (some-thing) slide** *informal* : to do nothing about (something, such as another person's mistake or bad behavior) • *You were late this morning. I'll let it slide this time, but don't let it happen again.*

²**slide** *n* [C] **1** : a movement to a lower or worse state or condition • *a slide in the stock market* • *her slide into depression* **2** : an act of moving along or over a surface by sliding • *The car hit a patch of ice and went into a slide.* **3** : a structure with a slippery surface that children slide down **4** *baseball* : the act of diving toward a base to avoid being tagged out • *a slide into home plate* **5** : a small piece of film with an image on it that can be shown on a wall or screen by using a projector • *They showed us slides from their vacation in Europe.* **6** : a piece of glass that holds an object to be looked at under a microscope **7** : a part of a musical instrument or a machine that is moved backward or forward • *the slide of a trombone*

slid·er /ˈslaɪdə/ *n* [C] **1** *baseball* : a fast pitch that curves slightly in the air **2** : something that slides

slide rule *n* [C] : an old-fashioned instrument that is like a ruler with a middle piece that slides back and forth and that is used to do calculations

sliding scale *n* [C] : a system in which the amount that people are required to pay changes according to different situations or conditions • *Patients at the clinic pay on a sliding scale based on their income.*

¹**slight** /ˈslaɪt/ *adj* **1** : very small in degree or amount • *a slight adjustment/fever* **2** : thin and not very strong • *a slight woman* — **not in the slightest** : not at all : not in the least • *"Does it bother you?" "Not in the slightest."* — **slight·ly** /ˈslaɪtli/ *adv*

²**slight** *vb* [T] : to treat (someone) with disrespect • *I'm sure he didn't mean to slight you.* — **slight** *n* [C] • *a deliberate slight* — **slight·ing** /ˈslaɪtɪŋ/ *adj* • *a slighting remark*

¹**slim** /ˈslɪm/ *adj* **slim·mer**; **-est** **1** : thin in an attractive way • *She looked slim and fit.* **2** : small in amount, size, or degree • *a slim chance of winning* — **slim·ly** *adv*

²**slim** *vb* **slimmed**; **slim·ming** **1** [T] : to make (something) thinner • *She started exercising to slim her thighs.* **2** [I] *Brit* : ²DIET • *I'll skip dessert; I'm slimming.* — **slim down** [*phrasal vb*] **1** : to become thinner • *He looks like he's slimmed down.* **2** *slim down (something)* or *slim (some-thing) down* : to make (something) smaller • *slim down the company's advertising budget* — **slim·mer** /ˈslɪmə/ *n* [C] *Brit*

slime /ˈslaɪm/ *n* [U] : a thick, slippery liquid • *Green slime covers the surface of the pond.*

slimy /ˈslaɪmi/ *adj* **slim·i·er**; **-est** **1** : covered with slime or resembling slime • *a slimy rock* • *a slimy liquid* **2** *informal* : very dishonest, bad, or offensive • *a slimy businessman* • *slimy behavior*

¹**sling** /ˈslɪŋ/ *vb* **slung** /ˈslʌŋ/; **sling·ing** [T] **1** : to throw (something) with a forceful sweeping motion • *She slung the bag over her shoulder.* • *(figurative) They slung insults at each other.* **2** : to hang (something) loosely • *His guitar was slung low around his neck.*

²**sling** *n* [C] **1** : a piece of cloth that hangs around your neck and is used to support an injured arm or hand • *His arm was in a sling.* **2** : a strap, net, rope, etc., that is used to carry or lift things • *a leather rifle sling* • *We attached the sling to the crane.* **3** : a strap usually with a pocket in the middle that is used to throw something (such as a stone) — **slings and arrows** : the problems and criticisms that are experienced in someone's life • *Politicians must be willing to endure/suffer the slings and arrows of public life.*

sling·shot /ˈslɪŋˌʃɑːt/ *n* [C] *US* : a Y-shaped stick with a rubber band attached to it that is used for shooting small stones

slink /ˈslɪŋk/ *vb* **slunk** /ˈslʌŋk/ *also US* **slinked**; **slink·ing** [I] : to move in a way that does not attract attention especially because you are embarrassed, afraid, or doing something wrong • *He slinked away in shame.*

¹**slip** /ˈslɪp/ *vb* **slipped**; **slip·ping** **1** [I] : to slide out of the proper position • *The ring slipped off my finger.* • *My foot slipped and I fell.* = *I slipped and fell.* **2** [T/I] : to move easily across or over something • *The drawer should just slip into place.* • *Help me slip the cover over the piano.* **3** [T/I] : to move into or out of a place without being noticed • *We'll slip out the back door.* **4** [T] : to put on or take off a piece of clothing quickly or easily • *He slipped off his shoes.* **5** [T] **a** : to put or place (something) somewhere in a quiet or secret way • *He slipped the key into his pocket.* • *He managed to slip in* [=include] *a few jokes during his speech.* **b** : to give (something) to someone in a quiet or secret way • *He slipped the envelope to his secretary.* **6** [I] : to happen or pass without being noticed • *Time keeps slipping away.* • *Some errors do slip past us.* **7** [I] **a** : to go from one state or condition to another • *The patient slipped into a coma.* **b** : to move into a lower or worse state or condition • *I can't believe he beat me. I*

must be slipping. ▪ *Test scores slipped this year.* 8 [T] : to escape (someone) : to get away from (someone) ▪ *The thief slipped his pursuers.* — **let (something) slip or let slip (something)** : to say (something that you did not want to say) by mistake ▪ *He let slip that he's looking for a better job.* — **slip out** [phrasal vb] : to be said by mistake ▪ *I didn't intend to tell them. It just slipped out.* — **slip up** [phrasal vb] informal : to make a mistake ▪ *Make sure you don't slip up again.* — **slip your mind/memory** informal : to be forgotten ▪ *Her birthday slipped my mind.* [=I forgot about her birthday]

²**slip** n [C] **1 a** : a small piece of paper ▪ *He wrote the number on a slip of paper.* **b** : a piece of paper that has a specified use or purpose ▪ *a deposit/betting slip* **2** : a mistake ▪ *a careless slip* **3** : a movement to a lower or worse state or condition ▪ *a slip in the ratings* **4** : the act of losing your balance and falling ▪ *a slip on the ice* **5** : a piece of woman's underwear that is like a thin dress or skirt and that is worn under a dress or skirt **6** : a place for a ship or boat in the water between two piers — **a slip of the tongue** : something that is said by mistake — **give (someone) the slip** informal : to escape (someone) : to get away from (someone) ▪ *She ran from the police and gave them the slip.*

slip·cov·er /ˈslɪpˌkʌvɚ/ n [C] US : a loose, removable cloth cover for a piece of furniture

slip·knot /ˈslɪpˌnɑːt/ n [C] : a knot that can slide along the rope around which it is made and that is tightened by pulling on one end

slip·page /ˈslɪpɪʤ/ n [C/U] formal **1** : a movement downward : an act of moving into a lower or worse condition or state ▪ *a/some slippage in sales* **2** : the act of sliding or slipping ▪ *The boot's sole prevents slippage.*

slipped disc also chiefly US **slipped disk** n [C] medical : an injury to the spine in which one of the connecting parts between the bones slips out and causes back pain

slip·per /ˈslɪpɚ/ n [C] : a light, soft shoe that is easily put on and taken off and that is worn indoors

slip·pery /ˈslɪpɚi/ adj **slip·per·i·er; -est** **1** : difficult to stand on, move on, or hold because of being smooth, wet, icy, etc. ▪ *a slippery floor* **2** : not easy to understand or identify in an exact way ▪ *slippery concepts/notions* **3** informal : not able to be trusted : TRICKY ▪ *slippery politicians*

slip road n [C] Brit : a short road that is used to get on or off a major road or highway

slip·shod /ˈslɪpˈʃɑːd/ adj : very careless or poorly done or made ▪ *slipshod construction*

slip-up /ˈslɪpˌʌp/ n [C] : a careless mistake ▪ *We were late because of a slipup in the schedule.*

slit /ˈslɪt/ vb **slit; slit·ting** [T] : to make a long, narrow cut or opening in (something) with a sharp object ▪ *I slit the bag open at the top.* ▪ *She tried to **slit her wrists**.* [=to kill herself by cutting her wrists] — **slit** n [C] ▪ *The skirt has a slit* [=a long, narrow cut or opening] *on one side.*

slith·er /ˈslɪðɚ/ vb [I] : to move by sliding your entire body back and forth ▪ *The snake slithered through the garden.* — **slith·ery** /ˈslɪðɚi/ adj : a slithery snake

sliv·er /ˈslɪvɚ/ n [C] : a small, thin piece that has been cut, torn, or broken from something larger ▪ *a sliver of wood/cake* ▪ (figurative) *a sliver of hope*

slob /ˈslɑːb/ n [C] informal + disapproving : a person who is lazy and dirty or messy

slob·ber /ˈslɑːbɚ/ vb [I] : to let saliva or liquid flow from your mouth ▪ *The puppy slobbered all over me.*

slog /ˈslɑːg/ vb **slogged; slog·ging** [T/I] informal **1** : to work at something in a steady, determined way ▪ *She slogged (her way) through her work.* **2** : to walk slowly usually with heavy steps ▪ *He slogged (his way) through the deep snow.* — **slog** n [singular] ▪ *a long, hard slog through the snow*

slo·gan /ˈsloʊgən/ n [C] : a word or phrase that is easy to remember and is used by a group or business to attract attention ▪ *advertising/campaign slogans*

sloop /ˈsluːp/ n [C] : a small sailboat with one mast

¹**slop** /ˈslɑːp/ vb **slopped; slop·ping** **1** [T/I] : to spill or splash ▪ *Water slopped (over the edge) as he handed her the glass.* ▪ *Huge waves slopped water into the boat.* **2** [T] US : to feed slop to (an animal) ▪ *slop the pigs*

²**slop** n **1** [U, plural] : food that is fed to pigs and other animals **2** [U] informal : soft, wet food that is very unappealing ▪ *I won't eat that slop!*

¹**slope** /ˈsloʊp/ n [C] **1 a** : ground that slants downward or upward ▪ *a steep/gentle slope* **b** : an area of land on a mountain that is used for skiing ▪ *a ski slope* **2** : an upward or downward slant ▪ *the slope of a ramp*

²**slope** vb **sloped; slop·ing** [I] **1** : to have a downward or upward slant ▪ *The ground sloped downward.* **2** : to lean or slant to the left or right ▪ *His handwriting slopes to the left.*

slop·py /ˈslɑːpi/ adj **slop·pi·er; -est** **1** : not careful or neat ▪ *sloppy work/handwriting* **2** : containing or involving a lot of liquid or too much liquid ▪ *sloppy food/kisses* — **slop·pi·ly** /ˈslɑːpəli/ adv — **slop·pi·ness** n [U]

slosh /ˈslɑːʃ/ vb **1** [I] : to walk through water, mud, etc., in a forceful and noisy way ▪ *The children sloshed through the puddle.* **2** [T/I] of a liquid : to move in a noisy or messy way ▪ *Water sloshed in the bottom of the boat as it rocked.*

sloshed /ˈslɑːʃt/ adj, slang : very drunk ▪ *They were/got sloshed last night.*

¹**slot** /ˈslɑːt/ n **1** : a long, thin opening ▪ *a coin slot* **2 a** : a period of time that is available or used for a particular occurrence, event, etc. ▪ *The doctor has an open slot at 2 p.m.* ▪ *a different **time slot*** **b** : a place or position in an organization, group, etc. ▪ *We have an open slot in the*

marketing department. **3** *US* : SLOT MA-CHINE ▪ *He likes to play the slots.*

²**slot** /'slɑːt/ *vb* **slot·ted; slot·ting 1** [*T*] : to put (something) into a space which is made for it ▪ *He slotted the wood into the groove.* **2** [*I*] : to fit easily into something ▪ *Her ideas slot neatly into the theory.*

sloth /'slɑːθ/ *n* **1** [*U*] *formal* : the quality or state of being lazy **2** [*C*] : a type of animal that lives in trees in South and Central America and that moves very slowly

sloth·ful /'slɑːθfəl/ *adj, formal* : LAZY ▪ *slothful people/behavior*

slot machine *n* [*C*] **1** : a machine used for gambling that starts when you put coins into it and pull a handle or press a button **2** *Brit* : VENDING MACHINE

slotted *adj* : having a slot or slots ▪ *a slotted spoon*

¹**slouch** /'slaʊtʃ/ *vb* [*I*] : to walk, sit, or stand lazily with your head and shoulders bent forward ▪ *Sit up straight. Please don't slouch.*

²**slouch** *n* **1** [*singular*] : a way of walking, sitting, or standing with the head and shoulders bent forward ▪ *She walks with a slouch.* **2** [*C*] *informal* : a lazy or worthless person ▪ *She's no slouch when it comes to cooking.* [=she's a very good cook]

slough /'slu:, *Brit* 'slaʊ/ *n* [*singular*] : a sad or hopeless condition ▪ *a slough of depression/frustration*

slov·en·ly /'slʌvənli/ *adj* **1** : messy or untidy ▪ *slovenly clothes/habits* **2** : done in a careless way ▪ *slovenly thinking*

¹**slow** /'sloʊ/ *adj* **1 a** : not moving quickly : not able to move quickly ▪ *a slow runner/speed* **b** : not happening quickly : taking more time than is expected or wanted ▪ *a slow increase/process* **c** : not operating quickly ▪ *a slow computer* **d** : not doing something quickly ▪ *They were slow to respond.* : not able to do something quickly ▪ *a slow reader/learner* **e** : not allowing someone or something to move quickly ▪ *a slow racetrack/route* **2** : not easily able to learn and understand things ▪ *He was quiet, and some people thought he was a little slow.* **3** : not very busy or interesting ▪ *Business is slow during the summer.* **4** of a clock or watch : showing a time that is earlier than the correct time ▪ *The clock is (five minutes) slow.* — **a slow start** ✧ Someone or something that has *a slow start* is not successful at first but does well eventually. ▪ *The team got off to a slow start but is playing well now.* — **slow·ly** /'sloʊli/ *adv* : moving/drive slowly ▪ *Things are slowly getting better.* ▪ *We're getting the work done, slowly but surely.* — **slow·ness** *n* [*U*]

²**slow** *adv* : in a slow way or at a low speed ▪ *go/drive slow*

³**slow** *vb* **1 a** [*I*] : to begin to move at a lower speed ▪ *The car slowed (down/up) and gradually came to a stop.* ▪ *You've been working too hard. You need to slow down and take it easy for a while.* **b** [*T*] : to make (something) move at a lower speed ▪ *The extra weight slowed (down/up) the truck.* **2 a** [*I*] : to become slower

▪ *a slowing economy* ▪ *Business slowed (down/up) after the holidays.* ▪ **Slow down!** *You're talking so fast I can hardly understand you.* **b** [*T*] : to make (something) slower ▪ *They tried to slow (down/up) the process.*

slow-down /'sloʊˌdaʊn/ *n* [*C*] : a decrease in the speed at which something is moving or happening ▪ *an economic slowdown*

slow motion *n* [*U*] : a way of showing action that has been filmed or photographed at a speed that is slower than the actual speed ▪ *They showed the goal in slow motion.* — **slow-mo·tion** /'sloʊˌmoʊʃən/ *adj* ▪ *a slow-motion replay*

slow-poke /'sloʊˌpoʊk/ *n* [*C*] *US, informal* : a person who moves, acts, or works very slowly

slow-wit·ted /'sloʊˈwɪtəd/ *adj* : slow to learn or understand things ▪ *a slow-witted person*

sludge /'slʌdʒ/ *n* [*U*] **1** : thick, soft, wet mud **2** : a soft, thick material that is produced in various industrial processes (such as in the treatment of sewage)

¹**slug** /'slʌg/ *n* [*C*] **1** : a small, soft creature that is like a snail without a shell **2** *US* : a small piece of metal that is fired from a gun : BULLET ▪ *a .45 slug* **3** *US, informal* : a disc shaped like a coin that is used illegally instead of a coin in a machine **4** *US* : a hard punch with the fist ▪ *a slug to the jaw* **5** *informal* : a small amount of liquor taken in one swallow ▪ *a slug of whiskey*

²**slug** *vb* **slugged; slug·ging** [*I*] *informal* : to hit (someone or something) hard with your fist, a bat, etc. ▪ *She slugged him.* ▪ (*baseball*) *He slugged two home runs.* — **slug it out** *informal* : to fight or compete over something until one side wins ▪ *The companies are slugging it out in court.*

slug·ger /'slʌgɚ/ *n* [*C*] **1** : a boxer who punches hard **2** *baseball* : a batter who hits many home runs

slug·gish /'slʌgɪʃ/ *adj* : moving slowly or lazily ▪ *a sluggish lizard/stream*

¹**sluice** /'slu:s/ *n* [*C*] **1** : an artificial passage for water to flow through with a gate for controlling the flow **2** : a device (such as a floodgate) used for controlling the flow of water

²**sluice** *vb* **sluiced; sluic·ing** [*T*] : to wash or spray (something or someone) with a stream of water ▪ *He sluiced (down) the floor.*

¹**slum** /'slʌm/ *n* [*C*] : an area of a city where poor people live and the buildings are in bad condition

²**slum** *vb* **slummed; slum·ming** [*I*] *informal* : to spend time in places or conditions that are much worse than your usual places or conditions ▪ *He's been slumming (it) in cheap hotels.*

slum·ber /'slʌmbɚ/ *vb* [*I*] *literary* : SLEEP ▪ *The children quietly slumbered.* — **slumber** *n* [*C/U*] ▪ *She fell into (a) deep slumber.* [=*sleep*]

slumber party *n* [*C*] *US* : a party where one or more people (usually girls) stay overnight at one person's house

slum·lord /'slʌmˌloɚd/ *n* [*C*] *chiefly US,*

disapproving : a person who owns a building with apartments that are in bad condition and rents them to poor people

¹**slump** /ˈslʌmp/ *vb* [I] **1 a** : to sit or fall down suddenly and heavily ▪ *He slumped down into the chair.* **b** : to move down or forward suddenly ▪ *His shoulders slumped forward in disappointment.* **2** : to decrease suddenly and by a large amount ▪ *Prices have slumped.* — **slumped** /ˈslʌmpt/ *adj* ▪ *He was/sat slumped in front of the TV all day.*

²**slump** *n* [C] **1** : a sudden decrease in prices, value, amount, etc. ▪ *a market slump* **2** : a period of time when someone or something is doing poorly ▪ *The team has been in a slump ever since they traded their best player.*

slung *past tense and past participle of* ¹SLING

slunk *past tense and past participle of* SLINK

¹**slur** /ˈslɚ/ *vb* **slurred; slur·ring** [T] **1** : to say (something) in an unclear way especially because you are drunk or tired ▪ *She was slurring her words/speech.* **2** : to say critical and unfair things about (someone or someone's character) ▪ *They tried to slur him by lying about his war record.*

²**slur** *n* [C] : an insulting remark about someone or someone's character ▪ *a racial/ethnic slur*

slurp /ˈslɚp/ *vb* [T] *informal* : to eat or drink (something) noisily or with a sucking sound ▪ *slurping soup/tea* — **slurp** *n* [C]

slush /ˈslʌʃ/ *n* [U] : partly melted snow ▪ *a sidewalk covered with slush* — **slushy** /ˈslʌʃi/ *adj* **slush·i·er; -est** ▪ *slushy snow*

slush fund *n* [C] : an amount of money that is kept secretly for illegal or dishonest purposes

slut /ˈslʌt/ *n* [C] *informal + offensive* : a woman who has many sexual partners — **slut·ty** /ˈslʌti/ *adj* **slut·ti·er; -est**

sly /ˈslaɪ/ *adj* **sli·er** *or* **sly·er; sli·est** *or* **sly·est** **1** : clever in a dishonest way ▪ *a sly criminal/scheme* **2** : showing that you know a secret ▪ *a sly smile* — **on the sly** *informal* : in a secret way ▪ *They've been meeting each other on the sly.* — **sly·ly** *adv* — **sly·ness** *n* [U]

sm. *abbr* small

S–M *or* **S/M** /ˌɛsəndˈɛm/ *abbr* sadomasochism

¹**smack** /ˈsmæk/ *vb* [T] **1** : to slap or hit (someone or something) hard ▪ *I was so angry I felt like smacking someone.* **2** *US, informal* : to kiss (someone) loudly ▪ *She smacked him on the cheek.* — **smack of** [*phrasal vb*] : to seem to contain or involve (something unpleasant) ▪ *That suggestion smacks of hypocrisy.* — **smack your lips** : to close and open your lips noisily especially before or after eating or drinking

²**smack** *n* **1** [C] : a hard slap or hit ▪ *I felt like giving him a smack.* **2** [C] *informal* : a loud kiss ▪ *She gave him a smack on the cheek.* **3** [U] *slang* : HEROIN

³**smack** *adv, informal* : exactly or directly ▪ *The ball hit me smack in the face.*

smack–dab /ˈsmækˈdæb/ *adv, US, informal* : exactly or directly ▪ *a tree smack-dab in the center of the lawn*

¹**small** /ˈsmɑːl/ *adj* **1** : little in size ▪ *a small house/room* **2** : few in number or little in amount ▪ *a small crowd/party/number* ▪ *a small chance of success* **3** : not very important ▪ *a small matter/mistake* **4** : very young ▪ *I loved the playground when I was small.* ▪ *a small boy* **5** : involving or including few people, things, etc. ▪ *a small company* **6** : LOWERCASE **7** : very soft and quiet ▪ *a small voice* **8** : foolish or ashamed ▪ *He felt very small to be caught cheating.* — **in no small measure/part** : to a great degree : largely or mostly ▪ *A child's happiness is due in no small part to its parents.* — **small·ish** /ˈsmɑːlɪʃ/ *adj* — **small·ness** /ˈsmɑːlnəs/ *n* [U]

²**small** *n* — **the small of the/your back** : the lower part of your back ▪ *I felt a pain in the small of my back.*

small change *n* [U] : coins that are not worth a lot of money ▪ *a pocket full of small change*

small fry *n, informal* **1** *US* **a** [C] : a child ▪ *when I was just a small fry* **b** [U] : CHILDREN ▪ *fun activities for the small fry* **2** [U] : people or things that are not important ▪ *Big businesses are not concerned with the small fry.*

small intestine *n* [C] : the long, narrow upper part of the intestine in which food is digested after it leaves the stomach

small–mind·ed /ˈsmɑːlˈmaɪndəd/ *adj, disapproving* **1** : not interested in new or different ideas ▪ *small-minded people* **2** : typical of a small-minded person ▪ *a small-minded attitude*

small potatoes *n* [U] *US, informal* : someone or something that is not important or impressive ▪ *These changes are small potatoes.*

small·pox /ˈsmɑːlˌpɑːks/ *n* [U] : a serious disease that causes fever and a rash and often death

small print *n* [U] *chiefly Brit* : FINE PRINT

small–scale /ˈsmɑːlˈskeɪl/ *adj* **1** : involving few people or things ▪ *a small-scale production* **2** : covering or involving a small area ▪ *a small-scale network/map*

small talk *n* [U] : informal, friendly conversation about unimportant subjects ▪ *They made small talk while waiting for the meeting to start.*

small–time /ˈsmɑːlˈtaɪm/ *adj* : not very important or successful ▪ *a small-time thief*

smarmy /ˈsmɑɚmi/ *adj* **smarm·i·er; -est** *informal + disapproving* : behaving in a way that seems polite, kind, or pleasing but is not genuine or believable ▪ *a smarmy politician*

¹**smart** /ˈsmɑɚt/ *adj* **1** *chiefly US* **a** : very good at learning or thinking about things : INTELLIGENT ▪ *He's a smart guy.* **b** : showing intelligence or good judgment : WISE ▪ *a smart investment* **2** *informal + disapproving* : RUDE, IMPOLITE ▪ *He gave her a smart answer.* ▪ *Don't get smart with me.* **3** : stylish and fashionable — *somewhat old-fashioned in U.S.*

English • *a smart dresser* **4** : very neat and clean — somewhat old-fashioned in U.S. English • *He looks smart in his new suit.* **5** : controlled by computers and able to do things that seem intelligent • *smart bombs* — **smart·ly** *adv* — **smart·ness** *n* [U]

²smart *vb* [I] **1** : to cause or feel a sudden sharp pain • *"Ouch! That smarts!" • Her eyes were smarting from the smoke.* **2** : to be upset about something • *He's still smarting at/from/over losing the match.*

smart·al·eck /ˈsmɑɚtˌælɪk/ *n* [C] *informal + disapproving* : a person who says things that are clever or funny but that are also disrespectful or rude — **smart-aleck** *or* **smart-al·ecky** /ˈsmɑɚtˌælɪki/ *adj* • *a smart-alecky comment*

smart card *n* [C] : a plastic card (such as a credit card) that has a small computer chip for storing information

smart·en /ˈsmɑɚtn̩/ *vb* — **smarten up** [*phrasal vb*] **1** *US* : to become smarter • *He told me to smarten up and pay attention to the teacher.* **2** *smarten (someone or something) up or smarten up (someone or something)* : to make (someone or something) smarter • *Someone needs to smarten him up before he gets in trouble.* • *They smartened up the room.* [=made the room neat and attractive]

smarts /ˈsmɑɚts/ *n* [plural] *US, informal* : INTELLIGENCE • *He's got the smarts to do the job.*

smarty *or* **smart·ie** /ˈsmɑɚti/ *n, pl* **smart·ies** [C] *US, informal* : SMART-ALECK

¹smash /ˈsmæʃ/ *vb* **1** [T/I] : to break (something) into many pieces • *He smashed the vase with a hammer. • The vase fell and smashed to pieces.* • *I smashed in the window.* **2** [T/I] : to hit (something) very hard • *The car smashed into the rail. • She smashed the ball deep into the opposite corner of the court.* • *They smashed down the door.* [=hit and knocked down the door] **3** [T] : to destroy (something) completely • *He smashed the world record.* **4** [T] : to crash (a vehicle) • *He smashed (up) his car.*

²smash *n* [C] **1** : someone or something that is very successful or popular • *The movie is a smash (hit).* **2** : the sound made when something hits a surface very violently • *a loud smash* **3** : a hard downward hit in tennis or other games **4** *Brit* : ²CRASH **2** • *a car smash*

smashed /ˈsmæʃt/ *adj, not before a noun, slang* : very drunk

smash·ing /ˈsmæʃɪŋ/ *adj, old-fashioned* : very good or impressive • *(chiefly Brit) You look smashing in that dress.*

smat·ter·ing /ˈsmætərɪŋ/ *n* [singular] : a small amount of something • *She knows a smattering of German.*

¹smear /ˈsmiɚ/ *n* [C] **1** : a dirty mark, spot, etc., made by touching or rubbing something **2** *medical* : a very small sample of skin, blood, etc., that someone examines with a microscope • *a blood smear* **3** : an untrue story about a per-

son that is meant to hurt that person's reputation • *a deliberate smear* • *a smear campaign*

²smear *vb* **1** [T] : to make (something) dirty by rubbing it with something else • *The children smeared the window with fingerprints.* **2** [T/I] : to spread (something) over a surface • *She smeared jam on her toast.* • *Water smeared the ink so I could barely read the letter.* • *Her mascara smeared when she cried.* **3** [T] : to make untrue statements about someone in order to hurt that person's reputation • *political opponents smearing each other*

smear test *n* [C] *Brit* : PAP SMEAR

¹smell /ˈsmɛl/ *n* **1** [C] : the quality of a thing that you can sense with your nose • *the smell of onions/perfume* **2** [U] : the ability to notice or recognize smells • *Dogs have a keen sense of smell.*

²smell *vb* **smelled** *or Brit* **smelt** /ˈsmɛlt/; **smell·ing** **1 a** [T/I] : to use your nose to sense smells • *She smelled the flowers.* **b** [T] : to notice something because of its smell • *I smell gas.* **2 a** [linking vb] : to have a particular smell • *This car smells like mold.* • *That soup smells good.* • *(figurative) Something doesn't smell* [=seem] *right about this deal.* — sometimes + *of* • *He smelled of alcohol.* **b** [I] : to have a bad smell • *These sneakers smell.* **3** [T] : to sense or detect (something) : to think that (something) is going to happen • *Our team began to smell victory.* • *I smell trouble.* — **smell a rat** *see* ¹RAT

smelling salts *n* [plural] : a chemical that has a strong smell and that is used to wake people up after they faint

smelly /ˈsmɛli/ *adj* **smell·i·er; -est** : having a bad smell • *smelly cheese/feet*

¹smelt /ˈsmɛlt/ *n, pl* **smelts** *or* **smelt** [C] : a type of small fish that can be eaten

²smelt *vb* [T] : to melt rock that contains metal in order to get the metal out • *smelting iron ore* — **smelt·er** /ˈsmɛltɚ/ [C]

³smelt *Brit past tense and past participle of* ²SMELL

smid·gen *also* **smid·geon** *also chiefly Brit* **smid·gin** /ˈsmɪdʒən/ *or US* **smidge** /ˈsmɪdʒ/ *n* [singular] *informal* : a small amount • *a smidgen of ice cream*

¹smile /ˈsmajəl/ *n* [C] : an expression on your face that makes the corners of your mouth turn up and that shows happiness, amusement, affection, etc. • *He greeted me with a big smile.* • *She gave me a smile.* • *a smile of satisfaction* — *all smiles* : happy and smiling • *She was all smiles as she opened the present.*

²smile *vb* **smiled; smil·ing** **1** [I] : to make a smile • *The kids smiled for the camera.* • *She smiled at me.* **2** [T] : to show or express (something) by a smile • *Both parents smiled their approval.* — *smile on/upon* [phrasal vb] : to make (someone or something) have good luck or success • *Fortune smiled on us.* [=we were lucky]

smil·ey /ˈsmaɪli/ *adj* : happy and cheerful : smiling a lot • *a smiley kid*

smirk /ˈsmɚk/ *vb* [I] : to smile in an unpleasant way because you are pleased with yourself, glad about someone else's trouble, etc. ▪ *She smirked when they announced the winner.* — **smirk** *n* [C]

smite /ˈsmaɪt/ *vb* **smote** /ˈsmoʊt/; **smitten** /ˈsmɪtn̩/ *or* **smote**; **smit·ing** [T] *literary + old-fashioned* **1** : to hurt, kill, or punish (someone or something) ▪ *smite the enemy* **2** : to hit (someone or something) very hard ▪ *He smote the ball mightily.*

smith /ˈsmɪθ/ *n* [C] : a person who makes tools, horseshoes, etc., with iron : BLACKSMITH

smith·er·eens /ˌsmɪðəˈriːnz/ *n* [*plural*] *informal* : small broken pieces : tiny bits ▪ *The car was* **blown to smithereens**. [=was completely destroyed by an explosion]

smit·ten /ˈsmɪtn̩/ *adj* **1** : in love with someone or something ▪ *He was* **smitten** *with her from the moment he saw her.* ▪ *I was* **smitten** *by his good looks.* **2** : suddenly affected by something ▪ *He was* **smitten** *by disaster.* ▪ *She was* **smitten** *with terror.*

smock /ˈsmɑːk/ *n* [C] **1** : a light, loose, long shirt usually worn over your regular clothing to protect it from getting dirty ▪ *an artist's smock* **2** : a long shirt usually worn by women

smog /ˈsmɑːg/ *n* [U] : a cloud of dirty air from cars, factories, etc., that is usually found in cities — **smog·gy** /ˈsmɑːgi/ *adj* **smog·gi·er**; **-est** ▪ *smoggy cities*

¹**smoke** /ˈsmoʊk/ *n* **1** [U] : the cloud of black, gray, or white gases and dust that is produced by burning something ▪ *cigarette smoke* **2 a** [C] *informal* : a cigarette, cigar, etc. ▪ *Can I bum a few smokes off you?* **b** [*singular*] : the act of smoking something ▪ *He went outside for a smoke.* [=to smoke a cigarette, cigar, etc.] — **go up in smoke 1** : to burn up completely ▪ *Her house went up in smoke.* **2** *informal* : to end or disappear completely ▪ *Our dreams went up in smoke.* — **where there's smoke, there's fire** (*chiefly US*) *or* **there's no smoke without fire** — used to say that if people are saying that someone has done something wrong there is usually a good reason for what they are saying

²**smoke** *vb* **smoked**; **smok·ing 1** [T/I] : to suck the smoke from a cigarette, cigar, pipe, etc., into your mouth and lungs and then exhale it ▪ *smoking a cigarette* ▪ *Do you mind if I smoke in here?* **2** [T] : to produce smoke ▪ *That old car smokes when you start it up.* **3** [T] : to use smoke to flavor and preserve (meat, cheese, or fish) ▪ *We smoke our hams over hickory.* ▪ *smoked salmon* — **smoke out** [*phrasal vb*] **smoke (someone or something) out** *or* **smoke out (someone or something)** : to force (someone or something) to leave a place by filling the place with smoke ▪ (*figurative*) *trying to smoke out* [=*find out*] *the truth* — **smok·er** /ˈsmoʊkə/ *n* [C]

smoke alarm *n* [C] : a device that makes a loud and harsh noise when smoke fills a room — called also *smoke detector*

smoke·house /ˈsmoʊkˌhaʊs/ *n* [C] : a building where meat or fish is given flavor and kept from spoiling by the use of smoke

smoke·less /ˈsmoʊkləs/ *adj* : not producing or containing smoke ▪ *smokeless powder*

smoke screen *n* [C] : something that you do or say to hide something or to take attention away from something ▪ *The truth was hidden behind a smoke screen of lies.*

smoke·stack /ˈsmoʊkˌstæk/ *n* [C] : a tall chimney on a factory, ship, etc., for carrying smoke away

smoking gun *n* [*singular*] : a piece of evidence that clearly proves something ▪ *This document is the smoking gun that proves that he was lying.*

smoky *also* **smok·ey** /ˈsmoʊki/ *adj* **smok·i·er**; **-est 1** : filled with smoke ▪ *a smoky bar* **2** : having a flavor, taste, or appearance of smoke ▪ *smoky bacon* ▪ *a smoky blue color* **3** : very attractive or sexy ▪ *a smoky voice* — **smok·i·ness** /ˈsmoʊkinəs/ *n* [U]

smol·der (*US*) *or Brit* **smoul·der** /ˈsmoʊldə/ *vb* [I] **1** : to burn slowly without flames but usually with smoke ▪ *a smoldering fire* **2** *literary* **a** : to feel a strong emotion but keep it hidden ▪ *He smoldered with lust.* **b** : to be felt strongly by someone without being directly shown or expressed ▪ *Anger smoldered in my heart.*

smooch /ˈsmuːtʃ/ *vb* [T/I] *informal* : to kiss ▪ *They smooched while sitting on the porch swing.* — **smooch** *n* [C]

¹**smooth** /ˈsmuːð/ *adj* **1 a** : having a flat, even surface : not rough ▪ *smooth skin* ▪ *The surface is* **(as) smooth as silk**. [=very smooth] **b** : not having any lumps ▪ *smooth gravy* **2** : happening or done without any problems ▪ *a smooth journey/process* **3** : even and regular without sudden movements ▪ *a smooth golf swing* ▪ *Our flight was very smooth.* **4** *informal* : relaxed, confident, and pleasant in a way that may be intended to deceive people ▪ *I don't trust him—he's too smooth.* ▪ *He's a* **smooth talker**. [=he says flattering things] **5** : not sharp, bitter, or unpleasant ▪ *a smooth wine* — **smooth sailing** see SAILING — **smooth·ly** *adv* — **smooth·ness** *n* [U]

²**smooth** *vb* [T] **1** : to make (something) smooth ▪ *He smoothed his tie (out).* ▪ *She smoothed back/down her hair.* **2** : to remove problems or difficulties from a situation ▪ *They smoothed the way for a quick end to the dispute.* [=they made it easier to achieve a quick end to the dispute] ▪ *She has helped* **smooth a path** [=make it easier] *for more women to run for office.* ▪ *We'll help* **smooth away** *any legal trouble.* ▪ *She tried to smooth things out with her daughter.* — **smooth over** [*phrasal vb*] **smooth (something) over** *or* **smooth over (something)** : to make (a disagreement, problem, difficulty, etc.) seem less serious than it really is ▪ *She smoothed over the objections to his candidacy.*

smooth·ie *or* **smoothy** /ˈsmuːði/ *n*, *pl* **-ies** [C] **1** : a person who has a relaxed, polite, and confident way of speaking and behaving but who may not seem honest or sincere ▪ *He's a real smoothie around women.* **2** : a thick, cold drink that is made of fruit mixed with milk, yogurt, or juice

smor·gas·bord /'smɔɚgəsˌbɔɚd/ *n* [*singular*] **1** : a meal with many different foods that are placed on a large table so that people can serve themselves **2** : a large mixture of many different things ▪ *a smorgasbord of options*

smote *past tense and past participle of* SMITE

smoth·er /'smʌðɚ/ *vb* [T] **1** : to kill (someone) by covering the face so that breathing is not possible **2** : to cover (something or someone) thickly or completely ▪ *She smothered the fire with a blanket to try to put it out.* ▪ *The potatoes were smothered in gravy.* ▪ *She smothered him with/in kisses.* ▪ (*figurative*) *She smothered her son with love/affection.* [=she gave her son a lot of love/affection in a way that prevented him from feeling free to live his own life] **3** : to try to stop yourself from doing (something) ▪ *smother a yawn*

smoulder *Brit spelling of* SMOLDER

¹**smudge** /'smʌdʒ/ *n* [C] : a dirty mark, spot, etc.

²**smudge** *vb* **smudged**; **smudg·ing** **1** [T] : to make a dirty mark, spot, etc., on (something) ▪ *His face was smudged with grease.* **2 a** [I] : to become blurry and unclear by being touched or rubbed ▪ *Charcoal drawings smudge easily.* **b** [T] : to make (something) blurry or unclear by touching or rubbing it ▪ *Try not to smudge the ink.*

smug /'smʌg/ *adj* **smug·ger**; **smug·gest** *disapproving* : having or showing the annoying quality of people who feel very pleased or satisfied with their abilities, achievements, etc. ▪ *a smug person/smile* — **smug·ly** *adv* — **smug·ness** *n* [U]

smug·gle /'smʌgəl/ *vb* **smug·gled**; **smug·gling** [T] : to move (someone or something) from one country to another illegally and secretly ▪ *smuggling drugs/immigrants across the border* — **smug·gler** /'smʌglɚ/ *n* [C] ▪ *drug smugglers*

smut /'smʌt/ *n* [U] *informal + disapproving* : language, pictures, or stories that deal with sex in a way that is offensive — **smut·ty** /'smʌti/ *adj* **smut·ti·er**; **-est** ▪ *a smutty magazine*

¹**snack** /'snæk/ *n* [C] : a small amount of food eaten between meals ▪ *a snack of chips and dip*

²**snack** *vb* [I] *informal* : to eat a small amount of food between meals ▪ *I'll just snack on an apple if I'm hungry.*

sna·fu /snæ'fuː/ *n* [C] *chiefly US, somewhat informal* : a problem that makes a situation difficult or confusing ▪ *a scheduling snafu*

¹**snag** /'snæg/ *n* [C] **1** : an unexpected problem or difficulty ▪ *We hit a snag with our travel plans.* **2** : a sharp or broken part that sticks out from a smooth surface ▪ *I caught my sleeve on a snag and*

tore it. **3** : a thread that sticks out from a piece of cloth **4** : a dead tree or tree stump that is still standing up

²**snag** *vb* **snagged**; **snag·ging** [T] **1** : to catch and tear (something) on something sharp ▪ *I snagged my sweater on a nail.* **2** *US, informal* : to catch, capture, or get (something or someone) by quick action or good luck ▪ *The police snagged the suspect as he was trying to run away.*

snail /'sneɪl/ *n* [C] : a small animal that lives in a shell that it carries on its back, that moves very slowly, and that can live in water or on land — **at a snail's pace** : very slowly ▪ *The work is progressing at a snail's pace.*

snail mail *n* [U] *informal + humorous* : ordinary mail that is delivered by a postal system : mail that is not e-mail

¹**snake** /'sneɪk/ *n* [C] **1** : an animal that has a long, thin body and no arms or legs **2** *chiefly US, informal* : a bad person who tells lies and betrays other people ▪ *He's a dirty snake!* — **snaky** /'sneɪki/ *adj*

²**snake** *vb* **snaked**; **snak·ing** [T/I] : to move like a snake : to follow a twisting path with many turns ▪ *The road snakes through the mountains.* ▪ *He snaked his way through the crowd.*

¹**snap** /'snæp/ *vb* **snapped**; **snap·ping** **1** [T/I] : to break quickly with a short, sharp sound ▪ *The branch snapped (off) and fell to the ground.* ▪ *She snapped the twig in two.* **2** [T/I] : to move into a specified position with a short, sharp sound ▪ *The pieces snap easily into place.* **3** [T] : to close (something) with a fastener and especially with a snap ▪ *She snapped her handbag shut.* ▪ *He snapped (up) his jacket.* **4** [T] : to turn (something) on or off with a switch ▪ *snap on/off the lights* **5** [T/I] : to make or cause (something) to make a short, sharp sound ▪ *The campfire snapped and crackled.* ▪ *snap a whip* **6** [T/I] : to use your thumb and fingers to make a short, sharp sound ▪ *He snapped his fingers to the beat.* **7** [T] *informal* : to take a photograph of someone or something ▪ *tourists snapping pictures* **8** [T/I] : to speak using short, angry sentences or phrases — usually + *at* ▪ *They argued and snapped at each other.* ▪ *"Leave me alone!" he snapped.* **9** [I] : to suddenly no longer be able to control your emotions ▪ *She snapped under the pressure of the job.* **10** [T] *US, informal* : to cause the end of (a series of wins, losses, etc.) ▪ *They snapped a 10-game losing streak.* [=they won a game after losing 10 games] **11** [T] *American football* : to pass (the ball) back between your legs to a teammate and especially to the quarterback at the start of a play ▪ *The center snapped the ball.* **12** [I] : to try to bite someone or something suddenly and quickly ▪ *The dog snapped at a fly.* — **snap out of** [*phrasal vb*] **snap out of** or **snap (someone) out of** *informal* : to stop being in or to cause (someone) to stop being in (an unhappy condition or mood, a daydream, etc.) ▪ *She needs to snap out of her depression.* ▪ *Come on, snap out of it!* — **snap up** [*phrasal vb*] **snap (something**

or someone) up or **snap up (something or someone)** : to buy or take (something or someone) quickly or eagerly ▪ *Shoppers came to snap up bargains after the holidays.*

²**snap** *n* 1 [C] : a sudden, short, sharp sound caused by something breaking or moving into a new position ▪ *We heard the snap of a branch.* 2 [C] : the act of snapping your fingers or the sound made when you snap your fingers ▪ *He got my attention with a snap of his fingers.* 3 [C] *US* : a device that fastens something by closing or locking with a short, sharp sound; *especially* : a set of two metal or plastic pieces that fit tightly together when you press them ▪ *pockets with snaps* 4 [C] : a thin, hard cookie 5 [*singular*] *US, informal* : something that is very easy to do ▪ *The recipes are a snap (to prepare).* 6 [*singular*] *US, informal* : a small amount of time ▪ *I'll be ready in a snap.* 7 [C] : a sudden brief period of cold weather ▪ *a cold snap* 8 [C] *American football* : the act of snapping the ball back to a teammate and especially to the quarterback at the start of a play

³**snap** *adj, always before a noun* : done or made suddenly or without careful thought ▪ *a snap decision*

snap·drag·on /ˈsnæpˌdrægən/ *n* [C] : a tall plant that has many colorful flowers

snap·per /ˈsnæpə/ *n* 1 [C/U] : a type of fish that lives in the ocean and that is eaten as food 2 [C] *American football* : the player who snaps the ball

snapping turtle *n* [C] : a large American turtle that has strong jaws and that is sometimes used for food

snap·py /ˈsnæpi/ *adj* **snap·pi·er**; **-est** *informal* 1 a : exciting or lively ▪ *snappy colors/tunes* b : moving or able to move quickly ▪ *a snappy pace* ▪ *Clean your room, and make it snappy!* [=do it quickly] 2 : fashionable or stylish ▪ *a snappy dresser* 3 : clever and funny ▪ *a snappy* [=*witty*] *joke/remark* ▪ *The show is well-acted, and the dialogue is snappy.* 4 : feeling or showing irritation ▪ *She was snappy with me.* — **snap·pi·ly** /ˈsnæpəli/ *adv*

snap·shot /ˈsnæpˌʃɑːt/ *n* [C] : an informal photograph that is taken quickly

¹**snare** /ˈsneə/ *n* [C] 1 : a device that has a loop which gets smaller when the end of it is pulled and that is used to catch animals ▪ *a rabbit snare* 2 : a position or situation from which it is difficult to escape ▪ *caught in the snare of drug addiction*

²**snare** *vb* **snared**; **snar·ing** [T] 1 : to catch in a snare or trap ▪ *They snared a rabbit.* ▪ *Turtles often get snared in the nets.* ▪ *(figurative) The mayor got snared in a scandal.* 2 : to win or get (something) by skillful action or good luck ▪ *I was lucky enough to snare the job.*

snare drum *n* [C] : a drum of a medium size that is played with drumsticks

¹**snarl** /ˈsnɑrəl/ *vb* [T/I] 1 : to become twisted together or to cause (something) to become twisted together ▪ *Her hair snarls easily.* ▪ *(figurative) The accident snarled (up) traffic.* 2 : to growl in an

angry or threatening way ▪ *The dog snarled at me.* ▪ *"Get back to work," she snarled.*

²**snarl** *n* [C] 1 : a twisted knot of hairs, thread, etc. 2 : a situation in which you can no longer move or make progress ▪ *a traffic snarl* 3 : an act of growling and showing the teeth ▪ *a dog's snarl*

¹**snatch** /ˈsnætʃ/ *vb* [T] 1 : to take (something) quickly or eagerly ▪ *She snatched the ball out of the air.* ▪ *She snatched (up) the last copy of the book.* ▪ *He snatched a few moments of rest.* 2 : to take (something or someone) suddenly from a person or place ▪ *A man snatched her purse.* ▪ *She snatched the toy away.* — **snatch at** [*phrasal vb*] : to grab or try to grab (something) quickly or eagerly ▪ *(figurative) She snatched at the opportunity to play the role.* — **snatch·er** /ˈsnætʃə/ *n* [C] ▪ *a purse snatcher*

²**snatch** *n* [C] : a small part of something ▪ *I only heard snatches of the conversation.* — **in snatches** : for short periods of time ▪ *sleeping in snatches*

snaz·zy /ˈsnæzi/ *adj* **snaz·zi·er**; **-est** *informal* : attractive and stylish ▪ *a snazzy car/dresser*

¹**sneak** /ˈsniːk/ *vb* **sneaked** or *chiefly US* **snuck** /ˈsnʌk/; **sneak·ing** 1 [I] : to move quietly and secretly in order to avoid being noticed ▪ *He sneaked past the guard.* 2 [T] : to take or bring (something) secretly and often quickly ▪ *She sneaked some cigars through customs.* ▪ *I sneaked a note to my friend in class.* ▪ *Can I sneak a look/peek at your quiz answers?* — **sneak up on** [*phrasal vb*] 1 : to approach (someone) quietly and secretly in order to avoid being noticed ▪ *Don't sneak up on me like that!* 2 : to approach, happen, or develop without being noticed ▪ *My birthday snuck up on me this year.*

²**sneak** *n* [C] *US, informal* : a person who acts in a secret and usually dishonest way

³**sneak** *adj, always before a noun* : done while others are not paying attention ▪ *a sneak attack*

sneak·er /ˈsniːkə/ *n* [C] *US* : a shoe with a rubber sole that is designed for people to wear while running, playing sports, etc.

sneaking *adj, always before a noun* 1 : not openly expressed ▪ *He had a sneaking admiration for his opponent.* 2 ◇ If you have a **sneaking feeling/suspicion**, you think that something might be true or might happen even though you have no definite reason to think so. ▪ *I have a sneaking feeling/suspicion that we're going to have a test today.*

sneak preview *n* [C] : a special showing of a movie, play, product, etc., before it becomes available to the general public ▪ *a sneak preview of the new film*

sneaky /ˈsniːki/ *adj* **sneak·i·er**; **-est** 1 : behaving in a secret and usually dishonest manner ▪ *a sneaky person* 2 : done in a secret and dishonest manner ▪ *a sneaky trick*

sneer /ˈsniə/ *vb* 1 [I] : to smile or laugh at someone or something with an expression on your face that shows dislike and a lack of respect ▪ *She sneered at me in disgust.* **2** [T/I] : to express dislike and a lack of respect in a very open way ▪ *Critics sneered at his first novel.* ▪ *"You're a fool," she sneered. — "They're crazy," he said with a sneer.* — **sneer·ing·ly** /'snɪrɪŋli/ *adv*

sneeze /'sniːz/ *vb* **sneezed; sneez·ing** [I] : to suddenly and loudly force air out through your nose and mouth as a reaction to dust, a sickness, etc. ▪ *Flowers make me sneeze.* ▪ *(figurative, informal) The award is nothing to sneeze at.* [=the award is important, impressive, etc.] — **sneeze** *n* [C]

snick·er /'snɪkə/ *vb* [I] *chiefly US* : to laugh quietly in a way that shows disrespect ▪ *They snickered at my outfit.* — **snicker** *n* [C]

snide /'snaɪd/ *adj* : unkind or insulting in an indirect way ▪ *a snide remark/tone* — **snide·ly** *adv*

sniff /'snɪf/ *vb* **1 a** [I] : to take air into your nose in short, loud breaths ▪ *She sniffed and wiped her nose with a tissue.* **b** [T/I] : to smell (something or someone) by taking air in through your nose in short breaths ▪ *The cat sniffed (at) the food and walked away.* **c** [T] : to take (something) into your body by inhaling it through your nose in order to get intoxicated ▪ *sniffing glue* **2 a** [T] : to discover or find (something) by smelling ▪ *dogs that are trained to sniff out drugs* **b** [I] : to search *for* something by smelling ▪ *(figurative) The detective sniffed (around) for clues.* **3** [T] : to say (something) in a way that shows dislike, disappointment, etc. ▪ *"I guess you don't need my help," she sniffed.* — **sniff at** [*phrasal vb*] : to show dislike or disapproval of (something) because you think it is not good, important, etc. ▪ *It's not a big profit, but it's not to be sniffed at.* = *It's nothing to sniff at.* — **sniff** *n* [C] ▪ *Give this flower a sniff.* ▪ *Take a sniff of this flower.* — **sniff·er** /'snɪfə/ *n* [C]

snif·fle /'snɪfəl/ *vb* **snif·fled; snif·fling** **1** [I] : to take air into your nose in short, loud breaths because you are sick or have been crying ▪ *He has been sniffling for a week now.* **2** [T] : to say (something) while crying or sniffling ▪ *"You just don't like me," she sniffled.* — **sniffle** *n* [C] ▪ *(informal) I have (a case of) the snif·fles.* [=a mild cold that causes you to sniffle a lot]

snig·ger /'snɪgə/ *vb* [I] *chiefly Brit* : SNICKER — **snigger** *n* [C]

snip /'snɪp/ *vb* **snipped; snip·ping** [T/I] : to cut (something) with scissors — *snipping pictures out of magazines* — **snip** *n* [C] ▪ *She removed the dead flowers with a snip of her scissors.*

snipe /'snaɪp/ *vb* **sniped; snip·ing** **1** [I] : to shoot at someone from a hidden place ▪ *Enemy fighters sniped at them.* **2** [T/I] : to criticize someone or something in a harsh or unfair way ▪ *The candidates sniped at each other.* — **snip·er** /'snaɪpə/ *n* [C] ▪ *He was shot by a sniper.* — **sniping** *n* [U]

snip·pet /'snɪpət/ *n* [C] : a small part of

something ▪ *I heard only a snippet of their conversation.* ▪ *snippets from her new novel*

snip·py /'snɪpi/ *adj* **snip·pi·er; -est** *US, informal* : feeling or showing irritation ▪ *Don't get snippy with me.*

snit /'snɪt/ *n* [*singular*] *US, informal* : a very annoyed and angry state usually because of something minor ▪ *He left in a snit.* ▪ *She had a snit* [=became angry] *when she saw the mess.*

snitch /'snɪtʃ/ *vb, informal* **1** [I] *disapproving* : to tell someone in authority about something wrong that someone has done ▪ *He snitched to the police.* ▪ *She snitched on me when I skipped school.* **2** [T] : to take or steal (something that is not very valuable) ▪ *He snitched a dime from me.* — **snitch** *n* [C] ▪ *Who's the snitch who called the police?*

sniv·el /'snɪvəl/ *vb, US* **-eled** *or Brit* **-elled;** *US* **-el·ing** *or Brit* **-el·ling** [T/I] : to complain or cry in an annoying way ▪ *He's sniveling about his problems again.* ▪ *a sniveling coward*

snob /'snɑːb/ *n* [C] *disapproving* : someone who tends to criticize, reject, or ignore people who have less money, less education, etc. ▪ *an intellectual snob* — **snob·bish** /'snɑːbɪʃ/ *adj* ▪ *a snobbish critic/attitude* — **snob·bish·ly** *adv* — **snob·bish·ness** *n* [U] — **snob·bism** /'snɑːˌbɪzəm/ *n* [U] — **snob·by** /'snɑːbi/ *adj* **snob·bi·er; -est** ▪ *a snobby brat*

snob·bery /'snɑːbəri/ *n* [U] *disapproving* : the behavior or attitude of snobs ▪ *the snobbery of some wine connoisseurs*

sno–cone *variant spelling of* SNOW CONE

snog /'snɑːg/ *vb* **snogged; snog·ging** [T/I] *Brit, informal* : to kiss for a long time ▪ *They were snogging (each other).* — **snog** *n* [*singular*]

¹**snook·er** /'snʊkə, *Brit* 'snuːkə/ *n* [U] : a version of the game of pool that is played chiefly in Britain

²**snooker** *vb* [T] *informal* **1** *US* : to trick or deceive (someone) ▪ *I think we've been snookered.* **2** *Brit* : to prevent (someone) from doing or achieving something ▪ *They wanted to build a museum but were snookered* [=thwarted] *by city regulations.*

snoop /'snuːp/ *vb* [I] *informal* : to look for private information about someone or something ▪ *I caught her snooping (around) in my desk drawers.* — **snoop** *n* [C] ▪ *She accused him of being a snoop.* [=accused him of snooping] — **snoop·er** *n* [C] — **snoop·ing** *n* [U]

snooty /'snuːti/ *adj* **snoot·i·er; -est** *informal + disapproving* : having or showing arrogance ▪ *a snooty girl/attitude* — **snoot·i·ness** /'snuːtinəs/ *n* [U]

snooze /'snuːz/ *vb* **snoozed; snooz·ing** [I] *informal* : to sleep lightly especially for a short period of time : DOZE ▪ *She was snoozing on the sofa.* — **snooze** *n* [*singular*] ▪ *take/catch a snooze* [=nap] ▪ *(US, figurative) The novel is a real snooze.* [=it is very dull or boring]

¹**snore** /'snoə/ *vb* **snored; snor·ing** [I] : to breathe noisily while sleeping ▪ *My husband snores.* — **snor·er** *n* [C] — **snoring** *n* [U]

²**snore** n [C] **1** : an act of snoring or the sound made when someone is snoring • *a loud snore* **2** US, informal : something that is dull and boring • *The movie was a real snore.*

¹**snor·kel** /ˈsnoɚkəl/ n [C] : a special tube that makes it possible to breathe while you are swimming with your head underwater

²**snorkel** vb, US **-keled** or Brit **-kelled**; US **-kel·ing** or Brit **-kel·ling** [I] : to swim while using a snorkel • *We went snorkeling in the Caribbean.* — **snor·kel·er** (US) or Brit **snor·kel·ler** n [C]

snort /ˈsnoɚt/ vb **1** [I] : to force air noisily through your nose • *He snorted like a pig.* **2** [T/I] : to express dislike, disapproval, anger, or surprise by snorting • *She snorted at his suggestion.* **3** [T] : to take (a drug) into your body by inhaling it through your nose • *snorting cocaine* — **snort** n [C] • *a snort of laughter* • *a snort of cocaine* [=an amount of cocaine inhaled by snorting]

snot /ˈsnɑːt/ n, informal + impolite **1** [U] : mucus from the nose **2** [C] disapproving : a rude and annoying person • *an obnoxious little snot*

snot·ty /ˈsnɑːti/ adj **snot·ti·er**; **-ti·est** informal **1** : rude, annoying, and often arrogant • *a snotty reply/person* **2** : covered or filled with mucus • *a snotty nose* — **snot·ti·ness** /ˈsnɑːtinəs/ n [U]

snout /ˈsnaʊt/ n [C] : the long nose of some animals (such as pigs)

¹**snow** /ˈsnoʊ/ n [C/U] : soft, white pieces of frozen water that fall to the ground from the sky • *We got 12 inches of snow.* [=12 inches of snow fell on the ground] • *A light/heavy snow was falling.*

²**snow** vb [I] — used with it to say that snow is falling • *It snowed all day.* — **snowed in** also Brit **snowed up 1** : unable to leave a place because a lot of snow is falling or has fallen • *They were snowed in for a week.* **2** : blocked with snow • *The road was snowed in.* — **snowed under** : having to deal with too much of something • *He was snowed under with e-mail.* [=he had a lot of e-mails to respond to]

¹**snow·ball** /ˈsnoʊˌbɑːl/ n [C] : a ball of snow that someone makes usually for throwing • *a snowball fight* [=a playful fight in which people throw snowballs at each other] • (*figurative, informal*) *He doesn't have a snowball's chance in hell of winning.* [=he has no chance of winning]

²**snowball** vb [I] : to increase, grow, etc., at a faster and faster rate • *Problems snowball when they are ignored.*

snow·bank /ˈsnoʊˌbæŋk/ n [C] : a pile of snow especially along the side of a road • *The car slid into a snowbank.*

snow·blow·er /ˈsnoʊˌbloʊɚ/ n [C] : a machine that picks up snow from a driveway, sidewalk, etc., and throws it aside

snow·board /ˈsnoʊˌboɚd/ n [C] : a board like a wide ski that is used for sliding down hills of snow while standing — **snowboard** vb [I] • *We went snowboarding.* — **snow·board·er** n [C]

snow·bound /ˈsnoʊˌbaʊnd/ adj **1** : unable to leave a place because a lot of snow is falling or has fallen • *We were snowbound for a week.* **2** : blocked with snow • *snowbound roads*

snow·capped /ˈsnoʊˌkæpt/ adj : having the top covered with snow • *snowcapped mountains*

snow cone or **sno–cone** /ˈsnoʊˌkoʊn/ n [C] US : a cone-shaped paper cup that contains very small pieces of ice flavored with a sweet syrup

snow day n [C] US : a day when schools are closed because a lot of snow is falling

snow·drift /ˈsnoʊˌdrɪft/ n [C] : a hill of snow that is formed by wind • *The car was buried in a snowdrift.*

snow·fall /ˈsnoʊˌfɑːl/ n [C/U] : an amount of snow that falls in a particular period of time • *The yearly snowfall here is over 30 feet!* • *The area is expecting (a) heavy snowfall tonight.*

snow·flake /ˈsnoʊˌfleɪk/ n [C] : a small piece of snow

snow·man /ˈsnoʊˌmæn/ n, pl **-men** /-ˌmɛn/ [C] : a figure made of snow that is shaped to look like a person • *We made/built a snowman.*

snow·mo·bile /ˈsnoʊmoʊˌbiːl/ n [C] : a vehicle used for traveling on snow or ice — **snow·mo·bil·er** /ˈsnoʊmoʊˌbiːlɚ/ n [C] — **snow·mo·bil·ing** /ˈsnoʊmoʊˌbiːlɪŋ/ n [U]

snow pea n [C] US : a type of pea whose flat outer part and seeds may be eaten

snow·plow (US) or Brit **snow·plough** /ˈsnoʊˌplaʊ/ n [C] : a piece of metal that is attached to the front of a vehicle and used for clearing snow from a road, driveway, etc.; also : a vehicle that has a snowplow attached

snow·shoe /ˈsnoʊˌʃuː/ n [C] : a light, wide frame that is attached to your shoe to make it easier to walk on soft snow — **snowshoe** vb **-shoed**; **-shoe·ing** [I] • *We snowshoed through the woods.*

snow·storm /ˈsnoʊˌstoɚm/ n [C] : a storm with a large amount of falling snow

snow·suit /ˈsnoʊˌsuːt/ n [C] : a jacket and matching pants that is worn by children over their regular clothes when they go outdoors in very cold weather

snow tire n [C] US : a special tire that gives a vehicle better control on snow and ice

snow–white /ˈsnoʊˈwaɪt/ adj : completely white • *snow-white hair*

snowy /ˈsnoʊi/ adj **snow·i·er**; **-est 1** : having a lot of snow • *a snowy day* **2** : covered in snow • *snowy streets/fields*

Snr abbr, Brit senior • *Dave Smith Snr*

snub /ˈsnʌb/ vb **snubbed**; **snub·bing** [T] **1** : to ignore (someone) in a deliberate and insulting way • *She snubbed me in the hallway.* **2** : to not accept or attend (something) as a way to show disapproval • *He snubbed their job offer.* — **snub** n [C]

snuck past tense and past participle of ¹**SNEAK**

¹**snuff** /ˈsnʌf/ vb [T] **1** : to cause (a candle, cigarette, etc.) to stop burning by pressing it with your fingers, covering it,

etc. ▪ *She snuffed (out) the candle.* **2** *informal* **a** : to cause the end of (something) ▪ *Their hopes were snuffed (out).* **b** : to kill (someone) ▪ *a gangster who was/got snuffed (out) by a rival* — **snuff** *Brit, informal* : to die ▪ *He snuffed it at a young age.*

²**snuff** *n* [*U*] : a type of tobacco that is chewed, placed against the gums, or inhaled into the nose ▪ *a pinch of snuff* — **up to snuff** *US, informal* : good enough ▪ *My skills weren't up to snuff.*

snuf·fle /ˈsnʌfəl/ *vb* **snuf·fled**; **snuf·fling** [*I*] : to breathe loudly because you have a cold or have been crying ▪ *The child was snuffling in his room.*

snug /ˈsnʌg/ *adj* **snug·ger**; **snug·gest** **1** : fitting closely and often too tightly ▪ *The shoes/clothes are too snug.* **2** : providing or enjoying warmth, shelter, and comfort ▪ *The kids are snug in their beds.* — **snug·ly** *adv*

snug·gle /ˈsnʌgəl/ *vb* **snug·gled**; **snug·gling** [*I*] : to lie or sit close together in a comfortable position ▪ *The puppy snuggled up against me.* ▪ *We snuggled (together) under a blanket.*

¹**so** /ˈsoʊ/ *adv* **1 a** : to a degree that is suggested or stated ▪ *The library is so large (that) you could get lost in it.* ▪ *How can you be so cruel?* ▪ *Don't eat so fast.* [=eat more slowly] ▪ *Would you be so kind as to help me?* [=would you please help me?] ▪ *Sailing is not so much a science as an art.* [=sailing is more of an art than a science] ▪ *The play was impressive—(all) the more so* [=it was even more impressive] *because the students had written it themselves.* **b** : very or extremely ▪ *He looked so handsome in his suit.* ▪ *I am so excited!* ▪ *Not so long ago* [=a short time ago], *she was the nation's best gymnast.* ▪ *Thank you so (very) much for your help.* ▪ *That was so much fun!* **c** *informal* : without any doubt — used to make a statement more forceful ▪ *I so don't believe you.* ▪ *Her hairstyle is so 1980s.* [=it looks like the hairstyles that were popular in the 1980s] ▪ *I can only move so fast.* ▪ *I have never seen so many stars.* ▪ *There is still so much to do.* **3** : in the same way ▪ *She was a hard worker and so was her father.* [=and her father was too] ▪ *"I'm going to the concert." "So am I."* [=I am also going] ▪ *"I wish I had more time." "So do I."* [=I do too] ▪ *(US, informal)* *"I really like her music." "So don't I."* [=I do too] **4** : in the way that is stated or suggested ▪ *The clock struck midnight, and so began a new year.* ▪ *It (just) so happens that I know her son.* [=I happen to know her son] **5** *informal* : most certainly ▪ *"I never said that" "You did so."* — **and so forth/on** : and other things often of the same or similar kind ▪ *I told her about my family, my hopes and fears, (and so on) and so forth.* — **even so** see ²EVEN — **ever so** see EVER — **every so often** see EVERY — **how so** see ¹HOW — **never so much as** see NEVER — **so far** see ¹FAR — **so help me (God)** see ¹HELP — **so long** see ²LONG — **so much** : an amount, price,

etc., that is not stated or known ▪ *You are charged so much a mile when renting a vehicle.* ▪ *You can only believe so much* [=you can only believe some] *of what he says.* — **so much as** — used after a negative word to stress the smallness of an amount or effort ▪ *They ended their date without so much as a hug.* — **so much for** *informal* — used to say that something has ended, was not successful, etc. ▪ *Well, it's raining. So much for our perfect weather.* ▪ *Well, so much for that idea.* [=that idea was not successful] — **so much so (that)** : to the extent that ▪ *The twins look alike—so much so that* [=the twins look so alike that] *even their parents sometimes confuse them.* — **so much the better** see ³BETTER — **so to speak** see SPEAK

²**so** *pron* — used to refer to something that has just been stated or suggested ▪ *"Has she left?" "I believe so."* [=I believe she has left] ▪ *If you have not yet returned the form, please do so now.* [=please return it now] ▪ *They're going to help us move, or so they said.* ▪ *I didn't like the dress, and I told her so.* [=told her I didn't like it] ▪ *I might be late. If so* [=if I am late], *please start without me.* ▪ *Fold the paper like so.* [=like this] ▪ *If they insist on going, so be it.* [=I can do nothing to stop them] ▪ *"Today is the first day of winter." "Why, so it is."* — **if I may say so** see ¹SAY — **or so** — used to say that a number, amount, etc., is not exact ▪ *Tickets cost $20 or so.*

³**so** *conj* **1** : and therefore ▪ *I don't want to go, so I won't.* **2** — used to say the reason for something ▪ *Please be quiet so (that) I can study.* **3** — used in speech to introduce a statement or question ▪ *So, how did the test go?* ▪ *So, as I was saying, the car is used but in good condition.* **4** — used in speech to say in a somewhat rude or annoyed way that something is unimportant ▪ *So I'm late. Who cares!* ▪ *"I'm taller than you!" "So?"* ▪ *She had a glass of wine—so what?* [=why should anyone object to that?] **5** — used in speech to say that you have just become aware of someone or something ▪ *So, that's who did it!* — **so as** see ²AS — **so long as** see ²LONG

⁴**so** *adj, not before a noun* : agreeing with actual facts : TRUE ▪ *You are saying things that are just not so.* ▪ *I heard you cheated—is that so?* — **just so** see ²JUST

⁵**so** *n* [*U*] *music* : SOL

So. *or* **so.** *abbr* south *or* southern

SO *abbr* significant other

¹**soak** /ˈsoʊk/ *vb* **1 a** [*T/I*] : to put (something) in a liquid for a period of time ▪ *Soak the beans (in water) overnight.* **b** [*I*] : to take a long bath ▪ *He soaked in the tub.* **c** [*T*] : to make (someone or something) very wet with water or another liquid ▪ *I was/got soaked by the rain.* ▪ *My clothes were soaked through.* [=made completely wet] **2** [*I*] *of a liquid* : to enter or pass *through* or *into* something ▪ *Sweat soaked through his shirt.* — **soak in** [*phrasal vb*] *of a liquid* : to enter something by a gradual process ▪ *Pour water on the soil and allow it to soak in.* ▪

(figurative) He sat quietly, letting her words soak in. — **soak up** [phrasal vb] **soak up (something)** or **soak (something) up** 1 : to take in (liquid) : ABSORB ▪ The rag soaked up most of the water. 2 : to enjoy feeling or experiencing (something pleasant) in usually a slow or relaxed way ▪ We went to the beach to soak up some sun. 3 : to learn and remember (something) quickly ▪ soaking up new information 4 : to use a large amount of (money, supplies, etc.) ▪ This project is soaking up resources.

²**soak** n [singular] 1 : an act of leaving something in a liquid for a long time ▪ This shirt needs a good soak to get out the stains. 2 informal : a long bath ▪ a nice, hot soak in the tub

soaked /'soʊkt/ adj : made completely wet by water or another liquid ▪ a soaked towel ▪ a blood-soaked bandage

soak·ing /'soʊkɪŋ/ n [singular] 1 : ²SOAK 1 2 : an act of making someone or something very wet ▪ We got a soaking [=got soaked] from a rain shower. — **soaking** adj ▪ I was soaking [=completely wet] after walking home in the rain. ▪ I was soaking wet.

so-and-so /'soʊwən,soʊ/ n, pl **so-and-sos** or **so-and-so's** /'soʊwən,soʊz/ [U] informal — used when the name of a person is unknown or not important ▪ She likes telling us that so-and-so is getting married or divorced or something.

¹**soap** /'soʊp/ n 1 [C/U] : a substance that is used for washing something ▪ Wash your hands with soap and water. ▪ a bar of soap ▪ dish/laundry soap [=detergent] 2 [C] informal : SOAP OPERA — **soapy** /'soʊpi/ adj **soap·i·er; -est**

²**soap** vb [T] : to rub soap over or into (someone or something) ▪ He soaped (up) the car.

soap·box /'soʊp,bɑːks/ n [C] : a box or small platform that someone stands on to give a speech ▪ *(figurative)* She needs to get off her soapbox and stop telling people what to do.

soap opera n [C] : a TV show that has continuing stories about the daily lives of a group of people ▪ *(figurative)* My life is a soap opera. [=my life has a lot of dramatic events and problems]

soap·stone /'soʊp,stoʊn/ n [U] : a type of soft stone ▪ a soapstone sculpture

soar /'soɚ/ vb [I] 1 : to increase very quickly in amount or price ▪ The temperature soared to 100 degrees. ▪ soaring popularity 2 a : to fly or sail often at a great height by floating on air currents ▪ The eagle soared above us. b : to rise quickly upward to a great height ▪ The rocket soared into the sky. ▪ *(figurative)* Her spirits soared. [=she became very happy and excited]

sob /'sɑːb/ vb **sobbed; sob·bing** 1 [I] : to cry noisily while taking in short, sudden breaths ▪ sobbing uncontrollably 2 [T] : to say (something) while sobbing ▪ "I hate you," she sobbed. — **sob** n [C]

¹**so·ber** /'soʊbɚ/ adj 1 : not drunk ▪ I'm driving tonight, so I have to stay sober. ▪ She has been sober for three years. ▪ she stopped drinking alcohol three years

ago] 2 : having or showing a very serious attitude or quality ▪ a sober conversation 3 : plain in color ▪ a sober gray suit — **so·ber·ly** adv

²**sober** vb [T] : to make (someone) serious or thoughtful ▪ He was sobered by the experience. — **sober up** [phrasal vb] **sober up** or **sober (someone) up** : to become sober or less drunk or to make (a drunk person) sober or less drunk ▪ You need to sober yourself up before you go. — **so·ber·ing** /'soʊbərɪŋ/ adj ▪ a sobering fact/experience

so·bri·ety /sə'brajəti/ n [U] 1 : the state of not being drunk ▪ The police gave him a sobriety test. 2 formal : the quality of being serious ▪ the sobriety of the situation

so·bri·quet also **sou·bri·quet** /'soʊbrɪ,keɪ/ n [C] formal : NICKNAME

sob story n [C] informal : a sad story about yourself that you tell in order to make people feel sorry for you ▪ He told us one of his sob stories.

soc. abbr 1 society 2 sociology

so-called /'soʊ'kɑːld/ adj, always before a noun 1 — used to indicate the name that is commonly or usually used for something ▪ the so-called mad cow disease 2 — used to indicate a name or description that you think is not really right or suitable ▪ I was lied to by a so-called friend. [=by someone who is not really my friend]

soc·cer /'sɑːkɚ/ n [U] : a game played between two teams of 11 players in which a round ball is moved toward a goal usually by kicking ▪ playing soccer ▪ a soccer ball — called also (Brit) football

soccer mom n [C] US, informal : a mother usually from the middle class who brings her children to soccer games and similar activities

so·cia·ble /'soʊʃəbəl/ adj 1 : liking to be with and talk to other people ▪ sociable people who enjoy having parties 2 : involving or allowing friendly and pleasant social relations ▪ a sociable evening — **so·cia·bil·i·ty** /,soʊʃə'bɪləti/ n [U]

¹**so·cial** /'soʊʃəl/ adj 1 a : relating to or involving activities in which people spend time talking to each other or doing enjoyable things with each other ▪ social events/skills ▪ She has a busy social life. [=she spends a lot of time doing social things] b : liking to be with and talk to people ▪ I'm not feeling very social this evening. 2 : of or relating to people or society in general ▪ social institutions like marriage and family ▪ social issues/problems 3 : tending to form relationships and live together in groups ▪ Bees are social insects. 4 always before a noun : of, relating to, or based on rank in a particular society ▪ She says her family's social status is middle class. — **so·cial·ly** /'soʊʃəli/ adv

²**social** n [C] : an informal social event for members of a group ▪ The club has socials every month.

social climber n [C] disapproving : someone who tries to gain a higher social position or status

so·cial·ism /'soʊʃə,lɪzəm/ n [U] : a way

1119

socialite • sodium chloride

of organizing a society in which major industries are owned and controlled by the government — **so·cial·ist** /'soʊʃə-lɪst/ n [C] — **socialist** or **Socialist** adj : a socialist country/government — **so·cial·is·tic** /ˌsoʊʃəˈlɪstɪk/ adj

so·cial·ite /'soʊʃəˌlaɪt/ n [C] : someone who often attends social events for wealthy people

so·cial·ize also Brit **so·cial·ise** /'soʊʃə-ˌlaɪz/ vb **-ized**; **-iz·ing** 1 [I] : to talk to and do things with other people in a friendly way • socializing with coworkers after work 2 [T] formal : to teach (someone) to behave in a way that is acceptable in society • Children are socialized by their parents. — **so·cial·i·za·tion** also Brit **so·cial·i·sa·tion** /ˌsoʊʃələ-ˈzeɪʃən, Brit ˌsəʊʃəˌlaɪˈzeɪʃən/ n [U]

social science n [C] : an area of study that relates to human society • Economics is a social science. — **social scientist** n [C]

social security or **Social Security** n [U] 1 : a program in which the government provides money to people who are unable to work because they are old, disabled, or unemployed • Social Security benefits/tax — abbr. SS 2 : money that is paid out through a social security program • She is living on social security (checks).

Social Security number n [C] : a number that is given to each citizen of the U.S. by the government and that is used for official forms and records — abbr. SSN

social studies n [plural] : a course of study that deals with human relationships and the way society works

social work n [U] : the work done by someone who works for an organization that helps people who have financial or family problems — **social worker** n [C]

so·ci·ety /səˈsajəti/ n, pl **-et·ies** 1 [U] : people in general thought of as living together in organized communities with shared laws, traditions, and values • Poverty hurts society as a whole. 2 [C/U] : the people of a particular country, area, time, etc. • ancient societies • the poorer members of (our) society • the values of Western society 3 [U] : people who are fashionable and wealthy • society ladies/parties • men from high society 4 [C] : a group of people who work together or regularly meet because of common interests, beliefs, or activities • a literary/historical society — **so·ci·e·tal** /sə-ˈsajətl/ adj, formal : societal problems

so·cio·eco·nom·ic /ˌsoʊsijoʊˌɛkə-ˈnɑːmɪk/ adj, formal : of, relating to, or involving a combination of social and economic factors • Their socioeconomic backgrounds are very different. — **so·cio·eco·nom·i·cal·ly** /ˌsoʊsijoʊˌɛkə-ˈnɑːmɪkli/ adv

so·ci·ol·o·gy /ˌsoʊsiˈɑːlədʒi/ n [U] : the study of society, social institutions, and social relationships — abbr. soc. — **so·cio·log·i·cal** /ˌsoʊsijəˈlɑːdʒɪkəl/ adj —

so·cio·log·i·cal·ly /ˌsoʊsijəˈlɑːdʒɪkli/ adv — **so·ci·ol·o·gist** /ˌsoʊsiˈɑːlədʒɪst/ n [C]

so·cio·path /'soʊsijəˌpæθ/ n [C] : someone who behaves in a dangerous or violent way towards other people without feeling guilty — **so·cio·path·ic** /ˌsoʊsijəˈpæθɪk/ adj

¹**sock** /'sɑːk/ n [C] 1 : a piece of clothing that is worn on your foot • a pair of wool socks • (figurative, informal) This song will **blow/knock your socks off.** [=you will enjoy this song very much] • (figurative, informal) Tell him to **put a sock in it.** [=to stop talking] 2 : a hard hit with the fist • She gave him a sock in the jaw.

²**sock** vb [T] informal : to hit (someone or something) hard • She socked him in the jaw. • (figurative) He socked us with a huge lawsuit. — **sock away** [phrasal vb] **sock away (something)** or **sock (something) away** US, informal : to save (something) by putting it in a safe place • He had been socking away money for years. — **socked in** US : affected by bad weather conditions that prevent people from leaving • The airport was socked in by fog. — **sock it to** informal : to do or say something to (someone) in a strong and forceful way • He really socked it to her.

sock·et /'sɑːkət/ n [C] 1 a : OUTLET 4 • Plug the lamp into the socket. b : an opening on a piece of electrical equipment into which a plug, light bulb, etc., fits • Screw the light bulb into the socket. 2 : a hollow part in a bone that holds an eye, a tooth, or another bone • the hip socket

socket wrench n [C] US : a tool that has a part which fits over the end of a bolt or nut and is used to turn it

So·crat·ic /səˈkrætɪk/ adj, formal : of or relating to the ancient Greek philosopher Socrates • the Socratic method of asking questions to discover the truth

sod /'sɑːd/ n [C/U] chiefly US : the upper layer of soil that is made up of grass and plant roots or a piece of this layer • laying sod in the yard

so·da /'soʊdə/ n 1 [U] : SODA WATER • Scotch and soda 2 [C/U] chiefly US : SODA POP • I ordered fries and a soda. • a soda can — see also BAKING SODA

soda fountain n [C] chiefly US : a counter usually in a store at which cold drinks, types of ice cream, etc., are prepared and served

soda pop n [C/U] US : a drink consisting of soda water, flavoring, and a sweet syrup

soda water n [C/U] : water that has bubbles in it and that is often used to make other drinks

sod·den /'sɑːdn/ adj : very heavy and wet • sodden sandbags/fields

so·di·um /'soʊdijəm/ n [U] : a white element that is found in salt, baking soda, and other compounds

sodium bicarbonate n [U] : BAKING SODA

sodium chlo·ride /-ˈkloɚˌaɪd/ n [U] technical : the chemical compound that forms salt

sod·o·my /ˈsɑːdəmi/ *n* [U] : anal sex with someone — **sod·o·mize** *also Brit* **sod·o·mise** /ˈsɑːdəˌmaɪz/ *vb* -**mized**; -**miz·ing** [T] *chiefly Brit*

so·fa /ˈsoʊfə/ *n* [C] : a long and comfortable piece of furniture on which a person can sit or lie down

sofa bed *n* [C] : a sofa that can be folded out to form a bed

soft /ˈsɑːft/ *adj* **1** : not hard or firm ▪ *a soft mattress* **2** : smooth and pleasant to touch ▪ *soft skin/fur* **3 a** : having a very light or pale color ▪ *soft colors* **b** *of light* : not bright or harsh ▪ *soft lighting* ▪ *a soft glow* **4 a** : gentle in manner ▪ *a soft touch/kiss* **b** : not strong or very forceful ▪ *a soft [=gentle] breeze* **c** : having a low, gentle sound ▪ *a soft voice* **5** : having a curved or rounded outline ▪ *soft rolling hills* **6** *disapproving* : not strict, harsh, or critical enough ▪ *The mayor is soft on crime.* **7 a** : not physically strong ▪ *He had grown soft from years of inactivity.* **b** : not brave or tough ▪ *She used to love adventure, but she has* **gone/gotten soft.** **8** : sympathetic and kind ▪ *He has a soft heart.* **9** : relating to matters that are not serious or important ▪ *soft news stories* **10** *of an illegal drug* : not as strong or harmful to the health as other drugs ▪ *Marijuana is a soft drug.* **11** *of water* : not containing many minerals ▪ *soft water* **12** : sounding like the "c" in "ace" or the "g" in "gem" ▪ *The "c" in "cell" is soft, but the "c" in "cabbage" is hard.* — **soft in the head** *informal* : stupid or crazy ▪ *Have you* **gone soft in the head?** *[=are you crazy?]* — **soft·ly** *adv* — **soft·ness** /ˈsɑːftnəs/ *n* [*singular*]

soft·ball /ˈsɑːftˌbɑːl/ *n* **1** [U] : a sport that is similar to baseball and that is played with a ball that is larger and softer than a baseball ▪ *playing softball* ▪ *softball teams* **2** [C] : the ball that is used in softball **3** [C] *US* : a question that is very easy to answer ▪ *All the questions in the interview were softballs.*

soft·cov·er /ˈsɑːftˌkʌvər/ *n* [C/U] *US* : a book that has a flexible cover ▪ *The novel is available in softcover.*

soft drink *n* [C] : a cold drink that is usually sweet, does not contain alcohol, and is often sold in bottles or cans

soft·en /ˈsɑːfən/ *vb* **1** [T/I] : to become less hard or firm or to make (something) less hard or firm ▪ *Allow the butter to soften.* ▪ *The heat softened (up) the wax.* **2** [T] : to make (something) less dry or rough ▪ *The lotion softens dry skin.* **3 a** [T] : to make (something) less harsh, extreme, etc. ▪ *The company softened its stance on dating in the workplace.* **b** [I] : to become less harsh, extreme, etc. ▪ *His criticism of the mayor has softened.* **c** [T] : to make (something) less painful, forceful, or harmful ▪ *The grass softened my fall.* ▪ *(figurative) Management tried to* **soften the blow** *of the layoffs by offering early retirement packages.* **4** [T] : to make (something) seem rounder or less sharp ▪ *Her new haircut softens her features.* — **soften up** [*phrasal vb*] **soften (someone) up** *or* **soften up (someone)** **1** : to treat (someone) very well or kindly

in order to make that person more likely to help you, give you something, etc. ▪ *He tried to soften her up by buying her flowers.* **2** : to weaken (an enemy) through military attacks ▪ *They used artillery to soften up the enemy's defenses.* — **soft·en·er** /ˈsɑːfənər/ *n* [C] ▪ *a skin softener*

soft·heart·ed /ˈsɑːftˌhɑɚtəd/ *adj* : having feelings of kindness and sympathy for other people ▪ *He looks tough, but he's really very softhearted.* ▪ *She's too softhearted to fire anyone.*

soft·ie *or* **softy** /ˈsɑːfti/ *n, pl* **soft·ies** [C] *informal* : a kind person ▪ *He may look tough, but he's really a softie.*

soft money *n* [U] *chiefly US* : money that is given to a political party rather than to a particular candidate

soft–ped·al /ˈsɑːftˈpɛdl/ *vb, US* -**aled** *or Brit* -**alled**; *US* -**al·ing** *or Brit* -**al·ling** [T] *chiefly US, informal* : to treat or describe (something) as less important than it really is ▪ *soft-pedal an issue*

soft rock *n* [U] : rock music with a gentler sound and slower beat than hard rock

soft sell *n* [*singular*] : a way of selling something that uses persuasion rather than aggressive pressure ▪ *a soft-sell approach to marketing*

soft–soap /ˈsɑːftˈsoʊp/ *vb* [T] *Brit, informal* : to try to persuade (someone) to do something by using praise, kind words, etc. ▪ *Don't be soft-soaped into going out with him.*

soft–spo·ken /ˈsɑːftˈspoʊkən/ *adj* : having a gentle, quiet voice or manner ▪ *a soft-spoken teacher*

soft spot *n* [C] **1** : a strong liking *for* someone or something ▪ *He has a soft spot for children.* **2** : a weak point that can be attacked ▪ *a soft spot in our defenses*

soft toy *n* [C] *Brit* : STUFFED ANIMAL

soft·ware /ˈsɑːftˌweɚ/ *n* [U] : the programs that run on a computer and perform certain functions ▪ *antivirus software* ▪ *software programs*

soft·wood /ˈsɑːftˌwʊd/ *n* **1** [C/U] : the wood of a tree that is soft and easy to cut ▪ *softwood lumber* **2** [C] : a tree that produces softwood ▪ *pines, firs, and other softwoods*

softy *variant spelling of* SOFTIE

sog·gy /ˈsɑːgi/ *adj* **sog·gi·er**; -**est** **1** : completely wet and usually soft ▪ *soggy bread* **2** *informal* : RAINY ▪ *soggy weather* — **sog·gi·ness** /ˈsɑːginəs/ *n* [U]

soh /ˈsoʊ/ *n* [U] *chiefly Brit, music* : SOL

¹soil /ˈsojəl/ *n* **1** [C/U] : the top layer of earth in which plants grow ▪ *The soil in this area is very fertile.* ▪ *poorly drained soils* **2** [U] *formal + literary* : the land of a particular country ▪ *their* **native soil** *[=the place they are originally from]* **3** [U] : a place where something begins or develops ▪ *Poor areas can be* **fertile soil** *for crime. [=there is often a lot of crime in poor areas]*

²soil *vb* [T/I] *formal* : to become dirty or make (something) dirty ▪ *The ink soiled* *my shirt.* ▪ *soiled diapers* ▪ *(figurative) He refused to* **soil his hands.** [=do anything dishonest or wrong]

soi·ree *or* **soi·rée** /swɑːˈreɪ/ *n [C]* : a formal party that is usually at night ▪ *a soiree at a fancy hotel*

so·journ /ˈsoʊˌdʒɚn/ *n [C] formal* : a period of time when you stay in a place as a traveler or guest ▪ *a two-week sojourn in the mountains* — **sojourn** *vb [I] formal* ▪ *We sojourned for two weeks at a resort.*

sol /ˈsoʊl/ *n [U] music* : the fifth note of a musical scale ▪ *do, re, mi, fa, sol, la, ti*

so·lace /ˈsɑːləs/ *n [U, singular] formal* : someone or something that gives comfort to a person who is sad, upset, etc. ▪ *Her presence was a great solace for/to me.* ▪ *We took/found solace in his words.*

so·lar /ˈsoʊlɚ/ *adj, always before a noun* **1** : of or relating to the sun ▪ *a solar eclipse* **2** : produced by or using the sun's light or heat ▪ *solar energy*

so·lar plex·us /ˈsoʊlɚˈplɛksəs/ *n* — **the solar plexus** : the area on the front of your body just below the ribs ▪ *He punched him in the solar plexus.*

solar system *n* **1 the solar system** : our sun and the planets that move around it **2** [C] : a star other than our sun and the planets that move around it

sold *past tense and past participle of* SELL

sol·der /ˈsɑːdɚ, *Brit* ˈsɒldə/ *n [U]* : a mixture of metals that is melted and used to join metal parts together — **solder** *vb [T]* ▪ *She solders wires* [=uses solder to attach wires] *onto circuit boards.*

¹sol·dier /ˈsoʊldʒɚ/ *n [C]* : a member of an army ▪ *Many soldiers were wounded in combat.* ▪ *British/German soldiers* — **sol·dier·ly** /ˈsoʊldʒɚli/ *adj* ▪ *soldierly virtues*

²soldier *vb* — **soldier on** [*phrasal vb*] : to continue to do something or to try to achieve something even though it is difficult ▪ *We soldiered on to the end.*

sold–out /ˈsoʊldˈaʊt/ *adj* : having all the tickets sold completely ▪ *a sold-out concert*

¹sole /ˈsoʊl/ *adj, always before a noun* **1** : only or single ▪ *the sole owner/survivor* **2** : belonging only to the person or group specified ▪ *He has sole jurisdiction of the area.* — **sole·ly** /ˈsoʊlli/ *adv* ▪ *You will be held solely responsible for any damage.* ▪ *She did not write solely* [=just, only] *for money.*

²sole *n* **1** [C] **a** : the bottom part of the foot **b** : the part of a shoe, boot, etc., that touches the ground ▪ *thick rubber soles* **2** [C/U] : a type of ocean fish that is eaten as food ▪ *fillet of sole*

soled /ˈsoʊld/ *adj, of a shoe* : having a particular type of sole ▪ *thick-soled boots*

sol·emn /ˈsɑːləm/ *adj* **1** : very serious or formal in manner, behavior, or expression ▪ *a solemn occasion/voice* **2** : sad and serious ▪ *A solemn crowd gathered around the grave.* **3** : done or made sincerely ▪ *a solemn oath/vow* — **sol·em·ni·ty** /səˈlɛmnəti/ *n [U] formal* — **sol·emn·ly** *adv*

so·lic·it /səˈlɪsət/ *vb, formal* **1 a** [T/I] : to ask for (money, help, etc.) from people, companies, etc. ▪ *The organization is soliciting (for) donations.* **b** [T] : to ask (a

person or group) for money, help, etc. ▪ *special interest groups that solicit Congress for funds* **2** [T] : to offer to have sex with (someone) in return for money ▪ *prostitutes soliciting customers* — **so·lic·i·ta·tion** /səˌlɪsəˈteɪʃən/ *n [C/U] formal* ▪ *solicitations for donations* — **so·lic·it·ing** *n [U]* ▪ *No soliciting is allowed.*

so·lic·i·tor /səˈlɪsətɚ/ *n [C]* **1** *US* : a person whose job involves trying to persuade people to buy things, donate money, etc. **2** : a lawyer in Britain who assists people in legal matters and who can represent people in lower courts of law **3** *US* : a chief law officer of a city, town, or government department

solicitor general *n [C]* : a law officer who assists an attorney general

so·lic·i·tous /səˈlɪsətəs/ *adj, formal* : showing concern or care for someone's health, happiness, etc. ▪ *I appreciated his solicitous inquiry about my health.* — **so·lic·i·tous·ly** *adv* — **so·lic·i·tude** /səˈlɪsəˌtuːd, *Brit* səˈlɪsəˌtjuːd/ *n [U] formal* ▪ *He expressed solicitude for my health.*

¹sol·id /ˈsɑːləd/ *adj* **1** : firm or hard ▪ *When ice melts, it passes from a solid to a liquid form.* ▪ *I was glad to get off the plane/boat and back on solid ground.* ▪ *The pond was frozen solid.* **2** : not hollow ▪ *a solid rubber ball* **3 a** *always before a noun* : made entirely from the specified material ▪ *The ring is solid gold.* **b** : consisting only of the color specified or only of one color ▪ *She wore a striped skirt with a solid shirt.* **4** : having no breaks, spaces, or pauses ▪ *a solid line* ▪ *We talked for three solid hours.* ▪ *(figurative) The hotel is booked solid through fall.* **5 a** : good and able to be trusted to do or provide what is needed ▪ *a good, solid player/performance* **b** : having a strong basis : good and dependable ▪ *solid advice/evidence* ▪ *a solid alibi/reason* ▪ *The company is (as) solid as a rock.* [=it is in very good condition] **6** : strong and well-made ▪ *solid furniture* **7** *geometry* : having length, width, and height ▪ *a solid geometric figure* — **sol·id·i·ty** /səˈlɪdəti/ *n [U]* — **sol·id·ly** *adv* — **sol·id·ness** *n [U]*

²solid *n* **1** [C] : a solid substance : a substance that is not a gas or a liquid **2** [C] *geometry* : an object that has length, width, and height **3** [*plural*] : foods that are not liquid ▪ *She couldn't eat solids after the surgery.*

sol·i·dar·i·ty /ˌsɑːləˈderəti/ *n [U]* : a feeling of unity between people who have the same interests, goals, etc. ▪ *national solidarity*

so·lid·i·fy /səˈlɪdəˌfaɪ/ *vb* **-fies; -fied; -fy·ing** [T/I] **1** : to make (something) solid or hard or to become solid or hard ▪ *Hot wax solidifies as it cools.* **2** : to make (a plan, project, etc.) stronger and more certain or to become stronger and more certain ▪ *The findings helped to solidify our position.* — **so·lid·i·fi·ca·tion** /səˌlɪdəfəˈkeɪʃən/ *n [U]*

so·lil·o·quy /səˈlɪləkwi/ *n, pl* **-quies** [C/U] : a long speech that a character in a play makes to an audience

sol·i·taire /ˈsɑːləˌteɚ/ *n* **1** [U] *chiefly US*

: a card game that is played by one person 2 [C] : a single jewel that is set alone in a piece of jewelry • *a diamond solitaire bracelet*

sol·i·tary /ˈsɑːləˌteri, *Brit* ˈsɒlətri/ *adj* 1 a : without anyone or anything else • *a solitary traveler* • *I couldn't hear a single, solitary word of what he said.* b : done by a person who is alone • *a solitary walk on the beach* 2 : separate from other people or things • *a solitary house on top of a hill* 3 : tending to live or spend time alone • *a solitary man/creature*

solitary confinement *n* [U] : the state of being kept alone in a prison cell away from other prisoners • *He spent a month in solitary confinement.*

sol·i·tude /ˈsɑːləˌtuːd, *Brit* ˈsɒləˌtjuːd/ *n* [U] : a state or situation in which you are alone usually because you want to be • *the peace and solitude of the woods*

¹**so·lo** /ˈsoʊloʊ/ *n, pl* **-los** [C] : a piece of music that is performed by one singer or musician • *a guitar solo* — **so·lo·ist** /ˈsoʊloʊwɪst/ *n* [C]

²**solo** *adj, always before a noun* 1 : done without another person • *a student pilot's first solo flight* 2 : involving or done by a single performer instead of a group • *a solo career/performance* — **solo** *adv* • *She is traveling solo.* [=by herself]

³**solo** *vb* **-los; -loed; -lo·ing** [I] 1 : to perform a piece of music without another singer or musician • *She solos during the concert.* 2 : to fly an airplane without an instructor

sol·stice /ˈsɑːlstəs/ *n* [C] : one of the two times during the year when the sun is farthest north or south of the equator ✧ The **summer solstice** occurs around June 22 and the **winter solstice** occurs around December 22.

sol·u·ble /ˈsɑːljəbəl/ *adj* 1 : capable of being dissolved in a liquid • *soluble fiber* 2 *formal* : capable of being solved or explained • *a soluble problem* — **sol·u·bil·i·ty** /ˌsɑːljəˈbɪləti/ *n* [U]

so·lu·tion /səˈluːʃən/ *n* 1 a [C] : something that solves a problem • *There is no simple solution to the crisis.* b [U] : the act of solving something • *a problem that has resisted solution* [=that no one has been able to solve] 2 [C] a : a correct answer to a problem, puzzle, etc. • *figuring out the solution to a math problem* b : an explanation for something that is difficult to understand • *find a solution to a crime/mystery* 3 a [C/U] : a liquid in which something has been dissolved • *a solution of baking soda and water* b [U] : the act or process of dissolving a solid, liquid, or gas in a liquid • *the solution of sucrose in water*

solve /ˈsɑːlv/ *vb* **solved; solv·ing** [T] 1 : to find a way to deal with and end (a problem) • *We are working to solve the problem.* 2 a : to find the correct answer to (something) • *She solved the riddle.* b : to find the correct explanation for (something) • *The mystery/crime/case has been solved.* — **solv·able** /ˈsɑːlvəbəl/ *adj* — **solv·er** *n* [C]

¹**sol·vent** /ˈsɑːlvənt/ *adj* : able to pay debts • *He couldn't stay solvent after losing his business.* — **sol·ven·cy** /ˈsɑːlvənsi/ *n* [U] • *measuring a borrower's solvency*

²**solvent** *n* [C/U] *technical* : a liquid substance that is used to dissolve another substance • *turpentine and other solvents*

som·ber (*US*) *or Brit* **som·bre** /ˈsɑːmbə/ *adj, formal* 1 : very sad and serious • *a somber mood* 2 : having a dull or dark color • *a somber suit* — **som·ber·ly** *adv* — **som·ber·ness** *n* [U]

som·bre·ro /sɑmˈbreroʊ/ *n, pl* **-ros** [C] : a type of hat with a very wide brim that is often worn in Mexico

¹**some** /ˈsʌm, səm/ *adj, always before a noun* 1 — used to refer to a person or thing that is not known, named, or specified • *Some birds cannot fly.* • *Some guy called while you were out.* • *For some reason, the lights went out.* 2 a : of an unspecified amount or number • *Can I have some raisins/water?* b : of a fairly large amount or number • *We met some years ago.* 3 *informal* a — used to express approval • *That was some game!* b — used to express disapproval, disappointment, etc. • *You have some nerve* [=a lot of nerve] *to say that!* • *You forgot to invite him? Some friend you are!* [=you're not a good friend]

²**some** /ˈsʌm/ *pron* : an unspecified amount or number of people or things • *Some of the apples are bruised.* • *Most birds can fly but some cannot.* • *Some* [=some people] *say that patience is a virtue.* • *I'm making coffee; do you want some?* — **and then some** *informal* : and more in addition to that • *I ran a mile and then some.*

³**some** /ˈsʌm, ˌsʌm/ *adv* 1 — used to indicate that a number is approximate • *Some 80 people* [=about 80 people] *attended.* 2 : to an unspecified amount or degree • (*US, informal*) *He needs to grow up some before he can live on his own.* • *Would you like some more ham?*

¹**some·body** /ˈsʌmˌbʌdi/ *pron* : a person who is not known, named, or specified • *Somebody left you a message.* • *Somebody has to do it.* • *They gave the job to somebody else.*

²**somebody** *n, pl* **-bod·ies** [C] : an important person — usually singular • *I want to be somebody when I grow up.*

some·day /ˈsʌmˌdeɪ/ *adv* : at some time in the future • *Someday we'll buy a house.* • *someday next week*

some·how /ˈsʌmˌhaʊ/ *adv* : in a way that is not known or certain • *Somehow* (*or other/another*) *we got lost.*

some·one /ˈsʌmˌwʌn/ *pron* : ¹**SOMEBODY** • *Someone left you a message.*

some·place /ˈsʌmˌpleɪs/ *adv, US* : **SOMEWHERE** • *Should we eat here or go someplace else?*

som·er·sault /ˈsʌmɚˌsɑːlt/ *n* [C] : a forward or backward movement of your body on the ground or in the air that is made by bringing your feet over your head • *She turned/performed/did a somersault.* — **somersault** *vb* [I] • *The diver somersaulted in midair.*

¹**some·thing** /ˈsʌmˌθɪn/ *pron* 1 : a thing that is not known, named, or specified • *Something came in the mail for you.* • *I*

have something to tell you. ▪ *Her job has something to do with* [=it relates to] *computers.* ▪ *Is there something* [=anything] *wrong?* ▪ *Do you want pizza or something else?* [=or a different thing] ▪ *(informal) Can I get you a soda or something?* [=or a different thing] ▪ *I got you a little something* [=a small or inexpensive thing] *for your birthday.* **2** : a person or thing that is important or worth noticing ▪ *That waterfall is really something!* ▪ *He went to college to make something of himself.* [=become successful] **3** : an amount that is more than a specified number ▪ *His friends are all twentysomething.* [=between the ages of 20 and 29] **4** — used to make a statement or description less forceful or definite ▪ *He is something of an expert.* [=he is an expert to some degree] — **something else** *informal* : a person or thing that is special or impressive ▪ *She really is something else.* — **start something** see ¹START

²**something** *adv* **1** : somewhat or slightly ▪ *He looks something like his father.* **2** *informal* — used before an adjective to add emphasis ▪ *He snores something awful/terrible.* [=very loudly] — **something fierce** see FIERCE

¹**some·time** /ˈsʌmˌtaɪm/ *adv* **1** : at an unspecified time in the future ▪ *We should get together sometime (soon).* **2** : at an unspecified or unknown time in the past ▪ *A burglar broke in sometime during the night.*

²**sometime** *adj, always before a noun* **1** *formal* — used to say what someone or something was in the past ▪ *the sometime* [=former] *prime minister* **2** *US* — used to say what someone sometimes does or is ▪ *He is a pianist and sometime teacher of music.*

some·times /ˈsʌmˌtaɪmz/ *adv* : at certain times : OCCASIONALLY ▪ *Sometimes I take the bus to work.* ▪ *We all make mistakes sometimes.*

some·way /ˈsʌmˌweɪ/ *adv* : SOMEHOW ▪ *We'll do it someway.*

¹**some·what** /ˈsʌmˌwʌt/ *adv* : in a small amount or degree ▪ *He was somewhat taller than I expected.*

²**somewhat** *pron* — used to make a statement or description less forceful or definite ▪ *We have somewhat of a problem.* [=we have a slight/minor problem]

¹**some·where** /ˈsʌmˌweɚ/ *adv* **1** : in, at, or to a place not known, named, or specified ▪ *She lives somewhere in the city.* ▪ *Do you want to go somewhere else?* **2** : close to a specified number, time, or amount ▪ *We left somewhere around nine o'clock.* ▪ *Somewhere between 300 and 500 people attended.* — **get somewhere** *informal* : to make progress ▪ *The work has been slow, but we're finally getting somewhere.*

²**somewhere** *n* [U] : a place not known, named, or specified ▪ *looking for somewhere to park the car*

son /ˈsʌn/ *n* **1** [C] : a male child ▪ *They have two sons and a daughter.* ▪ *(figurative) a native son of* [=a boy/man who is from] *our town* — sometimes used to address a younger man or boy ▪ *Slow*

down, son. **2** *the Son* : Jesus Christ ▪ *the Father, the Son, and the Holy Spirit*

so·nar /ˈsoʊˌnɑɚ/ *n* [U] : a device used for finding things that are underwater by using sound waves

so·na·ta /səˈnɑːtə/ *n* [C] *music* : a piece of music written for one or two instruments that has usually three or four large sections ▪ *a piano/cello sonata*

song /ˈsɑːŋ/ *n* **1** [C] : a short piece of music with words that are sung ▪ *He sang a love song.* **2** [U] : the act of singing ▪ *She burst/broke into song.* [=began singing] **3** [C/U] : a series of musical sounds that are produced by a bird or an animal (such as a whale) ▪ *the song of a sparrow* — **for a song** *chiefly US, informal* : for a very small amount of money ▪ *This old car can be bought/had for a song.*

song·bird /ˈsɑːŋˌbɚd/ *n* [C] : a bird that produces a series of musical sounds

song·writ·er /ˈsɑːŋˌraɪtɚ/ *n* [C] : a person who writes the words or music to songs — **song·writ·ing** /ˈsɑːŋˌraɪtɪŋ/ *n* [U]

son·ic /ˈsɑːnɪk/ *adj, always before a noun* : of or relating to sound, sound waves, or the speed of sound ▪ *sonic waves*

sonic boom *n* [C] : a very loud noise that is produced when an aircraft travels faster than the speed of sound

son–in–law /ˈsʌnənˌlɑː/ *n, pl* **sons–in–law** /ˈsʌnzənˌlɑː/ [C] : the husband of your daughter

son·net /ˈsɑːnət/ *n* [C] : a poem made up of 14 lines that rhyme in a fixed pattern

son of a gun *n, pl* **sons of guns** *US, informal* **1** [C] : a person (especially a man) or thing that you are annoyed with ▪ *That son of a gun never called me.* **2** — used to express mild surprise, disappointment, etc. ▪ *Son of a gun, I lost a button.*

sono·gram /ˈsɑːnəˌgræm/ *n* [C] *US, technical* : ULTRASOUND 2b ▪ *The sonogram showed that the fetus was developing normally.*

so·no·rous /ˈsɑːnərəs/ *adj, formal* : having a sound that is deep, loud, and pleasant ▪ *a deep, sonorous voice* — **so·nor·i·ty** /səˈnɔːrəti/ *n, pl* **-ties** [C/U]

soon /ˈsuːn/ *adv* **1 a** : at a time that is not long from now ▪ *I'll see you soon.* ▪ *The soonest I can get there is Friday.* ▪ *We'll find out soon enough.* ▪ *We need to fix this problem sooner rather than later.* [=we need to fix it soon] **b** : in a short time after something happens ▪ *We soon realized that it was a joke.* ▪ *She found a job soon after graduation.* ▪ *Call me as soon as* [=call me immediately when] *you get there.* ▪ *I had no sooner opened the door when the phone rang.* [=the phone rang immediately after I opened the door] ▪ *I asked for more copies. No sooner said than done.* [=immediately gave me more copies] **2** : QUICKLY ▪ *How soon can you finish the job?* ▪ *I'll get there as soon as I can.* ▪ *I will let you know as soon as possible.* ▪ *The sooner* [=more quickly] *we get the pipe fixed, the better.* = *We need to get the pipe fixed, the sooner the better.* — **sooner or later** : at an unspecified time in the future

: EVENTUALLY ▪ *Sooner or later, we'll have to tell her the truth.* — **too soon** : before the time that is proper, preferred, or specified ▪ *It's too soon to know what will happen.* ▪ *The plumber arrived, and not a moment too soon.* [=just in time] — **would sooner** or **would just as soon** — used to indicate what you want or prefer to do, have, etc. ▪ *He would sooner* [=would rather] *lose everything than admit that he was wrong.* ▪ *I'd just as soon stay home.*

soot /'sʊt/ *n* [U] : a black powder that is formed when wood, coal, etc., is burned — **sooty** /'sʊti/ *adj* **soot·i·er**; **-est** ▪ *the worker's sooty hands*

soothe /'su:ð/ *vb* **soothed**; **sooth·ing** [T] **1** : to cause (someone) to be calmer, less angry, etc. ▪ *She sang to soothe the baby.* **2 a** : to cause (a part of the body) to feel better ▪ *This cream soothes aching muscles.* **b** : to cause (pain) to go away or become less severe ▪ *Nothing can soothe their pain.*

soothing *adj* : producing feelings of comfort or relief ▪ *a soothing massage* ▪ *soothing words* — **sooth·ing·ly** *adv*

sooth·say·er /'su:θ,sejə/ *n* [C] *old-fashioned* : someone who makes predictions about the future

¹sop /'sɑ:p/ *n* [C] *disapproving* : something that is done or given to someone in order to prevent trouble, gain support, etc. ▪ *Critics say that the proposed tax cut is a sop to wealthy voters.*

²sop *vb* **sopped**; **sop·ping** — **sop up** [*phrasal verb*] **sop up (a liquid)** or **sop (a liquid) up** : to remove (a liquid) from a surface by using soft paper, bread, etc. ▪ *He sopped up the gravy with bread.*

soph. *abbr* sophomore

so·phis·ti·cat·ed /sə'fɪstə,keɪtəd/ *adj* **1 a** : having or showing a lot of experience and knowledge about the world and about culture, art, etc. ▪ *sophisticated tastes/travelers* **b** : attractive to fashionable or sophisticated people ▪ *a sophisticated restaurant* **2** : highly developed and complex ▪ *sophisticated technologies* — **so·phis·ti·cate** /sə'fɪstɪkət/ *n* [C] ▪ *urban sophisticates* [=sophisticated urban people] — **so·phis·ti·ca·tion** /sə,fɪstə'keɪʃən/ *n* [U] ▪ *I admire her style and sophistication.*

soph·ist·ry /'sɑ:fəstri/ *n* [U] *formal* : the use of reasoning or arguments that sound correct but are actually false

soph·o·more /'sɑ:f,mooə/ *n* [C] *US* : a student in the second year of high school or college ▪ *She's a sophomore.* = *She's in her sophomore year.*

soph·o·mor·ic /,sɑ:f'mɔrɪk/ *adj, US, disapproving* : foolish and immature ▪ *sophomoric behavior/jokes*

sop·o·rif·ic /,sɑ:pə'rɪfɪk/ *adj, formal* : causing a person to need sleep ▪ *a soporific drug*

sop·ping /'sɑ:pɪŋ/ *adj, informal* : completely wet ▪ *His clothes were sopping from the rain.* ▪ *a sopping wet* sponge

sop·py /'sɑ:pi/ *adj* **sop·pi·er**; **-est 1** *US* : very wet ▪ *soppy towels* **2** *Brit, informal* : sad or romantic in a foolish or exaggerated way ▪ *soppy* [=(US) *sappy*] *love songs*

¹so·pra·no /sə'prænoʊ, sə'prɑ:noʊ/ *adj, always before a noun* **1** : relating to the highest female singing voice ▪ *the soprano tones* **2** : having a high sound range ▪ *a soprano saxophone*

²soprano *n, pl* **-nos** [C] **1** : the highest voice part in a singing group **2** : the highest female singing voice or a person with this voice ▪ *an opera soprano*

sor·bet /soʊ'beɪ/ *n* [C/U] : a frozen sweet dessert that is made usually from fruit or fruit juices ▪ *a raspberry sorbet*

sor·cer·er /'soəsərə/ *n* [C] : a person who practices sorcery

sor·cer·ess /'soəsərəs/ *n* [C] : a woman who practices sorcery

sor·cery /'soəsəri/ *n* [U] : the use of magical powers that are obtained through evil spirits : WITCHCRAFT

sor·did /'soədəd/ *adj, formal* **1** : very bad or dishonest ▪ *sordid business deals* **2** : very dirty ▪ *sordid living conditions*

¹sore /'soə/ *adj* **sor·er**; **-est 1** : feeling or affected by pain ▪ *My back is sore.* ▪ *The patient has a sore throat.* **2** *always before a noun* : causing emotional pain or distress ▪ *That's a sore subject.* **3** *chiefly US, informal* : angry or upset ▪ *She is sore at me.* ▪ *He's a sore loser.* [=he becomes very upset or angry when he loses] — **a sight for sore eyes** see ¹SIGHT — **stick/stand out like a sore thumb** *informal* : to be very noticeable in usually a bad way ▪ *I stuck out like a sore thumb at the party.* — **sore·ness** *n* [U]

²sore *n* [C] : a sore or painful spot on the body ▪ *He has a sore on his lip.*

sore·ly /'soəli/ *adv* : very much ▪ *You will be sorely missed.*

sor·ghum /'soəgəm/ *n* [U] : a kind of tropical grass that is grown for food

so·ror·i·ty /sə'rorəti/ *n, pl* **-ties** [C] : an organization of female students at a U.S. college ▪ *She pledged/joined a sorority.*

sor·rel /'sorəl/ *n* **1** [C] : a reddish-brown horse ▪ *a sorrel mare* **2** [U] : a plant that has sour juice and that is used in cooking

sor·row /'sɑroʊ/ *n* **1** [U] : a feeling of sadness or grief caused especially by the loss of someone or something ▪ *I felt sorrow at/over the death of my friend.* **2** [C] : a cause of grief or sadness ▪ *a life filled with joys and sorrows* ▪ *He went to the bar to drown his sorrows.* [=to forget about the things that were making him sad by getting drunk] — **sor·row·ful** /'sɑrəfəl/ *adj* ▪ *sorrowful eyes* — **sor·row·ful·ly** *adv*

sor·ry /'sɑri/ *adj* **sor·ri·er**; **-est 1** : feeling sorrow or regret ▪ *I'm sorry if/that I offended you.* ▪ *I'm sorry for your loss.* ▪ *She was crying and he felt sorry for her.* [=he felt sympathy for her] ▪ *It's not necessary to lock the door, but (it's) better (to be) safe than sorry.* [=it's good to be cautious] **2 a** — used to express polite regret ▪ *Sorry, but I disagree.* **b** — used to introduce disappointing or bad news in a polite way ▪ *I'm sorry, but we can't come.* **c** — used as an apology for a minor fault or offense (such as bumping into someone) ▪ *Sorry. I didn't see you standing there.* ▪ *I forgot to buy the milk.* **Sorry**

about that. [=I'm sorry] **d** — used as a polite way of asking someone to repeat something spoken ▪ *Sorry? I missed what you said.* **3** *always before a noun* : very bad or poor ▪ *a sorry excuse* **b** : causing feelings of disappointment or pity ▪ *I dragged my sorry self out of bed.*

¹**sort** /ˈsoɚt/ *n* **1** [C] : a group of people or things that have some shared quality ▪ *What sort of car do you drive?* **2** [*singular*] : a person of a particular type ▪ *He's not a bad sort.* **3** [C] *technical* : the act of separating things and putting them in a particular order : the act of sorting things ▪ *The program did a numeric sort of the data.* — **all sorts of** : a large variety of (things or people) ▪ *The movie appeals to all sorts of people.* — **of sorts** or **of a sort** : in some ways but not entirely or exactly ▪ *It was a vacation of sorts.* — **of the sort** : like the person or thing mentioned ▪ *"You said you didn't like him." "I said nothing of the sort."* [=I didn't say that at all] — **out of sorts 1** : somewhat angry or unhappy ▪ *My boss is out of sorts today.* **2** : somewhat ill ▪ *I'm feeling a little out of sorts.* — **sort of** *informal* : to some small degree : slightly or somewhat ▪ *I feel sort of foolish.* ▪ *"Did you enjoy the movie?" "Sort of."*

²**sort** *vb* [T] **1** : to separate and put (people or things) in a particular order ▪ *sorting data/mail* ▪ *I sorted out the mess in the attic.* **2** *Brit, informal* : to deal with (something or someone) in a successful way ▪ *We need to get this problem sorted.* [=sorted out] — **sort out** [*phrasal vb*] **sort (something or someone) out** or **sort out (something or someone) 1** : to understand or find (something) by thinking ▪ *I'm trying to sort out a way to do it.* **2** : to find an answer or solution for (something) ▪ *He's getting his problems sorted out.* **3** ◆ If something *sorts itself out*, it stops being a problem without anyone having to do anything. ▪ *I'm hoping things will sort themselves out.* **4** : to solve the problems of (someone) ▪ *I just need a little more time to sort myself out.* **5** *Brit, informal* : to deal with (someone who is causing problems) in a forceful way ▪ *I told my brother they were bullying me, and he promised to sort them out (for me).* — **sort through** [*phrasal vb*] : to look at things and put them in a particular order ▪ *He sorted through the papers.* — **sort·er** *n* [C]

sorta /ˈsoɚtə/ — used in writing to represent the sound of the phrase *sort of* when it is spoken quickly ▪ *"It's sorta cold out," she said.*

sor·tie /ˈsoɚti/ *n* [C] : a sudden attack

SOS /ˌɛs.oʊˈɛs/ *n* [*singular*] : a signal used by ships and airplanes to call for help

so-so /ˈsoʊˈsoʊ/ *adj, informal* : neither very good nor very bad : fair or average ▪ *The reviews were only so-so.* ▪ *a so-so performance*

soubriquet *variant spelling of* SOBRIQUET

souf·flé /suˈfleɪ/ *n* [C/U] : a food that is made with eggs, flour, and other ingredients and that is baked until it becomes very light and fluffy ▪ *cheese soufflés*

sought *past tense and past participle of* SEEK

sought–after *adj* : wanted by many people and hard to get or find ▪ *the most sought-after artists*

soul /ˈsoʊl/ *n* **1** [C] **a** : the spiritual part of a person that is believed to give life to the body ▪ *the souls of the dead* **b** : a person's deeply felt moral and emotional nature ▪ *the guilt that he felt in the inner recesses of his soul* **2** [U] : the ability of a person to feel sympathy for others, to appreciate beauty, etc. ▪ *She has no soul.* **3** [C] : a human being ▪ *a brave/gentle soul* ▪ *There wasn't a soul* [=there wasn't anyone] *in sight.* **4** [U] : a quality that gives emotional force to a performance, a work of art, etc. ▪ *His music lacks soul.* **5** [U] : SOUL MUSIC ▪ *My favorite types of music are jazz and soul.* **6** [*singular*] : the most important part of something that makes it effective, valuable, etc. ▪ *Our employees are the heart and soul of our company.* — **body and soul** *see* BODY — **sell your soul (to the devil)** *see* SELL — **soul·less** /ˈsoʊlləs/ *adj*

soul food *n* [U] : the type of food traditionally eaten by African-Americans in the southern U.S.

soul·ful /ˈsoʊlfəl/ *adj* : full of or expressing feeling or emotion ▪ *soulful music/eyes* — **soul·ful·ly** *adv*

soul mate *n* [C] **1** : a person who completely understands you and is perfectly suited to be in a loving relationship with you ▪ *She married her soul mate.* **2** : a person who has the same beliefs and opinons as another person ▪ *They are ideological soul mates.*

soul music *n* [U] : a popular style of music that was created by African-Americans

soul–search·ing /ˈsoʊlˌsɚtʃɪŋ/ *n* [U] : the activity of thinking seriously about your feelings and beliefs in order to make a decision or to understand the reasons for your own behavior ▪ *I needed to do some soul-searching.*

¹**sound** /ˈsaʊnd/ *n* **1** [C/U] : something that is heard ▪ *the sound of thunder/laughter* ▪ *a loud, buzzing sound* [=noise] ▪ *devices used to record sound* **2** [U] : the speech, music, etc., that is heard as part of a broadcast, film, or recording ▪ *The film was good, but the sound was poor.* **3** [C] : the particular musical style of an individual, a group, or an area ▪ *I like the band's sound.* **4** [U] : the idea that is suggested when something is said or described ▪ *"The doctor wants to do more tests." "I don't like the sound of that."* [=that sounds bad/serious] — **By/from the sound of it,** *you may have poison ivy.* **5** [C] : a long and narrow area of water that connects two larger areas ▪ *Long Island Sound* — **sound·less** /ˈsaʊndləs/ *adj*

²**sound** *vb* **1 a** [T] : to cause (something) to make a sound or to be heard or make ▪ *sound a trumpet/horn* **b** [T] : to make (something) known by making a sound ▪ *They sounded the alarm.* **c** [I] : to make a sound ▪ *The buzzer sounded.* **2** [*linking*]

vb] : to seem to be something when heard ▪ *You sound tired.* : to seem to be something when heard about ▪ *Their plan sounds good to me.* ▪ *It sounds to me as if they won't be coming.* ▪ *The movie sounds as though it might be good.* ▪ *That sounds like a good idea.* **3** [*T*] *technical* : to measure the depth of the water in a lake, ocean, etc. — **sound like 1** : to have a voice that is like the voice of (someone else) ▪ *Your brother sounds just like you.* **2** : to say something that is like what is commonly said by (someone else) ▪ *You sound just like Mom when you say that.* — **sound off** [*phrasal vb*] **1** : to say your opinions in a very direct and often angry way ▪ *She sounded off about the unequal pay raises.* **2** *US* : to count out loud the steps you take while marching ▪ *The troops were sounding off during their exercises.* — **sound out** [*phrasal vb*] **1 sound (something) out** *or* **sound out (something)** : PRONOUNCE 1a ▪ *Sound out each syllable of the word.* **2 sound (someone or something) out** *or* **sound out (someone or something)** : to try to find out the opinions of someone by asking questions ▪ *polls that sound out public opinion*

³**sound** *adj* **1 a** : in good condition ▪ *The bridge is structurally sound.* **b** : in good health ▪ *a sound body* ▪ *(law) He was found to be of sound mind.* [=*sane*] **2** : showing good judgment ▪ *a sound argument* ▪ *sound reasoning/advice* **3** always before a noun : complete or thorough ▪ *She has a sound understanding of the system's structure.* **4** : deep and restful ▪ *a sound sleep* ▪ *a sound sleeper* [=someone who sleeps deeply] — **sound·ly** /ˈsaʊndli/ *adv* ▪ *I slept soundly.* ▪ *an argument soundly based on logic* ▪ *We were soundly* [=*thoroughly*] *beaten/defeated.* — **sound·ness** *n* /ˈsaʊndnəs/ *n* [*U*]

⁴**sound** *adv, of sleep* : deeply and completely ▪ *He was sound asleep.*

sound barrier *n* — **the sound barrier** : the large increase in air resistance that occurs as an aircraft nears the speed of sound ▪ *a plane that is able to break the sound barrier* [=to travel faster than the speed of sound]

sound bite *n* [*C*] : a short recorded statement that is broadcast on a TV or radio news program ▪ *sound bites from campaign speeches*

sounding board *n* [*C*] : a person or group with whom you discuss ideas to see if the ideas are good ▪ *My friend is my sounding board for new ideas.*

sound·proof /ˈsaʊndˌpruːf/ *adj* : not allowing sound to enter or leave ▪ *a soundproof room/wall* — **soundproof** *vb* [*T*] ▪ *soundproof a room*

sound system *n* [*C*] : equipment that is used to play music through speakers

sound·track /ˈsaʊndˌtræk/ *n* [*C*] : the sounds and especially the music recorded for a movie ▪ *a song on the movie's soundtrack*

sound wave *n* [*C*] : a wave that is formed when a sound moves through the air

¹**soup** /ˈsuːp/ *n* [*C/U*] : a food made by cooking vegetables, meat, or fish in a large amount of liquid ▪ *a delicious (bowl of) chicken soup*

²**soup** *vb* — **soup up** [*phrasal vb*] **soup (something) up** *or* **soup up (something)** *informal* : to increase the power of (something) ▪ *soup up a car's engine*

soup-çon /ˈsuːpˌsɑːn/ *n* [*C*] : a small amount of something ▪ *a soupçon of salt*

soup kitchen *n* [*C*] : a place that gives meals to poor people

soupy /ˈsuːpi/ *adj* **soup·i·er; -est 1** : resembling soup ▪ *The gravy is too soupy.* **2** *informal* : very foggy or cloudy ▪ *soupy weather*

¹**sour** /ˈsawɚ/ *adj* **1** : having an acid taste that is like the taste of a lemon ▪ *a sour apple/pickle/taste* **2** : having the unpleasant taste or smell of food that is no longer fresh ▪ *a sour odor* ▪ *The milk had turned/gone sour.* **3** : unpleasant or unfriendly ▪ *He made a sour face.* ▪ *Their relationship ended on a sour note.* [=ended unpleasantly] **4** *informal* : bad or wrong ▪ *Their investment went sour.* — **sour on** *informal* : having a bad opinion of (something) ▪ *She was sour on politics.* — **sour·ly** *adv* — **sour·ness** *n* [*U*]

²**sour** *n* [*C*] : an alcoholic drink that has a sour taste ▪ *a whiskey sour*

³**sour** *vb* **1** [*I*] *of food* : to lose freshness and become sour ▪ *The milk soured.* **2** [*T/I*] : to become or cause (someone or something) to become unpleasant or unfriendly ▪ *Her disposition has soured.* ▪ *The experience soured him.* **3** [*T*] : to make (something good) less pleasant or enjoyable ▪ *The team's victory was soured by injuries.* — **sour on** [*phrasal vb*] **sour on** *or* **sour (someone) on** *US* : to stop or cause (someone) to stop liking or being interested in (something) ▪ *Investors have soured on (buying) the company's stock.*

source /ˈsoɚs/ *n* [*C*] **1** : someone or something that provides what is wanted or needed ▪ *a town's water/power source* ▪ *His job is the family's main source of income.* **2** : the cause of something (such as a problem) ▪ *The delays are a source of concern.* **3** : a person, book, etc., that gives information ▪ *A government source spoke to the press today.* ▪ *a reference source* **4** : the beginning of a stream or river of water ▪ *the source of the Nile*

sour cream *n* [*U*] : a thick cream that has a sour flavor ▪ *He put sour cream on his baked potato.* — called also *(Brit)* **soured cream**

sour·dough /ˈsawɚˌdoʊ/ *n* [*U*] : a type of dough that has a slightly sour taste ▪ *sourdough bread*

sour grapes *n* [*plural*] *informal* : unfair criticism that comes from someone who is disappointed about not getting something ▪ *His remarks are nothing but sour grapes.*

south /ˈsaʊθ/ *n* **1** [*U*] : the direction that is to your right when you are facing the rising sun ▪ *The town is 20 miles to the south (of here).* ▪ *The wind blew from the south.* **2 the south** *or* **the South** : regions or countries south of a certain point ▪ *The birds migrate from the South.*; *especially* : the southern part of the U.S.

The American Civil War was between the North and the South. — **down south** *informal* : in or to the southern part of a country or region • *She spent a few years down south.* — **south** *adj* • *South America* • *a south wind* [=a wind that comes from the south] — **south** *adv* • *Turn south onto Elm Street.* • *(US, figurative, informal) The company's profits have gone/headed south.* [=gone into a worse state]

south·bound /ˈsaʊθˌbaʊnd/ *adj* : going or heading south • *a southbound train/highway*

south·east /ˌsaʊθˈiːst/ *n* **1** [U] : the direction between south and east **2** *the* **southeast** *or the* **Southeast** : the southeastern part of a country or region; *especially* : the southeastern part of the U.S. — **southeast** *adj* • *southeast Europe* • *a southeast wind* [=a wind that comes from the southeast] — **south·east** *adv* • *We headed southeast.* — **south·east·ern** /ˌsaʊθˈiːstən/ *adj* • *the southeastern corner of the state*

south·east·er·ly /ˌsaʊθˈiːstəli/ *adj* **1** : located in or moving toward the southeast • *sailing in a southeasterly direction* **2** : blowing from the southeast • *southeasterly winds*

south·er·ly /ˈsʌðəli/ *adj* **1** : located in or moving toward the south • *sailing in a southerly direction* **2** : blowing from the south • *a southerly wind*

south·ern /ˈsʌðən/ *adj* **1** : located in or toward the south • *southern Spain* **2 a** : of or relating to the south • *southern cities* **b** **Southern** : of or relating to the people born, raised, or living in the southeastern U.S. • *A Southern accent*

south·ern·er *or* **South·ern·er** /ˈsʌðənə/ *n* [C] : a person born, raised, or living in the south

south·ern·most /ˈsʌðənˌmoʊst/ *adj* : furthest to the south • *the southernmost tip of the island*

south·paw /ˈsaʊθˌpɑː/ *n* [C] *informal* : someone who is left-handed; *especially* : a left-handed baseball pitcher or boxer

South Pole *n* — **the South Pole** : the most southern point of the Earth

south·ward /ˈsaʊθˌwəd/ *also chiefly Brit* **south·wards** /ˈsaʊθˌwədz/ *adv* : toward the south • *birds flying southward* — **southward** *adj*

south·west /ˌsaʊθˈwɛst/ *n* **1** [U] : the direction between south and west **2** *the* **southwest** *or the* **Southwest** : the southwestern part of a country or region; *especially* : the southwestern part of the U.S. • *These plants grow in the Southwest.* — **southwest** *adj* • *southwest France* • *a southwest wind* [=a wind blowing from the southwest] — **south·west** *adv* • *traveling southwest* — **south·west·ern** /ˌsaʊθˈwɛstən/ *adj* • *southwestern Arizona*

south·west·er·ly /ˌsaʊθˈwɛstəli/ *adj* **1** : located in or moving toward the southwest • *moving in a southwesterly direction* **2** : blowing from the southwest • *a southwesterly wind*

sou·ve·nir /ˌsuːvəˈnɪə/ *n* [C] : something that is kept as a reminder of a place you have visited, an event you have been to, etc. • *I kept my concert ticket stub as a souvenir (of the show).* • *a souvenir shop*

¹**sov·er·eign** /ˈsɑːvrən/ *n* [C] **1** *formal* : a king or queen • *a Spanish sovereign* **2** : a British gold coin that was used in the past

²**sovereign** *adj, formal* **1 a** : having unlimited power or authority • *a sovereign prince* **b** : not limited • *the sovereign power of a king* **2** : having the authority to govern itself • *a sovereign nation* **3** *US* : highest and most important • *a sovereign duty*

sov·er·eign·ty /ˈsɑːvrənti/ *n* [U] **1** : unlimited power over a country • *He claimed sovereignty over the nation.* **2** : a country's independent authority and the right to govern itself • *national sovereignty*

so·vi·et /ˈsoʊviˌɛt/ *n* **1** [C] : an elected council in the former U.S.S.R. **2** *Soviets* [*plural*] *chiefly US* : the people and especially the leaders of the former U.S.S.R. • *The plan was opposed by the Soviets.*

Soviet *adj* : of or relating to the former U.S.S.R. or its people • *the Soviet government*

¹**sow** /ˈsoʊ/ *vb* **sowed**; **sown** /ˈsoʊn/ *or* **sowed**; **sow·ing** [*T/I*] **1** : to plant seeds in an area of ground • *sowing (the fields with) corn* **2** [*T*] : to cause (fear, doubt, etc.) to affect many people • *Threats of war have sown fear* [=made many people afraid] *in the region.* • *sowing the seeds of suspicion/doubt* [=making people have suspicions/doubts] — **reap what you sow** see REAP — **sow your (wild) oats** : to have many sexual relationships particularly when you are young • *a young man who is sowing his wild oats* — **sow·er** /ˈsoʊə/ *n* [C]

²**sow** /ˈsaʊ/ *n* [C] : a fully grown female pig

soy /ˈsɔɪ/ *n* [U] *US* : soybeans and the food products that are made from soybeans • *the health benefits of soy* • *soy milk* [=a drink that resembles cow's milk but that is made from soybeans]

soya /ˈsɔjə/ *n* [U] *Brit* : SOY

soy·bean /ˈsɔɪˌbiːn/ *n* [C] *US* : the bean of an Asian plant that contains a large amount of protein and that is used as a food — called also *(Brit)* **soya bean**

soy sauce *n* [U] : a brown sauce that is made from soybeans and used especially in Chinese and Japanese cooking — called also *(Brit)* **soya sauce**

spa /ˈspɑː/ *n* [C] **1 a** : a place where people go to swim in, bathe in, or drink the water from a spring **b** : a place where people go to improve their health and appearance by exercising, relaxing, etc. **2** *US* : a bathtub in which a pump causes hot water and air bubbles to move around your body

¹**space** /ˈspeɪs/ *n* **1 a** [U] : the amount of an area, room, surface, etc., that is empty or available for your use • *the space behind the couch* • *Those boxes take up a lot of space.* • *Is there enough space on the disk to save the files?* **b** [C/U] : an area that is used or available for a specific purpose • *a parking space* • *storage space* **2 a** [C/U] : an empty area between things • *She has*

a space between her front teeth. • *There isn't much space between our houses.* **b** [*U, plural*] : an area of land with no buildings on it • *an area with a lot of open space* • *the wide open spaces of the western U.S.* **3** [*U*] : OUTER SPACE • *sent the satellite into space* • *space exploration* **4** [*U*] : the limitless area in which all things exist and move • *the movement of sound waves through space* **5** [*C*] : a period of time • *a short space of time* [=a short time] • *They finished in/within the space of an hour.* [=within an hour] **6** [*C/U*] **a** : a blank area separating written or printed words or lines • *There should be a space after the comma.* • *Let's leave more space between the paragraphs.* **b** : a blank part or section on a document where something can be written • *There is (a) space at the bottom for your phone number.* **7** [*U*] **a** : the freedom and time to behave and think as you want to without being controlled or influenced by someone else • *I need more space in our relationship.* **b** : the amount of space between you and another person that makes you feel comfortable being near that person • *You're invading my space.* [=you're too close to me] **8** [*C*] : an available seat on a bus, train, etc. • *There are no spaces left on the bus.* — **stare/gaze (off) into space** : to look straight ahead without looking at anything specific • *He just sat there, staring into space.*

²**space** *vb* **spaced; spac·ing** [*T*] **1** : to place or arrange (things) so that there is a particular amount of space between them • *Space (out) the poles evenly.* **2** : to separate (things) by particular periods of time • *They spaced (out) the births of their children.* — **space out** [*phrasal vb*] *informal* : to stop paying attention • *I spaced out for a minute and didn't hear what she said.*

space–age /ˈspeɪsˌeɪdʒ/ *adj, informal* : very modern • *a space-age machine/design*

space bar *n* [*C*] : the wide key at the bottom of a computer keyboard or typewriter that is used to make a space

space·craft /ˈspeɪsˌkræft, *Brit* ˈspeɪsˌkrɑːft/ *n, pl* **spacecraft** [*C*] : a vehicle that is used for travel in outer space

spaced out *adj, informal* : unable to think clearly or to pay attention to what is going on around you • *I was tired and pretty spaced out.*

space·flight /ˈspeɪsˌflaɪt/ *n* [*C/U*] : flight into outer space in a spacecraft

space heater *n* [*C*] *US* : a small device that is used for heating a room

space·man /ˈspeɪsˌmæn/ *n, pl* **-men** /-ˌmɛn/ [*C*] **1** *informal* : ASTRONAUT **2** *in stories* : a visitor to Earth from outer space • *spacemen from Mars*

space probe *n* [*C*] : a device that is used to obtain information from outer space and send it back to Earth

space·ship /ˈspeɪsˌʃɪp/ *n* [*C*] : SPACECRAFT

space shuttle *n* [*C*] : a spacecraft that carries people into outer space and back to Earth

space station *n* [*C*] : a large spacecraft in which people live for long periods of time

space suit *n* [*C*] : a special suit that is designed to keep astronauts alive in outer space

space walk *n* [*C*] : an activity in which an astronaut does work outside a spacecraft while it is in outer space

spac·ey /ˈspeɪsi/ *adj* **spac·i·er; -est** *informal* : SPACED OUT • *I'm a little spacey today.*

spac·ing /ˈspeɪsɪŋ/ *n* [*U*] : the amount of space between letters, words, or lines on a printed page • *The spacing between characters should be even.*

spa·cious /ˈspeɪʃəs/ *adj* : having a large amount of space • *a spacious room/office/house* — **spa·cious·ly** *adv* — **spa·cious·ness** [*U*]

spade /ˈspeɪd/ *n* **1** [*C*] : a tool with a heavy metal blade attached to a handle that is used for digging **2 a** [*C*] : a playing card that is marked with a black shape that looks like a pointed leaf • *two hearts, one club, and three spades* **b** [*plural*] : the suit in a deck of playing cards that consists of spades • *the queen of spades* — **call a spade a spade** : to speak in an honest and direct way • *Why don't you just call a spade a spade and say that he's a liar?* — **in spades** : in large amounts • *His hard work was rewarded in spades.*

spade·work /ˈspeɪdˌwɜːk/ *n* [*U*] : difficult work that is done especially to prepare for something • *Her assistants did the spadework before the trial.*

spa·ghet·ti /spəˈɡɛti/ *n* [*U*] : pasta in the shape of long, thin strings

spaghetti western *n* [*C*] : a movie about the old American West that was produced in Italy • *the spaghetti westerns of the 1960s*

spake /ˈspeɪk/ *archaic past tense of* SPEAK

spam /ˈspæm/ *n* [*U*] *informal* : e-mail that is not wanted and that consists mostly of advertising • *tips to reduce spam* • *a spam filter* [=software that identifies and blocks spam] — **spam** *vb* **spammed; spam·ming** [*T*] • *That company keeps spamming me.* [=keeps sending me spam]

Spam /ˈspæm/ *trademark* — used for a type of meat that is sold in cans

¹**span** /ˈspæn/ *n* [*C*] **1** : the period of time between two dates or events • *a 25-year span* = *a span of 25 years* • *a brief time span* **2** : the part of a bridge or other structure that goes across a space from one support to another **3** : the width of something from one side to the other • *the span of his shoulders*

²**span** *vb* **spanned; span·ning** [*T*] **1** : to continue throughout (a period of time) • *His singing career spanned three decades.* **2** : to cover or include (a wide area, a large number of things, etc.) • *Their empire once spanned several continents.* **3** : to cross over (something) • *A bridge spans the river.*

span·dex /'spæn,deks/ *n* [*U*] : a material that stretches easily and is used especially in sports clothing

span·gle /'spæŋgəl/ *n* [*C*] : a small, shiny piece of metal or plastic that is used to decorate clothing ▪ *costumes with gold spangles* — **spangle** *vb* **span·gled; span·gling** [*T*] ▪ *spangled costumes*

Span·iard /'spænjəd/ *n* [*C*] : a person born, raised, or living in Spain

span·iel /'spænjəl/ *n* [*C*] : a type of small dog that has long ears and a soft coat

Span·ish /'spænɪʃ/ *n* **1** [*U*] : the language of Spain, Mexico, and many countries in Latin America **2** *the Spanish* : the people of Spain — **Spanish** *adj*

Spanish moss *n* [*U*] : a type of American plant that has long gray strands and that hangs down from the branches of trees

spank /'spæŋk/ *vb* [*T*] : to hit (someone) on the buttocks with your hand as a form of punishment ▪ *parents who spank their children* — **spank·ing** *n* [*C*] ▪ *My mom gave me a spanking.* [=spanked me]

spank·ing /'spæŋkɪŋ/ *adv, informal* : VERY ▪ *spanking new sneakers*

span·ner /'spænə/ *n* [*C*] *Brit* : ¹WRENCH 1 ▪ *(figurative, informal)* The bank put/ threw a spanner in the works [=caused our plans to fail or to not work properly] by denying the loan.

¹**spar** /'spɑɚ/ *vb* **sparred; spar·ring** [*I*] **1** : to box with someone as a form of training or practice **2** : to argue with someone in a friendly way ▪ *They sparred playfully over whose team was better.*

²**spar** *n* [*C*] : a thick pole or similar structure that supports something (such as the sails of a ship or the wing of an aircraft)

¹**spare** /'speɚ/ *adj* **spar·er; spar·est 1** *always before a noun* **a** : kept as something extra that can be used if it is needed ▪ *spare parts* ▪ *a spare tire/bedroom/set* **b** : available to be used in whatever way you want ▪ *Do you have any spare cash/ change?* [=any extra cash/change that you could give to me] ▪ *He likes to ski in his spare time.* [=the time when he is not working] **2** : somewhat thin ▪ *He has a spare frame.* **3** : simple or plain ▪ *a spare style of writing*

²**spare** *vb* **spared; spar·ing** [*T*] **1 a** : to choose not to punish or harm (someone) ▪ *No one knows why he spared their lives.* [=why he didn't kill them] **b** : to not destroy or harm (something) ▪ *Somehow the storm spared our house.* **2** : to prevent (someone or something) from experiencing or being affected by something unpleasant, harmful, etc. ▪ *Our church was spared the fate of many others that have been closed.* ▪ *He spared them the embarrassment of a public apology.* **3** : to give (time, money, etc.) to someone ▪ *Can you spare (me) a few minutes?* [=can you spend a few minutes with me?] ▪ *If you could spare a cup of sugar, it would save me a trip to the store.* **4** : to not do or provide (something) ▪ *Nothing was spared by the hotel* [=the hotel provided everything possible] *to make us comfort-*

able. ▪ *We will spare no effort.* [=we will do everything we can] ▪ *When they go on vacation, they spare no expense.* [=they do not worry about spending too much money] **5** : to use or give out (something) in small amounts ▪ *More pancakes, please, and don't spare the syrup.* [=give me a lot of syrup] — **spare someone's feelings** : to avoid doing or saying something that will hurt someone emotionally ▪ *He didn't tell her everything because he wanted to spare her feelings.* — **spare (someone) the details** : to not tell someone all the unpleasant or boring details about something ▪ *"I drank too much last night and got sick." "Please, spare me the details."* — **to spare** ◇ If you have money, time, etc., *to spare*, you have more than enough money, time, etc. ▪ *I have no money to spare* [=I do not have enough money] *for such things.* ▪ *He got there with (only) minutes/seconds to spare.* [=he got there only minutes/seconds before he needed to] ▪ *He got there with time to spare.* [=he got there early]

³**spare** *n* [*C*] **1** : something extra that is kept to be used if it is needed ▪ *"I've lost the key." "That's all right. I have a spare."* ▪ *Most cars come with spares.* [=spare tires] **2** *bowling* : the achievement of knocking down all 10 pins with the first two balls ▪ *He got a strike and two spares.*

spare·rib /'speɚ,rɪb/ *n* [*C*] : a piece of meat from a pig that includes a rib

spar·ing /'sperɪŋ/ *adj* : not using or giving a lot of something ▪ *an artist who is sparing in her use of color* — **spar·ing·ly** *adv* ▪ *He used the funds sparingly.*

¹**spark** /'spɑɚk/ *n* **1 a** : a small piece of burning material that comes from a fire or is produced by rubbing or hitting two hard objects together ▪ *A spark from the fireplace set the rug on fire.* **b** : a short, bright flash of electricity between two points **2** [*U*] : a quality that makes someone or something enjoyable, interesting, successful, etc. ▪ *The TV series has lost its spark.* **3** [*C*] : a small amount of something ▪ *a spark of hope/humor* **4** [*C*] : an action, occurrence, etc., that causes something larger to happen ▪ *His death was the spark that ignited the revolution.* — **sparks fly** ◇ When *sparks fly*, it means that two people are either having an argument with each other or are sexually attracted to each other. ▪ *Sparks flew when they first met.*

²**spark** *vb* **1** [*T*] : to cause (something) to start or happen ▪ *The question sparked (off) a debate.* ▪ *The book sparked her interest in history.* **2** [*I*] : to produce sparks ▪ *The wires made contact and sparked.*

¹**spar·kle** /'spɑɚkəl/ *vb* **spar·kled; spar·kling** [*I*] **1** : to produce small flashes of light ▪ *sparkling jewels* **2** : to perform very well ▪ *The dancers sparkled on stage.* **3** : to be or become bright and lively ▪ *Her eyes sparkled with pride.* ▪ *sparkling wit*

²**sparkle** *n* **1** [*C/U*] : a small flash of bright light ▪ *the sparkle of a diamond* **2** [*U*] : a lively quality ▪ *the sparkle in her eyes*

spar·kler /ˈspɑɚklɚ/ n [C] : a type of fire-work that throws off very bright sparks as it burns

spark plug n [C] : a part of an engine that produces a spark that makes the fuel burn

sparky /ˈspɑɚki/ adj **spark·i·er; -est** chiefly Brit, informal : lively and energet-ic ▪ a sparky heroine/conversation

sparring partner n [C] **1** : someone a boxer spars with for training **2** : a per-son that you have serious but friendly ar-guments with ▪ political sparring partners

spar·row /ˈsperoʊ/ n [C] : a common type of small bird that usually has brown or gray feathers

sparse /ˈspɑɚs/ adj **spars·er; -est** : present only in small amounts ▪ Reli-able data is sparse.; especially : thinly covering an area ▪ sparse vegetation — **sparse·ly** adv ▪ a sparsely populated area — **sparse·ness** n [U]

spar·tan also **Spar·tan** /ˈspɑɚtn̩/ adj : very bare and simple : lacking the things that make life comfortable or more pleasant ▪ They lived in spartan con-ditions.

spasm /ˈspæzəm/ n [C] **1** : a sudden un-controlled and often painful tightening of a muscle ▪ back/muscle spasms **2** : a sudden and usually brief occurrence of something you cannot control ▪ coughing spasms ▪ spasms of guilt

spas·mod·ic /spæzˈmɑːdɪk/ adj **1** : re-lating to or caused by a spasm ▪ spasmod-ic jerks **2** : happening suddenly and briefly at different times ▪ spasmodic ac-tivity — **spas·mod·i·cal·ly** /spæz-ˈmɑːdɪkli/ adv

spas·tic /ˈspæstɪk/ adj **1** medical : relat-ing to or affected with spasms ▪ a spastic colon **2** informal : having movements like spasms : clumsy or awkward ▪ spas-tic fingers/dancing

¹spat past tense and past participle of ¹SPIT

²spat /ˈspæt/ n [C] **1** : a short argument about something that is not important **2** : a cloth or leather covering for the an-kle and foot that men wore over their shoes in the past ▪ a pair of spats

spate /ˈspeɪt/ n [C] : a large number of things that appear or happen in a short period of time ▪ a spate of forest fires — **in spate** chiefly Brit : filled with water flow-ing very fast ▪ The river/stream was in spate due to heavy rains.

spa·tial /ˈspeɪʃəl/ adj, technical : of or re-lating to space and the relationship of objects within it ▪ the spatial dimensions of a room — **spa·tial·ly** adv

¹spat·ter /ˈspætɚ/ vb [T/I] : to cause drops of a liquid to be thrown forcefully in dif-ferent directions ▪ A passing car spattered mud on my coat. ▪ His clothes were spat-tered with paint. ▪ trying to prevent paint for spattering

²spatter n [C/U] : a mark made when something wet hits a surface ▪ spatters of paint ▪ an area of paint spatter

spat·u·la /ˈspætʃələ/ n [C] **1** US **a** : a kitchen tool that has a handle which is bent upward and a wide, thin blade used for lifting and turning foods on a hot sur-face **b** : a kitchen tool that has a long

handle and short, soft blade and that is used especially for mixing, spreading, etc. **2** : a kitchen tool similar to a knife that has a flexible blade and that is used for mixing, spreading, etc.

¹spawn /ˈspɑːn/ vb **1** [I] : to produce or lay eggs in water — used of animals such as fish or frogs ▪ Salmon spawn in late summer or fall. **2** [T] : to produce or create (something) ▪ The health-food craze spawned a huge industry.

²spawn n [U] : the eggs of a fish or frog

spay /ˈspeɪ/ vb [T] : to remove the sex or-gans of (a female animal) ▪ Our cat has been spayed.

speak /ˈspiːk/ vb **spoke** /ˈspoʊk/; **spo-ken** /ˈspoʊkən/; **speak·ing 1 a** [I] : to say words in order to express your thoughts, feelings, opinions, etc., to someone : to talk to someone ▪ She and I spoke this morning. ▪ They were speaking in Japanese. ▪ I need to speak to you. ▪ I spoke with him on the phone. ▪ They're not **on speaking terms.** [=they're not friendly and do not speak to each other] ▪ The res-taurant isn't too expensive, **comparatively/relatively speaking.** [=when compared to other restaurants] **b** [I] : to talk about a particular subject or person ▪ He still speaks about/of his ex-wife with affection. ▪ The company is doing well, **financially speaking.** [=is doing well financially] **c** [T] : to say (something) to someone ▪ She was speaking the truth. ▪ Do not **speak a word** of this to anyone. [=do not tell any-one about this] **2** [T/I] : to use your voice to say words ▪ He has laryngitis and can't speak. ▪ You're speaking too fast. ▪ He spoke the poem out loud. **3** [T] : to use (a particular language) to talk to some-one ▪ He can speak German. ▪ The Spanish-speaking population. ▪ I can't **speak a word** of French. [=I do not know any French] **4** [I] : to make or give a speech ▪ She was asked to speak at the conference. — **so to speak** — used to indicate that you are using words in an unusual or figurative way rather than a literal way ▪ We need to be on the same wavelength, so to speak. — **speak for** [phrasal vb] **1** : to express the thoughts or opinions of (someone) ▪ They chose him to speak for the group. ▪ "We don't want any dessert." "Speak for yourself. I want some." ▪ (figurative) The facts **speak for themselves.** [=the facts clearly show what is true] **2** chiefly US : to show that (something or someone) does or does not deserve to be praised, admired, etc. ▪ The test results speak well/poorly for our school system. **3 be spoken for** : to not be available because of already being claimed by someone else or in a relation-ship with someone else ▪ I'm sorry. This seat is spoken for. — **speak of** [phrasal vb] **1** : to talk or write about (someone or something) ▪ Speaking of Jill, where is she? ▪ In the letter, he spoke of feeling ill. ▪ He speak well/highly of her. **2** chiefly US : to show that (someone or something) does or does not deserve to be praised, admired, etc. ▪ The success of the business **speaks well** of their judgment. [=shows that their judgment is good] — **speak**

out [*phrasal vb*] : to express an opinion in an open way ▪ *Protesters spoke out against the decision.* — **speak up** [*phrasal vb*] 1 : to speak loudly and clearly ▪ *"Speak up. I can't hear you."* 2 : to speak at a meeting, in a class, etc. ▪ *If you have any questions, now is the time to speak up.* 3 : to express an opinion openly ▪ *She is always ready to speak up for animal rights.* — **speak volumes** see VOLUME — **speak your mind** see ¹MIND — **to speak of** : worth mentioning or noticing ▪ *There was no progress to speak of.*

speak·er /ˈspiːkə/ *n* 1 [*C*] : someone who speaks a particular language ▪ *speakers of French* = *French speakers* 2 [*C*] : someone who talks about something to a group of people ▪ *a public speaker* ▪ *She was invited to be a guest speaker* [=to give a speech] *at the conference.* 3 **the Speaker** : the person who controls the discussions in a legislature ▪ *the Speaker of the House (of Representatives)* 4 [*C*] : someone who is speaking ▪ *improper grammar used by a writer or speaker* 5 [*C*] : the part of a radio, television, computer, etc., that changes electric signals into sound

¹**spear** /ˈspiɚ/ *n* [*C*] 1 : a weapon that has a long straight handle and a sharp point 2 : a new part of a plant that is thin and pointed ▪ *spears of grass* ▪ *asparagus spears*

²**spear** *vb* [*T*] : to push a spear or other pointed object into (something) ▪ *spear a fish*

spear·head /ˈspiɚˌhɛd/ *n* [*C*] : a person, thing, or group that organizes or leads something ▪ *She was the spearhead of the campaign for better schools.* — **spearhead** *vb* [*T*] ▪ *She spearheaded the campaign.*

spear·mint /ˈspiɚˌmɪnt/ *n* [*U*] : a plant that has a strong and pleasant flavor and smell and that is grown especially for its oil

spec /ˈspɛk/ *n* 1 [*C/U*] : SPECIFICATION ▪ *design specs* ▪ *(US) parts built according to spec* 2 [*plural*] *informal* : eyeglasses or spectacles — **on spec** : without having a definite buyer or customer but with the hope or expectation of finding one when work is completed ▪ *He built the house on spec.*

¹**spe·cial** /ˈspɛʃəl/ *adj* 1 : different from what is normal or usual ▪ *a special occasion/guest* ▪ *special treatment/circumstances* ▪ *The movie was nothing special.* [=was not particularly good] 2 : especially important or loved ▪ *a special friend* ▪ *He makes her feel special.* 3 *always before a noun* **a** : more than is usual ▪ *Pay special attention to the last paragraph.* **b** : additional or extra ▪ *a special edition of a newspaper* ▪ *a camera with many special features* 4 *always before a noun* : relating to or intended for a particular purpose ▪ *a special diet* ▪ *special knowledge/skills* ▪ *To clean the oven, I had to wear special gloves.*

²**special** *n* [*C*] 1 : a television or radio program that is not part of a regular series ▪ *a one-hour special on whales* 2 : a meal that is not on a restaurant's usual menu ▪ *Today's lunch special is chili.* 3 : SALE 2 ▪ *They were having a special on paper towels so I stocked up.*

special delivery *n* [*U*] : a special service that delivers mail more quickly than usual for an extra fee

special education *n* [*U*] : classes for children who have special needs because of physical or learning problems — called also *special ed*

special effect *n* [*C*] : an image or sound that is created in television, radio, or movies to represent something real (such as an explosion) or imaginary (such as a monster) ▪ *The movie has spectacular special effects.*

special interest *n* [*C*] *chiefly US* : a group that tries to influence the people who run a government in order to help a particular business, cause, etc. ▪ *political contributions made by special interests* ▪ *special interest groups*

spe·cial·ism /ˈspɛʃəˌlɪzəm/ *n* [*C*] *Brit* : a particular subject or area of study or practice ▪ *a doctor whose specialism is in blood disorders*

spe·cial·ist /ˈspɛʃəlɪst/ *n* [*C*] : a person who has special knowledge and skill relating to a particular job, area of study, etc. ▪ *a specialist in international law* ▪ *an eye specialist* [=a doctor who deals with health problems relating to eyes]

spe·ci·al·i·ty /ˌspɛʃiˈæləti/ *n, pl* **-ties** [*C*] *chiefly Brit* : SPECIALTY

spe·cial·ize *also Brit* **spe·cial·ise** /ˈspɛʃəˌlaɪz/ *vb* **-ized; -iz·ing** [*I*] : to limit your business or area of study to one specific subject ▪ *My mechanic specializes in repairing foreign cars.* — **spe·cial·i·za·tion** *also Brit* **spe·cial·i·sa·tion** /ˌspɛʃələˈzeɪʃən, *Brit* ˌspɛʃəˌlaɪˈzeɪʃən/ *n* [*C/U*]

specialized *also Brit* **specialised** *adj* : made or used for one particular purpose, job, etc. ▪ *specialized regions of the brain* ▪ *specialized gear/skills*

spe·cial·ly /ˈspɛʃəli/ *adv* 1 : for a special purpose ▪ *dresses made specially for a wedding* ▪ *specially trained troops* 2 : to a special or unusual degree ▪ *I was specially pleased with your gift.* 3 : in a special manner ▪ *I don't want to be treated specially.*

special needs *n* [*plural*] : mental, emotional, or physical problems in a child that require a special setting for education ▪ *a child with special needs* ▪ *special-needs students/teachers*

spe·cial·ty /ˈspɛʃəlti/ *n, pl* **-ties** [*C*] *US* 1 : something that a person or place is known for making or producing very well ▪ *Eggs are my dad's specialty.* 2 : an area of study or business that a person specializes in or has special knowledge of ▪ *The doctor's specialty is skin problems.*

spe·cies /ˈspiːʃiz/ *n, pl* **species** [*C*] 1 *biology* : a group of animals or plants that are similar and can produce young among animals or plants ▪ *There are approximately 8,000 species of ants.* ▪ *an endangered/threatened species* 2 : a particular group of things or people that belong together or have some shared quality ▪ *the different species of criminals*

spe·cif·ic /spɪˈsɪfɪk/ *adj* **1** *always before a noun* : special or particular • *Is there anything specific you want for dinner?* • *a specific interest/concern* **2** : clearly and exactly presented or stated : precise or exact • *specific instructions/examples* • *Can you be more specific? What exactly did he say?* **3** : relating *to* a particular person, situation, etc. — *problems specific to this project* — **spe·cif·i·cal·ly** /spɪˈsɪfɪkli/ *adv* • *I specifically told her not to bother you.* • *The show is aimed specifically at a female audience.* — **spec·i·fic·i·ty** /ˌspɛsəˈfɪsəti/ *n* [U] *formal* • *the specificity of her instructions*

spec·i·fi·ca·tion /ˌspɛsəfəˈkeɪʃən/ *n* [C] : a detailed description of work to be done or materials to be used in a project • *the architect's specifications for a new building* • *It will be built to your specifications.* [=according to your specific instructions]

spec·i·fy /ˈspɛsəˌfaɪ/ *vb* **-fies; -fied; -fy·ing** [T] : to name or mention (someone or something) exactly and clearly • *Specify the color and quantity when you order.* • *The instructions do not specify what kind of screws to use.* • *We arrived at the specified time.*

spec·i·men /ˈspɛsəmən/ *n* [C] **1 a** : something (such as an animal or plant) collected as an example of a particular kind of thing • *a museum specimen* **b** : a small amount or piece of something that can be tested or examined • *a urine/blood specimen* **2** : a notable example of something • *The church is a magnificent specimen of baroque architecture.*

spe·cious /ˈspiːʃəs/ *adj, formal* : appearing to be true but actually false • *a specious argument* — **spe·cious·ly** *adv* — **spe·cious·ness** *n* [U]

speck /ˈspɛk/ *n* [C] : a very small piece or amount • *a speck of dust/humor*

speck·le /ˈspɛkəl/ *n* [C] : a small mark of color • *a banana with brown speckles*

speck·led /ˈspɛkəld/ *adj* : covered with many small marks • *speckled trout* • *a gold-speckled scarf*

spec·ta·cle /ˈspɛktɪkəl/ *n* **1** [C] : something that attracts attention because it is very impressive or unusual • *The photo exhibit was quite a spectacle.* **2** [plural] *old-fashioned* : GLASSES, EYEGLASSES • *He peered through his spectacles.* — **make a spectacle of yourself** : to do something in front of other people that is very embarrassing

spec·tac·u·lar /spɛkˈtækjələ/ *adj* : causing wonder and admiration : very impressive • *a spectacular sunset/catch/recovery* — **spec·tac·u·lar·ly** *adv*

spec·ta·tor /ˈspɛkˌteɪtə/ *n* [C] : a person who watches an event, game, etc., often as part of an audience • *The spectators cheered the racers on.*

spec·ter (*US*) *or chiefly Brit* **spec·tre** /ˈspɛktə/ *n* [C] *literary* : a ghost or spirit of a dead person — **the specter of**

(something) : something bad that might happen in the future • *the specter of war*

spec·trum /ˈspɛktrəm/ *n, pl* **spec·tra** /ˈspɛktrə/ *or* **spec·trums** [C] **1 a** : the group of colors that a ray of light can be separated into including red, orange, yellow, green, blue, and violet : the colors that can be seen in a rainbow **b** *technical* : an entire range of light waves, radio waves, etc. **2** : a complete range of different opinions, people, etc. • *The city's population represents a broad/wide spectrum of society.*

spec·u·late /ˈspɛkjəˌleɪt/ *vb* **-lat·ed; -lat·ing** **1** [T/I] : to think about something and make guesses about it • *She could only speculate about/on her friend's motives.* • *Scientists speculate that the illness is caused by a virus.* **2** [I] : to invest money in ways that could produce a large profit but that also involve a lot of risk • *speculating on the stock market* — **spec·u·la·tion** /ˌspɛkjəˈleɪʃən/ *n* [C/U] — **spec·u·la·tive** /ˈspɛkjələtɪv/ *adj* • *A speculative mind/investment* • *His conclusions are highly speculative.* — **spec·u·la·tive·ly** *adv* — **spec·u·la·tor** /ˈspɛkjəˌleɪtə/ *n* [C] • *financial speculators*

sped *past tense and past participle of* ²SPEED

speech /ˈspiːtʃ/ *n* **1** [C] : a spoken expression of ideas, opinions, etc., that is made by someone who is speaking in front of a group of people • *She has to make/give/deliver a speech at the convention.* **2** [U] : the ability to speak • *a speech impediment* [=a condition that makes it difficult to speak normally] • *They fought for freedom of speech.* = *They fought for the right to/of free speech.* [=they fought for the legal right to express their opinions freely] **3** [U] : spoken language • *Many words are more common in speech than in writing.* **4** [C] : the manner or style of speaking that is used by a particular person or group • *His speech was slurred.*

speech·less /ˈspiːtʃləs/ *adj* : unable to speak because of anger, surprise, etc. • *I was speechless with shock/anger.* • *Your story left me speechless.*

¹speed /ˈspiːd/ *n* **1** [C/U] : the rate at which someone or something moves or travels • *a speed of 40 miles per hour* • *The truck was gaining/gathering speed.* [=was going faster] • *He was running at full/top speed.* [=as fast as possible] **2** [C/U] : the rate at which something happens or is done • *The work was done with remarkable speed.* • *He types at a speed of about 50 words per minute.* **3** [U] : the quality of being quick • *They did the work with speed and ease.* **4** [C] : a gear in a vehicle or bicycle • *a three-speed bicycle* • *The car has four speeds.* **5** [U] *informal* : an illegal drug that makes a person feel more excited and full of energy — **up to speed** : having the latest information about something • *Let me bring you up to speed on our plans.* [=let me tell you about the changes in our plans] : having the knowledge that is needed to do or understand something • *It took time for the new secretary to get up to speed.* [=to learn the job]

²speed *vb* **sped** /ˈspɛd/ *or* **speed·ed;
speed·ing** **1** [*I*] : to move fast • *A car was speeding down/up the street.* **2** [*T*] : to move (someone or something) somewhere very quickly • *An ambulance sped her to the hospital.* . **3** [*I*] : to drive faster than the legal speed limit • *Don't speed.* • *I got a ticket for speeding.* **4** [*T*] : to cause (something) to happen faster • *trying to speed the process (along)* — **speed up** [*phrasal vb*] **speed up** *or* **speed up (something or someone)** *or* **speed (something or someone) up** : to become faster or to make (something or someone) faster • *The car suddenly sped up.* • *speed the process up* • *They're working too slowly. How can we speed them up?* —
speed·er /ˈspiːdə/ *n* [*C*]

speed·boat /ˈspiːˌboʊt/ *n* [*C*] : a motorboat that can go very fast

speed bump *n* [*C*] : a low raised ridge across a road or parking lot that causes people to drive more slowly

speed demon *n* [*C*] *chiefly US, informal* : someone or something that moves or works very fast • *The new cook is a regular speed demon.*

speed limit *n* [*C*] : the highest speed at which you are allowed to drive on a particular road • *The speed limit here is 55 mph.*

speed·om·e·ter /spɪˈdɑːmətə/ *n* [*C*] : an instrument in a car, truck, etc., that indicates how fast the vehicle is going

speedy /ˈspiːdi/ *adj* **speed·i·er; -est** : moving or able to move quickly • *a speedy car/boat* **2** : happening quickly • *a speedy recovery* — **speed·i·ly** /ˈspiːdəli/ *adv* — **speed·i·ness** /ˈspiːdinəs/ *n* [*U*]

¹spell /ˈspɛl/ *vb* **spelled** *or chiefly Brit* **spelt** /ˈspɛlt/; **spell·ing** *chiefly US* [*T/I*] : to say, write, or print the letters of (a word or name) • *Please spell (out) your full name.* **2** [*T*] : to have or lead to (a particular result or effect) • *Her boss's resignation spelled the end to her troubles.* [=her troubles ended when her boss resigned] • *Their carelessness could spell trouble/disaster for all of us.* **3** [*T*] *chiefly US* : to take the place of (someone) for a period of time • *When they're taking care of their grandson, they spell* [=relieve] *each other throughout the day.* — **spell out** [*phrasal vb*] **spell (something) out** *or* **spell out (something)** : to explain the details of (something) clearly • *The contract spelled out the terms of his employment.* — **spell·er** /ˈspɛlə/ *n* [*C*] • *She is a bad/good speller.* [=she is bad/good at spelling words]

²spell *n* **1** [*C*] **a** : a group of secret words that are believed to have magic power • *a magic spell* **b** : magic that is performed by saying a group of secret words • *The witch cast a spell on/over the children.* • *Drinking the potion will break the spell.* [=end the magic] • *She was under a spell.* [=affected by magic] **2** [*singular*] : a quality that attracts or influences someone or something in a powerful or seemingly magical way • *The sound of the phone ringing broke the spell of the music.* • *She has fallen under his spell.* **3** [*C*] : a short period of time marked by a particular activity or condition • *a dizzy/fainting spell* • *a spell of rainy weather*

spell·bind·ing /ˈspɛlˌbaɪndɪŋ/ *adj* : holding your attention completely : extremely interesting, entertaining, etc. • *a spellbinding speaker/performance*

spell·bound /ˈspɛlˌbaʊnd/ *adj* : giving all of your attention and interest to something or someone • *The children were (held/kept) spellbound by the puppet show.*

spell–check·er /ˈspɛlˌtʃɛkə/ *n* [*C*] : a computer program that finds and corrects misspelled words in documents, e-mail, etc.

spell·ing /ˈspɛlɪŋ/ *n* **1** [*U*] : the act of forming words from letters • *His spelling is good.* • *a spelling mistake/test* **2** [*C*] : the way in which a word is correctly spelled • *The words "made" and "maid" sound alike but have different spellings.*

spelling bee *n* [*C*] *chiefly US* : a contest in which contestants spell words aloud and are removed from the contest when they spell a word wrong

spelt *chiefly Brit past tense and past participle of* **¹SPELL**

spend /ˈspɛnd/ *vb* **spent** /ˈspɛnt/;
spend·ing **1** [*T/I*] : to use (money) to pay for something • *I spent $30 on his birthday gift.* • *He spends lavishly on vacations.* • *I don't have much money to spend.* **2** [*T*] : to allow (time) to pass in a particular place or while doing a particular activity • *I spent my summer at the beach.* **3** [*T*] : to use (energy or effort) to do something • *I wish he spent as much (of his) effort/energy on studying as he does on video games.* — **spend the night** ✧ If you sleep at a place for a night, you *spend the night* there. If you **spend the night with** someone, or if you and someone else **spend the night together**, you stay with someone overnight and have sex with that person.

spend·er /ˈspɛndə/ *n* [*C*] : a person who spends money • *big spenders* [=people who spend lots of money]

spending money *n* [*U*] : extra money that you can spend on whatever you want

spend·thrift /ˈspɛndˌθrɪft/ *n* [*C*] : a person who spends money in a careless or wasteful way

spent /ˈspɛnt/ *adj* **1** : used up and no longer useful • *spent fuel* **2** *somewhat formal* : tired and drained of energy • *By the end of the race I was spent.*

sperm /ˈspəm/ *n, pl* **sperm** *also* **sperms** *biology* **1** [*C*] : a cell that is produced by the male sexual organs and that combines with the female's egg in reproduction — called also *sperm cell* **2** [*U*] : SEMEN

sperm bank *n* [*C*] : a place where sperm are collected, stored, and then used to help women become pregnant

sper·mi·cide /ˈspəməˌsaɪd/ *n* [*C/U*] : a substance that is used to kill sperm in order to prevent pregnancy — **sper·mi·cid·al** /ˌspɜːmə'saɪdəl/ *adj*

sperm whale *n* [C] : a type of whale that has a very large head and is hunted for its fat and oil

spew /'spjuː/ *vb* [T/I] : to flow out or cause (something) to flow out in a fast and forceful way • *Smoke and ashes spewed from the volcano.* • *The faucet was spewing dirty water.* • (*figurative*) *They spewed (out) an endless stream of questions.*

sphere /'sfiɚ/ *n* [C] **1 a** : a round object • *a glass sphere* **b** *geometry* : a three-dimensional shape that looks like a ball **2** *somewhat formal* : an area of influence or activity • *the domestic sphere* • *jobs in the public/private sphere* — **spher·i·cal** /'sfirɪkəl, 'sferɪkəl/ *adj* • *a spherical object*

sphinc·ter /'sfɪŋktɚ/ *n* [C] *medical* : a ring-shaped muscle that surrounds a body opening and that can·tighten to close the opening

sphinx *or* **Sphinx** /'sfɪŋks/ *n* [C] *in ancient Greek and Egyptian stories* : a creature with the body of a lion and the head of a person; *also* : something (such as a statue) in the shape of a sphinx

spic-and-span *or* **spick-and-span** (*chiefly US*) *also chiefly Brit* **spick and span** *or* **spic and span** /ˌspɪkən'spæn/ *adj* : very clean and neat • *He keeps the house spic-and-span.*

¹spice /'spaɪs/ *n* [C/U] : a substance (such as pepper or nutmeg) that is used in cooking to add flavor to food and that comes from a dried plant and is usually a powder or seed **2** [U] : something that adds interest or excitement • *The elaborate costumes added spice to the performance.* • *Variety is the spice of life.* [=variety makes life more interesting]

²spice *vb* **spiced; spic·ing** [T] **1** : to flavor (food) with spices • *I spiced the chicken with ginger.* • *a heavily spiced dish* **2** : to add interest or excitement to (something) — usually + *up* • *We need to spice up our relationship.*

spicy /'spaɪsi/ *adj* **spic·i·er; -est 1** *of food* : flavored with or containing strong spices : flavored with or containing spices and especially ones that cause a burning feeling in your mouth • *This salsa is too spicy for me.* **2** : exciting and somewhat shocking • *a spicy story/scandal* — **spic·i·ness** /'spaɪsinəs/ *n* [U]

spi·der /'spaɪdɚ/ *n* [C] : a small creature that has eight legs and usually creates a web of sticky threads in which it catches insects for food

spi·der web /'spaɪdɚˌwɛb/ *n* [C] *US* : a network of sticky threads made by a spider and used as a resting place and a trap for food — called also *spider's web, web*

spi·dery /'spaɪdɚi/ *adj* : long and thin like the legs of a spider • *spidery arms and legs* • *spidery handwriting*

spiel /'spiːl/ *n* [C] *informal* : a fast speech that someone has often said before and that is usually intended to persuade people to buy something, agree to something, etc. • *a salesman's spiel*

spiffy /'spɪfi/ *adj* **spiff·i·er; -est** *chiefly US, informal* : neat, stylish, and attractive • *a spiffy uniform*

spig·ot /'spɪgət/ *n* [C] **1** : a device that controls the flow of liquid from a large container • *the spigot on a beer keg* **2** *US* : FAUCET; *especially* : an outdoor faucet

¹spike /'spaɪk/ *n* **1** [C] : a long, thin rod that ends in a point and is often made of metal • *a railroad spike* [=a large nail used to attach rails to railroad ties] **2** [C] : a sudden, rapid increase in something • *There's been a spike in traffic since the new grocery store opened.* **3 a** [C] : a metal point attached to the bottom of shoes worn by athletes in some sports • *I need to replace the spikes on my golf shoes.* **b** [*plural*] : shoes having spikes • *a pair of spikes* **4** [C] : a long, narrow group of flowers that grow on one stem

²spike *vb* **spiked; spik·ing 1** [T] : to add alcohol or drugs to (food or drink) • *Someone spiked the punch.* **2** [I] *chiefly US* : to increase greatly in a short period of time • *Gas prices have spiked (upward).* **3** [T] *sports* **a** : to hit (a volleyball) sharply downward toward the ground • *She spiked the ball and scored the winning point.* **b** *US* : to throw (a ball) sharply downward • *After he scored a touchdown, he spiked the ball in the end zone.* **4** [T] : to form (something) into spikes or points • *She spikes her hair.* **5** [T] : to pierce or cut (someone or something) with a sharp point or spike • *The second baseman was spiked by the runner.* [=injured by the spikes on the runner's shoes]

¹spill /'spɪl/ *vb, chiefly US* **spilled** /'spɪld/ *or chiefly Brit* **spilt** /'spɪlt/; **spill·ing 1 a** [T] : to cause or allow (something) to fall, flow, or run over the edge of a container usually in an accidental way • *I accidentally spilled coffee all over my suit.* • *The bag ripped open and spilled (out) its contents all over the floor.* **b** [I] : to fall or flow over the edge of a container • *Milk spilled (out) onto the table.* **2** [I] : to move or spread out into a wider place or area • *After the movie the crowd spilled (out) into/onto the street.* **3** [T] *US, informal* : to tell (a secret) to someone • *Come on, spill it. Who gave you the money?* — **cry over spilled/spilt milk** see ¹CRY — **spill blood** see BLOOD — **spill over** [*phrasal vb*] **1** : to be completely covered or filled with something • *The platter was spilling over with fruit.* **2** : to spread and begin to affect other people, areas, etc. • *The stress at work began to spill over into other aspects of his life.* — **spill the beans** see BEAN — **spill your guts** see ¹GUT

²spill *n* [C] **1** : an accident in which liquid is spilled or an amount of liquid that is spilled • *Please clean up the spill on the floor.* • *an oil spill* **2** : an accidental act of falling • *He took a spill* [=he fell] *while skiing.*

spill·age /'spɪlɪdʒ/ *n* [C/U] *formal* : an occurrence in which something is spilled accidentally • *The design of the mug prevents spillage.*

¹spin /'spɪn/ *vb* **spun** /'spʌn/; **spin·ning 1** [T/I] : to turn or cause someone or something to turn around repeatedly • *The Earth spins on its axis.* • *The boy was* *spinning a top.* • *He grabbed her and* **spun** *her around.* [=and turned her around quickly] • *He suddenly* **spun around.** [=turned around quickly] **2** [*I*] : to seem to be moving around in a way that makes you feel dizzy or sick • *I tried to stand up, but the room was spinning.* • *My head was spinning.* [=I was dizzy] • *All of that information* **made my head spin.** [=made me feel confused] **3** [*T/I*] : to draw out and twist fibers of cotton, wool, etc., into yarn or thread • *They spun the wool into yarn.* **4** [*T*] *of insects* : to form (something) by producing a fluid that quickly hardens into a thread • *a spider spinning its web* **5** [*T*] : to tell (a story, especially a story that you create by using your imagination) • **spinning yarns** [=telling stories] *about his adventures* • *She* **spun a tale** [=made up a story] *about her car breaking down to explain why she was late.* **6** [*T*] : to describe (something) in a certain way in order to influence what people think about it • *Both parties tried to spin the debate as a victory for their candidate.* — **spin off** [*phrasal vb*] **spin off** or **spin (something) off** or **spin off (something)** : to create something new (such as a new television show or company) by basing it on or taking it from something that already exists • *The show was so popular that it spun off a new series.* [=a new series was created based on the show] — **spin out** [*phrasal vb*] **1** *US, of a vehicle* : to slide and turn around quickly in an uncontrolled way • *The truck spun out on a patch of ice.* **2 spin (something) out** or **spin out (something)** *chiefly Brit* : to make (something) last for a very long time • *They're trying to spin out the debate.* **3 spin out of control a** : to move in a way that is not controlled • *The rocket spun out of control and crashed.* **b** : to keep getting worse in a way that is hard to stop or fix • *Her drinking problem is spinning out of control.* — **spin·ner** /ˈspɪnɚ/ *n* [*C*]

²**spin** *n* **1** [*C/U*] **a** : the act of turning around and around : an act of spinning • *the direction of the Earth's spin* • *The ice-skater executed graceful jumps and spins.* • *The plane went into a spin.* • *(figurative) Her head was all* **in a spin.** [=she was very confused] **b** : a rapid turning motion given to a ball by someone who throws or hits it • *She put (a) spin on the ball/shot.* **2** [*U, singular*] : a way of describing or talking about something that is meant to influence other people's opinion of it • *Each author puts a new/different spin on the story.* **3** [*C*] *informal* : a short trip in a vehicle • *He took me for a spin in his new car.*

spin·ach /ˈspɪnɪtʃ/ *n* [*U*] : a plant with dark green leaves that are eaten as a vegetable

spi·nal /ˈspaɪnl̩/ *adj* : of, relating to, or affecting the spine • *a spinal injury*

spinal column *n* [*C*] *technical* : BACKBONE

spinal cord *n* [*C*] : the large group of nerves that runs through the center of the spine and carries messages between the brain and the rest of the body

spin·dle /ˈspɪndl̩/ *n* [*C*] **1 a** : a thin rod or stick with pointed ends that is used in making yarn **b** : the long, thin pin on a spinning wheel that is used to make thread **2** : something shaped like a long, thin rod; *especially* : a long, thin part of a machine which turns around something or around which something turns

spin·dly /ˈspɪndli/ *adj* **spin·dli·er; -est** : long and thin and usually weak • *spindly legs*

spin doctor *n* [*C*] *informal* : a person (such as a political aide) whose job involves trying to control the way something (such as an important event) is described to the public in order to influence what people think about it

spine /ˈspaɪn/ *n* **1** [*C*] : the row of connected bones down the middle of the back : BACKBONE **2** [*C*] : a sharp, pointed part on an animal or plant • *cactus spines* **3** [*U*] *informal* : courage or strength • *They lack the spine to do what needs to be done.* **4** [*C*] : the part of a book to which the pages are attached — **up/down your spine** ◇ If something sends a chill/shiver **up/down your spine** or if *a chill/shiver runs up/down your spine*, you become frightened, thrilled, etc. • *Her performance sent a chill up my spine.*

spine–chill·ing /ˈspaɪnˌtʃɪlɪŋ/ *adj* : very exciting, thrilling, or frightening • *a spine-chilling scream*

spine·less /ˈspaɪnləs/ *adj* **1** *disapproving* : lacking courage or strength • *a spineless coward* **2** : having no spine or spines • *Jellyfish are spineless.*

spine–tin·gling /ˈspaɪnˌtɪŋɡəlɪŋ/ *adj* : very exciting, thrilling, or frightening • *spine-tingling suspense*

spin·na·ker /ˈspɪnɪkɚ/ *n* [*C*] : a large triangular sail on a boat that is used when the wind is blowing from behind

spinning wheel *n* [*C*] : a machine that was used in the past for making yarn or thread

spin–off /ˈspɪnˌɑːf/ *n* [*C*] **1** : a television program, movie, book, etc., that is based on characters from another television program, movie, book, etc. • *The comic book is a spin-off of the movie.* **2** : a new company created by a large company **3** : something useful that results from work done to produce something else • *spin-offs of space research*

spin·ster /ˈspɪnstɚ/ *n* [*C*] *old-fashioned + often disapproving* : an unmarried woman who is past the usual age for marrying and is considered unlikely to marry — **spin·ster·hood** /ˈspɪnstɚˌhʊd/ *n* [*U*]

spiny /ˈspaɪni/ *adj* **spin·i·er; -est** : having or covered with many sharp, pointed parts • *a spiny fish*

¹**spi·ral** /ˈspaɪrəl/ *n* [*C*] **1** : a circular curving line that goes around a central point while getting closer to or farther away from it • *The glider flew in a wide spiral over the field.* **2** : a situation in which something continuously increases, decreases, or gets worse • *a spiral of problems* • *Gas prices continued their* **upward**

spiral. [=gas prices got higher] ▪ *His drug use drove him into a downward spiral.*

²**spiral** *vb, US* **-raled** *or Brit* **-ralled;** *US* **-ral·ing** *or Brit* **-ral·ling** [*I*] **1** : to move in a circle around a central point while getting closer to or farther away from it ▪ *Smoke spiraled up from the chimney.* **2** : to greatly increase, decrease, or get worse in a continuous and usually fast and uncontrolled way ▪ *Prices have been spiraling upward/downward.* ▪ *spiraling* [=rapidly increasing] *costs*

³**spiral** *adj, always before a noun* : winding or circling around a central point ▪ *a spiral seashell/staircase*

spire /'spajɚ/ *n* [*C*] : a tall, narrow, pointed structure on the top of a building ▪ *church spires*

¹**spir·it** /'spirɪt/ *n* **1 a** [*C/U*] : the force within a person that is believed to give the body life, energy, and power ▪ *Yoga is healthy for both body and spirit.* **b** [*C*] : the inner quality or nature of a person ▪ *He has a youthful/generous spirit.* **2** [*C*] : a person ▪ *He was a proud spirit.* ▪ *They are kindred spirits.* [=people with similar interests or concerns] **3 a** [*C*] : GHOST **1** ▪ *evil spirits* **b the Spirit** : HOLY SPIRIT **4 a** [*C/U*] : a desire or determination to do something ▪ *His many disappointments never broke his spirit.* ▪ *an athlete with a lot of skill and spirit* **b** [*U*] : enthusiastic loyalty ▪ *The students showed their school spirit by having a rally to support the football team.* **5** [*singular*] : the attitude or feeling that a person has or people have about something ▪ *He didn't approach the work in/with the right spirit.* ▪ *a spirit of cooperation* ▪ *"I know I can do it if I keep trying." "Yeah, that's the spirit!"* [=that's the right attitude to have] **6** [*plural*] : feelings of happiness or unhappiness ▪ *Spirits were low* [=people were unhappy] *after our team lost again.* ▪ *We need to do something to lift your spirits.* [=to make you feel better/happier] ▪ *Everyone was in high/low spirits.* [=was happy/unhappy] ▪ *He's in good spirits.* [=happy and positive] **7** [*U*] : the real meaning or intention of something ▪ *understanding the spirit of the law* **8** [*plural*] : strong alcoholic drinks : LIQUOR

²**spirit** *vb* [*T*] : to carry (someone or something) away secretly ▪ *The singer was spirited away in a limousine.* ▪ *The funds were spirited away to another account.*

spir·it·ed /'spirɪtɚd/ *adj* : full of courage or energy : very lively or determined ▪ *a spirited discussion* ▪ *a spirited young lady*

spir·it·less /'spirɪtləs/ *adj* : lacking courage, energy, or cheerfulness ▪ *a spiritless performance*

spirit level *n* [*C*] *chiefly Brit* : ¹LEVEL 5

¹**spir·i·tu·al** /'spirɪtʃəwəl/ *adj* **1** : of or relating to a person's spirit ▪ *spiritual growth/needs* **2** : of or relating to religion or religious beliefs ▪ *spiritual leaders/songs* — **spir·i·tu·al·i·ty** /,spirɪtʃə-'wæləti/ *n* [*U*] ▪ *a man of deep spirituality* [=a very religious man] — **spir·i·tu·al·ly** *adv* ▪ *spiritually strong*

²**spiritual** *n* [*C*] : a religious folk song that was sung originally by African-Americans in the southern U.S.

spir·i·tu·al·ism /'spirɪtʃəwə,lɪzəm/ *n* [*U*] : a belief that the spirits of dead people can communicate with living people — **spir·i·tu·al·ist** /'spirɪtʃəwəlɪst/ *n* [*C*]

¹**spit** /'spɪt/ *vb* **spat** /'spæt/ *or chiefly US* **spit; spit·ting 1 a** [*I*] : to force saliva from your mouth ▪ *He spit/spat in my face.* **b** [*T*] : to force (food, liquid, etc.) from your mouth — *often + out* ▪ *He took a taste of the soup and quickly spat/spit it out.* **2** [*T*] : to say (something) in a quick and angry way ▪ *"You make me sick!" he spat.* — **spit it out** *informal* — used to tell someone to say something that he or she does not want to say or is having a hard time saying ▪ *"Come on, spit it out! What happened?"*

²**spit** *n* **1** [*U*] : the liquid produced in your mouth : SALIVA **2** [*C*] : a thin pointed rod or stick that is used for holding meat over a fire to cook it

spit·ball /'spɪt,bɑːl/ *n* [*C*] *US* **1** : a small piece of paper that is chewed and rolled into a ball so that it can be thrown or shot at someone **2** *baseball* : an illegal pitch in which the ball is made wet with saliva or sweat

spite /'spait/ *n* [*U*] : a desire to harm, anger, or defeat another person especially because you feel that you have been treated wrongly in some way ▪ *an act of spite* ▪ *You only denied his request out of (pure) spite.* — **in spite of** : without being prevented by (something) : DESPITE — used to say that something happens or is true even though there is something that might prevent it from happening or being true ▪ *He failed the test in spite of all his studying.* ▪ *She went ahead in spite of the snow.* — **in spite of yourself** : even though you do not want to or expect to ▪ *I ended up having a good time in spite of myself.*

²**spite** *vb* **spit·ed; spit·ing** [*T*] : to deliberately annoy, upset, or hurt (someone) ▪ *He only did it to spite me.*

spite·ful /'spaitfəl/ *adj* : having or showing a desire to harm, anger, or defeat someone ▪ *a spiteful person/remark* — **spite·ful·ly** *adv*

spitting image *n* [*C*] : someone who looks very much like someone else ▪ *She is the spitting image of her mother.*

spit·tle /'spɪtl/ *n* [*U*] : the liquid produced in your mouth : saliva or spit

¹**splash** /'splæʃ/ *vb* **1** [*I*] *of a liquid* : to move, fall, or hit something in a noisy or messy way ▪ *The water splashed onto the floor.* **2 a** [*T/I*] : to cause (a liquid) to move in a noisy or messy way ▪ *She splashed cold water on her face.* ▪ *The kids love splashing (around) in the pool.* **b** [*T*] : to make (someone or something) wet with large drops of a liquid ▪ *She splashed her face with cold water.* **3** [*T*] : to mark (something) with patches of color or light ▪ *The canvas was splashed with bold colors.* — **splash across/over** [*phrasal verb*] **splash (something) across/ over** : to put (a photograph, news headline, etc.) in a place or position where it will be easily seen by many people ▪ *The scandal was splashed across the front page.* ▪ *Her picture was splashed (all) over*

the news. — **splash out** [*phrasal vb*] **splash out** *or* **splash out (something)** *or* **splash (something) out** *Brit, informal* : to spend a lot of money • *We can't afford to splash out that much money.*

²**splash** *n* **1** [*C*] **a** : the sound made when someone or something hits liquid or when liquid hits something • *He listened to the gentle splash of the waves against the boat.* • *The bird dived into the pond with a splash.* **b** : the movement of liquid when something hits it • *I was hit by the splash when a truck drove through the puddle.* **2** [*C*] : a mark or spot made when a liquid is splashed on something • *You've got splashes of mud on your pants.* **3** [*C*] : a small area of bright color or light • *a splash of color* **4** [*singular*] *informal* : a small amount of liquid • *coffee with a splash of cream* — **make a splash** *informal* : to attract a lot of attention in an exciting way • *The director is making a splash in Hollywood.*

splashy /ˈsplæʃi/ *adj* **splash·i·er**; **-est** : having a bright or exciting quality that attracts attention • *splashy colors/ads*

splat·ter /ˈsplætɚ/ *vb* **1** [*I*] **a** *of a liquid* : to move, fall, or hit something in large drops • *Rain splattered against the windows.* **b** *of something that comes liquid* : to hit something and break apart • *A bug splattered against the car's windshield.* **2** [*T*] **a** : to cause (a liquid) to move or fall in large drops • *You're splattering paint everywhere.* **b** : to make (something) wet or dirty with large drops of liquid • *My clothes were splattered with paint.* — **splatter** *n* [*C/U*] • *I had paint splatters on my jeans.*

splay /ˈspleɪ/ *vb* [*T/I*] : to move your legs, fingers, etc.) out and apart from each other • *He sat with his legs splayed apart/out.*

spleen /ˈspliːn/ *n* **1** [*C*] : an organ located near your stomach that destroys worn-out red blood cells and produces white blood cells **2** [*U*] *literary* : feelings of anger • *I listened while she vented her spleen.* [=expressed her anger]

splen·did /ˈsplɛndəd/ *adj* **1** : very impressive and beautiful • *a splendid view* **2** : very good : EXCELLENT • *I have some splendid news.* — **splen·did·ly** *adv*

splen·dor (*US*) *or Brit* **splen·dour** /ˈsplɛndɚ/ *n* **1** [*U*] : great and impressive beauty • *The palace had lost much of its original splendor.* **2** [*plural*] : things that are very beautiful or impressive • *the splendors of the countryside*

splice /ˈsplaɪs/ *vb* **spliced**; **splic·ing** [*T*] **1** : to join ropes, wires, etc., by weaving or twisting them together **2** : to join (pieces of film, magnetic tape, etc.) by connecting their ends together — **splice** *n* [*C*] • *a film splice*

splint /ˈsplɪnt/ *n* [*C*] : a piece of wood, metal, plastic, etc., that is used to hold a broken bone in the correct position while it heals

¹**splin·ter** /ˈsplɪntɚ/ *n* [*C*] : a thin, sharp piece of wood, glass, etc., that has broken off a larger piece

²**splinter** *vb* [*T/I*] **1** : to break (something) into small pieces or splinters • *The*

impact of the crash splintered the glass. **2** : to divide or split a group of people into smaller groups • *The group splintered off to form a third political party.*

splinter group *n* [*C*] : a group of people that has separated from a larger group (such as a political party)

¹**split** /ˈsplɪt/ *vb* **split**; **split·ting** **1** [*T/I*] : to break apart or into pieces especially along a straight line • *The board split in two.* • *split (up) a log* **2** [*T/I*] **a** : to separate or divide into parts or groups • *The class split (up) into small groups.* • *Two of the band members split off to form their own band.* • *The river splits the town in two.* **b** : to separate or divide into groups that disagree • *The church split into moderate and conservative factions.* • *The budget issue has split (up) the town.* **3** [*T*] : to divide (money, food, etc.) among two or more people or things • *Why don't we split a pizza for dinner?* • *The prize money was split (up) evenly.* **4** [*T/I*] : to cut, rip, or tear (something) especially along a straight line • *I split my lip when I fell.* • *His pants split when he bent over.* **5** [*T/I*] *informal* : to end or cause the end of a relationship • *My parents split when I was little.* • *She split up with her husband.* • *Personality conflicts split up the band.* **6** [*I*] *informal* : to leave quickly • *It's late. We should split.* — **split hairs** see HAIR

²**split** *n* [*C*] : a narrow break, tear, or crack • *There's a split down the back of your jacket.* **2** [*C*] : a division or separation in a group that is caused by a disagreement • *a split between liberals and conservatives* **3** [*singular*] **a** : a part of something that has been divided • *Here's your split of the proceeds.* **b** : the act of dividing something among two or more people or things • *We agreed to a fifty-fifty split of the money.* [=we agreed to divide the money equally]

split–lev·el /ˈsplɪtˈlɛvəl/ *adj* : divided so that the floor in one part is about halfway between two floors in the other part • *a split-level house*

split personality *n* [*C*] : a condition in which a person behaves in two very different ways at different times

split second *n* [*singular*] : a very short period of time • *In a split second, it was all over.* — **split–second** *adj, always before a noun* • *a split-second decision* [=a decision made very quickly]

splitting headache *n* [*C*] : a very bad headache

splotch /ˈsplɑːtʃ/ *n* [*C*] *chiefly US* : a large spot or mark of dirt, paint, etc. • *splotches of ink/rust* — **splotchy** /ˈsplɑːtʃi/ *adj* **splotch·i·er**; **-est** • *splotchy skin*

splurge /ˈsplɚdʒ/ *vb* **splurged**; **splurg·ing** [*I*] *informal* : to spend more money than usual on something for yourself • *We decided to splurge on a bottle of good wine for dinner.* — **splurge** *n* [*C*] *informal* • *a shopping splurge*

splut·ter /ˈsplʌtɚ/ *vb* **1** [*I*] : to make a series of short, loud noises like the noises of someone who is struggling to breathe • *The old lawn mower spluttered* [=*sputtered*] *to life.* [=noisily started working]

2 [T/I] : to say (something) in short, confused phrases ▪ *When I demanded an explanation, he just stood there spluttering.* — **splutter** *n* [C]

¹**spoil** /'spɔjəl/ *vb* **spoiled** *or chiefly Brit* **spoilt** /'spɔjəlt/; **spoil·ing** 1 [T] : to have a bad effect on (something) : to ruin (something) ▪ *The fight spoiled the party.* ▪ *Don't spoil your appetite by snacking too much.* ▪ *I spoiled the sauce by adding too much garlic.* 2 [I] : to decay or lose freshness especially because of being kept too long ▪ *The milk/fruit was beginning to spoil.* 3 [T] **a** *disapproving* : to have a bad effect on (someone) by allowing too many things to or by not correcting bad behavior ▪ *Her grandparents spoil her.* ▪ *a spoiled brat* **b** : to treat (someone) very well ▪ *The hotel spoils their guests with excellent service.* ▪ *She always spoils me on my birthday.* — **(be) spoiling for** : to have a strong desire for (something) ▪ *They are spoiling for a fight/rematch.*

²**spoil** *n* [C] *formal* 1 : something stolen or taken by thieves, soldiers, etc. ▪ *the spoils of war* 2 : something valuable or desirable that someone gets by working or trying hard ▪ *the spoils of victory*

spoil·age /'spɔjlɪdʒ/ *n* [U] *technical* : the process or result of decaying ▪ *Milk should be refrigerated to prevent spoilage.*

spoil·er /'spɔjlɚ/ *n* [C] 1 : a person or thing that spoils something: such as **a** : a political candidate who cannot win but who prevents another candidate from winning by taking away votes **b** *chiefly US* : a person or team that surprisingly defeats a competitor that is expected to win **c** : information about the things that happen in a movie, book, etc., that spoils the surprise or suspense for someone who has not seen it or read it yet ▪ *The review contains a few spoilers, so don't read it if you haven't seen the movie.* 2 **a** : a long narrow part on the back of an automobile that prevents it from lifting off the road at high speeds **b** : a part of an airplane's wing that may be raised to control the amount of lift produced by the wing

spoil·sport /'spɔjəl,spoɚt/ *n* [C] *informal* : someone who spoils other people's fun or enjoyment

spoilt *chiefly Brit past tense and past participle of* ¹SPOIL

¹**spoke** *past tense of* SPEAK

²**spoke** /'spoʊk/ *n* [C] : one of the bars that connect the center of a wheel to the rim

¹**spo·ken** /'spoʊkən/ *past participle of* SPEAK

²**spoken** *adj* 1 : using speech and not writing ▪ *a spoken statement* ▪ *the spoken language* 2 : speaking in a specified manner ▪ *a soft-spoken person* [=a person who speaks softly]

spokes·man /'spoʊksmən/ *n, pl* **-men** /-mən/ [C] : a person who speaks for or represents someone or something ▪ *a company spokesman* ▪ *a spokesman for AIDS awareness*

spokes·per·son /'spoʊks,pɚsn̩/ *n, pl* **spokes·peo·ple** /'spoʊks,pi:pəl/ [C] : SPOKESMAN

spokes·wom·an /'spoʊks,wʊmən/ *n, pl* **-wom·en** /'spoʊks,wɪmən/ [C] : a woman who speaks for or represents someone or something ▪ *the company's spokeswoman*

¹**sponge** /'spʌndʒ/ *n* 1 : a piece of light natural or artificial material that becomes soft when it is wet, and is able to take in and hold liquid, and is used for washing or cleaning ▪ *a kitchen sponge* 2 : a type of sea animal from which natural sponges are made

²**sponge** *vb* **sponged; spong·ing** 1 [T] : to clean or wipe (something) with a sponge ▪ *She sponged up the spilt milk.* ▪ *He sponged off his face.* 2 [T/I] *informal* + *disapproving* : to get money, food, etc., from (someone) without doing or paying anything in return ▪ *She always sponges meals from us.* ▪ *She lives at home and sponges off her parents.* — **spong·er** /'spʌndʒɚ/ *n* [C]

sponge cake *n* [C/U] : a very light cake made with flour, eggs, and sugar

spongy /'spʌndʒi/ *adj* **spong·i·er; -est** : soft and full of holes or water : resembling a sponge ▪ *spongy bread*

¹**spon·sor** /'spɑːnsɚ/ *n* [C] 1 **a** : a person or organization that pays the cost of an activity or event in return for the right to advertise during the activity or event ▪ *the sponsors of a TV show* ▪ *corporate sponsors* **b** : a person or organization that gives someone money for participating in a charity event (such as a race) **c** : an organization that gives money to an athlete for training, clothes, equipment, etc., in return for the right to use the athlete for advertising ▪ *Her sponsors include a major sneaker company.* 2 **a** : someone who takes the responsibility for someone or something ▪ *The senator is a sponsor of the proposed bill.* **b** : a person who teaches and guides someone in religious or spiritual matters ▪ *She was my sponsor at my confirmation.*

²**sponsor** *vb* [T] : to be a sponsor for (something or someone) ▪ *The radio station sponsored the concert.* ▪ *She sponsored the new tax bill.*

spon·sor·ship /'spɑːnsɚ,ʃɪp/ *n* 1 [C/U] : an arrangement in which a sponsor agrees to give money to someone or something ▪ *You cannot race without sponsorship.* ▪ *corporate sponsorships* 2 [U] : the act of sponsoring someone or something ▪ *They protested the tobacco company's sponsorship of the tournament.*

spon·ta·ne·ous /spɑːn'teɪnijəs/ *adj* 1 : done or said in a natural and often sudden way and without a lot of thought or planning ▪ *spontaneous laughter* ▪ *a spontaneous decision* 2 : doing things that have not been planned but that seem enjoyable and worth doing at a particular time ▪ *He's spontaneous and fun.* — **spon·ta·ne·i·ty** /,spɑːntə'nejəti/ *n* [U] *the spontaneity* [=the spontaneous quality] *of their behavior* — **spon·ta·ne·ous·ly** *adv*

spoof /'spu:f/ *n* [C] : a humorous movie,

book, etc., that copies something in a silly and exaggerated way ▪ *a spoof of/on Shakespeare's play* — **spoof** *vb* [*T*] ▪ *The movie spoofs horror films.*

¹**spook** /'spuːk/ *n* [*C*] *informal* **1** : GHOST 1 **2** *chiefly US* : SPY 1 ▪ *a CIA spook*

²**spook** *vb* [*T/I*] *chiefly US, informal* : to become frightened or to make (a person or animal) frightened ▪ *The noise spooked the cat.* ▪ *The horse spooked and ran away.*

spooky /'spuːki/ *adj* **spook·i·er; -est** : strange and frightening ▪ *a spooky old house*

spool /'spuːl/ *n* [*C*] : a round object that is made to have thread, wire, tape, etc., wrapped around it ▪ *a spool of film*

¹**spoon** /'spuːn/ *n* [*C*] : an eating or cooking tool that has a small shallow bowl attached to a handle — see also GREASY SPOON

²**spoon** *vb* [*T*] : to move or pick up (food) with a spoon ▪ *He spooned the ice cream into a bowl.*

spoon–feed /'spuːn,fiːd/ *vb* **-fed** /-,fɛd/; **-feed·ing** [*T*] **1** : to feed (someone) with a spoon ▪ *She spoon-fed the baby.* **2** *disapproving* : to give someone information in a way that requires or allows no further thinking or effort ▪ *The students are being spoon-fed facts and dates without having any opportunity for discussion.*

spoon·ful /'spuːn,fʊl/ *n* [*C*] : as much as a spoon can hold ▪ *one spoonful of sugar*

spo·rad·ic /spə'rædɪk/ *adj* : happening often but not regularly : not constant or steady ▪ *sporadic gunfire/fighting* — **spo·rad·i·cal·ly** /spə'rædɪkli/ *adv*

spore /'spoɚ/ *n* [*C*] *biology* : a cell made by some plants that is like a seed and can produce a new plant

¹**sport** /'spoɚt/ *n* **1 a** [*C*] : a contest or game in which people do certain physical activities according to a specific set of rules and compete against each other ▪ *My favorite sports are tennis and volleyball.* ▪ *the sport of boxing* ▪ *Do you play any sports?* ▪ *I like watching sports on TV.* ▪ *Baseball is a team sport.* [=a sport played by teams] **b** [*U*] *Brit* : sports in general ▪ *He's not interested in sport.* [=(*US*) *sports*] **2** [*C/U*] : a physical activity that is done for enjoyment ▪ *Ice-skating with friends is my favorite sport.* ▪ *He hunts and fishes for sport.* **3** [*C*] **a** — used with *good*, *bad*, etc., to say if someone has behaved politely or not after losing a game or contest ▪ *He lost but he was a good sport about it.* [=he was not rude or angry about losing] ▪ *Don't be a poor sport.* [=don't be angry or rude if you lose] **b** *informal + old-fashioned* : someone who is kind or generous ▪ *Be a (good) sport and let him play with you.*

²**sport** *adj, always before a noun* **1** : done for enjoyment rather than as a job or for food for survival ▪ *sport fishing/hunting* **2** *chiefly US* : participating in an activity for enjoyment rather than as a job or for food for survival ▪ *a sport fisherman*

³**sport** *vb* [*T*] : to wear (something) in a way that attracts attention ▪ *She was sporting a bright red hat.*

sport coat *n* [*C*] *US* : a man's coat that is like the top part of a suit but is less formal — called also *sports coat*, *sports jacket*, (*US*) *sport jacket*

sport·ing /'spoɚtɪŋ/ *adj, always before a noun* **1** : of, relating to, or used in sports ▪ *sporting events/dogs* ▪ (*US*) *a store that sells sporting goods* = *a sporting goods store* **2** : fairly good ▪ *He should be given a sporting chance* [=a fair chance] *to succeed.* **3** *chiefly Brit* : done or behaving in a way that treats the other people in a sport or competition fairly ▪ *It wasn't very sporting of you to trip him.*

sports /'spoɚts/ *adj, always before a noun* : of, relating to, or suitable for sports ▪ *a sports team* ▪ *sports equipment/facilities*

sports car *n* [*C*] : a low, small car that seats two people and that is made for fast driving

sports·cast /'spoɚts,kæst, *Brit* 'spɔːts-,kɑːst/ *n* [*C*] *US* : a television or radio broadcast of a sports event or of news about sports — **sports·cast·er** /'spoɚts,kæstɚ, *Brit* 'spɔːts,kɑːstɚ/ *n* [*C*]

sports coat *n* [*C*] : SPORT COAT

sports day *n* [*C*] *Brit* : FIELD DAY

sport shirt *n* [*C*] *US* : an informal shirt; *especially* : POLO SHIRT — called also *sports shirt*

sports jacket *n* [*C*] : SPORT COAT

sports·man /'spoɚtsmən/ *n, pl* **sports·men** /'spoɚtsmən/ [*C*] **1** *US* : a man who participates in outdoor activities like hunting and fishing **2** *chiefly Brit* : a man who participates in sports

sports·man·like /'spoɚtsmən,laɪk/ *adj* : fair, respectful, and polite toward other players when participating in a sport ▪ *sportsmanlike behavior*

sports·man·ship /'spoɚtsmən,ʃɪp/ *n* [*U*] : fair play, respect for opponents, and polite behavior by someone who is competing in a sport or other competition ▪ *She showed good/bad/poor sportsmanship.*

sports shirt *n* [*C*] : SPORT SHIRT

sports·wear /'spoɚts,weɚ/ *n* [*U*] **1** : clothes that people wear for playing sports **2** *chiefly US* : comfortable clothes that people wear for informal activities

sports·wom·an /'spoɚts,wʊmən/ *n, pl* **-wom·en** /-,wɪmən/ [*C*] : a woman who participates in sports

sports·writ·er /'spoɚts,raɪtɚ/ *n* [*C*] : someone who writes about sports for a newspaper, magazine, etc.

sport–util·i·ty vehicle /'spoɚtjuː'tɪləti-/ *n* [*C*] : SUV

sporty /'spoɚti/ *adj* **sport·i·er; -est** **1** : attractive and suitable for informal wear ▪ *a sporty jacket* **2** : having the qualities or appearance of a sports car ▪ *a sporty convertible* **3** *chiefly Brit* : liking sports : active in and good at sports ▪ *sporty children*

¹**spot** /'spɑːt/ *n* [*C*] **1 a** : a small area of a surface that is different from other areas ▪ *The wood has some rough spots.* ▪ *The dog is black with a white spot on its chest.* **b** : a small amount of a substance that is on something ▪ *The tablecloth had a couple of spots.* ▪ *a spot of grease* **2** : a particular space or area : PLACE ▪ *a quiet spot*

by the river ▪ *a parking/vacation spot* ▪ *This is a good spot to stop the movie.* **3** : a particular position or situation ▪ *The talk show has been moved to a daytime spot.* ▪ *He's trying out for a spot on the team.* ▪ *When the truth came out, they found themselves in an awful spot.* ▪ *You put me in a tight spot.* [=in a difficult situation] **4** : an appearance on a television or radio program ▪ *a guest spot on a popular sitcom* **5** : a short announcement or advertisement on television or radio ▪ *advertising spots* **6** *Brit* : a small amount of something ▪ *a spot of trouble/lunch/tennis* — **hit the spot** *informal, of food or drink* : to be very enjoyable or satisfying ▪ *That dinner really hit the spot.* — **on the spot 1** : right away at the place that has been mentioned : IMMEDIATELY ▪ *When the boss saw him stealing, he was fired on the spot.* **2** : at the place where something is happening ▪ *She was on the spot reporting on the fire.* **3** : in a difficult or dangerous situation ▪ *The question put me on the spot.*

²**spot** *vb* **spot·ted; spot·ting** [T] **1** : to see or notice (someone or something that is difficult to see or find) ▪ *She spotted a deer in the woods.* ▪ *He spotted a typo.* **2** *US* **a** : to give (an opponent) a specified advantage at the beginning of a race, game, etc., in order to make a competition more even ▪ *They spotted us five points, and we still lost.* **b** *informal* : to lend (someone) a small amount of money ▪ *Can you spot me five bucks?* **3** *American football* : to put (the football) at the appropriate place on the field in preparation for the next play ▪ *The official spotted the ball at the 10-yard line.* **4** : to mark (something) with spots ▪ *His pants were spotted with mud.* — **spot·ter** /ˈspɑːtɚ/ *n* [C]

spot–check /ˈspɑːtˌtʃɛk/ *vb* [T/I] : to check (something) quickly for problems ▪ *She spot-checked the data) for errors.* — **spot check** *n* [C]

spot·less /ˈspɑːtləs/ *adj* : perfectly clean ▪ *a spotless kitchen* ▪ *(figurative) a spotless reputation* — **spot·less·ly** *adv* ▪ *The house is spotlessly clean.*

¹**spot·light** /ˈspɑːtˌlaɪt/ *n* **1** [C] **a** : a device that directs a narrow, bright beam of light on a small area **b** : the area of light created by a spotlight ▪ *The actor stood in the spotlight.* **2 the spotlight** : public attention or notice ▪ *a baseball star who hates the spotlight* ▪ *celebrities who are always in the spotlight*

²**spotlight** *vb* **-light·ed** *or* **-lit; -light·ing** [T] **1** : to shine a spotlight on (someone or something) ▪ *She was spotlighted as she sang her solo.* **2** : to give special attention to (something) ▪ *The news spotlighted the city's financial problems.*

spot–on /ˈspɑːtˈɑːn/ *adj, chiefly Brit, informal* : exactly correct or accurate ▪ *The weather forecast was spot-on.*

spot·ted /ˈspɑːtəd/ *adj* : marked with spots ▪ *a spotted cat*

spot·ty /ˈspɑːti/ *adj* **spot·ti·er; -est 1** *chiefly US* : good in some parts or at some times but not others ▪ *Her work has*

been spotty. **2** : marked with spots ▪ *a spotty photograph* ▪ *(Brit) a spotty* [=pimply] *youth*

spouse /ˈspaʊs/ *n* [C] : someone who is married : a husband or wife ▪ *my brothers and sisters and their spouses* — **spou·sal** /ˈspaʊzəl/ *adj, always before a noun* ▪ *spousal abuse/consent*

¹**spout** /ˈspaʊt/ *vb* [T/I] **1** : to shoot out with force ▪ *Blood spouted (out) from the wound.* ▪ *The well was spouting oil.* **2** : to say or talk about (something) in a way that is boring or annoying ▪ *He started spouting (off) poetry.* ▪ *He was spouting off about his adventures.*

²**spout** *n* [C] **1** : a tube, pipe, or hole out of which a liquid flows ▪ *the spout of a teakettle* **2** : a sudden strong stream of liquid ▪ *a spout of water*

sprain /ˈspreɪn/ *vb* [T] : to injure (a joint) by twisting it in a sudden and painful way ▪ *I sprained my wrist.* ▪ *a sprained ankle* — **sprain** *n* [C] ▪ *an ankle sprain*

sprang *past tense of* ²**SPRING**

¹**sprawl** /ˈsprɑːl/ *vb* [I] **1** : to lie or sit with your arms and legs spread wide apart ▪ *He sprawled (out) on the couch.* **2** : to spread or develop in an uneven or uncontrolled way ▪ *The bushes were sprawling along the road.* ▪ *a sprawling city* — **sprawled** /ˈsprɑːld/ *adj* ▪ *She lay sprawled across the bed.*

²**sprawl** *n* [singular] : a group of things (such as buildings) that cover an area in an uneven and ugly way ▪ *a sprawl of stores and restaurants* — see also URBAN SPRAWL

¹**spray** /ˈspreɪ/ *n* **1 a** [C/U] : a liquid substance that is used or applied by being forced out of a container in a stream of very small drops ▪ *A nasal/nose spray should help you breathe better.* ▪ *a can of hair spray* **b** [C] : the act of spraying something ▪ *a quick spray of perfume* **2** [U] : very small drops of water moving through the air ▪ *sea spray* **3** [C] : a stream of liquid in the form of very small drops ▪ *a spray of water* ▪ *(figurative) a spray of bullets* **4** [C] **a** : a branch of a plant that usually has flowers and is used as a decoration ▪ *a spray of apple blossoms* **b** : an attractive arrangement of flowers ▪ *a spray of roses*

²**spray** *vb* **1** [T] **a** : to put a stream of small drops of liquid on (someone or something) ▪ *She sprayed herself with perfume.* ▪ *The crops were sprayed (with a pesticide).* **b** : to put (something) on a surface or into the air using a special container that produces a stream of small drops of liquid ▪ *The boys sprayed graffiti on the wall.* ▪ *She sprayed some perfume into the air.* **2** [I] : to flow out in a stream of very small drops ▪ *The soda sprayed from the bottle.* **3** [T] : to shoot many bullets at someone or something ▪ *The gunmen sprayed the house with bullets.* = *The gunmen sprayed bullets into the house.* — **spray·er** *n* [C] ▪ *a paint sprayer*

spray can *n* [C] : a can that contains a liquid (such as paint) that can be sprayed

spray paint *n* [C/U] : paint that is sprayed onto a surface from a can that you can hold in one hand — **spray-paint** vb [T] • *I spray-painted the table.*

¹spread /'sprɛd/ vb **spread; spread·ing**
1 [T] : to open, arrange, or place (something) over a large area • *The newspaper was spread across his lap.* • *Her notes were spread (out) all over the desk.* • *We spread fertilizer on our yard.* **2 a** [T] : to become larger or to affect a larger area : to move into more places • *The fire spread quickly through the building.* • *Computer technology has spread into all fields of work.* **b** [T] : to cause (something) to be present in more places throughout a large area • *Flies spread diseases.* **3 a** [I] : to pass from person to person • *The rumor spread quickly.* **b** [T] : to cause (something) to become known by many people • *He was spreading lies about her.* • *People are spreading the word* [=telling others] *about his book.* **4** [T/I] : to move parts of your body outward or away from each other • *The bird spreads (out) its wings.* • *Spread your fingers wide apart.* • *There's no room on the couch to spread out.* **5** [I] of a smile or other facial expression : to appear and slowly grow more apparent • *A smile slowly spread across her face.* **6** [T] : to put a layer of (something) on top of something else • *He spread butter on the bread.* = *He spread the bread with butter.* **7** [T] : to divide up (something) over a period of time or among members of a group • *The payments are spread (out) over a period of six years.* • *You should spread the wealth.* [=share your money or good fortune with others] — **spread out** [phrasal vb] : to move apart from the other members of a group • *The police spread out to search the area faster.* — **spread your wings** see ¹**WING** — **spread·er** /'sprɛdə/ n [C]

²spread n **1** [U] : growth or increase that causes something to cover a larger area, affect a larger number of people, etc. • *the spread of infection* **2** [C/U] : a soft food that is spread on bread, crackers, etc. • *crackers and (a) cheese spread* **3** [C] : the total distance between the two outer edges of something • *the spread of a bird's wings* **4** [C] informal : a large meal • *We always have a huge spread for Thanksgiving.* **5** [C] : an advertisement, a series of photos, etc., that covers two or more pages in a newspaper or magazine • *a two-page spread* **6** [C] US : **BEDSPREAD** **7** [C] US : a large farm or ranch • *He bought a spread of 100 acres.*

spread·sheet /'sprɛd,ʃiːt/ n [C] **1** : a computer program that calculates numbers and organizes information in columns and rows **2** : a document that has columns and rows which are used to calculate numbers and organize information

spree /'spriː/ n [C] : a short period of time when you do a lot of something • *a shopping/crime spree*

sprig /'sprɪg/ n [C] : a small twig or stem that has leaves or flowers on it • *a sprig of parsley*

spright·ly /'spraɪtli/ adj **spright·li·er;**

-est : full of life and energy • *a sprightly old woman* — **spright·li·ness** n [U]

¹spring /'sprɪŋ/ n **1** [C/U] : the season between winter and summer • *We've had a rainy spring.* • *spring colors/flowers* **2** [C] : a twisted or coiled piece of metal that returns to its original shape when it is pressed down or stretched • *the springs of a mattress* — see also **BOX SPRING** **b** [U] : the ability of something to return to its original shape when it is pressed down, stretched, etc. • *The cushion has lost its spring.* **3** [C] : a source of water coming up from the ground • *a mineral spring* **4** [singular] : a lively and energetic quality • *She had a spring in her step.*

²spring vb **sprang** /'spræŋ/ *or* **sprung** /'sprʌŋ/; **sprung; spring·ing** [I] **1** : to move or leap suddenly forward or upward • *He sprang out of his seat and ran to the door.* **2** : to move quickly to a different position • *The lid sprang open/shut.* • *The branch sprang back and hit her.* — **spring a leak** : to start to leak • *The boat/pipe sprang a leak.* — **spring a surprise** : to do, ask, or say something that is not expected • *The teacher sprang a surprise on us and gave a quiz.* — **spring a trap** : to capture someone or something with a trap • *Police sprang a trap on the drug smugglers.* — **spring for** [phrasal vb] US, informal : to pay for (something) • *I'll spring for dinner.* — **spring from** [phrasal vb] informal : to start from or be caused by (something) • *The idea sprang from a dream I had.* — **spring into/to action/life** : to become suddenly very active and energetic • *They sprang into action as soon as they received their orders.* • *The crowd sprang to life.* — **spring on** [phrasal vb] **spring (something) on (someone)** : to surprise (someone) with (something) • *The teacher sprang a test on us.* — **spring to mind** see ¹**MIND** — **spring up** [phrasal vb] : to grow or appear suddenly • *The weeds sprang up overnight.* — **tears spring to your eyes** ◇ *If tears spring to your eyes,* you suddenly start to cry.

spring·board /'sprɪŋ,boɚd/ n [C] **1** : a strong, flexible board that is used for jumping very high in gymnastics or diving **2** : something that helps you start an activity or process • *The news served as a springboard for a class discussion.*

spring fever n [U] : a feeling of wanting to go outdoors and do things because spring is coming and the weather is getting warmer

spring onion n [C] chiefly Brit : **GREEN ONION**

spring roll n [C] : **EGG ROLL**

spring·time /'sprɪŋ,taɪm/ n [U] : the season of spring • *It's beautiful here in (the) springtime.* [=in the spring]

springy /'sprɪŋi/ adj **spring·i·er; -est** **1** : returning to an original shape when pressed down, stretched, etc. • *a springy bed* **2** : having or showing lively and energetic movement • *He walks with a springy step.*

¹sprin·kle /'sprɪŋkəl/ vb **sprin·kled; sprin·kling** **1** [T] : to drop or spread small pieces or amounts of something over something • *He sprinkled water on the plants.* • *She sprinkled cheese on the pasta.* = *She sprinkled the pasta with cheese.* • (figurative) *The essay is sprinkled with quotations.* **2** [*I*] *US* : to rain lightly • *It's sprinkling a little.*

²**sprinkle** *n* **1** [*singular*] : a light rain • *a sprinkle of rain* **2** [*singular*] : a small amount that is sprinkled on something • *pasta with a sprinkle of parsley* **3** [*plural*] *US* : tiny candies that are put on top of a sweet food (such as ice cream) • *chocolate sprinkles*

sprin·kler /ˈsprɪŋklɚ/ *n* [*C*] : a device that is used to spray water

sprin·kling /ˈsprɪŋklɪŋ/ *n* [*singular*] : a small amount that is sprinkled on something • *She put a sprinkling of parsley on the pasta.* • (figurative) *a sprinkling of suggestions*

¹**sprint** /ˈsprɪnt/ *vb* [*I*] : to run or go very fast for a short distance • *He sprinted to class.* — **sprint·er** *n* [*C*]

²**sprint** *n* **1** [*C*] : a race over a short distance at a very fast speed **2** [*singular*] : a short period of running or going very fast • *He made a sprint for the finish line.*

sprite /ˈspraɪt/ *n* [*C*] : a small creature that has magical powers : an elf or fairy • *a water sprite*

spritz /ˈsprɪts/ *vb* [*T*] *US* : to spray (something) quickly • *spritz the plants with water* — **spritz** *n* [*C*]

spritz·er /ˈsprɪtsɚ/ *n* [*C*] : a drink made of wine mixed with soda water

sprock·et /ˈsprɑːkət/ *n* [*C*] : a wheel that has a row of teeth around its edge which fit into the holes of something (such as a bicycle chain or a piece of film) and cause it to turn when the wheel turns; *also* : any one of the teeth on such a wheel

¹**sprout** /ˈspraʊt/ *vb* **1** [*T/I*] : to produce new leaves, buds, etc. • *seeds sprouting in the spring* • *The tree is sprouting leaves.* **2** [*T/I*] : to grow or develop (something) • *The deer sprouted horns.* • *Hair sprouted on his face.* **3** [*I*] : to appear suddenly and in large numbers • *New restaurants are sprouting up around the city.*

²**sprout** *n* **1** [*C*] : a new leaf, bud, etc., that is growing on a plant **2** [*plural*] *chiefly US* : very young plants that come from alfalfa or bean seeds and that are used as a vegetable **3** [*C*] *chiefly Brit* : BRUSSELS SPROUT

¹**spruce** /ˈspruːs/ *n, pl* **spruc·es** *also* **spruce** **1** [*C*] : a type of tree that has long, thin needles instead of leaves and that stays green throughout the year **2** [*U*] : the wood of a spruce tree

²**spruce** *vb* **spruced; spruc·ing** — **spruce up** [*phrasal vb*] **spruce (someone or something) up** *or* **spruce up (someone or something)** : to make (someone or something) look cleaner, neater, or more attractive • *We spruced up the room with a fresh coat of paint.*

³**spruce** *adj* **spruc·er; -est** *somewhat old-fashioned* : neat, clean, or stylish in appearance • *He looked very spruce in his new suit.*

sprung *past tense and past participle of* ²SPRING

spry /ˈspraɪ/ *adj* **spri·er** *or* **spry·er** /ˈspraɪɚ/; **spri·est** *or* **spry·est** /ˈspraɪəst/ : full of life and energy • *a spry old man*

spud /ˈspʌd/ *n* [*C*] *informal* : POTATO

spun *past tense and past participle of* ¹SPIN

spunk /ˈspʌŋk/ *n* [*U*] *informal* : spirit, courage, and determination • *That girl has a lot of spunk.* — **spunky** /ˈspʌŋki/ *adj* **spunk·i·er; -est** • *a spunky girl*

¹**spur** /ˈspɚ/ *n* **1** [*C*] : a sharp pointed object that is attached to the heel of a horse rider's boot and that is pressed into the horse's side to make the horse go faster **2** [*singular*] : something that makes you want to do something or that causes something to happen • *The reward was offered as a spur to greater work/achievement.* — **on/at the spur of the moment** ◇ If something is done *on/at the spur of the moment*, it is done immediately without planning. • *We decided on the spur of the moment to go to the beach.*

²**spur** *vb* **spurred; spur·ring** [*T*] **1** : to encourage (someone) to do or achieve something • *The reward spurred them (on) to work harder.* **2** : to cause (something) to happen or to happen more quickly • *Lower interest rates should spur economic growth.* **3** : to urge (a horse) to go faster by pushing spurs into its sides • *He spurred the horse onward.*

spu·ri·ous /ˈspjɚijəs/ *adj* **1** : not genuine, sincere, or authentic • *spurious gems/kindness* **2** : based on false ideas or bad reasoning • *spurious claims* — **spu·ri·ous·ly** *adv*

spurn /ˈspɚn/ *vb* [*T*] *literary* : to refuse to accept (someone or something) • *She spurned their offer.* • *a spurned lover*

spur–of–the–moment *adj, always before a noun* : done suddenly and without planning • *a spur-of-the-moment decision*

¹**spurt** /ˈspɚt/ *vb* **1** [*T/I*] : to pour out or come out quickly and suddenly • *Water spurted from the broken pipe.* • *His nose spurted blood.* **2** [*I*] : to move at a fast speed for a short distance • *He spurted for the finish line.*

²**spurt** *n* [*C*] **1** : an amount of liquid, flame, etc., that comes out of something suddenly • *a spurt of water/blood* **2** : a short period of greatly increased effort, activity, or development • *a spurt of hard work* • *When he was 11, he had a **growth spurt**.* • *They worked on the house in **spurts**.* **3** *US* : a short period of time • *They played well for a brief spurt but then started losing again.*

sput·ter /ˈspʌtɚ/ *vb* **1** [*I*] : to make loud sounds like explosions • *The motor sputtered and died.* **2** [*T/I*] : to speak quickly or in a confused way because you are upset, surprised, etc. • *He was sputtering with rage.* — **sputter** *n* [*C*]

¹**spy** /ˈspaɪ/ *n, pl* **spies** [*C*] **1** : a person who tries secretly to get information about a country or organization for another country or organization • *a spy for the CIA* • *a spy plane* [=a plane used for spying] **2** : someone who secretly

watches the movement or actions of other people ▪ *My coworker is a spy for the boss.*

²**spy** *vb* **spies; spied; spy·ing** 1 [*I*] : to try secretly to get information about a country, organization, etc. ▪ *spying for a foreign government* — often + *on* ▪ *They were accused of spying on a rival company.* 2 [*T*] : to see or notice (someone or something) ▪ *She spied a friend in the crowd.* — **spy on** [*phrasal vb*] : to watch (someone) secretly ▪ *He spies on his neighbors.*

spy·ware /ˈspaɪˌweɚ/ *n* [*U*] : computer software that secretly records information about the way you use your computer

sq. *abbr* square

squab·ble /ˈskwɑːbəl/ *vb* **squab·bled; squab·bling** [*I*] : to argue loudly about things that are not important ▪ *The children were squabbling over the toys.* — **squabble** *n* [*C*]

squad /ˈskwɑːd/ *n* [*C*] 1 : a part of a police force that deals with a specific type of crime ▪ *the bomb/vice squad* 2 : a small organized group of soldiers ▪ *an infantry squad* 3 : a group of people who are involved in a particular activity ▪ *a rescue/cheerleading squad*

squad car *n* [*C*] : POLICE CAR

squad·ron /ˈskwɑːdrən/ *n* [*C*] : a military unit consisting of soldiers, ships, or aircraft

squal·id /ˈskwɑːləd/ *adj* 1 : very dirty and unpleasant ▪ *living in squalid conditions* 2 : immoral or dishonest ▪ *a squalid affair* — **squal·id·ness** *n* [*U*]

¹**squall** /ˈskwɑːl/ *n* [*C*] : a sudden violent wind often with rain or snow ▪ *a snow squall*

²**squall** *vb* [*I*] : to cry loudly ▪ *a squalling baby*

squa·lor /ˈskwɑːlɚ/ *n* [*U*] : very bad and dirty conditions ▪ *living in squalor*

squan·der /ˈskwɑːndɚ/ *vb* [*T*] : to use (something) in a foolish or wasteful way ▪ *She squander her money.* ▪ *squander an opportunity*

¹**square** /ˈskweɚ/ *n* [*C*] 1 : a four-sided shape that is made up of four straight sides that are the same length and that has four right angles ▪ *Cut the brownies into squares.* ▪ *a square of tile/cloth* 2 : any of the squares on a board for playing chess, checkers, etc. 3 *mathematics* : the number that results from multiplying a number by itself ▪ *The square of 2 is 4.* [=2 x 2 = 4] 4 : an open area in a village, city, etc., where two or more streets meet ▪ *the main/town/market square* 5 *informal + disapproving* : someone who does not like or try unusual things that are exciting, interesting, etc. ▪ *He's such a square.* 6 *technical* : a flat tool that is used to mark or check angles ▪ *a carpenter's square*

²**square** *adj* **squar·er; squar·est** 1 a : shaped like a square ▪ *a square box/ room* b : forming a right angle ▪ *a square corner* 2 — used to describe a measurement that is produced by multiplying something's length and width ▪ *one square foot* [=an area that is one foot

long and one foot wide] 3 : shaped more like a right angle than a curve ▪ *a square jaw* 4 : honest and fair ▪ *a square deal* 5 *informal + disapproving* — used to describe someone who does not like or try unusual things that are exciting, interesting, etc. ▪ *He's nice but he's kind of square.* 6 *informal* : having nothing owed by either side : EVEN ▪ *Here's your money. Now we're square.*

³**square** *vb* **squared; squar·ing** [*T*] 1 : to make (something) square ▪ *square (off) the boards* 2 *mathematics* : to multiply (a number) by itself ▪ *3 squared by itself equals 9.* [=3 x 3 = 9] 3 : to pay money that is owed for (something) ▪ *We squared (up) our accounts.* — **square away** [*phrasal vb*] **square** (something) **away** *or* **square away** (something) *US* : to put (something) in an organized and proper state or condition ▪ *I got my work squared away before I left.* — **square off** [*phrasal vb*] 1 : to get into the position of two people who are going to fight each other ▪ *The two men squared off.* 2 : to fight or compete ▪ *The two teams will square off again tomorrow.* ▪ *They squared off against each other in the election/match/debate.* — **square up** [*phrasal vb*] : to turn so that you are facing something or someone directly ▪ *They squared up (with/to each other) for a fight.* — **square with** [*phrasal vb*] 1 : to agree with (something) ▪ *Your story doesn't square with the facts.* 2 **square** (something) **with** a : to make (something) agree with (something) ▪ *How can they square what they've done with what they've said?* b : to get agreement about or approval of (something) from (someone) ▪ *I need to square it with my parents.*

⁴**square** *adv* : in a direct way ▪ *Look (at) me square in the eye.*

square dance *n* [*C*] : a dance for four couples that begins with each couple facing one of the other couples so that the four couples form a square — **square dancer** *n* [*C*] — **square dancing** *n* [*U*] ▪ *We like to go square dancing.*

square knot *n* [*C*] *US* : a strong and simple type of knot

square·ly /ˈskweɚli/ *adv* 1 : in a direct and honest way ▪ *face a problem/issue squarely* 2 : EXACTLY, RIGHT ▪ *The dart hit the target squarely in the middle.* ▪ *Look me squarely in the eye.* 3 : in a way that makes direct contact ▪ *He hit the ball squarely.*

square meal *n* [*C*] : a full or complete meal ▪ *I eat three square meals a day.*

square one *n* [*U*] : the beginning stage or starting point ▪ *We had to go back to square one.* [=we had to start over]

square root *n* [*C*] *mathematics* : a number that produces a specified number when it is multiplied by itself ▪ *The square root of 9 is 3.*

¹**squash** /ˈskwɑːʃ/ *vb* 1 [*T*] : to press (something) into a flat or flatter shape ▪ *squash a bug* ▪ *The tomatoes got squashed.* 2 [*T*] : to stop (something) from continuing by doing or saying something ▪ *squash a rumor* 3 [*T/I*] : to move into a space that is very tight or crowded ▪ *We*

all squashed into the backseat. ▪ *We were squashed between the table and wall.*

²**squash** *n* **1** *pl* **squash** *or* **squash·es** [C/U] : a type of vegetable (such as a pumpkin) that has a usually hard skin and that is eaten cooked **2** [U] : a game played by two people with rackets and a rubber ball in a court with four walls **3** *pl* **squashes** [C/U] *Brit* : a drink made with fruit juice, sugar, and water ▪ *a glass of lemon squash*

squashy /ˈskwɑːʃi/ *adj* **squash·i·er; -est** *chiefly Brit* : soft and easy to press into a different shape ▪ *a squashy cushion*

¹**squat** /ˈskwɑːt/ *vb* **squat·ted; squat·ting** [I] **1** : to bend your knees and lower your body so that you are close to your heels or sitting on your heels ▪ *She squatted (down) to pick up the paper.* **2** : to live in a building or on land without the owner's permission and without paying — **squat·ter** /ˈskwɑːtə/ *n* [C] ▪ *Squatters were living in the building.*

²**squat** *n* **1** [C] : a position in which your knees are bent so that you are close to your heels or sitting on your heels **2** [U] *US slang* : the least amount : anything at all ▪ *I don't know squat about it.* : nothing at all ▪ *The car is worth squat.* **3** [C] *chiefly Brit* : an empty building that squatters live in

³**squat** *adj* **squat·ter; squat·test** : short and thick ▪ *a squat man/building*

squawk /ˈskwɑːk/ *vb* [I] **1** *of a bird* : to make a short, harsh cry **2** : to complain or protest loudly or with strong feeling ▪ *The customers squawked about the high prices.* — **squawk** *n* [C]

squeak /ˈskwiːk/ *vb* [I] **1** : to make a short, high-pitched cry or noise ▪ *The mouse/wheel/door squeaked.* ▪ *a squeaking sound* **2** : to almost lose or fail but to finally succeed, win, etc. ▪ *They squeaked into the finals.* ▪ *The bill squeaked through the Senate.* [=it barely got enough votes to be accepted] — **squeak** *n* [C] ▪ *She gave a squeak.* — **squeaky** /ˈskwiːki/ *adj* **squeak·i·er; -est** ▪ *a squeaky door/voice*

squeaky–clean *adj* **1** : completely clean ▪ *squeaky-clean hair/glass* **2** : not connected with or involving anything morally wrong ▪ *a squeaky-clean reputation/image*

squeal /ˈskwiːl/ *vb* **1** [I] : to make a long, high-pitched cry or noise ▪ *The pigs were squealing.* ▪ *The children squealed with/in delight.* ▪ *The car squealed to a stop.* **2** [I] *informal + disapproving* : to tell someone in authority about something wrong that someone has done ▪ *She squealed (on us) to the teacher/police.* **3** [T] : to say (something) in a high and excited voice ▪ *"Let me go," she squealed.* — **squeal** *n* [C] ▪ *a squeal of brakes* — **squeal·er** *n* [C] *informal + disapproving* ▪ *I didn't tell on you. I'm no squealer.*

squea·mish /ˈskwiːmɪʃ/ *adj* **1 a** : afraid to deal with or do things that might hurt or offend people ▪ *You can't be squeamish about firing people.* **b** : nervous or doubtful ▪ *I'm squeamish about eating raw fish.* **2** : easily shocked, offended, or disgusted ▪ *I'm too squeamish to watch*

horror movies. **3** : having a sick feeling in the stomach : QUEASY ▪ *She gets squeamish at the sight of blood.* — **squea·mish·ness** *n* [U]

squee·gee /ˈskwiːˌdʒiː/ *n* [C] : a tool that has a blade of rubber attached to a handle and that is used for spreading or wiping liquid on, across, or off a surface (such as a window or floor) — **squeegee** *vb* **-geed; -gee·ing** [T] ▪ *He squeegeed the (water off the) window.*

¹**squeeze** /ˈskwiːz/ *vb* **squeezed; squeez·ing** **1** [T/I] : to press together the parts and especially the opposite sides of (something) ▪ *Squeeze the bottle/tube.* ▪ *He squeezed her hand.* ▪ *Don't squeeze too hard.* ▪ *She squeezed her eyes shut.* [=she closed her eyes very tightly] **2** [T] : to get or remove (something) by squeezing something ▪ *squeeze the juice from an orange* **3** [T] : to pull back on (a gun's trigger) with your finger ▪ *He took aim and squeezed the trigger.* **4** [T/I] : to move into or through a small or crowded space ▪ *squeeze past/by someone* ▪ *squeeze through an opening* ▪ *We all squeezed into the elevator.* ▪ *We can squeeze one more person in.* ▪ *They squeezed all the activities into one day.* **5** [T] : to barely succeed at getting or doing (something) ▪ *The police squeezed a confession from her.* ▪ *The team squeezed out a victory.* **6** [T] **a** : to decrease the amount of (something, such as money) ▪ *Rising costs have squeezed profits.* **b** : to cause financial problems for (a business or organization) ▪ *Rising costs have squeezed the industry.* — **squeeze in** [*phrasal vb*] **squeeze (someone or something) in** *or* **squeeze in (someone or something)** : to find time for (someone or something) ▪ *I can squeeze you in at one o'clock.* — **squeeze out** [*phrasal vb*] **squeeze out (someone or something)** *or* **squeeze (someone or something) out** : to force (someone or something) out of a position, place, etc. ▪ *These big stores have squeezed out the smaller shops.*

²**squeeze** *n* **1** [*singular*] : a situation in which people or things are crowded together ▪ *It'll be a (tight) squeeze, but we can all fit.* **2** [C] : an act of squeezing something ▪ *She gave his hand a squeeze.* **3** [C] : a small amount that is gotten or removed from something by squeezing it ▪ *a squeeze of lemon/lime* **4 a** [C] : a situation in which there is not enough of something ▪ *a housing squeeze* [=shortage] **b** **the squeeze** *informal* : a situation that causes feelings of stress and pressure ▪ *We are really feeling the squeeze since I lost my job.* ▪ *The government is putting the squeeze on tax evaders.*

squelch /ˈskwɛltʃ/ *vb* [T] *US* : to stop (something) from continuing by doing or saying something ▪ *squelch a rumor*

squid /ˈskwɪd/ *n, pl* **squid** *or* **squids** [C] : a sea animal that has a long, thin, soft body and 10 long arms

squig·gle /ˈskwɪɡəl/ *n* [C] : a short, wavy line ▪ *He drew a bunch of squiggles.* — **squig·gly** /ˈskwɪɡli/ *adj* **squig·gli·er; -est** ▪ *squiggly lines*

squint /ˈskwɪnt/ *vb* **1** [I] : to look at

something with your eyes partly closed ▪ *She had to squint to read the small print.* **2** [*T*] : to cause (your eyes) to partly close ▪ *I squinted my eyes.* **3** [*I*] *chiefly Brit* : to have a medical condition that makes your eyes unable to look in the same direction — **squint** *n* [*singular*] ▪ *His gaze narrowed into a squint.* ▪ (*chiefly Brit*) *She was born with a squint.* — **squinty** /'skwɪnti/ *adj* **squint·i·er; -est** ▪ *squinty eyes*

squire /'skwajɚ/ *n* [*C*] **1** : a young man in the Middle Ages who helped a knight before eventually becoming a knight himself **2** : a man in the past in England who owned most of the land in a village or district in the country

squirm /'skwɚm/ *vb* [*I*] : to make a lot of twisting movements because you are nervous, uncomfortable, bored, etc. ▪ *The baby squirmed in my arms.* ▪ *The children squirmed with delight.* — **squirmy** /'skwɚmi/ *adj* **squirm·i·er; -est**

¹**squir·rel** /'skwɚrəl, *Brit* 'skwɪrəl/ *n, pl* **squir·rels** *also* **squirrel** [*C*] : a small animal with a long tail and soft fur that lives in trees

²**squirrel** *vb, US* **-reled** *or Brit* **-relled**; *US* **-rel·ing** *or Brit* **-rel·ling** — **squirrel away** [*phrasal vb*] **squirrel away (something)** *or* **squirrel (something) away** : to put (something) in a safe or secret place especially for future use ▪ *She squirreled a lot of money away.*

¹**squirt** /'skwɚt/ *vb* **1 a** [*T*] : to suddenly force (a liquid) out through a small opening ▪ *She squirted ketchup on her fries.* **b** [*I*] *of a liquid* : to suddenly be forced out through a small opening ▪ *Juice from the lemon squirted into my eye.* **2** [*T*] : to make (someone or something) wet with a stream of liquid ▪ *He squirted me with (water from) the hose.*

²**squirt** *n* [*C*] **1** : a small amount of liquid that is produced by squeezing or squirting something ▪ *a squirt of lemon (juice)* **2** *informal* : an annoying person who is small and usually young ▪ *an annoying little squirt*

squish /'skwɪʃ/ *vb* **1** [*T*] : to press (something) into a flatter shape ▪ *squish a bug* **2** [*T/I*] : to move into a space that is tight or crowded ▪ *We squished together to make more room.* ▪ *We were all squished together.* **3** [*I*] : to make the sound that is made when something very wet is pressed, stepped on, etc. ▪ *His wet shoes squished when he walked.* — **squishy** /'skwɪʃi/ *adj* **squish·i·er; -est** ▪ *The ground was wet and squishy.*

Sr. (*chiefly US*) *or Brit* **Sr** *abbr* **1** senior ▪ *John Smith, Sr.* **2** sister

SS *abbr* **1** saints **2** Social Security **3** steamship

SSN *abbr* Social Security number

st *abbr, Brit* stone ▪ *She weighs 7st 5lbs.* [=7 stone and 5 pounds]

St. (*chiefly US*) *or Brit* **St** *abbr* **1** saint **2** street

-st *symbol* — used in writing after the number 1 for the word *first* ▪ *He's in the 1st* [=*first*] *grade.* ▪ *It's her 21st birthday.*

¹**stab** /'stæb/ *n* [*C*] **1** : a wound made by a pointed weapon (such as a knife) ▪ *a*

stab to the heart ▪ *a stab wound/victim* **2** : a sudden, strong feeling of physical or emotional pain ▪ *a stab of pain/regret/doubt/fear* **3** *informal* : an attempt to do something successfully ▪ *She took/made a stab at solving the problem.* ▪ *Let me give it a stab.* = *Let me have a stab at it.* — **a stab in the back** : an act of betrayal ▪ *What she did was a real stab in the back.*

²**stab** *vb* **stabbed; stab·bing 1** [*T*] : to wound (someone or something) with a pointed weapon ▪ *He stabbed her with a knife.* **2** [*T/I*] : to quickly push a pointed object into or toward someone or something ▪ *He stabbed (at) the meat with a fork.* = *He stabbed the fork into the meat.* — **stab (someone) in the back** : to hurt (someone who trusts you) by not giving help or by doing something morally wrong : to betray (someone) ▪ *I trusted him and he stabbed me in the back.* — **stab·bing** /'stæbɪŋ/ *n* [*C*] ▪ *a fatal stabbing* — **stabbing** *adj, always before a noun* ▪ *a stabbing death/victim* ▪ *a stabbing* [=*sharp*] *pain*

sta·bi·lize *also Brit* **sta·bi·lise** /'steɪbə‑ˌlaɪz/ *vb* **-lized; -liz·ing 1** : to become stable or to make (something) stable: such as **a** [*T/I*] : to stop quickly changing, increasing, etc. ▪ *The population has stabilized.* ▪ *Prices have stabilized.* ▪ *efforts to stabilize prices* **b** [*T*] : to make (something) less easily moved ▪ *We used ropes to stabilize the platform.* ▪ *stabilize a patient's heartbeat* — **sta·bi·li·za·tion** *also Brit* **sta·bi·li·sa·tion** /ˌsteɪbələ'zeɪʃən, *Brit* ˌsteɪbəˌlaɪ'zeɪʃən/ *n* [*U*] — **sta·bi·liz·er** *also Brit* **sta·bi·lis·er** /'steɪbəˌlaɪzɚ/ *n* [*C*]

¹**sta·ble** /'steɪbəl/ *adj* **sta·bler; sta·blest 1 a** : in a good state or condition that is not easily changed or likely to change ▪ *a stable community/government/economy* ▪ *a stable income/family* **b** *medical* : not getting worse or likely to get worse ▪ *The patient is stable.* **2** : not easily moved ▪ *The ladder doesn't seem very stable.* **3** : emotionally or mentally healthy ▪ *a mentally/emotionally stable person* **4** *technical* : having a chemical structure or physical state that does not change easily ▪ *a stable compound* — **sta·bil·i·ty** /stə'bɪləti/ *n* [*U*] ▪ *the country's economic stability* ▪ *the patient's mental stability* ▪ *Test the ladder for stability.*

²**stable** *n* [*C*] : a building in which horses are kept, fed, and cared for ▪ *She rode the horse back to the stable(s).*

³**stable** *vb* **sta·bled; sta·bling** [*T*] : to put or keep (a horse) in a stable ▪ *She stabled the horse.*

stac·ca·to /stə'kɑːtoʊ/ *adj, music* : short and not sounding connected ▪ *staccato notes/chords*

¹**stack** /'stæk/ *n* **1** [*C*] : a group of things that are put one on top of the other : PILE ▪ *He arranged the letters in stacks.* ▪ *a stack of dishes* **2** [*C*] : a large amount of something ▪ *They have stacks of money.* ▪ *a stack of work* : SMOKESTACK **4 the stacks** : the rows of shelves where books are stored in a library ▪ *looking in the stacks*

²**stack** *vb* **1** [T/I] : to arrange (things) in a usually neat pile • *stacking (up) firewood* • *She stacked the plates in the cupboard.* **2** [T] : to cheat at a card game by arranging (a deck of cards) in a special way • *They accused him of stacking the deck.* ✧ If the *cards/odds are stacked against* you, you are in an unfair or bad situation in which you are not likely to win, succeed, etc. If you *stack the odds in your favor*, you arrange things to make it easier for you to win, succeed, etc. — *stack up* [*phrasal vb*] **1** : to increase in number or amount to a total that is difficult to deal with • *My bills are stacking up.* **2** : to be good enough or equally good • *This camera doesn't stack up. = This camera doesn't stack up well against the others.* [=it is not as good as the others]

sta·di·um /ˈsteɪdijəm/ *n* [C] : a very large building that has a field surrounded by rows of seats and that is used especially for sports events

staff /ˈstæf, *Brit* ˈstɑːf/ *n, pl* **staffs** or **staves** /ˈsteɪvz/ **1** *pl* **staffs a** [C/U] : a group of people who work for an organization or business • *The staff is/are at a meeting.* • *the sales/kitchen staff* • *a staff of 40 (people)* • (*US*) *There are 100 people on staff.* [=working as members of the staff] • *a staff member/meeting* **b** [C] : a group of military officers who help a commanding officer with planning and managing • *the general's staff* **2** *pl* **staves** [C] : a long stick that is carried as a symbol of authority • *a bishop's staff* **3** *pl* **staves** [C] *music* : the five horizontal lines and the spaces between them on which music is written — called also **stave** — **staff** *vb* [T] • *The office is fully staffed.* • *The organization is staffed by volunteers.* [=the workers in the organization are volunteers] — **staff·er** /ˈstæfɚ/ *n* [C] *US* • *newspaper staffers* [=staff members]

staff sergeant *n* [C] : an officer in the army, air force, or marines with a rank above a sergeant

stag /ˈstæg/ *n, pl* **stags** or **stag** [C] : an adult male deer — **go stag** *US* : to go to a party or other social event by yourself • *He's going stag to the party.*

¹**stage** /ˈsteɪdʒ/ *n* **1** [C] : a particular point or period in the growth or development of something • *an early/late stage of the disease* • *the first/last stage of the plan* **2 a** [C/U] : a raised platform in a theater, auditorium, etc., where the performers stand • *He walked out onto the stage.* = *He took the stage.* • *He was on stage for the entire show.* **b** [U] : the art or profession of acting and especially of acting in theaters • *a star of stage and screen* • *go on the stage* [=become an actor] • *a stage actor/play* **3** [*singular*] : a place or area of activity in which the things that happen are watched by many people • *the national political stage* [=national politics] **4** [C] : a section of a rocket that has its own fuel and engine • *a three-stage missile* — **in stages** : in a series of separate steps • *The changes were made in stages.* — **set the stage (for something)** : to make (something) possible or likely • *Her early training set the stage for her later success.*

²**stage** *vb* **staged; stag·ing** [T] **1** : to produce (a performance) on a stage • *stage a play* **2 a** : to organize and produce (a public event) • *stage a protest/demonstration* **b** : to arrange or do (something intended to get public attention) • *stage a hunger strike* **3** : to succeed in doing or making (something) • *The singer staged a comeback.*

stage·coach /ˈsteɪdʒˌkoʊtʃ/ *n* [C] : a large carriage pulled by horses that was used in the past to carry passengers and mail along a regular route

stage fright *n* [U] : a nervous feeling felt by someone who is going to appear in front of an audience

stage·hand /ˈsteɪdʒˌhænd/ *n* [C] : someone who prepares the scenery, lights, etc., for a performance on a stage

stag·ger /ˈstægɚ/ *vb* **1** [T/I] : to move or cause (someone) to move unsteadily from side to side • *She staggered over to the sofa.* • *a punch that staggered him* **2** [T] : to shock or surprise (someone) very much • *Their indifference staggers me.* **3** [T] : to arrange (things) in a series of different positions or times • *stagger work shifts* — **stagger** *n* [C] • *He walked with a stagger.* — **stag·ger·ing** /ˈstægərɪŋ/ *adj* • *The storm caused a staggering amount of damage.* — **stag·ger·ing·ly** *adv*

stag·ing /ˈsteɪdʒɪŋ/ *n* [C/U] : the performance of a play on a stage • *She has acted in several stagings of the play.*

stag·nant /ˈstægnənt/ *adj* **1** : not flowing • *stagnant water/air* **2** : not active, changing, or progressing • *a stagnant economy*

stag·nate /ˈstægˌneɪt/ *vb* **-nat·ed; -nat·ing** [I] : to stop developing, progressing, moving, etc. • *Their relationship is stagnating.* • *a puddle of stagnating water* — **stag·na·tion** /stægˈneɪʃən/ *n* [U]

stag party *n* [C] : a party for men only that is usually on the night before a man's wedding — called also (*Brit*) **stag night**

staid /ˈsteɪd/ *adj* : serious, boring, or old-fashioned • *a staid and solemn man/manner* — **staid·ness** *n* [U]

¹**stain** /ˈsteɪn/ *vb* **1 a** [T/I] : to leave a mark on something • *The red wine stained the carpet.* **b** [I] : to be marked or damaged by a stain • *This fabric stains easily.* **2** [T] : to use a special liquid to change the color of (something) • *He stained the wood a dark cherry color.* **3** [T] : to damage or spoil (something) • *The accusations stained his reputation.*

²**stain** *n* [C] **1** : a mark made on a surface, a piece of clothing, etc., that is very hard or impossible to remove • *a juice/wine/grass stain* • *She has a stain on her shirt.* **2** : a special liquid that is used to change the color of something (such as wood or cloth) **3** : something that damages a person's reputation • *a stain on her honor/reputation* — **stain·less** /ˈsteɪnləs/ *adj* • *a stainless reputation*

stained glass n [U] : colored glass that is used to make pictures and patterns in windows

stainless steel n [U] : a type of steel that does not rust

stair /'steɚ/ n 1 [plural] : a series of steps that go from one level or floor to another ▪ She ran/fell down the stairs. ▪ at the foot/bottom of the stairs ▪ The stairs lead to the roof. ▪ **a flight/set of stairs** 2 [C] : one of the steps in a set of stairs ▪ the bottom stair 3 [singular] literary : STAIRCASE ▪ climbing the stair

stair·case /'steɚ,keɪs/ n [C] : a set of stairs and its supporting structures ▪ a wooden staircase

stair·way /'steɚ,weɪ/ n [C] : a set of stairs that go from one level or floor to another ▪ I took the stairway up to the third floor.

stair·well /'steɚ,wɛl/ n [C] : a space in a building where stairs are located

¹**stake** /'steɪk/ n 1 [C] : a pointed stick or post that is pushed into the ground ▪ **the stake** : a post that a person was tied to and burned on in the past as punishment ▪ Joan of Arc was burned at the stake. 3 [plural] : something (such as money) that you could win or lose ▪ a poker game with high stakes 4 [C] : an interest or share in something ▪ They have a stake in the company. [=they own part of the company] ▪ We all have a stake in the economy. [=the economy affects us all] — **at stake** : in a position to be lost or gained ▪ Thousands of jobs/dollars/lives are at stake. ▪ My reputation is at stake. — **pull up stakes** US, informal : to leave your job or home ▪ She decided to pull up stakes and start over.

²**stake** vb staked; stak·ing [T] 1 : to risk the loss of (something) ▪ She staked all her money on the race. ▪ He staked his reputation on the plan's success. ▪ I'm sure it was him. **I would stake my life on it.** 2 : to support (something) with stakes ▪ She staked the tomato plants. — **stake out** [phrasal vb] **stake (something) out** or **stake out (something)** 1 : to mark the limits of (an area) with stakes ▪ stake out a mining area 2 : to watch (a place) secretly ▪ The police staked out the building. 3 : to state (your opinion) in a very clear and definite way ▪ He staked out his position on this issue in a speech he gave last month. — **stake (out) a/your claim** : to say or show that you believe you should have something or that you deserve something ▪ They staked their claim to the land. — **stake-out** /'steɪk,aʊt/ n [C] ▪ The police were **on a stakeout.**

sta·lac·tite /stə'læk,taɪt, Brit 'stælək,taɪt/ n [C] : a pointed piece of rock that hangs down from the roof of a cave

sta·lag·mite /stə'læg,maɪt, Brit 'stæləg,maɪt/ n [C] : a pointed piece of rock that sticks up from the floor of a cave

stale /'steɪl/ adj stal·er; -est 1 a of food : no longer fresh ▪ stale food/bread b : having an unpleasant taste or smell ▪ stale air/water ▪ a room filled with stale smoke 2 : not interesting or new ▪ stale news/jokes

stale·mate /'steɪl,meɪt/ n [C/U] 1 : a contest, dispute, etc., in which neither

side can gain an advantage or win ▪ The debate ended in (a) stalemate. ▪ trying to break the stalemate 2 : a situation in chess in which a player cannot successfully move any of the pieces and neither player can win — **stalemate** vb -mat·ed; -mat·ing [T] ▪ He was stalemated by the opposition.

¹**stalk** /'stɑːk/ n [C] 1 : a thick or tall stem of a plant ▪ a flower stalk ▪ celery stalks 2 : a thin, upright object or part that supports or connects something ▪ the stalk of a goblet

²**stalk** vb 1 [T] a : to follow (an animal or person) by moving slowly and quietly ▪ Lions stalked the herd. ▪ She was stalked by the killer. b : to go through (a place or area) while hunting ▪ hunters stalking the woods for deer ▪ (figurative) A killer stalks the city streets. 2 [T] : to follow, watch, and bother (someone) constantly in a way that is frightening, dangerous, etc. ▪ Her ex-husband was stalking her. 3 [I] : to walk in a stiff or proud manner ▪ She angrily stalked out of the room. — **stalk·er** /'stɑːkɚ/ n [C] ▪ She was threatened by a stalker. ▪ a deer stalker

¹**stall** /'stɑːl/ n 1 [C] : a small open counter or partially enclosed structure where things are displayed for sale ▪ a food/souvenir/market stall 2 [C] : an enclosed area in a building where a farm animal is kept ▪ She cleaned the horses' stalls. 3 [C] : a seat in a church that is wholly or partly enclosed ▪ choir stalls 4 [C] chiefly US : a small, enclosed area with room for one person in a bathroom ▪ a shower/toilet/bathroom stall 5 [singular] : a situation in which an engine suddenly stops or an airplane suddenly stops flying ▪ an engine stall ▪ The plane went into a stall.

²**stall** vb [T/I] 1 of an engine : to stop suddenly because of a problem ▪ The engine stalled. ▪ Don't stall the engine. 2 : to avoid doing something or to delay someone in a deliberate way ▪ Stop stalling and answer the question. ▪ Try to stall them until I get there. 3 : to stop progressing or developing ▪ Budget problems stalled the project. ▪ His career has stalled. 4 of an airplane : to stop flying suddenly and begin to fall ▪ The plane nearly stalled. ▪ The pilot almost stalled the airplane.

stal·lion /'stæljən/ n [C] : an adult male horse and especially one that is used for breeding

stal·wart /'stɑːlwɚt/ adj, formal 1 : very loyal and dedicated ▪ stalwart fans/supporters 2 : physically strong ▪ stalwart fortifications — **stalwart** n [C] ▪ party stalwarts [=people who support a political party very loyally] — **stal·wart·ly** adv

sta·men /'steɪmən/ n [C] botany : the part of a flower that produces pollen

stam·i·na /'stæmənə/ n [U] : physical or mental strength that allows you to continue doing something for a long time ▪ Do you have the/enough stamina to finish the job?

stam·mer /'stæmɚ/ vb [T/I] : to speak with many pauses and repetitions because you have a speech problem or because you are very nervous, frightened, etc. • *He stammered an excuse.* — **stammer** *n* [*singular*] • *speaking with a stammer*

¹**stamp** /ˈstæmp/ *n* [C] **1 a** : a small piece of paper that you buy and then stick to an envelope or package to pay the cost of mailing it — called also *postage stamp* **b** : a small piece of paper that is attached to something and that shows that a tax or fee has been paid **2 a** : a device or tool used for stamping something **b** : the mark made by such a device • *There was a time/date stamp on the letter.* • *(figurative) His manner gave/lent his words the stamp of authority.* • *(figurative) She gave the plan her* **stamp of approval**. [=she approved it] • *(figurative) He put/left his stamp on the process.* [=he affected the process in some important way] **3** : the act of bringing your foot down heavily and noisily • *an angry stamp of his foot*

²**stamp** *vb* **1** [T] : to bring (your foot) down heavily and noisily • *He stamped his foot in anger.* **2** [I] : to walk heavily and noisily • *He stamped* [=stomped] *out of the room.* **3** [T] **a** : to use a special device (called a stamp) to put a design, word, etc., on something • *She stamped the bill "paid."* • *stamp the date on a letter* = *stamp a letter with the date* **b** : to form (something) with a device that presses down on a material and cuts out shapes • *newly stamped coins* **4** [T] : to attach a postage stamp to (something) • *stamp a letter* • *a stamped envelope* — **stamp on** [*phrasal vb*] **1** : to step heavily on (something) with your foot • *She accidentally stamped on my toe.* **2** : to end (something) in a forceful way • *The city council stamped on the proposal.* — **stamp out** [*phrasal vb*] **stamp (something) out** or **stamp out (something) 1** : to stop or destroy (something) • *stamp out smallpox/corruption* **2** : to stop (something) from burning by stepping on it forcefully • *stamp out a fire/cigarette*

¹**stam·pede** /stæmˈpiːd/ *n* [C] **1** : an occurrence in which a large group of frightened or excited animals or people run together in a wild and uncontrolled way • *a buffalo stampede* • *a stampede to the exits* **2** : a situation in which a lot of people try to do the same thing at the same time • *a stampede of new applicants*

²**stampede** *vb* **-ped·ed; -ped·ing 1 a** [I] : to run away in a large group especially because of fear • *The cattle stampeded.* **b** [T] : to cause (animals) to run away in a large group • *The gunshot stampeded the cattle.* **2** [T] : to cause (a person or group) to do something suddenly and without proper thought • *Don't let yourself be stampeded into this decision.*

stamping ground *n* [C] *Brit* : STOMPING GROUND

stance /ˈstæns, *Brit* ˈstɑːns/ *n* [*singular*] **1** : a publicly stated opinion • *He has changed his stance on this issue.* **2** : a way of standing • *a casual/relaxed stance*

stanch (*chiefly US*) or **staunch** /ˈstɑːntʃ/ *vb* [T] : to stop something (especially blood) from flowing • *stanch the (flow of) blood* • *stanch a wound* [=stop the flow of blood from a wound]

stan·chion /ˈstæntʃən/ *n* [C] : a strong, upright pole that is used to support something

¹**stand** /ˈstænd/ *vb* **stood** /ˈstʊd/; **standing 1** [I] **a** : to be in an upright position with all of your weight on your feet • *She stood in/near the doorway.* • *He was standing next to me.* • *There were no seats so we had to stand.* • *The deer stood still.* • *We had to* **stand in line** *for tickets.* • *People were just* **standing around**, *waiting.* **b** : to move onto your feet from a sitting or low position • *He stood (up) to greet her.* • *Please stand for the national anthem.* **2 a** [I] : to be in an upright position • *A shovel stood in the corner.* **b** [T] : to put (something or someone) in an upright position • *She stood the ladder (up) against the wall.* **3** [I] **a** : to be in a particular place or position • *The house stands on a hill.* • *(figurative) Go ahead and leave. I won't* **stand in your way**. [=try to stop you] • *(figurative) Nothing can* **stand in the way** *of our happiness.* **b** : to remain in a place or position without moving or being moved • *The plane stood on the runway.* • *water standing in pools* **4** [I] : to be a specified height • *He stands six feet two (inches tall).* **5** [I] : to be in a particular state or situation • *Where do we* **stand** *financially?* [=what is our financial condition?] • *She* **stands** *accused of murder.* **6** [I] : to have a particular belief or opinion about something • *They* **stand** *divided.* [=they disagree] • *She* **stands for/against** [=supports/opposes] *the bill.* • *Where do you* **stand** [=what is your opinion] *on this matter?* • *From where I stand, it makes no sense.* **7** [I] : to have a particular rank or position within a group • *The team still stands first in the division.* **8** [I] : to continue to be at a specified number or amount • *The home run record stands at 73.* **9** [I] : to not be changed : to remain valid or effective • *The decision/record still stands.* **10** [I] : to exist at the present time • *You must leave or leave our offer as it stands.* • *As things stand, we can't meet the deadline.* **11** [I] : to be in a position in which you are likely to gain or lose something • *We stand to make/lose a lot of money.* **12** [T] **a** : to accept (something or someone unpleasant) without complaint • *How can you stand her?* • *He couldn't stand the pain.* • *I couldn't stand waiting.* = *I couldn't stand to wait.* • *His behavior was more than I could stand.* • *I couldn't stand the thought/idea of moving again.* **b** — used to say that someone strongly dislikes a person or thing • *I can't stand him.* • *She can't stand cooking.* = *She can't stand to cook.* **13** [T] : to not be harmed by (something) : WITHSTAND • *These plants can stand very cold temperatures.* • *His plays have stood the test of time.* [=his plays are still read/performed] **14** [T] : to be helped by (something) • *You could stand some sleep.* • *He could stand losing a few pounds.* = *He could stand to lose a few pounds.* [=he should lose a few

pounds] **15** [*I*] *Brit* : to be a candidate in an election for a particular office ▪ *He is standing* [=(*US*) *running*] *for a seat in Parliament.* **16** [*T*] *Brit, informal* : to pay for (a meal or drink) ▪ *I'll stand a meal for you.* = *I'll stand you a meal.* — **stand a chance** *see* ¹CHANCE — **stand alone 1** : to not be helped or supported by others ▪ *She stood alone in her opposition to the plan.* **2** : to be better than all others ▪ *For sound quality, this system stands alone.* — **stand aside** [*phrasal vb*] **1** : to move to the left or right within one or a few steps ▪ *Please stand aside and let me pass.* **2** : to allow something to happen ▪ *I'm not going to stand aside and watch you ruin your life.* — **stand back** [*phrasal vb*] **1** : to take a few steps backwards ▪ *The police told us to stand back.* **2** : to stop doing something or being involved in something for a time ▪ *It's time to stand back and reevaluate.* — **stand behind** [*phrasal vb*] : to support (someone or something) ▪ *I'll stand behind you no matter what you decide to do.* — **stand by** [*phrasal vb*] **1** : to stand or be present without taking any action ▪ *How can you stand by and do nothing?* **2** : to be ready or available for use ▪ *Operators are standing by* (*to take your calls*). **3 a** : to support or defend (something) ▪ *He stands by what he said earlier.* **b** : to act in the way that is required by (a belief, promise, etc.) ▪ *She stood by her promise.* **4** : to remain loyal to (someone) : to continue to support (someone) ▪ *They promised to stand by each other.* — **stand down** [*phrasal vb*] *Brit* : to leave a job, duty, etc. ▪ *He stood down as Mayor.* — **stand firm** : to refuse to change your decision, position, etc. ▪ *The judge stood firm in her ruling.* — **stand for** [*phrasal vb*] **1** : to have (a specified meaning) ▪ *"FYI" stands for "for your information."* **2** : to support (something) ▪ *Our party has always stood for reform.* **3** : to allow (something) to continue to happen ▪ *I will not stand for this nonsense.* — **stand guard/watch** : to stand in a position and guard against possible danger, threats, etc. ▪ *A soldier stood guard by the door.* — **stand in** [*phrasal vb*] : to take the place of someone who is away for a time ▪ *He asked me to stand in* (*for him*). — **stand on your head/hands** : to be in a position in which your legs and feet are straight up in the air and your weight is supported by your head or hands ▪ *She can stand on her head/hands.* — **stand or fall** — used to say that the future or success of someone or something depends on another person or thing ▪ *We* (*will*) *stand or fall by their decision.* — **stand out** [*phrasal vb*] **1** : to be easily seen or noticed ▪ *His bright tie made him stand out* (*in the crowd*). **2** : to be better or more important than other people or things in a way that is easily noticed ▪ *a student who stands out above/from the rest* ▪ *Two facts stand out from her testimony.* ▪ *His performance really stood out.* **3** : to stick out from a surface ▪ *The hat made her ears stand out.* — **stand tall** : to stand with your body very straight ▪ *(US,*

figurative) *We can stand tall and take pride in our accomplishments.* — **stand to reason** *see* ¹REASON — **stand trial** : to be on trial in a court of law ▪ *stand trial for murder* — **stand up** [*phrasal vb*] **1** : to remain valid or acceptable when tested or examined ▪ *evidence that will stand up in court* **2 stand (someone) up** *informal* : to fail to meet or keep an appointment with (someone) ▪ *You stood me up!* **3 stand up for** : to defend (someone or something) against attack or criticism ▪ *He stood up for his friend/rights.* ▪ *You should stand up for yourself.* **4 stand up to a** : to refuse to accept bad treatment from (someone) ▪ *She stood up to the bully.* **b** : WITHSTAND 1 ▪ *These boots have stood up to a lot of abuse.* — **stand your ground** *see* ¹GROUND

²**stand** *n* **1** [*C*] : a strongly held opinion about something ▪ *What is your stand on this issue?* ▪ *take a firm/strong stand for/against something* **2** [*C*] : a strong effort to defend yourself or oppose something ▪ *They are prepared to make a stand against the enemy.* ▪ *students making a stand against the war* **3** [*C*] : a partially enclosed structure where things are sold or displayed ▪ *a hot-dog/vegetable/roadside stand* ▪ *display stands* ▪ *He set up a stand at the fair.* **4** [*C*] : a device that holds an object in an upright position ▪ *an umbrella stand* ▪ *a bicycle/microphone stand* **5** [*C*] : a raised platform for people to stand on **6 the stands** : the rows of seats in a stadium that people sit in ▪ *The ball was hit into the stands.* **7 the stand** : the place where a witness testifies in court ▪ *She lied while on the (witness) stand.* ▪ *Please take the stand.* **8** [*C*] *chiefly US* : a series of performances, games, etc., that are at a particular place for a period of time ▪ *The magician was booked for a three-night stand.* **9** [*C*] : a group of plants growing close together ▪ *a stand of pines*

stand-alone /'stændə,loʊn/ *adj* : able to operate without control from another system, company, etc. ▪ *stand-alone computers/businesses*

¹**stan·dard** /'stændəd/ *n* **1 a** [*C/U*] : a level of quality, achievement, etc., that is considered acceptable or desirable ▪ *high/low standards of quality* ▪ *industry standards* ▪ *His work is not up to our standards.* = *His work is not up to standard.* = *His work is below standard.* **b** [*plural*] : ideas about morally correct and acceptable behavior ▪ *high moral standards* **2** [*C*] : something that is very good and that is used to judge the quality of other things ▪ *This book is the standard by which all others are judged.* **3** [*C*] : a fixed official unit of measurement ▪ *a standard of weight* **4** [*C*] : a flag that is used in official ceremonies **5** [*C*] : a song that has been sung by many different artists ▪ *an old standard*

²**standard** *adj* **1** : regularly and widely used, seen, or accepted : not unusual or special ▪ *a standard approach/procedure* ▪ *the standard features* ▪ *a door of standard width* **2** : generally accepted and used because of high quality or excellence

standard reference works **3** : accepted and used by most of the educated speakers and writers of a language ▪ *standard spelling/English*

stan·dard-bear·er /ˈstændəd₁berə/ *n* [C] *formal* **1** : the leader of an organization, movement, etc. **2** : someone who carries a flag or banner

stan·dard·ize *also Brit* **stan·dard·ise** /ˈstændə₁daɪz/ *vb* **-ized; -iz·ing** [T] : to change (things) so that they are similar and consistent ▪ *He standardized our procedures.* ▪ *standardized tests* — **stan·dard·i·za·tion** *also Brit* **stan·dard·i·sa·tion** /₁stændədəˈzeɪʃən, *Brit* ₁stændə₁daɪˈzeɪʃən/ *n* [U]

standard of living *n* [*singular*] : the amount of wealth, comfort, and possessions that a person or group has ▪ *People in that area enjoy a high standard of living.* ▪ *raise/lower/improve our standard of living*

standard time *n* [U] : the official time of a particular region or country

stand·by /ˈstænd₁baɪ/ *n, pl* **stand·bys** /ˈstænd₁baɪz/ [C] : a person or thing that is available especially in emergencies ▪ *More police officers were sent as standbys.* — **on standby 1** : ready or available for action or use ▪ *The officers were put on standby.* **2** : ready to travel if a ticket becomes available ▪ *We're on standby for the next flight.* — **standby** *adj,* always before a noun ▪ *standby tickets/passengers*

stand-in /ˈstænd₁ɪn/ *n* [C] : a person or thing that takes the place of someone or something else for a period of time ▪ *He was the boss's stand-in during her illness.*

¹**stand·ing** /ˈstændɪŋ/ *adj,* always before a noun **1 a** : used in or for standing ▪ *a standing position* **b** : done while in a standing position ▪ *a standing jump* **2** : not flowing : STAGNANT ▪ *standing water* **3** : remaining at the same level or amount until canceled ▪ *Their standing offer is $1,499.* **4** : continuing to exist or be used for an unlimited period of time ▪ *standing armies/committees* ▪ *a standing invitation* ▪ *It's a standing joke of ours.* [=a joke that we often make]

²**standing** *n* **1** [C] : the position or rank of someone in a group ▪ *He improved his standing with the voters.* [=he got the voters to rank him more highly] ▪ *a lawyer of high standing* ▪ (*chiefly US*) *a member in/of good standing* **2** [*plural*] *US, sports* : a list that shows the positions of the players or teams in a competition ▪ *The team has moved up in the standings.* **3** [U] : length of existence : DURATION ▪ *a marriage of many years' standing*

standing room *n* [U] : space available for people to stand after all seats are filled ▪ *There was standing room only at the concert.*

stand·off /ˈstænd₁ɑːf/ *n* [C] : an argument, contest, etc., in which there is no winner ▪ *The two governments are currently in a standoff over who has rights to the land.*

stand·off·ish /₁stændˈɑːfɪʃ/ *adj* : not friendly toward other people ▪ *She is a bit standoffish.*

stand·out /ˈstænd₁aʊt/ *n* [C] *US* : a person or thing that is better or more important than others ▪ *a standout among the products/candidates* ▪ *a standout candidate/performance*

stand·point /ˈstænd₁pɔɪnt/ *n* [C] : a way in which something is thought about or considered : POINT OF VIEW ▪ *From an economic standpoint, the policy is sound.*

stand·still /ˈstænd₁stɪl/ *n* [*singular*] : a state in which all activity or motion is stopped ▪ *Production is at a standstill.* ▪ *The accident brought traffic to a standstill.*

stand-up /ˈstænd₁ʌp/ *adj,* always before a noun **1 a** : done by a performer who is standing alone on a stage ▪ *stand-up comedy* **b** : performing stand-up comedy ▪ *a stand-up comedian/comic* **2** *US, informal* : very good, loyal, etc. ▪ *He's a real stand-up (kind of) guy.* — **stand-up** *n* [C/U] ▪ *a comic doing stand-up* [=stand-up comedy]

stank *past tense of* ¹STINK

stan·za /ˈstænzə/ *n* [C] : a group of lines in a poem : VERSE

staph /ˈstæf/ *n* [U] *medical* : a group of bacteria that cause many common illnesses ▪ *a staph infection*

¹**sta·ple** /ˈsteɪpəl/ *n* [C] **1** : a piece of wire or metal in the shape of a U that is used for attaching things ▪ *Fasten the pages together with staples.* ▪ *The notice was attached to the wall with staples.* **2** : an important food that is eaten very often ▪ *staples like bread and milk* ▪ *Rice is the staple of their diet.* **3** : something that is used widely and often ▪ *His writings are a staple of economic theory.* — **staple** *adj,* always before a noun ▪ *such staple items as flour and sugar* ▪ *staple crops like wheat and rice* ▪ *the birds' staple diet* [=the foods that they eat most often]

²**staple** *vb* **sta·pled; sta·pling** [T] : to attach (something) with staples ▪ *I stapled the pages (together).* ▪ *The notice had been stapled to the wall.* — **sta·pler** /ˈsteɪplə/ *n* [C] ▪ *The stapler jammed when I tried to use it.*

¹**star** /ˈstɑɚ/ *n* [C] **1** : any one of the objects in space that are made of burning gas and that look like points of light in the night sky ▪ *gazing up at the stars* ▪ *The stars are out.* [=are not hidden by clouds] ▪ *sleeping outside under the stars* **2** : a star or planet especially in a certain position that is believed in astrology to influence people's lives ▪ *I was born under a lucky star.* [=I was born lucky] ▪ *I guess romance isn't in the stars* [=isn't going to happen] *for me.* ▪ *You can thank your lucky stars* [=you are lucky] *that no one was hurt.* **3 a** : something with five or more points that represents a star ▪ *The teacher gave me a gold star.* [=a gold sticker in the shape of a star] ▪ *I put a star* [=asterisk] *next to his name.* **b** : a symbol that is shaped like a star and that is used as part of a rating system ▪ *Critics gave the movie/restaurant four stars.* **4 a** : the most important and well-known performer in a movie, play, etc. ▪ *She's the star of the show.* **b** : an extremely famous and successful performer or athlete ▪ *That film made him a star.* ▪ *base-*

ball/football/track stars ▪ *a movie/rock/ pop star* ▪ **star** *athletes* **c** : a person who is very successful, important, etc. ▪ *He is* **a rising star** [=he is becoming successful] *in politics.* ▪ *a* **star** *student* ▪ *She was the* **star** *witness at the trial.* ▪ *The pandas are the zoo's* **star** *attraction.* — **reach for the stars** : to try to do something that is very difficult and impressive — **see stars** : to see flashes of light usually because you have been hit on the head ▪ *I hit my head so hard that I saw* **stars.** ▪ **star·less** /ˈstɑɚləs/ *adj* ▪ *a cloudy, star- less sky* — **star·like** /ˈstɑɚˌlaɪk/ *adj* ▪ *starlike flowers*

²**star** *vb* **starred; star·ring** **1 a** [*I*] : to play the most important role in a movie, play, etc. ▪ *He has* **starred** *in many films.* ▪ *She had the* **starring** *role.* **b** [*T*] : to have (someone) as the most important per- former ▪ *The new TV series* **stars** *a famous movie actress.* **2** [*T*] : to mark (some- thing) with a star or other symbol ▪ *This hotel is* **starred** *in the guidebook.*

star·board /ˈstɑɚbəd/ *n* [*U*] : the side of a ship or aircraft that is on the right when you are looking toward the front ▪ *The ship turned to* **starboard.** — **star- board** *adj*

¹**starch** /ˈstɑɚtʃ/ *n* **1** [*C/U*] : a substance that is found in certain foods (such as bread, rice, and potatoes) **2** [*U*] : a pow- der or liquid that contains starch and is used to make clothing stiff — **starchy** /ˈstɑɚtʃi/ *adj* **starch·i·er; -est** ▪ *starchy foods*

²**starch** *vb* [*T*] : to make (clothing) stiff by using starch ▪ *a starched collar*

star·dom /ˈstɑɚdəm/ *n* [*U*] : the state of being a very famous performer ▪ *an ac- tress who has achieved movie* **stardom**

stare /ˈsteɚ/ *vb* **stared; star·ing** [*I*] : to look at someone or something for a long time often with your eyes wide open ▪ *She* **stared** *out the window.* ▪ *They* **stared** *at him in amazement.* ▪ *It's rude to* **stare** *(at people).* ▪ *The solution was* **staring** *right at me.* = (*US*) *The solution was* **staring** *me in the face/eyes.* [=the so- lution was obvious] — **stare down** (*US*) or *Brit* **stare out** [*phrasal vb*] **stare (someone) down/out** or **stare down/out (someone)** : to look directly into some- one's eyes without fear until he or she looks away — **stare** *n* [*C*] ▪ *a blank stare* [=a look showing that someone does not know or understand something]

star·fish /ˈstɑɚˌfɪʃ/ *n* [*C*] : a sea animal that has five arms and that looks like a star

¹**stark** /ˈstɑɚk/ *adj* **1** : having a very plain and often cold or empty appearance ▪ *a stark room/landscape* **2** : unpleasant and difficult to accept or experience ▪ *the stark reality of death* ▪ *She described the crimes in stark detail.* ▪ *a stark reminder of our own mortality* **3** : very obvious ▪ *His criticism of the movie stands in stark con- trast to the praise it has received from oth- ers.* — **stark·ly** *adv* — **stark·ness** *n* [*U*]

²**stark** *adv* : completely or fully ▪ *He was* **stark** *naked.* ▪ *That noise is driving me*

stark raving mad. = (*Brit*) *That noise is driving me* **stark staring mad.**

star·let /ˈstɑɚlət/ *n* [*C*] : a young movie actress

star·light /ˈstɑɚˌlaɪt/ *n* [*U*] : the light pro- duced by stars

star·ling /ˈstɑɚlɪŋ/ *n* [*C*] : a dark brown or black bird that is common in Europe and the U.S.

star·lit /ˈstɑɚˌlɪt/ *adj* : lighted by the stars ▪ *a starlit sky*

star·ry /ˈstɑri/ *adj* **star·ri·er; -est** **1** : full of stars ▪ *a starry sky* **2** : having a shape like a star ▪ *starry flowers* **3** : in- cluding many famous actors, athletes, etc. ▪ *a starry cast* **4** : shining brightly ▪ *starry eyes*

star·ry–eyed /ˈstɑriˌaɪd/ *adj* : having hopes and desires that are not realistic or practical ▪ *starry-eyed lovers*

Stars and Stripes *n* — **the Stars and Stripes** : the flag of the United States

star·struck /ˈstɑɚˌstrʌk/ *adj* : feeling or showing great interest in and admiration for famous people ▪ *starstruck fans*

star–stud·ded /ˈstɑɚˌstʌdəd/ *adj* : hav- ing many famous actors, athletes, etc. ▪ *a star-studded cast*

¹**start** /ˈstɑɚt/ *vb* **1 a** [*T/I*] : to do the first part of something : to begin doing some- thing ▪ *They* **started** *clearing debris.* ▪ *He* **started** *his speech (out) with a joke.* ▪ *She* **started** *studying music at the age of five.* ▪ *As soon as you're ready, we'll* **start.** ▪ **start** *fresh/again/over* ▪ *We had better get* **start- ed.** ▪ *We had to* **start** *from scratch.* [=be- gin from a point at which nothing had been done yet] ▪ *Her book is a good* **start- ing** *point for beginners.* **b** [*T*] : to begin to work on, produce, or give attention to (something) ▪ *Did you* **start** *(reading) the book yet?* **c** [*T*] : to cause (something) to begin ▪ *We* **started** *the meeting at 6:30.* : to cause (something) to begin in a spec- ified way ▪ *He* **starts** *every day with a cup of coffee.* **d** [*T*] : to begin to have a feel- ing, thought, etc. ▪ *She* **started** *feeling diz- zy.* = *She* **started** *to feel dizzy.* **e** [*T/I*] : to begin working at a new job or going to school ▪ *I* **start** *(my new job) next week.* **2 a** [*T/I*] : to begin to happen, to exist, to be done, etc. ▪ *The fire* **started** *in the cel- lar.* ▪ *When does school* **start?** ▪ *It* **started** *to rain.* = *It* **started** *raining.* ▪ *The movie is* **starting** *now.* ▪ *Starting next week, all staff must wear ID tags.* **b** [*T*] : to cause (something) to exist or happen ▪ *He* **start- ed** *a business.* ▪ **start** *a tradition* ▪ **start** *a fight/argument* ▪ **start** *a family* [=begin to have children] **3 a** [*I*] : to begin to func- tion or operate ▪ *The car/engine won't* **start.** **b** [*T*] : to cause (something) to be- gin to function or operate ▪ *She* **started** *the car.* **4** [*T*] : to begin the use of (something) ▪ **start** *a new roll of tape* **5** [*I*] **a** : to begin at a specified place or in a specified way ▪ *The English alphabet* **starts** *with A and ends with Z.* ▪ *The trail* **starts** *here.* **b** : to have a specified quali- ty, identity, job, etc., at the beginning ▪ *It* **started** *(off) as a simple idea.* ▪ *She* **started** *(out) as a sales assistant.* **6** [*I*] : to begin to move toward a particular place or in a particular direction ▪ *We'll* **start** *for home*

soon. • *He started toward the door.* **7** [I] — used to indicate the beginning of a range, series, etc. • *Salaries start at around $30,000.* • *What is the* **starting salary** *for the job?* **8 a** [T/I] : to participate in a game or contest at its beginning • *She started (the race) but didn't finish.* • *the* **starting lineup** [=the players who will be playing when the game begins] • *the* **starting pitcher b** [T] : to put (someone or something) into a game or contest at its beginning • *The coach started him at quarterback.* • *start* [=enter] *a horse in a race* **9** [T] : to cause (someone) to begin doing something • *Her questions started me thinking.* : to cause (someone) to begin in a particular way, at a particular level, etc. • *Don't start him talking about the war!* = **Don't get him started on the war!** **10** [I] : to move suddenly and quickly because you are surprised or frightened • *The loud noise made him start.* — **start in** [phrasal vb] *chiefly US, informal* **1** : to start doing a particular activity or action • *She started in on another book.* **2 start in on** : to criticize (someone) about something • *My dad started in on me about not having a job.* — **start off** [phrasal vb] **1 start off or start (something) off or start off (something)** : to start or cause (something) to start in a specified way • *He started off by introducing himself.* • *She started off (her run) at a slow jog.* • *The day started off badly.* • *We started the season off with a win.* **2** : to have a specified quality, identity, job, etc., at the start • *She started off as a sales assistant.* **3** : to begin an important period in your life or career • *newlyweds who are just starting off* **4** : to begin to move toward a particular place or in a particular direction • *She started off for work.* **5 start (someone) off or start off (someone)** : to cause (someone) to begin doing a particular activity or action • *He started her off with some easy questions.* — **start on** [phrasal vb] **1** : to begin doing (something) • *Did you start on your homework yet?* **2 start (someone) on** : to cause (someone) to start doing or using (something) • *The doctor started him on antibiotics.* — **start out** [phrasal vb] **1** : to begin in a specified way • *He started out by introducing himself.* • *The day started out hot and humid.* • *She started out wanting to be a doctor.* **2** : to have a specified quality, identity, job, etc., at the start • *It started out as a simple idea.* **3** : to begin an important period in your life or career • *She started out on a career in teaching.* **4** : to begin to travel • *They started out in the morning.* **5** : to have a particular place as a beginning point • *The parade starts out at the school.* — **start over** [phrasal vb] *chiefly US* **1 start over or start (something) over** : to begin doing something again • *I'm sorry, but you'll have to start (all) over (again).* • *She started (her life) over in a new city.* **2** : to begin to happen again • *In the spring, the cycle starts (all) over (again).* — **start something** also **start anything** *informal* : to do something that causes trouble • *She is always trying to start some-*

thing. • *Don't start anything.* — **start up** [phrasal vb] **1** : to begin to happen or exist • *More new businesses are starting up.* **2 start up or start (something) up or start up (something)** : to begin to function or to make (something) begin to function • *The engine won't start up.* • *He started the car up.* — **to start with** **1** — used to introduce the first statement in a series of statements • *I don't think we should buy it. To start with, we can't afford it.* **2** : at the beginning • *He didn't like his job to start with.*

²**start** *n* **1** [C] : the time at which something begins • *the start of the season/race* • *It was clear* **from** *the (very) start that she had talent.* • *The game was close* **from start to finish.** **2** [C] : the first part of an activity, development, event, etc. • *We missed the start of the game.* • *Their marriage is/got off to a good/bad start.* **3** [C] : the first opportunity to begin a career • *She gave him his start in the business.* **4** [C] : the act of starting something • *She got an early start.* • *They wanted to* **make a fresh/new start.** [=start a new life] • *He made a start on dinner.* **5** [singular] : a brief, sudden action or movement • *She gave a start when he tapped her on the shoulder.* • *He woke with a start.* **6 the start** : the place where a race begins

start·er /ˈstɑɚtɚ/ *n* [C] **1** : a player, horse, etc., that is in a game or race at its beginning **2** : someone who gives the signal for a race to start **3** : a device that is used for starting an engine • *the car's starter* **4** : someone or something that starts an activity, process, etc. • *The question was a good conversation starter.* • *a starter kit for building a model car* **5** *chiefly Brit* : APPETIZER — **for starters** — used to introduce the first statement in a series of statements • *"Why don't you like him?" "Well, for starters, he was rude to my parents."*

star·tle /ˈstɑɚtl̟/ *vb* **star·tled; star·tling** **1** [T] : to surprise or frighten (someone) suddenly and usually not seriously • *You startled me.* • *I was startled by the noise.* **2** [I] : to move or jump suddenly because something surprises or frightens you • *The cat startles easily.*

star·tling /ˈstɑɚtl̟ɪŋ/ *adj* : very surprising, shocking, or frightening • *a startling discovery* — **star·tling·ly** *adv*

start–up /ˈstɑɚtˌʌp/ *n* [C] : a new business • *fund/launch a start-up (company)*

star·va·tion /stɑɚˈveɪʃən/ *n* [U] : suffering or death caused by having nothing to eat or not enough to eat • *They died from/of starvation.*

starve /ˈstɑɚv/ *vb* **starved; starv·ing** **1** [I] : to suffer or die from lack of food • *Those people are starving.* • *starving children* • *They starved to death.* [=died from lack of food] **2** [T] : to cause (a person or animal) to suffer or die because of lack of food • *They tried to starve their enemies into submission.* • *starving yourself to lose weight* **3 a** [I] *chiefly US* : to want or need something very much • *Those children are starving for attention.* **b** [T] : to not give (someone or something) enough of something that is wanted or needed ▪ *Those children have been* **starved of** *attention.* ▪ (*chiefly US*) *Those children are* **starved for** *attention.* — be **starving/starved** *chiefly US, informal* : to be very hungry ▪ *When are we eating? I'm starving!*

stash /'stæʃ/ *vb* **stashed; stash·ing** [*T*] *informal* : to put (something) in a secret or hidden place ▪ *The gifts were stashed in the closet.* ▪ *She stashed some money away.* — **stash** *n* [*C*] *informal* : a drug stash [=an amount of drugs that is kept hidden] ▪ *a stash of money/food/guns*

sta·sis /'steɪsəs/ *n* [*U*] *formal* : a state or condition in which things do not change, move, or progress ▪ *economic stasis*

¹stat /'stæt/ *n* [*C*] *US, informal* : STATISTIC ▪ *baseball stats*

²stat *adv* : **¹**IMMEDIATELY 2 — used chiefly in medicine ▪ *Get this patient to the operating room, stat!*

¹state /'steɪt/ *n* **1** [*C*] **a** : a way of living or existing ▪ *Happiness is the state or condition of being happy.* ▪ *a state of readiness* **b** : the overall physical condition of something ▪ *The building is in a sorry state.* ▪ *The car is in a* **good/bad state of repair.** [=in good/bad condition] **c** : your physical or mental condition ▪ *He was in quite a state.* [=he was very upset, worried, angry, etc.] ▪ *a state of shock/confusion* ▪ *the state of her health* ▪ *an altered state of consciousness* ▪ *her mental/emotional state* = *her* **state of mind** ▪ *She was in no (fit) state* [=too sick, drunk, etc.] *to drive.* **d** : the characteristics of a situation ▪ *the current state of the economy* ▪ *We are in a* **state of war.** [=we are at war] **2** [*C*] : the fact of being a liquid, solid, or gas ▪ *water in a gaseous state* **3** [*C*] **a** : NATION 1a ▪ *African/Arabic states* ▪ *the member states of the United Nations* **b** : a particular kind of government or politically organized society **4** **a** [*C*] : a region of a country that is controlled by the country's central government but that has the authority to make its own laws about certain things ▪ *the 50 states of the U.S.* ▪ *state and federal laws* ▪ *state lines/borders* **b the States** *informal* : the United States of America ▪ *visiting friends in the States* **5** [*U*] : the government of a country ▪ *matters of state* [=government business] ▪ *the separation of church and state* ▪ *The President made a state visit to China.* ▪ *the (U.S.)* **Department of State** = *the* **State Department** [=the part of the U.S. government that is responsible for how the U.S. deals with other countries] — **lie in state** ✧ When the body of a famous leader *lies in state,* it is displayed in a public place so that people can view it and show respect. — **state·hood** /'steɪt,hʊd/ *n* [*U*] ▪ *Alaska and Hawaii achieved statehood in 1959.*

²state *vb* **stat·ed; stat·ing** [*T*] **1** : to express (something) formally in speech or writing ▪ *state your name* ▪ *state an opinion/fact* ▪ *He stated his objections for the record.* ▪ *She accused me of* **stating the obvious.** [=telling people things they already knew] **2** : to give (information,

instructions, etc.) in writing ▪ *The rules clearly state that you can only draw one card.*

state·house /'steɪt,haʊs/ *n* [*C*] : the building in which the legislature of a U.S. state meets and works

state·ly /'steɪtli/ *adj* **state·li·er; -est** : very impressive in appearance, manner, or size ▪ *a stately building* — **state·li·ness** *n* [*U*]

state·ment /'steɪtmənt/ *n* **1** [*C*] : something that you say or write in a formal or official way ▪ *His office issued/released an official statement concerning his health.* ▪ *I disagree with your earlier statement.* ▪ *a signed/sworn statement from a witness* ▪ *The police took the witness's statement.* = *The witness* **made a statement** *to the police.* **2** [*C*] : an opinion, attitude, etc., that you express through the things you do ▪ *The boycott was a political statement.* ▪ *The government* **made a statement** *by increasing fines.* ▪ *The painting makes a strong/clear statement.* **3** [*C*] : a document which shows amounts of money that you have received, spent, etc. ▪ *a statement of expenses* ▪ *a* **bank/financial statement** **4** [*U, singular*] : the act or process of stating something in speech or writing ▪ *She began with a statement of her beliefs.*

state-of-the-art *adj* : using or having the most modern methods, knowledge, or technology ▪ *state-of-the-art procedures* ▪ *The system is state-of-the-art.*

state·room /'steɪt,ru:m/ *n* [*C*] : a private room on a ship or on a railroad car

state·side *or* **State·side** /'steɪt,saɪd/ *adv* : in or to the U.S. ▪ *He's been living in England for several years but he's returning stateside next month.* — **stateside** *or* **Stateside** *adj* ▪ *It was the band's first stateside tour.*

states·man /'steɪtsmən/ *n, pl* **-men** /-mən/ [*C*] : a usually wise, skilled, and respected government leader ▪ *a great/eminent statesman* — **states·man·like** /'steɪtsmən,laɪk/ *adj* — **states·man·ship** /'steɪtsmən,ʃɪp/ *n* [*U*]

¹stat·ic /'stætɪk/ *adj* **1** : showing little or no change, action, or progress ▪ *a static population* ▪ *static* [=*still*] *images* **2** : of, relating to, or producing static electricity ▪ *a static charge*

²static *n* [*U*] : unwanted noise caused in a radio or television receiver by electricity or by conditions in the atmosphere

static electricity *n* [*U*] : electricity that collects on the surface of something and can cause a mild shock if you touch it

¹sta·tion /'steɪʃən/ *n* [*C*] **1** : a place where buses, trains, etc., regularly stop so that passengers can get on and off ▪ *a subway station* **2** : a place where someone does a job or waits for a task ▪ *a nurse's/nursing station* ▪ *sailors manning their battle stations* **3** *old-fashioned* : a person's social or official position ▪ *He married above his station.* ▪ *her station in life* **4** : a building, area, etc., where a certain kind of work or activity is done ▪ *a research/space/weather station* **5** : a place that provides a certain kind of service to the public ▪ *Stop for gas at the next* station. [=(US) gas station] ▪ *Officers brought him to the station.* [=police station] **6** : a company that makes radio or television broadcasts ▪ *a TV station* ▪ *What station is the game on?*

²**station** vb [T] **1** : to assign (someone) to a station or position : POST ▪ *The troops were stationed at the border.* **2** : to put (yourself) in a place and stay there for a period of time ▪ *He stationed himself by the door.*

sta·tion·ary /'steɪʃəˌneri, *Brit* 'steɪʃənri/ *adj* **1** : not moving ▪ *shooting at stationary targets* **2** : not changing ▪ *a stationary population*

sta·tio·nery /'steɪʃəˌneri, *Brit* 'steɪʃənri/ *n* [U] **1** : materials (such as paper, pens, and ink) that are used for writing or typing ▪ *a store that sells stationery = a stationery store* **2** : paper that is used for writing letters and that usually has matching envelopes ▪ *business stationery*

station wagon *n* [C] *US* : a car that has a large open area behind the back seat instead of a trunk and that has a door at the back — called also *(US)* **wagon**, *(Brit)* **estate car**

sta·tis·tic /stə'tɪstɪk/ *n* **1** [C] : a number that represents a piece of information ▪ *statistics about unemployment rates* ▪ *basketball statistics* **2** [U] : a type of mathematics that deals with the study of statistics — **sta·tis·ti·cal** /stə'tɪstɪkəl/ *adj* ▪ *statistical evidence* — **sta·tis·ti·cal·ly** /stə'tɪstɪkli/ *adv*

stat·is·ti·cian /ˌstætə'stɪʃən/ *n* [C] : a person who collects and studies statistics

stat·ue /'stæˌtʃuː/ *n* [C] : a figure usually of a person or animal that is made from stone, metal, etc. ▪ *bronze statues*

stat·u·esque /ˌstætʃə'wɛsk/ *adj* : tall and beautiful ▪ *a statuesque young woman*

stat·u·ette /ˌstætʃə'wɛt/ *n* [C] : a small statue

stat·ure /'stætʃɚ/ *n* [U] **1** : the level of respect that people have for a successful person, organization, etc. ▪ *I was honored to work with a writer of his stature.* [=a writer who is so highly respected] **2** *somewhat formal* : a person's height ▪ *a woman of short stature* [=a short woman]

sta·tus /'steɪtəs, 'stætəs/ *n* **1 a** [C/U] : the position or rank of someone or something when compared to others in a society, organization, group, etc. ▪ *his high (social) status* ▪ *her status in the community* ▪ *They want to maintain the city's status as a tourist attraction.* **b** [U] : high position or rank in society ▪ *a man of status and wealth* **2** [C/U] : the official position of a person or thing according to the law ▪ *They were given refugee status.* **3** [C] : the current state of someone or something ▪ *What is the status of the project?* ▪ *a status report*

status quo /-'kwoʊ/ *n* [singular] : the current situation : the way things are now ▪ *maintaining the status quo*

status symbol *n* [C] : something (such as an expensive car) that you own and that shows that you are wealthy or have a high social status

stat·ute /'stæˌtʃuːt/ *n* **1** [C/U] : a written law that is formally created by a govern-

ment ▪ *The legislature passed the statute.* ▪ *activities that are prohibited/protected by statute* **2** [C] : a written rule or regulation ▪ *college/university statutes*

stat·u·to·ry /'stætʃəˌtori, *Brit* 'stætʃətri/ *adj, law* **1** : of or relating to formal laws or statutes ▪ *statutory acts* **2** : controlled or determined by a law or rule ▪ *the statutory age of retirement*

¹**staunch** *variant spelling of* STANCH

²**staunch** /'stɑːntʃ/ *adj, always before a noun* : very devoted or loyal to a person, belief, or cause ▪ *She is a staunch advocate of women's rights.* ▪ *He's a staunch believer in the value of exercise.* ▪ *a staunch supporter* — **staunch·ly** *adv*

¹**stave** /'steɪv/ *n* [C] **1** : one of the narrow strips of wood that form the sides of a barrel **2** : a long wooden stick : STAFF 3 *chiefly Brit* : STAFF 3

²**stave** *vb* **staved** *also* **stove** /'stoʊv/; **stav·ing** — **stave in** [phrasal vb] **stave in** *or* **stave (something) in** *or* **stave in (something)** : to be broken or crushed inward or to break or crush (something) inward ▪ *The hull of the boat stove in when it hit the rocks.* ▪ *The rocks stove in the hull.* — **stave off** [phrasal vb] **stave (someone or something) off** *or* **stave off (someone or something)** : to keep (someone or something) away usually for a short time ▪ *He's trying to stave off his creditors.* ▪ *eating crackers to stave off hunger*

staves *plural of* STAFF

¹**stay** /'steɪ/ *vb* **1 a** [I] : to continue to be in the same place or with the same person or group for a period of time : REMAIN ▪ *Please stay nearby.* ▪ *He is staying with the team.* ▪ *We stayed home last night.* ▪ *Go to your room and stay there.* ▪ *I'll stay around for a bit longer.* ▪ *You go on ahead. I'll stay behind to clean up.* **b** [I, linking vb] : to continue to be in a specified state, condition, or position : REMAIN ▪ *She stayed angry all night.* ▪ *I couldn't stay awake.* ▪ *The store stays open until six o'clock.* ▪ *Despite his injury, he stayed in the game.* ▪ *They stayed friends.* [=continued to be friends] **2** [I] : to live in a place as a guest for a short period of time ▪ *stayed overnight in a hotel* ▪ *You can stay with us. = You can stay at our house.* **3** [T] : to give a legal order that stops or delays (something) ▪ *The judge agreed to stay the execution.* — **stay away** [phrasal vb] : to not go near someone or something ▪ *couldn't stay away for long* ▪ *Stay away from my girlfriend!* ▪ *I try to stay away from* [=avoid] *caffeine.* — **stay in** [phrasal vb] : to stay inside or at home ▪ *We're staying in tonight.* — **stay off** [phrasal vb] **1** : to avoid (something) ▪ *Let's stay off the subject of politics.* **2** : to not go on (something) ▪ *Please stay off the grass.* — **stay on** [phrasal vb] **1** : to continue to work at a job ▪ *She retired but stayed on as a consultant.* **2** : to continue taking (a medication, drug, etc.) ▪ *I have to stay on the antibiotics for two weeks.* — **stay out** [phrasal vb] **1 a** : to avoid going into (a place) ▪ *Get out and stay out!* ▪ *Stay out of my room.* **b stay out of** : to avoid becoming involved in

(something) • *Try to stay out of trouble.*
2 : to spend time away from home • *She stayed out dancing all night.* — **stay over** [*phrasal vb*] : to sleep at another person's house for the night • *Can she stay over tonight?* — **stay the course** : to continue with a process, effort, etc., even though it is difficult • *We'll succeed if we just stay the course.* — **stay the night** : to sleep at another person's house for the night • *They stayed the night (at our house).* — **stay up** [*phrasal vb*] : to continue to be awake past the time when you usually go to bed • *He stayed up until midnight.* — **stay with** [*phrasal vb*] **1** : to continue to influence or affect (someone) • *The tragedy has stayed with her.* **2** : to continue using or doing (something) • *This method works, so we'll stay with it.* **3** : to keep even with (someone) in a race, competition, etc. • *The other runners struggled to stay with the leader.*

²**stay** *n* [*C*] **1** : an occasion in which you spend time at a place as a guest or visitor • *Have a pleasant stay. = Enjoy your stay.* **2** : a legal order that stops or delays something • *a stay of execution* **3 a** : a rope or wire that supports a pole, a ship's mast, etc. • *the stays on a tent* **b** : a piece of stiff plastic, bone, etc., that provides shape to clothing • *a corset stay*

std. *abbr* standard

STD /ˌɛsˌtiːˈdiː/ *n* [*C*] : any one of various diseases that you can get by having sex with a person who has the disease ◇ *STD* is an abbreviation for "sexually transmitted disease."

stead /ˈstɛd/ *n* — **in someone's/something's stead** *formal* : in the place of someone or something • *She conducted the meeting in his stead.* • *One empire died, and another arose in its stead.* — **stand someone/something in good stead** *formal* : to be useful or helpful to someone or something • *His language skills will stand him in good stead when he is traveling.*

stead·fast /ˈstɛdˌfæst, *Brit* ˈstɛdˌfɑːst/ *adj* : very devoted or loyal : not changing • *steadfast friends* • *He was steadfast in his support.* — **stead·fast·ly** *adv* — **stead·fast·ness** /ˈstɛdˌfæstnəs, *Brit* ˈstɛdˌfɑːstnəs/ *n* [*U*]

¹**steady** /ˈstɛdi/ *adj* **stead·i·er; -est** **1** : held firmly in one place or position • *Keep the camera steady.* • *a steady hand/gaze* • *He wasn't very steady on his feet.* **2** : not changing as time passes • *Prices have remained steady.* • *a steady job* • *They do a steady business.* • *a steady relationship* • *a **steady** boyfriend/girlfriend* **3** : happening or developing in a continuous and usually gradual way • *a steady increase* • *steady progress* • *There was a steady rain all day.* • *a **steady** stream of donations* **4** : not nervous or excited • *Her voice was calm and steady.* **5** : dependable or reliable • *a steady worker/friend* — **steady on** *Brit, informal* — used to tell someone to be calm, reasonable, etc. • *Steady on, now. It's not as bad as that.* — **stead·i·ly** /ˈstɛdəli/ *adv* — *Wages have steadily increased.* — **steadi·ness** /ˈstɛdinəs/ *n* [*U*]

²**steady** *vb* **stead·ies; stead·ied; steady·ing** : to make (something or someone) steady or to become steady: such as **a** [*T*] : to keep (something or someone) from moving, falling, etc. • *She steadied the gun/camera.* • *He held the rail to **steady** himself.* **b** [*T/I*] : to cause (something) to stop increasing, decreasing, etc. • *She took medication to steady her heart rate.* • *Prices have steadied.* — **steady your nerves** : to make yourself calm or calmer • *She took a drink to try to steady her nerves.*

³**steady** *adv* : in a steady way • *Hold the camera steady.* — **go steady** *informal + old-fashioned* : to have a lasting romantic relationship with one person • *Do you want to go steady (with me)?*

steak /ˈsteɪk/ *n* **1** [*C/U*] : a thick, flat piece of meat and especially beef **2** [*C*] : a thick, flat piece of fish • *a tuna/swordfish steak* **3** [*U*] *Brit* : beef that is cut into small pieces and used for stews, casseroles, etc. • *steak and kidney pie*

¹**steal** /ˈstiːl/ *vb* **stole** /ˈstoʊl/; **sto·len** /ˈstoʊlən/; **steal·ing** **1** **a** [*T/I*] : to take (something) in a way that is wrong or illegal • *They stole thousands of dollars.* • *Someone stole my car. = My car was stolen.* • *a stolen watch* • *He accused the boy of stealing.* **b** [*T*] : to wrongly take and use (another person's idea, words, etc.) • *He stole my idea.* **2** [*T*] : to get (something that is difficult to get) usually a quick and often secret way • *I stole a nap this afternoon.* • *He stole a glance at her.* • *She stole a kiss from him.* [=kissed him quickly and suddenly] **3** [*T*] : to get more attention than others during (a performance, scene, etc.) • *He **stole** the show. = His performance stole the show.* **4 a** [*T/I*] *baseball* : to reach (a base) safely by running to it from the previous base when the ball has not been hit by a batter • *He stole second (base).* **b** [*T*] *sports* : to take (the ball, puck, etc.) from another player • *(basketball) He stole the ball/pass.* **5** [*I*] : to come or go quietly or secretly • *They stole out of the room.* • *She stole away silently.* — **steal a march on** see ²MARCH

²**steal** *n* [*C*] **1** *informal* : something that is being sold at a low price • *This car is a steal at only $5,000.* **2 a** *baseball* : the act of stealing a base • *He has 40 steals this season.* **b** *sports* : the act of taking the ball, puck, etc., from another player

stealth /ˈstɛlθ/ *n* [*U*] : a secret, quiet, and clever way of moving or behaving • *The fox uses stealth to hunt its prey.* — **stealth·i·ly** /ˈstɛlθəli/ *adv* — **stealthy** /ˈstɛlθi/ *adj* **stealth·i·er; -est** • *stealthy movements* • *a stealthy burglar*

¹**steam** /ˈstiːm/ *n* [*U*] **1 a** : the hot gas that is created when water is boiled **b** : steam that is created by a machine and kept under pressure to provide power • *The boat/train runs on steam.* • *The damaged ship returned to port **under its own steam**.* [=by using its own power] • *a steam(-powered) engine* **2** : very small drops of water that form on a surface when warm moist air is cooled down • *He wiped the steam from the mirror.* **3**

informal : the strength, force, or energy needed to continue, to go faster, etc. • *Sales have lost steam.* [=slowed down] • *The campaign quickly gained/gathered steam.* [=became more successful] • *I was making good progress, but then I ran out of steam.* • *The project is picking up steam.* [=beginning to move ahead faster] • *The campaign is going full steam ahead.* [=with as much speed and power as possible]— **let/blow off (some) steam** *informal* : to get rid of energy or anger by doing something active • *I went jogging to let off some steam.*

²**steam** *vb* **1** [*I*] : to produce steam • *a steaming bowl of soup* **2** [*T*] : to cook, heat, or treat (something) with steam • *steam carrots* • *steamed vegetables* **3** [*T/I*] : to cause (a window, mirror, etc.) to become covered with small drops of water • *Their breath steamed (up) the windows.* • *My glasses (were/got) steamed up.* **4** [*I*] **a** : to move by using power produced by steam • *The ship steamed up the river.* **b** : to move forward in a quick and forceful way • *Our plans are steaming ahead.*

steam·boat /'sti:m,bout/ *n* [*C*] : a boat that is powered by steam

steamed /'sti:md/ *adj, not before a noun, chiefly US, informal* : angry or irritated • *He got all steamed up about it.*

steam·er /'sti:mɚ/ *n* [*C*] **1** : a container in which food is cooked with steam **2** : a boat or ship that is powered by steam

steam·ing /'sti:mɪŋ/ *adj, informal* **1** : very hot • *steaming (hot) weather* **2** : very angry • *She was steaming.* = *She was steaming mad.*

steam·roll·er /'sti:m,roulɚ/ *n* [*C*] : a large, heavy machine that is used for making a road or other surface flat

steam·ship /'sti:m,ʃɪp/ *n* [*C*] : a ship that is powered by steam

steam shovel *n* [*C*] *US* : a large machine that is powered by steam and that is used for digging large holes

steamy /'sti:mi/ *adj* **steam·i·er; -est** **1** : full of steam or warm, moist air • *steamy* [=hot and humid] *weather* **2** : sexually exciting • *a steamy love scene*

steed /'sti:d/ *n* [*C*] *literary* : a horse that a person rides • *a knight's noble steed*

¹**steel** /'sti:l/ *n* **1** [*U*] **a** : a strong, hard metal made of iron and carbon • *steel bars* **b** : the industry that makes steel • *She came from a steel town* [=a town where steel is made] *in Pennsylvania.* **2** **a** [*U*] *literary* : things (such as weapons) that are made of steel • *the clash of steel* **b** [*singular*] : the part of something that is made of steel • *the steel of a knife* **c** [*C*] : a device or tool that is made of steel • *a sharpening steel* [=a steel rod for sharpening knives] **3** [*U*] — used to describe something or someone that is very strong • *a grip of/like steel* • *a man of steel*

²**steel** *vb* — **steel yourself** : to make (yourself) ready for something difficult or unpleasant • *He steeled himself for the interview.*

steel wool *n* [*U*] : long threads of metal

that are wound together to form a rough pad which is used for cleaning and polishing things

steel·work·er /'sti:l,wɚkɚ/ *n* [*C*] *US* : a person who works at a place where steel is made

steely /'sti:li/ *adj* **steel·i·er; -est** **1** : very strong and determined often in a cold or unfriendly way • *steely determination* • *She gave him a steely gaze.* **2** : resembling steel especially in color • *steely gray clouds*

¹**steep** /'sti:p/ *adj* **1** : rising or falling very sharply • *a steep slope/hillside* • *The stairs are very steep.* **2** : going up or down very quickly • *a steep drop/increase* **3** : very high • *Their prices/rates are pretty steep.* — **steep·ly** *adv* • *Prices rose/fell steeply.* — **steep·ness** *n* [*U*]

²**steep** *vb* [*T/I*] : to put (something) in a liquid for a period of time • *Steep the tea.* • *The tea steeped for several minutes.* — **steep in** [*phrasal vb*] **1 steep (someone) in** : to make (someone) know and understand a lot about (something) • *She was steeped in the classics.* • *He steeped himself in the language.* **2** — used to say that there is a lot of something in a place, time, etc. • *a country that is steeped in tradition*

stee·ple /'sti:pəl/ *n* [*C*] : a tall, pointed tower on a church

stee·ple·chase /'sti:pəl,ʧeɪs/ *n* [*C*] **1** : a race in which people riding horses jump over fences, water, etc. **2** : a race in which runners jump over fences and water

¹**steer** /'stiɚ/ *vb* **1 a** [*T/I*] : to control the direction in which a car, ship, etc., moves • *He steered his car carefully into the parking space.* • *navigators steering by the stars* **b** [*I*] — used to describe how easy or difficult it is to steer a vehicle • *The car steers well.* **2** [*I*] : to be moved or guided in a particular direction or along a particular course • *The boat steered out to sea.* **3** [*T*] **a** : to direct or guide the movement or progress of (something) • *She steered the bill through the legislature.* • *He steered the team to victory.* **b** : to cause (someone) to act in a particular way • *I won't steer you wrong.* [=give you bad advice] — **steer clear** *US* : to keep away from someone or something completely • *He's in a bad mood. You'd better steer clear (of him).* • *I try to steer clear of that subject.*

²**steer** *n* [*C*] : a male cow that has had its sex organs removed and is raised for meat

steer·ing /'stiɚɪŋ/ *n* [*U*] : the mechanical parts of a car, boat, etc., that are used to control its direction • *There's a problem with the boat's steering.*

steering wheel *n* [*C*] : a wheel in a vehicle that the driver turns to steer the vehicle

stel·lar /'stɛlɚ/ *adj* **1** *technical* : of or relating to the stars • *stellar light* **2** : very good : EXCELLENT • *a stellar performance*

¹**stem** /'stɛm/ *n* [*C*] **1 a** : the long and thin part of a plant that rises above the soil and supports the leaves and flowers

b : the long, thin part of a fruit, leaf, flower, etc., that connects it to its plant ▪ *a cherry stem*   **2** : a long and thin part ▪ *the stem of a wine glass* — **stemmed** /ˈstɛmd/ *adj* ▪ *long-stemmed roses*

²**stem** *vb* **stemmed; stem·ming** [*T*]   **1** : to stop the progress or spread of (something) ▪ *The doctor stemmed the flow of blood.* ▪ *laws meant to* **stem the tide** *of illegal immigration*   **2** : to remove the stem from (a fruit, leaf, flower, etc.) ▪ *She stemmed the berries.* — **stem from** [*phrasal vb*] : to come from or be caused by (something or someone) ▪ *a health problem that stems from an old injury* ▪ *His love of the outdoors stems from his father.*

stench /ˈstɛntʃ/ *n* [*singular*] : a very bad smell : STINK ▪ *the stench of rotting meat*

sten·cil /ˈstɛnsəl/ *n* [*C*]   **1** : a piece of paper, metal, etc., that has a design, letter, etc., cut out of it ▪ *painted a border on the wall with a stencil* ▪ *letter/number stencils*   **2** : a design or a print that is made with a stencil ▪ *The walls are decorated with a vine stencil.* — **stencil** *vb*, *US* **-ciled** *or Brit* **-cilled;** *US* **-cil·ing** *or Brit* **-cil·ling** [*T*] ▪ *stencil numbers on a mailbox* ▪ *She stenciled the walls with a decorative pattern.*

ste·nog·ra·phy /stəˈnɑːɡrəfi/ *n* [*U*] : a method used for writing down the words that someone says very quickly by using a special type of writing (called shorthand) — **ste·nog·ra·pher** /stəˈnɑːɡrəfə/ *n* [*C*] ▪ *He works as a courtroom stenographer.* — **steno·graph·ic** /ˌstɛnəˈɡræfɪk/ *adj*

¹**step** /ˈstɛp/ *n*   **1** [*C*] **a** : a movement made by lifting your foot and putting it down in a different place ▪ *She took one step forward/backward.*   **b** : the distance covered in one step ▪ *The edge of the cliff was three steps to my left.*   **2** [*singular*] : the way that someone walks ▪ *She walked with a quick/light step.*   **3** [*C*] : one of a series of actions that are done to achieve something ▪ *a major/important step towards independence* ▪ *We are taking steps to correct the situation.*   **4** [*C*] : a stage in a process ▪ *She's one step nearer/closer to graduation.* ▪ *We'll guide you through the process* **step by step.**   **5** [*C*] : a level or rank in a scale ▪ *a step above/below average*   **6** [*C*] : the flat piece of wood, stone, etc., that forms one of the levels of a staircase ▪ *They sat on the steps in front of the house.*   **7** [*C*] : a movement or pattern of movements made by someone who is dancing ▪ *dance steps* — **a/one step ahead of**   **1** : better prepared than (someone or something) ▪ *She is always one step ahead of me.*   **2** : able to avoid being caught or found by (someone or something) ▪ *staying one step ahead of the police/law* — **fall into step** : to begin walking or marching with the same rhythm as another person or group of people ▪ *He fell into step beside her.* — **in step**   **1** : with the same rhythm as someone or something ▪ *dancing in step with the music*   **2** : matching or agreeing *with* someone or something ▪ *She's in step with people her age.* [=she has

the same ideas, problems, etc., as other people her age] — **mind/watch your step**   **1** : to walk carefully ▪ *It's slippery, so watch your step.*   **2** : to speak or behave carefully ▪ *Watch your step with me, young lady.* — **out of step**   **1** : not moving with the same rhythm as someone or something ▪ *One of the dancers was out of step.*   **2** : not matching or agreeing with someone or something ▪ *Her fashion sense is completely out of step (with current styles).*

²**step** *vb* **stepped; step·ping** [*I*]   **1** : to move in a specified direction by lifting your foot and putting it down in a different place ▪ *I stepped onto/off the bus.* : to move somewhere by walking ▪ *Please step into my office.*   **2** : to put your foot down ▪ *step on a nail* ▪ *step in a puddle* — **step aside/down** [*phrasal vb*] : to leave a job or official position ▪ *He stepped down as president.* — **step back** [*phrasal vb*] : to stop doing something or being actively involved in something for a time ▪ *You need to step back and take time to work through this.* — **step forward** [*phrasal vb*] : to give or offer help, information, etc. ▪ *He stepped forward to identify the robber.* — **step in** [*phrasal vb*] : to become involved in an activity, discussion, etc., in order to prevent trouble or provide help ▪ *She stepped in and took charge.* — **step into** [*phrasal vb*] : to take a particular role or do a particular task ▪ *She stepped into the role/position of director.* — **step on it** *or US* **step on the gas** *informal* : to drive faster ▪ *Step on it, they're getting away!* — **step out** [*phrasal vb*] *US* : to briefly leave a place ▪ *I stepped out for a moment.* — **step out of line** *informal* : to disobey rules or behave badly ▪ *If you step out of line, you'll get kicked off the team.* — **step up** [*phrasal vb*]   **1** : to increase in amount or speed ▪ *Production has stepped up.*   **2 a** : to say openly or publicly that you are the person who should get something or who can do something ▪ *She stepped up to volunteer.*   **b** : to do better ▪ *The team's best player is injured, so someone else needs to step up.*   **3** **step (something) up** *or* **step up (something)**   **a** : to increase the amount or speed of (something) ▪ *stepping up production*   **b** : to improve (something) ▪ *He needs to step up his performance.*

step·broth·er /ˈstɛpˌbrʌðə/ *n* [*C*] : the son of your stepmother or stepfather

step–by–step /ˌstɛpbaɪˈstɛp/ *adj*   **1** : showing or explaining each stage in a process ▪ *step-by-step directions*   **2** : happening or done in a series of steps or stages : GRADUAL ▪ *a step-by-step approach*

step·child /ˈstɛpˌtʃajəld/ *n, pl* **-chil·dren** [*C*] : a stepson or stepdaughter

step·daugh·ter /ˈstɛpˌdɑːtə/ *n* [*C*] : your wife's or husband's daughter by a past marriage or relationship

step·fa·ther /ˈstɛpˌfɑːðə/ *n* [*C*] : a man that your mother marries after her marriage to or relationship with your father has ended

step·lad·der /ˈstɛpˌlædə/ *n* [*C*] : a ladder

that has wide, flat steps and two pairs of legs which are connected at the top and that opens at the bottom so that it can stand without being attached to or supported by something else

step·moth·er /ˈstɛpˌmʌðɚ/ n [C] : a woman that your father marries after his marriage to or relationship with your mother has ended

step·par·ent /ˈstɛpˌpɛrənt/ n [C] : someone that your mother or father marries after the marriage to or relationship with your other parent has ended

steppe /ˈstɛp/ n [C] : a large, flat area of land with grass and very few trees especially in eastern Europe and Asia

step·ping–stone /ˈstɛpɪŋˌstoʊn/ n [C] 1 : a large, flat stone that you step on to cross a stream 2 : something that helps you get or achieve something ▪ He regarded his first job as a stepping-stone to a better career.

step·sis·ter /ˈstɛpˌsɪstɚ/ n [C] : the daughter of your stepmother or stepfather

step·son /ˈstɛpˌsʌn/ n [C] : your wife's or husband's son by a past marriage or relationship

¹**ste·reo** /ˈstɛrijoʊ/ n, pl **-re·os** 1 [C] : a piece of electronic equipment that plays the radio, CDs, etc., and that uses two speakers for the sound 2 [U] : a way of recording and playing back sound so that the sound comes from two directions ▪ broadcasting **in stereo**

²**stereo** adj : of or relating to a system that directs sound through two speakers ▪ stereo headphones/equipment

¹**ste·reo·type** /ˈstɛrijəˌtaɪp/ n [C] : an often unfair and untrue belief that many people have about all people or things with a particular characteristic ▪ racial/cultural stereotypes — **ste·reo·typ·i·cal** /ˌstɛrijəˈtɪpɪkəl/ adj ▪ He's the stereotypical absentminded professor. [=he's a professor who is absentminded in the way that people often think of professors as being] — **ste·reo·typ·i·cal·ly** /ˌstɛrijəˈtɪpɪkli/ adv

²**stereotype** vb **-typed; -typ·ing** [T] : to believe unfairly that all people or things with a particular characteristic are the same ▪ It's not fair to stereotype a group of people based on one person you don't like.

ster·ile /ˈstɛrəl, Brit ˈstɛˌrajəl/ adj 1 : not able to produce crops or plants ▪ sterile soil/fields 2 a : not able to produce children, young animals, etc. ▪ sterile offspring b : not able to grow or develop ▪ sterile eggs 3 : clean and free of bacteria and germs ▪ sterile needles 4 : not producing or containing new ideas, useful results, etc. ▪ a sterile debate/subject 5 : very plain and not interesting or attractive ▪ a sterile building/room — **ste·ril·i·ty** /stəˈrɪləti/ n [U]

ster·il·ize also Brit **ster·il·ise** /ˈstɛrəˌlaɪz/ vb **-ized; -iz·ing** [T] 1 : to clean (something) by destroying germs or bacteria ▪ sterilize the dental instruments 2 : to make (someone or something) unable to produce children, young animals, etc. ▪ sterilize your cat/dog — **ster·il·i·za·tion**

also Brit **ster·il·i·sa·tion** /ˌstɛrələˈzeɪʃən, Brit ˌstɛrəˌlaɪˈzeɪʃən/ n [C/U]

¹**ster·ling** /ˈstɚlɪŋ/ n [U] 1 : silver that is 92 percent pure — called also **sterling silver** 2 : British money ▪ a drop in the value of sterling

²**sterling** adj 1 : made of silver that is 92 percent pure ▪ a sterling bracelet 2 : very good ▪ a sterling example of democracy

¹**stern** /ˈstɚn/ adj 1 a : very serious especially in an unfriendly way ▪ a stern judge/warning b : expressing strong disapproval or criticism ▪ He gave me a stern look. 2 : not likely to change or become weaker ▪ stern resolve — **stern·ly** adv — **stern·ness** /ˈstɚnnəs/ n [U]

²**stern** n [C] : the back part of a boat or ship

ster·num /ˈstɚnəm/ n [C] technical : BREASTBONE

ste·roid /ˈstɛˌrɔɪd/ n [C] 1 : a natural substance that is produced in the body 2 : ANABOLIC STEROID ▪ a steroid user/abuser

stetho·scope /ˈstɛθəˌskoʊp/ n [C] medical : an instrument that is used for listening to someone's heart or lungs

¹**stew** /ˈstuː, Brit ˈstjuː/ n, pl **stews** [C/U] : a dish of vegetables and usually meat cooked in hot liquid for a long time — **in a stew** informal : excited, worried, or confused ▪ He got himself in a stew over nothing.

²**stew** vb 1 [T/I] : to cook (something) slowly in hot liquid ▪ stew the meat ▪ a can of stewed tomatoes 2 [I] : to be upset or worried ▪ She's been stewing over/about what he said for days.

stew·ard /ˈstuːwɚd, Brit ˈstjuːwəd/ n [C] 1 : a person and especially a man whose job is to serve meals and take care of passengers on a train, airplane, or ship 2 a : someone who protects or is responsible for money, property, etc. ▪ teaching our children to be good stewards of the land b : a person whose job is to manage the land and property of another person 3 chiefly Brit : someone who is in charge of a race, contest, or other public event — **stew·ard·ship** /ˈstuːwɚdˌʃɪp, Brit ˈstjuːwədˌʃɪp/ n [U] ▪ the stewardship of their investments/estate

stew·ard·ess /ˈstuːwɚdəs, Brit ˈstjuːwədəs/ n [C] somewhat old-fashioned : a woman whose job is to serve meals and take care of passengers on a train, airplane, or ship

¹**stick** /ˈstɪk/ n 1 [C] : a cut or broken branch or twig ▪ a pile of sticks 2 [C] a : a long, thin piece of wood, metal, plastic, etc., that is used for a particular purpose ▪ a measuring/hiking stick b : a long, thin object that is used for hitting or moving a ball or puck in a game ▪ a hockey stick 3 [C] a : something that is long and thin like a stick ▪ carrot/celery sticks ▪ a stick of dynamite b : a long piece of something that is usually wrapped in paper, plastic, etc. ▪ a stick of gum/butter 4 **the sticks** informal : an area in the country that is far away from towns and cities ▪ living in the sticks 5 [C] informal : punishment or the threat

of punishment that is used to try to persuade someone to do something ✧ This sense of *stick* is often contrasted with *carrot*, which refers to the reward or advantage someone will get if they do something. ▪ *They say that a carrot works better than a stick.* — **get on the stick** *US, informal* : to start working hard at something that you have been avoiding doing — **the short end of the stick** *chiefly US, informal* : unfair or unfavorable treatment ▪ *She got the short end of the stick in the deal.* — **the wrong end of the stick** *chiefly Brit, informal* : an incorrect understanding of something ▪ *You've got (hold of) the wrong end of the stick. He didn't push me; I fell.*

²**stick** *vb* **stuck** /ˈstʌk/; **stick·ing** **1 a** [*T*] : to push (something usually sharp or pointed) into something ▪ *stick a toothpick in/into a sandwich* **b** [*I*] *of something usually sharp or pointed* : to go partly into something ▪ *The thorn stuck in the dog's paw.* : to be partly inside something ▪ *I saw a letter sticking out of his pocket.* **2** [*T*] *informal* : to put (something or someone) in a specified place ▪ *He stuck the pencil behind his ear.* ▪ *The dog stuck its head out the window.* ▪ *The girl stuck her finger in the batter.* **3 a** [*T*] *informal* : to attach (something) to a surface with glue, tape, pins, etc. ▪ *stick a stamp on a letter* **b** [*I*] : to become attached to the surface of something ▪ *Two pages had stuck together.* ▪ *The biscuits stuck to the pan.* **4** [*I*] : to become difficult or impossible to move from a place or position ▪ *Her foot stuck in the mud.* ▪ *(figurative) His words stuck in my mind.* [=I remembered his words] — **stick around** [*phrasal vb*] *informal* : to stay somewhere especially in order to wait for something or someone ▪ *Stick around. The band should start playing soon.* — **stick by** [*phrasal vb*] : to continue to support or be loyal to (someone or something) ▪ *She stuck by him throughout the trial.* — **stick it to** *US, informal* : to treat (someone) harshly or unfairly ▪ *businesses that stick it to consumers by charging high fees* — **stick like glue** *informal* **1** : to stay very firmly attached to something ▪ *If the egg dries, it will stick like glue.* **2** : to stay very close to someone ▪ *Her dog stuck to her like glue.* — **stick out** [*phrasal vb*] **1** : to extend outward beyond an edge or surface ▪ *His ears stick out.* **2 stick out (something) or stick out** : to extend (something, such as a body part) outward ▪ *She stuck out her tongue.* **b** *informal* : to continue doing (something unpleasant or difficult) ▪ *Our team was down by 20 points, but we stuck it out* [=stayed and watched the game] *until the end.* **3** : to be easily seen, recognized, or noticed ▪ *You certainly stick out with that orange hat.* ▪ *Two facts stick out from her testimony.* — **stick to** [*phrasal vb*] : to continue doing or using (something) especially when it is difficult to do so ▪ *She stuck to her story/plan.* : to not change (a deci-

sion, belief, etc.) ▪ *I will stick to my promise/word.* — **stick together** *informal* : to continue to support each other ▪ *We need to stick together.* — **stick up** [*phrasal vb*] **1** : to extend upward above a surface ▪ *The baby's hair sticks (straight) up.* **2 stick up for** *informal* : to defend (someone) against attack or criticism ▪ *She stuck up for herself.* — **stick with** [*phrasal vb*] *informal* **1** : to continue using or doing (something) ▪ *You need to find a job and stick with it.* : to not change (a decision, belief, etc.) ▪ *He is sticking with his decision.* **2 stick (someone) with** : to force (someone) to deal with (something or someone unpleasant) ▪ *He stuck me with the bill.* [=made me pay the bill] ▪ *I was stuck with washing dishes.* **3 a** : to stay close to (someone) in a race or competition ▪ *The challenger stuck with the champion until the very last round.* **b** : to stay near (someone) in order to gain knowledge, protection, etc. ▪ *Stick with me, kid, and you'll learn something!* **c** : to be remembered by someone for a very long time ▪ *That experience stuck with her.*

stick·er /ˈstɪkɚ/ *n* [*C*] : a piece of paper with a picture or writing on it and a sticky substance on its back that is used to attach it to a surface

stick figure *n* [*C*] : a drawing that shows the head of a person or animal as a circle and all other parts as usually straight lines

sticking point *n* [*C*] : something that people disagree about and that prevents progress from being made in discussions ▪ *The length of the contract has become a sticking point in the negotiations.*

stick-in-the-mud /ˈstɪkənðəˌmʌd/ *n* [*C*] *informal* + *disapproving* : someone who has old-fashioned ideas or who does not like trying new or exciting things

stick·ler /ˈstɪklɚ/ *n* [*C*] : a person who believes that something is very important and should be done or followed all the time ▪ *He's a stickler for the rules.*

stick·pin /ˈstɪkˌpɪn/ *n* [*C*] *US* : a decorative pin that is worn on a jacket or used to hold the ends of a necktie in place

stick shift *n* [*C*] *US* **1** : a device in a car that you move into different positions in order to change the car's gears **2** : a car that has a stick shift : MANUAL ▪ *Do you know how to drive a stick shift?*

stick-to-it-ive-ness /ˌstɪkˈtuːwətɪvnəs/ *n* [*U*] *US, informal* : the quality that allows someone to continue trying to do something even though it is difficult or unpleasant : PERSEVERANCE

sticky /ˈstɪki/ *adj* **stick·i·er; -est** **1** : covered in a substance that things stick to ▪ *sticky fingers/hands* **2** *of a substance* : tending to have things attach to it : tending to have things stick to it ▪ *The sap is sticky.* **3** *informal* : unpleasantly warm and humid ▪ *a sticky day* ▪ *The weather was hot and sticky.* **4** *informal* : difficult or unpleasant ▪ *a sticky situation* — **stick·i·ness** /ˈstɪkinəs/ *n* [*U*]

¹**stiff** /ˈstɪf/ *adj* **1 a** : difficult to bend or move ▪ *stiff hairs/bristles/fabric* ▪ *The brush was as stiff as a board.* [=very stiff]

b : painful to move or use • *stiff muscles* • *a stiff back/neck* **2** : thick and difficult to stir or pour • *stiff batter* **3** : difficult, strict, or severe • *a stiff penalty/fine* • *stiff competition* **4** : not graceful, relaxed, or friendly • *a stiff manner* : too formal • *stiff writing/dialogue* **5** : very expensive • *a stiff price* **6** : strong and forceful • *a stiff wind/breeze* **7** : containing a lot of alcohol • *a stiff drink/cocktail* — **stiff upper lip** : a calm and determined attitude in a difficult situation • *She kept a stiff upper lip through the whole ordeal.* — **stiff·ly** *adv* — **stiff·ness** *n* [U]

²**stiff** *adv, informal* : very much • *She was scared/bored stiff.* — **frozen stiff** **1** : completely stiff because of being wet and frozen • *The shirt was frozen stiff.* **2** *informal* : extremely cold • *I was frozen stiff by the time I got indoors.*

³**stiff** *n* [C] *informal* **1** : the body of a dead person **2** *US* **a** : a person who you think is lucky, unlucky, etc. • *You lucky stiff!* **b** : an ordinary or dull person *(disapproving)* *His friends are a bunch of stiffs.* • *I'm just an average working stiff.*

⁴**stiff** *vb* [T] *US, informal* : to not give as much money as you should give to (someone) • *He stiffed the waiter on the tip.*

stiff·en /ˈstɪfən/ *vb* **1** [I] : to stop moving and become completely still especially because of fear, anger, etc. • *She stiffened when he grabbed her shoulder.* **2** [I] : to become painful to move or use • *My muscles stiffened (up) the next day.* **3** [T/I] : to become more severe or strong or to make (something) more severe or strong • *The wind stiffened.* • *He stiffened his resolve.* **4** [T] : to make (something, such as cloth) difficult to bend or move • *stiffen a shirt with starch* — **stiff·en·er** /ˈstɪfənər/ *n* [C]

sti·fle /ˈstaɪfəl/ *vb* **sti·fled; sti·fling** **1** [T] **a** : to not allow yourself to do or express (something) • *stifle a cry/yawn* **b** : to stop (someone) from doing or expressing something • *He felt stifled by the school's rules.* **2** [T] : to make (something) difficult or impossible • *Too many regulations stifle innovation.* **3 a** [I] : to be unable to breathe easily • *We were stifling in the hot, tiny room.* **b** [T] : to make (someone) unable to breathe easily or unable to breathe easily • *He was almost stifled by the smoke.*

stifling *adj* **1** : making it difficult to breathe • *The heat was stifling.* : very hot and humid • *a stifling day* **2** : not allowing something to be done or expressed • *stifling rules/regulations/requirements* — **stifling** *adv* • *stifling hot* [=very hot] *weather*

stig·ma /ˈstɪgmə/ *n* [*singular*] : negative and often unfair beliefs that a group of people have about something • *the stigma of being poor = the stigma of poverty*

stig·ma·tize *also Brit* **stig·ma·tise** /ˈstɪgmə,taɪz/ *vb* **-tized; -tiz·ing** [T] *usually disapproving* : to describe or regard (something, such as a characteristic or group of people) in a way that shows strong disapproval • *Society stigmatizes welfare recipients.*

sti·let·to /stəˈlɛtoʊ/ *n, pl* **-tos** *or* **-toes** [C] **1 a** : a woman's shoe with a very high, thin heel **b** : the heel of a stiletto **2** : a knife with a thin, pointed blade

¹**still** /ˈstɪl/ *adv* **1** : happening or existing before now and continuing into the present — used to say that an action or condition continues • *He still lives there.* • *She's still upset.* • *Is the food still hot?* **2** : in spite of that — used to say that something happens or is true even though there is something that might prevent it from happening or being true • *I tried again and still I failed.* **3** : without moving • *Stand/Sit still.* **4** : to a greater extent or degree — used to add force to words like *more, better, bigger,* etc. • *a still more difficult problem = a problem that is more difficult still* • *still bigger/better/longer* **5** : in addition — used for emphasis • *He won still* [=*yet*] *another game.*

²**still** *adj* **1 a** : not moving • *still water* **b** : lacking motion or activity • *a hot, still day* [=a day without wind] **2** *photography* — used to describe an ordinary photograph that does not show movement • *still photographs* **b** : relating to or used for still photographs • *a class in still photography* • *a still camera* **3** *chiefly Brit* : of a liquid : not having bubbles • *still wine* — **still·ness** *n* [U]

³**still** *vb, literary* **1** [T] : to make (something) less severe or strong • *Her words stilled our fears/apprehensions.* **2** [T/I] : to stop moving or to cause (something) to stop moving • *The water stilled at last.* • *river waters stilled by dams* **3** [T] : to stop (something) from continuing • *The report has not stilled debate about whether the procedure is safe.*

⁴**still** *n* **1** [U] *literary* : quiet or silence • *the still of the evening/woods* **2** [C] : PHOTOGRAPH; *specifically* : a photograph of actors or scenes from a movie **3** [C] : a device that is used for making strong alcoholic drinks • *a whiskey still* — **the still of the night** *literary* : the time late at night when it is very quiet and dark

still-birth /ˈstɪl,bəθ/ *n* [C] : the birth of a dead baby

still-born /ˈstɪlˈboən/ *adj, of a baby* : dead at birth

still life *n, pl* ~ **lifes** [C] : a painting, drawing, etc., of a carefully arranged group of objects (such as flowers and fruit)

stilt /ˈstɪlt/ *n* [C] **1** : one of a set of upright posts that are used to hold a building up above water or the ground **2** : one of a pair of long poles with platforms for your feet that you can stand on to walk high above the ground • *a circus performer walking on stilts*

stilt·ed /ˈstɪltəd/ *adj* : awkward especially because of being too formal • *stilted speech/language*

stim·u·lant /ˈstɪmjələnt/ *n* [C] **1** : something (such as a drug) that makes you more active or gives you more energy • *Caffeine is a stimulant.* **2** : something that causes more activity • *The movie was a stimulant to discussion.*

stim·u·late /ˈstɪmjə,leɪt/ *vb* **-lat·ed; -lat-**

ing [T] 1 : to make (something) more active ▪ *Caffeine stimulates the heart.* : to cause or encourage (something) to happen or develop ▪ *a hormone that stimulates growth* 2 : to make (a person) excited or interested in something ▪ *He was stimulated by their discussion.* ▪ *a stimulating conversation* — **stim·u·la·tion** /ˌstɪmjəˈleɪʃən/ n [U]

stim·u·lus /ˈstɪmjələs/ n, pl **stim·u·li** /ˈstɪmjəˌlaɪ/ [C] 1 : something that causes something else to happen, develop, or become more active ▪ *an economic stimulus plan* 2 : something that causes a change or a reaction ▪ *Heat and light are physical stimuli.*

¹**sting** /ˈstɪŋ/ vb **stung** /ˈstʌŋ/; **sting·ing** 1 [T/I] of an insect, plant, or animal : to hurt (someone) by piercing the skin with a sharp, pointed part that usually contains poison ▪ *I was/got stung by a bee.* 2 [T/I] : to cause a quick, sharp pain ▪ *The cold rain stung my eyes.* 3 a [I] : to feel a quick, sharp pain ▪ *The smoke made our eyes sting.* b [T/I] : to cause (someone) to feel emotional or mental pain ▪ *His words stung (me).*

²**sting** n 1 [singular] : a quick, sharp pain ▪ *When you get the shot, you'll feel a little sting.* ▪ (figurative) *He'll eventually overcome the sting of being rejected.* 2 [C] : an injury caused when an insect or animal stings you ▪ *a bee sting* 3 [C] : a complicated and clever plan that is meant to deceive someone especially in order to catch criminals ▪ *They were caught in a drug sting.* 4 [C] Brit ◆ STINGER

sting·er /ˈstɪŋɚ/ n [C] chiefly US : a pointed part on an insect and animal that is used to sting someone

sting·ray /ˈstɪŋˌreɪ/ n [C] : a type of fish that has a large, flat body and a long tail with spines on it

stin·gy /ˈstɪndʒi/ adj **stin·gi·er**; **-est** disapproving 1 : not liking or wanting to give or spend money ▪ *a stingy old miser* : not generous ▪ *He is stingy with compliments.* 2 : small in size or amount ▪ *stingy portions of food* — **stin·gi·ness** /ˈstɪndʒinəs/ n [U]

¹**stink** /ˈstɪŋk/ vb **stank** /ˈstæŋk/ or **stunk** /ˈstʌŋk/; **stunk**; **stink·ing** [I] 1 : to have a very bad smell ▪ *Something stinks in here.* ▪ *His clothes stank of fish.* ▪ (figurative) *Something stinks about his story.* [=something about his story does not seem true or honest] 2 informal a : to do something very poorly ▪ *I stink at golf.* b : to be very low in quality ▪ *The movie stunk.* c : to be very unpleasant, unfair, etc. ▪ *It stinks that you can't stay longer.* — **stink up** (US) or Brit **stink out** [phrasal vb] **stink (something) up/out** or **stink up/out (something)** : to give a very bad smell to (something) ▪ *His cigars stink up the house.*

²**stink** n [singular] 1 : a very bad smell ▪ *the stink of garbage* 2 informal : a situation in which someone complains in a very angry and often public way ▪ *He caused/raised a stink about the changes.*

stink·er /ˈstɪŋkɚ/ n [C] informal 1 : somewhat old-fashioned : a person or thing

that is disliked ▪ *He is a dirty stinker.* 2 : something (such as a book or film) that is very bad ▪ *Her latest movie is a real stinker.*

stink·ing /ˈstɪŋkɪŋ/ adj 1 : having a very bad smell ▪ *Put out that stinking cigar.* 2 always before a noun, informal — used for emphasis when you are angry ▪ *I hate this stinking job.*

stinky /ˈstɪŋki/ adj **stink·i·er**; **-est** informal : having a very bad smell ▪ *stinky feet*

¹**stint** /ˈstɪnt/ n [C] : a period of time spent doing a certain job or activity ▪ *a four-year stint in the army*

²**stint** vb [I] : to use or give something in limited amounts ▪ *She doesn't stint on spices.* [=she uses a lot of spices] ▪ *He can be stinting with praise.*

sti·pend /ˈstaɪˌpɛnd/ n [C] : a usually small amount of money that is paid regularly to someone ▪ *a weekly stipend*

stip·u·late /ˈstɪpjəˌleɪt/ vb **-lat·ed**; **-lat·ing** [T] : to demand or require (something) as part of an agreement ▪ *The rules stipulate that players must wear uniforms.*

stip·u·la·tion /ˌstɪpjəˈleɪʃən/ n [C/U] : something that is required as part of an agreement ▪ *We agreed to the deal with the stipulation that she pay the expenses herself.*

¹**stir** /ˈstɚ/ vb **stirred**; **stir·ring** 1 [T] : to mix (something) by making circular movements in it with a spoon or similar object ▪ *She stirred her coffee.* 2 [T/I] : to move or cause (someone or something) to move after being still ▪ *He never stirred from the couch* [=he stayed on the couch] *all day.* ▪ *The breeze stirred the leaves on the tree.* 3 a [I] : to be active or busy ▪ *People were stirring inside the shop.* b [T] : to cause (someone or something) to be active ▪ *stir the imagination* ▪ *He stirred himself to action.* 4 [T] : to cause (an emotion or reaction) ▪ *The story stirred (up) deep emotions within him.* — **stir up** [phrasal vb] **stir up (someone or something)** or **stir (someone or something) up** 1 : to cause (someone) to feel a strong emotion and a desire to do something ▪ *The speech stirred up the crowd.* 2 a : to cause (something) to move up into and through the air or water ▪ *The workers stirred up a lot of dust.* b : to cause (something, usually something bad or unpleasant) to happen ▪ *stir up trouble*

²**stir** n [singular] 1 : a state of excitement, anger, or surprise among a group of people ▪ *His comments caused quite a stir.* 2 : a small movement ▪ *the stir of the leaves in the breeze* 3 : the act of stirring something with a spoon or similar object ▪ *She gave the sauce a stir.*

stir–fry /ˈstɚˈfraɪ/ vb **-fries**; **-fried**; **-fry·ing** [T] : to fry (something) quickly over high heat while stirring it constantly ▪ *stir-fried chicken* — **stir–fry** /ˈstɚˈfraɪ/ n, pl **-fries** [C/U] ▪ *We had (a) chicken stir-fry for dinner.*

¹**stir·ring** /ˈstɚɪŋ/ adj : causing strong feelings ▪ *a stirring speech*

²**stirring** n [C] : the beginning of a motion,

activity, feeling, idea, etc. ▪ *We felt the first stirrings of hope when we heard the news.*

stir·rup /ˈstɚrəp, *Brit* ˈstɪrəp/ *n* [C] : one of two loops that are attached to a saddle for the rider's feet

¹**stitch** /ˈstɪtʃ/ *n* [C] **1** : a piece of thread that is passed through a piece of material with a needle **2** *medical* : a special piece of thread that is used to hold a large cut or wound closed ▪ *His cut required six stitches.* **3** : a single loop of thread or yarn that is wrapped around a tool (such as a knitting needle) and is linked to other loops to make fabric — *a stitch informal* ◇ If you *are not wearing a stitch, do not have a stitch on,* etc., you are naked. — *a stitch in time (saves nine)* ◇ The phrase *a stitch in time (saves nine)* means that it is better to fix a problem when it is small than to wait and let it become a bigger problem. — *in stitches informal* : laughing very hard ▪ *He had me in stitches.*

²**stitch** *vb* [T] **1** : SEW ▪ *He stitched a patch onto his coat.* ▪ *She stitched together the pieces of fabric.* **2** : to make (something, such as a design) out of stitches ▪ *Her initials were stitched on the pillowcase.* — *stitch up* [*phrasal vb*] : *stitch (someone or something) up* or *stitch up (someone or something)* : to use a needle and thread to close a large cut or wound on someone ▪ *The doctor stitched him up.* = *The doctor stitched up his wound.*

¹**stock** /ˈstɑːk/ *n* **1** [C/U] : the supply of goods available for sale in a store ▪ *That camera is* **out of stock**. ▪ *Do you have more light bulbs* **in stock**? ▪ *They carry a* **large/small stock** *of computer software.* **2** [C/U] : a supply of something that is available for use ▪ *an ample stock of food* **3** [C/U] : a share of the value of a company which can be bought, sold, or traded as an investment ▪ *Most of her money is invested in stocks.* ▪ *Do you own any stock?* ▪ *a stock certificate* **4** [C] : the part of a gun that is held against your shoulder **5** [U] : the country or group of people that a person comes from ▪ *He is of Irish stock.* [=his family comes originally from Ireland] **6** [U] : LIVESTOCK **7** [U] : liquid in which meat, fish, or vegetables have been cooked and then removed and which is used to make soups, sauces, etc. ▪ *a cup of chicken/beef stock* **8** [U] *US* : confidence or faith in someone or something ▪ *He* **placed/put a lot of stock** [=had a lot of trust] *in her ability to get the job done.* **9** [U] — used to describe how popular or unpopular someone or something is at a particular time ▪ *The mayor's* **stock** *with voters is high/low right now.* **10** [*plural*] : a wooden frame with holes in it for a person's feet, hands, or head that was used in the past as a form of punishment — *lock, stock, and barrel* see ¹LOCK — *take stock* : to carefully think about something in order to make a decision about what to do next ▪ *We need to* **take stock** (*of things*) *and formulate a plan.*

²**stock** *vb* [T] **1** : to have a supply of (something) in a store for sale ▪ *Do you stock this item?* **2** : to fill (something, such as a room or a building) with a supply of food, drinks, etc. ▪ *a well-stocked kitchen* — *stock up* [*phrasal vb*] : to get a large quantity of something so that you will have it for later use ▪ *We stocked up (on food).*

³**stock** *adj, always before a noun* **1 a** : regularly used or included with something ▪ *stock patterns/designs* **b** : commonly used and not original or interesting ▪ *stock answers/characters* **2** : usually available for sale in a store ▪ *stock sizes*

stock·ade /stɑːˈkeɪd/ *n* [C] : a line of tall posts that are set in the ground and used as a barrier to protect or defend a place

stock·bro·ker /ˈstɑːkˌbroʊkɚ/ *n* [C] : someone whose job is to buy and sell shares of stock for other people

stock car *n* [C] : a car used for racing that has the same basic structure as a car normally sold to the public but has a more powerful engine, a stronger frame, etc.

stock exchange *n* [C] : a system or place where shares of various companies are bought and sold

stock·hold·er /ˈstɑːkˌhoʊldɚ/ *n* [C] *US* : someone who owns stock in a company : SHAREHOLDER

stock·ing /ˈstɑːkɪŋ/ *n* [C] **1** : a long covering for the foot and leg ▪ *a pair of wool stockings* **2** : ¹SOCK 1 **3** : a decorative pouch shaped like a large sock that is used for holding gifts at Christmas — *in your stockinged/stocking feet* : wearing socks but not shoes ▪ *Don't go outside in your stocking feet!*

stock–in–trade /ˌstɑːkənˈtreɪd/ *n* [U] : something that someone or something does or makes very well and often ▪ *Ballads were her stock-in-trade.*

stock market *n* **1** [U] : the business or activity of buying and selling stocks ▪ *We lost money in the stock market.* ▪ **playing the stock market** [=buying and selling stocks] **2** [C] : a system for buying and selling stocks or a place where stocks are bought and sold ▪ *International stock markets saw declines at the end of the trading day.*

stock·pile /ˈstɑːkˌpajəl/ *n* [C] : a large supply of something that is kept for future use ▪ *a stockpile of ammunition/weapons* — *stockpile vb* -piled; -piling [T] ▪ *They stockpiled food for the winter.*

stock·room /ˈstɑːkˌruːm/ *n* [C] : a storage area for the supplies and goods that are used or sold in a business

stock–still /ˈstɑːkˈstɪl/ *adj, not before a noun* : not moving at all ▪ *He stood/stayed stock-still.*

stock·yard /ˈstɑːkˌjɑɚd/ *n* [C] *chiefly US* : an enclosed area where farm animals (such as cattle) are kept so they can be slaughtered, sold, or shipped

stodgy /ˈstɑːdʒi/ *adj* **stodg·i·er; -est** *disapproving* **1 a** : having very old-fashioned opinions, attitudes, etc. ▪ *a stodgy old man* **b** : too plain or dull to be interesting ▪ *stodgy clothes* **2** *Brit, of* food : unpleasantly heavy and causing you to feel very full ▪ *a stodgy meal* — **stodg·i·ness** /ˈstɑːdʒinəs/ *n* [U]

¹**sto·ic** /ˈstoʊɪk/ *or* **sto·i·cal** /ˈstoʊɪkəl/ *adj* : showing no emotion especially when something bad is happening ▪ *a stoic person/expression* — **sto·i·cal·ly** /ˈstoʊɪkli/ *adv*

²**stoic** *n* [C] : a person who accepts what happens without complaining or showing emotion — **sto·i·cism** /ˈstoʊəˌsɪzəm/ *n* [U] ▪ *She endured his criticism with her usual stoicism.*

stoke /ˈstoʊk/ *vb* **stoked; stok·ing** [T] **1** : to stir or add fuel to (something that is burning) ▪ *stoke the fire/coals/furnace/flames* **2** : to increase the amount or strength of (something) ▪ *The news has stoked concerns about possible layoffs.* — **stok·er** /ˈstoʊkɚ/ *n* [C]

stoked *adj, not before a noun, US slang* : very excited ▪ *He was stoked to see her.*

¹**stole** *past tense of* ¹STEAL

²**stole** /ˈstoʊl/ *n* [C] : a long, wide piece of clothing that is usually worn across the shoulders ▪ *a mink stole*

stolen *past participle of* ¹STEAL

stol·id /ˈstɑːləd/ *adj* : not easily excited or upset ▪ *a stolid person/face* — **stol·id·ly** *adv*

¹**stom·ach** /ˈstʌmək/ *n* [C] **a** : the organ in your body where food goes after you swallow it ▪ *I've had enough to eat. My stomach is full.* **b** : the part of your body that contains the stomach ▪ *She punched him in the stomach.* [=belly] **2** [U] : the desire, courage, etc., that is needed to do or accept something difficult or unpleasant — usually used in negative statements ▪ *He has no stomach for controversy.* — **a strong/weak stomach** ✧ If you have *a strong stomach*, you are not bothered by things that many people find disgusting, shocking, or offensive. If you have *a weak stomach*, you are easily bothered by disgusting, shocking, or offensive things. — **on a full stomach** : after eating a lot of food ▪ *Don't go swimming on a full stomach.* — **on an empty stomach** : with nothing in your stomach ▪ *Take this medication on an empty stomach.* — **sick to your stomach** see ¹SICK — **turn your stomach** ✧ Something that *turns your stomach* or *makes your stomach turn* makes you feel ill or uncomfortable usually because it is offensive or disgusting.

²**stomach** *vb* [T] **1** : to accept or experience (something unpleasant) without becoming sick, upset, etc. ▪ *I could barely stomach the smell.* **2** : to eat (something) without getting a sick or unpleasant feeling in your stomach ▪ *I can't stomach raw onions.*

stom·ach·ache /ˈstʌməkˌeɪk/ *n* [C/U] : pain in or near your stomach ▪ *I have a stomachache.*

stomp /ˈstɑːmp/ *vb* **1** [I] : to walk or move with very heavy or noisy steps ▪ *He stomped out of the room.* **2** [T] *chiefly US* : to put (your foot) down forcefully and noisily ▪ *He stomped his foot.* — **stomp on** [*phrasal vb*] : to step on (something or someone) very forcefully ▪

He stomped on the bug. — **stomp out** [*phrasal vb*] **1** : to stop or destroy (something) ▪ *trying to stomp out* [=*stamp out*] *corruption* **2** : to stop (something) from burning by stepping on it forcefully ▪ *She stomped out her cigarette.*

stomp·ing ground /ˈstɑːmpɪŋ-/ *n* [C] *US* : a place where someone likes to go or often goes ▪ *We enjoyed going back home and visiting our old stomping grounds.*

¹**stone** /ˈstoʊn/ *n* **1** [U] : a hard substance that comes from the ground and is used for building, carving, etc. ▪ *a wall made of stone = a stone wall* **2** [C] **a** : a small piece of rock ▪ **b** : a piece of rock used for a particular purpose ▪ *His birthdate and date of death were carved on the stone.* **3** [C] : a jewel ▪ *precious stones* **4** [C] : a small, hard object that sometimes forms in a part of the body (such as the kidney) **5** [C] *chiefly Brit* : ¹PIT 8 **6** *pl* **stone** [C] *Brit* : a British unit of weight equal to 14 pounds (6.35 kilograms) ▪ *He weighs 12 stone.* — abbr. **st** — **a stone's throw** : a short distance ▪ *She lives a stone's throw away.* — **carved/etched/set/written in stone** : permanent or not able to be changed ▪ *These new rules are not carved in stone.* — **leave no stone unturned** : to make every possible effort to find someone or something ▪ *They left no stone unturned in the search for the documents.*

²**stone** *vb* **stoned; ston·ing** [T] **1** : to throw stones at (someone or something) ▪ *Rioters stoned the building.* **2** : to kill (someone) by throwing stones ▪ *He was stoned to death.* **3** *Brit* : ²PIT 3 ▪ *stone a peach*

³**stone** *adv* : totally or completely ▪ (*US*) *They sat there, stone silent.* ▪ *The soup was stone cold.* ▪ *He was stone broke.* [=he had no money at all] ▪ *I thought I had gone stone-deaf.*

Stone Age *n* — **the Stone Age** : the oldest period in which human beings are known to have existed ▪ *tools/weapons from the Stone Age* ▪ (*figurative*) *political ideas from the Stone Age* [=outdated ideas]

stoned /ˈstoʊnd/ *adj, informal* : intoxicated by a drug (such as marijuana) ▪ *He got/was stoned on pot.*

stone·wall /ˈstoʊnˌwɑːl/ *vb* [T/I] : to refuse or fail to answer questions, to do what has been requested, etc., especially in order to delay or prevent something ▪ *They were just stonewalling for time.* ▪ (*chiefly US*) *trying to stonewall the media/investigation*

stone·work /ˈstoʊnˌwɚk/ *n* [U] : a structure or part of a structure that is built of stone ▪ *The stonework on this house is over 100 years old.*

stony /ˈstoʊni/ *adj* **ston·i·er; -est 1** : full of stones ▪ *stony soil* **2** : made of stone or hard like stone ▪ *a stony material* **3** : showing no emotion or friendliness ▪ *stony silence* — **ston·i·ly** /ˈstoʊnəli/ *adv*

stood *past tense and past participle of* ¹STAND

stooge /ˈstuːdʒ/ *n* [C] **1** *disapproving* : a weak or unimportant person who is controlled by a powerful person, organization, etc. • *a government stooge* **2** : a performer in a show who says and does foolish things that other performers make jokes about

stool /'stu:l/ *n* [*C*] **1 a** : a seat that fits one person and that has no back or arms • *a bar stool* **b** : FOOTSTOOL **2** *medical* : a piece of solid waste that is released from the body

stool pigeon *n* [*C*] *chiefly US, informal* : a criminal who gives the police information about other criminals

¹stoop /'stu:p/ *vb* [*I*] **1** : to bend down or over • *She stooped down to hug the child.* **2** : to walk or stand with your head and shoulders bent forward • *He tends to stoop as he walks.* **3** : to do something that is not honest, fair, etc. • *She would never stoop to lying.*

²stoop *n* **1** [*singular*] : a bend or curve forward of your back and shoulders • *He walks with a slight stoop.* **2** [*C*] *US* : a raised area (such as a porch, platform, or stairway) at the entrance to a house or building — **stooped** /'stu:pt/ *adj*

¹stop /'sta:p/ *vb* **stopped; stop·ping 1 a** [*I*] : to not move, walk, run, etc., after doing so before • *The bus stopped at the corner.* • *He stopped to pick up a penny.* • *We stopped for lunch.* **b** [*T*] : to cause (someone or something) to not move, walk, etc., after doing so before • *Stop that man!* • *She stopped the car and turned back.* **2** [*T/I*] : to not do something that you have been doing before : to not continue doing something • *We've been working all morning. It's time to stop and take a break.* • *I stop work at 5 o'clock.* • *Stop arguing/talking/running.* • *He said he was unhappy with some of his employees, but he stopped short of naming which ones.* [=but he did not say which ones] **b** [*T*] : to make (someone or something) no longer do something • *I'm leaving and you can't stop me.* • *(US) I couldn't stop him from crying.* = *(Brit) I couldn't stop him crying.* **3** [*T*] : to cause (something) to end • *The teacher stopped the fight.* **4** [*I*] : to end • *The music stopped.* • *The rain finally stopped.* **5** [*I*] : to suddenly not work or function • *The engine just stopped.* **6** [*T*] : to close, block, or fill (a hole) • *He stopped his ears with his fingers.* [=he put his fingertips in his ears so that he couldn't hear] — usually + *up* • *The sink is stopped up with food.* — **stop at nothing** — used to say that someone will do anything to achieve a goal or purpose • *She will stop at nothing to get what she wants.* — **stop by** [*phrasal vb*] *informal* : to visit someone briefly • *Feel free to stop by anytime.* — **stop in** [*phrasal vb*] *informal* **1** : to visit someone briefly • *Please stop in sometime.* **2** *Brit* : to stay at home • *I'm stopping in tonight.* — **stop off** [*phrasal vb*] *informal* : to go or stay somewhere briefly while traveling to another place • *I'll stop off (at the station) to pick up some milk.* — **stop over** [*phrasal vb*] *informal* : to go to or stay in a place while traveling to another place • *The plane stops over in Chicago before going on to Seattle.*

²stop *n* [*C*] **1** : an act of stopping or a state of being stopped • *a sudden stop* • *The car came/skidded/slowed to a stop.* • *Negotiations brought a stop to* [=ended] *the conflict.* • *We need to put a stop to* [=end] *these rumors.* **2 a** : a place that you visit or go to for a short period of time during a journey • *His first stop will be Washington, D.C.* **b** : a short period of time during which you stop or stay at a place during a journey • *an overnight stop in Chicago* • *I need to make a stop at the grocery store.* **3 a** : the place where a bus or train regularly stops on a route to let passengers get on and off • *a bus stop* **b** *US* : a place on a road (such as an intersection) where traffic must stop • *a four-way stop* • *a stop sign* [=a sign telling drivers to stop and wait until they can continue safely] — **pull out all the stops** *informal* : to do everything possible in order to do or achieve something • *When he throws a party, he pulls out all the stops.*

stop·gap /'sta:p₁gæp/ *n* [*C*] : someone or something that is intended to be used for a short time and then replaced by someone or something better • *a stopgap solution*

stop·light /'sta:p₁laɪt/ *n* [*C*] *US* : TRAFFIC LIGHT

stop·over /'sta:p₁oʊvɚ/ *n* [*C*] : a brief period of time when you stop at a place during a journey • *We had a six-hour stopover in Atlanta.*

stop·page /'sta:pɪdʒ/ *n* [*C*] **1** : the act of stopping something • *the stoppage of payments* **2** : a situation in which workers stop working for a period of time as a protest • *work stoppages* **3** *sports* : an occurrence in which play is stopped during a game • *The penalty caused a stoppage in play.*

stop·per /'sta:pɚ/ *n* [*C*] **1** : someone or something that stops something • *crime stoppers* **2** : something that is used to block an opening • *a wine/bottle stopper* — **stopper** *vb* [*T*] • *a stoppered bottle*

stop·watch /'sta:p₁wa:tʃ/ *n* [*C*] : a watch that can be started and stopped very quickly and that is used for measuring the amount of time that is taken to do something (such as to run a race)

stor·age /'stɔrɪdʒ/ *n* [*U*] **1 a** : space where you put things when they are not being used • *The house has plenty of storage* (*space*). **b** : the state of being kept in a place when not being used • *getting our furniture out of storage* • *He put some things in storage.* **2** : the act of putting something that is not being used in a place where it is available, where it can be kept safely, etc. : the act of storing something • *the storage of nuclear waste* • *data storage*

¹store /'stɔɚ/ *vb* **stored; stor·ing** [*T*] **1 a** : to put (something that is not being used) in a place where it is available, where it can be kept safely, etc. • *She stores her jewels in a safe.* • *The grain was stored (away) for the winter.* **b** : to collect and put (something) into one location for future use • *The body stores (up) fat.* **2** : to place (information) in a person's memory or a computer's memory ▪ *studying how our brains store memories* ▪ *The file is stored (away) on the backup drive.*

²**store** *n* **1** [C] **a** : a building or room where things are sold ▪ *a grocery/furniture/pet/candy store* **usage** see ¹SHOP 1A **b** : a large building in which something is kept for future use ▪ *a grain/weapons store* **2** [C] : a large amount or supply of something that is kept for future use ▪ *a store of wood/information* **3** [*plural*] : things that are collected and kept for future use ▪ *medical/military stores* **4** [U] — used to say that something is regarded as having a lot of value or importance ▪ *Our family sets/lays great store by tradition.* [=our family values tradition very highly] — **in store** : in a state of being ready or prepared to happen or be done ▪ *We have a big surprise in store for you.* — used to talk about what will happen to someone in the future ▪ *I wonder what the future holds in store for us.* = *I wonder what lies in store for us in the future.* [=I wonder what will happen to us in the future]

store-bought /'stoɚˌbɑːt/ *adj, US* : bought at a store or shop and not made at home ▪ *store-bought cookies*

store-house /'stoɚˌhaʊs/ *n* [C] **1** : a building where goods are kept for future use ▪ WAREHOUSE **2** : a large amount or supply of something ▪ *a storehouse of information/knowledge*

store-keep-er /'stoɚˌkiːpɚ/ *n* [C] *US* : someone who owns or manages a store or shop ▪ SHOPKEEPER

store-room /'stoɚˌruːm/ *n* [C] : a room or space where things are stored

storey *chiefly Brit* spelling of ²STORY

sto-ried /'storid/ *adj, always before a noun* : having an interesting history ▪ *a storied castle/player/leader* : interesting because of stories that relate to it ▪ *her storied past/career*

stork /'stoɚk/ *n* [C] : a large bird that has long legs and a long bill and neck

¹**storm** /'stoɚm/ *n* [C] **1** : an occurrence of bad weather in which there is a lot of rain, snow, etc., and often strong winds ▪ *It looks like a storm is coming.* **2 a** : a sudden occurrence of something in large amounts ▪ *a storm of publicity* **b** : a situation in which many people are angry, upset, etc. ▪ *His comments kicked/whipped/stirred up a storm.* [=his comments upset people] — **take (something) by storm** **1** : to quickly become very successful or popular in (a particular place) or among (a particular group) ▪ *He took the art world by storm.* **2** : to attack and capture (a place) suddenly by using a lot of force or a large number of people ▪ *The soldiers took the castle by storm.* — **the calm/lull before the storm** : a period of quiet that comes before a time of activity, excitement, violence, etc. ▪ *The college was quiet, but it was the calm before the storm. Thousands of students would arrive later.* — **up a storm** *informal* — used to say that something is being done with a lot of energy or enthusiasm ▪ *They danced/sang*

up a storm. — **weather the storm** or **ride out the storm** : to deal with a difficult situation without being harmed or damaged too much ▪ *It was a difficult time but they managed to ride out the storm.*

²**storm** *vb* **1** [I] — used with *it* to say that a storm (sense 1) is happening ▪ *It stormed all night.* **2** [T/I] : to attack (something) suddenly with a lot of force or with a large number of people ▪ *Police stormed the building.* ▪ *The army stormed ashore.* **3** [I] : to go quickly and in an angry, loud way ▪ *He stormed out of the room.* **4** [T/I] : to shout loudly and angrily ▪ *She stormed at her parents and ran to her room.*

storm cloud *n* [C] : a dark cloud which shows that a storm is coming

storm door *n* [C] *US* : a second door that is placed outside the usual outside door of a building for protection against cold and bad weather

storm drain *n* [C] : a drain that carries water (such as rainwater) away from a street, parking lot, etc.

storm trooper *n* [C] : a member of a group of specially trained and violent soldiers especially in Nazi Germany during World War II

storm window *n* [C] *US* : a second window that covers the usual outside window of a building for protection against cold and bad weather

stormy /'stoɚmi/ *adj* **storm-i-er; -est** **1** : relating to or affected by a storm ▪ *stormy skies/weather* **2** : full of anger, shouting, etc. ▪ *They have a stormy relationship.* — **storm-i-ness** /'stoɚminəs/ *n* [U]

¹**sto-ry** /'stori/ *n, pl* **-ries** **1** [C] : a description of how something happened ▪ *a movie based on a true story* ▪ *He told us stories about his childhood.* ▪ *"Why are you late?" "It's a long story."* [=it is too complicated to explain] ◆ The phrase *the story goes* is used to say that you are telling a story that you heard from other people. ▪ *The story goes* [=people say] *that after he died, he haunted the house.* **2** [C] : a description of imaginary events that is told as a form of entertainment ▪ *a horror/detective story* ▪ *a bedtime story* [=a story that you read or tell a child at bedtime] **3** [C] : something that is reported in a newspaper, on television, etc. ▪ *a news story* ▪ *The magazine ran a story* [=printed an article] *about the scandal.* **4** [C] : a description of the most important events in someone's life ▪ *She told him her life story.* [=she told him about the things that had happened in her life] **5 a** [C] : SITUATION 1 ▪ *We lost power, and it's the same story throughout the city.* [=people throughout the city also lost power] ▪ *She got good grades in math, but English was another story.* [=she did not do well in English] ▪ *It's the same old story* [=things have not changed] *with her— she just can't keep a job.* **b** **the story** *somewhat informal* : basic information about someone or something ▪ *What's the story with that guy?* [=what can you tell me about that guy?] **6** [C] **a** : a lie that

someone tells • *You shouldn't tell stories.* **b** : an explanation or excuse and especially one that is not true • *The police don't believe his story.* — compare ²STORY

²**story** *also chiefly Brit* **sto·rey** /'stori/ *n, pl* **-ries** [C] : a group of rooms or an area that forms one floor level of a building • *a five-story building* [=a building that has five stories/floors] — compare ¹STORY

sto·ry·book /'stori,bʊk/ *n* [C] : a book of stories for children — **storybook** *adj, always before a noun* • *a storybook ending/romance* [=an ending/romance that is like something in a storybook]

sto·ry·tell·er /'stori,tɛlɚ/ *n* [C] : someone who tells or writes stories — **sto·ry·tell·ing** /'stori,tɛlɪŋ/ *n* [U]

¹**stout** /'staʊt/ *adj* **1** : thick and strong • *stout legs* **2** : having a large body that is wide with fat or muscles • *a short, stout man* **3** *a literary* : brave and strong • *a stout heart/leader* **b** *formal* : forceful and determined • *a stout defense* — **stout·ly** *adv*

²**stout** *n* [C/U] : a very dark, heavy beer

stout·heart·ed /'staʊt,hɑɚtəd/ *adj, literary* : brave and determined • *a stout-hearted soldier*

¹**stove** /'stoʊv/ *n* [C] **1** *chiefly US* : a flat piece of kitchen equipment for cooking that usually has four devices (called burners) which become hot when they are turned on and that often is attached to an oven — called also *(Brit)* **cooker** **2** : a device that burns fuel for heating or cooking • *a wood-burning/gas stove*

²**stove** *past tense and past participle of* ²STAVE

stove·top /'stoʊv,tɑːp/ *n* [C] *US* : the top of a stove

stow /'stoʊ/ *vb* [T] : to put (something that is not being used) in a place where it is available, where it can be kept safely, etc. : STORE • *He stowed his gear in a locker.* • *The supplies were stowed (away) below deck.* — **stow away** [*phrasal vb*] : to hide on a ship, airplane, etc., in order to travel without paying or being seen • *He stowed away on a merchant ship.*

stow·away /'stoʊə,weɪ/ *n* [C] : someone who hides on a ship, airplane, etc., in order to travel without paying or being seen

strad·dle /'strædl/ *vb* **strad·dled; strad·dling** [T] **1** : to sit or ride with a leg on either side of (something) • *straddled a stool/horse* **2 a** : to be on both sides of (something) • *Campsites straddled the river.* • *(figurative) Their music straddles the line between rock and jazz.* **b** : to have parts that are in (different places, regions, etc.) • *Turkey straddles Asia and Europe.* **3** : to agree with or seem to agree with two opposite sides of (something) • *She straddled the issue.*

strafe /'streɪf/ *vb* **strafed; straf·ing** [T] : to attack (something) with machine guns from low-flying airplanes • *The planes strafed the town.*

strag·gle /'strægəl/ *vb* **strag·gled; strag·gling** [I] **1** : to walk slowly into or from a place in a way that is not continuous or organized • *The children strag-*

gled in from outside. **2** : to move away or spread out from others in a disorganized way • *She straggled behind the rest of the group.* — **strag·gler** /'stræglɚ/ *n* [C] • *People waited for the stragglers to finish the race.*

strag·gly /'strægli/ *adj* **strag·gli·er; -est** : growing or hanging in an untidy way • *a straggly beard*

¹**straight** /'streɪt/ *adj* **1** : not having curves, bends, or angles • *a straight line/edge* • *straight hair* **2** : vertical or level • *The picture isn't quite straight.* **3** *always before a noun* : following one after the other in order • *He has won three straight* [=consecutive] *tournaments.* **4** : honest and direct • *a straight answer* • *They're not being straight with you.* **5** *always before a noun* **a** : including only two people or things • *a straight exchange/swap* **b** : not including any things or parts of a different kind • *a straight romance novel* **2** : *(US)* *She got straight A's last year.* [=she got an A in every class] • *(US) a straight-A student* **6** *not before a noun* : agreeing with what is true or what is stated to be true • *We have to get our stories straight or the police will get suspicious.* • *You need to get your facts straight.* [=you need to get your facts correct] **7** *not before a noun, informal* : having nothing owed by either side • *You pay for your ticket, and I'll consider us straight.* **8** : behaving in a way that is socially correct and acceptable • *(disapproving) She's too straight and needs to lighten up.* • *(informal) He tried to* **go straight** [=stop being a criminal] *after he left prison.* **9** *informal* : HETEROSEXUAL • *He's gay but has a lot of straight friends.* **10** *US, of alcoholic drinks* : without ice or water added • *I like my bourbon/whiskey straight.* • *a martini* **straight up** — **straight·ness** *n* [U]

²**straight** *adv* **1** : in a straight or direct way • *She looked him straight in the eye.* • *The tunnel goes straight through the mountain.* • *The library is straight ahead.* • *He was so drunk he couldn't walk straight.* **2** : in or into a vertical position • *Sit up straight and don't slouch.* **3 a** : without any delay • *She came straight home from school.* **b** : without interruption • *They worked for three days straight.* **4** : in an honest and direct way • *Tell me straight: did you do it or didn't you?* • *Are you dealing/playing straight with me?* [=are you being honest with me?] **5** : in the usual, normal, or correct way • *She was so drunk she couldn't see straight.* • *It's so noisy I can't think straight.* — **straight off** *US, informal* : ¹IMMEDIATELY **2** • *I knew straight off that she was lying.* — **straight out** *informal* : in a very direct way • *I asked him straight out if he was doing drugs.*

³**straight** *n* [C] **1** *informal* : HETEROSEXUAL • *gays and straights* **2** : a straight part of a race course : STRAIGHTAWAY • *He overtook them on the straight.* **3** : a hand of playing cards in poker that contains five cards in a series (such as a five, a six, a seven, an eight, and a nine) — **the straight and narrow** *informal* : the way

of living that is honest and morally proper ▪ *His wife keeps him* **on the straight and narrow.**

straight arrow *n* [C] *US, informal* : a person who is very honest and morally proper

¹**straight·away** /ˌstreɪtəˈweɪ/ *adv* : without any delay : IMMEDIATELY ▪ *He found the information straightaway.*

²**straight·away** /ˈstreɪtəˌweɪ/ *n* [C] *chiefly US* : a straight part of a race course

straight·en /ˈstreɪtn/ *vb* **1** [T/I] : to make (something) straight or to become straight ▪ *He straightened (out) the wire.* ▪ *The river curves and then straightens (out) again.* **2** [T] : to make (something) organized or tidy ▪ *He straightened (out) the papers on his desk.* ▪ *They straightened (up) the house after the party.* — **straighten out** [*phrasal vb*] **1 straighten out (something or someone) or straighten (something or someone) out** **a** : to deal with (something) successfully ▪ *straighten out a problem* **b** : to improve the behavior of (someone) ▪ *Boarding school will straighten her out.* **2 straighten out or straighten out (something) or straighten (something) out** : to improve in behavior or condition ▪ *He straightened out (his life) after joining the army.* — **straighten up** [*phrasal vb*] **1** : to move your body to an upright position ▪ *Straighten up. There's no excuse for slouching.* **2** *US* : to improve in behavior ▪ *You need to straighten up, young man.* — **straighten·er** /ˈstreɪtnə/ *n* [C/U]

straight face *n* [C] : a face that shows no emotion and especially no amusement ▪ *She lied with a straight face.* ▪ *It was hard to* **keep a straight face.** [=to not laugh or smile] — **straight-faced** /ˈstreɪtˈfeɪst/ *adj*

straight flush *n* [C] : a hand of playing cards in poker that contains five cards of the same suit in a series (such as a five, a six, a seven, an eight, and a nine of clubs)

straight·for·ward /ˌstreɪtˈfoɚwəd/ *adj* **1** : easy to do or understand ▪ *straightforward instructions* **2** : honest and open ▪ *He was straightforward with us.* — **straight·for·ward·ly** *adv*

straightjacket *variant spelling of* STRAITJACKET

straightlaced *variant spelling of* STRAITLACED

straight man *n* [C] : a member of a comedy team who says things that allow a partner to make jokes

straight shooter *n* [C] *US, informal* : a person who is very honest

¹**strain** /ˈstreɪn/ *n* **1** [C/U] **a** : a feeling of stress and worry that you have because you are trying to do too much, are dealing with a difficult problem, etc. ▪ *The work was a strain on me.* ▪ *The work* **put/placed a strain** *on me.* [=it has been stressful for me] ▪ *the strain of working and going to school full-time* ▪ *She has been* **under (a lot of) strain** *lately.* **b** : something that is very difficult to deal with and that causes harm or trouble ▪ *Debt has been a* **(source of) strain** *on our marriage.* **2** [C/U] : a force that pulls or stretches something : STRESS ▪ *There was*

too much strain on the cables. **3** [C/U] : an injury to a body part or muscle that is caused by too much tension, effort, or use ▪ *a leg/muscle strain* **4 a** [C] : a group of closely related plants or animals ▪ *a strain of bacteria* **b** [*singular*] *formal + literary* : a small amount of something ▪ *There was a strain of sadness in her voice.* **5** [*plural*] *formal* : the musical sounds of someone or something ▪ *the strains of the harp*

²**strain** *vb* **1** [T] : to injure (a body part or muscle) by too much tension, use, or effort ▪ *I strained my back.* ▪ *strain a muscle* **2** [T/I] : to try very hard to do or get something ▪ *He was straining for air.* [=struggling to breathe] ▪ *I strained to open the jar.* ▪ *straining to hear* **3 a** [T/I] : to be pulled or stretched in a forceful way ▪ *His muscles strained under the weight.* ▪ *People were* **straining their necks** [=were lifting their heads as high as they could by stretching their necks] *to see the fight.* **b** [I] : to pull hard on or push hard against something ▪ *The dog strained at its leash.* ▪ *His belly strained against the buttons of the shirt.* **4** [T] : to cause problems or trouble for (something) ▪ *The disagreement strained their relationship.* **5** [T] : to separate a liquid from solid pieces by using a special device (called a strainer) ▪ *He strained the pasta.* = *He strained the water from the pasta.* — **strain yourself 1** : to injure yourself by making your muscles do too much work ▪ *Don't strain yourself trying to move the couch.* **2** : to put a lot of physical or mental effort into doing something ▪ *Don't strain yourself trying to think of the answer.*

strained /ˈstreɪnd/ *adj* **1** : feeling or showing the effect of too much work, use, effort, etc. ▪ *Her voice sounded strained.* **2** : not natural and sincere ▪ *a strained smile* **3** : not friendly and relaxed ▪ *Their relationship was strained.*

strain·er /ˈstreɪnə/ *n* [C] : a kitchen device that has many small holes and that is used to hold back solid pieces while a liquid passes through

strait /ˈstreɪt/ *n* **1** [C] : a narrow passage of water that connects two large bodies of water ▪ *the Straits of Gibraltar* **2** [*plural*] : a very difficult situation ▪ *The economy is in desperate/dire straits.*

strait·ened /ˈstreɪtnd/ *adj, always before a noun, formal* : not having enough money ▪ *living in* **straitened circumstances**

strait·jack·et *also* **straight·jack·et** /ˈstreɪtˌdʒækət/ *n* [C] : a jacket that has long arms which can be tied together behind someone's back and that is used to control the movements of a violent prisoner or patient

strait·laced *or* **straight·laced** /ˈstreɪtˈleɪst/ *adj* : very proper in manners, morals, or opinion ▪ *She is very straitlaced.*

¹**strand** /ˈstrænd/ *n* [C] **1** : a thin piece of thread, wire, hair, etc. **2** : something that is long like a string ▪ *a strand of pearls/DNA* **3** : one of the parts of something that is very complicated ▪ *strands of evidence* **4** : a shore or beach

²**strand** *vb* [T] **1** : to leave (a person or

animal) in a place without a way of leaving it ▪ *He was stranded on a deserted island.* **2** : to cause (something, such as a boat or a sea animal) to become stuck on land ▪ *The ship was stranded on the sandbank.* ▪ *a stranded whale*

strange /ˈstreɪndʒ/ *adj* **strang·er; strang·est** **1** : different from what is usual, normal, or expected : odd or unusual ▪ *strange behavior* ▪ *a strange person* ▪ *a strange-looking person* **2** : not known, heard, or seen before : UNFAMILIAR ▪ *a strange city/country* **3** *not before a noun* : not entirely comfortable or well ▪ *I began to feel strange, and then I fainted.* — **strange·ness** /ˈstreɪndʒnəs/ *n [U]*

strange·ly /ˈstreɪndʒli/ *adv* **1** : in a strange way ▪ *acting strangely* ▪ *The house seemed strangely familiar to her.* **2** — used to say that something is strange or surprising ▪ *Strangely (enough), he never asked my name.*

strang·er /ˈstreɪndʒɚ/ *n [C]* **1** : someone who you have not met before or do not know ▪ *He is a (complete/total/perfect) stranger to me.* **2** : someone who has not experienced something ▪ *He is a stranger to losing.* [=he does not know what losing is like] — usually used in negative statements ▪ *She is no stranger to controversy.* [=she has been involved in controversy before] **3** : someone who is in a new and unfamiliar place ▪ *I'm a stranger to the area.*

stran·gle /ˈstræŋgəl/ *vb* **stran·gled; stran·gling** [*T*] **1** : to kill (a person or animal) by squeezing the throat ▪ *He used a rope to strangle her (to death).* **2** : to stop (something) from growing or developing ▪ *Weeds strangled the plant.* — **stran·gler** /ˈstræŋglɚ/ *n [C]* — **stran·gu·la·tion** /ˌstræŋgjəˈleɪʃən/ *n [U]* ▪ *The cause of death was strangulation.*

strangled *adj* — used to describe a cry or other sound that stops suddenly or that seems strained because of tightness in the throat ▪ *a strangled cry/sob/voice*

stran·gle·hold /ˈstræŋgəlˌhoʊld/ *n [C]* : a force or influence that stops something from growing or developing ▪ *The state has a stranglehold on the city's finances.*

¹**strap** /ˈstræp/ *n [C]* : a narrow and usually flat piece of a material that is used for fastening, holding together, or wrapping something ▪ *a watch strap*

²**strap** *vb* **strapped; strap·ping** [*T*] : to fasten (someone or something) by using a strap ▪ *We strapped our snowshoes on.* ▪ *She strapped the children in* [=fastened the children's seat belts] *and drove away.*

strap·less /ˈstræpləs/ *adj* : made or worn without straps over the shoulders ▪ *a strapless evening gown*

strapped *adj, informal* : not having enough money ▪ *financially strapped* ▪ *I'm strapped for cash.*

strapping *adj, always before a noun, of a person* : tall, strong, and healthy ▪ *a strapping young man*

strata *plural of* STRATUM

strat·a·gem /ˈstrætədʒəm/ *n [C] formal* : a trick or plan for deceiving an enemy or for achieving a goal ▪ *a clever stratagem*

stra·te·gic /strəˈtiːdʒɪk/ *also* **stra·te·gi·cal** /strəˈtiːdʒɪkəl/ *adj* **1** : of or relating to a general plan that is created to achieve a goal in war, politics, etc., usually over a long period of time ▪ *strategic planning/warfare/maneuvers* ▪ *strategic nuclear weapons* [=powerful nuclear weapons that are designed to be used against targets that are chosen as part of a general plan to defeat an enemy rather than in an attempt to win a specific battle] **2** : useful or important in achieving a plan or strategy ▪ *a strategic location* — **stra·te·gi·cal·ly** /strəˈtiːdʒɪkli/ *adv*

strat·e·gist /ˈstrætədʒɪst/ *n [C]* : a person who is skilled in making plans for achieving a goal ▪ *military/political/campaign strategists*

strat·e·gy /ˈstrætədʒi/ *n, pl* **-gies** **1** [*C*] : a careful plan or method for achieving a particular goal usually over a long period of time ▪ *They are proposing a new strategy for treating the disease with a combination of medications.* **2** [*U*] : the skill of making or carrying out plans to achieve a goal ▪ *a specialist in campaign/military strategy*

strat·i·fied /ˈstrætəˌfaɪd/ *adj* **1** : arranged or formed in layers ▪ *stratified rock* **2** : divided into social classes ▪ *stratified societies* — **strat·i·fi·ca·tion** /ˌstrætəfəˈkeɪʃən/ *n [C/U]* ▪ *social stratifications*

strato·sphere /ˈstrætəˌsfiɚ/ *n* — *the* **stratosphere** **1** : the upper layer of the Earth's atmosphere that begins about 7 miles (11 kilometers) above the Earth's surface and ends about 30 miles (50 kilometers) above the Earth's surface **2** : a very high position, level, or amount ▪ *His career is headed for the stratosphere.*

stra·tum /ˈstreɪtəm, *Brit* ˈstrɑːtəm/ *n, pl* **stra·ta** /ˈstreɪtə, *Brit* ˈstrɑːtə/ [*C*] **1** : one of usually many layers of a substance ▪ *a rock stratum* **2** : a level of society made up of people of the same rank or position ▪ *different social strata*

straw /ˈstrɑː/ *n* **1 a** [*U*] : the dry stems of wheat and other grain plants ▪ *a bed/pile of straw* ▪ *a straw hat/mat* **b** [*C*] : a single dry stem of a grain plant ▪ *chewing on a straw* **2** [*C*] : a thin tube used for sucking up a drink — **clutch/grasp at straws** : to try to solve a problem by doing things that probably will not help ▪ *I didn't think it would work, but at that point I was grasping at straws.* — **draw straws** *see* ¹DRAW — *the* **final/last straw** *or* *the* **straw that breaks/broke the camel's back** : the last in a series of bad things that happen to make someone very upset, angry, etc. ▪ *It had been a difficult week, so when the car broke down, it was the last straw.*

straw·ber·ry /ˈstrɑːˌberi, *Brit* ˈstrɔːbri/ *n, pl* **-ries** [*C*] : a soft, juicy red fruit that grows on a low plant with white flowers

straw poll *n [C]* : an informal and unofficial poll or vote that is done to get information about what people think about something — called also *(US)* **straw vote**

¹**stray** /ˈstreɪ/ vb [I] : to go in a direction that is away from a group or from the place where you should be ▪ *Two cows strayed into the woods.* ▪ *The airplane strayed off course.* ▪ *She strayed from the group and got lost.* ▪ *(figurative) The discussion strayed from the original topic.* ▪ *(figurative) a straying husband* [=a husband who has sexual relations with a woman who is not his wife]

²**stray** adj, always before a noun **1** of an animal : lost or having no home ▪ *a stray cat/dog* **2** : separated from another or others of the same kind ▪ *a stray sock* **3** : not in or coming in the proper or intended place ▪ *a few stray hairs* ▪ *a stray bullet*

³**stray** n [C] : an animal (such as a cat or dog) that is lost or has no home

¹**streak** /ˈstriːk/ n [C] **1** : a long, thin mark that is a different color from its background **2** : a quality that is noticeable especially because it is different from a person's other qualities ▪ *a streak of stubbornness = a stubborn streak* ▪ *She has a mean streak.* [=a tendency to be mean] **3** : a period of repeated success or failure ▪ *a lucky streak* ▪ *a winning/losing streak* [=a series of wins/losses] **4** : a long, narrow area or flash of light ▪ *a streak of lightning/light*

²**streak** vb **1** [T] : to make long lines of a different color on or in (something) ▪ *Tears streaked her face.* ▪ *Her hair is streaked with gray.* **2** [I] : to go or move very quickly ▪ *A shooting star streaked across the sky.*

streak·er /ˈstriːkɚ/ n [C] : a person who runs through a public place naked in order to get attention

streaky /ˈstriːki/ adj **streak·i·er; -est** **1** : having or showing streaks ▪ *streaky windows* **2** chiefly US : good or successful at some times and bad or unsuccessful at others ▪ *a streaky player/golfer*

¹**stream** /ˈstriːm/ n [C] **1** : a natural flow of water that is smaller than a river ▪ *a mountain stream* **2** : any flow of liquid or gas ▪ *a stream of cold air* **3** : a continuous flow of people or things ▪ *an endless stream of traffic*

²**stream** vb **1** [I] : to move in a steady flow ▪ *Tears streamed down his cheeks.* ▪ *Cold air streamed in through the window.* **2** of the body or a body part **a** [T/I] : to produce a liquid continuously and often in large amounts ▪ *Her eyes were streaming (with) tears.* **b** [I] : to be or become wet with a liquid ▪ *His face streamed with sweat.* **3** [I] : to come or flow continuously to a place in large numbers ▪ *People streamed into the hall.* **4** [I] : to move freely in one direction especially in wind or water ▪ *Her long hair streamed behind her as she ran.*

stream·er /ˈstriːmɚ/ n [C] **1** : a long, narrow piece of colored paper or plastic that is used as a decoration **2** : a long, narrow flag

stream·line /ˈstriːmˌlaɪn/ vb **-lined; -lin·ing** [T] **1** : to design or make (something, such as a boat or car) with a smooth shape which makes motion through water or air easier ▪ *The manufacturer has streamlined the car's design.*

2 : to make (something) simpler, more effective, or more productive ▪ *streamline production/operations* — **stream·lined** /ˈstriːmˌlaɪnd/ adj ▪ *a very streamlined car/design*

street /ˈstriːt/ n [C] **1** : a road in a city or town that has houses or other buildings on one or both sides ▪ *a busy/residential street* ▪ *a street address/map* ▪ *our neighbor down the street* [=our neighbor who lives farther down on our street] ▪ *They live across the street (from us).* [=they live across from us on the other side of the street] ▪ *He was living on the street(s).* [=was homeless] ▪ *street people* [=homeless people] — often used in names ▪ *We live at 156 Elm Street.* **2** informal : a poor part of a city where there is a lot of crime — usually plural ▪ *the raw language of the streets* — **streets ahead of** Brit, informal : much better than (other people or things) ▪ *She is streets ahead of the other students.* — **the man in the street** see ¹**MAN** — **up someone's street** Brit, informal : suited to someone's tastes or abilities ▪ *The job is right up his street.* [=(chiefly US) right up his alley]

street·car /ˈstriːtˌkɑɚ/ n [C] US : a vehicle that travels on streets on metal tracks and that is used for carrying passengers — called also *(chiefly Brit)* **tram**

street·light /ˈstriːtˌlaɪt/ n [C] : a light on a tall pole next to a public road — called also *street lamp*

street·walk·er /ˈstriːtˌwɑːkɚ/ n [C] : a prostitute who finds customers by walking around in the streets

strength /ˈstrɛŋkθ/ n **1** [U] : the quality or state of being physically strong ▪ *I don't have enough strength to lift the box by myself.* ▪ *muscular/physical strength* ▪ *She hit the ball with all her strength.* [=she hit the ball as hard as she could] **2** [U] : the ability to resist being moved or broken by a force ▪ *the strength and durability of the material* **3** [U] : the quality that allows someone to deal with problems in a determined and effective way ▪ *moral strength* ▪ *His determination shows real strength of character.* ▪ *Her inner strength is an inspiration to us all.* **4** [C] : a quality or feature that makes someone or something effective or useful ▪ *We talked about the strengths and weaknesses* [=the good parts and bad parts] *of the movie.* **5** [U] : the power or influence of a group, organization, etc. ▪ *The country has great military/economic strength.* ▪ *negotiating from a position of strength* [=from a strong position] **6** [U] — used to describe how strong or deeply held an emotion or opinion is ▪ *I was impressed by the strength of her convictions.* **7** [C/U] — used to describe how powerful something is ▪ *the strength of the wind* **8** [U] : the number of people in a group, army, team, etc. ▪ *The team is at full strength again.* [=the team has all its players again] ▪ *We're only at half strength today.* [=only half the usual number of people are here today] ▪ *(chiefly Brit) The team is under/below strength today.* [=the team does not have all of its players today] **9** [U] **a** : the value of a country's money when it is compared to money from other countries ▪ *the strength of the U.S. dollar* **b** : the financial condition of something ▪ *the strength of the economy/market* — **on the strength of** : because of the influence of (something) ▪ *I saw the film on the strength of his recommendation.*

strength·en /'strɛŋkθən/ *vb* **1** [T] : to make (someone or something) stronger, more forceful, more effective, etc. ▪ *These exercises will strengthen your stomach muscles.* ▪ *strengthening the immune system* **2** [I] : to become stronger, more forceful, more effective, etc. ▪ *The storm has strengthened.* **3** [T/I] *of money* : to increase in value when compared to money from other countries ▪ *The Canadian dollar is strengthening against the U.S. dollar.* ▪ *The trade restrictions strengthened the pound.*

stren·u·ous /'strɛnjəwəs/ *adj* : requiring or showing great energy and effort ▪ *strenuous exercise* ▪ *strenuous efforts* — **stren·u·ous·ly** *adv*

strep throat /'strɛp-/ *n* [U] *US, medical* : a painful infection of the throat caused by streptococcus bacteria — called also **strep**

strep·to·coc·cus /ˌstrɛptə'kɑːkəs/ *n, pl* **-coc·ci** /-'kɑːˌkaɪ/ [C] *medical* : a type of bacteria that causes diseases in people and animals

¹**stress** /'strɛs/ *n* **1 a** [U] : a state of mental tension and worry caused by problems in your life, work, etc. ▪ *She exercises as a way of reducing/relieving stress.* **b** [C/U] : something that causes strong feelings of worry or anxiety ▪ *I've been under (a lot of) stress at work lately.* ▪ *the stresses and strains of her job* **2** [C/U] : physical force or pressure ▪ *To reduce the amount of stress on your back, bend your knees when you lift something heavy.* **3** [U] : special importance or attention that is given to something ▪ *The teacher laid/put stress on the need for good study habits.* **4** [C/U] : greater loudness or force given to a syllable of a word in speech or to a beat in music ▪ *The stress is on the first syllable.*

²**stress** *vb* **1** [T] : to give special attention to (something) ▪ *He stressed the importance of exercising regularly.* **2** [T] : to pronounce (a syllable or word) in a louder or more forceful way than other syllables or words ▪ *When she said, "We need lots of money," she stressed the word "lots."* **3** [T/I] *US, informal* : to feel very worried or anxious about something ▪ *The decision isn't worth stressing over.* ▪ *My job is stressing me.* [=stressing me out] — **stress out** [*phrasal vb*] **stress out** or **stress (someone) out** or **stress (someone)** *informal* : to feel very worried or anxious or to make (someone) feel very worried or anxious ▪ *Work is stressing him out.*

stressed /'strɛst/ *adj* **1** : feeling very worried or anxious ▪ *He was stressed (out) about the deadline.* **2** *technical* : having a lot of physical pressure or force on it ▪ *stressed beams*

stress fracture *n* [C] *medical* : a crack on the surface of a bone caused by repeated pressure

stress·ful /'strɛsfəl/ *adj* : making you feel worried or anxious ▪ *a stressful situation/event/job*

stress test *n* [C] : a test to show how strong something is; *especially* : a medical test to show how strong and healthy your heart is during a period of exercise

¹**stretch** /'strɛtʃ/ *vb* **1 a** [T] : to make (something) wider or longer by pulling it ▪ *Don't yank on my sweater. You'll stretch it.* **b** [I] : to become longer or wider when pulled ▪ *The material/fabric stretches.* **2** [T/I] **a** : to put your arms, legs, etc., in positions that make the muscles long and tight ▪ *He stretched and yawned.* ▪ *She stretched her arms above her head.* **b** : to extend your arm, leg, etc., in order to reach something ▪ *She stretched over me to open the window.* ▪ *Her hand stretched (out) toward him.* = *She stretched her hand toward him.* [=she reached toward him with her hand] **3** [T] : to pull (something) so that it becomes flat and smooth and goes across a surface or area ▪ *A big banner was stretched across the doorway.* **4** [I] **a** : to continue for a specified distance ▪ *The cornfields stretch for miles.* — used to describe how long something is ▪ *The horse's tail stretches three and a half feet from base to end.* **b** : to continue over a period of time ▪ *Her interest in art stretches back to her childhood.* [=she has been interested in art since she was a child] **5** [T] : to say something that is not exactly true ▪ *He was stretching the truth.* [=exaggerating] ▪ (*informal*) *It's stretching it/things to say that she enjoys his visits.* [=she doesn't really enjoy his visits] **6** [T] : to cause or force (something) to be used for a longer time or for more purposes than originally planned or expected ▪ *They were forced to stretch (out) their food supplies.* **b** : to cause (something, such as a rule) to have a meaning or purpose that is different from what was originally intended ▪ *stretching the rules* [=doing something that is not really allowed by the rules] **c** — used figuratively in various phrases ▪ *Her bad behavior is stretching my patience (to the limit).* [=is causing me to lose patience] ▪ *His explanation stretches credulity.* [=is hard to believe] **7** [T] : to require (someone) to use a lot of effort, ability, skill, etc., in order to succeed ▪ *The work doesn't stretch me intellectually.* [=the work is too easy for me] — **stretch out** [*phrasal vb*] **stretch out** or **stretch (yourself) out** : to extend your body in a flat position ▪ *She stretched out on the bed.* — **stretch your legs** *informal* : to stand up and walk especially after sitting for a long period of time

²**stretch** *n* **1** [C] : a continuous area or length of land or water ▪ *an open stretch of highway/road* **2** [C] **a** : a continuous period of time ▪ *She reads for hours at a stretch.* [=at one time without stopping] **b** *informal* : a period of time spent in prison ▪ *He just got out of prison after a*

six-year stretch. **3** [C/U] : an act of stretching your body or part of your body ▪ *I always do some stretches before I exercise.* **4** **the stretch** : the final straight part of a race course before the finish line ▪ *The horses are in the (final) stretch.* ▪ *(figurative)* They won some crucial games down the stretch. [=in the last part of the season] **5** [U] : the ability to be stretched without breaking or being torn ▪ *material with a lot of stretch* **6** [*singular*] *chiefly US* **a** : something that requires a special effort to be done ▪ *Playing that role was not much of a stretch for her.* **b** : a statement, description, etc., that is not strictly true or accurate ▪ *Some people think it's a stretch to call fishing a sport.* — **at full stretch** *Brit, informal* : with as much effort as possible ▪ *The medical team worked at full stretch.* — **by any/no stretch of the imagination** — used to emphasize that something is not true, does not happen, etc. ▪ *He's not wealthy by any stretch of the imagination.* [=not wealthy at all]

stretch·er /ˈstrɛtʃɚ/ *n* [C] : a device that is made of a long piece of thick cloth stretched between two poles and that is used for carrying an injured or dead person — **stretcher** *vb* [T] *Brit* ▪ *The injured player was stretchered* [=carried on a stretcher] *off the field.*

stretchy /ˈstrɛtʃi/ *adj* **stretch·i·er**; **-est** : able to stretch and then return to the original size and shape ▪ *a stretchy fabric/shirt*

strew /ˈstruː/ *vb* **strewed**; **strewed** or **strewn** /ˈstruːn/; **strew·ing** [T] : to spread or scatter things over or on the ground or some other surface ▪ *She strewed the birdseed on the ground.* ▪ *The toys were strewed around the room.* [=were lying in different places in the room] ▪ *The park was strewn with litter.* [=there was litter scattered throughout the park]

strick·en /ˈstrɪkən/ *adj* : powerfully affected by disease, sorrow, etc. ▪ *stricken by/with embarrassment* ▪ *disease-stricken villages*

strict /ˈstrɪkt/ *adj* **1** — used to describe a command, rule, etc., that must be obeyed ▪ *strict rules/laws* **2** : demanding that people obey rules or behave in a certain way ▪ *a strict parent/teacher* **3 a** : carefully obeying the rules or principles of a religion or a particular way of life ▪ *a strict Hindu/vegetarian* **b** : complete or thorough ▪ *strict secrecy* **4** : exact or precise ▪ *He's not a volunteer in the strict/strictest sense (of the word)* [=he is not really a volunteer] *because he receives a small stipend.* — **strict·ly** /ˈstrɪktli/ *adv* ▪ *Smoking is strictly forbidden/prohibited.* ▪ *Strictly speaking, the book is not a novel but a series of short stories.* — **strict·ness** /ˈstrɪktnəs/ *n* [U]

stric·ture /ˈstrɪktʃɚ/ *n* [C] *formal* : a law or rule that limits or controls something ▪ *strictures on/against the sale of weapons*

¹**stride** /ˈstraɪd/ *vb* **strode** /ˈstroʊd/; **strid·den** /ˈstrɪdn̩/; **strid·ing** /ˈstraɪdɪŋ/ [I] : to walk with very long steps ▪ *She strode across the room.*

²**stride** *n* [C] **1** : a long step ▪ *She crossed the room in only a few strides.* **2** : a way of walking ▪ *She entered the room with a confident stride.* **3** : a change or improvement that brings someone closer to a goal ▪ *The patient is making strides toward a complete recovery.* — **break (your) stride** *chiefly US* : to stop walking or running in a regular and steady way ▪ *He caught the ball without breaking stride.* ▪ *(figurative)* She went from college to her first job without breaking stride. — **hit your stride** (US) or Brit **get into your stride** : to begin to do something in a confident and effective way after starting slowly ▪ *Both teams seem to have hit their stride.* — **off stride** ✧ If you are walking or running and someone or something (*chiefly US*) **throws/knocks you off (your) stride** or (*chiefly Brit*) **puts you off your stride**, you are unable to continue walking or running steadily. ▪ *I bumped into him and threw/knocked him off his stride.* ▪ *(figurative)* She was thrown off stride by the unexpected question. — **take (something) in stride** (US) or Brit **take (something) in your stride** : to deal with (something difficult or upsetting) in a calm way ▪ *She has taken the news in stride.*

stri·dent /ˈstraɪdn̩t/ *adj* **1** : sounding harsh and unpleasant ▪ *a strident voice* **2** : expressing opinions or criticism in a very forceful and often annoying or unpleasant way ▪ *strident critics* — **stri·den·cy** /ˈstraɪdn̩si/ *n* [U] — **stri·dent·ly** *adv*

strife /ˈstraɪf/ *n* [U] *formal* : very angry or violent disagreement between two or more people or groups ▪ *political/religious strife*

¹**strike** /ˈstraɪk/ *vb* **struck** /ˈstrʌk/; **struck** *also* **strick·en** /ˈstrɪkən/; **strik·ing** /ˈstraɪkɪŋ/ **1** [T] : to hit (someone or something) in a forceful way ▪ *The car struck the tree.* ▪ *He was struck by lightning.* ▪ *A bolt of lightning struck him dead.* [=struck him and killed him] **b** : to cause (something) to hit something in a forceful way ▪ *She struck the cymbals together.* **c** : to hit (someone or something) with your hand, a weapon, etc. ▪ *The killer struck him with a blunt object.* **2** [I] : to attack someone or something suddenly ▪ *The snake was about to strike.* ▪ *He struck at her with a knife.* ▪ *(figurative)* The proposed law strikes at the foundations of our democracy. **3** [T/I] : to affect (someone or something) suddenly in a bad way ▪ *He was stricken with a high fever.* ▪ *When disaster strikes, will you be prepared?* **4** [T] : to cause (someone) to be in a certain condition suddenly ▪ *He was struck deaf/blind.* [=became deaf/blind] **5** [T] **a** : to cause someone to feel (a strong emotion) suddenly ▪ *Her words struck fear into the hearts of her listeners.* **b** : to affect (someone) with a strong emotion ▪ *He was struck with horror.* **6** [T] : to cause (something) to happen or exist ▪ *He needs to strike a better balance between his work life and his family life.* [=he needs to spend less time at work and more time with his family] **7**

[T] : to be thought of by (someone) suddenly • *It suddenly struck me* [=I realized suddenly] *that I would never see her again.* • *It strikes me* [=I realize] *that there is a larger issue at stake.* **8** [T] : to cause (someone) to think about someone or something in a particular way • *Her comment struck me as odd.* [=her comment seemed odd to me] **9** [I] *of a group of workers* : to refuse to work until your employer does what you want • *The teachers are threatening to strike.* [=go on strike] • *They are striking for an increase in pay.* **10** [T/I] *of a clock* : to make the time known by making a sound • *The clock struck one.* • *The clock struck as they entered the room.* **11** [T] : to cause (a match) to start burning by rubbing it against a surface **12** [T] : to make (an agreement) • *The two parties have struck a bargain/deal.* **13** [T] : to remove (something) *from* (something) • *The clause has been stricken from the contract.* **14** [T] : to find or discover (something) especially by digging • *They struck oil/gold.* • *(figurative) The studio struck gold* [=was very successful] *with their latest film.* **15** [T] : to place yourself in (a particular position, posture, etc.) • *She struck a dramatic pose.* **16** [T] : to play (a note, chord, etc.) on a musical instrument by using your fingers on keys or strings • *He struck the song's opening chords.* • *(figurative) She struck the right note/tone with her speech.* [=she said things that appealed to her audience] **17** [I] : to begin to walk or go in a particular direction • *He struck off through the woods.* • *We struck out for/toward our campsite.* **18** [T] : to make (a coin, medal, etc.) by pressing an image into a piece of metal • *The coins were struck in 1789.* — **be struck by** *informal* : to be very impressed by or pleased with (something or someone) • *We were struck by the beauty of the landscape.* — **strike a chord** see CHORD — **strike a nerve** see NERVE — **strike back** [*phrasal vb*] : to try to hurt someone who has hurt you or treated you badly • *He angrily struck back at his critics.* — **strike down** [*phrasal vb*] **1** **strike (someone) down** : to make (someone) unable to work, act, or function in the usual way • *She was struck down by an injury.* **b** : to cause (someone) to die suddenly • *He was struck down by a heart attack.* **2** **strike (something) down** or **strike down (something)** *chiefly US, law* : to say officially that (something) is no longer legally valid • *The court struck down the law.* — **strike it rich** *informal* : to become rich suddenly — **strike/upon** [*phrasal vb*] : to find or discover (something) especially suddenly • *He struck on an idea.* — **strike out** [*phrasal vb*] **1** *baseball* **a** **strike (someone) out** or **strike out (someone)** *of a pitcher* : to cause (a batter) to be out by pitching three strikes • *The pitcher struck out the batter.* **b** *of a batter* : to make an out by getting three strikes • *The batter struck out.* **2** **strike (something) out** or **strike out (something)** : to remove (something) from a document : DELETE

• *The editor struck out the last paragraph.* **3** *US, informal* : to be unsuccessful • *"Did you get her phone number?" "No, I struck out."* **4** : to begin a course of action • *She struck out on her own after graduation.* **5** : to try to hit someone or something suddenly • *He struck out wildly at the police officers.* **6** : to make a sudden and angry attack against someone • *She struck out at her critics.* — **strike up** [*phrasal vb*] **1 a** : to begin to play (a piece of music) • *The band struck up a waltz.* **b** : to cause (an orchestra, a band, etc.) to begin playing • *The conductor struck up the band.* **2** **strike up (something)** *also* **strike (something) up** : to begin (something) • *We struck up a conversation/friendship.* — **strike while the iron is hot** : to do something while you still have a good chance to succeed

²**strike** *n* **1** [C/U] : a period of time when workers stop work in order to force an employer to agree to their demands • *a teachers' strike* • *The workers are on strike.* • *Workers are threatening to go (out) on strike.* **2** [C] : a military attack • *an air strike* [=an attack by aircraft] **3** [C] : the act of hitting something with force • *a lightning strike* [=an occurrence in which the ground is struck by lightning] **4** [C] *baseball* : a pitch that passes through a certain area over home plate without being hit and that counts against the batter • *The first pitch was a ball but the next two pitches were strikes.* **5** [C] *chiefly US* : something that makes someone or something less likely to be accepted, approved, successful, etc. • *Her poor attendance was a strike against her.* **6** [C] *bowling* : the achievement of knocking down all 10 pins with the first ball • *She made/bowled a strike.* **7** [C] : a discovery of something valuable (such as oil) • *an oil strike* — **strik·er** /ˈstraɪkɚ/ *n* [C]

strike·break·er /ˈstraɪkˌbreɪkɚ/ *n* [C] : a person who is hired to replace a worker who is on strike or who continues to work during a strike

strik·ing /ˈstraɪkɪŋ/ *adj* **1** : unusual or extreme in a way that attracts attention • *a striking resemblance/contrast* **2** : very attractive especially in an unusual or interesting way • *her striking good looks* — **strik·ing·ly** *adv*

¹**string** /ˈstrɪŋ/ *n* **1** [C/U] : a long, thin piece of twisted thread that you use to attach things, tie things together, or hang things **2** [C] : a group of objects that are connected with a string, wire, chain, etc. • *a string of pearls* **3** [C] **a** : a series of similar things • *He owns a string of movie theaters.* **b** : a series of events which follow each other in time • *a string of robberies* **4** [C] : a long, thin piece of tightly stretched wire or other material (such as nylon) that is used to produce sounds in a musical instrument • *guitar/piano/violin strings* **5** [U] *chiefly US* : a group of players on a team that play together because they have similar abilities • *the first/second string of a football team* **6** [*plural*] : things that you have to do, give, etc., if you accept something (such

as a gift or an offer) ▪ *They offered her the job with no strings attached.* [=with no conditions] **7** [C] : a long, thin piece of nylon or other material that is stretched tightly across a tennis racket or similar object — **pull strings** : to use the influence that you have with important people to get or achieve something ▪ *His father pulled (some) strings to get him the job.* — **pull the strings** : to control someone or something often in a secret way ▪ *His brother is the person pulling the strings behind the operation.*

²**string** *vb* **strung** /'strʌŋ/; **string·ing** [T] **1** : to put (things) together on a string, thread, chain, etc. ▪ *string beads* **2** : to place or hang (things) in a line or series ▪ *They strung wires from tree to tree.* **3** : to tie, hang, or fasten (something) with string ▪ *She strung the key around her neck.* **4** : to attach strings to (a musical instrument, tennis racket, etc.) — **string along** [*phrasal vb*] **string (someone) along** : to continue to deceive or trick (someone) for a long time ▪ *He strung us along with false promises.* — **string out** [*phrasal vb*] **string (something) out** or **string out (something)** : to make (something) take longer than it should ▪ *You're just stringing this out to avoid leaving.* — **string together** [*phrasal vb*] **string (something) together** or **string together (something)** : to combine (different things) into something that is complete, useful, etc. ▪ *The filmmaker strung together several interviews.* : to create (something) by putting different things together ▪ *She managed to string together a coherent argument.*

string bean *n* [C] *chiefly US* **1** : a type of long, thin green bean **2** *informal* : a very tall thin person

stringed instrument /'strɪŋd-/ *n* [C] : a musical instrument (such as a guitar, violin, or piano) that has strings

strin·gent /'strɪndʒənt/ *adj* : very strict or severe ▪ *stringent rules* — **strin·gen·cy** /'strɪndʒənsi/ *n* [U] — **strin·gent·ly** *adv*

string·er /'strɪŋə/ *n* [C] : a journalist who writes stories for a newspaper but is not on the regular staff

stringy /'strɪŋi/ *adj* **string·i·er; -est** **1** : containing long, thin pieces that are like string and that are hard to chew ▪ *a stringy piece of meat* **2** *of hair* : long, thin, and dirty ▪ *stringy hair* **3** : having long, thin muscles ▪ *stringy arms* — **string·i·ness** *n* [U]

¹**strip** /'strɪp/ *n* [C] **1** : a long, narrow piece of something ▪ *a strip of paper/land* **2** *US* : a road that has a lot of shops, restaurants, etc., along it ▪ *the Las Vegas strip* **3** : AIRSTRIP **4** : COMIC STRIP

²**strip** *vb* **stripped; strip·ping 1 a** [*T/I*] : to remove your clothing ▪ *He stripped (himself) down to his underwear.* [=he took all his clothes off except for his underwear] ▪ *The prisoners were told to strip naked.* **b** [T] : to take the clothes of (someone) ▪ *The prisoners were stripped naked.* **c** [I] : to remove your clothing in a sexually exciting way while someone is watching ▪ *She gets paid to strip at the*

club. **2** [T] : to remove an outer covering or surface from something ▪ *strip the bark from a tree = strip a tree of its bark* **3** [T] : to remove everything (such as furniture or equipment) from (a room, building, car, etc.) ▪ *They stripped the room when they left.* **4** [T] : to separate (a machine or piece of equipment) into parts for cleaning or repair ▪ *They stripped (down) the engine.* **5** [T] : to take (something) away from someone in a forceful way ▪ *The pageant winner was stripped of her crown/title.* [=she was forced to give up her crown/title] ▪ *Their rights were stripped away.* **6** [T] : to damage part of a screw or gear so that it does not work properly ▪ *Pushing too hard will strip the screw.* — **strip away** [*phrasal vb*] **strip (something) away** or **strip away (something)** **1** : to remove (something that covers a surface) ▪ *strip away the bark of a tree* **2** : to remove (unimportant material) from something ▪ *The editor stripped away repetitive sections of the essay.* — **strip·per** /'strɪpə/ *n* [C/U] ▪ *She worked as a stripper in a nightclub.*

stripe /'straɪp/ *n* [C] **1** : a long, narrow line of color ▪ *gray stripes on a black background* **2** : a piece of material worn on the arm of a military uniform to show the rank of the person wearing the uniform **3** : a particular type of person or thing ▪ *classes for artists of all stripes* [=for all kinds of artists] — **earn your stripes** : to do something which shows that you deserve to be accepted and respected by the other people in a field or profession ▪ *She has yet to earn her stripes as a reporter.* — **striped** /'straɪpt/ *adj* ▪ *a striped shirt*

strip mall *n* [C] *US* : a long building that is divided into separate shops which usually have outside entrances and which share a parking lot

strip mine *n* [C] : a mine that is dug by removing the surface of a large piece of land one section at a time — **strip–mine** *vb* **-mined; -min·ing** [T] ▪ *a region where coal is strip-mined*

strip search *n* [C] : an act of removing someone's clothing to see if that person is hiding illegal drugs, weapons, etc. — **strip–search** *vb* [T] ▪ *They were strip-searched at the airport.*

strip–tease /'strɪp,tiːz/ *n* [C] : a performance in which someone removes clothing in a sexually exciting way

strive /'straɪv/ *vb* **strove** /'stroʊv/ *also* **strived; striv·en** /'strɪvən/ *or* **strived; striv·ing** [I] *formal* : to try very hard to do or achieve something ▪ *She strives for perfection.* — **striv·er** /'straɪvə/ *n* [C]

strobe light /'stroʊb-/ *n* [C] : a bright light that flashes on and off very quickly

strode *past tense of* ¹STRIDE

¹**stroke** /'stroʊk/ *n* **1** [C] *medical* : a serious illness caused when a blood vessel in your brain suddenly breaks or is blocked ▪ *He had/suffered a stroke.* ▪ *a stroke patient* **2** [C] **a** : an act of hitting a ball or the movement made to hit a ball during a game ▪ *a backhand stroke* **b** *golf* : an act of hitting the ball that is counted as

part of a player's score • *He is ahead by two strokes.* **3** [C] **a** : one of a series of repeated movements of your arms in swimming or rowing that you make to move yourself or the boat through the water • *the stroke of an oar* **b** : a style of swimming • *She knows the four basic strokes.* **4** [C] : one of a series of repeated movements by something that goes up and down or back and forth • *the stroke of a piston* **5** [C] : an act of hitting someone or something with a stick, whip, etc. • *a stroke of the whip* **6** [C] : a gentle movement of your hand over or along something • *Pet the cat with soft strokes.* **7** [C] : a single act of moving a pen or brush when it is being used to write or paint • *the strokes of a painter's brush* **8** [C] : one of the sounds made by a clock or bell to indicate a particular time • *the first stroke of the clock at midnight* **b** [singular] : an exact time • *They arrived at the stroke of midnight.* [=at exactly midnight] **9** [C] : a single decisive action • *She solved our problems in one stroke.* **10** [C] : something good, lucky, etc., that happens or is thought of suddenly • *Finding this place was a stroke of luck.* • *The plan was a stroke of inspiration/genius.* [=a great idea] **11** [C] : a bright flash • *a stroke of lightning*

²**stroke** *vb* **stroked; strok·ing** [T] **1** : to move your hand over (someone or something) gently and in one direction • *She stroked the cat's fur.* **2** *chiefly US, informal* : to say nice things to (someone) in order to get approval, agreement, etc. • *Her clients expect her to stroke their egos.*

stroll /ˈstroʊl/ *vb* [T/I] : to walk slowly in usually a pleasant and relaxed way • *They strolled along/down/across the street.* • *We strolled the streets of the village.* — **stroll** *n* [C] • *He went for a stroll in/through the park.*

stroll·er /ˈstroʊlɚ/ *n* [C] **1** *US* : a small carriage with four wheels that a baby or small child can ride in while someone pushes it — called also (*Brit*) *pushchair* **2** : someone who is strolling • *strollers on the beach*

strong /ˈstrɑːŋ/ *adj* **stron·ger** /ˈstrɑːŋgɚ/; **stron·gest** /ˈstrɑːŋgəst/ **1** : having great physical power and ability • *a strong kid* • *strong muscles* • *He's as strong as an ox.* **2** : not easy to break or damage • *strong walls/furniture* **3** : HEALTHY • *The patient is feeling a little stronger.* **4** : very noticeable • *a strong accent/resemblance* **5** : having great power or force • *a strong wind* **6 a** : very powerful in action or effect • *a strong drug* **b** : having a powerful and sometimes unpleasant taste or smell • *strong cheese/smell* **7** : containing a large amount of an important ingredient (such as alcohol) • *a strong drink* **8** : having a lot of power or influence • *a strong leader* **9** : likely to persuade or convince people that something is true, real, correct, etc. • *a strong argument/case* **10** : very confident and able to deal with difficult situations • *a strong personality* **11** : felt, believed, or expressed in a very definite

and powerful way • *strong opinions/desires* **12** : powerful and effective in supporting something, opposing something, etc. • *a strong opponent of the proposal* **13** : well established and likely to continue • *strong traditions/friendships* **14** : likely to succeed or to happen • *a strong candidate/possibility* **15 a** : great in number • *There was a strong turnout for the election.* [=many people voted] **b** — used to indicate the number of people in a large group • *The army was ten thousand strong.* **16 a** : having a value that is great or that is increasing • *The dollar is strong.* **b** : in a good financial condition • *The economy is strong.* **17** : very forceful and sometimes obscene or offensive • *She used some strong language.* [=she swore] **18** : very bright • *strong colors/light* — **come on strong** see COME — **going strong** : very active, healthy, or successful • *He's 92 years old and still going strong.* — **strong on 1** : very good at (something) • *She's strong on vocabulary but not grammar.* **2** : containing a lot of (something) • *The explanation was strong on detail.* — **strong·ly** /ˈstrɑːŋli/ *adv*

strong–arm /ˈstrɑːŋˌɑɚm/ *adj, always before a noun* : using force or threats to make someone do what is wanted • *strong-arm tactics* — **strong–arm** *vb* [T] • *She strong-armed us into cooperating.*

strong·hold /ˈstrɑːŋˌhoʊld/ *n* [C] **1** : an area dominated by a particular group • *The state is a Republican stronghold.* **2** : a protected place where the members of a military group stay and can defend themselves against attacks • *The rebels retreated to their mountain stronghold.*

strong suit *n* [singular] : something that a person does well — often used in negative statements • *Cooking is not my strong suit.*

strong–willed *adj* : very determined to do something even if other people say it should not be done • *strong-willed children*

strove *past tense of* STRIVE

struck *past tense and past participle of* ¹STRIKE

struc·tur·al /ˈstrʌktʃərəl/ *adj, always before a noun* : relating to the way something is built or organized • *The house suffered no structural damage.* — **struc·tur·al·ly** *adv*

¹**struc·ture** /ˈstrʌktʃɚ/ *n* **1** [C] **a** : the way that something is built, arranged, or organized • *the structure of a plant* **b** : the way that a group of people are organized • *a solid family structure* **2** [C] : something (such as a house, bridge, etc.) that is built by putting parts together and that usually stands on its own • *a brick/steel structure* **3** [U] : the quality of something that is carefully planned, organized, and controlled • *The novel lacks structure.*

²**structure** *vb* **-tured; -tur·ing** [T] : to arrange or organize (something) in a particular way • *She structured the essay chronologically.*

stru·del /ˈstruːdl̩/ *n* [C/U] : a German

pastry made of thin dough rolled up with fruit filling and baked • *apple strudel*

¹strug·gle /ˈstrʌgəl/ *vb* **strug·gled; strug·gling** [*I*] **1** : to try very hard to do, achieve, or deal with something that is difficult or that causes problems • *She's struggling to survive.* • *They struggled against injustice.* **2 a** : to move with difficulty or with great effort • *She struggled up the hill.* **b** : to try to move yourself, an object, etc., by making a lot of effort • *He struggled to get free of the wreckage.* He struggled to fight with someone in order to get something • *They struggled over the gun.* **3** : to be doing something without success • *He is struggling in math class.* • *a struggling artist* — **strug·gler** /ˈstrʌglə/ *n* [*C*]

²struggle *n* **1** [*C*] : a long effort to do, achieve, or deal with something that is difficult or that causes problems • *the struggle for survival* • *They got into a power struggle.* [=a fight for control] **2** [*C*] : a physical fight between usually two people • *There was no sign of a struggle.* **3** [*singular*] : something that is difficult to do or achieve • *Getting her to listen was a struggle.*

strum /ˈstrʌm/ *vb* **strummed; strum·ming** [*T*] **1** : to play (an instrument) by moving your fingers across the strings • *strummed a guitar/banjo* **2** : to play (music) on a guitar, banjo, etc., by moving your fingers over the strings • *strum a tune* — **strum·mer** *n* [*C*]

strung *past tense and past participle of* ²STRING

strung out *adj, informal* : strongly affected by an illegal drug • *strung out on heroin*

¹strut /ˈstrʌt/ *vb* **strut·ted; strut·ting** [*I*] : to walk in a confident and proud way • *She strutted across the stage.* — **strut your stuff** *informal* : to proudly show your abilities • *The show gives young actors a chance to strut their stuff.* — **strut·ter** *n* [*C*]

²strut *n* **1** [*C*] : a long, thin piece of wood or metal used for support in a building, vehicle, etc. **2** [*singular*] : a proud and confident walk

strych·nine /ˈstrɪkˌnaɪn/ *n* [*U*] : a poisonous substance that can be used in very small amounts as a medicine

¹stub /ˈstʌb/ *n* [*C*] **1** : a short part left after a larger part has been broken off or used up • *a pencil stub* **2** : a part of a ticket that is kept by the person who uses the ticket • *a ticket stub* **3** : a piece of paper that is attached to a check and has information (such as the amount and the date) printed on it • *a check stub*

²stub *vb* **stubbed; stub·bing** [*T*] : to put out (a cigarette) by pressing it down against something • *He stubbed his cigarette out in/on the ashtray.* — **stub your toe** : to hurt your toe by hitting it against something

stub·ble /ˈstʌbəl/ *n* [*U*] **1** : short hairs growing from the face of a man who has not shaved very recently **2** : the short ends of crops left in the ground after the crops have been cut down — **stub·bled**

/ˈstʌbəld/ *adj* • *his stubbled chin* — **stub·bly** /ˈstʌbəli/ *adj* • *a stubbly beard*

stub·born /ˈstʌbən/ *adj* **1** : refusing to change your ideas or to stop doing something • *a stubborn child/attitude* • **She has a stubborn streak.** [=she is often stubborn] • *He's* **(as) stubborn as a mule.** [=very stubborn] **2** : difficult to deal with, remove, etc. • *a stubborn stain/infection* — **stub·born·ly** *adv* — **stub·born·ness** /ˈstʌbənnəs/ *n* [*U*]

stub·by /ˈstʌbi/ *adj* **stub·bi·er; -est** : short and thick • *a stubby tail*

stuc·co /ˈstʌkoʊ/ *n* [*U*] : a type of plaster used for decoration or to cover the outside walls of houses — **stuc·coed** /ˈstʌkoʊd/ *adj* • *stuccoed walls*

¹stuck /ˈstʌk/ *adj, not before a noun* **1 a** : difficult or impossible to move from a position • *The ring is stuck on my finger.* • *The door keeps* **getting stuck.** • (*figurative*) *He's* **stuck in his ways.** [=he's unwilling to change his ways of doing or thinking about things] • (*figurative*) *The song is* **stuck in my head.** [=I keep hearing the song over and over again in my head] **b** : in a place or situation that is difficult or impossible to get out of • *The car was stuck in the mud.* • *I was stuck at the office all day.* • *I got stuck in traffic.* **c** : forced to keep or deal with someone or something unpleasant • *We're stuck with this old sofa that nobody wants.* • *I got stuck washing dishes.* **2** *informal* : unable to think of a solution, an idea, etc. • *I'm stuck. Can you help me?* • *I'm stuck on this math problem.* • *If you're* **stuck for ideas,** *I can help.* — **stuck on** *informal* : loving or admiring someone foolishly or too much • *He's stuck on her.* • *She is stuck on herself.* [=stuck-up]

²stuck *past tense and past participle of* ²STICK

stuck–up /ˈstʌkˈʌp/ *adj, informal* : acting unfriendly towards other people because you think you are better than they are • *stuck-up rich people*

¹stud /ˈstʌd/ *n* **1 a** [*C/U*] : a male animal (such as a horse) kept for breeding • *retired racehorses being used as studs* • *a horse that has been* **put out to stud b** [*C*] *informal* : a very attractive and masculine man • *She ran off with some young stud.* **2** [*C*] *US* : one of the upright pieces of wood that are used to build the frame of a wall **3** [*C*] **a** : a small metal knob that is used for decoration • *a belt with silver studs* **b** : a small metal object used as a clothing fastener or for decoration • *shirt studs* **c** : a small piece of jewelry that is attached through a hole in part of a person's body (such as an ear) • *diamond studs*

²stud *vb* **stud·ded; stud·ding** [*T*] : to decorate or cover (something) with many small items • *a gown studded with jewels* • (*figurative*) *Bright stars studded the sky.*

stu·dent /ˈstuːdn̩t, *Brit* ˈstjuːdn̩t/ *n* [*C*] **1** : a person who attends a school, college, or university • *a high school student* • *a student athlete* **2** : a person who studies something — + *of* • *a student of human nature*

student body n [C] : the students at a school ▪ The school has a large student body. [=a large number of students]

stud·ied /ˈstʌdid/ adj 1 : carefully thought out or prepared ▪ a studied response 2 : done deliberately ▪ a studied insult

stu·dio /ˈstuːdiˌoʊ, Brit ˈstjuːdiˌoʊ/ n, pl -dios [C] 1 : the building or room where an artist works 2 : a place where people go to learn, practice, or study singing, dancing, acting, etc. 3 a : a place where movies are made b : a company that makes movies ▪ Hollywood studios 4 : a place where radio or television programs are broadcast 5 : a place where music is recorded 6 : a small apartment that has a main room, a small kitchen, and a bathroom

stu·di·ous /ˈstuːdijəs, Brit ˈstjuːdiəs/ adj 1 : very serious about studying, reading, learning, etc. ▪ a studious child 2 : very careful and serious ▪ a studious effort to obey the rules — **stu·di·ous·ly** adv — **stu·di·ous·ness** n [U]

¹**study** /ˈstʌdi/ n, pl stud·ies 1 [C/U] : the activity or process of learning about something by reading, memorizing facts, attending school, etc. ▪ Becoming a doctor requires years of study. ▪ She will return to her studies after vacation. ▪ You can design your own course of study. [=you can choose the subjects you will study] 2 a [C] : an area of learning taught in a school — usually plural ▪ literary/American/women's studies b [singular] : something that a person studies or gives attention to ▪ She has made a study of [=studied] the problem. 3 [C] a : an organized experiment in which many things are looked at, measured, recorded, etc., in order to learn more about something ▪ a study of childhood obesity b : a report or publication based on a study ▪ The study of the new drug will be published next year. 4 [C] : a quiet room in someone's home for reading, writing, etc. 5 [singular] US : a person who learns or memorizes something ▪ He's a quick study. [=he learns things quickly] — **under study** : being studied ▪ The proposal is under study.

²**study** vb studies; stud·ied; study·ing 1 [T/I] : to read, memorize facts, attend school, etc., in order to learn about a subject ▪ He is studying music. ▪ Did you study for the test? 2 [T] a : to give careful attention to (something) ▪ She studied his face. b : to conduct an organized experiment in order to learn more about (something) ▪ The effects of the drug have never been thoroughly studied.

¹**stuff** /ˈstʌf/ n [U] 1 informal a : materials, supplies, or equipment ▪ She got out the cooking stuff. b : a group or pile of things that are not specifically described ▪ Pick that stuff up off the floor. 2 informal — used to refer to something when you do not need to name exactly what it is ▪ She wears cool stuff. ▪ The stuff he says is just not true. ▪ TVs and stereos and stuff (like that) [=and other similar things] ▪ Get out on that stage and do your stuff. [=do the things that you are able to do

well] ▪ When it comes to gardening, she really knows her stuff. [=knows a lot] ▪ The competition gives performers a chance to show their stuff. [=show what they can do] 3 informal — used to speak in a general way about something that is talked about, written about, etc. ▪ There's some fascinating stuff in this book. 4 informal — used to describe the quality of a performance, experience, etc. ▪ The early chapters are pretty dull stuff. [=are uninteresting] 5 informal : actions or behavior of a particular kind ▪ He does stuff that bugs his parents. 6 : personality or character ▪ He's a wimp but his brother is made of sterner/tougher stuff. [=his brother is a stronger/tougher person] ▪ She has the right stuff to succeed. 7 : the material that something is made of ▪ The floor tiles are made of very tough stuff. ▪ (figurative) He has the stuff of greatness. [=the qualities that can make a person great] ▪ (figurative) Her partying became the stuff of legend. [=became legendary] — **strut your stuff** see ¹STRUT

²**stuff** vb [T] 1 : to fill (something) so that there is no room for anything else ▪ He stuffed his pockets with candy. 2 : to push (something) quickly and carelessly into a small space ▪ He stuffed candy into his pockets. 3 : to put a seasoned mixture of food into (something that is being cooked) ▪ stuff a turkey 4 : to fill the skin of (a dead animal) so that it looks the way it did when it was alive ▪ He had the deer's head stuffed. — **stuff it** informal — used as an angry and rude way to say that you do not want something or are not interested in something ▪ When they offered me the job I told them to stuff it. — **stuff yourself** or **stuff your face** informal + often disapproving : to eat a large amount of food ▪ They stuffed themselves with pizza.

stuffed /ˈstʌft/ adj 1 not before a noun : not hungry any more ▪ "Would you like dessert?" "No, thanks. I'm stuffed." 2 : filled with mucus because of illness ▪ My nose is stuffed (up). = I'm (all) stuffed up. ▪ a stuffed (up) nose — **get stuffed** chiefly Brit, informal — used as an angry and rude way to tell someone to go away or to leave you alone

stuffed animal n [C] US : a toy in the shape of an animal that usually has fake fur and is filled with soft material

stuffed shirt n [C] informal + disapproving : a person who behaves in a very formal way and expects to be treated as someone very important

stuff·ing /ˈstʌfɪŋ/ n 1 [U] : soft material that is used to fill a pillow, cushion, etc. 2 [C/U] : a seasoned mixture of food that is put inside another food and cooked — **knock the stuffing out of** informal : to cause (someone) to lose energy and confidence ▪ Losing his job really knocked the stuffing out of him.

stuffy /ˈstʌfi/ adj stuff·i·er; -est 1 : lacking fresh air ▪ a stuffy room 2 : filled with mucus because of illness ▪ a stuffy nose 3 informal + disapproving

: very formal, serious, or old-fashioned ▪ *a stuffy judge* — **stuff·i·ness** /'stʌfinəs/ *n* [U]

stul·ti·fy /'stʌltəˌfaɪ/ *vb* **-fies; -fied; -fy·ing** [T] *formal* : to cause (someone or something) to become dull, slow, etc. ▪ *The government has been stultified by bureaucracy.* — **stultifying** *adj*

stum·ble /'stʌmbəl/ *vb* **stum·bled; stum·bling** [I] **1** : to hit your foot on something when you are walking or running so that you fall or almost fall ▪ *I stumbled on the uneven pavement.* **2** : to walk in an awkward way ▪ *He stumbled drunkenly across the room.* **3 a** : to speak or act in an awkward way ▪ *She stumbled through an apology.* **b** : to begin to have problems after a time of success ▪ *The economy has stumbled again.* **4** : to find or learn about something unexpectedly ▪ *I stumbled across/on/upon this book.* ▪ *stumble onto the truth* — **stumble** *n* [C]

stumbling block *n* [C] : something that stops you from doing what you want to do ▪ *My plans hit a stumbling block.*

¹**stump** /'stʌmp/ *n* [C] **1** : a part that remains after something has been broken off, removed, worn down, etc. ▪ *the stump of a tooth* **2** : the part of a tree that remains in the ground after the tree is cut down **3** : the part of an arm or leg that remains after most of it has been cut off **4** *cricket* : one of the three sticks that form a wicket — **on the stump** : traveling around and giving speeches during a campaign for election to a political office ▪ *candidates who are on the stump*

²**stump** *vb* **1** [T] : to be too difficult for (someone) to answer ▪ *The question stumped me.* ▪ *This problem has me stumped.* [=I do not know the solution] **2** [T/I] *US* : to go to different places and make speeches during a political campaign ▪ *Several candidates have been stumping (in) the state.*

stumpy /'stʌmpi/ *adj* **stump·i·er; -est** : short and thick ▪ *stumpy legs*

stun /'stʌn/ *vb* **stunned; stun·ning** [T] **1** : to surprise or upset (someone) very much ▪ *We were stunned by the news.* **2** : to cause (someone) to suddenly become very confused, very dizzy, or unconscious ▪ *weapons that can stun people temporarily*

stung *past tense and past participle of* ¹STING

stunk *past tense and past participle of* ¹STINK

stun·ner /'stʌnɚ/ *n* [C] *informal* **1** : a very attractive person ▪ *His wife is a real stunner.* **2** : something that amazes or shocks people ▪ *The jury's decision was a stunner.*

stunning *adj* **1** : very surprising or shocking ▪ *a stunning decision/discovery* **2** : very beautiful or pleasing ▪ *a stunning gown/view* — **stun·ning·ly** *adv*

¹**stunt** /'stʌnt/ *vb* [T] : to stop (someone or something) from growing or developing ▪ *Poor soil can stunt a plant's growth.*

²**stunt** *n* [C] **1** : something that is done to get attention or publicity ▪ *a publicity*

stunt **2** : a difficult and often dangerous action ▪ *airplane stunts; especially* : a difficult action or scene that is done by actors in a movie ▪ *a star actor who does/performs his own stunts* — **pull a stunt** *informal* : to do something foolish or dangerous

stunt·man /'stʌntˌmæn/ *n, pl* **-men** /-ˌmɛn/ [C] : a man who takes an actor's place during the filming of stunts and dangerous scenes

stunt·wom·an /'stʌntˌwʊmən/ *n, pl* **-wom·en** /-ˌwɪmən/ [C] : a woman who takes an actor's place during the filming of stunts and dangerous scenes

stu·pe·fy /'stuːpəˌfaɪ, *Brit* 'stjuːpəˌfaɪ/ *vb* **-fies; -fied; -fy·ing** [T] : to cause (someone) to become confused or unable to think clearly ▪ *I was stupefied by their decision.* — **stu·pe·fac·tion** /ˌstuːpəˈfækʃən, *Brit* ˌstjuːpəˈfækʃən/ *n* [U] — **stupefied** *adj* ▪ *They looked at her with stupefied expressions on their faces.* — **stupefying** *adj*

stu·pen·dous /stʊˈpɛndəs, *Brit* stjuːˈpɛndəs/ *adj* : so large or great that it amazes you ▪ *stupendous wealth* — **stu·pen·dous·ly** *adv*

stu·pid /'stuːpəd, *Brit* 'stjuːpəd/ *adj* **1** : having or showing a lack of ability to learn and understand things ▪ *a stupid person* ▪ *He had a stupid expression on his face.* **2** : not sensible or logical ▪ *It was stupid of me to do that.* ▪ *a stupid decision* **3** *informal* — used to refer to something in an angry or irritated way ▪ *My stupid car won't start.* — **stu·pid·i·ty** /stʊˈpɪdəti, *Brit* stjuːˈpɪdəti/ *n, pl* **-ties** [C/U] — **stu·pid·ly** *adv*

stu·por /'stuːpɚ, *Brit* 'stjuːpə/ *n* [C] : a condition in which someone is not able to think normally because of being drunk, drugged, tired, etc. ▪ *a drunken stupor*

stur·dy /'stɚdi/ *adj* **stur·di·er; -est** **1** : strongly made ▪ *sturdy furniture* **2** : strong and healthy ▪ *a sturdy body* **3** : having or showing mental or emotional strength ▪ *sturdy self-reliance* — **stur·di·ly** /'stɚdəli/ *adj* — **stur·di·ness** /'stɚdinəs/ *n* [U]

stur·geon /'stɚdʒən/ *n* [C/U] : a type of large fish that is eaten as food

stut·ter /'stʌtɚ/ *vb* [T/I] : to have a speech problem that causes you to repeat the beginning sound of some words ▪ *a child who stutters* ▪ *He stuttered something that I didn't understand.* — **stutter** *n* [*singular*] ▪ *He has a stutter.* ▪ *He speaks with a stutter.* — **stut·ter·er** /'stʌtərɚ/ *n* [C]

sty /'staɪ/ *n, pl* **sties** *also* **styes** [C] **1** : a place where pigs are kept : PIGSTY **2** *or* **stye** *medical* : a painful, swollen red area on the edge of an eyelid

¹**style** /'staɪəl/ *n* **1** [C/U] : a particular way in which something is done, created, or performed ▪ *a unique singing/writing style* ▪ *The room was decorated in (a) modern style.* **2** [C] : a particular form or design of something ▪ *a style of architecture* ▪ *clothing styles* **3** [C] : a way of behaving or of doing things ▪ *an abrasive management style* ▪ *I like your style.* **4** [U] : a particular way of living ▪ *He has*

been living in high style. [=the way rich people live] **5** [U] : the quality that makes things attractive, fashionable, etc. ▪ *He has a real sense of style.* ▪ *a woman of style* [=a stylish woman] **6** [U] : an easy and graceful manner ▪ *She handled the situation with style.* **7** [C] : the way that written words are spelled, capitalized, etc. ▪ *Each newspaper had its own style.* ▪ *a style guide* — **in style 1** : popular or fashionable ▪ *clothes that are in style* **2** : in a way that is impressive or admired because it shows talent, good taste, etc. ▪ *She likes to travel in style.* — **out of style** : not popular or fashionable ▪ *a fad that has fallen/gone out of style* — **sty·lis·tic** /staɪˈlɪstɪk/ *adj* : *stylistic changes/differences* — **sty·lis·ti·cal·ly** /staɪˈlɪstɪkli/ *adv*

²**style** *vb* **styled; styl·ing** [T] **1** *formal* : to give (yourself) a name or title even if you do not really deserve it ▪ *She styles herself a "spiritual adviser."* **2** : to give a particular shape to (someone's hair) ▪ *She cuts and styles hair.* **3** : to design (something) for a particular purpose ▪ *clothing styled for teenagers*

styling *n* [U] : the way in which something is designed ▪ *a car with sleek styling*

styl·ish /ˈstaɪlɪʃ/ *adj* : following the popular style : FASHIONABLE ▪ *stylish clothes* ▪ *a stylish dresser* — **styl·ish·ly** *adv*

styl·ist /ˈstaɪlɪst/ *n* [C] **1** : a person whose job is to make something (such as a person's hair) look attractive ▪ *a hair stylist* **2** : a person known for writing, singing, etc., in a particular style ▪ *a fine prose/song stylist*

styl·ized *also Brit* **styl·ised** /ˈstajə₁laɪzd/ *adj* : made to look like a style or pattern rather than the way it would really look in nature ▪ *stylized floral motifs*

sty·lus /ˈstaɪləs/ *n, pl* **sty·li** /ˈstaɪˌlaɪ/ *also* **sty·lus·es** /ˈstaɪləsəs/ [C] **1** : ¹NEEDLE 4 **2** : a tool used long ago for writing on clay or wax tablets **3** : a small tool that is used to write or touch buttons on a computer

sty·mie /ˈstaɪmi/ *vb* **-mied; -mie·ing** [T] : to stop (someone) from doing something or to stop (something) from happening ▪ *Progress has been stymied by lack of money.*

Sty·ro·foam /ˈstaɪrəˌfoʊm/ *trademark* — used for a type of light plastic

suave /ˈswɑːv/ *adj* **suav·er; -est** : behaving in a relaxed, confident, and pleasant way in social situations ▪ *a suave businessman* — **suave·ly** *adv* — **sua·vi·ty** /ˈswɑːvəti/ *n* [U]

¹**sub** /ˈsʌb/ *n* [C] *informal* **1** : someone who does the job of another person when that person is not able to do it : SUBSTITUTE ▪ *The team's subs need to be versatile.* **2** : SUBMARINE 1 **3** *US* : SUBMARINE SANDWICH

²**sub** *vb* **subbed; sub·bing** [I] : to take the place of another person ▪ *Smith subbed for Jones at halftime.*

sub- *prefix* **1** : under : beneath : below ▪ *subfreezing* **2 a** : at a lower rank or secondary level ▪ *substation* **b** : division or smaller part of ▪ *subtopic*

sub·atom·ic /ˌsʌbəˈtɑːmɪk/ *adj* **1**

: smaller than an atom ▪ *subatomic particles* **2** : of or relating to the inside of an atom ▪ *subatomic physics*

sub·com·pact /ˈsʌbˌkɑːmˌpækt/ *n* [C] *US* : a very small car

sub·con·scious /ˌsʌbˈkɑːnʃəs/ *adj* : existing in the part of the mind that a person is not aware of ▪ *subconscious desires* — **subconscious** *n* [U] ▪ *Those feelings had been hidden in her subconscious.* — **sub·con·scious·ly** *adv*

sub·con·ti·nent /ˌsʌbˈkɑːntɪnənt/ *n* [C] : a large area of land that is a part of a continent — used especially to refer to the area that includes India, Pakistan, and Bangladesh ▪ *the Indian subcontinent*

sub·con·tract /ˌsʌbˈkɑːnˌtrækt/ *vb* [T/I] : to hire another person or company to do part of a job that you have been hired to do ▪ *Parts of the project were subcontracted (out) to specialists.* — **sub·con·trac·tor** /ˌsʌbˈkɑːnˌtræktɚ/ *n* [C]

sub·cul·ture /ˈsʌbˌkʌltʃɚ/ *n* [C] : a group that has beliefs and behaviors that are different from the main groups within a culture or society ▪ *a subculture of local artists* — **sub·cul·tur·al** /ˌsʌbˈkʌltʃərəl/ *adj*

sub·di·vide /ˌsʌbdəˈvaɪd/ *vb* **-vid·ed; -vid·ing** [T] **1** : to divide (something) into several or many smaller parts ▪ *subdivide a house into several apartments* **2** *US* : to divide (a piece of land) into smaller areas on which houses will be built ▪ *The land was subdivided into building lots.* — **sub·di·vi·sion** /ˈsʌbdəˌvɪʒən/ *n* [C/U] : *a subdivision of land* ▪ (*US*) *She lives in a subdivision.* [=an area of land that has been divided into smaller areas on which houses are built]

sub·due /səbˈduː, *Brit* səbˈdjuː/ *vb* **-dued; -du·ing** [T] **1** : to get control of (a violent or dangerous person or group) by using force, punishment, etc. ▪ *subdue a violent drunk* **2** : to get control of (something, such as a strong emotion) ▪ *subdue your fears*

sub·dued /səbˈduːd, *Brit* səbˈdjuːd/ *adj* : not strong, loud, intense, etc. ▪ *a subdued manner/voice*

sub·ed·i·tor /ˌsʌbˈɛdətɚ/ *n* [C] *Brit* : COPY EDITOR

sub·freez·ing /ˌsʌbˈfriːzɪŋ/ *adj, chiefly US* : colder than the temperature at which water freezes ▪ *subfreezing temperatures*

sub·hu·man /ˌsʌbˈhjuːmən/ *adj* **1** : not having or showing the level of kindness, intelligence, etc., that is expected of normal human beings ▪ *subhuman murders* **2** : not suitable for human beings ▪ *subhuman conditions*

¹**sub·ject** /ˈsʌbˌdʒɪkt/ *n* [C] **1** : the person or thing that is being discussed or described ▪ *Death is a difficult subject to talk about.* ▪ *an excellent book on the subject of linguistics* ▪ *We got on/onto the subject of work.* [=we started talking about work] ▪ *He kept getting off the subject.* [=talking about other things] ▪ *I changed the subject.* [=started a new topic of conversation] ▪ *I dropped the subject.* [=stopped talking about that topic] **2** : an area of knowledge that is studied in school ▪

Chemistry is my favorite subject. **3** : a person or thing that is being dealt with in a particular way — + *of* • *He was the subject of a criminal investigation.* **4** : someone or something that is shown in a photograph, painting, etc. • *a photographer's favorite subject* **5** : a person or animal that is used in an experiment, study, etc. • *a test subject* **6** *grammar* : a noun, noun phrase, or pronoun that performs the action of a verb in a sentence • *"He" is the subject (of the verb "kissed") in the sentence "He kissed me."* **7** : a person who lives in a country that is ruled by a king or queen • *British subjects*

²**sub·ject** /'sʌbdʒɪkt/ *adj* : under the control of a ruler • *subject peoples* • *They were subject to the emperor.* — **subject to 1** : affected by or possibly affected by (something) • *All purchases are subject to tax.* • *The schedule is subject to change.* [=the schedule might change] **2** : likely to do, have, or suffer from (something) • *He is subject to panic attacks.* **3** : dependent on something else to happen or be true • *Rooms are $100 a night, subject to availability.*

³**sub·ject** /səb'dʒɛkt/ *vb* — **subject to** [*phrasal vb*] **subject (someone or something) to** : to cause or force (someone or something) to experience (something harmful, unpleasant, etc.) • *They were subjected to torture.* — **sub·jec·tion** /səb'dʒɛkʃən/ *n* [U]

sub·jec·tive /səb'dʒɛktɪv/ *adj* **1** *philosophy* : relating to the way a person experiences things in his or her own mind • *subjective perceptions* **2** : based on feelings or opinions rather than facts • *a subjective decision* — **sub·jec·tive·ly** *adv* — **sub·jec·tiv·i·ty** /ˌsʌbˌdʒɛk'tɪvəti/ *n* [U]

subject matter *n* [U] : the information or ideas that are discussed or dealt with in a book, movie, etc. • *The film's subject matter is disturbing.*

sub·ju·gate /'sʌbdʒɪˌgeɪt/ *vb* **-gat·ed; -gat·ing** [T] *formal* : to defeat and gain control of (someone or something) by the use of force • *a people subjugated by invaders* — **sub·ju·ga·tion** /ˌsʌbdʒɪ'geɪʃən/ *n* [U]

¹**sub·junc·tive** /səb'dʒʌŋktɪv/ *adj, grammar* : of or relating to the verb form that is used to express suggestions, wishes, uncertainty, possibility, etc. • *In "I wish it were Friday," the verb "were" is in the subjunctive mood.*

²**subjunctive** *n, grammar* **1** **the subjunctive** : the form that a verb or sentence has when it is expressing a suggestion, wish, uncertainty, possibility, etc. • *"I wish it were not so" is in the subjunctive.* **2** [C] : a subjunctive verb or sentence

sub·let /'sʌbˈlɛt/ *vb* **-let; -let·ting** [T/I] **1** : to allow someone to use (an apartment, house, etc., that you are renting) for a period of time in return for payment • *He plans to sublet (his apartment).* **2** : to use (an apartment, house, etc., that is rented by someone) in return for payment • *She agreed to sublet my apartment.* — **sublet** *n* [C]

sub·lime /sə'blaɪm/ *adj* **1** : very beauti-

ful or good • *Her paintings are sublime.* **2** : complete or extreme • *sublime ignorance* — **the sublime** : something that is very beautiful or good • *They have brought ordinary food to the level of the sublime.* — **sub·lime·ly** *adv*

sub·lim·i·nal /sʌb'lɪmənəl/ *adj* : relating to things that influence your mind in a way that you do not notice • *an ad containing subliminal messages* • *subliminal advertising* — **sub·lim·i·nal·ly** *adv*

sub·ma·chine gun /ˌsʌbmə'ʃiːn-/ *n* [C] : a small, light machine gun

sub·ma·rine /'sʌbməˌriːn/ *n* [C] **1** : a ship that can operate underwater • *nuclear submarines* **2** *US* : SUBMARINE SANDWICH

submarine sandwich *n* [C] *US* : a sandwich that is made by splitting a long roll and filling it with meat, cheese, etc.

sub·merge /səb'məːdʒ/ *vb* **-merged; -merg·ing 1** [T] : to cover (someone or something) with a liquid • *The town was submerged by the flood.* **2** [I] : to go underwater • *The divers prepared to submerge.* **3** [T] : to make (yourself) fully involved in an activity or interest • *He submerged himself in his work.*

sub·mers·ible /səb'məːsəbəl/ *adj* : able to be used underwater • *a submersible pump*

sub·mis·sion /səb'mɪʃən/ *n* **1 a** [C/U] : an act of giving a document, proposal, piece of writing, etc., to someone so that it can be considered or approved • *the electronic submission of tax returns* **b** [C] : something that is submitted • *Over 5,000 submissions were received.* **2** [U] : the state of being obedient • *submission to God's will* • *The prisoners were beaten into submission.*

sub·mis·sive /səb'mɪsɪv/ *adj* : willing to obey someone else • *submissive children/behavior* — **sub·mis·sive·ly** *adv*

sub·mit /səb'mɪt/ *vb* **-mit·ted; -mit·ting 1** [T] : to give (a document, proposal, etc.) to someone so that it can be considered or approved • *Submit your application no later than July 1st.* **2** [I] : to stop trying to fight or resist something • *He refused to submit (to their demands).* **3** [T] *formal* : to offer (something) as an opinion or suggestion • *I submit that his guilt has not been proven.*

sub·nor·mal /ˌsʌb'noəməl/ *adj, technical* : lower or smaller than normal • *subnormal temperatures*

¹**sub·or·di·nate** /sə'boədənət/ *adj* **1** : in a position of less power or authority than someone else • *a subordinate officer* • *The priests are subordinate to the bishops.* **2** : less important than someone or something else • *a subordinate concern*

²**subordinate** *n* [C] : someone who has less power or authority than someone else • *She treats her subordinates well.*

³**sub·or·di·nate** /sə'boədəˌneɪt/ *vb* **-nat·ed; -nat·ing** [T] *formal* : to think of or treat (someone or something) as less important than someone or something else • *His personal life has been subordinated to his career.* — **sub·or·di·na·tion** /sə-ˌboədə'neɪʃən/ *n* [U]

sub·par /ˈsʌbˌpɑɚ/ adj, US : below a usual or normal level ▪ a subpar performance

sub-plot /ˈsʌbˌplɑːt/ n [C] : a plot that is related to but less important than the main plot of a story

sub·poe·na /səˈpiːnə/ n [C] law : a written order that commands someone to appear in court to give evidence — **subpoena** vb -naed; -na·ing [T] ▪ He was subpoenaed [=ordered to appear in court] to testify.

sub·scribe /səbˈskraɪb/ vb -scribed; -scrib·ing [I] 1 : to pay money to get a publication or service regularly ▪ I subscribe to that magazine. 2 : to agree to buy shares in a company ▪ She subscribed for 100 shares. — **subscribe to** [phrasal vb] : to agree with or support (an opinion, theory, etc.) ▪ I don't subscribe to that idea. — **sub-scrib·er** n [C]

sub·scrip·tion /səbˈskrɪpʃən/ n [C/U] : an agreement that you make with a company to get a publication or service regularly and that you usually pay for in advance ▪ a magazine/newspaper subscription ▪ I'm going to renew/cancel my subscription.

sub·sec·tion /ˈsʌbˌsɛkʃən/ n [C] : a part of a section especially of a legal document

sub·se·quent /ˈsʌbsəkwənt/ adj, formal : happening or coming after something else ▪ Subsequent studies confirmed their findings. ▪ events subsequent to the war — **sub·se·quent·ly** /ˈsʌbsəˌkwɛntli/ adv ▪ She graduated from college and subsequently [=afterward] moved to New York.

sub·ser·vi·ent /səbˈsɚvijənt/ adj 1 : very willing or too willing to obey someone else ▪ a subservient wife ▪ She refused to be subservient to her husband. 2 formal : less important than something or someone else ▪ Your rights are not subservient to mine. — **sub·ser·vi·ence** /səbˈsɚvijəns/ n [U]

sub·set /ˈsʌbˌsɛt/ n [C] technical : a group of things, people, etc., that is part of a larger group ▪ A subset of the patients experienced side effects.

sub·side /səbˈsaɪd/ vb -sid·ed; -sid·ing [I] 1 : to become less strong or intense ▪ The pain subsided. 2 : to move down to a lower level ▪ The flood finally subsided.

¹**sub·sid·iary** /səbˈsɪdiˌeri, Brit səbˈsɪdiəri/ adj 1 : not as important as something else ▪ a subsidiary issue 2 : owned or controlled by another company ▪ a subsidiary corporation

²**subsidiary** n, pl -iar·ies [C] : a company that is owned or controlled by another company

sub·si·dize also Brit **sub·si·dise** /ˈsʌbsəˌdaɪz/ vb -dized; -diz·ing [T] : to help someone or something pay for the costs of (something) ▪ The state subsidizes housing for low-income families. ▪ subsidized agriculture — **sub·si·di·za·tion** also Brit **sub·si·di·sa·tion** /ˌsʌbsədə-ˈzeɪʃən, Brit ˌsʌbsəˌdaɪˈzeɪʃən/ n [U]

sub·si·dy /ˈsʌbsədi/ n, pl -dies [C] : money that is paid usually by a government to keep the price of a product or service low or to help a business or or-ganization to continue to function ▪ housing/farm subsidies

sub·sist /səbˈsɪst/ vb — **subsist on** [phrasal vb] : to use (something) as a way to stay alive ▪ The villagers subsist primarily on rice and fish.

sub·sis·tence /səbˈsɪstəns/ n [U] : the amount of food, money, etc., that is needed to stay alive ▪ Farming is their means of subsistence. ▪ **subsistence farming/agriculture** [=farming that provides just enough food to live on]

sub·son·ic /ˌsʌbˈsɑːnɪk/ adj : slower than the speed of sound ▪ subsonic aircraft/speeds

sub·spe·cies /ˈsʌbˌspiːʃiz/ n [C] : a group of related plants or animals that is smaller than a species

sub·stance /ˈsʌbstəns/ n 1 [C] a : a material of a particular kind ▪ hazardous substances ▪ a powdery substance b : a drug that is considered harmful and whose use is controlled by law or made illegal ▪ He had a history of substance abuse. ▪ a controlled substance [=a drug that you need permission from a doctor to use] 2 [U] a : the quality of being meaningful, useful, or important ▪ The book lacks substance. b : the quality of being true or believable ▪ These rumors are without substance. [=are not true] 3 [U] : the most basic or necessary part or quality of something ▪ the substance of my argument ▪ These two books differ in style and substance. [=content] — a man/woman/person of substance literary : a person who is rich and powerful ▪ She married a man of substance.

sub·stan·dard /ˌsʌbˈstændɚd/ adj : below what is considered standard, normal, or acceptable ▪ substandard housing

sub·stan·tial /səbˈstænʃəl/ adj 1 : large in amount, size, or number ▪ a substantial number of people ▪ a substantial amount of money 2 : strongly made ▪ a substantial house 3 of food : enough to satisfy hunger ▪ a substantial meal

sub·stan·tial·ly /səbˈstænʃəli/ adv 1 : very much ▪ He makes substantially more money. 2 : in a general or basic way ▪ The methods are substantially the same.

sub·stan·ti·ate /səbˈstænʃiˌeɪt/ vb -at·ed; -at·ing [T] formal : to prove the truth of (something) ▪ He offered no evidence to substantiate his claim. — **sub·stan·ti·a·tion** /səbˌstænʃiˈeɪʃən/ n [U]

¹**sub·sti·tute** /ˈsʌbstəˌtuːt, Brit ˈsʌbstə-ˌtjuːt/ n [C] 1 : a person or thing that takes the place of someone or something else ▪ a sugar/meat substitute ▪ Watching the movie is a poor substitute for reading the book. 2 US : SUBSTITUTE TEACHER — **substitute** adj, always before a noun ▪ a substitute mother/father

²**substitute** vb -tut·ed; -tut·ing 1 [T] : to put or use (someone or something) in place of someone or something else ▪ If cream is unavailable, you can substitute milk (for the cream). 2 [I] : to do the job of someone else or serve the function of something else ▪ She'll be substituting for the regular teacher today. 3 [T] : to replace (one person or thing) with another

• *They substituted real candles with electric ones.* = *Real candles were substituted by/with electric ones.* — **sub·sti·tu·tion** /ˌsʌbstəˈtuːʃən, *Brit* ˌsʌbstəˈtjuːʃən/ *n* [C/U] • *The cookbook has a list of substitutions for ingredients that may be hard to find.*

substitute teacher *n* [C] *US* : a teacher who teaches a class when the usual teacher is not available

sub·stra·tum /ˈsʌbˌstreɪtəm/ *n, pl* **-stra·ta** /-ˌstreɪtə/ [C] : a layer of something (such as soil or rock) that is under another layer • *(figurative) the city's social substrata*

sub·ter·fuge /ˈsʌbtəˌfjuːdʒ/ *n* [C/U] *formal* : the use of tricks especially to hide, avoid, or get something • *a clever subterfuge* • *They obtained the documents by/through subterfuge.*

sub·ter·ra·nean /ˌsʌbtəˈreɪnijən/ *adj, formal* : located or living under the surface of the ground • *subterranean caverns*

sub·ti·tle /ˈsʌbˌtaɪtl/ *n* [C] **1** : words that appear on the screen during a movie, video, or television show and that are translations of what the actors are saying • *a Chinese film with English subtitles* **2** : a title that comes after the main title of a book and that often gives more information about the contents of the book — **subtitle** *vb* **-ti·tled; -ti·tling** [T] • *Subtitle a film.* — *a subtitled movie*

sub·tle /ˈsʌtl/ *adj* **sub·tler; sub·tlest 1** : hard to notice or see • *a subtle difference/change* **2** : not showing your real purpose • *subtle hints* **3** : having or showing skill at recognizing and understanding things that are not obvious • *She has a subtle mind.* — **sub·tly** /ˈsʌtli/ *adv*

sub·tle·ty /ˈsʌtlti/ *n, pl* **-ties 1** [U] : the quality or state of being subtle • *The movie lacks subtlety.* **2** [C] : a small detail that is usually important but not obvious — usually plural • *the subtleties of social interaction*

sub·to·tal /ˈsʌbˌtoʊtl/ *n* [C] : the sum of a set of numbers that is then added to another number or set of numbers • *Your subtotal is $14, and with tax, that will be $14.70.*

sub·tract /səbˈtrækt/ *vb* [T/I] : to take (a number or amount) from another number or amount • *If we subtract 5 from 9, we get 4.* • *The children learned how to add and subtract.*

sub·trac·tion /səbˈtrækʃən/ *n* [U] mathematics : the act or process of subtracting one number from another • *The children learned addition and subtraction.*

sub·trop·ics /ˌsʌbˈtrɑːpɪks/ *n* — **the subtropics** : parts of the world that are close to the tropics — **sub·trop·i·cal** /ˌsʌbˈtrɑːpɪkəl/ *adj* • *a subtropical region*

sub·urb /ˈsʌˌbɚb/ *n* [C] : a town or other area where people live in houses near a larger city • *a suburb of Chicago* • *She lives in the suburbs.* [=one of the suburbs near a city] — **sub·ur·ban** /səˈbɚbən/ *adj* • *a suburban family/house*

sub·ur·ban·ite /səˈbɚbəˌnaɪt/ *n* [C] : a person who lives in a suburb

sub·ur·bia /səˈbɚbijə/ *n* [U] : suburbs in general • *a common problem in suburbia*; *also* : people who live in suburbs • *the values of suburbia*

sub·ver·sive /səbˈvɚsɪv/ *adj* **1** : secretly trying to ruin or destroy a government, political system, etc. • *subversive groups/activities* **2** : criticizing something in a clever and indirect way in order to make it weaker or less effective • *a subversive sense of humor* — **subversive** *n* [C] • *a group of subversives* [=subversive people]

sub·vert /səbˈvɚt/ *vb* [T] *formal* **1** : to secretly try to ruin or destroy a government, political system, etc. • *They conspired to subvert the government.* **2** : to make (something) weaker or less effective • *trying to subvert the electoral process* — **sub·ver·sion** /səbˈvɚʒən/ *n* [C/U]

sub·way /ˈsʌbˌweɪ/ *n* [C] **1** *chiefly US* : a system of underground trains in a city • *I took/rode the subway to midtown.* • *a subway car/station* **2** *Brit* : a road or passage for walking under a road, set of railroad tracks, etc.

sub·ze·ro /ˌsʌbˈzirou/ *adj* : below zero degrees • *subzero temperatures*

suc·ceed /səkˈsiːd/ *vb* **1** [I] **a** : to do what you are trying to do • *She hopes to succeed* [=do well] *at her job.* • *He will never succeed in this business.* **b** : to happen in the planned or desired way • *The plan just might succeed.* **2 a** [T] : to come after (something) in a series • *The new model will succeed the current one next spring.* **b** [T/I] : to get a particular job, position, or title after the person who had it before you has retired, died, etc. • *She will succeed him as chair of the committee.* • *James I succeeded to the throne* [=became king] *in 1603.*

suc·ceed·ing /səkˈsiːdɪŋ/ *adj* : coming after something • *now and for succeeding decades*

suc·cess /səkˈsɛs/ *n* **1** [U] **a** : the fact of getting or achieving wealth, respect, or fame • *Success came easily to him.* • **the secret of my success** [=why I am successful] **b** : the correct or desired result of an attempt • *Did you have any/much success?* [=did you succeed?] • *The project met with little success.* [=was not successful] • *He tried to do it but without success.* **2** [C] : someone or something that is successful • *The play was an immediate success.* [=it was immediately popular]

suc·cess·ful /səkˈsɛsfəl/ *adj* **1** : having the correct or desired result • *a successful attempt* **2** : having gotten or achieved wealth, respect, or fame • *a successful businesswoman* — **suc·cess·ful·ly** *adv*

suc·ces·sion /səkˈsɛʃən/ *n* **1** [U] : the act of getting a title or right when someone else dies or is no longer able or allowed to have it • *His succession to the throne occurred in 1603.* [=he became king in 1603]; *also* : the process by which this happens • *royal succession* **2** [C] : a series of people or things that come one after the other • *a succession of visitors* — **in succession** : following one after the other • *She listed the names in* **quick/rapid succession.**

suc·ces·sive /sək'sɛsɪv/ adj, always before a noun : following one after the other in a series • the third successive day — **suc·ces·sive·ly** adv

suc·ces·sor /sək'sɛsɚ/ n [C] : a person who has a job, position, or title after someone else • the successor to the throne

success story n [C] : a successful person or thing • That company is one of this area's biggest success stories.

suc·cinct /sə'sɪŋkt/ adj : using few words to state or express an idea • a succinct description — **suc·cinct·ly** adv

suc·cor (US) or Brit **suc·cour** /'sʌkɚ/ n [U] literary : something that you do or give to help someone • giving succor to those in need — **succor** (US) or Brit **succour** vb -cored; -cor·ing [T] • succoring those in need

suc·co·tash /'sʌkəˌtæʃ/ n [U] US : a cooked dish consisting of corn and lima beans

suc·cu·lent /'sʌkjələnt/ adj 1 : full of juice • a succulent steak/orange 2 of plants : having thick, heavy leaves or stems that store water • Cacti are succulent plants. — **suc·cu·lence** /'sʌkjələns/ n [U] — **succulent** n [C] • cacti and other succulents

suc·cumb /sə'kʌm/ vb [I] somewhat formal 1 : to stop trying to resist something • You must not succumb (to the pressure/temptation). 2 : to die • She eventually succumbed (to cancer).

¹**such** /'sʌtʃ/ adj 1 always before a noun — used to say that something is great in degree, quality, or number • I've been such a fool! [=I've been very foolish] • Why are you in such a rush? • The building had deteriorated to **such a degree** [=so much] that they had to tear it down. • I was surprised that the town had changed to **such an extent** [=so much] 2 not before a noun — used to say that something has a quality that results in something specified • The evidence is **such as to** leave no doubt. = The evidence is **such that** there can be no doubt. 3 always before a noun : of the kind specified • She has published her first sci-fi novel and hopes to write more such novels. • "Can I talk to Mary?" "I'm sorry. There is no such person here." [=there is no one named Mary here] • I've never heard of **such a thing!** • "You will apologize at once!" "I'll do **no such thing!**" [=I will not apologize] • There is **no such thing as** having too many friends. [=you cannot have too many friends] • She said she was too busy **or some such** nonsense. [=or something similar]

²**such** pron, somewhat formal 1 : that kind or type of person or thing • It is a serious problem and should be treated **as such**. [=as a serious problem] 2 : something previously stated or specified • We were outnumbered and surrounded. Such being the case [=since that was the case], we had to surrender. • If you have a receipt, please enclose a copy of such. [=a copy of the receipt] — **and such** : and things of that kind • Pens, pencils, markers, and such are in this drawer. — **as such** 1 : of the usual or expected kind •

I have no boss as such [=there is no one who is actually my boss], but I do have to answer to my clients. 2 : by, of, or in itself — used to indicate that something is being considered by itself and not along with other things • There's nothing wrong with chocolate as such, but it's best to eat it in moderation. — **such is life** : life is like that and cannot be changed • We've had our share of problems, but such is life.

³**such** adv 1 somewhat informal — used to make a description more forceful • She wears such stylish clothes. [=her clothes are very stylish] • We had such a good time! 2 : to the degree that is specified or understood • I have never seen such a large cat! — **ever such** see EVER — **such as** 1 — used to introduce an example or series of examples • You will need a form of identification, such as a driver's license. • "I have my reasons for not wanting to go." "Such as?" [=give me an example] 2 : of the specified kind • Questions such as the one you've asked are difficult to answer. — **such as it is** — used to say that something is not very good in quality or condition • Welcome to my humble home—such as it is.

¹**such and such** adj, always before a noun : not named or specified • people from such and such areas • If you were born in **such and such** a year . . .

²**such and such** pron : something that is not specified • If you earn such and such per year, then . . .

such·like /'sʌtʃˌlaɪk/ adj, always before a noun, chiefly Brit : sharing qualities or characteristics : SIMILAR • rakes, shovels, and suchlike things

suck /'sʌk/ vb 1 a [T] : to pull (liquid, air, etc.) into your mouth especially while your lips are forming a small hole • sucking milk through a straw b [T/I] : to pull on (something in your mouth) with the muscles of your lips and mouth • a child sucking (on) his thumb c [T/I] : to let (candy, medicine, etc.) stay in your mouth as it melts • I sucked (on) a cough drop. 2 [T] a : to pull (something) with the force of moving water, air, etc. • The tide almost sucked us out to sea. b : to remove (something) from an area or substance by pulling it with the force of moving water, air, etc. • These plants suck moisture from the soil. • The vacuum cleaner sucked up the dirt. 3 [T] : to make (part of your body) flatter or tighter by pulling your muscles inward — + in • He sucked in his gut. [=pulled in his stomach so he would seem thinner] 4 [T] : to cause (someone) to become involved or interested in something — + in or into • Their exciting lifestyle sucked me in. • Many people got sucked into the scheme. 5 [I] informal + sometimes impolite a : to be very bad or unpleasant • You lost your job? That sucks. b : to do something very badly • I suck at golf [=I play golf badly] — **suck up** [phrasal vb] 1 informal + disapproving : to try to get the approval of someone in authority by saying and doing helpful and friendly things that are not sincere • She's always sucking up to the boss. 2 **suck it up** US, *informal* : to do or deal with something unpleasant by making a special effort • *I know you don't want to see him, but you'll just have to suck it up and be polite.*

¹suck·er /'sʌkə/ *n [C]* **1** *informal* : a person who is easily tricked or deceived • *There's a sucker born every minute.* [=there are many people who are easily tricked or deceived] **2** *informal* : a person who is very strongly attracted to a particular type of thing or person — + *for* • *He's a sucker for women with dark hair.* **3** *chiefly US, informal* : an annoying person or thing • *I got the other window open, but I can't get this sucker* [=this window] *to budge.* **4** : a part of an animal's body that is used for sucking or for attaching to things • *the suckers on an octopus's arms* **5** : a new branch that grows from the base of a plant **6** *US, informal* : LOLLIPOP

²sucker *vb* — **sucker into** [*phrasal vb*] **sucker (someone) into** *US, informal* : to deceive or trick (someone) in order to make that person do (something) • *How did I get suckered into (doing) this?*

suck·le /'sʌkəl/ *vb* **suck·led**; **suck·ling** [*T*] : to give (a baby or young animal) milk from a breast or from an udder • *a cat suckling her kittens*

su·crose /'suːˌkroʊs/ *n [U] technical* : a type of sugar that is found in most plants and that is commonly used for cooking and baking

suc·tion /'sʌkʃən/ *n [U]* : the act or process of removing the air, water, etc., from a space in order to pull something into that space or in order to cause something to stick to a surface • *The vacuum cleaner picks up dirt by suction.*; *also* : the force with which the air, water, etc., in a space is removed • *a vacuum cleaner with enough suction to do the job*

suction cup *n [C]* : a round, shallow cup made of a flexible material (such as rubber) that you attach to a surface by pressing the cup against the surface until the air between the cup and surface is removed

sud·den /'sʌdn/ *adj* : happening, coming, or done very quickly in a way that is usually not expected • *a sudden change/decision/urge* • *sudden fame* — **all of a sudden** : SUDDENLY • *All of a sudden, it started raining.* — **sud·den·ness** /'sʌdnnəs/ *n [U]*

sudden death *n [U] sports* : a period of extra play that is added when teams or players are tied at the end of normal play and that ends as soon as one team or player scores a point or gains the lead • *We won 27–24 in sudden death.* • *a sudden-death play-off*

sud·den·ly /'sʌdnli/ *adv* : very quickly in usually an unexpected way • *Suddenly the lights went out.* • *She suddenly decided to quit her job.*

suds /'sʌdz/ *n [plural]* : bubbles that form on top of water that contains soap — **sud·sy** /'sʌdzi/ *adj* **suds·i·er**; **-est** • *sudsy water*

sue /'suː, *Brit* 'sjuː/ *vb* **sued**; **su·ing** [*T/I*] : to use a legal process against a person, company, or organization that has treat-

ed you unfairly or hurt you in some way : to bring a lawsuit against someone or something • *They have threatened to sue (the company) for damages.* [=to sue to get money for the unfair treatment, damage, etc., that they have suffered] • *His wife is suing (him) for divorce.*

suede /'sweɪd/ *n [U]* : soft leather that has been rubbed on one side to make a surface that looks and feels like velvet • *a suede jacket*

su·et /'suːwət/ *n [U]* : a type of hard fat that is found in beef and mutton

suf·fer /'sʌfə/ *vb* **1** [*T/I*] : to experience pain, illness, or injury • *He died instantly and did not suffer.* • *She suffers from arthritis.* • *She suffered an injury.* **2** [*T/I*] : to experience something unpleasant • *We suffered a great deal during the war.* • *The team suffered a defeat.* • *He broke the law, so he has to suffer the consequences.* **3** [*I*] : to become worse because of being badly affected by something • *He was working so hard that his health began to suffer.* — **suf·fer·er** /'sʌfərə/ *n [C]* • *asthma sufferers*

suf·fer·ing /'sʌfərɪŋ/ *n* **1** [*U*] : pain that is caused by injury, illness, loss, etc. • *ways to alleviate human suffering* **2** [*plural*] : feelings of pain • *the sufferings of the dying*

suf·fice /sə'faɪs/ *vb* **-ficed**; **-fic·ing** [*I*] : to be or provide as much as is needed • *You don't need to write a letter. A phone call will suffice.* — **suffice (it) to say** — used to say that you could give more information about something but that the statement that follows is enough • *Suffice to say, she has a lot of work to do with four children.*

suf·fi·cient /sə'fɪʃənt/ *adj, somewhat formal* : ENOUGH • *A brisk walk is sufficient to raise your heart rate.* • *A 15 percent tip is sufficient.* — **suf·fi·cien·cy** /sə'fɪʃənsi/ *n, pl* **-cies** [*C/U*] — **suf·fi·cient·ly** *adv* • *Her health has improved sufficiently to allow her to return to work.*

suf·fix /'sʌfɪks/ *n [C]* : a letter or a group of letters that is added to the end of a word to change its meaning or to form a different word • *The word "smokeless" is formed by adding the suffix "-less" to the noun "smoke."*

suf·fo·cate /'sʌfəˌkeɪt/ *vb* **-cat·ed**; **-cat·ing** **1 a** [*I*] : to die because you are unable to breathe • *Don't put your head in a plastic bag—you could suffocate.* • *(figurative) I'm suffocating in this job.* [=I can't express myself, act freely, etc., in this job] **b** [*T*] : to kill (someone) by making breathing impossible • *The victims were suffocated.* • *(figurative) Anger and resentment slowly suffocated their marriage.* **2** [*I*] : to be uncomfortable because there is not enough fresh air • *We were suffocating in the stuffy room.* — **suf·fo·ca·tion** /ˌsʌfə'keɪʃən/ *n [U]*

suf·frage /'sʌfrɪdʒ/ *n [U]* : the right to vote in an election • *women who fought for suffrage*

suf·frag·ette /ˌsʌfrɪ'dʒɛt/ *n [C]* : a woman who worked to get voting rights for women in the past when women were not allowed to vote

suf·frag·ist /ˈsʌfrɪdʒɪst/ n [C] : a person in the past who worked to get voting rights for people who did not have them

suf·fuse /səˈfjuːz/ vb -fused; -fus·ing [T] literary : to spread over or fill (something) • *The room was suffused with morning light.*

¹**sug·ar** /ˈʃʊgɚ/ n **1 a** [U] : a sweet substance that comes from plants and is used to make foods sweeter • *Do you take sugar in your coffee?* • *a lump/cube/packet of sugar* **b** [C] : the amount of sugar in one spoonful, lump, packet, etc. • *coffee with two sugars* **2** [C] technical : any one of various substances that are found in plants and that your body uses or stores for energy • *simple/complex sugars*

²**sugar** vb [T] : to put sugar on or in (something) • *She sugared her coffee.* • *heavily sugared tea* [=tea with a lot of sugar added]

sugar beet n [C] : a white beet that is grown for the sugar in its root

sug·ar·cane /ˈʃʊgɚˌkeɪn/ n [U] : a tall grass that is grown in warm places as a source of sugar

sug·ar·coat /ˈʃʊgɚˌkoʊt/ vb [T] : to talk about or describe (something) in a way that makes it seem more pleasant or acceptable than it is • *She doesn't sugarcoat her opinions.* • *a sugar-coated version of history*

sug·ary /ˈʃʊgɚi/ adj **1** : tasting like sugar or containing a lot of sugar • *sugary breakfast cereals* **2** disapproving : showing or expressing a pleasant emotion in a way that seems excessive and false • *a sugary ballad*

sug·gest /səˈdʒɛst/ vb [T] **1** : to mention (something) as a possible thing to be done, used, thought about, etc. • *I suggest (that) you call the store.* • *She suggested several solutions.* **2** : to say that (someone or something) is good or deserves to be chosen • *Who would you suggest for the job?* **3** : to show that (something) is likely or true • *The evidence suggests arson as the cause of the fire.* **4** : to say (something) in an indirect way • *Are you suggesting (that) he cheated?* — **suggest itself** somewhat formal, of an idea, plan, etc. : to be thought of • *No good solution suggested itself.* [=I was unable to think of a good solution]

sug·gest·ible /səˈdʒɛstəbəl/ adj : likely to believe that what someone says is true or may be true • *a very/highly suggestible person*

sug·ges·tion /səˈdʒɛstʃən/ n **1** [C] **a** : an idea about what someone should do or how someone should behave • *May I offer/make a suggestion?* • *I am open to suggestions.* [=willing to hear new ideas] **b** : something that is said in an indirect way • *I'm shocked at the suggestion that he cheated.* **2 a** [C/U] : an action, quality, appearance, etc., that seems to indicate the presence or existence of something • *There was a/some suggestion of boredom in his voice.* **b** [C] : a very small amount of something • *chocolate with a (slight) suggestion of pepper* **3** [U] : the process by which you make people think or feel something by saying, expressing, or

showing something that is related only indirectly • *The director relies on the power of suggestion rather than explicitly showing the murder.* — **at/on someone's suggestion** : because someone said that you should • *On his suggestion, I applied for the job.* • *She went to Germany at my suggestion.*

sug·ges·tive /səˈdʒɛstɪv/ adj **1 a** : bringing thoughts, memories, or feelings into the mind — + of • *music suggestive of a past era* **b** : showing or seeming to show something — + of • *symptoms suggestive of AIDS* **2** : causing or tending to cause sexual feelings or excitement • *a suggestive nightgown* — **sug·ges·tive·ly** adv

¹**sui·cid·al** /ˌsuːˈsaɪdl̩/ adj **1** : wanting to kill yourself • *suicidal psychiatric patients* : showing a desire to kill yourself • *suicidal thoughts* **2** : very dangerous : likely to cause your death • *a suicidal mission* : likely to cause great harm to yourself • *Supporting a tax increase would be politically suicidal.*

¹**sui·cide** /ˈsuːwəˌsaɪd/ n **1 a** [C/U] : the act of killing yourself because you do not want to continue living • *Authorities have ruled the death a suicide.* • *He committed suicide.* [=he killed himself] • *He attempted suicide.* [=he tried to kill himself] **b** [C] : a person who commits suicide • *Her father was a suicide.* [=he killed himself] **2** [U] : an action that ruins or destroys your career, social position, etc. • *Accepting that kind of support is political suicide.*

²**suicide** adj, always before a noun : of or relating to suicide • *a suicide attempt* • *He left a suicide note.* [=a note explaining why he killed himself] • *a suicide pact* [=an agreement between two or more people to kill themselves at the same time] • *a suicide bomber* [=a person who commits suicide by exploding a bomb in order to kill other people]

¹**suit** /ˈsuːt/ n **1** [C] : a set of clothes that usually consists of a jacket and a skirt or pair of pants that are made out of the same material **2** [C] : a set of clothes or protective covering that is worn for a special purpose or under particular conditions • *a gym suit* • *a suit of armor* **3** [C/U] : LAWSUIT • *a civil/criminal suit* • *He filed/brought (a) suit* [=started legal proceedings] *against her.* **4** [C] : all the cards that have the same symbol in a pack of playing cards • *The trump suit is hearts/clubs/diamonds/spades.* **5** [C] informal + disapproving : a person who has an important job in an office and who wears a suit • *Get back to work. The suits just walked in.* — **birthday suit** see BIRTHDAY — **follow suit** see FOLLOW

²**suit** vb [T] **1 a** : to provide what is required or wanted by or for (someone or something) • *The restaurant offers meals to suit* [=please] *all tastes.* • *He only helps out when it suits him.* [=when he wants to] **b** : to be proper or suitable for (someone or something) • *The job suits her.* **2** : to be attractive on (someone) • *The dress suits her.* — **suit up** [phrasal vb] US : to put on a uniform or special clothing •

The players are suiting up for the game. — **suit yourself** *informal* : to do what you want to do — used especially to tell people that they can do what they want even though you do not think it is what they should do ▪ *"I don't want to go." "Suit yourself. We'll go without you."* — **suited** /ˈsuːtəd/ *adj* ▪ *The land is well suited for farming.* ▪ *Who is best/most suited to the job?*

suit·able /ˈsuːtəbəl/ *adj* : having the qualities that are right, needed, or appropriate for something ▪ *The dress was a suitable choice.* ▪ *The movie is not suitable for children.* — **suit·abil·i·ty** /ˌsuːtə-ˈbɪləti/ *n* [U] — **suit·ably** /ˈsuːtəbli/ *adv*

suit·case /ˈsuːtˌkeɪs/ *n* [C] : a large case that you use to carry your clothing and possessions when you are traveling ▪ *pack a suitcase*

suite /ˈswiːt/ *n* [C] **1 a** : a group of rooms that is used for one purpose ▪ *a suite of offices* **b** : a group of rooms in a hotel that is used by one person, couple, family, etc. ▪ *She checked into a suite.* **2** : a piece of music that is made up of many short pieces that are taken from a larger work (such as a ballet) ▪ *the Nutcracker Suite* **3** *chiefly Brit* : a set of matching pieces of furniture for a room ▪ *a bedroom suite*

suit·or /ˈsuːtɚ/ *n* [C] *old-fashioned* : a man who wants to marry a particular woman ▪ *She had many suitors.*

sul·fate (*US*) *or chiefly Brit* **sul·phate** /ˈsʌlˌfeɪt/ *n* [C/U] *chemistry* : a salt that is formed when sulfuric acid reacts with another chemical element ▪ *copper sulfate*

sul·fide (*US*) *or chiefly Brit* **sul·phide** /ˈsʌlˌfaɪd/ *n* [C/U] *chemistry* : a compound that contains sulfur and one or more other chemical elements

sul·fur (*US*) *or chiefly Brit* **sul·phur** /ˈsʌlfɚ/ *n* [U] : a yellow chemical element that has a strong, unpleasant odor when it is burned and that is used in making paper, gunpowder, medicine, etc. — **sul·fu·rous** (*US*) *or chiefly Brit* **sul·phu·rous** /ˈsʌlfərəs/ *adj*

sul·fu·ric acid (*US*) *or chiefly Brit* **sul·phu·ric acid** /ˌsʌlˈfjɚɪk-/ *n* [U] *chemistry* : a very strong type of acid

sulk /ˈsʌlk/ *vb* [I] : to be angry or upset about something and to refuse to discuss it with other people ▪ *He is sulking in his room.* — **sulk** *n* [C] ▪ *He is in a sulk.* [=he is sulking]

sulky /ˈsʌlki/ *adj* **sulk·i·er; -est 1** : angry or upset about something and refusing to discuss it with others ▪ *She is sulky today.* ▪ *a sulky mood* **2** : often quiet and angry or upset ▪ *a sulky child*

sul·len /ˈsʌlən/ *adj* **1** — used to describe an angry or unhappy person who does not want to talk, smile, etc. ▪ *a sullen teenager/mood* **2** *literary* : gray and dark ▪ *a sullen sky/morning* — **sul·len·ly** *adv* — **sul·len·ness** /ˈsʌlənnəs/ *n* [U]

sul·ly /ˈsʌli/ *vb* **-lies; -lied; -ly·ing** [T] *formal* : to damage or ruin the good quality of (something) ▪ *The scandal sullied her reputation.*

sulphate, sulphide, sulphur, sul-

phuric acid *chiefly Brit* spellings of SULFATE, SULFIDE, SULFUR, SULFURIC ACID

sul·tan /ˈsʌltn/ *n* [C] : a king or ruler of a Muslim state or country

sul·try /ˈsʌltri/ *adj* **sul·tri·er; -est 1** : very hot and humid ▪ *a sultry day* **2** : attractive in a way that suggests or causes feelings of sexual desire ▪ *a sultry woman/dress/voice* — **sul·tri·ness** /ˈsʌltrinəs/ *n* [U]

¹sum /ˈsʌm/ *n* **1** [C] : an amount of money ▪ *We spent large sums (of money) repairing the house.* ▪ *a small/modest sum (of money)* **2** [C] **a** : the result of adding two or more numbers together ▪ *The sum of 5 and 7 is 12.* **b** : a simple problem in mathematics — usually plural ▪ *schoolchildren doing sums* **3** [*singular*] : the whole amount of something ▪ *Working odd summer jobs has been the sum of my experience.* [=has been all the experience I've had] — **in sum 1** : as a brief statement of the most important information in a piece of writing or speech ▪ *In sum, we need a better public health-care system.* **2** : in a few words ▪ *The movie was, in sum, entertaining as well as educational.* — **sum and substance** : the general or basic meaning of something said or written ▪ *What is the sum and substance of the argument?* — **sum of its parts** ◇ Something that is *greater/better/more than the sum of its parts* is better or more effective as a team, combination, etc., than you would expect it to be when you look at the different parts that form it.

²sum *vb* **summed; sum·ming** — **sum up** [*phrasal vb*] **1 sum up** *or* **sum up (something)** *or* **sum (something) up** : to tell (information) again using fewer words ▪ *She sums up the main arguments of the essay in the final paragraph.* **2 sum up (someone or something)** *or* **sum (someone or something) up a** : to describe or show the most important parts or qualities of (someone or something) in a brief or simple way ▪ *The article nicely sums up her career.* **b** : to describe (someone or something) using few words ▪ *The word "lazy" sums him up pretty well.* ▪ *"So, you don't want to go because you think it will be boring?" "That just about sums it up."*

su·mac /ˈʃuːˌmæk, ˈsuːˌmæk/ *n* [C/U] : a type of tree, bush, or vine that has many small leaves and produces red or white berries

sum·ma·rize (*US*) *also Brit* **sum·ma·rise** /ˈsʌməˌraɪz/ *vb* **-rized; -riz·ing** [T/I] : to tell (information) again using fewer words ▪ *I would like to take a moment to summarize (the facts that I presented earlier).* ▪ *To summarize, we need better schools.* — **sum·ma·ri·za·tion** *also Brit* **sum·ma·ri·sa·tion** /ˌsʌmərəˈzeɪʃən, *Brit* ˌsʌmərˈaɪˈzeɪʃən/ *n* [C/U]

¹sum·ma·ry /ˈsʌməri/ *n, pl* **-ries** [C] : a brief statement that gives the most important information about something ▪ *He concluded the report with a brief summary.* — **in summary** : as a brief statement of the most important information in a piece of writing or speech ▪ *In summary, we need a better public health-care system.*

²**summary** *adj, always before a noun* 1 : using few words to give the most important information about something ▪ *a summary account/report* 2 *formal* : done quickly in a way that does not follow the normal process ▪ *a summary court proceeding* — **sum·mar·i·ly** /səˈmɛrəli/ *adv, formal* ▪ *He was summarily dismissed.*

sum·ma·tion /səˈmeɪʃən/ *n* [C] 1 *formal* : a brief description of the most important information about something ▪ *We gave a summation of our discovery.* 2 *US, law* : a final speech made by a lawyer in a court of law to give a summary of the main arguments in a case ▪ *The attorneys made their final summations.*

¹**sum·mer** /ˈsʌmɚ/ *n* [C/U] : the warmest season of the year that is after spring and before autumn ▪ *What are your plans for (this) summer?* ▪ *We visited them two summers ago.* ▪ *a summer job/vacation/camp* — **sum·mery** /ˈsʌmɚi/ *adj* ▪ *summery weather*

²**summer** *vb* [I] : to spend the summer in a particular place ▪ *We summer in Maine.*

sum·mer·house /ˈsʌmɚˌhaʊs/ *n* [C] 1 *chiefly Brit* : a covered structure in a garden or park that is used as a resting place in summer 2 **summer house** : a house that someone lives in during the summer ▪ *a summer house by the lake* — called also *summer home*

summer school *n* [C/U] : special classes that are taught at a school during the summer

summer squash *n* [C/U] *US* : a long, usually yellow vegetable that is a type of squash

sum·mer·time /ˈsʌmɚˌtaɪm/ *n* [U] : the season of summer ▪ *in the summertime*

sum·mit /ˈsʌmət/ *n* [C] 1 a : the highest point of a mountain ▪ *the summit of Mount Everest* ▪ the highest level ▪ *the summit of his career* 2 : a meeting or series of meetings between the leaders of two or more governments ▪ *an economic summit* ▪ *a summit meeting*

sum·mon /ˈsʌmən/ *vb* [T] *formal* 1 a : to order (someone) to come to a place ▪ *The queen summoned him to the palace.* b : to order (someone) to appear in a court of law ▪ *She was summoned to (appear in) court.* 2 : to ask for (someone or something) to come ▪ *She summoned a doctor.* 3 : to get (the courage, energy, strength, etc., that you need to do something) by making a special effort ▪ *He finally summoned (up) the courage to ask her on a date.* 4 : to ask or order a group of people to come together for (a meeting) ▪ *The president summoned a meeting/conference.* — **summon up** [*phrasal vb*] : to bring (a memory, feeling, image, etc.) into the mind ▪ *Visiting his old house summoned up memories of his childhood.*

sum·mons /ˈsʌmənz/ *n* 1 [C/U] *law* : an official order to appear in a court of law ▪ *He was served with a summons (to appear in court).* ▪ *a writ/service of summons*

2 [C] : an official order to appear at a particular place ▪ *a royal summons*

su·mo /ˈsuːˌmoʊ/ *n* [U] : a Japanese form of wrestling that is performed by very large men ▪ *sumo wrestlers*

sump pump *n* [C] *US* : a pump that removes water from underneath a house or building

sump·tu·ous /ˈsʌmpʃəwəs/ *adj* : very expensive, rich, or impressive ▪ *a sumptuous banquet* — **sump·tu·ous·ly** *adv* — **sump·tu·ous·ness** *n* [U]

sum total *n* — **the sum total** : the whole amount ▪ *That's the sum total of what I know about cars.* [=that's all I know about cars]

¹**sun** /ˈsʌn/ *n* 1 a **the sun** also **the Sun** : the star that the Earth moves around and that gives the Earth heat and light ▪ *The sun is shining.* b [C] : any star that has planets which move around it ▪ *distant suns* 2 [U] : sunshine or sunlight ▪ *The plant needs full sun.* [=it should not be in the shade] ▪ *We went to the beach to get/catch some sun.* [=to spend time in the sunlight] — **in the sun** ◇ If someone or something has a **day/moment/time** (etc.) **in the sun**, that person or thing is popular during a period of time. ▪ *The singer is still waiting for his day in the sun.* — **under the sun** : in the world — used to emphasize the large number of things that are being mentioned ▪ *We talked about everything under the sun.*

²**sun** *vb* sunned; sun·ning [T/I] : to sit or lie in the light of the sun especially in order to make your skin darker ▪ *They were sunning (themselves) by the pool.*

Sun. *abbr* Sunday

sun·bathe /ˈsʌnˌbeɪð/ *vb* -bathed; -bath·ing [I] : to sit or lie in the sunlight especially in order to make your skin darker ▪ *They were sunbathing on the beach.* — **sun·bath·er** /ˈsʌnˌbeɪðɚ/ *n* [C]

sun·beam /ˈsʌnˌbiːm/ *n* [C] : a ray of sunlight

sun·block /ˈsʌnˌblɑːk/ *n* [C/U] : a lotion that you put on your skin to prevent sunburn by completely blocking out the sun's rays

sun·burn /ˈsʌnˌbɚn/ *n* [C/U] : a condition in which your skin becomes sore and red from too much sunlight ▪ *a bad sunburn* ▪ *Sunscreen prevents sunburn.*

sun·burned /ˈsʌnˌbɚnd/ *adj* : sore and red from too much sunlight ▪ *a sunburned nose*

sun·dae /ˈsʌnˌdeɪ/ *n* [C] : a dessert of ice cream that is topped with a sweet sauce, nuts, whipped cream, etc. ▪ *a hot-fudge sundae*

Sun·day /ˈsʌnˌdeɪ/ *n* [C/U] : the day of the week between Saturday and Monday ▪ *She visited me last Sunday.* ▪ *I arrived on Sunday.* ▪ *Sunday brunch* — abbr. **Sun.** — **Sun·days** *adv* ▪ *He works Sundays.* [=he works every Sunday]

Sunday school *n* [C/U] : a school especially for children that is held on Sunday for religious education

sun·di·al /ˈsʌnˌdajəl/ *n* [C] : a device that is used to show the time of day by the position of the sun and that consists of a plate with markings like a clock and an object with a straight edge that casts a shadow onto the plate

sun·down /'sʌn₁daʊn/ n [U] chiefly US : SUNSET ▪ Passover ends at sundown.

sun·dry /'sʌndri/ adj, always before a noun, formal : made up of different things ▪ sundry [=various] items — all and sundry formal : every person ▪ It was clear to all and sundry that something was wrong.

sun·flow·er /'sʌn₁flawɚ/ n [C] : a tall plant that has very large yellow flowers and that produces seeds which can be eaten ▪ sunflower seeds/oil

sung past tense and past participle of SING

sun·glass·es /'sʌn₁glæsəz, Brit 'sʌn₁glɑːsəz/ n [plural] : glasses with dark lenses that protect the eyes from the sun ▪ a pair of sunglasses

sunk past tense and past participle of ¹SINK

sunk·en /'sʌŋkən/ adj 1 always before a noun : lying at the bottom of a sea, lake, layer, etc. ▪ a sunken ship 2 : curving inward because of illness, age, etc. ▪ sunken [=hollow] cheeks 3 always before a noun : lying or built at a lower level than the surrounding area ▪ a sunken living room

sun·less /'sʌnləs/ adj : having little light from the sun ▪ a sunless room/day

sun·light /'sʌn₁laɪt/ n [U] : the light of the sun ▪ Sunlight streamed through the windows.

sun·lit /'sʌn₁lɪt/ adj : lighted by the sun ▪ a sunlit room

sun·ny /'sʌni/ adj sun·ni·er; -est 1 : having plenty of bright sunlight ▪ a sunny room/day ▪ sunny weather 2 : cheerful and happy ▪ a sunny smile/disposition

sun·rise /'sʌn₁raɪz/ n 1 [U] : the time when the sun appears above the horizon in the morning ▪ We were up before/at sunrise. 2 [C/U] : the colors that are in the sky when the sun slowly appears above the horizon ▪ a beautiful sunrise

sun·roof /'sʌn₁ruːf/ n [C] : a part of the roof of a car or truck that can be opened to let air and light in

sun·room /'sʌn₁ruːm/ n [C] US : a room in a house that has a lot of windows and glass to let sunlight in

sun·screen /'sʌn₁skriːn/ n [C/U] : a lotion that you put on your skin to prevent sunburn by blocking out some of the sun's rays

sun·set /'sʌn₁sɛt/ n 1 [U] : the time when the sun goes below the horizon in the evening ▪ We arrived just before sunset. ▪ We worked from sunrise to sunset. 2 [C/U] : the colors that are in the sky when the sun slowly goes below the horizon ▪ the golden light of sunset

sun·shine /'sʌn₁ʃaɪn/ n [U] 1 : warmth and light from the sun ▪ Enjoy the sunshine! 2 informal : a feeling of happiness ▪ She brought sunshine into our lives. ▪ She was a ray of sunshine. [=she made others feel happier and more cheerful]

sun·tan /'sʌn₁tæn/ n [C] : a browning of the skin that is caused by the sun's rays ▪ She has a nice suntan. [=tan] — suntan lotion — sun·tanned /'sʌn₁tænd/ adj ▪ suntanned bodies/faces

sun·up /'sʌn₁ʌp/ n [U] chiefly US : SUNRISE ▪ We will meet at sunup.

¹su·per /'suːpɚ/ adj, informal : extremely good ▪ She's a super cook. ▪ The party was super.

²super adv, US, informal : very or extremely ▪ She's super nice/rich/smart.

³super n [C] US, informal : SUPERINTENDENT 3

super- prefix 1 : bigger, better, or more important than others of the same kind ▪ superhuman 2 : superior in position or rank ▪ a military superpower

su·perb /su'pɚb/ adj : extremely good ▪ They've done a superb job. — **su·perb·ly** adv ▪ a superbly gifted writer

Super Bowl service mark — used for the annual championship game of the National Football League

su·per·charged /'suːpɚ₁tʃɑɚdʒd/ adj, informal : filled with energy, tension, or emotion ▪ a supercharged atmosphere

su·per·cil·ious /₁suːpɚ'sɪlijəs/ adj, formal + disapproving : having or showing the proud and unpleasant attitude of people who think that they are better or more important than other people ▪ a supercilious professor

su·per·com·put·er /'suːpɚkəm₁pjuːtɚ/ n [C] : a large and very fast computer

su·per·ego /₁suːpɚ'iː₁goʊ/ n, pl -egos [C] psychology : a part of a person's mind that relates to attitudes about what is right and wrong and to feelings of guilt

su·per·fi·cial /₁suːpɚ'fɪʃəl/ adj 1 : concerned only with what is obvious or apparent : not thorough or complete ▪ superficial changes/solutions 2 : affecting or involving only the outer part or surface ▪ superficial damage/wounds ▪ These similarities/differences are only superficial. 3 disapproving : not caring about or involving important matters or deep emotions ▪ He thinks she's a rather superficial. [=shallow] — **su·per·fi·ci·al·i·ty** /₁suːpɚ₁fɪʃi'æləti/ n [U] — **su·per·fi·cial·ly** /₁suːpɚ'fɪʃəli/ adv

su·per·flu·ous /su'pɚfluwəs/ adj, formal : beyond what is needed ▪ a superfluous word/detail ▪ Further discussion seemed superfluous.

su·per·he·ro /'suːpɚ₁hiroʊ/ n, pl -roes [C] : a fictional character who has amazing powers (such as the ability to fly) ▪ comic-book superheroes

su·per·high·way /₁suːpɚ'haɪ₁weɪ/ n [C] US : a large and wide highway used for traveling at high speeds over long distances

su·per·hu·man /₁suːpɚ'hjuːmən/ adj : greater than normal human power, size, or ability ▪ superhuman strength/courage/powers

su·per·im·pose /₁suːpɚɪm'poʊz/ vb -posed; -pos·ing [T] : to place or lay (something) over something else ▪ superimposed images ▪ (figurative) We should not superimpose our values onto other cultures. [=we should not try to make other cultures adopt/accept our values]

su·per·in·ten·dent /₁suːpɚɪn'tɛndənt/ n [C] 1 : a person who directs or manages a place, department, organization, etc. ▪ a park superintendent 2 : a high rank in a police department or a person who has this rank **3** *US* : a person who is in charge of cleaning, maintaining, and repairing a building

¹su·pe·ri·or /sʊˈpɪrijɚ/ *adj* **1 a** : high or higher in quality ▪ *superior products/results* ▪ *The new model is (vastly/far) superior to the old one.* **b** : great or greater in amount, number, or degree ▪ *The army was overwhelmed by superior numbers.* **2** *disapproving* **a** : better than other people ▪ *He only helps us because it makes him feel superior.* **b** : having or showing the attitude of people who think that they are better or more important than other people : ARROGANT ▪ *a superior manner/tone* **3** *always before a noun* : high or higher in rank ▪ *your superior officer* — su·pe·ri·or·i·ty /sʊˌpɪriˈorəti/ *n* [*U*] ▪ *one product's superiority over another* ▪ *a false sense of superiority* ▪ *the country's technological/economic superiority*

²superior *n* [*C*] : a person of higher rank or status than another ▪ *Report any problems to your immediate superior.*

su·per·la·tive /sʊˈpɚlətɪv/ *adj* **1** *grammar* : of or relating to the form of an adjective or adverb that is used to indicate the greatest degree of a particular quality ▪ *The superlative form of "nice" is "nicest."* **2** *somewhat formal* : of very high quality ▪ *a superlative performance* — superlative *n* [*C*] *grammar* ▪ *"Simplest" is the superlative of "simple."*

su·per·man /ˈsuːpɚˌmæn/ *n, pl* -men /-ˌmɛn/ [*C*] : a man who is very strong, successful, etc.

su·per·mar·ket /ˈsuːpɚˌmɑɚkət/ *n* [*C*] : a store where customers can buy a variety of foods and usually household items ▪ *I made a quick trip to the supermarket.*

su·per·mod·el /ˈsuːpɚˌmɑːdl̩/ *n* [*C*] : a very famous and successful fashion model

su·per·nat·u·ral /ˌsuːpɚˈnætʃərəl/ *adj* : of, relating to, or seeming to come from magic, a god, etc. ▪ *supernatural powers/phenomena/beings* — the supernatural : things that cannot be explained by science and seem to involve ghosts, spirits, magic, etc. ▪ *a belief in the supernatural*

su·per·pow·er /ˈsuːpɚˌpawɚ/ *n* [*C*] : an extremely powerful nation ▪ *economic/military superpowers*

su·per·sede /ˌsuːpɚˈsiːd/ *vb* -sed·ed; -sed·ing [*T*] : to take the place of (someone or something that is old, no longer useful, etc.) ▪ *This edition supersedes the previous one.*

su·per·son·ic /ˌsuːpɚˈsɑːnɪk/ *adj* : faster than the speed of sound ▪ *a supersonic airplane*

su·per·star /ˈsuːpɚˌstɑɚ/ *n* [*C*] : an extremely famous and successful performer, athlete, etc. ▪ *a Hollywood/football superstar*

su·per·sti·tion /ˌsuːpɚˈstɪʃən/ *n* [*C/U*] : a belief that certain events or things will bring good or bad luck ▪ *It is a common superstition that a black cat crossing your path is bad luck.*

su·per·sti·tious /ˌsuːpɚˈstɪʃəs/ *adj* : of,

relating to, or influenced by superstition ▪ *superstitious practices/beliefs* ▪ *He's very superstitious.*

su·per·store /ˈsuːpɚˌstoɚ/ *n* [*C*] : a very large store that sells a wide variety of goods ▪ *an electronics superstore*

su·per·struc·ture /ˈsuːpɚˌstrʌktʃɚ/ *n* [*C*] : the part of a structure (such as a ship or bridge) that is above the lowest part

su·per·vise /ˈsuːpɚˌvaɪz/ *vb* -vised; -vis·ing [*T*] : to watch and direct (someone or something) ▪ *She supervises a staff of 30 workers.* ▪ *a supervised study period*

su·per·vi·sion /ˌsuːpɚˈvɪʒən/ *n* [*U*] : the action or process of watching and directing what someone does or how something is done ▪ *Parental supervision is recommended.* ▪ *The medication should be taken under a doctor's supervision.*

su·per·vi·sor /ˈsuːpɚˌvaɪzɚ/ *n* [*C*] : a person who supervises someone or something ▪ *I had a meeting with my supervisor.* ▪ *an office/factory supervisor* — su·per·vi·so·ry /ˌsuːpɚˈvaɪzɚri/ *adj* ▪ *a supervisory position/role*

su·per·wom·an /ˈsuːpɚˌwʊmən/ *n, pl* -wom·en /-ˌwɪmən/ [*C*] : a woman who is very strong, successful, etc.

sup·per /ˈsʌpɚ/ *n* **1** [*C/U*] : the evening meal — used especially to refer to an informal meal that you eat at home ▪ *It's almost time for supper.* **2** [*C*] *chiefly US* : a social event especially for raising money that takes place in the evening and includes a meal ▪ *a church supper* **3** [*C/U*] *chiefly Brit* : a light meal or snack that is eaten late in the evening

sup·plant /səˈplænt/ *vb* [*T*] : to take the place of (someone or something that is old or no longer used or accepted) ▪ *Videos have been supplanted by DVDs.*

sup·ple /ˈsʌpl̩/ *adj* sup·pler /ˈsʌplɚ/; -plest /-pləst/ **1** of a body or body part : able to bend or twist easily ▪ *Stretching helped to keep him supple.* [=limber] **2** : soft and able to bend or fold easily ▪ *supple leather/skin* — sup·ple·ness /ˈsʌpl̩nəs/ *n* [*U*]

sup·ple·ment /ˈsʌpləmənt/ *n* [*C*] **1** : something that is added to something else in order to make it complete ▪ *dietary/vitamin supplements* **2** : an extra part that is added to a book or newspaper ▪ *an advertising/literary supplement* — supplement *vb* [*T*] ▪ *He supplements* [=adds to] *his income by selling his paintings.* — sup·ple·men·ta·tion /ˌsʌpləˌmɛnˈteɪʃən/ *n* [*U*]

sup·ple·men·tal /ˌsʌpləˈmɛntl̩/ *adj, chiefly US* : added to something else to make it complete ▪ *supplemental information/income*

sup·ple·men·ta·ry /ˌsʌpləˈmɛntəri/ *adj* : SUPPLEMENTAL ▪ *supplementary materials*

sup·pli·er /səˈplajɚ/ *n* [*C*] : a person or company that supplies goods or services ▪ *food/drug/paper suppliers*

¹sup·ply /səˈplaɪ/ *n, pl* -plies **1** [*C/U*] : the amount of something that is available to be used ▪ *the nation's food/oil supply* ▪ *Doctors are in short supply.* [=there are not enough doctors] **2** [*plural*] : things (such as food, equipment, fuel,

etc.) that are needed for a particular purpose and that will be used by a particular person or group ▪ *basic medical supplies* ▪ *art/office/cleaning supplies* **3** [*U*] : the quantities of goods or services that are offered for sale at a particular time or at one price ▪ *When demand increases, will supply increase, too?*

²**supply** *vb* **-plies; -plied; -ply·ing** [*T*] : to provide someone or something with (something that is needed or wanted) ▪ *You'll have to supply your own food.* ▪ *He kept us supplied with the latest news.*

supply and demand *n* [*U*] : the amount of goods and services that are available for people to buy compared to the amount of goods and services that people want to buy ▪ *If the company produces less of a product than the public wants, the law of supply and demand says that the company can charge more for the product.*

¹**sup·port** /səˈpoət/ *vb* [*T*] **1** : to agree with or approve of (someone or something) ▪ *I completely support your decision.* ▪ *He supports the legislation/war.* **2 a** : to give help or assistance to (someone or something) ▪ *The charity supports needy families.* **b** : to provide what is needed by (someone or something) ▪ *The planet's atmosphere cannot support human life.* **c** : to provide the money that is needed by or for (someone or something) ▪ *She has two children to support.* **3** : to hold (something or someone) up ▪ *The roof is supported by pillars.* **4** : to help show that (something) is true ▪ *Their claims are not supported by the evidence.* **5** *chiefly Brit* : to be a fan of (a sports team) ▪ *She supports both teams.*

²**support** *n* **1** [*U*] : approval of someone or something ▪ *There isn't much support for the proposal.* [=few people support the proposal] ▪ *The team gets a lot of support from its fans.* **2** [*U*] **a** : the act of helping someone by giving love, encouragement, etc. ▪ *Thank you for your love and support.* ▪ *Her friends were there to provide moral support.* [=to give her encouragement] **b** : help that is given in the form of money or other valuable things ▪ *They had no means of support.* [=source of income] — see also CHILD SUPPORT **c** : the act of helping someone by giving information or services ▪ *She called technical/tech support.* [=a department or person that helps people with computer problems] ▪ *the company's support staff* **3 a** [*C*] : something that holds a person or thing up and stops that person or thing from falling down ▪ *the bridge's supports* **b** [*U*] : the act of holding something up ▪ *He grabbed the railing for support.* **4** [*U*] : evidence which shows that something is true ▪ *The results give support to the hypothesis.* — **in support of 1** : in a way that shows approval of (something) ▪ *A majority voted in support of the bill.* **2** : in order to support (something) ▪ *He presented evidence in support of his hypothesis.* [=evidence that helps to prove his hypothesis]

sup·port·er /səˈpoətɚ/ *n* [*C*] : a person

who supports someone or something ▪ *the proposal's supporters* ▪ *the team's loyal supporters*

support group *n* [*C*] : a group of people who have similar experiences and concerns and who meet in order to provide emotional help, advice, and encouragement for one another ▪ *a support group for recovering alcoholics*

sup·port·ive /səˈpoətɪv/ *adj* : giving help or encouragement to someone ▪ *She has very supportive parents.*

sup·pose /səˈpouz/; *supposed* is pronounced səˈpous when followed by *to*/ *vb* **-posed; -pos·ing** [*T*] **1** : to think of (something) as happening or being true in order to imagine what might happen ▪ *Just suppose for a moment that you agreed with me.* ▪ *Supposing he refuses to help, what do we do then?* **2 a** : to believe (something) to be true ▪ *Who do you suppose* [=*think*] *will win?* **b** : to believe (something) to be possible ▪ *"Do you suppose it's true?" "Yes, I suppose it is."* ▪ *I suppose you're right.* ✧ The phrase **I suppose (so)** is used as a way of agreeing or saying "yes" when you are not certain or not very excited or interested. ▪ *"Do you want to come along?" "I suppose so."* [=*I guess so*] ✧ The phrase **I suppose not** is used as an informal way of agreeing with a negative statement or of saying "no." ▪ *"That wasn't a very smart thing to do, was it?" "I suppose not."* — **be supposed 1 a** : to be expected to *do* something ▪ *She was supposed to be here an hour ago.* **b** : to be intended or expected *to be* (something) ▪ *The party was supposed to be a surprise.* **c** — used to show that you are angry or offended by something; followed by *to + verb* ▪ *What's that supposed to mean?* [=what do you mean by that comment?] **2** — used to say what someone should do or is allowed to do; followed by *to + verb* ▪ *You are supposed to listen to your parents.* ▪ *Are you supposed to be here?* **3** — used to indicate what people say about someone or something; followed by *to + verb* ▪ *She is supposed to be the best doctor in town.* [=people say that she's the best doctor in town]

sup·posed /səˈpouzəd/ *adj, always before a noun* — used to say that a statement or description is probably not true or real even though many people believe that it is ▪ *a supposed cure for cancer* ▪ *supposed experts*

sup·pos·ed·ly /səˈpouzədli/ *adv* : according to what someone has said or what is generally believed to be true or real ▪ *These detergents are supposedly better for the environment.* ▪ *Supposedly, she left a message on my answering machine. I never got it.*

sup·po·si·tion /ˌsʌpəˈzɪʃən/ *n* [*C/U*] : an idea or theory that you believe is true even though you do not have proof ▪ *just (an) idle supposition*

sup·press /səˈprɛs/ *vb* [*T*] **1** : to end or stop (something) by force ▪ *suppressing a rebellion* **2** : to keep (something) secret ▪ *The governor tried to suppress the news.* ▪ *The judge may suppress the evidence.* [=not allow the evidence to be used at a trial] **3 a :** to not allow yourself to feel, show, or be affected by (an emotion) ▪ *I had to suppress the urge to tell him what I really thought.* **b :** to stop yourself from doing something that might bother other people ▪ *She tried to suppress a cough/laugh.* [=tried not to cough/laugh] **4 :** to slow or stop the growth, development, or normal functioning of (something) ▪ *The pill suppresses your appetite.* — **sup·pres·sion** /səˈprɛʃən/ *n* [*U*] ▪ *political suppression* ▪ *the suppression of evidence*

sup·pres·sant /səˈprɛsnt/ *n* [*C*] : a drug that prevents or controls something ▪ *cough/appetite suppressants*

su·prem·a·cist /səˈprɛməsɪst/ *n* [*C*] : a person who believes that one group of people is better than all other groups and should have control over them ▪ *racial/religious/cultural supremacists* ▪ *white supremacists*

su·prem·a·cy /səˈprɛməsi/ *n* [*U*] : the quality or state of having more power, authority, or status than anyone else ▪ *military/economic supremacy*

su·preme /səˈpriːm/ *adj* **1 :** highest in rank or authority ▪ *She reigns supreme* [=is the best] *in tennis.* **2 :** greatest or highest possible ▪ *a problem of supreme importance* — **su·preme·ly** *adv* ▪ *supremely* [=extremely] *confident/boring/imaginative*

supreme court *or* **Supreme Court** *n* [*singular*] : the highest court of law in a country or U.S. state ▪ *The case went all the way to the (U.S.) Supreme Court.*

su·pre·mo /səˈpriːmoʊ/ *n, pl* **-mos** [*C*] *Brit, informal* : a person who has the most authority or power in a particular activity ▪ *a banking supremo*

Supt. (*US*) *or chiefly Brit* **Supt** *abbr* superintendent

sur·charge /ˈsɚˌtʃɑɚdʒ/ *n* [*C*] : an amount of money that must be paid in addition to the regular price ▪ *a $20 fuel surcharge*

¹**sure** /ˈʃɚ, *Brit* ˈʃɔː/ *adj* **sur·er; -est 1** *not before a noun* : convinced or certain ▪ *I am sure (that) everything will be fine.* ▪ *Are you sure about this?* **2 :** not allowing any doubt or possibility of failure ▪ *One sure way to improve your health is to stop smoking.* ▪ *It's a **sure thing** that they'll win.* [=it is certain that they'll win] **3** — used to say that something will definitely happen or that someone will definitely do something; usually followed by *to* + *verb* ▪ *I'll be sure to call when I get home.* **4 :** known to be true or correct ▪ *Nothing else is sure.* ▪ *One thing is (for) sure, we'll never eat there again.* [=we certainly will never eat there again] **5 a :** firm or solid ▪ *a sure hold/grip* ▪ *(figurative) He lacks a sure grasp of the issue.* [=he does not understand the issue well] **b :** calm, steady, and confident ▪ *the sure hands of a surgeon* — **be sure** — used to tell someone not to forget to do something ▪ *Be sure to lock the door when you leave.* — **for sure :** without a doubt ▪ *No one knows for sure* [=for certain] *what happened.* ▪ *"We don't want that to happen again." "That's for sure!"* [=that is certainly true] — **make sure :** to find out

or do something so that you have no doubt about whether something is true, correct, will happen, etc. ▪ *Make sure (that) you turn the oven off.* — **sure of yourself 1 :** confident in your abilities ▪ *He was never very sure of himself as a comedian.* **2** *somewhat disapproving* : overly confident or arrogant ▪ *They seem awfully sure of themselves.* — **sure thing** *informal* — used to say "yes" or to agree to a request or suggestion ▪ *"Can you be here in five minutes?" "Sure thing."* — **to be sure** *formal* — used to say that you admit that something is true ▪ *It will be challenging, to be sure, but I am confident that we will succeed.* — **sure·ness** /ˈʃɚnəs, *Brit* ˈʃɔːnəs/ *n* [*U, singular*]

²**sure** *adv, informal* **1 a** — used to say "yes" or to agree to a request or suggestion ▪ *"Can you help me with this?" "Sure."* [=certainly] **b** — used to disagree with a negative statement or situation ▪ *"I don't think he's coming." "Sure he is. He's just a little late."* **2** — used to emphasize that you agree with the first part of the statement that you are about to make ▪ *Sure, she's talented, but she's no superstar.* **3** *US* — used as an informal way to accept someone's thanks ▪ *"Thank you for your help." "Sure."* [=you're welcome] **4** *US* — used for emphasis ▪ *I sure am tired.* ▪ (*impolite*) *I sure as hell hope you know what you're doing!* — **sure enough** — used to say that what happened was not surprising or unexpected ▪ *We were finally ready to go outside, and sure enough, it started to rain.*

sure·fire /ˈʃɚˌfajɚ, *Brit* ˈʃɔːˌfajə/ *adj*, always before a noun, informal : certain not to fail ▪ *The movie is a surefire hit/success.*

sure·foot·ed /ˈʃɚˈfʊtəd, *Brit* ˈʃɔːˈfʊtəd/ *adj* : not likely to slip or fall when walking, climbing, or running ▪ *a surefooted athlete* ▪ *(figurative) a surefooted leader* [=a confident leader who is not likely to make mistakes]

sure·ly /ˈʃɚli, *Brit* ˈʃɔːli/ *adv* **1 :** in a confident way ▪ *She answered quickly and surely.* **2** *formal* : without a doubt : CERTAINLY ▪ *He will surely be missed.* **b** — used in negative statements to show surprise that something could be true ▪ *Surely you haven't forgotten my name!*

¹**surf** /ˈsɚf/ *vb* **1** [*I*] : to ride on ocean waves using a special board ▪ *He learned to surf when he was living in California.* **2** [*T/I*] : to look for information or other interesting things on the Internet ▪ *surfing (on) the Internet/Web* — **surf·er** *n* [*C*] — **surf·ing** *n* [*U*] ▪ *She went surfing yesterday.*

²**surf** *n* [*U*] : large waves that fall on the shore and the white foam and sound that they produce ▪ *the roar of the surf*

¹**sur·face** /ˈsɚfəs/ *n* [*C*] **1 :** an outside part or layer of something ▪ *The bowl has a shiny/textured surface.* **2 :** the upper layer of an area of land or water ▪ *the Earth's surface* ▪ *Bubbles rose/floated to the surface (of the water).* ▪ *(figurative) On the surface the plan seems simple.* [=the plan seems simple when we first look at it but may be more complicated when

we find out more] **3** : a flat or curved side of an object ▪ *each surface of the box*; **especially** : the flat, top part of an object that you can work on ▪ *kitchen work surfaces*

²**surface** *vb* **-faced; -fac·ing 1** [*I*] : to rise to the surface of water ▪ *The submarine surfaced.* **2** [*I*] : to appear or become obvious after being hidden or not seen ▪ *The information surfaced many years later.* **3** [*T*] : to put a surface on (something, such as a road) ▪ *The road needs to be surfaced again.*

surf·board /'sɚf,boɚd/ *n* [*C*] : a long, light, narrow board that is used for surfing

¹**surge** /'sɚdʒ/ *vb* **surged; surg·ing** [*I*] **1** : to move very quickly and suddenly in a particular direction ▪ *We all surged toward the door.* ▪ (*figurative*) *Thoughts were surging through his mind.* **2** : to suddenly increase to an unusually high level ▪ *Housing prices have surged in recent months.* ▪ *surging oil costs*

²**surge** *n* [*C*] **1** : a sudden, large increase ▪ *a surge of excitement/popularity* **2** : a sudden movement of many people ▪ *There was a sudden surge toward the door.* **3** : a sudden increase in the amount of electricity that is flowing through an electrical circuit ▪ *an electrical/power surge*

sur·geon /'sɚdʒən/ *n* [*C*] : a doctor who performs surgery ▪ *a brain/heart surgeon*

sur·gery /'sɚdʒəri/ *n, pl* **-ger·ies 1** [*C/U*] : medical treatment in which a doctor cuts into someone's body in order to repair or remove damaged or diseased parts ▪ *He's a specialist in brain surgery.* ▪ *She is recovering from her surgery.* [=*operation*] ▪ *The patient is still in surgery.* [=*still being operated on*] **2** [*U*] *chiefly US* : the area in a hospital where surgery is performed ▪ *The patient was taken directly to surgery.* **3** *Brit* **a** [*C*] : a place where a doctor or dentist treats people **b** [*U*] : OFFICE HOURS

sur·gi·cal /'sɚdʒɪkəl/ *adj, always before a noun* **1** : of, relating to, or used during the process of performing a medical operation ▪ *a surgical procedure/treatment* ▪ *surgical instruments/gloves/masks* **2** : very careful and accurate ▪ *The work was done with surgical precision.* — **sur·gi·cal·ly** /'sɚdʒɪkli/ *adv* ▪ *The tumor will have to be surgically removed.*

surgical spirit *n* [*U*] *Brit* : RUBBING ALCOHOL

sur·ly /'sɚli/ *adj* **sur·li·er; -est** : rude and unfriendly ▪ *surly customers*

sur·mise /sɚ'maɪz/ *vb* **-mised; -mis·ing** [*T*] *formal* : to form an opinion about something without definitely knowing the truth : GUESS ▪ *We can only surmise what happened.* — **surmise** *n* [*C/U*]

sur·mount /sɚ'maʊnt/ *vb* [*T*] *formal* **1** : to deal with (a problem or a difficult situation) successfully ▪ *She has had to surmount many obstacles in her career.* **2** : to be placed at the top of (something) ▪ *a chain-link fence that is surmounted* [=*topped*] *by barbed wire*

sur·name /'sɚ,neɪm/ *n* [*C*] : the name that is shared by the people in a family ✧

In English, your surname comes after your first name and middle name.

sur·pass /sɚ'pæs, *Brit* sɚ'pɑːs/ *vb* [*T*] : to be better or greater than (someone or something) ▪ *She surpassed* [=*exceeded*] *our expectations.*

sur·plus /'sɚpləs/ *n* [*C/U*] : an amount that is more than the amount that is needed ▪ *If there is any surplus, it will be divided equally.* ▪ *a surplus of workers* ▪ *a $3 million budget surplus* [=*$3 million more than what is needed to pay for all planned expenses*] — **surplus** *adj* ▪ *The government bought the surplus grain/food/supplies.* ▪ (*Brit, formal*) *His services had become surplus to requirements.* [=*no longer needed*]

¹**sur·prise** /sɚ'praɪz/ *n* **1** [*C*] **a** : an unexpected event, piece of information, etc. ▪ *What a pleasant surprise to see you!* ▪ *The news was a (complete/total) surprise to everyone.* [=*everyone was surprised by the news*] **b** : an unexpected gift, party, etc. ▪ *I have a special surprise for you.* **2** [*U*] : the feeling caused by something that is unexpected or unusual ▪ *Imagine our surprise when he suddenly quit.* ▪ *Much to our surprise, she refused.* [=we were very surprised when she refused] **3** — used as an interjection ▪ *Surprise! Happy Birthday!* — **catch/take (someone or something) by surprise** : to happen to (someone or something) unexpectedly ▪ *The question caught him by surprise.* [=surprised him]

²**surprise** *vb* **-prised; -pris·ing** [*T*] **1** : to cause (someone) to feel surprised ▪ *The results surprised me.* **2** : to find, attack, or meet (someone or something) unexpectedly ▪ *A police officer surprised the burglars.*

³**surprise** *adj, always before a noun* : not expected : causing a feeling of surprise ▪ *a surprise visit/success* ▪ *We threw him a surprise party.*

surprised *adj* : having or showing the feeling that people get when something unexpected or unusual happens : feeling or showing surprise ▪ *She had a surprised expression on her face.* ▪ *Are you surprised at/by/about what happened?* ▪ *They were surprised to see us.*

surprising *adj* : unexpected or unusual ▪ *It's not surprising that he doesn't want to go.* ▪ *A surprising number of people were there.* — **sur·pris·ing·ly** /sɚ'praɪzɪŋli/ *adv*

sur·re·al /sə'riːl/ *adj* : very strange or unusual ▪ *a surreal* [=*dreamlike*] *atmosphere/experience*

sur·re·al·ism /sə'riːjə,lɪzəm/ *n* [*U*] : a 20th-century art form in which an artist or writer combines unrelated images or events in a very strange and dreamlike way — **sur·re·al·ist** /sə'riːjəlɪst/ *n* [*C*] — **surrealist** *adj* — **sur·re·al·is·tic** /sə,riːjə'lɪstɪk/ *adj*

¹**sur·ren·der** /sə'rɛndɚ/ *vb* **1** [*T/I*] : to agree to stop fighting, hiding, resisting, etc., because you know that you will not win or succeed ▪ *The enemy finally surrendered after three days of fighting.* ▪ *The suspect surrendered himself (to the police).* ▪ (*figurative*) *She surrendered to*

temptation and ordered dessert. [=she gave in to temptation] **2** [*T*] : to give the control or use of (something) to someone else • *He surrendered* [=handed over] *his weapon to the police.*

²**surrender** *n* [*singular*] **1** : an agreement to stop fighting, hiding, resisting, etc., because you know that you will not win or succeed • *They demanded an unconditional surrender.* • *(figurative) a surrender to desire* **2** : the act of giving the control or use of something to someone else • *the surrender of territory*

sur·rep·ti·tious /ˌsərəpˈtɪʃəs/ *adj* : done in a secret way • *a surreptitious glance/relationship* — **sur·rep·ti·tious·ly** *adv*

sur·ro·ga·cy /ˈsɚrəgəsi/ *n* [*U*] : the practice by which a woman becomes pregnant and gives birth to a baby in order to give it to someone who cannot have children

sur·ro·gate /ˈsɚrəgət/ *n* [*C*] **1** : a person or thing that takes the place or performs the duties of someone or something else • *He could not attend the meeting, so he sent his surrogate.* **2** : SURROGATE MOTHER — **surrogate** *adj, always before a noun* • *She considered them her surrogate family.*

surrogate mother *n* [*C*] : a woman who agrees to become pregnant in order to give the baby to someone who cannot have children

sur·round /səˈraʊnd/ *vb* [*T*] **1** : to be on every side of (someone or something) • *The lake is surrounded by cottages.* **2** : to move close to (someone or something) on all sides often in order to stop a person from escaping • *Police surrounded the house.* **3** : to be closely related or connected to (something) • *There's a lot of uncertainty surrounding the decision.* **4** *of a family, group, etc.* : to always be near (someone) • *As a child she was surrounded by/with family.* — **surround yourself with** (*someone or something*) : to cause (certain types of people or things) to be near you • *He surrounds himself with very talented people.*

sur·round·ing /səˈraʊndɪŋ/ *adj, always before a noun* : near or around someone or something • *the surrounding area/neighborhood/land*

sur·round·ings /səˈraʊndɪŋz/ *n* [*plural*] : the places, conditions, or objects that are around you • *We're becoming familiar with our new surroundings.*

sur·veil·lance /səˈveɪləns/ *n* [*U*] : the act of carefully watching someone or something especially in order to prevent or detect a crime • *government surveillance of suspected terrorists* • *The police kept her under surveillance.* [=watched her closely]

¹**sur·vey** /ˈsɚˌveɪ/ *n, pl* **-veys** [*C*] **1** : an activity in which many people are asked a question or a series of questions in order to gather information about what most people do or think about something : POLL • *a survey on American drinking habits* **2** : an act of studying something in order to make a judgment about it • *a quick survey of the new regulations* **3** : an act of measuring and exam-

ining an area of land • *a land survey* **4** : a general description of or report about a subject or situation • *a survey* [=overview] *of current events* • *a survey course/class* [=a class/course that gives an introduction to a subject]

²**sur·vey** /səˈveɪ/ *vb* **-veys; -veyed; -vey·ing** [*T*] **1** : to ask (many people) a question or a series of questions in order to gather information about what most people do or think about something • *64 percent of the people surveyed said that the economy was doing well.* **2** : to look at and examine all parts of (something) • *The teacher surveyed the room.* **3** : to measure and examine (an area of land) • *Engineers surveyed the property.* **4** *Brit* : to examine (a building) to make sure it is in good condition • *The house must be surveyed.* [=(US) inspected]

sur·vey·or /səˈveɪjɚ/ *n* [*C*] **1** : someone whose job is to measure and examine an area of land • *a land surveyor* **2** *Brit* : someone whose job is to examine buildings

sur·viv·al /səˈvaɪvəl/ *n* [*U*] : the state or fact of continuing to live or exist especially in spite of difficult conditions • *Small businesses are fighting/struggling for survival.* • *survival skills/techniques* • *The doctor said her chance of survival* [=chance that she would get better and continue to live] *was about 50 percent.* — **survival of the fittest** **1** : NATURAL SELECTION **2** — used to refer to a situation in which only the people or things that are strongest, most skillful, etc., are able to succeed or to continue to exist • *In the business world, it's survival of the fittest.*

sur·vive /səˈvaɪv/ *vb* **-vived; -viv·ing** [*I*] **a** : to continue to live • *I don't see how any creature can survive under those conditions.* • *The plant survives on very little water.* **b** : to continue to exist • *Only a few written records survive from those times.* **2** [*T*] : to remain alive after the death of (someone) • *Only his son survived him.* • *She is survived by her three children.* **3** [*T*] **a** : to continue to be alive or to exist after (something) • *The fruit trees didn't survive the harsh winter.* **b** : to continue to function, succeed, etc., in spite of (something) • *He survived a political scandal and was reelected.* • *helpful hints for surviving the holidays*

sur·vi·vor /səˈvaɪvɚ/ *n* [*C*] **1** : a person who continues to live after an accident, illness, someone else's death, etc. • *a Holocaust/cancer survivor* • *There were no survivors.* • *She died and left no survivors.* [=none of her family members were alive after she died] **2** : someone or something that continues to exist, function, compete, etc. • *The survivors of the first round of competition will meet today in the second round.* **3** : someone who is able to keep living or succeeding despite a lot of problems • *There's no question about it—he's a survivor.*

sus·cep·ti·ble /səˈsɛptəbəl/ *adj* : easily affected, influenced, or harmed by something • *The virus can infect susceptible in-*

dividuals. ▪ *He is very susceptible to colds.* — **sus·cep·ti·bil·i·ty** /sə̩sɛptə'bɪləti/ *n* [U, singular]

su·shi /'suːʃi/ *n* [U] : a Japanese dish of cold cooked rice shaped in small cakes and topped or wrapped with pieces of raw fish or other ingredients

¹**sus·pect** /sə'spɛkt/ *vb* [T] **1 a** : to think that (someone) is possibly guilty of a crime or of doing something wrong ▪ *The police suspect him of murder.* ▪ *a suspected arsonist* [=a person who is suspected of being an arsonist] **b** : to think that (something) is possibly the cause of something bad ▪ *The pesticide is suspected of causing cancer.* **c** : to think that (a crime) has possibly been committed ▪ *The fire chief suspects arson.* **2** : to think that (something, especially something bad) possibly exists, is true, will happen, etc. ▪ *We suspected a trap.* ▪ *"We haven't done our homework." "I suspected as much."* **3** : to have feelings of doubt about (something) ▪ *I have reason to suspect her sincerity.*

²**sus·pect** /'sʌˌspɛkt/ *n* [C] : a person who is believed to be possibly guilty of committing a crime ▪ *a murder suspect* ▪ *a possible/prime suspect in the kidnapping*

³**sus·pect** /'sʌˌspɛkt/ *adj* : not able to be trusted : causing feelings of doubt or suspicion ▪ *The witness's claim was suspect.* [=dubious, questionable] ▪ *a suspect odor*

sus·pend /sə'spɛnd/ *vb* [T] **1** : to force (someone) to leave a job, position, or place for a usually short period of time as a form of punishment ▪ *The police officers were suspended without pay.* **2 a** : to stop (something) for a usually short period of time ▪ *The city suspended bus service during the storm.* **b** : to make (something) invalid or ineffective for a usually short period of time ▪ *He's driving with a suspended license.* **3** : to hang something so that it is free on all sides except at the point of support ▪ *They suspended the lantern from the ceiling.* ▪ *a wire suspended between two poles* [=hung so that it is attached at each end to a pole]

suspended sentence *n* [C] *law* : a legal arrangement in which a person who has been found guilty of a crime is not sentenced to jail but may be sentenced for that crime at a future time if he or she commits another crime during a specified period ▪ *The judge handed down a suspended sentence.*

sus·pend·er /sə'spɛndə/ *n* **1** [*plural*] *US* : straps that are used for holding up pants and that go over a person's shoulders — called also (*Brit*) **braces 2** [C] *Brit* : GARTER 2

suspender belt *n* [C] *Brit* : GARTER BELT

sus·pense /sə'spɛns/ *n* [U] : a feeling or state of nervousness or excitement caused by wondering what will happen ▪ *The suspense builds as the story progresses.* ▪ *I don't know who won and the suspense is killing me.* [=I am very anxious to know who won] ▪ *She kept him in suspense.* [=waiting anxiously] — **sus-**

pense·ful /sə'spɛnsfəl/ *adj* ▪ *a suspenseful story/situation/movie*

sus·pen·sion /sə'spɛnʃən/ *n* **1** [C/U] : the act of forcing someone to leave a job, position, or place for a usually short period of time as a form of punishment ▪ *He was angry about his suspension from the team.* ▪ *He's under suspension.* **2** [U, singular] : the act of stopping or delaying something for a usually short period of time ▪ *(a) suspension of peace talks* **3** [C/U] : the act of making something invalid or ineffective for a usually short period of time ▪ *a 30-day license suspension* **4** [U] *technical* : the parts of a vehicle that connect the body to the tires and allow the vehicle to move more smoothly over uneven surfaces ▪ *the car's front/rear suspension*

sus·pi·cion /sə'spɪʃən/ *n* **1** [U] : a feeling that someone is possibly guilty of a crime or of doing something wrong ▪ *He is under suspicion of* [=suspected of] *selling illegal drugs.* ▪ *He was arrested on suspicion of robbery.* [=he was arrested because the police suspect that he committed a robbery] **2** [C] : a feeling that something bad is likely or true ▪ *I have a sneaking suspicion that those cookies aren't really homemade.* **3** [C/U] : a feeling of doubt ▪ *They regard the new policies with suspicion.* ▪ *I have my suspicions about his motives.*

sus·pi·cious /sə'spɪʃəs/ *adj* **1** : causing a feeling that something is wrong or that someone is behaving wrongly ▪ *suspicious activity/behavior* ▪ *The suspicious vehicle was reported to police.* **2** : having or showing a feeling that something is wrong or that someone is behaving wrongly ▪ *Officials are suspicious about her death.* ▪ *His behavior made me suspicious.* ▪ *The dog is suspicious of strangers.* [=the dog does not trust strangers] — **sus·pi·cious·ly** *adv* ▪ *acting/behaving suspiciously*

suss /'sʌs/ *vb* [T] *Brit, informal* : to find or discover (something) by thinking — usually + *out* ▪ *They had to suss out* [=figure out] *whether he was telling the truth.* ▪ *I think I've got him sussed out.* [=I understand what kind of person he is]

sus·tain /sə'steɪn/ *vb* [T] **1** : to provide what is needed for (something or someone) to exist, continue, etc. ▪ *The planet cannot sustain* [=support] *life.* ▪ *a period of sustained* [=continuing] *economic growth* **2** *formal* : to deal with or experience (something bad or unpleasant) ▪ *The army sustained heavy losses.* **3** *law* : to decide or state that (something) is proper, legal, or fair ▪ *The lawyer's objection was sustained.*

sus·tain·able /sə'steɪnəbəl/ *adj* **1** : able to be used without being completely used up or destroyed ▪ *sustainable energy resources* **2** : involving methods that do not completely use up or destroy natural resources ▪ *sustainable agriculture/farming/techniques* **3** : able to last or continue for a long time ▪ *sustainable development/growth* — **sus·tain·abil·i·ty** /sə-

ˌsteɪnəˈbɪləti/ *n* [U] — **sus·tain·ably** /səˈsteɪnəbli/ *adv*

sus·te·nance /ˈsʌstənəns/ *n* [U] *formal* : something (such as food) that keeps someone or something alive • *The village depends on the sea for sustenance.*

su·ture /ˈsuːtʃɚ/ *n* [C] *medical* : a stitch or a series of stitches used to close a cut or wound

SUV /ˌɛsˌjuːˈviː/ *n, pl* **SUVs** [C] : a large vehicle that is designed to be used on rough surfaces but that is often used on city roads or highways — called also *sport-utility vehicle*

svelte /ˈsvɛlt/ *adj* : thin in an attractive or graceful way : SLENDER • *a svelte young actor*

SW *abbr* southwest, southwestern

¹**swab** /ˈswɑːb/ *n* [C] **1** : a small piece of soft material sometimes on the end of a small stick that is used for applying medicine, cleaning a wound, etc. • *a cotton swab* **2** : a small amount of material taken with a swab as a sample from a person's body • *The doctor took a throat swab.*

²**swab** *vb* **swabbed; swab·bing** [T] **1** : to wipe or clean (something) with a swab • *swab a cut with disinfectant* **2** : ²MOP 1 • *sailors swabbing the decks*

swad·dle /ˈswɑːdl̩/ *vb* **swad·dled; swad·dling** [T] : to wrap (someone, especially a baby) tightly with a blanket, pieces of cloth, etc. • *He swaddled the baby in a blanket.*

swag·ger /ˈswæɡɚ/ *n* [C] : a way of walking or behaving that shows you have a lot of confidence • *walks with a swagger* — **swagger** *vb* [I] • *He swaggered in like he owned the place.*

¹**swal·low** /ˈswɑːloʊ/ *vb* **1 a** [T/I] : to take (something) into your stomach through your mouth and throat • *He swallowed the grape whole.* • *Chew your food before you swallow.* **b** [I] : to move the muscles in your throat as if you are swallowing something often because you are nervous • *The boss said, "Come in." I swallowed hard and walked in.* **2** [T] : to flow over and cover (something) completely • *The wave swallowed (up) the boat.* • (*figurative*) *He was swallowed (up) by the crowd.* [=he disappeared into the crowd] **3** [T] *informal* : to accept or believe (something) • *Her story is pretty hard to swallow.* **4** [T] : to not allow yourself to show or be affected by (an emotion) • *She had to swallow her pride and ask for help.*

²**swallow** *n* [C] **1** : an amount that is swallowed at one time : the act of swallowing something • *She took a swallow of water to wash down the pill.* • *He drank it in/with one swallow.* **2** : a small bird that has long wings and a deeply forked tail

swam *past tense of* ¹SWIM

¹**swamp** /ˈswɑːmp/ *n* [C/U] : land that is always wet and often partly covered with water — **swampy** /ˈswɑːmpi/ *adj* **swamp·i·er; -est** • *swampy land*

²**swamp** *vb* [T] **1** : to cover (something) with water • *The boat sank after it was swamped by waves.* **2** : to cause (someone or something) to have to deal with a

very large amount of things or people at the same time • *I'm swamped with work right now.* [=I'm extremely busy right now] • *In the summer, the town is swamped with/by tourists.*

swan /ˈswɑːn/ *n* [C] : a large usually white bird that lives on or near water and that has a very long and graceful neck

swank /ˈswæŋk/ *adj, chiefly US* : SWANKY • *a swank club/hotel/restaurant*

swanky /ˈswæŋki/ *adj* **swank·i·er; -est** *informal* : very fashionable and expensive • *a swanky club/hotel/restaurant*

swan song *n* [C] : the last performance or piece of work by an actor, athlete, writer, etc. • *This tournament will be her swan song.* [=this will be her last tournament]

¹**swap** *also Brit* **swop** /ˈswɑːp/ *vb* **swapped; swap·ping** [T/I] *informal* **1** : to trade or exchange (things) • *He swapped chairs with me.* = *We swapped chairs.* • *I liked her blue notebook and she liked my red one, so we swapped.* **2** : to replace (something) with something else • *He swapped (out) his hard drive for a bigger one.*

²**swap** *n* [C] : an act of giving or taking one thing in return for another thing • *They made the swap in secret.* • *an even swap*

swarm /ˈswoɚm/ *n* [C] : a very large number of insects moving together • *a swarm of bees/mosquitoes/ants/locusts* • (*figurative*) *The tourists arrived in swarms.*

swarm *vb* **1** [I] : to move in a large group • *Bees were swarming near the hive.* • *Spectators swarmed into the stadium.* **2 a** [I] : to be surrounded or filled with a large group of insects, people, etc., moving together • *The island was swarming with tourists.* **b** [T] : to surround (something or someone) with a large group • *The movie star was swarmed by adoring fans.*

swar·thy /ˈswoɚði/ *adj* **swar·thi·er; -est** : having dark skin • *a swarthy man/complexion*

swas·ti·ka /ˈswɑːstɪkə/ *n* [C] : a symbol in the form of a cross with its ends bent at right angles all in the same direction ✧ *The swastika was used as a symbol of the German Nazi Party.*

swat /ˈswɑːt/ *vb* **swat·ted; swat·ting** [T] : to hit (someone or something) with a quick motion • *She swatted the fly with a magazine.* — **swat** *n* [C] • *She gave the ball a swat.* [=she swatted the ball]

SWAT /ˈswɑːt/ *n* [U] *chiefly US* : a police or military unit that is specially trained to handle very dangerous situations • *a SWAT team*

swatch /ˈswɑːtʃ/ *n* [C] : a small piece of cloth that is used as a sample for choosing colors, fabrics, etc. • *fabric swatches*

swath /ˈswɑːθ/ *or* **swathe** /ˈswɑːð/ *n* [C] **1** : a long, wide strip of land • *wide swathes of green countryside* **2** : an area of grass or grain that has been cut or mowed • *He cut a swath through the field.* • (*figurative*) *The tornado cut a swath through the county.*

¹**sway** /ˈsweɪ/ *vb* **1** [I] : to move slowly back and forth • *branches swaying in the*

breeze **2** [*T*] : to cause (someone) to agree with you or to share your opinion • *The lawyer tried to* **sway** *the jury.* • *He can be easily* **swayed.**

²**sway** *n* [*U*] **1** : a slow movement back and forth • *the* **sway** *of her hips* **2** : a controlling force or influence • *He has come/fallen* **under the sway** *of the enemy.* • *The ancient Romans* **held sway** *over most of Europe.*

¹**swear** /ˈsweɚ/ *vb* **swore** /ˈswoɚ/; **sworn** /ˈswoɚn/; **swear·ing** **1** [*T/I*] **a** : to state (something) very strongly and sincerely • *I* **swear** *(that) I saw it.* • *I could have* **sworn** *that I left my keys on the counter.* [=I was sure I left my keys on the counter] • *I didn't do anything wrong. I* **swear.** **b** : to promise very strongly and sincerely to do or not do something • *He swore revenge on the killers.* • *I* **swear to God,** *I'll never do that again.* **2** [*I*] : to use offensive words when you speak • *Don't* **swear** *in front of the children.* • *The other driver* **swore** *at me.* **3** [*T/I*] : to make a formal or official promise especially in a court of law • *I do solemnly* **swear** *to tell the whole truth.* **4** [*T*] : to cause (someone) to make a promise • *Witnesses are* **sworn** *to tell the truth.* — *I* **swear** *informal* — used for emphasis • *I* **swear,** *every time I see her she's got a new boyfriend.* — **swear by** [*phrasal vb*] : to have or express a lot of confidence in (something) • *She* **swears by** *this diet.* — **swear in** [*phrasal vb*] **swear (someone) in** *or* **swear in (someone)** : to place (someone) in a new office or position by having an official ceremony in which that person makes a formal promise to do the work properly, to be honest and loyal, etc. • *The new president will be* **sworn in** *tomorrow.* — **swear off** [*phrasal vb*] *chiefly US* : to stop doing, having, or being involved in (something) • *She tried to* **swear off** *chocolate.*

²**swear** *n* [*C*] *US, informal* : SWEARWORD • *He said a* **swear.**

swear·word /ˈsweɚˌwɚd/ *n* [*C*] : an offensive word • *a movie filled with* **swearwords**

¹**sweat** /ˈswɛt/ *vb* **sweat** *or* **sweat·ed**; **sweat·ing** **1** [*I*] : to produce a clear liquid from your skin when you are hot or nervous • *He* **sweats** *a lot when he exercises.* • (*informal*) *He was* **sweating like a pig.** [=sweating a lot] **2** [*I*] *informal* : to work very hard • *They* **sweated** *and saved so their children could go to college.* • *He* **sweated** *over the wording of his speech for several days.* **3** [*T/I*] *informal* : to worry or be nervous about something • *We'll let them* **sweat it out** *for a while longer.* • *"I'm sorry I'm late." "That's OK. Don't* **sweat** *it."* • *Don't* **sweat the small stuff.** [=don't worry about minor things] • *They were* **sweating over** [=worrying about] *their test scores.* — **sweat blood** *see* BLOOD — **sweat bullets** *US, informal* : to be very nervous or worried • *I was* **sweating bullets** *while I waited.* — **sweat out** [*phrasal vb*] **sweat out (something)** *or* **sweat (something) out** *informal* **1** : to wait nervously until the end of (something) • *It was a close game, and the*

fans were really **sweating it out** *at the end.* **2** *US* : to get or achieve (something, such as a victory) by working very hard • *He managed to* **sweat out** *a narrow victory in the semifinals.*

²**sweat** *n* **1** [*U*] : the clear liquid that forms on your skin when you are hot or nervous • *The runners were dripping with* **sweat.** **2** [*C*] : the state or condition of someone who is sweating • *We* **worked up a sweat.** [=we were sweating] • *I* **broke into a sweat.** [=I began to sweat] **3** [*U*] : hard work • *We built this house with our blood and* **sweat.** **4** [*plural*] *US, informal* : SWEATPANTS — **break a sweat** (*US*) *or Brit* **break sweat** : to begin to sweat • *He loaded all five boxes without* **breaking a sweat.** • (*figurative*) *She answered all the questions without* **breaking a sweat.** [=very easily] — **by the sweat of your brow** : by doing hard, physical work • *He earned his money by the* **sweat of his brow.** — **no sweat** *informal* : with little or no difficulty : EASILY • *"Can you move that for me?" "Sure, no* **sweat."**

sweat·er /ˈswɛtɚ/ *n* [*C*] : a warm usually knitted piece of clothing for the upper part of your body: such as **a** : one that is put on by pulling it over your head — called also (*Brit*) *jumper* **b** *US* : one that opens like a jacket — called also *cardigan*

sweat·pants /ˈswɛtˌpænts/ *n* [*plural*] *chiefly US* : pants made from a thick, soft material that are worn mostly when you are exercising

sweat·shirt /ˈswɛtˌʃɚt/ *n* [*C*] : a piece of clothing for the upper part of your body that is made from a thick, soft material

sweat·shop /ˈswɛtˌʃɑːp/ *n* [*C*] : a place where people work long hours for low pay in poor conditions • *clothing made in* **sweatshops**

sweat suit *n* [*C*] *US* : clothing that consists of a matching sweatshirt and sweatpants

sweaty /ˈswɛti/ *adj* **sweat·i·er**; **-est** **1** : causing you to sweat • *a hot and* **sweaty** *afternoon* **2** : wet with sweat • **sweaty** *palms/clothes*

swede /ˈswiːd/ *n* [*C/U*] *Brit* : RUTABAGA

Swede /ˈswiːd/ *n* [*C*] : a person born, raised in, or living in Sweden

¹**sweep** /ˈswiːp/ *vb* **swept** /ˈswɛpt/; **sweep·ing** **1 a** [*T*] : to remove (dust, dirt, etc.) from a surface with a broom or brush or with a quick movement of your hand, fingers, etc. • *He* **swept** *the crumbs off/from the table.* **b** [*T/I*] : to remove dust, dirt, etc., from (something) with a broom or brush • *She* **swept** *(up) the floor.* • *I need to* **sweep** *(out) the kitchen.* **2 a** [*I*] : to move or pass quickly, forcefully, or smoothly • *Fires* **swept** *through the forest.* • (*figurative*) *She* **swept to victory.** **b** [*I*] : to move or walk in a smooth, quick, and impressive way • *The star* **swept** *into the room.* **c** [*T*] : to push or move (something) quickly or forcefully • *He* **swept** *the curtains aside.* **d** [*T*] : to push, carry, or lift (someone or something) with great force • *The debris was* **swept** *out to sea by the tide.* • *He* **swept** *her (up) into his arms.* • (*figurative*) *We were* **swept**

along/away by her enthusiasm. **3** [*I*] *of a feeling or emotion* : to be felt suddenly ▪ *Fear swept over/through her.* [=she suddenly felt afraid] **4** [*T*] : to pass over (all of an area or place) in a continuous motion ▪ *A searchlight swept the area.* **5** [*T*] : to become very popular or common suddenly in (a particular place) ▪ *the latest craze sweeping the nation* **6** [*T*] **a** : to win everything that can be won in (something, such as an election) in an easy or impressive way ▪ *The opposition party swept the election.* **b** *US, sports* : to win all of the games in a series of games against another team ▪ *They swept the series/doubleheader.* **7** [*T*] : to brush or pull (your hair) away from your face ▪ *She swept her hair up/back.* — **sweep aside** [*phrasal vb*] **sweep (something) aside** *or* **sweep aside (something)** : to treat (something) as not important ▪ *He swept aside questions about his son's arrest.* — **sweep away** [*phrasal vb*] **sweep (something) away** *or* **sweep away (something)** : to destroy or remove (something) completely ▪ *Floods swept away several houses.* — **sweep (someone) off his/her feet** : to make (someone) suddenly become very attracted to you in a romantic way ▪ *He swept her off her feet.* — **sweep (something) under the rug** (*US*) *or chiefly Brit* **sweep (something) under the carpet** : to hide (something that is illegal, embarrassing, or wrong) ▪ *This is not something we can just sweep under the rug.* — **sweep the board** *chiefly Brit* : to win everything that can be won in a competition ▪ *She swept the board at the awards ceremony.* — **sweep·er** /ˈswiːpɚ/ *n* [*C*] ▪ *a street sweeper* [=a machine that sweeps the streets]

²**sweep** *n* **1** [*C*] : an act of cleaning an area with a broom or brush ▪ *I gave the floor/room a quick sweep.* [=swept the floor/room quickly] **2** [*C*] : a long, smooth movement often in a wide curve ▪ *a sweep of his hand* **3** [*singular*] : everything that is included in something ▪ *the whole sweep of American history* **4** [*C*] : a search for something over a large area ▪ *The search party made a sweep of the forest.* **5** [*C*] *US, sports* : an occurrence in which one team wins all the games in a series of games against another team ▪ *a World Series sweep* **6** [*plural*] *US* : a time during the year when television stations try to see which shows are the most popular in order to decide how much can be charged for advertising ▪ *sweeps week/month*

sweeping *adj* **1** : including or involving many things ▪ *sweeping changes/reforms* **2** *disapproving* : too general : including or involving too many things or people ▪ *sweeping claims/generalizations*

sweep·stakes /ˈswiːpˌsteɪks/ *n* [*plural*] : a race or contest in which the winner receives all the prize money

¹**sweet** /ˈswiːt/ *adj* **1** : containing a lot of sugar ▪ *sweet desserts* **2** : very gentle, kind, or friendly ▪ *He's a sweet guy.* ▪ *It was sweet of her to help us.* **3 a** : having a very pleasant smell, sound, or appear-

ance ▪ *a sweet fragrance/scent* ▪ *sweet music/voices* **b** : clean and fresh ▪ *sweet air* ▪ *The water from the well is sweet.* **c** *US* : not salty or salted ▪ *sweet butter* **4** : making you feel happy or pleased ▪ *Victory/success/revenge is sweet.* ▪ *"Good night and sweet dreams."* [=I hope you will sleep well and have pleasant dreams] **5** *chiefly US, informal* : very good or impressive ▪ *a sweet job offer* ▪ *"I got free tickets." "Sweet!"* — **short and sweet** see ¹SHORT — **sweet·ness** /ˈswiːtnəs/ *n* [*U*]

²**sweet** *n* **1 a** [*C*] : a food that contains a lot of sugar ▪ *I'm trying to cut down on sweets.* **b** [*C*] *Brit* : a piece of candy ▪ *a bag of sweets* **c** [*C/U*] *Brit* : a sweet food served at the end of a meal : DESSERT **2** [*U*] *old-fashioned* — used to address someone you love ▪ *Good morning, my sweet*

sweet corn *n* [*U*] **1** *US* : a kind of corn (sense 1) that contains a lot of sugar **2** *sweetcorn Brit* : CORN 1b

sweet·en /ˈswiːtn̩/ *vb* [*T*] **1** : to make (something) sweet or sweeter in taste ▪ *She sweetened her coffee.* **2** : to make (something) more valuable or attractive ▪ *Let's see if we can't sweeten the deal.* — **sweet·en·er** /ˈswiːtnɚ/ *n* [*C/U*] ▪ *She uses (an) artificial sweetener instead of sugar.*

sweet·heart /ˈswiːtˌhɑɚt/ *n* [*C*] **1 a** *somewhat old-fashioned* : a person you love very much ▪ *childhood/college sweethearts* **b** — used to address someone you love ▪ *Sweetheart, what's the matter?* **2** : a kind or helpful person ▪ *He is such a little sweetheart.*

sweet·ie /ˈswiːti/ *n, informal* **1 a** [*C*] : a person you love very much ▪ *My sweetie and I will be at the party.* **b** — used to address someone you love ▪ *"How are you, sweetie?"* **2** : a kind or helpful person ▪ *She's a total/real sweetie.*

sweet·ly /ˈswiːtli/ *adv* **1** : in a kind or loving way ▪ *She smiled sweetly.* **2** : smelling or tasting sweet ▪ *a sweetly scented candle* **3** : in a pleasant or appealing way ▪ *sweetly melodious music*

sweet pepper *n* [*C*] : a pepper (sense 2) that has a mild flavor and that can be eaten raw or cooked ▪ *a red/green sweet pepper*

sweet potato *n* [*C/U*] : a large root of a tropical plant that has orange skin and orange flesh, that is eaten as a vegetable, and that tastes sweet

sweet–talk /ˈswiːtˌtɑːk/ *vb* [*T*] : to say nice things to (someone) in order to persuade that person to do something ▪ *He tried to sweet-talk her into doing his work for him.*

sweet tooth *n* [*singular*] *informal* : a liking for sweet foods ▪ *He's always had a sweet tooth.* [=he has always liked sweets]

¹**swell** /ˈswɛl/ *vb* **swelled; swelled** *or* **swol·len** /ˈswoʊlən/; **swell·ing** **1** [*I*] : to become larger than normal ▪ *Her broken ankle swelled (up).* **2** [*T*] : to make (something) larger or more full than normal ▪ *Heavy rains swelled the river.* **3** [*T/I*] : to increase in size or num-

ber • *The population has swelled/swollen in recent years.* • *Immigrants have swelled the population.* **4** [*I*] : to become louder • *The music swelled.* **5** [*I*] : to feel an emotion strongly • *His heart swelled with pride.* [=he felt very proud] — **a swelled head** see ¹HEAD — **swollen** *adj* • *a swollen ankle* • *a swollen river*

²**swell** *n* **1** [*C*] : an upward and downward movement of the water in the sea • *heavy ocean swells* **2** [*singular*] : an increase in size, number, loudness, feeling, etc. • *a swell in the population* • *the swell of the music* • *a swell of enthusiasm/fear/hope*

³**swell** *adj, US, informal + old-fashioned* : very good • *He's a swell guy.*

swell·ing /ˈswɛlɪŋ/ *n* [*C/U*] : an area on someone's body that is larger than normal because of an illness or injury • *There was a/some swelling above her eye.*

swel·ter /ˈswɛltɚ/ *vb* [*I*] : to be very hot and uncomfortable • *We were sweltering in the summer heat.* — **swel·ter·ing** /ˈswɛltərɪŋ/ *adj* • *a sweltering* [=very hot] *summer day*

swept *past tense and past participle of* ¹SWEEP

swerve /ˈswɚv/ *vb* **swerved; swerv·ing** [*I*] : to change direction suddenly especially to avoid hitting someone or something • *The car swerved.* [=turned] • *He swerved toward a tree.*

¹**swift** /ˈswɪft/ *adj* **1** : happening or done quickly or immediately • *a swift kick/response* **2** : moving or able to move very fast • *a swift horse/runner* **3** *US, informal* : smart or intelligent • *She's nice, but she's not too swift.* — **swift·ly** *adv* — **swift·ness** /ˈswɪftnəs/ *n* [*U*]

²**swift** *n* [*C*] : a small bird that has long, narrow wings

swig /ˈswɪg/ *vb* **swigged; swig·ging** [*T*] *informal* : to swallow a lot of (a drink) • *swigging* [=gulping] *water from a bottle* — **swig** *n* [*C*] • *He took a swig of beer.*

¹**swill** /ˈswɪl/ *vb* [*T*] *informal* : to drink (something) quickly in large amounts • *swilling* (*down*) *their beer*

²**swill** *n* [*U*] : food for animals (such as pigs) made from scraps of food and water • (*figurative*) *I refuse to eat this swill.* [=garbage]

¹**swim** /ˈswɪm/ *vb* **swam** /ˈswæm/; **swum** /ˈswʌm/; **swim·ming 1 a** [*I*] : to move through water by moving your arms and legs • *She swam across the pool.* • *I can't swim.* **b** [*T*] : to move through or across (an area of water) by swimming • *He swam the English Channel.* **c** [*I*] *of a fish, bird, etc.* : to move through or over water • *Ducks swam in/on the pond.* **2** [*I*] : to be completely covered with a liquid • *The potatoes were swimming in butter/gravy.* **3** [*I*] **a** : to feel dizzy or unable to think clearly because you are sick, confused, etc. • *My head was swimming.* **b** : *of something you are looking at* : to seem to be moving around because you are tired, sick, etc. • *The room swam before my eyes.* — **sink or swim** see ¹SINK — **swimming** *n* [*U*] • *I am going swimming later today.*

²**swim** *n* [*C*] : an act or period of swimming • *a quick swim* • *Would you like to go for a swim?* — **in/into the swim (of things)** *informal* : involved in an activity or informed about a situation • *When he gets into the swim of things, he'll be much happier.*

swim·mer /ˈswɪmɚ/ *n* [*C*] : a person who swims or is swimming • *There were a few swimmers at the lake this morning.*

swimming costume *n* [*C*] *Brit* : SWIMSUIT

swimming hole *n* [*C*] *US* : a place in a river, pond, etc., where people swim

swim·ming·ly /ˈswɪmɪŋli/ *adv, informal* : very well • *Everything's going swimmingly.*

swimming pool *n* [*C*] : a large structure that is filled with water and that is used for swimming • *Our neighbors have a swimming pool in their backyard.*

swimming trunks *n* [*plural*] : special shorts that men and boys wear for swimming

swim·suit /ˈswɪmˌsuːt/ *n* [*C*] : special clothing that women and girls wear for swimming

swim·wear /ˈswɪmˌweɚ/ *n* [*U*] : special clothing worn for swimming

swin·dle /ˈswɪndl̩/ *vb* **swin·dled; swin·dling** [*T*] : to take money or property from (someone) by using lies or tricks • *He swindled elderly women out of their savings.* — **swindle** *n* [*C*] • *an insurance swindle* — **swin·dler** /ˈswɪndlɚ/ *n* [*C*]

swine /ˈswaɪn/ *n, pl* **swine** [*C*] **1** : ¹PIG **1** • *a herd of swine* **2** *informal* : a very bad person • *You filthy swine!*

¹**swing** /ˈswɪŋ/ *vb* **swung** /ˈswʌŋ/; **swing·ing 1** [*T/I*] : to move backward and forward or from side to side while hanging from something • *She sat on the edge of the table, swinging her legs.* **2** [*T/I*] : to move with a smooth, curving motion • *The door swung open/shut.* • *He swung himself* (*up*) *into the truck.* **3** [*T/I*] : to move (your arm, a tool, etc.) with a quick, curving motion especially to try to hit something • *swinging a bat/hammer/ax* • *He swung at me* [=tried to hit me with his fist] *for no reason.* **4** [*I*] : to move back and forth on a special type of seat (called a swing) • *a playground where kids go to swing* **5** [*T/I*] : to turn or move quickly in a particular direction • *The road swings* (*around*) *to the left.* • *She swung the car into the driveway.* **6 a** [*I*] : to change suddenly from one state or condition to another • *Sales swung up sharply at the end of the year.* • *They have to swing into action.* [=to start doing something quickly] **b** [*T*] : to change or influence (something) in an important way • *His performance swung the game in our favor.* **7** [*T*] *informal* : to do or manage (something) successfully • *If he can swing it, he'll visit next month.* **8** [*I*] *informal* : to be lively or exciting • *The party was swinging.* — **swing by/over** [*phrasal vb*] *US, informal* : to make a brief visit • *I'll swing by* [=*stop by*] *after work.* — **swing the balance** : to change a situation so that one person, group, etc., is more able or likely to succeed

than another ▪ *Her experience could swing the balance in her favor.* — **swinger** /'swɪŋɚ/ *n* [C]

²**swing** *n* **1** [C] **a** : an act of moving something with a quick, sweeping motion ▪ *a swing of the hammer* ▪ *her golf swing* [=the way she swings a golf club] ▪ *Some drunk took a swing at me.* [=tried to hit me] **b** : the movement of something that swings backward and forward or from side to side ▪ *the swing of a pendulum* **2** [C] : a usually sudden change from one state or condition to another ▪ *big swings in the stock market* ▪ *mood swings* [=sudden changes in your mood] **3** [C] : a seat that hangs from ropes or chains and that moves back and forth ▪ *The kids were playing on the swings.* ▪ *a porch swing* **4** [U] : a style of jazz music that has a lively rhythm and that is played mostly for dancing — **in full swing** : at the highest level of activity ▪ *The party was in full swing by the time we arrived.* — **in/into the swing of** *informal* : fully involved and comfortable with (a regular activity, process, etc.) ▪ *After a while, she got into the swing of her job.* [=she got used to her job and was able to do it well] ▪ *I should be (back) in the swing of things in a few days.*

³**swing** *adj, always before a noun* **1** : of or relating to the style of jazz music called swing ▪ *a swing band* **2** : not certain to vote for a particular candidate or party in an election and therefore often able to decide the result of the election ▪ *swing voters/states*

swinge·ing /'swɪndʒɪŋ/ *adj, Brit* **1** : very large and difficult to deal with ▪ *swingeing fines/penalties/taxes* **2** : very critical or severe ▪ *swingeing criticism*

swinging door *n* [C] *US* : a door that can be pushed open from either side and that swings shut when it is released — called also *(Brit)* **swing door**

swing set *n* [C] *US* : a wooden or metal structure that has swings hanging from it and that may have a slide or other things attached to it for children to play on

swing shift *n* [C] *US* : a scheduled period of work that begins in the afternoon and ends at night ▪ *He works the swing shift.*

¹**swipe** /'swaɪp/ *vb* **swiped**; **swip·ing** **1** [T/I] : to reach toward and try to hit (something) with a swinging motion ▪ *The cat swiped (at) the dog.* **2** [T] *informal* : to steal (something) ▪ *She swiped my idea/wallet.* **3** [T] : to pass (a credit card, ATM card, etc.) through a machine that reads information from it ▪ *Please swipe your credit card.*

²**swipe** *n* [C] : a swinging movement of a person's hand, an animal's paw, etc., that is done in an attempt to hit something ▪ *a swipe of the cat's paw* ▪ *He took a swipe at the ball.* [=he swung at the ball and tried to hit it] ▪ *(figurative) She took a swipe at* [=criticized] *her former company in her speech.*

¹**swirl** /'swɚl/ *vb* [T/I] : to move in circles or to cause (something) to move in circles ▪ *She swirled the drink (around) in her*

glass. ▪ *(figurative) Rumors are swirling about/around them.* [=there are a lot of rumors about them]

²**swirl** *n* [C] **1** : a twisting or swirling movement, form, or object ▪ *swirls of color* ▪ *ice cream with chocolate swirls* **2** : a state of busy movement or activity ▪ *the swirl of events*

¹**swish** /'swɪʃ/ *vb* [T/I] : to move with or cause (something) to move with a soft sweeping or brushing sound ▪ *The horse's tail swished back and forth.* ▪ *The horse swished its tail back and forth.* — **swish** *n* [singular] ▪ *a swish of the horse's tail*

²**swish** *adj, Brit, informal* : fashionable and expensive : SWANKY ▪ *a swish hotel*

¹**Swiss** /'swɪs/ *adj* : of or relating to Switzerland or its people ▪ *the Swiss ski team*

²**Swiss** *n* — **the Swiss** : the people of Switzerland ▪ *the traditions of the Swiss*

Swiss cheese *n* [U] : a type of cheese that is hard and pale yellow and that has many large holes

¹**switch** /'swɪtʃ/ *n* [C] **1** : a small device that starts or stops the flow of electricity to a lamp, a machine, etc., when it is pressed or moved up and down ▪ *She flicked a switch and turned the lamp/lights on.* ▪ *a light switch* ▪ *He threw the switch to stop the machine.* **2** : a sudden change from one thing to another ▪ *There has been a switch in plans.* [=the plans have changed] ▪ *"He says he'll do it." "Well, that's a switch."* [=that's something unusual] **3** : a thin stick that can be easily bent

²**switch** *vb* **1** [T/I] : to make a change from one thing to another ▪ *He kept switching back and forth between topics.* ▪ *Why did you switch jobs?* **2** [T/I] : to make a change from one thing to another by turning or pushing a button or moving a switch, lever, etc. ▪ *He switched (over) to a different channel.* ▪ *Stop switching channels.* **3** [T] : to change or replace (something) with another thing ▪ *They switched places/positions/roles/sides.* — **switch gears** see ¹**GEAR** — **switch off/on** [*phrasal vb*] **switch (something) off/on** or **switch off/on (something)** : to turn off/on (something) by turning or pushing a button or moving a switch, lever, etc. ▪ *He switched off the light/lamp.* ▪ *I switched on the TV.*

switch·back /'swɪtʃˌbæk/ *n* [C] : a road, trail, etc., that has many sharp turns for climbing a steep hill

switch·blade /'swɪtʃˌbleɪd/ *n* [C] *chiefly US* : a knife that has a blade inside the handle which springs out when a button is pressed — called also *(Brit)* **flick-knife**

switch·board /'swɪtʃˌboɚd/ *n* [C] : a system used to connect telephone calls with many separate phone lines in a building ▪ *Angry callers flooded/jammed the company's switchboard.* [=made telephone calls to the company]

switch-hit·ter /'swɪtʃˈhɪtɚ/ *n* [C] *baseball* : a batter who bats right-handed against a left-handed pitcher and left-handed against a right-handed pitcher

¹**swiv·el** /'swɪvəl/ *n* [C] : a device that joins two parts so that one of the parts can turn or spin while the other part

does not move • *a swivel chair* [=a chair with the seat mounted on a swivel so that it turns freely]

²**swivel** *vb, US* **-eled** *or Brit* **-elled**; *US* **-eling** *or Brit* **-el·ling** [*T/I*] : to turn around • *She swiveled in her seat.* • *The owl swiveled* [=twisted] *its head around.*

swollen *see* ¹SWELL

swoon /ˈswuːn/ *vb* [*I*] **1** : to become very excited about someone or something • *Teenage girls swooned over the band's lead singer.* **2** *old-fashioned* : ²FAINT • *She swooned from fright.* — **swoon** *n* [*singular*] *old-fashioned* • *She fell into a swoon.*

swoop /ˈswuːp/ *vb* [*I*] **1** : to fly down through the air suddenly • *A hawk swooped down and caught a rabbit.* **2** : to arrive at a place suddenly and unexpectedly • *The police swooped in and captured him.* — *in/at one fell swoop see* ³FELL — **swoop** *n* [*C*] • *the swoop of a hawk*

swop *Brit spelling of* SWAP

sword /ˈsoɚd/ *n* [*C*] : a weapon with a long metal blade that has a sharp point and edge — *cross swords see* ²CROSS

sword·fish /ˈsoɚdˌfɪʃ/ *n* [*C*] : a very large fish that lives in the ocean, that has a long, pointed upper jaw which looks like a sword, and that is eaten as food

swore *past tense of* ¹SWEAR

¹**sworn** *past participle of* ¹SWEAR

²**sworn** /ˈswoɚn/ *adj, always before a noun* **1** — used to describe people who have openly stated their feelings, opinions, etc. • *a sworn conservative* • *They are sworn enemies/friends.* **2** : made or given by someone who has made a formal promise to tell the truth • *sworn testimony/statements*

swum *past participle of* ¹SWIM

swung *past tense and past participle of* ¹SWING

syc·a·more /ˈsɪkəˌmoɚ/ *n* [*C*] **1** : a tree of the eastern and central U.S. that has light-brown bark that peels off in thin flakes **2** : a type of European maple tree with five-pointed leaves

sy·co·phant /ˈsɪkəfənt/ *n* [*C*] *formal + disapproving* : a person who praises powerful people in order to get their approval — **sy·co·phan·tic** /ˌsɪkəˈfæntɪk/ *adj* • *sycophantic praise/flattery*

syl·lab·ic /səˈlæbɪk/ *adj, linguistics* : of or relating to syllables • *syllabic accent/stress*

syl·la·ble /ˈsɪləbəl/ *n* [*C*] : any one of the parts into which a word is naturally divided when it is pronounced • *"Doctor"* is a *two-syllable word.*

syl·la·bus /ˈsɪləbəs/ *n, pl* **-bi** /-ˌbaɪ/ *or* **-bus·es** [*C*] : a list of the topics or books that will be studied in a course

sym·bi·o·sis /ˌsɪmbiˈoʊsəs/ *n, pl* **-o·ses** /-ˌoʊˌsiːz/ [*C/U*] **1** *biology* : the relationship between two different kinds of living things that live together and depend on each other • *The bacteria exist in (a) symbiosis with the plant's roots.* **2** *formal* : a relationship between two people or groups that work with and depend on each other • *There is (a) symbiosis be-*

tween celebrities and the media. — **sym·bi·ot·ic** /ˌsɪmbiˈɑːtɪk/ *adj* • *a symbiotic relationship*

sym·bol /ˈsɪmbəl/ *n* [*C*] **1** : an action, object, event, etc., that expresses or represents a particular idea or quality • *The flag is a symbol of our country.* **2** : a letter, group of letters, character, or picture that is used instead of a word or group of words • *The company's symbol* [=logo] *is a red umbrella.*

sym·bol·ic /sɪmˈbɑːlɪk/ *adj* **1** : expressing or representing an idea or quality without using words • *The lighting of the candles is symbolic.* • *a symbolic act/gesture* [=an act/gesture that is intended as a symbol of something but that does not have any real effect] • *The dove is symbolic of peace.* **2** : relating to or being used as a symbol • *The sharing of the wine has symbolic meaning.* — **sym·bol·i·cal·ly** /sɪmˈbɑːlɪkli/ *adv*

sym·bol·ism /ˈsɪmbəˌlɪzəm/ *n* [*U*] **1** : the use of symbols to express or represent ideas or qualities in literature, art, etc. • *a story filled with religious symbolism* **2** : the particular idea or quality that is expressed by a symbol • *What is the symbolism of the lion in the picture?* [=what does the lion symbolize in the picture?]

sym·bol·ize *also Brit* **sym·bol·ise** /ˈsɪmbəˌlaɪz/ *vb* **-ized**; **-iz·ing** [*T*] : to be a symbol of (something) • *She came to symbolize the women's movement in America.*

sym·met·ri·cal /səˈmɛtrɪkəl/ *also* **symmet·ric** /səˈmɛtrɪk/ *adj* : having sides or halves that are the same • *a symmetrical design/pattern* — **sym·met·ri·cal·ly** /səˈmɛtrɪkli/ *adv*

sym·me·try /ˈsɪmətri/ *n* [*U*] : the quality of something that has two sides or halves that are the same or very close in size, shape, and position • *the symmetry of the human body*

sym·pa·thet·ic /ˌsɪmpəˈθɛtɪk/ *adj* **1** : feeling or showing concern about someone who is in a bad situation • *She is very sympathetic to/toward the poor.* **2** *not before a noun* : having or showing support for or approval of something • *He was not sympathetic to/toward their cause.* [=he did not support their cause] **3** : having pleasant or appealing qualities • *The book doesn't have any sympathetic* [=likable] *characters.* — **sym·pa·thet·i·cal·ly** /ˌsɪmpəˈθɛtɪkli/ *adv*

sym·pa·thize *also Brit* **sym·pa·thise** /ˈsɪmpəˌθaɪz/ *vb* **-thized**; **-thiz·ing** [*I*] **1** : to feel sorry for someone who is in a bad situation • *I sympathize with you.* **2** : to feel or show support for or approval of something • *She sympathized with their cause.* — **sym·pa·thiz·er** *also Brit* **sym·pa·this·er** *n* [*C*] • *the group's sympathizers* [=supporters]

sym·pa·thy /ˈsɪmpəθi/ *n, pl* **-thies** **1** [*C/U*] : the feeling that you care about and are sorry about someone else's trouble, grief, misfortune, etc. • *I have no sympathy for her.* • *My deepest sympathies go out to them.* **2** [*U, plural*] : a feeling of support for something ▪ *Her sympa- thies are/lie with the rebels.* **3** [U] : a state in which different people share the same interests, opinions, goals, etc. ▪ *There was no sympathy between them.*

sym·phon·ic /sɪmˈfɑːnɪk/ *adj* : of or re- lating to a symphony or symphony or- chestra ▪ *symphonic music*

sym·pho·ny /ˈsɪmfəni/ *n, pl* **-nies** [C] **1** : a long piece of music that is usually in four large, separate sections and that is performed by an orchestra **2** : SYM- PHONY ORCHESTRA

symphony orchestra *n* [C] : a large or- chestra of musicians who play classical music together and are led by a conduc- tor ▪ *the Chicago Symphony Orchestra*

sym·po·sium /sɪmˈpoʊzijəm/ *n, pl* **-sia** /-zijə/ *or* **-siums** [C] *formal* : a formal meeting at which experts discuss a par- ticular topic ▪ *a symposium on cloning*

symp·tom /ˈsɪmptəm/ *n* [C] **1** : a change in the body or mind which indi- cates that a disease is present ▪ *cold/flu symptoms* ▪ *a symptom of depression* **2** : a sign of something bad ▪ *Corporate lay- offs are a symptom of financial trouble.*

symp·tom·at·ic /ˌsɪmptəˈmætɪk/ *adj* **1** *medical* **a** : showing that a particular disease is present ▪ *A fever and runny nose are symptomatic of the flu.* [=are symp- toms of the flu] **b** : relating to or show- ing symptoms of a disease ▪ *The patient was not symptomatic.* [=did not have any symptoms] **2** *formal* : showing the exis- tence of a particular problem ▪ *The child's behavior is symptomatic of an un- stable home life.*

syn·a·gogue /ˈsɪnəˌɡɑːɡ/ *n* [C] : a build- ing that is used for Jewish religious ser- vices

syn·apse /ˈsɪˌnæps/ *n* [C] *biology* : the place where a signal passes from one nerve cell to another — **syn·ap·tic** /səˈnæptɪk/ *adj*

sync *also* **synch** /ˈsɪŋk/ *n* — **in sync** : in a state in which two or more people or things move or happen together at the same time and speed ▪ *The dancers moved in sync.* ▪ *(figurative)* The President *is not in sync with* [=does not under- stand] *the people.* — **out of sync** : in a state in which two or more people or things do not move or happen together at the same time and speed ▪ *The soundtrack was out of sync so they stopped the film.* ▪ *(figurative)* His actions are com- pletely *out of sync with our goals.*

syn·chro·nize *also Brit* **syn·chro·nise** /ˈsɪŋkrəˌnaɪz/ *vb* **-nized;** **-niz·ing** **1** [T] : to cause (things) to agree in time or to make (things) happen at the same time and speed ▪ *They synchronized their watches.* [=they adjusted their watches so that they all showed the same time] **2** [I] : to happen at the same time and speed ▪ *The sound and picture have to syn- chronize (with each other).* — **syn·chro- ni·za·tion** *also Brit* **syn·chro·ni·sa- tion** /ˌsɪŋkrənəˈzeɪʃən/ *n* [U]

¹**syn·di·cate** /ˈsɪndɪkət/ *n* [C] **1 a** : a group of people or businesses that work together ▪ *A syndicate owns the company.* **b** : a group of people who are involved in

organized crime ▪ *a crime syndicate* **2** : a group of newspapers that are man- aged by one company ▪ *a newspaper syn- dicate*

²**syn·di·cate** /ˈsɪndəˌkeɪt/ *vb* **-cat·ed;** **-cat·ing** [T] : to sell (a piece of writing, comic strip, series of TV or radio pro- grams, etc.) to many different newspa- pers, magazines, or stations at the same time ▪ *His column is syndicated in all the major newspapers.* ▪ *The sitcom has been syndicated nationally.* — **syn·di·ca- tion** /ˌsɪndəˈkeɪʃən/ *n* [U] ▪ *The show is now in syndication.* [=reruns of the show are being shown on different stations that have paid to show them]

syn·drome /ˈsɪnˌdroʊm/ *n* [C] : a disease or disorder that involves a particular group of signs and symptoms ▪ *a rare syndrome* ▪ *psychological syndromes*

syn·er·gy /ˈsɪnədʒi/ *n, pl* **-gies** [C/U] *technical* : the increased effectiveness that results when two or more people or businesses work together ▪ *two compa- nies that have found (a) synergy*

syn·o·nym /ˈsɪnəˌnɪm/ *n* [C] **1** : a word that has the same meaning as another word in the same language ▪ *"Small" and "little" are synonyms.* = *"Small" is a syn- onym of "little."* **2** : a word, name, or phrase that very strongly suggests a par- ticular idea, quality, etc. ▪ *His name has become a synonym for oppression.*

syn·on·y·mous /səˈnɑːnəməs/ *adj* **1** : having the same meaning ▪ *"Small" and "little" are synonymous (words).* [=are syn- onyms] **2** *not before a noun* : very strongly associated *with* something ▪ *The company's name is synonymous with quality.* — **syn·on·y·mous·ly** *adv* ▪ *words that are used synonymously*

syn·op·sis /səˈnɑːpsəs/ *n, pl* **syn·op- ses** /səˈnɑːpˌsiːz/ [C] *formal* : a short de- scription of the most important informa- tion about something ▪ *a plot synopsis* [=summary]

syn·tax /ˈsɪnˌtæks/ *n* [U] *linguistics* : the way in which words are put together to form phrases, clauses, or sentences ▪ *"I saw that she a cookie ate" shows incorrect syntax.* — **syn·tac·tic** /sɪnˈtæktɪk/ *or* **syn·tac·ti·cal** /sɪnˈtæktɪkəl/ *adj*

syn·the·sis /ˈsɪnθəsəs/ *n, pl* **-the·ses** /-θəˌsiːz/ **1** [C] *formal* : something that is made by combining different things (such as ideas, styles, etc.) ▪ *The band's sound is a synthesis of jazz and rock mu- sic.* **2** [C/U] *technical* : the production of a substance by combining simpler substances through a chemical process ▪ *the synthesis of water from hydrogen and oxygen*

syn·the·size *also Brit* **syn·the·sise** /ˈsɪnθəˌsaɪz/ *vb* **-sized;** **-siz·ing** [T] **1** *formal* **a** : to make (something) by combining different things ▪ *a theory syn- thesized from traditional and modern phi- losophies* **b** : to combine (things) in or- der to make something new ▪ *He syn- thesized old and new ideas.* **2** *technical* : to make (something) from simpler sub- stances through a chemical process ▪ *Sci- entists synthesize new drugs.*

syn·the·siz·er *also Brit* **syn·the·sis·er**

/ˈsɪnθəˌsaɪzɚ/ *n* [C] : an electronic machine that produces and controls sound and is used especially in music and for reproducing speech • *The band used a synthesizer.*

¹**syn·thet·ic** /sɪnˈθɛtɪk/ *adj* : not natural • *synthetic drugs/chemicals/rubber* — **syn·thet·i·cal·ly** /sɪnˈθɛtɪkli/ *adv* • *The fibers are synthetically produced.*

²**synthetic** *n* [C] : something made by combining different artificial substances • *The shirt is made of synthetics.*

syph·i·lis /ˈsɪfələs/ *n* [U] *medical* : a very serious disease that is spread through sexual intercourse

syphon *variant spelling of* SIPHON

sy·ringe /səˈrɪndʒ/ *n* [C] : a device made of a hollow tube and a needle that is used to force fluids into or take fluids out of the body

syr·up /ˈsɪrəp/ *n* **1** [U] : a sweet, thick liquid made of sugar and water with flavoring or medicine added to it • *chocolate syrup* **2** [C/U] : a sweet, thick liquid made from the juice of a fruit or plant • *She poured syrup on her pancakes.* — **syr·upy** /ˈsɪrəpi/ *adj* • *a syrupy liquid*

sys·tem /ˈsɪstəm/ *n* **1** [C] : a group of related parts that move or work together • *a system of rivers* • *a security/telephone/heating system* **2** [C] **a** : a group of a person or animal thought of as an entire group of parts that work together • *No drugs were found in his system.* **b** : a group of organs that work together to perform an important function of the body • *the digestive/reproductive/respiratory system* **3** [C] : a way of managing, controlling, organizing, or doing something that follows a set of rules or a plan • *the legal system* • *Under the new system, students will have to pass an exam to graduate.* • *a democratic system of government* **4 the system** *disapproving* : a powerful government or social organization that controls people's lives • *You can't beat the system.* — **all systems (are) go** *see* ²GO — **get it out of your system** *informal* **1** : to do something that you have been wanting to do so that you no longer feel a strong desire to do it **2** : to get rid of a strong emotion (such as anger) by doing something • *I was upset, so I went for a walk to get it out of my system.*

sys·tem·at·ic /ˌsɪstəˈmætɪk/ *adj* : using a careful system or method • *a systematic approach* • *a systematic study of the evidence* — **sys·tem·at·i·cal·ly** /ˌsɪstəˈmætɪkli/ *adv*

sys·tem·a·tize *also Brit* **sys·tem·a·tise** /ˈsɪstəməˌtaɪz/ *vb* **-tized; -tiz·ing** [T] *formal* : to make (something) into a system or to organize (something) by using a system • *systematize a process* • *systematizing data*

sys·tem·ic /sɪˈstɛmɪk/ *adj* **1** *formal* : of or relating to an entire system • *The problem seems to be systemic.* **2** *medical* : of, relating to, or affecting the entire body • *a systemic disease*

T

¹**t** *or* **T** /ˈtiː/ *n, pl* **t's** *or* **ts** *or* **T's** *or* **Ts** /ˈtiːz/ [C/U] : the 20th letter of the English alphabet • *a word that begins with (a) t* — **to a T** *informal* : in a perfect or exact way • *Her new car fits/suits/suits her to a T.*

²**t** *abbr* **1** temperature **2** time **3** ton **4** *T* transitive

ta /ˈtɑː/ *interj, Brit, informal* — used to say "thank you"

TA *abbr* **1** *US* teaching assistant **2** *Brit* Territorial Army

¹**tab** /ˈtæb/ *n* [C] **1 a** : a small, flat piece on a box, envelope, etc., that can be put into a hole in order to hold two parts together • *Insert the tab into this slot to close the box.* **b** : a small, flat piece that sticks out from the edge of something (such as a folder) and allows you to identify and find it easily • *a notebook with index tabs* **c** *US* : a small piece of metal, plastic, etc., that is pulled in order to open or close something • *the tab on a can of soda* **2** *US, informal* : a record of the things that a customer has ordered and will pay for later • *a $200 bar tab* • *She offered to pick up the tab.* [=pay the bill] **3** : TAB KEY — **keep tabs on** *informal* : to carefully watch (someone or something) in order to learn what that person or thing is doing • *We are keeping tabs on their movements.*

²**tab** *vb* **tabbed; tab·bing** [T] **1** : to put a small, identifying tab on something • *a tabbed notebook* [=a notebook with index tabs] **2** *US, informal* : to say that (someone or something) will do something or have a particular role or purpose • *She was tabbed (as) the favorite to win.* • *an amount of money tabbed for maintenance*

Ta·bas·co /təˈbæskoʊ/ *trademark* — used for a spicy sauce made from hot peppers

tab·by /ˈtæbi/ *n, pl* **-bies** [C] : a cat that has dark and light stripes or spots on its fur

tab·er·na·cle /ˈtæbəˌnækəl/ *n* **1** [C] : a place of worship that is used by some Christian groups **2** [C] : a box in which the holy bread and wine are kept in a Catholic church **3 the Tabernacle** : a small tent that was used as a place of worship by the ancient Israelites

tab key *n* [C] : a key on the keyboard of a typewriter or computer that is used to move several spaces at a time

¹**ta·ble** /ˈteɪbəl/ *n* [C] **1** : a piece of furniture that has a flat top and one or more

legs ▪ *sitting at/around the dining/dinner table* ▪ *She reserved a table for two at the restaurant.* ▪ *a billiard/poker table* **2** : a group of people who are sitting at a table ▪ *He had the attention of the entire table.* **3** : a collection of information that is arranged in rows and columns ▪ *The table shows the salary of each employee.* — **lay/ put (all/all of) your cards on the table** see ¹CARD — **on the table** : able to be considered or discussed ▪ *All options are on the table.* — **run the table** *chiefly US, pool, billiards, etc.* : to hit all the remaining balls into pockets without missing — **table of contents** see ¹CONTENT — **turn the tables** : to change a situation completely so that you have an advantage over someone who previously had an advantage over you ▪ *He turned the tables on his attacker.* — **under the table** — used to describe a situation in which a worker is being paid in a secret and illegal way in order to avoid paying taxes ▪ *He's working/paid under the table.*

²**table** *vb* **ta·bled; ta·bling** [T] **1** *US* : to decide not to discuss (something) until a later time ▪ *The group tabled the issue until the next meeting.* **2** *Brit* : to formally present (something) for discussion ▪ *She tabled the motion in Parliament.*

tab·leau /ˈtæˌbloʊ/ *n, pl* **tab·leaux** *also* **tab·leaus** /ˈtæˌbloʊz/ [C] : a scene that is created on a stage by a group of people who do not speak or move ▪ *The play opens with a tableau of a scene from the Bible.*

ta·ble·cloth /ˈteɪbəlˌklɑːθ/ *n* [C] : a cloth that is placed on a table before other objects are placed on it

table salt *n* [U] : the type of salt that is usually on a table for people to use while they are dining

ta·ble·spoon /ˈteɪbəlˌspuːn/ *n* [C] **1 a** : a spoon for measuring ingredients that holds an amount equal to ½ fluid ounce or three teaspoons **b** : TABLESPOONFUL **2** : a fairly large spoon that is used for serving or eating food

ta·ble·spoon·ful /ˈteɪbəlˌspuːnˌfʊl/ *n, pl* **-spoon·fuls** /-ˌspuːnˌfʊlz/ *or* **-spoons·ful** /-ˌspuːnzˌfʊl/ [C] : the amount that a tablespoon will hold — abbr. *tb., tbs., tbsp.*

tab·let /ˈtæblət/ *n* [C] **1** : a flat piece of stone, clay, or wood that has writing on it **2** : a small usually round piece of medicine ▪ *aspirin tablets* **3** *chiefly US* : ¹PAD 2 ▪ *a writing/drawing tablet*

table tennis *n* [U] : a game in which players stand at opposite ends of a table and use wooden paddles to hit a small plastic ball to each other across a net

ta·ble·top /ˈteɪbəlˌtɑːp/ *n* [C] : the surface of a table

ta·ble·ware /ˈteɪbəlˌweə/ *n* [U] *formal* : dishes, glasses, knives, forks, etc., that are used for serving and eating food

table wine *n* [C/U] : a wine that is used for ordinary meals

tab·loid /ˈtæˌblɔɪd/ *n* [C] : a small newspaper that contains many photographs and stories about famous people and other less serious news items ▪ *the British tabloids* ▪ *tabloid news*

¹**ta·boo** /təˈbuː/ *adj* : not acceptable to talk about or do ▪ *Sex is a taboo subject for them.*

²**taboo** *n, pl* **-boos** [C] : a rule against doing or saying something in a particular culture or religion ▪ *religious/social taboos* ▪ *Marrying relatives is a taboo in many cultures.*

tab·u·lar /ˈtæbjələ/ *adj* : arranged in rows or columns in a table ▪ *data displayed in tabular form*

tab·u·late /ˈtæbjəˌleɪt/ *vb* **-lat·ed; -lating** [T] : to arrange information in an organized way so that it can be studied, recorded, etc. ▪ *The machine tabulates the votes.* — **tab·u·la·tion** /ˌtæbjəˈleɪʃən/ *n* [U]

ta·chom·e·ter /tæˈkɑːmətə/ *n* [C] *technical* : a device that measures how fast something (such as a wheel) is turning

tac·it /ˈtæsət/ *adj, formal* : expressed or understood without being directly stated ▪ *tacit agreement/approval* — **tac·it·ly** *adv*

tac·i·turn /ˈtæsəˌtən/ *adj, formal* : tending to be quiet : not speaking frequently ▪ *a taciturn young man*

¹**tack** /ˈtæk/ *n* [C] **a** : a small, sharp nail usually with a wide, flat head **b** *US* : THUMBTACK **2 a** [C/U] : the direction that a ship or boat is sailing in as it moves at an angle to the direction of the wind ▪ *We were sailing on (a/the) port tack.* [=with the wind coming from the port/ left side] **b** [C] : a change in direction while sailing ▪ *a tack from port to starboard* **3** [U, singular] : a way in which you do something or try to do something ▪ *Let's try a new/different tack.* ▪ *They changed tack.* **4** [C] : a loose stitch that is used to hold pieces of cloth together before sewing them tightly together — **get down to brass tacks** see BRASS

²**tack** *vb* **1** [T] : to fasten or attach (something) with tacks ▪ *A message was tacked on/to the board.* **2** [T] : to add on or attach (something) in a quick or careless way ▪ *They tacked one more provision onto the deal.* **3** [I] : to turn a ship or boat so that the wind is coming at it from the opposite side ▪ *We tacked toward the harbor.*

¹**tack·le** /ˈtækəl/ *n* **1** [U] : equipment that is used for a particular activity (especially fishing) ▪ *a box for fishing tackle* **2** [C] : the act of tackling another player in football, rugby, etc. ▪ *He made the tackle.* **3** [C] *American football* **a** : either one of two players on the offensive team who play in positions on the line of scrimmage next to the guards **b** : either one of two players on the defensive team who play in positions near the center of the line of scrimmage **4** [C/U] : an arrangement of ropes and wheels used for lifting or pulling something heavy

²**tackle** *vb* **tack·led; tack·ling** [T] **1 a** : to forcefully seize (someone) and cause that person to fall to the ground ▪ *The police officer tackled him as he tried to escape.* **b** *American football or rugby* : to force (the player with the ball) to fall to the ground **c** *soccer, field hockey, etc.* : to try to get the ball from (an opposing

player) **2** : to deal with (something difficult) • *I'll tackle that problem later.* — **tack·ler** /'tækələ/ *n* [C]

tacky /'tæki/ *adj* **tack·i·er**; **-est** **1** : slightly wet and sticky • *The paint is still tacky.* **2** *informal* **a** : having a cheap and ugly appearance : not tasteful or stylish • *tacky clothes/wallpaper* **b** *chiefly US* : not socially proper or acceptable • *a tacky comment* — **tack·i·ness** /'tækinəs/ *n* [U]

ta·co /'tɑːkoʊ/ *n, pl* **-cos** [C] : a Mexican food that consists of a folded and usually fried tortilla that is filled with meat, cheese, lettuce, etc.

tact /'tækt/ *n* [U] : the ability to do or say things without offending or upsetting other people • *The peace talks required great tact by the leaders.* — **tact·ful** /'tæktfəl/ *adj* • *a tactful person/response* — **tact·ful·ly** /'tæktfəli/ *adv* — **tact·less** /'tæktləs/ *adj* • *a tactless question* [=a question that tends to offend or upset people] — **tact·less·ly** *adv*

tac·tic /'tæktɪk/ *n* **1** [C] : an action that is planned and used to achieve a particular goal • *We may need to change tactics.* • *a tactic for solving crimes* • *a delaying tactic* **2** [*plural*] : the activity or skill of organizing and moving soldiers and equipment in a military battle • *naval tactics* — **tac·ti·cal** /'tæktɪkəl/ *adj* • *a tactical maneuver/advantage/decision* — **tac·ti·cal·ly** /'tæktɪkli/ *adv*

tac·ti·cian /tæk'tɪʃən/ *n* [C] : someone who is good at making plans in order to achieve particular goals • *a brilliant political/military tactician*

tac·tile /'tæktl, *Brit* 'tæk,taɪl/ *adj, formal* : relating to the sense of touch • *visual and tactile experiences*

tad /'tæd/ *n* — **a tad** *informal* **1** : a small amount • *Move a tad to the right.* **2** : very slightly • *I'm a tad nervous.*

tad·pole /'tæd,poʊl/ *n* [C] : a small creature that becomes an adult frog or toad, that has a rounded body and a long tail, and that lives in water

tae kwon do *or* **Tae Kwon Do** /'taɪ-ˈkwɑːnˈdoʊ/ *n* [U] : a style of fighting that originated in Korea and that uses kicks and punches but no weapons

taf·fe·ta /'tæfətə/ *n* [U] : a shiny type of cloth that is used especially to make dresses

taf·fy /'tæfi/ *n, pl* **-fies** [C/U] *US* : a type of soft and chewy candy

¹**tag** /'tæg/ *n* **1** [C] : a small piece of cloth, paper, metal, etc., that is attached to something and that has information written on it • *a dog's identification/ID tags* • *luggage tags* **2** [U] : a children's game in which one player is called "it" and chases the other players to try to touch one of them and make that player "it" **3** [C] *baseball* : the act of causing a base runner to be out by touching the runner with the ball • *The catcher made the tag for the out.* **4** [C] *computers* : a piece of computer code that is used to identify a particular type of text • *HTML tags*

²**tag** *vb* **tagged**; **tag·ging** [T] **1** : to put a tag on (something) • *The items were*

tagged for the sale. **2** : to touch (a player) in a game of tag • *Tag! You're it!* **3** *baseball* : to cause (a base runner) to be out by touching him or her with the ball • *She was tagged out by the catcher.* — **tag along** [*phrasal vb*] *informal* : to go somewhere with someone • *"I'm going to the store." "May I tag along with you?"* — **tag·ger** /'tægə/ *n* [C]

tag sale *n* [C] *US* : GARAGE SALE

tag team *n* [C] : a team of two or more professional wrestlers who take turns fighting during a match • (*figurative*) *a political tag team*

tai chi *or* **t'ai chi** *or* **Tai Chi** *or* **T'ai Chi** /'taɪˈʧiː/ *n* [U] : a Chinese form of exercise that uses very slow and controlled movements

¹**tail** /'teɪl/ *n* **1** [C] : the part of an animal's body that extends from the animal's back end • *a monkey with a long tail* **2** [C] **a** : a long piece that extends from the back end or bottom of something • *a comet's tail* **b** : the back end of an airplane, helicopter, etc. **3** [*plural*] : the side of a coin that is opposite the side which shows a picture of a person's head • *Is it heads or tails?* [=did the coin land with heads or tails facing up?] **4** [*plural*] : TAILCOAT • *He wore a top hat and tails.* **5** [*singular*] *informal* : a person (such as a detective) who follows or watches someone • *They put a tail on the suspect.* [=they had someone follow the suspect] — **not make head or/nor tail of** see ¹HEAD — **on someone's tail** *informal* : following closely behind someone • *The sheriff was hot on their tails.* — **turn tail** *informal* : to turn around and run away from danger, trouble, etc. — **with your tail between your legs** : with a feeling of being embarrassed or ashamed especially because you have been defeated • *He went home with his tail between his legs.*

²**tail** *vb* [T] *informal* : to follow (someone) closely • *The police were tailing a suspect.* — **tail off** [*phrasal vb*] : to become smaller or quieter in a gradual way • *Our productivity tailed off last year.* • *Her voice tailed off.*

tail·back /'teɪl,bæk/ *n* [C] **1** *American football* : HALFBACK 1 **2** *Brit* : a situation in which the flow of traffic is blocked and a long line of vehicles forms

tail·bone /'teɪl,boʊn/ *n* [C] : the small bone at the end of the spine

tail·coat /'teɪl,koʊt/ *n* [C] : a formal jacket that is worn by a man and that has a short front and a long back which divides into two pieces

tailed /'teɪld/ *adj* : having a tail of a specified type • *a white-tailed deer* • *long-tailed monkeys*

tail end *n* — **the tail end** : the last part of something • *the tail end of summer*

¹**tail·gate** /'teɪl,geɪt/ *n* [C] *chiefly US* : a door at the back of a vehicle (such as a pickup truck) that opens downward

²**tailgate** *vb* **-gat·ed**; **-gat·ing** **1** [T/I] : to drive too closely behind another vehicle • *Someone was tailgating me.* **2** [I] *US* : to have a tailgate party

tailgate party *n* [C] *US* : a party in which

people serve food and drinks from the back end of their vehicles usually in a parking lot before or after a football game, a concert, etc.

tail·light /ˈteɪlˌlaɪt/ n [C] : a red light at the back of a vehicle

¹tai·lor /ˈteɪlə/ n [C] : a person who makes men's clothes that are measured to fit a particular person

²tailor vb [T] **1** : to make (clothing that is measured to fit a particular person) ▪ I had my suit tailored. ▪ a tailored suit **2** : to make or change (something) so that it meets a special need or purpose ▪ They tailored the show for/to younger audiences.

tai·lor–made /ˌteɪləˈmeɪd/ adj **1** : made by a tailor ▪ a tailor-made suit **2** : made or seeming to have been made for a particular person or purpose ▪ The job is tailor-made for him.

tail·pipe /ˈteɪlˌpaɪp/ n [C] chiefly US : ²EXHAUST 2

tail·spin /ˈteɪlˌspɪn/ n [singular] **1** : a condition in which an airplane is falling rapidly while turning around and around ▪ The plane went into a tailspin. **2** : a state in which something quickly becomes much worse ▪ Stock prices are in a tailspin.

tail·wind /ˈteɪlˌwɪnd/ n [C] : a wind that blows in the same direction as something (such as an airplane) that is moving forward

¹taint /ˈteɪnt/ vb [T] **1** : to hurt or damage the good condition of (something) ▪ Their relationship was tainted with/by jealousy. **2** : to make (something) dangerous or dirty especially by adding something harmful or undesirable to it ▪ The water is tainted by bacteria/pesticides. ▪ tainted food

²taint n [singular] : something that causes a person or thing to be thought of as bad, dishonest, etc. ▪ a career damaged by the taint of scandal

¹take /ˈteɪk/ vb **took** /ˈtʊk/; **tak·en** /ˈteɪkən/; **tak·ing** **1** [T] **a** : to carry or move (something) to a place ▪ She took her things to her room. ▪ You had better take an umbrella with you. **b** : to carry and give (something) to a person ▪ Take this note to your teacher. = Take your teacher this note. **c** : to carry, move, or lead (someone) to a place ▪ This bus takes you downtown. ▪ He was taken to the hospital. ▪ Her office is upstairs. I can take you there. ▪ (figurative) He took her to court. [=sued her] **2** [T] : to begin to hold (someone or something) with your fingers, arms, etc. ▪ I took the pen and signed my name. ▪ He took her by the hand. = He took her hand. **3** [T] : to remove (something) from a place, a person's hand, etc. ▪ She took the letter (from him) and read it. ▪ He took a beer from the fridge. ▪ We'll have to take some blood from your arm. **4** [T] **a** : to get (something) : to gain possession of (something) ▪ That man took [=stole] my purse! ▪ We will take [=seize, capture] the city at dawn. ▪ She took [=borrowed] her dad's car for the day. ▪ Military leaders **took control of** the government. **b** : to claim (someone

or something) as your own ▪ I'm sorry. This seat's taken. [=someone else is planning to sit in this chair] ▪ Is he single or is he taken? [=is he someone else's boyfriend?] **5** [T] : to cause (someone) to be your prisoner ▪ They were **taken prisoner/captive/hostage**. **6** [T] : to cause (someone's life) to end ▪ The plane crash **took** the lives of the people on board. ▪ He **took his own life**. [=he killed himself] **7** [T] **a** : to borrow or use (something that was created by a different person or used in a different place) ▪ a quotation **taken** from Shakespeare ▪ The builders took their inspiration from [=they were inspired by] the Acropolis in Athens. **b** : to begin to have (a particular shape, form, or arrangement) ▪ The plan is finally starting to **take form/shape**. **8** [T] : to choose (something) ▪ He'll have the fish and I'll take the chicken. ▪ You can have either one. **Take your pick**. [=choose whichever one you want] **9** [T] **a** : to accept or receive (something) as payment or as a response ▪ Do you take credit cards? ▪ She was taking bribes. ▪ (Brit) The pub takes [=(US) takes in] lots of money. ▪ I insist that you come, and I **won't take no for an answer!** ▪ I'll give you $500 for the camera, and that's my best offer. **Take it or leave it**. **b** : to accept (blame, credit, etc.) ▪ I take full responsibility for the error. ▪ I did the work and he took all the credit. **10** [T] : to accept (someone) into a club, school, etc. ▪ The doctor's office is not taking [=accepting] any new patients. **11** [T] : to have enough room for (someone or something) ▪ I think the elevator will take a few more people. **12** [T] **a** : to need or require (something) ▪ What size shoe do you take? ▪ It took four people to move the couch. ▪ What would it take to get you to buy this car? ▪ The bridge will take several years to finish. ▪ What size batteries does the flashlight take? ▪ The car takes diesel. **b** ✧ The phrase **it takes two (to tango)** is used to say that two people or groups are needed in order to do something. ▪ Both of you will be punished for fighting. It takes two, you know. **13** [T] : to do or perform (something) ▪ take a walk/tour/shower/nap/bite ▪ I failed the test and had to take it again. ▪ Take a look at this. ▪ How old do you think I am? Take a guess. **14** [T] : to get (a drug, pill, etc.) into your body by swallowing it, breathing it in, etc. ▪ take medicine/pills ▪ She stopped **taking drugs**. [=using illegal drugs] **15** [T] : to sit or stand in (a particular place) ▪ Please take a seat. ▪ I took my place next to her at the table. ▪ The actors took their places on the stage. = The actors took the stage. ▪ She took the (witness) stand. **16** [T] : to create or record (a picture or image) ▪ The camera takes great pictures. ▪ They took an X-ray of my leg. ▪ The police took his fingerprints. **17** [T] **a** : to find out (something) ▪ The nurse took my temperature. ▪ The seamstress took our measurements. ▪ I'll take your name and number and call you back. **b** : to create (a list or a record of information) ▪ take notes during class ▪ take an inventory/census **18** [T] **a** : to travel using (a road, vehicle, etc.) ▪ *We took the highway/train into the city.* **b** : to turn toward (a particular direction) ▪ *Take a right at the next stoplight.* ▪ *We took a wrong turn* [=turned in the wrong direction] *and got lost.* **19** [*T*] : to move on or over (something) in a particular way ▪ *She took the curve too fast and the car skidded.* **20** [*T*] **a** : to agree to do or have (a job, role, etc.) ▪ *He took a job as a janitor.* ▪ *She takes an active role* [=she is actively involved] *in her child's education.* ▪ *The governor took office* [=became governor] *in 2006.* **b** *Brit* : to lead (a person, class, or religious service) ▪ *She took a class of eight children.* **21** [*T*] : to study or participate in (something) ▪ *She takes piano lessons.* ▪ *He's taking French (classes).* **22** [*T*] : to use (something) for a particular purpose ▪ *Let me take this opportunity to thank you.* ▪ *taking new measures to reduce crime* ▪ *I suggest you take his advice.* ▪ *They never took the time* [=bothered] *to get to know her.* **23** [*T*] : to accept control of (something) ▪ *She was chosen to take charge/ control of the organization.* ▪ *I'll get you started, and you take it from there.* **24** [*T*] : to deal with or consider (something) ▪ *The governor took questions from reporters.* ▪ *Let's take first things first.* ▪ *I'm still recovering and need to take (it) one day at a time.* **25** [*T*] **a** : to understand or think about (something or someone) in a certain way ▪ *She takes herself too seriously.* ▪ *He said that I was tall, and I took it as a compliment.* ▪ *Try not to take it personally.* [=to be offended or upset by it] ▪ *Can't you take a hint/ joke?* ▪ *I take it that you didn't get my message.* ▪ *Excuse me. I took you for* [=mistakenly thought you were] *an old friend of mine.* **b** : to react to (someone or something) in a certain way ▪ *He took the news pretty badly/hard.* [=he was very upset by the news] **26** [*T*] : to think about (something or someone) as an example ▪ *They just want attention. For instance, take the way they wear their hair.* **27** [*T*] : to believe (something that someone tells you) ▪ *Take it from me.* [=believe me] *He would love to join you.* ▪ *I'll take your word for it.* [=I will believe that what you say is true] **28** [*T*] **a** : to begin to have (an opinion, interest, etc.) ▪ *take a position on an issue* ▪ *She has taken an interest in politics.* ▪ *She refuses to take sides* [=to agree with or support one person or group and not another] *on the issue.* **b** : to ask people to participate in (a survey, poll, etc.) ▪ *Let's take a vote about what we should do.* **29** [*T*] : to experience (a feeling or emotion) ▪ *Please don't take offense.* ▪ *He takes pride in his work.* ▪ *I take comfort in the fact that others have gone through the same thing.* ▪ *(US) He and I both took ill/sick* [=became ill] *after eating the fish.* **30** [*T*] **a** : to experience or be affected by (something unpleasant) ▪ *Everyone had to take a pay cut.* ▪ *He took a punch to the head.* **b** : to experience (something bad or unpleasant) without being seriously harmed ▪ *These boots can take a lot of punishment.* **c** : to accept

the difficulty or unpleasantness of (something or someone) without complaining or making changes ▪ *I can't take this noise anymore!* ▪ *I won't take that kind of rudeness from anyone.* **31** [*T*] : to become known by (someone) in a certain way ▪ *Her reaction took me by surprise.* [=surprised me] ▪ *The band is taking the country by storm.* [=becoming very popular throughout the country] **32** [*T*] : to be liked or enjoyed by (someone) ▪ *He was quite taken by/with her.* [=he liked her very much] **33** [*T*] : to be the cause of (damage, suffering, etc.) ▪ *taking revenge against someone* ▪ *The war took a toll on* [=did a lot of damage to] *the economy.* **34** [*T*] **a** : to win or get (something) in a game, contest, etc. ▪ *She took (home) first place/prize in the contest.* ▪ *The number 20 car took the lead.* **b** : to beat or defeat (someone) in a game, fight, etc. ▪ *I think I can take him.* **35** [*T*] : to cause (something) to move to a particular level or area of activity ▪ *They took the company public.* **36** [*T*] : to go to a place for (shelter, cover, etc.) ▪ *taking refuge in a cave* **37** [*I*] : to be effective or become established ▪ *The lesson he had tried to teach them didn't take.* [=they didn't learn the lesson] **38** [*T*] *grammar* : to be used with (something) ▪ *Transitive verbs take an object while intransitive verbs do not.* **39** [*T*] *mathematics* : SUBTRACT ▪ *When you take two (away) from five, you get three.*

In addition to the phrases shown below, *take* occurs in many idioms that are shown at appropriate entries throughout the dictionary. For example, *take the cake* can be found at ¹CAKE.

— **take aback** [*phrasal vb*] **take (someone) aback** : to surprise or shock (someone) ▪ *He was taken aback by her answer.* — **take action** : to do something : to act in order to get a particular result ▪ *If we fail to take action, many people could be hurt.* ▪ *She took legal action against* [=she sued] *the company.* — **take after** [*phrasal vb*] : to be or look like (someone, such as a parent) ▪ *He takes after his father in height and build.* — **take a lot out of you** ◇ If something *takes a lot out of you* or (*Brit*) *takes it out of you*, it requires a lot of work or energy and causes you to feel tired. ▪ *That interview really took a lot out of me.* — **take apart** [*phrasal vb*] **take apart (something)** or **take (something) apart 1** : to remove or separate the parts of (something) ▪ *taking apart rifles and putting them back together again* **2** : to talk about the different parts of (an idea, story, etc.) often in order to criticize it ▪ *She takes apart the theory and shows its weaknesses.* — **take away** [*phrasal vb*] **1 take away (someone or something)** or **take (someone or something) away** : to cause (someone or something) to go away, to no longer exist, to no longer be held, etc. ▪ *"Take him away!" said the queen.* He tried to take the ball away from the dog. ▪ *Her parents took away her driving privileges.* ▪ *The* *beautiful view* **took my breath away.** [=it made me feel surprised and excited] **2 take away (something) or take (something) away a** : to remember (something) for possible use in the future • *What lesson can we take away from this?* **b** *Brit* : to buy (food that is cooked in a restaurant) and carry it to another place • *pizza to take away* [=(US) *pizza for take-out*] **3 take away from** : to reduce the value or importance of (something) • *The ugly door takes away from the beauty of the house.* — **take back** [*phrasal vb*] **take back (something or someone) or take (something or someone) back a** : to return (something or someone) • *Take back the toys (to the store) for a refund.* • *I took him back (to his) home.* **b** : to accept or receive (something or someone) again • *They'll take back the dress if you have the receipt.* **c** : to say that you did not really mean (something that you said) • *He refused to take back what he said.* **2 take (someone) back** : to cause (someone) to remember a time or event • *a song that takes you back to your childhood* — **take down** [*phrasal vb*] **take down (something) or take (something) down 1** : to remove (something) from the place where it is hanging or standing • *She took the books down from the shelf.* **2** : to write (something) • *I took her phone number down on a napkin.* — **take in** [*phrasal vb*] **1 take in (someone) or take (someone) in a** : to allow (a person or animal) to stay in your house, hotel, etc. • *The homeless shelter takes in women and children.* • *taking in stray cats* **b** : to take (someone) to a police station • *The suspects were taken in for questioning.* **c** : to trick or deceive (someone) • *He was taken in by a man who said he was collecting money for a charity.* **2 take in (something) or take (something) in a** : to make (a piece of clothing) smaller or shorter • *I lost weight and had to take in my pants.* **b** *US* : to receive (something) as payment or earnings • *The restaurant takes in* [=(*Brit*) *takes*] *thousands of dollars a night.* **c** : to allow (water, air, etc.) to enter your body • *She took in the salty sea air.* **d** : to look at and think about (something) • *We sat taking in the view.* **e** : to learn about and try to understand (something) • *It's hard to take all this information in at once.* — **take it upon/on yourself** : to do something that needs to be done even though no one has asked you to do it • *I took it upon myself to organize the meeting.* — **take long** : to require or use a long amount of time • *It didn't take long to realize that something was wrong.* • *Hurry up. You're taking too long.* — **take note/notice** : to notice or pay attention to something • *She took note of the exact time.* • *The news made them sit up and take notice.* [=suddenly give full attention to something] — **take off** [*phrasal vb*] **1 a** : to suddenly go somewhere • *She took off without saying goodbye.* • *Where did you take off to?* [=where did you go?] **b take off after** *US* : to start to chase (someone or something) • *My dog*

took off after a rabbit. **2** : to begin to fly • *The plane's about to take off.* **3** : to quickly become very successful or popular • *Business is starting to take off.* **4 take off (something) or take (something) off a** : to remove (something) • *I took my boots/makeup off.* • *This diet will take inches off your waist.* • **Take your hands off me.** [=stop touching or holding me] • *I can't take my eyes off it.* [=I cannot stop looking at it] • *Hiring more teachers would help take the pressure off our staff.* **b** : to reduce the price of something by (a specified amount) • *They took $3,000 off the car's price.* **c** : to spend (an amount of time) away from a job or activity • *He took the day off (work) and went to the beach.* **5 take (someone) off** : to tell (someone) to stop using or doing (something) • *The doctor took her off the drug.* • *He was taken off the project.* — **take on** [*phrasal vb*] **take on (something or someone) or take (something or someone) on 1 a** : to begin to deal with (something) • *taking on new responsibilities/challenges* • *He was asked to take on an important assignment.* **b** : to begin to have (a particular quality or appearance) • *Her writings took on new meaning after her death.* • *stories in which animals take on human attributes* **2 a** : to fight or struggle with (someone or something) • *Police are taking on the city's drug dealers.* **:** to criticize or argue against (someone or something) • *She's not afraid to take on her critics.* **b** : to compete against (a person, team, etc.) • *She took him on in a game of tennis.* **c** : to allow (someone or something) to enter • *The train took on a few more passengers.* • *The ship sprang a leak and began to take on water.* **3** : to accept (someone) as an employee, client, etc. • *She took him on as an assistant.* — **take out** [*phrasal vb*] **1 take (something) out or take out (something) a** : to remove (something) from a thing, place, or person • *She had her tonsils taken out.* • *take out the nails* : to move (something) from the place that held, enclosed, or hid it • *Please take out a pencil and begin the test.* **b** : to make the arrangements, payments, etc., that are required for (something) • *All drivers must take out insurance on their vehicles.* • *take out a mortgage* • *take an ad out in the newspaper* **c** : to borrow or rent (something) from a store, library, etc. • *She took out books from the library.* **d** : to destroy (something) • *taking out enemy targets* **2 take (someone) out or take out (someone) a** : to go with (someone you have invited) to a restaurant, party, etc. • *Can I take you out (on a date) sometime?* • *They took us out for/to lunch.* **b** : to cause (a person or team) to no longer be part of a competition • *We were taken out in the first round.* **3 take (something) out on** : to treat someone badly because you feel angry, frustrated, etc. • *I'm sorry you didn't get the job, but don't take it out on me.* [=don't treat me badly because you are disappointed] — **take over** [*phrasal vb*] **take over or take over (something) or take (something) over 1** : to start doing (something that someone has stopped doing) ▪ *Take over (driving) for me for a while.* **2 :** to become the person who has control of (something) ▪ *She took over the company last year.* — **take through** [*phrasal vb*] **take (someone) through :** to tell (someone) how (something) happens or is done by explaining the details of each step ▪ *Take me through that day hour by hour.* — **take to** [*phrasal vb*] **1 :** to go to or into (a place) ▪ *They took to the hills/streets.* **2 :** to begin to like (someone or something) ▪ *He tried skiing and took to it immediately.* ▪ (*informal*) *They don't* **take (too) kindly to** [=they don't like] *strangers around here.* **3 :** to begin (doing something) as a habit ▪ *He took to drinking after he lost his job.* **4 take (something) to :** to use (something) to do something to (someone or something) ▪ *I need to take a mop to* [=I need to mop] *this floor.* — **take up** [*phrasal vb*] **1 take up or take up (something) or take (something) up :** to continue (something) after you or another person stops ▪ *She took up the story where he left off.* **2 :** to fill (an area, amount of time, etc.) completely or almost completely ▪ *The couch takes up half of the room.* ▪ *The entire day was taken up by/with meetings.* **3 take up (something) or take (something) up a :** to begin studying or practicing (something) ▪ *I was thinking about taking up skiing/photography.* ▪ *She took up the guitar.* **b :** to begin to deal with (a problem, an issue, etc.) ▪ *She has taken up the cause of global warming.* **c :** to begin to have (a new job, home, etc.) ▪ *He will take up his post next week.* ▪ *She took up residence in Paris.* **d :** to begin to use (something) ▪ *They took up hammers and went to work on the roof.* ▪ *They took up arms to defend their country.* **e :** to make (something, such as a piece of clothing) shorter ▪ *taking up a pair of pants* **f :** to lift and remove (something) ▪ *We took up the carpet.* **g :** to gather (money, clothes, etc.) from many different people or places ▪ *taking up a collection for the homeless* **4 take (someone) up on :** to make an agreement with (someone) to accept (an offer) ▪ *"Can I buy you a drink?" "Sure, I'll take you up on that."* ▪ *We took the company up on its offer to replace the computer for free.* **5 take (something) up with :** to talk about (something) with (someone) ▪ *If you have a problem, please take it up with the manager.* **6 :** to begin a friendly or romantic relationship with (someone) ▪ *She took up with a younger man.* — **taker** /ˈteɪkɚ/ *n* [*C*] ▪ *I have two tickets for sale. Any takers?*

²**take** *n* [*C*] **1 a :** the way that a person thinks about or understands something ▪ *What's your take on it?* [=what do you think about it?] **b :** a particular way of dealing with or treating something ▪ *a modern take on Dickens' story* **2 :** a scene that is filmed or a song that is recorded at one time without stopping ▪ *It took us 20 takes to get the scene right.* **3** *informal* **:** the amount of money that is earned or received ▪ *a take of 1 million*

dollars — **on the take** *informal* **:** illegally accepting bribes ▪ *a senator who is on the take*

take·away /ˈteɪkəˌweɪ/ *n* **1** *Brit* **a** [*U*] **: TAKEOUT 1 b** [*C*] **: TAKEOUT 2 2** [*C*] *sports* **:** an act of taking the ball or puck from a player on the other team

take–home pay /ˈteɪkˌhoʊm-/ *n* [*U*] **:** the amount of money that a person earns after taxes and other amounts have been subtracted ▪ *She grosses $40,000 a year but her take-home pay is about $25,000.*

taken *past participle of* ¹TAKE

take–no–prisoners *adj, always before a noun, US, informal* **:** very tough and aggressive ▪ *take-no-prisoners politics*

take–off /ˈteɪkˌɑːf/ *n* **1** [*C/U*] **:** the moment when an airplane, helicopter, etc., leaves the ground and begins to fly ▪ *ready for takeoff* **2** [*C*] **:** the beginning of a jump ▪ *a high jumper's flawless takeoff* **3** [*C*] **a :** a performance in which someone copies the way another person speaks, moves, etc., in usually a humorous way ▪ *He did a perfect takeoff* [=imitation] *of our teacher.* **b** *chiefly US* **:** ¹PARODY 1 ▪ *a funny takeoff on/of a quiz show*

take–out /ˈteɪkˌaʊt/ *n, US* **1** [*U*] **:** food that is cooked in a restaurant and taken by a customer to be eaten in another place ▪ *We ordered some Chinese takeout.* **2** [*C*] **:** a restaurant that sells takeout ▪ *She works in a Chinese takeout.* — **take-out** *adj, always before a noun, US* ▪ *take-out food/restaurants*

take·over /ˈteɪkˌoʊvɚ/ *n* [*C*] **:** an occurrence in which a person, company, etc., takes control of something ▪ *a takeover of the government by the military* ▪ *The company is trying to protect itself from a hostile takeover.* [=an attempt to buy a company when the people who own the company do not want to sell it]

take–up /ˈteɪkˌʌp/ *n* [*U, singular*] *Brit* **:** the rate at which something offered is accepted by people ▪ *Take-up of our products has been high.*

tak·ings /ˈteɪkɪŋz/ *n* [*plural*] *chiefly Brit* **:** the amount of money that is earned **: TAKE** ▪ *They donated the takings to charity.*

talc /ˈtælk/ *n* [*U*] **: TALCUM POWDER**

tal·cum powder /ˈtælkəm-/ *n* [*U*] **:** a soft, white powder that is used to make your skin feel dry and smooth

tale /ˈteɪl/ *n* [*C*] **1 :** a story about imaginary events **:** an exciting or dramatic story ▪ *The movie is a stirring tale of courage.* **2 :** a story about someone's actual experiences ▪ *He told us tales about his experiences during the war.* **3 :** a false story that is told to deceive someone ▪ *Are you telling tales? Or is that the truth?*

tal·ent /ˈtælənt/ *n* [*C/U*] **1 :** a special ability that allows someone to do something well ▪ *a singer with lots of talent* ▪ *athletic/artistic/musical talent* ▪ *He has a talent for getting into trouble.* [=he often gets into trouble] ▪ *a talent show/contest* **2 :** a talented person or group ▪ *She is a special talent.* — **tal·ent·ed** /ˈtæləntəd/ *adj* ▪ *a talented actor/athlete*

tal·is·man /ˈtæləsmən/ n [C] : a ring, stone, etc., that is believed to have magic powers

¹talk /ˈtɑːk/ vb **1 a** [T/I] : to say words in order to express your thoughts, feelings, etc., to someone ▪ *He never talks at the meetings.* ▪ *Don't talk to your mother that way.* ▪ *She still talks about her ex-boyfriend.* **b** [I] : to have a conversation or discussion with someone ▪ *We need to talk.* ▪ *They were talking in Spanish.* ▪ *We talked on the phone.* ▪ *Both sides in the dispute are now willing to talk.* ▪ *It's been two weeks since their argument, and they're still not talking (to each other).* ▪ *I could hear her talking to herself as she studied.* ▪ *The teacher talked with him about his poor grades.* **c** [T] : to have a conversation about (something) ▪ *They were talking baseball/politics.* ▪ *We talked shop.* [=talked about work] **2** [I] : to use your voice to say words : SPEAK ▪ *She had laryngitis and couldn't talk.* ▪ *No talking during the performance, please!* **3** [I] : to talk about the personal lives of other people ▪ *If you keep acting like that, people are going to talk.* **4** [I] : to tell secret information to someone ▪ *The police forced him to talk.* **5** [I] : to give information without speaking ▪ *They were talking to each other in sign language.* ▪ *The computer is talking to the printer.* **6** [T] : to talk until (someone or something) is in a specified state ▪ *He talked himself hoarse.* [=he talked so much that his voice became hoarse] ▪ *We talked the night away.* [=we talked throughout the night] **7** [I] : to criticize someone ✧ This sense of *talk* is often used in phrases like **look who's talking**, **you're one to talk**, and **you should talk** to say that someone should not criticize another person because he or she has the same faults as that other person. ▪ *"She's too skinny." "You're one to talk. You need to gain weight, too."* **8** [T] *informal* — used to describe or suggest the size or amount of something ▪ *To fix the car, you're talking at least $500.* — **know what you are talking about** see ¹KNOW — **now you're talking** *informal* — used to say that someone has said or suggested something that you think is good, worth doing, etc. ▪ *"You don't want hamburgers. Well, how about steak?" "Yeah, now you're talking."* — **talk a blue streak** see ¹BLUE — **talk about 1** ✧ The phrase **what are you talking about?** can be used to show that you are confused, worried, etc., about something that someone has just said. ▪ *What are you talking about? I did what you told me to do.* **2** *informal* — used to emphasize the size, amount, or extent of something ▪ *Talk about rain! I've never seen it rain like this in my entire life!* — **talk a good game** *informal* : to say things that make people believe that you can do something or that something is true about you ▪ *They talk a good game, but they're not a very good team.* — **talk around** also chiefly Brit **talk round** [phrasal vb] : to avoid talking about (something) especially because it is difficult, unpleasant, or embarrassing ▪

They've been talking around the issue. — **talk back** [phrasal vb] : to answer (someone) in a rude way that does not show proper respect ▪ *Don't talk back (to your parents).* — **talk down** [phrasal vb] **1 talk down to** : to talk to (someone) in an overly simple way ▪ *Don't talk down to me. I'm not stupid.* **2 talk down (something or someone)** or **talk (something or someone) down** : to cause (the price of something) to be lower by talking to someone ▪ *She managed to talk down his asking price for the car.* : to convince (someone) to lower the price of something ▪ *She talked him down 500 dollars.* — **talk into** [phrasal vb] **talk (someone) into** : to convince or persuade (someone) to do something by talking about the good reasons for doing it ▪ *The salesman talked us into buying the car.* — **talk of** [phrasal vb] : to speak or write about (someone or something) ▪ *It was the first time she talked of going to law school.* ▪ *(Brit) Talking of Jill, where is she?* — **talk out** [phrasal vb] **talk out (something)** or **talk (something) out** : to talk about (something) in order to find a solution ▪ *Try talking out the problem.* — **talk out of** [phrasal vb] **1 talk (someone) out of** : to persuade or convince (someone) not to do (something) by talking about the good reasons for not doing it ▪ *He talked her out of quitting school.* **2 talk (yourself) out of** or **talk your way out of** : to avoid (something unpleasant or undesirable) by saying things to make other people forgive or excuse you ▪ *She talked her way out of trouble.* — **talk over** [phrasal vb] **talk (something) over** or **talk over (something)** : to discuss (something) with someone in order to make a decision or reach an agreement ▪ *I need to talk the offer over with my wife, first.* — **talk someone's ear off** US, *informal* : to talk to someone for a very long time — **talk the talk** : to say that you will do things ▪ *Sure, she talks the talk, but can she walk the walk?* [=she says that she will do things, but will she actually do them?] — **talk through** [phrasal vb] **1 talk (someone) through** : to help (someone) understand or do something by explaining its steps in a careful way ▪ *The woman on the phone talked me through the procedure.* **2 talk (something) through** : to discuss (something) with someone in order to make a decision or reach an agreement ▪ *Have you talked this through with your family?* — **talk trash** see ¹TRASH — **talk turkey** see TURKEY — **talk up** [phrasal vb] **talk up (someone or something)** or **talk (someone or something) up** : to describe (someone or something) in a favorable way ▪ *The salesperson talked up the car's safety features.*

²talk n **1** [C/U] : the act of talking about something with another person ▪ *After a long talk about our relationship, we decided to get married.* ▪ *When they get together, the talk* [=conversation] *always turns to baseball.* ▪ *The boss would like to* **have a talk with** *you.* **2** [C] : a speech or lecture ▪ *He gave a talk on organic farming.* **3** [C] : a formal discussion between two or more groups that are trying to reach an agreement about something • *talks on nuclear disarmament* **4** [*U*] : a particular way of speaking • *I will not allow that kind of talk in my house.* **5** [*U*] : discussion about what might happen • *There has been some talk of* [=people have been saying that there will/may be] *further delays.* **6** [*U*] : the things people say about what they want to do or are going to do • *She was* **all talk** *(and no action).* [=she talked about doing things but never actually did them] • *Talk is cheap.* [=it is easy to say that you will do something] *I need to see results.* — **talk the talk** see ¹TALK — **the talk of the town** : a person or thing that many people in a town, city, etc., are talking about in an interested or excited way • *The new restaurant is the talk of the town.*

talk·a·tive /'tɑːkətɪv/ *adj* : tending to talk a lot or to enjoy having conversations with people • *a talkative boy/mood*

talk·er /'tɑːkɚ/ *n* [*C*] : a person who talks in a particular way or who talks a lot • *She's a great/fast talker.* • *He's not much of a talker.*

talk·ing–to /'tɑːkɪŋˌtuː/ *n* [*singular*] *informal* : an angry or serious conversation in which you criticize someone's behavior • *We gave our son a good/stern talking-to about his poor grades.*

talk radio *n* [*U*] *chiefly US* : radio programs in which people talk about politics, sports, etc.

talk show *n* [*C*] : a radio or TV program in which usually well-known people talk about something or are interviewed

tall /'tɑːl/ *adj* **1** : greater in height than the average person, building, etc. • *My dad is quite tall.* • *the world's tallest building/trees* **2** *always after a noun* : having a specified height • *She is five feet tall.* • *The building is six stories tall.* [=high] — **stand tall** see ¹STAND — **walk tall** see ¹WALK

tall order *n* [*singular*] *informal* : something that is very difficult to do • *Finishing the project on time will be a tall order (to fill).*

tall tale *n* [*C*] : a story that is very difficult to believe

¹**tal·ly** /'tæli/ *n, pl* **-lies** [*C*] **1** : a record of scores, votes, money, etc. • *He was declared the winner after the final tally.* • *He kept a daily/running tally* [=account] *of his expenses.* **2** *US, informal* : a score or point made in a game or sport • *the game-winning tally*

²**tally** *vb* **-lies; -lied; -ly·ing** **1** [*T*] : to record and count or calculate (something) • *He tallied (up) his expenses.* **2** [*I*] : to agree or match • *The old numbers don't tally with the new numbers.*

Tal·mud /'tɑːlˌmʊd/ *n* — **the Talmud** : the writings that declare Jewish law and tradition — **Tal·mu·dic** /tæl'muːdɪk/ *adj* • *Talmudic scholars*

tal·on /'tælən/ *n* [*C*] : one of the sharp claws on the feet of some birds • *the owl's talons*

ta·ma·le /tə'mɑːli/ *n* [*C*] : a Mexican food that consists of meat or beans rolled in cornmeal and wrapped in a corn husk

tam·bou·rine /ˌtæmbə'riːn/ *n* [*C*] : a small musical instrument that is held in one hand and played by shaking or hitting it with the other hand

¹**tame** /'teɪm/ *adj* **tam·er, -est** **1 a** : not wild : trained to obey people • *a tame elephant* **b** : not afraid of people • *The island's birds are quite tame.* **2** : not exciting or interesting • *a tame political campaign* **3** : gentle and obedient • *a tame audience* — **tame·ly** *adv* — **tame·ness** *n* [*U*]

²**tame** *vb* **tamed; tam·ing** [*T*] **1** : to make (an animal) tame • *trying to tame a horse* **2** : to make (something) less wild : to bring (something) under control • *taming the Wild West* • *ways to tame inflation* — **tam·er** *n* [*C*] • *a lion tamer*

tamp /'tæmp/ *vb* [*T*] : to press (something) down by hitting it lightly • *He tamped (down) the soil with his foot.*

tam·per /'tæmpɚ/ *vb* — **tamper with** [*phrasal vb*] : to change or touch (something) especially in a way that causes damage or harm • *Someone tampered with the lock/evidence.*

tam·per-proof /'tæmpɚˌpruːf/ *adj* : designed so that tampering cannot occur • *pills that come in tamperproof packaging*

tam·pon /'tæmˌpɑːn/ *n* [*C*] : a piece of soft material that is placed in the vagina to absorb menstrual blood

¹**tan** /'tæn/ *n* **1** [*C*] : SUNTAN • *I got a tan on my vacation.* **2** [*C/U*] : a light brown color

²**tan** *vb* **tanned; tan·ning** **1** [*T/I*] : to become or cause (skin) to become darker especially from being exposed to the sun's rays • *The sun tanned her skin.* • *My skin tans easily.* = *I tan easily.* **2** [*T*] : to change (the skin of an animal) into leather by a chemical process • *tan the hides*

³**tan** *adj* **1** : having skin that has been made darker by being exposed to the sun's rays • *She is tan.* **2** : having a light brown color • *a tan coat*

tan·dem /'tændəm/ *n* **1** : TANDEM BICYCLE **2** *chiefly US* : a group of two people or things that work together or are associated with each other • *The team has a tandem of talented guards.* — **in tandem** *of two people, groups, or things* : working or happening together or at the same time • *The two products can be used alone or in tandem.* • *They're working in tandem with scientists from England.*

tandem bicycle *n* [*C*] : a bicycle built for two riders with one sitting behind the other

tang /'tæŋ/ *n* [*singular*] : a strong, sharp taste or smell • *chicken with a tang of citrus* — **tangy** /'tæŋi/ *adj* **tang·i·er, -est** • *a tangy sauce*

tan·gent /'tændʒənt/ *n* [*C*] *geometry* : a line that touches a sphere or circle at only one point — **go off on a tangent** (*US*) or *Brit* **go off at a tangent** : to start talking about something that is only slightly or indirectly related to the original subject

tan·gen·tial /tæn'dʒɛnʃəl/ *adj* **1** *formal* : slightly or indirectly related to something • *Their romance is tangential to the* *book's main plot.* **2** *geometry* : relating to a tangent : in or along a tangent ▪ *tangential force* — **tan·gen·tial·ly** *adv*

tan·ger·ine /ˈtændʒəˌriːn/ *n* **1** [C] : a small, sweet fruit that is like an orange with a loose skin **2** [U] : a deep orange-yellow color

tan·gi·ble /ˈtændʒəbəl/ *adj* **1** : easily seen or recognized ▪ *tangible benefits/results* **2** : able to be touched or felt ▪ *tangible objects/assets* — **tan·gi·bil·i·ty** /ˌtændʒəˈbɪləti/ *n* [U]

¹**tan·gle** /ˈtæŋgəl/ *vb* **tan·gled; tan·gling** [T/I] : to become or cause (something) to become twisted together ▪ *My hair tangles easily.* ▪ *Her foot was tangled (up) in the cord.* ▪ *tangled yarn* ▪ *(figurative) He got tangled up in legal problems.* — **tangle with** [phrasal vb] informal : to fight or argue with (someone or something) ▪ *He's not someone I would want to tangle with.*

²**tangle** *n* [C] **1** : a twisted knot of hair, thread, etc. **2** : a state of disorder or confusion ▪ *a legal/financial tangle* **3** informal : a fight or disagreement ▪ *He got into a tangle with police.*

tan·go /ˈtæŋgoʊ/ *n, pl* **-gos** [C] : a Latin-American dance in which couples make long pauses ▪ *dancing a/the tango* — **tan·go** *vb* [I] ▪ *learning how to tango* ▪ *(figurative) In a fight, it takes two to tango.* [=two people are needed to fight]

¹**tank** /ˈtæŋk/ *n* [C] **1** **a** : a container for holding a liquid or gas ▪ *a fuel/gas/fish tank* **b** : the amount that a tank will hold ▪ *We used up a tank of gas.* **2** : a military vehicle that moves on two large metal belts and that is covered in heavy armor — **in/into the tank** US, informal : in or into a very bad state or condition ▪ *The economy is in the tank right now.* — **tank·ful** /ˈtæŋkˌfʊl/ *n* [C] ▪ *a tankful of gas*

²**tank** *vb* [I] US, informal : to be very unsuccessful : to fail completely ▪ *The movie tanked.*

tank·er /ˈtæŋkɚ/ *n* [C] : a vehicle (such as a ship or truck) that is designed to carry liquids

tank top *n* [C] US : a shirt that has no sleeves or collar and usually has wide shoulder straps

tan·nin /ˈtænən/ *n* [C/U] : a reddish acid that occurs in various foods and drinks (such as wine)

tan·ning /ˈtænɪŋ/ *n* [U] : the act or process of darkening your skin by exposing it to the bright light of the sun or a special type of lamp

tan·ta·lize also Brit **tan·ta·lise** /ˈtæntəˌlaɪz/ *vb* **-lized; -liz·ing** [T] : to cause (someone) to feel interest or excitement about something that is very attractive, appealing, etc. ▪ *the tantalizing aroma of baking bread* — **tan·ta·liz·ing·ly** also Brit **tan·ta·lis·ing·ly** *adv*

tan·ta·mount /ˈtæntəˌmaʊnt/ *adj* : equal to something in value, meaning, or effect ▪ *His statement was tantamount to an admission of guilt.*

tan·trum /ˈtæntrəm/ *n* [C] : an uncontrolled expression of childish anger ▪ *When he doesn't get his way, he has/*throws a (temper) tantrum. [=he gets very angry and behaves like a child]

Tao /ˈdaʊ/ *n* [U] : the source and guiding principle of all reality according to Taoism

Tao·ism /ˈdaʊˌɪzəm/ *n* [U] : a Chinese philosophy based on the writings of Lao-tzu that stresses living simply and honestly and in harmony with nature — **Tao·ist** /ˈdaʊɪst/ *n* [C]

¹**tap** /ˈtæp/ *vb* **tapped; tap·ping** **1** [T/I] : to hit (someone or something) lightly especially with a small sound ▪ *He was tapping the desk with a pencil.* ▪ *He tapped her (on the) shoulder to get her attention.* **2** [T/I] : to hit (your fingers, feet, etc.) against something lightly ▪ *tapping a pencil on a desk* ▪ *Her foot was tapping to (the beat of) the music.* **3** [T/I] : to take or use money, knowledge, etc., from a source ▪ *tap (into) the nation's resources* ▪ *(figurative) The story taps into powerful emotions.* **4** [T] : to make liquid flow from something by attaching a spigot or tap or by making or opening a hole ▪ *tap a keg* ▪ *tapping (sap from) maple trees* **5** [T] : to place a device on (someone's phone) in order to secretly listen to telephone calls ▪ *The FBI tapped his phone.* **6** [T] : to get something useful or valuable from (someone) ▪ *He tried to tap me for a loan.* **7** [T] chiefly US : to choose (someone) for a particular job, honor, etc. ▪ *She was tapped for treasurer. = She was tapped to be treasurer.*

²**tap** *n* [C] **1** : a light hit or touch or the sound that it makes ▪ *There was a tap at the door.* ▪ *I felt a tap on my shoulder.* **2** : a device for controlling the flow of a liquid or gas from a pipe or container ▪ *turn on/off the tap* [=faucet] ▪ *the tap* [=spigot] *on a beer keg* **3** : a device that allows someone to secretly listen to phone conversations ▪ *They put a tap on her phone.* — **on tap** **1** : served from a barrel ▪ *beer on tap* **2** : available whenever you need it ▪ *The hotel has Internet service on tap.* **3** US : planned or scheduled to happen ▪ *What's on tap for this weekend?*

tap dance *n* [C] : a kind of dance in which you wear special shoes with metal plates on the heels and toes and make tapping sounds with your feet — **tap–dance** *vb* **-danced; -dancing** [I]

¹**tape** /ˈteɪp/ *n* **1** [U] : a long, narrow piece of material that is sticky on one side and that is used to attach things **2** **a** [U] : a thin piece of plastic that is coated with magnetic material on which information may be stored ▪ *The show/song was recorded on tape.* **b** [C] : something recorded on tape ▪ *a tape of the concert* **c** [C] : CASSETTE ▪ *She stuck a tape in the VCR.* **3** [U] : a long, thin piece of plastic, paper, or cloth ▪ *The crime scene was marked off with yellow police tape.*

²**tape** *vb* **taped; tap·ing** [T] **1** : to attach (something) using tape ▪ *She taped a note to/on the door.* **2** : to fasten, tie, or cover (something) with tape ▪ *Tape the box shut.* ▪ *I taped (up) the ends of the wire.* **3** : to record (something) on magnetic tape ▪ *The show is taped before a live audience.*

• *a taped interview* **4** *chiefly US* : to wrap (an injured body part) tightly with long pieces of special cloth • *The doctor taped (up) her ankle.*

tape deck *n* [C] : a machine that plays and records sounds on magnetic tape

tape measure *n* [C] : a long, thin piece of plastic, cloth, or metal that is marked with inches, centimeters, etc., and that is used for measuring things

¹**ta·per** /ˈteɪpɚ/ *vb* [I] : to become gradually smaller toward one end • *leaves that taper to a point* — **taper off** [*phrasal vb*] : to become gradually less and less : to decrease slowly • *Production has been tapering off.* — **tapered** *adj* • *tapered slacks*

²**taper** *n* [C] : a long, thin candle

tape–re·cord /ˌteɪprɪˈkoɚd/ *vb* [T] : to make a recording of (something) on magnetic tape • *tape-record a concert*

tape recorder *n* [C] : a machine used to record and play sound on magnetic tape

tape recording *n* [C] : ¹TAPE 2b

tap·es·try /ˈtæpəstri/ *n, pl* **-tries** [C] : a heavy cloth that has designs or pictures woven into it and that is used for wall hangings, curtains, etc.

tape·worm /ˈteɪpˌwɚm/ *n* [C] : a long, flat worm that lives in the intestines of people and animals

tap·i·o·ca /ˌtæpiˈoʊkə/ *n* [U] **1** : a type of small, white grain **2** : a dessert made by cooking tapioca grains — called also *tapioca pudding*

ta·pir /ˈteɪpɚ/ *n, pl* **tapir** or **ta·pirs** [C] : an animal that is like a pig and that lives in tropical America and southeast Asia

taps /ˈtæps/ *n* [*plural*] *US, military* : a song played on a bugle at military funerals and as a signal for soldiers to go to bed

tap water *n* [U] : water that comes through pipes from the public water system

¹**tar** /ˈtaɚ/ *n* [C/U] **1** : a very thick, black, sticky liquid that becomes hard when it cools and that is used especially for road surfaces **2** : a sticky substance that is formed by burning tobacco • *low-tar cigarettes*

²**tar** *vb* **tarred; tar·ring** [T] : to cover (something) with tar • *tar a roadway* — **tar and feather (someone)** : to cover (someone) with tar and then with feathers as an old-fashioned punishment • (*figurative*) *If I don't get home in time, Mom will tar and feather me.*

ta·ran·tu·la /təˈræntʃələ/ *n* [C] : a large, hairy spider that lives in warm regions

tar·dy /ˈtaɚdi/ *adj* **tar·di·er; -est** *formal* **1** : slow in moving, acting, or happening • *tardy progress* • *a tardy payment/arrival* **b** : arriving or doing something late • *tardy students* • *She was tardy to/for work.* — **tar·di·ly** /ˈtaɚdəli/ *adv* — **tar·di·ness** /ˈtaɚdinəs/ *n* [U]

¹**tar·get** /ˈtaɚgət/ *n* [C] **1** : something that you are trying to do or achieve • *We failed to meet/reach this month's sales targets.* [=goals] • *Our target amount for the fund-raiser is $2,500.* **2** : a place, thing,

or person at which an attack is aimed • *Planes struck at key military targets.* • *a target for/of criticism* • *Tourists are often easy targets for thieves.* • (*figurative*) *Men in this age group are prime targets for heart disease.* **3** : the person or group that someone is trying to influence, sell something to, etc. • *Their target audience/market is teenagers.* **4** : something (such as a round board with circles on it) that you try to hit with arrows, bullets, etc. • *aiming/firing/shooting at a moving target* — **off target 1** : not correct or accurate • *You're way off target.* **2** : not likely to reach a goal • *We are off target in terms of sales.* — **on target 1** : correct or accurate • *His predictions are on target.* **2** : likely to reach a goal • *We are on target to meet this month's sales goals.*

²**target** *vb* [T] **1** : to aim an attack at someone or something • *The missiles were targeted at major cities.* • *Thieves often target tourists.* • *drugs that target cancer cells* **2** : to direct an action, message, etc., at someone or something • *The commercial is targeted at children.* • *government programs that target low-income areas*

tar·iff /ˈterəf/ *n* [C] **1** : a tax on goods coming into or leaving a country **2** *chiefly Brit* : a list of prices charged by a hotel, restaurant, company, etc.

tar·mac /ˈtaɚˌmæk/ *n* — **the tarmac** : the area covered by pavement at an airport • *airplanes on the tarmac*

¹**tar·nish** /ˈtaɚnɪʃ/ *vb* **1** [T/I] : to become or cause (metal) to become dull • *Silver tarnishes easily.* **2** [T] : to damage or ruin the good quality of (a person's reputation, image, etc.) • *His actions tarnished the family's good name.*

²**tarnish** *n* [U, *singular*] : a dull surface on metal

ta·ro /ˈtɑroʊ, ˈteroʊ/ *n, pl* **-ros** [C/U] : a tropical plant with a thick root that can be boiled and eaten

tar·ot /ˈteroʊ/ *n* [*singular*] : a set of cards with pictures and symbols that is used to see what will happen in the future • *tarot cards*

tarp /ˈtaɚp/ *n* [C] *US* : TARPAULIN

tar·pau·lin /taɚˈpɑlən/ *n* [C] : a large piece of plastic, canvas, etc., that is used to cover things and keep them dry

tar·ra·gon /ˈterəˌgɑn/ *n* [U] : a small herb that is used to flavor food

¹**tar·ry** /ˈteri/ *vb* **-ries; -ried; -ry·ing** [I] *literary* : to be slow in going : LINGER • *We tarried over breakfast.*

²**tar·ry** /ˈtɑri/ *adj* **1** : covered with tar • *a tarry surface* **2** : dark or thick like tar • *a tarry substance*

¹**tart** /ˈtaɚt/ *n* [C] **1** : an open pie that usually has a sweet filling (such as fruit or custard) **2** *informal* : ¹PROSTITUTE

²**tart** *adj* **1** : having a sharp or sour taste • *a tart apple* **2** : having a sharp and unkind quality • *a tart reply* — **tart·ly** *adv* — **tart·ness** *n* [U]

³**tart** *vb* — **tart up** [*phrasal vb*] **tart (someone) up** *informal* : to try to make (yourself or someone else) attractive by wearing fancy clothes, makeup, etc. • *She*

tarted herself up for the party. • (Brit, figurative) old ideas tarted up to look new

tar·tan /'tɑɑtn̩/ n 1 [C] : a traditional Scottish cloth pattern of stripes that cross each other to form squares 2 [C/U] : fabric with a tartan pattern

tar·tar /'tɑɑtə/ n [U] : a hard substance that forms on teeth

tar·tar sauce (US) or Brit **tar·tare sauce** /'tɑɑtə-/ n [U] : a sauce that is made of mayonnaise and chopped pickles and that is often served with fish

¹**task** /'tæsk/ n [C] : a piece of work for someone to do • accomplishing a difficult task • This is no easy task. • I'm concentrating on the task at hand. [=the work I'm doing right now] — take (someone) to task : to criticize (someone) harshly • She took me to task for wasting time.

²**task** vb [T] : to give (someone) a piece of work to do • She was tasked with decorating the room.

task·bar /'tæsk,bɑɑ/ n [C] : a narrow band across the bottom of a computer screen that shows which programs are running and which documents are open

task force n [C] : a group of people who deal with a specific problem • a crime-fighting task force

task·mas·ter /'tæsk,mæstə, Brit 'tɑːsk-,mɑːstə/ n [C] : a person who assigns work to other people

tas·sel /'tæsəl/ n [C] : a decoration made of a bunch of strings fastened at one end • shoes with tassels — **tas·seled** (chiefly US) or chiefly Brit **tas·selled** /'tæsəld/ adj • tasseled pillows

¹**taste** /'teɪst/ n 1 [C] : the sweet, sour, bitter, or salty quality of a thing that you can sense when it is in your mouth • The wine had a slightly bitter taste. • the sour taste of vinegar • (figurative) The experience left a bad taste in my mouth. [=it made me feel bad, disgusted, etc.] 2 [U] : the ability to taste flavors • The illness affected her sense of taste. 3 [C] : a small amount of food or drink • May I have a taste of your soup? 4 [singular] : something (such as a brief experience) that gives you some knowledge about what something is like • her first taste of success • That first storm was just a taste of things to come. 5 [C/U] : the feelings that each person has about what is appealing, attractive, etc. • She has developed/acquired a taste for red wine. • You and I have different tastes. • They have expensive tastes. [=they like expensive things] • The music is too loud for my taste. • The movie appeals to popular taste. [=is liked by many or most people] • Whether you like the music or not is purely a matter of taste. 6 [U] : the ability to choose what is appealing, attractive, appropriate, or enjoyable • The way he dresses shows that he has no taste. • She has good/poor taste in music. • The joke was in (very) bad/poor taste. = The joke wasn't in good taste. [=the joke was offensive] — to taste : in an amount that results in the taste that you want • Salt the stew to taste.

²**taste** vb **tast·ed**; **tast·ing** 1 [linking vb] : to have a particular taste • The milk tastes bad/sour. • The wine tastes like vine-

gar. • a sweet-tasting fruit 2 [T] **a** : to sense the flavor of (something that you are eating or drinking) • Can you taste the garlic in the sauce? **b** : to put a small amount of (food or drink) in your mouth in order to find out what its flavor is • I tasted the tea and put more sugar in it. **c** : EAT • I haven't tasted anything since yesterday. 3 [T] : to experience (something) • The team has yet to taste victory/defeat.

taste bud n [C] : one of many small spots on your tongue that let you taste things

taste·ful /'teɪstfəl/ adj : done or chosen with a knowledge of what is attractive, appropriate, or enjoyable • tasteful decorations — **taste·ful·ly** adv • The room was tastefully decorated. — **taste·ful·ness** n [U]

taste·less /'teɪstləs/ adj 1 : not having much flavor • a nearly tasteless soup 2 : not having or showing good taste : rude or offensive • a tasteless joke — **taste·less·ly** adv — **taste·less·ness** n [U]

taste·mak·er /'teɪst,meɪkə/ n [C] : a person whose judgments about what is good, fashionable, etc., are accepted and followed by many other people

tast·er /'teɪstə/ n [C] 1 : a person who tastes foods or drinks to test their quality 2 Brit, informal : a small amount of something that you can try to see if you like it • The magazine printed a taster of the novel.

tasting n [C] : a social event at which something is sampled and tasted • a wine tasting

tasty /'teɪsti/ adj **tast·i·er**; **-est** 1 : having a good flavor • a tasty meal 2 informal : very appealing or interesting • tasty gossip — **tast·i·ness** /'teɪstinəs/ n [U]

tat /'tæt/ n [U] Brit, informal : items that are cheap and poorly made • shops full of tat [=junk] — see also TIT FOR TAT

ta–ta /,tæ'tɑː/ interj, chiefly Brit, informal : GOODBYE

ta·ter /'teɪtə/ n [C] informal : POTATO

tat·tered /'tætəd/ adj : old and torn • a tattered flag/book • (figurative) the tattered remains of her image

tat·ters /'tætəz/ n [plural] : clothes that are old and badly torn • They were dressed in tatters. • (figurative) After the war, the economy was/lay in tatters.

tat·tle /'tætl/ vb **tat·tled**; **tat·tling** [I] chiefly US, informal : to tell a parent, teacher, etc., about something bad or wrong that another child has done • He tattled on her. — **tat·tler** /'tætlə/ n [C]

tat·tle·tale /'tætl̩,teɪl/ n [C] chiefly US, informal + disapproving : a child who tattles on another child

tat·too /tæ'tuː/ n, pl **-toos** [C] 1 : a picture, word, etc., that is drawn on a person's skin by using a needle and ink 2 Brit : an outdoor performance in the evening with music and marching by members of the military — **tattoo** vb [T] • He had a heart tattooed on his arm. [=he had a tattoo of a heart on his arm]

tat·ty /'tæti/ adj **tat·ti·er**; **-est** informal : old and in poor condition • a tatty sweater

taught past tense and past participle of TEACH

taunt /ˈtɑːnt/ vb [T] : to say insulting things to (someone) in order to make that person angry ▪ *The boys taunted each other.* — **taunt** n [C] — **taunt·er** n [C]

Tau·rus /ˈtorəs/ n **1** [U] : the second sign of the zodiac that comes between Aries and Gemini and has a bull as its symbol **2** [C] : a person born between April 20 and May 20

taut /ˈtɑːt/ adj **1** : very tight from being pulled or stretched ▪ *The rope was pulled taut.* **2** : firm and strong ▪ *taut muscles* **3** : very tense ▪ *taut nerves* — **taut·ly** adv — **taut·ness** n [U]

tav·ern /ˈtævən/ n [C] : a place where alcoholic drinks are served : BAR

taw·dry /ˈtɑːdri/ adj **taw·dri·er; -est** disapproving **1** : having a cheap and ugly appearance ▪ *tawdry decorations* **2** : morally low or bad ▪ *The scandal was a tawdry affair.* — **taw·dri·ness** /ˈtɑːdrinəs/ n [U]

taw·ny /ˈtɑːni/ adj : having a brownish-orange color ▪ *tawny fur*

¹**tax** /ˈtæks/ n [C/U] : an amount of money that a government requires people to pay according to their income, the value of their property, etc., and that is used to pay for the things done by the government ▪ *raise/cut taxes* ▪ *a tax on tobacco products* ▪ *What was your income before/after tax?* ▪ *tax laws*

²**tax** vb [T] **1 a** : to require (someone) to pay a tax ▪ *taxing the wealthy* ▪ *You are taxed according to your income.* **b** : to require someone to pay a tax on (something) ▪ *All income/property is taxed.* **2** : to require a lot from (something or someone) ▪ *You're taxing my patience.* [=making me lose my patience] ▪ *puzzles that tax your brain* ▪ *have a vacation without taxing your budget* [=without spending a lot of money] ▪ *a very taxing job/journey* — **tax with** [phrasal vb] **tax (someone) with** formal : to accuse (someone) of (something) ▪ *She taxed them with carelessness.* — **tax·able** /ˈtæksəbəl/ adj ▪ *taxable income* — **tax·a·tion** /tækˈseɪʃən/ n [U] ▪ *taxation on capital gains* — **tax·er** n [C]

¹**taxi** /ˈtæksi/ n, pl **tax·is** /ˈtæksiz/ [C/U] : a car that carries passengers to a place for an amount of money that is based on the distance traveled ▪ *We took a taxi to the airport.*

²**taxi** vb **taxis** or **tax·ies; tax·ied; taxi·ing 1** [I] of an airplane : to move on wheels along the ground ▪ *The plane taxied to the runway.* **2** [T/I] : to cause an airplane to taxi ▪ *The pilot taxied (the plane) out to the runway.*

taxi·cab /ˈtæksiˌkæb/ n [C/U] : ¹TAXI

taxi·der·my /ˈtæksəˌdəmi/ n [U] : the activity of preparing the skins of dead animals so that they look like they did when they were alive — **taxi·der·mist** /ˈtæksəˌdəmist/ n [C]

taxi stand n [C] US : a place where taxis park while waiting to be hired — called also (Brit) **taxi rank**

tax·on·o·my /tækˈsɑːnəmi/ n, pl **-mies**

[C/U] technical : the process or system of describing the way different living things are related by putting them in groups ▪ *plant taxonomy* — **tax·o·nom·ic** /ˌtæksəˈnɑːmɪk/ adj — **tax·o·nom·i·cal·ly** /ˌtæksəˈnɑːmɪkli/ adv — **tax·on·o·mist** /tækˈsɑːnəmɪst/ n [C]

tax·pay·er /ˈtæksˌpejə/ n [C] : a person who pays taxes

tb. abbr tablespoon; tablespoonful

TB /ˌtiˈbiː/ n [U] : TUBERCULOSIS

TBA abbr to be announced — used to indicate that the time, place, etc., of something will be announced at a later time ▪ *The meeting will be next Monday at 2:00, location TBA.*

T–ball /ˈtiːˌbɑːl/ n [U] sports : a form of baseball for young children in which the ball is hit off a tee

TBD abbr, US to be determined — used to indicate that the time, place, etc., of something has not yet been decided ▪ *The game has been postponed, time TBD.*

T–bone /ˈtiːˌboun/ n [C] : a thick piece of beef that contains a T-shaped bone — called also **T-bone steak**

tbs. or **tbsp.** abbr tablespoon; tablespoonful

TD /ˈtiːˈdiː/ n [C] American football, informal : TOUCHDOWN

tea /ˈtiː/ n **1** [C/U] : a drink that is made by soaking the dried leaves of a plant in hot water ▪ *a cup of (herbal/mint) tea* **2** [U] : the dried leaves that are used in making tea ▪ *a bag of tea = a tea bag* **3** [C/U] Brit **a** : a light meal or snack that usually includes tea and that is served in the late afternoon ▪ *Let's meet for tea.* **b** : a cooked meal that is served in the early evening — **not your cup of tea** see ¹CUP

tea break n [C] chiefly Brit : COFFEE BREAK

tea cake n [C] : a small, flat cake that is eaten with tea

teach /ˈtiːtʃ/ vb **taught** /ˈtɑːt/; **teach·ing 1** [T/I] : to cause or help a person or animal to learn about a subject, to do an activity, etc., by giving lessons ▪ *She teaches (English) at the high school.* ▪ *teaching a child to read/swim* ▪ *I taught my dog to retrieve sticks.* **2** [T] : to show someone how to behave, think, etc. ▪ *Someone needs to teach her right and wrong.* ▪ *The experience taught us that money doesn't mean everything.* **3** [T] informal : to cause (someone) to know the unpleasant results of something ▪ *He got punished. That'll teach him to lie to me.* [=show him that he should not lie to me again] ▪ *She wanted to teach them a lesson.* [=show them not to do something again] — **you can't teach an old dog new tricks** see ¹DOG

teach·able /ˈtiːtʃəbəl/ adj **1** : able and willing to be taught ▪ *teachable students* **2** : allowing something to be taught or learned easily ▪ *The book's style makes it very teachable.*

teach·er /ˈtiːtʃə/ n [C] : a person or thing that teaches something ▪ *Experience is a good teacher.; especially* : a person whose job is to teach students about certain subjects ▪ *a language/math/science teacher*

teaching *n* **1** [*U*] : the job or profession of a teacher ▪ *He went into teaching after college.* ▪ *the teaching profession* **2** [*C*] : the ideas and beliefs that are taught by a person, religion, etc. ▪ *the teachings of Confucius/Christianity*

teaching assistant *n* [*C*] *US* : a graduate student who teaches classes at a college or university — abbr. *TA*

tea cloth *n* [*C*] *Brit* : DISH TOWEL

tea·cup /'tiːˌkʌp/ *n* [*C*] : a small cup used for drinking tea

tea·house /'tiːˌhaʊs/ *n* [*C*] : a restaurant where tea and other refreshments are served

teak /'tiːk/ *n* [*U*] : the strong, hard wood of a tree that grows in southeast Asia — called also *teakwood*

tea·ket·tle /'tiːˌkɛtl/ *n* [*C*] *US* : a covered container that is used for boiling water and that has a handle and a spout

teal /'tiːl/ *n, pl* **teal** *or* **teals** **1** [*C*] : a small duck found in Europe and America **2** [*U*] : a dark greenish-blue color — called also *teal blue*

¹**team** /'tiːm/ *n* [*C*] **1** : a group of people who compete in a sport, game, etc., against another group ▪ *a basketball/gymnastics/bowling team* ▪ *He is the best player on his team.* ▪ *She is the team captain.* ▪ *Baseball is a team sport.* [=a sport played by teams] ▪ *Our team is losing.* = (*Brit*) *Our team are losing.* ▪ (*US*) *He is on a team.* = (*Brit*) *He is in a team.* **2** : a group of people who work together ▪ *We worked as a team to put out the fire.* ▪ *a team of lawyers* ▪ *The project was a team effort.* **3** : a group of two or more animals used to pull a wagon, cart, etc. ▪ *a team of horses*

²**team** *vb* [*T*] : to bring or join together (people or things) ▪ *a show that teams professional singers with amateurs* ▪ *They teamed up (with one another) to finish the job quickly.*

team·mate /'tiːmˌmeɪt/ *n* [*C*] : a person who is on the same team as someone else ▪ *She's very popular among her teammates.*

team player *n* [*C*] : someone who cares more about helping a group or team to succeed than about his or her individual success ▪ *She's not a team player.*

team·ster /'tiːmstɚ/ *n* [*C*] *US* : someone who drives a truck as a job

team·work /'tiːmˌwɚk/ *n* [*U*] : the work done by people who work together as a team ▪ *They credit good teamwork for their success.*

tea party *n* [*C*] : a social gathering at which tea is served

tea·pot /'tiːˌpɑːt/ *n* [*C*] : a pot that is used for making and serving tea and that has a spout and handle — **a tempest in a teapot** see TEMPEST

¹**tear** /'teɚ/ *vb* **tore** /'toɚ/; **torn** /'toɚn/; **tear·ing** **1** [*T/I*] : to separate (something) into parts by pulling it, cutting it, etc. : to rip, split, or open (something) quickly or violently ▪ *He tore the letter in half.* ▪ *They began tearing their presents*

open. ▪ *Tear along the dotted line.* ▪ *He tore apart the tickets and handed one to me.* ▪ *The dog tore the pillow to pieces/shreds.* **2** [*T/I*] : to make (a hole or opening) in a piece of clothing, a piece of paper, etc. ▪ *She tore a hole in her sock.* ▪ *His pants tore at the seam.* **3** [*T*] : to cut or injure (skin, a muscle, etc.) ▪ *He tore a ligament in his knee.* ▪ *a torn muscle* ▪ *She fell and tore the skin on her elbow.* **4** [*T*] : to remove (something) quickly or violently ▪ *They tore out the old cabinets.* ▪ *He tore the page out of the magazine.* ▪ *I tore off a piece of bread and ate it.* ▪ *Open up or we'll tear down this door!* ▪ *The cop grabbed him, but he managed to tear himself loose/free.* [=to pull himself away from the cop] **5** [*I*] : to go or move very quickly ▪ *The kids tore into the house and up the stairs.* ▪ *He went tearing down the street on his bicycle.* ▪ *The fire tore through the forest.* **6** [*T*] : to damage or harm (something, such as a country) very badly ▪ *a country torn by war* = *a war-torn country* **7** [*T*] : to cause (someone) to feel confused, upset, etc., especially about making a choice or decision ▪ *I'm still torn between these two choices.* ▪ *She was torn by conflicting loyalties.* — **tear apart** [*phrasal vb*] **tear (something or someone) apart** *or* **tear apart (something or someone)** **1** : to completely destroy (something) by tearing it into pieces ▪ *I couldn't open the box nicely, so I tore it apart.* ▪ (*figurative*) *We can't agree, and it's tearing our family apart.* **2** : to criticize (someone or something) in a harsh way ▪ *She tore the movie apart.* — **tear at** [*phrasal vb*] : to attack and pull pieces from (something) in a violent way ▪ *Wolves tore at the dead deer.* ▪ (*figurative*) *They are always tearing at each other's throats.* [=always arguing with and harshly criticizing each other] — **tear away** [*phrasal vb*] **tear (someone or something) away** : to cause (someone) to leave or move away from something ▪ *She couldn't tear him away from the TV.* — **tear down** [*phrasal vb*] **tear down (something)** *or* **tear (something) down** : to completely destroy (a building, wall, etc.) ▪ *They tore down the old hospital and built a new one.* — **tear into** [*phrasal vb*] *informal* **1** : to begin doing (something) in a very quick or forceful way ▪ *The kids tore into the pizza.* [=quickly began eating the pizza] **2** : to criticize (someone or something) in a harsh way ▪ *The critics tore into the movie.* — **tear (someone) limb from limb** see LIMB — **tear (someone or something) to pieces/shreds** : to criticize (someone or something) in a harsh way ▪ *They tore my idea to pieces.* — **tear up** [*phrasal vb*] **tear up (something)** *or* **tear (something) up** **1** : to completely destroy (something) by tearing it into pieces ▪ *I tore the letter up and threw it away.* ▪ (*figurative*) *They tore up his old contract and gave him a new one.* **2** : to break apart and remove pieces of (something) ▪ *The city tore the street up to fix a broken water main.* **3** *chiefly US, informal* : to perform very well on or in (something) ▪ *They were tearing up the dance floor.* — compare ⁴TEAR

²**tear** *n* [C] : a hole or opening in something that is made by cutting it or tearing it ▪ *The nail left a tear in his jacket.* ▪ *She suffered a muscle tear.* — **on a tear** *US, informal* : having great success over a period of time ▪ *The team has been on a tear.* [=has been playing very well] — **wear and tear** see ²WEAR — compare ³TEAR

³**tear** /'tiɚ/ *n* [C] : a drop of liquid that comes from your eyes especially when you cry ▪ *She wiped the tears from her eyes.* ▪ *crying/weeping tears of joy* ▪ *tear-filled eyes* ▪ *That song brings a tear to my eye.* [=makes me cry a little] ▪ *She suddenly burst into tears.* [=started to cry] ▪ *He looked like he was close to tears.* [=going to cry soon] ▪ *Come now. Dry your tears.* [=stop crying] ▪ *I tried to fight back the tears.* [=I tried not to cry] ▪ *I couldn't hold back my tears.* [=I could not stop myself from crying] ▪ *The memory brought on a flood of tears.* ▪ *We were laughing so hard that we were in tears.* [=tears were coming out of our eyes] ▪ *The audience was moved/reduced to tears by her song.* [=her song made everyone cry] — **end in tears** : to have an ending in which people are crying or unhappy ▪ *Our discussions about money always seem to end in tears.* — **shed tears** : to cry or weep ▪ *I never saw him shed a single tear.* — compare ²TEAR

⁴**tear** *vb* [I] : to fill with tears ▪ *His eyes started tearing (up).* — compare ¹TEAR

tear·away /'terə,weɪ/ *n* [C] *Brit, informal* : a young person who behaves badly and who does dangerous, foolish, or illegal things

tear·drop /'tiɚ,drɑːp/ *n* [C] **1** : ³TEAR **2** : something that is pointed at the top and round at the bottom ▪ *diamond teardrop earrings*

tear·ful /'tiɚfəl/ *adj* **1** : filled with tears ▪ *tearful eyes* **2** : happening with tears ▪ *a tearful goodbye* — **tear·ful·ly** *adv*

tear gas *n* [U] : a gas that makes people unable to see by causing their eyes to be filled with tears — **tear·gas** /'tiɚ,gæs/ *vb* **-gas·ses; -gassed; -gas·sing** [T] ▪ *The protesters were teargassed by the police.*

tear·jerk·er /'tiɚ,ʤɚkɚ/ *n* [C] *informal* : a story, song, movie, etc., that makes you cry or feel very sad

tea·room /'tiː,ruːm/ *n* [C] : a small restaurant that serves light meals

teary /'tiri/ *adj* **tear·i·er; -est** **1** : filled with tears ▪ *teary eyes* **2** : happening with tears ▪ *a teary farewell*

teary–eyed *adj* : having eyes that are wet with tears ▪ *I got a little teary-eyed at the end of the movie.*

¹**tease** /'tiːz/ *vb* **teased; teas·ing** **1** [T/I] : to laugh at and criticize (someone) in a way that is either friendly and playful or cruel and unkind ▪ *We were teasing each other about our different tastes in music.* ▪ *Don't get angry. I was just/only teasing!* **2** [T] : to annoy or bother (an animal) ▪ *tease a dog* **3** [T] *US* : to make (hair)

look fuller or bigger by combing it in a special way **4** [T/I] : to make (someone) feel excitement or interest about something you might do or say without actually doing it or saying it ▪ *Stop teasing (us) and say what the surprise is.* **5** [T] : to remove or separate (thin pieces of something) slowly and carefully ▪ *tease apart strands of rope* ▪ (*figurative*) *They're trying to tease out* [=*find out*] *the details of the accident.* — **teas·ing** *adj* ▪ *a teasing tone of voice* — **teas·ing·ly** /'tiːzɪŋli/ *adv*

²**tease** *n* [C] : a person who teases other people; *especially* : a person who seems to be sexually interested in someone but who is not serious about having a sexual relationship

teas·er /'tiːzɚ/ *n* [C] **1** : a person who teases other people **2** : something that is done, offered, or shown to make people want something or want to see something that will be offered or shown at a later time ▪ *a teaser for the movie* **3** *Brit* : BRAINTEASER

tea·spoon /'tiː,spuːn/ *n* [C] **1** : a small spoon that is used especially for eating soft foods and stirring drinks **2 a** : a spoon that is used by cooks for measuring dry and liquid ingredients and that holds an amount equal to ⅙ fluid ounce or ⅓ tablespoon **b** : the amount that a teaspoon will hold : TEASPOONFUL ▪ *a teaspoon of sugar* — abbr. *tsp.*

tea·spoon·ful /'tiː,spuːn,fʊl/ *n, pl* **-spoon·fuls** /-,spuːn,fʊlz/ *or* **-spoons·ful** /-,spuːnz,fʊl/ [C] : the amount that a teaspoon will hold ▪ *a teaspoonful* [=*teaspoon*] *of salt* — abbr. *tsp.*

teat /'tɪt, 'tiːt/ *n* [C] **1** : the part of a female animal (such as a cow) through which a young animal receives milk **2** *Brit* : NIPPLE 2

tea·time /'tiː,taɪm/ *n* [U] *Brit* : the usual time for the afternoon meal known as tea

tea towel *n* [C] *chiefly Brit* : DISH TOWEL

tech /'tɛk/ *n* **1** [C] *informal* : TECHNICIAN ▪ *lab/computer techs* **2** [U] *informal* : TECHNOLOGY ▪ *tech companies* **3** [U] : a technical school — used in the shortened forms of names of technical schools ▪ *Georgia Tech*

tech·ie /'tɛki/ *n* [C] *informal* : someone who knows a lot about technology ▪ *computer techies*

tech·ni·cal /'tɛknɪkəl/ *adj* **1 a** : relating to the practical use of machines or science in industry, medicine, etc. ▪ *The network was experiencing technical difficulties/problems.* **b** : teaching practical skills rather than ideas about literature, art, etc. ▪ *a technical school/college* **2 a** : having special knowledge especially of how machines work or of how a particular kind of work is done ▪ *a technical expert/consultant/adviser* **b** : relating to the special skills or techniques needed to do a particular job or activity ▪ *a pianist/painter with good technical skills* **3** : involving special knowledge, language, etc., that is used or understood by experts but usually not by others ▪ *technical writing/terms* ▪ *the more technical de-*

tails/aspects of their research **4** : according to a very strict explanation of a rule, fact, etc. ▪ *a technical violation of the law* ▪ *argue over a minor technical point* [=*technicality*]

tech·ni·cal·i·ty /ˌtɛknəˈkæləti/ *n, pl* **-ties** [C] **1** : a small detail in a rule, law, etc., and especially one that forces an unwanted or unexpected result ▪ *She lost because of a technicality.* = *She lost on a technicality.* **2** : something that is understood by experts but usually not by other people ▪ *the technicalities of programming*

tech·ni·cal·ly /ˈtɛknɪkli/ *adv* **1 a** : according to a very strict explanation of a rule, fact, etc. ▪ *It took a minute to do. Well, technically it took 53 seconds. Technically, a tomato is a fruit, not a vegetable.* **b** : according to or among experts ▪ *A map maker is (more) technically known as a cartographer.* **2** : in a way that relates to the use of special techniques or skills ▪ *a performance that was technically good but uninspired*

tech·ni·cian /tɛkˈnɪʃən/ *n* [C] : a person whose job relates to the practical use of machines or science in industry, medicine, etc. ▪ *X-ray/laboratory technicians*

tech·nique /tɛkˈniːk/ *n* **1** [C] : a way of doing something by using special knowledge or skill ▪ *techniques for relieving stress* **2** [U] : the way that a person performs basic physical movements or skills ▪ *a dancer with excellent technique*

tech·no /ˈtɛkˌnoʊ/ *n* [U] : a type of electronic dance music that has a fast beat

tech·nol·o·gy /tɛkˈnɑːlədʒi/ *n, pl* **-gies** **1** [U] : the use of science in industry, engineering, etc., to invent useful things or to solve problems ▪ *Recent advances in medical technology have saved many lives.* **2** [C/U] : a machine, piece of equipment, method, etc., that is created by technology ▪ *innovative/advanced technologies* — **tech·no·log·i·cal** /ˌtɛknəˈlɑːdʒɪkəl/ *also US* **tech·no·log·ic** /ˌtɛknəˈlɑːdʒɪk/ *adj* ▪ *technological advances/developments* — **tech·no·log·i·cal·ly** /ˌtɛknəˈlɑːdʒɪkli/ *adv*

tec·ton·ics /tɛkˈtɑːnɪks/ *n* [U] *geology* : the structure of the Earth's surface and the ways in which it changes shape over time — see also PLATE TECTONICS — **tec·ton·ic** /tɛkˈtɑːnɪk/ *adj* ▪ *tectonic plates/forces*

teddy bear *n* [C] : a stuffed animal shaped like a bear

te·dious /ˈtiːdijəs/ *adj* : boring and too slow or long ▪ *tedious work* — **te·dious·ly** *adv* — **te·dious·ness** *n* [U]

te·di·um /ˈtiːdijəm/ *n* [U] : the quality or state of being tedious or boring ▪ *I took a day off to relieve the tedium of work.*

¹**tee** /ˈtiː/ *n* [C] **1 a** : a small peg on which a golf ball is placed so that it can be hit **b** : an object that is used for holding a football in position so that it can be kicked **c** *chiefly US* : a post on which a baseball is placed so that a child can hit the ball with a bat in T-ball **2** : the area from which a golf ball is first hit to start play on a hole — **to a tee** : in a perfect

or exact way ▪ *The car fits/suits her to a tee.* [=*to a T*]

²**tee** *vb* **-teed**; **-tee·ing** [T] : to place (a ball) on a tee ▪ *She teed (up) the ball.* — **tee off** [*phrasal vb*] **1** : to hit a golf ball for the first time on a hole or in a round ▪ *We teed off at 8 a.m.* **2 tee off (someone)** or **tee (someone) off** *US, informal* : to make (someone) angry ▪ *That really tees me off.*

teem /ˈtiːm/ *vb* — **teem with** [*phrasal vb*] : to have many (people or animals) moving around inside ▪ *The river is teeming with fish.* ▪ (*figurative*) *a mind teeming with ideas* — **teem·ing** /ˈtiːmɪŋ/ *adj* ▪ *the city's teeming streets*

teen /ˈtiːn/ *n* [C] : TEENAGER — **teen** *adj, always before a noun* ▪ *a teen magazine/movie* ▪ *teen* [=*teenage*] *pregnancy*

teen·age /ˈtiːnˌeɪdʒ/ *adj, always before a noun* **1** or **teen·aged** /ˈtiːnˌeɪdʒd/ : between 13 and 19 years old ▪ *teenage boys/girls* **2** : relating to people who are between 13 and 19 years old ▪ *teenage* [=*teen*] *rebellion*

teen·ag·er /ˈtiːnˌeɪdʒər/ *n* [C] : someone who is between 13 and 19 years old

teens /ˈtiːnz/ *n* [*plural*] : the numbers 13 through 19 ▪ *The temperature is in the teens.*; *especially* : the years 13 through 19 in a century or a person's lifetime ▪ *a girl in her teens* [=*a teenage girl*]

teen·sy /ˈtiːnsi/ *adj* **teen·si·er; -est** *informal* : very small

tee·ny /ˈtiːni/ *adj* **tee·ni·er; -est** *informal* : very small ▪ *a teeny piece of cake* ▪ *I'm a teeny bit nervous.* ▪ *a teeny little/tiny bug*

teeny·bop·per /ˈtiːniˌbɑːpər/ *n* [C] *informal + old-fashioned* : a girl who is about 11 to 13 years old and who listens to popular music and likes current fashions

teepee *variant spelling of* TEPEE

tee shirt *variant spelling of* T-SHIRT

tee·ter /ˈtiːtər/ *vb* [I] : to move in an unsteady way back and forth or from side to side ▪ *The pile of books teetered and fell to the floor.* ▪ (*figurative*) *a bird that is teetering on the edge/brink of extinction* [=*almost extinct*]

teeth *plural of* TOOTH

teethe /ˈtiːð/ *vb* **teethed**; **teeth·ing** [I] : to have the first set of teeth begin to grow ▪ *The baby is starting to teethe.*

teething troubles *n* [*plural*] *Brit* : GROWING PAINS — called also *teething problems*

tee·to·tal·er (*chiefly US*) *or chiefly Brit* **tee·to·tal·ler** /ˈtiːˈtoʊtlər/ *n* [C] : someone who never drinks alcohol — **tee·to·tal** /ˈtiːˈtoʊtl/ *adj, Brit* ▪ *a teetotal store owner*

TEFL /ˈtɛfəl/ *abbr, chiefly Brit* teaching English as a foreign language

Tef·lon /ˈtɛˌflɑːn/ *trademark* — used for a substance that is used especially for nonstick coatings on cooking pans

tel *abbr* telephone; telephone number

tele·cast /ˈtɛlɪˌkæst, Brit ˈtɛlɪˌkɑːst/ *vb* **-cast; -cast·ing** [T] : to broadcast (a program) by television ▪ *The game was telecast live.* — **telecast** *n* [C] ▪ *a live telecast of the game*

tel·e·com /ˈtɛlɪˌkɑːm/ *n* **1** [C] : a telecommunications company ▪ *a major* *telecom* **2** [*U*] : the telecommunications industry • *telecom companies/services*

tele·com·mu·ni·ca·tions /ˌtɛlɪkəˌmjuːnəˈkeɪʃənz/ *n* [*plural*] : the technology of sending and receiving signals, images, etc., over long distances by telephone, television, satellite, etc. • *telecommunications companies/equipment* • *the telecommunications industry*

tele·com·mute /ˈtɛlɪkəˌmjuːt/ *vb* **-mut·ed; -mut·ing** [*I*] : to work at home by using a computer connection to a company's main office • *employees who telecommute* — **tele·com·mut·er** *n* [*C*]

tele·con·fer·enc·ing /ˈtɛlɪˌkɑːnfrənsɪŋ/ *n* [*U*] : the use of telephones and video equipment to have a meeting with people who are in different places

tele·gen·ic /ˌtɛləˈdʒɛnɪk/ *adj* : tending to look good or seem likable on television • *a telegenic politician*

tele·gram /ˈtɛləˌgræm/ *n* [*C*] : a message that is sent by telegraph — called also *wire*

¹**tele·graph** /ˈtɛləˌgræf, *Brit* ˈtɛlɪˌgrɑːf/ *n* **1** [*U*] : an old-fashioned system of sending messages over long distances by using wires and electrical signals • *I sent the message by telegraph.* **2** [*C*] : a device used for sending or receiving messages by telegraph

²**telegraph** *vb* **1 a** [*T/I*] : to send (a message) by telegraph • *He telegraphed a message to her.* **b** [*T*] : to send a telegram to (someone) • *Please telegraph me when you get there.* **2** [*T*] : to make (something that you are about to do or say) obvious or apparent by the way you move, look, etc. • *Her face telegraphed bad news.*

telegraph pole *n* [*C*] *Brit* : TELEPHONE POLE

tele·mar·ket·ing /ˌtɛləˈmɑːrkətɪŋ/ *n* [*U*] *chiefly US* : the activity or job of selling goods or services by calling people on the telephone • *a job in telemarketing* — **tele·mar·ket·er** /ˌtɛləˈmɑːrkətɚ/ *n* [*C*]

te·lep·a·thy /təˈlɛpəθi/ *n* [*U*] : a way of communicating thoughts directly from one person's mind to another person's mind without using words or signals — **tele·path·ic** /ˌtɛləˈpæθɪk/ *adj* : *telepathic communication* — **tele·path·i·cal·ly** /ˌtɛləˈpæθɪkli/ *adv*

¹**tele·phone** /ˈtɛləˌfoʊn/ *n* **1** [*U*] : a system that uses wires and radio signals to send sounds (such as people's voices) over long distances : PHONE • *We spoke by telephone.* • *I have to make a telephone call.* • *You can order it over the telephone.* **2** [*C*] : a device that is connected to a telephone system and that you use to listen or speak to someone who is somewhere else : PHONE • *The telephone is ringing.* • *I was hired to answer the telephones.* • *a cellular telephone* [=*cell phone*] — **on the telephone 1** : using a telephone to talk to someone • *She's (talking) on the telephone.* [=*on the phone*] **2** *Brit* : connected to a telephone system • *the percentage of households on the telephone*

²**telephone** *vb* **-phoned; -phon·ing** [*T/I*] : to speak or try to speak to (someone)

using a telephone • *He telephoned (me) to say that he was going to be late.*

telephone book *n* [*C*] : PHONE BOOK

telephone booth *n* [*C*] *chiefly US* : PHONE BOOTH

telephone box *n* [*C*] *Brit* : PHONE BOOTH

telephone directory *n* [*C*] : PHONE BOOK

telephone number *n* [*C*] : PHONE NUMBER

telephone pole *n* [*C*] *chiefly US* : a tall wooden pole that supports the wires of a telephone system

te·le·pho·nist /təˈlɛfənɪst/ *n* [*C*] *Brit* : OPERATOR 2

tele·pho·to lens /ˌtɛləˈfoʊtoʊ-/ *n* [*C*] : a lens for a camera that makes things that are far away appear to be closer

tele·prompt·er /ˈtɛləˌprɑːmptɚ/ *n* [*C*] *chiefly US* : a machine that helps someone who is speaking to an audience or on television by showing the words that need to be said

¹**tele·scope** /ˈtɛləˌskoʊp/ *n* [*C*] : a device shaped like a long tube that you look through in order to see things that are far away

²**telescope** *vb* **-scoped; -scop·ing** [*I*] : to become shorter by having one section slide inside another somewhat larger section • *an antenna that telescopes*

tele·scop·ic /ˌtɛləˈskɑːpɪk/ *adj* **1** : made or seen with a telescope • *telescopic observations/images* **2** : having the power to make objects that are far away appear to be closer • *a telescopic lens* **3** : able to become longer or shorter by having sections that slide inside one another • *a telescopic antenna*

tele·thon /ˈtɛləˌθɑːn/ *n* [*C*] : a long television program that tries to raise money for a charity by asking people to call during the program and make a donation

tele·vise /ˈtɛləˌvaɪz/ *vb* **-vised; -vis·ing** [*T*] : to broadcast (something) by television • *The speech was televised live.*

tele·vi·sion /ˈtɛləˌvɪʒən/ *n* **1** [*U*] : an electronic system of sending images and sounds by a wire or through space • *satellite or cable television* [=*TV*] **2** [*C*] : a piece of equipment with a screen that receives images and sounds sent by television • *turn on/off the television* [=*TV*, (*chiefly Brit*) *telly*] **3** [*U*] : programs that are broadcast by television • *We don't watch much television.* **4** [*U*] : the television broadcasting industry • *He's a star of stage, screen, and television.* — **on (the) television** : broadcast by television : being shown by television • *What's on the television tonight?*

television set *n* [*C*] : TELEVISION 2

tele·work·ing /ˈtɛləˌwɚkɪŋ/ *n* [*U*] *chiefly Brit* : the activity of working at home and communicating with customers or other workers by using a computer, telephone, etc. — **tele·work·er** /ˈtɛləˌwɚkɚ/ *n* [*C*]

tell /ˈtɛl/ *vb* **told** /ˈtoʊld/; **tell·ing 1** [*T*] **a** : to say or write (something) to (someone) • *tell a story* • *Tell her your name.* • *I won't tell anyone your secret.* = *I won't tell your secret to anyone.* • *Tell me about your* *trip.* ▪ *I told them how to open it.* ✧ This sense of *tell* is often used informally to emphasize a statement. ▪ *It's wrong,* ▪ **I tell you.** ▪ **I'm telling you,** *I wasn't there.* ▪ **Let me tell you (something):** *you can't buy love.* **b :** to say (a word or words) to (someone) ▪ *Tell your mom hello for me.* **2** [*T/I*] **a :** to give information to (someone) by speaking or writing ▪ *Tell me when they get here.* ▪ *"I know the answer." "Don't tell me.* [=don't say what the answer is] *I want to guess."* ▪ *"Who called?" "I'm not telling."* **b :** to let (someone) know a secret ▪ *Promise not to tell anyone." "Your secret is safe with me. I'll never tell."* **3** [*T*] **:** to express (something) by speaking ▪ *telling stories/jokes* ▪ **tell a lie** ▪ *I'm telling the truth.* ▪ *I hated the movie,* **to tell the truth.** [=to say what I really think] ▪ **Truth be told** [=to say what the truth is], *the food was pretty bad.* **4** [*T*] **:** to give (someone) an instruction or command ▪ *I was told to go.* ▪ *Don't tell me what to do.* ▪ *Do what I tell you.* = **Do as you're told.** **5** [*T/I*] **:** to inform others that someone has done something wrong or behaved badly — used especially by children ▪ *If you do that, I'll tell (Mom/Dad/the teacher).* **6** [*T*] **:** to give information to (someone or something) by doing a particular action or making a particular sound ▪ *That light tells you the device is on.* **7** [*T*] **:** to make (something) known to (someone) ▪ *Her smile told me everything I needed to know.* ▪ *What does the evidence tell us?* **8** [*T*] **:** to see or understand the differences between two people or things ▪ *I can't* **tell a/the difference between** them. = *I can't* **tell which is which.** ▪ *He's old enough to* **tell right from wrong.** [=to know what things are good and what things are bad] **9** [*T/I*] **:** to see or know (something) with certainty ▪ *"This bill is fake." "Really? How can you tell?" "I can tell by the quality of the paper."* ▪ *It's hard to tell if she's serious.* ▪ *You can never tell what she'll do.* ▪ *You might win the raffle—you never can tell.* ▪ *As far/near as I can tell, it's working.* It seems to be working — **all told** see ²ALL — **don't tell me** *informal* **1** — used to show that you already know what someone is going to say especially because he or she often says such things ▪ *"I have a favor to ask." "Don't tell me—You need to borrow more money, don't you?"* **2** — used to express surprise and disappointment ▪ *"Don't tell me you lost it?!" "No, it's right here."* — **I/I'll tell you what** *informal* — used to introduce a suggestion or to emphasize a statement ▪ *(I'll) Tell you what—you can borrow the car if you fill it up with gas.* — **I told you (so)** *informal* — used to say to someone that you were right about something especially when that person disagreed with you — **tell against** [*phrasal vb*] *Brit* : to be a disadvantage to (someone) ▪ *His appearance will tell against him in court.* — **tell apart** [*phrasal vb*] **tell (someone or something) apart** : to identify (people or things that look similar to each other) ▪ *It's hard to tell the twins apart.* — **tell it like it is** *US, infor-*

mal : to speak about unpleasant things in an honest way ▪ *I don't want to offend anyone; I'm just telling it like it is.* — **tell me** — used in speech to introduce a question ▪ *Tell me, is there a subway nearby?* — **tell of** [*phrasal vb*] *formal + literary* **1** : to describe (something) ▪ *The explorer's journals tell of a vast wilderness.* **2 tell (someone) of** : to talk to (someone) about (something) ▪ *He told us of his plans.* — **tell off** [*phrasal vb*] **tell (someone) off** or **tell off (someone)** *informal* **1** *US* : to yell at or insult (someone who did or said something that made you angry) ▪ *She told him off for spreading rumors about her.* **2** *Brit* : to criticize (someone) in an angry way from a position of authority ▪ *The teacher told us off for talking during class.* — **tell on** [*phrasal vb*] *informal* : to tell someone in authority about the bad behavior or actions of (someone) ▪ *Please don't tell on me.* — **tell time** or **tell the time** see ¹TIME — **there's no telling** — used to say that it is impossible to know something with certainty ▪ *There's no telling how long it will take.* — **you're telling me** *informal* — used to say that you already know and completely agree with something that was just said ▪ *"This hot weather is brutal." "You're telling me."*

tell-all /ˈtɛlˌɑːl/ *n* [*C*] : a book that contains new and usually shocking information about someone or something ▪ *a tell-all biography*

tell-er /ˈtɛlɚ/ *n* [*C*] **1** : a person who tells something (such as a story) to someone else ▪ *a teller of tales* **2** : a person who works in a bank and whose job is to receive money from customers and pay out money to customers

tell-ing /ˈtɛlɪŋ/ *adj* **1** : producing a strong or important effect ▪ *The most telling moment in the case was when the victim took the stand.* **2** : giving information about someone or something without intending to ▪ *Her response was very telling.* [=it showed how she really felt] — **tell-ing-ly** *adv*

tell-tale /ˈtɛlˌteɪl/ *adj, always before a noun* : indicating that something exists or has occurred ▪ *Slurred speech is usually a telltale sign of intoxication.*

tel-ly /ˈtɛli/ *n, pl* **-lies** [*C/U*] *chiefly Brit, informal* : TELEVISION

temp /ˈtɛmp/ *n* [*C*] **1** *chiefly US, informal* : TEMPERATURE ▪ *the outside temp* **2** : someone who works at a place for a limited and usually short period of time : a temporary worker — **temp** *vb* [*I*] ▪ *She was temping* [=working as a temp] *in an office.*

¹**tem-per** /ˈtɛmpɚ/ *n* **1 a** [*C*] : the tendency of someone to become angry ▪ *She has a bad/quick/terrible temper.* ▪ *Learn to* **control your temper.** **b** [*U, singular*] : a state of being angry ▪ *a fit of temper* **2** [*C*] : calmness of mind : COMPOSURE ▪ *I* **lost my temper** [=got angry] *(with him).* **3** [*singular*] **a** : the way that a person is feeling at a particular time : MOOD ▪ *He is* **in a foul temper.** **b** : the usual attitude, mood, or behavior of a person or

animal ▪ *She has an even temper.* [=she does not easily become angry, upset, etc.]

²tem·per */vb* [T] **1** *formal* : to make (something) less severe or extreme ▪ *He tempered criticism with words of encouragement.* **2** *technical* : to cause (something) to become hard or strong by heating it and cooling it ▪ *tempered steel/glass*

tem·per·a·ment /ˈtɛmprəmənt/ *n* [C/U] : the usual attitude, mood, or behavior of a person or animal ▪ *people with nervous/artistic/poetic temperaments*

tem·per·a·men·tal /ˌtɛmprəˈmɛntl̩/ *adj* **1 a** : likely to become upset or angry ▪ *a temperamental child* **b** : unpredictable in behavior or performance ▪ *The car is temperamental.* **2** : of or relating to someone's usual attitude, mood, or behavior ▪ *our temperamental differences* — **tem·per·a·men·tal·ly** *adv*

tem·per·ate /ˈtɛmprət/ *adj* **1** : having temperatures that are not too hot or too cold ▪ *temperate climates/forests* **2** *formal* : emotionally calm and controlled ▪ *a temperate person/discussion* **3** *old-fashioned* : avoiding behavior that goes beyond what is normal, healthy, or acceptable ▪ *a temperate* [=*moderate*] *drinker*

tem·per·a·ture /ˈtɛmprəˌtʃʊɚ/ *n* **1** [C/U] : a measurement that indicates how hot or cold something is ▪ *Water boils at a temperature of 212°F.* ▪ *There was a sudden fall/drop in temperature.* [=it got colder] ▪ **room temperature** [=the temperature of a room that is comfortable] **2 a** [*singular*] : a measurement of the heat in a person's body ▪ *the normal body temperature of 98.6°F* ▪ *She took his temperature.* [=used a thermometer to find out if he had a fever] **b** [C] : a level of heat that is above what is normal for the human body : FEVER ▪ *I have a temperature.* = *I'm running a temperature.*

tem·pest /ˈtɛmpəst/ *n* [C] *literary* : a violent storm ▪ (*figurative*) *a tempest of controversy/emotions* — **a tempest in a teapot** *US* : a situation in which people are upset or angry about something that is not very important

tem·pes·tu·ous /tɛmˈpɛstʃəwəs/ *adj* : full of strong emotions (such as anger or excitement) ▪ *a tempestuous romance/relationship*

tem·plate /ˈtɛmplət/ *n* [C] **1** : a shape or pattern that is cut out of a hard material (such as metal or plastic) and used to make the same shape and pattern in other pieces of material **2** *computers* : a computer document that has the basic format of something (such as a business letter, chart, graph, etc.) and that can be used many different times

tem·ple /ˈtɛmpəl/ *n* [C] **1 a** : a building for worship ▪ *Buddhist/Hindu/Jewish/Mormon temples* **b** : a meeting place for the members of a local group that is part of a larger organization ▪ *a Masonic temple* **2** : the small, flat area on each side of your forehead

tem·po /ˈtɛmpoʊ/ *n, pl* **-pos** [C/U] **1** : the speed at which a musical piece is played or sung ▪ *a song with a fast/upbeat*

tempo **2** : the speed at which something moves or happens : PACE ▪ *We walked at a fast tempo.*

tem·po·rary /ˈtɛmpəˌreri/ *adj* **1** : continuing for a limited amount of time ▪ *a temporary job* **2** : intended to be used for a limited amount of time ▪ *a temporary solution* — **tem·po·rari·ly** /ˌtɛmpəˈrerəli/ *adv*

tempt /ˈtɛmpt/ *vb* [T] : to cause (someone) to do or want to do something even though it may be wrong, bad, or unwise ▪ *She tried to tempt us into buying a more expensive car.* ▪ *I'm tempted to say yes, but I'm not completely sure.* ▪ *He tempted me with the offer of more money.* — **tempt fate** : to do something that is very risky or dangerous

temp·ta·tion /tɛmpˈteɪʃən/ *n* **1** [C/U] : a strong urge or desire to have or do something ▪ *I resisted the temptation to snack.* ▪ **give in to temptation** **2** [C] : something that causes a strong urge or desire to have or do something : something that tempts you ▪ *the temptations of the city*

tempt·ing /ˈtɛmptɪŋ/ *adj* : causing an urge or desire to have or do something ▪ *a tempting offer* — **tempt·ing·ly** *adv*

tempt·ress /ˈtɛmptrəs/ *n* [C] : a woman who makes a man want to have sex with her

ten /ˈtɛn/ *n* **1** [C] : the number 10 **2** [C] : the tenth in a set or series ▪ *page ten* **3** [U] : ten o'clock ▪ *It's almost ten.* **4** [C] **a** *US* : a ten-dollar bill ▪ *Do you have any fives or tens?* **b** *Brit* : a ten-pound note **5** [*singular*] : something that is the best ▪ *The meal was a (perfect) ten.* — **ten** *adj* ▪ *ten guests/choices* — **ten** *pron* ▪ *Ten* (*of them*) *passed the test.*

te·na·cious /təˈneɪʃəs/ *adj* **1 a** : not easily stopped or pulled apart ▪ *a tenacious grip* **b** : continuing for a long time ▪ *a tenacious effort* **2** : very determined to do something ▪ *a tenacious* [=*persistent*] *competitor* — **te·na·cious·ly** *adv* — **te·nac·i·ty** /təˈnæsəti/ *n* [U] ▪ *She fought with great tenacity.*

ten·an·cy /ˈtɛnənsi/ *n* [U] *formal* : the right to use another person's land, house, etc., for a short period of time ▪ *He was granted tenancy of the farm.*

ten·ant /ˈtɛnənt/ *n* [C] : a person, business, group, etc., that pays to use another person's property

tend /ˈtɛnd/ *vb* **1** [I] **a** — used to describe what often happens or what someone often does or is likely to do; followed by *to* + *verb* ▪ *He tends to slouch.* ▪ *People in my family tend to be tall.* [=most people in my family are tall] **b** — used to describe a quality that someone or something often has or is likely to have; + *toward* or *towards* ▪ *Her style tends toward the informal.* [=tends to be informal] **2** [T/I] : to give your attention to and take care of (something or someone) ▪ *Please tend the store while I'm away.* ▪ *well-tended gardens* ▪ *tending to* (*the*) *business*

ten·den·cy /ˈtɛndənsi/ *n, pl* **-cies** [C] **1** : a quality that makes something likely to happen or that makes someone likely to think or behave in a particular way ▪

The door has a tendency to get stuck. [=the door often gets stuck] ▪ *her tendency to overreact* **2** : a way of behaving, proceeding, etc., that is developing and becoming more common ▪ *The economy's has shown a tendency toward inflation.*

¹**ten·der** /ˈtɛndɚ/ *adj* **1** : very loving and gentle ▪ *tender words* **2** *of food* : easy to chew or bite ▪ *a tender steak* **3** : painful when touched ▪ *a tender elbow* **4** : easily damaged : delicate and weak ▪ *tender young plants* **5** (*figurative*) *a tender* [=sensitive] *ego* — **tender loving care** : extra attention to make someone or something look or feel better ▪ *a house that needs some tender loving care* — **tender (young) age** : a very young age ▪ *She left home at the tender young age of 14.* — **ten·der·ly** *adv* ▪ *He kissed her tenderly.* — **ten·der·ness** *n* [U]

²**tender** *vb* **1** [T] *formal* : to give or offer (something, such as a payment or a letter) ▪ *She tendered his resignation.* **2** [I] *Brit* : to offer to do work or to provide goods for a particular price : to make a bid for something ▪ *tender for* [=(US) bid for] *a job/contract*

³**tender** *n* [C] **1** : an offer made for acceptance ▪ *a tender of payment* **2** : a small piece of chicken meat that is usually cooked by being breaded and fried ▪ *chicken tenders*

ten·der·heart·ed /ˈtɛndɚˈhɑɚtəd/ *adj* : very gentle and kind ▪ *a tender-hearted woman*

ten·der·ize *also Brit* **ten·der·ise** /ˈtɛndəˌraɪz/ *vb* **-ized; -iz·ing** [T] : to make (meat) softer before cooking it so that it is easier to cut and eat — **ten·der·iz·er** *also Brit* **ten·der·is·er** /ˈtɛndəˌraɪzɚ/ *n* [C/U]

ten·der·loin /ˈtɛdɚˌlɔɪn/ *n* [C/U] : a piece of very tender meat from the back of a cow or pig ▪ *beef/pork tenderloin*

ten·di·ni·tis *also* **ten·do·ni·tis** /ˌtɛndə-ˈnaɪtəs/ *n* [U] *medical* : a painful condition in which a tendon in your arm, leg, etc., becomes inflamed

ten·don /ˈtɛndən/ *n* [C] : a tough piece of tissue in your body that connects a muscle to a bone

ten·dril /ˈtɛndrəl/ *n* [C] **1** : the thin stem of a climbing plant that attaches to walls, fences, etc. **2** : something that is thin and curly ▪ *tendrils of hair/smoke*

ten·e·ment /ˈtɛnəmənt/ *n* [C] : a large building that has apartments or rooms for rent and that is usually in a poor part of a city — called also *tenement house*

te·net /ˈtɛnət/ *n* [C] *formal* : a belief or idea that is very important to a group ▪ *the central tenets of a religion*

Tenn. *abbr* Tennessee

ten·ner /ˈtɛnɚ/ *n* [C] *Brit, informal* : a ten-pound note

ten·nis /ˈtɛnəs/ *n* [U] : a game that is played by two people or two pairs of people on a special court (called a tennis court) where they hit a small ball back and forth over a net using rackets

tennis shoe *n* [C] : a low shoe that is worn while playing sports (such as tennis) or exercising : SNEAKER

¹**ten·or** /ˈtɛnɚ/ *n* **1** [C] : the highest adult

male singing voice; *also* : a singer who has such a voice **2** [*singular*] : the general or basic quality or meaning of something ▪ *I was surprised by the angry tenor* [=tone] *of the letter.*

²**tenor** *adj, always before a noun* : having a range that is lower than an alto and higher than a baritone ▪ *a tenor sax/saxophone*

¹**tense** /ˈtɛns/ *adj* **tens·er; -est 1** : nervous and not able to relax ▪ *Why are you so tense?* **2** : showing or causing nervousness ▪ *a tense situation/meeting* **3** : not relaxed but hard and tight ▪ *tense muscles* — **tense·ly** *adv* — **tense·ness** *n* [U]

²**tense** *vb* **tensed; tens·ing 1** [T/I] : to make (a muscle) hard and tight ▪ *She tensed her shoulders.* ▪ *Her shoulders tensed (up).* **2** [I] : to become nervous or tense ▪ *He tensed up and missed the putt.*

³**tense** *n* [C/U] *grammar* : a form of a verb that is used to show when an action happened ▪ *Change the tense of the verb.*

ten·sion /ˈtɛnʃən/ *n* **1** [U] **a** : a feeling of nervousness that makes you unable to relax ▪ *nervous tension* **b** : a feeling of nervousness, excitement, or fear that is created in a movie, book, etc. ▪ *dramatic tension* **2** [C/U] : a state in which people, groups, countries, etc., disagree with and feel anger toward each other ▪ *Political tensions in the region make it unstable.* ▪ *There was a lot of tension at the meeting.* **3** [C/U] : a difficult situation caused by the opposite needs or effects of two different ideas, desires, etc. ▪ *the tension between the desire to reduce risk and the desire to increase profits* **4** [U] : the degree to which something is stretched ▪ *muscle tension* [=tightness]

tent /ˈtɛnt/ *n* [C] : a portable shelter that is used outdoors, is made of cloth (such as canvas or nylon), and is held up with poles and ropes ▪ *Let's pitch the tent* [=put our tent up, set our tent up] *here.*

ten·ta·cle /ˈtɛntɪkəl/ *n* [C] **1** : one of the long, flexible arms of an animal (such as an octopus) that are used for grabbing things and moving **2** [*plural*] *often disapproving* : power or influence that reaches into many areas ▪ *the tentacles of organized crime*

ten·ta·tive /ˈtɛntətɪv/ *adj* **1** : not done with confidence ▪ *a tentative smile* **2** : not definite : still able to be changed ▪ *tentative plans* — **ten·ta·tive·ly** *adv* ▪ *The meeting is tentatively scheduled for noon.* — **ten·ta·tive·ness** *n* [U]

ten·ter·hooks /ˈtɛntɚˌhʊks/ *n* — **on tenterhooks** : waiting nervously for something to happen ▪ *I've been on tenterhooks since I applied for the job.*

¹**tenth** /ˈtɛnθ/ *n* **1** [*singular*] : the number 10 in a series ▪ *the tenth of May* **2** [C] : one of 10 equal parts of something ▪ *I paid a tenth of what you paid.*

²**tenth** *adj* : occupying the number ten position in a series ▪ *our tenth wedding anniversary* — **tenth** *adv* ▪ *the tenth largest country*

ten·u·ous /ˈtɛnjəwəs/ *adj* : not certain,

definite, or strong • *He has a tenuous grasp/grip/hold on reality.* — **ten·u·ous·ly** *adv*

ten·ure /ˈtɛnjɚ/ *n* **1** [C] : the amount of time that a person holds a job, office, or title • *her 12-year tenure with the company* **2** [U] : the right to keep a job (especially the job of being a professor at a college or university) for as long as you want to have it • *He got tenure last year.* — **ten·ured** /ˈtɛnjɚd/ *adj, US* • *a tenured professor*

te·pee *or* **tee·pee** /ˈtiːpiː/ *n* [C] : a tent that is shaped like a cone and that was used in the past by some Native Americans as a house

tep·id /ˈtɛpəd/ *adj* **1** : not hot and not cold : WARM • *a tepid bath* **2** : not energetic or excited • *a tepid performance*

te·qui·la /təˈkiːlə/ *n* [C/U] : a strong, clear alcoholic drink from Mexico

¹**term** /ˈtɚm/ *n* **1** [C] **a** : a word or phrase that has an exact meaning • *scientific/technical terms* **b** **terms** [*plural*] : the particular kinds of words used to describe someone or something • *He spoke about them in glowing terms.* • *She expressing her opinion in no uncertain terms.* [=in very strong and clear language] **2** [C] **a** : the length of time during which a person has an official or political office • *the governor's second term* • *her term of/in office* [=the time when she was in office] **b** : the length of time during which someone is in a prison, jail, etc. • *a jail/prison term* **c** : the length of time during which something (such as a contract) continues • *The term of the contract is 60 months.* **3** [C] : one of the parts of the school year • *His grades improved last term.* **4** [*plural*] : the conditions or rules that limit something (such as an agreement or a contract) • *the terms of a contract* **5** [*plural*] — used to describe the kind of relationship that people have with each other • *He's on good terms with his ex-wife.* [=he and his ex-wife are friendly with each other] • *They're no longer on speaking terms.* [=they are no longer speaking to each other] **6** [U] *medical* : the time at which a pregnancy of normal length ends • *She carried the baby to term.* = *She carried the baby full term.* [=to the natural end of the pregnancy] — **come to terms** **1** : to reach an agreement • *The two sides have not been able to come to terms (with each other).* **2** : to learn how to accept or live with something that is difficult or painful — + *with* • *coming to terms with the demands of a job* — **in terms of** — used to indicate the specific thing that is being described, thought of, etc. • *The car is great in terms of gas mileage.* [=the car's gas mileage is great] — **on your (own) terms** : according to your own wishes • *If I agree to help, it will only be on my terms.* — **term of address** see ²ADDRESS

²**term** *vb* [T] : to give a particular name or description to (something) • *The project was termed a success.*

¹**ter·mi·nal** /ˈtɚmənl/ *adj* **1** **a** : causing death eventually • *a terminal* [=*fatal*] *ill-*

ness/disease **b** : having an illness that cannot be cured and that will soon lead to death • *a terminal patient* **2** *informal* : very bad or severe • *terminal boredom* **3** : forming or coming at the end of something • *branches that end in a terminal bud* — **ter·mi·nal·ly** *adv* • *He is terminally ill.* [=he has a terminal illness]

²**terminal** *n* [C] **1** **a** : a building where buses or trains regularly stop so that passengers can get on and off : STATION **b** : a building at an airport where people get on and off airplanes **2** : a computer or a combination of a keyboard and a video display that is connected to a system and used for entering or receiving data **3** : a part on a piece of electrical equipment where you make an electrical connection • *a battery terminal*

ter·mi·nate /ˈtɚməˌneɪt/ *vb* **-nat·ed;** **-nat·ing** *formal* **1** [I] : to end in a particular way or at a particular place • *The rail line terminates in Boston.* **2** [T] : to cause (something) to end • *terminate a pregnancy/contract* **3** [T] *US* : to take a job away from (someone) : FIRE • *He was terminated last month.* — **ter·mi·na·tion** /ˌtɚməˈneɪʃən/ *n* [C/U]

ter·mi·nol·o·gy /ˌtɚməˈnɑːlədʒi/ *n, pl* **-gies** [C/U] : the special words or phrases that are used in a particular field • *legal/medical terminology*

ter·mite /ˈtɚˌmaɪt/ *n* [C] : a kind of soft, white insect that lives in groups, eats wood, and causes a lot of damage to wooden structures

term paper *n* [C] *US* : a long essay that usually requires research and that is written by a student as part of a course or class

tern /ˈtɚn/ *n* [C] : a kind of bird that lives near the ocean and has long wings and a tail with two points

ter·race /ˈtɛrəs/ *n* **1** [C] : a flat area created on the side of a hill and used especially for growing crops **2** [C] : a flat area next to a building where people can sit and relax **3** [C] *Brit* : a row of houses that are joined together **4** **the terraces** [*plural*] *Brit* : a section of a stadium with wide steps where people stand to watch soccer matches — **ter·raced** /ˈtɛrəst/ *adj* • *a terraced hillside* — **ter·rac·ing** /ˈtɛrəsɪŋ/ *n* [U]

ter·ra·cot·ta /ˌtɛrəˈkɑːtə/ *n* [U] : a reddish clay that is used for pottery and tiles

ter·rain /təˈreɪn/ *n* [C/U] : land of a particular kind • *driving over rough terrain*

ter·res·tri·al /təˈrɛstriəl/ *adj* **1** : relating to or occurring on the earth • *terrestrial life forms* **2** *technical* : living or growing on land instead of in water or air • *terrestrial birds*

ter·ri·ble /ˈtɛrəbəl/ *adj* **1** : very shocking and upsetting • *a terrible disaster/crime* **2** : very bad or unpleasant • *terrible music/food* • *a terrible mistake* • *I woke up feeling terrible.* [=very sick]

ter·ri·bly /ˈtɛrəbli/ *adv* **1** : very or extremely • *terribly sad/important* • *I miss you terribly.* [=very much] **2** : in a very bad or unpleasant way • *I like tennis, but I play terribly.* [=very badly]

ter·ri·er /'terijə/ *n* [C] : a type of small dog originally used for hunting

ter·rif·ic /tə'rifik/ *adj* **1** *informal* : extremely good : EXCELLENT ▪ *a terrific idea* ▪ *They did a terrific job.* ▪ *I feel terrific.* **2** : causing a feeling of surprise or wonder ▪ *a terrific snowstorm* — **ter·rif·i·cal·ly** /tə'rifikli/ *adv* ▪ *terrifically exciting*

ter·ri·fy /'terə,faı/ *vb* **-fies; -fied; -fy·ing** [T] : to cause (someone) to be extremely afraid ▪ *Big dogs terrify me.* — **terrified** *adj* ▪ *I was/felt terrified.* [=extremely afraid] — **terrifying** *adj* ▪ *a terrifying ordeal* — **ter·ri·fy·ing·ly** *adv*

ter·ri·to·ri·al /,terə'torijəl/ *adj* **1** : of or relating to land or water that is owned or controlled by a government ▪ *territorial boundaries* ▪ *a territorial dispute* [=a disagreement about who controls a particular territory] **2** — used to describe animals or people that try to keep others away from an area that they use or control ▪ *the human tendency to be territorial*

Territorial Army *n* — **the Territorial Army** : a part of the military forces of Britain that is made up of people who are not professional soldiers but are given military training for a period of time each year — *abbr. TA*

territorial waters *n* [*plural*] : the part of the ocean near a country's coast that is legally controlled by that country

ter·ri·to·ry /'terə,tori, *Brit* 'terətri/ *n, pl* **-ries** **1 a** [C/U] : an area of land that belongs to or is controlled by a government ▪ *disputed territories* ▪ *entering enemy territory* **b** [C] : one of the parts of the United States that is not a state ▪ *Guam is a U.S. territory.* **c** [C] : any one of the large parts that some countries are divided into ▪ *Canada's Yukon Territory* **2** [C/U] : an area that an animal or group of animals owns and defends **3** [U] : an area of land or water ▪ *We've covered a lot of territory today.* [=we have traveled a long distance] ▪ *(figurative) As the conversation turned to politics, I knew we were heading into* **dangerous territory.** **4** [C] : an area that someone is responsible for when doing a job ▪ *a sales rep's territory* — **come/go with the territory** : to be a natural part of a particular situation, position, or area of work ▪ *Of course players get injured sometimes. It comes with the territory.*

ter·ror /'terə/ *n* **1** [U, *singular*] : a very strong feeling of fear ▪ *The sound fills me with terror.* ▪ *They fled in terror* **2** [C/U] : something that causes very strong feelings of fear ▪ *the terrors of war* **3** [U] : violence that is committed by a person, group, or government in order to frighten people and achieve a political goal ▪ *a regime that rules by terror* ▪ *a war on terror* [=terrorism] **4** [C] *informal* : a child who behaves very badly ▪ *Their kids are holy terrors.* — **hold no terror/terrors** ◇ If something holds no terror/terrors for you, you are not afraid of it.

ter·ror·ism /'terə,rızəm/ *n* [U] : the use of violent acts to frighten the people in an area as a way of trying to achieve a political goal ▪ *acts of terrorism* — **ter·ror·ist** /'terərıst/ *n* [C] ▪ *a suspected terrorist* [=a person who uses or supports terrorism] — **terrorist** *adj, always before a noun* ▪ *terrorist activities/attacks/organizations*

ter·ror·ize *also Brit* **ter·ror·ise** /'terə,raız/ *vb* **-ized; -iz·ing** [T] : to cause (someone) to be extremely afraid ▪ *neighborhoods terrorized by gangs*

ter·ry cloth /'teri-/ *n* [U] : a type of soft, thick cloth with many tiny loops on its surface that is often used to make towels — called also **terry**

terse /'təs/ *adj* : brief and direct in a way that may seem rude or unfriendly ▪ *a terse statement/summary* — **terse·ly** *adv* — **terse·ness** *n* [U]

ter·ti·ary /'tə,ʃi,eri, *Brit* 'tə:ʃəri/ *adj, formal* : third in order, importance, or value ▪ *our tertiary goals*

TESOL /'ti:sɑl/ *abbr* **1** *US* Teachers of English to Speakers of Other Languages **2** teaching English to speakers of other languages

¹test /'test/ *n* [C] **1** : a set of questions or problems that are designed to measure a person's knowledge, skills, or abilities ▪ *a math/history test* ▪ *a driver's/driving test* [=a test that is used to see if someone is able to safely drive a car] ▪ *test questions/scores* **2 a** : a careful study of a part of the body or of a substance taken from the body ▪ *a vision/hearing test* [=a test that shows how well you see/hear] ▪ *a blood test* ▪ *a drug test* [=a test that examines a person's blood or urine for evidence of illegal drugs] **b** : a careful study of a small amount of water, soil, air, etc., in order to see if its quality is good, to find out if it contains a dangerous substance, etc. ▪ *routine water tests* **3** : a planned and usually controlled act or series of acts that is done to learn something, to see if something works properly, etc. ▪ *lab/laboratory tests* ▪ *a test of a new vaccine* **4** : something (such as a difficult situation or task) that shows how strong or skilled someone or something is ▪ *a test of will/strength/character* **5** *Brit, sports* : TEST MATCH — **put (someone or something) to the test** : to cause (someone or something) to be in a situation that shows how strong, good, etc., that person or thing really is ▪ *A trip through the desert will put the truck to the test.* — **stand the test of time** : to continue to be important, respected, etc., for a long period of time ▪ *art that has stood the test of time*

²test *vb* **1** [T] : to use a set of questions or problems to measure someone's skills, knowledge, or abilities ▪ *The exam will test you on your knowledge of trees.* **2** [T/I] : to examine a part of the body or a substance taken from the body ▪ *testing athletes for illegal drugs* ▪ *She tested positive/negative for AIDS.* **3** [T/I] : to examine a small amount of water, soil, air, etc., in order to see if its quality is good, if it contains a dangerous substance, etc. ▪ *testing soil for traces of lead = testing for the presence of lead in soil* **4** [T] : to use (something) in a planned and usually controlled way in order to see if it works properly ▪ *The vaccine has not yet been tested on humans.* **5** [T] : to show how strong, good, etc., someone or something is in a difficult situation ▪ *Life's ordeals test us.* ▪ *You're testing my patience.* [=you are starting to make me annoyed or upset] — **test the waters** *also* **test the water** : to do something to find out if people like or approve a possible plan, product, etc., so that you can make a decision about it ▪ *She's testing the waters for a presidential bid.* — **test·er** /ˈtɛstə/ *n* [*C*]

tes·ta·ment /ˈtɛstəmənt/ *n* **1** [*C/U*] : proof or evidence that something exists or is true ▪ *Her success is (a) testament to the power/strength of determination.* **2** [*C*] *law* : the legal instructions in which you say who should receive your property, possessions, etc., after you die : WILL ▪ *a person's last will and testament*

test drive *n* [*C*] : an occurrence in which you drive a car that you do not own to see if you like it and would like to buy it ▪ *I took the car for a test drive.* — **test-drive** *vb* **-drove; -driv·en; -driv·ing** [*T*] ▪ *I test-drove the car.*

tes·ti·cle /ˈtɛstɪkəl/ *n* [*C*] : one of two small organs that are located in a sack of skin (called the scrotum) in men and male animals and that produce sperm and male hormones — **tes·tic·u·lar** /tɛˈstɪkjələ/ *adj*

tes·ti·fy /ˈtɛstəˌfaɪ/ *vb* **-fies; -fied; -fy·ing** [*T/I*] **1 a** : to talk and answer questions about something especially in a court of law while formally promising that what you are saying is true ▪ *Three witnesses were called to testify at the trial.* ▪ *She testified that she'd seen the defendant there.* **b** : to talk about or say (something) in an honest and confident way ▪ *I can (personally) testify that their food is excellent.* ▪ *people who testify to her generosity* [=who say that she is a generous person] **2** : to show that something is true or real ▪ *These statistics testify to the fact that the program is working.* [=show that the program is working]

tes·ti·mo·ni·al /ˌtɛstəˈmoʊnijəl/ *n* [*C*] **1 a** : a written or spoken statement in which you say that you used a product or service and liked it ▪ *product testimonials* **b** : a written or spoken statement that praises someone's work, skill, character, etc. ▪ *He received a glowing testimonial from his former boss.* **2** : an event at which someone is honored ▪ *They held a testimonial in her honor.* — **testimonial** *adj*

tes·ti·mo·ny /ˈtɛstəˌmoʊni/ *n, pl* **-nies** [*C/U*] **1** : something that someone says especially in a court of law while formally promising to tell the truth ▪ *The jury heard 10 days of testimony.* ▪ *the personal testimonies of survivors* **2** : proof or evidence that something exists or is true — + *to* ▪ *It's (a) testimony to her persistence that she worked at it for so long.*

test match *n* [*C*] *chiefly Brit, sports* : a game or series of games of cricket or rugby played by teams from different countries

tes·tos·ter·one /tɛˈstɑːstəˌroʊn/ *n* [*U*] *medical* : a hormone that occurs naturally in men and male animals

test pilot *n* [*C*] : a pilot who flies new aircraft in order to see how well they work

test run *n* [*C*] : an occurrence in which a product or procedure is tried in order to see if it works correctly : TRIAL RUN

test tube *n* [*C*] : a glass container that is shaped like a tube which is closed at one end and that is used especially in science experiments

tes·ty /ˈtɛsti/ *adj* **tes·ti·er; -est** : becoming angry or annoyed easily ▪ *She's a little testy today.* — **tes·ti·ly** /ˈtɛstəli/ *adv* — **tes·ti·ness** /ˈtɛstinəs/ *n* [*U*]

tet·a·nus /ˈtɛtnəs/ *n* [*U*] *medical* : a dangerous disease that is caused by bacteria that usually enter the body through a cut or wound ✧ Tetanus causes muscles and especially muscles in the jaw to become stiff.

tetchy /ˈtɛtʃi/ *adj* **tetch·i·er; -est** *chiefly Brit* : becoming angry or annoyed easily ▪ *a tetchy mood*

tête-à-tête /ˌtɛtɑːˈtɛt/ *n* [*C*] : a private conversation between two people

teth·er /ˈtɛðə/ *n* [*C*] : a rope or chain that is used to tie an animal to a post, wall, etc., so that it will stay in a particular area — **tether** *vb* [*T*] ▪ *The dog was tethered to the fence.* ▪ *(figurative) I was tethered to my desk all day.*

Tex. *abbr* Texas

Tex–Mex /ˈtɛksˈmɛks/ *adj, always before a noun* : relating to Mexican-American culture, music, or food of the kind that exists especially in southern Texas ▪ *a Tex-Mex restaurant*

¹**text** /ˈtɛkst/ *n* **1** [*U*] : the original words of a piece of writing or a speech ▪ *The full text of the speech is online.* **2** [*U*] : the words that make up the main part of a book, magazine, newspaper, Web site, etc. ▪ *The book is mostly pictures with very little text.* **3** [*C*] **a** : a book or other piece of writing; *especially* : one that is studied ▪ *an ancient religious text* **b** *US* : TEXTBOOK ▪ *a psychology text* **4 a** [*U*] : data handled by a computer, cell phone, etc., that is mostly in the form of words ▪ *a text file* **b** [*C*] : TEXT MESSAGE ▪ *I sent her a text.*

²**text** *vb* [*T/I*] : to send someone a text message ▪ *I texted her.* — **text·er** /ˈtɛkstə/ *n* [*C*] — **text·ing** /ˈtɛkstɪŋ/ *n* [*U*]

¹**text·book** /ˈtɛkstˌbʊk/ *n* [*C*] : a book about a particular subject that is used in the study of that subject especially in a school

²**textbook** *adj, always before a noun* : very typical ▪ *a textbook* [=classic, perfect] *case/example*

tex·tile /ˈtɛkˌstajəl, ˈtɛkstl/ *n* **1** [*C*] : a fabric that is woven or knit ▪ *a textile factory* **2 textiles** [*U*] : the businesses that make textiles ▪ *a job in textiles*

text message *n* [*C*] : a short message that is sent electronically to a cell phone or other device — called also *text* — **text messaging** *n* [*U*] ▪ *I use my cell phone for text messaging.* [=for sending text messages]

tex·tu·al /ˈtɛkstʃəwəl/ *adj* : relating to or based on a piece of writing (such as a book or magazine) ▪ *textual analysis*

tex·ture /ˈtɛkstʃə/ *n* [*C/U*] **1** : the way

that something feels when you touch it ▪ *wood with a rough/smooth texture* **2** : the way that a food or drink feels in your mouth ▪ *a rich/silky texture* — **tex·tur·al** /ˈtɛkstʃərəl/ *adj*

tex·tured /ˈtɛkstʃərd/ *adj* : having a surface that was designed so that it is not smooth ▪ *textured fabrics*

Th. *abbr* Thursday

-th *or* **-eth** *adj suffix* — used in writing after numbers other than 1, 2, and 3 ▪ *100th = hundredth* ▪ *a 5th-grade teacher* ▪ *the eighth of April*

¹than /ˈðæn, ðən/ *conj* **1** — used to introduce the second or last of two or more things or people that are being compared; used with the comparative form of an adjective or adverb ▪ *Ten is less than 20.* ▪ *She's older than I am.* = *(somewhat formal)* *She's older than I.* ▪ *Losing weight is easier said than done.* [=is difficult to do] ▪ *I would rather eat out than cook tonight.* — see also *other than* at ¹OTHER, *rather than* at RATHER **2** — used to say that something happens immediately after something else ▪ *No sooner had I spoken than he appeared.* [=he appeared immediately after I spoke]

²than *prep* : when compared to — used with pronouns in the objective case (*me, her, him, them*, and *us*) in the same way ▪ that the conjunction *than* is used with pronouns in the subjective case (*I, she, he, they*, and *we*) ▪ *She's older than she.* [=older than I (am)] ▪ *I'm taller than him.* [=taller than he (is)]

---

usage Some people consider the use of *than* as a preposition to be incorrect. It is very common, however, especially in the phrase **than me.**

— *none other than* see ¹NONE

thank /ˈθæŋk/ *vb* [*T*] : to tell (someone) that you are grateful for something that he or she has done or given ▪ *I thanked her for (giving me) the gift.* — **have (someone or something) to thank for** — used to say that someone or something is responsible for something ▪ *The city has the mayor to thank for its current problems/success.* — **thank God/goodness/heaven(s)/the Lord** — used to express happiness or relief that something did or did not happen ▪ *Thank God you weren't hurt.* — **thank you 1** — used to thank someone ▪ *"Here's your change." "Thank you." "You're welcome."* ▪ *Thank you (very much) for your help.* **2** — used to politely accept or refuse an offer ▪ *"Can I carry that for you?" "Thank you (very much)."* ▪ *"Would you like another one?" "Yes, thank you."* [=yes, please] ▪ *"Can I carry that for you?" "No, thank you. I'll do it myself."* **3** — used to tell someone in a somewhat annoyed way that you do not want help or advice ▪ *I can do it myself, thank you (very much).*

thank·ful /ˈθæŋkfəl/ *adj* **1** : glad that something has happened or not happened, that something or someone exists, etc. ▪ *I was thankful to hear the good news.* ▪ *We have a lot to be thankful for.* **2** : of,

relating to, or expressing thanks ▪ *thankful words* — **thank·ful·ness** *n* [U]

thank·ful·ly /ˈθæŋkfəli/ *adv* : in a way that makes you feel thankful ▪ *Thankfully, no one was hurt.* [=I am glad/thankful that no one was hurt]

thank·less /ˈθæŋkləs/ *adj* **1** : difficult and not valued by other people ▪ *a thankless task/job* **2** : not showing or feeling thanks ▪ *thankless people*

thanks /ˈθæŋks/ *n* [*plural*] **1** : a good feeling that you have towards someone who has helped you, given something to you, etc. ▪ *I want express my thanks* [=gratitude] *(to you) for your generosity.* **2** : something done or said to express thanks ▪ *We should give thanks (to God) for all the good things in our lives.* **3** — used as a less formal way to say "thank you" ▪ *"Here's your change." "Thanks." "You're welcome."* ▪ *Thanks for coming.* **4** — used like "thank you" as a polite way of accepting or refusing an offer ▪ *"Do you want another one?" "Thanks."* [=yes, please] ▪ *"Do you want another one?" "No, thanks."* ▪ *"Would you like a ride?" "Thanks, but no thanks. I'll walk."* — **no thanks to** : without the help of (someone or something) ▪ *The vote passed, no thanks to the mayor.* [=even though the mayor did not help or want it to pass] — **thanks a bunch/lot/million** *informal* : thank you very much ▪ *Wow, this is great! Thanks a million!* — often used in an ironic way to say that you are not pleased that someone has done or said something ▪ *"I'm boring? Thanks a lot!"* — **thanks to** : with the help of (someone or something) : because of (someone or something) ▪ *Thanks to a new technique, patients typically recover from the surgery in only a few days.* — often used in an ironic way ▪ *Thanks to you we have to start over again.*

thanks·giv·ing /ˌθæŋksˈgɪvɪŋ/ *n* [U] **1** *Thanksgiving* : the fourth Thursday in November in the U.S. or the second Monday in October in Canada celebrated as a legal holiday for people to be thankful for what they have — called also *Thanksgiving Day* **2** *formal* : a prayer that expresses thanks to God ▪ *a hymn of thanksgiving*

thank–you /ˈθæŋkˌju:/ *n* [C] : something that you give or do to show thanks ▪ *The party is a thank-you for all the work you've done.* ▪ *a thank-you note/letter/gift*

¹that /ˈðæt, ðət/ *pron, pl* **those** /ˈðoʊz/ **1 a** — used to indicate which person, thing, fact, or idea is being shown, pointed to, or mentioned ▪ *That is my book.* ▪ *Those are my shoes.* ▪ *"What kind of tree is that?" "That is a maple."* ▪ *Is that your dad (standing) over there?* ▪ *You did what was right, and that makes me proud.* ▪ *"The meeting is canceled." "Who told you that?" usage* see ¹THIS **b** — used to refer to a time, action, or event that was just mentioned ▪ *Why did you do that?* ▪ *I brushed my teeth, and after that I went to bed.* ▪ *"I hate you!" she screamed. And with that* [=after saying that] *she stormed out of the room.* **c** — used to refer to the one that is farther away or less familiar ▪ *This is* my hat and that is yours. ▪ *Those are nice, but I like these better.* **2** *somewhat formal* **a** : the kind or thing described or identified ▪ *The aluminum parts are much lighter than those made from steel.* [=much lighter than the parts made from steel] ▪ *a planet with an atmosphere like that of the Earth* [=an atmosphere like the Earth's atmosphere] **b** : the kind or thing stated previously ▪ *"There is the matter of your raise (to discuss)." "Yes, there is that."* **3** *those* somewhat formal : a particular group of people ▪ *Let's take a vote. All those in favor, say "aye."* ▪ *There are those who think she should resign.* **4** — used to introduce a group of words that limits the meaning of a noun especially to a specific person, place, or thing ▪ *Is it me that you're looking for?* ▪ *Describe the person that* [=who, (*formal*) *whom*] *you saw.* ▪ *The movie that we watched was a drama.* ▪ *You were born the same year that I was.* ▪ *There is nothing that you can do about it now.*

> **usage** *That* in this sense is often omitted in informal English. ▪ *You were born the same year (that) I was.* ▪ *Open the wine (that) our guests brought.* When it is the subject of a verb, however, it is always included. ▪ *The person that won the race also won last year.*

— all that 1 *informal* **a** : everything of the kind stated or suggested ▪ *She had money, fame, and all that.* **b** : more things of the same kind ▪ *The store sells computers, cell phones, and all that* [=and other such things] **2** : the stated or suggested degree, amount, etc. — usually used in negative statements ▪ *It wasn't as bad as all that.* [=it was better than you said it was] — see also *all that* at ²ALL — **at that 1** — used when giving more information about something or someone that was just mentioned; usually used in the phrase *and a bad/good (etc.) one* **at that** ▪ *She's a lawyer, and a very talented one at that.* **2** : without adding or doing anything more ▪ *Let's just say it's complicated, and* **leave it at that.** = *Let's let it go* **at that.** [=let's not say anything more about it] — **for all that** : in spite of something just mentioned ▪ *She practiced and practiced, but for all that she still failed.* — **that is** or **that is to say 1** — used when giving more accurate or specific information about someone or something that was just mentioned ▪ *We—that is to say my wife and I—will attend the wedding.* **2** — used when giving information that affects something previously mentioned ▪ *We plan on going to the concert—that is, if tickets are still available.* — **that is all** or **that's all 1** — used to say that something is finished or completed ▪ *"Do you need anything else?" "No, thanks, that's all." ▪ They're (just) different, that's all.* [=I am not saying anything more than that they are different] **2** — used to say that something is all that is needed or wanted ▪ *I went there to visit friends and that's all.* ▪ *That's all I wanted to do there]* — **that is that** or **that's that** — used to say that a decision or situation

cannot be changed ▪ *I'm not going and that's that.* — **that's it** see ¹IT — **that's life** — used to say that something unpleasant or difficult is a normal part of life ▪ *Sometimes you try your hardest and still don't succeed. That's life.*

²that *conj* **1** — used to introduce a clause that is the subject or object of a verb ▪ *That he said no is not surprising.* ▪ *I never said that I was afraid.* ▪ *The reason for his absence is that he is ill.* **2** — used to introduce a clause that completes or explains the meaning of a previous noun or adjective or of the pronoun *it* ▪ *There is a chance that it might rain.* ▪ *It's not surprising that he said no.* ▪ *It's clear that he needs our help.* **3** — used to introduce a clause that states a reason or purpose ▪ *I'm glad that you're here.* ▪ *She was saving money* **so that** *she could buy a car.* **4** — used especially after a phrase beginning with *so* or *such* to introduce a clause that states a result ▪ *She was so dizzy that she fell down.* ▪ *He was in such a rush that he forgot to take his hat.*

> **usage** *That* in senses 1, 2, 3, and 4 is often omitted in informal English, except when it is used at the beginning of a sentence. ▪ *I never said (that) I was afraid.* ▪ *I'm glad (that) you're here.* ▪ *Carry it with both hands so (that) you don't drop it.* ▪ *She was so dizzy (that) she fell down.*

— in that see ²IN — **not that** — used to say that something that may seem true is not true ▪ *Some people lie to get out of jury duty. Not that I ever would, of course.* [=I would never lie to get out of jury duty]

³that *adj, always before a noun, pl* **those 1** — used to indicate which person, thing, or idea is being shown, pointed to, or mentioned ▪ *That boy hit me.* ▪ *Those books are mine.* ▪ *Hand me that wrench.* ▪ *I like that idea.* ▪ *I got home on that day.* **2** — used to indicate the one that is farther away or less familiar ▪ *Do you want this one or that one?* ▪ *Are you talking about these shoes, or those shoes over there?* — **that way 1** : in the manner described or suggested ▪ *What makes her act that way?* **2** : in or into the condition described or suggested ▪ *He's very successful and it's easy to see how he got that way.*

⁴that /ˈðæt/ *adv* **1 a** : to the degree that is stated or suggested ▪ *"It was awful." "Was it really that bad?" "Yes, it was that bad."* ▪ *What would you do with that much money?* ▪ *I've never been that sad.* [=as sad as I was then] ▪ *I can't throw the ball that far.* ▪ (*Brit, informal*) *They were that* [=so] *poor they couldn't buy food.* **b** : to the degree or extent indicated by a gesture ▪ *It's about that* [=this, so] *tall.* **2** *informal* : to a great degree : VERY — usually used in negative statements ▪ *"When did it happen?" "Not that long ago."*

thatch /ˈθætʃ/ *n* **1** [U] : dried plant material (such as straw or leaves) that is used to make the roof of a building **2** [*singular*] : a thick mass of hair on a person's head ▪ *her thatch of dark brown hair* — **thatched** /ˈθætʃt/ *adj* ▪ *a thatched* *roof* [=a roof made of thatch] ▪ *a thatched cottage* [=a cottage with a roof made of thatch]

¹thaw /ˈθɑː/ *vb* **1** [T/I] : to stop being frozen or to cause (something) to stop being frozen ▪ *The ice on the pond is beginning to thaw.* [=*melt*] ▪ *You have to thaw the meat (out).* = *The meat has to thaw (out).* **2** [I] *of weather* : to become warm enough that snow and ice melt ▪ *The weather is beginning to thaw.* **3** [T/I] : to return to a normal temperature after being very cold ▪ *Our cold fingers eventually thawed (out).* **4** [T/I] : to become more friendly and less angry ▪ *Relations between the countries have thawed.*

²thaw *n* [C] **1** : a period of weather that is warm enough to melt ice and snow ▪ *the spring thaw* **2** : a situation in which a relationship becomes more friendly and less angry ▪ *a thaw in international relations*

the /ðə *before consonant sounds,* ði *before vowel sounds,* ˈðiː *when said with emphasis/ definite article* **1** — used to indicate a person or thing that has already been mentioned or seen or is clearly understood from the situation ▪ *I'll take the red one.* ▪ *The teacher gave a quiz.* ▪ *She's the boss.* ▪ *Tell the truth.* ▪ *What is the matter/ problem?* **2 a** — used to refer to things or people that are common in daily life ▪ *talk on the telephone* ▪ *go to the doctor* **b** — used to refer to things that occur in nature ▪ *The sky is getting dark.* ▪ *The planets revolve around the sun.* ▪ *We talked about the weather.* **3 a** — used to refer to a particular unit or period of time ▪ *the best movie of the year* ▪ *during the winter* ▪ *in the future/past/present* ▪ *a style popular during the 1980s* **b** *Brit* — used to indicate the day on which something happened or will happen ▪ *He left five days later, on the Sunday.* [=(US) on Sunday] **4** — used before the name of a specific person, place, event, work of art, etc. ▪ *the President of the United States of America* ▪ *the Mississippi River* ▪ *the Renaissance* **5** — used to indicate which person or thing you are referring to or discussing ▪ *It's the correct answer.* ▪ *the fastest runner* ▪ *I never have the time to read.* ▪ *the English language* ▪ *the poet Virgil* ▪ *the west coast of Africa* **6** — used in titles after a person's name ▪ *Alexander the Great* ▪ *Elizabeth the Second* **7** — used before an ordinal number ▪ *the Fourth of July* ▪ *the first time* **8 a** — used before a singular noun to refer in a general way to people or things of a particular kind ▪ *useful tips for the beginner* [=for beginners] ▪ *The cobra is a poisonous snake.* [=cobras are poisonous snakes] **b** — used to indicate the type of musical instrument someone plays ▪ *She plays the guitar.* **c** — used before an adjective that is being used as a noun to refer to all of the people or things that have a particular quality ▪ *the rich/homeless* ▪ *the British* ▪ *the living and the dead* **d** — used before a plural noun to indicate that every person or thing of the kind specified is included ▪ *the Greeks and the Romans* ▪ *The newspapers covered the story.* **e** —

used before the plural form of a person's last name to indicate that all the members of the family are included ▪ *the Smiths* **9 a** — used to indicate that a person or thing is the best of its kind ▪ *This is the life.* [=this is a very enjoyable way to live, spend time, etc.] ▪ *He is the person* [=the right person] *for the job.* **b** — used to indicate the most famous person having a particular name ◊ This sense of *the* is emphasized in speech. ▪ *"I met Julia Roberts." "You met the Julia Roberts, the famous actress?"* **10** — used to refer in a general way to a specific type of activity ▪ *the law* ▪ *the publishing industry* ▪ *I love the opera/cinema.* **11 a** — used to refer to a part of your body or clothing ▪ *How's the* [=*your*] *arm feeling?* ▪ *She led him by the* [=*his*] *hand.* **b** *informal* — used before a noun that refers to a person's family, job, health, etc. ▪ *How is the* [=*your*] *family?* ▪ *Is the job going well?*

the·a·ter *(US) or chiefly Brit* **the·a·tre** /ˈθiːjətər/ *n* **1** [C] **a** : a building where plays, shows, etc., are performed on a stage **b** *US* : a building or room in which movies are shown ▪ *a movie theater* **2** [U] **a** : plays in general or as a form of entertainment ▪ *the theater of 16th-century England* ▪ *a theater critic* **b** : the art or activity of performing in or producing plays on a stage ▪ *a course in American theater* ▪ *a theater troupe/company* **3** [C] : a large area where there is a war ▪ *the Pacific theater (of operations) in World War II* **4** [C] *Brit* : OPERATING ROOM

the·ater·go·er *(US) or chiefly Brit* **the·atre·go·er** /ˈθiːjətərˌgowər/ *n* [C] : a person who often goes to the theater to see plays

the·at·ri·cal /θiˈætrɪkəl/ *adj* **1** : of or relating to the theater ▪ *theatrical costumes/ ambitions* **2** : behaving or done in a way that is meant to attract attention and that is often not genuine or sincere ▪ *a theatrical gesture/bow* — **the·at·ri·cal·ly** /θiˈætrɪkli/ *adv*

the·at·rics /θiˈætrɪks/ *n* [*plural*] *chiefly US, often disapproving* : ways of behaving and speaking that are like a performance on a stage and are intended to attract attention ▪ *courtroom theatrics*

thee /ˈðiː/ *pron, old-fashioned + literary* — used as a singular form of "you" when it is the object of a verb or preposition ▪ *"I take thee at thy word . . . "* —Shakespeare, *Romeo and Juliet* (1594–95)

theft /ˈθɛft/ *n* [C/U] : the act or crime of stealing ▪ *car thefts* ▪ *He was guilty of theft.*

their /ˈðeɚ, ðɚ/ *adj, always before a noun, possessive form of* THEY **1** : relating to or belonging to certain people, animals, or things ▪ *the furniture in their house* ▪ *The birds have left their nest.* : made or done by certain people, animals, or things ▪ *They did their best.* ▪ *I listened to their conversation.* **2** : his or her : his : her : its — used to refer to a single person whose sex is not known or specified ▪ *Each person reacts to their environment differently.*

theirs /ˈðeɚz/ *pron* **1** : that which belongs to or is connected with them : their one : their ones ▪ *The computer is theirs.* [=the computer belongs to them; it is their computer] ▪ *She is a friend of theirs.* [=she is their friend] **2** : his or hers — used to refer to a single person whose sex is not known or specified ▪ *I will do my part if everybody else does theirs.*

them /ˈðɛm, ðəm/ *pron, objective form of* THEY **1** — used to refer to certain people, animals, or things as the objects of a verb or preposition ▪ *I haven't met them yet.* **2** : him or her — used to refer to a single person whose sex is not known or specified ▪ *The teacher said that if anyone admitted to the prank, she wouldn't punish them.* [=she wouldn't punish that person]

the·mat·ic /θɪˈmætɪk/ *adj* : of or relating to a theme ▪ *the thematic development in the story* — **the·mat·i·cal·ly** /θɪˈmætɪkli/ *adv*

theme /ˈθiːm/ *n [C]* **1** : the main subject that is being discussed or described in a piece of writing, a movie, etc. ▪ *the album's themes of love and loss* **2 a** : a particular subject or issue that is discussed often or repeatedly ▪ *The deficit was a dominant theme in the election.* **b** : the particular subject or idea on which the style of something (such as a party or room) is based ▪ *a party with a Hawaiian luau theme* **3** *music* **a** : the main melody that is repeated in a piece of music **b** : THEME SONG **4** *US* : a short piece of writing by a student on a particular subject : ESSAY — **themed** /ˈθiːmd/ *adj, always before a noun* ▪ *a Hawaiian-themed party*

theme park *n [C]* : an amusement park where the rides and attractions are based on a particular theme (sense 2b)

theme song *n [C]* : a song that is played at the beginning and end of a television show, movie, etc.

them·selves /ðɛmˈsɛlvz/ *pron* **1** — used as the object of a verb or preposition to refer to people, animals, or things that have already been mentioned ▪ *They are getting themselves ready.* ▪ *They did most of it themselves.* ▪ *people who are unable to care for themselves* ▪ *They kept their plans to themselves.* [=they kept their plans secret] — often used for emphasis ▪ *They were young once themselves.* **2** : himself or herself — used to refer to a single person whose sex is not known or specified ▪ *Nobody should blame themselves.* **3** : their normal or healthy selves ▪ *They were themselves again after a night's rest.* — **by themselves** **1** : without any help from other people ▪ *They solved the problem by themselves.* **2** : with nobody else : ALONE ▪ *They toured the city by themselves.*

¹then /ˈðɛn/ *adv* **1** : at that time : at the time mentioned ▪ *It was then believed (that) the Earth was flat.* ▪ *Just then he walked in.* **2 a** — used to indicate what happened or happens next ▪ *He stood, then walked away.* ▪ *First the clowns come out, (and) then the elephants (come out).* **b** — used to indicate what should be done next ▪ *Take your first right, (and) then turn left at the light.* **3** — used to

indicate what must be true or what must or should happen if something else is true or happens ▪ *If it rains, then we can't go.* ▪ *"It's raining." "Then we can't go."* ▪ *"He confessed." "The case is closed, then."* ▪ *If you want it, then take it.* ▪ *Hurry, then, if you want to catch the bus.* ▪ *What if there should be a fire?* **What then?** [=what will happen then?] ✧ *Then* is often omitted following *if.* ▪ *If it rains, (then) we can't go.* **b** — used to say or ask about what appears to be true based on what has happened or been said ▪ *Your mind is made up, then?* **c** — used to say what has been agreed to or decided ▪ *OK, then, I'll see you at seven o'clock.* **d** *somewhat formal* — used to make a final statement that refers back to the things that have just been mentioned or described ▪ *These, then, are the things you must do.* **4** — used after words like *all right* and *OK* at the beginning of a statement ▪ *All right, then, let's get started.* — **and then some** see ²SOME — **but then** see ¹BUT — **(every) now and then** see ¹NOW — **then and there** or *chiefly Brit* **there and then** : immediately at that place ▪ *I made up my mind then and there.*

²then *n [singular]* : that time ▪ *Since then, I've been more careful.* ▪ *They'll announce their decision next week. Until then, we'll just have to wait.* ▪ *They were friends from then on.*

³then *adj, always before a noun* : existing at or belonging to the time mentioned ▪ *She was appointed by Utah's then governor.* [=by the person who was Utah's governor at that time]

thence /ˈðɛns/ *adv, formal* : from that place ▪ *Their travels took them to the Bahamas, thence south to Venezuela.*

thence·forth /ˈðɛnsˌfoəθ/ *adv, formal* : from that time forward ▪ *He was determined thenceforth to dedicate himself to his studies.*

the·oc·ra·cy /θiˈɑːkrəsi/ *n, pl* **-cies** **1** *[U]* : a form of government in which a country is ruled by religious leaders **2** *[C]* : a country that is ruled by religious leaders — **the·o·crat·ic** /ˌθiːjəˈkrætɪk/ *adj* ▪ *a theocratic government/regime*

theo·lo·gian /ˌθiːjəˈloʊdʒən/ *n [C]* : a person who is an expert on theology

the·ol·o·gy /θiˈɑːlədʒi/ *n, pl* **-gies** **1** *[U]* : the study of religious faith, practice, and experience **2** *[C]* : a system of religious beliefs or ideas ▪ *Christian/Muslim/Jewish theology* — **theo·log·i·cal** /ˌθiːjəˈlɑːdʒɪkəl/ *adj* ▪ *theological studies/arguments*

the·o·rem /ˈθiːjərəm/ *n [C] technical* : a formula or statement that can be proved from other formulas or statements ▪ *mathematical theorems*

the·o·ret·i·cal /ˌθiːjəˈrɛtɪkəl/ *also* **the·o·ret·ic** /ˌθiːjəˈrɛtɪk/ *adj* **1** : relating to what is possible or imagined rather than to what is known to be true or real ▪ *The idea is purely theoretical at this point.* ▪ *a theoretical argument/possibility* **2** : relating to the general principles or ideas of a subject rather than the practical uses of those ideas ▪ *theoretical physics* — **the·o·**

ret·i·cal·ly /ˌθiːjəˈrɛtɪkli/ adv ▪ It's theoretically possible but very unlikely.

the·o·re·ti·cian /ˌθiːjərəˈtɪʃən/ n [C] : THEORIST

the·o·rist /ˈθiːjərɪst/ n [C] : a person who forms theories about something ▪ political theorists

the·o·rize also Brit **the·o·rise** /ˈθiːjəˌraɪz/ vb -rized; -riz·ing [T/I] : to think of or suggest ideas about what is possibly true or real ▪ theorizing about/on the possibility of life on other planets

the·o·ry /ˈθiːjəri/ n, pl -ries 1 [C/U] : an idea or set of ideas that is intended to explain facts or events ▪ a scientific theory ▪ theories on/about evolution 2 [C] : an idea that is suggested or presented as possibly true but that is not known or proven to be true ▪ Her method is based on the theory that all children want to learn. ▪ There are a number of different theories about the cause of the disease. 3 [U] : the general principles or ideas that relate to a particular subject ▪ music theory — in theory 1 — used to say what should happen or be true if a theory is correct ▪ In theory, their skills should improve. 2 — used to say that something seems to be true or possible as an idea but may not actually be true or possible ▪ I agree with you in theory, but realistically I don't think we have the time to do that.

ther·a·peu·tic /ˌθɛrəˈpjuːtɪk/ adj 1 : producing good effects on your body or mind ▪ the therapeutic benefits of yoga 2 : of or relating to the treatment of illness ▪ the therapeutic effects of radiation

ther·a·pist /ˈθɛrəpɪst/ n [C] 1 : a person trained in methods of treating illnesses especially without the use of drugs or surgery 2 : a person who helps people deal with mental or emotional problems by talking about those problems : a person trained in psychotherapy ▪ a family therapist

ther·a·py /ˈθɛrəpi/ n, pl -pies 1 [C/U] : the treatment of physical or mental illnesses ▪ cancer therapy ▪ new drug therapies 2 [U] : PSYCHOTHERAPY

¹**there** /ˈðeə/ adv 1 a : in that place : at that location ▪ Put the package there on the table. ▪ She was sitting there a minute ago. ▪ Hello. Is Pat there? ▪ When will you be there? ▪ I used to live there. ▪ So there you are. I've been looking for you. ▪ Ah, there's the book I've been looking for. ▪ That clock there once belonged to my grandmother. b : to or into that place ▪ We should get there by noon. 2 a : at that point in a process, activity, story, etc. ▪ Stop right there, before you say something you'll regret. b : in that particular matter ▪ There is where I disagree with you. 3 a — used with the verb be at the beginning of a sentence that makes a statement about a situation or asks about a situation ▪ There's still a lot for us to do. ▪ There are many things to be considered. ▪ There is a person waiting to see you. [=a person is waiting to see you] ▪ Is there a gas station nearby? b — used to introduce a sentence in which the subject comes after the verb ▪ There used to be a school here. ▪ Once upon a time, there

lived a beautiful princess. 4 informal — used to address a person or animal ▪ Well, hello there. ▪ Say there, do you have the time? — have been there — used to say that you have experienced the same thing that someone else has experienced ▪ I know how you feel. I've been there (before) myself. — neither here nor there see ¹HERE — out there informal — used to say that someone or something exists ▪ There are a lot of crazy drivers out there. — there's . . . for you see ¹FOR — there you are or there you go informal 1 — used to tell someone that you have given them what they asked for ▪ There you are, sir. That will be $3 for the coffees. ▪ "Could you pass the salt?" "Sure, there you go." 2 — used to indicate that something is completed or done in a satisfactory way ▪ Wait, I want to fix your tie. There you go. — there you have it informal — used to indicate that something is completed or done in a satisfactory way ▪ There you have it. The mystery is solved. — you have me there or there you have me see HAVE 18b

²**there** adj, not before a noun : capable of being relied on for support or help ▪ My dad has always been there for me. [=has always helped me when I needed his help] — not all there see ²ALL

³**there** interj 1 — used to attract attention ▪ There, look at that. 2 — used to show satisfaction, approval, or encouragement ▪ There, it's finished at last. ▪ There, I told you so. — so there informal — used to say in a somewhat rude, angry, or childish way that you have stated your opinion or decision and will not change it ▪ Well, I don't want to be your friend, either. So there! — there, there — used to tell someone not to be worried or unhappy ▪ There, there, don't cry. Everything will be OK.

⁴**there** n [U] 1 : that place ▪ Get away from there. 2 : that point ▪ I'll get everything ready, and you take it from there.

there·abouts /ˌðeərəˈbaʊts/ also US **there·about** /ˌðeərəˈbaʊt/ adv : near or around that place, time, amount, etc. ▪ He lives on Maple Street or thereabouts. ▪ It happened in 1977 or thereabouts.

there·af·ter /ðeəˈræftə, Brit ðeəˈɑːftə/ adv, formal : after that ▪ She returned shortly thereafter.

there·by /ðeəˈbaɪ/ adv, formal : by means of that act, those words, that document, etc. ▪ He signed the contract, thereby forfeiting his right to the property.

there'd /ˈðeəd/ — used as a contraction of there had or there would ▪ There'd [=there had] never been a case like it before. ▪ I knew there'd [=there would] be trouble.

there·fore /ˈðeəˌfoə/ adv, somewhat formal : for that reason : because of that ▪ The cell phone is thin and light and therefore very convenient to carry around. ▪ Payment was received after it was due; therefore, you will be charged a late fee.

there·in /ðeəˈrɪn/ adv, formal 1 : in or into that place or thing ▪ The insurance covers the apartment and all the property therein. 2 : in that statement, fact, or detail ▪ *They have to make a decision soon.* **Therein lies the problem.** [=that is why there is a problem]

there·of /ðeⱥˈʌv/ *adv, formal* : of the thing that has been mentioned ▪ *a will or any part thereof* [=any part of a will] ▪ *The problem is money, or (a/the)* **lack thereof**.

there·on /ðeⱥˈɑːn/ *adv, formal* : on the thing that has been mentioned ▪ *The highway and structures thereon are being repaired.*

there's /ˈðeⱥz, ðəz/ — used as a contraction of *there is* or *there has* ▪ *There's* [=there is] *a lot more to do.* ▪ *There's* [=there has] *never been any reason to doubt him.*

there·up·on /ˈðeⱥrəˌpɑːn/ *adv, formal* : immediately after that ▪ *The committee reviewed the documents and thereupon decided to accept the proposal.*

¹**ther·mal** /ˈθɚməl/ *adj* **1** : of, relating to, or caused by heat ▪ *thermal energy* **2** : designed to keep you warm by preventing heat from leaving your body ▪ *thermal underwear* **3** : having hot water flowing out of the ground ▪ *thermal springs* — **ther·mal·ly** *adv*

²**thermal** *n* **1** [*C*] : a rising current of warm air that is produced when the sun heats an area of the ground **2** [*plural*] *Brit* : thermal clothing or underwear

ther·mo·dy·nam·ics /ˌθɚmoʊˌdaɪˈnæmɪks/ *n* [*U*] *technical* : a science that deals with the action of heat and related forms of energy — **ther·mo·dy·nam·ic** /ˌθɚmoʊˌdaɪˈnæmɪk/ *adj*

ther·mom·e·ter /θɚˈmɑːmətɚ/ *n* [*C*] : an instrument used for measuring temperature ▪ *The thermometer says it's 80 degrees outside.*

ther·mo·nu·cle·ar /ˌθɚmoʊˈnuːklijɚ, *Brit* ˌθɚːməʊˈnjuːkliə/ *adj, technical* : of or relating to the changes in the nucleus of atoms that happen at extremely high temperatures ▪ *a thermonuclear reaction*

ther·mos /ˈθɚməs/ *n* [*C*] : a container that keeps liquids hot or cold for long periods of time

ther·mo·stat /ˈθɚməˌstæt/ *n* [*C*] : a device that automatically adjusts the temperature of a room, machine, etc., to a desired level ▪ *I set the thermostat to 68 degrees.*

the·sau·rus /θɪˈsɔrəs/ *n, pl* **-sau·ri** /-ˈsɔˌaɪ/ *or* **-sau·rus·es** /-ˈsɔrəsəz/ [*C*] : a book in which words that have the same or similar meanings are grouped together

these *plural of* THIS

the·sis /ˈθiːsəs/ *n, pl* **the·ses** /ˈθiːˌsiːz/ [*C*] **1** : a long piece of writing on a particular subject that is done to earn a degree at a university ▪ *a master's/doctoral thesis on the effects of global warming* **2** *formal* : a statement that someone wants to discuss or prove ▪ *We disagreed with the basic thesis of the report.*

thes·pi·an /ˈθɛspijən/ *n* [*C*] *formal + sometimes humorous* : ACTOR ▪ *a renowned thespian and director*

they /ˈðeɪ/ *pron* **1** : those people, animals, or things ▪ *They dance very well.* **2** — used to refer to people in a general way or to a group of people who are not

specified ▪ *You know what they say: you only live once.* ▪ *She's as hardworking as they come.* [=she's very hardworking] ▪ *They took away his license.* **3** : he or she — used to refer to a single person whose sex is not known or specified ▪ *Everyone can go if they want to.*

they'd /ˈðeɪd/ — used as a contraction of *they had* or *they would* ▪ *They admitted that they'd* [=they had] *been foolish.* ▪ *They'd* [=they would] *love to go but won't be able to.*

they'll /ˈðeɪl, ðɛl/ — used as a contraction of *they will* ▪ *They'll be arriving soon.*

they're /ˈðeⱥ, ðɚ/ — used as a contraction of *they are* ▪ *They're not here yet.*

they've /ˈðeɪv/ — used as a contraction of *they have* ▪ *They've already left.*

¹**thick** /ˈθɪk/ *adj* **1 a** : having a large distance between the top and bottom or front and back surfaces : not thin ▪ *a thick book/wall* ▪ *He wore thick glasses.* [=glasses with thick lenses] ▪ *a thick slice of bread* ▪ *a thick wool sweater* ▪ *He was* **thick around the middle.** [=fat around his waist] **b** : having a specified thickness ▪ *The planks were two inches thick.* **2** : growing closely together and in a large amount ▪ *thick fur/hair* **3** : difficult to see through : DENSE ▪ *thick black smoke* **4** *of a liquid* : not flowing easily ▪ *thick gravy/sauce/syrup* **5 a** *of speech or the voice* : difficult to understand ▪ *Her voice was thick with emotion.* **b** *of a person's accent* : very easy to notice ▪ *He spoke with a thick accent.* **6** *informal* : STUPID 1 ▪ *They were too thick to understand what I was saying.* ▪ *Why can't he get it through his thick head that I don't like him?* **7** *not before a noun* **a** *chiefly US* : existing in great numbers or large amounts ▪ *Tension was thick in the office.* [=there was a lot of tension in the office] **b** : having great numbers or a large amount of something ▪ *The air was thick with mosquitoes.* **8** *not before a noun, informal* : having a close and friendly relationship ▪ *They were (as)* **thick as thieves.** [=very close and secretive] — **blood is thicker than water** see BLOOD — **thick·ly** /ˈθɪkli/ *adv* ▪ *thickly sliced mushrooms* ▪ *a thickly settled neighborhood*

²**thick** *adv* **1** : in a way that makes thick pieces, layers, etc. ▪ *Slice the roast thick.* **2** : in great numbers ▪ *Apples hung thick on the trees.* ▪ *Suggestions were coming in* **thick and fast.**

³**thick** *n* — **in the thick of** : in the most active or intense part of (something) ▪ *a soldier in the thick of (the) battle* — **through thick and thin** : through many difficult times over a long period ▪ *She stood by me through thick and thin.*

thick·en /ˈθɪkən/ *vb* [*T/I*] : to make (something) thick or thicker or to become thick or thicker ▪ *I thickened the gravy with flour.* ▪ *The fog thickened.* — **thick·en·er** /ˈθɪkənɚ/ *n* [*C*]

thick·et /ˈθɪkət/ *n* [*C*] : a group of bushes or small trees that grow close together ▪ *(figurative) a tangled thicket of laws*

thick–head·ed /ˈθɪkˌhɛdəd/ *adj, informal* : STUPID 1 ▪ *a thick-headed decision/ fool*

thick·ness /ˈθɪknəs/ *n* **1 a** [C/U] : the distance between the top and bottom or front and back surfaces of something : a measurement of how thick something is ▪ *The plank measures two inches in thickness.* **b** [U] : the quality of being thick ▪ *I added flour to increase the gravy's thickness.* **2** [C] : a layer or sheet of some material ▪ *a single thickness of canvas*

thick·set /ˈθɪkˌsɛt/ *adj* : having a short, thick body ▪ *a thickset man*

thick–skinned /ˈθɪkˌskɪnd/ *adj* **1** : having a thick skin ▪ *a thick-skinned orange* **2** : not easily bothered by criticism or insults ▪ *Politicians need to be thick-skinned.*

thief /ˈθiːf/ *n, pl* **thieves** /ˈθiːvz/ [C] : a person who steals something ▪ *a car thief*

thiev·ery /ˈθiːvəri/ *n* [U] *formal* : the act of stealing ▪ *They accused him of thievery.*

thiev·ing /ˈθiːvɪŋ/ *n* [U] *somewhat old-fashioned* : the act or activity of stealing ▪ *They finally found out about his thieving.*
— **thieving** *adj, always before a noun* ▪ *You thieving liar!*

thigh /ˈθaɪ/ *n* [C] : the part of your leg that is above the knee

thim·ble /ˈθɪmbəl/ *n* [C] : a small metal or plastic cap used in sewing to protect the finger that pushes the needle

¹**thin** /ˈθɪn/ *adj* **thin·ner**; **-nest 1** : having a small distance between the top and bottom or front and back surfaces : not thick ▪ *a thin line/wall/layer* ▪ *a thin slice of ham* **2** : not having a lot of extra flesh on the body : not fat ▪ *She is very/too thin.* ▪ *thin legs* **3 a** : not growing closely together ▪ *a thin stand of trees* : not growing in a large amount ▪ *thin hair* **b** : having less than the usual, original, or needed number or amount ▪ *Attendance was thin.* ▪ *My patience was wearing/running thin.* [=I was becoming less patient] **4** *of a liquid* : flowing very easily ▪ *thin gravy* **5** : having less oxygen than normal ▪ *a thin atmosphere* **6** : easy to see through ▪ *a thin mist* **7** : not large or impressive ▪ *She has a thin lead in the polls.* **8** : not very good, useful, etc. : WEAK ▪ *His argument wore thin.* ▪ *His argument wore thin.* **9** *of a voice* : weak and high ▪ *a high, thin voice* — **disappear/ vanish into thin air** : to disappear completely in a way that is mysterious — **on thin ice** see ¹ICE — **out of thin air** — used to say that someone or something appears in a sudden and unexpected way ▪ *He appeared out of thin air.* — **through thick and thin** see ³THICK — **thin·ness** /ˈθɪnnəs/ *n* [U]

²**thin** *vb* **thinned**; **thin·ning** [T/I] : to make (something or someone) thin or thinner or to become thin or thinner ▪ *The crowd thinned as the night went on.* ▪ *He added more water to thin the gravy.* ▪ *His hair is thinning.* = *He has thinning hair.* ▪ *She's thinned (down) a lot in the past year.*

³**thin** *adv* **thin·ner**; **-nest** : in a way that makes thin pieces, layers, etc. ▪ *She sliced the cheese thin.*

thine /ˈðaɪn/ *pron, old-fashioned + literary* : YOURS ▪ *May God's blessings be thine.* — **thine** *adj*

thing /ˈθɪŋ/ *n* **1** [C] **a** : an object whose name is not known or stated ▪ *What is that thing on the floor?* ▪ *I can't see a thing* [=can't see anything] *without my glasses.* **b** : an object, animal, quality, etc., of a specified kind ▪ *Put the cleaning/cooking things away.* ▪ *We must respect all living things.* ▪ *She loves all things chocolate.* [=anything made out of chocolate] ▪ *Her voice is a thing of beauty.* [=her voice is beautiful] ▪ *Those problems are a thing of the past.* [=they no longer exist] ▪ *The drawer has pens, paper clips, and things (like that).* **c** : a particular event, occurrence, or situation ▪ *Birth is a miraculous thing.* ▪ *It was the worst thing that could have happened.* ▪ *Let's just forget about the whole thing and move on.* ▪ *It is one thing to say you're sorry but (it is) another (thing) to actually mean it.* ▪ *It's a good thing (that) no one was injured.* **2** [plural] : objects that belong to a person ▪ *Are all your things packed?* **3** [C] : an action that is done, that will be done, or that needs to be done ▪ *I have many things to do today.* ▪ *That was a mean/ thoughtful thing to do.* ▪ *Don't worry about a thing.* [=anything] *I'll take care of everything.* **4** [C] : an activity ▪ *I like hiking, biking—that sort of thing.* ▪ *(informal) They spent the evening doing guy things.* [=the kinds of things that guys/men like to do] ▪ *(informal) Dancing is his thing.* [=he enjoys dancing and does it well] ▪ *The students are allowed to do their own thing.* [=do the activities that they want to do] ▪ *Just do your thing* [=do what you usually do] *and pretend I'm not here.* **5** [plural] : the conditions that exist at a particular time and in a particular place ▪ *Things are improving.* ▪ *How are things with the new baby?* ▪ *As things stand now, we can't afford a new car.* ▪ *All things considered, the party went very well.* **6** [C] : a fact or piece of information about something or someone ▪ *There is one more thing I'd like to ask you.* ▪ *We are always arguing, but the (funny) thing is, I think I love him.* ▪ *I make excellent chili. The thing is to pick the right peppers.* [=to make excellent chili, you need to pick the right peppers] ▪ *The thing with/about him is that he is not reliable.* ▪ *Forget what he said—it doesn't mean a thing.* [=it has no meaning or importance; it's not true] ▪ *I know a thing or two about cars.* = *I know some things about cars.* **7** [C] : a thought, idea, or opinion ▪ *That was a terrible thing to say.* **8** [singular] : a reason for something ▪ *I can't stand being around him. For one thing, he smokes. For another, he's rude.* ▪ *OK, here's the thing: I don't have enough money to go to college.* ▪ *I'm sorry I didn't call you. The thing is, I've been really busy lately.* **9** [C] *informal* : a strong feeling of liking or disliking something or someone ▪ *She has a/this ·thing about/with snakes.* [=she is afraid of snakes] ▪ *My teacher has this/a thing against me.* [=my teacher dislikes me] ▪ *He has a thing for* [=he likes] *women with red hair.* **10 the thing a** : the item that is the most fashionable or popular ▪ *Long skirts are the thing (to wear) this sea-*

son. **b** : the fashionable or proper way of behaving, talking, or dressing ▪ *It's the thing to buy products made from recycled materials.* — **all/other things being equal** *formal* — used to say what should happen or be true if two situations, products, etc., are different in a specified way but not in other ways ▪ *All things being equal, a person with a PhD should be getting a higher salary than someone with only a Master's degree.* — **all things to all people/men** : a person or thing that makes all people happy by giving them what they want or need ▪ *She was criticized for trying to be all things to all people in her campaign.* — **first thing** see ¹FIRST — **first things first** see ¹FIRST — **last thing** see ²LAST — **make a big thing** *informal* ✧ If you *make a big thing (out) of (something)* or *make a big thing about (something),* you act as if something is very important or serious when it is not. ▪ *It was a minor error, but she made a big thing out of it.* — **of all things** — used to emphasize that the thing you are referring to is the thing you would least expect ▪ *The coach is making the football team take, of all things, ballet classes.* — **one of those things** *informal* — used to refer to a bad or unfortunate experience that happened and to say that such experiences happen to everyone ▪ *I missed the train and had to take a later one. It was just one of those things, I guess.* — **see things** see SEE — **sure thing** see ¹SURE — **the real thing** : something that is genuine and not a copy or imitation ▪ *The diamond turned out to be the real thing.*

thing·am·a·jig *or* **thing·um·a·jig** /ˈθɪŋə-məˌdʒɪg/ *n* [C] *informal* : something whose name you have forgotten or do not know ▪ *It's one of those thingamajigs that can give you driving directions.*

thing·um·my /ˈθɪŋəmi/ *n, pl* **-mies** [C] *chiefly Brit, informal* : THINGAMAJIG

thingy /ˈθɪŋi/ *n, pl* **thing·ies** [C] *informal* : THINGAMAJIG

think /ˈθɪŋk/ *vb* **thought** /ˈθɑːt/; **think·ing** **1** [T/I] : to believe that something is true, that a particular situation exists, that something will happen, etc. ▪ *She thinks (that) she knows the answer.* ▪ *I never thought (that) I would become a teacher.* ▪ *It was once thought (that) the Earth was flat.* = *The Earth was once thought to be flat.* ▪ *People are more difficult than they think.* ▪ *"Has she accepted the job?" "I (don't) think so."* ▪ *Am I right in thinking (that) you used to work there?* ▪ *You would think (that) the school would have dictionaries in the classrooms.* [=the school should have dictionaries in the classroom] ▪ *Do you think (that) you could give me a ride to the airport?* [=could you give me a ride to the airport?] **2** [T/I] : to have an opinion about someone or something ▪ *It's hot in here, don't you think?* [=don't you agree?] ▪ *People think (that) he is one of the greatest singers of all time.* = *He is thought to be one of the greatest singers of all time.* ▪ *Where do you think (that) we should eat?* ▪ *What did you*

think about/of the movie? [=did you like or dislike the movie?] ▪ *He thinks of himself as a good writer.* ▪ *The hiring committee thought highly of her.* [=had a high opinion of her] ▪ *Is he right? I think not/so.* [=I don't/do believe that he is] **3** [T/I] : to form or have a particular thought in your mind ▪ *"He's handsome," she thought (to herself).* ▪ *You should try to think pleasant thoughts.* ▪ *I was thinking (of/about) what it would be like to be a doctor.* ▪ *Why do you always think the worst?* ▪ *Just think (of/about) how nice it would be to live here.* **4** [T/I] : to use your mind to understand or decide something ▪ *Think before you answer the question.* ▪ *The game teaches students how to think.* ▪ *Let me think. Where did I see your car keys?* ▪ *Give me a minute to think (about) what to do.* ▪ *You're awfully quiet. What are you thinking?* **5** [T] : to remember (something) ▪ *Can you think where you put it?* ▪ *She never thinks to call home.* **6** [T] : to have thoughts about possibly doing (something) ▪ *I think I'll give him a call today.* **7** [T] **a** — used to make a statement or suggestion less definite ▪ *They used to live here, I think.* [=I believe that they used to live here, although I'm not sure] ▪ *I thought maybe we could go for a walk in the park.* **b** — used to politely ask someone to do something or give you something ▪ *Do you think (that) you could give me a ride to the airport?* [=could you give me a ride to the airport?] **c** — used in questions that show anger or surprise about what someone has done or is doing ▪ *Where do you think you're going?* [=where are you going?] *No one gave you permission to leave.* — **come to think of it** see COME — **don't even think about (doing) it** *informal* — used to tell someone in a forceful way that something is not allowed ▪ *It's illegal to park here. Don't even think about it!* — **not think anything of** : to not think of (something) as being important or unusual ▪ *I didn't think anything of it at the time—but it turned out to be important.* — **not think much of** : to not like (someone or something) very much ▪ *They didn't think much of my idea.* — **think again** *informal* — used to say that what someone believes, expects, etc., is not true or will not happen ▪ *If you think you can get away with this, think again.* [=you are wrong] — **think ahead** : to prepare for a future event or situation by thinking about what might happen ▪ *We should have thought ahead and brought an umbrella.* — **think aloud** or **think out loud** : to say your thoughts so that other people can hear them — **think back** [*phrasal vb*] : to think about something that happened in the past ▪ *Thinking back to my childhood, I remember summers at the beach.* — **think better of** : to decide not to do (something) after thinking further about it ▪ *She was going to make a comment but thought better of it.* — **think big** see ²BIG — **think fit** see ¹FIT — **think for yourself** : to form opinions and make decisions without help from other people — **think less of**

: to not respect (someone) as much as you did before : to have a worse opinion of (someone) ▪ *I hope you don't think (any) less of me after what happened.* — **think nothing of** **1** : to not hesitate at all about (doing something that other people think is very difficult or dangerous) ▪ *She thinks nothing of running 10 miles.* **2 think nothing of it** — used as a polite response when someone has apologized to you or thanked you ▪ *"Thanks for the ride." "Think nothing of it—I was going in this direction anyway."* — **think out** [*phrasal vb*] **think out (something)** or **think (something) out** : to think about (something) in an effort to find a solution, make a decision, etc. ▪ *He spent hours thinking out the solution to the physics problem.* ▪ *Your argument is well thought out.* — **think outside the box** see ¹BOX — **think over** [*phrasal vb*] **think (something) over** or **think over (something)** : to think about (something) especially in an effort to understand or make a decision about it ▪ *I've thought over what you said, and you're right.* — **think through** [*phrasal vb*] **think (something) through** or **think through (something)** : to think about all the different parts or effects of (something) especially in an effort to understand or make a decision about it ▪ *We have thought through the matter and have come to a decision.* — **think twice** *informal* : to think seriously about whether you really want to do something ▪ *I'd think twice about/before doing that if I were you.* — **think up** [*phrasal vb*] **think up (something)** or **think (something) up** *informal* : to use your mind to form or invent (something) ▪ *Quick! We have to think up an excuse.* — **to think** — used to express surprise or shock ▪ *To think (that) he lied to you!* — **think·a·ble** /ˈθɪŋkəbəl/ *adj* — **think·er** /ˈθɪŋkɚ/ *n* [C]

think tank *n* [C] : an organization that consists of a group of people who think of new ideas on a particular subject or who give advice about what should be done

thin·ly /ˈθɪnli/ *adv* **1** : in a way that makes thin pieces, layers, etc. ▪ *thinly sliced carrots* **2** : with very few people or things close together ▪ *a thinly populated area* **3** : in a weak way that does not seem sincere ▪ *He smiled thinly.* **4** : in a way that does not completely hide something ▪ *The book is a thinly disguised autobiography.*

thin·ner /ˈθɪnɚ/ *n* [C] : a liquid (such as turpentine) that is added to paint to make it thinner and able to flow more easily

thin–skinned /ˈθɪnˌskɪnd/ *adj* **1** : having a thin skin ▪ *a thin-skinned fruit* **2** : easily bothered by criticism or insults ▪ *He's too thin-skinned for a career in show business.*

¹third /ˈθɚd/ *adj, always before a noun* **1** : occupying the number three position in a series ▪ *C is the third letter in the alphabet.* **2** : next to the second in importance or rank ▪ *I won third prize.* — **third**

adv ▪ *She finished third in the race.* ▪ *the third highest mountain*

²third *n* **1** [*singular*] : something that is third ▪ *We arrived on the third of October.* [=on October 3] ▪ *The win was his third of the year.* **2** [C] : one of three equal parts of something ▪ *She divided the cookie into thirds.* ▪ *Rent costs two-thirds of my paycheck.* **3** [U] *baseball* : THIRD BASE ▪ *He stole third.* **4** [C] *Brit* : an undergraduate degree of the lowest level from a British university

third base *n* [*singular*] *baseball* : the base that must be touched third by a base runner ▪ *a runner on third base* — **third baseman** /-ˈbeɪsmən/ *n* [C]

third class *n* **1** [U] **a** : the level of service on a train, ship, etc., that is the cheapest ▪ *seats in third class* **b** : a class of mail in the U.S. that includes advertisements **2** [*singular*] *Brit* : an undergraduate degree of the lowest level given by a British university

third–class *adj* : of or relating to third class ▪ *We'll be traveling in the third-class cabin.* ▪ (US) *third-class mail* — **third-class** *adv* ▪ *travel third-class*

third degree *n* — **the third degree** *informal* : a long and intense period of questioning ▪ *The police gave him the third degree.* [=they questioned him intensely]

third–degree *adj, always before a noun* **1** *US, of a crime* : deserving the mildest punishment ▪ *third-degree murder* **2** : causing severe injury ▪ *third-degree burns*

third·ly /ˈθɚdli/ *adv* — used to introduce a statement that is the third statement in a series ▪ *Thirdly, a dictionary provides examples of usage.*

third party *n* [C] *law* : someone who is not one of the two main people involved in a legal agreement but who is still affected by it in some way

third person *n* [U] **1** *grammar* : a set of words or forms (such as pronouns or verb forms) that refer to people or things that the speaker or writer is not addressing directly ▪ *"He," "she," and "it" are third person pronouns.* **2** : a writing style that uses third person pronouns and verbs ▪ *a story written in the third person*

third–rate *adj* : of very low quality ▪ *a third-rate writer* ▪ *The meal was third-rate.*

third world or **Third World** *n* [*singular*] *sometimes offensive* : the countries of the world that are very poor and that have very few industries

¹thirst /ˈθɚst/ *n* **1 a** [U, *singular*] : an uncomfortable feeling that is caused by the need for something to drink ▪ *a powerful thirst* ▪ *He quenched his thirst.* [=he had a drink] **b** [U] : a very great need for something to drink ▪ *He died of/from thirst.* **2** [*singular*] *literary* : a strong desire *for* something ▪ *a thirst for knowledge*

²thirst *vb* [I] *literary* : to have or feel a strong desire ▪ *She thirsts for/after justice.*

thirsty /ˈθɚsti/ *adj* **thirst·i·er; -est** **1 a** : having an uncomfortable feeling because you need something to drink : feeling thirst ▪ *a thirsty child* ▪ *The salty food was making her thirsty.* **b** : needing wa-

ter ▪ *thirsty plants* **2** *not before a noun, literary* : feeling a strong desire or need for something ▪ *thirsty for knowledge* —
thirst·i·ly /ˈθɚstəli/ *adv*

thir·teen /ˌθɚˈtiːn/ *n* [C] : the number 13 — **thirteen** *adj* ▪ *thirteen students* — **thirteen** *pron* — **thir·teenth** /ˌθɚˈtiːnθ/ *n* [C] — **thirteenth** *adj* — **thirteenth** *adv*

thir·ty /ˈθɚti/ *n, pl* **-ties** **1** [C] : the number 30 **2** [*plural*] **a** : the numbers ranging from 30 to 39 ▪ *The temperature is in the high thirties.* **b** : a set of years ending in digits ranging from 30 to 39 ▪ *He is in his thirties.* ▪ *old photographs from the (nineteen) thirties* [=from 1930–1939] — **thir·ti·eth** /ˈθɚtijəθ/ *n* [C] — **thirtieth** *adj* — **thirty** *adj* ▪ *thirty days* — **thirty** *pron* — **thir·ty·ish** /ˈθɚtijɪʃ/ *adj* ▪ *He looks thirtyish.* [=about 30 years old]

¹**this** /ˈðɪs, ðəs/ *pron, pl* **these** /ˈðiːz/ **1** : the person or thing that is present or near in place or time or that has just been mentioned ▪ *These are my friends.* ▪ *Anything would be better than this.* ▪ *This is the most fun I've had in years!* **2** : the thing that is closest to you or that is being shown to you ▪ *This is my jacket and that's yours.* ▪ *Those sunglasses are nice, but I like these better.* **3** : the present time ▪ *We expected you to return before this.* **4** : the following idea : what is stated in the following sentence or phrase ▪ *How about this: you stay here while I go to the store?* ▪ *If you think that's funny, wait until you hear this!* [=I will tell you another thing that is even funnier] ▪ *What's this I hear about you getting engaged?* [=I heard that you got engaged. Is it true?] — **like this** see ²LIKE — **this and that** also chiefly Brit **this, that, and the other** *informal* : several different things ▪ *We started talking about this and that.* — **this is it** — used to say that a very important thing is about to be done, a very important event is about to happen, etc. ▪ *This is it, men. Let's take home the championship!*

²**this** *adj, always before a noun, pl* **these** **1** — used to indicate the person or thing that is present or near in place or time or that has just been mentioned ▪ *This cake is delicious.* ▪ *I'm not sure I understand this theory of yours.* ▪ *This kind of behavior will not be tolerated in the classroom.* ▪ *The problem usually goes away on its own, but* **in this case** *you may need to see a doctor.* ▪ *In* **this regard/respect**, *the two books are very similar.* **2** — used to indicate the thing that is closest to you or that is being shown to you ▪ *This jacket's mine and that's yours.* ▪ *I like these sunglasses better than those.* **3** — used to indicate the present period of time or a period of time that is near the present time ▪ *How are you feeling this morning?* ▪ *Is she coming home this week or next (week)?* ▪ *You're just friends with him?* **All this time** *I thought you were dating him.* ▪ *It's hard to find good help* **these days.** **4** : stated in the following sentence or phrase ▪ *How about this idea: you stay here while I go to the store?* **5** — used to introduce someone or something that

has not been mentioned yet ▪ *We both had this sudden urge to go shopping.*

³**this** /ˈðɪs/ *adv* **1** : to the degree or extent that is suggested in the present situation ▪ *I haven't had this much fun in ages!* ▪ *They didn't expect this many people to come to the party.* **2** : to the degree or extent indicated by a gesture ▪ *He's about this tall.*

this·tle /ˈθɪsəl/ *n* [C] : a wild plant that has sharp points on its leaves and purple, yellow, or white flowers

thith·er /ˈθɪðɚ/ *adv, old-fashioned + literary* : to that place ▪ *traveling* **hither and thither** [=here and there]

thong /ˈθɑːŋ/ *n* [C] **1** : a long thin strip of material (such as leather) that is used to attach something **2** : a kind of women's underpants that has only a thin strip of material in the back **3** *US* : FLIP-FLOP 1

tho·rax /ˈθoɚˌæks/ *n, pl* **tho·rax·es** or **tho·ra·ces** /ˈθoɚəˌsiːz/ [C] *technical* **1** : the part of an animal's body between the neck and the waist **2** : the middle section of an insect's body — **tho·rac·ic** /θəˈræsɪk/ *adj* ▪ *the thoracic cavity*

thorn /ˈθoɚn/ *n* [C] **1** : a sharp point on the stem of some plants (such as roses) **2** *Brit* : a tree or bush that has thorns — **a thorn in the/your side** : a person or thing that repeatedly annoys you or causes problems for you ▪ *He's been a thorn in my side for years.*

thorny /ˈθoɚni/ *adj* **thorn·i·er; -est** **1** : having a lot of thorns ▪ *thorny bushes* **2** : very difficult or complicated ▪ *a thorny issue*

thor·ough /ˈθɚroʊ/ *adj* **1** : including every possible part or detail ▪ *a thorough investigation* ▪ *a thorough understanding of the rules* **2** : careful about doing something in an accurate and exact way ▪ *a thorough worker* **3** *always before a noun, chiefly Brit* : complete or absolute ▪ *a thorough disgrace* — **thor·ough·ly** *adv* ▪ *I thoroughly enjoyed the performance.* ▪ *He studied the proposal thoroughly.* — **thor·ough·ness** *n* [U]

thor·ough·bred /ˈθɚrəˌbrɛd/ *n* [C] **1** : an animal (especially a horse) whose parents are from the same breed **2 Thoroughbred** : a type of fast horse used mainly for racing

thor·ough·fare /ˈθɚrəˌfeɚ/ *n* [C] : a main road

thor·ough·go·ing /ˌθɚrəˈgoʊwɪŋ/ *adj* : including every possible detail ▪ *a thoroughgoing analysis*

those *plural of* THAT

¹**thou** /ˈðaʊ/ *pron, old-fashioned + literary* — used as a singular form of "you" when it is the subject of a verb ▪ *"Thou shalt have no other gods before me."* —Exodus 20:3 (KJV)

²**thou** /ˈθaʊ/ *n, pl* **thou** [C] *US, informal* : a thousand dollars ▪ *She earns more than a hundred thou a year.*

¹**though** /ˈðoʊ/ *conj* : ALTHOUGH ▪ *Though it was raining, we went hiking.* — **as though** see ²AS — **even though** see ²EVEN

²**though** *adv* — used when you are saying something that is different from or con-

thought • threaten

trasts with a previous statement ▪ *She was happy. Not for long, though.* [=however]

¹thought past tense and past participle of THINK

²thought /ˈθɑːt/ n 1 [C] : an idea, opinion, picture, etc., that is formed in your mind : something that you think of ▪ *My first thought was that something must have changed.* ▪ *She had a sudden thought.* = *A sudden thought occurred to her.* ▪ *Do you have any thoughts about/on the subject?* 2 a [U] : the act or process of thinking ▪ *She was lost/deep in thought.* b [U] : the act of carefully thinking about the details of something ▪ *I'll give the idea some thought.* ▪ *They should have put more thought into the proposal.* c [singular] : the act of thinking about the feelings or situations of other people ▪ *He has no thought for anyone but himself.* 3 [U] : a way of thinking that is characteristic of a particular group, time period, etc. ▪ *Western thought* ▪ *modern economic thought* ▪ *There are two main* **schools of thought** [=systems of thinking] *on the topic.* — **food for thought** see FOOD — **perish the thought** see PERISH

thought·ful /ˈθɑːtfəl/ adj 1 : serious and quiet because you are thinking ▪ *a thoughtful expression* ▪ *He looked thoughtful.* 2 : done or made after careful thinking ▪ *a thoughtful explanation* 3 : showing concern for the needs or feelings of other people ▪ *a thoughtful gesture/person* ▪ *That's very thoughtful of you.* — **thought·ful·ly** /-fəli/ adv — **thought·ful·ness** n [U]

thought·less /ˈθɑːtləs/ adj : not showing concern for the needs or feelings of other people ▪ *thoughtless comments* ▪ *a selfish and thoughtless person* — **thought·less·ly** adv — **thought·less·ness** n [U]

thou·sand /ˈθaʊzənd/ n 1 pl **thousand** [C] : the number 1,000 2 [plural] : an amount that is more than 2,000 ▪ *Thousands (and thousands) of people visited the shrine.* 3 [C] : a very large number — usually plural ▪ *I've done this thousands of times.* ▪ **a picture is worth a thousand words** see ¹WORTH — **thousand** adj, always before a noun ▪ *a thousand miles* — **thou·sandth** /ˈθaʊzəndθ/ n [C] ▪ *a/one thousandth of a second* [=¹⁄₁₀₀₀ second] — **thousandth** adj ▪ *the thousandth person to join*

thrall /ˈθrɑːl/ n — **in thrall** literary : in a state of being controlled or strongly influenced by someone or something ▪ *He was completely in thrall to her.* = *He was completely in her thrall.*

thrash /ˈθræʃ/ vb 1 [T] : to hit (someone or something) very hard with a stick, whip, etc. ▪ *He thrashed me with his belt.* 2 [T] informal : to defeat (someone or something) very easily or completely ▪ *The team thrashed them last week.* 3 [I] : to move about violently ▪ *Something was thrashing around/about in the water.* — **thrash out** [phrasal vb] **thrash (something) out** or **thrash out (something)** : to talk about (something) in order to make a decision, find a solution,

etc. ▪ *They had a meeting to thrash out their problems.* : to produce (an agreement, a plan, etc.) by a lot of discussion ▪ *thrash out a plan* — **thrash·ing** /ˈθræʃɪŋ/ n [C] ▪ *He gave the prisoner a thrashing.*

¹thread /ˈθrɛd/ n 1 [C/U] : a long, thin piece of cotton, silk, etc., used for sewing ▪ *a spool of thread* ▪ *A thread was hanging from her coat.* 2 [C] literary : a long, thin line of something ▪ *a thread of smoke* 3 [C] : the raised line that winds around a screw 4 [singular] : an idea, feeling, etc., that connects the different parts of something (such as a story) ▪ *The stories share a common thread.* ▪ *I found it hard to follow the thread of the conversation.* 5 [C] computers : a series of related messages that are written on an Internet message board — **hang by a thread** see ¹HANG — **pick up the threads** informal : to begin something again after a long time ▪ *I'm hoping to pick up the threads of our relationship.*

²thread vb 1 [T] : to put (a thread, string, etc.) through a hole in something ▪ *thread a needle* ▪ *She threaded her shoelace through the holes.* 2 [T] : to put (film or tape) into a movie camera, tape recorder, etc. ▪ *thread film through a camera* 3 [T/I] : to move forward by turning and going through narrow spaces ▪ *Waiters threaded (their way) through the crowd.* 4 [T] : to put (something) on a thread ▪ *thread beads*

thread·bare /ˈθrɛdˌbeɚ/ adj 1 : very thin and in bad condition from too much use ▪ *a threadbare carpet/suit* 2 : not very effective, interesting, etc., because of being used too often ▪ *a threadbare joke*

threat /ˈθrɛt/ n 1 [C/U] : a statement saying you will be harmed if you do not do what someone wants you to do ▪ *He used violence and threats to get what he wanted.* ▪ *bomb/death threats* ▪ *He carried out his threat.* [=he did the thing that he threatened to do] ▪ *She said she would quit, but it was an idle/empty threat.* [=she did not mean it] ▪ *an action done under threat* [=done by someone who has been threatened with harm] 2 a [C] : someone or something that could cause trouble, harm, etc. ▪ *The country is a serious threat to world peace.* b [C/U] : the possibility that something bad or harmful could happen ▪ *We can't ignore the threat posed by nuclear weapons.* ▪ *a country under threat of civil war*

threat·en /ˈθrɛtn̩/ vb 1 [T] : to say that you will harm someone or do something unpleasant or unwanted especially in order to make someone do what you want ▪ *The mugger threatened him with a gun.* ▪ *The workers have threatened to strike.* = *The workers have threatened a strike.* ▪ *He threatened to kill her.* = *He threatened her life.* 2 [T/I] **a** : to be something that is likely to cause harm to (someone or something) ▪ *a marriage threatened by financial problems* **b** — used to say that something bad or harmful appears likely or possible ▪ *The clouds were threatening rain.* [=the clouds made it appear that it was likely to rain] — **threat·en·ing** /ˈθrɛtn̩ɪŋ/ *adj* ▪ *a threatening comment* — **threat·en·ing·ly** /ˈθrɛtn̩ɪŋli/ *adv*

three /ˈθriː/ *n* **1** [*C*] : the number 3 **2** [*C*] : the third in a set or series ▪ *the three of hearts* **3** [*U*] : three o'clock ▪ *It's almost three.* — **three** *adj* ▪ *three weeks* — **three** *pron* ▪ *Three (of them) failed the test.*

3–D /ˈθriːˈdiː/ *n* — **in 3-D** : made in a way that causes an image to appear to be three-dimensional ▪ *The movie is in 3-D.* — **3–D** *adj* ▪ *a 3-D painting*

three–dimensional *adj* : having or seeming to have length, width, and depth ▪ *a three-dimensional object/image*

three R's *n* — **the three R's** : the basic subjects of reading, writing, and arithmetic that are taught in school to young children

three·some /ˈθriːsəm/ *n* [*C*] : a group of three people or things ▪ *a threesome of reporters*

thresh /ˈθrɛʃ/ *vb* [*T/I*] : to separate the seeds of corn, wheat, etc., from the plant by using a special machine or tool ▪ *threshing wheat* — **thresh·er** /ˈθrɛʃɚ/ *n* [*C*]

thresh·old /ˈθrɛʃˌhould/ *n* [*C*] **1** : a piece of wood, metal, or stone that forms the bottom of a door ▪ *He stepped across the threshold.* **2** : the point or level at which something begins or changes ▪ *If your income rises above a certain threshold, your tax rate also rises.* ▪ *He has a high pain threshold.* = *He has a high threshold for pain.* [=he does not feel pain as easily as other people] ▪ *young people on/at the threshold of adulthood*

threw *past tense of* ¹THROW

thrice /ˈθraɪs/ *adv, old-fashioned* : three times ▪ *She was thrice married.*

thrift /ˈθrɪft/ *n* [*U*] **1** *old-fashioned* : careful use of money so that it is not wasted ▪ *Through hard work and thrift they sent all of their children to college.* **2** *US* : a business like a bank that is used for saving money — called also *thrift institution*

thrift shop *n* [*C*] *US* : a store that sells used goods and especially used clothes and that is often run by a charity — called also *thrift store*

thrifty /ˈθrɪfti/ *adj* **thrift·i·er; -est** : managing or using money in a careful or wise way ▪ *a thrifty shopper* — **thrift·i·ness** /ˈθrɪftinəs/ *n* [*U*]

¹**thrill** /ˈθrɪl/ *vb* [*T/I*] : to feel or cause (someone) to feel very excited or happy ▪ *Her performance thrilled the audience.* ▪ *I was thrilled by their decision.* ▪ *Crowds thrilled at/to the sights and sounds of the circus.*

²**thrill** *n* [*C*] **1** : a feeling of great excitement or happiness ▪ *The thrill is gone from our marriage.* ▪ *the thrill of victory* ▪ *What do people do for thrills* [=excitement] *around here?* ▪ *She got the thrill of her life from seeing the Queen.* [=seeing the Queen was very exciting] ▪ *They get their thrills from drag racing.* **2** : a very exciting or enjoyable event or experience ▪ *What a thrill it was to see the Queen!* ▪ (*US*) *a movie with a lot of thrills and chills* [=exciting and scary parts]

thrilled /ˈθrɪld/ *adj, not before a noun* : very excited and happy ▪ *I'm so thrilled to see you.* ▪ *I'm not thrilled about/with her decision.*

thril·ler /ˈθrɪlɚ/ *n* [*C*] : a novel, movie, etc., that is full of exciting action, mystery, adventure, or suspense

thrill·ing /ˈθrɪlɪŋ/ *adj* : very exciting ▪ *a thrilling discovery* — **thrill·ing·ly** /ˈθrɪlɪŋli/ *adv*

thrive /ˈθraɪv/ *vb* **thrived** *or old-fashioned* **throve** /ˈθrouv/; **thrived** *also old-fashioned* **thriv·en** /ˈθrɪvən/; **thriv·ing** /ˈθraɪvɪŋ/ [*I*] : to grow or develop successfully ▪ *Business is thriving.* ▪ *plants that thrive in the desert* ▪ *a thriving economy* — **thrive on** [*phrasal vb*] : to do well in a situation in which you experience (attention, stress, etc.) ▪ *She thrives on attention.*

throat /ˈθrout/ *n* [*C*] **1** : the tube inside the neck that leads to the stomach and lungs ▪ *His throat was sore.* **2** : the front part of the neck ▪ *He grabbed her by the throat.* — **a lump in your throat** see ¹LUMP — **at each other's throats** : very angry with each other : having a serious fight or argument ▪ *Workers and management have been at each other's throats.* — **force/ram/shove (something) down someone's throat** *informal* : to force someone to accept or like (something) ▪ *She was always forcing her opinions down his throat.* — **jump down someone's throat** *informal* : to respond angrily to someone ▪ *He jumped down my throat when I suggested a different plan.*

throaty /ˈθrouti/ *adj* **throat·i·er; -est** *of a sound* : deep or rough : made in the back of the throat ▪ *a throaty laugh*

throb /ˈθrɑːb/ *vb* **throbbed; throb·bing** [*I*] **1** : to feel a pain that starts and stops quickly and repeatedly ▪ *Her finger throbbed with pain.* ▪ *My head is throbbing.* = *I have a throbbing headache.* **2** : to beat with a strong, steady rhythm ▪ *He could hear his heart throbbing.* ▪ *The music throbs with a Caribbean beat.* — **throb** *n* [*singular*] ▪ *a sudden throb of pain*

throes /ˈθrouz/ *n* [*plural*] : painful emotions, sensations, or feelings ▪ *the throes of childbirth* — **in the throes of** : experiencing (something painful) ▪ *He was in the throes of a messy divorce.*

throne /ˈθroun/ *n* **1** [*C*] : the special chair for a king, queen, or other powerful person **2** **the throne** : the position of king or queen ▪ *the heir to the throne* ▪ *He ascended the throne* [=became king] *after the death of his father.*

¹**throng** /ˈθrɑːŋ/ *n* [*C*] : a large group of people ▪ *throngs of shoppers*

²**throng** *vb* [*T/I*] : to go to (a place) in a large group or in large numbers ▪ *The island was thronged with tourists.* = *Tourists thronged the island.* ▪ *Shoppers thronged to the mall.* ▪ *Fans thronged* [=crowded] *around him.*

¹**throt·tle** /ˈθrɑːtl̩/ *n* [*C*] *technical* : a device that controls the flow of fuel to an

engine — **at full throttle** : as fast as possible • *driving/proceeding at full throttle*

²**throttle** *vb* **throt·tled; throt·tling** [*T*] **1** : to choke or strangle (someone) • *I'm so mad I could throttle him!* **2** : to not allow (something) to grow or develop • *policies that throttle creativity* — **throttle back** [*phrasal vb*] **throttle back** or **throttle back (something)** or **throttle (something) back** : to reduce the amount of fuel flowing to an engine by adjusting the throttle • *He throttled back to 45 mph.*

¹**through** /ˈθru/ *prep* **1** : into one side and out the other side of (something) • *She looked through the binoculars.* • *The bullet went through the wall.* **2** : from one side or end to another side or end of (something) • *He walked through the door.* • *She could see a figure through the fog.* • *I looked through the window.* **3** — used to describe movement within a place or area • *We rode our bikes through the woods.* • *birds gliding through the air* **4** — used to indicate the path that someone or something moves along to get somewhere • *Cold air was getting in through a crack in the wall.* **5** : without stopping for (a traffic signal, a stop sign, etc.) • *He got caught driving through a red light.* **6 a** : by using (someone or something) • *The leaders communicated through interpreters.* • *I learned of the job opening through her.* [=she told me about the job opening] **b** : by doing (something) • *He learned to cook through watching his mother in the kitchen.* **c** : because of (something) • *The company's profits increased through improved sales.* • *knowledge that is gained through life experience* **7** : over all the parts of (something) • *The illness swept through the town.* • *He went through his notes before the exam.* **8** : from the beginning to the end of (something) • *She worked through the summer.* • *All through her life, she dreamed of going up into outer space.* **9** *US* — used to indicate the numbers, days, etc., that are included in a range • *The store is open Monday through Friday.* [=is open Monday, Tuesday, Wednesday, Thursday, and Friday] • *Read chapters 2 through 5 for homework.* **10** — used to say that you have survived or completed something • *We're through the worst part of the storm.* [=the worst part of the storm has ended] **11** : to a state of official acceptance or approval by (an organization) • *The vote got the bill through the legislature.*

²**through** *adv* **1** : from one side or end to the other • *Let these people go through.* **2** : over the whole distance • *The package was shipped through to New Orleans.* **3** : from the beginning to the end • *Read the essay through and tell me what you think.* • *The teacher stopped the movie halfway through.* [=when it was half finished] **4** : without stopping • *The light was red, but he drove straight through.* **5** : to the end : until something is completed or achieved • *I need time to think this problem through.* • *He intended to see the project through.* **6** : in or to every part • *Her clothes were wet through.* • *He is a*

gentleman **through and through.** **7** *of a phone call* : in connection with the person you are calling • *The operator put me through to him.* • *I called, but I couldn't get through.*

³**through** *adj* **1** *not before a noun, chiefly US* : having reached the end of an activity, job, relationship, etc. : FINISHED • *I'm not through yet. I have one more topic to discuss.* • *If you're through using the phone, I'd like to use it next.* • *Lisa and I are through.* • *His career is through.* — often + *with* • *She is almost through with law school.* • *I'm through with him.* **2** *always before a noun* : allowing passage from one end to the other • *a through street* **b** : going the whole distance without stopping • *The left lane is for through traffic only.*

¹**through·out** /θruˈaʊt/ *prep* **1** : in or to every part of (something) • *She has traveled throughout the world.* **2** : during an entire (situation or period of time) • *It rained throughout the day.*

²**throughout** *adv* **1** : in or to every part • *The house is painted white throughout.* **2** : from the beginning to the end • *He had a difficult year, but his supporters remained loyal throughout.*

through·put /ˈθruˌpʊt/ *n* [*C/U*] *technical* : the amount of material, data, etc., that enters and goes through a machine, system, etc. • *The network can handle large throughputs.*

throughway *variant spelling of* THRU-WAY

throve *old-fashioned past tense of* THRIVE

¹**throw** /ˈθroʊ/ *vb* **threw** /ˈθru/; **thrown** /ˈθroʊn/; **throw·ing** **1** [*T/I*] : to cause (something) to move out of your hand and through the air by quickly moving your arm forward • *She threw the ball to first base.* • *Throw me the car keys.* = *Throw the car keys to me.* • *Let's see how far you can throw.* **2** [*T*] : to put (something) in a particular place in a careless or forceful way • *She threw her coat on the bed.* • *He threw (down) the newspaper in disgust.* **3** [*T*] : to cause (someone or something) to move suddenly or forcefully to, away from, or into a particular place or position • *The wrestler threw his opponent to the mat.* • *She was thrown from the horse.* • *The storm threw the boat against a reef.* • *She threw herself into his arms.* • *He threw back his head in laughter.* • *She threw her leg over the arm of the chair.* • *He threw open the window to get some air.* **4** [*T*] *sports* : to perform an action that involves throwing a ball • *(American football) The quarterback threw a pass/touchdown.* • *(baseball) The pitcher threw a curve to him.* = *The pitcher threw him a curve.* • *(baseball) She threw* [=pitched] *a shutout.* **5 a** [*T/I*] : to send (something) from your hand in a way that causes it to move forward and turn over many times along a surface • *She threw* [=rolled] *the dice on the table.* • *He threw the bowling ball.* **b** [*T*] : to get (a number or score) by throwing dice or a bowling ball • *She threw a six/spare.* **6** [*T*] : to cause or force (someone or something) to suddenly be in a particular

state, condition, or position • *The discovery threw the previous theory into (a state of) doubt.* • *He was thrown into prison.* • *When the factory closed, the workers were thrown out of their jobs.* [=the workers lost their jobs] **7** [T] : to try to hit someone with your fist • *He threw a punch.* **8** [T] : to move (a switch) to an on or off position • *She threw the switch.* **9** [T] : to organize and hold (a party) • *Let's throw her a party.* = *Let's throw a party for her.* **10** [T] : to lose (a game or contest) in a deliberate way • *He was suspected of throwing the boxing match.* **11** [T] : to express strong emotions in an uncontrolled way • *The child was throwing a tantrum/fit.* **12** [T] : to use (your effort, influence, money, etc.) in order to accomplish something • *Lobbyists are throwing their weight/influence behind the legislation.* [=they are using their influence to support the legislation] — often + *into* • *She threw everything she had into winning the match.* [=she tried as hard as she could to win the match] **13** [T] : to direct (a question, look, etc.) at someone • *She threw him an evil look.* • *He threw the question back at me.* [=he asked me the same question that I asked him] **14** [T] *informal* : to confuse or surprise (someone) • *The tricky wording of the contract didn't throw her.* • *His resignation really threw me.* **15** [T] : to cause (something, such as a shadow) to appear on a surface • *The tree threw a shadow across the lawn.*

In addition to the phrases shown below, *throw* occurs in many idioms that are shown at appropriate entries throughout the dictionary. For example, *throw down the gauntlet* can be found at GAUNTLET and *throw light on* can be found at ¹LIGHT.

— **throw away** [phrasal vb] **throw away (something)** or **throw (something) away** **1** : to put (something that is no longer useful or wanted) in a trash can, garbage can, rubbish bin, etc. • *Throw that candy wrapper away, please.* **2 a** : to use (something) in a foolish or wasteful way • *He threw all of his money away on gambling.* **b** : to foolishly fail to use (something) • *You had a chance to do something great, and you threw it away.* — **throw in** [phrasal vb] **throw in (something)** or **throw (something) in** **1** : to add (something) to what you are selling without asking for more money • *If you buy two, we'll throw in a third (for free)!* **2** : to add (something) to the effort or activity of a group • *She threw in some money for the gift.* — **throw off** [phrasal vb] **1 throw off (something)** or **throw (something) off** **a** : to quickly remove (a piece of clothing) • *He threw his robe off and jumped into the shower.* **b** : to get rid of (a quality, condition, etc., that you do not want) • *He threw off his inhibitions.* **c** : to cause (something) to be incorrect • *A decimal point in the wrong place threw his calculations off.* **d** : to send (light, smoke, etc.) out from a source • *The woodstove throws off a lot of heat.* **2**

throw off (someone) or **throw (someone) off** **a** : to cause (someone) to be confused or uncertain about something • *The professor was thrown off during her lecture by a ringing cell phone.* **b** : to get away from (someone who is trying to catch you) • *He managed to throw off his pursuers by swimming across the river.* — **throw on** [phrasal vb] **throw on (something)** or **throw (something) on** **1** : to quickly put on (a piece of clothing) • *She threw on her coat and ran out the door.* **2** : to cause (something) to work by moving a switch • *He threw on the lights.* — **throw out** [phrasal vb] **1 throw out (something)** or **throw (something) out** **a** : to put (something that is no longer useful or wanted) in a trash can, garbage can, etc. • *She threw out a pair of old shoes.* **b** : to refuse to accept or consider (something) • *His testimony was thrown out by the judge.* **c** : to suggest or mention (something) • *She threw out a couple of ideas for improving the Web site.* **d** : to send (light, smoke, etc.) out from a source • *The woodstove throws out a lot of heat.* **2 throw (someone) out** or **throw out (someone)** **a** : to force (someone) to leave a place, game, etc. • *She got thrown out of school for cheating.* **b** *baseball* : to cause (a player) to be out by throwing the ball to the base that the player is running to • *The shortstop threw the runner out at second.* — **throw together** [phrasal vb] **1 throw together (something)** or **throw (something) together** : to make (something) by joining or combining things in a quick and usually careless way • *He threw a meal together for his friends.* **2 throw together (people)** or **throw (people) together** : to bring (people) together usually in an unexpected way • *People of different occupations were thrown together for the jury.* — **throw up** [phrasal vb] **1 throw up** or **throw up (something)** or **throw (something) up** *informal* : to have the food, liquid, etc., that is in your stomach come out through your mouth : VOMIT • *She said she felt sick and then threw up.* • *The patient was throwing up blood.* **2 throw up (something)** or **throw (something) up** **a** : to raise or lift (something) quickly or suddenly • *He threw up the window.* **b** : to build (something) quickly • *The house was thrown up almost overnight.* **c** *chiefly Brit* : to leave (your job, home, etc.) • *She suddenly threw up* [=quit] *her job.* **d** *Brit* : to cause (something) to be known • *The study has thrown up some surprising results.* — **throw yourself into** : to begin doing or working on (something) with great energy and determination • *He threw himself into (composing/performing) his music.* — **throw·er** /ˈθroʊwɚ/ *n* [C]

²**throw** *n* [C] **1** : an act of throwing something (such as a ball) • *The quarterback made a perfect throw.* **2** : the distance over which something is thrown or could be thrown • *a discus throw of 200 feet* **3** : a loose blanket or cloth that is put on a sofa, chair, etc. — **a stone's throw** see

¹STONE — *a throw* Brit, informal : for each one : APIECE ▪ *Tickets cost £25 a throw.*

throw·a·way /ˈθroʊəˌweɪ/ adj, always before a noun **1** : made to be thrown away after use ▪ *throwaway containers* **2** : made or said with very little thought ▪ *a throwaway remark* **3** : tending to throw things away instead of keeping them and using them again ▪ *a throwaway culture/society*

throw·back /ˈθroʊˌbæk/ n [C] : a person or thing that is similar to someone or something from the past or that is suited to an earlier time ▪ *The band's music is a throwback to the 1980s.*

thrown past participle of ¹THROW

throw rug n [C] chiefly US : a small rug that can be easily moved

thrum /ˈθrʌm/ vb thrummed; thrum·ming [I] : to make a low, steady sound ▪ *The engine thrummed.* — **thrum** n [singular]

thrush /ˈθrʌʃ/ n **1** [C] : a type of bird that is brown with a spotted breast **2** [U] **a** : a disease that occurs mostly in babies and children, that is caused by a fungus, and that produces white patches in the mouth and throat **b** chiefly Brit : YEAST INFECTION

¹**thrust** /ˈθrʌst/ vb thrust; thrust·ing **1** [T] : to push (someone or something) with force : SHOVE ▪ *He thrust his hands into his pockets.* ▪ *She thrust him aside and walked past him.* **2** [I] : to make a sudden, strong, forward movement at someone or something with a weapon ▪ *He thrust at me with his sword.* — **thrust on/upon** [phrasal vb] **thrust (something) on/upon** : to force (someone) to have or accept (something) ▪ *Fame was thrust upon her.* [=she became famous even though she did not try or want to be famous]

²**thrust** n **1** [C] : a forward or upward push ▪ *a single thrust of his sword* **2** [singular] : the main point or purpose of something ▪ *the (main) thrust of the argument/article/research* **3** [U] technical : the force produced by an engine that causes an aircraft, rocket, etc., to move forward — **cut and thrust** see ²CUT

thru·way also **through·way** /ˈθruːˌweɪ/ n [C] US : a large highway that can be entered and left only at certain places ▪ *the New York State Thruway*

¹**thud** /ˈθʌd/ vb thud·ded; thud·ding [I] : to hit or beat with a loud, dull sound ▪ *The ball thudded against the side of the house.* ▪ *Her heart was thudding against her rib cage.*

²**thud** n [C] : a loud, dull sound made especially when a heavy object hits something ▪ *The book hit the floor with a thud.*

thug /ˈθʌg/ n [C] : a violent criminal ▪ *a gang of thugs* — **thug·gish** /ˈθʌgɪʃ/ adj ▪ *thuggish violence*

¹**thumb** /ˈθʌm/ n [C] **1** : the short, thick finger on the side of your hand ▪ *I accidentally cut my thumb.* — see also GREEN THUMB **2** : the part of a glove or mitten that covers a thumb — **all thumbs** (US) or Brit **all fingers and thumbs** : extremely awkward or clumsy

▪ *I'm all thumbs when it comes to wrapping packages.* — **rule of thumb** see ¹RULE — **stick out like a sore thumb** see ¹SORE — **twiddle your thumbs** see TWIDDLE — **under someone's thumb** : under someone's control or influence ▪ *He kept the employees under his thumb.*

²**thumb** vb [T/I] informal : to get a ride in a passing vehicle by sticking out your arm with your thumb up as you stand on the side of the road : HITCHHIKE ▪ *I thumbed a ride to school.* — **thumb through** [phrasal vb] : to turn the pages of (a book, magazine, etc.) quickly ▪ *I thumbed through a magazine while I waited.* — **thumb your nose at** : to show that you do not like or care about (something) ▪ *She thumbed her nose at my suggestions.*

¹**thumb·nail** /ˈθʌmˌneɪl/ n [C] **1** : the hard covering at the end of a thumb **2** : a very small copy of a larger picture on a computer

²**thumbnail** adj : very short or brief ▪ *a thumbnail sketch of the poet*

thumb·print /ˈθʌmˌprɪnt/ n [C] : the pattern of marks made by pressing your thumb on a surface

thumb·tack /ˈθʌmˌtæk/ n [C] US : a short pin that has a large, flat head and that is used to attach papers, pictures, etc., to a wall or bulletin board — called also (Brit) **drawing pin**

¹**thump** /ˈθʌmp/ vb **1** [T/I] : to hit or beat with a loud, deep sound ▪ *The boat thumped against the side of the pier.* ▪ *My heart was thumping inside my chest.* ▪ *I thumped* [=pounded] *him on the back.* **2** [I] : to walk or run with loud, heavy steps ▪ *She thumped up the stairs.*

²**thump** n [C] **1** : a loud, deep sound made especially when a heavy object hits something ▪ *The ball landed with a thump.* **2** : an act of hitting someone or something ▪ *I gave him a (good) thump on the back.*

thump·ing /ˈθʌmpɪŋ/ adj, chiefly Brit, informal : very large, great, etc. ▪ *She won the election by a thumping 79 percent.* ▪ *a thumping lie* — **thumping** adv ▪ *We had a thumping* [=very] *good time.*

¹**thun·der** /ˈθʌndɚ/ n **1** [U] : the very loud sound that comes from the sky during a storm : the sound that follows a flash of lightning ▪ *Thunder boomed/crashed.* **2** [singular] : a loud noise that sounds like thunder ▪ *the distant thunder of cannon fire* — **steal someone's thunder** : to prevent someone from having success or getting a lot of attention, praise, etc., by doing or saying whatever that person was planning to do or say

²**thunder** vb **1** [I] : to produce thunder ▪ *It was raining and thundering all night.* **2** [I] : to make a loud sound like the sound of thunder ▪ *Guns thundered in the distance.* **3** [T] : to shout (something) very loudly ▪ *The crowd thundered its approval.*

thun·der·bolt /ˈθʌndɚˌboʊlt/ n [C] : a flash of lightning that makes a loud sound of thunder and that hits someone or something

thun·der·clap /ˈθʌndərˌklæp/ *n* [C] : a very loud, sharp sound of thunder

thun·der·cloud /ˈθʌndərˌklaʊd/ *n* [C] : a large, dark cloud that produces lightning and thunder

thun·der·head /ˈθʌndərˌhɛd/ *n* [C] *chiefly US* : a very large cloud appearing before a thunderstorm

thun·der·ous /ˈθʌndərəs/ *adj* : making a loud noise like the sound of thunder • *thunderous applause* — **thun·der·ous·ly** *adv*

thun·der·show·er /ˈθʌndərˌʃawɚ/ *n* [C] *US* : a brief storm with lightning and thunder

thun·der·storm /ˈθʌndərˌstoɚm/ *n* [C] : storm with lightning and thunder

thun·der·struck /ˈθʌndərˌstrʌk/ *adj* : feeling sudden and great surprise or shock • *She was thunderstruck when her parents told her she was adopted.*

thun·dery /ˈθʌndəri/ *adj, Brit* : producing or likely to produce thunder • *thundery showers/weather*

Thurs. *or* **Thur.** *abbr* Thursday

Thurs·day /ˈθɚzˌdeɪ/ *n* [C/U] : the day of the week between Wednesday and Friday • *He was late last Thursday.* • *I'll arrive (on) Thursday.* = (Brit) *I'll arrive on the Thursday.* — abbr. *Thurs.* or *Thur.* or *Th.* — **Thurs·days** /ˈθɚzˌdeɪz/ *adv* • *The class meets Thursdays.* [=every Thursday]

thus /ˈðʌs/ *adv, formal* **1** : in this way or manner : like this • *The judge expressed it thus: "Our obligation is to discover the truth."* **2** : because of this or that : THEREFORE • *This detergent is highly concentrated and thus you will need to dilute it.* — **thus far** see ¹FAR

thwack /ˈθwæk/ *vb* [T] : to hit (someone or something) hard with a loud sound • *A book fell off the shelf and thwacked me on the head.* — **thwack** *n* [C] • *The book hit the floor with a thwack.*

thwart /ˈθwoɚt/ *vb* [T] : to prevent (someone) from doing something or to stop (something) from happening • *She thwarted his plans.* • *He was thwarted in his evil plans.*

thy /ˈðaɪ/ *adj, old-fashioned + literary* : YOUR — used when speaking to a single person • *". . . thou shalt love thy neighbor as thyself."* —Leviticus 19:18 (KJV)

thyme /ˈtaɪm/ *n* [U] : a sweet-smelling herb with small leaves that is used in cooking

thy·roid /ˈθaɪˌrɔɪd/ *n* [C] : a small gland in the neck that affects growth

thy·self /ðaɪˈsɛlf/ *pron, old-fashioned + literary* : YOURSELF — used when speaking to a single person • *Know thyself.*

ti /ˈtiː/ *n* [U] : the seventh note of a musical scale • *do, re, mi, fa, sol, la, ti*

ti·ara /tiˈɛrə, Brit tiˈɑːrə/ *n* [C] **1** : a crown worn by the pope **2** : a small crown that is decorated with jewels and that is worn by women or girls on special occasions

tic /ˈtɪk/ *n* [C] **1** : a small repeated movement of a muscle especially in the face that cannot be controlled • *a facial tic* **2** : a word or phrase that someone frequently says or an action that someone frequently does without intending to • *a nervous tic*

¹**tick** /ˈtɪk/ *n* **1** [*singular*] : a small, quick sound that is made by a machine and that often occurs in a series to produce a rhythm • *the tick of a clock* **2** [C] : a very small insect that attaches itself to the skin of larger animals or people and drinks their blood **3** [C] *chiefly Brit* : a mark ✓ that is used to show that something (such as an item on a list) has been noted, done, etc. : CHECK • *Put a tick next to your name.*

²**tick** *vb* **1** [I] : to make a small, quick, and often rhythmic tapping sound • *a ticking clock/watch* **2** [I] : to continue to work or function in a normal way • *His old heart is still ticking.* **3** [T] *chiefly Brit* : to mark (something) with a written tick (✓) : CHECK • *Tick (off) the box next to your choice.* — **tick away/by/past** [*phrasal vb*] *of time* : to pass or go by • *Time is ticking away.* • *The hours slowly ticked by.* — **tick off** [*phrasal vb*] **tick (someone or something) off** *or* **tick off (someone or something)** **1** *US, informal* : to make (someone) angry • *She was ticked off by the rude salesclerk.* **2** *Brit* : to criticize (someone) strongly • *His mother ticked him off for his behavior.* **3 a** *US* : to say the name of (someone or something) as part of a list • *He ticked off all the reasons for his decision.* **b** : to count or mark things as they pass • *We are ticking off the days until vacation.* — **tick over** [*phrasal vb*] **1** *chiefly Brit, of a vehicle's engine* : to run at a very low speed **2** *Brit* : to run or proceed in a steady but slow way • *"How's business?" "Oh, just ticking over."* — **what makes someone tick** *informal* : the feelings, opinions, etc., that are parts of someone's personality • *I've always wondered what makes people like that tick.*

ticked /ˈtɪkt/ *or* **ticked off** *adj, not before a noun, US, informal* : very angry or upset • *I was ticked off at him.*

tick·er /ˈtɪkɚ/ *n* [C] **1** : a machine that receives and prints out stock prices and other news on long, thin pieces of paper **2** *informal* : HEART • *Exercise is good for your/the ticker.*

¹**tick·et** /ˈtɪkət/ *n* **1** [C] : a piece of paper that allows you to see a show, participate in an event, travel on a vehicle, etc. • *We bought tickets for/to the opera.* • *a bus ticket* **2** [C] : a card or piece of paper that shows that you are participating in a contest, raffle, etc. • *a winning lottery ticket* **3** [C] : a piece of paper that officially tells you that you have driven or parked your car improperly and that you will have to pay a fine • *I got a ticket for speeding.* **4** [C] *Brit* : a piece of paper that is attached to an item in a store and that gives information about its price, size, etc. **5** [*singular*] *chiefly US* : a list of the candidates supported by a political party in an election • *the Republican/Democratic ticket* **6** [*singular*] : something that makes it possible to get or achieve something that you want • *The novel was his ticket to fame and fortune.*

7 the ticket *informal* : the thing that is needed or wanted • *Compromise, now that's the ticket.* [=that's what we need]

²**ticket** *vb* [T] **1** *chiefly US* : to give (a driver) a ticket for driving or parking improperly • *He was ticketed for speeding.* **2** : to give or sell a ticket to (someone) • *methods used for ticketing airline passengers*

tick·le /ˈtɪkəl/ *vb* **tick·led; tick·ling 1** [T] : to try to make (someone) laugh by lightly touching a very sensitive part of the body • *Her little brother screamed with laughter as she tickled him.* **2** [T/I] : to have or cause a slightly uncomfortable feeling on a part of your body • *The tag on the sweater tickled his neck.* • *My nose started to tickle.* **3** [T] : to please or amuse (someone or something) • *We were tickled by the invitation.* — **tickled pink** *informal* : very happy or amused • *I was tickled pink to see her.* — **tickle the ivories** see IVORY — **tickle your fancy** *informal* : to interest or attract you • *Do you see anything on the menu that tickles your fancy?* — **tickle** *n* [C] • *He gave her neck a tickle.* [=he tickled her neck]

tick·lish /ˈtɪklɪʃ/ *adj* **1** : sensitive and easily tickled • *My feet are very ticklish.* **2** : difficult to deal with : requiring special care • *Religion can be a very ticklish subject.*

tic–tac–toe *or* **tick–tack–toe** /ˌtɪkˌtæk-ˈtoʊ/ *n* [U] *US* : a game in which one player draws Xs and another player draws Os inside a set of nine squares and each player tries to be the first to fill a row of squares with either Xs or Os — called also (*Brit*) **noughts and crosses**

tid·al /ˈtaɪdl/ *adj* : of or relating to tides : rising and falling at regular times • *tidal currents*

tidal wave *n* [C] **1** : a very high, large wave in the ocean that is often caused by strong winds or an earthquake **2** : a very large amount of something • *a tidal wave of emotion*

tid·bit (*US*) /ˈtɪdˌbɪt/ *or Brit* **tit·bit** /ˈtɪt-ˌbɪt/ *n* [C] **1** : a small piece of food **2** : a small piece of news or interesting information • *I heard a juicy tidbit about your brother.*

tid·dler /ˈtɪdlə/ *n* [C] *Brit, informal* **1** : a small fish **2** : a small and unimportant person or thing • *The company is no tiddler.*

¹**tide** /ˈtaɪd/ *n* **1** [C] : the regular upward and downward movement of the level of the ocean that is caused by the pull of the Sun and the Moon on the Earth • *Is the tide coming in or going out?* = *Is the tide rising or falling?* • *The boat got swept away in/by the tide.* **2** [*singular*] : the way in which something is changing or developing • *the tide of public opinion* • *The team was on a losing streak, but then the tide turned and they started winning.* **3** [*singular*] : something that increases over time • *We have to do something to stem the tide of violence.* [=to stop the violence from continuing and increasing]

²**tide** *vb* **tid·ed; tid·ing** — **tide over** [*phrasal vb*] **tide (someone) over** : to give (someone) what is needed to get through

a short period of time • *He had a snack to tide himself over until dinner.*

tid·ings /ˈtaɪdɪŋz/ *n* [*plural*] *old-fashioned* : NEWS • *good/glad tidings*

¹**ti·dy** /ˈtaɪdi/ *adj* **ti·di·er; -est 1** : clean and organized • *a tidy kitchen* **2** : keeping things clean and organized • *He is a tidy person.* **3** *informal, of an amount of money* : fairly large • *a tidy sum/salary*

²**tidy** *vb* **-dies; -died; -dy·ing** [T/I] : to make (something) clean and organized • *We need to tidy (up) the house.* — **tidy away** [*phrasal vb*] **tidy (something) away** *or* **tidy away (something)** *Brit* : to put (something) in its proper place • *I tidied all the loose papers away.*

¹**tie** /ˈtaɪ/ *vb* **tied; ty·ing** /ˈtaɪɪŋ/ **1 a** [T] : to attach (someone or something) to something with a string, rope, etc. • *His kidnappers tied him to a chair.* • *They had him tied down on a stretcher.* **b** [T] : to pass (a string, ribbon, etc.) around itself in a way that attaches it to something or holds it in place : to make a knot or bow in (something) • *He tied (up) his shoelaces/necktie.* • *He tied the ropes together.* • *He tied the rope to a tree branch.* • *tie a bow/knot* **c** [T/I] : to close or hold (something) with a string, rope, etc., that is attached to it or wrapped around it • *You need to tie your shoe.* • *The apron ties (up) in the back.* **2** [T/I] **a** : to make the score of a game or contest equal • *She tied (up) the score/game with a late goal.* • *a tied game/score* **b** : to achieve the same score, time, etc., as (a person, a record, etc.) • *I had the lead but he tied me.* • *Her time tied the world record.* • *He tied (her) for first place.* **3** [T] : to connect (someone or something) to another person or thing • *The rise in crime has been tied to drug dealing.* **4** [T] : to cause or require (someone) to be somewhere, do something, etc. • *His responsibilities tie him to this area.* • *She was tired of being tied to the same routine.* — **fit to be tied** see ¹FIT — **tie down** [*phrasal vb*] **tie (someone) down** *or* **tie down (someone)** : to limit the freedom of (someone) • *You're too young to be tied down with so much responsibility.* — **tie in** [*phrasal vb*] **1** : to be related or connected to something — + *to* or *with* • *The book's illustrations tie in to/with the story.* **2 tie in (something)** *or* **tie (something) in** : to connect (something) to something else — + *to* or *with* • *The teacher tied in what we learned last week with today's lesson.* — **tie off** [*phrasal vb*] **tie off (something)** *or* **tie (something) off** : to fasten, hold, or close (something) by tying a knot or bow at its end • *I finished knitting the last row and tied off the yarn.* — **tie the knot** see ¹KNOT — **tie up** [*phrasal vb*] **tie (something or someone) up** *or* **tie up (something or someone) 1** : to deal with (something) in order to complete something • *We're almost finished, but we still have a few final details to tie up.* = *We still have to tie up some loose ends.* **2** *US* : to prevent the use or progress of (something) • *He tied up the phone for an hour.* • *Traffic was tied up for miles.* • *The money was tied up in stocks.* [=the money could

not be used because it was invested in stocks] **3** : to tie rope, tape, etc., around the body, arms, or legs of (someone) in order to keep that person from moving or escaping ▪ *The robbers tied up the clerk.* **4** : to prevent (someone) from doing other things or from going to a particular place ▪ *Meetings tied me up all day.* ▪ *She was tied up in traffic.*

²tie *n* [*C*] **1** : NECKTIE ▪ *He was wearing a suit and tie.* — see also BOW TIE **2** : a string, ribbon, etc., that is used for fastening, joining, or closing something **3 a** : an interest, experience, feeling, etc., that is shared by people or groups and that forms a connection between them ▪ *The company has close ties to conservative groups.* ▪ *She has severed all ties with the company.* **b** : a responsibility that limits a person's freedom to do other things ▪ *He was not ready to accept the ties of family life.* **4 a** : the final result of a game, contest, etc., in which two or more people or teams finish with the same number of points, votes, etc. ▪ *The game ended in a tie.* = *The game was a tie.* ▪ *There was a tie for second place.* ▪ *a tie to break the tie.* ▪ *a tie score* **5** *US* : one of the heavy pieces of wood to which the rails of a railroad are fastened — called also (*Brit*) *sleeper* **6** *Brit* : a match in a sports competition (such as a soccer or tennis tournament) in which the loser is eliminated

tie·break·er /ˈtaɪˌbreɪkɚ/ *n* [*C*] : something (such as an extra period of play or an extra question) that is used to decide a winner when a game, contest, etc., has ended with a tied score

tie–dye /ˈtaɪˌdaɪ/ *vb* **-dyed; -dye·ing** [*T*] : to decorate (fabric or clothing) by tying parts of it with knots, strings, etc., and soaking it in different colors of dye ▪ *a tie-dyed shirt*

tier /ˈtiɚ/ *n* [*C*] **1** : a row or layer of things that is above another row or layer ▪ *the theater's top tier (of seats)* **2** : a particular level in a group, organization, etc. ▪ *the lowest tier of management*

tie–up /ˈtaɪˌʌp/ *n* [*C*] *chiefly US* : a situation in which something (such as traffic) becomes very slow or stops because of a problem, accident, etc. ▪ *a traffic tie-up*

tiff /ˈtɪf/ *n* [*C*] : a small fight or argument about something that is not important

ti·ger /ˈtaɪgɚ/ *n* [*C*] : a large, wild cat that has a coat of usually yellow or orange fur and black stripes and that lives in Asia

¹tight /ˈtaɪt/ *adj* **1** : fastened, attached, or held in a position that is not easy to move ▪ *a tight lid* ▪ *a tight knot/grip* **2** : fitting very close to your body ▪ *tight jeans* **3** : flat or firm from being pulled or stretched ▪ *a tight wire* ▪ *Pull the ribbon tight and make a bow.* **4** : tense or stiff : not relaxed ▪ *Her muscles were tight.* ▪ *a tight smile* **5** : having parts that are very close together ▪ *The cat was curled into a tight ball.* **6** : not having or allowing much room or time ▪ *a tight space/sched-*

ule **7** : close or equal in score, progress, or ability ▪ *a tight race/game* **8** : not allowing much freedom : strict about controlling what happens ▪ *She kept a tight hand/reign on the business.* ▪ *tight security* ▪ *He's pretty tight* [=*stingy*] *with his money.* **9** : difficult or awkward ▪ *They were in a tight spot financially.* **10** : low in supply ▪ *Money is tight.* ▪ *a tight job market* [=a situation in which there are few jobs] **11** : having a close relationship ▪ *She's tight with the boss.* **12** : curving or changing direction suddenly ▪ *a tight* [=*sharp*] *bend in the road* **13** *informal* + *old-fashioned* : very drunk ▪ *getting tight at a bar* — **run a tight ship** see ¹SHIP — **tight·ly** *adv* ▪ *The shirt fits tightly around the arms.* ▪ *Hold on tightly to the railing.* — **tight·ness** *n* [*U*]

²tight *adv* : in a tight way ▪ *Hold on tight. Is the door shut tight?* — **sit tight** see SIT — **sleep tight** see ¹SLEEP

tight·en /ˈtaɪtn̩/ *vb* [*T/I*] : to make (something) tight or tighter or to become tight or tighter ▪ *She tightened her hold on the handle.* ▪ *His jaw muscles tightened.* ▪ *They tightened (up) security.* — **tighten your belt** see ¹BELT

tight end *n* [*C*] *American football* : a player on the offensive team who plays in a position on the line of scrimmage and who blocks and sometimes catches passes

tight·fist·ed /ˈtaɪtˈfɪstəd/ *adj, disapproving* : not wanting to spend or give money ▪ *a tightfisted owner*

tight–knit /ˈtaɪtˈnɪt/ *adj* — used to describe a group of people who care about each other and who are very friendly with each other ▪ *a tight-knit family*

tight–lipped /ˈtaɪtˈlɪpt/ *adj* : not willing to speak about something ▪ *He remained tight-lipped about his plans.*

tight·rope /ˈtaɪtˌroʊp/ *n* [*C*] : a tightly stretched rope or wire high above the ground that a performer walks on, does tricks on, etc. ▪ *a tightrope walker* ▪ (*figurative*) *Soldiers* **walk a tightrope** *between life and death every day.*

tights /ˈtaɪts/ *n* [*plural*] **1** : a piece of clothing that is worn especially by girls, women, and dancers, that fits closely over the feet, legs, and waist, and that is made of a thicker material than pantyhose **2** *Brit* : PANTYHOSE

tight·wad /ˈtaɪtˌwɑːd/ *n* [*C*] *informal* + *disapproving* : a person who does not like to spend or give money

ti·gress /ˈtaɪgrəs/ *n* [*C*] : a female tiger

tike *variant spelling of* TYKE

'til *or* **til** *variant spelling of* ¹TILL

til·de /ˈtɪldə/ *n* [*C*] : a mark ~ used in some languages (such as Spanish and Portuguese) to show that the letter *n* is pronounced /nj/ or that a vowel is pronounced in a different way

¹tile /ˈtajəl/ *n* **1** [*C/U*] : a usually flat piece of hard clay, stone, or other material that is used for covering walls, floors, roofs, etc. ▪ *ceramic tiles* **2** [*C*] : a small, flat piece that is used in some board games

²tile *vb* **tiled; til·ing** [*T*] : to cover (something) with tiles ▪ *tile the bathroom floor* ▪ *a tiled roof*

¹till *or* **'til** *also* **til** /'til, təl/ *prep* : UNTIL ▪ *We won't finish till next week.* — **till** *or* **'til** *also* **til** *conj* ▪ *They kept playing till it got dark.*

²till /'til/ *vb* [*T*] : to prepare (soil, land, etc.) for growing crops ▪ *The farmers tilled the soil.* — **till·able** /'tiləbəl/ *adj* ▪ *tillable land*

³till *n* [*C*] **1** : a drawer for keeping money in a store or bank **2** *Brit* : CASH REGISTER

till·er /'tilɚ/ *n* [*C*] **1** : a person who tills land **2** : a tool used for tilling land **3** : a handle that is used to steer a boat by turning the rudder

¹tilt /'tilt/ *vb* **tilt·ed; tilt·ing** **1** [*T/I*] : to lift or move (something) so that one side is higher than another side ▪ *Tilt the glass as you pour in the beer.* ▪ *The steering wheel can tilt downward.* **2** [*T*] : to move (your head, chin, etc.) up, down, or to one side ▪ *Her head was tilted to the side.*

²tilt *n* [*C*] : the state of having one side higher than the other ▪ *He gave a tilt of his head.* [=he tilted his head] — **(at) full tilt** : as fast as possible ▪ *running at full tilt*

tim·ber /'tımbɚ/ *n* **1** [*U*] : a : trees that are grown in order to produce wood **b** — used as an interjection to warn people nearby that a cut tree is about to fall **2** [*C*] : a large piece of wood that is used to form a part of a building ▪ *the roof's timbers* **3** [*U*] *chiefly Brit* : wood that is used to make something ▪ *a chair made of sturdy timber*

tim·ber·land /'tımbɚˌlænd/ *n* [*C/U*] *US* : land that is covered with trees that are grown in order to produce wood

timber yard *n* [*C*] *Brit* : LUMBERYARD

tim·bre /'tæmbɚ/ *n* [*C/U*] : the quality of the sound made by a particular voice or musical instrument

¹time /'taım/ *n* **1** [*U*] : the thing that is measured as seconds, minutes, hours, days, years, etc. ▪ *The time passed slowly.* ▪ *a short amount/period of time* ▪ *Memory fades as time goes by/on.* ▪ *In the course of time* [=as time passed], *people forgot.* ▪ *Her opinion improved over/with time.* [=as time passed] ▪ *a time span* [=period] *of 20 years* **2** a [*singular*] : a particular minute or hour shown by a clock ▪ *What time is it?* ▪ *The time is 6:15.* ▪ *Call me at any time.* **b** [*U*] : the time in a particular area or part of the world ▪ *It's 2:00 p.m. local time.* **3** a [*C/U*] : the part of a day, week, month, or year when something usually happens or is scheduled to happen ▪ *It's party time!* ▪ *vacation time* **b** [*C*] : a particular part of a day, week, month, or year ▪ *We were in Italy this time last year.* ▪ *It's unusually hot for this time of year.* [=season] **4** [*C*] : an occurrence of an action or event ▪ *I've seen that movie several times.* ▪ *Do you remember the time we got lost?* ▪ *I buckle my seatbelt each and every time I ride in a car.* ▪ *I'll come by the next time I'm in town.* ▪ *The last time I saw him* [=the most recent time that I saw him] *was at his wedding.* ▪ *I'll do it one last/more time.* ▪ *For the last time, please stop!* = *This is the last time I'm going to tell you: please stop!* ▪ *"This time you've gone too far!" he said.* ▪ *She beats*

me at chess *nine times out of ten.* [=for every ten games we play, she beats me nine times] ▪ *They lost again, but they're determined to win the next time around/round.* ▪ *One time* [=once] *I came home two hours late and nobody noticed.* **5** a [*singular*] : the period of time when something happens ▪ *Perhaps we can meet at another time.* ▪ *She had left by the time I arrived.* ▪ *She has lived here from the time* [=since] *she was seven years old.* ▪ *At no time did the defendant ask for a lawyer.* [=the defendant never asked for a lawyer] ▪ *It was raining at the time of the accident.* ▪ *He was elected pope in 1978, at which time he took the name John Paul.* **b** [*C*] : the exact moment when a particular event happens or is scheduled to happen ▪ *The patient's time of death was 2:15 a.m.* ▪ *my departure/arrival times* [=the times when I am scheduled to depart/arrive] **6** [*C/U*] : a period of minutes, hours, days, weeks, etc., when something is happening or someone is doing something ▪ *I can't remember a time that/when I've been happier.* ▪ *She helped me in my time of need.* [=when I needed help] ▪ *I lived there for a time in my early twenties.* ▪ *No one spoke to us the entire/whole time we were there.* ▪ *It happened a long time ago.* ▪ *How could you think about food at a time like this?* ▪ *At one time* [=during one period of time in the past], *20 people lived together in this house.* ▪ *At the present time* [=right now], *we don't have an answer.* = *We don't have an answer at this time.* ▪ *I met him some time ago.* [=at some point in the past] ▪ *She has been living there for (quite) some time.* [=for a somewhat long time] ▪ *I get sick if I sit in the back seat of a car for any length of time.* [=for more than a very small amount of time] **7** [*U*] : the number of minutes, days, weeks, etc., before something happens ▪ *The movie is coming out in two months' time.* [=is coming out two months from now] ▪ *It's just a matter of time before someone gets hurt.* [=someone will get hurt eventually] ▪ *The police will catch him. It's only a question of time.* [=the police will catch him eventually] **8** [*U*] : the amount of time that is used, needed, available, or allowed for a particular activity or for someone to do something ▪ *You must complete the exam within the time allotted.* ▪ *This new system will save time.* [=will be faster] ▪ *He spends all his time watching TV.* ▪ *Stop wasting time.* [=doing nothing or doing something that is not useful] ▪ *There's no time to explain. I'll have to tell you why later.* ▪ *They wasted no time in decorating their new apartment.* [=they started decorating it immediately] ▪ *We have to hurry. There's no time to lose.* [=we have little time, so we cannot waste any of it] ▪ *What do you do in your free/spare time?* [=when you are not working] ▪ *We played games to pass/kill the time.* [=we played games to cause time to seem to go by more quickly] ▪ *We ran out of time and didn't finish the project.* ▪ *Time's up.* [=the allowed period of time has ended] ▪ *They finished with time to spare.* [=they finished early] ▪ *She has a lot of time on her hands.* [=time when she is not busy] ▪ *He can't manage to find (the) time to exercise.* **9** [*C/U*] : the right moment to do something or for something to happen ▪ *This is no time for jokes.* ▪ *The perfect time to buy a new car* ▪ *Am I calling at a bad time?* [=are you too busy to talk to me?] ▪ *"Should we do it now?" "Sure. There's no time like the present."* [=let's do it now] ▪ *There comes a time when children leave their parents and start families of their own.* ▪ *an idea whose time has come* [=an idea that is ready to be used] **10** [*C*] : the quality of a person's experience on a particular occasion or during a particular period ▪ *We all had a good/great/lovely time at the concert.* [=we enjoyed the concert very much] ▪ *Their music helped me get through some difficult/hard/rough/tough times in my life.* ▪ *I had the time of my life.* [=had a lot of fun] ▪ *They've been having a hard time finding an apartment.* **11** [*C*] : a specific period in the past ▪ *The bridge was built around the time of World War I.* ▪ *The biography was titled "The Life and Times of Napoleon."* ▪ *I've seen a lot of crazy things in my time.* [=during my life] ▪ *She was a legend in her own time.* [=she was very famous and admired while she was still alive] ▪ *tools used in medieval/ancient/prehistoric times* ▪ *In earlier times, this road was a trade route.* ▪ *farming methods used in times past* [=in the past] ▪ *the greatest actor of our time* [=of the present day] ▪ *Life was very different at that time.* [=then] ▪ *People have been creating art since time immemorial.* [=for a very long time] **12** [*plural*] **a** : the conditions experienced by a group of people now or during a particular period in the past ▪ *The country is facing some difficult times.* **b** : the styles, events, or ideas that are popular or important in a culture now or at a particular period in the past ▪ *Companies must change/evolve/move with the times or risk losing their customers.* ▪ *In this business, you have to keep up with the times.* [=change as conditions change] ▪ *Times have changed since then.* ▪ *Come on. Get with the times.* [=understand and change to fit what is now happening and accepted in the culture] ▪ *Their methods are behind the times.* [=outdated] **13** [*C*] : a period or stage in a person's life ▪ *I'm at a time in my life when I don't care much about my appearance.* **14 a** [*singular*] : the number of months, years, etc., that a person spends at a particular place or in a particular group or organization ▪ *I enjoyed my time at Harvard.* **b** [*singular*] : the number of months or years that an active member of the military is required to stay in the army ▪ *She plans on going to college after she serves her time in the army.* ▪ *an ex-soldier who did his time* [=fought, served] in Vietnam **c** [*U*] *informal* : the number of days, months, or years that a person must stay in prison ▪ *She's doing time for armed robbery.* ▪ *(US) He could be facing hard time.* [=a long or difficult prison sentence] **15** [*C*] : the seconds, minutes, etc., it takes to do

something (such as finish a race) ▪ *She ran the mile in a time of 5 minutes and 15 seconds.* **16** [*U*] : the minutes, hours, or days that a person works or is required to work for a company ▪ *She has been putting in a lot of time at the office.* ▪ *I took time off (work) to go to the dentist.* ▪ *(US) Employees need to make personal calls on their own time, not on company time.* **17** [*plural*] — used to say how much bigger, smaller, faster, etc., something is than something else ▪ *She earns five times as much money as I do.* ▪ *Their original investment has paid for itself many times over.* **18** [*U*] *music* **a** : the rate of speed at which a piece of music is performed ▪ *We clapped in time to* [=in a way that matched the speed of] *the music.* **b** : the way that beats are grouped together in a piece of music ▪ *a dance performed in 4/4 time* — **against time** ✧ If you are *racing/working (etc.) against time* or are in a *race against time*, you are doing something quickly because you have only a small amount of time. — **ahead of time** : earlier than a time or event ▪ *She read the report ahead of time to prepare for the meeting.* — **ahead of your/its time** ✧ If you are *ahead of your time* or if your ideas, creations, etc., are *ahead of their time*, you are too advanced or modern to be understood or appreciated during the time when you live or work. — **(all) in good time** : when the appropriate moment arrives ▪ *I'll let him know in good time.* — **all (of) the time 1** : ALWAYS ▪ *You can't be right all of the time.* **2** *informal* : very often or frequently ▪ *My sisters argue all of the time.* **3** *usually all the time* : since something began ▪ *I knew the truth all the time.* — **any time (now)** : very soon ▪ *The train should be arriving any time now.* — **a sign of the times** see ¹SIGN — **a stitch in time (saves nine)** see ¹STITCH — **at all times** : ALWAYS ▪ *The system is kept running at all times.* — **at a time 1** : during one particular moment ▪ *I can only do one thing at a time.* [=at once] ▪ *Please speak one at a time.* [=so that only one person is speaking at any time] **2** : during one period of time without stopping ▪ *She can sit and read for hours at a time.* **3** ✧ If you *take one day at a time* or *take it/things one day at a time,* you make progress in a slow and careful way by dealing with each day as it comes. — **at the same time 1** : during the same moment ▪ *She was driving, eating, and talking on the phone all at the same time.* **2** — used to introduce a statement that adds to and differs from a preceding statement ▪ *The new regulations will help the environment. At the same time* [=on the other hand], *they may be a burden to businesses.* — **at times** : SOMETIMES ▪ *I worry about you at times.* — **before your time 1** — used to say that something happened before you were born or before you were involved in some activity ▪ *You wouldn't know about that. It was before your time.* **2** ✧ If you become old *before your time,* you look and feel older than you are. **3** ✧ If you *die before* *your* time, you die at a younger age than you should. — **behind the times** : not having or showing knowledge of current ideas or styles ▪ *The entire country is behind the times when it comes to protecting the environment.* — **be living on borrowed time** see BORROW — **bide your time** see BIDE — **buy time** see ¹BUY — **call time** US, sports : to ask for or order a time-out ▪ *The coach/referee called time.* — **for the time being** : during the present time but possibly not in the future ▪ *For the time being, this car suits all of our family's needs.* — **from time to time** : SOMETIMES ▪ *She visits us from time to time.* — **give (someone) a hard time** see ¹HARD — **half the time** *informal* : very often ▪ *Half the time I have no idea what you are talking about.* — **have time** 1 : to be able to use an amount of time for a particular purpose ▪ *"Did you eat lunch?" "No, I didn't have time."* [=I was too busy] ▪ *We don't have time for this nonsense!* 2 : to like or be willing to spend time dealing with (something or someone) ▪ *I have no time for liars.* — **in no time** : very quickly or soon ▪ *We'll be done in no time.* — **in the nick of time** see ¹NICK — **in time** 1 : before something happens : early enough ▪ *We arrived in time to catch the last train.* ▪ *I'll be home in time for dinner.* 2 : when an amount of time has passed ▪ *Things will get better in time.* [=eventually] — **in your own (good) time** : at the time that is right or appropriate for you and not sooner ▪ *He'll make a decision in his own good time.* — **it's about time** *informal* — used to say often in an annoyed way that something should have happened sooner ▪ *It's about time you got here!* — **it's high time** see ¹HIGH — **keep time** 1 *of a watch or clock* : to show the correct time ▪ *My watch keeps good/perfect time.* 2 *music* : to perform music at the correct speed ▪ *The conductor helps the orchestra keep time (to the music).* — **make good time** : to travel somewhere quickly ▪ *They made good time on their trip.* — **make time** : to cause an amount of time to be available for an activity ▪ *I'll have to make (the) time to get it done.* ▪ *No matter how busy he was, Grandpa always made time for us.* — **most of the time** or **most times** : USUALLY ▪ *Most times, this method works well.* — **ninety/ninety-nine (etc.) percent of the time** : USUALLY ▪ *He's right ninety percent of the time.* — **not give someone the time of day** ◊ If you do *not* **give someone the time of day**, you do not give that person any attention or help. — **of all time** : that has ever lived or existed ▪ *the greatest basketball player of all time* — **once upon a time** see ¹ONCE — **(only) time will tell** — used to say that the results of a situation will be known only after a certain amount of time has passed ▪ *"Will he be OK?" "I don't know. Only time will tell."* — **on time** : at a time that is not late ▪ *We arrived right on time.* [=exactly at the right time] — **play for time** see ¹PLAY — **stand the test of time** see ¹TEST — **take (the) time to do**

something : to use an amount of time in order to do something important ▪ *They never took the time to get to know her.* — **take time** ◊ People say that something **takes some/no (etc.) time** to describe how much time is needed for something to happen or be done. ▪ *Things like this take time.* [=cannot be done quickly] ▪ *It may take some time for the medication to wear off.* ▪ *It'll take no time at all.* = *It will take very little time.* — **take your time** : to do something slowly or without hurrying ▪ *There's no need to hurry. Take your time.* — **tell time** (US) or Brit **tell the time** : to be able to know what time it is by looking at a clock ▪ *My son is just learning to tell time.* — **the whole time** : during the entire period of time ▪ *I knew the truth the whole time.* — **time after time** or **time and again** or **time and time again** : frequently or repeatedly ▪ *Time after time, we see this happen with our patients.* — **time flies** — used to say that time passes quickly ▪ *Time flies when you're having fun.* — **time is money** see MONEY — **time is (not) on your side** ◊ If *time is on your side,* you have a good chance of success because you can wait until a situation improves. If *time is not on your side,* your chance of success is less because you have to do something very soon. — **until such time as** *formal* : UNTIL ▪ *He will be suspended from work until such time as this matter has been resolved.* — **your (own) sweet time** *chiefly US, informal* ◊ If you do something **in your (own) sweet time** or you **take your (own) sweet time** about doing something, you do it slowly even though other people want you to do it more quickly.

²**time** *vb* **timed; tim·ing** [T] **1** : to choose the hour, day, month, etc., when (something) will happen ▪ *They timed their vacation to coincide with the festival.* ▪ *It was a poorly timed visit.* [=the visit happened at an unfortunate or inconvenient time] **2** : to cause (something) to happen at a certain moment ▪ *She timed the shot perfectly.* **3** : to measure the amount of time needed by someone to do something ▪ *timing a horse race*

time and a half *n* [U] : a rate of pay that is equal to what a worker usually earns for an hour plus half of that amount ▪ *We get paid time and a half for overtime.*

time bomb *n* [C] **1** : a bomb that is set to explode at a particular moment **2** : a person or situation that will probably become dangerous or harmful in the future ▪ *If we ignore the problem, we'll be sitting on a ticking time bomb.*

time capsule *n* [C] : a container that is filled with things from the present time and that is meant to be opened by people at some time in the future

time clock *n* [C] : a special clock that is used to record the times when an employee starts and stops working

time-con·sum·ing /ˈtaɪmkənˌsuːmɪŋ, Brit ˈtaɪmkənˌsjuːmɪŋ/ *adj* : using or needing a large amount of time ▪ *time-consuming chores*

time frame *n* [C] : a period of time that is

used or planned for a particular action or project ▪ *We finished the project within the established time frame.*

time·hon·ored (*US*) *or Brit* **time·hon·oured** /ˈtaɪmˌɑːnəd/ *adj, always before a noun* : existing and respected for a long time ▪ *time-honored traditions*

time·keep·er /ˈtaɪmˌkiːpə/ *n* [*C*] **1** : a person who controls or records official times during a race, game, etc. **2** *Brit* — used in the phrases *good timekeeper* and *bad/poor timekeeper* to say that someone is or is not good about arriving at the correct or expected time ▪ *We expect our employees to be good timekeepers.*

time·lapse /ˈtaɪmˌlæps/ *adj, always before a noun* — used to describe a way of filming something in which many photographs are taken over a long period of time and are shown quickly in a series so that a slow action appears to happen quickly ▪ *time-lapse photography*

time·less /ˈtaɪmləs/ *adj* **1** : staying beautiful or fashionable as time passes ▪ *the timeless beauty of the sea* **2** : lasting forever ▪ *timeless truths*

time·ly /ˈtaɪmli/ *adj* **time·li·er; -est** : happening at the correct or most useful time ▪ *a timely decision* ▪ *She always replies* **in a timely fashion/manner.** — **time·li·ness** *n* [*U*]

time machine *n* [*C*] *in stories* : a machine that allows people to travel to a time in the past or future

time–out /ˈtaɪmˈaʊt/ *n* [*C/U*] **1** : a short period of time during a sports event when the game stops and the players rest or talk to their coach ▪ *The coach called (a) time-out.* **2** : a short period of time when you stop doing something so that you can rest or do something else ▪ *Let's take (a) time-out.* **3** *US* : a short period of time when a child must sit quietly as punishment for behaving badly ▪ *give a child a time-out*

time·piece /ˈtaɪmˌpiːs/ *n* [*C*] *formal* : a clock or watch ▪ *an expensive German timepiece*

tim·er /ˈtaɪmə/ *n* [*C*] **1** : a device that makes a sound when a certain amount of time has passed ▪ *The timer is set to go off in 15 minutes.* **2** : a device that can be set to turn something on or off at a certain time ▪ *The sprinkler/light is on a timer.*

times /ˈtaɪmz/ *prep* : multiplied by ▪ *Two times two is/equals four.*

time·ta·ble /ˈtaɪmˌteɪbəl/ *n* [*C*] **1** : a plan of things that need to be done and the times they will be done ▪ *What's your timetable for completing the work?* **2** *chiefly Brit* : a list of the times when something is expected to leave or arrive ▪ *a bus/train timetable* [=(*US*) *schedule*] **3** *Brit* : a written or printed list of activities and the times when they will be done ▪ *There have been a few changes to the class timetable.* [=(*US*) *schedule*] — **time·table** *vb* **-tabled; -tabling** [*T*] *chiefly Brit* ▪ *The meeting is timetabled* [=scheduled] *for 10 a.m.*

time warp *n* [*C*] : a feeling, state, or place in which time seems to stop, go back-

ward, etc. ▪ *Walking into the castle was like entering a time warp.*

time·worn /ˈtaɪmˌwoən/ *adj* **1** : in bad condition because of age ▪ *timeworn houses* **2** : no longer interesting or effective because of being old or used too often ▪ *a timeworn joke/excuse*

time zone *n* [*C*] : any one of the world's 24 divisions that has its own time ▪ *We flew west and landed in a different time zone.*

tim·id /ˈtɪməd/ *adj* : feeling or showing a lack of courage or confidence ▪ *a timid person/smile* — **ti·mid·i·ty** /təˈmɪdəti/ *n* [*U*] — **tim·id·ly** /ˈtɪmədli/ *adv*

tim·ing /ˈtaɪmɪŋ/ *n* [*U*] **1** : the time when something happens or is done especially when it is thought of as having a good or bad effect on the result ▪ *The timing of the sale was perfect.* **2** : the ability to choose the best moment for some action, movement, etc. ▪ *an athlete with impeccable timing*

tim·o·rous /ˈtɪmərəs/ *adj, formal* : easily frightened ▪ *a timorous child* — **tim·o·rous·ly** *adv*

tin /ˈtɪn/ *n* **1** [*U*] : a soft, shiny, bluish-white metal that has many different uses **2** [*C*] **a** : a container or plate made of metal ▪ *a pie tin* **b** : a decorative metal box with a cover or lid ▪ *a tin of tobacco* **c** *chiefly Brit* : ²CAN 1a ▪ *sardine tins* **d** *Brit* : ¹PAN ▪ *a roasting tin* — **tin** *adj*

tinc·ture /ˈtɪŋktʃə/ *n* [*C*] *technical* : a medicine that is made of a drug mixed with alcohol ▪ *medicinal tinctures*

tin·der /ˈtɪndə/ *n* [*U*] : dry material (such as wood or grass) that burns easily and can be used to start a fire : KINDLING

tin·der·box /ˈtɪndəˌbɑːks/ *n* [*C*] **1** : a box that holds tinder **2 a** : a structure that would burn very quickly if it caught on fire ▪ *The old house is a tinderbox.* **b** : a place or situation that could suddenly become very violent ▪ *The campus was a tinderbox on the verge of a riot.*

tine /ˈtaɪn/ *n* [*C*] : one of the thin, pointed parts on a fork

tin·foil /ˈtɪnˌfɔjəl/ *n* [*U*] : a thin sheet of shiny metal that is used especially for cooking or storing food ▪ *Wrap the leftovers in (a piece of) tinfoil.*

¹tinge /ˈtɪndʒ/ *n* [*C*] : a slight color, flavor, or quality ▪ *a tinge of color/regret*

²tinge *vb* **tinged; tinge·ing** [*T*] **1** : to give a small amount of color to (something) ▪ *The sky was tinged with red.* **2** : to give a small amount of some quality to (something) ▪ *The day was tinged with sadness.*

tin·gle /ˈtɪŋgəl/ *vb* **tin·gled; tin·gling** [*I*] **1** : to have a feeling like the feeling of many small sharp points pressing into your skin ▪ *My arm/leg was numb and tingling.* **2** : to feel an emotion (such as excitement) very strongly ▪ *I was tingling* **with excitement.** — **tingle** *n* [*C*] — **tin·gly** /ˈtɪŋgəli/ *adj* **tin·gli·er; -est** ▪ *a tingly sensation*

¹tin·ker /ˈtɪŋkə/ *vb* [*I*] : to try to repair or improve something (such as a machine) by making small changes or adjustments to it • *He was tinkering (with the car) in the garage.* — **tin·ker·er** /ˈtɪŋkərə/ *n* [C]

²**tinker** *n* [C] : a person who in the past traveled to different places and sold or repaired small items (such as pots and pans)

tin·kle /ˈtɪŋkəl/ *vb* **tin·kled; tin·kling** **1** [T/I] : to make sounds like the sounds of a small bell • *The ice tinkled in the glass.* • *He tinkled a small bell.* **2** [I] *informal* : URINATE — used especially by small children • *The little boy said he had to tinkle.* — **tinkle** *n* [C] • *the tinkle of the bell*

tinned /ˈtɪnd/ *adj, Brit* : preserved in a metal or glass container : CANNED • *tinned ham*

tin·ny /ˈtɪni/ *adj* **tin·ni·er; -est** : having a high and unpleasant sound • *a tinny voice*

tin·sel /ˈtɪnsəl/ *n* [U] **1** : thin strips of shiny metal or paper that are used as decoration • *decorate a Christmas tree with tinsel* **2** : something that seems attractive or appealing but is of little worth • *the tinsel and glitter of Hollywood*

tint /ˈtɪnt/ *n* **1** [C] : a small amount of color • *a photo with a yellowish tint* **2 a** [C/U] : dye used to change the color of hair **b** [*singular*] : an act of changing the color of hair by using dye • *She got a red tint at the salon.* — **tint** *vb* [T] • *She got her hair tinted.* • *tinted glasses/windows*

ti·ny /ˈtaɪni/ *adj* **ti·ni·er; -est** : very small • *a tiny bird/hole/problem*

¹**tip** /ˈtɪp/ *vb* **tipped; tip·ping** **1** [T/I] : to turn or move something so that it is not straight or level • *He tipped his chair back.* • *The glass tipped and the water spilled out.* **2** [T/I] : to give an extra amount of money to someone who performs a service for you • *tip a waiter* **3** [T] *sports* : to hit or push (a moving ball or puck) lightly so that it changes direction • *The hockey player tipped the puck into the net.* — **tip off** **1** *of a basketball game* : START • *The game is scheduled to tip off at 7:00 p.m.* **2 tip (someone) off** *or* **tip off (someone)** : to give useful or secret information to (someone) • *Someone tipped off the police.* — **tip over** [*phrasal vb*] **tip over** *or* **tip (something) over** *or* **tip over (something)** : to fall over or to cause (something) to fall over • *The glass tipped over.* • *He tipped the lamp over.* — **tip the scales 1** *or* **tip the balance** : to change a situation so that one person, group, etc., is more able or likely to succeed • *Experience tips the scales in her favor.* **2 tip the scales at** : to have (a specified weight) • *He tips the scales at [=weighs] 285 pounds.* — **tip up** [*phrasal vb*] **tip (something) up** *or* **tip up (something)** : to move or cause (something) to move so that one end is lifted up • *She tipped up the lid of the box.* — **tip your cap/hat 1** : to touch your hat or cap or to lift it off your head as a way of greeting or saying goodbye to someone • *He tipped his hat to her.* **2** — used informally to say that you admire or respect someone • *I tip my hat to you for all your hard work.* — **tip your hand** : to show what you are planning to do • *The company tipped its hand about its decision.* — **tip·per** /ˈtɪpə/ *n* [C]

²**tip** *n* **1** [C] : the end of something that is usually long and thin • *the tip of a finger/pencil/ski* **2** [*singular*] : the act of touching your hat or cap or lifting it off your head as a way of greeting or saying goodbye to someone • *He said goodbye with a tip of his hat.* **3** [C] : an extra amount of money that you give to someone who performs a service for you • *I left/gave the waitress a good tip.* **4** [C] **a** : a piece of advice or useful information • *household cleaning tips* **b** : a piece of information given by a person who has special or secret knowledge about something • *an insider's tip on when to sell the stock* • *I got a hot tip about a great new restaurant.* **5** [C] *Brit* **a** : a place where rubbish is left : DUMP **b** *informal* : a very messy place : DUMP • *This place is a real tip!* — **on the tip of your tongue 1** ◇ If a word, name, etc., is *on the tip of your tongue*, you know it but cannot remember it. **2** ◇ If a statement is *on the tip of your tongue*, you nearly say it but decide not to say it. — **the tip of the iceberg** see ICEBERG

tip–off /ˈtɪpˌɑːf/ *n* [C] **1 a** : a warning that something (such as a crime) is going to happen • *The police received a tip-off about the robbery.* **b** : a clear sign or indication of something • *His frown was a tip-off that something was wrong.* **2** *basketball* : the start of a game when the ball is thrown in the air and a player from each team jumps up and tries to get the ball

tip·ster /ˈtɪpstə/ *n* [C] : a person who gives useful information to someone • *An anonymous tipster reported the crime.*

tip·sy /ˈtɪpsi/ *adj* **tip·si·er; -est** *informal* : slightly drunk • *I got a little tipsy at the party.*

¹**tip·toe** /ˈtɪpˌtoʊ/ *n* — **on tiptoe** *or* **on (your) tiptoes** : with your toes touching the ground and your heels raised up • *standing/walking on tiptoe* — **tiptoe** *adv* • *standing tiptoe*

²**tiptoe** *vb* **-toed; -toe·ing** [I] : to walk with your heels raised up and only your toes touching the ground • *He tiptoed quietly out of the room.* — **tiptoe around** [*phrasal vb*] : to avoid talking about (something) • *tiptoe around a subject*

tip–top /ˈtɪpˈtɑːp/ *adj, informal* : very good • *The car is in tip-top shape.*

ti·rade /ˈtaɪreɪd/ *n* [C] : a long and angry speech • *The coach directed a tirade at the team after the loss.*

¹**tire** /ˈtajə/ *vb* **tired; tir·ing** [T/I] : to become tired or to make (someone) tired • *The pitcher seems to be tiring.* • *The long hike tired (out) the younger children.* — **tire of** [*phrasal vb*] : to become bored by (something) • *She never tires of listening to music.* — **tiring** *adj* • *tiring work*

²**tire** (*US*) *or Brit* **tyre** /ˈtajə/ *n* [C] : a rubber ring that usually contains air and that fits around the wheel of a car, bicycle, etc. • *a flat tire*

tired *adj* **1** : feeling a need to rest or sleep • *I'm too tired to go out tonight.* • *tired muscles* **2** : bored or annoyed by something because you have heard it, seen it, done it, etc., for a long time — + *of* ▪ *Are you tired of your job?* ▪ *I'm* **sick and tired of** [=very tired of] *your complaining.* **3** *disapproving* : used over and over again ▪ *a tired excuse/joke* — **tiredness** *n* [U]

tire·less /ˈtajələs/ *adj* : working very hard with a lot of energy for a long time ▪ *a tireless worker/advocate* — **tire·less·ly** *adv*

tire·some /ˈtajəsəm/ *adj* : causing you to feel bored, annoyed, or impatient ▪ *a tiresome lecture* — **tire·some·ly** *adv*

'tis /ˈtɪz, təz/ *old-fashioned + literary* — used as a contraction of "it is" ▪ *'Tis the season to be jolly.*

tis·sue /ˈtɪʃu/ *n* **1** [C] : a piece of soft and very thin paper that is used especially for cleaning ▪ *She wiped her nose with a tissue.* **2** [U, *plural*] : the material that forms the parts in a plant or animal ▪ *a sample of brain/lung/muscle tissue* ▪ *the body's tissues* **3** [U] : TISSUE PAPER ▪ *a box wrapped in tissue*

tissue paper *n* [U] : thin paper used especially for covering or wrapping something

ti·tan /ˈtaɪtn/ *n* [C] **1** *Titan* : one of a family of giants in Greek mythology **2** : an extremely large and powerful person, company, etc. ▪ *media titans*

ti·tan·ic /taɪˈtænɪk/ *adj* : very great in size, force, or power ▪ *a titanic explosion/struggle*

ti·ta·ni·um /taɪˈteɪnijəm/ *n* [U] : a very strong and light silvery metal

titbit *Brit spelling of* TIDBIT

tit for tat /ˌtɪtfɚˈtæt/ *n* [U, *singular*] : a situation in which you do something to harm someone who has done something harmful to you ▪ *a tit for tat between two rival politicians* — **tit–for–tat** *adj*

tithe /ˈtaɪð/ *n* [C] : an amount of money that a person gives to a church which is usually equal to ⅒ of that person's income

tit·il·late /ˈtɪtl̩ˌeɪt/ *vb* **-lat·ed; -lat·ing** [T/I] : to interest or excite (someone) in an enjoyable and often sexual way ▪ *a film that titillates (its audience)* ▪ *titillating gossip* — **tit·il·la·tion** /ˌtɪtl̩ˈeɪʃən/ *n* [U]

ti·tle /ˈtaɪtl̩/ *n* **1** [C] : the name given to a book, song, movie, etc., to identify or describe it **2** [C] : a published book ▪ *one of our best-selling titles* **3** [C] : a word or name that describes a person's job in a company or organization ▪ *Her title is Vice President of Marketing.* **4** [C] : a word (such as *Sir* or *Doctor*) or an abbreviation (such as *Mr.* or *Dr.*) that is used with someone's name to show that person's rank, profession, or marital status **5** [C] : the status or position of being the champion in a sport or other competition ▪ *He holds the heavyweight boxing title.* **6** *law* [U] : a legal right to the ownership of property ▪ *The court ruled that he had title to the land.* **b** [C] : a document which shows that someone owns property ▪ *the car's title* — **title** *vb* **ti·tled; ti·tling** [T] ▪ *She titled the book "The Story of My Life."*

titled *adj* : having a title (such as "Lord" or "Lady") ▪ *a member of the titled ranks*

tit·ter /ˈtɪtɚ/ *vb* [I] : to laugh in a quiet and nervous way ▪ *Some audience members tittered nervously.* — **titter** *n* [C]

tit·u·lar /ˈtɪtʃələ/ *adj* **1** : having an important or impressive title but not having the power or duties that usually go with it ▪ *a titular ruler* **2** : having the name of the character that is featured in the title of a movie, play, etc. ▪ *the titular role in Hamlet* [=the role of Hamlet in the play *Hamlet*]

tiz·zy /ˈtɪzi/ *n* [*singular*] *informal* : a state in which you feel very worried, upset, and confused ▪ *She's always getting in/into a tizzy over minor things.*

TLC /ˌtiːˌɛlˈsiː/ *n* [U] *informal* : care and attention that is given to make someone feel better, to improve the bad condition of something, etc. ▪ *an old house that needs some TLC* ◇ *TLC* is an abbreviation of "tender loving care."

TM *abbr* trademark

TN *abbr* Tennessee

TNT /ˌtiːˌɛnˈtiː/ *n* [U] : a very powerful explosive

¹to /ˈtuː, tə/ *prep* **1** — used to indicate that the following verb is in the infinitive form ▪ *I like to swim.* — often used by itself in place of an infinitive verb when the verb is understood ▪ *You can go if you want to.* [=if you want to go] **2 a** — used to indicate the place, person, or thing that someone or something moves toward ▪ *We are flying to London tomorrow.* **b** — used to indicate the place where someone participates in a particular activity ▪ *Where do you go to school?* **3** — used to indicate the direction of something ▪ *I live a mile to the south of here.* **4** — used to indicate the limit or range of something ▪ *The water was up to my waist.* ▪ *men from 18 to 30 years of age* ▪ *To my knowledge, she has never visited Paris.* [=I do not know of any time when she visited Paris] ▪ *I'll do it to the best of my ability.* [=as well as I can] **5 a** — used to indicate a particular result or end ▪ *The school was converted to an apartment building.* ▪ *He was sentenced to death.* **b** : according to (something) ▪ *Add salt to taste.* [=add as much salt as you want according to your taste] **6 a** — used to indicate the end of a particular period of time ▪ *He works from nine to five.* **b** : before the start of (something, such as an hour or event) ▪ *It is ten to six.* [=it is 10 minutes before 6 o'clock] **7 a** — used to indicate the person or thing that receives an object or action ▪ *Give the letter to me.* ▪ *Let me introduce you to my sister.* **b** : in honor of (someone or something) ▪ *Let us drink to the bride and groom.* **8 a** — used to indicate how people or things are related, connected, etc. ▪ *She is married to my cousin.* ▪ *the key (that goes) to this door* **b** : in response to (something) ▪ *The answer to your question is no.* **9** — used to indicate the thing that causes something to happen ▪ *She lost her mother to cancer.* [=her mother died of cancer] **10** — used when one person or thing is being compared to another ▪ *He prefers a* good book to a movie. ▪ *We won the game ten to six.* [=we had ten points and the other team had six] **11** — used to indicate that something is attached to or touches something else ▪ *He tied the dog's leash to the post.* **12** — used to indicate the thing that contains or includes a certain number or amount of something ▪ *The pencils come ten to a box.* [=there are ten pencils in each box] **13** — used to indicate the sound that people hear while they do something or while something happens ▪ *Children were dancing to the music.* **14 a** : in the opinion of (someone) ▪ *The plan is agreeable to all of us.* **b** : from the point of view of (someone) ▪ *Their marriage is news to me.* [=I did not know about their marriage] — **to yourself** — used with *have* to say that you are the only one who is using something or who is in a place ▪ *I finally had the computer (all) to myself.*

²**to** /'tuː/ *adv* **1** : into a state of being awake or conscious ▪ *He brought her to* [=made her conscious again] *with smelling salts.* ▪ *He came to* [=became conscious] *an hour after the accident.* **2** *chiefly Brit* : into a position that is closed or almost closed ▪ *The wind blew the door to.* — **to and fro** : forward and backward ▪ *The baby rocked to and fro in the swing.* : from one place to another ▪ *The boat was tossed to and fro by the waves.*

toad /'toʊd/ *n* [C] : a small animal that looks like a frog but has dry skin and lives on land

toad·stool /'toʊd,stuːl/ *n* [C] : a kind of fungus that is similar to a mushroom and that is often poisonous

toady /'toʊdi/ *n, pl* **toad·ies** [C] *informal + disapproving* : a person who praises and helps powerful people in order to get their approval ▪ *She's a real toady to the boss.* — **toady** *vb* **toadies; toad·ied; toady·ing** [I] ▪ *She's always toadying to the boss.*

¹**toast** /'toʊst/ *n* **1** [U] : bread that has been sliced and then made crisp and brown by heat ▪ *a piece of toast* **2** [C] : an occurrence in which words are said that honor someone, express good wishes, etc., and people take a drink to show that they agree with what has been said ▪ *He made/proposed/drank a toast to the bride and groom.* — **be toast** *informal* : to be in a lot of trouble ▪ *If anyone finds out about this, we're toast.* : to be completely ruined, defeated, etc. ▪ *His career is toast.* — **the toast of** : a person who is very popular in (a particular place) or among (a particular group of people) ▪ *She is the toast of the town.*

²**toast** *vb* [T] **1 a** : to make (food) crisp and brown by heat ▪ *Toast the bread.* **b** : to warm (yourself or part of your body) by being close to a fire or some other source of heat ▪ *He toasted his feet by the fire.* **2** : to drink a toast to (someone) ▪ *We toasted the bride and groom.*

toast·er /'toʊstɚ/ *n* [C] : an electrical device used for toasting bread

toaster oven *n* [C] *US* : a small oven in which food is toasted, heated, or cooked

toasty /'toʊsti/ *adj* **toast·i·er; -est** *US, informal* : comfortably warm ▪ *The room was toasty.*

to·bac·co /tə'bækoʊ/ *n* [U] **1** : a plant that produces leaves which are smoked in cigarettes, pipes, etc. **2** : the leaves of the tobacco plant used for smoking or chewing ▪ *chewing/pipe tobacco* **3** : products (such as cigars or cigarettes) that are made from tobacco ▪ *the tobacco industry*

to·bac·co·nist /tə'bækənɪst/ *n* [C] : a person who sells tobacco and tobacco products (such as cigarettes)

to·bog·gan /tə'bɑːgən/ *n* [C] : a long, light sled that has a curved front and that is used for sliding over snow and ice — **toboggan** *vb* [I] ▪ *The kids tobogganed down the hill.*

¹**to·day** /tə'deɪ/ *n* [U] **1** : this day ▪ *Is today a holiday?* ▪ *today's newspaper* **2** : the present time ▪ *the computers of today*

²**today** *adv* **1** : on, during, or for this day ▪ *I have an appointment today.* **2** : at the present time; NOWADAYS ▪ *I worry about children today.*

tod·dle /'tɑːdl̩/ *vb* **tod·dled; tod·dling** [I] *of a young child* : to walk with short, unsteady steps ▪ *The little boy toddled across the room.*

tod·dler /'tɑːdlɚ/ *n* [C] : a young child who is just learning to walk

to–do /tə'duː/ *n* [*singular*] *informal* : excited or angry activity that is usually not necessary or wanted ▪ *They're making a big to-do about nothing.*

¹**toe** /'toʊ/ *n* [C] **1** : one of the five separate parts at the end of your foot ▪ *I accidentally stepped on her toe.* **2** : the part of a shoe or sock that covers the front part of your foot ▪ *My sock has a hole in the toe.* — **keep (someone) on their toes** *informal* : to cause someone to be alert and prepared to deal with problems ▪ *This job really keeps me on my toes.* — **step on someone's toes** (*US*) *or Brit* **tread on someone's toes** *informal* : to do something that upsets or offends someone ▪ *I don't want to step on anyone's toes.*

²**toe** *vb* **toed; toe·ing** — **toe the line** : to do what you are told or required to do even though you do not want to do it ▪ *We expect you to toe the line if you want to stay here.*

TOEFL /'toʊfəl/ *trademark* — used for a test of the language skills of people who have learned English as a foreign language

toe·hold /'toʊ,hoʊld/ *n* [C] **1** : a place where your toes may be placed when you are climbing a cliff, a mountain, etc. **2** : a position that makes it possible to begin an activity or effort ▪ *He helped me get a toehold in the business.*

toe·nail /'toʊ,neɪl/ *n* [C] : the hard covering at the end of a toe

toff /'tɑːf/ *n* [C] *Brit, informal + disapproving* : a person who belongs to a high social class

tof·fee /'tɑːfi/ *n* [U] : a hard, sticky candy made by boiling sugar and butter together

to·fu /ˈtoʊˌfuː/ n [U] : a soft, white food made from soybeans and often used in vegetarian cooking instead of meat — called also **bean curd**

to·ga /ˈtoʊgə/ n [C] : a long, loose piece of clothing that was worn by people in ancient Rome

¹to·geth·er /təˈgɛðɚ/ adv **1** : with each other ▪ They went to the party together. ▪ They have been in business together since 1971. **2** : in or into one group, mixture, piece, etc. ▪ Mix the ingredients together. **3** : in a close relationship ▪ She got back together with her old boyfriend. **4** : so that two or more people or things touch ▪ The doors banged together. **5** : at the same time ▪ They all cheered together. **6 a** : to each other ▪ Add the numbers together. **b** : considered as a whole ▪ All together there were 15 of us. usage see AL-TOGETHER — **come together** see COME — **get together, get your act together** see GET — **hold together** see ¹HOLD — **pull together** see ¹PULL — **throw to-gether** see ¹THROW — **together with** : in addition to (someone or something) ▪ The fingerprint together with the other evidence proved that he was there.

²together adj, informal : confident, organized, and able to deal with problems in a calm and skillful way ▪ She's always so to-gether.

to·geth·er·ness /təˈgɛðɚnəs/ n [U] : a state or feeling of closeness and happiness among people who are together as friends, family members, etc. ▪ family to-getherness

tog·gle /ˈtɑːgəl/ n [C] **1** : a small piece of wood, plastic, metal, etc., that is pushed through a loop or hole to fasten one part of something to another part **2** computers : a setting that can be switched between two different options by pressing a single key, making a single choice from a menu, etc. — **toggle** vb

tog·gled; tog·gling [I] computers ▪ The program lets you toggle [=switch] easily be-tween two different views.

toggle switch n [C] : a switch that turns the flow of electricity to a machine on and off

togs /ˈtɑːgz/ n [plural] Brit, informal : CLOTHES ▪ fancy togs

¹toil /ˈtojəl/ n [U] formal + literary : work that is difficult and unpleasant and that lasts for a long time ▪ days of toil and sweat

²toil vb [I] formal + literary **1** : to work very hard for a long time ▪ workers toiling in the fields **2** : to move slowly and with a lot of effort ▪ toiling up a steep hill — **toil·er** /ˈtojlɚ/ n [C]

toi·let /ˈtojlət/ n [C] **1** : a large bowl attached to a pipe that is used for getting rid of bodily waste and then flushed with water ▪ flush the toilet ▪ a toilet brush/seat/bowl **2** chiefly Brit : BATHROOM ▪ a pub-lic toilet **3** old-fashioned : the act or process of washing and dressing yourself ▪ a woman at her toilet

toilet paper n [U] : thin, soft paper used to clean yourself after you have used the toilet — called also **toilet tissue**

toi·let·ries /ˈtojlətriz/ n [plural] : things

(such as soap, lotions, etc.) that are used to clean yourself and make yourself look neat

toilet training n [U] : the process of teaching a small child to use the toilet — **toilet train** vb [T] ▪ toilet train a child

toilet water n [U] : a kind of perfume that consists mostly of water and does not have a strong scent

¹to·ken /ˈtoʊkən/ n [C] **1** : a round piece of metal or plastic that is used instead of money in some machines ▪ a bus/subway token **2** : something that is a symbol of a feeling, event, etc. ▪ The gift is a token of my affection/gratitude. **3** Brit : GIFT CERTIFICATE ▪ a book/record/gift token — **by the same token** : in the same way — used to introduce a statement that says something more and often something different about the same situation referred to by a previous statement ▪ The result was disappointing, but by the same token, it could have been much worse.

²token adj, always before a noun, disap-proving **1** — used to describe some-thing that is done with very little effort and only to give the appearance that an effort is being made ▪ a token effort/ges-ture **2** : included in a group only to pre-vent criticism that people of a particular kind are being unfairly left out ▪ The ad campaign features a few token minorities.

to·ken·ism /ˈtoʊkəˌnɪzəm/ n [U] : the practice of doing something (such as hir-ing a person who belongs to a minority group) only to prevent criticism and give the appearance that people are being treated fairly

told past tense and past participle of TELL

tol·er·able /ˈtɑːlərəbəl/ adj **1** : unpleas-ant but able to be accepted or tolerated ▪ a tolerable level of pain **2** : good enough to be accepted but not very good ▪ a tol-erable effort — **tol·er·ably** /ˈtɑːlərəbli/ adv

tol·er·ance /ˈtɑːlərəns/ n **1** [U, singular] : willingness to accept feelings, habits, or beliefs that are different from your own ▪ religious tolerance ▪ a tolerance for/of oth-er lifestyles **2** [C/U] : the ability to ac-cept, experience, or survive something harmful or unpleasant ▪ I don't have much tolerance for cold weather. [=I dis-like cold weather] **3** [C/U] medical : your body's ability to become adjusted to something (such as a drug) so that its effects are experienced less strongly ▪ Some patients develop (a) greater toler-ance for the drug's effects.

tol·er·ant /ˈtɑːlərənt/ adj **1** : willing to accept feelings, habits, or beliefs that are different from your own ▪ a tolerant soci-ety ▪ They are tolerant of each other's dif-ferences. **2** : able to allow or accept something that is harmful, unpleasant, etc. ▪ These plants are tolerant of hot cli-mates. [=are able to live and grow in hot climates] — **tol·er·ant·ly** adv

tol·er·ate /ˈtɑːləˌreɪt/ vb **-at·ed; -at·ing** [T] **1** : to allow (something that is bad, unpleasant, etc.) to exist, happen, or be done ▪ Our teacher will not tolerate bad grammar. **2** : to experience (something harmful or unpleasant) without being

harmed ▪ *These plants tolerate heat well.*
3 : to accept the feelings, behavior, or beliefs of (someone) ▪ *I don't like my boss, but I tolerate him.* — **tol·er·a·tion** /ˌtɑːləˈreɪʃən/ *n* [U]

¹**toll** /ˈtoʊl/ *n* [C] **1 a** : an amount of money that you are required to pay for the use of a road or bridge ▪ *collect/pay a toll* ▪ *a toll road/bridge* **b** *chiefly US* : an amount of money paid for a long-distance telephone call **c** : the number of people who are killed or injured in an accident, disaster, war, etc. ▪ *The full/final toll of the disaster is not yet known.* **2 a** : the sound of bells being rung slowly ▪ *The toll of the bells sounded throughout the village.* **b** : a single sound made by a ringing bell ▪ *He counted the tolls of the bell.* — **take a toll** or **take its toll** : to have a serious, bad effect on someone or something ▪ *If you keep working so hard, the stress will eventually take its toll (on you).*

²**toll** *vb* [T/I] : to ring slowly ▪ *Church bells tolled.* ▪ *The bells were tolled.*

toll·booth /ˈtoʊlˌbuːθ/ *n* [C] : a small building where you pay a toll to use a road or bridge

toll call *n* [C] *US* : a long-distance telephone call for which you must pay an extra amount of money

toll–free /ˈtoʊlˈfriː/ *adj, US* : allowing you to make a long-distance telephone call without having to pay a toll ▪ *a toll-free call/number* — **toll–free** *adv*

toll·gate /ˈtoʊlˌgeɪt/ *n* [C] : a place where the driver of a vehicle must pay a toll to go through a gate that blocks a road

toll·house /ˈtoʊlˌhaʊs/ *n* [C] : a building where you pay a toll to use a road or bridge

toll plaza *n* [C] : PLAZA 3b

tom /ˈtɑːm/ *n* [C] **1** : TOMCAT **2** : a male turkey

tom·a·hawk /ˈtɑːmɪˌhɑːk/ *n* [C] : a small ax used as a weapon by Native Americans

to·ma·to /təˈmeɪtoʊ, *Brit* təˈmɑːtoʊ/ *n, pl* **-toes** [C] : a round, soft, red fruit that is eaten raw or cooked ▪ *crushed tomatoes* ▪ *tomato soup/sauce/paste/juice*

tomb /ˈtuːm/ *n* [C] : a building or chamber above or below the ground in which a dead body is kept

tom·boy /ˈtɑːmˌbɔɪ/ *n* [C] : a girl who enjoys things that people think are more suited to boys — **tom·boy·ish** /ˈtɑːmˌbɔɪʃ/ *adj*

tomb·stone /ˈtuːmˌstoʊn/ *n* [C] : GRAVESTONE

tom·cat /ˈtɑːmˌkæt/ *n* [C] : a male cat

Tom, Dick, and Har·ry /ˌtɑːmˌdɪkənd-ˈheri/ *n* — **any/every Tom, Dick, and Harry** *informal* : any person ▪ *We don't just give jobs to every Tom, Dick, and Harry who walks in here.*

tome /ˈtoʊm/ *n* [C] *formal* : a very large, thick book

tom·fool·ery /ˌtɑːmˈfuːləri/ *n* [U] *old-fashioned* : playful or silly behavior

¹**to·mor·row** /təˈmɑroʊ/ *n* **1** [U] : the day after today ▪ *Tomorrow is a school day.* ▪ *tomorrow's meeting* **2** [U, *singular*] : the future ▪ *Who knows what tomorrow*

may bring? ▪ *hoping for a better tomorrow* — **like there's no tomorrow** : in a quick and careless way without any thought about the future ▪ *He's spending money like there's no tomorrow.*

²**tomorrow** *adv* : on, during, or for the day after today ▪ *I'll do it tomorrow.*

ton /ˈtʌn/ *n* [C] **1** *pl also* **ton a** *US* : a unit for measuring weight that equals 2,000 pounds (907 kilograms) **b** *Brit* : a unit for measuring weight that equals 2,240 pounds (1,016 kilograms) **2** *informal* : a large amount ▪ *I have a ton of work to do.* ▪ *Her purse weighs a ton.* — **like a ton of bricks** see ¹BRICK

ton·al /ˈtoʊnl/ *adj* **1** *technical* : of or relating to musical or color tones ▪ *tonal variations* **2** *music* : having or based in a particular key ▪ *tonal music* — **to·nal·i·ty** /toʊˈnæləti/ *n, pl* **-ties** [C/U] — **ton·al·ly** *adv*

¹**tone** /ˈtoʊn/ *n* **1** [C] **a** : the quality of a person's voice ▪ *a friendly tone* ▪ *Don't use that rude tone of voice with me.* **b** : the quality of a sound produced by a musical instrument or singing voice ▪ *the low tones of an organ* **2** [C] **a** : a quality, feeling, or attitude expressed by the words that someone uses in speaking or writing ▪ *The speech had religious tones.* **b** : the general quality of a place, situation, etc. ▪ *The seriousness of his opening words set the tone for/of the meeting.* [=established that the meeting would be serious] **3** [C] **a** : a shade of color ▪ *a dark tone of blue* ▪ *the soft tones of the painting* **b** : a small amount of a color ▪ *gray with a bluish tone* **4** [U] : strength and firmness of the muscles or skin ▪ *These exercises help build muscle tone.* **5** [U] : the highness or lowness of a spoken syllable ▪ *a rising/falling tone* **6** [C] : a sound made as a signal by a machine (such as an answering machine) ▪ *Please leave a message after the tone.* **7** [C] *music* **a** : a sound of a particular pitch and vibration ▪ *the different tones [=notes] of a musical scale* **b** *chiefly Brit* : WHOLE STEP

²**tone** *vb* **toned; ton·ing** [T] : to give strength and firmness to (muscles, skin, etc.) ▪ *exercising to tone (up) your stomach muscles* — **tone down** *or* **tone down (something)** *phrasal vb* **tone (something) down** *or* **tone down (something)** **1** : to make (something) less forceful, offensive, or harsh ▪ *Please tone down your language.* **2** : to make (something) less bright or colorful ▪ *She toned down her wardrobe.*

tone–deaf /ˈtoʊnˌdɛf/ *adj* : unable to hear the difference between musical notes or sing the right musical notes

tongs /ˈtɑːŋz/ *n* [*plural*] : a tool used for lifting or holding objects that is made of two long pieces connected at one end or in the middle ▪ *a pair of ice/salad tongs*

tongue /ˈtʌŋ/ *n* **1 a** [C] : the soft, movable part in the mouth that is used for tasting and eating food and in human beings for speaking ▪ *The hot soup burned my tongue.* **b** [C/U] : the tongue of an animal (such as an ox or sheep) that is eaten as food **2** [C] : LANGUAGE ▪ *He spoke in a foreign tongue.* — see also

MOTHER TONGUE **3** [C] : a particular way or quality of speaking ▪ *His sharp/ quick tongue is going to get him into trouble someday.* ▪ *Watch your tongue!* [=don't say rude or offensive things] **4** [C] : something that is shaped like a tongue ▪ *tongues of fire/flame* **5** [C] : a long flap that is under the laces or buckles of a shoe **6** [C] : a long, raised part at the end of a board that extends out and fits into a long cut (called a groove) in another board — *a slip of the tongue* see ²SLIP — *bite your tongue* see ¹BITE — *Cat got your tongue?* see CAT — *get your tongue around* *informal* ✧ If you cannot *get your tongue around* a word or phrase, you have difficulty saying it. — *hold your tongue* see ¹HOLD — *loosen someone's tongue* see LOOSEN — *on the tip of your tongue* see ²TIP — *roll/trip off the tongue* : to be easy to say or pronounce ▪ *The name just rolls off the tongue.* — *speak in tongues* ✧ Someone who is *speaking in tongues* is saying strange words that no one can understand, especially as part of a religious experience. — *speak/talk with (a) forked tongue* see FORKED — *tongues (are) wagging* ✧ If something *sets/gets tongues wagging* or if *tongues are wagging*, people are talking a lot about something. ▪ *Their engagement set tongues wagging.*

tongue in cheek *adv* : in a way that is not serious and that is meant to be funny ▪ *The interview was done tongue in cheek.* — **tongue–in–cheek** *adj*

tongue–lash·ing *n* [C] *informal* : a severe scolding ▪ *She gave him a tongue-lashing.*

tongue–tied /ˈtʌŋˌtaɪd/ *adj* : unable to speak because you are nervous or shy ▪ *She became tongue-tied whenever he was around.*

tongue twister *n* [C] : a word, name, phrase, or sentence that is hard to say ▪ *Her name is a real tongue twister.*

ton·ic /ˈtɑːnɪk/ *n* **1** [C/U] : a type of water that has bubbles in it, has a bitter taste, and is often used in alcoholic drinks ▪ *gin and tonic* — called also *tonic water* **2** [C] **a** : something that makes you feel healthier and more relaxed ▪ *To her, music is a tonic.* **b** : a medicine that brings you back to a normal physical or mental condition ▪ *an herbal tonic* **c** *somewhat old-fashioned* : a liquid that is used on your hair to make it healthier ▪ *a hair tonic*

¹**to·night** /təˈnaɪt/ *n* [U] : this night or the night following this day ▪ *Tonight will be rainy.*

²**tonight** *adv* : on this night or on the night following this day ▪ *He's leaving tonight.*

ton·nage /ˈtʌnɪdʒ/ *n* [C/U] **1** : the size of a ship or the total weight that it carries in tons **2** : the total weight or amount of something in tons

ton·sil /ˈtɑːnsəl/ *n* [C] : either one of the pair of round, soft parts on the inside of your throat ▪ *He had his tonsils out.* [=had an operation to remove his tonsils]

ton·sil·lec·to·my /ˌtɑːnsəˈlɛktəmi/ *n, pl*

-**mies** [C] *medical* : an operation to remove a person's tonsils

ton·sil·li·tis /ˌtɑːnsəˈlaɪtɪs/ *n* [U] *medical* : a condition in which a person's tonsils are painful and swollen

tony /ˈtoʊni/ *adj* **ton·i·er; -est** *US, informal* : very expensive and fashionable ▪ *tony restaurants*

too /ˈtuː/ *adv* **1** *usually at the end of a sentence or clause* : ALSO ▪ *We sold the house and the furniture too.* ▪ *"I'm hungry." "Me too."* **2** *always before an adjective or adverb* : more than what is wanted, needed, acceptable, possible, etc. ▪ *The soup is too hot.* ▪ *You gave me too many cards.* ▪ *You're talking too fast.* ▪ *Thank you for your donation. You are too kind.* [=you are very kind] ▪ *Her efforts were too little, too late.* [=her efforts were not enough and not soon enough to make a difference] ▪ *She knew all/only too well* [=unfortunately, she knew very well] *what he would say.* **3** : very or extremely — used in negative statements ▪ *She's not doing too well.* ▪ *He was none too pleased* [=he was not pleased] *to see me.* **4** *chiefly US, informal* : most certainly ▪ *"You're not strong enough to lift that box." "I am too." "I am too."* [=yes, I am]

took *past tense of* ¹TAKE

¹**tool** /ˈtuːl/ *n* [C] **1** : something (such as a hammer, saw, shovel, etc.) that you hold in your hand and use for a particular task **2 a** : something that is used to do a job or activity ▪ *Words are a writer's tools.* **b** : something that helps to get or achieve something ▪ *The Internet has become an important research tool.* **3** *disapproving* **a** : someone or something that is used or controlled by another person or group ▪ *a politician who is just a tool of special interests* **b** *informal* : a foolish person who can easily be used or tricked by others ▪ *He's such a tool.*

²**tool** *vb* **1** [I] *US, informal* : to drive or ride in a vehicle ▪ *We tooled along/up/ down the highway.* **2** [T] : to shape, form, or finish (something) with a tool ▪ *tool a design on a leather belt* — **tooled** *leather*

tool·bar /ˈtuːlˌbɑɚ/ *n* [C] : a row of icons on a computer screen that allow you to do various things when you are using a particular program

tool·box /ˈtuːlˌbɑːks/ *n* [C] : a box for storing or carrying tools

tool kit *n* [C] : a set of tools

toot /ˈtuːt/ *vb* [T/I] : to make a short, high sound with a horn or whistle ▪ *She tooted (her horn) at me as she drove past.* — *toot your own horn* see ¹HORN — **toot** *n* [C]

tooth /ˈtuːθ/ *n, pl* **teeth** /ˈtiːθ/ **1** [C] : one of the hard white objects inside the mouth that are used for biting and chewing ▪ *Brush your teeth.* ▪ *She sank her teeth into* [=bit] *the apple.* **2** [C] : a sharp or pointed object that sticks out of something and is part of a row of similar objects ▪ *the teeth of a saw/comb* **3** [*plural*] : the power that makes something effective ▪ *The labor union showed that it has teeth.* — *by the skin of your teeth* see ¹SKIN — *cut a tooth, cut your*

teeth see ¹*CUT* — *fly in the teeth of* see ¹*FLY* — *get your teeth into* or chiefly US *sink your teeth into* : to become fully involved in (something) ▪ *He finally has a project he can get his teeth into.* — *grit your teeth* see ²*GRIT* — *in the teeth of* **1** or *into the teeth of* : directly against (a strong wind, storm, etc.) ▪ *sailing in/into the teeth of the wind* **2** : despite (something) ▪ *A shopping mall was built in the teeth of fierce opposition.* — *like pulling teeth* — used to say that something is very difficult and frustrating ▪ *Getting him to make a decision is like pulling teeth.* — *long in the tooth informal* : no longer young : OLD ▪ *Isn't she a little long in the tooth for those kinds of antics?* — *set your teeth on edge* ◇ If a sound, taste, etc., *sets your teeth on edge*, it makes your body feel tense or uncomfortable. — *tooth and nail* : with a lot of effort and determination ▪ *They fought tooth and nail.* — *to the teeth* : fully or completely ▪ *They were armed to the teeth.* [=they had a lot of weapons] —
tooth·less /ˈtuːθləs/ *adj* ▪ *a toothless person/smile*

tooth·ache /ˈtuːθˌeɪk/ *n* [C/U] : pain in or near a tooth ▪ *He has a toothache.*

tooth·brush /ˈtuːθˌbrʌʃ/ *n* [C] : a brush for cleaning your teeth

tooth·paste /ˈtuːθˌpeɪst/ *n* [U] : a substance that is used for cleaning teeth ▪ *a tube of toothpaste*

tooth·pick /ˈtuːθˌpɪk/ *n* [C] : a short, pointed stick used for removing small pieces of food from between your teeth

toothy /ˈtuːθi/ *adj* **tooth·i·er**; **-est** : having or showing many teeth ▪ *a toothy grin*

toots /ˈtuːts/ *n* [U] US slang, old-fashioned — used to address a woman or girl ▪ *How are you, toots?* ◇ *Toots* is often used in a joking way but may be considered offensive.

¹**top** /ˈtɑːp/ *n* **1 a** [C] : the highest part, point, or level of something ▪ *the top of the stairs/mountain* **b** [C] : an upper surface or edge of something ▪ *a table with a glass top* **c** [C] : something that covers the upper part or opening of something ▪ *The box's top had been removed.* **d** [U] : the highest position in rank, success, or importance ▪ *He is at the top of his profession.* ▪ *He graduated at the top of his/the class.* [=his grades were among the highest in his class] ▪ *The order came straight from the top.* [=from the person with the most authority or power] **2** [C] : a piece of clothing that is worn on the upper part of your body ▪ *a blue silk top* **3** [U] *informal* : the beginning ▪ *We'll have another news update for you at the top of the hour.* [=at the start of the next hour] ▪ *Let's rehearse the scene from the top.* ▪ *Let's take it from the top.* [=start from the beginning of a scene, song, etc.] **4** [*singular*] : the first half of an inning in baseball ▪ *the top of the sixth inning* **5** [U] *chiefly Brit* : the part of something (such as a street) that is farthest away ▪ *Try the shop at the top of the road.* **6** [C] : a child's toy that can be made to spin very quickly — *at the top of your voice/lungs* : in the loudest

way possible ▪ *They were shouting at the top of their lungs.* — *blow your top* see ¹*BLOW* — *come out on top* : to win a competition, argument, etc. ▪ *He's confident that he'll come out on top when all the votes have been counted.* — *from top to bottom* : in a very thorough way ▪ *We cleaned/searched the house from top to bottom.* — *off the top of your head informal* : immediately by thinking quickly about something ▪ *I can't remember her name off the top of my head.* — *on top* **1** : on the highest part or surface of something ▪ *vanilla ice cream with chocolate sauce on top* **2** *chiefly Brit* : winning a game or competition ▪ *The team was on top after the first half.* — *on top of* **1** : on the highest or upper part of (something or someone) ▪ *The house sits on top of a hill.* **2** : doing the things that are needed to deal with (something) ▪ *"Can you get this done by next week?" "Don't worry. I'm on top of it."* ▪ *She is on top of her game.* [=she is performing well] **3** : aware of what is happening in (a particular area of activity) ▪ *She tries to keep/stay on top of current events.* **4** : very close to or near (someone or something) ▪ *The deadline is on top of us.* ▪ *The houses are built right on top of each other.* **5** : in addition to (something) ▪ *On top of everything else, he lost his job.* — *on top of the world informal* : in a very successful or happy state ▪ *The newlyweds were on top of the world.* — *over the top informal* : beyond what is expected, usual, normal, or appropriate ▪ *His performances are always over the top.*

²**top** *adj, usually before a noun* **1** : located at the highest part or position ▪ *the top shelf* **2** : highest in rank, success, or importance ▪ *a top student* ▪ *Safety is our top concern.* **3** : highest in quality, amount, or degree ▪ *the car's top speed*

³**top** *vb* **topped; top·ping** [T] **1** : to be or become more than (a particular amount) ▪ *Album sales topped 500,000.* **2** : to be in the highest position on (a list) because of success ▪ *The song topped the charts.* **3** : to do or be better than (someone or something) ▪ *He topped his previous record.* **4** : to cover or form the top of (something) ▪ *A fresh layer of snow topped the mountains.* ▪ *She topped the pizza with cheese and mushrooms.* ▪ *a cup of hot chocolate topped (off) with whip cream* **5** : to cut off the top of (something) ▪ *top a tree* **6** *literary* : to reach the top of (something) ▪ *We topped the hill.* — *top off* [*phrasal vb*] *top off (something)* or *top (something) off* **1** : to end (something) usually in an exciting or impressive way ▪ *The victory tops off the coach's successful career.* **2** *US* : to fill (something) completely with a liquid ▪ *I top off a mug.* — *top out* [*phrasal vb*] : to reach the highest amount or level and stop increasing ▪ *Interest rates are expected to top out at 15 percent.* — *top up* [*phrasal vb*] *top up (something)* or *top (something) up Brit* : to fill (something) completely with a liquid ▪ *top up a glass of water* — *to top it (all) off* (US) or chiefly Brit *to top it all* — used to indicate a fi-

nal thing that happened that was even better, worse, etc., than what happened before ▪ *The car was filthy when she returned it to me, and to top it all off, there was almost no gas left in the tank.*

to·paz /'toʊˌpæz/ *n* [C/U] : a clear yellow to brownish-yellow stone that is used as a jewel

top brass *n* [U] *informal* : BRASS 4 ▪ *Navy top brass met earlier today.*

top·coat /'tɑːpˌkoʊt/ *n* [C] **1** *somewhat old-fashioned* : a long coat the is worn in cold weather **2** : the last layer of paint that is put on a surface

top dollar *n* [U] : the highest amount of money that something costs or that someone earns ▪ *She paid top dollar* [=a lot of money] *for the tickets.*

top hat *n* [C] : a tall, usually black hat that is worn by men on very formal occasions

top–heavy /'tɑːpˌhɛvi/ *adj* **1** : likely to fall over because the top part is too large and heavy for the bottom part ▪ *a top-heavy truck* **2** : having too many people whose job is to manage workers and not enough ordinary workers ▪ *a top-heavy corporation*

to·pi·ary /'toʊpiˌeri, *Brit* 'təʊpiəri/ *n* [U] : plants (such as trees and bushes) that are cut or grown into decorative shapes ▪ *a topiary garden; also* : the art of shaping plants in this way

top·ic /'tɑːpɪk/ *n* [C] : someone or something that people talk or write about : SUBJECT ▪ *We discussed a wide range of topics.* ▪ *a topic of conversation*

top·i·cal /'tɑːpɪkəl/ *adj* **1** : dealing with things that are important, popular, etc., right now ▪ *topical issues/humor* **2** *medical* : made to be put on the skin ▪ *topical drugs/lotions* — **top·i·cal·ly** /'tɑːpɪkli/ *adv* — **top·i·cal·i·ty** /ˌtɑːpəˈkæləti/ *n* [U]

top·less /'tɑːpləs/ *adj* **1** *of a woman* : wearing no clothing on the upper body ▪ *topless dancers* **2** : done while not wearing any clothing on the upper body ▪ *topless sunbathing* **3** : having or allowing topless women ▪ *a topless beach* — **topless** *adv*

top·most /'tɑːpˌmoʊst/ *adj, always before a noun* : highest in position or importance ▪ *the topmost step* ▪ *the country's topmost leaders*

top–notch /'tɑːpˈnɑːtʃ/ *adj, informal* : of the best quality ▪ *The hotel offers top-notch service.*

to·pog·ra·phy /təˈpɑːgrəfi/ *n* [U] *technical* **1** : the art or science of making maps that show the height, shape, etc., of the land in a particular area **2** : the features (such as mountains and rivers) in an area of land ▪ *The map shows the topography of the island.* — **to·pog·ra·pher** /təˈpɑːgrəfɚ/ *n* [C] — **to·po·graph·ic** /ˌtɑːpəˈgræfɪk/ *or* **to·po·graph·i·cal** /ˌtɑːpəˈgræfɪkəl/ *adj*

top·ping /'tɑːpɪŋ/ *n* [C/U] : a food that is added to the top of another food ▪ *pizza toppings*

top·ple /'tɑːpəl/ *vb* **top·pled; top·pling 1** [T/I] : to cause (something) to become unsteady and fall ▪ *Wind toppled the tree.*

▪ *The pile of books toppled over.* **2** [T] **a** : to remove (a government or a leader) from power ▪ *The rebels toppled the dictator.* **b** *US* : to win a victory over (someone or something) in a war, contest, etc. ▪ *The company has toppled its competition.*

top–ranking *adj, always before a noun* : having the highest rank ▪ *a top-ranking school*

¹tops /'tɑːps/ *adj, not before a noun, informal* : highest in quality, ability, popularity, or importance ▪ *He is tops in his field.*

²tops *adv, informal* : at the very most ▪ *It takes me 15 minutes tops* [=no more than 15 minutes] *to do the dishes.*

top secret *adj* : kept completely secret by high government officials ▪ *a top secret mission*

top·side /'tɑːpˌsaɪd/ *adv* : on or onto the deck of a ship ▪ *Let's go topside.*

top·soil /'tɑːpˌsojəl/ *n* [U] : the upper layer of soil in which plants have most of their roots

top·sy–tur·vy /ˌtɑːpsiˈtɚvi/ *adv* : in or into great disorder or confusion ▪ *Her life was turned topsy-turvy when her husband left her.* — **topsy–turvy** *adj*

To·rah /'torə/ *n — the Torah* **1** : the wisdom and law contained in Jewish sacred writings and oral tradition **2** : the first five books of the Jewish Bible that are used in a synagogue for religious services

¹torch /'toɚtʃ/ *n* [C] **1** : a long stick with material at one end that burns brightly ▪ *the Olympic torch* **2** : BLOWTORCH **3** *Brit* : FLASHLIGHT — **carry a torch** : to continue to have romantic feelings for someone who does not love you ▪ *Is she still carrying a torch for him?* — **carry the torch** : to support or promote a cause in an enthusiastic way ▪ *His children continue to carry the torch for justice.* — **pass the torch** *chiefly US* ◇ If you **pass the torch (on)** or **pass on the torch**, you give your job, duties, etc., to another person. ▪ *He is retiring and passing the torch on to his successor.*

²torch *vb* [T] : to set fire to (something, such as a building) deliberately ▪ *An arsonist torched the warehouse.*

tore *past tense of* ¹TEAR

¹tor·ment /'toɚˌmɛnt/ *n* **1** [U] : extreme physical or mental pain ▪ *inner torment* **2** [C] : something that causes extreme physical or mental pain ▪ *The mosquitoes were a constant torment.*

²tor·ment /toɚˈmɛnt/ *vb* [T] : to cause (someone or something) to feel extreme physical or mental pain ▪ *He was tormented by thoughts of death.* ▪ *Stop tormenting* [=annoying, teasing] *your sister!* — **tor·men·tor** /toɚˈmɛntɚ/ *n* [C]

torn *past participle of* ¹TEAR

tor·na·do /toɚˈneɪdoʊ/ *n, pl* **-does** *or* **-dos** [C] : a violent and destructive storm in which powerful winds move around a central point ▪ *in the path of a tornado*

¹tor·pe·do /toɚˈpiːdoʊ/ *n, pl* **-does** [C] : a bomb that is shaped like a tube and that is fired underwater

²torpedo *vb* **-does; -doed; -do·ing** [T] **1** : to hit or sink (a ship) with a torpedo ▪

The submarine torpedoed the battleship.
2 *somewhat informal* : to destroy or stop (something) completely ▪ *He torpedoed the plan.*

tor·pid /ˈtoɚpəd/ *adj, formal* : having or showing very little energy or movement ▪ *a torpid state ▪ a torpid economy*

tor·por /ˈtoɚpɚ/ *n* [*singular*] *formal* : a state of not being active and having very little energy ▪ *The news aroused him from his torpor.*

torque /ˈtoɚk/ *n* [U] *technical* : a force that causes something to rotate ▪ *An automobile engine delivers torque to the driveshaft.*

tor·rent /ˈtorənt/ *n* [C] **1** : a large amount of water that moves very quickly in one direction ▪ *a raging torrent ▪ The rain came down in torrents.* **2** : a large amount of something that is released suddenly ▪ *a torrent of criticism/e-mail*

tor·ren·tial /təˈrɛnʃəl/ *adj, always before a noun* : coming in a large, fast stream ▪ *torrential rains/flooding*

tor·rid /ˈtorəd/ *adj* **1** : very hot and usually dry ▪ *torrid weather* **2** : showing or expressing very strong feelings especially of sexual or romantic desire ▪ *a torrid love affair*

tor·so /ˈtoɚsoʊ/ *n, pl* **-sos** [C] : the main part of the human body not including the head, arms, and legs

tort /ˈtoɚt/ *n* [C] *law* : an action that wrongly causes harm to someone but that is not a crime and that is dealt with in a civil court

tor·tel·li·ni /ˌtoɚtəˈliːni/ *n, pl* **tortellini** *also* **tor·tel·li·nis** [C] : pasta in the form of small, ring-shaped cases containing meat, cheese, etc.

tor·til·la /toɚˈtiːjə/ *n* [C] : a round, thin Mexican bread that is usually eaten hot with a filling of meat, cheese, etc.

tor·toise /ˈtoɚtəs/ *n* [C] : a kind of turtle that lives on land

tor·toise·shell /ˈtoɚtəˌʃɛl/ *n* [C/U] : the usually brown and yellow shell of a turtle that is used to make decorations

tor·tu·ous /ˈtoɚtʃəwəs/ *adj* **1** : having many twists and turns ▪ *a tortuous path* **2** : complicated, long, and confusing ▪ *a tortuous explanation* — **tor·tu·ous·ly** *adv*

¹**tor·ture** /ˈtoɚtʃɚ/ *n* [U] **1** : the act of causing severe physical pain as a form of punishment or as a way to force someone to do or say something ▪ *the torture of prisoners ▪ a torture chamber/device* **2** : a very painful or unpleasant experience ▪ *Waiting is torture for me.*

²**torture** *vb* **-tured; -tur·ing** [T] **1** : to cause (someone) to experience severe physical pain especially as a form of punishment or to force that person to do or say something ▪ *The prisoners had been repeatedly tortured.* **2** : to cause (someone) to feel very worried, unhappy, etc. ▪ *Don't torture yourself over the mistake.* — **tor·tur·er** /ˈtoɚtʃərɚ/ *n* [C]

tor·tur·ous /ˈtoɚtʃərəs/ *adj* : causing great pain or suffering ▪ *torturous hardship*

To·ry /ˈtori/ *n, pl* **-ries** [C] *informal* : a member of the British Conservative Party — **Tory** *adj*

¹**toss** /ˈtɑːs/ *vb* **1** [T] : to throw (something) with a quick, light motion ▪ *I tossed the ball to him.* = *I tossed him the ball.* **2** [T] : to move or lift (a part of your body) quickly or suddenly ▪ *He tossed his head back.* **3** [T/I] : to move (something) back and forth or up and down ▪ *Waves tossed the ship about.* ▪ *The ship tossed on the waves.* **4** [T] : to stir or mix (something) lightly ▪ *Toss the salad.* **5** [T/I] : to cause (something) to turn over by throwing it into the air ▪ *toss a coin* — **toss and turn** : to move about and turn over in bed because you are unable to sleep ▪ *I tossed and turned all night.* — **toss back** [*phrasal vb*] **toss back (something)** *or* **toss (something) back** *informal* : to drink (something) quickly ▪ *He tossed back a shot of whiskey.* — **toss in** [*phrasal vb*] **toss in (something)** *or* **toss (something) in** : to add (something) to what you are selling without asking for more money ▪ *I'll even toss in a free upgrade.* — **toss off** [*phrasal vb*] *informal* **toss (something) off** *or* **toss off (something)** **1** : to produce (something) quickly and without much effort ▪ *He tossed off a new poem.* **2** : to drink (something) quickly ▪ *She tossed off a shot of whiskey.* — **toss out** [*phrasal vb*] *US* **1** **toss (something) out** *or* **toss out (something)** **a** : to put (something) in a trash can, garbage can, etc. ▪ *It's time to toss out* [=*throw out*] *those bananas.* **b** : to refuse to accept or consider (something) ▪ *His testimony was tossed out by the judge.* **c** : to mention (something) as a possible thing to be done, thought about, etc. ▪ *She tossed out a couple of suggestions.* **2** **toss (someone) out** *or* **toss out (someone)** : to force (someone) to leave a place ▪ *They tossed him out of the bar.*

²**toss** *n* [C] **1** : the act of throwing or tossing something with a quick, light motion ▪ *a quick toss to first base* **2** : the act of throwing a coin up into the air in order to make a decision about something based on which side of the coin is shown after it lands ▪ *She won the toss.* **3** : the act of moving your head suddenly upward and backward ▪ *a toss of her head* — **not give a toss** *Brit, informal* : to not care at all about something ▪ *He doesn't give a toss about our problems.*

toss–up /ˈtɑːsˌʌp/ *n* [*singular*] : a situation in which there is no clear right choice or in which what will happen is not known ▪ *The election is a toss-up.*

¹**tot** /ˈtɑːt/ *n* [C] *informal* : a young child

²**tot** *vb* **tot·ted; tot·ting** — **tot up** [*phrasal vb*] **tot (something) up** *or* **tot up (something)** *Brit, informal* : to add numbers together to find out the total ▪ *He totted up* [=*totaled*] *the bill.*

¹**to·tal** /ˈtoʊtl/ *adj* **1** : complete or absolute ▪ *total chaos/control/freedom* **2** : after everything or everyone is counted ▪ *the total amount of the bill*

²**total** *n* [C] : the number or amount of everything counted ▪ *The total is 64.*

³**total** *vb, US* **-taled** *or Brit* **-talled;** *US* **-tal·ing** *or Brit* **-tal·ling** [*T*] **1 a :** to produce (a total) when added together ▪ *Donations totaled $120.* **b :** to add numbers together to find out the total ▪ *He totaled (up) the bill.* **2** *US* **:** to damage (something) so badly that it is not worth repairing ▪ *He totaled the car.*

to·tal·i·tar·i·an /toʊˌtæləˈterijən/ *adj* **:** controlling the people of a country in a very strict way with complete power that cannot be opposed ▪ *a totalitarian regime* — **to·tal·i·tar·i·an·ism** /toʊˌtæləˈterijəˌnɪzəm/ *n* [*U*]

to·tal·i·ty /toʊˈtæləti/ *n* [*U*] **:** the whole or entire amount of something ▪ *the totality of human knowledge* — **in its/their totality :** with nothing left out ▪ *The exhibit is best viewed in its totality.*

to·tal·ly /ˈtoʊtli/ *adv* **:** completely or entirely ▪ *He was totally naked.* ▪ *a totally new method*

tote /ˈtoʊt/ *vb* **tot·ed; tot·ing** [*T*] **:** carry (something) ▪ *He's always toting tools around.* — **tot·er** /ˈtoʊtɚ/ *n* [*C*]

tote bag *n* [*C*] **:** a large bag used for carrying things

to·tem /ˈtoʊtəm/ *n* [*C*] **1 a :** something (such as an animal or plant) that is the symbol for a family, tribe, etc., especially among Native Americans **b :** a usually carved or painted figure that represents such a symbol **2 :** a person or thing that represents an idea ▪ *Livestock are a totem of success in that culture.*

totem pole *n* [*C*] **1 :** a tall usually wooden pole that is carved and painted with symbols, figures, or masks which represent different Native American tribes **2** *US, informal* — used to describe someone's position or level in a company or organization ▪ *She's low on the company's totem pole.* [=she does not have an important position]

tot·ter /ˈtɑːtɚ/ *vb* [*I*] **1 :** to move or walk in a slow and unsteady way ▪ *He tottered off to bed.* **2 :** to become weak and likely to fail or collapse ▪ *a tottering company*

tou·can /ˈtuːˌkæn/ *n* [*C*] **:** a tropical American bird that has bright feathers and a very large beak

¹**touch** /ˈtʌtʃ/ *vb* **1** [*T/I*] **:** to put your hand, fingers, etc., on someone or something ▪ *Do not touch the statue.* ▪ *Look but don't touch.* ▪ *Touch your toes.* ▪ *Stop touching me!* **2** [*T/I*] **:** to be in contact with (something) ▪ *His head almost touches the ceiling.* ▪ *Don't let the wires touch (each other).* **3** [*T*] **a :** to change or move (something) ▪ *Don't touch anything before the police come.* **b :** to harm (someone or something) ▪ *I won't let anyone touch you.* **4** [*T*] **a :** to deal with or work on (something) ▪ *I haven't touched my essay yet.* **b :** to become involved with (someone or something) ▪ *Since the scandal, no team will touch him.* ▪ *(figurative) I wouldn't touch that job with a ten-foot pole.* **5** [*T*] **:** to eat, drink, or use (something) ▪ *You haven't touched your food.* ▪ *They didn't have to touch their savings.* ▪ *Alcohol? I never touch the stuff.* **6** [*T*] **a :** to affect, involve, or influence (someone) ▪ *a matter that touches every-*

one ▪ *a teacher who touched the lives of many students* **b :** to cause (someone) to feel sympathy, gratitude, etc. ▪ *Their kindness touched him.* ▪ *a story that touched our hearts* **7** [*T*] **:** to be as good as (someone or something) ▪ *No other athlete can touch her.* **8** [*T*] *chiefly Brit* **:** to reach (a particular level or amount) ▪ *temperatures touching 38 degrees* — **touch a nerve** see NERVE — **touch down** [*phrasal vb*] **:** ²LAND 1a ▪ *The plane touched down at 3:15.* — **touch off** [*phrasal vb*] **touch off (something) or touch (something) off :** to cause (something) to start suddenly ▪ *The verdict touched off riots.* — **touch on/upon** [*phrasal vb*] **1 :** to mention (something) briefly ▪ *The report touches on many important points.* **2 :** to almost be (something) ▪ *actions that touch on treason* — **touch up** [*phrasal vb*] **touch up (something) or touch (something) up :** to improve (something) by making small changes ▪ *touch up a photograph*

²**touch** *n* **1** [*C*] **:** the act of touching someone or something ▪ *He felt a touch on his arm.* ▪ *sending emails with/at the touch of a button* **2** [*U*] **:** the sense that allows you to be aware of physical things by touching them ▪ *your sense of touch* ▪ *The surface was hot/smooth to the touch.* **3** [*singular*] **:** the quality of a thing that is experienced by feeling or touching it ▪ *the touch [=feel] of silk* **4** [*C*] **:** a small detail that is added to improve or complete something ▪ *The flowers add a nice touch to the room.* ▪ *putting the final touches on a letter* **5** [*singular*] **:** a quality that can be seen in the way something is done ▪ *service with a personal touch* — **a touch :** to a small extent ▪ SLIGHTLY ▪ *She aimed a touch too low and missed.* — **a touch of :** a small amount of (something) ▪ *Add a touch of vinegar.* ▪ *I have a touch of the flu.* — **in touch 1 :** in a state in which people communicate with each other ▪ *We kept/stayed in touch after college.* ▪ *I'll be/get in touch (with you).* [=I will contact you] **2 a :** the state of being aware of what is happening, how people feel, etc. ▪ *keeping/staying in touch with the latest research* **b :** the state of being aware of a particular part of your character ▪ *He is in touch with his sensitive side.* — **lose touch 1 :** to stop communicating with each other ▪ *They moved to different cities and lost touch.* ▪ *I lost touch with her.* **2 :** to stop knowing what is happening, how people feel, etc. ▪ *We're losing touch with our history.* ▪ *She has lost touch with reality.* [=she believes things that are not true] — **lose your touch :** to no longer be able to do things that you were able to do in the past ▪ *His last album flopped; he must be losing his touch.* — **out of touch 1 :** not communicating with each other ▪ *We've been out of touch for some time.* **2 :** in a state of not knowing what is happening, how people feel, etc. ▪ *He is out of touch with younger voters.*

touch and go *adj, informal* — used to describe a situation in which no one is sure what will happen and there is a chance that the result will be bad ▪ *It was touch and go there for a while, but the patient survived.*

touch·down /'tʌʃˌdaʊn/ *n* [*C*] **1** *American football* : a score worth six points that is made by carrying the ball over the opponent's goal line or by catching the ball while standing in the end zone ▪ *He scored a touchdown.* ▪ *throw a touchdown (pass)* **2** : the moment when an airplane or spacecraft touches the ground at the end of a flight

tou·ché /tuˈʃeɪ/ *interj* — used to admit that someone has made a clever or effective point

touched /'tʌʃt/ *adj, not before a noun* **1** : having a small amount of something ▪ *His hair was touched with gray.* **2** : feeling emotional because you are grateful or pleased ▪ *She was touched that he cared.* ▪ *I was very touched by their story.*

touch·ing /'tʌʃɪŋ/ *adj* : causing feelings of sadness or sympathy ▪ *a deeply/very touching story* — **touch·ing·ly** *adv*

touch·line /'tʌʃˌlaɪn/ *n* [*C*] : either one of the lines that mark the long sides of the playing field in rugby or soccer

touch·stone /'tʌʃˌstoʊn/ *n* [*C*] : a trait or characteristic that is used to judge the quality of something ▪ *Good service is one touchstone of a first-class restaurant.*

touchy /'tʌʃi/ *adj* **touch·i·er; -est** **1** : easily hurt or upset by the things that people think or say about you : SENSITIVE ▪ *He's touchy about his weight.* **2** : likely to cause people to become upset ▪ *a touchy subject* — **touch·i·ness** /'tʌʃinəs/ *n* [*U*]

touchy–feely /ˌtʌʃiˈfiːli/ *adj, informal + usually disapproving* : tending to show emotions very openly ▪ *touchy-feely people*

¹**tough** /'tʌf/ *adj* **1** : very difficult to do or deal with ▪ *a tough job/problem/choice* ▪ *She had a tough time in college.* ▪ *It was tough to quit smoking.* ▪ *It's been a tough year for us.* = *This year has been tough on us.* **2 a** : physically and emotionally strong ▪ *tough soldiers* **b** : physically strong and violent ▪ *tough criminals* **3 a** : strong and not easily broken or damaged ▪ *tough fibers/material* **b** : difficult to cut or chew ▪ *tough meat* **4** : very strict ▪ *a tough law/policy* ▪ *a tough boss/teacher* ▪ *getting tough on crime* **5** : having a lot of crime or danger ▪ *a tough neighborhood* **6** : hard to influence or persuade ▪ *a tough negotiator* **7** *informal* : unfortunate in a way that seems unfair ▪ *It's tough that he lost that job.* — often used in an ironic way ▪ *He failed the test? Tough! He should have studied more.* — **tough** *adv* ▪ *play/talk tough* [=in a way that shows you are strong or strict] — **tough·ly** *adv* — **tough·ness** *n* [*U*]

²**tough** *vb* — **tough it out** *informal* : to deal with a difficult situation by being determined and refusing to quit ▪ *Can you tough it out until the end of the game?*

tough·en /'tʌfən/ *vb* [*T/I*] **1** : to make (something) stricter or to become stricter ▪ *toughen (up) antidrug laws* ▪ *The laws have toughened up.* **2** : to make (some-

one) stronger or to become stronger ▪ *The experience toughened him (up).* ▪ *You need to toughen up.*

tough·ie /'tʌfi/ *n* [*C*] *informal* : a difficult problem or question ▪ *The last question was a toughie.*

tough love *n* [*U*] : love or concern that is expressed in a strict way especially to make someone behave responsibly

tou·pee /tuˈpeɪ/ *n* [*C*] : a small wig that is worn by a man to cover a bald spot on his head

¹**tour** /'tʊɚ/ *n* **1** [*C*] **a** : a journey through the different parts of a country, region, etc. ▪ *We went on a tour of Italy.* ▪ *a sightseeing tour* ▪ *We hired a **tour guide**.* **b** : an activity in which you go through a place in order to see and learn about it ▪ *go on a tour* ▪ *take a tour* ▪ *She gave us a tour of the house/museum.* **2** [*C/U*] : a series of related performances, competitions, etc., that occur at different places over a period of time ▪ *a golf/book/concert tour* ▪ *The band is **on tour**.* **3** [*C*] : a period of time during which a soldier, sailor, etc., is on duty or in a certain place ▪ *during his tour in Vietnam* ▪ *serving a tour of duty*

²**tour** *vb* [*T/I*] **1** : to make a journey or trip through an area or place ▪ *We toured the city/museum.* **2** : to travel from place to place to perform, give speeches, etc. ▪ *The band/show is touring (the country).*

tour de force /ˌtʊɚdəˈfoɚs/ *n* [*singular*] : a very skillful and successful effort or performance ▪ *The book/film is a tour de force.*

tour·ism /'tʊɚˌɪzəm/ *n* [*U*] **1** : the activity of traveling to a place for pleasure ▪ *The city is trying to encourage/promote tourism.* **2** : the business of providing hotels, restaurants, etc., for people who are traveling ▪ *the tourism industry*

tour·ist /'tʊrɪst/ *n* [*C*] : a person who travels to a place for pleasure ▪ *The museums attract a lot of tourists.* ▪ *a tourist attraction* — **touristy** /'tʊrəsti/ *adj, informal* ▪ *often disapproving* ▪ *avoid the touristy areas* [=areas that are appealing to tourists]

tourist class *n* [*U*] : the cheapest seats on an airplane or the cheapest rooms on a ship or in a hotel

tour·na·ment /'tʊɚnəmənt/ *n* [*C*] **1** : a sports competition or series of contests that involves many players or teams ▪ *a basketball/golf/tennis tournament* **2** : a contest of skill and courage between soldiers or knights in the Middle Ages

tour·ney /'tʊɚni/ *n, pl* **-neys** [*C*] *chiefly US, informal* : TOURNAMENT 1

tour·ni·quet /'tʊɚnɪkət/ *n* [*C*] : a bandage, strip of cloth, etc., that is tied tightly around an injured arm or leg to stop or slow bleeding

tou·sle /'taʊzəl/ *vb* **tou·sled; tou·sling** [*T*] : to make (someone's) hair untidy ▪ *She tousled the boy's hair.*

¹**tout** /'taʊt/ *vb* **1** [*T*] : to talk about (something or someone) as being very good, effective, etc. ▪ *ads touting the drug's effectiveness* ▪ *a stock touted by experts* ▪ *She is being touted as a possible*

candidate. **2** [T/I] *Brit* : to try to persuade people to buy your goods or services ▪ *vendors touting their wares* ▪ *They were touting for business.* **3** [T/I] *Brit* : ²SCALP 2 ▪ *touting (tickets) outside a stadium*

²**tout** *n* [C] **1** *US* : a person who sells information about which horses are likely to win the races at a racetrack **2** *Brit* : a person who buys tickets for an event and resells them at a much higher price ▪ *ticket touts* [=(*US*) *scalpers*]

¹**tow** /ˈtoʊ/ *vb* [T] : to pull (a vehicle) behind another vehicle with a rope or chain ▪ *The car was towed to the garage.*

²**tow** *n* [C] : the act of towing a vehicle ▪ *We need a tow.* — **in tow** *or* **under tow** *or Brit* **on tow** — used to describe a situation in which one vehicle, boat, etc., is being pulled by another ▪ *a car with a boat in tow* ▪ (*figurative*) *a woman with seven children in tow*

to·ward /ˈtoʊəd, ˈtoəd/ *or* **to·wards** /ˈtoʊədz, ˈtoədz/ *prep* **1 a** : in the direction of (something or someone) ▪ *The bus is heading toward town.* ▪ *She took a step toward the door.* ▪ *He leaned towards me.* **b** — used to indicate the direction faced by something ▪ *Turn the chair toward the window.* **2 a** : near (a particular place) ▪ *They live out towards the edge of town.* **b** : not long before (a particular time) ▪ *towards the end of the month* **3** : in a process that is intended to produce or achieve (something) ▪ *a step toward peace* **4** : in regard to (something or someone) ▪ *a positive attitude toward life* ▪ *She was very kind towards them.* **5** : as part of the payment for (something) ▪ *We put $100 toward a new sofa.*

tow-away zone /ˈtoʊəˌweɪ-/ *n* [C] *US* : an area where a parked car will be towed

tow·el /ˈtawəl/ *n* [C] : a piece of cloth used for drying things ▪ *She dried her face with a towel.* ▪ (*figurative, informal*) *I wasn't ready to throw in the towel.* [=*quit*] — **towel** *vb*, *US* **-eled** *or Brit* **-elled**; *US* **-el·ing** *or Brit* **-el·ling** [T/I] ▪ *He toweled (off) his hair.*

¹**tow·er** /ˈtawə/ *n* [C] : a tall, narrow building or structure ▪ *a bell/clock/radio tower* ▪ *the church tower*

²**tower** *vb* — **tower above/over** [*phrasal vb*] : to be much taller than (someone or something) ▪ *He towers over his sister.* ▪ *The skyscrapers tower above the city.*

tow·er·ing /ˈtawərɪŋ/ *adj, always before a noun* **1** : very tall ▪ *towering skyscrapers* **2** : very powerful or intense ▪ *He flew into a towering rage.* **3** : very great or impressive ▪ *a towering performance*

tow-head·ed /ˈtoʊˌhɛdəd/ *adj, US, informal + old-fashioned* : having very light blond hair ▪ *a towheaded child*

town /ˈtaʊn/ *n* **1** [C] : a place where people live that is larger than a village but smaller than a city ▪ *a small town in Georgia* ▪ *the town of Jackson, Kentucky* ▪ *town officials* **2 a** [C] : the people in a town ▪ *The whole town was at the parade.* **b the town** : the government of a town ▪ *The town increased taxes.* **3** [U] : the business and shopping center of a town ▪

driving into town **4** [U, *singular*] : the town where someone lives ▪ *He left town.* [=*moved away*] ▪ *The circus is coming to town.* ▪ *the best restaurant in town* ▪ *I'll be in town* [=*in your town*] *next week.* ▪ *She's from out of town.* ▪ *We spent last night (out) on the town.* = *We hit the town last night.* [=we went to the bars, restaurants, etc.] ▪ (*figurative, informal*) *She really went to town (on the decorations).* [=she decorated very thoroughly and enthusiastically]

town hall *n* [C] : a town government's main building

town house *n* [C] **1** *US* : a house that is attached to a similar house by a shared wall **2** : a house in a town or city owned by someone who also has a house in the country

towns·folk /ˈtaʊnzˌfoʊk/ *n* [*plural*] : TOWNSPEOPLE

town·ship /ˈtaʊnˌʃɪp/ *n* [C] : a unit of local government in the U.S.

towns·peo·ple /ˈtaʊnzˌpiːpəl/ *n* [*plural*] : the people who live in a town or city

tow truck *n* [C] : a truck with special equipment on the back of it to tow away vehicles

tox·ic /ˈtɑːksɪk/ *adj* : POISONOUS ▪ *toxic fumes/substances* — **tox·ic·i·ty** /tɑːkˈsɪsəti/ *n, pl* **-ties** [C/U] *technical* ▪ *a chemical with low toxicity* [=a chemical that is not very poisonous]

tox·i·col·o·gy /ˌtɑːksəˈkɑːlədʒi/ *n* [U] *technical* : the study of poisonous chemicals, drugs, etc., and how living things react to them — **tox·i·col·o·gist** /ˌtɑːksəˈkɑːlədʒɪst/ *n* [C]

toxic waste *n* [C/U] : unwanted poisonous chemicals that are the result of manufacturing or industry ▪ *dumping toxic waste(s)*

tox·in /ˈtɑːksən/ *n* [C] : a poisonous substance and especially one that is produced by a living thing

¹**toy** /ˈtoɪ/ *n* [C] **1** : something a child plays with ▪ *a plastic/wooden/stuffed toy* **2** : something that an adult buys or uses for enjoyment ▪ *Her latest toy is a new TV.* **3** : a person who is controlled or used by someone else ▪ *She's just his toy.* — **toy·like** /ˈtoɪˌlaɪk/ *adj*

²**toy** *vb* — **toy with** [*phrasal vb*] **1 a** : to think about (something) briefly and not very seriously ▪ *I toyed with the idea.* **b** : to move or touch (something) with your fingers often without thinking ▪ *She toyed with her hair while she talked on the phone.* **2** : to deal with or control (someone or something) in a clever and usually unfair way ▪ *Don't toy with my emotions.* = *Don't toy with me.*

³**toy** *adj, always before a noun* **1 a** : of, for, or relating to toys ▪ *a toy store* ▪ *Put your toys back in the toy box/chest.* **b** : of a kind that is meant for a child to play with ▪ *toy cars/trains* **2** : of the smallest kind of a particular breed ▪ *a toy poodle*

¹**trace** /ˈtreɪs/ *n* [C] **1** : a very small amount of something ▪ *a trace of cinnamon in the cake* ▪ *She spoke without a trace of irony.* ▪ *trace amounts of pesticide* **2** : a mark or object which shows that

someone or something was in a particular place ▪ *Scientists found traces of a campsite.* ▪ *They left no trace (of evidence) behind.* ▪ *He disappeared/vanished without a trace.*

²**trace** *vb* **traced; trac·ing** **1** [*T*] **a** : to draw the outline of (something) ▪ *The children traced their hands.*; *especially* : to copy (a design or picture) by putting a thin piece of paper that you can see through over it and drawing on top of it **b** : to draw (something) especially in a careful way ▪ *She traced (out) the letters of her name.* ▪ *tracing circles in the sand* **2** [*T*] : to follow the path or line of (something) ▪ *She traced the edge of the book with her finger.* **3** [*T/I*] : to find out where something came from ▪ *The engine noise was traced to a loose bolt.* ▪ *The police traced the call to a pay phone.* ▪ *words that can be traced back to Latin* = *words that trace back to Latin* **4** [*T*] : to describe or study the way (something) happened over time ▪ *tracing the development of art* **5** [*T*] : to try to find (someone or something) by collecting and studying evidence ▪ *tracing missing persons* — **trace·able** /ˈtreɪsəbəl/ *adj*

trac·er /ˈtreɪsɚ/ *n* [*C*] : a type of bullet that shows its path through the air by creating smoke or light

tra·chea /ˈtreɪkijə, *Brit* trəˈkiːjə/ *n*, *pl* **-che·ae** /-kiˌiː, *Brit* -ˈkiːjiː/ *or* **-che·as** [*C*] *medical* : a long tube in your neck and chest that carries air into and out of your lungs — called also *windpipe* — **tra·che·al** /ˈtreɪkijəl/ *adj*

tra·che·o·to·my /ˌtreɪkiˈɑːtəmi/ *n*, *pl* **-mies** [*C*] *medical* : an emergency operation in which a cut is made in the trachea so that a person can breathe

¹**track** /ˈtræk/ *n* **1** [*C*] : a mark left on the ground by a moving animal, person, or vehicle — usually plural ▪ *moose/tire tracks* **2** [*C*] : a path or trail that is made by people or animals walking through a field, forest, etc. **3** [*C*] : a pair of metal bars that a train, trolley, or subway car rides along ▪ *the train/railroad tracks* **4** [*C*] : an often circular path or road that is used for racing ▪ *a dog/horse track* **5** [*U*] *US* : TRACK AND FIELD ▪ *He ran track in high school.* ▪ *a track team* **6** [*C*] : a rod or bar that is used to hold a curtain or a door that slides open **7** [*C*] : the course along which someone or something moves or proceeds ▪ *the track of a storm/missile* **8** [*C*] : a song on a record, CD, etc. ▪ *tracks 6 and 11* ▪ *the title track* [=the song with the same title as the album] **b** : a separate recording of each instrument or voice in a song ▪ *the drum/vocal track* — **cover your tracks** : to hide anything that shows where you have been or what you have done so that no one can find or catch you ▪ *The culprits covered their tracks well and left little evidence at the crime scene.* — **in your tracks** ◇ If you stop or are stopped *in your tracks*, you stop doing something suddenly or immediately. ▪ *He stopped/froze in his tracks, turned, and came back.* — **keep track** : to be aware of how something is changing, what someone is

doing, etc. ▪ *There's so much going on that it's hard to keep track.* = *It's hard to keep track of what's going on.* — **lose track** : to stop being aware of how something is changing, what someone is doing, etc. ▪ *With so much going on, it's easy to lose track.* ▪ *I lost track of the time.* — **make tracks** *informal* : to leave a place quickly ▪ *Here comes your mom—I'd better make tracks.* — **off track** : away from the main point, thought, etc. ▪ *Let's not get off track.* — **on the right/wrong track** : following a course that will lead to success/failure ▪ *Your design is not perfect, but you're on the right track.* — **on track** : happening the way that you expect or want things to happen ▪ *The project is on track.* ▪ *I had to get my life back on track.* — **the wrong side of the tracks** : the part of a town, city, etc., where poor people live

²**track** *vb* **1** [*T*] **a** : to follow and try to find (an animal) by looking for signs that show where it has gone ▪ *He tracked the deer for a mile.* **b** : to follow and find (someone or something) especially by looking at evidence ▪ *The detectives tracked the killer to Arizona.* ▪ *They tracked him down in Arizona.* ▪ *trying to track down the cause of the disease* **2** [*T*] **a** : to follow or watch the path of (something) ▪ *tracking a storm/missile* ▪ *a tracking device/system* **b** : to watch or follow the progress of (someone or something) ▪ *I started tracking my expenses.* ▪ *The study tracked the patients for five years.* **3** [*I*] *US* : to move in a certain way or in a certain direction ▪ *tracking north for 40 miles* **4** [*T*] *US* : to make marks by bringing (dirt, mud, etc.) indoors on your feet ▪ *Don't track mud into the house!* — **track·er** *n* [*C*] ▪ *an animal tracker*

track and field *n* [*U*] *US* : a sport in which athletes participate in different running, jumping, and throwing contests — **track–and–field** /ˌtrækənˈfiːld/ *adj*

track record *n* [*C*] : the things that someone or something has done or achieved in the past regarded especially as a way to judge that person or thing is likely to do in the future ▪ *They have a good/bad/proven track record.*

tract /ˈtrækt/ *n* [*C*] **1** : a system of body parts that has a particular purpose ▪ *the digestive/urinary/respiratory tract* **2** : an area of land ▪ *a 200-acre tract (of land)* **3** : a small book that expresses a group's political or religious ideas

trac·ta·ble /ˈtræktəbəl/ *adj, formal* **1** : easily managed or controlled ▪ *making problems more tractable* **2** : willing to learn or be guided by another ▪ *a tractable child/horse*

tract house *n* [*C*] *US* : a house that is one of many similar houses built on an area of land

trac·tion /ˈtrækʃən/ *n* [*U*] **1 a** : the force that causes a moving thing to stick against the surface it is moving along ▪ *Ice caused the car/tires to lose traction.* **b** : the power that is used to pull something ▪ *steam traction* **2** *medical* : a way of treating broken bones in which a device gently pulls the bones back into

place ▪ *She was in traction for three weeks.*
3 *informal* : the support, interest, etc., that is needed for something to succeed or make progress ▪ *The bill failed to* **gain/get traction** *in the Senate.*

trac·tor /ˈtræktə/ *n* [C] **1** : a large vehicle that is used to pull farm equipment **2** *US* : a short, heavy truck that is designed to pull a large trailer

tractor–trailer *n* [C] *US* : SEMITRAILER 2

¹**trade** /ˈtreɪd/ *n* **1 a** [U] : the activity or process of buying, selling, or exchanging goods or services ▪ *foreign/international trade* ▪ *trade agreements* **b** [U, *singular*] : the amount of things or services that are bought and sold ▪ *Trade accounts for half of our gross national product.* **2** [C] : the act of exchanging one thing for another ▪ *making a fair/good trade* **3** [C/U] : a job; *especially* : a job that requires special skills and that is done by using your hands ▪ *learning a new trade* ▪ *I am a carpenter/beautician* **by trade.** [=I work as a carpenter/beautician] ▪ *acquiring the* **tools of the/your trade** [=the set of tools or skills that are necessary for a particular kind of work] ▪ *She showed us a* **trick of the/her trade.** [=a quick or clever way of doing something that she learned as part of her job] **4** [C] : a certain kind of business or industry ▪ *the tourist/drug trade* ▪ *a trade association/publication*

²**trade** *vb* **trad·ed; trad·ing 1 a** [T/I] : to give something to someone and receive something in return ▪ *Do you want to trade (with me)?* ▪ *I traded seats with her.* = *We traded seats.* ▪ *I'll trade (you) my chips for your popcorn.* ▪ *trading jokes/secrets/insults* ▪ *I would love to* **trade places** *with him.* [=to be in his situation] **b** [T] *US, sports* : to give (one of your players) to another team in exchange for one of their players ▪ *He was traded to the Yankees.* **2** [T] : to stop using (one thing) and start using another ▪ *I traded my pen for a pencil.* **3 a** [I] : to buy, sell, or exchange goods or services ▪ *The countries trade with each other.* ▪ *They* **trade in** *illegal weapons.* **b** [T/I] : to buy and sell stocks, bonds, etc. ▪ *Their firm trades (in) bonds.* ▪ *The stock is trading at $71 a share.* — **trade down/up** [*phrasal vb*] : to sell something you own and buy a similar thing that costs less/more money ▪ *They traded down to a smaller house.* ▪ *trade up to a luxury car* — **trade in** [*phrasal vb*] **trade (something) in** *or* **trade in (something)** : to sell (something) back to a business as part of your payment for something else ▪ *Trade in your car and get $3,000 towards a new car!* — **trade off** [*phrasal vb*] **1** *US* : to take turns doing something ▪ *When you get tired, I'll trade off with you.* = *We can trade off.* **2** : to give up (something) in order to have something else ▪ *The car trades off power for greater fuel efficiency.* — **trade on** [*phrasal vb*] : to get an advantage from (something) ▪ *He trades on his good looks.* — **trading** *n* [U] ▪ *Trading was slow at the stock market today.* ▪ *a trading company/partner*

trade–in /ˈtreɪdˌɪn/ *n* [C] : something

(such as a car) that you sell to a business as part of your payment for something new ▪ *We got $3,000 for our trade-in.*

trade·mark /ˈtreɪdˌmɑɚk/ *n* [C] **1** : something (such as a word) that identifies a particular company's product and cannot be used by another company without permission ▪ *"Kleenex" is a registered trademark.* — abbr. **TM 2** : a characteristic quality or way of behaving, speaking, etc. ▪ *Courtesy is the company's trademark.* ▪ *her trademark smile* — **trade·marked** /ˈtreɪdˌmɑɚkt/ *adj* ▪ *a trademarked name*

trade name *n* [C] **1** : BRAND NAME **2** : the name of a business

trade–off /ˈtreɪdˌɑːf/ *n* [C] **1** : a situation in which you must choose between or balance two things that cannot be had at the same time ▪ *a trade-off between safety and speed* **2** *US* : something that you do not want but must accept in order to have something else ▪ *The job's biggest trade-off is having to work long hours.*

trad·er /ˈtreɪdɚ/ *n* [C] : a person who buys, sells, or exchanges goods ▪ *a stock/fur trader*

trade show *n* [C] : a large gathering in which different companies in a particular field or industry show their products to possible customers

trades·man /ˈtreɪdzmən/ *n, pl* **-men** /-mən/ [C] **1** : a person who works in a job that requires special skill or training ▪ *electricians, plumbers, and other tradesmen* **2** *chiefly Brit* : someone who sells or delivers goods; *especially* : STOREKEEPER

trades·peo·ple /ˈtreɪdzˌpiːpəl/ *n* [*plural*] **1** : people who work in a trade ▪ *tradespeople like plumbers and electricians* **2** *Brit* : shopkeepers or merchants

trade union *n* [C] *Brit* : LABOR UNION

trading card *n* [C] : a card that usually has pictures of and information about someone (such as an athlete) and that is part of a set which you collect by exchanging cards with other people

tra·di·tion /trəˈdɪʃən/ *n* **1** [C/U] : a way of thinking, behaving, or doing something that has been used by the people in a particular group for a long time ▪ *cultural/family traditions* ▪ *an ancient/time-honored tradition* ▪ *Will our children* **carry on the/our traditions?** ▪ *They* **follow the traditions** *of their ancestors.* = *They follow tradition.* ▪ *We* **broke with tradition** *and had a small wedding.* ▪ **By tradition,** *the celebration begins at midnight.* ▪ *a politician* **in the (great/grand) tradition** *of Franklin Delano Roosevelt* [=a politician who has qualities like those of Franklin Delano Roosevelt] **2** [U] : the stories, beliefs, etc., that have been part of the culture of a group of people for a long time ▪ *According to tradition, the goddess lives beneath the mountain.*

tra·di·tion·al /trəˈdɪʃənəl/ *adj* **1 a** : based on a way of thinking, behaving, or doing something that has been used by the people in a particular group, family, society, etc., for a long time ▪ *It is traditional to eat turkey on Thanksgiving.* ▪

She wore a traditional Japanese kimono.
b : typical or normal in a particular type of person or thing ▪ *We got a traditional bank loan with a fixed interest rate.* **2** : not new, different, or modern ▪ *I prefer a more traditional style of furniture.* ▪ *traditional beliefs/values* — **tra·di·tion·al·ly** *adv*

tra·di·tion·al·ist /trə'dɪʃənəlɪst/ *n* [C] : a person who believes that older ways of doing or thinking about things are better than newer ways ▪ *conservative/religious traditionalists* — **tra·di·tion·al·ism** /trə'dɪʃənəlˌɪzəm/ *n* [U]

¹traf·fic /'træfɪk/ *n* [U] **1** : all the vehicles driving along a certain road or in a certain area ▪ *rush hour traffic* ▪ *Traffic is backed up.* ▪ *a traffic accident* **2** : the movement of airplanes, ships, etc., along routes ▪ *air traffic* **3** : the amount of people who pass through a certain place or travel in a certain way ▪ *a walkway for pedestrian/foot traffic* **4** *computers* : the number of people who visit a Web site or use a system ▪ *increasing traffic to our site* **5** : the buying and selling of illegal goods or services ▪ *Drug traffic across the border has increased.* — **traf·ficked** /'træfɪkt/ *adj* ▪ *a heavily trafficked bridge/site* [=a bridge/site that has a lot of traffic]

²traffic *vb* **-ficked; -fick·ing** [I] : to buy or sell something especially illegally ▪ *a gang that traffics in drugs* — **traf·fick·er** /'træfɪkɚ/ *n* [C] ▪ *a drug trafficker* — **trafficking** *n* [U] ▪ *drug trafficking*

traffic circle *n* [C] *US* : a circular area where two or more roads meet and on which all vehicles must go in the same direction — called also (*US*) *rotary,* (*Brit*) *roundabout*

traffic cop *n* [C] : a police officer who directs traffic or gives fines to people who break traffic laws

traffic jam *n* [C] : a situation in which a long line of vehicles on a road have stopped moving or are moving very slowly ▪ *I got stuck in a traffic jam.*

traffic light *n* [C] : an electric lamp that usually has a red, a green, and a yellow light and that is used to control traffic ▪ *Take a left at the traffic light(s).*

traffic ticket *n* [C] : TICKET 3

trag·e·dy /'trædʒədi/ *n, pl* **-dies** **1 a** [C/U] : a very bad event that causes great sadness and often involves someone's death ▪ *Her son's death was a terrible tragedy.* ▪ *The situation ended in tragedy.* **b** [C] : a very sad, unfortunate, or upsetting situation ▪ *It is a tragedy that so few victims get help.* **2 a** [C] : a play, movie, etc., that is serious and has a sad ending ▪ *"Hamlet" is one of Shakespeare's best-known tragedies.* **b** [U] : plays, movies, etc., that are tragedies ▪ *Greek tragedy*

trag·ic /'trædʒɪk/ *adj* **1** : causing strong feelings of sadness usually because someone has died in a way that seems very shocking, unfair, etc. ▪ *a tragic accident/death* **2** : involving very sad or serious topics ▪ *a tragic play* : of or relating to tragedy ▪ *tragic characters* — **trag·i·cal·ly** /'trædʒɪkli/ *adv* ▪ *He died tragically.*

¹trail /'treɪl/ *vb* **1 a** [T] : to pull (something) behind you especially on the

ground ▪ *The dog was trailing its leash.* **b** [I] : to be pulled behind someone or something ▪ *The dog's leash was trailing along/on the ground.* **2** [T/I] : to walk or move slowly as you follow behind (someone or something) ▪ *He trailed us up the mountain.* ▪ *Her children* **trailed (along) behind/after** (*her*). **3** [T/I] : to be behind in a race or competition ▪ *He is trailing* (*his opponent*) *in the polls.* ▪ *We were trailing* (*them*) *by 3 runs.* **4** [T] : to follow and watch or try to catch (someone or something) ▪ *trail a fox/suspect* **5** [I] : to move, flow, or extend slowly in a thin line ▪ *Smoke trailed (away) from the chimney.* **6** [I] : to hang down to the ground ▪ *The curtains trailed onto the floor.* — **trail away/off** [*phrasal vb*] — used to say that someone's voice becomes softer and softer and then stops ▪ *She trailed off in mid-sentence.* ▪ *Her voice trailed off.*

²trail *n* [C] **1** : a path through a forest, field, etc. ▪ *a bike/ski/hiking trail* **2** : the marks, signs, smells, etc., that are left behind by someone or something ▪ *He left (behind) a trail of blood/crumbs.* ▪ *following a trail* ▪ *The dogs/police were* (**hot**) **on her trail.** [=following her (closely)] ▪ *The* **trail went cold.** [=the trail could no longer be found] **3** : a route that someone follows to go somewhere or achieve something ▪ *the trail to success* ▪ *The candidates are on the* **campaign trail.** [=are going to different places during the campaign] — **hit the trail** *chiefly US* : to begin a journey ▪ *We should hit the trail by 8:00.*

trail·blaz·er /'treɪlˌbleɪzɚ/ *n* [C] : a person who makes, does, or discovers something new and makes it acceptable or popular ▪ *one of the trailblazers of jazz* — **trail·blaz·ing** /'treɪlˌbleɪzɪŋ/ *adj*

trail·er /'treɪlɚ/ *n* [C] **1** : a long platform or box with wheels that is pulled behind a truck or car and used to transport things **2** *chiefly US* **a** : a vehicle that can be pulled by a truck or car and that can be parked and used as an office, vacation home, etc. **b** : MOBILE HOME **3** : a selected group of scenes that are shown to advertise a movie : PREVIEW

trailing *adj* **1** : having stems that hang downward or rest on the ground ▪ *trailing plants/vines* **2** : forming the back or last part of something ▪ *the trailing edge of the airplane's wing*

¹train /'treɪn/ *n* **1** [C/U] : a connected group of railroad cars ▪ *a freight/passenger train* ▪ *take/catch a train* ▪ *traveling by train* ▪ *a train station* ▪ *train tracks* **2** [C] : an orderly series of events, actions, or ideas ▪ *a train of events* ▪ *I lost my* **train of thought.** [=I forgot what I was thinking about] **3** [C] *technical* : a series of moving machine parts (such as gears) for controlling motion ▪ *the car's drive train* **4** [C] : a part of a long dress that trails behind the woman who is wearing it ▪ *the bride's train* — **in train** *Brit, formal* : in an active state or condition ▪ *a process that had been in train for decades*

²train *vb* **1** [T/I] : to teach (someone) the skills needed to do a job, task, etc. ▪ *He was trained as a chef.* ▪ *My boss is* *training me on the new equipment.* ▪ **highly trained** *professionals* **b** [*I*] : to be taught the skills needed to do a job, task, etc. ▪ *I'm training to be/become a nurse.* ▪ *He's training as a chef.* **2** [*T*] : to cause (someone or something) to develop an ability or skill ▪ *You can train yourself to relax.* **3 a** [*I*] : to try to make yourself stronger, faster, or better at doing something before competing ▪ *She's training for the Olympics.* **b** [*T*] : to help (someone) to prepare for an event or competition ▪ *He trains Olympic athletes.* **4** [*T*] : to teach (an animal) to obey commands ▪ *She trained her dog to sit.* **5** [*T*] : to make (a plant) grow in a particular direction ▪ *train a vine* **6** [*T*] : to aim or point (something) toward something or in a particular direction ▪ *We trained our eyes on the horizon.* [=we looked toward the horizon] — **train·able** /ˈtreɪnəbəl/ *adj* — **train·ing** /ˈtreɪnɪŋ/ *n* [*U*] ▪ *Employees receive* **on-the-job** *training.* ▪ *She's* **in training** *for the Olympics.* ▪ *a training manual*

train·ee /treɪˈniː/ *n* [*C*] : a person who is being trained for a job ▪ *management trainees*

train·er /ˈtreɪnɚ/ *n* [*C*] **1** : a person who trains athletes or animals ▪ *She hired a personal trainer.* **2** *US* : a person who treats the injuries of the members of a sports team **3** *Brit* : SNEAKER

training shoe *n* [*C*] *chiefly Brit* : SNEAKER

training wheels *n* [*plural*] *US* : a small pair of extra wheels that are added to a child's bicycle while the child is learning to ride it

traipse /ˈtreɪps/ *vb* **traipsed**; **traips·ing** [*I*] *informal* : to walk or go somewhere ▪ *I'm too old to go traipsing around Europe.*

trait /ˈtreɪt, *Brit* ˈtreɪ/ *n* [*C*] *formal* : a quality that makes one person or thing different from another ▪ *personality traits*

trai·tor /ˈtreɪtɚ/ *n* [*C*] : a person who betrays his or her own country, friends, etc. ▪ *a traitor who sold military secrets to the enemy* ▪ *He turned traitor.* — **trai·tor·ous** /ˈtreɪtərəs/ *adj*

tra·jec·to·ry /trəˈdʒɛktəri/ *n, pl* **-ries** [*C*] : the curved path along which a rocket, bullet, etc., moves through air or space ▪ *the trajectory of the missile* ▪ *(figurative) her career's trajectory*

tram /ˈtræm/ *n* [*C*] **1** *US* : a vehicle that runs on a track or on rails and that usually carries groups of people for a short distance ▪ *an airport tram* **2** *chiefly Brit* : STREETCAR

tram·mel /ˈtræməl/ *vb, US* **-meled** *or Brit* **-melled**; *US* **-mel·ing** *or Brit* **-mel·ling** [*T*] *formal* : to limit or restrict (something or someone) unfairly ▪ *laws that trammel our rights*

¹**tramp** /ˈtræmp/ *vb* **1** [*I*] : to walk or step heavily ▪ *Workmen were tramping through the house all day.* **2** [*T/I*] : to walk for a long distance or time ▪ *tramping through the woods*

²**tramp** *n* **1** [*C*] : a person who travels from place to place and does not have a home or much money **2** [*C*] *chiefly US, disapproving* : a woman who has sex with

many different men **3** [*C*] : ²HIKE **1** ▪ *a tramp through the woods* **4** [*singular*] : the sound made by someone walking heavily ▪ *the tramp of boots*

tram·ple /ˈtræmpəl/ *vb* **tram·pled**; **tram·pling** [*T/I*] **1** : to cause damage or pain by walking or stepping heavily on something or someone ▪ *The workmen trampled (on) my flowers.* ▪ *They were trampled to death by the crowd.* **2** : to treat other people's rights, wishes, or feelings as if they are not important ▪ *They are trampling (on) our rights.*

tram·po·line /ˌtræmpəˈliːn/ *n* [*C*] : a piece of equipment that has a sheet of strong cloth attached by springs to a metal frame and that is used for jumping up and down for exercise or as a sport

trance /ˈtræns/ *n* [*C*] **1** : a state that is like being asleep except that you can move and respond to questions and commands ▪ *She put him in a trance.* ▪ *He fell/went into a trance.* **2** : a state in which you are not aware of what is happening around you ▪ *staring out the window* **in a trance**

tran·ny /ˈtræni/ *n, pl* **-nies** [*C*] *US, informal* : TRANSMISSION 3

tran·quil /ˈtræŋkwəl/ *adj* : quiet and peaceful ▪ *a tranquil life/sea/village* — **tran·quil·i·ty** (*US*) *or chiefly Brit* **tran·quil·li·ty** /trænˈkwɪləti/ *n* [*U*] ▪ *peace and tranquility* — **tran·quil·ly** *adv*

tran·quil·ize *also Brit* **tran·quil·lise** /ˈtræŋkwəˌlaɪz/ *vb* **-ized**; **-iz·ing** [*T*] : to use a drug to cause (a person or animal) to become very relaxed and calm ▪ *They tranquilized the bear with a dart.* — **tran·quil·iz·er** *also Brit* **tran·quil·lis·er** /ˈtræŋkwəˌlaɪzɚ/ *n* [*C*] ▪ *a patient who is on/taking tranquilizers*

trans·act /trænˈzækt/ *vb* [*T*] *somewhat formal* : to do (business) with another person, company, etc. ▪ *transact a real estate deal*

trans·ac·tion /trænˈzækʃən/ *n* **1** [*C*] : a business deal ▪ *business/commercial/bank transactions* **2** [*U*] : the act or process of doing business with another person, company, etc. ▪ *the transaction of business*

trans·at·lan·tic /ˌtrænsətˈlæntɪk/ *adj* **1** : going across the Atlantic Ocean ▪ *a transatlantic cable/voyage* **2** : located on the other side of the Atlantic Ocean ▪ *our transatlantic friends* **3** : involving people or countries on both sides of the Atlantic Ocean ▪ *a transatlantic conspiracy*

trans·ceiv·er /trænˈsiːvɚ/ *n* [*C*] : a radio that can send and receive messages

tran·scend /trænˈsɛnd/ *vb* [*T*] *formal* : to rise above or go beyond the normal limits of (something) ▪ *music that transcends cultural boundaries* ▪ *She transcended* [=overcame] *her suffering.* — **tran·scen·dence** /trænˈsɛndəns/ *n* [*U*] — **tran·scen·dent** /trænˈsɛndənt/ *adj, formal* ▪ *a transcendent experience/performance* — **tran·scen·den·tal** /ˌtrænsɛnˈdɛntl̩/ *adj*

tran·scen·den·tal·ism /ˌtrænsɛnˈdɛntəˌlɪzəm/ *n* [*U*] : a philosophy which says that thought and spiritual things are more real than ordinary human experience and material things — **tran·scen·den·tal·ist** /ˌtræn͵sɛnˈdɛntəlɪst/ n [C]

trans·con·ti·nen·tal /ˌtræns͵kɑːntəˈnɛntl̩/ adj : going across a continent • a transcontinental flight

tran·scribe /trænˈskraɪb/ vb -**scribed**; -**scrib·ing** [T] **1 a** : to make a written copy of (something) • transcribe a letter/document **b** : to write down (something that is spoken) • transcribe a speech **2** : to rewrite (music, text, etc.) in a different form • transcribe books into braille — **tran·scrib·er** n [C]

tran·script /ˈtrænˌskrɪpt/ n [C] **1** : a written, printed, or typed copy of words that have been spoken • a transcript of a show/speech • a court transcript **2** US : an official record of a student's grades • a college transcript

tran·scrip·tion /trænˈskrɪpʃən/ n **1** [U] : the act or process of making a transcript of words that have been spoken • an error in transcription **2** [C] : TRANSCRIPT 1

trans·du·cer /trænsˈduːsɚ, Brit trænsˈdjuːsə/ n [C] technical : a device that changes power from one form to another

tran·sept /ˈtrænˌsɛpt/ n [C] : the shorter area that goes across and sticks out from the long part of a church and that gives the church the shape of a cross when it is viewed from above

trans fat /ˈtræns-, ˈtrænz-/ n [C/U] technical : a type of fat that is bad for your health

¹**trans·fer** /trænsˈfɚ/ vb -**ferred**; -**fer·ring** **1** [T] : to move or cause (someone or something) to move from one place to another • The patient was transferred to a different hospital. • transfer a (phone) call • a metal that transfers heat • The virus is transferred by fleas. • (law) He transferred the property/rights to his son. **2** [T/I] : to use (an idea, a skill, etc.) or be used for a new or different purpose • She was able to transfer her skills to her new job. • Her skills transferred well. **3 a** [I] : to stop going to one school and begin going to another • She transferred from/to another high school. **b** [T/I] : to move to a different place or job for the same employer • I (was) transferred to the sales department. **4** [T/I] : to change from one plane, bus, train, etc., to another • We transferred (planes) in Chicago. — **trans·fer·able** also **trans·fer·ra·ble** /trænsˈfɚrəbəl/ adj • transferable skills/credits • These tickets are not transferable. [=they cannot be given to another person] — **trans·fer·ence** /trænsˈfɚrəns, ˈtrænsͺfɚrəns/ n [U] • transference of energy/heat

²**trans·fer** /ˈtrænsͺfɚ/ n **1 a** [C/U] : an act or process of moving someone or something from one place to another • a transfer of the prisoner • heat/data transfer • a transfer of property from father to son **b** [C] : a process by which one method, system, etc., is replaced by another • making a transfer to the new system **2** [C] : an act of moving from one job or location to another for the same company • My transfer to the home office has

been approved. **3** [C] US : a student who has moved from one school to another • She's a transfer (student) from the junior college. **4** [C] chiefly Brit : DECAL **5** [C] chiefly US : a ticket that allows a passenger on a bus or train to continue traveling on another bus or train

trans·fig·ure /trænsˈfɪɡjɚ, Brit trænsˈfɪɡə/ vb -**ured**; -**ur·ing** [T] literary : to change the appearance of (something or someone) • a transfigured landscape

trans·fix /trænsˈfɪks/ vb [T] formal : to cause (someone) to sit or stand without moving because of surprise, interest, etc. • He stood transfixed by her gaze.

trans·form /trænsˈfoɚm/ vb [T] : to change (something) completely and usually in a good way • The paint completely transformed the room. • The factory was transformed into an art gallery. • The Internet has transformed our business. — **trans·for·ma·tion** /ˌtrænsfɚˈmeɪʃən/ n [C/U] • undergoing (a) transformation — **trans·for·ma·tive** /trænsˈfoɚmətɪv/ adj, formal • a transformative experience/force

trans·form·er /trænsˈfoɚmɚ/ n [C] technical : a device that changes the voltage of an electric current

trans·fu·sion /trænsˈfjuːʒən/ n [C/U] : a medical treatment in which someone's blood is put into the body of another person • Without a (blood) transfusion her chances of survival were slim. • the transfusion of blood

trans·gress /trænsˈɡrɛs/ vb [T/I] formal : to disobey a command or law • transgressing the rules — **trans·gres·sion** /trænsˈɡrɛʃən/ n [C] • a minor transgression — **trans·gres·sor** /trænsˈɡrɛsɚ/ n [C]

¹**tran·sient** /ˈtrænziʲənt/ adj, formal **1** : not lasting long • transient joys **2** : staying somewhere only a short time • a transient population — **tran·sience** /ˈtrænziʲəns/ n [U] — **transiently** adv

²**transient** n [C] chiefly US : a person who does not have a permanent home and who stays in a place for only a short time

tran·sis·tor /trænˈzɪstɚ/ n [C] : a small device that is used to control the flow of electricity in radios, computers, etc.

transistor radio n [C] : a small radio that has transistors

tran·sit /ˈtrænsət/ n [U] **1** : the act of moving people or things from one place to another • The goods are in transit. [=in the process of being transported] **2** US : MASS TRANSIT

tran·si·tion /trænˈzɪʃən/ n [C/U] : a change from one state or condition to another • a transition of power/ownership/management • making/undergoing a smooth transition • The company is in transition. [=it is changing] — **tran·si·tion·al** /trænˈzɪʃənəl/ adj • a transitional government — **transition** vb [I] chiefly US • The company is transitioning to new management.

tran·si·tive /ˈtrænsətɪv/ adj, grammar, of a verb : having or taking a direct object • a transitive verb • In "I like pie," the verb "like" is transitive. — **tran·si·tive·ly** adv

tran·si·to·ry /ˈtrænsəˌtori, Brit ˈtræn-**

zətri/ *adj* : lasting only for a short time : TEMPORARY 1 ▪ *a transitory phase*

trans·late /træns'leɪt, 'trænz,leɪt/ *vb* -lat·ed; -lat·ing 1 [T/I] : to change words from one language into another language ▪ *Will you translate for me?* ▪ *translating Japanese into English* ▪ *The word translates as "hello."* ▪ *translate a book/document* 2 [T] : to explain (something) in a way that is easier to understand ▪ *Can you translate this jargon?* 3 [I] : to have the same meaning ▪ *Your 5 percent salary increase translates to/into about $3,000.* 4 [T/I] : to change (something) into a different form ▪ *Translate your ideas into action.* ▪ *The play translated well to the big screen.* — **translate into** [*phrasal vb*] : to lead to (something) as a result ▪ *Competition often translates into lower prices.* — **trans·lat·able** /træns-'leɪtəbəl/ *adj* — **trans·la·tion** /træns-'leɪʃən/ *n* [C/U] ▪ *a rough/loose translation of the phrase* ▪ *reading a Russian novel in translation* [=in translated form] ▪ *The joke loses something in translation.* [=it is not as funny when it is translated into another language]

trans·la·tor /træns'leɪtɚ, 'trænz,leɪtɚ/ *n* [C] : a person who changes words in one language into a different language

trans·lit·er·ate /træns'lɪtə,reɪt/ *vb* -at·ed; -at·ing [T] : to write words or letters in the characters of another alphabet — **trans·lit·er·a·tion** /træns,lɪtə'reɪʃən/ *n* [C/U]

trans·lu·cent /træns'lu:sn̩t/ *adj* : not completely clear but clear enough to allow light to pass through ▪ *translucent glass* — **trans·lu·cence** /træns'lu:sn̩s/ or **trans·lu·cen·cy** /træns'lu:sn̩si/ *n* [U]

trans·mis·si·ble /træns'mɪsəbəl/ *adj* : able to be spread to other people, animals, etc. ▪ *transmissible diseases/infections*

trans·mis·sion /træns'mɪʃən/ *n* 1 a [U] : the act or process of sending electrical signals to a radio, TV, computer, etc. ▪ *data/voice transmission* b [C] : something that is transmitted ▪ *a fax/satellite transmission* 2 [U] : the act or process by which something is spread or passed from one person or thing to another ▪ *the transmission of disease/knowledge* 3 [C/U] : the part of a vehicle that uses the power produced by the engine to turn the wheels ▪ *My car has a manual transmission.* ▪ *an automatic transmission*

trans·mit /træns'mɪt/ *vb* -mit·ted; -mit·ting 1 [T/I] : to send (information, sound, etc.) in the form of electrical signals to a radio, TV, computer, etc. ▪ *transmitting and receiving data* ▪ *The radio transmits on two frequencies.* 2 [T] : to give or pass (information, values, etc.) from one person to another ▪ *transmit knowledge* 3 [T] : to cause (a virus, disease, etc.) to be given to others ▪ *a disease transmitted by ticks* 4 [T] : to allow (light, heat, etc.) to pass through ▪ *Glass transmits light.* — **trans·mit·ta·ble** /træns'mɪtəbəl/ *adj*

trans·mit·ter /træns'mɪtɚ, 'trænz,mɪtɚ/ *n* [C] 1 : a device that sends out radio or television signals 2 : a person or thing that causes something to be spread to others ▪ *transmitters of the disease*

trans·mute /træns'mju:t/ *vb* -mut·ed; -mut·ing [T/I] *formal* : to completely change the form, appearance, or nature of (someone or something) ▪ *Her art transmutes* [=transforms] *trash into a thing of beauty.* — **trans·mu·ta·tion** /,trænsmju'teɪʃən/ *n* [C/U]

trans·na·tion·al /,træns'næʃənl̩/ *adj* : operating in or involving more than one country ▪ *transnational corporations/crime*

trans·oce·an·ic /,træns,oʊʃi'ænɪk/ *adj* : crossing the ocean ▪ *transoceanic flights*

tran·som /'trænsəm/ *n* [C] 1 *US* : a small window that is above a door or larger window 2 : a stone or wooden bar above a door or window

trans·par·en·cy /træns'perənsi/ *n, pl* -cies 1 [U] : the quality of being transparent ▪ *the transparency of glass* ▪ *the transparency of their motives* 2 [C] : a piece of thin, clear plastic with pictures or words printed on it that can be viewed on a large screen by shining light through it

trans·par·ent /træns'perənt/ *adj* 1 : able to be seen through ▪ *transparent glass* 2 a : easy to notice or understand : OBVIOUS ▪ *a transparent lie* ▪ *Their motives were transparent.* b : honest and open : not secretive ▪ *transparent business dealings* — **trans·par·ent·ly** *adv*

tran·spire /træn'spajɚ/ *vb* -spired; -spir·ing [I] *formal* 1 : to happen ▪ *What transpired at the meeting?* ▪ *the events that transpired on that day* 2 : to become known ▪ *It transpired that they had met previously.* [=we found out that they had met previously]

trans·plant /,træns'plænt/ *vb* 1 [T/I] : to remove (a plant) from the ground or from a pot and move it to another place ▪ *She carefully transplanted the seedlings.* 2 [T] *medical* : to remove an organ or other part from the body of one person and put it into the body of another person ▪ *transplant a kidney* ▪ *a transplanted heart* 3 [T/I] : to move (a person or animal) to a new home : RELOCATE ▪ *The group transplanted the beavers to another part of the state.* ▪ *a New Yorker who transplanted to Seattle* — **trans·plant** /'træns,plænt/ *n* [C/U] ▪ *a successful heart transplant* ▪ *Her body rejected the transplant.* ▪ *a Southern transplant who moved to New York* — **trans·plan·ta·tion** /,træns,plæn'teɪʃən/ *n* [C/U]

trans·pon·der /træn'spɑːndɚ/ *n* [C] *technical* : a device that receives and sends out a radio signal and that shows the location of an airplane, satellite, etc.

¹**trans·port** /,træns'poɚt/ *vb* [T] 1 : to carry (someone or something) from one place to another ▪ *A van transported us to and from the airport.* ▪ *transporting goods in crates* 2 : to cause (someone) to imagine that he or she is in a different place or time ▪ *The movie transports us to another world.* — **trans·port·able** /,træns'poɚtəbəl/ *adj* — **trans·port·er** /træns'poɚtɚ/ *n* [C]

²**trans·port** /'træns,poɚt/ *n* 1 [U]

: TRANSPORTATION 1 • *the transport of goods* **2** [C] **a** : a ship that is made for carrying soldiers or military equipment • *a troop transport* **b** : an airplane that is used to carry people or goods • *supersonic transports* **3** [U] *chiefly Brit* : TRANSPORTATION 2 • *public transport*

trans·por·ta·tion /ˌtrænspəˈteɪʃən/ *n* [U] **1** *chiefly US* : the act or process of moving people or things from one place to another • *the transportation of troops/supplies* **2** *chiefly US* **a** : a way of traveling from one place to another place • *I was left without (a means of) transportation.* • *air/ground transportation* **b** : a system for moving passengers or goods from one place to another • *the city's public transportation* [=a public system of trains, buses, etc.]

trans·pose /trænsˈpoʊz/ *vb* -posed; -pos·ing [T] **1** : to change the position or order of (two things) • *I accidentally transposed the numbers.* **2** : to write or perform (a piece of music) in a different key • *a melody transposed to the key of C* — **trans·po·si·tion** /ˌtrænspəˈzɪʃən/ *n* [C/U]

trans·sex·u·al /trænˈsɛkʃəwəl/ *n* [C] : a person who tries to look, dress, and act like a member of the opposite sex — **transsexual** *adj*

trans·verse /trænsˈvɚs/ *adj, technical* : lying or made across something • *a transverse incision* — **trans·verse·ly** *adv*

trans·ves·tite /trænsˈvɛsˌtaɪt/ *n* [C] : a person who likes to dress like a person of the opposite sex — **trans·ves·tism** /trænsˈvɛsˌtɪzəm/ *n* [U]

¹trap /ˈtræp/ *n* [C] **1** : a device that is used for catching animals • *a bear/lobster trap* **2 a** : something that is used or done to stop or capture someone • *lay/set a trap to catch the thief/enemy* • *I walked/stumbled into a trap.* **b** : a situation in which someone is tricked into doing or saying something • *Credit card companies were accused of laying/setting traps for consumers.* **c** : a bad position or situation from which it is difficult to escape • *Don't fall into the trap of relying too much on technology.* **3** *US, golf* : SAND TRAP **4** *slang* : MOUTH • *I disagreed, but I kept my trap shut.* • *Shut your trap!* **5** *US, technical* : a bend in a pipe that prevents gas from passing through the pipe

²trap *vb* **trapped; trap·ping** [T] **1** : to catch (an animal) in a trap • *trapping mice/bears* **2** : ³CORNER 1 • *The police trapped the robber in an alley.* **3 a** : to cause (a person or animal) to be unable to move or escape • *She was trapped in/inside the elevator.* **b** : to force (someone) to stay in a bad or unpleasant situation • *He felt trapped in his job/marriage.* **4** : to fool or trick (someone) into doing or saying something • *He trapped the witness into admitting that she had lied.* **5** : to stop (something) from escaping or being lost • *trap heat/fumes*

trap·door /ˈtræpˌdoɚ/ *n* [C] : a door that covers or hides an opening in a floor or ceiling

tra·peze /trəˈpiːz/ *n* [C] : a short bar that

is hung high above the ground by two ropes and that is used to perform athletic tricks • *circus performers who swing on the trapeze*

trap·e·zoid /ˈtræpəˌzoɪd/ *n* [C] *geometry* : a four-sided shape that has two sides that are parallel and two sides that are not parallel — **trap·e·zoi·dal** /ˌtræpəˈzoɪdl/ *adj*

trap·per /ˈtræpɚ/ *n* [C] : someone who catches animals in traps • *18th-century fur trappers*

trap·pings /ˈtræpɪŋz/ *n* [*plural*] : the visible signs of something • *She enjoyed all the trappings of success/wealth.*

¹trash /ˈtræʃ/ *n* [U] **1** *US* : things that are no longer useful or wanted and that have been thrown away • *Take out the trash, please.* **b** : a container where people put things that are being thrown away • *I put/threw it in the trash.* **2** *informal* : something that is very low in quality • *How can you read that trash?* **3** *chiefly US, informal + disapproving* : someone who has very low social status or who is not respected • *They treated him like trash.* — **talk trash** *US, informal* : to say insulting things especially to an opponent • *He was talking trash during the game.*

²trash *vb* [T] *informal* **1** *US* : to throw away (something) • *It couldn't be fixed, so I trashed it.* **2** : to cause great damage to (something) • *The office had been trashed.* **3** : to criticize (someone or something) very harshly • *Critics trashed the film.*

trash can *n* [C] *US* : a container that holds materials that have been thrown away — called also (*Brit*) **dustbin,** (*Brit*) **litter bin**

trash talk *n* [U] *US, informal* : insulting comments that are made especially to an opponent in a contest, game, etc. — **trash–talk** /ˈtræʃˌtɑːk/ *vb* [T/I] • *He's always trash-talking (the other players).*

trashy /ˈtræʃi/ *adj* **trash·i·er; -est** *informal + disapproving* **1** : not decent or respectable • *trashy novels/outfits/women* **2** : very low in quality • *trashy TV programs*

trau·ma /ˈtrɑːmə/ *n* [C/U] **1** : a very unpleasant experience that causes someone to have mental or emotional problems usually for a long time • *the traumas she suffered during her childhood* **2** *medical* : a serious injury to a person's body • *an accident victim with (a) severe head trauma* — **trau·mat·ic** /trəˈmætɪk/ *adj* • *a traumatic experience/childhood* • *a traumatic brain injury* — **trau·mat·i·cal·ly** /trəˈmætɪkli/ *adv*

trau·ma·tize *also Brit* **trau·ma·tise** /ˈtrɑːməˌtaɪz/ *vb* -tized; -tiz·ing [T] : to cause (someone) to suffer emotional trauma • *He was traumatized by the experience.*

tra·vail /trəˈveɪl/ *n* **1** [C] *formal* : a difficult experience or situation • *the political travails of the President* **2** [U] *literary* : painful or difficult work or effort • *They finally succeeded after many months of travail.*

¹trav·el /ˈtrævəl/ *vb, US* **-eled** *or Brit*

-elled; *US* **-el·ing** *or Brit* **-el·ling** **1 a**
[*I*] : to go to a place and especially one
that is far away ▪ *The birds travel south for
the winter.* ▪ *He travels frequently.* ▪ *travel
around Europe by bus/car/train* ▪
(*figurative*) *My mind traveled back to* [=I
began thinking about] *my childhood.* **b**
[*T*] : to go through or over (a place) during a trip or journey ▪ *traveling the countryside* **2** [*I*] : to move from one place to
another ▪ *The car was traveling at a high
speed.* ▪ *The pain traveled down his back.* ▪
the way that sound travels **3** [*I*] : to
spread or be passed from one place or
person to another ▪ *The news traveled
fast.* **4** [*I*] : to spend time with a particular group or kind of people ▪ *He travels
with a rough crowd.* **5** [*I*] *basketball* : to
take more steps while holding a basketball than the rules allow ▪ *The referee
called her for traveling.* — **trav·eled**
(*US*) *or Brit* **trav·elled** /ˈtrævəld/ *adj* ▪ *a
heavily traveled road* — **trav·el·er** (*US*)
or Brit **trav·el·ler** /ˈtrævələ/ *n* [*C*]

²**travel** *n* **1** [*U*] : the act or activity of
traveling ▪ *She enjoys foreign travel.* ▪
train/rail/air travel ▪ *travel books/expenses*
2 [*plural*] : trips or journeys to distant
places ▪ *their travels in foreign lands*

travel agency *n* [*C*] : a business that
helps to make arrangements for people
who want to travel — **travel agent** *n*
[*C*] ▪ *He's a travel agent.*

traveler's check (*US*) *or Brit* **traveller's
cheque** *n* [*C*] : a check that is paid for in
advance and that may be used like cash

trav·el·ing (*US*) *or Brit* **trav·el·ling**
/ˈtrævəlɪŋ/ *adj, always before a noun* **1**
: going to different places instead of staying in one place ▪ *a traveling circus/sales-
man* **2 a** : relating to the activity of
traveling ▪ *traveling expenses* ▪ *a traveling
companion* [=a person who travels with
you somewhere] **b** : designed to be
used by someone who is traveling ▪ *a
traveling alarm clock*

trav·el·ogue *also US* **trav·el·og** /ˈtrævə-
ˌlɑːg/ *n* [*C*] : a speech, movie, or piece of
writing about someone's travels

tra·verse /trəˈvɚs/ *vb* **-versed; -vers-
ing** [*T*] *formal* : to move across (an area)
▪ *ships traversing the ocean* — **tra·verse**
/ˈtrævɚs, trəˈvɚs/ *n* [*C*] ▪ *making a dangerous traverse across a glacier*

trav·es·ty /ˈtrævəsti/ *n, pl* **-ties** [*C*]
: something that is shocking, upsetting,
or ridiculous because it is not what it is
supposed to be ▪ *The investigation was a
travesty.* ▪ *The trial was a travesty of justice.*

trawl /ˈtrɑːl/ *vb* [*T/I*] **1** : to catch fish by
pulling a large net along the bottom of
the ocean ▪ *trawling the ocean floor* **2**
: to search through (something) in order
to find someone or something ▪ *He
trawled (through) the files for clues.* —
trawl *n* [*C*] ▪ *a boat pulling a trawl (net)*
— **trawl·er** /ˈtrɑːlɚ/ *n* [*C*] ▪ *the captain
of a trawler*

tray /ˈtreɪ/ *n* [*C*] : a thin, flat, and often
rectangular piece of plastic, metal, etc.,
that has low sides and that is used for
carrying or holding things ▪ *carrying trays
of food* ▪ *an ice cube tray*

treach·er·ous /ˈtrɛtʃərəs/ *adj* **1** : not
able to be trusted ▪ *a treacherous ally/en-
emy* : showing that someone cannot be
trusted ▪ *a treacherous act of betrayal* **2**
: very dangerous and difficult to deal
with ▪ *treacherous waters/terrain* ▪ *a
treacherous hike* — **treach·er·ous·ly**
adv

treach·ery /ˈtrɛtʃəri/ *n, pl* **-er·ies** **1** [*U*]
: harmful things that are done usually se-
cretly to a friend, your country, etc. ▪ *a
tale of treachery* **2** [*C*] : an act of harming someone who trusts you ▪ *She was
hurt by her husband's treacheries.*

trea·cle /ˈtriːkəl/ *n* [*U*] *Brit* : MOLASSES
— **trea·cly** /ˈtriːkəli/ *adj* **trea·cli·er;
-est**

¹**tread** /ˈtrɛd/ *vb* **trod** /ˈtrɑːd/ *also* **tread-
ed; trod·den** /ˈtrɑːdn̩/ *or* **trod; treading** **1** [*I*] : to walk ▪ *Don't tread on the
grass.* ▪ (*figurative*) *She goes where others fear to tread.* [=does things that other
people are afraid to do] ▪ (*figurative*) *I advise you to tread lightly.* [=to proceed
carefully] **2** [*T*] : to walk on or along
(something) ▪ *treading the halls* ▪
(*figurative*) *treading a fine line between
justice and revenge* **3** [*T*] : to form (a
path) by walking ▪ *They have trodden a
path in the woods.* **4** [*T*] : to crush or
press (something) with your feet ▪ *Don't
tread dirt into the rug.* — **tread water 1**
: to float upright in deep water by moving your legs and arms forward and
backward **2** : to stay in a situation without making any progress ▪ *I'm just treading water financially right now.*

²**tread** *n* [*C*] **1** : the pattern of lines on the
surface of a tire or on the bottom of a
shoe or boot ▪ *The treads of our tires/
boots were badly worn.* **2** : the part of a
stair that you step on **3** : ¹STEP 2 ▪ *walking with a light/heavy tread*

tread·mill /ˈtrɛdˌmɪl/ *n* [*C*] : a machine
used for exercising which has a large belt
that moves around while a person walks
or runs on it

trea·son /ˈtriːzn̩/ *n* [*U*] : the crime of trying to overthrow your country's govern-
ment or of helping your country's enemies during war ▪ *He is guilty of treason.*
— **trea·son·able** /ˈtriːzənəbəl/ *adj* ▪
treasonable acts — **trea·son·ous**
/ˈtriːzənəs/ *adj* ▪ *treasonous behavior*

¹**trea·sure** /ˈtrɛʒɚ/ *n* **1** [*U*] : money, jewels, gold, etc., that is hidden or kept in a
safe place ▪ *the pirates' buried/sunken/
hidden treasure* **2** [*C*] : something that
is very special, important, or valuable ▪ *a
box of old childhood treasures* ▪ *The
Grand Canyon is a national treasure.*

²**treasure** *vb* **-sured; -sur·ing** [*T*] : to value (something) very much ▪ *I treasure
our friendship.* ▪ *my most treasured possession*

treasure chest *n* [*C*] : a large box that is
filled with gold, jewels, etc.

treasure house *n* [*C*] : a place where
there are many valuable things ▪ *Books
are treasure houses of knowledge.*

treasure hunt *n* [*C*] **1** : an act of
searching for treasure **2** : a game in

which players try to find objects that have been hidden — **treasure hunter** n [C]

trea·sur·er /ˈtrɛʒərə/ n [C] : someone who is officially in charge of the money that is taken in and paid out by a government, business, etc. ▪ *She is treasurer of the club.*

treasure trove n [C] : a collection of valuable things ▪ *Divers found a treasure trove of gold.* ▪ *The book is a treasure trove of useful information.*

trea·sury /ˈtrɛʒəri/ n, pl **-sur·ies** [C] **1** : the place where the money of a government, club, etc., is kept ▪ *stealing from the nation's treasury* **2** : a group of valuable things ▪ *a treasury of ideas/facts* — **(the) Treasury** : the government department that is in charge of handling a country's money ▪ *the U.S. Secretary of the Treasury* = *the Treasury Secretary* — called also the *Treasury Department*

¹treat /ˈtriːt/ vb **1** [T] : to deal with or think about (something) especially in a particular way ▪ *She treats the issue in her book.* ▪ *He treated it as a joke.* ▪ *This situation must be treated with care.* **2** [T] : to think of and act toward (someone or something) in a specified way ▪ *treat animals kindly/cruelly* ▪ *Treat your elders with respect.* ▪ *She treats everyone as an equal.* ▪ *They treated me like a queen/criminal/child.* ▪ *He treated me like dirt.* [=he was very rude, unkind, etc., to me] **3** a [T/I] : to pay for someone's food, drink, or entertainment ▪ *Let's go out to dinner. I'll treat.* ▪ *They treated us to lunch.* **b** [T] : to provide (someone) with something pleasant or amusing ▪ *He treated us to a song.* **c** [T] : to buy or get something special and enjoyable for (yourself) ▪ *He treated himself to some ice cream.* **4** [T] **a** : to give medical care to (a person or animal) ▪ *treat a patient* ▪ *She was treated for dehydration.* **b** : to deal with (an illness) in order to make someone better or healthy ▪ *The infection was treated with antibiotics.* **5** [T] : to put a chemical or other substance on or in (something) in order to protect it, preserve it, clean it, etc. ▪ *Has the water/wood been treated?* ▪ *The crops were treated with a pesticide.* — **treat·able** /ˈtriːtəbəl/ adj, medical ▪ *a treatable condition*

²treat n [C] **1** : an occurrence in which you pay for someone's food, drink, or entertainment ▪ *Let's go out to dinner. It'll be my treat.* **2** : something pleasant or amusing that is unusual or unexpected ▪ *It was a treat to see her again.* **3** US : something that tastes good and that is not eaten often ▪ *freshly baked treats* ▪ *I gave the dog a treat.* — **a treat** Brit, informal : very well or very good ▪ *The plan worked/looked a treat.* ▪ *The food went down a treat.* [=tasted very good]

trea·tise /ˈtriːtəs/ n [C] : a book, article, etc., that discusses a subject carefully and thoroughly ▪ *a treatise on education*

treat·ment /ˈtriːtmənt/ n **1** [U] : the way that you act toward someone or something ▪ *the humane treatment of prisoners* ▪ *She received special/preferential treat-*

ment *from teachers.* [=teachers were kinder to and less strict with her than with other students] **2** a [U] : the way that you deal with or discuss a subject ▪ *the book's careful treatment of the issue* **b** [C] : something that deals with or discusses a subject ▪ *Previous treatments of this topic have ignored some key issues.* **3** [C/U] : medical care that treats a disease, injury, etc. ▪ *The patient/condition required medical treatment.* ▪ *cancer treatments* **4** [C] : something that you use or do to feel and look healthy or attractive ▪ *a skin/beauty treatment* **5** [C/U] : a process in which a substance is put on or in something in order to protect it, clean it, etc. ▪ *a treatment that protects wood* ▪ *a waste/sewage treatment plant*

trea·ty /ˈtriːti/ n, pl **-ties** [C] : an official agreement that is made between two or more countries or groups ▪ *a peace treaty* [=an agreement to stop fighting a war]

¹tre·ble /ˈtrɛbəl/ n, music **1** [C/U] : the highest range of sounds used in music ▪ *Turn down the treble.* **2** [C] : a voice or instrument that has the highest range of sound

²treble adj **1** always before a noun, music : having or indicating a high sound or range ▪ *the treble clef* ▪ *a treble voice* **2** chiefly Brit : ³TRIPLE

³treble vb **tre·bled; tre·bling** [T/I] chiefly Brit : ¹TRIPLE 1 ▪ *She trebled her earnings.* ▪ *Prices have trebled.*

tree /ˈtriː/ n [C] : a usually tall plant that has a thick, wooden stem and many large branches ▪ *a pine/oak/apple tree* — see also FAMILY TREE — **not see the forest for the trees** (US) or US **miss the forest for the trees** or Brit **not see the wood for the trees** : to not understand or appreciate a larger situation, problem, etc., because you are considering only a few parts of it ▪ *This investment would be good for the company, but he's so concerned about saving money that he can't see the forest for the trees.* — **treed** /ˈtriːd/ adj : a heavily treed area [=an area in which there are many trees] — **tree·less** /ˈtriːləs/ adj ▪ *a treeless plain* — **tree·like** /ˈtriːˌlaɪk/ adj

tree house n [C] : a small house that is built among the branches of a tree

tree–lined adj : having trees on both sides ▪ *a tree-lined street*

tree·top /ˈtriːˌtɑːp/ n [C] : the highest part of a tree ▪ *from the highest treetops*

trek /ˈtrɛk/ vb **trekked; trek·king** [I] **1** : to walk usually for a long distance ▪ *We trekked up six flights of stairs.* **2** : to go on a long or difficult journey especially by walking ▪ *They went trekking in the Himalayas.* — **trek** n [C] ▪ *a trek across the country*

trel·lis /ˈtrɛləs/ n [C] : a wooden frame that is used as a support for climbing plants

trem·ble /ˈtrɛmbəl/ vb **trem·bled; trembling** [I] **1** : to shake slightly because you are afraid, excited, etc. ▪ *My hands/voice trembled as I began to speak.* ▪ *trembling with fear* **2** : to shake slightly because of some force ▪ *The house trembled as the train went by.* **3** : to be afraid or nervous ▪ *I tremble to think of it. = I tremble at the thought of it.* — **tremble** *n* [C] — usually singular ▪ *I felt a tremble as the train went by.*

tre·men·dous /trɪˈmɛndəs/ *adj* **1** : very large or great ▪ *He has a tremendous amount of energy/talent.* ▪ *a tremendous problem* **2** : WONDERFUL ▪ *That song was tremendous.* — **tre·men·dous·ly** *adv* ▪ *tremendously successful*

trem·or /ˈtrɛmɚ/ *n* [C] **1** : a shaking movement of the ground before or after an earthquake ▪ *We felt several small tremors.* **2** : a slight shaking that is caused by nervousness, illness, etc. ▪ *I heard a tremor in her voice.* ▪ *a disease that causes tremors*

trem·u·lous /ˈtrɛmjələs/ *adj, formal + literary* **1** : shaking slightly because of nervousness, illness, etc. ▪ *tremulous hands/voices* **2** : feeling or showing a lack of confidence or courage ▪ *a tremulous person/smile*

trench /ˈtrɛntʃ/ *n* [C] **1** : a long, narrow hole that is dug in the ground; *especially* : one that is used as protection for soldiers ▪ *soldiers who fought in the trenches in World War I* **2** : a long, narrow hole in the ocean floor

tren·chant /ˈtrɛntʃənt/ *adj, formal* : very strong, clear, and effective ▪ *a trenchant analysis/essay/wit* — **tren·chant·ly** *adv*

trench coat *n* [C] : a usually long raincoat with a belt

trend /ˈtrɛnd/ *n* [C] **1** : a way of behaving, proceeding, etc., that is becoming more common ▪ *the latest/current trend in fashion* ▪ *a disturbing/growing trend toward obesity in children* ▪ *He set/started a (new) trend.* **2** : something that is currently popular or fashionable ▪ *fashion trends* — **trend·set·ter** /ˈtrɛndˌsɛtɚ/ *n* [C] ▪ *She's a trendsetter.* — **trend·set·ting** /ˈtrɛndˌsɛtɪŋ/ *adj* ▪ *a trendsetting designer*

trendy /ˈtrɛndi/ *adj* **trend·i·er; -est** *sometimes disapproving* : currently popular or fashionable ▪ *trendy clothes/restaurants* — **trend·i·ness** /ˈtrɛndinəs/ *n* [U]

trep·i·da·tion /ˌtrɛpəˈdeɪʃən/ *n* [U] *formal* : a feeling of fear that causes you to hesitate ▪ *He had/felt some trepidation about signing the contract.*

¹**tres·pass** /ˈtrɛˌspæs, *Brit* ˈtrɛspəs/ *vb* [I] **1** : to go on someone's land without permission ▪ *The sign said "No Trespassing."* ▪ *The hunters trespassed on his land.* **2** *old-fashioned* : to do something that hurts or offends someone ▪ *those who trespass against us* — **tres·pass·er** *n* [C]

²**tres·pass** /ˈtrɛspəs/ *n* **1** [C/U] *law* : the crime of going on someone's land without permission ▪ *He was arrested for trespass.* **2** [C] *old-fashioned* : a sin or other wrong or improper act ▪ *Forgive us our trespasses.*

tress·es /ˈtrɛsəz/ *n* [*plural*] *literary* : a woman's long hair ▪ *her golden tresses*

tres·tle /ˈtrɛsəl/ *n* [C] : a structure that is used especially for supporting railroad tracks over a valley, river, etc.

T. rex /ˈtiːˈrɛks/ *n* [C] : TYRANNOSAURUS

tri- *prefix* : three : having three parts ▪ *triangle* ▪ *tricycle*

tri·ad /ˈtraɪˌæd/ *n* [C] : a group of three usually related people or things ▪ *a triad of symptoms*

tri·age /ˈtriːˌɑːʒ/ *n* [U] *medical* : the process of deciding which patients should be treated first based on how sick or seriously injured they are ▪ *doing triage in the ER*

¹**tri·al** /ˈtraɪəl/ *n* **1** [C/U] : a formal meeting in a court in which evidence about crimes, disagreements, etc., is presented to a judge and often a jury so that decisions can be made according to the law ▪ *civil/criminal trials* ▪ *a murder trial* ▪ *He got/had/received a fair trial.* ▪ *a trial by jury = a jury trial* ▪ *She is awaiting trial.* ▪ *She will stand/face trial* [=be tried] *for murder.* ▪ *He was brought to trial.* [=tried] ▪ *The case never came to trial.* ▪ *a man who is/goes on trial for murder* [=who has evidence against him presented in a court to a judge and often a jury to decide if he is guilty of murder] **2** [C] **a** : a test of the quality, value, or usefulness of a drug, medical device, etc. ▪ *drug/clinical trials* **b** : TRYOUT ▪ *the Olympic trials* **3** [C] : a difficult task, situation, etc., that shows how patient, strong, or trusting you are ▪ *Recovering from her injury was a real trial of strength.* **b** : something or someone that is difficult to deal with ▪ *the trials and tribulations* [=difficult experiences, problems, etc.] *of the settlers* — **trial and error** : a process in which you find out the best way to do something by trying different ways until one is successful ▪ *learning by/through trial and error*

²**trial** *adj, always before a noun* : relating to or used in a test that is done for a period of time to see if something is worth buying, using, etc. ▪ *a 30-day free trial period* ▪ *You can use it on a trial basis.* [=for a short period of time]

trial run *n* [C] : TEST RUN

tri·an·gle /ˈtraɪˌæŋgəl/ *n* [C] **1** : a shape that is made up of three lines and three angles **2** : something that is shaped like a triangle ▪ *She cut the sandwiches into triangles.* — **tri·an·gu·lar** /traɪˈæŋgjələ/ *adj*

tri·an·gu·la·tion /traɪˌæŋgjəˈleɪʃən/ *n* [U] *technical* : a method of finding a distance or location by measuring the distance between two points and then measuring the angles between each point and a third unknown point — **tri·an·gu·late** /traɪˈæŋgjəˌleɪt/ *vb* -**lat·ed; -lat·ing** [T] ▪ *triangulate a building's location*

tri·ath·lon /traɪˈæθlən/ *n* [C] *sports* : a long-distance race that has three parts (such as swimming, bicycling, and running) — **tri·ath·lete** /traɪˈæθˌliːt/ *n* [C]

tribe /ˈtraɪb/ *n* [C] : a group of people that includes many families and relatives who have the same language, customs, and beliefs ▪ *Native American tribes* ▪ *nomadic tribes* ▪ *(figurative, informal)* a tribe *of artists with wild hair* — **trib·al** /ˈtraɪbəl/ *adj* : *tribal culture/groups* — **trib·al·ly** *adv* — **tribes·man** /ˈtraɪbzmən/ *n, pl* -**men** /-mən/ [C] —

tribes·peo·ple /ˈtraɪbzˌpiːpəl/ n [plural] — **tribes·wom·an** /ˈtraɪbzˌwʊmən/ n, pl **-wom·en** /-ˌwɪmən/ [C]

trib·u·la·tion /ˌtrɪbjəˈleɪʃən/ n, formal 1 [U] : unhappiness, pain, or suffering • a source of tribulation 2 [C] : an experience that causes someone to suffer • the trials and tribulations [=difficult experiences, problems, etc.] of growing up

tri·bu·nal /traɪˈbjuːnl/ n [C] : a kind of court that has authority in a specific area • an international tribunal

trib·u·tary /ˈtrɪbjəˌteri, Brit ˈtrɪbjətri/ n, pl **-tar·ies** [C] : a stream that flows into a larger stream or river or into a lake

trib·ute /ˈtrɪˌbjuːt/ n 1 [C] : something that you say, give, or do to show respect or affection for someone • The concert was a tribute to the musician. • **paying tribute** to someone 2 [singular] : something that proves the good quality or effectiveness of something • Her success is a tribute to her skills.

trice /ˈtraɪs/ n — **in a trice** chiefly Brit : in a small amount of time • I'll be there in a trice.

tri·cep /ˈtraɪˌsɛp/ n [C] : TRICEPS

tri·ceps /ˈtraɪˌsɛps/ n, pl **triceps** [C] : a large muscle along the back of the upper arm — usually plural • My triceps are sore.

¹trick /ˈtrɪk/ n [C] 1 : an action that is meant to deceive someone • It was a trick to persuade her to give him money. 2 : something done to surprise or confuse someone and to make other people laugh • She enjoys playing tricks on her friends. 3 : a clever and skillful action that someone performs to entertain or amuse people • magic/card/circus tricks 4 : a clever and effective way of doing something • I know a good trick for removing stains from clothes. 5 : something that causes confusion or that makes something seem different from what it actually is • He was so tired his mind was playing tricks on him. [=he could not think clearly] • The paint looked blue, but it was just a trick of the light. [=the light made the paint appear blue] 6 : the cards that are played in one round of a card game • She won the last three tricks. — **do the trick** informal : to produce a desired result : to solve a problem • One small adjustment will do the trick. — **every trick in the book** ◇ If you try every trick in the book, you do everything you can to achieve something. • He tried/used every trick in the book to get the car started, but nothing worked.

²trick vb [T] : to deceive (someone) • He tricked her by wearing a disguise. • He was **tricked into** buying the car. • He bought the car because he was deceived. • She was **tricked out** of her savings. [=she lost her savings because she was deceived] — **trick out** [phrasal vb] 1 **trick (someone) out** : to dress (someone or yourself) in an unusual way • She was tricked out in a brightly colored costume. 2 **trick (something) out** or **trick out (something)** : to decorate (something) • The room was tricked out with ribbons and streamers.

trick·ery /ˈtrɪkəri/ n [U] : the use of tricks to deceive or cheat someone • He resorted to trickery to get what he wanted.

trick·le /ˈtrɪkəl/ vb **trick·led**; **trick·ling** [I] 1 : to flow or fall in drops • Tears trickled down her cheeks. 2 : to move or go slowly in small numbers or amounts • People trickled into the theater. • Donations have been trickling in. — **trickle** n [singular] • the trickle of water • Sales have slowed to a trickle.

trick or treat n [U] : a custom on Halloween in which children knock on people's doors and say "trick or treat" when the doors are opened to ask for candy — **trick–or–treat·er** n [C] • trick-or-treaters dressed up in costumes — **trick–or–treat·ing** n [U] • The kids went trick-or-treating

trick·ster /ˈtrɪkstɚ/ n [C] : someone who tricks or deceives people • a sly trickster

tricky /ˈtrɪki/ adj **trick·i·er**; **-est** 1 : using or likely to use dishonest tricks • a tricky salesman 2 : requiring skill or caution : difficult to do or deal with • a tricky question — **trick·i·ness** /ˈtrɪkinəs/ n [U]

tri·cy·cle /ˈtraɪsəkəl/ n [C] : a three-wheeled vehicle that a person rides by pushing on foot pedals

tri·dent /ˈtraɪdənt/ n [C] : a spear that has three points and that looks like a large fork

tried past tense and past participle of ¹TRY

tri·er /ˈtrajɚ/ n [C] : someone who tries very hard to do something

¹tri·fle /ˈtraɪfəl/ n [C] : something that does not have much value or importance • There's no reason to argue over such trifles. — **a trifle** : to a small degree • SLIGHTLY • The music is a trifle too loud.

²trifle vb **tri·fled**; **tri·fling** — **trifle with** [phrasal vb] : to treat or deal with (someone or something) in a way that shows a lack of proper respect or seriousness • You shouldn't trifle with their feelings. • She is not someone to be trifled with.

tri·fling /ˈtraɪfəlɪŋ/ adj : having little value or importance • trifling details

¹trig·ger /ˈtrɪgɚ/ n [C] 1 : a lever on a gun that you pull to fire the gun • He pulled/squeezed the trigger. 2 : something that causes something else to happen • The faulty wire was the trigger for the explosion.

²trigger vb [T] 1 : to cause (something) to start functioning • Smoke triggered the fire alarm. • **trigger a bomb** [=cause a bomb to explode] 2 : to cause (something) to start or happen • The power outage was triggered by heavy rains.

trig·ger–hap·py /ˈtrɪgɚˌhæpi/ adj, informal + disapproving : eager to fire a gun • trigger-happy hunters

trig·o·nom·e·try /ˌtrɪgəˈnɑːmətri/ n [U] : a branch of mathematics that deals with relationships between the sides and angles of triangles — **trig·o·no·met·ric** /ˌtrɪgənəˈmɛtrɪk/ also **trig·o·no·met·ri·cal** /ˌtrɪgənəˈmɛtrɪkəl/ adj

trike /ˈtraɪk/ n [C] informal : TRICYCLE

trill /ˈtrɪl/ n [C] 1 : the sound of going quickly back and forth many times between two musical notes that are close to each other **2** : a quick high sound that is repeated ▪ *She pronounces her r's with a trill.* — **trill** *vb* [T/I] ▪ *She trills her r's.*

tril·lion /'trɪljən/ *n, pl* **trillion** *or* **trillions** **1** : the number 1,000,000,000,000 ▪ *a/one/two trillion (of them)* ▪ *a hundred trillion = 100 trillion* ▪ *a trillion dollars* **2** : a very large amount or number ▪ *trillions (and trillions) of cells* — **tril·lionth** /'trɪljənθ/ *adj* — **trillionth** *n* [C]

tril·o·gy /'trɪlədʒi/ *n, pl* **-gies** [C] : a series of three novels, movies, etc., that involve the same characters or themes

¹**trim** /'trɪm/ *vb* **trimmed; trim·ming** [T] **1 a** : to cut (something) off something else : to remove (something) by cutting ▪ *She trimmed off/away the dead branches.* **b** : to make (something) neat by cutting it ▪ *He trimmed his mustache.* **2** : to make the size, amount, or extent of (something) smaller ▪ *They need to trim the budget.* **3** : to decorate (something) especially around the edges with ribbons, ornaments, etc. ▪ *We trimmed the Christmas tree.* ▪ *a pillow trimmed in/with lace* **4** : to adjust (a boat's sails) in order to move faster — **trim down** [*phrasal vb*] : to become thinner ▪ *He trimmed down over the summer.* — **trim·mer** /'trɪmɚ/ *n* [C]

²**trim** *adj* **trim·mer; trim·mest 1** : neat and orderly ▪ *a trim lawn* **2** : slim and healthy ▪ *He keeps fit and trim by biking.* — **trim·ly** *adv*

³**trim** *n* **1** [C] : an act of trimming something ▪ *He went to the barber for a trim.* **2** [C/U] : material that is used for decorating something especially around its edges ▪ *a skirt with (a) lace trim* ▪ *The house is gray with black trim.* [=the material around the doors, windows, etc., is black]

tri·mes·ter /traɪˈmɛstɚ/ *n* [C] **1** : a period of three months; *especially* : one of three periods into which a- woman's pregnancy is often divided **2** *US* : one of three periods into which an academic year is sometimes divided

trim·mings /'trɪmɪŋz/ *n* [*plural*] **1** : something that is added to complete a dish or meal ▪ *a feast with turkey and all the trimmings* [=all the other foods that are typically served with turkey] **2** : pieces removed from something by trimming it ▪ *hedge/meat trimmings* **3** *US* : something added as a decoration especially around the edges ▪ *a hat with leather trimmings*

trin·i·ty /'trɪnəti/ *n, pl* **-ties 1 the Trinity** *Christianity* : the Father, the Son, and the Holy Spirit existing as one God — called also *the Holy Trinity* **2** [C] : a group of three people or things ▪ *an unholy trinity of criminal organizations*

trin·ket /'trɪŋkət/ *n* [C] : a piece of jewelry or an ornament that has little value

trio /'triːjoʊ/ *n, pl* **tri·os** [C] **1** : a group of three singers or musicians who perform together ▪ *a jazz trio* **2** : a group of three people or things ▪ *a trio of novels*

¹**trip** /'trɪp/ *n* [C] **1 a** : a journey to a place ▪ *a trip around the world* ▪ *She took a trip to Europe.* ▪ *a day trip* [=a journey in which you go to visit a place and then return to your home on the same day] ▪ *She is on a business trip.* [=she is traveling as part of her work] **1 b** : a short journey to a store, office, etc., for a particular purpose ▪ *He made a trip to the dentist.* **2** *informal* : the experience of strange mental effects (such as seeing things that are not real) that is produced by taking a very powerful drug (such as LSD) ▪ *He was on an acid trip.*

²**trip** *vb* **tripped; trip·ping 1 a** [I] : to hit your foot against something while you are walking or running so that you fall or almost fall ▪ *He tripped over the curb.* ▪ *She tripped on the stairs.* **1 b** [T] : to cause (someone who is walking or running) to fall or almost fall ▪ *He tried to trip me.* ▪ *He got tripped up by the wires on the floor.* **2** [T] : to cause (an alarm, a switch, etc.) to be turned on often in an accidental way ▪ *Burglars smashed in the window and tripped the alarm.* **3** [I] *informal* : to experience strange mental effects (such as seeing things that are not real) after taking a very powerful drug (such as LSD) ▪ *They were tripping on acid.* — **trip up** [*phrasal vb*] **trip up (someone)** *or* **trip (someone) up** : to cause (someone) to make a mistake ▪ *He tried to trip up the cashier as she counted his change.*

tripe /'traɪp/ *n* [U] **1** : the stomach of an animal (such as a cow or ox) that is eaten as food **2** : something that is worthless, unimportant, or of poor quality ▪ *How can you watch this tripe?* [=rubbish]

¹**tri·ple** /'trɪpəl/ *vb* **tri·pled; tri·pling 1** [T/I] : to become or cause (something) to become three times as great or as many ▪ *The town's population has tripled in size.* ▪ *He tripled his winnings.* **2** [I] *baseball* : to hit a triple ▪ *He tripled to right field.*

²**triple** *n* [C] *baseball* : a hit that allows the batter to reach third base

³**triple** *adj* **1** : three times bigger in size or amount ▪ *She got a new job with triple the salary of her old one.* ▪ *a triple espresso* **2** *always before a noun* : having three parts or including three people or things ▪ *a triple murder* — **tri·ply** /'trɪpli/ *adv*

triple play *n* [C] *baseball* : a play in which the team in the field causes three runners to be put out

trip·let /'trɪplət/ *n* [C] : one of three babies that are born at the same time to the same mother

trip·li·cate /'trɪplɪkət/ *n* — **in triplicate** : in three copies ▪ *File the forms in triplicate.*

tri·pod /'traɪˌpɑːd/ *n* [C] : a support or stand for a camera, telescope, etc., that has three legs

trip·per /'trɪpɚ/ *n* [C] *chiefly Brit* : a person who takes a short trip to an interesting place ▪ *a day tripper* [=a person who goes on a short trip that lasts for less than a full day]

trip·tych /'trɪpˌtɪk/ *n* [C] : a picture, painting, etc., that has three panels placed next to each other

trite /'traɪt/ *adj* **trit·er; -est** : not interesting or effective because of being used too often ▪ *trite expressions* — **trite·ness** *n* [U]

¹**tri·umph** /ˈtraɪəmf/ n **1** [C] : a great or important victory, success, or achievement • *They earned/gained a magnificent triumph over/against the invading army.* • *Quitting smoking was a personal triumph for her.* • *The bridge is an engineering triumph.* **2** [U] : the very happy and joyful feeling that comes from victory or success • *a shout/feeling of triumph* • *They stood atop the mountain in triumph.*

²**triumph** vb [I] : to achieve victory especially in a long or difficult contest • *She likes stories where good triumphs over evil.*

tri·um·phal /traɪˈʌmfəl/ adj : of, relating to, or honoring a triumph : celebrating a victory or success • *a triumphal procession/arch*

tri·um·phant /traɪˈʌmfənt/ adj **1** : resulting in victory or success • *The boxer made a triumphant return to the ring.* **2** : celebrating victory or success • *a triumphant shout* — **tri·um·phant·ly** adv

tri·um·vi·rate /traɪˈʌmvərət/ n [C] : a group of three people who share a position of authority or power

triv·ia /ˈtrɪvijə/ n [U] **1** : unimportant facts or details • *She doesn't pay attention to such trivia.* **2** : facts about people, events, etc., that are not well-known • *He is an expert on baseball trivia.* • *trivia questions*

triv·i·al /ˈtrɪvijəl/ adj : not important • *trivial matters* • *a trivial sum of money* — **triv·i·al·i·ty** /ˌtrɪviˈæləti/ n, pl **-ties** [C/U] • *We shouldn't spend time on such trivialities.* [=trivial things]

triv·i·al·ize also Brit **triv·i·al·ise** /ˈtrɪvijəˌlaɪz/ vb **-ized; -iz·ing** [T] usually disapproving : to make (something) seem less important or serious than it actually is • *The news story trivialized the problem.*

trod past tense and past participle of ¹TREAD

trod·den past participle of ¹TREAD

¹**troll** /ˈtroʊl/ n [C] in stories : a creature that looks like a very large or very small ugly person

²**troll** vb [T/I] : to fish with a hook and line that you pull through the water • *They trolled for fish.*

trol·ley /ˈtrɑːli/ n, pl **-leys** [C] **1** a US : an electric vehicle that runs along the street on tracks — called also (US) trolley car **b** : a vehicle that is pulled along tracks on the ground by a moving cable or that hangs from a moving cable — called also (US) trolley car **2** chiefly Brit **a** : a metal basket on wheels used to hold groceries while you are shopping **b** : a table with wheels used especially for serving food • *a dessert trolley* [=(US) cart]

trom·bone /trɑmˈboʊn/ n [C] : a large brass musical instrument that you blow into and that has a tube that you slide in and out to play different notes — **trom·bon·ist** /trɑmˈboʊnɪst/ n [C]

tromp /ˈtrɑːmp/ vb [I] US, informal : ¹TRAMP 1 • *We tromped over/through the grass.*

¹**troop** /ˈtruːp/ n **1** a [C] : a group of soldiers • *Where is his troop heading?* **b** [plural] : soldiers in a group • *enemy troops* • *a plan to withdraw troops* **2** [C] : a group of people or things • *a troop of*

enthusiastic children **3** [C] : a group of Boy Scouts or Girl Scouts

²**troop** vb [I] : to walk somewhere in a group • *The kids trooped off to school.*

troop·er /ˈtruːpɚ/ n [C] **1** : a low-ranking soldier **2** US : a state police officer

tro·phy /ˈtroʊfi/ n, pl **-phies** [C] **1** : an object (such as a large cup or sculpture) that is given as a prize for winning a competition • *a bowling trophy* **2** : something that you keep or take to show that you were successful in hunting, war, etc. • *hunting trophies*

trop·ic /ˈtrɑːpɪk/ n **1** [singular] : either one of the two imaginary lines that circle the Earth to the north and south of the equator ❖ **The Tropic of Cancer** is 23½ degrees north of the equator and the **Tropic of Capricorn** is 23½ degrees south of the equator. **2** **the tropics** [plural] : the part of the world that is near the equator where the weather is very warm • *a vacation in the tropics* — **trop·i·cal** /ˈtrɑːpɪkəl/ adj • *tropical forests/plants* • *a tropical climate/country*

¹**trot** /ˈtrɑːt/ vb **trot·ted; trot·ting** [I] **1** of a horse : to move at a speed faster than walking by stepping with each front leg at the same time as the opposite back leg • *A horse trotted past us.* **2** a : to run at a slow, steady pace • *The batter trotted around the bases after hitting a home run.* **b** : to move quickly : HURRY • *She trotted off to help.* — **trot out** [phrasal vb] **trot (something) out** or **trot out (something)** informal + disapproving : to say (something that has been said before) as an excuse, explanation, etc. • *Don't trot out that old excuse again.*

²**trot** n [singular] **1** : a horse's way of moving that is faster than a walk but slower than a gallop • *The horse went into a trot.* **2** : a person's way of running slowly • *He set off at a trot.* — **on the trot** Brit, informal : following one after another • *He won the race three times on the trot.* [=in a row]

trou·ba·dour /ˈtruːbəˌdoɚ/ n [C] : a writer and performer of songs or poetry in the Middle Ages

¹**trou·ble** /ˈtrʌbəl/ n **1** [C/U] : problems or difficulties • *The new system is giving me trouble.* • *He was having trouble with his homework/computer.* • *I had a little trouble finding the place.* • *financial troubles* • *gangs looking to make/cause trouble* **2** [U] a : a situation that is difficult or has a lot of problems • *The company is in financial trouble.* **b** : a situation that occurs if you do something wrong or break a rule and which will make someone angry or cause you to be punished • *He's always getting in/into trouble at school.* • *He promised to keep/stay out of trouble.* • *He will be in trouble with his mom if he's late.* **3** [singular] : a bad feature, characteristic, quality, etc. • *His trouble is that he's lazy.* • *The trouble with driving into the city is finding a place to park.* **4** [U] : extra effort or work • *You didn't have to go to all that trouble for me.* • *Thank you for taking the trouble to write.* • *I decided that upgrading the soft-*

ware was more trouble than it's worth. • *If it's no trouble, could you bring us some more coffee?* — **ask for trouble** see ASK

²**trouble** *vb* **trou·bled; trou·bling** [*T*] **1** : to make (someone) feel worried or upset • *I'm troubled by his strange behavior.* **2** *formal* : to disturb or bother (someone) • *I don't mean to trouble you, but I have a question.* • **Don't trouble yourself** [=I don't need your help], *I can handle it.* **3** : to cause (someone) to feel pain • *My back has been troubling* [=*bothering*] *me again.* **4** : to make an effort *to do* something • *I wish you'd at least troubled to call.*

troubled *adj* **1** : worried or anxious • *a troubled expression/look* **2** : having many problems • *a troubled child/student*

trou·ble·mak·er /ˈtrʌbəlˌmeɪkɚ/ *n* [*C*] : a person who causes trouble • *He was a troublemaker in high school.*

trou·ble·shoot·er /ˈtrʌbəlˌʃuːtɚ/ *n* [*C*] **1** : a person who finds and fixes problems in machinery, computers, etc. **2** : a person who tries to find solutions to problems or end disagreements • *a financial troubleshooter* — **trou·ble·shoot·ing** /ˈtrʌbəlˌʃuːtɪŋ/ *n* [*U*]

trou·ble·some /ˈtrʌbəlsəm/ *adj* : causing problems or worry : causing trouble • *a troublesome infection/child*

trouble spot *n* [*C*] : a place where violence or war often happens • *one of the world's trouble spots*

trough /ˈtrɑːf/ *n* [*C*] **1** : a long, shallow container from which animals (such as cows, pigs, etc.) eat or drink • *a water trough* **2** : a long, low area between waves or hills

trounce /ˈtraʊns/ *vb* **trounced; trounc·ing** [*T*] : to defeat (someone or something) easily and thoroughly • *Their opponents trounced them in the final game.*

troupe /ˈtruːp/ *n* [*C*] : a group of actors, singers, etc., who work together • *an acting/dance troupe*

troup·er /ˈtruːpɚ/ *n* [*C*] *informal* **1** : an actor or other performer who is very experienced and reliable **2** : someone who works very hard, is very reliable, and does not complain when there are problems

trou·sers /ˈtraʊzɚz/ *n* [*plural*] : PANTS 1 — **trou·ser** /ˈtraʊzɚ/ *adj, always before a noun* • *a trouser leg*

trouser suit *n* [*C*] *Brit* : PANTSUIT

trout /ˈtraʊt/ *n, pl* **trout** *also* **trouts** [*C/U*] : a common fish that lives in rivers and lakes and is often used as food

trove /ˈtroʊv/ *n* [*C*] see TREASURE TROVE

trow·el /ˈtraʊəl/ *n* [*C*] **1** : a small tool with a curved blade that is used for digging holes **2** : a small tool with a flat blade that is used for spreading and smoothing mortar or plaster

tru·ant /ˈtruːwənt/ *n* [*C*] : a student who misses school without permission — **tru·an·cy** /ˈtruːwənsi/ *n, pl* **-cies** [*C/U*] • *the problem of truancy in schools*

truce /ˈtruːs/ *n* [*C*] : an agreement between enemies or opponents to stop fighting, arguing, etc., for a certain period of time • *They called/proposed a truce.*

¹**truck** /ˈtrʌk/ *n* [*C*] **1 a** : a very large,

heavy vehicle that is used to move large or numerous objects • *a delivery truck* **b** : a vehicle that is larger than a car and that has an open back with low sides : PICKUP **2** : a piece of equipment that has wheels and handles and that you push or pull to move heavy objects **3** *Brit* : a railroad car that is open at the top

²**truck** *vb* [*T*] *US* : to transport (something) in a truck • *They trucked food to the market.* • *Produce is trucked in from local farms.*

truck·er /ˈtrʌkɚ/ *n* [*C*] *US* : a person whose job is to drive a truck

tru·cu·lent /ˈtrʌkjələnt/ *adj* : easily annoyed or angered and likely to argue • *a truculent person* — **truc·u·lence** /ˈtrʌkjələns/ *n* [*U*]

trudge /ˈtrʌdʒ/ *vb* **trudged; trudg·ing** [*I*] : to walk slowly and heavily because you are tired or working very hard • *trudging through the snow* — **trudge** *n* [*singular*]

¹**true** /ˈtruː/ *adj* **tru·er; -est** **1** : agreeing with the facts : not false • *a true statement/story* • *Is it true that you were planning to go without me?* • *He can be stubborn, but that is true of many people.* [=many people can be stubborn] **2** *always before a noun* : real or genuine • *His true character was revealed.* • *She let him know her true feelings.* **3** : having all the expected or necessary qualities of a specified type of person or thing • *He's a true artist/gentleman.* **4** : completely loyal or faithful • *true friends* • *He's always been true to his wife.* **5** : placed or done correctly or perfectly • *His aim was true.* [=he hit the target] **6** *always before a noun* : rightful, legal, or official • *He is the true king.* **7** — used to admit that something is correct or true • *"It would cost a lot less if we did it ourselves." "(That's) True."* — **come true** : to become real : to happen in the way that you wished or dreamed • *Their prediction came true.* • *The trip abroad was a dream come true.* — **show your true colors** see ¹COLOR — **too good to be true** see ¹GOOD — **true to life** : realistic and natural • *The author's characters are true to life.* — **true to yourself** : acting in a way that agrees with your beliefs or values • *He's always true to himself.* [=he always does what he thinks is right] — **true to your word** : doing what you said you would do : keeping your promise • *He said he would help, and he was true to his word.*

²**true** *adv* : in a straight line • *The bullet traveled straight and true.*

true–blue *adj* **1** *US* : completely faithful and loyal • *a true-blue patriot/friend* **2** *Brit, informal* : loyal to the ideas of the British Conservative party • *true-blue Tories*

true–life /ˈtruːˈlaɪf/ *adj, always before a noun* : based on a real story and not imaginary • *a true-life movie*

truf·fle /ˈtrʌfəl/ *n* [*C*] **1** : a type of fungus that grows under the ground and that is used in cooking **2** : a kind of chocolate candy with a soft center

tru·ism /ˈtruːˌɪzəm/ *n* [*C*] : a true statement that is very commonly heard

tru·ly /ˈtruːli/ *adv* **1** : in an honest manner : SINCERELY ▪ *I truly believe they can do it.* ▪ *She's truly sorry.* **2** : in truth : actually or really ▪ *This is truly a different situation.* **3** : without question or doubt ▪ *It's truly hot out today.* — **yours truly 1** — used at the end of a letter and before the writer's signature **2** *humorous* — used to refer to yourself ▪ *"Who is in charge here?" "Yours truly."* [=I am]

¹trump /ˈtrʌmp/ *n* **1** [C] : a card from the suit that has been chosen as the most valuable for a particular card game ▪ *a trump card* **2** [U, *plural*] : the suit whose cards are the most valuable for a particular card game ▪ *Diamonds are trumps.* — **come/turn up trumps** *Brit, informal* : to do or provide what is necessary in order to succeed ▪ *The team turned up trumps in the second half and won the game.*

²trump *vb* [T] **1** : to play a trump card to beat (another card) ▪ *She trumped my ace to win the trick.* **2** : to do better than or be more important than (someone or something) ▪ *Their offer for the house was trumped by a higher bid.*

trumped–up /ˈtrʌmptˈʌp/ *adj* : deliberately done or created to make someone appear guilty ▪ *She was arrested on trumped-up charges.*

¹trum·pet /ˈtrʌmpət/ *n* [C] **1** : a brass musical instrument that you blow into and that has three buttons which you press to play different notes **2** : something shaped like a trumpet ▪ *the trumpet of a flower* — **blow your own trumpet** *Brit, informal* : to talk about yourself or your achievements especially in a way that shows that you are proud or too proud

²trumpet *vb* **1** [T] : to praise (something) loudly and publicly especially in a way that is annoying ▪ *He likes to trumpet his own achievements.* **2** [I] : to make a sound like a trumpet ▪ *The elephant trumpeted loudly.*

trum·pet·er /ˈtrʌmpətɚ/ *n* [C] : a person who plays a trumpet

trun·cate /ˈtrʌŋˌkeɪt/ *vb* **-cat·ed; -cat·ing** [T] *formal* : to make (something) shorter ▪ *The essay was truncated before it was published.* ▪ *a truncated discussion* — **trun·ca·tion** /trʌŋˈkeɪʃən/ *n* [U]

trun·cheon /ˈtrʌnʃən/ *n* [C] *Brit* : NIGHTSTICK

trun·dle /ˈtrʌndl̩/ *vb* **trun·dled; trun·dling** [T/I] : to roll on wheels slowly and noisily ▪ *She trundled her suitcase into the room.* ▪ *Trucks trundled through town.*

trunk /ˈtrʌŋk/ *n* **1** [C] : the thick main stem of a tree **2** [C] : the main part of the human body not including the head, arms, and legs **3** [C] : the main or central part of something ▪ *the trunk of an artery* **4** [C] *US* : the enclosed space in the back of a car for carrying things ▪ *The spare tire is in the trunk.* — called also *(Brit)* **boot 5** [C] : a large, strong box used for holding clothes or other things especially for traveling **6** [C] : the long, flexible nose of an elephant **7** [*plural*] **a** : SWIMMING TRUNKS **b** : shorts worn by a boxer

trunk road *n* [C] *Brit* : a main road

¹truss /ˈtrʌs/ *vb* [T] **1** : to tie up (someone) tightly ▪ *The thieves trussed (up) the guards.* **2** : to tie together the wings or legs of (a turkey, chicken, etc.) for cooking ▪ *She stuffed and trussed the duck.*

²truss *n* [C] : a strong frame of beams, bars, or rods that supports a roof or bridge

¹trust /ˈtrʌst/ *n* **1** [U] : belief that someone or something is reliable, good, honest, effective, etc. ▪ *Our relationship is founded on mutual love and trust.* ▪ *She has no trust in the security of online banking.* ▪ *He placed/put his trust in us.* ▪ *She betrayed my trust.* **2 a** [C/U] : an arrangement in which someone's property or money is legally held or managed by someone else or by an organization (such as a bank) for usually a set period of time ▪ *He created a trust for his children.* ▪ *The property will be held in trust until her 18th birthday.* **b** [C] : an organization that results from the creation of a trust ▪ *a charitable trust* **3** [C] *chiefly US* : a group of companies that work together to try to control an industry by reducing competition **4** [U] : responsibility for the safety and care of someone or something ▪ *The child was committed to his trust.* ▪ *We left our pets in the trust of* [=in the care of] *our neighbor while we were gone.* — **take something on trust** : to believe that something you have been told is true or correct even though you do not have proof of it

²trust *vb* [T] **1** : to believe that someone or something is reliable, true, good, honest, effective, etc. ▪ *They don't trust each other.* ▪ *I trust him to do the right thing.* ▪ *a parent, teacher, or someone else you trust* ▪ *I don't trust that ladder.* [=I don't think that ladder is safe] ▪ *You should trust your instincts/judgment* ▪ *and do what you think is right.* **2** : to hope or expect that something is true or will happen — often used to politely tell someone what you think they should do ▪ *I trust that you'll pay me for the broken window.* — **trust in** [*phrasal vb*] *formal* : to have a strong belief in the goodness or ability of (someone or something) ▪ *trust in God* ▪ *It is important to trust in yourself and your abilities.* — **trust to** [*phrasal vb*] **1** : to rely on (luck, chance, etc.) to get what you want or need ▪ *All we can do is hope for the best and trust to luck.* **2 trust (something) to** : to give the responsibility of (something) to (someone) ▪ *They trusted the care of their daughter to us while they were away.* — **trust with** [*phrasal vb*] **trust (someone) with** : to allow (someone) to have or use (something) ▪ *They trusted their son with the family car.*

trust·ee /ˌtrʌˈstiː/ *n* [C] **1** : a person or organization that has been given responsibility for managing someone else's property or money through a trust ▪ *trustees to the estate* **2** : a member of a group that manages the money of an organization ▪ *the museum's board of trustees*

trust·ing /ˈtrʌstɪŋ/ *adj* : tending to believe that other people are honest, good, etc. • *a naive and trusting person*

trust·wor·thy /'trʌst,wɜði/ *adj* : able to be relied on to do or provide what is needed or right : deserving of trust • *trustworthy friends* — **trust·wor·thi·ness** *n* [U]

trusty /'trʌsti/ *adj, always before a noun* **trust·i·er; -est** : able to be depended on • *my trusty pocketknife*

truth /'truːθ/ *n, pl* **truths** /'truːðz, 'truːθs/ **1** *the truth* : the real facts about something : the things that are true • *Are you telling (me) the truth?* • *You have to face the simple/hard truth that we failed.* • *Do you swear to tell the whole truth and nothing but the truth?* • *I know you think I don't care, but nothing could be further from the truth.* [=that is absolutely not true] • *To tell (you) the truth, I liked her first book better than this one.* • *I told her I liked the restaurant but, (the) truth be told/known, the food was pretty bad.* **2** [U] : the quality or state of being true • *There's no truth in anything he says.* • *She said she was feeling fine, but in truth* [=*actually*] *she was very ill.* **3** [C] : a statement or idea that is true or accepted as true • *basic/universal truths about human nature* — **moment of truth** see ¹MOMENT

truth·ful /'truːθfəl/ *adj* : telling or expressing the truth : HONEST • *They are truthful (people).* • *a truthful answer* • *The movie is truthful to actual events.* [=it shows what actually happened] — **truth·ful·ly** /'truːθfəli/ *adv* — **truth·ful·ness** *n* [U]

¹try /'traɪ/ *vb* **tries; tried; try·ing 1** [T/I] : to make an effort to do something • *You can do it if you try hard enough.* • *I was only trying to help!* • *Try to relax.* = *Try and relax.* • *If you don't succeed the first time, try, (and) try again.* • *I tried my best/hardest, but I just couldn't do it.* **2** [T] : to do or use (something) in order to see if it works or will be successful • *He tried (out) a few things to remove the stain, but nothing worked.* • *If you want to lose weight, try exercising more.* • *I tried (opening) the door, but it was locked.* • *You should try (out) a different approach.* **3** [T] **a** : to do or use (something) in order to find out if you like it • *He never wants to try anything new.* • *I tried skiing for the first time last winter.* • *She has tried (out) many different jobs but can't find one she likes.* **b** : to taste (food or drink) to find out what it is like • *You should try the cake. It's excellent.* **4** [T] : to test how good, strong, etc., something or someone is • *You are trying my patience.* [=you are making me lose my patience and become angry] **5** [T] **a** : to examine and make a decision about (a legal case) • *The case was tried in a federal court.* **b** : to have a trial to decide if someone is innocent or guilty • *He was tried for murder.* [=he was put on trial for murder] — **try for** [*phrasal vb*] : to make an attempt or effort to get (something) • *She tried for the job and got it.* — **try on** [*phrasal vb*] **try on** (something) or **try** (something) **on** : to put on (a piece of

clothing, a pair of shoes, etc.) in order to see how it fits and looks • *This is the fifth dress you've tried on.* — **try out** [*phrasal vb*] *chiefly US* : to compete for a position on an athletic team or a part in a play • *He tried out for the golf team.* — **try your hand** see ¹HAND

²try *n, pl* **tries** [C] **1** : an effort or attempt to do something • *I doubt it will work, but it's worth a try.* • *Nice try. I'm sure you'll do better next time.* • *"I can't open this jar." "Let me have a try at it."* • *You should give skydiving a try.* **2** *rugby* : a play in which points are scored by touching the ground with the ball behind the opponent's goal line • *He scored a try.*

trying *adj* : difficult to deal with • *These are trying times.* • *He can be very trying.*

try·out /'traɪ,aʊt/ *n* [C] *US* : a test of someone's ability to do something that is used to see if he or she should join a team, perform in a play, etc. • *Open tryouts for the team are next Monday.*

tryst /'trɪst/ *n* [C] *literary* : a meeting by lovers at a secret time or place

tsar, tsarina *variant spellings of* CZAR, CZARINA

T–shirt *also* **tee shirt** /'tiː,ʃɚt/ *n* [C] : a shirt that has short sleeves and no collar and that is usually made of cotton

tsp. *abbr* teaspoon, teaspoonful

tsu·na·mi /su'nɑːmi/ *n* [C] : a very high, large wave in the ocean that is usually caused by an earthquake under the sea and that can cause great destruction when it reaches land

Tu. *abbr* Tuesday

tub /'tʌb/ *n* [C] **1** : a wide container used to hold something • *a tub of butter/water* **2** *US* : BATHTUB • *The bathroom has a shower and tub.*

tu·ba /'tuːbə, *Brit* 'tjuːbə/ *n* [C] : a large brass musical instrument that is played by blowing air into it and that produces low tones

tub·by /'tʌbi/ *adj* **tub·bi·er; -est** *informal* : short and somewhat fat • *a tubby kid*

tube /'tuːb, *Brit* 'tjuːb/ *n* **1** [C] **a** : a long, hollow object that is used especially to control the flow of a liquid or gas • *She was breathing oxygen through a tube.* **b** : an object shaped like a pipe • *a tube of lipstick* **2** [C] : a soft, long, narrow container that has a small opening at one end and that contains a soft material which can be pushed out by squeezing • *a tube of toothpaste* **3** [C] : thin, long, hollow part within an animal or plant • *bronchial/pollen tubes* **4** *the tube US, informal* : the television • *What's on the tube tonight?* **5** [U] *Brit* : the system of trains that run underground in London • *It's easy to get around London on the tube.* • *a tube station* — **go down the tubes** *informal* **1** : to fail or become ruined • *His health is going down the tubes.* **2** : to be wasted or lost • *All my hard work went down the tubes.*

tu·ber /'tuːbə, *Brit* 'tjuːbə/ *n* [C] : a short, thick, round stem that is a part of certain plants (such as the potato), that grows underground, and that can produce a new plant — **tu·ber·ous** /'tu:bərəs, Brit 'tju:bərəs/ adj • *tuberous roots*

tu·ber·cu·lo·sis /tu₁bəkjə'lousəs, Brit tju₁bɜː'kjə'lousəs/ n [U] : a serious disease that mainly affects the lungs — called also TB — **tu·ber·cu·lar** /tʊ'bɜːkjələ, Brit tjuː'bɜːkjələ/ adj • *a tubercular cough* — **tu·ber·cu·lous** /tʊ'bəkjələs, Brit tjuː'bɜːkjələs/ adj • *a tuberculous patient*

tu·bu·lar /'tu:bjələ, Brit 'tju:bjələ/ adj 1 : having the form of a tube • *tubular flowers/pasta* 2 : made of a tube or tubes • *a tubular chair*

¹**tuck** /'tʌk/ vb 1 [T] : to push the end of (something) into or behind something in order to hold it in place, make it look neat, etc. • *Tuck in your shirt.* [=push the bottom of your shirt into the waist of your pants or skirt] • *She tucked in the flap of the envelope.* • *The sheets were tucked tightly under the mattress.* 2 [T] a : to put (something) in a particular place usually to hide it, hold it, or make it safe • *She tucked her hair up under her hat.* • *The dog tucked its tail between its legs and slinked away.* — often + away • *He keeps his coin collection tucked away in the closet.* b — used as *tucked* to indicate the quiet or hidden place where something is located • *They live in a log cabin tucked (away) among the trees.* 3 [T/I] Brit, informal : to eat with pleasure • *He tucked away a big lunch.* • *We tucked in as soon as the food was served.* — *We all tucked into the delicious food.* — **tuck in** or chiefly Brit **tuck up** [phrasal vb] **tuck (someone) in/up** : to make (someone) comfortable in bed by moving the blankets to the right positions • *I tucked him in and kissed him good night.*

²**tuck** n [C] 1 : a fold that is sewn into a piece of clothing or fabric 2 : an operation to remove extra skin or fat from a part of the body • *a tummy tuck* — see also *nip and tuck* at ²NIP

tuck·er /'tʌkə/ vb — **tucker (someone) out** or **tucker out (someone)** US, informal : to cause (someone) to become very tired • *Raking the leaves tuckered me out.* • *We were tuckered out by the hard work.*

Tues. or **Tue.** abbr Tuesday

Tues·day /'tu:z₁deɪ, Brit 'tju:z₁deɪ/ n [C/U] : the day of the week between Monday and Wednesday • *I had lunch with her last Tuesday.* • *I'll arrive (on) Tuesday.* = (Brit) *I'll arrive on the Tuesday.* — abbr. **Tues.**, **Tue.**, or **Tu.** — **Tues·days** /'tu:z₁deɪz, Brit 'tju:z₁deɪz/ adv • *He works late Tuesdays.* [=every Tuesday]

tuft /'tʌft/ n [C] : a small bunch of feathers, hairs, grass, etc., that grow close together • *tufts of grass* — **tuft·ed** /'tʌftəd/ adj • *The fox has tufted ears.*

¹**tug** /'tʌg/ vb **tugged**; **tug·ging** [T/I] : to pull something with a quick, forceful movement • *She tugged the rope.* • *I felt someone tugging on/at my sleeve.*

²**tug** n [C] 1 : a quick pull • *She gave the rope a tug.* 2 : a strong pulling force • *the tug of gravity* • *(figurative) The tug of city life drew him from his country home.* 3 : TUGBOAT

tug·boat /'tʌg₁boʊt/ n [C] : a small, powerful boat that is used for pulling and pushing ships

tug-of-war /₁tʌgəv'woə/ n, pl **tugs-of-war** 1 [singular] : a contest in which two teams pull against each other at opposite ends of a rope 2 [C] : a struggle between two people or groups to win control or possession of something • *The countries are in a tug-of-war over control of the region.*

tu·ition /tə'wɪʃən, Brit tjuː'ɪʃən/ n [U] : money that is paid to a school for the right to study there • *an increase in tuition* • *tuition fees*

tu·lip /'tu:ləp, Brit 'tju:ləp/ n [C] : a large, bright flower that is shaped like a cup and that grows in the spring

tulle /'tu:l/ n [U] : a light, thin type of cloth that is like a net and that is used for veils, evening dresses, etc.

tum /'tʌm/ n [C] Brit, informal : your stomach or belly

tum·ble /'tʌmbəl/ vb **tum·bled**; **tum·bling** [I] 1 a : to fall down suddenly and quickly • *He tripped and tumbled to the ground.* • *The statue came tumbling down during the riots.* b : to fall forward while turning over • *She slipped and tumbled down the hill.* 2 : to fall suddenly in amount, value, etc. • *Stock prices tumbled.* 3 : to move in a fast, confused, or uncontrolled way • *Water tumbled over the rocks.* 4 : to roll or turn your body across the ground or through the air while performing a series of athletic movements • *tumbling acrobats* — **tumble** n [C] • *She took a tumble down the stairs.* [=she fell down the stairs] • *The value of the stock has taken a tumble.*

tum·ble·down /'tʌmbəl₁daʊn/ adj, always before a noun : in bad condition : ready to fall down • *a tumbledown shack*

tumble dryer or **tumble drier** n [C] Brit : a machine used for drying clothes after they are washed

tum·bler /'tʌmblə/ n [C] 1 : a glass used for drinking that has a flat bottom and no stem or handle 2 : a person who performs athletic movements that involve rolling or turning along the ground or through the air • *circus tumblers* [=acrobats]

tum·ble·weed /'tʌmbəl₁wi:d/ n [C/U] : a plant found especially in the North American desert that breaks away from its roots and is blown across the ground by the wind

tum·my /'tʌmi/ n, pl **-mies** [C] informal : your stomach or belly • *She woke up with a tummy ache.* [=a stomachache]

tu·mor (US) or Brit **tu·mour** /'tu:mə, Brit 'tju:mə/ n [C] : a mass of tissue found in or on the body that is made up of abnormal cells • *a brain tumor*

tu·mult /'tu:₁mʌlt, Brit 'tju:₁mʌlt/ n [C/U] formal 1 : a state of noisy confusion or disorder • *We had to shout to be heard over the tumult.* • *The country was in tumult.* 2 : a state of great mental or emotional confusion • *emotional tumult = a tumult of emotions*

tu·mul·tu·ous /tʊ'mʌltʃəwəs, Brit tjuː-

ˈmʌltʃəwəs/ *adj* **1** : loud, excited, and emotional ▪ *tumultuous applause* **2** : involving a lot of violence, confusion, or disorder ▪ *the nation's tumultuous past*

tu·na /ˈtuːnə, *Brit* ˈtjuːnə/ *n, pl* **tuna** also **tunas** **1** [*C*] : a large fish that lives in the ocean and is eaten as food **2** [*U*] : the meat of a tuna that is eaten as food ▪ *a can of tuna* ▪ *tuna salad* — called also *tuna fish*

tun·dra /ˈtʌndrə/ *n* [*C/U*] : a large area of flat land in northern parts of the world where there are no trees and the ground is always frozen

¹**tune** /ˈtuːn, *Brit* ˈtjuːn/ *n* [*C*] : a series of musical notes that produce a pleasing sound when played or sung ▪ *dance tunes* ▪ *He played a delightful tune* [=*melody*] *on the piano.* ▪ *a catchy tune* [=*song*] — **call the tune** *informal* : to be in charge or control of something ▪ *She called the tune all through the meeting.* — **change your tune** *or* **sing a different tune** *informal* : to change the way you talk or think about something ▪ *He bragged that the test was easy, but when he saw his grade he changed his tune.* — **in tune** **1** : in a state in which the correct musical sound is played or sung ▪ *The guitar was in tune.* **2** : in a state in which people or things agree with one another ▪ *The president and his followers were clearly in tune (with each other).* ▪ *Her formal clothing was in tune with the occasion.* — **out of tune** **1** : in a state in which the correct musical sound is not played or sung ▪ *The piano was out of tune.* **2** : in a state in which people or things do not agree with one another ▪ *His speech was out of tune with our concerns.* — **to the tune of** **1** : using the tune of (a particular song) ▪ *Amusing lyrics were sung to the tune of* [=to the music of the song] *"New York, New York."* **2** *informal* — used to emphasize a large amount of money ▪ *A telecommunications company funded the event to the tune of* [=at a cost of] *several million dollars.*

²**tune** *vb* **tuned; tun·ing** **1** [*T*] : to adjust (a musical instrument) so that it makes the correct sound when played ▪ *The piano needs to be tuned.* **2** [*T*] : to make small changes to (something) in order to make it work better ▪ *The mechanic tuned (up) the engine.* **3** [*T/I*] : to adjust (a radio or television) so that it receives a broadcast clearly ▪ *The televisions in the store were tuned (in) to the same channel.* ▪ *He tuned (in) to the news channel.* — **stay tuned** : to keep watching a television show or listening to a radio broadcast ▪ *Stay tuned for a news update.* ▪ (*figurative*) *Stay tuned for a new version of the software.* [=a new version of the software will be available soon] — **tune in** [*phrasal vb*] **1** : to watch a television show or listen to a radio broadcast ▪ *Millions of listeners/viewers tuned in for coverage of the presidential debate.* **2** **be tuned in** : to understand and be aware of something ▪ *He was tuned in to the needs of his staff.* — **tune out** [*phrasal vb*] *informal* **tune out** *or* **tune (someone or something) out** *or* **tune out (someone or**

something) : to ignore or not listen to (someone or something) ▪ *After just five minutes of listening to the lecture, he began to tune out.* ▪ *She tuned out the noise and concentrated on her work.*

tune·ful /ˈtuːnfəl, *Brit* ˈtjuːnfəl/ *adj* : having a pleasant musical sound ▪ *a tuneful melody*

tune·less /ˈtuːnləs, *Brit* ˈtjuːnləs/ *adj* : not having a pleasant musical sound ▪ *tuneless humming*

tun·er /ˈtuːnə, *Brit* ˈtjuːnə/ *n* [*C*] **1** : a person who tunes musical instruments ▪ *a piano tuner* **2** : an electronic device that changes radio signals into sounds or images ▪ *televisions with digital tuners*

tune-up /ˈtuːnˌʌp, *Brit* ˈtjuːnˌʌp/ *n* [*C*] *chiefly US* : a process in which small changes are made to something (such as an engine) in order to make it work better ▪ *My car needs a tune-up.*

tung·sten /ˈtʌŋstən/ *n* [*U*] : a hard metal that is used to make the thin wire in light bulbs and to harden other metals (such as steel)

tu·nic /ˈtuːnɪk, *Brit* ˈtjuːnɪk/ *n* [*C*] **1** : a loose piece of clothing usually without sleeves that reaches to the knees and that was worn by men and women in ancient Greece and Rome **2** : a long shirt or jacket that reaches to or just below the hips

tuning fork *n* [*C*] : a metal device that has two long points, that produces a particular note when it is hit, and that is used to tune musical instruments

¹**tun·nel** /ˈtʌnl/ *n* [*C*] : a passage that goes under the ground, through a hill, etc. ▪ *The train goes through a tunnel in the mountain.* — **(a) light at the end of the tunnel** see ¹**LIGHT**

²**tunnel** *vb, US* **-neled** *or Brit* **-nelled;** *US* **-nel·ing** *or Brit* **-nel·ling** [*T/I*] : to make a tunnel ▪ *Insects tunneled into the tree.* ▪ *The prisoners tunneled their way out.* [=escaped by digging a tunnel]

tunnel vision *n* [*U*] **1** *medical* : a condition in which you can see things that are straight ahead of you but not to the side **2** *often disapproving* : a tendency to think only about one thing and to ignore everything else ▪ *His tunnel vision made sensible discussions on political issues nearly impossible.*

tur·ban /ˈtəbən/ *n* [*C*] : a head covering that is worn especially by men in some parts of the Middle East and in southern Asia and that is made of a long cloth wrapped around the head

tur·bine /ˈtəbən/ *n* [*C*] : an engine that has a part with blades that are caused to spin by pressure from water, steam, or air

tur·bo·charg·er /ˈtəboʊˌtʃɑədʒə/ *n* [*C*] : a device that supplies air to an engine at a higher pressure than normal to increase the engine's power — **tur·bo·charged** /ˈtəboʊˌtʃɑədʒd/ *adj* ▪ *a turbocharged engine*

tur·bu·lence /ˈtəbjələns/ *n* [*U*] **1** : sudden, violent movements of air or water ▪ *The plane hit some turbulence during our* *flight.* **2** : a state of confusion, violence, or disorder ▪ *political/emotional turbulence*

tur·bu·lent /ˈtərbjələnt/ *adj* **1** : moving in an irregular or violent way ▪ *turbulent waters* **2** : full of confusion, violence, or disorder ▪ *a turbulent relationship* — **tur·bu·lent·ly** *adv*

tu·reen /təˈriːn, Brit tjuˈriːn/ *n* [C] : a deep bowl with a cover that is used for serving food (such as soup)

¹turf /ˈtərf/ *n* **1 a** [U] : the upper layer of ground that is made up of grass and plant roots ▪ *a piece of turf* [C/U] *Brit* : a square piece of turf cut out of the ground that is used for making lawns **2** [C/U] : a material that looks like grass and that is used especially to cover athletic fields ▪ *playing on artificial turf* **3** [C/U] : an area or a place that you control or that feels like your home ▪ *gangs defending their turfs* ▪ *(figurative) He was on unfamiliar turf when the discussion turned to sports.* ▪ *The team played on home turf.*

²turf *vb* — **turf out** *also* **turf off** [*phrasal vb*] **turf (someone) out/off** *or* **turf out/off (someone)** *Brit, informal* : to force (someone) to leave a place or position ▪ *His landlord turfed him out.*

tur·gid /ˈtərdʒəd/ *adj, formal, disapproving* : very complicated and difficult to understand ▪ *turgid prose*

tur·key /ˈtərki/ *n, pl* **tur·keys** *or* **turkey** **1 a** [C] : a large American bird that is related to the chicken and that is hunted or raised by people for its meat **b** [U] : the meat of the turkey used as food ▪ *roasted/smoked turkey* **2** [C] *US, informal* : a stupid or foolish person — **talk turkey** *chiefly US, informal* : to speak with someone in a plain, clear, or honest way ▪ *It's time to talk turkey about the problems in our relationship.* — see also COLD TURKEY

tur·moil /ˈtərˌmojəl/ *n* [U, *singular*] : a state of confusion or disorder ▪ *His life has been in (a) constant turmoil.*

¹turn /ˈtərn/ *vb* **1** [T/I] : to move around a central point ▪ *The Earth turns on its axis.* ▪ *We spun the top and watched it turn around in circles.* ▪ *He turned the key/doorknob and opened the door.* ▪ *Turn the steering wheel to the left.* **2** [T/I] **a** : to cause your body or a part of your body to face a different direction ▪ *They turned and walked away.* ▪ *The patient turned (himself) onto his side.* ▪ *She turned her face away.* **b** : to cause (something or a side of something) to face an opposite or different direction ▪ *Turn the picture (around) so that I can see it.* ▪ *turn a page.* ▪ *He turned up/down the collar of his jacket.* **3** [T/I] : to move or begin to go in a different or opposite direction ▪ *A car turned into the driveway.* ▪ *Turn right onto Main Street.* ▪ *He turned the light in the direction of the noise.* ▪ *The bicyclists turned the corner* [=they rode around the corner] *at full speed.* ▪ *The river turns east up ahead.* ▪ *The tide is turning.* **4** [T/I] : to change into a different state or form ▪ *The leaves turn* [=change color] *in the fall.* ▪ *The milk has turned.* [=has become

sour] ▪ *His luck turned, and he lost all his winnings.* ▪ *The water turned to ice.* ▪ *The witch turned the prince into a frog.* **5 a** [*linking vb*] : to change to a different state, condition, etc. : BECOME ▪ *The milk has turned sour.* ▪ *It was beginning to turn dark outside.* ▪ *an actress turned director* [=an actress who became a director] **b** [T] : to cause (someone or something) to change in a specified way ▪ *The events of his life had turned* [=made] *him bitter.* ▪ *The sun turned her skin (a) golden brown.* **c** [*linking vb*] : to reach a particular age ▪ *She turned two years old last week.* **6** [T] : to change the volume, temperature, channel, etc., of (something) by pressing a button, moving a switch, etc. ▪ *Turn the TV to channel 4.* ▪ *He turned the oven to 400 degrees.* ▪ *The lights in the room had been turned low.* **7** [T] : to direct (your thoughts, attention, etc.) toward or away from something ▪ *She turned her attention to the child.* **8** [T] : to earn (a profit) ▪ *He turned a quick profit.* **9** [T] : to perform (a particular action) ▪ *The team turned a double play to end the inning.* ▪ *turn a cartwheel* **10** [T] : to injure (your ankle) by moving it in an unnatural way ▪ *She turned* [=twisted] *her ankle.*

> In addition to the phrases shown below, *turn* occurs in many idioms that are shown at appropriate entries throughout the dictionary. For example, *turn a blind eye* can be found at ¹BLIND and *turn the tables* can be found at ¹TABLE.

— **turn against** [*phrasal vb*] **1 turn against (someone or something)** *or* **turn (someone) against (someone or something)** : to stop or cause (someone) to stop supporting or being friendly to (someone or something) ▪ *The senator turned against the war.* ▪ *He tried to turn our friends against us.* **2 turn (something) against (someone)** : to use (something) in a way that harms (someone) ▪ *She started turning my argument against me.* — **turn around** *or chiefly Brit* **turn round** [*phrasal vb*] **1 turn around** *or* **turn around (something)** *or* **turn (something) around** : to cause a vehicle to travel in the opposite direction ▪ *We turned (the car) around in someone's driveway.* **b** : to change something in a way that makes it better or more successful ▪ *The new CEO has really turned the company around in the past year.* ▪ *The company has turned around.* **2 turn around and (do something)** *informal* : to act in an unexpected or surprising way by doing (something specified) ▪ *He just turned around and left school.* [=he just suddenly left school] — **turn away** [*phrasal vb*] **turn away (someone)** *or* **turn (someone) away** : to refuse to allow (someone) to enter a place ▪ *The homeless shelter will not turn away people in need.* — **turn back** [*phrasal vb*] **1 a** : to move in the opposite direction in order to return to a place ▪ *The sun is setting. It's time to turn back.* **b** : to return to an earlier place or time ▪ *Turn back to the* *first page.* ▪ *Once you start the process, there's no turning back.* [=you must continue] **2 turn back (someone or something)** *or* **turn (someone or something) back** : to force (someone or something) to move in an opposite direction ▪ *They fought to turn back the enemy.* ▪ *If I could* **turn back (the hands of) time** [=return to a condition that existed in the past]*, I would.* — **turn down** [*phrasal vb*] **turn down (something or someone)** *or* **turn (something or someone) down 1** : to lower the volume, temperature, etc., of something by pressing a button, moving a switch, etc. ▪ *Please turn down the heat/ volume.* ▪ *The lights were turned down low.* **2** : to say no to (someone or something) especially in a polite way ▪ *She turned down the offer.* ▪ *I asked her out, but she turned me down.* — **turn in** [*phrasal vb*] **1** : to enter a place by turning from a road or path ▪ *Here's the house. You can turn in up there.* **2** : to go to bed ▪ *It's time to turn in.* **3 turn (something) in** *or* **turn in (something)** a *chiefly US* : to give (something) to a person who will review or accept it ▪ *He turned in his application/homework.* **b** : to return (something that you have borrowed, found, etc.) ▪ *Please turn in the art supplies when you're finished with them.* **c** : to perform or produce (something) ▪ *She turned in a fine performance.* **4 turn (someone) in** : to give control of or information about (someone) to the police or some other authority ▪ *His girlfriend threatened to turn him in.* ▪ *The escaped prisoner* **turned himself in** (to the police). — **turn (someone or something) loose** see ¹LOOSE — **turn off** [*phrasal vb*] **1** : to go in a direction that moves you away from a straight course or main road ▪ *They turned off onto the wrong road.* **2 turn off (something or someone)** *or* **turn (something or someone) off** a : to stop the operation or flow of (something) by pressing a button, moving a switch, etc. ▪ *She turned off the heat/ lights/water.* **b** *informal* : to cause a strong feeling of dislike in (someone) ▪ *People who smoke turn me off.* — **turn on** [*phrasal vb*] **1 turn on (something or someone)** *or* **turn (something or someone) on** a : to cause (something) to work or flow by pressing a button, moving a switch, etc. ▪ *She turned on the heat/ lights/water.* ▪ (*figurative*) *She turned the tears on* [=she started crying] *to get their sympathy.* **b** *informal* : to cause (someone) to feel excitement or enjoyment ▪ *What kind of music turns you on?* **2 turn (someone) on to** : to cause (someone) to use or become interested in (something) for the first time ▪ *She turned him on to water-skiing.* **3** : to attack or criticize (someone or something) in a sudden or unexpected way ▪ *The dog suddenly turned on its owner.* **4** : to be determined or decided by (something) ▪ *The outcome of the election turns on* [=depends on] *how well the candidates perform in the next debate.* — **turn out** [*phrasal vb*] **1** : to leave your home in order to participate in or do something ▪ *Few peo-*

ple turned out for the election. **2** : to happen, end, or develop in a particular way ▪ *The wedding turned out well.* ▪ *Things don't always turn out the way you want them to.* ▪ *She turned out to be right.* = *It turned out that she was right.* ▪ *He didn't want to turn out (to be) like his father.* **3 turn out (something)** *or* **turn (something) out** a : to cause (a lamp, flashlight, etc.) to no longer produce light by pushing a button, moving a switch, etc. ▪ *Who turned out the lights?* **b** : to produce (something) ▪ *The factory turns out parts for car engines.* **c** : to cause (something, such as a pocket) to become inside out ▪ *He turned out his pockets to show that they were empty.* **d** : to empty the contents of (something) especially for cleaning or organizing ▪ *She turned out the drawer.* **4 turn (someone) out** *or* **turn out (someone)** : to force (someone) to leave a place or position ▪ *The landlord turned them out from/of the apartment for not paying the rent.* — **turn over** [*phrasal vb*] **1 turn over (someone or something)** *or* **turn (someone or something) over** : to move or cause (someone or something) to move and face the opposite direction ▪ *She turned over (in bed) to see what time it was.* ▪ *The kayak turned over in the rapids.* ▪ *turn the paper over* **2** *of an engine* : to start to work ▪ *The engine would not turn over.* **3 turn over (something)** *or* **turn (something) over** *US, sports* : to allow the other team to get possession of (a ball) ▪ *The quarterback turned the ball over.* **4 turn (someone or something) over to** *or* **turn over (someone or something) to** : to give the control or responsibility of (someone or something) to (someone) ▪ *I am turning the job/property over to you.* ▪ *The suspect was turned over to the police.* **5 turn over (something) in your mind** *or* **turn (something) over in your mind** : to think about (something) in order to understand it or make a decision ▪ *She kept turning over the problem in her mind.* — **turn to** [*phrasal vb*] **1** : to go to (someone or something) for support, information, etc. ▪ *I was all alone and had no one to turn to.* ▪ *She turned to a friend for help.* ▪ *Turn to the handout for the exact figures.* ▪ *She became depressed and turned to drugs.* [=began using drugs] **2** : to become involved in or begin to deal with (something) ▪ *He turned to a life of crime.* ▪ *The conversation turned to politics.* — **turn up** [*phrasal vb*] **1 a** : to be found usually unexpectedly ▪ *New evidence has turned up.* ▪ *The missing person eventually turned up dead.* **b turn up (something)** *or* **turn (something) up** : to find or discover (something) ▪ *Did you turn up anything interesting?* **2** : to happen unexpectedly ▪ *Something is always turning up to prevent us from getting together.* **3 a** : to arrive at a place ▪ *I was surprised when John turned up at the ceremony.* **b** : to appear in a place ▪ *Her name is always turning up in the newspapers.* **4 turn up (something)** *or* **turn (something) up** a : to increase the volume, temperature, etc., of something by pressing a button, moving a switch, etc. ▪ *I turned up the heat/volume.* **b** : to make (a skirt, a pair of pants, etc.) shorter ▪ *These pants need to be turned up a little.*

²**turn** *n* [*C*] **1** : an opportunity or responsibility to do or use something before or after other people ▪ *You have to wait your turn in line.* ▪ *Can I please have/take a turn on your bike?* ▪ *Whose turn is it to do the dishes?* **2** : an act of turning something around a central point ▪ *Give the wheel another turn.* **3** : an act of changing the direction that someone or something is facing or moving in ▪ *I made/took a right turn onto Main Street.* ▪ *a quick turn of her head* **4** : a change in the state or condition of something ▪ *The stock market took a sharp downward turn.* ▪ *Business took a turn for the worse/better.* [=*became worse/better*] ▪ *There has been a dramatic turn of events.* [=*something important and surprising has happened*] **5** : a place where a road, path, etc., changes direction ▪ *a turn in the road* **6** : an act that affects someone in a particular way ▪ *He did me a nasty turn.* ▪ *One good turn deserves another.* [=*if someone does something nice for you, you should do something nice for that person*] **7** *old-fashioned* : a short walk or ride ▪ *They took a turn through the park.* — **at every turn** : in a constant or continuous way : each time a person tries to do something ▪ *They opposed her at every turn.* — **by turns** — used to describe different things that happen one after another ▪ *The book was praised and criticized by turns.* — **done to a turn** *Brit* : cooked, performed, etc., in a perfect way ▪ *The chicken was done to a turn.* — **in turn 1** : following one after another in a particular order ▪ *The algae feeds the fish, which in turn become food for larger sea animals.* **2** : as a result ▪ *I supported him and expected that he, in turn, would support me.* — **out of turn 1** : not at the time you are expected to do something according to a set order ▪ *She rolled the dice out of turn.* **2** : at a wrong or improper time or place ▪ *Excuse me for speaking out of turn* [=*for speaking when it is not proper for me to speak*]*, but I don't believe you are treating him fairly.* — **take turns** also *Brit* **take it in turns** ✧ If people *take turns* doing or using something or *take it in turns* to do or use something, they do or use it one after another in order to share the responsibility or opportunity of doing or using it. ▪ *We take turns washing the dishes.* — **the turn of the century** : the beginning of a new century ▪ *at the turn of the 19th/last century* — **turn of mind** : a way of thinking ▪ *He has a philosophical/inquiring turn of mind.* — **turn of phrase** : a way of saying or describing something ▪ *a nice turn of phrase*

turn·about /ˈtənəˌbaʊt/ *n* [*C*] : TURN-AROUND 2 ▪ *a sharp turnabout in oil prices* — **turnabout is fair play** *US* — used to say that if someone does something to harm you, it is fair for you to do something to harm that person

turn·around /ˈtənəˌraʊnd/ also *Brit*

turn·round /ˈtənˌraʊnd/ *n* [*C*] **1** : the time it takes someone to receive, deal with, and return something ▪ *The turnaround for most orders is/takes 24 hours.* **2** : a complete change from a bad situation to a good situation, from one way of thinking to an opposite way of thinking, etc. ▪ *The company has achieved a remarkable turnaround in the past year.* ▪ *a turnaround in public opinion*

turn·coat /ˈtənˌkoʊt/ *n* [*C*] *disapproving* : a person who stops being a member of a group in order to join another group that opposes it : TRAITOR ▪ *a political turncoat*

turning point *n* [*C*] : a time when an important change happens ▪ *Winning that game was the turning point of the team's season.*

tur·nip /ˈtənəp/ *n* [*C/U*] : a round, light-colored root of a plant that is eaten as a vegetable; *also* : the plant that produces such a root

turn·off /ˈtənˌɑːf/ *n* [*C*] **1** : a road that allows vehicles to leave a highway **2** *informal* : something that you dislike or that causes you to stop being interested in or attracted to someone or something ▪ *His strong cologne was a real turnoff.*

turn–on /ˈtənˌɑːn/ *n* [*C*] : something that you like or that causes you to be interested and excited ▪ *Classical music is one of his turn-ons.* ▪ *sexual turn-ons*

turn·out /ˈtənˌaʊt/ *n* [*C*] **1** : the number of people who go to or participate in something ▪ *There was a good/large turnout at the meeting.* ▪ *heavy voter turnouts* **2** *US* : an area next to a road where vehicles can stop

turn·over /ˈtənˌoʊvə/ *n* **1** [*C/U*] : the amount of money that is received in sales by a store or company ▪ *an annual turnover of one million dollars* **2** [*C/U*] : the rate at which people leave a place, company, etc., and are replaced by others ▪ *The store has a high employee turnover (rate).* ▪ *We've had a lot of turnover recently.* **3** [*C/U*] : the rate at which the goods in a store are sold and replaced by other goods ▪ *(a) rapid inventory turnover* **4** [*C*] *US, sports* : an occurrence in which the team that has the ball loses it to the other team because of an error or a minor violation of the rules ▪ *He forced/committed a turnover.* **5** [*C*] : a type of small pie that has one half of the crust folded over the other half and that is filled with fruit, meat, or a vegetable ▪ *an apple turnover*

turn·pike /ˈtənˌpaɪk/ *n* [*C*] *US* : a major road that you must pay to use

turn·round /ˈtənˌraʊnd/ *n* [*C*] *Brit* : TURNAROUND

turn signal *n* [*C*] : one of the lights on a vehicle that flash to indicate that the vehicle is turning left or right — called also [*Brit*] *indicator*

turn·stile /ˈtənˌstajəl/ *n* [*C*] : a gate at an entrance that has arms which turn around and that allows only one person at a time to pass through

turn·ta·ble /ˈtənˌteɪbəl/ *n* [*C*] **1** : the part of a record player that turns the record 2 : a platform that is used to turn vehicles (such as railroad cars) around

turn–up /ˈtənˌʌp/ n [C] Brit : ¹CUFF 2

tur·pen·tine /ˈtəpənˌtaɪn/ n [U] : a type of oil with a strong smell that is used to make paint thinner and to clean paint brushes

tur·pi·tude /ˈtəpəˌtuːd, Brit ˈtəːpəˌtjuːd/ n [U] formal : a very evil quality or way of behaving • moral turpitude

tur·quoise /ˈtəˌkɔɪz, ˈtəˌkwɔɪz/ n [U] 1 : a bluish-green stone used in jewelry 2 : a bluish-green color

tur·ret /ˈtərət/ n [C] 1 : a small tower on a building • a castle with turrets 2 : the part on a military tank, airplane, or ship from which guns are fired

tur·tle /ˈtətl̩/ n [C] : a reptile that lives mostly in water and that has a hard shell which covers its body

tur·tle·neck /ˈtətl̩ˌnɛk/ n [C] US : a high collar that covers most of your neck even when the collar is folded over itself; also : a shirt or sweater with this kind of collar • She wore a turtleneck under her jacket. — called also (Brit) polo neck

tush /ˈtʊʃ/ n [C] US, informal + humorous : the part of the body that you sit on : BUTTOCKS

tusk /ˈtʌsk/ n [C] : a very long, large tooth that sticks out of the mouth of an animal (such as an elephant, walrus, or boar)

tus·sle /ˈtʌsəl/ vb **tus·sled**; **tus·sling** [I] : to fight or struggle with someone especially by grabbing or pushing • The two players tussled for the ball. — **tussle** n [C] • a tussle with a security guard

tu·te·lage /ˈtuːtəlɪdʒ, Brit ˈtjuːtəlɪdʒ/ n [U] formal 1 : the teaching of an individual student by a teacher • He studied music under the tutelage of his father. [=he was taught music by his father] 2 : an act of guarding or protecting something • an African nation formerly under British tutelage

tu·tor /ˈtuːtə, Brit ˈtjuːtə/ n [C] 1 : a teacher who works with one student • I got a math tutor to help me with my homework. 2 Brit : a teacher at a British university who works with one student or a small group of students — **tutor** vb [T/I] • She spent her evenings tutoring her son in math. [=helping her son study math]

tu·to·ri·al /tuˈtɔriəl, Brit tjuˈtɔːriəl/ n [C] 1 : a book, computer program, etc., that teaches someone how to do something • a tutorial on how to install the software 2 : a class taught by a tutor • a physics tutorial for undergraduates

tu·tu /ˈtuːˌtuː/ n [C] : a short skirt that is made of many layers of material and that is worn by a ballerina

tux /ˈtʌks/ n [C] chiefly US, informal : TUXEDO

tux·e·do /ˌtʌkˈsiːdoʊ/ n, pl **-dos** or **-does** [C] chiefly US : a formal suit for a man; especially : a formal black suit worn with a white shirt and a black bow tie — called also (Brit) dinner suit

TV /ˈtiːˈviː/ n [C/U] : TELEVISION

TV dinner n [C] : a cooked meal that is frozen and packaged and that needs only to be heated before it is eaten

twang /ˈtwæŋ/ n [C] 1 : the typical sound of the speech of people from a certain place; especially : a sound that seems to be produced through the nose as well as the mouth • a Southern/nasal twang 2 : a harsh, quick sound made by pulling something (such as a wire) tight and then letting it go • the twang of a guitar — **twang** vb [T/I] • twanging the strings of a guitar

tweak /ˈtwiːk/ vb [T] 1 : to change (something) slightly in order to improve it • Software developers are tweaking the program. 2 : to injure (a part of your body) slightly • He tweaked his ankle. 3 : to pinch and pull (something) with a sudden movement • His grandmother tweaked his cheek. — **tweak** n [C] • The software still needs a few tweaks. [=small improvements]

twee /ˈtwiː/ adj, chiefly Brit, informal + disapproving : sweet or cute in a way that is silly or sentimental • The movie was a bit twee for my taste.

tweed /ˈtwiːd/ n 1 [C/U] : a rough, woolen cloth that is woven with different colored threads • a tweed suit 2 [plural] : tweed clothing (such as a suit) • an elderly man dressed in tweeds — **tweedy** /ˈtwiːdi/ adj **tweed·i·er**; **-est**

¹**tween** /ˈtwiːn/ prep, literary : BETWEEN

²**tween** n [C] US : a boy or girl who is 11 or 12 years old • a movie that appeals to tweens

tweet /ˈtwiːt/ vb [I] : to make a short, high sound • Birds were tweeting in the trees. — **tweet** n [C] • the tweets of the birds

twee·zers /ˈtwiːzəz/ n [plural] : a small tool that is made of two narrow pieces of metal which are joined at one end and that is used to hold, move, or pull very small objects • She used (a pair of) tweezers to take a splinter out of her finger.

twelfth /ˈtwɛlfθ/ n 1 [singular] : number 12 in a series • the twelfth of the month 2 [C] : one of 12 equal parts of something • a twelfth of the population — **twelfth** adj • the twelfth day — **twelfth** adv • He finished twelfth in the race.

twelve /ˈtwɛlv/ n 1 [C] : the number 12 2 [C] : the 12th in a set or series • question twelve 3 [U] : twelve o'clock • I have lunch at twelve. — **twelve** adj • twelve days — **twelve** pron • All twelve (of them) came to the party.

twen·ty /ˈtwɛnti/ n, pl **-ties** 1 [C] : the number 20 2 [plural] : the numbers ranging from 20 to 29 • The temperature is in the low twenties. b : a set of years ending in digits ranging from 20 to 29 • She's in her twenties. • the gangsters of the twenties [=1920–1929] 3 [C] a US : a twenty-dollar bill • All I have is a twenty. b Brit : a twenty-pound note — **twen·ti·eth** /ˈtwɛntiəθ/ n [C] — **twentieth** adj • their twentieth anniversary — **twenty** adj • twenty days — **twenty** pron

twen·ty–four seven or **24–7** or **24/7** /ˈtwɛntiˈfoəˈsɛvən/ adv, informal : all the time : twenty-four hours a day and seven days a week • The store is open 24/7.

twen·ty–twen·ty or **20/20** /ˈtwɛnti-

'twenti/ *adj* : having the normal ability to see things without glasses ▪ *She has 20/20 vision.*

twerp /'twəp/ *n* [C] *informal* : someone who is stupid or annoying

twice /'twaɪs/ *adv* **1** : two times : on two occasions ▪ *He has rehearsals twice a month.* ▪ *I've been there at least twice.* **2** : doubled in amount or degree ▪ *The house is twice as large as our old one.* ▪ *He must be twice her age.* — **think twice** see THINK

twid·dle /'twɪdl/ *vb* **twid·dled; twid·dling** [T/I] : to turn (something) back and forth slightly ▪ *She twiddled (with) her pen while she talked on the phone.* — **twiddle your thumbs** *informal* : to waste time while you wait for something to happen ▪ *I was just twiddling my thumbs until the phone rang.*

'twig /'twɪg/ *n* [C] : a small branch of a tree or bush

²twig *vb* **twigged; twig·ging** [T/I] *Brit, informal* : to understand (something) suddenly ▪ *He twigged that something was wrong.*

twi·light /'twaɪ,laɪt/ *n* **1** [U] **a** : the light from the sky at the end of the day when night is just beginning **b** : the period when day is ending and night is beginning ▪ *We had to stop working at twilight.* [=dusk] **2** [*singular*] : a period when something is ending ▪ *He's in the twilight (years) of his career.* [=the last part of his career]

twill /'twɪl/ *n* [U] : cloth that is made in a way that produces a pattern of diagonal lines ▪ *cotton twill pants*

'twin /'twɪn/ *n* [C] **1** : either one of two babies that are born at the same time to the same mother ▪ *Sarah and her brother are twins.* ▪ *I didn't know she had a twin.* [=a sister/brother who is her twin] **2** : either one of two similar things that form a pair ▪ *I found one glove but I can't find its twin.* [=I can't find the other glove]

²twin *adj, always before a noun* **1** — used to describe children who are twins ▪ *my twin brother* [=my brother who is my twin] ▪ *twin girls* **2** : made up of two similar things that are used together ▪ *a twin-engine airplane* [=an airplane that has two engines] **3** : forming one of a pair ▪ *the twin goals of reducing oil use and protecting the environment*

³twin *vb* **twinned; twin·ning** [T] : to bring (two things) together in close association ▪ *Research is twinned* [=coupled] *with technology.* ▪ *two cultures with a twinned destiny*

twin bed *n* [C] *US* : a bed that is big enough for only one person

'twine /'twaɪn/ *n* [U] : a string made of two or more threads twisted together

²twine *vb* **twined; twin·ing** [T/I] : to twist or wrap around (someone or something) ▪ *The tree was twining its branches around the chimney.* ▪ *Ivy twines around the columns.*

twinge /'twɪndʒ/ *n* [C] **1** : a sudden and usually slight pain ▪ *I felt a twinge in my leg.* **2** : a sudden slight feeling or emotion ▪ *a twinge of guilt/sadness*

'twin·kle /'twɪŋkəl/ *n* [*singular*] : a quick, unsteady movement of light ▪ *the twinkle of a candle* — **a twinkle in your eye** : a friendly or happy expression in your eyes ▪ *He talks about his children with a twinkle in his eye.* — **in the twinkle of an eye** *informal* : very quickly : in a very short time ▪ *She was back in the twinkle of an eye.* — **twin·kly** /'twɪŋkəli/ *adj* **-kli·er; -est** ▪ *twinkly lights*

²twinkle *vb* **twin·kled; twin·kling** [I] **1** : to shine with an unsteady light ▪ *Stars twinkle in the night sky.* ▪ *twinkling lights* **2** *of the eyes* : to have a friendly or happy expression ▪ *Her eyes twinkled with excitement.*

twin·kling /'twɪŋkəlɪŋ/ *n* — **in a twinkling** or **in the twinkling of an eye** : very quickly : in a very short time ▪ *He was back in a twinkling.*

twirl /'twəl/ *vb* **1** [T/I] : to turn or spin around and around ▪ *The cheerleaders jumped and twirled.* ▪ *twirl a baton* **2** [T] : to twist or wrap (something) around something ▪ *He twirled the noodles around his fork.* — **twirl** *n* [C] ▪ *The dancers executed perfect twirls.* — **twirl·er** /'twələ/ *n* [C] ▪ *baton twirlers*

'twist /'twɪst/ *vb* **1** [T] : to bend or turn (something) ▪ *The toy can be twisted into different shapes.* ▪ *The antenna was twisted out of shape.* **2** [T/I] : to turn (something) in a circular motion with your hand ▪ *twist a dial* ▪ *twist off a bottle cap* **3** [T] : to pull or break off (something) by turning it ▪ *He twisted a small branch off the tree.* **4** [I] : to turn your body or a part of your body around ▪ *He twisted around to face me.* **5** [T] : to hurt (your ankle, knee, etc.) by turning it too far ▪ *I twisted my ankle.* **6** [T] : to combine several threads or wires by wrapping them around one another ▪ *Twist the wire ends together.* **7** [T/I] : to wrap or wind (something) around something ▪ *She twisted her hair around her finger.* ▪ *Ivy twisted around the columns of the porch.* **8** [T] : to change the meaning of (something) unfairly ▪ *He was twisting the facts.* ▪ *He twisted my words.* [=he repeated what I said in a way that had a different meaning] **9** [I] : to curve or change direction suddenly ▪ *a twisting path* ▪ *The road along the coast twists and turns.* — **twist someone's arm 1** : to grab someone's arm and bend it in order to cause pain **2** *informal* : to try to force someone to do something ▪ *My wife really had to twist my arm to get me to apologize to my boss.*

²twist *n* [C] **1** : an act of turning or twisting ▪ *a twist of the wrist* ▪ *The jar should open with a twist of the lid.* **2** : a turn, curve, or bend in a road, river, etc. ▪ *The coastal road had many twists and turns.* **3 a** : an unexpected or strange occurrence ▪ *The plot has many twists.* ▪ *a strange twist of fate* **b** : something new created by changing something slightly ▪ *It's a new twist on an old recipe.* **4** : a small piece of lemon or lime peel used to flavor a drink ▪ *a diet cola with a twist of lemon*

twist·ed /ˈtwɪstəd/ *adj* : strange and unpleasant • *a twisted sense of humor*

twist·er /ˈtwɪstə/ *n* [C] *US, somewhat informal* : TORNADO

twist tie *n* [C] *US* : a small piece of wire that you use to close something (such as a plastic bag) by twisting the ends together

twit /ˈtwɪt/ *n* [C] *informal* : a stupid or foolish person

twitch /ˈtwɪtʃ/ *vb* **1** [I] : to make a slight, sudden movement that is not controlled or deliberate • *His left leg twitched.* **2** [T] : to move or pull (something) with a sudden motion • *The rabbit twitched its ears.* — **twitch** *n* [C] • *sudden muscle twitches* — **twitchy** /ˈtwɪtʃi/ *adj* **twitch·i·er; twitch·i·est**

¹**twit·ter** /ˈtwɪtə/ *vb* **1** [T/I] : to make fast and usually high sounds • *The birds were twittering in the trees.* **2** [I] : to talk in a quick, informal way about unimportant things • *What are those people twittering about?*

²**twitter** *n* [C] **1** : the short, high sounds that birds make **2** : a light, silly laugh — **in a twitter** *informal* : very nervous or excited about something • *She was all in a twitter about the birthday party.*

two /ˈtuː/ *n, pl* **twos** **1** [C] : the number 2 **2** [C] : the second in a set or series • *page two* **3** [U] : two o'clock • *It was two in the morning.* — **a bird in the hand is worth two in the bush** see BIRD — **in two** : into two equal parts : in half • *He cut the apple in two.* — **it takes two (to tango)** see ¹TAKE 12b — **of two minds** see ¹MIND — **put two and two together** : to make a correct guess based on what you have seen or heard • *You weren't home so I put two and two together and went back to your office to find you.* — **two cents** see CENT — **two left feet** see ¹FOOT — **two** *adj* • *two days* — **two** *pron* • *There are two (of them) left.*

two–bit /ˈtuːˈbɪt/ *adj, always before a noun, informal* : not very important or valuable • *a two-bit thief/town*

two–by–four /ˌtuːbaɪˈfoɚ/ *n* [C] *US* : a piece of wood that has been cut to be long and straight so that it can be used for building things and that is about 2 inches thick and 4 inches wide

two–edged sword *n* [C] : DOUBLE-EDGED SWORD

two–faced /ˈtuːˈfeɪst/ *adj, informal + disapproving* : saying different things to different people in order to get their approval instead of speaking and behaving honestly • *a two-faced liar*

two–fold /ˈtuːˈfoʊld/ *adj* **1** : twice as much or as many • *a twofold increase* **2** : having two parts • *The aims of the study are twofold.* — **two–fold** /ˈtuːˈfoʊld/ *adv* • *Our funding increased twofold.*

two–hand·ed /ˈtuːˈhændəd/ *adj* **1** : using or needing both hands • *a two-handed sword/catch* **2** : needing two people • *a two-handed saw*

two·some /ˈtuːsəm/ *n* [C] : a group of two people or things

two–way *adj* **1** : moving or allowing movement in both directions • *two-way traffic* • *a two-way street* **2** : involving

two people or groups • *Communication is a two-way process.* • *Trust between two people is a two-way street.* [=trust requires effort from both people] **3** : made to send and receive messages • *a two-way radio*

TX *abbr* Texas

ty·coon /taɪˈkuːn/ *n* [C] : a very wealthy and powerful business person • *an oil tycoon*

tying *present participle of* ¹TIE

tyke *also* **tike** /ˈtaɪk/ *n* [C] *informal* : a small child

¹**type** /ˈtaɪp/ *n* **1** [C] : a particular kind or group of things or people • *What type of food do you like?* • *various types of trees* • *Allergies of this type are common.* **2** [C] : a particular kind of person • *She's an outdoors type.* [=she loves hiking, camping, etc., in the outdoors] • *He's not her type.* [=he is not the kind of man she is attracted to] • *Her mother is not the type to complain.* **3** [U] **a** : printed letters • *italic type* **b** : small metal blocks that are used for printing letters and numbers on paper • *lead type*

²**type** *vb* **typed; typ·ing** **1** [T/I] : to write with a computer keyboard or typewriter • *How fast can you type?* • *type (up) a memo* **2** [T] *technical* : to find out what group something is in • *The lab will type this blood sample.* [=will determine what type of blood the sample is]

type·cast /ˈtaɪpˌkæst, *Brit* ˈtaɪpˌkɑːst/ *vb* **-cast; -cast·ing** [T] : to always give (an actor or actress) the same kind of role : to cause people to think that (an actor or actress) should always play the same kind of role • *Her television work typecast her as a helpless victim.* • *He feared being typecast as a criminal.*

type·face /ˈtaɪpˌfeɪs/ *n* [C] : a set of letters, numbers, etc., that are all in the same style and that are used in printing : FONT

type·writ·er /ˈtaɪpˌraɪtə/ *n* [C] : a machine that prints letters or figures on a sheet of paper when a person pushes its keys

type·writ·ing /ˈtaɪpˌraɪtɪŋ/ *n* [U] **1** : the use of a typewriter **2** : writing done with a typewriter

type·writ·ten /ˈtaɪpˌrɪtn/ *adj* : written by using a typewriter or a computer • *five typewritten pages*

ty·phoid /ˈtaɪˌfoɪd/ *n* [U] : a serious disease that is passed from one person to another in dirty food or water — called also *typhoid fever*

ty·phoon /taɪˈfuːn/ *n* [C] : an extremely large, powerful, and destructive storm that occurs especially in the region of the Philippines or the China Sea

ty·phus /ˈtaɪfəs/ *n* [U] : a serious disease that is carried by small insects that live on the bodies of people and animals and that causes high fever, headache, and a dark red rash — called also *typhus fever*

typ·i·cal /ˈtɪpɪkəl/ *adj* : normal for a person, thing, or group • *a typical example/response* • *It was typical of her to be late.* • *It was a typical night for us.* — **typ·i·cal·ly** /ˈtɪpɪkli/ *adv* • *The recitals typically* [=usually] *last one hour.* • *Typically, I or-*

der steak when I eat there. ▪ **They serve typically American food.** [=the kind of food that is usual/typical in America]

typ·i·fy /ˈtɪpəˌfaɪ/ vb **-fies; -fied; -fy·ing** [T] 1 : to be a good or typical example of (something) ▪ **His heroic actions typified the courage of all the firefighters at the scene.** ▪ **He typifies [=represents] what a professional athlete should be.** 2 : to be a usual or typical part or feature of (something) ▪ **His movies are typified by complex plots and exciting action sequences.**

typ·ist /ˈtaɪpɪst/ n [C] : a person who uses a typewriter or a computer keyboard ▪ **She's a good/poor typist.** [=she types well/badly]

ty·po /ˈtaɪpoʊ/ n, pl **-pos** [C] informal : a mistake (such as a misspelled word) in typed or printed text

ty·pog·ra·phy /taɪˈpɑːgrəfi/ n [U] 1 : the work of producing printed pages from written material 2 : the style, arrangement, or appearance of printed letters on a page — **ty·pog·ra·pher** /taɪˈpɑːgrəfɚ/ n [C] — **ty·po·graph·i·cal** /ˌtaɪpəˈgræfɪkəl/ also **ty·po·graph·ic** /ˌtaɪpəˈgræfɪk/ adj ▪ typographical errors — **ty·po·graph·i·cal·ly** /ˌtaɪpəˈgræfɪkli/ adv

ty·ran·ni·cal /təˈrænɪkəl/ adj : using power over people in a way that is cruel and unfair ▪ a tyrannical dictatorship/boss — **ty·ran·ni·cal·ly** /təˈrænɪkli/ adv

tyr·an·nize also Brit **tyr·an·nise** /ˈtɪrəˌnaɪz/ vb **-niz·es; -nized; -niz·ing** [T/I] : to use power to treat (people) in a cruel and unfair way ▪ a government that tyrannizes its own people ▪ **He tyrannizes over his employees.**

ty·ran·no·sau·rus /təˌrænəˈsorəs/ n [C] : a very large meat-eating dinosaur — called also T. rex, tyrannosaurus rex /-ˈrɛks/

tyr·an·ny /ˈtɪrəni/ n, pl **-nies** 1 [C/U] : cruel and unfair treatment by people with power over others ▪ the tyranny of slavery ▪ a nation ruled by tyranny ▪ **the tyranny of the majority** [=a situation in which a group of people are treated unfairly because their situation is different from the situation of most of the people in a democratic country] 2 [C] : a government in which all power belongs to one person ▪ **The king sought an absolute tyranny over the colonies.**

ty·rant /ˈtaɪrənt/ n [C] 1 : a ruler who has complete power over a country and who is cruel and unfair 2 : someone who uses power in a cruel and unfair way ▪ **Our boss is a real tyrant.**

tyre Brit spelling of ²TIRE

ty·ro /ˈtaɪˌroʊ/ n, pl **-ros** [C] : a person who has just started learning or doing something : a beginner or novice ▪ **Most of the people in the class were tyros like me.**

tzar, tzarina variant spellings of CZAR, CZARINA

U

u or **U** /ˈjuː/ n, pl **u's** or **U's** /ˈjuːz/ [C/U] : the 21st letter of the English alphabet ▪ a word that starts with (a) u

U abbr 1 uncountable — used in this dictionary to indicate a noncount noun 2 **U.** university

ubiq·ui·tous /juˈbɪkwətəs/ adj : seeming to be seen everywhere ▪ ubiquitous advertisements/celebrities — **ubiq·ui·ty** /juˈbɪkwəti/ n [U]

ud·der /ˈʌdɚ/ n [C] : the bag-shaped part of a cow, goat, etc., that hangs below the belly and produces milk

UFO /ˌjuːˌɛfˈoʊ/ n, pl **UFO's** or **UFOs** /ˌjuːˌɛfˈoʊz/ [C] : a flying object in the sky that some people believe could be a spaceship from another planet ✧ UFO is as an abbreviation of "unidentified flying object."

ugh /ˈʌg/ interj, informal — used to show that you are annoyed, disgusted, or upset about something ▪ **Ugh, I can't stand that movie.**

ug·ly /ˈʌgli/ adj **ug·li·er; -est** 1 a : not pretty or attractive ▪ an ugly person/color/house b : unpleasant to hear ▪ an ugly sound/voice 2 : offensive or disgusting ▪ an ugly racial slur 3 : very bad or unpleasant ▪ an ugly situation/temper ▪ **Things could get/turn ugly.** — **ug·li·ness** /ˈʌglinəs/ n [U]

ugly duckling n [C] : a person or thing that is not attractive or successful but that is likely to become attractive or successful in the future ▪ **The house is an ugly duckling, but it has a lot of potential.**

uh /ˈʌ/ interj, chiefly US, informal — used when you hesitate because you are not sure about what to say ▪ **"What time is it?" "Uh, I'm not sure."**

UHF abbr ultra high frequency ✧ Ultra high frequency radio waves are used for broadcasting television and some types of radio signals. ▪ UHF television stations

uh–huh /ˌʌˈhʌ but spoken nasally/ interj, informal — used to show that you agree or understand ▪ **"Is that your dog?" "Uh-huh."** [=yeah, yes]

uh–oh /ˈʌˌoʊ with a stop between the vowels/ interj, chiefly US, informal — used when you realize that you are in a bad situation, that you have made a mistake, etc. ▪ **Uh-oh, we're in trouble!**

uh–uh /ˈʌˌʌ but spoken nasally/ interj, chiefly US, informal — used to say no or to emphasize a negative answer to a question, request, or offer ▪ **"Are you going to the party?" "Uh-uh. I have to study."**

UK also **U.K.** abbr United Kingdom

uku·le·le /ˌjuːkəˈleɪli/ n [C] : a musical instrument that is like a small guitar with four strings

ul·cer /ˈʌlsə/ *n* [C] *medical* : a painful, sore area inside or outside the body ▪ *a stomach ulcer*

ul·cer·ate /ˈʌlsəˌreɪt/ *vb* **-at·ed; -at·ing** [I] *medical* : to form an ulcer ▪ *an ulcerated wound* [=a wound that has formed an ulcer]

ul·te·ri·or /ˌʌlˈtirijə/ *adj* : kept hidden in order to get a particular result ▪ *She has an ulterior motive* [=a secret reason] *for helping us.*

ul·ti·mate /ˈʌltəmət/ *adj, always before a noun* **1** : happening or coming at the end of a process, series of events, etc. ▪ *our ultimate destination* ▪ *the ultimate outcome/result* ▪ *Our ultimate aim/goal/purpose is to increase production.* **2** : greatest or most extreme — used to say that something or someone is the greatest or most extreme example of a particular type of thing or person ▪ *the ultimate betrayal/challenge/hero* **3** — used to refer to the original or basic source or cause of something ▪ *the river's ultimate source* ▪ *the ultimate cause of the problem* **4** : most distant in space or time ▪ *the ultimate reaches of the universe* ▪ *the ultimate in* : the greatest or most extreme form or example of (something) ▪ *This car is the ultimate in safety.* [=this car is as safe as a car can be]

ul·ti·mate·ly /ˈʌltəmətli/ *adv* **1** : at the end of a process, period of time, etc. ▪ *He ultimately agreed to do it.* **2** : in the central or most important way ▪ *Ultimately, it's a question of who is more popular.*

ul·ti·ma·tum /ˌʌltəˈmeɪtəm/ *n, pl* **-tums** *or* **-ta** /-tə/ [C] : a promise or threat that force or punishment will be used if someone does not do what is wanted ▪ *She was given an ultimatum—work harder or lose her job.*

ul·tra- /ˈʌltrə/ *prefix* **1** : beyond ▪ extremely : more than is usual ▪ *ultramodern* **2** *technical* : beyond the range or limits of ▪ *ultrasonic*

ul·tra·ma·rine /ˌʌltrəməˈriːn/ *n* [U] : a very bright blue color — **ultramarine** *adj*

ul·tra·son·ic /ˌʌltrəˈsɑːnɪk/ *adj* — used to describe sounds that are too high for humans to hear ▪ *ultrasonic frequencies*

ul·tra·sound /ˈʌltrəˌsaʊnd/ *n* **1** [U] : a type of sound that is too high for humans to hear **2** a [C/U] *medical* : a method of producing images of the inside of the body by using a machine that produces sound waves which are too high to be heard **b** [C] : an image that is made using ultrasound

ul·tra·vi·o·let /ˌʌltrəˈvajələt/ *adj, technical* — used to describe rays of light that cannot be seen and that are slightly shorter than the rays of violet light ▪ *ultraviolet light/radiation*

um /ˈʌm *or a prolonged* m *sound*/ *interj* — used when you hesitate because you are not sure about what to say ▪ *"Are you coming to the party?" "Um, I think so."*

um·bil·i·cal cord /ˌʌmˈbɪlɪkəl-/ *n* [C] : a long, narrow tube that connects an unborn baby to the placenta of its mother

um·brage /ˈʌmbrɪdʒ/ *n* [U] *formal* : a feeling of being offended by what some-

one has said or done ▪ *He took umbrage at the remark.* [=was offended by the remark]

um·brel·la /ˌʌmˈbrelə/ *n* [C] **1** : a device that is used for protection from the rain and sun **2** : a group or organization that includes many smaller groups ▪ *an umbrella corporation* **3** : something that includes several or many different things ▪ *I bought an umbrella policy that insures my car, jewelry, and house.*

um·laut /ˈuːmˌlaʊt/ *n* [C] : a mark placed over a vowel (such as a *u* in German) to indicate a specific pronunciation

um·pire /ˈʌmˌpajə/ *n* [C] : a person who controls play and makes sure that players act according to the rules in a sports event (such as a baseball game or tennis match) — **umpire** *vb* **-pired; -pir·ing** [T/I] ▪ *Who umpired (the game)?*

ump·teen /ˈʌmpˌtiːn/ *adj, informal* : very many ▪ *I have umpteen things to do today.* — **ump·teenth** /ˈʌmpˌtiːnθ/ *adj*

UN *also* **U.N.** *abbr* United Nations

un- /ˌʌn/ *prefix* **1** : not ▪ *unhappy* ▪ *unwise* **2** : opposite of ▪ *unethical* ▪ *unorthodox* **3** : do the opposite of ▪ *undress* ▪ *unfold* **4** : remove (a specified thing) from ▪ *uncork a wine bottle*

un·abashed /ˌʌnəˈbæʃt/ *adj* : not embarrassed or ashamed about openly expressing strong feelings or opinions ▪ *an unabashed supporter/admirer* — **un·abash·ed·ly** /ˌʌnəˈbæʃədli/ *adv*

un·abat·ed /ˌʌnəˈbeɪtəd/ *adj* : continuing at full strength or force without becoming weaker ▪ *Her popularity remains unabated.*

un·able /ˌʌnˈeɪbəl/ *adj, not before a noun* : not able to do something ▪ *I was unable to afford the trip.*

un·abridged /ˌʌnəˈbrɪdʒd/ *adj* : not shortened by leaving out some parts ▪ *an unabridged dictionary*

un·ac·cept·able /ˌʌnɪkˈseptəbəl/ *adj* : not pleasing or welcome ▪ *unacceptable behavior/ideas* — **un·ac·cept·ably** /ˌʌnɪkˈseptəbli/ *adv*

un·ac·com·pa·nied /ˌʌnəˈkʌmpənid/ *adj* **1 a** : without another person : ALONE ▪ *Unaccompanied children are not allowed in the store.* **b** : not together with something specified ▪ *a lot of talk unaccompanied by any action* **2** *music* : played or sung without another musical instrument or singer ▪ *an unaccompanied solo*

un·ac·count·able /ˌʌnəˈkaʊntəbəl/ *adj, formal* **1** : strange or mysterious ▪ *She has shown an unaccountable reluctance to accept their offer.* **2 a** : not required to explain actions or decisions ▪ *He is unaccountable to the voters.* **b** : not required to be responsible for something ▪ *Despite everything, she remains unaccountable for her mistakes.* — **un·ac·count·ably** /ˌʌnəˈkaʊntəbli/ *adv* ▪ *She looked unaccountably upset.* [=upset for a reason that was difficult to understand]

un·ac·count·ed /ˌʌnəˈkaʊntəd/ *adj* — **unaccounted for** — used to say that what happened to someone or something is not known ▪ *The money remains* *unaccounted for.* [=no one knows what happened to the money]

un·ac·cus·tomed /ˌʌnəˈkʌstəmd/ *adj, formal* **1** : not usual or common ▪ *They responded with unaccustomed speed.* **2** : not familiar with something so that it does not seem normal or usual ▪ *She was unaccustomed to fame.*

un·ac·knowl·edged /ˌʌnɪkˈnɑːlɪʤd/ *adj* : not recognized, accepted, or admitted ▪ *He had a largely unacknowledged role in the campaign.*

un·ac·quaint·ed /ˌʌnəˈkweɪntəd/ *adj* **1** : not having knowledge about something ▪ *I am unacquainted with her books.* **2** : not knowing each other in a personal or social way ▪ *He was unacquainted with my brother.*

un·adorned /ˌʌnəˈdoɚnd/ *adj* : not decorated or fancy ▪ *an unadorned room*

un·adul·ter·at·ed /ˌʌnəˈdʌltəˌreɪtəd/ *adj* **1** : not having anything added ▪ *unadulterated foods* **2** : complete and total ▪ *unadulterated happiness*

un·af·fect·ed /ˌʌnəˈfɛktəd/ *adj* **1** : not influenced or changed ▪ *Her concentration was unaffected* [=was not affected] *by the noise.* **2** : genuine, sincere, or natural ▪ *He has a friendly and unaffected manner.*

un·afraid /ˌʌnəˈfreɪd/ *adj, not before a noun* : not afraid ▪ *He is unafraid of failure.*

un·aid·ed /ˌʌnˈeɪdəd/ *adj* : without help : not aided ▪ *patients who can get out of bed unaided*

un·alien·able /ˌʌnˈeɪlijənəbəl/ *adj, chiefly US, formal* : impossible to take away or give up : INALIENABLE ▪ *unalienable rights*

un·al·ter·able /ˌʌnˈɑːltərəbəl/ *adj* : not capable of being changed or altered ▪ *unalterable conditions*

un·al·tered /ˌʌnˈɑːltəd/ *adj* : not changed or altered ▪ *an unaltered landscape/photograph*

un·am·big·u·ous /ˌʌnæmˈbɪgjəwəs/ *adj* : clearly expressed or understood ▪ *unambiguous evidence* — **un·am·big·u·ous·ly** *adv*

un–Amer·i·can /ˌʌnəˈmɛrɪkən/ *adj* : not agreeing with American values, principles, or traditions ▪ *un-American activities*

unan·i·mous /juˈnænəməs/ *adj* **1** : agreed to by everyone ▪ *a unanimous vote/decision* **2** *not before a noun* : having the same opinion ▪ *We were unanimous in our approval of the report.* [=we all approved the report] — **una·nim·i·ty** /ˌjuːnəˈnɪməti/ *n* [U] — **unan·i·mous·ly** *adv*

un·an·nounced /ˌʌnəˈnaʊnst/ *adj* : surprising and unexpected ▪ *an unannounced visit/test*

un·an·swer·able /ˌʌnˈænsərəbəl/ *adj* **1** : not capable of being answered ▪ *an answerable question* **2** : impossible to prove wrong ▪ *an unanswerable argument*

un·an·swered /ˌʌnˈænsəd/ *adj* **1** : without a reply ▪ *Our questions went unanswered.* **2** *US, sports* : scored during a time when an opponent fails to score ▪ *The team scored 20 unanswered points in the third quarter.*

un·apol·o·get·ic /ˌʌnəˌpɑːləˈʤɛtɪk/ *adj* : not feeling or showing regret or shame : not apologetic ▪ *She was unapologetic about her remarks.* ▪ *an unapologetic liberal/conservative*

un·ap·peal·ing /ˌʌnəˈpiːlɪŋ/ *adj* : not attractive or appealing ▪ *an unappealing choice/color/taste*

un·ap·pre·ci·at·ed /ˌʌnəˈpriːʃiˌeɪtəd/ *adj* : not given the respect or thanks that is deserved : not appreciated ▪ *I feel unappreciated at work.*

un·armed /ˌʌnˈɑɚmd/ *adj* **1** : not having a weapon : not armed ▪ *an unarmed guard* **2** : not using or involving a weapon ▪ *unarmed robbery/combat*

un·ashamed /ˌʌnəˈʃeɪmd/ *adj* : not feeling or showing shame or guilt : not ashamed ▪ *He is unashamed of his patriotism.* — **un·asham·ed·ly** /ˌʌnəˈʃeɪmədli/ *adv*

un·as·sail·able /ˌʌnəˈseɪləbəl/ *adj, formal* : not able to be doubted, attacked, or questioned ▪ *an unassailable fact/truth*

un·as·sist·ed /ˌʌnəˈsɪstəd/ *adj* **1** : without help or assistance ▪ *He is unable to walk unassisted.* **2** *sports* : done without help from another player ▪ *an unassisted double play*

un·as·sum·ing /ˌʌnəˈsuːmɪŋ, Brit ˌʌnəˈsjuːmɪŋ/ *adj, approving* : not having or showing a desire to be noticed, praised, etc. : MODEST ▪ *an unassuming guy/home/neighborhood*

un·at·tached /ˌʌnəˈtæʧt/ *adj* **1** : not married, engaged, or in a serious romantic relationship ▪ *He is currently unattached.* **2** : not joined to another building ▪ *an unattached garage*

un·at·tend·ed /ˌʌnəˈtɛndəd/ *adj* : not cared for or watched ▪ *Do not leave your child unattended.*

un·at·trac·tive /ˌʌnəˈtræktɪv/ *adj* : not beautiful, interesting, or pleasing : not attractive ▪ *an unattractive woman/man/idea* — **un·at·trac·tive·ly** *adv*

un·au·tho·rized *also Brit* **un·au·tho·rised** /ˌʌnˈɑːθəˌraɪzd/ *adj* : without permission : not authorized ▪ *an unauthorized use of government vehicles*

un·avail·able /ˌʌnəˈveɪləbəl/ *adj* : not available ▪ *The shoes are unavailable in certain sizes.* ▪ *She was unavailable for comment.* — **un·avail·abil·i·ty** /ˌʌnəˌveɪləˈbɪləti/ *n* [U]

un·avoid·able /ˌʌnəˈvoɪdəbəl/ *adj* : not able to be prevented or avoided ▪ *an unavoidable accident* — **un·avoid·ably** /ˌʌnəˈvoɪdəbli/ *adv*

un·aware /ˌʌnəˈweɚ/ *adj* : not having knowledge about something : not aware ▪ *They were unaware that they were being watched.* ▪ *We were unaware of the problem.*

un·awares /ˌʌnəˈweɚz/ *adv* : without warning — used to describe something that happens without being expected ▪ *The rainstorm caught us unawares.* ▪ *She was taken unawares* [=taken by surprise] *by the sudden change in plans.*

un·bal·ance /ˌʌnˈbæləns/ *vb* **-anced; -anc·ing** [T] : to cause (something or someone) to stop being balanced, steady, stable, etc. ▪ *The tax cuts will unbalance the budget.*

un·bal·anced /ˌʌnˈbælənst/ *adj* 1 : not in a state of balance : not balanced ▪ *The weight was unbalanced.* ▪ *an unbalanced diet* 2 : not completely sane ▪ *mentally unbalanced people*

un·bear·able /ˌʌnˈberəbəl/ *adj* : too bad, harsh, or extreme to be accepted or endured ▪ *unbearable pain* — **un·bear·ably** /ˌʌnˈberəbli/ *adv*

un·beat·able /ˌʌnˈbiːtəbəl/ *adj* 1 : not capable of being defeated ▪ *an unbeatable team* 2 : very good or excellent ▪ *unbeatable prices*

un·beat·en /ˌʌnˈbiːtn̩/ *adj* : not defeated : not beaten ▪ *The team is unbeaten this season.*

un·be·com·ing /ˌʌnbɪˈkʌmɪŋ/ *adj* 1 : not attractive : not becoming ▪ *an unbecoming dress* 2 *formal* : not appropriate or acceptable for a person in a particular job or position ▪ *conduct unbecoming (to/of) an officer* [=not appropriate for an officer]

un·be·knownst /ˌʌnbɪˈnoʊnst/ *or* **un·be·known** /ˌʌnbɪˈnoʊn/ *adj* — **unbeknownst/unbeknown** to : without being known about by (someone) ▪ *Unbeknownst to us, he had entered the room.* [=we did not know/realize that he had entered the room]

un·be·liev·able /ˌʌnbəˈliːvəbəl/ *adj* 1 : difficult or impossible to believe ▪ *an unbelievable story* 2 — used to describe something that is so good, bad, etc., that it is difficult to believe ▪ *The pain was unbelievable.* ▪ *an unbelievable performance* — **un·be·liev·ably** /ˌʌnbəˈliːvəbli/ *adv*

un·bend /ˌʌnˈbend/ *vb* **-bent** /-ˌbent/; **-bend·ing** 1 [*T/I*] : to make (something) straight or to become straight ▪ *He was bending and unbending his fingers.* 2 [*I*] : to stop being serious or tense : RELAX ▪ *He unbent a little at the party.*

un·bend·ing /ˌʌnˈbendɪŋ/ *adj, sometimes disapproving* : not willing to change an opinion, decision, etc. ▪ *unbending determination*

un·bi·ased /ˌʌnˈbajəst/ *adj* : treating all people and groups equally and fairly : not biased ▪ *an unbiased judge/opinion*

un·blem·ished /ˌʌnˈblemɪʃt/ *adj* 1 : not having any unwanted marks or blemishes ▪ *unblemished skin* 2 : not harmed or damaged in any way ▪ *an unblemished reputation for honesty*

un·blink·ing /ˌʌnˈblɪŋkɪŋ/ *adj* 1 : not blinking ▪ *unblinking eyes* 2 : looking at or describing something in a very honest and accurate way ▪ *unblinking honesty* — **un·blink·ing·ly** *adv*

un·block /ˌʌnˈblɑːk/ *vb* [*T*] : to stop (something) from being blocked ▪ *unblock a drain*

un·born /ˌʌnˈboɚn/ *adj* : not yet born ▪ *her unborn child*

un·bound·ed /ˌʌnˈbaʊndəd/ *adj* : not limited in any way ▪ *unbounded enthusiasm/joy*

un·bowed /ˌʌnˈbaʊd/ *adj, literary* : not defeated or willing to admit defeat ▪ *He was unbowed by failure.*

un·break·able /ˌʌnˈbreɪkəbəl/ *adj* : not

able to be broken ▪ *an unbreakable bond of friendship*

un·bri·dled /ˌʌnˈbraɪdl̩d/ *adj, formal + literary* : not controlled or limited ▪ *unbridled enthusiasm*

un·bro·ken /ˌʌnˈbroʊkən/ *adj* 1 : not damaged or broken ▪ *unbroken eggs* 2 : CONTINUOUS 1 ▪ *eight hours of unbroken sleep*

un·buck·le /ˌʌnˈbʌkəl/ *vb* **-buck·led**; **-buck·ling** [*T*] : to open the buckle of (something, such as a belt) ▪ *She unbuckled her seat belt.*

un·bur·den /ˌʌnˈbɚdn̩/ *vb* [*T*] : to take a problem or burden away from (someone or something) ▪ *They tried to unburden her of her worries/troubles.* — **unburden yourself** : to talk about something that is causing you to feel worried, guilty, etc. ▪ *He welcomed the opportunity to unburden himself.*

un·but·ton /ˌʌnˈbʌtn̩/ *vb* [*T*] : to open the buttons of (something) ▪ *He unbuttoned his coat/shirt.*

un·called–for /ˌʌnˈkɑːldˌfoɚ/ *adj* : not necessary or appropriate ▪ *His jealousy is completely uncalled-for.*

un·can·ny /ˌʌnˈkæni/ *adj* : strange or unusual in a way that is surprising or difficult to understand ▪ *an uncanny resemblance* — **un·can·ni·ly** /ˌʌnˈkænəli/ *adv*

un·car·ing /ˌʌnˈkerɪŋ/ *adj* : not feeling or showing concern for someone or something ▪ *an uncaring attitude*

un·ceas·ing /ˌʌnˈsiːsɪŋ/ *adj* : never stopping : not ceasing ▪ *unceasing efforts/vigilance* — **un·ceas·ing·ly** /ˌʌnˈsiːsɪŋli/ *adv*

un·cer·e·mo·ni·ous /ˌʌnˌserəˈmoʊnijəs/ *adj* : happening or done very suddenly and quickly with no effort to be careful or polite ▪ *His unceremonious dismissal by the new boss surprised everybody.* — **un·cer·e·mo·ni·ous·ly** *adv*

un·cer·tain /ˌʌnˈsɚtn̩/ *adj* : not certain: such as **a** : not exactly known or decided : not definite or fixed ▪ *an uncertain quantity* **b** : not sure ▪ *I'm uncertain about my plans.* **c** : not definitely known ▪ *The cause of the fire is uncertain.* **d** : likely to change ▪ *uncertain weather* — **in no uncertain terms** : in a very clear and direct way ▪ *She told me in no uncertain terms to never say that word again!* — **un·cer·tain·ly** *adv*

un·cer·tain·ty /ˌʌnˈsɚtn̩ti/ *n, pl* **-ties** 1 [*U*] : the quality or state of being uncertain : DOUBT ▪ *There is some uncertainty about the company's future.* 2 [*C*] : something that is doubtful or unknown ▪ *life's uncertainties*

un·chal·lenged /ˌʌnˈtʃæləndʒd/ *adj* : not questioned or doubted ▪ *an unchallenged authority*

un·changed /ˌʌnˈtʃeɪndʒd/ *adj* : not changed ▪ *Their plans remain unchanged.*

un·chang·ing /ˌʌnˈtʃeɪndʒɪŋ/ *adj* : not changing : staying the same ▪ *unchanging traditions*

un·char·ac·ter·is·tic /ˌʌnˌkerəktəˈrɪstɪk/ *adj* : not typical or usual ▪ *an uncharacteristic outburst* — **un·char·ac·ter·is·ti·cal·ly** /ˌʌnˌkerəktəˈrɪstɪkli/ *adv*

un·char·i·ta·ble /ˌʌnˈtʃerətəbəl/ *adj*

: very harsh in judging others ▪ *an uncharitable critic*

un·chart·ed /ˌʌnˈtʃɑːtəd/ *adj* : not recorded or located on a map, chart, or plan ▪ *an uncharted island* ▪ *(figurative) The discussion moved into uncharted territory/waters.* [=moved into a new and unknown area]

un·checked /ˌʌnˈtʃɛkt/ *adj* : not stopped, slowed, or controlled ▪ *unchecked power*

un·civ·i·lized also Brit **un·civ·i·lised** /ˌʌnˈsɪvəˌlaɪzd/ *adj* : not civilized ▪ *uncivilized behavior* ▪ *an uncivilized form of punishment*

un·cle /ˈʌŋkəl/ *n* **1** [C] : the brother of your father or mother or the husband of your aunt ▪ *I have three uncles and two aunts.* ▪ *my Uncle David* **2** US, informal — used as a word that you say when you are being hurt in a fight to show that you admit being defeated and do not want to continue fighting ▪ *He was forced to cry/say uncle.* [=forced to surrender]

un·clean /ˌʌnˈkliːn/ *adj* **1** : not clean : dirty ▪ *unclean living conditions* **2** : morally bad ▪ *unclean thoughts/desires*

un·clear /ˌʌnˈkliɚ/ *adj* **1** : difficult to understand ▪ *unclear instructions* ▪ *The cause of the disease is unclear.* **2** : confused or uncertain about something ▪ *I'm a little unclear about what to do.*

un·clench /ˌʌnˈklɛntʃ/ *vb* [T/I] : to move (something) out of a tightly closed position and make it less tense ▪ *He unclenched his fist/jaw.*

Un·cle Sam /ˌʌŋkəlˈsæm/ *n* [U] informal : the American government, nation, or people pictured or thought of as a person ▪ *Uncle Sam wants you to join the Army!*

Uncle Tom /ˌʌŋkəlˈtɑːm/ *n* [C] disapproving : a black person who is eager to win the approval of white people and willing to cooperate with them

un·clog /ˌʌnˈklɑːg/ *vb* **-clogged; -clogging** [T] : to open (something) so things can pass or flow through ▪ *unclog a drain*

un·clothed /ˌʌnˈkloʊðd/ *adj*, formal : not wearing clothes : NAKED ▪ *an unclothed body*

un·coil /ˌʌnˈkojəl/ *vb* [T/I] : to make (something that is curled or coiled) straight ▪ *uncoil a rope*

un·com·fort·able /ˌʌnˈkʌmfətəbəl/ *adj* **1 a** : causing a feeling of physical discomfort ▪ *an uncomfortable chair* **b** : feeling physical discomfort ▪ *You look uncomfortable in that chair.* **2 a** : causing a feeling of being embarrassed or uneasy ▪ *an uncomfortable silence* **b** : feeling embarrassed or uneasy ▪ *She's uncomfortable being in the spotlight.* — **un·com·fort·ably** /ˌʌnˈkʌmfətəbli/ *adv*

un·com·mon /ˌʌnˈkɑːmən/ *adj* **1** : not often found or seen : UNUSUAL ▪ *uncommon plants/animals* **2** : not ordinary : remarkable or exceptional ▪ *uncommon athletic abilities* ▪ *a soldier of uncommon courage* — **un·com·mon·ly** *adv*

un·com·mu·ni·ca·tive /ˌʌnkəˈmjuːnəˌkeɪtɪv, ˌʌnkəˈmjuːnəkətɪv/ *adj* : not tending or liking to talk or give out information ▪ *an uncommunicative person*

un·com·plain·ing /ˌʌnkəmˈpleɪnɪŋ/ *adj,*

approving : accepting, doing, or dealing with something difficult or unpleasant without complaining ▪ *an uncomplaining worker* — **un·com·plain·ing·ly** /ˌʌnkəmˈpleɪnɪŋli/ *adv*

un·com·pli·cat·ed /ˌʌnˈkɑːmpləˌkeɪtəd/ *adj* : easy to understand, do, or use ▪ *an uncomplicated machine/story*

un·com·pro·mis·ing /ˌʌnˈkɑːmprəˌmaɪzɪŋ/ *adj* : not willing to change a decision, opinion, method, etc. ▪ *uncompromising standards of excellence*

un·con·cerned /ˌʌnkənˈsɚnd/ *adj* : not worried or upset : not concerned ▪ *She's unconcerned about/with that issue.*

un·con·di·tion·al /ˌʌnkənˈdɪʃənl/ *adj* : not limited in any way : complete and absolute ▪ *an unconditional surrender* ▪ *unconditional love* — **un·con·di·tion·al·ly** *adv*

un·con·firmed /ˌʌnkənˈfɚmd/ *adj* : not supported by evidence ▪ *an unconfirmed rumor/report*

un·con·nect·ed /ˌʌnkəˈnɛktəd/ *adj* : not related or connected ▪ *two unconnected events*

un·con·scio·na·ble /ˌʌnˈkɑːnʃənəbəl/ *adj, formal* **1** : extremely bad, unfair, or wrong ▪ *unconscionable cruelty* **2** : going far beyond what is usual or proper ▪ *unconscionable delays*

¹**un·con·scious** /ˌʌnˈkɑːnʃəs/ *adj* **1** : not awake especially because of an injury, drug, etc. ▪ *He was knocked unconscious by a fall.* **2** : not aware of something ▪ *He is unconscious of his mistake.* **3** : not intended or planned ▪ *an unconscious mistake* — **un·con·scious·ly** *adv* — **un·con·scious·ness** *n* [U]

²**unconscious** *n* [U] : the part of the mind that a person is not aware of but that is often a powerful force in controlling behavior

un·con·sti·tu·tion·al /ˌʌnˌkɑːnstəˈtuːʃənl, ˌʌnˌkɑːnstəˈtjuːʃənl/ *adj* : not allowed by the constitution of a country or government ▪ *The law may be unconstitutional.* — **un·con·sti·tu·tion·al·i·ty** /ˌʌnˌkɑːnstəˌtuːʃəˈnæləti, Brit ˌʌnˌkɑːnstəˌtjuːʃəˈnæləti/ *n* [U] — **un·con·sti·tu·tion·al·ly** *adv*

un·con·trol·la·ble /ˌʌnkənˈtroʊləbəl/ *adj* : not able to be controlled ▪ *uncontrollable anger/children/urges* — **un·con·trol·la·bly** /ˌʌnkənˈtroʊləbli/ *adv*

un·con·trolled /ˌʌnkənˈtroʊld/ *adj* : happening or done without being stopped, slowed, or controlled ▪ *uncontrolled bleeding/growth/spending*

un·con·ven·tion·al /ˌʌnkənˈvɛnʃənl/ *adj* : very different from the things that are used or accepted by most people : not conventional ▪ *unconventional thinking/methods/people* — **un·con·ven·tion·al·ly** *adv*

un·con·vinced /ˌʌnkənˈvɪnst/ *adj, not before a noun* : not completely sure or certain about something ▪ *I was unconvinced that he was guilty.*

un·con·vinc·ing /ˌʌnkənˈvɪnsɪŋ/ *adj* : not able to make you believe that something is true, real, or acceptable ▪ *an unconvincing argument*

un·cooked /ˌʌnˈkʊkt/ *adj* : not cooked

: RAW • *uncooked meat*

un·co·op·er·a·tive /ˌʌnkoʊˈɑːprətɪv/ *adj* : not willing to do what someone wants or asks for • *uncooperative children*

un·co·or·di·nat·ed /ˌʌnkoʊˈoɚdəˌneɪtəd/ *adj* **1** : not able to move different parts of your body together well or easily • *I'm too uncoordinated to be a good dancer.* **2** : not well organized • *uncoordinated efforts*

un·cork /ˌʌnˈkoɚk/ *vb* [T] **1** : to remove a cork from (a bottle) • *uncork a bottle of wine* **2** *informal* : to allow (something that was contained or controlled) to come out, escape, etc. • *The incident uncorked years of pent-up anger and frustration.*

un·cor·rob·o·rat·ed /ˌʌnkəˈrɑːbəˌreɪtəd/ *adj* : not supported or proved by evidence • *uncorroborated evidence/testimony*

un·count·able /ˌʌnˈkaʊntəbəl/ *adj* : not able to be counted : not countable • *an uncountable number of insects* • (*grammar*) *an* **uncountable noun** [=a noun that refers to something that cannot be counted; a noncount noun]

un·couth /ˌʌnˈkuːθ/ *adj* : behaving in a rude way : not polite or socially acceptable • *uncouth language/behavior/people*

un·cov·er /ˌʌnˈkʌvɚ/ *vb* [T] **1** : to remove a cover from (something) • *Uncover the pot.* **2** : to find or become aware of (something that was hidden or secret) • *Police uncovered a criminal plot.*

un·crit·i·cal /ˌʌnˈkrɪtɪkəl/ *adj* : not expressing or willing to express appropriate criticism or disapproval • *uncritical support* • *an uncritical newspaper article* — **un·crit·i·cal·ly** /ˌʌnˈkrɪtɪkli/ *adv*

unc·tu·ous /ˈʌŋktʃəwəs/ *adj, formal + disapproving* — used to describe someone who speaks and behaves in a way that is meant to seem friendly and polite but that is obviously not sincere • *an unctuous hostess*

un·cut /ˌʌnˈkʌt/ *adj* : not cut: such as **a** : allowed to continue growing • *an uncut forest* **b** : not cut into a different shape • *an uncut diamond* **c** : not shortened or edited • *the uncut version of the film*

un·dam·aged /ˌʌnˈdæmɪdʒd/ *adj* : not harmed or damaged in any way • *The package arrived undamaged.*

un·daunt·ed /ˌʌnˈdɑːntəd/ *adj* : not afraid to continue doing something or trying to do something even though there are problems, dangers, etc. • *She was undaunted by the challenges.*

un·de·cid·ed /ˌʌndɪˈsaɪdəd/ *adj* **1** : not having made a decision • *undecided voters* • *She was undecided about what to do.* **2** : not yet settled or resolved • *The question is still undecided.*

un·de·feat·ed /ˌʌndɪˈfiːtəd/ *adj* : not having or including any losses or defeats • *an undefeated team/season*

un·de·fined /ˌʌndɪˈfaɪnd/ *adj* : not shown or described clearly • *an undefined amount of money*

un·de·mand·ing /ˌʌndɪˈmændɪŋ, *Brit* ˌʌndɪˈmɑːndɪŋ/ *adj* : not requiring much time, effort, etc. : not demanding • *an undemanding job/guest*

un·de·ni·able /ˌʌndɪˈnajəbəl/ *adj* : clearly true : impossible to deny • *an undeniable fact* — **un·de·ni·ably** /ˌʌndɪˈnajəbli/ *adv*

un·de·pend·able /ˌʌndɪˈpendəbəl/ *adj* : not able to be trusted or relied on : not dependable • *an undependable car/employee*

¹**un·der** /ˈʌndɚ/ *prep* **1** : in or to a lower place than (something) : UNDERNEATH • *sitting under a tree* • *The ball rolled under the car.* **2** : guided or managed by (a person or group) • *The cafe is under new management.* • *She has 12 employees (working) under her.* **3** : controlled or affected by (something) • *She's under a lot of pressure/stress.* • *The work was done under the direction/guidance/supervision of an architect.* [=an architect directed/guided/supervised the work] • *He's under a doctor's care.* [=being treated by a doctor] • *driving while under the influence of alcohol* [=driving while drunk] **4** : in a particular state or condition : affected by a particular process • *The police put her* **under arrest.** [=the police arrested her] • *The house is* **under construction.** [=is now being built] • *The incident is currently under investigation.* [=is being investigated] • *His suggestion is still under discussion/consideration/review.* **5** : according to (something) • *Under the terms of the lease, rent will be due on the first of each month.* **6** : within the group that has (a particular title or label) • *The purchase is listed under "debits."* **7** — used to say that a particular name is used to indicate something • *The table is reserved under my last name.* **8** : less or lower than (a certain age, amount, etc.) • *children under the age of 14* • *We arrived in under an hour.* • *It costs under $10.* **9** : hidden below (an outward appearance) • *Under that rough exterior, he is a gentle man.*

²**under** *adv* **1 a** : in or into a position that is below or beneath something • *He turned under his shirt's collar.*; *especially* : in a position that is below the surface of water • *The whale surfaced briefly then dove under again.* **b** : in a forward direction that passes below something • *The bridge was too low for the ship to sail under.* **2** : less than an expected or stated number or amount • *A score of 60 is needed to pass; anything under is failing.* • *children aged five and under* [=children who are five years old and younger] **3** : into an unconscious state • *They had to put me under for surgery.* — **go under** see ¹GO

under- *prefix* **1** : below • *undercurrent* • *undershirt* **2** : less than an expected or correct number or amount • *underpaid* • *undercook*

un·der·achiev·er /ˌʌndɚəˈtʃiːvɚ/ *n* [C] : someone (such as a student or athlete) who does not perform as well or work as hard as he or she can — **un·der·achieve** /ˌʌndɚəˈtʃiːv/ *vb* **-achieved;** **-achiev·ing** [I] • *Many students underachieve during their senior year.*

un·der·ac·tive /ˌʌndɚˈæktɪv/ *adj* : not active enough • *an underactive thyroid*

un·der·age /ˌʌndəˈeɪdʒ/ *adj* : too young to do something legally ▪ *an underage driver* ▪ *underage drinking* [=drinking by someone who is underage]

¹**un·der·arm** /ˈʌndəˌɑɚm/ *adj* **1** *always before a noun* : placed on or along the armpit ▪ *underarm deodorant* **2** *Brit* : UNDERHAND ▪ *an underarm throw* — **un·der·arm** /ˌʌndəˈɑɚm/ *adv, Brit* ▪ *He threw the ball underarm.*

²**un·der·arm** /ˈʌndəˌɑɚm/ *n* [C] : ARMPIT

un·der·bel·ly /ˈʌndəˌbɛli/ *n, pl* **-lies** **1** [C] : the bottom part of an object or an animal's body ▪ *the underbelly of an airplane* — usually singular **2** [*singular*] : an area that is easy to attack or criticize ▪ *the army's underbelly*

un·der·brush /ˈʌndəˌbrʌʃ/ *n* [U] *chiefly US* : plants, bushes, and small trees growing under larger trees in a forest

un·der·car·riage /ˈʌndəˌkerɪdʒ/ *n* [C] **1** *chiefly US* : the supporting structures of a car, truck, etc. **2** : LANDING GEAR

un·der·class /ˈʌndəˌklæs, Brit ˈʌndəˌklɑːs/ *n* [C] : a social class made up of people who are very poor and have very little power or chance to improve their lives ▪ *the suffering of the underclass*

un·der·class·man /ˌʌndəˈklæsmən, Brit ˌʌndəˈklɑːsmən/ *n, pl* **-men** /-mən/ [C] *US* : a student in the first or second year of high school or college

un·der·clothes /ˈʌndəˌkloʊz/ *or* **un·der·cloth·ing** /ˈʌndəˌkloʊðɪŋ/ *n* [*plural*] *formal* : UNDERWEAR

un·der·coat /ˈʌndəˌkoʊt/ *n* [C] : a coat of paint that is put on a surface to prepare it for another coat of paint

un·der·cook /ˌʌndəˈkʊk/ *vb* [T] : to not cook (food) enough ▪ *The chicken was undercooked.*

un·der·cov·er /ˌʌndəˈkʌvə/ *adj* : done or working in a secret way in order to catch criminals or collect information ▪ *an undercover investigation/officer/agent* — **undercover** *adv* ▪ *an agent who is working undercover*

un·der·cur·rent /ˈʌndəˌkɚrənt/ *n* [C] **1** : a flow of water that moves below the surface of the ocean or a river **2** : a hidden feeling or tendency that is usually different from the one that is easy to see or understand ▪ *undercurrents of resentment*

un·der·cut /ˌʌndəˈkʌt/ *vb* **-cut; -cut·ting** [T] **1** : to offer to sell things or work for a lower cost than (another person or company) ▪ *They undercut the competing store by 10 percent.* **2** : to make (something) weaker or less effective ▪ *Her behavior undercuts her credibility.*

un·der·de·vel·oped /ˌʌndədɪˈvɛləpt/ *adj* **1** : not developed to a normal size or strength ▪ *a baby with underdeveloped lungs* **2** *of a country, society, etc.* : having many poor people and few industries ▪ *underdeveloped nations*

un·der·dog /ˈʌndəˌdɑːg/ *n* [C] : a person, team, etc., that is expected to lose a contest or battle ▪ *I always root for the underdog instead of the favorite.*

un·der·done /ˌʌndəˈdʌn/ *adj* : not cooked completely or enough ▪ *The chicken was underdone.*

un·der·dress /ˌʌndəˈdrɛs/ *vb* [T/I] : to dress in clothes that are too informal or not warm enough for an occasion ▪ *I don't want to underdress for the party.* ▪ *She was underdressed.*

un·der·es·ti·mate /ˌʌndəˈɛstəˌmeɪt/ *vb* **-mat·ed; -mat·ing** [T] **1** : to estimate (something) as being less than the actual size, quantity, or number ▪ *We underestimated the cost.* **2** : to think of (someone or something) as being lower in ability, influence, or value than that person or thing actually is ▪ *Her talent has always been underestimated.* — **un·der·es·ti·mate** /ˌʌndəˈɛstəmət/ *n* [C] ▪ *an underestimate of the cost* — **un·der·es·ti·ma·tion** /ˌʌndəˌɛstəˈmeɪʃən/ *n* [C/U]

un·der·ex·pose /ˌʌndəɪkˈspoʊz/ *vb* **-posed; -pos·ing** [T] : to allow too little light to fall on (film in a camera) when you are taking a photograph ▪ *an underexposed picture* — **un·der·ex·po·sure** /ˌʌndəɪkˈspoʊʒə/ *n* [U]

un·der·fed /ˌʌndəˈfɛd/ *adj* : not given enough food to eat ▪ *The cat looked underfed.*

un·der·foot /ˌʌndəˈfʊt/ *adv* **1** : below your feet ▪ *The ground was slippery underfoot.* **2** : near your feet so as to make movement difficult ▪ (*figurative*) *It can be hard to clean the house with five children underfoot.*

un·der·fund·ed /ˌʌndəˈfʌndəd/ *adj* : not having enough money to do what is needed ▪ *The school system is badly underfunded.*

un·der·gar·ment /ˈʌndəˌgɑɚmənt/ *n* [C] *somewhat old-fashioned* : a piece of underwear

un·der·go /ˌʌndəˈgoʊ/ *vb* **-goes; -went** /-ˈwɛnt/; **-gone** /-ˈgɑːn/; **-go·ing** [T] : to experience or endure (something) ▪ *She will have to undergo an operation.*

un·der·grad /ˈʌndəˌgræd/ *n* [C] *chiefly US* : UNDERGRADUATE

un·der·grad·u·ate /ˌʌndəˈgrædʒəwət/ *n* [C] : a student at a college or university who has not yet earned a degree ▪ *a group of college undergraduates*

¹**un·der·ground** /ˈʌndəˌgraʊnd/ *adj* **1** : located or occurring below the surface of the ground ▪ *underground parking garages* **2** *always before a noun* : secret and usually illegal ▪ *an underground deal* **3** *always before a noun* : of, relating to, or produced in a social and artistic world that is different and separate from the main part of society ▪ *the city's underground music scene* — **un·der·ground** /ˌʌndəˈgraʊnd/ *adv* ▪ *animals that live underground* ▪ *The political party went underground* [=started working in secret] *after the new government took power.*

²**un·der·ground** /ˈʌndəˌgraʊnd/ *n* **1** [U, *singular*] *Brit* : SUBWAY **1** ▪ *the London Underground* **2 the underground** : a group of people who secretly work to oppose or overthrow a government

un·der·growth /ˈʌndəˌgroʊθ/ *n* [U] : UNDERBRUSH

un·der·hand /ˈʌndəˌhænd/ *adj* **1** *US* : made with the hand brought forward and upward from below the shoulder ▪

an underhand throw 2 chiefly Brit : UN-DERHANDED 1 • an underhand deal/tac-tic — **underhand** adv, US • Throw the ball underhand.

un·der·hand·ed /ˌʌndəˈhændəd/ adj 1 chiefly US : done in a secret and dishon-est way : intended to deceive or trick someone • underhanded tactics/methods 2 US : UNDERHAND 1 • an underhand throw — **underhanded** adv, US • She threw the ball underhand.

un·der·lie /ˌʌndəˈlaɪ/ vb -lies; -lay /-ˈleɪ/; -lain /-ˈleɪn/; -ly·ing [T] 1 : to lie or be located under (something) • A tile floor underlies the rug. 2 : to form the basis or foundation of (an idea, a process, etc.) • A theme of revenge underlies much of her writing.

un·der·line /ˈʌndəˌlaɪn/ vb -lined; -lin-ing [T] 1 : to draw a line under (some-thing) • His name was underlined in the book. 2 : to emphasize (something) • The accident underlines our need for bet-ter safety procedures.

un·der·ling /ˈʌndəlɪŋ/ n [C] disapproving : a person of low rank who works for a more powerful person • the boss's under-lings

un·der·ly·ing /ˌʌndəˈlajɪŋ/ adj 1 — used to identify the idea, cause, problem, etc., that forms the basis of something • an underlying cause of the accident • an underlying problem/disease 2 : lying un-der or below something • the ocean and the underlying rock

un·der·mine /ˌʌndəˈmaɪn/ vb -mined; -min·ing [T] : to make (someone or something) weaker or less effective usu-ally in a secret or gradual way • She un-dermined my authority.

un·der·neath /ˌʌndəˈniːθ/ prep 1 : be-low or beneath (something) : UNDER • She slipped a note underneath the door. • The ball rolled underneath the car. 2 : on the bottom of (something) • There was gum stuck underneath the table. 3 : hidden below (an outward appearance) • Underneath her calm exterior she was very nervous. — **the underneath** chiefly Brit : the bottom surface of something • The plate had a name stamped on the un-derneath. — **underneath** adv • He wore a white sweater with a red shirt under-neath.

un·der·nour·ished /ˌʌndəˈnɚɪʃt/ adj : not getting enough food or not getting enough healthy food for good health and growth • undernourished children

underpaid past tense of UNDERPAY

un·der·pants /ˈʌndəˌpænts/ n [plural] 1 US : underwear that people wear on the lower part of their bodies 2 Brit : underpants for men and boys

un·der·pass /ˈʌndəˌpæs, Brit ˈʌndəˌpɑːs/ n [C] : a place where a road or railroad crosses under another road or railroad

un·der·pay /ˌʌndəˈpeɪ/ vb -paid /-ˈpeɪd/; -pay·ing [T/I] : to pay too little for something • She underpaid for her meal. • underpaid workers

un·der·priv·i·leged /ˌʌndəˈprɪvələdʒd/ adj : having less money, education, etc., than the other people in a society : poor or disadvantaged • underprivileged stu-dents — **the underprivileged** : under-privileged people • trying to help the un-derprivileged

un·der·rate /ˌʌndəˈreɪt/ vb -rat·ed; -rat-ing [T] : to rate or value (someone or something) too low • She underrated his ability. — **underrated** adj • an under-rated restaurant/singer

un·der·score /ˌʌndəˈskoə/ vb -scored; -scor·ing [T] 1 : to emphasize (some-thing) or show the importance of (some-thing) • The President's visit underscores the administration's commitment to free trade. 2 : UNDERLINE 1 • underscore a word

un·der·sea /ˌʌndəˈsiː/ adj, always before a noun : found, done, or used below the surface of the sea • undersea cables/ves-sels

un·der·sec·re·tary /ˌʌndəˈsɛkrəˌteri, Brit ˌʌndəˈsɛkrətri/ n, pl -tar·ies [C] : a high-ranking government official who serves under a department secretary or other high official • the U.S. Undersec-retary of Defense

un·der·shirt /ˈʌndəˌʃɚt/ n [C] US : a shirt that has no collar and sometimes no sleeves and that is worn as underwear

un·der·shorts /ˈʌndəˌʃoəts/ n [plural] : underpants for men or boys

un·der·side /ˈʌndəˌsaɪd/ n 1 [C] : the bottom side or part of something • the underside of the table 2 [singular] : a part of life, a city, etc., that is hidden and usually unpleasant • Hollywood's dark underside

un·der·signed /ˈʌndəˌsaɪnd/ n — **the undersigned** formal : the person whose name is signed or the people whose names are signed at the end of a docu-ment • We, the undersigned, object to the recent rulings.

un·der·sized /ˌʌndəˈsaɪzd/ adj : smaller than the usual size • He is undersized for a basketball player.

un·der·staffed /ˌʌndəˈstæft, Brit ˌʌndə-ˈstɑːft/ adj : not having enough workers • The office was understaffed. • an under-staffed hospital

un·der·stand /ˌʌndəˈstænd/ vb -stood /-ˈstʊd/; -stand·ing 1 [T/I] : to know the meaning of (something, such as the words that someone is saying or a lan-guage) : COMPREHEND • Do you under-stand English? • I don't understand these directions. 2 [T] : to know how (some-thing) works or happens • They under-stand local politics. • We still don't fully understand the causes of the disease. 3 a [T] : to know how (someone) thinks, feels, or behaves • She understands chil-dren. b [T/I] : to feel sympathy for someone's feelings or situation • I under-stand your feelings about him. • They will understand if you need some time off. 4 [T] a : to think or believe (something) • She was **given to understand** [=she was led to believe] that the job was hers. — used to say what you believe to be true based on what you have heard, read, etc. • I understand that they will arrive today. b — used to say that something is agreed to or accepted and does not need to be discussed • It's **understood** [=we all know/

accept] *that more time will be needed.* **5** [T] : to think that (something) has a particular meaning • *I understood the letter to be a refusal.*

un·der·stand·able /ˌʌndəˈstændəbəl/ *adj* **1** : normal and reasonable for a particular situation • *an understandable feeling/reaction/error* **2** : able to be understood • *He can make scientific concepts understandable to the general public.* — **un·der·stand·ably** /ˌʌndəˈstændəbli/ *adv*

¹un·der·stand·ing /ˌʌndəˈstændɪŋ/ *n* **1** [U, singular] : the knowledge and ability to judge a particular situation or subject • *He has a thorough/full understanding of the subject.* • *She has little understanding of our situation.* **2** [singular] : an informal agreement • *We have an understanding that whoever cooks doesn't have to do the dishes.* **3** [U] : a willingness to understand people's behavior and forgive them • *She treats them with kindness and understanding.* **4** [singular] : your belief about something based on what you have heard, read, etc. • *My understanding was that you were going to help.* [=I thought that you were going to help] — **on the understanding that** — used to say that something is done, accepted, etc., because you have been told that something else will happen or is true • *She agreed to do the work on the understanding that she would be paid now.*

²understanding *adj* : showing sympathy and kindness • *an understanding husband/wife*

un·der·state /ˌʌndəˈsteɪt/ *vb* **-stat·ed; -stat·ing** [T] : to say that (something) is smaller, less important, etc., than it really is • *understate an issue/problem*

un·der·stat·ed /ˌʌndəˈsteɪtəd/ *adj* : expressed or done in a quiet or simple way • *an understated style/performance*

un·der·state·ment /ˌʌndəˈsteɪtmənt/ *n* **1** [C] : a statement that makes something seem smaller, less important, etc., than it really is • *To say that I didn't like the book is an understatement.* [=I hated the book] **2** [U] : the practice of describing things in a way that makes them seem smaller, less important, etc., than they really are • *He has a knack for understatement.*

understood *past tense and past participle of* UNDERSTAND

un·der·study /ˈʌndəˌstʌdi/ *n, pl* **-stud·ies** [C] : an actor who prepares to take the part of another actor if that actor is unable to perform

un·der·take /ˌʌndəˈteɪk/ *vb* **-took** /-ˈtʊk/; **-tak·en** /-ˈteɪkən/; **-tak·ing** [T] *formal* **1** : to begin or attempt (something) • *undertake a task/journey/search* **2** : to agree or promise to do (something) • *He undertook to raise his sister's child.*

un·der·tak·er /ˈʌndəˌteɪkə/ *n* [C] : a person whose job is to arrange and manage funerals

un·der·tak·ing /ˈʌndəˌteɪkɪŋ/ *n* **1** [C] : an important or difficult task or project • *a new creative undertaking* **2** [U] : the business of an undertaker • *a career in undertaking* **3** [C] *Brit, formal* : a promise or agreement to do or not do some-

thing • *The newspaper gave an undertaking* [=promised] *not to disclose his identity.*

un·der·tone /ˈʌndəˌtoʊn/ *n* [C] **1** : a low or quiet voice • *She spoke in an undertone.* **2** : a quality, meaning, etc., that is present but not clear or obvious • *The play is a comedy with dark undertones.* **3** : a color that you can see in small amounts • *The fabric is a brown with undertones of red.*

undertook *past tense and past participle of* UNDERTAKE

un·der·tow /ˈʌndəˌtoʊ/ *n* [C] : a current in the sea or ocean that is below the surface and that moves away from the shore

un·der·used /ˌʌndəˈjuːzd/ *adj* : not used enough : not fully used • *underused land/ talents*

un·der·val·ue /ˌʌndəˈvælju/ *vb* **-val·ued; -val·u·ing** [T] **1** : to place too low a value on (something) • *Experts undervalued the stock.* **2** : to fail to give enough importance to (something) • *Her work was undervalued.*

un·der·wa·ter /ˌʌndəˈwɑːtə/ *adj* : located, used, done, or happening below the surface of water • *underwater caves/volcanoes* • *underwater photography* — **underwater** *adv* • *swimming underwater*

under way *or* **un·der·way** /ˌʌndəˈweɪ/ *adv* **1** : in or into motion • *The ship finally got under way.* [=began sailing] **2** : happening now • *Preparations are already under way.*

un·der·wear /ˈʌndəˌweə/ *n* [U] : clothing that is worn next to your skin and under other clothing

un·der·weight /ˌʌndəˈweɪt/ *adj* : weighing less than the normal or expected amount • *She is dangerously/slightly underweight.*

underwent *past tense of* UNDERGO

un·der·whelm /ˌʌndəˈwɛlm/ *vb* [T] *somewhat humorous* : to fail to impress (someone) • *I was underwhelmed by the evidence/performance.* [=the evidence/ performance did not impress me] — **un·der·whelm·ing** /ˌʌndəˈwɛlmɪŋ/ *adj* • *an underwhelming performance*

un·der·world /ˈʌndəˌwɜːld/ *n* [singular] **1** : the world of crime and criminals • *an underworld spy* **2 the underworld** : the place where dead people go in Greek myths

un·der·write /ˈʌndəˌraɪt/ *vb* **-wrote** /-ˌroʊt/; **-writ·ten** /-ˌrɪtn/; **-writ·ing** [T] **1** *formal* : to give money to support (something, such as a new business) and agree to be responsible for any losses if it fails • *underwrite an expedition/project* **2** *technical* : to agree to pay for a certain kind of loss or damage by offering (an insurance policy) • *underwrite a homeowner's policy* — **un·der·writ·er** /ˈʌndəˌraɪtə/ *n* [C] • *an insurance underwriter*

un·de·served /ˌʌndɪˈzɜːvd/ *adj* : not earned or deserved • *undeserved promotion/reputation*

un·de·serv·ing /ˌʌndɪˈzɜːvɪŋ/ *adj* **1** : not having qualities that deserve praise, support, etc. • *The author chose to write about an undeserving subject.* • *He left all his money to his undeserving children.* **2**

not before a noun — used to say that someone should not have or be given something • *He is **undeserving** of the criticism he has received.*

un·de·sir·able /ˌʌndɪˈzaɪrəbəl/ *adj* : bad, harmful, or unpleasant • *an undesirable behavior/habit* : not worth having or getting : not desirable • *an undesirable job* — **undesirable** *n [C]* • *The bar attracts a lot of undesirables.* [=dangerous or immoral people] — **un·de·sir·ably** /ˌʌndɪˈzaɪrəbli/ *adv*

un·de·vel·oped /ˌʌndɪˈvɛləpt/ *adj* **1** : not used for building, farming, industry, etc. • *undeveloped land/areas* **2** : having many poor people and a low level of industrial production : not developed • *an undeveloped nation* **3** : not fully grown or developed • *undeveloped skills*

un·dies /ˈʌndiz/ *n [plural] informal* : UNDERWEAR; *especially* : underpants or panties • *a pair of undies*

un·dig·ni·fied /ˌʌnˈdɪgnəˌfaɪd/ *adj* : not serious or formal : not dignified • *undignified behavior*

un·dis·ci·plined /ˌʌnˈdɪsəplənd/ *adj* : behaving in a way that is not properly controlled, organized, serious, etc. : lacking discipline • *undisciplined children*

un·dis·closed /ˌʌndɪsˈkloʊzd/ *adj* : not made known to the public • *They were paid an undisclosed amount.*

un·dis·cov·ered /ˌʌndɪsˈkʌvəd/ *adj* : not having been found or noticed : not discovered • *undiscovered territory*

un·dis·guised /ˌʌndəsˈkaɪzd/ *adj, of a feeling* : not concealed or hidden • *undisguised fear/hatred*

un·dis·mayed /ˌʌndɪsˈmeɪd/ *adj* : not worried or upset • *He was undismayed by the setbacks.*

un·dis·put·ed /ˌʌndɪsˈpjuːtəd/ *adj* **1** : definitely true : not doubted or questioned • *an undisputed fact* **2** : accepted by everyone • *the undisputed leader/champion*

un·dis·turbed /ˌʌndɪsˈtɜːbd/ *adj* **1** : not moved, changed, touched, etc., by anyone or anything • *an undisturbed forest/tomb* **2** : not upset or affected by something • *She was undisturbed by the changes.*

un·di·vid·ed /ˌʌndəˈvaɪdəd/ *adj* **1** : complete or total • *You have my undivided attention.* **2** : not separated into smaller parts • *an undivided property*

un·do /ˌʌnˈduː/ *vb* **-does** /-ˈdʌz/; **-did** /-ˈdɪd/; **-done** /-ˈdʌn/; **-do·ing** [T] **1** : to open or release (something) • *undo a belt/button/zipper* **2** : to change or stop the effect of (something) : REVERSE • *You can't undo the past.* • *The damage cannot be undone.* **3** *formal* : to cause the failure of (someone or something). • *He was undone by greed.* — see also UNDONE

un·do·ing /ˌʌnˈduːwɪŋ/ *n [singular]* **1** : something that causes someone's failure, ruin, etc. • *My quick temper was my undoing.* **2** : a state of failure, ruin, etc. • *His greed lead to his undoing.*

un·done /ˌʌnˈdʌn/ *adj, not before a noun* **1** : not fastened or tied • *My shoelace has come undone.* **2** : not done • *There were still some tasks left undone.*

un·doubt·ed /ˌʌnˈdaʊtəd/ *adj* : definitely true or existing : not doubted • *an undoubted truth/fact* — **un·doubt·ed·ly** *adv* • *She was undoubtedly the best athlete in the school.*

un·dreamed of /ˌʌnˈdriːmd-/ *also chiefly Brit* **un·dreamt of** /ˌʌnˈdrɛmt-/ *adj* : much more or better than you thought was possible • *opportunities undreamed of 10 years ago* • *an undreamed-of opportunity*

un·dress /ˌʌnˈdrɛs/ *vb* **1** [T/I] : to take your clothes off • *She undressed (herself) and climbed into bed.* • *He got undressed.* [=took off his clothes] **2** [T] : to remove the clothes of (someone) • *She undressed the children for bed.*

un·due /ˌʌnˈduː-/ *Brit* /ˌʌnˈdjuː-/ *adj, always before a noun, formal* : more than is reasonable or necessary • *undue pressure/influence*

un·du·late /ˈʌndʒəˌleɪt, *Brit* ˈʌndjəˌleɪt/ *vb* **-lat·ed; -lat·ing** [I] *formal* : to move or be shaped like waves • *undulating hills* — **un·du·la·tion** /ˌʌndʒəˈleɪʃən, *Brit* ˌʌndjəˈleɪʃən/ *n [C]*

un·du·ly /ˌʌnˈduːli, *Brit* ˌʌnˈdjuːli/ *adv, formal* : to an extreme, unreasonable, or unnecessary degree : EXCESSIVELY • *The punishment was unduly harsh.*

un·dy·ing /ˌʌnˈdaɪɪŋ/ *adj, always before a noun* : lasting forever • *undying gratitude/love*

un·earth /ˌʌnˈɜːθ/ *vb* [T] **1** : to find (something) that was buried in the earth • *unearth buried treasure* **2** : to find or discover (something) that was hidden or lost • *unearth a secret*

un·earth·ly /ˌʌnˈɜːθli/ *adj* **1** : very strange, unnatural, and frightening • *an unearthly scream* **2** *Brit* : unreasonably early or late • *She was up at an/some unearthly hour.*

un·ease /ˌʌnˈiːz/ *n [U]* : a feeling of worry or unhappiness • *A feeling of unease came over her.*

un·easy /ˌʌnˈiːzi/ *adj* **1** : worried or unhappy about something • *I'm (feeling) uneasy about/with the change.* **2** : likely to change or end • *an uneasy truce/alliance/relationship* **3** : awkward and uncomfortable • *an uneasy silence* — **un·eas·i·ly** /ˌʌnˈiːzəli/ *adv* — **un·eas·i·ness** *n [U]*

un·ed·u·cat·ed /ˌʌnˈɛdʒəˌkeɪtəd/ *adj* : having or showing little or no formal schooling • *an uneducated man*

un·emo·tion·al /ˌʌnɪˈmoʊʃənl/ *adj* : not emotional : not showing emotion • *an unemotional voice/manner/person*

un·em·ployed /ˌʌnɪmˈplɔɪd/ *adj* : having no job : not employed • *unemployed workers* • *I'm currently unemployed.* — **the unemployed** : people who have no jobs • *centers for the unemployed*

un·em·ploy·ment /ˌʌnɪmˈplɔɪmənt/ *n [U]* **1** : the state of not having a job • *My unemployment lasted about six months.* **2** : the total number of people who do not have jobs in a particular place or area • *high/low unemployment* • *an unemployment rate of six percent* **3** *US* : money paid by the government to someone who does not have a job ▪ *She was receiving/collecting unemployment for a few months.* — called also **unemployment benefits**, (*Brit*) **unemployment benefit**, (*US*) **unemployment compensation**

un·end·ing /ˌʌnˈɛndɪŋ/ *adj* : lasting forever ▪ *an unending quest/supply*

un·en·dur·able /ˌʌnɪnˈdʊrəbəl, *Brit* ˌʌnɪnˈdjʊərəbəl/ *adj* : too unpleasant, painful, etc., to accept or endure ▪ *unendurable pain/stress/suffering*

un·en·light·ened /ˌʌnɪnˈlaɪtnd/ *adj* : not having or showing a good understanding of how people should be treated ▪ *unenlightened people/comments*

un·en·thu·si·as·tic /ˌʌnɪnˌθuːziˈæstɪk, *Brit* ˌʌnɪnˌθjuːziˈæstɪk/ *adj* : having or showing a lack of excitement or interest : not enthusiastic ▪ *an unenthusiastic response*

un·en·vi·able /ˌʌnˈɛnvijəbəl/ *adj* : very bad or unpleasant ▪ *an unenviable position/task*

un·equal /ˌʌnˈiːkwəl/ *adj* **1** : giving more advantages, power, etc., to some people and less to other people for unfair reasons ▪ *unequal justice/treatment* ▪ *the unequal distribution of wealth/resources* **2** : different in number, degree, quality, size, etc. ▪ *unequal amounts* **3** *not before a noun* : not able to do what is needed ▪ *She felt unequal to the job.* [=she felt that she could not do the job] — **un·equal·ly** *adv*

un·equaled *also chiefly Brit* **un·equalled** /ˌʌnˈiːkwəld/ *adj* : better than all others ▪ *an unequaled achievement/talent*

un·equiv·o·cal /ˌʌnɪˈkwɪvəkəl/ *adj, formal* : not showing or allowing any doubt ▪ *unequivocal evidence* ▪ *Her answer was an unequivocal yes/no.* — **un·equiv·o·cal·ly** /ˌʌnɪˈkwɪvəkli/ *adv*

un·err·ing /ˌʌnˈɛrɪŋ, ˌʌnˈ ɝɪŋ/ *adj, formal* : always right and accurate : making no errors ▪ *an unerring sense of good taste* — **un·err·ing·ly** *adv*

un·eth·i·cal /ˌʌnˈɛθɪkəl/ *adj* : morally bad ▪ *unethical behavior/methods* — **un·eth·i·cal·ly** /ˌʌnˈɛθɪkli/ *adv*

un·even /ˌʌnˈiːvən/ *adj* : not even: such as **a** : not level, flat, or smooth ▪ *an uneven surface/texture* **b** : not following a regular pattern : IRREGULAR ▪ *uneven heating/drying* ▪ *His breathing was uneven.* **c** : better in some parts than in others ▪ *an uneven performance* **d** : unequal or unfair ▪ *an uneven distribution of wealth* **e** : more likely to be won easily by one side than the other ▪ *an uneven match* **f** : ODD 5a ▪ *an uneven number of students* — **un·even·ly** *adv* — **un·even·ness** /ˌʌnˈiːvənnəs/ *n* [U]

un·event·ful /ˌʌnɪˈvɛntfəl/ *adj* : having nothing exciting, interesting, or unusual happening : not eventful ▪ *an uneventful vacation/day/life* — **un·event·ful·ly** *adv*

un·ex·cep·tion·al /ˌʌnɪkˈsɛpʃənəl/ *adj* : not unusually good, interesting, etc. ▪ *an unexceptional student/writer*

un·ex·pect·ed /ˌʌnɪkˈspɛktəd/ *adj* : not expected ▪ *unexpected consequences/results/guests* — **un·ex·pect·ed·ly** *adv* ▪

Guests arrived unexpectedly.

un·ex·plained /ˌʌnɪkˈspleɪnd/ *adj* : having no known reason or cause ▪ *an unexplained death/illness*

un·fail·ing /ˌʌnˈfeɪlɪŋ/ *adj* **1** : never changing or becoming weaker even in difficult times ▪ *unfailing loyalty/support/optimism* **2** : always providing enough of what is needed ▪ *an unfailing supply* — **un·fail·ing·ly** *adv* ▪ *He is unfailingly* [=always] *polite.*

un·fair /ˌʌnˈfeɚ/ *adj* : treating people in a way that favors some over others : not fair, honest, or just ▪ *an unfair trial* ▪ *unfair advantages* ▪ *Life is often unfair.* — **un·fair·ly** *adv* — **un·fair·ness** *n* [U]

un·faith·ful /ˌʌnˈfeɪθfəl/ *adj* **1** : having a sexual relationship with someone who is not your wife, husband, or partner ▪ *an unfaithful husband* ▪ *She has been unfaithful to him.* **2** : not accurate ▪ *an unfaithful translation* — **un·faith·ful·ness** *n* [U]

un·fa·mil·iar /ˌʌnfəˈmɪljɚ/ *adj* : not frequently seen, heard, or experienced ▪ *an unfamiliar face/place/word* ▪ *The language is unfamiliar to him.* [=he does not know the language at all] — **unfamiliar with** : not having any knowledge of (something) ▪ *I'm unfamiliar with that subject.* — **un·fa·mil·iar·i·ty** /ˌʌnfəˌmɪlˈjerəti/ *n* [U]

un·fash·ion·able /ˌʌnˈfæʃənəbəl/ *adj* : not currently popular or stylish : not fashionable ▪ *unfashionable shoes*

un·fas·ten /ˌʌnˈfæsn̩, *Brit* ˌʌnˈfɑːsən/ *vb* [T] : to make (something) loose : UNDO ▪ *unfasten a belt/buckle/button*

un·fath·om·able /ˌʌnˈfæðəməbəl/ *adj, literary* : impossible to understand ▪ *unfathomable reasons/motives/behavior*

un·fa·vor·able (*US*) *or Brit* **un·fa·vour·able** /ˌʌnˈfeɪvɚəbəl/ *adj* **1** : likely to cause problems or difficulties ▪ *unfavorable weather* **2** : expressing disapproval ▪ *unfavorable comments/reviews* — **un·fa·vor·ably** (*US*) *or Brit* **un·fa·vour·ably** /ˌʌnˈfeɪvɚəbli/ *adv*

un·fazed /ˌʌnˈfeɪzd/ *adj* : not confused, worried, or shocked by something that has happened ▪ *She was unfazed by the delay.*

un·feel·ing /ˌʌnˈfiːlɪŋ/ *adj* : not kind or sympathetic toward other people ▪ *a cold and unfeeling person* — **un·feel·ing·ly** *adv*

un·feigned /ˌʌnˈfeɪnd/ *adj* : not false or pretended : GENUINE ▪ *unfeigned enthusiasm*

un·fet·tered /ˌʌnˈfɛtɚd/ *adj, formal* : not controlled or restricted ▪ *unfettered access*

un·fin·ished /ˌʌnˈfɪnɪʃt/ *adj* : not completed : not finished ▪ *an unfinished building* ▪ *unfinished furniture* [=furniture made of wood that has not yet been stained or varnished] ▪ *You and I have some unfinished business to deal with.*

un·fit /ˌʌnˈfɪt/ *adj* **1** : not proper, suitable, or acceptable ▪ *The movie is unfit for children.* ▪ *The food was unfit to eat.* **2** : not having the necessary qualities, skills, mental health, etc., to do something ▪ *an unfit parent* ▪ *He's unfit for* *army service.* **3** : not physically healthy : not in good physical condition ▪ *She is overweight and unfit.*

un·flag·ging /ˌʌnˈflæɡɪŋ/ *adj* : not decreasing or becoming weaker : remaining strong ▪ *her unflagging energy/enthusiasm*

un·flap·pa·ble /ˌʌnˈflæpəbəl/ *adj* : not easily upset : unusually calm in difficult situations ▪ *He has a reputation for being unflappable.*

un·flat·ter·ing /ˌʌnˈflætərɪŋ/ *adj* : making someone or something look or seem worse or less attractive ▪ *an unflattering color/description*

un·flinch·ing /ˌʌnˈflɪntʃɪŋ/ *adj* **1** : staying strong and determined even when things are difficult ▪ *unflinching dedication* **2** : looking at or describing something or someone in a very direct way ▪ *The movie takes an unflinching look at the war.* — **un·flinch·ing·ly** *adv*

un·fo·cused *or Brit* **un·fo·cussed** /ˌʌnˈfoʊkəst/ *adj* : not focused: such as **a** : not relating to or directed toward one specific thing ▪ *an unfocused essay* **b** : not looking at anything specific ▪ *an unfocused gaze*

un·fold /ˌʌnˈfoʊld/ *vb* **1** [*T/I*] : to spread or cause (something) to spread or straighten out from a folded position ▪ *The couch unfolds to form a bed.* **2** [*I*] : to happen as time passes ▪ *We watched the drama unfold on live television.* **3** [*I*] : to be told or made known ▪ *Their relationship becomes more complex as the story unfolds.*

un·fore·see·able /ˌʌnˌfoɚˈsiːjəbəl/ *adj* : impossible to predict or expect ▪ *unforeseeable problems*

un·fore·seen /ˌʌnˌfoɚˈsiːn/ *adj* : not predicted or expected : UNEXPECTED ▪ *unforeseen consequences/problems*

un·for·get·ta·ble /ˌʌnfɚˈɡɛtəbəl/ *adj* : very special, unusual, beautiful, etc., and therefore difficult or impossible to forget ▪ *an unforgettable experience/night* — **un·for·get·ta·bly** /ˌʌnfɚˈɡɛtəbli/ *adv*

un·for·giv·able /ˌʌnfɚˈɡɪvəbəl/ *adj* : so bad that it can never be forgiven ▪ *an unforgivable crime/sin* — **un·for·giv·ably** /ˌʌnfɚˈɡɪvəbli/ *adv*

un·for·giv·ing /ˌʌnfɚˈɡɪvɪŋ/ *adj* **1** : not willing to forgive other people ▪ *an unforgiving person/attitude* **2** : very harsh or difficult ▪ *an unforgiving climate/environment*

un·formed /ˌʌnˈfoɚmd/ *adj* : not fully or completely developed ▪ *an unformed thought/idea*

un·for·tu·nate /ˌʌnˈfoɚtʃənət/ *adj* **1** : not fortunate: such as **a** : having bad luck : UNLUCKY ▪ *the unfortunate victim* **b** : coming or happening by bad luck ▪ *an unfortunate experience/result* ▪ *It's unfortunate that he wasn't here.* **2** : not appropriate or desirable ▪ *an unfortunate choice of words* — **unfortunate** *n* [*C*] *literary* ▪ *a group of poor unfortunates* [=unfortunate people]

un·for·tu·nate·ly /ˌʌnˈfoɚtʃənətli/ *adv* — used to say that something bad or unlucky has happened ▪ *Unfortunately, we were late.* ▪ *"Would you like to have dinner with us?" "I can't, unfortunately. I have to work."*

un·found·ed /ˌʌnˈfaʊndəd/ *adj, formal* : not based on facts or proof ▪ *unfounded claims/rumors/fears*

un·friend·ly /ˌʌnˈfrɛndli/ *adj* **un·friend·li·er**; **-est** : not friendly ▪ *unfriendly people/nations* ▪ *an unfriendly greeting/stare* — **un·friend·li·ness** /ˌʌnˈfrɛndlinəs/ *n* [*U*]

un·ful·filled /ˌʌnfʊlˈfɪld/ *adj* **1** : not yet achieved ▪ *an unfulfilled dream/promise* **2** : not feeling happy and satisfied about life ▪ *She's bored and unfulfilled at her job.*

un·ful·fill·ing /ˌʌnfʊlˈfɪlɪŋ/ *adj* : not providing happiness or satisfaction ▪ *an unfulfilling job/relationship*

un·fun·ny /ˌʌnˈfʌni/ *adj, disapproving* : not funny ▪ *unfunny jokes*

un·furl /ˌʌnˈfɚl/ *vb* [*T/I*] : to cause (something that is folded or rolled up) to open ▪ *unfurl a flag/banner* ▪ *We watched as the banner unfurled.*

un·fur·nished /ˌʌnˈfɚnɪʃt/ *adj* : without furniture ▪ *an unfurnished apartment*

un·gain·ly /ˌʌnˈɡeɪnli/ *adj* : moving in an awkward or clumsy way : not graceful ▪ *a large, ungainly animal* — **un·gain·li·ness** *n* [*U*]

un·glued /ˌʌnˈɡluːd/ *adj* — **come un·glued** *US, informal* **1** : to become extremely upset or angry ▪ *She came unglued when they refused her request.* **2** : to fail suddenly or completely ▪ *Their marriage came unglued.*

un·god·ly /ˌʌnˈɡɑːdli/ *adj* **un·god·li·er**; **-est 1** *somewhat old-fashioned* **a** : not believing in or respecting God ▪ *ungodly people* **b** : immoral or evil ▪ *ungodly behavior* **2** *always before a noun* : very bad or shocking ▪ *an ungodly* [=extremely large] *amount of money* ▪ *Who would call at this ungodly hour?* [=who would call so late/early?] — **un·god·li·ness** /ˌʌnˈɡɑːdlinəs/ *n* [*U*]

un·gra·cious /ˌʌnˈɡreɪʃəs/ *adj, formal* : not polite or respectful : not gracious ▪ *an ungracious response* — **un·gra·cious·ly** *adv*

un·gram·mat·i·cal /ˌʌnɡrəˈmætɪkəl/ *adj* : not following the rules of grammar ▪ *an ungrammatical sentence*

un·grate·ful /ˌʌnˈɡreɪtfəl/ *adj* : not feeling or showing thanks for favors, gifts, etc. ▪ *an ungrateful child* — **un·grate·ful·ly** *adv* — **un·grate·ful·ness** *n* [*U*]

un·guard·ed /ˌʌnˈɡɑːdəd/ *adj* **1** : speaking carelessly without thinking about what you are saying ▪ *an unguarded remark* **2** : not protected or watched over ▪ *an unguarded border*

un·ham·pered /ˌʌnˈhæmpɚd/ *adj* : allowed to move, progress, or happen without difficulties or obstacles ▪ *She enjoyed a season unhampered by injury.*

un·hap·pi·ly /ˌʌnˈhæpəli/ *adv* **1** : without happiness : in an unhappy manner ▪ *They were unhappily married.* **2** : in a way that is unfortunate or unlucky ▪ *Unhappily, many of the passengers got seasick.*

un·hap·py /ˌʌnˈhæpi/ *adj* **un·hap·pi·er**; **-est 1** : sad, depressed, or disappointed : not happy ▪ *I can see that he's unhappy.*

He was unhappy with the hotel. ▪ *The children were unhappy about going back to school.* **2** : causing or involving feelings of sadness : not pleasant or joyful ▪ *an unhappy childhood/marriage* **3** : not appropriate or lucky ▪ *an unhappy choice of career/words* — **un·hap·pi·ness** *n* [U]

un·harmed /ˌʌnˈhɑɚmd/ *adj, not before a noun* : safe or unhurt : not harmed ▪ *They escaped from the fire unharmed.*

un·healthy /ˌʌnˈhɛlθi/ *adj* **un·health·i·er; -est** : not healthy ▪ *an unhealthy person* ▪ *unhealthy eating habits* ▪ *a financially unhealthy company* ▪ *an unhealthy relationship*

un·heard /ˌʌnˈhɚd/ *adj* **1** : not given attention ▪ *The students' concerns went unheard.* [=were ignored] **2** : not heard or listened to ▪ *a previously unheard recording*

un·heard-of /ˌʌnˈhɚdˌʌv/ *adj* : not known to have existed or happened before : very unusual ▪ *In those days, indoor plumbing was almost unheard-of.* ▪ *It's not unheard-of for a patient's condition to improve this quickly.*

un·heed·ed /ˌʌnˈhiːdəd/ *adj* : heard or noticed but then ignored or not followed ▪ *Her warnings went unheeded.* [=were ignored]

un·help·ful /ˌʌnˈhɛlpfəl/ *adj* : giving no help : not helpful or useful ▪ *unhelpful advice* — **un·help·ful·ly** *adv*

un·her·ald·ed /ˌʌnˈhɛrəldəd/ *adj, formal* **1** : not getting the praise or appreciation that is deserved ▪ *Our goalie is one of the unheralded players on our team.* **2** : happening without any warning ▪ *an unheralded visit*

un·hes·i·tat·ing /ˌʌnˈhɛzəˌteɪtɪŋ/ *adj* : done, made, or shown quickly and immediately without waiting or hesitating ▪ *an unhesitating reply* — **un·hes·i·tat·ing·ly** *adv*

un·hinge /ˌʌnˈhɪndʒ/ *vb* **-hinged; -hinging** [T] : to make (someone) very upset or mentally ill ▪ *He was unhinged by grief.*

un·hitch /ˌʌnˈhɪtʃ/ *vb* [T] : to disconnect (something) that is attached to something else by a knot, hook, or hitch ▪ *We unhitched the trailer from the car.*

un·ho·ly /ˌʌnˈhoʊli/ *adj* **1** : not showing respect for a god or a religion ▪ *an unholy attitude* **2** — used to describe people or groups that are working together for a bad purpose ▪ *an unholy alliance between politicians and lobbyists* **3** *always before a noun, informal* : shockingly or surprisingly bad, large, etc. ▪ *Our finances are an unholy mess.*

un·hook /ˌʌnˈhʊk/ *vb* [T] **1** : to remove (something) from a hook ▪ *He unhooked the fish from the line.* **2** : to open or remove (something that is attached with hooks) ▪ *She unhooked the gate.*

un·hur·ried /ˌʌnˈhɚrid/ *adj* : not happening or done quickly or too quickly : relaxed and calm ▪ *strolling along at an unhurried pace*

un·hurt /ˌʌnˈhɚt/ *adj, not before a noun* : not hurt ▪ *They were unhurt in the crash.*

UNICEF /ˈjuːnəˌsɛf/ *abbr* United Nations Children's Fund ◆ UNICEF is an organization created by the United Nations

to help children in poor countries around the world.

uni·corn /ˈjuːnəˌkoɚn/ *n* [C] : an imaginary animal that looks like a horse and has a straight horn growing from the middle of its forehead

uni·cy·cle /ˈjuːnɪˌsaɪkəl/ *n* [C] : a vehicle that is similar to a bicycle but has only one wheel

un·iden·ti·fi·able /ˌʌnaɪˌdɛntəˈfajəbəl/ *adj* : impossible to identify ▪ *an unidentifiable substance*

un·iden·ti·fied /ˌʌnaɪˈdɛntəˌfaɪd/ *adj* : not known or identified ▪ *an unidentified person* ▪ *an unidentified flying object* [=UFO]

¹**uni·form** /ˈjuːnəˌfoɚm/ *n* [C/U] : a special kind of clothing that is worn by all the members of a group or organization ▪ *a school/police/baseball uniform* ▪ *soldiers in (full) uniform* [=wearing uniforms] — **uni·formed** /ˈjuːnəˌfoɚmd/ *adj* ▪ *uniformed officers/police/soldiers*

²**uniform** *adj* : not varying or changing : staying the same at all times, in all places, or for all parts or members ▪ *The cookies should be uniform in size.* = *The cookies should be of uniform size.* — **uni·for·mi·ty** /ˈjuːnəˈfoɚməti/ *n* [U, singular] ▪ *There is little uniformity among the states in voting procedures.* [=different states have different voting procedures] — **uni·form·ly** *adv* ▪ *uniformly high standards*

uni·fy /ˈjuːnəˌfaɪ/ *vb* **-fies; -fied; -fy·ing** [T] : to cause (people or things) to be joined or brought together : UNITE ▪ *The creation of the national railroad system unified the country.* — **uni·fi·ca·tion** /ˌjuːnəfəˈkeɪʃən/ *n* [U] ▪ *the unification of Germany*

uni·lat·er·al /ˌjuːnɪˈlætərəl/ *adj* : involving only one group or country ▪ *a unilateral cease-fire* — **uni·lat·er·al·ly** *adv*

un·imag·in·able /ˌʌnəˈmædʒənəbəl/ *adj* : not possible to imagine : beyond what you would normally imagine ▪ *the unimaginable horrors of war* ▪ *This technology would have been unimaginable five years ago.* — **un·imag·in·ably** /ˌʌnəˈmædʒənəbli/ *adv*

un·imag·i·na·tive /ˌʌnəˈmædʒənətɪv/ *adj* : not having or showing an ability to think of new and interesting ideas : not imaginative ▪ *an unimaginative writer/book*

un·im·peach·able /ˌʌnɪmˈpiːtʃəbəl/ *adj, formal* : not able to be doubted or questioned ▪ *a person of unimpeachable integrity* — **un·im·peach·ably** /ˌʌnɪmˈpiːtʃəbli/ *adv*

un·im·por·tant /ˌʌnɪmˈpoɚtn̩t/ *adj* : not important ▪ *unimportant details/matters*

un·im·pressed /ˌʌnɪmˈprɛst/ *adj, not before a noun* : not feeling that someone or something is very good or special : not impressed ▪ *He was unimpressed by/with their arguments.*

un·im·pres·sive /ˌʌnɪmˈprɛsɪv/ *adj* : not deserving attention, admiration, or respect : not impressive ▪ *an unimpressive performance*

un·in·formed /ˌʌnɪnˈfoɚmd/ *adj* : not having knowledge or information about something • *Many Americans are sadly uninformed about politics.*

un·in·hab·it·a·ble /ˌʌnɪnˈhæbətəbəl/ *adj* : not safe or suitable to be lived in • *an uninhabitable wasteland/building*

un·in·hab·it·ed /ˌʌnɪnˈhæbətəd/ *adj, of a place* : not lived in by people • *a small uninhabited island*

un·in·hib·it·ed /ˌʌnɪnˈhɪbətəd/ *adj* : able to express thoughts and feelings freely • *a very uninhibited person*

un·in·i·ti·at·ed /ˌʌnɪˈnɪʃiˌeɪtəd/ *n* — **the uninitiated** : people who do not have knowledge of or experience with something • *For the uninitiated, let me explain how this device works.* — **uninitiated** *adj* • *an uninitiated observer*

un·in·jured /ˌʌnˈɪndʒəd/ *adj* : not hurt or injured • *The driver of the car died but the passengers were uninjured.*

un·in·spired /ˌʌnɪnˈspajəd/ *adj* : not very good or clever • *She gave an uninspired performance.*

un·in·spir·ing /ˌʌnɪnˈspaɪrɪŋ/ *adj* : not causing people to want to do or create something • *an uninspiring public speaker*

un·in·sured /ˌʌnɪnˈʃəd/ *adj* : not having insurance : not insured • *uninsured drivers*

un·in·tel·li·gent /ˌʌnɪnˈtɛlədʒənt/ *adj* : not intelligent • *unintelligent people/observations*

un·in·tel·li·gi·ble /ˌʌnɪnˈtɛlədʒəbəl/ *adj* : impossible to understand • *He left an unintelligible message on my voice mail.*

un·in·tend·ed /ˌʌnɪnˈtɛndəd/ *adj* : not planned as a purpose or goal • *The proposed bill could have unintended consequences.*

un·in·ten·tion·al /ˌʌnɪnˈtɛnʃənl/ *adj* : not done in a way that is planned or intended • *an unintentional omission/error* — **un·in·ten·tion·al·ly** *adv*

un·in·ter·est·ed /ˌʌnˈɪntrəstəd/ *adj* : not wanting to learn more about something or become involved in something : not interested • *She seemed uninterested in our problems.*

un·in·ter·est·ing /ˌʌnˈɪntrəstɪŋ/ *adj* : dull and boring • *an uninteresting topic*

un·in·ter·rupt·ed /ˌʌnˌɪntəˈrʌptəd/ *adj* : not interrupted, stopped, or blocked • *eight hours of uninterrupted* [=*continuous*] *sleep* • *an uninterrupted view of the ocean*

un·in·vit·ed /ˌʌnɪnˈvaɪtəd/ *adj* : not asked or expected to come or to do something with others • *an uninvited guest* • *She showed up uninvited.*

un·in·vit·ing /ˌʌnɪnˈvaɪtɪŋ/ *adj* : not appealing or attractive • *The house was dark and uninviting.*

union /ˈjuːnjən/ *n* **1** [C] : an organization of workers formed to protect the rights and interests of its members • *union members/leaders/officials* — called also (US) *labor union*, (Brit) *trade union* **2** [U] : an act of joining two or more things together • *a perfect union of Eastern and Western music* **3** [*singular*] : a group of states or nations that are ruled by one government or that agree to work together • *the European Union* **4** *the Union* **a** : the United States • *Utah joined the Union in 1896.* ◇ *The State of*

the Union address is a yearly speech given by the U.S. President to Congress and the people to tell them about important things that are affecting the country. **b** : the group of northern states that supported the federal government during the American Civil War • *One brother fought for the Union and one for the Confederacy.* — often used as *Union* before another noun • *Union soldiers* **5** [C] : an organized group of people, businesses, etc., that have the same purpose or interest • *the American Civil Liberties Union* **6** [C/U] *formal* : the act of getting married or of causing two people to be married • *the union of two people in marriage*

union·ize *also Brit* **union·ise** /ˈjuːnjəˌnaɪz/ *vb* **-ized**; **-iz·ing** **1** [I] : to form or join a labor union • *Workers are fighting for the right to unionize.* **2** [T] : to help (people) form or join a labor union • *Organizers unionized the staff.* — **union·i·za·tion** *also Brit* **union·i·sa·tion** /ˌjuːnjənəˈzeɪʃən, Brit ˌjuːnjəˌnaɪˈzeɪʃən/ *n* [U]

Union Jack *n* — **the Union Jack** : the national flag of the United Kingdom

unique /juˈniːk/ *adj* **1** — used to say that something or someone is unlike anything or anyone else • *His talents make him truly unique.* **2** : very special or unusual • *a unique opportunity* • *a unique feature/characteristic* **3** : belonging to or connected with only one particular thing, place, or person • *a species unique to this region* [=*a species that occurs only in this region*] — **unique·ly** *adv* • *a uniquely American tradition* — **unique·ness** *n* [U]

uni·sex /ˈjuːnəˌsɛks/ *adj, always before a noun* : designed for or used by both men and women • *unisex clothing*

uni·son /ˈjuːnəsən/ *n* — **in unison** ◇ If people do something *in unison*, they do it together at the same time. • *singing/playing in unison* • *The children recited the alphabet in unison.* If people **work/act in unison**, they work together to achieve something. • *Residents and police are working in unison to make the neighborhood safer.*

unit /ˈjuːnət/ *n* [C] **1** : a single thing, person, or group that is a part of something larger • *The family is the basic unit of society.* • *an army unit* **2** : a part of a hospital where a particular type of care is provided • *the intensive care unit* **3** : a particular amount of length, time, money, etc., that is used as a standard for counting or measuring • *Feet and meters are units of length.* • *units of measurement* **4** : a part of a school course or textbook with a particular subject • *Our class is finishing the unit on World War I.* **5** *US, education* : an amount of work used for measuring a student's progress towards earning a degree in a school, college, etc. • *Each unit of credit represents 120 classroom hours.* **6** *business* : an individual item of one of the products that a company makes and sells • *Last year the company sold 200,000 units of that particular model of car.* **7** : a machine or part of a machine or system that has a particular use • *an air-conditioning unit* • *the computer's* **central processing unit** **8** : one of a number of apartments in a building • *The building has eight units.*

Uni·tar·i·an Uni·ver·sal·ist /ˌjuːnə-ˈterijən,juːnəˈvɜːsəlɪst/ *n [C]* : a person who belongs to a religion that allows its members to freely choose their own religious beliefs and that supports liberal social action — **Unitarian Uni·ver·sal·ism** /-ˌjuːnəˈvɜːsəˌlɪzəm/ *n [U]*

unite /juˈnaɪt/ *vb* **unit·ed; unit·ing** **1** *[T/I]* : to join together to do or achieve something • *Party members united in support of their candidate.* • *We were united by a common purpose.* **2 a** *[T]* : to cause (two or more people or things) to be joined together and become one thing • *A treaty united the independent nations.* • *They were united in marriage on Sunday, August 24.* **b** *[I]* : to become joined together as one thing • *The sperm and egg unite to form an embryo.* — **unit·er** /juˈnaɪtɚ/ *n [C]*

united *adj* **1** : involving people or groups working together to achieve something • *a united campaign against drug abuse* **2** : made up of members who share the same purpose, interest, etc. • *a united Europe* — often used in the names of countries and organizations • *the United States of America*

United Nations *n* — **the United Nations** : an international organization that helps to solve world conflicts peacefully — abbr. *UN* or *U.N.*

unit trust *n [C] Brit* : MUTUAL FUND

uni·ty /ˈjuːnəti/ *n* **1** *[U, singular]* : the state of being in full agreement : HARMONY • *political/national unity* **2** *[U]* : a way of combining the parts in a work of art or literature so that they seem to belong together • *His paintings lack unity.*

Univ. *abbr* University

uni·ver·sal /ˌjuːnəˈvɜːsəl/ *adj* **1** : done or experienced by everyone • *universal human emotions* • *an idea with universal appeal* : existing or available for everyone • *universal health care* **2** : existing or true at all times or in all places • *universal truths/laws* — **uni·ver·sal·i·ty** /ˌjuːnəvɚˈsæləti/ *n [U]* — **uni·ver·sal·ly** *adv* • *a universally recognized/accepted truth*

uni·verse /ˈjuːnəˌvɚs/ *n* **1 the universe** : all of space and everything in it including stars, planets, galaxies, etc. **2** *[C]* : an area of space or a world that is similar to but separate from the one that we live in • *a parallel/alternate universe* **3** *[singular]* : the people, places, experiences, etc., that are associated with a particular person, place, or thing • *The college campus is its own little universe.* • *Her son is the* **center of her universe.** [=the most important part of her life]

uni·ver·si·ty /ˌjuːnəˈvɚsəti/ *n, pl* **-ties** *[C/U]* : a school that offers courses leading to a degree (such as a bachelor's, master's, or doctoral degree) and where research is done • *public/private universities* • *Harvard University* • *university students/professors* • (*Brit*) *Did she go* **to uni-**

versity? [=did she study at a university?] — abbr. *U., Univ.*

un·just /ˌʌnˈdʒʌst/ *adj, formal* : not fair or deserved • *unjust punishment* — **un·just·ly** *adv*

un·jus·ti·fi·able /ˌʌnˈdʒʌstəˌfajəbəl/ *adj* : not able to be defended, excused, or accepted • *an unjustifiable expense* — **un·jus·ti·fi·ably** /ˌʌnˈdʒʌstəˌfajəbli/ *adv*

un·jus·ti·fied /ˌʌnˈdʒʌstəˌfaɪd/ *adj* : unnecessary and not right or fair • *The shooting of the unarmed suspect was unjustified.*

un·kempt /ˌʌnˈkɛmpt/ *adj* : not neat or orderly : messy or untidy • *an unkempt lawn*

un·kind /ˌʌnˈkaɪnd/ *adj* : not friendly, pleasant, helpful, etc. : not kind • *an unkind remark* • *How could you be so unkind?* • *He was unkind to her.* [=he treated her badly] — **un·kind·ly** *adv* • *He was treated unkindly.* • *Judges tend to* **look unkindly on/upon** [=disapprove of] *repeat offenders.* — **un·kind·ness** /ˌʌnˈkaɪndnəs/ *n [U]*

un·know·able /ˌʌnˈnowəbəl/ *adj* : not able to be known • *an unknowable God*

un·know·ing /ˌʌnˈnowɪŋ/ *adj, always before a noun* : not aware of what is really happening • *She became an unknowing accomplice to the crime.* — **un·know·ing·ly** /ˌʌnˈnowɪŋli/ *adv*

¹un·known /ˌʌnˈnoʊn/ *adj* **1** : not known • *a disease of unknown cause/origin* **2** : not famous or well-known • *an unknown artist*

²unknown *n* **1 the unknown** : a place, situation, or thing that you do not know about or understand • *a fear of the unknown* **2** *[C]* : a person who is not famous or well-known • *An unknown played the lead.* **3** *[C]* : something that is not known or not yet discovered • *We're facing too many unknowns.*

un·law·ful /ˌʌnˈlɑːfəl/ *adj, formal* : not allowed by the law : ILLEGAL • *an unlawful search*

un·lead·ed /ˌʌnˈlɛdəd/ *adj* : not containing lead • *unleaded gasoline*

un·learn /ˌʌnˈlɚn/ *vb [T]* : to forget and stop doing (something, such as a habit) in a deliberate way because it is bad or incorrect • *It is hard to unlearn bad habits.*

un·leash /ˌʌnˈliːʃ/ *vb [T]* : to allow or cause (something very powerful) to happen suddenly • *The editorial unleashed a flood of angry responses.*

un·leav·ened /ˌʌnˈlɛvənd/ *adj* : flat because of being made without yeast, baking powder, etc. • *unleavened bread*

un·less /ənˈlɛs/ *conj* — used to say what will happen, be done, or be true if something else does not happen, is not done, or is not true • *Unless something is done, the species will become extinct.* • *I won't have an operation unless surgery is absolutely necessary.* [=I will only have an operation if surgery is absolutely necessary] • *"Will I have to pay?" "Not unless* [=only if] *you want to."*

¹un·like /ˌʌnˈlaɪk/ *prep* **1** : different from (something or someone) • *She's unlike anyone I've ever met.* • *a texture* **not** *unlike*

[=similar to] *that of silk* **2** : not typical of (someone) • *It's unlike her to be late.* **3** — used to indicate how someone or something is different from other people or things • *Unlike most mammals, the platypus lays eggs.*

²**unlike** *adj, somewhat formal* : not similar • *a comparison of unlike things*

un·like·ly /ˌʌnˈlaɪkli/ *adj* **un·like·li·er; -est** **1** : not likely — used to say that something probably will not happen or is not true • *an unlikely story* [=a story that is hard to believe] • *It is unlikely that she will recover. = She is unlikely to recover.* **2** always before a noun : not seeming to be right or suited for a purpose • *an unlikely ally/candidate/combination* — **un·like·li·hood** /ˌʌnˈlaɪkliˌhʊd/ *n* [U]

un·lim·it·ed /ˌʌnˈlɪmətəd/ *adj* **1** : without any limits or restrictions • *unlimited access* • *a ticket good for unlimited travel* **2** : not limited in number or amount • *Her funds seem to be unlimited.*

un·list·ed /ˌʌnˈlɪstəd/ *adj* : not appearing on an official list; *especially, chiefly US* : not appearing in a telephone book • *an unlisted* [=(Brit) *ex-directory*] *phone number*

un·load /ˌʌnˈloʊd/ *vb* **1** [T/I] : to remove something (such as cargo) from a truck, ship, etc. • *unload a truck/car* • *I have to unload the groceries (from the car).* **2** [T] : to allow (someone) to leave a train, ship, etc. • *The train stopped to unload passengers.* **3** [T] *informal* : to get rid of (something or someone) quickly • *trying to unload* [=*sell*] *an old car* **4** [T] : to take something out of a device • *unload a gun* [=remove the bullets from a gun] • *unload the dishwasher* **5** [I] *US, informal* : to express a strong feeling (such as anger) in a very forceful way • *It's not fair to unload on them like that.*

un·lock /ˌʌnˈlɑːk/ *vb* [T] **1** : to open the lock on (something) • *unlock the car/door* **2** : to find out about (something that was secret or unknown) • *unlocking the secrets of DNA* **3** : to make (something) available for use • *unlock a computer with a password*

un·lov·able /ˌʌnˈlʌvəbəl/ *adj* : not having attractive or appealing qualities • *an unlovable character*

un·lucky /ˌʌnˈlʌki/ *adj* **un·luck·i·er; -est** **1** : having bad luck • *an unlucky person* **2** : causing bad luck • *an unlucky number* **3** : resulting from bad luck • *an unlucky accident* — **un·luck·i·ly** /ˌʌnˈlʌkəli/ *adv* • *Unluckily* [=*unfortunately*] *for her, it rained.*

un·made /ˌʌnˈmeɪd/ *adj* — used to describe a bed that looks untidy because it has been slept in and its blankets and sheets have not been neatly arranged to cover the mattress • *an unmade bed*

un·man·age·able /ˌʌnˈmænɪʤəbəl/ *adj* : difficult to deal with or control • *unmanageable children/hair* — **un·man·age·ably** /ˌʌnˈmænɪʤəbli/ *adv*

un·manned /ˌʌnˈmænd/ *adj* : not carrying or done by a person • *an unmanned spacecraft*

un·marked /ˌʌnˈmɑːkt/ *adj* : not having any marks or signs that show what some-

thing is • *an unmarked grave*

un·mar·ried /ˌʌnˈmerid/ *adj* : not married • *an unmarried* [=*single*] *man/woman*

un·mask /ˌʌnˈmæsk, Brit ˌʌnˈmɑːsk/ *vb* [T] : to reveal the true identity or nature of (someone or something) • *He was unmasked as a spy.*

un·matched /ˌʌnˈmæʧd/ *adj* : better than all others • *unmatched quality*

un·men·tion·able /ˌʌnˈmenʃənəbl/ *adj* : too offensive, shocking, or embarrassing to talk about or mention • *unmentionable words*

un·mer·ci·ful /ˌʌnˈmɚsɪfəl/ *adj* : very harsh or cruel : MERCILESS • *an unmerciful attack/critic* — **un·mer·ci·ful·ly** /ˌʌnˈmɚsɪfli/ *adv*

un·met /ˌʌnˈmet/ *adj* : not satisfied or fulfilled • *unmet needs*

un·mis·tak·able /ˌʌnməˈsteɪkəbəl/ *adj* : not capable of being mistaken or misunderstood • *an unmistakable odor* — **un·mis·tak·ably** /ˌʌnməˈsteɪkəbli/ *adv*

un·mit·i·gat·ed /ˌʌnˈmɪtəˌgeɪtəd/ *adj, always before a noun* : complete and total — usually used to describe something bad • *The party was an unmitigated disaster.*

un·moved /ˌʌnˈmuːvd/ *adj* : not feeling pity, sympathy, or admiration for someone or something • *He was unmoved by their pleas.*

un·named /ˌʌnˈneɪmd/ *adj* **1** — used to indicate that a person's name is not mentioned or known • *an unnamed source/official* **2** : not having a name • *an unnamed stream*

un·nat·u·ral /ˌʌnˈnæʧ[ə]rəl/ *adj* **1** : different from how things usually are in the physical world or in nature • *an unnatural color* • *deaths from unnatural causes* [=deaths caused by things other than old age or disease] **2** : different from what is normal in a way that is seen as wrong, disturbing, etc. • *She has an unnatural obsession with money.* **3** : not real • *The movie's dialogue sounds unnatural.* [=*fake*] — **un·nat·u·ral·ly** *adv*

un·nec·es·sary /ˌʌnˈnesəˌseri, Brit ˌʌnˈnesəsri/ *adj* : not needed or necessary • *an unnecessary delay/risk* — **un·nec·es·sar·i·ly** /ˌʌnˌnesəˈserəli, Brit ˌʌnˈnesəsrəli/ *adv*

un·nerve /ˌʌnˈnɚv/ *vb* **-nerved; -nerv·ing** [T] *somewhat formal* : to make (someone) feel afraid or upset and unable to think clearly • *Seeing her there unnerved me.* — **un·nerv·ing** *adj* • *an unnerving encounter* — **un·nerv·ing·ly** /ˌʌnˈnɚvɪŋli/ *adv*

un·no·ticed /ˌʌnˈnoʊtəst/ *adj* : not seen or noticed • *His efforts went (largely) unnoticed.*

un·ob·served /ˌʌnəbˈzɚvd/ *adj* : not seen or noticed • *an unobserved problem*

un·ob·tain·able /ˌʌnəbˈteɪnəbəl/ *adj* : not possible to get or achieve • *an unobtainable outcome*

un·ob·tru·sive /ˌʌnəbˈtruːsɪv/ *adj* : not attracting attention in a way that bothers you • *an unobtrusive waiter* — **un·ob·tru·sive·ly** *adv* • *sitting unobtrusively in a corner*

un·oc·cu·pied /ˌʌnˈɑːkjəˌpaɪd/ *adj* : not

being used, filled up, or lived in : EMPTY • *an unoccupied house*

un·of·fi·cial /ˌʌnəˈfɪʃəl/ *adj* : not official: such as **a** : not formally chosen by an official decision or vote • *the group's unofficial leader* **b** : not done or made in a formal way by someone in a position of authority • *unofficial estimates* — **un·of·fi·cial·ly** *adv*

un·opened /ˌʌnˈoʊpənd/ *adj* : not opened • *an unopened package*

un·or·ga·nized *also Brit* **un·or·ga·nised** /ˌʌnˈɔəgəˌnaɪzd/ *adj* **1** : not arranged in an orderly way • *unorganized photos* **2** : not part of a formal organization (such as a labor union) • *unorganized workers*

un·orig·i·nal /ˌʌnəˈrɪdʒənl/ *adj* : not new or different • *an unoriginal idea* : not able to think of or make new and creative things • *an unoriginal thinker*

un·or·tho·dox /ˌʌnˈɔəθəˌdɑːks/ *adj* : different from what is usually done or accepted • *unorthodox views/opinions/beliefs*

un·pack /ˌʌnˈpæk/ *vb* [T/I] : to take something out of a suitcase, box, etc. • *unpack clothes (from a suitcase)* • *I was too tired to unpack (my suitcase).*

un·paid /ˌʌnˈpeɪd/ *adj* **1** : needing to be paid • *unpaid bills/taxes* **2** : done or taken without payment • *an unpaid leave of absence* **3** : not receiving money for work that is done • *an unpaid consultant*

un·par·al·leled /ˌʌnˈperəˌleld/ *adj, formal* **1** : never seen or experienced before : UNIQUE • *an unparalleled opportunity* **2** : better or greater than anyone or anything else • *unparalleled success*

un·par·don·able /ˌʌnˈpɑədnəbəl/ *adj, formal* : too bad to be forgiven • *unpardonable sins/offenses*

un·paved /ˌʌnˈpeɪvd/ *adj, chiefly US* : not covered with a hard, smooth surface • *unpaved roads*

un·planned /ˌʌnˈplænd/ *adj* : not planned or expected • *an unplanned pregnancy*

un·play·able /ˌʌnˈpleɪəbəl/ *adj* : not able to be played, played on, or played with • *an unplayable DVD/guitar*

un·pleas·ant /ˌʌnˈplɛznt/ *adj* **1** : not pleasant or enjoyable • *an unpleasant smell/odor* • *unpleasant weather* **2** : not friendly • *unpleasant people* — **un·pleas·ant·ly** *adv* — **un·pleas·ant·ness** *n* [U]

un·plug /ˌʌnˈplʌg/ *vb* **-plugged; -plugging** [T] : to disconnect (something) from an electrical source or another device by removing its plug • *unplug a lamp*

un·plugged /ˌʌnˈplʌgd/ *adj, informal* : sung or performed without electrical instruments • *an unplugged concert*

un·pop·u·lar /ˌʌnˈpɑːpjələ/ *adj* : not liked by many people • *I was unpopular in high school.* • *an unpopular policy* **2** : not shared by most people • *unpopular opinions* — **un·pop·u·lar·i·ty** /ˌʌnˌpɑːpjəˈlerəti/ *n* [U]

un·prec·e·dent·ed /ˌʌnˈprɛsəˌdɛntəd/ *adj* : not done or experienced before • *This level of growth is unprecedented.*

un·pre·dict·able /ˌʌnprɪˈdɪktəbəl/ *adj*

1 : not capable of being known before happening or being done • *unpredictable results/behavior* **2** : not always behaving in a way that is expected • *an unpredictable person* — **un·pre·dict·abil·i·ty** /ˌʌnprɪˌdɪktəˈbɪləti/ *n* [U] — **un·pre·dict·ably** /ˌʌnprɪˈdɪktəbli/ *adv*

un·pre·pared /ˌʌnprɪˈpeəd/ *adj* : not ready to deal with something • *I was unprepared for the test.*

un·pre·ten·tious /ˌʌnprɪˈtɛnʃəs/ *adj* : not having or showing the unpleasant quality of people who want to be regarded as more impressive, successful, or important than they really are : not pretentious • *an unpretentious woman/restaurant* — **un·pre·ten·tious·ly** *adv* — **un·pre·ten·tious·ness** *n* [U]

un·prin·ci·pled /ˌʌnˈprɪnsəpəld/ *adj* : not having or showing concern for what is right • *an unprincipled politician*

un·print·able /ˌʌnˈprɪntəbəl/ *adj* : too offensive or shocking to be printed or published • *unprintable words*

un·pro·duc·tive /ˌʌnprəˈdʌktɪv/ *adj* : not giving good, steady, or useful results • *The talks were unproductive.*

un·pro·fes·sion·al /ˌʌnprəˈfɛʃənl/ *adj* : not having or showing the experience, skill, etc., that is expected of or appropriate in a person who is trained to do a job well • *unprofessional conduct* — **un·pro·fes·sion·al·ly** /ˌʌnprəˈfɛʃənəli/ *adv*

un·prof·it·able /ˌʌnˈprɑːfətəbəl/ *adj* **1** : not making money • *an unprofitable company* **2** : not producing good or helpful results or effects • *an unprofitable discussion*

un·prom·is·ing /ˌʌnˈprɑːməsɪŋ/ *adj* : not likely to be successful or good • *an unpromising start*

un·prompt·ed /ˌʌnˈprɑːmptəd/ *adj* : done or said by someone who has not been asked or reminded to do or say anything • *an unprompted offer*

un·pro·nounce·able /ˌʌnprəˈnaʊnsəbəl/ *adj* : impossible or very difficult to say • *an unpronounceable name*

un·pro·tect·ed /ˌʌnprəˈtɛktəd/ *adj* **1** : not guarded or kept from something that can cause harm or damage • *unprotected wilderness* **2** of sexual activity : done without using anything (such as a condom) that can prevent unwanted pregnancy or the spread of disease (such as AIDS) • *unprotected sex*

un·prov·able /ˌʌnˈpruːvəbəl/ *adj* : not able to be proved or shown to be true • *an unprovable claim/assertion*

un·proved /ˌʌnˈpruːvd/ *adj* : UNPROVEN

un·prov·en /ˌʌnˈpruːvən/ *adj* : not tested and shown to be true, good, or useful • *scientifically unproven treatments*

un·pub·lished /ˌʌnˈpʌblɪʃt/ *adj* **1** : not prepared, printed, and sold as or as part of a book, magazine, newspaper, etc. • *an unpublished manuscript* **2** — used to describe a writer whose works have not yet been published • *an unpublished poet*

un·pun·ished /ˌʌnˈpʌnɪʃt/ *adj* : not punished • *Their crime must not be allowed to go unpunished.*

un·qual·i·fied /ˌʌnˈkwɑːləˌfaɪd/ *adj* **1** : not having the skills, knowledge, or experience needed to do a particular job or activity ▪ *an unqualified candidate* **2** : complete or total ▪ *The show was an unqualified success.* [=it was successful in every way]

un·ques·tion·able /ˌʌnˈkwɛsʧənəbəl/ *adj* : not able to be questioned or doubted ▪ *a person of unquestionable integrity* — **un·ques·tion·ably** /ˌʌnˈkwɛsʧənəbli/ *adv* ▪ *The book is unquestionably* [=*certainly*] *a masterpiece.*

un·ques·tioned /ˌʌnˈkwɛsʧənd/ *adj* : not doubted or questioned ▪ *Her honesty is unquestioned.*

un·ques·tion·ing /ˌʌnˈkwɛsʧənɪŋ/ *adj* : given completely and without asking questions or expressing doubt ▪ *unquestioning loyalty/obedience*

un·quote /ˈʌnˌkwoʊt/ *n* — used in speech with *quote* to show that you are exactly repeating someone else's words ▪ *She said that she can't deal with quote, "the real world," unquote.* ▪ *He called me a quote, unquote "rotten liar."*

un·rat·ed /ˌʌnˈreɪtəd/ *adj, US* : not having a special mark (such as PG or R) which shows that a movie is appropriate for a specific audience ▪ *an unrated film*

un·rav·el /ˌʌnˈrævəl/ *vb* **-els**; *US* **-eled** *or Brit* **-elled**; *US* **-el·ing** *or Brit* **-el·ling** **1** [*T/I*] : to cause the separate threads of something to come apart ▪ *unravel a rope* ▪ *The ends of the rope are unraveling.* **2** [*T*] : to find the correct explanation for (something that is difficult to understand) ▪ *unraveling the secrets/mysteries of DNA* **3** [*I*] : to fail or begin to fail ▪ *Their plans unraveled when she lost her job.*

un·read /ˌʌnˈrɛd/ *adj* : not read ▪ *an unread book*

un·read·able /ˌʌnˈriːdəbəl/ *adj* **1** : unable to be read or understood ▪ *The computer file is unreadable.* **2** : too difficult, badly written, etc., to be worth reading ▪ *an unreadable novel*

un·re·al /ˌʌnˈriːjəl/ *adj* **1** : not real : artificial or fake ▪ *The town seemed unreal, like a movie set.* **2** *informal* : very strange or unusual ▪ *I think it's unreal that he survived the accident.* **3** *informal* — used to describe something that is so good, bad, etc., that it is difficult to believe ▪ *The pain was unreal.*

un·re·al·is·tic /ˌʌnˌriːjəˈlɪstɪk/ *adj* **1** : not able to see things as they really are ▪ *an unrealistic person* **2** : based on what is wanted or hoped for rather than on what is possible or likely ▪ *unrealistic expectations/demands* **3** : not showing people and things as they are in real life ▪ *an unrealistic movie* — **un·re·al·is·tic·al·ly** /ˌʌnˌriːjəˈlɪstɪkli/ *adv*

un·rea·son·able /ˌʌnˈriːznəbəl/ *adj* : not fair, sensible, or appropriate ▪ *unreasonable people/demands/prices* — **un·rea·son·ably** /ˌʌnˈriːznəbli/ *adv* ▪ *unreasonably high standards*

un·rec·og·niz·able *also Brit* **un·rec·og·nis·able** /ˌʌnˈrɛkɪɡˌnaɪzəbəl/ *adj* : not able to be identified or recognized ▪ *After the accident, the car was unrecognizable.*

un·rec·og·nized *also Brit* **un·rec·og·nised** /ˌʌnˈrɛkɪɡˌnaɪzd/ *adj* **1** : not given deserved attention or notice ▪ *The art-*

ist's work went unrecognized in his lifetime. **2** : not known about ▪ *a previously unrecognized problem*

un·re·cord·ed /ˌʌnrɪˈkɔɚdəd/ *adj* **1** : not written down ▪ *an unrecorded vote* **2** : not recorded on a record, CD, etc. ▪ *an unrecorded song/musician*

un·re·fined /ˌʌnrɪˈfaɪnd/ *adj* **1** : still in the natural and original state or form ▪ *unrefined oil/metal/sugar* **2** *disapproving* : not having or showing good education and manners ▪ *a crass, unrefined person*

un·re·hearsed /ˌʌnrɪˈhɚst/ *adj, chiefly US* : not practiced or prepared in advance ▪ *an unrehearsed performance*

un·re·lat·ed /ˌʌnrɪˈleɪtəd/ *adj* **1** : not part of the same family ▪ *We have the same last name, but we're unrelated.* **2** : not connected in any way to someone or something else ▪ *unrelated events*

un·re·lent·ing /ˌʌnrɪˈlɛntɪŋ/ *adj* **1** : not slowing down, stopping, or growing weaker ▪ *unrelenting pressure/criticism* **2** — used to describe someone who does something in a constant and determined way without stopping or becoming less forceful ▪ *an unrelenting crusader* — **un·re·lent·ing·ly** *adv*

un·re·li·able /ˌʌnrɪˈlajəbəl/ *adj* **1** : not able to be trusted to do or provide what is needed or promised ▪ *an unreliable car* [=a car that breaks down often] **2** : not believable or trustworthy ▪ *an unreliable witness/report* — **un·re·li·ably** /ˌʌnrɪˈlajəbli/ *adv*

un·re·mark·able /ˌʌnrɪˈmɑɚkəbəl/ *adj* : not worthy of special attention or notice : ORDINARY ▪ *The day was unremarkable.* — **un·re·mark·ably** /ˌʌnrɪˈmɑɚkəbli/ *adv*

un·re·mit·ting /ˌʌnrɪˈmɪtɪŋ/ *adj, formal* : not stopping or growing weaker ▪ *unremitting efforts/hostility/pain* — **un·re·mit·ting·ly** *adv*

un·re·pen·tant /ˌʌnrɪˈpɛntnt/ *adj* : not sorry for something wrong that you have done ▪ *an unrepentant sinner*

un·rep·re·sen·ta·tive /ˌʌnˌrɛprɪˈzɛntətɪv/ *adj* : not showing what a group of people or things is truly like ▪ *an unrepresentative sample/minority*

un·re·quit·ed /ˌʌnrɪˈkwaɪtəd/ *adj* : not shared or returned by someone else ▪ *unrequited love*

un·re·served /ˌʌnrɪˈzɚvd/ *adj* **1** : not kept for use only by a particular person or group ▪ *unreserved seating* **2** : not limited in any way ▪ *unreserved admiration/support*

un·re·solved /ˌʌnrɪˈzɑːlvd/ *adj* : still needing an answer, a solution, or an ending ▪ *unresolved issues*

un·re·spon·sive /ˌʌnrɪˈspɑːnsɪv/ *adj* **1** : not replying or reacting to someone's question, request, demand, etc. ▪ *an unresponsive bureaucracy* **2** *medical* : not reacting or able to react in a normal way when touched, spoken to, etc. ▪ *The victim was unresponsive.*

un·rest /ˌʌnˈrɛst/ *n* [*U*] : a situation in which many of the people in a country are angry and hold protests or act violently ▪ *The country has experienced years of civil/social/political unrest.*

un·re·strained /ˌʌnrɪˈstreɪnd/ adj : not controlled or limited • *unrestrained growth/enthusiasm*

un·re·strict·ed /ˌʌnrɪˈstrɪktəd/ adj : not controlled or limited in any way • *I was granted unrestricted access to the documents.* • *an unrestricted view*

un·re·ward·ing /ˌʌnrɪˈwoɚdɪŋ/ adj : not giving you a good feeling that you have done something valuable, important, etc. • *unrewarding work*

un·ripe /ˌʌnˈraɪp/ adj, of food : not fully grown or developed : not yet ready to eat • *unripe fruit*

un·ri·valed (US) or Brit **un·ri·valled** /ˌʌnˈraɪvəld/ adj : better than anyone or anything else • *Her athletic records are unrivaled.*

un·roll /ˌʌnˈroʊl/ vb [T/I] : to make (something that has been rolled) flat : to smooth out (something that is rolled up) • *unroll a scroll/rug*

un·ruf·fled /ˌʌnˈrʌfəld/ adj : not upset or disturbed • *She was unruffled despite the delays.*

un·ruly /ˌʌnˈruːli/ adj, disapproving : difficult to control • *unruly children/hair* — **un·rul·i·ness** n [U]

un·safe /ˌʌnˈseɪf/ adj **un·saf·er**; **-est** **1** : able or likely to cause harm, damage, or loss • *The water is unsafe for drinking.* = *It is unsafe to drink the water.* **2** : not giving protection from danger, harm, or loss • *working under unsafe conditions* **3** : not protected from danger, harm, or loss • *I feel unsafe in that neighborhood.* — **un·safe·ly** adv

un·said /ˌʌnˈsɛd/ adj : thought but not spoken out loud or discussed • *Some things are better left unsaid.*

un·san·i·tary /ˌʌnˈsænəˌteri, Brit ˌʌnˈsænətri/ adj : dirty and likely to cause disease • *working under unsanitary conditions*

un·sat·is·fac·to·ry /ˌʌnˌsætəsˈfæktəri/ adj : not good enough • *unsatisfactory results*

un·sat·is·fied /ˌʌnˈsætəsˌfaɪd/ adj **1** : not dealt with in a way that provides what is needed or wanted • *an unsatisfied curiosity/hunger* **2** : not pleased or happy about what has happened or been done • *an unsatisfied customer*

un·sat·is·fy·ing /ˌʌnˈsætəsˌfajɪŋ/ adj : not providing what is needed or wanted • *an unsatisfying meal*

un·sat·u·rat·ed /ˌʌnˈsætʃəˌreɪtəd/ adj : used to describe a type of oil or fat that is found in foods and that is better for your health than other types • *unsaturated fats*

un·sa·vory (US) or Brit **un·sa·voury** /ˌʌnˈseɪvəri/ adj : unpleasant or offensive • *unsavory characters*

un·scathed /ˌʌnˈskeɪðd/ adj, not before a noun : not hurt, harmed, or damaged • *She emerged from the wreckage unscathed.*

un·sched·uled /ˌʌnˈskɛˌdʒuːld, Brit ˌʌnˈʃɛˌdjuːld/ adj : not planned for a certain time • *an unscheduled departure*

un·sci·en·tif·ic /ˌʌnˌsajənˈtɪfɪk/ adj : not done in a way that agrees with the methods of science • *an unscientific survey/poll* — **un·sci·en·tif·i·cal·ly** /ˌʌnˌsajənˈtɪfɪkli/ adv

un·scram·ble /ˌʌnˈskræmbəl/ vb **-scram·bled**; **-scram·bling** [T] : to change (something, such as a message or an electronic signal) from a form that cannot be understood to a form that can be properly displayed, heard, read, etc. • *unscramble a satellite signal*

un·screw /ˌʌnˈskruː/ vb **1** [T/I] : to loosen and remove (something) by turning it • *unscrew a light bulb* • *The lid unscrews easily.* **2** [T] : to remove the screws from (something) • *Unscrew the cover before you remove it.*

un·script·ed /ˌʌnˈskrɪptəd/ adj : not written or planned at an earlier time • *unscripted comments*

un·scru·pu·lous /ˌʌnˈskruːpjələs/ adj : doing things that are wrong, dishonest, or illegal • *an unscrupulous businessman*

un·sea·son·able /ˌʌnˈsiːznəbəl/ adj, of weather : not normal for that time of year • *unseasonable weather/temperatures* — **un·sea·son·ably** /ˌʌnˈsiːznəbli/ adv • *unseasonably cool/warm*

un·seat /ˌʌnˈsiːt/ vb [T] : to remove (someone or something) from a position of power or authority • *He unseated an incumbent senator.*

un·se·cured /ˌʌnsɪˈkjɚd/ adj : not protected against risk or loss • *an unsecured loan*

un·seem·ly /ˌʌnˈsiːmli/ adj, formal : not proper or appropriate for the situation • *rude and unseemly behavior*

un·seen /ˌʌnˈsiːn/ adj : not seen or able to be seen • *unseen dangers* — **sight unseen** see ¹SIGHT

un·self·ish /ˌʌnˈsɛlfɪʃ/ adj : having or showing more concern for other people than for yourself • *unselfish behavior/people* — **un·self·ish·ly** adv — **un·self·ish·ness** n [U]

un·sen·ti·men·tal /ˌʌnˌsɛntəˈmɛntl/ adj : based on, influenced by, or resulting from reason or thought rather than feelings or emotions • *an unsentimental decision*

un·set·tle /ˌʌnˈsɛtl/ vb **-set·tled**; **-set·tling** [T] : to make (someone) nervous, worried, or upset • *Changes unsettle her.*

un·set·tled /ˌʌnˈsɛtld/ adj **1** : feeling nervous, upset, or uncomfortable • *unsettled investors* • *an unsettled stomach* **2** : not lived in by people • *a region that is still largely unsettled* [=not settled] **3** : not yet finally decided or dealt with • *an unsettled question* **4** : likely to change • *unsettled weather*

un·set·tling /ˌʌnˈsɛtlɪŋ/ adj : making you upset, nervous, worried, etc. • *unsettling news*

un·shak·able or **un·shake·able** /ˌʌnˈʃeɪkəbəl/ adj : too strong to be changed, weakened, or destroyed • *an unshakable faith/belief*

un·shak·en /ˌʌnˈʃeɪkən/ adj, formal : not changed or weakened • *unshaken confidence/faith*

un·shav·en /ˌʌnˈʃeɪvən/ adj : not shaved or not recently shaved • *an unshaven man/face*

un·sight·ly /ˌʌnˈsaɪtli/ adj : not pleasant

to look at ▪ *an unsightly scar*

un·signed /ˌʌnˈsaɪnd/ *adj* **1 a** : not having a signature ▪ *an unsigned note* **b** : published without the name of the writer ▪ *an unsigned editorial* **2** : not having a contract with a professional sports team, music company, etc. ▪ *an unsigned pitcher*

un·skilled /ˌʌnˈskɪld/ *adj* : not having or requiring special skills or training ▪ *unskilled laborers ▪ unskilled jobs*

un·smil·ing /ˌʌnˈsmaɪlɪŋ/ *adj, somewhat formal* : not smiling ▪ *They were tense and unsmiling.*

un·so·cia·ble /ˌʌnˈsoʊʃəbəl/ *adj* : not liking to be with other people ▪ *an unsociable man*

un·so·cial /ˌʌnˈsoʊʃəl/ *adj, Brit* : occurring at times that prevent you from being with your friends and family ▪ *a job with unsocial hours*

un·so·lic·it·ed /ˌʌnsəˈlɪsətəd/ *adj* : not asked for : given or received without being requested ▪ *unsolicited advice*

un·solved /ˌʌnˈsɑːlvd/ *adj* : not yet solved : never solved ▪ *an unsolved crime* — **un·solv·able** /ˌʌnˈsɑːlvəbəl/ *adj*

un·so·phis·ti·cat·ed /ˌʌnsəˈfɪstəˌkeɪtəd/ *adj* **1** : not having or showing a lot of experience and knowledge about the world and about culture, art, literature, etc. ▪ *unsophisticated people/tastes* **2** : not highly developed or complex ▪ *unsophisticated weapons*

un·sound /ˌʌnˈsaʊnd/ *adj* **1** : not based on truth or logic : not showing good judgment ▪ *unsound arguments* **2** : poorly built or in bad condition ▪ *The roof is structurally unsound.*

un·speak·able /ˌʌnˈspiːkəbəl/ *adj* **1** : very bad or evil ▪ *unspeakable crimes* **2** : impossible to describe in words ▪ *moments of unspeakable beauty* — **un·speak·ably** /ˌʌnˈspiːkəbli/ *adv*

un·spec·i·fied /ˌʌnˈspɛsəˌfaɪd/ *adj* : not named or mentioned ▪ *an unspecified amount of money*

un·spec·tac·u·lar /ˌʌnspɛkˈtækjələ/ *adj* : not spectacular or special ▪ *The team has had an unspectacular season.*

un·spoiled /ˌʌnˈspɔɪld/ *or chiefly Brit* **un·spoilt** /ˌʌnˈspɔɪlt/ *adj* **1** : still wild and not changed by people ▪ *unspoiled beaches* **2** : not affected by the special attention you are receiving because of fame or success ▪ *He's completely unspoiled by success.*

un·spo·ken /ˌʌnˈspoʊkən/ *adj* : expressed or understood without being directly stated ▪ *an unspoken agreement*

un·sport·ing /ˌʌnˈspoɚtɪŋ/ *adj, chiefly Brit* : not done or behaving in a way that treats the other people in a sport or competition fairly ▪ *unsporting behavior*

un·sports·man·like /ˌʌnˈspoɚtsmənˌlaɪk/ *adj* : not fair, respectful, and polite toward other players when participating in a sport ▪ *unsportsmanlike conduct*

un·sta·ble /ˌʌnˈsteɪbəl/ *adj* : not stable: such as **a** : likely to change ▪ *unstable prices* **b** : not emotionally or mentally healthy ▪ *She's mentally unstable.* **c** : not held in a secure position ▪ *an unstable ladder*

un·steady /ˌʌnˈstɛdi/ *adj* : not steady: such as **a** : not standing or moving in a steady and balanced way ▪ *walking with an unsteady gait* **b** : shaking or moving because of nervousness, weakness, etc. ▪ *Her voice was unsteady.* **c** : not happening or proceeding in a smooth and constant way ▪ *a period of unsteady growth* — **un·stead·i·ly** /ˌʌnˈstɛdəli/ *adv* — **un·stead·i·ness** /ˌʌnˈstɛdinəs/ *n [U]*

un·stop·pa·ble /ˌʌnˈstɑːpəbəl/ *adj* : not able to be stopped ▪ *unstoppable momentum*

un·stressed /ˌʌnˈstrɛst/ *adj* : not having an accent or a stress ▪ *an unstressed syllable*

un·struc·tured /ˌʌnˈstrʌktʃəd/ *adj* : not organized or planned in a formal way ▪ *unstructured play*

un·stuck /ˌʌnˈstʌk/ *adj* : able to move freely : no longer stuck ▪ *trying to get the car unstuck* — **come unstuck** *Brit, informal* : to fail ▪ *Their marriage has come unstuck.*

un·styl·ish /ˌʌnˈstaɪlɪʃ/ *adj* : not stylish or fashionable ▪ *unstylish clothes*

un·sub·stan·ti·at·ed /ˌʌnsəbˈstænʃiˌeɪtəd/ *adj, formal* : not proven to be true ▪ *unsubstantiated claims*

un·suc·cess·ful /ˌʌnsəkˈsɛsfəl/ *adj* : not having or producing success ▪ *an unsuccessful musician/attempt* — **un·suc·cess·ful·ly** *adv*

un·suit·able /ˌʌnˈsuːtəbəl/ *adj* : not having the qualities that are right, needed, or appropriate for something ▪ *She's an unsuitable candidate for the job.*

un·suit·ed /ˌʌnˈsuːtəd/ *adj* : not having the qualities that are right, needed, or appropriate for something or someone ▪ *She's unsuited for the job.* ▪ *He is unsuited to academic life.*

un·sung /ˌʌnˈsʌŋ/ *adj* : not given attention and praise that is deserved for doing good things ▪ *He is one of the unsung heroes of the civil rights movement.*

un·sure /ˌʌnˈʃoɚ/ *adj* : not certain about something ▪ *We're unsure (of) how to proceed.* — **unsure of yourself** : not confident about what to do or say ▪ *She was unsure of herself as a child.*

un·sur·passed /ˌʌnsəˈpæst, Brit ˌʌnsəˈpɑːst/ *adj, somewhat formal* : better or greater than anyone or anything else ▪ *unsurpassed beauty*

un·sur·pris·ing /ˌʌnsəˈpraɪzɪŋ/ *adj* : not causing surprise because you expected it ▪ *an unsurprising fact* — **un·sur·pris·ing·ly** *adv*

un·sus·pect·ed /ˌʌnsəˈspɛktəd/ *adj* : not known to exist ▪ *an unsuspected heart condition* : not suspected ▪ *His real motives were unsuspected by others.*

un·sus·pect·ing /ˌʌnsəˈspɛktɪŋ/ *adj* : not knowing about or expecting something bad that is going to happen or that could happen ▪ *unsuspecting victims*

un·sus·tain·able /ˌʌnsəˈsteɪnəbəl/ *adj* : not able to last or continue for a long time ▪ *unsustainable logging/fishing*

un·swayed /ˌʌnˈsweɪd/ *adj* — used to say that someone's opinion has not changed despite efforts to change it ▪ *I* *tried to convince him, but he remained unswayed.*

un·sweet·ened /ˌʌnˈswiːtn̩d/ *adj* : not having sugar or another sweetener added • *unsweetened tea*

un·swerv·ing /ˌʌnˈswɚvɪŋ/ *adj* : not changing or becoming weaker : always staying strong • *unswerving loyalty*

un·sym·pa·thet·ic /ˌʌnˌsɪmpəˈθɛtɪk/ *adj* 1 : not feeling or showing concern about someone who is in a bad situation • *an unsympathetic judge* 2 *not before a noun* : not having or showing support for or approval of something • *I'm unsympathetic to/toward their cause.* [=I don't support their cause] 3 : not having pleasant or appealing qualities • *an unsympathetic character*

un·tamed /ˌʌnˈteɪmd/ *adj* : wild and not controlled by people • *untamed animals*

un·tan·gle /ˌʌnˈtæŋgəl/ *vb* **-tan·gled; -tan·gling** [*T*] : to separate (things that are twisted together) • *untangle ropes* : to remove the twists or knots in (something) • *untangling a child's hair* • *(figurative) untangle a mystery*

un·tapped /ˌʌnˈtæpt/ *adj* : available but not used • *untapped resources*

un·test·ed /ˌʌnˈtɛstəd/ *adj* : not yet shown to be good, strong, etc., by being used, placed in a difficult situation, etc. • *an untested theory*

un·think·able /ˌʌnˈθɪŋkəbəl/ *adj* : impossible to imagine or believe • *moving at an unthinkable speed* : too bad or shocking to be thought of • *unthinkable cruelty* — **the unthinkable** : something that you cannot accept, believe, or imagine; *especially* : something that is so bad that you do not want to think about it • *And then, the unthinkable happened: the roof collapsed.*

un·think·ing /ˌʌnˈθɪŋkɪŋ/ *adj* : done or said in a foolish or careless way without thinking about the possible effects • *unthinking remarks* : behaving in a foolish or careless way without careful thought • *unthinking consumers* — **un·think·ing·ly** *adv*

un·ti·dy /ˌʌnˈtaɪdi/ *adj* 1 **a** : not neat or clean • *an untidy desk* **b** : not having neat or clean habits • *untidy roommates* 2 : not done in an organized and pleasant way • *an untidy divorce* — **un·ti·di·ness** /ˌʌnˈtaɪdinəs/ *n* [*U*]

un·tie /ˌʌnˈtaɪ/ *vb* **-tied; -ty·ing** 1 [*T/I*] : to undo the knots in or of (something) • *untie your shoelaces/shoes* • *untie a rope* • *The knot untied easily.* 2 [*T*] : to remove the rope, string, etc., that attaches (something or someone) to something • *She untied the horse from the post.*

¹un·til /ən̩ˈtɪl/ *prep* 1 : up to (a particular time) — used to indicate the time when a particular situation, activity, or period ends • *I stayed until morning.* • *from May until July* • **Until then,** *I'd been single.* • *I kept working up until dinnertime.* 2 — used to indicate the time when something will happen, become true, etc. • *We don't open until ten.* • *It won't be ready until tomorrow.*

²until *conj* : up to the time or point that •

We played until it got dark. • *Wait until I call.*

un·time·ly /ˌʌnˈtaɪmli/ *adj* 1 : happening or done sooner than the proper or expected time • *her untimely death* 2 : happening or done at a time that is not suitable or appropriate • *an untimely comment/interruption*

un·tir·ing /ˌʌnˈtaɪrɪŋ/ *adj* : working very hard with a lot of energy for a long time • *She is an untiring advocate for the poor.* • *untiring efforts*

un·to /ˈʌntu/ *prep, old-fashioned* — used in the past like "to" • *They remained faithful unto* [=until] *death.*

un·told /ˌʌnˈtoʊld/ *adj* 1 : not told or made public • *untold secrets* 2 : too many to count or too much to measure • *untold riches*

un·touch·able /ˌʌnˈtʌtʃəbəl/ *adj* 1 : too powerful or important to be punished, criticized, etc. • *a mayor who believed that he was untouchable* 2 : too good to be equaled by anyone else • *an untouchable record*

un·touched /ˌʌnˈtʌtʃt/ *adj* : not touched: such as **a** : not changed : still in the original state or condition • *untouched wilderness* **b** : not eaten or drunk • *He left his food untouched.* **c** : not emotionally affected by something • *She was untouched by his declarations of love.*

un·to·ward /ˌʌnˈtoʊwɚd, ˌʌnˈtoɚd/ *adj, formal* 1 : bad or unfavorable : not good • *untoward side effects* 2 : not proper or appropriate • *There was nothing untoward about his appearance.*

un·trained /ˌʌnˈtreɪnd/ *adj* : without formal training • *untrained employees* • *The error was not obvious to the untrained eye.*

un·tram·meled (*US*) *or Brit* **un·tram·melled** /ˌʌnˈtræməld/ *adj, formal* : not limited or restricted • *untrammeled greed*

un·true /ˌʌnˈtruː/ *adj* 1 : not true : FALSE • *untrue statements* 2 *literary + old-fashioned* : not loyal to someone or something • *a lover who is untrue*

un·trust·wor·thy /ˌʌnˈtrʌstˌwɚði/ *adj* : not able to be trusted • *an untrustworthy person*

un·truth /ˌʌnˈtruːθ/ *n* [*C*] *formal* : a statement that is not true : LIE • *a blatant untruth*

un·truth·ful /ˌʌnˈtruːθfəl/ *adj* : not telling the truth • *untruthful reports/witnesses*

un·tucked /ˌʌnˈtʌkt/ *adj, chiefly US* : not tucked into something (such as your pants) • *an untucked shirt*

un·turned /ˌʌnˈtɚnd/ *adj* — **leave no stone unturned** see ¹STONE

un·typ·i·cal /ˌʌnˈtɪpɪkəl/ *adj* : not usual or normal • *untypical behavior*

un·used /ˌʌnˈjuːzd/ *adj* : not being used : not having been used before • *unused disk space* — **un·used to** /ˌʌnˈjuːst-/ : not familiar or comfortable with (something) : not used to (something) • *I'm unused to crowds.*

un·usu·al /ˌʌnˈjuːʒəwəl/ *adj* 1 : not normal or usual • *unusual occurrences/behavior* • *It's not unusual for me to work late.* 2 : different or strange in a way that attracts attention • *an unusual car/design* 3 : not commonly seen, heard, etc. ▪ *an unusual name/flower*

un·u·su·al·ly /ˌʌnˈjuːʒəwəli/ *adv* **1** : to a great degree : VERY ▪ *an unusually large dog* **2** : in a way that is not normal or usual ▪ *You're unusually quiet this morning.*

un·vary·ing /ˌʌnˈverijɪŋ/ *adj* : always the same ▪ *an unvarying routine*

un·veil /ˌʌnˈveɪl/ *vb* [T] **1** : to show or reveal (something) to others for the first time ▪ *The company will unveil its newest product today.* **2** : to remove a cover from (something) so that people can see it ▪ *unveil a statue* — **un·veil·ing** /ˌʌnˈveɪlɪŋ/ *n* [C] ▪ *the unveiling of a statue*

un·waged /ˌʌnˈweɪdʒd/ *adj, Brit* : not earning or paying wages ▪ *unwaged students/work*

un·want·ed /ˌʌnˈwɑːntəd/ *adj* : not wanted or needed ▪ *an unwanted pregnancy*

un·war·rant·ed /ˌʌnˈworəntəd/ *adj, formal* : not necessary or appropriate ▪ *Your anger is unwarranted.*

un·wary /ˌʌnˈweri/ *adj* : not aware of and careful about possible problems, dangers, etc. ▪ *unwary buyers*

un·washed /ˌʌnˈwɑːʃt/ *adj* : not clean ▪ *unwashed hair/dishes*

un·wa·ver·ing /ˌʌnˈweɪvərɪŋ/ *adj* : continuing in a strong and steady way ▪ *unwavering loyalty/bravery/support*

un·wed /ˌʌnˈwed/ *adj* : not married ▪ *an unwed mother*

un·wel·come /ˌʌnˈwelkəm/ *adj* : not wanted or welcome ▪ *unwelcome news* ▪ *an unwelcome guest*

un·well /ˌʌnˈwel/ *adj, formal* : not feeling well : SICK ▪ *I am sorry she is feeling unwell.*

un·whole·some /ˌʌnˈhoʊlsəm/ *adj* **1** : not good for your health ▪ *unwholesome foods* **2** : not mentally or morally good and normal ▪ *unwholesome thoughts*

un·wieldy /ˌʌnˈwiːldi/ *adj* : difficult to handle, control, or deal with because of being large, heavy, or complex ▪ *a large, unwieldy box*

un·will·ing /ˌʌnˈwɪlɪŋ/ *adj* **1** : not wanting to do something ▪ *She was unwilling to help us.* **2** *always before a noun* : made to do something that you do not want to do ▪ *He was an unwilling participant.* — **un·will·ing·ly** *adv* — **un·will·ing·ness** *n* [U]

un·wind /ˌʌnˈwaɪnd/ *vb* **-wound** /-ˈwaʊnd/; **-wind·ing** **1** [T/I] : to undo the end of something (such as a piece of string) that is wound in a roll, coil, etc., so that it becomes straight ▪ *unwind thread from a spool* **2** [I] : to relax and stop thinking about work, problems, etc. ▪ *trying to unwind after a hard day*

un·wise /ˌʌnˈwaɪz/ *adj* : not intelligent or wise ▪ *an unwise decision* — **un·wise·ly** *adv*

un·wit·ting /ˌʌnˈwɪtɪŋ/ *adj, always before a noun* **1** : not aware of what is really happening ▪ *an unwitting victim* **2** : not intended or planned ▪ *an unwitting mistake* — **un·wit·ting·ly** *adv*

un·work·able /ˌʌnˈwərkəbəl/ *adj* : not able to be done well or successfully ▪ *an unworkable plan*

un·world·ly /ˌʌnˈwərldli/ *adj* : having or showing a lack of experience or knowledge of the world ▪ *an unworldly young man*

un·wor·thy /ˌʌnˈwərði/ *adj* **un·wor·thi·er**; **-est** *formal* **1** : not good enough to deserve something or someone ▪ *She thought he was unworthy of his promotion.* **2** : not appropriate or acceptable for a good or respected person ▪ *unworthy thoughts/feelings* ▪ *actions unworthy of a gentleman*

unwound *past tense and past participle of* UNWIND

un·wrap /ˌʌnˈræp/ *vb* **-wrapped**; **-wrap·ping** [T] : to remove the covering that is around something ▪ *unwrap a gift/bandage*

un·writ·ten /ˌʌnˈrɪtn/ *adj* : spoken or understood without being written ▪ *an unwritten rule/agreement*

un·yield·ing /ˌʌnˈjiːldɪŋ/ *adj* **1** : not changing or stopping ▪ *unyielding opposition/devotion* **2** : not flexible or soft ▪ *the hard, unyielding ground* — **un·yield·ing·ly** *adv*

un·zip /ˌʌnˈzɪp/ *vb* **-zipped**; **-zip·ping** [T] : to open (something) by using a zipper ▪ *He unzipped his jacket.*

¹**up** /ˈʌp/ *adv* **1 a** : from a lower to a higher place or position ▪ *The land rises up from the valley.* ▪ *Pull up your socks.* = *Pull your socks up.* ▪ *Pick your clothes up off the floor.* **b** : in a high position or place ▪ *He held up his hand.* ▪ *What's going on up there?* **2** : toward the sky or ceiling ▪ *She looked up at the stars.* **3** : from beneath the ground or water to the surface ▪ *The dolphin came up for air.* ▪ *pulling up weeds* **4 a** : to or toward the north ▪ *She flew up from Florida.* ▪ *The weather is colder up north.* **b** *informal* : to or toward a place that is thought of as above or away from another place ▪ *She went up to the cabin for the weekend.* ▪ *Come on up and see us.* **5 a** : to or toward a place that is close to someone or something ▪ *I walked up to her and said "hello."* ▪ *Pull up a chair.* **b** : to or toward a more forward position ▪ *We moved up to the front of the line.* **6** : in or into a vertical or upright position ▪ *Stand up.* ▪ *Sit up. Don't slouch.* ▪ *She helped him up (from his seat).* **7** : out of bed ▪ *What time did you get up this morning?* ▪ *I stayed up late.* [=I went to sleep late in the night] **8 a** : with greater force ▪ *Speak up. I can't hear you.* **b** : to a higher or greater level, amount, or rate ▪ *Turn the volume/heat up.* ▪ *The price of oil went up.* ▪ *children 9 years old and up* [=and older] **9** : into a better or more advanced position or state ▪ *She worked her way up in the firm.* **10** : in or into a working or usable state ▪ *Put the tents up first.* **11** : to someone's attention especially for discussion or consideration ▪ *bring up an issue* ▪ *Her contract is coming up for negotiation.* **12** : so as to be done or completed ▪ *Fill up the gas tank.* ▪ *I still have some work to finish up.* ▪ *She used up all the tape.* ▪ *cleaning up the kitchen* **13** : so as to be closed ▪ *seal up a package* ▪ *zip up a jacket* **14** : into pieces or parts ▪ *She tore/cut up the paper.* **15** : into a state of activity or ex-

citement ▪ *She stirred up the crowd.* **16** : to a stop ▪ *He pulled the car up at the curb.* **17** : for each player or team : APIECE ▪ *The score is two up.* — **up and down 1** : repeatedly in one direction and then the opposite direction ▪ *He paced up and down in the waiting room.* **2** : from a lower position to a higher position several times ▪ *jumping up and down* — **up close** see ³CLOSE

²**up** *adj* **1** *not before a noun* **a** : in a high place or position ▪ *It's up on the top shelf.* **b** : raised so as to be opened ▪ *The window is up.* **c** : risen above the horizon ▪ *The sun is up.* **d** : risen from beneath the ground or water to the surface ▪ *The tulips are up.* **e** : in a forward place or position ▪ *Your key is up at the front desk.* ▪ *Our seats were up near the stage.* **2** *not before a noun* **a** : out of bed ▪ *Is she up yet?* **b** : AWAKE ▪ *I was up all night.* **3** *not before a noun* : higher than usual ▪ *Gas prices are up.* ▪ *Attendance has been up.* ▪ *Profits are* **up** *on last year.* [=are higher than they were last year] **4** *always before a noun* : moving or going to a higher level ▪ *the up escalator* **5** *not before a noun, informal* : happening : going on ▪ *I can tell something's up by the look on her face.* ▪ *"Can I talk to you for a minute?" "Sure. What's up?"* [=what do you want to talk to me about?] ▪ *(US) "Hi, Jim. What's up?"* [=what's new?] *"Not much."* — often + *with* ▪ *What's up with you? Why are you so grumpy?* **6** *not before a noun* : having more points than an opponent ▪ *The team was up (by) two runs.* **7** *not before a noun* : operating or functioning ▪ *The network is up again.* = *The network is* **up and running** *again.* **8** *not before a noun* : beginning your turn in an activity ▪ *Get ready. You're up next.* **9** *not before a noun, of time* : at an end ▪ *Put your pencils down. Time is up.* [=the allowed amount of time has ended] ▪ *The president's term is nearly up.* [=has nearly ended] **10** *not before a noun* : happy or excited ▪ *She was feeling down, but now she's up again.* **11** *informal* : having a lot of knowledge about something ▪ *She's always* **up** *on the latest fashions.* **12** *Brit, of a road* : having the surface broken because repairs are being done ▪ *They've had the road up for weeks.* — **up against 1** : placed so as to be touching (something) ▪ *The bed is up against the wall.* **2** : confronted with ▪ *problems we're up against* [=problems we have to deal with] — **up against it** *informal* : in a difficult situation ▪ *With hardly any money or time left, we are really up against it!* — **up and about** *or chiefly US* **up and around** : out of bed and doing things ▪ *I didn't expect you to be up and around this early.* — **up and down** *informal* : sometimes good and sometimes bad ▪ *They have an up and down relationship.* — **up for 1** *informal* : wanting to have or do (something) ▪ *Are you up for watching a movie?* **2 a** — used to say that someone or something is or will be involved in a particular process and especially one that leads to a decision ▪ *The budget is up for discussion in today's meeting.* ▪ *She's up for reelection*

next year. [=she will be trying to get re-elected next year] **b** — used to say that something is available to be bought ▪ *items that are* **up for sale/auction** [=items being sold/auctioned] — **up to 1 a** : capable of performing or dealing with (something) ▪ *She feels up to the challenge.* **b** : good enough for (something) ▪ *Her performance wasn't up to her usual standards.* [=wasn't as good as it usually is] ▪ *(Brit) My Spanish* **isn't up to much.** [=I don't speak Spanish well] **2** : doing something especially in a way that is secret and with intentions that are bad ▪ *They're up to something, but I don't know what.* ▪ *She's* **up to no good.** **3** — used to say who is responsible for making a choice or decision ▪ *The amount of your donation is entirely up to you.* **4 a** — used to indicate the place or level that is reached by something ▪ *The water was up to our knees.* **b** : to or at (a specified amount, level, etc.) ▪ *Estimates for repairing the car ran from $500 up to $1,000.* **c** : as many or as much as (a specified number or amount) ▪ *The car holds up to six people.* **5** : during the time or period before ▪ *Up to* [=*until*] *that time they had been fairly successful.* — **up to here** *informal* — used to show that you have too much of something to deal with or that you are very annoyed by something and will not accept any more of it ▪ *I've had it up to here with your nonsense!* [=I have had to deal with too much of your nonsense] — **up to par** see PAR — **up to snuff** see ²SNUFF — **up to speed** see ¹SPEED — **up to your ears** see EAR — **up to your eyeballs** see ¹EYEBALL

³**up** *prep* **1** : to, toward, or at a higher point on (something) ▪ *climb up a ladder* ▪ *She walked her bike up the hill.* **2** : along the course or path of (something) ▪ *Go up the street and turn left.* ▪ *The ship sailed up the coast.* ▪ *pacing up and down the hall* — **up until** *or* **up till** : during the time or period before ▪ *Up until now, everything has gone very well.*

⁴**up** *n* [C] : a period or state of success, happiness, etc. ▪ *We have had our ups and downs.* — **on the up** *chiefly Brit* : moving toward an improved or better state ▪ *Sales are on the up.* [=sales are increasing] — **on the up and up** *informal* **1** *US* : honest and legal ▪ *Let's keep everything on the up and up.* **2** *Brit* : becoming more successful ▪ *a team that's on the up and up*

⁵**up** *vb* **upped** /ˈʌpt/; **up·ping** [T] : to make (something) higher ▪ *The restaurant upped* [=*increased*] *its prices.* — **up and** *informal* : to do something specified in a sudden and unexpected way ▪ *One day, he just upped and left.* ✧ *In U.S. English,* **up** *and is often used instead of* **ups** *and or* **upped** *and.* ▪ *One day, he just upped and left.* [=he just suddenly left] — **up the ante** see ¹ANTE

up-and-com·ing /ˌʌpəndˈkʌmɪŋ/ *adj* : becoming more successful, important, and well known ▪ *an up-and-coming actor*

up·beat /ˈʌpˌbiːt/ *adj* : positive and cheerful ▪ *a story with an upbeat ending*

up·braid /ˌʌpˈbreɪd/ *vb* [T] *formal* : to speak in an angry or critical way to (someone who has done something wrong) ▪ *She upbraided [=scolded] him for not offering to help his grandfather.*

up·bring·ing /ˈʌpˌbrɪŋɪŋ/ *n* [C] : the care and teaching given to a child by parents or other people ▪ *I had a sheltered/religious/privileged upbringing.*

up·chuck /ˈʌpˌtʃʌk/ *vb* [T/I] *US, informal* : VOMIT ▪ *I felt like I was about to upchuck.*

up·com·ing /ˈʌpˌkʌmɪŋ/ *adj* : happening or appearing soon ▪ *the upcoming election/holiday*

¹**up·date** /ˌʌpˈdeɪt/ *vb* **-dat·ed; -dat·ing** [T] **1 a** : to change (something) by including the most recent information ▪ *I need to update my résumé.* **b** : to make (something) more modern ▪ *She wants to update her wardrobe.* ▪ *an updated version of a classic story* **2** : to give (someone) the most recent information about something ▪ *He updated us on his mother's health.*

²**up·date** /ˈʌpˌdeɪt/ *n* [C] **1** : a report that includes the most recent information about something ▪ *a weather update = an update on the weather* **2** : a change or addition to computer software that includes the most recent information

up·draft /ˈʌpˌdræft, *Brit* ˈʌpˌdrɑːft/ *n* [C] *technical* : an upward flow of air

up·end /ˌʌpˈɛnd/ *vb* [T] **1** : to cause (something) to be upside down : to turn (something) over ▪ *I upended my bag and dumped everything out.* **2** : to cause (someone) to fall down or be turned over ▪ *A giant wave upended the surfers.* ▪ *(US, figurative) The new regulations could upend the entire industry.*

up–front /ˌʌpˈfrʌnt/ *adj* **1** : honest and direct ▪ *I was up-front about my financial position.* **2** — used to refer to money that is paid in advance ▪ *up-front fees* — see also *up front* at ¹FRONT

¹**up·grade** /ˌʌpˈɡreɪd/ *vb* **-grad·ed; -grad·ing** **1 a** [T] : to make (something) better by including the most recent information or improvements ▪ *This course will help you to upgrade your computer skills.* ▪ *They've upgraded the quality of their service.* **b** [I] : to choose to have or use something more modern, useful, etc. ▪ *upgrade to a larger car* **2** [T/I] : to get something (such as a seat on an airplane or a room in a hotel) that is better than what you had originally ▪ *We were able to upgrade to first class.* **3** [T] : to give (someone or something) a higher rank or grade ▪ *The restaurant was upgraded from three to four stars.* — **up·grad·able** *or* **up·grade·able** /ˌʌpˈɡreɪdəbəl/ *adj* ▪ *upgradable hardware*

²**up·grade** /ˈʌpˌɡreɪd/ *n* [C] **1** : an area or surface that goes upward : an upward slope ▪ *a gradual upgrade* **2** : an occurrence in which one thing is replaced by something better, newer, more valuable, etc. ▪ *software/equipment upgrades*

up·heav·al /ˌʌpˈhiːvəl/ *n* [C/U] : a major change or period of change that causes a lot of conflict, confusion, anger, etc. ▪ *major political upheavals* ▪ *a period of cul-*

tural and social upheaval

¹**up·hill** /ˈʌpˈhɪl/ *adv* : toward the top of a hill or mountain ▪ *riding a bicycle uphill*

²**up·hill** /ˈʌpˌhɪl/ *adj* **1** : going or sloping up toward the top of a hill or mountain ▪ *an uphill climb* **2** *always before a noun* : difficult to do, deal with, etc. ▪ *This project has been an uphill battle/fight/struggle from the start.*

up·hold /ˌʌpˈhoʊld/ *vb* **-held** /-ˈhɛld/; **-hold·ing** [T] **1** : to support or defend (something, such as a law) ▪ *He took an oath to uphold the Constitution.* **2** : to judge (a legal decision) to be correct ▪ *The Court of Appeals upheld her conviction.* — **up·hold·er** *n* [C]

up·hol·ster /ˌʌpˈhoʊlstɚ/ *vb* [T] : to put a covering of cloth, leather, etc., on (a piece of furniture, such as a couch or chair) ▪ *They upholstered the couch with/in a floral fabric.* — **up·hol·stered** *adj* ▪ *an upholstered chair* — **up·hol·ster·er** /ˌʌpˈhoʊlstərɚ/ *n* [C]

up·hol·stery /ˌʌpˈhoʊlstəri/ *n* [U] : the cloth, leather, etc., that covers a couch, chair, etc. ▪ *a car with leather upholstery*

up·keep /ˈʌpˌkiːp/ *n* [U] : the care or maintenance of buildings, equipment, etc. ▪ *the cost of a car's/house's upkeep* ▪ *The yard requires very little upkeep.*

up·land /ˈʌplənd/ *n* [C] : a region of high land especially far from the sea ▪ *the uplands of eastern Turkey* — **upland** *adj, always before a noun* ▪ *an upland forest/species*

¹**up·lift** /ˌʌpˈlɪft/ *vb* [T] : to make (someone) happy or hopeful ▪ *music that uplifts the soul*

²**up·lift** /ˈʌpˌlɪft/ *n* **1** [*singular*] : an increase in amount or number ▪ *an uplift in prices/sales* **2** [U, *singular*] : an increase in happiness or hopefulness ▪ *searching for spiritual uplift*

up·lift·ed /ˌʌpˈlɪftəd/ *adj* **1** : raised or turned upward ▪ *uplifted faces/hands* **2** : made happier or more hopeful ▪ *uplifted spirits*

up·lift·ing /ˌʌpˈlɪftɪŋ/ *adj* : causing happy and hopeful feelings ▪ *uplifting music*

up·load /ˌʌpˈloʊd/ *vb* [T] *computers* : to move or copy (a file, program, etc.) from a computer or device to a usually larger computer or computer network ▪ *upload files to the Internet* — **up·load** /ˈʌpˌloʊd/ *n* [C] ▪ *a data upload*

up·mar·ket /ˈʌpˈmɑːkət/ *adj* : made for or appealing to people who have a lot of money ▪ *upmarket restaurants/shops*

up·on /əˈpɑːn/ *prep, formal* **1** : ¹ON ▪ *He placed the vase upon the table.* ▪ *immediately upon arrival* ▪ *behavior that is frowned upon* **2** — used to say that someone or something is very close or has arrived ▪ *The holidays are nearly upon us.* **3** — used to emphasize something that is repeated many times ▪ *layer upon layer [=many layers] of paint* ▪ *thousands upon thousands of people*

¹**up·per** /ˈʌpɚ/ *adj, always before a noun* **1 a** : located above another or others of the same kind ▪ *the tree's upper branches* ▪ *upper and lower front teeth* ▪ *the upper stories/floors of the tower* ▪ *temperatures in the upper 20s* **b** : located at or near the

top ▪ *the upper left-hand corner of the page* ▪ *upper body strength* [=strength in the arms, shoulders, neck, and back] ▪ *the upper atmosphere* **2** : located toward the north ▪ *upper Manhattan* **3** : above another or others in position, rank, or order ▪ *upper management* ▪ *the upper middle class* — **stiff upper lip** see ¹STIFF

²**upper** *n* [C] **1** : the parts of a shoe or boot above the sole ▪ *leather uppers* **2** *informal* : a drug that gives you more energy : AMPHETAMINE

up·per·case /ˌʌpəˈkeɪs/ *adj* : having as its typical form A, B, C rather than a, b, c : CAPITAL ▪ *uppercase letters* ▪ *uppercase D* — compare LOWERCASE — **uppercase** *n* [U] ▪ *letters written in uppercase*

upper class *n* [C] : a social class that is above the middle class ▪ *a member of the upper class* — **upper-class** *adj* ▪ *upper-class families*

up·per·class·man /ˌʌpəˈklæsmən, *Brit* ˌʌpəˈklɑːsmən/ *n, pl* **-men** /-mən/ [C] *US* : a student in the third or fourth year of high school or college

upper crust *n* — **the upper crust** *informal* : UPPER CLASS ▪ *the wealthy upper crust* — **upper-crust** *adj* ▪ *upper-crust schools*

upper hand *n* — **the upper hand** : the position of having power or being in control in a particular situation ▪ *He had the upper hand in the negotiations.*

up·per·most /ˈʌpəˌmoʊst/ *adj* : highest in position or importance ▪ *the uppermost* [=topmost] *branches of the tree* — **uppermost** *adv*

up·pi·ty /ˈʌpəti/ *adj, informal + disapproving* : acting as if you are more important than you really are, do not have to do what you are told to do, etc. ▪ *Don't get uppity with me.*

up·raised /ˌʌpˈreɪzd/ *adj* : raised or lifted up ▪ *He danced with his arms upraised.*

¹**up·right** /ˈʌpˌraɪt/ *adj* **1 a** : positioned to be straight up : VERTICAL ▪ *an upright posture* ▪ *Put your seat back in the upright position.* **b** — used to describe something that is tall rather than wide ▪ *an upright freezer* **2** : always behaving in an honest way ▪ *an upright citizen* — **upright** *adv* ▪ *walking/standing upright* ▪ *She sat bolt upright.* [=she sat up straight] *in bed.*

²**upright** *n* [C] **1** : a board or pole placed in a vertical position to support something **2** *American football* : GOALPOST ▪ *He kicked the ball through the uprights.*

up·ris·ing /ˈʌpˌraɪzɪŋ/ *n* [C] : a usually violent effort by many people to change the government or leader of a country ▪ *an armed uprising*

up·riv·er /ˌʌpˈrɪvə/ *adv* : toward the start of a river ▪ *The salmon swim upriver* [=*upstream*] *to spawn.*

up·roar /ˈʌpˌroə/ *n* [C/U] : a situation in which many people are upset, angry, or disturbed by something ▪ *The proposal caused an uproar.* ▪ *The town was in an uproar over the proposed jail.*

up·roar·i·ous /ˌʌpˈrorijəs/ *adj* **1** : very noisy ▪ *uproarious laughter* **2** : extremely funny ▪ *an uproarious comedy* — **uproar·i·ous·ly** *adv*

up·root /ˌʌpˈruːt/ *vb* [T] **1** : to pull (a plant and its root) completely out of the ground ▪ *Many trees were uprooted by the storm.* **2** : to remove (something) completely ▪ *trying to uproot racism* **3** : to make (someone) leave home and move to a different place ▪ *Taking the job would mean uprooting my family.*

up·scale /ˈʌpˈskeɪl/ *adj, US* : relating to or appealing to people who have a lot of money ▪ *an upscale neighborhood* — **upscale** *adv* ▪ *The brand is going/moving upscale.*

¹**up·set** /ˌʌpˈsɛt/ *adj* **1** : angry or unhappy ▪ *I was feeling upset by/about the whole experience.* ▪ *She was too upset to speak to him.* ▪ *I'm upset that you didn't call.* **2** ✧ If you have an **upset stomach**, you have an unpleasant feeling in your stomach because of illness or because of something you have eaten.

²**up·set** /ˌʌpˈsɛt/ *vb* **-set; -set·ting** [T] **1** : to make (someone) unhappy, worried, etc. ▪ *Her remark really upset me.* ▪ *A lot of people were upset by the court's decision.* **2** : to cause an unpleasant feeling in (your stomach) ▪ *Spicy food upsets my stomach.* **3** : to cause (something) to be unable to continue in the expected way ▪ *His sudden arrival upset* [=*disrupted*] *my plans.* **4** : to defeat (someone who was expected to defeat you) ▪ *She was upset in the election.* **5** : to cause (something) to fall ▪ *I bumped the table and upset a lamp.* — **upset the apple cart** *informal* : to do something that changes or spoils a plan, situation, system, etc. — **upsetting** *adj* ▪ *a very upsetting situation*

³**up·set** /ˈʌpˌsɛt/ *n* **1** [C] : an occurrence in which a game, contest, etc., is won by a person or team that was expected to lose ▪ *Her victory in the election was a big upset.* **2** [C/U] : an unpleasant feeling of illness in your stomach ▪ *foods that cause stomach upset* **3** [C/U] : a period of worry and unhappiness caused by something that has happened ▪ *a period of emotional upset*

up·shot /ˈʌpˌʃɑːt/ *n* — **the upshot** : the final result or outcome of a process, discussion, etc. ▪ *The upshot of the decision is that the park will be closed.*

¹**up·side** /ˈʌpˌsaɪd/ *n* [C] : a part of something that is good or desirable ▪ *One upside to the new house is its location.*

²**up·side** /ˈʌpˌsaɪd/ *prep, US, informal* : on or against the side of (something) ▪ *She smacked him upside the head.* [=she hit/slapped him on the side of his head]

upside down /ˈʌpˌsaɪdˈdaʊn/ *adv* : with the top at the bottom and the bottom at the top : placed so that the end that should be at the top is at the bottom ▪ *You hung the picture upside down!* — **turn (something) upside down** *informal* : to make (something) very untidy ▪ *I turned the room upside down looking for my car keys.* ▪ (*figurative*) *My whole world was turned upside down when she died.* — **upside-down** *adj* ▪ *That flag is upside-down.*

¹**up·stage** /ˈʌpˈsteɪdʒ/ *adv* : toward the back part of a stage ▪ *The actor moved upstage.*

²**up·stage** /ˌʌpˈsteɪdʒ/ vb **-staged; -staging** [T] : to take attention away from (someone or something else, such as another performer) ▪ *The children upstaged the adult performers.* [=people watched the children more than the adults]

up·stairs /ˌʌpˈsteɚz/ adv **1** : on or to a higher floor of a building ▪ *My in-laws live upstairs.* **2** *informal* : in the head : mentally or intellectually ▪ *Some say he's a little slow upstairs.* [=he's mentally slow] — **the upstairs** : the upper floors of a building ▪ *We've decided to rent out the upstairs.* — **upstairs** adj, always before a noun ▪ *the upstairs bathroom*

up·stand·ing /ˌʌpˈstændɪŋ/ adj : honest and respectable ▪ *upstanding members of the community*

up·start /ˈʌpˌstɑɚt/ n [C] **1** *disapproving* : a person who has recently begun an activity, become successful, etc., and who does not show proper respect for older and more experienced people ▪ *a young upstart who thinks he knows more than the boss* **2** *chiefly US* : a newly successful person, business, etc. ▪ *upstart Internet companies*

up·state /ˈʌpˈsteɪt/ n [U] *US* : the northern part of a state — **up·state** /ˈʌpˌsteɪt/ adj, always before a noun ▪ *upstate New York* — **up·state** /ˈʌpˈsteɪt/ adv ▪ *They moved upstate.*

up·stream /ˈʌpˈstriːm/ adv : in the direction opposite to the flow in a stream, river, etc. : toward the source of a stream, river, etc. ▪ *swimming upstream*

up·surge /ˈʌpˌsɚdʒ/ n [C] : a rapid or sudden increase or rise ▪ *a recent upsurge in crime* ▪ *an upsurge of anger*

up·swing /ˈʌpˌswɪŋ/ n [C] : a situation in which something is increasing or becoming better ▪ *an upswing in profits* ▪ *Business is on the upswing.* [=improving]

up·take /ˈʌpˌteɪk/ n **1** [U, singular] *technical* : the process by which something is taken in by the body, a plant, etc. ▪ *a rapid uptake of liquid* **2** [U] *informal* : the ability to learn new things, to understand what is happening or being said, etc. ▪ *She's pretty quick/slow on the uptake.* [=she understands things quickly/slowly]

up·tem·po /ˈʌpˌtempoʊ/ adj : played very fast : having a fast tempo ▪ *up-tempo music*

up·tick /ˈʌpˌtɪk/ n [C] *US* : a small increase or rise ▪ *an uptick in sales/hiring*

up·tight /ˈʌpˈtaɪt/ adj **1** : nervous or worried and tending to become upset about something that does not make other people upset ▪ *There's no reason to get so uptight about the delay.* **2** : unable or unwilling to relax and express feelings openly ▪ *Some people are very uptight about sex.*

up-to-date adj **1** : including the latest information ▪ *up-to-date maps* **2** : based on or using the newest information, methods, etc. ▪ *up-to-date* [=modern] *methods*

up-to-the-minute adj **1** : including the very latest information ▪ *up-to-the-minute news* **2** : based on or using the newest information, methods, etc. ▪ *up-to-the-minute equipment*

up·town /ˈʌpˈtaʊn/ n [C] *chiefly US* : the part of a city or town that is away from the central part ▪ *They took a taxi from uptown to downtown.* — **uptown** adv, *chiefly US* ▪ *I live uptown.* — **uptown** adj, always before a noun ▪ *uptown Manhattan*

up·turn /ˈʌpˌtɚn/ n [C] : an increase or improvement ▪ *an upturn in sales*

up·turned /ˈʌpˌtɚnd/ adj **1** : turned so that the bottom part is on top : turned upside down ▪ *an upturned boat* **2** : turned or directed upward ▪ *upturned faces*

¹**up·ward** (*chiefly US*) /ˈʌpwɚd/ or *chiefly Brit* **up·wards** /ˈʌpwɚdz/ adv **1** : from a lower place or level to a higher place or level ▪ *The path climbed upward.* **2** : toward the ceiling, sky, etc. ▪ *He pointed upward.* **3** : toward a higher or better condition or position ▪ *moving upward in the corporate world* **4** : to a larger amount : to a higher number ▪ *Prices shot upward.* — **upwards of** also *US* **upward of** : more than (an amount or number) ▪ *upwards of half a million people*

²**upward** adj, always before a noun **1** : moving or going from a lower place or level to a higher place or level ▪ *upward movement/flow* ▪ *an upward curve* **2** : moving or going toward the ceiling, sky, etc. ▪ *the plant's upward growth* — **up·ward·ly** adv

upwardly mobile adj : moving or able to move into a higher social or economic position ▪ *upwardly mobile professionals* — **upward mobility** n [U] ▪ *a job with upward mobility*

up·wind /ˈʌpˈwɪnd/ adv : in the direction that is opposite to the direction of the wind ▪ *standing upwind of the fire* — **upwind** adj ▪ *the upwind side of the fire*

ura·ni·um /juˈreɪnijəm/ n [U] : a radioactive element that is used to make nuclear energy and nuclear weapons

Ura·nus /ˈjɚrənəs, juˈreɪnəs/ n [singular] : the planet that is seventh in order from the sun

ur·ban /ˈɚbən/ adj : of or relating to cities and the people who live in them ▪ *urban housing/voters*

ur·bane /ˌɚˈbeɪn/ adj : polite and confident ▪ *witty and urbane people/dialogue* — **ur·bane·ly** adv ▪ *urbanely witty dialogue*

ur·ban·i·za·tion also *Brit* **ur·ban·i·sa·tion** /ˌɚbənəˈzeɪʃən/ n [U] : the process by which towns and cities are formed and become larger as more and more people begin living and working in central areas ▪ *rapid urbanization* — **ur·ban·ize** also *Brit* **ur·ban·ise** /ˈɚbəˌnaɪz/ vb **-ized; -iz·ing** [T/I] ▪ *The country/region is rapidly urbanizing.*

urban legend n [C] : a story about an unusual event or occurrence that many people believe is true but that is not true — called also *urban myth*

urban renewal n [U] : a process by which old buildings or buildings that are in bad condition in part of a city are replaced or repaired ▪ *an area undergoing urban renewal*

urban sprawl n [U] : a situation in which large stores, groups of houses, etc., are built in an area around a city that formerly had few people living in it

ur·chin /'ɚtʃən/ n [C] **1** old-fashioned : a usually poor and dirty child who annoys people or causes minor trouble • a street urchin **2** : SEA URCHIN

¹urge /'ɚdʒ/ vb **urged; urg·ing** [T] **1** : to ask people to do or support (something) in a way that shows that you believe it is very important • He is continually urging reform. **2** : to try to persuade (someone) in a serious way to do something • an editorial urging readers to vote **3** : to use force or pressure to move (someone or something) in a particular direction or at a particular speed • A hand on her back urged her forward. — **urge on** [phrasal vb] **urge (someone or something) on** : to encourage (someone or something) to move ahead, to do something, etc. • riders urging their horses on

²urge n [C] : a strong need or desire to have or do something • He fought the urge to cry/laugh. • creative/sexual urges

ur·gent /'ɚdʒənt/ adj **1** : very important and needing immediate attention • We've come to deliver an urgent message. • an urgent appeal for assistance **2** : showing that something is very important and needs immediate attention • An urgent voice told us to leave the building immediately. — **ur·gen·cy** /'ɚdʒənsi/ n [U] • the urgency of the problem — **ur·gent·ly** adv • Volunteers are urgently needed.

urging n [U] : the act of trying to persuade someone in a serious way to do something • At the urging of her teacher, she chose to pursue a career in journalism.

uri·nal /'jɚrənəl/, Brit ju'raɪnl/ n [C] : a toilet that is attached to a wall especially in a public bathroom for men to urinate into

uri·nary /'jɚrəˌneri, Brit 'jʊərənri/ adj, always before a noun, medical **1** : relating to the parts of the body in which urine is produced and through which urine passes • the urinary bladder/tract **2** : relating to or used for urine • a urinary catheter

uri·nate /'jɚrəˌneɪt/ vb **-nat·ed; -nat·ing** [I] medical : to send urine out of the body — **uri·na·tion** /ˌjɚrə'neɪʃən/ n [U]

urine /'jɚrən/ n [U] medical : waste liquid that collects in the bladder before leaving the body

URL /ˌjuːˌaɚ'ɛl/ n [C] computers : the letters and symbols (such as http://www.Merriam-Webster.com) that are the address of a Web site ◊ URL is an abbreviation of "Uniform Resource Locator."

urn /'ɚn/ n [C] **1** : a container that is often shaped like a vase with a closed top and that is used to hold the ashes of someone who has been cremated **2** : a closed container with a faucet near the bottom which is used to serve hot drinks • a coffee urn

us /'ʌs/ pron, objective form of WE **1** — used to refer to the speaker and another person or group of people as the object of a verb or preposition • It was nice of you to invite us. • They promised the mon-

ey to us. • Someone please help us! • All of us [=we all] will be affected by these changes. **2** : people in general • Does God walk among us? **3** Brit, informal : ME • Give us a kiss.

U.S. or **US** abbr United States (of America)

U.S.A. or **USA** abbr United States of America

us·able /'juːzəbəl/ adj : capable of being used : in good enough condition to be used • Is any of this junk usable?

USAF abbr United States Air Force

us·age /'juːsɪdʒ/ n **1** [U] **a** : the act of using something • drug usage among college students **b** : the way that something is used • rough usage **c** : the amount of something that is used • reducing water/energy usage **d** : how often something is used • increasing usage of the nation's highways **2** [C/U] : the way that words and phrases are used in a language • an uncommon usage • differences between British and American usage • a usage manual/guide/dictionary

USB /ˌjuːˌɛs'biː/ n [U] computers : a system for connecting a computer to another device (such as a printer, keyboard, or mouse) by using a special kind of cord • a USB cable/port ◊ USB is an abbreviation of "Universal Serial Bus."

USDA abbr United States Department of Agriculture

¹use /'juːz/ vb **used; us·ing 1** [T] : to do something with (an object, machine, person, method, etc.) in order to accomplish a task, do an activity, etc. • The machine is easy to use. • Use this knife to cut the bread. • She used the money for college. • After the accident, she could no longer use her legs. • He used his time there well/wisely. • The word "place" can be used as a noun or verb. • Maybe if we **use our heads** [=think carefully], we can figure this out. **2** [T] : to take (something) from a supply in order to function or to do a task • a new kind of light bulb that uses very little electricity • Did you use (up) all the eggs? • The car uses a lot of gas. **3** [T] — used to say that something is needed or to ask if something is needed or wanted; usually used with can or could • Can you use this lamp? I don't want it anymore. • The house could use [=it needs] a coat of paint. • I sure could use some help. **4 a** [T] : to eat, drink, etc., (something) regularly • She stopped using alcohol/drugs a year ago. **b** [I] informal : to take illegal drugs regularly • How long has he been using? **5** [T] **a** : to treat (someone) well in order to get something for yourself • She was just using me (for my money). **b** : to treat (someone who is generous or helpful) unfairly • After driving them all over the place, I began to feel used. — **use up** [phrasal vb] **use up (something)** or **use (something) up** : to take (all of something) from a supply • She quickly used up (all of) her inheritance. • Don't use up (all) the hot water. — see also USED, USED TO

²use /'juːs/ n **1** [U] **a** : the act of using something • The knife is dull from constant use. [=from being used very often over a period of time] • *illegal drug use* • *the author's use of irony in the novel* **b** : the state of being used • *The computer is currently **in** use.* [=is currently being used] • *When did the word first **come into** use?* [=when was the word first used?] • *Typewriters have practically **gone out of** use.* [=almost no people use typewriters anymore] **2 a** [C] : a way in which something is or can be used • *a tool with many uses* • *Doctors have found a new use for the drug.* • *The technique **has its uses**.* [=the technique is useful in some ways] **b** [*singular*] : a way to use something or someone • *Do you have a/any use for this old computer?* **3** [U] : the opportunity or right to use something • *I have the use of her car* [=I am allowed to use her car] *while she is away.* • *The pool is **for the use of** hotel guests only.* [=only hotel guests are allowed to swim in the pool] **4** [U] — used to say that something or someone is or is not helpful or useful • *It's too small to be of use.* • *Go home and rest. You're no use to us if you're sick.* [=you cannot help us if you're sick] • *He's been of no use at all to me.* [=he hasn't helped me at all] • *There's **no use** (in) worrying about the past.* [=worrying about the past will not help, make anything better, etc.] • *"You should talk to her." "What's the use?* [=talking to her will not help] *She's won't change her mind."* **5** [U] : the ability or power to use something • *He lost (the) use of his legs in a car accident.* — **have no use for** *or* **not have any use for** : to not like or value (someone or something) • *I'm a logical person. I have no use for sentimentality.* — **it's no use** — used to say that something you have tried to do cannot be done • *It's no use —the door won't open.* — **make use of** : to use (something) • *She made use of the money to pay for college.* • **make good/better use of** *spare time* [=use spare time in a better and more productive way] — **put (something) to (good) use** : to use (something) in an effective way • *I'm putting my new skills to use.* [=using my new skills] • *We'll put the money to good use.* [=we'll do something good with it]

used /ˈjuːzd/ *adj* **1** : having been used before • *a used tissue* • *a much-used excuse* **2** : having had a previous owner • *a used car/book*

¹**used to** /ˈjuːstə/ *adj* : familiar with something so that it seems normal or usual • *I'm not used to driving this car.* • *He is used to criticism.* = *He is used to being criticized.* • *She **got** used to the weather.*

²**used to** *vb* [*modal vb*] — used to say that something existed or repeatedly happened in the past but does not exist or happen now • *I used to write more often.* [=in the past I wrote more often] • *He never used to smoke.* [=he never smoked in the past]

---

usage **Used to** is usually used in the form *use to* when it occurs with *did.* • *Did you **use** to work there?* [=did you work there in the past?] • *He didn't **use** to smoke.*

---

use·ful /ˈjuːsfəl/ *adj* : helping to do or achieve something • *a useful invention/tool/skill* • *useful suggestions/advice* • *It can be useful to know CPR.* • *The therapy is useful as a treatment for diabetes.* = *The therapy is useful in treating diabetes.* • *I tried to **make myself** useful.* [=to be helpful; to do something helpful] — **use·ful·ly** *adv* — **use·ful·ness** *n* [U]

use·less /ˈjuːsləs/ *adj* : not at all useful : not doing or able to do what is needed • *a dull, useless knife* : not producing or able to produce the effect you want • *a useless attempt at fixing it* • *It's useless trying to change her mind.* = *It's useless to try to change her mind.* — **use·less·ly** *adv* — **use·less·ness** *n* [U]

us·er /ˈjuːzɚ/ *n* [C] **1** : a person or thing that uses something • *computer users* • *Enter your **user** name.* [=the name or word that you use to identify yourself when you want to use a computer program or the Internet] **2** : a person who frequently uses illegal drugs • *I never knew she was a (drug) user.*

us·er–friend·ly /ˌjuːzɚˈfrɛndli/ *adj* : easy to use or understand • *user-friendly software* — **us·er–friend·li·ness** *n* [U]

¹**ush·er** /ˈʌʃɚ/ *n* [C] : a person who leads people to their seats in a theater, at a wedding, etc.

²**usher** *vb* [T] : to lead (someone) to a place • *A nurse ushered us into the hospital room.* — **usher in** [*phrasal vb*] **usher in (something)** *also* **usher (something) in** **1** : to happen at the beginning of (something, such as a period of activity) and usually to help cause it • *a discovery that ushered in a period of change* [=that marked the beginning of a period of change] **2** : to celebrate the beginning of (something) • *a celebration to usher in the New Year*

USMC *abbr* United States Marine Corps

USS *abbr* United States ship — used in the names of U.S. naval vessels • *(the) USS Constitution*

U.S.S.R. *abbr* Union of Soviet Socialist Republics

¹**usu·al** /ˈjuːʒəwəl/ *adj* : done, found, or used most of the time or in most cases : normal or regular • *He took his usual route to work.* • *my usual activities/methods* • *She's not my usual doctor.* • *It's (not) usual to charge a fee for delivery.* — **as usual** : in the way that happens or exists most of the time or in most cases • *We had to wait as usual.* — **be your usual self** : to behave in the way you usually do • *Is anything wrong? You're not your usual self today.* — **business as usual** see BUSINESS

²**usual** *n* — **the usual** *informal* **1** : what happens or is done most of the time • *"What have you been doing lately?" "Oh, you know. The usual."* [=the things I usually do] **2** : what someone chooses to eat or drink most of the time — used especially in restaurants, bars, etc. • *"What'll it be, Joe?" "I'll have the usual, please."*

usu·al·ly /ˈjuːʒəwəli/ *adv* — used to describe what happens or exists most of the time or in most cases • *The trip usually takes an hour.* • *I usually work on Satur-*

days. ▪ *Usually, there are no problems.*

usurp /juˈsəp, Brit juˈzɜːp/ vb [T] *formal* : to take and keep (something, such as power) in a forceful or violent way and especially without the right to do so ▪ *attempts to usurp the throne* — **usurp·er** /juˈsəpə, Brit juˈzɜːpə/ n [C]

usu·ry /ˈjuːʒəri/ n [U] *formal + disapproving* : the practice of lending money and requiring the borrower to pay a high amount of interest

UT *abbr* Utah

uten·sil /juˈtɛnsəl/ n [C] : a simple and useful device that is used for doing tasks in a person's home and especially in the kitchen ▪ *cooking/kitchen utensils*

uter·us /ˈjuːtərəs/ n, pl **uteri** /ˈjuːtəˌraɪ/ *also* **uter·us·es** [C] *medical* : the organ in women and some female animals in which babies develop before birth — called also **womb** — **uter·ine** /ˈjuːtəˌraɪn, ˈjuːtərən/ adj ▪ *the uterine lining*

util·i·tar·i·an /juˌtɪləˈterijən/ adj **1** : made to be useful rather than to be decorative or comfortable ▪ *utilitarian furniture/objects* **2** *philosophy* : of or relating to utilitarianism

util·i·tar·i·an·ism /juˌtɪləˈteriəˌnɪzəm/ n [U] *philosophy* : the belief that a morally good action is one that helps the greatest number of people

¹util·i·ty /juˈtɪləti/ n, pl **-ties** **1** [U] *formal* : the quality or state of being useful ▪ *I question the utility [=usefulness] of the procedure.* **2** [C] **a** : a service (such as a supply of electricity or water) that is provided to the public — usually plural ▪ *Many of these people are in danger of having their utilities shut off.* [=of no longer getting electricity, water, etc., in their homes] **b** : a company that provides electricity, water, etc. : PUBLIC UTILITY ▪ *Notify the utility (company) if there's an outage.* **3** [C] *computers* : a computer program that does a specific task ▪ *an antivirus utility* [=a computer program that prevents/removes viruses]

²utility adj, always before a noun **1** : designed for general use ▪ *a utility bag/knife/truck* — see also SPORT-UTILITY VEHICLE **2** *sports* : able to be used in

several different positions or roles ▪ *a utility infielder*

uti·lize *also Brit* **uti·lise** /ˈjuːtəˌlaɪz/ vb **-lized; -liz·ing** [T] *formal* : to use (something) for a particular purpose ▪ *Many of the library's resources are not utilized by townspeople.* — **uti·li·za·tion** *also Brit* **uti·li·sa·tion** /ˌjuːtələˈzeɪʃən/ n [U]

¹ut·most /ˈʌtˌmoʊst/ adj, always before a noun **1** : greatest or highest in degree, number, or amount ▪ *a matter of the utmost importance/urgency* **2** *formal* : farthest or most distant ▪ *the utmost limit*

²utmost n [singular] : the highest point or degree that can be reached ▪ *It's designed to provide the utmost in comfort.* ▪ *We did our utmost* [=did all that we could] *to help.* ▪ *We had to push ourselves to the utmost to finish the job in time.*

uto·pia *or* **Uto·pia** /juˈtoʊpijə/ n [C/U] : an imaginary place in which the government, laws, and social conditions are perfect — **uto·pi·an** /juˈtoʊpijən/ adj ▪ *a utopian community/vision*

¹ut·ter /ˈʌtər/ adj, always before a noun : complete and total ▪ *The situation descended into utter chaos.* ▪ *She showed an utter lack of interest in what he was saying.* ▪ *That argument is (complete and) utter nonsense.* — **ut·ter·ly** adv ▪ *I was utterly convinced that she was wrong.*

²utter vb [T] **1** : to make (a particular sound) ▪ *She uttered a cry of pleasure/pain.* **2** : to say (something) ▪ *Don't utter a word* [=say anything] *about this to anyone.*

ut·ter·ance /ˈʌtərəns/ n, *formal* **1** [C] : something that a person says ▪ *public utterances* **2** [U] : the act of saying something ▪ *give utterance to an idea*

U–turn /ˈjuːˌtɜːn/ n [C] **1** : a turn that you make while driving a car, walking, etc., that causes you to begin going in the opposite direction : a 180-degree turn ▪ *The driver made/did a quick U-turn and headed back north.* **2** *informal* : a complete change of ideas, plans, etc. ▪ *She did/made a U-turn when she found out the price.*

V

¹v *or* **V** /ˈviː/ n, pl **v's** *or* **V's** /ˈviːz/ **1** [C/U] : the 22nd letter of the English alphabet ▪ *The word "vest" starts with* (*a*) *v.* **2** [C] : the Roman numeral that means five ▪ *XXV* [=25]

²v *abbr* **1** *or* **v.** versus — used between two names that are opposed in a contest or court case ▪ *Brown v. Board of Education* **2** V volt ▪ *a 60 V bulb*

VA *abbr* **1** Veterans Administration **2** Veterans Affairs ▪ *a VA hospital* **3** Virginia

va·can·cy /ˈveɪkənsi/ n, pl **-cies** [C] **1**

formal : a job or position that is available to be taken ▪ *filling vacancies at the company* **2** : a room in a hotel, motel, etc., that is available for use ▪ *There were no vacancies at the hotel.*

va·cant /ˈveɪkənt/ adj **1** : not filled, used, or lived in ▪ *These lockers/seats/ apartments are vacant.* ▪ *a vacant lot* [=a piece of land that is not being used] **2** *formal, of a job or position* : available to be taken by someone ▪ *The position will become vacant next year.* **3** : showing no indication of what someone is thinking, feeling, etc. • *a vacant stare/smile/look* — **va·cant·ly** *adv* • *smiling vacantly*

va·cate /ˈveɪˌkeɪt/ *vb* **-cat·ed; -cat·ing** [T] *formal* : to leave (a job, seat, hotel room, etc.) • *She vacated her position.* • *Vacate the premises.*

¹**va·ca·tion** /veɪˈkeɪʃən/ *n* **1** [C/U] *US* : a period of time that a person spends away from home, school, or business usually in order to relax or travel • *We had a good vacation.* • *I'll be on vacation next week.* **2** [U] *chiefly US* : the number of days or hours per year for which an employer agrees to pay workers while they are not working • *I get three weeks vacation a year.* **3** [C] *US* : a time when schools, colleges, and universities are closed • *spring/summer vacation*

²**vacation** *vb* [I] *US* : to go somewhere during a vacation • *They are vacationing in Italy.*

va·ca·tion·er /veɪˈkeɪʃənɚ/ *n* [C] *US* : a person who takes a vacation somewhere • *summer vacationers*

vac·ci·nate /ˈvæksəˌneɪt/ *vb* **-nat·ed; -nat·ing** [T] *medical* : to give (a person or an animal) a vaccine • *They are/got vaccinated (against measles).* — **vac·ci·na·tion** /ˌvæksəˈneɪʃən/ *n* [C/U]

vac·cine /vækˈsiːn/ *n* [C/U] *medical* : a substance that is usually injected into a person or animal to protect against a particular disease • *the polio vaccine*

vac·il·late /ˈvæsəˌleɪt/ *vb* **-lat·ed; -lat·ing** [I] *formal* : to repeatedly change your opinions or desires • *She has vacillated on this issue.* — **vac·il·la·tion** /ˌvæsəˈleɪʃən/ *n* [C/U]

vac·u·ous /ˈvækjəwəs/ *adj, formal* : lacking meaning, importance, or substance • *a vacuous movie/comment* — **va·cu·i·ty** /væˈkjuːwəti/ *n* [U]

¹**vac·u·um** /ˈvæˌkjuːm/ *n* [C] **1** : an empty space in which there is no air or other gas • *The pump created a vacuum inside the bottle.* • *(figurative) Her death created/left a vacuum* [=left an empty place] *in our lives.* • *(figurative) The riots did not happen in a vacuum.* [=they were affected by other events or influences] **2** : VACUUM CLEANER

²**vacuum** *vb* [T/I] : to use a vacuum cleaner • *I vacuumed (the living room).*

vacuum cleaner *n* [C] : an electrical machine that cleans floors by sucking up dirt

vag·a·bond /ˈvæɡəˌbaːnd/ *n* [C] : a person who travels from place to place and does not have a home or much money

va·ga·ries /ˈveɪɡəriz/ *n* [plural] *formal* : changes that are difficult to predict or control • *the vagaries of the weather*

va·gi·na /vəˈdʒaɪnə/ *n* [C] : the passage in a woman's or female animal's body that leads from the uterus to the outside of the body — **va·gi·nal** /ˈvædʒənl/ *adj*

va·grant /ˈveɪɡrənt/ *n* [C] : a person who has no place to live and no job and who asks people for money — **va·gran·cy** /ˈveɪɡrənsi/ *n* [U] • *He was arrested and charged with vagrancy.*

vague /ˈveɪɡ/ *adj* **vagu·er; -est 1** a : not clear in meaning • *vague instructions* b : not thinking or expressing

your thoughts clearly or precisely • *He was vague about what happened.* [=he did not say exactly what happened] **2** a : not completely formed or developed • *I had only a vague idea/recollection of who he was.* b : not clearly or strongly felt • *a vague sense of uneasiness* **3** : not able to be seen clearly • *vague figures in the distance*

vague·ly /ˈveɪɡli/ *adv* **1** : somewhat or slightly • *He looked vaguely familiar.* **2** : in a way that is not clearly stated or expressed • *talking vaguely about the future* **3** : in a way which shows that you are not paying attention • *She smiled vaguely.* — **vague·ness** *n* [U]

vain /ˈveɪn/ *adj* **1** : CONCEITED • *She is vain about her long hair.* **2** : having no success • *a vain attempt to escape* — **in vain 1** : without success • *He tried in vain to get the baby to sleep.* **2** : in a way that does not show proper respect • *He took God's name in vain.* [=used God's name in a disrespectful way] — **vain·ly** *adv*

va·lance /ˈvæləns/ *n* [C] *chiefly US* : a short curtain or frame placed on top of a window

val·e·dic·to·ri·an /ˌvælədɪkˈtorijən/ *n* [C] *US* : the student who has the highest grades in a graduating class and who gives a speech at graduation ceremonies • *She was the valedictorian of her class.*

val·e·dic·to·ry /ˌvæləˈdɪktəri/ *adj, formal* : saying goodbye in a formal way • *a valedictory address/speech*

val·en·tine /ˈvælənˌtaɪn/ *n* [C] **1** : a card or gift that you give usually to someone you love on Valentine's Day **2** *or* **Valentine** : a person who you give a valentine to • *Won't you be my Valentine?*

Valentine's Day *n* [singular] : February 14 observed as a time for sending valentines — called also *Saint Valentine's Day*

va·let /ˈvæˌleɪ/ *n* [C] **1** *US* : a person who parks cars for guests at a hotel, restaurant, etc. • *using a hotel's valet parking/service* [=a service in which you can have your car parked by a valet] **2** : a man's personal male servant

val·iant /ˈvæljənt/ *adj, somewhat formal* : very brave or courageous • *her valiant battle with cancer* — **val·iant·ly** *adv*

val·id /ˈvæləd/ *adj* **1** : fair or reasonable • *valid concerns/points* **2** : acceptable according to the law • *You must present valid identification.*

val·i·date /ˈvæləˌdeɪt/ *vb* **-dat·ed; -dat·ing** [T] **1** : to state or show that something has been checked and is legal or official • *The court validated the contract.* • *Customs officers validated our passports (by stamping them).* **2** : to show that something is real, reasonable, or correct • *The claims cannot yet be validated.* — **val·i·da·tion** /ˌvæləˈdeɪʃən/ *n* [U]

va·lid·i·ty /vəˈlɪdəti/ *n* [U] : the state or quality of being acceptable, real, or correct • *the validity of the contract/findings*

Val·ium /ˈvælijəm/ *trademark* — used for a drug that helps to reduce anxiety and stress

val·ley /ˈvæli/ *n, pl* **-leys** [C] **1** : an area of low land between hills or mountains

2 : a low period, point, or level • *There are peaks and valleys* [=high and low periods] *in sales.*

val·or (*US*) or *Brit* **val·our** /ˈvælə/ *n* [*U*] *literary* : courage or bravery • *the nation's highest award for valor*

val·u·able /ˈvæljəbəl/ *adj* 1 : worth a lot of money • *The watch is very valuable.* 2 : very useful or helpful • *valuable advice* • *a valuable member of the staff* 3 : important and limited in amount • *Please don't waste my time; it is very valuable.*

val·u·ables /ˈvæljəbəlz/ *n* [*plural*] : small things that you own that are worth a lot of money • *I keep my valuables in a safe.*

val·u·a·tion /ˌvæljəˈweɪʃən/ *n* 1 [*C/U*] : the act or process of judging the price or value of something • *(a) valuation of a company's assets* 2 [*C*] : the estimated value of something • *home valuations*

¹**val·ue** /ˈvælju/ *n* 1 [*C/U*] : the amount of money that something is worth • *property values* • *a decline/decrease/drop in value* • *The vase has little value.* 2 [*C/U*] : something that can be bought for a low or fair price • *This car is a good value (for the/your money).* 3 [*C/U*] : usefulness or importance • *the value of a good education* • *He uses offensive language for (its) shock value.* [=in order to shock people] 4 [*C*] : a strongly held belief about what is valuable, important, or acceptable • *cultural/religious values* 5 [*C*] : a mathematical quantity that is represented by a letter • *If x + 3 = 5, what is the value of x?* — **of value** 1 : worth a lot of money • *They stole everything of value.* 2 : useful or important • *He had nothing of value to say.* [=nothing he said was important]

²**value** *vb* **val·ued; val·u·ing** [*T*] 1 : to make a judgment about the amount of money that something is worth • *The ring was valued at $250.* 2 : to think that (someone or something) is important or useful • *He values her advice/opinions.* • *a valued* [=*valuable*] *employee*

value-added tax *n* [*U*] : a tax that is added to products at each stage of their production — called also *VAT*

value judgment *n* [*C*] : a personal opinion about how good or bad someone or something is • *making value judgments*

valve /ˈvælv/ *n* [*C*] 1 : a mechanical device that controls the flow of liquid, gas, etc., by opening and closing • *Turn off the house's main water valve.* 2 *medical* : a structure in the heart, stomach, etc., that temporarily stops the flow of fluid or that allows fluid to move in one direction only • *a heart valve*

vam·pire /ˈvæmˌpajə/ *n* [*C*] *in stories* : a dead person who leaves the grave at night to bite and suck the blood of living people

vampire bat *n* [*C*] : a bat from Central and South America that sucks the blood of people and animals

van /ˈvæn/ *n* [*C*] 1 : a vehicle that is used for transporting goods • *a delivery/moving van* 2 *US* : a vehicle that is larger than a car, that is shaped like a box, and that is used for transporting people or things 3 *Brit* : a railroad car for carrying goods or baggage

van·dal /ˈvændl/ *n* [*C*] : a person who deliberately destroys or damages property — **van·dal·ism** /ˈvændəˌlɪzəm/ *n* [*U*] • *He was arrested for vandalism.* — **van·dal·ize** *also Brit* **van·dal·ise** /ˈvændəˌlaɪz/ *vb* **-ized; -iz·ing** [*T*] • *Our car was vandalized.*

van·guard /ˈvænˌgɑːd/ *n* 1 [*C*] : the group of people who are the leaders of an action or movement in society, politics, art, etc. • *She was in the vanguard of the feminist movement.* 2 **the vanguard** : the soldiers, ships, etc., that are at the front of a fighting force that is moving forward

va·nil·la /vəˈnɪlə/ *n* [*U*] : a dark substance that is made from a kind of bean and that is used to flavor food • *1 teaspoon vanilla (flavoring/extract)* • *vanilla ice cream*

van·ish /ˈvænɪʃ/ *vb* [*I*] 1 : to disappear entirely without a clear explanation • *She vanished without a trace.* = *She vanished into thin air.* • *He pulled a vanishing act* [=he suddenly left or disappeared] *when it was time to pay.* 2 : to stop existing • *Dinosaurs vanished from the face of the earth.*

van·i·ty /ˈvænəti/ *n, pl* **-ties** 1 [*U*] : the quality of being vain or conceited • *The handsome actor's vanity was well-known.* 2 [*C*] *US* **a** : a table with a mirror in front of which you sit while putting on makeup, jewelry, etc. **b** : a bathroom cabinet that is covered by a sink and a countertop

van·quish /ˈvæŋkwɪʃ/ *vb* [*T*] *literary* : to defeat (someone) completely in a war, battle, etc. • *vanquished enemies/foes*

van·tage point /ˈvæntɪʤ-/ *n* [*C*] : a position from which something is viewed or considered • *From our vantage point, it is difficult to imagine why she did it.*

va·pid /ˈvæpəd/ *adj, formal* : dull or boring • *a song with vapid lyrics* — **va·pid·i·ty** /væˈpɪdəti/ *n* [*U*]

va·por (*US*) or *Brit* **va·pour** /ˈveɪpə/ *n* [*C/U*] : a substance that is in the form of a gas or that consists of very small drops or particles mixed with the air • *water vapor*

va·por·ize *also Brit* **va·por·ise** /ˈveɪpəˌraɪz/ *vb* **-ized; -iz·ing** [*T/I*] : to change or cause (something) to change into a vapor • *Heat vaporized the liquid.* — **va·por·i·za·tion** *also Brit* **va·por·i·sa·tion** /ˌveɪpərəˈzeɪʃən, Brit ˌveɪpəˌraɪˈzeɪʃən/ *n* [*U*] — **va·por·iz·er** *also Brit* **va·por·is·er** /ˈveɪpəˌraɪzə/ *n* [*C*]

¹**var·i·able** /ˈverijəbəl/ *adj* : able or likely to change or be changed • *a variable interest rate* — **var·i·abil·i·ty** /ˌverijəˈbɪləti/ *n* [*U*]

²**variable** *n* [*C*] 1 : something that changes or that can be changed • *economic variables* 2 *mathematics* : a quantity that can have any one of a set of values

var·i·ance /ˈverijəns/ *n* 1 [*C/U*] formal : an amount of difference or change • *(a) slight variance between/in the results* 2 [*C*] *law* : an official decision or document that allows someone to do something that is not usually allowed by the rules • *He had to get a zoning variance to* *add a garage on to his house.* — **at variance** *formal* : not in agreement • *Their statements are at variance with ours.*

var·i·ant /ˈverijənt/ *n* [C] **1** : something that is different in some way from others of the same kind • *a new variant of the disease* **2** : one of two or more different ways to spell or pronounce a word • *regional/spelling variants* — **variant** *adj* • *variant spellings*

var·i·a·tion /ˌveriˈeɪʃən/ *n* **1** [C/U] : a change in the form, position, condition, or amount of something • *variations in temperature* **2** [C] : something that is similar to something else but different in some way • *a variation on a familiar theme*

var·i·cose vein /ˈverəˌkoʊs-/ *n* [C] *medical* : a vein that is abnormally swollen

var·ied /ˈverid/ *adj* : including many different things • *varied diets/interests*

va·ri·e·ty /vəˈrajəti/ *n, pl* **-et·ies** **1** [*singular*] : a number or collection of different things or people • *a wide/great variety of topics/people/problems* **2** [U] : the quality or state of having or including many different things • *My diet/life lacks variety.* **3** [C] : a particular kind of person or thing • *two varieties of apples*

var·i·ous /ˈverijəs/ *adj* — used to refer to several different or many different things, people, etc. • *various colors/options* — **var·i·ous·ly** /ˈverijəsli/ *adv* • *He is variously described as a hero and a villain.*

var·nish /ˈvaɚnɪʃ/ *n* **1** [C/U] : a liquid that is spread on a surface and that dries to form a hard, shiny coating • *floor varnish* **2** [U] : the hard, shiny coating that is produced by varnish • *Don't scratch the varnish.* — **varnish** *vb* [T] • *He varnished the table.*

var·si·ty /ˈvaɚsəti/ *n, pl* **-ties** [C/U] *US* : the main team of a college, school, or club in a particular sport • *I made varsity this year.* • *the varsity track team*

vary /ˈveri/ *vb* **var·ies; var·ied; vary·ing** **1** [I] : to be different or to become different • CHANGE • *The law varies by state.* • *The rooms vary in size.* • *varying degrees of success* **2** [T] : to change (something) so that it is not always the same • *I try to vary my diet.*

vas·cu·lar /ˈvæskjələ/ *adj* : of or relating to veins, arteries, etc. • *the human vascular system*

vase /ˈveɪs, *Brit* ˈvɑːz/ *n* [C] : a container that is used for holding flowers or for decoration • *a vase of roses*

va·sec·to·my /vəˈsɛktəmi/ *n, pl* **-mies** [C] *medical* : a surgery that prevents a man from producing sperm when he has sex

Vas·e·line /ˌvæsəˈliːn/ *trademark* — used for petroleum jelly

vast /ˈvæst, *Brit* ˈvɑːst/ *adj* : very great in size, amount, or extent • *a vast amount of knowledge* • *the vast majority of people* — **vast·ly** *adv* • *vastly different experiences* — **vast·ness** /ˈvæstnəs, *Brit* ˈvɑːstnəs/ *n* [U] • *the vastness of the ocean*

vat /ˈvæt/ *n* [C] : a large container used especially for holding liquids

VAT /ˌviːˌeɪˈtiː/ *n* [U] : VALUE-ADDED TAX

Vat·i·can /ˈvætɪkən/ *n* — **the Vatican** **1** : the place in Rome where the Pope lives and works **2** : the government of the Roman Catholic Church • *a Vatican official*

vaude·ville /ˈvɑːdvəl/ *n* [U] *US* : a type of entertainment that was popular in the U.S. in the late 19th and early 20th centuries and that had many different performers doing songs, dances, and comic acts • *a vaudeville performer/show* — **vaude·vil·lian** /ˌvɑːdˈvɪljən/ *n* [C]

¹vault /ˈvɑːlt/ *n* [C] **1** : a locked room where money or valuable things are kept • *a bank vault* **2** : a room or chamber in which a dead person is buried **3** : an instance of vaulting over something • *performing a difficult vault*

²vault *vb* [T/I] **1** : to jump over (something) especially by using your hands or a pole to push yourself upward • *She vaulted (over) the fence.* **2** *chiefly US* : to move suddenly and quickly into a better position • *He vaulted into the lead.* — **vault·er** /ˈvɑːltɚ/ *n* [C]

vault·ed /ˈvɑːltəd/ *adj* : built in the form of an arch • *vaulted ceilings*

vaunt·ed /ˈvɑːntəd/ *adj* : often praised • *the team's vaunted defense*

vb *abbr* verb

VCR /ˌviːˌsiːˈaɚ/ *n* [C] : a machine that is used to make and watch video recordings of TV programs, movies, etc.

VD *abbr* venereal disease

've /v *after vowels,* əv *after consonants*/ — used as a contraction of *have* • *I've* [=I have] *been busy.*

veal /ˈviːl/ *n* [U] : the meat of a young cow that is used for food

veer /ˈviɚ/ *vb* [I] : to change direction quickly or suddenly • *The car veered off the road.* • *(figurative) The story veers toward the ridiculous.*

¹veg /ˈvɛdʒ/ *vb* **veg·es; vegged; veg·ging** [I] *informal* : VEGETATE • *We vegged out in front of the TV.*

²veg *n, pl* **veg** [C/U] *chiefly Brit, informal* : VEGETABLE **1** • *meat and two veg*

veg·an /ˈviːgən/ *n* [C] : a person who does not eat any food that comes from animals and who often also does not use animal products (such as leather)

veg·e·ta·ble /ˈvɛdʒtəbəl/ *n* [C] **1** : a plant or plant part that is eaten as food • *fruits and vegetables* • *vegetable soup* **2** *sometimes offensive* : a person who is unable to talk, move, etc., because of severe brain damage • *The accident had left him a vegetable.*

veg·e·tar·i·an /ˌvɛdʒəˈterijən/ *n* [C] : a person who does not eat meat — **vegetarian** *adj* • *a vegetarian diet* — **veg·e·tar·i·an·ism** /ˌvɛdʒəˈterijəˌnɪzəm/ *n* [U]

veg·e·tate /ˈvɛdʒəˌteɪt/ *vb* **-tat·ed; -tat·ing** [I] : to spend much time doing things that do not require much thought or effort • *vegetating in front of the TV*

veg·e·ta·tion /ˌvɛdʒəˈteɪʃən/ *n* [U] : plants that cover a particular area • *the vegetation of the jungle*

veg·gie /ˈvɛdʒi/ *n* [C] *informal* **1** *chiefly US* : VEGETABLE **1** • *Eat your veggies.* **2** *chiefly Brit* : VEGETARIAN

ve·he·ment /ˈviːjəmənt/ *adj* : showing

strong and often angry feelings ▪ *a vehement critic* ▪ *vehement opposition* — **ve·he·mence** /ˈviːjəməns/ *n* [U] — **ve·he·ment·ly** *adv* ▪ *He vehemently denied the accusation.*

ve·hi·cle /ˈviːjəkəl/ *n* [C] **1** : a machine that is used to carry people or goods from one place to another ▪ *cars, trucks, and other vehicles* ▪ *a stolen vehicle* **2** : the thing that allows something to be passed along, expressed, achieved, or shown ▪ *art as a vehicle for self-expression*

ve·hic·u·lar /viˈhɪkjələ/ *adj* **1** : of, relating to, or designed for vehicles ▪ *vehicular traffic* **2** : caused by or resulting from the operation of a vehicle ▪ *vehicular homicide*

¹**veil** /ˈveɪl/ *n* [C] **1** : a piece of cloth or net worn usually by women over the head and shoulders and often over the face ▪ *a bridal veil* **2** : something that covers or hides something else ▪ *a veil of secrecy*

²**veil** *vb* [T] : to hide or partly hide (something) ▪ *The sun was veiled by clouds.*

veiled /ˈveɪld/ *adj* **1** : having or wearing a veil ▪ *a veiled hat* **2** : expressed in a way that is not clear or direct ▪ *a thinly veiled threat*

vein /ˈveɪn/ *n* **1** [C] : any one of the tubes that carry blood to the heart **2** [C] : a long, narrow opening in rock filled with gold, silver, etc. ▪ *a vein of gold/ore* **3** [C] : any one of the thin lines that can be seen on the surface of a leaf or on the wing of an insect **4** [*singular*] : a particular style, quality, etc. ▪ *stories in the romantic vein*

Vel·cro /ˈvɛlˌkroʊ/ *trademark* — used for a nylon fabric that can be fastened to itself

ve·loc·i·ty /vəˈlɑːsəti/ *n, pl* **-ties** [C/U] : ¹SPEED 1 ▪ *moving at high velocities*

ve·lour /vəˈlʊə/ *n* [U] : a type of cloth that resembles velvet

vel·vet /ˈvɛlvət/ *n* [C/U] : a soft type of cloth that has short raised fibers on one side — **velvet** *adj* ▪ *a velvet dress*

vel·vety /ˈvɛlvəti/ *adj* : soft and smooth ▪ *velvety hair*

ven·det·ta /vɛnˈdɛtə/ *n* [C] : a series of acts done to harm a disliked person or group ▪ *He has a vendetta against her.* [=he is trying to cause trouble for her]

vending machine *n* [C] : a machine that you put money into in order to buy food, cigarettes, etc.

ven·dor /ˈvɛndə/ *n* [C] **1** : a person who sells things especially on the street ▪ *a hot dog vendor* **2** : a business that sells a particular type of product ▪ *software vendors*

ve·neer /vəˈnɪə/ *n* **1** [C/U] : a thin layer of wood or other material that is attached to the surface of something ▪ *a dresser with (a) mahogany veneer* **2** [*singular*] : a way of behaving or appearing that gives other people a false idea of your true feelings or situation ▪ *her happy veneer*

ven·er·a·ble /ˈvɛnərəbəl/ *adj, formal* : old and respected ▪ *a venerable institution*

ven·er·ate /ˈvɛnəˌreɪt/ *vb* **-at·ed; -at·ing**

[T] *formal* : to feel or show deep respect for (someone or something) ▪ *a writer venerated by generations of admirers* — **ven·er·a·tion** /ˌvɛnəˈreɪʃən/ *n* [U]

ve·ne·re·al disease /vəˈnirijəl-/ *n* [C/U] : a disease that is passed from one person to another through sexual intercourse — *abbr. VD*

ve·ne·tian blind /vəˈniːʃən-/ *n* [C] : a covering for a window made of strips of wood, plastic, or metal that can be turned to block out or let in light

ven·geance /ˈvɛndʒəns/ *n* [U] : the act of doing something to hurt someone because that person did something that hurt you or someone else ▪ *inflicting vengeance on a killer* — **with a vengeance** : with great force or effort ▪ *She set to work with a vengeance.*

venge·ful /ˈvɛndʒfəl/ *adj* : feeling or showing a desire to harm someone who has harmed you ▪ *a vengeful former employee*

ven·i·son /ˈvɛnəsən/ *n* [U] : the meat of a deer

ven·om /ˈvɛnəm/ *n* [U] **1** : poison that is produced by an animal and used to kill or injure another animal **2** : a very strong feeling of anger or hatred ▪ *He spewed venom against his rival.* — **ven·om·ous** /ˈvɛnəməs/ *adj* ▪ *venomous snakes* ▪ *a venomous attack/comment*

¹**vent** /ˈvɛnt/ *vb* **1** [T] *US* : to allow (smoke, gas, etc.) to go out through an opening ▪ *Open the windows to vent the fumes.* **2** [T/I] : to express (an emotion) usually in a loud or angry manner ▪ *She vented (her frustrations) by kicking the car.*

²**vent** *n* [C] : an opening through which steam, smoke, etc., can go into or out of a room, machine, or container ▪ *a heating vent* **2** [*singular*] : an opportunity or a way to express a strong emotion that you have not openly shown ▪ *find a vent for his frustration* — **give vent to** : ¹VENT 2 ▪ *He gave vent to his annoyance.*

ven·ti·late /ˈvɛntəˌleɪt/ *vb* **-lat·ed; -lat·ing** [T] : to allow fresh air to enter and move through (a room, building, etc.) ▪ *a poorly ventilated room* — **ven·ti·la·tion** /ˌvɛntəˈleɪʃən/ *n* [U]

ven·ti·la·tor /ˈvɛntəˌleɪtə/ *n* [C] *medical* : RESPIRATOR 2

ven·tri·cle /ˈvɛntrəkəl/ *n* [C] *technical* : one of two sections of the heart that pump blood out to the body

ven·tril·o·quist /vɛnˈtrɪləkwɪst/ *n* [C] : a performer who speaks in a way that makes it appear that the words are being said by a large doll

¹**ven·ture** /ˈvɛntʃə/ *vb* **-tured; -tur·ing 1** [I] : to go somewhere that is unknown, dangerous, etc. ▪ *We ventured out into the woods.* **2** [I] : to start to do something new or different that usually involves risk ▪ *venturing on/upon a new project* **3** [T] : to do, say, or offer a suggestion, opinion, etc., even though you are not sure about it ▪ *venture a guess* — **nothing ventured, nothing gained** — used to say that it is worth trying to do something because you might succeed even though success is not certain

²**venture** n [C] : a new activity, project, business, etc., that typically involves risk ▪ *a joint business venture*

ven·ue /'vɛn.juː/ n [C] : the place where an event takes place ▪ *a sports/music venue* ▪ *the venue of the trial*

Ve·nus /'viːnəs/ n [singular] : the planet that is second in order from the sun

ve·rac·i·ty /vəˈræsəti/ n [U] formal : the quality of being true, accurate, or honest ▪ *We questioned the veracity of his statements.*

ve·ran·da or **ve·ran·dah** /vəˈrændə/ n [C] : PORCH 1

verb /'vɝb/ n [C] grammar : a word (such as *jump, think, happen,* or *exist*) that expresses an action, an occurrence, or a state of being

ver·bal /'vɝbəl/ adj 1 : relating to or consisting of words ▪ *She has strong verbal skills.* [=she is good at writing and speaking] ▪ *verbal abuse* [=harsh and insulting language] 2 : spoken rather than written ▪ *verbal agreements/instructions* — **ver·bal·ly** adv

ver·bal·ize also Brit **ver·bal·ise** /'vɝbə‑ˌlaɪz/ vb **‑ized; ‑iz·ing** [T] : to express (something) in words ▪ *She couldn't verbalize her feelings.*

ver·ba·tim /vɝˈbeɪtəm/ adj : in exactly the same words ▪ *a verbatim account of what was said* [=an account that gives the exact words that were spoken] — **ver·batim** adv ▪ *She recited the poem verbatim.*

ver·bose /vɝˈboʊs/ adj, formal : using more words than are needed ▪ *He is a verbose speaker.*

ver·dant /'vɝdnt/ adj, literary : green with growing plants ▪ *verdant fields*

ver·dict /'vɝdɪkt/ n [C] 1 law : the decision made by a jury in a trial ▪ *The verdict was not guilty.* 2 : a judgment or opinion about something ▪ *The critic's verdict about the show was positive.*

¹**verge** /'vɝdʒ/ n — **on the verge of** : at the point when (something) is about to happen or is very likely to happen ▪ *a company on the verge of bankruptcy* [=close to going bankrupt] ▪ *I was on the verge of tears.* [=almost crying]

²**verge** vb **verged; verg·ing** — **verge on** [phrasal vb] : to come near to being (something) ▪ *comedy that verges on farce* [=that is almost farce]

ver·i·fy /'vɛrəˌfaɪ/ vb **‑fies; ‑fied; ‑fy·ing** [T] : to prove, show, find out, or state that (something) is true or correct ▪ *We could not verify the rumor.* ▪ *He verified that the item was in stock.* — **ver·i·fi·able** /ˌvɛrəˈfajəbəl/ adj ▪ *a verifiable claim* — **ver·i·fi·ca·tion** /ˌvɛrəfəˈkeɪʃən/ n [U] ▪ *He received verification of the change.*

ver·i·ta·ble /'vɛrətəbəl/ adj, always before a noun — used to emphasize a description ▪ *The island is a veritable paradise.*

ver·min /'vɝmən/ n [plural] : small insects and animals that are sometimes harmful to plants or other animals ▪ *roaches, mice, and other vermin*

ver·mouth /vɝˈmuːθ/ n [U] : a type of flavored wine that is often mixed with other alcoholic drinks

ver·nac·u·lar /vɚˈnækjələ/ n [C] : the language of ordinary speech rather than formal writing ▪ *the vernacular of teenagers*

ver·nal /'vɝnl/ adj, formal : of, relating to, or occurring in the spring ▪ *vernal breezes* ▪ *the vernal equinox*

ver·sa·tile /'vɝsətl̩, Brit 'vɝsəˌtajəl/ adj 1 : able to do many different things ▪ *a versatile athlete* 2 : having many different uses ▪ *a versatile tool/outfit* — **ver·sa·til·i·ty** /ˌvɝsəˈtɪləti/ n [U]

verse /'vɝs/ n 1 [U] : POETRY 1 ▪ *a tale written in verse* 2 [C] : a part of a poem or song ▪ *the song's second verse* 3 [C] : one of the parts of a chapter of the Bible — **chapter and verse** see CHAPTER

versed /'vɝst/ adj : having knowledge about something ▪ *He is well versed in French cooking.*

ver·sion /'vɝʒən, Brit 'vɝʃən/ n [C] 1 : a story or description that is different in some way from another person's story or description ▪ *Let me tell you my version of what happened.* 2 : a form of something (such as a product) that is different in some way from other forms ▪ *an older version of the software*

ver·sus /'vɝsəs, 'vɝsəz/ prep 1 — used to indicate the two people, teams, etc., that are competing against each other or that are opposed to each other in a legal case ▪ *I felt like it was me versus* [=against] *the world.* ▪ *the State versus John Smith* — abbr. *vs., v.* 2 — used to indicate two things, choices, etc., that are being compared or considered ▪ *a choice of going out versus staying home*

ver·te·bra /'vɝtəbrə/ n, pl **‑brae** /‑ˌbreɪ/ or **‑bras** [C] technical : one of the small bones that are linked together to form the backbone

ver·te·brate /'vɝtəbrət/ n [C] biology : an animal that has a backbone — **vertebrate** adj

ver·ti·cal /'vɝtɪkəl/ adj : going straight up ▪ *a shirt with vertical stripes* — **vertical** n [C] — **ver·ti·cal·ly** /'vɝtɪkli/ adv

ver·ti·go /'vɝtɪˌgoʊ/ n [U] : a feeling of dizziness caused especially by being in a very high place

verve /'vɝv/ n [U] : great energy and enthusiasm ▪ *She played with skill and verve.*

¹**very** /'vɛri/ adv 1 : to a great degree — used for emphasis before adjectives and adverbs ▪ *a very hot day* ▪ *a very small number/amount* ▪ *Check very carefully.* ▪ *The food wasn't very good.* ▪ *"Were you surprised?" "Yes, very."* 2 — used to emphasize the exactness of a description ▪ *We left the very next day.* — **very good** see ¹GOOD — **very much so** — used to say "yes" or to say that you agree with something ▪ *"Were you surprised?" "Yes, very much so."* — **very well** 1 somewhat old-fashioned — used to say that you agree with something ▪ *Oh, very well. Do as you please.* 2 : reasonably or properly ▪ *I can't very well show up uninvited.* [=it would be improper for me to show up uninvited]

²**very** adj, always before a noun 1 — used to emphasize that you are talking about

one specific thing or part and not another • *There's the very book I was looking for.* • *They are meeting at this very moment.* [=right now] **2** : not having anything added or extra • *You could try to help, at the very least* [=you could at least try to help] **3** — used to emphasize that something belongs to or is part of a particular person or thing • *He disappeared before our very eyes!* • *a room of my very own* [=a room I do not have to share]

ves·sel /ˈvɛsəl/ *n* [C] **1** *formal* : a ship or large boat • *a fishing/sailing vessel* **2** *old-fashioned* : a container for holding liquids • *a drinking vessel*

¹vest /ˈvɛst/ *n* [C] **1** *US* : a sleeveless piece of clothing with buttons down the front that is worn over a shirt and under a suit jacket **2** : a special piece of clothing that you wear on your upper body for protection or safety • *a bulletproof vest* • *(US) a life vest* — **close to the vest** see ²CLOSE

²vest *vb* [T] *formal* : to give (someone) the legal right or power to do something or to own land or property • *I am fully vested in the company pension plan.* [=I have earned the right to get a full pension when I retire]

vested interest *n* [C] : a personal or private reason for wanting something to be done or to happen • *She has a vested interest in seeing the business sold.*

ves·ti·bule /ˈvɛstəˌbjuːl/ *n* [C] *formal* : an entrance hall inside a building

ves·tige /ˈvɛstɪdʒ/ *n* [C] *formal* : the last small part that remains of something that existed before • TRACE • *He is still clinging to the last vestiges of his power.*

¹vet /ˈvɛt/ *n* [C] **1** : VETERINARIAN • *I took my dog to the vet.* **2** *US, informal* : VETERAN • *a World War II vet*

²vet *vb* **vet·ted; vet·ting** [T] **1** : to investigate (someone) to see if they should be given a job • *They vetted her before offering her the job.* **2** : to check (something) carefully to make sure it is acceptable • *The book was vetted by two editors.*

vet·er·an /ˈvɛtərən/ *n* [C] **1** : someone who fought in a war as a soldier, sailor, etc. • *a Navy veteran* **2** : someone who has a lot of experience in a particular activity, job, etc. • *a teaching veteran* • *a 10-year veteran of the team* — **veteran** *adj* • *a veteran politician/player*

Veterans Day *n* [C/U] : a holiday observed on November 11 in the U.S. to honor veterans of the armed forces

vet·er·i·nar·i·an /ˌvɛtərəˈnɛrijən/ *n* [C] *chiefly US* : a person who is trained to give medical care to animals — called also *vet*, *(Brit, formal) veterinary surgeon*

vet·er·i·nary /ˈvɛtərəˌnɛri, Brit ˈvɛtnri/ *adj* : relating to the medical care of animals • *veterinary medicine*

¹ve·to /ˈviːtoʊ/ *n, pl* **-toes** [C] **1** : a decision by a person in authority to not allow or approve something • *Congress may override the President's veto (of the bill/law).* **2** [U] : the right or power of a person to use a veto • *The President chose to exercise his veto (power).*

²veto *vb* **-toes; -toed; -to·ing** [T] **1** : to refuse to allow (a bill) to become a law • *The President vetoed the bill.* **2** : to refuse to allow or accept (a plan, suggestion, etc.) • *She vetoed our vacation plans.*

vex /ˈvɛks/ *vb* [T] *old-fashioned* : to annoy or worry (someone) • *This problem has vexed her for years.* — **vexing** *adj* • *a vexing problem*

VHF *abbr* very high frequency — used for a range of radio waves that is used in broadcasting, communications, and navigation

via /ˈvaɪə, ˈviːjə/ *prep* **1** : by going through (a particular place) • *She flew to Los Angeles via Chicago.* **2** : by using (something or someone) • *tracking via satellite*

vi·a·ble /ˈvaɪjəbəl/ *adj* **1 a** : capable of being done or used • *a viable solution/alternative* **b** : capable of succeeding • *Is she a viable candidate?* **2** *technical* : capable of living or of developing into a living thing • *viable seeds/eggs* — **vi·a·bil·i·ty** /ˌvaɪjəˈbɪləti/ *n* [U]

vi·a·duct /ˈvaɪjəˌdʌkt/ *n* [C] : a long, high bridge over a valley

vi·al /ˈvajəl/ *n* [C] : a very small glass or plastic container

vibe /ˈvaɪb/ *n* [C] *informal* : a feeling that someone or something gives you • *I got a good/bad vibe from her.*

vi·brant /ˈvaɪbrənt/ *adj* **1** : having or showing great life, activity, and energy • *a vibrant personality/city* **2** : bright, strong, or loud • *vibrant colors/music* — **vi·bran·cy** /ˈvaɪbrənsi/ *n* [U] — **vi·brant·ly** *adv*

vi·brate /ˈvaɪˌbreɪt, Brit vaɪˈbreɪt/ *vb* **-brat·ed; -brat·ing** [T/I] : to move back and forth or from side to side with very short, quick movements • *The engine was vibrating.*

vi·bra·tion /vaɪˈbreɪʃən/ *n* **1** [C/U] : a series of small, fast movements back and forth or from side to side • *vibration(s) from the engine* **2** [plural] *informal* : a feeling that someone or something gives you • *giving off good/bad vibrations* [=vibes]

vi·bra·tor /ˈvaɪˌbreɪtɚ, Brit vaɪˈbreɪtə/ *n* [C] : an electronic device that vibrates and that is used especially for massage or sexual pleasure

vic·ar /ˈvɪkɚ/ *n* [C] **1** : a priest in the Church of England who is in charge of a church and the area around it **2** *US* : a pastor's assistant in an Episcopalian or Lutheran church

vi·car·i·ous /vaɪˈkɛrijəs/ *adj* : experienced by watching or hearing about someone else rather than by doing something yourself • *a vicarious thrill/joy* — **vi·car·i·ous·ly** *adv* • *She lived vicariously through her children.*

¹vice /ˈvaɪs/ *n* **1** [C] : a moral flaw or weakness • *He thought gambling was a vice.* **2** [C] : a minor bad habit • *Eating too much is my vice.* **3** [U] : criminal activities that involve sex or drugs • *the vice squad* [=police officers who investigate crimes involving sex or drugs]

²vice *Brit spelling of* VISE

vice-chan·cel·lor /ˌvaɪsˈtʃænslɚ, Brit ˌvaɪsˈtʃɑːnslə/ *n* [C] **1** : a person who has a rank just below that of a chancellor **2** : the person who runs a British university

vice president also **vice–president** n [C] : a person whose rank is just below that of the president of a country, business, etc. • a former Vice President of the United States — **vice presidency** n [C]

vice ver·sa /ˌvaɪsˈvɚsə/ adv — used to say that the opposite of a statement is also true • She influenced his career, and vice versa. [=and he also influenced her career]

vi·cin·i·ty /vəˈsɪnəti/ n [singular] : the area around or near a particular place • She lives in Boston, or somewhere in that/ the vicinity. [=somewhere near there] — **in the vicinity of 1** : in the area that is close to (a place) • He lives in the vicinity of the school. **2** : close to or around (an amount) • a salary in the vicinity of $100,000

vi·cious /ˈvɪʃəs/ adj **1** : very violent and cruel • a vicious attack/battle **2** : very dangerous • a vicious dog **3** : having or showing very angry or cruel feelings • vicious gossip **4** informal : very bad or severe • a vicious headache — **vi·cious·ly** adv — **vi·cious·ness** n [U]

vicious circle n [singular] : a situation in which one problem causes another problem that makes the first problem worse • We're trapped in a vicious circle. — called also vicious cycle

vi·cis·si·tudes /vəˈsɪsəˌtuːdz, Brit vəˈsɪsəˌtjuːdz/ n [plural] formal : the many changes or problems that happen over time • the vicissitudes of life

vic·tim /ˈvɪktəm/ n [C] **1** : a person who has been hurt or killed by someone else • a victim of abuse • a murder victim **2** : someone or something that is harmed by an unpleasant event (such as an illness or accident) • a victim of a hoax • a tornado victim — **fall victim to 1** : to be hurt or killed by (someone or something) • She fell victim to a serial killer. **2** : to be affected badly by (something) • schools falling victim to budget cuts

vic·tim·ize also Brit **vic·tim·ise** /ˈvɪktəˌmaɪz/ vb **-ized; -iz·ing** [T] **1** : to treat (someone) cruelly or unfairly • They were victimized because of their religion. **2** chiefly US : to harm or commit a crime against (someone) • people who are victimized by thieves/theft [=people who are robbed] — **vic·tim·i·za·tion** also Brit **vic·tim·i·sa·tion** /ˌvɪktəməˈzeɪʃən, Brit ˌvɪktəˌmaɪˈzeɪʃən/ n [U]

vic·tor /ˈvɪktɚ/ n [C] formal : WINNER **1** • Who will emerge the victor? [=who will win?]

Vic·to·ri·an /vɪkˈtorijən/ adj **1** : relating to or typical of the period from 1837–1901 when Queen Victoria ruled England • a Victorian house • the Victorian age **2** : similar to the old-fashioned moral values that were typical during the time of Queen Victoria • Victorian attitudes toward sex

vic·to·ri·ous /vɪkˈtorijəs/ adj : having won a victory or having ended in a victory • the victorious army/side • Who will emerge victorious? [=who will win?] —

vic·to·ri·ous·ly adv

vic·to·ry /ˈvɪktəri/ n, pl **-ries 1** [C/U] : success in defeating an opponent or enemy • the thrill of victory • a victory speech • The passage of the law was a great victory for their cause. **2** [C] : the act of defeating an opponent or enemy • the team's fifth straight victory

¹**vid·eo** /ˈvɪdijoʊ/ n, pl **-eos 1** [C] : a movie, TV show, event, etc., that has been recorded onto a videocassette, DVD, etc., so that it can be watched on a TV or computer screen • Let's rent a video. • the show we saw on the Internet • home videos [=recordings made by ordinary people using a video camera] **2** [U] : VIDEOTAPE • watching a movie on video **3** [C] : a recorded performance of a song in which visual images are shown together with the music • She released her new music video on the Internet. **4** [U] : the images seen in a recording or broadcast • The audio is OK but there's a problem with the video. **5** [C] Brit : VCR

²**video** adj, always before a noun **1** : of or relating to the images seen in a recording or broadcast • the video portion of the broadcast **2** : of, relating to, or involving videos that are shown on a TV or computer screen • video equipment • a short video clip

video camera n [C] : a camera that is used to create videos by recording moving images and sounds onto a videotape, computer disk, etc.

vid·eo·cas·sette /ˌvɪdijoʊkəˈsɛt/ n [C/U] : a plastic case that holds videotape and that is played using a VCR

vid·eo·con·fer·enc·ing /ˌvɪdijoʊˈkɑːnfrənsɪŋ/ n [U] : a method of holding meetings that allows people who are in different cities, countries, etc., to hear and see each other on computer or TV screens — **vid·eo·con·fer·ence** /ˌvɪdijoʊˈkɑːnfrəns/ n [C]

video game n [C] : an electronic game in which players control images on a TV or computer screen

vid·eo·tape /ˈvɪdijoʊˌteɪp/ n [U] : tape on which movies, TV shows, etc., can be recorded. — **videotape** vb **-taped; -tap·ing** [T] • We videotaped the show.

vie /ˈvaɪ/ vb **vied; vy·ing** /ˈvajɪŋ/ [I] : to compete with others in an attempt to get or win something • They vied (with each other) for her attention.

¹**view** /ˈvjuː/ n **1** [C] : an opinion or way of thinking about something • her political views = her views on/about politics • In my view the plan will fail. [=I think that the plan will fail] • He takes the view [=he believes] that the economy will improve. **2** [C] : the things that can be seen from a particular place • a scenic/spectacular view • a room with a view [=a room that allows you to see a beautiful or interesting scene from your window] **3** [C/U] — used to say that something can or cannot be seen • You're blocking my view. • The ship disappeared from view. • The robbery was committed in (full) view of some tourists. — **in plain view** see ¹PLAIN — **in view of 1** : when thinking

about or considering (something) ▪ *His current support is surprising in view of his earlier opposition.* **2** : because of (something) ▪ *In view of your late payment, you'll have to pay a fine.* — **on view** : available to be seen ▪ *His paintings are on view* [=are being displayed] *at the museum.* — **with a view to** : with the hope or goal of (doing something) ▪ *reorganizing a department with a view to making it more efficient*

²**view** *vb* [T] **1** : to look at (something) carefully ▪ *viewing the evidence in a court case* **2** : to see or watch (a movie, a TV show, etc.) ▪ *The program was viewed by millions of people.* **3** : to think about (someone or something) in a particular way ▪ *Students viewed the new rules with contempt.* — **view·ing** /ˈvjuːwɪŋ/ *n* [C] ▪ *the first viewing of a film*

view·er /ˈvjuːwə/ *n* [C] : a person who watches TV ▪ *viewers of the evening news*

view·point /ˈvjuːˌpoɪnt/ *n* [C] : POINT OF VIEW ▪ *a story told from the viewpoint of a child*

vig·il /ˈvɪdʒəl/ *n* [C/U] : an event or a period of time when a person or group quietly waits, prays, etc., especially at night ▪ *They held a candlelight vigil for the killer outside the prison.* [=they held candles and waited for him to be executed or pardoned] ▪ *She kept vigil at his bedside.* [=she sat beside his bed]

vig·i·lant /ˈvɪdʒələnt/ *adj* : carefully noticing problems or signs of danger ▪ *a vigilant parent* — **vig·i·lance** /ˈvɪdʒələns/ *n* [U] — **vig·i·lant·ly** *adv*

vig·i·lan·te /ˌvɪdʒəˈlænti/ *n* [C] : a person who is not a police officer but who tries to catch and punish criminals ▪ *vigilante groups*

vig·or (US) or Brit **vig·our** /ˈvɪgə/ *n* [U] : strength, energy, or determination ▪ *She defended her beliefs with vigor.* — **vim and vigor** see VIM

vig·or·ous /ˈvɪgərəs/ *adj* **1** : healthy and strong ▪ *She remained vigorous into her nineties.* **2** : done with great force and energy ▪ *a vigorous argument/debate* ▪ *20 minutes of vigorous exercise* — **vig·or·ous·ly** *adv*

Vi·king /ˈvaɪkɪŋ/ *n* [C] : a member of a group of people who attacked the coasts of Europe in the 8th to 10th centuries A.D. ▪ *a Viking ship*

vile /ˈvajəl/ *adj* **vil·er; -est** **1** : evil or immoral ▪ *vile acts* **2** : very bad or unpleasant ▪ *a vile odor* ▪ *She has a vile temper.* — **vile·ly** *adv* — **vile·ness** *n* [U]

vil·i·fy /ˈvɪləˌfaɪ/ *vb* **-fies; -fied; -fy·ing** [T] *formal* : to say or write very harsh and critical things about (someone or something) ▪ *He was vilified in the press.* — **vil·i·fi·ca·tion** /ˌvɪləfəˈkeɪʃən/ *n* [U]

vil·la /ˈvɪlə/ *n* [C] **1** : a large house or estate that is usually located in the country **2** : a house that you can rent and live in when on vacation ▪ *a seaside villa*

vil·lage /ˈvɪlɪdʒ/ *n* [C] : a small town in the country ▪ *fishing/mining villages* [=villages in which most people fish/mine as a job] **2** : the people who live in a village ▪ *Entire villages come to see the parade.*

vil·lag·er /ˈvɪlɪdʒə/ *n* [C] : a person who lives in a village

vil·lain /ˈvɪlən/ *n* [C] **1** : a character in a story, movie, etc., who does bad things ▪ *comic-book heroes and villains* **2** : someone or something that is blamed for a problem or difficulty ▪ *Don't try to make me the villain.* **3** Brit, informal : ²CRIMINAL

vil·lain·ous /ˈvɪlənəs/ *adj* : very bad or evil ▪ WICKED ▪ *a villainous attack/criminal*

vil·lainy /ˈvɪləni/ *n* [U] *formal* : evil behavior or actions ▪ *a story of villainy and betrayal*

vim /ˈvɪm/ *n* — **vim and vigor** (US) or Brit **vim and vigour** : energy and enthusiasm ▪ *full of vim and vigor*

vin·ai·grette /ˌvɪnɪˈgrɛt/ *n* [C/U] : a mixture of oil, vinegar, and seasonings that is used as a salad dressing

vin·di·cate /ˈvɪndəˌkeɪt/ *vb* **-cat·ed; -cat·ing** [T] **1** : to show that (someone) is not guilty ▪ *She was vindicated by the evidence.* **2** : to show that (someone or something that has been criticized or doubted) is correct, true, or reasonable ▪ *He felt vindicated when the truth became known.* — **vin·di·ca·tion** /ˌvɪndəˈkeɪʃən/ *n* [U, singular]

vin·dic·tive /vɪnˈdɪktɪv/ *adj, disapproving* : having or showing a desire to hurt someone who has hurt or caused problems for you ▪ *a bitter and vindictive person* — **vin·dic·tive·ness** *n* [U]

vine /ˈvaɪn/ *n* [C] : a plant that has very long stems and that grows along the ground or up and around something

vin·e·gar /ˈvɪnɪgə/ *n* [C/U] : a sour liquid that is used to flavor or preserve foods or to clean things — **vin·e·gary** /ˈvɪnɪgəri/ *adj*

vine·yard /ˈvɪnjəd/ *n* [C] : a field where grapes are grown

vin·tage /ˈvɪntɪdʒ/ *adj, always before a noun* **1** — used to describe a wine of high quality that was produced in a particular year ▪ *a selection of vintage wines* **2** — used to describe something that is not new but that is valued because of its good condition, attractive design, etc. ▪ *vintage clothing/cars*

vi·nyl /ˈvaɪnl/ *n* [U] : a plastic material that is used to make records, flooring, etc. ▪ *vinyl siding/tablecloths*

vi·o·la /viˈoʊlə/ *n* [C] : a musical instrument that is like a violin but slightly larger

vi·o·late /ˈvaɪəˌleɪt/ *vb* **-lat·ed; -lat·ing** [T] **1 a** : to do something that is not allowed by (a law, rule, etc.) ▪ *He violated his parole.* **b** : to interfere with or ignore (a person's rights, privacy, etc.) in an unfair or illegal way ▪ *My rights were violated.* [=I was treated unfairly] **2** *formal* : ¹RAPE ▪ *He attacked and violated her.* — **vi·o·la·tion** /ˌvaɪəˈleɪʃən/ *n* [C/U] ▪ *human rights violations* ▪ *a violation of the law* ▪ *acting in violation of the law* [=in a way that is illegal] — **vi·o·la·tor** /ˈvaɪəˌleɪtə/ *n* [C]

vi·o·lence /ˈvaɪələns/ *n* [U] **1** : the use of physical force to harm someone, to damage property, etc. ▪ *an act of violence*

• **domestic violence** [=acts or threats of physical harm that happen in the home] **2** : great destructive force or energy ▪ *the violence of the storm*

vi·o·lent /ˈvajələnt/ *adj* **1** : using or involving the use of physical force to cause harm or damage to someone or something ▪ *a violent crime/protest* : showing violence ▪ *violent movies* **2** : caused by physical force or violence ▪ *She suffered a violent death.* **3 a** : trying to physically attack someone because of anger ▪ *The patient became violent.* **b** : likely to physically attack other people ▪ *violent criminals* **4** : very forceful or intense ▪ *a violent argument* **5** : very powerful and able to cause damage ▪ *violent storms/winds* — **vi·o·lent·ly** *adv* ▪ *We were violently attacked.* ▪ *She became violently ill.* [=she vomited]

vi·o·let /ˈvajələt/ *n* **1** [C] : a plant that has small bluish-purple or white flowers **2** [C/U] : a bluish-purple color — **violet** *adj*

vi·o·lin /ˌvajəˈlɪn/ *n* [C] : a musical instrument that has four strings and that you usually hold under your chin and play with a bow

vi·o·lin·ist /ˌvajəˈlɪnɪst/ *n* [C] : a person who plays the violin

VIP /ˌviːˌaɪˈpiː/ *n, pl* **VIPs** /ˌviːˌaɪˈpiːz/ [C] *informal* : a very important person ▪ *I was treated like a VIP.*

vi·per /ˈvaɪpə/ *n* [C] : a type of poisonous snake

vi·ral /ˈvaɪrəl/ *adj* : caused by a virus ▪ *viral diseases/infections*

¹**vir·gin** /ˈvɚdʒən/ *n* [C] **1** : a person who has not had sex **2** : a person who does not have experience in a particular activity, job, etc. ▪ *a political virgin*

²**virgin** *adj* **1** : never having had sex ▪ *a virgin bride* **2** : not affected by human activity ▪ *virgin forests/snow* **3** *of olive oil* : obtained from the first light pressing of olives ▪ *extra virgin olive oil* **4** : used or worked for the first time ▪ *virgin wool/timber* — **virgin territory** : an experience or situation that is new for someone ▪ *This is virgin territory for us.*

vir·gin·al /ˈvɚdʒənl/ *adj* **1** : having a young, pure, and innocent quality ▪ *a virginal young girl* **2** : not changed from a natural or original condition ▪ *wood in its virginal state*

vir·gin·i·ty /vɚˈdʒɪnəti/ *n* [U] : the state of never having had sex ▪ *He lost his virginity.* [=he had sex for the first time]

Vir·go /ˈvɚgoʊ/ *n, pl* **-gos** **1** [U] : the sixth sign of the zodiac that comes between Leo and Libra and that has a Virgin as its symbol **2** [C] : a person born between August 23 and September 22 ▪ *Are you a Virgo?*

vir·ile /ˈvɪrəl, Brit ˈvɪˌraɪl/ *adj* : having or suggesting qualities that are associated with men and that are usually considered attractive in men ▪ *virile young athletes* — **vi·ril·i·ty** /vəˈrɪləti/ *n* [U]

vir·tu·al /ˈvɚtʃəwəl/ *adj, always before a noun* **1** : very close to being something without actually being it ▪ *Her victory is a virtual certainty.* [=she almost certainly will win] **2** : existing or occurring on

computers or on the Internet ▪ *virtual shopping*

vir·tu·al·ly /ˈvɚtʃəwəli/ *adv* : very nearly : almost entirely ▪ *The stadium was virtually empty.* ▪ *I remember virtually everything he said.*

virtual reality *n* [U] : an artificial world created by a computer that is affected by the actions of a person who is experiencing it

vir·tue /ˈvɚtʃuː/ *n* **1** [U] : morally good behavior or character ▪ *leading a life of virtue* [=living virtuously] **2** [C] : a good and moral quality ▪ *Patience is a virtue.* **3** [U] : the good result that comes from something ▪ *She learned the virtue of hard work.* [=that hard work is important and valuable] **4** [C] : an advantage or benefit ▪ *One of the virtues of this job is the flexible hours.* — **by virtue of** : because of (something) ▪ *She can participate by virtue of her being a former employee.*

vir·tu·o·so /ˌvɚtʃuˈoʊsoʊ/ *n, pl* **-sos** **-si** /-siː/ [C] : a person who does something in a very skillful way ▪ *a piano virtuoso* — **virtuoso** *adj, always before a noun* ▪ *She gave a virtuoso performance.*

vir·tu·ous /ˈvɚtʃəwəs/ *adj* : morally good ▪ *a virtuous man* ▪ *virtuous behavior* — **vir·tu·ous·ly** *adv* — **vir·tu·ous·ness** *n* [U]

vir·u·lent /ˈvɪrələnt/ *adj* **1** : full of hate or anger ▪ *virulent racists/racism* **b** : extremely harsh or strong ▪ *virulent criticism* **2** : extremely dangerous and deadly and usually spreading very quickly ▪ *a virulent disease* — **vir·u·lence** /ˈvɪrələns/ *n* [U] — **vir·u·lent·ly** *adv*

vi·rus /ˈvaɪrəs/ *n* [C] **1** : an extremely small living thing that causes a disease and that spreads from one person or animal to another ▪ *the AIDS virus* **2** : a disease or illness caused by a virus ▪ *a stomach virus* **3** *computers* : a program that is designed to harm a computer by deleting data, ruining files, etc., and that can be spread secretly from one computer to another ▪ *The software checks your hard drive for viruses.*

vi·sa /ˈviːzə/ *n* [C] : an official mark or stamp on a passport that allows someone to enter or leave a country usually for a particular reason ▪ *a work/student visa*

vis·age /ˈvɪzɪdʒ/ *n* [C] *literary* : a person's face ▪ *his smiling visage*

vis·cer·al /ˈvɪsərəl/ *adj* : coming from strong emotions and not from logic or reason ▪ *Her visceral reaction was to yell at the other driver.* — **vis·cer·al·ly** *adv*

vis·cous /ˈvɪskəs/ *adj, of a liquid* : thick or sticky — **vis·cos·i·ty** /vɪˈskɑːsəti/ *n, pl* **-ties** [C/U] ▪ *a liquid with (a) high/low viscosity*

vise (*US*) *or Brit* **vice** /ˈvaɪs/ *n* [C] : a tool that is attached to a table and that has two flat parts that can be closed to hold something very firmly — **vise-like** (*US*) *or Brit* **vice-like** /ˈvaɪsˌlaɪk/ *adj* ▪ *He had a viselike* [=very firm] *grip.*

vis·i·bil·i·ty /ˌvɪzəˈbɪləti/ *n* [U] **1** : the ability to see or be seen — used to describe how far you are able to see because of weather conditions, darkness, etc. ▪ *The fog was very heavy and visibility* *was low/poor.* **2** : the quality or state of being known to the public • *increasing the company's visibility*

vis·i·ble /'vɪzəbəl/ *adj* **1** : able to be seen • *The ship was not visible through the fog.* **2** : easily seen or understood : OBVIOUS • *a visible change in his mood* **3** : known to or noticed by the public • *a highly visible politician* — **vis·i·bly** /'vɪzəbli/ *adv* • *He was visibly upset.*

vi·sion /'vɪʒən/ *n* **1** [*U*] : the ability to see • *She has good/poor vision.* • *a vision test* **2** [*C*] : something that you dream or see in your mind • *the architect's vision for the new building* • *The idea came to me in a vision.* **3** [*C/U*] : a clear idea about what should happen or be done in the future • *a leader with (a) vision* **4** [*C*] : a beautiful person or thing • *She was a vision (of beauty).*

vi·sion·ary /'vɪʒəˌneri, *Brit* 'vɪʒənri/ *adj* **1** : having or showing clear ideas about what should happen or be done in the future • *a visionary leader* **2** : having or showing a powerful imagination • *a visionary poet* — **visionary** *n, pl* **-ar·ies** [*C*] • *She's a visionary in her field.*

¹**vis·it** /'vɪzət/ *vb* **1 a** [*T/I*] : to go somewhere to spend time with (a friend, relative, etc.) • *She is visiting (with) her aunt in New York.* **b** [*T*] : to go somewhere to see and talk to (someone) in an official way • *He is visiting a client in Phoenix.* **c** [*T*] : to go to see (a doctor, dentist, etc.) • *She visits her doctor regularly.* **2** [*T*] : to go to (a place) for pleasure, as part of your job, etc. • *I would like to visit Rome someday.* **3** [*T*] : to go to (a Web site) on the Internet • *Be sure to visit our Web site.* — **visit with** [*phrasal vb*] *US* : to spend time talking informally with (someone) • *I got to visit with her for a few minutes.*

²**visit** *n* [*C*] : an occasion when someone visits a person or place • *Is this your first visit to the U.S.?* • *a doctor's visit = a visit to the doctor's office* • *We had a visit from the company president.* • *He paid a visit to his parents.*

vis·i·ta·tion /ˌvɪzəˈteɪʃən/ *n* **1** [*U*] *law* : the act of visiting or the right to visit your children after you are divorced and while they are living with their other parent • *He has visitation rights on the weekends.* **2** [*C*] *US* : a time before a dead person is buried when people may view the body • *Visitation is from 8:00 to 10:00 a.m.*

vis·it·ing /'vɪzətɪŋ/ *adj* **1** — used to describe someone (such as a teacher) who goes to work for a limited time at a different school, college, etc. • *a visiting professor* **2** *sports* : playing on the field or court of an opponent • *the visiting team*

vis·i·tor /'vɪzətə/ *n* [*C*] : someone who visits a person or place • *We are expecting visitors.* • *The museum gets hundreds of visitors each day.*

vi·sor /'vaɪzə/ *n* [*C*] **1** : a piece on the front of a helmet that you can pull down to protect your face **2** *US* : the part of a hat or cap that sticks out in front to protect or shade your eyes **3** : a flat, stiff piece of material on the inside of a car above the windshield that you can pull

down to shade your eyes

vis·ta /'vɪstə/ *n* [*C*] : a large and beautiful view of an area • *mountain vistas*

¹**vi·su·al** /'vɪʒəwəl/ *adj* : relating to seeing or to the eyes • *a visual impairment* • *the visual arts* [=painting, film, etc.] — **vi·su·al·ly** *adv* • *He is visually impaired.* [=he cannot see well]

²**visual** *n* [*C*] : a picture, chart, film, etc., that is used to make something more appealing or easier to understand • *Include visuals in your presentation.*

visual aid *n* [*C*] : a picture, chart, film, etc., that makes something easier to understand

vi·su·al·ize *also Brit* **vi·su·al·ise** /'vɪʒəwəˌlaɪz/ *vb* **-ized; -iz·ing** [*T*] : IMAGINE **1** • *I can't visualize her as a parent.* — **vi·su·al·i·za·tion** *also Brit* **vi·su·al·i·sa·tion** /ˌvɪʒəwələˈzeɪʃən, *Brit* ˌvɪʒəwəˌlaɪˈzeɪʃən/ *n* [*C/U*]

vi·tal /'vaɪtl/ *adj* **1** : extremely important • *He had a vital role in the project.* • *matters vital to national defense* • *Your cooperation is vital.* = *Your cooperation is of vital importance.* **2** *always before a noun* : needed by your body in order to keep living • *your heart, lungs, and other vital organs* — **vi·tal·ly** *adv* • *vitally important*

vi·tal·i·ty /vaɪˈtæləti/ *n* [*U*] **1** : a lively or energetic quality • *the vitality of youth* • *A shopping mall would bring new vitality to the area.* **2** : the power or ability of something to continue to exist, be successful, etc. • *the economic vitality of our cities*

vi·tal·ize /'vaɪtəˌlaɪz/ *vb* **-ized; -iz·ing** [*T*] *chiefly US* : to give life or energy to (something) • *Will cutting taxes vitalize the economy?*

vi·tals /'vaɪtlz/ *n* [*plural*] *US, informal* : VITAL SIGNS

vital signs *n* [*plural*] : important body functions (such as breathing and heartbeat) that are measured to see if someone is alive or healthy • *Check the patient's vital signs.*

vi·ta·min /'vaɪtəmən, *Brit* 'vɪtəmən/ *n* [*C*] **1** : a natural substance that helps your body to be healthy • *a cereal with added vitamins and minerals* • *a good source of vitamin C/D/A/E* **2** : a pill containing vitamins • *Take your vitamins.*

vit·ri·ol /'vɪtrijəl/ *n* [*U*] *formal* : harsh and angry words • *His speech was full of vitriol.* — **vit·ri·ol·ic** /ˌvɪtriˈɑːlɪk/ *adj* • *a vitriolic debate*

vi·va·cious /vəˈveɪʃəs/ *adj* : happy and lively • *a vivacious young woman* — **vi·vac·i·ty** /vəˈvæsəti/ *n* [*U*]

viv·id /'vɪvəd/ *adj* **1** *of a picture, memory, etc.* : seeming like real life because it is very clear, bright, or detailed • *a vivid description/memory* • *He has a very vivid imagination.* [=he can imagine things very clearly and easily] **2** : very bright in color • *a vivid red* — **viv·id·ly** *adv* • *I remember it vividly.* — **viv·id·ness** *n* [*U*]

vix·en /'vɪksən/ *n* [*C*] **1** : a female fox **2** *informal* : a sexually attractive woman

V-neck /'viːˌnɛk/ *n* [*C*] : a shirt, sweater, etc., with a neck that has an opening shaped like the letter V ▪ *a V-neck sweater*

vo·cab·u·lary /vou'kæbjə,leri, *Brit* vəu-'kæbjələri/ *n, pl* **-lar·ies** 1 [*C*] : the words that make up a language ▪ *the basic vocabulary of English* 2 [*C/U*] : all of the words known and used by a person ▪ *improving your vocabulary* [=learning new words] ▪ *He has a large/limited vocabulary.* [=he knows and uses many/few words] 3 [*C/U*] : words that are related to a particular subject ▪ *the vocabulary of the Internet* 4 [*C/U*] : a set of forms or elements that are used for expression in an art, in music, etc. ▪ *architectural vocabulary*

vo·cal /'voukəl/ *adj* 1 : of, relating to, or produced by the voice ▪ *music with vocal and instrumental parts* 2 : expressing opinions in a public and forceful way ▪ *She is a vocal critic of the new law.* — **vo·cal·ly** *adv*

vocal cords *n* [*plural*] : the thin pieces of folded tissue in your throat that help you to make sounds with your voice

vo·cal·ist /'voukəlɪst/ *n* [*C*] : SINGER ▪ *a pop vocalist*

vo·cal·ize *also Brit* **vo·cal·ise** /'voukə,laɪz/ *vb* **-ized; -iz·ing** *formal* 1 [*T*] : to express (something) by speaking words ▪ *vocalizing your thoughts/feelings* 2 [*T/I*] : to make a sound with the voice ▪ *a baby vocalizing (sounds)* — **vo·cal·i·za·tion** *also Brit* **vo·cal·i·sa·tion** /,voukələ-'zeɪʃən, *Brit* ,vəukə,laɪ'zeɪʃən/ *n* [*C/U*]

vocals /'voukəlz/ *n* [*plural*] : the parts of a piece of music that are sung ▪ *He played the guitar and sang (the) vocals.*

vo·ca·tion /vou'keɪʃən/ *n* 1 [*C*] : a strong desire to spend your life doing a certain kind of work ▪ *people who follow a religious vocation* 2 [*C/U*] : the work that a person does or should be doing ▪ *Architecture was her true vocation.*

vo·ca·tion·al /vou'keɪʃənl/ *adj* : relating to the skills, training, etc., that you need for a particular job ▪ *vocational schools/courses that teach auto repair*

vo·cif·er·ous /vou'sɪfərəs/ *adj* : expressing feelings or opinions in a very loud or forceful way ▪ *He was vociferous in his support/criticism of the plan.* : expressed in a very loud or forceful way ▪ *vociferous support* — **vo·cif·er·ous·ly** *adv*

vod·ka /'vɑːdkə/ *n* [*C/U*] : a strong, clear alcoholic drink originally from Russia

vogue /'voug/ *n* [*C/U*] : something that is fashionable or popular in a particular time and place ▪ *the current vogue for spicy food* ▪ *Short skirts are in vogue right now.*

¹voice /'vɔɪs/ *n* 1 [*C/U*] : the sounds that you make with your mouth and throat when you are speaking, singing, etc. ▪ *He has a deep voice.* ▪ *speaking in a loud/high/timid/quiet voice* ▪ *a voice on the radio* ▪ *Please keep your voice down.* [=speak quietly] ▪ *He never raised his voice.* [=spoke loudly or harshly] ▪ *I don't like your tone of voice.* [=the way you are speaking to me] 2 a [*U*] : the ability to speak ▪ *I lost my voice.* b [*C*] : the ability to sing ▪ *She has a terrific voice.* 3 a [*singular*] : a right or way to express

your wishes, opinions, etc. ▪ *giving people a voice in local politics* b [*C*] : a wish, opinion, etc., that you express openly or publicly ▪ *Listen to the voice of the people.* c [*C*] : a thought or feeling that comes to you ▪ *A little voice in my head told me not to trust him.* d [*C*] : a person who expresses a wish, opinion, etc. ▪ *She was the voice of reason in our group.* [=she stopped us from doing foolish things] 4 [*C*] *grammar* : a verb form that shows whether the subject of a sentence does or receives the action of the verb ▪ *"I do it" is in the active voice.* ▪ *"It is done by me" is in the passive voice.* — **find your voice** see ¹FIND — **to give voice to** *formal* : to express (a thought, feeling, etc.) to someone ▪ *Therapy allowed her to give voice to her fears.* — **with one voice** — used to say that all the people in a group say the same thing together, express the same opinion, etc. ▪ *They spoke with one voice on* [=they all agreed about] *the need to reduce taxes.*

²voice *vb* **voiced; voic·ing** [*T*] : to express (something) in words ▪ *He voiced concern* [=he said he felt concern] *about them.*

voiced *adj* : having a voice of a particular kind ▪ *a deep-voiced man*

voice·less /'vɔɪsləs/ *adj* : not large or powerful enough to be noticed by the government, the media, etc. ▪ *a voiceless minority*

voice mail *n* [*U*] : a system in which callers can leave recorded messages for you over the telephone ▪ *Leave a message on my voice mail.*; *also* [*C*] : a message left using this system ▪ *I left her a voice mail.*

¹void /'vɔɪd/ *adj, law* : having no legal force or effect ▪ *The contract was declared null and void.* — **void of** : not having (something that is expected or wanted) ▪ *He is void of charm.*

²void *n* [*C*] : a large empty space ▪ *the great voids between galaxies* ▪ (*figurative*) *Her death left a void in my life.*

³void *vb* [*T*] *law* : to make (something) invalid ▪ *The judge voided the contract.*

voi·là *or* **voi·la** /vwɑ'lɑː/ *interj* — used when something is being presented or shown to someone ▪ *Add oil and vinegar to the lettuce, and voilà—you have a salad.*

vol. *abbr* volume — used in titles ▪ *The Works of Shakespeare, Vol. I*

vol·a·tile /'vɑːlətl, *Brit* 'vɒlə,tajəl/ *adj* 1 a : likely to change in a very sudden or extreme way ▪ *The stock market can be volatile.* b : having or showing extreme or sudden changes of emotion ▪ *a volatile temper/woman* 2 : likely to become dangerous or out of control ▪ *a volatile situation* — **vol·a·til·i·ty** /,vɑːlə'tɪləti/ *n* [*U*]

vol·can·ic /vɑːl'kænɪk/ *adj* 1 : of, relating to, or produced by a volcano ▪ *a volcanic eruption* 2 *informal* : very angry or violent ▪ *volcanic emotions*

vol·ca·no /vɑːl'keɪnou/ *n, pl* **-noes** *or* **-nos** [*C*] : a mountain with a hole in the top or side that sometimes sends out rocks, ash, lava, etc., often in an explosion ▪ *an active volcano* [=a volcano that is erupting now or will erupt soon]

vo·li·tion /vooˈlɪʃən/ *n* [U] *formal* : the power to make your own choices or decisions ▪ *He left the company of his own volition.* [=because he wanted to]

vol·ley /ˈvɑːli/ *n, pl* **-leys** [C] **1** *sports* : a shot or kick made by hitting a ball before it touches the ground ▪ *(tennis)* a *backhand volley* **2** : a large number of bullets, stones, etc., that are shot or thrown at the same time ▪ *a volley of arrows* **3** : a lot of comments, questions, etc., that are directed at a person very quickly ▪ *a volley of criticism*

vol·ley·ball /ˈvɑːliˌbɑːl/ *n* **1** [U] : a game in which two teams of players hit a large ball back and forth over a high net **2** [C] : the ball used to play volleyball

volt /ˈvoʊlt/ *n* [C] : a unit for measuring the force of an electrical current ▪ *a nine-volt battery* — abbr. *V*

volt·age /ˈvoʊltɪdʒ/ *n* [C/U] : the force of an electrical current that is measured in volts ▪ *a high-voltage area*

vol·u·ble /ˈvɑːljəbəl/ *adj, formal* : talking a lot in an energetic and rapid way ▪ *a voluble host* — **vol·u·bly** /ˈvɑːljəbli/ *adv*

vol·ume /ˈvɑːlˌjuːm/ *n* **1** [U] : the amount of sound that is produced by a TV, radio, etc. ▪ *Turn up/down the volume.* **2** [C/U] : an amount of something ▪ *a high/large volume of sales* **3** [C/U] : the amount of space that is filled by something ▪ *We measure the items by weight, not by volume.* **4** [C] **a** : a book that is part of a series or set of books ▪ *The first volume of the series was good.* **b** : one of the magazines, newspapers, etc., in a series ▪ *The article appears in volume 19, number 4.* — **speak volumes** : to show something very clearly ▪ *Your decision speaks volumes* [=says a lot] *about your character.*

vo·lu·mi·nous /vəˈluːmənəs/ *adj, formal* **1 a** : very large ▪ *a voluminous room* **b** : having large amounts of fabric ▪ *a voluminous skirt* **2** : having very many words or pages ▪ *a voluminous report* — **vo·lu·mi·nous·ly** *adv*

vol·un·tary /ˈvɑːlənˌteri, *Brit* ˈvɒləntri/ *adj* **1** : done or given because you want to ▪ *voluntary retirement* ▪ *He was charged with voluntary manslaughter.* **2** : doing work without being paid ▪ *She works for them on a voluntary basis.* [=she works as a volunteer for them] **3** : able to be controlled consciously ▪ *voluntary body movements* — **vol·un·tar·i·ly** /ˌvɑːlənˈterəli, *Brit* ˈvɒləntrəli/ *adv*

¹**vol·un·teer** /ˌvɑːlənˈtiɚ/ *n* [C] **1** : a person who chooses to join the military **2** : a person who does work without getting paid to do it ▪ *The school was built by volunteers.* — **volunteer** *adj* ▪ *a volunteer army/organization*

²**volunteer** *vb* **1** [T/I] : to offer to do something or give something without being forced to or without getting paid to do it ▪ *I volunteered to do the job.* = *I volunteered for the job.* ▪ *I volunteered my services.* ▪ *He would not volunteer any information.* **2** [I] : to choose to join the military ▪ *He volunteered for military service.* **3** [T] : to say that someone will do something without asking if he or she wants to do it ▪ *She volunteered me to babysit.* [=she said I would babysit without asking me if I wanted to]

vo·lup·tu·ous /vəˈlʌptʃəwəs/ *adj, of a woman* : having a shapely and attractive body ▪ *a voluptuous movie star* — **vo·lup·tu·ous·ness** *n* [U]

¹**vom·it** /ˈvɑːmət/ *vb* [T/I] : to have the food, liquid, etc., that is in your stomach come out through your mouth because you are sick ▪ *The dog vomited on the floor.* ▪ *vomiting blood*

²**vomit** *n* [U] : the food, liquid, etc., that comes out of your mouth when you vomit

voo·doo /ˈvuːˌduː/ *n* [U] : a religion that is practiced chiefly in Haiti — **voodoo** *adj* ▪ *a voodoo priest/curse/doll*

vo·ra·cious /vəˈreɪʃəs/ *adj* : having or showing a tendency to eat very large amounts of food ▪ *He has a voracious appetite.* ▪ *(figurative) I'm a voracious reader.* — **vo·ra·cious·ly** *adv*

vor·tex /ˈvoɚˌteks/ *n, pl* **vor·ti·ces** /ˈvoɚtəˌsiːz/ *also* **vor·tex·es** /ˈvoɚˌteksəz/ [C] *technical* : a mass of spinning air, liquid, etc., that pulls things into its center

¹**vote** /ˈvoʊt/ *vb* **vot·ed; vot·ing 1** [I] : to make an official choice for or against someone or something by casting a ballot, raising your hand, etc. ▪ *Citizens will vote today for their new governor.* ▪ *Congress voted 121 to 16 to pass the bill.* ▪ *She voted against/for the proposal.* **2** [T] **a** : to make (something) legal by a vote ▪ *They voted the bill into law.* **b** : to choose (someone or something) for an award by voting ▪ *He was voted Bachelor of the Year.* **3** [T] : to suggest (something) for others to agree or disagree with ▪ *I vote that we have pizza for dinner.* — **vote down** [*phrasal vb*] **vote** (something) **down** *or* **vote down** (something) : to defeat or reject (something) by voting ▪ *The proposal was voted down.* — **vote in** [*phrasal vb*] **vote** (someone) **in** *or* **vote in** (someone) : to elect (someone) to an office or position ▪ *She was voted in* (as vice president). — **vote on/onto** [*phrasal vb*] **vote** (someone) **on/onto** : to decide by a vote that (someone) will be allowed to become a member of (a group, team, etc.) ▪ *She was voted on/onto the team.* — **vote out** [*phrasal vb*] **vote** (someone) **out** *or* **vote out** (someone) : to decide by a vote that (someone) will no longer have an office or position ▪ *She was voted out* (of office). — **vote with your feet** : to show your dislike of a particular place or situation by leaving and going somewhere else ▪ *Many former customers voted with their feet and stopped coming.* — **vote with your wallet/pocketbook 1** : to vote in a way that helps you financially **2** : to show what you like and dislike by choosing where to shop and what to buy ▪ *Customers will vote with their wallets.* — **vot·er** /ˈvoʊtɚ/ *n* [C] — **voting** *n* [U] ▪ *The polls are now open for voting.*

²**vote** *n* **1 a** [C] : the official choice that you make in an election, meeting, etc., by casting a ballot, raising your hand,

etc. ▪ *He got 56 percent of the votes.* ▪ *People waited in line to* **cast their votes**. **b** [*singular*] : the result of voting ▪ *She won by a vote of 206 to 57.* **2** **the vote** **a** : the legal right to vote ▪ *In 1920, American women won the vote.* **b** : the whole group of people in an area who have the right to vote ▪ *helping to* **get out the vote** [=to persuade people to go vote] **c** : the total number of votes made in an election ▪ *He won 10 percent of the vote.* **d** : a particular group of people who have the right to vote ▪ *the youth/business vote* **3** [*singular*] : an occurrence in which a group of people make a decision about something by voting ▪ *Let's take a vote.* ▪ *The issue will be* **put to a vote**.

vote of confidence *n* [C] **1** : a formal process in which people vote in order to indicate whether or not they support a leader, government, etc. **2** : a statement or action that shows continuing support and approval for someone ▪ *He was given a vote of confidence by the President.* [=the President said that he has confidence in him]

vote of no confidence *n* [C] : a formal vote by which people indicate that they do not support a leader, government, etc.

voting booth *n* [C] *chiefly US* : a small, enclosed area in which a person stands while casting a vote — called also (*Brit*) polling booth

voting machine *n* [C] : a machine that you use to cast a vote and that records and counts all of the votes cast

vo·tive candle /ˈvoʊtɪv-/ *n* [C] : a small candle that is sometimes used in religious ceremonies

vouch /ˈvaʊtʃ/ *vb* — **vouch for** [*phrasal vb*] : to say that (someone or something) is honest, true, or good ▪ *I can vouch for the document's authenticity.* ▪ *We'll vouch for him.*

vouch·er /ˈvaʊtʃɚ/ *n* [C] : a document that gives you the right to get a product, service, etc., without paying for it ▪ *a travel/airline voucher*

vow /ˈvaʊ/ *n* [C] : a serious promise to do something or to behave in a certain way ▪ *marriage/wedding vows* ▪ *The mayor made/took a vow to reduce crime.* — **vow** *vb* [T] ▪ *The mayor vowed to reduce crime.*

vow·el /ˈvawəl/ *n* [C] **1** : a speech sound

made with your mouth open and your tongue not touching your teeth, lips, etc. **2** : a letter (such as *a, e, i, o, u,* and sometimes *y* in English) that represents a vowel

¹**voy·age** /ˈvojɪdʒ/ *n* [C] : a long journey to a distant or unknown place especially over water or through outer space ▪ *a voyage to America/Mars* ▪ *(figurative)* a spiritual voyage

²**voyage** *vb* **-aged; -ag·ing** [I] : to take a long journey usually by ship or boat ▪ *voyaging to distant lands* — **voy·ag·er** /ˈvojɪdʒɚ/ *n* [C]

voy·eur /vɔɪˈɚ/ *n* [C] **1** : a person who gets sexual pleasure from secretly watching other people have sex **2** : a person who likes seeing and talking or writing about something that is considered to be private ▪ *political voyeurs* — **voy·eur·ism** /vɔɪˈɚˌɪzəm/ *n* [U] — **voy·eur·is·tic** /ˌvɔjəˈrɪstɪk/ *adj*

VP *abbr* vice president

vs *or* **vs.** *abbr* versus ▪ *the Red Sox vs. the Yankees* ▪ *Brown vs. Board of Education*

Vt *or* **VT** *abbr* Vermont

vul·gar /ˈvʌlgɚ/ *adj, disapproving* : not having or showing good manners, good taste, or politeness ▪ *a vulgar man* ▪ *vulgar jokes/language* — **vul·gar·i·ty** /ˌvʌlˈgerəti/ *n, pl* **-ties** [C/U] ▪ *the vulgarity of his language* ▪ *uttering vulgarities* [=vulgar words]

vul·ner·a·ble /ˈvʌlnərəbəl/ *adj* **1** : easily hurt or harmed physically, mentally, or emotionally ▪ *a vulnerable young woman* ▪ *The patient will be* **vulnerable to** *infection after surgery.* **2** : open to attack, harm, or damage ▪ *The troops were in a vulnerable position.* ▪ *Your computer is* **vulnerable to** *viruses.* — **vul·ner·a·bil·i·ty** /ˌvʌlnərəˈbɪləti/ *n, pl* **-ties** [C/U]

vul·ture /ˈvʌltʃɚ/ *n* [C] **1** : any one of several large birds that eat dead animals and have a small and featherless head **2** *disapproving* : a person who tries to take advantage of someone who is in a very bad situation ▪ *The media vultures have started circling.*

vul·va /ˈvʌlvə/ *n, pl* **vul·vas** *or* **vul·vae** /ˈvʌlˌviː/ [C] : the parts of the female sexual organs that are on the outside of the body

vying *present participle of* **VIE**

¹w or **W** /'dʌbəl,ju:/ n, pl **w's** or **ws** or **W's** or **Ws** /'dʌbəl,ju:z/ [C/U] : the 23rd letter of the English alphabet • *a word that starts with (a)* w

²w or **W** abbr **1** watt **2** west, western **3** width

WA abbr Washington

wac·ko /'wækoʊ/ n, pl **wack·os** [C] US, informal : a person who is crazy or very strange and unusual — **wacko** adj • wacko [=crazy] ideas

wack·y /'wæki/ adj **wack·i·er; -est** informal : amusing and very strange • wacky ideas/people — **wack·i·ness** /'wækinəs/ n [U]

¹wad /'wɑːd/ n [C] **1** : a small mass or ball of soft material • a wad of cotton/gum **2 a** : a thick roll or folded pile of paper money or papers • a wad of $20 bills **b** US, informal : a large amount of money • He spent a wad on clothes.

²wad vb **wad·ded; wad·ding** [T] chiefly US : to crush or press (something) into a small, tight ball • He wadded up the paper and threw it in the trash.

wad·dle /'wɑːdl/ vb **wad·dled; wad·dling** [I] : to walk with short steps while moving from side to side like a duck • The geese waddled across the yard. — **waddle** n [singular]

wade /'weɪd/ vb **wad·ed; wad·ing** [T/I] **1** : to walk through water • We waded into the ocean. • They waded the river. [=they walked across the river] **2** : to move or proceed with difficulty or determination • It took weeks to wade through all the evidence. • We waded (our way) through the crowd. • She waded right into their argument. — **wad·er** /'weɪdɚ/ n [C]

wa·fer /'weɪfɚ/ n [C] **1** : a thin, crisp cracker **2** : a round, thin piece of bread eaten during the Christian Communion ceremony **3** : a small, round, thin object • silicon wafers

¹waf·fle /'wɑːfəl/ n [C] : a crisp cake with a pattern of deep squares on both sides that is made by cooking batter in a special device (called a waffle iron)

²waffle vb **waf·fled; waf·fling** [I] informal **1** US : to be unable or unwilling to make a clear decision about what to do • Her opponent has accused her of waffling on the important issues. **2** Brit : to talk or write a lot without saying anything important or interesting • His uncle was waffling (on) about politics.

waffle iron n [C] : a device used to cook waffles

waft /'wɑːft/ vb [T/I] : to move lightly through the air • Music wafted softly into the room. • A breeze wafted the scent of roses towards our table. — **waft** n [C] • a waft of perfume

¹wag /'wæg/ vb **wagged; wag·ging** [T/I] : to move something from side to side or forward and backward repeatedly • The dog wagged its tail. • The dog's tail began to wag. — **tongues (are) wagging** see TONGUE — **wag** n [C] • the wag of a dog's tail

¹wage /'weɪdʒ/ n [C] : an amount of money that a worker is paid based on the number of hours, days, etc., that are worked • an hourly wage of $14 • The table and chairs cost two weeks' wages.

²wage vb **waged; wag·ing** [T] : to start and continue (a war, battle, etc.) in order to get or achieve something • They waged (a) war against the government.

wa·ger /'weɪdʒɚ/ n [C] : ¹BET 1, 2 • He has a wager on the game. • I placed/made a wager on the horse. [=I bet money on the horse] — **wager** vb [T/I] • She wagered [=bet] $50 on the game.

wag·gle /'wægəl/ vb **wag·gled; wag·gling** [T/I] : to move up and down or from side to side repeatedly • She waggled her finger at me. — **waggle** n [singular]

wag·on /'wægən/ n [C] **1** : a vehicle with four wheels that is used for carrying heavy loads or passengers and that is usually pulled by animals (such as horses) **2** : a small, low vehicle with four wheels that children play with **3** US : STATION WAGON — **on/off the wagon** informal ✧ A person who is on the wagon has stopped drinking alcohol. A person who had stopped drinking alcohol but has started again has **fallen off the wagon**.

waif /'weɪf/ n [C] : a young person who is thin and appears to have no home — **waif·ish** /'weɪfɪʃ/ adj • a waifish girl

wail /'weɪl/ vb **1** [I] : to make a loud, long cry of sadness or pain • The child started wailing after she stumbled and fell. **2** [I] : to make a long, high sound • a wailing siren **3** [T] : to complain in a loud voice • "I don't want to go!" he wailed. — **wail** n [C] • a wail of sadness • the wail of a siren

waist /'weɪst/ n [C] **1** : the middle part of your body between the hips and chest • He put his arm around her waist. **2** : the part of a piece of clothing that fits around your waist • pants with an elastic waist

waist·band /'weɪst,bænd/ n [C] : the strip of fabric at the top of a piece of clothing that fits around your waist • shorts with an elastic waistband

waist·coat /'wɛskət/ n [C] chiefly Brit : VEST

waist·line /'weɪst,laɪn/ n [C] **1** : the distance around the narrowest part of your waist • dieting to reduce your waistline **2** : the part of a piece of clothing that covers your waist • The dress has a small waistline.

¹wait /'weɪt/ vb **1** [I] : to stay in a place until an expected event happens, until someone arrives, until it is your turn to do something, etc. ▪ *I hate waiting in long lines.* ▪ *I'm waiting to use the bathroom.* ▪ *Wait a minute. I need to tie my shoe.* ▪ **Wait** *for me! I'll go with you.* ▪ *We were* **waiting** *around for hours.* ▪ *I'm sorry to have* **kept** *you waiting.* **2** [T/I] : to not do something until something else happens ▪ *Wait! Don't start the engine yet.* ▪ *We waited for the sun to set before starting the fire.* ▪ *We'll wait until you come back to start the movie.* ▪ *You'll have to* **wait your turn.** [=wait until it is your turn] **3** [I] : to remain in a state in which you expect something will happen, arrive, be found out, etc. ▪ *I have waited for this opportunity for a long time.* ▪ *She waited for his answer.* ▪ *We are waiting to hear back from the doctor.* ▪ *I have to* **wait and see** *whether or not I got the job.* **4** [I] : to be done or dealt with at a later time ▪ *The other issues will have to wait until our next meeting.* **5** [I] : to be in a place ready to be dealt with, taken, etc. ▪ *It's time to come inside. Dinner is waiting.* ▪ *A package is waiting for you at home.* — **can't wait** or **can hardly wait** ◆ If you *can't wait* or *can hardly wait*, you are very excited about doing something or eager for something to happen or begin. ▪ *The concert is tomorrow, and we can hardly wait!* ▪ *I can't wait to try your apple pie.* — **wait a minute/moment/second** **1** — used to tell someone to stop and wait briefly ▪ *Wait a minute. I need to tie my shoe.* **2** — used to interrupt someone or something because you have noticed, thought of, or remembered something ▪ *Wait a second—that's not what she said.* — **wait at table** *Brit, formal* : to serve food or drinks as a waiter or waitress — **wait on** *also* **wait upon** [*phrasal vb*] **1 a** : to serve food or drinks as a waiter or waitress to (someone) ▪ *The hostess waits on tables/people when the restaurant is crowded.* **b** : to provide service to (a customer) ▪ *He is busy waiting on customers.* **c** : to act as a servant to (someone) ▪ *He seems to expect his wife to wait on him.* **2** *chiefly US* : to wait for (someone or something) to arrive or happen ▪ *We waited on him, but he never came.* — **wait out** [*phrasal vb*] **wait (something) out** or **wait out (something)** : to stay in one place until the end of (something) ▪ *We waited out the storm in our hotel room.* — **wait tables** *US* : to serve food or drinks as a waiter or waitress ▪ *She has a job waiting tables.* — **wait until/till** — used to emphasize that a future event is going to be very surprising, important, etc. ▪ *Wait till you see their new house. It's just beautiful!* — **wait up** [*phrasal vb*] **1** : to delay going to bed while you wait for someone to arrive ▪ *I'll be late; don't wait up (for me).* **2** *chiefly US, informal* : to stop moving forward so that someone who is behind you can join you ▪ *Hey, wait up (for me)! I'm going with you.*

²**wait** *n* [C] : a period of time when you must wait ▪ *He had a long wait in line.* — **lie in wait** : to hide and wait for the right moment to make an attack ▪ *The killer was lying in wait for him.*

wait·er /ˈweɪtɚ/ *n* [C] : a man who serves

food or drinks to people in a restaurant

wait·ing game /ˈweɪtɪŋ-/ *n* [*singular*] : a situation in which you wait to see what happens before you decide what to do ▪ *Until they make their decision, we're just playing a waiting game.*

waiting list *n* [C] : a list that contains the names of people who are waiting for something ▪ *The country club has a two-year waiting list to become a member.*

waiting room *n* [C] : a room in a hospital, doctor's office, etc., where people can sit down and wait

wait·ress /ˈweɪtrəs/ *n* [C] : a woman who serves food or drinks to people in a restaurant — **waitress** *vb* [I] ▪ *She waitressed while going to college.*

wait·staff /ˈweɪtˌstæf, *Brit* ˈweɪtˌstɑːf/ *n* [C] *US* : the group of waiters and waitresses who work at a restaurant ▪ *The waitstaff was/were very helpful.*

waive /ˈweɪv/ *vb* **waived; waiv·ing** [T] : to officially say that you will not use or require something that is usually allowed or required ▪ *She waived her right to a lawyer.*

waiv·er /ˈweɪvɚ/ *n* [C] **1** : the act of choosing not to use or require something that is usually allowed or required ▪ *a criminal defendant's waiver of a jury trial* **2** : an official document indicating that someone has given up or waived a right or requirement ▪ *He signed an insurance waiver before surgery.*

¹**wake** /ˈweɪk/ *vb* **woke** /ˈwoʊk/ *also* **waked** /ˈweɪkt/; **wo·ken** /ˈwoʊkən/ *or* **waked** *also* **woke; wak·ing** [T/I] : to become or cause (a person or animal) to become awake after sleeping ▪ *She can never remember her dreams upon waking (up).* ▪ *A loud crash woke me (up).* — **wake up** [*phrasal vb*] **1** : to become fully awake and energetic ▪ *It takes a couple cups of coffee for me to wake up in the morning.* **2 wake up** or **wake (someone) up** : to become or cause (someone) to become aware of something ▪ *He finally started to wake up and take care of his health.* — often + *to* ▪ *The study woke us up to the importance of regular exercise.*

²**wake** *n* [C] **1** : a time before a dead person is buried when people gather to remember the person who has died and often to view the body **2** : the track left by a boat moving through the water — **in someone's or something's wake** — used to say what is left behind by someone or something ▪ *He went from job to job, leaving a trail of broken promises in his wake.* — **in the wake of** — used to say what happens after and often as a result of something ▪ *Safety regulations were improved in the wake of the oil spill.*

wak·en /ˈweɪkən/ *vb* [T/I] *formal* : ¹WAKE ▪ *She was wakened by the telephone.*

wake–up call *n* [C] **1** : a telephone call that a hotel makes to your room to wake you up **2** : something that makes you fully understand a problem, danger, or need ▪ *His diagnosis of cancer was a wake-up call to all of us about the dangers of smoking.*

¹**walk** /ˈwɑːk/ *vb* **1 a** [I] : to move with your legs at a speed that is slower than

running ▪ *We walked around the city.* ▪ *He turned and walked away.* **b** [T] : to go with (someone) to a place by walking ▪ *I'll walk you to your car.* **c** [T] : to take (an animal) for a walk ▪ *He walks the dog at least three times a day.* **d** [T] : to cause (something) to move with you while walking ▪ *She walked her bike up the hill.* **2** [T] : to pass over, through, or along (something) by walking ▪ *We walked four miles.* ▪ *It is not safe to walk the streets at night.* **3** *baseball* **a** [I] of a *batter* : to get to first base by not swinging at four pitches that are balls ▪ *She walked her first time at bat.* **b** [T] of a *pitcher* : to cause (a batter) to go to first base by throwing four pitches that are balls ▪ *He walked the first batter.* — **walk away** [*phrasal vb*] **1** : to decide not to do or be involved in something ▪ *If you don't like the deal, you can walk away.* ▪ *You can't walk away from your responsibilities!* **2 walk away with** *informal* : to win (something) especially in an easy way ▪ *He walked away with first place.* — **walking on air** see ¹AIR — **walk in on** [*phrasal vb*] : to enter a room and interrupt (someone or something) ▪ *She walked in on the meeting.* — **walk off with** [*phrasal vb*] *informal* **1** : to steal (something) ▪ *He walked off with $500,000 worth of jewelry.* **2** : to win (something) especially in an easy or impressive way ▪ *They walked off with the state championship.* — **walk on eggshells** or *US* **walk on eggs** *informal* : to be very careful about what you say or do ▪ *She is very touchy, so you have to walk on eggshells around her.* — **walk out** [*phrasal vb*] **1 a** : to leave somewhere suddenly especially as a way of showing disapproval ▪ *A group of angry parents walked out (of the meeting).* **b** : to go on strike ▪ *The workers walked out over a wage dispute.* **2 walk out on** *informal* : to leave (someone or something) suddenly and unexpectedly ▪ *He walked out on* [=abandoned] *his wife and children.* — **walk over** [*phrasal vb*] *informal* : to treat (someone) very badly ▪ *Don't let people walk (all) over you! Stand up for yourself!* — **walk tall** : to walk or behave in a way that shows you feel proud and confident ▪ *After that performance, she can walk tall.* — **walk the walk** *informal* : to do the things that you say you will do ▪ *Don't talk the talk unless you can walk the walk!* [=don't say that you can do something unless you can actually do it] — **walk through** [*phrasal vb*] **1** : to do (something) slowly or without much effort ▪ *We walked through the whole dance routine, then practiced each section.* **2 walk (someone) through** : to help (someone) do (something) by going through its steps slowly ▪ *He walked me through the process.*

²**walk** *n* [C] **1** : an act of walking : an act of going somewhere by walking ▪ *a short walk to the restaurant* ▪ *a quarter mile walk* ▪ *It's a nice day to go for a walk.* ▪ *We took a walk along the beach.* = (*Brit*) *We had a walk along the beach.* ▪ *He took the dog for a walk.* **2** : a place or path for

walking ▪ *Many exotic plants can be found along the walk.* **3** : BASE ON BALLS **4** : a particular way of walking ▪ *His walk is just like his father's.* — **all walks of life** or **every walk of life** — used to refer to people who have many different jobs or positions in society ▪ *People from all walks of life came to the carnival.* — **walk in the park** *US, informal* : something that is pleasant or easy ▪ *Being a firefighter is no walk in the park.*

walk·er /ˈwɑːkɚ/ *n* [C] **1 a** : someone who walks especially for exercise **b** : someone who walks in a specified way ▪ *He is a fast/slow walker.* **2** : a frame that is designed to support a baby or an injured or elderly person who needs help walking

walk·ie-talk·ie /ˌwɑːkiˈtɑːki/ *n* [C] : a small radio for receiving and sending messages

walk-in /ˈwɑːkˌɪn/ *adj, always before a noun* **1** : large enough to be walked into ▪ *a walk-in closet* **2 a** : able to be visited without an appointment ▪ *a walk-in clinic* **b** : visiting a place without an appointment ▪ *walk-in customers*

¹**walk·ing** /ˈwɑːkɪŋ/ *n* [U] : the activity of walking for exercise ▪ *She goes walking in the park.*

²**walking** *adj, always before a noun* **1** : suitable for walking ▪ *walking shoes* **2** : capable of being easily walked ▪ *The store is within walking distance.* [=is close enough so that you can walk there] **3** *humorous* : in human form ▪ *He is a walking encyclopedia/dictionary.* [=he knows so much that he's like a human encyclopedia/dictionary]

walking papers *n* [*plural*] *US, informal* — used to say that someone has been ordered to leave a place, job, etc. ▪ *His boss gave him his walking papers.* [=his boss fired him]

walking stick *n* [C] : a stick that is used to help someone to walk

walk-on /ˈwɑːkˌɑːn/ *n* [C] : a minor part in a play or movie ▪ *a walk-on part/role*

walk·out /ˈwɑːkˌaʊt/ *n* [C] **1** : a strike by workers ▪ *Workers staged a walkout to protest poor conditions in the factory.* **2** : the act of leaving a meeting or organization as a way of showing disapproval

walk·up /ˈwɑːkˌʌp/ *n* [C] *US* : a tall apartment or office building that does not have an elevator; *also* : an apartment or office in such a building ▪ *He rents a fifth-floor walk-up.*

walk·way /ˈwɑːkˌweɪ/ *n* [C] : a passage or path for walking ▪ *a covered walkway*

¹**wall** /ˈwɑːl/ *n* [C] **1** : a structure of brick, stone, etc., that surrounds an area or separates one area from another ▪ *A stone wall marks off their property.* ▪ *the walls of the ancient city* ▪ (*figurative*) *a wall of water/sound* **2** : the structure that forms the side of a room or building ▪ *She hung posters on the walls of her room.* **3** : the outer layer of something that is hollow ▪ *plant cell walls* — **bang is to/against the wall** see ¹BACK — **climbing the walls** see ¹CLIMB — **drive (someone) up a/the wall** *informal* : to make (someone) irritated, angry, or cra-

zy • *Your constant tapping is driving me up the wall!* — **go to the wall** *informal* **1** *US* : to make every possible effort to achieve something, to win, etc. • *He's prepared to go to the wall to defend his beliefs.* **2** *Brit* : to fail because of a lack of money • *The company has gone to the wall.* — **hit a/the wall** *informal* : to reach a point at which you find it very difficult or impossible to continue • *Her tennis career hit a wall after the injury.* — **the writing/handwriting is on the wall** *or* **see/read the writing/handwriting on the wall** — used to say that it is clear that something bad will probably happen soon • *No one told him he was going to be fired, but he could see the writing on the wall.*

²**wall** *vb* — **wall in** [*phrasal vb*] **wall (something) in** *or* **wall in (something)** : to surround (something) with a wall or with something that is like a wall • *They walled the garden in with rows of thick shrubs.* — **wall off** [*phrasal vb*] **wall (something) off** *or* **wall off (something)** : to separate (something) from the area around it with a wall • *The school walled off the playground from the parking lot.* — **wall up** [*phrasal vb*] **wall (something) up** *or* **wall up (something)** : to close off (an opening) by filling it with stone, brick, etc. • *They walled up the doorway of the abandoned house.*

wal·la·by /ˈwɑːləbi/ *n, pl* **wal·la·bies** *also* **wallaby** [*C*] : an Australian animal that is like a small kangaroo

wall·board /ˈwɑːlˌboɚd/ *n* [*U*] *US* : DRYWALL

walled /ˈwɑːld/ *adj, always before a noun* : surrounded by a wall • *a walled city*

wal·let /ˈwɑːlət/ *n* [*C*] : a small folding case that holds paper money, credit cards, etc. • (*figurative*) *Consumers are watching their wallets.* [=are not spending a lot of money] — **vote with your wallet** see ¹VOTE

wall·flow·er /ˈwɑːlˌflawɚ/ *n* [*C*] *informal* : a person who is shy or unpopular and who stands or sits apart from other people at a dance or party

wal·lop /ˈwɑːləp/ *vb* [*T*] *informal* : to hit (someone or something) very hard • *She walloped the ball.* — **wallop** *n* [*singular*] • *She gave the ball a wallop.*

wal·low /ˈwɑːloʊ/ *vb* [*I*] **1** : to spend time experiencing or enjoying something without making any effort to change your situation, feelings, etc. — usually + *in* • *wallowing in luxury/self-pity* **2** : to roll about in deep mud or water • *elephants wallowing in the river*

wall·pa·per /ˈwɑːlˌpeɪpɚ/ *n* [*C/U*] : thick decorative paper used to cover the walls of a room • *They hung wallpaper in the room.* — **wallpaper** *vb* [*T*] • *They wallpapered the room.*

Wall Street /ˈwɑːl-/ *n* [*U*] : a street in New York City where the New York Stock Exchange and many major financial businesses are located • *Stocks rose on Wall Street today.* — used to refer to the powerful people and businesses of Wall Street that play an important role in the U.S. economy • *The company's bank-*

ruptcy was extremely troubling to Wall Street.

wall–to–wall *adj* **1** : covering the entire floor of a room • *wall-to-wall carpeting* **2** *informal* : filling an entire space or time • *The beach was wall-to-wall (with) sunbathers.*

wal·nut /ˈwɑːlˌnʌt/ *n* **1** [*C*] : a type of tree that produces large nuts which can be eaten **2** [*C*] : the nut of a walnut tree **3** [*U*] : the wood of a walnut tree • *a table made of walnut*

wal·rus /ˈwɑːlrəs/ *n, pl* **walrus** *or* **wal·rus·es** [*C*] : a large animal that lives on land and in the sea in northern regions and that has flippers and long tusks

¹**waltz** /ˈwɑːlts/ *n* [*C*] : a dance in which a couple moves in a regular series of three steps; *also* : the music used for this dance

²**waltz** *vb* **1** [*T/I*] : to dance a waltz • *He waltzed with his daughter.* **2** [*I*] : to move or walk in a lively and confident manner • *He came waltzing into the room.* **3** [*I*] : to succeed at something easily • *He waltzed through the tournament.* — **waltz off with** [*phrasal vb*] : to take or get (something) especially in an easy way • *The actress waltzed off with several awards.*

wam·pum /ˈwɑːmpəm/ *n* [*U*] : beads, polished shells, etc., used in the past by Native Americans as money and decorations

wan /ˈwɑːn/ *adj* **1** : looking sick or pale • *a wan complexion* **2** : having a weak quality : FEEBLE • *She gave a wan smile.* — **wan·ly** *adv*

wand /ˈwɑːnd/ *n* [*C*] **1** : a long, thin stick used by a magician or during magic tricks • *a magic wand* **2** : a long, thin electronic device used to gather or enter information • *a security wand*

wan·der /ˈwɑːndɚ/ *vb* **1** [*T/I*] : to move around or go to different places usually without having a particular purpose or direction • *They wandered down the street.* • *Don't let the children wander too far (off).* • *Students were wandering (around) the halls.* • *wandering sailors/streams* **2** [*I*] : to go away from a path, course, etc. • *He wandered away from the trail and got lost.* • (*figurative*) *We are wandering from our original plan.* • (*figurative*) *The speech was boring and my attention/mind began to wander.* [=I began to think about other things besides the speech] — **wander** *n* [*singular*] *chiefly Brit* • *Let's have/take a wander.* = *Let's go for a wander.* [=let's take a walk] — **wan·der·er** /ˈwɑːndərɚ/ *n* [*C*] — **wan·der·ing** /ˈwɑːndərɪŋ/ *n* [*C*] • *He describes his wanderings in the book.*

wan·der·lust /ˈwɑːndɚˌlʌst/ *n* [*U, singular*] : a strong desire to travel

¹**wane** /ˈweɪn/ *vb* **waned**; **wan·ing** [*I*] **1** : of the moon : to appear to become thinner or less full • *The moon waxes and then wanes.* **2** : to become smaller or less • *The scandal caused her popularity to wane.*

²**wane** *n* — **on the wane** : becoming smaller or less • *Her popularity was on the wane.*

wan·gle /ˈwæŋgəl/ *vb* **wan·gled**; **wan-**

gling [T] *informal* : to get (something) by clever methods or by persuading someone ▪ *He wangled a free ticket to the show.*

wan·na /ˈwɑːnə/ — used in writing to represent the sound of the phrase *want to* when it is spoken ▪ *I don't wanna go.*

wan·na·be *also* **wan·na·bee** /ˈwɑːnəˌbiː/ *n* [C] *informal* : someone who tries to look or act like a particular person or type of person ▪ *an actress wannabe* ▪ *a wannabe pop star*

¹**want** /ˈwɑːnt/ *vb* **1** [T] : to desire or wish for (something) ▪ *Do you want more coffee?* ▪ *She wanted more time to finish the test.* ▪ *You can choose whichever color you want.* ▪ *She wants to go to college.* ▪ *You can do whatever you want to (do).* **2** [T] **a** : to need (something) ▪ *Our house wants painting.* **b** : to be without (something needed) : LACK ▪ *He doesn't want self-confidence.* [=he has a lot of self-confidence] ▪ *She will never want for friends.* [=she will always have friends] **3** [T] **a** : to wish or demand to see or talk to (someone) ▪ *The police want him for questioning.* ▪ *You're wanted on the phone.* [=someone wants to speak to you on the phone] **b** : to desire (someone) *to do something* ▪ *I just want him to be honest with me.* **c** : to seek (someone) in order to make an arrest ▪ *The suspect is wanted for murder.* ▪ *one of the nation's most wanted criminals* **4** [I] *informal* : to desire to move or be in or out of a place ▪ (*chiefly US*) *The cat wants in/out.* [=the cat wants to go inside/outside] ▪ (*figurative*) *She wanted in on the deal.* [=she wanted to be included in the deal] **5** [T] *informal* — used to give advice about what someone should do or be ▪ *You want to be very careful when you pull out of the parking lot.* ▪ *We might want to leave early.* **6** [T] : to feel sexual desire for (someone) ▪ *You can tell that he wants her.*

²**want** *n* **1** [U, *singular*] *formal* : the state or condition of not having any or enough of something : LACK ▪ *He is suffering from (a) want of adequate sleep.* **2** [C] : something that is desired or needed ▪ *The company caters to the wants and needs of its customers.* **3** [U] : the state or condition of being poor ▪ *people who are living in want* — **for (the) want of** : because of not having or doing (something) ▪ *For want of a better name, let's call it "Operation One."* ▪ *Her failure to get the information was not for want of trying.* [=was not because she didn't try] — **in want of** : in the condition of wanting or needing (something) ▪ *The house is in want of repairs.*

want ad *n* [C] *US* : a notice in a newspaper, magazine, etc., that lets people know about something that you want to buy or sell, a job that is available, etc. ▪ *She checked the want ads to find a new job.*

want·ing /ˈwɑːntɪŋ/ *adj* : not having all that is needed or expected : LACKING ▪ *The plan was wanting.* ▪ *He was not wanting in confidence.*

wan·ton /ˈwɑːntn̩/ *adj* **1** : showing no

thought or care for the rights, feelings, or safety of others ▪ *wanton cruelty toward animals* ▪ *a wanton disregard for his friend's feelings* **2** : not limited or controlled ▪ *a life of wanton luxury* **3** *old-fashioned* : not sexually moral or respectable ▪ *a wanton woman* — **wan·ton·ly** *adv* — **wan·ton·ness** /ˈwɑːntn̩nəs/ *n* [U]

war /ˈwoɚ/ *n* **1** [C/U] : a state or period of fighting between countries or groups ▪ *They fought a war over the disputed territory.* ▪ *a time of war* ▪ *The countries were at war (with each other).* ▪ *The President decided against going to war.* [=starting a war] **2** [C/U] : a situation in which people or groups compete with or fight against each other ▪ *countries conducting trade wars* **3** [C] : an organized effort by a government or other large organization to stop or defeat something that is viewed as dangerous or bad ▪ *the war on/against cancer/drugs* — **all's fair in love and war** see ¹FAIR — **declare war** see DECLARE — **war of nerves** see NERVE — **war of words** see ¹WORD

war·ble /ˈwoɚbəl/ *vb* **war·bled; war·bling** **1** [I] *of a bird* : to sing a song that has many different notes ▪ *Birds were warbling in the trees.* **2** [T] *humorous* : to sing (something) especially with a high or shaky voice ▪ *warble a tune* — **warble** *n* [C]

war·bler /ˈwoɚblɚ/ *n* [C] : any one of many different kinds of small singing birds that live in America and Europe

war chest *n* [C] **1** : an amount of money that can be used by a government to pay for a war **2** : an amount of money intended for a specific purpose ▪ *the company's marketing war chest*

war crime *n* [C] : an act committed during a war that violates international law usually because it is cruel, unfair, etc. — **war criminal** *n* [C]

¹**ward** /ˈwoɚd/ *n* [C] **1 a** : a section in a hospital for patients needing a particular kind of care ▪ *a cancer/maternity ward* **b** *US* : a section in a prison ▪ *a maximum security ward* **2** : one of the sections into which a city or town is divided for the purposes of an election ▪ *the council representative from Ward 22* **3** : a person (such as a child) who is protected and cared for by a court or guardian ▪ *wards of the state/court*

²**ward** *vb* — **ward off** [*phrasal vb*] **ward (something) off** *or* **ward off (something)** : to avoid being hit or affected by (something) ▪ *ward off a blow/cold*

war·den /ˈwoɚdn̩/ *n* [C] **1** : a person who is in charge of or takes care of something ▪ *a park warden* ▪ *a game warden* [=a person who makes sure that hunting and fishing laws are obeyed] **2** *US* : an official who is in charge of a prison **3** *Brit* : any one of various officials at a British college

ward·er /ˈwoɚdɚ/ *n* [C] *Brit* : a person who works as a guard in a prison

ward·robe /ˈwoɚˌdroʊb/ *n* [C] **1 a** : a collection of clothes that a person owns or wears ▪ *She has a new summer wardrobe.* **b** : the clothes worn by actors in films, plays, etc. **2** : a room, closet, or chest where clothes are kept

ware /ˈweɚ/ n **1** [U] : things that are made from a particular material or that are designed for a particular use — usually used in combination • *cookware/ glassware* **2** [plural] : things that are being sold by someone • *She sold her wares at the market.*

ware·house /ˈweɚˌhaʊs/ n [C] : a large building used for storing goods

war·fare /ˈwoɚˌfeɚ/ n [U] **1** : military fighting in a war • *guerrilla/nuclear warfare* **2** : activity that is done as part of a struggle between competing groups, companies, etc. • *gang/industrial warfare*

war·head /ˈwoɚˌhɛd/ n [C] : the part of a missile that contains the explosive • *nuclear warheads*

war·horse /ˈwoɚˌhoɚs/ n [C] : a person (such as a soldier or politician) with a lot of experience in a field • *the Democratic warhorse in the Senate*

war·like /ˈwoɚˌlaɪk/ adj **1** : liking or tending to fight in wars or to start wars • *a warlike nation/tribe* **2** : showing or suggesting that a country, group, etc., is ready or eager to fight a war • *a warlike attitude/statement*

war·lock /ˈwoɚˌlɑːk/ n [C] : a man who has magical powers and practices witchcraft

war·lord /ˈwoɚˌloɚd/ n [C] : a leader of a military group who fights against other groups or governments

¹warm /ˈwoɚm/ adj **1 a** : somewhat hot : not cool or cold • *warm weather* • *We sat by the fire to stay/keep warm.* **b** : causing or allowing you to feel warm • *warm clothing* **2** : feeling or showing friendship and affection • *a warm welcome* • *She has a warm and friendly nature.* **3** : close to finding something, solving a puzzle, etc. • *Keep going; you're getting warm.* **4 a** : having a yellow, orange, or red color • *warm colors* **b** of sound : rich and full • *the warm sound of the cello* — **warm·ness** /ˈwoɚmnəs/ n [U]

²warm vb [T/I] : to become warm or to make (someone or something) warm • *He warmed his hands in front of the fire.* • *I'll warm (up) the leftovers.* • *Air rises when it warms.* — **warm to** [phrasal vb] **1** : to begin to feel affection for (someone) • *She quickly warmed (up) to her guests.* **2** : to begin to be interested in or excited about (something) • *It took them a while to warm (up) to the idea.* — **warm up** [phrasal vb] **1** : to become warmer • *The days are starting to warm up.* **2** **warm up or warm (something) up or warm up (something) a** : to do exercises in order to prepare for some activity (such as a sport) • *You should always warm up before you begin to run.* • *The singer warmed up her voice before the concert.* **b** : to become ready for use or cause (a machine) to become ready for use after being started or turned on • *The engine needs to warm up for a couple of minutes.* • *He warmed up the car.* **3** **warm (someone) up or warm up (someone)** : to entertain (people) before a show begins • *The comedian warmed up*

the audience before the concert. — **warm your heart** : to cause you to have pleasant feelings of happiness • *It warms my heart to see them together again.*

warm–blood·ed /ˈwoɚmˈblʌdəd/ adj, biology : having a body temperature that does not change when the temperature of the environment changes • *warm-blooded animals*

warmed–over /ˈwoɚmdˈoʊvɚ/ adj, US **1** disapproving : not fresh or new • *warmed-over ideas* **2** : heated again • *warmed-over stew*

warm·er /ˈwoɚmɚ/ n [C] : a device, piece of clothing, etc., that is used to keep something warm • *hand/leg warmers*

warm·heart·ed /ˈwoɚmˈhaɚtəd/ adj : having or showing kindness, sympathy, and affection • *a warmhearted person/ gesture*

warm·ly /ˈwoɚmli/ adv **1** : in a very friendly way • *They greeted us warmly.* **2** : in a way that keeps you warm • *She was warmly dressed.*

war·mon·ger /ˈwoɚˌmʌŋɚ, ˈwoɚˌmɑːŋɚ/ n [C] disapproving : a person who wants a war or tries to make other people want to start or fight a war — **war·mon·ger·ing** /ˈwoɚˌmʌŋgərɪŋ, ˈwoɚˌmɑːŋgərɪŋ/ n [U] • *The press accused him of warmongering.* — **warmongering** adj

warm spot n [singular] chiefly US : a strong liking for someone or something • *She has a warm spot for her old classmates.*

warmth /ˈwoɚmθ/ n [U] **1** : the quality or state of being warm in temperature • *I could feel the warmth of the fireplace.* **2** : the quality or state of being kind or friendly • *She enjoyed the warmth of their praise.*

warm–up /ˈwoɚmˌʌp/ n [C] chiefly US **1** : an exercise or set of exercises done to prepare for a sport or other activity • *She did a five-minute warmup before running.* • *He injured himself during warmups.* **2** : something done before something else to prepare an audience, a group, etc., for the next thing • *This presentation is just a warmup for the big session tomorrow.*

warn /ˈwoɚn/ vb [T/I] **1** : to tell (someone) about possible danger or trouble • *I was warned about the difficulties of the job.* • *She warned me that the store was hot.* • *"This won't be easy," he warned.* • *The book warns about/of the dangers of not getting enough exercise.* **2** : to tell (someone) to do or not to do something in order to avoid danger or trouble • *I warned him to be careful.* • *She warns against making changes too quickly.* — **warn off** [phrasal vb] **warn (someone) off** : to tell (someone) to go or stay away in order to avoid danger or trouble • *They warned us off their land.*

warn·ing /ˈwoɚnɪŋ/ n **1** [C/U] : an action, a statement, etc., that tells someone about possible danger or trouble • *She issued a stern warning about/against making changes too quickly.* • *We had no warning of the dangers that were ahead of us.* • *The storm struck without warning.* • *The policeman fired a warning shot.* • *Fall-*

*ing prices may be a **warning sign** of a recession.* [=may indicate that a recession is coming] **2** [*C*] : a statement that tells a person that bad or wrong behavior will be punished if it happens again ▪ *I was stopped for speeding, but the policeman just gave me a warning.*

¹warp /ˈwoɚp/ *vb* **1** [*T/I*] : to twist or bend (something) into a different shape ▪ *The wood was warped by moisture.* ▪ *The heat caused the wood to warp.* **2** [*T*] *disapproving* : to cause (a person's opinions, thoughts, etc.) to be changed in a way that is wrong or unnatural ▪ *His prejudices warped his judgment.* ▪ *a vicious criminal with a warped mind*

²warp *n* **1** [*C*] : a twist or curve in something that is usually flat or straight ▪ *There's a warp in the floorboards.* **2** [*U*] *technical* : the threads that run up and down on a loom or in a woven fabric

war paint *n* [*U*] : paint put on the face, arms, etc., by Native Americans before going into battle

war-path /ˈwoɚˌpæθ, *Brit* ˈwɔːˌpɑːθ/ *n* — **on the warpath** *informal* : angry and ready to fight with, criticize, or punish someone ▪ *The boss is on the warpath today because the project is behind schedule.* ▪ *Her supporters went on the warpath.*

war-plane /ˈwoɚˌpleɪn/ *n* [*C*] : a military airplane that has guns or missiles

¹war-rant /ˈworənt/ *n* [*C*] *law* : a document issued by a court that gives the police the power to do something ▪ *The police had a warrant for his arrest.*

²warrant *vb* [*T*] **1** : to require or deserve (something) ▪ *This report warrants careful study.* ▪ *The punishment he received was not warranted.* **2 a** : to make a legal promise that a statement is true ▪ *The seller warrants that the car has no defects.* **b** : to give a guarantee or warranty for (a product) ▪ *The tires are warranted for 40,000 miles.*

warrant officer *n* [*C*] : an officer of middle rank in various branches of the armed forces

war-ran-ty /ˈworənti/ *n, pl* **-ties** [*C*] : a written statement that promises the good condition of a product and states that the maker is responsible for repairing or replacing the product usually for a certain period of time after its purchase ▪ *The stereo came with a three-year warranty.*

war-ren /ˈworən/ *n* [*C*] **1** : a series of underground tunnels where rabbits live **2** : a building or place with many connected rooms, passages, etc. ▪ *a warren of narrow hallways*

war-ring /ˈworɪŋ/ *adj* : involved in a war, conflict, or disagreement ▪ *warring nations/factions*

war-rior /ˈworijɚ/ *n* [*C*] : a person who fights in battles and is known for having courage and skill ▪ *a brave warrior*

war-ship /ˈwoɚˌʃɪp/ *n* [*C*] : a military ship that has many weapons and is used for fighting in wars

wart /ˈwoɚt/ *n* [*C*] **1** : a small, hard lump on the skin caused by a virus **2** : a defect or fault ▪ *She loved him, **warts and all**.* [=she loved him even though he had

many faults] — **warty** /ˈwoɚti/ *adj* ▪ *warty skin*

wart-hog /ˈwoɚtˌhɑːg/ *n* [*C*] : a type of wild hog that lives in Africa

war-time /ˈwoɚˌtaɪm/ *n* [*U*] : a time when a country is involved in a war ▪ *Many goods were rationed during/in wartime.* ▪ *wartime leaders*

wary /ˈweri/ *adj* **war-i-er; -est** : not having or showing complete trust in someone or something that could be dangerous or cause trouble ▪ *Investors are wary about/of putting money into stocks.* — **war-i-ly** /ˈwerəli/ *adv*

was *past tense of* BE

¹wash /ˈwɑːʃ/ *vb* **1** [*T/I*] : to clean (something) with water and usually soap ▪ *wash clothes/dishes* ▪ *wash your hair/hands* ▪ *Tell the kids to wash* [=to wash their hands, faces, etc.] *before eating.* **2** [*T/I*] : to carry (something) or be carried by the movement of water ▪ *The flooding washed sand all over the area.* ▪ *The pollution washes into rivers from nearby factories.* ▪ *A sailor was washed overboard* [=knocked off the ship and into the water] *during the storm.* ▪ *The bridge was washed away by flooding.* ▪ *Heavy rain washed away the grass seed.* **3** [*I*] : to move by flowing ▪ *Water washed over the deck of the ship.* ▪ *(figurative) I felt relief washing over me.* **4** [*I*] *informal* : to be believable or acceptable ▪ *That story/excuse won't wash.* — **wash down** [*phrasal vb*] **wash (something) down** *or* **wash down (something)** **1** : to clean (something) with water ▪ *They washed down the walls.* **2** : to drink something after eating (food) ▪ *The kids washed down their cookies with milk.* — **wash off** [*phrasal vb*] **wash (something) off** *or* **wash off (something)** : to clean (something) by using water ▪ *Wash the mud off the bikes.* = *Wash off the muddy bikes.* **2** : to be able to be removed or cleaned by washing ▪ *This makeup washes off easily.* — **wash out** [*phrasal vb*] **1** : to be able to be removed or cleaned by washing ▪ *The wine stain won't wash out.* **2** **wash (something) out** *or* **wash out (something)** **a** : to clean the inside of (a cup, pot, etc.) with water ▪ *wash out the cups* **b** : to damage or carry away (something) by the force of moving water ▪ *The flooding river washed out the bridge/road.* **c** : to cause (something, such as a sports event) to be stopped or canceled because of rain ▪ *The game was washed out.* — **wash up** [*phrasal vb*] **1** : to be carried by the movement of water to the shore ▪ *Trash washed up on the beach after the storm.* **2** *US* : to wash your hands, face, etc. ▪ *I need to wash up.* **3** *chiefly Brit* : to wash the dishes after a meal ▪ *I cooked dinner and he washed up afterwards.* — **wash your hands of** : to say or decide that you will no longer deal with or be responsible for (someone or something) because you are angry, disgusted, etc. ▪ *I've tried to help them and they won't listen to me, so I'm washing my hands of the whole mess.*

²wash *n* **1** [*C*] : an act of washing something ▪ *My car needs a wash.* **2** [*singular*]

: a group of clothes, towels, etc., that are being washed or that are going to be washed ▪ *My jeans are in the wash.* **3** [*singular*] : the movement of water ▪ *We could hear the wash of the waves against the rocks.* **4** [*C*] : a thin layer of paint **5** [*C*] : a liquid used for cleaning ▪ *an antibacterial skin wash* **6** [*singular*] *US, informal* : a situation in which losses and gains balance each other ▪ *You won the first game and I won the second, so* **it's a wash.** — **it will all come out in the wash** *informal* **1** — used to say that a problem is not serious and will be solved in the future **2** — used to say that the truth will be known in the future ▪ *No one knows who was responsible, but surely it will all come out in the wash.*

wash·able /ˈwɑːʃəbəl/ *adj* : able to be washed without being damaged ▪ *a washable silk* ▪ *The skirt is* **machine washable.** [=able to be washed in a washing machine]

wash·ba·sin /ˈwɑːʃˌbeɪsn/ *n* [*C*] **1** : a large bowl for water that is used to wash your hands and face **2** *chiefly Brit* : a bathroom sink

wash·board /ˈwɑːʃˌboɚd/ *n* [*C*] : a board with ridges on its surface that was used in the past for washing clothes by rubbing wet clothes against it

wash·cloth /ˈwɑːʃˌklɑːθ/ *n* [*C*] *US* : a small piece of cloth that you use to wash your face and body

washed–out /ˈwɑːʃˈaʊt/ *adj* **1** of a color : not bright : very light or faded ▪ *washed-out colors* **2** : very tired and without energy ▪ *I felt washed-out after working all night.*

washed–up /ˈwɑːʃˈʌp/ *adj* : no longer successful, popular, or needed ▪ *a washed-up actor*

wash·er /ˈwɑːʃɚ/ *n* [*C*] **1** : a thin, flat ring that is made of metal, plastic, or rubber and that is used to make something (such as a bolt) fit tightly or to prevent rubbing **2** *informal* : WASHING MACHINE

wash·ing /ˈwɑːʃɪŋ/ *n* **1** [*C*] : an act of washing something with water and soap ▪ *The shirt needs a washing.* **2** [*U*] *Brit* : clothes, towels, etc., that need to be washed or that are being washed ▪ *His mother still does his washing.* [=laundry]

washing machine *n* [*C*] : a machine used for washing clothes

washing–up *n* [*U*] *Brit* **1** : the activity of washing dishes, pans, etc. **2** : dirty dishes, pans, etc., that need to be washed ▪ *a pile of washing-up*

wash·out /ˈwɑːʃˌaʊt/ *n* [*C*] *informal* : a complete failure ▪ *He was a washout as a professional golfer.* **2** : an event, game, etc., that is canceled because of rain ▪ *The game was a washout.*

wash·rag /ˈwɑːʃˌræg/ *n* [*C*] *US* : WASHCLOTH

wash·room /ˈwɑːʃˌruːm/ *n* [*C*] *chiefly US* : a bathroom in a public building

wash·stand /ˈwɑːʃˌstænd/ *n* [*C*] : a small table used especially in the past in a bedroom to hold the things you need for washing your face and hands

wash·tub /ˈwɑːʃˌtʌb/ *n* [*C*] : a tub used

especially in the past for washing dirty clothes, towels, etc.

wasn't /ˈwʌznt/ — used as a contraction of *was not* ▪ *It wasn't important.*

wasp /ˈwɑːsp/ *n* [*C*] : a black-and-yellow flying insect that can sting

WASP /ˈwɑːsp/ *or* **Wasp** *n* [*C*] *US, often disapproving* : an American whose family originally came from northern Europe and especially Britain and who is considered to be part of the most powerful group in society ◆ *WASP* is an abbreviation of "White Anglo-Saxon Protestant."

wasp·ish /ˈwɑːspɪʃ/ *adj* **1** : easily annoyed ▪ *a waspish temper* : showing annoyance ▪ *waspish comments* **2** : very thin ▪ *her waspish waist*

wast·age /ˈweɪstɪdʒ/ *n* [*U*] : loss of something by using too much of it or using it in a way that is not necessary or effective ▪ *a large amount of wastage* ▪ *food/water wastage*

¹**waste** /ˈweɪst/ *n* **1 a** [*U*] : loss of something valuable that occurs because too much of it is being used or because it is being used in a way that is not necessary or effective ▪ *The current system causes a lot of waste.* ▪ *reducing/avoiding waste* **b** [*singular*] : an action or use that results in the unnecessary loss of something valuable ▪ *These old computers are still useful. It seems like such a waste to throw them away.* ▪ *a* **waste of money/time** [=a bad use of money/time] **c** [*U, singular*] : a situation in which something valuable is not being used or is being used in a way that is not appropriate or effective ▪ *That role was a waste of her talents.* ▪ *It's a shame to see all that food* **go to waste.** [=not be used] **2** [*C/U*] : material that is left over or that is unwanted after something has been made, done, used, etc. ▪ *hazardous waste* ▪ *waste removal* **3** [*U*] : the solid and liquid substances that are produced by the body : feces and urine ▪ *a waste treatment plant* **4** [*plural*] *literary* : a large, empty area of land ▪ WASTELAND ▪ *the frozen wastes of the tundra* — **lay waste to** see ¹LAY

²**waste** *vb* **wast·ed**; **wast·ing** [*T*] **1** : to use (something valuable) in a way that is not necessary or effective ▪ *He wastes his money on useless gadgets.* ▪ *I think he's just wasting my time.* **2** : to use (something or someone) in a way that does not produce a valuable result or effect ▪ *We can't afford to waste this opportunity.* ▪ *She's wasting her talent.* ▪ *My efforts were wasted.* **3** *slang* : to kill or murder (someone) ▪ *Someone wasted him.* — **waste away** [*phrasal vb*] : to become thinner and weaker because of illness or lack of food — **waste no time** : to do something quickly ▪ *We wasted no time getting our tickets.* — **waste not, want not** — used to say that if you never waste things you will always have what you need — **waste your breath** see BREATH — **wast·er** /ˈweɪstɚ/ *n* [*C*]

³**waste** *adj, always before a noun* : of, relating to, or being material that is left over or unwanted after something has been made, done, used, etc. ▪ *waste material/ water*

waste·bas·ket /ˈweɪstˌbæskət, Brit ˈweɪstˌbɑːskət/ n [C] US : a small container for trash — called also *wastepaper basket*

wast·ed /ˈweɪstəd/ adj 1 : not used, spent, etc., in a good, useful, or effective way ▪ *a wasted effort/opportunity* 2 : very thin because of sickness or lack of food ▪ *Her body was thin and wasted.* 3 *informal* : very drunk or affected by drugs ▪ *He was/got wasted.*

waste disposal unit n [C] Brit : GARBAGE DISPOSAL

waste·ful /ˈweɪstfəl/ adj : using more of something than is needed ▪ *a wasteful use of natural resources* ▪ *a wasteful person/ expenditure* — **waste·ful·ly** adv

waste·land /ˈweɪstˌlænd/ n [C] 1 : land where nothing can grow or be built ▪ *a desert wasteland* 2 : an ugly and often ruined place or area ▪ *an industrial wasteland*

waste·pa·per /ˈweɪstˌpeɪpɚ/ n [U] : paper that you throw away because it has been used or is not needed

wastepaper basket n [C] : WASTEBASKET

¹**watch** /ˈwɑːtʃ/ vb 1 [T/I] a : to look at (someone or something) and pay attention to what is happening ▪ *I fell asleep watching television.* ▪ *What movie are you watching?* ▪ *She sat and watched the children play.* ▪ *Keep watching to see what happens next.* ▪ *He was being watched by the police.* b : to give your attention to (a situation, an event, etc.) ▪ *People are watching this presidential race very closely.* 2 [T] : to care for (someone or something) for a period of time in order to make sure that nothing bad or unwanted happens ▪ *Will you watch my things (for me) until I get back?* ▪ *He watched the baby while I made dinner.* ▪ *Watch yourself* [=be careful] *up on the roof.* 3 [T] a : to try to control (something) ▪ *She tries to watch her weight.* [=she tries not to gain weight] ▪ *The doctor told him that he has to watch what he eats.* b : to be careful about (something) ▪ *Watch your step. These stairs are slippery.* ▪ *Watch what you're doing! You almost hit me.* ▪ *Watch your language/mouth/tongue, young lady!* [=don't say rude or inappropriate things] 4 [T] : to make sure that something bad or unwanted does not happen ▪ *You will want to watch that it doesn't happen again.* ▪ *Watch (that) you don't fall!* — **watch for** [phrasal vb] 1 : to look for (someone or something that you expect to see) ▪ *Are you watching for your parents? They should be here any minute.* ▪ *She watched for the bus from inside her house.* 2 : to look for (something that you want to get or use) ▪ *She is always watching for sales.* — **watch it** informal — used to tell someone to be careful ▪ *Watch it! You nearly hit me!* — **watch out** [phrasal vb] : to be aware of something dangerous ▪ *If you don't watch out, you could fall.* ▪ *Watch out for that car!* — **watch over** [phrasal vb] : to take care of (someone or something) ▪ *The shepherds watched over their sheep.* ▪ *She believed that angels were watching over her.* —

watch someone's back see ¹BACK — **watch your back** see ¹BACK — **watch your p's and q's** see ¹P — **watch your step** see ¹STEP — **you watch** informal — used to tell someone that you think something will probably happen ▪ *She'll change her mind again, you watch.* [=I think she'll change her mind again] — **watch·er** /ˈwɑːtʃɚ/ n [C]

²**watch** n 1 [C] : a device that shows what time it is and that you wear on your wrist or carry in a pocket ▪ *He glanced/ looked at his watch.* 2 [U, singular] a : the act of giving your attention to someone or something especially in order to make sure that nothing bad or unwanted happens ▪ *The guards kept a close watch over the prisoner.* ▪ *We are continuing to keep watch on the situation.* b : the act of looking for someone or something that you expect to see ▪ *She kept watch outside while the others robbed the bank.* ▪ *The police told residents to keep a watch out for a black van.* ▪ *When you're driving in winter, you should always be on the watch for ice on the roads.* 3 a [C/U] : a period of time when a person or group is responsible for guarding or protecting someone or something ▪ *My watch ends in an hour.* ▪ *Two guards were on/standing watch.* b [C] : a group of people who guard or protect someone or something for a period of time ▪ *A fresh group of soldiers relieved the morning/night watch.* c [C] : the period of time during which someone is in charge of something ▪ *"Will anything go wrong?" "Not on my watch!"* 4 [C] US : a quick announcement from an official source which tells people that severe weather conditions could occur very soon ▪ *a winter storm watch*

watch·able /ˈwɑːtʃəbəl/ adj : worth watching ▪ *a watchable film*

watch·band /ˈwɑːtʃˌbænd/ n [C] US : a strap or band that holds your watch on your wrist

watch·dog /ˈwɑːtʃˌdɑːg/ n [C] 1 : a dog that is trained to guard a place 2 : a person or organization that makes sure that companies, governments, etc., are not doing anything illegal or wrong ▪ *consumer/environmental watchdogs*

watch·ful /ˈwɑːtʃfəl/ adj : watching the actions of someone or something closely ▪ *We need to be more watchful of our children.* ▪ *The supervisor keeps a watchful eye on the workers.* [=the supervisor closely watches the workers]

watch·mak·er /ˈwɑːtʃˌmeɪkɚ/ n [C] : a person or company that makes or repairs watches or clocks

watch·man /ˈwɑːtʃmən/ n, pl -men /-mən/ [C] : a person whose job is to watch and guard property at night or when the owners are away ▪ *a night watchman*

watch·word /ˈwɑːtʃˌwɚd/ n [C] : a word or phrase that expresses a rule that a particular person or group follows : SLOGAN ▪ *"Safety" is our watchword.*

¹**wa·ter** /ˈwɑːtɚ/ n 1 [U] : the clear liquid that has no color, taste, or smell, that falls from clouds as rain, that forms

streams, lakes, and seas, and that is used for drinking, washing, etc. ▪ *a glass of water* ▪ *There's water dripping from the ceiling.* ▪ **drinking water** [=water that is safe for drinking] ▪ *The house has hot and cold* **running water**. [=water carried by pipes inside a building] **2** [*U*] : an area of water (such as a lake, river, or ocean) ▪ *deep/shallow water* ▪ *A stick was floating on/in the water.* **3** [*plural*] : a specific area of water; *especially* : an area of seawater ▪ *coastal/frigid/international waters* ▪ *(figurative) The company is moving into* **uncharted waters** [=new and unknown areas] *with its Internet marketing campaign.* **4** [*U*] : methods of travel that involve boats and ships ▪ *They came by water.* — **a fish out of water** see ¹FISH — **blood is thicker than water** see BLOOD — **dead in the water** see ¹DEAD — **hold water** *informal* : to be possible or believable ▪ *Her argument doesn't hold water.* — **in deep water** see ¹DEEP — **keep your head above water** see ¹HEAD — **pour/throw cold water on** : to say that you do not like (an idea, suggestion, etc.) in a way that stops other people from liking it or acting on it ▪ *He wanted to buy a new car, but I poured/threw cold water on that idea.* — **test the waters/water** see ²TEST — **tread water** see ¹TREAD — **water breaks** (*US*) or *Brit* **waters break** — used to describe the sudden release of fluid from a pregnant woman's body that indicates her baby will be born soon ▪ *Her waters broke early.* — **water under the bridge** : something that happened in the past and is no longer important or worth arguing about ▪ *We had our differences in the past, but that's all water under the bridge now.*

²**water** *vb* **1** [*T*] : to pour water on (something) ▪ *water the lawn/garden/plants* **2** [*T*] : to give (an animal) water to drink ▪ *They fed and watered the horses.* **3** [*I*] *of the eyes* : to produce tears ▪ *My eyes watered as I chopped the onion.* **4** [*I*] *of the mouth* : to become wet with saliva especially because you want to eat or taste something ▪ *Just smelling chocolate makes my mouth water.* — **water down** [*phrasal vb*] **water (something) down** or **water down (something) 1** : to make (an alcoholic drink) weaker by adding water to it ▪ *Someone watered down the punch.* **2** *disapproving* : to make (something) less effective, powerful, etc. ▪ *The movie watered down the lessons of the book.*

water bed *n* [*C*] : a bed that has a mattress which is made of rubber or plastic and is filled with water

wa·ter·bird /ˈwɑːtəˌbɚd/ *n* [*C*] : a bird that swims and lives in or near water ▪ *gulls, ducks, and other waterbirds*

wa·ter·borne /ˈwɑːtəˌboɚn/ *adj* : spread or carried by water ▪ *waterborne diseases*

water buffalo *n* [*C*] : a large animal like a cow with long horns that lives in Asia and is often used to pull plows

water chestnut *n* [*C*] : the white root of a plant that grows in water and that is often used in Chinese cooking

wa·ter·col·or (*US*) or *Brit* **wa·ter·col·our** /ˈwɑːtəˌkʌlə/ *n* **1** [*U*, *plural*] : a type of paint that is mixed with water ▪ *a landscape done in watercolor* ▪ *He works in watercolors.* **2** [*C*] : a picture painted with watercolors ▪ *an exhibition of watercolors*

water cooler /ˈwɑːtəˌkuːlə/ *n* [*C*] : a machine that cools and stores water for drinking and that is usually found in offices and public buildings

wa·ter·course /ˈwɑːtəˌkoɚs/ *n* [*C*] *formal* : a river, stream, etc.

wa·ter·craft /ˈwɑːtəˌkræft, *Brit* ˈwɔːtəˌkrɑːft/ *n* [*C/U*] : a ship or boat

wa·ter·cress /ˈwɑːtəˌkrɛs/ *n* [*U*] : a plant that grows in water and that has small, round leaves which are often used in salads

watered–down *adj* : made to be less effective, powerful, etc. ▪ *a watered-down version of the original proposal*

wa·ter·fall /ˈwɑːtəˌfɑːl/ *n* [*C*] : an area in a stream or river where running water falls down from a high place (such as over the side of a cliff)

water fountain *n* [*C*] **1** *chiefly US* : a machine that produces a small stream of water for drinking **2** : FOUNTAIN 1

wa·ter·fowl /ˈwɑːtəˌfawəl/ *n*, *pl* **waterfowl** : a duck or similar bird that swims and lives in or near water

wa·ter·front /ˈwɑːtəˌfrʌnt/ *n* [*C*] : the land or the part of a town next to the water of an ocean, lake, etc. ▪ *a concert on the waterfront* ▪ *waterfront property*

water hole *n* [*C*] : a small pool, pond, or lake used by animals for drinking — called also *watering hole*

watering can *n* [*C*] : a container that is used to pour water on plants

watering hole *n* [*C*] **1** *humorous* : a place (such as a bar) where people gather to drink **2** : WATER HOLE

water lily *n* [*C*] : a plant that grows in water with round, floating leaves and large flowers

wa·ter·logged /ˈwɑːtəˌlɑːgd/ *adj* : filled or soaked with water ▪ *a waterlogged boat* ▪ *waterlogged clothes/soil*

wa·ter·mark /ˈwɑːtəˌmaɚk/ *n* [*C*] : a design or symbol (such as the maker's name) that is made in a piece of paper and that can be seen when the paper is held up to the light

wa·ter·mel·on /ˈwɑːtəˌmɛlən/ *n* [*C/U*] : a large, round fruit that has hard, green skin, sweet, red, juicy flesh, and black seeds

water moccasin *n* [*C*] : a poisonous snake found in the southern U.S. that lives on land and in water

water park *n* [*C*] : an amusement park with rides that involve water and areas where people can play or swim in water

water pistol *n* [*C*] : a toy pistol that shoots a stream of water

water polo *n* [*U*] : a game that is played in water by two teams of swimmers who try to score by throwing a ball into a goal

wa·ter·pow·er /ˈwɑːtəˌpawə/ *n* [*U*] : the power that comes from moving water and that is used to run machinery or make electricity

¹**wa·ter·proof** /'wɑːtəˌpruːf/ adj : designed to prevent water from entering or passing through • *waterproof boots* — **waterproof** vb [T] • *He waterproofed the deck by applying sealer to it.*

²**waterproof** n [C] chiefly Brit : RAINCOAT

wa·ter·re·pel·lent /ˌwɑːtərɪˈpɛlənt/ adj : WATER-RESISTANT

wa·ter·re·sis·tant /ˌwɑːtərɪˈzɪstənt/ adj : designed to not be easily harmed or affected by water or to not allow water to pass through easily • *water-resistant fabric*

wa·ter·shed /'wɑːtəˌʃɛd/ n [C] **1 :** a time when an important change happens • *The protests mark a watershed in the history of the country.* • *a watershed year/event* **2 a :** a line of hills or mountains from which rivers drain **b** chiefly US : the area of land that includes a particular river or lake and all the rivers, streams, etc., that flow into it **3** Brit : the time of day after which television programs not appropriate for children may be broadcast

wa·ter·ski /'wɑːtəˌskiː/ vb [I] : to ski on the surface of water while holding onto a rope that is attached to a motorboat moving at high speed — **water ski** n [C] • *a pair of water skis* — **wa·ter·ski·er** /'wɑːtəˌskiːjə/ n [C] — **wa·ter·ski·ing** /'wɑːtəˌskiːjɪŋ/ n [U]

water table n [C] technical : the highest underground level at which the rocks and soil in a particular area are completely wet with water • *Heavy rainfall has caused the water table to rise.*

wa·ter·tight /ˌwɑːtəˈtaɪt/ adj **1 :** put or fit together so tightly that water cannot enter or pass through • *a watertight seal* **2 :** too strong or effective to fail or to be defeated • *a watertight alibi/case*

water tower n [C] : a tower with a large container for storing water that is usually supplied to buildings located near it

wa·ter·way /'wɑːtəˌweɪ/ n [C] : a canal, river, etc., that is deep and wide enough for boats and ships to travel through

wa·ter·wheel /'wɑːtəˌwiːl/ n [C] : a usually large wooden or metal wheel that is turned by the force of water flowing against it

wa·ter·works /'wɑːtəˌwəːks/ n [plural] : a system for supplying water to a city or town that includes pipes, pumps, etc.

wa·tery /'wɑːtəri/ adj **1 :** containing or filled with water or a similar liquid • *The pollen made her eyes watery.* **2** of a liquid : very thin and similar to water in appearance, taste, etc. • *watery soups/drinks*

watt /'wɑːt/ n [C] : a unit for measuring electrical power • *a 40-watt light bulb* — abbr. *W*

watt·age /'wɑːtɪdʒ/ n [U] : the amount of electrical power measured in watts that something (such as a light bulb) uses • *Use a bulb with low wattage.*

¹**wave** /'weɪv/ vb **waved**; **wav·ing** **1** [T/I] : to move your hand or something held in your hand usually in a repeated motion in order to signal or greet someone • *We waved to our friends through the window.* • *They waved at us.* • *We waved goodbye* [=waved as a way of saying goodbye] *to them and drove away.* • *We offered to help but he waved us off.* [=he waved as a way of telling us that he did not want help] • *We tried to wave down a taxi.* [=to get a taxi to stop for us by waving at its driver] **2** [I] : to float, shake, or move back and forth because of wind • *Flags were waving in the breeze.* **3** [T] : to move (something) back and forth • *The magician waved his magic wand.* • *wave a flag* • *The robber waved a pistol at the clerk.* **4** [I] of hair : to curl slightly • *His hair waves naturally.* — **wave aside** [phrasal vb] **wave (something) aside** or **wave aside (something) :** to refuse to consider or respond to (something) • *The officer waved aside my questions.*

²**wave** n [C] **1 :** an area of moving water that is raised above the main surface of an ocean, a lake, etc. • *ocean waves* — see also TIDAL WAVE **2 :** something that has the shape or movement of a wave • *She has a wave in her hair.* • *Waves of warm air washed over us.* **3 :** a usually repeated movement of your hand or of something held in your hand especially as a signal or greeting • *He gave me a wave.* [=he waved to/at me] • *a kiss and a wave goodbye* [=a wave that you use to say goodbye] **4 a :** a period of time in which a particular type of activity is being done commonly or repeatedly • *a crime wave* — see also HEAT WAVE **b :** a large number of people or things that do something together, are seen together, etc. • *a new wave of immigrants* — see also NEW WAVE **5 a :** a strong feeling that affects someone suddenly • *A wave of fatigue swept over me.* **b :** a strong feeling or attitude that is shared by many people at the same time • *a wave of nostalgia* **6** technical : an amount of energy (such as light) that moves in a shape resembling a wave • *light waves* — **make waves** informal : to do something that causes people to notice you • *He's making waves in the music industry.; especially* : to cause trouble or annoy people by complaining • *I'm tempted to complain, but I don't want to make waves.* — **the wave of the future** : an idea, product, way of thinking, etc., that will become very popular in the future • *These new video games are the wave of the future.*

wave·length /'weɪvˌlɛŋkθ/ n [C] **1** technical : the distance from one wave of energy to another as it is traveling from one point to another point • *light/radio wavelengths* **2** informal — used especially in the phrases **on the same wavelength** and **on a different wavelength** to say that people share or do not share a way of thinking • *She is on a different wavelength than I am.*

wa·ver /'weɪvə/ vb [I] **1 :** to be uncertain about what you think about something or someone • *people who are still wavering between the two candidates* • *They never wavered in their support.* **2 :** to become unsteady • *During a long lecture my attention will sometimes waver.* [=I will sometimes think about other things]

wavy /'weɪvi/ adj **wav·i·er; -est :** having

the curving shape of a wave or of many waves ▪ *wavy hair/lines*

¹**wax** /ˈwæks/ *n* **1** [C/U] : a hard substance that becomes soft when it is heated and that is used to make candles, crayons, polish, etc. ▪ *floor waxes* ▪ *car wax* [=a substance used to polish cars] ▪ *a wax candle* **2** [U] : a natural sticky substance that is produced inside the ear : EARWAX — **wax-like** /ˈwæksˌlaɪk/ *adj*

²**wax** *vb* **1** [T] **a** : to treat or polish (something) by rubbing it with wax ▪ *wax a car* **b** : to remove hair from (a part of the body) by putting hot wax on it and then pulling the wax off ▪ *She waxes her eyebrows/legs.* **2** [I] **a** *of the moon* : to appear to become larger or more full ▪ *The moon waxes and then wanes.* **b** : to increase in amount, size, etc. ▪ *Interest in the story waxes and wanes depending on other news.* **3** *always followed by an adjective* [*linking vb*] : to talk or write about something in a specified way ▪ *He waxed nostalgic about his childhood.* [=he talked/wrote nostalgically about his childhood]

wax bean *n* [C] *US* : a kind of bean whose long yellow seed cases are eaten as a vegetable

wax-en /ˈwæksən/ *adj, literary* : made of or seeming to be made of or covered in wax ▪ *waxen figurines* ▪ *flowers with waxen* [=smooth and shiny] *petals* ▪ *a pale, waxen face*

wax paper *or* **waxed paper** *n* [U] *US* : paper that is covered with wax in order to prevent water and other substances from passing through it and that is often used to wrap food

waxy /ˈwæksi/ *adj* **wax·i·er; -est** : seeming to be made of or covered in wax ▪ *a plant with waxy leaves* ▪ *a waxy surface/substance*

¹**way** /ˈweɪ/ *n* **1** [C] **a** : how someone or something behaves, appears, feels, etc. ▪ *I like the way she looks/dresses/laughs.* ▪ *The steak was cooked the way I like it.* ▪ *That's no way to talk to him.* ▪ *It's a tragedy in more ways than one.* [=for more than one reason] ▪ **The way things are going** [=if things continue to happen like this], *I may lose my job.* ▪ *We lost, but that's the way it/life goes sometimes.* [=bad or disappointing things happen sometimes] **b** : a method or system that can be used to do something ▪ *We'll try doing it your way first.* ▪ *one way to look at the problem* ▪ *There's no way of knowing what will happen.* ▪ **One way or another,** *it's going to happen.* ▪ **Where there's a will, there's a way.** [=if you have the desire and determination to do something, you can find a method for accomplishing it] **2** [C] : a person's usual habits, actions, qualities, etc. ▪ *He has a charming way about him.* ▪ *He is set in his ways.* [=unwilling to change his habits, behaviors, etc.] **3** [C] **a** : the series of roads, paths, etc., that can be used to go from one place to another ▪ *We took the long way home.* — often used figuratively to refer to a series of actions, procedures, etc., that can be used to achieve something ▪ *One way around the problem of*

poor sales is to lower prices. ▪ *They* **smoothed the way** *for an end to the dispute.* [=they made an end to the dispute easier and more likely] **b** : a road, path, etc. ▪ *We found the way that leads to the lake.* ▪ *They live* **across the way** *from us.* **c** : a door, opening, etc., that is used for going into or out of a place ▪ *This door is the only way out of the room.* ▪ *(figurative)* *There is no (clear/simple) way out of this situation.* ▪ *(figurative)* trying to **take the easy way out** [=trying to avoid having to do something difficult] **4** [C] **a** : the route along which someone or something is moving or intends to move ▪ *A tree fell and blocked our way.* ▪ *You're in* **my/the way.** [=you are blocking my path] ▪ **Get out of my/the way!** **b** — used with *her, his, their, its, your,* and *our* to describe someone or something that is moving forward, going somewhere, etc. ▪ *We pushed our way through the crowd.* ▪ *The river winds/snakes its way through the valley.* ▪ *He bought his way into the college.* [=he used money to get himself accepted as a student at the college] ▪ *She talked her way past the guard.* **5** [C] **a** : a specified or indicated direction ▪ *They went that way.* ▪ *Look both ways before crossing the street.* **b** — used with *her, his, their, its, your,* and *our* to say that someone or something is moving toward or coming to a particular person or thing ▪ *A storm is heading our way.* ▪ *Some bad luck had come his way.* **6** [*singular*] : a distance ▪ *a long way from here* [=far from here] ▪ *(figurative) He has a* **way to go** [=a long time to wait] *before the test results are in.* — see also WAYS **7** [*singular*] *informal* : the area or region where someone lives ▪ *The weather has been rainy out our way.* [=out where we live] **8** [C] **a** : a particular part of something that is being thought about or discussed ▪ *Her computer is superior to mine in* **every way.** [=it is completely superior] ▪ **In many ways,** *their stories are the same.* [=their stories are the same to a great degree] ▪ **In some ways** *the movie is brilliant, but* **in other ways** *it's horrible.* ▪ *That's true,* **in a way.** [=it is partly true] ▪ **In no way** *am I like him.* [=I am not at all like him] **b** : a manner of thinking about or considering something ▪ *I started looking at the problem in a different way.* **9** [*singular*] : the situation that exists ▪ *People are angry but it doesn't have to be that way.* ▪ *Business is good, and we want to keep it that way.* ▪ *That's just the* **way things are.** **10** [C] : one of usually two possible decisions, actions, or results ▪ *The election could not have gone any other way.* ▪ *I will take the bus or train, but* **either way** *I will be there tonight.* ▪ *You can't* **have it both ways.** ▪ *I don't care* **one way or the other.** **11** [C] : one of a specified number of usually equal parts into which something is divided ▪ *The money was divided three ways.* — **all the way 1** : to the full or entire extent ▪ *We sat all the way in the back.* **2** : throughout an entire process or period of time ▪ *She was with him all the way through his candidacy.* **3** : to the fullest and most complete extent ▪ *I am with you all the way.* **4** : over an entire distance ▪ *She ran all the way there.* ▪ *You came all this way just to see me?* — **by the way** — used in speech to introduce a statement or question that may or may not relate to the current topic of conversation ▪ *By the way, I like your shoes.* — **by way of 1** : by traveling through (a place) ▪ *She came here from China by way of England.* **2** : for the purpose of giving, making, or doing (something specified) ▪ *She said that many people are trying to improve their diets, and she mentioned her own family by way of example.* [=as an example] — **change your ways** : to improve your behavior, habits, or beliefs ▪ *If you want to live a long life, you'd better change your ways!* — **clear the way 1** : to make the area through which someone or something is trying to pass open and able to be used ▪ *She directed traffic to clear the way for the ambulance.* **2** : to allow something to happen or develop ▪ *The truce would clear the way for further talks.* — **give way 1** : to break apart and fall down ▪ *The roof gave way* [=collapsed] *under heavy snow.* **2** *formal* : to stop trying to fight or resist something ▪ *After several hours of debate, the opposition finally gave way.* **3** : to be replaced by something specified ▪ *Our frustration soon gave way to anger.* **4** *Brit* : to allow another car or person to go ahead of you or in front of you ▪ *Cars must give way* [=(US) yield] *to pedestrians.* — **go all the way** *informal* **1** *sports* : to win a championship, title, etc. ▪ *The team could go all the way this year.* **2** : to have sex with someone ▪ *Did you go all the way (with him/her)?* — **go either way** — used to say that either of two possible results is likely to occur and that neither is more likely than the other ▪ *The game could go either way.* — **go out of your way** : to make a special effort to do something ▪ *She went out of her way to help me.* — **go someone's way 1** : to travel in the same direction as someone ▪ *Are you going my way?* **2** : to happen in a way that helps someone ▪ *Things haven't been going my way lately.* — **go your own way** : to do the things that you want to do rather than doing the things that other people expect you to do ▪ *She always went her own way.* — **have a way of ✧** If someone or something *has a way of* being or doing something, the person or thing often has that characteristic or is frequently does that thing. ▪ *She has a way of exaggerating* [=she often exaggerates] *about her job.* — **have a way with** : to be able to use (something) or to deal with (something or someone) well ▪ *She has a way with kids/dogs.* ▪ *He has a way with words.* [=he is good with words] — **have/get your (own) way** : to get or do what you want to get or do despite the desires, plans, etc., of other people ▪ *If I had my way, we would leave at 6:00.* — often disapproving ▪ *a spoiled child who always gets his (own) way* ▪ *All right.* **Have it your way.** [=do what you want to do] — **have your way with** : to do exactly

what you want to do to or with (something or someone); *especially* : to have sex with (someone) ▪ *He has had his way with many women.* — **in any way, shape, or form** : under any circumstances or conditions ▪ *That behavior is not acceptable in any way, shape, or form.* — **in the way** *or* **in someone's or something's way** : making it more difficult for a person to do something ▪ *I felt that I was just in their way.* ▪ *We have important issues to deal with, but these petty arguments keep getting in the way.* ▪ *We won't let anything stand in the way of progress!* — **in the way of** — used to indicate the type of thing that is being described, thought of, etc. ▪ *They offered him little in the way of emotional support.* [=they did not give him much emotional support] — **lose your way** : to become lost ▪ *I lost my way while hiking.* ▪ *(figurative) The political party has lost its way and isn't connecting with voters anymore.* — **make way** : to create a path or open space so that someone or something can use it ▪ *The houses were torn down to make way for a shopping center.* ▪ *Make way! I'm coming through!* — **make your way** : to move forward usually by following a path ▪ *He made his way to the stage.* ▪ *(figurative) She set out to make her way in the world.* — **no two ways about it** — used to say that something is definitely true ▪ *They were rude—(there are) no two ways about it.* — **no way** *informal* **1** — used to say that you will definitely not do something ▪ *There is no way I'm going to swim with a shark.* ▪ *"Do you want to try skydiving?" "No way."* **2** *US* — used to show that you are very surprised by something or do not believe that something is true ▪ *"He's 40 years old." "No way!"* — **on the way** *or* **on someone's or something's way 1** : in a state of development ▪ *More layoffs are on the way.* **2** : moving from one place to another place ▪ *The package is on its way.* ▪ *I must be on my way.* [=I must leave now] **3** : changing from one level or condition to another level or condition ▪ *House prices are on their way up.* [=are increasing] — **on the way out** *or* **on someone's or something's way out 1** : leaving a place or position ▪ *She closed the door on her way out.* ▪ *There are rumors that the CEO is on the way out.* **2** : becoming no longer popular ▪ *That style is on its way out.* — **out of the way 1** : far from other places that are well-known ▪ *The cottage is quiet and out of the way.* **2** : done or dealt with completely ▪ *She got her homework out of the way early.* **3** : unusual or remarkable ▪ *There is nothing out of the way about the plan.* — **see your way (clear) to** : to be willing to (do something) ▪ *Could you see your way clear to lend/lending me a few dollars?* — **the other way around** *also chiefly Brit* **the other way round 1** : in the opposite position, direction, or order ▪ *You put the fork on the right and the knife on the left. They should be the other way around.* **2** — used to say that the opposite situation is true ▪ *"I thought he want-*

ed a divorce." "No, it was the other way around." [=she wanted a divorce] — the **way** informal **1** — used to say what someone's way of speaking, behaving, etc., seems to suggest ▪ *The way he talks, you would think he ran the company.* **2** — used to say that something happens or is done with the same attitude, at the same pace, etc., as something else ▪ *They replace their cars the way* [=like] *other people replace shoes.* — **the way/ways of the world** : how things happen or how people behave ▪ *Success comes easier for some people. That's just the way of the world.* — **way of life 1** : the habits, customs, and beliefs of a particular person or group of people ▪ *modern and traditional ways of life* **2** : an important activity, job, etc., that affects all parts of someone's life ▪ *For me, tennis is not just a sport, it's a way of life.* — **way to go** *US, informal* — used to tell someone that he or she has done something well ▪ *Nice job, guys! Way to go!*

²**way** *adv, informal* **1** : very far ▪ *He is way ahead of the other runners.* ▪ *They live way out in the country.* ▪ *I am way behind with my work.* **2** : by a great amount ▪ *I ate way too much.* **3** *US* : VERY ▪ *They are way cool.* — **way back** : from a time in the distant past ▪ *way back in the 1960s* ▪ *We are friends from way back.* [=we have been friends for a long time]

way·far·er /ˈweɪˌferɚ/ *n* [C] *literary* : a person who travels from place to place usually by walking

way·lay /ˈweɪˌleɪ/ *vb* **-laid** /-ˌleɪd/; **-lay·ing** [T] **1** : to stop (someone who is going somewhere) ▪ *I was waylaid by reporters.* **2** : to attack (someone or something) without warning from a hidden place ▪ *Gangs sometimes waylay travelers on that road.*

way–out /ˈweɪˈaʊt/ *adj, informal* : very strange or unusual ▪ *way-out ideas*

ways /ˈweɪz/ *n* [singular] *US, informal* : a distance ▪ *We're a long ways* [=way] *from home.* ▪ *We still have a ways to go.* [=a long way to go] ▪ *(figurative) The wedding is a long ways off.* [=it is far in the future]

way·side /ˈweɪˌsaɪd/ *n* [C] : the land next to a road or path ▪ *Flowers grew along the wayside.* ▪ *a wayside inn/restaurant* — **by the wayside** : into a state of no longer being considered, used, etc. ▪ *Our plans have fallen/gone by the wayside.* [=we have dropped/abandoned our plans]

way station *n* [C] *US* : a place where people can stop for rest, supplies, etc., during a long journey

way·ward /ˈweɪˌwɚd/ *adj* **1** : tending to behave in ways that are not socially acceptable ▪ *a wayward teenager* **2** : not going or moving in the intended direction ▪ *a wayward throw*

we /ˈwiː/ *pron* **1** — used to refer to the speaker and another person or group of people as the subject of a verb ▪ *We had a party.* **2 a** — used to refer to the company, business, organization, etc., that the speaker works for or is involved with ▪ *We are open until noon.* **b** *formal* — used like *I* by a king or queen ▪ *"We welcome you," said the queen to her visitors.*

3 : people in general ▪ *We must learn to forgive.*

weak /ˈwiːk/ *adj* **1** : having little physical power or ability : not strong ▪ *He was too weak to stand up.* ▪ *weak eyes/eyesight/ankles/lungs* **2** : having little power or force ▪ *a weak punch/voice* **3** : not able to handle weight, pressure, or strain ▪ *a weak rope* **4** *disapproving* **a** : having little power or influence ▪ *a weak leader* **b** : not able to make good decisions or deal with difficult situations ▪ *a sign of a weak character* ▪ *In a weak moment* [=during a brief time when I had bad judgment] *I told them my secret.* **5 a** : lacking enough or the usual amount of an important ingredient ▪ *This tea is weak.* [=it has little tea flavor] **b** : not powerful in action or effect ▪ *a weak drug* ▪ *a weak radio signal* **6** : not likely to persuade or convince people that something is true, real, correct, etc. ▪ *a weak argument/case/excuse* **7** : not having enough skill or ability ▪ *The team is weak on defense.* **8** : not effective ▪ *a weak attempt at humor* **9** : showing little confidence or enthusiasm ▪ *a weak smile* **10 a** : having a value that is small or is not increasing ▪ *The dollar is weak.* **b** : in a poor financial condition ▪ *a weak economy* **11** : dull or pale ▪ *weak colors/light* **12** : smaller than the usual size ▪ *a man with a weak chin* — **a weak stomach** see ¹STOMACH — **the weak** : weak people ▪ *the weak and the powerful* — **weak at/in the knees** : so nervous or powerfully affected that it is difficult for you to stand ▪ *She said hello and I went weak in the knees.* — **weak·ly** *adv* ▪ *smiling weakly*

weak·en /ˈwiːkən/ *vb* **1** [T] : to make (something or someone) weaker, less forceful, less effective, etc. ▪ *The disease weakens the immune system.* ▪ *efforts to weaken environmental laws* **2** [I] : to become weaker, less forceful, less effective, etc. ▪ *The disease causes the immune system to weaken.* **3** [T/I] *of money* : to decrease in value when compared to money from other countries ▪ *Lower interest rates have weakened the dollar.*

weak·ling /ˈwiːklɪŋ/ *n* [C] *disapproving* : a weak person ▪ *a 90-pound weakling*

weak·ness /ˈwiːknəs/ *n* **1** [U] : the quality or state of being weak ▪ *muscle weakness* ▪ *a sign of weakness* ▪ *the weakness of the economy* **2** [C] : a quality or feature that prevents someone or something from being effective or useful ▪ *the student's strengths and weaknesses* **3** [C] **a** : something that you like so much that you are often unable to resist it ▪ *Chocolate is my greatest weakness.* **b** : a strong feeling of desire for something ▪ *He has a weakness for desserts.*

wealth /ˈwɛlθ/ *n* **1** [U] : a large amount of money and possessions ▪ *a family that has acquired great wealth* **2** [singular] : a large amount or number ▪ *I was impressed by the wealth of choices.* ▪ *Libraries offer a wealth of information.* — **share/spread the wealth** : to share your money, goods, etc., with other people ▪ *If your garden is overflowing, spread* *the wealth.* [=give some of what is growing in your garden to other people]

wealthy /ˈwɛlθi/ *adj* **wealth·i·er; -est**
: having a lot of money and possessions
: RICH ▪ *a wealthy businessman* ▪ *a wealthy suburb/neighborhood* — **the wealthy** : wealthy people ▪ *policies that benefit the wealthy* — **wealth·i·ness** /ˈwɛlθinəs/ *n* [U]

wean /ˈwiːn/ *vb* [T] : to start feeding (a child or young animal) food other than its mother's milk ▪ *The calves are weaned at an early age.* — **wean from/off** [*phrasal vb*] **wean (someone or something) from/off** : to make (someone or something) stop doing or using (something) ▪ *I'm weaning myself off cigarettes.* — **wean on** [*phrasal vb*] **wean (someone) on** : to have (someone) see, use, or experience (something) often especially from a young age ▪ *kids weaned on television*

weap·on /ˈwɛpən/ *n* [C] 1 : something (such as a gun, knife, club, or bomb) that is used for fighting or attacking someone or for defending yourself when someone is attacking you ▪ *a deadly weapon* ▪ *weapons of mass destruction* [=weapons that can destroy entire cities, regions, etc.] 2 : something (such as a skill, idea, or tool) that is used to win a contest or achieve something ▪ *a new weapon in the fight against cancer*

weap·on·ry /ˈwɛpənri/ *n* [U] : WEAPONS ▪ *high-tech weaponry*

¹wear /ˈweɚ/ *vb* **wore** /ˈwoɚ/; **worn** /ˈwoɚn/; **wear·ing** [T] 1 a : to use or have (something) as clothing ▪ *He was wearing jeans.* b : to use or have (something) on your body ▪ *I don't wear glasses/perfume.* ▪ *Were you wearing a seat belt?* c : to grow or arrange (your hair) in a particular way ▪ *She wears her hair in a ponytail.* 2 : to have or show (some expression, such as an emotion or facial expression) especially on your face ▪ *She was wearing a frown/smile.* 3 a : to cause (something) to become thinner, weaker, etc., because of continued use over time ▪ *The carpet was badly worn.* b : to cause (something) to form gradually because of use ▪ *A path had been worn into the grass.* 4 : to make (someone) very tired ▪ *soldiers worn by the strain of war* — **wear away** [*phrasal vb*] **wear away or wear (something) away or wear away (something)** : to gradually disappear or to cause (something) to gradually disappear or become thinner, smaller, etc., because of use ▪ *The paint on the sign had worn away.* ▪ *The table's finish was worn away.* — **wear down** [*phrasal vb*] **wear (someone) down or wear down (someone)** 1 : to make (someone) tired or weak ▪ *The pressure at work was wearing her down.* 2 : to convince (someone) to do what you want by trying again and again ▪ *She wore her parents down and they agreed to let her go to the party.* — **wear off** [*phrasal vb*] : to gradually decrease, disappear, or stop ▪ *The painkillers wore off slowly.* — **wear on** [*phrasal vb*] 1 : to annoy or bother (someone) ▪ *Their constant talking was wearing on me.*

2 : to continue in a way that seems slow ▪ *as the day wore on* — **wear out** [*phrasal vb*] 1 **wear (someone) out or wear out (someone)** : to make (someone) tired ▪ *She was worn out from exercising.* 2 **wear out or wear (something) out or wear out (something)** : to become or to cause (something) to become thinner, weaker, or no longer useful because of use ▪ *The tires wore out after 60,000 miles.* ▪ *The tape was worn out.* — **wear the pants** (*US*) *or Brit* **wear the trousers** : to be the leader ▪ *She wears the pants in our family.* — **wear thin** 1 : to become weak or ineffective ▪ *My patience is wearing thin.* [=I was becoming annoyed/upset] 2 : to become ineffective or uninteresting because of being too familiar or used too often ▪ *His charm began to wear thin.* 3 : to become thin because of use ▪ *The rug is wearing thin.* — **wear through** [*phrasal vb*] **wear through (something) or wear (something) through** : to use (something) so much that a hole develops in it ▪ *I've worn through two pairs of shoes at this job.* — **wear well** 1 : to remain in good condition after being used ▪ *a fabric that wears well* 2 *informal + humorous* : to look younger than you are ▪ *For 70, she's wearing well.* — **wear·able** /ˈwerəbəl/ *adj* — **wear·er** *n* [C]

²wear *n* [U] 1 a : the act of using something as clothing ▪ *shoes for everyday wear* b : the act of using something ▪ *The deck can withstand years of wear.* 2 : clothing that is designed for a specified kind of person, occasion, or use ▪ *children's/active/evening wear* 3 : damage that is caused by use ▪ *The carpet is showing signs of wear.* — **wear and tear** : damage that happens to something when it is used for a period of time ▪ *normal wear and tear* — **worse for wear** ✧ Someone or something that is **slightly/somewhat/much (etc.) (the) worse for wear** looks worse after doing or experiencing something. ▪ *He came out of basic training only slightly the worse for wear.*

wea·ri·some /ˈwirisəm/ *adj* : causing you to feel bored, annoyed, or impatient : TIRESOME ▪ *his usual wearisome complaints/stories* — **wea·ri·some·ly** *adv*

¹wea·ry /ˈwiri/ *adj* **wear·i·er; -est** 1 : needing rest or sleep : TIRED ▪ *I need to rest my weary eyes.* 2 : bored or annoyed by something because you have seen it, heard it, done it, etc., many times or for a long time ▪ *I'm weary of fighting.* ▪ *I've grown weary of his stories.* 3 *literary* : causing you to feel tired ▪ *a long, weary journey* — **wea·ri·ly** /ˈwirəli/ *adv* — **wea·ri·ness** /ˈwirinəs/ *n* [U]

²weary *vb* **-ries; -ried; -ry·ing** [T] *somewhat formal* : to make (someone) very tired ▪ *The work wearies me sometimes.* — **weary of** [*phrasal vb*] : to stop being interested in (something) ▪ *He wearied of their questions.*

¹wea·sel /ˈwiːzəl/ *n, pl* **weasel** *or* **weasels** [C] 1 : a small animal that has a thin body and brown fur and that eats small birds and other animals 2 *informal* : a dishonest person who cannot be trusted

²**weasel** vb, US -seled or Brit -selled; US -sel·ing or Brit -sel·ling — **weasel into** [phrasal vb] chiefly US, informal : to get into (a place or situation) by being dishonest, by persuading someone in a clever way, etc. ▪ She weaseled (herself) into the position of manager. — **weasel out of** [phrasal vb] chiefly US, informal : to avoid doing (something) by being dishonest, by persuading someone in a clever way, etc. ▪ He weaseled (his way) out of helping me.

¹**weath·er** /ˈwɛðə/ n [U, plural] : the temperature and other outside conditions (such as rain, cloudiness, etc.) ▪ How's the weather? ▪ severe/foul/mild/hot/cold weather ▪ a weather report/forecast ▪ (Brit) She rides her bike in all weathers. [=in any kind of weather] ▪ (figurative) They had some stormy weather [=they had some problems] in their marriage. — **under the weather** : feeling ill ▪ I'm (feeling) a little under the weather today.

²**weather** vb [T/I] **1** : to change in color, condition, etc., because of the effects of the sun, wind, rain, etc., over a long period of time ▪ The wood has weathered over the years. ▪ weathered cedar **2** : to deal with or experience (something dangerous or unpleasant) without being harmed or damaged too much ▪ They weathered a storm at sea. ▪ He has weathered the criticism well.

weath·er–beat·en /ˈwɛðəˌbiːtn̩/ adj **1** : toughened or colored by the effects of the sun, wind, rain, etc. ▪ their weather-beaten faces **2** : worn and damaged by the effects of the sun, wind, rain, etc. ▪ a weather-beaten barn

weath·er·man /ˈwɛðəˌmæn/ n, pl -men /-ˌmɛn/ [C] : a man who reports and forecasts the weather

weath·er·proof /ˈwɛðəˌpruːf/ adj **1** : not able to be changed or damaged by the effects of the sun, wind, rain, etc. ▪ weatherproof materials **2** : able to protect someone or something from the effects of the sun, wind, rain, etc. ▪ a weatherproof coat — **weatherproof** vb [T] ▪ He weatherproofed his shoes.

weather stripping n [U] US : long, thin pieces of material that are used to seal a door or window around its edges — **weather–strip** vb -stripped; -stripping [T] ▪ He weather-stripped the doors and windows.

weath·er vane /ˈwɛðəˌveɪn/ n [C] : an object that is usually put on the top of a roof and that has an arrow that turns as the wind blows to show the direction of the wind

¹**weave** /ˈwiːv/ vb wove /ˈwoʊv/ or weaved; woven /ˈwoʊvən/ or weaved; weav·ing ◇ Wove is the usual past tense and woven the usual past participle for senses 1, 2, and 4. Weaved is the usual past tense and past participle for sense 3. **1** [T/I] : to make something (such as cloth) by crossing threads or long pieces of material over and under each other ▪ weave cloth/baskets **2** [T] : to create something (such as a story) by combining different things in usually a complicated way ▪ The author wove (together) an exciting tale of adventure and romance. **3** [T/I] : to move from side to side while going forward ▪ The car was weaving in and out of traffic. ▪ He weaved his way through the crowd. **4** [T] of a spider : to create (a web) ▪ a spider weaving its web — **weav·er** /ˈwiːvə/ n [C]

²**weave** n [C] : a pattern in a woven cloth : a particular way of weaving cloth ▪ a twill/open weave

web /ˈwɛb/ n **1** [singular] : WORLD WIDE WEB ▪ surfing the Web ▪ a Web browser/page **2** [C] : SPIDER WEB ▪ (figurative) a web of lies **3** [C] : a complicated arrangement or pattern of things ▪ a web of city streets **4** [C] : an area of skin that is between the fingers or toes of an animal or bird

webbed /ˈwɛbd/ adj : having pieces of skin that connect all the toes on a foot ▪ the webbed feet of ducks

web·bing /ˈwɛbɪŋ/ n [U] : strong and tightly woven material that is used in strips to support, catch, or hold things ▪ the webbing of a baseball glove

web·cam /ˈwɛbˌkæm/ n [C] : a small video camera that is used to show live images on a Web site

Web·mas·ter /ˈwɛbˌmæstə, Brit ˈwɛbˌmɑːstə/ n [C] : a person whose job is to create and maintain a Web site

Web page n [C] : a page of words, pictures, etc., that is shown on a Web site

Web site or **web·site** /ˈwɛbˌsaɪt/ n [C] : a place on the World Wide Web that contains information about a person, organization, etc., and that usually consists of many Web pages joined by hyperlinks ▪ Visit our Web site at www.Merriam-Webster.com.

wed /ˈwɛd/ vb wed·ded also wed; wed·ding **1** [T/I] somewhat formal + old-fashioned : MARRY ▪ They will wed in the fall. **2** [T] : to bring or join (two things) together ▪ The novel weds tragedy and comedy.

we'd /ˈwiːd/ — used as a contraction of we had or we would ▪ We'd [=we had] better be going. ▪ We said we'd [=we would] try harder.

Wed. abbr Wednesday

wed·ded adj **1** formal : MARRIED ▪ your lawfully wedded husband ▪ (humorous) wedded bliss [=the happiness experienced by people who are married] **2** : very closely involved in or connected to something ▪ He was wedded to his work.

wed·ding /ˈwɛdɪŋ/ n [C] : a ceremony at which two people are married to each other ▪ The wedding will be at 2:00 p.m. ▪ a wedding dress

wedding ring n [C] : a ring that you wear as a sign that you are married

¹**wedge** /ˈwɛdʒ/ n [C] **1** : a piece of wood, metal, etc., with one pointed end and one thicker end that is used to split something, to fit into a space, to separate two things stuck together, etc. ▪ A wedge held the door open. **2** : something that is shaped like a triangle or wedge ▪ a lemon wedge **3** : a golf club that is used for hitting short, high shots — **drive a wedge between** : to cause disagreement or anger between (people who had been

friendly before) ▪ *The fight drove a wedge between them.*

²**wedge** *vb* **wedged; wedg·ing** [T] **1** : to force (someone or something) into a very small or narrow space ▪ *She wedged her foot into the crack.* ▪ *I wedged myself into the car's back seat.* **2** : to use a wedge or similar object to keep (something, such as a door or window) in an open or closed position ▪ *She wedged the door open.*

wed·lock /ˈwɛdˌlɑːk/ *n* [U] : the state of being married ▪ *Their child was born out of wedlock.* [=they were not married when their child was born]

Wednes·day /ˈwɛnzˌdeɪ/ *n* [C/U] : the day of the week between Tuesday and Thursday ▪ *last/next Wednesday* ▪ *The paper is due (on) Wednesday.* — abbr. *Wed.* or *Weds.;* see also ASH WEDNESDAY — **Wednes·days** /ˈwɛnzˌdeɪz/ *adv* ▪ *He works late Wednesdays.* [=every Wednesday]

Weds. *abbr* Wednesday

wee /ˈwiː/ *adj* **1** *chiefly Scotland + Ireland* : very small or very young ▪ *a wee lad* **2** : very early ▪ *the wee hours* — *a wee bit informal* : by a very small amount or to a very small degree ▪ *She's a wee bit late.*

¹**weed** /ˈwiːd/ *n* **1** [C] : a plant that grows very quickly where it is not wanted and covers or kills more desirable plants **2** [U] *informal* : MARIJUANA ▪ *smoking weed*

²**weed** *vb* [T] : to remove weeds from (an area of land) ▪ *weed a garden* — **weed out** [*phrasal vb*] **weed (someone or something) out** *or* **weed out (someone or something)** : to remove (people or things that are not wanted) from a group ▪ *weeding out errors*

weedy /ˈwiːdi/ *adj* **weed·i·er; -est 1** : full of weeds ▪ *a weedy garden* **2** *Brit, informal* : looking thin and weak ▪ *a weedy little man*

week /ˈwiːk/ *n* **1** [C/U] : a period of seven days usually thought of as beginning on Sunday ▪ *the last week of the month* ▪ *I can meet you sometime next week.* ▪ *I volunteer here once a week.* [=once every week] **2** [C] : any period of seven days in a row ▪ *The baby is two weeks old.* ▪ *I arrived a week ago.* ▪ *We'll meet again (on) a week from Tuesday.* = (Brit) *We'll meet again on Tuesday week.* **3** [C] : the days from Monday through Friday when people usually work ▪ *We're open from 9 to 5 all week.* — **week in and week out** *also* **week in, week out** : every week for many weeks ▪ *He worked week in and week out with no vacation.*

week·day /ˈwiːkˌdeɪ/ *n* [C] : any day of the week except Saturday and Sunday — **week·days** /ˈwiːkˌdeɪz/ *adv, chiefly US* ▪ *We're open weekdays from 9 to 5.*

¹**week·end** /ˈwiːkˌɛnd/ *n* [C] : Saturday and Sunday ▪ *What are you doing this weekend?* ▪ *I kept busy during the weekend.* ▪ *The office is closed on weekends.* ▪ *Next Friday is a holiday, so we'll have a long weekend.*

²**weekend** *vb* [U] : to spend the weekend at a specified place ▪ *They weekend on the*

coast. — **week·end·er** /ˈwiːkˌɛndɚ/ *n*

week·long /ˈwiːkˌlɑːŋ/ *adj* : lasting for a week ▪ *a weeklong training session*

¹**week·ly** /ˈwiːkli/ *adj* **1** : happening, done, or made every week ▪ *weekly meetings* **2** : published once every week ▪ *a weekly magazine* **3** : of or relating to one week ▪ *a weekly paycheck* — **weekly** *adv* ▪ *We are paid weekly.* [=once every week]

²**weekly** *n, pl* **-lies** [C] : a magazine or newspaper that is published once every week

week·night /ˈwiːkˌnaɪt/ *n* [C] : any evening except Saturday and Sunday evening ▪ *The news is on every weeknight at 6 p.m.* — **week·nights** /ˈwiːkˌnaɪts/ *adv, chiefly US* ▪ *We watch the news weeknights at 6 p.m.*

weep /ˈwiːp/ *vb* /ˈwiːp/ *or* **wept** /ˈwɛpt/; **weep·ing** [T/I] **1** *somewhat formal* : to cry because you are very sad or are feeling some other strong emotion ▪ *She wept with joy/relief.* ▪ *He wept bitter tears of disappointment.* **2** : to produce a liquid slowly ▪ *The wound was weeping pus.* [=pus was slowly coming out from the wound]

weepy /ˈwiːpi/ *adj* **weep·i·er; -est** *informal* : crying or likely to cry ▪ *feeling weepy*

wee·vil /ˈwiːvəl/ *n* [C] : a small insect that eats grains and seeds and that can ruin crops

weft /ˈwɛft/ *n* [*singular*] *technical* : the threads that run from side to side on a loom or in a woven fabric

weigh /ˈweɪ/ *vb* **1 a** [T] : to find how heavy (someone or something) is ▪ *She weighed herself.* **b** [*linking vb*] : to have a specified weight ▪ *I weigh 180 pounds.* ▪ *This box weighs a ton.* [=is very heavy] **2** [T] : to think carefully about (something) : CONSIDER ▪ *weigh the pros and cons* ▪ *He's weighing his options.* **3** [I] : to be considered in a specified way when a person or thing is being judged ▪ *Her experience weighs in her favor.* — **weigh down** [*phrasal vb*] **weigh (someone or something) down** *or* **weigh down (someone or something)** **1** : to make (someone or something) heavier and less able to move easily ▪ *My backpack weighed me down.* **2** : to cause (someone) to accept or deal with something difficult or unpleasant ▪ *I'm feeling weighed down by all the work I have to do.* — **weigh in** [*phrasal vb*] **1 weigh in** *or* **weigh (someone) in** *or* **weigh in (someone)** : to be weighed or to weigh (someone) before competing in a fight, race, etc. ▪ *When will the jockeys weigh in?* **2** : to have a specified weight ▪ *He weighs in at 240 pounds.* [=he weighs 240 pounds] **3** *informal* : to give your opinion about something ▪ *She weighed in with her opinion.* ▪ *Did she weigh in on the plan?* — **weigh on** [*phrasal vb*] : to make (someone or something) sad, depressed, or worried ▪ *The news is really weighing on me.* — **weigh out** [*phrasal vb*] **weigh (something) out** *or* **weigh out (something)** : to measure and remove a certain weight of (something) • *He weighed out 20 pounds of rice.* — **weigh up** [*phrasal vb*] **weigh (someone) up** or **weigh up (someone)** : to look at and listen to (someone) in order to make a judgment about that person's character, abilities, etc. • *She watched him closely, weighing him up.*

weigh-in /ˈweɪˌɪn/ *n* [*C*] : an occurrence in which an athlete is weighed before an event • *the pre-fight weigh-in*

¹**weight** /ˈweɪt/ *n* **1** [*U*] **a** : a measurement that indicates how heavy a person or thing is • *Her weight is 105 pounds.* **b** : the heaviness of a person or thing • *The roof collapsed under the weight of the snow.* • *She gained/lost (some) weight.* [=became heavier/lighter] • *He is trying to watch his weight* [=to lose weight or to not gain weight] **2** [*C*] **a** : a heavy object that is lifted during exercising • *a 10-pound weight* • *He lifts weights.* **b** : a heavy object that is used to press something down or to or hold something in place **3** [*C*] : a unit of measurement (such as a pound, kilogram, etc.) used for showing how heavy someone or something is • *weights and measures* **4** [*singular*] **a** : something that causes worry or sadness • *Well, that's a weight off my mind/shoulders.* [=that's a relief] **b** : a difficult responsibility • *He bore the weight of having to tell them the bad news.* **5** [*U*] **a** : the influence or power someone or something has over other people or things • *Several senators put/threw their weight behind the bill.* [=used their influence to support the bill] • *(disapproving) He likes to throw his weight around.* **b** : the power to influence the opinions of other people • *Her opinion carries a lot of weight with me.* — **pull your own weight** : to do the things that you should be doing as part of a group of people who are working together • *You have to pull your own weight around here.*

²**weight** *vb* [*T*] : to put a weight on (something) to make it heavier or to keep it from moving • *I weighted (down) the fishing line with a lead sinker.*

weight·ed /ˈweɪtəd/ *adj* **1** : held in place or made heavier by a weight • *a weighted fishing line* **2** — used to say that something favors or does not favor a particular person, group, etc. • *The system is weighted against them.* • *The tax law is weighted toward people with high incomes.* = *The tax law is weighted in favor of people with high incomes.*

weight·less /ˈweɪtləs/ *adj* : having no weight or seeming to have no weight • *floating weightless* — **weight·less·ness** *n* [*U*]

weight lifting *n* [*U*] : the activity of lifting weights for exercise or in competition — **weight lifter** *n* [*C*]

weighty /ˈweɪti/ *adj* **weight·i·er; -est** **1** : HEAVY • *a weighty bag/book* **2** : very important and serious • *a weighty issue/topic* **3** : having the power to influence the opinions of other people • *a weighty figure in the art world*

¹**weird** /ˈwiəd/ *adj* : unusual or strange • *a*

weird person/noise — **weird·ly** *adv* — **weird·ness** *n* [*U*]

²**weird** *vb* — **weird out** [*phrasal vb*] **weird (someone) out** or **weird out (someone)** *US, informal* : to make (someone) feel strange or uncomfortable • *That movie weirded me out.*

weirdo /ˈwiədoʊ/ *n, pl* **weird·os** [*C*] *informal + disapproving* : a strange or unusual person

¹**wel·come** /ˈwɛlkəm/ *interj* — used as a friendly greeting to someone who has arrived at a place • *Welcome home/back!*

²**welcome** *adj* **1** : giving someone happiness or pleasure • *welcome news* • *a welcome change/sight* **2** — used to say that you are happy to have someone come to and stay in a place (such as your home) • *You're always welcome here.* **3 a** — used to say that someone can have or take something because you do not want it yourself • *If she wants this old desk, she's welcome to it.* **b** — used to say that someone can certainly do or use something if he or she wants to • *Anyone is welcome to use the pool.* [=anyone can use the pool] — **you're welcome** — used as a response to someone who has thanked you • *"Thanks for the ride." "You're welcome."*

³**welcome** *vb* **-comed; -com·ing** [*T*] **1** : to greet (someone) in a warm and friendly manner • *She welcomed me into her home.* **2** : to receive or accept (something) with happiness or pleasure • *We welcome your comments/suggestions.*

⁴**welcome** *n* [*C*] : the way in which someone is greeted • *He received a warm/hero's welcome.* — **outstay/overstay your welcome** or **wear out your welcome** : to be no longer welcome to stay in a place because you have stayed too long, been impolite, etc. • *After a week, she felt she had worn out her welcome.*

welcome mat *n* [*C*] *US* : a small rug that is placed by the door of a person's house, apartment, etc., for guests to wipe their feet on before entering — **put/roll/throw out the welcome mat** : to welcome someone in a warm and friendly way • *They rolled out the welcome mat for us.*

weld /ˈwɛld/ *vb* [*T/I*] : to join pieces of metal by heating the edges until they begin to melt and then pressing them together • *welding beams together* • *(figurative) His style of painting welds impressionism with surrealism.* — **weld** *n* [*C*] • *a strong weld* — **weld·er** /ˈwɛldə/ *n* [*C*]

wel·fare /ˈwɛlˌfeə/ *n* [*U*] **1** : a government program for poor or unemployed people that helps pay for their food, housing, medical costs, etc. • *He is on welfare.* [=receiving government assistance] • *welfare benefits/programs/payments* • *(chiefly US, figurative) corporate welfare* [=money or aid given by the government to help a large company] **2** : the state of being happy, healthy, or successful • *I'm concerned about your welfare.*

¹**well** /ˈwɛl/ *adv* **bet·ter** /ˈbɛtə/; **best** /ˈbɛst/ **1 a** : in a successful way • *The*

plan worked well. ▪ *I did well on the test.* ▪ *You got a perfect score! Well done!* **b :** in a skillful way ▪ *She sings well.* ▪ *The essay is well written.* **c :** in a good, proper, or positive way ▪ *She doesn't treat me very well.* **d :** in a kind, friendly, or generous way ▪ *They always speak well of you.* ▪ *I wish her well.* [=I hope that she succeeds] ▪ *He means well.* [=he has good intentions] ▪ *The company did well by me.* [=the company treated me well] **2 :** completely or fully ▪ *We are well aware of the problem.* ▪ *I knew him well.* **3 :** to a great degree or extent ▪ *The temperature was well above average.* **4 a** — used for emphasis to say that something is or is not proper, appropriate, etc. ▪ *She's angry, and well she should be.* [=she has a good reason to be angry] — usually used with *can, could, may,* or *might* ▪ *I couldn't very well just leave!* ▪ *And what, one might/may well ask, makes this car worth its high price?* **b :** very possibly — usually used with *could, may,* or *might* ▪ *You could very well be right.* **c :** without doubt or question ▪ *He can well afford to be generous.* ▪ *As you well know, I don't like her.* ▪ *You know perfectly well how to do it.* **5 a** ◆ To **live well** is to live in the comfortable and enjoyable way of people who have a lot of money, possessions, etc. ▪ *He lived very well in retirement.* **b** ◆ To **marry well** is to marry someone who has high social status, wealth, etc. — **as well 1 as well (as) :** in addition to someone or something else ▪ *You bought a new car? I bought one as well.* [=also] ▪ *She plays softball as well as basketball.* **2 a** — used in phrases like **might as well** and **may as well** to say that something should be done or accepted because it cannot be avoided or because there is no good reason not to do it ▪ *You might as well tell them the truth.* **b** — used to say that something else could have been done with the same result ▪ *The party was so dull that I might (just) as well have stayed home.* **3 :** in the same way ▪ *You know as well as I do* [=you and I both know] *that we can't afford that car.*

²**well** *adj* **better; best 1 :** HEALTHY ▪ *He is not well.* ▪ *I don't feel very well.* ▪ *I hope you get well soon.* **2** *not before a noun* **:** in a good or satisfactory state ▪ *I hope all is well with you.* ▪ *We almost didn't make it here, but all's well that ends well.* [=everything ended in a good way] ▪ *I should have left/let well (enough) alone.* [=I should not have tried to make the situation better] **3** *not before a noun, formal* **:** wise, sensible, or reasonable ▪ *It might be well for you to leave now.* — **all very well or all well and good** — used to say that something may seem proper, good, or reasonable by itself but that there are other things that also have to be considered ▪ *They say we have to improve our schools. That's all very well, but how can we find the money to do it?* — **just as well** see ²JUST — **very well** see ¹VERY

³**well** *interj* **1** — used to show that you are unsure about something you are saying ▪ *They are, well, not what you'd expect.*

▪ *"How old is he?" "Well, I don't really know."* **2** — used to show that you accept something even though you are not happy about it ▪ *"I'm sorry about the mixup." "Well, that's OK."* ▪ *"I'm busy this week." "Oh, well, maybe we can try again next week."* **3** — used when you are trying to persuade someone or to make someone feel less upset, worried, etc. ▪ *Well, maybe it won't be that bad.* **4** — used when you are saying in a mild way that you disapprove of or disagree with something ▪ *Well, I still think my way is better.* **5** — used to show that you are waiting for someone to say or do something ▪ *Well, what have you decided?* **6** — used to say that something has ended or to make a final statement about something ▪ *Well, we'd better get going.* **7** — used to begin a story or explanation or to continue one that was interrupted ▪ *You know Tom, don't you? Well, I saw him today.* **8** — used to express happiness or relief ▪ *"The doctor says it's nothing serious." "Well, thank goodness!"* **9** — used to express surprise or annoyance ▪ *Well, well, what do we have here?* **10** — used when you want to correct a previous statement ▪ *Everyone—well, almost everyone—was there.*

⁴**well** *n* [C] **1 :** a deep hole made in the ground through which water can be removed **2 :** OIL WELL

⁵**well** *vb* [I] *of a liquid* **:** to rise to a surface and flow out ▪ *Tears of joy welled up in her eyes.* [=her eyes filled with tears of joy] ▪ *(figurative) Anger welled up inside him.* [=he became angry]

we'll /ˈwiːl, ˈwɪl/ — used as a contraction of *we will* ▪ *We'll be waiting.*

well–ad·just·ed /ˌwɛləˈdʒʌstəd/ *adj* **:** able to deal with other people in a normal or healthy way ▪ *a well-adjusted adult*

well–ad·vised /ˌwɛlədˈvaɪzd/ *adj* **:** wise or sensible ▪ *You'd be well-advised to accept their offer.* [=you should accept their offer]

well–ap·point·ed /ˌwɛləˈpɔɪntəd/ *adj, formal* **:** having all the furniture, equipment, etc., that you need ▪ *a well-appointed apartment*

well–ba·lanced /ˌwɛlˈbælənst/ *adj* **:** having good or equal amounts of all the necessary parts of something ▪ *a well-balanced meal/diet* ▪ *a well-balanced account of the event*

well–be·haved /ˌwɛlbɪˈheɪvd/ *adj* **:** behaving in a polite or correct way ▪ *a well-behaved dog/child*

well–be·ing /ˈwɛlˈbiːjɪŋ/ *n* [U] **:** the state of being happy, healthy, or successful ▪ *Meditation can increase a person's sense of well-being.* ▪ *the economic well-being of the state*

well–bred /ˈwɛlˈbrɛd/ *adj, somewhat old-fashioned* **:** having or showing good manners ▪ POLITE ▪ *a well-bred child*

well–built /ˈwɛlˈbɪlt/ *adj* **1 :** built to be strong or to work well ▪ *a well-built house/car/system* **2 :** physically strong or attractive ▪ *He's well-built.*

well–con·nect·ed /ˌwɛlkəˈnɛktəd/ *adj* **:** having important and powerful friends

▪ *a well-connected lawyer*

well–de·fined /ˌwɛldɪˈfaɪnd/ *adj* : easy to see or understand ▪ *a well-defined boundary/policy*

well–de·vel·oped /ˌwɛldɪˈvɛləpt/ *adj* : large, advanced, or complete : fully developed ▪ *well-developed muscles*

well–dis·posed /ˌwɛldɪˈspoʊzd/ *adj, formal* : having a favorable or friendly feeling about someone or something ▪ *He is well-disposed to/toward the idea.*

well–done /ˈwɛlˈdʌn/ *adj* : cooked completely ▪ *a well-done steak*

well–dressed /ˌwɛlˈdrɛst/ *adj* : wearing attractive or fashionable clothes ▪ *a well-dressed man*

well–earned /ˈwɛlˈɚnd/ *adj* : fully deserved ▪ *a well-earned reputation/rest*

well–fed /ˈwɛlˈfɛd/ *adj* : having plenty of food to eat ▪ *well-fed pets*

well–found·ed /ˌwɛlˈfaʊndəd/ *adj* : based on good reasoning, information, or judgment ▪ *well-founded fears/advice*

well–groomed /ˌwɛlˈgruːmd/ *adj* : having a clean, neat appearance ▪ *The men were well-groomed.*

well–heeled /ˌwɛlˈhiːld/ *adj* : WEALTHY ▪ *well-heeled investors*

well–in·formed /ˌwɛlɪnˈfoɚmd/ *adj* 1 : having a lot of knowledge about current topics, a particular situation, etc. ▪ *a well-informed doctor* 2 : based on facts ▪ *a well-informed decision/opinion*

well–in·ten·tioned /ˌwɛlɪnˈtɛnʃənd/ *adj* : WELL-MEANING ▪ *well-intentioned advice*

well–kept /ˈwɛlˈkɛpt/ *adj* 1 : always having a neat, tidy, and attractive appearance ▪ *well-kept houses/lawns* 2 : known by only a few people ▪ *a well-kept secret*

well–known /ˈwɛlˈnoʊn/ *adj* : known by many people ▪ *a well-known writer/fact*

well–liked /ˈwɛlˈlaɪkt/ *adj* : liked by many people ▪ *a well-liked restaurant*

well–made /ˈwɛlˈmeɪd/ *adj* : made in an effective, strong, or skillful way ▪ *well-made furniture*

well–man·nered /ˌwɛlˈmænɚd/ *adj, formal* : POLITE ▪ *a well-mannered child*

well–mean·ing /ˌwɛlˈmiːnɪŋ/ *adj* : having or showing a desire to do something good but often producing bad results ▪ *well-meaning relatives/advice*

well–meant /ˌwɛlˈmɛnt/ *adj* : based on a desire to do something good but often producing bad results ▪ *well-meant advice*

well·ness /ˈwɛlnəs/ *n* [U] *chiefly US* : the quality or state of being healthy ▪ *a wellness center/program* [=a center/program that helps you become healthy]

well–nigh /ˈwɛlˈnaɪ/ *adv, formal* : almost or nearly ▪ *well-nigh perfect/impossible*

well–off /ˈwɛlˈɑːf/ *adj* **better off**; **best off** 1 : WEALTHY ▪ *a well-off family* 2 : in a good position or situation — usually used as **better off** ▪ *You might be better off in a different career.*

well–oiled /ˌwɛlˈɔjəld/ *adj* : working in a proper and successful way ▪ *a well-oiled political machine*

well–read /ˌwɛlˈrɛd/ *adj* : having gained a lot of knowledge by reading ▪ *a well-read scholar*

well–round·ed /ˌwɛlˈraʊndəd/ *adj* 1 : educated in many different subjects ▪ *well-rounded students* 2 : including many different things ▪ *a well-rounded education/diet*

well–spo·ken /ˌwɛlˈspoʊkən/ *adj* 1 : speaking well, politely, or appropriately ▪ *a well-spoken woman* 2 : spoken in an appropriate and proper way ▪ *well-spoken words*

well·spring /ˈwɛlˌsprɪŋ/ *n* [C] : a good source of something ▪ *a wellspring of information*

well–timed /ˈwɛlˈtaɪmd/ *adj* : done or happening at a good or suitable time : TIMELY ▪ *a well-timed announcement*

well–to–do /ˌwɛltəˈduː/ *adj* : WEALTHY ▪ *a well-to-do family*

well–trod·den /ˈwɛlˈtrɑːdn̩/ *adj* : walked on by many people ▪ *a well-trodden path* ▪ *(figurative) The book covers some well-trodden ground.*

well–wish·er /ˈwɛlˌwɪʃɚ/ *n* [C] : someone who wants another person to be happy, successful, etc. ▪ *Dozens of well-wishers gathered to say goodbye to him.*

well–worn /ˈwɛlˈwoɚn/ *adj* 1 : having been used or worn a lot and no longer in good condition ▪ *well-worn shoes* 2 : not interesting or effective because of being used too often ▪ *a well-worn quotation*

welsh /ˈwɛlʃ/ *vb* — **welsh on** [*phrasal vb*] *informal + disapproving* : to fail or refuse to do (something that you said you would do) ▪ *He welshed on his loan.* [=he did not repay his loan]

Welsh /ˈwɛlʃ/ *n* 1 [U] : the language of the Welsh people 2 **the Welsh** : the people of Wales — **Welsh** *adj* ▪ *Welsh literature*

welt /ˈwɛlt/ *n* [C] : a usually large bump or red area on your skin

wel·ter /ˈwɛltɚ/ *n* [*singular*] *formal* : a large and confusing number or amount ▪ *a welter of problems*

wel·ter·weight /ˈwɛltɚˌweɪt/ *n* [C] : a fighter in a class of boxers who weigh up to 147 pounds (67 kilograms)

wench /ˈwɛntʃ/ *n* [C] *old-fashioned + humorous* : a young woman; *especially* : a young woman who is a servant

wend /ˈwɛnd/ *vb* [T/I] *literary* : to move from one place to another ▪ *We wended (our way) through the narrow streets.*

went *past tense of* ¹GO

wept *past tense and past participle of* WEEP

were *see* BE

we're /ˈwiɚ, wɚ/ — used as a contraction of *we are* ▪ *We're here.*

weren't /ˈwɚrənt/ — used as a contraction of *were not* ▪ *We weren't expecting to win.*

were·wolf /ˈweɚˌwʊlf/ *n, pl* **-wolves** /-ˌwʊlvz/ [C] *in stories* : a person who sometimes changes into a wolf

¹**west** /ˈwɛst/ *n* 1 [U] : the direction where the sun sets : the direction that is the opposite of east ▪ *The storm approached from the west.* 2 **the west** or **the West** : regions or countries west of a certain point: such as **a** : a western part of the U.S. ▪ *the American West* **b** : North America and Western Europe ▪

policies foreign to the West

²**west** *adj* **1** : located in or toward the west ▪ *the west coast* **2** : coming from the west ▪ *a west wind*

³**west** *adv* : to or toward the west ▪ *They live just west of here.* — **out West** *or* **out west** *US, informal* : in or to the western part of a country or region ▪ *heading out west*

west·bound /ˈwɛstˌbaʊnd/ *adj* : going toward the west ▪ *a westbound train*

west·er·ly /ˈwɛstɚli/ *adj* **1** : located or moving toward the west ▪ *the lake's westerly shore* **2** : blowing from the west ▪ *westerly winds*

¹**west·ern** /ˈwɛstɚn/ *adj* **1** : located in or toward the west ▪ *the western U.S.* **2** *Western* : of or relating to the countries of North America and Western Europe ▪ *the Western world* **3** : of or relating to the American West ▪ *western movies* — see also COUNTRY AND WESTERN — **west·ern·most** /ˈwɛstɚnˌmoʊst/ *adj*

²**western** *n* [C] : a story, movie, or television show about life in the American West in the late 19th century; *especially* : a movie about cowboys

West·ern·er /ˈwɛstɚnɚ/ *n* [C] **1** : a person born, raised, or living in North America or Western Europe **2** : a person born, raised, or living in the western U.S.

west·ern·ize *or* **West·ern·ize** *also Brit* **west·ern·ise** /ˈwɛstɚnaɪz/ *vb* **-ized; -iz·ing** [T/I] : to cause (someone or something) to have the qualities or characteristics that are associated with Western Europe and North America ▪ *westernized cities/countries* — **west·ern·i·za·tion** *or* **West·ern·i·za·tion** *also Brit* **west·ern·i·sa·tion** /ˌwɛstɚnəˈzeɪʃən, Brit ˌwɛstənaɪˈzeɪʃən/ *n* [U]

west·ward /ˈwɛstwɚd/ *also chiefly Brit* **west·wards** /ˈwɛstwɚdz/ *adv* : toward the west ▪ *The settlers moved westward.* — **westward** *adj*

¹**wet** /ˈwɛt/ *adj* **wet·ter; wet·test 1** : covered or soaked with water or another liquid : not dry ▪ *wet clothes/towels/leaves* ▪ *His clothes were dripping/soaking/sopping wet* [=very wet] **2** : RAINY ▪ *a cold, wet morning* **3** *of paint, plaster, etc.* : not yet dry ▪ *wet cement* **4** *US, informal* : allowing alcoholic beverages to be sold or drunk ▪ *a wet state/county* — **all wet** *US, informal* : completely wrong ▪ *His argument was all wet.* — **get your feet wet** : to begin doing a new job, activity, etc., in usually a slow and simple way in order to become more familiar with it ▪ *She's getting her feet wet at her new job.* — **wet behind the ears** *informal* : young and not experienced ▪ *The reporter was still wet behind the ears.* — **wet·ly** *adv* — **wet·ness** *n* [U]

²**wet** *vb* **wet** *or* **wet·ted; wet·ting** [T] **1** : to cause (something) to become wet ▪ *She wet (down) the grass with a hose.* **2** : to make (a bed or your clothes) wet by urinating ▪ *The little boy wet his pants.* ▪ *The girl still wets the bed.* [=still urinates while sleeping in bed]

³**wet** *n* [C] *Brit, informal* + *disapproving* : a person who belongs to the Conservative

Party and who has moderate or liberal ideas

wet blanket *n* [C] *informal* : a person who makes it difficult for other people to enjoy themselves by complaining, by showing no enthusiasm, etc.

wet·land /ˈwɛtˌlænd/ *n* [C] : an area of land (such as a marsh or swamp) that is covered with shallow water — usually plural ▪ *protecting the wetlands*

wet suit *n* [C] : a piece of clothing that is made of rubber and that is worn by swimmers, divers, etc., when they are in cold water in order to keep their bodies warm

we've /ˈwiːv/ — used as a contraction of *we have* ▪ *We've got to go.*

¹**whack** /ˈwæk/ *vb* **1** [T/I] *informal* : to hit (someone or something) with great force ▪ *She whacked him on the head.* **2** [T] *US slang* : to murder or kill (someone) ▪ *He got whacked by mobsters.*

²**whack** *n, informal* **1** [C] **a** : the act of hitting someone or something with great force ▪ *She gave him a whack on the head.* **b** : the sound made when something is hit hard ▪ *The books hit the floor with a whack.* **2** [U] *Brit* : a share or portion of something ▪ *paying full whack* [=full price] — **(all) in one whack** *US, informal* : at one time ▪ *We spent $5,000 all in one whack.* — **have/take a whack at** *US, informal* : to try to do (something) ▪ *She took a whack at solving the puzzle.* — **out of whack** *US, informal* : not working properly ▪ *The garage door is out of whack.*

whacked–out *also* **wacked–out** /ˈwæktˌaʊt/ *adj, US slang* **1** : unusual or different in usually an amusing way ▪ *a whacked-out* [=wacky] *world* **2** : acting strangely because of the effects of drugs or alcohol ▪ *They were whacked-out on drugs.*

¹**whale** /ˈweɪl/ *n, pl* **whale** *or* **whales 1** [C] : an often very large animal that lives in the ocean and that is a mammal rather than a fish **2** [*singular*] *informal* : something that is very big, important, good, etc. — + *of* ▪ *a whale of a job/problem* [=a very big job/problem] ▪ *We had a whale of a time.* [=a great time]

²**whale** *vb* **whaled; whal·ing** *US, informal* **1** [T] : to hit (something) with great force and energy ▪ *He whaled the ball over the fence.* **2** [I] : to attack or hit someone or something repeatedly ▪ *She whaled on him* [=pounded on him] *with her fists.* ▪ *He was whaling into his employees.* [=angrily criticizing his employees]

whal·er /ˈweɪlɚ/ *n* [C] **1** : a person who hunts for whales **2** : a ship that is used for hunting whales

whal·ing /ˈweɪlɪŋ/ *n* [U] : the job or business of hunting whales ▪ *the whaling industry*

wham /ˈwæm/ *interj* — used to imitate the sound of a loud, sudden noise or to say that something happened very quickly ▪ *Everything was fine until wham!—all hell broke loose.*

wham·my /ˈwæmi/ *n, pl* **-mies** [C] *informal* : something (such as a magical spell) that causes someone to have bad luck ▪

They **put the whammy on him.** [=caused him to have bad luck] — see also DOUBLE WHAMMY

wharf /ˈwoɚf/ *n, pl* **wharves** /ˈwoɚvz/ *also* **wharfs** [*C*] : a flat structure that is built along the shore of a river, ocean, etc., so that ships can load and unload cargo or passengers

¹**what** /ˈwɑːt, ˈwʌt/ *pron* **1 a** — used to ask for information about someone or something ▪ *What is your name?* ▪ *What happened?* ▪ *What else did he say?* **b** — used to describe a question ▪ *Please ask them what they want for dinner.* **2 a** — used to ask someone to say something again because you have not clearly heard or understood it ▪ *What did you say?* = (*informal*) *What?* — often used to show surprise about the thing that someone has just said ▪ *She did what?!* **b** *informal* — used to express surprise, excitement, etc. ▪ *What, no breakfast?* **3 a** : that which : the one or ones that ▪ *"Do you have any other sizes?" "No, only what you see here."* **b** : the kind that : the same as ▪ *The speech was what we expected.* ▪ *My memory isn't what it used to be.* [=it is not as good as it used to be] **c** : something that ▪ *He was holding what appeared to be a gun.* **d** : the thing or things that ▪ *What you need is a vacation.* ▪ *Do what you're told.* ▪ *He knows what he should do.* ▪ *I don't know what to think.* ▪ *She has what it takes* [=she has the skills and personality] *to do the job.* ▪ *Guess what happened to me today!* **e** : anything or everything that : WHATEVER ▪ *Take what you need.* **4** *informal* — used to direct attention to something that you are about to say ▪ *I'll tell you what I'm going to do: I'm going to let you have it for 30 percent off.* ▪ *"You know what—you're right."* — **or what** *informal* **1** — used to ask about what is happening, being done, etc. ▪ *Are you ready or what?* **2** — used to ask if someone agrees with you ▪ *Is this fun or what?* — **say what** see ¹SAY — **what about 1 a** : does that include (someone) : how about (someone) ▪ *"We're all going out." "What about Pat?"* **b** : how does that affect (someone or something) ▪ *"You can throw this one away." "What about the others?" "Those I want to keep."* **2** — used to make a suggestion about what could be done ▪ *What about* [=how about] *coming with us?* **3** — used to ask someone to tell you something in response to the thing that you have just said ▪ *I like skiing and hiking.* **What about you?** [=what sports do you like?] — **what . . . for** : for what purpose or reason ▪ *What did you do that for?* ▪ *What is this switch for?* [=what does this switch do?] ▪ *"The boss wants to see you." "What for?"* [=why?] — **what have you** *informal* : any of the other things that might also be mentioned ▪ *They sell paper clips, pins, and/or what have you.* — **what if 1** : what would happen if ▪ *What if it rains?* **2** : what does it matter if — used to say that something is not important ▪ *"They might find out." "So what if they do?"* — **what of 1** *formal* : how does that affect (someone or something) ▪

What of those who cannot pay? **2** : why does (something) matter ▪ *"Did you approve this request?" "Yes. What of it?"* — **what's it to you?** *informal* : why do you want to know — used to respond in a somewhat angry or annoyed way to a question that you do not want to answer ▪ *"How much do they pay you?" "Why? What's it to you?"* — **what's more** : in addition ▪ *Her boyfriend is intelligent and handsome; what's more, he respects her.* — **what's up?** *US, informal* — used as a friendly greeting ▪ *"Hi. What's up?"* — **what's what** *informal* : the true state of things ▪ *She knows what's what when it comes to fashion.* [=she knows a lot about fashion] — **what's with** or **what's up with** *informal* **1** : what is the reason for (something) ▪ *(So) what's with the hat?* [=why are you wearing that hat?] ▪ *He told me to go away. What's up with that?* **2** : what is wrong with (someone or something) ▪ *What's (up) with him?*

²**what** *adj, always before a noun* **1** — used to ask someone to indicate the identity or nature of someone or something ▪ *What book did you read?* **2** — used to say that someone or something is remarkable for having good or bad qualities ▪ *What a good idea!* ▪ *Remember what fun we had?* **3** — used to refer to an amount that someone has, uses, etc. ▪ *He gambled away what (little) money he had left.*

³**what** *adv* : in what way ▪ *What* [=how] *does it matter?* ▪ *What does she care?* [=why is it important to her?] — **so what** *informal* — used to say that something said or done is not important ▪ *She has a drink now and then—so what?* — **what with** — used to introduce the part of a sentence that indicates the cause of something ▪ *What with school and sports, she's always busy.*

what all *pron, informal* : WHATNOT

what·cha·ma·call·it /ˈwɑːtʃəməˌkɑːlət, ˈwʌtʃəməˌkɑːlət/ *n* [*C*] *US, informal* : something whose name you have forgotten or do not know : THINGAMAJIG ▪ *I can't find the whatchamacallit that holds the door open.*

¹**what·ev·er** /wɑtˈɛvɚ, wʌtˈɛvɚ/ *pron* **1** : anything or everything that ▪ *Take whatever you need.* **2** : no matter what ▪ *Whatever he says, don't believe him.* ▪ *Whatever you do, don't press that button!* **3** — used in questions that express surprise or confusion ▪ *Whatever did she mean (by that)?* **4** *informal* : WHATNOT ▪ *I enjoy all kinds of sports—skiing, biking, (or) whatever.*

²**whatever** *adj* **1** *always before a noun* **a** : all the ▪ *Take whatever supplies you need.* **b** : any ▪ *She will buy it at whatever price.* : any . . . that ▪ *We will take whatever action is needed.* **c** — used to refer to something that is not known ▪ *For whatever reason, he refused to go.* **2** *not before a noun* : of any kind or amount at all : WHATSOEVER ▪ *There's no evidence whatever to support your theory.*

³**whatever** *adv, informal* — used to show that something said or done is not impor-

tant • *We could go to a movie, watch TV—whatever.*

what·not /'wɑːt,nɑːt, 'wʌt,nɑːt/ *pron, informal* : any of the other things that might also be mentioned • *They sell paper clips, pins, and/or whatnot.*

what's–her–name *also US* **what's–her–face** *n* [*singular*] *informal* : a woman whose name you have forgotten or do not know • *I just bumped into what's-her-name from the bank.*

what's–his–name *also US* **what's–his–face** *n* [*singular*] *informal* : a man whose name you have forgotten or do not know • *I think she's still dating what's-his-name.*

what·so·ev·er /,wɑːtsə'wɛvɚ, ,wʌtsə-'wɛvɚ/ *adj, not before a noun* : of any kind or amount at all • *There's no evidence whatsoever* [=whatever] *to support your theory.*

wheat /'wiːt/ *n* [*U*] **1** : a kind of grain that is used to make flour for breads, cookies, etc. **2** *US* : bread that is made from wheat flour • *a turkey sandwich on wheat*

wheat germ *n* [*U*] : the center part of a grain of wheat which is eaten often as a source of vitamins and protein

whee·dle /'wiːdl/ *vb* **whee·dled; wheedling** [*T/I*] *often disapproving* : to persuade someone to do something or to give you something by saying nice things • *He wheedled a lot of money from her.* • *He wheedled his way into his current job.*

¹wheel /'wiːl/ *n* **1** [*C*] **a** : one of the round parts underneath a car, wagon, etc., that rolls and allows something to move **b** : a hard, round object that turns and causes machinery or a mechanical device to move • (*figurative*) *You could almost see the wheels turning in his head.* [=you could almost see him thinking about what to do] **2** [*C*] : STEERING WHEEL • *She fell asleep at the wheel.* [=while she was driving] • *He got behind the wheel* [=in the driver's seat] *and sped off.* • *She offered to take the wheel.* [=offered to drive] **3** [*C*] : something that is round like a wheel or that turns like a wheel • *a wheel of cheddar cheese* **4** [*C*] **a** : an essential or functioning part of an organization, process, etc. — usually plural • *the wheels of government* **b** *informal* : an important person in an organization • *He's a big wheel at the company.* **5** [*plural*] *slang* : CAR • *a nice set of wheels* — **a/the squeaky wheel gets the grease/oil** — used to say that someone who complains or causes problems is more likely to receive attention or help than someone who stays quiet and does not cause problems — **wheels come/fall off** *informal* ◇ If the **wheels come/fall off**, someone or something fails in a sudden or unexpected way. • *The team was doing well at first, but then the wheels fell off.*

²wheel *vb* **1** [*T*] **a** : to move (someone or something) on a vehicle that has wheels • *She wheeled me into the operating room.* **b** : to push (something) that has wheels on it • *Our waiter wheeled out a small dessert cart.* **2** [*I*] : to turn

quickly and face a different direction • *She wheeled around in her chair to face him.* **3** [*I*] : to move in a circle or curve • *Seagulls wheeled overhead.* — **wheel and deal** : to make deals or agreements in business or politics in a skillful and sometimes dishonest way • *There was a lot of wheeling and dealing going on at the convention.*

wheel·bar·row /'wiːl,beroʊ/ *n* [*C*] : a cart with two handles and usually one wheel that is used for carrying heavy loads of dirt, rocks, etc.

wheel·chair /'wiːl,tʃeɚ/ *n* [*C*] : a chair with wheels that is used by people who cannot walk

wheeled /'wiːld/ *adj* **1** : having wheels • *a wheeled vehicle* **2** : having a specified number of wheels • *a four-wheeled vehicle*

wheel·er /'wiːlɚ/ *n* [*C*] : a vehicle that has a specified number of wheels • *an 18-wheeler* [=a large truck with 18 wheels]

wheel·er–deal·er /,wiːlɚ'diːlɚ/ *n* [*C*] *informal* : a person who makes deals in business or politics in a skillful and sometimes dishonest way • *a political wheeler-dealer*

wheel·house /'wiːl,haʊs/ *n* [*C*] : an enclosed area on a boat or ship where a person stands to steer

wheel·ie /'wiːli/ *n* [*C*] : an action in which a bicycle, motorcycle, etc., is balanced for a short time on its rear wheel • *He did a wheelie on his bike.*

¹wheeze /'wiːz/ *vb* **wheezed; wheez·ing** [*I*] **1** : to breathe loudly and with difficulty • *He was hacking and wheezing all night.* **2** : to make a sound like a person who is breathing with difficulty • *The car's motor wheezed and stalled.*

²wheeze *n* [*C*] **1** : the sound made by a person who is having difficulty breathing or a similar sound • *the wheeze of an engine* **2** *Brit, informal* : a clever idea or joke • *a good wheeze* — **wheezy** /'wiːzi/ *adj* **wheez·i·er; -est** • *a wheezy cough*

¹when /'wɛn/ *adv* **1** : at what time • *When will you return?* • *He asked me when I last saw her.* • *When is the next show?* **2** **a** : at, in, or during which • *It was a time when life was simpler.* **b** : at or during which time • *We're still waiting for the test results, when we'll decide our next move.* **3** *informal* : at a former and usually less successful time • *I can say I knew you when.* [=I knew you before you were famous or successful]

²when *conj* **1** **a** : at or during the time that • *When I was in school, we didn't have computers.* **b** : just after the time that • *Call me when you get home.* **c** : at any or every time that • *I cry when I hear that song.* **2** **a** — used to say what happens, is true, or can be done in a particular situation • *I take the bus when it rains.* • *When and if he comes, you can ask him.* = *If and when he comes, you can ask him.* **b** — used to ask why or how something is done in the situation that exists • *Why buy a newspaper when you can read the news online for free?* **3** : the time or occasion at or in which • *Tomorrow is when we must decide.*

³**when** *pron* : what or which time ▪ *You need the report by when?*

whence /ˈwɛns/ *adv, old-fashioned + literary* : from where ▪ *They returned to the land (from) whence they came.*

¹**when·ev·er** /wɛˈnɛvɚ/ *conj* : at any or every time that ▪ *You may leave whenever you wish.*

²**whenever** *adv* : at any time ▪ *You can come tomorrow or whenever.*

¹**where** /ˈweɚ/ *adv* **1 a** : at or in what place ▪ *Where are my keys?* ▪ *Where are you from?* — sometimes + *at* in very informal speech ▪ *Where's the party at?* **b** : to what place ▪ *Where are we going (to)?* ▪ **Where to, Miss?** [=what place do you want to go to?] **2** : when or at what point ▪ *Where does the story get interesting?* **3** : how or in what way ▪ *Where am I wrong?* **4** : to what goal or result ▪ *Where will this course of action lead us?* — **where it's at** *informal* **1** : the best or most exciting or interesting place to be ▪ *Los Angeles is where it's at if you want to get into the film industry.* **2** : a subject, field of interest, etc., that is very popular or important ▪ *Education is where it's at in politics.*

²**where** *conj* **1 a** : at or in the place that ▪ *Please stay where you are.* **b** : to or in what place ▪ *It doesn't matter to me where we eat.* ▪ *She didn't know where to go.* **c** : the place that ▪ *I know where his house is.* **d** : that is the place in which ▪ *the town where we live* **2** : to or in whatever place ▪ WHEREVER ▪ *I can go where I want.* ▪ *Sit where you like.* **3 a** — used to refer to a particular point in a story, process, etc. ▪ *The project is at a point where the end is in sight.* **b** — used to refer to a particular part of what is being discussed ▪ *That's where you're wrong.* **4** : in a situation in which ▪ *We must be careful where children are concerned.*

¹**where·abouts** /ˈweɚ əˌbaʊts/ *adv* : near what place ▪ *Whereabouts* [=where] *does he live?*

²**whereabouts** *n* [*plural*] : the location of a person or thing ▪ *Her present whereabouts are/is unknown.*

where·as /weɚˈæz/ *conj* **1** — used to make a statement that describes how two people, groups, etc., are different ▪ *He has brown eyes whereas his children have green eyes.* **2** *law* : since it is true that — usually used at the beginning of a statement in an official document ▪ *Whereas the citizens of the state of Virginia have a right to . . .*

where·by /weɚˈbaɪ/ *conj* : by which ▪ *They created a program whereby single parents could receive greater financial aid.*

where·fore /ˈweɚˌfoɚ/ *adv* — used in the past to mean "why" ▪ *"Wherefore art thou Romeo?"* [=why are you Romeo?] —Shakespeare, *Romeo and Juliet* (1594–95) — **the whys and (the) wherefores** see ³WHY

¹**where·in** /weɚˈɪn/ *adv, formal* : in what way ▪ *Wherein was I wrong?* : in what way ▪ *Wherein lies the secret to his success?*

²**wherein** *conj, formal* **1 a** : in which ▪ *the city wherein he lives* : during which ▪ *There was a period in her life wherein she*

took no active part in politics. **2** : in what way ▪ *He showed me wherein I was wrong.*

where·of /weɚˈʌv, weɚˈɑːv/ *conj, formal + old-fashioned* : of what ▪ *I know where-of I speak.*

where·up·on /ˈweɚ əˌpɑːn/ *conj, formal* : at which time — used to say that something happens directly after something else and often as a result of it ▪ *He graduated from high school in 1986, whereupon he joined the navy.*

¹**wher·ev·er** /weɚˈɛvɚ/ *adv* **1** : in what place ▪ WHERE — used in questions that express surprise or confusion ▪ *Wherever have you been?* **2** : in, at, or to any place ▪ *"Where should I put this?" "Just put it wherever."*

²**wherever** *conj* **1** : at, in, or to any place that ▪ *We can go wherever you like.* **2** : in any situation in which ▪ *Wherever* [=whenever] *(it is) possible, I try to help out.*

where·with·al /ˈweɚwɪˌðɑːl, ˈweɚwɪˌθɑːl/ *n* [U] : the money, skill, etc., that is needed to get or do something ▪ *financial wherewithal* ▪ *He lacks the wherewithal to finish the project.*

whet /ˈwɛt/ *vb* **whet·ted**; **whet·ting** [T] : to make (something, such as a person's appetite or curiosity) sharper or stronger ▪ *We had some wine to whet our appetites.*

wheth·er /ˈwɛðɚ/ *conj* **1 a** : if it is or was true that ▪ *I don't know whether they were invited.* **b** : if it is or was better ▪ *She was uncertain whether to go or stay.* **2** — used to indicate choices or possibilities ▪ *It doesn't matter whether you pay by cash or check.* ▪ *We're going whether or not you decide to come along.* [=we're going if you decide to come with us and we're going if you decide not to come with us]

whet·stone /ˈwɛtˌstoʊn/ *n* [C] : a stone used for sharpening knives, blades, etc.

whew /a whistling sound, often read as ˈhwuː, ˈhjuː/ *interj* — used to indicate that you are surprised, relieved, or hot ▪ *"Whew! It's hot in here."*

whey /ˈweɪ/ *n* [U] : the watery part of milk that forms after the milk becomes thick and sour

¹**which** /ˈwɪtʃ/ *adj* : what one or ones of a group : what particular one or ones — used to indicate what is being shown, pointed to, or mentioned ▪ *He knew which people had paid and which hadn't.* ▪ *Which way should we turn?* — **every which way** see EVERY

²**which** *pron* **1** : what one or ones out of a group — used to indicate or ask what is being shown, pointed to, or mentioned ▪ *They could not decide which of road to take.* ▪ *Which of those houses do you live in?* **2 a** — used to introduce an additional statement about something that has already been mentioned ▪ *She plays squash, which is similar to racquetball.* **b** — used after a preposition to refer again to something that has already been mentioned ▪ *The exhibit is on view here for three months, after which it travels to another city.* **c** — used to introduce a group of words that limits the meaning of a noun to a specific place or thing ▪

This is a matter which [=that] requires further study. — **which is which** — used to say that you are unsure about the identity of each member of a group • *The two words sound alike, so it's hard to remember which is which.*

which·ev·er /ˌwɪtʃˈɛvɚ/ *pron* : whatever one or ones out of a group • *We can go on Tuesday or Friday, whichever you prefer.* — **whichever** *adj* • *Choose whichever one you want.*

¹**whiff** /ˈwɪf/ *n*   **1** [C] : a slight smell of something • *a whiff of perfume*   **2** [*singular*] : a slight trace or indication • *I detected a whiff of sarcasm in her voice.*

²**whiff** *vb, US, informal*   **1** [T] : to notice (a smell) • *He whiffed a strong odor of perfume.*   **2** [T/I] *baseball* : to strike out or to cause (a batter) to strike out • *The batter whiffed.* • *The pitcher whiffed the batter.* • *The pitcher whiffed [=struck out] three batters in a row.*

Whig /ˈwɪg/ *n* [C]   **1** : a member or supporter of a British political group of the 18th and early 19th centuries   **2** : an American who supported independence from Great Britain during the American Revolution   **3** : a member or supporter of an American political party of the 19th century that was formed to oppose the Democrats

¹**while** /ˈwajəl/ *conj*   **1** : during the time that • *They met while they were in college.* • *Can I get you anything while I'm at the store?*   **2** — used to make a statement that describes how two people, groups, etc., are different • *While some people think his comedy is funny, others find him offensive.*   **3** : in spite of the fact that : ALTHOUGH • *While (he is) respected, the mayor is not liked.*

²**while** *n* [*singular*] : a period of time • *It took them a while to find out what was causing the problem.* • *Why don't we stay here (for) a while?* • *It has been quite a while since I last saw her.* • *He was thinking all the while* [=during that entire time] *of quitting his job.* — **(every) once in a while** see ¹ONCE — **worth your while** : worth doing • *If you help me, I'll make it worth your while.*

³**while** *vb* **whiled; whil·ing** — **while away** [*phrasal vb*] **while away (time)** *or* **while (time) away** : to spend (time) doing something pleasant and easy • *We whiled away the afternoon with a walk around the garden.*

whilst /ˈwajəlst/ *conj, chiefly Brit, formal* : ¹WHILE

whim /ˈwɪm/ *n* [C] : a sudden wish, desire, decision, etc. • *the whims of fashion* • *He quit his job on a whim.* [=because of a sudden decision]

whim·per /ˈwɪmpɚ/ *vb*   **1** [I] : to make a quiet crying sound • *The puppy was whimpering.*   **2** [T/I] : to complain in a weak or annoying way • *She whimpered about having to get up early.* — **whimper** *n* [C] • *She accepted their decision without a whimper.* [=without complaining]

whim·si·cal /ˈwɪmzɪkəl/ *adj* : unusual in a playful or amusing way : not serious • *whimsical behavior/decorations/humor* — **whim·si·cal·ly** /ˈwɪmzɪkli/ *adv*

whim·sy *also US* **whim·sey** /ˈwɪmzi/ *n* [U] : a playful or amusing quality • *Her outfit had a touch of whimsy.*

whine /ˈwaɪn/ *vb* **whined; whin·ing**   **1** [T/I] : to complain in an annoying way • *He's always whining about the weather.* • *They were whining that the office was too cold.*   **2** [I]   **a** : to make a high, crying sound • *The dog was whining.*   **b** : to make a high and unpleasant sound that continues for a long time • *The electric saw whined as it cut through the wood.* — **whine** *n* [C] • *the loud whine of the saw* — **whin·er** *n* [C] • *They're all a bunch of whiners.* — **whiny** *or* **whin·ey** /ˈwaɪni/ *adj* **whin·i·er; -est** • *a whiny child/voice*

whinge /ˈwɪndʒ/ *vb* **whinged; whing·ing** *or* **whinge·ing** [I] *Brit, informal* : to complain in an annoying way : WHINE — **whing·er** *n* [C]

whin·ny /ˈwɪni/ *vb* **-nies; -nied; -ny·ing** [I] *of a horse* : to make a gentle, high sound — **whinny** *n, pl* **-nies** [C]

¹**whip** /ˈwɪp/ *n* [C]   **1** : a long, thin piece of leather or similar material that is attached to a handle and that is used for hitting a person as punishment or to hit an animal (such as a horse) to make it move faster   **2** : a member of a legislature (such as the U.S. Congress or the British Parliament) who is appointed by a political party to make sure that other members are present when votes are taken and that they do the things they are expected to do • *the Republican/Democratic/Labour whip* — **crack the whip** see ¹CRACK

²**whip** *vb* **whipped; whip·ping**   **1** [T] : to hit (a person or animal) with a whip or with something that is like a whip • *The sailor was whipped for disobeying orders.*   **2** [T] : to move (something) to a different position or remove (something) from a place quickly and forcefully • *He suddenly whipped out a gun.* • *He whipped off his jacket.*   **3** [T/I] : to move or cause (something) to move quickly or forcefully • *The flag was whipping in the strong wind.* • *The wind whipped the ship's sails.* • *The shortstop whipped the ball to first base.*   **4** [T] *informal* : to defeat (someone) easily • *He always whips me at tennis.*   **5** [T] : to mix or beat a food (such as cream or an egg) very quickly • *She whipped the cream.* • *whipped butter/potatoes* — **whip into** [*phrasal vb*] **whip (someone) into** : to cause (a person or a group of people) to be in (a desired state) • *The speaker whipped the crowd into a frenzy.* • *Her coach whipped her into shape.* — **whip through** [*phrasal vb*] *informal* : to do (something) very quickly • *She whipped through her chores.* — **whip together** [*phrasal vb*] **whip (something) together** *or* **whip together (something)** *informal* : to produce or prepare (something) very quickly • *She whipped together a quick lunch.* — **whip up** [*phrasal vb*] **whip (someone or something) up** *or* **whip up (someone or something)**   **1** : to excite (someone or something) • *His speech whipped up the crowd.*   **2** *informal*   **a** : to cause or create (something) • *She was trying to whip up some enthusiasm.*

b : to produce or prepare (a meal) very quickly • *whip up a snack*

whip·lash /ˈwɪpˌlæʃ/ *n* [*U*] : an injury to the neck that is caused by a sudden backward movement of the head

whipping boy *n* [*C*] : someone or something that often is blamed for problems caused by other people • *The coach has become the whipping boy for all of the team's problems.*

whir *also* **whirr** /ˈwər/ *n* [*C*] : the sound made by something that is spinning very fast • *the whir of a fan* — **whir** *also* **whirr** *vb* **whirred; whir·ring** [*I*] • *I could hear the engine whirring.*

¹**whirl** /ˈwərəl/ *vb* **1** [*I*] : to move or go in a circle or curve especially with force or speed • *The cars were whirling around the track.* **2 a** [*T/I*] : to turn rapidly in circles : SPIN • *Her dance partner whirled her around.* • *whirling winds* **b** [*I*] : to turn quickly and suddenly • *She whirled around in surprise.* **3** [*I*] : to be dizzy or confused • *My head was whirling.*

²**whirl** *n* **1** [*C*] **a** : a fast turning movement • *He gave the crank a whirl.* **b** : something that is turning quickly in circles • *a whirl of dust* **2** [*singular*] : a state of busy movement or activity • *a whirl of activity* • *She got caught up in the social whirl.* [=busy social activity] **3** [*singular*] : a dizzy or confused mental state • *My head was in a whirl.* — **give (something) a whirl** *informal* : to attempt or try (something) • *He thought he'd give acting a whirl.*

whirl·pool /ˈwərəlˌpuːl/ *n* [*C*] : an area of water that moves very fast in a circle • *(figurative) She has experienced a whirlpool of emotions.* [=a confusing mixture of emotions]

whirl·wind /ˈwərəlˌwɪnd/ *n* **1** [*C*] : a very strong wind that moves in a spinning or swirling motion **2** [*singular*] : something that involves many quickly changing events, feelings, etc. • *He attended a whirlwind of meetings.* • *an emotional whirlwind* — **whirlwind** *adj, always before a noun* • *a whirlwind romance* [=a romance that happens very quickly]

whirly·bird /ˈwəliˌbəd/ *n* [*C*] *US, informal* : HELICOPTER

¹**whisk** /ˈwɪsk/ *n* [*C*] : a cooking tool that is made of curved wire and that is used to stir or beat eggs, sauces, etc.

²**whisk** *vb* [*T*] **1** : to stir or beat (eggs, sauces, etc.) with a whisk or fork • *Whisk the eggs with the cream until the mixture thickens.* **2** : to move or take (someone or something) to another place very quickly • *The taxi whisked me to the airport.*

whisk broom *n* [*C*] *US* : a small broom or brush with a short handle that you use especially to clean clothes

whis·ker /ˈwɪskər/ *n* **1** [*C*] : a hair that grows on a man's face • *He shaved off his whiskers.* **2** [*C*] : any one of the long, stiff hairs that grow near the mouth of some animals • *a cat's whiskers* **3** [*singular*] *informal* : a very small distance or amount • *He won/lost the race by a whisker.* — **whis·kered** /ˈwɪskəd/ *adj* • *a whiskered animal/chin*

whis·key (*chiefly US + Ireland*) *or chiefly Brit* **whis·ky** /ˈwɪski/ *n, pl* **-keys** *or* **-kies** [*C/U*] : a strong alcoholic drink made from a grain (such as rye, corn, or barley)

¹**whis·per** /ˈwɪspər/ *vb* **1** [*T/I*] : to speak very softly or quietly • *He whispered (something) in/into her ear.* • *"I'll be right back," she whispered.* **2** [*I*] : to produce a quiet sound • *A breeze whispered through the trees.* — **whis·per·er** /ˈwɪspərər/ *n* [*C*]

²**whisper** *n* [*C*] **1 a** : a very soft and quiet way of speaking • *She spoke in a whisper.* **b** : a soft and quiet sound • *the whisper of the wind* **2** : RUMOR • *I've heard whispers that she might quit.* **3** : a very small amount of something • *a whisper of smoke*

¹**whis·tle** /ˈwɪsəl/ *n* [*C*] **1 a** : a small device that makes a very high and loud sound when a person blows air through it • *The policeman blew his whistle.* **b** : a device through which air or steam is forced to produce a very high and loud sound • *a factory/train whistle* — see also BELLS AND WHISTLES **2** : a high and loud sound made by forcing air through your lips or teeth • *He gave a whistle.* [=he whistled] **3** : a sound made by blowing • *the whistle of the teakettle* — **blow the whistle** : to tell police, reporters, etc., about something that has been kept secret • *He blew the whistle on the company's illegal hiring practices.* — **clean as a whistle** *informal* : very clean • *We scrubbed the old boat until it was (as) clean as a whistle.* — **wet your whistle** *US, informal* : to have a drink

²**whistle** *vb* **whis·tled; whis·tling** **1** [*T/I*] : to make a high sound by blowing air through your lips or teeth • *He whistled for a cab.* • *He whistled a happy tune.* **2** [*I*] : to produce a high and loud sound by forcing air or steam through a device • *The teakettle started to whistle.* **3** [*I*] : to move, pass, or go very fast with a high sound • *A bullet whistled past me.*

whis·tle–blow·er /ˈwɪsəlˌbloʊə/ *n* [*C*] : a person who tells police, reporters, etc., about something that has been kept secret • *a whistle-blower who has revealed the corporation's illegal activities*

whis·tle–stop /ˈwɪsəlˌstɑːp/ *adj, always before a noun, US* : relating to or involving a series of appearances by a politician in different communities during an election campaign • *a whistle-stop campaign/tour*

whit /ˈwɪt/ *n* [*singular*] *informal + old-fashioned* : a very small amount • *He didn't care a whit about the money.*

¹**white** /ˈwaɪt/ *adj* **whit·er; -est** **1 a** : having the color of fresh snow or milk • *white socks/hair/rice* **b** : light or pale in color • *He turned white when he heard the news.* **2** : of or relating to a race of people who have light-colored skin and who come originally from Europe • *a white* [=Caucasian] *male* • *He came from a white middle-class background.* **3** *Brit* : served with cream or milk • *white coffee/tea* — **white·ness** /ˈwaɪtnəs/ *n* [*U*]

²**white** *n* **1** [*C/U*] : the very light color of

fresh snow or milk **2 a** [*U*] : white clothing • *nurses dressed in white* [=in white uniforms] **b** [*plural*] : white clothes used to play sports • *tennis whites* **3** [*C*] : a white or light-colored thing or part: such as **a** : the white part of the eye **b** : the clear or white substance around the yolk of an egg • *egg whites* **4** [*C*] : a person belonging to a race of people who have light-colored skin : a white person — usually plural • *His policies are supported by both blacks and whites.*

white blood cell *n* [*C*] : a clear or colorless cell in the blood that protects the body from disease

white-col·lar /ˈwaɪtˈkɑːləʳ/ *adj* : done in an office instead of a factory, warehouse, etc. • *white-collar jobs* : relating to or having jobs that are done in an office • *white-collar workers* — compare BLUE-COLLAR — **white-collar crime** : crime that typically involves stealing money from a company and that is done by people who have important positions in the company • *Embezzlement is a white-collar crime.*

white elephant *n* [*C*] : something that requires a lot of care and money and that gives little profit or enjoyment • *The run-down historic building has been the city's white elephant.*

white flag *n* [*C*] : a flag used to show that you want to stop fighting or to indicate defeat • *(figurative) They raised/waved the white flag* [=admitted defeat] *soon after the election results came in.*

White·hall /ˈwaɪtˌhɑːl/ *n* [*U*] *Brit* : a wide street in London where there are many government buildings — used to refer to the British government • *There has been no response from Whitehall about the claims.*

white–hot /ˈwaɪtˈhɑːt/ *adj* : extremely hot • *white-hot metal* • *(figurative) white-hot enthusiasm*

White House *n* — **the White House 1** : the place in Washington, D.C., where the U.S. President lives **2** : the executive branch of the U.S. government • *The White House announced the new appointments to the Cabinet.* • *White House staffers*

white lie *n* [*C*] : a lie about a small or unimportant matter that someone tells to avoid hurting another person

whit·en /ˈwaɪtn̩/ *vb* [*T/I*] : to make (something) white or whiter or to become white or whiter • *The toothpaste whitens teeth.* • *His hair whitened as he aged.*

white pages *n* — **the white pages** or **the White Pages** *US* : the part of a phone book that lists the names, addresses, and phone numbers of people and businesses

white trash *n* [*U*] *US, informal + offensive* : poor white people who are not well educated

white·wall /ˈwaɪtˌwɑːl/ *n* [*C*] *US* : a tire on a car that has a white band near the rim of the wheel

¹**white·wash** /ˈwaɪtˌwɑːʃ/ *n* **1** [*U*] : a white liquid mixture used for making walls, fences, etc., whiter **2** [*C*] *disapproving* : a planned effort to hide a dis-

honest, immoral, or illegal act or situation : COVER-UP • *The official report is believed to be a whitewash written to conceal the truth.*

²**whitewash** *vb* [*T*] **1** : to make (something) whiter by painting it with whitewash • *They whitewashed the fence.* **2** : to prevent people from learning the truth about (something dishonest, immoral, or illegal) • *a book that tries to whitewash the country's past* **3** *chiefly Brit* : to defeat (an opponent) easily by winning every game, point, etc. • *She was whitewashed 8–0.*

white water *n* [*U*] : water in part of a river that looks white because it is moving very fast over rocks — **white-wa·ter** /ˈwaɪtˌwɑːtəʳ/ *adj* • *whitewater rafting*

whith·er /ˈwɪðəʳ/ *adv, old-fashioned + literary* : to what place • *He grew up in New York City whither his family had immigrated in the early 1920s.* — sometimes used in questions to ask what the future of something will be • *Whither cancer research?*

whit·tle /ˈwɪtl̩/ *vb* **whit·tled; whit·tling** [*T*] : to cut small pieces from (a piece of wood) • *whittle a branch* : to make or shape (something) from a piece of wood by cutting small pieces from it • *She whittled a walking stick from a branch.* — **whittle away** [*phrasal vb*] **whittle (something) away** or **whittle away (something)** : to reduce or get rid of (something) slowly • *I'm trying to whittle away a few pounds.* — **whittle down** [*phrasal vb*] **whittle (something) down** or **whittle down (something)** : to gradually make (something) smaller by removing parts • *We whittled the list down to four people.*

¹**whiz** *(chiefly US)* or *Brit* **whizz** /ˈwɪz/ *vb* **whiz·zes; whizzed; whiz·zing** [*I*] *informal* **1** : to move quickly while making a buzzing or humming sound • *Bullets whizzed overhead.* **2** : to pass by quickly • *He whizzed past us on skates.*

²**whiz** *(chiefly US)* or *Brit* **whizz** *n, pl* **whiz·zes** [*C*] **1** : a humming or buzzing sound made by something moving quickly • *We could hear the whiz of the bullets.* **2** *informal* : someone who is very good at something • *He's a whiz at math.* • *a computer whiz kid* [=a smart young person who knows a lot about computers]

who /ˈhuː/ *pron* **1 a** : what or which person or people — used when you do not know the name or identity of a person or group of people that you are talking about or asking about • *Who will be at the meeting?* • *I didn't know who he was.* **b** — used to question a person's character or authority • *Who do you think you are?* [=what gives you the right to say or do this?] **c** — used in questions that are meant to say that no one would or would not do something, know something, etc. • *"Are they coming?" "Who knows?"* [=no one knows; I don't know] **2** — used after a noun or pronoun to show which group of people you are talking about • *The people who conducted the study were extremely professional.* **3** — used to introduce an additional statement about someone who has already been mentioned ▪ *The former president of the company, who is retired now, expanded the product line.* — **who's who** 1 *or* **who is who** : information about the people who make up a group ▪ *I'm still learning who's who around the office.* 2 : a list of the names of the important and well-known people in a particular field ▪ *The guest list reads like a who's who of the publishing industry.*

whoa /ˈwoʊ/ *interj* 1 — used to command a horse to stop moving 2 — used to tell someone to slow down or stop and think about something ▪ *Whoa. Take a deep breath and tell me what's wrong.* 3 — used to show that you are surprised or impressed ▪ *Whoa, that's a cool car.*

who'd /ˈhuːd/ — used as a contraction of *who would* or *who had* ▪ *Who'd* [=who would] *have thought he could do it?* ▪ *We didn't know who'd* [=who had] *done it.*

who·dun·it (*chiefly US*) *or Brit* **who·dun·nit** /huˈdʌnət/ *n* [C] *informal* : a novel, play, or movie about a murder where you do not know who committed the murder until the end

who·ev·er /huˈɛvɚ/ *pron* 1 : whatever person : any person at all ▪ *Whoever wants to come along is welcome to join us.* ▪ *A prize will be given to whoever solves the riddle.* 2 — used in questions that express surprise or confusion ▪ *Whoever can that be?*

¹**whole** /ˈhoʊl/ *adj* 1 a *always before a noun* : complete or full : not lacking or leaving out any part ▪ *The whole* [=*entire*] *family went on the trip.* ▪ *The whole house was remodeled.* ▪ *She read the whole book in one day.* ▪ *I felt like the luckiest girl in the whole wide world.* b : having all the parts : not divided or cut into parts or pieces ▪ *a whole egg/chicken* ▪ *whole strawberries* 2 a : great or large in size, extent, etc. ▪ *The community center offers a whole range of programs.* ▪ *There's a whole set of criteria to consider.* b — used for emphasis before a noun ▪ *She missed the whole point of the story.* ▪ *He doesn't seem to have a whole lot of* [=*much*] *respect for other people's feelings.* ▪ *Things are looking a whole lot* [=*much*] *brighter now.* — **whole·ness** *n* [U]

²**whole** *n* [C] : something that is full or complete — usually singular ▪ *The whole of my day was spent in meetings.* [=I spent the entire day in meetings] ▪ *He felt he was part of a greater whole.* [=something much larger and greater than himself] — **as a whole** : as a complete unit — used to make a statement that relates to all the parts of something ▪ *Language as a whole is constantly evolving.* — **in whole** *law* : to the full or entire extent ▪ *The contract can be voided in whole or in part.* [=the entire contract can be voided or a part of the contract can be voided] — **on the whole** 1 — used to say what you think is true, what should be done, etc., when you consider a situation in a general way ▪ *On the whole, I think the project is going well.* 2 : in general : in most cases ▪ *On the whole, new parents reported that*

they were adapting very well to parenthood.

³**whole** *adv* 1 : entirely or completely ▪ *a whole new system* 2 : in one piece that has not been cut into parts ▪ *We cooked the chicken whole.*

whole·heart·ed /ˈhoʊlˈhɑɚtəd/ *adj* : having or showing no doubt or uncertainty about doing something, supporting someone, etc. ▪ *wholehearted devotion/support* — **whole·heart·ed·ly** *adv*

whole meal *adj, Brit* : WHOLE WHEAT ▪ *whole meal bread*

whole note *n* [C] *US* : a musical note equal in time to two half notes or four quarter notes

whole number *n* [C] *mathematics* : a number (such as 0, 1, 2, 3, etc.) that is not a negative and is not a fraction

¹**whole·sale** /ˈhoʊlˌseɪl/ *n* [U] : the business of selling things in large amounts to other businesses rather than to individual customers

²**wholesale** *adj* 1 : relating to the business of selling things in large amounts to other businesses rather than to individual customers ▪ *a wholesale grocer/dealer* ▪ *wholesale prices* 2 : affecting large numbers of people or things ▪ *The poor economy has caused wholesale layoffs in many industries.* — **wholesale** *adv* ▪ *They bought the supplies wholesale.*

³**wholesale** *vb* **-saled; -sal·ing** 1 [*T*] : to sell (things) to other businesses rather than to individual customers ▪ *The company wholesales clothing to boutiques in the area.* 2 [*I*] : to be sold to other businesses for a specified price ▪ *a product that wholesales at/for $10 a pound* — **whole·sal·er** /ˈhoʊlˌseɪlɚ/ *n* [C] ▪ *book wholesalers*

whole·some /ˈhoʊlsəm/ *adj* 1 : helping to keep your body healthy ▪ *a wholesome diet/snack* 2 : morally good ▪ *wholesome people/values* — **whole·some·ness** *n* [U]

whole step *n* [C] *US, music* : a difference in pitch that is equal to ⅙ of an octave

whole wheat *adj* : made from wheat from which no part (such as the bran) has been removed ▪ *whole wheat bread*

whol·ly /ˈhoʊlli/ *adv, formal* : completely or fully ▪ *The claim is wholly without merit.*

whom /ˈhuːm/ *pron, objective case of* WHO — used in formal writing or speech ▪ *To whom am I speaking?* ▪ *The person to whom we spoke was very helpful.* = *The person whom we spoke to was very helpful.* ▪ *Whom did you speak to?* ▪ *His brother, with whom he is very close, works for the same company.* — **To whom it may concern** see ²CONCERN

whom·ev·er /huˈmɛvɚ/ *pron, objective case of* WHOEVER — used in formal writing or speech ▪ *You can invite whomever you please.*

whoop /ˈhuːp, ˈwuːp/ *vb* [*I*] *informal* : to shout loudly in an enthusiastic or excited way ▪ *The children whooped with joy.* — **whoop it up** *informal* : to celebrate and have fun in a noisy way ▪ *My pals and I whooped it up at the concert.* — **whoop** *n*

[C] • *loud cheers and whoops of joy/excitement*

whoop·ee /ˈwʊpi/ *interj* — used to express enthusiasm • *Whoopee! I passed the entrance exam!*

whoop·ing cough /ˈhuːpɪŋ-/ *n* [U] : a disease that usually affects children and that causes severe coughing and difficult breathing

whoops *also* **woops** /ˈwʊps/ *interj* — used to express surprise or distress or to say that you have done or said something wrong • *Whoops* [=*oops*]*, I slipped!*

whoosh /ˈwʊʃ/ *vb* [I] : to move very quickly with the sound of quickly flowing air or water • *Water whooshed down the pipe.* — **whoosh** *n* [C] • *a whoosh of hot air*

whop·per /ˈwɑːpɚ/ *n* [C] *informal* 1 : something that is very large and impressive • *That's a whopper of a diamond ring.* 2 : a big lie • *He told us a real whopper.*

whop·ping /ˈwɑːpɪŋ/ *adj, always before a noun, informal* : very large, impressive, etc. • *The play was a whopping success.*

whore /ˈhoɚ/ *n* [C] *somewhat old-fashioned* : PROSTITUTE

whorl /ˈwɚl/, ˈwoɚl/ *n* [C] : something that turns or goes around in a circle • *a whorl of smoke*

who's /ˈhuːz/ — used as a contraction of *who is* or *who has* • *Who's* [=*who is*] *in charge here?* • *a student who's* [=*who has*] *always been interested in math*

¹**whose** /ˈhuːz/ *adj* 1 — used in questions to ask who owns something, has something, etc. • *Whose bag is it?* • *I wonder whose story was chosen.* 2 — used to show which person or thing you are talking about • *The gentleman whose phone was stolen was very upset.* • *the book whose cover is torn* 3 — used to give more information about a person or thing that has already been mentioned • *My roommate, whose sister is an actress, gets lots of requests for autographs.*

²**whose** *pron* : that or those belonging to a person • *Whose are these?* [=*who is the owner of these?*]

¹**why** /ˈwaɪ/ *adv* 1 : for what reason or purpose • *Why are you laughing?* • *Why is the sky blue?* • *"I can't go out tonight." "Why not?"* 2 — used to offer a suggestion or to say that a course of action is not necessary • *If you don't want to go, why not just say so?* • *Why don't you come over for dinner?* [=*we would like to have you over for dinner*]

²**why** *conj* 1 : the cause, reason, or purpose for which • *I know why he did it.* 2 : for which • *Give me one good reason why I should stay.*

³**why** *n* — **the whys and (the) wherefores** : the reasons for something • *She explained the whys and the wherefores of the price increase.*

⁴**why** *interj, somewhat old-fashioned* — used at the beginning of a statement especially to express surprise • *Why, I can't imagine such a thing!* • *"Do you know him?" "Why, yes! We know him quite well."*

WI *abbr* Wisconsin

Wic·ca /ˈwɪkə/ *n* [U] : a religion that is

characterized by belief in the existence of magical powers in nature — **Wic·can** /ˈwɪkən/ *adj* • *Wiccan rituals* — **Wiccan** *n* [C] • *a group of Wiccans*

wick /ˈwɪk/ *n* [C] : a string or piece of material in a candle or lamp that is lit for burning

¹**wick·ed** /ˈwɪkəd/ *adj* 1 a : morally bad : EVIL • *a wicked person/act* b *informal* : having or showing slightly bad thoughts in a way that is funny or not serious • *a wicked grin* • *a wicked sense of humor* 2 *informal* : very bad or unpleasant • *a wicked case of food poisoning* 3 *informal* : very good • *He throws a wicked fastball.* — **wick·ed·ly** *adv* — **wick·ed·ness** *n* [U]

²**wicked** *adv, US, informal* : very or extremely • *It's wicked funny!*

wick·er /ˈwɪkɚ/ *n* [U] : thin twigs or sticks that are woven together to make furniture and baskets • *a wicker chair* [=a chair made from wicker] • *wicker baskets*

wick·et /ˈwɪkət/ *n* [C] 1 *US* : a curved wire that the ball must be hit through in the game of croquet 2 *cricket* a : a set of three wooden sticks at which the ball is bowled b : the rectangular area of ground that is between the two wickets

wick·et·keep·er /ˈwɪkətˌkiːpɚ/ *n* [C] *cricket* : the player who stands behind the wicket to catch the ball

¹**wide** /ˈwaɪd/ *adj* **wid·er; wid·est** 1 a : extending a great distance from one side to the other : not narrow • *a wide road/smile* b : measured from side to side : having a specified width • *The desk is three feet wide.* 2 : opened as far as possible • *Her eyes were wide with wonder.* 3 : including or involving a large number of people or things • *a wide range of options* • *The dishes are available in a wide assortment of colors.* [=in many colors] • *The book appealed to a wide audience.* 4 : extending throughout a specified area • *an industry-wide decrease in production* 5 : away from a target • *His shot was wide and landed in the rough.* • *The shot was wide of the goal.* [=the shot missed the goal]

²**wide** *adv* 1 : at a great distance : FAR • *The poles were placed wide apart.* 2 : to the side of something by a large distance • *The shot landed wide (of the target).* 3 : to the fullest extent : as fully as possible • *He opened his eyes/mouth wide.* • *They spread the map out wide.* • *His mouth was wide open.* • *wide open spaces* • *It was late, but the children were still wide awake.* [=not tired at all] — **far and wide** *see* ¹FAR

wide–eyed /ˈwaɪdˌaɪd/ *adj* 1 : having your eyes wide open especially because of surprise or fear • *He stared at me, wide-eyed in astonishment.* 2 : having or showing a lack of experience or knowledge • *wide-eyed innocence*

wide·ly /ˈwaɪdli/ *adv* 1 : over or through a wide area : in or to many places • *They traveled widely.* • *widely scattered towns* • *Their products are widely available.* 2 : to a great extent • *widely different opinions* 3 : by a large number of people • *a* widely known poet • *Her books are widely read.*

wid·en /ˈwaɪdn/ *vb* [T/I] : to make (something) wide or wider or to become wide or wider • *widen a road/lead* • *Her eyes widened in surprise.*

wide·out /ˈwaɪdˌaʊt/ *n* [C] *American football* : WIDE RECEIVER

wide receiver *n* [C] *American football* : a player on the offensive team who specializes in catching passes

wide·spread /ˈwaɪdˈsprɛd/ *adj* : common over a wide area or among many people • *There is widespread interest in the election.*

wid·ow /ˈwɪdoʊ/ *n* [C] : a woman whose husband has died — see also BLACK WIDOW — **wid·ow·hood** /ˈwɪdoʊˌhʊd/ *n* [U]

wid·owed /ˈwɪdoʊd/ *adj* — used to describe a woman whose husband has died or a man whose wife has died • *her widowed mother/father* • *She was widowed by the war.* [=her husband was killed in the war]

wid·ow·er /ˈwɪdoʊwər/ *n* [C] : a man whose wife has died

width /ˈwɪdθ/ *n* 1 [C/U] : a measurement of how wide something is • *She measured the length and width of the room.* 2 [C] : a measured and cut piece of material (such as cloth) • *a width of fabric*

wield /ˈwiːld/ *vb* [T] 1 : to hold (a tool, weapon, etc.) in your hands so that you are ready to use it • *The man was wielding a gun.* 2 : to have and use (power, influence, etc.) • *He wields a great deal of influence over his students.* — **wield·er** *n* [C]

wie·ner /ˈwiːnə/ *n* [C] *US, informal* : HOT DOG 1

wife /ˈwaɪf/ *n, pl* **wives** /ˈwaɪvz/ [C] : a married woman : the woman someone is married to • *We met him and his wife.*

wife·ly /ˈwaɪfli/ *adj, old-fashioned* : of, relating to, or suitable for a wife • *wifely affection*

wig /ˈwɪg/ *n* [C] : artificial hair that you wear on your head because you are bald or in order to change your appearance • *She was wearing a blonde wig.* — **flip your wig** see ¹FLIP

wig·gle /ˈwɪgəl/ *vb* **wig·gled; wig·gling** [T/I] : to move up and down or from side to side with short quick motions • *She wiggled her hips/toes.* • *The puppy wiggled with excitement.* — **wiggle** *n* [C] • *She gave her hips a wiggle.*

wig·wam /ˈwɪgˌwɑːm/ *n* [C] : a round tent that was used in the past by Native Americans as a house or shelter

¹wild /ˈwaɪld/ *adj* 1 **a** *of an animal* : living in nature without human control or care • *wild animals* **b** *of a plant* : growing or produced in nature : not grown by people • *wild blueberries* **c** *of land* : not changed by people • *wild places high in the mountains* 2 : uncontrolled and dangerous • *He was wild with anger.* 3 : very enthusiastic or excited • *wild laughter* • *The crowd went wild.* 4 : going far beyond what is normal or usual • *a wild story/idea* • *The company was suc-*

cessful *beyond my wildest dreams/fantasies.* [=much more successful than I ever thought possible] 5 : noisy and disorganized • *a wild party/protest* 6 : made without knowledge or information • *a wild guess* 7 *of a playing card* : able to represent any other playing card • *In this game, jokers are wild.* 8 : done without accuracy or control • *a wild throw/pitch* 9 : very stormy or violent • *a wild sea/storm* — **be wild about** : to like (someone or something) very much • *She's wild about her new boyfriend.* — **wild·ly** /ˈwaɪldli/ *adv* • *behaving wildly* • *wildly* [=*extremely*] *popular* — **wild·ness** /ˈwaɪldnəs/ *n* [U]

²wild *n* 1 **the wilds** : a large area of land where people do not live and where plants, trees, etc., grow freely : WILDERNESS • *They hiked through the wilds of Maine.* 2 **the wild** : a wild, free, or natural place, state, or existence • *The plants were collected from the wild.*

³wild *adv* : without being controlled • *These plants grow wild on the roadside.* — **run wild** : to run, go, behave, etc., in a wild and uncontrolled way • *His imagination ran wild.*

wild boar *n* [C] : BOAR 2

wild card *n* [C] 1 : a playing card that can represent any other card in a game 2 : a person or thing that could affect a situation in a way that cannot be predicted • *Taxes are the wild card in this election.* 3 *sports* : a player or team chosen to fill a place in a competition after the regularly qualified players or teams have all been decided 4 *usually* **wildcard** : a symbol (such as ? or *) that is used in a computer search to represent any letter or number

wild·cat /ˈwaɪldˌkæt/ *n* [C] : a kind of cat that lives in the wilderness

wildcat strike *n* [C] : a strike that is started by a group of workers without the approval of their union

wil·de·beest /ˈwɪldəˌbiːst/ *n, pl* **wil·de·beests** *also* **wildebeest** [C] : a large African animal that has long curving horns

wil·der·ness /ˈwɪldənəs/ *n* [C] : a wild and natural area in which few people live • *She enjoys hikes through the wilderness.* • *(figurative) a bureaucratic wilderness*

wild·fire /ˈwaɪldˌfajə/ *n* [C] : a fire in a wild area (such as a forest) that is not controlled and that can burn a large area very quickly — **like wildfire** *informal* : very quickly • *The new fad spread like wildfire.*

wild·flow·er /ˈwaɪldˌflawə/ *n* [C] : a flower that grows in natural places without being planted by people

wild·fowl /ˈwaɪldˌfawəl/ *n* [U] : birds (such as ducks and geese) that live in the wild especially near water and are often hunted

wild goose chase *n* [C] : a difficult and long search for something that is not important or that cannot be found • *The boss sent me on a wild goose chase.*

wild·life /ˈwaɪldˌlaɪf/ *n* [U] : animals living in nature : wild animals • *an area with abundant wildlife* • *wildlife protection*

Wild West *n* — **the Wild West** : the

western United States in the past when there were many cowboys, outlaws, etc. ▪ *stories about the Wild West*

wiles /ˈwajəlz/ *n* [*plural*] : clever tricks that you use to get what you want ▪ *She used her feminine wiles to influence his decision.*

¹**will** /ˈwɪl, wəl/ *vb, past tense* **would** /ˈwʊd, wəd/ *present tense for both singular and plural* **will**; *negative* **will not** *or* **won't** /ˈwoʊnt/ [*modal vb*] **1** — used to say that something is expected to happen in the future ▪ *We will leave tomorrow.* ▪ *Tomorrow will be partly cloudy.* ▪ *Who do you think will win?* **2 a** — used to say that you want something ▪ *I will* [=(*more commonly*) *I'll*] *have a hamburger and fries.* **b** — used to say that you are willing to do something ▪ *Yes, I will marry you.* **3** — used to ask someone to do something ▪ *Will you help me with my homework?* **4** — used to give a command or to say what must happen or not happen ▪ *Everyone will leave immediately!* **5 a** — used to say that something is likely or certain to be true ▪ *The gray house on the left will be theirs.* [=must be theirs] ▪ *Ask anyone and they will tell you the same thing.* **b** — used to describe a situation that is continuing ▪ *He won't stop bothering me.* [=he refuses to stop bothering me] **6** — used to say that something usually happens or that a person or thing usually does something ▪ *The dog will growl if you get too close to it.* ▪ *Accidents will happen.* [=accidents sometimes happens; it isn't possible to avoid all accidents] — compare ³WILL, ⁴WILL

²**will** /ˈwɪl/ *n* **1** [*C*] *law* : a legal document in which a person states who should receive his or her possessions after he or she dies ▪ *In her will, she asked that her money be donated to the church.* ▪ *He made/prepared/wrote a will only days before his death.* **2** [*C/U*] : a strong desire or determination to do something ▪ *She never lost her will to live.* ▪ *He has the will to succeed.* ▪ *She has a strong will.* = *She has a will of iron.* = *She has an iron will.* ▪ *He won the battle/clash of wills with his wife.* [=he got what he wanted] ▪ *"Do you think she can finish on time?" "She can if she really wants to.* **Where there's a will, there's a way."** — see also FREE WILL **3** [*U*] : a person's choice or desire in a particular situation ▪ *a government that reflects the will of the people* ▪ *He was forced to do it against his will.* [=even though he did not want to do it] ▪ *She chose to go against her parents' will.* [=to do something that her parents did not want her to do] — **at will** : when you want or in a way that you want ▪ *She is free to come and go at will.* — see also ILL WILL

³**will** /ˈwɪl/ *vb, present tense for both singular and plural* **will** [*T*] : to want or desire (something) ◇ This verb is only used in the simple present tense. ▪ *You can say what you will* [=you can say whatever you want to say]*, but I will always love her.* ▪ *Imagine, if you will, life without computers.* — compare ¹WILL, ⁴WILL

⁴**will** /ˈwɪl/ *vb* **wills; willed; will·ing** [*T*] **1** : to cause or try to cause something to

happen by using the power of your mind ▪ *She was haunted by the thought that she had willed his death.* [=that she had caused his death by wishing that he would die] ▪ *He willed himself to stay awake.* **2** : to want or intend (something) to happen ▪ *It will happen if God wills it.* **3** *law* : to state in a will that (your property) will be given to a particular person, organization, etc., after you die ▪ *He willed his entire estate to the church.* — compare ¹WILL, ³WILL

will·ful *or chiefly Brit* **wil·ful** /ˈwɪlfəl/ *adj, disapproving* **1** : refusing to change your ideas or opinions or to stop doing something ▪ *a stubborn and willful child* **2** : done deliberately : INTENTIONAL ▪ *willful disobedience* — **will·ful·ly** *adv* — **will·ful·ness** *n* [*U*]

wil·lies /ˈwɪliz/ *n* — **the willies** *informal* : a nervous feeling ▪ *Hearing noises at night gives me the willies.*

will·ing /ˈwɪlɪŋ/ *adj* **1** : not refusing to do something : READY ▪ *I am willing to help.* ▪ *We're ready and willing to make the trip.* **2** : doing something or ready to do something without being persuaded ▪ *He was a willing participant in the crime.* **3** : done, made, or given by choice ▪ *a willing sacrifice* — **will·ing·ly** /ˈwɪlɪŋli/ *adv* ▪ *They acted willingly.* — **will·ing·ness** *n* [*U*]

wil·low /ˈwɪloʊ/ *n* [*C*] : a tree that has long, narrow leaves and strong, thin branches that are used to make baskets

wil·lowy /ˈwɪləwi/ *adj* : tall, thin, and graceful ▪ *a willowy dancer/body*

will·pow·er /ˈwɪlˌpawɚ/ *n* [*U*] : the ability to control yourself : strong determination that allows you to do something difficult (such as to lose weight or quit smoking) ▪ *He conquered his drinking problem through sheer willpower.*

wil·ly–nil·ly /ˌwɪliˈnɪli/ *adv* **1** : in a careless and unplanned way ▪ *They decided willy-nilly to change the rules.* **2** : in a way that does not allow any choices or planning ▪ *We are being forced willy-nilly to accept their decision.*

wilt /ˈwɪlt/ *vb* **1** [*T/I*] *of a plant* : to bend over because of not having enough water ▪ *The roses were wilting.* ▪ *The hot weather wilted the plants.* **2** [*I*] **a** : to become weak and tired especially because of hot weather ▪ *The crowd wilted in the heat.* **b** : to lose energy, confidence, effectiveness, etc. ▪ *He wilted under the pressure.*

wily /ˈwaɪli/ *adj* **wil·i·er; -est** : very clever ▪ *a wily negotiator* ▪ *wily tactics*

¹**wimp** /ˈwɪmp/ *n* [*C*] *informal* : a weak person who lacks confidence, courage, etc. ▪ *I was too much of a wimp to confront him.* — **wimpy** /ˈwɪmpi/ *adj* **wimp·i·er; -est** ▪ *I was too wimpy to confront him.*

²**wimp** *vb* — **wimp out** [*phrasal vb*] *informal* : to fail to do something because you are too afraid, weak, etc. ▪ *He wanted to ask her to the dance but he wimped out.*

¹**win** /ˈwɪn/ *vb* **won** /ˈwʌn/; **win·ning 1 a** [*T/I*] : to achieve victory in a fight, contest, game, etc. ▪ *They won the game/battle/war.* ▪ *She won the election/argument.* ▪ *They played well, but they didn't win.* ▪

Okay, you win. [=I agree to do what you want] **b** [T] : to get (something, such as a prize) by achieving victory in a fight, contest, game, etc. ▪ *She won a tennis trophy.* **2** [T] : to get (something) by effort ▪ *She won praise for her hard work.* ▪ *His perseverance won him the job.* **3** [T] : to persuade (someone) to like you or to choose you ▪ *She broke up with him, but he's determined to win her back.* [=to persuade her to be his girlfriend again] ▪ *He'll do anything to win her heart.* [=to get her to fall in love with him] — **can't win** *informal* — used to say that success is not possible for someone in a particular situation ▪ *I feel like I can't win. Nothing I do seems to make any difference.* — **win out** *also Brit* **win through** [*phrasal vb*] : to achieve victory or success after dealing with many difficulties ▪ *It was a challenge, but we won out in the end.* — **win over** [*phrasal vb*] **win (someone) over** : to persuade (someone) to accept and support something (such as an idea) after opposing it ▪ *They eventually won him over with some persuasive arguments.*

²win *n* [C] : an act of achieving victory especially in a game or contest : VICTORY ▪ *The team has 8 wins and 4 losses so far.*

wince /ˈwɪns/ *vb* **winced; winc·ing** [I] : to have an expression on your face for a very short time which shows that you are embarrassed or in pain ▪ *She winced (in pain) when she hit her elbow.* — **wince** *n* [C]

winch /ˈwɪntʃ/ *n* [C] : a machine that has a rope or chain and that is used for pulling or lifting heavy things — **winch** *vb* [T] ▪ *They winched the car out of the lake.*

¹wind /ˈwɪnd/ *n* **1** [C/U] : a natural movement of air outside ▪ *A light wind rustled the leaves.* ▪ *northerly/strong winds* ▪ *There isn't much wind today.* **2** [C] : something that has force or influence ▪ *the changing/shifting winds of political opinion* ▪ *The winds of change have begun to blow.* [=change is going to happen] **3** [U] : the ability to breathe normally ▪ *The fall knocked the wind out of me.* [=made me unable to breathe normally for a brief time] — see also SECOND WIND **4** [U] *Brit* : gas in the stomach or intestines ▪ *Certain foods give me wind.* [=(US) gas] **5** [plural] : musical instruments (such as flutes and horns) that are played by blowing air into them : wind instruments — **break wind** : to pass gas out of the anus — **catch/get wind of (something)** : to hear about (something private or secret) ▪ *They got wind of our plans.* — **in the wind** : about to happen ▪ *Change is in the wind.* — **like the wind** : very fast ▪ *He ran like the wind.* — **take the wind out of someone's sails** : to cause someone to lose confidence or energy ▪ *The news really took the wind out of their sails.* — **throw/fling/cast caution to the wind** see ¹CAUTION

²wind /ˈwaɪnd/ *vb* **wound** /ˈwaʊnd/; **wind·ing 1** [T/I] *of a river, road, etc,* : to follow a series of curves and turns ▪ *The river winds (its way) through the valley.* ▪ *winding roads* **2** [T] : to wrap (something, such as a string) around

something ▪ *He wound twine around the box.* **3** [T] : to turn a knob, handle, etc., on something (such as a clock) several times so that it can work ▪ *wind (up) a clock* — **wind down** [*phrasal vb*] **1** : to end gradually ▪ *The party was winding down.* **2** : to relax and stop thinking about work, problems, etc. : UNWIND ▪ *I intend to wind down with a good book this weekend.* — **wind up** [*phrasal vb*] **1** **wind up** *or* **wind (something) up** *or* **wind up (something)** : to end ▪ *The meeting should be winding up soon.* ▪ *It's time to wind up the meeting.* **2** : to reach or come to a place, situation, or condition that was not planned or expected ▪ *After a wrong turn, we wound up in an unfamiliar neighborhood.* ▪ *They wound up* [=ended up] *being millionaires.* — **wind·er** /ˈwaɪndɚ/ *n* [C]

wind·bag /ˈwɪndˌbæɡ/ *n* [C] *informal + disapproving* : a person who talks too much

wind·blown /ˈwɪndˌbloʊn/ *adj* **1** : carried through the air by the wind ▪ *windblown pollen* **2** : made messy by the wind ▪ *windblown hair*

wind·break /ˈwɪndˌbreɪk/ *n* [C] : something (such as a fence or group of trees) that protects an area from the wind

Wind·break·er /ˈwɪndˌbreɪkɚ/ *trademark* — used for a light jacket that protects you from the wind

wind·chill /ˈwɪndˌtʃɪl/ *n* [U] *chiefly US* : the effect that wind has of making air feel colder than it actually is — called also *windchill factor*

wind·ed /ˈwɪndəd/ *adj* : unable to breathe easily or normally because you have been running, climbing, etc. ▪ *We were winded* [=out of breath] *after the long climb.*

wind·fall /ˈwɪndˌfɑːl/ *n* [C] : an unexpected amount of money that you get as a gift, prize, etc. ▪ *They received a windfall because of the tax cuts.*

wind instrument *n* [C] : a musical instrument (such as a flute, horn, or organ) that is played by blowing air through it

wind·mill /ˈwɪndˌmɪl/ *n* [C] : a structure that has parts which are turned around by the wind and that is used to produce power, pump water, etc.

win·dow /ˈwɪndoʊ/ *n* **1** [C] **a** : an opening in a wall, door, etc., that usually contains a sheet of glass ▪ *She opened a window to let in some air.* ▪ *I looked out the window and saw a deer.* ▪ *(figurative) This knowledge opens a window into your opponent's mind.* [=allows you to see what your opponent is thinking] **b** : a sheet of glass that covers an opening in a building, vehicle, etc. ▪ *He broke a window.* **c** : an opening in a wall through which business is conducted ▪ *a ticket window* **2** [C] : a part of something that you can see through ▪ *the window in an envelope* **3** [C] : an area or box on a computer screen that shows a program that is currently running ▪ *Close all the windows and restart the computer.* **4** [singular] : a period of time during which something can happen ▪ *The window of opportunity* [=the time during which there is a chance to do something] has closed/ended. — **go out the window** *informal* : to stop being used or thought about • *By that point in the argument, reason had gone out the window.* — **throw (something) out the window** *informal* : to stop using or thinking about (something) • *We can throw that idea out the window.* — **win·dow·less** /ˈwɪndoʊləs/ *adj*

window dressing *n* [U] *disapproving* : something that is intended to make a person or thing seem better or more attractive but that does not have any real importance or effect • *These changes are important. They're not just window dressing.*

win·dow·pane /ˈwɪndoʊˌpeɪn/ *n* [C] : a piece of glass that covers an opening in a window

window shade *n* [C] *US* : a roll of cloth or plastic that is hung at the top of a window and that can be pulled down to cover the window

win·dow-shop /ˈwɪndoʊˌʃɑːp/ *vb* **-shopped; -shop·ping** [I] : to walk in front of stores and look at the products displayed in the windows without buying anything • *I like to window-shop when I'm in the city.* — **window shopper** *n* [C] — **window-shopping** *n* [U] • *We went window-shopping last weekend.*

win·dow·sill /ˈwɪndoʊˌsɪl/ *n* [C] : a narrow shelf that is attached to the bottom of a window

wind·pipe /ˈwɪndˌpaɪp/ *n* [C] : the tube in your neck and chest that carries air into and out of your lungs

wind·proof /ˈwɪndˌpruːf/ *adj* : not allowing wind to enter or move through • *a windproof jacket*

wind·screen /ˈwɪndˌskriːn/ *n* [C] *Brit* : WINDSHIELD

windscreen wiper *n* [C] *Brit* : WINDSHIELD WIPER

wind·shield /ˈwɪndˌʃiːld/ *n* [C] *US* : the window at the front of a car, truck, etc., that protects the driver and passengers — called also (*Brit*) *windscreen*

windshield wiper *n* [C] *US* : a long, thin piece of rubber on a metal frame that moves back and forth and pushes water, snow, etc., off the surface of a windshield — called also (*Brit*) *windscreen wiper*

wind·surf /ˈwɪndˌsɔːf/ *vb* [I] : to ride along the surface of the water while standing on a long, narrow board that has a sail attached — **wind·surf·er** *n* [C]

wind·swept /ˈwɪndˌswɛpt/ *adj* **1** : exposed to strong winds • *windswept mountaintops* **2** : made messy by the wind • *windswept hair*

wind tunnel *n* [C] : a long, narrow room through which air is blown in order to test the effects of wind on an airplane, car, etc.

¹**wind·up** /ˈwaɪndˌʌp/ *n* [*singular*] **1** : the things that are done at the end of an event, a process, etc. • *the windup of the negotiations* **2** *baseball* : the movements that a pitcher makes before the ball is

thrown • *He went into the/his windup, then threw the pitch.*

²**windup** *adj, always before a noun* : having a motor that is given power when someone turns a handle • *windup toys*

wind·ward /ˈwɪndwəd/ *adj* : located on the side that is facing the direction that the wind is blowing from • *the windward side of the mountain* — **windward** *n* [U] • *sailing to windward* [=toward the wind]

windy /ˈwɪndi/ *adj* **wind·i·er; -est** **1** : having a lot of wind • *a windy day/place* **2** : using too many words • *a long, windy speech*

¹**wine** /ˈwaɪn/ *n* **1** [C/U] **a** : an alcoholic drink made from the juice of grapes • *a glass/bottle of wine* **b** : an alcoholic drink made from plants or fruits other than grapes • *rice/apple wine* **2** [U] : a dark reddish-purple color

²**wine** *vb* **wined; win·ing** — **wine and dine** : to entertain (someone) at a restaurant with good food, wine, etc. • *The company wined and dined the prospective clients.*

win·ery /ˈwaɪnəri/ *n, pl* **-er·ies** [C] : a place where wine is made

wine steward *n* [C] *chiefly US* : a waiter in a restaurant who is in charge of serving wine

¹**wing** /ˈwɪŋ/ *n* **1** [C] **a** : a part of an animal's body that is used for flying or gliding • *a bird's wing* **b** : the wing of a bird and especially a chicken used as food • *We ordered some wings.* **2** [C] : one of usually two long, flat parts of an airplane that extend from the sides and make it possible for the airplane to fly **3** [C] : a particular section of a large building • *The guest room is in the east wing.* **4 the wings** : the areas on the sides of a stage where performers wait before going onto the stage • *She was standing in the wings, waiting for her cue.* • (*figurative*) *The issue has been lurking/waiting in the wings* [=waiting to be dealt with] *for several years.* **5** [C] : a particular part of a large organization or group • *the conservative wing of the party* **6** [C] *sports* : a person who plays on the offense in a position that is towards the sides of the playing area in sports like hockey and soccer • *The left/right wing passed the ball to the center.* — called also **winger** **7** [C] *Brit* : FENDER 1 — **on the wing** : in flight • *The birds were on the wing.* [=were flying] — **spread your wings** : to become more independent and confident : to try doing new things • *College gave her a chance to spread her wings.* — **take (someone) under your wing** : to help, teach, or take care of (someone who is younger or has less experience than you) • *She took me under her wing and showed me how things were done.* — **take wing** : to begin to fly • *The ducks took wing and flew away.* • (*figurative*) *Let your imagination take wing.* — **wing·less** /ˈwɪŋləs/ *adj*

²**wing** *vb* **1** [T/I] : to travel to a place by flying there • *She winged (her way) to Paris.* [=she flew to Paris] **2** [T] *US, informal* : to throw (something) forcefully • *She winged the ball over to first base.* **3**

[T] *US, informal* : to touch or hit (someone or something) especially in the arm or wing while moving past : GRAZE • *The soldier was winged by a stray bullet.* —

wing it *informal* : to do or try to do something without much practice or preparation • *I hadn't practiced the part, so I got up there and winged it.*

wing commander *n* [C] : a high-ranking officer in the British air force

winged /'wɪŋd/ *adj* : having wings • *winged insects*

wing·er /'wɪŋɚ/ *n* [C] : ¹WING 6

wing·span /'wɪŋˌspæn/ *n* [C] : the distance from the tip of one wing of a bird or airplane to the tip of the other wing • *The hawk has a wingspan of about three feet.*

wing·tip /'wɪŋˌtɪp/ *n* [C] **1** : the pointed end of a wing • *a bird with black wingtips* **2** *US* : a type of usually leather shoe that is worn by a man and that has an extra piece of leather that covers the toe

¹**wink** /'wɪŋk/ *n* [C] **1** : an act of closing and opening one eye very quickly often as a way of giving a secret signal or private message to someone • *He gave me a wink.* [=winked at me] **2** *informal* : a very short amount of time • *She said hello, and* **(as) quick as a wink** [=instantly], *she was gone.* • *I didn't get a wink of sleep last night. = I didn't sleep a wink last night.* [=I didn't sleep at all last night]

²**wink** *vb* [T/I] : to close and open one eye quickly as a signal to someone • *He winked (at me) and said that he understood.*

win·ner /'wɪnɚ/ *n* [C] **1** : someone or something that wins a contest, prize, etc. • *the winners and losers of the court case* • *the grand prize winner* [=the person who has won the grand prize] **2** *informal* : a very good or successful person or thing • *She's a real winner.* • *That idea's a winner.* **3** *sports* : the final goal, point, etc., that wins a game • *She scored the winner.* = *She scored the game-winner.*

win·ning /'wɪnɪŋ/ *adj* **1** *always before a noun* : relating to or producing a win • *She scored the winning goal.* **2** : pleasing or attractive to other people • *a winning smile/personality/combination* — **win·ning·ly** /'wɪnɪŋli/ *adv* • *He smiled winningly.*

win·nings /'wɪnɪŋz/ *n* [*plural*] : money that is won in a game or contest • *The contestant's winnings totaled $25,000.*

win·now /'wɪnoʊ/ *vb* [T] **1** : to remove (people or things that are less important, desirable, etc.) from a larger group or list • *The least qualified applicants were winnowed out of the initial pool.* : to make (a list of possible choices) smaller by removing the less desirable choices • *The list of candidates has been winnowed (down) to five.*

wino /'waɪnoʊ/ *n, pl* **win·os** [C] *informal + disapproving* : a person who has no place to live and who is often drunk

win·some /'wɪnsəm/ *adj, formal* : cheerful, pleasant, and appealing • *a winsome smile*

¹**win·ter** /'wɪntɚ/ *n* [C/U] : the coldest season of the year that is after autumn and

before spring • *They spend winters in Florida.* • *She traveled there two winters ago.* • *in early/late winter* • *the last day of winter* • *winter coats/weather*

²**winter** *vb* [I] : to spend the winter in a particular place • *My family winters in Florida.*

win·ter·ize /'wɪntɚˌraɪz/ *vb* **-ized; -iz·ing** [T] *US* : to make (something) able to resist the effects of winter weather • *winterize cars by adding antifreeze and putting on snow tires*

winter squash *n* [C/U] *US* : any one of several vegetables that are grown until their shell and seeds are hard and that can be stored for several months

win·ter·time /'wɪntɚˌtaɪm/ *n* [U] : the season of winter • *in the wintertime*

win·try /'wɪntri/ *also* **win·tery** /'wɪntɚi/ *adj* **win·tri·er; -est 1** : relating to, happening during, or typical of winter • *wintry days/weather* **2** *literary* : not cheerful or friendly • *a wintry welcome*

win–win /'wɪn'wɪn/ *adj, always before a noun* : providing a good result for everyone involved • *a win-win situation/deal*

¹**wipe** /'waɪp/ *vb* **wiped; wip·ing** [T] **1** : to clean or dry (something) by using a towel, your hand, etc. • *Would you wipe the dishes (off)?* • *She wiped her eyes with a tissue.* **2** : to remove (something) by rubbing • *Wipe (away) your tears.* • *Wipe (off) the spots from the wine glasses.* • *(figurative) She has wiped the entire conversation from her mind.* [=she has forgotten the entire conversation] **3** : to move (something) over a surface • *He wiped his hand across his forehead.* **4** *chiefly Brit* : to completely remove recorded material from (a tape or disk) • *You can wipe* [=erase] *the tape/disk and use it again.* — **wipe down** [*phrasal vb*] **wipe (something) down** *or* **wipe down (something)** : to clean (a surface) by rubbing it with a cloth • *He wiped down the counters with a wet cloth.* — **wipe out** [*phrasal vb*] **1** *US, informal* : to fall down violently especially when riding a bicycle, surfing, skiing, etc. • *The cyclist wiped out coming around the curve.* **2** **wipe (someone or something) out** *or* **wipe out (someone or something)** : to kill or destroy (someone or something) completely • *Drought wiped out our crops.* • *Doctors think they can wipe out the disease.* **3** **wipe (someone) out** : to make (someone) very tired • *That game wiped me out.* • *I am completely wiped out.* — **wipe the slate clean** : to forget all the things that have happened or been done and start doing something again : to start again from the very beginning • *She wishes she could wipe the slate clean and start over in a different career.* — **wipe up** [*phrasal vb*] **wipe (something) up** *or* **wipe up (something)** : to use a cloth to remove (something) from a surface • *Please wipe up that spill.*

²**wipe** *n* [C] **1** : a small, wet cloth that is used for cleaning • *disposable wipes* **2** : an act of cleaning or drying something by using a towel, your hand, etc. • *I gave the table a quick wipe.*

wipe·out /'waɪpˌaʊt/ *n* [C] *US* : a sudden,

violent fall by someone who is riding a bicycle, surfing, skiing, etc. ▪ *The surfer had a nasty wipeout.*

wip·er /'waɪpɚ/ n [C] : WINDSHIELD WIPER

¹**wire** /'waɪɚ/ n **1** [C/U] : a thin, flexible thread of metal ▪ *The flowers were bound together with a wire.* ▪ *copper/aluminum wire* ▪ *a wire rack/fence* **2** [C] : a thread of metal that is covered with plastic, rubber, etc., and used to send or receive electricity or electrical signals ▪ *telephone wires* **3** [*singular*] *US* : a small microphone that is worn under clothing in order to secretly record a conversation ▪ *The undercover officer wore a wire to her meeting with the drug dealer.* **4** *chiefly US* [C] : TELEGRAM ▪ *They just received a wire from their daughter.* **5 the wire** *US* : a thin piece of string that the winner of a race breaks through at the end of the race ▪ *She was ahead by two seconds at the wire.* ▪ (*figurative*) *The election went/came (right) down to the wire.* [=the election was not decided until the very end] — **get/have your wires crossed** *informal* : to fail to understand each other : to be confused because each person has a different idea about what is happening or being said ▪ *We got our wires crossed there—I thought you were asking me something else.* — **under the wire** *chiefly US* : at the end of the time when it is still possible to do something ▪ *Her application got/came in just under the wire.* [=just in time] — **wire to wire** *chiefly US, sports* : from the beginning of a race, game, etc., until the end ▪ *He led the race (from) wire to wire.*

²**wire** vb **wired; wir·ing** [T] **1 a** : to provide (a building, room, etc.) with wires for a particular service or for electricity ▪ *The house will be wired next week.* **b** : to connect (a device) to another device by using wires ▪ *You can wire the generator to a car battery.* **2** : to use wire to close or hold (something) ▪ *Her jaw was wired shut after the accident.* **3 a** : to send (money) by using electronic methods ▪ *She wired the money home to Canada.* **b** *chiefly US* : to send a telegram to (someone) ▪ *Please wire me when you get there.*

wired adj **1** *chiefly US, informal* : very excited or full of nervous energy ▪ *No more caffeine for me, I'm pretty wired.* **2** : connected to the Internet ▪ *a wired classroom*

wire fraud n [U] : the crime of stealing money by using computers, telephones, etc.

wire·less /'waɪɚləs/ adj **1** : not using wires to send and receive electronic signals ▪ *a wireless microphone* **2** : of or relating to the use of radio waves to send and receive electronic signals ▪ *wireless Internet access* ▪ *wireless communications*

wire service n [C] : a news organization that sends news stories to many newspapers, magazines, etc.

wire·tap /'waɪɚˌtæp/ n [C] : a device that allows someone to secretly listen to phone conversations ▪ *Federal agents put a wiretap on his phone.* — **wiretap** vb

-tapped; -tap·ping [T] ▪ *The FBI wiretapped his phone.*

wire wool n [U] *Brit* : STEEL WOOL

wiring n [U] : the system of wires that carry electricity in a particular place, device, etc. ▪ *The wiring in the house needs to be replaced.*

wiry /'waɪɚri/ adj **wir·i·er** /'waɪrijɚ/; **-est** **1** : very thin but strong and muscular ▪ *a man with long, wiry arms* **2** : stiff like wire ▪ *the dog's wiry coat/fur*

Wis. or **Wisc.** abbr Wisconsin

wis·dom /'wɪzdəm/ n [U] **1 a** : knowledge that is gained by having many experiences in life ▪ *She has gained a lot of wisdom over the years.* **b** : the natural ability to understand things that most other people cannot understand ▪ *a young person of great wisdom* **c** : knowledge of what is proper or reasonable ▪ *He had the wisdom to stop before he said too much.* : good sense or judgment ▪ *I fail to see the wisdom in doing that.* **2** : advice or information given to a person ▪ *He shared a valuable bit of wisdom with his daughter.* — **in someone's (infinite) wisdom** — used in an ironic way to say that someone has made a foolish choice or decision ▪ *He decided, in his infinite wisdom, that it would be better to sell the house than to keep it.*

wisdom tooth n [C] : one of four large teeth in the back of your mouth that do not appear until you are an adult

¹**wise** /'waɪz/ adj **wis·er; -est** **1** : having or showing wisdom or knowledge usually from learning or experiencing many things ▪ *a wise old woman* ▪ *a wise saying* ▪ *He is wise in the ways of the world.* **2** : showing good sense or judgment ▪ *You were wise to ask permission first.* ▪ *a wise choice* **3** *US, informal* : saying things that are rude or insulting ▪ *Don't you get wise with me, young man!* — **a word to the wise** see ¹WORD — **none the wiser** or **not any the wiser** **1** : not knowing or understanding anything more about something ▪ *We're still none the wiser about the true cause of the accident.* **2** also **never the wiser** — used to describe someone who is not at all aware of something that has happened ▪ *We left early, and no one was any the wiser.* [=no one noticed that we had left] — **wise to** *informal* : not fooled by (someone or something) ▪ *I'm wise to you.* = *I'm wise to what you're doing.* [=I know what you're doing] : aware of (something, especially something dishonest) ▪ *She got wise to his scheme.* — **wise·ly** adv

²**wise** vb **wised; wis·ing** — **wise up** [*phrasal vb*] *informal* **1** : to become aware of what is really happening ▪ *They finally wised up to the fact that they were being cheated.* **2** : to start to think and act in a more intelligent way ▪ *They could lose everything they have if they don't wise up.*

-wise /ˌwaɪz/ combining form **1 a** : in the position or direction of ▪ *lengthwise* **b** : in the manner of ▪ *moving crabwise* [=moving like a crab] **2** *informal* : with regard to : CONCERNING ▪ *She has made some bad choices career-wise.* [=has made some bad choices about her career] ▪ *Health-wise, I'm doing fine.*

wise·crack /'waɪz,kræk/ *n* [C] *informal* : a funny and smart comment or joke ▪ *He was making wisecracks during the entire movie.* — **wisecrack** *vb* [I] ▪ *a wisecracking waitress*

wise guy /'waɪz,gaɪ/ *n* [C] *informal, chiefly US* : a person who says or does things that are funny but also annoying or somewhat rude ▪ *Quit being a wise guy.*

¹wish /'wɪʃ/ *vb* **1** [T] : to want (something) to be true or to happen ▪ *I wish (that) you were here.* ▪ *He was wishing (that) she would leave him alone.* **2** [T] *formal* : to want or ask to do (something) ▪ *You may use the telephone, if you wish.* ▪ *Ms. Jones wishes to see you.* ▪ *You can do as you wish.* [=you can do whatever you want to do] **3** [T] **a** : to want (someone) to be in a particular state ▪ *I wish him well.* [=I hope that good things happen to him] ▪ *She wished him dead.* ▪ *I wish you no harm.* [=I don't want you to be harmed] **b** : to say that you hope someone will have happiness, health, etc. ▪ *We wish you a Merry Christmas.* ▪ *I wish you luck.* **4** [I] : to hope for something that usually cannot be had ▪ *He wished for a second chance.* ▪ *I couldn't wish for a better friend than you.* [=you are the best friend I could have] ▪ *She wished for a pony and blew out the candles on her birthday cake.* — **I wish** *or* **don't I wish** *informal* — used to say that you want something to happen but that you know it will probably not happen ▪ *"Will you be getting the job?" "Don't I wish!"* — **wish away** [*phrasal vb*] **wish (something) away** *or* **wish away (something)** : to cause (something) to stop or go away just by wanting it to stop or go away ▪ *You can't just wish your problems away.* — **wish on** [*phrasal vb*] **wish (someone or something) on** : to want (someone) to have or be affected by (someone or something bad or unpleasant) ▪ *I wouldn't wish that terrible illness on anyone.* [=I wouldn't want anyone to have that terrible illness] — **you wish** *or* **don't you wish** *informal* — used to tell people in a rude way that it is unlikely that they will get what they want ▪ *Give you a kiss? You wish.*

²wish *n* **1** [C] : a desire for something to happen or be done : a feeling of wanting to do or have something ▪ *Please respect my wishes and leave me alone.* ▪ *It is my wish that my estate go to my granddaughter.* ▪ *I have no wish to interfere in your plans.* ▪ *It was her dying wish to see them married.* [=it was the last thing she wanted before she died] ▪ *She went against her parents' wishes.* [=did something her parents did not want her to do] **2** [C] : an act of thinking about something that you want and hoping that you will get it or that it will happen in some magical way ▪ *Close your eyes and make a wish.* [=wish for something] ▪ *I got my wish.* = *My wish came true.* [=I got what I wished for] **3** [*plural*] : good thoughts or feelings directed toward a person ▪ *Send her my good/best wishes.* ▪ *Best wishes!*

wish·bone /'wɪʃ,boʊn/ *n* [C] : a bone that is at the front of a bird's chest and that is shaped like a V ✧ When a chicken or turkey is eaten, its *wishbone* is traditionally dried and held by two people who each make a wish and pull the bone apart. The person who gets the bigger piece of the bone is supposed to get his or her wish.

wish·ful /'wɪʃfəl/ *adj* : showing a belief that something will happen or succeed even though it is not likely to happen or succeed ▪ *The idea that the enemy will surrender is nothing more than wishful thinking.*

wishing well *n* [C] : a well that people throw coins into while making a wish

wish list *n* [C] : a list of things that someone would like to have ▪ *That book is on my wish list.*

wishy–washy /'wɪʃi,wɑ:ʃi/ *adj* **-wash·i·er; -est** *disapproving* : not having or showing strong ideas or beliefs about something ▪ *a wishy-washy answer/politician*

wisp /'wɪsp/ *n* [C] **1** : a thin streak of smoke, mist, etc. ▪ *a wisp of smoke* **2** : a thin thread or strand of something ▪ *A few wisps (of hair) framed the sides of her face.* **3** : a small amount of something ▪ *There was a wisp of a smile on her lips.* **4** : a small and thin person ▪ *She is a wisp of a girl.*

wispy /'wɪspi/ *adj* **wisp·i·er; -est** : very thin or light ▪ *wispy clouds* ▪ *a wispy mustache*

wis·te·ria /wɪ'stirijə/ *n* [C/U] : a plant that grows as a thick vine with large bunches of purple or white flowers

wist·ful /'wɪstfəl/ *adj* : having or showing sad thoughts and feelings about something that you want to have or do and especially about something that made you happy in the past ▪ *He had a wistful look on his face.* — **wist·ful·ly** *adv* — **wist·ful·ness** *n* [U]

wit /'wɪt/ *n* **1** [U] : an ability to say or write things that are clever and usually funny ▪ *She is full of wit and vivacity.* ▪ *The book is a collection of his wit and wisdom.* **2** [C] : a person who is known for making clever and funny remarks ▪ *She was a famous writer and wit.* **3 a** [*plural*] : the ability to think or reason ▪ *He learned to live by his wits.* [=to survive by doing clever and sometimes dishonest things] ▪ *She kept her wits about her.* [=remained calm and able to think clearly] ▪ *(chiefly US)* The chess champion will **match wits** [=compete] *with a computer.* **b** **the wit** : the ability to make good decisions ▪ *She had the wit to leave before the situation got any worse.* — **at (your) wit's end** *(chiefly US)* *or* **at (your) wits' end** : upset and unable to think of what needs to be done ▪ *I've spent six hours trying to fix my computer, but now I'm at my wit's end.* — **out of your wits** *informal* — used for emphasis with verbs like *scare* and *frighten* ▪ *I was scared out of my wits!* [=I was very scared] — **to wit** *formal* — used before stating the specific thing or example being discussed ▪ *This can only mean two* *things, to wit: that he lied, or that he is wrong.*

witch /ˈwɪtʃ/ n [C] **1** : a woman who is thought to have magic powers **2** : a person who practices magic as part of a religion (such as Wicca) **3** *informal* : a very unpleasant woman — **witch·y** /ˈwɪtʃi/ *adj* **witch·i·er, -est** *a witchy old woman*

witch·craft /ˈwɪtʃˌkræft, Brit ˈwɪtʃˌkrɑːft/ n [U] : magical things that are done by witches : the use of magical powers obtained especially from evil spirits • *The villagers blamed their problems on witchcraft.*

witch doctor n [C] : a person in some cultures who is believed to have magic powers and to be able to cure illness and fight off evil spirits, curses, etc.

witch hunt n [C] *disapproving* : the act of unfairly looking for and punishing people who are accused of having opinions that are believed to be dangerous or evil

with /ˈwɪθ, ˈwɪð/ prep **1** — used to say that people or things are together in one place • *Do you have your books with you?* • *The children are home with their father.* • *The doctor will be with you shortly.* [=the doctor will come to see you soon] • *We barely escaped with our lives.* [=we almost died when trying to escape] **2** — used to say that people or things are doing something together or are involved in something • *He went to the store with her.* • *I need to speak with you.* • *We are in competition with other companies.* **3** : having (a particular characteristic, possession, etc.) • *a boy with green eyes* [=a boy who has green eyes] • *people with pets* • *a class with 20 students* **4** : using (something specified) • *She opened the door with her key.* • *The sauce is made with milk and cheese.* • *He entertained the crowd with a few jokes.* **5** — used to refer to the feeling, thought, quality, etc., that someone has or experiences when doing something • *They accepted the offer with certain conditions.* • *You acted with great courage.* **6** — used to indicate the cause of something • *She was red with embarrassment.* • *He was sick with the flu.* **7** — used to indicate a related fact or situation • *He stood there with his hat in his hand.* • *Our products have been designed with you in mind.* • *With her on our team, there's no way we can lose.* **8** — used to indicate the specific thing or person that is being referred to • *Please be careful with those boxes.* • *They are on friendly terms with their neighbors.* **9** — used to say that someone has a relationship with a person, organization, etc. • *He has been with the same woman for 35 years.* **10** — used to say that someone or something is the object of attention, behavior, or a feeling • *I'm in love with you.* • *He is happy with his new job.* **11** : in the performance, condition, behavior, or quality of (something or someone) • *What's the problem with your car?* • *What's the matter with you? Are you upset about something?* • *(informal) What's with her?* [=why is she acting so strangely?] **12** : in opposition to or against (someone) • *The boys were fighting/arguing with each other.* **13** : so

as to be separated from (someone or something) • *I hated to part with my dolls.* **14 a** — used to say that you agree with or understand someone • *Are you still with me?* [=are you still listening to me and understanding what I am saying?] **b** : supporting the beliefs or goals of (someone) : on the side of (someone) • *You're either with us or against us.* **15** : in the opinion or judgment of (someone) • *It's fine with us if you want to come, too.* **16** : as successfully as (someone) • *He can ski with the best of them.* [=he can ski as well as the best skiers] **17** — used to say that things happen at the same time • *The birds returned with the arrival of spring.* **18** : in a way that changes according to (something) • *The pressure varies with the depth.* **19** : in the same direction as (something) • *We were sailing with the wind.* **20** — used to say that someone or something is included in a total number or amount • *It costs $10.35 with tax.* **21** : in spite of (something) • *They love the team, with all its faults.* **22** — used to indicate the object of an adverb in a type of command • *Away with her.* [=take her away from here] — **with it** *informal* **1** : in a state in which you are thinking clearly and are aware of what is happening • *I had just woken up and wasn't quite with it yet.* • *Come on, now. Get with it.* **2** : knowing a lot about current styles, ideas, or events • *You have to be pretty with it if you want to talk to them about politics.* — **with that** : immediately after doing or saying that • *She said goodbye. And with that, she was gone.*

with·draw /wɪðˈdrɑː, wɪθˈdrɑː/ vb **-drew** /-ˈdruː/; **-drawn** /-ˈdrɑːn/; **-draw·ing** **1** [T] : to remove (money) from a bank account • *She withdrew $200 from her checking account.* **2** [T] : to take (something) back • *The company withdrew the job offer.* • *The pills were withdrawn from the market because they were unsafe.* **3** [I] : to stop participating in something • *The injury forced him to withdraw from the tournament.* **4** [T/I] : to leave a place, room, area, etc. • *The troops were forced to withdraw (from the battlefield).* • *The troops were withdrawn from the front line.* • *After dinner, we withdrew to the library.* **5** [I] : to stop spending time with other people • *She withdrew from other people as she grew older.* **6** [T] : to take (something) back, away, or out • *He withdrew* [=removed] *his hand from the doorknob.*

with·draw·al /wɪðˈdrɑːəl, wɪθˈdrɑːəl/ n **1** [C] **a** : an act of taking something away • *a withdrawal of support/troops* **b** : an act of ending your involvement in something • *He announced his withdrawal from the campaign.* **2** [C/U] : the act of taking money out of a bank account • *She made a withdrawal of $100 from her checking account.* **3** [U] **a** : the act or process of stopping the use of an addictive drug • *his withdrawal from heroin* **b** : the physical and mental problems that occur for a period of time after a person stops using an addictive drug • *She expe-*

rienced symptoms of nicotine withdrawal after she quit smoking.

with·drawn /wɪθˈdrɑːn, wɪθˈdrɔːn/ *adj* : very quiet and usually shy ▪ *He became more withdrawn after his brother's death.*

with·er /ˈwɪðɚ/ *vb* [*I*] *of a plant* : to become dry and weak ▪ *The plants withered and died.* ▪ *(figurative) Our hopes have withered (away).*

with·ered /ˈwɪðɚd/ *adj* 1 *of a plant* : dry and weak ▪ *withered leaves* 2 : thin and wrinkled because of illness, old age, etc. ▪ *an old man with a withered face*

with·hold /wɪθˈhould, wɪðˈhould/ *vb* **-held** /-ˈheld/; **-hold·ing** [*T*] 1 : to hold (something) back ▪ *You can withhold the fee until the work is complete.* ▪ *The witness's name was withheld.* 2 : to refuse to provide (something) ▪ *She was accused of withholding evidence.* 3 *US* : to take out (an amount of money for taxes) from someone's income ▪ *She has $20 withheld from her paycheck every week.*

¹**with·in** /wɪˈðɪn, wɪˈθɪn/ *prep* 1 : inside (something) ▪ *They live within the city limits.* ▪ *sounds coming from within his apartment* ▪ *changes within the company* 2 : before the end of (a particular period of time) ▪ *Scientists predict that a cure will be found within (the next) five years.* ▪ *He entered the house, and within seconds, he was surrounded by children.* 3 : less than (a particular distance) from something or someone ▪ *Everything I need is within a few miles of my apartment.* ▪ *I keep my dictionary within (easy) reach* [=close enough to reach] *on my desk.* ▪ *The hotel is within sight of the ocean.* [=you can see the ocean from the hotel] 4 : not beyond the limits of (something) ▪ *Let's try to stay within our/the budget.* ▪ *It is within the realm of possibility* [=it is possible], *but it is not likely.* 5 — used to say how close someone is or was to doing or achieving something ▪ *She is within two hundred votes of being elected.* 6 : in the thoughts or character of (someone) ▪ *She searched within herself for the truth.*

²**within** *adv, formal* 1 : inside something ▪ *We could hear sounds coming from within.* 2 : in someone's inner thoughts, feelings, etc. ▪ *They were outwardly calm but nervous within.*

with·out /wɪˈðaʊt, wɪˈθaʊt/ *prep* 1 : not having or including (something) ▪ *Do you take your coffee with or without sugar?* ▪ *Without water, there would be no life on Earth.* ▪ *a world without war* ▪ *They fought without fear.* ▪ *We kept trying without success.* 2 — used to say that someone is not with or is not involved with another person or group ▪ *He went to the store without her.* ▪ *Please don't make a decision without me.* 3 : not using (something specified) ▪ *Try doing the math without a calculator.* 4 : not doing something specified ▪ *They left without (even) saying goodbye.* ▪ *Even without studying, she answered all of the questions correctly.* — **do without** *see* ¹DO — **go without** *see* ¹GO — **without** *adv* ▪ *Do you take your coffee with sugar or without?*

with·stand /wɪθˈstænd, wɪðˈstænd/ *vb* **-stood** /-ˈstʊd/; **-stand·ing** [*T*] 1 : to not be harmed or affected by (something) ▪ *These pots can withstand high temperatures.* 2 : to deal with (something) successfully ▪ *They withstood attacks from many critics.*

wit·less /ˈwɪtləs/ *adj* 1 : very foolish or stupid ▪ *a witless blunder/fool* 2 *not before a noun, informal* : very much ▪ *We were bored/scared witless.* [=extremely bored/scared]

¹**wit·ness** /ˈwɪtnəs/ *n* 1 [*C*] **a** : a person who sees something (such as a crime) happen ▪ *a murder witness = a witness to a murder* **b** *law* : a person who makes a statement in a court about what he or she knows or has seen ▪ *a witness for the defense/prosecution* 2 [*C*] : a person who is present at an event and can say that it happened ▪ *There must be two witnesses present when she signs the document.* 3 [*U*] *US* : a statement of a person's religious beliefs ▪ *They gave witness to their faith.* [=declared their belief in a god or religion] — **bear witness** 1 : to show that something exists or is true ▪ *His success bears witness to the value of hard work.* 2 *formal* : to make a statement saying that you saw or know something ▪ *She was accused of bearing false witness.* [=saying that she saw something that she did not really see] — **be witness to** : to see (something) happen ▪ *We have been witness to many changes in recent years.*

²**witness** *vb* [*T*] 1 : to see (something) happen ▪ *Several people witnessed the accident.* 2 *law* : to be present at (an event) in order to be able to say that it happened ▪ *He witnessed the signing of her will.* 3 : to be the time or place when (something) happens ▪ *The past decade has witnessed many new advances in medical research.* 4 — used to say that something is an example of or is proof of something ▪ *The economy is improving— witness the decrease in unemployment.* [=the decrease in unemployment shows that the economy is improving] ▪ *The event was a success, as witnessed by* [=as shown by] *the high turnout.*

wit·ter /ˈwɪtɚ/ *vb* [*I*] *Brit, informal* : to talk for a long time about something that is not important or interesting ▪ *She was wittering (on) about her health problems.*

wit·ti·cism /ˈwɪtəˌsɪzəm/ *n* [*C*] : a clever or funny remark ▪ *a collection of famous witticisms*

wit·ty /ˈwɪti/ *adj* **wit·ti·er**; **-est** : funny and clever ▪ *a witty writer/remark* — **wit·ti·ly** /ˈwɪtəli/ *adv* — **wit·ti·ness** /ˈwɪtinəs/ *n* [*U*]

wives *plural of* WIFE

wiz /ˈwɪz/ *n, pl* **wiz·zes** [*C*] *US, informal* : WIZARD ▪ *She's a spelling wiz.* [=she's very good at spelling]

wiz·ard /ˈwɪzɚd/ *n* [*C*] 1 : a person who is skilled in magic or who has magical powers 2 : a person who is very good at something ▪ *a math wizard*

wiz·ard·ry /ˈwɪzɚdri/ *n* [*U*] 1 : the magical things done by a wizard 2 : something that is very impressive in a way that seems magical ▪ *the wizardry of modern technology*

wiz·ened /ˈwɪzənd/ *adj* : dry and wrinkled usually because of old age ▪ *the old man's wizened face*

wk *abbr* week

w/o *abbr* without

wob·ble /ˈwɑːbəl/ *vb* **wob·bled**; **wob·bling** [*I*] **1** : to move with an unsteady side-to-side motion ▪ *The vase wobbled but didn't fall over.* **2** : to be or become unsteady or unsure ▪ *They have been wobbling in their support of the bill.* — **wobble** *n* [*singular*] — **wob·bly** /ˈwɑːbəli/ *adj* **wob·bli·er**; **-est** ▪ *a wobbly table/voice*

woe /ˈwoʊ/ *n* **1** [*U*] : a feeling of great pain or sadness ▪ *a tale of woe* [=a sad story] **2** [*plural*] : problems or troubles ▪ *The city's traffic woes are well-known.* ▪ *financial woes* — **woe is me** — used in a humorous way to say that you are sad or upset about something

woe·be·gone /ˈwoʊbɪˌgɑːn/ *adj* : looking or feeling very sad ▪ *His face had a woebegone expression.*

woe·ful /ˈwoʊfəl/ *adj* **1** : very sad ▪ *a woeful story* **2** : very bad ▪ *woeful grades* — **woe·ful·ly** *adv*

wok /ˈwɑːk/ *n* [*C*] : a pan that is shaped like a bowl and that is used especially for cooking Chinese food

woke *past tense and past participle of* ¹WAKE

woken *past participle of* ¹WAKE

¹**wolf** /ˈwʊlf/ *n, pl* **wolves** /ˈwʊlvz/ [*C*] : a large wild animal that is similar to a dog and that often hunts in groups ▪ *a pack of wolves* — **a wolf in sheep's clothing** : a person who appears to be friendly or helpful but who really is dangerous or dishonest — **cry wolf** *see* ¹CRY — **throw someone to the wolves** : to put someone in a position that allows them to be criticized or treated badly without any defense or protection — **wolf·ish** /ˈwʊlfɪʃ/ *adj* ▪ *a wolfish grin*

²**wolf** *vb* [*T*] : to eat (something) very quickly ▪ *The kids were wolfing (down) their food.*

wolf·hound /ˈwʊlfˌhaʊnd/ *n* [*C*] : a type of large dog that was used for hunting wolves and other large animals in the past

wom·an /ˈwʊmən/ *n, pl* **wom·en** /ˈwɪmən/ **1** [*C*] : an adult female human being ▪ *a group of men and women* ▪ *women's basketball* ▪ *the town's first woman mayor* **2** [*C*] : a woman who has a specified job or position ▪ *a cleaning woman* ▪ *a saleswoman* **3** [*U*] : all women thought of as a group ▪ *a celebration of woman* [=women] **4** [*C*] *informal* : the girlfriend, wife, or lover of a man ▪ *the new woman in his life*

wom·an·hood /ˈwʊmənˌhʊd/ *n* [*U*] **1** : the state or condition of being an adult woman and no longer a girl ▪ *a young girl on the verge of womanhood* **2** : women in general ▪ *The book is a celebration of womanhood.*

wom·an·iz·er *also Brit* **wom·an·is·er** /ˈwʊməˌnaɪzɚ/ *n* [*C*] *disapproving* : a man who has sexual relationships with many women — **wom·an·ize** *also Brit* **wom·an·ise** /ˈwʊməˌnaɪz/ *vb* **-ized**; **-iz-**ing [*I*] ▪ *He has been accused of womanizing.*

wom·an·kind /ˈwʊmənˌkaɪnd/ *n* [*U*] : all women thought of as one group ▪ *for the benefit of all womankind*

wom·an·ly /ˈwʊmənli/ *adj* : having or showing qualities (such as beauty or gentleness) that are expected in a woman ▪ *a womanly radiance* ▪ *womanly curves*

womb /ˈwuːm/ *n* [*C*] : UTERUS

women *plural of* WOMAN

wom·en·folk /ˈwɪmənˌfoʊk/ *n* [*plural*] *old-fashioned + humorous* : the women of a family or community ▪ *cowboys fighting to protect their womenfolk*

women's room *n* [*C*] *US* : LADIES' ROOM

won *past tense and past participle of* ¹WIN

¹**won·der** /ˈwʌndɚ/ *n* **1** [*C*] : something or someone that is very surprising, beautiful, amazing, etc. ▪ *The Grand Canyon is one of the natural wonders of the world.* ▪ *the wonders of science* **2** [*U*] : a feeling caused by seeing something that is very surprising, beautiful, amazing, etc. ▪ *She gazed up at the tall buildings in wonder.* **3** [*singular*] : something that is surprising or hard to believe ▪ *It's a wonder* [=it is surprising] *that we made it this far.* — **do/work wonders** : to help or improve something greatly ▪ *A vacation will do wonders for your mood.* — **no wonder** or **small/little wonder** — used to say that something is not surprising ▪ *It's no wonder you're hungry; you didn't have any breakfast.* — **wonders never cease** *humorous* — used to say that you are happy and surprised by something good that has happened ▪ *He was on time again. Wonders never cease!*

²**wonder** *vb* **1** [*T/I*] : to think about something with curiosity ▪ *Have you ever wondered why the sky is blue?* ▪ *I wonder if he's going to change jobs.* ▪ *I was wondering about that.* **2** [*T*] — used to ask a question or make a polite request ▪ *I wonder if you could tell me where the post office is?* **3** [*I*] : to feel surprise or amazement ▪ *Sometimes his behavior makes me wonder.* ▪ *We stood and wondered at the impressive display of lights.*

wonder drug *n* [*C*] : a very effective drug ▪ *a new wonder drug for treating arthritis*

won·der·ful /ˈwʌndɚfəl/ *adj* : extremely good ▪ *That's wonderful news!* ▪ *a wonderful meal/party* — **won·der·ful·ly** *adv*

won·der·land /ˈwʌndɚˌlænd/ *n* [*C*] : a place that is filled with things that are beautiful, impressive, or surprising ▪ *The garden was a floral wonderland.*

won·der·ment /ˈwʌndɚmənt/ *n* [*U*] : a feeling of being surprised or amazed ▪ *He felt a sense of wonderment.*

won·drous /ˈwʌndrəs/ *adj* : causing wonder or amazement ▪ *a wondrous display* — **won·drous·ly** *adv*

wonk /ˈwɑːŋk/ *n* [*C*] *US, informal + sometimes disapproving* : a person who knows a lot about the details of a particular field and often talks a lot about that subject ▪ *the policy wonks in the government*

won·ky /ˈwɑːŋki/ *adj* **won·ki·er**; **-est** *informal* **1** *US, sometimes disapproving*

: having or showing a lot of interest in and knowledge about the details of a particular subject ▪ *a wonky bureaucrat* **2** *Brit* **a** : not straight or steady ▪ *a wonky [=wobbly] chair* **b** : not working correctly ▪ *a wonky knee*

¹**wont** /ˈwɑːnt, *Brit* ˈwəʊnt/ *adj, not before a noun, formal* : having a tendency to do something ▪ *Some people are wont to blame others for their faults.*

²**wont** *n* [*U*] *old-fashioned* : a usual habit or way of behaving ▪ *He enjoyed a drink after work, as is his wont.*

won't /ˈwoʊnt/ : will not ▪ *I won't see him today.*

woo /ˈwuː/ *vb* [*T*] **1** *old-fashioned* : to try to have a romantic relationship with (someone) ▪ *He wooed her with flowers and dinner.* **2** : to try to attract (a customer, voter, worker, etc.) ▪ *the store's efforts to woo new customers*

wood /ˈwʊd/ *n* **1** [*U*] : the hard substance that makes up the stems and branches of trees and shrubs ▪ *a block of wood* ▪ *This baseball bat is made out of wood.* ▪ *wood paneling/floors* **2 a** *or* **woods** [*C*] : an area of land covered with many trees ▪ *Their house is near a small wood.* ▪ *a thick woods* **b** **woods** [*U, plural*] : a thick growth of trees and bushes that covers a wide area ▪ *He went for a hike in the woods.* ▪ *The woods are a dangerous place for walking.* **3** [*C*] : a golf club with a large head that was made of wood in the past but is now usually made of metal ▪ *She hit a wood off the tee.* — **knock on wood** (*US*) *or chiefly Brit* **touch wood** ◇ People say *knock on wood* or *touch wood* and often hit or touch something made of wood as a way to prevent bad luck after they have just said that something good has happened, that they are in a good situation, etc. ▪ *I've never broken a bone, knock on wood.* — **neck of the woods** see ¹NECK — **not see the wood for the trees** see TREE — **out of the wood/woods** : in a position free from danger or difficulty ▪ *Her health is getting better but she's not out of the woods yet.*

wood·chuck /ˈwʊdˌtʃʌk/ *n* [*C*] : a small, furry North American animal that lives in the ground — called also *groundhog*

wood·cock /ˈwʊdˌkɑːk/ *n, pl* **woodcocks** *or* **woodcock** [*C*] : a brown bird that has a short neck and long bill and that is often hunted

wood·ed /ˈwʊdəd/ *adj* : covered with trees ▪ *a wooded area*

wood·en /ˈwʊdn̩/ *adj* **1** : made of wood ▪ *a wooden crate/fence/spoon* **2** : awkward or stiff ▪ *wooden acting/dialogue*

wood·land /ˈwʊdlənd/ *n* [*C/U*] : land covered with trees and bushes ▪ *The lake was surrounded by (a) dense woodland.* ▪ *The woodlands stretch for miles.* ▪ *woodland creatures*

wood·peck·er /ˈwʊdˌpɛkɚ/ *n* [*C*] : a bird that has a very hard beak which it uses to make holes in trees to get insects for food

wood·shed /ˈwʊdˌʃɛd/ *n* [*C*] : a small building used for storing firewood

woodsy /ˈwʊdzi/ *adj* **woods·i·er; -est**

US, informal **1** : covered with trees ▪ *a woodsy area* **2** : relating to or suggesting the forest ▪ *a woodsy smell*

wood·wind /ˈwʊdˌwɪnd/ *n* **1** [*C*] : any one of the group of musical instruments that includes flutes, clarinets, oboes, bassoons, and saxophones ▪ *woodwind instruments* ▪ *the woodwind section of an orchestra* **2** [*plural*] : the section of a band or orchestra that plays woodwind instruments

wood·work /ˈwʊdˌwɚk/ *n* [*U*] **1** : the parts of a room or house (such as window frames or stairs) that are made of wood ▪ *decorative woodwork* **2** *Brit* : WOODWORKING — **come/crawl out of the woodwork** *disapproving* ◇ If people **come/crawl out of the woodwork**, they appear suddenly, usually because they see an opportunity to get something for themselves. — **into the woodwork** — used in phrases like *fade into the woodwork* to describe someone or something that is not noticed or that seems to disappear ▪ *a shy man who seems to fade into the woodwork at parties*

wood·work·ing /ˈwʊdˌwɚkɪŋ/ *n* [*U*] *US* : the skill or work of making things out of wood — **wood·work·er** /ˈwʊdˌwɚkɚ/ *n* [*C*]

woody /ˈwʊdi/ *adj* **wood·i·er; -est** **1** : having stems and branches that are made of wood ▪ *woody plants* : made of wood ▪ *tall woody stems* **2** : similar to wood ▪ *a woody texture/smell* **3** *informal* : having many trees ▪ *a woody piece of land*

woof /ˈwʊf/ *n* [*C*] : the sound made by a dog — **woof** *vb* [*I*] ▪ *The dog woofed.*

wool /ˈwʊl/ *n* [*U*] **1** : the soft, thick hair of sheep and some other animals **2** : cloth or clothing made of wool ▪ *I never wear wool.* ▪ *wool socks/blankets/sweaters* **3** *chiefly Brit* : long, thick thread made of wool and used for knitting ▪ *a ball of wool* [=(*US*) *yarn*] — **pull the wool over someone's eyes** *informal* : to hide the truth from someone ▪ *He was too clever to let them pull the wool over his eyes.*

wool·en (*US*) *or Brit* **wool·len** /ˈwʊlən/ *adj, always before a noun* : made of wool ▪ *woolen blankets*

wool·ens (*US*) *or Brit* **wool·lens** /ˈwʊlənz/ *n* [*plural*] *somewhat old-fashioned* : clothes made of wool ▪ *He wore his best woolens.*

¹**wool·ly** *also* **wooly** /ˈwʊli/ *adj* **wool·li·er; -est** **1** : covered with wool ▪ *a woolly animal* **2** *chiefly Brit, informal* : made of wool or resembling wool ▪ *a woolly hat* **3** *chiefly Brit* : confused and unclear ▪ *a woolly argument* — **wool·li·ness** *n* [*U*]

²**wool·ly** /ˈwʊli/ *n, pl* **-lies** [*C*] *chiefly Brit, informal* : a warm piece of clothing (such as a sweater) made of knitted wool ▪ *winter woollies*

woolly mammoth *n* [*C*] : ¹MAMMOTH

woo·zy /ˈwuːzi/ *adj* **woo·zi·er; -est** : slightly dizzy, sick, or weak ▪ *She was already feeling woozy after her first drink.* — **woo·zi·ness** *n* [*U*]

¹**word** /ˈwɚd/ *n* **1** [*C*] : a sound or combination of sounds that has a meaning and is spoken or written ▪ *"Please" is a useful*

word. • *What is the French word for car?*
2 [C] : something that a person says •
*You can't believe a word (of what) she
says.* [=you can't believe anything she
says] • *Describe the experience in your
own words.* • *Could I have a word with
you?* [=could I talk with you briefly?] •
They gave me • **word of warning.** [=they
warned me] • *Don't say/breathe a word*
[=don't talk] *about this to anyone.* • *He is
a* **man of few words.** [=he doesn't talk
very much] • *I've been asked to* **say a few
words.** [=make a short speech or state-
ment] **3** [singular] : an order or command • *She gave the word to begin.* **4** [U,
singular] : news or information • *(Is
there) Any word on how they are?* • *They
sent word* [=sent a message] *that they'd
be late.* • **Word has it** [=I have heard] *that
they are engaged.* • *The police* **put/got the
word out** [=let people know] *that they
were looking for him.* **5** [singular] : a
promise to do something • *I'll be there. I
give you my word.* [=I promise] • *You'd
better* **keep your word.** • *He is a* **man of
his word.** [=he always keeps his promis-
es] • *I can't go back on my word.* [=I can't
break my promise] • *You'll have to* **take
my word for it.** [=you'll have to believe
me] • *She was* **true to her word.** [=she did
what she said she would do] **6** [plural]
: angry remarks • *Words were exchanged.*
[=people said angry things to each other]
• *He had words* [=had an argument] *with
his boss.* — *a picture is worth a thousand words* see 1WORTH — *a word in
someone's ear chiefly Brit* : a remark
that is made privately to someone • *May
I have a word in your ear?* [=may I speak
to you privately?] — *a word to the
wise* — used to say that you are about
to give someone advice or a warning • *A
word to the wise: never sign a contract
without reading it first.* — *by word of
mouth* : by being told by another person
• *We found this hotel by word of mouth.* —
eat your words see EAT — *from the
word go informal* : from the beginning •
The show was a success from the word go.
— *get a word in edgewise* see EDGE-
WISE — *good word* : a favorable comment • *Please put in a good word for me*
[=say something good about me] *when
you talk to the boss.* — *hang on someone's every word* see 1HANG — *in a
word* : very briefly — used to indicate
that you are saying something by using
only one word or by using as few words
as possible • *Our answer, in a word, is no.*
— *in other words* — used to introduce
a statement that repeats what has been
said in a different and usually a simpler
or more exact way • *"She said the movie
was a bit predictable." "In other words, she
didn't like it."* — *in so many words also
in as many words* : in exactly those
words or in exactly that way — usually
used in negative statements • *"Did he say
he wouldn't do it?" "Not in so many
words, but that was the impression I got."*
— *lost for words* see 2LOST — *mark
my words* see 2MARK — *put words in/
into someone's mouth* : to suggest
that someone said or meant something

that he or she did not say or mean • *Don't
put words in my mouth. I wasn't defending
his actions, despite what you may think.*
— *say the word* : to give an order •
*When you want to leave (just) say the
word.* — *take the words right out of
someone's mouth* : to say exactly what
someone was thinking • *I agree! You took
the words right out of my mouth!* — *the
last/final word* **1** : the final thing said
in an argument or a discussion • *Her decision is the final word on the matter.* •
Why do you always have to **have the last
word?** [=to be the last person to speak]
2 : the power to make a final decision •
The judge will have the last word. **3** *informal* : the most modern or best one of its
kind • *This is the last word in wireless
phones.* — *(upon) my word somewhat
old-fashioned* — used to express surprise
• *My word, what a beautiful dress!* — *war
of words* : an argument in which people
or groups criticize and disagree with
each other publicly and repeatedly for
usually a long time • *Rival groups have
engaged in a war of words over the new
law.* — *word for word* : in the exact
words • *He gave the same speech word for
word yesterday.* — *word of honor* ✧
Your *word of honor* is your promise that
you will do something, that something is
true, etc. • *I give you my word of honor
that I will pay the money back.* — **wordless** /'wədləs/ *adj* • *a wordless agreement*
— **word·less·ly** *adv*

²**word** *vb* [T] : to say (something) in a particular way by choosing which words to
use • *Could we word the headline differently?* • *The request was worded carefully.*

word·ing /'wədɪŋ/ *n* [U] : the words that
are used to say something • *What's the
exact wording of the agreement?*

word·play /'wəd,pleɪ/ *n* [U] : playful or
clever use of words • *witty wordplay*

word processing *n* [U] : the production
of printed pages of writing (such as business letters) that can be stored and printed by using computer equipment • *software used for word processing = word
processing software*

word processor *n* [C] **1** : a computer
used for creating, storing, and printing
text **2** : software used on a computer to
perform word processing

wordy /'wədi/ *adj* **word·i·er; -est** *disapproving* : using or containing too many
words • *The script was too wordy.*

wore *past tense of* 1WEAR

¹**work** /'wək/ *vb* **1 a** [T/I] : to have a job •
Her husband doesn't work. • *She works
part-time.* • *He works two jobs.* **b** [T/I]
: to do things as part of your job • *She
worked through lunch to get the report
done.* • *I work for him.* [=I am his employ-
ee] • *He works about 60 hours a week.* •
She is used to **working long hours.** **c** [T]
: to do work in, on, or at (an area, event,
etc.) • *farmers working the fields* **2 a** [I]
: to do something that involves physical
or mental effort • *She is working in the
garden.* • *We worked hard on this project.*
b [T] : to force (someone or something)
to do something that involves physical or
mental effort • *This exercise works the*

muscles in your chest. ▪ *The coach worked her team hard during practice.* **3** [*T*] : to use and control (something) ▪ *I don't know how to work your cell phone.* **4** [*I*] : to perform or operate in the correct way ▪ *The computer isn't working (properly).* **5** [*I*] **a** : to have the intended effect or result ▪ *The medicine seems to be working.* **b** : to have a particular effect or result ▪ *Red curtains would work well in this room.* ▪ *I think you'll get the job. Being bilingual definitely* **works in your favor.** [=it helps or benefits you] ▪ *Her lack of experience* **worked against her.** [=it made her less likely to succeed] **6** [*T*] : to cause (something) to happen ▪ *I'll do my best, but I can't* **work miracles.** [=I can't make miracles happen] ▪ *a brilliant chef who* **works magic** [=does special or remarkable things] *in the kitchen* **7** [*T/I*] : to move (something) into or out of a particular position slowly or with difficulty ▪ *The knot worked (itself) loose.* [=became loose] **8** [*T*] : to bring (something) into a desired shape or form by cutting it, pressing it, etc. ▪ *Work the dough with your hands.* **9** [*T*] : to talk to and try to gain the friendship or support of (the people in a group) ▪ *a politician who knows how to* **work a crowd/room** — **work around** *or chiefly Brit* **work round** [*phrasal vb*] **1** : to organize things or proceed in a way that avoids (something) ▪ *We'll just have to find a way to work around the problem.* **2** **work around/round to** : to start talking or writing about (something) after talking or writing about other things ▪ *He eventually worked around to the subject/issue.* — **work at** [*phrasal vb*] : to make an effort to do (something) better ▪ *He needs to work at his handwriting.* — **work in** [*phrasal vb*] **1** **work (something) in** *or* **work in (something)** **a** : to add or include (something) in a conversation, essay, etc. ▪ *During the speech, he worked in a few jokes.* **b** : to stir or mix (something) into something ▪ *Work in the blueberries.* **2** **work (someone or something) in** *US* : to make an amount of time available for (someone or something) ▪ *My schedule is pretty full, but I think I can work you in.* [=fit you in] — **work into** [*phrasal vb*] **1** **work (something) into** **a** : to add or include (something) in (something) ▪ *You should work more fresh fruit into your diet.* **b** : to stir or mix (something) into (something) ▪ *Work the blueberries into the mixture.* **2** **work (someone) into** : to gradually cause (someone) to be in (an excited, angry, or frightened state) ▪ *He worked himself into a panic.* — **work it/things** *informal* : to arrange your activities in a particular way so that it is possible for something to happen or be done ▪ *I'll try to work things so that I can come to your party.* — **work off** [*phrasal vb*] **work off (something)** *or* **work (something) off** **1** : to pay (a debt) by working ▪ *She worked off her loan.* **2** : to lose or get rid of (something) by physical activity ▪ *Jogging is a great way to work off stress.* — **work on** [*phrasal vb*] **1 a** : to be in the process of making

(something), doing (something), etc. ▪ *The director is working on a new movie.* ▪ *He is in the garage working on* [=fixing] *the car.* **b** **work on doing (something)** : to make an effort to do (something) ▪ *You have to work on controlling your temper.* **2** : to try to influence or persuade (someone) to do something ▪ *She is working on them to change their votes.* — **work out** [*phrasal vb*] **1** : to perform athletic exercises in order to improve your health or physical fitness ▪ *She works out at the gym twice a week.* **2 a** : to happen, develop, or end in a desired or successful way ▪ *Our plan worked out perfectly.* **b** : to happen, develop, or end in a particular way or to have a particular result ▪ *Despite some difficulties, everything worked out well.* ▪ *How is your new job working out?* [=how are things going with your new job?] ▪ *With tax, it* **works out at/to** [=cost] *just over $115.* **3** **work out (something)** *or* **work (something) out** **a** : to find or create (a solution, plan, etc.) by thinking ▪ *We worked out a plan to save money.* **b** : to use mathematics to solve (something) ▪ *She worked out the problem on a piece of paper.* — **work over** [*phrasal vb*] **work (someone) over** *informal* : to hurt (someone) by hitting, kicking, etc. ▪ *Someone worked him over* [=beat him up] *pretty good.* — **work through** [*phrasal vb*] : to deal with (something that is difficult or unpleasant) successfully ▪ *He saw a psychologist to help him work through his depression.* — **work up** [*phrasal vb*] **1** **work (someone) up** : to make (someone) feel very angry, excited, upset, etc. ▪ *Don't work yourself up again.* **2** **work up (something)** *or* **work (something) up** **a** : to produce (something) by physical or mental effort ▪ *I worked up a sweat at the gym.* **b** *chiefly Brit* : to improve your skill at (something) or increase your knowledge of (something) ▪ *I need to work up my French for the exam.* **c** *chiefly Brit* : to develop or expand (something) ▪ *He worked up the short story into a novel.* **3** **work up to** : to reach (a rate, level, etc.) by gradually increasing in speed, intensity, etc. ▪ *The ship gradually worked up to full speed.* — **work wonders** see ¹WONDER — **work your way** : to move yourself into or out of a particular position slowly or with difficulty ▪ *I worked my way to the center of the crowd.* ▪ (*figurative*) *She slowly worked her way to the top of the company.* ✧ If you **work your way through college/school,** you have a job that helps you pay for your expenses while you go to college/school.

²**work** *n* **1** [*U*] **a** : a job or activity that you do regularly especially in order to earn money ▪ *She is trying to find work.* ▪ *She plans to* **return to work** [=start working her job again] *soon.* ▪ *What* **line of work** *are you in?* = *What do you do for work?* **b** : the place where you do your job ▪ *She's not home. She's at work.* **2** [*U*] : the things that you do especially as part of your job ▪ *I have a lot of work to do.* ▪ *administrative/secretarial work* **3** [*U*] **a** : physical or mental effort that is used to

perform a job or achieve a goal ▪ *Hard work is the key to success.* ▪ b : the process or activity of working ▪ *He plans to start work on a new novel soon.* ▪ *You need to* **get down to work**. [=start working] ▪ *She* **set to work** [=started working] *on the project immediately.* ❖ Phrases like **good work, nice work**, etc., are used to tell people that they have done something very well. ▪ *"I finished the project ahead of schedule." "Good work!"* **4** a [U] : something that is produced or done by someone ▪ *The cabinets are the work of a skilled carpenter.* [=they were made by a skilled carpenter] ▪ b [C/U] : something that is produced by a writer, musician, artist, etc. ▪ *I love this painter's work.* ▪ *literary works* ▪ *The painting is a work in progress.* [=it is not yet finished] **5** [*plural*] : roads, bridges, dams, and similar structures ▪ *engineering works from the 19th century* **6 works** [C] : a factory ▪ *a steel works* — used with both singular and plural verbs ▪ *The local steel works has/have shut down.* **7 the works** : the moving parts of a machine ▪ *the works of a clock* ▪ *(figurative) The office used to be very efficient, but the new regulations have* **gummed up the works**. [=made the work more difficult and slow] **8 the works** *informal* : everything ▪ *a pizza with the works* [=with all the available toppings] **— at work 1** a : actively doing work ▪ *The boss kept us hard at work.* ▪ *We're at* **work on the new project**. b : doing your regular job ▪ *He's on vacation, but he'll be back at work soon.* **2** : having an effect or influence ▪ *She felt that a higher power was at work.* **— have your work cut out for you** ❖ If you *have your work cut out for you*, the thing you have to do is very difficult, and you have to work very hard to achieve it. **— in the works** *informal* : in the process of being prepared, developed, or completed ▪ *Her next movie is already in the works.* **— in work** *Brit* : having a regular job ▪ *the percentage of people who are in work* [=people who have jobs] **— make short/quick/light work of 1** : to make it possible for (something) to be done quickly or easily ▪ *This new snow shovel makes short work of clearing off the driveway.* ❖ The expression **many hands make light work** means that people can do things more quickly and easily when they work together. **2** : to finish (something) or defeat (someone) quickly or easily ▪ *She made short work of her opponents.* **— out of work** : without a regular job ▪ *The factory closed and left/put 5,000 people out of work.*

work·able /ˈwɚkəbəl/ *adj* : able to be used successfully ▪ *a workable plan/solution*

work·a·day /ˈwɚkəˌdeɪ/ *adj, always before a noun* : not unusual or interesting : ORDINARY ▪ *workaday life/activities/ concerns*

work·a·hol·ic /ˌwɚkəˈhɑːlɪk/ *n* [C] : a person who is always working, thinking about work, etc.

work·bench /ˈwɚkˌbɛntʃ/ *n* [C] : a long

table that people use when they are working with tools

work·book /ˈwɚkˌbʊk/ *n* [C] : a book that contains problems or exercises and that students use to practice what they are learning in a class

work·day /ˈwɚkˌdeɪ/ *n* [C] *chiefly US* **1** : a day on which you work at a job ▪ *On workdays I usually wake up at six o'clock.* **2** : the period of time in a day during which you work at a job ▪ *an 8-hour workday*

worked up *adj, not before a noun, informal* : very angry, excited, or upset about something ▪ *What is she so worked up about?*

work·er /ˈwɚkɚ/ *n* [C] **1** a : a person who does a particular job to earn money ▪ *office/factory/construction/postal workers* ▪ *a full-time/part-time worker* b : a person who is actively involved in a particular activity ▪ *aid/rescue/research workers* **2** : a person whose job does not involve managing other people ▪ *The workers went on strike.* **3** : a person who works in a particular way ▪ *a hard/fast/ good worker* **4** : a type of bee, ant, etc., that does most of the work in a colony of insects ▪ *worker bees*

workers' compensation *n* [U] *US* : a system of insurance that pays an employee who cannot work because he or she has been injured while working — called also *workers' comp*

work·force /ˈwɚkˌfoɚs/ *n* [*singular*] **1** : the group of people who work for a particular organization or business ▪ *a workforce of 2,400 people* **2** : the number of people in a country or area who are available for work ▪ *the nation's workforce*

work·horse /ˈwɚkˌhoɚs/ *n* [C] : a dependable person, machine, etc., that does a lot of work

work·house /ˈwɚkˌhaʊs/ *n* [C] *Brit* : POORHOUSE

work·ing /ˈwɚkɪŋ/ *adj, always before a noun* **1** : having a job ▪ *working mothers* [=mothers who also have paying jobs] ▪ *working people* [=people who are not rich and powerful and who have jobs that usually do not pay a lot of money] **2** a : of or relating to a person's job ▪ *poor working conditions* ▪ *regular/flexible working hours* b : suitable to be worn while working ▪ *working clothes/boots* **3** a : doing work ▪ *a working farm* b : relating to the work done by a machine, system, etc. ▪ *Everything is in (good) working order/condition.* [=is working properly] **4** : good enough to be used or useful although not perfect ▪ *I have a working knowledge of German.* [=I can read and understand German fairly well] **5** — used to describe something that is used while work is being done on something (such as a project) and that may be changed later ▪ *a working title/hypothesis*

working class *n* — **the working class** *also Brit* **the working classes** : the class of people who earn money by doing usually physical work and who are not rich or powerful — **working–class** *adj, al-*

ways before a noun ▪ *a working-class family*

work·ings /ˈwəkɪŋz/ *n* [*plural*] **1** : the moving parts that are inside a machine ▪ *the clock's inner workings* **2** : the ways in which something works ▪ *the inner workings of government*

work·load /ˈwəkˌloʊd/ *n* [C] : the amount of work that is expected to be done ▪ *a heavy workload*

work·man /ˈwəkmən/ *n, pl* **-men** /-mən/ [C] : a skilled worker (such as an electrician or carpenter)

work·man·like /ˈwəkmənˌlaɪk/ *adj* : done with the skill expected of a good worker or performer but usually not in a very exciting or impressive way ▪ *a workmanlike job/performance*

work·man·ship /ˈwəkmənˌʃɪp/ *n* [U] : the quality of the work that is done by someone ▪ *He admires good workmanship.*

work of art *n, pl* **works of art** [C] **1** : a painting, sculpture, etc., that is created to be beautiful or to express an important idea or feeling **2** : something that is attractive and skillfully made ▪ *The cake was a real work of art.*

work·out /ˈwəkˌaʊt/ *n* [C] : a period of physical exercise that you do in order to improve your fitness, ability, or performance ▪ *Her workout includes running on the treadmill and lifting weights.*

work·place /ˈwəkˌpleɪs/ *n* [C] : the office, factory, etc., where people work ▪ *a clean, comfortable workplace*

work·room /ˈwəkˌruːm/ *n* [C] : a room used for doing work usually inside a store ▪ *a tailor's workroom*

work·sheet /ˈwəkˌʃiːt/ *n* [C] **1** : a piece of paper that contains printed exercises and problems to be done by a student **2** : a printed form that is used in planning or calculating something ▪ *a tax worksheet*

work·shop /ˈwəkˌʃɑːp/ *n* [C] **1** : a place where things are made or repaired ▪ *a carpenter's workshop* **2** : a class or series of classes in which a small group of people learn the methods and skills used in doing something ▪ *a photography workshop*

work·sta·tion /ˈwəkˌsteɪʃən/ *n* [C] **1** : an area that has the equipment needed for one person to do a particular job **2** : a computer that is connected to a computer network

work·top /ˈwəkˌtɑːp/ *n* [C] *Brit* : ¹COUNTER 2a

work·week /ˈwəkˌwiːk/ *n* [C] *US* : the total amount of hours or days that you spend working at a job in one week ▪ *a 5-day/40-hour workweek*

world /ˈwəld/ *n* **1 a the world** : the Earth and all the people and things on it ▪ *the countries/people/languages of the world* ▪ *people from (all) around/across the world* = *people from all over the world* **b** [C] : a part of the world and the people and things that exist there ▪ *the industrialized world* ▪ *the English-speaking world* **2** [C] : human society ▪ *the history of the world* ▪ *ambitious students who want to change the world* ◇ **The real world** is the

world where everyone lives, works, and deals with everyday problems. ▪ *After college, she went out into the real world and got a job.* **3 the world** : the people in the world ▪ *She felt that the world was against her.* ▪ *It's a private matter. Please don't tell* ***the whole world*** *about it!* ◇ **The outside world** refers to the people who live outside of a particular place or who do not belong to a particular group. ▪ *The prisoners have little contact with the outside world.* **4** [C] **a** : a particular kind of interest, activity, or social situation, or the people who are involved in it ▪ *the business and financial worlds* **b** : a group of things of a particular type ▪ *the animal/plant world* **c** : a particular environment ▪ *the natural world* **5** [C] **a** : a particular part of human life and experience ▪ *the physical/material/spiritual world* **b** : the life and experiences of a particular person ▪ *His (whole/entire) world fell apart when his wife left him.* **6** [C] : a planet where there is life : a planet that is like Earth ▪ *stories about other worlds* **7** [*singular*] *informal* : a great amount of something ▪ *He's in a world of trouble.* ▪ *A vacation would do you a world of good.* **8 the world** : all that is important : EVERYTHING ▪ *She means the world to me.* [=she is extremely important to me] ▪ *He thinks the world of you.* [=he thinks very highly of you] — **a world away from** : completely different from (something) ▪ *The village is a world away from the hustle and bustle of the city.* — **come down in the world** : to become less wealthy, successful, etc. ▪ *He has really come down in the world.* — **dead to the world** see ¹DEAD — **for all the world** : in every way : EXACTLY ▪ *The copy looked for all the world like the original.* — **for the world** *informal* : for any reason — used to make a statement more forceful ▪ *I wouldn't miss your wedding for the world.* — **in the world** *informal* : among many possibilities — used to make a question or statement more forceful ▪ *What in the world are you talking about?* ▪ *This is the best apple pie in the world.* — **in your own world** or **in a world of your own** ◇ If you **are/live in a world of your own** or **are/live in your own (little) world**, you spend so much time thinking about something that you do not notice what is happening around you. — **(it's a) small world** — used to show surprise when you meet someone you know at an unexpected place or find out that you share a friend, acquaintance, etc., with another person ▪ *You know him, too? Wow, it's a small world.* — **move up in the world** : to become more wealthy, successful, etc. ▪ *He has really moved up in the world.* — **not long for this world** : about to die soon ▪ *His grandfather is not long for this world.* — **on top of the world** see ¹TOP — **out of this world** *informal* : EXCELLENT ▪ *This apple pie is out of this world.* — **set the world on fire** *also chiefly Brit* **set the world alight** *informal* : to be very successful and attract a lot of attention ▪ *The company is doing all right, but they* *haven't exactly set the world on fire.* — *the best of all (possible) worlds* : the best possible situation ▪ *The current economic situation is the best of all possible worlds for investors.* — *the best/worst of both worlds* ✧ When you have *the best of both worlds*, you have all the advantages of two different situations and none of the disadvantages. When you have *the worst of both worlds*, you have all the disadvantages of two different situations and none of the advantages. ▪ *I have the best of both worlds—a wonderful family and a great job.* — *the (whole) world over* : everywhere in the world ▪ *His books have entertained readers the world over.* — *the world is your oyster* see OYSTER — *world (is) coming to* ✧ People say that they *don't know what the world is coming to* or they ask *What is the world coming to?* when they are shocked or disgusted by something that has happened. — *world revolves around* 1 ✧ If you think *the world revolves around you*, you think that your own life, problems, etc., are more important than other people's. 2 ✧ If *your world revolves around someone or something*, that person or thing is extremely important in your life. ▪ *Their world revolves around their children.* — *world(s) apart* ✧ If something is a *world apart from* something else, or if two people or things are *worlds apart*, they are completely different. ▪ *The place where she lives now is a world apart from the small town where she grew up.*

world–class *adj* : among the best in the world ▪ *a world-class athlete*

world–famous *adj* : famous throughout the world ▪ *a world-famous scientist*

world·ly /ˈwɚldli/ *adj* 1 *always before a noun* : of or relating to the human world and ordinary life rather than to religious or spiritual matters ▪ *worldly goods/pleasures* 2 : having a lot of practical experience and knowledge about life and the world ▪ *a worldly woman* — **world·li·ness** *n* [U]

world·ly–wise /ˈwɚldliˌwaɪz/ *adj* : having or showing a lot of experience and knowledge about life and the world ▪ *He is very worldly-wise for someone so young.*

World Series *n, pl* **World Series** [C] *baseball* : the annual championship of the major leagues in the United States

world·view /ˈwɚldˌvjuː/ *n* [C] : the way someone thinks about the world ▪ *a scientific/religious/cultural worldview*

world war *n* [C/U] : a war involving many nations of the world ▪ *the First World War = World War I* [=the war that was fought mainly in Europe from 1914 to 1918] ▪ *the Second World War = World War II* [=the war that was fought mainly in Europe and Asia from 1939 to 1945]

world–wea·ry /ˈwɚldˌwiri/ *adj* : no longer having or showing excitement or interest in life ▪ *a world-weary young man*

world·wide /ˈwɚldˈwaɪd/ *adj* : happening or existing in all parts of the world ▪ *worldwide network* — **worldwide** *adv* ▪ *The disease affects millions of people worldwide.*

World Wide Web *n* — *the World Wide Web* : the part of the Internet that you can look at with a special program (called a browser) and that is made up of many documents which are linked together — abbr. *www* — called also *the Web*

¹**worm** /ˈwɚm/ *n* 1 [C] : a long, thin animal that has a soft body with no legs or bones and that often lives in the ground 2 [C] : the young form of some insects that looks like a small worm 3 [*plural*] : an infection or a disease caused by tiny worms that live inside the body of an animal or person ▪ *Our dog has worms.* 4 [C] *computers* : a computer virus that causes damage to computers connected to each other by a network — *can of worms* see ²CAN — **worm·like** /ˈwɚmˌlaɪk/ *adj* — **wormy** /ˈwɚmi/ *adj* **worm·i·er; -est**

²**worm** *vb* 1 [T/I] : to move or proceed by twisting and turning ▪ *He slowly wormed (his way) through the crowd.* 2 [T] : to give (an animal) medicine that destroys the small worms that live inside it and cause illness ▪ *worm a puppy* — *worm into* [*phrasal vb*] *worm (your way or yourself) into informal* : to get (yourself) into (a desired position, situation, etc.) in a gradual and usually clever or dishonest way ▪ *I wormed my way into this job.* — *worm out of* [*phrasal vb*] *informal* 1 *worm (something) out of* : to get (information) from (someone) by asking many questions, by using clever methods of persuasion, etc. ▪ *She wormed the truth out of him.* 2 *worm out of* or *worm (your way) out of* : to avoid doing (something) in usually a clever or dishonest way ▪ *He somehow wormed his way out of doing the work.*

worn *past participle of* ¹WEAR

worn–out /ˈwoɚnˈaʊt/ *adj* 1 *of a thing* : too old or damaged from use to be used any longer ▪ *a pair of worn-out jeans* 2 : very tired ▪ *I'm worn-out after that hike.*

wor·ried /ˈwɚrid/ *adj* : feeling or showing fear and concern because you think that something bad has happened or could happen ▪ *We were worried that we would arrive late.* ▪ *She's always worried about money.* ▪ *She had a worried look on her face.* ▪ *We've been worried sick!* [=extremely worried] — **wor·ried·ly** /ˈwɚridli/ *adv*

wor·ri·er /ˈwɚrijɚ/ *n* [C] : a person who worries too much or who worries about unimportant things

wor·ri·some /ˈwɚrisəm/ *adj, chiefly US* : causing people to worry ▪ *worrisome news*

¹**wor·ry** /ˈwɚri/ *vb* **-ries; -ried; -ry·ing** 1 [T/I] : to feel or show fear and concern because you think that something bad has happened or could happen ▪ *We didn't want you to worry (about us).* ▪ *Don't worry. You'll be fine.* ▪ *I worry that the children don't get enough exercise.* ▪ *The nurse said her condition was nothing to worry about.* [=was not serious] 2 [T] : to make (someone) anxious or upset ▪ *His poor health worries me.* — *not to worry informal* — used to say that there

is no cause for concern or worry ▪ *"It looks like we're almost out of milk." "Not to worry. I'll get some more this afternoon."*

²worry *n, pl* **-ries** **1** [U] : a feeling of concern about something bad that might happen ▪ *His high blood pressure is cause for worry.* ▪ *I was sick with worry.* [=extremely worried] **2** [C] : a problem or concern ▪ *Our greatest worry is that she'll get lost.* ▪ *His money worries* [=difficulties] *are over.*

wor·ry·wart /ˈwɜriˌwoɑt/ *n* [C] *US, informal* : a person who worries too much or who worries about things that are not important

¹worse /ˈwɜs/ *adj, comparative form of* **¹BAD** **1** : lower in quality ▪ *His grades got worse. Her first book was bad, but her second one is* ***even worse.*** **2** : less pleasant, attractive, appealing, effective, useful, etc. ▪ *You have even worse luck than I do.* ▪ *Cheer up.* ***Things could be worse.*** ▪ *He broke the vase but* ***what is worse,*** *he lied to me about it.* ▪ *My car broke down, and* ***to make matters worse,*** *I can't afford to fix it.* [=the situation is even worse because I can't afford to fix it] **3** : more serious or severe ▪ *Her symptoms have gotten/grown worse.* **4 a** : in poorer health than before ▪ *I feel worse today than I felt yesterday.* **b** : less happy or pleased ▪ *After we talked, I felt even worse.* **5** : less appropriate or acceptable ▪ *You couldn't have picked a worse time to ask for a raise.* **6** : less morally right or good ▪ *It may be no worse to cheat than to steal.* **7** : less skillful ▪ *I've gotten worse at golf.* — *from bad to worse* see **¹BAD** — *worse for wear* see **²WEAR**

²worse *adv, comparative form of* **BADLY** **1** : in a worse way ▪ *You drive worse than he does.* **2** — used to say that what is going to be described is worse than what was mentioned before ▪ *I got into an accident and suffered a cut on my arm. (Even) Worse, my car was totaled.* — *could do worse* — used to say that a particular choice, action, etc., is not a bad one ▪ *You could do worse than to vote for her.*

³worse *n* [U] : something that is worse ▪ *Her accusations don't bother me. I've been accused of worse.* ▪ *The patient's condition* ***took a turn for the worse.*** [=became worse] — *for better or (for) worse* see **³BETTER** — *if (the) worse comes to (the) worst* see **³WORST**

wors·en /ˈwɜsn/ *vb* [T/I] : to make (something) worse or to become worse ▪ *Yelling is only going to worsen the problem.* ▪ *The situation has worsened.*

worse off *adj* **1** : having less money and possessions ▪ *He was worse off financially than he was before.* **2** : in a worse position ▪ *If you quit school, you'll be worse off.*

¹wor·ship /ˈwɜʃəp/ *vb* **-shipped** *also US* **-shiped**; **-ship·ping** *also US* **-ship·ing** **1** [T] : to honor or respect (someone or something) as a god ▪ *Many ancient cultures worshipped the sun and moon.* **2** [T/I] : to show respect and love for God or for a god especially by praying, having religious services, etc. ▪ *They worship at*

this temple. ▪ *I worship God in my own way.* **3** [T/I] : to love or honor (someone or something) very much or too much ▪ *He worships* [=idolizes] *his brother.* — **wor·ship·per** *also US* **wor·ship·er** *n* [C]

²worship *n* [U] **1** : the act of showing respect and love for God or for a god especially by praying with other people ▪ *Worship services are held daily.* ▪ *a* ***place/house of worship*** [=a church, synagogue, etc.] **2** : excessive admiration for someone ▪ *the media's worship of celebrities*

wor·ship·ful /ˈwɜʃəpfəl/ *adj* : feeling or showing great admiration and love for someone or something ▪ *worshipful fans*

¹worst /ˈwɜst/ *adj, superlative form of* **¹BAD** **1 a** : worse than all others ▪ *the worst movie I've ever seen* **b** : least skillful, talented, or successful ▪ *the worst singer I've ever heard* **2** : least appropriate, useful, or helpful ▪ *She called at the worst possible moment.* — ***in the worst way*** *US, informal* : very much ▪ *I want a new bike in the worst way.* — *worst of all* — used to refer to the least pleasant or appealing part of something that has many bad parts ▪ *I forgot my backpack, was late for class, and worst of all, I studied the wrong material for the test.*

²worst *adv, superlative form of* **BADLY** : in a way that is worse than all others ▪ *My sister was hurt worst.* ▪ *the worst-dressed celebrity*

³worst *n* **1** *the worst* : the worst person or thing ▪ *That movie was the worst! What's the worst that can happen? They warned us to* ***expect/fear the worst.*** [=assume that something very bad would happen] : the worst group of people or things ▪ *This city's schools are the worst in the nation.* : the worst part of something ▪ *Even in the worst of times, she was hopeful.* **2** [*singular*] : someone's or something's least effective or pleasant condition — used in phrases like *at your worst* and *at its worst* ▪ *This is politics at its worst.* ▪ *He's at his worst when he's drunk.* — *at worst* — used to refer to a result, condition, etc., that is the worst one possible ▪ *At worst, you'll have to pay a fine.* — *bring out the worst in* ◇ If someone or something *brings out the worst in you,* that person or thing causes you to use or show your worst qualities. ▪ *Competition brings out the worst in some people.* — *get the worst of it* : to lose a fight, argument, battle, etc. — *if (the) worst comes to (the) worst* or *if (the) worst comes to (the) worst also if worse comes to (the) worst* or *if worse comes to worse* : if the worst possible thing happens ▪ *If worst comes to worst, you can always ask me for help.*

wor·sted /ˈwʊstəd/ *n* [U] : a type of cloth or yarn made from wool ▪ *a suit made of worsted*

¹worth /ˈwɜθ/ *prep* **1 a** — used to indicate the value of something ▪ *This painting is worth a fortune.* **b** : having money and possessions equal in value to (an amount) ▪ *an actor worth several million dollars* **2** : good, valuable, or important enough for (something) ▪ *This book is* worth reading. ▪ *That meal was* **worth every penny.** ▪ *I promise this will be* **worth your while.** [=will be a good/useful thing for you to do] ▪ *The repairs cost a lot of money, but they were* **worth it.** — **a picture is worth a thousand words** — used to say that it is often easier to show something in a picture than to describe it with words — **for all something or someone is worth** : as much as possible or with as much effort as possible ▪ *I ran for all I was worth.* [=as fast as I could] — **for what it's worth** — used to say that you are not sure how helpful something you are about to say will be ▪ *For what it's worth, I don't think he meant to insult you.*

²**worth** *n* [U] **1** : an amount of something that has a specified value, that lasts for a specified length of time, etc. — + *of* ▪ *40 dollars' worth of gas* ▪ *a week's worth of food* **2** : the amount of money that something is worth : VALUE ▪ *The worth of the stocks has increased.* **3** : usefulness or importance ▪ *He has* **proved his worth** *to the team.* ▪ **your money's worth** see MONEY

worth·less /ˈwəθləs/ *adj* **1 a** : having no financial value ▪ *worthless stocks* **b** : having no use, importance, or effect ▪ *The boots may be nice, but they're worthless if they don't fit you.* **2** : having no good qualities ▪ *a worthless coward* — **worth·less·ness** *n* [U]

worth·while /ˈwəθˌwajəl/ *adj* : worth doing or getting ▪ *a worthwhile investment/cause*

¹**wor·thy** /ˈwəði/ *adj* **wor·thi·er; -est** **1** : good and deserving respect, praise, or attention ▪ *a worthy cause/opponent* **2** : having enough good qualities to be considered important, useful, etc. ▪ *The suggestion is worthy of consideration.* ▪ *The voters will decide if he is worthy to become governor.* — **wor·thi·ness** /ˈwəðinəs/ *n* [U]

²**worthy** *n, pl* **-thies** [C] : an important or respected person — often used in a joking or disapproving way to refer to people who think of themselves as important ▪ *The party was attended by the mayor and a large group of local worthies.*

would /ˈwʊd, wəd, əd/ *vb* [*modal vb*] **1** — used to indicate what someone said or thought about what was going to happen or be done ▪ *She said she would be leaving soon.* [=she said, "I will be leaving soon"] ▪ *They knew (that) I would enjoy the trip.* **2** — used to talk about a possible situation that has not happened or that you are imagining ▪ *You would look good in a tuxedo.* ▪ *If you lived closer, I would see you every day.* **3** — used with *have* to talk about something that did not happen or was not done ▪ *She would have won the race if she hadn't tripped.* **4** — used to say what you think someone should do or to ask for someone's opinion about what to do ▪ *I would take the train if I were you.* ▪ *What would you do?* **5** — used to say that you want to do or have something ▪ *We would like to help.* [=we want to help] ▪ *I* **would rather** *have ice cream than cake.* = (more commonly)

I'd rather have ice cream than cake. ▪ *I* **would sooner** *die than be enslaved.* **6** — used to ask a polite question or to make a polite request, offer, invitation, etc. ▪ *Would you care for some tea?* ▪ *Would it be all right if we left a little early?* ▪ *I would like to see the menu.* **7 a** — used to say that you are willing to do something ▪ *I would be glad to help.* = *I'd be glad to help.* **b** — used in negative statements to say that someone was not willing to do something ▪ *He would not help us.* = (more commonly) *He wouldn't help us.* [=he refused to help us] **8** — used to express a wish ▪ *I wish that he would call.* = *I wish he'd call.* **9** — used to express your opinion ▪ *I would hate to have that job.* **10** — used to talk about something that always or often happened in the past ▪ *When she still lived here, we would eat lunch together every day.* **11** — used with *so (that)* to explain why something was done ▪ *We left early so we would be sure to arrive on time.* **12** — used to say what you think is probably true ▪ *I would hope that he was telling the truth.* **13** — used to say that something is possible or likely ▪ *I think the pool would* [=could] *hold 20,000 gallons of water.* **14** — used to express your displeasure with behavior that you think is typical of someone ▪ *"He said that it was your fault." "He would say that, wouldn't he? What a jerk."* **15** *old-fashioned + literary* — used to say that you wish something were true, had happened, etc. ▪ *I would that he had lived.* = *Would that he had lived.* — **how would I/we know** — used to say that you do not know the answer to a question and are surprised that you were asked it ▪ *"Where did they go?" "How would I know?"*

would-be /ˈwʊdˌbiː/ *adj, always before a noun* — used to describe someone who hopes to be a particular person or type of person ▪ *a would-be poet/writer*

wouldn't /ˈwʊdn̩t/ — used as a contraction of *would not* ▪ *I wouldn't call him if I were you.*

would've /ˈwʊdəv/ — used as a contraction of *would have* ▪ *I would've come earlier if I'd known.*

¹**wound** /ˈwuːnd/ *n* [C] **1** : an injury that is caused when a knife, bullet, etc., cuts or breaks the skin ▪ *a knife/stab/gunshot/bullet wound* **2** : a feeling of sadness, anger, etc., that is caused by something bad that has happened to you ▪ *emotional wounds* — **lick your wounds** see ¹LICK

²**wound** *vb* [T] **1** : to injure (someone or something) by cutting or breaking the skin ▪ *Four people were wounded in the explosion.* **2** : to cause (someone) to feel emotional pain ▪ *I was wounded by her remarks.* ▪ *Losing the match* **wounded his pride/ego.**

³**wound** /ˈwaʊnd/ *past tense and past participle of* ²WIND

wound·ed /ˈwuːndəd/ *adj* **1** : injured by a weapon ▪ *a wounded soldier* **2** : feeling emotional pain ▪ *a wounded nation* ▪ *wounded pride* — **the wounded** : people who have been wounded ▪ *carrying the wounded off the battlefield*

wound up /ˈwaʊndˈʌp/ *adj, not before a noun, informal* : nervous or excited • *Don't get the kids all wound up.*

wove *past tense of* ¹WEAVE

woven *past participle of* ¹WEAVE

¹**wow** /ˈwaʊ/ *interj* — used to show that you are very surprised or pleased • *Wow! This is delicious!*

²**wow** *vb* [T] *informal* : to impress or excite (someone) very much • *Her performance wowed the critics.*

wrack /ˈræk/ *vb* [T] : to cause (someone or something) to suffer pain or damage : RACK • *She is wracked by/with guilt.* [=she feels very guilty]

wran·gle /ˈræŋgəl/ *vb* **wran·gled; wran·gling** **1** [I] : to argue angrily with someone • *They were wrangling over/about money.* **2** [T] *US, informal* : to get (something) by clever methods or by persuading someone • *He managed to wrangle a couple of tickets to the concert.* — **wrangle** *n* [C] • *a bitter wrangle over money*

wran·gler /ˈræŋglɚ/ *n* [C] *US* : a person who takes care of horses on a ranch : COWBOY

¹**wrap** /ˈræp/ *vb* **wrapped; wrap·ping** **1** [T] **a** : to cover (something) by winding or folding a piece of material around it • *wrapping presents* • *Please wrap (up) this box for me.* • *She wrapped the baby in a blanket.* • *The handle was wrapped with tape.* **b** : to wind or fold (something) around something else • *She wrapped a scarf around her neck.* **c** : to put (your arms, legs, etc.) around someone or something • *I wrapped my arms around her.* **2** [I] : to go *around* something • *The line of people went out the door and wrapped around the corner.* **3** [T/I] : to finish filming a movie or television show or one of its scenes • *Let's wrap this scene (up).* • *The movie should wrap soon.* — **wrap (someone) around your (little) finger** *informal* : to have complete control over (someone) • *She has him wrapped around her little finger.* — **wrap up** [*phrasal vb*] **1 wrap (something) up** *or* **wrap up (something)** *or* **wrap up** : to finish or end (something) • *Let's wrap this meeting up.* • *The meeting wrapped up at four o'clock.* **2 wrapped up in** ◇ If you are *wrapped up in* something, you are fully involved or interested in it. • *I was (completely) wrapped up in my work, so I didn't hear you come in.*

²**wrap** *n* **1** [U] : material used for covering or wrapping something • *holiday gift wrap* **2** [C] : a piece of clothing that is wrapped around a person's shoulders, waist, etc. **3** [C] : a thin piece of bread that is rolled around a filling of meat, vegetables, etc. • *a chicken/veggie wrap* **4** [C] : a bandage that you wear around a part of your body to treat or prevent an injury • *a leg/elbow wrap* — **it's a wrap** *or* **that's a wrap** — used to say that the filming of a movie or television show or one of its scenes is finished • *It's a wrap, folks. We can go home now.* — **under wraps** *informal* : known to only a few people • *The name of the movie is being kept under wraps.*

wrap·around /ˈræpəˌraʊnd/ *adj, always before a noun* : going all or most of the way around something • *a wraparound porch*

wrap·per /ˈræpɚ/ *n* [C] : a thin piece of paper, plastic, etc., that covers or surrounds something to protect it • *a candy bar wrapper*

wrapping *n* [C/U] : a thin piece of paper, plastic, fabric, etc., that covers or surrounds something to protect it • *She tore the wrapping off the present.*

wrapping paper *n* [U] : paper that is used to wrap gifts

wrap–up /ˈræpˌʌp/ *n* [C] *US* : ¹SUMMARY • *a wrap-up of the game*

wrath /ˈræθ, *Brit* ˈrɒθ/ *n* [U] *formal + old-fashioned* : extreme anger • *the wrath of the gods* — **wrath·ful** /ˈræθfəl, *Brit* ˈrɒθfəl/ *adj*

wreak /ˈriːk/ *vb* [T] : to cause (something very harmful or damaging) • *The hurricane wreaked destruction/havoc on the island.*

wreath /ˈriːθ/ *n, pl* **wreaths** /ˈriːðz, ˈriːθs/ [C] **1** : an arrangement of leaves or flowers in the shape of a circle that is worn or placed as a sign of honor or victory **2** : an arrangement of leaves, flowers, fruits, etc., in the shape of a circle that is used for decoration • *a Christmas wreath*

wreathe /ˈriːð/ *vb* **wreathed; wreath·ing** [T] *literary* : to surround or cover (something) • *mountaintops wreathed in clouds* • *(figurative) She was wreathed in glory.*

¹**wreck** /ˈrɛk/ *n* [C] **1** : a vehicle, airplane, etc., that has been badly damaged or destroyed • *Firefighters pulled him from the (car) wreck.* **2** *US* : an accident in which a car, airplane, train, etc., is badly damaged or destroyed • *a car/train/plane wreck* **3** *informal* : a person who is very tired, ill, worried, or unhappy • *The stress made her a wreck.* • *I am a* **nervous wreck.** **4** *informal* : something that is not in good condition • *The house is a wreck.*

²**wreck** *vb* [T] **1** : to damage (something) so badly that it cannot be repaired • *I wrecked my car.* **2** : to ruin or destroy (something) • *The affair wrecked his marriage/career.* **3** : to destroy (a ship) by crashing it into something • *The ship was wrecked off the coast of Ireland.*

wreck·age /ˈrɛkɪdʒ/ *n* [U] : the broken parts of a vehicle, building, etc., that has been badly damaged or destroyed • *Rescue workers sifted through the wreckage of the building.*

wreck·er /ˈrɛkɚ/ *n* [C] **1** *US* : TOW TRUCK **2** : someone or something that destroys something • *a home-wrecker* [=someone who has an affair with a married person and causes that person's marriage to fail]

wren /ˈrɛn/ *n* [C] : a small bird with brown feathers and a short tail that points upward

¹**wrench** /ˈrɛntʃ/ *n* **1** [C] *US* : a tool consisting of a handle with one end designed to hold, twist, or turn an object (such as a bolt or nut) — called also *(Brit)* span-

ner 2 [C] : a violent twisting or pulling movement ▪ *a wrench of the wheel* **3** [*singular*] *chiefly Brit* : something unpleasant that happens and that causes you to feel emotional pain ▪ *It was a wrench to say goodbye to them.* — **throw a wrench into the works** *US, informal* : to damage or change (something) in a way that ruins it or prevents it from working properly ▪ *We were ready to buy the car, but the bank threw a wrench into the works by delaying the loan.*

²**wrench** *vb* **1** [*T/I*] : to twist and pull with a sudden violent motion ▪ *I tried to wrench (myself) free from his grip.* ▪ (*figurative*) *I have trouble wrenching myself away from a good book.* ▪ (*figurative*) *an emotionally wrenching experience* [=a very sad/painful experience] **2** [*T*] : to injure (a part of your body) by making a violent twisting motion ▪ *He wrenched his back lifting a heavy box.* **3** [*T*] : to take (something) by using force ▪ *She wrenched the toy from his grasp.*

wrest /ˈrɛst/ *vb* [*T*] **1** : to pull (something) away *from* someone by using violent twisting movements ▪ *She wrested the weapon (away) from her attacker.* **2** : to take (something) *from* someone with much effort ▪ *He tried to wrest control of the company from his uncle.*

wres•tle /ˈrɛsəl/ *vb* **wres•tled; wres•tling** [*T/I*] **1** : to fight by holding and pushing instead of by hitting, kicking, or punching ▪ *She wrestled with her attacker.* ▪ *She wrestled him to the ground.* [=she held on to him and forced him to fall to the ground] **2** : to struggle to move, deal with, or control something ▪ *She wrestled with her luggage.* ▪ *He wrestled a drug habit for many years.* ▪ *wrestling with an issue/problem*

wres•tling /ˈrɛslɪŋ/ *n* [*U*] : a sport in which two people try to throw, force, or pin each other to the ground — **wres•tler** /ˈrɛslɚ/ *n* [*C*] : *a professional wrestler*

wretch /ˈrɛtʃ/ *n* [*C*] **1** : a very unhappy or unlucky person ▪ *The poor wretch lost his job.* **2** : a very bad or unpleasant person ▪ *an ungrateful wretch*

wretch•ed /ˈrɛtʃəd/ *adj* **1** : very unhappy, ill, etc. ▪ *poor, wretched children* ▪ *She looks wretched.* **2** : very bad or unpleasant ▪ *wretched poverty/conditions* **3** : very poor in quality or ability ▪ *a wretched performance* — **wretch•ed•ly** *adv* — **wretch•ed•ness** *n* [*U*]

wrig•gle /ˈrɪɡəl/ *vb* **wrig•gled; wrig•gling** [*I*] **1** : to twist from side to side with small quick movements like a worm ▪ *They wriggled out of their wet clothes.* **2** : to move forward by twisting and turning ▪ *The snake wriggled across the path.* — **wriggle out of** [*phrasal vb*] *informal + often disapproving* : to avoid doing (something that you do not want to do) in some clever or dishonest way ▪ *She tried to wriggle out of the contract.*

wring /ˈrɪŋ/ *vb* **wrung** /ˈrʌŋ/; **wring•ing** /ˈrɪŋɪŋ/ [*T*] **1** : to twist and squeeze (wet cloth, hair, etc.) to remove water ▪ *I wrung the towel (out) and hung it up to dry.* **2** : to get (something) *out of* or *from* someone or something with a lot of

effort ▪ *They tried to wring every last dollar of profit out of the company.* ▪ *I finally managed to wring an apology from her.* **3** : to twist and break (an animal's neck) in order to kill the animal ▪ *wring a chicken's neck* — **wring your hands** : to twist and rub your hands together because you are nervous or upset ▪ *She was wringing her hands and pacing back and forth.*

wring•er /ˈrɪŋɚ/ *n* [*C*] : a machine used for squeezing water out of clothes that have been washed — **through the wringer** *informal* : through a series of very difficult or unpleasant experiences ▪ *Those poor people have really gone/been through the wringer.* = *They've been put through the wringer.*

¹**wrin•kle** /ˈrɪŋkəl/ *n* [*C*] **1** : a small line or fold that appears on your skin as you grow older **2** : a small fold in the surface of clothing, paper, etc. ▪ *I ran my hands over my skirt to smooth out the wrinkles.* ▪ (*figurative*) *We still have to iron out a few wrinkles* [=fix a few small problems] *in the schedule.* **3** *informal* **a** : a surprising or unexpected occurrence in a story or series of events ▪ *Here's the latest wrinkle in the story—we find out that the villain is actually the hero's father!* **b** : a clever technique, trick, or idea ▪ *He has added some new wrinkles to his game.* — **wrin•kly** /ˈrɪŋkli/ *adj* **wrin•kli•er; -est** ▪ *wrinkly* [=*wrinkled*] *skin*

²**wrinkle** *vb* **wrin•kled; wrin•kling** [*T/I*] : to develop wrinkles or to cause (something) to develop wrinkles ▪ *Try not to wrinkle your trousers.* ▪ *Linen clothing wrinkles easily.* ▪ *His brow wrinkled as he thought about the question.*

wrinkled *adj* : having many wrinkles ▪ *wrinkled skin/clothes*

wrist /ˈrɪst/ *n* [*C*] : the part of your body where your hand joins your arm ▪ *I sprained my wrist.* — **a slap on the wrist** *see* ²SLAP

wrist-watch /ˈrɪst₊wɑːtʃ/ *n* [*C*] : a watch that you wear on a strap or band around your wrist

¹**writ** /ˈrɪt/ *n* [*C*] *law* : a document from a court ordering someone to do something or not to do something ▪ *The judge issued a writ of execution.*

²**writ** *old-fashioned past participle of* WRITE — **writ large 1** : shown in a clear way ▪ *His nervousness was writ large on his face.* **2** : on a very large scale ▪ *National politics are just local politics writ large.*

write /ˈraɪt/ *vb* **wrote** /ˈroʊt/; **writ•ten** /ˈrɪtn̩/; **writ•ing** **1** [*T/I*] : to form letters or numbers on a surface with a pen, pencil, etc. ▪ *children learning to read and write* ▪ *Please write your name at the top of each sheet.* ▪ *The note was written in blue ink.* **2** [*T*] **a** : to create (a book, poem, story, etc.) by writing words on paper, on a computer, etc. ▪ *She wrote an article/essay.* **b** : to produce (a written document, agreement, rule, etc.) by writing ▪ *I wrote (her) a check for $200.* ▪ *They wrote (up) a contract.* **c** : to write (a piece of music) ▪ *a performer who writes her own songs* **3** [*T/I*] : to express or state (something) in a book, story, essay, letter, etc. ▪ *He wrote, "I love you."* ▪ *She writes about* *politics.* **4** [*T/I*] : to communicate with someone by sending a letter, e-mail, etc. ▪ *I wish you would write* (*to me*) *more often.* ▪ *I wrote a letter to him.* = *I wrote him a letter.* = (*US*) *I wrote him.* **5** [*I*] : to do the work of writing books, news articles, stories, etc. ▪ *He writes for the local newspaper.* — **nothing to write home about** *informal* : not very good or appealing ▪ *The food at that restaurant is nothing to write home about.* — **write back** [*phrasal vb*] **write back** or **write** (*someone*) **back** : to send someone a letter, e-mail, etc., in response to one that was sent to you ▪ *He wrote back* (*to me*) *as soon as he got my card.* — **write down** [*phrasal vb*] **write** (*something*) **down** or **write down** (*something*) : to write (something) on a piece of paper ▪ *Please write your phone number down for me.* — **write in** [*phrasal vb*] **1** : to send a letter to a newspaper, a company, the government, etc., to express an opinion or to ask a question ▪ *Dozens of people wrote in to the newspaper to complain about the story.* **2 write** (*something or someone*) **in** or **write in** (*something or someone*) **a** : to write (something) on a form ▪ *She wrote in "Latina" under/beside "race or ethnicity."* **b** *US* : to vote for (someone who is not on the official list of candidates) by writing that person's name in a special place on the ballot ▪ *Several hundred voters wrote her in on the ballot.* — **write into** [*phrasal vb*] **write** (*something*) **into** : to add (something new) to (a contract, law, etc.) ▪ *A bonus was written into the contract.* — **write off** [*phrasal vb*] **write** (*something or someone*) **off** or **write off** (*something or someone*) **a** : to say officially that (money that is owed to you) will not be paid or does not need to be paid ▪ *The government has agreed to write off the debt.* **b** : to take away (an amount) from the total amount that is used to calculate taxes ▪ *You might be able to write off* [=*deduct*] *the cost of the computer on your taxes.* **c** : to consider (something or someone) to be lost, hopeless, unimportant, etc. ▪ *Don't write off the team yet.* **2 write off for** (*something*) *chiefly Brit* : to make a request for (something) by sending a letter ▪ *She wrote off for a free sample.* — **write out** [*phrasal vb*] **1 write** (*something*) **out** or **write out** (*something*) **a** : to put (something) in writing on a piece of paper ▪ *I wrote out the directions.* **b** : to write the required information on (a check, receipt, etc.) ▪ *I wrote out a check for $200.* **2 a write** (*someone*) **out of** : to change a document (such as a will) so that (someone) is not included ▪ *She wrote me out of her will.* **b write** (*someone*) **out of** or **write out** (*someone*) : to remove (a character) from a story by having the character die, disappear, etc. ▪ *They wrote her character out of the show.* — **write up** [*phrasal vb*] **write** (*something or someone*) **up** or **write up** (*something or someone*) **1** : to describe (something) in a detailed written account ▪ *A music critic wrote up the concert.* **2** *US* : to produce an official document that reports (some-

one) to an authority to be punished ▪ *The teacher wrote him up for tardiness.* — **write your own ticket** *informal* ✧ If you can *write your own ticket,* you can choose to do whatever you want or to go wherever you want because you have excellent or special skills or abilities. — **wrote the book on** *informal* — used to say that someone is an expert on a particular subject ▪ *She wrote the book on long-distance swimming.*

write-in /ˈraɪtˌɪn/ *n* [*C*] *US* **1** : a candidate in an election whose name is not printed on the ballot and whose name must be written on the ballot by voters ▪ *He ran as a write-in.* ▪ *a write-in candidate* **2** : a vote for someone who is not on an election's official list of candidates ▪ *The election commission decided that write-ins would not be counted.*

writ-er /ˈraɪtə/ *n* [*C*] **1** : someone whose work is to write books, poems, stories, etc. ▪ *my favorite writer* ▪ *a writer of horror stories* **2** : someone who has written something ▪ *The writer of the best essay will win a prize.*

write-up /ˈraɪtˌʌp/ *n* [*C*] : a written description or review of something ▪ *There's a write-up of the restaurant in the paper.*

writhe /ˈraɪð/ *vb* **writhed; writh-ing** [*I*] : to twist your body from side to side ▪ *She was writhing in pain.*

writ-ing /ˈraɪtɪŋ/ *n* **1** [*U*] **a** : the activity or work of writing books, poems, stories, etc. ▪ *He teaches creative writing.* **b** : the way that you use written words to express your ideas or opinions ▪ *The novel's plot is okay, but the writing is horrible.* ▪ *a unique writing style* **2** [*U, plural*] : books, poems, essays, letters, etc. ▪ *the writings of Benjamin Franklin* **3** [*U*] : words, numbers, or symbols that have been written or printed on something ▪ *Japanese/Chinese/Arabic writing* **4** [*U*] **a** : the activity or skill of forming letters and numbers with a pen, pencil, etc. ▪ *Having a broken finger made writing difficult.* **b** : the particular way in which someone writes letters and numbers : HANDWRITING ▪ *Her writing is illegible.* — **in writing** : in the form of a letter or a document ▪ *The agreement needs to be in writing.* — **the writing is on the wall** or **see/read the writing on the wall** see ¹WALL

writing desk *n* [*C*] : a desk with a flat surface for writing on

written *past participle of* WRITE

¹wrong /ˈrɑːŋ/ *adj* **1 a** : not agreeing with the facts or truth ▪ *the wrong answer* ▪ *I dialed the wrong number.* [=an incorrect telephone number] **b** *not before a noun* : speaking, acting, or judging in a way that does not agree with the facts or truth ▪ *I was wrong* [=mistaken] *about the price.* ▪ *You're wrong; the answer is six.* ▪ *It's wrong to assume that she'll help you.* **2** : not suitable or appropriate for a particular purpose, situation, or person ▪ *These shoes are the wrong size.* ▪ *I made the wrong decision.`* **3** *not before a noun* : not in a proper, good, or normal state or condition — used to describe a situation in which there is a problem ▪ *There's something wrong with my car.* [=my car is not working properly] ▪ *You look unhappy. What's wrong?* **4** : not morally or socially correct or acceptable ▪ *Stealing is wrong.* **5** *US* — used to refer to the side of something that is not meant to be on top, in front, or on the outside ▪ *He had his socks on wrong side out.* — **put a foot wrong** see ¹FOOT — **the wrong end of the stick** see ¹STICK — **the wrong side of the tracks** see ¹TRACK — **wrong·ly** *adv* ▪ *She was wrongly accused.* ▪ *Many people, rightly or wrongly, believe that the economy will soon improve.* — **wrong·ness** *n* [U]

²**wrong** *adv* **1** : in a way that does not agree with the facts or truth ▪ *Her name was spelled wrong on the form.* **2** : in a way that is not suitable, proper, etc. ▪ *You're doing it wrong.* — **get (someone or something) wrong** : to fail to understand (someone or something) correctly ▪ *She got the instructions wrong.* ▪ *Don't get me wrong—I like his parents. They're just a little too strict.* — **go wrong 1** : to happen or proceed in a way that causes a bad result ▪ *Something went wrong with the experiment.* **2** : to make a mistake ▪ *I followed the instructions and the computer still doesn't work. Where did I go wrong?*

³**wrong** *n* **1** [U] : behavior that is not morally good or correct ▪ *People who do wrong* [=do bad things] *should be punished.* ▪ *He's old enough to know the difference between right and wrong.* = *He's old enough to know right from wrong.* **2** [C] : a harmful, unfair, or illegal act ▪ *She is seeking compensation for the wrongs that she suffered.* — **do (someone) wrong** *informal + old-fashioned* : to treat (someone) badly or unfairly ▪ *Her ex-boyfriend did her wrong.* — **in the wrong** : in the position or situation of being wrong

Each person thinks that the other was in the wrong. — **two wrongs don't make a right** — used to say that if someone hurts you, you should not hurt that person in return

⁴**wrong** *vb* [T] : to treat (someone) badly or unfairly ▪ *We should forgive those who have wronged us.*

wrong·do·er /ˈrɑːŋˌduːwɚ/ *n* [C] : a person who does something that is morally or legally wrong — **wrong·do·ing** /ˈrɑːŋˌduːwɪŋ/ *n* [C/U] ▪ *He denied any wrongdoing.*

wrong·ful /ˈrɑːnfəl/ *adj* : not legal, fair, or moral ▪ *wrongful conduct* ▪ (*law*) *a wrongful death* [=a death caused by someone's mistake or improper act] — **wrong·ful·ly** *adv*

wrong-head·ed /ˈrɑːŋˈhɛdəd/ *adj* : having or showing opinions or ideas that are wrong ▪ *wrongheaded people/policies*

wrote *past tense of* WRITE

wrought /ˈrɑːt/ *adj, formal + old-fashioned* : carefully formed or worked into shape ▪ *carefully wrought essays*

wrought iron *n* [U] : a kind of iron that is often used to make decorative fences, furniture, etc.

wrung *past tense and past participle of* WRING

wry /ˈraɪ/ *adj* **1** : humorous in a clever and often ironic way ▪ *wry humor/remarks* **2** : showing both amusement and a feeling of being tired, annoyed, etc. ▪ *a wry smile/grin* — **wry·ly** *adv*

wuss /ˈwʊs/ *also* **wus·sy** /ˈwʊsi/ *n, pl* **wuss·es** *also* **wus·sies** [C] *slang* : a weak or cowardly person ▪ *Don't be such a wuss.*

WV *or* **W VA** *abbr* West Virginia

WW *abbr* World War

www *abbr* World Wide Web

WY *or* **Wyo.** *abbr* Wyoming

¹**x** *or* **X** /ˈɛks/ *n, pl* **x's** *or* **xs** *or* **X's** *or* **Xs** /ˈɛksəz/ **1** [C/U] : the 24th letter of the English alphabet ▪ *a word that starts with (an) x* **2** [C] : the Roman numeral that means ten ▪ *XX* [=20] **3** [U] *mathematics* **a** — used to represent an unknown quantity ▪ *What is the value of x in the equation x – 4 = 3?* **b** — used as a symbol for multiplication ▪ *2 × 3 = 6* [=2 times 3 equals 6; 2 multiplied by 3 is 6] **4** [U] — used as a symbol between the numbers of a measurement ▪ *The room is 10' x 12'.* [=10 feet by 12 feet; two of the room's walls are 10 feet long and two walls are 12 feet long]

²**x** *vb* **x–es** *also* **x's** *or* **xes** /ˈɛksəz/; **x–ed** *also* **x'd** *or* **xed** /ˈɛkst/; **x–ing** *or* **x'ing** /ˈɛksɪŋ/ — **x out** [*phrasal vb*] **x (something) out** *or* **x out (something)** : to draw an x or a series of x's through (something) to show that it is wrong or not

wanted ▪ *x out a mistake*

X /ˈɛks/ — used in the past as a special mark to indicate that no one under the age of 17 in the U.S. or 18 in the U.K. was allowed to see a particular movie in a movie theater ▪ *The movie was rated X.* = *The movie was X-rated.* ▪ (*figurative*) *X-rated language* [=obscene or offensive language]

X chromosome *n* [C] : a type of chromosome that is found in pairs in the cells of female mammals and is found with the Y chromosome in the cells of male mammals

xe·no·pho·bia /ˌzɛnəˈfoʊbijə, ˌziːnəˈfoʊbijə/ *n* [U] : fear or hatred of strangers or foreigners — **xe·no·phobe** /ˈzɛnəˌfoʊb, ˈziːnəˌfoʊb/ *n* [C] — **xe·no·pho·bic** /ˌzɛnəˈfoʊbɪk, ˌziːnəˈfoʊbɪk/ *adj*

Xe·rox /ˈzirəˌɑːks/ *trademark* — used for

a machine that makes paper copies of printed pages, pictures, etc.

xe·rox /'zɪəˌɑːks/ *vb* [T/I] : to copy (something, such as a document) by using a special machine (called a copier) ▪ *I'll xerox the form for you.*

xl *or* **XL** *abbr* extra large ▪ *The shirt comes in S, M, L, and XL.*

Xmas /'krɪsməs, 'ɛksməs/ *n* [C/U] *informal* : CHRISTMAS — used especially on signs and in advertisements

X-ray /'ɛksˌreɪ/ *n* **1** [*plural*] *technical* : powerful invisible rays that can pass through various objects and that make it possible to see inside things (such as the human body) **2** *also* **x-ray** [C] : an image that is created by using X-rays and that is usually used for medical purposes **3** *also* **x-ray** [C] : a medical examination that involves using X-rays ▪ *I went to the hospital for an X-ray on my foot.* — **x-ray** *or* **X-ray** /'ɛksˌreɪ/ *vb* [T] ▪ *I had my foot x-rayed.*

xy·lo·phone /'zaɪləˌfoʊn/ *n* [C] : a musical instrument that has a set of wooden bars of different lengths that are hit with hammers

Y

y *or* **Y** /'waɪ/ *n, pl* **y's** *or* **ys** *or* **Y's** *or* **Ys** /'waɪz/ **1** [C/U] : the 25th letter of the English alphabet ▪ *"Yes" starts with (a) y.* **2** *the* **Y** *US, informal* : the YMCA or the YWCA ▪ *I'm going to the Y.*

-y *also* **-ey** /i/ *adj suffix* **1 a** : full or having a lot of something ▪ *dirty hands* **b** : having the qualities of something ▪ *waxy* **2 a** : tending to do something ▪ *chatty* ▪ wanting or needing to do something ▪ *sleepy* **b** : causing or performing a specified action ▪ *curly hair* [=hair that curls]

yacht /'jɑːt/ *n* [C] : a large boat that is used for racing or pleasure

yacht·ing /'jɑːtɪŋ/ *n* [U] : the activity or sport of sailing in a yacht ▪ *We went **yachting**.*

¹ya·hoo /jɑ'huː/ *interj* — used to express excitement or joy ▪ *Yahoo! We won!*

²ya·hoo /'jeɪˌhuː, 'jɑːˌhuː/ *n, pl* **-hoos** [C] *informal* : a person who is very rude, loud, or stupid ▪ *a bunch of rowdy yahoos*

¹yak /'jæk/ *n, pl* **yaks** *also* **yak** [C] : a large animal that has long hair and curved horns

²yak *vb* **yakked; yak·king** [I] *informal* : to talk in a loud way often for a long time ▪ *He was yakking (away) on his cell phone.*

y'all /'jɑːl/ *US, informal* — used as a contraction of *you all* ▪ *Where are y'all from?* ❖ *Y'all* is used mainly in the southern U.S. to address two or more people.

yam /'jæm/ *n* [C] **1** : a long, thick root of a tropical plant that is eaten as a vegetable **2** *US* : SWEET POTATO

yam·mer /'jæmɚ/ *vb* [I] *informal* : to talk in an annoying way usually for a long time ▪ *yammering (on) about work*

yang /'jɑːŋ, 'jæŋ/ *n* [U] in Chinese philosophy : the male principle of the universe that is considered light and active — *the **yin and yang*** see YIN

yank /'jæŋk/ *vb* **1** [T/I] : to suddenly pull (something) in a quick, forceful way ▪ *She yanked (on) the dog's leash.* **2** [T] : to quickly or suddenly remove (something or someone) ▪ *The show was yanked off the air.* [=was suddenly canceled] — **yank someone's chain** see ¹CHAIN —

yank *n* [C] ▪ *Give the rope a yank.* [=yank the rope]

Yank /'jæŋk/ *n* [C] *informal* : a person from the U.S. : YANKEE

Yan·kee /'jæŋki/ *n* [C] **1** : a person born or living in the U.S. — often used to show disapproval or as an insult ▪ *The signs said "Yankee Go Home."* **2** *US* : a person born or living in the northern U.S. ▪ *a southern girl who married a Yankee* **3** : a soldier who fought on the side of the northern states during the American Civil War

¹yap /'jæp/ *vb* **yapped; yap·ping** [I] **1** *of a dog* : to bark in high, quick sounds **2** *informal* : to talk in a loud and annoying way ▪ *She's yapping on the phone again.*

²yap *n* [C] **1** : a dog's high, quick bark **2** *US slang* : MOUTH ▪ *Shut your yap.*

yard /'jɑːrd/ *n* [C] **1** *US* : an outdoor area that is next to a house and is usually covered by grass ▪ *children playing in the yard* [=(Brit) garden] ▪ *the back/front yard* **2** : the land around a building ▪ *the prison yard* **3** : an area with buildings and equipment that is used for a particular activity ▪ *a rail yard* [=a place where railroad cars are kept] **4** : a unit of measurement equal to 3 feet (0.9144 meters) or 36 inches ▪ *10 yards of rope* ▪ *The football player ran for 35 yards.* ▪ *40 square yards of carpeting* — abbr. **yd.** — *the whole nine yards chiefly US, informal* : EVERYTHING ▪ *For Thanksgiving dinner we had turkey, potatoes—the whole nine yards* [=all the foods that are traditionally served]

yard·age /'jɑːrdɪdʒ/ *n* [U] **1** : an amount of something measured in yards ▪ *fabric yardage* **2** *American football* : the number of yards a team moves the ball down the field ▪ *We lost yardage on that play.*

yard line *n* [C] *American football* : any one of the lines on a football field that are one yard apart and that show the distance to the nearest goal line ▪ *He was tackled on the 20-yard line.*

yard sale *n* [C] *US* : GARAGE SALE

yard·stick /'jɑːrdˌstɪk/ *n* [C] **1** : a tool that is one yard long and is used to measure things **2** : a rule or idea about what is desirable that is used to judge or measure something • *The test scores aren't an adequate yardstick for judging a student's ability.*

yar·mul·ke /ˈjɑːməkə, ˈjɑːməlkə/ *n* [C] : a small round cap that is worn by some Jewish men and boys

yarn /ˈjɑɚn/ *n* **1** [C/U] : a long, thin piece of cotton, wool, etc., that is thicker than thread and that is used for knitting and weaving **2** [C] : a very surprising or unusual story • *a storyteller spinning yarns about his adventures*

yawn /ˈjɑːn/ *vb* [I] **1** : to open your mouth wide while taking in breath usually because you are tired or bored • *Students were yawning in class.* **2** *of an opening, hole, etc.* : to be deep, large, etc. • *A chasm yawned below us.* — **yawn** *n* [C] • *trying to stifle a yawn* [=trying not to yawn]

yawn·er /ˈjɑːnɚ/ *n* [C] *US, informal* : something that is very boring • *The show was a real yawner.*

yawn·ing /ˈjɑːnɪŋ/ *adj* : very large or wide open • *a yawning hole/gap/deficit*

yay /ˈjeɪ/ *interj* — used to express joy, approval, or excitement • *Yay! We won!*

Y chromosome *n* [C] *biology* : a chromosome that is found with the X chromosome in the cells of male mammals

yd. *abbr* yard

¹ye /ˈjiː/ *pron, old-fashioned* : YOU • *"... Seek and ye shall find ..."* —Luke 11:9 KJV

²ye /ˈjiː/ *definite article, old-fashioned* : THE — used especially in the names of stores, businesses, etc. • *Ye Old Tavern*

yea /ˈjeɪ/ *n* [C] *formal* : a yes vote • *We counted seven yeas and two nays.*

yeah /ˈjɛə/ *adv, informal* **1** : ¹YES • *"Are you sure?"* **"Yeah, I'm sure."** • *Yeah, I agree.* **2** — used in speech to show that you are surprised by or disagree with what someone has said • *"I'm from Maine."* **"Oh yeah?** *I didn't know that."* • *"You're a bad golfer."* **"Oh yeah?** *Let's see you do better."* **3** — used in speech to express disbelief • *"I've never lied."* **"Yeah, right/sure."** [=I do not believe you]

year /ˈjiɚ/ *n* [C] **1** : a unit of time that is equal to 12 months or 365 or sometimes 366 days • *He quit a year ago.* • *The job pays $45,000 a/per year.* • *We haven't won in years.* • *She has changed over the years.* [=during several/many years] • *The park is open all year round.* [=the entire year] **2** : the regular period of 12 months that begins in January • *She was born in the year 1967.* • *It'll be done by the end of the year.* • *last year* [=the year before this one] • *next year* [=the year after this one] • *the movie of the year* [=the best movie in a specific year] **3** — used to refer to the age of a person • *She's 14 years old.* • *a six-year-old boy* **4** : a period of time when a particular event, process, etc., happens or is done • *The school year runs* [=the school operates] *from September to June.* • *The fiscal year begins in October and ends in September.* • *her sophomore year of college* — **put years on** : to cause (someone) to look or feel older • *That job has put years on him.* —

take years off : to cause someone to look or feel younger • *The diet has taken years off (her appearance).*

year·book /ˈjiɚˌbʊk/ *n* [C] **1** : a book about a particular topic that is published each year • *an auto industry yearbook* **2** *US* : a book that is published by a school each year and that shows the activities at the school during that year

year–end /ˈjiɚˈɛnd/ *adj, always before a noun* : made or done at the end of the year • *a year-end sale/report*

year·long /ˈjiɚˈlɑːŋ/ *adj, always before a noun* : lasting one year • *a yearlong study*

year·ly /ˈjiɚli/ *adj* **1** : happening, done, or made once each year • *my yearly checkup* **2** : of or relating to one year • *your yearly income* [=the income you receive each year] — **yearly** *adv* • *The report is published yearly.* [=once each year]

yearn /ˈjɚn/ *vb* [I] : to feel a strong desire for something or *to do* something • *prisoners yearning for freedom = prisoners yearning to be free* — **yearn·ing** /ˈjɚnɪŋ/ *n* [C] • *a yearning* [=a strong desire] *to travel*

year–round /ˈjiɚˈraʊnd/ *adj, always before a noun* : active, present, or done throughout the year • *the island's year-round residents* — **year–round** *adv* • *The park is open year-round.* [=all year]

yeast /ˈjiːst/ *n* [U] : a type of fungus that is used in making alcoholic drinks and in baking to help make dough rise — **yeasty** /ˈjiːsti/ *adj* **yeast·i·er; -est** • *yeasty bread*

yeast infection *n* [C] *US, medical* : a disease that affects the vagina and that is caused by a fungus

¹yell /ˈjɛl/ *vb* **1** [T/I] : to say (something) very loudly especially because you are angry, surprised, or are trying to get someone's attention • *Someone yelled (out) my name.* • *"Look out!" she yelled.* • *Stop yelling at me!* **2** [I] : to make a sudden, loud cry • *She yelled (out) in pain.* — **yell·er** *n* [C]

²yell *n* [C] : a sudden, loud cry • *a yell of joy/triumph* • *(informal)* **Give me a yell** [=call me; let me know] *if you need anything.*

¹yel·low /ˈjɛloʊ/ *adj* **1** : having the color of the sun or of ripe lemons • *a yellow car* • *The door was yellow.* **2** *informal* : COWARDLY • *He was too yellow to fight.* — **yel·low·ish** /ˈjɛloʊɪʃ/ *adj*

²yellow *n* [C/U] : the color of the sun or of ripe lemons • *(a) pale/bright yellow*

³yellow *vb* [T/I] : to become yellow or to cause (something) to become yellow • *The paper had yellowed with age.*

yellow fever *n* [U] *medical* : a serious disease that causes fever and that is passed from one person to another by the bite of mosquitoes

yellow jacket *n* [C] *US* : a flying insect that has yellow marks on its body and that can sting you

yellow pages *n* — **the yellow pages** or **the Yellow Pages** : a phone book or part of a phone book that is printed on yellow paper and that lists the names, addresses, and phone numbers of businesses, organizations, etc., according to what they sell or provide ✧ In British English, *Yellow Pages* is a trademark.

yelp /ˈjɛlp/ *vb* [*I*] : to make a quick, high cry or bark ▪ *The dog yelped in pain.* — **yelp** *n* [*C*] ▪ *She gave/made a yelp when I pinched her.*

yen /ˈjɛn/ *n, pl* **yen** **1** [*C*] : the basic unit of money of Japan ▪ *It costs 300 yen.* **2** [*C*] : a coin or bill representing one yen ▪ *a handful of yen* **3** [*singular*] : a strong desire *for* something or *to do* something ▪ *a yen for spicy food* ▪ *a yen to travel*

yep /ˈjɛp/ *adv, informal* : ¹YES ▪ *Yep, that's right.*

¹yes /ˈjɛs/ *adv* **1** — used to give a positive answer or reply to a question, request, or offer ▪ *"Are you ready?" "Yes." ▪ "I want this room cleaned up. Do you understand?" "Yes, sir/ma'am." ▪ "Do you want some coffee?" "Yes, please/thanks."* [=I would like some coffee] ▪ *I asked her out and she said yes.* **2** — used to express agreement with an earlier statement or to say that something is true ▪ *Yes, I see your point. ▪ "The concert was good." "Yes, but it was too crowded."* **3** — used to introduce a statement that corrects or disagrees with an earlier negative statement ▪ *"He wasn't there." "Yes, he was." ▪ "You can't do that!" "Oh, yes I can."* **4** — used to emphasize a statement or to make it more precise ▪ *It was amusing, yes, but also very moving.* **5** *informal* — used to express excitement, enthusiasm, or relief ▪ *"We won!" "Yes!"* **6** — used to indicate uncertainty or polite interest ▪ *Yes? Can I help you? ▪ "Mr. Jones?" "Yes?" "You have a phone call."* **7** — used to show you have remembered something ▪ *Where was I? Oh, yes. I was telling you about the dance.*

²yes *n, pl* **yes·es** or **yes·ses** [*C*] : a positive reply : an answer of yes ▪ *She answered all the questions with yeses and nos.*

yes–man /ˈjɛsˌmæn/ *n, pl* **-men** /-ˌmɛn/ [*C*] *disapproving* : a person (especially a man) who agrees with everything that someone says in order to gain that person's approval ▪ *corporate yes-men*

¹yes·ter·day /ˈjɛstɚˌdeɪ/ *n* **1** [*U*] : the day before today ▪ *Yesterday's game was canceled. ▪ Yesterday was our anniversary. ▪ I saw her the day before yesterday.* [=two days ago] **2** [*C*] : a time in the past ▪ *the cars of yesterday*

²yesterday *adv* : on, during, or for the day before today ▪ *It rained yesterday. ▪ I called early/late yesterday morning. ▪ It's been years since we met, but it seems like only yesterday.* [=it seems as if we just met] — **wasn't born yesterday** see BORN

yes·ter·year /ˈjɛstɚˌjiɚ/ *n* — **of yesteryear** : from a long time ago ▪ *radio shows of yesteryear*

¹yet /ˈjɛt/ *adv* **1 a** : until now : so far ▪ *We have not won a game yet.* = *We have yet to win a game. ▪ It's his best book yet.* **b** : at this time : so soon as now ▪ *Are we there yet? ▪ It's not time to eat yet. ▪ "Are you ready?" "No, not yet." ▪ Has he left yet?* = (*US, informal*) *Did he leave yet?* **2 a** : in addition — used for emphasis ▪ *They made up yet another excuse.* **b** : to a

greater extent or degree ▪ *The situation has become yet more complicated.* **3** : at a later time ▪ *It's still early. He may yet join us.* — **as (of) yet** : until now : so far ▪ *As yet he has not heard the result.* — **just yet** see ²JUST — **the best is yet to come/be** see ³BEST — **yet again** : for another time : AGAIN ▪ *I was late yet again.*

²yet *conj* : ¹BUT ▪ *simple yet elegant clothing* ▪ *She played well, yet she didn't win.* [=although she played well, she didn't win] ▪ *He was smiling, and yet I knew he was unhappy.*

yew /ˈjuː/ *n* [*C*] : an evergreen tree or bush with stiff needles and small red berries

Yid·dish /ˈjɪdɪʃ/ *n* [*U*] : a language based on German that was originally spoken by Jews of central and eastern Europe — **Yiddish** *adj* ▪ *Yiddish expressions*

¹yield /ˈjiːld/ *vb* **1** [*T*] **a** : to produce or provide (a plant, crop, etc.) ▪ *an apple tree that yields large fruit* **b** : to produce (something) as a result of time, effort, or work ▪ *New methods have yielded (up) some promising results.* **c** : to produce (a profit, an amount of money, etc.) ▪ *The tax is expected to yield millions.* **2** [*I*] : to agree to do or accept something that you have been resisting ▪ *The company yielded to the protesters' demands.* **3** *formal* **a** [*T/I*] : to give (someone) the chance to speak at a public meeting ▪ *I yield (the floor) to the Senator from Maine.* **b** [*I*] : to stop trying to fight someone or something ▪ *The enemy refused to yield.* [=give up] **4** [*I*] : to bend, stretch, or break because of physical force or pressure ▪ *Ripe fruit should yield slightly to pressure.* [=ripe fruit should be just a little bit soft] ▪ *The heavy weight caused the rope to yield.* **5** [*T/I*] *US* : to allow another car or person to go ahead of you or in front of you ▪ *The driver failed to yield (the right of way).*

²yield *n* [*C*] **1** : the amount of something that is produced by a plant, farm, etc. ▪ *the average yield per tree* **2** : the profit made from an investment ▪ *stocks with high-percentage yields*

yield·ing /ˈjiːldɪŋ/ *adj* **1** : tending to do or willing to do what other people want ▪ *a gentle, yielding temperament* **2** : bending or stretching easily ▪ *a soft and yielding material*

yikes /ˈjaɪks/ *interj, informal* — used to express a feeling of fear or surprise ▪ *Yikes! It's midnight already?*

yin /ˈjɪn/ *n* [*U*] *in Chinese philosophy* : the female principle of the universe that is considered dark and passive — **the yin and yang** *chiefly US* : the two opposite sides or parts of something ▪ *learning about the yin and yang of politics*

yip /ˈjɪp/ *vb* **yipped**; **yip·ping** [*I*] *US, of a dog* : to bark in high, quick sounds

yip·pee /ˈjɪpi/ *interj, informal* — used to express delight or joy ▪ *Yippee! We're on vacation!*

YMCA /ˌwaɪˌɛmˌsiːˈeɪ/ *n* — **the YMCA** : an international organization that provides social programs, recreation, etc., for the people in a community — called also (*US, informal*) **the Y** ✧ **YMCA** is an abbreviation of "Young Men's Christian Association."

yo /ˈjou/ *interj, US, informal* — used to attract someone's attention, as a greeting, etc. ▪ *Yo! What's up?*

yob /ˈjɑːb/ *n [C] Brit, informal* : a teenage boy or young man who does noisy and sometimes violent things as part of a group or gang

yo·del /ˈjoudl/ *vb* **-dels;** *US* **-deled** *or Brit* **-delled;** *US* **-del·ing** *or Brit* **-del·ling** [*T/I*] : to sing loudly while changing back and forth between a natural pitch and a higher pitch — **yodel** *n [C]* ▪ *a loud yodel* — **yo·del·er** (*US*) *or Brit* **yo·del·ler** /ˈjoudlə/ *n [C]*

yo·ga /ˈjougə/ *n [U]* **1** : a system of exercises for mental and physical health **2** *Yoga* : a Hindu philosophy that teaches a person to experience inner peace by controlling the body and mind

yo·gurt *also Brit* **yo·ghurt** /ˈjougət/ *n [C/U]* : a food that is made when bacteria is added to milk ▪ *blueberry/frozen yogurt*

yoke /ˈjouk/ *n* **1** [*C*] : a bar or frame that is attached to the heads or necks of two work animals (such as oxen) so that they can pull a plow or heavy load **2** [*singular*] *formal + literary* : something that causes people to be treated cruelly and unfairly especially by taking away their freedom ▪ *the yoke of tyranny* — **yoke** *vb* **yoked; yok·ing** [*T*] ▪ *two oxen yoked together* ▪ (*figurative*) *He was yoked to his job.*

yo·kel /ˈjoukəl/ *n [C] informal* — used as an insulting word for a person who lives in a small town or in the country and is regarded as stupid

yolk /ˈjouk/ *n [C/U]* : the yellow part in the center of an egg

Yom Kip·pur /joumkɪˈpuə/ *n [U]* : a Jewish holiday in September or October during which Jews do not eat or drink anything and pray to ask for forgiveness for mistakes made during the year

yon·der /ˈjɑːndə/ *adv, old-fashioned + literary* : at or in that place ▪ *the trees over yonder* — **yonder** *adj* ▪ *from yonder tower* [=from the tower over there]

yore /ˈjoə/ *n* — **of yore** *literary* : of the past ▪ *in days of yore*

York·shire pudding /ˈjoəkʃə-/ *n [C/U]* : a baked British food that is made from eggs, flour, and milk and that is usually served with meat

you /ˈjuː, jə/ *pron* **1** — used to refer to the person or group of people that is being addressed as the subject of a verb or as the object of a verb or preposition ▪ *You are right.* ▪ *I love you.* ▪ *What did she tell you?* ▪ *What do you mean?* **2** — used to refer to any person or to people in general ▪ *The work is hard, but you get used to it.* ▪ *How do you change a tire?* [=what is the proper way to change a tire?] **3** *informal* — used to address someone directly ▪ *You in the red shirt! Come here!* ▪ *You fool!* ▪ *Calm down, you two.* — **you and yours** : you and your family or the people you care about ▪ *Best wishes to you and yours for a happy holiday.*

you–all /juˈɑːl, ˈjɑːl/ *pron, US, informal* — used mainly in the southern U.S. to address two or more people ▪ *How are you-all* [=y'all] *doing?*

you'd /ˈjuːd, jəd/ — used as a contraction of *you had* or *you would* ▪ *If you'd* [=you had] *tried harder, we might have won.* ▪ *You'd* [=you would] *like this movie.*

you–know–who *n [U] informal* — used in speech to refer to someone who is not named but is known to both the hearer and speaker ▪ *We're planning a party for you-know-who.*

you'll /ˈjuːl, jəl/ — used as a contraction of *you will* ▪ *I hope you'll come to the party.*

¹**young** /ˈjʌŋ/ *adj* **youn·ger** /ˈjʌŋgə/ **-gest** /-gəst/ **1** : in an early stage of life, growth, or development : not yet old ▪ *young children* ▪ *a young tomato plant* ▪ *He's a nice young man.* ▪ *You look young for your age.* ▪ *She died young.* ▪ *my younger brother* ▪ *He surfed when he was young.* = *He surfed in his younger days.* ▪ *They're still young at heart.* [=they think and act like young people] ▪ (*informal, humorous*) *If we want to travel, we should do it soon. We're not getting any younger, you know.* [=we are getting older and may not have much more time to do the things we want to do] **2** : recently produced, started, etc. ▪ *a young* [=new] *company* ▪ *young wine/cheese* ▪ *The season is young.* — **the younger** — used in comparing the ages of two people who are members of the same family ▪ *He's the younger of her two sons.* — **young·ish** /ˈjʌŋɪʃ/ *adj* ▪ *a youngish* [=fairly young] *man*

²**young** *n* **1** **the young** : young people ▪ *music that appeals to the young* **2** [*plural*] : young animals, birds, etc. ▪ *a bird feeding her young* — **young and old** : young and old people ▪ *a story for young and old* [=a story that will appeal to people of all ages]

young·ster /ˈjʌŋstə/ *n [C]* : a young person ▪ *a shy youngster*

your /ˈjoə, jə/ *adj, always before a noun, possessive form of* YOU **1** : relating to or belonging to you ▪ *Your garden is beautiful.* ▪ *Wash your hands.* ▪ *Finish your homework.* **2** — used to refer to any person or to people in general ▪ *She's not your* [=a] *typical teenager.* ▪ *Exercise is good for your* [=one's] *health.* **3** — used in the titles of royalty, judges, etc. ▪ *Your Majesty/Honor*

you're /ˈjoə, jə/ — used as a contraction of *you are* ▪ *You're going too fast.*

yours /ˈjoəz/ *pron* **1** : that which belongs to you : your one : your ones ▪ *This book is yours.* [=this is your book] ▪ *Yours is the book on the left.* [=your book is the one on the left] ▪ *The choice is yours.* ▪ *Is he a friend of yours?* [=is he your friend?] **2** — used at the end of an informal letter ▪ *Yours, David* — **you and yours** see YOU — **yours ever** *or* **ever yours** see EVER — **yours sincerely** *or* **sincerely yours** see SINCERELY — **yours truly** see TRULY

your·self /joəˈsɛlf/ *pron* **1** — used as the object of a verb or preposition when the person being addressed has already been mentioned or is the object of a command ▪ *Be careful or you might hurt yourself.* ▪ *You're making a fool of yourself.* ▪ *(You can) Judge for yourself.* ▪ *Behave yourself.* — often used for emphasis ▪ *You told them yourself, remember?* **2** : your normal or healthy self ▪ *You're not yourself today. Is something wrong?* — **be yourself** : to act or behave as you normally do ▪ *Just be yourself.* — **by yourself** **1** : without any help ▪ *You fixed the car (all) by yourself?* **2** : with nobody else ▪ *Do you like living by yourself?*

your·selves /jəˈsɛlvz/ *pron* **1** — used as the object of a verb or preposition to refer to a group of people who are being addressed with a command or after that group has already been mentioned ▪ *Behave yourselves.* ▪ *(You can) Judge for yourselves.* ▪ *You should be proud of yourselves.* — often used for emphasis ▪ *You should have done it yourselves.* **2** : your normal or healthy selves ▪ *You'll feel more like yourselves after a rest.* — **by yourselves** **1** : without any help ▪ *I can't believe you did it by yourselves!* **2** : with nobody else ▪ *You boys aren't old enough to go to the mall by yourselves.*

youth /ˈjuːθ/ *n, pl* **youths** /ˈjuːðz/ **1** [*U, singular*] : the time of life when someone is young ▪ *She had a troubled youth.* ▪ *He spent his youth in Ohio.* ▪ *youth groups/clubs* **2** [*U*] : the time when something is new and not yet established ▪ *an industry still in its youth* **3** [*C*] : a teenage boy or young man ▪ *Four youths started the fire.* **4 the youth** : young people ▪ *the youth of today*

youth·ful /ˈjuːθfəl/ *adj* **1** : having or showing the freshness or energy of someone who is young ▪ *youthful good looks* ▪ *a youthful 50-year-old* **2** : having or showing the innocence, hope, etc., of someone who is young ▪ *youthful optimism/inexperience* — **youth·ful·ness** [*U*]

youth hostel *n* [*C*] : HOSTEL

you've /ˈjuːv, jəv/ — used as a contraction of *you have* ▪ *I think you've solved the problem.*

yowl /ˈjawəl/ *vb* [*I*] : to make a loud, long cry of grief, pain, or distress ▪ *He was yowling in pain.* — **yowl** *n* [*C*]

¹**yo–yo** /ˈjoʊˌjoʊ/ *n, pl* **yo–yos** [*C*] : a round toy that has two flat sides with a string attached to its center, that is held in your hand, and that is made to go up and down by unwinding and rewinding the string with a movement of your wrist

²**yo–yo** *vb* **yo–yos; yo–yoed; yo–yo·ing** [*I*] : to move repeatedly and quickly up and down or from a higher level to a lower level ▪ *Her weight has yo-yoed in recent years.*

yr. *abbr* **1** year **2** your

YT *abbr* Yukon Territory

yu·an /ˈjuːˌwɑːn/ *n, pl* **yuan** [*C*] : the basic unit of money in China; *also* : a coin or bill worth one yuan

yuck /ˈjʌk/ *interj, informal* — used to express disgust ▪ *Yuck, I hate meat loaf.*

yucky *also US* **yuk·ky** /ˈjʌki/ *adj* **yuck·i·er** *also* **yuk·ki·er; -est** *informal* : unpleasant and disgusting ▪ *yucky food*

Yule /ˈjuːl/ *n* [*C/U*] *old-fashioned* : CHRISTMAS ▪ *the Yule season*

Yule·tide /ˈjuːlˌtaɪd/ *n* [*C/U*] *literary* : the Christmas season ▪ *Yuletide cheer*

yum·my /ˈjʌmi/ *adj* **yum·mi·er; -est** *informal* : DELICIOUS 1 ▪ *a yummy dessert*

yup /ˈjʌp/ *adv, informal* : ¹YES ▪ *"It's cold out, isn't it?" "Yup, it sure is."*

yup·pie /ˈjʌpi/ *n, pl* **-pies** [*C*] *often disapproving* : a young college-educated adult who has a job that pays a lot of money ▪ *a store for yuppies*

YWCA /ˌwaɪˌdʌbəljuːˌsiːˈeɪ/ *n* — **the YWCA** : an international organization that provides social programs, recreation, etc., for the people and especially the women in a community — called also (*US, informal*) the **Y** ◊ *YWCA* is an abbreviation of "Young Women's Christian Association."

Z

z *or* **Z** /ˈziː, *Brit* ˈzɛd/ *n, pl* **z's** *or* **zs** *or* **Z's** *or* **Zs** /ˈziːz, *Brit* ˈzɛdz/ [*C/U*] : the 26th letter of the English alphabet ▪ *a word that begins with (a) z*

za·ny /ˈzeɪni/ *adj* **za·ni·er; -est** *informal* : very strange and silly ▪ *zany comedians/humor* — **za·ni·ness** /ˈzeɪninəs/ *n* [*U*]

zap /ˈzæp/ *vb* **zapped; zap·ping** *informal* **1** [*T*] **a** : to attack, destroy, or kill (someone or something) quickly ▪ *The flowers were zapped by the cold weather.* ▪ *(figurative) He was zapped* [=*hit*] *with a fine.* **b** : to hit (someone or something) with electricity ▪ *Lightning zapped the tree.* **2** [*T*] *informal* : to heat or cook (something) in a microwave oven ▪ *She zapped the muffin in the microwave to*

heat it. **3** [*T/I*] : to change what you are watching on television by using an electronic device (called a remote control) ▪ *We tape the show so we can zap (through) the commercials.* **4 a** [*I*] : to move quickly or suddenly ▪ *Pain zapped through his ankle.* **b** [*T*] : to send (something or someone) quickly from one place to another through electronic means ▪ *He can zap the file to the office from his laptop.*

zeal /ˈziːl/ *n* [*U*] : a strong feeling of interest and enthusiasm that makes someone very eager or determined to do something ▪ *religious zeal*

zeal·ot /ˈzɛlət/ *n* [*C*] *often disapproving* : a person who has very strong feelings about something and who wants other people to have those feelings ▪ *political/ religious zealots*

zeal·ous /ˈzɛləs/ *adj* : feeling or showing strong and energetic support for a person, cause, etc. ▪ *zealous fans/supporters* — **zeal·ous·ly** *adv*

ze·bra /ˈziːbrə, *Brit* ˈzɛbrə/ *n, pl* **ze·bras** *also* **zebra** [C] : an African animal that looks like a horse and has black and white stripes covering its body

zebra crossing *n* [C] *Brit* : CROSSWALK

zeit·geist /ˈzaɪtˌɡaɪst/ *n* [*singular*] : the general beliefs, ideas, and spirit of a time and place ▪ *the zeitgeist of 1960s America*

Zen /ˈzɛn/ *n* [U] : a Japanese form of Buddhism that emphasizes meditation — called also *Zen Buddhism*

ze·nith /ˈziːnəθ, *Brit* ˈzɛnəθ/ *n* [*singular*] **1** *formal* : the strongest or most successful period of time ▪ *the zenith* [=the highest point] *of her career* **2** *technical* : the highest point reached in the sky by the sun, moon, etc.

¹**ze·ro** /ˈzirou/ *n, pl* **ze·ros** *also* **ze·roes** **1** [C/U] : the number 0 **2** [U] : the temperature shown by the zero mark on a thermometer ▪ *The temperature is 10° above/below zero.* **3** [U] : nothing at all ▪ *Her contribution to the project was close to zero.* ▪ (*informal*) *I know zero about art.*

²**zero** *adj* : not any ▪ *zero inflation* ▪ (*informal*) *He has zero chance of winning.* = *His chances of winning are zero.* ▪ *experiments conducted in zero gravity* [=a condition in which there is no gravity] ▪ *a policy of zero tolerance* [=a policy that punishes anyone who breaks a rule or commits a crime as severely as possible]

³**zero** *vb* **zeroes**; **ze·roed**; **ze·ro·ing** [T] *technical* : to set (a measuring device, such as a scale) so that it reads 0 ▪ *zero the scale* — **zero in on** [*phrasal vb*] **1** : to direct all of your attention to (someone or something) ▪ *Scientists are zeroing in on a cure.* **2** : to aim a gun, camera, etc., directly at (someone or something) ▪ *He zeroed in on her with the camera.*

zero hour *n* [U] : the time at which an event (such as a military attack) is scheduled to begin

zero–sum game *n* [*singular*] : a situation in which one person or group can win or gain something only by causing another person or group to lose it ▪ *Dividing up the budget is a zero-sum game.*

zest /ˈzɛst/ *n* **1** [U, *singular*] **a** : lively excitement ▪ *the zest of youth* ▪ *She has a real zest for life.* [=she enjoys life very much] **b** : a lively quality that increases enjoyment, excitement, or energy ▪ *His humor added (a certain) zest to the performance.* **2** [U] : small pieces of the skin of a lemon, orange, or lime that are used to flavor food ▪ *a tablespoon of lemon zest* — **zest·ful** /ˈzɛstfəl/ *adj* — **zest·ful·ly** *adv*

zesty /ˈzɛsti/ *adj* **zest·i·er**; **-est** *chiefly US* **1** : having a strong, pleasant, and somewhat spicy flavor ▪ *a zesty sauce* **2** : lively and pleasing ▪ *zesty humor*

¹**zig·zag** /ˈzɪɡˌzæɡ/ *n* [C] : a line that has a series of short, sharp turns or angles to

one side and then the other ▪ *a zigzag pattern*

²**zigzag** *vb* **-zagged**; **-zag·ging** [I] : to move along a path that has a series of short, sharp turns or angles to one side and then the other ▪ *A dirt road zigzags up the hill.*

zilch /ˈzɪltʃ/ *n* [U] *informal* : nothing at all ▪ *I know zilch about art.*

zil·lion /ˈzɪljən/ *n* [C] *informal* : a very large number ▪ *a zillion problems* ▪ *zillions of ants*

zinc /ˈzɪŋk/ *n* [U] : a bluish-white metal that is very common and is used especially to make brass and as a protective coating for things made of iron and steel

¹**zing** /ˈzɪŋ/ *n* [U] *informal* : a quality that makes something exciting, interesting, etc. ▪ *a sauce with a little extra zing*

²**zing** *vb, informal* **1** [I] : to move very quickly and make a humming sound ▪ *The bullets zinged past our ears.* **2** [T] *US, informal* : to insult or criticize (someone) in a sharp, clever, or playful way ▪ *We spent the evening cracking jokes and zinging each other.*

zing·er /ˈzɪŋɚ/ *n* [C] *US, informal* : a quick and clever comment that criticizes or insults someone

zin·nia /ˈzɪnijə/ *n* [C] : a plant that is grown in gardens for its brightly colored flowers

Zi·on·ism /ˈzajəˌnɪzəm/ *n* [U] : political support for the creation and development of a Jewish homeland in Israel — **Zi·on·ist** /ˈzajənɪst/ *n* [C] — **Zionist** *adj*

¹**zip** /ˈzɪp/ *vb* **zipped**; **zip·ping** **1** [T/I] : to close, open, or connect something with a zipper ▪ *He zipped (up) his jacket.* ▪ *The bag zips shut.* **2** [I] : to move or act very quickly ▪ *We zipped through the store.* ▪ *Cars were zipping past us.* **3** [T] *computers* : COMPRESS 3 ▪ *zip a file*

²**zip** *n* **1** [U] *informal* **a** : energy and excitement ▪ *The performance lacked zip.* **b** : speed of movement ▪ *a car with plenty of zip* **2** [U] *US, informal* **a** : nothing at all ▪ *I know zip about art.* **b** : a score of zero ▪ *We won the game 7-zip.* **3** [C] *Brit* : ZIPPER ▪ *The zip was stuck.* **4** *or* **ZIP** [C] *US* : ZIP CODE

zip code *or* **ZIP code** *n* [C] *US* : a group of numbers that is used in the U.S. as part of an address to identify a mail delivery area (such as a town or a part of a city — compare POSTCODE

zip·per /ˈzɪpɚ/ *n* [C] *US* : a device that is made of two rows of metal or plastic teeth and another piece that slides over the teeth to make them fit together or come apart and that is used to fasten clothing, open or close bags, etc. ▪ *The zipper was stuck.* — called also (*Brit*) **zip** — **zipper** *vb* [T] ▪ *She zippered* [=zipped] *the bag shut.* — **zip·pered** /ˈzɪpəd/ *adj* ▪ *a purse with a zippered compartment*

zit /ˈzɪt/ *n* [C] *informal* : PIMPLE

zo·di·ac /ˈzoudiˌæk/ *n* — **the zodiac** : an imaginary area in the sky that the sun, moon, and planets appear to travel through ◇ The zodiac is divided into 12 parts (called signs of the zodiac) which have special names and symbols and are believed by some people to have influence over people and events.

zom·bie /ˈzɑːmbi/ n [C] **1** informal : a person who moves very slowly and is not aware of what is happening especially because of being very tired ▪ If I don't go to bed early I'll be a zombie tomorrow. **2** : a dead person who is able to move because of magic according to some religions and in stories, movies, etc. ▪ a scary film about zombies

¹zone /ˈzoʊn/ n [C] **1** : an area that is different from other areas in a particular way ▪ an earthquake zone [=an area where earthquakes occur] ▪ a combat/danger/war zone ▪ a no-parking zone [=an area where parking is not allowed] **2** : one of the sections in a city or town that is used for a particular purpose ▪ a business/residential zone [=district]

²zone vb zoned; zon·ing [T] : to officially say that (a section in a city, town, etc.) can be used for a particular purpose (such as business or housing) ▪ This area is zoned for residential development. ▪ commercially zoned land — **zone out** [phrasal vb], informal : to stop paying attention because you are tired, bored, etc. ▪ I zoned out during the movie.

zone defense (US) also Brit **zone defence** n [U] chiefly US, sports : a way of playing defense in football, basketball, etc., by having each player on a team guard a certain area of the field or court

zoned out adj, US, informal : not thinking clearly or paying attention to what is happening around you because you are tired, drugged, etc. ▪ He was zoned out on drugs.

zoning n [U] : a system of rules used to control where businesses and homes are built in a city or town ▪ zoning laws

zonked /ˈzɑːŋkt/ adj, informal : very tired or affected by alcohol or drugs ▪ She was zonked (out) from the trip.

zoo /ˈzuː/ n, pl **zoos** **1** [C] : a place where many kinds of animals are kept so that people can see them **2** [singular] informal : a place, situation, or group that is crowded, loud, and uncontrolled ▪ The classroom was a zoo after recess.

zoo·keep·er /ˈzuːˌkiːpɚ/ n [C] : a person who takes care of the animals in a zoo

zo·ol·o·gy /zoʊˈɑːlədʒi/ n [U] : the branch of science that involves the study of animals and animal behavior — **zoo·log·i·cal** /ˌzoʊəˈlɑːdʒɪkəl/ adj — **zo·ol·o·gist** /zoʊˈɑːlədʒɪst/ n [C]

¹zoom /ˈzuːm/ vb [I] **1** informal **a** : to move quickly ▪ Cars zoomed down the highway. **b** : to move quickly upward ▪ a zooming rocket ▪ She zoomed to the top of her profession. **2** informal : to increase suddenly ▪ Sales have zoomed (up) in recent months. — **zoom in** [phrasal vb] ✧ When a camera or photographer zooms in, the lens of the camera is adjusted so that the image seems to be bigger and closer. ▪ The camera zoomed in on her face. ▪ (figurative) We're trying to zoom in on the cause of the problem. [=to see and understand the exact cause of the problem] — **zoom out** [phrasal vb] ✧ When a camera or photographer zooms out, the lens of the camera is adjusted so that the image seems to be smaller and farther away. ▪ The camera zoomed out to show a wider view of the scene.

²zoom n **1** [C] : ZOOM LENS **2** [singular] informal : the loud sound of a vehicle that is moving very fast ▪ The truck went by with a zoom.

zoom lens n [C] : a camera lens that can make the size of the image become larger and smaller : a camera lens that can zoom in and zoom out

zuc·chi·ni /zuˈkiːni/ n, pl **zucchini** or **zuc·chi·nis** [C/U] US : a dark green vegetable with smooth soft skin

Irregular Verbs

The following list shows the infinitive, past-tense, and past-participle forms for the irregular verbs in this dictionary. All verbs with the same final element are grouped together; thus, *outdo, overdo, redo,* and *undo* all appear immediately after *do* rather than in alphabetical order.

A regular English verb forms its past tense and past participle by adding *-ed* to its infinitive: for example, *trust* ("We trust her"), *trusted* ("In those days we trusted her"), *trusted* ("We have always trusted her"). A verb is considered regular if, when the *-ed* is added,

- the infinitive's final consonant is doubled (*stop, stopped, stopped*)
- its final silent *-e* is dropped (*die, died, died*)
- its final *-y* changes to *-i-* (*hurry, hurried, hurried*)
- its final *-c* changes to *-ck-* (*panic, panicked, panicked*)

A verb is considered irregular if

- either the past tense or the past participle lacks *-ed* (*swim, swam, swum; mean, meant, meant*)
- either the past tense or the past participle has a variant form that lacks *-ed* (*burn, burned* or *burnt, burned* or *burnt*)

INFINITIVE	PAST	PAST PARTICIPLE
be	was, were	been
bear	bore	borne
*forbear	forbore	forborne
beat	beat	beaten *or chiefly US* beat
*browbeat	browbeat	browbeaten
begin	began	begun
bend	bent	bent
*unbend	unbent	unbent
beseech	besought *or* beseeched	besought *or* beseeched
bet	bet *also* betted	bet *also* betted
bid (to express)	bade *or* bid	bidden *or* bid
*forbid	forbade *or* forbad	forbidden
bid (to offer)	bid	bid
*outbid	outbid	outbid
bind	bound	bound
bite	bit	bitten
bleed	bled	bled
blow	blew	blown
break	broke	broken
*housebreak	housebroke	housebroken
breed	bred	bred
bring	brought	brought
build	built	built
*rebuild	rebuilt	rebuilt
burn	burned *or* burnt	burned *or* burnt
burst	burst *also* bursted	burst *also* bursted
bust	busted *also Brit* bust	busted *also Brit* bust
buy	bought	bought
cast	cast	cast
*broadcast	broadcast	broadcast
*forecast	forecast *also* forecasted	forecast *also* forecasted
*recast	recast	recast
*telecast	telecast	telecast
*typecast	typecast	typecast
catch	caught	caught
cc	cc'd	cc'd

INFINITIVE	PAST	PAST PARTICIPLE
choose	chose	chosen
cling	clung	clung
clothe	clothed *also* clad	clothed *also* clad
come	came	come
*become	became	become
*overcome	overcame	overcome
cost	cost	cost
creep	crept	crept
cut	cut	cut
*undercut	undercut	undercut
deal	dealt	dealt
dig	dug	dug
dive	dived *or chiefly US* dove	dived *or chiefly US* dove
do	did	done
*outdo	outdid	outdone
*overdo	overdid	overdone
*redo	redid	redone
*undo	undid	undone
draw	drew	drawn
*overdraw	overdrew	overdrawn
*withdraw	withdrew	withdrawn
dream	dreamed *or* dreamt	dreamed *or* dreamt
drink	drank	drunk
drive	drove	driven
*test-drive	test-drove	test-driven
dwell	dwelled *or* dwelt	dwelled *or* dwelt
eat	ate	eaten
*overeat	overate	overeaten
fall	fell	fallen
*befall	befell	befallen
feed	fed	fed
*bottle-feed	bottle-fed	bottle-fed
*spoon-feed	spoon-fed	spoon-fed
feel	felt	felt
fight	fought	fought
find	found	found
fit (to be right)	fitted *or chiefly US* fit	fitted *or chiefly US* fit
flee	fled	fled
fling	flung	flung
fly	flew	flown
forsake	forsook	forsaken
freeze	froze	frozen
get	got	got *or US* gotten
*beget	begot *also* begat	begotten *or* begot
*forget	forgot	forgotten *or* forgot
gild	gilded *or* gilt	gilded *or* gilt
give	gave	given
*forgive	forgave	forgiven
go	went	gone
*forgo	forwent	forgone
*undergo	underwent	undergone
grind	ground	ground
grow	grew	grown
*outgrow	outgrew	outgrown
*overgrow	overgrew	overgrown
hang	hung *or* hanged	hung *or* hanged
*overhang	overhung	overhung
have	had	had
hear	heard	heard
*overhear	overheard	overheard
heave	heaved	heaved
hew	hewed	hewed *or* hewn
hide	hid	hidden *or* hid

INFINITIVE	PAST	PAST PARTICIPLE
hit	hit	hit
hold	held	held
*behold	beheld	beheld
*uphold	upheld	upheld
*withhold	withheld	withheld
hurt	hurt	hurt
keep	kept	kept
kneel	knelt *also chiefly US* kneeled	knelt *also chiefly US* kneeled
knit	knit *or* knitted	knit *or* knitted
know	knew	known
lay	laid	laid
*inlay	inlaid	inlaid
*overlay	overlaid	overlaid
*waylay	waylaid	waylaid
lead	led	led
*mislead	misled	misled
lean	leaned *or Brit* leant	leaned *or Brit* leant
leap	leapt *or* leaped	leapt *or* leaped
learn	learned *also chiefly Brit* learnt	learned *also chiefly Brit* learnt
leave	left	left
lend	lent	lent
let	let	let
*sublet	sublet	sublet
lie	lay	lain
*underlie	underlay	underlain
light	lighted *or* lit	lighted *or* lit
*spotlight	spotlighted *or* spotlit	spotlighted *or* spotlit
lose	lost	lost
make	made	made
*remake	remade	remade
mean	meant	meant
meet	met	met
mow	mowed	mowed *or* mown
pay	paid	paid
*overpay	overpaid	overpaid
*prepay	prepaid	prepaid
*repay	repaid	repaid
*underpay	underpaid	underpaid
plead	pleaded *or* pled	pleaded *or* pled
prove	proved	proved *or chiefly US* proven
*disprove	disproved *or chiefly US* disproven	disproved *or chiefly US* disproven
put	put	put
*input	inputted *or* input	inputted *or* input
*output	outputted *or* output	outputted *or* output
quit	quit *also* quitted	quit *also* quitted
read	read	read
*lip-read	lip-read	lip-read
*misread	misread	misread
*proofread	proofread	proofread
rend	rent *also US* rended	rent *also US* rended
rid	rid *also* ridded	rid *also* ridded
ride	rode	ridden
*override	overrode	overridden
ring (to sound)	rang	rung
rise	rose	risen
*arise	arose	arisen
run	ran	run
*outrun	outran	outrun
*overrun	overran	overrun
*rerun	reran	rerun
saw	sawed	sawed *or Brit* sawn
say	said	said

INFINITIVE	PAST	PAST PARTICIPLE
see	saw	seen
*foresee	foresaw	foreseen
*oversee	oversaw	overseen
seek	sought	sought
sell	sold	sold
*outsell	outsold	outsold
*oversell	oversold	oversold
send	sent	sent
set	set	set
*beset	beset	beset
*inset	inset	inset
*offset	offset	offset
*reset	reset	reset
*upset	upset	upset
sew	sewed	sewn *or* sewed
shake	shook	shaken
shave	shaved	shaved *or* shaven
shear	sheared	sheared *or* shorn
shed	shed	shed
shine	shone *or chiefly US* shined	shone *or chiefly US* shined
*outshine	outshone *or* outshined	outshone *or* outshined
shoe	shod *also chiefly US* shoed	shod *also chiefly US* shoed
shoot	shot	shot
*overshoot	overshot	overshot
show	showed	shown *or* showed
shrink	shrank *or* shrunk	shrunk *or* shrunken
shut	shut	shut
sing	sang *or* sung	sung
sink	sank *or* sunk	sunk
sit	sat	sat
*babysit	babysat	babysat
*resit	resat	resat
slay	slew *also* slayed	slain
sleep	slept	slept
*oversleep	overslept	overslept
slide	slid	slid
*backslide	backslid	backslid
sling	slung	slung
slink	slunk *also US* slinked	slunk *also US* slinked
slit	slit	slit
smell	smelled *or Brit* smelt	smelled *or Brit* smelt
smite	smote	smitten
sneak	sneaked *or chiefly US* snuck	sneaked *or chiefly US* snuck
sow	sowed	sown *or* sowed
speak	spoke	spoken
*bespeak	bespoke	bespoken
speed	sped *or* speeded	sped *or* speeded
spell	spelled *or chiefly Brit* spelt	spelled *or chiefly Brit* spelt
*misspell	misspelled *or chiefly Brit* misspelt	misspelled *or chiefly Brit* misspelt
spend	spent	spent
*misspend	misspent	misspent
spill	*chiefly US* spilled *or chiefly Brit* spilt	*chiefly US* spilled *or chiefly Brit* spilt
spin	spun	spun
spit	spat *or chiefly US* spit	spat *or chiefly US* spit
split	split	split
spoil	spoiled *or chiefly Brit* spoilt	spoiled *or chiefly Brit* spoilt
spread	spread	spread
spring	sprang *or* sprung	sprung
stand	stood	stood
*misunderstand	misunderstood	misunderstood
*understand	understood	understood

INFINITIVE	PAST	PAST PARTICIPLE
*withstand	withstood	withstood
stave	staved *also* stove	staved *also* stove
steal	stole	stolen
stick	stuck	stuck
sting	stung	stung
stink	stank *or* stunk	stunk
strew	strewed	strewed *or* strewn
stride	strode	stridden
strike	struck	struck *also* stricken
string	strung	strung
*hamstring	hamstrung	hamstrung
strive	strove *also* strived	striven *or* strived
swear	swore	sworn
*forswear	forswore	forsworn
sweat	sweat *or* sweated	sweat *or* sweated
sweep	swept	swept
swell	swelled	swelled *or* swollen
swim	swam	swum
swing	swung	swung
take	took	taken
*mistake	mistook	mistaken
*overtake	overtook	overtaken
*partake	partook	partaken
*retake	retook	retaken
*undertake	undertook	undertaken
teach	taught	taught
tear (to rip)	tore	torn
tell	told	told
*foretell	foretold	foretold
*retell	retold	retold
think	thought	thought
*rethink	rethought	rethought
thrive	thrived *or old-fashioned* throve	thrived *also old-fashioned* thriven
throw	threw	thrown
*overthrow	overthrew	overthrown
thrust	thrust	thrust
tread	trod *also* treaded	trodden *or* trod
wake	woke *also* waked	woken *or* waked *also* woke
*awake	awoke	awoken
wear	wore	worn
weave	wove *or* weaved	woven *or* weaved
*interweave	interwove	interwoven
wed	wedded *also* wed	wedded *also* wed
weep	wept	wept
wet	wet *or* wetted	wet *or* wetted
win	won	won
wind	wound	wound
*rewind	rewound	rewound
*unwind	unwound	unwound
wring	wrung	wrung
write	wrote	written
*ghostwrite	ghostwrote	ghostwritten
*rewrite	rewrote	rewritten
*underwrite	underwrote	underwritten